THE SIXTH MENTAL MEASUREMENTS YEARBOOK

EARLIER PUBLICATIONS IN THIS SERIES

Edited by Oscar Krisen Buros

EDUCATIONAL, PSYCHOLOGICAL, AND PERSONALITY TESTS OF 1933 AND 1934

*

EDUCATIONAL, PSYCHOLOGICAL, AND PERSONALITY TESTS OF 1933, 1934, AND 1935

*

EDUCATIONAL, PSYCHOLOGICAL, AND PERSONALITY TESTS OF 1936

*

THE NINETEEN THIRTY-EIGHT MENTAL MEASUREMENTS YEARBOOK

*

THE NINETEEN FORTY MENTAL MEASUREMENTS YEARBOOK

*

THE THIRD MENTAL MEASUREMENTS YEARBOOK

*

THE FOURTH MENTAL MEASUREMENTS YEARBOOK

*

THE FIFTH MENTAL MEASUREMENTS YEARBOOK

*

TESTS IN PRINT

THE SIXTH MENTAL MEASUREMENTS YEARBOOK

Edited by

OSCAR KRISEN BUROS

Visiting Professor of Education
University College, University of East Africa
Nairobi, Kenya

THE GRYPHON PRESS
HIGHLAND PARK · NEW JERSEY
1965

DESIGNED BY LUELLA BUROS

 PUBLISHED BY THE GRYPHON PRESS
220 MONTGOMERY STREET, HIGHLAND PARK, NEW JERSEY 08904

MANUFACTURED BY QUINN & BODEN COMPANY, INC., RAHWAY, NEW JERSEY
PRINTED IN THE UNITED STATES OF AMERICA

To the memory of

TRUMAN LEE KELLEY

Table of Contents

* * * * *

Contributing Test Reviewers

* * * * *

IRA E. AARON, Professor of Education, University of Georgia, Athens, Georgia

CLIFFORD R. ADAMS, Professor of Psychology, The Pennsylvania State University, University Park, Pennsylvania

C. J. ADCOCK, Associate Professor of Psychology, Victoria University of Wellington, Wellington, New Zealand

DOROTHY C. ADKINS, Professor of Psychology, The University of North Carolina, Chapel Hill, North Carolina

J. STANLEY AHMANN, Professor of Psychology and Head of the Department, Colorado State University, Fort Collins, Colorado

LEWIS E. ALBRIGHT, Assistant Director, Employee Relations Research, Standard Oil Company (Indiana), Chicago, Illinois

ANNE ANASTASI, Professor of Psychology, Fordham University, New York, New York

O. F. ANDERHALTER, Professor of Education, and Director, Bureau of Institutional Research, St. Louis University, St. Louis, Missouri

HOWARD R. ANDERSON, Senior Consulting Editor, High School Department, Houghton Mifflin Company, Boston, Massachusetts

JAMES M. ANDERSON, Research Consultant, Institute of Therapeutic Psychology, Santa Ana, California

KENNETH E. ANDERSON, Dean, School of Education, The University of Kansas, Lawrence, Kansas

E. ANSTEY, Chief Psychologist, Civil Service Commission, London, England

ALEXANDER W. ASTIN, Director of Research, American Council on Education, Washington, D.C.

MARY C. AUSTIN, Professor of Education, Western Reserve University, Cleveland, Ohio

J. DOUGLAS AYERS, Associate Professor of Educational Psychology, University of Alberta, Edmonton, Alberta, Canada

ANDREW R. BAGGALEY, Professor of Psychology, Temple University, Philadelphia, Pennsylvania

IROL WHITMORE BALSLEY, Professor of Office Administration and Head of the Department, Louisiana Polytechnic Institute, Ruston, Louisiana

RICHARD S. BARRETT, Associate Professor of Management Engineering and Psychology, New York University, New York, New York

THOMAS C. BARRETT, Assistant Professor of Education, The University of Wisconsin, Madison, Wisconsin

ROBERT H. BAUERNFEIND, Associate Professor of Education, Northern Illinois University, DeKalb, Illinois

KENNETH L. BEAN, Clinical Psychologist, Veterans Administration Hospital, Knoxville, Iowa

HAROLD P. BECHTOLDT, Professor of Psychology, University of Iowa, Iowa City, Iowa

WESLEY C. BECKER, Professor of Psychology, University of Illinois, Urbana, Illinois

H. R. BEECH, Lecturer in Psychology, Institute of Psychiatry, The Maudsley Hospital, University of London, London, England

JOHN ELDERKIN BELL, Program Director, National Institute of Mental Health, United States Public Health Service, San Francisco, California

GEORGE K. BENNETT, President, The Psychological Corporation, New York, New York

P. M. BENTLER, United States Public Health Service Fellow, Department of Psychology, Stanford University, Stanford, California

RALPH F. BERDIE, Professor of Psychology, and Director, Student Counseling Bureau, University of Minnesota, Minneapolis, Minnesota

HARRY D. BERG, Professor, Office of Evaluation Services, Michigan State University, East Lansing, Michigan

EMMETT ALBERT BETTS, Research Professor, University of Miami, Coral Gables, Florida

WILLIAM C. BINGHAM, Lecturer in Education, Rutgers, The State University, New Brunswick, New Jersey

L. B. BIRCH, Senior Lecturer in Educational Psychology, Institute of Education, University of Sheffield, Sheffield, England

ÅKE BJERSTEDT, Professor of Education, University of Lund, Lund, Sweden

DONALD B. BLACK, Professor of Education, University of Alberta, Edmonton, Alberta, Canada

HILLEL BLACK, Senior Editor, Saturday Evening Post, New York, New York

JOHN D. BLACK, Director, Counseling and Testing Center, and Consulting Associate Professor of Psychology, Stanford University, Stanford; and President, Consulting Psychologists Press, Inc., Palo Alto; California

C. B. BLAKEMORE, Lecturer in Psychology, Institute of Psychiatry, The Maudsley Hospital, University of London, London, England

EMERY P. BLIESMER, Director, McGuffey Reading Clinic, University of Virginia, Charlottesville, Virginia

PAUL BLOMMERS, Professor of Education, University of Iowa, Iowa City, Iowa

HAROLD BORKO, Human Factors Scientist, Advanced Technology and Research Directorate, System Development Corporation, Santa Monica, California

MORTON BORTNER, Chief Psychologist, Department of Physical Medicine and Rehabilitation, New York Medical College, New York, New York

JOHN E. BOWERS, Director of Testing, Office of Admissions and Records, University of Illinois, Urbana, Illinois

ARTHUR H. BRAYFIELD, Executive Officer, American Psychological Association, Washington, D.C.

M. ALAN BRIMER, Senior Research Fellow in Education, University of Bristol, Bristol, England

NELSON BROOKS, Associate Professor of French, Yale University, New Haven, Connecticut

CHARLES M. BROWN, Associate Professor of Education, and Director, The Reading Center, University of Southern California, Los Angeles, California

JAMES E. BRYAN, Training Administrator, United States Public Health Service, Division of Foreign Quarantine, United States Quarantine Station, Staten Island, New York

MIRIAM M. BRYAN, Associate Director of Test Development, Educational Testing Service, Princeton, New Jersey

N. DALE BRYANT, Executive Director, Study Center for Learning Disabilities, State University of New York at Albany and Albany Medical College, Albany, New York

THOMAS C. BURGESS, Associate Professor, Counseling Center, Portland State College, Portland, Oregon

ALVIN G. BURSTEIN, Associate Professor of Psychology, Neuropsychiatric Institute, University of Illinois College of Medicine, Chicago, Illinois

DAVID P. CAMPBELL, Associate Professor of Psychology, and Director, Center for Interest Measurement Research, University of Minnesota, Minneapolis, Minnesota

DONALD T. CAMPBELL, Professor of Psychology, Northwestern University, Evanston, Illinois

DUGAL CAMPBELL, Assistant Professor of Psychology, Queen's University, Kingston, Ontario, Canada

J. A. CAMPBELL, Professor of Chemistry and Chairman of the Department, Harvey Mudd College, Claremont, California

JOEL T. CAMPBELL, Research Psychologist, Educational Testing Service, Princeton, New Jersey

JOHN B. CARROLL, Professor of Educational Psychology, Harvard University, Cambridge, Massachusetts

ROBERT C. CHALLMAN, Clinical Psychologist, 301 Kenwood Parkway, Minneapolis, Minnesota

HENRY CHAUNCEY, President, Educational Testing Service, Princeton, New Jersey

STANLEY CLARK, Professor of Education, University of Saskatchewan, Saskatoon, Saskatchewan, Canada

WILLIS W. CLARK, Executive Vice President, California Test Bureau, Monterey, California

W. V. CLEMANS, Director, Test Department, Science Research Associates, Inc., Chicago, Illinois

DOROTHY M. CLENDENEN, Assistant Director, Test Division, The Psychological Corporation, New York, New York

RICHARD W. COAN, Professor of Psychology, University of Arizona, Tucson, Arizona

WILLIAM E. COFFMAN, Director of Research and Development, College Board Programs Division, Educational Testing Service, Princeton, New Jersey

BERTRAM D. COHEN, Professor of Psychology, and Director of Clinical Training, Rutgers, The State University, New Brunswick, New Jersey

JACOB COHEN, Professor of Psychology, New York University, New York, New York

WILLIAM W. COOLEY, Program Director, University of Pittsburgh Project Talent Office, Pittsburgh, Pennsylvania

WILLIAM R. CRAWFORD, Office of Research in Medical Education, University of Illinois College of Medicine, Chicago, Illinois

JOHN O. CRITES, Associate Professor of Psychology, University of Iowa, Iowa City, Iowa

LEE J. CRONBACH, Professor of Education and Psychology, Stanford University, Stanford, California

DOUGLAS P. CROWNE, Associate Professor of Psychology, University of Connecticut, Storrs, Connecticut

THOMAS E. CULLITON, JR., Assistant Professor of Education, University of Illinois, Urbana, Illinois

W. GRANT DAHLSTROM, Professor of Psychology, The University of North Carolina, Chapel Hill, North Carolina

RICHARD H. DANA, Professor of Psychology, University of South Florida, Tampa, Florida

CHARLOTTE CROON DAVIS, Test Research Service, Bronxville, New York

PAUL C. DAVIS, Dean and Professor of Psychology, Los Angeles Pacific College, Los Angeles, California

STANLEY E. DAVIS, Reading and Study Skills Counseling Director, University Counseling Center, The Ohio State University, Columbus, Ohio

LESTER W. DEARBORN, Director, Counseling Service, 316 Huntington Avenue, Boston, Massachusetts

GABRIEL DELLA-PIANA, Associate Professor of Educational Psychology, University of Utah, Salt Lake City, Utah

GEORGE D. DEMOS, Associate Dean—Counseling and Testing, and Associate Professor of Educational Psychology, California State College at Long Beach, Long Beach, California

CLARENCE DERRICK, Professor of English, and Chairman, Humanities Department, University of Florida, Gainesville, Florida.

LOUIS M. DICARLO, Professor of Audiology and Speech Pathology, Syracuse University, Syracuse, New York

CHARLES F. DICKEN, Assistant Professor of Psychology, San Diego State College, San Diego, California

JEROME E. DOPPELT, Assistant Director, Test Division, The Psychological Corporation, New York, New York

N. M. DOWNIE, Professor of Psychology, Purdue University, Lafayette, Indiana

PAUL L. DRESSEL, Director of Institutional Research, Michigan State University, East Lansing, Michigan

PHILIP H. DUBOIS, Professor of Psychology, Washington University, St. Louis, Missouri

HAROLD B. DUNKEL, Professor of Education, The University of Chicago, Chicago, Illinois

S. S. DUNN, Assistant Director, Australian Council for Educational Research, Hawthorn, Victoria, Australia

MARVIN D. DUNNETTE, Professor of Psychology, University of Minnesota, Minneapolis, Minnesota

WALTER N. DUROST, Associate Professor of Education, University of New Hampshire, Durham, New Hampshire

RALPH D. DUTCH, Principal Lecturer in Educational Psychology, Aberdeen College of Education, Aberdeen, Scotland

HENRY S. DYER, Vice President, Educational Testing Service, Princeton, New Jersey

ROBERT L. EBEL, Professor of Education, Michigan State University, East Lansing, Michigan

ALLEN L. EDWARDS, Professor of Psychology, University of Washington, Seattle, Washington

WILLIAM J. EICHMAN, Chief, Psychology Service, Veterans Administration Hospital, Salem, Virginia

DOROTHY EICHORN, Associate Research Psychologist, and Administrator, Harold E. Jones Child Study Center, Institute of Human Development, University of California, Berkeley, California

WILLIAM ELLER, Professor of Education, State University of New York at Buffalo, Buffalo, New York

ALBERT ELLIS, Consulting Psychologist, 333 West 56th Street, New York, New York

MAX D. ENGELHART, Director, Division of Institutional Research and Evaluation, Department of Higher Education, Chicago Public Schools, Chicago, Illinois

GERALD L. ERICKSEN, Assistant Professor of Psychology, St. Olaf College, Northfield, Minnesota

LAWRENCE W. ERICKSON, Associate Professor of Education, University of California, Los Angeles, California

LEONARD D. ERON, Professor of Psychology, University of Iowa, Iowa City, Iowa

BARBARA F. ESSER, Professional Associate, Educational Testing Service, Princeton, New Jersey

H. J. EYSENCK, Institute of Psychiatry, The Maudsley Hospital, University of London, London, England

PAUL R. FARNSWORTH, Professor of Psychology, Stanford University, Stanford, California

LEONARD S. FELDT, Professor of Education, University of Iowa, Iowa City, Iowa

GEORGE A. FERGUSON, Professor of Psychology, McGill University, Montreal, Quebec, Canada

LEONARD W. FERGUSON, Program Director, Research Division, Life Insurance Agency Management Association, Hartford, Connecticut

WARREN G. FINDLEY, Professor of Education, and Coordinator of Educational Research, University of Georgia, Athens, Georgia

SEYMOUR FISHER, Research Professor of Psychology, and Director, Psychopharmacology Laboratory, Boston University School of Medicine, Boston, Massachusetts

WAYNE D. FISHER, Assistant Professor of Education in Russian, and Associate Coordinator of the Master of Arts in Teaching Program in Russian, The University of Chicago, Chicago, Illinois

JOHN C. FLANAGAN, President, American Institute for Research; and Professor of Psychology, University of Pittsburgh; Pittsburgh, Pennsylvania

W. G. FLEMING, Assistant Director, Department of Educational Research, Ontario College of Education, University of Toronto, Toronto, Ontario, Canada

JOHN P. FOLEY, JR., President, J. P. Foley and Company, Inc., New York, New York

BERTRAM R. FORER, Consulting Psychologist, and Executive Editor, Journal of Projective Techniques and Personality Assessment, Suite 307, 8833 Sunset Boulevard, Los Angeles, California

FRANK J. FORNOFF, Head, Science Section, Test Development Division, Educational Testing Service, Princeton, New Jersey

ELIZABETH D. FRASER, Professor of Psychology, University of Aberdeen, Aberdeen, Scotland

NORMAN FREDERIKSEN, Director of Research, Educational Testing Service, Princeton, New Jersey

JOHN W. FRENCH, Professor of Psychology, and College Examiner, New College, Sarasota, Florida

ROBERT L. FRENCH, Vice President for Research and Testing, Science Research Associates, Inc., Chicago, Illinois

BENNO G. FRICKE, Associate Professor of Psychology, and Chief, Evaluation and Examinations Division, The University of Michigan, Ann Arbor, Michigan

GUSTAV J. FROEHLICH, Director, Bureau of Institutional Research, University of Illinois, Urbana, Illinois

EDWARD B. FRY, Professor of Education, Rutgers, The State University, New Brunswick, New Jersey

EDWARD J. FURST, Associate Professor of Psychology, The Ohio State University, Columbus, Ohio

ERIC F. GARDNER, Professor of Education and Psychology, and Chairman, Department of Psychology, Syracuse University, Syracuse, New York

J. RAYMOND GERBERICH, Visiting Professor of Education, University of Maryland, College Park, Maryland

CECIL A. GIBB, Professor of Psychology, The Australian National University, Canberra City, Australia

JAMES R. GLENNON, Director, Employee Relations Research, Standard Oil Company (Indiana), Chicago, Illinois

GOLDINE C. GLESER, Professor of Psychology, University of Cincinnati Medical School, Cincinnati, Ohio

MARVIN D. GLOCK, Professor of Educational Psychology, Cornell University, Ithaca, New York

BERT A. GOLDMAN, Associate Professor of Education, and Associate, Counseling Service, State University of New York at Albany, Albany, New York

LEO GOLDMAN, Associate Professor of Education, Brooklyn College, Brooklyn, New York

LEONARD D. GOODSTEIN, Professor of Psychology, and Director, University Counseling Service, University of Iowa, Iowa City, Iowa

LEONARD V. GORDON, Chief, Behavioral Evaluation Research Laboratory, U.S. Army Personnel Research Office, Washington, D.C.

HARRISON G. GOUGH, Professor of Psychology, University of California, Berkeley, California

RUSSEL F. GREEN, Associate Professor of Psychology, The University of Rochester, Rochester, New York

RICHARD E. GROSS, Associate Professor of Education, Stanford University, Stanford, California

WILSON H. GUERTIN, Associate Professor of Education and Psychology, University of Florida, Gainesville, Florida

JOHN H. HAEFNER, Professor of Social Studies Education, University of Iowa, Iowa City, Iowa

ELIZABETH HAGEN, Professor of Psychology and Education, Teachers College, Columbia University, New York, New York

MILTON E. HAHN, Professor of Psychology, University of California, Los Angeles, California

WALLACE B. HALL, Assistant Research Psychologist, Institute of Personality Assessment and Research, University of California, Berkeley, California

E. W. HAMILTON, Head, Department of Mathematics, State College of Iowa, Cedar Falls, Iowa

ROBERT A. HARPER, Consulting Psychologist, 3000 Connecticut Avenue, N.W., Washington, D.C.

PHILIP L. HARRIMAN, Professor of Psychology, Bucknell University, Lewisburg, Pennsylvania

ALBERT J. HARRIS, Professor of Education, and Director, Office of Research and Evaluation, Division of Teacher Education, The City University of New York, New York, New York

DALE B. HARRIS, Professor of Psychology and Head of the Department, The Pennsylvania State University, University Park, Pennsylvania

JESSE G. HARRIS, JR., Professor of Psychology and Chairman of the Department, University of Kentucky, Lexington, Kentucky

THEODORE L. HARRIS, Professor of Educational Psychology and Education, The University of Wisconsin, Madison, Wisconsin

J. THOMAS HASTINGS, Director, Office of Educational Testing; University Examiner; and Professor of Educational Psychology; University of Illinois, Urbana, Illinois

RICHARD S. HATCH, Vice President, Dunnette, Kirchner and Associates, Inc., Minneapolis, Minnesota

MARY R. HAWORTH, Associate Professor of Medical Psychology, University of Nebraska College of Medicine, Omaha, Nebraska

JAMES R. HAYDEN, Superintendent of Schools, New Bedford Public Schools, New Bedford, Massachusetts.

DAVID K. HEENAN, Associate Professor, Office of Evaluation Services, Michigan State University, East Lansing, Michigan

LLOYD H. HEIDGERD, Assistant Professor of Natural Science, Michigan State University, East Lansing, Michigan

ALFRED B. HEILBRUN, JR., Associate Professor of Psychology, University of Iowa, Iowa City, Iowa

A. W. HEIM, Medical Research Council, The Psychological Laboratory, University of Cambridge, Cambridge, England

WILLIAM H. HELME, Supervisory Research Psychologist, United States Army Personnel Research Office, Washington, D.C.

JOHN K. HEMPHILL, Director, Developmental Research Division, Educational Testing Service, Princeton, New Jersey

WILLIAM HERED, Associate Professor of Chemistry, Indiana University, Gary, Indiana; and Examiner, University of Chicago, Chicago, Illinois

DAVID O. HERMAN, Staff Psychologist, The Psychological Corporation, New York, New York

ALBERT N. HIERONYMUS, Professor of Education and Psychology, University of Iowa, Iowa City, Iowa

JOHN R. HILLS, Director, Testing and Guidance, The University System of Georgia, Atlanta, Georgia

C. B. HINDLEY, Research Psychologist, Centre for the Study of Human Development, Institutes of Education and Child Health, University of London, London, England

MARSHALL S. HISKEY, Professor of Educational Psychology, and Director, Educational Psychological Clinic, University of Nebraska, Lincoln, Nebraska

MARJORIE P. HONZIK, Lecturer in Psychology, and Associate Research Psychologist, Institute of Human Development, University of California, Berkeley, California

KENNETH D. HOPKINS, Associate Professor of Educational Psychology, University of Southern California, Los Angeles, California

JOHN E. HORROCKS, Professor of Psychology, The Ohio State University, Columbus, Ohio

CYRIL J. HOYT, Professor of Educational Psychology, University of Minnesota, Minneapolis, Minnesota

KENNETH B. HOYT, Professor of Education, University of Iowa, Iowa City, Iowa

LLOYD G. HUMPHREYS, Professor of Psychology and Head of the Department, University of Illinois, Urbana, Illinois

JOHN D. HUNDLEBY, Research Assistant Professor of Psychology, University of Illinois, Urbana, Illinois

STEPHEN HUNKA, Assistant Professor of Educational Psychology, University of Alberta, Edmonton, Alberta, Canada

ARTHUR R. JENSEN, Associate Professor of Educational Psychology, and Associate Research Psychologist, Institute of Human Learning, University of California, Berkeley, California

FRANK B. JEX, Professor of Educational Psychology, University of Utah, Salt Lake City, Utah

RICHARD T. JOHNSON, Assistant Professor of Education, Rutgers, The State University, New Brunswick, New Jersey

H. GWYNNE JONES, Senior Lecturer in Psychology, St. George's Hospital Medical School, London, England

KENNETH J. JONES, Research Associate, Graduate School of Education, Harvard University, Cambridge, Massachusetts

WORTH R. JONES, Professor of Education, University of Cincinnati, Cincinnati, Ohio

C. E. JURGENSEN, Assistant Vice President, Personnel, Minneapolis Gas Company, Minneapolis, Minnesota

WALTER KATKOVSKY, Associate Professor of Psychology, Fordham University, New York, New York

MARTIN KATZ, Assistant Director, Evaluation and Advisory Service, Educational Testing Service, Princeton, New Jersey

RAYMOND A. KATZELL, Professor of Psychology and Head of the Department, New York University, New York, New York

WALTER V. KAULFERS, Professor of Education, University of Illinois, Urbana, Illinois

J. A. KEATS, Reader in Psychology, University of Queensland, Brisbane, Queensland, Australia

E. LOWELL KELLY, Professor of Psychology, The University of Michigan, Ann Arbor, Michigan

WILLIAM E. KENDALL, Director, Personnel and Marketing Research Division, The Psychological Corporation, New York, New York

JAMES E. KENNEDY, Associate Professor of Psychology, University of Wisconsin, Madison, Wisconsin

WILLARD A. KERR, Professor of Psychology, Illinois Institute of Technology, Chicago, Illinois

GILBERT C. KETTELKAMP, Professor of Education, University of Illinois, Urbana, Illinois

ALBERT J. KINGSTON, Professor of Education, University of Georgia, Athens, Georgia

WAYNE K. KIRCHNER, Manager, Personnel Research, Minnesota Mining and Manufacturing Company, St. Paul, Minnesota

PHILIP M. KITAY, Professor of Psychology, Adelphi University, Garden City, New York

PAUL M. KJELDERGAARD, Assistant Professor of Education, Harvard University, Cambridge, Massachusetts

BENJAMIN KLEINMUNTZ, Associate Professor of Psychology, Carnegie Institute of Technology, Pittsburgh, Pennsylvania

MILTON V. KLINE, Consulting Psychologist, 345 West 58th Street, New York, New York

PHILIP H. KRIEDT, Associate Director of Personnel Research, The Prudential Insurance Company, Newark, New Jersey

JOHN D. KRUMBOLTZ, Associate Professor of Education and Psychology, Stanford University, Stanford, California

ALBERT K. KURTZ, Fulbright Lecturer, Ein Shams University, Cairo, United Arab Republic

CHARLES R. LANGMUIR, Director of Special Projects, The Psychological Corporation, New York, New York

Peter A. Lappan, Jr., Assistant Professor of Mathematics, Lehigh University, Bethlehem, Pennsylvania

William S. Larson, Professor of Music Education and Chairman of the Department, The Eastman School of Music, The University of Rochester, Rochester, New York

J. S. Lawes, Senior Lecturer in Education, Westminster College, North Hinksey, Oxford, England

Wilbur L. Layton, Professor of Psychology and Head of the Department, Iowa State University, Ames, Iowa

S. G. Lee, Professor of Psychology, University of Leicester, Leicester, England

D. Welty Lefever, Professor of Education, University of Southern California, Los Angeles, California

Irvin J. Lehmann, Associate Professor in Evaluation Services, Michigan State University, East Lansing, Michigan

Eugene E. Levitt, Professor of Clinical Psychology, Indiana University School of Medicine, Indianapolis, Indiana

Philip M. Levy, Lecturer in Psychology, Institute of Education, University of Birmingham, Birmingham, England

Seymour Levy, Manager, Personnel Research and Manpower Development, The Pillsbury Company, Minneapolis, Minnesota

John Liggett, Senior Lecturer in Psychology, University College of South Wales and Monmouthshire, University of Wales, Cardiff, Wales

James C. Lingoes, Associate Professor of Psychology, The University of Michigan, Ann Arbor, Michigan

Paul R. Lohnes, Associate Professor of Education, State University of New York at Buffalo, Buffalo, New York

Peter G. Loret, Program Director, Educational Testing Service, Princeton, New Jersey

Margaret F. Lorimer, Associate Professor, Office of Institutional Research, Michigan State University, East Lansing, Michigan

Maurice Lorr, Chief, Outpatient Psychiatric Research Laboratory, Veterans Benefits Office; and Lecturer in Psychology, Catholic University of America; Washington, D.C.

Kenneth Lovell, Lecturer in Educational Psychology, University of Leeds, Leeds, England

William H. Lucio, Professor of Education, University of California, Los Angeles, California

Robert W. Lundin, Professor of Psychology, The University of the South, Sewanee, Tennessee

David T. Lykken, Associate Professor of Psychiatry and Psychology, University of Minnesota, Minneapolis, Minnesota

Howard B. Lyman, Associate Professor of Psychology, University of Cincinnati, Cincinnati, Ohio

Boyd R. McCandless, Professor of Education and Psychology; Director, University School Clinic Complex; and Chairman, Department of Special Education; Indiana University, Bloomington, Indiana

Arthur S. McDonald, Professor of Education, and Director of Reading Services, Marquette University, Milwaukee, Wisconsin

Christine McGuire, Assistant Director, Research in Medical Education, University of Illinois College of Medicine, Chicago, Illinois

Arthur C. MacKinney, Associate Professor of Psychology, Iowa State University, Ames, Iowa

Saunders Mac Lane, Max Mason Distinguished Service Professor of Mathematics, The University of Chicago, Chicago, Illinois

Kenneth F. McLaughlin, Specialist, Appraisal of the Individual, United States Office of Education, Washington, D.C.

Jonathon C. McLendon, Professor of Social Science Education, Florida Atlantic University, Boca Raton, Florida

Thomas W. Mahan, Jr., Consultant in Guidance, Connecticut State Department of Education, Hartford, Connecticut

George G. Mallinson, Dean, School of Graduate Studies, Western Michigan University, Kalamazoo, Michigan

Jacqueline V. Mallinson, Assistant Professor of Science, Western Michigan University, Kalamazoo, Michigan

Winton H. Manning, Associate Professor of Psychology, Texas Christian University, Fort Worth, Texas

Melvin R. Marks, Professor of Business Administration, The University of Rochester, Rochester, New York

Bertram B. Masia, Assistant Professor of Education, The University of Chicago, Chicago, Illinois

Samuel T. Mayo, Associate Professor of Education, Loyola University, Chicago, Illinois

Richard S. Melton, Assistant Director, Test Development Division, Educational Testing Service, Princeton, New Jersey

GERALD A. MENDELSOHN, Assistant Professor of Psychology, University of California, Berkeley, California

PHILIP R. MERRIFIELD, Director, Bureau of Educational Research, Kent State University, Kent, Ohio

JACK C. MERWIN, Professor of Educational Psychology, and Assistant Director, Student Counseling Bureau, University of Minnesota, Minneapolis, Minnesota

DONALD L. MEYER, Assistant Professor of Education, Syracuse University, Syracuse, New York

WILLIAM B. MICHAEL, Professor of Education and Psychology, University of California, Santa Barbara, California

T. R. MILES, Professor of Psychology, University College of North Wales, Bangor, Wales

JOHN E. MILHOLLAND, Professor of Psychology, The University of Michigan, Ann Arbor, Michigan

JASON MILLMAN, Assistant Professor of Educational Psychology and Measurement, Cornell University, Ithaca, New York

ARTHUR MITTMAN, Associate Professor of Education, University of Oregon, Eugene, Oregon

JOSEPH E. MOORE, Regents Professor of Psychology, Georgia Institute of Technology, Atlanta, Georgia

TERENCE MOORE, Research Psychologist and Lecturer, Centre for the Study of Human Development, University of London Institute of Education, London, England

G. A. V. MORGAN, Former Principal Psychologist, North Wales Child Guidance Service, Denbighshire, Wales

COLEMAN MORRISON, Assistant Professor of Education, Rhode Island College, Providence, Rhode Island

FRANCES CROOK MORRISON, Associate Professor of Education, State University of New York at Albany, Albany, New York

C. SCOTT MOSS, Mental Health Consultant, National Institute of Mental Health, United States Public Health Service, San Francisco, California

ALLYN MILES MUNGER, Associate Director, Personnel and Marketing Research Division, The Psychological Corporation, New York, New York

BERNARD I. MURSTEIN, Associate Professor of Psychology, Connecticut College, New London, Connecticut

SHELDON S. MYERS, Head, Mathematics Section, Test Development Division, Educational Testing Service, Princeton, New Jersey

THEODOR F. NAUMANN, Associate Professor of Psychology, Central Washington State College, Ellensburg, Washington

LEO NEDELSKY, Professor of Physical Sciences, University of Chicago, Chicago, Illinois

CHARLES O. NEIDT, Professor of Psychology, Colorado State University, Fort Collins, Colorado

CLARENCE H. NELSON, Professor, Office of Evaluation Services, Michigan State University, East Lansing, Michigan

T. ERNEST NEWLAND, Professor of Educational Psychology, University of Illinois, Urbana, Illinois

ROBERT C. NICHOLS, Program Director, National Merit Scholarship Corporation, Evanston, Illinois

JOHN NISBET, Professor of Education, University of Aberdeen, Aberdeen, Scotland

STANLEY NISBET, Professor of Education, University of Glasgow, Glasgow, Scotland

VICTOR H. NOLL, Professor of Education, Michigan State University, East Lansing, Michigan

WARREN T. NORMAN, Associate Professor of Psychology, The University of Michigan, Ann Arbor, Michigan

ROBERT D. NORTH, Associate Director, Educational Records Bureau, New York, New York

DONALD W. OLIVER, Associate Professor of Education, Harvard University, Cambridge, Massachusetts.

JACOB S. ORLEANS, Professor of Psychology, University of Nevada, Southern Regional Division, Las Vegas, Nevada

DAVID B. ORR, Senior Research Scientist, American Institute for Research; and Director of School and Survey Research, University of Pittsburgh Project Talent Office; Washington, D.C.

WILLIAM A. OWENS, Professor of Psychology, Purdue University, Lafayette, Indiana

C. ROBERT PACE, Professor of Higher Education, University of California, Los Angeles, California

ELLIS BATTEN PAGE, Professor of Education, and Director, Bureau of Educational Research and Service, University of Connecticut, Storrs, Connecticut

Osmond E. Palmer, Professor, Office of Evaluation Services, Michigan State University, East Lansing, Michigan

Jean Maier Palormo, Head, Industrial Test Research, Science Research Associates, Inc., Chicago, Illinois

Jerome D. Pauker, Assistant Professor of Clinical Psychology, Medical School, University of Minnesota, Minneapolis, Minnesota

David A. Payne, Assistant Professor of Education, Syracuse University, Syracuse, New York

R. W. Payne, Associate Professor of Psychology, Queen's University, Kingston, Ontario, Canada

Donald R. Peterson, Professor of Psychology, and Director, Psychological Clinic, University of Illinois, Urbana, Illinois

Theodore G. Phillips, Assistant Dean, Amundsen Branch, Chicago City Junior College, Chicago, Illinois

Douglas A. Pidgeon, Deputy Director, National Foundation for Educational Research in England and Wales, Slough, Bucks, England

John Pierce-Jones, Professor of Educational Psychology, The University of Texas, Austin, Texas

Ellen V. Piers, Associate Professor of Psychology, The Pennsylvania State University, University Park, Pennsylvania

A. E. G. Pilliner, Senior Lecturer in Education, University of Edinburgh, Edinburgh, Scotland

Paul Pimsleur, Director, The Listening Center, The Ohio State University, Columbus, Ohio

Gus P. Plessas, Associate Professor of Education, Sacramento State College, Sacramento, California

Lynnette B. Plumlee, Personnel Research and Testing Division, Sandia Corporation, Albuquerque, New Mexico

Robert C. Pooley, Professor of English, University of Wisconsin, Madison, Wisconsin

Lyman W. Porter, Associate Professor of Psychology, University of California, Berkeley, California

Ray G. Price, Professor of Business Education, University of Minnesota, Minneapolis, Minnesota

M. L. Kellmer Pringle, Director, National Bureau for Co-operation in Child Care, London, England

S. Rachman, Lecturer in Psychology, Institute of Psychiatry, University of London, London, England

John A. Radcliffe, Senior Lecturer in Psychology, University of Sydney, Sydney, Australia

Alton L. Raygor, Associate Professor of Educational Psychology, and Coordinator, Reading and Study Skills Center, University of Minnesota, Minneapolis, Minnesota

William R. Reevy, Associate Professor of Psychology, State University of New York, Cortland, New York

Ralph M. Reitan, Professor of Psychology (Neurology), and Director, Section of Neuropsychology, Indiana University Medical Center, Indianapolis, Indiana

Roger A. Richards, Assistant Professor of English, Jersey City State College, Jersey City, New Jersey

James H. Ricks, Jr., Assistant Director, Test Division, The Psychological Corporation, New York, New York

C. Alan Riedesel, Assistant Professor of Education, Pennsylvania State University, University Park, Pennsylvania

James P. Rizzo, Mathematics Instructor, The Lawrenceville School, Lawrenceville, New Jersey

Holland Roberts, Director, Academic Freedom Committee, P.O. Box 5503, San Francisco, California

H. Alan Robinson, Assistant Professor of Education, The University of Chicago, Chicago, Illinois

Helen M. Robinson, William S. Gray Research Professor of Reading, The University of Chicago, Chicago, Illinois

Paul C. Rosenbloom, Professor of Mathematics, Institute of Technology, and Director, Minnesota School Mathematics and Science Center, University of Minnesota, Minneapolis, Minnesota

Benjamin Rosner, Director, Test Development Division, Educational Testing Service, Princeton, New Jersey

Alan O. Ross, Chief Psychologist, Pittsburgh Child Guidance Center, Pittsburgh, Pennsylvania

Paul F. Ross, Industrial Psychologist, Imperial Oil Limited, Toronto, Ontario, Canada

John W. M. Rothney, Professor of Education, University of Wisconsin, Madison, Wisconsin

HAROLD L. ROYER, Associate Professor of Accounting, University of Miami, Coral Gables, Florida

ARTHUR B. ROYSE, Lecturer in Psychology, The University of Hull, Hull, England

STANLEY I. RUBIN, Coordinator, Assessment Services, Personnel Research and Development Corporation, Cleveland, Ohio

FLOYD L. RUCH, President, Psychological Services, Inc., Los Angeles, California

DAVID G. RYANS, Director, Bureau of Educational Research, University of Hawaii, Honolulu, Hawaii

EVERETT B. SACKETT, Dean, College of Liberal Arts, University of New Hampshire, Durham, New Hampshire

H. BRADLEY SAGEN, Assistant Professor of Education, University of Iowa, Iowa City, Iowa

H. J. SANTS, Lecturer in Education, University College of North Wales, Bangor, Wales

BERT R. SAPPENFIELD, Professor of Psychology, Montana State University, Missoula, Montana

IRWIN G. SARASON, Associate Professor of Psychology, University of Washington, Seattle, Washington

JOHANN M. SCHEPERS, Senior Research Officer, National Institute for Personnel Research, Johannesburg, Republic of South Africa

WILLIAM SCHOFIELD, Professor of Psychology, University of Minnesota, Minneapolis, Minnesota

WILLIAM B. SCHRADER, Director of Statistical Analysis, Educational Testing Service, Princeton, New Jersey

HERBERT SCHUELER, Director of Teacher Education, Hunter College of the City University of New York, New York, New York

DOUGLAS G. SCHULTZ, Associate Professor of Psychology, Western Reserve University, Cleveland, Ohio

HAROLD A. SCHULTZ, Professor of Art Education, University of Illinois, Champaign, Illinois

D. H. SCHUSTER, Staff Psychologist, Collins Radio Company, Cedar Rapids, Iowa

RICHARD E. SCHUTZ, Professor of Education, and Director, Testing Service, Arizona State University, Tempe, Arizona

MARIETTE SCHWARZ, Associate in Foreign Languages, Educational Testing Service, Princeton, New Jersey

HAROLD SEASHORE, Director, Test Division, The Psychological Corporation, New York, New York

STANLEY J. SEGAL, Associate Professor of Psychology, and Director, Student Counseling Center, State University of New York at Buffalo, Buffalo, New York

S. B. SELLS, Professor of Psychology, and Director, Institute of Behavioral Research, Texas Christian University, Fort Worth, Texas

BORIS SEMEONOFF, Reader in Psychology, University of Edinburgh, Edinburgh, Scotland

LAURANCE F. SHAFFER, Professor of Psychology and Education, Teachers College, Columbia University, New York, New York

MARION F. SHAYCOFT, Senior Research Scientist, American Institute for Research; and Director of Measurement Research, University of Pittsburgh Project Talent Office; Pittsburgh, Pennsylvania

JOHN C. SHERWOOD, Professor of English, University of Oregon, Eugene, Oregon

BENJAMIN SHIMBERG, Director of Educational Relations, Cooperative Test Division, Educational Testing Service, Princeton, New Jersey

DONALD E. P. SMITH, Associate Professor of Education, and Chief, Reading Improvement Service, The University of Michigan, Ann Arbor, Michigan

I. MACFARLANE SMITH, Principal Lecturer (Research), Garnett College for Training Technical Teachers, London, England

ROBERT J. SOLOMON, Vice President, Educational Testing Service, Princeton, New Jersey

GEORGE D. SPACHE, Professor of Education, and Head, Reading Laboratory and Clinic, University of Florida, Gainesville, Florida

BERNARD SPOLSKY, Assistant Professor of Education, McGill University, Montreal, Quebec, Canada

OTFRIED SPREEN, Assistant Research Professor of Neurology, University of Iowa, Iowa City, Iowa

ROBERT E. STAKE, Associate Director, Office of Educational Testing, University of Illinois, Urbana, Illinois

JOHN M. STALNAKER, President, National Merit Scholarship Corporation, Evanston, Illinois

JULIAN C. STANLEY, Professor of Educational Psychology, and Director, Laboratory of Experimental Design, University of Wisconsin, Madison, Wisconsin

RUSSELL G. STAUFFER, Professor of Education, and Director, The Reading Study Center, University of Delaware, Newark, Delaware

JOHN E. STECKLEIN, Director, Bureau of Institutional Research, University of Minnesota, Minneapolis, Minnesota

HARRY L. STEIN, Professor of Education, and Director of Graduate Studies in Education, University of British Columbia, Vancouver, British Columbia, Canada

JACK M. STEIN, Professor of German, Harvard University, Cambridge, Massachusetts

WILLIAM STEPHENSON, Professor of Psychology, University of Missouri, Columbia, Missouri

NAOMI STEWART, Formerly Staff Associate, Educational Testing Service, Princeton, New Jersey

LAWRENCE J. STRICKER, Research Psychologist, Educational Testing Service, Princeton, New Jersey

NORMAN D. SUNDBERG, Professor of Psychology, University of Oregon, Eugene, Oregon

DONALD E. SUPER, Professor of Psychology and Education, Teachers College, Columbia University, New York, New York

JOHN SUTHERLAND, Principal Lecturer in Education, Moray House College of Education, Edinburgh, Scotland

EDWARD O. SWANSON, Assistant Professor, and Senior Student Personnel Worker, University of Minnesota, Minneapolis, Minnesota

ABRAHAM J. TANNENBAUM, Associate Dean, Graduate School of Education, Yeshiva University, New York, New York

ERWIN K. TAYLOR, President, Personnel Research and Development Corporation, Cleveland, Ohio

PAUL W. THAYER, Director of Human Resources Research, Life Insurance Agency Management Association, Hartford, Connecticut

WILLIAM N. THETFORD, Associate Professor of Medical Psychology, College of Physicians and Surgeons of Columbia University, New York, New York

ALBERT S. THOMPSON, Professor of Psychology and Education, Teachers College, Columbia University, New York, New York

ROBERT L. THORNDIKE, Professor of Education, and Head, Department of Psychological Foundations and Services, Teachers College, Columbia University, New York, New York

DAVID V. TIEDEMAN, Professor of Education, Harvard University, Cambridge, Massachusetts

AGATHA TOWNSEND, Consultant, Educational Records Bureau, New York, New York

ARTHUR E. TRAXLER, Executive Director, Educational Records Bureau, New York, New York

HAROLD C. TRIMBLE, Professor of Mathematics Education, Ohio State University, Columbus, Ohio

MARY E. TURNBULL, Formerly Head of Test Production, Educational Testing Service, Princeton, New Jersey

WILLIAM W. TURNBULL, Executive Vice President, Educational Testing Service, Princeton, New Jersey

CLARENCE E. TURNER, Professor of Romance Languages, Rutgers, The State University, New Brunswick, New Jersey

LEONA E. TYLER, Professor of Psychology, University of Oregon, Eugene, Oregon

FORREST L. VANCE, Administrative Officer, American Psychological Association, Washington, D.C.

B. H. VAN ROEKEL, Professor of Education, Michigan State University, East Lansing, Michigan

DONALD J. VELDMAN, Associate Professor of Educational Psychology, University of Texas, Austin, Texas

MAGDALEN D. VERNON, Professor of Psychology, University of Reading, Reading, England

PHILIP E. VERNON, Professor of Educational Psychology, Institute of Education, University of London, London, England

WIMBURN L. WALLACE, Director, Professional Examinations Division, The Psychological Corporation, New York, New York

NORMAN E. WALLEN, Associate Professor of Educational Psychology, University of Utah, Salt Lake City, Utah

MOREY J. WANTMAN, Director of Advisory and Instructional Programs, Educational Testing Service, Princeton, New Jersey

CHARLES F. WARNATH, Associate Professor of Psychology, and Director, Counseling Center, Oregon State University, Corvallis, Oregon

WILLARD G. WARRINGTON, Director, Office of Evaluation Services, Michigan State University, East Lansing, Michigan

JOHN G. WATKINS, Chief, Clinical Psychologist, Veterans Administration Hospital, Portland, Oregon

HAROLD WEBSTER, Associate Research Psychologist, Center for the Study of Higher Education, University of California, Berkeley, California

HENRY WEITZ, Associate Professor of Education, and Director, Bureau of Testing and Guidance, Duke University, Durham, North Carolina

EMMY E. WERNER, Assistant Professor of Child Development, University of California, Davis, California

ALEXANDER G. WESMAN, Associate Director, Test Division, The Psychological Corporation, New York, New York

GEORGE WESTBY, Professor of Psychology, University College of South Wales and Monmouthshire, University of Wales, Cardiff, Wales

DEAN K. WHITLA, Director, Office of Tests, Harvard University, Cambridge, Massachusetts

JERRY S. WIGGINS, Associate Professor of Psychology, University of Illinois, Urbana, Illinois

J. ROBERT WILLIAMS, Director, Child Study Clinic, and School Psychologist, Public Schools, Kankakee, Illinois

WARREN W. WILLINGHAM, Director of Evaluation Studies, Georgia Institute of Technology, Atlanta, Georgia

J. RICHARD WILMETH, Associate Professor of Sociology, University of Iowa, Iowa City, Iowa

HERBERT D. WING, Principal, City of Sheffield Training College, Sheffield, England

GEORGE P. WINSHIP, JR., Professor of English, King College, Bristol, Tennessee

ROBERT D. WIRT, Professor of Psychology, Child Development, and Psychiatry, University of Minnesota, Minneapolis, Minnesota

LEROY WOLINS, Associate Professor of Psychology and Statistics, Iowa State University, Ames, Iowa

FRANK B. WOMER, Associate Professor of Education, and Test Consultant, Bureau of School Services, The University of Michigan, Ann Arbor, Michigan

WAYNE S. ZIMMERMAN, Test Officer, Los Angeles State College, Los Angeles, California

Preface

* * * * *

THE first publication in this series, *Educational, Psychological, and Personality Tests of 1933 and 1934,* appeared 30 years ago. This and the succeeding two publications, issued in 1936 and 1937, were simply bibliographies of recently published tests. The first volume to include critical reviews of tests, *The Nineteen Thirty-Eight Mental Measurements Yearbook,* was published in 1938.

Thus a generation of test users has never known what it is to select and use tests without the help of the critical reviews in the *Mental Measurements Yearbooks.* Since they have never known anything else, most test users take the *Mental Measurements Yearbooks* for granted. On the other hand, to others it seems extraordinary that hundreds of the most competent testing specialists speak so candidly about the professional work of their fellow workers in testing in order to permit test users to select tests with greater discrimination. Readers of the test reviews in the *Mental Measurements Yearbooks* should keep in mind that testing specialists cannot be praised too highly for making this test-the-tests service available to test users and, incidentally, to others interested in, or effected by, test results. At the same time, it is discouraging that relatively few tests escape adverse criticism. As a result, lay critics of testing are able to use the MMY's to support many of their charges against currently used testing practices. These lay critics do not take the MMY's for granted; nor do they praise testing specialists for their efforts to improve testing practices by providing frankly critical test reviews. On the contrary, the reaction of most lay critics of testing is likely to be similar to the view expressed by Martin L. Gross when, in discussing the marked disagreements among psychologists regarding the value of personality testing, he wrote:

> The most surprising insight into this discord and fratricidal back-biting can be found in the *Mental Measurements Yearbooks,* a tester's bible where colleagues get the rare professional opportunity to dissect each other's test inventories within the secure bounds of a review not unlike the familiar ones in the Sunday book section. A study of the *Yearbook* (which has had five editions in a generation) is an eye-opener for the uninitiated skeptic. If some of the articles were put into the framework of science, say chemistry, they would read like works of professional chemists wrangling over whether valences and elements exist and whether compounds can actually be created in a test tube.[1]

Unfortunately, the rank and file of test users do not appear to be particularly alarmed that so many tests are either severely criticized or described as having no known validity. Although most test users would probably agree that many tests are either worthless or misused, they continue to have the utmost faith in their own particular choice and use of tests regardless of the absence of supporting research or even of the presence of negating research. When I initiated this test reviewing service in 1938, I was confident that frankly critical re-

1 GROSS, MARTIN L. *The Brain Watchers,* p. 205. New York: Random House, Inc., 1962. Pp. x, 305. * For reviews, see B215.

views by competent specialists representing a wide variety of viewpoints would make it unprofitable to publish tests of unknown or questionable validity. Now, 27 years and five *Mental Measurements Yearbooks* later, I realize that I was too optimistic. Although many test users undoubtedly are selecting and using tests with greater discrimination because of the MMY's, there are many who are not. Despite unfavorable reviews in the MMY's, the publication and use of inadequately validated tests seem to be keeping pace with the population explosion. After editing hundreds of reviews for this volume, I feel more confident than ever of the correctness of the following three paragraphs quoted from the Introduction to *Tests in Print:*

At present, no matter how poor a test may be, if it is nicely packaged and if it promises to do all sorts of things which no test can do, the test will find many gullible buyers. When we initiated critical test reviewing in *The 1938 Yearbook,* we had no idea how difficult it would be to discourage the use of poorly constructed tests of unknown validity. Even the better informed test users who finally become convinced that a widely used test has no validity after all are likely to rush to use a new instrument which promises far more than any good test can possibly deliver. Counselors, personnel directors, psychologists, and school administrators seem to have an unshakable will to believe the exaggerated claims of test authors and publishers. If these users were better informed regarding the merits and limitations of their testing instruments, they would probably be less happy and less successful in their work. The test user who has faith—however unjustified—can speak with confidence in interpreting test results and in making recommendations. The well informed test user cannot do this; he knows that the best of our tests are still highly fallible instruments which are extremely difficult to interpret with assurance in individual cases. Consequently, he must interpret test results cautiously and with so many reservations that others wonder whether he really knows what he is talking about. Children, parents, teachers, and school administrators are likely to have a greater respect and admiration for a school counselor who interprets test results with confidence even though his interpretations have no scientific justification. The same applies to psychologists and personnel directors. Highly trained psychologists appear to be as gullible as the less well trained school counselors. It pays to know only a little about testing; furthermore, it is much more fun for everyone concerned—the examiner, the examinee, and the examiner's employer.

We realize that the preceding paragraph may seem out of place in a test bibliography. Nevertheless, we are permitting it to stand. It probably reflects our discouragement at the little progress which has been made toward using tests more intelligently since we first started to publish frankly critical test reviews in *The 1938 Yearbook.* It is difficult to allocate the blame for the lack of greater progress. We think, however, that the major blame rests with test users. The better test publishers would like to make more moderate claims for their tests. Unfortunately, test buyers don't want tests which make only moderate claims. Consequently, even the best test publishers find themselves forced by competition to offer test users what they want. Bad usage of tests is probably more common than good usage. Must it always be this way? We are afraid so.

Although we think that test users will enjoy administering and interpreting tests more if they do not read the reviews which the tests have received in the MMY's, we hope that they will turn in ever increasing numbers to the MMY's and consider the reviews carefully. Some of the reviews are conflicting and some are not particularly good reviews. But on the whole, the reviews represent the best and most authoritative source of critical information about currently published tests. If at times some reviews seem hypercritical, keep in mind that we have reason to believe that for every reviewer who is overly critical, there are at least ten reviewers who pull their punches in assessing a test. It is, of course, more pleasant and more profitable to speak well of the work of others.[2]

FUTURE PLANS

Despite my discouragement over the slowness with which progress in the selection and use of tests is taking place, the thought that this cooperative test reviewing service might be terminated with this volume fills me with apprehension. Consequently, although the task of preparing each MMY seems to become successively more demanding, I feel compelled to continue the series, at least until the service is taken over by others who can give the project adequate support. As a result, work on *The Seventh Mental Measurements Yearbook* is already under way.

I stated in the Preface of *The Fifth Yearbook* that the cost in time and money of preparing the MMY's was becoming too great to permit us to continue to give extensive review coverage of new tests without sacrificing some of the other features which characterized the first five *Mental Measurements Yearbooks.* I stated that the major economy would be made by omitting bibliographies covering the construction, validation, and use of specific tests. Since every reference listed in these bibliographies has been located and examined by me, the preparation of the bibliographies was a tremendous drain upon my time. The second announced economy was to be the elimination of our extensive listing and review coverage of tests in other English-speaking countries. The first appreciative reviews of *The Fifth Yearbook* caused me to change my mind about these economies. I had not realized that there

2 Buros, Oscar Krisen. *Tests in Print: A Comprehensive Bibliography of Tests for Use in Education, Psychology, and Industry,* pp. xxiii–xxiv. Highland Park, N.J.: Gryphon Press, 1961. Pp. xxix, 479. *

would be so much concern over the discontinuance of the bibliographies of test references, and, to a lesser extent, over the discontinuance of reviews of foreign tests. Instead of economizing, therefore, *The Sixth Yearbook* has been expanded in both size and quality. The most important improvement—and a very costly one—in this volume is the inclusion of information on the status of all tests listed in *Tests in Print* but not otherwise included in this volume. For the first time, this *Mental Measurements Yearbook* lists all tests known to be in print as of the time the manuscript was completed.

No important economies are planned for *The Seventh Yearbook*. Certainly there is no intention of discontinuing the bibliographies for specific tests. We may, however, discontinue giving references to abstracts in *Psychological Abstracts* and *Dissertation Abstracts* unless we receive information that these abstract references are being found sufficiently useful to justify the labor and cost involved.

I had hoped to prepare a new edition of *Tests in Print* immediately following each new MMY. The latest edition of TIP would then serve not only as a comprehensive bibliography of all tests in print in the English-speaking world, but it would also serve as a master index to the contents of all MMY's published to date. Unfortunately, because of the poor sales of *Tests in Print,* a new edition to include the contents of *The Sixth Yearbook* will not be prepared. However, for the most efficient use of the first six MMY's, *Tests in Print* will continue to be essential.

In discussing future plans in *The Fifth Yearbook,* I stated that the MMY's would not continue to grow in size. This announcement also turned out to be wrong. *The Sixth Yearbook* has 32.6 per cent more pages than *The Fifth Yearbook.* The percentage increase in the number of words is even greater since this volume contains proportionately more 6 point composition (references) and more 8 point composition (test entries, book entries, and indexes) than *The Fifth Yearbook;* the rest of the text is set in 10 point with 1 point leading.

ACKNOWLEDGMENTS

The preparation and publication of this volume represents the combined efforts of many hundreds of individuals. To all these, I owe a debt of great gratitude. One of my most satisfying rewards has been my relationships with test reviewers. Their willingness to undertake the thankless task of writing frankly critical reviews with the hope of improving testing practices has made this series possible. Most reviewers consider that they have an obligation to the profession to review for the MMY regardless of other commitments upon their time. My warmest thanks go to these reviewers who have contributed so generously of their time. I also wish to express my thanks to the many persons who helped me in my search for competent reviewers, to the test publishers who supplied us with specimen sets for review, and to the editors who gave permission to reprint excerpts from reviews in their journals.

The American Psychological Association facilitated our work by supplying galley proofs of *Psychological Abstracts* to permit us to make the latest possible references to abstracts in *PA*. University Microfilms assisted by providing copies of *Dissertation Abstracts* to permit us to refer to abstracts in *DA*.

I have been fortunate in having an especially competent editorial and secretarial staff—all of whom worked with painstaking care to make this publication as accurate as possible. My assistant editor, Miss Barbara A. Peace, has done a tremendous job assisting me in every phase of the work. I cannot speak too highly of the quality of her work. Two of my former students—Alfred E. Hall of Carnegie Institute of Technology and Roger A. Richards of Jersey City State College—gave me much needed assistance by serving as part time editorial associates. During a period when the task of editing test reviews was more than we could handle, Mrs. Sonia Johnson also served on the editorial staff. The secretarial staff doubled as editorial assistants—preparing indexes, checking copy, and proofreading. Mrs. Doris G. McCan, a veteran of the last four MMY's, has been of great comfort to me because of her painstaking accuracy and sensitivity for style. Mrs. Margaret F. Hammond and Mrs. Minnie Yale have assisted me on the last two MMY's; I am grateful to them for the thoroughness with which they have done their work. Miss Alice Hirschman, the only full time member of the secretarial staff, has demonstrated a real flair as an editorial secretary and assistant. Mrs. Jean

Anderson, the most recent addition to the secretarial staff, has given valuable help wherever needed. All members of the secretarial staff have performed a variety of duties: typing, copyreading, index making, proofreading, and filing. I also wish to express my gratitude to Rajendra Kumar Rongong for the assistance he gave us during his year of graduate study in testing. Finally, I want to acknowledge my indebtedness to the veteran who has labored with me in secretarial, editorial, typographic, and business capacities on all of the publications issued in this series over the past thirty years—my wife, Luella.

I wish to thank Rutgers University for the assistance which it has given me by providing office space for the editorial staff in the Graduate School of Education. The facilities of the University Library were used extensively by me. I especially wish to express my appreciation to Henry C. Herge, Dean of the Graduate School of Education during the period this volume was being prepared, for his encouragement and appreciation of my work.

The publication of *The Sixth Mental Measurements Yearbook* coincides with my early retirement from Rutgers University. Until June 1966, I shall be Visiting Professor of Education, University of East Africa, Nairobi, Kenya. The editorial office of the MMY has been moved to my home: 220 Montgomery Street, Highland Park, New Jersey 08904. Despite the location of offices in different continents for the next year, close liaison will permit the initial stages of work on the preparation of the next MMY to proceed very nearly as usual. All correspondence regarding the MMY should be sent to the editorial office in Highland Park, New Jersey.

DEDICATION

For the second time, the dedication of a *Mental Measurements Yearbook* is being used to honor an outstanding scholar in mental measurements. It gives me great pleasure to dedicate this volume to the memory of one who was a giant among us, Truman Lee Kelley. Even today, all test users and test specialists would find it profitable to read his *Interpretation of Educational Measurements* [3] written thirty-eight years ago. The "jangle" fallacy which Kelley warned us about in 1927 is even more rampant today than it was in 1927.

OSCAR KRISEN BUROS

Nairobi, Kenya
June 1, 1965

3 KELLEY, TRUMAN LEE. *Interpretation of Educational Measurements.* Yonkers, N.Y.: World Book Co., 1927. Pp. xiii, 363. *

Introduction

* * * * *

THIS volume is the tenth in a series of publications[1] designed to assist test users in education, industry, psychiatry, and psychology to locate, choose, and use tests with greater ease and discrimination. A concise history of the first eight publications—spanning the 24-year period 1935 to 1959—was presented by Charles R. Langmuir in the December 1960 issue of *Contemporary Psychology*. Since this historical review is reprinted in the section Books and Reviews of this volume—along with excerpts from other representative reviews of *The Fifth Mental Measurements Yearbook*—the earlier publications will be described only briefly here.

It was 35 years ago that I first began to think about the need for establishing a "Bureau of Standards" to test the tests. At that time, and many times since, I made unsuccessful attempts to enlist the financial support needed to launch a test consumers research organization. It was because of this goal that I undertook the task of preparing my first bibliography of recently published tests, a 44-page pamphlet entitled *Educational, Psychological, and Personality Tests of 1933 and 1934,* published in 1935. The following year a cumulated issue of 83 pages, covering the years 1933, 1934, and 1935, was published. The third bibliography, published in 1937, listed only tests published, revised, or supplemented in the year 1936. Its size, however, increased to 141 pages because of the inclusion of a bibliography of books on testing and closely related areas along with excerpts of the critical portions of the reviews which these books had received in professional journals.

Encouraged by the warm reception given to the reprinting of critical excerpts from reviews of measurement books, I decided to initiate a test reviewing service. Since I had been unsuccessful in getting financial support to establish a research organization to test the tests, I settled for a less costly project—a series of

1 BUROS, OSCAR K. *Educational, Psychological, and Personality Tests of 1933 and 1934.* Rutgers University Bulletin, Vol. 11, No. 11; Studies in Education, No. 7. New Brunswick, N.J.: School of Education, Rutgers University, May 1935. Pp. 44. Paper. Out of print. *
BUROS, OSCAR K. *Educational, Psychological, and Personality Tests of 1933, 1934, and 1935.* Rutgers University Bulletin, Vol. 13, No. 1; Studies in Education, No. 9. [Highland Park, N.J.: Gryphon Press], July 1936. Pp. 83. Paper. $0.50. * For reviews, see 40:B856, 38:B325, and 36:B46.
BUROS, OSCAR K. *Educational, Psychological, and Personality Tests of 1936: Including a Bibliography and Book Review Digest of Measurement Books and Monographs of 1933–36.* Rutgers University Bulletin, Vol. 14, No. 2A; Studies in Education, No. 11. [Highland Park, N.J.: Gryphon Press], August 1937. Pp. 141. Paper. $0.60. * For reviews, see 40:B857 and 38:B326.
BUROS, OSCAR KRISEN, EDITOR. *The Nineteen Thirty-Eight Mental Measurements Yearbook of the School of Education, Rutgers University.* New Brunswick, N.J.: Rutgers University Press, 1938. Pp. xv, 415. Out of print. * For reviews, see 40:B858. (Xerographic prints of this yearbook may be ordered from University Microfilms, Inc., 313 North First St., Ann Arbor, Mich.)
BUROS, OSCAR KRISEN, EDITOR. *The Nineteen Forty Mental Measurements Yearbook.* Highland Park, N.J.: Gryphon Press, 1941. Pp. xxv, 674. Out of print. * For reviews, see 4:B70 and 3:788. (Xerographic prints of this yearbook may be ordered from University Microfilms, Inc., 313 North First St., Ann Arbor, Mich.)
BUROS, OSCAR KRISEN, EDITOR. *The Third Mental Measurements Yearbook.* Highland Park, N.J.: Gryphon Press, 1949. Pp. xv, 1047. $18.00. * For reviews, see 4:B71.
BUROS, OSCAR KRISEN, EDITOR. *The Fourth Mental Measurements Yearbook.* Highland Park, N.J.: Gryphon Press, 1953. Pp. xxv, 1163. $20.00. * For reviews, see 5:B84.
BUROS, OSCAR KRISEN, EDITOR. *The Fifth Mental Measurements Yearbook.* Highland Park, N.J.: Gryphon Press, 1959. Pp. xxix, 1292. $22.50. * For reviews, see B104.
BUROS, OSCAR KRISEN, EDITOR. *Tests in Print: A Comprehensive Bibliography of Tests for Use in Education, Psychology, and Industry.* Highland Park, N.J.: Gryphon Press, 1961. Pp. xxix, 479. $7.00. * For reviews, see B105.

yearbooks which would present frankly critical test reviews written by specialists representing a great variety of disciplines and viewpoints. Although test reviews are commonplace today, the introduction of frankly critical test reviews in *The Nineteen Thirty-Eight Mental Measurements Yearbook* proved to be a milestone in the history of testing. The story of the angry reactions of hurt test authors and publishers is presented in the Introduction of *The Nineteen Forty Mental Measurements Yearbook.* It is only in recent years that all but a few test authors and publishers have come to accept critical reviews of their tests as inevitable and proper. (There are still some small publishers who refuse to give us any information whatsoever about their tests and even refuse to sell tests to us.)

The Nineteen Thirty-Eight Mental Measurements Yearbook, a 430-page volume published in 1938, presented 331 original test reviews by 133 reviewers. *The Nineteen Forty Mental Measurements Yearbook,* a 699-page volume published in 1941, presented 503 original test reviews by 250 reviewers. After a long delay because of World War II, *The Third Mental Measurements Yearbook,* a 1,062-page volume, was published in 1949 with 713 original test reviews by 320 reviewers. *The Fourth Mental Measurements Yearbook,* a 1,185-page volume published in 1953, presented 596 original test reviews by 308 reviewers. *The Fifth Mental Measurements Yearbook,* a 1,321-page volume published in 1959, presented 698 original test reviews by 350 reviewers. A grand total of 2,841 original test reviews have appeared in the first five yearbooks.

The first two MMY's listed only a few references to the various articles, books, and theses dealing with the construction, validity, and use of specific tests. Bibliographies which aimed to be as comprehensive as possible were introduced for the first time in *The Third Yearbook.* The third, fourth, and fifth yearbooks present 3,368, 4,417, and 6,468 references, respectively; a grand total of 14,253 references appeared in these three volumes.

The first four MMY's included excerpts of the critical comments made in all book and test reviews which could be located. *The Third Yearbook,* for example, included excerpts from 851 reviews appearing in 135 journals. In *The Fourth Yearbook,* there were excerpts from 811 reviews in 121 journals. *The Fifth Yearbook,* however, introduced the policy of excerpting only selected reviews representing a cross section of the best reviews located; it presented excerpts from 583 reviews in 81 journals.

Each *Mental Measurements Yearbook* supplements rather than replaces earlier yearbooks. Consequently, after the publication of *The Fifth Yearbook* it became necessary at times to consult all of the first five MMY's to locate information wanted. Furthermore, there was no way to determine whether a test listed in an earlier volume was still in print. Primarily to overcome these two difficulties, *Tests in Print: A Comprehensive Bibliography of Tests for Use in Education, Psychology, and Industry* was published in the fall of 1961. This volume presents listings of all tests known to be in print in early 1961, and title listings of all tests once listed in an MMY but now out of print. It also presents cross references to all reviews which a particular test has received in the various MMY's. For each test, the reviewers are named and the number of references and excerpts to be found in the MMY's reported. Thus, *Tests in Print* also serves as a master index to the contents of the first five *Mental Measurements Yearbooks.* Readers interested in further information about *Tests in Print* should read in the section Books and Reviews in this volume the excerpts from reviews which TIP received in professional journals. For effective use of *The Mental Measurements Yearbooks,* it is essential that *Tests in Print* continue to be used.

OBJECTIVES

The objectives of *The Mental Measurements Yearbooks* have remained basically unchanged since their first statement in *The Nineteen Forty Yearbook.* The objectives of the section Tests and Reviews in this and other yearbooks in the series are as follows:

(*a*) to make readily available comprehensive and up-to-date bibliographies of recent tests published in all English-speaking countries; (*b*) to make readily available hundreds of frankly critical test reviews, written by persons of outstanding ability representing various viewpoints, which will assist test users to make more discriminating selections of the standard tests which will best meet their needs; (*c*) to make readily available comprehensive and accurate bibliographies of references on the construction, validation, use, and limitations of specific tests; (*d*) to impel authors and publishers to place fewer but better tests on the market and to provide test users with detailed and accurate information on the construction, validation, uses, and limitations of their tests at the time they are first placed on the market; (*e*) to suggest to test users better methods of arriving at their own appraisals of both standard and nonstandard tests in light of their particular values and needs; (*f*) to stimulate cooperating reviewers—and others to a lesser extent—to reconsider and think through more carefully their beliefs and values relevant to testing; (*g*) to inculcate upon test users a keener awareness of both the values and dangers which may accompany the use of standard tests; and (*h*) to impress test users with the desirability of suspecting all standard tests—even though prepared by well known authorities—unaccompanied by detailed data on their construction, validation, use, and limitations.

The objectives of the section Books and Reviews in this and other yearbooks in the series are:

(*a*) to make readily available comprehensive and up-to-date bibliographies of recent books on measurements and closely associated fields published in all English-speaking countries; (*b*) to make readily available evaluative excerpts from hundreds of book reviews appearing in a great variety of journals in this country and abroad in order to assist test users to make more discriminating selections of books for study and purchase; (*c*) to stimulate readers to develop more critical attitudes toward what they read; (*d*) to make readily available important and provocative statements which, though appearing in book reviews, have considerable value entirely apart from a consideration of the book under review; (*e*) to point out books which are not being reviewed but which probably merit review; (*f*) to improve the quality of book reviews by stimulating review editors to make greater efforts to choose competent reviewers who will contribute frankly critical reviews; and (*g*) to improve the quality of book reviews by stimulating reviewers "to take their responsibilities more seriously" by refusing to review books which they cannot appraise competently and honestly.

As I have indicated in the Preface, when I first formulated the above objectives more than a quarter of a century ago I was too optimistic in my expectations. Some progress has undoubtedly been made. Future progress toward the attainment of these objectives—particularly objectives *b, d, e, f, g,* and *h* of the section Tests and Reviews, and objectives *b* and *c* of the section Books and Reviews—will depend largely upon test users.

GUIDING PRINCIPLES

In addition to the above-stated objectives, the MMY's have been founded on a certain set of beliefs with respect to why critical reviews of tests are necessary, what sort of people ought —and ought not—to be asked to review tests, and in what ways publishers should be held responsible for the kinds of test materials submitted for review. The principles which guided me in initiating test reviews in *The Nineteen Thirty-Eight Yearbook* and in selecting reviewers and editing reviews for that volume are essentially the same as those which guide me today. Briefly, these principles may be stated as follows: (*a*) Because of the technical nature of standardized tests, most test users cannot, on their own, make an intelligent assessment of a test's validity in a given situation for a given purpose. (*b*) Just as an ill person wants to believe in the efficacy of a drug, the typical test user wants to believe in the validity of a test. If the claims for a test are accepted as true, decisions can be made in a "scientific" manner. If such claims are questioned, the would-be test user is forced to rely upon his unaided judgment. (*c*) Most commercially marketed tests are poorly constructed, inadequately validated, and of unknown value. Even the best of the tests tend to make some claims not supported by research data. (*d*) The test reviews in the MMY's should reflect a great variety of views and disciplines. (*e*) Each test should receive multiple reviews in order to get a better representation of different viewpoints. (*f*) Reviewers should use their own criteria in evaluating tests. (*g*) Test publishers should present whatever information they want test reviewers to consider in the manuals and technical reports which are routinely sold with their tests. (*h*) Reviewers should not be asked to review tests by their former teachers or by past or present colleagues. (Although I have taken considerable pains to avoid the selection of reviewers likely to be biased in reviewing a test for these reasons, I know that selection errors have occasionally been made.)

I can think of only three guiding principles which have been discarded or deliberately broken at times—all of them principles related to the selection of reviewers. In *The Nineteen Thirty-Eight Yearbook* I avoided asking employees of test publishers to review tests. As test publishers began to employ more and more testing specialists, I began to ask the testing specialists working for test publishers to review tests which were not directly competitive with their own tests. But even this practice proved too restrictive. In order to get the most competent persons available to review particular tests, I have had to invite more and more employees of test publishers to review tests. Their reviews are by and large among the best in this volume.

In a similar manner, I once avoided asking test authors to review tests which might be considered in direct competition with their own tests. The practice also proved too restrictive. At times it meant that I was ruling out the best informed persons as possible reviewers. Consequently, there have been deliberate exceptions to this rule.

Finally, in the earlier MMY's I attempted to avoid selecting as reviewers of a particular test persons who were known to believe that the test was useless. To a lesser extent, I avoided selecting as reviewers persons who were known to be devotees of a particular test. Nevertheless, in the case of projective techniques, I originally selected reviewers only from among persons interested in projective techniques. Because of this practice and because many psychologists interested in personality assessment refuse to review projective tests, the reviews of projective tests in the earliest yearbooks were loaded in favor of such tests. To correct this bias, I began to make an increasing number of exceptions. For example, when I asked H. J. Eysenck to review the Rorschach in *The Fifth Yearbook* I knew that his review would be unfavorable. As a result of these exceptions, I am confident that the present review coverage of tests—especially projective tests—reflects more closely the variety of views with which particular tests are regarded by professional workers of recognized standing.

THE SIXTH YEARBOOK

The Sixth Mental Measurements Yearbook, covering the period 1959 to mid-1964, is a completely new work which supplements rather than replaces earlier volumes in the series. Like previous volumes, *The Sixth Yearbook* consists of three main parts: the test section, the book section, and the indexes.

TESTS AND REVIEWS

The section Tests and Reviews, the most important part of the volume, has been greatly expanded. It presents extensive listings for 1,219 tests, 795 critical test reviews by 396 reviewers, 97 excerpts from reviews of tests which first appeared in 30 journals, and 8,001 references for specific tests.

The number of tests listed, 1,219, represents 27.4 per cent more entries than the number in *The Fifth Yearbook*. The test classification scheme used is essentially the same as that used in previous volumes in the series. A separate subcategory has been added for diagnostic reading tests in the reading section; such tests previously appeared in the miscellaneous subcategory of the reading section. The subcategory courtship and marriage is also new to the MMY's, having first appeared in *Tests in Print*. In the specific vocations subcategory under vocations, we have gone back to *The Fourth Yearbook* practice of subdivision into specific occupational areas. Table 1 presents statistics

Table 1

Sixth MMY Tests by Major Classifications

Classification	Number	Percentage
Personality	196	16.1
Vocations	179	14.7
Intelligence	131	10.7
Miscellaneous	108	8.9
English	99	8.1
Mathematics	96	7.9
Reading	87	7.1
Foreign Languages	77	6.3
Science	74	6.1
Social Studies	61	5.0
Business Education	29	2.4
Achievement Batteries	28	2.3
Sensory-Motor	27	2.2
Multi-Aptitude	16	1.3
Fine Arts	11	.9
Total	1,219	100.0

on the number and percentage of tests in each of the 15 major classifications of tests. Personality, the area in which our assessment procedures have the least validity, is represented by the largest number of tests—196 or 16.1 per cent. Tests of personality, vocations, and intelligence make up 41.5 per cent of the total. Although achievement and multi-aptitude batteries make up only 3.6 per cent of the total, tests in these two categories are probably administered to more examinees than the tests in any one of the other categories. Because of this wide usage, a great deal of space has been given to the review coverage of achievement and multi-aptitude batteries.

The recency of publication of the tests in *The Sixth Yearbook* is shown in Table 2. More than half of the tests, 51.5 per cent, are new tests not previously listed in a *Mental Measurements Yearbook;* 36.5 per cent are tests which have been revised or supplemented since they were last listed; and only 12.0 per cent are old tests—that is, tests which have not been revised or supplemented since they were last listed in a *Mental Measurements Yearbook*. The 628 new

Table 2

Percentage of Tests New and Revised or Supplemented by Major Classifications

Classification	Number of Tests	Percentage New	Percentage Revised	Percentage Total
Personality	196	52.6	23.5	76.0
Vocations	179	65.9	26.3	92.2
Intelligence	131	45.0	38.2	83.2
Miscellaneous	108	61.1	28.7	89.8
English	99	49.5	41.4	90.9
Mathematics	96	51.0	42.7	93.7
Reading	87	40.2	46.0	86.2
Foreign Languages	77	67.5	26.0	93.5
Science	74	37.8	58.1	95.9
Social Studies	61	37.7	54.1	91.8
Business Education	29	44.8	48.3	93.1
Achievement Batteries	28	21.4	64.3	85.7
Sensory-Motor	27	63.0	18.5	81.5
Multi-Aptitude	16	37.5	62.5	100.0
Fine Arts	11	36.4	45.5	81.9
Total	1,219	51.5	36.5	88.0

tests are indicated by stars preceding their titles; the 445 revised or supplemented tests are indicated by asterisks preceding their titles. The percentage of new tests ranges from 21.4 for achievement batteries to 67.5 for foreign languages. The percentage of revised or supplemented tests ranges from 18.5 for sensory-motor to 64.3 for achievement batteries. A total of 1,073 tests, 88.0 per cent, are new, revised, or supplemented since the publication of *The Fifth Yearbook*. The percentage of new, revised, or supplemented tests ranges from 76.0 for personality tests to 100 for multi-aptitude batteries.

The 1,219 tests for which full entries are given include the following categories: (*a*) All tests known to have been published (new, revised, or supplemented) in English-speaking countries during the period 1959 to mid-1964. (*b*) Tests published prior to 1959 but not previously included in an MMY. (*c*) Tests published prior to 1959 for which at least seven new references had been located. Most of these tests have not been reviewed in this volume because of adequate review coverage in earlier volumes. (*d*) Tests published prior to 1959 but selected for reviewing. This last category includes tests which were listed in earlier MMY's but not reviewed, tests which received only one review in previous volumes, tests which needed further reviewing in light of current knowledge and competing tests, and a few pioneer tests of historical interest. The pioneer tests reviewed, listed in order of original publication, are: *Kent-Rosanoff Free Association Test* (1910), *Otis Group Intelligence Scale* (1918), *Monroe's Standardized Silent Reading Tests* (1919), and *Pressey Classification and Verifying Tests* (1922). (*e*) Selected tests which are not commercially available but are widely used under restricted conditions. This category includes such tests as the College Entrance Examination Board tests, *National Merit Scholarship Qualifying Test,* and *Medical College Admission Test.* (*f*) Selected testing programs and series of tests. Special mention should be made of the following reviews of testing programs and test series: *The Affiliation Testing Program for Catholic Secondary Schools* (see 758), *College Entrance Examination Board Admissions Testing Program* (see 760), *Secondary School Admission Tests* (see 24), *Sequential Tests of Educational Progress* (see 25), and *National Teacher Examinations* (see 700).

In addition to listing 1,219 tests, the section Tests and Reviews presents for every category of tests references to the *Tests in Print* entry numbers of all other tests in the same category which are not listed in *The Sixth Yearbook* but may be found in *Tests in Print.* For each of these other tests, information is given as to whether the test was in print, out of print, or of unknown status as of mid-1964. All test publishers were asked to indicate whether or not their tests were in print as of mid-1964. In the few cases where no reply was received to repeated requests for information, we have described the test as "status unknown." The addition of these references provides the reader with a comprehensive bibliography of all tests known to be in print as of mid-1964.

REVIEWERS

A total of 396 persons have cooperated to make this volume possible by contributing original reviews of tests. The review coverage by major categories is presented in Table 3.

An examination of the list of cooperating reviewers on pages xi–xxii of this volume will reveal the extremely wide range of interests and specialties represented among the reviewers. Most of the reviewers are college teachers in education and psychology: 124 are instructors in education or educational psychology; 122 are instructors in psychology; 51 are employees of test publishers; 27 work in test construction and research bureaus in colleges; 18 are college instructors in business administration, English, foreign languages, mathematics, science, or sociology; 15 are research psychologists not affiliated with colleges; 13 are

Table 3

Review Coverage in *The Sixth Yearbook*

Classification	Number of Reviews	Number of Tests Reviewed	Percentage of Tests: 1 or More Reviews	Percentage of Tests: 2 or More Reviews
Personality	210	125	63.8	38.3
Intelligence	114	76	58.0	28.2
Vocations	90	59	33.0	16.8
Reading	72	43	49.4	32.2
English	49	36	36.4	12.1
Mathematics	49	37	38.5	12.5
Achievement Batteries	44	22	78.6	64.3
Science	37	26	35.1	14.9
Miscellaneous	35	28	25.9	6.5
Foreign Languages	25	19	24.7	7.8
Social Studies	22	18	29.5	6.6
Multi-Aptitude	21	11	68.7	56.2
Fine Arts	11	8	72.7	27.3
Business Education	10	8	27.6	6.9
Sensory-Motor	6	6	22.2	0
Total	795	522	42.8	20.9

industrial psychologists; 13 are clinical psychologists not affiliated with colleges; and the remaining 32 hold miscellaneous other positions. The distribution of reviewers by countries follows: United States, 343; Great Britain, 34; Canada, 11; Australia, 4; New Zealand, 1; Republic of South Africa, 1; Sweden, 1; and United Arab Republic, 1. The relative distribution of reviewers among countries is very nearly the same as the relative distribution of tests among countries.

Over half of the reviewers, 213 or 53.8 per cent, are new reviewers. Of the 183 old reviewers, only 7 have reviewed for all six MMY's, 14 for five MMY's, 33 for four MMY's, 47 for three MMY's, and 82 for two MMY's. Ages are available for 262 of the reviewers. Their ages range from 30 to 73 years with quartiles 40, 46, and 53. The quartiles for new reviewers are 37, 41, and 44; the quartiles for old reviewers are 45, 52, and 58.

In addition to the 795 test reviews written specifically for *The Sixth Yearbook,* the section Tests and Reviews includes excerpts of the critical comments made in 97 test reviews originally published in 30 journals. No effort has been made to reprint excerpts from all test reviews located. We have excerpted only the reviews which seemed to be of sufficiently high quality to justify reprinting. Even though we have been more selective than in previous MMY's, the number of excerpted test reviews is almost exactly double the number presented in *The Fifth Yearbook*. This is a reflection of the increasing number of test reviews to be found in journals, a trend which is likely to accelerate during the next few years.

This volume lists 8,001 references on the construction, uses, and limitations of specific tests—23.7 per cent more references than were included in *The Fifth Yearbook*. All published references have been examined to make sure that they warrant being listed as references. These bibliographies are more selective than those usually prepared by test authors and publishers; references which merely mention a test or give cursory attention to it are not included. The bibliographies are limited to articles, books, and theses written in English.

BOOKS AND REVIEWS

The section Books and Reviews lists 527 books, 8.6 per cent more than *The Fifth Yearbook,* on measurements and closely related fields. Four hundred fifty three, or 86.0 per cent, are new books which have not been previously listed in a *Mental Measurements Yearbook;* 39, or 7.4 per cent, are books which have been revised since they were last listed in an MMY; and only 35, or 6.6 per cent, are books which were also listed in *The Fifth Yearbook*.

In the first four MMY's, the critical portions of all reviews located for books on testing were reprinted as review excerpts. In order to give more space to test reviews, this practice of excerpting all reviews was discontinued in *The Fifth Yearbook*—only a representative selection of the reviews were chosen for excerpting. In this volume there has been even a more drastic reduction in the space devoted to excerpts from book reviews. *The Sixth Yearbook* presents only 377 excerpts, 29.5 per cent less than *The Fifth Yearbook,* from 70 journals. Excerpts are presented for 193 books, 36.6 per cent of all books listed; 82 of these books have one excerpt, 61 have two excerpts, 36 have three excerpts, 6 have four excerpts, and 5 have five or more excerpts. Despite our search of over two hundred journals, no reviews worth excerpting were found for approximately two-thirds of the books.

INDEXES

As have earlier volumes, *The Sixth Yearbook* contains five indexes. Important improvements, however, have been made in the Title Index and the Classified Index. The Title Index not only lists the titles of the 1,219 tests and the 527 books for which full entries are given in this volume but also lists the titles of 952 other tests known to be in print as of mid-1964. The titles for these 952 tests are followed by references to the corresponding entry numbers in *Tests in Print*. The total number of tests known to be in print as of mid-1964 is 2,171. *The Sixth Yearbook* presents extensive information on 56.1 per cent of these tests and indicates where in *Tests in Print* information about the remaining 43.9 per cent may be found. Table 4 presents statistics on the number of tests in print in each of the major classifications of tests. The percentage which the tests in this volume are of all tests in print in the same category ranges from 39.3 for fine arts to 80.0 for multi-aptitude batteries.

Table 4

Tests in Print as of Mid-1964 by Major Classifications

Classification	Tests in 6th MMY	Tests in TIP	Total	Percentage in 6th MMY
Personality	196	116	312	62.8
Vocations	179	128	307	58.3
Intelligence	131	112	243	53.9
Miscellaneous	108	121	229	47.2
Mathematics	96	105	201	47.8
English	99	85	184	53.8
Reading	87	77	164	53.0
Foreign Languages	77	43	120	64.2
Science	74	35	109	67.9
Social Studies	61	45	106	57.5
Sensory-Motor	27	30	57	47.4
Business Education	29	21	50	58.0
Achievement Batteries	28	13	41	68.3
Fine Arts	11	17	28	39.3
Multi-Aptitude	16	4	20	80.0
Total	1,219	952	2,171	56.1

The usefulness of the Classified Index has been greatly increased by including in it a complete listing of all tests known to be in print as of mid-1964. Two alphabetical sequences of test titles are presented for each classification of tests. The first sequence lists the entry numbers and titles of tests to be found in this volume along with names of the reviewers, if any. The second sequence lists the *Tests in Print* entry numbers and titles of other tests in print.

SUGGESTIONS TO REVIEWERS

A sheet entitled "Suggestions to Reviewers" was enclosed with each letter inviting a person to review. The suggestions given are essentially the same as those sent to reviewers for earlier yearbooks. To properly understand the viewpoint from which the test reviews were written, readers are urged to study the following "Suggestions to Reviewers."

1) Reviews should be written with the following major objectives in mind:

a) To provide test users with carefully prepared appraisals of tests for their guidance in selecting and using tests.

b) To stimulate progress toward higher professional standards in the construction of tests by commending good work, by censuring poor work, and by suggesting improvements.

c) To impel test authors and publishers to present more detailed information on the construction, validity, reliability, uses, and possible misuses of their tests.

2) Reviews should be concise, the average review running from 500 to 1000 words in length. The average length of the reviews written by one person should not exceed 800 words. Except for reviews of achievement batteries, multi-factor batteries, and tests for which a literature review is to be made, longer reviews should be prepared only with the approval of the editor.

3) Reviews should be frankly critical, with both strengths and weaknesses pointed out in a judicious manner. Descriptive comments should be kept to the minimum necessary to support the critical portions of the review. Criticism should be as specific as possible; implied criticisms meaningful only to testing specialists should be avoided. Reviews should be written primarily for the rank and file of test users. An indication of the relative importance and value of a test with respect to competing tests should be presented whenever possible. If a reviewer considers a competing test better than the one being reviewed, the competing test should be specifically named.

4) If a test manual gives insufficient, contradictory, or ambiguous information regarding the construction, validity, and use of a test, reviewers are urged to write directly to authors and publishers for further information. Test authors and publishers should, however, be held responsible for presenting adequate data in test manuals—failure to do so should be pointed out. For comments made by reviewers based upon unpublished information received personally from test authors or publishers, the source of the information should be clearly indicated.

5) Reviewers will be furnished with the test entries which will precede their reviews. Information presented in the entry should not be repeated in reviews unless it is done for evaluative purposes.

6) The use of sideheads is optional with reviewers.

7) Each review should conclude with a paragraph presenting a concise summary of the reviewer's overall evaluation of the test. The summary should be as explicit as possible. Is the test the best of its kind? Is it recommended for use? If other tests are better, which of the competing tests is best?

8) A separate review should be prepared for each test. Each review should begin on a new sheet. The test and forms reviewed should be clearly indicated. Your name, title, position, and address should precede each review, e.g.: John Doe, Professor of Education and Psychology, University of Maryland, College Park, Maryland. The review should begin a new paragraph immediately after the address.

9) All reviews should be typed *double spaced* and *in triplicate. Two copies* of each review should be submitted to THE MENTAL MEASUREMENTS YEARBOOK; *one copy* should be retained by the reviewer.

10) If for any reason a reviewer thinks he is not in a position to write a frankly critical review in a scholarly and unbiased manner, he should request the editor to substitute other tests for review.

11) Reviewers may not invite others to collaborate with them in writing a review unless permission is secured from the editor.

12) Most tests will be reviewed by two or more persons in order to secure better representation of various viewpoints. Noncritical content which excessively

overlaps similar material presented by another reviewer may be deleted. Reviews will be carefully edited, but no important changes will be made without the consent of the reviewer. Galley proofs (unaccompanied by copy) will be submitted to reviewers for checking.

13) The editor reserves the right to reject any review which does not meet the minimum standards of the yearbook series.

14) Each reviewer will receive a complimentary copy of THE SIXTH MENTAL MEASUREMENTS YEARBOOK.

HOW TO USE THIS YEARBOOK

The reader who wishes to get the maximum help in as brief a time as possible from *The Sixth Mental Measurements Yearbook* should read the following suggestions and explanations. This should be done even though the reader has had experience using earlier volumes.

1) *Table of Contents.* The Table of Contents should be consulted first to get an overall picture of the volume's contents and the classification plan used. The Table of Contents lists all the main headings, subheadings, and subsubheadings under which tests are classified in the section Tests and Reviews. The numbers referred to in the Table of Contents are page numbers, not entry numbers. Elsewhere in the volume, all references are to entry numbers.

2) *Classified Index of Tests.* After examining the Table of Contents, the reader may find it profitable to turn to the Classified Index of Tests at the end of this volume. The Classified Index, an expanded table of contents of the section Tests and Reviews, presents a complete list of all tests and reviewers in this volume. In addition, it presents a classified list of all in print tests which are *not* in this yearbook. It is, therefore, a classified bibliography of all tests known to be in print as of mid-1964.

3) *Page and Entry Numbers.* Confusion of page and entry numbers is probably responsible for more difficulty in using the MMY's than is any other characteristic of the volumes. Readers are urged, therefore, to keep in mind that page numbers appear in the running heads next to the *inside* margins; entry numbers (i.e., the numbers assigned to specific tests and books) appear in the running heads next to the *outside* margins. The entry numbers on facing pages represent the first and last tests or books listed on those pages. The Table of Contents refers to page numbers—the numbers next to the inside margins. Cross references and indexes refer to entry numbers—the numbers next to the outside margins. Except when using the Table of Contents, the reader will have no need to use page numbers.

4) *Stars, Asterisks, and Ellipses.* A star (★) preceding a title indicates a new test or book not previously listed in an MMY. An asterisk (*) preceding a title indicates a test or book which has been revised or supplemented in some way since last listed in an MMY. An asterisk following an entry for a test, book, or reference indicates that the entry was prepared from a first-hand examination of the publication in question. Asterisks and ellipses in quotations and excerpts indicate omissions; asterisks indicate a break in the continuity of reading, and ellipses indicate continuity of reading.

5) *Citations for Cross References.* Cross references to reviews and references in this and earlier volumes are frequently made. Cross references should be interpreted thus: "see 416" refers to test entry 416 in this volume; "see B387" refers to book entry B387 in this volume; "see 5:632" refers to test entry 632 in *The Fifth Mental Measurements Yearbook;* "see 40:193" refers to entry 193 in *The Nineteen Forty Mental Measurements Yearbook;* and "see 36:B210" refers to book entry B210 in *Educational, Psychological, and Personality Tests of 1936.*

6) *Test Entries.* For each test, an attempt has been made to present in 8 point type the following information in the order given.

a) TITLE. Test titles are printed in boldface type. Secondary or series titles are set off from main titles by a colon. Titles are always presented exactly as reported in the test materials. When the titles on the test booklet and manual differ, the better known title is given in boldface; the second title is generally given in italic type within the entry. Entry titles which differ from those reported in the test materials (generally because no definitive title is used) are enclosed in brackets. Stars (★) precede titles of tests which have never before been listed in an MMY; asterisks (*) precede titles of tests which have been revised or supplemented since their last MMY listing.

b) DESCRIPTION OF THE GROUPS FOR WHICH THE TEST IS INTENDED. The grade, chronological age, or semester range, or the employment category is usually given. "Grades 1.5–2.5, 2–3, 4-12, 13–17" means that there are four test booklets: a booklet for the middle of the first grade through the middle of the second grade, a booklet for the beginning of the second grade through the end of the third grade, a booklet for grades 4 through 12 inclusive, and a booklet for undergraduate and graduate students in colleges and universities. "First, second semester" means that there are two test booklets: one covering the work of the first semester, the other covering the work of the second semester. "1, 2 semesters" indicates that the second booklet covers the work of the two semesters. Short dashes separate years and months. For example, "ages 10-2 to 11-11" means ages 10 years 2 months to 11 years 11 months;

"grades 4-6 to 5-9" means the sixth month in the fourth grade through the ninth month in the fifth grade. Commas are used to separate levels. "High school and college" denotes a single test booklet for both levels; "High school, college" denotes two test booklets, one for high school and one for college.

c) DATE OF COPYRIGHT OR PUBLICATION. The inclusive range of copyright dates (or publication dates if not copyrighted) for the various forms, accessories, and editions of a test is reported. When the publication date differs from the copyright date, both dates are given; e.g., "1948, c1946-48" means that the test was copyrighted both in 1946 and in 1948 but was not published until 1948. When publication or copyright dates do not appear on the materials and the date has been secured through correspondence with the publisher, it is enclosed in brackets.

d) PART SCORES. The number of part scores is presented along with their titles or descriptions of what they presumably represent.

e) INDIVIDUAL OR GROUP TEST. All tests are group tests unless otherwise indicated.

f) MACHINE SCORABLE TESTS. Tests which may be scored by scoring machines which may be purchased or for which machine scoring services are available independently of the test publisher are marked in one of the following ways: "IBM" means either that the test may be scored by *IBM Test Scoring Machine* (see 669) or that it may be scored by *IBM Optical Mark Scoring Reader* (see 668); "Digitek" means that the test may be scored by *Digitek Optical Test Scoring and Document Scanning System* (see 661); "Grade-O-Mat" means that the test may be scored by *Grade-O-Mat* (see 666); "Hankes" means that *Hankes Answer Sheets* and scoring services (see 667) are available; "MRC" means that Measurement Research Center answer sheets and scoring services (see 670) are available; and "NCS" means that National Computer Systems answer sheets and scoring services (see 671) are available. "IBM" may refer to either IBM 805 or IBM 1230 answer sheets; no attempt has been made to specify which type answer sheet is available. Some publishers have developed special types of answer sheets and scoring services which are available only for their own tests; such machine scorable features are not mentioned at this point in the entry but are noted in the price information given for answer sheets. As entries for *The Sixth Yearbook* were being prepared, many publishers—most of the larger ones—were in the process of revising and expanding upon the machine scoring accessories available for their tests. For up-to-date information on machine scoring features, the latest catalogs of test publishers should be consulted.

g) FORMS, PARTS, AND LEVELS. All available forms, parts, and levels are listed with the most recent date of publication.

h) PAGES. The number of pages on which print occurs is reported for test booklets, manuals, technical reports, profiles, and other nonapparatus accessories. Blank pages and pages containing only material not related to the test (e.g., advertising pages and pages containing only printer's marks) have not been counted. Self-covers have been counted only when the cover is not duplicated by a title page inside.

i) RELIABILITY AND VALIDITY. The complete absence of data in a test manual is indicated. It was originally intended to include in the entries the statement "reliability data for raw scores only" wherever appropriate. However, since it soon became apparent that almost all tests still report only raw score reliability data rather than data on reliability of normed scores, the idea of including such a statement was abandoned.

j) COST. Both test package and specimen set prices are given. A statement such as "$3 per 35 tests" means that all accessories are included unless otherwise indicated by the reporting of separate prices for accessories. Such a statement also means 35 tests of one level, one edition, or one part unless we say otherwise. Discounts that may be available for purchasing in large quantities and special discounts that may be available to professional groups are not reported. Specimen set prices mean specimen sets of all levels, all editions, all parts—but not all forms—unless otherwise indicated. Price information is believed to be correct as of mid-1964. Although every precaution has been taken to ensure accuracy, some prices may be in error and other prices may have changed. For full and up-to-date information on test prices, the latest catalogs of test publishers should be consulted.

k) TIME. The number of minutes of actual working time allowed examinees and the approximate length of time needed for administering a test are reported whenever obtainable. The latter figure is always enclosed in parentheses. Thus, "50(60) minutes" indicates that the examinees are allowed fifty minutes of working time and that a total of sixty minutes is needed to administer the test. When the time necessary to administer a test is not reported or suggested in the test materials but has been obtained through correspondence with the test publisher or author, the time is enclosed in brackets.

l) AUTHOR. For most tests, all authors are reported. In the case of tests which appear in a new form each year, only authors of the most recent forms are listed. Names are reported exactly as printed on test booklets. Names of editors are generally not reported.

m) PUBLISHER. The name of the publisher or distributor is reported for each test. Publishers' names which do not appear on the test materials are enclosed in brackets. For addresses of publishers and distributors, see the Publishers Directory and Index.

n) SUBENTRIES. Levels, editions, subtests, or parts of a test which are available in separate booklets are presented as subentries with titles set in small capitals. Sub-subentries are indented with titles set in italic type.

7) *Test References.* All known references—published articles and books and unpublished doctoral theses—on the construction, validity, use, and limitations of each test are reported in 6 point type immediately after the test entry. These references are arranged in chronological order by year of publication and alphabetically by authors within years. The test bibliographies are believed to be fairly complete through 1963; a dozen or so references for 1964 are also included. In order to assist students who wish to do selected reading on a particular test, references are given to abstracts in *Dissertation Abstracts* and in *Psychological Abstracts.* For example, "(*DA* 33:6843)" refers to a thesis abstract beginning on page 6843 in volume 33 of *Dissertation Abstracts;* and "(*PA* 37:416)" refers to abstract number 416 in volume 37 of *Psychological Abstracts.* References are numbered consecutively through all MMY volumes.

References which appeared in earlier volumes are referred to but are not repeated. For example, "1–5. See 5:791" means that the first five references for the test will be found under entry 791 in *The Fifth Yearbook.*

8) *Original Test Reviews.* Original reviews of a particular test are set in 10 on 11 point type and are arranged in alphabetical order by reviewers. Cited references which are also references for the test under review are indicated by the use of italic numbers in parentheses. Cited references which are not among the test references are indicated by the use of superscripts which refer to footnotes. At times, it will be necessary to consult an earlier MMY for the reference cited. Within test reviews only full titles of published tests are italicized; short titles and titles of unpublished tests are set in Roman.

9) *Excerpted Test Reviews.* Excerpts from test reviews first published elsewhere are set in 10 on 11 point type immediately after the original test reviews in alphabetical order by journal.

10) *References to Other Test Reviews.* Cross references to other reviews in earlier yearbooks of the same or earlier editions of tests and to related reviews in this volume are set in 10 on 11 point italic type following the original and excerpted reviews.

11) *References to Other Tests in Print.* Following the last test listed under a given heading, references are made to the *Tests in Print* entry numbers of other tests in the same category. For each of the tests to which references are made, information is given as to whether the test is in print, out of print, or of unknown status. The titles of all tests in print as of mid-1964 are presented in the Classified Index of Tests at the end of this volume.

12) *Book Entries.* The books listed in the section Books and Reviews are arranged in alphabetical order by authors with anonymous books arranged alphabetically by title preceding the others. Rather complete bibliographic information is given for each book. When publishers in two countries are reported, the country of origin is indicated by the first listed publisher. The book entries, like the test entries, are set in 8 point type. Wherever available, references to abstracts to be found in *Psychological Abstracts* are also presented.

13) *Classified Index of Books.* A roughly classified index presented at the beginning of the section Books and Reviews will assist the reader to locate books on a particular subject. In addition to using this index, readers are urged to skim over titles and excerpts in search for books of interest.

14) *Book Reviews.* Excerpts from book reviews first published elsewhere are set in 10 on 11 point type and are arranged under each book in alphabetical order by journals.

15) *References to Other Book Reviews.* References to reviews of the same or earlier editions of books either in this volume or in earlier volumes are given in 10 on 11 point italic type following the excerpted reviews.

16) *Catchwords.* The running heads include catchwords to assist readers in the location of particular materials. These catchwords are presented on right-hand pages. For the section Tests and Reviews, catchwords consist of the first test classification represented on the facing pages; for the section Books and Reviews catchwords consist of the first author represented on the facing pages.

17) *Indexes.* The book contains five indexes: the previously mentioned Classified Index of Tests, in which all tests in print in a given area are grouped for quick reference; the Periodical Directory and Index, the major purpose of which is to serve as a key to the abbreviations used for journal titles from which excerpts have been taken; the Publishers Directory and Index, which furnishes the addresses of test and book publishers; the Index of Titles, wherein any test or book included in *The Sixth Yearbook* and any other test in print as of mid-1964 can be quickly located if its exact title is known; and the Index of Names, which lists the names of all reviewers, authors, editors, and others mentioned in test entries, book entries, references, reviews, cross references, and footnotes. Detailed information on the use of each index is contained in the italic matter preceding the index.

THE SIXTH MENTAL MEASUREMENTS YEARBOOK

Tests and Reviews

* * * * *

ACHIEVEMENT BATTERIES

REVIEWS BY *Dorothy C. Adkins, J. Stanley Ahmann, J. Douglas Ayers, Robert H. Bauernfeind, George K. Bennett, Miriam M. Bryan, Willis W. Clark, George D. Demos, Paul L. Dressel, Walter N. Durost, Henry S. Dyer, Max D. Engelhart, Warren G. Findley, J. Thomas Hastings, James R. Hayden, Kenneth D. Hopkins, Thomas W. Mahan, Jr., Jack C. Merwin, Jason Millman, Charles O. Neidt, Victor H. Noll, Robert D. North, Jacob S. Orleans, Ellis Batten Page, Everett B. Sackett, Harold Seashore, Marion F. Shaycoft, Robert J. Solomon, John E. Stecklein, David V. Tiedeman, Arthur E. Traxler, Willard G. Warrington, Alexander G. Wesman, and Frank B. Womer.*

[1]

★**The American College Testing Program Examination.** Grade 12 and junior college students preparing to transfer to 4-year colleges; 1959–63; tests administered 4 times a year (February, April, June, November) at participating colleges and centers established by the publisher; 5 scores: English usage, mathematics usage, social studies reading, natural sciences reading, composite; MRC; Forms 4-AC and 4-BR (32 pages) used in 1962–63 program; 2 new forms published annually; supervisor's manual, 1963–64 edition ('60, 20 pages); interpretive booklet for colleges, 1962–63 edition ('60, 38 pages); interpretive booklet for students, 1963–64 edition ('60, 34 pages); technical report, 1960–61 edition ('60, 24 pages); student information bulletin, 1962–63 edition ('62, 140 pages); general information bulletin ('63, 37 pages); manual for interpreting research reports to individual colleges ('62, 42 pages) by D. P. Hoyt and E. F. Lindquist; manual for participating in 1963 research service ['63, 41 pages]; manual for interpreting 1963 research reports ('63, c1962–63, 53 pages) by D. P. Hoyt and E. F. Lindquist; examination fee: $4; fee includes reporting of scores to the student, his high school, and 3 colleges designated at time of application, and follow-up reporting of research and predictive validity data to participating colleges and high schools; 180(210) minutes; American College Testing Program. *

REFERENCES

1. *How to Pass High on the American College Testing Program Exams.* New York: Arco Publishing Co., Inc., 1960. Pp. iv, 128, plus supplements. *
2. PETERS, FRANK R., AND PLOG, EUGENIA L. "The Effectiveness of the ACT for Selection and Placement at the Ohio State University." *Ed Res B* 40:232–41+ D '61. *
3. SWANSON, EDWARD O., AND BERDIE, RALPH F. "Predictive Validities in an Institute of Technology." *Ed & Psychol Meas* 21:1001–8 w '61. * Errata: 22:258 su '62.
4. JONES, REGINALD L. "A Study of the Validity of the Pre-Engineering Ability Test." *Ed & Psychol Meas* 22:393–6 su '62. * (*PA* 37:3879)
5. STATON, JON TOM. *The Relationship of Selected Factors to Academic Success for Beginning Freshmen.* Doctor's thesis, University of Oklahoma (Norman, Okla.), 1962. (*DA* 23:1564)
6. ULLMAN, ROBERT WARREN. *A Comparison of the Predictive Abilities of the ACT and GST With Respect to the Five State Universities of Ohio.* Doctor's thesis, Western Reserve University (Cleveland, Ohio), 1962.
7. BURNS, RICHARD LEO. *An Investigation of the Value of the American College Testing Program, the Scholastic Aptitude Test and the Purdue Placement Tests as Predictors of Academic Success of Purdue University Freshmen.* Doctor's thesis, Purdue University (Lafayette, Ind.), 1963. (*DA* 24:1477)
8. KAMMANN, RICHARD A. "Aptitude, Study Habits, and Reading Improvement." *J Develop Read* 6:77–86 w '63. *
9. LESTER, ROBERT ANDREW. *The Relationship of SVIB and ACT Scores to Differential Academic Achievement.* Doctor's thesis, University of Minnesota (Minneapolis, Minn.), 1963. (*DA* 24:1076)
10. LINDQUIST, E. F. "An Evaluation of a Technique for Scaling High School Grades to Improve Prediction of College Success." *Ed & Psychol Meas* 23:623–46 w '63. *
11. MICHAEL, WILLIAM B.; CATHCART, ROBERT; ZIMMERMAN, WAYNE S.; AND MILFS, MILO. "Gains in Various Measures of Communication Skills Relative to Three Curricular Patterns in College." *Ed & Psychol Meas* 23:365–74 su '63. * (*PA* 38:1384)

12. ORGEL, JOSEPH RANDOLPH. *Preparing for American College Test Program Examinations.* Cambridge, Mass.: Educators Publishing Service, 1963. Pp. vi, 314. *
13. TRUMP, PAUL L. "The American College Testing Program." *J Nat Assn Women Deans & Counselors* 27:40–3 O '63. *
14. YAGER, ROBERT E., AND DESSEL, NORMAN F. "Selection Criteria for High Ability Science Students." *J Ed Res* 57: 193–6 D '63. *

MAX D. ENGELHART, *Director, Division of Institutional Research and Evaluation, Department of Higher Education, Chicago Public Schools, Chicago, Illinois.* [Review of Forms 4-AC and 4-BR.]

During its first year of operation (1959–1960) approximately 120,000 "college-bound" high school seniors took the ACT battery and reports of their scores were sent to 368 participating colleges (plus over 600 other colleges) in 19 states. During the school year 1962–1963 over 350,000 students completed the tests, and reports of their scores were sent to over 725 colleges or universities requiring or recommending the tests as a means of obtaining data useful in admission of students, in placement, in guidance, and in awarding scholarships or loans. In 28 states, colleges participated through affiliated state programs. The three-hour ACT test battery is administered on four Saturdays in November, February, April, and June in more than a thousand test centers, most of them on college campuses in all 50 states, the District of Columbia, and at American schools overseas.

Within two to four weeks after each testing date, reports of scores are sent to each of three colleges designated by the student; within three to four weeks, two reports are sent to the student's high school, one for the school and one for the student himself. A college having participated in the ACT Research Service receives predictive grade indices for English, mathematics, social studies, natural sciences, and for overall grade point average of each prospective student based on weighted combinations of his ACT scores only. Another five predictive indices are also reported based on weighted combinations of the student's ACT scores and junior year high school course marks in the same areas. In addition, the participating college receives local norm data also useful in estimating levels of achievement to be expected of students after admission. The information given in this and the preceding paragraph should give the reader some idea of the impressive magnitude of the ACT program.

The *Third, Fourth,* and *Fifth Mental Measurements Yearbooks* contain reviews of the *Iowa Tests of Educational Development,* the USAFI *Tests of General Educational Development,* and the *National Merit Scholarship Qualifying Test,* tests partly or wholly similar in character to the ACT examination. It is interesting to compare the judgments concerning content and construct validity reported in these reviews, for example the judgments of Herbert Conrad, Benno Fricke, and Warren Findley, with the section entitled "Rationale of the ACT Tests" in the ACT Technical Report, 1960–1961 Edition. After noting that factorially pure tests of the differential aptitude type tend to neglect "the *complexity* of the criterion itself, or the *interactions* among the specific traits involved," the technical report argues that "what really matters in determining college success is not so much what specific skills and knowledges the student has mastered independently, but rather *how well he can use all of them—in proper combination*—in an integrated attack upon complicated problems." It is further argued that "nearly all of the most widely accepted tests used to predict academic success consist in large part of this kind of exercise: comprehensive reading passages, and functional and practical problems involving complex arithmetic reasoning." It is claimed that "the ACT tests also provide a broader coverage of educational skills than do most other tests of scholastic aptitude" and the ACT English Usage Test is cited in this connection.

Tests of the general educational development type are often accused of neglecting measurement of student possession of knowledge. In the "Rationale of the ACT Tests," however, it is contended:

> Tests of this character *do* place a high and definite premium on the possession of a rich store of knowledge, but they do so indirectly rather than directly. The tests are not constructed to measure the acquisition of subject matter content *per se.* The questions do not call directly for specific information. Rather, they test the student's ability to use *whatever* knowledge he possesses in the solution of complex problems.

The author of this review is in general agreement with the philosophy expressed in the "Rationale of the ACT Tests." The spectrum of aptitudes, skills, abilities, and achievements which might be measured in predicting success on the college level ranges from such purely "psychological" tests as figure analogies, number series, and the like to tests of subject matter knowledge. The emphasis on generalized school-learned abilities seems to be a legitimate compromise, although one can regret possible injustice to students more capable of nonverbal reasoning than of reasoning in verbal symbols. This reviewer has no misgivings with reference to measurement of subject matter knowledge. Such knowledge is measured by the ACT tests to the extent that it can be measured for students of varied high school learning experiences. One has only to take the ACT tests, as this reviewer has done, to realize the extent to which knowledge functions. This is evident not only in responding to the "background" items of the social studies and natural science tests but in responding to the items relevant to the reading selections and to the items of the English and mathematics tests also. Similarly, if introspection is to be trusted, one feels that intelligence is functioning as well!

Each edition of the ACT examination is published as a single 32-page booklet containing four subtests possibly best described by quoting from the pamphlet Using the ACT Scores on Your Campus.

TEST 1. ENGLISH USAGE TEST. This 80-item, 50-minute test "measures the student's educational development in the use of the basic elements of correct and effective writing: punctuation, capitalization, diction, phraseology, and organization of ideas. The test consists of several written exercises into which a number of errors or inappropriate expressions have been inserted. The student's task is to identify the instances of improper English usage and to choose the most acceptable substitutes. Approximately 75 per cent of the items are concerned with the appropriateness of words and phrases, paragraphing, word order, effectiveness of various constructions, diction, style, organization of ideas, and general facility with the language. The remaining items are concerned with formal correctness of punctuation, capitalization, and grammar."

TEST 2. MATHEMATICS USAGE TEST. This 40-item, 50-minute test "measures the student's educational development in the use of mathematical principles for solving quantitative problems and in the interpretation of graphs and charts. The test is composed of two general kinds of problems: (*a*) quantitative reasoning based on timely situations and (*b*) formal exercises in geometry, first-year algebra, and advanced arithmetic. The reasoning problems are drawn from a variety of areas—industry, business and finance, home management, the social sciences, and the natural sciences—and cover such topics as proportions and percentages, costs and profits, interest, and interpretation of graphs and tables. Exercises include such problems as solving first-degree equations in one and two unknowns, simplifying algebraic expressions, substituting in formulas, working with roots and powers, factoring quadratics, computing areas of polygons, applying the Pythagorean theorem, and understanding angular relationships."

TEST 3. SOCIAL STUDIES READING TEST. This 52-item, 40-minute "educational development test measures the student's ability to read materials from the social studies with critical understanding and to do the types of reasoning and problem solving characteristic of these fields. * Typical reading passages are concerned with topics and problems within the field of the social studies—political science, economics, sociology, geography, American and world history, psychology, and anthropology. The discussions center on important aspects, theories, and controversies within these fields and emphasize relevant concepts, terminology, and styles of writing. * The general skills tested include (*a*) recognizing and taking into account the author's biases and points of view, (*b*) evaluating the evidence and distinguishing between facts and opinions, (*c*) grasping the implied meanings, and (*d*) detecting the techniques of the demagogue and recognizing false or specious logic."

Also included are 14 items evaluating understanding of important concepts or recall of important facts to which the student responds on the basis of his prior knowledge.

TEST 4. NATURAL SCIENCE READING TEST. This 52-item, 40-minute "educational development test measures the student's ability to interpret and evaluate reading materials in the natural sciences. * Typical reading passages, for example, present summaries of the procedures and outcomes of one or more simple experiments. The student, in responding to the specific items, is required to demonstrate his understanding of the purposes of the experiments, the hypothesis tested by each, the logical relationships among them, and valid conclusions or generalizations that can be inferred from the series of experiments as a whole. Other passages present materials that are assumed to be unfamiliar to most high school students; the student's task is to demonstrate his ability to assimilate and master the new materials."

This test also includes 16 items relevant to important facts and concepts to be answered on the basis of prior knowledge.

The persons employed in writing items for the ACT examinations are provided with "specifications" to direct their efforts. Those for the English Usage Test first describe the form of the test—units consisting of prose passages with underlined and numbered portions in left-hand columns with correspondingly numbered alternative versions in an adjacent column. It is also indicated here that effectiveness of expression is to be given greater weight than correctness of expression and that items should "contain more than one factor to consider in obtaining the correct answer." (This is a condition entailed by the exercise form and may not be inherently desirable.) The instructions concerning selection of prose passages and the detailed suggestions concerning form and content of items are, within the limitations of the exercise form, generally excellent. Item writers for the English Usage Test must find the "Style Guide for English Usage Items" extremely helpful, since it provides a model which they can follow. Also generally commendable are the specifications available to the item writers of the other subtests. In the case of the social studies and the natural science specifications, separate instructions are provided for "reading" and "background" items. Especially noteworthy for their emphasis on measurement of intellectual skills transcending knowledge are the instructions relevant to the reading items in the social studies and natural science tests. For example, one section of the social studies specifications suggests that the items "should call for evidence of the following abilities" and among the eight listed are the abilities to "recognize the writer's position," "evaluate evidence and differentiate fact from opinion," and "detect inconsistencies in argument."

Concerning the effectiveness of the various subtests, the most serious question in this reviewer's judgment is whether the English usage subtests of Forms 4-AC and 4-BR do have the content validity to be expected from the description of this test earlier quoted and from the definitions in the specifications given the item writers. There appears to be excessive emphasis on circumlocutions at the expense of crucial items on diction, grammatical usage, logical comparisons, and sentence construction. There is little provision of problems concerning paragraphing, sentence placement, and other aspects of organization. While problems relevant to restrictive and nonrestrictive elements are well represented, there are relatively few other punctuation problems. The correct answer to one item contains a pronoun with no antecedent. The double presentation of the reading passages (once without and once with accompanying questions) might be justified if used to present organization problems, but, as given, the procedure is needlessly time consuming in a test where speed is so evidently a factor to the critic who administers the test to himself.

But beyond questions of specific content is the question whether this exercise form adequately or optimally measures student writing ability. While it "is designed to approximate a situation in which a student is revising a prose composition," no evidence is given to show that the skills involved are the same skills required in revising one's own composition, or indeed that such revision is in any case the major subskill of writing. Nor is it certain that most college English teachers give more weight to effectiveness than to correctness of expression. Studies are badly needed to determine the relative validity of this type of English exercise in comparison with scores on writing samples and on other types of objective tests addressed to specific subskills of writing.[1] The present writer does not prejudge the outcome of such studies, but does venture to say that in such a complex and rapidly developing field as the objective measurement of writing ability we should not be asked to accept content and construct validity claims on mainly deductive grounds.

Although Using the ACT Scores on Your Campus gives admirably full treatment to the use of optimally weighted scores on all of the ACT tests alone or in combination with high school marks in placing English composition students at appropriate levels of instruction, unfortunately no similar guidance is given for the placement of students in either remedial or developmental reading classes. It seems likely that some weighted combination of the English and social studies scores, or scores and high school marks, could be used for this purpose; but, if so, the proper weighting remains to be worked out.

The mathematics tests of Forms 4-AC and 4-BR satisfactorily cover the topics listed in the description of this test earlier quoted. The distribution of content over advanced arithmetic, geometry, and first year algebra with the last-named receiving the greatest emphasis is also appropriate. Numerous items are stated in the phraseology of industry, of business, of the home, or of science, though what effect this has on students is uncertain. The items do seem to "emphasize mathematics reasoning ability rather than memorization of formulas, mere knowledge of techniques, or computational skill," though the latter are necessary rather than sufficient factors in successful response. All of the 40 multiple choice items have five listed responses and often the fifth answer is "Not given." Very few of the items can be easily answered from trial of the various responses. One example of means of discouraging solution by trial of answers is the listing of pos-

1 Like, for example, the research recently conducted by Educational Testing Service for the College Entrance Examination Board. See Noyes, Edward S. "Essay and Objective Tests in English." *Col Board R* 49:7–11 w '63. *

sible values of X rather than values of both X and Y as responses to an item concerning simultaneous equations. Only actual solution of the equations is certain to produce the correct answer. The items are well written from the standpoint of form with the problem in the item stem and the answers plausible. This test should be very useful in sectioning beginning college mathematics classes and in placement or counseling of students. The test is not designed for differential prediction or advanced placement. ACT is developing another mathematics test to supplement this one for the latter purpose.

The content of the Social Studies Reading Test of Forms 4-AC and 4-BR deals almost exclusively with political science, economics, and American and world history, although one or two of the readings have relevance to sociology or psychology. It is possible that this emphasis better reflects the high school learning experiences of students than would greater emphasis on sociology, geography, psychology, and anthropology. Measurement of the general skills earlier mentioned emphasizes the ability "to grasp implied meanings" to a far greater extent than the abilities "to evaluate evidence" or "to recognize false or specious logic and to detect inconsistencies in argument." Excellent items requiring interpretation of data were present in the earlier Forms 2-BR and 3-AC. It is hoped that more such items will appear in future forms. Many excellent items in the 1962–63 forms require the student to infer the points of view, attitudes, and values, though not the biases, of writers of the various passages and to forecast consequences of different courses of action. It is gratifying to find in each form items evaluating student knowledge of sources of social studies information. In general, the four-response multiple choice items are extremely well written. The problem is in the stem and the listed answers are plausible and of parallel construction. In the case of only one or two items in each form does this reviewer question the keyed answer. As stated above, one should hope in future forms for more items emphasizing interpretation of data and more items concerned with the ability to "recognize the writer's position," "to evaluate evidence and differentiate fact from opinion," "to detect inconsistencies in argument," and other skills enumerated in the specifications for this test.

The items of the Natural Science Reading Test of Forms 4-AC and 4-BR are fairly evenly distributed over the fields of biology, chemistry, and physics, though most of the physics items are among the background ones. There are a few such items in elementary astronomy. Apart from content, it is this reviewer's judgment that this test quite effectively fulfills the purpose of assessing "the student's understanding of the methods of science, the nature of experimentation, the processes by which scientists develop new understandings and insights, and the logical steps scientists follow in arriving at conclusions and generalizations." The utilization of such series of items should motivate teachers to include these understandings among the real objectives of their instruction and motivate students to realize their importance. Again, the four-response multiple choice items are very well written, with the problems in the stems and the alternatives plausible and of parallel construction. This reviewer was especially impressed by certain items containing paired statements in their stems and responses that require the student to identify the relationship between the given pair of statements.

In developing new forms of the test, "tryout" units are administered to large representative samples of students who are also taking corresponding subtests of the *Iowa Tests of Educational Development* as part of the annual fall testing program in Iowa. These scores become the criteria for Flanagan discrimination indices. The item analysis data also include the per cents electing each response including the correct one. While the use of an external criterion is indeed valuable in production of forms, both item difficulty and item discrimination data based on representative samples of ACT examinees would also be useful in evaluating current forms and in planning new ones.

The raw scores of the ACT tests are equated to corresponding standard scores of the *Iowa Tests of Educational Development* whose scale for all four high school grades in the Iowa high school population originally had mean 15 and standard deviation 5. The use of this scale and the ITED data for very large and representative samples of twelfth grade students makes possible the reporting of national ACT percentile rank norms for such students. National percentile rank norms are also reported for the very large number of "college-bound" high school seniors actually taking the ACT tests. The differences between the two populations are strikingly revealed in the norm tables: for example, a standard score of 20 (the composite standard score of all four subtests) has a percentile rank of 75 in the first population and of 48 in the second according to the 1957 national (ITED) data and 1961–62 ACT data. Similar tables of norm data relevant to college-bound high school seniors of a given state are available to colleges participating in affiliated state programs. Most important are the local norms and other data provided colleges utilizing the Research Service.

A college or university reporting to the Research Service data (for example grade-point averages for all freshman courses in English, mathematics, social studies, and natural science, or marks in single specific courses in these areas) for 200 or more students who took the ACT prior to admission "routinely" receives 105 simple correlation coefficients, 15 multiple correlation coefficients, 50 regression weights, 65 means and standard deviations, 40 frequency distributions and percentile ranks, 10 expectancy tables, and 10 computational tables. Recently the colleges participating in the Research Service can also report data obtained from up to five instruments other than the ACT examination to determine how these instruments compare with the ACT in predictive power, or how they might augment its predictive power. All of this testifies to the wonders of modern electronic test scoring and data processing.

The odd-even reliability coefficients [2] of the four subtests of Form 4-AC obtained for a sample 990 high school seniors taking this form are .90, .89, .86, and .83 for English, mathematics, social studies, and natural sciences, respectively. The reliability of the composite standard score is .95. In standard score units, the corresponding standard errors of measurement are, respectively, 1.54, 2.13, 2.15, 2.45, and 1.03. The intercorrelations of the four tests based on the same data are as follows: English and mathematics, .53; English and social studies, .63; English and natural sciences, .58; mathematics and social studies, .55; mathematics and natural sciences, .64; social studies and natural sciences, .68.

These substantial intercorrelations indicate the need for caution in offering advice in counseling which is essentially the making of differential predictions. Those responsible for the ACT program wisely emphasize this in the section on student counseling in Using the ACT Scores on Your Campus. "The question of the relative suitability of a student for various curriculums or majors is an extremely complex one, and involves considerations beyond ACT information (such as the student's goals, interests, values, personality characteristics, occupational opportunities; the college's educational and training requirements and philosophies)."

Colleges participating in the Research Service by contributing criterion data in the form of grade-point averages in the various areas are provided, *on the basis of these local data,* with multiple correlations and multiple regression weights for each of the ACT tests and for high school marks earned by their entrants in the same field. (One averages the predictions of success, for example, in mathematics by averaging the predicted grade point averages separately obtained from the four ACT subtests and from the corresponding four high school marks.) Such extensive use of local data is a notable advance in measurement practice. Some idea of the predictive validity of the "five best-weighted combinations....of each of the four ACT test scores and four corresponding high school course grades" can be gained from the following summary of frequency distributions of multiple correlation coefficients based on 1962 data of 132 participating colleges.

	English	Mathematics	Social Studies	Natural Sciences	All Subjects
90th Percentile	.72	.68	.69	.70	.74
50th Percentile	.63	.55	.61	.60	.67
10th Percentile	.51	.42	.51	.48	.58

In an earlier paragraph this reviewer suggested research relevant to the English Usage Test. The data reported above suggest other important problems. To what extent do college teachers include as instructional objectives the types of intellectual skills measured, or specified for measurement, by the ACT tests? To what extent do college teachers evaluate such skills in their determinations of course marks? Does such measurement or evaluation by college teachers characterize the colleges where validity coefficients are relatively high? What kinds of measurements of achievement in determining course marks characterize the colleges

2 The data reported in this paragraph were obtained from personal correspondence with the publisher.

where the validity coefficients are relatively low? More efficient prediction of college or university performance will depend as much or more on improvement of college evaluation of performance as on improvement of such prediction instruments as the ACT.

In concluding this review mention should be made, or again be made, of the very competently written supporting materials: the ACT General Information Bulletin, Using the ACT Scores on Your Campus, the ACT Technical Report, 1960–1961 Edition, the Manual of Instructions for Participating in the ACT Research Service—1963, the Manual of Intrepretation for 1963 Research Service Reports, the Sample Report of Results for Midstate University, the Supervisor's Manual, and the booklets of information for students. A common criticism of literature of this kind has to do with "exaggerated claims." The materials referred to do not deserve such criticism. While the authors describe with justified pride what has been accomplished, this is balanced by appropriate admonitions with reference to caution in the interpretation of ACT data in admissions, placement, and counseling. This is especially evident in the booklet Using the ACT Scores on Your Campus and the Manual of Interpretation for 1963 Research Service Reports. Both are also among the best of materials contributing to intelligent use of test data.

While this reviewer has noted what seem to him certain limitations of Forms 4-AC and 4-BR, on the whole those responsible for the American College Testing Program deserve high praise for its development.

WARREN G. FINDLEY, *Professor of Education, and Coordinator of Educational Research, University of Georgia, Athens, Georgia.* [Review of Forms 2-AC, 2-BR, 4-AC, and 4-BR.]

The American College Testing Program is a secure program of tests for college admission, designed to serve primarily, though not exclusively, state university systems. Although launched only in 1959, it claims to serve one or another college testing program for 29 of the 50 states. Analysis of the 1962–63 Student Information Bulletin confirms this, showing that in 16 states the tests are almost universally required by state system colleges, in 5 other states the tests are uniformly recommended, while in the remainder one or more special programs (e.g., out-of-state candidates and scholarship candidates) are serviced by the ACT program. Inevitably the program is to be compared with the programs of the College Entrance Examination Board. The fact that it provides healthy competition for this long-established and otherwise virtually monopolistic examination service is the best answer to the occasional complaint of too much "external" testing in the high schools of the country.

The American College Testing Program is to be discussed in terms of (*a*) the nature of the tests themselves, (*b*) the score reporting services, and (*c*) the research services.

THE TESTS. Viewed in terms of the tests themselves, the ACT program "is but the lengthened shadow" of E. F. Lindquist. An accurate account of the history of the educational development tests from which the ACT examination is derived by direct descent is presented succinctly and graphically in the ACT Technical Report, 1960–61 Edition. The *Iowa Tests of Educational Development,* launched with the fall testing program for Iowa high schools in 1942, became the source of the USAFI *Tests of General Educational Development* during World War II, and in 1958 became the basis of the *National Merit Scholarship Qualifying Test* and the *National Educational Development Tests.* If we carry the history back one step farther, we see all these tests issuing from the Iowa testing program, whose tests for grades 3–9 first became available for general purchase as the *Iowa Every-Pupil Tests of Basic Skills* in 1940, after a decade of use in Iowa elementary schools. These are tests of basic learning skills comprising (*a*) reading skills, (*b*) arithmetic skills, (*c*) language usage skills, and (*d*) work-study skills. Like the tests being discussed here they are miniature worksamples of learning skills involved in school work. The 1942 high school tests, however, involved a decision not to attempt to extend the testing of these basic skills to higher levels along similar lines, as is the case with other batteries like the *California Achievement Tests* and the *Sequential Tests of Educational Progress,* but to respond to the demand of schoolpeople for continuous measurement of general educational development on through junior college with a second pattern of miniature worksamples of more complex learning skills appropriate to this higher level of study.

The subtests of the *American College Test-*

ing Program Examination are English usage (80 items, 50 minutes), mathematics usage (40 items, 50 minutes), social studies reading (52 items, 40 minutes), and natural sciences reading (52 items, 40 minutes). The test of English usage measures correctness and effectiveness of expression in multiple choice form. The test of mathematics "usage" includes (*a*) "word problems" in arithmetic and (*b*) formal exercises in algebra and geometry, in approximately equal proportions. The two reading tests in each battery contain reading passages that are appropriate to the field but that the examinees are not likely to have encountered in their reading. In addition, each reading test in the four test booklets furnished for examination contained 12–16 questions not based on the reading, but to be answered by direct recall of knowledge or by application of recalled knowledge to a problem or situation. The individual questions show a high level of craftsmanship in their construction.

This reviewer accepts the authors' view that a debate over whether such tests are of "aptitude" or "achievement" is quite unprofitable. It is proper to accept a "content and process" analysis of the test exercises as evidence of their being proper worksamples of college work and to rest the case for their usefulness on their ability to predict grades in college work for that reason. The composite score obtained by adding or averaging the four scores meets this requirement nicely and compares well with competing indices like the sum of scores on the two parts of the *College Entrance Examination Board Scholastic Aptitude Test*.

One may well quarrel, however, with the implied reliability and differential significance of the four part scores. In describing the scales and norms in the Technical Report, it is carefully explained that "On theoretical and empirical grounds, it was determined that a reliability of 0.91 for a single grade population was required to permit useful differentiation in the multiscore description of individual students" in developing the original forms of the *Iowa Tests of Educational Development*. However, the same Technical Report shows that the reliabilities (using the Spearman-Brown split-half technique) for the four ACT tests vary from .83 to .88. Moreover, the lowest reliabilities tend to be found for the two reading tests (.83 to .86) while the highest intercorrelations for the four tests are between the reading tests (.70 to .77). This lack of clear differentiation and specialization of meaning for the two reading scores results in a higher correlation between social studies reading and grade-point average in natural science (.496) than between natural science reading and GPA in natural science (.457) for 705 students in "Midstate University" in the illustrative statistical report included to guide interpretation of such reports. This high intercorrelation of separate reading scores and corresponding failure to differentiate achievement in the curriculum fields for which they are named and on whose content they are based seems to this reviewer best interpreted as evidence of the stubbornly unitary character of reading ability at the college entrance level. This would imply the merit of combining the content of the two reading tests into a composite measure of ability to read college textbook material, perhaps redistributing the time allotments among the resulting three-part battery of tests and bringing all to approximately the .91 standard mentioned earlier. The *Scholastic Aptitude Test* verbal score clearly exceeds this standard, while SAT mathematics approaches it.

An alternative solution might be to expand the sections of the two reading tests that depend on direct recall of knowledge, making them more differentially descriptive, but at the possible loss of the predictiveness inherent in the interpretation of reading passages. Finally, one might question the price paid in time allotted to the English Usage Test (50 minutes) for the value gained in predicting college achievement in English. The data for the 132 colleges receiving reports from the 1962 Research Service indicate that the present test is highly predictive of GPA in English, but probably because freshman English in these colleges is 50 per cent or more English composition and relatively unselected populations of college freshmen show wide variability of talent and much room for improvement in usage.

In sum, the test content is excellent and the composite score is predictive of college achievement. The separate tests are logically designed, but do not justify the implied claim of differential prediction.

SCORE REPORTING SERVICES. Scores for each of the four tests are reported on a scale for which 15 represents the average November score for senior year of unselected high school seniors, and 5 is the standard deviation of such scores. Unselected high school seniors are the most meaningful reference group that could have been chosen, and reference of scores to a standard date of examination removes a small source of systematic bias, which is advisable. The resulting scales from 0 to 36 have the merit of not being subject to confusion with other standard scales. They have the disadvantage of suggesting the existence of an absolute scale of performance starting at zero, although no claim is made for such a property of the scales.

Score reports for each examinee go to the college(s) of his choice, to his high school, and to him via the high school. In these respects the services parallel those offered by the College Entrance Examination Board. The student's interpretative booklet includes information about choosing a college that reflects the late closing dates for admission to state universities as compared to those of the more selective institutions generally served by the College Board. Otherwise, both programs provide the same types of illustrative examples and both allow for dissemination of reports to students and their parents through the trained counselors at the high school.

The individual student's score report, pasted into the interpretative booklet, reports (*a*) standard score equivalents for each of his test scores and (*b*) the high school grades he reported on his answer sheet for corresponding subjects. Agreements and discrepancies between these standard scores and grades in the same subject area constitute a fruitful source for study and for counseling. From tables in the interpretative booklet the student may also determine the percentile equivalents of his test scores for college bound seniors, as well as for seniors generally.

The booklet Using the ACT Scores on Your Campus is a well organized and clearly presented statement directed to college administrators and admissions officers. It offers specific suggestions and illustrations of uses of ACT results, presumably needed and wanted by the cooperating colleges (e.g., use of results in selective admissions, advanced placement, scholarship awards, sectioning, counseling). This is to be contrasted with a more diverse set of materials and procedures provided by the College Entrance Examination Board to its test program users. In part, this stems from the newness and simplicity of the ACT offering, which corresponds most closely with the *Scholastic Aptitude Test* of the College Board, and which thus far lacks counterparts of the Board's achievement tests, advanced placement tests, and college scholarship service.

In addition to standard scores, national and ACT percentile equivalents, and high school grades, colleges that participate in the research services (described below) receive on each student's score report predicted GPA's for each subject area and overall, based on (*a*) test scores alone, and (*b*) composites of test scores and grades. This feature alone saves the institutions time and costs far in excess of the cost of supplying the research data required for the research service. This must be accounted an important value unique to the ACT program.

Examination dates in November, February, April, and June neatly dovetail with College Board dates in December, January, March, May, and July. Both services report scores to the colleges and high schools within approximately a month of testing.

In sum, score reporting services are adequate and clear and appropriate to the college clientele served. In addition, they offer a predictive service that is both efficient and extremely valuable.

RESEARCH SERVICES. The unique and truly remarkable feature of the American College Testing Program is the extensive offering of helpful research services available to colleges using the program. This free service to colleges requires that the total group of students, or any subgroup for which an analysis is requested, shall number at least 200 for whom records can be supplied. The minimum required "record" is an overall GPA for each student. Additional data, generally reported, include GPA's in the curriculum fields of English, mathematics, social studies, and natural sciences. Individual institutions may submit a different set of four additional criteria for each subgroup, if they wish, and beginning in 1963 may obtain analytical results for three local items of predictive information (e.g., scores on local tests or interest inventories, data other than grades supplied by high schools).

The illustrative statistical reports and the accompanying manual for interpreting them are models of clarity and completeness. A typical statistical report to the college shows for that institution (*a*) correlations of each ACT test and the composite score with GPA in the four major fields and the overall GPA, plus the multiple correlation and standard error of estimate for predicting each criterion from all four test scores, (*b*) corresponding correlations for high school grades in the four major subject areas and overall high school average with the same GPA criteria, and (*c*) correlations for composites of test scores and high school grades with GPA, subject area by subject area, and overall.

Even more directly useful are expectancy tables showing per cents of students with various predicted GPA's who may be expected to earn GPA's of 1.0 or above, 2.0 or above, 3.0 or above, or 4.0, in each major subject area and overall, when predictions are based on (*a*) test scores alone and (*b*) special composites of scores and grades. Corresponding computation tables are offered for use by the local admissions office for evaluating the scores and grades of late applicants not evaluated statistically in the score reporting service. A further step that would be useful to high school counselors would be for the Research Service, with the approval of the using colleges, to produce a document covering these colleges comparable to the Counselor's Guide for Georgia Colleges, published by the Office of Testing and Guidance of the Regents of the University System of Georgia. Simplified prediction equation procedures described in that guide allow high school counselors to compute a predictive composite for each college, based on high school average and entrance test scores and involving only the multiplication and addition of whole numbers, for use in entering an expectancy table of the sort provided here.

Additional tables show the college the frequency distributions and local percentile equivalents of (*a*) the four ACT scores and the composite, (*b*) predicted GPA in the four subject areas and overall, based on ACT scores only, and (*c*) predicted GPA for the same five criteria, based on ACT scores and high school grades. Finally, each college receives summary data for all cooperating colleges showing (*a*) frequency distributions of the various correlations with GPA of individual ACT tests, unweighted ACT composites, optimally weighted ACT scores, optimally weighted composites of high school grades, and weighted composites of ACT scores and high school grades; and (*b*) percentile equivalents for all men and women tested in the 1961–62 programs for 650 ACT colleges.

The myriad institutional researches in which these data would prove helpful are described and illustrated in the manual. The perennial problem of equivalence of course grades, the effectiveness of sectioning, and comparison with previous classes or other colleges are but a few. It would be difficult to overstate the value in immediate practical usefulness of this research information.

SUMMARY. The American College Testing Program offers a secure college-admissions testing service based on well-conceived and well-built tests, an efficient score reporting service, a valuable time- and cost-saving predictive service, and a richly useful free research service. All parts of the program are supported by clear, helpful interpretative materials. The ACT program thus offers a constructive competitive alternative to much of the College Entrance Examination Board's program of services. Points of exception raised in this review should be taken as intended as "praising with faint damns."

Personnel & Guid J 41:814–9 My '63. David V. Tiedeman. [Review of Form 1-AC.] * The ACT Program is a big and solid business. Is the ACT Program a good business? That is the question examined in this review. * THE EXAMINATION * In the English Usage Test the student replies to 80 questions concerning the possible improvement of various parts of four passages. * With 50 minutes available for answering 80 items, students must react to eight items every five minutes. Included in the rate is the time necessary to read each of four passages, first in its entirety—and with its mistakes—and then to locate the task in its passage and with its alternative possibilities. With allowance for these tasks, the student probably has to tick off two items per minute. Although the *Technical Report* (p. 23) notes that about 90 per cent of students attempted one of the last five items of the test, I consider the task to be a demanding one and suspect that the confidence which stems from deliberation over reply is not gained by many who take the test. My suspicion is strengthened by the further fact that students are directed—in this test as in the other three—to complete the test even by guessing because the score will be the number of right responses. The "fact" of completion of a test is therefore not well established by the procedure used. The ACT Examination was deliberately constructed in the tradition of the *Iowa Tests of Educational Development* (ITED), the *Tests of General Educational Development* of the United States Armed Forces Institute (USAFI-GED), and the *National Merit Scholarship Qualifying Test* (NMSQT). Those responsible for this test of English usage can therefore point to a decade or two of experience with such a test. Nevertheless I suggest that consideration be given to eliminating the initial presentation of each of the four passages. Reading of these initial passages is slowed both by a search for the tasks which are to be tackled later and which are not therein identified, and by identification of the deliberately placed errors which wrench the reader from the directed set of reading for general meaning. In short, it seems like an investment of time with slight return particularly when the type of printing of the passage where tasks are identified is so much easier to read. The Mathematics Usage Test consists of 40 items which are to be answered in 50 minutes. The timing on this test seems appropriate for the power test it is intended to be. The test requires reasoning with quantities presented in structures characterizing geometry and introductory algebra and the interpretation of data presented in graph or chart. * The Social Studies Reading Test contains 52 items which are to be answered in 40 minutes. Thirty-seven of the items ask questions about one of four passages. These passages seem to be about political science and economics in Form 1-AC but the report to colleges suggests that sociology, geography, American and world history, psychology, and anthropology are also represented in the sections on this test. Perhaps the subjects missing in the passages are held to be present because the test also has 15 items which are to be answered without reference to a reading passage. In Form 1-AC political science, particularly the American system of government, and economics again receive heaviest attention in this type of item, however. Sociology is represented by only one item and the student doesn't need to know too much about the locations of places around the world to answer any of these items. Psychology and anthropology also receive scant attention. * the test gives little indication of the store of knowledge about social studies which a student has at his command. Actually the ACT Program lays no claim to fulfilling this latter task and no blame is intended in my remark. However, I am here laying grounds for later discussion of the course placement uses which the ACT Program claims the Examination can fulfill. The Natural Sciences Reading Test also presents 52 items which are to be completed in 40 minutes along with the reading of four passages. Fifteen of the 52 items are also to be answered without recourse to a reading passage as is the case with the test in the reading of social studies. The passages provide data and the student is required to examine assumptions, methods, and statements, and to reach conclusions. The questions which do not make direct reference to the four longer reading passages are surprisingly parallel to those accompanying such passages. By this I mean that those questions deal largely with the making of inferences rather than with memory of another's inferences. STATISTICAL CHARACTERISTICS * Although the probable error is larger in the ACT Examination than in ITED, each test has a reliability (*TR,* p. 16) which is probably adequate for individual use in admitting students to college. Higher reliability might be in order when precise ability placement is needed, however. The ACT provides norms in terms of both students in the twelfth grade and college-bound students. The norms for the former group were obtained by equi-percentile equating with a comprehensive sample of students involved in norming the ITED. The norms for the latter group were simply computed for the high school seniors tested in 1959–1960. * Logically the claim for the validity of the ACT Examination rests on the correspondence of the tasks it requires and the tasks required for accomplishment in college. There is little doubt in my mind that the ACT Examination requires the exercise of reason in the several media in which the understanding of knowledge is founded. I therefore think that the composite score in the ACT Examination provides a good indication of scholastic aptitude for college work as is claimed. * It seems fair to say....that the ACT Program provides indices of relevance to the selection of applicants applying for admission to college which equal, and may even slightly excel, the best. The accuracy of this statement—particularly the attribution of superiority—does rest upon the inclusion of reported high school grades in the ACT Program, of course. SUPPORTING

MATERIALS * Advertising....materials which are intended for the public seem of high standard and modest claim. The ACT Program reaches high schools by way of a bulletin for administrators * Information is given in the bulletin quite concisely and accurately and makes the obligations and rights of participation very plain. The ACT Program's early contact with a student is through its *Student Information Bulletin* * A large part of the *Bulletin* is devoted to a list by state of what seem to be all the colleges and universities in the United States. The careful student can identify the colleges in this list which require or recommend participation in the ACT Program. The student next meets the ACT Program through the Examination which is given on Saturdays at college centers under secure conditions. Within a month, the student and his high school each get a copy of a label which reports five standard scores for the student. The student is to affix his scores to his *Student's Booklet* which defines the test scores, helps the student convert his scores to percentiles, and tries to get the student to compare his test scores with his grades, to assess his interests, and to choose a college. It is surprising that the student is only now told how to choose a college because by then his scores reside in three colleges "of his choice." Is this hope of ACT expressed too late? Also, can a student really compare his test scores and grades without conversion by equi-percentile or regression methods? Here lie two weaknesses of the *Booklet* in my judgment. Colleges receive *The American College Testing Program, Inc.* (1960) which explains the structure of the Program and the services which the Program will provide a college *without charge.* * This manual also provides a table for ascertaining presumably comparable scores on the CEEB *Scholastic Aptitude Test* from scores on the ACT. The table in the 1960–1961 edition of this manual derives from a similar conversion of NMSQT to SAT. Since ACT derives from NMSQT, this procedure is probably satisfactory. It would make an admissions officer using ACT as a substitute for SAT more comfortable, however, if he knew that the correlation between ACT and SAT was high—on the order of magnitude of the reliability coefficient of the SAT in fact. Professionals can view the ACT Program through *Technical Report* (1960–1961 Edition) and *Interpreting the 1961 ACT Research Reports* (with accompanying "Sample Report of Results for Midstate University, Midstate, USA"). These reports are of high technical competence and provide all that is necessary for understanding the ACT Examination. The *Interpretation* also represents a contribution to the professional literature on the selection of variables for prediction of freshman grades in college. EVALUATION: ACCEPT INDEX OF SCHOLASTIC APTITUDE. The ACT Examination is beyond much question in its technical aspects. Design, items, accuracy and speed of scoring, scales, norms, reports, and manuals—the ACT Program exemplifies excellence in each of these regards. I have no doubt that the ACT Examination is a good test of scholastic aptitude—particularly when it is used in conjunction with the marks the student reports on each of four recent major courses in high school. EVALUATION: BUT THINK BEFORE PLACING. The ACT Examination provides scores on four tests as well as the composite score. Part scores are supposed to be useful both in guidance while in high school and placement upon arrival in college. * The ACT requires reasoning in the media of English, mathematics, natural science, and social studies. I have agreed that such reasoning is required in college and represents aptitude for collegiate study. I do not agree that these indications that a student can do collegiate work because he probably has done similar work in high school also suggest that he has done advanced work in college. For instance, students who are relatively high on the English test are likely to be relatively high in their grade in freshman English. The tests provide no indication that the student has completed freshman English, however. Therefore, a college would do well to use an achievement test of English in connection with placement in English courses. In making this statement, I presume, of course, that college courses are established on the basis of prerequisite knowledge, not ability—or at least predominantly on the basis of prerequisites and only secondarily on the basis of ability. A college sectioning primarily on ability will probably find that the ACT Examination, or many other tests of scholastic aptitude for that matter, is useful. EVALUATION: AND DEMAND RESPONSIBILITY! * The ACT Program is a non-profit educational corporation chartered in the State of Iowa. A Board of Directors is elected by coordinators of state testing programs in 19 states. Services are purchased from both Measurement Research Center and Science Research Associates and both corporations are represented on the Board of Directors of the ACT Program, Inc. * The students are the customers. Fees are assessed only on students. Neither high schools nor colleges pay anything. The ACT Program attempts to provide extensive service for its customers. Therefore, scores are sent to colleges where the student directs them even if the college is not participating. Furthermore, scores are sent to students with a complex and stimulating *Booklet* even if the collegiate plans of a student have emerged with adequate prior service of a counselor. Selective college admission is somewhat mistrusted at the present time and the Directors of ACT therefore ought to review their policy of sending ACT scores to colleges indiscriminately as they now do. A college should have the right to refuse to deal with students through the ACT Examination without direct explanation to the student. It is the responsibility of the ACT Program, not the college, to control this. Furthermore, public understanding of guidance service is not yet so clear that a guidance program can unequivocally withstand all of the undifferentiated claims and directions of a prestige program such as ACT. The Directors of the ACT Program could therefore also be more helpful to those who counsel by recognizing that counselors are employed in some high schools. A different *Student Information Bulletin* and *Student's Booklet* could lighten the work and increase public trust of employed (and hence probably certificated) counselors.

[2]

***American School Achievement Tests.** Grades 1, 2–3, 4–6, 7–9; 1941–63; 4 levels; 2–4 parts (parts 1–3 of Forms D, E, F are essentially the same as Forms A, B, C copyrighted 1941–43); parts 1–4 available as separates; 1960 restandardization referred to in publisher's 1964 catalog applies to intermediate and advanced levels only; postage extra; Canadian norms supplement available for grades 2–9; Willis E. Pratt, Robert V. Young (parts 1–3), Miriam E. Wilt (*a*), and Clara Cockerille (part 4); Bobbs-Merrill Co., Inc. *

a) PRIMARY BATTERY I. Grade 1; 1941–56; 5 scores: reading (word recognition, word meaning, total), numbers, total; Forms D ('55), E ('55, some printings copyrighted 1956), (6 pages); manual ('55, 12 pages); $4 per 35 self-marking tests; 50¢ per specimen set; (35) minutes in 2 sessions.

b) PRIMARY BATTERY 2. Grades 2–3; 1941–58; 9 scores: reading (sentences and words, paragraphs, total), arithmetic (computation, problems, total), language, spelling, total; Forms D ('55), E ('56), F ('57, some printings copyrighted 1955), G ('58, some printings copyrighted 1955); separate parts (4 pages) 1 (reading), 2 (arithmetic, language, spelling); manual ('58, c1955–58, 13 pages); $5.75 per 35 sets of both parts; 50¢ per specimen set; 65(85) minutes in 2 sessions.

c) INTERMEDIATE BATTERY. Grades 4–6; 1942–61; 11 scores: same as for primary battery 2 plus social studies, science; 2 editions: self-marking, machine scorable; manual ('61, 17 pages); *self-marking edition:* Forms D (parts 1–3, '55; 4, '57), E (parts 1–2, '56, some printings copyrighted 1955; 3, '56; 4, '57), F ('57), G ('58, some printings of parts 1–2 copyrighted 1955); separate parts (4 pages) 1 (reading), 2 (arithmetic), 3 (language and spelling), 4 (social studies and science); $8.50 per 35 sets of parts 1–4 (complete battery); $7 per 35 sets of parts 1–3 (partial battery); 75¢ per specimen set of complete battery; 50¢ per specimen set of partial battery; *machine scorable edition:* IBM; Form DM; partial battery ('60, 16 pages); separate part 4 ('57, 4 pages); no directions for administering with separate answer sheets; separate answer sheets must be used; $5 per 35 tests of partial battery; $6.50 per 35 sets of complete battery (partial battery and part 4); $2 per 35 IBM scorable answer sheets for partial battery; $3 per 35 sets of IBM scorable answer sheets for complete battery; 80¢ per set of scoring stencils for partial battery; $1.20 per set of scoring stencils for complete battery; 155(200) minutes in 4 sessions for complete battery.

d) ADVANCED BATTERY. Grades 7–9; 1947–63; 11 scores: same as for intermediate battery; 2 editions: self-marking, machine scorable; manual ('63, 17 pages); *self-marking edition:* Forms D (parts 1–2, '55, some printings of part 2 copyrighted 1956; 3, '56; 4, '57), E (parts 1–3, '56; 4, '57), F ('57), G ('58); separate parts 1–4 (titles as for intermediate level): *machine scorable edition:* IBM; Form DM; partial battery ('55, c1947–55, 16 pages); part 4 ('60, c1957–60, 4 pages); no directions for administering with separate answer sheets; prices same as for intermediate battery; 177(220) minutes in 4 sessions for complete battery.

ROBERT H. BAUERNFEIND, *Associate Professor of Education, Northern Illinois University, DeKalb, Illinois.*

The *American School Achievement Tests* provide a variety of achievement scores for pupils in grades 1–9. The tests are presented in four levels, with varying curricular emphases at each level.

In terms of usual test publishing mechanics, these tests reflect careful work. The directions for administering the tests are well written; the test problems have been carefully edited; and the scoring keys appear to be accurate. There is, however, a question about the purposes these tests would serve.

The series is intended to serve as a schoolwide achievement testing program for children in grades 1–9—perhaps in similar fashion to the annual achievement measures provided by the *Iowa Tests of Basic Skills* or the *Sequential Tests of Educational Progress.* But the present series has several limitations such that it cannot really do the job that the ITBS or STEP series can do. Some of these limitations are: (*a*) There is no evidence of continuity of the grade equivalent or age equivalent norms from one level to the next. Thus, any efforts to study pupil growth from one level to the next would appear to be treacherous. (*b*) The basis of the grade equivalent and age equivalent norms at all grade levels is quite vague, and there are no reported studies relating the norms to the norms of other publishers' standardized tests. With an inadequate description of the norms, and in the absence of norms-comparison studies, this reviewer doubts that a school could study these grade equivalent scores with confidence that a national perspective was being brought to bear on the test findings. (*c*) No intertest correlation studies are reported; such data would be most useful in judging the extent to which the several test scores are providing relatively unique information about each pupil tested.

If we agree that the format and the present state of research of these tests largely preclude their use in schoolwide achievement testing programs, we may still ask whether individual teachers might want to use individual tests for occasional and incidental measures of their pupils' achievements. Following, briefly, are this reviewer's comments in answer to this question.

Number Concepts, grade 1: This is quite a clever test of quantitative concepts—arithmetic terms, counting problems, identifying geometric figures, simple addition and subtraction problems. The test scores are probably not especially reliable, but a study of a pupil's right answers and wrong answers might be very helpful to a first grade teacher who chooses to give this test to her class.

Word Recognition, grade 1: This test requires the pupil to recognize the printed word corresponding to the word read aloud by his teacher. The test is too short for reliable measurement (only 24 items); but, like the number concepts test, a simple study of pupils' right and wrong answers could be useful.

Word Meaning, grade 1: This test requires the pupil to recognize the printed word corresponding to a given picture. This test also is too short for reliable measurement (only 24 items), but might well be useful for informal studies of pupils' right and wrong answers.

Word Meaning, grades 2–9: These are essentially tests of reading vocabulary—synonyms, antonyms, and sentence completion problems. The tests are a little short (30–40 items), but they might still serve well to classify pupils in terms of verbal ability.

Paragraph Meaning, grades 2–9: These are, by and large, excellent tests of reading comprehension. Each paragraph is short but fairly involved. Some test questions require the pupil to identify a key fact in the paragraph; others require him to draw inferences and conclusions from the paragraph.

Arithmetic Computation, grades 2–9: These appear to be useful tests of computational skills. The tests require a minimum of reading, which is highly desirable; but the printed format of some of the test items is cramped and confusing.

Arithmetic Problems, grades 2–9: These tests are seriously short (12–24 items), and with this length they cannot provide reliable measures for most selection or classification purposes. One might add these scores to the arithmetic computation scores for a total arithmetic achievement score, but the reading loading of the verbal problems would complicate interpretations of such a total arithmetic score. On balance, it seems best to suggest that the arithmetic problems tests not be used, except possibly for informal studies of pupils' right answers and wrong answers.

Grammar, grades 2–9: All test authors find it difficult to develop lifelike tests of language usage skills using a multiple choice format; but these tests seem more remote than most. Many of the problems are presented in a simple true-false format, and the format of other problems is crowded and confusing. This reviewer can find little to commend this test for use by teachers.

Spelling, grades 2–9: The spelling tests require the pupil to recognize the correct spelling of a word from four possible spellings. The distractors represent common spelling errors; the tests are reasonably long; and these tests would appear to be useful to classroom teachers.

Social Studies, grades 4–9: These are, by and large, pretty sterile tests of memorized information. Few items require problem-attack or reasoning skills; and it is difficult to estimate the behavioral differences between a high-scoring pupil and a low-scoring pupil, except that the former is probably a better memorizer. Before a teacher elects to use these tests, this reviewer would urge him to consider the more dynamic social studies tests in the *Sequential Tests of Educational Progress* as alternatives.

Science, grades 4–9: The same comments as above apply to the science tests. Again, the STEP series should be considered for science tests that appear to represent consistently worthwhile outcomes of a school's instructional programs.

In summary, the *American School Achievement Tests* have not been researched or published in such a way that they could be readily used in schoolwide achievement testing programs. In this sense, the series is not really competitive with the ITBS or other broad every-pupil achievement test batteries. On the other hand, several of the tests in the series are quite well developed and might prove useful to individual teachers working with individual pupils.

This reviewer would also suggest to the Bobbs-Merrill staff that this battery may be in a *cul de sac* for the wrong reasons. Most recurring criticisms of these tests—especially those pertaining to their short length and complicated format—seem to be functions of the publisher's rigid system of forcing each test into a carbon-scoring format. If the carbon-scoring format were abandoned, the test authors would be free to (*a*) lengthen certain tests as needed, (*b*) present the test items in a less crowded way, and (*c*) arrange a plan whereby all tests could be marked on a single answer sheet—for example, an MRC answer sheet. The program would then be amenable to systematic research; and, subsequently, it could become useful as a basic battery for schoolwide achievement testing programs. In their present format, however, these tests appear to be useful only for occasional and informal studies of pupils' right and wrong answers.

FRANK B. WOMER, *Associate Professor of Education, and Test Consultant, Bureau of School Services, The University of Michigan, Ann Arbor, Michigan.*

The *American School Achievement Tests* (ASAT) are an old test series that was revised rather extensively in 1955 and restandardized in 1958, and again in 1960 for the Intermediate and Advanced Batteries. Previous reviews covered the materials currently available with the exception of a new manual for the Intermediate Battery, copyright in 1961, a new manual for the Advanced Battery, copyright in 1963, and a machine scorable edition of one form of each of these batteries. This review will concentrate upon the new intermediate and advanced level manuals.

Previous reviewers have been fairly consistent in their remarks. They tended to be favorably impressed by the test items and item selection procedures, but pointed out the traditional, factual nature of those items. There were some favorable and some unfavorable comments on test format and ease of use of the materials. There were generally unfavorable comments on the statement of purposes of the tests, on low reliabilities at certain grade levels, on inadequate standardization, and on a failure to provide sufficient evidence of statistical characteristics of the tests.

The new manuals are "new" to the extent of only about 2 pages out of 17. The rest is identical to the 1958 manuals and, except for the addition of Form G data to various tables, to the 1955 editions. The lack of newness is best illustrated by a failure of the editor to change many numbers in the intermediate level manual that were correct in the previous edition but are not correct in the 1961 edition. In describing the test battery, the "new" manual refers to "three parts" of the ASAT tests. But in 1957 a fourth part (Social Studies and Science) was added to the tests. The "new" manual refers at several points to the "three forms" (D, E, and F) and the "other two forms" of the tests. But in 1958 a fourth form (G) was added. In at least seven places the "new" manual should have been corrected, but was not. The advanced level manual does not show these errors.

Another example of sloppy editing with the intermediate level manual is the use of roman numerals in the Table of Contents and List of Tables, while not using any numerical designation for chapters in the manual proper and using arabic numbers for the tables. Again, these items are correct in the advanced level manual.

The only change in test reliability data is the addition of split-half coefficients for Form G (the previous manuals covered only Forms D, E, and F) and Forms D, E, and F of Part 4, Social Studies and Science. The coefficients for Form G, intermediate level, range from .788 for Arithmetic Computation to .950 for Arithmetic Problems. The coefficients for Form G, advanced level, range from .818 to .943. Several of these coefficients are too low to be considered adequate for individual use; several are satisfactory.

No new evidence of test validity is presented. The claims continue to rest primarily upon curricular or content validity.

The new manuals continue to claim that the items are "so perfectly balanced in one form with corresponding items in the other three forms that the same age and grade norms were found for all four forms." Previous reviewers were skeptical of this point, and this reviewer is skeptical also. Such perfection is difficult to imagine.

The major addition to the new manuals is a section called Grade and Age Norms, which reports the restandardization of the ASAT in 1961. One major criticism of the previous ASAT was its standardization. The restandardization involved pupils in either 50 or 32 or 30 or 28 states. "The children tested....were selected on a randomized basis and stratified with respect to geographical location, size of community, school enrollment, and grade assignment." It appears that sampling procedures followed generally accepted practices, which is a distinct improvement over the previous hit-or-miss procedures. One disturbing element, however, is the confusion over how many states and communities actually were involved in the restandardization. On page 14 of the intermediate level manual, column 1, it is stated that "In order to restandardize the ASAT, these tests were given to a sampling of students in all fifty states." But on page 14, column 2, it states "Thirty-two states....were represented in the sample." If one counts the number of states from the listing of states and communities, one gets 28 states, not 32 or 50. The count of 28 is misleading, however, since the name of one state, North Carolina, is omitted, although the communities of Charlotte and Cherryville are listed. This would seem to make 29, but another state, Louisiana, must be subtracted because, even though it is listed in the sample, a footnote says "scores not tabulated." The advanced level manual claims both 50 and 32 states. It does list 32 but two states must be eliminated because of "scores not tabulated." Such editorial errors should never have gotten into print.

Other criticisms that seem worthy of mention are: (*a*) No test means or standard deviations are given in either manual. (*b*) No percentiles have been developed in spite of previous criticisms and in spite of the known limitations of grade equivalent scores. (*c*) There is no discussion of the uses (and misuses) of grade equivalent scores. (*d*) Expected chance scores for certain tests are dangerously high when changed to grade equivalents; e.g., the expected chance raw score of 10 (40 items) on Arithmetic Computation, intermediate level, yields a grade equivalent of 4.0. (*e*) Expected chance scores for the advanced level are not so bad. The highest ones yield grade equivalents of 5.9 (Social Studies) and 5.5 (Arithmetic Problems). (*f*) The advanced level manual claims "The revised norms....are approximately the same as those which were established in 1955 and in 1958. With the nationwide restandardization, a slight revision will be found in the Table of Norms." However, comparison of the grade norms in the 1958 and 1963 manuals shows that some of the differences are scarcely "slight." For example, a raw score of 22 on the science test corresponded to a grade norm of 8.9 in the 1958 standardization and 7.2 in the 1960 standardization. Many other examples of this type could be cited.

In summary, one might say that the items of the ASAT, while quite traditional and factual in nature, seem to be relatively sound. The restandardization of the intermediate and advanced levels seems to follow accepted sampling procedures. Previous criticisms of low reliability at certain levels still are valid. Previous criticisms of inadequate statistical evidence of the value of these tests still are valid. Editing of the new intermediate level manual seems worse than before but the advanced level manual is better. The high grade equivalents obtainable by some chance scores are a serious flaw. There seems to be little reason for any school to elect to use the *American School Achievement Tests* when test series such as the *Iowa Tests of Basic Skills, Metropolitan Achievement Tests, SRA Achievement Series, California Achievement Tests,* and *Stanford Achievement Test* are available.[1]

For reviews by J. Raymond Gerberich and Virgil E. Herrick, see 5:1; for a review by Ralph C. Preston of an earlier edition, see 4:1; for reviews by Walter W. Cook and Gordon N.

[1] A statement about the joint standardization of the *American School Achievement Tests* and the *American School Intelligence Test* is made in this reviewer's review of that intelligence test.

Mackenzie (with Glen Hass), see 3:1. For reviews of subtests, see 5:174, 5:455–6, and 5:620.

[3]

***California Achievement Tests, 1957 Edition With 1963 Norms.** Grades 1–2, 2.5–4.5, 4–6, 7–9, 9–14; 1934–63; 11 scores: reading vocabulary, reading comprehension, reading total, arithmetic reasoning, arithmetic fundamentals, arithmetic total, mechanics of English, spelling, language total, total, handwriting; IBM and Grade-O-Mat for grades 4–14; 2–4 forms ('63, c1957–63, identical with tests copyrighted in 1957 except for profile and, in junior high level Form X, revision of the reading subtest); 5 levels; tests in reading, language, and arithmetic available as separates; manual ('63, c1957–63, 53–70 pages) for each level; technical report ('57, 48 pages) on 1957 edition with 1957 norms; questions and answers ('61, 18 pages); individual profile ('63, 2 pages) for each level; school profile-record sheet ('63, 2 pages); no norms for grades 13–14; separate answer sheets or cards may be used in grades 4–14; 15¢ per set of IBM answer sheets; 27¢ per set of Scoreze answer sheets; 9¢ per set of Cal-Cards; 12¢ per set of Grade-O-Mat scorable punch-out cards; 60¢ per set of either IBM answer sheet or Cal-Card hand scoring stencils; 2¢ per individual profile; 10¢ per school profile-record sheet; postage extra; technical report free; 75¢ per specimen set of *a* or *b;* $1 per specimen set of *c, d,* or *e;* postpaid; can be administered in 2 sessions; Ernest W. Tiegs and Willis W. Clark; California Test Bureau. *

a) LOWER PRIMARY. Grades 1–2; Forms W, X, ('63, c1957–63, 29 pages); $5.60 per 35 tests; 89(110) minutes.

b) UPPER PRIMARY. Grades 2.5–4.5; Forms W, X, ('63, c1957–63, 30 pages); $5.95 per 35 tests; 124(145) minutes.

c) ELEMENTARY. Grades 4–6; IBM and Grade-O-Mat; Forms W, X, Y, Z, ('63, c1957–63, 34 pages); $6.65 per 35 tests; $1.20 per set of machine scoring stencils; 160(175) minutes.

d) JUNIOR HIGH LEVEL. Grades 7–9; IBM and Grade-O-Mat; Forms W, X, Y, Z, ('63, c1957–63, 38 pages); $6.65 per 35 tests; $1.20 per set of machine scoring stencils; 178(190) minutes.

e) ADVANCED. Grades 9–14; IBM and Grade-O-Mat; Forms W, X, Y, ('63, c1957–63, 47 pages); $6.65 per 35 tests; $1.40 per set of machine scoring stencils; 178(190) minutes.

REFERENCES

1. See 40:1193.
2–4. See 3:15.
5–12. See 4:2.
13–22. See 5:2.
23. WRIGHT, HAROLD THEODORE, JR. *A Study of the Achievement Status of the Ohio Eighth Year Tests.* Doctor's thesis, Indiana University (Bloomington, Ind.), 1957. (*DA* 18:934)
24. WILSON, JOHN A. R. "Differences in Achievement Attributable to Different Educational Environments." *J Ed Res* 52:83–93 N '58. * (*PA* 33:10949)
25. GARLOCK, J. C., AND HARSH, J. R. "A Comparative Study of Four Commonly Used Achievement Tests." *Calif J Ed Res* 11:147–54 S '60. * (*PA* 35:7117)
26. OSBORNE, R. T. "Racial Differences in Mental Growth and School Achievement: A Longitudinal Study." *Psychol Rep* 7:233–9 O '60. * (*PA* 35:2782)
27. RUPIPER, OMER JOHN. "Multiple Factor Analysis of Academic Achievement: A Comparative Study of Full-Blooded Indian and White Children." *J Exp Ed* 28:177–205 Mr '60. *
28. FINDLEY, WARREN G. "Use and Interpretation of Achievement Tests in Relation to Validity." *Yearb Nat Council Meas Ed* 18:23–34 '61. *
29. ROTH, ROBERT M., AND GILBERT, JEAN. "AF: A New Approach to the Concept of Achievement." *J Ed Res* 55:90–2 O '61. *
30. STAKE, ROBERT E. "'Overestimation' of Achievement With the California Achievement Test." *Ed & Psychol Meas* 21:59–62 sp '61. * (*PA* 36:1KL59S)
31. WOLINS, LEROY; MACKINNEY, A. C.; AND STEPHANS, PAUL. "Factor Analyses of High School Science Achievement Measures." *J Ed Res* 54:173–7 Ja '61. * (*PA* 35:7129)
32. NORMAN, RALPH D.; CLARK, BETTY P.; AND BESSEMER, DAVID W. "Age, Sex, IQ, and Achievement Patterns in Achieving and Nonachieving Gifted Children." *Excep Child* 29:116–23 N '62. * (*PA* 37:7159)
33. PARSLEY, KENNETH M., JR., AND POWELL, MARVIN. "Achievement Gains or Losses During the Academic Year and Over the Summer Vacation Period: A Study of Trends in Achievement by Sex and Grade Level Among Students of Average Intelligence." *Genetic Psychol Monogr* 66:285–342 N '62. * (*PA* 37:7198)
34. TAYLOR, EDWARD A., AND CRANDALL, JAMES H. "A Study of the 'Norm-Equivalence' of Certain Tests Approved for the California State Testing Program." *Calif J Ed Res* 13:186–92 S '62. *
35. ANDERSON, HARRY, JR., AND LETON, DONALD A. "Optimum Grade Classification With the California Achievement Test Battery." *Ed & Psychol Meas* 23:135–43 sp '63. * (*PA* 38:2664)
36. BOBBE, CAROL; CAMPBELL, WILLIAM; LAMBERTI, ELAINE; AND SHEPPARD, CHARLES. "A Correlation Analysis in Testing." *Ed* 83:375–8 F '63. *
37. CASSEL, RUSSELL N. "Comparing 8th Grade CAT Scores and 9th Grade ITED Scores." *Psychol Rep* 12:53–4 F '63. * (*PA* 38:3198)
38. FINLEY, CARMEN J. "A Comparison of the California Achievement Test, Metropolitan Achievement Test and Iowa Test of Basic Skills." *Calif J Ed Res* 14:79–88 Mr '63. * (*PA* 38:1422)
39. LETON, DONALD A.; ANDERSON, HARRY E., JR.; AND STIER, JULIUS H. "Factors of Achievement as Defined by the California Achievement Tests." *J Exp Ed* 32:65–71 f '63. *
39a. KENNEDY, WALLACE; VAN DE RIET, VERNON; AND WHITE, JAMES C., JR. *A Normative Sample of Intelligence and Achievement of Negro Elementary School Children in Southeastern United States.* Monographs of the Society for Research in Child Development, Vol. 28, No. 6. Lafayette, Ind.: Child Development Publications, 1963. Pp. 112.*
40. SAXTON, GEORGE H.; BLACKMAN, LEONARD S.; AND TRETAKOFF, MAURICE I. "Achievement Measurement and Academic Grade Placement in Educable Mental Retardates." *Am J Mental Def* 67:748–50 Mr '63. * (*PA* 38:1279)
41. SMITH, W. N. "Differential Prediction of Two Test Batteries." *J Ed Res* 57:39–42 S '63. *

JACK C. MERWIN, *Professor of Educational Psychology, and Assistant Director, Student Counseling Bureau, University of Minnesota, Minneapolis, Minnesota.*

The 1957 edition of the *California Achievement Tests* is the latest revision of an achievement test series which started in 1934 under the title *Progressive Achievement Tests.* Major changes in content from the 1950 version were made in the two reading tests and the mechanics of English tests at the elementary, junior high, and advanced levels. A major change in structure was the splitting of the primary level battery of the 1950 tests into two batteries called Upper Primary and Lower Primary. These tests are revisions, rather than completely new tests, some items from the 1950 tests being retained in the 1957 version.

The 1957 Technical Report states that one of the main purposes of the 1957 tests is to continue the aim of earlier work on this series "to develop a battery of diagnostic tests rather than another survey-type battery yielding but single subject area scores." To this end the authors limit themselves to the areas of reading, arithmetic, and language. For the advanced battery, proposed for grades 9 to 14, the authors label the quantitative section "mathematics" rather than arithmetic but it is largely arithmetic in content.

The manuals note that the curricular placement and emphasis on the skills covered by these tests varies from school to school and that for many secondary school students instruction will be negligible for skills covered by some of the subtests. All school systems will have a degree of concern for developing the skills tested by these batteries. However, most junior and senior high schools, and many elementary schools, will find that a large portion of the objectives of their instruction are not sampled by these tests.

Each battery yields a set of scores which are to be plotted on the grade placement diagnostic profile chart developed for that battery. These scores vary in number from 21 for the lower primary battery to 27 for the three upper level batteries, with some subsection scores which are based on as few as 10 to 15 items. Other scores are based on combinations of the scores from the subsections, culminating in an overall battery score. As a further aid to the proposed diagnostic use of the results of the tests a sheet entitled "Diagnostic Analysis of Learning Difficulties" is provided. Items are grouped by content on these sheets, though single items are listed in some cases. It is proposed that a study of these sheets, when completed, will provide a basis for more extensive diagnosis and the identification of more specific problems than is possible through the use of the subsection scores alone.

A school considering the use of any test battery should be concerned with the reliability of *each* score obtained from the battery. For these batteries, the reliability coefficients reported at each grade level for the three total scores and six subscores are satisfactory. At the other extreme the manuals appropriately caution that the use of small numbers of items for diagnosis should be made only with the intention of identifying areas of possible concern for further exploration. This warning is particularly appropriate for the use of the diagnostic analysis sheet. The reliability of the subsection scores remains in question.

The caution regarding the use of small numbers of items for diagnosis certainly applies to subsection scores based on as few as 10 to 15 items. The authors provide space for plotting these scores as points on a grade placement scale, in spite of the statement in the manual that, "The reliability of individual sections does not justify attaching specific grade placement values to the section scores." This statement implies that information about the reliability, or unreliability, of these scores does exist. Such information should be made available to potential users. Accepting the validity of the statement, these scores should not be plotted on the grade placement profile. Teachers may appropriately recognize the limited sampling and probable low reliability of classifications on the diagnostic analysis sheet but many will be led to ignore the unreliability of subsection scores which they plot on diagnostic profiles.

The content validity of these tests for a school system must be assessed in light of the instructional objectives of that system. This requires a careful analysis of the items of the tests for each grade level to be tested. A school may find that the lower level batteries cover a relatively large portion of their objectives for the early elementary grades and that the higher level batteries cover a lesser portion of the objectives of their instruction.

Coefficients of correlation between subtests of this battery and the most nearly comparable subtests from the *Stanford Achievement Test* and the *Metropolitan Achievement Tests* are reported as evidence of "construct" validity. These coefficients are uniformly high, indicating that the skills sections from those batteries and the *California Achievement Tests* may be tapping similar skills.

The most recent norming of these tests took place in 1963. The tests were administered concurrently with the 1963 S-Form of the *California Short-Form Test of Mental Maturity,* to somewhat over 15,000 students, the number per grade ranging from 968 to 1481. It is reported that the students are from "(1) independent class units from seven geographic regions representing forty-nine states, and (2) complete school systems, including all students in Grades 1 through 12 from five school systems located in the northeastern, eastern, central, and western areas of the United States." It would be helpful to the prospective user if the information concerning the composition of the norm sample provided in the battery manuals were supplemented by a more detailed description such as that provided for the last norming in the 1957 Technical Report.

Prior to developing norms, two restrictions were imposed: only the scores for students with chronological ages within plus or minus nine months of the mean age for a grade were included for each grade and "statistical procedures" incorporating the CTMM Short-Form scores were used to adjust the "obtained performance" to get a normal distribution of mental ability within each grade.

Five sets of norms are provided for the 10 main scores obtained from each battery. They include grade norms, percentile ranks, standard scores, and stanines based on "low" and "high" levels of each grade, and "Anticipated Achievement Grade Placements" provided in tables for intervals of two or three months of actual grade placement. The teacher is most likely to be unfamiliar with the anticipated achievement grade placements and should not use them without careful study of their characteristics.

The idea behind the anticipated achievement grade placement norms is commendable. The potential user should recognize that these norms cannot be used unless the CTMM Short-Form has also been administered. If he is willing to use both batteries he should carefully study the characteristics of these norms prior to application. The 1963 manuals have a somewhat better description of the use of the two batteries and these norms than appeared in the 1957 manuals. For example, the statement that these norms "may be considered as the test performance which the student would be expected to attain," is more appropriate than the statement from earlier manuals that "they may be considered as the test performance which the student should attain." However, statements which imply that these norms present an opportunity for comparison with scores of other students having the same CA, MA, IQ, and actual grade placement remain in the new manuals and are misleading. A student's anticipated achievement is determined only by his raw score on the CTMM Short-Form and his actual grade placement. The student's chronological age is not a factor in determining his anticipated achievement.

The Diagnostic Profile Sheet is well designed and provides a convenient method for summarizing a student's performance on these tests. It should be noted, however, that interpretation is limited to within test comparisons across students. To make legitimate intraindividual comparisons (e.g., is his standing in arithmetic better than in English) requires knowledge of the intercorrelations of the tests and these are pointedly not reported because the authors feel that they "add little."

Unfortunately, scales for plotting the grade placement of subscales of reportedly low reliability remain on the new profile sheet. If the scores for these short sections are to appear on the profile it would be less misleading if they were not plotted, as is the case with the subsections of the 1963 S-Form of the companion CTMM.

The test booklets and extensive materials provided to help teachers interpret scores are presented in an attractive, readable format. The manuals and auxiliary materials provided for both student diagnosis and class summary are extensive and well written. These materials provide much individual item information, as well as suggestions for interpretation of the scores.

In summary, this is a well constructed set of tests, though, as an achievement battery, coverage is limited. Much information about the tests and aids for interpreting the results are provided in the test manuals. This material should be carefully studied and understood prior to administration of the tests. Scores from the subsections should not be plotted on the diagnostic profile and interpretation across the scores for an individual student should await the provision of information concerning the reliability of the differences between these scores. Schools that are seeking an achievement battery to test just the three general skills areas covered by these batteries and who find from a study of the items that the content coverage is relevant to their instructional objectives may find these batteries of tests useful.

ROBERT D. NORTH, *Associate Director, Educational Records Bureau, New York, New York.*

The five levels of the 1957 edition of the *California Achievement Tests* provide articulated, normative evaluation of reading, arithmetic, and language achievement in the grade range of 1–14. The scores for the parts, sections, and total battery may be converted to grade placement scores, percentile ranks, standard scores, and stanines. Among the meritorious features of this test series are its excellent and extensive accessory materials, its normative linkage with the *California Short-Form Test of Mental Maturity* to facilitate comparisons between achievement and academic aptitude, its diagnostic aids, and its provisions for economical, efficient scoring and reporting services.

The publisher has evidently gone to considerable trouble and expense to compile 1963 norms for the 1957 edition in coordination with the norming of the 1963 edition of the *California Short-Form Test of Mental Maturity,* but, except for the junior high level reading test, has not revised the contents of the achievement test booklets in any way. Conspicuously lacking, therefore, is any coverage of "modern" mathematics, which is beginning to appear in the curriculum of many schools. Curriculum changes of this nature may cause achievement tests published in 1957 to become outmoded soon.

The 1963 norms for the *California Achievement Tests* are based on modal-age groups (18 months age range per grade) drawn from a stratified national sample of 15,351 pupils. To gauge the effects of the renorming on the grade placement scores, the reviewer took the raw score values that yielded grade placements of 4.9, 6.9, and 8.9, respectively, on the 1957 norms and found their corresponding grade placements on the 1963 norms. The results for the six subtests are shown below.

Table 1
1957 and 1963 Grade Score Equivalents for Identical Raw Scores

1957 Grade Score	1963 Grade Scores					
	Reading		Arithmetic		Language	
	Vocabulary	Comprehension	Reasoning	Fundamentals	Mechanics	Spelling
4.9	4.4	4.5	4.85	4.95	4.5	4.65
6.9	6.1	6.4	6.4	6.9	6.3	5.7
8.9	8.7	8.9	8.8	8.85	8.8	9.5

Judging from these data, grade equivalent scores on the reading and language subtests for the elementary grades will tend to be lower on the 1963 norms than they were on the 1957 norms. On the reading vocabulary subtest, the raw scores that formerly yielded grade equivalents of 4.9 and 6.9 now correspond to grade equivalents that are lower by five months and eight months, respectively. No appreciable change is evident, however, in the end-of-year grade equivalent norms for either of the arithmetic subtests at the fourth grade level, for the arithmetic fundamentals subtest at the sixth grade level, or for any of the subtests except spelling at the eighth grade level. It is interesting to find that the spelling raw score that yielded a grade equivalent of 8.9 on the 1957 norms now gives a grade equivalent of 9.5, or six months higher, on the 1963 norms. In this reviewer's opinion, the normative changes that are in the direction of reflecting higher standards of educational achievement (i.e., a lower grade equivalent for a given raw score) seem to be more in keeping with the current trend of change in pupils' test performances than are those that go in the opposite direction.

In conjunction with the renorming of the test, the procedure for computing grade scores on the total battery was changed. Instead of averaging the reading, arithmetic, and language grade placement scores to get a total battery grade score as before, the subtest raw scores are now added to obtain a total battery raw score, which is then converted as a separate score. With this new procedure, the subtests will influence the total battery scores in proportion to their standard deviations. Consequently, a subtest such as Arithmetic Fundamentals of the upper primary level, which apparently has a standard deviation more than double that of any of the other subtests in that battery, may tend to distort the total battery scores. From the measurement point of view, this change in the scoring procedure does not seem to be advantageous.

In addition to the IBM and Scoreze answer forms that were previously available for the elementary, junior high, and advanced levels, punch-out cards and Cal-Cards are now obtainable for these levels. The punch-out cards can be scored locally by the relatively inexpensive Grade-O-Mat machine. For the Cal-Cards, the publisher offers complete data processing services, including right response records that list the correct responses of each student. These records are designed to be used in conjunction with the "Diagnostic Analysis of Learning Difficulties" sheet to find the achievement strengths and weaknesses of individuals and class groups.

No revision of the 1957 Technical Report had been published by the time this review was being prepared, but some revised reliability data are reported for four of the five levels in the 1963 edition of the separate manuals. The Kuder-Richardson formula 21 reliabilities of the junior high level apparently have not been recomputed, since the coefficients and the standard deviations for a group of 200 eighth grade pupils are the same in the 1957 and 1963 manuals. These reliabilities are .83 for spelling, .84 for arithmetic reasoning, and between .90 and .95 for the other parts and the subtest total scores.

The Kuder-Richardson formula 21 reliabilities reported in the 1963 manuals for the primary, elementary, and advanced batteries are based on single-grade groups ranging in size from 115 to 384 pupils. No information about the procedures used for drawing these samples is given, nor is any explanation offered for the small sizes of the samples. As compared with the corresponding Kuder-Richardson reliabilities reported for groups of 200 pupils in the 1957 Technical Report, the newly reported reliabilities for the six parts are lower by an average of about .06 for the lower primary level and higher by an average of about .09 for the upper primary level and .03 for the elementary level. The changes in the reliabilities for these three levels are evidently attributable mainly to the differences between the standard deviations of the 1957 and 1963 samples, since none of the standard errors of measurement for the subtests have changed by as much as one raw score point. The average part score reliability of the advanced level for the eleventh grade is about the same for the 1957 and 1963 samples.

The reported reliabilities for the total reading, total arithmetic, and total language scores are satisfactory, in general, falling in the range of .86 to .96. The reliabilities fall below .80, however, for reading comprehension, arithmetic reasoning, and spelling in the lower primary level, spelling in the upper primary level, and arithmetic reasoning in the elementary level. Caution should therefore be observed in using these subtest scores at these levels for individual evaluation or diagnostic purposes other than as guides. The estimated reliabilities for the total battery scores for all five levels are consistently high, ranging from .95 to .98. These reliability estimates were obtained by applying the Spearman-Brown formula to the average reliability of the six subtests, equally weighted, of each level.

Validity data are given in the 1957 Technical Report in terms of correlations with other test scores, item analysis statistics, and other criteria. While this type of validity information is helpful, schools will no doubt want to make their validity appraisals mainly in terms of the relation between the tests' coverage and their curriculum objectives.

In this reviewer's opinion, the 1957 edition of the *California Achievement Tests* is suitable for use by schools that want to focus their achievement measurement and diagnosis on the traditional, fundamental skills and content in the areas of reading vocabulary and comprehension, arithmetic, and English. If coordinated evaluation of a more intensive or extensive nature is desired, consideration might well be given to test series such as the *Stanford Achievement Test* for the elementary grades or, for the junior and senior high school grades, the separate-subject achievement tests published by the Cooperative Test Division of Educational Testing Service.

For a review by Charles O. Neidt, see 5:2; for reviews by Warren G. Findley, Alvin W. Schindler, and J. Harlan Shores of the 1950 edition, see 4:2; for a review by Paul A. Witty of the 1943 edition, see 3:15; for reviews by C. W. Odell and Hugh B. Wood of an earlier edition, see 40:1193; for a review by D. Welty Lefever, see 38:876 (1 excerpt). For reviews of subtests, see 251, 5:177, 5:468, 4:151, 4:411, 4:530, 40:1292, 40:1459, 40:1563, 38:893, and 38:1110.

[4]

California Basic Skills Tests. Grades 4-6, 7-9; 1933-54; hand scoring edition of Forms AA and DD of the *California Achievement Tests, 1950 Edition* (see 4:2; for the 1957 edition, see 3) except for the spelling tests which are from the *Progressive Achievement Tests* (see 3:15); 10 scores: vocabulary, reading comprehension, total reading, arithmetic reasoning, arithmetic fundamentals, total arithmetic, mechanics of English and grammar, spelling, total language, total; 2 levels; manual ('54, 28 pages) for each level; $5.60 per 35 tests, postage extra; 50¢ per specimen set of either level, postpaid; Ernest W. Tiegs and Willis W. Clark; California Test Bureau. *
a) ELEMENTARY. Grades 4-6; Form 2 ('54, 23 pages); (120) minutes in 2 sessions.
b) INTERMEDIATE. Grades 7-9; Forms 1, 2, ('54, 31 pages); (155) minutes in 2 sessions.

ROBERT D. NORTH, *Associate Director, Educational Records Bureau, New York, New York.*

The *California Basic Skills Tests* are hand scoring vestiges of the 1950 edition of the *California Achievement Tests* and their forerunners, the *Progressive Achievement Tests.* They consist of reading, arithmetic, and language subtests, with section and part subdivisions, each yielding a separate score.

Grade placement values for all the scores, including the total, are given in scale form on the profile on the back of the test booklet. Tables in the manual give the grade placement and percentile values for the section and total battery scores. The norms were derived from those of the 1950 edition of the *California Achievement Tests* by equating procedures, and they have not been brought up to date. Normative interpretation of the results of these tests may therefore be seriously misleading.

A unique feature of these tests is a provision for appraising the pupils' handwriting on the spelling part of the test by comparing it with specimens that have been assigned grade placement values. The handwriting rating does not affect the total battery score, however.

The 1963 California Test Bureau catalog describes the tests as useful instruments for teachers who want to see and analyze pupils' answers as they are written in the test booklets, particularly in the areas of arithmetic, spelling, and punctuation, where the items are of the open-ended type, rather than multiple choice. A "Diagnostic Analysis of Learning Difficulties" chart is printed on the inside back cover of each test booklet to help the teacher make an item-by-item analysis of the pupil's difficulties in areas where his scores indicate weaknesses.

As a classroom teacher's aid for appraising pupils' strengths and weaknesses in the basic skills, this obsolescent test series may still have some merit. For normative evaluations, however, newer batteries such as the 1957 edition of the *California Achievement Tests* should be used instead.

Apparently the publisher is allowing the basic skills test to "phase out" since one of the two forms (Form 1) of the elementary level is no longer in print, and there is no indication that new forms or new editions are being prepared.

For reviews by Warren G. Findley, Alvin W. Schindler, and J. Harlan Shores of the 1950 edition, see 4:2; for a review by Paul A. Witty of the 1943 edition, see 3:15; for reviews by C. W. Odell and Hugh B. Wood of an earlier edition, see 40:1193; for a review by D. Welty Lefever, see 38:876 (1 excerpt). For reviews of subtests, see 4:151, 4:411, 4:530, 40:1292, 40:1459, 40:1563, 38:893, and 38:1110.

[5]

★Canadian Test of General Information (CTGI). Grade 10; 1963; one of 4 tests of the *Canadian Test Battery,* grade 10; girls' Form G, boys' Form B, (10 pages); 2 editions of manual: hand scoring (8 pages), machine scoring (9 pages); supplementary data (6 pages) for the battery; battery profile (1 page); separate answer sheets or cards must be used; $1.25 per 25 tests; $1 per set of 50 answer sheets and hand scoring manual; 20¢ per hand scoring stencil; 20¢ per 15 battery profiles; 50¢ per set of 25 IBM answer cards (machine scoring through the Department of Educational Research only); 10¢ per machine scoring manual; 50¢ per specimen set; $2.15 per battery specimen set; postage extra; 60(70–75) minutes; Department of Educational Research, Ontario College of Education, University of Toronto; distributed by Guidance Centre (machine scoring manual and answer cards must be purchased from the Department of Educational Research). *

REFERENCES

1. D'OYLEY, VINCENT R. *Technical Manual for the Canadian Tests: Statistical Data on the Carnegie Study Tests of Academic Aptitude and Achievement in Grades 8, 9, and 10 in Ontario Schools and Grades 7 and 8 in Toronto Schools.* Carnegie Study of Identification and Utilization of Talent in High School and College, Bulletin No. 4. Toronto, Canada: Department of Educational Research, Ontario College of Education, University of Toronto, 1964. Pp. viii, 50. *

2. D'OYLEY, VINCENT R. *Testing: The First Two Years of the Carnegie Study 1959 to 1961: Analysis of Scores by Course, Sex, and Size of Municipality.* Carnegie Study of Identification and Utilization of Talent in High School and College, Bulletin No. 6. Toronto, Canada: Department of Educational Research, Ontario College of Education, University of Toronto, 1964. Pp. ix, 53. *

J. DOUGLAS AYERS, *Associate Professor of Educational Psychology, University of Alberta, Edmonton, Alberta, Canada.*

The Fifth Mental Measurements Yearbook contains only one reference to an information test and that for use by life insurance companies. It was not reviewed due to its restricted nature. This is rather surprising since information tests are probably better predictors of vocational choice than current inventories, particularly in the earlier years of high school.

The *Canadian Test of General Information* is one of a large number of achievement and aptitude tests that were administered several years ago, as part of a Carnegie study, to nearly all students in Ontario who started grade 9 in September 1959. There are two forms, one for boys and one for girls, both consisting of 140 items, about 74 per cent of which are identical.

This test, in common with all other tests in the battery, has a one hour time limit. Such a time limit appears difficult to justify when 30 to 35 minutes would be generous.

The manual contains no data on item analysis, reliability, or validity, but supplementary data supplied by the publisher indicate that the split-half reliability for 200 cases on the boys' form has been found to be .95 and for 200 cases on the girls' form, .93. In a random sample of 500, the correlations of the boys' form with grade 10 marks varies from .32 for mathematics to .50 for social studies. For 500 girls the correlations vary from .29 for mathematics to .44 for English. These predictive validities probably add no information to the other aptitude and achievement tests used in the Carnegie survey.

The manual provides no evidence of content validity, although it is indicated that the test covers 10 "school" topics, not all of which are mutually exclusive: famous people, general, physical and health, music and art, current events, history, science, government and politics, geography, and literature. Apparently content validity is implied by listing the items that fall in each of these categories. However, most areas that are apt to have predictive validity, such as medicine, electronics, auto mechanics, and outdoors, are excluded.

The percentile norms are based on some 32,000 boys and 31,000 girls who were in grade 10 in 1960–61, apparently all the students in Ontario schools. The 1963 edition of the test included some very slight changes in the current events items that are apparently not sufficient to change the norms significantly. There are no Canadian norms. In fact, at the grade 10 level, the provincial school systems in Canada are sufficiently different that Ontario norms are not appropriate.

The directions for administration are adequate. The test may be administered with a separate answer sheet which has a hand scored key or with answer cards which are scored by the publishers. The directions in the test booklet itself, however, refer repeatedly to answer cards and this may cause some confusion when the hand scored answer sheet is used.

In summary, the *Canadian Test of General Information* is not Canadian. It is unnecessarily long; and it provides only one score based on school-related general information.

ROBERT J. SOLOMON, *Vice President, Educational Testing Service, Princeton, New Jersey.*

The *Canadian Test of General Information* was developed for use in the Carnegie Study of Identification and Utilization of Talent in High School and College. The Study, supported by the Carnegie Corporation, is being conducted by the staff of the Department of Educational Research of the Ontario College of Education. It is a longitudinal study of the approximately 90,000 students who in 1959 were enrolled in the ninth grade in the Ontario schools. This five year survey will follow each student to one year beyond completion of secondary school or, if he leaves school before reaching that level, for one year of employment. The objectives of the study include: enlarging the knowledge of the abilities required for success in Canadian schools and colleges, providing information for improving high school curricula and college admissions requirements, identifying able students and studying ways of encouraging their educational careers, and developing better instruments for measuring characteristics related to educational or occupational success.

The test was developed for use in the second year of the Study. It was developed in two forms, one for tenth grade boys and one for tenth grade girls. According to the manual, the 1963 edition that is currently available is, except for minor revisions, essentially the same as the first edition (1961). The only differences between the 1961 and 1963 editions are that five current events items in the girls' form and six in the boys' form have been revised for the later edition. Technical data are available only for the 1961 edition but, because of the slight differences between the editions, the test authors believe that the data are applicable to the 1963 edition.

The boys' and girls' forms each contain 140 five-choice items of the typical general information item type construction. The test requires a total of approximately 75 minutes for administration. The students are given 60 minutes working time to complete the test; approximately 15 minutes are needed for instructions. Answer cards, answer sheets, and scoring stencils have been developed to enable the test to be scored either by machine or by hand. There are separate answer keys for each form. The score is the number of items answered correctly.

Each form includes items on 10 topics (famous people, literature, physical and health, government and politics, science, music and art, geography, current events, history, and general), with all of the items on a topic grouped together. However, the topics are not ordered in the same way in the boys' form as in the girls' form. Also, neither the number nor the content of the items devoted to each topic is the same for boys as for girls. For example, questions 109–125 (17 questions) are devoted to geography in the girls' form; questions 80–94 (15 questions) are devoted to the same topic in the boys' form; and only 11 geography items are common to the two forms. Moreover, there are some interesting but unexplained differences in option order and option content between items with the same stem. Of the total number of 140 items in each form, about 100 items are common to both. Items included in only one of the forms were selected on the basis of differences between the sexes as indicated in the analysis of tryout results. It would be interesting to know more about how the tryout influenced the number, the order, and the content of the items selected for each form.

As should be expected in any general information test, the appropriateness and the difficulty of the questions in this test must be considered in terms of the population for which it was intended and the time when it was developed and administered. The test contains a significant number of questions that are relevant for a population of Canadian tenth graders but would not be for tenth graders in the United States. Also, several questions no longer have a correct response or have changed markedly in difficulty as a result of recent events. This is, of course, a problem in the development and use of all general information tests and, indeed, some achievement tests.

The norms provided are based on the performance of 32,041 boys and 31,055 girls in grade 10 in Ontario who took the 1961 edition of the test in April 1961. The norms are given in terms of the percentile rank for each raw score obtained in the 1961 administration. In that administration, scores on the boys' form ranged from 13 to 127 (140 the possible maximum); the median was 65. On the girls' form scores ranged from 15 to 123; the median was 63. Although fewer than 4 per cent of the items were changed from the 1961 edition to the 1963 edition, it is difficult to know to what extent the revisions and, more important, the passage of time have affected the appropriateness of the 1961 norms for the 1963 edition.

In general, using data from the 1961 edition, both forms seem appropriate for the groups for which they were intended. Also, both forms seem reasonably parallel to one another statistically. The means and standard deviations of scores on the boys' form and girls' form are 67.47, 23.29 and 67.30, 20.20, respectively, indicating that the tests were somewhat too difficult for the population. Approximately 3 per cent of the scores are at or below the mean chance score. Although no data on speededness are given, examination of the test and the accompanying data suggests that the test is probably not speeded.

The reliabilities of the forms are good; the split-halves reliabilities are .95 for the boys' form and .93 for the girls' and the standard errors of measurement are 5.21 and 5.34, respectively. Information on validity is available in terms of correlations, based on a random sample of 500, between grade 10 test scores and grade 10 school marks in English, French, mathematics, science, and social studies. They range from a high of .50 for boys' scores with social studies grades to a low of .29 for girls' scores with mathematics grades.

This test appears to have been a useful instrument for the study in which it was employed and it may be useful to other researchers in Canadian education or, possibly, comparative education. In its present state, however, it is unlikely to have wider utility.

[6]

***Closed High School Placement Test.** End of grade 8; 1955–63; replaces the "open" series called *High School Placement Test* published in 1955–59; various titles used by publisher; IBM; new form of *a* issued annually; 1–3 tests; manual ('62, 17 pages); technical report ('63, 21 pages); distribution restricted to participating schools; separate answer sheets must be used; tests rented only; examination fee: $1.10 per student, postpaid; fee includes scoring service; 134(180) minutes including optional tests; Scholastic Testing Service, Inc. *

a) 1963 CLOSED HIGH SCHOOL PLACEMENT TEST. 7 scores: verbal ability, quantitative ability, ability total, reading, arithmetic, language, composite; form 1963 ('62, 21 pages); 104(130) minutes.

b) RELIGION TEST FOR CLOSED HIGH SCHOOL PLACEMENT BATTERY. For Catholic schools; optional; 1 form ('61, 5 pages); supplementary manual ('61, 1 page); 15(20) minutes.

c) MECHANICAL COMPREHENSION TEST FOR CLOSED HIGH SCHOOL PLACEMENT BATTERY. Optional; 1 form ('61, 7 pages); supplementary manual ('63, 1 page, identical with manual copyrighted in 1961); 15(20) minutes.

MARION F. SHAYCOFT, *Senior Research Scientist, American Institute for Research; and Director of Measurement Research, University of Pittsburgh Project Talent Office; Pittsburgh, Pennsylvania.* [Review of the 1962 and 1963 tests.]

DESCRIPTION OF BATTERY. This is a battery intended for use at the end of the eighth grade, as an aid in selection and placement at the beginning high school level. The nine tests of the basic battery yield seven scores, as follows: three "general abilities" scores—verbal ability (sum of scores on Same-Opposites, Letter Patterns, and Logical Reasoning), quantitative ability (sum of scores on Numerical Reasoning, Figure Analogies, and Number Patterns), and total ability (sum of verbal ability and quantitative ability); three basic skills and achievement scores, each based on a separate test (Arithmetic, Reading, Language); and a composite for the battery (sum of the general ability score and the three basic skills and achievement scores). Two optional tests are also available: religion (for use in parochial schools) and mechanical comprehension.

EVALUATION OF BATTERY ORGANIZATION. Several relatively simple changes might be made in the organization and scoring scheme outlined above that would increase the usefulness of some of the scores by improving their reliability or factorial purity or both. For instance, while Letter Patterns is unobjectionable as a component of the "Total Ability" score, it seems quite out of place as a component of "Verbal Ability." Letter Patterns is a letter series test of the usual type, and is quite similar in the abilities it requires to Number Patterns, which consists of traditional number series items. The assumption of the test authors that the mere fact that discrete letters of the alphabet are involved instead of numbers makes a test "verbal" probably has the result of increasing the correlation between the "Verbal Ability" and "Quantitative Ability" scores, thus reducing their usefulness as separate measures.

The utility of scores derived from Arithmetic and Numerical Reasoning could also be improved. The two parts of the arithmetic subtest—Computation (40 items) and Reasoning (20 items)—are not separately scored. And scores on Numerical Reasoning, whose 15 items are of about the same type as those in the Arithmetic Reasoning subtest, are swallowed up in the quantitative ability score, and not separately reported. The reasons given for not reporting separate arithmetic reasoning and computation scores are that the test users don't want them and that such scores would be based on too few items for adequate reliability. These arguments are weak. Separate measures are worthwhile, since the skills required in arithmetic reasoning are correlationally quite different from those used in computation. And 40 well constructed computation items surely should be enough to yield a reasonably reliable score. After all, four of the present scores (quantitative ability, reading, mechanical comprehension, and religion) are based on only 45 items each. Furthermore if the reasoning part of the arithmetic test were combined with the numerical reasoning test the resultant 35-item arithmetic reasoning score should have a useful degree of reliability.

This type of reorganization would have the disadvantage that if the 15 numerical reasoning items continued to be a part of the "Quantitative Ability" and "Total Ability" scores, these "ability scores" would not be experimentally independent of the "achievement score" in arithmetic reasoning. This, however, seems of little moment, since the battery is apparently intended more for practical operational use than for research on the relation between something called "ability scores" and something else called "achievement scores"—a distinction that is largely an artificial one anyhow (unlike the distinction between computation skill and reasoning ability).

EVALUATION OF TEST CONTENT. Logical Reasoning and Numerical Reasoning and the reasoning section of the arithmetic test appear to have fewer defective items than the other tests, although the wording could be somewhat improved on a few items in Logical Reasoning.

Same-Opposites has a few somewhat questionable items with no clearly defensible answer.

Clerical errors in marking the questions to the items in Letter Patterns could undoubtedly be reduced, and reliability improved, by routine matching of option letter and option, wherever the latter is A, B, C, or D. For instance, item 51 in the 1963 test has the following options: a) C b) U c) D d) B; instead of a) U b) B c) C d) D. Letter Patterns item 57 (1962 test) has two answers. (The test author forgot that geometric series are just as legitimate a concept as arithmetic series.)

Two items in Number Patterns seem to lack defensible answers.

In Figure Analogies (1963 test) item 72 seems to have no defensible answer, but items 64 and 62 have two apiece, as does item 75 in the 1962 test.

Most of the arithmetic computation items seem in good shape. It strikes this reviewer as unfortunate, however, that five of the items (three in the 1963 and two in the 1962 tests) use the infantile "R" notation to represent remainders in the answers to division problems. Surely an eighth grade student should not be expected to harbor the notion that 19,603 divided by 68 equals something absurdly called 288 R19 rather than $288\frac{19}{68}$ or 288.28. If he has had the bad luck to have been indoctrinated with this kind of misinformation in an earlier grade, he should have discarded it by the time he is ready to enter high school because it surely will not help him in his high school mathematics—and for the same reasons it has no place in a high school placement test.

Most of the items in Language are of acceptable quality, although more attention might have been paid to sampling of content. There are several instances of two parallel items testing the identical point twice in the same test while many other points of equal or greater importance went untested. And the test includes usage items on points on which authorities disagree as to whether there *is* any preferred usage. The test places considerable emphasis on the technicalities of formal grammar—for instance whether a particular word is classified as a relative adverb, a compound relative pronoun, or a distributive pronoun. Many educators would undoubtedly regard this stress as excessive. To this reviewer it appears that the testing time devoted to this aspect could be better used to test objectives which have wider acceptance and in which more eighth graders would have received instruction. Language, like most of the other tests in the battery, has its share of incorrectly keyed items.

So much for the tests that have a few bad items but consist mostly of adequate items. We now come to Reading, which, particularly in the 1963 edition, has an appallingly large percentage of items for which getting the correct answer is dependent more on chance than on anything else. Close to a third of the items in the 1963 form have either no clear answer, two or three defensible answers, an incorrectly keyed answer, an answer that can be neither determined nor inferred from the passage, or an answer based on a passage that is so badly written that it says one thing and means another. Furthermore, some of the items test visual perception much more than reading comprehension. For instance, one item actually requires the student to get an exact count of the number of capital letters in the passage!

The optional test of mechanical comprehension is the type of test in which the problem is posed in terms of diagrams. Like so many of the other tests in the battery this one could be improved by correcting the keying of some items, editing other items more carefully (for instance eliminating "None of these" as an option in items for which it doesn't make sense), providing a correct answer for items that lack one, and eliminating some items completely that have little or nothing to do with mechanical comprehension. For instance, the two items that require nothing except knowledge of the definition of symmetry might be appropriate in a mathematics test, or even an art appreciation test, but surely they are out of place in a mechanical comprehension test—as is the item whose answer must be determined computationally (from the formula for area of a circle) rather than visually, because the accompanying diagrams were not drawn to scale.

RELIABILITY AND SPEEDEDNESS. Odd-even reliability coefficients and K-R 20's are presented for all seven of the basic scores though not for the two optional tests. The coefficients are mostly in the .80's except the ones for the composite scores, which are in the .90's. The Technical Report quite properly states that to the extent that the tests are speeded, the odd-even coefficients are overestimates. It neglects to point out, however, that the same limitation is applicable to K-R 20's, and erroneously implies that K-R 20's are lower-bound estimates even for speeded tests. Data on the percentage of students attempting at least 75 per cent of the items indicate that in the 1963 test the quantitative ability and arithmetic scores depend to a substantial degree on speed, and that it is also a limited factor on the other tests. Quite apart from the issue of speededness, the reliability coefficients for the reading test are spuriously high because these items are not all experimentally independent. This could have been controlled in the split-half procedure by keeping all the items for a passage in the same half-test.

Improvement of the general level of item quality could probably improve the reliability of all tests substantially without lengthening the battery. Improvements could be made in the printing format that would permit increasing the number of options from four per item in most cases to five, without increasing either the testing time or the number of pages. This, too, would improve test reliability.

NORMS. Raw scores and percentile ranks are reported for all seven scores. In addition the total ability score is converted to a deviation IQ, and grade equivalents are reported for the three basic skills scores (reading, arithmetic, and language). The norms appear to be carefully obtained. Preliminary norms are derived each year from an equipercentile equating to the previous year's test, on a split sample of approximately 2,500 students. These preliminary norms are then checked against new norms obtained from a stratified sample consisting of 25,000 students. (Stratification is on the basis of sex, school size, location, and rural versus urban community type.)

MANUALS AND TECHNICAL REPORTS. The Manual of Directions and the Technical Report for each new edition are quite good on the whole, except for the inaccuracies noted above that the latter contains in its discussion of reliability coefficients and a little vagueness in the description of the way the deviation IQ's were developed. The manual contains excellent discussions of the limitations of IQ's and grade equivalent norms. Each Technical Report contains a thorough description of the norming procedure. It also presents numerous validity coefficients, both concurrent and predictive. The criteria are various intelligence tests, achievement tests, and for predictive validity, high school course grades.

SUMMARY. Commendable effort has obviously gone into maintaining good norms and determining validity coefficients for the test. There is undoubtedly a useful function to be served by a "secure" battery of this general sort, suitable for the beginning high school level. It is unfortunate that the *Closed High School Placement Test* does not serve the purpose better. With a little reorganization of its scores, better distribution of the two hours of testing time among the various tests, and considerably more attention to the item writing and editing phases, it could.

In its present form the test could still be useful in some school systems—particularly in ones whose curricula involve the same kinds of emphasis as the test content—for instance the heavy stress on formal grammar. But users *must* bear the battery's limitations in mind—particularly the weaknesses of the score yielded in a very important area, reading.

JAMES R. HAYDEN, *Superintendent of Schools, New Bedford Public Schools, New Bedford, Massachusetts.*

For a "program designed specifically to meet the problem of selection and/or placement at the beginning high school level" the authors have used two subtests resembling the SAT plus a combination of other subtests which give the usual information found in the majority of achievement test batteries now on the market. The meritorious objective of obtaining uniform placement information on students arriving from many sources is aided by complete scoring and reporting services on a closed type of test battery that is rented not sold. Its norms are annually revised through a method of equating to national norms based upon performance of a stratified sample of 25,000 individuals tested one year earlier. While it is not specifically stated in the description of the sample, other material furnished the prospective customer states that the norms are based on approximately 75,000 students graduating from Catholic elementary schools.

Both the 1962 and 1963 editions were available for review and considerable improvement was noted in both the technical manuals and the tests themselves. The format of the 1963 test is improved with larger illustrations, better type, different placement of responses, and more space between lines. Both tests are generally similar in item content, with most changes in Test 7 (Reading). Most items are challenging, providing a range from easy to good ceiling items.

Only supplementary manuals with no statistical data are available for the religion and mechanical comprehension tests, which makes it difficult to judge their validity or reliability. Item 45 in the religion test which refers to "non-Catholic worship" seemed unduly ambiguous in the light of current developments and practices of prominent Catholic hierarchy.

Means and standard deviations are reported in addition to statistics which give odd-even and Kuder-Richardson formula 20 reliability coefficients. In spite of the fact that in Table 3 in the 1962 Technical Report three coefficients are in the low 80's, in the 1963 Technical Report seven coefficients are now in the low 80's and, with the exception of four subscores, all are lower than the earlier version. The fact that *n* equalled 3,670 in 1962 and but 1,433 in 1963 could well be a partial explanation. However, very definite directions are given in both manuals as to just how these subscores should be weighted when placing the student in English, mathematics, or social science sections. The only cautions are given when the use of scores in "guidance" is discussed. The reviewer contends these cautions are valid whenever using the subscores and that placement is a valid and definite part of guidance. Table 6 in the 1963 version indicates speededness is more of a factor than before. This is admitted and plans are made to correct same in the 1964 version. This candor is refreshing and commendable.

The manual has a good format for the ease of a person administering the test, in fact much better than the supplementary directions for the religion or mechanical tests. Included in the manual are valuable and clearly explained uses of IQ scores. A commendable feature is the use of the deviation IQ score. Grade equivalents are also well explained with special references as to their shortcomings. In fact, if the user will read this section carefully, he may well decide not to use them at all.

In summary, this is a specific attempt to meet a specific need, probably most suited to private schools. Evidence is presented to show that research is continuing to improve the product each year. While the authors admit the composite score is most useful for selection purposes, greater caution should be given concerning the interpretation of the profile of subscores. It is hoped that future technical reports will omit the obvious sales type of talk, e.g., "considerable consultation with top authorities" and "an extensive survey of the most frequently used textbooks." Let's tell who and what in a technical report or omit it entirely. It is further hoped that when the user is told that a stratified sample is used the sample could be described in some detail so that comparisons with the using group could be made. When offering proof of concurrent validity, seven small groups are described quite well in contrast to the stratified sample. The authors say, "The importance of checking national norms cannot be overestimated." But, how can the user check the publisher's norms if the samples are not adequately described in the first place?

For reviews by William C. Cottle and Robert A. Jones of the 1955 "open" test, see 5:15.

[7]

Cooperative General Achievement Tests. Grades 9–12 and college entrants; 1937–56; 3 tests; IBM; Forms XX ('53, revision of Form X), YZ ('55, c1948–51, revision of Forms Y and Z, identical with test copyrighted in 1951); manual ('56, 16 pages); high school norms same as those published in 1938; separate answer sheets must be used; $4 per 25 tests; $1 per 25 IBM answer sheets; 25¢ per scoring stencil; $1 per specimen set; postage extra; 40(50) minutes for any one test; Cooperative Test Division. *

a) TEST 1, SOCIAL STUDIES. Manual uses the subtitle *A Test of General Proficiency in the Field of Social Studies;* Forms XX, YZ, (8 pages); Jeanne M. Bradford (XX).

b) TEST 2, NATURAL SCIENCE. Manual uses the subtitle *A Test of General Proficiency in the Field of Natural Science;* Forms XX, YZ, (7 pages); Paul J. Burke (XX).

c) TEST 3, MATHEMATICS. Manual uses the subtitle *A Test of General Proficiency in the Field of Mathematics;* Form XX (8 pages), YZ (10 pages); Paul J. Burke (XX).

REFERENCES

1–9. See 4:5.
10–21. See 5:6.
22. JEX, FRANK B. *University of Utah Studies in the Prediction of Academic Success.* University of Utah Research Monographs in Education, Vol. 1, No. 1. Salt Lake City, Utah: the University, July 1957. Pp. ix, 51. *
23. BERRY, CHARLES A., AND JONES, ARLYNNE L. "A Further Note on the Predictive Value of the National Freshman Testing Program." *Negro Ed R* 11:120–5 Jl '60. *
24. THOMSEN, STEPHEN J. "Academic Achievement and Institutional Testing Program Scores: A Longitudinal Study of One Class at a Liberal Arts College." *Proc W Va Acad Sci* 33:120–3 N '61. * (*PA* 36:5KL20T)
25. WILLIAMS, JOHN E., AND JOHNSTON, ROBERT A. "The Area Tests of the Graduate Record Examination as a Partial Criterion of Academic Success." *J Exp Ed* 32:95–100 f '63. *

WILLARD G. WARRINGTON, *Director, Office of Evaluation Services, Michigan State University, East Lansing, Michigan.*

Since the introduction of the *Cooperative General Achievement Tests* in 1937, several new forms have been developed. This review is concerned with Form XX, dated 1953, Form YZ, dated 1955, and the Examiner's Manual, dated 1956. These specific dates are mentioned for two purposes.

First, since the tests are designed "to measure proficiency in three major fields of study: social studies, natural sciences, and mathematics" and "to cover the portion of each area which is commonly included in the high school curriculum," surely they should be revised fairly frequently to be functional. The usefulness of 8- to 10-year old tests of this type is suspect. This point seems to be particularly relevant for the past 8- or 10-year period during which so much has happened in the educational domain. The financial problems involved in recommending more frequent test revisions are recognized. However, test publishers must assume some obligation for keeping their tests current or they should withdraw from the testing arena. It should be said that this reviewer does not feel that the *Cooperative General Achievement Tests* are drastically or uniquely antiquated. But on the other hand they certainly do not sparkle with new and imaginative materials. More frequent revisions would allow for a gradual introduction of the newer developments in the areas being tested.

Secondly, since Forms XX and YZ have been in existence for several years, it is not surprising that *The Fifth Mental Measurements Yearbook* contains a very thorough review by Max D. Engelhart of these same forms. The present reviewer, finding practically nothing in Engelhart's review with which to disagree, sees little point in duplicating that report here. Consequently, this review will only briefly describe the tests; the reader who wishes a more detailed review is advised to read the one prepared by Engelhart.

These tests are designed for use "at the end of the twelfth grade level or at the beginning of the college freshman level." Each of the tests requires 40 minutes working time and each is divided into two parts. Part 1 is concerned with definitions of terms and concepts; Part 2 involves comprehension and interpretation. Part 1 items are discrete and self contained; Part 2 items generally refer to reading passages, charts, diagrams, or maps. While Part 2 items involve critical thinking skills they also draw on background knowledge not presented in the test.

The item format is good, directions are specific, item coverage is adequate, and the material seems to have been well edited. There are a few items with ambiguities or weak or duplicating alternatives but, in general, the results of the development of these forms by selecting the better items from earlier forms are evident.

While the two parts of each test are timed separately only total scores for each area are used. Time limits are 15 minutes for Part 1 and 25 minutes for Part 2. Data reported in the manual indicate that these time limits are adequate for Social Science and Natural Science but insufficient for completion of the mathematics test. In this regard the manual reports a disturbing explanation: "there is reason to believe that much of the drop-out is due to the attitude of those who find mathematics difficult; they are quite willing to leave the later, more difficult items unanswered. To the extent that this argument is correct, the provision of more time would not result in higher scores, nor is the test accurately described as speeded." Now the reviewer does not necessarily agree or disagree with this argument as stated. Rather, his objections pertain to the fact that this is a testable argument and surely before eight years have elapsed some data could have been collected to support or reject the argument, data which then should have resulted in a revision or addition to the manual. Here again some responsibility on the part of the publisher seems lacking.

In general, however, the manual is well done. Instructions for administration and scoring of the tests are brief but adequate. Specific and relevant information concerning possible uses and limitations of the tests are presented. The section on interpretation of scores is a little sketchy. The reviewer would have liked more information as to the nature of the scaled scores and the comparability of such scores for different tests and different forms of the same test. Also, under the discussion on reliability some mention should have been made of the problems of interpreting differences among the scores for a given student on the three tests. Granted no manual can give a complete course in tests and measurements, but an effort should be made to minimize errors in those areas most susceptible to overinterpretation.

The statistical characteristics of the tests are generally discussed in a straightforward but rather sketchy fashion. While the test publisher needs to be wary of over selling his product, he can also err by too limited a discussion of the implication of his data.

The manual is probably strongest with respect to the information on validity. Here the prospective test user is given specific information as to the content of the various parts of the tests as well as correlations and predictive validity data. One validity table may be criticized, however, for citing data obtained in 1947–48; this table obviously refers to an earlier form.

Undoubtedly the tables of normative data represent the weakest aspect of the manual. For example, college freshman norms are based on Form YZ only, no breakdown by sex is shown, and the time of testing is unspecified. From a positive standpoint, the descriptions of the normative sample and the actual listing of the colleges involved are very commendable. The percentile norms for high school students are even more inadequate. These norms are based on data collected "in the late 1930's" with later form norms being equated to previous norms. In the opinion of this reviewer these norms are highly suspect and probably virtually useless. In view of the limited and questionable normative material, much more emphasis should have been placed upon the value of local norms.

To maintain proper perspective, the reader must remember that this review has deliberately focused on extending and elaborating upon criticisms not covered extensively in the previously mentioned review. As an overall evaluation of the tests, this reviewer feels that these tests, while somewhat pedestrian in nature, are good solid instruments with positive features that considerably outweigh the weaknesses and limitations discussed above. This battery should be particularly useful in situations where it is possible to develop and utilize local normative data since most of the criticisms mentioned in this review refer less to the tests themselves than to the supporting data provided by the publisher.

This reviewer is of the opinion that test publishers have a responsibility to demonstrate careful and thorough development of their tests and, in addition, a responsibility to provide sufficient supporting data so that the reasonably competent user can adequately interpret the test results. Since many achievement test publishers fail miserably with respect to this second responsibility, the criticisms and opinions offered here are directed as much toward achievement test publishers in general as toward the publishers of the *Cooperative General Achievement Tests.*

For a review by Max D. Engelhart, see 5:6; for a review by Paul L. Dressel of earlier forms, see 4:5; for a review by John V. McQuitty, see 3:3. For reviews of individual tests, see 3:316, 3:548, and 3:596.

[8]

***Eighth Grade Test.** Grade 8; 1934–63; 5 scores: English, arithmetic, science, history, total; new form (8 pages) usually issued annually; forms from previous testing programs also available for review purposes; no manual; mimeographed directions for administration (1 page); no data on reliability; Ohio norms for new forms available following testing program; 25¢ per test for new form; 10¢ per test for old forms; postpaid; 120(135) minutes; Ohio Scholarship Tests. *

REFERENCES

1. WRIGHT, HAROLD THEODORE, JR. *A Study of the Achievement Status of the Ohio Eighth Year Tests.* Doctor's thesis, Indiana University (Bloomington, Ind.), 1957. (*DA* 18:934)

[8a]

***General Scholarship Test for High School Seniors.** Grade 12; 1930–63; test administered each November in Ohio at centers established by publisher; new form issued each year; 6 scores: English, history, mathematics, science, reading-vocabulary, total; MRC; 1 form ('63, 15 pages); form issued in January 1961 available for review purposes; directions for administering ['63, 4 pages]; no data on reliability and validity; examination fee: $1; fee includes reporting of scores to 3 schools or scholarship agencies; 15¢ per copy of January 1961 form; cash orders postpaid; 150(155) minutes; Ohio Scholarship Tests. *

REFERENCES

1. WOOD, RAY GEORGE. *The Ohio General Scholarship Test for High School Seniors, 1930–33, Inclusive: Its Diagnostic, Motivating, and Predictive Functions.* Doctor's thesis, Ohio State University (Columbus, Ohio), 1935.
2. ULLMAN, ROBERT WARREN. *A Comparison of the Predictive Abilities of the ACT and GST With Respect to the Five State Universities of Ohio.* Doctor's thesis, Western Reserve University (Cleveland, Ohio), 1962.

For a review by C. C. Ross of the 1947 form, see 3:14.

[9]

***The Graduate Record Examinations: The Area Tests.** Grades 14–17; 1954–61; available only in the Institutional Testing Program; for more complete information, see 762; 3 scores: social science, humanities, natural science; 210(240) minutes; Educational Testing Service. *

REFERENCES

1. LANNHOLM, GERALD V. "Development of a College-Level General Achievement Battery." *Yearb Nat Council Meas Used Ed* 12:44–9 pt 1 '55. *
2. WRIGHT, JOHN C., AND SCARBOROUGH, BARRON B. "The Interrelationship of Area Test Scores and Cooperative General Culture Test Scores." *J Ed Psychol* 48:460–3 N '57. * (*PA* 33:2203)
3. MICHAEL, WILLIAM B.; JONES, ROBERT A.; AND GIBBONS, BILLIE D. "The Prediction of Success in Graduate Work in Chemistry From Scores on the Graduate Record Examination." *Ed & Psychol Meas* 20:859–61 w '60. * (*PA* 35:3957)
4. THOMSEN, STEPHEN J. "Academic Achievement and Institutional Testing Program Scores: A Longitudinal Study of One Class at a Liberal Arts College." *Proc W Va Acad Sci* 33:120–3 N '61. * (*PA* 36:5KL20T)
5. JOHNSON, JANET WILDMAN. *An Investigation of Relationships Between College and Senior Student Characteristics and Performance on the Aptitude and Area Tests of the Graduate Record Examination at the George Washington University.* Doctor's thesis, George Washington University (Washington, D.C.), 1962.
6. MABERLY, NORMAN CHARLES. *The Validity of the Graduate Record Examinations as Used With English-Speaking Foreign Students.* Doctor's thesis, University of Southern California (Los Angeles, Calif.), 1962. (*DA* 23:2424)
7. TULLY, G. EMERSON. "Screening Applicants for Graduate Study With the Aptitude Test of the Graduate Record Examinations." *Col & Univ* 38:51–60 f '62. *
8. MABERLY, NORMAN C. "The Validity of the Graduate Record Examinations as Used With English-Speaking Foreign Students." *Ed & Psychol Meas* 23:785–8 w '63. *
8a. PEMBERTON, W. A. *Ability, Values, and College Achievement.* University of Delaware Studies in Higher Education, No. 1. Newark, Del.: the University, 1963. Pp. xii, 77. * (*PA* 38:6573)
9. WILLIAMS, JOHN E., AND JOHNSTON, ROBERT A. "The Area Tests of the Graduate Record Examination as a Partial Criterion of Academic Success." *J Exp Ed* 32:95–100 f '63. *

PAUL L. DRESSEL, *Director of Institutional Research, Michigan State University, East Lansing, Michigan.* [Review of Forms JGR1, JGR2, and JGR3.]

The Area Tests of the *Graduate Record Examinations* are designed "to assess the broad outcomes of education in the liberal arts." These tests, as is true of the Aptitude Test and the Advanced Tests which form the other two components of the series, are secure examinations.

The Area Tests cover three broad fields: social science (100 items), humanities (75 items), and science (75 items). Every student participating in the program takes all three tests, which have a time limit of 70 minutes each and which are all included in the same booklet. Separate answer sheets are used. The questions are all multiple choice, although many variants are used.

The tests are described as emphasizing "the abilities and understandings which are important to the individual's effectiveness as a member of society." Basic concepts and the ability to interpret and apply them rather than recall of specific facts are required. The questions have been chosen to represent goals of liberal or general education shared by most colleges offering a liberal education. Constructing a test to these specifications is a difficult task and the appraisal of the extent of success with the task is equally difficult.

The reviewer has worked with general education programs in many colleges and has assisted in the development of examinations in many courses in which the emphasis has been placed on an examination meeting these specifications. Associated with him in these efforts were many of the persons who served on the examination committees responsible for developing these tests. This alone would lead the reviewer to expect good tests. As a second approach, the reviewer undertook to read and attempt to answer a large proportion of the items in each of the three fields of each form of the tests. This venture leads to the conclusion that the test items definitely do emphasize application, thought, and judgment. A basic knowledge of essential facts and principles is necessarily required but seldom is rote recall of even this basic knowledge the focal point of an item. Many of the items can readily be answered by an individual who has read widely and can apply his knowledge.

Reference has been made to variety in the test items. Paragraph material, graphs, tables of data, pictures, maps, and a music score have been introduced as the basis for significant and realistic questioning. One surmises that even low performing students may find the taking of the test an interesting and stimulating task. No attempt was made to classify the questions according to the Bloom taxonomy as was done by Bloom himself in a previous review of these same tests (see 5:10). His analysis, however, bears out the present reviewer's judgment that much more than factual recall is involved in the majority of the items in these tests. The reviewer concludes that the tests are appropriate measures of broad liberal or general education outcomes.

A second problem in developing such tests is to decide at which class level they should be used or to so develop them that they are useful at all levels. It is claimed by the Educational Testing Service that the Area Tests are suitable in difficulty for a wide range of student abilities and that they may be administered at any college level from beginning freshmen to graduating seniors. Such a characteristic is highly desirable in tests of this type, for educational experiences in all of the four years of college should contribute to a broad liberal education. Accordingly, a test usable at all levels can be invaluable in assessing starting points of students and their progress at each of several stages. Statistical reports prepared by the ETS provide norms which make possible some examination of this feature of the Area Tests even though these data are based on earlier forms of the tests. The means exhibited in the following table, although based upon several different groups of institutions, show that progressively higher scaled scores are made by students at advancing class levels.

Table 1

Mean Scaled Scores on the GRE Area Tests at Various College Levels

Level	Social Science	Humanities	Science
Freshman	342	393	409
Sophomore	392	437	444
Junior	426	457	453
Senior	440	463	455
First Year Graduate	464	471	468

Source: The means for seniors are weighted means of the 1955 and 1959 means presented in *The Performance of Senior Classes in Seventy-Nine Colleges on the Graduate Record Examinations Area Tests in 1955 and 1959* (September 1961). All other means are from *The Graduate Record Examinations Scores for Supplementary Reference Groups* (February 1959).

Scaled scores of this type have been so adjusted that the mean for the basic reference group is about 500 and the standard deviation about 100. To secure maximal score range, the items selected are so gauged in difficulty that the mean corresponds to successful performance by seniors on approximately one half of the items. Since there are 100 items in the social science test (75 in each of the two others) this means that some classes of entering freshmen taking the tests might average little more than 10 to 15 items right out of the 100 on the social science test, a performance very close to a chance level. This may be a discouraging experience for new students unless the situation is explained to them. One may also question whether these freshmen thereby reveal what they know or what they do not know.

Other available evidence demonstrates that, in repeated testings of the same students, significant gains are made from one year to another. The greatest gains appear between the initial freshman testing and repetition at the close of the sophomore year. This is consistent with the common pattern in higher education which devotes much of the first two years to acquiring a broad general education. The data also demonstrate that majors in disciplines falling in any one of the broad areas tend to record the larger gains. Both characteristics give additional confidence in the worth of the tests.

Analytical data on the current forms of the tests, although not yet published, were made available to the reviewer. Form JGR1 reliabilities of .88 for Social Science, .84 for Humanities, and .89 for Natural Science based on 370 seniors correspond closely to those reported for earlier forms. At least 97 per cent of the students finished three quarters of each test. Intercorrelations of Social Science and Humanities approximate .38 to .52; those for Social Science and Natural Science, .44 to .57; and those for Humanities and Natural Science, .37 to .49. Thus the statistical characteristics appear adequate.

The Area Tests must be regarded as the best available instruments for measuring broad liberal-general education outcomes.

Everett B. Sackett, *Dean, College of Liberal Arts, University of New Hampshire, Durham, New Hampshire.* [Review of Forms JGR1, JGR2, and JGR3.]

"These tests," in the words of the Handbook for Deans and Examiners, "provide for a comprehensive appraisal of the college student's orientation in three principal areas of human culture: social science, humanities, and natural science * The Area Tests emphasize the abilities and understandings which are important to the individual's effectiveness as a member of society; thus, the questions are intended to test the student's grasp of basic concepts and his ability to apply them * the tests have been aimed beyond the details of specific courses in an attempt to reach toward those goals of education which are shared generally by the college offering instruction in the liberal arts."

To accomplish this goal in half a day of paper and pencil testing is an ambitious undertaking. The test items are multiple choice with five alternatives, except for less than half a dozen with fewer alternatives. Compared with the typical test, these are expansive in the statement of each item. The social science and natural science tests average fewer than nine items per 8½ by 11 inch page. The humanities test averages fewer than five items per page. Included in Forms JGR1 and JGR2 is an excellent color reproduction of a masterpiece of a painting from the collection of the Metropolitan Museum of Art. Form JGR3 has two such reproductions. The item writers have done well in making each alternative answer seem reasonable while providing one on which experts would usually agree as being best.

Just what emphasis should be given the various disciplines in order to achieve a balanced measure of each of the three areas covered in these tests is open to debate. Certainly no faculty committee would agree unanimously. Rather than to say that the balance is good or bad, the reviewer classified the test items by discipline to enable the reader to form his own judgment. The distribution is nearly uniform from form to form. Some of the items were themselves somewhat interdisciplinary, and some were classified as "miscellaneous."

The percentage distribution of items in social science approximates: economics, 28; government, 26; history, 19; sociology, 15; geography, 6; psychology, 1; and miscellaneous, 5. In humanities it is: literature, 26; art, 24; music, 20; philosophy, 18; architecture, 9; and miscellaneous, 3. In science it is: biology, 38; physics, 16; chemistry, 15; geology, 15; astronomy, 10; and miscellaneous, 6.

It will be noted that mathematics is omitted,

something of a disadvantage in this day of increasing emphasis on this discipline in liberal education. Also missing, as would be expected in an objective test, is measurement of that basic aim of liberal education, ability to organize and express one's thoughts.

How successful is the endeavor "to test the student's grasp of basic concepts and his ability to apply them"? Using Form JGR2 as a sample, the reviewer attempted to classify the items by what may be loosely termed the mental processes involved. The Prospectus for Students lists as objectives 8 such processes for the social science test, 8 for the humanities, and 10 for the natural sciences. (These were listed in *The Fifth Mental Measurements Yearbook* in the review by Benjamin S. Bloom; see 5:10.) The present reviewer's classifying was obviously subjective. Many items did not fall neatly into a single category, which is commendable for a test of this nature. Repeating the classifying after a lapse of several days, a substantial number of items were placed in a category different from that to which they had first been assigned.

Because of the approximate nature of this classifying, it would be misleading to report it numerically. In the social science test, "acquaintance with basic facts and trends" receives most emphasis. About equally treated are "understanding of fundamental terms and concepts" and "ability to draw warranted conclusions." "Understanding of cause-and-effect relationships" and "ability to recognize the adequacy of data" receive some attention. The items which appear to have been intended to test "ability to compare and contrast points of view" really require, rather, acquaintance with the beliefs of certain notable men.

For the humanities test, recall of facts is not listed in the Prospectus as an objective, but the reviewer does not see how else ability to match the name of an author with the title of one of his works, for example, can be classified. This ranked with ability "to recognize the nature, use, and importance of medium and technique" in receiving most attention in this test. Ability "to interpret verbal and other modes of expression and to compare texts" ranks nearly as high as these two. In the reviewer's judgment, the other mental processes listed as objectives for the humanities test would be of only incidental help in selecting answers.

Of the 10 objectives listed for the natural science test, the reviewer classified well over two thirds of the items as measuring ability "to understand and interpret basic principles and concepts" and "to be able to recall, use, and interpret common symbols and terms." A few items bear on the abilities "to understand symbolic, graphic, and verbal presentations and to be able to translate from one to another," "to identify the implications of changed conditions in a situation," and "to recognize the limitations of scientific procedures." If the other abilities listed as objectives are tested, it is incidentally.

The student who has had thorough courses in the disciplines covered by the Area Tests should do well on them. The one who does not have broad knowledge of the vocabularies, the facts, and the methods of these disciplines could not do well no matter how great his skill in the various mental processes theoretically involved. Were it otherwise, the tests might be tests of intelligence or of reading ability, but hardly of a liberal education. Such being the case, these tests are useful in determining the breadth of the individual's "liberal education," whether obtained in the classroom or by his own efforts.

Being a relic of the pre-computer age of statistics, the reviewer approaches with caution comment on the extensive statistical analyses of the Area Tests supplied by ETS. Observations can be drawn from some of the less sophisticated statistics, however.

Eighty per cent of the students tested reached almost all of the items. From an examination of the tests, it is the reviewer's judgment that those failing to finish were the less well informed who, for this reason, would need to spend time puzzling out answers which would come quickly to a well-informed student.

Intercorrelations among the tests are commendably low, ranging from .37 to .57. Reliability coefficients, on the other hand, are much higher, ranging from .78 to .89.

Correlations of the verbal section of the GRE Aptitude Test with the social science and humanities tests are higher than of the Area Tests with each other, running for Forms JGR1 and JGR2 between .70 and .76. Natural Science correlates with the verbal score at only .50 and with the quantitative score at .61 to .64. Social Science correlates with the quantitative score at .49 and Humanities at only .36.

The table of norms furnished with the tests

is based on the scores of 3,035 seniors in 21 colleges of respectable reputation. Supplementary norms are also available for college freshmen, sophomores, juniors, and graduate students. A special service is available from ETS enabling an institution to get scores for comparative purposes from an individually selected group of other colleges which have given the tests. The norms for seniors indicate that the student's major field makes little difference in his showing on Social Science, whereas humanities majors do better than others on Humanities and science majors do better than others on Natural Science.

Allowing for what might be termed the "Madison Avenue effect" in the expansiveness of the claims made in the quotation at the beginning of this review, it is judged that these tests do come close, at least, to accomplishing their purpose. As suggested in the report of a recent study (*9*), these tests have some advantage over the grade-point average in evaluating a college graduate's general knowledge. They would be useful in comparing the breadth of information and comprehension of the students in one college with those in similar institutions or in comparing different groups of students within the same institution. Were they to be used regularly for such purposes, there would be the danger present in any widely used standardized achievement test that they would influence curricular emphasis in spite of the effort to avoid details and to reach toward goals shared generally.

For reviews by Benjamin S. Bloom and Frederick B. Davis of earlier forms, see 5:10. For a review of the testing program, see 5:601.

[10]

***The Gray-Votaw-Rogers General Achievement Tests.** Grades 1–3, 4–6, 7–9; 1934–63; IBM for grades 4–9; 4 forms; 3 levels; $3.75 per 25 tests for grades 1–3, 4–6; $4 per 25 tests for grades 7–9; separate answer sheets may be used in grades 4–9; 8¢ per IBM answer sheet; 60¢ per set of scoring stencils; $1.50 per 100 profiles for any one level; 25¢ per specimen set of any one level; cash orders postpaid; Hob Gray, David F. Votaw, Sr., and J. Lloyd Rogers; Steck Co. *

a) PRIMARY. Grades 1–3; 1934–63; 6 scores: reading comprehension, reading vocabulary, spelling, arithmetic reasoning, arithmetic computation, total; Forms A ('61), B ('61), C ('63), D ('63), (20 pages); manual ('63, 12 pages); profile ('61, 1 page); (70–80) minutes in 2 sessions.

b) INTERMEDIATE. Grades 4–6; 1934–62; 10–11 scores: same as for primary level plus elementary science, language, literature (optional), social studies, health and safety; IBM; Forms A ('60), B ('60), C ('62), D ('62), (32 pages); combined manual ('62, 29 pages) for this and advanced level; profile ('60, 1 page); 147–161(170) minutes in 2–4 sessions.

c) ADVANCED. Grades 7–9; 1934–62; 10–11 scores: same as for intermediate level; IBM; Forms A ('60), B ('60), C ('62), D ('62), (40 pages); combined manual ('62, 29 pages) for this and intermediate level; profile ('60, 1 page); 147–161(170) minutes in 2–4 sessions.

REFERENCES

1. See 40:1187.
2–4. See 3:9.
5. See 5:11.

KENNETH D. HOPKINS, *Associate Professor of Educational Psychology, University of Southern California, Los Angeles, California.*

PRACTICAL FEATURES. The GVR achievement series has several important practical features, especially testing time and cost. In these respects, it is superior to its competitors. The sacrifices necessitated by these practical characteristics are, however, reflected in other respects as will be seen in later discussions.

Although separate answer sheets are available for the intermediate and advanced batteries, the tests are definitely oriented toward booklet marking; e.g., only directions for booklet administration are given in the manual.

The manuals for the advanced and intermediate batteries are combined; separate manuals would minimize confusion and error and would simplify the user's task of locating desired information.

The quality of printing, paper, and other physical characteristics of the tests are excellent.

ADMINISTRATION AND SCORING. The general suggestions for administering the tests are helpful and well founded. There are several unanswered questions, however, regarding certain of the specific directions. Although two to four sittings are recommended, no data are given to insure the equivalence of scores obtained under different arrangements. No mention is made as to which method was used in the standardization procedures.

Except for the primary battery, in which only booklet marking is used, a separate IBM answer sheet is available. No empirical findings are presented, however, to support the assumption that such a variation does not provide significantly different results. Also lacking is a description of which method was used in the standardization procedures.

The manual for the intermediate and advanced levels may allow too much freedom to the test administrator regarding instructions to examinees. This possibility is especially evident if separate answer sheets are used, in which case the administrator must improvise from the booklet-marking instructions. Such lack of structure causes the tests to deviate, to some extent, from the true meaning of "standardized," and makes the accruing results more difficult to interpret.

The examinees are instructed not to skip items; this attempt to minimize the gambling response style is commendable, but the assumption that the minimized response set variance is greater than the concomitant increased chance variance should be buttressed by empirical findings.

It is appropriately recommended that high achieving sixth grade classes be given the advanced battery and, conversely, that low achieving seventh grade classes be given the intermediate tests.

STANDARDIZATION. The sample on which the norms were derived is, unfortunately, not carefully described. It was composed of 21,202, 23,082, and 19,822 pupils for the primary (1–3), intermediate (4–6), and advanced (7–9) batteries, respectively. There is no discussion of the number, size, and socio-economic characteristics of the participating school districts. The sampling procedures (except for per cent by broad geographical regions) are also omitted. In addition, no mention is made of the degree of selectivity introduced by noncooperating schools.

NORMS. Scaled scores, educational grade scores (grade equivalents), and end-of-year percentile ranks are provided. Suggestions are also given if national stanines are desired. These are inadequate since, for some unidentified reason, the percentages of scores within the stanine ranges do not correspond with normal values, e.g., instead of the expected 11 per cent in stanines 1 and 2 or 8 and 9, only 5.3 per cent is found.

Following each test a conversion table is provided in which raw scores are converted to "scaled scores." The exact nature of the scaled scores and the basis on which they were derived are not explained. The manual states that these scores "conform to the natural educational growth curve; that is, two consecutive grades at the higher levels show less difference in achievement than two consecutive grades at lower levels due to the leveling of the rate of educational growth curve in higher grades." Such a general, conclusive statement regarding the nature of educational growth is not documented and certainly not widely accepted for all achievement areas. The manual also contains an exaggerated claim that a student with a given scaled score for each of the tests "has uniform achievement in all the divisions." From the normative data, however, for illustrative purposes it was determined that if a fourth grade child was one standard deviation above the mean, he would receive a scaled score of 56 in arithmetic computation but a score of 62 in literature.

In addition to the results from each subtest appearing on the individual profile chart, a pupil's total average achievement, chronological age, educational age, and school grade are plotted. The inclusion of CA in the profile is a commendable feature which facilitates the identification of over-aged and under-aged pupils who may be deserving of special attention. The usefulness of the "educational age" is, on the other hand, questionable, since there seems to be an implication of a direct correlation between age and achievement within grades which, in practice, has been found to be negligible after the primary grades.

RELIABILITY. Reliability coefficients were determined by the split-half method corrected by the Spearman-Brown formula on the data from "three typical school systems." There is no further description of the "typical" districts except for a comment that the variability in them was less than that of the national sample, from which the manual concludes that the reliability coefficients are conservative. When the SD values for the national sample were used in conjunction with these reliability coefficients, however, the values for the standard errors of measurement were virtually identical with those from the three "typical" districts, thus showing that the reliability estimates are not conservative as claimed.

The authors have continued to use the split-half method of reliability assessment, even though they have been repeatedly criticized by MMY reviewers for not providing evidence confirming the assumed lack of speed variance.

Reliability estimates were not determined by grade, as would be appropriate, but by battery. Students in grades 1–3, 4–6, and 7–9 were pooled, a practice which tends to exaggerate the meaningful reliability of the tests since the variance is expanded. For the intermediate and advanced levels, reliability by grade was subsequently estimated from a formula. No data, however, are given to confirm the formula's assumption of constant standard errors of measurement for each grade level within a battery. The formula used is in error; the reliability coefficients should not be squared. It is regrettable that where individual grade reliabilities are needed most they are missing, i.e., in the primary grades the combined variabilities are considerably greater than individual grade variability. Applying the same approximation approach used for the other batteries to estimate reliability coefficients for the separate primary grades yielded reliability coefficients as low as .70 (in arithmetic computation) in grade 1, and .80 (in spelling) in grade 2—markedly different from the values of .95 to .98 given for the combined grades.

It is noteworthy that some data on practice effects are given, however, the units (raw score or grade equivalents) are not provided.

VALIDITY. The items of the tests were based upon "course content usually included in the various courses of study," materials from superior teachers, textbooks in current use, and curriculum bulletins from state departments. Much more careful and explicit elaboration of the above statements would have assisted in evaluating the content validity of the tests, especially from the local school district's point of view.

Items were tried out and discarded or retained on the basis of grade differentiation and item difficulty. It is unfortunate that data on item statistics are not given.

Evidence for concurrent validity is given by correlations between test scores of students in one school with a "composite measure of achievement based upon two school-wide objective measures, class marks, and teacher judgments." No discussion as to how the above were combined into a composite is offered. More seriously, the correlations are given for grades 4–6 and 7–9 pooled rather than by grades, thus causing the resulting values, although high, to be difficult to interpret.

Although the manual indicates that the tests may be given for individual diagnosis, such would not seem to be justified since the high correlations between subtests make the corresponding difference scores quite unreliable.

The vocabulary on some of the non-reading tests seems heavy at times for an independent assessment, especially for grades 1 and 4. The expected chance scores on most tests are high enough to suggest caution in individual use and interpretation, especially at grades 1 (reading), 4 (all tests), and 7 (arithmetic reasoning). Many of the tests seem unduly influenced by speed.

THE SUBTESTS. Each of the 10 subtests will be briefly described and discussed below and, in some cases, compared with its competitors.

The elementary science test is a 12-minute test composed of short, direct, and generally factual, three-choice items. The average number of words per item, including options, is about 16, very similar to the value for the science test of the *Stanford Achievement Test,* about one half the value for the science items on the *Metropolitan Achievement Tests,* and about one fourth the value for *Sequential Tests of Educational Progress: Science.*

The language test is a 14-minute test of basic grammatical usage composed of a series of very short, two-choice items in which the proper wording is selected.

The literature test is a 14-minute optional test composed of short, highly factual, four-choice items that average about 16 words in length. The test should be studied carefully for curricular validity before local adoption.

The spelling test is a 15-minute test in which the examinee selects which (if any) of the four words per item is misspelled, except for the primary battery, which very appropriately uses the dictation method.

The reading vocabulary test is a 10-minute test in which one of four words (usually a synonym) is selected to complete the given sentence. Items appear to be well constructed and to have high examinee appeal.

The reading comprehension test is a 14-minute test composed of short stories followed by three to six questions each. To complete the test, an examinee must complete two to three items per minute, which is more than in the reading subtest of any major competing battery. (The advanced test requires an average reading rate of 122 words per minute, even without considering needed time for deliberating and responding.)

The social studies test is a 15-minute test composed principally of short, factual items pertaining to American history, geography, and map and graph reading.

The health and safety test is a 12-minute test composed of short, direct questions relating primarily to elementary physiology. This test would have little curricular relevance in many districts. Many items could appropriately appear on a science test.

The arithmetic reasoning test is a series of short and direct, yet thought provoking and interesting, problems cast into a lifelike situation. Frequent use of pictorial material enhances the appeal of the test. Unfortunately, examinees are required to read 25 per cent more words per minute at both the intermediate and advanced levels than on any major competing test. Although the primary test is attractively presented in recall format, the relatively heavy vocabulary load would seem to preclude its use at grade 1.

The arithmetic computation test is a 12–18 minute recall test for the primary level that samples processes ranging from simple addition and subtraction through simple multiplication and division. The intermediate test continues through fractions, the advanced through areas of circles, etc. Only a fast worker would probably complete the problems in the time allotted.

SUMMARY. The chief advantages of the GVR achievement tests are found in their low cost and minimal demand for testing time. Major problems and unanswered questions are encountered regarding standardized administration, sampling procedures for the norming group, the method of determining reliability, the lack of data on form equivalence, the emphasis on speed, and the uncritical and sometimes unwarranted favorable self-description found in the manuals.

Little is offered to the user to insure proper interpretation. The reviewer impressionistically feels that several of the tests have potential merit which would become evident if the emphasis moved away from the practical advantages, if more time were allowed, if better norming procedures were developed, and if the batteries did not attempt to span so many grades, especially at the primary level. It is unfortunate that many of the problems indicated by previous MMY reviews were not heeded. It is also unfortunate that no mention or attention seems to have been paid to the technical recommendations of the APA, the AERA, and the NCME.

VICTOR H. NOLL, *Professor of Education, Michigan State University, East Lansing, Michigan.*

The review of this battery referred to by previous reviewers (see 5:11) is that of Anderhalter in *The Fourth Mental Measurements Yearbook* (see 4:12). Checking this review against the latest edition leaves the present reviewer with the conviction that nearly all, if not all, that Anderhalter wrote at that time still applies. The organization and content remain essentially the same. The features he commended are still there and still commendable; some of the weaknesses he pointed out at that time have been corrected; most remain and they are still faults.

The format was good and has been made more attractive; directions for administering and scoring are quite satisfactory; the basis for norms has been improved in that the normative population has been greatly enlarged and presumably made much more representative. More information should be given on selection of the population with respect to such factors as type of community, socio-economic levels, racial origin, etc. Claims of validity rest primarily on a rather general statement to the effect that the tests are based upon course content usually included in the various courses of study. No information is given regarding the particular courses of study, textbooks, or other curriculum materials and guides consulted. Reference is made to item analysis but no statistics are supplied on either difficulty indexes or discriminating values of items. For the present edition, information given regarding what is referred to as "concurrent validity" seems of doubtful value, since it is too general to be clearly interpreted. The criticisms expressed in previous reviews regarding reliability have been partially met, though it probably would have been preferable to determine reliability coefficients for each grade separately rather than estimating them from reliability coefficients obtained for a three-grade range. The use of the split-halves technique for speeded tests, which many in the battery appear to be, has been continued. The claim that the tests may be used for diagnostic purposes is hardly justified in the generally accepted meaning of this term.

In this edition a type of score referred to as "scaled scores" has been introduced. This type of score is said to apply to all levels and forms, to have a range from 0 to 99, and to conform to the "natural educational growth curve." However, no information as to the nature of the units of these scaled scores nor how they or the "natural educational growth curve" were actually derived is given in the manuals. Correspondence with one of the authors on the matter did not result in clarification for this reviewer. Presumably scaled scores are some type of standard score. It would be very helpful to have more information about them.

The manuals for the new edition have been expanded to include tables of end-of-year percentile ranks for subtest scores for each grade; equivalence table of scores on this edition with scores on previous editions; and reference to the use of separate answer sheets with the intermediate and advanced batteries.

A rough check of content indicates that many of the items in the new edition are, in fact, new items; at least, they were not noted in the immediately preceding edition. The incorporation of new, up-to-date content is highly desirable and commendable. It suggests that the revision was, indeed, more than simply a renorming of an old test. The scoring of the spelling and arithmetic computation tests in the intermediate and advanced batteries has been made more objective, an improvement in convenience, at least.

It is probably inevitable in such an extensive series of tests that some questionable items will not be eliminated. For example, in Primary Form A this item appears: "In Roman numerals X = 10, V = 5 and I = 1. Write 24 in Roman numerals." If the object is to test knowledge of the Roman numeral system, the first part of the item should probably not be given. On the other hand, if the purpose is to test ability to use information given, how is the pupil to know that 4 is written IV (according to the key) and not IIII? In the same form, a matching item under reading comprehension has as one part "I am a bird—I can fly." Among the choices are pictures of a robin, a hen, and a duck; all three are birds and all three can fly. In Intermediate Form B appear such items as "The best way to keep from taking colds is to (1) take vitamin pills (2) take patent medicines (3) obey health rules every day (4) get vaccinated." The medical profession would like to know the answer to this one! Again, "You probably do not need to see an eye doctor if you read a book best at a distance of (1) 8 inches (2) 10 inches (3) 15 inches (4) 25 inches." Such items seem highly questionable on more than one count. In Advanced Form A we find under social studies, "Some sugar is made from (1) beans (2) beets (3) barley (4) bran." Aside from its ambiguity, one might wonder why this item appears under social studies.

It is not the reviewer's desire to be picayunish in criticizing items. However, these were found without making any particular effort to scan every item. They lead one to speculate as to how many such items might be found in the entire battery. The most serious aspect of this is, of course, the lowering of the quality of the instrument. There is, however, another consideration of perhaps equal concern. Pouncing upon items such as these is the delight of the Grosses and the Hoffmans. They seize upon them and, it must be admitted, they have some justification. More than a few such items in a comprehensive achievement battery are inexcusable. They lead one to the almost inescapable conclusion that proper care and attention to detail was lacking in constructing, editing, and trying out of items. To the extent that this is so, it constitutes grist for the mill of critics, friendly (which this reviewer is) or otherwise.

On the whole, while the battery shows certain improvements over previous editions, it leaves one with the definite impression of not meeting the highest standards of workmanship and of not being the equal of the best achievement batteries now available, such as the *Stanford Achievement Test* or the *Iowa Tests of Basic Skills*.

ELLIS BATTEN PAGE, *Professor of Education, and Director, Bureau of Educational Research and Service, University of Connecticut, Storrs, Connecticut.*

The Graw-Votaw-Rogers achievement tests were well and extensively reviewed by Anderhalter in *The Fourth Yearbook,* and by Findley in *The Fifth Yearbook.* For continuing characteristics of the battery, the present reviewer endorses observations already made, refers the reader to those reviews, and will here describe and comment upon the newest editions of the GVR.

This is a huge barrage of tests, from primary through junior high level. Each of the three levels, Primary (grades 1–3), Intermediate (4–6), and Advanced (7–9), has its own four separate forms, with numerous subtests as noted above. Testing at the primary level will take less than two class periods and at the upper levels about four class periods. For shorter testing at the upper levels, a shorter selection is recommended from among the full battery, and the manual reports an extremely high correlation of the overall scores from short-term testing with the overall scores of the complete batteries. In this reporting, however, as elsewhere in the manual, the statistical discussion is questionable.

TEST CONTENT. The primary battery contains the following tests: Reading Vocabulary, Reading Comprehension, Spelling, Arithmetic Reasoning, and Arithmetic Computation. These tests employ large print suitable for beginning readers and, where appropriate, attractive black and white pictures. Answers are marked directly in the primary booklets, which are then scored by hand. Answers are objective and easy to grade. In general, material appears interesting and grade appropriate, but a personal inspection of the primary content is not altogether satisfying. The last portion of the Form C Reading Comprehension, for example, contains items which seem to measure arithmetic reasoning about as much as reading skill. Some of the answer choices offered, too, might be rather equivocal to the primary child (since they were highly debatable to the reviewer!). Similarly, items in the arithmetic reasoning section appear generally quite dependent on reading skills and, if a first grader had poor reading ability, his "arithmetic reasoning" would surely not be fairly assessed. For these two tests, then, the scores do not seem very pure. This impression is reinforced by finding that tables show arithmetic reasoning to be more highly correlated with the reading tests than with arithmetic computation. It is difficult to compare such intercorrelations with the reliability coefficients of the tests, however, because of regrettably different procedures employed in their computation.

At the intermediate and advanced levels, the elementary science portion is reported by the publisher to test scientific vocabulary, and also "a higher level of understanding," such as "understanding of cause-and-effect and application of principles." Inspection reveals that most items are of the common knowledge sort, representing a variety of subjects often studied in general science courses. For each question, there are three possible choices.

The language portion at these levels is a test of correct English usage in which the student is offered a choice of only two single words or two two-word alternatives with which to complete each sentence. Which option the student selects will depend partly upon underlying grammatical rules, but more upon the usage he hears about him among his family and peers.

The literature test represents the publisher's "sampling from standard sources," such as "anthologies of children's literature," and is aimed at assessing students' "proper familiarity with children's classics and with recognized modern books, stories, and poems." Low scores, in the view of the publisher, could reflect that "appropriate books" are unavailable or unread, or that students have failed to understand their reading. The test is not itself a test of reading ability, but of familiarization with literature. The present reviewer does not know how to judge the content of this test. On Intermediate Form C, he would have known for certain about 14 answers out of 44 asked in the literature section, and this performance would have earned a percentile rank of around 10 at the fourth grade (chance choices and guided guessing would of course have raised the score). The more classic works for young people, and those holding a high reputation with sophisticated adults and parents of the general public, are relatively poorly represented compared with more minor and transitory works. This emphasis is in opposition to the publisher's policy, as stated in the intermediate-advanced manual, which is that "ephemeral forms of knowledge and information should be minimized in an achievement test." The intermediate literature test is, therefore, not to be taken too seriously as a measure of high cultural interest in the child, though presumably it does reflect some currently popular reading curricula in many schools.

For an intermediate and advanced measure of Spelling, the GVR has moved from a dictation organization to a recognition or proof reading test. The authors' research is said to have indicated that there is a high correlation between scores from recognition and dictation tests and that the recognition test provides more discrimination among superior spellers. This change from earlier editions also permits the entire battery (from fourth grade on) to be machine scored and analyzed.

Intermediate Reading Vocabulary consists of items in which synonyms of some stem word are selected from among four choices. Reading Comprehension consists of 34 questions on the substance of six original readings, using three-choice items. Intermediate Social Studies could be termed a general information test with a heavy emphasis on North American history, and this emphasis probably corresponds with curricular patterns in most schools of this country. The health and safety section evaluates general knowledge about the human body and about personal hygiene. Tests 9 and 10 are, respectively, measures of arithmetic reasoning and arithmetic computation. The reasoning test is aimed to include "fundamental concepts basic to recent developments and changes in the methods of teaching mathematical reasoning," and is constructed to be "of minimum computational difficulty after the student has thought through the relationships involved." Arithmetic Computation is aimed at testing such fundamental processes as placing decimal points, making estimates, and applying computation to symbols as well as to numbers.

The advanced level tests are about the same in design as the intermediate tests, except for more difficult content, and therefore they will not be separately described.

VALIDITY. The publishers state that the tests are based upon content "usually included in the various courses of study." Principals were asked to suggest "superior" teachers, and these teachers were then asked for course outlines. Textbooks in current use were studied, say the publishers, as were curriculum bulletins from state departments and reports of state committees on curriculum materials. In the preparation of preliminary test items consultants were brought in from among the ranks of "outstanding teachers and supervisors." All of this help is very anonymous, as it is in most publishers' descriptions of the construction of achievement items. The content of achievement tests has not yet been conceptualized clearly as a sampling problem by most publishers and there is seldom clear explanation of where the items originated. This characteristic remains a defect of this battery as well as of most other batteries available.

Selection from among the original store of items is more fully explained, at least for the intermediate and advanced items, but still not explained adequately for review purposes. All of the items for a given subtest were apparently administered to students in rather massive tests (apparently eight times the length of the published forms for these subtests), and the results were analyzed for growth in percentage of correct response from grade to grade. Items which failed to show such growth were eliminated. The purpose of such elimination, to exclude ephemeral material which is learned and forgotten, is admirable, but the procedure leaves unanswered questions. About three hundred students of each intermediate and advanced grade were apparently used, from "five school systems," but no details are given of sampling procedures used in selecting these systems. If they were systems conveniently close to the authors, and therefore homogeneous in certain curricular trends, the item discrimination indices so developed would not necessarily be repeated in the nation at large.

A sort of concurrent validity was measured at one school (586 students in grades 4–9) by comparing the "scores on this test" with "a composite measure of achievement based on two school-wide objective measures, class marks, and teacher judgments." For the intermediate level the correlation of the GVR with this composite measure is reported to be .95, and for the advanced level .91. Like other statistical data reported, however, the manner of combining scores and computing such figures is so undefined as to render meaningless any coefficient obtained. Correspondence with the publishers failed to obtain much more complete information than that contained in the Manual of Directions and Interpretations.

RELIABILITY. Reliability coefficients are reported, as are inter-test correlations. Reliabilities, which are of course desired to be high, were computed by split-half techniques for three grades at a time, and then apparently scaled to more modest coefficients by correcting for size of standard deviation. On the other hand, subtest intercorrelations, which are of course desired to be small, were computed grade by grade. What effects these different procedures have on the reported coefficients are again obscure. Also, to measure the inter-level "continuity of scale," correlation coefficients are given between the intermediate and advanced batteries administered to the same group of sixth and seventh graders. These are apparently uncorrected coefficients based upon the combined sixth and seventh grades and are, therefore, misleadingly high (about as high as the split-half reliabilities reported for those same tests). And in any case, such correlations do not themselves constitute exact evidence for the desired "continuity of scale." Such evidence would rather be found in the actual similarity of grade-equivalent results, and these are not reported.

NORMING. Percentile rank equivalents for the intermediate and advanced tests are given for each grade and for each subtest. These "national" norms are based upon 23,082 students at the intermediate level and 19,822 at the advanced level. Since there are 6 grades and 4 forms for each, the norm groups consist of perhaps about 1,750–2,000 per form per grade. The percentage distribution of the sample "among six regions into which the nation was divided" was: North (including Alaska) (17.6), East (9.7), Central (19.6), South (20.6), Southwest (16.2), and West (including Hawaii) (16.3). No account is given of the sampling procedure used to obtain representativeness in this norm population or of any statistical weighting to compensate for apparent gross biasing in the norms, nor are these regions better defined elsewhere in the manual. It is fairly well known that the East, as usually defined, is both populous and high in educational achievement. On the other hand, the South and Southwest, as usually defined, are rather sparsely settled and somewhat lower in cognitive test scores. In absence of more information it must be assumed that statistical compensations were not appropriately made for these contributions and that the "national" norms are biased in a low direction. Therefore, the net effect of using such norms in the usual district is probably to show an artificially high national "achievement" of the students tested, and this effect is perhaps not unpopular with some school administrators. But without more sampling information, even the extent of any such bias is not assessable. This seems a serious shortcoming, but the GVR tests, it should be noted, are not the only ones on the market today which perhaps carry such distorted norms.

The matching of the various forms at the intermediate and advanced levels was done as follows. After items were selected (about twice as many as were eventually to be used), they were administered to about 300 students at each grade level. On the basis of such preliminary administration, items were arranged according to discovered difficulty and "broken into" four forms "of equal mean difficulty and equal variability of difficulty." Even so, this matching of parallel forms for difficulty was not perfect, judged by the scaled score equivalents provided by the publisher and the empirical distributions from their norming population. The reviewer happened to notice one subtest in which a certain raw score would earn a percentile rank 37 points higher than would the same raw score on a different (presumably matched) form (Advanced Elementary Science, Forms A and D, 30 right) though such disparity is surely uncommon.

In general, the publisher's handling of statistical information has improved since Findley's review was published in *The Fifth Yearbook,* but it has not yet caught up with the expectations of today's professional workers.

TESTING MATERIALS. Materials provided seem attractive and clear, printed on good paper. The tests are all designed for direct marking of the booklets, but this characteristic probably does not lead to much difficulty when separate answer sheets are employed at the upper two levels. The instructions to the proctors seem clear and easy to follow, and administration is uncomplicated. A number of brief suggestions for use of test scores are given and these are generally sound, though so briefly explained as possibly not to help the workers who most need it.

SUMMARY. Notwithstanding the rather severe criticism above, the GVR batteries are clear and convenient in testing procedures and usually reasonable and rather interesting in test content. It is uncertain to what extent any profile from a battery is a meaningful description of a child's national position or an accurate prediction of his relative future strengths and weaknesses. Yet these ambiguities are shared by many other achievement test batteries currently available. The weaknesses of the GVR reflect the future needs of the commercial testing movement itself: to reanalyze the basis of achievement test content, to move norming out into the arena of public inspection, and to report statistical data in ways calculated better to illuminate true test characteristics.

For reviews by Warren G. Findley and Douglas E. Scates of an earlier edition, see 5:11; for a review by Oliver F. Anderhalter, see 4:12; for a review by Roland L. Beck, see 3:9; for reviews by Joseph E. Moore and C. C. Ross, see 40:1187.

[11]

★**High School Classification Examination.** Grades 8–9; 1957–63; test, under the title *High School Entrance Examination,* and all accessories of the 1963 program used first in the Cooperative Entrance Examination Program for High Schools conducted by three Catholic dioceses; 9 scores: verbal, numerical, reasoning, aptitude total, arithmetic, reading, English, achievement total, total; MRC; new form released each spring following use as a make-up examination in the diocesan program; Form 7B ('63, 14 pages) used in 1963 program; examiner's manual ('62, c1961–62, 8 pages); optional pupil preparation handbook ('62, c1961–62, 29 pages); reliability and validity data based upon earlier forms and upon Catholic school students only; norms (based upon the diocesan program) available upon request; separate answer sheets must be used; examination fee, $1 per student; fee includes scoring service; 40¢ per pupil preparation handbook; 60¢ per specimen set of previous year's examination; postage extra; 125(150) minutes in 2 sessions; Harcourt, Brace & World, Inc. *

REFERENCES

1. GRUBER, EDWARD C. *How to Score High on the Catholic High School Entrance Examination.* New York: Arco Publishing Co., Inc., 1962. Pp. 117, plus supplements. *

THOMAS W. MAHAN, JR., *Consultant in Guidance, Connecticut State Department of Education, Hartford, Connecticut.* [Review of Form 7B.]

This test battery represents another effort in the development of screening and placement devices for the selective secondary school and is roughly analogous to college entrance examinations. In this regard it has considerable to recommend it: it is a "secure" test with new forms developed each year; there are alternate forms available in a given year for make-up or retest purposes; the second form developed each year is made empirically equivalent to the earlier form and a conversion table provided for comparison of raw scores; there is a Handbook for Pupils which describes the tests, gives sample items and hints for success. In addition, the instrument attempts to provide a measure of both aptitude and achievement as well as a total score sum of the two. The test item types and content, though not unusual in any way, reflect those found in aptitude and achievement batteries and show considerable diversity.

The test was originally developed in connection with the Cooperative Entrance Examination Program sponsored by the Catholic Archdiocese of New York and the manual, norms, and pupil handbook presently available for general use are those utilized in that program. This immediately places some restriction on the applicability of the data reported in the manual to other types of high schools. However, the publisher's intent that the results be utilized for a ranking of applicants according to the school's own preference in regard to aptitude, achievement, or total score is not affected by this situation.

Yet certain other questions are raised by this entire procedure. The need for the establishment of the validity of the instrument remains. The manual reports some evidence, in studies with relatively small *n*'s, to show that the aptitude score correlates highly (.79 to .89 in a series of studies) with the *Otis Quick-Scoring Mental Ability Tests: Gamma Test,* the total score moderately with the *Preliminary Scholastic Aptitude Test* given three years later (.55 with PSAT Verbal; .57 with PSAT Mathematical), and the total score moderately with ninth grade first semester grades (from .27 with algebra to .59 with history). It is somewhat disconcerting that neither the size of the sample nor a description of the school (in regard to comprehensiveness, grading system, etc.) is provided for these last correlations. This leaves the prospective test user wondering why he should utilize this battery, particularly in light of this statement in the manual: "It is clear that the Entrance Examination scores were, on the average, as effective predictors of first-year achievement as Gamma IQ's." And the Otis Gamma is more economical in time and money! The relevance of this problem is accentuated by the lack of information about item selection or analysis.

Actually, the final justification of the *High School Classification Examination* will lie in its use as a diagnostic instrument. With its effort to provide general aptitude and achievement measures along with subtest scores in each of these areas, the test may be able to provide the high school administrator with information useful for grouping, for planning of remedial and developmental programs, and for the more appropriate development of varying curricula in a comprehensive high school. But at present the data provided by the publisher are not adequate for this purpose. Standard scores providing direct comparability of subtests are needed as well as validity coefficients based on well described, differing populations, and improvement of the reliability of some of the subtests. School systems themselves should be counseled in the research use of the information provided.

At the present time the reviewer wonders what advantage this instrument provides for general selection or classification purposes over a measure of general ability. Nonetheless, the test appears to have promise. The rationale behind its construction, its reported split-half reliability, the annual empirical derivation of norms (if only the sample could be broken down and described), the relative independence of the subtests (unfortunately no data are reported on the independence of the aptitude and achievement sections), the experimental equivalence of the two forms each year, and the stated recognition of the cooperating school's responsibility for evolving its own approach to utilization of the test data are all welcome and commendable. Perhaps as the instrument receives wider usage the deficiencies noted will be corrected. Now, use of the *High School Classification Examination* demands some empirical research by the user and an awareness that the data for each year's test in regard to such critical factors as validity and reliability can be calculated only after the test has been administered. Still, it may be better to recognize and accept this situation than to assume that coefficients reported 20 years ago on some other test are meaningful and applicable to a given, here-and-now population.

DAVID V. TIEDEMAN, *Professor of Education, Harvard University, Cambridge, Massachusetts.* [Review of Form 7B.]

The publisher offers the *High School Classification Examination* both for the selection of applicants for admission to secondary schools and for the later placement of those admitted. Two new forms a year, only one of which was to have been a released form of the secure examination of the diocesan program, were promised for use of the general public but the demand has so far not justified preparation of a form other than that used in the Cooperative Entrance Examination Program.

Form 7B (1963) of the *High School Classification Examination* was offered for review. Other forms of the test were not provided for comparison. Hence no judgment of comparability of tests in the series can be offered. Also, since the statistical information about the test is so far limited to that accumulated in the diocesan program, this review can deal with the test only in those terms.

The aptitude section of the test provides scores for verbal ability, numerical ability, and reasoning ability. Verbal ability is assessed in terms of 60 items requiring the identification of a synonym of the word in the stem. The five options available in each item are alternately identified as a to e and f to k. This alternation, which is characteristic of all sections of the test, probably helps the student keep his place as he marks his answer sheet. The word "competent" is twice used as a stem in the verbal ability section. Despite the fact that the options of the two items are different except for the answer, this seems like an unusual practice and may be only inadvertent.

The section on numerical ability requires both reasoning with numbers and algebraic operations. The section has much in common with the problem part of the arithmetic section. There undoubtedly is overlap in these two sections (intercorrelation reported as .59) despite the urging in the Handbook for Pupils that the section on numerical ability aims at ingenuity and facility with numbers while the part on problems involves computation. I found myself computing as well as being ingenious and computing as I tackled both of these portions of the test.

There are 25 items in the section on reasoning ability. The items require the discovery of pattern in series of numbers or letters or both and the choice among four options of the number or letter which is logically next in the series.

The test provides, and the program reports, an aptitude score as the sum of scores on the sections for verbal, numerical, and reasoning abilities. The score on items such as are in these sections is in the tradition of the measurement of intelligence as it is manifested in scholastic ability. The high correlation of the aptitude score and of the total score with scores, respectively, on the Beta and Gamma Tests of the *Otis Quick-Scoring Mental Ability Tests* as reported in the manual bear witness to this judgment. The publisher has a long tradition of well respected instruments of measurement in the area of scholastic ability and this test is true to that tradition. In fact, the statement in the manual that some of the items were "drawn from other published or unpublished tests" suggests that this examination may have more in common with the *Otis Quick-Scoring Mental Ability Tests* than the mere capability of the students with items of the kind in both tests. It would be wise to reflect on this similarity in considering the use of the test. It is after all another of several tests of scholastic aptitude intended for use in grades 8 and 9.

A feature of the test intended to distinguish it from the general line of aptitude tests is the inclusion of three sections of achievement items. It is this aspect of the test which is recommended both for use with the aptitude section in the selection of students for admission to high school and for use in the placement of students once admitted. In this latter use, the manual is ambiguous on the kind of placement which is possible and on the separate or combined use of the achievement section or sections in undertaking the task. I presume it will become clear as I proceed that this is a claim for the test which I consider ill-founded at the present time.

The arithmetic section has 20 items which can be answered largely through computation and 20 problems which require the construction of an attack before computation. The five options available for the items of the section always contain the option, "not given." This helps to insure that the student is accurate in his computations. The single score obtained for the section combines the student's ability in computation and problem attack. The section is definitely limited to the assessment of arithmetical operations, however, and no effort is made to test for aspects of the logic of numbers which pupils are acquiring through some of the modern curricula in mathematics.

The reading section consists of six passages of increasing length and presumably of increasing difficulty, each followed by from four to eight questions. Students could have fun with the test, if they dared, by reading the questions before they read the passage. Several of the 35 questions can be answered from general information without reading the passage. The prior knowledge of the questions is also helpful in locating only the small quantity of specific information which is relevant to the questions. The test is supposed to measure comprehension and probably does to some small extent. Looking at the test through the questions rather than through the passage, however, certainly causes one to wonder what is really measured. Since it is claimed that most students complete most items in most sections, it would appear that the reading section does not measure speed of reading. Also, the reading score and the verbal ability score are the most highly related scores in the test according to the single study of the matter which is reported in the manual. Perhaps this suggests the real meaning of "reading."

The use of grammatical terms is tested by 30 items in the first part of the English section and the use of words in context is tested by 30 items in the last part of the section. The score on the test is for the section as a whole despite its divided nature. I am not a student of English but it does seem possible that the equal emphasis on grammar and word usage as represented in this section may be more a diocesan definition of English than a secular definition. The test is fairly traditional and makes no concession to present discussions on the place of linguistics and of literature in the English curriculum.

The sum of scores in arithmetic, reading, and English represents the achievement score reported for the test. The sum of the aptitude and achievement scores is reported as the total score. Presumably, the total score figures in the selection of applicants for admission to high school. The achievement score and the aptitude score, with attention being given to the components of these subtotals, constitute the information available for the placement of admitted students. Placement of whom in what, however?

The test is available for placement purposes but neither logic nor statistic is offered to specify the divisions of students needed or possible. In the high school grades, the total score on the test might well serve to construct sections of students which are reasonably homogenous in general scholastic ability. However, I seriously doubt that the achievement tests could be used alone to construct, in any subject, sections of students which would pass muster long with either pupil or teacher. Each of the achievement tests is short. Their content is fairly traditional. Furthermore, each of the tests correlates as much with a test in the aptitude section as tests in either area do among themselves. (The manual, after reporting intercorrelations of the section scores, says that "there is not any great degree of overlap among the subtests" when it has just previously stated that correlations of this same magnitude between the total score on the test and grades in courses clearly indicate that the test is an effective predictor of first-year achievement. Seek and ye shall find!) Also, the corrected split-half reliability coefficients of the section scores range from .43 to .90. Finally, the standard errors of measurement suggest that fine distinctions in ability among the norm groups should not be attempted. Within these limitations, classification could be attempted but it should be quite clear that a school department is going to have to work its way through the problem of placement with this test largely through its own intelligence.

The standard administration of the examination in the diocesan program, the scoring of the examinations almost simultaneously at the Measurement Research Center, and the capacity of MRC to provide percentile norms in the process of scoring the examinations, all combine to make the problem of norming the examination of no consequence to the Cooperative Entrance Examination Program, the prime user of the examination. Furthermore, the selection of students who participate in this program solely in terms of their immediate competition without reference to a standard of aptitude (except for a percentile of the immediate group) also makes the problem of comparability of the examination from testing to testing and from year to year of no consequence so long as the general content of the examination is kept parallel from one examination to another. For these reasons, I offer no objection to the procedures employed in the diocesan program.

Outside of the closed system, however, the matters of comparability and of norms are of consequence, both in the guidance of students and in admission. For this reason, users intending to take advantage of the present general availability of the *High School Classification Examination* should reflect carefully on the questions of comparability and norms before purchasing the test. The present norms are for the diocesan program. This is a closed system with little opportunity for comparison in the more general framework of educational testing. Therefore, there seems little basis available for a non-diocesan school to use the test other than for selection of its students.

In sum, the test is well in the mold of tests of scholastic aptitude. It is a secure test which undoubtedly has been of good advantage in the diocesan program of selection to high school. It provides a good practice handbook for pupils desiring to prepare for the examination. It is of restricted content and concept as a test of achievement, however. Furthermore, it is of doubtful value as a placement instrument even within diocesan schools because of the high generality and low reliability of scores of the achievement sections. Consequently, there seems little to recommend the test to the general school audience except those who want to experiment with what is merely another test of scholastic aptitude.

[12]

***High School Fundamentals Evaluation Test.** Grades 9–12; 1955–59; 6 scores: reading vocabulary, reading comprehension, history and social studies, science, mathematics, total; IBM; Forms A ('55), B ('55), C ('59), D ('59), (39–40 pages); manual ('59, 12 pages); profile ['59, 1 page]; $4 per 25 tests; separate answer sheets may be used; $1.25 per 50 hand scoring answer sheets; 15¢ per key; 4¢ per IBM answer sheet; 30¢ per set of scoring stencils; $1.50 per 100 profiles; 25¢ per specimen set; cash orders postpaid; 120(180) minutes in 3 sessions; David F. Votaw, Sr.; Steck Co. *

REFERENCES

1. VOTAW, DAVID F., SR. "Variability of Fundamentals on the Basis of Their Acquisition Independently by Gifted Students." *Yearb Nat Council Meas Used Ed* 16:160–3 '59. *

GEORGE D. DEMOS, *Associate Dean—Counseling and Testing, and Associate Professor of Educational Psychology, California State College at Long Beach, Long Beach, California.*

Despite the fact that the author undoubtedly expended tremendous energy in developing this achievement test, one cannot help but note that the test has been a case of "too little, too soon." That is, perhaps the greatest weakness with the battery is that there simply has not been enough done to indicate its merits and potential uses to recommend its use in high schools at this time. It seems to the reviewer that when one attempts to compete with such well known, studied, and researched tests as the *Iowa Tests of Educational Development*, the *Sequential Tests of Educational Progress*, and the *California Achievement Tests*, one must be ready not only to expend a great amount of effort but he must be heavily endowed with both finances and staff, and have the cooperation of schools and agencies throughout the country as well.

Whether or not the publishers, the Steck Company, will be able to compete in this market is very problematical. Unless they are able to do so, and put forth the much needed additions, the test does not have much to recommend it for use at this time. Aside from this fact, the test has several serious weaknesses.

Schools involved in various aspects of the norming were located in Alabama, Arkansas, Florida, Georgia, Mississippi, Missouri, and Texas. No information is given with regard to how and why these schools were selected, what the schools were like, why only predominantly schools of southern states were selected, etc. A host of other questions regarding the norm population needs to be spelled out much more explicitly. The author refers to his norm population as a national norm group. The small number of students, schools, and states involved in the study could hardly make it a national norm group. Local norms are frequently preferred for larger high schools, but no instructions or suggestions are given as to how, why, and when local norms can be provided. Examples and much more specific information and elaboration are needed.

The manual indicates two kinds of validation—content validity and concurrent validity. In one of the two concurrent validity studies reported, the manual indicates that of 13 gifted students who were located by the test in a Texas high school, only one failed to be confirmed as gifted by "the faculty or personnel director." No indication is given as to how "gifted" was defined, what criteria were used by the faculty or personnel director, and why such a small sample was utilized in this study. To refer to a study with such limited data says little for the validity of the test. The other concurrent validity study reports correlations between the grade-point average and test scores for 138 students in a Texas high school. The correlations between the subtests and the school grades range from .42 (in history and social studies) to .73 (in reading comprehension). Very sketchy data, however, are given regarding the specifics of the study, namely, data are missing on what course grades were used, what grade levels were utilized, and whether or not nonacademic course grades were included in the overall grade-point average (physical education, shop courses, home economics, etc.). No studies are reported as to the usefulness of this test in either predicting college success or predicting success in specific subject areas in high school.

One of the desirable aspects of the battery centers around the time allotment feature. The author indicates that in fixing the testing time for each subdivision, "three time elements were used experimentally, the last one being practically unlimited. The time limit finally adopted was the one beyond which little or no additional score gain appeared." This, in effect, makes the test a power rather than a speed test which is a desirable feature in achievement testing, in view of some of the recent research dealing with rigorous time limits and their deleterious effects on certain students. Correlations between the scores made on the finally adopted time limits and those made on the most liberal time limit are all very high: .97 to .99.

The reliability coefficients reported range from .62 at grade 9 to a high of .97 for grades 9–12 combined. The correlations reported are means of four of the six possible intercorrelations between the four forms. The failure to report the original correlations is unfortunate.

Many of the multiple choice items present only three choices. Since no correction factor for guessing is involved, a spuriously high score can be obtained by chance. At least four alternatives should be given.

No information is given to teachers, counselors, and administrators to show how the listed purposes of the test can be carried out. No examples, suggestions, case materials, charts, and so on are given to aid them in the proper usage of the battery. An expansion of this area is certainly needed.

In summary, the *High School Fundamentals Evaluation Test* is in dire need of considerable "evaluation of fundamentals" itself. The reviewer cannot see how this test in its present form can possibly compete with existing superior tests on the market such as the ITED, STEP, and CAT.

JASON MILLMAN, *Assistant Professor of Educational Psychology and Measurement, Cornell University, Ithaca, New York.*

DESCRIPTION. There are four forms to the *High School Fundamentals Evaluation Test,* two of which have been published since the test was reviewed in *The Fifth Mental Measurements Yearbook*. All the forms have the same organization, format, and general content.

This achievement test is designed to measure "'strong' and 'weak' areas in the individual student" and "in the scholastic program" as well as to assess "achievement evaluation of the entire high school" and to locate gifted students. It consists of five subtests. The reading vocabulary subtest consists of 50 key words, each followed by four other words; the student must choose the word most like the key word. The reading comprehension subtest contains a number of short prose selections and a poem, all of which should be unfamiliar to the student. The majority of the items of this subtest measure the ability to note details; a number require the student to read between the lines. The remaining three subtests primarily test the knowledge of specific information. Names and dates are emphasized in the history and social studies subtest, definitions of technical terms in the science subtest, and routine arithmetical and algebraic calculations in the mathematics subtest. The test is primarily one of power rather than speed.

EVALUATION. The appropriateness of any achievement test depends upon the qualities one wishes to measure. One questions whether most educators are primarily interested in the student's knowledge of the specific facts called for throughout this test. Those who are interested in testing a deeper understanding and application of principles would be well advised to select one of the more popular test batteries, such as the *Sequential Tests of Educational Progress*.

Many of the items are open to criticism. Interpretation questions on the reading comprehension subtest, such as item 31 of Form A, sometimes have no best answer. One series of questions on this subtest, items 35–40 of Form B, appears to measure knowledge of high school physics rather than reading comprehension. Another item, "The width of the United States in terms of degrees of latitude is approximately (1) 10 degrees, (2) 20 degrees, (3) 30 degrees, (4) 40 degrees," is outdated now that Alaska and Hawaii have become states. The correct width, 25 degrees, makes options 2 and 3 equally correct.

Norms are expressed both in percentile ranks and in an "arbitrary score scale," which varies according to grade. For each grade, the norms are based upon the scores of approximately 600 students from only nine high schools in seven southern states. These norms seem meaningless and are likely to give a false impression of the individual's and of the school's achievement.

Use of the "arbitrary scale scores" as recommended will not permit "discovery of 'strong' and 'weak' areas in the individual student." A tenth grader, equally bright in reading comprehension and in science, would be likely to have a higher "arbitrary scale score" in the former subtest, as it is less tied to any specific curricular experience. One might conclude from such a result that the student is better in reading comprehension than in science. The same limitation keeps the test from fulfilling another recommended purpose: "discovery of 'strong' and 'weak' areas in the scholastic program." A school with highly able students would probably conclude that its worst area, in the ninth and tenth grades, was science. The students would not have had the specific training in physics and chemistry necessary to attain a high score on the science subtest. The lack of any norms of school averages and the inadequacy of the individual norms make it difficult to attain another purpose of the test: "general achievement evaluation of the entire high school."

The equivalent-form reliabilities of the total scores and of the history and social studies subtest are quite high. The reliabilities of the other subtests are in the .80's for grades 11 and 12, and usually only in the .70's for grades 9 and 10. Consequently, if schools use the test scores in educational decisions about individuals, they should retest borderline cases with another form, especially in the ninth and tenth grades.

SUMMARY. The *High School Fundamentals Evaluation Test* is an achievement battery which measures recall of specific details in several areas. Its norms are unacceptable and probably should not be used. Its reliability is satisfactory, especially in the higher grades. Schools that are particularly interested in the factual emphasis of the test and are willing to restrict themselves to within-school and within-subject comparisons, may find the test of value.

For reviews by Victor H. Noll and Verner M. Sims, see 5:14.

[13]

Iowa Tests of Basic Skills. Grades 3–9; 1955–56; 15 scores: vocabulary, reading comprehension, language (5 scores), work-study skills (4 scores), arithmetic skills (3 scores), total; IBM and MRC; Forms 1 ('55), 2 ('56), (96 pages); teacher's manual ('56, 04 pages) for use with MRC answer sheets; teacher's manual ('56, 23 pages) for use with IBM answer sheets; administrator's manual ('56, 111 pages); profile ('55, 1 page); pupil report folder ('55, 4 pages); separate answer sheets must be used; 84¢ per test; $3.36 per set of 35 MRC answer sheets, teacher's MRC manual, and 35 pupil report folders; 45¢ per hand scoring stencil for MRC answer sheets (machine scoring service, by Measurement Research Center, Inc., may be arranged through the publisher); $5.76 per set of 35 IBM answer sheets, teacher's MRC manual, and teacher's IBM manual; hand and machine scoring stencils for IBM answer sheets: $1.47 per set for grades 3–5, $1.68 per set for grades 6–9; 90¢ per 35 profiles; 90¢ per 35 pupil report folders; 90¢ per administrator's manual; $2.25 per specimen set; postage extra; 279(315) minutes in 4 sessions; E. F. Lindquist, A. N. Hieronymus, and others; Houghton Mifflin Co. *

REFERENCES

1. BARRY, BARBARA A. *A Comparison of the Metropolitan Achievement Test and the Iowa Tests of Basic Skills in Grade Four in a Typical New England Town.* Master's thesis, Boston University (Boston, Mass.), 1958.

2. ORTON, KENNETH DALLAS. *An Empirical Study of Annual Gains in the Iowa Tests of Basic Skills at Various Achievement Levels.* Doctor's thesis, State University of Iowa (Iowa City, Iowa), 1958. (*DA* 19:1657)

3. SCANNELL, DALE PAUL. *Differential Prediction of Academic Success From Achievement Test Scores.* Doctor's thesis, State University of Iowa (Iowa City, Iowa), 1958. (*DA* 19:2007)

4. CROFT, ELLA JOYCE. "Prediction of Clothing Construction Achievement of High School Girls." *Ed & Psychol Meas* 19:653–5 w '59. * (*PA* 34:6562)

5. HAGE, DEAN S., AND STROUD, JAMES B. "Reading Proficiency and Intelligence Scores, Verbal and Nonverbal." *J Ed Res* 52:258–62 Mr '59. * (*PA* 34:4813)

6. KNIEF, LOTUS M., AND STROUD, JAMES B. "Intercorrelations Among Various Intelligence, Achievement, and Social Class Scores." *J Ed Psychol* 50:117–20 Je '59. * (*PA* 35:779)

7. OAKES, FREDERICK, JR. *The Contribution of Certain Variables to the Academic Achievement of Gifted Seventh Grade Students in an Accelerated General Science Curriculum.* Doctor's thesis, New York University (New York, N.Y.), 1959. (*DA* 20:4002)

8. GARLOCK, J. C., AND HARSH, J. R. "A Comparative Study of Four Commonly Used Achievement Tests." *Calif J Ed Res* 11:147–54 S '60. * (*PA* 35:7117)

9. HARBILAS, JOHN N. *The Iowa Tests of Basic Skills and the SRA Primary Mental Abilities as Predictors of Success in Seventh Grade Science.* Master's thesis, Stetson University (DeLand, Fla.), 1960.

10. MARIGLIO, ANGELO J. *A Pilot Study of the Relation of the Work Study Skills Scores of the Iowa Tests of Basic Skills to the Semester Grades of Citizenship Education of Selected Ninth Grade Students.* Master's thesis, Niagara University (Niagara University, N.Y.), 1960.

11. SCANNELL, DALE P. "Prediction of College Success From Elementary and Secondary School Performance." *J Ed Psychol* 51:130–4 Je '60. * (*PA* 35:3987)

12. ANDERSON, VAYDEN. *A Study of Results When the Iowa Tests of Basic Skills Are Administered to Selected Low Achievers in the Fifth and Sixth Grades.* Master's thesis, Winona State College (Winona, Minn.), 1961.

13. CHATURVEDI, VIPULA. *An Investigation Into the Generality of Composite Scores on the Iowa Test of Basic Skills.* Master's thesis, State University of Iowa (Iowa City, Iowa), 1961.

14. GNAUCK, JOHANNA, AND KACZKOWSKI, HENRY. "Prediction of Junior High School Performance." *Ed & Psychol Meas* 21:485–8 su '61. * (*PA* 36:2KL85G)

15. TAYLOR, EDWARD A., AND CRANDALL, JAMES H. "A Study of the 'Norm-Equivalence' of Certain Tests Approved for the California State Testing Program." *Calif J Ed Res* 13:186–92 S '62. *

16. WOMER, FRANK B. "BJMP Test Project Establishes Local Norms." *Mich Ed J* 39:522–3+ Ap '62. *

17. FINLEY, CARMEN J. "A Comparison of the California Achievement Test, Metropolitan Achievement Test and Iowa Test of Basic Skills." *Calif J Ed Res* 14:79–88 Mr '63. * (*PA* 38:1422)

For reviews by Virgil E. Herrick, G. A. V. Morgan, and H. H. Remmers, see 5:16 (1 excerpt).

[14]

***The Iowa Tests of Educational Development.** Grades 9–12; 1942–63; 10 scores: understanding of basic social concepts, general background in the natural sciences, correctness and appropriateness of expression, ability to do quantitative thinking, ability to interpret reading materials in the social studies, ability to interpret reading materials in the natural sciences, ability to interpret literary materials, general vocabulary, subtotal, use of sources of information; IBM and MRC; 2 editions; separate answer sheets must be used; postage extra; prepared under the direction of E. F. Lindquist and Leonard S. Feldt (*a*); Science Research Associates, Inc. *

a) [SRA-SCORED SINGLE BOOKLET EDITION.] 1942–63; MRC; Forms X-4, Y-4, ('60, 65 pages); examiner's manual ('62, c1949–62, 31 pages); administrator's manual ('63, c1949–63, 31 pages); teachers' and counselors' manual, eighth revision ('63, c1949–62, 72 pages); college planning manual, second edition ('57, 64 pages); student profile leaflet, sixth edition ('61, c1958, 2 pages); prospectus, third edition ('62, 21 pages); tests rented only; fee: $1.25 per student; fee includes scoring service; $1 per prospectus; $1.50 per specimen set; 464(540) minutes in 2 days for full length version, 329(405) minutes in 9 sessions for class period version.

b) [SCHOOL-SCORED SEPARATE BOOKLET EDITION.] 1942–61; IBM; Forms X-3S, Y-3S, ('52, 7–9 pages for most tests); 9 tests in separate booklets (titles are the same as scores listed above); examiner's manual ('58, c1947–57, 23 pages); general manual ('59, c1951–59, 37 pages); student profile leaflet, sixth edition ('61, c1958, 2 pages); student profile card (no date, 4 pages); interpretive charts ('59, 1 page each): percentile score profile chart, standard score profile chart, frequency distribution of scores chart, scores made by selected students chart, growth and relation to national norms chart, achievement status chart; no data on reliability; $2.40 per 20 tests; $5 per 100 IBM answer sheets; 50¢ per scoring stencil; 90¢ per 20 profile leaflets; $2 per 20 sets of profile cards; 50¢ per pad of 20 copies of any one interpretive chart (includes enlarged demonstration chart); $3 per specimen set of all 9 tests; 55–65(60–75) minutes for most tests in full length version, 40(45) minutes for most tests in class period version.

REFERENCES

1–3. See 4:17.

4–12. See 5:17.

13. HANSMEIER, THOMAS W. *A Study of the Relationship Between Twelfth Grade Performance on the Iowa Tests of Educational Development and Freshman-in-College Grade Point Index.* Master's thesis, Iowa State Teachers College (Cedar Falls, Iowa), 1957.

14. SCANNELL, DALE PAUL. *Differential Prediction of Academic Success From Achievement Test Scores.* Doctor's thesis, State University of Iowa (Iowa City, Iowa), 1958. (*DA* 19:2007)

15. KACZKOWSKI, HENRY R. "Using Expectancy Tables to Validate Test Procedures in High School." *Ed & Psychol Meas* 19:675–7 w '59. * (*PA* 34:6536)

16. O'NEILL, RALPH C. "Predicting College Success With the ITED." *Calif J Ed Res* 10:86–9+ Mr '59. * (*PA* 34:2113)

17. ROBERTSON, JAMES R. *Predicting Success at Highland High School From the Iowa Test of Educational Development.* Master's thesis, University of Utah (Salt Lake City, Utah), 1959.

18. CASSEL, RUSSELL N., AND STANCIK, EDWARD J. "Fac-

torial Content of the Iowa Tests of Educational Development and Other Tests." *J Exp Ed* 29:193–6 D '60. *

19. HANSMEIER, THOMAS W. "The Iowa Tests of Educational Development as Predictors of College Achievement." *Ed & Psychol Meas* 20:843–5 w '60. * (*PA* 35:3983)

20. PONDER, MARIAN. *Standard Score Gains on the Iowa Tests of Educational Development and the Correlation of Scores With the High School Marks in the Same Field.* Master's thesis, Drake University (Des Moines, Iowa), 1960.

21. SCANNELL, DALE P. "Prediction of College Success From Elementary and Secondary School Performance." *J Ed Psychol* 51:130–4 Je '60. * (*PA* 35:3987)

22. BENTALL, GRACE. *Determination of Critical Levels of Reading Ability for High School Students as Measured by Course Marks and Achievement Test Results.* Doctor's thesis, University of Oregon (Eugene, Ore.), 1961. (*DA* 22:1458)

23. CASSEL, RUSSELL N., AND HADDOX, GENEVIEVE. "Comparing Reading Competency With Personality and Social Insight Test Scores." *Calif J Ed Res* 12:27–30 Ja '61. * (*PA* 36:1KJ27C)

24. CASSEL, RUSSELL N., AND STANCIK, EDWARD J. "California Test of Mental Maturity b Weights for Predicting a Composite Score on the Iowa Tests of Educational Development." *J Genetic Psychol* 98:119–26 Mr '61. * (*PA* 35:7074)

25. CONNELL, DOROTHEA B. *A Study of the Relationships of Tenth Grade Students' Scores on the New York State Junior High School Survey Test in Mathematics and the Quantitative Thinking Test of the ITED Battery.* Master's thesis, Niagara University (Niagara University, N.Y.), 1961.

26. DARROW, HARRIET DRISKELL. *The Relationship of Certain Factors to Performance of Elementary Student Teachers With Contrasting Success Records in Student Teaching.* Doctor's thesis, Indiana University (Bloomington, Ind.), 1961. (*DA* 22:3934)

27. MCADAMS, HENRY EDWARD. *The Prediction of General and Differential Achievement in Two Samples of Junior College Students.* Doctor's thesis, University of Southern California (Los Angeles, Calif.), 1961. (*DA* 22:3524)

28. WOLD, ARNOLD A. *A Study of the Relationship Between the Iowa Tests of Educational Development and College Freshman Scholarship.* Master's thesis, State University of South Dakota (Vermillion, S.D.), 1961.

29. POLING, E. GORDON. *A Study of the Achievement of Students in South Dakota High Schools of Selected Enrollments.* Doctor's thesis, State University of South Dakota (Vermillion, S.D.), 1962. (*DA* 23:1610)

30. STEINBACH, RALEIGH REINHART. *A Comparison of the I.T.E.D. Scores of Selected South Dakota Ninth Grade Pupils Grouped According to Grades per Teacher in Elementary Schools Attended.* Doctor's thesis, State University of South Dakota (Vermillion, S.D.), 1962. (*DA* 23:1238)

31. TRAXLER, ROGER J. *A Comparison of the Iowa Tests of Educational Development Scores and Chemistry and Physics Grades in High School.* Master's thesis, Winona State College (Winona, Minn.), 1962.

32. CAPLAN, STANLEY W.; RUBLE, RONALD A.; AND SEGEL, DAVID. "A Theory of Educational and Vocational Choice in Junior High School." *Personnel & Guid J* 42:129–35 O '63. *

33. CASSEL, RUSSELL N. "Comparing 8th Grade CAT Scores and 9th Grade ITED Scores." *Psychol Rep* 12:53–4 F '63. * (*PA* 38:3198)

34. DURFLINGER, GLENN W. "Academic and Personality Differences Between Women Students Who Do Complete the Elementary Teaching Credential Program and Those Who Do Not." *Ed & Psychol Meas* 23:775–83 w '63. *

35. YAGER, ROBERT E., and DESSEL, NORMAN F. "Selection Criteria for High Ability Science Students." *J Ed Res* 57:193–6 D '63. *

ELLIS BATTEN PAGE, *Professor of Education, and Director, Bureau of Educational Research and Service, University of Connecticut, Storrs, Connecticut.* [Review of the SRA-Scored Single Booklet Edition.]

The ITED battery is one of the most widely used measures of achievement ever designed. According to the 1962 prospectus for the centrally scored edition, the battery is used to test one and a half million students, and there are reasons to predict the number will rise. The ITED is on some counts one of a number of nearly perfect instruments (within the philosophy and assumptions and present skills guiding achievement test development), and its quality as well as its popularity justify a scrutiny of certain testing practices of which it is an outstanding exemplar.

The battery comes in a complete and glossy package. Nine tests measure four curricular areas. Testing materials include densely packed, attractive, optically efficient procedures. Regular output to the schools includes a profile of percentiles for each student, a list report of scores, a confidential summary of the school's averages and local percentiles and frequency distributions. These report services appear well organized and systematic. Here as in other programs, services surpass the dreams of a few years ago.

This edition marks the advent of two new forms of the ITED, X-4 and Y-4. These were developed with completely new items in an effort to modernize test content. Items were selected with a number of statistical considerations to assure that X and Y are equivalent and fairly comparable in interpretation with previous editions of the tests. A general impression is that the new subtests are more difficult than the former editions, and this fact may make for further difficulties of a kind later considered. The battery may be administered either as a full length version requiring four half days of testing or as a somewhat shorter class period version requiring nine class periods. Efforts have been taken to assure that these versions, though obviously differing slightly in reliability due to length, will be comparable in interpretation.

The administrator's manual provides the publisher's rationale for validity, the most vexed question in achievement testing. The publishers suggest an individual kind of face validity. The Manual for the School Administrator urges the user to "Put yourself in the student's place and take the tests. In this way the user himself can decide what skills are demanded of his students and what proficiencies they must develop to obtain high scores. The user may then decide whether or not these abilities are desirable outcomes of a program of general education." The authors add, "there is no adequate statistical substitute for a commonsense evaluation of this kind." This claim seems debatable. With our improving techniques for measuring values, choices, and preferences, we could probably do much better in professional assessment of achievement test validity than to rely upon the random individual judgment. For example, if school administrators are seriously the group who should evaluate the test content, their best judgments should at least be pooled in various ways to reduce judgmental error. But perhaps panels of subject matter specialists are more appropriate judges. In any case, it may be asking too much for test publishers to explore these ways of evaluation, and it should perhaps be the task of commercially uninvolved professionals in educational measurement.

The publishers correctly state that the tests do not measure the outcome of taking specific courses, but rather what a student has learned in school and out throughout his educational career (and we could add, throughout his life). But the problem of proper achievement test content remains a large one.

Predictive validity rests upon the correlation of prior editions of the ITED with later school and college success, and tables are provided showing correlations from the .40's to the .70's or higher between ITED composite scores and rank in high school graduating class, average high school grades in specific courses, high school grade-point averages, and college freshman grades. The publishers argue with justification that it does not make much sense to say that concurrent correlation between the tests and school marks is evidence of *validity* of achievement tests. Such a practice would assume that the school or college grades are *superior* as a measure of achievement, and it could be argued that grades are *inferior* measures on a number of counts. The point seems equally true about predictive, as about concurrent, validity. All reported coefficients are in the usually high ranges.

Within-grade split-half reliabilities for all tests are reported, ranging in the .80's and .90's, with reliabilities for the composite reaching a striking .98 or .99.

The standard scores of the ITED are based upon the error of measurement, with the probable error of any score equal to one standard score point. In other words, a teacher who bothers to note the standard score may, considering only split-half reliability of the kind used, have confidence at the 50 per cent level that the "true score" (in this special sense) of any given student is not more than one point away from that reported. This is surely a valid, if a somewhat arbitrary, basis for constructing a psychological scale, but such confidence of the teacher or counselor may still be misplaced. If the 50 per cent interval estimates of "true" scores were based upon test-retest reliability, for instance, then the probability would be less than .50 of being within one point of the standard score on the present scale. And what teachers really mean when they speak of faith in a test score is something like faith in different forms, or different tests, or even behavioral goals. Of course, the same false confidence may creep into the use of percentile bands such as are reported for certain other tests. It is well to realize that test scores, given measurement errors, are not really the firm points they are sometimes assumed to be. But what is often lost sight of by the teacher is that, in any practical sense, the usual percentile bands, based upon split-half reliability, are much too restrictive as well. In any validity sense, a real probable-error "band" would be huge indeed.

One of the most vexing problems in any battery concerns the meaning of peaks and valleys in the individual profile. Some psychometrists have for some batteries pointed out that differences in standard scores for the individual student are not always meaningful, reflecting random error from the lower reliability of the shorter subtest scores. (See Stanley's review of the SCAT battery, 5:322.) ITED has attempted to sidestep this criticism by computing, by analysis of variance procedures, a "coefficient of discriminating power" which is said to be "the average value of the reliability of the difference between scores," and which is found to be .70. But action of chance in the subtest ordering, as pointed out by Eric Gardner in an earlier review of ITED (see 4:17), is still very large, and the common variance measured by some general factors is also large.

An example of the action of chance may be easily gathered from the publisher's tables for raw scores, standard scores, and percentiles for the nine tests of Form X-4. If a ninth grade, first semester student did not read *any* items but only made random choices throughout the battery, he would on the average receive percentile scores for the nine tests as follows: 12, 15, 16, 24, 33, 30, 21, 19, and 13. This chance student would have, therefore, a rather interesting profile which would cause most counselors to consider seriously some particular study field. In this case, these interesting differences in percentile scores do *not* measure anything different from one subtest to another, except subtest difficulty. An occasional argument of test publishers is that students do not typically choose their answers randomly. But here is a potential variable in test administration which may be, if it is not now, seriously disturbing to test interpretation. If a proctor or counselor at one school urges his students to guess blindly where there is no clear preference for any choice, and another proctor does not, the first group will on the average do much better than the second, especially in those difficult technical areas. The solution is not a so-called correction for guessing, since this has pitfalls as well. Rather it is to adjust test difficulty and span and administration so that a chance score is indeed a zero percentile. But this solution, if realized, would probably entail certain other problems, such as testing inefficiency for the middle and upper groups. Or perhaps a partial solution would be to build some optical computer logic which would depreciate obviously patterned test responses. In the meantime, the test user should realize, in spite of the publisher's "coefficient of discriminating power," how unreliable some profile differences may be, especially among the younger and weaker scholars, or among others who may be testwise about guessing.

The percentile rank norms for the new SRA-scored editions are based upon a nationwide testing in the Fall of 1962. (Norms for the school-scored forms are based on 1957 testing.) The population sampled includes "all students in grades 9 through 12 in regular daily attendance at public high schools throughout the continental United States," regardless of the form of these schools (four-year or various junior high and high school arrangements). It does not include students in private schools, denominational schools, or teacher training schools associated with colleges or universities. This population was stratified by region and size of student body and then sampled randomly within strata. In this way 136 school systems were tested in 39 states, contributing 51,098 students. This is slightly under the sample of 1 per cent per stratifying category which the publishers had originally sought, but seems a most respectable sample for any reasonable purposes. Where certain types of public schools were not represented in true proportion to the total population, the sample was statistically augmented or reduced to adjust the norms more accurately. A number of different kinds of norms are available. For instance, the canny administrator may compare his own schools with either a national population of students or with a national population of *schools*. His choice might depend on his audience, his political purpose, or his professional conscience.

In summary, the ITED is a modern battery of subject area tests designed in conformity with good canons of test construction, supplied with high quality norms and statistical information, and reported in an easily disseminable and usable form. With some reservations about profile differences, it measures what it measures very well. Whether it measures the right thing, however, seems at present an unresolved question. But the competent ITED battery did not invent the perplexing problems concerning the relationship of national testing programs to national educational purpose, and it does not deserve the blame more than any other.

ALEXANDER G. WESMAN, *Associate Director, Test Division, The Psychological Corporation, New York, New York.*

The *Iowa Tests of Educational Development* were prepared to "provide a comprehensive and dependable description of the general educational development of the high school student. * With respect to all broad aspects of educational development that are readily measurable, the *Iowa Tests of Educational Development* meet this need. * [The tests] emphasize ultimate and lasting outcomes of the whole program of education. * [They are] not.... limited to the temporary and immediate outcomes of instruction in individual subjects." Thus, the announced goals more directly resemble those of the *Sequential Tests of Educational Progress* (STEP) than those of more directly curriculum-oriented batteries like the *Stanford Achievement Test* or the *Metropolitan Achievement Tests*.

To achieve these goals, nine tests are employed drawing on the subject matter of four broad curricular areas: social studies, natural sciences, general mathematics, and English. Social studies is represented by two tests: a 90-item conventional test called Understanding of Basic Social Concepts and an 80-item reading test called Ability to Interpret Reading Materials in the Social Studies. Two parallel tests represent natural sciences, each with the same respective number of items. The single mathematics test consists of 53 problems and is called Ability to Do Quantitative Thinking. English is broadly represented by tests of Correctness and Appropriateness of Expression (99 items), Ability to Interpret Literary Materials (80 items), General Vocabulary (75 items), and Use of Sources of Information (60 items). There is also a composite score including eight of the tests (all but Use of Sources of Information). The 707 items and 26 reading passages require almost eight hours of working time, or two full school days (9:00 A.M. to 3:35 P.M.) of testing. A "class period" version takes five and one half working hours over two less crowded days.

The required investment of pupil and school time would seem to make it mandatory for administrators to consider whether or not there is adequate return for the expenditure involved. Among the specific questions to be answered are: How much information are we getting? How useful is the information for direct improvement of the pupil's education? Might equally good information about the student's ability be obtained in less time, or more varied useful information in the same amount of time? If the information is obtained for the pupil in one year, is there enough change in the abilities appraised to justify testing with the same instruments the following year and the year after that—for four years if the manual's recommendations are followed; or would new and different information about the pupil be a more profitable investment? When schools are being accused from within and from without of overtesting, such questions may not be lightly dismissed.

On the whole the tests are prepared with satisfactory technical competence. There has been a genuine effort to include items which call for the ability to generalize, to apply in new situations what has previously been learned in other settings, and to derive information from newly presented materials. The success of this effort varies from test to test; Understanding of Basic Social Concepts and General Background in the Natural Sciences are liberally sprinkled with "fact" items, as is Use of Sources of Information. The vocabulary test and the spelling portion of the correctness and appropriateness test are conventional measures of these fields of knowledge. Accordingly, it is primarily in the three reading tests, and perhaps in the mathematics test, that the student's ability to generalize and apply principles is challenged.

The scoring and reporting services which are an integral part of the SRA-scored program (half the Manual for the School Administrator is devoted to preparations to be made for testing, checking in materials, shipping test materials, using a grid on the answer sheet, and the like) are attractive; they should save schools the otherwise heavy burden of scoring the tests and preparing rosters. Moreover, a school system which wishes to have basic statistics computed for various groups to be studied may order these statistics as part of the reporting service. Hopefully, the availability of these computational services will increase the likelihood that administrators will devote serious attention to the results of the testing program.

The widespread use of this battery indicates that a great many school administrators have been impressed with the ITED program. Test specialists are unlikely to find comparable satisfactions. One source of dissatisfaction is the lack of restraint exercised in putting forth claims; that the claims are sometimes inconsistent with one another appears not to have acted as a deterrent. Thus, the tests are proposed to school administrators "to provide a dependable and objective base for evaluating the curriculum programs of individual high schools" and to "point up any need for curriculum revision that may exist"; for teachers and counselors the tests "will be useful in educational guidance and in the adaptation of instruction to individual needs." These virtues are professed despite the information that the tests were "not constructed on the basis of an analysis of the content of any specific high school courses."

Further, the tests "are designed for administration to all students in the school, regardless of their grade classification or course registration," even though they "measure education development in [only] four major curricular areas." Again, though the tests are presumably independent of the curriculum, "there is some advantage in giving the tests early in the school year, in order that....the measures may be influenced as little as possible by the temporary results of current instruction." The reader who brings into apposition these conflicting statements from the various pamphlets and manuals must be pardoned his confusion.

The claims go on and on. The battery, we are told, "identifies students for possible grouping and/or special project assignments"; it "makes it easier to adapt instruction and guidance to each student's unique and changing needs." It measures "the knowledge and skills the student has accumulated from all [sic] of his in-school and out-of-school experiences." It will help the student "make up your mind how to distribute your efforts in your schoolwork." These are but a few of the benefits purported, in the various manuals, brochures, pamphlets, and bulletins, to flow from the use of tests. The claims are overwhelming; unhappily, they are largely unsubstantiated.

What about the tests as tests? The "heart of the battery consists," we are told, "particularly of tests 5 through 7. Tests 5, 6, and 7 measure the ability to interpret reading materials in the social studies, the natural sciences, and literature." In effect, then, we have here three reading tests drawing on content from three curricular areas. The list of skills the tests are intended to measure is very similar to the lists of skills to which the standard single reading tests are also addressed. The closest approach to uniqueness is found in those passages and items of the natural science reading test which deal with reports of experiments. No equally distinguishing characteristics appear in the other two reading tests. One need not gainsay the indisputable importance of reading as a central skill to question whether 240 items and three hours are appropriate expenditures; one hour or less is ordinarily sufficient to obtain satisfactory measures of a high school student's speed and level of comprehension.

The specific content of certain of the individual tests is to be reviewed by other contributors to this yearbook. This reviewer is impelled to express the wish that more careful editorial attention had been devoted to some of the items. For example, in Form Y-4 of the quantitative thinking test an item reads, "The first four values in a series of numbers written according to a set scheme are" and this is followed by *five* numbers. In the same booklet, the social studies reading test contains purported excerpts from five writers, numbered I, II, II [sic], IV, and V. Since the correct answer to the second item on this passage is "Writer III" and one of the misleads is Writer II, the student may well be perplexed. It is also somewhat disconcerting to find, in the basic social concepts test, an item stem which concludes with "What explanation may be offered for this?" Literally, of course, *any* explanation may be *offered*. This may appear to be "nit picking," but anti-test critics make much of such lapses. One has come to expect more attentive care than is displayed in these and similar instances.

Perhaps the most serious deficiency of the ITED program is the failure to provide the kind of statistical data to which the interested potential user is entitled. There is no single manual to which one may refer for basic information; one must flit back and forth among the Manual for the School Administrator, the Manual for Teachers and Counselors, a bulletin on using the ITED for college planning, and the scoring keys (the only source for raw score to scale score conversion). The end product of this flitting is, unhappily, frustration.

The Manual for the School Administrator contains two reliability tables, the correlation coefficients being of the odd-even variety. One of these tables refers to Form X and Form Y; no further identification is provided. It appears most unlikely that the exact same coefficients would have been obtained for Forms X-1, X-2, and X-3, or for Y-1, Y-2, and Y-3. The reader should not be asked to assume that these coefficients apply to the particular form with which he is concerned. No information is presented, either, as to the means and standard deviations associated with these coefficients. Presumably the coefficients refer to the full-length versions of the battery; in that case, no data are presented for the shorter class-period versions. A school which used these tests could not readily judge whether or not these coefficients were based on a more heterogeneous group than its own, and might therefore be larger than would be the case for that school.

Absence of basic information also characterizes the other reliability table; again, no means or standard deviations are provided. This table does identify the forms studied as X-4 and Y-4 and presents odd-even reliability coefficients for the full-length and class-period versions. A comparison of these coefficients will leave the reader more than a little puzzled; the full-length versions appear to be no more reliable than their class-period portions! No coefficient for the full-length version is as much as .05 larger than that of the class-period segment; in fact, in several instances the coefficients for the shorter versions are larger than those for the full-length. Undoubtedly, there is a reasonable explanation for these unreasonable data; one may assume, perhaps, that the standard deviations of scores for the groups which took the shorter versions were larger than those for the groups which took the full-length version. If so, the importance of reporting standard deviations is cogently illustrated. As reported, the coefficients range between .81 and .96 for the individual tests for a single grade; the composite score reliability is estimated as .98.

Much is made, in the Manual for the School Administrator, of the care taken to assure representativeness of the norms sample for the 1957 standardization. It is entirely likely that the group used for the development of norms compares favorably with samples used for competing test batteries. The presentation of the data, however, is most unfortunate. Tables derived from U.S. Office of Education census data are presented as percentages. Tables showing similar breakdowns by region, community size, and grade for the ITED norms are shown as frequencies. When these frequencies are translated into percentages, discrepancies between census data and the norms tables are revealed to be of considerable size. For example, the census proportion of high school students in the East South Central region, in small communities, is reported as 65 per cent; only 26 per cent were obtained for the ITED standardization. Similar discrepancies appear for other portions of the sample. It is not the reviewer's contention that these discrepancies mean that the normative sample is poor. Had the manual simply described the sample obtained in objective fashion, there would probably be little cause to comment. It is because the manual places the stress it does, with implicit claims, that the discrepancies become noteworthy.

What of validity, that most central quality of a test? Validity of the ITED, we are told, cannot be described on any quantitative, objective basis. The tests are declared, however, to have predictive guidance value; the demonstration of predictive usefulness does call for evaluation, by validity coefficients or similar evidence against the criteria which the tests purportedly predict. In the Manual for the School Administrator, no coefficients appear; nor are any to be found in the Manual for Teachers and Counselors. In the latter, there is the statement that the composite score serves quite well as a predictor of academic success as measured by school marks, and reference is made to "studies summarized in Part III of the Manual for the School Administrator." But studies are *not* summarized in the manual referred to—at least, not in the 1962 edition made available to the reviewer. Instead, one is again referred—this time to a special bulletin, Using the Iowa Tests of Educational Development for College Planning.

The latter bulletin reports validity coefficients for the composite score against freshman performance in a number of colleges; most of the coefficients reported are very respectable. (The presence of standard deviation data for some of the studies is most welcome.) The validity coefficients suggest, as one should expect from a battery of such length, that the composite score is a good predictor of college grades. The relationship of ITED twelfth grade composite and quantitative thinking scores to College Board scores is also reported, and is appreciable (r = .80 to .87). No data from earlier grade (more useful) administrations of the ITED are cited. The bulletin notes that ITED provides limited discrimination above SAT scores of 550. This is perhaps not unexpected, since ITED is presumably aimed at average students, not only the college-bound. At the same time, the usefulness of the ITED for counseling with respect to the more selective colleges is accordingly limited.

One section of the bulletin which should be of appreciable interest to counselors of college-bound students presents the ITED profiles of high school students who subsequently were graduated from college in various major fields; within each field, separate profiles are shown for students who earned "A," "B," and "C" averages. Though limited to Iowa colleges, and though some of the n's are inevitably small, the follow-up study as a whole is very much a noteworthy contribution. One cannot help but wish that here, since means and standard deviations for the separate tests are reported and criterion grades were obviously at hand, validity coefficients had also been computed; they have not.

This kind of failure to present relevant data, even when these have clearly been available, typifies the program. It is well-nigh impossible to understand why more information concerning the tests and their use does not appear in a comprehensive manual. Millions of students have taken these tests in recent years; opportunities for extensive research are practically built into the reporting services offered to the schools. Why, one wonders, have these opportunities been so neglected? Why are there not long tables of validity coefficients for each of the tests against appropriate criteria? Why are there not test-retest data from successive administrations—the schools are urged to test the same students four times during their high school years. Where are the tables of intercorrelation with other tests? Where is the evidence that sufficient growth occurs in the abilities measured by these tests to justify urging schools to duplicate testing year after year?

The *Iowa Tests of Educational Development* are among the most widely sold tests. According to the publisher's announcements, over a million and a half high school students take this battery each year. The very size of the program emphasizes the obligation of the authors and the publisher to provide superior tests, complete documentation of psychometric characteristics, substantiation of claims, and a body of research data consistent with such widespread usage. Too much of this obligation is unfulfilled.

Because the *Iowa Tests of Educational Development* include three reading tests, and because there is absence of evidence that full-length versions have more to offer than class period versions, this reviewer feels the battery is inefficient. Nevertheless, a school system may deem what is measured by the tests (as distinguished from what is claimed for them) is worth obtaining as testimony of certain kinds of achievement; in that case, administration of the battery once during a student's career would be warranted. Until evidence is presented that noteworthy gains occur from one year to the next, the reviewer believes that expenditure for retesting is wasteful; the time and money might better be devoted to testing for other abilities, aptitude or achievement, which will yield new and useful information.

ADDENDUM. In late February 1964, several months after the above review had been submitted to the editor, the publishers made available a revised Manual for the School Administrator, dated December 1963. The revised manual contains a more satisfactory discussion of the topic of validity (except for cavalier treatment of "concurrent" validity), but the evidence offered to document validity of the ITED is still most disappointingly meager, especially in view of the extraordinary wealth of opportunity to do and report studies of this characteristic. Means and standard deviations are still conspicuous by their absence from all tables in the manual; thus, the interpretation of tables of reliability, intercorrelation, and correlation with scholastic aptitude tests remains ambiguous. Tables reporting reliability data are similar to those presented earlier, and subject to much the same criticism. The discussion of the standardization population differs from the earlier discussion; it is more elaborate, but no more satisfactory. In the circumstances, the reviewer is not impelled to modify appreciably the general conclusions represented in the original review.

For reviews by J. Murray Lee and Stephen Wiseman of Form Y-3S and earlier forms, see 5:17; for a review by Eric F. Gardner of earlier forms, see 4:17; for reviews by Henry Chauncey, Gustav J. Froehlich, and Lavone A. Hanna, see 3:12. For reviews of separate tests, see 579, 876, and 969.

[15]

***Metropolitan Achievement Tests.** Grades 1.5, 2, 3–4, 5–6, 7–9, 9–12; 1931–64; IBM and MRC for grades 5–12; 6 levels; subtests for grades 2–9 in reading, for grades 3–9 in arithmetic, for grades 5–12 in science and social studies, and for grades 9–12 in mathematics and language available as separates; interpretive manual ('62, 121 pages) for *a–e;* interpretive manual ('64, c1962–64, 16 pages) for *f;* individual profile ('60, 1 page) for each level except *f;* profile ('63, 2 pages) for *f;* profile directions ('60, 2 pages) for *a–e;* cumulative record card ['61, 1 page] for *a–e;* 70¢ per 35 individual profiles; $2 per 35 cumulative record cards; $1.20 per interpretive manual for *a–e* (interpretive manual for *f* included in price of tests); $8 per 100 MRC answer sheets (grades 5–12 only); $1.60 per set of hand scoring stencils for MRC answer sheets; $2 per 100 sets of Harbor answer cards (scored only by Measurement Research Center, Inc.); postage extra; IBM and MRC machine scoring services available; Walter N. Durost, (for *a–e*) Harold H. Bixler, Gertrude H. Hildreth, Kenneth W. Lund, and J. Wayne Wrightstone, and (*f* only) William H. Evans, James D. Leake, Howard A. Bowman, Clarke Cosgrove, and John G. Read; Harcourt, Brace & World, Inc. *

a) PRIMARY I BATTERY. Grade 1.5; 1931–62; 4 scores: word knowledge, word discrimination, reading, arithmetic concepts and skills; Forms A ('60, c1958), B ('59), C ('61), (16 pages); directions for administering ('59, 24 pages); $6.25 per 35 tests; 80¢ per specimen set (without interpretive manual); 85(115) minutes in 4 sessions.

b) PRIMARY 2 BATTERY. Grade 2; 1932–62; 7 scores: word knowledge, word discrimination, reading, spelling, arithmetic (concepts and problem solving, computation, total); Forms A ('60, c1958), B ('59), C ('61), (19 pages); directions for administering ('59, 24 pages); $8 per 35 tests; 80¢ per specimen set (without interpretive manual); 100(125) minutes in 4 sessions.

c) ELEMENTARY BATTERY. Grades 3–4; 1932–62; 9 scores: word knowledge, word discrimination, reading, spelling, language (usage, punctuation and capitalization, total), arithmetic (computation, problem solving and concepts); Forms A ('60, c1958), B ('59), C ('61), D ('62), (19 pages); directions for administering ('59, 19 pages); $8 per 35 tests; 80¢ per specimen set (without interpretive manual); 147(177) minutes in 5 sessions.

d) INTERMEDIATE BATTERY. Grades 5–6; 1932–62; IBM and MRC (except Form DM, IBM only); 2 batteries, 2 editions of each; $1.60 per 35 optional arithmetic worksheets for the machine scorable edition of either battery.

1) *Partial Battery.* 11 scores: word knowledge, reading, spelling, language (usage, parts of speech, punctuation and capitalization, total), language study skills, arithmetic (computation, problem solving and concepts), social studies study skills; 2 editions; directions for administering ('59, 20–24 pages) for each edition; *hand scored edition:* Forms A ('60, c1958), B ('59), C ('61), D ('62), (24 pages); $9 per 35 tests; *machine scorable edition:* Forms AM ('60, c1958), BM ('59), CM ('61), DM ('62), (24 pages); separate answer sheets must be used; $9.80 per 35 tests; $5 per 35 sets of IBM answer sheets; $1 per set of scoring stencils for IBM answer sheets; 80¢ per specimen set (without interpretive manual); 197(227) minutes in 5 sessions.

2) *Complete Battery.* 13 scores: same as for partial battery plus social studies information, science; 2 editions; directions for administering ('59, 20–24 pages) for each edition; *hand scored edition:* Forms A ('60, c1958), B ('59), C ('61), D ('62), (31 pages); $11 per 35 tests; *machine scorable edition:* Forms AM ('60, c1958), BM ('59), CM ('61), DM ('62), (32 pages); separate answer sheets must be used; $12 per 35 tests; $6.75 per 35 sets of IBM answer sheets; $1.40 per set of scoring stencils for IBM answer sheets; $1 per specimen set (without interpretive manual); 237(267) minutes in 5 sessions.

e) ADVANCED BATTERY. Grades 7–9; 1932–62; IBM and MRC (except Form DM, IBM only); 2 batteries, 2 editions of each; $1.60 per 35 optional arithmetic worksheets for the machine scorable edition of either battery.

1) *Partial Battery.* 12 scores: same as for intermediate partial battery plus kinds of sentences under language; 2 editions; details same as for intermediate partial battery except: 207(237) minutes in 5 sessions.

2) *Complete Battery.* 14 scores: same as for intermediate complete battery plus kinds of sentences under language; 2 editions; details same as for intermediate complete battery except: 247(277) minutes in 5 sessions.

f) HIGH SCHOOL BATTERY. Grades 9–12; 1962–64; 11 scores: reading, spelling, language, language study skills, social studies (study skills, vocabulary, information), mathematics (computation and concepts, analysis and problem solving), science (concepts and understandings, information); IBM and MRC; Forms AM ('62, 32 pages), BM ('63, 30 pages); directions for administering ('62, 15 pages); norms booklet ('62, 8 pages); profile ('63, 2 pages); separate answer sheets must be used; $10.50 per 35 tests; $5.85 per 35 sets of IBM answer sheets; $1.20 per set of scoring stencils for IBM answer sheets; $1 per specimen set (with interpretive manual); 282(316) minutes.

REFERENCES

1–3. See 40:1189.
4–10. See 3:13.
11–20. See 4:18.
21. NEMZEK, CLAUDE L., AND DE HEUS, JOHN H. "The Prediction of Academic and Non-Academic Marks in Junior High Schools." *Sch & Soc* 50:670–2 N 18 '39. * (*PA* 14:1598)
22. DUROST, WALTER N., AND PRESCOTT, GEORGE A. "An Improved Method of Comparing a Capacity Measure With an Achievement Measure at the Elementary School Level." *Ed & Psychol Meas* 12:741–55 w '52. * (*PA* 27:6151)
23. TILTON, J. W. "Factors Related to Ability-Profile Unevenness." *Ed & Psychol Meas* 13:467–73 au '53. * (*PA* 28:4951)
24. MILLER, VELMA J. *A Critical Analysis of Standardized Vocabulary Tests to Determine Those Most Valid for Use With the Macmillan Readers.* Master's thesis, Bowling Green State University (Bowling Green, Ohio), 1954.
25. SMITH, OTTO BAMBER. *Predicting Grade Success of High School Students in Radio and Drafting.* Master's thesis, Alabama Polytechnic Institute (Auburn, Ala.), 1955.
26. TAIT, ARTHUR T. "A Comparative Study of Five Major Achievement Tests." *Calif J Ed Res* 6:99–106 My '55. * (*PA* 30:1633)
27. SCOTT, HELEN E., AND WILSON, GUY M. "A Critical Examination of Spelling Words in One Speller in Relation to Four Standardized Tests in Spelling." *J Ed Res* 49:331–43 Ja '56. * (*PA* 31:3658)
28. BARRY, BARBARA A. *A Comparison of the Metropolitan Achievement Test and the Iowa Tests of Basic Skills in Grade Four in a Typical New England Town.* Master's thesis, Boston University (Boston, Mass.), 1958.
29. SHACHOY, GORDON R. "A Study of the Metropolitan Achievement Test Results of Educable Girls in Residence at the Rome State School." *Am J Mental Def* 62:622–4 Ja '58. *
30. NORTH, ROBERT D. "Trial Use of the 1959 Edition of the Metropolitan Achievement Tests in Some ERB Member Schools." *Ed Rec B* 74:61–74 Jl '59. * (*PA* 35:1288)
31. NORTH, ROBERT D. "An Appraisal of Independent School Results on the Primary Levels of the Metropolitan Achievement Tests, 1959 Edition." *Ed Rec B* 77:55–66 Jl '60. *
32. JUNGEBLUT, ANN. "An Analysis of the 1960 Fall Independent School Program Results on the Metropolitan Achievement Tests, 1959 Edition, Form A." *Ed Rec B* 78:61–7 F '61. *
33. TAYLOR, EDWARD A., AND CRANDALL, JAMES H. "A Study of the 'Norm-Equivalence' of Certain Tests Approved for the California State Testing Program." *Calif J Ed Res* 13:186–92 S '62. *
34. FINLEY, CARMEN J. "A Comparison of the California Achievement Test, Metropolitan Achievement Test and Iowa Test of Basic Skills." *Calif J Ed Res* 14:79–88 Mr '63. * (*PA* 38:1422)
35. MITCHELL, BLYTHE C. "A Comparison of the Achievement-Intelligence Relationship for Pupils With That for School Systems." *J Ed Res* 57:172–80 D '63. *
36. WEINER, MAX, AND TOBIAS, SIGMUND. "Chance Factors in the Interpretation of Group Administered Multiple-Choice Tests." *Personnel & Guid J* 41:435–7 Ja '63. * (*PA* 39:1771)

PAUL L. DRESSEL, *Director of Institutional Research, Michigan State University, East Lansing, Michigan.* [Review of the High School Battery.]

THE TESTS AND TEST ITEMS. Test 1, Reading, consists of four reading selections followed by a number of questions testing several abilities, including that of determining the appropriate meaning of a word in a given context. The reviewer found no difficulty in most of these items in selecting the right meaning prior to reading the selection. Some students, however, might not know the meaning of the words tested and have to infer meaning from the context—one aspect of the objective.

On Test 2, Spelling, the student marks spellings as correct, incorrect, or don't know. He is also asked to spell correctly on a worksheet the words he believes to be misspelled, although there is no adjustment for this in scoring. Here, as elsewhere, the student is given no intimation as to whether he will be penalized if he guesses instead of using the "don't know" response.

Test 3, Language, Parts B2 and C, and Test 4, Language Study Skills, present from seven to nine lettered alternative answers to following items. The answer sheet contains five responses including "Right," three responses designated by letters referring to the initial list, and the ubiquitous DK (don't know). If the item is thought not to be right, anyone not possessing a photographic memory must either check each of the three alternatives by looking for and rereading the lettered response, or reread the full statements of alternatives until the presumed right one is found and then check to see if its lettered designation appears on the answer sheet. Certainly there are procedures which make more effective use of time even though they may require more space.

Test 5, Part A, Reading Maps, includes several items which seem to have but slight relation to the map provided. For example, a student with any recollection of locations would hardly need a map to determine the direction of Tokyo from Moscow. Surely no map is needed to decide what direction a submarine must go upon leaving the North Pole!

In Test 5, Part B, Reading Tables, Charts and Graphs, some questions about change or increase may cause alert students some difficulty since the wording does not make clear whether absolute or percentage change is to be the basis for the answer. A series of three questions about stock quotations waste the test taker's time because the possible answers are not in alphabetical order as they are in the quotations.

No special comments are required on any of the other tests. The questions exhibit no unusual features, but they are competently done. Although a large number of specific objectives are listed and tested, the emphasis is clearly on skills and on factual knowledge. As is always the case, individual students lacking specific knowledge might by shrewd guessing arrive at answers, but items carefully constructed to require critical thinking of all students are not to be found. The test content adheres closely to the patterns established in earlier forms of the tests, raising some question as to how the test is updated to keep abreast of new curricular developments.

ADMINISTRATION AND INTERPRETATION. The instructions for giving and scoring the test are detailed and clear; there will be no difficulty in these regards.

The Guide for Interpreting speaks of "curricular validity" and "content validity." Under the first, assurance is given that analyses have been made of current textbooks, courses of study, and formulations of goals of instruction. Under the second, these assurances are reiterated, and the test authors are also reported to have developed a detailed outline or blueprint for each test specifying objectives, content areas or topics, and proportionate emphasis. The blueprints, regrettably, are not exhibited.

Generally, the information given for interpretation is adequate. Much is made of the age-controlled norms which are provided, although, in fact, the norm group differs but little from the total sample. Reference is repeatedly made to norms for college preparatory groups but these were not included, and indeed are apparently not yet available. Test norms are also provided for Otis Gamma IQ's by grade for the age-controlled sample.

TECHNICAL CHARACTERISTICS. Extensive data on item analyses, test reliabilities, and test intercorrelations are provided. Reliabilities are generally adequate except for Test 9, Mathematical Analysis and Problem Solving, which yields only a reliability of .77 to .78 for Form AM and .70 to .84 for Form BM. This test contains fewer items (30) than any other test. The test should be lengthened if reliability cannot be increased by more careful selection of items, or possibly Test 8, Mathematical Computation and Concepts, and Test 9 should be combined to yield a more satisfactory reliability. Indeed, the question may be raised more generally as to whether separate scores and norms should be used for each of the 11 tests. Test 4, Language Study Skills, with a reliability of .79 to .83 and Test 5, Social Studies Study Skills, with a reliability of .79 to .87 are intercorrelated to the extent, .66. Can these, then, be regarded as really distinctive? Like questions could be raised with other combinations.

ITEM VALIDATION TECHNIQUES. According to the authors, one of the criteria for item selection was "the ability of an item to distinguish between students at successive grade levels." Such a statement implies that items were so selected as to insure a greater percentage of correct responses as the grade level is increased. Superficially, one might conclude that such an increase is consistent with the objectives of the test and accept the technique without further investigation. However, several problems worthy of consideration are introduced by the use of this technique. First, items of mere recall of specific factual information that might be emphasized in grade 9 but not used and forgotten by grade 12 students would not be included in the test. On the whole, this is a beneficial effect. The effect of a lack of a common sequence of topics in any field of study in the high schools is not entirely clear, but a reasonable conclusion would seem to be that this technique would tend to eliminate some of the material commonly covered in the high school but not presented in a generally accepted sequence. A study of the test on Mathematical Computation and Concepts reveals either that the authors have attempted to circumvent this problem by the inclusion of many elementary concepts and a few more advanced concepts from algebra and trigonometry, or that this pattern is a result of this selection criterion.

Another problem arising as a result of such an item selection technique is the determination of the level of item difficulty to be used. Research has shown that an item difficulty of .50 for uncorrelated items provides the maximum discrimination if the examinees are to be divided into only two groups. The objective of the present battery is to discriminate between grade level as well as achievement levels within grades. Therefore, a rectangular distribution would be preferred instead of a point distribution clustered about a .50 item difficulty level. It appears from the content of the test that a rectangular distribution has been used. It is to be noted, however, that the mean item difficulty on Test 5 for grade 11 is .525 and drops to .518 for grade 12. Thus, the extent to which the selection criterion under discussion was utilized for Test 5 is subject to question.

Again, the content of the mathematics sections reveals that little attention has been given to some of the materials presented in the newer mathematics curricula. Whether items of this sort did not stand up under the criteria of selection or whether they were not even introduced in the tryout materials is uncertain. If the curriculum materials were introduced in the beginning mathematics courses but were not part of the experience of advanced students, the demand for a higher percentage of right answers at advanced grades would operate to eliminate such items.

COMPARISON WITH THE ESSENTIAL HIGH SCHOOL CONTENT BATTERY. The publisher also offers the *Essential High School Content Battery,* published in 1950–51 under the authorship of David P. Harry and Walter N. Durost. The Essential battery yields 4 subscores, mathematics, science, social studies, and English, in contrast to the 11 scores of the Metropolitan battery. In fact, however, the two batteries are comparable in design and content. The use of 11 tests for which norms have been determined instead of 4 will provide the user with greater opportunity for analysis of achievement within more specific areas of study, such as spelling achievement compared to reading achievement. However, as has been noted earlier, this apparent additional information may be misleading because of high intercorrelations among some of the additional sections.

The reading test in the Metropolitan battery utilizes four reading selections in contrast to one reading selection in the Essential battery. Vocabulary testing is interspersed throughout the reading test of the Metropolitan battery instead of in a separate section in the Essential test. Also included in the Essential battery is a section on literature acquaintance which does not appear in the present battery. Language usage, capitalization and punctuation, and spelling are covered in a comparable manner in both batteries.

The social studies section in the Metropolitan battery contains a test of study skills, one on social studies vocabulary, and a social studies information test. The Essential social studies test consists of 10 parts with a total of 90 items. The social studies sections of the two batteries are comparable both in content and design. The test on map reading, previously quite inadequate, has been somewhat improved in the Metropolitan battery.

If, indeed, a function of testing which merits

consideration is the improvement of instruction and the curriculum then it must necessarily follow that changes in instruction and the curriculum should be reflected in the design and content of the tests. A comparison of the mathematics test in the Essential battery and the post-Sputnik era Metropolitan battery reveals striking similarities between the two tests. Each test includes just one item on trigonometry, several items dealing with problems of percentages, proportions, operations with fractions, both common and decimal, mensuration, geometric theorems, algebraic operations, and some items from elementary analytic geometry. There is little difference in the structure or content of the two mathematics tests. Apparently, no attempt has been made to include concepts from new mathematics curricula such as developed by the School Mathematics Study Group, the University of Illinois Commission on School Mathematics, and other groups which have attempted revisions of the high school mathematics curriculum.

The science test in the Metropolitan battery represents a change in terminology from the Essential battery but the changes made are quite superficial in that the same basic content is included in each with the Metropolitan test utilizing present-day terminology.

Differences exist between the two batteries in the approach to an interpretation and use of results. The newer test provides age-controlled norms along with grade norms while the older test utilizes school norms as well as individual norms. Norms are also provided in the Essential battery for purposes of comparing achievement of students who are taking academic and scientific courses with those students taking commercial and general courses. If it could be assumed that each test adequately covers the curriculum of the high schools and if it could be further assumed that there exists a curriculum common to all high schools then the use of school norms would be justifiable. In light of the great diversity of curricular organization and content, it would appear that the use of school norms results in superficial if not misleading comparisons. The decision of the authors of the Metropolitan battery to discontinue the use of school norms and to rely upon individual norms for an interpretation of results is a judicious one. Otherwise, the current test cannot be regarded as a significant improvement over the earlier one.

SUMMARY. The tests of the High School Battery of the *Metropolitan Achievement Tests* probably do reflect the traditional curricular emphases of many secondary schools and they fairly adequately test the basic skills and knowledge which they undertook to cover. Their greatest utility would seem to be for guidance or as a general survey of competencies at the beginning of the secondary school program. Neither in content level nor in the range of cognitive objectives are the tests adequate to provide direction to secondary school teachers in improvement of instruction and the curriculum. Either the *Iowa Tests of Educational Development* or the *Sequential Tests of Educational Progress* would be more suitable to the latter purpose as well as serving the survey and guidance functions.

HENRY S. DYER, *Vice President, Educational Testing Service, Princeton, New Jersey.*

A comprehensive achievement test battery may reflect in its content either what the curriculum ought to be or what it is. In the case of the *Metropolitan Achievement Tests,* the publisher appears to have been at considerable pains to turn out a series of tests reflecting what he thinks the curriculum is, or perhaps *was* during the period that the tests were in preparation.

According to the Manual for Interpreting, "The authors reviewed expert pronouncements concerning the goals of elementary [and secondary] education, current research on the nature of essential skills, such as reading and the work-study skills, representative courses of study, and several widely-used textbook series in the various branches." Some evidence of the extent of this background work is provided in the Manual for Interpreting, especially with respect to the content sources of tests of word knowledge and spelling. References to the source materials for the other tests are somewhat vague: e.g., "In preparing the content for the Social Studies Information Test and the Science Test, exhaustive analyses were made of courses of study in terms of content as well as of purposes or aims." The "current research on the nature of essential skills" is presumably covered, for the pre-high school tests, by 21 titles in the appendix concerned with reading and another 6 titles concerned with arithmetic. The high school Guide for Interpreting provides no comparable information.

Be this as it may, one can probably assume with some confidence that a reasonably serious effort was made to determine the kinds of learning materials to which pupils are most commonly exposed and to shape the tests around these materials. In the tests for the three upper levels (i.e., grades 5 through 12), the outcome of this effort is disconcerting to the present reviewer. It suggests that the schools are still putting a massive emphasis on the rote learning of information and skills and paying little heed to the development of those more complex cognitive processes normally associated with the maturing mind.

In the three batteries designed for grades 1 to 4, the prime emphasis is, as it must be, on the basic skills involved in reading and arithmetic. In each of the three batteries for grades 5 to 12, however, this reviewer could find no more than one fourth of the items (and this is probably stretching a point) which make any demands on a pupil's ability to reason and solve problems. Two thirds of the remainder call for the simplest kind of factual recall and the rest for demonstration of such routine skills as are to be found in spelling, punctuation, and computation.

Judging from the item content of the *Metropolitan Achievement Tests,* one would suppose that the present curricular ferment in mathematics, the sciences, the social studies, and English has had no effect whatever on actual practice in the schools. Perhaps this is so, but in view of the test publication dates, it is hard to know for sure whether it is the school curriculum or the test battery that is out of date. Because of the inevitable time lag in curriculum reform, there are no doubt still a great many schools, probably a majority, that will find the content validity of the Metropolitan tests sufficient for their purposes. In brief, these are conservative tests aimed at a conservative curriculum where such notions as "process" and "the art of discovery" have not yet contaminated teaching practice.

Given this conceptual framework for the tests, most of the items seem likely to contribute reasonably well to the measurement of the narrow kind of achievement called for. Some of the item types show an inventiveness on the part of the testmakers that one might wish had been allowed to extend more deeply into the basic structure of the tests.

The format of the items varies considerably depending on the nature of the material and on whether a separate answer sheet is to be used. In the five pre-high school batteries, the authors have used short answer items in preference to multiple choice items whenever feasible (e.g., in arithmetic computation questions). In those circumstances where this mode of response is not feasible, they have tried to retain some of the advantages of the short answer form by having the pupil supplement his multiple choice response with a written answer that is not scored. For example, after indicating that a word is misspelled or a given usage is grammatically wrong, the pupil writes down what he conceives to be the correct spelling or the correct usage. This technique may have value for the teacher who wishes to dig into the response data for purposes of individual diagnosis. Whether it adds anything to the validity of the response that is actually scored remains unknown.

In the reading comprehension questions for the later grades, and to some extent for the earlier grades as well, the authors make a deliberate attempt to get at a number of the specific elements in the reading process which have been identified in factor studies: ability to recognize the main idea or purpose of a reading passage, ability to draw correct inferences from the material presented, ability to perceive and understand details, ability to recognize the correct meaning of words in the context of the passage. This attempt is laudable. Its execution, however, strikes this reviewer as more than necessarily wooden. There tends to be a sameness in the phrasing of the item stems as one proceeds from one set of questions to the next. Over and over again one reads, "The best name for this story is....," "One can infer from this article that....," "In this story the word xxx means," etc. The danger from this repetitiveness arises not so much from the tedium it is likely to bring to the testing situation as from the notion it is likely to implant in the minds of pupils and teachers that effective reading is something one achieves by following a standard formula. This is not to say that the reading tests are inadequate for differentiating the capable from the incapable reader. They probably do this very well. They might have done it better if more imagination had been brought to the phrasing of the questions.

A new kind of reading exercise is introduced

into the high school battery. It is one that requires the pupil to remember as well as to interpret what he reads. It is not known how much this exercise adds to the validity of the reading section as a whole. On its face, however, the exercise makes sense as a sample of the kind of reading behavior normally expected of students. One wonders why the same sort of test exercise should not be introduced at the earlier grades.

The amount of information reported on the statistical characteristics of the items in these tests seems far from adequate. Although it is claimed that "for most subtests, an item discrimination index was....computed," no data summarizing these indices are given for the pre-high school batteries. One such table giving "mean item validities" for the two high school forms is included, but even here the numbers are given without any description of how they were derived or how the sample of 372 cases was drawn. They are therefore meaningless. Similarly, although it is stated that data on item difficulties were collected for each grade, the only such data reported are for the high school tests and one form of the intermediate level arithmetic subtest. Statistical information of this sort, while certainly not in itself sufficient for assessing the quality of the tests, is nevertheless fundamental if one is to have any idea of the degree to which the individual items are contributing to the measurement process. The failure to summarize such item statistics as are available and to indicate precisely where they are not available is unfortunate.

The data on the reliability of the tests appear adequate, though the form in which they are reported for the five pre-high school batteries leaves something to be desired. The Guide for Interpreting, which describes the characteristics of the high school battery, carries a table that is something of a model of completeness and interpretability. The Manual for Interpreting, which describes the characteristics of the five pre-high school batteries, carries a similar table, but this latter table omits three kinds of information required for interpretation of the reliability coefficients, namely, the raw score range, the mean, and the standard deviation for each of the samples used in estimating the reliabilities. If the publisher was aware of the need for this kind of information in the high school manual, how did he come to overlook it in the pre-high school manual?

Nevertheless, on the strength of such data as are presented, it seems reasonable to suppose that most of the tests are adequately reliable for the measurement of individuals. Some appear to fall a bit short, however, particularly the test of "Mathematical Analysis and Problem Solving" in the High School Battery, the test of social studies skills in the Intermediate Battery, and certain of the language subtests in the Advanced Battery. The low reliabilities reported for some of the subtest scores prompt the question whether it is wise to encourage their use at all. The fact that they are there and that space on the report forms is provided for entering them is more than likely to lure teachers into the illusion that the tests have more individual diagnostic value than the uncertainty of the subscores warrants.

Much thought and effort apparently went into the development of usable national norms for these tests, but like all such norms, there can be no guarantee that they mean anything. The following quotation from the Guide for Interpreting exemplifies the usual problem:

> In accord with these specifications, the country was divided into eight census districts and invitations were issued to communities randomly selected from within these districts. A total of 29 school systems in 19 states *accepted the invitation* * [italics added].

It is inconceivable to this reviewer that any norms sample, however large or diverse, which depends upon the willingness of the participants to "accept the invitation" can be in any way representative of the national population of school children or school systems. And no statistical finagling whatever can make up for the unknown bias. It is difficult for this reviewer to understand why test publishers in general continue to waste so much time, money, and ingenuity on the impossible problem of trying to produce "national norms." The most that such efforts can yield is a convenient but arbitrary scale for rendering the scores across tests more or less comparable. One requires a highly varied reproducible sample for this purpose, but it is not necessary that the sample should be "accurately representative of the national school population," even if it could be. It is high time that test publishers ceased perpetuating the myth that the so called "grade equivalent scale" has any useful normative meaning. The very notion of a "grade" in any general sense is a glaring example of the fallacy of misplaced concreteness. Accordingly, such statements as the following can only mislead the test user into untenable comparisons.

> Stanines and percentile ranks are particularly appropriate for comparison of a pupil's score with the scores of other pupils of similar grade placement * Grade equivalents are especially appropriate for the interpretation of class, school, and system averages.

It is to the credit of the publishers of the *Metropolitan Achievement Tests* that they urge on the test user the desirability of developing his own local stanines and percentile ranks. The advice would have been more effective if the notion "national" stanines and percentiles had been avoided.

The Manual for Interpreting, which accompanies the pre-high school batteries, is a compendious document. It contains much shrewd advice for organizing test data for effective use. As indicated above, however, it fails to report some of the basic kinds of data needed for the evaluation of the tests. It also encourages the reader to commit such ancient mistakes as that of comparing a student's "capacity," as measured by an intelligence test, with his "achievement" as measured by this achievement battery. The Guide for Interpreting, which accompanies the high school tests, is less than one sixth the size of the Manual for Interpreting; it is short on the shrewd advice; it contains more useful data for evaluating the tests; but it encourages some of the same fallacious interpretations of scores. Both booklets appear to this reviewer to be attempts at an impossible compromise. On the one hand, they contain much of the true doctrine of measurement; on the other hand, they tend to tell the test consumer what he expects to hear, even when such expectations rest upon misconceptions of the possible.

WARREN G. FINDLEY, *Professor of Education, and Coordinator of Educational Research, University of Georgia, Athens, Georgia.*

The 1959–62 series of this battery is a direct lineal descendant of earlier editions, dating back as far as 1931. This means, of course, that it shares their virtues and defects in various measures. Since this reviewer had the privilege of reviewing the 1947 series at some length in an earlier yearbook, he will not repeat comments made there in full, but will attempt to comment on new features and changes.

The most notable new feature is the addition of a High School Battery for grades 9–12. In keeping with a trend among all major publishers, Harcourt, Brace and World has now undertaken to provide continuous measurement from grade 1 through grade 12 of progress in mastering basic skills and common learnings. The pattern of tests in the High School Battery is a natural sequel to the evolving pattern of tests for the skills and areas of substantive knowledge that characterizes the forms at successive levels from primary up. This resolution of the problem of providing useful continuity of measurement into senior high school lies between the extremes represented by the uniform pattern of tests, time limits, and numbers of items characteristic of the *Sequential Tests of Educational Progress,* and the abrupt shift from an elementary school pattern to a distinctly different secondary school pattern characteristic of the *Iowa Tests of Basic Skills* (or the *SRA Achievement Tests*) and the *Iowa Tests of Educational Development.* In the Metropolitan tests continuity is achieved in the broad areas of language arts, mathematics, and, for grades 5–12, science and social studies. It is to be regretted that norms are not provided for the total scores for each of these large blocks of the curriculum, particularly at the high school level. The authors may protest that the shifting composites are sufficiently different to produce uncertainty about the comparability of such curriculum area scores on the forms at successive levels. Yet, this is done for the area of language usage at all levels at which that composite is tested. Moreover, scores on these large blocks would consistently meet the criterion of a reliability of .91 at a single grade level, while the shorter component tests have reliabilities generally in the range .80 to .88 at the high school level and one or more reported scores at each level fail to meet the higher standard.

The manual for the 1947 series was hailed for its clarity, completeness, and direct usefulness. The interpretative manual for the present series is even better, approaching in quality and scope a textbook in educational measurement, with particular application to the *Metropolitan Achievement Tests.* It may well be prescribed reading for all who will use the tests at any level.

The chapter headings in the table of contents indicate the scope and quality: Metropolitan Achievement Tests, Their Development and

Purpose; Giving Metropolitan Achievement Tests; Interpreting the Scores on Metropolitan Achievement Tests; Using Metropolitan Achievement Tests for the Improvement of Instruction; Validity of Metropolitan Achievement Tests; The What and Why of Reliability; Comparing Capacity (School Learning Ability) and Achievement; Item Analysis as a Means of Improving Instruction; Identifying and Dealing with the Educationally Disabled Child in a Skills Area; Planning and Administering a School Testing Program; Using Metropolitan Achievement Tests in Administration and Supervision; and Using Metropolitan Achievement Tests in Guidance.

The discussion of interpreting grade scores and that of relating capacity and achievement are particularly well done. A wholesome caution pervades all of the explanation. A constructive new note is the suggestion that batteries be used flexibly, at higher or lower grade levels than normally indicated, whenever a system, school, or class is markedly superior or inferior.

The High School Battery depends largely on this manual for interpretation but has its own brief manual containing interpretative data especially related to that battery and its development. In view of this interdependence of batteries and interpretative manuals, one may look forward to a single integrated manual when next the series is revised. Minor frustrations, like repeated reference in the high school interpretative manual to a nonexistent Table 3 in the Booklet of Norms, can be resolved at the same time.

The stanine as an index for describing the relative accomplishments of individual pupils is persuasively presented. (Stanines are scores reported on a scale from 1 to 9 with mean 5 and standard deviation 2.) Anyone who has taught educational measurement will testify that both percentiles and *T*-scores, as two-digit numbers, lend themselves to confusion with per cent right on a test, which stanines avoid. And stanines have the further advantage of representing a range rather than a point. Of course, this range is arbitrary, but one stanine point equals the standard error of measurement of a score with a reliability of .75, and is about one and a half times the standard error of measurement of a score with a reliability of .90, for the standardization group. So we can say with confidence that any individual student's true level of accomplishment will not be more than one stanine point higher or lower than found for him in each subject. In fact, if we adopt the practice of adding plus or minus signs to stanine scores as we do to letter grades, we can say confidently of stanines followed by plus that the student's true level is at that stanine or the one above, while for stanines followed by minus we can say with equal confidence that the student's true level is at that stanine or the one below. Conversely, as pointed out in the manual, we can say that differences of 2 stanines or more between two individuals in the same subject or between two subjects for the same individual are substantial and should be taken seriously, while differences of 1 stanine point or less may be regarded as negligible.

Those who are unhappy about the too ready use of a single measure of general mental ability as evidence of learning capacity in all subjects, as is this reviewer, will be pleased with the complementary emphasis on "composite prognostic scores," based entirely on achievement scores or including a measure of general mental ability as one factor in the composite. Those composites that are based on achievement scores alone serve the additional function of providing measures of general achievement as of the date of testing, measures shown in the manual to predict similar composites a year later with a correlation of about .90, as compared with a correlation of only .80 between widely used group measures of general mental ability given a year apart.

Finally, the discussion of planning the school testing program presents briefly, but clearly, a plan of administrative organization, an emphasis on annual fall testing of achievement, and in-service training arrangements that should be generally helpful. It fits well this reviewer's experience in a large city system.

It is a tribute to the functional organization of the accessory materials that the norms for interpreting the test results are built into the interpretative materials themselves—class record sheet, class analysis sheet, individual profile chart, directions for scoring, and directions for administering—so, except at the high school level, there is no separate booklet of norms to which one need refer. The various types of norms are all there, but they are where they are needed in the interpretative process, and their sound use is clearly propounded in the basic Manual for Interpreting. Adequate modern normative sampling procedures underlie the norms presented.

The criticism of earlier editions for stressing outmoded instructional objectives is largely met by this present series. In fact, this reviewer is prepared to reverse earlier judgments that this series is limited in this way. The change has come about to a large extent because instructional practice generally has moved forward during the decade since the 1947 series so that the avowed intent to "insure the validity of the tests by basing them on thoroughgoing analyses of the textbooks, courses of study, and expert formulations of the goals of instruction" in the various subject areas has had the effect of producing tests in keeping with current best thought regarding objectives. In 1947, for example, when the test was similarly designed to reflect common instructional practice, it was possible to criticize the series for failure to measure important study skills; in 1959–62, the study skills are not only represented adequately, but are subdivided functionally to associate dictionary use and knowledge of sources of information with language arts, while reading of maps and interpretation of charts, tables, and graphs are put with the social studies.

This new look is evident at other levels and in other areas. The larger pages (8⅜ by 10⅞ inches) and attractive use of color provide a distinctive format for each level. At the primary levels, evident effort has been put into making the test experience a happy one for the pupils and the results directly useful to the classroom teacher. Pupils are invited to color balloons, balls, or tops on the front cover before beginning the test. A word discrimination test, in addition to a word knowledge test, adds to the analytical value of the results in planning reading instruction and in identifying individual pupils warranting detailed diagnosis. The test of arithmetic concepts and skills is primarily oral and pictorial, requiring only the reading and writing of single digits in simple problems of addition and subtraction in the Primary 1 Battery, and the reading of simple sentences in only 5 out of 72 items in the Primary 2 Battery. Thereby the results give functional evidence of arithmetic competence uncontaminated by reading, happily unlike arithmetic tests in primary batteries of so many earlier tests.

So far as competences in arithmetic are measured at successively higher levels, the authors appear content with establishing the fact that items employed in the machine scorable tests result in measures that are valid equivalents of free response tests. Although the separate arithmetic part scores reported for the Elementary, Intermediate, and Advanced Batteries are quite reliable, composites would consistently meet the .91 criterion even for the High School Battery, where the part score reliabilities are only .70 to .89. Of course, the user may strike an average of grade equivalents for the two scores at each of the three levels first mentioned and may average standard scores at all levels, but this is effectively discouraged by failure to leave a space for it on the class record sheet. For sectioning and guidance, there is a need for such composites, even though the instructional value of subscores should be preserved.

Reading is now measured at all levels in convenient, natural multiple choice form, from the level of sentences chosen to be descriptive of pictured objects, actions, or situations at the Primary 1 level to progressively longer and more abstract paragraphs and articles followed by questions of content, intent, and inference. A balance is struck between pleasure- and study-type reading, and the study-type reading is evenly distributed over the subject fields. One is tempted to protest the use in the primary tests of repetitive simple sentences, after the manner of primary readers. Beyond this, the reading materials tend to be neither more nor less interesting than those the examinee will encounter in normal reading.

Spelling, which first appears in the Primary 2 Battery, involves spelling in response to dictation at that level and in the Elementary Battery. An interesting objective adaptation used at the three higher levels requires the examinee to mark each key word (presented in context) R for right, W for wrong, and DK for don't know, and then to put down his corrected spelling for each word he has marked as incorrectly spelled. He is scored only for his objective R and W responses, but the added list of corrected spellings helps the teacher analyze his learning problems. The possibility of extending this objective approach to lower levels might well be explored, with the examiner reading each item aloud while the examinee follows the text in his test booklet.

This would virtually eliminate the influence of the examinee's general reading competence but leave the exercises in the natural form of recognizing and correcting wrong spellings.

This reviewer would question the use of the DK response option in the spelling and several of the language usage sections of the tests. The test publishers report that extensive studies show that scores earned on this item type are highly correlated with scores made on free response or other natural item types appropriate to measurement in each subarea. The fact remains that testwise examinees who reject the DK option entirely because it cannot possibly earn credit for knowledge will have a systematic advantage over examinees who accept this as a natural alternative when they do not feel sure of the correctness of R or W as a response. An unrepresentative sample of six elementary principals yielded the information that in two of the schools the pupils had been taught by their teachers to disregard the DK option. This feature of the item type seems needlessly to introduce into upper level scores for spelling and language the type of systematic distortion that leads us to advise against use of scores from interest inventories in selection procedures. Granted that the item type under discussion does not permit the examinee to falsify the record by favorable self-report of his knowledge of particular items—he still DK's—yet by adopting a response set that systematically rejects this response he cumulatively records right responses his more forthright competitor voluntarily denies himself and earns a spuriously high score for his knowledge when the test is scored simply for number of correct responses. It would be safer and simpler to offer only R and W and score R-W.

Language usage is measured first in the Elementary Battery, intended for general use in grades 3 and 4. At each level on through the High School Battery, the separately measured skills of (*a*) knowing correct usage and (*b*) applying accepted rules of punctuation and capitalization, are included in a total language score, being joined by various other special emphases at successive levels, such as "parts of speech," "kinds of sentences," "grammar," "understanding correct usage," and "sentence style and structure." These eclectic combinations are evidently designed to help teachers evaluate instructional outcomes stressed at different school levels, but their variability is further complicated by an annoying shifting of sequence so that, for example, "Punctuation and Capitalization" is Part B, C, B, and A at successive battery levels. The authors appear to vacillate between considerations of "naturalness," which is allowed to dictate the format of the spelling test, and "separate measurement with unnatural, uncapitalized content" in measuring capitalization and punctuation. This reviewer feels a better purpose would be served if "naturalness" were allowed to predominate throughout and all types of usage errors—except spelling which testmakers generally find more efficient to measure separately—were to be spread through continuous copy as in other published batteries. Analysis of error types can then be accomplished by special procedures for teachers to apply to group the item results, as in the manner of the Scoreze answer sheet available with the *California Achievement Tests*, or item classifications given in manuals for other batteries. If the trends in teaching English move further in the direction of stressing structure, a next edition of this test might well include two chief subscores, "correct and effective expression" and "understanding of language structure."

Meanwhile, we must note that even our most "natural" procedures in this area are pale substitutes for measurement of the true art of writing. The College Entrance Examination Board's English composition test often contains "interlinear" exercises, exercises that consist of substantial selections of garbled prose on which the examinee is asked to indicate any needed corrections and that the scorer evaluates in terms of a predetermined key, disregarding corrections proposed by the examinee except at the "key" points. No publisher seems to have found a way of working this procedure into an achievement battery, but it has the advantage of meeting two criticisms of the multiple choice type of items in that it requires the examinee to (*a*) find where corrections are needed and (*b*) supply the corrections needed. Exercises of this type or short essays rated globally, as in the STEP Essay Test, may constitute the next step forward in the evolution of achievement batteries. Indeed, the criticism that standardized testing regularly omits emphasis on writing needs to be met head-on by ingenuity in appraising writing within standardized batteries.

The sections on social studies and science are

introduced, appropriately, at the intermediate level, intended primarily for grades 5 and 6. In the Intermediate and Advanced Batteries, the social studies information section is divided equally among geography, history, and civics, but only a total score is reported; in the High School Battery a separate subscore for social studies vocabulary is broken out, while questions sampling the social studies broadly are miscellaneously organized—for example, Lincoln, Churchill, freedom of the press, the Louisiana Purchase, and Little Rock, in that order—to yield a separate social studies information score. As noted earlier, a separate test of social studies skills is in the battery at the three highest levels. This allows the user to combine it in his thinking either with the scores for social studies information or language study skills.

A single score for science is derived from the Intermediate and Advanced Batteries, while separate scores for (*a*) scientific concepts and understandings and (*b*) science information are provided in the High School Battery. No subgrouping of items has been attempted in any of these batteries to bring together items related to the physical versus the biological sciences, or any other natural subdivision of the content. As in the social studies test, this produces a "miscellaneous" effect that appears unnecessary and undesirable.

The individual items are generally clear and well constructed. Students should have little trouble understanding and following directions. A flaw, in the eyes of this reviewer, is failure to group separately items involving "not," "least," or other negative terms that call for choice of a negative sort. Most students naturally seek a "right" or "best" answer, so that negatively worded items need to be grouped at the beginning or end of sections to avoid confusion in responding to them. This reviewer also prefers using all capitals rather than italics, e.g., NOT rather than *not,* to make such words stand out as they need to.

The tests are generally satisfactory as regards speededness except at the high school level. Using this reviewer's rule of thumb (that a test is speeded if the average score earned by those in the highest grade for which the test is recommended is less than half way from the chance score to the maximum possible score), the following tests appear speeded: reading in the Primary 1 Battery; word knowledge and reading in the Primary 2 Battery; spelling, language, social studies information, and social studies skills in the Intermediate Battery; and the two social studies measures in the Advanced Battery. By this criterion 9 of the 11 tests in the High School Battery appear speeded. If these tests are not speeded, they are excessively difficult for general measurement in high school.

Although all tests at all levels provide ample scales for reflecting superior achievement, measurement of poor learners is generally inadequate. At the Primary 1 level the chance grade scores on word knowledge, word discrimination, and reading are 1.3, 1.3, and 1.6, respectively, and at the Primary 2 level, the corresponding values are 1.8, 1.6, and 2.0. All these values are a half grade or less below the minimum grade level for which norms are offered. At the elementary level, four tests (word knowledge, word discrimination, reading, and total language) have chance scores within a half grade of 3.0, the lowest level for which interpretative data are offered. In the case of language, a random marking yields a grade score of 3.5. The arithmetic problem solving and concepts test yields a chance grade score of 2.3, less than a full grade below 3.0. At the intermediate level, the spelling test yields a chance grade score of 5.3 if the DK option is not used, while the corresponding figure for language is 4.3. The remainder of the tests at the intermediate level yield chance grade scores between one and two grades below the minimum grade level for which norms are offered, except for the two arithmetic tests which require largely free response so that for these tests the chance scores are more than two grades below the minimum level. At the advanced level, only the spelling test yields a chance grade score less than one grade below the minimum level for which the test is normed. All the other tests at the advanced level yield chance grade scores more than two grades below the lowest grade level for which norms are offered. At the high school level an incomplete survey shows that the stanine values corresponding to the chance scores for the first three tests—reading, spelling, and language—are 2, 4, and 3, respectively, at grade 9, and 1, 3, and 2, respectively, even at grade 12. Granted that one should expect a gradual broadening of the scale, it is not too much to ask that the Elementary, Intermediate, and High School Batteries measure up to the standards achieved by the Advanced Battery. The Primary 1 and 2 Batteries should yield chance grade scores of 1.0 for every test if they are to be accepted as dependable measures of deficiencies in learning. The fact that spelling and language tests prove least satisfactory for measuring poor learners at the higher levels is due partially to ignoring the DK (don't know) option in computing chance scores, but this is essential in view of teacher reaction reported above and in the light of real experience with other tests where inadequate provision for measuring poor learners has resulted in equivocal scores. Also, although the authors have been commended for suggesting flexible use of tests so that poor learners may be examined by lower level tests, this is not yet common practice and calls for prior judgments of need for testing at lower levels that are not always available.

Special note should be made of the great flexibility of the test materials themselves. Not only are the Intermediate and Advanced Batteries available in both regular booklets, in which students mark their answers, and in separate answer sheet editions, but partial batteries omitting the social studies and science sections of these batteries may be purchased if a school or system prefers to restrict standardized testing to skills and measure outcomes in the substantive areas by local tests. Furthermore, separate test booklets for reading and arithmetic are available from the Elementary, Intermediate, Advanced, and High School Batteries and separate booklets for science and social studies are available from the Intermediate, Advanced, and High School Batteries. These separate booklets become increasingly important as we face the prospect of more departmentalized approaches in the middle and upper elementary grades. Finally, the separate answer sheet editions permit use of either the standard IBM answer sheet or the answer sheet of the Measurement Research Center at the State University of Iowa. The latter form permits use of MRC to score the tests rapidly and to provide simultaneously a wealth of summarizing and analytical data.

A light rap on the wrist should probably be added for advertising the batteries as "a test series of unequaled usefulness." Unexcelled perhaps, but not unequaled. Better to leave those terms to Madison Avenue and its toothpaste ads.

SUMMARY. This latest edition of the *Metropolitan Achievement Tests* is to be applauded for scope, both vertical and horizontal, for the quality of individual test questions, for the measurement of important outcomes, for careful standardization, for clear and attractive format, and for efficient accessory materials, but especially for the outstanding Manual for Interpreting. Limitations have been indicated in the item types used to measure proficiency in spelling and language and in the inadequacy of measuring poor learners. In final summary, nevertheless, this is a superior test series representative of the high quality and usability of modern achievement tests, with as fine an interpretative manual as is to be found.

For a review by Warren G. Findley of the 1947 edition, see 4:18; for reviews by E. V. Pullias and Hugh B. Wood of an earlier edition, see 40:1189; for reviews by Jack W. Dunlap, Charles W. Odell, and Richard Ledgerwood, see 38:874. For reviews of the subtests, see 627, 797, 877, and 970; for reviews of earlier editions, see 4:416, 4:543, 40:1458.1, 40:1551, 38:892, and 38:1105.

[16]

***National Achievement Tests.** Grades 4-6, 7-9; 1954-62; 4 scores: language, mathematics, social studies-science-health, total; 2 levels; no data on reliability of total scores; 25¢ per manual; 50¢ per specimen set of either level; postage extra; Lester D. Crow, Alice Crow, and William H. Bristow (*b*); [Psychometric Affiliates]. *

a) INTERMEDIATE BATTERY. Grades 4-6; 1957-62; IBM; Forms B ('58, 20 pages), A ('60, c1957-60, 16 pages, identical with test copyrighted in 1957 except for revision in 1 item and change in item order and response procedure); manual ('62, 4 pages); $6.50 per 25 tests; 100(115) minutes.

b) ADVANCED BATTERY. Grades 7-9; 1954-57; Form A ('55, 24 pages); manual ('57, 4 pages, identical with manual copyrighted in 1955); no norms for total score; $6.65 per 25 tests; 105(120) minutes.

For a review by William E. Coffman, see 5:19.

[17]

★**National Educational Development Tests.** Grades 9-10; 1959-63; tests administered annually in March and November by individual schools; 6 scores: English usage, mathematics usage, social studies reading, natural sciences reading, word usage, total; two new forms issued annually; 1963 form ('63, c1959-63, 40 pages) used in spring 1963 program; fall 1963 form ('63, c1960, 44 pages) used in fall 1963 program; supervisor's manual ('63, c1959-63, 16 pages); revised interpretive manual ('63, c1962, 24 pages); technical report ('63, c1961, 11 pages); student interpretive booklet ('63, 23 pages); student information bulletin ('63, c1960, 13 pages); percentile rank norms are those for "equivalent" scores on the *Iowa Tests* *of Educational Development,* 1957 testing; separate DocuTran answer sheets must be used; examination fee: $1 per student; fee includes scoring service; 170(215) minutes; E. F. Lindquist, Leonard S. Feldt, and others; Science Research Associates, Inc. *

WILLIS W. CLARK, *Executive Vice President, California Test Bureau, Monterey, California.* [Review of the spring 1963 edition.]

The *National Educational Development Tests* (NEDT) consist of five tests covering broad aspects of students' general educational development. These tests are said to have been modified and adapted for use in the NEDT program from the nine tests of the *Iowa Tests of Educational Development* which were first used in 1942. The NEDT edition for spring 1963, which was administered on March 5 and 9, 1963 to over 400,000 ninth and tenth grade students, is the subject of this review.

The five tests, which are contained in a single booklet, are as follows: English usage (76 items, 40 minutes); mathematics usage (40 items, 40 minutes); social studies reading (48 items, 35 minutes); natural sciences reading (48 items, 35 minutes); and word usage (88 items, 20 minutes). The manual for test administration is adequate and complete. Proctor duties and seating arrangements are clearly stated, and specific instructions to be read to students are provided.

Test scores are reported for each student in terms of standard scores which have a median of 12 for grade 9 and of 13 for grade 10 and standard deviations of 5 for each grade. The percentile ranks equivalent to the various standard scores are also given. The standard score system was derived from an equating of raw scores from the 1959 NEDT to the ITED standard score system. The relation of normalized standard scores, or *T* scores, to percentiles could well have been added so that the test data could be interpreted in the most widely approved method, based on median 50 and standard deviation 10.

The data are furnished for each student in an alphabetical list and on a "Presscore" label which the student uses to prepare his individual profile. He is instructed to record his standard scores on the six scales and to locate each score on the profile. Below each profile scale is the standard error of measurement for the subtest, rounded to the nearest whole number. The student is instructed to draw a line one standard error above and below his standard score. This area is then shaded to represent his "bands of confidence" of NEDT score results. Students are told that the middle line of the shaded area represents their scores "at the time you took the test." The "bands of confidence" allow "for the chance that you might do better....or not....as well" next time.

The authors of NEDT are aware of the correct meaning of standard errors of measurement. This reviewer favors reporting obtained scores as the best evidence of probable "true score." The interpreter should be aware of the proper interpretation of standard error of measurement. Rounding off the standard errors decreases the accuracy of the "bands of confidence" by varying amounts for the five component parts. (The rounded standard errors for the subtests and the composite are 2, 3, 2, 3, 2, and 1, while the actual standard errors for grade 9 are 1.59, 2.84, 2.29, 2.87, 1.63, and .91.) The procedure of establishing a "band of confidence" of plus and minus one standard error takes into account only 68 per cent of possible score variation and omits consideration of 32 per cent, 16 per cent of which will be higher and 16 per cent lower than the blocked off area on the profile.

Reliability coefficients for a sample of 200 ninth grade students were computed by Kuder-Richardson formula 20 and by the odd-even correlation corrected to full length by the Spearman-Brown prophecy formula. These reliabilities range from .76 to .92 for the subtests and .96 for the composite score. The technical report comments on some evidence of speededness resulting in these estimates being somewhat high. Coefficients of stability obtained by correlating 1959 and 1960 NEDT batteries with about 500 students show correlations of the various subtests a year apart ranging from .68 to .88 with a correlation of .91 for the composite score.

The validity data reported were obtained by a study of test results and teacher's grades. Correlations between ninth grade marks and test scores ranged from .40 to .66 for the subtests and from .64 to .71 for the composite; tenth grade marks correlated from .24 to .69 for the subtests and from .60 to .62 for the composite. These data were obtained by use of the 1959 edition. Assuming that the 1963 edition is equivalent to the 1959 edition (no evidence on this point was available to the reviewer), these validity correlations are fairly good, since the maximum correlation that could be expected is .70 to .75.

This reviewer concludes that the 1963 NEDT tests are carefully prepared. The norms indicate that the items tend to be difficult for typical high school students since the mean correct raw scores are considerably less than one half of the total items. For grade 9 the average difficulty of tests ranges from 28 to 38 per cent correct; for grade 10 average difficulty ranges from 31 to 41 per cent correct. The tests will undoubtedly be frustrating and discouraging for the bottom half of the class because of difficulty, speededness, and frequent admonitions of "do not waste time." Also, this reviewer prefers to consider the obtained score as the best evidence of the student's probable true score; one standard error of measurement each direction from the obtained score does not actually show the range of possible true scores, but only 68 per cent of the possible scores.

From the guidance point of view the measurement data provided by the NEDT should be useful in predicting success in academic subjects, but the data would be much more useful if multiple regression equations were available to show the relationship of test results to currently used scholarship or college entrance examinations.

The interpretative manual proposes that a scatterplot be prepared to show the relation of total grade averages to composite score percentiles. This would indicate for which pupils there was disagreement between the two criteria. From the instructional point of view this reviewer believes it would be more useful if an outline of the specific objectives of the test items were provided to give the teachers an idea of needs for remedial instruction. This type of information is given in some manuals for achievement tests, especially those in basic skills.

ARTHUR E. TRAXLER, *Executive Director, Educational Records Bureau, New York, New York.* [Review of the spring 1963 edition.]

The *National Educational Development Tests* compose what might be called a "semi-controlled" battery of tests of developed abilities important in the academic work of ninth and tenth grade pupils. The test materials and scoring services are sold as a "package" at the rate of one dollar for each pupil tested. Although a new form of the test is prepared each year, users are instructed to destroy used test booklets after each administration. However, the degree of secrecy surrounding the use of these tests, whose instructional and guidance uses are stressed, is not so great as that which characterizes the use of certain other controlled tests, particularly those whose main function is that of selection for purposes of admission and placement.

The five tests in the battery—English usage, mathematics usage, social studies reading, natural sciences reading, and word usage—are published in a single booklet of some forty pages. Responses to the total of 300 items in the battery are recorded on the two sides of an answer sheet, which also has space for a name grid. Different colored answer sheets are used for grades 9 and 10.

FORMAT AND PRINTING. The printing of the spring 1963 edition is fairly clear, but it could be improved. The tests are set in 10-point type with poor background contrast, and partly on this account some of the reading passages may present a rather severe visual task for some 14- and 15-year-old pupils. One is inclined to wonder why this edition is printed in brown ink on light tan paper, when black on white, or practically any other color on white, would provide better contrast and thus probably increase legibility.

The response positions on the answer sheet are set close together, as is true of virtually all Lindquist-designed answer sheets. This fact does not, in the experience of this reviewer, lead to eye strain in taking the test, as might be feared. However, the close setting of the response positions does make it difficult for the student to align answer sheet with test booklet and to keep the right place on the answer sheet.

TEST CONSTRUCTION FEATURES. The foregoing comments on test format are perhaps minor and unimportant (although the points raised may not be unimportant to the pupils taking the tests). In any event, these comments should not be given undue weight, for the NEDT battery contains many admirable features. The content and structure of the tests are, for the most part, excellent. Lindquist and his associates are masters of the art of writing test items, and their skill is clearly evident in all parts of the battery.

The English Usage Test presents a series of

passages, each followed by items which allow the subject to indicate whether no change should be made or whether certain suggested changes would improve the passage. Most of these are four-choice items, but some are two- or three-choice. The fact that no correction formula is used makes it feasible to vary the number of choices from one item to another. The first choice in each item is NO CHANGE, printed in all capitals, in contrast to the use of lower case for the other choices. While this arrangement seems rather dubious at first, the writer believes, from taking the test, that it does not cause undue emphasis to be placed on the first choice.

The Mathematics Usage Test consists of 40 five-choice items which tend to test application of mathematical facts rather than the facts as such. Performance on the test seems not to be influenced to any extent by "new mathematics."

The Social Studies Reading Test and the Natural Sciences Reading Test seem well designed to test thinking, understanding, and ability to interpret and apply what is read. This is particularly true of the latter test, which, if the reliability were higher, would be one of the best tests of reading scientific material which the writer has seen. Both the Social Studies Reading Test and the Natural Sciences Reading Test were designed as power tests, and, from the standpoint of depth of reading required, they do, in fact, test power. However, there appears to be a considerable speed element in both tests in that it would be difficult for a moderately capable reader to finish either one within the 35 minute time limit.

In the Word Usage Test, each test word is presented in a phrase or short sentence, a fact which this reviewer applauds as a welcome contrast to the many vocabulary tests in which test words are presented out of context. Most of the correct choices are well chosen, although one might take mild exception to one or two of them. *Creek,* for example, is not a good synonym for *bayou* (item 38).

SUPPLEMENTARY MATERIALS. In addition to the test booklets, answer sheets, and supervisor's manual for test administration, the test is accompanied by a number of supplementary materials: a student information booklet, a booklet for students and their parents entitled "You and the National Educational Development Tests," an interpretive manual, and a technical report. The first two booklets are well designed to give the student and his parents useful information about the tests and to ease tensions concerning them.

The interpretive manual explains the meaning and some of the uses of the scores for administrators, teachers, and counselors. It also contains percentiles for ninth and tenth grade pupils for the standard scores on each of five parts of the test and the composite score. The standard score range is from 0 to 36, but the effective range for grades 9 and 10 seems to be about 0 to 28. The mean and standard deviation of the standard scores were set at 15 and 5, respectively, for the standardization group.

A lack in the information given is either a distribution of the original raw scores of the standardization group or a table for translating raw scores into standard scores, or vice versa. Since the report of results comes complete with standard scores and percentiles, this information is not needed by users, but it *is* needed by critics of the test battery. In view of the fact that no correction for chance factors is used, one can be rather sure that a considerable proportion of the scores fall within the chance range and are, therefore, indicative of nothing. Without some way of determining the raw scores equivalent to given standard scores, one cannot say how large this proportion is.

The results for an individual pupil may be shown graphically on a profile form which appears with an explanation in the booklet, "You and the National Educational Development Tests." This graphic record is designed to show not only the pupil's standard score on each part of the test and his composite score but also, by means of a shaded area, the standard error of measurement for each score. This profile form is somewhat reminiscent of the "percentile band" concept of Educational Testing Service, but the reviewer believes it is to be preferred to the ETS procedure in that the standard scores obtained by the pupil are retained, while, at the same time, the user is reminded that the scores are subject to a certain degree of error.

STATISTICAL INFORMATION. Much valuable statistical information is given in the technical manual and this is kept up to date. For the spring 1963 edition, the Kuder-Richardson and Spearman-Brown odd-even reliabilities indicate that the composite score, the word usage score, and the English usage score are reliable enough for use with individual pupils. The scores of individual pupils on the other parts can be used with less confidence, and this is particularly true of the natural sciences reading score, where all reported reliabilities are in the .70's. The low reliability of this part seems surprising in view of the apparently high content validity. The explanation is probably found in a table which reports means and standard deviations for the raw scores of ninth and tenth grade groups. The mean, even for the tenth grade, is below 15 out of 48 raw score points, and it is to be noted that this mean was obtained for scores uncorrected for guessing. The science test is clearly too hard for the ninth and tenth grades, and it seems likely that a good many of the items are nonfunctioning, thus lowering the reliability. The Mathematics Usage Test is, likewise, very difficult for these grades.

The reported correlations of the NEDT with grades are about what one would expect. Most of them are within the range .40 to .60. For 406 parochial school ninth grade pupils, the reported correlation between composite score and grade-point average is .68, which approaches the upper limit of correlations between test scores and a criterion as lacking in reliability as grades frequently are.

SUMMARY AND RECOMMENDATION. The NEDT is designed to measure educational development in five areas—English, mathematics, social studies, natural sciences, and vocabulary. Many of its features are similar to those of the *Iowa Tests of Educational Development,* but it is planned for a more limited range—grades 9 and 10. The reading passages are well chosen, and most of the test items are expertly constructed. The format and printing of the test booklet and answer sheets are good but less than ideal. The supplementary materials for pupils and parents are well designed. The norms seem nationally representative. The scores are uncorrected for guessing and involve a considerable chance factor, but not enough information is given about the raw scores to enable one to say how serious this fact is. The results are reported in terms of standard scores and percentiles, which may be graphed on a profile form. The scores show satisfactory correlation with school grades. The composite scores are highly reliable and the scores on two of the five parts are reliable enough for use in the guidance of individual pupils, while the scores on the other three parts are of somewhat doubtful reliability for individual use. The test materials and scoring and reporting services are sold as a "package" for one dollar a student. The test seems well worth the investment for any school desiring to appraise the developed abilities of its ninth and tenth grade pupils in the areas covered by this battery.

ALEXANDER G. WESMAN, *Associate Director, Test Division, The Psychological Corporation, New York, New York.* [Review of the spring 1963 edition.]

The *National Educational Development Tests* are a "secure" battery for grades 9 and 10, patterned after the *Iowa Tests of Educational Development.* The five tests which comprise the NEDT are: English usage (four reading passages on which 76 items are based); mathematics usage (40 items); social studies reading (six reading passages, 48 items); natural science reading (five reading passages, 48 items); and word usage (88 items). A composite score is reported as well as scores for each of the five separate measures. Working time is 170 minutes; thus the battery can be administered in approximately three and a quarter to three and a half hours.

The two chief differences between the NEDT and ITED are: (*a*) the NEDT omits one of the reading tests (Ability to Interpret Literary Materials) and the three direct "knowledge" tests (Understanding of Basic Social Concepts, General Background in the Natural Sciences, and Use of Sources of Information); and (*b*) the average difficulty of the items of NEDT is apparently greater, in keeping with the enunciated purpose of identifying superior students.

According to its accompanying manuals and interpretive accessories, the NEDT battery was also developed to measure "the cumulative effects of educational experience over an extended period of time. It is designed to provide helpful information for guidance of all [sic] students at a time when they can best use this information" and also to "measure the student's ability to attack significant problems found both in school and in the total cultural environment." Other purported virtues are claimed: the composite score "is related to....ability to succeed in academic pursuits"; "teachers and counselors are assisted in identifying those students who seem especially fitted to attend college, those who have the ability for special courses, and those who could profit from extra help"; "others use the [NEDT] data primarily in individual counseling." Moreover, "Educational development tests measure as directly as possible in the test situation the complex skills and abilities required for effective problem solving. * the scores have a direct and obvious relation to the student's educational progress—a relation that may be readily grasped by the instructional staff, the student, and his parents."

That the five tests actually accomplish these laudable goals is doubtful. One who has seen the *National Merit Scholarship Qualifying Test* (another ITED outgrowth) will more readily accept another stated *raison d'etre* for the NEDT. "The National Educational Development Tests came into being after a number of educators expressed the need for a ninth- and tenth-grade testing program offering information and services comparable to those provided for eleventh-grade students by the National Merit Scholarship Qualifying Test."

The individual tests are styled like their counterparts in the ITED (and the NMSQT); the same item types are used. The Word Usage Test and two of the reading tests employ four-choice items, the mathematics test has five-choice items (the fifth being "not given" in most instances), and the English Usage Test has two-, three-, and four-choice items, with "no change" as an option in each one. As noted above, in keeping with the announced intent to make the tests primarily applicable to superior students, the average item difficulty is rather high. Unhappily, some of this difficulty results from irrelevant characteristics.

For example, the Mathematics Usage Test makes use of graphs which require the examinee to perform visual discriminations so fine as to confuse whether it is graph reading or vision which is being measured; at least 4 of the 40 items are highly vulnerable on this charge. Since 4 raw score points are apparently at least two thirds of a standard deviation, an important proportion of a student's score may be determined by his ability to see ultra-fine visual differences. (One must infer, rather than compute, the significance of 4 raw score points; no table translating raw scores to standard scores or percentiles appears in the manuals or on the scoring key).

The Social Studies Reading Test has at least two items (items 4 and 8) with more than one correct answer. The Word Usage Test frequently calls for relatively remote meanings; in at least one instance (item 45) there are two good answers and in one (item 34) the examinee is asked to accept "satisfactory" as equivalent to "valid." (Is a test with "satisfactory" sales *ipso facto* "valid"?)

It is in the English Usage Test, however, that the examinee is likely to find most perplexity. Here, the student is required to decide whether an indicated change, or no change at all, should be made in a sentence fragment. His choice is to be made not only on the basis of correctness of the English, but on the basis of style as well. Even if one were to accept the keying of every item (and this reviewer would insist that several are debatable), the conscientious examinee must find decision making a slow, arduous, and unsettling process. It is regrettable that greater editorial care and appropriate compassion for the student were not exercised.

That difficult tests have been prepared is abundantly clear; that the attained difficulty is optimal is not. Table 7 of the Technical Report reveals that the average difficulty of the mathematics items for ninth graders is .29; since there is apparently no correction formula applied, the chance expectancy would be .25. Thus, the average raw score of 11.47 reported for a presumably representative group of ninth grade students is only three and a half raw score points above a chance score of 8. A worse situation occurs for the Natural Sciences Reading Test: the average score of these ninth grade students is only one and a third points above the expected chance score. One must question both the efficiency and the effectiveness of tests which display this characteristic; clearly, the tests are too difficult for the proper measurement of a large proportion of the group for which they were designed.

As with the ITED program, the presentation of relevant psychometric data for NEDT leaves much to be desired. It is acknowledged in the Technical Report that "there is some evidence....that a speed factor exists in the 1963 battery" and, further, that "the reported split-half and Kuder-Richardson Formula 20 estimates of reliability are probably somewhat high." Nonetheless, not only are these presented as "the reliability data" but standard errors of measurement based on the K-R estimates are also presented—and without a warning to the reader that these are also "somewhat" spurious. Moreover, computation of these standard errors utilizes K-R estimates based on one sample and standard deviations based on a different sample; this procedure does little to enhance confidence in the meaningfulness of the standard errors.

The reported internal consistency estimates of reliability range from .71 for (ninth grade) natural science reading to .97 for (tenth grade) composite score. Two additional sets of reliability estimates are presented: correlation of the 1959 battery with similar tests of ITED (range, .63 to .90) and test-retest with a year intervening for the 1959 and 1960 NEDT batteries (range, .68 to .91). Comparison of n's among the several tables suggests that the students used in the NEDT-ITED study were also the ones on whom the tables of intercorrelation coefficients are based.

As one might expect from the nature of the tests, intercorrelation coefficients among the five parts are rather large (the smallest is .53, the largest, .78), indicating that there is considerable overlap in what is measured by the several tests. The reliability coefficients included in the tables of intercorrelation among the subtests should not have been reported in these tables—not only because "spurious" reliability coefficients are used, but also because the reliability coefficients are not based on the same students to whom the coefficients of intercorrelation apply. Why the data are presented in this way is difficult to understand.

Validity data are reported for three schools, for grades in four courses, and for grade-point average at the ninth and tenth grade levels. Expected variation in validity is found from school to school and from course to course; some of the reported coefficients are above .60, others are in the .20's and .30's. In most instances, the best prediction is associated with the composite score. A disappointing aspect of the validity tables is the omission of coefficients which would complete the tables. For example, no data are included for natural sciences reading or mathematics usage scores versus English grades or social studies grades, nor for word usage scores versus any course except English. It has been well established by research with other test batteries that important predictive relationships may be found between tests and course grades for which there may not be surface relevance. Since the data for investigating these relationships were obviously available and since most current devices for treating data of this kind would yield a full matrix of the necessary statistics with little or no effort, it is difficult to understand why incomplete tables, with selected coefficients only, should be presented. It is to be hoped that future manuals will fill in the gaps. This point is underscored by Table 3 of the 1963 technical manual, in which concurrent measurement data show mathematics usage scores correlating with English grades to the extent of .53 (equal to that for the Word Usage Test) and English usage scores correlating .59 with mathematics grades, as compared with .52 for the natural sciences reading scores versus mathematics grades—but the analogous coefficients are not chosen for presentation in the predictive validity tables!

Table 3, cited above, also contains correlation data for Henmon-Nelson IQ's and NEDT scores. The correlation coefficient for NEDT composite score and Henmon-Nelson IQ in this group is reported as .76. This study contains the only instance of correlation of NEDT with other tests (correlation with ITED should not be counted—these are not really "other tests"). One must deplore the absence of such data; surely students in the NEDT program have been administered other achievement or aptitude tests in the same or adjacent grades. It would be informative, for example, to see how similar the results might be for scores on a standard reading test and those on the reading tests included in the NEDT. Correlation with other tests is a common approach to understanding the nature of any test and is perhaps especially important when a battery like the NEDT is being studied.

The absence of appropriate supporting data for the NEDT is unfortunate. At the least, it is frustrating to the knowledgeable reviewer who is unable to interpret properly such evidence as does appear. If he is of a skeptical turn of mind, he may wonder whether the omission is intended to prevent him from spotting deficiencies in the data or unfavorable evidence concerning the tests. Even if he is more favorably inclined and pardons the omissions as innocent oversights, he must nevertheless ask some fundamental questions concerning the usefulness of the tests and legitimacy of the claims.

The tests are proposed for use in guidance

of "all students"; the heavy loading of reading measurement limits their efficiency for this purpose. Furthermore, aside from the matter of efficiency, the content of the tests is restricted when compared with that of competing batteries such as the Stanford or Metropolitan achievement tests on the one hand, or of a comprehensive aptitude battery on the other. Moreover, the suggestion that the tests be used for *all* students is forcefully refuted by the data in the manual: the tests are obviously too difficult to provide proper measurement for a large number—in some instances almost half—of the students in the grades at which the tests are used. Thus, any claims of serving a broad guidance function, or of general utility for a school, are simply not tenable. The claim that the composite score is as good a predictor of college success as are standard scholastic aptitude measures is probably justified, despite the inadequacy of supporting documentation. Here, however, the matter of efficiency cannot be ignored. Standard scholastic aptitude tests require far less expenditure of time and money. If the NEDT is to be justified on this score alone, it must be demonstrated to be a much better predictor to compensate for its costliness. This superiority has not been (and, the reviewer believes, *could not* be) demonstrated.

The one unchallenged claim, then, is that for those students who will later take the *National Merit Scholarship Qualifying Test,* the NEDT provides a realistic practice session. A school system which yields to immoderate pressures to the extent of feeling a need to provide specific practice for NMSQT may find the NEDT a suitable device. Most school systems, it is to be hoped, will conclude that they cannot afford this extravagance; far better value may be obtained, for the three and a half hours or the dollar per student expended, by obtaining more varied information in the same amount of time or equally useful information in less time. The NEDT is ineffective for most students, inefficient for virtually all.

[18]

***National Merit Scholarship Qualifying Test.** Second semester juniors and first semester seniors seeking college scholarships; 1955–63; tests administered annually in March by individual schools; 7 scores: English usage, mathematics usage, social studies reading, natural sciences reading, word usage, selection score (total), composite (average); MRC; two new forms issued annually; Forms A, B, ('63, 40 pages) used in 1963 program; supervisor's manual ('63, 16 pages); interpretive manual ('63, 41 pages); 1963–64 student information bulletin ('62, 34 pages); interpretive handbook for students ('63, 48 pages); program guide ('63, 61 pages); technical report ('62, 23 pages); separate answer sheets must be used; examination fee: $1 per student; fee includes scoring service; postage extra; 170(200) minutes; Science Research Associates, Inc. *

REFERENCES

1. HOLLAND, JOHN L. "Prediction of Scholastic Success for a High Aptitude Sample." *Sch & Soc* 86:290–3 Je 21 '58. *
2. ALDRIDGE, BILLY G. *A Study of the Relationship of Fundamental Skills Measured by the National Merit Scholarship Qualifying Test to Natural Sciences Reading Ability.* Master's thesis, University of Kansas (Lawrence, Kan.), 1959.
3. BOND, HORACE MANN. "Talent and Toilets." *J Negro Ed* 28:3–14 w '59. *
4. DIRKS, A. W. *A Study of Questionnaire Responses From 5703 Kansas High School Participants and Non-Participants in the National Merit Scholarship Qualifying Test Program.* Doctor's thesis, University of Kansas (Lawrence, Kan.), 1959. (*DA* 20:2657)
5. ALDRIDGE, BILLY G., AND ANDERSON, KENNETH E. "A Study of the Relationship of Fundamental Skills Measured by the *National Merit Scholarship Qualifying Test* to Natural Sciences Reading Ability." *Sch Sci & Math* 60:439–44 Je '60. *
6. ANDERSON, KENNETH E., AND ALDRIDGE, BILLY. "Parental Attitude and Teacher Influence on College Attendance as Related to National Merit Scholarship Test Scores." *Sci Ed* 44:176–8 Ap '60. *
7. ANDERSON, KENNETH E., AND ALEY, TILGHMAN. "Humanistic and Science Composite Scores as Related to Intellectual Curiosity and Persistence." *Sci Ed* 44:171–6 Ap '60. *
8. ANDERSON, KENNETH E., AND ALEY, TILGHMAN. "Relationship of Self-Rating Items on Intellectual Curiosity and Persistence to National Merit Scholarship Test Scores." *Sch & Soc* 88:356–7 O 8 '60. *
9. TARR, HARRY A. *How to Pass National Merit Scholarship Tests.* New York: Arco Publishing Co., Inc., 1960. Variously paged. *
10. WILSON, CHARLES CHASE. *The Relationship of Achievement as Measured by the National Merit Scholarship Qualifying Test to Curriculum and Educational Factors in Selected Nebraska High Schools.* Doctor's thesis, University of Nebraska (Lincoln, Neb.), 1961. (*DA* 22:805)
11. WOMER, FRANK B. "The Need for the National Merit Scholarship Qualifying Test: A Michigan Study." *Personnel & Guid J* 41:218–21 N '62. * (*PA* 37:7180)
12. LEVINE, HAROLD G., AND LYONS, WILLIAM A. "Comparability of Scores on Three Examinations Sponsored by External Agencies in Secondary Schools in New York State." *Personnel & Guid J* 41:596–601 Mr '63. *

DOROTHY C. ADKINS, *Professor of Psychology, The University of North Carolina, Chapel Hill, North Carolina.*

Some criticisms to which the *National Merit Scholarship Qualifying Test* have been heir are attributable to the fact that its perpetrators have embraced two conflicting purposes. One is to provide a battery of tests optimally suited to selecting a small percentage of college scholarship recipients from among high school students who have some hopes of obtaining a scholarship. The other is to provide a battery of tests useful for educational and vocational guidance for eleventh graders in general.

If two groups of equally competent specialists set out to develop test batteries to accomplish these different objectives independently, the resulting tests might indeed tap very similar patterns of abilities. The scholarship selection battery, however, would place more emphasis on a final composite score with as good predictive power as possible for overall college scholarship at the upper echelons of ability, while the diagnostic battery would evidence more attention to relatively independent abilities. Moreover, the scholarship tests would be substantially more difficult than the guidance tests for high school juniors. In addition, they would be planned for high school seniors.

Evidence of incompatible purposes permeates the brochures accompanying the National Merit Scholarship Program. The operational objectives of the program are said to be "to discover exceptionally talented young people * to work with corporations, foundations and other organizations, and with individuals, in establishing scholarship programs * to conduct research related to the foregoing." Yet the materials abound with suggestions that the high school junior might well take the test for guidance purposes, whether or not he is likely to qualify for a scholarship, and that he differentially interpret his score profile.

The first SRA edition of NMSQT, published in 1958, was an adaptation of five of the nine *Iowa Tests of Educational Development*. The subsequent editions, also, have been planned to represent equivalent forms of the ITED tests. Although the circumstances surrounding the initiation of the NMSQ program in 1958 may have excused the adaptation of an existing test battery geared to other needs, to understand the continuation of such a plan over the ensuing years for a multi-million dollar program entailing the testing of now some 600,000 students annually is difficult.

Throughout the materials is repetitive insistence that the NMSQT is a test of educational development, not a test of academic aptitude. Neither by arguments that at times border on sophistry nor by empirical comparisons with other tests are the authors able to justify this claim. Indeed, were they to do so, this reviewer would be tempted to assert that their goal and its achievement were ill-advised. For, if a distinction between the two types of tests did exist, tests for selection of college students of great promise should be academic aptitude tests. This is especially true since other features of the final selection include subjective evaluation of high school achievement and other factors that may lead to modification of predictions of college achievement based upon aptitude alone. Like a previous reviewer (Benno G. Fricke), this one definitely rejects the arguments and purported evidence that the NMSQT is other than an academic aptitude test.

Inspection of the subtests reveals that they are not very different from tests that are regarded as aptitude tests. The first, English usage, is a 40-minute, four-choice test of 76 items. The subject responds to numbered sections of several passages by indicating whether they should remain as stated or be replaced by suggested substitute wordings or punctuations. (The subject is directed to read the entire passage presented first without underlining, but this device seems only to waste time and has little bearing upon the responses.) A few questions about paragraphing, topic sentences, etc., are also included. Test 2, mathematics usage, is based primarily upon elementary algebra but also slightly upon plane geometry. Forty five-choice items are to be answered in 40 minutes. (A relatively minor technical flaw is that "Not Given" is used as the fifth choice for a number of items but constitutes the correct answer less often than would be expected by chance, e.g., two times for 21 such items in one form examined.) Tests 3 and 4, Social Science Reading Test and Natural Science Reading Test, each consist of 51 four-choice items for a 35-minute time limit. Some 7 to 13 questions are supposedly based upon a single paragraph with content in one of the areas in question. In some cases, almost all the questions can be answered by a knowledgeable subject without reference to the supposedly relevant paragraph. A few questions can be answered only on the basis of knowledge not contained at all in the paragraph. In general, however, these appear to be much like other reading tests. Test 5, Word Usage Test, contains 88 four-choice items and has a 20-minute time limit. The key word is imbedded in context, a device that often seems to create a disadvantage when it comes to writing discriminating distracters.

The tests appear to be satisfactorily reliable by the odds-even and Kuder-Richardson 20 approaches, although the reliability of the mathematics and natural sciences tests probably could be improved. The median reliability estimate of the composite or total score for the several forms is reported as .97, both for samples representative of high school juniors and those representative of Merit Program participants. One might wonder why alternative forms reliability estimates could not have been obtained and must regard as unimpressive the authors' argument that this would have entailed immediate retesting of the students.

(The authors' suggestion that the test-retest method would have been among the appropriate methods if the tests were somewhat too long for the less able students is questionable at best.)

For a sample representative of all high school juniors, the test intercorrelations range from .63 to .78, while for a sample representative of Merit Program participants they range from .49 to .78. The English usage and mathematics usage tests are the least related to each other. Most persons interested in the possibility of meaningful differential diagnosis would regard the correlations between the two reading tests for the two samples reported, .76 and .71, to be somewhat more than moderate. The interpretive manual remarks that these tests "are probably more independent than they appear to be from their correlations." Cited as evidence are the partial correlation coefficients of .52, with the English Usage Test partialed out, and .43, with the Word Usage Test partialed out. These may provide evidence that the abilities *underlying* the tests are more independent than the test data reveal. It is the test scores, however, that the unwary student plots on his profile.

Undergraduates in measurement courses are commonly taught that score distributions for the purpose of selecting a small percentage of scholarship recipients should be markedly skewed in the positive direction. The 1962 NMSQT selection scores (and doubtless the earlier ones as well), however, are negatively skewed for the some 600,000 students "making at least tentative plans for college." The average item difficulty values, based upon samples representative of Merit Program participants, are .50, .45, .50, .45, and .60, respectively, for the five subtests. Although it is stated, for example, that the Word Usage Test "measures the student's understanding of the meanings of words at advanced levels of difficulty," both inspection of the test and the statistical data show that the test should be more difficult. This is also true of the other tests.

The data on validity are disappointing. For various samples of college freshmen and various test forms, correlations with scholarship for two or three quarters range from about .35 to about .59. One would prefer more direct evidence that those in the finalist group do better in college than those scholarship aspirants not in the finalist group. We might even hope eventually to have validity data on the *entire* selection process, which includes committee judgments about academic marks, the quality of courses taken, school recommendations, student activities, biographical statements, and so on. Is the college scholarship of those finalists selected by the committees significantly better than that of those finalists not selected but who nevertheless go to college? Do the scholarship winners, as determined from among the finalists by committee selection, do better in college than those not among the finalists? Does the committee process yield more valid predictions than a statistical combination of aptitude test scores, high school marks, and other relatively objective indices? The relevant validity questions for a scholarship selection program pertain only slightly to the question of whether the aptitude test predicts college scholarship for a group that ranges widely in ability. They should have more to do with the extent to which the most talented are being selected. Research on whether the selection devices are as efficient as possible would also be worthwhile.

The NMSQT would be more useful for the counseling of eleventh graders if it either emphasized only the total score or at most part scores for verbal and quantitative abilities or if it contained subtests more independent of each other. It would be more suitable for the selection of scholarship recipients if it were designed to provide maximum discrimination among high school seniors at the upper level of academic aptitude.

George K. Bennett, *President, The Psychological Corporation, New York, New York.*

When important social and financial benefits are contingent upon a single test score, there is an obligation to use a test of the highest quality. When an eminent philanthropic institution endorses a testing instrument for "guidance" purposes on a national scale, that instrument should be representative of the best current practice. In both respects the *National Merit Scholarship Qualifying Test* is unsatisfactory.

The National Merit Scholarship Program is one of great size and of major significance to education in the United States. In March of 1962, nearly 600,000 high school juniors from more than 16,000 secondary schools took one of the two forms (Form A on a weekday or Form B on a Saturday) of the *National Merit Scholarship Qualifying Test* (NMSQT).

Somewhat more than 11,000 of these individuals gained scores high enough to attain the status of "Semifinalist." The next 29,000 were designated "Commended students." Each semifinalist was encouraged (*a*) to obtain the endorsement of his school and have his record submitted to the National Merit Scholarship Corporation, (*b*) to validate his NMSQT scores by taking the *College Entrance Examination Board Scholastic Aptitude Test,* (*c*) to complete a biographical form, and (*d*) to provide the National Merit Scholarship Corporation (NMSC) with confidential financial information. In each year at least 97 per cent of the semifinalists have satisfied these requirements and become "Finalists." All Merit Scholars are selected from the group of finalists. In 1962, National Merit Scholarships were awarded from the funds of NMSC to 409 finalists, while 632 others received sponsored scholarships from funds provided by 151 external sponsors who participated in the NMSC program. The average value of these scholarships was about $3,400 per recipient over the four-year period, or a total of somewhat more than three and a half million dollars. In addition, 181 individuals qualified for scholarships but chose to accept grants from other sources and were designated as "Honorary Merit Scholars." Supplementary payments are made to many of the institutions which Merit Scholars attend.

The process of selection of recipients is described in the NMSC Annual Report for 1962:

> Recipients of National Merit Scholarships are chosen [from among the Finalists] by the National Merit Scholarship Selection Committee, composed of experts in college admissions and financial aid. This committee also selects the winners of sponsored Merit Scholarships whenever a sponsor requests. The winners of other sponsored Merit Scholarships are chosen by the sponsors from the pool of qualified Finalists.

A list of all semifinalists is published and receives wide circulation. The 1962 NMSC Annual Report estimates that about half of each year's semifinalists receive unsolicited offers of financial aid to attend college. Many others are invited to participate in honors programs.

Each commended student receives a letter of commendation issued by NMSC and signed by his secondary school principal. It is estimated that 40 per cent of this group are offered aid from outside sources. In every case, cards with name, address, and test scores are sent to the indicated institutions of first and second choice for both semifinalist and commended students.

Taking into consideration the highly competitive aspect of gaining admission to the college of one's choice and the great advantage of being awarded the accolade for intellectual talent by NMSC, it is no wonder that so many secondary school students find it desirable to pay the dollar per head charged by the Corporation's contractor for preparing, printing, and processing the qualifying test. As a sort of consolation prize for the 94 per cent of competitors who do not reach the commended scholar level, the NMSQT is recommended as an aid to guidance.

Each year, two new forms of the NMSQT are prepared. Since 1958, all of the forms have been patterned after the *Iowa Tests of Educational Development.* In each form there are five subtests covering English usage, mathematics usage, social studies reading, natural sciences reading, and word usage. Fricke, in his MMY review of the 1958 form (5:20), makes a number of points, among which are the following: (*a*) that the test is too easy, since the average student "got 56% of the items right"; (*b*) that the intercorrelation among the subtest scores is high; (*c*) that the reliabilities of the subtest scores, especially in the social and natural sciences subtests, are low; and (*d*) that the quality of the items could be improved.

From the information given in the technical report in 1962 and from scrutiny of the 1963 test forms, it would appear that the changes since 1958 are relatively minor. Taking Fricke's points in the order given above:

a) The present level of difficulty for the National Merit Scholarship candidate population is slightly higher, the mean item difficulty now being .53 as contrasted to .56 some years ago.

b) The intercorrelation among part scores is now higher, the median being .61 against the .54 which Fricke reports.

c) The reliabilities of the subtests appear to have been improved; the coefficients for social studies reading and natural sciences reading are now reported as .90 and .87, respectively (odd-even). It is unfortunate that no alternate form reliability coefficient is available, since the degree of speededness is unknown, although presumably small, and the structure of the English usage, social studies reading, and natural sciences reading subtests is such that groups of questions relate to single passages. In such circumstances, there is ordinarily a tendency for the proportion of right answers among the questions relating to a single selection to be influenced by the student's grasp of the material presented, with a consequent inflation of the estimate of reliability by the split-half method.

d) Item quality remains unimpressive. The present reviewer was greatly perturbed by the third reading passage in the natural sciences subtest (Form A, 1963) in which a table of planetary temperatures based only upon solar radiation is given. In this table, the temperature of the earth is given as −17° F., while that of Venus is given as −47° F. Since Venus is appreciably nearer to the sun, it is obvious that the relative temperatures must be incorrect, and it would seem that a bright high school junior who was aware of this fact might block in responding to some questions relating to this paragraph. To comment further on test content, the English usage section requires the correction of passages ostensibly representative of the writing of high school students. The instructions include the admonition, "Correct, appropriate English consistent with the general tone and style of the whole passage is required. In many of the questions, more than one of the suggested revisions is grammatically correct. In such cases, choose the expression that fits the passage most effectively. Be sure to consider *all* the suggested revisions before making your choice." This would seem to put the respondents in a sort of quandary, since it can be assumed that even experts might disagree as to the order of desirability among correct alternatives.

The primary purpose of the NMSQT is to identify those individuals who are to be designated as semifinalists and, somewhat incidentally, those who will be given letters of commendation. For this purpose, the test should discriminate with maximum accuracy at the level where these dichotomies occur. The data furnished cast grave doubts on the suitability of this test for this purpose. To begin with, the experimental items are tried out in conjunction with the annual fall testing program for Iowa high schools. The experimental items comprise supplementary 20-minute tests, and the discrimination indices are computed against the criterion of the similar subtest of the ITED used in that program. Quoting from the 1962 technical report,

> The indexes of difficulty were used in conjunction with the discrimination coefficients to adjust the over-all level of difficulty of each subtest, and to create a fairly flat distribution of item difficulties within a relatively narrow range centering on approximately 50 per cent for maximum discrimination among the NMSQT population.

In terms of standard scores, the ITED produces a mean of 15 with a standard deviation of 5 based on the performance of representative second semester juniors. Those who take the NMSQT obtain a mean score of 20.5 with a standard deviation of 5.15. Thus, the mean of the National Merit Scholarship group is approximately 1 standard deviation superior to that of representative high school juniors. However, the 10,000 persons who become semifinalists constitute the topmost 2 per cent of the National Merit Scholarship candidate population, and consequently have a lower score limit two standard deviations above the contestant group mean. It would seem difficult to select items appropriate for identification of this superior group by experimental trial upon a population whose mean is almost 3 standard deviations lower. Furthermore, the philosophy, quoted above, of selecting items with "difficulties within a relatively narrow range centering on approximately 50 per cent," will tend to produce a test with maximum discrimination near the middle of the range rather than near its upper end. The consequence of this approach is apparent in the relatively low ceilings of all the subtests except mathematics usage; and it is particularly evident in the Word Usage Test where the mean raw score (Form A, 1962) of the NMSQT representative sample is 52.45, and the standard deviation is 16.69, so that a perfect score for the 88 items included is only a shade more than 2 standard deviations beyond the mean. This would appear to indicate that a National Merit Scholarship candidate possessing a really superior vocabulary could not demonstrate it in such a manner as to offset a low score in one of the other subtests.

What is referred to as the "selection score" is the sum of the previously described standard scores on the five subtests of the NMSQT. Four of these subtests have a heavy loading of verbal content, while the Mathematics

Usage Test enjoys a reasonable degree of independence. The consequence of this arrangement is to weight verbal skills four times as heavily as mathematics usage, a practice which perhaps is reasonable if one is seeking liberal arts candidates but which necessarily penalizes those whose special strengths are in mathematics and physical science.

The second purpose of the NMSQT, and the one which is advanced as the justification for its use on an every-pupil basis, is its value as a guidance instrument. A battery of tests for this purpose should have low intercorrelations among its parts, and the parts should display different orders of validity with different socially important criteria. Admittedly, these are difficult goals to attain, but the four verbal sections of the test do not achieve the kind of differentiation which is currently possible. A curious recognition of this appears in the following paragraphs of the technical report:

In all four samples it is evident that the English Usage and Mathematics Usage tests are the least related to each other, as one might readily hypothesize. Some of the other tests, such as Social Studies Reading and Natural Sciences Reading, appear to be moderately related. These tests, however, are probably more independent than they appear from their correlations. One important but frequently overlooked factor affecting the correlation coefficient is heterogeneity with respect to a third variable. If each of two variables is causally related to a third variable, the heterogeneity of the third variable will tend to produce a correlation between two variables. The technique of partial correlation can be used to obtain an estimate of the correlation between two variables unaffected by the influence of the third variable, because the partial-correlation coefficient represents an estimate of what the correlation would be if the third variable were controlled or held constant.

In Table 11, Form A, the correlation between Social Studies Reading (Test 3) and Natural Sciences Reading (Test 4) is found to be .76. If the influence of English Usage ability (Test 1) is partialed out, the partial-correlation coefficient ($r_{34.1}$) is only .52. Similarly, if the effect of Word Usage ability (Test 5) is partialed out, the partial-correlation coefficient ($r_{34.5}$) is .43.

When correlations between the Social Studies Reading and Natural Sciences Reading tests were calculated for groups having the same initial ability in English Usage and Word Usage, it was found that the correlations were substantially lowered because the causal effect of the third (heterogeneous) variable was removed. Thus it is evident that the relation between Social Studies Reading and Natural Sciences Reading is inflated because of the range of the students' initial abilities in English Usage or Word Usage.

Both MMY reviewers of the 1958 edition point out the hazard of attempting guidance on the basis of such a combination of related variables, and Fricke goes on to say that "two good reliable tests measuring verbal and mathematical abilities would be satisfactory from the statistical and selection points of view." The present reviewer heartily endorses this conclusion. He is also unable to understand why the National Merit Scholarship Corporation has not directed some portion of its very considerable research capability toward the improvement of its basic instrument of selection.

The NMSQT has some commendable attributes. It samples aspects of ability which are important to college success. It yields a reliable total score, as any test of 300 items should. It is reasonably valid as a predictor of college grades when administered to an incoming freshman class. One can feel confident that those scoring at the 98th percentile have better than average prospects of attaining high grades and other academic distinctions. At the same time, the content and difficulty level of the test would seem to place a premium on a kind of academic docility which may favor the collegiate counterparts of Madison Avenue's man in the gray flannel suit, while operating to the disadvantage of the candidate with more brilliance and imagination but less conformity to the goals of the typical American high school.

The NMSQT is, then, minimally adequate for selection purposes, largely inadequate for guidance. It seems unfortunate that so frail a foundation is provided for so noble an edifice as the National Merit Scholarships.

J. Thomas Hastings, *Director, Office of Educational Testing; University Examiner; and Professor of Educational Psychology; University of Illinois, Urbana, Illinois.*

The tests used in the National Merit Scholarship Program in 1958 were reviewed in *The Fifth Mental Measurements Yearbook.* Those reviews very ably covered the descriptive information on content and psychometric characteristics of the 1958 *National Merit Scholarship Qualifying Test* (referred to from here on as the NMSQT). Each year two "comparable" new forms have been developed. Although the current review treats mainly the forms used with high school juniors in the spring of 1963, references are made to the earlier tests, their materials, and the reviewers' comments concerning them.

It is important for the secondary school user (and for the "measurement specialist" reader or writer of reviews) to realize that this test is not available in the open market but is imbedded in a program of talent selection which involves far more than the test. Furthermore, in many communities there are social pressures exerted for the school to enter the program. This context alters the usual questions which face the school in deciding to use or not use a given test battery. "How does this test compare with others which we might use instead?" is changed to "Is the test sufficiently good for the basic purpose to allow us to participate without being a party to unreasonable error?" The question of whether this test is good enough to allow us to use the scores in guidance to supplement what we already know is quite a different question than whether this particular battery is better for our purchase than those others to use as a part of guidance.

This reviewer believes that, in terms of the questions appropriate to the context of a program such as this, the characteristics of NMSQT and the quality and completeness of the descriptive and interpretive materials which accompany it allow for a very clear affirmative answer. Put another way, the decision to enter or not to enter the National Merit Program should not be negative because of the test used in it. Also, the decision whether, if a school is in the program, to use the results as a supplement to guidance information or to "throw them away" should be answered—on the basis of test characteristics and interpretive aids—in favor of use. To say that the scores should be used cautiously in counseling is to invoke a platitude applicable to all test scores. To tell what cautions need to be observed is partly the job of an interpretive manual and partly the job of teacher and counselor trainers. The question of "How well does this manual do that job?" is treated briefly toward the end of this review.

The five subtests of NMSQT are very much the same as their 1958 predecessors in terms of format, content, and mode. This is good from at least one standpoint: Continuation of highly similar tests from year to year allows for an accumulation of data which are needed in assessing the instrument for selection and for counseling purposes, e.g., facts concerning the predictive quality of the 1960 tests are generally applicable to the 1963 tests. The tests are very similar to five of the subtests in the *Iowa Tests of Educational Development* (ITED), as was stated in the earlier reviews, and to the tests which have been developed more recently for the American College Testing Program (ACT). Although the latter are "secure" tests, as is NMSQT, the reader may examine copies of ITED to satisfy himself on the content validity of the NMSQT subtests.

This parallelism in content—not in specific items—may well make the user wonder whether students who take one or two of the batteries do better on a remaining one than do students who have not taken them. This reviewer found no information treating this question. Although inferences from studies of the "warm-up" effect of taking tests which are similar in mode and content support the idea that the effect is small at best, the National Merit Scholarship Corporation and the NMSQT publishers (as well as the publishers of ITED and ACT) have some responsibility for demonstrating to the users the practical effects in this instance.

Earlier reviewers complained rightly that the number of alternatives for items varied from two to five. Four-choice items are used in all of the 1963 subtests except the Mathematics Usage Test, which consists of five-choice items. Both of the 5th MMY reviewers pled for more careful editorial work; the present tests seem to be in good shape on this count.

There are real changes since 1958 in the descriptive and interpretive material furnished for the tests. There are now data on the grade-point behavior in college of students who took the NMSQT in the second semester of the junior year in high school. There are also correlations between NMSQT scores and scores on other widely used tests. Both sets of correlations cover several different groups and several different subject areas or tests. The coefficients are reasonably high, with the best GPA predictors being the verbal subtests and the composite score (in the .40's and .50's with most groups). The highest "other tests" relationships are with the Minnesota Scholastic Aptitude Test (a shortened form of the *Ohio State University Psychological Test*) and the *College Entrance Examination Board Scholastic Aptitude Tests*. The NMSQT-MSAT coefficient, using composite, is reported as .78;

the coefficient for SAT verbal with the 1961 NMSQT "verbal" is .92; and the comparable figure for mathematics parts is .90.

Earlier reviewers pointed out the lack of independence among subtests and the consequent dangers in interpreting differences within a student's profile. The highest intercorrelation reported for the 1962 forms is between social studies reading and word usage, .78; the two reading tests of 1962 Form A run a close second with .71. The lowest correlation is between English usage and mathematics usage, .49. Both split-half reliability and Kuder-Richardson 20 reliability coefficients are presented for the 1962 forms. Each is .97 for composite, .94 for word usage, and from .80 to .91 for the other subtests. These figures suggest that the problems of interpreting profile differences as real still exist, but it should be pointed out that the 1963 profile encourages the use of "bands" (one standard error each side of score) for interpretation purposes. This is certainly a STEP toward less dangerous interpretation of subscores.

The controversy concerning whether NMSQT assesses "educational development" or "scholastic aptitude" still can be waged. The answer at this time is probably a matter of taste. The National Merit Scholarship Program errs, this reviewer believes, only in making non-data-based statements which suggest that the test results can indicate remedial work in the senior year (not cramming) which can seriously effect improvement in the student's exercise of "reasoning and problem-solving abilities required for success in college." If these basic intellectual accomplishments have been developed over years of schooling, it seems doubtful that a remedial course or two in the senior year will really correct deficiencies. Instructional research on this point would be helpful.

In summary, a number of the faults pointed out by earlier reviews have been corrected or lessened. The interpretive publications are well written and contain data which are meaningful to the careful and trained user. The quality of administration instructions and test editing ranges from very, very good to excellent. For selection purposes the NMSQT does a good job; for guidance purposes the test and materials compare favorably with other available batteries.

For reviews by Benno G. Fricke and Roger T. Lennon of the 1958 test, see 5:20.

[19]

*__Public School Achievement Tests.__ Grades 3–8; 1928–61; subtests in reading, arithmetic computation, and arithmetic reasoning available as separates; 7 scores: reading, arithmetic computation, arithmetic reasoning, language usage, spelling, grammar (grades 6–8 only), total; Forms 1 ('59, 23 pages), 2 ('61, 24 pages); tests identical with tests copyrighted in 1928 except for addition of the grammar subtest in both forms (identical with grammar subtest from the grades 6–8 level of the battery which was also copyrighted in 1928 but is no longer available), wording changes in 7 items of Form 2, and format of Form 2; manual ('59, 20 pages, essentially the same—including norms—as 1928 manual); manual also covers 4 additional subtests from an earlier battery (history, geography, nature study, health) which are no longer included in the battery or available separately; no data on reliability of subscores; $3.85 per 35 tests; 25¢ per manual; 50¢ per specimen set; postage extra; 140(180) minutes in 5 sessions for grades 3–5, 160(200) minutes in 6 sessions for grades 6–8; Jacob S. Orleans; Bobbs-Merrill Co., Inc. *

REFERENCES

1. Wilson, Guy M., and Parsons, A. Rebecca. "Critical Examination of a Standardized Spelling Test." *Ed Adm & Sup* 15:494–8 O '29. * (*PA* 4:903)
2. Pullias, Earl V. "Commercial Standardized Tests," pp. 65–80. In his *Variability in Results From New-Type Achievement Tests.* Duke University Studies in Education, No. 2. Durham, N.C.: Duke University Press, 1937. Pp. 100. * (*PA* 11:5966)

For reviews by Herbert S. Conrad and E. V. Pullias, see 40:1194.

[20]

★**Pupil Record of Educational Progress.** Grades 6–9; 1961, c1960–61; a single booklet combination of 4 achievement tests (English, mathematics, social studies reading, science reading), the grades 6–9 level of *SRA Tests of Educational Ability* (only the total IQ score is reported), and the grades 6–9 level of *Your Educational Plans;* tests administered during periods established by the publisher (September 15–October 15 or March 15–April 15) or at other times at increased cost; Form Y ('61, 50 pages); manual ('61, c1960–61, 49 pages); profile ['61, 2 pages, 1 of which is the answer sheet for the free-response items of YEP]; pupil's interpretive booklet ['61, 4 pages]; school summary report folder ['61, 4 pages]; separate DocuTran answer sheets must be used; tests rented only; fee: $1 per student during regular testing periods, $1.35 per student at other times; fee includes scoring service; postage extra; (390) minutes in 2–6 sessions; Science Research Associates, Inc. *

George D. Demos, *Associate Dean—Counseling and Testing, and Associate Professor of Educational Psychology, California State College at Long Beach, Long Beach, California.*

The *Pupil Record of Educational Progress* (PREP) was designed to measure development in four educational areas: English, mathematics, social studies, and science. Along with the achievement battery (extracted from certain aspects of language, reasoning, and quantitative skills), a TEA (*SRA Tests of Educational Ability*) or IQ score is formed.

Also accompanying the achievement and IQ measures is a section with the unlikely name of YEP (*Your Educational Plans*), an aspect of the test specifically designed for future educational and vocational planning by teachers and counselors. In addition to the PREP, TEA, and YEP scores, the authors develop other terms such as "Granines" (Grade/Stanine), "Presscore," and others, all of which give the impression that Madison Avenue may have found its way into test development. Other phrases throughout the many booklets and pamphlets that come with the test also indicate a great concern with the salability of the test. For example, the "Fact Sheet" on PREP contains the following statements. "*Something for everybody.* In the reporting information [sic] is something for the student, the parent, the counselor, the classroom teacher and the administrator. * *Cost.* The cost of the PREP battery is *amazingly* low [reviewer's italics], in view of the wealth of information furnished."

The reviewer could not help but feel that SRA had gone somewhat overboard on developing test terms and services which were well market-researched with catchy phrases—trying deliberately to develop a marketable test—but there seemed to be a minimum of effort in areas that would have made the battery more meaningful and practicable, such as validity and reliability studies.

The fact that the manual has a brief paragraph near the back dealing with validity, with meager, sketchy studies done primarily with the TEA IQ's, and a modicum of data available on norms and reliability also gives one the impression that the test simply does not have the kind of substance necessary to make the kind of predictions advertised.

The authors state that PREP is the only battery combining ability (TEA), achievement, and educational plans (YEP) information in one package. The reviewer, after carefully perusing these features of the battery, is not convinced that it is desirable to combine these three features into one battery. Granted, it is commendable to consider educational plans and aspiration levels and the host of other demographic data in attempting to provide this information for counselors to work with in helping the student plan his future career. There is, however, considerable evidence—the work of Rothney, Hoyt, and Super in particular—which suggests that many difficulties arise in attempting to indicate career choice at the junior high school level. The reviewer fears that making commitments towards educational and career objectives too early can inhibit exploration and development of wise vocational choices at a later date. It may be unfair to infer that this will necessarily take place upon using the YEP; however, it is very probable that in the hands of some poorly trained counselors and teachers it may preclude the optimal use of such guidance information.

The reviewer also feels that perhaps the test is mixing objective and subjective data in a way that can be confusing to many users. For instance, the manual on the YEP states that "potential drop-outs, at all ability levels, can be located quickly." Coupled with the usage of such information as the educational level of the father and the mother, financial need, family type, high school program preference, aspirations, and so on, this approach may be providing the kind of data that is not in line with certain counseling philosophies. More data are necessary on its proper and successful usage. A variety of personality tests, problem checklists, and general information sheets, in conjunction with brief interviews, may serve the same purpose at less cost and with less time involved.

After perusing the test booklet itself, it is easy to see that the test is highly verbal and very dependent on reading skills. The sections dealing with mathematics, social studies, and science are heavily weighted along verbal lines with lengthy word problems which appear to make these tests more reading comprehension tests than mathematics or science achievement tests *per se*. The test does not appear capable of competing with the *Sequential Tests of Educational Progress* (STEP). The rather unattractive test booklet with its off-white color also makes it difficult to read.

On the other hand, there are some counselors, teachers, and administrators who will undoubtedly view this test as a significant contribution in the testing movement for the very reasons that this reviewer criticized it negatively. It is certainly conceivable that the PREP battery with TEA and YEP will, with additional follow-up research, additions, and corrections, prove to be a valuable tool particularly in the area of guidance and counseling at the junior high school level.

In the test's present state, however, there appear to be too many unanswered questions for it to be strongly recommended.

JACK C. MERWIN, *Professor of Educational Psychology, and Assistant Director, Student Counseling Bureau, University of Minnesota, Minneapolis, Minnesota.*

The *Pupil Record of Educational Progress* (PREP) program is a testing, data processing, and reporting service. It involves the administration of four "educational development" tests, an IQ test, and a questionnaire. The program is offered under three alternative plans, all of which require that the tests be scored and reported by the publisher. Under plan A all materials are rented, under plan B the school purchases the booklets, and plan C, which also involves the purchase of booklets, is offered for schools who wish to use the intelligence and achievement sections alone.

This program is a package service which combines a variety of information about pupils in grades 6 through 9. The convenience of the procedure developed for securing and reporting data of several different types is an attractive feature of this program. However, the information reported out of any data processing procedure, regardless of the speed with which the information is made available or the attractiveness of the report form, can be no better than the basic data obtained from the instruments used. Much information needed to judge adequately the value of data obtained by the instruments used in this program is not available, and some of the information that is available suggests that they are of limited value.

EDUCATIONAL DEVELOPMENT TESTS. The educational development section of PREP offers four tests labeled "English," "mathematics," "social studies," and "science." Each yields a single score and these are combined to obtain a composite score.

The English test is composed of three reading passages with items which vary in number from 18 to 21 per passage. Each item consists of an underlined word or set of words in the passage with one to three possible substitutions and "no change" as alternatives from which the student is to pick the correct answer. The vertical distance on the test booklet page between the underlined part of the passage and the location of the item responses which refer to it is quite large for some items and might be troublesome for sixth graders. An apparent attempt to remedy this in the second passage was to space out the paragraphs on the page.

The mathematics test has 50 items, 23 of which are graph and table interpretation items. All items have four alternatives with "none of these" as the fourth response on 32 items. Some of the items in this test are completely inexcusable in a published test. To illustrate, one item asks which of three measurements (one a measurement of time, one a measurement of distance, and one a measurement of weight) would be "most exact," with "none of these" as a distractor. Another item asks which of three numbers is "about" the true answer and has "none of these" as a distractor. Following a circle graph which shows the per cent of allowance two students "spend," is a question which states an amount spent which contradicts the graph and asks about the amount "allotted," which is apparently supposed to come from the graph.

The social studies test is a 50-item reading test with three reading passages, each of which precedes 11 to 20 four-choice items. Twenty three of the items involve the selection of an alternative which means "most nearly" the same thing as a word underlined in the passage. The authors have chosen to use a small number of reading passages with a relatively large number of items on each reading passage. This approach obviously limits sampling across reading passages.

The test for "science" has three reading passages with 16 to 18 items on each passage. Twenty six of the 50 items are of the word meaning type. According to the manual, this test "draws heavily upon the pupil's science background and his ability to comprehend reading passages dealing with scientific information." One of the three reading passages is entitled "A Simple Machine." The contents of this passage will probably have been studied by some, but not all, pupils at any one grade level before they take this test. Thus some students will find that they can answer certain items without reading the passage even though they are told, "This is a test to see how well you can read science material with understanding."

The scores from the four tests are combined

to obtain a composite score which the manual describes as "the best predictor of success in high school or college." There is no evidence provided to support this statement.

The manual states that predictive validity data based on students tested with Form X (which has now been withdrawn) in the fall of 1960 and spring of 1961, and pupils tested with Form Y in the fall of 1961 and the spring of 1962 will be reported "as soon as school grades for these pupils can be obtained." No such information was available at the time this review was prepared.

The means, standard deviations, Kuder-Richardson formula 21 reliability coefficients, and standard errors of measurement for Form X are reported for each grade level. These data are apparently based on the norm sample which included only school systems testing in all four grades. The 16 coefficients reported range from .62 to .86 with a median value of .76. The standard errors of measurement range from 3.3 to 3.8. The differences in the means for adjacent grade levels vary from 1.9 to 4.5 raw score units. These small mean gains raise serious questions about the extent to which the tests are measuring, if at all, "educational development" as set forth in the objectives of schools. How meaningful differences of this magnitude can be must also be assessed in light of the relatively large standard errors of measurement.

Corrected split-half reliability coefficients based on a "sample representative of the PREP standardization sample" numbering 668 students are reported. The median of the 16 within-grade coefficients is .82. The split-half coefficients reported for the composite scores vary from .92 in grade 6 to .95 in grade 9. Interform reliability coefficients reported are based on students from a single school which had considerably higher mean scores than the norm group. The interform correlation coefficients for the four tests range from .68 to .82 for this group.

Can the tests in this battery be used to provide useful differential information about educational development in the four areas by which they are entitled? A hypothesis that such information would be minimal could be made on the basis of the highly verbal content of the tests. The high intercorrelations among the tests, reported for each grade level, support such a hypothesis. Of the 24 intercorrelations reported for Form X the lowest is .54, the highest .78, and the median .62. The 16 correlation coefficients between the subtests and composite score range from .79 to .91 with a median value of .86. The extent of these interrelationships casts serious doubt on the value of the four test scores as measures of differential educational development.

The norms provided are based on students from 54 schools whose mean composite score on the *Iowa Tests of Educational Development* is reported to be at approximately the 50th percentile of ITED national pupil norms. The distribution of the mean grade 9 ITED composite scores for the standardization schools is given, although the percentiles reported are not designated as either individual or school mean percentiles. Based on a four-way geographic split of the United States, population percentages and percentages in the sample differ by three to four percentage points. As noted above, the norms are based on only those schools which tested students in all four grades.

The norms reported are of two types. One is percentile within-semester, within-grade. The other is labeled a "granine," and is comprised of a digit which states the grade in which the student took PREP and a number following a slash which is a stanine. While norms are provided for each semester of each grade, 6 through 9, none of the report forms for granines include the designation of a semester on which the figures are based. A "Chart for Profiling PREP Scores" is provided for each individual and the school must complete the profiling on these charts. The manual states that a difference of two stanines between scores may be viewed as statistically significant. The relatively large standard errors of measurement and the high intercorrelations between tests, raises a serious question of the meaningfulness of the profiles. Within a test, a difference of two stanines can be based on a difference of only 2 to 7 raw score points. With standard errors of measurement of 3.3 to 3.8, the rule of thumb of viewing a difference of 2 stanines on the profile as statistically significant appears questionable at best. The high intercorrelations will seriously limit the possibility of the identification of differential "educational development."

TESTS OF EDUCATIONAL ABILITY. The *SRA Tests of Educational Ability* for grades 6–9 are composed of five separately timed parts labeled "Language 1," a classification test, "Language 2," a synonyms test, "Reasoning 1," a number series test, "Reasoning 2," a letter series test, and "Quantitative," an arithmetic test. The subtests vary in number of items from 15 to 30. The subtest scores are combined and manipulated to obtain an intelligence quotient which the manual states "is the ratio of a pupil's mental age to his chronological age at the time of testing multiplied by 100." According to the manual the IQ's range from 70 to 140 and the "national average is 100." They also report a "percentile-in-age." It is reported that the "TEA raw scores were assigned grade and age values by direct equi-percentile equating to the grade and age values of the composite score of the *SRA Achievement Series*" for grades 6–9. The norms are based on 10,660 pupils in 154 schools in 107 school systems from "all parts of the country." The number of pupils included varies from a little under 1,800 in grade 9 to a little over 3,300 in grade 6. The data on the norm sample is extremely brief and inadequate. With very little information about the groups used, reliability coefficients for the TEA 6–9 are reported in terms of both split-half coefficients and Kuder-Richardson formula 21 coefficients. The coefficients reported for the total score range from .93 to .95 and subtest reliability estimates reported vary from .65 to .91. While there is a nod in the direction of acknowledging that the split-half estimates are probably a "little high" in view of the speed factor operating in the reasoning and quantitative subtests, no acknowledgement is made that the K-R 21 coefficients would also be affected by the speed factor.

Validity information on this test is very limited and inadequate. The longest of the few short paragraphs on validity is devoted to the reporting of correlations between the TEA IQ's and scores from tests of general academic ability; coefficients reported range from .69 to .88. Information about the samples needed to interpret these coefficients is not provided. Correlations between the TEA total score and *SRA Achievement Series* composite score are reported to be .84 and .89, although there is no designation as to whether these are predictive or concurrent validity indices. One short paragraph is devoted to the correlation between TEA total score and teacher grade averages recorded two months after the administration of the TEA. The two coefficients reported are .73 for grade 6 and .50 for grade 9. There is no information about the variance of the groups used for these two studies, or whether the teachers had knowledge of the scores at the time of grading. Both pieces of information would be relevant to the interpretation of these coefficients.

YOUR EDUCATIONAL PLANS. The third part of this program involves an inventory entitled *Your Educational Plans* which, according to the manual, provides "a concise yet rich inventory of facts and attitudes about a pupil's educational plans as reported by the pupil." *Your Educational Plans* (YEP) is comprised of 3 open-end questions and 38 multiple choice questions related to the students' plans for schooling beyond high school, his parents' and siblings' education, his perception of how his parents feel about his going to college, what his closest friend is likely to do in high school and whether that friend will go to college. Twenty three of the responses are coded on the Counselor's Worksheet. The other questions are asked "to develop a mental set on the part of the pupil." This latter is not elaborated in any way, except to say that the counselor may want to repeat these questions in a counseling session.

The Counselor's Worksheet from *Your Educational Plans* involves the grouping of students into four categories: planning college preparatory program—definite, planning college preparatory program—indefinite, not planning college preparatory program—indefinite, not planning college preparatory program—definite. Within each group, the report form contains for each student his IQ or achievement composite percentile and a separate index of favorability toward continuing education derived from the response to each of 23 items. The manual states that an index of "1" is favorable for continuing schooling beyond high school, "2" is somewhat less favorable, "and so on." With no information about the validity of these indexes, it would be at best speculative that they might provide the school with dependable information it did not already have available.

SUMMARY. The apparent objective of the PREP program to provide a service for collating information of different types is commendable. The attempt to find a substitute for the usual grade norms is also commendable. Unfortunately, there is little evidence to suggest that the instruments employed will provide meaningful data as a basis with which to initiate these procedures.

The content of some of the tests of "educational development" leaves much to be desired. The small mean gains from one grade level to the next cast serious question on the curricular validity of these tests and the high intercorrelations cast serious doubt on the likely value of the tests for identifying differential development. There is no information on the validity of the indexes reported on the Counselor's Worksheet and no basis on which to believe they provide any more information than simple knowledge of the responses. Until positive evidence bearing on these points is available, it is important that schools not become blinded to these important considerations by the seeming efficiency of processing and convenience of forms offered through PREP.

[21]

***SRA Achievement Series.** Grades 1–2, 2–4, 4–6, 6–9 (grades 1–2, 2–4, 4.7–6.6, 6.7–8.3, 8.4–9.9 for Forms C and D); 1954–64; IBM for grades 4–9; 2 editions; teacher's handbook ['64, c1955, 47 pages] for both editions; 50¢ per teacher's handbook; postage extra; Louis P. Thorpe, D. Welty Lefever, and Robert A. Naslund; Science Research Associates, Inc. *

a) FORMS A AND B. Grades 1–2, 2–4, 4–6, 6–9; 1954–64; subtests in arithmetic, reading, language arts (grades 2–9 only), and work-study skills (grades 4–9 only) available as separates; 4 levels; school administrator's manual ('58, c1955–56, 32 pages); technical supplement, second edition ('57, 45 pages); pupil progress and profile charts ('59, c1955–59, 4 pages); interpretation charts ('59, 1 page each): percentile profile chart, grade equivalent profile chart, frequency distribution chart, scores made by selected students chart, achievement status chart; prospectus ('62, 20 pages); 90¢ per 20 pupil progress and profile charts; 50¢ per pad of 20 copies of any one interpretation chart (including 1 enlarged demonstration chart); 50¢ per school administrator's manual; $1 per technical supplement; $1 per prospectus; $1.50 per specimen set of any one level.

1) *Grades 1–2.* 1958–61; 7 scores: reading (verbal-pictorial associations, language perception, comprehension, vocabulary), arithmetic (concepts, reasoning, computation); Form A ('58); 2 tests: reading (29 pages), arithmetic (17 pages); examiner's manual ('58, revised '61, 21 pages); mimeographed technical data supplement ('59, 3 pages); $3.50 per 20 reading tests; $2.50 per 20 arithmetic tests; 225(340) minutes in 7 sessions.

2) *Grades 2–4.* 1955–60; 8 scores: arithmetic (reasoning, numerical concepts, computation), language arts (capitalization-punctuation, grammatical usage, spelling), reading (comprehension, vocabulary); Forms A ('55), B ('57); 3 tests: arithmetic (15 pages), language arts (14 pages), reading (15 pages); a fourth subtest, language perception, is out of print; examiner's manual, third edition ('60, c1955–60, 27 pages); $2 per 20 tests; 50¢ per hand scoring stencil; 275(390) minutes in 7 sessions.

3) *Grades 4–6.* 1954–63; 11 scores: references, charts, reading comprehension, vocabulary, capitalization and punctuation, grammatical usage, spelling, arithmetic (reasoning, concepts, computation), total; IBM; Forms A ('55), B ('56), (63 pages); *SRA-scored materials:* examiner's manual ('61, c1954–61, 40 pages); reporting service manual, third edition ('63, c1961, 24 pages) for this and the grades 6–9 battery; separate DocuTran answer sheets must be used; fee: 60¢ to $1 per student; minimum fee includes loan of test materials, scoring, list report of scores, report of average scores, report of local percentile norms and frequency distributions, and pupil progress and profile charts; item analysis data and other services included in higher fees; *school- or SRA-scored materials:* examiner's manual, second edition ('56, c1954–56, revised '60, 39 pages); separate IBM scorable answer folders must be used; test materials may either be purchased ($10 per 20 tests, $2 per 20 IBM scorable answer folders, $4 per set of machine scoring stencils, $2 per set of hand scoring stencils) or rented (price included in scoring service fee); fee: 40¢ to 70¢ per student when test materials are purchased separately, 60¢ to $1 per student including rental of test booklets; 352 (445) minutes in 6 sessions.

4) *Grades 6–9.* Details same as for grades 4–6 except: Forms A, B, (71 pages); examiner's manual for SRA-scored materials (36 pages); $3 per set of machine scoring stencils; 305(370) minutes in 5 sessions.

b) FORMS C AND D. Grades 1–2, 2–4, 4.7–6.6, 6.7–8.3, 8.4–9.9; 1955–64; subtests in arithmetic (grades 1–4 only), reading (grades 1–4 only), language arts (grades 2–4 only), and work-study skills (grades 4.7–9.9 only) available as separates; 5 levels; test coordinator's manual ('64, c1961–64, 64 pages); pupil progress and profile charts ('64, c1955–64, 4 pages) for grades 1–4, 4–9; 90¢ per 20 pupil progress and profile charts; 50¢ per test coordinator's manual; $2 per specimen set of 1) and 2); $3 per specimen set of 3).

1) *Grades 1–2.* 1958–64; 10 scores: reading (verbal-pictorial association, language perception, comprehension, vocabulary, total), arithmetic (concepts, reasoning, computation, total), total; Forms C ('58, revised '63), D ('63); 2 tests: reading (36 pages; Form C is essentially the same as the 1958 Form A except for typography, art work, revision or wording changes in 16 items, 1 new item, and changes in item order), arithmetic (21 pages; Form C is essentially the same as the 1958 Form A except for typography, art work, vocabulary changes in most orally presented items, and option order changes in one-third of the items); examiner's manuals (45 pages): Form C ('58, revised '64), Form D ('63, c1958–63, revised '64); $3.50 per 20 reading tests; $2.50 per 20 arithmetic tests; 225(340) minutes in 7 sessions.

2) *Grades 2–4.* 1955–64; 12 scores: language arts (capitalization and punctuation, grammatical usage, spelling, total), arithmetic (concepts, reasoning, computation, total), reading (comprehension, vocabulary, total), total; Forms C ('55, revised '63), D ('57, revised '63), (59 pages); tests are revisions, with approximately 24 per cent new items, of Forms A and B published in 1955 and 1957, respectively; examiner's manual ('64, c1955–64, 43 pages) for each form; $5.50 per 20 tests; 260(365) minutes in 7 sessions.

3) *Multilevel Edition.* Grades 4.7–6.6, 6.7–8.3, 8.4–9.9; 1955–64; 14 or 17 scores: social studies, science, language arts (capitalization and punctuation, grammatical usage, spelling, total), arithmetic (reasoning, concepts, computation, total), reading (comprehension, vocabulary, total), total, work-study skills (references, charts, total)—optional; IBM; Forms C, D, ('63, 94 pages); 3 levels (called blue, green, and red levels, after color of answer sheet used) in a single booklet; work-study skills supplement: Forms C, D, ('63, 32 pages); separate examiner's manuals for use with DocuTran answer sheets ('63, 43 pages), IBM 805 answer sheets ('64, c1963–64, 40 pages), IBM 1230 answer sheets ('64, c1963–64, 42 pages); manual on how to use the test results ('64, c1961–64, 34 pages); conversion tables booklet ('64, 38 pages) for each level; pupil progress and profile charts ('64, c1955–64, 4 pages); separate IBM or DocuTran answer sheets must be used; *school-scored materials:* $16 per 20 tests of the basic battery; $6 per 20 work-study skills supplements; $18 per 100 sets of IBM 805 answer sheets; $3.50 per set of scoring stencils and conversion tables booklet for any one level; $14 per 100 sets of IBM 1230 answer sheets, set of master answer sheets for machine scoring, and conversion tables booklet for any one level; $2 per set of hand scoring stencils and conversion tables booklet for any one level; $8 per 100 DocuTran answer sheets; $2 per set of hand scoring templates and conversion tables booklet for any one level; 90¢ per 20 pupil progress and profile charts; 50¢ per examiner's manual; 50¢ per how-to-use manual; *SRA-scored materials:* test materials may either be purchased (materials and prices as given above) or rented (price included in scoring service fee); fee: 40¢ to 80¢ per student for basic battery when test materials are purchased separately (60¢ to $1 when work-study skills test is included), 60¢ to $1 per student for basic battery including rental of test booklets (80¢ to $1.20 when work-study skills test is included); minimum fees include scoring, list report of scores, report of average scores, and pupil progress and profile charts; local percentile norms, frequency distributions, item analysis data, and other services included in higher fees; 310(363) minutes in 3 sessions for basic battery, 70(80) minutes for work-study skills supplement.

REFERENCES

1. Garlock, J. C., and Harsh, J. R. "A Comparative Study of Four Commonly Used Achievement Tests." *Calif J Ed Res* 11:147–54 S '60. * (*PA* 35:7117)

2. Findley, Warren G. "Use and Interpretation of Achievement Tests in Relation to Validity." *Yearb Nat Council Meas Ed* 18:23–34 '61. *

3. Taylor, Edward A., and Crandall, James H. "A Study of the 'Norm-Equivalence' of Certain Tests Approved for the California State Testing Program." *Calif J Ed Res* 13:186–92 S '62. *

Jacob S. Orleans, *Professor of Psychology, University of Nevada, Southern Regional Division, Las Vegas, Nevada.* [Review of Forms A and B.]

The *SRA Achievement Series* has been reviewed in earlier editions of *The Mental Measurements Yearbooks.* The present review deals only with the reliability of interpretations of individual pupil's scores.

The publication of another battery of achievement tests when there are already several good ones on the market should be welcomed if for no other reason than that the greater the competition the greater the likelihood of a high level of product. The *SRA Achievement Series* offers a great deal of information in the Technical Supplement, 1957 Edition, concerning the method of planning the tests, the sources of content, preparation of items, and standardization, and extensive data on validity, reliability, and related matters.

The reliability coefficients (Kuder-Richardson coefficients of consistency) appear to be reasonably high. Of the 91 correlations reported for individual tests for individual grades, 4 are .900 or above, 64 are between .800 and .899, 20 are between .700 and .799, and 3 are below .700. However, the same table reports grade means and standard errors which, when translated into months of grade as shown in the grade equivalent norms, throw an entirely different light on the meaningfulness of the test scores.

The standard error of an arithmetic computation score for the second grade is 2.2 months (of a 10-month school year). The standard error of a score ranges from 3.5 months to 3.9 months for second grade capitalization-punctuation, grammatical usage, arithmetic concepts, and arithmetic reasoning; third grade arithmetic computation; and fourth grade arithmetic computation. The standard error of a score ranges from 4.4 months to 4.8 months for second grade vocabulary and comprehension, and for fifth grade comprehension. The 52 other standard errors reported range from 5.3 months to 34.6 months.

In other words in 52 of the 62 possible scores (by test and grade level) the scores of one third of the pupils may be expected to be in error by at least a half of a school year. In only one instance would a third of the scores be in error by more than (only) .2 of a school year. One can hardly become enthusiastic about the value of a battery of achievement tests when the measures it provides are subject to such large errors, particularly since the major value of a battery of achievement tests is for administrative purposes.

The authors have furnished a great deal of information concerning the preparation and standardization of the series, making an impressive presentation of the validity of the content and the appropriateness of the procedures for standardization. The weakness of the tests probably derives from the fact that in the case of most tests at a given battery level the mean score for the lowest grade level for the battery is high and the differences between the grade norms are very small. In reading comprehension (battery for grades 2–4) the mean score for grade 2 is 25.89 and for grade 4 is 33.67. Two years of achievement in reading comprehension are represented by 7.78 points of raw score. The elimination of some of the easier items and substitution for them of items of appropriate difficulty could increase the spread of scores representing two years of achievement to double the present spread.

Similarly, a comparison of the mean scores for grades 6 and 9 on the battery for those levels reveals that three years of achievement is represented by 9.35 raw score points in reading comprehension, 11.12 in vocabulary, 6.74 in punctuation-capitalization, 7.22 in grammatical usage, 8.62 in spelling, 12.80 in arithmetic reasoning, 9.29 in arithmetic concepts, and 12.61 in computation. With standard errors of a score averaging over 3 points it is easy to see why the standard errors at this level are all over .6 year, many being well over a year.

Until the standard errors of the scores are reduced to useful proportions, it is difficult to see how the *SRA Achievement Series* can take its place along with some of the other elementary school achievement batteries.

For reviews by Warren G. Findley and Worth R. Jones of Forms A and B of the tests for grades 2–9, see 5:21. For reviews of Forms A and B of the subtests, see 632, 808, 5:200, 5:483, 5:649, 5:668, and 5:696.

[22]

***SRA High School Placement Test.** Entering ninth grade students; 1957–63; 6 scores: educational ability, reading achievement, arithmetic achievement, language arts achievement, total, Catholic religion (optional); new form issued annually for use in large diocesan systems in the same year, for use in small diocesan systems the following year, and for use in non-Catholic schools the next following year; 3 tests in use in 1963: Series 64K ('62, c1960–62, 34 pages), Series 63K ('61, 34 pages), Series 63A ('60, 34 pages); optional religion test ('60, 8 pages) by John A. McMahon and Albert Meyer; separate examiner's manuals ('61, c1960–61, 32 pages, identical except for time allotments) for Series K, Series A and K; manual for religion test ('61, 13 pages); mimeographed technical reports ('63) for Series 63A and 63K (37 pages), 63K and 64K (64 pages); profile leaflet ('61, 4 pages); separate DocuTran answer sheets must be used; tests loaned only; examination fee (with or without religion test): $1.10 per student, postage extra; fee includes scoring service and reporting of normed scores and local norms; 185(230) minutes for Series 64K, 175(215) minutes for Series 63K and 63A, 30(35) minutes for religion test; Science Research Associates, Inc. *

REFERENCES

1. GRUBER, EDWARD C. *How to Score High on the Catholic High School Entrance Examination.* New York: Arco Publishing Co., Inc., 1962. Pp. 117, plus supplements. *

2. BAUERNFEIND, ROBERT H., AND BLUMENFELD, WARREN S. "A Comparison of Achievement Scores of Public-School and Catholic-School Pupils." *Ed & Psychol Meas* 23:331–6 su '63. * (*PA* 38:1418)

3. BAUERNFEIND, ROBERT H., AND BLUMENFELD, WARREN S. "A Comparison of Achievement Scores of Public-School and Parochial-School Pupils." Abstract. *Yearb Nat Council Meas Ed* 20:165 '63. *

WALTER N. DUROST, *Associate Professor of Education, University of New Hampshire, Durham, New Hampshire.* [Review of Series 64K.]

This test is intended primarily for a restricted population of parochial schools to be used in determining the acceptability of the student for the ninth grade or for placing him in appropriate instructional divisions at the beginning of the grade.[1] The test has been published annually for a number of years, but with considerable inconsistency in content from year to year. The writer will limit himself largely to the most recent of the forms made available for review, namely, Series 64K.

Chapter 1 of the technical report covering Series 63K and 64K begins, "The SRA High School Placement Test (HSPT) is designed to predict academic success of entering ninth grade students." As if this were not a sufficient task, the report also says that the test may be used for selection of students in schools that limit enrollment, for placement of incoming ninth grade students, for homogeneous grouping, for identifying students with superior ability, for identification of students with special instructional needs, and for evaluation of achievement. Although six possible uses are mentioned, only three are really different, namely, selection out of a large unselected body of students seeking admission to high school, placement, and evaluation of achievement. Of these three, only the first two can be claimed as possible uses of this instrument with any degree of validity. Therefore, the most vital evaluation of this instrument must be done in terms of the extent to which it succeeds in its primary purpose, namely, predicting success in Catholic high schools.

1 Since the new test constructed each year is used first in parochial schools and since the test apparently finds its primary use in this connotation, no attention has been paid to its possible public school use.

THE TEST. In terms of the primary stated purpose of predicting success in high school the selection of subtests for inclusion in the battery makes fairly good sense to the writer. It is desirable to combine a mental ability measure with tests of school achievement, especially in the skills areas for predicting subsequent school success. The only questionable test is Language Arts. It has been the writer's experience that tests in spelling and language usage have the lowest correlation of any skills test with school learning aptitude and yet the results as reported in the technical report for Series 64K would indicate that this is not true in this particular battery. This may be a characteristic of the curriculum in the parochial schools, but this is only a guess. The total amount of testing time involved is certainly long enough to give as good a prediction of success as can be obtained from objective test results.

The quality of the item writing leaves much to be desired. The test could be greatly improved by some very careful editing. The item form used in the word reasoning subtest is unnecessarily restrictive. Out of the 20 items included, only 2 of the key words are nouns; the others are adjectives or verbs and in some cases one must derive from the context whether the word is intended in the adjectival or the verbal sense. The synonyms given are often times defensible only because they are the best of the possible alternatives and not because they are precisely equivalent to the key word. For example: "old" is not a very good synonym for "archaic" and the word "archaic" would never be used as applying to a bridge as in the context; "antiquated" possibly or even "ancient" but not "archaic." Consider the following item: "a slanderous statement" with the suggested correct answer being "harmful." To slander is to speak disparagingly with the intent to defame. It may or may not be harmful depending upon whether or not the truth or falsity of the slander is established. Or consider "with volcanic force" with the correct answer being "powerful." To be sure, a volcanic force is powerful, but so are many other forces, such as atomic and tornadic. It is this type of multiple choice item which feeds the fires of lay criticism of testing, especially by those who start out with a bias against objective tests and seek to find illustrations to serve their purpose.

Of all the tests in the educational ability section, the one on arithmetical reasoning seems to be the least defensible. This battery is intended to be used at the end of the eighth grade or the beginning of the ninth grade. Even a casual observation of this subtest is sufficient to show that a knowledge of algebra is essential or at least tremendously helpful. Perhaps 50 per cent of those taking the test will have had algebra at the eighth grade level. For the rest of the students, struggling through this subtest, attempting to derive the answers by empirical cut-and-try methods, will certainly be a much more difficult task.

In the reading test, the first story or paragraph in this form has to do with the fictional character Paul Bunyan and the first question asks when the action in the story took place. The alternatives given are the 1600's, 1700's, 1800's, 1900's. The article implies that the Paul Bunyan stories emerged from the early logging camps of Wisconsin and one could perhaps, if he had a sufficient knowledge of American history, conclude that the 1800's must be the correct answer. However, this answer is not to be obtained from anything in the paragraph itself. The second item is introduced with the stem "According to this story, both Paul Bunyan and Davy Crockett can be described as....". The correct answer is supposed to be "legendary." In the story itself, there is the following sentence: "Following is an example of the exploits that have made Paul Bunyan the Davy Crockett of the somber North Woods." This is the sole reference to Davy Crockett. With only this meager information, the student would have every right to mark "loggers" or "brave" as equally correct responses.

The multiple choice form used for the arithmetic section of the test is particularly unsuited for the purpose and the great majority of these items can be answered by estimation without any actual computation. Consider this item: "24 is three-fourths of a. 18 b. 32 c. 72 d. None of these." Obviously, 24 cannot be three fourths of 18 since it is larger than 18. It obviously cannot be three fourths of 72 since it is less than half of 72. This leaves 32 and "None of these" as the only possible alternatives. It is not much of a task to see that 24 is indeed three fourths of 32. One might argue that this is an early item in the test and thus intentionally easy. However, consider item 40:

"If insurance costs $1.10 per $100, what is the premium on $8700?" At an even $1.00 per hundred, the premium would be $87.00. With this information alone, it is obvious that there is no answer to compete with $95.70 unless it is "None of these." Adding 10¢ per hundred, or $8.70, gives the answer $95.70 and eliminates "None of these."

The writer would conclude that by and large the item writing is about average, but that the test betrays the need for careful editing which it obviously did not get. Only if the ablest students take the test in the spirit of "what answer did the author intend to be considered right" instead of "what answer or answers can be defended as correct alternatives" would they score well on the test.

As to the mechanical arrangement involved, certainly the booklets are nicely printed with ample white space, but in many instances this white space has not been used effectively to improve the item impact. For example, in the word reasoning test there is plenty of room to use different kinds of stems which would have made it possible to test nouns more frequently than was done.

Quite frequently a subtest ends on an even numbered page which leaves the directions for the next test exposed. Thus a student who finishes a given test before time is called is allowed the advantage of studying the directions for the next test. This may make little or no difference if the tests truly are power tests, but the evidence on this point is confusing.

DIRECTIONS FOR ADMINISTRATION. On the whole, the Examiner's Manual for Series K seems to be well organized and reasonably clear and explicit. The writer searched diligently through the manual for some indication that the test was to be broken up into several sittings. Certainly the implication of the directions is that the pupils would be tested without a major break since the total testing time listed, excluding any optional test but including 5 minute breaks between tests, is 3 hours and 50 minutes. This seems to be an excessively long period to expect children of this level to attend to a task such as this.

The writer was pleased to see that the directions for preparing materials for return to the publisher for scoring indicate the need for scanning the answer sheets to detect weak or inadequate marking and double marked answers. No scoring machine, no matter how sophisticated, can compensate for poorly marked original documents. However, one of the directions as regards double marked answers reads, "Check to see that only one choice has been marked for each question." No directions are given as to what to do if double marked items are detected. Are the double marks to be erased or left alone? If they are to be left alone without any designation on the answer sheet that the responses are suspect, why check for double marked items? The writer's experience is that 3 or more double marked items in a single test of 50 or 60 items effectively nullifies the test and should cause the test to be thrown out as invalid. This can be particularly serious if the ablest students have resolved their feeling that a particular item is ambiguous by marking the two or three choices which they think can be defended.

SCORES AND NORMS. It would seem wise to combine scores on the subtests to obtain some kind of weighted composite score which in turn could be used to predict some kind of composite criterion or even some specific criterion according to high school subject. The writer can find no effective treatment or even reasonably good discussion of this problem in the materials made available to him for study. Provision is made for averaging the grade equivalents of the three achievement tests. However, grade equivalents are notoriously unsatisfactory as units because the standard deviations ordinarily vary greatly from subject to subject and from level to level. Many students may get totally unrealistic values, running up into grade values beyond the junior high school where there is no continuity of curriculum and the term "grade equivalent" as applying to specific subjects loses all meaning.

It is difficult to understand the omission of the educational ability measure from the composite, if this is intended to be the single best predictive measure to be derived from the battery. The writer is not advocating an elaborate statistical treatment of this subject. Weights derived, for example, by using a multiple regression equation against the criterion in one situation may not apply in another situation which superficially seems the same. (The problem of the bouncing betas.) It would be sufficient to express all of the scores in some kind of simple standard score and to assign judged weights to these components in terms of their judged importance for predicting success. Such judged weights could then be cross-validated against a number of samples to see to what extent reasonably good predictions were obtained. A considerable number of correlations are reported between the composite and a subject matter criterion but these are not particularly impressive.

Much time is spent in the technical report describing the procedure for obtaining norms. In view of the restricted uses for the tests, the entire problem of obtaining norms is largely an academic one. The tests are not normed adequately. Adequate norms would require administration to large groups of parochial school pupils. It is quite unsatisfactory to norm by equating to a test intended for general distribution (the *SRA Achievement Series*) in the public schools of the country even if the tests are quite similar. There is considerable reference to the equipercentile method of equating, but no discussion of how this operates and what its limitations are. The so-called grade equivalent norms reported are worse than useless because their applicability for selection purposes in the parochial school setting is open to serious question.

Unless the writer is misreading the text, a serious technical error was made in obtaining IQ equivalents for the educational ability score by equating to the *Otis Quick-Scoring Mental Ability Tests*. In the technical manual, it is reported that Otis IQ's were available for 899 students who took Form A of the educational ability subtest. No information is given as to how old these mental ability data were. The IQ's thus obtained were converted to mental ages by multiplying each respondent's IQ by his chronological age in months and dividing by 100. Raw scores on the educational ability test were then equated to these up-dated mental ages by the equipercentile method. The statement is then made that ratio IQ's may be found by reversing this process, namely, by dividing the respondent's mental age equivalent by his chronological age and that this procedure will yield IQ's comparable to Otis IQ's. Reference is made to the 1954 manual for Otis Beta. An examination of this manual indicates that tables of mental ages are given separately for Forms CM and DM and for Forms EM and FM. However, the Otis IQ's are *not* derived by the ratio method as suggested, but are derived by determining the deviation of a pupil's score from the norm for his age and adding or subtracting this deviation from 100. The Otis manual further states that the standard deviations of Beta IQ's have been found to range from 10 to 17 points and that, in one study of 32,000 pupils, the standard deviation was found to be 16.2 on the intermediate level of *Otis Self-Administering Tests of Mental Ability,* not the Otis Beta. The fact that the sample size is so large indicates that this obviously is a population of several grades not a single grade or age, although no specific information is given on this point. Otis further states that " 'Beta IQ's' tend to be somewhat less dispersed than IQ's obtained by the division method from group tests in general."

The method of up-dating mental age equivalents by multiplying a chronological age by the intelligence quotient is highly suspect in any case since it assumes that the mental age norm line (the line of relation between test score and age) is a straight line, which it never is, especially for children approaching the teenage level. But what is more serious is that the tables of mental ages in the Otis manual were contrived from the normative data solely to provide mental ages for those who wanted these values for their own sake and not as a method of computing the IQ. To make this more specific, consider the fact that the highest score on the Beta Test for which any age norm is given is 57, this score being assigned age equivalents from 17–6 to 17–11 inclusive. However, reference to the tables of mental ages indicates that a score of 57 has a mental age of 15–4!

TECHNICAL DATA. A substantial amount of data is presented regarding reliability but, in most instances, some essential information is lacking so that one cannot quite "nail down" all of the necessary facts to evaluate the data reported. If these data are taken at their face value, the reliability coefficients are within the expected limits judging from other evidence. Certainly the total score on the battery would be sufficiently reliable for the primary purpose of selection for grade 9 as well as the subsidiary purposes of organizing the school into relatively homogeneous groups for instructional purposes.

The technical report reports briefly an experiment to determine the possible effect of the change from the IBM 805 answer sheet to the more compact DocuTran sheet currently used with the test. The result of this experiment based upon 2,600 students indicated no significant difference between score distributions or means of the groups using each answer sheet. In view of the multiplicity of answer documents currently in use, this piece of information as to the transferability from one type of answer document to another is an important addition to our knowledge. This finding is probably generalizable to the answer sheets issued by the Measurement Research Center at Iowa since the MRC and DocuTran sheets are very similar in configuration.

The ultimate validation of this battery is something which must be done for each indigenous or homogeneous school system having a curriculum which is generally prescribed for all students within the population in question. The big problem in prediction is, as always, the matter of the criterion. Low correlations between test scores and performance in school may be due far more to the criterion than to the instrument used for predictive purposes. Research of this sort is time consuming and expensive, although the availability of electronic data processing equipment can do a great deal to simplify studies which in the past would have been quite out of the question. A number of validity studies are reported in the technical report. However, since validity is specific to the local situation theoretically, this is primarily a problem for those who *use* the test rather than for the publisher, except that SRA has the facilities to encourage far more local research if the local communities have the knowledge, desire, and financial means to support such investigation.

CONCLUSION. All reviewers necessarily approach the task of reviewing a test by comparing it with some hypothetical but nonexistent perfect product. This has the effect of making reviews seem more negative than they should be. Except for the serious inappropriateness of the arithmetical reasoning test as a part of the so-called educational ability section, most of the criticisms leveled at this test probably could be leveled at almost any test of similar nature. The preparation and editing of test items is a difficult task calling for great patience and great skill and knowledge. When single purpose tests with a limited life span are being prepared, some leniency should perhaps be shown. It is much easier to be critical than it is to be constructive in suggesting how the end product could be improved. Although the reviewer certainly cannot give this test his unqualified approval, he must conclude by saying it is not a bad test as such tests go.

CHARLES O. NEIDT, *Professor of Psychology, Colorado State University, Fort Collins, Colorado.* [Review of Series 63A, 63K, and 64A.]

The *SRA High School Placement Test* is designed for use with entering ninth grade students for general selection, placement, grouping, identification of superior students, identification of pupils with special instructional needs, and the evaluation of achievement. The HSPT yields six scores: educational ability expressed as IQ or percentile equivalent; four achievement measures (reading, arithmetic, language arts, and composite) expressed as grade equivalents or percentile equivalents; and Catholic religion (optional) expressed as a stanine score. The educational ability test and the three achievement subtests are bound in single booklets with detailed instructions to the pupil for using SRA DocuTran answer sheets.

The 60-item educational ability test includes four sections: word reasoning (word meaning), arithmetic reasoning (number problems), verbal analogies, and number reasoning (number series). Although no individual item statistics are reported, this test appears to be a satisfactory measure of general scholastic aptitude. Kuder-Richardson formula 20 reliability is reported as .89 ($n = 521$) and test-retest reliability as .91 ($n = 55$).

Derived scores on the educational ability test are expressed as IQ's or as percentile equivalents. The mental age equivalents on which to base IQ's were obtained by equating raw scores on the educational ability test to mental age equivalents based on *Otis Quick-Scoring Mental Ability Test* results for 899 pupils. From this distribution the percentile equivalents were derived. Conversion of the educational ability raw score directly to a derived IQ would seem to this reviewer to be a more straightforward procedure than conversion of the raw score to mental age followed by division by the subject's chronological age. Nevertheless, substitution of the present educational ability test for the *Purdue Non-Language Test* which was included in the 1957 edition of the HSPT is a definite improvement for the purposes for which this test is intended.

The achievement subtests of the *SRA High School Placement Test* consist of generally well constructed items, although no individual item statistics are shown. While the arithmetic subtest is quite detailed, it appears to have a rather low ceiling for pupils who have experienced an enriched mathematics curriculum.

In the Technical Report on Series 63A and 63K, six tables are included showing the relation of Series 63K scores to various other measures of pupil achievement such as course marks. The contents of these tables are duplicated in the Technical Report on Series 63K and 64K (except for typographical errors) with the implication that these results could encompass Series 64K. In the opinion of this reviewer such a practice is misleading and undesirable. In general, however, the correlations with course marks shown in the technical reports are relatively high.

Norms for the achievement subtests of each current series are based on the 1960 edition of the HSPT. The 1960 edition norms, in turn, were based on the 1955 standardization of the grades 6–9 level of the *SRA Achievement Series*. The 1955 standardization sample of approximately 4,500 eighth and ninth graders was carefully stratified according to national census data. The 1960 HSPT edition was patterned in form and content after the corresponding subtests in the achievement series and was equated by an equipercentile procedure with the 1955 norms. Each year the new series is equated with the 1960 norms after administration of the new form and the 1960 form to 1,000 to 1,500 pupils. For Series 63A, these pupils were all from the Chicago area. Representative as the 1955 sample may have been, changes in curricula and in population characteristics after nine years warrant a new standardization for this test if interpretation is to be accurate. In addition, since the test is used primarily in parochial schools, consideration should be given to normative data based on performance of pupils within such schools.

Almost all studies reported show significant sex differences for the four achievement subtest scores, the mean scores of girls tending to be higher than those of boys. This difference is noted even when the mean educational ability scores of boys are higher than those of girls. Careful inspection of item statistics classified by sex, or the preparation of separate norms, seem warranted by such a consistent difference.

Perhaps the greatest shortcoming of the *SRA High School Placement Test* is the failure to include a measure of science achievement. Increased emphasis on elementary science in recent years dictates that such an evaluation be undertaken if all the purposes for which this test is designed are to be achieved.

The optional Catholic Religion Test is designed to measure the student's understanding of the facts and principles of the Catholic religion. It is appropriately emphasized in the separate manual for this test that the test is not a measure of devoutness. In the only concurrent validity study cited, the test correlated .60 with religion grades for 262 eighth grade pupils. It appears that the test may be rather heavily loaded with verbal ability components, since correlations of .77 with the HSPT reading subtest, .60 with the arithmetic subtest, .64 with the language arts subtest, and .77 with the composite score for 591 pupils were obtained. No relationship between scores on the religion test and measures of mental ability are reported.

In summary, Series 63A, 63K, and 64K of the *SRA High School Placement Test* represent improvements over earlier editions. Addition of a science subtest would be highly desirable to assure that the HSPT parallels modern curricula. Consideration should also be given to establishing new norms for the test. Greater emphasis on item statistics and prepublication analysis of current forms would be appropriate. The test is designed to fill a unique educational need and with continued improvement will make a substantial contribution.

For reviews by Cyril J. Hoyt (with W. Wesley Tennyson) and William W. Turnbull of the 1957 and 1958 tests, see 5:22.

[23]

***Scholastic Achievement Series.** Grades 1.5–2.5, 2.5–3, 4–6, 7–9; 1953–59; various titles used by publisher; for Catholic schools; 11–13 scores: English (total and 2–4 subscores), spelling, arithmetic (total and 2 subscores), religion (total and 3 subscores); IBM for grades 4–9; 4 levels; subtests for grades 2.5–9 in English-spelling, arithmetic, and religion available as separates; $4 per 20 tests; separate answer sheets may be used in grades 4–9; $3 per 20 sets of IBM scorable answer sheets; 50¢ per specimen set of any one level; postage extra; Oliver F. Anderhalter, R. Stephen Gawkoski, and John O'Brien; Scholastic Testing Service, Inc. *

a) PRE-PRIMARY BATTERY. Grades 1.5–2.5; 1955; Form A (15 pages); manual (15 pages); (65–75) minutes.

b) PRIMARY BATTERY. Grades 2.5–3; 1953–59; Forms A ('53), B ('55), (16 pages); manual ('59, 12 pages); (85–95) minutes.
c) ELEMENTARY BATTERY. Grades 4–6; 1954–58; IBM; Forms A ('54, 28 pages), B ('55, 31 pages); manual ('58, 21 pages, technical data and norms same as in 1955 manual); 60¢ per set of scoring stencils; (145) minutes.
d) ADVANCED BATTERY. Grades 7–9; 1954–59; IBM; Forms A, B, ('54, 28 pages); manual ('59, 22 pages, technical data and norms same as in 1955 manual); 48¢ per set of scoring stencils; (145) minutes.

J. STANLEY AHMANN, *Professor of Psychology and Head of the Department, Colorado State University, Fort Collins, Colorado.*

The *Scholastic Achievement Series* is a battery of tests designed for elementary schools which are operated under the jurisdiction of the Roman Catholic Church. Four levels are available, each including four achievement tests. These tests are intended to measure pupil knowledge with respect to English, spelling, arithmetic, and religion.

The principal unique feature of this battery of tests is the attempt to measure the pupil's knowledge of the Catholic religion. This is the principal justification for developing a separate series of tests for Catholic elementary schools. The content of the test has been determined by study of the course content of a sample of elementary schools which the authors believe to be geographically representative of the nation with respect to Catholic schools. Little evidence to support this belief is provided.

The tests have changed little since they were originally published in 1953–1955. Consequently, the detailed reviews published in *The Fifth Mental Measurements Yearbook* are quite pertinent and should be studied. In general, these reviews raise questions concerning (*a*) the degree of content validity of these tests, in particular the English tests and in some respects the arithmetic tests, (*b*) the amount of information provided with respect to the development of the tests and the interpretation of the scores yielded, (*c*) the less than satisfactory format of some of the tests, and (*d*) the representativeness of the standardization population. In only minor instances does this reviewer disagree with these criticisms.

An even more basic question, however, is the question of the appropriateness of developing a set of standardized achievement tests in the basic skills area for exclusive use in the Catholic elementary schools. Such a tailor-made battery could be considered a manifestation of provincialism which is not in the best interest of education in this country. On what pedagogical or philosophical grounds can one support the contention that the measurement of the command of the basic skills of pupils enrolled in Catholic schools requires special achievement tests such as those included in the *Scholastic Achievement Series?* Unless a satisfactory answer can be given to the foregoing question, the merits of the tests must be judged in terms of the qualities of widely used standardized achievement tests in the area of the basic skills. These tests will provide a high standard for comparison purposes.

In addition to the questions raised in earlier reviews with respect to the degree of content validity of the English and arithmetic tests, doubts must be raised as to suitability of the degree of content validity of the religion tests. This well could be the most serious validity question of all, since the religion tests are the major unique contribution made by the entire battery.

The authors admit that the content of the religion tests was difficult to establish because of the great variation in grade placement of content which was found. Although three general areas, namely, creed, commandments, and sacraments, were usually included during successive three year periods beginning at the fourth grade, the location of the grade placement of specific points within these categories evidently is not firmly established. It is inevitable, therefore, that the degree of content validity is in doubt. Probably it is low for some schools. Hence, particular care must be taken in terms of the interpretation of the test scores in this area at the upper grade levels. No tables of specifications are shown.

Evidently the content in religion is more stable below third grade. The authors found that the "*First Communion Catechism* is the essence of the content in over 75% of the courses of study screened." On the other hand, vocabulary problems are serious in the religion test in the preprimary and primary battery. Variations in religious instruction which yield variations in command of terminology could produce distressing variations in test scores. For example, even such a relatively minor variation as the use of the expressions "Holy Spirit" rather than "Holy Ghost" could cause a first grade pupil a needless problem with respect to the item 7 in Test 8, Form A, of the preprimary test. This illustrates how the degree of content validity can shift in small but important ways as a result of terminology variations.

All of the religion tests were copyrighted between 1953 and 1955. This means that, at this writing, the analysis of content occurred at least 10 years ago. Yet far reaching changes have taken place in the instructional materials and methods of teaching religion in the Catholic elementary schools. Certainly these changes are sufficiently important to cause the authors to restudy immediately the content included in the religion tests.

SUMMARY. The principal justification for the use of the *Scholastic Achievement Series* is that the tests included are uniquely suited for Catholic elementary schools. If the religion tests are ignored, this justification is weak. Certainly the recent revision of the *Stanford Achievement Test* as well as the original edition of the *Iowa Tests of Basic Skills,* to name just two batteries, are undoubtedly superior to the *Scholastic Achievement Series* in their ability to measure a pupil's command of the basic skills. If the principal justification for the *Scholastic Achievement Series* is the religion test, then it seems logical to use the separate booklets for that test when it is possible to do so. Even this test, however, can be challenged vigorously in terms of its degree of content validity. Instructional materials in the area of religion are being modernized, and even the methods of teaching religion are changing in a number of Catholic schools. To the degree this is occurring, the grade placement of the content is unstable and the degree of content validity seriously drops in the case of the administration of this test in at least some of the schools for which it is designed. Carefully designed tables of specifications would be most helpful in the content validity study with respect to these tests.

THOMAS W. MAHAN, JR., *Consultant in Guidance, Connecticut State Department of Education, Hartford, Connecticut.*

The basis for the development of this achievement battery is the assumption on the part of the publisher that existing instruments did not and could not validly assess the curricular outcomes of the Catholic elementary school system and that a new test whose content was closely geared to the offerings of the Catholic schools was needed. The *Scholastic Achievement Series* is the result of this belief and it has been published after a survey of the curricular content in Catholic schools "representing 46% of the dioceses in the country." Although the intent to provide instruments relevant to the educational goals of a school or school system is both important and desirable, the publisher presents no real evidence that the *Scholastic Achievement Series* does more validly assess the curricular goals. At no place in the manuals does there appear comparative data with other achievement batteries which have enjoyed wide usage in the Catholic elementary schools nor is there any evidence, other than the survey of content referred to above, to justify the assumed homogeneity of Catholic schools in varying sections of the country and differing socioeconomic regions. A study of the tests included in the series reveals only the religion test as unique in any way and leaves the reviewer puzzled over the omission of reading, social studies, and study skills from the battery.

The procedure for item selection is well described in the manuals, although a more comprehensive tabular description of the relationship of items to total score and of the item level of difficulty would considerably enhance this section. Also very commendable is the provision of three measures of the reliability of each of the subtests for the Primary, Elementary, and Advanced Batteries. Yet this, too, is somewhat obscured by the use of the median "single-year coefficient"; since the grade span is small, the data for each grade level would be more meaningful. In this connection, it appears that the manuals assume a level of sophistication which may not be realistic; for example, the standard error of measurement is clearly given for each subtest, but no clear description is provided of the meaning of this figure. Again, a profile sheet is provided for plotting each pupil's scores on the various tests, but the profile sheet is graduated in terms of grade equivalents in spite of the publisher's statement in the manual that "such results [i.e., grade equivalent scores] can be misleading unless percentile ranks corresponding to such equivalents are considered." The very fact that the profile sheet is so constructed will lead many to assume that grade equivalent scores in various areas are comparable while the normative data explicitly contradict this.

The major weakness in the test is the lack of validity data. The manuals for the various levels present the evidence for item validity in terms of difficulty indices and higher median scores at higher grade levels. This, along with the statement of content sampling, is the major claim to validity. Only in the manual for the Advanced Battery is any data presented for concurrent validity. Here there is some evidence of moderate correlation with mental ability tests ($n = 163$) and with reading comprehension. Also presented are the correlations of the four tests (English, arithmetic, religion, and spelling) with the letter grades in these subjects for 70 eighth grade subjects; the correlations here range from .52 to .61. The small size of the sample and the vagueness of the criteria reduce the meaningfulness of these data.

All in all, this achievement series does not at the present time appear to have established its intended usefulness for evaluating the outcomes of the Catholic elementary system. Its major claim to uniqueness is the inclusion of a religion test which will probably prove very useful to the intended users. The other tests are not unique in form or content, their range of content seems somewhat restricted, and there is no evidence that they are more valid in assessing the curricular outcomes of Catholic education than are other instruments which provide more comprehensive technical information. The need for much expanded evidence of concurrent validity, for further item analyses in terms of validity criteria, and for reports of the homogeneity versus heterogeneity of the Catholic schools in comparison with public schools must be satisfied. In addition, improved interpretative data should be made available before this instrument can be assumed to be meeting the demand for increased curricular relevance which led to its development.

For reviews by William E. Coffman and James R. Hayden, see 5:23. For reviews of subtests, see 5:201 and 5:484.

[24]

★Secondary School Admission Tests: General School Ability and Reading Test. Students in grades 6–11 who are applying for admission to independent secondary schools; 1957–63; tests administered 3 times annually (December, February, April) at centers established by the publisher; test consists of secure forms of the *Cooperative School and College Ability Tests* and *Reading Comprehension: Cooperative English Test,* [*1960 Revision*]; 7 scores: verbal, quantitative, ability total, vocabulary, speed of comprehension, level of comprehension, reading total; IBM; Form KST ('62, c1961–62, 29 pages) used in 1962–63 program; bulletin of information for candidates ('63, 30 pages); score interpretation manual ('63, 26 pages); examination fee: $7; fee includes reporting of scores to 1–6 schools designated at the time of testing; reports to additional schools free on application; scores not reported to candidates; 110(125) minutes; program administered for the Secondary School Admission Test Board; Educational Testing Service. *

REFERENCES

1. SPAULDING, GERALDINE. "Some Data on the Relation Between the Junior Scholastic Aptitude Test and the General School Ability Test Used in the Secondary School Admission Test Program." *Ed Rec B* 79:62–4 Jl '61. *

CHARLES O. NEIDT, *Professor of Psychology, Colorado State University, Fort Collins, Colorado.* [Review of Forms JST and KST.]

The *Secondary School Admission Tests* consist of two tests in a single booklet, a General School Ability Test and a Reading Test. They are designed for "helping to select students for admission to grades 7 through 12." From the six subtests comprising these two tests, seven scores are derived. The three scores derived from the ability test are: verbal (sentence completion and synonyms subtests); quantitative (arithmetic computation and arithmetic reasoning subtests); and total (all four subtests). The four scores derived from the Reading Test are: vocabulary (a synonyms-type subtest); speed of comprehension (a 60-item paragraph comprehension subtest); total reading (average of the vocabulary and speed of comprehension scores); and level of comprehension score (first 30 of the 60 paragraph comprehension items of the speed of comprehension subtest). All applicants are administered the same tests, regardless of grade level.

The tests are the basic components of a school admissions program, the policies for which are determined by the Secondary School Admission Test Board, an association of 50 independent secondary schools. The program is administered by the Educational Testing Service. Participating schools are charged yearly fees of $25 or more depending on the number of score reports sent to them. Candidates pay a fee of $7 to take the tests which are administered at more than 300 test centers in the United States and abroad. The tests are administered three times during the year. Candidates may have their scores sent to as many as six participating schools for the regular fee. Scores are not reported to candidates or their parents, but may be discussed with them by school officials.

Since the *Secondary School Admissions Tests* are part of a program, several kinds of documents have been prepared for prospective participants and members of the program. These range from attractively printed brochures describing the general aspects of the program to mimeographed summaries containing distributions of the characteristics of participating schools and candidates. Reference to several of these sources is necessary for a total comprehension of the tests and the program. Although all materials are interrelated, three documents other than the printed tests are pertinent to this review and will be discussed individually: the Score Interpretation Manual, a statistical report on Form JST, and a report on the predictive validity of forms used in 1959 and 1960.

SCORE INTERPRETATION MANUAL. The Educational Testing Service has prepared an "interpretive manual" for use by schools participating in the program. The manual is straightforward, lucid, and unusually readable. Discussions of procedures for constructing local norms for using General School Ability Test scores as predictors of school marks as well as of College Board scores are excellent. Explanations of concepts embodied in norms and in the precision of scores for comparison are also above average in clarity and readability. Although the manner in which scaled scores are to be used is described clearly in the manual, no explanation of the relationship between raw scores and scaled scores is made. In the norm tables appended to the manual, percentile ranks corresponding to scores of a national sample of public school students (but not for the program norms) are reported as decimals for the first and last ranks in the distribution. Such a procedure seems to this reviewer to be unnecessary.

TEST ANALYSIS OF FORM JST. Analyses of results based on approximately 12,000 cases in grades 6 through 11 are included in this report. As might be expected, the test differentiates most effectively among eighth and ninth graders, and is somewhat difficult for sixth graders and somewhat easy for tenth and eleventh graders. Considering the range of abilities represented in the total group, the score distributions for each grade level are surprisingly symmetrical.

The remainder of the data reported are based on scores for 320 sixth grade pupils and 370 eighth and ninth grade pupils. Kuder-Richardson formula 20 reliability coefficients for these groups range from .79 for level of comprehension to .89 for aptitude total at the sixth grade level, and from .78 for level of comprehension to .92 for aptitude total at the combined eighth and ninth grade level. In view of the extensive use of the tests for admission decisions at both the eighth and ninth grade levels, however, it would be appropriate to have reliability data available for each of these grade levels separately as well as for the others which the test covers.

Examination of the intercorrelations among the nonreported subtest scores indicates that the three measures of verbal ability (sentence completion, synonyms, and the vocabulary subtest of the Reading Test) have high intercorrelations in relation to their reliabilities. For example, the sentence completion section correlates .68 with synonyms and the reliabilities are .73 and .66, respectively, for the sixth grade level. For the eighth-ninth grade level, the intercorrelation is .80 and the reliabilities are .79 and .78. Reference is made in the report to the high intercorrelation between the vocabulary subtest of the Reading Test and the other two measures of verbal ability. Three possibilities for improving the situation are suggested in this report; pooling the vocabulary section with the other two subtests, replacing the vocabulary section with other type items, and lengthening the level of comprehension subtest. This reviewer concurs that all three possibilities are appropriate and would suggest further scrutiny of the two subtests composing the verbal score.

It will be recalled that the speed of comprehension score of the Reading Test consists of performance on paragraph comprehension type items and that performance on the first 30 of these items yields the level of comprehension score. The correlation between these two measures is .83 for grade 6 and .81 for grades 8 and 9. It is noted that these correlation coefficients are spuriously high since the speed score contains the level score also. From a test analysis standpoint, it would be appropriate to know the correlation between performance on the first 30 items and the corresponding performance on the last 30 items. The procedure of obtaining two reading measures for the 60 items is an efficient one, but more evidence is necessary to support its validity.

Data relating to internal consistency of item responses and to the range of chance scores for each subtest are adequate. Similar analyses for each grade level covered by these tests, however, would be desirable.

REPORT ON PREDICTIVE VALIDITY. This report contains the results of a study on the effectiveness of SSAT scores obtained in 1959 and 1960 for predicting the academic success of ninth grade boys at two independent schools. Effectiveness of the test scores in predicting ninth grade averages is compared with predictions obtained using previous school averages and age as predictors of the same criteria.

Some discrepancies between schools and, in one school, between years are noted in the predictive effectiveness of the tests. Based on samples of 1959 and 1960 entrants, respectively, correlations of .52 and .51 for one school and .68 and .41 for the other were obtained between ability total scores and overall ninth grade averages. As might be expected, combinations of test scores and previous grade average increased predictive effectiveness somewhat (to .57 for one school and .59 for the other for the 1959 and 1960 samples combined) but age contributed little to increasing effectiveness in predicting overall averages. Correlations between the test scores and various other criteria (English and mathematics averages) suggest that the test scores have satisfactory, although not uniformly high, predictive effectiveness.

GENERAL COMMENTS. Inspection of Form JST and Form KST reveals that their format is attractive, the directions are generally clear, and the specially prepared answer sheet is easy to use. The individual items in the subtests appear to be well constructed and to have plausible distractors. This reviewer feels, however, that the predictive effectiveness of the total test could be enhanced by sampling a greater variety of items. Restricting the quantitative sections to basic arithmetic computation and problem solving skills seems unduly severe. In addition, two subtests measuring knowledge of synonyms seem unnecessary.

In summary, the *Secondary School Admission Tests* are the result of sound although limited test construction procedures and analyses. They are designed to fill a particular need of independent schools and, with modifications based on additional analyses, they offer promise of making an excellent contribution to the selection process.

DAVID V. TIEDEMAN, *Professor of Education, Harvard University, Cambridge, Massachusetts.* [Review of Forms JST and KST.]

The General School Ability Test (GSAT) and the Reading Test are jointly issued as the *Secondary School Admission Tests* (SSAT). The tests are offered three days per year as secure tests. They are taken by students applying for admission to one or more of approximately 300 independent secondary schools. However, the tests are set by members of the 50 independent secondary schools which comprise the Secondary School Admission Test Board. Educational Testing Service administers the program. Other secondary schools may participate in the program for a small fee. There are approximately 25,000 students who now annually take the examination.

The GSAT consists of four sections which are combined to form a score of verbal and numerical abilities as well as a total score. The verbal ability score consists of responses to an equal number (30) of items requiring the identification of one of five words appropriate to the context of a sentence or the identification among five options of the synonym of the word in the stem. The numerical ability score consists of the answers to an equal number (25) of arithmetical computations and arithmetical problems.

The GSAT is in the tradition of the *Cooperative School and College Ability Test.* Opinion about that test is now generally available and needs no augmentation here. The GSAT is one of several tests which permit the anticipation of general performance in school as well as testmakers have so far been able to accomplish such anticipation.

The Reading Test is in two parts, vocabulary and reading comprehension. The latter section is scored in its entirety as an indicator of speed of comprehension and in its first 30 questions as an indicator of level of comprehension. The total reading score is an average of the vocabulary and speed of comprehension scores. The 60 items in the vocabulary section require identification of the synonym of the stem as is true of the 30 items in the third section of the GSAT. The reading scores come from the answers to 60 questions based on the information provided in one of the twelve or more paragraphs which must be read in order to answer the questions. I have commented (see my review of test 11 in this volume) that the reading section of the *High School Classification Examination* (HSCE) has several questions which can be answered without reading the paragraphs on which they are presumably based. This possibility also exists in the Reading Test of the SSAT. The independence seems less marked in the SSAT than it did in the HSCE, however. This may be due merely to the ease of the reading test in the HSCE because the HSCE is intended for pupils in grades 8 and 9 while the SSAT serves the admission requirements of students who take the test while enrolled in any one of the grades from 6 to 11.

The Reading Test of SSAT is in the tradition of the test of reading comprehension of the Cooperative Test Division. Therefore I shall not comment more specifically on this well known form of reading test. It does seem slightly incongruous, however, that this rather thorough test of reading skill is recommended only as an admission instrument in the SSAT program while its shorter counterpart in the HSCE is offered for both the selection of students and their classification once they are admitted to a high school.

While the GSAT and the Reading Test are each worthy in their own right, they are slightly grotesque when wed. The grotesqueness arises from the synonym section which appears in both the GSAT and the Reading Test as a separate test with different names. (The directions in the vocabulary section seem more appropriate than they do in the synonym section, too.) The result is that about four tenths of the answers to the test can be for synonym questions and the report acts as if these are different subtests.

The Test Analysis of Form JST of SSAT indicates that the Educational Testing Service is aware of the redundancy in the two sections of the test. The analysis reports that the correlation between the verbal and vocabulary scores of the test is practically 1.00 when allowance is made for the unreliability of the two scores. The analysis merely poses the question, however; it does not indicate an answer. It is true that admission to a selective school is always a delicate matter. Care and accuracy in decisions of this nature are therefore of great importance and even of some consequence. This fact may alone justify the continued redundancy in use of synonyms. Synonyms do provide a good way to assess potential scholastic ability. It does seem, however, that the Educational Testing Service would be able to solve this problem even if it meant a reduction in the number of synonym items which were to determine the total score on the test. If no other kinds of items were to be substituted for those eliminated, a shorter test would require less time of the student and might perhaps be offered for a smaller fee.

The publisher has studied the relationship between scores on the test and the grades which admitted students made in the ninth grade of two of the independent schools which participate in the program. The total score on the test prior to entry correlated with the grade average at the school at the end of the year at a level of approximately .55. The correlation of the previous grade average with the average in the independent school one year later was on the order of .40. The regression combination of the two variables brought the correlation to about .60. These results held in three of the four instances reported. The data for the replication of results in one of the schools were much less impressive. The cause of the difference could not be ascertained.

The results on the predictive validity of the test are well within expectation. The previous grade record is also a bit of information worthy of careful scrutiny in this process of deciding on admission, at least if a school is interested in the grades which its students make as freshmen. However, it is a bit surprising that the income from this program and the probable interest which it generates among applicants so far brings only one study of predictive validity from the publisher to the reviewer. The predictive validity of the test seems to be no better known than is that of one of its competitors, the *High School Classification Examination.*

The psychometric properties (other than predictive validity) of the test have been studied rather carefully. The Educational Testing Service has recently satisfied itself (and me) about the capacity of the test to be discriminating over its range from grade 6 to 11.

Furthermore, speed does not seem to figure in the test except in the speed of comprehension subtest in which it is intentionally placed. The total scores on the test and each of its two aspects have reliability coefficients which make possible somewhat fine discrimination among subjects when necessary. The reliability of the separate scores justifies only coarser discriminations, however. In general, guidance on the basis of sectional scores can be done only in terms of rather gross distinctions. The scales on the test are constructed with care and offer the possibility of comparability within section from test to test. The scale is placed in an unusual range, however; namely from about 240 to about 360.

The policy governing participation in the program does not authorize the report of scores to the students who are the ones who pay for them. Scores are reported to the school in which the student is registered when he takes the examination if the school requests such a report. A Score Interpretation Manual is provided which will undoubtedly help the admission officers of the schools which participate in the program. The manual will also be of some slight help to the counselor or principal of the school which the applicant is attending when he applies. The interpretations of such officers will be limited to designation of the student's rank among all applicants and to the likelihood of obtaining a particular score on the CEEB *Scholastic Aptitude Test,* however. Short shrift indeed for him who pays and tries. But perhaps this is necessary in admission to independent secondary school because the transition may not always please the school the student is leaving, and the school the student is leaving may not always enjoy the trust of the student and his parent.

The SSAT are indeed sound psychometric instruments which seem to be performing as expected in an admission program which is long established. The length, kind, and craftsmanship of the tests seem satisfactory except for the problem of possible redundancy due to an inordinate reliance upon a knowledge of synonyms. This problem is known to Educational Testing Service and may soon be solved. The problem is indeed in need of resolution. The test is not offered for purposes of classification or guidance although it could probably be used in these ways with the assembly of relatively little other information. But then the magnitude of the fee would probably cause concern from potential institutional users.

The independent schools pride themselves on their capacity to be different. They are sometimes envied for this capacity. Perhaps they might do a little to earn this envy in the psychometric field. At the present time the aspects of the admission program revealed to me appear of hoary tradition. I was not greatly excited although I am admittedly not incensed either.

[25]

***Sequential Tests of Educational Progress.** Grades 4–6, 7–9, 10–12, 13–14; 1956–63; IBM and Grade-O-Mat; also called STEP; 7 tests: reading, writing, mathematics, science, social studies, listening, essay; Forms A, B, ('57) of each test except essay test (Forms A, B, C, D); 4 levels; directions ('57, 12 pages) for all tests except listening and essay tests; directions ('57, 22–24 pages, separate booklet for each form) for listening test; examiner's handbooks ('57, 34 pages, separate booklet for each level) for essay test; interpretive manuals ('57, 29–32 pages, separate booklet for each test except essay test); battery technical report ('57, 58 pages); 1958 SCAT-STEP supplement ('58, 32 pages); 1962 SCAT-STEP supplement ('62, 49 pages); 1963 SCAT-STEP supplement of urban norms ('63, 16 pages); teacher's guide ('59, 85 pages); STEP-SCAT profile ('57, 2 pages); STEP-SCAT student report ('58, 4 pages); no data on reliability of Form B; separate answer sheets must be used (except with essay test); $4 per 20 tests (except essay test); $1 per 20 essay tests; $1 per 20 IBM scorable answer sheets; 25¢ per scoring stencil; $2 per 20 Scribe answer sheets (see 763 for scoring service); see 666 for prices of Grade-O-Mat cards; $1 per 20 profiles; $1 per 20 student reports; $1 per pad of 50 score distribution sheets; $1 per directions for listening test; $1 per handbook for essay test; $1 per interpretive manual; $1 per technical report; $1 per supplement; $1 per teacher's guide; postage extra; $1.25 per essay test specimen set; $3 per combined specimen set (with interpretive manual for one test only) of reading, writing, and listening or mathematics, science, and social studies; $5 per battery specimen set (with interpretive manual for one test only); cash orders postpaid; descriptive booklet free; 35(40) minutes for essay test, (90–100) minutes for listening test, 70(90–100) minutes for any other test; Cooperative Test Division. *

REFERENCES

1. Traxler, Arthur E. "Some Data on the Results of the Sequential Tests of Educational Progress (STEP), Level 3, Form A, for Small Groups of Pupils in Two Independent Schools for Girls." *Ed Rec B* 72:69–73 Jl '58. * (*PA* 33:11035)

2. Bartlett, Claude J., and Baumeister, Alfred A. "Prediction of Classroom Discipline Problems." *Excep Child* 27:216–8+ D '60. * (*PA* 36:4JO16B)

3. Garlock, J. C., and Harsh, J. R. "A Comparative Study of Four Commonly Used Achievement Tests." *Calif J Ed Res* 11:147–54 S '60. * (*PA* 35:7117)

4. Hills, John R.; Emory, Linda B.; Franz, Gretchen; and Crowder, Dolores Garcia. "Admissions and Guidance Research in the University System of Georgia." *Personnel & Guid J* 39:452–7 F '61. * (*PA* 35:7102)

5. Fortna, Richard O. "A Factor-Analytic Study of the Cooperative School and College Ability Tests and Sequential Tests of Educational Progress." *J Exp Ed* 32:187–90 w '63. *

6. Wellck, A. A. "Statewide Tests and Academic Success at the University of New Mexico." *Personnel & Guid J* 42:403–5 D '63. *

HAROLD SEASHORE, *Director, Test Division, The Psychological Corporation, New York, New York.*

In *The Fifth Mental Measurements Yearbook* the *Sequential Tests of Educational Progress* received 37 pages of critical review. Jackson and Layton used 12 pages to describe and evaluate the battery as a whole and comment on each part. The seven separate tests were accorded 24 pages of detailed assessment. One journal review was reproduced.

The 1959 reviews probably were written in STEP's second year. The present reviewer can avoid considerable redundancy by endorsing the 1959 reports. Anyone currently interested in using the STEP battery should read the accounts in *The Fifth MMY,* especially those by Jackson and Layton. They are basic. The present reviewer is responsible for a general over-view as of late 1963; other reviewers will deal with the seven parts of the series.

To remind the reader of the structure of this battery, the components will be outlined. For six areas—Reading, Writing, Science, Mathematics, Listening, and Social Studies—there are two *forms* (A and B) for each of four *levels* (1, 2, 3, and 4). Appropriate and normal grades to which the levels are administered are as follows: 1, grades 13–14; 2, grades 10–12; 3, grades 7–9; 4, grades 4–6. The manuals observe that it is permissible to deviate from this pattern. For example, a slow grade 7 group or grade 7 pupil might be examined with level 4 tests. Since grade designations do not appear on the test copies and the same answer sheet is used for all the tests, mixtures of levels and forms can be used in the same testing session, the administrators having determined in advance which particular test, level, or form each student is to take. Of course, only one form of the orally presented listening test can be given in one room in one period. The format of booklets, answer sheets, and directions which permit this flexibility is a strong feature of the test battery. The Essay Tests are somewhat different in format, since the student writes in his test booklet. There are four forms at each level.

This complex of tests, levels, and forms to embrace grade 4 through the second year of college necessarily requires quite an inventory of "pieces." The specimen set includes 64 different test booklets for the seven areas, well-identified by color and titles. There are 48 different keys used for hand scoring and for IBM 805 scoring. The Essay Tests have no objective keys but are scored by comparison with model essays in the Handbooks. The printing and layout of items are excellent. One IBM 805 answer sheet is usable with each of the 48 different tests, all but the Essay Test. Even though this scheme places more responsibility on students and teachers to identify properly the test, level, and form, the "universal" STEP answer sheet is clever and commendable. There is also a Scribe answer sheet which provides on two sides for six of the seven STEP tests plus SCAT.

The basic administrative and technical manuals (21 in all) seem not to have been changed. All but one bear the 1957 date; one appeared in 1959. (Even in 1963 a pink errata sheet dated 1961 was included in the reviewer's specimen set.) There is a general manual entitled STEP: Directions for Administering and Scoring which serves five tests. Essay and Listening present sufficiently special problems of administering and scoring to require separate treatment. The Essay Test requires four separate manuals (one for each level) and Listening eight (one for each level and form). Thus there are 13 different administration and scoring booklets which a school must keep track of if STEP is used widely in the system. One teacher administering one form of all seven tests to one grade must have on hand at least three different administrative guides. When she later tries to interpret and understand the scores, she will need at least eight additional booklets, discussed below. The teacher might not wish to study the Technical Report.

It is understandable that Listening will require eight different scripts for the two forms at each of four levels. These are presented in eight 24-page booklets with semi-hard covers, 192 pages in all. In each one of these only the 13 pages of orally presented script are specific to the form or level; the other pages are identical for all levels and forms, except for about a half dozen lines which are special for level 4. Two books of 64 pages could embrace Form A and B content for levels 1 and 2 and a similar manual would do for levels 3 and 4. Consider the four Essay manuals. Each is 36 pages including the covers. In these, only 11 or 12 pages are specific to the *level;* the remaining content is identical for all levels and forms.

One 64-page manual would do the whole job now spread out over 144 pages.

The other five tests are administered from instructions in one well-written booklet called STEP: Directions for Administering and Scoring. The examiner is adequately informed. The directions are so general that the teacher makes no references to the title or content of the particular test being administered and the one sample item is the very same for every test at every level. The purpose of this generality is to permit giving any mixture of levels, forms, and tests in any room at the same time. With no further exploration of the nature of the content or the structure of the items, students plunge directly into the test. This seems to be plausible for tests like Reading and Mathematics, but the first items in Writing are like none that students, especially those in lower grades, will have seen before. This reviewer, however, has a preference for directions which clearly help the student understand the structure of the items so that his score is maximally dependent on his responses to substance. This reviewer suspects that, except in counseling centers, such mixtures of *areas* in one period are unlikely to occur very often; however, two *levels* of a given test area might be used fairly often when a wide range of performance is expected in one grade group.

To provide information for interpreting scores, understanding the tests themselves, and facilitating local utilization of data, there is a separate Manual for Interpreting Scores for each of six tests. These six 36-page manuals have about 15 pages in common—covers, blank pages, general information, and a five-page listing of schools which cooperated on norms. Each manual has about one page listing professional contributors, about half of each list being common to all lists. The *unique* material —that describing each particular test and the norms for each test—requires only seven pages. Then, there are about 13 pages of material which are almost identical in all six manuals. The differences arise mainly because profiles of four students are used and different comments are needed as each test is discussed. The well-chosen cases are the same in all six documents. However, the discussions are geared to general principles which are stated in nearly identical paragraphs. The topics discussed are relevant and well presented. With a modest amount of rewriting, these interpretive sections could be made common to all six tests. It is estimated that in place of six 36-page interpretive manuals, one single manual of not over 64 pages would do the job.

As the reader will have gathered, this reviewer is taken aback by the sheer number of pieces of manuals and handbooks one needs for a complete specimen set of STEP. It is understandable that the editors were torn between producing a few comprehensive manuals and technical documents and, on the other hand, having a plan whereby a given teacher on a given day in a given classroom would need only the precise materials for giving the test to be administered in that period. While this latter goal is desirable, the "five foot shelf" of STEP documents does not seem necessary to serve that goal. Just how many times must a teacher in grade 6 read the answer to this question, "What is a percentile rank?" Why must she read it in seven manuals? And how does she know that the manuals are essentially duplicates unless she, like this reviewer, reads the whole collection? And, as a matter of practicality, why must she check tables in seven different books to verify the percentile bands a clerk may have posted on a particular student's record form? It is hoped that potential users of STEP do not judge the quality of the battery by poundage of two-color printing. These eminent tests should stand on their own psychometric feet. In general the STEP manuals include functional information. They just overpower one with redundancy.

The 1957 Technical Report is still a basic document for six tests. The technical data for the Essay Tests are in separate manuals. Three Supplements, embracing both SCAT and STEP, have appeared as well as a Teacher's Guide (1959). The 1958 Supplement contains mainly validation data for SCAT. Data on STEP for college sophomores tested in the spring are presented. These norms are based on scores of 146 students, 2 from each of 73 colleges, from among the 97 colleges which had contributed fall data three semesters before; these sparse data were statistically extrapolated to estimate norms based on the 97 colleges. Another section presents tables on the reliability of differences between scores on five STEP tests and the SCAT parts at the college level. The 920-case sample is generally below average on the five tests, the percentile equivalents of the means ranging from 14 to 67. One validity study in grade 7 in one school is reported; it is not clear whether this is a study of predictive or concurrent validity.

The 1962 Supplement is also mostly devoted to SCAT. For STEP there is a table of grade 8 norms on Science for suburban schools with high socioeconomic standards; a reliability study based on alternate forms of Reading in grade 8, and a table of estimated spring norms for grade 12, with no information as to its derivation. There are also several pages which reproduce in convenient form the tables, originally appearing only on the keys, by which one changes raw scores to converted scores.

The 1963 Supplement is concerned with comparing scores from urban schools (tested in January-February 1962) with scores from the 1956 (fall) normative sample. The differences are small, favoring urban schools. The report spells out the pitfalls in sampling, smoothing, etc., which are involved. No mention is made of the proportions of the national norms which came from large cities. One wonders why the 1956–57 data were not used to tease out large city, middle urban, and rural differences. Two to three classrooms in each of four grades (5, 7, 9, and 11) in 59 cities (over 100,000 population) were tested so that one fifth took each of five STEP tests; Listening was given to additional whole classes in 40 schools. Norms for the other grades were interpolated and extrapolated. The actual number of cases is not stated.

By late 1963, then, the tests and manuals were unchanged and a modest amount of additional information was released. There is little evidence that the publisher has reacted to the Jackson and Layton criticisms in the 1959 MMY. Some of the specific criticisms having to do with the manuals and the adequacy of communicating information to the user could well have led to revisions and addenda. The present reviewer will not raise all of these questions again, preferring to focus on only a few matters.

Layton raised serious questions about the system of converted scores which leads neither to comparability of scores nor to unequivocal evidence of growth in a student. His comments were indeed cogent. Regrettably, neither refinement in the scaling of the actual converted scores nor evidence of practicality of the whole plan has been reported. A rationale for plotting and recording growth has not yet been presented.

What new data are there on reliability and validity? Earlier reviewers questioned the sole use of the K-R 20 formula, especially since it was used with means and standard deviations for all cases and item statistics for only 100 cases. In the supplements there are three limited and minor reports on reliability for some grades and one report on a college level sample. It is not difficult to compute coefficients for fair samples based on odd-even items or alternate form testing.

The earlier reviews called for more evidence of validity. They asked for prediction studies and also studies relating STEP scores to other test data. The Technical Report (1957) does give elaborate data on the relation of each STEP component to the SCAT parts and total. However, there still are no tables of intercorrelations of the STEP tests below the college level—a sort of basic table which users expect for any battery. True, such data were hard to come by during the 1956–57 standardizing because each normative case took only part of the battery. But since that time there must have been at least a few hundred school systems which could provide scores for students who took the entire battery, and for whom scores on some other tests and grade records were also available. For example, for several years ETS has had available statewide data on STEP for one or more grades in one large state. Surely ETS can afford to draw a proper 1,000-case state sample and print a table of intercorrelations. Surely in some school system, STEP by now has been repeated two, three, or four years later so that growth of students and stability of scores could be documented. The annotated bibliographies do describe some validity studies.

The style and structure of items have a direct bearing on the *efficiency* of a test. To accomplish their announced purposes, the authors of the STEP series were led to express many of the test items in somewhat wordy "situational" type of items. In Reading, of course, paragraphs are necessary and the number of responses per minute of testing time becomes a factor to cope with in developing a reliable test. For the other STEP tests, one can raise the question as to how far one should go in wording items so as to simulate real life problems. The extensive use of much reading to introduce a set of items does not automatically make these tests more sensitive measures of educational development or of power to apply knowledge. The scores on the tests might well reflect reading ability as much as ability to recall and utilize previous specific learnings. In 1959 Jackson, without denying the utility of the chosen item patterns, expressed the need for more straightforward, factual items. One might even argue that sensing the nature of a test problem without a situational crutch might sometimes reflect a higher order of learning and understanding. It is possible to write terse items which tap more than simple memory. With briefer items a test could be more efficient. Either the same number of items in less time would yield equally reliable scores, or more items in the same time would yield more reliable scores. In the end, of course, validity is the crucial matter. Content validity should increase with more extensive sampling of the subject field which would insure more coverage and reduce the effects of idiosyncratic selection of items.

The issue here is not one of the quality of the STEP items *per se* but rather one of how much is lost compared to what is gained by the STEP approach. As Layton pointed out, once the pattern was set, the use of simpler items for some purposes seems to have been foreclosed. This reviewer has seen no empirical evidence that the "wordy item" approach with fewer responses by examinees per unit of time is more valid than the less wordy, leaner approach. In grades 7–9, STEP Mathematics presents 50 items in 70 minutes. The *Metropolitan Achievement Test* for the same grades includes 93 arithmetic items in 70 minutes and with at least equal reliability of score. Similarly, STEP Writing presents 60 items in 70 minutes, yielding one score. Metropolitan has tests for spelling, several aspects of language usage, and language study skills, with a total of 165 items in 62 minutes, yielding three scores, each one as reliable as the single STEP Writing score.

The stated goals of STEP are congruent with the goals of many educators. Educators should not, however, be lulled by a reassuring statement of goals into accepting an instrument without asking for empirical evidence that the elaborated form of items is really a more valid way of attaining these goals. And, for others, the goals themselves may be a consideration. For example, spelling competence is a respected grade 8 goal, but STEP Writing barely checks on this competence. Test users should be concerned with efficiency of item structure *vis à vis* the practicality of testing time and empirical evidence of reliability and validity. Research studies are called for. Let there be a battle between proponents of the "lean item" and the "fat item" approaches until we have good answers. Suppose the five comparable parts of the Metropolitan and STEP batteries prove to be so highly correlated that the economy of 233 minutes versus 350 minutes becomes a valuable consideration. Let there be comparative studies to tease out the efficiency of *item structure* as well as of *item content* in diagnostic and predictive situations.

Those who standardize achievement tests are faced with the serious problem of getting enough cases to yield representative and stable normative data. Layton has pointed out the problems which ETS met. The documentation of the procedures is excellent even though one might be unhappy about the limited sampling both as to number of cases and number of schools. Given small samples and gaps in data, the publishers applied generally acceptable statistical adjustments. The norms for the STEP series may be adequate and may stand the test of time for a decade, but educators still express anxiety about their adequacy. By now, ETS might well have published a follow-up study based on some proper sampling of the more than a million students who have taken the battery in whole or in major part. Since many of these papers are scored by ETS, the data have been available. By now, good norms based on *school means* also should have appeared, especially since the manuals stress the role of STEP for assessing schools.

This tendency to be satisfied with statistical manipulations of small samples shows up in the 1959 supplementary manual entitled Teacher's Guide. It is concerned with suggestions as to how teachers can tally frequencies and compute the percentage of pupils passing each item. After discussing how this is to be done for one's own class, the Guide refers the teachers to 65 pages of tables which state, among other things of considerably greater importance, the percentage of cases passing each item in the normative population. Instead of using large samples of real cases for each grade, statistical adjustments are made. For example, for level

3, a sample of 100 cases from the grade 8 normative sample was used to determine the percentage of pupils passing each item. The stability of these values is suspect. Then, the percentages for the adjacent grades, 7 and 9, were determined by estimating growth and making adjustments of the grade 8 percentages. How much faith should a teacher place in comparisons of the percentage of her 35 pupils passing each item with these grossly estimated values so derived? Some readers might question the value of the whole exercise which is proposed to the teachers, but if it is to be undertaken the teacher should have good numbers to start with. Another table enables the teacher to estimate significance of differences in performance on items by her own class and by the random, small grade 8 sample adjusted crudely for grades 7 and 9.

The Teacher's Guide and the separate Handbooks and Manuals for Interpreting do contain a great amount of practical discussion as to how teachers can make use of the data about their students. Warnings about overinterpreting appear. Details are given as to how to develop local norms tables and to determine percentile bands. The writing ranges from informal to formal and at the right places. In general, these documents are well written and, apart from the redundancy discussed earlier, well planned and attractively printed. This reviewer must express serious doubts about the value and propriety of the plans for teachers to discuss items in detail with their students; but if a school wants to do this, the procedures are sketched for the teacher.

The *Sequential Tests of Educational Progress* are indeed an important battery for assessing the general aspects of educational development. The publisher is to be commended again for presenting much statistical detail so fully and usually very clearly. The main shortcoming is the failure to carry forward the job of documentation—especially when answer sheets for more than a million students have been available and ETS has such a competent group of psychometric specialists with access to the most modern computer facilities.

Whether the *basic idea* of STEP will dominate the field remains to be seen. STEP and the *Iowa Tests of Educational Development* represent a common trend away from achievement tests which bear a close relation to the curriculum. Doubtless there is a place for these measures of general development or common learnings, but it is hoped there will always be a demand for, and competent production of, more specific achievement tests. The mood of the times is again to ask how well students perform in more clearly defined curricula; for this STEP is not adequate. Well standardized tests of basic computational skill in grades 5 and 7 and of spelling in grade 9, for example, should still be available. The mathematical and science achievements measured in STEP and ITED at the high school level really cannot tell a school or a teacher much about the efficiency and quality of local teaching in, say, a course in algebra or physics. One test can hardly be equally functional in measuring growth of students in radically non-common tracks who study shop arithmetic, commercial arithmetic, and college preparatory mathematics. The resolution of this dilemma probably is best sought in a variety of approaches to measuring learning. The global approach of the STEP and ITED batteries should not be allowed to monopolize the scene just because they present a seemingly easy method of measuring achievement-in-general. STEP has a role in solving some of the measurement problems of schools, but schoolmen should be aware that the organization and content of STEP preclude its use as a sufficient basis for evaluating the effectiveness of their curriculum and staff and the growth of individual pupils. For those educators who understand and accept these limitations, STEP can be a serviceable instrument.

JOHN E. STECKLEIN, *Director, Bureau of Institutional Research, University of Minnesota, Minneapolis, Minnesota.*

The *Sequential Tests of Educational Progress* (STEP) were based on four assumptions: (*a*) "The primary goal of the whole educational process is the development of the individual student." (*b*) "Education is a continuous and cumulative process." (*c*) "The focus of education is upon development of critical skills and understandings." (*d*) "The success of education is to be measured in terms of the individual student's ability to apply his school-learned skills in solving new problems."

From its inception then, STEP was not designed to be a conventional achievement test to measure specific course learning, but rather a test to determine the extent to which individuals had acquired certain critical skills and understandings which might have been the result of a number of courses and other experiences. The authors did not intend to imply that factual knowledge of a specific field was irrelevant, but that the tests "would emphasize broad understandings and abilities to utilize learned skills in solving new problems rather than abilities to handle only the facts of 'lesson material.' "

The reviewers in *The Fifth Mental Measurements Yearbook* stated that the test publishers had undertaken a tremendous task in developing and designing the STEP battery. One of them also pointed out that reviews at that time might be unduly critical because the STEP series was still in an early stage of development and many of the criticisms made at that time might be found to be unwarranted several years hence. For this reason it seems appropriate to list the major criticisms noted in the earlier reviews, both for reaction by the present reviewer, and to indicate the extent to which the test publisher has since taken these criticisms into account. Only those criticisms which applied to the total test battery will be discussed here, because each of the tests in the STEP battery is reviewed specifically elsewhere.

Since the series was reviewed in *The Fifth Mental Measurements Yearbook,* three SCAT-STEP supplements (for 1958, 1962, and 1963) have been published, as well as a Teacher's Guide. These materials provided the basis for the reviewer's analysis of the extent to which previous criticisms have been answered or warrant modification.

The test publishers have provided additional information concerning the following major criticisms which were made in one or both of the two reviews of this test in *The Fifth Mental Measurements Yearbook:*

a) No statistical evidence of validity was presented except correlations with SCAT.

A limited amount of additional evidence concerning the predictive validity of the STEP is presented in the 1958 and 1962 SCAT-STEP Supplements. The evidence is spotty and inconclusive, however. Findings ranged from correlation coefficients of .74 for STEP Science with science grades of seventh graders to .38 for the science test with overall grades of freshmen in a women's college. Similarly STEP Reading correlated .74 with average grades of seventh graders, and .27 with first semester grades of junior college transfer students in education. Validity coefficients for other tests used at different grade levels ranged from .35 to .71.

Careful and systematic validity studies are still needed.

b) Reliability estimates were obtained only from internal analyses based on single administrations of Form A tests. No reliability coefficients were provided for Form B tests. The additional information about the equivalence of forms promised by the test authors should have been collected and published before the battery was published.

Some new data are presented on the reliability of the tests but in only one instance are data provided for a Form B test (Reading, Form 3B). In this one instance the reliability coefficients were as high as or higher than those for Form 3A.

Comparisons of the computation of the reliability coefficient using the Spearman-Brown split-half, the K-R 21, and alternate form showed no appreciable difference in values, all being in the high .80's or low .90's, for level 3 Reading. Other studies, involving Listening for grades 7, 8, and 9, and Mathematics for grades 4 and 12, produced Spearman-Brown reliability coefficients of .71, .72, .85, .42, and .87, respectively.

Reliabilities of differences between scores on the several tests (Form A) are also reported, based on a sample of 920 students in the National College Freshman Testing Program.

Some of the Form A tests are not as reliable as would be desirable. It is regrettable that empirical evidence of the reliability of the Form B tests is still lacking six years after the test was published. Even more serious is the lack of information about the equivalence of the two forms.

c) Data on intercorrelations among the tests of the STEP series are needed because it would appear that the similarity among certain kinds of items in some of the tests is so great that these correlations might be uncomfortably high.

Intercorrelations among five of the STEP tests, presented in the 1958 supplement, ranged from .47 (Writing versus Mathematics) to .79 (Reading versus Writing). As might be expected with a test of this type, high correlations are found between Reading and each of the other tests—even Mathematics, with a correlation of .55.

The evidence supports the suspicion expressed above—that there is a high element of communality among the five tests.

d) The high correlation between STEP scores and SCAT scores suggests that the two instruments "come so close to measuring the same thing as to cast doubt on the value of administering both to the same students."

New studies show consistently high correlations between STEP and SCAT scores. The high correlation coefficients of STEP scores with SCAT scores do indeed raise serious questions about the duplication of measurability of the two instruments. A validity study reported in the 1958 supplement produced a correlation between STEP Reading and SCAT of .81—approximately the same level reported in the earlier technical report. It is probably not unexpected that STEP Reading would have a high correlation with all of the other tests except Mathematics because of the highly verbal nature of test items that are designed to measure general education. On the other hand when one finds correlations between the STEP tests and SCAT Quantitative all above .60 but one, and with the SCAT Verbal ranging from .498 to .83, one cannot help but wonder if the two types of tests are really appreciably different, or if they may not both be heavily saturated with a "*g*" factor.

e) The finding of some ambiguous items in Form 1B prevented the equating of Forms 1A and 1B. The norms and the revised form of 1B should be thoroughly studied before publication and data collected to support the conclusion that norms for Form 1A will be suitable for a revised Form 1B.

According to the 1958 SCAT-STEP Supplement, Form 1B of Writing was edited, equated, and published in 1958, based on a special testing program conducted in the fall of 1957. The vertical equating of Form 1B was based on the horizontal equating of Form 1B to 1A, however (see comment in item *t*).

f) There is an unjustified tendency to substitute the measurement of understanding and application of knowledge for the measurement of acquisition of factual information.

No change in test content. The present reviewer disagrees that the step taken was "unjustified." The avowed purpose of the test was to measure the student's ability to apply his knowledge to solve problems.

g) In the process of developing a test which provided continuity of measurement over a span of several grades, differentiated measurement at the several instructional levels had to be sacrificed; thus the test fails to sample both content and emphases that are considered important at certain grade levels.

The present reviewer considers this criticism inappropriate in view of the fact that the STEP battery was specifically designed not to measure particular content emphases at particular grade levels, but rather certain skills and understanding that would tend to cut across all grade levels. It does not therefore seem valid to criticize the test on this point.

h) Tests of specific study skills, such as the ability to interpret charts, graphs, tables, to read maps, etc., have been omitted from the battery.

It is true that certain specific study skills have been omitted from this test just as certain objectives are omitted from any test. It is impossible for any test to cover all of the possible kinds of skills and understandings that a teacher might consider important. Those that were identified were selected by a group of experts who apparently felt that the kinds of skills cited above as omissions were not as important as those skills and understandings that were included.

No new data, explanations, or information were found by the reviewer on the following criticisms, although some may have eluded his search. Statements of support or contradiction, or other comments by the present reviewer are included where appropriate.

i) The lack of utility of the converted scores is cited and questions are raised as to the reason for their inclusion. The suggestion is made that their inclusion plus the sequential character of the tests provides an impression of continuity of measurement which does not exist.

The reviewer agrees with the criticism concerning the questionable utility of the converted scores and the need for them. It would seem that the conversion from raw scores to percentile bands could be accomplished without the intermediate use of converted scores.

The serious criticism raised in the previous yearbook concerning the "impression of continuity of measurement" appears to hold up on subsequent examination. No additional data have been presented by the publishers of a longitudinal nature to provide a scale of scores that could be used to demonstrate continuous growth by a single group of students taking the different tests at different levels. Nor have data been provided to demonstrate whether or not the increments in the score units, when based on a single population of students moving through the various grades and taking the various STEP tests, were more or less consistent than the increments derived from the converted score bands reported in the technical manual, when such bands were compared between the various pairs of successive grade levels. Certainly if the test is intended to measure an on-going set of skills and understandings throughout the students' educational program, it does not seem unrealistic to insist that the publisher demonstrate the nature of normative growth from level to level as a basis for individual or group comparison by teachers using the tests.

j) Any comparison of growth or gains in scores from level to level even for the same test will be meaningless for this test battery, because no normative standards are available.

No additional information available. It would seem that it would be useful for the test publishers to report some longitudinal data concerning the gains in scores which can be shown by the utilization of this battery. In the absence of such information or other kinds of normative standards, the appraisal of growth from level to level by particular individuals or classes is indeed difficult.

k) The descriptive and analytical information about the normative sample is inadequate, making it impossible to determine the kinds of biases that might be reflected in the normative statistics.

No additional data were provided about the original normative sample. The criticism is well founded. Detailed information is essential about normative groups if test users are to understand fully the proper use of the norms.

New normative information was reported in the 1963 supplement, however, based on the results of an administration of the test to students in schools in cities with populations of 100,000 or more. Comparisons were made of norms based on this urban group with the earlier reported national norms. The publishers point out that the superiority of the urban norms shown by this comparison may reflect some bias resulting from the failure of a large proportion of these large city systems to agree to cooperate.

The extreme difficulty of obtaining large scale normative data for any test, but particularly for a test battery of such magnitude as the STEP, should be acknowledged. All the more reason, however, for the publisher to provide complete information about the normative sample that is used.

l) The norms are based on an "availability" sample and no data are provided to tell the test user what sort of biases have resulted by giving the tests only in those schools in the selected sample that were willing to give them. In addition, it is not clear whether the normative samples were representative of the nine regions of the United States or only represented four regions.

The present reviewer doubts that there is any other kind of a sample than one that is available. Either someone gives permission to administer a test or he does not. However, this state of affairs does not relieve a test publisher of the responsibility of attempting to assess possible biases resulting from certain refusals to give the test.

No clarification of the second point was found. The description of the normative samples is rather confusing, and although the participating schools and nine regions are listed, no data are given to show the proportionate representation of the nine regions among the four used to indicate the distribution of the sample. Finally, since geographic identifications were made, and since significant differences are frequently found in the achievement levels of students in different geographic regions, one wonders why regional norms were not developed. Even in the new set of urban norms, geographic analyses would be enlightening.

m) The sample "was [so] severely underrepresentative of large colleges and universities" that the weighting procedures used may not have adequately corrected for the underrepresentation.

No additional data presented. This may or may not be a serious criticism; additional norms data on large universities would be helpful in deciding the question.

n) A sample of only 50 schools is an inadequate sample upon which to base a school norm.

The criticism is well taken. While school norms are highly desirable, and too often ignored, such norms should be based on a large enough sample to assure stable representation, whether for a small geographic region or the nation as a whole. Again geographic school norms would be useful, but in their absence, a sample larger than 50 (or 42, as was actually used in one case) is necessary to represent adequately the nation as a whole.

o) "There are no two successive grades for which the STEP norms are based on exactly the same schools, while the samples for the different levels presumably do not overlap at all."

It is not clear to the present reviewer why random grade sampling was used to obtain norms in preference to a saturation technique using several grade levels in a common set of schools. Such a procedure would have provided normative data for given grade levels within a set of school systems, as well as data on successive levels within and between the same systems.

p) No evidence was provided as to the comparability of the time during the school year at which the national administrations were given and norms are reported for a fall testing only.

No additional data provided.

q) The pair of percentiles for each score interval is less useful and perhaps more misleading than if a single percentile had been given with the band of error merely indicated.

The present reviewer suspects that whether a band or single percentile is preferable is largely a matter of opinion and personal preference. Arguments can be presented for the utilization of both, although there is much to commend the idea of the percentile band as a means of clearly emphasizing to the uninitiated teacher the uncertainty of a precise numerical score.

r) The adequacy of samples of 100 in determining item difficulty and discrimination indices is questionable.

The present reviewer is inclined to feel that, despite the obvious simplicity of taking samples of 100, present day computer techniques should make it feasible to use a much larger proportion of the total groups tested in determining difficulty and discrimination statistics, thus forestalling such criticisms.

s) No cross validation was carried out to determine whether the item statistics for items on the alternate forms tended to correspond as nearly as possible to the desired distribution of the item difficulties for the item mid-grade for which the level was designed.

No additional information provided. Such analyses would be helpful in supporting the technical quality of the battery.

t) It is risky to assume that Form B could be vertically equated automatically simply because it has been horizontally equated to Form A. The magnitude of the errors involved in the equating procedures may be compounded in such a process.

The present reviewer agrees. Evidence of the successful application of this technique in developing other tests should at least be given, if no trial statistics are available for this battery to support the vertical equating of the two forms.

u) The STEP appears to be a superior battery on all counts ranging from the technical aspects of construction to the matter of preparation of test booklets and readable manuals. However, because many school people still view the requirement of knowledge of subject matter as a primary and desirable aim of education, the battery may prove to be completely unsuitable for use by some individuals. The STEP series may represent too much of a swing of the pendulum to the opposite direction from measurement of information and fact, even though the functions upon which the battery has been based, have been clearly identified and competently measured.

This supposition may very well be true, but the present reviewer feels that the STEP battery was never intended to replace other kinds of tests that might be more suited to individual grade levels or subject areas of measurement of specific subject areas. However, it can be extremely useful as a supplementary test that will measure the growth of skills that permeate the entire spectrum of education.

A Teacher's Guide was published in 1959 designed to assist the teacher in making maximum use of the STEP results. The Guide contains item by item analyses of what each test in the series was intended to measure, suggestions for using the results of specific STEP tests instructionally, and a case study suggesting how the STEP testing program and the special instructional aims of the teachers might be integrated. This very readable guide will probably be found quite useful by teachers who are concerned about using STEP test results diagnostically. Work charts and conversion tables are provided to make the process easier, and specific examples are illustrated to make the process more intelligible. The Teacher's Guide is an imaginative and well-developed contribution to the set of materials that accompanies the STEP.

In summary, the present reviewer believes that the battery represents an ambitious and significant venture in testing that is worthy of praise. The concept of the sequential test, the test materials, and much of the technical data are of the highest order.

Much more experimentation with the STEP battery is needed, however, and the publishers should be exhorted to pull together some of the loose statistical ends relating to the validity and reliability of the instrument. They should also be urged to make some longitudinal studies of the utilization of this battery to obtain more definitive information about its effectiveness in measuring true growth of the kinds of skills and understanding selected for measurement. Furthermore, since the STEP was apparently designed for use in conjunction with the SCAT, this intention might be made the subject of a critical review prompted by the high correlation found between scores on the two instruments.

For reviews by Robert W. B. Jackson and Wilbur L. Layton, see 5:24 (1 excerpt). For reviews of individual tests, see 292, 590, 810, 882, 971, 5:206, 5:207, 5:438, 5:578, 5:653, 5:716, and 5:792.

[26]

***Stanford Achievement Test, [1964 Revision].** Grades 1.5–2.5, 2.5–3.9, 4–5.5, 5.5–6.9, 7–9; 1923–64; 1953 revision (see 5:25) still available; subtests in (grades 4–9) spelling and language, arithmetic, reading, and (grades 5.5–9) science and social studies available as separates; IBM and MRC for grades 4–9; 5 levels; reliability data for one form (unspecified) only; separate answer sheets may be used for grades 4–9; 80¢ per specimen set of *a* or *b;* $1 per specimen set of *c, d,* or *e;* postage extra; Truman L. Kelley, Richard Madden, Eric F. Gardner, and Herbert C. Rudman; Harcourt, Brace & World, Inc. *

a) PRIMARY I BATTERY. Grades 1.2–2.5; 6 scores: word reading, paragraph meaning, vocabulary, spelling, word study skills, arithmetic; Forms W, X, ('64, 12 pages); manual ('64, 32 pages); $5.65 per 35 tests; 60¢ per key; (127–160) minutes in 5 sessions.

b) PRIMARY 2 BATTERY. Grades 2.5–3.9; 8 scores: word meaning, paragraph meaning, science and social studies concepts, spelling, word study skills, language, arithmetic computation, arithmetic concepts; Forms W ('64), X ('64, c1963–64), (16 pages); manual ('64, 32 pages); $5.80 per 35 tests; 85¢ per key; (185–235) minutes in 7 sessions.

c) INTERMEDIATE I BATTERY. Grades 4–5.5; 8 (partial battery) or 10 (complete battery) scores: word meaning, paragraph meaning, spelling, word study skills, language, arithmetic computation, arithmetic concepts, arithmetic applications, (complete battery only) social studies, science; IBM and MRC; manual ('64, 24 pages); supplementary directions ['64, 1 page each] for use with IBM answer sheets, MRC answer sheets; $8 per 100 MRC answer sheets; $1.60 per set of hand scoring stencils for MRC answer sheets (machine scoring service, by Measurement Research Center, Inc., may be arranged through the publisher).

1) *Complete Battery.* Forms W ('64), X ('64, c1963-64), (31 pages); $9.75 per 35 tests; $1 per key; $5 per 35 sets of IBM answer sheets; $1 per set of scoring stencils; 261(300) minutes in 7 sessions.

2) *Partial Battery.* Form W ('64, 23 pages); $8.25 per 35 tests; 75¢ per key; $3.50 per 35 sets of IBM answer sheets; 80¢ per set of scoring stencils; 201(230) minutes in 5 sessions.

d) INTERMEDIATE 2 BATTERY. Grades 5.5-6.9; 7 (partial battery) or 9 (complete battery) scores: same as for Intermediate 1 Battery except for omission of word study skills; IBM and MRC; manual ('64, 26 pages); supplementary directions ['64, 1 page each] for use with IBM answer sheets, MRC answer sheets; $8 per 100 MRC answer sheets; $1.60 per set of hand scoring stencils for MRC answer sheets (machine scoring service, by Measurement Research Center, Inc., may be arranged through the publisher).

1) *Complete Battery.* Forms W ('64), X ('64, c1963-64), (31 pages); $9.75 per 35 tests; $1 per key; $5.25 per 35 sets of IBM answer sheets; $1.20 per set of scoring stencils; 267(303) minutes in 7 sessions.

2) *Partial Battery.* Form W ('64, 22 pages); prices same as for Intermediate 1 Partial Battery; 192 (219) minutes in 5 sessions.

e) ADVANCED BATTERY. Grades 7-9; 6 (partial battery) or 8 (complete battery) scores: same as for Intermediate 1 Battery except for omission of word meaning and word study skills; IBM and MRC; manual ('64, 27 pages); supplementary directions ['64, 1 page each] for use with IBM answer sheets, MRC answer sheets; prices same as for Intermediate 2 Battery.

1) *Complete Battery.* Forms W ('64), X ('64, c1963-64), (32 pages); 255(287) minutes in 6 sessions.

2) *Partial Battery.* Form W ('64, 20 pages); 178(201) minutes in 4 sessions.

REFERENCES

1-34. See 3:18.
35-54. See 4:25.
55-73. See 5:25.
74. HAYES, SAMUEL P. "A New Series of Stanford Achievement Tests Adapted for Use with Blind and Partially Seeing Pupils." *Int J Ed Blind* 5:44-5 D '55. *
75. HAYES, SAMUEL P. "Is Achievement Testing Practical in the Primary Grades?" *Int J Ed Blind* 5:51-4 Mr '56. *
76. HARPER, R. J. C. "Reading and Arithmetic Reasoning: A Partial Correlation and Multiple Regression Analysis." *Alberta J Ed Res* 3:81-6 Je '57. * (*PA* 33:4569)
77. COFFMAN, WILLIAM E. "Patterns of Growth in Basic Skills in Two Elementary School Classrooms Over a Four-Year Period." *Yearb Nat Council Meas Used Ed* 17:141-51 '60. *
78. STUMPF, JOHN C. *The Correlation Between the Wechsler Intelligence Scale for Children and Reading Scores From the Standard Achievement Test.* Master's thesis, University of Utah (Salt Lake City, Utah), 1960.
79. DAVIS, CARL J., AND NOLAN, CARSON Y. "A Comparison of the Oral and Written Methods of Administering Achievement Tests." *Int J Ed Blind* 10:80-2 Mr '61. * (*PA* 37:6968)
80. FINDLEY, WARREN G. "Use and Interpretation of Achievement Tests in Relation to Validity." *Yearb Nat Council Meas Ed* 18:23-34 '61. *
81. HASCALL, EDWARD O. "Predicting Success in High School Foreign Language Study." *Personnel & Guid J* 40:361-7 D '61. * (*PA* 36:4KL61H)
82. HOWELL, JOHN J., AND WEINER, MAX. "Note on the Equivalence of Alternate Forms of an Achievement Test." *Ed & Psychol Meas* 21:309-13 su '61. * (*PA* 36:2KL09H)
83. TAYLOR, EDWARD A., AND CRANDALL, JAMES H. "A Study of the 'Norm-Equivalence' of Certain Tests Approved for the California State Testing Program." *Calif J Ed Res* 13:186-92 S '62. *
84. BIRCH, JANE R.; STUCKLESS, E. ROSS; AND BIRCH, JACK W. "An Eleven Year Study of Predicting School Achievement in Young Deaf Children." *Am Ann Deaf* 108:236-40 Mr '63. * (*PA* 37:8132)
85. MITCHELL, BLYTHE C. "A Comparison of the Achievement-Intelligence Relationship for Pupils With That for School Systems." *J Ed Res* 57:172-80 D '63. *
86. SCOTT, CARRIE M. "Intelligence and Gain in Reading as Related to Gains in the Sub-Tests of the Stanford Achievement Test." *J Ed Res* 56:494-6 My-Je '63. *

MIRIAM M. BRYAN, *Associate Director of Test Development, Educational Testing Service, Princeton, New Jersey.*

The 1964 edition of the *Stanford Achievement Test* constitutes the fourth extensive revision of this pioneer among standardized test batteries. During its more than 40 years, how responsive has the test been to curricular changes at the elementary school level and to innovations and refinements in test theory and practice? To what extent have successive editions offered technical improvements over earlier editions? How does the latest edition compare with its predecessors and with currently competing test batteries?

HISTORY OF THE TEST. The first edition of the test was published in 1923 in two parallel forms, Forms A and B. A Primary Examination for grades 2 and 3 included tests of reading, arithmetic, and spelling; an Advanced Examination for grades 4 through 8 included tests of reading, arithmetic, nature study and science, history and literature (a rather strange combination), language usage, and spelling. In the Primary Examination the paragraph meaning test required the pupil to write in words to complete paragraphs, and the word meaning test presented multiple choice definitions or classifications among which the pupil made a selection; the sentence meaning test was of the "Is green a color?" type of exercise with all questions answered "Yes" or "No"; the arithmetic test included computation and reasoning (simple problem solving) tests; and the spelling test was in the form of a dictation exercise. For the Advanced Examination the reading, arithmetic, and spelling tests took the same form as did the primary tests (indeed, every item in the Primary Examination was repeated, and in the same order, in the Advanced Examination); the nature study and science test and the history and literature test were made up of items which were strictly factual; and the language usage test offered two-choice items covering grammatical constructions and word choice. The reading and arithmetic tests were published also as separate tests.

The item writing had been preceded by an analysis of textbooks and courses of study and studies of subject difficulties. The items were rated by a panel of judges before assembly for pretesting, and only those items retained for the final forms that showed in the pretesting a steady increase from grade to grade in per cent of pupils passing them. The test was meticulously edited in terms of item writing standards of the day.

Since the invention of the scoring machine was still many years away, the test was devised for administration in the test booklet and for hand scoring with a variety of formulas (for the eight separate tests in the Advanced Examination five different formulas were used) to insure the proper weighting of the separate test scores. A modest but complete Manual of Directions provided directions for administering and scoring the test as well as information concerning the construction of the test, reliability coefficients and probable errors of scores, directions for the use of the norms, and suggestions for the utilization of test results.

While some of the achievement tests predating the *Stanford Achievement Test* had been of high quality, many more had not. Furthermore, tests in various subjects had been constructed independently of each other by different authors and normed on different school populations at different periods of the school year. With the *Stanford Achievement Test,* tests in the subject areas covered were devised for the first time by the same group of authors and the norms on all the tests were similarly derived (the publishers pointed with pride to the fact that the batteries were standardized and equated on the basis of scores of 1,500 pupils), thus making readily obtainable a pupil's score in one subject that could be compared with his score in other subjects. For the first time also, age norms as well as grade norms were supplied, thus making possible the derivation of an educational quotient. Is it any wonder that this finely conceived and well constructed test, accompanied by such complete accessory materials and interpretative data, and boasting reliability coefficients by age for the separate tests for the most part in the high .80's and .90's, should have been accepted so enthusiastically and with so much confidence by school people?

In 1925 the norms were revised on the basis of a sample of 2,000 additional cases from a population of nearly 10,000 cases, a revised Manual of Directions was printed, and an Educational Profile Chart was provided on the cover page of the test books. With these exceptions, no revisions were made until 1929, when five new forms, Forms V, W, X, Y, and Z, were announced, bearing the name *New Stanford Achievement Test.* These were published between 1929 and 1931, both as separate tests and in battery form.

Several revisions made in these forms are worthy of note: (*a*) The Advanced Examination was extended upward to measure ninth grade ability, with consequent changes in the paragraph meaning, arithmetic, and spelling tests to provide adequate coverage of ninth grade subject matter content (this an acknowledgment of the testing needs of the fast-multiplying junior high schools serving grades 7, 8, and 9). (*b*) The single test for history and literature was divided and two separate tests, one in history and civics and one in literature, were devised; and the test in nature study and science was discontinued and in its place a test in geography and one in physiology and hygiene inserted (these substitutions made in order to provide scores more directly applicable to different school subjects). (*c*) The sentence meaning test was discontinued because the two other reading tests appeared to be covering the subject adequately (this in an effort to keep testing time as low as possible). (*d*) Two columns per page were used rather than one in order to shorten the length of the line to conform with the results of scientific investigations of eye movements and to simplify scoring. (*e*) The number of different formulas used for the scoring of the Advanced Examination was reduced to three, and for both batteries raw scores with equivalent grade score values were printed across the bottoms of the test pages to make more automatic the conversion of scores.

The items for these forms, a majority of them new, were constructed and selected with the same kind of careful planning, prejudging, and pretesting that had accompanied the development of the first edition. The new forms were equated to the old so that the same norms could apply, and the norms for all of the tests were equated to each other in such a way that a particular score for a given age or grade had the same meaning for all tests. With the provision of five forms, and with the inclusion again of the Primary Examination in the Advanced Examination, it now became possible not only to construct a profile of relative achievement in the different school subjects but also to make growth studies.

With this edition, a Guide for Interpreting the tests was published in addition to Directions for Administering (the manual). The guide contained more detailed information than the manual concerning the construction, validity, and reliability of the tests; the norms; and the interpretation and uses of test results. It was the most comprehensive document for test users assembled to date. The rationale for the predominantly factual nature of the content tests in this series, written for the guide by the eminent test authors, is probably representative of the thinking of the time:

> Modern educational practice is emphasizing the development of the interpretive abilities of the pupils by means of project teaching and other methods of creating thought-provoking situations with which the pupils must deal. The authors of these tests are in full sympathy with this movement. In so far as the testing of this function is concerned, however, they believe that most of the so-called "thought-questions" found in current tests have no special claim to that title. * Indeed, there seems to be no way to determine in an objective manner from the form of a statement whether or not it is especially provocative of thought.

With the appearance of the 1929 edition, boasting total score reliabilities ranging from .92 to .98 at the various grade levels, the *Stanford Achievement Test* entered a period of widespread popularity which it was to enjoy almost alone for another decade. True, the *Iowa High School Content Examination,* appearing in 1924, and the *Public School Achievement Tests,* published in 1928, took away the distinction which it had previously enjoyed as the only achievement test battery, but only the latter battery was designed for use at the elementary level and it presented no competition to a battery representing the ultimate in achievement testing for the time. And of the half dozen batteries for elementary schools that appeared in the 1930's, only the *Metropolitan Achievement Tests* and the *Progressive Achievement Tests* offered any serious competition.

With the addition of a School Summary Record in 1930, and a third revision of the manual in 1931, the test continued without further change until 1940, when the second major revision occurred. Actually, this was not so much a revision as the construction of five forms, with approximately 80 per cent of the items entirely new. Forms D, E, F, G, and H, with the *New* dropped from the name, appeared from 1940 to 1943 in batteries at three levels: a Primary Battery for grades 2 and 3; an Intermediate Battery for grades 4 through 6; and an Advanced Battery for grades 7 through 9.

The nature of the tests was somewhat changed in the new forms. The tests in the Primary Battery remained the same in name; they no longer, however, consisted of the easier materials from the other batteries, but were designed specifically to fit the content of the second and third grades. In the Intermediate Battery and the Advanced Battery, two social studies tests, one for history and one for geography, replaced the tests labeled geography, and history and civics in the previous edition, and the science test was reinstated. At all levels the spelling test changed from a dictation exercise to a list of words presented in illustrative sentences. The tests at the two upper levels were made available in complete and partial batteries, the literature, social studies, and science tests being omitted in the partial batteries.

This time the Primary Battery was printed in primer-size type, a real improvement in format. To facilitate administration and scoring, the format of six of the tests in the Intermediate and Advanced Batteries, Word Meaning, Language Usage, Literature, Social Studies 1 and 2, and Elementary Science, all completely objective, was changed to permit scoring with a perforated key; and the format of four of the tests, Paragraph Meaning, Spelling, Arithmetic Computation, and Arithmetic Reasoning, requiring the writing of words or numbers, was changed to permit scoring with a strip key. No effort was made to adapt any of the batteries to machine scoring, but separate subtests having substantially the same material as the Intermediate and Advanced Batteries were later made available in machine scorable editions.

Once again, according to the Directions for Administering, the test content had been arrived at as a result of analysis of curricula and textbooks and prejudging by subject matter specialists. Differences in content from the previous editions were, however, obvious only in arithmetic, where changes in placement of topics were made in the Primary and Intermediate Batteries, and the arithmetic computation test in the Advanced Battery was expanded to present charts and graphs and simple algebra and geometry. The tests in other content fields were still concerned with strictly factual information of the most traditional type, the history tests concentrating on political, economic, and military events, the science tests heavily weighted with the content of health and nature study, and the literature tests concerned largely with identification of authors, characters, and plots.

The most impressive feature of the 1940 revision was the norming program involving the testing of approximately 300,000 pupils in 173 communities in 32 states, from which a random sample of 50,955 cases was drawn. The publisher's assertion that "it is believed that the sample on which the norms....are based represents a more adequate sample of the national elementary school population than has heretofore been obtained for any test, either intelligence or achievement" was not to be disputed.

An innovation was the provision of norms based upon the average scores of modal age groups, from which accelerated or retarded pupils had been eliminated, as well as norms based upon the complete population. Again, scores were equated to scores on preceding forms to permit comparison of results on the old and new forms. With this edition also a Class Record and Class Analysis Chart was introduced.

Reviews of the *Stanford Achievement Test* appeared for the first time in *The Third Mental Measurements Yearbook*. The reviews were largely favorable. The most severe criticism was directed at the content tests, not only because of the lack of detailed information in the manual regarding sources of material, but also for the narrow coverage, with high factual emphasis, and for low reliabilities, ranging from .71 to .84. The most favorable comment was directed at the highly reliable tests in the skill areas (mostly above .90) and the generally comprehensive Directions for Administering (the manual), especially the section dealing with the interpretation of scores. In the words of one reviewer, the *Stanford Achievement Test* had still "not been surpassed as tests of the skill subjects."

The 1940 edition was reviewed again in *The Fourth Mental Measurements Yearbook*. In the four years between yearbooks, no revisions had been made in the tests, and, indeed, the Guide for Interpreting the 1940 edition, referred to many times in the 1940 manual, had never appeared. This time the reviews were somewhat less favorable. While the reviewer of the complete battery felt that the test still represented "some of the best practice in this field of testing," another reviewer felt that while it had originally represented "the best in the then recognized principles of test construction," it was being "surpassed by more recently developed achievement tests." Most reviewers criticized the lack of detailed information regarding the validity of the items, and most were agreed that from the point of view of the curriculum, the content tests were "not representative of sound, generally approved practice."

Of the achievement batteries available by this time (1953), more serious competition was coming from the *Metropolitan Achievement Tests* and the *Progressive Achievement Tests,* and a newcomer in commercial competition, the *Iowa Every-Pupil Tests of Basic Skills,* appearing in 1940, was becoming a real threat. In due respect to the *Stanford Achievement Test,* however, it must be emphasized that none of the other popular test batteries included tests of the content type, for which the *Stanford Achievement Test* took the most criticism; and the content tests of the less widely used batteries were very similar to those in the *Stanford Achievement Test.*

The test appeared in its fourth edition, designated as the 1953 revision, between 1953 and 1956. This time there were four almost entirely new batteries: the Primary Battery for grades 1.9 to 3.5; the Elementary Battery for grades 3 and 4; the Intermediate Battery for grades 5 and 6; and the Advanced Battery for grades 7, 8, and 9. The test was offered in five different forms, Forms J, K, L, M, and N, which were hand scorable; and three forms of the Intermediate and Advanced Batteries were presented in special editions, designated as Forms JM, KM, and LM, designed for use with separate answer sheets of either the IBM or the MRC type, which could be hand or machine scored. The Intermediate and Advanced Batteries were once again offered as complete and partial batteries, the latter limited to the tests in the skill areas. All tests were also available as separates.

In addition to almost entirely new content and the adaptability of certain forms at the two higher levels for machine scoring, the 1953 revision differed from earlier editions in a number of ways. (*a*) The provision of four batteries rather than three made it possible to reduce the range of achievement covered by any one battery and permitted testing, with the Primary Battery, at the end of grade 1, whereas previous editions had not been intended for use before grade 2. (*b*) Items of the objective type were introduced into the paragraph meaning test in the Primary Battery, the pupil no longer being required to supply his own answer but to select his answer from among four choices and underline it. (*c*) The language test, presented in all batteries from the Elementary Battery on, included items in capitalization, punctuation, and sentence sense in addition to items on grammatical constructions and word choice. (*d*) In the arithmetic reasoning test at all levels, a section on meanings was added, with the items ranging from simple pictorial items testing number concepts and understanding of terms in the Primary Battery to items testing the informational background of pupils and their understanding of the number system at the higher levels. (*e*) The two social studies tests of the 1940 edition were combined into a single social studies test covering facts of history, geography, and community life. (*f*) The literature test was dropped completely because of the wide diversity of literature curricula from school to school. (*g*) A study skills test, designed to measure ability to read charts, graphs, tables, and maps, and to use the dictionary and other sources of information, was introduced in the Intermediate and Advanced Batteries in recognition of the increased attention being devoted to those skills in schools.

In the 1953 revision the only non-objective test still remaining was the spelling test in the Primary and Elementary Batteries, still a dictation exercise. And the language test in all batteries from the Elementary Battery on was the only test still scored with a correction for guessing (this in spite of the fact that pupils were not advised against "wild guessing").

The actual test construction, according to the Directions for Administering (the manual), was preceded by the usual analyses of textbooks and courses of study and this time, in addition, by an analysis of research literature pertaining to "children's concepts, experiences, and vocabulary at successive ages or grades." At all stages in the developmental process, the manual emphasized, heavy reliance was again placed on the judgment of subject matter specialists in the various areas. With all of this preparatory work, it is surprising that trends in curricular emphases and teaching methods do not seem to have been reflected to any considerable extent in any of the tests but arithmetic and study skills; and the trend toward the teaching of meanings and understandings was certainly not reflected in any large proportion of the items in the social studies and science tests which were still principally concerned with measuring factual knowledge. This quotation from the authors regarding the content of the social studies test is of interest:

> The items in the test measure primarily social studies content or information. The authors make no apology for this fact although they are well aware of the many other objectives of social studies instruction in the grades. The authors believe that all of the content which they have included....is appropriate to the understanding of life and as a background for worthy attitudes and behaviors as anyone might define them. No attempt has been made in this test to measure these other outcomes, including the ability to think critically in the area of the social studies, the development of worthy human relations, etc., either because they cannot be measured adequately in a reasonable testing time and space or because they are not susceptible of paper-and-pencil measurement.

The *Taxonomy of Educational Objectives: The Classification of Educational Goals: Handbook 1, The Cognitive Domain,* was still, of course, to make its appearance, full of suggestions that critical thinking could be measured under the conditions described by the authors.

While not in a class with the comprehensive handbooks and technical reports accompanying some of the newer tests, the Directions for Administering the 1953 edition was still an adequate manual. In addition to test descriptions and directions for administering and scoring the tests, it presented detailed suggestions for the interpretation of scores, the usual practical suggestions for using test results, and information about the construction and standardization of the tests. Modal-age grade norms were again provided for the interpretation of individual scores, and total-age grade norms were presented for the interpretation of group averages; in addition, percentile norms based on modal-age grade groups were provided for the first time for beginning, middle, and end-of-year testing. (As with the various previous editions, scores on the 1953 revision were directly comparable to scores on earlier forms.) For use in the study of relative rates of growth in the functions covered by the various tests, true changes in variability in the functions over the range of elementary grades, and related problems, K-scales, with score units approximately equal throughout the entire range of grade scores, were also supplied.

Again the description of the standardization program was most impressive. Described by the publishers as "what was undoubtedly the most broadly representative national normative group ever obtained for such a program," it involved altogether 460,000 pupils in 340 school systems in 38 states, the whole group carefully balanced with respect to geographical distribution, size of school system, and type of community. The publisher's description could not be refuted. The estimates of reliability, ranging from .66 to .96, with a median value of approximately .88, were also impressive.

The reviews of the 1953 revision which appeared in *The Fifth Mental Measurements Yearbook* were mixed. With mild objections to some aspects of them, the tests in the skills areas were generally favorably, although only mildly favorably, commented upon. The social studies and science tests were criticized as dealing with miscellaneous knowledge rather than with problem-solving skills, critical understandings, and applications of learning. The manual was criticized again for the absence of detailed information regarding the validity of items, and for the lack of data on intercorrelations among the subtests of the various batteries and the failure to make mention of the multitude of studies involving the test that had been carried on during the three decades of its history, reports of many of which were available as supplementary material. The reviews in this Yearbook, easily the least enthusiastic in the history of the test, are exemplified by this excerpt from one review:

> All in all, the *Stanford Achievement Test* impresses this reviewer as a useful, plodding, dependable workhorse that can serve the middle-of-the-road school system well. Its content represents no thought provoking or imaginative innovations, from the standpoint of what leaders in curriculum development might nowadays desire. * The authors have perhaps been too cautious about getting too far ahead of the schools, with the possible consequence that they may be holding many schools back from advances which might with more encouragement be made. * the Stanford is perhaps not taking its rightful share of the leadership role to which decades of use in American schools have made it heir.

And how did the competing batteries fare in *The Fifth Mental Measurements Yearbook?* Of the eight other elementary level batteries reviewed (the *Metropolitan Achievement Tests* were this time not among them), three were considered by their reviewers to have very little to recommend them—thus promising to offer little competition to the Stanford; three, the *California Achievement Tests* (successor to the *Progressive Achievement Tests*), the *SRA Achievement Series,* and the *Scholastic Achievement Series,* received, like the Stanford, mildly favorable reviews—thus promising to offer some competition to the Stanford; one, the *Sequential Tests of Educational Progress,* received mixed reviews from lukewarm to highly favorable; and one, the *Iowa Tests of Basic Skills,* received generally enthusiastic reviews—these two batteries promising to provide the greatest competition to the oldest battery of them all.

THE 1964 REVISION. The 1964 *Stanford Achievement Test* is the product of five years of research and developmental work. The program is described by the publishers as having been undertaken "to provide for American schools a comprehensive test series for grades 1–9 that measures dependably what is actually being taught today—that is convenient to administer and score—that provides up-to-date norms and other workable aids for interpreting and applying test results." According to the publisher also, "Recent, extensive curriculum research and item analysis assure that the test reflects current instructional goals, materials, and methods," and that appropriate weight is given "both to traditional objectives and to recent curriculum trends." In an effort to determine whether the 1964 revision does indeed provide the type of measure described here and whether this measure is a better one than has been provided by previous forms, this reviewer has made a comprehensive study of all forms of the test at all levels from the first edition to the 1964 revision.[1]

While four forms, Forms W, X, Y, and Z, of the 1964 revision are scheduled for publication, only one form, Form W, has actually been published as this review is being written.[2] At the primary 1 and 2 levels, however, additional forms of certain of the tests which are read

1 In the examination of the 1964 revision the reviewer has had the assistance of four department chairmen in the Test Development Division at Educational Testing Service: Frank Fornoff, Science; Fred Godshalk, Humanities; Dana Kurfman, Social Studies; and Sheldon Myers, Mathematics. The discussion of the content of the new tests is based very largely upon their critical reviews.

2 The second form mentioned in the entry preceding the review, Form X, appeared too late to be considered.—Editor.

orally have already been printed in the appropriate Directions for Administering (for the Primary 1 Battery, Forms X and Y of the vocabulary test, the spelling test, the test of word study skills, and the arithmetic test; for the Primary 2 Battery, Forms X and Y of the test of science and social studies concepts, the spelling test, the test of word study skills, and the test of arithmetic concepts).

Aside from the organization in five, rather than four, batteries, which provide better at-grade coverage of content and skills, the 1964 revision differs from the 1953 revision in the following ways: (*a*) All of the items are new, except for some very simple items in the lowest battery (like 2 + 2, for example) which of necessity appear in almost every edition. (*b*) In the Primary 1 Battery a word reading test, which measures ability to analyze a word without the aid of context clues, has replaced the word meaning test. The new test employs a multiple choice type of item in which the pupil selects from a group of four words the word that stands for a picture. (*c*) At the primary 1, primary 2, and intermediate 1 levels, a word study skills test has been introduced. This test includes multiple choice items designed to test auditory perception of beginning and ending sounds, phonics, and phonograms (rhyming words). (*d*) In the Primary 1 Battery a single arithmetic test consists of parts on measures, problem solving, and number concepts; in the Primary 2 Battery there are two separate arithmetic tests—one on computation and one on concepts; in the Intermediate 1 and 2 Batteries and the Advanced Battery there are three separate tests measuring computation, concepts, and applications. (*e*) The measurement of science and social studies now begins at grade 2.5 (Primary 2 Battery), rather than at grade 5, through a detailed "specialized vocabulary test" of science and social studies concepts. (*f*) Rather than a single study skills test, two such tests, one with the language test and one with the social studies test, are now included at the intermediate and advanced levels.

FORMAT. The tests and the Directions for Administering for each level (the manuals) are presented in booklets measuring approximately 8½ by 11 inches, the booklets at each level combining black and white and a distinctive color. While the use of color in test materials has never particularly appealed to this reviewer, it is used here so judiciously as to make the physical appearance and readability of both the test booklets and manuals outstanding; as used here also, it has the further advantage of making it very easy to distinguish between the materials at the various levels. Test booklets and manuals are both printed on paper of a quality much superior to that of previous editions. The cover page of each test booklet provides space for personal information about the pupil and a place for recording the grade score, percentile rank, and stanine for each test in the battery. The test booklets at the primary 1 and 2 levels are designed so that the answers must be marked directly in the booklets. The same test booklet for the intermediate and advanced levels may be used irrespective of whether the answers are marked in the test booklets, on IBM answer sheets, or on MRC answer sheets or cards. The intermediate and advanced tests are also available in partial batteries, and some of the tests are also published as separate booklets.

CONTENT. *Language Tests.* Of the several tests in the various batteries, those concerned with word reading, word meaning, paragraph meaning, vocabulary, spelling, word study skills, and language can all properly be grouped together as "language" tests. They will here be reviewed as such.

By and large, one can hardly help being impressed at the outset by each of these tests in each of the batteries in which they appear. They are most carefully prepared, meticulously presented both to the pupil and to the teacher, organized logically and completely—without haste, with nothing left to conjecture or chance. One wonders, however, whether perhaps the thoroughness has gotten somewhat out of hand in the matter of length and detail.

While one is inclined to take most aspects of the tests on faith because of the obvious competence of the producers, three questions may be raised: (*a*) Is it necessary, or advisable from the standpoint of integrated language instruction, to fragment the language testing process into so many parts above the primary 1 level? Since capitalization and punctuation, for example, can be tested with a single format that can yield reliable subscores, would it not make better sense to combine these aspects of the pure "mechanics" of writing? In the Intermediate 1 Battery, for example, there are 10 separately timed, although not all separately scored, tests (or subtests) in language: word meaning, paragraph meaning, spelling, phonics, syllabication, usage, punctuation, capitalization, dictionary skills, and sentence sense. This is thorough indeed. (*b*) Are these power tests or speed tests? No information on speededness is contained in the Directions for Administering, except for the statement that the time limits "are generous and calculated to give practically all pupils sufficient time to attempt all questions which they are capable of answering correctly." At the intermediate 1 level, which seems a good halfway point, the pupil's tasks include the following: (1) in the word meaning test, to choose, in 10 minutes, the answer to 38 four-choice items, with the stem word presented in single sentence context; (2) in the paragraph meaning test, to read 29 "paragraphs" (three or four are single sentences) and a total of about 1,500 words, and to make responses to 60 four-choice questions or sentence completion type items in 30 minutes; (3) in the phonics subtest, to compare, in 12 minutes, an indicated sound included in each of 36 stem words with somewhat similar words in sets of three, of the type—Ball: balloon, brought, bat. (*c*) What is the predictive validity of the bits and pieces of separately-timed tests? In other words, aside from the validity referred to in the manual as "*content,* or *curricular,* validity," has any attempt been made to relate these separate measures to other evaluations of language skill? Is it sufficient for an achievement battery of this sort merely to follow "appropriate courses of study and textbooks" in deciding upon test outline, or should an experimental rather than an authoritative basis be established?

The reviewer's answers to these questions follow: (*a*) The fragmentation of this testing both follows and supports a theory of language learning that may be less than logically or psychologically sound, and that must make language instruction the dull thing that it has become for great numbers of pupils before they reach high school. (*b*) To read 1,500 words of essentially disconnected "story" or explanation (in the 29 paragraphs) and, for 60 items, to react to rather searching questions about them or to select a missing word to suit the context, all in the period of 30 minutes, is well-nigh impossible for the majority of pupils at this grade level. A speeded test cannot be justified as an achievement test of discrete skills. If the pupil is as thorough as the testmaker, he will not finish and his score will not reflect the total accomplishment of which he is capable. Speededness will, on the other hand, confirm other measures of "intelligence"—but that is not the stated purpose of this battery. (*c*) *What* has been acquired of communication skill should be tested, rather than how the acquisition has been accomplished. If we use the fairly standardized separation of communications skill into listening, speaking, reading, and writing, the kind of testing that comes out is materially different from the 10 tests of the intermediate 1 level. A listening test, for example, is an especial lack at this level, particularly because it would perform diagnostic functions that are untapped by tests of such things as word study skills (phonics and syllabication) and dictionary skills. (This is not to be interpreted as a criticism of the tests of word study skills and dictionary skills, but rather as a question of their relative importance in the testing of language competence as compared to tests of other skills. On the contrary, both tests are extremely well contrived to serve the rather narrow functions for which they were designed.)

Four or five rather minor points for comment on the language tests remain. The problem of an objective test of spelling has still not been solved. What correlation is there between the spelling that a pupil does in free writing or the copying of dictated passages and the measure used here (determining which word in each of 50 four-word groups is incorrectly spelled)? It cannot be very high, and must show some startling discrepancies in the case of a few pupils. There are people who spell well orally and do not make mistakes in their own writing, who are trapped by seeing a word misspelled in print. There is the further "testing question" of the forced choice of one word always wrong, and three always right, in each set of four words.

Then there is the matter, in the language usage section, of treating usage with the instruction to decide upon the basis of "standard written English." Unfortunately, the sentences chosen are brief, simple, and contextually conversational. It seems unlikely that a valid measure of the pupil's ability to *write* good English results from such sentences as "I wish I 1 can 2 could go with you," "We 1 done 2 did the lesson yesterday," "Where did you put 1 you're 2 your coat?," and "I 1 got 2 have to go now." For a language usage test the reviewer favors the type of exercise in which the pupil is required to find the error, if one exists, rather than to supply an answer selected from given choices.

In the paragraph meaning test in both the Primary 1 and 2 Batteries, the reviewer wonders why the pupil is asked to draw a line through the correct response rather than to underline it or encircle it, the act of drawing a line through it seeming to "rule out" rather than "rule in" the choice. Beyond the primary 1 level, the paragraph meaning test, in which since 1923 the pupil has demonstrated his comprehension of the paragraph by selecting the proper word for each omission in the paragraph from four choices offered him, now includes a small number of paragraphs about which multiple choice questions are asked. This the reviewer is glad to see—and wishes there were more such paragraphs. The technique of filling in blanks with words necessarily limits the range of comprehension abilities which can be measured to getting the facts or details; it does not allow for the measurement of ability to get main ideas, to follow directions, to draw conclusions, to recognize motives, and the like.

In spite of all these questions and comments, the language tests remain impressive. Perhaps there are good *other* answers to the questions raised here and good reasons why suggestions similar to those offered here have previously been considered and rejected.

Arithmetic Tests. The several arithmetic tests in the new edition appear to be a marked improvement over the corresponding tests in previous editions. The typography, the art work, and the well conceived items go together to make these tests pleasant to look at and interesting to take.

If any question is to be raised regarding the items themselves, it is to ask why the choices are not consistently presented in more logical order—particularly choices involving numbers, which might better have been given in ascending or descending order than in the almost haphazard order in which they now appear in about 50 per cent of the items involving such choices. In one of the manuals there is an example of some confusion. A note on page 22 of the primary 2 manual appears to refer to "numerals" as if the word were synonymous to "number": "Some pupils are taught that these [numbers] are *numerals* rather than numbers. Use the word which your pupils use."

The content of the arithmetic tests through the Intermediate 2 Battery, though of high quality, does not reflect enough of the widespread contemporary trends in the elementary curriculum. Noticeably missing at these lower levels are such areas as the number line, inequalities, some of the structure of the number system, and properties of numbers (odd and even, divisibility, etc.). Strangely, the Primary 1 and 2 Batteries appear to have greater content breadth than the Intermediate 1 and 2 Batteries.

The Advanced Battery reflects more than the other batteries the influences of contemporary changes in the mathematics curriculum, particularly in Test 5, Arithmetic Concepts, where the following newer topics are tested: divisibility, short cut computation by factoring, commutative and distributive properties, prime numbers, and numerations in other bases. In the tests on arithmetic applications in the Intermediate and Advanced Batteries, pragmatic contexts or settings are provided by brief sentences followed by a cluster of five or six questions. Another aspect of these tests which merits attention is the emphasis throughout on the important area of interpretation of data in tabular and graphic form.

The full breadth of mathematics from grade 1 through grade 9 is not covered by these five batteries, nor do they claim to measure beyond the area of arithmetic. However, some simple geometry and measurement occurs in the Primary 1 and 2 Batteries and some algebra, solid geometry, and logical reasoning occurs in the Advanced Battery. In providing a measure of that phase of the traditional mathematics curriculum known by the general term "arithmetic," the 1964 *Stanford Achievement Test* continues to be outstanding among tests of its kind.

Social Studies Tests. With a social studies test included in each battery from the Intermediate 1 Battery on, the 1964 edition offers an opportunity for the evaluation of social studies achievement for grades 4 through 9. In addition, certain social studies concepts and information are included with science in a test in the Primary 2 Battery (although the low reliability coefficients reported for the test make it unsuitable for serious use). The social studies tests make an important contribution to the measurement of significant social studies objectives. Each of these tests includes a content section and a study skills section. Most of the content questions are based upon the history, geography, and civics taught in intermediate and junior high school social studies. The study skills sections contain sets of questions dealing with such varied materials as tables, graphs, maps, political posters, bibliographies, book indexes, and library index cards.

In the content section of each test, most questions require an understanding of important social studies generalizations or relationships rather than the recall of discrete facts. Teachers who attempt to develop understanding of the various aspects of human interdependence and such relationships as hold between man and his physical environment will find much to please them in the tests. However, an explicit statement of these and other objectives measured by the tests would be of help to school systems in deciding whether the tests are appropriate for their social studies program.

Perhaps it is this lack of direction which objectives can provide that permitted the inclusion of an occasional seemingly irrelevant question. For example, in the Advanced Battery (item 14) students are asked to indicate what follows if they do not ask questions of adults ("They miss good chances to learn"). In item 39 of the same test students are asked to identify "commercial competition" as the major problem facing American symphony orchestras. There likewise seems to be little reason for the inclusion of a few attitudinal questions in tests which are primarily measures of achievement in the cognitive domain. Item 14 in the Intermediate 1 Battery is such a question. It asks what Sue should do during a test when many pupils are looking at other pupils' papers. Naturally she should "refuse to look at others' papers."

One consequence of writing social studies questions dealing with significant generalizations is a tendency to overgeneralize, to supply simple answers to complex questions. Thus, although the intended answer seems to be clear, often another option is equally acceptable. In the Advanced Battery test, item 34, which is concerned with the causes of problems of group living, would seem to be as correctly answered by "a failure to adjust properly to changing conditions" (choice 7) as by "intense rivalry between groups" (choice 6), the designated key. In item 44 of the same test, the looseness of the word "suggest" in the stem ("The contributions of George Washington Carver, Simon Bolívar, Mohandas K. Gandhi, and Sun Yat-sen suggest that—") would seem to make "national culture is unrelated to individual potential" (choice 7) as acceptable as "any cultural group may produce great men" (choice 5), the indicated key. In item 20, unless the Baltic Sea is construed to be an ocean, "Poland" (choice 5) qualifies as well as "Switzerland" (choice 6) as a "European country which has no ocean harbors."

Just as the content section of each test for the most part does an excellent job of testing important conceptual outcomes, the study skills sections will provide a good indication of pupil progress in graph and map reading. The most unusual of these exercises is the set of maps in the Intermediate 2 Battery. In answering the questions, pupils are required to relate information from three different kinds of maps of the same hypothetical area. A map exercise such as this, which interrelates the rainfall, production, political, and physical characteristics of an area, can be a model for improving the use of maps in social studies classrooms.

Included in the study skills sections of the intermediate 2 and advanced social studies tests are make-believe political posters. The questions based on these posters are excellent for measuring an important dimension of student understanding of politics, but they are not likely to measure what is normally thought of as study skills. Again, they are fine models for teaching and evaluating the development of political understanding.

Perhaps the most serious reservation about the study skills sections concerns the lack of questions requiring inferences from the data which are given. It might be expected that students who have reached junior high school should be evaluated on their ability to extrapolate and reach conclusions from data presented to them in tabular and graphic form. However, these sections are tests of study skills, not of critical thinking, and they perform their function well.

Science Tests. Science questions are contained in all of the batteries of the 1964 edition except the Primary 1 Battery. In the Primary 2 Battery the questions are part of the subtest that includes both science and social studies questions. The questions are dictated by the teacher; only the choices are printed in the test booklet.

The listed purposes of the Primary 2 Battery science questions are to measure knowledge of synonyms, simple definitions, and "ready associations," and "higher-level comprehension of the concepts represented by words, and fullness of understanding of terms." Science content for this test is described as being about evenly distributed among the three categories of physical science, life science, and the attitudes and methods of scientists. The purposes have probably been realized insofar as they can be for the grades covered, but the content specifications have not: only 1 of the 19 science questions in Form W could possibly be classified as dealing with the attitudes and methods of scientists, and certainly no more than 2 of the 19 questions in either Form X or Form Y could be so classified. The distribution of questions between the physical sciences and the biological sciences is not the same for the several forms but does approximate half for each.

The objectives about which the science tests in the other batteries have been designed are as follows: (*a*) the ability to see the application of the principles of science in our environment and everyday activities, (*b*) knowledge of the facts and generalizations from the various branches of the natural sciences, and (*c*) some knowledge of the scientific method. A check of the batteries indicates that the numbers of questions designed for each of the first two objectives are about the same and that about 10 per cent of the questions are related to the third objective.

The content coverage for the tests in the Intermediate 1 and 2 Batteries and in the Advanced Battery is given in detail in the manuals. The emphasis is about the same for each of the batteries. A bit more than half of the questions deal with physical and earth sciences, a bit fewer than half with biological sciences. In general, the specifications seem adequate for science tests for the grades involved, although in the upper tests some questions measuring understanding of graphs and of experimental results would have been desirable.

All of the questions are short; the testing time of 25 minutes for 56 to 60 questions in the intermediate and advanced level tests has made short questions necessary. The abilities probed might have been somewhat more sophisticated if some of the questions could have been a bit longer.

When one considers the individual questions, it is easy to be critical. A number of the questions would have profited from more review by competent science specialists. Among the weaknesses noted in the questions are the following: A glacier may be a large body of ice but a large body of ice is not necessarily a glacier (Primary 2 Battery, Form W, item 3). Thermometers are not properly said to measure weather (Intermediate 1 Battery, item 7). "Germ" seems a rather unscientific word to use in science tests (Advanced Battery, item 31). The level at which a boat floats depends not only on the size but also on the weight (Intermediate 1 Battery, item 31). The "weakness" of a spring is not commonly said to be determined by how tightly it is wound (Intermediate 1 Battery, item 45; Advanced Battery, item 6). Chickens must not be birds since "birds are valuable to us because they often eat insects," not because they "lay eggs" (Intermediate 1 Battery, item 8). A dry cell is called a battery (Primary 2 Battery, Form W, item 16). One question (Intermediate 1 Battery, item 49; Intermediate 2 Battery, item 28) requires the pupil to indicate whether proteins or carbohydrates provide the "most calories" without any indication as to whether this is most calories per gram or most calories in one's total diet for a day. The statement that "molten material comes from a volcano," not from a pipeline, may not disturb grade school pupils, but it is careless science (Primary 2 Battery, Form Y, item 12). A few of the biological questions lapse into teleology. With few exceptions, one has no trouble selecting the answers to the questions, but all too often one wishes for more careful wording in order that science may not be unnecessarily distorted.

The items have been meticulously edited insofar as the basic principles for item writing are concerned. Only in the Intermediate 1 Battery is there a small lapse in test assembly. Here the placement of two items one directly after the other presents a situation in which the stem of the second question guides the pupil away from one incorrect alternative in the first question: "All metals are able to....resist rust" (item 33). "If an iron gate is to be kept from rusting...." (item 34).

The pattern of item difficulty, while it is not wholly unsatisfactory, seems to be not wholly satisfactory either. For the Advanced Battery, for example, 31 questions right out of 60 questions corresponds to a grade equivalent of 7.2 and 33 questions right corresponds to a grade equivalent of 8.0. This for a test designed for grades 7, 8, and 9! The science tests in the Intermediate Batteries are more satisfactory in this respect, from five to nine questions being required to raise by a year the grade equivalent within the grade range for which the batteries are intended. In the Primary 2 Battery, the combined science and social studies test seems to involve more serious measurement problems than do the upper level batteries. More of the science questions seem to be overly sophisticated either in wording or in content than appears to be true of the social studies questions. The chance score on the test is 13 questions correct, and a rights score of 17 corresponds to a grade equivalent of 2.6 while a rights score of 22 corresponds to a grade equivalent of 3.6. It seems doubtful that scores on this test show much about science achievement.

Reviewers of previous editions of the science tests have been most critical of the fact that the questions tested little more than recall of factual information. They have implied, however, that the nature of much of the instruction in science in the grades covered by these tests may be largely to blame for weakness of the content of the questions. They have urged the test authors to go beyond existing course objectives and content with questions that will influence curriculum revision rather than perpetuate mediocre courses of instruction. Science curricula have improved since the last revision of the tests and so have the science questions. But while the questions in the new edition do probe higher abilities than have the questions in earlier forms, they probably do not probe far enough to make a significant contribution toward better science education.

RELIABILITY AND VALIDITY. The manuals present for each test at each grade level for which a given battery is intended both split-half reliability coefficients corrected by the Spearman-Brown formula and Kuder-Richardson estimates. Each of these is based on a sample of 1,000 cases from each grade "drawn randomly from 76 school systems testing in all grades 1–9 in national standardization." Along with these are presented the standard errors of measurement. The 74 split-half coefficients range from .66 (for the test of science and social studies concepts in grade 2) to .95 (for the arithmetic test in grade 1 and the language test in grade 6). The 74 K-R 20 coefficients range from .71 (again for the test of science and social studies concepts in grade 2) to .95 (again for the arithmetic test in grade 1). The median value of both sets of coefficients is approximately .88. All but 11 of the split-half coefficients and all but 11 of the K-R 20 coefficients are .85 or higher. Fourteen of the 22 lower coefficients are on one or another of the arithmetic tests, and 13 of the 14 are for arithmetic tests in the Intermediate 2 and Advanced Batteries. This may well reflect the turmoil of the present period of transition from traditional to modern mathematics, particularly in the upper elementary grades.

The test is recommended for use in the analysis of group differences among school subjects and also of the differences in the abilities of individual pupils in the various subjects for purposes of planning individualized instruction, grouping pupils for instructional purposes, determining and evaluating rate of progress, and evaluating achievement. It is further recommended for use in the study of strengths and weaknesses for a grade or a school or a system as a whole, in evaluating instructional methods and materials, and as a source of information on which to base curriculum changes. The average estimates of reliability, ranging from .88 to .90, indicate that the test may appropriately serve these purposes (except for the science and social studies concepts test in the Primary 2 Battery). The authors wisely caution against the use of part scores within a given subject area for individual diagnostic purposes.

The manuals contain little information concerning the validity of the test. They merely state that the authors "sought to insure content validity by examining appropriate courses of study and textbooks as a basis for determining the skills, knowledges, understandings, etc. to be measured." A previous reviewer has commented that to the extent that achievement tests continue to be based on what has been taught instead of what should be taught, they hinder curriculum revision. There is no doubt but that standardized achievement tests, while they are not designed to do so, do tend to have some effect upon curriculum. However, the reviewer would argue that while achievement tests should reflect the ultimate in modern school practice, they cannot anticipate reforms in content or curriculum without sacrificing claim to current content or curricular validity.

ADMINISTRABILITY. The Directions for Administering (the manual) which accompanies each battery makes the task of administering and scoring the tests a comparatively simple one. The directions to the teacher for giving the tests and to the pupils for taking them are quite clear and complete. For most tests the time limits seem ample. On the basis of information gleaned from the raw score-grade score conversion tables, however, speed is likely to be a factor in some of the language tests, notably at the Intermediate 1 Battery level; in at least one of the arithmetic tests, the test in arithmetic applications, in the Advanced Battery; in some of the social studies tests, notably at the intermediate 1 and advanced levels; and in at least one of the science tests, the test in the Intermediate 1 Battery. The format of the test booklets, the answer sheets, the scoring keys, and the Class Record and Class Analysis Chart seems planned for efficient use. In the Primary 1 and 2 Batteries, where answers must be recorded directly in the test booklet, scoring is perforce by hand. For all other batteries scoring may be by hand or by machine.

INTERPRETABILITY. Scores on the 1964 *Stanford Achievement Test* may be translated into grade scores, grade equivalents, and percentile ranks, as with the 1953 revision, and into stanines, an innovation for the new edition. All the norms are based on "the total enrollment in regular classes at each grade level except for a small group markedly atypical as to age."

For all batteries the "grade scores" (grade equivalents without the decimal point) corresponding to each raw score are conveniently found in the conversion table at the end of each test and on the back of the IBM keys. The grade score is translated into a grade equivalent by simply placing a decimal point before the last digit. Since the grade norms are based on the performance of pupils in grades 1 through 9 tested in the standardization program, grade scores up to 96 are considered "to reflect accurately the achievement of pupils of the designated grade status in the various subjects." Beyond 96, the manual warns, the grade scores, derived by a process of extrapolation, are fictitious and "cannot be interpreted as signifying the performance typical of pupils of the indicated grade placement."

Percentile ranks corresponding to grade scores on each of the tests in each battery are given for three different testing dates—roughly for beginning, middle, and end-of-year testing. Like the previous reviewer, this reviewer hails the provision of percentile norms but is disappointed that they are still geared to the grade norms, which have so much less merit.

In addition, stanines (values in a simple 9-point scale of normalized scores) are also presented. Like the percentile norms, these are geared to the grade scores. While stanines are becoming increasingly popular as interpretative statistics and are now supplied with at least two other standardized achievement test batteries, the reviewer is torn between hailing their provision as a quick and easy means of combining and averaging scores and regretting their provision because of the large amount of information regarding score differences which is lost in the conversion of scores to such a simple scale.

A profile chart, which appears on the front page of each test booklet and is also printed separately, allows for the recording of grade scores and percentile ranks, and the plotting of a point on the stanine scale for each test in the battery to produce a graph which will, in the words of the manual, "permit ready identification of areas of strength and weakness, and the magnitude of the departure from typical performance in the various subjects." To illustrate the reason for the misgivings regarding the ability of the stanines to provide this kind of information, the reviewer offers the scores of a hypothetical Mary Smith completing the eighth grade. Mary's grade equivalents on the Advanced Battery are as follows: 9.6 in paragraph meaning, 9.6 in spelling, 9.8 in language, 8.4 in arithmetic computation, 8.2 in arithmetic concepts, 8.5 in arithmetic applications, 8.0 in social studies, and 8.3 in science. Obviously Mary's achievement in the language arts is much better than it is in the other subject matter areas; however, since each of these grade scores would be converted to a stanine of 5, Mary's profile would be expressed in a straight line. Now, if Mary had had only two more questions correct in paragraph meaning and one more question correct in spelling and language, and one less question correct on each of the other five tests, her stanine scores would have been 6 for the language tests and 4 for the other tests, resulting in a somewhat different looking profile. For a more accurate identification of areas of strength and weakness, the reviewer would be inclined to concentrate on the percentile ranks.

The manual suggests that if, for a pupil, class, or school, "it is desired to obtain an average grade score for all the tests in the battery," the median may be found by ranking the eight test scores in order of magnitude and then averaging the fourth and fifth scores. No suggestions are offered as to how this battery median is to be interpreted in any other way than as an average grade score.

From the Intermediate 1 Battery on, part scores (raw scores) corresponding to the 25th, 50th, and 75th percentiles for parts of the language and social studies tests are given. The manuals indicate that while the scores on the parts are sufficiently reliable for use in the diagnosis of group performance, they should not be used for the diagnosis of the performance of any individual pupil. Reliability estimates for these part scores are not given.

Finally, for the Intermediate 1 Battery on, there are tables which permit the interpretation of a pupil's level of achievement as indicated by his grade scores in relation to his general mental ability as measured by the *Otis Quick-Scoring Mental Ability Tests*. These are based on Otis and Stanford data from the 1963 standardization. Comparisons of scores on the Stanford with scores on other ability tests cannot be made from these tables.

CONCLUSION. With the publication of *The Sixth Mental Measurements Yearbook* the *Stanford Achievement Test* is more than 40 years old. In its 1964 edition it is presented in batteries at five different levels as compared with two in 1923, thus offering much better at-grade content than could possibly have been offered by the original test.

In spite of the fact that new tests have been introduced from time to time and new items from revision to revision, the content of the 1964 edition appears to be not too different from the content of the original edition. Some change, but very little, has taken place in the word meaning, paragraph meaning, and language tests, a little more change in the social studies and science tests, and probably the greatest change in the arithmetic tests which still, however, favor the traditional rather than the modern mathematics program. Insofar as the content is concerned, the test is probably best described as reflecting curricular changes positively but rather cautiously.

The items for every edition of the test have been written with considerable concern for accuracy of content and precision of form. In the 1964 edition there is evidence that the authors have overcome to some extent their long-standing conviction that items of the objective type cannot adequately measure higher intellectual abilities and skills or attitudes and behaviors; however, the items are still largely concerned with factual knowledge. The social studies and science tests, particularly, would benefit from greater emphasis on items designed to test critical thinking in the areas covered by the tests.

The change from the strongly subjective test of 1923 to the strongly objective test of 1964 has been steady but slow, with the *Stanford Achievement Test* a little bit behind its competitors during the past two decades. In the 1964 edition only the Primary 1 and 2 Batteries are not completely objective and machine scorable.

The Directions for Administering (the manuals), while containing useful information regarding the development of the tests and practical aids to the interpretation of test results, cannot be described as being particularly comprehensive. The discriminating test user, familiar with the comprehensive manuals and technical reports supplied for competing test batteries, will want more complete and detailed information than is currently supplied regarding the development of the series, the standardization sample, reliability and validity, intercorrelations among subtests, item difficulty values, equivalence of forms, and the like. A recent promotional piece promises both a technical supplement that will provide this information and guides for teachers, one for each battery, that will contain more helpful material on interpretation of scores, content of each subtest, illustrative profile charts and class analysis charts, and recommendations for the classroom use of test results. These publications should be placed high on the publisher's priority list.

Despite the many questions raised and suggestions offered, the reviewer would still rate the 1964 edition of the *Stanford Achievement Test* high among standardized achievement test batteries designed for use at the elementary school level. The new edition is in many ways superior to its predecessors and in some ways to its current competitors, although the degree of superiority is sometimes disappointing in terms of its auspicious start and its long history. For two reasons quite beyond any consideration of its quality, the Stanford will, without doubt, offer keen competition to most other standardized achievement tests currently available for use at the elementary school level: (*a*) it offers a means of continuous measurement from grade 1 through grade 9, which some of its competitors do not, and (*b*) many test users have come to feel comfortable in working with it as a result of long experience.

For the prospective test user who is looking for an achievement test which offers a means of continuous measurement through the elementary grades, the reviewer does not hesitate to recommend the *Stanford Achievement Test* over its competitors, with the possible exception of the *Metropolitan Achievement Tests,* which are similar to the Stanford in content and format and offered by the same publisher for use in grades 1 through 12. For use from grades 3 and 4 on, the relative merits of the Stanford and its competitors should be considered carefully. If testing is to be confined to the skill areas, the reviewer would personally prefer the *Iowa Tests of Basic Skills* to the Stanford and to its competitors on the basis of content and format and the kind and amount of data available for the use and interpretation of results, but the Stanford would be a close second choice. If the content areas are to be covered as well, the choice would, in the reviewer's opinion, be between the Stanford with its largely content-based approach and the *Sequential Tests of Educational Progress* emphasizing the ability to apply to the solution of new problems school-learned skills and understandings. Here instructional objectives would need to be the determining factor.

Personnel & Guid J 43:178–84 O '64. Robert E. Stake and J. Thomas Hastings. * In the Manual....for the 1964 Edition it is stated that periodic revision is undertaken [for a number of stated purposes] * These statements deserve attention. What is taught in the schools does change and is changing at an increasing rate. Before constructing these tests the authors carefully reviewed textbooks, curriculum guides, and classroom practices in the late 1950's. (But, maximum annual sales of these tests are expected in the late 1960's.) Even with careful projections, periodic revision does not "insure that the content of the tests is attuned to what is actually being taught." What students of a given grade can do changes, too. Each year, by small increments, students do many things better than students of the preceding year. In the general literature on educational quality of the curriculum one can find allusions to regular increases in norms over years. Other things being equal, the more out-of-date the test, the better the appearance of a local group against the national norms. If a user is more concerned with the appearance of his group (to teachers, boards, and other citizens) than about the accuracy of test interpretation, the reviewers suggest that he use one of the achievement batteries on which the norms are less current than they *now* are on the 1964 Stanford. The third and fourth reasons....for revising the tests [to keep abreast of improvements in measurement theory and to avoid the dangers of familiarity of test content of the earlier edition] are, at best, not important. * There are technological innovations, such as optical machine scoring, which can make the new edition more convenient to use; but the application of new theories and techniques do not characterize this battery nor any of its competitors. As for the fourth reason, with the 1953 Tests available in five forms, the dangers of overfamiliarity of test content have been avoidable. * In his 1959 review, Gage complimented the Stanford publisher for resisting the swing to "gaudy, multicolor fanciness" (5:25). The 1964 Edition is multicolored, with different paper, with new type style, i.e., with new fanciness. To the best knowledge of the present reviewers, there is no evidence that attractive format influences examinee performance. Perhaps motivation is increased; perhaps fatigue is lessened. We just do not know. Considering what we do know, however, new format, protection from overfamiliarity of test content, and unspecified improvements in measurement theory and technique do not justify replacing 1953 tests with 1964 tests. For many schools, the revised content and revised norms *do* justify the replacement. *Test Content.* The 1964 Edition is stratified in five levels for Grades 1–9. At each level, verbal comprehension and skills in rhetoric and quantification are emphasized. For younger pupils there is considerable attention to phonics; for older pupils there are many items devoted to concepts taught in general science, social studies, and advanced arithmetic classes. * The Manuals....are well organized to help local officials decide on the appropriateness of content. The 1964 batteries are longer than the 1953 batteries—increased from 213 to 255 minutes for the advanced level, for example. For junior high school students, the extra time permits more thorough measurement of language skills, an extended consideration of science, and a newly added assessment of arithmetic concepts. For second-grade students (spring testing), the extra time permits much more testing of arithmetic and language skills and a newly added assessment of social studies concepts. The stratification of Grades 1–9 in five levels instead of the four used in 1953 is more than an incidental change. The intent was to reduce the range of achievement to be covered by any one subtest. However, just the opposite occurred in some cases. For example, fourth-grade scores on Paragraph Meaning running from 25 per cent of the items correct to 75 percent in 1953 represented a range of 2.8 grade equivalents whereas in 1964 these scores represent a range of 4.0 grade equivalents. The 1964 item content in this case is more heterogeneous, not more homogeneous. With beginning second graders, the intended result obtains. The 25–75 percent difficulty range represents more than 1.5 grade equivalents in 1953 but less than 1.0 grade equivalents in 1964. The 1964 Primary I tests should do a better job of measuring the achievement of children who are *achieving* at the second-grade level than do the 1953 Primary tests. But the reduced-range achievement test is not necessarily a better test for all children in the class. For pupils "at-grade," more items would contribute to effective measurement; but for pupils "above-grade" or "below-grade," fewer items would contribute. The typical class of elementary-school children includes a range of achievement of several years. Often there is extra concern for the children not "at-grade." Although the narrow-range test probably will have a little higher reliability coefficient, some children are sure to be tested less well with it. The tests will not be revised in the immediate future, but the Manuals are sure to be modified and enlarged. A splendid opportunity faces the authors—an opportunity to develop a new approach to within-grade heterogeneity. They might try a new "package plan" by which, for example, a school purchasing Intermediate II tests would automatically receive some Intermediate I and Advanced tests with the suggestion to use these for retesting the top-scoring and bottom-scoring students. Individual students would be more thoroughly tested, and teachers would be assured that test publishers are aware of the heterogeneity problem. *The Content Dilemma.* Authors of achievement tests....face a perplexing decision in weighting skill and content-comprehension to obtain a single achievement score. Since skill and comprehension are not factorially equivalent, any single achievement score affected by both represents an arbitrary combination. For any given achievement test, there will be users who are unhappy because content has been emphasized so much and users who are unhappy because skill has been emphasized so much. * The authors of the Stanford Tests, then and now, have sought some middle ground, attempting to measure verbal comprehension and expression abilities and to tap some body of content to which most U.S. students have been exposed at least briefly. Previous editions have been criticized in professional reviews (4:25, 5:25) mainly because the items seemed to deal too much with content knowledge, not enough with problem-solving, transfer, and ability to evaluate. On the other hand, the teacher doing the universally recommended content analysis of the items has been more likely to criticize the tests because they did not contain enough of the "right" content. The authors are hard-put to write a single test which will please such conflicting critics. It appears to these reviewers that "it is more impossible to write a perfect, standardized, content-oriented achievement test than to write a perfect, standardized, skill-oriented achievement test." Curriculum content is changing rapidly. It is a bit pretentious to suggest that the test content approved in 1959 will be suitable test content in 1969. Today's curriculum projects and instructional research projects are making the curriculum less standard. Some schools will introduce a topic at Grade 10 whereas other schools may introduce the same topic at Grade 6. The latter school is probably following a different sequence of learning, not merely accelerating the same sequence. In the future, individual pupils, as well as individual communities, will utilize widely differing materials, in different sequences, generating different content backgrounds. In the *Seventh Mental Measurements Yearbook* (1970?) all of the achievement-battery reviewers may agree that the assumption of a standard content is not sound even for all the students in a single class, much less for all the classes of a nation. The dilemma is not resolved by a statement that there always will be some common content to tap. Choice of curricular content is not just a matter of "what things" but also how those things are perceived. In the current Stanford Intermediate I Science section, item 7 shows three thermometers. To answer the item sensibly, one must *assume* that the scale is the same on all three. One of the objectives of some of the new science work is to teach that scales such as the temperature scale are arbitrary. The examinee who is alert to "scaling facts" may be confused by an item which ignores them. At some point in time, school administrators will become convinced that nationally standardized achievement tests with single-continuum, grade-oriented achievement scores are not compatible with local instructional practice. They probably will insist instead on a continuous program of "diagnostic" testing, using tests for keeping inventory of "what all is known and understood." It may continue to be reasonable to indicate that a student can spell certain English words better than 80 percent of the children in the nation's third-grade classes, but it probably will be unreasonable to summarize understanding of social science concepts with a single score. The content dilemma perhaps will be resolved by using locally assembled tests, by delimiting content, by de-emphasizing total scores, and by abandoning grade-equivalent notions. *Item Quality.* * Almost all items appear to be new. Spelling and language items for the fourth grade and higher remain proofreading rather than recall items. Item format has been changed on several subtests. The replacement of horizontal arrays of item alternatives (considered a commendable feature by a 1940 reviewer) with vertical arrays in some subtests has permitted longer, more complex response alternatives. * Almost certainly there will be better measurement of understanding of complex social relationships with the 1964 Edition. The major portion of the Advanced Study Skills items are now placed in the Social Studies section. Many of the correct responses to these items will reflect competence gained in science and mathematics classes. The items are good items which tease out skills more general than the subtest title, Social Studies, would suggest. Compared to those of the 1953 Edition, items for the 1964 Edition seem to be more difficult. On several of the advanced-form subtests, getting 75 percent of the items correct results in a 1964 grade score much above the 1953 grade score for 75 percent correct. Item content of the mathematics and science sections was scrutinized for two purposes: to judge the quality of the item writing and to note any representation of new curricula. The physical sciences, per se, were covered better than they had been in 1953, with less emphasis on hygiene and kitchen clatter, more emphasis on physics and chemistry. Too large a number of items in the science section need further editing. * The few items about scientists and the scientific method promote the stereotype of science as antiseptic, laboratory-based, clear-minded—a questionable notion which probably is being taught in the classroom. At least some science curriculum projects are trying to create a different perception. Schools so inclined would be better advised to try the TOUS tests, available for experimental uses from the Educational Testing Service. The impact of new curricula was more apparent in the Advanced and Intermediate mathematics items than in the science items. There is a new emphasis on intuitive equation-solving, place value, and symbolic notation. There is a noticeable replacement of operator commands (+, ÷) for word commands (add, divide). The new items appear to be more difficult. Although these tests do not go "as far" as some mathematics education people would like, the user is reminded of the forthcoming supplementary test of modern mathematics concepts. In the primary level tests little attention is given to modern mathematics concepts. * *Scoring.* * scoring aids packaged with the Stanford Tests are very helpful. * For Grade 4 and above, answer sheets for machine scoring are available, one form for the conventional IBM 805 scoring machine and a different form for scoring at the Measurement Research Center (MRC), Iowa City, Iowa. The 805 answer sheets have been in use for several years, and it is generally agreed that fourth graders are able to make appropriate marks with reasonably few clerical errors. Stanford 805 answer sheets are arranged so that raw scores are to be written in by the machine operator, with subsequent recording of grade scores from the appropriate table and percentile ranks from another table. This procedure increases the likelihood of errors in selecting and reading tables and is time-consuming. * The MRC answer sheet is a high-density sheet to be used with optical scoring machines. There is evidence that such sheets can be handled by Junior High examinees, but there is a disturbing lack of clarity about results with fourth-grade pupils. * *Test Interpretation.* The arrangement for profiling students' scores on the front of the test booklet or on a separate sheet is attractive. The method of profiling is easy to execute, and the use of stanines affords a simplicity which some profile sheets lack. * Profiles do not insure accurate interpretation, of course. In fact, profiles are often over-interpreted. Patterns and differences are seen which the "hard data would attribute to chance." Furthermore, stanines involve a rounding error which could contribute to over-interpretation in many instances. The Manual for the Stanford would be better insurance against over-interpretation if it contained information on the intercorrelations among subtests together with some discussion of the relationships between test intercorrelation, reliability, and the interpretation of profiles. The authors and publisher.... should be commended for including...the grade score standard errors of measurement (SEM). * it would have been quite helpful if they had included some examples of the use of the SEM in interpreting a set of scores. The Manual provides essential data clearly but does not go far enough toward helping teachers and counselors use the tests properly. * Only a smattering of technical specifications are available at this writing. The "Technical Manual" is supposed to be available by January 1, 1965. The decision to release the tests without a full statement of the norming, reliability, and validity is not a commendable decision. In this case users are protected somewhat by the reputation of these authors and the publisher. In the past the Stanford Achievement Tests have been developed with all due heed to appropriate psychometric principles. Split-half and Kuder-Richardson 20 coefficients of reliability....for each subtest for each grade....are generally as high as those for any of the currently available, standardized achievement tests. * For "knowledge of validity" the authors include a description of the sampling of content, and they put all emphasis upon the user's judgment regarding appropriateness of content for his school. Certainly content validity is extremely important for achievement tests. Once again, however, the authors might have added much help with little additional data by reporting the correlations between subscores on the achievement tests and scores on the Otis...., which they administered to all of the norming group. It is true that the main labor involved would be connected with interpreting such correlations to less-than-well-trained readers, but the data would increase "knowledge of validity." * In the existing Manual at each level the authors have a short paragraph in the section on "Interpreting Scores, Norms" on the procedure for finding a "median battery score." They do not say this procedure is justified. They merely say, in effect, that one should do it this way *if* he desires to do it. The reviewers' experience with multiple-test reports is that far too many school people want a single average—even though the subtests measure very different things. If the tests are highly correlated, the subscores are not very meaningful; if the tests are not highly correlated, median battery scores are apt to be more misleading than helpful for the majority of educational uses. The reviewers feel that 1964 would have been a good year in which to start advising against the use of the median battery score instead of clearing the computational path toward such an ambiguous statistic. * *Summary.* Teachers, counselors, and administrators who were satisfied with the 1953 Stanford Achievement Tests are likely to be satisfied with the 1964 Edition. Not much has been changed, and most of the changes seem to be improvements. School people who have supported innovation in curriculum are likely to have reservations about the item content and the emphasis on grade-equivalent scores. Users should beware of the attractiveness and ease of construction of the profiles since the use of stanines and the size of intercorrelations may aid over-interpretation. Perhaps the greatest general fault is that the authors still seem to assume a minimum responsibility for the education of test users. A more conceptually instructive Manual would be appreciated. Since the Stanford Tests are structured for content rather than predictive validity, counselors will find little ground in the current Manual for recommending them. A forthcoming "Technical Manual" should put the Stanford Tests in better psychometric perspective. The norms are "fresh" and should be more useful now than at any time in the future. It seems safe to conclude that, if local instructors endorse the content coverage, the Stanford Tests will do as effective a job of measuring elementary-school achievement as any standardized battery currently available.

For a review by N. L. Gage of the 1953 revision, see 5:25; for reviews by Paul R. Hanna (with Claude E. Norcross) and Virgil E. Herrick of the previous edition, see 4:25; for reviews by Walter W. Cook and Ralph C. Preston, see 3:18. For reviews of subtests of the 1953 and earlier editions, see 5:487, 5:656, 5:698, 5:799, 4:419, 4:555, 4:593, 3:503, and 3:595.

[27]

Wide Range Achievement Test: Reading, Spelling, Arithmetic From Kindergarten to College, 1946 Edition. Ages 5 and over; 1940–46; 3 scores: reading, spelling, arithmetic; individual; 1 form ('46, 4 pages); manual ('46, 24 pages); $3.60 per 50 tests; 80¢ per manual; 90¢ per specimen set; postpaid; (20–45) minutes; Joseph Jastak and Sidney Bijou; distributed by Psychological Corporation. *

REFERENCES

1. Bijou, Sidney W. "A Genetic Study of the Diagnostic Significance of Psychometric Patterns." *Am J Mental Def* 47:171–7 O '42. * (*PA* 17:939)
2. Landisberg, Selma. "A Personality Study of Institutionalized Epileptics." *Am J Mental Def* 52:16–22 Jl '47. * (*PA* 22:2267)
3. Rabin, Albert, and Geiser, Eugene. "The Achievement of Schizophrenics, Other Psychotics, and Non-Psychotics in Basic School Subjects." *J General Psychol* 41:125–9 Jl '49. * (*PA* 24:2719)
4. Jastak, Joseph. "Wide Range Achievement Tests," pp. 772–81. (*PA* 27:8038) In *Contributions Toward Medical Psychology: Theory and Psychodiagnostic Methods, Vol. II.* Edited by Arthur Weider. New York: Ronald Press Co., 1953. Pp. xi, 459–885. *
5. Diller, Juliet C. "A Comparison of the Test Performances of Male and Female Juvenile Delinquents." *J Genetic Psychol* 86:217–36 Je '55. * (*PA* 30:7485)
6. Topetzes, Nick John. "A Program for the Selection of Trainees in Physical Medicine." *J Exp Ed* 25:263–311 Je '57. * (*PA* 33:7024)
7. Scherer, Isidor W. "The Prediction of Academic Achievement in Brain Injured Children." *Excep Child* 28: 103–6 O '61. *
8. Smith, Bessie S. "The Relative Merits of Certain Verbal and Non-Verbal Tests at the Second-Grade Levels." *J Clin Psychol* 17:53–4 Ja '61. * (*PA* 37:3595)
9. Cassel, Robert H.; Johnson, Anna P.; and Burns, William H. "The Order of Tests in the Battery." *J Clin Psychol* 18:464–5 O '62. * (*PA* 39:5042)
10. Clawson, Aileen. "Relationship of Psychological Tests to Cerebral Disorders in Children: A Pilot Study." *Psychol Rep* 10:187–90 F '62. * (*PA* 37:1655)
11. Hopkins, Kenneth D.; Dobson, James C.; and Oldridge, O. A. "The Concurrent and Congruent Validities of the Wide Range Achievement Test." *Ed & Psychol Meas* 22: 791–3 w '62. * (*PA* 37:7188)
12. Lawson, John R., and Avila, Donald. "Comparison of Wide Range Achievement Test and Gray Oral Reading Paragraphs Reading Scores of Mentally Retarded Adults." *Percept & Motor Skills* 14:474 Je '62. * (*PA* 37:3581)
13. Fortenberry, Warren D., and Broome, Billy J. "Comparison of the Gates Reading Survey and the Reading Section of the Wide Range Achievement Test." *J Develop Read* 7:66–8 au '63. *
14. Matthews, Charles G., and Reitan, Ralph M. "Relationship of Differential Abstraction Ability Levels to Psychological Test Performances in Mentally Retarded Subjects." *Am J Mental Def* 68:235–44 S '63. * (*PA* 38:6430)
15. Saxton, George H.; Blackman, Leonard S.; and Tretakoff, Maurice I. "Achievement Measurement and Academic Grade Placement in Educable Mental Retardates." *Am J Mental Def* 67:748–50 Mr '63. * (*PA* 38:1279)

For reviews by Paul Douglas Courtney, Verner M. Sims, and Louis P. Thorpe, see 3:21.

[Other Tests]

For tests not listed above, see the following entries in *Tests in Print:* 3, 7, 10, 12–3, 17–8, 22–3, 34, 40, and 43–4; out of print: 9, 19–20, 28–9, and 41.

BUSINESS EDUCATION

Reviews by *Irol Whitmore Balsley, Lawrence W. Erickson, Melvin R. Marks, Jacob S. Orleans, Ray G. Price, Harold L. Royer, Edward O. Swanson, and Henry Weitz.*

[28]

***Business Education: National Teacher Examinations.** College seniors and teachers; 1956–63; for more complete information, see 700; IBM; 80(90) minutes; Educational Testing Service. *

For reviews of the testing program, see 700; 5:538, and 4:802.

[29]

★Business Education: Teacher Education Examination Program. College seniors preparing to teach secondary school; 1957; an inactive form of *Business Education: National Teacher Examinations;* for more complete information, see 709; IBM; 80(95) minutes; Educational Testing Service. *

For a review of the testing program, see 5:543. For reviews of the National Teacher Examinations, *see 700, 5:538, and 4:802.*

[30]

***Business Fundamentals and General Information Test: National Business Entrance Tests.** Grades 11–16 and adults; 1938–62; 4 forms: General Testing Series Form 19-51 ('55), Official Testing Series Forms 18-41 ('54), 20-61 ('59), 21-71 ('60); for further information, see the battery entry, 33;

Joint Committee on Tests of the United Business Education Association and the National Office Management Association (Forms 19-51 and 18-41 only); National Business Education Association. *

For reviews by Vera M. Amerson and C. C. Upshall of the 1946 form, see 3:369. For reviews of the complete battery, see 33, 5:515, and 3:396.

[31]

★General Business: Every Pupil Scholarship Test. High school; 1959–61; 3 forms: April '59, January '61, April '61, (2–4 pages); general directions sheet ['63, 2 pages]; no data on reliability; 4¢ per test; 4¢ per scoring key; postage extra; 40(45) minutes; Bureau of Educational Measurements. *

RAY G. PRICE, *Professor of Business Education, University of Minnesota, Minneapolis, Minnesota.*

The Every Pupil Scholarship Test is a series of tests used to determine levels of achievement for students in Kansas but also available to out-of-state users. *General Business* is one of the tests in this series. The April 1959 form consists of 100 items; Part 1 has 45 true-false items; Part 2, 25 multiple choice items; and Part 3, 30 matching items. The January 1961 and April 1961 forms each contain 75 multiple choice items. The scoring is quite easy and objective. Each item is worth one point.

Unfortunately, no data on reliability or validity was reported for any form of the test. Lacking this information, it is difficult, if at all possible, for the prospective user to judge its value as a measuring instrument.

Also missing was the manual that usually accompanies a published test and which contains such information as (*a*) the purpose of the test; (*b*) source of content and method of preparation; (*c*) statistical evidence of validity and reliability; and (*d*) suggestions for using the test results.

Supposedly, each of the three test forms covers the essential material presented in a general business course. The basis used for selecting the content, however, is not clear. For example, in the April 1959 form only two items out of 100 pertain to insurance. The January 1961 form, on the other hand, contains 23 items on insurance out of a total of 75. This seems to indicate a lack of balance in covering the content of the general business course. In addition, the test items tend to emphasize specific details and a knowledge of facts rather than general understanding, reasoning ability, and critical discrimination. But perhaps, it is only fair to say that the test may be a reflection of the way the average general business course is taught.

Nevertheless, the test *General Business* is a worthy effort. Furthermore, the two later forms (January and April, 1961) are a vast improvement over the earlier form. Properly revised, the test could be developed into a useful measuring instrument that is greatly needed.

[32]

***General Office Clerical Test (Including Filing): National Business Entrance Tests.** Grades 11–16 and adults; 1948–62; 4 forms (8–10 pages plus accessories); General Testing Series Form 19-53 ('55), Official Testing Series Forms 18-43 ('54), 20-63 ('59), 21-73 ('60); for further information, see the battery entry, 33; Joint Committee on Tests of the United Business Education Association and the National Office Management Association (Forms 19-53 and 18-43 only); National Business Education Association. *

REFERENCES

1. HAMILTON, HERBERT A. *Relationship of Success in Beginning General Clerical Occupations to Achievement in the Information and Skill Aspects of General Office Clerical Division of the National Business Entrance Tests Series.* Doctor's thesis, New York University (New York, N.Y.), 1951.

For reviews by Arnold E. Schneider and C. C. Upshall of the 1946 form, see 3:379. For reviews of the complete battery, see 33, 5:515, and 3:396.

[33]

***National Business Entrance Tests.** Grades 11–16 and adults; 1938–62; formerly called *National Clerical Ability Tests* and *United-NOMA Business Entrance Tests;* 3 series; 6 tests (also listed separately); no data on reliability; no adult norms; Joint Committee on Tests of the United Business Education Association and the National Office Management Association (for 1800, 1900, and short forms only); National Business Education Association. *

a) [GENERAL TESTING SERIES.] 1938–59; 1 form; 6 tests; directions for administering ('55, 4 pages); correction manual ['55, 15 pages]; norms ['59, 1 page]; 50¢ per test; 50¢ per set of directions for administering and correction manual (free with orders of $3 or more); $3 per specimen set; cash orders postpaid.

1) *Machine Calculation Test.* 1941–59; Form 19-54 ('55, 7 pages); 120(130) minutes.

2) *Typewriting Test.* 1941–59; Form 19-56 ('55, 4 pages plus accessories); 120(130) minutes.

3) *Business Fundamentals and General Information Test.* 1938–59; Form 19-51 ('55, 8 pages); separate answer sheets must be used; 45(55) minutes.

4) *Bookkeeping Test.* 1938–59; Form 19-52 ('55, 7 pages plus accessories); 120(130) minutes.

5) *General Office Clerical Test (Including Filing).* 1948–59; Form 19-53 ('55, 10 pages plus accessories); 120(130) minutes.

6) *Stenographic Test.* 1938–59; Form 19-55 ('55, 2 pages plus accessories); manual ('55, 11 pages); 90(130) minutes.

b) [SHORT FORM SERIES.] 1938–55; 1 form ('55); 2 tests; no norms; 50¢ per test, cash orders postpaid.

1) *Stenographic Test.* 1938–55; 1 form (2 pages plus accessories); directions sheet ('55, 2 pages); 45(65) minutes.
2) *Typewriting Test.* 1941–55; 1 form (4 pages); no manual; 45(55) minutes.
c) [OFFICIAL TESTING SERIES.] 1938–62; administered only at NBET Centers which may be established in any community; 3 forms; 6 tests; directions for administering 1800 forms ('54), 2000 forms ('59), 2100 forms ('60), (4 pages); norms for 1800 forms ['56, 1 page], 2000 forms ['62, 2 pages], 2100 forms ['62, 1 page]; postpaid; fee includes scoring, reporting, and consultation services.
1) *Machine Calculation Test.* 1941–62; Forms 18-44 ('54, 7 pages), 20-64 ('59, 4 pages), 21-74 ('60, 7 pages); examination fee, $1; 60(70) minutes for Form 20-64, 120(130) minutes for Forms 18-44 and 21-74.
2) *Typewriting Test.* 1941–62; Forms 18-46 ('54), 20-66 ('55), 21-76 ('60), (4 pages plus accessories); examination fee, $1; 60(70) minutes for Form 20-66, 120(130) minutes for Forms 18-46 and 21-76.
3) *Business Fundamentals and General Information Test.* 1938–62; Forms 18-41 ('54), 20-61 ('59), 21-71 ('60), (8 pages); separate answer sheets must be used; available free when one or more of the tests in the series are ordered; 40(50) minutes for Form 20-61, 45(55) minutes for Forms 18-41 and 21-71.
4) *Bookkeeping Test.* 1938–62; Forms 18-42 ('54), 20-62 ('59), 21-72 ('60); examination fee, $1; 60(70) minutes for Form 20-62, 120(130) minutes for Forms 18-42 and 21-72.
5) *General Office Clerical Test (Including Filing).* 1948–62; Forms 18-43 ('54, 10 pages plus accessories), 20-63 ('59, 8 pages plus accessories), 21-73 ('60, 10 pages plus accessories); examination fee, $1.25; 60(70) minutes for Form 20-63, 120(130) minutes for Forms 18-43 and 21-73.
6) *Stenographic Test.* 1938–62; Forms 18-45 ('54), 20-65 ('59), 21-75 ('60), (11 pages); manual for Forms 18-45 ('54, 11 pages), 20-65 ('59, 8 pages), 21-75 ('60, 11 pages), examination fee, $1.25; 60(90) minutes for Form 20-65, 90(130) minutes for Forms 18-45 and 21-75.

REFERENCES

1–9. See 40:1476.
10. See 4:453.
11. CRISSY, WILLIAM J., AND WANTMAN, M. J. "Measurement Aspects of the National Clerical Ability Testing Program." *Ed & Psychol Meas* 2:37–46 Ja '42. * (*PA* 16:2441)
12. NELSON, JOHN HOWARD. *A Study of the Relationships Between Achievement on the National Business Entrance Tests and the Job Performance of Beginning Stenographers and Typists.* Doctor's thesis, New York University (New York, N.Y.), 1951.
13. LILES, PARKER. "National Business Entrance Tests Motivate Business Students." *Bus Ed Forum* 14:22+ F '60. *
14. SLAUGHTER, ROBERT E. "The National Business Entrance Tests," pp. 338–46. In *Evaluation of Pupil Progress in Business Education.* The American Business Education Yearbook, Vol. 17, 1960. New York: New York University Bookstore, 1960. Pp. x, 399. *
15. BAIRD, MARGARET W. "National Business Entrance Tests: Personal Experience." *J Bus Ed* 36:287–8 Ap '61. *
16. NATALE, GLORIA MARIE. *Measurement Aspects of the National Business Entrance Tests.* Doctor's thesis, Columbia University (New York, N.Y.), 1963. (*DA* 24:1887)

MELVIN R. MARKS, *Professor of Business Administration, The University of Rochester, Rochester, New York.* [Review of Series 1900, 2000, and 2100.]

The NBE tests are offered in a General Testing Series and an Official Testing Series. Each series includes six tests: bookkeeping, general office clerical, machine calculation, stenography, typewriting, and "business fundamentals and general information." On the positive side the five specific tests appear to have adequate face validity for their subject matter. Unfortunately, no other positive points can be made by this reviewer. The format and number of items in the tests of the General Testing Series and the long forms of the Official Testing Series are identical, and the item content is highly similar. Thus, in appearance, they seem to be parallel forms. However, the publisher says that they have different purposes and that "careful consideration should be made of the purpose intended when ordering these tests." What are these purposes? "Tests in the Official Testing Series are available solely for administration at National Business Entrance Testing Centers * Included at no extra charge are the scoring, reporting, and consultation services * The General Testing Series is used in schools for grading purposes and in preparing students for the Official Testing Series. Business also makes use of the General Testing Series for employment and placement purposes." This distinction in purpose does not appear to be one which would be accepted by most sophisticated users of tests. It is not a distinction which in any way bears upon the content, reliability, validity, or usefulness of the tests. Thus, as far as the reviewer is concerned the Official Series represents only an additional service, not a different kind of test, and the implication that the Official Series is "better" is not warranted.

The adverse comments on the NBET appearing in *The Fifth Yearbook* could well stand as written for the current presentation of the tests. Additionally, the publishers furnished a copy of an exhaustive critique by Alexander Wesman made for the Joint Committee on Tests. Except for some favorable comments on face validity, the critique is almost wholly adverse (although, admittedly, the review is said to have deliberately concentrated on negative criticisms). Presumably this critique was available to the NBEA before the current versions of the NBET were released. The less than enthusiastic response of the reviewers to the almost complete lack of data on reliability and predictive validity has not persuaded the test publisher to remedy the deficiencies. A leaflet describing the tests offers the following under the heading "What about reliability and validity?": (*a*) that the tests are "prepared by testing specialists and business educators.... [and] reviewed by qualified office executives"; (*b*) that "several graduate research studies have been made relating to the tests and their effectiveness in predicting successful employment and adjustments in office occupations"; and (*c*) that "Persons interested in further evaluations of the NBETests are referred to recent editions of the 'Mental Measurements Yearbook.'" None of these "data" are useful answers to the questions on reliability and validity. This reviewer wrote to the publishers, pointing out the deficiencies. The reply referred again to the dissertations, but did not quote figures. The Wesman review referred to above was critical of the dissertation findings as to both technique and interpretation.

The point has been made that the General and Official Testing Series appear to contain parallel forms. The normative data bear out this assumption with respect to each of the six subtests, although the Official Testing Series appears to be slightly more difficult. It may be that in the process of revision (the Official Testing Series forms are said to be "revisions and improved versions" of General Testing Series forms) the Official Series has unintentionally been made more difficult. In any case, since new forms are introduced without any accompanying statement on the degree to which difficulty, parallelism, reliability, and validity have been held constant, the use of the word "improved" is not warranted.

Some additional adverse comments are in order. (*a*) There is no rationale for the complicated scoring procedure. (*b*) There is no rationale for the differential weighting of items within subtests or the differential weights of the subtests. (*c*) There is no indication that the intended weights have been realized by compensating for varying standard deviations of the tests or for their contributions to prediction of job performance. (*d*) There is frequent duplication of content areas between subtests; for example, numerical skills are required in several subtests. (*e*) Some subtests are so short (20 items) that their reliabilities may be seriously questioned.

Percentile rank on the Business Fundamentals and General Information Test seems to be regarded as a criterion for evaluating performance on the other tests. The user is told that if the examinee achieves a higher percentile rank on a skill test than on the fundamentals test "the quality of instruction, and level of achievement would be judged better than average," and conversely. This attribution of what may be random variation, or genuine intraindividual differences (for example, test specificity) to the inferred relationship between a general and a specific measure displays considerable naïveté.

In summary, while it may be true that the NBET could be useful in the evaluation of achievement in business education or for the prediction of office performance, the verdict of this reviewer is *not proven,* and thus the tests cannot be recommended for these purposes.

For reviews by Edward N. Hay, Jacob S. Orleans, and Wimburn L. Wallace, see 5:515; for a review by Paul S. Lomax of the 1946 forms, see 3:396. For reviews of individual tests, see 55, 5:506, 5:508, 5:511, 5:514, 5:522, 5:526, 3:368–9, 3:379, 3:384, 3:391, and 3:394.

[Other Tests]

For tests not listed above, see the following entries in *Tests in Print:* 48 and 52; out of print: 49.

BOOKKEEPING

[34]

***Bookkeeping: Every Pupil Scholarship Test.** High school; 1926–64; new form (2–4 pages) usually issued each January and April; forms from previous testing programs also available; general directions sheet ['63, 2 pages]; no data on reliability; norms for new forms available following testing program; 4¢ per test; 4¢ per scoring key; postage extra; 40(45) minutes; Bureau of Educational Measurements. *

[35]

***Bookkeeping: Minnesota High School Achievement Examinations.** High school; 1952–63; series formerly called *Midwest High School Achievement Examinations;* new form issued each May; norms available in June following release of new form; Form F ('63, 6 pages) used in 1963 testing; no specific manual; series manual ('63, 4 pages); series norms ['63, 4 pages]; series cumulative profile ('62, 2 pages); no data on reliability; no description of normative population; 12¢ per test; $2.50 per 100 profiles; postage extra; 20¢ per specimen set, postpaid; 60(65) minutes; American Guidance Service, Inc. *

HAROLD L. ROYER, *Associate Professor of Accounting, University of Miami, Coral Gables, Florida.* [Review of Form F.]

The coverage of this bookkeeping examination is fairly representative of the theory in first year high school bookkeeping. However, the examination could certainly be improved upon by including some questions or problems about the worksheet, computation of inventories, bank reconciliation, and petty cash, and by having several problems on the computation of depreciation. Several questions aim at breadth of coverage, but none aims at depth.

The examination is composed of 118 questions divided into 13 units as follows: general principles (32 questions); statements (12 questions); adjusting and closing entries (7 questions); special journals (8 questions); problems relating to sales and purchases (5 questions); payroll and taxes (6 questions); depreciation (6 questions); bad debts (6 questions); notes and interest (6 questions); accrued expense and income (5 questions); partnerships, corporations, and cooperatives (10 questions); banking services (5 questions); and "Problems" (10 questions). The problem section is not sufficiently representative either in scope or weight.

There is very little evidence of any attempt to work on validity. A number of the questions have several responses; items 4, 8, and 28 have more than one answer. Item 29 is answerable in a way which is at variance with the scoring key. Items 39 and 41 should have better accounting terminology for their answers. Neither at the beginning nor at any point throughout the examination is there a sample question.

The percentile norms are worked out for each new form of the examination, but we do not know how many examinations were given to base the norms upon. No information is given concerning the geographical distribution of the examinees on whom the norms are based, nor the types of schools from which they come—public or private, general or commercial.

The examination may serve the purpose of the teacher who wants a very general test at the end of the semester or at the end of the school year. There are not enough questions or problems in a single unit to obtain detailed information and to diagnose a student's ability to work the worksheet and make the statements.

For a review by I. David Satlow of earlier forms, see 5:504.

[36]

***Bookkeeping Test: National Business Entrance Tests.** Grades 11–16 and adults; 1938–62; 4 forms: General Testing Series Form 19-52 ('55), Official Testing Series Forms 18-42 ('54), 20-62 ('59), 21-72 ('60); for further information, see the battery entry, 33; Joint Committee on Tests of the United Business Education Association and the National Office Management Association (Forms 19-52 and 18-42 only); National Business Education Association. *

For reviews by Harvey A. Andruss and Ray G. Price of the 1946 form, see 3:368. For reviews of the complete battery, see 33, 5:515, and 3:396.

[37]

***First-Year Bookkeeping: Every Pupil Test.** 1 year high school; 1939–64; new form (4 pages) usually issued each April; forms from previous testing programs also available; general directions sheet ('63, 2 pages); no data on reliability; Ohio norms for new forms available following testing program; 5¢ per test; 3¢ per scoring key; postpaid; 40(45) minutes; Ohio Scholarship Tests. *

[Other Tests]

For tests not listed above, see the following entries in *Tests in Print:* 55, 58–9, and 61–2; out of print: 63.

MISCELLANEOUS

[38]

★Commercial Law: Every Pupil Scholarship Test. High school; 1951; 1 form (2 pages); general directions sheet ['63, 2 pages]; no data on reliability; 4¢ per test; 4¢ per scoring key; postage extra; 40(45) minutes; Bureau of Educational Measurements. *

[39]

***Machine Calculation Test: National Business Entrance Tests.** Grades 11–16 and adults; 1941–62; earlier tests called *Key-Driven Calculating Machine Ability Test;* 4 forms: General Testing Series Form 19-54 ('55), Official Testing Series Forms 18-44 ('54), 20-64 ('59), 21-74 ('60); for further information see the battery entry, 33; Joint Committee on Tests of the United Business Education Association and the National Office Management Association (Forms 19-54 and 18-44 only); National Business Education Association. *

For a review by Dorothy C. Adkins, see 5:514; for a review by Elizabeth Fehrer of the 1946 form, see 3:384. For reviews of the complete battery, see 33, 5:515, and 3:396.

[Other Tests]

For tests not listed above, see the following entry in *Tests in Print:* 66.

SHORTHAND

[40]

★APT Dictation Test. Stenographers; 1955; 1 form (33⅓ rpm record); comparison script (1 page); no data on reliability; no norms; distribution restricted to clients; $12.50 per set of testing materials, postage extra; 4[10] minutes; Associated Personnel Technicians, Inc. *

[41]

★Byers' First-Year Shorthand Aptitude Tests. First year students in grades 9–13 and business school; 1959; 6 scores: total and 5 scores listed below; 1 form; 2 parts; manual (13 pages); no data on reliability; no norms for college or business school students; 50¢ per set of both parts; 50¢ per manual (free with 10 or more sets of both parts); postage extra; Edward E. Byers; Allied Publishers, Inc. *

a) PART 1. 2 scores: phonetic perception, retention ability; orally administered in part; 1 form (3 pages); 35(40) minutes.

b) PART 2. 3 scores: observation aptitude, pattern from parts, hand dexterity; 1 form (13 pages); 35(40) minutes.

REFERENCES

1. BYERS, EDWARD ELMER. *Construction of Tests Predictive of Success in First-Year Shorthand.* Doctor's thesis, Boston University (Boston, Mass.), 1958. (*DA* 19:1610)

EDWARD O. SWANSON, *Assistant Professor, and Senior Student Personnel Worker, University of Minnesota, Minneapolis, Minnesota.*

Shorthand is "a rapid method of writing by substituting characters or symbols for letters, words, etc." (*Webster's New Collegiate Dictionary*) and is synonymous with "stenography." The Byers' test purports to measure aptitude for utilizing this method and "to predict success in first-year shorthand." The tests "were constructed for use as prognostic testing instruments that would assist in the (1) placement of beginning shorthand students, (2) early identification of unqualified students, and (3) improvement of effective classroom instruction." No effort was made "to measure functional factors concerned with transcription or vocational success."

The test consists of five subtests entitled Phonetic Perception (writing, in regular spelling, words listed by phonetic spelling), Retention Ability (a digit to letter substitution task when a string of digits are read orally to the examinees), Observation Aptitude (choosing a given pattern of symbols from five patterns when curves and straight lines in the pattern are reversed), Pattern From Parts (marking a diagonal for missing letters from a paragraph with the letters strung out equally spaced), and Hand Dexterity (marking as many as possible of prescribed patterns on a dotted field in a 20-second time period). The five tests are divided into two parts, each requiring about 35 minutes to administer.

The tasks were arrived at by observation of processes of shorthand, interviews with shorthand teachers and students, reviews of other shorthand tests, and surveys of writing and research on shorthand prognosis.

These shorthand tests appear to be overelaborate attempts to match armchair-derived component functions of the shorthand process with similarly derived tasks that will supposedly measure these functions. Each test author has the prerogative of defining what domain is to be measured, but he is also bound to present validation data for his approach. The manual presents no reliability data and the most meager of validity data. Even necessary descriptive data are lacking (sample sizes, means, and standard deviations).

Validity information consists of three multiple correlation coefficients between the test and "shorthand accomplishment tests (partial transcription of seven dictated letters, each requiring 2½ minutes to dictate, with dictation rates ranging from 45 to 75 words a minute) administered at the end of one year of shorthand study." No sample sizes are given, and the groups are *not* described. Presumably the multiple correlation coefficients are each obtained by combining the five subtests in optional statistical fashion but the manual does not make this clear, simply stating the subtest scores are weighted in order to produce the highest possible multiple correlations. Neither a table of zero order intercorrelations nor of beta weights is presented; consequently, the reader cannot decide which subtests carry what weights in the regression equations. Outside of the sentence quoted, the reader will learn nothing about the criterion measure. No concurrent validities are shown. Though the author presumably derived his ideas in part by reference to other shorthand tests, he did not see fit to relate results of his tests to results of other shorthand tests or to factor tests of a similar nature.

A norms table for a high school group is presented for an averaged "Z" score of the five subtests. No description of the high school sample is given, neither its size nor its representativeness. How the "Z" scores (ranging from 86 to 928) were derived is totally unexplained. No suggested cutting points for selecting or possibly sectioning shorthand students are given.

Because of the nature of the tasks presented, two of the tests appear difficult to administer and score. Retention Ability requires 56 timed intervals ranging from 6 seconds to 11 seconds and Hand Dexterity requires 16 intervals of 20 seconds each. This hardly recommends these tests for easy administration particularly since speed is an important part of the task involved. Retention Ability requires each substituted letter to be correct for the item to be counted as correct, while Hand Dexterity requires a scorer's judgment as to whether a pattern drawn is accurate enough to be counted correctly.

The symbols for Observation Aptitude are poorly printed, the lines appearing blurred, the squares not quite square, and the circles not quite circular. A reasonably good draftsman and use of the photo-offset process would have permitted a considerably better printing job. Directions in the manual do not have clearly differentiated breaks between the finish of one subtest and the start of another.

The reviewer cannot recommend this test. No descriptive statistics, poor validity data, no information about intercorrelations of the subtests, no description of the criterion group and the criterion measure, no evidence on test reliability, and insufficient norm information all combine to make a flat non-recommendation necessary.

[42]

***First-Year Shorthand: Every Pupil Test.** 1 year high school; 1938–64; test booklet titles vary; new form (4 pages) usually issued each April; forms from previous testing programs also available; general directions sheet ('63, 2 pages); no data on reliability; Ohio norms for new forms available following testing program; 25¢ per set of teacher's dictation sheets, postpaid; 30(45) minutes; Ohio Scholarship Tests. *

[43]

Personnel Research Institute Test of Shorthand Skills. Stenographers; 1951–54; title on test is *Otis and Laurent Test of Shorthand Skills;* 2 scores: transliteration, transcription; Forms A, B, ('51, 2 pages); manual ('54, 6 pages); tentative norms; 15¢ per test; 50¢ per set of scoring key and manual; $1 per specimen set; postage extra; (20–35) minutes; [Jay L. Otis and Harry Laurent]; Personnel Research Institute. *

IROL WHITMORE BALSLEY, *Professor of Office Administration and Head of the Department, Louisiana Polytechnic Institute, Ruston, Louisiana.*

The authors recommend in the manual, published in 1954, that this test be used only for preliminary screening, since a "minimum of data is available with respect to its validity, and norms are based on relatively small samples." Apparently, no further attempt at validation has been made in the past nine years.

Since Forms A and B are of the same design, specific comments will be made regarding Form A only.

The first part of the test consists of a business letter presented in printed form with space under each line of copy for the testee to write the shorthand outlines for the words. There is no explanation in the manual of the procedure used to select the vocabulary for the letter or to decide upon the length of it.

The testee is timed on his writing of the shorthand notes, and his time is recorded in minutes and seconds. No maximum amount of time to be allowed is stated. In scoring the first part, only the time taken to write the shorthand is considered. The completeness or accuracy of the shorthand notes is disregarded. The material consists of 332 actual words, or 384 words using the Gregg 1.4 syllable standard word.

The second part of the test requires the testee to supply 60 selected words or phrases (70 actual words) in a partially completed printed transcript of the letter, using his own shorthand notes previously written from print. In Form A, this partial transcript contains approximately 52 per cent of the letter. The 21 per cent of the transcript to be filled in by the testee is indicated by single-line markings; the remaining 27 per cent, indicated by double-line markings, is not to be filled in.

In speaking of the suitability of this type of test, the authors state that "In an analysis of shorthand skills preparatory to actual test construction, it was found that the primary difference distinguishing the skilled from the mediocre stenographer appeared to be not so much in speed of taking down the shorthand (transliteration) as in accuracy in reading the notes after they had been taken (transcription) * It was found, however, that the speed of transliteration of printed material was related to the rate of transliteration of orally presented material." No explanation of the nature of the analysis that led to these conclusions is given.

Teachers of shorthand would be likely to challenge such conclusions for at least two reasons. First, in the writing-shorthand-from-print test, a basic element is missing that is present in the writing-shorthand-from-dictation test. The shorthand writer is not required to carry in his memory the dictated message as he writes the outlines. Second, he has the opportunity to go back over the printed copy several times if need be to fill in outlines that he could not think of in the first writing.

In taking dictation in an office situation, the rate at which a stenographer can take dictation and transcribe the notes accurately is of importance. This test provides no measure of dictation rate the testee can take. If the assumption is made that the testee can take dictation at the rate at which he is able to write the message from the printed copy, the rates indicated by the times recorded in the manual for the validation groups would be vastly different from what they are.

For in the decile norms for Form A, the time required by employed stenographers in the 1st tenth was 4 minutes, 20 seconds or less; in the 10th tenth, more than 8 minutes, 50 seconds. The time required by the advanced students in the 1st tenth was 5 minutes, 45 seconds or less; in the 10th tenth, more than 8 minutes, 45 seconds. According to these figures, only the testees in the 1st tenth of the advanced students would be taking dictation in excess of 70 words a minute and only testees in the 1st tenth of employed stenographers would be taking dictation in excess of 75 words a minute. The mean rate in each group would be less than 60 words a minute. It must be remembered, also, that these recorded times give no indication of the completeness or accuracy of the shorthand written. A testee could be very weak, quit trying in a few minutes, and have a high score on this aspect of the test.

The second part of the test is designed to measure the testee's ability to transcribe his shorthand notes. The real measure of the adequacy of a person's shorthand skill is, of course, his ability to transcribe completely and accurately. This process involves skill not only in reading shorthand notes but also in applying rules of grammar and punctuation, in spelling, in word usage, and in typing the transcript. Skill in typing the transcript is not, of course, measured in any way. Skill in reading shorthand notes is measured on the basis of transcribing less than 20 per cent of the dictation. The scorer of a test paper is directed to consider as an error any mistake in spelling or in hyphenation. There are four hyphenated words in Form A. No measure of ability to apply rules of grammar and punctuation is provided. Thus, it is evident that much of the transcription process is not measured by this test.

The authors state that since Forms A and B differ in difficulty, they have provided separate norms for the two forms. They explain that the norms given are not based on large samples and are not representative of a wide variety of training institutions or stenographic employers.

In establishing the correlation between scores on the various aspects of the test and final grades of advanced stenographic students, the authors used small numbers of cases, between 36 and 45. In no instance was the absolute correlation greater than .63 for the second part of the test or .53 for the first part.

In establishing the correlation between scores on the various aspects of the test and words-per-minute rate for employed stenographers, the authors used a total of 50 cases. The highest absolute correlation with accuracy of transcription was .25; and with speed of transliteration, .56. These figures arouse suspicion concerning the statement of the authors that the correlations between test scores and final grades "indicate satisfactory validity for both the rights and the time scores."

In summary, this test is of little value for its stated purpose. The customary dictation test used in the classroom would be a more valid test; and, incidentally, it (like this test) can be administered by a person who does not know any shorthand system.

[44]

★**Revised Standard Graded Tests for Stenographers.** High school and business school; 1958–59, c1956–59; 4 scores: mailability, speed of transcription, accuracy of transcription, accuracy of typing; Form A ('59); instructions and script ('59, 14 pages); no data on reliability; no norms; instructions and script free; [45] minutes; H. M. Overley; the Author. * (Test withdrawn.)

[45]

★**Shorthand Test: Individual Placement Series (Area IV).** Adults; 1960; Forms A, B, (2 pages); also available on 33⅓ rpm record; no manual; no data on reliability; no description of normative population; $10 per 25 tests; $10 per record containing both forms; $2 per specimen set without record; $12 per specimen set with record; postpaid; (20–25) minutes; J. H. Norman; the Author. *

[46]

★**Stenographic Dictation Test.** Applicants for stenographic positions; 1962–64; 6 forms ['62, 2 mimeographed pages]; forms 60A and 60B (60 wpm), 80A and 80B (80 wpm), 100A and 100B (100 wpm); practice sheet (1 page); manual ('64, 8 pages); no data on reliability; $35 per 25 tests; specimen set loaned for rental fee of $5, which may be applied to purchase price; postpaid; (20–30) minutes for test; McCann Associates. *

[47]

***Stenographic Test: National Business Entrance Tests.** Grades 11–16 and adults; 1938–62; earlier tests called *Stenographic Ability Tests;* 5 forms (2 pages plus accessories): General Testing Series Form 19-55 ('55), Official Testing Series Forms 18-45 ('54), 20-65 ('59), and 21-75 ('60), Short Form ('55); for further information, see the battery entry, 33; Joint Committee on Tests of the United Business Education Association and the National Office Management Association (except Forms 20-65 and 21-75); National Business Education Association. *

REFERENCES

1. Nelson, John Howard. *A Study of the Relationships Between Achievement on the National Business Entrance Tests and the Job Performance of Beginning Stenographers and Typists.* Doctor's thesis, New York University (New York, N.Y.), 1951.

For a review by Edward B. Greene, see 5:522; for reviews by Ann Brewington and Elizabeth Fehrer of the 1946 form, see 3:391. For reviews of the complete battery, see 33, 5:515, and 3:396.

[48]

★Test of Dictation Speed. Stenographers; 1958; 1 form ('58, 4 pages); no manual; directions sheet ['58, 1 page]; no data on reliability; no norms; $3 per 25 tests, postage extra; 50¢ per specimen set, postpaid; (5) minutes; Richardson, Bellows, Henry & Co., Inc. *

[Other Tests]

For tests not listed above, see the following entries in *Tests in Print:* 70–1, 74–5, 78, 80, 82, and 84; out of print: 69 and 83; status unknown: 79.

TYPEWRITING

[49]

***First-Year Typewriting: Every Pupil Test.** High school; 1938–64; 2 scores: speed, performance; new form (4 pages) usually issued each April; forms from previous testing programs also available; general directions sheet ('63, 2 pages); no data on reliability; Ohio norms for new forms available following testing program; 5¢ per test; 3¢ per scoring key; postpaid; 35(40) minutes; Ohio Scholarship Tests. *

[50]

★[McCann Typing Tests.] Applicants for typing positions; 1961–64; 3 scores: speed, accuracy, total; Form A, B, C, ('61, 2 pages); mimeographed manual ('64, 14 pages); no data on reliability; no norms for part scores; $35 per 10 tests; specimen set loaned for rental fee of $5, which may be applied to purchase price; postpaid; 5(10) minutes for practice test, 10(25) minutes for test; McCann Associates. *

[51]

SRA Typing Skills. Grades 9–12 and adults; 1947; 2 scores: speed, accuracy; Forms A, B, (4 pages); preliminary manual (4 pages); no data on reliability; $2.45 per 20 tests; 50¢ per specimen set; postage extra; 10(15) minutes; Marion W. Richardson and Ruth A. Pedersen; Science Research Associates, Inc. *

REFERENCES

1. Skula, Mary, and Spillane, Robert F. "Validity Information Exchange, No. 7-016: D.O.T. Code 1-37.32, Typist." *Personnel Psychol* 7:147–8 sp '54. *
2. Ash, Philip. "Validity Information Exchange, No. 13-07, Stenographers, Typists, General Clerks, and Secretaries." *Personnel Psychol* 13:456 w '60. *

Lawrence W. Erickson, *Associate Professor of Education, University of California, Los Angeles, California.*

The *SRA Typing Skills* test is described in the manual as consisting of "a business letter, approximately 225 words long, which is copied by the examinee as often as possible in a 10-minute period." The test, however, is little more than a 10-minute straight-copy test with only a salutation and a complimentary close included with the body of the letter. The typist is confronted with none of the placement problems involved in typing letters. The work sheet includes a lined box within which the salutation is to be typed. The body of the letter starts two spaces below this point. The typist is directed to copy the material line for line, with no changes and no erasures. Other lined boxes, appropriately placed on the work sheet, are provided for any repetition of the material.

There are other limitations of the test. It does not measure such essential attributes of a good typist as the abilities to make decisions in placement of material on the page, to type from rough-draft copy, to arrange material in tabulated or tabular form, and to proofread typed copy.

The typist's speed is scored in terms of net words per minute, with a 10-word (50 stroke) penalty for each error. Research has shown that such a penalty is unrealistic—it does not adequately express the "true" cost of an error. The manual gives some helpful suggestions for interpreting speed scores in relation to the accuracy ratio, which is determined by dividing the net stroking rate by the gross stroking rate.

No information is given in the manual as to the validity of the test other than to say, "It yields results which are closely related to those obtained on mutilated [*sic*] copy, tabular materials, hand-written drafts, etc." No evidence is provided for this statement. To the best knowledge of this reviewer, there is no research which would indicate that straight-copy skill automatically transfers to problem-and-production typing situations which characterize office work. As stated in the manual, "much research needs to be done in this field, particularly in determining standards on tests given for actual employment purposes."

The manual also states that the test is available in two equated forms. This statement seems to be true only to the extent that Form A and Form B of the test include similar copy (a so-called business letter). No evidence is given as to the method used to equate the copy. The usual procedure followed by authors of typewriting materials is to determine the syllabic intensity of the material. A syllabic intensity study of the copy on both forms was made by this reviewer. The copy of Form A has the following syllabic intensity: paragraph 1, 1.64; paragraph 2, 1.66; paragraph 3, 1.77; paragraph 4, 1.80. The syllabic intensity of the copy of Form B is as follows: paragraph 1, 1.61; paragraph 2, 1.58; paragraph 3, 1.57; paragraph 4, 1.60. To the extent that syllabic intensity is a measure of the difficulty of copy, the two forms of this test are not of the same difficulty. The examinees would, in all probability, make somewhat higher speed scores on Form B.

The chief attribute of the test is that the directions for the examinee are simple and clear; so are the directions for administering and scoring.

In summary, it is the judgment of this reviewer that this test measures straight-copy copying skill only. To the extent that this type of skill transfers to office typing situations, the test may be a helpful selection device. As an initial screening device, the test has merit since it is easy to administer and it can be given in a minimum of time. However, the same results could be obtained by having the examinee type from regular straight-copy material which can be secured at a lower cost. If this test is used, this reviewer recommends that examinees be allowed to erase. Such practice is realistic in terms of office work and provides evidence as to the proofreading ability and erasing skill of the examinee. The words-a-minute rate, obtained under these conditions, would be more nearly a measure of the typist's skill.

Jacob S. Orleans, *Professor of Psychology, University of Nevada, Southern Regional Division, Las Vegas, Nevada.*

description. Each form consists of (*a*) a practice exercise in which the examinee types some 165 words of the instructions; and (*b*) a letter for the typing of which 10 minutes are allowed, the examinee to type the letter over if time is still available. The letter has about 260 "words," a word being defined as 5 strokes (including one space).

The test is in the form of a long sheet accordion folded into eight pages, the backs of the pages being blank. The instructions and the letter to be typed take a little more than one and one half pages. The rest is a work sheet on which the examinee is to type the letter line for line, starting with the salutation in a box provided for that purpose. Margins are furnished for both elite and pica type. Space is designated for as many as three typings of the letter.

administration and scoring. Examinees competent to take this test should have no difficulty carrying out the instructions properly under an experienced examiner. Detailed instructions and suggestions are given concerning the testing room, lighting, materials needed, and timing. The scoring is simple and is in accord with standard techniques for determining number of words per minute and number of errors. The instructions for scoring are detailed and clear. The scoring method produces for each examinee the following three measures: total number of strokes; net speed (number of words a minute); and accuracy ratio. The authors furnish nomographs for finding both net speed score and accuracy ratio.

norms. The test is designed "for the proper selection and placement of stenographic personnel." The prospective employer should know what typing speed and accuracy level the job demands. The test scores will tell whether the applicant meets the demands of the job. It would seem helpful to have available distributions of scores, both speed and accuracy, for typical groups of applicants for specified levels of typing jobs.

evaluation. No data are furnished on validity or reliability. No information is provided on how the test was prepared. There is no evidence that the letters used in the two forms are satisfactory for the purpose and no information as to how the letters were selected. It would seem to be a simple matter to administer Forms A and B, or the same form again after an interval of a week or two, to the same group of examinees and to compute a reliability coefficient. To publish and distribute the test without such readily obtainable information means that the authors and publisher regard such information as unnecessary or irrelevant.

The examinee who completes the standard letter before the time is up types it over again. No evidence is offered that this procedure is more valid or produces more reliable measures than typing new context throughout the 10 minutes. It might be noted that provision is made on the work sheet for a maximum of not quite 80 words a minute (with perfect accuracy).

SRA Typing Skills has all the earmarks of a clever usable test, concerning which almost no data are made available to the prospective user. Apparently the user is expected to accept the test on faith as a valid and reliable instrument.

[52]

★**The Tapping Test: A Predictor of Typing and Other Tapping Operations.** High school; 1959–63; 1 form ('59, 12 pages); manual ('63, 24 pages); $5.50 per 25 tests; $2.50 per 25 sets of color tablets; postage extra; $1.50 per specimen set, postpaid; (30) minutes; John C. Flanagan, Grace Fivars (manual), Shirley A. Tuska (manual), and Carol F. Hershey (manual); Psychometric Techniques Associates. *

REFERENCES

1. FLANAGAN, JOHN C.; FIVARS, GRACE; AND TUSKA, SHIRLEY A. "Predicting Success in Typing and Keyboard Operation." *Personnel & Guid J* 37:353–7 Ja '59. * (*PA* 35:1319)

2. KIRCHNER, WAYNE K., AND BANAS, PAUL. "Prediction of Key-Punch Operator Performance." *Personnel Adm* 24:23–6 Ja–F '61. *

RAY G. PRICE, *Professor of Business Education, University of Minnesota, Minneapolis, Minnesota.*

This rather elaborate aptitude test was developed "to predict ability to operate a typewriter or other keyboard machines." Specifically, the test is designed to measure two of the aptitudes needed in learning to type, "the ability to tap quickly and accurately with one finger at a time by controlling each finger separately and independently" and the ability "to learn to respond with a particular finger on perceiving a letter, number, or other type of symbol."

The 12-page test booklet contains 3 pages of instructions and practice exercises and 9 pages of timed test material. In preparation for the test, the examinee attaches felt pads to the tips of eight fingers (thumbs are not used). Each pad is then moistened with a different color so that when the fingers are tapped on a piece of paper, colored dots are produced. A letter is assigned to each finger, beginning with A for the little finger of the left hand and ending with H for the right hand little finger.

The first aptitude is measured by having the examinee tap "as fast as possible making dots in a series of circles, using each of the four fingers of each hand in succession." The second aptitude, the ability to associate a particular finger with a symbol, is measured by having the examinee "tap the appropriate finger to spell out simple words in short performance exercises." The dots are to be within a circle. In fact, tapping inside a circle is an important element of the test. A dot more than half outside the circle is considered an error.

The test requires approximately 30 minutes to administer. Two thirds of this time is devoted to instructions and preparations such as applying dots and color. Actual testing time is only about 10 minutes. Each page of the test consists of either a separately timed section or an example problem. The nine timed pages are arranged in order of increasing difficulty. A complete manual of instructions accompanies the test. Reliability coefficients indicate that the test conforms to accepted standards as a measuring instrument.

As a screening instrument for use in selecting students for typewriting instruction, the *Tapping Test* has merit. Its greatest potential use, however, is in the selection of trainees to be prepared as typists in government, business, and the armed services. In the secondary schools, where it is generally accepted that typewriting should be available to all students, the chief value of the test would be to aid in grouping students according to ability. But on the basis of evidence indicating a high relationship between initial key striking ability and success in typewriting as measured by straight copy tests or teachers' grades in typewriting, one might justifiably question the need for this intricate procedure involving felt pads, paint tablets, and tapping dots inside circles rather than having examinees tap the actual keys of a typewriter.

Certainly one could seriously question whether an instrument prepared to predict ability to operate a typewriter would also predict ability to operate "other keyboard machines" since no evidence is cited to confirm that such a relationship actually exists. This is not to say that the *Tapping Test* lacks validity as a predictor of ability to operate keyboard machines other than the typewriter but neither can its predictive value for this purpose be assumed. Even though some teachers of typewriting believe that a positive relationship exists between playing the piano and operating the typewriter, research evidence does not bear this out.

HENRY WEITZ, *Associate Professor of Education, and Director, Bureau of Testing and Guidance, Duke University, Durham, North Carolina.*

This test is designed to provide a basis for estimating a student's chances of developing, through training, skill in typing or other keyboard machine operations. The data reported in the manual and elsewhere seem to suggest that this purpose can be achieved.

The test requires the examinee to tap in coded sequences with four fingers of each hand in small circles printed on the test booklet. By covering the fingers with color-coded inked pads, the taps are recorded in scorable form on the booklet. This rather ingenious method of recording tapping responses is explained fully in the manual and in some detail in an article by Flanagan, Fivars, and Tuska (*1*).

Predictive validity coefficients with typing course grades and words per minute as criteria range from .05 to .73 with average validity coefficients for a number of studies hovering in the area .35 to .40. This suggests that the use of the test score would make some contribution to predicting performance and might aid in the selection of students. Charts are provided relating test performance to typing course achievement. These might provide suggestions for tentative cutoff scores for selection. Users of the test, however, would be well advised to establish local criteria.

Reliability data, based on groups of students at various levels of training in typing classes, suggest that the instrument is sufficiently reliable for individual prediction. Corrected split-half coefficients for fairly homogeneous groups range from .84 to .95 with an average of .90. Evidence is presented to indicate that the score on this test is relatively independent of intelligence and that typing skill is also independent of intelligence. It is probable, therefore, that the test may be a useful independent measure of unique job elements.

This seems to be a very promising test of the ability to learn to type. It appears to be relatively easy to administer and score. The instructions for administration, scoring, and interpreting the scores are well written and should make these psychometric chores as painless as possible. With further standardization, the test should be especially effective when candidates for a typing course in a school exceed the available facilities. By logical extension, it would seem that the test would be useful in estimating the trainability of keypunch operators and other personnel for similar keyboard operating tasks. If this turns out to be true, the test would have considerable value as part of an employment test battery.

[53]

★Test of Typing Speed. Applicants for clerical positions; 1958–63; 2 scores: net speed, accuracy; forms A, B, ('58, 5 pages, forms not differentiated on test booklets); manual ['63, 3 unnumbered pages]; no data on reliability; tentative norms; $3 per 25 tests, postage extra; 50¢ per specimen set, postpaid; 5(10) minutes; Richardson, Bellows, Henry & Co., Inc. *

[54]

***Typewriting I and II: Every Pupil Scholarship Test.** 1 or 2 years high school; 1928–64; new form (4 pages) usually issued each January and April; forms from previous testing programs also available; general directions sheet ['63, 2 pages]; no data on reliability; norms for new forms available following testing program; 4¢ per test; 4¢ per scoring key; postage extra; 36(40) minutes; Bureau of Educational Measurements. *

[55]

***Typewriting Test: National Business Entrance Tests.** Grades 11–16 and adults; 1941–62; earlier tests called *Typing Ability Test;* 5 forms: General Testing Series Form 19-56 ('55), Official Testing Series Forms 18-46 ('54), 20-66 ('55), and 21-76 ('60), Short Form ('55); for further information see the battery entry, 33; Joint Committee on Tests of the United Business Education Association and the National Office Management Association (except Forms 20-66 and 21-76); National Business Education Association. *

REFERENCES

1. NELSON, JOHN HOWARD. *A Study of the Relationships Between Achievement on the National Business Entrance Tests and the Job Performance of Beginning Stenographers and Typists.* Doctor's thesis, New York University (New York, N.Y.), 1951.

LAWRENCE W. ERICKSON, *Associate Professor of Education, University of California, Los Angeles, California.* [Review of Forms 19-56, 20-66, 21-76, and the Short Form.]

This problem-and-production typing skill test covers such typical office typing tasks as typing letters, filling in forms, arranging statistical material in tabular form, addressing envelopes, typing from rough draft copy, and other related activities. To the extent that such activities are a measure of the kind of work that the typist will be expected to do in the office, these are good tests for use in the final selection process after applicants have been screened initially by a test which is more easily administered and scored, such as a straight-copy, timed typing test.

The tests are realistic, in terms of office typing work, in that the examinee is called upon to solve placement problems, to follow various directions, to erase and correct errors, to divide words correctly at the ends of lines, and to make other decisions relating to work of the kind found in an on-the-job situation. Since typing errors are to be corrected by erasing, an evaluation can be made of the erasing skill and proofreading ability of the examinee. This is a far more realistic testing practice than that of penalizing the examinee 10 words (50 strokes) for each error made in the copy and determining speed in terms of net words per minute.

The directions are clear and concise, and they are of a kind that test the skill and problem solving ability of the examinee. The directions in the Administrator's Manual are also easy to follow. Probably the greatest limitation of Forms 19-56 and 21-76 is that either test takes two hours to administer. However, on the basis of such a test, the examiner would have information which would enable him to make an intelligent evaluation of the examinee's production typing skill. A typist selected by this testing procedure could be expected to succeed on the job, all other things being equal. Form 20-66, however, can be administered in 60 minutes. A short form is also available which can be administered in 45 minutes.

An excellent Correction Manual is furnished for each of the tests. Despite this fact, another limitation of the tests is the time it would take to score the completed work properly. However, this would be time well spent in terms of improved selection of qualified office typists.

The publisher states that several graduate research studies have been made on the effectiveness in predicting successful employment and adjustment in office occupations. However, no data on the correlation of the test results with job success are cited. Such statistical data would be welcomed by test users, if indeed job success can be predicted from a single test such as this. A battery of tests covering various aspects of office work would, in all probability, be a better indicator of job success.

The greatest shortcomings of these tests are the time it takes to administer them and the subjectivity which may occur in the evaluation and scoring. The latter problem may be partially solved by careful training of persons who do the scoring. The directions for the examinees would be improved if more emphasis were given to the fact that copy containing uncorrectable errors will be considered as unacceptable, with no points being allowed for it in the scoring. This may lead the examinee to exercise greater care and caution and thereby increase the reliability of the test. Similarly, the tests might yield the same results if the test materials were shortened somewhat so that a production timed typing sample of, say, 30 minutes could be used. This would enable the examiner to give and score a test in less than an hour. Production rates could be determined which would be somewhat more objective than the point-scoring system now used with these tests.

In summary, these tests of typing production skill are much better indicators of the typing skill needed in an office situation than is the straight-copy test which is frequently used as a selection device. As indicated above, a straight-copy test may well be used as an initial screening device, with one of the typing tests of the *National Business Entrance Tests* being used as a final selection device.

For a review by Clifford E. Jurgensen, see 5:526; for reviews by E. G. Blackstone and Beatrice J. Dvorak of the 1946 form, see 3:394. For reviews of the complete battery, see 33, 5:515, and 3:396.

[56]

★Typing Test: Individual Placement Series (Area IV). Adults; 1959; Forms C, D, (2 pages); scoring instructions-norms (2 pages) for each form; no data on reliability; no description of normative population; $10 per 25 tests; 50¢ per scoring instructions-key; $2 per specimen set; postpaid; 5(15) minutes; J. H. Norman; the Author. *

[Other Tests]

For tests not listed above, see the following entries in *Tests in Print:* 86, 89, 92, 96, and 98; out of print: 85 and 87-8.

CHARACTER AND PERSONALITY

REVIEWS BY *C. J. Adcock, Lewis E. Albright, Anne Anastasi, Alexander W. Astin, Andrew R. Baggaley, Richard S. Barrett, Kenneth L. Bean, Wesley C. Becker, H. R. Beech, John Elderkin Bell, P. M. Bentler, Åke Bjerstedt, John D. Black, C. B. Blakemore, Harold Borko, Arthur H. Brayfield, Thomas C. Burgess, Alvin G. Burstein, Donald T. Campbell, Dugal Campbell, Joel T. Campbell, Dorothy M. Clendenen, Richard W. Coan, Bertram D. Cohen, Jacob Cohen, John O. Crites, Lee J. Cronbach, Douglas P. Crowne, W. Grant Dahlstrom, Richard H. Dana, Charles F. Dicken, Marvin D. Dunnette, Ralph D. Dutch, Allen L. Edwards, William J. Eichman, Leonard D. Eron, H. J. Eysenck, Paul R. Farnsworth, Seymour Fisher, Bertram R. Forer, Norman Frederiksen, Robert L. French, Eric F. Gardner, Cecil A. Gibb, James R. Glennon, Goldine C. Gleser, Leonard D. Goldstein, Harrison G. Gough, Wilson H. Guertin, Wallace B. Hall, Philip L. Harriman, Dale B. Harris, Jesse G. Harris, Jr., J. Thomas Hastings, Richard S. Hatch, Mary R. Haworth, Alfred B. Heilbrun, Jr., William H. Helme, John K. Hemphill, Marshall S. Hiskey, John D. Hundleby, Arthur R. Jensen, Walter Katkovsky, E. Lowell Kelly, Philip M. Kitay, Paul M. Kjeldergaard, Benjamin Kleinmuntz, Milton V. Kline, Wilbur L. Layton, S. G. Lee, Eugene E. Levitt, John Liggett, James C. Lingoes, Maurice Lorr, David T. Lykken, Boyd R. McCandless, Winton H. Manning, Gerald A. Mendelsohn, T. R. Miles, Terence Moore, G. A. V. Morgan, C. Scott Moss, Allyn Miles Munger, Bernard I. Murstein, Theodor F. Naumann, Robert C. Nichols, Warren F. Norman, David B. Orr, Jerome D. Pauker, R. W. Payne, Donald R. Peterson, John Pierce-Jones, M. L. Kellmer Pringle, John A. Radcliffe, Ralph M. Reitan, Alan O. Ross, John W. M. Rothney, Floyd L. Ruch, H. Bradley Sagen, Bert R. Sappenfield, Irwin G. Sarason, Johann M. Schepers, William Schofield, Stanley J. Segal, S. B. Sells, Boris Semeonoff, Laurance F. Shaffer, Otfried Spreen, William Stephenson, Lawrence J. Stricker, Norman D. Sundberg, William N. Thetford, Robert L. Thorndike, Leona E. Tyler, Forrest L. Vance, Donald J. Veldman, Philip E. Vernon, Norman E. Wallen, John G. Watkins, Harold Webster, Henry Weitz, George Westby, Jerry S. Wiggins, J. Robert Williams, and Robert D. Wirt.*

NONPROJECTIVE

[57]

A-S Reaction Study: A Scale for Measuring Ascendance-Submission in Personality. College and adults; 1928–39; separate forms (8 pages) for men ('28), women ('39); manual, second edition ('39, 16 pages); $3.40 per 35 tests; 60¢ per complete specimen set; postage extra; (20) minutes; Gordon W. Allport and Floyd H. Allport; Houghton Mifflin Co. *

REFERENCES

1–19. See 40:1198.
20–30. See 3:23.
31–45. See 5:28.
46. READER, NATALIE, AND ENGLISH, HORACE B. "Personality Factors in Adolescent Female Friendships." *J Consult Psychol* 11:212–20 Jl–Ag '47. * (*PA* 22:261)
47. SKIFF, STANLEY CUBE. *A Study of Some Relationships Between Personality Traits and Learning Ability.* Doctor's thesis, University of Kentucky (Lexington, Ky.), 1950. (*DA* 20:3861)
48. RAY-CHOWDHURY, K., AND GANDHI, J. S. "Allport's Ascendance-Submission Reaction Study in Indian Situation: II, Ascendance-Submission Trait Difference Among Three Groups of Women Chosen on the Basis of Three Different Provinces They Belong To." *Indian Psychol B* 3:22–3 Ja '58. * (*PA* 33:9983)
49. RAY-CHOWDHURY, K., AND HUNDAL, PIARA SINGH. "Allport's Ascendance-Submission Reaction Study of Indian Situation: I, Ascendance-Submission Trait Difference Among Three Groups of Men Chosen on the Basis of Three Different Provinces They Belong To." *Indian Psychol B* 3:11–22 Ja '58. * (*PA* 33:9984)
50. FLANAGAN, J. J., JR., AND HERR, V. V. "Ascendance-Submission and the Psychogalvanic Response to Mild Stress." *Psychol Rep* 5:289–92 Je '59. * (*PA* 34:2760)
51. MANN, RICHARD D. "A Review of the Relationships Between Personality and Performance in Small Groups." *Psychol B* 56:241–70 Jl '59. * (*PA* 34:4194)
52. BRONZAFT, A.; HAYES, R.; WELCH, L.; AND KOLTUV, M. "Relationships Between Extraversion, Neuroticism, and Ascendance." *J Psychol* 50:279–85 O '60. * (*PA* 35:6475)
53. BRONZAFT, ARLINE; HAYES, ROSLYN; WELCH, LIVINGSTON; AND KOLTUV, MYRON. "Relationship Between PGR and Measures of Extraversion, Ascendance, and Neuroticism." *J Psychol* 50:193–5 O '60. * (*PA* 35:6522)
54. PARAMESWARAN, E. G., AND OLIVER, A. G. "An Ascendance-Submission Inventory for Use With Adolescents (A Preliminary Investigation)." *Indian J Psychol* 36:149–54 D '61. * (*PA* 37:6684)
55. BROWER, JULIAN LEWIS. *Patient-Personnel Interpersonal Choice on a State Mental Hospital Ward.* Doctor's thesis, University of Buffalo (Buffalo, N.Y.), 1962. (*DA* 23:2982)
56. PARAMESWARAN, E. G., AND SUNDARAM, K. "Item Validity of the A. S. Reaction Test for Use With Adolescent." *Indian J Psychol* 37:107–14 S '62. * (*PA* 38:8430)

WARREN T. NORMAN, *Associate Professor of Psychology, The University of Michigan, Ann Arbor, Michigan.*

The principal criticism one can make of this device is that no effort has been made by the authors and publisher in the past 25 years to bring the item content and psychometric characteristics of the test up to date. With regard to item content, the situations are biased, as they always have been, toward college environs and some are described in what would be considered today rather stilted language even by persons with college experience.

But more crucial to the user is the second matter which includes the absence of current data on such things as norms based on pertinent subpopulations, validities against independent external criteria, relationships to other closely related, as well as presumably unrelated, dimensions, and the ability of respondents to fake or "slant" responses in one or another direction. The test has been used extensively in the last two decades and much of the information required to modernize the manual and the test is readily available in scattered published sources. A carefully executed normative study employing an appropriately stratified sampling scheme would go a long way to augment these numerous but more limited and diverse research findings.

On the positive side, the test has done yeoman service in research investigations of personality functioning and development. Strangely enough, however, it seems to have been particularly unsuccessful in certain social psychological applications where it would seem to be most relevant. For example, in the identification of leaders in small groups both the Ascendance scale of the *Guilford-Zimmerman Temperament Survey* and the Dominance scale of Cattell's *Sixteen Personality Factor Questionnaire* have yielded positive results whereas the *A-S Reaction Study* has not (*51*). Nor has the general concept of dominance or ascendance, however measured, been found to relate as one might expect to other aspects of performance in small groups, except possibly to conforming behavior and to task activity.

In a more positive vein, scores on the test have been found (*a*) to distinguish between grossly dissimilar occupational groups that one would expect to differ on ascendance-submission, (*b*) to be unrelated to measured intelligence, and (*c*) to be slightly to moderately correlated with educational achievement and neuroticism (both negatively) and with extroversion and persistence (both positively). Reliabilities between .85 and .96 have been reported for the two forms of this test. But, as noted earlier, all of these results are based on research done over 25 years ago and the operating characteristics of this device may well have changed in the interim.

In brief, as a short, crude device for assessing a major dimension (or related cluster of traits), the *A-S Reaction Study* has filled an important need in personality and social psychological research during the last three and one half decades, though with limited success. But it is time at least to recalibrate this instrument or preferably to completely rebuild it if it is to be of continued service. Alternatively, it might be better simply to withdraw it from the market in deference to other devices more recently standardized—especially some of the multivariate instruments that provide, simultaneously, comparable standard scores on several relatively independent attributes of each respondent. The day when much can be learned from measures on only one or a few attributes of a person has passed. In the more sophisticated and complex research being done today in the areas of personality and social phenomena, multivariate instruments, standardized on a single (though carefully stratified) normative sample, are to be preferred to patchwork batteries of simpler devices with their separate and idiosyncratic bases of interpretation.

For a review by William U. Snyder, see 3:23; for a review by Doncaster G. Humm of the 1928 edition, see 40:1198; for a review by Doncaster G. Humm of an out of print revision for business use, see 40:1199.

[58]

***Activity Vector Analysis.** Ages 16 and over; 1948–63; test booklet title is *Placement Analysis;* personality characteristics related to job success; 6 scores: aggressiveness, sociability, emotional adjustment, social adaptability, intelligent behavior, activity level; Forms A ('62, c1945–62), B ('62), C ('62), (3 pages); general information ('62, 15 pages); manual ('63, 43 looseleaf pages); directions for administering ['62, 1 page]; directions for scoring ['62, 1 page]; manual of correlation tables ('58, 161 looseleaf pages); profile ('62, 1 page) for each form; looseleaf Manual for Job Activity Rating includes separately copyrighted sections on job analysis ('56, 26 pages) and Jarsort procedure of job profile determination ('62, 9 pages), illustrative job analysis form ['56, 7 pages], 10 blank Jarsort profiles ('60, 2 pages), and 10 Jarsort correlation forms ('60, 2 pages); Jarsort cards ('60, 60 cards); distribution restricted to persons who have completed a training course offered by the publisher; quotations on course fee available on request; test materials must be purchased separately; postage extra; French and Spanish editions available; (5–10) minutes; Walter V. Clarke Associates, Inc.; AVA Publications, Inc. *

REFERENCES

1–11. See 5:29.
12. FARRINGTON, ALLEN D. "Validity Information Exchange, No. 11-29: D.O.T. Code 8–19.01, Laborer, Process (Textile)." *Personnel Psychol* 11:586 w '58. *
13. HAMMER, CHARLES HOWARD. *A Validation Study of the Activity Vector Analysis.* Doctor's thesis, Purdue University (Lafayette, Ind.), 1958. (*DA* 19:1108)
14. MERENDA, PETER F., AND CLARKE, WALTER V. "AVA Validity for Textile Workers." *J Appl Psychol* 43:162–5 Je '59. * (*PA* 34:6653)
15. MERENDA, PETER F., AND CLARKE, WALTER V. "Activity Vector Analysis Validity for Life Insurance Salesmen." *Eng & Ind Psychol* 1:1–11 sp '59. * (*PA* 34:4884)
16. MERENDA, PETER F., AND CLARKE, WALTER V. "Factor Analysis of a Measure of 'Social Self.'" *Psychol Rep* 5:597–605 D '59. * (*PA* 34:5021)
17. MERENDA, PETER F., AND CLARKE, WALTER V. "A Further Note on Self-Perceptions of Management Personnel and Line Workers." *Eng & Ind Psychol* 1:49–54 su '59. * (*PA* 35:5398)

18. MERENDA, PETER F., AND CLARKE, WALTER V. "Personality Profiles of Self-Made Company Presidents—A Second Look." *Eng & Ind Psychol* 1:95–101 au '59. * (*PA* 35:1353)
19. MERENDA, PETER F., AND CLARKE, WALTER V. "The Predictive Efficiency of Temperament Characteristics and Personal History Variables in Determining Success of Life Insurance Agents." *J Appl Psychol* 43:360–6 D '59. * (*PA* 34:8503)
20. MERENDA, PETER F., AND CLARKE, WALTER V. "Test-Retest Reliability of Activity Vector Analysis." *Psychol Rep* 5:27–30 Mr '59. * (*PA* 34:150)
21. MERENDA, PETER F.; FARRINGTON, ALLEN D.; AND CLARKE, WALTER V. "Prediction of Performance of Textile Workers." *Eng & Ind Psychol* 1:120–7 w '59. * (*PA* 35:4064)
22. MERENDA, PETER F., AND CLARKE, WALTER V. "Multiple Inferential Selves of Male and Female College Students." *J Psychol Studies* 11:206–12 My–Je '60. * (*PA* 34:7408)
23. MERENDA, PETER F.; CLARKE, WALTER V.; AND KESSLER, SYDNEY. "AVA and the Kessler PD Scale as Measures of Passive-Dependency." *J Clin Psychol* 16:338–41 Jl '60. * (*PA* 36:2HF38M)
24. MERENDA, PETER F.; MUSIKER, HAROLD R.; AND CLARKE, WALTER V. "Relation of the Self-Concept to Success in Sales Management." *Eng & Ind Psychol* 2:69–77 su '60. * (*PA* 37:2052)
25. MERENDA, PETER F., AND CLARKE, WALTER V. "Influence of College Experience on the Self-Concepts of Young Male Job Applicants." *J Psychol Studies* 12:49–60 Mr '61. *
26. MERENDA, PETER F.; CLARKE, WALTER V.; AND HALL, CHARLES E. "Cross-Validity of Procedures for Selecting Life Insurance Salesmen." *J Appl Psychol* 45:376–80 D '61. * (*PA* 37:2053)
27. MERENDA, PETER F.; CLARKE, WALTER V.; MUSIKER, HAROLD R.; AND KESSLER, SYDNEY. "AVA and KPDS as Construct Validity Coordinates." *J Psychol Studies* 12:35–42 Ja '61. *
28. DUNNETTE, MARVIN D., AND KIRCHNER, WAYNE K. "Validities, Vectors, and Verities." *J Appl Psychol* 46:296–9 Ag '62. * (*PA* 37:3088, title only)
29. LOCKE, EDWIN A., AND HULIN, CHARLES L. "A Review and Evaluation of the Validity Studies of Activity Vector Analysis." *Personnel Psychol* 15:25–42 sp '62. * (*PA* 37:3114)
30. MERENDA, PETER F., AND CLARKE, WALTER V. "Rejoinder to 'Validities, Vectors, and Verities' by Marvin D. Dunnette and Wayne K. Kirchner." *J Appl Psychol* 46:300–2 Ag '62. * (*PA* 37:3092)
31. MERENDA, PETER F., AND CLARKE, WALTER V. "Comparison of Concepts of Multiple Inferential Selves Between Clinical Psychologists and School Guidance Counselors." *J Clin Psychol* 19:355–9 Jl '63. *
32. MERENDA, PETER F., AND CLARKE, WALTER V. "Forced-Choice vs. Free-Response in Personality Assessment." *Psychol Rep* 13:159–69 Ag '63. * (*PA* 38:6089)

LEWIS E. ALBRIGHT, *Assistant Director, Employee Relations Research, Standard Oil Company (Indiana), Chicago, Illinois.*

The *Activity Vector Analysis* (AVA) is a self-report adjective checklist used to measure several aspects of personality. The test was designed for use in business and industry. The subject first checks those adjectives which he believes anyone has ever used in describing him, then marks the list again to indicate the words which he feels are truly descriptive of himself. There is no time limit. Three forms of the test now exist. Revised Form A has 81 items; new Forms B and C each have 84 items.

The rationale on which the AVA is based is that all behavior can be described in terms of Aggressiveness, Sociability, Emotional Adjustment, and Social Adaptability. The test is scored on these four scales (vectors) plus "Activity Level" (total number of words checked). These dimensions were isolated initially by means of a cluster analysis of the 81 words and later verified by factor analysis. Despite these statistical niceties, can anyone seriously believe that only four factors (or vectors) are sufficient to account for *all* human behavior? Apparently even the test author is dubious since he has identified a fifth vector, named "social intelligence," which consists of words found to discriminate high and low scorers on an Otis test of mental ability. It is not clear, however, to what extent this vector is used in the interpretation of the test profile.

The manual states that in constructing the original 81-word AVA form, all derogatory words were eliminated. Remaining, however, are terms such as "scairdy cat," "argumentative," and "conformist" which can hardly be considered flattering and are certainly less desirable than other words in the same list such as "pleasant," "decisive," and "admirable." In short, there could still be great differences in social desirability of the words which could be contaminating whatever is being measured.

Reliability of the AVA is given in three ways for each vector: split-half, test-retest, and parallel forms. The split-half coefficients have been stepped up by the Spearman-Brown formula and are all in the 90's. The test-retest reliabilities range from .62 for Vector 3 to .75 for Activity Level (mean retest interval was one year). These coefficients suggest that the test has only a fair degree of stability over time. The parallel forms coefficients (given only for the new Forms B and C) look satisfactory until one realizes that these are, in fact, not parallel forms, but variations of the same form because many of the same words are used on both. This reviewer counted at least 30 words common to *all three forms*. The overlap of each pair of forms is even greater; therefore, if the parallel forms coefficients were computed without removal of the common elements (as appears to be the case), these values are spurious and misleading.

The manual includes no norms whatever—a gross omission in view of the fact that the test has been given to hundreds of thousands of people in industry. (It should be mentioned, however, that standard scores are provided on profile cards for each form, but their usefulness is limited due to the fact that only Certified AVA Analysts may interpret the instrument.) Similarly, nothing is said about the possible fakability of this instrument. The entire validity issue is handled by referring the reader to an annotated bibliography of both published and unpublished investigations, mostly conducted by Walter V. Clarke, the author and publisher, and his associates. After a thorough examination of the published articles, this reviewer agrees with Locke and Hulin (*29*), who concluded in their critique of these same studies that "AVA has failed to demonstrate any practical utility as a *selection device* in industry. Nearly all the studies involved incorrect validation procedures....or erroneous interpretation of the actual data. In the only study in which there was both correct procedure and a sufficiently large N, the authors reported inconclusive results." It should be noted that Locke and Hulin were concerned primarily with the ability of the AVA, given at the time of hiring, to predict subsequent job performance (predictive validity). The instrument has, on occasion, shown some degree of concurrent validity (discrimination of presently employed workers—either in different occupational groups or more and less effective workers in the same occupational group). This feature might make the AVA useful as a counseling or placement tool rather than a selection device. Clarke and associates could make a contribution here by using their vast store of data to show us with which groups and under what circumstances the AVA can discriminate.

Accompanying the AVA is a card sorting method, called the JARsort procedure, for analyzing jobs in terms of AVA test profiles. Apparently, the user is to find the AVA pattern required by the *job,* then search for candidates whose AVA test scores match this pattern. An instruction manual, 60 cards, and a box for sorting the cards constitute the materials necessary for the JARsort analysis. The manual, called Manual for Job Activity Rating, describes the Job Activity Analysis method of job description based on observation and the SKILLsort card sort procedure (related to the publisher's *Measurement of Skill* battery) in addition to the JARsort procedure. Each JARsort card contains a statement describing a job element, for example, "Requires answering the telephone." The cards are to be sorted into a forced normal distribution of seven piles according to the importance of each element to the job in question. By some method not described, an AVA pattern shape has been determined for each card. The analyst computes an overall Universe Pattern Shape using the 20 most important job elements resulting from the sorting process. No data are presented to support the implied relationship of pattern shape to job success. It is claimed that with the JAR approach "one may rate and directly compare all jobs in both shop and office, from sweeper to president." Again no evidence is given to justify this claim; in this reviewer's opinion, many of the statements are so vague and general that they might indeed apply to all jobs and therefore be of no value for differentiating one job from another.

To summarize, the questionable reliability and validity data for the AVA make it unsuitable at present as a selection device in industry. It may have some use as a counseling or placement aid, but even here more evidence is needed before it could be recommended. With perhaps half a million or more AVA's given in industry to date, the authors must be in possession of all the information necessary to provide a conclusive test of the instrument if they would do so. If not, they may soon be able to construct a fourth test form—composed of derogatory terms used by reviewers in describing the AVA!

ALEXANDER W. ASTIN, *Director of Research, American Council on Education, Washington, D.C.*

Because of the unusual terminology associated with the *Activity Vector Analysis,* one needs to keep in mind just what the test is: a checklist of 81 adjectives (e.g., "persuasive," "timid," "tactful") which can be scored on four personality scales ("Vectors" 1–4). The scoring keys for the four scales were developed by internal consistency procedures: factor analyses and cluster analyses of item intercorrelations. These four scores provide the main basis for interpretation of the AVA profile, although two other scores are also available: V-5 (initially obtained by an item analysis against an Otis mental ability test) and the total number of adjectives checked ("Activity Level"). The subject is first asked to check those adjectives which have "ever been used by anyone in describing you." Using an identical list, he then checks each adjective "which you honestly believe is descriptive of you." The six AVA scores (Vectors 1–5 and Activity Level) can be obtained separately for the first list ("Column 1"), for the second list ("Column 2"), and for the sum of the two ("Resultant").

According to the manual, the AVA is a

"measuring device for determining the probable behavior of a normal individual in a given job situation." In a brochure distributed by the publisher, it is stated that the AVA enables the executive to make more accurate predictions about the consequences of hiring, placing, or promoting a given employee, and also gives him "valuable insight into the best methods of supervising his workers."

AVA, however, is not merely a personality inventory to be purchased and used by the trained industrial psychologist or personnel manager. The publisher states that any person who desires to interpret the AVA must first take a course (length varies but the cost of a two-week course may be as much as $975) in order to qualify as a "Certified Analyst." Interpretation of AVA profiles by anyone other than a Certified Analyst may result in "irreparable harm to the person concerned." In addition to training in interpretation of AVA profiles, this course includes training in a method of job analysis called the Job Activity Rating (JAR). The publisher provides a deck of Q-sort cards describing different job requirements, and a cardboard device containing seven bins labeled "least important" to "most important." The cards are to be sorted into a forced normal distribution in terms of their relative importance to the job in question. These "JARsorts" yield a profile of personality traits for the job which are to be compared with the worker's AVA test profile. A basic assumption in AVA analysis appears to be that the probability of job success is a direct function of the degree of congruence between the person's AVA profile and the JAR profile for the job.

The publisher also provides a supplementary booklet of AVA Correlation Tables which show correlations between every possible AVA and JAR profile. The analyst can also obtain a visual comparison between a given JAR profile and several AVA profiles at one time by using the "distribution" chart or one of the "polar tabulation" charts from the "AVA Pattern Universe." In the introductory section of this booklet the author presents his view that the pattern of AVA scores indicates the probable "directions" of a person's behavior. No supporting evidence for this assumption is actually presented.

The plastic hand scoring stencil included in the test materials is cleverly designed and appears to be convenient for scoring a few tests at a time. The likelihood of scoring error might be greatly increased, though, if a large number of tests are scored at one sitting, since the stencil's differently colored markings for the different scales require a continuous change of set on the part of the scorer.

The AVA manual appears to be deficient in several respects. For example, practically no information is presented on the meanings of the four scores (Vectors 1–4) except for the statement that the adjective clusters in an early version of the test "were suggestive of aggressive, sociable, stable, and avoidant behavior." The meanings of the Vector 5 and Activity Level scores are even more obscure. Corrected split-half reliabilities of an earlier form of the test are high, ranging from .92 to .97; retest coefficients over a one-year interval range from .62 to .75. No retest reliability data are given for current forms of the test.

It is difficult to determine from the manual just how the alternate forms (A, B, and C) of the AVA were derived. There is a considerable amount of item overlap among all three forms. One puzzling feature is that the same adjectives are often keyed differently in the different forms. A comparison of the hand scoring stencils revealed at least 15 discrepancies between Forms A and C in the scoring of identical items, 11 discrepancies in scoring between Forms A and B, and 3 discrepancies in scoring between Forms B and C.

These facts make it difficult to interpret the correlations between alternate Forms B and C given in Tables 4–6 of the manual. The high degree of item overlap would tend to inflate the correlations, but the discrepancies in scoring would serve to attenuate them. Some of the correlations between parallel scales in Forms B and C are, in fact, not significantly higher than correlations between certain nonparallel scales. Correlations of Forms B and C with Form A (which was involved in most of the scoring inconsistencies) are not given in the manual.

The last section of the AVA manual contains an annotated bibliography of studies, apparently as a substitute for a section on validity. Abstracts of the studies are vague and give the reader little information about either the construct validity of the scales or the potential usefulness of the AVA in practice. Quantitative results are often omitted and replaced by phrases such as "positive evidence of predictive validity," "statistically significant discriminant functions," or "substantially correct classifications."

This published research actually provides very little evidence on the validity of the AVA when used in the manner proposed by the publisher, i.e., when clinical predictions of job success are made by trained AVA analysts. In one study (*14, 21*), a single trained analyst was able to predict job performance of textile workers significantly better than chance. However, in a large scale selection study of life insurance salesmen (*7*), clinical predictions of job success made by AVA analysts were of no value. Interestingly enough, the AVA appears to have some validity for selecting life insurance salesmen when used actuarially (*19, 26*), although this finding does not seem to have persuaded the publisher to begin training his Analysts in the procedures of empirical test validation.

The author's attempt to develop objective methods for comparing worker traits (AVA) with job requirements (JAR) is commendable. What he has yet failed to do is to show that the two types of profiles are in fact comparable and useful in practice. It seems likely that the four factored AVA scales are not too different in meaning from some of the scales on other personality instruments which have been developed by internal analyses of item responses (e.g., the *Sixteen Personality Factor Questionnaire, Edwards Personal Preference Schedule,* and the *Guilford-Zimmerman Temperament Survey*). The AVA differs from these instruments, however, in that its publisher has made more extravagant claims for its validity in practical situations and has set down a rigid and costly set of conditions for its use. Under these circumstances, the potential user would seem justified in expecting much more evidence on validity than is presently available.

WINTON H. MANNING, *Associate Professor of Psychology, Texas Christian University, Fort Worth, Texas.*

The AVA is a controversial test which has, especially in the last two or three years, provoked considerable discussion among psychologists and others concerned with research in personnel selection and industrial psychology. Part of the controversy centers about the test itself, but the principal focus of criticism has been on the claims for validity made by the test developer and the relationship of these claims to alleged defects in experimental designs, and to the manner in which results have been statistically treated and discussed.

In previous reviews in *The Fifth Yearbook* and in critiques by others (*28, 29*) a number of characteristics of the research on the AVA reported by the test publisher and his associates have been identified. These include such criticisms as: (*a*) failure to distinguish between predictive and concurrent validity, (*b*) absence of concern about or failure to report when and under what conditions the AVA had been administered to subjects, (*c*) failure to provide cross validation before entering claims of predictive validity, (*d*) erroneous interpretations of data, (*e*) emphasis upon statistical significance when overlap between distributions is large, (*f*) tendency to equate statistical significance *per se* with practical validity, (*g*) failure to report procedures in sufficient detail to permit replication by other disinterested experimenters, (*h*) presentation of research in a style of reporting evidently designed less to inform than to overwhelm the naïve reader, and (*i*) the adoption of such trappings as titles for test administrators and gaudy names for accessory materials entirely inconsistent with conservative scientific practice.

After studying over two dozen articles concerned with the AVA this reviewer concluded that, sadly, these criticisms were in every instance amply supported.

A review of all the studies published on the AVA since 1959 is not warranted because the latter studies conform rather highly to the unfortunate pattern described above. Of particular interest, however, has been the question of cross validation, and hence, some discussion should be directed to two recent articles by Merenda and Clarke (*19*) and Merenda, Clarke, and Hall (*26*). It should be noted at the outset that only one adequately designed study involving cross validation of *predictive* validity of the AVA has been performed. This study (*7*) found that for selection of life insurance salesmen the AVA had no validity.

In the first of the above mentioned articles Merenda and Clarke report the results of a study of the efficacy of four AVA variables and five personal history variables in discriminating between 108 successful and 414 unsuccessful life insurance salesmen. It should be pointed out that this involved a follow-up of 522 subjects who had at least three years earlier been tested at the time of hiring, and that at that time the general agents, who evaluated the applicants, made use of the AVA in deciding whether to hire or not to hire the applicant. Further, the authors state that the general agents placed greater reliance on the AVA profiles than upon the personal history variables for the reason that "an integrated personality profile determined to be 'best' for life insurance salesmen was being used by the company....whereas no such profile was determined for the personal history variables." The authors note that this condition would serve to restrict the range of their AVA variables more than the personal history variables. They fail to consider the possibility that the decision to *fire or terminate* an "unsuccessful" employee might also be influenced by the AVA profile which evidently counted so heavily in the general agents' decisions as to whether or not to hire. An unsuccessful agent is defined as one who fails to reach production goals, has his contract terminated, or leaves the company within a three year period. Thus, it would seem that we are in the dark as to the extent to which the criterion of success or failure may or may not be contaminated. Nevertheless, a conclusion is ultimately reached by the authors that the AVA has validity, for the discriminant function is significant at the .001 level. This is accomplished despite the fact that, as reported by Dunnette and Kirchner (*28*), the multiple correlation is only .21, and that, at a minimum, 85 per cent of scores of successful salesmen are duplicated by unsuccessful salesmen. It would seem justified to point out the well known fact that a "significant" result may not always be a "salient" result.

Following this first study Merenda, Clarke, and Hall (*26*) report a cross validation of the discriminant function developed earlier. Although it is not mentioned, we assume that in this study of 535 agents the same conditions regarding administration of tests, comparison with a determined *"best"* profile, and the consequent influence of these factors on the general agents' decisions to hire (and perhaps to fire!) prevailed. The results showed, of course, some shrinkage. Using a phi coefficient as an indicator of predictive efficiency, the reviewer calculates a correlation in the validation sample of .11 between the dichotomized linear composite and the success-failure criterion. An analogous correlation of .09 would obtain in the cross validation sample. Of course, these are somewhat lower than would be found if the linear composite were treated continuously. It seems, in sum, however, that with the possibility of criterion contamination present and the low correlations which exist, there is little ground for concluding on the basis of this study that the AVA is a valid predictor of success as a life insurance agent.

Exhaustive discussion of the other studies seems pointless to the reviewer. It would be a dreary task to set it down on paper, and an even drearier one to read it. Also, no amplification is needed concerning Bennett's cogent remarks (see 5:29) on the precarious superstructure of mathematical hocus-pocus which surrounds the calculation of vector scores and profile indices. Unfortunately, the AVA is not alone guilty in this respect, for personality assessment instruments have many times exhibited a functional independence between scoring procedures and adequacy of observational foundations. In reflecting upon the evident enthusiastic adoption of the AVA by some naïve test givers, the story of St. Denis comes irresistibly to mind. As I recall, the martyred saint was observed to be stalking the streets of Paris carrying his severed head in his hands. When implored by an astonished passerby how he was able to do such a bewildering thing, the good saint is said to have replied, "It is only the first step which is difficult." To a dispassionate reader of the AVA literature, the meaning is obvious.

For reviews by Brent Baxter and George K. Bennett, see 5:29.

[59]

***The Adjustment Inventory.** Grades 9–16, adults; 1934–63; IBM; 1 form; 2 levels; postage extra; specimen set not available; (20–30) minutes; Hugh M. Bell; Consulting Psychologists Press, Inc. *

a) REVISED STUDENT FORM, RESEARCH EDITION (1962). Grades 9–16; 1934–63; 6 scores: home, health, submissiveness, emotionality, hostility, masculinity; 1 form ('62, 4 pages); manual ('63, c1962, 27 pages); profile ('62, 2 pages); separate answer sheets must be used; $3.25 per 50 tests; $3.75 per 50 IBM answer sheets; $2 per set of hand or machine scoring stencils; $1.25 per manual.

b) ADULT FORM. Adults; 1938–39; 6 scores: home, occupational, health, social, emotional, total; 1 form ('38, 4 pages); manual ['38, 4 pages]; $3 per 25 tests; separate answer sheets may be used; $2.20 per 50

IBM answer sheets; 50¢ per set of hand scoring stencil and manual; $1.75 per machine scoring stencil. *c)* [ORIGINAL] STUDENT FORM. Grades 9–16; 1934–39; 5 scores: home, health, social, emotional, total; 2 editions; manual ['34, 4 pages]; tentative norms.

1) [*Regular Edition.*] 1934–39; 1 form ('34, 4 pages); $3 per 25 tests; separate answer sheets may be used; $2.20 per 50 IBM answer sheets; 50¢ per set of hand scoring stencil and manual; $1.75 per set of machine scoring stencils.

2) [*IBM Test-Answer Sheet Edition.*] 1939; $3.75 per 50 tests; $2.50 per set of machine scoring stencils.

REFERENCES

1–15. See 40:1200.
16–119. See 4:28.
120–145. See 5:30.
146. SCHOLL, GERALDINE. "Some Notes on the Use of Two Personality Tests With Visually Handicapped Students." *New Outlook Blind* 47:287–95 D '53. *
147. HOLMES, JACK A. "Factors Underlying Major Reading Disabilities at the College Level." *Genetic Psychol Monogr* 49:3–95 F '54. * (*PA* 28:8982)
148. RISHER, CHARITY CONRAD. *Some Characteristics Which Differentiate Between Academically Successful and Unsuccessful College Business Students.* Doctor's thesis, University of Missouri (Columbia, Mo.), 1958. (*DA* 19:2006)
149. MATHUR, KRISHNA. "Relationship of Socio-Economic Status to Personality Adjustment Among the High School Boys and Girls at Aligarh." *Indian Psychol B* 4:30–1 Ja '59. *
150. STRUNK, ORLO, JR. "Interest and Personality Patterns of Preministerial Students." *Psychol Rep* 5:740 D '59. * (*PA* 34:5635)
151. WINTHROP, HENRY. "Self-Images of Personal Adjustment vs. the Estimates of Friends." *J Social Psychol* 50:87–99 Ag '59. * (*PA* 35:3516)
152. DANA, RICHARD H., AND BAKER, DAVID H. "High School Achievement and the Bell Adjustment Inventory." *Psychol Rep* 8:353–6 Ap '61. * (*PA* 36:1KL53D)
153. DAS, RHEA S. "Validity Information Exchange, No. 14-05: D.O.T. Code 2-66.01, Police Lieutenant." *Personnel Psychol* 14:459–61 w '61. *
154. DEAN, DWIGHT G. "Romanticism and Emotional Maturity: A Preliminary Study." *Marriage & Family Living* 23:44–5 F '61. * (*PA* 36:3HF44D)
155. LOCKWOOD, DORIS H., AND GUERNEY, BERNARD, JR. "Identification and Empathy in Relation to Self-Dissatisfaction and Adjustment." *J Abn & Social Psychol* 65:343–7 N '62. *
156. VORREYER, WARREN J. "Relationship of Selected Adjustment Factors, College Ability, and Achievement to Drop-Outs and Nondrop-Outs of College Freshmen." *J Ed Res* 56:362–5 Mr '63. *

FORREST L. VANCE, *Administrative Officer, American Psychological Association, Washington, D.C.* [Review of Revised Student Form.]

This revision of the Bell *Adjustment Inventory* provides a total face lifting for this venerable member of the first generation of objectively scored personality questionnaires. The manual provides extensive theoretical discussion and devotes considerable space to interpretive guidelines, features that are in happy contrast to the perfunctory, sink-or-swim introductory materials provided with many devices.

The inventory proper consists of 200 questions to be answered by a "yes," "no," or "?," as on earlier forms. New items have been added, however, and scores are now obtained on scales labeled "hostility" and "masculinity-femininity" as well as the four variables present in the original (1934) edition. In the construction of these new scales, Bell's strategy continues to be a three stage sequence: (*a*) writing items that seem appropriate; (*b*) eliminating items that fail to correlate with the scale as a whole; and (*c*) validating the surviving scale against external criteria (expert ratings, similar scales, life history data). This results in an instrument that yields scores that reflect an individual's subjective impression of his own adjustment in areas determined by the author, *plus* an element of predictive information concerning the probable nature of independent evaluations of his adjustment in these same areas.

Data in the manual indicate that the Bell differentiates very well between groups judgmentally identified as high and low on the dimensions named in the individual scales. No information is given concerning amount of overlap between the high and low distributions, but values of t for six validation studies (one for each of the six scales) have a median of approximately 6.0, with a range of 2.7 to 32.6, the latter for 316 men versus 347 women on masculinity-femininity. Aside from the masculinity-femininity study, the degrees of freedom associated with these t values range from 39 to 100, making it evident that very wide differences are involved.

Concurrent validity is demonstrated by correlations between the Bell and other inventories. Except for masculinity-femininity, the relationships presented in the manual are astonishingly high. For some reason, Bell masculinity-femininity scores correlate only .13 for men and .38 for women with MF scores on the *Minnesota Multiphasic Personality Inventory*. The remaining relationships range from .72, between Bell submissiveness and Allport ascendance-submission, to an astronomical .93 between Bell emotionality and the related score on Thurstone's *Personality Schedule*. As would be expected from this validity information, the reported reliabilities of the Bell scales are high. Yet, the odd-even reliabilities, corrected upward by the Spearman-Brown prophecy formula, are all in the .80's. One can only conclude that the very high correlations reported with some other scales are probably maximal estimates and not likely to be replicated frequently.

The normative sampling for this instrument

is rather scanty. Percentile norms are given for 295 high school boys and 372 girls. College norms are based on 316 men and 347 women. None of the high school sample comes from any community east of Ashtabula, Ohio, and the college group is from Rochester, Minnesota, and points west. Furthermore, the high school norms combine students in grades 10, 11, and 12, and the college norms are based on a composite of freshmen, sophomores, and juniors.

In general, the Revised Student Form of the Bell *Adjustment Inventory* is supported by sufficient validity data to justify trial use as a screening device. It should go without saying that such use requires that evidence of specific validity must be obtained for the purpose involved. Such local validity is possibly less crucial where the instrument is used only as a source of counseling hypotheses, which will be checked by other information. Still, even in this situation, one would be professionally remiss to continue the use of any instrument unless it leads to correct hunches with some determinable and significant frequency.

J Counsel Psychol 11:98–9 sp '64. Laurence Siegel. * The current revision has been newly normed for high school and college students. However, the normative groups are quite small (approximately 300 for each sex) and far from representative. * On the whole, the revision of this inventory is not likely either to encourage or discourage more widespread use of the instrument.

For reviews by Nelson G. Hanawalt and Theodore R. Sarbin, see 4:28; for reviews by Raymond B. Cattell, John G. Darley, C. M. Louttit, and Percival M. Symonds of the original Student Form, and reviews by S. J. Beck, J. P. Guilford, and Doncaster G. Humm of the Adult Form, see 40:1200 (1 excerpt); for a review by Austin H. Turney of the Student Form, see 38:912.

[60]

The Alcadd Test. Adults; 1949; identification of alcoholic addicts and individuals with alcoholic problems; 6 scores: regularity of drinking, preference for drinking over other activities, lack of controlled drinking, rationalization of drinking, excessive emotionality, total; 1 form (4 pages); manual (2 pages); no data on reliability of subscores; $6.50 per 25 tests, postpaid; specimen set not available; (5–15) minutes; Morse P. Manson; Western Psychological Services. *

REFERENCES

1. MANSON, MORSE P. "A Psychometric Determination of Alcoholic Addiction." *Am J Psychiatry* 106:199–205 S '49. * (*PA* 24:3271)
2. BARILLAS, MARIO G. *A Study of the Validity and Reliability of the Alcadd Test as a Psychometric Instrument for the Identification of Male Alcoholics.* Master's thesis, Fordham University (New York, N.Y.), 1952.
3. MURPHY, DONAL G. *The Validity and Reliability of the Manson Evaluation and the Alcadd Test in the Identification of Female Alcoholics.* Master's thesis, Fordham University (New York, N.Y.), 1955.
4. MURPHY, DONAL G. "The Revalidation of Diagnostic Tests for Alcohol Addiction." *J Consult Psychol* 20:301–4 Ag '56. * (*PA* 31:8340)
5. CLARK, JAMES WARD. *Personality Syndromes in Chronic Alcoholism: A Factorial Study.* Doctor's thesis, Queen's University (Kingston, Ont., Canada), 1958. (Abstract: *Can Psychologist* 1:116–7)
6. SMART, REGINALD G. "A Critical Evaluation of the Alcadd Test." *O.P.A. Q* 14:70–5 D '61. *

DUGAL CAMPBELL, *Assistant Professor of Psychology, Queen's University, Kingston, Ontario, Canada.*

The Alcadd Test consists of a set of 65 questions on drinking behaviour (for example, "I get drunk about every pay-day"). The score on these questions, each answered either Yes or No, is intended to measure the extent to which a patient is controlled by his alcoholism. The questions are designed to measure five traits: regularity of drinking, preference for drinking over other activities, lack of controlled drinking, rationalization of drinking, and excessive emotionality.

Murphy (*4*) gave the test to four groups: active alcoholics, members of Alcoholics Anonymous, social drinkers, and abstainers. Critical ratios between all four groups were significant and from 80 to 100 per cent of the four groups were correctly identified using Manson's cut-off scores.

No systematic work has been reported for this test. Consequently the criticisms made in the original *Mental Measurements Yearbook* reviews (the five traits are subjective conceptions and have no objective analysis to warrant them, and it is not known how well the test will work with subjects who do not admit to alcoholism) remain unanswered. Until data relevant to these criticisms are obtained, the test appears to be of little practical value.

For reviews by Charles Honzik and Albert L. Hunsicker, see 4:30.

[61]

Attitude-Interest Analysis Test. Early adolescents and adults; 1936–38; also called *M-F Test;* masculinity-femininity; Form A ('36, 14 pages); manual ('38, 21 pages, out of print); $4.50 per 25 tests, postage extra; specimen set not available; (40–50) minutes; Lewis M. Terman and Catherine Cox Miles; McGraw-Hill Book Co., Inc. *

REFERENCES

1–20. See 3:24.

21. CERF, ARTHUR Z. "General Information, CE505GX3," pp. 676–7. In *Printed Classification Tests.* Edited by J. P. Guilford. Army Air Forces Aviation Psychology Program Research Reports, Report No. 5. Washington, D.C.: United States Government Printing Office, 1947. Pp. xi, 919. * (*PA* 22:4145)

22. HARDY, VIRGINIA T. "Relation of Dominance to Non-Directiveness in Counseling." *J Clin Psychol* 4:300–3 Jl '48. * (*PA* 23:179)

23. CARTER, LAUNOR, AND NIXON, MARY. "Ability, Perceptual, Personality, and Interest Factors Associated With Different Criteria of Leadership." *J Psychol* 27:377–88 Ap '49. * (*PA* 23:4183)

24. DE CILLIS, OLGA E., AND ORBISON, WILLIAM D. "A Comparison of the Terman-Miles M-F Test and the Mf Scale of the MMPI." *J Appl Psychol* 34:338–42 O '50. * (*PA* 26:294)

25. LEE, MARILYN C. *Relationship of Masculinity-Femininity to Tests of Mechanical and Clerical Abilities.* Master's thesis, University of Minnesota (Minneapolis, Minn.), 1950.

26. ROSS, ROBERT T. "Some Characteristics of the M-F Score." Abstract. *Am Psychol* 5:471 S '50. *

27. ARONSON, MARVIN LUCIUS. *A Study of the Freudian Theory of Paranoia by Means of a Group of Psychological Tests.* Doctor's thesis, University of Michigan (Ann Arbor, Mich.), 1951. (*Microfilm Abstr* 11:443)

28. BOTWINICK, JACK, AND MACHOVER, SOLOMON. "A Psychometric Examination of Latent Homosexuality in Alcoholism." *Q J Studies Alcohol* 12:268–72 Je '51. * (*PA* 26:390)

29. FISHER, SEYMOUR, AND HINDS, EDITH. "The Organization of Hostility Controls in Various Personality Structures." *Genetic Psychol Monogr* 44:3–68 Ag '51. * (*PA* 26:2889)

30. SHEPLER, BERNARD F. "A Comparison of Masculinity-Femininity Measures." *J Consult Psychol* 15:484–6 D '51. * (*PA* 26:7011)

31. VACCARO, JOSEPH J. *A Study of Psychological Factors That Contrast the Most and Least Efficient Psychiatric Aids in a Mental Hospital.* Doctor's thesis, Fordham University (New York, N.Y.), 1951.

32. FORD, C. FENTON, JR., AND TYLER, LEONA E. "A Factor Analysis of Terman and Miles' M-F Test." *J Appl Psychol* 36:251–3 Ag '52. * (*PA* 27:3551)

33. LEE, MARILYN C. "Relationship of Masculinity-Femininity to Tests of Mechanical and Clerical Abilities." *J Appl Psychol* 36:377–80 D '52. * (*PA* 27:6431)

34. PARKER, FREDERICK B. "A Comparison of the Sex Temperament of Alcoholic and Moderate Drinkers." *Am Sociol R* 24:366–74 Je '59. * (*PA* 34:4618)

35. STANEK, RICHARD J. "A Note on the Presumed Measures of Masculinity-Femininity." *Personnel & Guid J* 37:439–40 F '59. *

36. ENGEL, ILONA MARIA. *A Factor Analytic Study of Items From Five Masculinity-Femininity Tests.* Doctor's thesis, University of Michigan (Ann Arbor, Mich.), 1962. (*DA* 23:307)

For a review by Starke R. Hathaway, see 3:24; for excerpts from related book reviews, see 40:B1094, 38:B498, and 36:B256.

[62]

★Attitudes Toward Industrialization. Adults; 1959; community attitude toward industrial expansion; 1 form (1 page); manual (4 pages); $3 per 50 tests; $1 per specimen set (must be purchased to obtain manual); cash orders postpaid; (10) minutes; Donald E. Kaldenberg; Psychometric Affiliates. *

MARVIN D. DUNNETTE, *Professor of Psychology, University of Minnesota, Minneapolis, Minnesota.*

This is a short 18-item attitude scale designed to assess the attitudes of community groups toward industrial expansion. As the author states, "Rather intense interest and some controversy in Iowa on the issue [of industrial expansion] precipitated the present research. Controversy was expressed in speeches by state political leaders, newspaper editorials, and 'letters to the editor' from ordinary citizens."

The brief 4-page manual is unusually explicit in describing the development of the scale. An original pool of 97 statements was gleaned from the content of nine hours of tape recorded interviews. Twenty eight of the 97 items were discarded because of ambiguity after ratings on a 5-point scale by five psychologists. The remaining items were then administered to 110 Iowa State University students who responded to the items using the usual 5-step Likert response format. Both internal and external criteria were used to obtain internal consistency and validity coefficients for each of the statements. The external criterion consisted of each subject's status on eight background variables, such as father's occupation and population of home community, which enabled an *a priori* assignment of subjects into groups presumably favorably and unfavorably disposed toward industrialization. The final 18 items of the scale are those which possessed phi coefficients above .25 on both the internal and external criteria.

Unfortunately, the author computed reliability and validity estimates for the 18-item scale on the same group of subjects used for the item analyses, obtaining a corrected odd-even coefficient of .80 and a validity coefficient of .55 against the 8-item background criterion. It is evident, of course, that these fold-back coefficients cannot be relied on to be accurate estimates of the scale's reliability and validity when applied to an independently selected group of subjects; the scale should not have been released for publication until it had been tried out on such a group. Both the author and particularly the publisher should be chastised for not demanding this final and simple test of the scale's merit prior to its release for distribution and sale to the public.

Norms are provided for 100 Northwestern University and Illinois Institute of Technology students as well as for the original group of 110 Iowa State University students, but apparently reliability and validity data were *not* computed for the Northwestern and Illinois students.

In summary, *Attitudes Toward Industrialization* appears to be a well conceived and carefully developed scale directed toward measuring attitudes toward industrial expansion. It still needs to be cross validated, but even in its present form it constitutes a worthy research instrument which may well be tried out by investigators concerned with the general questions raised by the issue of industrialization.

[63]

★**The Ayres Space Test.** Ages 3 and over; 1962; brain damage; 3 scores: accuracy, time, accuracy less adjustment for time; individual; 1 form; record booklet (4 pages); mimeographed manual (27 pages); no norms for ages 11 and over; $30 per set of test materials including two formboards, blocks, pegs, 25 record booklets, and manual; $4.50 per manual; postpaid; specimen set not available; (20–30) minutes; A. Jean Ayres; Western Psychological Services. *

REFERENCES

1. Ayres, A. Jean. *Space Perception and Visualization in Cerebral Dysfunction.* Doctor's thesis, University of Southern California (Los Angeles, Calif.), 1961. (*DA* 22:1708)
2. Sleeper, Mildred L. *Correlation of Body Balance and Space Perception in Cerebral Palsied Individuals.* Master's thesis, University of Southern California (Los Angeles, Calif.), 1962.

Alvin G. Burstein, *Associate Professor of Psychology, Neuropsychiatric Institute, University of Illinois College of Medicine, Chicago, Illinois.*

This test, the author of which has had extensive experience as an occupational therapist, is intended "to measure space relations: namely, the speed of perception of stimuli composed largely of spatial elements, position in space or directionality, and space visualization"; the test "is designed particularly for use with subjects age three through adulthood who have or are suspected of having perceptual difficulty." The test manual clearly recommends the use of the test as part of a battery for the diagnosis of brain damage.

The testing materials consist of two formboards (one for diamond shaped, one for egg shaped blocks), eight blocks (four of each shape), and four wooden pegs. The four similarly shaped blocks differ in that each has a hole drilled in one of four different positions; thus, each formboard, with a change in the position of a peg, can become uniquely appropriate for a single block. The test consists of a series of 40 items in each of which the patient is presented with the formboard and two blocks. Difficulty is varied, increasing through the test, by increasing the similarity between the blocks to be discriminated and by varying the angles at which the constituent pieces are presented.

The item pool is, then, highly homogeneous. The scoring involves noting the accuracy and time involved in each choice.

Overall, the test is clearly in the tradition of well known formboard performance tests such as those in the Pintner-Paterson battery, and the Arthur, the Ferguson and Kent-Shakow formboards.

The apparent difference is in the simplicity of the required response, and the effort given to grading item difficulty without involving more than minimal motor skill. A further contribution is the recognition that the formboard task, familiar in developmental studies, might be of additional relevance to the study of the brain damaged.

In the absence of published research on the test, it is necessary to rely heavily on the manual for an assessment of the test's worth and, unfortunately, the manual appears inadequate for a device offered for applied clinical use.

Carelessness can be identified on several levels in the manual. The first example, excusable but by no means desirable, involves the sort of lapse that merely inconveniences the reader, e.g., mistaken references to page and table numbers, and careless writing of crucial definitions. An example displaying imprecision of definition has already been quoted in the first paragraph of this review; a second is the statement that, "Space is a quality an individual attributes to sensation." Whether the intent is to characterize the phenomenology or the ontogeny of spatial perception is not clear and is never clarified.

A second, and much more critical, level of carelessness is involved in the presenting of inadequate standardization data. For example, although the test is described as appropriate for patients "through adulthood," reported standardization data relevant to adults is limited to 26 cases with cerebral palsy, aged "17–44." Further, the standardization data for children appears somewhat questionable. Misleading reference is first made to a study in which the test was administered to 100 brain-damaged subjects and 100 subjects without brain damage. The age range is said to be 3 to 77 years, with a division into five age groups. It is further stated that "subjects were matched by mean age." It is unclear whether this means that the groups at each age division were so matched or whether the total groups were so matched. Even more important, the disposition of subjects across this very wide age range on a highly age-dependent performance task is not mentioned. Nor is there any attempt to specify degree, site, or variety of cerebral damage, despite the obvious importance of such factors. Also omitted is control of variables such as educational status and cultural background.

Initial reference to these data as misleading is based on the fact that though the data are presented in a section entitled "Population Used," they are based *not* on the use of the clinical form of the test, but on an earlier, much longer, experimental version of the test.

Basic normative data are apparently based on the scores of 15 male and 15 female children "at each year of age from 3–10 years." While the sample here would seem more nearly adequate in terms of numbers at each age level, lack of clarity persists in several places. For example, performance is to be evaluated in terms of standardized rather than raw scores. For one age group, the standard deviation of that group was used to achieve the desired conversion; mysteriously, for the remaining seven groups the standard deviation specific to the group was replaced by the geometric mean of the seven standard deviations, with no explanation for this peculiar computational divergence. Further, clinical comparisons are to be based on an "adjusted score" which is derived by reducing the accuracy score by differential amounts based on the time used by the S. Such an adjustment may, in fact, be quite reasonable, but no discussion of how the degree of adjustment was determined is presented.

Further carelessness exists at the level of specifying how the test is to be given. For example, with respect to timing, it seems quite unclear as to just where in a series of implicit or explicit trials and errors the examiner may decide that S has made a mistake "for keeps" and hence to interrupt the crucial timing. Reliable time scores correct to the second, required for scoring the adjusted scores, would seem most difficult to achieve.

The above listing of errors and ambiguities is not exhaustive, but is, in the reviewer's opinion, sufficient indication that this test, interesting as it may be, cannot in good faith be recommended for general clinical use. It is difficult to understand why the publisher and author have collaborated in producing the test so prematurely.

ALFRED B. HEILBRUN, JR., *Associate Professor of Psychology, State University of Iowa, Iowa City, Iowa.*

The *Ayres Space Test* includes 60 formboard items requiring relatively simple spatial discriminations. It is intended primarily as a diagnostic tool for detection of brain damage, although the manual suggests that its properties make it useful in a variety of other situations—in research, as an adjunct in therapy, and for training and retraining purposes. However, since there is no evidence presented to substantiate these rather extensive claims, they must be considered premature at best.

Items were selected by determining which spatial perception problems best discriminated between heterogeneous groups of brain damaged individuals and normals at five different age levels extending from 3 to 77 years. Despite the wide age span used for item derivation and the manual's contention that the test is intended for persons from 3 through adulthood, norms are provided only for ages 3 through 10. Apparently one reason for this is a ceiling effect which is reached by age 14. The norms are not only curtailed in range of years but also are minimally constituted with respect to numbers; there were but 30 children sampled at each year.

An even more glaring deficit in the manual is the almost total lack of validating evidence for the test as a predictor of brain pathology. Four studies are considered in the validation section. Two have no relevance to the detection of brain damage, and a third reports the performance of 7- to 10-year old cerebral palsied groups with n's ranging between 3 and 6. The fourth study of 50 brain damaged children is open to serious criticism if the test constructor used the same children for item derivation and for this validation study, since discrimination would be spuriously high. The failure of the manual to be explicit allows for such a conclusion.

Reliability is reported in terms of internal consistency coefficients, and these run high at each age level. A test-retest stability measure would have been preferable, especially since the similarity in task performance from item to item makes internal consistency almost a foregone conclusion. Stability of children's performance over a length of time is another matter.

As mentioned above, mean scores on the

test increase rapidly with age until a ceiling is reached, presumably around 14 years. A point which is completely neglected by the manual is the likelihood that test performance is substantially correlated with mental age and with IQ. If so and the Ayres test is to be seriously proposed as a diagnostic indicant of brain damage, then the relationship between intelligence and spatial perception should be considered somewhere in the normative procedures.

There certainly is room in the clinician's diagnostic battery for a simple, reliable, and valid test which will enhance his ability to detect brain pathology in children. This test may someday qualify in this regard, but the best that can be said now is that a great deal more work is necessary before a judgment can be rendered. The manual both claims too much and provides too little; it is obscure in some spots and redundant in others. In the opinion of this reviewer, much of the criticism of the test could have been averted if publication had been postponed until the rudimentary attributes of the test were more thoroughly investigated. Although the manual in no place mentions the preliminary status of this test, the test user would do well to employ the AST with considerable caution until its merits are more clearly established.

[64]

***Babcock Test of Mental Efficiency.** Ages 7 and over; 1930–62; formerly called *Babcock Test of Mental Deterioration;* record booklet title is *The Revised Examination for the Measurement of Efficiency of Mental Functioning;* individual; 10 scores: easy tests, repetition, initial learning, recall and recognition, motor A, motor B, perception time, easy continuous work, total efficiency (based on 8 previous scores), efficiency deviation; 1 form ('40); mimeographed manual ['62, 68 pages]; record booklet ('42, 8 pages); reliability data the same as reported in 1940; $20 per set of testing materials, 25 record booklets, and manual; $10 per 25 record booklets; $6.50 per manual; postpaid; (70) minutes; Harriet Babcock and Lydia Levy (test); Western Psychological Services. *

REFERENCES

1–14. See 40:1248.
15–35. See 3:71.
36–45. See 4:31.
46. BABCOCK, HARRIET. "Measuring the Efficiency Variable," pp. 741–50. (*PA* 27:7752) In *Contributions Toward Medical Psychology: Theory and Psychodiagnostic Methods, Vol. II.* Edited by Arthur Weider. New York: Ronald Press Co., 1953. Pp. xi, 459–885. *
47. HOOK, MARION EMERSON. *A Factorial Analysis of Some Tests of Mental Efficiency.* Doctor's thesis, Ohio State University (Columbus, Ohio), 1954. (*DA* 20:2375)
48. SHAPIRO, M. B., AND NELSON, E. H. "An Investigation of the Nature of Cognitive Impairment in Co-operative Psychiatric Patients." *Brit J Med Psychol* 28:239–56 pt 4 '55. * (*PA* 30:6185)
49. PAYNE, R. W.; MATTUSSEK, P.; AND GEORGE, E. I. "An Experimental Study of Schizophrenic Thought Disorder." *J Mental Sci* 105:627–52 Jl '59. * (*PA* 34:6384)
50. PAYNE, R. W., AND HEWLETT, J. H. G. Chap. 1, "Thought Disorder in Psychotic Patients," pp. 3–104. In *Experiments in Personality: Vol. 2, Psychodiagnostics and Psychodynamics.* Edited by H. J. Eysenck. London: Routledge & Kegan Paul Ltd., 1960. Pp. viii, 333. *
51. PAYNE, R. W. Chap. 6, "Cognitive Abnormalities," pp. 193–261. In *Handbook of Abnormal Psychology: An Experimental Approach.* Edited by H. J. Eysenck. New York: Basic Books, Inc., 1961. Pp. xvi, 816. * (*PA* 35:6719)

For reviews by D. Russell Davis and Seymour G. Klebanoff, see 4:31; for excerpts from related book reviews, see 3:72.

[65]

***Behavior Cards: A Test-Interview for Delinquent Children.** Delinquents having a reading grade score 4.5 or higher; 1941–50; individual; 1 form ('41, 150 cards); mimeographed manual, third edition ('50, c1941, 20 pages); record sheet ('41, 2 pages); $5.35 per set of cards, 25 record sheets, and manual; $1 per 25 record sheets; postage extra; (15–30) minutes; Ralph M. Stogdill; distributed by C. H. Stoelting Co. *

REFERENCES

1–3. See 3:25.
4. ZAKOLSKI, F. C. "Studies in Delinquency: I, Personality Structure of Delinquent Boys." *J Genetic Psychol* 74:109–17 Mr '49. * (*PA* 23:4925)

For reviews by W. C. Kvaraceus and Simon H. Tulchin, see 3:25.

[66]

★Billett-Starr Youth Problems Inventory. Grades 7–9, 10–12; 1961, c1953–61; problems checklist; 12 scores: physical health and safety, getting along with others, boy-girl relationships, home and family life, personal finance, interests and activities, school life, personal potentialities, planning for the future, mental-emotional health, morality and religion, total; 1 form ('61, c1953–58, 12 pages); 2 levels; manual ('61, 24 pages); no data on reliability; $4.70 per 35 tests; 40¢ per specimen set of both levels; postage extra; (70–80) minutes; Roy O. Billett and Irving S. Starr; Harcourt, Brace & World, Inc. *

REFERENCES

1. TRIFARI, THERESA ELEANOR. *The Identification of the Problems of Junior High School Youths and the Determination of the Relative Stability of These Problems.* Doctor's thesis, Boston University (Boston, Mass.), 1959. (*DA* 20:3638)

THOMAS C. BURGESS, *Associate Professor, Counseling Center, Portland State College, Portland, Oregon.*

The Billett-Starr inventory is a relatively long checklist consisting of 432 problems for the junior high school level and 441 problems for the senior high school level. Problems are arranged into the 11 areas listed above, with the number of problems per area ranging from 9 in the area of Personal Finance to 87 (or 88) in the area of School Life. Neither the rationale nor the procedure used to assign problems to these groups is mentioned. Problems within areas are arranged in an order designed to give continuity among related items.

Time required for completing the inventory is said to range from 26 to 120 minutes, though recommended time allowances (including time for directions) are 80 minutes for junior high school and 70 minutes for senior high school students. It is suggested that these somewhat excessive time requirements could be avoided in guidance classes by administering only one area at a time. While this procedure might be useful if the results are to be used only as a stimulus for class discussions, any reliance on the results for other purposes would be limited by the question of possible differences from what one might expect to obtain in a single session and reduced comparability with norms and the results reported by others. No data are presented to show that such results would be comparable, nor is the possibility of different results mentioned.

In responding to the inventory the student is asked to consider each item and to indicate whether it is no problem for him (NP), somewhat of a problem for him (S), or much of a problem for him (M) by crossing out one of these symbols. His score is simply a count of the number of problems marked M or S, the differences in the felt intensity of the problem being ignored. Total scores may be evaluated by reference to percentile norms for each sex at each level based on what appear to be reasonably appropriate groups. The authors take the reasonable position that the S and M responses should be considered by the counselor in making a study of an individual, but that to consider these different responses in routine scoring would unnecessarily complicate the tabulation and interpretation of the results.

Quartile norms based on the same groups are presented for each of the area scores. This seems a good idea, but examination of the norms reveals that for some areas the checking of as few as two problems will move the student from the bottom quarter to the top quarter of the distribution. Areas with so little differentiation between the top and bottom of the distribution would seem to be subject to considerable error, and should either be expanded by the addition of more popular problems in the area or should be combined with other related areas in the inventory.

The manual also gives useful frequency data on each item separately for boys and girls at each of the two levels.

An interesting feature of the inventory is the attempt to label certain items as indicators of "Very Serious" or "Urgent" problems. Items so labeled were those identified by the "consensus" of a jury of 20 specialists ("school counselors, school psychologists, directors of guidance, college professors of psychology, and the like"). Problems designated "Urgent" were judged to demand immediate attention. No indication is given of what was considered to constitute "consensus," a question which may be raised since consensus seems to have been reached on every item. And while judgments of a group of specialists provide a good starting point, further studies should be made to provide follow-up information on students who mark these items. To what extent do they tend to have serious problems? According to the item frequencies some of these items are checked by as many as 15 per cent in some of the groups of students sampled (no frequencies are reported for 7 of the 12 items rated "Urgent") suggesting a fairly high rate of false positive identifications may result.

The authors argue that the validity of the inventory "is to be determined largely by inspection of the instrument itself in light of the method used to obtain its content." Items were collected from students who were asked to write statements of their problems. These items were then sorted to eliminate overlapping and edited to eliminate ambiguity. The inventory "is a valid list of the problems of youth because it was derived from what young people themselves report as being their problems." This argument is supported by the normative data, by both the frequencies for items and the distributions of scores, which indicate that students do respond to the items. While this indicates that the items have been drawn from the domain of student problems it says nothing about how thoroughly this domain has been covered or how adequately it has been sampled. Furthermore, no external evidence of validity is given. There are no data on the relationship between responses to the inventory and any non-inventory behavior, problem diagnoses from case studies, or performance on any other standardized instrument. Such data should be gathered, both for the total score and for the 11 area scores.

No data are given on reliability. It is argued appropriately that the split-half estimate of reliability would be inappropriate because the content is not homogeneous. The retest method is rejected by the authors because the inventory is so long it would be too time consuming, because of the influence of memory over a short interval of time, and because of the probability of real changes in problems over any period long enough to eliminate the influence of memory. While there is merit in these arguments it would be preferable to have the estimates made and the data presented, and then to consider the shortcomings of the procedures in the light of obtained data—not in the darkness of absent data.

In summary, it would appear that this is a potentially useful checklist, but one on which more information is needed. It lacks, at this time, the completeness of information contained in the manual of the *SRA Youth Inventory* and the more voluminous validity data contained in the published research on the *Mooney Problem Check List.*

J. THOMAS HASTINGS, *Director, Office of Educational Testing; University Examiner; and Professor of Educational Psychology; University of Illinois, Urbana, Illinois.*

The areas of adjustment suggested by the 11 parts of this inventory are certainly of real concern to student and to educator alike. Perhaps a major contribution of the instrument is to focus the attention (however briefly) of teachers, counselors, administrators, and parents on these critical domains of problems. An instrument which looks like a test might do it when a pamphlet which looks like a sermon might not; "scores" on real youngsters may be more apt to motivate adults to attend to real problems than will generalized statements about such problems. The main difficulty, however, with considering this motivational-focusing effect as a contribution of the *Billett-Starr Youth Problems Inventory* is that there already were, at the time of its publication, three other similar instruments available: The *Mooney Problem Check List,* the *SRA Junior Inventory,* and the *SRA Youth Inventory.* It is true that the parts do not have exactly the same titles (problem areas) in all four instruments, but almost any topic in one can be found in the other two.

The task set the student in the Billett-Starr inventory is that of marking *each* of a series of statements (Junior Level, 432; Senior Level, 441) as either "NP," not a problem to him, or as a problem to him. If he believes the statement represents a problem, he is to designate whether it is a problem which worries him "some" or a problem which worries him "very much." This further discrimination may give some advantage over the Mooney and the SRA inventories—but certainly no data are presented to show that it does. Furthermore, the manual (page 7) recommends that no distinction be made between "problems marked S [some] and those marked M [much]" in scoring the test. Just following this suggestion is the statement that "neither of the two types of norms furnished....is broken down into the Some and Much classifications." Later on, Table 4 presents for each of the 11 parts the percentage (in "a representative sample of 6390 cases") of items marked "much" on a base of items marked as problems. The authors support having the respondents make the distinction—S and M—on the basis that it improves "the student's general attitude and the validity of his responses." No data are given to support this generalization, and yet such data could be acquired rather easily.

Validity is pinned to the validity of the statements as problems, i.e., all of the statements represent "real problems." This claim is supported by the assertion that all items are "based on the freely written statements of large numbers of students in junior and senior high schools." This basis is a necessary condition but certainly not sufficient—nor does it add anything new to the available instruments. A further statement is made to the effect that counselors report good agreement between the results from this instrument and information gained in personal interviews. The possible user should beware of basing a decision on such a claim unless he can find out more about the extent of agreement and the conditions of comparison.

No data are given in the manual concerning the reliability of the instrument. After explaining at great length why "the traditional approach to reliability is not applicable," the authors dismiss a need for test-retest data (after all, the user should be interested in the stability over time of the problems) with the statement that "this procedure would be unduly time-consuming." The user might be justified in replying that administering and "scoring" the inventory is certainly unduly time-consuming if no picture of stability of the problems is presented.

The one thing added to this inventory that does not appear in the earlier ones is a coding of items (in the inventory and in the norms) in terms of judged seriousness of each problem. The authors had 20 specialists—an unspecified mixture of counselors, school psychologists, professors of psychology, "and the like"—rate each statement on a 3-point scale: minor, in-between, and very serious problem. These same judges also marked a number of items at each level as "urgent." The very serious and the urgent problems are coded for the user. Since the ratings were made apart from application to any individual or context, it is probably preferable for the user to make his own judgments regarding these dimensions at the time of use. If he is incapable of making better judgments concerning seriousness for a particular student than were the judges who didn't know the student, he probably should not be using the instrument.

In summary, there is no evidence to indicate that the Billett-Starr inventory is better than the earlier published instruments of the same type; and since it has not been as widely used as the Mooney or the SRA inventories, it lacks some of the data available on them in the journals. It can be hoped that through controlled use of the instrument the authors will collect and publish the kinds of data which will make the inventory more useful to the general test buyer.

HENRY WEITZ, *Associate Professor of Education, and Director, Bureau of Testing and Guidance, Duke University, Durham, North Carolina.*

Billett and Starr have compiled a list of questions related to the concerns of youth, grouped them into 11 "problem areas," furnished a response system which is only occasionally unnecessarily confusing, applied a scoring system which requires only the ability to count, presented a set of "norms" which contribute little to the use of the instrument, and made the claim that the inventory "provides (1) information that contributes to the counselor's fuller understanding of each *individual* student, and (2) facts about the prevalence of certain problems within school or other community *groups*."

As in the case of other inventories of this sort, the present document drew its items from "the freely written statements of large numbers of students in junior and senior high schools." This appears to be the instrument's principal claim to validity.

No evidence of reliability is provided because, the authors insist, scores obtained on this kind of instrument may not be legitimately treated by the usual correlation analysis. They may well have a point here, yet other procedures could have been used to examine response consistency. The argument that "if the attitudes and feelings of any individual are subject to great variation over relatively short periods of time this is a very important fact to know about him even though it would mitigate against the conventional notion of reliability for the instrument," makes one wonder about the general utility of an instrument which is so subject to momentary fluctuations of mood. The counselor is urged to use the student's responses to gain some insight into the student's problems. If the authors' arguments about reliability hold, the counselor may be gaining insight into problems which have no lasting significance in the child's adjustment.

The manual provides abundant information on the mechanics of administering, scoring, and tallying responses for various uses, but it provides inadequate information on effective ways in which the instrument can be used and no evidence to support the recommended uses.

One device introduced in this test may have some promise. It involves identification by single and double dots printed in the booklet of those problems considered "very serious" and "urgent" by a jury of 20 specialists. Thirty six of the 432 items at the junior level and 41 of the 441 items at the senior level are identified as very serious or urgent. No evidence is given that these items can identify students with behavioral problems or that they can tell very much about the nature of the child's problem.

The student taking the test is asked to differentiate between problems which bother him somewhat and those which bother him a great deal. Little use is made of these differentiated responses since the scoring involves simply counting both kinds of responses together. The suggestion is made that the counselor may use the indicated severity of the problem as a guide to his counseling.

The *Billet-Starr Youth Problems Inventory* appears to do no more and, perhaps, very little less than, for example, the *Mooney Problem Check List* or the *SRA Youth Inventory.* It is to the credit of the authors of the present instrument that they have made no excessive claims for their inventory. Yet instruments of this sort suffer from a common ailment: they represent an elaborate and expensive procedure for securing unreliable answers to simple questions. The effective counselor does not require this sort of a crutch to gain understanding of his clients. The unskilled, inexperienced, or inept counselor should not be allowed to use such an instrument, for it is likely to retard his professional growth. The only possible use that might legitimately be made of instruments of this kind would be for preliminary large scale group surveys of student problems where individual interviews are impractical.

[67]

★Biographical Inventory for Students. Grades 12–13; 1955–62; for research use only; 10 scores: action, social activities, heterosexual activities, religious activities, literature-music-art, political activities, socioeconomic status, economic independence, dependence on home, social conformity; IBM; Form KDRD1 ('58, c1955–58, 14 pages); mimeographed manual ('62, c1955–58, 38 pages); separate answer sheets must be used; $2.50 per 25 tests; 25¢ per single copy; $1 per 25 IBM scorable answer sheets; scoring stencils must be prepared locally; $1 per manual; postage extra; (55–60) minutes; Laurence Siegel; distributed by Educational Testing Service. *

REFERENCES

1. SIEGEL, LAURENCE. "Note on a Biographical Inventory for Students." *J Counsel Psychol* 1:116–8 su '54. * (*PA* 29:3022)
2. SIEGEL, LAURENCE. "A Biographical Inventory for Students: I, Construction and Standardization of the Instrument." *J Appl Psychol* 40:5–10 F '56. * (*PA* 31:3079)
3. SIEGEL, LAURENCE. "A Biographical Inventory for Students: II, Validation of the Instrument." *J Appl Psychol* 40:122–6 Ap '56. * (*PA* 31:6128)
4. KAUSLER, DONALD H., AND LITTLE, NEAL D. "The BIS Dependency Scale and Grades in Psychology Courses." *J Counsel Psychol* 4:322–3 w '57. * (*PA* 33:6919)
5. KAUSLER, DONALD H., AND TRAPP, E. PHILIP. "Anxiety Level and Score on a Biographical Inventory." *J Appl Psychol* 42:305–7 O '58. * (*PA* 33:9755)
6. DUFF, O. LEE, AND SIEGEL, LAURENCE. "Biographical Factors Associated With Academic Over- and Underachievement." *J Ed Psychol* 51:43–6 F '60. * (*PA* 34:8398, 35:2261)

[68]

***Bristol Social-Adjustment Guides.** Ages 5–15; 1956–63; ratings by teachers or other adults; 3 scales and 1 supplementary key; 1 form ('56, 4 pages) of each scale; diagnostic form ('56, 1 page) for each scale; manual, second edition ('63, 63 pages); 8*s.* per 25 diagnostic forms; 25*s.* per manual; 3*s.* per specimen set of *a–c* (without manual); postage and purchase tax extra; (10–20) minutes per scale; D. H. Stott and E. G. Sykes (*a, b*); University of London Press Ltd. *

a) THE CHILD IN SCHOOL. 1956–63; separate editions for boys and girls; 12*s.* per 25 scales; 6*d.* per single copy; 3*s.* per set of scoring keys.

b) THE CHILD IN RESIDENTIAL CARE. 1956–63; 12*s.* per 25 scales; 6*d.* per single copy; 4*s.* per set of scoring keys.

c) THE CHILD IN THE FAMILY. 1956–63; life history chart ('56, 1 page); 17*s.* 6*d.* per set of 25 scales and 25 charts; 9*d.* per single copy of each; 2*s.* 6*d.* per scoring key.

d) DELINQUENCY PREDICTION INSTRUMENT. Boys ages 5–15; 1961–63; consists of a delinquency prediction key to be used with the diagnostic form for *The Child in School* scale and a teacher's questionnaire ('61, 1 page) for preliminary identification of pupils to be rated on the scale; manual ('61, 4 pages, also available as part of the manual for *a–c* above); no data on reliability; 2*s.* 6*d.* per 12 questionnaires; 3*d.* per single copy; 1*s.* per key; 9*d.* per separate manual; (10–15) minutes.

REFERENCES

1. STOTT, D. H. *Unsettled Children and Their Families.* London: University of London Press Ltd., 1956. Pp. 240. * (*PA* 32:3012)
2. STOTT, D. H. "Boys on Probation: Maladjusted or Normal." Abstract. *Adm Sci Q* 15:498–502 Je '59. *
3. LUNZER, E. A. "Aggressive and Withdrawing Children in the Normal School: 1, Patterns of Behaviour." *Brit J Ed Psychol* 30:1–10 F '60. *
4. STOTT, D. H. "Delinquency, Maladjustment and Unfavourable Ecology." *Brit J Psychol* 51:157–70 My '60. * (*PA* 35:1114)
5. STOTT, D. H. "A New Delinquency Prediction Instrument Using Behavioural Indications." *Int J Social Psychiatry* 6:195–205 au '60. * (*PA* 36:4JO95S)
6. STOTT, D. H. "The Prediction of Delinquency From Non-Delinquent Behaviour." *Brit J Delinq* 10:195–210 Ja '60. *
7. STOTT, D. H. "Relationship Between Delinquency, Non-Delinquent Social Maladjustment and Neighbourhood Factors." Abstract. *Acta Psychologica* 19:425 '61. *
8. CRAFT, MICHAEL; FABISCH, WALTER; STEPHENSON, GEOFFRY; BURNAND, GORDON; AND KERRIDGE, DAVID. "100 Admissions to a Psychopathic Unit." *J Mental Sci* 108:564–83 S '62. * (*PA* 38:2138)
9. PETRIE, I. R. J. "Residential Treatment of Maladjusted Children: A Study of Some Factors Related to Progress in Adjustment." *Brit J Ed Psychol* 32:29–37 F '62. * (*PA* 37:893)
10. STOTT, D. H. "The Bristol Guides." *Child Care* 16:76–8 Jl '62. *
11. STOTT, D. H. "Evidence for a Congenital Factor in Maladjustment and Delinquency." *Am J Psychiatry* 118:781–94 Mr '62. *
12. STOTT, D. H. "Delinquency Proneness and Court Disposal of Young Offenders." *Brit J Criminol* 4:37–42 Jl '63. *
13. STOTT, DENIS. "Truancy and Crime." *Scottish Ed J* 46:189–90 Mr 8 '63. *

G. A. V. MORGAN, *Former Principal Psychologist, North Wales Child Guidance Service, Denbighshire, Wales.*

BRISTOL SOCIAL-ADJUSTMENT GUIDES. The Guides are basically checklists of statements describing items of behaviour significantly related to the emotional adjustment of children from 5 to 15 years of age. The three forms of the Guides cover the areas of school, residential care, and home background.

It is envisaged that the Child in School and the Child in Residential Care will be completed by persons best acquainted with the child, usually the teacher in charge of the child. The observer is given freedom to select from scrambled items in paragraphs statements which describe the child. Completion of each Guide for one child takes 10–20 minutes, depending on the skill of the observer. Items checked are scored by means of a transparent key and scores are transferred to a diagnostic form. This procedure is estimated to take some seven minutes.

The Child in the Family clearly requires knowledge of both family and child, and the implication is that this Guide will need to be used by a social worker or other professionally qualified person. Interpretation of the check-list on the child is made in terms of similar evidence on parents and the relationship within the family. The observations are reduced to patterns and measured finally in terms of two components, the number and severity of adverse factors in the child's situation and the degree to which he is affected by these.

The Guides were empirically based on collections of statements, describing the various forms of maladjusted behaviour in children, made by workers with children in residential care. This led to the development of the Child in Residential Care and this in turn to similar work with teachers on the Child in School. The items in the Guides are concerned with behaviour *symptomatic of maladjustment,* not with *personality traits* (e.g., "maladjustment," rather than "neuroticism" or "introversion"). Although the statements in the Guides were collected and sifted quite empirically with respect to their ability to distinguish maladjusted children from "normal" controls, the authors made use of their "clinical" knowledge of the significance of various kinds of behaviour and their observed associations to identify and score various subgroups of items relating to "syndromes" of maladjusted response, e.g., the "withdrawn," "hostile," and "anxious for affection." To this extent, Stott's own theories and generalizations are built into the Guides. The manual describes mainly the development and evaluation of the Child in School, which appears to be the Guide at present in most use. Careful and skilful revisions of the sample items for all Guides are described, passing through five versions for the Child in School and four for the Child in Residential Care. Items were analysed statistically and revised or discarded. Of 195 items, 133 finally achieved high significance in discriminating between maladjusted and normal groups.

The author rejects the total score on maladjustment based on counting disturbed responses as meaningless, in view of the variations in forms of maladjusted response; the diagnostic form provides for "syndrome" scores. It seems a pity that an attitude scaling technique should not have been used to confirm the groupings of items and suggest optional weighting. It would have been profitable, too, to cross validate the items within the experimental group to avoid well known sampling fluctuation effects.

The question of the reliability of the Guides is a complex one. Consistency of assessment between observers, or by the same observer over a period of time, appears analogous to "reader reliability" in assessing written work. Yet the various aspects of reliability do not appear to have been systematically explored. Evidence on the reliability of the Guides is sparse. One would estimate that the retest reliability coefficient of the two forms of the Guide is about .80. On present evidence, they are useful for comparison of groups but will need to be interpreted with liberal limits of score in classifying and comparing individuals.

Since the Guides were developed from empirical "common sense" observations, the validity and generality of their definitions of maladjustment depend on the degree to which items are representative of varieties of maladjustment and the extent to which the criterion groups were representative. The author points out that the original categories of maladjustment on the Guides were influenced by his delinquency studies and there is evidence, from the distribution of items, that the associated groups of aggressive-anxious behaviour bulk larger than withdrawn or unforthcoming (timid and introverted) behaviour. Some forms of disturbed behaviour commonly found in referrals to child guidance clinics are probably less adequately sampled than aggressive and delinquent behaviour. The manual does not specify the way in which the criterion "maladjusted" group was chosen. A later reference showed that the first groups used for developing the Child in School were composed of groups of three children (normal, unsettled, and maladjusted) each chosen by 20 teachers from among their class. This seems to be a very small and subjective criterion group. It is not reported that children referred to child guidance clinics or other psychiatric help, likely to be among the most extreme of the maladjusted population, were used. At the final revision of the Child in School, 234 of 613 children were maladjusted, but no criterion for the choice for the maladjusted group is given. The maladjusted group was larger than the control group. This was necessary to allow for identification of subgroups, with respect to syndrome associations between items. Since, however, maladjusted children are in a minority in the general population, the degree of efficiency of discrimination in terms of the percentage of maladjusted children identified by any given range of score cannot be established, even though items discriminated between maladjusted and controls at a high level of significance. This is a criticism brought up by Stott himself (5) in discussing the need to adjust percentages to approximately correct numbers of those at risk, in deciding the efficacy of a predictive scale.

The validity of the Guides rests on their agreement with the usual criteria of what constitutes maladjustment. The available evidence in the manual shows consistent success in this in a wide variety of settings. For example, the reliability and validity of the Child in School and the Child in Residential Care were "moderately good" in showing agreement with ratings by the warden on children's behaviour and improvement over 18 months in a special school for maladjusted children, whereas various projective tests were by contrast poor (9). In a study by the National Foundation for Educational Research, poor readers were found to be significantly more withdrawn than matched good readers at the ages of 9–10 and significant improvement over a year could be measured pari-passu with reading.

In view of the lack of knowledge of exactly what "maladjustment" means and its limits and sampling variations, "standardization" of instruments such as the Guides presents some complications, as pointed out by the author. Data on the distribution of scores are available on a random sample of children of 7–8 years in Liverpool, on delinquent and nondelinquent boys of 9–14 years in Glasgow, and on "delicate" children of 8, 10, and 14 in London. These tables printed in the manual should have percentiles for various scores to be useful and, as far as possible, some indication should be given of limits indicating the normal range and severity of maladjustment. There is a need for a comprehensive standardization on adequately randomized samples.

The manual contains a considerable amount of useful information on the development, evaluation, and purpose of the Guides, but requires careful reading. It would be more convenient if one section were devoted to direct and specific instructions for completing and scoring each of the Guides.

When using the Child in the Family careful diagnostic work needs to be done. The family patterns described tend to reflect the more extreme forms of parental tension, rejection, and neglect likely to be related to the author's particular interests. It is not so clear whether some subtler, latent patterns of emotional involvement found in many disturbed children referred to child guidance clinics are adequately represented by this Guide. This seems to be a matter for experiment and development. One would be interested to know the degree to which the Child in the Family is known to or accepted by the professional workers who might profitably use it, and how it would be considered by them to supplement or replace the usual full case history.

In summary, The Bristol Guides are based on a pragmatic approach to maladjustment. Clinical workers will be sceptical of the descriptive and "symptomatic" approach, but the Guides to the Child in School and the Child in Residential Care appear to have a great deal to offer in helping the everyday observer sharpen his observations of children. The Guides have already played a valuable part in research and, unlike self-scored personality questionnaires, seem to work as effectively in the practical setting as in research. Despite their limitations, they have a useful contribution to make, and are capable of further development. They are probably used more widely in Britain than any other single assessment of personality outside those solely in professional use.

DELINQUENCY PREDICTION INSTRUMENT. This instrument was developed by Stott from observations that delinquents (boys of 9–14 on probation in Glasgow) showed significantly higher scores than "normal" controls on the Bristol Guides in such areas as hostility to adults and children, anxiety for affection, and lack of normal emotional involvement. Fifty four items from the Child in School Guide which occurred four times more frequently among delinquents were chosen to form the instrument, the items being roughly weighted in proportion to the differences in response.

The effectiveness of the instrument is expressed in terms of two ratios. One is the predictive range of the instrument in a "normal" mixed population of boys containing an average expected number of delinquents. The range, for any given score, specifies the number of delinquents who will be included, with normals, in the sample defined. A low criterion score will ensure that a majority of delinquents is brought into the sample, but at the cost of including a fairly large number of nondelinquents, and, conversely, a high criterion score will eliminate nondelinquents but also a significant number of delinquents. This is the usual dilemma of any selection procedure.

The second measure, the selectivity ratio, describes the efficiency of the instrument in isolating a group which has a high probability of being delinquent, that is, the proportion of the group defined by each score level who are likely to be delinquent.

The two criteria have curves which are in opposite directions. When a low score is used as a criterion the number of delinquents caught up along with normals will be large, but the actual proportion of delinquents in the group (or selectivity) will be low. Conversely, when a high score is used, a large number of actual or potential delinquents will be eliminated, but those in the group defined will have a high probability of being delinquent. The author discusses this issue rather more lucidly and at greater length in another reference (5) than in the manual to the Bristol Guides. He suggests as the best compromise the 50 per cent level of selectivity; this would detect 70 per cent of all delinquents.

A table is given in the manual representing range and selectivity ratios for given scores on the Delinquency Prediction Instrument. In addition, a table is given of prediction scores for individuals, in terms of the probability that an individual will be or become delinquent. To lighten work in screening delinquents, the author offers a list of six questions on delinquent and aggressive attitudes observed in schools; these are to be used by teachers in selecting children for full assessment on this instrument. This useful procedure is parallel to that proposed by Stott in his six questions for screening the children in a class likely to be sufficiently maladjusted to warrant fuller investigation with the Child in School Guide.

The author points out that, since the instrument provides an objective rating procedure and takes only 10–15 minutes per child, it is a simple and effective procedure for classifying children likely to be or become delinquents, particularly by contrast with the case histories and prediction tables based on a variety of weighted factors which are described by the Gluecks.[1] Stott criticizes the proportional effectiveness of such prediction tables in isolating delinquents from a natural mixed population. There is evidence that the Delinquency Prediction Instrument is sensitive to degrees of maladjustment or delinquency within the delinquent group as related to the number of further offences committed during probation, or recidivism. It is claimed that it isolates the psychological factors of delinquency even within areas varying widely in sociological factors related to delinquency.

The instrument has not been extended for routine use with girls or for use with boys outside the age range described. No reliability studies have been reported: it is clear that wide limits of score are needed to classify individuals with a high degree of accuracy. As far as the emotional aspects of predelinquent behaviour which can be described in school are concerned, the Delinquency Prediction Instrument appears to form a most useful addition to measures for the assessment and prediction of delinquency.

M. L. KELLMER PRINGLE, *Director, National Bureau for Co-operation in Child Care, London, England.*

The purpose of the *Bristol Social-Adjustment Guides* is, in the author's words, to "offer a method for detecting and diagnosing maladjustment, unsettledness or other emotional handicap in children of school age. They constitute a clinical instrument by which a comprehensive report of how the child behaves and reacts in real life can be furnished to the psychologist or psychiatrist, and a system for the interpretation of the behaviour. Educationally they are a means of judging whether a child is suffering from emotional difficulties, such as might be the cause of failure in school-work, or which might act as a warning sign of the possibility of delinquent-breakdown."

Adults familiar with the child are presented with a list of statements and are required to underline those which describe his habitual mode of response. No expert knowledge or

1 GLUECK, SHELDON, AND GLUECK, ELEANOR. *Unraveling Juvenile Delinquency*, pp. 257–62. New York: Commonwealth Fund, 1950. Pp. xv, 399. * (*PA* 25:2578)

insight is needed by the teacher or residential staff who are completing the Guides since the interpretations will be made by clinicians of one kind or another. It would seem, however, that the Guide relating to the Child in the Family is to be filled in by a trained social worker who also evaluates the results. All the Guides are couched in everyday, jargon-free language, describing readily observable behaviour; the completion of the schedules takes only 10 to 20 minutes. The method aims at providing a general statement about the social adjustment of a child which is as free as possible from the unreliability of subjective, personal judgment. Since only contemporary adjustment is being assessed, change and improvement, whether spontaneous or as a result of treatment, can be measured by obtaining another record after a period of time. Stott has deliberately refrained from expressing the diagnosis in terms of a quotient or score. This he considers "would be artificial because there are different ways of being maladjusted which are hardly comparable to one another." Rather, children are classified into three main groups—stable, unsettled, or maladjusted—or, according to the predominant behaviour pattern which they show, aggressive, withdrawn, etc. For research purposes, however, there is, in Stott's view, no objection to using a score derived either by simple counting or by some kind of weighting.

The manual falls between several stools. Teachers and house parents looking for a simple explanation of the aims of the Guides and for some suggestions to help with their completion (for example, on how to avoid a halo effect) are likely to be disappointed; even the first chapter, entitled "Explanations and Directions" is not only too technical but too detailed and long for this purpose. The staff of psychological services will wish for much greater clinical detail, for example, some case studies and profiles to illustrate patterns shown by unsettled and maladjusted children, respectively, or some explanation of how Stott arrived at his 12 "Patterns of Family-Situation." Research workers will regret that the discussion of "Methodology and Compilation" has been compressed into a mere 13 pages, 4 of which are devoted to a general consideration of current controversies regarding the nature of personality and its scientific measurement. Moreover, a curious method has been chosen for presenting this chapter. It begins with a list of 37 headings, such as "The conflict between Objectivists and the Understanders," "The Concept of 'proof,'" and "Weakness of sectional hypotheses." Only subsequently does it become apparent that each of them is being discussed in turn. Since they are not repeated at the beginning of the relevant section, one has to keep on going back to the beginning of the chapter to check on the topic under discussion. All readers will hope that the third edition will be revised so as to serve the conventional purposes of a manual more adequately; that the contents page will also contain page numbers and a list of the tables; and that certain obscure statements will be clarified (for example, "Experience with the Guide itself tends to even out discrepancies" on p. 8 or "In a few groups two 'normal' items are given, but this is to drain off a variety of normality which may otherwise be included in an 'unsettled' item"). It would also be useful to have all the various guides, diagnostic forms, and templates included in the manual.

As yet no comprehensive standardisation of the Guides on a randomized sample has been carried out. The results of a number of pilot studies are quoted which show significant differences between boys and girls in the incidence of maladjustment, as well as differences between delinquent and nondelinquent groups. Arguing that it is difficult to find some external validation for tests of social adjustment, Stott suggests that "some element of validation is achieved if the results tally with the assessments of teachers or others who know the children well in a day-to-day working relationship." This was found in a number of studies. Similarly, an adequate survey has not yet been made of the extent to which teachers' or house parents' recordings differ either among themselves or between each other. Again, there is some evidence from a number of experimental studies. In a project carried out by the National Foundation for Educational Research in England and Wales, pairs of teachers completed Guides independently for some 88 children; correlations between "maladjusted" scores were .76 and, between "unsettled" scores, .78. The Residential Guide was completed three times independently by nurses, rating 45 young adults who were patients in a hospital unit for psychopaths; the intercorrelations were .49, .58, and .55, respectively.

The Delinquency Prediction Instrument aims at diagnosing "delinquency-proneness." The author recommends that in the first place the teacher complete for every pupil the "preliminary sorting procedure"; this consists of six questions about the child which are answered by either "yes" or "no." "These questions are framed so as to cover the maladjusted attitudes which the prediction instrument show to be most conducive to delinquency." Then the full Bristol Guide is filled in for every child who receives one or more "yes" answers in the "preliminary sorting procedure." After this is scored, a delinquency prediction score is obtained by means of a transparent delinquency prediction key. Caution is urged in interpreting and in using this score since it has been derived from one study of Glasgow boys. At present no other data are available, either from boys in the same city or from other areas, nor have these predictive procedures been applied to girls.

In summary, the *Bristol Social-Adjustment Guides* are useful instruments for obtaining judgments of children's behaviour from teachers and house staff which will aid clinicians both in selecting children for individual examination and in diagnosing the nature of their difficulties. However, for the time being their greatest value lies in their being new research tools. Until adequate standardisation data become available, it would be unwise to recommend their widespread adoption as reliable instruments for the detection of maladjustment or for the prediction of delinquency. The present manual would benefit from being divided into two parts: a simple, concise manual giving directions for the use and scoring of the Guides and a much enlarged volume describing and giving data for all the pilot studies which preceded the present schedules, the theoretical and practical considerations which underlie them, and case studies of individual children and their families.

A.M.A. Arch Gen Psychiatry 1:556 N '59. Mary Engel. * On first blush, the "Bristol Social Adjustment Guides" seem to offer a quick, easy, and rather accurate technique, if not for understanding the dynamics of a child's disturbance, at least for selecting a potential patient from a large group of children. However, the various discussions, expositions, and arguments in the "Manual" give cause for concern over a number of issues conscientiously raised but too lightly dismissed. The authors pride themselves on their empirical approach, yet cannot resist making theoretical statements which not only are poorly integrated with the empirical attitude but also are mere restatements of rather well-known theoretical positions. For example, their discussion of "normal responses to unfavorable situations which ....get into a state of overreadiness" (p. 11) is simply a naïve expression of the concept of overuse of the defense mechanism. While the authors urge the reader to be "free of conceptual models" and accept the "empirical discipline [as] a counsel of perfection" (p. 15), they do not follow their own advice. Conceptual models are present in the "Manual"; only they are hidden and unrecognized. The "Bristol Social Adjustment Guides" have limitations for the American user in that the language of the items is often unfamiliar. It would be a difficult matter to rate a child on such items as "feckless," "seems to play daft," "spivvish dress," or "has stupid moods,"—the last being perhaps as good an example of linguistic difficulty as of the clearly judgmental nature of "objective" ratings in general.

Brit J Ed Psychol 30:187–8 Je '60. P. E. Vernon. * The Manual, though somewhat difficult to follow, is worthy of close attention from child psychologists and others interested in personality. Dr. Stott criticises both the rigidity of the "objectivist," with his fixed traits or types of personality, and the subjectivity of the clinician. All that he claims to supply is a series of records of behaviour in particular contexts, grouped under a number of syndromes or "attitudes" (Anxiety, Hostility to Adults, Restlessness, etc.) and graded for their seriousness in respect of unsettledness or maladjustment. Clearly, these can be of considerable value to the psychologist in the educational clinic, the teacher, or others concerned with maladjusted or delinquent children, in giving a codified, all-round picture of a child's personality. They represent a genuine attempt to get away from the artificiality of the objective, projective or questionnaire test, and the bias of the ordinary personality rating. Nevertheless, a number of doubts arise. First, how far can any observer, who has sufficient acquaintance with the child to answer the questions, avoid halo and subjectivity even in underlining such apparently concrete "bits of behaviour"? Dr. Stott provides some evidence of reliability (inter-observer agreement), but other studies of the problem reported in the literature are unpromising. Secondly, it is not easy to follow just why these particular categories were chosen, nor how the items were assigned to one rather than another. Quite legitimately, the author eschews any overall score or quotient for maladjustment, but one would like to know much more about the internal consistency of the categories and their overlapping. Thirdly, while frequency tables for the "School" symptoms are provided, it would be valuable to have something in the nature of norms for each category, and for different age groups. It seems unlikely that the same patterns of normality and abnormality occur in children all the way from 5 to 15 years. However, this type of information can well be collected by the author and others who use the Guides, and we will look forward to future reports. It is unfortunate that the cost, particularly of the Manual, is so high. *

J Child Psychol & Psychiatry 1:249 O '60. R. G. Andry. * In an age when we have become accustomed to tests which are usually easy to administer, to score and to interpret, Dr. Stott's new scales come as a mild shock. At first sight they appear complicated to the layman and over-simplified to the psychometrician, but they are easy to score and deserve to be considered, because they reveal at once the skilful touch of the clinician. * The author ....challenges bravely all those who, in the study of personality theory, demand rigorous quantification, "objectivity" and "proof," pointing out that it is high time that researchers returned sensibly to making factual statements about a person (e.g., whether he reverts to hostility when his need for attention is not met, etc.). The author seems to imply that before we can leap to describing personality in terms of a few "higher order factors," we should first concentrate on isolating many "lower-order" attitudinal trait-factors with more microscopic clinical care than is usual with psychometricians, who often reveal a lack of clinical knowledge. He does not recognize, however, that the function of a psychometrician is different from that of a clinician and that he often considers it his task to advance the behavioural sciences, by enabling people to perceive the uniformities underlying the rich variety of concrete life-situations. The author's sympathy with Tinbergen's theory of instinct is undisguised. At the same time he is far from decrying the need for a quantified or experimental approach. With propriety and insight Dr. Stott merely urges caution at this stage *vis-à-vis* the development of the still-growing plant of psychology. He concludes by advancing a concept of his own which he calls "situation attitude," as contrasted with the constancy of traits in various situations, which is often assumed. Rightly he does not pursue this further in this manual, whose function is to give the background to these interesting and rather skilfully devised inventories. One great lesson seems to emerge from this work: the need for clinician and psychometrician to team up as equal partners in tackling the thorny problem of evolving a theory of personality.

J Consult Psychol 24:99 F '60. Read D. Tuddenham. * a careful attempt to render more objective and precise the observations of teachers, social workers, and foster parents, with respect to children's social adjustment. The *Guides* are intended to save time for the psychologist by providing accounts of behavior more standardized and compact than anecdotal protocols, and more specific than impressionistic ratings. Since the *Guides* encourage accuracy in observing children and provide a system for classifying symptomatic behavior, they have a place also as aids in clinical training. Each *Guide* consists of numerous adjectives and phrases grouped by topic and scrambled as to desirability, though with negative indications in the majority. The observer simply underlines those terms which apply to the child concerned. * Their reliability (interrater agreement) in a preliminary study is given as around .76. More data are needed, but reliability is likely to depend as much upon the raters' skills and opportunities as upon the content of these forms. The validity of each item in differentiating between the stable and the maladjusted is presented, but without cross-validation. Normative data for the interpretation of total scores on each attitude are lacking. This is not a serious omission for American users who will need to develop their own norms anyway. Differences between the English and American languages constitute a more fundamental problem. The author's success in finding meaningful descriptive phrases drawn from the colloquial speech of nurses, teachers, etc., e.g., "spivvish dress," or "feckless," will occasionally create problems of understanding for Americans. Even clinical vocabulary has its differences—e.g., "unforthcomingness" for "shy," or "unsettled" for "mildly maladjusted." Those of us used to the euphemistic polysyllables of "psychopathic deviate" may feel decidedly self-conscious characterizing a child as a "knave." The *Guides,* in summary, will probably not achieve their potential value in this country until someone undertakes to translate them from the authors' English into ours.

Q J Exp Psychol 12:126 My '60. A. W. Heim. * Reliability is remarkably high for this field, correlations between pairs of teachers, for instance, being 0.78 for "unsettled scores" and 0.76 for "maladjusted scores." * Inevitably, a number of criticisms suggest themselves. There is, for instance, too much philosophizing and self-interested history in the Section called "Methodology and Compilation"; there is, also, an infuriating tendency to assume familiarity on the part of the reader with the particular jargon chosen; and certain sections of the Manual suggest that, despite six years' work, publication in this form may be slightly premature. In general, however, the Guides are impressive. Stott and Sykes have tackled a perplexing problem without underestimating its difficulties and without oversimplifying method or interpretation. It is one of the most hopeful attempts yet made in this important field.

[69]

★Cain-Levine Social Competency Scale. Mentally retarded children ages 5–13; 1963; rating scale based upon information obtained from parents; 5 scores: self-help, initiative, social skills, communication, total; 1 form (7 pages); manual (19 pages); mimeographed supplementary data (24 pages); $3.85 per 25 tests; $1 per specimen set; postage extra; supplementary data free on request; Leo F. Cain, Samuel Levine, and Freeman F. Elzey; Consulting Psychologists Press, Inc. *

MARSHALL S. HISKEY, *Professor of Educational Psychology, and Director, Educational Psychological Clinic, University of Nebraska, Lincoln, Nebraska.*

This scale is designed primarily for use with moderately retarded children or those who are frequently referred to as "trainable." Educational goals for such children are usually defined in terms of social competency behaviors. In the past there have been few, if any, specifically designed instruments of evaluation for assessing the development of retarded children. This scale is concerned with evaluation of the extent of development of learned skills which ultimately permit the child to achieve self-sufficiency and socially contributing behaviors. As such it will be welcomed by many who work closely with retarded children.

This scale is based on the assumption that the "child's development of social competency is reflected by" (*a*) "an increase of his manipulative abilities"; (*b*) his "moving from other-directed to self-initiated behavior"; (*c*) his changing "from self-oriented to other-oriented behavior"; and (*d*) an "increased ability to make himself understood." It utilizes four subtests: Self-Help, Initiative, Social Skills, and Communication.

"The Self-Help subscale (SH) is designed to estimate the child's manipulative ability, or motor skills." It is concerned "with motor performance *per se*" on the assumption that "the greater the....manipulative ability, the greater his independence."

The Initiative subscale (I) attempts "to measure the degree to which the child's behavior is self-directed." It assumes that "the child who must be directed to an activity is more dependent than the child who initiates that activity."

"The Social Skills subscale (SS) seeks to assess the degree to which the child engages in interpersonal relationships with other children and adults." It is hypothesized that "the more able a child is in relating to others and participating in group situations, the greater his independence."

"The Communication subscale (C) is designed to measure the degree to which a child makes himself understood." It is utilized on the assumption that "the child who makes his wants known is more independent than the child who does not."

Each of the 44 activities listed in the scale is followed by four or five descriptive statements which represent varying degrees of independence. They are printed in an expendable booklet with the items grouped by content rather than by subscale. Percentile ratings are available for each subtest and for the total social competency score.

The standardizing group consisted of 716 trainable mentally retarded children (414 males and 302 females) in the state of California. The subjects had intelligence quotients ranging from 25 through 59 with mental ages 2 through 7 and chronological ages 5 through 13. Tables for chronological ages 5 through 13 permit the user to determine a child's percentile rank relative to his age group. With the exception of the five year level, norms are listed at two year intervals, since mentally retarded children change and progress so slowly.

It should be emphasized that this is a *rating* device and not a scale that is administered directly to the child. The social competency rating is obtained by conducting an interview to determine the habitual or typical performance of the child in regard to each of the items. Since the items are social competency behaviors which are explicitly observable in the home it is suggested that the best respondent is usually the mother or the house parent. However, most of the behaviors are observable in the special class or school and may be rated by the teacher(s) for school evaluation purposes.

Validity of this instrument is based on the criteria of expert judges and an item analysis after tryout. Test-retest reliability coefficients were obtained by re-rating a random sample of 35 subjects after an interval of three weeks. The coefficients vary from .88 to .97 for the subscales, with the "total" listed as .98. Whereas these approaches to validity and reliability are appropriate under the circumstances, it must be recognized that they can be affected by the inconsistencies within the respondent or among respondents. Thus validity and reliability quotations should be accepted tentatively until more rigorous approaches can be utilized.

The manual is rather complete and the material is well presented. Part 2 gives a good word description of the derivation of the scale and the tables summarize the most important statistical information; further statistical data on individual items are available without charge from the publisher. Part 1 of the manual is concerned with the utilization of the scale and lists some very important considerations and cautions concerning respondents and the interviewing procedure. Since the interviewer does *not* read the description statements to the respondent the manual would be of even greater value to the user had it included some further examples of the general questions which could be utilized with each item.

It is unfortunate that the title of the scale does not make known that the scale is to be used with retarded children, or, even better yet, with the moderately retarded (trainable). Whereas the scale can show the status of any child in relation to the skills sampled, the percentile norms are established on children in the 25–59 IQ range. If utilized with a child with an intelligence quotient of 75 or 80, the percentile ratings could present a very distorted evaluation of the individual. One cannot assume that a scale such as this one will be employed only by individuals who are sufficiently sophisticated to avoid such pitfalls.

Perhaps the greatest value of this scale rests in the evaluation or recognition of the progress of the individual, rather than the possibility of comparing him with others. Likewise, it provides a limited method for identifying more specifically a child's tendency to improve somewhat rapidly in one area while showing little or no gain in another. Since these children progress so slowly, teachers and parents often become discouraged if positive changes are not identified.

The percentile ranks have specific advantages also. One can compare the child with other trainable children of his age in terms of overall social competence and also his relative status on each subscale. Such information can be helpful in grouping children and in planning future training for the individual. From a research standpoint the scale can be quite useful.

In summary, this scale is a much needed and useful instrument in the area of mental retardation. It is one of a very few attempts at a "standardization" on a group that is intellectually deficient. In the hands of a specially trained (professional) individual, it can provide pertinent and worthwhile information to parents, teachers, and researchers. As a new instrument and one which uses respondents to obtain the resulting ratings, it is in need of well designed follow-up studies relative to respondent variables.

[70]

★**The California Medical Survey (CMS).** Medical patients ages 10–18, adults; 1962; checklist of medical and psychological information; 18–23 scores: chronicity of illness, emotional conditions, familial background, basic medical information, psychiatric symptoms, specific disorder, medical background, genito-urinary, neuro-mus-skeletal, cardio-vas-blood, sensory, digestive, respiratory, 5 gynecologic scores

(Form W only), anxiety-stress, psychiatric, habits-traits, sexual-social, energy level; 2 levels; summary sheet (1 page); mimeographed manual (9 pages); no data on reliability and validity; no norms; $3 per 10 tests; $5 per 30 summary sheets; $2 per manual; postpaid; specimen set not available; (10–20) minutes; Harold L. Snow and Morse P. Manson; Western Psychological Services. *

a) CHILDREN'S FORM. Ages 10–18; Form C (4 pages).
b) ADULT FORMS. Adults; Forms M (for men), W (for women), (6 pages).

[71]

California Psychological Inventory. Ages 13 and over; 1956–60; 18 scores: dominance (Do), capacity for status (Ca), sociability (Sy), social presence (Sp), self-acceptance (Sa), sense of well-being (Wb), responsibility (Re), socialization (So), self-control (Sc), tolerance (To), good impression (Gi), communality (Cm), achievement via conformance (Ac), achievement via independence (Ai), intellectual efficiency (Ie), psychological-mindedness (Py), flexibility (Fx), femininity (Fe); IBM and NCS; 1 form ('56, 12 pages); manual ("re-issued 1960," c1957, 39 pages, same as earlier 1957 manual except for some omissions and additions of validity data); administrator's guide ('57, 15 pages, reprinted from manual); profiles ['57, 2 pages]; separate answer sheets must be used; $9.75 per counselor's kit of 5 tests, 25 hand scored answer sheets, 25 profiles, set of stencils, and manual; $6.25 per 25 tests; $3.75 per 50 sets of profiles and either hand scored or IBM answer sheets; $4.50 per set of hand scoring stencils; $6 per set of IBM scoring stencils; $3.25 per 50 NCS answer sheets (scored by National Computer Systems only, see 671); 75¢ per administrator's guide; $3 per manual; $1 per specimen set (includes abstract of manual); postage extra; scoring service available; Italian, French, and German editions available; (45–60) minutes; Harrison G. Gough; Consulting Psychologists Press, Inc. *

REFERENCES

1–33. See 5:37.
34. BARRON, FRANK. "The Disposition Toward Originality." *J Abn & Social Psychol* 51:478–85 N '55. * (*PA* 31:2533)
34a. HOLMEN, MILTON G.; KATTER, ROBERT V.; JONES, ANNE M.; AND RICHARDSON, IRVING F. "An Assessment Program for OCS Applicants." *HumRRO Tech Rep* 26:1–50 F '56. * (*PA* 31:8957)
35. GOWAN, J. C. "A Summary of the Intensive Study of Twenty Highly Selected Elementary Women Teachers." *J Exp Ed* 26:115–24 D '57. * (*PA* 33:4731)
36. HEUSINKVELD, EDWIN D. *A Study of the Relationship of Certain Scores on the California Psychological Inventory to Student Adjustment in a College Dormitory.* Master's thesis, State University of Iowa (Iowa City, Iowa), 1957.
37. JOHNSTON, ROY PAUL. *The Isolation of Social Personality Dimensions Through a Factor Analysis of the California Psychological Inventory.* Doctor's thesis, University of North Carolina (Chapel Hill, N.C.), 1957.
38. SANFORD, NEVITT; WEBSTER, HAROLD; AND FREEDMAN, MERVIN. "Impulse Expression as a Variable of Personality." *Psychol Monogr* 71(11):1–21 '57. * (*PA* 33:3336)
39. COULSON, ROGER WAYNE. *Relationships Among Personality Traits, Ability and Academic Efficiency of College Seniors.* Doctor's thesis, State University of Iowa (Iowa City, Iowa), 1958. (*DA* 19:1647)
40. DINITZ, SIMON; RECKLESS, WALTER C.; AND KAY, BARBARA. "A Self Gradient Among Potential Delinquents." *J Crim Law & Criminol* 49:230–3 S–O '58. * (*PA* 33:10646)
41. KELLY, E. LOWELL; MILLER, JAMES G.; MARQUIS, DONALD G.; GERARD, R. W.; AND UHR, LEONARD. "Personality Differences and Continued Meprobamate and Proclorperazine Administration." *A.M.A. Arch Neurol & Psychiatry* 80:241–6 Ag '58. * (*PA* 33:10420)
42. BENDIG, A. W. "Personality Variables Related to Individual Performance on a Cognitive Task." *J General Psychol* 60:265–8 Ap '59. * (*PA* 36:2HJ65B)
43. BRENGELMANN, J. C. "Differences in Questionnaire Responses Between English and German Nationals." *Acta Psychologica* 16(5):339–55 '59. * (*PA* 34:5788)
44. COHEN, LEONARD MARLIN. *The Relationship Between Certain Personality Variables and Prior Occupational Stability of Prison Inmates.* Doctor's thesis, Temple University (Philadelphia, Pa.), 1959. (*DA* 20:3375)
45. HOLLAND, JOHN L. "The Prediction of College Grades From the California Psychological Inventory and the Scholastic Aptitude Test." *J Ed Psychol* 50:135–42 Ag '59. * (*PA* 35:2796)
46. KEOGH, JACK. "Relationship of Motor Ability and Athletic Participation in Certain Standardized Personality Measures." *Res Q* 30:438–45 D '59. * (*PA* 35:4989)
47. KOENIG, KATHRYN, AND MCKEACHIE, W. J. "Personality and Independent Study." *J Ed Psychol* 50:132–4 Je '59. * (*PA* 35:1201)
48. MERRIMAN, J. BURTON. *The Relationship of Personality Traits to Motor Ability.* Doctor's thesis, State University of Iowa (Iowa City, Iowa), 1959. (*DA* 20:950)
49. OBST, FRANCES. "A Study of Selected Psychometric Characteristics of Home Economics and Non-Home Economics Women at the University of California, Los Angeles." *Calif J Ed Res* 10:180–4+ S '59. * (*PA* 34:7957)
50. TUDDENHAM, READ D. "Correlates of Yielding to a Distorted Group Norm." *J Personality* 27:272–84 Je '59. * (*PA* 34:4096)
51. WHITLOCK, GLENN EVERETT. *The Relationship Between Passivity of Personality and Personal Factors Related to the Choice of the Ministry as a Vocation.* Doctor's thesis, University of Southern California (Los Angeles, Calif.), 1959. (*DA* 20:2392)
52. ZEDEK, MEIRA E. "The Conditioning of Verbal Behavior With Negative Cultural Connotations." *J Personality* 27:477–86 D '59. *
53. BARNES, TED JOHN. *An Investigation of the Relationships Between Certain Personality Traits and Elements of Speaking Effectiveness.* Doctor's thesis, State University of Iowa (Iowa City, Iowa), 1960. (*DA* 20:4750)
54. BAY, JUNG HONG. *The Validity of Two Objective Measures of Academic Motivation.* Doctor's thesis, State University of Iowa (Iowa City, Iowa), 1960. (*DA* 20:4585)
55. BLOCK, JACK. "Commonality in Word Association and Personality." *Psychol Rep* 7:332 O '60. * (*PA* 35:2202)
56. BOGARD, HOWARD M. "Union and Management Trainees—A Comparative Study of Personality and Occupational Choice." *J Appl Psychol* 44:56–63 F '60. * (*PA* 34:7496)
57. DICKEN, CHARLES F. "Simulated Patterns on the California Psychological Inventory." *J Counsel Psychol* 7:24–31 sp '60. * (*PA* 35:2218)
58. GOUGH, HARRISON G. "Theory and Measurement of Socialization." *J Consult Psychol* 24:23–30 F '60. * (*PA* 34:7554)
59. GOWAN, JOHN C. "Intercorrelations of the California Psychological Inventory and the Guilford-Zimmerman Temperament Survey With Intelligence as Measured by the ACE." *Calif J Ed Res* 11:213–5 N '60. * (*PA* 35:4856)
60. HILL, ROBERT E., JR. "Dichotomous Prediction of Student Teaching Excellence Employing Selected CPI Scales." *J Ed Res* 53:349–51 My '60. *
61. HILLS, DAVID ALLEN. *The California Personality Inventory Flexibility Scale, Motivation Instructions, and Some Measures of Behavioral Rigidity.* Doctor's thesis, State University of Iowa (Iowa City, Iowa), 1960. (*DA* 21:2003)
62. JACKSON, DOUGLAS N. "Stylistic Response Determinants in the California Psychological Inventory." *Ed & Psychol Meas* 20:339–46 su '60. * (*PA* 35:6420)
63. KEIMOWITZ, ROBERT I., AND ANSBACHER, HEINZ L. "Personality and Achievement in Mathematics." *J Indiv Psychol* 16:84–7 My '60. * (*PA* 34:7392)
64. MAXWELL, MARTHA JANE. *An Analysis of the California Psychological Inventory and the American Council on Education Psychological Test as Predictors of Success in Different College Curricula.* Doctor's thesis, University of Maryland (College Park, Md.), 1960. (*DA* 21:549)
65. MERRIMAN, J. BURTON. "Relationship of Personality Traits to Motor Ability." *Res Q* 31:163–73 My '60. * (*PA* 36:1HA63M)
66. MITCHELL, JAMES V., JR., AND PIERCE-JONES, JOHN. "A Factor Analysis of Gough's California Psychological Inventory." *J Consult Psychol* 24:453–6 O '60. * (*PA* 35:4893)
67. SIMPSON, JON E.; DINITZ, SIMON; KAY, BARBARA; AND RECKLESS, WALTER C. "Delinquency Potential of Pre-Adolescents in High-Delinquency Areas." *Brit J Delinq* 10:211–5 Ja '60. *
68. VINCENT, CLARK E. "Unwed Mothers and the Adoption Market: Psychological and Familial Factors." *Marriage & Family Living* 22:112–8 My '60. *
69. BARNETTE, W. LESLIE, JR. "A Structured and a Semi-Structured Achievement Measure Applied to a College Sample." *Ed & Psychol Meas* 21:647–56 au '61. * (*PA* 36:4KL47B)
70. CRITES, JOHN O.; BECHTOLDT, HAROLD P.; GOODSTEIN, LEONARD D.; AND HEILBRUN, ALFRED B., JR. "A Factor Analysis of the California Psychological Inventory." *J Appl Psychol* 45:408–14 D '61. * (*PA* 37:1192)
71. DICKEN, CHARLES F. "Note on Biserial Correlation and the Validity of the California Personality Inventory." *J Counsel Psychol* 8:185–6 su '61. * (*PA* 36:3HC85D)
72. GOODSTEIN, LEONARD D.; CRITES, JOHN O.; HEILBRUN, ALFRED B., JR.; AND REMPEL, PETER P. "The Use of the California Psychological Inventory in a University Counseling

Service." *J Counsel Psychol* 8:147–53 su '61. * (*PA* 36: 3KI47G)
73. HEILBRUN, ALFRED B., JR. "Male and Female Personality Correlates of Early Termination in Counseling." *J Counsel Psychol* 8:31–6 sp '61. * (*PA* 36:3KI31H)
74. HILL, ROBERT E., JR. "An Investigation of the California Psychological Inventory Empirically Keyed for Dichotomous Prediction of Student Teacher Excellence." *Yearb Nat Council Meas Ed* 18:107–9 '61. *
75. HUNT, JAMES G. *A Study of Nonintellectual Factors Related to Academic Achievement Among College Seniors at Ball State Teachers College.* Doctor's thesis, Purdue University (Lafayette, Ind.), 1961. (*DA* 22:157)
76. JACKSON, DOUGLAS N., AND PACINE, LEONARD. "Response Styles and Academic Achievement." *Ed & Psychol Meas* 21:1015–28 w '61. *
77. LESSINGER, LEON M., AND MARTINSON, RUTH A. "The Use of the California Psychological Inventory With Gifted Pupils." *Personnel & Guid J* 39:572–5 Mr '61. * (*PA* 35: 7201)
78. MCKEE, JOHN P., AND TURNER, WALTER S. "The Relationship of 'Drive' Ratings in Adolescence to CPI and EPPS Scores in Adulthood." *Vita Hum* 4(1–2):1–14 '61. * (*PA* 36:1HF01M)
79. MAHONEY, THOMAS A.; JERDEE, THOMAS H.; AND NASH, ALLAN N. *The Identification of Management Potential: A Research Approach to Management Development.* Dubuque, Iowa: Wm. C. Brown Co., 1961. Pp. xiii, 79. *
80. MERRITT, MYRTLE AGNES. *The Relationship of Selected Physical, Mental, Emotional and Social Factors to the Recreational Preferences of College Women.* Doctor's thesis, State University of Iowa (Iowa City, Iowa), 1961. (*DA* 22:2675)
81. MUSSEN, PAUL. "Some Antecedents and Consequents of Masculine Sex-Typing in Adolescent Boys." *Psychol Monogr* 75(2):1–24 '61. * (*PA* 36:3FH24M)
82. NUGENT, FRANK A. "The Relationship of Discrepancies Between Interest and Aptitude Scores to Other Selected Personality Variables." *Personnel & Guid J* 39:388–95 Ja '61. * (*PA* 35:6212)
83. PIERCE, JAMES V. "Personality and Achievement Among Able High School Boys." *J Indiv Psychol* 17:102–7 My '61. * (*PA* 36:1KL02P)
84. RIGNEY, FRANCIS J., AND SMITH, L. DOUGLAS. *The Real Bohemia: A Sociological and Psychological Study of the "Beats."* New York: Basic Books, Inc., 1961. Pp. xxi, 250. * (*PA* 36:1GB50R)
85. SIEGMAN, ARON WOLFE. "A Cross-Cultural Investigation of the Relationship Between Ethnic Prejudice, Authoritarian Ideology, and Personality." *J Abn & Social Psychol* 63:654–5 N '61. * (*PA* 37:1085)
86. WEINBERG, NORRIS; MENDELSON, MYER; AND STUNKARD, ALBERT. "A Failure to Find Distinctive Personality Features in a Group of Obese Men." *Am J Psychiatry* 117:1035–7 My '61. *
87. CERBUS, GEORGE, AND NICHOLS, ROBERT C. "Personality Correlates of Picture Preferences." *J Abn & Social Psychol* 64:75–8 Ja '62. * (*PA* 37:3139)
88. CLARK, HOWARD GATES. *Prediction of Teacher and Peer Group Concepts of Ninth Grade High School Students With the California Psychological Inventory.* Doctor's research study No. 1, Colorado State College (Greeley, Colo.), 1962. (*DA* 23:3769)
88a. COBB, BART B. "Problems in Air Traffic Management: 2, Prediction of Success in Air Traffic Controller School." *Aerospace Med* 33:702–13 Je '62. *
88b. DATEL, WILLIAM E. "Socialization Scale Norms on Military Samples." *Mil Med* 127:740–4 S '62. *
89. DINITZ, SIMON; SCARPITTI, FRANK R.; AND RECKLESS, WALTER C. "Delinquency Vulnerability: A Cross Group and Longitudinal Analysis." *Am Sociol R* 27:515–7 Ag '62. * (*PA* 37:5447)
90. ENGEL, ILONA MARIA. *A Factor Analytic Study of Items From Five Masculinity-Femininity Tests.* Doctor's thesis, University of Michigan (Ann Arbor, Mich.), 1962. (*DA* 23:307)
91. FINK, MARTIN B. "Objectification of Data Used in Underachievement-Self Concept Study." *Calif J Ed Res* 13:105–12 My '62. * (*PA* 37:3883)
92. FOX, RONALD ERNEST. *Personality Patterns of Resident Psychotherapists.* Doctor's thesis, University of North Carolina (Chapel Hill, N.C.), 1962. (*DA* 23:4743)
93. GILMORE, SUSAN KAY. *A Study of Differences in Personality Patterns Between Pentecostal Groups of Differential Religious Emphases.* Master's thesis, University of Oregon (Eugene, Ore.), 1962. (*MA* 1:57)
94. HEILBRUN, ALFRED B., JR. "Psychological Factors Related to Counseling Readiness and Implications for Counselor Behavior." *J Counsel Psychol* 9:353–8 w '62. * (*PA* 39:2298)
95. HEILBRUN, ALFRED B., JR.; DANIEL, JOHN L.; GOODSTEIN, LEONARD D.; STEPHENSON, RICHARD R.; AND CRITES, JOHN O. "The Validity of Two-Scale Pattern Interpretation on the California Psychological Inventory." *J Appl Psychol* 46:409–16 D '62. * (*PA* 37:5637)
96. HILGARD, ERNEST R., AND LAUER, LILLIAN W. "Lack of Correlation Between the California Psychological Inventory and Hypnotic Susceptibility." *J Consult Psychol* 26: 331–5 Ag '62. * (*PA* 38:4432)
97. HIRT, MICHAEL L., AND COOK, RICHARD A. "Effectiveness of the California Psychological Inventory to Predict Psychiatric Determinations of Socialization." *J Clin Psychol* 18:176–7 Ap '62. * (*PA* 38:8519)
98. HOLLAND, JOHN L., AND ASTIN, ALEXANDER W. "The Prediction of the Academic, Artistic, Scientific, and Social Achievement of Undergraduates of Superior Scholastic Aptitude." *J Ed Psychol* 53:132–43 Je '62. * (*PA* 37:2010)
99. JOHNSON, RICHARD T., AND FRANDSEN, ARDEN N. "The California Psychological Inventory Profile of Student Leaders." *Personnel & Guid J* 41:343–5 D '62. * (*PA* 37:6624)
99a. KALIS, BETTY L.; TOCCHINI, JOHN J.; AND THOMASSEN, PAUL R. "Correlation Study Between Personality Tests and Dental Student Performance." *J Am Dental Assn* 64:656–70 My '62. *
100. KORMAN, MAURICE. "A Factorial Study of Judgmental Space." *Psychol Rep* 10:739–46 Je '62. * (*PA* 37:5651)
101. KORN, HAROLD A. "Differences Between Majors in Engineering and Physical Sciences on CPI and SVIB Scores." *J Counsel Psychol* 9:306–12 w '62. * (*PA* 39:2870)
102. LANIER, WILLIAM JETT. *The Predictive Value of Selected Personality and College Adjustment Instruments Used With the American College Testing Program.* Doctor's thesis, Purdue University (Lafayette, Ind.), 1962. (*DA* 23:2424)
103. LETON, DONALD A. "Personality Ratings of High School Students." *J Ed Res* 56:160–3 N '62. *
104. LETON, DONALD A., AND WALTER, SIDNEY. "A Factor Analysis of the California Psychological Inventory and Minnesota Counseling Inventory." *Calif J Ed Res* 13:126–33 My '62. * (*PA* 37:3446)
105. MACKINNON, DONALD W. "The Personality Correlates of Creativity: A Study of American Architects," pp. 11–39. (*PA* 37:4958) In *Personality Research.* Proceedings of the XIV International Congress of Applied Psychology, Vol. 2. Copenhagen, Denmark: Munksgaard, Ltd., 1962. Pp. 229. *
106. MILBRATH, LESTER W., AND KLEIN, WALTER W. "Personality Correlates of Political Participation." *Acta Sociologica* 6(1–2):53–66 '62. *
107. NELSON, JOHN ANDREWS, JR. *The California Psychological Inventory as a Predictor of the Behavior of the Secondary Student Teacher While Teaching.* Doctor's thesis, University of California (Berkeley, Calif.), 1962.
108. NICHOLS, ROBERT C. "Subtle, Obvious and Stereotype Measures of Masculinity-Femininity." *Ed & Psychol Meas* 22:449–61 au '62. * (*PA* 37:5014)
109. PIERCE-JONES, JOHN; MITCHELL, JAMES V., JR.; AND KING, F. J. "Configurational Invariance in the California Psychological Inventory." *J Exp Ed* 31:65–71 S '62. * (*PA* 37:8012)
110. PUMROY, DONALD K. "Relationship Between the Social Desirability Scale and the California Psychological Inventory." *Psychol Rep* 10:795–6 Je '62. * (*PA* 37:5015)
111. ROSENBERG, LEON A. "Idealization of Self and Social Adjustment." Abstract. *J Consult Psychol* 26:487 O '62. *
112. ROSENBERG, LEON A.; MCHENRY, THOMAS B.; ROSENBERG, ANNA MARIA; AND NICHOLS, ROBERT C. "The Prediction of Academic Achievement With the California Psychological Inventory." *J Appl Psychol* 46:385–8 D '62. * (*PA* 37:5670)
113. ROSENHAN, DAVID. "Naysaying and the California Psychological Inventory." *J Consult Psychol* 26:382–3 Ag '62. * (*PA* 38:4314)
114. SIEGMAN, ARON WOLFE. "Personality Variables Associated With Admitted Criminal Behavior." Abstract. *J Consult Psychol* 26:199 Ap '62. * (*PA* 37:5459)
115. STEWART, LOUIS H. "Social and Emotional Adjustment During Adolescence as Related to the Development of Psychosomatic Illness in Adulthood." *Genetic Psychol Monogr* 65:175–215 F '62. *
116. STRUMPFER, DEODANDUS J. W., AND NICHOLS, ROBERT C. "A Study of Some Communicable Measures for the Evaluation of Human Figure Drawings." *J Proj Tech* 26:342–53 S '62. * (*PA* 37:3240)
117. WINKELMAN, SIDRA LEVI. *California Psychological Inventory Profile Patterns of Underachievers, Average Achievers, and Overachievers.* Doctor's thesis, University of Maryland (College Park, Md.), 1962. (*DA* 23:2988)
118. YOUNG, CHARLES RAY. *Factors Associated With Achievement and Underachievement Among Intellectually Superior Boys.* Doctor's thesis, University of Missouri (Columbia, Mo.), 1962. (*DA* 23:2406)
119. AIKEN, LEWIS R., JR. "The Relationships of Dress to Selected Measures of Personality in Undergraduate Women." *J Social Psychol* 59:119–28 F '63. * (*PA* 38:910)
120. ALLER, FLORENCE D. "Some Factors in Marital Adjustment and Academic Achievement of Married Students." *Personnel & Guid J* 41:609–16 Mr '63. *
121. APPLEY, MORTIMER H., AND MOELLER, GEORGE. "Conforming Behavior and Personality Variables in College Women." *J Abn & Social Psychol* 66:284–90 Mr '63. * (*PA* 37:8237)
122. CANTER, FRANCIS M. "Simulation on the California Psychological Inventory and the Adjustment of the Simulator." *J Consult Psychol* 27:253–6 Je '63. * (*PA* 38:992)
123. CAPLAN, STANLEY W.; RUBLE, RONALD A.; AND SEGEL, DAVID. "A Theory of Educational and Vocational Choice in Junior High School." *Personnel & Guid J* 42:129–35 O '63. *

124. CAPRETTA, PATRICK J.; JONES, REGINALD L.; SIEGEL, LAURENCE; AND SIEGEL, LILA C. "Some Noncognitive Characteristics of Honors Program Candidates." *J Ed Psychol* 54:268–76 O '63. * (*PA* 38:4674)
124a. CARNEY, RICHARD E., AND MCKEACHIE, WILBERT J. "Religion, Sex, Social Class, Probability of Success, and Student Personality." *J Sci Study Relig* 3:32–42 f '63. *
125. COROTTO, LOREN V. "An Exploratory Study of the Personality Characteristics of Alcohol Patients Who Volunteer for Continued Treatment." *Q J Studies Alcohol* 24:432–42 S '63. *
126. DAHLKE, ARNOLD E., AND DANA, RICHARD H. "Intraindividual Verbal-Numerical Discrepancies and Personality." Abstract. *J Consult Psychol* 27:182 Ap '63. *
127. DICKEN, CHARLES. "Good Impression, Social Desirability, and Acquiescence as Suppressor Variables." *Ed & Psychol Meas* 23:699–720 w '63. * (*PA* 38:8516)
128. DICKEN, CHARLES F. "Convergent and Discriminant Validity of the California Psychological Inventory." *Ed & Psychol Meas* 23:449–59 au '63. * (*PA* 38:6090)
129. DURFLINGER, GLENN W. "Academic and Personality Differences Between Women Students Who Do Complete the Elementary Teaching Credential Program and Those Who Do Not." *Ed & Psychol Meas* 23:775–83 w '63. *
130. DURFLINGER, GLENN W. "Personality Correlates of Success in Student-Teaching." *Ed & Psychol Meas* 23:383–90 su '63. * (*PA* 38:1427)
131. FINK, MARTIN. "Cross Validation of an Underachievement Scale." *Calif J Ed Res* 14:147–52 S '63. * (*PA* 38:6642)
132. GOODSTEIN, LEONARD D., AND SCHRADER, WILLIAM J. "An Empirically-Derived Managerial Key for the California Psychological Inventory." *J Appl Psychol* 47:42–5 F '63. * (*PA* 37:8352)
133. KIRK, BARBARA A.; CUMMINGS, ROGER W.; AND HACKETT, HERBERT R. "Personal and Vocational Characteristics of Dental Students." *Personnel & Guid J* 41:522–7 F '63. *
134. KNAPP, ROBERT R. "Personality Correlates of Delinquency Rate in a Navy Sample." *J Appl Psychol* 47:68–71 F '63. * (*PA* 37:8179)
135. MITCHELL, JAMES V., JR. "A Comparison of the First and Second Order Dimensions of the 16 PF and CPI Inventories." *J Social Psychol* 61:151–66 O '63. * (*PA* 38:8499)
136. NICHOLS, ROBERT C., AND SCHNELL, RICHARD R. "Factor Scales for the California Psychological Inventory." *J Consult Psychol* 27:228–35 Je '63. * (*PA* 38:961)
137. PODELL, HARRIETT A. "Note on Successive Dimensional Analysis Applied to Affective, Cognitive, and Personality Traits." *Psychol Rep* 13:813–4 D '63. * (*PA* 38:8503)
138. SHURE, GERALD H., AND ROGERS, MILES S. "Personality Factor Stability for Three Ability Levels." *J Psychol* 55:445–56 Ap '63. * (*PA* 38:1001)
139. SILVERMAN, PAUL L. "Some Personality Correlates of Attributive Projection." *Percept & Motor Skills* 17:947–53 D '63. * (*PA* 38:6131)
140. SPRINGOB, H. KARL. "Relationship of Interests as Measured by the Kuder Preference Record to Personality as Measured by the California Psychological Inventory Scales." *Personnel & Guid J* 41:624–8 Mr '63. * (*PA* 39:1760)
141. STEWART, CHARLES ALLEN, JR. *Prediction of Academic Success in Selected United States Army Medical Field Service School Courses.* Doctor's thesis, University of Texas (Austin, Tex.), 1963. (*DA* 24:597)
142. TONRA, MARY FIDELIS. *Differentiation Between a Female Delinquent and a Female Non-Delinquent Group on the Socialization Scale of the California Psychological Inventory.* Master's thesis, Fordham University (New York, N.Y.), 1963.
143. WEBB, ALLEN P. "Sex-Role Preferences and Adjustment in Early Adolescents." *Child Develop* 34:609–18 S '63. *
144. WHITLOCK, GLENN E. "Role and Self Concepts in the Choice of the Ministry as a Vocation." *J Pastoral Care* 17:208–12 w '63. * (*PA* 38:9350)

E. LOWELL KELLY, *Professor of Psychology, The University of Michigan, Ann Arbor, Michigan.*

The CPI, as it is now widely known, was developed to make possible the comprehensive, multidimensional assessment of normal persons in a variety of settings. The resulting inventory, composed of 480 statements, is essentially self-administering for literate subjects who are instructed to respond to each item on a separate answer sheet, "True" or "False" according to whether they agree or disagree with a statement or feel that "it is" or "is not" true about them. Three types of answer sheets are available: one for hand scoring and two for machine scoring.

The inventory yields 18 raw scores; transferring them to a profile form provides for graphic conversion to standard scores with mean 50 and SD 10. The norms on one side of the profile sheet are based on over 6,000 males and those on the reverse side on over 7,000 female cases. While the author does not claim that these normative groups represent a random sample of the general population, he states that they include a wide range of ages, socioeconomic groups, and geographical areas.

In addition to these separate norms for males and females, the manual presents separate mean profiles for college and high school subjects of each sex. The manual also includes totals showing the raw score means and standard deviations of 30 special groups (19 male and 11 female) for each of the 18 scores.

As noted above, the inventory yields 18 scores: 11 of these are based on empirically derived scoring weights assigned to responses found to differentiate defined criterion groups; four of the scores are based on weights originally judged by the author as indicating the presence of a designated variable and refined by internal consistency analysis. The remaining three scores were also derived empirically to detect tendencies of subjects to fake (good or bad) or to respond in a manner which makes the other scores of doubtful validity.

The number of items contributing to the 18 scores varies from 22 to 56 (median = 37). Test-retest reliabilities based on 200 male prisoners retested after one to three weeks range from .49 to .87 with a median of .80. For high school subjects tested after one year, the median test-retest correlation is .65 for males and .68 for females. The manual does not report any reliability estimates based on a single administration, but presumably these would be higher than the test-retest consistency coefficients noted above, and hence sufficiently high for both group and individual use.

How many and what psychological variables are assessed by the CPI? According to the manual, there are 18 different characteristics, each with a name, and for each the author presents some evidence for some validity. For example, the first scale is called Dominance, abbreviated Do. Scoring weights for this scale were empirically determined on the basis of differential responses of high school students nominated as "most" and "least" dominant by their principals. In cross-validational samples, students nominated "most dominant" tend to score about one standard deviation higher than those nominated as "least dominant." The difference is significant at the .01 level for both boys and girls. Furthermore, Do scores were found to correlate .48 and .40 with staff ratings of dominance in two different assessment studies.

Similar evidence is presented for each of the 11 scales based on empirically derived response weights of contrasting groups. While the discrimination of extreme groups is less sharp than one might expect, and while one may not always agree with the author in his choice of name for the psychological continuum underlying certain of these scales, there is convincing evidence that each of the scales has some validity when judged against life performance criteria. This is true even for the scales developed on the basis of *a priori* weights and then refined through item analysis (internal consistency). Thus, Self-Acceptance (Sa) scores significantly differentiate between high school students rated as high and low on self-acceptance, and correlate positively (.32) with assessment staff ratings of "self-acceptance," negatively (−.57) with staff Q-sorting of the phrase, "Has a readiness to feel guilty."

Additional evidence of the functional validity of each of the scales is provided by a list of the adjectives indicating the way in which persons scoring high and low on each of the scales are seen by assessment staff members or peers in an assessment program. Thus even for Communality (Cm), based on the modal response to only 28 items and one of the least reliable of the 18 scales, high scoring persons are seen as "Dependable, moderate, tactful, reliable, sincere, patient, steady, and realistic; as being honest, conscientious; and as having common sense and good judgment." Low scorers, on the other hand, are seen as: "Impatient, changeable, complicated, imaginative, disorderly, nervous, restless, and confused; as being guileful and deceitful; inattentive and forgetful; and as having internal conflicts and problems."

Similarly, extensive lists of adjectives are provided to characterize the high and low ends of each of the 18 scales. These lists combined with the critical ratios showing the ability of each set of scores to differentiate between extreme groups gives the impression that the CPI measures a very large number of important personality variables. A crucial question, of course, is how many? The author does not imply that the 18 dimensions are independent but groups them into four categories as follows: (*a*) "Measures of Poise, Ascendancy, and Self-Assurance" (Do, Cs, Sy, Sp, Sa, and Wb); (*b*) "Measures of Socialization, Maturity, and Responsibility" (Re, So, Sc, To, Gi, and Cm); (*c*) "Measures of Achievement Potential and Intellectual Efficiency" (Ac, Ai, and Ie); and (*d*) "Measures of Intellectual and Interest Modes" (Py, Fx, and Fe).

Two factor analytic studies (*66, 70*) both indicate that most of the information contained in the 18 scores could be reflected in 4 or 5 scores. More important, both for users of the instrument and as indication of the hazards of not paying enough attention to the intercorrelations of the scales as reported in the manual, these studies both point to probably incorrect locations of certain of the scales in the author's classification. For example, for reasons which are not clear, Gough groups Wb (Sense of Well-being) in class (*a*) above and Ac (Achievement via Conformance) in class (*c*) even though his own data show that these two scales are intercorrelated to the extent of .58 for men and .66 for women and that both are more highly correlated with class (*b*) scales than with class (*a*) or (*c*) scales. The author was apparently more confident of his theorizing than of his empirical data!

Like most test authors, Gough tends to be somewhat more enthusiastic about and confident of the validity of his instrument than is justified by the evidence available. For example, the manual suggests that in interpretation, considerable weight be given to "interactions among scales," to patterns of profiles, and to "internal variability of the profile." While a logical case can be made for the probable validity of such interpretational inferences, the only evidence presented is a series of profile analyses of individual cases.

All in all, however, the CPI in this reviewer's opinion is one of the best, if not the best, available instruments of its kind. It was developed on the basis of a series of empirical studies and the evidence for the validity of its several scales is extensive. The manual is one of the most complete of any available and "wonders of wonders" reports intercorrelations of CPI scores with those of several other widely used tests of personality. Unfortunately, these data suggest that the CPI does not yield nearly as much information nor such unique information as the CPI scale names would imply. For example, about half of the 18 CPI scales correlate .50 or higher with scores on Bernreuter's *Personality Inventory* first published in 1931. By contrast, however, the intercorrelations of CPI and MMPI scales tend to be quite low in spite of the fact that the two inventories have some 200 items in common. Perhaps it is too much to ask of any test author or publisher, but this reviewer regrets that the manual does not indicate the correlation of the CPI scores with those derived from the most similar (and competitive!) inventories which also purport to yield a multidimensional profile of the normal personality albeit utilizing markedly different trait or factor labels.

The degree of professional acceptance of the CPI and its impact on personality research is reflected in the large number of references which have appeared since the last edition of the MMY.

For reviews by Lee J. Cronbach and Robert L. Thorndike, see 5:37 (1 excerpt).

[72]

★The California Q-Set: A Q-Sort for Personality Assessment and Psychiatric Research. Adults; 1961; observer ratings; Form 3 (110 cards); manual (166 pages, see *1* below); record sheet (1 page); $8.75 per set of cards and manual; $2.25 per set of cards; $1.75 per 25 record sheets; $6.75 per manual; postage extra; administration time not reported; Jack Block; distributed by Consulting Psychologists Press, Inc. *

REFERENCES

1. BLOCK, JACK. *The Q-Sort Method in Personality Assessment and Psychiatric Research.* Springfield, Ill.: Charles C Thomas, Publisher, 1961. Pp. ix, 161. * (*PA* 36:5HE61B)
2. MACKINNON, DONALD W. "The Personality Correlates of Creativity: A Study of American Architects," pp. 11-39. (*PA* 37:4958) In *Personality Research.* Proceedings of the XIV International Congress of Applied Psychology, Vol. 2. Copenhagen, Denmark: Munksgaard, Ltd., 1962. Pp. 229. *

ALLEN L. EDWARDS, *Professor of Psychology, University of Washington, Seattle, Washington.*

The *California Q-Set* consists of 100 carefully selected statements which are intended to provide "a comprehensive description, in contemporary psychodynamic terms, of an individual's personality." The statements are supposedly of sufficiently broad coverage that "ideally—and the set is not yet ideal—the items should permit the portrayal of any kind of psychopathology and of any kind of normality."

Personality descriptions are obtained by having an observer describe another person, using whatever information he has about the person, with the CQ-Set. The statements are sorted into nine categories, from most to least salient, with a fixed number of statements being assigned to each category. Satisfactory reliability of the personality descriptions can be obtained by having several observers describe the same person and then averaging their independently made Q-sorts to obtain a composite Q-sort.

The CQ-Set is not a test or scale which purports to measure any specific personality variable. Instead, it is a pool of items which, like those in the MMPI, can conceivably be used in the development of many different scales. Suppose, for example, that each of a number of psychiatrists describes his conception of a male paranoid with the CQ-Set. Their ratings can be combined to obtain a composite. The composite is called a criterion or defining Q-sort. If a given individual is described in terms of the CQ-Set, his Q-sort can be correlated with the criterion sort and the resulting correlation coefficient is regarded by Block as a score. A convenient table for converting the sum of squared discrepancies between the ratings of two Q-sorts into the correlation coefficient is given in Block's monograph. It is obvious that, by means of defining Q-sorts, as many different scales can be developed as there are concepts or variables about which professionally competent judges can show some degree of agreement in their Q-sorts of the concepts.

Three defining Q-sorts, based upon the judgments of nine clinical psychologists, are presented in the monograph: the optimally adjusted individual, the male paranoid, and the female hysteric. Presumably, if the Q-sort for a given individual has a high positive correlation with the optimally adjusted composite, he would be regarded as having a higher adjustment score than an individual whose Q-sort correlates only moderately with the composite—as adjustment is conceived by the nine clinical psychologists. It should be obvious that the defining Q-sort does *not* solve the problem of construct validity. If correlations with a defining Q-sort are to be interpreted as scores, then further research on construct validity is necessary.

Block implies that social desirability considerations are not involved when observer evaluations are obtained from professionally competent people, the use emphasized in the monograph. That this is not necessarily the case is indicated by a study by Kogan, Quinn, Ax, and Ripley,[1] a reference not cited by Block.

The reviewer had nine judges Q-sort the CQ-Set for social desirability. The composite social desirability sort was then correlated with the optimally adjusted sort. The resulting correlation coefficient was .88. Is "optimal adjustment," as conceived by clinical psychologists, more or less equivalent to "social desirability"?

In general, Block's monograph is a sound and complete treatment of Q-sorts as a means of obtaining observer evaluations. Various potential research applications of Q-sorts are described in sufficient detail that they may be tried by others. The monograph should be read by anyone interested in personality assessment. If one proposes to use a Q-sort to obtain personality descriptions, the CQ-Set is probably as good as, if not better than, any other available on the commercial market. The items are neatly printed on 2¼ by 3½ inch cards. The cards are sturdy and after nine Q-sorts showed little wear.

DAVID T. LYKKEN, *Associate Professor of Psychiatry and Psychology, University of Minnesota, Minneapolis, Minnesota.*

Many clinicians would agree, although admittedly in some cases not without a fight, that most current personality testing—as actually, clinically used—is not measurement at all. It is true that many of the available tests have, either in the course of their construction or through subsequent research, been shown to be able to differentiate among various diagnostic (or otherwise specifiable) groups, or able to estimate certain characterological or behavioral dimensions identified by, e.g., factor analysis, or to be correlated with some other criterion of interest. The practical reality, however, is that the predictions or estimates which these tests have been empirically proved to be able to make are not usually a sufficient basis for the important decisions which the clinician is required to make. Therefore, one finds the clinician making inferences from the test data for which there is no existing empirical support, inferences which are a necessary guide for the decisions which are required of him and the validity of which depends upon, among other things, his experience and skill.

Thus, in effect, the clinician commonly uses the test protocol as a surrogate for the subject; the test, so to speak, has interviewed the subject, has elicited from him a more-or-less standardized behavior sample which hopefully is rich in information relevant to a wide variety of questions. And an important advantage of the test, thus used, over other opportunities for sampling the behavior of the subject (in interviews, on the ward, in work or play situations, etc.) is that the observations of the test are provided in a codified, reasonably standardized form. Unlike the human observer, the test always remembers what it has seen and formulates its observations in the same clear, simple standard vocabulary every time. By way of contrast, the clinician, after he has interviewed his subject, must in a real sense score himself; he must consider what he has seen in the subject, decide what descriptive generalizations are warranted, and determine the relative degrees of confidence he is willing to place on each such facet. Whether this task is approached deliberately and systematically or not, it logically must be done somehow before the clinician can hope to bring to bear his knowledge and previous experience in formulating inferences based upon his observations or before he can communicate his impression of the subject to others.

Of the various devices which have been developed to assist the clinician in this difficult task of "self-scoring"—devices such as the structured interview, the standardized rating schedule, the adjective checklist, etc.—perhaps the most promising is the Q-sort. And the most skillfully designed and carefully developed standard set of Q-sort items now available in published form is the *California Q-Set,* the result of some 10 years of thoughtful planning on the part of Jack Block and his associates of the University of California at Berkeley. The CQ-Set consists of 100 items printed on 2¼ by 3½ inch cards for convenience of sorting. Some of the items describe the immediate

1 Kogan, William S.; Quinn, Robert; Ax, Albert F.; and Ripley, Herbert S. "Some Methodological Problems in the Quantification of Clinical Assessment by Q Array." *J Consult Psychol* 21:57-62 F '57. *

social persona of the subject: "Is an interesting, arresting person," "Is cheerful," "Is verbally fluent; can express ideas well." Others require an assessment of long term behavior trends or dispositions: "Expresses hostile feelings directly," "Is self-indulgent," "Is a genuinely dependable and responsible person." Many transcend sheer behavioral description and demand varying degrees of clinical insight: "Has a readiness to feel guilty," "Tends to project his own feelings and motivations onto others," "Handles anxiety and conflicts by, in effect, refusing to recognize their presence; repressive or dissociative tendencies." Overall, the items make little reference to psychiatric symptoms or abnormal phenomena; the CQ-Set is aimed at delineating general personality organization, whereas other instruments, such as the *Wittenborn Psychiatric Rating Scales,* might be more suited to differentiating syndromes of severe psychiatric illness.

The clinician describes his subject by sorting these 100 items along a nine point scale according to a forced quasi-normal distribution; that is, 5 items are to be placed in each of the extreme categories One and Nine, 8 items in Two and in Eight, 12 items in both Three and Seven, and so on. A complete sort requires in the neighborhood of 30 minutes. The placement of the items is to depend on the judge's estimate of the salience of the trait in question in relation to understanding the subject being described. That is, a trait is rated in terms of its importance in specifying the unique and essential characteristics of the subject, rather than according to how strong the trait is in him in relation to other people. Thus, for example, in Q-sorting an acute schizophrenic patient, an item such as "Appears to have a high degree of intellectual capacity" might well be rated in the middle range even though the subject was known to have an IQ of 160, since intellectual capacity is a relatively less important facet of the essential portrait of this particular subject.

This codified, standard-language distillation of the observer-subject interaction should have many uses in both research and clinical settings. Agreement between two or more judges rating the same subject can be easily measured by intercorrelating their Q-sorts to determine, for example, whether enough discrepancy exists to indicate that the subject in question should be studied further before decisions are reached about him. Item by item comparisons will help identify areas of disagreement. Two or more subjects may be compared either globally by intercorrelation or item by item. One promising technique is to combine the wisdom and varying perspectives of the members of a clinical or research team by averaging their Q-sorts of the same subject, thus hopefully producing a more valid assessment by the summation of veridical insights and the cancellation of "noisy" error. The Q-sort is a convenient datum for longitudinal or "P-type" studies of, e.g., developmental changes and progress of treatment, or it might be applied in reverse as a means of assessing clinical skill. Finally, of course, the Q-sort can be used as raw material for the development of specialized actuarial prediction tables or formulas. Imagine, for example, a diagnostic center where juvenile offenders are observed for a period of weeks by a team of psychologists, social workers, and attendants and whose function is to determine whether individual boys should best be sent home, to a work camp, to a psychiatric hospital, or to a high security prison. Within a reasonable time, a large file of consensus Q-sorts averaged over the members of the diagnostic team, together with follow-up data on the results of the disposition made, could be accumulated. From such a file, one could readily develop "criterion Q-sorts," e.g., by averaging across groups of individuals for whom the follow-up indicates that prison assignment would have been appropriate and against which subsequent cases could be compared; or, one could employ ordinary item analysis to construct recidivism scales and the like.

The "manual" designed to accompany the *California Q-Set* is in fact a hard-cover treatise which not only describes at length the development of the CQ-Set but which also contains a thorough and thoughtful appraisal of the Q-sort method generally by an authority in the field. The book is recommended reading for all clinicians and essential study for prospective users of the method.

As the foregoing will attest, this reviewer considers the Q-sort method to hold great promise for both clinical and research applications and has high regard for the contributions of Block and his associates in this area. This is not to say, however, that one cannot argue with certain of Block's views, nor would Block himself pretend that the present CQ-Set is unimprovable. While there is no room here for an extended critique, it seems appropriate to alert readers new to this field to at least some possible areas of controversy, beginning with perhaps the most basic issue of all: Is it possible with *any* standard set of items of manageable length to satisfactorily describe the essence of the individual personality? This is, of course, the old nomothetic-ideographic issue, which, in the reviewer's opinion, has yet to be adequately resolved. One line of argument can be adumbrated by noting that if individuality is in part a result of (learned) *structural* uniqueness, as evidenced by idiosyncratic behavior patterning (i.e., unique traits) or idiosyncratic systems of S-R relationships, then —to the extent that the behaviors one wants to predict are mediated by such unique aspects of structure—to that extent will *any* nomothetic assessment be found wanting. One means of answering this essentially empirical question is, of course, by exploring the limits of the nomothetic approach with the most sophisticated techniques available, among which the Q-sort method has to be included.

Block treats at length in the manual with the reasons which led him (*a*) to require sorters to allocate specific numbers of items to each of the nine scale categories and (*b*) to identify the sorting dimension as "salience" rather than asking, "Which of these items most accurately describe the subject?" or "How does the subject compare on these traits with people in general?" Block's arguments on these two closely related issues have considerable weight and rest in part upon specific research findings. Thus, against the complaint that "salience" is a subtle concept and especially difficult to rationalize in relation to many items of the CQ-Set, Block can point to repeated findings of retest reliabilities of .8 and .9; although judges may complain that they cannot sort some items for "salience," they do in fact sort all the items with remarkable consistency. On the matter of "forcing" the Q-distribution, Block refers to a study in which unforced sorting distributions were found to reflect peculiarities of the judges and contained no information about the subjects not available in forced sortings that were collected later. However, this one finding, based on a rather atypical sorting situation, needs considerable extension before it can be generalized to all sets of items, all judges, all subjects, and other sorting criteria than "salience." Nor, of course, does a high retest reliability guarantee validity—that the items being consistently sorted are also accurately reflecting the judge's clinical impression of the subject.

Finally, of course, one must consider the quality of the items themselves; does sorting the particular 100 items of the CQ-Set allow one to encapsulate the essence of the individual under study, to record all of the impressions and insights one feels he has in hand about the subject? When one first attempts to sort the CQ-Set, the selection of items almost inevitably seems arbitrary, and it is easy to be critical of their content and to think of additional or alternative items which "should obviously be included." In fact, the choice of these 100 items was not at all capricious but the result of careful editing, selection, and testing; the present set incorporates suggestions from over 50 clinicians who had experience with earlier versions. An important point to keep in mind here is that a descriptive dimension, property, or trait need not be the explicit subject of a specific Q-item in order for it to be expressable via the Q-sort as a whole; many attributes can be communicated by means of the configuration of pairs or groups of item placements so that, in principle at least, many times 100 descriptive properties can be captured in the Q-sorting of 100 well chosen (and perhaps relatively atomistic) items. Perhaps one should continue the analogy drawn earlier between the global, nomothetic personality description attempted by the Q-sort and the similarly global representation commonly read into protocols of personality tests like the MMPI. Modern psychometric practice considers responses to questionnaire items to be bits of behavior, the meaning of which devolves from the empirical item correlations. It is considered naïve to criticize (or to interpret) an MMPI item on the basis of its content. It may be that a similar attitude should govern one's evaluation of a Q-Set. Clearly, in both cases, every resource of logic, theory, prior experience, and clinical intuition should be utilized in generating the original item pool and formulating the rules of procedure in the "context of discovery" phase of test or Q-Set construction. But the ultimate evaluation of the end product must hang upon an empirical assessment of the instrument's properties and capacities.

The Q-sort method deserves the active and enlightened attention of all practicing clinicians and those whose research involves personality assessment. In the 10 years since Stephenson introduced the method, only a comparative handful of psychologists have been exploring its problems and possibilities and much remains to be learned. It seems likely that many workers will eventually find it most useful to develop their own set of items and a sorting procedure tailored to their particular application. One can expect many changes in technique and in theory as experience accumulates. In the meanwhile, Block's manual provides an excellent and provocative introduction to the method and his *California Q-Set* is the appropriate starting point at least for any potential user.

Arch Gen Psychiatry 7:230–1 S '62. Samuel J. Beck. [Review of the manual.] * should prove of much value to researchers employing the technique and to other investigators who are interested in results of researchers using the method but who are not experienced in using it. The book is at once both a primer of instruction for applying the basic procedures and an elucidation of the orienting statistical theory. Appendices supply supporting information, results, and tables. An extensive list of reading references will be helpful to the interested students.

Cont Psychol 8:389–90 O '63. John E. Exner, Jr. [Review of the manual.] The materials presented in this monograph provide a substantial argument supporting the usefulness in research of the general scaling procedure known as the Q-sort technique. The author, well grounded in his knowledge and experience with the technique, is admittedly interested in presenting this argument so as to discuss in turn the relative merits of a specific Q-sort, the California Q-set (CQ). Thus, the material becomes narrowed considerably in its total scope but nevertheless continues throughout to be thought provoking. Several of the frequently voiced criticisms of the Q-sort technique are dealt with in adequate depth and sufficient clarity to leave even the most negativistic reader somewhat impressed. * there are points in the text where the reader almost has the impression that if publication of the monograph had been delayed another year or two and subsequent data had been included, the entire impact of the material would have been significantly greater. The over-all description of the development and uses of the CQ set is quite good. The enormity of work devoted to its construction is very impressive and the care given to the rationale of the set is admirable indeed and could well serve as a model for the construction of other such sets. Even the decision to construct the CQ set as a forced-choice type, which ordinarily could open the door to much criticism, is based on solid reasoning to which most researchers would be agreeable. It seems realistic to suggest that if many of the earlier articles pertaining to the Q-sort technique contained the theoretical and practical thoroughness as is demonstrated in the construction of the CQ set, the entire status of the technique as a research tool could be much greater than is currently apparent. The arguments favoring the usefulness of the technique in general, and the CQ set in particular, in individual personality assessment are considerably less attractive and realistic than are the statements favoring its use as a research tool. * Possibly the most unfortunate aspect of the monograph is that it is too short. After struggling through arguments, and bits of data, all of which lend themselves quite well to the notion that the Q-sort technique is really worthwhile, the reader is left with little information concerning some of the most practical applications of the technique. For example, any teacher of clinical students could not help but be impressed by suggestions of how the technique can be helpful in evaluation of the degree to which personality appraisals agree. But alas, little elaboration is provided here. Also mentioned far too briefly is the applicability of the technique to the study of highly specific personality characteristics such as need achievement, reality testing, etc. A more thorough approach concerning the various applications of the technique would not only make the book more palatable, but could have easily made it useful as a good seminar text. In its present form it provides useful information to the reader but much of this information only serves to raise questions rather than answer them. Its full clarity is probably derived only if the reader has some previous familiarity with Q-sort. The author has done a very good job in light of his apparent objectives. But I wish the book were longer.

Ed & Psychol Meas 23:208–10 sp '63. Harold Borko. [Review of the manual.] * In this slim volume Block lucidly presents the details of the Q-sort procedure and the advantages of applying this method to the study of personality types and psychiatric classifications. * primarily concerned with a description and discussion of the special Q-sort procedure designated as the California Q-set * By describing the methods and rationale of these procedures Block has increased and updated our knowledge of the technique. By pointing out the kinds of research applications in which the Q-sort is appropriate, he has extended the range of its usefulness. Through having developed a comprehensive set of 100 items, he has made the California Q-set readily available for personality research. He has accomplished a great deal, and the monograph is recommended to those researchers who are interested in exploring the applicability of the Q-sort method for personality assessment.

[73]

California Test of Personality, 1953 Revision. Grades kgn–3, 4–8, 7–10, 9–16, adults; 1939–53; 16 scores: self-reliance, sense of personal worth, sense of personal freedom, feeling of belonging, withdrawing tendencies, nervous symptoms, total personal worth, social standards, social skills, anti-social tendencies, family relations, school relations, occupation relations, community relations, total social adjustment, total adjustment; IBM for grades 4 and over; Forms AA, BB, ('53, 8 pages); 5 levels; manual ('53, 32 pages); profile ('53, 1 page); $3.50 per 35 tests; separate answer sheets may be used; 5¢ per IBM answer sheet; 9¢ per Scoreze answer sheet; 20¢ per hand scoring stencil; 75¢ per machine scoring stencil; postage extra; 50¢ per specimen set of any one level, postpaid; (45–60) minutes; Louis P. Thorpe, Willis W. Clark, and Ernest W. Tiegs; California Test Bureau. *

a) PRIMARY. Grades kgn–3; 1940–53.
b) ELEMENTARY. Grades 4–8; 1939–53.
c) INTERMEDIATE. Grades 7–10; 1939–53.
d) SECONDARY. Grades 9–16; 1942–53.
e) ADULT. Adults; 1942–53.

REFERENCES

1–24. See 3:26.
25–117. See 5:38.
118. SERPENTO, SANTINO T. "The Personality Adjustment of a Seventh Grade Population in Relation to Reading Ability." *W Va Univ B* 24:137–43 Je '53. *
119. HOLMES, JACK A. "Factors Underlying Major Reading Disabilities at the College Level." *Genetic Psychol Monogr* 49:3–95 F '54. * (*PA* 28:8982)
120. ABRAMS, DOROTHY FRANCES. *A Comparative Study of the Dominant Personality Tendencies, as Shown by the California Test of Personality, of Selected Cerebral Palsied and Selected Physically Normal Children.* Doctor's thesis, New York University (New York, N.Y.), 1956. (*DA* 19:167)
121. SEWELL, WILLIAM H., AND HALLER, ARCHIE O. "Social Status and the Personality Adjustment of the Child." *Sociometry* 19:114–25 Mr '56. * (*PA* 31:5849)
122. RATLIFF, JOHN ALLEN. *A Comparison of Mothers' Estimates With the Measured Adjustments of Their Junior High School Children.* Doctor's thesis, University of Houston (Houston, Tex.), 1957. (*DA* 19:3218)
123. SEMLER, IRA JACKSON. *Relationship Among Various Measures of Pupil Adjustment.* Doctor's thesis, State University of Iowa (Iowa City, Iowa), 1957. (*DA* 17:2923)
124. BURCHINAL, LEE G. "Parents' Attitudes and Adjustment of Children." *J Genetic Psychol* 92:69–79 Mr '58. * (*PA* 36:1FG69B)
125. CALDWELL, EDWARD. *A Study of the Stability of Scores on a Personality Inventory Administered During College Orientation Week.* Doctor's thesis, Florida State University (Tallahassee, Fla.), 1958. (*DA* 19:1998)
126. CARTER, CLEO DORRIS. *The Relationship Between Personality and Academic Achievement (Reading and Arithmetic) of Seven Year-Olds.* Doctor's thesis, Indiana University (Bloomington, Ind.), 1958. (*DA* 19:1027)
127. KOLLMEYER, LOUIS ADOLPH. *The Relationship Between Children's Drawings and Reading Achievement, Personal-Social Adjustment, and Intelligence.* Doctor's thesis, University of Oregon (Eugene, Ore.), 1958. (*DA* 19:2269)
128. OXFORD, LAKE C. *A Study of Personal and Social Adjustment of Seventh Grade Boys and Girls as Influenced by Physical Size, Athletic Ability, Acceptance by Peers, and Acceptance of Peers.* Doctor's thesis, University of Maryland (College Park, Md.), 1958. (*DA* 20:3634)
129. REINBOLD, EMMA J. *A Study of the Relationship Between Emotional Adjustment and School Citizenship.* Doctor's thesis, Temple University (Philadelphia, Pa.), 1958. (*DA* 19:1956)
130. SMITH, PAUL MILTON, JR. *Personality Characteristics of Rural and Urban Southern Negro Children.* Doctor's thesis, Indiana University (Bloomington, Ind.), 1958. (*DA* 19:1019)
131. TERRELL, GLENN, JR., AND SHREFFLER, JOY. "A Developmental Study of Leadership." *J Ed Res* 52:69–72 O '58. * (*PA* 34:1063)
132. WILSON, JOHN A. R. "Differences in Achievement Attributable to Different Educational Environments." *J Ed Res* 52:83–93 N '58. * (*PA* 33:10949)
133. CALDWELL, EDWARD. "Stability of Scores on a Personality Inventory Administered During College Orientation Week." *Personnel & Guid J* 38:305–8 D '59. * (*PA* 35:1259)
134. EASTON, JUDITH C. "Some Personality Traits of Underachieving and Achieving High School Students of Superior Ability." *B Maritime Psychol Assn* 8:34–9 Ap '59. * (*PA* 34:4786)
135. JACKSON, PHILIP W., AND GETZELS, JACOB W. "Psychological Health and Classroom Functioning: A Study of Dissatisfaction With School Among Adolescents." *J Ed Psychol* 50:295–300 D '59. * (*PA* 34:8368, 36:1FH95J)
136. MATHIS, CLAUDE. "Note on the Susceptibility of the California Test of Personality to Faking." *Psychol Rep* 5:527 S '59. * (*PA* 38:4279)
137. MONTGOMERY, GRACE I. *The Use of the California Test of Personality in Identifying Children's Personality Problems.* Master's thesis, Central Washington College of Education (Ellensburg, Wash.), 1959.
138. MOORE, PHELMA NEWTON. *A Survey of the Orientation Problems Common to Entering Freshmen in Pan American College for the First Semester of the 1958–1959 School Year.* Doctor's thesis, University of Houston (Houston, Tex.), 1959. (*DA* 20:2103)
139. MUNSON, BYRON E. "Personality Differentials Among Urban, Suburban, Town, and Rural Children." *Rural Sociol* 24:257–64 S '59. * (*PA* 35:725)
140. NORMAN, RALPH D., AND DALEY, MARVIN F. "The Comparative Personality Adjustment of Superior and Inferior Readers." *J Ed Psychol* 50:31–6 F '59. * (*PA* 35:2003)
141. ROFFEE, DOROTHY T. *A Study of Personality Traits of Elementary School Stutterers as Revealed by the California Test of Personality.* Master's thesis, Boston University (Boston, Mass.), 1959.
142. SEWELL, WILLIAM H., AND HALLER, A. O. "Factors in the Relationship Between Social Status and the Personality Adjustment of the Child." *Am Sociol R* 24:511–20 Ag '59. *
143. WILSON, J. A. R. "Achievement, Intelligence, Age and Promotion Characteristics of the Students Scoring at or Below the Tenth Percentile on the California Test of Personality." *J Ed Res* 52:283–92 Ap '59. * (*PA* 34:4101)
144. CONDIT, ELROY J. *How High School Students Interpret Items of the California Test of Personality.* Master's thesis, Drake University (Des Moines, Iowa), 1960.
145. HORLICK, REUBEN S., AND MILLER, MAURICE H. "A Comparative Personality Study of a Group of Stutterers and Hard of Hearing Patients." *J General Psychol* 63:259–66 O '60. * (*PA* 35:3756)
146. ISCOE, IRA, AND COCHRAN, IRENE. "Some Correlates of Manifest Anxiety in Children." Abstract. *J Consult Psychol* 24:97 F '60. * (*PA* 34:8047)
147. LEHNER, GEORGE F. J. "Some Relationships Among Personal Adjustment Self-Ratings, Self-Scores, and Assigned 'Average' Scores." *J Psychol* 50:333–7 O '60. * (*PA* 35:6488)
148. LOWE, MARJORIE A. *An Analysis of the California Test of Personality Results and Other Data Contained From 22 Juvenile Delinquents.* Master's thesis, East Tennessee State College (Johnson City, Tenn.), 1960.
149. SEMLER, IRA J. "Relationships Among Several Measures of Pupil Adjustment." *J Ed Psychol* 51:60–4 Ap '60. * (*PA* 35:2741)
150. SNELLGROVE, JOHN LOUIS. *A Study of Relationships Between Certain Personal and Socio-Economic Factors and Underachievement.* Doctor's thesis, University of Alabama (University, Ala.), 1960. (*DA* 21:1859)

151. CLEVELAND, GERALD ARTHUR. *A Study of Certain Psychological and Sociological Characteristics as Related to Arithmetic Achievement.* Doctor's thesis, Syracuse University (Syracuse, N.Y.), 1961. (*DA* 22:2681)
152. DUNKLEBERGER, CLARENCE J., AND TYLER, LEONA E. "Interest Stability and Personality Traits." *J Counsel Psychol* 8:70–4 sp '61. * (*PA* 36:3FF70D)
153. HARRISON, MAHALAH J. *The Correlation Between the Children's Form of the Manifest Anxiety Scale and the California Test of Personality.* Master's thesis, University of Tennessee (Knoxville, Tenn.), 1961.
154. HILLS, JOHN R. "The Influence of Instructions on Personality Inventory Scores." *J Counsel Psychol* 8:43–8 sp '61. * (*PA* 36:3HF43H)
155. ROTH, ROBERT M. "The Adjustment of Negro College Students at Hampton Institute." *J Negro Ed* 30:72–4 w '61. *
156. SEROT, NAOMI M., AND TEEVAN, RICHARD C. "Perception of the Parent-Child Relationship and Its Relation to Child Adjustment." *Child Develop* 32:373–8 Je '61. * (*PA* 36:3FG73S)
157. SMITH, PAUL M., JR. "Personal and Social Adjustment of Negro Children in Rural and Urban Areas of the South." *Rural Sociol* 26:73–7 Mr '61. * (*PA* 36:1FF73S)
158. CLARK, EDWARD T., AND MURRAY, JOHN B. "Student Perceptions of Adjustment of Priest and Lay Professors." *Cath Ed R* 60:386–91 S '62. *
159. HALLER, A. O., AND WOLFF, CAROLE ELLIS. "Personality Orientations of Farm, Village, and Urban Boys." *Rural Sociol* 27:275–93 S '62. * (*PA* 37:2989)
160. HALLER, ARCHIBALD O., AND THOMAS, SHAILER. "Personality Correlates of the Socioeconomic Status of Adolescent Males." *Sociometry* 25:398–404 D '62. * (*PA* 38:4094)
161. KERN, WILLIAM H., AND PFAEFFLE, HEINZ. "A Comparison of Social Adjustment of Mentally Retarded Children in Various Educational Settings." *Am J Mental Def* 67:407–13 N '62. * (*PA* 37:5412)
162. MELLENBRUCH, P. L. "The Validity of a Personality Inventory Tested by Hypnosis." *Am J Clin Hypnosis* 5:111–4 O '62. * (*PA* 37:5234)
163. BUTTS, HUGH F. "Skin Color Perception and Self-Esteem." *J Negro Ed* 32:122–8 sp '63. *
164. GOFF, REGINA M. "Trait Identification as a Means of Predicting Academic Goal Attainment." *J Exp Ed* 31:297–302 Mr '63. *
165. PEAK, BOYD D. *The California Test of Personality: A Study of Validation.* Doctor's thesis, Florida State University (Tallahassee, Fla.), 1963. (*DA* 24:1281)
166. ROTH, ROBERT M. "A Method for Identifying Prospective Counselees in College." *J Ed Res* 56:275–6 Ja '63. *

For a review by Verner M. Sims, see 5:38; for reviews by Laurance F. Shaffer and Douglas Spencer of the original edition, see 3:26 (1 excerpt); for reviews by Raymond B. Cattell, Percival M. Symonds, and P. E. Vernon of the elementary and secondary levels, see 40:1213 (1 excerpt).

[74]

The Cassel Psychotherapy Progress Record. Mental patients; 1953; 3 ratings: emotional development, barrier vulnerability development, overall psychotherapy development; 1 form (8 pages); manual (41 pages); no data on reliability and validity; no norms; $10 per set of 25 forms and manual; postpaid; specimen set not available; Russell N. Cassel; Western Psychological Services. *

WILLIAM SCHOFIELD, *Professor of Psychology, University of Minnesota, Minneapolis, Minnesota.*

The *Cassel Psychotherapy Progress Record* (CPPR) "was designed to provide a standardized and objective means for recording and evaluating the progress of psychotherapy for individuals." Although the title and general format suggest that the CPPR is intended for general use by therapists of varying theoretical persuasion, it appears from the manual and the consistent reference to "clients" (rather than patients) that the author's orientation is to client-centered therapy. The CPPR consists of three scales on each of which the client is to be rated following each therapy contact. The "Overall Psychotherapy Development Scale" is described as the "basic record"; this 14-step scale bears a close resemblance to the 15-step scale of the same author's *Client-Centered Counseling Progress Record* (see 76).

The other two scales (each with 14 steps) are labeled: "The Emotional Development Scale" and "The Barrier Vulnerability Development Scale." With respect to the former, the manual states: "The emotional development of the client appears to progress from the stage of destructive feelings through stages of negative, neutral, positive feelings to feelings of client independence tempered by an interdependence type of vulnerability." The 14 steps of this scale are described in accordance with this theoretical progression. There is no reference to research findings substantiating that this is in fact the generalized sequence of expression of client feeling in psychotherapy.

The rationale of the Barrier Vulnerability Development Scale involves the notion of deliberate use of barriers by the therapist in order to provide "problem situations for client adaptation" and "an evaluation basis for determining progress and growth status" within therapy. Four kinds of barriers used in therapy are listed as: responsibility, time, hostility, and affection.

The manual includes 10 pages of discourse on the "nature of psychotherapy" and extended descriptions and definitions of the intended meanings of each of the 14 positions of each of the 3 scales. It is unfortunate that there are no concrete examples of client behavior that would be relevant to particular ratings. Certain of the ratings involve an appreciation of concepts (for example, "nucleus genetic emotional experience") that receive extremely abstract and ambiguous definition in the text; it is unlikely that these variables could be comfortably assimilated or reliably noted by a therapist not steeped in the author's approach to therapy. Overlap of the three scales is illustrated in the respective specification of step 14 for the emotional, barrier, and overall development scales: "Considerable independence of the client emerges"; "Self-acceptance and assumption of full responsibility"; and "Client-independence, self-reliance, and self-activity." No data are offered from any studies of the reliability with which these scales are applicable to a specified sample.

The provision of a simple graphic rating form on which to record the session-to-session progress of the psychotherapy patient would meet an important need of both the clinician and researcher. The development of a form of sufficient objectivity and generality to permit of reliable application by therapists of different schools would require more research than appears to have gone into the CPPR. Nevertheless, the CPPR could be useful, especially in supervision of neophyte therapists who were simultaneously being trained in Cassel's version of client-centered psychotherapy.

[74a]

★**The Child Behavior Rating Scale.** Grades kgn-3; 1960-62; ratings by teachers or parents; 6 adjustment scores: self, home, social, school, physical, total; 1 form ('62, 4 pages); manual ('62, 17 mimeographed pages); no data on reliability of subscores; $6 per 25 tests and manual; $1.50 per manual; postpaid; specimen set not available; [5-10] minutes; Russell N. Cassel; Western Psychological Services. *

[74b]

★**Children's Embedded Figures Test.** Ages 5-12; 1963; revision of the Goodenough-Eagle modification (see *2* below) of the *Embedded Figures Test;* for research use only; 1 form (25 cards plus demonstration and practice materials); manual (15 pages); single sets of test materials and manual free to persons planning research with the test; [10-20] minutes plus practice session; Stephen A. Karp and Norma L. Konstadt; Cognitive Tests. *

REFERENCES

1. GOODENOUGH, DONALD R., AND KARP, STEPHEN A. "Field Dependence and Intellectual Functioning." *J Abn & Social Psychol* 63:241-6 S '61. * (*PA* 37:1214)

2. GOODENOUGH, DONALD R., AND EAGLE, CAROL JOHNSON. "A Modification of the Embedded-Figures Test for Use With Young Children." *J Genetic Psychol* 103:67-74 S '63. *

[75]

★**The Children's Hypnotic Susceptibility Scale.** Ages 5-12, 13-16; 1963, c1962; downward extension of *Stanford Hypnotic Susceptibility Scale,* on which its content is based; individual; 2 levels: younger form, older form; manual ('63, c1962, 62 pages, including both forms and sample scoring and observation form); scoring and observation form (4 pages); no data on reliability; no norms; $5.50 per examiner's kit of manual and 25 scoring and observation forms; $6.50 per 50 scoring and observation forms; $2.25 per manual; postage extra; (50-60) minutes; Perry London; Consulting Psychologists Press, Inc. *

REFERENCES

1. LONDON, PERRY. "Hypnosis in Children: An Experimental Approach." *Int J Clin & Exp Hypnosis* 10:79-91 Ap '62. * (*PA* 37:3385)

2. MOORE, ROSEMARIE K., AND LAUER, LILLIAN W. "Hypnotic Susceptibility in Middle Childhood." *Int J Clin & Exp Hypnosis* 11:167-74 Jl '63. * (*PA* 38:6278)

C. SCOTT MOSS, *Mental Health Consultant, National Institute of Mental Health, United States Public Health Service, San Francisco, California.*

Based on the *Stanford Hypnotic Susceptibility Scale, The Children's Hypnotic Susceptibility Scale* is a standardized induction procedure for children 5 to 16 years. Part 1 of the Children's Scale parallels Forms A and B of the original scale. Nine of the 10 items of Part 2 are selected from among the items of the unpublished *Stanford Depth Scales.* In all cases items were rewritten to make them suitable for use with children. In addition, there are younger and older forms of the Children's Scale for ages 5-12 and 13-16 respectively, which differ only with respect to the level of wording of some of the instructions.

The purpose of the Children's Scale is "to discover the extent to which a child will respond to hypnotic suggestions which are made in a standard way and which permit a standard means for evaluating responses." At the same time it is recognized that effective use of the scale depends more on the ability of the investigator to establish effective relationships with children than upon experience in the use of hypnosis. "It is as nearly impossible to overstate the importance of getting and keeping good rapport in testing children as it is to overstate the importance of adhering to standard test procedures. Serious or persistent violation of either rule will invalidate the test results." The point to be emphasized is that, as with many psychological tests, the administration appears deceptively simple, and valid results require a high degree of psychological sophistication; for instance, in determination of when and how to deviate from the standardized instructions and what has been the precise effect of that departure.

A virtue of the Children's Scale is that it may be scored in terms of a single dichotomy of pass or fail, as is the *Stanford Hypnotic Susceptibility Scale,* or along a four-point continuum which provides a more refined index of the child's responses. A limitation is that little information is available in the manual on normative data, other than the statement that the scale had been administered to over 250 children. Who were these children and how were they obtained? It is suspected that a problem of volunteer bias would be manifest in that a uniqueness obtains in families where parents volunteer their children for hypnosis experiments.

In a later article London (*1*) reports that interscorer reliability ranged from .90 to .96, and retest reliability was found to be .92. London also reports on the simultaneous use of two scoring systems, one measuring *overt behavior,* the other measuring *subjective involvement,* an approach referred to in a footnote in the manual and reflective of concern over the genuineness of the behavior elicited by the hypnotic suggestions.

A fundamental question indeed is the nature of so-called hypnotic phenomena. As London recognizes, children are likely to respond with docility to the wishes of adult authority, and they may produce responses to the explicit demands and even implicit expectations of the examiner without, in fact, being hypnotized. A control group of well motivated young simulators might help clarify this question. In the later article referred to above, London found a linear relationship between age and role-playing ability ($r = .67$). He speculates that, to the extent a suspected curvilinear relationship of age and susceptibility actually exists, it may be a function of the confounding of simulation ability and motivation with hypnotic behavior.

In terms of the amount of normative data provided, publication of this scale may be viewed as premature. However, if the author's stated intent of encouraging other investigators to employ and report on standard procedures of hypnosis in children is fulfilled, the effort will have been worthwhile in view of the dearth of empirical studies of hypnotizability with children. A basic value of this scale is that it provides the possibility of a developmental perspective to studies of hypnotic susceptibility.

JOHN G. WATKINS, *Chief Clinical Psychologist, Veterans Administration Hospital, Portland, Oregon.*

This scale represents an extension of the approach used by Weitzenhoffer and Hilgard in the *Stanford Hypnotic Susceptibility Scales.* The London scale presents a "Younger Form" covering the age range 5–12, and an "Older Form" advised for ages 13–16. Each form is composed of 12 simpler items in Part 1 followed by 10 more difficult items in Part 2. The Part 1 items include postural sway, eye closure, hand lowering, arm immobilization, finger lock, arm rigidity, hands together, verbal inhibition, auditory hallucination, eye catalepsy, post-hypnotic suggestion, and amnesia. In Part 2 are found items of post-hypnotic suggestion (re-induction), visual and auditory hallucination, cold hallucination, anesthesia, taste hallucination, small hallucination, visual hallucination, age regression, dream, awakening, and post-hypnotic suggestion.

These represent essentially the same items found in the Stanford scale but reworded to be more appealing and understandable to children. It should be noted that many of these items have been historically considered as tests of suggestibility and have been reported by various earlier writers.[1] The Stanford scale, which was the original standardized instrument for measuring hypnotic susceptibility, was the product of considerable study and research by well known investigators in the field and is certainly the best validated test of this type currently available. Accordingly, the children's scale inherits both the assets which accrued to the carefully prepared Stanford work and the liabilities which may inhere in this kind of an approach aimed at objectifying hypnotic responses.

Perhaps the most credit should be given to the author's explicit and detailed instructions for administration. Clearly written, they cover not only all the physical conditions, equipment, props, etc., needed for giving the scale, but especially praiseworthy is the care given to alteration of wordings in order to adapt the items to the intellectual level and interests of children. In themselves they constitute a good verbatim presentation of techniques for inducing trance in young people. Since eye closure is initiated in the second item, and since all subsequent items are administered with the subject's eyes closed, the more inexperienced administrator can read the suggestions and thus present a standardized wording. The author wisely makes provision for individual differences and advises appropriate modifications as needed. A separate Scoring and Observation Form is available on which individual scoring can be noted.

An attempt at greater precision of scoring is proposed in that four levels of response for

1 DAVIS, LAWRENCE W., AND HUSBAND, RICHARD W. "A Study of Hypnotic Susceptibility in Relation to Personality Traits." *J Abn & Social Psychol* 26:175–82 Jl–S '31. * (*PA* 6:648)
FRIEDLANDER, J. W., AND SARBIN, T. R. "The Depth of Hypnosis." *J Abn & Social Psychol* 33:453–75 O '38. * (*PA* 13:1412)

each item, scored 3, 2, 1, and 0 are listed, each being specifically defined. Some of the items are timed and the Scoring and Observation Form provides space for timing the responses. In the original Stanford scale only the fact of response (scored plus or minus), not the degree of response, is required. The London scale permits either plus-minus or numerical scoring.

The greatest current deficiency in this scale is its lack of published standardization and normative data. In regards to this matter the author states: "At this writing, the present form....has been administered in standard fashion to over two hundred and fifty children of both sexes within the age range for which the test was developed. * Information from pilot studies clearly indicates that the scale is sufficiently reliable to warrant publication. Norms will be published at the earliest possible date."

In summary, the scale is a carefully prepared extension of the earlier well-designed Stanford scale adapted to the needs of children. As such it is a welcome addition to the few instruments of evaluation currently available in this area. However, the entire approach is based on a concept of the nature of hypnosis, which, although widely held, is not universally accepted. This is the view that hypnosis is a relatively stable state, and hypnotizability a behavior characteristic that remains fairly constant within any given individual. The Stanford studies [2] seem to bear out this contention. According to such a concept a given subject achieves his normal level of hypnosis under any standard approach, regardless of who administers the induction.

There are a number of workers in the field who maintain that hypnosis is more than a state, but a complex interpersonal relationship process, and that it is subject to such influences as transference and countertransference reactions.[3] According to this view the hypnotizability of a given subject would vary widely depending on the exact nature of the hypnotic relationship, the technique of induction used, the unconscious psychodynamic needs within the subject, and the personality and motivation of the hypnotist. From such a viewpoint a "standardized" approach to hypnotic induction leaves much to be desired. This second school of thought is closer to psychoanalytic theory and is espoused more by clinicians and "subjectivists." Final determination of the most appropriate form for hypnotic susceptibility scales must await more precise theoretical formulations as to the exact nature of hypnosis.

Am J Clin Hypnosis 5:336–7 Ap '63. André Weitzenhoffer. * According to the author: "The purpose of the *Children's Scale*....is to discover the extent to which a child will respond to hypnotic suggestions which are made in an entirely standard way and which permit a standard means for evaluating responses. The Children's Scale is thus a test of *typical* performance rather than one of *maximum* performance. Used properly, it should give reliable information about how susceptible a child is to attempts at hypnotic induction under certain typical conditions, *not* how susceptible he is to the application of a maximum effort at induction." * At first look the physical arrangement of the scale gives one the impression of a somewhat complicated device. However, this may not be as serious as it sounds upon actual application of the scale. This writer, admittedly, has not had an opportunity to use it. The author of the scale also emphasizes the fact that the ability to establish an effective relationship with children is of primary importance in the successful use of the scale. He considers previous experience with such tests as the *Stanford Binet* and the *Wechsler Intelligence Scale for Children* to be a considerable aid. This is clearly an inherent weakness in the scale which will probably limit its use by investigators, but it must be recognized that this probably is not so much a reflection upon the test instrument itself as a function of the nature of the population to be tested. The scale is the result of careful, thoughtful work by a well trained and serious investigator and has been shown to be both practical and useful. It has the virtue of not only being standardized, but of giving scores which can be related to scores obtained on adult populations by means of other standardized scales which are being increasingly used in research on hypnosis. It also demonstrates that it is fully possible to do hypnotic

2 Hilgard, Ernest R.; Weitzenhoffer, Andre M.; Landes, Judah; and Moore, Rosemarie K. "The Distribution of Susceptibility to Hypnosis in a Student Population: A Study Using the Stanford Hypnotic Susceptibility Scale." *Psychol Monogr* 75(8):1–22 '61. *
Hilgard, Ernest R.; Weitzenhoffer, Andre M.; and Gough, Philip. "Individual Differences in Susceptibility to Hypnosis." *Proc Nat Acad Sci* 44:1255–9 D '58. *
3 Kline, Milton V. *Freud and Hypnosis: The Interaction of Psychodynamics and Hypnosis.* New York: The Julian Press, Inc., 1958. Pp. xii, 210. *
Watkins, John G. Chap. 1, "Transference Aspects of the Hypnotic Relationship," pp. 5–24. In *Clinical Correlations of Experimental Hypnosis.* Edited by Milton V. Kline. Springfield, Ill.: Charles C Thomas, Publisher, 1963. Pp. xv, 524. *

research on children, and opens the door to further work of this kind. The Children's Scale, even more than the Stanford Scale will probably not have much appeal to medical practitioners for whom it probably would be of limited usefulness anyway; but it should prove a valuable instrument in academic research and must be considered a definite contribution to scientific hypnotism.

[76]

***Client-Centered Counseling Progress Record.** Adults and children undergoing psychotherapeutic counseling; 1950-60; form for rating progress in up to 40 counseling visits; 1 form ('59, 4 pages); manual ('60, 8 pages); no norms; $2 per 25 records, postage extra; $1 per specimen set, postpaid; [3-5] minutes; Russell N. Cassel; Associated Publishers. *

WILLIAM SCHOFIELD, *Professor of Psychology, University of Minnesota, Minneapolis, Minnesota.*

This is a simple, four-page pamphlet that affords the client-centered counselor a convenient grid on which to plot his estimate of the general clinical status of a client as revealed in each counseling session. A total of 40 sessions may be rated on a single form. The cover page provides for recording general identifying information and the back page is lined for the recording of "significant changes."

The status of the patient at a given interview is recorded on a single 15-step chart based largely on Rogers' theories of personality and the counseling process. The 15 steps are divided into 4 sections of the scale, each presumably reflecting a different major focus of the counseling process. These are labeled: "Developing Counseling Readiness," "Deeper Personality Layer—Negative Reflections," "Middle Personality Layer—Positive Reflections," and "Outer Personality Layer—Educational Process." Stages that exemplify each of these "layers," respectively, are: "Client decides on clinic or therapist for obtaining assistance, and makes the necessary arrangements"; "Client accepts own individuality, and is able to perceive differences in own various self worlds"; "Significant changes in various client self worlds, and with the 'perceived' self approaching the 'would be' self"; and "Re-education directed at an effective client goal-setting and goal-striving process."

The manual refers to the chart as a rating scale and the process of assigning the client's position for a particular interview is clearly a rating procedure; the format of the record suggests a rating continuum from early, and presumably poorer or "lower" (note the numeration), to "higher" and presumably better stages. The manual provides no information as to precisely how each of the stages was derived or, more important, as to how the sequence of stages was derived. Such ordering could well have been based on the rich research literature on nondirective, client-centered counseling, but there is no discussion of any specific research on which the rating continuum is based. While there is moderately extended discussion of the meaning and observations pertinent to each of the 15 stages, no data are offered as to the reliability with which this form can be applied in appraisal of a series of counseling sessions by independent evaluators. The statement that the record "is far superior to the traditional technique of using descriptive narrative summaries" suggests that it might be completely substituted for the latter. While such a quantified summary rating of therapy progress is a highly desirable addition to the usual clinical notes, the latter are not dispensable with respect to adequate professional records or for purposes of teaching or research.

For client-centered counselors, and especially for counselors in training, the use of such a standardized record form has distinct value in sensitizing the counselor to the need to appraise progress and clinical status of the counselee, in providing a graphic record which is useful for cross-case comparisons, and in enhancing awareness of the accumulation of sessions.

For a more elaborate version of a comparable recording instrument, see the *Cassel Psychotherapy Progress Record.*

[77]

The College Inventory of Academic Adjustment. College; 1949; 7 scores: curricular adjustment, maturity of goals and level of aspiration, personal efficiency-planning and use of time, study skills and practices, mental health, personal relations, total; 1 form (4 pages); manual (10 pages); $3 per 25 tests; 25¢ per set of manual and scoring stencils; 50¢ per specimen set; cash orders postpaid; (15-25) minutes; Henry Borow; [Consulting Psychologists Press, Inc.]. *

REFERENCES

1-3. See 4:34.
4. BURGESS, ELVA. *Personality Factors in Over- and Under-Achievers in Engineering.* Doctor's thesis, Pennsylvania State College (State College, Pa.), 1953.
5. MCCOULLOUGH, CHESTER A. *A Statistical Study of the Relationships Between Scores Obtained by 400 North Carolina College Students on the Mooney Problem Check List and the Borow College Inventory of Academic Adjustment.* Master's thesis, North Carolina College (Durham, N.C.), 1954.
6. SPENCER, GEORGE MINARD. *An Investigation of Some Non-*

Intellectual Factors Presumably Affecting the Academic Adjustment of College Students at Florida State University. Doctor's thesis, Florida State University (Tallahassee, Fla.), 1955. (*DA* 15:1436)

7. BURGESS, ELVA. "Personality Factors of Over- and Under-Achievers in Engineering." *J Ed Psychol* 47:89–99 F '56. * (*PA* 31:8811)

8. CHRISTENSEN, CLIFFORD M. "A Note on Borow's College Inventory of Academic Adjustment." *J Ed Res* 50:55–8 S '56. * (*PA* 31:6669)

9. MOORE, MARY ROWENA. *The Effects of Two Interview Techniques on Academic Achievement and Certain Non-Intellectual Factors Affecting Academic Success.* Doctor's thesis, Indiana University (Bloomington, Ind.), 1958. (*DA* 19:2853)

10. CURRAN, ANN MARIE. *Non-Intellective Characteristics of Freshman Underachievers, Normal Achievers, and Overachievers at the College Level.* Doctor's thesis, University of Connecticut (Storrs, Conn.), 1960. (*DA* 21:2584)

11. POPHAM, W. JAMES, AND MOORE, MARY R. "A Note on the Validity of Borow's College Inventory of Academic Adjustment." *J Ed Res* 54:115–7 N '60. *

12. POPHAM, W. JAMES, AND MOORE, MARY R. "A Validity Check on the Brown-Holtzman Survey of Study Habits and Attitudes and the Borow College Inventory of Academic Adjustment." *Personnel & Guid J* 38:552–4 Mr '60. * (*PA* 35:7094)

13. ALLEN, ROSCOE JACKSON. *An Analysis of the Relationship Between Selected Prognostic Measures and Achievement in the Freshman Program for Secretarial Majors at the Woman's College of the University of North Carolina.* Doctor's thesis, Pennsylvania State University (University Park, Pa.), 1961. (*DA* 23:122)

14. CENTI, PAUL. "Personality Factors Related to College Success." *J Ed Res* 55:187–8 D–Ja '62. *

15. LANIER, WILLIAM JETT. *The Predictive Value of Selected Personality and College Adjustment Instruments Used With the American College Testing Program.* Doctor's thesis, Purdue University (Lafayette, Ind.), 1962. (*DA* 23:2424)

LEONARD D. GOODSTEIN, *Professor of Psychology, and Director, University Counseling Service, University of Iowa, Iowa City, Iowa.*

The College Inventory of Academic Adjustment is a 90-item, self-administering questionnaire which presumably taps 6 areas of college adjustment: curricular adjustment (12 items), maturity of goals and level of aspiration (14 items), personal efficiency (16 items), study skills and practices (21 items), mental health (14 items), and personal relations (13 items). These items, which are quite obvious in content and hence easily faked, are answered directly in the test booklet, using the alternative responses of yes, no, or undecided, and are scored by means of a convenient, but time consuming, transparent overlay stencil. Scores are obtained for each of the six areas and are combined into a single unweighted total score. Percentile equivalents are available, separately for the sexes, for the total scores, and quartile norms are provided, again, by sex, for the six area scores.

The split-half reliability coefficients of the total score are .92 for males (n = 155) and .90 for females (n = 130), both coefficients corrected by the Spearman-Brown formula. The test-retest reliability coefficient of the total score is .92, while the test-retest reliability coefficients for the six area scores range from .81 to .89 (n = 130 females).

Five types of information are presented as validity data: (*a*) item selection procedures (items included in the inventory are those that statistically differentiated between groups of male and female overachievers and underachievers at Pennsylvania State College); (*b*) high interjudge agreement about which of the six areas the specific items tapped; (*c*) significant correlations between inventory scores and college grade point average (for 155 males these range from .16 for the personal relations score to .41 for the personal efficiency score); (*d*) mean differences between the inventory scores of 81 female overachievers and 67 female underachievers (these differences are statistically significant with the overachievers higher on the total and each of the area scores, except for the personal relations area); and (*e*) correlations between the several inventory scores and scores on Wrenn's *Study Habits Inventory,* Bell's *Adjustment Inventory,* and Bernreuter's *Personality Inventory,* most of which are said to be "in accord with logical expectation."

None of these validity data, however, bears directly upon the question of whether or not this inventory can serve as "a diagnostic aid in counseling," a major use professed for the test by its author. Clues as to sources of difficulty are presumably given by the six area scores but these rationally derived indices share considerable common variance as indicated by the table of intercorrelations presented in the manual (the r's range from .23 to .56 with median r .44). The theoretical implications of such intercorrelated area scores either for a theory of academic adjustment or for the practical problems of identifying the sources of a student's difficulties are largely ignored. While the author was not unaware of these problems, the 14 years since the publication of the manual have not seen any attempt to relieve the situation, either in the research literature or in a revision of the manual.

Even more serious is the failure to extend and update the norms. These norms appear to be based upon data collected between 1945 and 1948, approximately, and only involve the scores of 237 male students from two institutions and 454 female students from one institution. Considering the changes in the nature of the student body which have taken place over the past 15 or more years and what is now known about the diversity of student characteristics from institution to institution, these norms are grossly inadequate for any practical purpose.

Some of the inventory items, approximately 15 per cent by this reviewer's estimate, have a slightly archaic or moralistic flavor, for example, "Do you have a keen desire for success?" or "Are you guilty of not taking things seriously enough?" that limit the suggested usefulness of the individual item responses for providing "valuable diagnostic clues." The failure of the test publishers to provide machine scorable answer sheets in these days of high speed electronic test scoring machines is still another instance of how outdated this test has become. Under these circumstances, one must not only question the standards of the publisher in continuing to market the test but also those of users who might purchase it.

In summary, there is very little to recommend this inventory for use in any applied situation. There has been no attempt to cross-validate the findings of the original validation work (a criticism previously noted some ten years ago in the *Fourth Mental Measurements Yearbook,* see 4:34), both the test booklet and the manual are obviously dated, and there is very little recently reported evidence that would suggest this inventory is a useful one. College counselors and others seeking techniques for assessing the nonintellectual factors in collegiate achievement should look elsewhere.

For reviews by Lysle W. Croft and Harrison G. Gough, see 4:34.

[78]

Concept Formation Test. Normal and schizophrenic adults; 1940; individual; 1 form (a set of blocks); mimeographed instructions ['40, 4 pages]; no data on reliability and validity; no norms; $13.75 per set of testing materials, postage extra; (10–60) minutes; Jacob Kasanin and Eugenia Hanfmann; C. H. Stoelting Co. *

REFERENCES

1–19. See 3:27.
20–27. See 4:35.
28. PENNY, RONALD. "The Vigotsky Block Test: A Form of Administration." *Austral J Psychol* 3:65–83 D '51. * (*PA* 27:1184)
29. CORTER, HAROLD M. "Factor Analysis of Some Reasoning Tests." *Psychol Monogr* 66(8):1–31 '52. * (*PA* 27:4995)
30. SEMEONOFF, B., AND LAIRD, A. J. "The Vigotsky Test as a Measure of Intelligence." *Brit J Psychol, Gen Sect* 43:94–102 My '52. * (*PA* 27:1982)
31. HANFMANN, EUGENIA. "Concept Formation Test," pp. 731–40. (*PA* 27:7772) In *Contributions Toward Medical Psychology: Theory and Psychodiagnostic Methods, Vol. II.* Edited by Arthur Weider. New York: Ronald Press Co., 1953. Pp. xi, 459–885. *
32. LOVIBOND, S. H. "The Object Sorting Test and Conceptual Thinking in Schizophrenia." *Austral J Psychol* 6:52–70 Je '54. * (*PA* 29:6035)
33. BRESSLER, MILDRED BLOOM. *A Study of an Aspect of Concept Formation in Brain-Damaged Adults With Aphasia.* Doctor's thesis, New York University (New York, N.Y.), 1955. (*DA* 16:568)
34. EDRINGTON, THOMAS CRAIGHEAD. *A Revised Test of Concept Formation as Related to Intelligence and Interests.* Doctor's thesis, Tulane University (New Orleans, La.), 1955.
35. MILLER, ELEANOR O. "New Use for the Vigotsky Blocks." *J Clin Psychol* 11:87–9 Ja '55. * (*PA* 29:7304)
36. KRESS, ROY ALFRED, JR. *An Investigation of the Relationship Between Concept Formation and Achievement in Reading.* Doctor's thesis, Temple University (Philadelphia, Pa.), 1956. (*DA* 16:573)
37. O'NEILL, JOHN J., AND DAVIDSON, JOANN L. "Relationship Between Lipreading Ability and Five Psychological Factors." *J Speech & Hearing Disorders* 21:478–81 D '56. * (*PA* 31:4907)
38. VON HOLT, HENRY W., JR.; SENGSTAKE, CORD B.; SONODA, BEVERLY C.; AND DRAPER, WILLIAM A. "Orality, Image Fusions and Concept-Formation." *J Proj Tech* 24:194–8 Je '60. * (*PA* 35:4943)

For a review by Kate Levine Kogan (with William S. Kogan), see 4:35; for a review by O. L. Zangwill, see 3:27; for excerpts from related book reviews, see 3:28.

[79]

★Constant-Choice Perceptual Maze Attitude of Responsibility Test. Ages 4 and over; 1938–63; formerly called the *Line Centering Test;* "liking or disliking of required behavior"; 3 scores: intensity of quality (self-initiative), persistency of quality (self-importance), reaction tendencies (self-confidence); 1 form ('53, 4 pages); trial test ('53, 2 pages); administrative and scoring manual ('53, 16 pages); interpretive norms manual ('54, 118 pages); "personal testing" manual ['63, 56 unnumbered pages, including materials copyrighted 1958–63]; $25 per 50 sets of test and trial test; $1 per administration and scoring manual; $5 per interpretive norms manual; $5 per "personal testing" manual; $1.25 per 25 sets of various record and report forms; $2 per specimen set of test, trial test, and administration and scoring manual; postage extra; 3(15) minutes; John C. Park; the Author. *

[80]

Cornell Word Form 2. Adults; 1946–55; civilian edition of *Cornell Word Form* designed for use in military psychiatric screening; title on test is *C.W.F.-2;* psychosomatic and neuropsychiatric symptoms; 1 form ['55, 2 pages]; manual ('55, 8 pages, reprint of *11* below); $5 per 100 tests; specimen set free; postage extra; [5–15] minutes; Arthur Weider, Bela Mittelmann, David Wechsler, and Harold Wolff; Cornell University Medical College. *

REFERENCES

1–11. See 5:44.
12. *Personal Characteristics of Traffic-Accident Repeaters,* pp. 27–9. Saugatuck, Conn.: Eno Foundation for Highway Traffic Control, 1948. Pp. 64. *

S. B. SELLS, *Professor of Psychology, and Director, Institute of Behavioral Research, Texas Christian University, Fort Worth, Texas.*

This test is a revision of an earlier form developed by a Cornell Medical School research group (Weider, Mittelmann, Brodman, Wechsler, and Wolff) for military use in World War II. Its original purpose was for screening of psychologically unfit recruits at induction stations. It has subsequently been used productively in clinical, occupational, and military (including aviation) situations and in discriminating accident-free civilians from accident repeaters.

The form consists of 80 items, containing 80 stimulus words and 160 response words, 20 of the former and 24 of the latter from the Kent-Rosanoff list. Each item contains a stimulus word and two response choices, one of which is selected by the subject on the basis of "reminding" him most of the stimulus word. Some of the choices are fairly obvious. For example, to the stimulus word "sleep," the response words "comfort" and "restless" are given. In other cases, the implication is less apparent. For example, to the stimulus word "brother" the response words "man" and "my brother" are given. A number of neutral, filler items are dispersed among those that are intended to discriminate.

Although high validities have never been reported, published results with this instrument have been both consistent enough and discriminating enough to warrant consideration as a screening instrument. The items are highly sensitive to varying population characteristics, however, such as intelligence, education, occupation, and to the purposes of screening, in relation to test taking attitudes. It is therefore necessary to carry out thorough validation research and to standardize keys for any formal screening program in which it may be used. For this reason, inclusion in any informal clinical testing batteries may prove to be worthless, while at the same time, this pool of items may produce a valuable adjunct to a screening battery in competent psychometric hands.

[81]

★**Cotswold Personality Assessment P.A. 1.** Ages 11-16; 1960; manual subtitle is *A Study of Preferences and Values for Use in Schools and Clubs;* 6 scores: 3 preference scores (things, people, ideas) and 3 attitude scores (using one's hands, being with other people, talking about school); 1 form ['60, 8 pages]; manual ['60, 6 pages]; no norms for attitude scores; 9*d.* per test; 1*s.* per manual; postage extra; (40) minutes; C. M. Fleming; Robert Gibson & Sons (Glasgow), Ltd. *

REFERENCES

1. FLEMING, C. M. "A New Personality Test." *Indian Psychol B* 4:59-66 S '59. *

RALPH D. DUTCH, *Principal Lecturer in Educational Psychology, Aberdeen College of Education, Aberdeen, Scotland.*

This test is described as "an aid to the assessment of the personal characteristics of boys and girls as these are represented by predominating interests and prevailing values." The adolescent testee is asked to identify himself more or less strongly with various opinions and statements expressed by members of an imaginary youth club, and his total scores show the relative strength of his preferences and attitudes. The information thus obtained is described as having shown itself useful (*a*) in educational guidance, (*b*) in vocational guidance and selection, (*c*) in sociometric grouping in youth clubs. The test can be given to a group, with verbal explanations, or can be used as a self-administered individual test.

The first page of the test is used for recording a summary of the results and also for giving instructions to the subject. The wording of these instructions is important: "give 4 votes to the statements with which you agree very strongly, 3 to the next most sensible ones, 2 to the next, 1 to the ones with which you agree least, and 0 to those with which you do not agree at all." The use of the word "sensible" here seems unfortunate and may puzzle a testee with sufficient self knowledge to appreciate that the point of view with which he agrees very strongly is not necessarily the most "sensible," either for himself or for the imaginary character who is supposed to be putting it forward. Also, where does agreement stop and disagreement begin on a scale thus worded? In fact, these instructions can be read in so many different ways that one becomes immediately doubtful of the value of any averages or norms produced by the test.

The test divides into 9 subtests, arranged in 3 sections. In the first section the places for recording the answers to the 5 subtests are so arranged that the relative strength of the subject's preferences for "Things," "People," "Ideas" can easily be seen by adding the scores on three columns. Similarly, the results of the 3 subtests in the attitudes section appear in two columns—favourable and unfavourable. In the final subtest, a list of 45 common adolescent activities is presented and the subject is asked to record which of these he has engaged in, or would like to have engaged in, during the last fortnight.

The amount and type of standardisation varies between the three sections. The reliability of the test is good, with a split-half reliability coefficient of .88 for the whole test, and test-retest figures for the subtests varying between .81 and .93. As each testee could consistently follow his own interpretation, the reliability coefficient would not, of course, necessarily be impaired by any ambiguity in the instructions. The items on the "Preference" tests were carefully selected to give content validity, but no coefficients are quoted and we are merely told that "the validity of the whole was later confirmed by case studies." If the test is being used for guidance and selection, however, as is confirmed by the test author in a personal letter, this will not do, and some predictive validities, or at least a concurrent validity, will have to be provided. The testee's "preference" results can be expressed as a profile, which can then be compared with the scores (averages and standard deviations) of various groups of adolescents. These scores, however, are not presented in any systematic order and it is difficult to see the value of such a comparison, specially when the standard deviations are so large. The author herself, in the same letter, indicates belief that the main finding of the test is the extent of the overlap between groups. The results of the "attitudes" tests, the items on which were again "validated" by the opinion of judges, express the attitudes of the testee on a simple + or − scale, but in the absence of any norms whatsoever it is impossible to interpret an individual score. The items on the final subtest, which is linked to the "Preferences" section, were chosen from an item analysis of 700 pupils' interests. Nothing is claimed for this last test other than that its results are "often corroborative of the information given by the other tests."

Some general points about the whole test are: (*a*) The instructions seem ambiguous and the wording of many of the items is peculiar; e.g., one is asked to record an attitude towards "Managing people (like a bus conductor, a hospital sister, a lawyer, a doctor)"—hardly a homogeneous collection! (*b*) The tentative norms in the "preference" section show great overlapping between groups so the implication that a kind of tri-partite division can be made is unfortunate. (*c*) The danger of contamination by self delusion or the social desirability factor appears great, as in most self-rating inventories. The manual stresses the need for good "rapport" between examiner and subject, but this cuts down the area of the test's use drastically, and where this good relationship already exists it is doubtful if the test would be necessary. (*d*) If one is led by the numerical system of scoring, with a profile and tentative norms, to expect some kind of fairly rigorous quantitative assessment, then the test is disappointing.

In this reviewer's opinion the test, as it stands, is best suited not to provide numerical results but to elicit certain clues about personality or to start off a discussion. Used thus, the tester may find it useful as a basis for guidance and advice without scoring the results at all.

G. A. V. Morgan, *Former Principal Psychologist, North Wales Child Guidance Service, Denbighshire, Wales.*

This test falls into three parts: the measurement of interests and values based on preferences for dealing with things, people, and ideas; three attitude scales partly related to the above; and a checklist of leisure activities classified under the three preference headings. The latter was suggested by an item analysis of the activities reported by 700 pupils whose interests were known from their responses to the remainder of the test.

The assumption underlying the test is, as in the Allport-Vernon *Study of Values,* that consistent and permanent personal interests and values are reflected in preferences for particular activities and situations. As in the *Kuder Preference Record—Vocational* this indirect use of preferences is claimed to be useful in vocational guidance.

Items are arranged in five subtests such as "Talking About Wishes" and "Spending Money." There are 66 questions, with 22 items referring to each preference category. Responses are expressed, in a hypothetical "club" discussion, as a "vote" of from 0 to 4 for each item. This procedure is claimed to be attractive to adolescents. It seems doubtful whether rating over this range is natural or easy for unsophisticated subjects, as compared with a simple three-point scale. In fact, the average scores may conceal individual variation in range of response.

The test originated from the work of the author on the psychology of adolescents, backed by a considerable amount of unpublished research on their interests and attitudes done by students in the University of London from 1947 to 1958. Validation of the preference test by comparison of item scores with teachers' estimates of pupils' interests and case studies is satisfactory. Although the author suggests that the test might with modifications be given to "duller" adolescents or younger children, the test probably has a lower age and ability limit in terms of the reading level and the type of response required. All data given describe selected groups of secondary school children, that is, the upper 20 to 33 per cent in ability of age groups 11 to 16 years.

"Norms" are given only for the preference tests for ages 11 to 16, but mainly for 13-year-old groups. These norms consist of 15 school raw score means and standard deviations, which are useful only as a rough guide. No effective standards are available for age, sex, or type of school in terms of percentiles or standard scores. Variation among individual schools and types of school is quite marked. No data are given on the relative ability level or sociocultural background of the groups.

The manual could with effect have been more simply written. In its present form it is a manual for a research instrument, but not convenient for general use. The reviewer initially found difficulty in following the test from the manual: a minor irritation is the dual description of subtests by page letters and roman figures whereas the test form uses arabic figures. The section on interpretation of the test is brief and vague, leaving the interpretation in effect up to the test user. Despite apparent detail on the test's characteristics, insufficient data are given on the groups on which reliability and validity studies were carried out. "Personal communication" is quoted for important issues such as reliability, and background references are mainly to unpublished theses, many known to the reviewer, but not in general accessible.

The reliability data seem satisfactory for this kind of material and length of test. A split-half reliability coefficient for the whole test was .88, and test-retest coefficients (one month interval) ranged from .81 to .90 for preference and attitude subtests, based on small groups only in each instance. Since a profile of the three preference scores is proposed, the standard error of score differences should be available. A difference of seven between scores is suggested as "definitive," but this is a vague formulation.

The attitude scales, developed by means of a modified Thurstone-Chave technique, with neutral items omitted, are given scores from 4 to 0 to indicate degree of agreement with positive or negative statements. Total scores are based on the difference between positive and negative totals. Two of the scales corroborate to some extent the preference scores, but it is not clear how "attitude to school" is interpreted. The absence of norms makes interpretation of this part of the test difficult.

The main differentiation appears to be between interest in things and interest in people or ideas. This is more marked with age and among more intelligent pupils. The things-people dichotomy also probably, in the reviewer's opinion, reflects a social class variation in Britain. Girls tend to prefer activities related to people; boys to things. In general, the school means show a tendency for technical school boys to score higher on things and grammar school boys (academically superior) on people or ideas. This is also reflected by the small but useful correlations reported between preference for things and later success in technical and commercial secondary courses.

In summary, this test appears to be an interesting and useful research instrument; there is in Britain a scarcity of published tests of personal preferences and attitudes with the background of development of this one. It seems unlikely that it is, in its present form, suitable for routine individual guidance, as suggested in the manual. At the present stage of educational practice, it appears improbable too that it will be widely used in youth clubs or grammar schools where it might prove most useful.

[82]

★**Cowell Personal Distance Scale.** Grades 7–9; 1958–63; title on scale is *Confidential Personal Distance Ballot;* social distance ratings of classmates; 1 form ['58, 1 page]; directions ['63, 1 page]; norms ['58, 1 page] for boys only; $2 per pad of 50 scales, postpaid; specimen set free; (30) minutes; Charles C. Cowell; [Tri-State Offset Co.]. *

REFERENCES

1. COWELL, C. C., AND ISMAIL, A. H. "Validity of a Football Rating Scale and Its Relationship to Social Integration and Academic Ability." *Res Q* 32:461–7 D '61. *

2. COWELL, CHARLES C., AND ISMAIL, A. H. "Relationships Between Selected Social and Physical Factors." *Res Q* 33:40–3 Mr '62. * (*PA* 37:1917)

3. CLARKE, H. HARRISON, AND GREENE, WALTER H. "Relationships Between Personal-Social Measures Applied to 10-Year-Old Boys." *Res Q* 34:288–98 O '63. *

[83]

★**Cowell Social Behavior Trend Index.** Grades 7–9; 1958–61; social adjustment ratings by 3 teachers; 2 parts ['58, 1 page] completed 1 week apart: Form A (positive behavior), Form B (negative behavior); directions ['61, 1 page]; norms ['58, 1 page] for boys only; supplementary data ('58, 12 pages, reprint of *1* below); $2 per set of pads containing 100 copies of each part, postpaid; specimen set free; (30) minutes per part for rating 30 students; Charles C. Cowell; [Tri-State Offset Co.]. *

REFERENCES

1. COWELL, CHARLES C. "Validating an Index of Social Adjustment for High School Use." *Res Q* 29:7-18 Mr '58. * (*PA* 33:5979)
2. COWELL, CHARLES C., AND ISMAIL, A. H. "Relationships Between Selected Social and Physical Factors." *Res Q* 33:40-3 Mr '62. * (*PA* 37:1917)

[84]

★**Cree Questionnaire.** Industrial employees; 1957-59; creativity and inventiveness; 1 form ('57, 8 pages); manual ('59, 17 pages); no data on reliability; norms for males only; $6 per 20 tests, postage extra; $1 per specimen set, postpaid; (15-20) minutes; Thelma Gwinn Thurstone (test), John Mellinger (test), and Measurement Research Division, Industrial Relations Center, University of Chicago (manual); Education-Industry Service. *

ALLYN MILES MUNGER, *Associate Director, Personnel and Marketing Research Division, The Psychological Corporation, New York, New York.*

"The *Cree Questionnaire* is a semi-disguised test of creativity and inventiveness." It has been used with engineers, engineer supervisors, research development personnel, salesmen, craftsmen, and others. This test is a product of research initiated by the A C Spark Plug Division of General Motors and was carried out under the direction of L. L. Thurstone in the Psychometric Laboratory at the University of North Carolina.

Besides items written specifically for this test, items were also drawn from the *Thurstone Temperament Schedule.* The original validation was done on 283 men selected by the chief engineers at 18 General Motors divisions. Essentially, the chief engineers were asked to select, one by one, engineers whom they knew to be creative and at the same time to choose another group in the same department or type of work whom they definitely knew were not creative. This method of choosing a criterion group would maximize the differences to be expected in response to the items in the questionnaire.

There is no evidence in either the test manual or in the references secured from the authors that any attempt was made to study a hold-out group or cross validation group. This means that we have a study of concurrent validity performed on two extreme groups without any hypothesis of what should discriminate. This would tend to maximize the differences to be found in favor of the researcher. In all other data supplied on this test, the scores were combined with other parts of a test battery so that it was impossible to evaluate the questionnaire as a separate instrument.

In evaluating the entire battery, one must go along with the original authors in their statement that it must be used with extreme caution in any other but the original environment. It is to be appreciated that General Motors has seen fit to release this study. However, the potential user should not regard this as a test ready to select creative individuals, but rather as an experimental set of items with certain research findings which need to be studied in each new environment. The questionnaire is a good example of a well-designed experimental test and should be labeled as such.

THEODOR F. NAUMANN, *Associate Professor of Psychology, Central Washington State College, Ellensburg, Washington.*

The manual describes this instrument as a "semi-disguised test of creativity and inventiveness." The eight-page test booklet contains 145 items; for each item a Y, ?, or N is to be circled in the booklet. The questionnaire is untimed and can be completed in about 20 minutes. Raw scores are obtained by matching each part of the scoring sheet with the answer sections on the margins of the respective test booklet pages.

The norms and the section of the manual dealing with them are somewhat confusing. The 1959 manual lists separate standard scores for four groups of employees and for the combined total (n = 496). The "new norms" which have more recently been attached to the manual are nothing but the old "combined total." This makes most of the manual's paragraph on norms irrelevant. Reliability data are not given. The validity discussion deals only with a group of engineers dichotomized into inventors and noninventors.

This is a rather conventionally prepared questionnaire. The more recent methods of test development have apparently not been utilized. There is also no indication that the results of modern research on creativity have been seriously taken into account. The instrument should be considered as a research device usable for rough screening and only applicable to a limited population.

[84a]

★**Developmental Potential of Preschool Children.** Handicapped children ages 2-6; 1958-62; title on record form is *Educational Evaluation of Preschool Children;* subtitle on report form is *Inventory of Developmental Levels;* level and pattern of intellectual, sensory, and emotional functioning and "readiness to profit from an educational program"; individual; 1

form (a series of objects, toys, and test cards); manual ('58, 297 pages, see B230); directions for assembling and constructing test kit ('62, 8 pages); recording form ('62, 7 pages, reprinted from manual); report form ('62, 4 pages); test cards ('62, 6 cards); no data on reliability; $5 per set of 20 recording forms and 20 report forms; $5.50 per set of test cards; $2.25 per manual for assembling test kit; $8.75 per manual; postage extra; test materials, except for cards, must be assembled locally; (45–120) minutes in 1 or 2 sessions; Else Haeussermann; Grune & Stratton. *

REFERENCES

1. Haeussermann, Else. *Developmental Potential of Preschool Children: An Evaluation of Intellectual, Sensory, and Emotional Functioning.* New York: Grune & Stratton, Inc., 1958. Pp. xvii, 285. * (*PA* 34:2998)

For an excerpt from a review of the manual, see B230.

[85]

***Diplomacy Test of Empathy.** Business and industry; 1957–60; revision of *Primary Empathic Abilities* ('57); title on test is *Diplomacy Test of Empathic Ability;* 1 form ('60, 4 pages); manual ('60, 4 pages); separate answer sheets must be used; $9 per 50 tests; $2 per 50 answer sheets; $1 per specimen set (must be purchased to obtain manual and key); postage extra; (20–25) minutes; Willard A. Kerr; Psychometric Affiliates. *

REFERENCES

1. Smouse, Albert D.; Aderman, Morris; and Van Buskirk, Charles. "Three Empathy Measures as Correlates of Test and Rating Criteria." *Psychol Rep* 12:803–9 Je '63. * (*PA* 38:6035)

Arthur H. Brayfield, *Executive Officer, American Psychological Association, Washington, D.C.*

This test is representative of an interesting idea inadequately developed. Apparently the definition of empathy is the "ability to put yourself in the other person's position, establish rapport, and anticipate his reactions, feelings and behaviors."

The measurement approach is to use as items bits of miscellaneous factual information including verbal reactions of people to a variety of stimuli. Many of the items are based on findings from attitude surveys dealing with work factors, annoyances, and worries. Agreement with the actual results is assumed to index empathy. A sample item from the most and least answer format is: "Most and Least copies printed per issue: (*a*) Popular Mechanics, (*b*) McCalls, (*c*) Forbes." An example of the one answer format is: "Men aged 35 are most likely to worry about: (*a*) Work associates, (*b*) Work efficiency, (*c*) Health, (*d*) Morality of self."

The single odd-even reliability coefficient reported on 114 adults is .56. Norms for six groups, mainly from management, sales, and business generally, are presented. The groups are described only by broad job classification; no means and standard deviations are given.

Undoubtedly something is being measured here; it is difficult to say what. There are insufficient and inadequate data to believe that the construct "empathy" has been isolated. The publisher's catalog says that this test "measures ability to sell, to be persuasive, tactful, and diplomatic." There is only the most indirect and peripheral evidence for any such statement. The salary increase criterion is too hedged with technical issues to be relied upon. The group difference findings are incompletely reported and descriptive data are lacking; age, experience, socio-economic, and education variables are uncontrolled. The cleanest finding, in my view, is the correlation of .40 between scores and numbers of elective offices held, although again uncontrolled variables may be operative.

In short, here is a basically interesting notion. It merits careful, technically competent, and systematic follow-up. The present instrument should be labeled "For Research Only." The word diplomacy in the test title is meaningless and the personality theory outlined in the manual is naïve. These trappings should not distract the serious investigator, nor should they impress the prospective purchaser.

Richard S. Hatch, *Vice President, Dunnette, Kirchner and Associates, Inc., Minneapolis, Minnesota.*

The *Diplomacy Test of Empathy* purports to measure "profundity of understanding of others' feelings and tastes" through predictions by the examinee of the self-descriptions of a large variety of generalized "others," such as persons aged 25–29, the average man, employees, married men, men, women, people, fired people, old people, etc. In addition to this prediction type item, the examinee is asked to estimate such things as the ages at which children are likely to have front teeth missing, academic disciplines in which women receive most and fewest degrees, and the number of farm families owning their own homes in 1950. Scoring is presumably based on a comparison of examinees' predictions with actual self-descriptions by the "others" for whom the predictions were directed—although the test manual does not provide specific references to such test development research.

Most significant are the severe methodological errors and statistical artifacts associated with the measurement approach employed. It has been pointed out by Gage and Cronbach[1] that empathic measurement approaches of the type employed in this test present artifactually "linked" components. These are Assumed Similarity, Real Similarity, and Accuracy. The degree to which the examinee possesses attitudes similar to the "others" for whom he is predicting (Real Similarity) and the degree to which the examinee assumes that the "others" possess attitudes like his own (Assumed Similarity) dictate Accuracy. Research has repeatedly demonstrated that individuals tend to assume a high degree of similarity between their own self-descriptions and the self-descriptions of "others" toward whom they are predicting; consequently, the Real Similarity between the examinee's own attitudes and those possessed by the "others," a factor unrelated to any empathic sensitivity possessed by the examinee, will determine Accuracy. In this test the degree of Real Similarity between the examinee and the "others" is uncontrolled, as well as the degree to which examinees "assume similarity" with the generalized "others." No control of examinees' response sets has been attempted. Without statistical or procedural controls either in the scoring or in the design of the test itself, the responses to exercises of the type presented in this test are uninterpretable. Most probably, the test simply provides scores which closely reflect the degree with which examinees possess attitudes similar to those of the generalized "others" for whom they are predicting, and if so, it is unwarranted to characterize examinees scoring high on the test as "empathic" or differentially sensitive in their interpersonal perceptions of others' attitudes and preferences.

The test manual only provides information on validation studies by the author, and these are not referenced. The reviewer strongly recommends that potential users interested in personnel selection and placement carry out specific validation research within their own prediction environments before basing decisions of any consequence on the test. Interpretation of scores as provided by the manual is definitely not recommended.

Investigators of interpersonal perception may desire, for research purposes, the scores generated by the test, although the reliability of the test is somewhat unsatisfactory—the odd-even reliability being .56. This reviewer considers use of the test in experimental studies to be a waste of time in view of the test's reliance upon a methodologically inadequate approach to empathic measurement. Researchers in the area would do better to pursue more sophisticated measurement techniques and design new measures of this elusive "trait" than to perpetuate the measurement fallacies inherent in the approach incorporated in this test.

In summary, research on the measurement of interpersonal perception processes has not, as yet, yielded an acceptable approach to the construction of an "off-the-shelf" test of empathic sensitivity. Consequently, the reviewer is unaware of any valid standardized empathy test which might be recommended in lieu of the *Diplomacy Test of Empathy*. It is encouraging to note, however, that empathy has been successfully measured in the "laboratory." It is not unreasonable, then, considering the potential usefulness of this social skill, to expect early applications of methodologically acceptable empathic measurement approaches to the practical problems of personnel selection.

[1] GAGE, N. L., and CRONBACH, LEE J. "Conceptual and Methodological Problems in Interpersonal Perception." *Psychol R* 62:411–22 S '55. *

For a review by Robert L. Thorndike of the earlier test, see 5:99.

[86]

★Dynamic Personality Inventory. Ages 15 or 17 and over with IQ's of 80 and over; 1956–61; for research and experimental use only (not so labeled in distributor's catalog); 33 scores: hypocrisy, passivity, seclusion-introspection, orality, oral aggression, oral dependence, emotional independence, verbal aggression, impulsiveness, unconventionality, hoarding behavior, attention to details, conservatism, submissiveness, anal sadism, insularity, phallic symbol interest, narcissism, exhibitionism, active Icarus complex, passive Icarus complex, sensuality, Icarian exploits, sexuality, tactile impression enjoyment, creative interests, masculine sexual identification, feminine sexual identification, social role seeking, social activity interest, need to give affection, ego defense persistence, initiative; 1 form ('56, 7 pages); also available, in abbreviated form and without scores for orality, phallic symbol interest, and sexuality, under the title *Likes and Interests Test* ('56, 6 pages) for use with apprentices and employee applicants ages 15 and over; mimeographed temporary manual ('61, 8 pages); the interpretive manual which the temporary manual says will be available "shortly" is not yet available as of summer 1963; DPI score-norms sheets ('56, 6 sheets, separate sheets for male students, female students, general population males, general population females, male neurotics, female neurotics); LIT score-norms sheets ('56, 2 sheets, separate sheets for male apprentices, female technical college students); separate answer sheets must be used; 15*s.* per 25 tests of either title; 13*s.* per 100 answer sheets; 42*s.* 6*d.* per set of DPI scoring keys; 41*s.* per set of LIT scoring keys; 25*s.* per 100 score-norms sheets for any one population; 4*s.* per manual; 8*s.* per specimen set; prices include purchase tax; postpaid within U.K.; (40) minutes; T. G. Grygier; distributed by National Foundation for Educational Research in England and Wales. *

REFERENCES

1. BARRON, FRANK. "The Disposition Toward Originality." *J Abn & Social Psychol* 51:478–85 N '55. * (*PA* 31:2533)
2. GRYGIER, PATRICIA. "The Personality of Student Nurses: A Pilot Study Using the Dynamic Personality Inventory." *Int J Social Psychiatry* 2:105–12 au '56. * (*PA* 32:2238)
3. GRYGIER, T. G. "The Dynamic Personality Inventory: A Preliminary Notice." *B Nat Found Ed Res Engl & Wales* (9):39–42 Mr '57. *
4. GRYGIER, T. G. "Psychometric Aspects of Homosexuality." *J Mental Sci* 103:514–26 Jl '57. * (*PA* 32:5664)
5. GRYGIER, TADEUSZ. "Homosexuality, Neurosis and 'Normality': A Pilot Study in Psychological Measurement." *Brit J Delinq* 9:59–61 Jl '58. * (*PA* 33:10330)
6. GRYGIER, TADEUSZ. "Statistical and Psychoanalytical Criteria in the Development of the Dynamic Personality Inventory." *Rorsch Newsl* 3:5–7 Je '58. *
7. BEACH, LEE. "Rorschach Variables and Vocational Choice." *B Maritime Psychol Assn* 8:28–33 Ap '59. *

S. B. SELLS, *Professor of Psychology, and Director, Institute of Behavioral Research, Texas Christian University, Fort Worth, Texas.*

Although offered for sale for clinical, industrial selection, and other practical uses, this test, published in 1956, has available only a temporary manual, copyrighted in 1961. It has apparently enjoyed some considerable use in research, as indicated by a typewritten list of references, plus a list of 19 papers in preparation, submitted by the author. The 1961 manual cites no references.

The DPI is designed to provide a "general picture of personality organisation in developmental terms." It is psychoanalytic in conception and the author acknowledges the influence of M. H. Krout and J. Krout Tabin regarding theoretical principles of measurement. The inventory, which was originally a modification of the Krout-Tabin *Personal Preference Scale* (5:93) but has since been extensively modified, consists of 325 items, arranged nonsystematically, which are responded to in terms of like or dislike. Manual scoring by overlay stencils yields 33 scales (of from 8 to 24 items per scale, with a median of 12) that purport to measure "tendencies, sublimations, reaction-formations, and defence mechanisms associated with the various patterns of psychosexual development, with masculine and feminine identifications, with some patterns of mature interests, and with two aspects of ego-strength." The items consist of objects (hot milk, strong drinks, torrential rain), activities (diving, prolonged kissing, watching explosions), and concepts (keeping all foreigners out of the civil service, staying in familiar surroundings, a Negro family settling in a house opposite) that are associated with one or more of the "traits" measured. They are designed to stimulate imagination and subjects are instructed to give free rein to their imagination, assessing each item according to first reaction.

Psychometrically, this test is difficult to evaluate. While a careful reading of the items against the key suggests a considerable degree of face validity in terms of psychoanalytic rationale, this is insufficient except to give insight into the author's approach. Unfortunately, the temporary manual is not only of no help to the sophisticated critic, but rather quite frustrating. Under "Principles of Scale Construction," the author states that, over a dozen experimental editions were constructed, and "succeeding editions of the test were factorized, examined for internal consistency and repeat reliability, validated and cross-validated." No statements are included concerning factor structure. But the claims for the excellence of the test are extreme. Indeed, *most* of the scales now in use (many of the original ones were abandoned or empirically modified) are claimed to have satisfied the criteria of (*a*) adequate split-half reliability, (*b*) adequate retest reliability, (*c*) content validity in relation to theoretical formulation (the reviewer has termed this face validity), (*d*) concurrent validity with other personality measures, and (*e*) construct validity in factor-analytic studies. Five scales are acknowledged to be "experimental." The items are claimed to be (*a*) neither universally liked nor disliked, (*b*) highly and significantly correlated with their own scales and appropriately correlated with other scales, (*c*) not unduly highly correlated with conceptually unrelated scales, (*d*) relatively unaffected by social desirability, (*e*) stable in patterns of relationship on cross validation, (*f*) productive of emotional reactions and free associations in accordance with the test design, and (*g*) the mental processes interpretations have been analyzed.

Unfortunately no data are presented in support of most of these claims which would be considered extravagant in relation to any other personality test known to the reviewer. Some data are mentioned on reliability, which is said to average .75 for split-half and .80 for retest, but reliability data are not reported by scale. Since the scales range from 8 to 24 items, this is rather important. The validity discussion merely mentions correlations with "several hundred independent measures." Although industrial uses are recommended, no data are presented, and not even any claims of validity for such application.

The reviewer has sampled the references supplied by the author and there are a number of interesting results which lend partial support to the validity of various individual scales. For example, Barron (*1*) obtained borderline significance on the relation of measures of *anality* and originality. However, this is more than a giant step away from proof of the sweeping statements of the author. If data are available to substantiate his claims, he may have a magnificent test and he should make all haste to publish them. But it is doubtful that this is the case. The very nature of the psychoanalytic constructs that the test purports to measure raises questions of a more fundamental, theoretical nature, as well as measurement problems of definition, testability, and behavioral correlates that appear to be overwhelming.

At the same time, this test booklet may provide a fruitful research instrument for quantitative investigation of a more conventional (nonpsychoanalytic) nature. The pool of items is both interesting and novel and research with them may lead to new formulations of personality and motivational traits of considerable value.

[87]

***Edwards Personal Preference Schedule.** College and adults; 1953–59; 15 scores: achievement, deference, order, exhibition, autonomy, affiliation, intraception, succorance, dominance, abasement, nurturance, change, endurance, heterosexuality, aggression; IBM and NCS; 1 form ('54, 8 pages); revised manual ('59, 25 pages); answer sheet-profile ('59, c1954–59, 2 pages); separate answer sheets must be used; $3.50 per 25 tests; $2.50 per 50 hand scoring answer sheets; $2.40 per 50 IBM answer sheets; $3.25 per 50 NCS answer sheets (scored by National Computer Systems only, see 671); set of manual and keys: 60¢ with hand scoring template, $1.50 with set of hand scoring stencils for IBM answer sheets, $1.65 with set of machine scoring stencils; 75¢ per specimen set; postpaid; (40–55) minutes; Allen L. Edwards; Psychological Corporation. *

REFERENCES

1–50. See 5:47.
51. Bendig, A. W. "Manifest Anxiety and Projective and Objective Measures of Need Achievement." Abstract. *J Consult Psychol* 21:354 Ag '57. * (*PA* 33:1671, title only)
52. Bennis, Warren; Burke, Richard; Cutter, Henry; Harrington, Herbert; and Hoffman, Joyce. "A Note on Some Problems of Measurement and Prediction in a Training Group." *Group Psychother* 10:328–41 D '57. * (*PA* 33:5971)
53. Edwards, Allen L. *The Social Desirability Variable in Personality Assessment and Research.* New York: Dryden Press, Inc., 1957. Pp. xv, 108. * (*PA* 32:464)
54. Navran, Leslie, and Stauffacher, James C. "The Personality Structure of Psychiatric Nurses." *Nursing Res* 5:109–14 F '57. * (*PA* 34:2283)
55. Starr, Harold. *Personality Correlates of Time Estimation.* Doctor's thesis, Purdue University (Lafayette, Ind.), 1957. (*DA* 18:2217)
56. Wright, Calvin E. *Relations Between Normative and Ipsative Measures of Personality.* Doctor's thesis, University of Washington (Seattle, Wash.), 1957. (*DA* 18:1487)
57. Abe, Steven Kiyoshi. *Nisei Personality Characteristics as Measured by the Edwards Personal Preference Schedule and Minnesota Multiphasic Personality Inventory.* Doctor's thesis, University of Utah (Salt Lake City, Utah), 1958. (*DA* 19:2648)
58. Anderson, Darrell Edward. *Personality Variables and Verbal Conditioning.* Doctor's thesis, University of Nebraska (Lincoln, Neb.), 1958. (*DA* 19:1811)
59. Bendig, A. W. "Objective Measures of Needs and Course Achievement in Introductory Psychology." *J General Psychol* 59:51–7 Jl '58. * (*PA* 36:2KJ51B)
60. Bosdell, Betty Jane. *Perceptions of Guidance Services as Related to Personality Needs and Job Title.* Doctor's thesis, University of Illinois (Urbana, Ill.), 1958. (*DA* 19:1010)
61. Cabrer, Sebastian M. *Exploration of Behavioral Correlates of Perseveration.* Doctor's thesis, Purdue University (Lafayette, Ind.), 1958. (*DA* 19:1444)
62. Dilworth, Tom, IV. "A Comparison of the Edwards PPS Variables With Some Aspects of the TAT." Abstract. *J Consult Psychol* 22:486 D '58. * (*PA* 33:10321)
63. Dilworth, Tom, IV. *A Comparison of the Edwards Personal Preference Schedule Variables With Some Aspects of the Thematic Apperception Test.* Master's thesis, Southern Methodist University (Dallas, Tex.), 1958.
64. Gisvold, Darrell. "A Validity Study of the Autonomy and Deference Subscales of the EPPS." *J Consult Psychol* 22:445–7 D '58. * (*PA* 33:10092)
65. Himelstein, Philip; Eschenbach, Arthur E.; and Carp, A. "Interrelationships Among Three Measures of Need Achievement." *J Consult Psychol* 22:451–2 D '58. * (*PA* 33:9953)
66. Karr, Chadwick. *A Comparison of EPPS Scores Obtained From the Standard Forced-Choice Procedure and a Rating-Scale Procedure.* Doctor's thesis, University of Washington (Seattle, Wash.), 1958. (*DA* 19:3382)
67. Kelly, E. Lowell; Miller, James G.; Marquis, Donald G.; Gerard, R. W.; and Uhr, Leonard. "Personality Differences and Continued Meprobamate and Proclorperazine Administration." *A.M.A. Arch Neurol & Psychiatry* 80:241–6 Ag '58. * (*PA* 33:10420)
68. Levy, Leo. *A Study of Some Personality Attributes of Independents and Conformers.* Doctor's thesis, University of Washington (Seattle, Wash.), 1958. (*DA* 19:1823)
69. Marlowe, David. "Some Psychological Correlates of Field Independence." Abstract. *J Consult Psychol* 22:334 O '58. * (*PA* 34:1044)
70. Michel, John. *Non-Intellectual Dimensions of Performance in Reading.* Doctor's thesis, University of Texas (Austin, Tex.), 1958. (*DA* 19:2285)
71. Mitchell, Peter Michael. *Perceptual Correlates of Anxiety.* Doctor's thesis, Purdue University (Lafayette, Ind.), 1958. (*DA* 18:2213)
72. Moroney, Frances Mary. *Methods of Studying Self-Concepts of Teachers.* Doctor's thesis, Pennsylvania State University (University Park, Pa.), 1958. (*DA* 19:90)
73. Navran, Leslie, and Stauffacher, James C. "A Comparative Analysis of the Personality Structure of Psychiatric and Nonpsychiatric Nurses." *Nursing Res* 7:64–7 Je '58. *
74. Nimnicht, Glendon Perrin. *A Study of Successful Superintendents and Their Leadership Ability.* Doctor's thesis, Stanford University (Stanford, Calif.), 1958. (*DA* 19:720)
75. Nunnery, Michael Y. *A Study in the Use of Psychological Tests in Determining Effectiveness and Ineffectiveness Among Practicing School Administrators.* Doctor's thesis, University of Tennessee (Knoxville, Tenn.), 1958. (*DA* 19:1276)
76. Parker, Seymour. "Personality Factors Among Medical Students as Related to Their Predisposition to View the Patient as a 'Whole Man.'" *J Med Ed* 33:736–44 O '58. * (*PA* 34:3539)
77. Pepper, Roger S. *The Relationship Between Certain Dimensions of Psychological Need and the Achievement of First-Semester College Freshmen.* Doctor's thesis, University of Michigan (Ann Arbor, Mich.), 1958. (*DA* 19:732)
78. Sanders, Ella Moye. *The Relationship Between Verbal-Quantitative Ability and Certain Personality and Metabolic Characteristics.* Doctor's thesis, University of Texas (Austin, Tex.), 1958. (*DA* 19:2540)
79. Scheidel, Thomas M.; Crowell, Laura; and Shepherd, John R. "Personality and Discussion Behavior: A Study of Possible Relationships." *Speech Monogr* 25:261–7 N '58. * (*PA* 33:9990)
80. Thorpe, Jo Anne. "Study of Personality Variables Among Successful Women Students and Teachers of Physical Education." *Res Q* 29:83–92 Mr '58. * (*PA* 33:5974)
81. Verrill, Bernard Victor. *An Investigation of the Concept of Impulsivity.* Doctor's thesis, University of Houston (Houston, Tex.), 1958. (*DA* 19:183)
82. Vogel, Bertram. *Humor and Personality: A Study of the Relationship Between Certain Selected Aspects of Person-*

ality and the Preference for Aggressive or Non-Aggressive Written Humor. Doctor's thesis, New York University (New York, N.Y.), 1958. (*DA* 19:2157)
83. YADOFF, BERNARD. *An Attempt to Change Word Meaning and a Personality Test Score Through Semantic Generalization.* Doctor's thesis, University of Pittsburgh (Pittsburgh, Pa.), 1958. (*DA* 19:2161)
84. ZUCKERMAN, MARVIN, AND GROSZ, HANUS J. "Suggestibility and Dependency." Abstract. *J Consult Psychol* 22:328 O '58. * (*PA* 34:1435)
85. ANDREWS, JOHN H. M., AND BROWN, ALAN F. "Can Principals Exclude Their Own Personality Characteristics When They Rate Their Teachers?" *Ed Adm & Sup* 45:234–42 Jl '59. * (*PA* 34:6579)
86. ARKOFF, ABE. "Need Patterns in Two Generations of Japanese Americans in Hawaii." *J Social Psychol* 50:75–9 Ag '59. * (*PA* 35:3319)
87. BADAL, ALDEN WESLEY. *The Relationship of Selected Test Measures to Administrator Success in the Elementary School.* Doctor's thesis, Stanford University (Stanford, Calif.), 1959. (*DA* 20:1263)
88. BENDIG, A. W. "Comparative Validity of Objective and Projective Measures of Need Achievement in Predicting Students' Achievement in Introductory Psychology." *J General Psychol* 60:237–43 Ap '59. * (*PA* 36:2KL37B)
89. BENDIG, A. W. "Personality Variables Related to Individual Performance on a Cognitive Task." *J General Psychol* 60:265–8 Ap '59. * (*PA* 36:2HJ65B)
90. BURCHINAL, LEE G. "Adolescent Role Deprivation and High School Age Marriage." *Marriage & Family Living* 21:378–84 N '59. * (*PA* 36:2IQ78B)
91. CARON, ALBERT J., AND WALLACH, MICHAEL A. "Personality Determinants of Repressive and Obsessive Reactions to Failure-Stress." *J Abn & Social Psychol* 59:236–45 S '59. * (*PA* 34:3310)
92. COLEMAN, WILLIAM, AND COLLETT, DOROTHY MANLEY. "Development and Applications of Structured Tests of Personality." *R Ed Res* 29:57–72 F '59. * (*PA* 34:5604)
93. DICKEN, CHARLES F. "Simulated Patterns on the Edwards Personal Preference Schedule." *J Appl Psychol* 43:372–8 D '59. * (*PA* 34:7379)
94. EDWARDS, ALLEN L.; WRIGHT, CALVIN E.; AND LUNNEBORG, CLIFFORD E. "A Note on 'Social Desirability as a Variable in the Edwards Personal Preference Schedule.'" *J Consult Psychol* 23:558 D '59. * (*PA* 34:5607)
95. FRYE, ROLAND L., AND ADAMS, HENRY E. "Effect of the Volunteer Variable on Leaderless Group Discussion Experiments." *Psychol Rep* 5:184 Je '59. * (*PA* 34:2762)
96. GOODSTEIN, LEONARD D., AND HEILBRUN, ALFRED B., JR. "The Relationship Between Personal and Social Desirability Scale Values of the Edwards Personal Preference Schedule." Abstract. *J Consult Psychol* 23:183 Ap '59. * (*PA* 34:1365, title only)
97. HARDISON, JAMES, AND PURCELL, KENNETH. "The Effects of Psychological Stress as a Function of Need and Cognitive Control." *J Personality* 27:250–8 Je '59. * (*PA* 34:4071)
98. HEILBRUN, ALFRED B., JR., AND GOODSTEIN, LEONARD D. "Relationships Between Personal and Social Desirability Sets and Performance on the Edwards Personal Preference Schedule." *J Appl Psychol* 43:302–5 O '59. * (*PA* 34:5719)
99. HOOKER, WILLIAM DOUGLAS. *A Study of Certain Personal Characteristics and Attitudes of Full-Time and Part-Time Student Teachers and Certified Beginning Teachers.* Doctor's thesis, University of Texas (Austin, Tex.), 1959. (*DA* 20:2677)
100. HORST, PAUL, AND WRIGHT, CALVIN E. "The Comparative Reliability of Two Techniques of Personality Appraisal." *J Clin Psychol* 15:388–91 O '59. * (*PA* 36:1HC88H)
101. KAHN, SAMUEL. *The Relationship of Needs to Friendship Choices in Adolescence.* Doctor's thesis, Columbia University (New York, N.Y.), 1959. (*DA* 20:756)
102. KARR, CHADWICK. "Two Methods for Scoring Self-Rating Scales to Approximate Forced Choice Results." *Psychol Rep* 5:773–9 D '59. * (*PA* 34:4962)
103. KENNEY, RAYMOND CARROLL. *An Analysis of Self Perceptions in Counselor Trainees.* Doctor's thesis, University of Texas (Austin, Tex.), 1959. (*DA* 20:2677)
104. KLETT, C. JAMES, AND YAUKEY, DAVID W. "A Cross-Cultural Comparison of Judgments of Social Desirability." *J Social Psychol* 49:19–26 F '59. * (*PA* 35:4763)
105. KRUG, ROBERT E. "Over- and Underachievement and the Edwards Personal Preference Schedule." *J Appl Psychol* 43:133–6 Ap '59. * (*PA* 34:3439)
106. LEVONIAN, EDWARD; COMREY, ANDREW; LEVY, WILLIAM; AND PROCTER, DONALD. "A Statistical Evaluation of Edwards Personal Preference Schedule." *J Appl Psychol* 43:355–9 D '59. * (*PA* 34:7401)
107. LEWIS, WILLIAM A. "Emotional Adjustment and Need Satisfaction of Hospital Patients." *J Counsel Psychol* 6:127–31 su '59. * (*PA* 34:4315)
108. MARLOWE, DAVID. "Relationships Among Direct and Indirect Measures of the Achievement Motive and Overt Behavior." *J Consult Psychol* 23:329–32 Ag '59. * (*PA* 34:4394)
109. MERRILL, REED M., AND MURPHY, DANIEL T. "Personality Factors and Academic Achievement in College." *J Counsel Psychol* 6:207–10 f '59. * (*PA* 35:3935)
110. MILAM, JAMES ROBERT. *An Application of the Edwards Personal Preference Schedule to Problems in Psychopathology.* Doctor's thesis, University of Washington (Seattle, Wash.), 1959. (*DA* 20:1075)
111. MORTON, JOHN. "An Investigation Into the Effects of an Adult Reading Efficiency Course." *Occupational Psychol* 33:222–37 O '59. * (*PA* 34:6523)
112. NUNNERY, MICHAEL Y. "How Useful Are Standardized Psychological Tests in the Selection of School Administrators." *Ed Adm & Sup* 45:349–56 N '59. * (*PA* 35:7092)
113. PENA, CESAREO D. "Influence of Social Desirability Upon Rorschach Content." *J Clin Psychol* 15:313–6 Jl '59. * (*PA* 35:3436)
114. RITCHEY, RONALD E. *The Relationship Between Academic Achievement and the Personality Variables Measured by the Edwards Personal Preference Schedule.* Master's thesis, University of Nebraska (Lincoln, Neb.), 1959.
115. RODGERS, FRANK P. *A Psychometric Study of Certain Interest and Personality Variables Associated With Academic Achievement in a College Level Printing Curriculum.* Doctor's thesis, University of Buffalo (Buffalo, N.Y.), 1959. (*DA* 19:3219)
116. SCHUMACHER, CHARLES FREDRICK. *A Comparison of Three Methods for Keying Interest and Personality Inventories.* Doctor's thesis, University of Minnesota (Minneapolis, Minn.), 1959. (*DA* 20:370)
117. SHELDON, M. STEPHEN; COALE, JACK M.; AND COPPLE, ROCKNE. "Concurrent Validity of the 'Warm Teacher Scale.'" *J Ed Psychol* 50:37–40 F '59. * (*PA* 35:2810)
118. TREHUB, ARNOLD. "Ego Disjunction and Psychopathology." *J Abn & Social Psychol* 58:191–4 Mr '59. * (*PA* 34:1064)
119. TUCKER, WOODIE L. *The Relationship Between Personality Traits and Basic Skill in Typewriting.* Doctor's thesis, University of Pittsburgh (Pittsburgh, Pa.), 1959. (*DA* 20:1694)
120. TUDDENHAM, READ D. "Correlates of Yielding to a Distorted Group Norm." *J Personality* 27:272–84 Je '59. * (*PA* 34:4096)
121. WAGGONER, GLEN HASTINGS. *Administrator's Scores on Selected Standardized Tests and His Administrative Performance as Reported by Classroom Teachers.* Doctor's thesis, Stanford University (Stanford, Calif.), 1959. (*DA* 20:3169)
122. WALSH, RICHARD P. "The Effect of Needs on Responses to Job Duties." *J Counsel Psychol* 6:194–8 f '59. * (*PA* 35:3514)
123. WARD, PAUL LEWIS. *A Study of the Relationship of Evaluative Attitudes to Scholastic Ability and Academic Achievement.* Doctor's thesis, Ohio State University (Columbus, Ohio), 1959. (*DA* 20:3639)
124. WEISS, PETER; WERTHEIMER, MICHAEL; AND GROESBECK, BYRON. "Achievement Motivation, Academic Aptitude, and College Grades." *Ed & Psychol Meas* 19:663–6 w '59. * (*PA* 34:6575)
124a. WEYBREW, BENJAMIN B., AND MOLISH, H. B. "Approaches to the Study of Motivation of Officer Candidates for the Submarine Service." *U S Naval Med Res Lab Rep* 18:1–47 O '59. * (*PA* 34:8530)
125. ZUCKERMAN, MARVIN, AND OLTEAN, MARY. "Some Relationships Between Maternal Attitude Factors and Authoritarianism, Personality Needs, Psychopathology, and Self-Acceptance." *Child Develop* 30:27–36 Mr '59. * (*PA* 34:3176)
126. ATKINSON, JOHN W., AND LITWIN, GEORGE H. "Achievement Motive and Test Anxiety Conceived as Motive to Approach Success and Motive to Avoid Failure." *J Abn & Social Psychol* 60:52–63 Ja '60. * (*PA* 34:7132)
127. BAY, JUNG HONG. *The Validity of Two Objective Measures of Academic Motivation.* Doctor's thesis, State University of Iowa (Iowa City, Iowa), 1960. (*DA* 20:4585)
128. BERNBERG, RAYMOND E. "An Analysis of the Responses of a Male Prison Population to the Edwards Personal Preference Schedule." *J General Psychol* 62:319–24 Ap '60. * (*PA* 34:8097)
129. BERNHARDT, HAROLD E., JR. "'Intraception' Test Score and Psychiatry Grade as a Freshman and as a Sophomore Medical Student: A Validational Study of a Subscale of the Edwards Personal Preference Schedule." *Ed & Psychol Meas* 20:365–79 su '60. * (*PA* 35:6426)
130. BOYCE, RICHARD DUDLEY. *An Empirical Evaluation of Five Tests for Administrator Selection: The Composite Study.* Doctor's thesis, Stanford University (Stanford, Calif.), 1960. (*DA* 21:2546)
131. BROWN, DONALD JAMES. *An Investigation of the Relationships Between Certain Personal Characteristics of Guidance Counselors and Performance in Supervised Counseling Interviews.* Doctor's thesis, Ohio State University (Columbus, Ohio), 1960. (*DA* 21:810)
132. BUNIN, SANFORD MELVIN. *Non-Intellectual Dimensions of Some Academic Performance.* Doctor's thesis, University of Texas (Austin, Tex.), 1960. (*DA* 20:4586)
133. CHANCE, JUNE ELIZABETH, AND MEADERS, WILSON. "Needs and Interpersonal Perception." *J Personality* 28:200–9 Je '60. * (*PA* 35:2260)
134. CLARK, CHARLES MARVIN. *Changes in Response Patterns of Counseling Institute Trainees.* Doctor's thesis, Ohio State University (Columbus, Ohio), 1960. (*DA* 21:811)
135. DICKEN, CHARLES F. "Simulated Patterns on the

California Psychological Inventory." *J Counsel Psychol* 7:24–31 sp '60. * (*PA* 35:2218)
136. DIENER, CHARLES L. "Similarities and Differences Between Over-Achieving and Under-Achieving Students." *Personnel & Guid J* 38:396–400 Ja '60. *
137. DIVESTA, FRANCIS J., AND COX, LANDON. "Some Dispositional Correlates of Conformity Behavior." *J Social Psychol* 52:259–68 N '60. * (*PA* 35:4813)
138. DUNNETTE, MARVIN D., AND KIRCHNER, WAYNE K. "Psychological Test Differences Between Industrial Salesmen and Retail Salesmen." *J Appl Psychol* 44:121–5 Ap '60. * (*PA* 35:4029)
139. EBERT, FRANCIS JOHN. *An Empirical Evaluation of Five Tests for the Selection of Elementary School Principals.* Doctor's thesis, Stanford University (Stanford, Calif.), 1960. (*DA* 21:2548)
140. EDWARDS, ALLEN L.; HEATHERS, LOUISE B.; AND FORDYCE, WILBERT E. "Correlations of New MMPI Scales With Edwards SD Scale." *J Clin Psychol* 16:26–9 Ja '60. * (*PA* 36:1HF26E)
141. FELDMAN, MARVIN J., AND CORAH, NORMAN L. "Social Desirability and the Forced Choice Method." *J Consult Psychol* 24:480–2 D '60. * (*PA* 36:1HF80F)
142. FISKE, DONALD W. "Variability Among Peer Ratings in Different Situations." *Ed & Psychol Meas* 20:283–92 su '60. * (*PA* 35:6337)
143. FISKE, DONALD W.; HOWARD, KENNETH; AND RECHENBERG, WILLIAM. "The EPPS Profile Stability Coefficient." Abstract. *J Consult Psychol* 24:370 Ag '60. *
144. FORDYCE, WILBERT E., AND CROW, WILLIAM R. "Ego Disjunction: A Failure to Replicate Trehub's Results." *J Abn & Social Psychol* 60:446–8 My '60. * (*PA* 35:4954)
145. GARDNER, MARGARET SEYMOUR. *Factors Associated With Success in First Grade Teaching.* Doctor's thesis, Northwestern University (Evanston, Ill.), 1960. (*DA* 21:2609)
145a. GARDNER, RILEY W.; JACKSON, DOUGLAS N.; AND MESSICK, SAMUEL J. "Personality Organization in Cognitive Controls and Intellectual Abilities." *Psychol Issues* 2(8):1–149 '60. * (*PA* 36:2HA49G)
146. GUSTAFSON, MONTANE C. *Relationship Between Manifest Needs and Differential Achievement of High School Students.* Doctor's thesis, University of Nebraska (Lincoln, Neb.), 1960. (*DA* 20:4335)
147. GUSTAV, ALICE. "Use of Two Tests in Brief Counseling." *J Counsel Psychol* 7:228–9 f '60. *
148. HAINES, LEWIS EDGAR. *An Evaluation of the FIRO-B and the EPPS for Predicting College Roommate Compatibility.* Doctor's thesis, Washington State University (Pullman, Wash.), 1960. (*DA* 21:2173)
149. HEIST, PAUL. "Personality Characteristics of Dental Students." *Ed Rec* 41:240–52 Jl '60. * (*PA* 35:7081)
150. IZARD, CARROLL E. "Personality Characteristics Associated With Resistance to Change." *J Consult Psychol* 24:437–40 O '60. * (*PA* 35:4985)
151. IZARD, CARROLL E. "Personality Characteristics of Engineers as Measured by the Edwards Personal Preference Schedule." *J Appl Psychol* 44:332–5 O '60. * (*PA* 35:4016)
152. IZARD, CARROLL E. "Personality Similarity and Friendship." *J Abn & Social Psychol* 61:47–51 Jl '60. * (*PA* 35:2117)
153. IZARD, CARROLL E. "Personality Similarity, Positive Affect, and Interpersonal Attraction." *J Abn & Social Psychol* 61:484–5 N '60. * (*PA* 36:2GE84I)
154. JAMES, KENNETH RAYMOND. *An Empirical Evaluation of Five Tests for Administrator Selection in a Metropolitan School District.* Doctor's thesis, Stanford University (Stanford, Calif.), 1960. (*DA* 21:2556)
155. JOHNSON, RONALD ENGLE. *A Quantification and Measurement of Three Qualitative Changes in the Recall of Complex Verbal Materials.* Doctor's thesis, Ohio State University (Columbus, Ohio), 1960. (*DA* 21:2358)
156. KATZ, IRWIN; GLUCKSBERG, SAM; AND KRAUSS, ROBERT. "Need Satisfaction and Edwards PPS Scores in Married Couples." *J Consult Psychol* 24:205–8 Je '60. * (*PA* 35:6685)
157. KAZMIER, LEONARD JOHN. *Validation of a Technique for Predicting Over- and Under-Achievement Through Objective Testing.* Doctor's thesis, Ohio State University (Columbus, Ohio), 1960. (*DA* 21:2359)
158. KIRCHNER, WAYNE K.; DUNNETTE, MARVIN D.; AND MOUSLEY, NANCY. "Use of the Edwards Personal Preference Schedule in the Selection of Salesmen." *Personnel Psychol* 13:421–4 w '60. * (*PA* 36:1LD21K)
159. LUDEGREN, HERBERTA MARIE. *Personality Traits of Successful and Unsuccessful Women Counselors in Girls' Private and Agency Camps.* Doctor's thesis, State University of Iowa (Iowa City, Iowa), 1960. (*DA* 20:4579)
160. MARSHALL, SIMONE. "Personality Correlates of Peptic Ulcer Patients." *J Consult Psychol* 24:218–23 Je '60. * (*PA* 35:6970)
161. MERRILL, REED M. "Comparison of Education Students, Successful Science Teachers and Educational Administrators on the Edwards PPS." *J Ed Res* 54:38–40 S '60. *
162. MESSICK, SAMUEL. "Dimensions of Social Desirability." *J Consult Psychol* 24:279–87 Ag '60. * (*PA* 35:2211)
163. MILLER, SUTHERLAND, JR. *The Relationship of Personality to Occupation, Setting and Function.* Doctor's thesis, Columbia University (New York, N.Y.), 1960. (*DA* 21:3518)
164. MOGAR, ROBERT EDWARD. *Personality Correlates of Differential Performance in a Competitive Situation.* Doctor's thesis, State University of Iowa (Iowa City, Iowa), 1960. (*DA* 21:1631)
165. NEWMAN, JOSEPH, AND WISCHNER, GEORGE J. "The Performance of a Hospitalized Neuropsychiatric Sample on the Edwards Personal Preference Schedule." *J Clin Psychol* 16:99–100 Ja '60. * (*PA* 36:1HF99N)
166. NORRELL, GWEN, AND GRATER, HARRY. "Interest Awareness as an Aspect of Self-Awareness." *J Counsel Psychol* 7:289–92 w '60. * (*PA* 36:1HF89N)
167. RALEY, COLEMAN LAVAN. *Personality Traits of High-Academic Achievers at Oklahoma Baptist University, 1958–1959.* Doctor's thesis, University of Oklahoma (Norman, Okla.), 1960. (*DA* 20:2680)
168. REILLY, MARY ST. ANNE; COMMINS, WILLIAM D.; AND STEFIC, EDWARD C. "The Complementarity of Personality Needs in Friendship Choice." *J Abn & Social Psychol* 61:292–4 S '60. * (*PA* 35:4822)
169. RICHTER, PAUL D. *The Relationship of Personality Traits Measured by the Edwards Personal Preference Schedule to Ratings of Supervisory Success.* Master's thesis, Pennsylvania State University (University Park, Pa.), 1960.
170. SANDERS, ELLA M.; MEFFERD, ROY B., JR.; AND BOWN, OLIVER H. "Verbal-Quantitative Ability and Certain Personality and Metabolic Characteristics of Male College Students." *Ed & Psychol Meas* 20:491–503 au '60. * (*PA* 35:3550)
171. UHLINGER, CAROLYN A., AND STEPHENS, MARK W. "Relation of Achievement Motivation to Academic Achievement in Students of Superior Ability." *J Ed Psychol* 51:259–66 O '60. * (*PA* 36:1KL59U)
172. VAN DE CASTLE, R. L. "Perceptual Defense in a Binocular Rivalry Situation." *J Personality* 28:448–62 D '60. * (*PA* 35:5010)
173. WILSON, GORDON GILBERT. *Relationships Among Three Measured Levels of Personality Functioning: Self-Assessment, Fantasy, Coping Activity and Their Relationships to Ratings of Real-Life Behavior.* Doctor's thesis, University of Denver (Denver, Colo.), 1960. (*DA* 22:921)
174. WORELL, LEONARD. "EPPS N Achievement and Verbal Paired-Associates Learning." *J Abn & Social Psychol* 60:147–50 Ja '60. * (*PA* 34:7187)
175. ANDERSON, THELMA HILL. *Dimensions of the Characteristics Related to the High- and Low-Achievement of a Selected Group of Negro College Students.* Doctor's thesis, University of Oklahoma (Norman, Okla.), 1961. (*DA* 22:1082)
176. ARKOFF, ABE; MEREDITH, GERALD; AND JONES, RONALD. "Urban-Rural Differences in Need Patterns of Third Generation Japanese-Americans in Hawaii." *J Social Psychol* 53:21–3 F '61. * (*PA* 35:6260)
177. BAZNIK, CHARLES ARTHUR. *An Attempt by College Students to Assume the Need System of Veteran Teachers on the Edwards Personal Preference Schedule.* Doctor's thesis, University of Kansas (Lawrence, Kan.), 1961. (*DA* 22:2303)
178. BELL, TERREL HOWARD. *The Characteristics of Weber School District Teachers Who Had Negative and Positive Attitudes Toward a Major Change in the District's Instructional Program.* Doctor's thesis, University of Utah (Salt Lake City, Utah), 1961. (*DA* 22:1475)
179. BLUM, STUART H. "The Desire for Security: An Element in the Vocational Choice of College Men." *J Ed Psychol* 52:317–21 D '61. * (*PA* 38:3175)
180. BORGATTA, EDGAR F. "Mood, Personality, and Interaction." *J General Psychol* 64:105–37 Ja '61. * (*PA* 35:6415)
181. BORGATTA, EDGAR F., AND GLASS, DAVID C. "Personality Concomitants of Extreme Response Set (ERS)." *J Social Psychol* 55:213–21 D '61. * (*PA* 36:3HE13B)
182. BORGATTA, EDGAR F.; IN COLLABORATION WITH HENRY J. MEYER. "Make a Sentence Test: An Approach to Objective Scoring of Sentence Completions." *Genetic Psychol Monogr* 63:3–65 F '61. * (*PA* 35:6435)
183. CARLSON, EARL R. "Motivation and Set in Acquiring Information About Persons." *J Personality* 29:285–93 S '61. * (*PA* 37:3137)
184. CHRISTENSEN, C. M. "Use of Design, Texture, and Color Preferences in Assessment of Personality Characteristics." *Percept & Motor Skills* 12:143–50 Ap '61. * (*PA* 36:1HB43C)
185. COOK, DESMOND L.; LINDEN, JAMES D.; AND MCKAY, HARRISON E. "A Factor Analysis of Teacher Trainee Responses to Selected Personality Inventories." *Ed & Psychol Meas* 21:865–72 w '61. * (*PA* 36:5HF65C)
186. COPEMAN, JAMES; PASCOE, ROBERT; AND WARD, GEORGE, II. "The Edwards Personal Preference Schedule and Revised Cooperative English Test as Predictors of Academic Achievement." *Proc W Va Acad Sci* 33:124–6 '61. * (*PA* 36:5KL24C)
187. CORAH, NORMAN L. "A Factor Analytic Study of Edwards' Personal Preference Schedule." *Psychol Rep* 9:147–50 Ag '61. *
188. CRANDALL, VAUGHN J., AND PRESTON, ANNE. "Verbally Expressed Needs and Overt Maternal Behaviors." *Child Develop* 32:261–70 Je '61. * (*PA* 36:3FG61C)
189. DAY, BARBARA R. "A Comparison of Personality Needs of Courtship Couples and Same Sex Friendships." *Sociol & Social Res* 45:435–40 Jl '61. * (*PA* 36:3HJ35D)
190. DEMOS, GEORGE D., AND SPOLYAR, LUDWIG J. "Aca-

demic Achievement of College Freshmen in Relation to the Edwards Personal Preference Schedule." *Ed & Psychol Meas* 21:473–9 su '61. * (*PA* 36:2KL73D)

191. Dunkleberger, Clarence J., and Tyler, Leona E. "Interest Stability and Personality Traits." *J Counsel Psychol* 8:70–4 sp '61. * (*PA* 36:3FF70D)

192. Endler, Norman S. "Conformity Analyzed and Related to Personality." *J Social Psychol* 53:271–83 Ap '61. * (*PA* 36:1GE71E)

193. Garrison, Karl C., and Scott, Mary Hughie. "A Comparison of the Personal Needs of College Students Preparing to Teach in Different Teaching Areas." *Ed & Psychol Meas* 21:955–64 w '61. * (*PA* 36:5KM55G)

194. Gocka, Edward F., and Rozynko, Vitali. "Some Comments on the EPPS Disjunction Score." *J Abn & Social Psychol* 62:458–60 Mr '61. * (*PA* 36:4HF58G)

195. Heilbrun, Alfred B., Jr., and Goodstein, Leonard D. "Consistency Between Social Desirability Ratings and Item Endorsement as a Function of Psychopathology." *Psychol Rep* 8:69–70 F '61. * (*PA* 36:1HI69H)

196. Heilbrun, Alfred B., Jr., and Goodstein, Leonard D. "The Relationships Between Individually Defined and Group Defined Social Desirability and Performance on the Edwards Personal Preference Schedule." *J Consult Psychol* 25:200–4 Je '61. *

197. Heilbrun, Alfred B., Jr., and Goodstein, Leonard D. "Social Desirability Response Set: Error or Predictor Variable." *J Psychol* 51:321–9 Ap '61. * (*PA* 35:6430)

198. Heilizer, Fred. "A Scale of Compatibility and Incompatibility of Pairs of Needs." *Psychol Rep* 9:565–72 D '61. *

199. Hetlinger, Duane F., and Hildreth, Richard A. "Personality Characteristics of Debaters." *Q J Speech* 47:398–401 D '61. *

200. Howard, Maurice Lloyd. *A Study of Under-Achieving College Students With High Academic Ability From the Phenomenological Frame of Reference.* Doctor's thesis, University of Colorado (Boulder, Colo.), 1961. (*DA* 22:3040)

201. Jerry, Donald H. *References and Problems of Thirty High School Football Players and Thirty Non-Football Players.* Master's thesis, Ohio State University (Columbus, Ohio), 1961.

202. Kazmier, Leonard J. "Cross-Validation Groups, Extreme Groups, and the Prediction of Academic Achievement." *J Ed Psychol* 52:195–8 Ag '61. * (*PA* 38:3204)

203. Krug, Robert E., and Moyer, K. E. "An Analysis of the F Scale: II, Relationship to Standardized Personality Inventories." *J Social Psychol* 53:293–301 Ap '61. * (*PA* 36:1HC93K)

204. Lipetz, Milton E. "Reliability of EPPS Autonomy for Males and Females." *Psychol Rep* 8:456 Je '61. * (*PA* 36:2HF56L)

205. McKee, John P., and Turner, Walter S. "The Relationship of 'Drive' Ratings in Adolescence to CPI and EPPS Scores in Adulthood." *Vita Hum* 4(1–2):1–14 '61. * (*PA* 36:1HF01M)

206. Medley, Donald M. "Teacher Personality and Teacher-Pupil Rapport." *J Teach Ed* 12:152–6 Je '61. *

207. Milton, G. A., and Lipetz, Milton E. "EPPS Consistency Score: Inconsistency or Equality of Need?" *Psychol Rep* 8:310 Ap '61. * (*PA* 36:1HE10M)

208. Moore, Robert Burkland. *A Comparison of Test Performance and Current Status of Administrative Candidates in Twenty-Four School Districts.* Doctor's thesis, Stanford University (Stanford, Calif.), 1961. (*DA* 22:476)

209. Morgan, J. B. *Personality Variables of Industrial Arts Teachers.* Doctor's research study No. 1, Colorado State College (Greeley, Colo.), 1961. (*DA* 22:4225)

209a. Mussen, Paul. "Some Antecedents and Consequents of Masculine Sex-Typing in Adolescent Boys." *Psychol Monogr* 75(2):1–24 '61. * (*PA* 38:2479)

210. Nevis, Edwin C., and Parker, James W. "The Use of Published Norms in the Industrial Setting." *Personnel Psychol* 14:59–65 sp '61. * (*PA* 36:4LD59N)

211. Parker, Aileen Webber. *A Comparative Study of Selected Factors in the Vocational Development of College Women.* Doctor's thesis, Indiana University (Bloomington, Ind.), 1961. (*DA* 22:1087)

212. Peck, Joan H. *The Appropriateness of the Edwards Personal Preference Schedule for Use With Junior High School Students.* Master's thesis, University of Maryland (College Park, Md.), 1961.

213. Phares, E. Jerry, and Adams, Calvin K. "The Construct Validity of the Edwards PPS Heterosexuality Scale." *J Consult Psychol* 25:341–4 Ag '61. * (*PA* 37:1262)

213a. Redden, James W., and Scales, Eldridge E. "Nursing Education and Personality Characteristics." *Nursing Res* 10:215–8 f '61. *

213b. Reece, Michael M. "Personality Characteristics and Success in Nursing." *Nursing Res* 10:172–6 su '61. *

214. Satz, Paul, and Allen, Robert M. "A Study of the Edwards Personal Preference Schedule: Regional Normative Approach." *J Social Psychol* 53:195–8 Ap '61. * (*PA* 36:1HF95S)

215. Shanker, Prem. *The Contribution of EPPS Scores to Differential and Multiple Absolute Academic Prediction.* Doctor's thesis, University of Washington (Seattle, Wash.), 1961. (*DA* 22:2065)

216. Shaw, Merville C. "Need Achievement Scales as Predictors of Academic Success." *J Ed Psychol* 52:282–5 D '61. * (*PA* 38:3209)

217. Spilka, Bernard. "Social Desirability: A Problem of Operational Definition." *Psychol Rep* 8:149–50 F '61. * (*PA* 36:1HE49S)

218. Tolor, Alexander. "The Relationship Between Insight and Intraception." *J Clin Psychol* 17:188–9 Ap '61. * (*PA* 38:988)

219. Van Wagenen, Donald Richard. *The Relation of Selected Non-Intellectual Factors to Academic Achievement in Several College Groups.* Doctor's thesis, Syracuse University (Syracuse, N.Y.), 1961. (*DA* 23:539)

220. Wegner, Kenneth Walter. *An Analysis of Interest Patterns and Psychological Need Structures Related to L-I-D Response Patterns on the Strong Vocational Interest Blank for Women.* Doctor's thesis, University of Kansas (Lawrence, Kan.), 1961. (*DA* 22:3931)

221. Wright, Calvin E. "A Factor Dimension Comparison of Normative and Ipsative Measurements." *Ed & Psychol Meas* 21:433–44 su '61. * (*PA* 36:2HE33W)

222. Zuckerman, Marvin; Levitt, Eugene E.; and Lubin, Bernard. "Concurrent and Construct Validity of Direct and Indirect Measures of Dependency." *J Consult Psychol* 25:316–23 Ag '61. *

223. Abraham, Henry H. L. "The Suggestibility Personality: A Psychological Investigation of Susceptibility to Persuasion." *Acta Psychologica* 20(2):167–84 '62. * (*PA* 37:6862)

224. Armatas, James P., and Collister, E. Gordon. "Personality Correlates of SVIB Patterns." *J Counsel Psychol* 9:149–54 su '62. * (*PA* 37:6710)

225. Bendig, A. W., and Martin, Ann M. "The Factor Structure and Stability of Fifteen Human Needs." *J General Psychol* 67:229–35 O '62. * (*PA* 37:8001)

226. Borgatta, Edgar F. "The Coincidence of Subtests in Four Personality Inventories." *J Social Psychol* 56:227–44 Ap '62. * (*PA* 37:1247)

227. Brady, John Paul; Thornton, Douglas R.; Pappas, Nicholas; and Tausig, Theodore N. "Edwards Personal Preference Schedule Correlates of Operant Behavior." *J Clin Psychol* 18:224–6 Ap '62. * (*PA* 38:8476)

228. Bromer, John A.; Johnson, J. Myron; and Sevransky, Paul. "Validity Information Exchange, No. 15-02: D.O.T. Code 4-97.010, 4-75.120, 4-85.040, Craft Foremen Correspond to Foreman I; 5-91.875, 5-91.088, 5-91.091, 5-91.831, 5-91.812, Process, Production, and Warehouse Foremen Correspond to Foremen II." *Personnel Psychol* 15:107–9 sp '62. *

229. Brower, Julian Lewis. *Patient-Personnel Interpersonal Choice on a State Mental Hospital Ward.* Doctor's thesis, University of Buffalo (Buffalo, N.Y.), 1962. (*DA* 23:2982)

230. Cairns, Robert B., and Lewis, Michael. "Dependency and the Reinforcement Value of a Verbal Stimulus." *J Consult Psychol* 26:1–8 F '62. * (*PA* 37:4976)

231. Campbell, Joel T.; Otis, Jay L.; Liske, Ralph E.; and Prien, Erich P. "Assessments of Higher-Level Personnel: II, Validity of the Over-All Assessment Process." *Personnel Psychol* 15:63–74 sp '62. * (*PA* 37:3908)

231a. Crane, William J. "Screening Devices for Occupational Therapy Majors." *Am J Occup Ther* 16:131–2 My-Je '62. * (*PA* 37:4078)

232. Edwards, Allen L., and Diers, Carol Jean. "Social Desirability and Conflict." *J Social Psychol* 58:349–56 D '62. * (*PA* 37:6731)

233. Edwards, Allen L., and Walker, Jerald N. "Relationship Between Probability of Item Endorsement and Social Desirability Scale Value for High and Low Groups on Edwards' SD Scale." *J Abn & Social Psychol* 64:458–60 Je '62. * (*PA* 38:979)

234. Fenz, Walter D., and Arkoff, Abe. "Comparative Need Patterns of Five Ancestry Groups in Hawaii." *J Social Psychol* 58:67–89 O '62. * (*PA* 37:6539)

235. Ford, LeRoy H., Jr., and Sempert, Edith L. "Relations Among Some Objective Measures of Hostility, Need Aggression, and Anxiety." Abstract. *J Consult Psychol* 26:486 O '62. *

236. Forrest, D. W., and Lee, S. G. "Mechanisms of Defense and Readiness in Perception and Recall." *Psychol Monogr* 76(4):1–28 '62. * (*PA* 37:1339)

237. Francesco, E. "A Pervasive Value: Conventional Religiosity." *J Social Psychol* 57:467–70 Ag '62. * (*PA* 37:4855)

238. Fuster, Joachim M. "A Study of the Edwards Personal Preference Schedule on Indian College Students." *J Social Psychol* 57:309–14 Ag '62. * (*PA* 37:4814)

239. Garrison, Karl C., and Scott, Mary Hughie. "The Relationship of Selected Personal Characteristics to the Needs of College Students Preparing to Teach." *Ed & Psychol Meas* 22:753–8 w '62. * (*PA* 37:6732)

240. Goodman, Marvin. *A Pilot Study of the Relationship Between Degree of Expressed Self-Acceptance and Interspousal Need Structure in the Mate Selection Process.* Doctor's thesis, Michigan State University (East Lansing, Mich.), 1962. (*DA* 24:867)

241. Goodstein, Leonard D., and Heilbrun, Alfred B., Jr. "Prediction of College Achievement From the Edwards Personal Preference Schedule at Three Levels of Intellectual Ability." *J Appl Psychol* 46:317–20 O '62. * (*PA* 37:5661)

242. Grat, Edwin Casimer. *A Study of Personality Preferences of Student Speech Therapists on the Basis of the Edwards Personal Preference Schedule.* Master's thesis, University of Oregon (Eugene, Ore.), 1962. (*MA* 1:63)

243. Gray, James Terry. *Manifest Needs in Secondary Teachers, Accountants, and Mechanical Engineers: An Exploratory Study.* Doctor's thesis, University of Houston (Houston, Tex.), 1962. (*DA* 23:1413)

244. Gynther, Malcolm D., and Gertz, Boris. "Personality Characteristics of Student Nurses in South Carolina." *J Social Psychol* 56:277–84 Ap '62. * (*PA* 37:1256)

245. Gynther, Malcolm D.; Miller, Francis T.; and Davis, Hugh T. "Relations Between Needs and Behavior as Measured by the Edwards PPS and Inter-Personal Check List." *J Social Psychol* 57:445–51 Ag '62. * (*PA* 37:5063)

246. Hartley, Raymond E., and Allen, Robert M. "The Minnesota Multiphasic Personality Inventory (MMPI) and the Edwards Personal Preference Schedule (EPPS): A Factor Analytic Study." *J Social Psychol* 58:153–62 O '62. * (*PA* 37:6733)

247. Heilbrun, Alfred B., Jr. "Social Desirability and the Relative Validities of Achievement Scales." *J Consult Psychol* 26:383–6 Ag '62. * (*PA* 38:4310)

248. Heilizer, Fred, and Trehub, Arnold. "Relationships of the EPPS Need Profile Among Eight Samples." *J Clin Psychol* 18:461–4 O '62. * (*PA* 39:5178)

249. Hogue, J. Pierre; Otis, Jay L.; and Prien, Erich P. "Assessments of Higher-Level Personnel: VI, Validity of Predictions Based on Projective Techniques." *Personnel Psychol* 15:335–44 au '62. * (*PA* 37:7249)

250. Hull, J., and Zubek, John P. "Personality Characteristics of Successful and Unsuccessful Sensory Isolation Subjects." *Percept & Motor Skills* 14:231–40 Ap '62. *

251. Hutchins, Edwin B. "The Student and His Environment." *J Med Ed* 37:67–82 D '62. *

252. Izard, Carroll E. "Personality Change During College Years." Abstract. *J Consult Psychol* 26:482 O '62. *

253. Izard, Carroll E. "Personality Characteristics (EPPS), Level of Expectation, and Performance." Abstract. *J Consult Psychol* 26:394 Ag '62. * (*PA* 38:4311)

254. Karr, Chadwick. "Note on the Edwards Personal Preference Schedule and Between-Subjects Variance." *Psychol Rep* 10:55–8 F '62. * (*PA* 37:1258)

255. Katzell, Raymond A., and Katzell, Mildred E. "Development and Application of Structured Tests of Personality." *R Ed Res* 32:51–63 F '62. * (*PA* 37:1197)

256. Kemp, C. Gratton. "Counseling Responses and Need Structures of High School Principals and of Counselors." *J Counsel Psychol* 9:326–8 w '62. * (*PA* 39:1805)

257. Kirchner, Wayne K. "'Real-Life' Faking on the Edwards Personal Preference Schedule by Sales Applicants." *J Appl Psychol* 46:128–30 Ap '62. *

258. Korman, Maurice, and Coltharp, Frances. "Transparency in the Edwards Personal Preference Schedule." *J Consult Psychol* 26:379–82 Ag '62. * (*PA* 38:4313)

259. Lang, Gerhard; Sferra, Amedeo; and Seymour, Marjorie. "Psychological Needs of College Freshmen and Their Academic Achievement." *Personnel & Guid J* 41:359–60 D '62. * (*PA* 37:7193)

260. Lang, Peter J., and Lazovik, A. David. "Personality and Hypnotic Susceptibility." *J Consult Psychol* 26:317–22 Ag '62. * (*PA* 38:4433)

261. Levy, Leon H. "Age and Personal Need Correlates of Expectancy for Change." *Percept & Motor Skills* 15:351–6 O '62. * (*PA* 37:8033)

262. Lipetz, Milton E., and Milton, G. A. "Prediction of Autonomy Behavior From Situational Modifications of the EPPS n Autonomy Scale." *Psychol Rep* 11:487–93 O '62. * (*PA* 37:7984)

263. Locke, Lawrence F. "Performance of Administration Oriented Male Physical Educators on Selected Psychological Tests." *Res Q* 33:418–29 O '62. *

264. Longenecker, E. D. "Perceptual Recognition as a Function of Anxiety, Motivation, and the Testing Situation." *J Abn & Social Psychol* 64:215–21 Mr '62. * (*PA* 38:1723)

265. Lubin, Bernard; Levitt, Eugene E.; and Zuckerman, Marvin. "Some Personality Differences Between Responders and Non-Responders to a Survey Questionnaire." *J Consult Psychol* 26:192 Ap '62. * (*PA* 37:5013)

266. Mehlman, Benjamin. "Similarity in Friendships." *J Social Psychol* 57:195–202 Je '62. * (*PA* 37:3839)

267. Mogar, Robert E. "Competition, Achievement, and Personality." Abstract of doctor's thesis. *J Counsel Psychol* 9:168–72 su '62. * (*PA* 37:7197)

268. Mott, Carol Cowles. *A Study of Personality Variables Among Counselor Education Majors, Counselors, and Graduate Students in Administration, Curriculum, and Supervision as Shown by the Edwards Personal Preference Schedule.* Doctor's thesis, Florida State University (Tallahassee, Fla.), 1962. (*DA* 23:3779)

269. Patterson, C. H. "A Note on the Construct Validity of the Concept of Empathy." *Personnel & Guid J* 40:803–6 My '62. * (*PA* 37:3448)

270. Patterson, C. H. "Test Characteristics of Rehabilitation Counselor Trainees." *J Rehabil* 28:15–6 S–O '62. * (*PA* 37:6953)

271. Peckens, Russell George. *A Factor-Analytic Study of Edwards Personal Preference Schedule Need Scores as a Function of Age and Sex.* Doctor's thesis, University of Tennessee (Knoxville, Tenn.), 1962. (*DA* 23:3781)

272. Pulos, Lee; Nichols, Robert C.; Lewinsohn, Peter M.; and Koldjeski, Theodore. "Selection of Psychiatric Aides and Prediction of Performance Through Psychological Testing and Interviews." *Psychol Rep* 10:519–20 Ap '62. * (*PA* 37:3401)

273. Renzaglia, Guy A.; Henry, Donald R.; and Rybolt, Gaylord A., Jr. "Estimation and Measurement of Personality Characteristics and Correlates of Their Congruence." *J Counsel Psychol* 9:71–8 sp '62. * (*PA* 38:2704)

274. Saltz, Eli; Reece, Michael; and Ager, Joel. "Studies of Forced-Choice Methodology: Individual Differences in Social Desirability." *Ed & Psychol Meas* 22:365–70 su '62. * (*PA* 37:3180)

275. Scandrette, Onas. "Differential Need Patterns of Women Elementary and Secondary Level Student Teachers." *J Ed Res* 55:376–9 My '62. * (*PA* 37:5685)

276. Singh, Paras Nath; Huang, Sophia Chang; and Thompson, George G. "A Comparative Study of Selected Attitudes, Values, and Personality Characteristics of American, Chinese, and Indian Students." *J Social Psychol* 57:123–32 Je '62. * (*PA* 37:3847)

277. Smith, Ronald E. *Parents, Children, Preferences, and Achievement.* Master's thesis, Ohio State University (Columbus, Ohio), 1962.

278. Southworth, Horton Coe. *A Study of Certain Personality and Value Differences in Teacher Education Majors Preferring Early and Later Elementary Teaching Levels.* Doctor's thesis, Michigan State University (East Lansing, Mich.), 1962. (*DA* 23:1284)

279. Spangler, Donald P., and Thomas, Charles W. "The Effects of Age, Sex, and Physical Disability Upon Manifest Needs." *J Counsel Psychol* 9:313–9 w '62. *

280. Stefflre, Buford; King, Paul; and Leafgren, Fred. "Characteristics of Counselors Judged Effective by Their Peers." *J Counsel Psychol* 9:335–40 w '62. * (*PA* 39:2312)

281. Stuckey, June Elizabeth. *The Relationship of Academic Achievement to Selected Personality Needs.* Doctor's thesis, Ohio State University (Columbus, Ohio), 1962. (*DA* 24:185)

282. Super, Donald E., and Crites, John O. *Appraising Vocational Fitness by Means of Psychological Tests, Revised Edition,* pp. 537–55. New York: Harper & Row, Publishers, Inc., 1962. Pp. xv, 688. * (*PA* 37:2038)

283. Tolor, Alexander. "The Personality Need Structure of Psychiatric Attendants." *Mental Hyg* 46:218–22 Ap '62. *

284. Tutko, Thomas A., and Sechrest, Lee. "Conceptual Performance and Personality Variables." *J Consult Psychol* 26:481 O '62. * (*PA* 39:1766)

285. Uhlir, Gladys Ann. *The Prediction of Success in the Professional Preparation of Health and Physical Education Teachers.* Doctor's thesis, Columbia University (New York, N.Y.), 1962. (*DA* 24:646)

286. Vacek, William Lee. *Personality Variables of Freshmen College Majors With Emphasis on Industrial Arts.* Doctor's research study No. 1, Colorado State College (Greeley, Colo.), 1962. (*DA* 23:1285)

287. Vestre, Norris D. "The Relationship Between Verbal Conditionability and the Edwards Personal Preference Schedule." *J Clin Psychol* 18:513–5 O '62. * (*PA* 39:5186)

288. Vineyard, Edwin E.; Drinkwater, Ruby; and Dickison, Walter L. "Teacher Education and Pharmacy Students: A Comparison of Their Need Structures." *J Teach Ed* 13:409–13 D '62. *

289. Wiemann, Carl Barge, Jr. *Social Desirability and the Edwards Personal Preference Schedule.* Doctor's research study No. 1, Colorado State College (Greeley, Colo.), 1962. (*DA* 23:3789)

290. *Normative Information: Manager and Executive Testing.* New York: Richardson, Bellows, Henry & Co., Inc., May 1963. Pp. 45. *

291. Appley, Mortimer H., and Moeller, George. "Conforming Behavior and Personality Variables in College Women." *J Abn & Social Psychol* 66:284–90 Mr '63. * (*PA* 37:8237)

292. Banta, Thomas J., and Hetherington, Mavis. "Relations Between Needs of Friends and Fiancés." *J Abn & Social Psychol* 66:401–4 Ap '63. * (*PA* 37:7941)

293. Bendig, A. W., and Martin, Ann M. "The Factor Structure of Temperament Traits and Needs." *J General Psychol* 69:27–36 Jl '63. * (*PA* 38:4297)

294. Brewington, William Iven. *A Statistical Analysis of Low Achieving and High Achieving Freshman Chemistry Students at the University of Arkansas.* Doctor's thesis, University of Arkansas (Fayetteville, Ark.), 1963. (*DA* 24:570)

295. Carrier, Neil A. "Need Correlates of 'Gullibility.'" *J Abn & Social Psychol* 66:84–6 Ja '63. * (*PA* 37:5056)

296. Cook, Desmond L.; Lebold, William; and Linden, James D. "A Comparison of Factor Analyses of Education and Engineering Responses to Selected Personality Inventories." *J Teach Ed* 14:137–41 Je '63. *

297. GHEI, S. N. "The Reliability and Validity of Edwards Personal Preference Schedule: A Cross-Cultural Study." *J Social Psychol* 61:241–6 D '63. * (*PA* 38:8414)
298. GORDON, IRA J. "Personality Patterns of Volunteers for an Experimental Professional Education Program." *J Exp Ed* 32:115–21 f '63. *
299. GRAY, JAMES T. "Needs and Values in Three Occupations." *Personnel & Guid J* 42:238–44 N '63. *
300. HAAS, KURT. "Personality Needs of Academically Superior Students and Their Parents." *J Ed Res* 56:389–90 Mr '63. *
301. HARRIS, DOROTHY V. "Comparison of Physical Performance and Psychological Traits of College Women With High and Low Fitness Indices." *Percept & Motor Skills* 17:293–4 Ag '63. * (*PA* 38:8356)
302. HEILBRUN, A. B. "Evidence Regarding the Equivalence of Ipsative and Normative Personality Scales." *J Consult Psychol* 27:152–6 Ap '63. * (*PA* 37:7982)
303. HEILBRUN, ALFRED B., JR. "Configural Interpretation of the Edwards Personal Preference Schedule and the Prediction of Academic Performance." *Personnel & Guid J* 42:264–8 N '63. *
304. HEILBRUN, ALFRED B., JR. "Social Value–Social Behavior Inconsistency and Early Signs of Psychopathology in Adolescence." *Child Develop* 34:187–94 Mr '63. * (*PA* 38:5808)
305. HEILIZER, FRED. "An Ipsative Factor Analysis of the Ipsative EPPS." *Psychol Rep* 12:285–6 F '63. * (*PA* 38:2669)
306. IZARD, CARROLL E. "Personality Profile Similarity as a Function of Group Membership." *J Abn & Social Psychol* 67:404–8 O '63. * (*PA* 38:4193)
307. IZARD, CARROLL E. "Personality Similarity and Friendship: A Follow-Up Study." *J Abn & Social Psychol* 66:598–600 Je '63. * (*PA* 38:920)
308. KAMANO, DENNIS K. "Relationship of Ego Disjunction and Manifest Anxiety to Conflict Resolution." *J Abn & Social Psychol* 66:281–4 Mr '63. * (*PA* 37:8035)
309. KOLE, DELBERT M., AND MATARAZZO, J. D. "Intellectual and Personality Characteristics of Medical Students." Abstract. *J Med Ed* 38:138–9 F '63. *
310. KUHLEN, RAYMOND G. "Needs, Perceived Need Satisfaction Opportunities, and Satisfaction With Occupation." *J Appl Psychol* 47:56–64 F '63. * (*PA* 37:8347)
311. LEVITT, EUGENE E.; BRADY, JOHN PAUL; AND LUBIN, BERNARD. "Correlates of Hypnotizability in Young Women: Anxiety and Dependency." *J Personality* 31:52–7 Mr '63. *
312. LIND, AMY. "Measured Personality Characteristics of Occupational Therapy Graduates and Undergraduates at the University of North Dakota." *Univ N Dak Col Ed Rec* 48:69–73 F '63. *
313. MCDONALD, ROBERT L., AND GYNTHER, MALCOLM D. "Nonintellectual Factors Associated With Performance in Medical School." *J Genetic Psychol* 103:185–94 S '63. *
313a. MANHOLD, J. H.; SHATIN, LEO; AND MANHOLD, BEVERLY S. "Comparison of Interests, Needs, and Selected Personality Factors of Dental and Medical Students." *J Am Dental Assn* 67:601–5 O '63. *
314. MEHLMAN, MARY R., AND FLEMING, JAMES E. "Social Stratification and Some Personality Variables." *J General Psychol* 69:3–10 Jl '63. * (*PA* 38:4169)
315. MOLDOVAN, STANLEY. "Some Familial Antecedents of Personality Needs." *B Maritime Psychol Assn* 12:28–40 sp '63. * (*PA* 38:4244)
316. MORRIS, KENNETH TURNER. *A Comparative Study of Selected Needs, Values, and Motives of Science and Non-Science Teachers.* Doctor's thesis, University of Georgia (Athens, Ga.), 1963. (*DA* 24:2325)
317. NUNNALLY, JUM C., AND FLAUGHER, RONALD L. "Correlates of Semantic Habits." *J Personality* 31:192–202 Je '63. *
317a. PEMBERTON, W. A. *Ability, Values, and College Achievement.* University of Delaware Studies in Higher Education, No. 1. Newark, Del.: the University, 1963. Pp. xii, 77. * (*PA* 38:6573)
318. POOL, DONALD ALFRED. *The Relation of Personality Needs to Vocational Counseling Outcome.* Doctor's thesis, University of Texas (Austin, Tex.), 1963. (*DA* 24:1922)
319. RADCLIFFE, J. A. "Some Properties of Ipsative Score Matrices and Their Relevance for Some Current Interest Tests." *Austral J Psychol* 15:1–11 Ap '63. *
320. RYCHLAK, JOSEPH F. "Personality Correlates of Leadership Among First Level Managers." *Psychol Rep* 12:43–52 F '63. * (*PA* 38:2600)
321. SCHUMACHER, CHARLES F. "Interest and Personality Factors as Related to Choice of Medical Career." *J Med Ed* 38:932–42 N '63. *
322. SCHWARTZ, MILTON M.; JENUSAITIS, EDMUND; AND STARK, HARRY. "Motivational Factors Among Supervisors in the Utility Industry." *Personnel Psychol* 16:45–53 sp '63. * (*PA* 38:3327)
323. SCOTT, WILLIAM A. "Social Desirability and Individual Conceptions of the Desirable." *J Abn & Social Psychol* 67:574–85 D '63. * (*PA* 38:5953)
324. SUZIEDELIS, ANTANAS, AND STEIMEL, RAYMOND J. "The Relationship of Need Heirarchies to Inventoried Interests." *Personnel & Guid J* 42:393–6 D '63. * (*PA* 39:1761)
325. VAN EVRA, JUDY PAGE, AND ROSENBERG, B. G. "Ego Strength and Ego Disjunction in Primary and Secondary Psychopaths." *J Clin Psychol* 19:61–3 Ja '63. * (*PA* 39:2409)
326. WRIGHT, MORGAN W.; SISLER, GEORGE C.; AND CHYLINSKI, JOANNE. "Personality Factors in the Selection of Civilians for Isolated Northern Stations." *J Appl Psychol* 47:24–9 F '63. * (*PA* 37:8319)

JOHN A. RADCLIFFE, *Senior Lecturer in Psychology, University of Sydney, Sydney, Australia.*

This test is designed to assess the relative strengths of 15 manifest needs selected from Murray's need system. Each need is represented by nine statements. A statement from each need is paired twice with one from every other need (210 items). Additionally, to allow an indication of the consistency of a subject's responses, for each need one of these pairs is repeated (15 items). Another indication of the consistency of responses (the profile stability coefficient) is available by correlating the scores obtained on the first and second set of item pairings, but this assumes that the nine statements for each need have equivalent need content. Scale values for social desirability have been assigned to the 135 statements and within each item the two statements have approximately equal social desirability scale values. This design was introduced to attempt to control social desirability as a source of variance and is usually regarded as one of the particular merits of the test. The forced choice paired-comparison format of the EPPS requires that the total scores for each subject are constant so that the scores are ipsative. To allow interindividual comparisons and to allow for sex differences, centile rank norms (college and general adult) and *T* score norms (college only) based on large samples are presented for males and females separately. Internal consistency (n = 1,509; range .60 to .87; median .78) and one-week retest (n = 89; range .74 to .87; median .83) reliability coefficients are quoted, and Mann (45) has reported three-week retest coefficients (n = 96; range .55 to .87; median .73). Validity data in the manual are meagre.

The procedure here will be to review the evidence on the control of social desirability; to consider some technical features of the test, especially the equivalence of the statements within each need and the effects of ipsative scoring; to outline some of the conditions known to affect test scores; and to review the evidence on predictive, concurrent, and construct validity.

SOCIAL DESIRABILITY. Research on social desirability has been directed mainly towards investigating (*a*) the generality of the social desirability scale values originally obtained by Edwards (*21, 26–8, 44, 104*); (*b*) the degree of control of the influence of the social desirability stereotype on test scores by matching for social desirability the two statements in each item (*2, 28, 32, 36, 42–3, 45, 106*), especially considering the possibility that this pairing may introduce a new context that destroys the matching based upon judgments made singly (*37, 94, 141*); (*c*) whether personal desirability may be an additional source of influence on test scores (*36, 96, 98*); and (*d*) whether social desirability may involve idiosyncratic interpretations whose effects have been masked by attention to group averages only (*196–7*).

In relation to (*b*), it is now clear that judgments of social desirability are influenced by context (*141*), with the result that the statements in pairs do not retain the approximately equal social desirability scale values assigned to them singly (*37*). Edwards and others (*94*) have attempted to refute this latter finding by arguing that it was obtained with a sample of items removed from their original context in the test, and by demonstrating that, with the entire test, the correlation between the proportions choosing alternative A under normal and social desirability instructions is much lower (.69) than that obtained by Corah and others (.88). But it remains that the correlation is still substantial and that the argument about the relevance of context could apply equally to the difference in context between judgments of the statements singly and the judgment in pairs. Thus there now seems little doubt that the test design does not control the social desirability stereotype as much as was indicated by earlier studies that took no account of the effects of context (*2, 28, 32, 36, 42–3, 45*).

Regarding the role of personal desirability, investigators have concluded both that personal and social desirability are the same (*36*), and that they are different (*98*). That the personal and social desirability scale values of the 135 statements correlate .90 implies identity (*96*), but in a subsequent study (*98*) the same authors concluded that, although personal desirability makes a contribution to variance additional to that made by social desirability, it is insufficient "to represent a crucial flaw in Edwards' attempt to minimise desirability of verbal statements as an important source of performance variance." That a subject's profile correlation between normal versus personal desirability instructions does not differ from that between normal versus social desirability instructions also implies identity (*36*), but the inappropriate use of *T* scores for the profile correlations may well have obscured results here. The non-occurrence of similar profiles among the subjects under social desirability instructions in this latter study suggests that the social desirability ratings of statements may have idiosyncratic features, perhaps generated even by their grammatical form (*129*). This possibility is supported by the finding (*196*) that the item alternative rated as the more *individually* socially desirable was chosen (on the average) 67 per cent of the time, as compared with 56 per cent endorsement of the *group* defined more socially desirable alternative. From this and other evidence (*197*), Heilbrun and Goodstein concluded that social desirability is not a "response set" but a "content" variable and that both individually defined and group defined social desirability may affect scores on the EPPS.

Even aside from the need to recognise that the earlier generality ascribed to Edwards' social desirability scale values (*21, 26, 27, 28, 44*) may in fact be restricted to the United States (*104*), from the foregoing it is apparent that the design of the EPPS does not control the desirability of verbal statements as much as was originally believed. This does not necessarily constitute an intrinsic weakness of the test. The control of desirability alone, even if sufficient to allow test usage under a wide variety of conditions, would not guarantee any validity. Nor would the ineffectual control of desirability necessarily imply invalidity. Validity remains an empirical question in specified circumstances. However, it will be seen that the forced choice character of the items and the resultant ipsative scores introduce particular problems in the way of answering validity questions with the EPPS.

TECHNICAL FEATURES. In using nine statements for each need, Edwards assumes that each of the statements has equivalent need content, but he does not justify this assumption by presenting evidence on how the statements were selected. The only investigation of the equivalence of need statements that seems to have been made is that by Levonian et al. (*106*).

They believed that the assumption implies that for each need separately factor analysis of the item intercorrelations would produce, *inter alia*, a general factor, and they showed that their expectations were not confirmed. However, their expectations and analyses were misconceived. For each need, there are three types of pairs of items that may occur and yield item intercorrelations: (*a*) an "identical" pair, represented by the two "consistency" items and involving the same needs and the same statements; (*b*) a "fraternal" pair, represented by the items that produce the two separate row and column scores on the answer sheet (e.g., items 2 and 6, for Achievement), these items involving the same needs but, in general, different statements; and (*c*) an "unrelated" pair, which involves different needs and different statements. For each need, there will be one correlation between "identical" items, 14 between "fraternal" items, and, since there are 29 items for each need, 15 between "unrelated" items. Only the "identical" and "fraternal" item correlations can be expected to be non-zero. A meaningful general factor could not occur from such a peculiar correlation matrix, and factor analysis would seem a quite inappropriate technique. Consequently, as reported, the study by Levonian and others contributes no evidence on the equivalence of the statements because the 15 correlations that would be expected to be non-zero for each scale are not given.

So far there appear to be only two lines of evidence relevant to the equivalence of the statements; viz. the internal consistency coefficients and the profile stability coefficients given by Edwards in the manual. "Uncorrected" values of the former are more appropriate than "corrected" values. From Edwards' "corrected" values, the "uncorrected" values would range .43 to .71, with median .64, and would give a rough indication of what the correlation between "fraternal" items could be. Either some statements have little "equivalence" or the responses to them include considerable "error." Perhaps idiosyncratic conceptions of desirability are relevant here. Edwards reports subjects' profile stability coefficients ranging from zero to unity, with mean .74 and median approximately the same. Fiske and others (*143*) have reported similar values. Do low profile stability coefficients indicate non-equivalence of the statements for those subjects, or do they derive from inconsistency of responses? Edwards might have reported the correlation between consistency scores and profile stability coefficients. There is, then, need for more evidence on the equivalence of the statements.

The scores derived from the EPPS are ordinal ipsative scores, but surprisingly little attention has been paid to their implications (*48, 254, 319*). That Edwards makes no mention of ipsatization and lack of independence in the manual is particularly striking, because Clemans,[1] at Edwards' own university, made a detailed analysis of some of the features of deviational ipsative scores. Karr's (*102*) attempts to predict ipsative from normative scores are based on a dependence between the two that occurs only with deviational ipsative and not with ordinal ipsative scores (*319*), but in any case have no practical value. Stoltz (*48*) emphasizes the need for caution in the correlational use of ipsative scores, but in his suggested regression usage of the MMPI K-score for indirect ipsatization he seems to believe that the major aim of ipsatization with the EPPS is to remove social desirability variance. Rather the major aim seems to be to serve as a substitute for the lack of more direct measures of need strength. Heilbrun's conclusion (*302*) that ipsative and normative scores are substantially equivalent for making normative predictions does not seem justified by the correlations he obtained. Radcliffe (*319*) has considered some consequences of ordinal and deviational ipsative scoring. Those for ordinal ipsative scores of most relevance here are that the average intercorrelation among the EPPS scales will tend to $-1/(n-1) = -.071$ (which is the average of those reported by Edwards), and that the average correlation of the scales with any other variable will tend to zero. These consequences of lack of independence among the scores emphasize the necessity for cross validation (c.f. the higher absolute values of the scale intercorrelations reported by Allen, *14, 15, 34*). Additionally, Edwards fails to emphasize the need for care in the use of normative centile ranks and *T* scores based on EPPS ipsative scores. These centile ranks and *T* scores may be used meaningfully to compare an individual's relative strength on a need with that of others, but their use in a profile as he recommends seems inadvisable for the general

[1] CLEMANS, W. V. *An Analytical and Empirical Examination of Some Properties of Ipsative Measures.* Doctor's thesis, University of Washington (Seattle, Wash.), 1956.

test user. To take his sample profile as an example, Endurance does not have the lowest relative strength in the original profile, and yet it is markedly the lowest in the centile rank profile. Another example would be that the person with an average centile rank profile (50th centile rank on all needs) would not be a person in whom all needs had the same relative strength. In short, the rank orders of the needs may change considerably when the scores are expressed normatively, and it is questionable if this latter rank order is that which is of interest.

DEMOGRAPHIC DIFFERENCES. Scores are known to be affected by test taking attitudes and by cultural and other demographic factors. Singh and others (*276*) report that Koponen (*31*) found age, sex, educational level, income level, and geographic differences among his large sample of adults. Since Edwards' adult norms are taken from this sample, it would have been preferable had he at least reported the age and educational level. As it is, the interested user is required to order a microfilm from the test publisher.

High school norms are also available from the publisher. Reliabilities are lower and scale intercorrelations are higher with high school than with college subjects (*26*), and social desirability scale values in the items are less adequately matched (*28*). Occupational differences also occur and will be considered later. All cultural comparisons have used college students: Chinese and Indian (*276*), Southern Negroes (*23*), Japanese American (*21, 86*). Some of the obtained differences are inconsistent (*21, 86*), but some make good sense and possibly attest to the Schedule's research potential. For example, compared with white college norms, both male and female Southern Negroes are higher on Deference, Order, Abasement, and Endurance, and lower on Exhibition, Autonomy, Affiliation, Dominance, and Heterosexuality. But when instructed to simulate a "good impression," college students increased their scores on Deference, Order, Endurance, and Achievement, and decreased them on Autonomy, Heterosexuality, Aggression, Change, Succorance, and Exhibition (*93*), giving a pattern something like that of the Southern Negro! High needs for Order, Dominance, and Change can also be successfully simulated, and the nature of the simulated patterns clearly reflects the non-independence of the scales, the correlations between the rank order of the changes and that of the scale intercorrelations for the relevant scales being .85, .55, and .03, respectively (*93*). Equivalent correlations calculated by this reviewer and based on the scale intercorrelations reported by Allen (*15*) are .81, .58, and .79. This evidence on "fakability" augurs ill for the test's use in any selection situation.

VALIDITY. In considering validity data, account needs to be taken that the average correlation of the scales with another variable must tend to zero. This requires that "significant" correlations that are "predicted" be given more credence than those "discovered," and that even the former should be replicated. On predictive validity nothing of any merit has been obtained. Two studies (*59, 111*) have reported approximately .40 correlation of Achievement with course results, but one study (*186*) reported zero correlation. Bernhardt (*129*) did not obtain an expected correlation between Intraception and psychiatry course grades. It may be, as Heathers suggests in the manual, that the EPPS contributes to "understanding the client" and to "stimulating discussions....[that] are frequently very fruitful," but there is nothing to indicate that the Schedule has any other counseling use.

Data on concurrent validity fall under two main heads: (*a*) correlations with other "motivational" or "interest" measures; and (*b*) correlations with inventory and self-rating measures of personality traits. The limited available evidence (*39*) shows little meaningful relation between any EPPS scale and an "interest area" on the *Strong Vocational Interest Blank*. When EPPS scores are treated normatively there seems no doubt that they are not related to "projective" motivational measures derived from the TAT or the French Insight Test (*46, 51, 65, 69, 108, 117, 222*), and it seems unlikely that this is due to scorer unreliability with the projective tests (*65*). Nor do EPPS variables seem likely to have any relations with scores derived from the *Rosenzweig Picture-Frustration Study* (*22*). Only one study has followed what seems to be the more correct procedure, the rank order correlation for each subject between the relative strengths of the need measures on the two tests (*62*). But again there was no relationship. Melikian (*46*) suggests that the EPPS and the TAT measure at different levels, while Marlowe (*108*) believes that "social learning theory" would require the obtained zero relationship. Interpretations of these findings will be left to the reader's predilections.

Expectations concerning correlations of EPPS scales with rating or inventory measures of personality traits present a problem. In the manual Edwards does not make clear what he expects himself. He says that correlations with the Taylor MAS and the *Guilford-Martin Personnel Inventory* are in the expected direction, but he does not comment on their low magnitude, seeming in fact to imply that smallness is desirable because otherwise the correlations would indicate contamination of the EPPS by social desirability. Ignoring for the moment complications introduced by ipsative scoring, the optimal expectation would seem to be "moderate" correlation of an EPPS scale with a similarly named personality trait. Since both motives and traits typically are inferred from the same data—what the individual does, says he does, or says he would do—some correlation would be expected. But too high correlation would negate the virtues of the EPPS variables as "motivational" measures. If .50 is accepted as a "moderate" correlation, then moderate correlations have been obtained between Aggression and Guilford-Martin Agreeableness scores (manual); between combined measures of "dependency" derived from the EPPS and the MMPI, respectively (*222*); and, within "mothers" but not within "non-mothers," between some EPPS scales and the Hostility-Rejection scale of the Parental Attitude Research Inventory (*125*). With these exceptions, studies involving the *Guilford-Martin Personnel Inventory* (manual), *Guilford-Zimmerman Temperament Survey* (*185, 203*), *California Test of Personality* (*39*), MMPI (*15*), Gough's Hr scale (*89*), hostility scales (*235*), and self ratings (*45*) have not produced moderate correlations. Two factor analyses (*185, 203*) agree rather well on the factors extracted, primarily intra-inventory and intra-EPPS factors in both cases. EPPS scales and personality inventories, then, do not share the expected common variance. But the effects of ipsatization may have intruded here. When normatively used, deviational ipsative scoring typically will reduce positive and increase negative correlation with another variable (*319*). Since it removes overall between-subjects variance (*254*) and at least partially removes general factor covariance in the deviational case (*319*), it might be expected to have similar effects with ordinal scores. It is likely, then, that intrasubject profile correlations of the EPPS variables with measures of similarly named traits would be a more appropriate procedure. This has been used only between EPPS variables and self rankings on the same variables. There were substantial individual differences in the correlations. Edwards comments that these differences were probably due largely to difficulties in interpreting the statements. A similar procedure with inventory measures might hold more promise.

Most of the evidence on the use of the EPPS scales relates to their construct validity, and any assistance that it offers to their interpretation depends on opinions on the source of the hypotheses tested or on the plausibility of any differences observed. This review merely will indicate the kinds of research that have been carried out and will make little attempt at evaluation. Achievement is related to paired-associates verbal learning (*174*) but not to the solution of crossword puzzles (*89*). Heterosexuality affects preference for pictures involving "sexual elements," but not selective memory for sexual material (*213*). Areas of investigation that have produced conflicting results have been the use of EPPS scales to classify conforming and dependent subjects in the study of conforming and dependent behaviour (*18, 64, 192, 291*); the similarity of need patterns of friends and courtship couples (*152, 189, 266, 292, 307*); and the relationship between EPPS defined ego-disjunction and degree of psychopathology (*118, 144*). Demographic factors probably need to be controlled in the use of this ego-disjunction measure (*194*). Since ego-disjunction and manifest anxiety interact to prolong conflict resolution (*308*), the fact that ego-disjunction was not found to be related to conflict intensity (*118*) may have been due in part to the use of *T* scores and the failure to allow for demographic factors. Some EPPS scales, notably Intraception, are related to "gullibility" (*295*) and there are some unimpressive relationships with some of the "semantic habit" scales (*317*). Hypnotisable women are emotionally unstable, anxious, and dependent, when "dependency" is derived from Autonomy, Dominance, and Aggression, but not when it is derived from Deference, Succorance, and Abasement (*311*).

Physiological and other data suggest that persons with a high verbal and low quantitative ability pattern have introverted characteristics, and their high Autonomy would not be inconsistent with this (*170*). EPPS scores are unrelated to success at withstanding sensory isolation (*250*), seeking rhinoplasty,[2] volunteering for participation in leaderless group discussions (*95*), to "field independence" (*69*), and to being a member of the personnel of a hospital ward having a "satisfied" atmosphere (*20*). Differences between second and third generation Japanese Americans tend to be consistent with an acculturation interpretation (*86*). The score patterns of prison inmates (*128*) and differences between high school and college students are plausible (*26*), but those between "accurate" and "inaccurate" judges of personality are not markedly so (*133*). Likes and dislikes of "job duties" (*122*), being a "warm teacher" (*117*), and electing to teach in different educational fields (*193*) have been reported to be related to EPPS scores. Achievement is one of the major sources of motivation of dental students (*149*); psychiatry students have high Intraception (*129*); basic airmen (*40*) have some plausible score patterns; and engineers and engineering students differ from liberal arts and science students (*41, 151*). The most studied occupational group has been nurses (*50, 54, 222, 244*), but the only characteristic that has withstood replication has been low Dominance. With some of these reported differences the possible role of stereotype simulation cannot be overlooked. Perhaps the most consistent evidence comes from studies of overachievers (*41, 105*). Though there are some differences that were not replicated in the two studies, both report that overachievers have higher Achievement and Order and lower Affiliation than underachievers, and that high aptitude students have high Dominance and low Abasement, Deference, and Order.

SUMMARY. In all, the evidence on the use of the EPPS remains "spotty." Some of the most convincing evidence lies in occupational and other demographic differences, but failure to achieve the desired control of social desirability and evidence on simulation of responses raise doubts that these differences reflect actual characteristics of the persons. On correlational evidence, the EPPS measures relatively unique aspects of the person (whatever they may be) but interpretation here is obscured by the effects of ipsative scoring. There is nothing to suggest that the counselor will find the *Edwards Personal Preference Schedule* particularly useful, except possibly to "stimulate discussion." Its record so far in the testing of psychological hypotheses is unimpressive, though the fault here may of course be with the "hypotheses" themselves. It may be that future research that takes better account of the role of ipsative scoring will permit the EPPS to become a useful addition to the psychologist's test repertoire, but this remains to be seen, and for the time being it must be regarded primarily as a research tool.

2 MEYER, EUGENE; JACOBSEN, WAYNE E.; EDGERTON, MILTON T.; AND CANTER, ARTHUR. "Motivational Patterns in Patients Seeking Elective Plastic Surgery: 1, Women Who Seek Rhinoplasty." *Psychosom Med* 22:193–201 My–Je '60. * (*PA* 35:4998)

LAWRENCE J. STRICKER, *Research Psychologist, Educational Testing Service, Princeton, New Jersey.*[1]

Since its appearance a decade ago, the *Edwards Personal Preference Schedule* (EPPS) has been very widely used and has generated a tremendous amount of research. This popularity stems from the theoretical relevance and potential usefulness of the personality variables that it is intended to measure—15 of Murray's needs—and its attempt to minimize the effects of social desirability response style, in the light of Edwards' (*1*) well known finding that the rated social desirability of a set of personality items correlated .87 with their frequency of endorsement.

CONSTRUCTION. The paired comparison method was used in constructing the EPPS. Each need was represented by nine items. The items for each need were paired with items from the other needs that had similar average social desirability ratings. Each pair of needs is compared twice in this way, and 210 pairs of items are needed for this purpose. The EPPS provides three kinds of scores: scores for each need (the number of times that the need was chosen as being more descriptive than the other needs); a consistency score (agreement in responses on 15 pairs of items that are identical); and a profile stability score (the correlation between the score profiles for the two halves of the inventory).

1 Only those studies of the EPPS that are published and are based on the administration of the standard form of the inventory are cited in this review. Unless otherwise indicated, the .05 level of significance is employed.

Some of the procedures used in constructing the EPPS may have limited or altered its meaning in unforeseen ways:

a) The paired comparison method produces ipsative scores, reflecting intraindividual differences, rather than the normative scores, reflecting interindividual differences, which are usually encountered in personality inventories. The current (third) edition of the manual surprisingly does not mention this feature of the EPPS scores, even though the psychological meaning of variables is so radically affected by being placed in an ipsative format (depending, in large part, on the particular nature and sheer number of the other ipsative scales in that format) that ipsative variables and their normative counterparts may have very little in common.

A normative score reflects the absolute level of the variable; an ipsative score reflects the level of the variable relative to the other variables in the ipsative format. Hence, two people with the same normative score on a variable may differ markedly in their ipsative scores on that same variable because of differences on one or more of the other variables that are included in the ipsative format.

The relative, within-individual, meaning of ipsative scores complicates interpretations of relationships between an ipsative variable and a normative variable because such relationships, in effect, take a form such as "those who are high on a particular variable relative to all the other variables are also higher (or lower) on a particular normative variable."

More importantly, the precise extent of the relationships between ipsative and normative variables is affected by statistical properties of ipsative scales. Hence, although the typical statistical indexes reported, such as correlation coefficients, accurately describe these relationships, these indexes may not describe the corresponding relationships between the same normative variables and the normative counterparts of the ipsative variables. The two relevant statistical properties of ipsative scales are as follows: when a set of ipsative scales has equal variances, the correlations of the set with any normative variable sum to zero; and these positive correlations tend to be lower and the negative correlations tend to be higher than the corresponding correlations for normative scales. As an illustration of this effect, the mean of the correlations reported in the manual between the EPPS scales and the Cooperativeness, Agreeableness, and Objectivity scales of the *Guilford-Martin Personnel Inventory* are −.06, .00, and −.16, respectively (*319*).

A related property of ipsative scales affects their interrelationships: the mean intercorrelation of a set of ipsative scales is $-1/(n-1)$, n being the number of scales. This value for the EPPS (*319*) is −.071, precisely the mean of the intercorrelations reported in the manual.

b) The use of the nine items in each scale in 28 comparisons with the other need items—eight are used three times each and the ninth is used four times—produced item overlap between and within scales.

An item overlaps between its own scale and the other scale with which it is compared because the endorsement of this item increases the score on its own scale and decreases the score on the other scale; the rejection of this item has the opposite effect. This artifact is not inherent in the paired comparison method, for the item could be used in a comparison with another item but not contribute to the score on its own scale if it is endorsed. The between-scale overlap precludes an accurate assessment of the interrelationships among the scales (*106*).

Similarly, there is item overlap within a scale because the nine items on a scale enter into a total of 28 comparisons, all of which contribute to the score for that scale. This overlap inflates internal-consistency reliability estimates.[2]

c) It is uncertain that the sets of nine items reflect the needs that they are intended to measure or, even if they do, that each set represents the same level of its need. These items appear to have been selected entirely on two bases: that their content manifestly reflected the needs, and that their social desirability ratings were appropriate. No data exist concerning the validity of the sets of items, but it is known that their internal-consistency reliability is low; the lower-bound Kuder-Richardson formula 21 estimates for the scales range from .13 to .75, with a median of .52 (*225*). Moreover, there are no data about the extent to which the sets of items represent equal levels of their needs, which is a prerequisite if the strength of needs within a person is to be ordered accurately. The ordering of two needs, for example, would obviously be inaccurate if one was represented

2 Messick, Samuel. "Review of *The Social Desirability Variable in Personality Assessment and Research* by Allen L. Edwards." *Ed & Psychol Meas* 19:451–4 au '59. *

by an item (or set of items) reflecting a high level of the need, but the other need was represented by an item (or set of items) reflecting a much lower level of the need.

d) Matching the items on the basis of average social desirability ratings of *unpaired* items may reduce social desirability as a response determinant, even though such matching is not as precise as matching on the basis of average social desirability ratings of *paired* items, but it cannot eliminate this tendency entirely in view of the multidimensionality of social desirability judgments (*162*).

INTERCORRELATIONS. The intercorrelations of the scales reported in the manual and obtained in other studies (*14, 26, 128, 145a, 185, 221*) are generally low. However, these results do not necessarily support the manual's conclusion that "the variables being measured by the EPPS are relatively independent" in view of the distortion produced by the ipsative nature of the scores (*48, 319*), as indicated previously. This ipsatization also makes it difficult to interpret factor and cluster analyses of the EPPS (*145a, 185, 203, 221, 226, 246*).

RELIABILITY. The reliability of most of the EPPS scales is roughly comparable to that of other personality inventories, but the reliability of some of the scales may be so low as to vitiate their usefulness. Test-retest reliability estimates, based on a three-week interval, ranged from .55 to .87, with a median of .73 (*45*). The other available reliability estimates are not as readily interpretable. The test-retest reliability estimates, based on a one-week interval, that are reported in the manual (the median is .79) and by Horst and Wright (*100;* the median is .80) may be affected by memory factors because of the short length of time involved. Moreover, the split-half reliability coefficients reported in the manual (the median is .78) and elsewhere (*26, 204*) are inflated by the previously described duplication of items within each scale.

NORMS. The norms in the current edition of the manual are excellent. Norms are presented for college students (based on a total of 760 males and 749 females drawn from a number of colleges throughout the country) and adults (based on 4,031 males and 4,932 females who participated in a nationwide survey of heads of households). These adult norms reflect one of the few instances in which norms for any personality inventory are based on a truly representative national sample of adults. In addition, norms based on 799 male and 760 female high school students exist (*26*), but are not reported in the manual.

VALIDITY. The validity data reported in the manual are scanty and inadequate. Only five studies—all unpublished—are described, and not always in sufficient detail, despite the vast number of relevant published studies (some of which are cited in the manual's bibliography). While the sheer number of these studies precludes a review of them all, the results bearing on some of the more important issues concerning the validity of the EPPS will be considered. The bulk of these studies involve the relationship of the EPPS with one or more normative variables, and, hence, are affected by the previously described limitations that are imposed on such relationships by the statistical properties of ipsative scores.

SELF-REPORT MEASURES. The relationships of the EPPS with self-report measures of the same needs—self-ratings or scores on projective tests and personality inventories—have been investigated in several studies.

The studies of self-ratings generally find moderate relationships between the EPPS and self-ratings. In Q-type analyses, the means of the EPPS scores and the means of the corresponding self-ratings correlated −.03 (*2*) and .56 (*258*). Moreover, the correlation between the EPPS scores and corresponding self-ratings, when computed on an individual basis, ranged from −.59 to .90, with a median of .39 (*273*). In R-type analyses, EPPS scores and real-self ratings were significantly related for 10 to 14 scales, and the median correlations ranged from .26 to .35 (*45, 258, 273*). EPPS scores and ideal-self ratings were significantly related for one scale (*45*).

The most relevant of the studies that compare the EPPS with projective tests and other personality inventories concern instruments which yield scores for the same needs found on the EPPS. These instruments include the *Thematic Apperception Test* (TAT), and various modifications of it, as well as the *Adjective Check List*. Most of these studies concern the relationship of the Achievement scale of the EPPS with two need achievement measures modeled after the TAT—McClelland's and the French Test of Insight. Almost without exception, these studies find that the EPPS Achievement scale is not significantly related to the other measures. The EPPS scale was significantly related ($r = .26$) to the McClelland measure in one study (*124*), but not in five others[3] (*46, 51, 65, 216*). It was significantly related ($r = .51$) to the French Test of Insight in one of four groups in one study (*216*), but not related at all in two other studies (*65, 126*). Less is known about the correspondence between the other need scales of the EPPS and the need scores on the TAT. In a Q-type analysis, the average rho was .15 between the score profiles on the two instruments, when the correlations were computed separately for each individual (*62*). And, in an R-type analysis, a dependency measure—a composite of Abasement, Autonomy, Deference, Dominance, and Succorance scores—on the two instruments was not significantly related (*222*). In the one study of the *Adjective Check List,* the means of the EPPS scores and the means of the *Adjective Check List* scores correlated .60 when the real self was described, and .57 and .64 when the ideal self was described (*42*).

NONTEST MEASURES OF UNDERLYING CONSTRUCTS. The relationships of the EPPS with a variety of non-test variables which reflect one or more of the constructs that the EPPS is intended to measure have been investigated in a great many studies.

Two studies bear directly on the need for achievement variable and support the finding that the EPPS Achievement scale was unrelated to standard measures of need for achievement. In one study (*126*), high scorers on the EPPS Achievement scale *avoided* intermediate risks in a ring toss game more than low scorers, and the two groups did not differ significantly in the time that they spent on a final course examination. In contrast, need for achievement theory predicts that those with high need for achievement should *prefer* such risks and spend more time on the examination, and these predictions were confirmed by the French Test of Insight. In a second study (*253*), level of expectation—the subjects' predictions of their scores on a course examination—was significantly related to only one scale—Endurance—and only for men and not women.

Studies of interpersonal influence—conformity, suggestibility, and hypnotizability—bear directly on the construct validity of the Autonomy and Deference scales.

The results of studies of one form of interpersonal influence—conformity in an Asch-type situation—are generally negative, and the few positive findings are not replicable. One scale was significantly related to conformity in two of the studies that reported the results for all EPPS scales (*137, 291*); none of the EPPS scales were so related in the third study (*192*); and in a fourth study (*120*), which used the .10 level of significance, one scale was significantly related to conformity for males and three for females. In a fifth study (*64*), which just reported the results for the Autonomy and Deference scales, the first scale was significantly (and negatively) related to conformity. Finally, a sixth study (*18*) found no significant difference in conformity between those classified as high on dependency (high on the Deference scale and low on the Autonomy scale) and those classified as low on dependency (low on the Deference scale and high on the Autonomy scale). Moreover, only the Achievement scale was significantly (and negatively) related to conformity in more than one (*120, 137*) of the first five studies.

The results of studies of other forms of interpersonal influence—suggestibility and hypnotizability—are contradictory. Postural sway was significantly (and positively) related to Deference and Affiliation in a study (*260*) that reported the results for all scales, but it was significantly (and negatively) related to only the Autonomy scale in a study (*84*) that reported the results for three scales—Autonomy, Deference, and Succorance. A related phenomenon, hypnotic susceptibility, was not significantly related to any of the EPPS scales in the Lang and Lazovik study (*260*), but another study (*311*) found that hypnotizable subjects were significantly lower than refractory subjects on one dependency measure—a composite of the Aggression, Autonomy, and Dominance scales—although the two groups did not differ significantly on another dependency measure—a composite of the Abasement, Deference, and Succorance scales.

Studies of dependency also bear on the construct validity of the Deference and Autonomy scales, as well as others. There is almost no agreement in the results of these studies, which employ behavioral variables—verbal condition-

3 McClelland, David C. Chap. 1, "Methods of Measuring Human Motivation," pp. 7–42. In *Motives in Fantasy, Action, and Society: A Method of Assessment and Study.* Edited by John W. Atkinson. Princeton, N.J.: D. Van Nostrand Co., Inc., 1958. Pp. xv, 873. *

ing, performance decrement following stress, and seeking help—as well as peer ratings.

In one study of verbal conditioning (*230*), those classified as high in dependency (on the basis of the Deference and Autonomy scales) were more conditionable when aggressive words were reinforced, but the two dependency groups did not differ significantly in conditionability when dependency words were reinforced. And in a second study (*287*), which reinforced pronouns, the more conditionable subjects were significantly higher on the Deference scale and significantly lower on the Autonomy scale, as well as being significantly higher on the Affiliation, Abasement, and Order scales and significantly lower on the Achievement and Dominance scales.

In studies of decrement in performance as a result of stress, those classified as high in dependency (on the basis of the Deference and Autonomy scales) had a significantly greater decrement than those classified as low in dependency in one study (*18*), but did not differ significantly in a second study (*97*).

In studies of the tendency to ask the experimenter for help on a hard task after being instructed that such help would be provided on request, those classified as high in dependency (on the basis of the Deference and Autonomy scales) asked for more help than those classified as low in dependency in one study (*18*), but the two groups did not differ significantly in this tendency in a second study (*230*).

In a study of peer ratings, those rated as either dependent, submissive, or conforming were significantly higher than those rated as rebellious on the Abasement, Deference, and Succorance scales and significantly lower on the Aggression, Autonomy, and Dominance scales (*50*).

Relatively little evidence exists about the construct validity of the other EPPS scales, but some relevant studies do concern four scales—Dominance, Change, Abasement, and Aggression.

The validity of the Dominance scale is supported by a study in which management personnel were rated for leadership by observers and peers on the basis of the subjects' performance in a simulated business situation and group discussion; the observers' ratings correlated positively with the Dominance and Intraception scales and negatively with the Abasement and Nurturance scales, and the peers' ratings correlated positively with the Dominance and Aggression scales and negatively with the Abasement and Nurturance scales (*320*).

Support for the validity of the Change scale comes from the finding that expectation of change correlated positively with the Change and Intraception scales, and correlated negatively with the Deference and Dominance scales (*261*).

On the other hand, the validity of the Abasement scale is questioned by the finding that those male students who predicted, on the first day of a course, that their final course grade would be *lower* and those who predicted that it would be *higher* than their grade-point average for the previous semester differed significantly in the scores on the Abasement scale, but the difference was in the wrong direction (those predicting higher course grades had higher Abasement scores); and the two female groups did not differ significantly in their Abasement scores (*197*).

Similarly, the meaning of the Aggression scale is challenged by the finding that those scoring high and those scoring low on that scale did not differ significantly in their perception of aggressive words in a binocular rivalry situation or in their acceptance of aggressive Rorschach percepts (*172*).

ACADEMIC ACHIEVEMENT AND OCCUPATIONAL PERFORMANCE. Relatively little is known about the ability of the EPPS to predict socially important variables. Most of the available data concern the relationship of the EPPS to academic performance—academic achievement (e.g., grade-point average) and "over-under achievement" (e.g., grade-point average with ability held constant)—or occupational performance. The academic performance findings, in addition to their bearing on the predictive validity of the EPPS, are relevant to the construct validity of the Achievement scale, and probably the Endurance scale as well.

Academic achievement was significantly (and positively) related to the Achievement scale in seven samples (*59, 111, 124, 239, 253*), but not in three others (*126, 253, 264*)—the median of the reported correlations was .35. In the studies that report the results for other scales (*59, 111, 129, 239, 253*), only the Abasement and Change scales were significantly (and negatively) related to achievement in more than one of the samples (*59, 239, 253*).

The results concerning over-under achievement are less consistent. This variable was significantly related to the Achievement scale in five samples (*41, 105, 197, 241, 267*), but not in nine others (*109, 190, 197, 216, 241, 247, 267*). In those studies which also report the results for the other scales, five scales were significantly related to over-under achievement in two or three of the eight samples—positively related scales were Dominance (*109, 267*), Order (*41, 105*), and Endurance (*105, 109*); negatively related ones were Affiliation (*41, 105, 109*) and Change (*41, 109*).

Studies of occupational performance have found some scattered relationships with the EPPS scales. Three of these studies concern nurses or hospital aides. Compared with those student nurses who were classified by their supervisors as "poor" in terms of their overall desirability as a nurse, those who were classified as "good" were significantly lower on the Order scale and significantly higher on the Dominance scale (*244*); nurses and aides in satisfied and dissatisfied wards did not differ significantly on any of 12 EPPS scales (all but the Change, Endurance, and Heterosexuality scales) that were investigated (*20*); and the efficiency ratings of psychiatric employees only correlated significantly (and positively) with one scale—Autonomy (*272*). The other studies concern performance in industrial settings. Four of the EPPS scales' correlations with managers' ratings of selling effectiveness were significant for either retail salesmen or industrial salesmen—the Dominance scale was significantly correlated (r = .29 and .32) for both groups (*138*); overall performance ratings of foremen correlated significantly with three EPPS scales—positively with Endurance (r = .27), and negatively with Nurturance (r = −.32) and Succorance (r = −.32) (*228*); and, in a study of telephone employees who had worked at isolated Arctic stations, those who received the highest ratings by their supervisors on work and social adjustment were significantly higher on the Deference and Order scales, and significantly lower on the Aggression scale (*326*).

SOCIAL DESIRABILITY RESPONSE STYLE AND FAKING. In view of the importance of social desirability as a response determinant and the special precautions taken in constructing the EPPS to minimize the effects of this response style, how much does it affect the EPPS? Studies of this issue have been carried out at the item level and the score level.

At the item level, a substantial tendency exists to endorse the more socially desirable item in each pair of EPPS items, but it is not as great as that endorsement tendency on unpaired items. The obtained correlations, ranging from .37 to .69, in studies reported in the manual and elsewhere (*28, 53, 94, 196*) of the relationship between the difference in social desirability ratings of the items in each pair and their frequency of endorsement are in contrast with the correlation of .87 between social desirability ratings and frequency of endorsement of unpaired items originally obtained by Edwards (*1*). In addition to a tendency to endorse the more socially desirable item in each pair, there is a related tendency to endorse the more personally desirable (the desirability of a trait in oneself rather than its desirability in others) item (*98*).

In contrast to the trend of these other studies, the correlations, computed separately for each item pair, between choice of item within the pair and a social desirability response style (SD) scale clustered around zero; and the number of times that the more socially desirable item in each pair was chosen was not significantly correlated with the score on the SD scale (*43*).

At the score level, the average EPPS score for each scale correlated −.01 (*2*) and .46 (*258*) with the average social desirability rating of the need and .63 and .56 with the average personal desirability rating of the need (*42*). More to the point, none of the correlations between EPPS score profiles and social desirability ratings of the needs, when computed separately for each individual, were significant (*2*).

Also at the score level, an independent measure of social desirability response style was significantly related to several of the EPPS scales in three studies, but these relationships were generally lower than corresponding relationships of this response style with personality inventories that use a true-false or a yes-no format, such as the MMPI (cf., *11*). The difference in magnitude of these relationships, however, may be due, at least in part, to the statistical properties of ipsative scores described earlier. A study reported in the manual found that the Edwards SD scale significantly correlated with two scales—Endurance (r = .32) and Succorance ($r = -.32$); another study (*11*), using the same SD scale, found that it correlated significantly with four scales—Dominance ($r = .51$), Exhibitionism ($r = .28$), Abasement ($r = -.46$), and Aggression ($r = -.26$); and a third study (*32*) found that another measure of this response style—the difference between performance on the standard Manifest Anxiety Scale and a forced choice version of it—correlated significantly with five scales—Achievement ($r = -.24$), Autonomy ($r = -.29$), Abasement ($r = .29$), Endurance ($r = .32$), and Aggression ($r = -.25$).

Also relevant to the issue of social desirability response style, as well as the general issue of faking, are studies that compare normal performance on the EPPS with performance under conditions where the subjects attempt to make a desirable impression, either as a result of explicit instructions or situational pressures.

In studies where subjects were instructed to choose socially desirable or personally desirable responses, there was only slight inter-subject agreement in score profiles—the average rho was .25 (*36*) and .14 (*274*)—but in a study in which subjects were instructed to make a "good impression" there was substantial inter-subject agreement—the average rho was .58 (*93*). While the first two studies, though not the third, indicate that *group* standards of social desirability have been eliminated from the EPPS, other findings in these two studies indicate that *individual* standards of social desirability remain. In the Borislow study (*36*), the mean of the correlations, computed separately for each individual, between the score profile when the EPPS was taken originally with standard instructions and the score profile when it was taken again with social desirability or personal desirability instructions was significantly lower than the mean of the correlations between the score profiles for a control group that took the EPPS both times with standard instructions. And in the Saltz study (*274*), there was high intra-subject agreement between the score profiles for the two halves of the EPPS—the median was .70 of the rhos computed separately for each individual.

Other evidence points to the existence of group standards on the EPPS. Instructions to make a good impression produced significant mean changes on 11 scales, and separate instructions to simulate high Change, high Order, and high Dominance produced significant changes on 10, 11, and 12 scales, respectively (*93*); Air Force trainees who were told that instructors would see their test results differed significantly on eight scales from trainees who responded anonymously (*40*); and applicants for retail sales jobs differed significantly on four scales from those already employed on such jobs, but applicants for industrial sales jobs did not significantly differ on any scale from those already employed on such jobs (*257*).

The consistency and profile stability scores generally do not detect such explicit attempts to make a good impression. In the Borislow study (*36*) neither measure differed significantly between the standard condition and either the social desirability or personal desirability conditions; and in the Dicken study (*93*) the consistency score did not differ between the standard condition and either the Good Impression or Order conditions, although it did differ between the standard condition and both the Dominance and Change conditions. Furthermore, the consistency and profile stability scores were not significantly correlated in the standard condition of the Borislow study.

SUMMARY. The EPPS set out to measure an interesting set of variables and its construction represented an important attempt to minimize the effects of social desirability response style. Its reliance on a paired comparison format, however, has complicated interpretations of the resulting ipsative scores and appraisals of their statistical relationships. Moreover, its development apparently concentrated on the control of the response style to the neglect of other validity considerations. As a result, although the influence of the response style was reduced—the EPPS is affected by it, but less so than most other personality inventories—a decade of research into the validity of the EPPS offers little justification for assuming that its scales measure the constructs that they are intended to reflect, or that, with the important exception of the link between the Achievement scale and academic achievement, the scales are useful in predicting socially important variables. Consequently, the likelihood of obtaining meaningful measures of personality variables within the normal range would seem to be greater if, instead of the EPPS, any of several personality inventories whose construction focused particularly on the validity of their scales was employed. Such inventories include the *Guilford-Zimmerman Temperament Survey* and the 16 PF, both of which use the traditional true-false or yes-no format. If an inventory of this kind is employed, it would be wise to administer the inventory with a standard measure of social desirability response style so as to be able to gauge its effects on the results obtained.

J Consult Psychol 23:471 O '59. Edward S. Bordin. [Review of 1959 revision of manual.] This revision of the 1954 manual....differs in only minor respects from the original. The directions for administration now include a section on machine scoring; a general adult sample now provides an additional norm group; the bibliography has been expanded from 9 to 82 references, most of the new references representing studies in which the EPPS figured. The general adult sample is less than adequate for normative purposes because it consists of a nationwide sample of male and female household heads who are members of a consumer purchase panel used for market surveys. It is not clear what this means with regard to its possible biases with respect to age, education, and class status. The mean scores of this sample vary from those in the other norm group, college students. But there is no effort to analyze the significance of these differences for the validity of the test. In fact, it is astonishing that no effort was made to summarize the relevance of the large body of studies in the bibliography to the test's validity and reliability. The reviews of the first manual pointed to its deficiencies with regard to validating evidence. One wonders why the author and publisher bothered to offer a revision which revises so little and is so unresponsive to criticism.

For reviews by Frank Barron, Åke Bjerstedt, and Donald W. Fiske, see 5:47 (2 excerpts.)

[88]

The Ego Strength Q-Sort Test. Grades 9–16 and adults; 1956–58; 6 scores: ego-status, social status, goal setting and striving, good mental health, physical status, total; 1 form ('58, 4 pages, essentially the same as form copyrighted in 1956); manual ('58, 53 pages); no data on reliability; $9 per examiner's kit of 25 tests, 2 item sheets (from which sort slips for 2 examinees may be prepared), manual, stencils, and sorting board; $3 per 25 tests; cash orders postpaid; (50–90) minutes; Russell N. Cassel; Psychometric Affiliates. *

REFERENCES

1. CASSEL, RUSSELL N. "Comparing the Effectiveness of the Ego-Strength Q-Sort Test by Use of R- and Q-Methodologies." *J Genetic Psychol* 94:161–8 Je '59. *
2. CASSEL, RUSSELL N., AND HARRIMAN, B. LYNN. "A Comparative Analysis of Personality and Ego Strength Test Scores for In-Prison, Neuro-Psychiatric and Typical Individuals." *J Ed Res* 53:43–52 O '59. * (*PA* 35:810)
3. BAILEY, MATTOX A.; WARSHAW, LEON; AND COHEN, JACOB. "An Obverse Factor Analytic Study of Values in Psychologists, Psychiatrists, Social Workers and Nurses." *J Clin Psychol* 19:120–4 Ja '63. * (*PA* 39:1650)

ALLEN L. EDWARDS, *Professor of Psychology, University of Washington, Seattle, Washington.*

The total score on the ESQT is based upon the correlation between the ratings assigned to the 60 items by a subject and a standard set of ratings. The standard ratings are based upon the judgments of six different groups. Since a simple averaging of the mean ratings assigned by each group was used in establishing the standard ratings, the chaplains ($n = 31$) and psychologists ($n = 25$) contribute to the standard ratings to the same degree as delinquent and wayward girls ($n = 100$) and typical secondary male youth ($n = 200$).

Evidence is presented, in the form of point-biserial coefficients ranging from .22 to .60, that differences occur between the mean correlations (total scores) when various groups are compared. No information is provided concerning the test-retest stability of the total score nor is any information given concerning the stability of the five part scores. One of the part scores, Physical Status, is based upon the ratings assigned to only two items. Low correlations, between −.28 and .16 are reported between total score and three other proposed measures of ego strength. The part scores have similarly low correlations with the other ego strength measures, the highest in absolute value being −.36 between Social Status and the Es scale of the MMPI.

Scoring keys are provided for each of the six original groups of judges in addition to the standard set of ratings for the combined groups. However, at least one of these keys, that for ordained ministers, contains irregularities in the number of items assigned to each of the rating categories. For example, 7 items are supposed to be assigned to category 4, but the manual shows 10 items in this category for ordained ministers.

The items in the ESQT were typed on an 8½ by 11 inch page and then photographed. The original typing was bad and the reproduction is worse. Furthermore, the items are on thin paper and the cards or items are so small, approximately ¾ by 2 inches, that they are awkward to handle.

The scoring stencil for the total score is not in alignment with the test booklet in which the Q-sort is recorded. In addition, the standard ratings on the scoring stencil opposite a given item number are not always the same as the ratings given in the manual. For example, the manual assigns a rating of 11 to item 55, whereas this rating appears opposite item 56 on the scoring stencil. This occurs because the rating assigned item 47 is misplaced.

The manual contains no references to any published research with the ESQT. This reviewer can find nothing in the manual which would lead to his recommendation of the test's use as a measure of ego strength.

Harrison G. Gough, *Professor of Psychology, University of California, Berkeley, California.*

This test consists of 60 statements (e.g., "continued recognized progress towards personal goals," "adjusts to progressive change readily," "knows how to relax and practices it," and "gets a fair share of the luxuries of life relative to group") which the subject is asked to Q-sort into 11 categories of specified frequency (1, 3, 5, 7, etc.). The continuum of judgment underlying the sorting is the presumed relevance of each statement to "happiness." The 60 items were selected from an original library of 4,275 and maintain the same relative balance among five themes (ego status, social status, goal setting, mental health, and physical health) as observed among the full set of items.

The principal score on the test is the correlation of an individual's sorting of the items with the modal sorting derived from an unweighted average of the mean placements of each item by six samples; these original samples are described in the manual as "federal reformatory prisoners" ($n = 200$); "delinquent and wayward girls" ($n = 100$); "typical secondary male youth" ($n = 200$); "typical secondary female youth" ($n = 100$); "chaplains (all religious faiths)" ($n = 31$); and "research psychologists" ($n = 25$).

The operations defining the scoring key, it is clear, are similar to those used to define such indices as Rorschach P, Rosenzweig's Group Conformity Ratio, the F scale on the MMPI (except that F is scored for uncommon responses), and the Cm or communality scale of the *California Psychological Inventory*. The basic presumption concerning the total score on the ESQT, therefore, is that it is a measure of conventionality, conformance to modal standards, and the internalization of manifest norms.

Unfortunately, the manual carries no hint of these theoretical implications and, in fact, in its continual emphasis on total score as a measure of "ego strength," does violence to them. This review's first conclusion, therefore, is that the ESQT is flawed by an inherent confusion between ego strength and conformity.

This basic deficiency is augmented by other errors and misconceptions almost too numerous to list, and by a manual which is so inadequate and badly written that one wonders why either publisher or author would permit it to be released. As illustrations of the latter point, consider the following passages:

> It is presumed that an individual can live only his or her own life, and that only he or she, in the final analysis, can forge for their own happiness.
>
> It [happiness] falls on a continuum scale which ranges in scope from that of an individual with a "passive and vegetable" like existence of a feeble-minded and apathetic type, through that of the truly happy person, to that of a person with a hyper-mania, non-satiable, effervescing, and additive type of manifestations....
>
> The diversity of human beings with respect to what constitutes happiness is rather unique from one person to the other, and, therefore, is infinite in scope.

Singular subjects with plural verbs, plural subjects with singular verbs, misspellings, incorrect uses of prepositions, solecisms, and barbarisms abound in the text of the manual. These are not technical errors, to be sure, but it is nonetheless embarrassing to think of psychological testing being represented by a manual as poorly written as this one.

With respect to technical errors, there is a very unsatisfactory handling of the validity problem. The Cronbach-Meehl convention of defining four types of validity is dutifully followed, but is misunderstood. Construct validity is seen merely as "the relationship between scores on the ESQT and scores....for other tests" (p. 15), and "prediction validity" (*sic*) is allegedly demonstrated by showing discriminations between (*a*) hospitalized and non-hospitalized airmen; and (*b*) schizophrenic patients and unselected adults.

The data presented do nothing to allay the

anxieties aroused by these conceptual misunderstandings. In a sample of 200 adults, the total score on the ESQT correlated −.19 with Barron's ego strength scale, −.03 with Taylor's scale for manifest anxiety, +.25 with the *Army General Classification Test,* and +.04 with last school grade completed. Other correlations ranging from −.44 to +.16 are also cited, but are either with relatively unknown instruments (e.g., the "Ego Strength Rating Scale by B. Hartman," $r = -.28$), or with instruments whose validity is not unequivocally established (*Cassel Group Level of Aspiration Test,* first goal, $r = -.12$).

In addition to the total score (the correlation of an individual sorting with the modal sorting), separate scores may also be obtained for the five clusters of items (Ego Status, Social Status, Goal Setting and Striving, Mental Health, and Physical Status), and standard score conversions are provided. No evidence on the reliability of these part scores is offered, and one must doubt whether two of these scores (Ego Status with 10 items, and Physical Status with 2 items) could meet minimum standards. Evidence on the reliability of the total score is also lacking, although the reviewer's expectation is that a sort-resort correlation for a 60-item deck would be adequate.

Perhaps the most fundamental deficiency in the manual, considering that the test is a Q-sort deck, is the absence of a table giving intercorrelations among the 60 items and mean placements of each one (although these latter can be to some extent inferred from the scoring key). In an optimum Q-deck, one which maximizes differences among people and in which all items are functional, the intercorrelations among items should be at a minimum and the mean placement of items in a large and heterogeneous sample should converge on the middle step of the Q-distribution. If the mean placement of an item is near either extreme of the continuum, the item is by definition weak as a differentiator; if two items are highly correlated there is redundancy of response. There is no evidence in the manual that these two basic technical points were considered in the selection and evaluation of items.

More problems could be raised, but enough has been said to lead to an overall summary. The reviewer wishes to apologize for the harshness of his judgment, but can see no way of avoiding the conclusion that this test is clearly below minimal publication standards. Its basic variable is misunderstood and misidentified, evidence on validity is unconvincing and inadequate, and reliability is totally neglected. Even the Q-sort method, on which the test is based, appears to be misconceived, as essential technical information pertaining to this deck is neither discussed nor presented. A Q-sort test of ego strength might indeed be developed, and the work already done on this test could constitute a first step toward such a goal, but as it stands, this instrument is not ready for publication and commercial release.

[89]

***Embedded Figures Test.** Ages 10 and over; 1950–62; individual; 1 form ['57, 32 cards, may also be administered as a short form using only 12 cards]; manual ('50, 15 pages, reprint of *1* below); supplementary instructions and data ['62, 6 hectographed sheets]; college norms only; $3 per set of testing materials, postpaid; (15–25) minutes; Herman A. Witkin; the Author. *

REFERENCES

1–9. See 5:49.
10. BAUMAN, GERALD. *The Stability of the Individual's Mode of Perception, and of Perception-Personality Relationships.* Doctor's thesis, New York University (New York, N.Y.), 1951.
11. LINTON, HARRIET B. *Relations Between Mode of Perception and Tendency to Conform.* Doctor's thesis, Yale University (New Haven, Conn.), 1952.
12. ROSENFELD, IRWIN JOSEPH. *Mathematical Ability as a Function of Perceptual Field-Dependency and Certain Personality Variables.* Doctor's thesis, University of Oklahoma (Norman, Okla.), 1958. (*DA* 19:880)
13. DANA, RICHARD H., AND GOOCHER, BUELL. "Embedded-Figures and Personality." *Percept & Motor Skills* 9:99–102 Je '59. * (*PA* 38:4299)
14. GARDNER, RILEY W.; HOLZMAN, PHILIP S.; KLEIN, GEORGE S.; LINTON, HARRIET B.; AND SPENCE, DONALD P. "Cognitive Control: A Study of Individual Consistencies in Cognitive Behavior." *Psychol Issues* 1(4):1–186 '59. * (*PA* 35:2266)
15. BIERI, JAMES. "Parental Identification, Acceptance of Authority, and Within-Sex Differences in Cognitive Behavior." *J Abn & Social Psychol* 60:76–9 Ja '60. * (*PA* 34:7526)
16. DANA, RICHARD H., AND GOOCHER, BUELL. "Pessimism Reaffirmed: A Reply to Witkin." *Percept & Motor Skills* 11:243–4 D '60. * (*PA* 35:2206)
17. GARDNER, RILEY W.; JACKSON, DOUGLAS N.; AND MESSICK, SAMUEL J. "Personality Organization in Cognitive Controls and Intellectual Abilities." *Psychol Issues* 2(8):1–149 '60. * (*PA* 36:2HA49G)
18. MEUX, MILTON OTTO. *The Role of Reasoning and Spatial Abilities in Performance at Three Difficulty Levels of the Embedded Figures Task.* Doctor's thesis, University of Illinois (Urbana, Ill.), 1960. (*DA* 21:1625)
19. WITKIN, HERMAN A. "'Embedded Figures and Personality': A Reply." *Percept & Motor Skills* 11:15–20 Ag '60. * (*PA* 35:3447)
20. GOODENOUGH, DONALD R., AND KARP, STEPHEN A. "Field Dependence and Intellectual Functioning." *J Abn & Social Psychol* 63:241–6 S '61. * (*PA* 37:1214)
21. ISCOE, IRA, AND CARDEN, JOYCE ANN. "Field Dependence, Manifest Anxiety, and Sociometric Status in Children." Abstract. *J Consult Psychol* 25:184 Ap '61. * (*PA* 36:4FF84I)
22. LEAGUE, BETTY JO, AND JACKSON, DOUGLAS N. "Activity and Passivity as Correlates of Field-Independence." *Percept & Motor Skills* 12:291–8 Je '61. * (*PA* 36:2HJ91L)
23. LOEFF, RICHARD. *Embedding and Distracting Field Contexts as Related to the Field Dependence Dimension.* Master's thesis, Brooklyn College (New York, N.Y.), 1961.
24. WITKIN, HERMAN A. "Cognitive Development and the Growth of Personality." *Acta Psychologica* 18(4):245–57 '61. * (*PA* 36:5HJ45W)
25. KARP, STEPHEN A. *A Factorial Study of Overcoming Embeddedness in Perceptual and Intellectual Functioning.* Doctor's thesis, New York University (New York, N.Y.), 1962.
26. LONGENECKER, E. D. "Perceptual Recognition as a Function of Anxiety, Motivation, and the Testing Situation." *J Abn & Social Psychol* 64:215–21 Mr '62. * (*PA* 38:1723)

27. STEWART, HORACE F., JR. *A Study of the Relationship Between Certain Personality Measures and Hallucinoidal Visual Imagery.* Doctor's thesis, University of Florida (Gainesville, Fla.), 1962. (*DA* 24:827)
28. WITKIN, H. A.; DYK, R. B.; FATERSON, H. F.; GOODENOUGH, D. R.; AND KARP, S. A. *Psychological Differentiation: Studies of Development.* New York: John Wiley & Sons, Inc., 1962. Pp. xii, 418. * (*PA* 37:819)
29. COPPINGER, NEIL W.; BORTNER, RAYMAN W.; AND SAUCER, RAYFORD T. "A Factor Analysis of Psychological Deficit." *J Genetic Psychol* 103:23-43 S '63. * (*PA* 39:174)
30. ELKIND, DAVID; KOEGLER, RONALD R.; AND GO, ELSIE. "Field Independence and Concept Formation." *Percept & Motor Skills* 17:383-6 O '63. * (*PA* 38:5349)
31. FISHBEIN, GERALD M. "Perceptual Modes and Asthmatic Symptoms: An Application of Witkin's Hypothesis." *J Consult Psychol* 27:54-8 F '63. * (*PA* 37:8205)
32. GOODENOUGH, DONALD R., AND EAGLE, CAROL JOHNSON. "A Modification of the Embedded-Figures Test for Use With Young Children." *J Genetic Psychol* 103:67-74 S '63. *
33. KARP, STEPHEN A.; POSTER, DOROTHY C.; AND GOODMAN, ALAN. "Differentiation in Alcoholic Women." *J Personality* 31:386-93 S '63. *

HARRISON G. GOUGH, *Professor of Psychology, University of California, Berkeley, California.*

This test consists of 24 complex colored figures, derivations of those used by Gottschaldt in the 1920's in his work on the influence of experience on perception. Each complex figure contains one of eight simple figures. In administering the test, a card on which a complex figure appears is shown to the subject for 15 seconds, and he is asked to describe it. Then a card containing the simple figure embedded in that complex figure is shown for 10 seconds. Following this, the complex figure is again presented and the subject's task is to find the simple figure and to trace it with a blunt stylus.

The score on each item is the time taken to find the embedded figure. A maximum of five minutes per card is allowed, after which a failure is recorded and the next card is presented. Reexamination of the simple figure is permitted when requested, for 10-second periods; the time record is held in abeyance during any such interval.

The items differ considerably in difficulty, ranging from mean times of 10 seconds to over two minutes for college males, and for failure rates from 0 to 27 per cent for college females. For the full test, mean time scores are reported of 16 minutes 39 seconds and 23 minutes 4 seconds for adult males and females, and 58 minutes 4 seconds and 62 minutes 16 seconds for 10-year-old boys and girls. Reliability coefficients, whether by the odd-even, test-retest, or analysis of variance method, are excellent, the median coefficient in 10 studies being .905.

Although the test is viewed by its author as related to such well known devices as the Kohs blocks, Guilford's tests of adaptive flexibility, and Wechsler's subtests for block design, picture completion, and object assembly, it is not interpreted as an index of general ability. Its diagnostic implications, on the contrary, are seen as related to (*a*) field independence, (*b*) cognitive clarity, (*c*) an analytic versus global perceptual mode, and (*d*) a general disposition to articulate and structure experience. These notions, it should be observed, are not just ad hoc comments on the apparent nature of the test, but are basic theoretical principles arising from a vast amount of careful and convincing experimentation by Witkin and his associates. Indeed, one of the most attractive features of this test is its firm anchoring in a systematic context of theory and empirical evidence.

There is no question concerning the importance of the approach to cognitive testing represented by this device. From Gottschaldt in the 1920's, through Thurstone in the 1940's, to 1950 when Witkin's first paper on the embedded figures test appeared, one can discern the gradual crystallizing of a concept of measurement of truly fundamental significance. This reviewer has no doubt but that within 15 to 20 years the embedded figure kind of content will be as basic in cognitive test batteries as analogies, progressions, spatial manipulations, and quantitative analyses are today. There are also the exciting potentialities of a test of this type for cross-cultural usage.

The importance of the innovative trend exemplified by Witkin's test, therefore, cannot be overemphasized; but this does not mean that the test as it stands is free from flaws and imperfections. One major difficulty is the lack of a manual. Witkin's paper "Individual Differences in Ease of Perception of Embedded Figures" (*1*) is distributed with the test materials, and a later paper, "Cognitive Development and the Growth of Personality" (*24*) is also available. The former is an excellent research report and the latter a stimulating exposition of theory, but neither is a test manual. Information which a manual would contain—e.g., intercorrelations among items, correlations of the EFT with other well established cognitive measures, norms for various groups, correlations with utilitarian criteria such as school grades and job success, and the meaning and dependability of scores obtained in retesting—is lacking.

A second area of difficulty concerns the unwieldiness of the test in its present form.

Experimentation with group forms is needed, as there seems to be no reason in principle for insisting on individual testing. Group testing would probably require a shift from time to error scores, but again there seems to be no compelling theoretical rationale for use of time scores. A shorter maximum time per item (e.g., two minutes) would do away with the hour-long and frustrating sessions which occur with some frequency among children and which are not unknown even with adults. A conventional item versus total score internal consistency analysis might also permit a reduction in length by elimination of undifferentiating items. All of these modifications—toward a shorter test with briefer time allotments and in a group test format—would make for a more serviceable, wieldy, and convenient device. They should all be attainable without loss of any intrinsic validity.

A third need is for a parallel form of this test. Learning during the test itself must be appreciable, and it is doubtful whether the test could be given more than once to adults. Yet the function being measured is almost by definition a growth function calling for longitudinal assessment. At least two equivalent forms are therefore necessitated.

A fourth issue concerns Witkin's present opinion that this test assesses a cognitive mode (analytical structuring) while being more or less independent of the general level of intellectual ability. On the basis of extensive work with R. S. Crutchfield's adaptation of Gottschaldt's figures (Crutchfield's test is somewhat comparable to Witkin's), this reviewer is of the opinion that the embedded figures procedure does assess intellectual ability and that, were studies conducted, Witkin's EFT would in fact reveal significant correlations with such tests as the Henmon-Nelson, Raven's matrices, Cattell's culture-fair test, and similar instruments in widespread usage. At the same time, and here in agreement with Witkin, the reviewer sees the EFT as not merely synonymous with these other indices, but as an instrument which assesses a new and important facet of the cognitive domain.

The intention of these comments is entirely constructive. Witkin's use of the hidden figures technique to test cognitive and perceptual modes is a development of fundamental significance. Although in its current form the instrument is crude and unwieldy, there is every reason to believe that it can be improved and simplified and that parallel forms can be developed. With such technical improvement, the test will provide a worthy and auspicious addition to psychology's list of valid devices of measurement.

Leona E. Tyler, *Professor of Psychology, University of Oregon, Eugene, Oregon.*

Since World War II various researchers have been studying individual differences in perception, cognitive style, or cognitive control principles. (The same domain has been variously labeled by different workers at different times.) This research effort has had a theoretical rather than a practical orientation, and none of the tests have been placed on the market for general use. It is unlikely that procedures such as Witkin's Tilting Room-Tilting Chair will ever be employed very widely as practical testing procedures because of the elaborate equipment they require. But the *Embedded Figures Test* (EFT), Witkin's adaptation of the Gottschaldt figures, is a convenient and usable instrument. It consists of 24 complex geometrical figures, some in black and white and some in color, presented to the subject on separate cards. His task is to locate in the complex figure a simple figure he has previously been shown. His score for each item is the time it takes him to do this. The test can be used with children as well as with adults.

The trait or characteristic measured by this test was labeled field dependence in the first major report by Witkin and associates (*2*), field articulation in factor analytic studies carried on by Gardner and others (*14*), psychological differentiation by Witkin and his coworkers in their more recent study of children (*28*). The fact that EFT showed significant and generally high correlations with most of the scores based on tests of bodily orientation (the Tilting Room-Tilting Chair, Rotating Room, and Rod and Frame test) indicated that all of these procedures must make some similar demand upon subjects. What subjects who did well with them seemed to have was the ability to analyze a complex configuration and then to respond to some parts of it, ignoring others. Subsequent studies showed that this ability was related to temperament or personality characteristics as well as to the spatial aspects of intelligence. Field-dependent persons, those having great difficulty with EFT as well as with the body orientation tests, showed up as more passive and anxious about control of body impulses, with lower self esteem and less well differentiated body images than those who did well. Females scored significantly more field dependent than males.

The reliability coefficients reported in the studies in which the EFT has been used indicate that, whatever this trait is, individuals manifest it consistently on different parts of the test and at different times. Test-retest coefficients for men and women, even with a three year interval between administrations, were .89. Stability coefficients over shorter intervals and split-half coefficients have tended to run even higher.

Since there has been no attempt to publish the EFT and make it available to regular consumers of tests, no manual has been issued. If one wishes to use EFT in a research undertaking, Witkin sends a reprint of his 1950 paper (*1*), which contains instructions and essential information, along with some dittoed material based on other studies. But in order to use the test intelligently a researcher really needs to read in their entirety the books and monographs to which reference has been made earlier in this review.

Until or unless more extensive norms and more readily available technical information are developed, EFT is not a practical instrument for diagnosis or selection purposes. Perhaps the time has now come for special studies in which its utility in clinics, counseling offices, and personnel departments is assessed. The characteristics to which it points would seem to be important enough to justify this effort.

[90]

★**Emo Questionnaire.** Adults; 1958–60; 14 scores: rationalization, inferiority feelings, fear and anxiety, N vector (total of preceding 3 scores), depression, projection, unreality, withdrawal, Z vector (total of preceding 4 scores), hostility, sex, organic response, total diagnostic, buffer score; 1 form ('58, 8 pages); manual ('59, 37 pages); report form ('60, 4 pages); no data on reliability of current form; $7.50 per 20 tests; postage extra; $1 per specimen set, postpaid; (20–30) minutes; George O. Baehr (test), Melany E. Baehr (test), and Measurement Research Division, Industrial Relations Center, University of Chicago (manual); Education-Industry Service. *

REFERENCES

1. Pishkin, Vladimir; Olson, Lois O.; and Jacobs, Durand F. "An Objective Attempt to Analyze Emotional Interactions Between Psychiatric Patients and Nursing Staff." *J Clin Psychol* 17:383–9 O '61. * (*PA* 38:8804)

Bertram D. Cohen, *Professor of Psychology, and Director of Clinical Training, Rutgers, The State University, New Brunswick, New Jersey.*

This paper-and-pencil questionnaire was devised for both industrial placement and clinical diagnostic purposes. Group or individual administration techniques are feasible. The scores may be used as an adjunctive device in the selection of industrial personnel (i.e., to screen potentially effective workers) or as a basis for individualized personality description. The items are grouped into a series of specific "diagnostic" categories such as "hostility," "fear and anxiety," and "depression." These categories, in turn, are grouped into three composite scores: total diagnostics, neurotic vector, and psychotic vector. Finally, the system includes three kinds of scores for each diagnostic category or composite vector: frequency of response, intensity of response, and conformity of response.

Although the authors offer industrial selection and placement as important purposes of the test, the major attempts at validity determination concern comparison of the scores of presumably normal industrial workers with those of hospitalized psychiatric patients, mostly schizophrenic. The results show that the test (particularly the conformity of response scores) can discriminate reliably between these groups, and holds up on cross-validation. Also, in an independent study (*1*), scores on the test successfully differentiated nursing personnel from a hospitalized patient group. The major shortcoming of this work is the lack of validity criteria that are genuinely relevant to the industrial situations within which the test is intended to apply. It is hardly sufficient to know that industrial workers score differently most of the time from hospitalized psychotic patients, even if all other variables (e.g., age, sex, etc.) had been adequately controlled.

For certain clinical purposes, there are some indications that the test and its special scoring methods may be of some specific value. The authors report studies indicating that scores differentiate between psychiatric patients who showed "steady progress" and those who "suffered a temporary relapse during the course of treatment." The test has also been used to determine the relative effectiveness of individual psychotherapy, group therapy, and combined individual and group therapy.

As for individual personality description, there are as yet no grounds for evaluating the usefulness of the test. The apparent content validity of the diagnostic category items is all one would have to go on.

In summary, the main feature of this test that might prove intriguing to test users is the use of "intensity" and "conformity" measures along with the more traditional frequency counts employed in most personality inventories. Further work with more practical and relevant criterion groups and situations is clearly necessary before the test can be considered a viable competitor among personality inventories.

W. GRANT DAHLSTROM, *Professor of Psychology, The University of North Carolina, Chapel Hill, North Carolina.*

This instrument is advanced for use in industry, hospitals, and private clinical practice for two applications: screening of emotional health problems and individual personality diagnosis. Different scoring procedures are utilized for these two purposes but the manual provides the interpretive guidelines for screening use only. For individual personality appraisal the manual recommends that the protocol and score sheet from the subject be sent to the test author for interpretation (fee unspecified).

The test booklet contains 140 items out of 230 originally developed (and presumably scaled for the 14 component scores) in a previous test by G. O. Baehr, the Baehr Discontentment Scale (1951). The items surviving in this test were pruned for hospital related experiences. The test is represented to the subject as a measure of how well he understands himself. The format of the present instrument calls for a judgment about each item first as having happened to the subject within the last month or not, and then requests an additional four-step rating of the subject's reactions to the items that are relevant. These ratings range from "pleased" to "troubled very much" to describe each particular experience. Thus the test subject is able to describe his current range of experiences and his recent reactions to these experiences without being trapped into continuing to respond to some previously true test item as currently characteristic of him merely because of an arbitrary tense of some verb. The range of content among the items is wide but some subjects may be forced to deny a number of items if they have been confined in a hospital, prison, or some other special environment during the preceding month. The authors indicate that nine or more items must be admitted and rated to provide a valid basis for screening, but nearly a fourth of one hospitalized group of 87 patients and over 10 per cent of an industrial employee sample failed to meet this minimum completion standard. If these trends are typical, this could be a serious source of invalidity in practical application.

Two additional checks are provided for guardedness in test response: first, the number of items rated "not affected" (earning a scale value of 2) in intensity; second, the total number of answers given to the 30 buffer items scattered throughout the booklet. No data are provided on how well these measures rule out undesirable test response sets in screening or diagnosis.

Three different scoring systems are employed: frequency of item endorsements, intensity of item ratings of endorsed items, and deviations from typical patterns of item intensity judgments for the various content areas. These scoring steps are not handled by separate scoring stencils (as in the SVIB) but the authors attempt to provide all of these data reduction procedures on a single score sheet. The result is utterly chaotic, making it next to impossible to get a record free of clerical errors and computational blunders. Since the manual does not provide the interpreter with any basis for drawing inferences from these various scores once they have been derived, the scoring procedure is a masterful study in frustration. One would certainly be tempted to send the protocol to the author before scoring rather than after.

Reliability data on this test form are not available. The stability of one score from the original test (intensity score) over a day's time for 86 neurotic patients is reported as .84 prior to treatment. No information is provided to judge the effect of removal of 90 items upon even this score. No validation data are provided for the separate component scales or even on how they were derived. In the manual, validation but not cross validation data are given for screening hospitalized and nonhospitalized male adults. Eleven "Emotional Disturbance Indicators" are reported. For the groups on which the indices were established, the best separation occurs using intensity response patterns as Emotional Disturbance Indicators. The criterion of presence of one or more such indicators identified 77.3 per cent of 66 hospitalized cases as unhealthy and falsely called 22.4 per cent of 107 industrial workers emotionally disturbed. Even without the inevitable shrinkage were these separations to be applied to a sample of 1,000 adults with, at the outside, about 200 of them having some emotional illness, the results would not be very favorable. Using the criterion of presence of one or more Emotional Disturbance Indicators based on intensity responses, the *Emo Questionnaire* would screen out as disturbed 155 of the 200 sick ones (missing 45); of the 800 normals, 179 would be called sick. So, more of the cases labeled "sick" would be normal than sick (179:155).

On the available evidence, this instrument, with its current scoring format, cannot be recommended for the uses proposed. As a screening device it is lengthy to administer, laborious to score, and too sensitive to defensiveness and false positive errors. As an individual diagnostic device it carries the same burdens of scoring problems but these are magnified at least threefold and, in addition, it is devoid of all evidence of validity and all interpretive material for diagnostic use. In its present format, it is hard to see how the *Emo Questionnaire* could be utilized even for research purposes.

[91]

***The Empathy Test.** Ages 13 and over; 1947–61; Forms A ('47), B Revised ('61, c1951), C ('54, adaptation of Form A for Canadian use), (1 page); manual ('55, 4 pages); $3 per 50 tests; $1 per specimen set (must be purchased to obtain manual); cash orders postpaid; (10–15) minutes; Willard A. Kerr and Boris J. Speroff; Psychometric Affiliates. *

REFERENCES

1–20. See 5:50.
21. WOLFSON, BEATRICE NATALIE. *A Study of Personality Variables, as Measured by Certain Instruments, That May Differentiate School Guidance Counselors From Classroom Teachers.* Doctor's thesis, University of Connecticut (Storrs, Conn.), 1958. (*DA* 19:2816)
22. GLENNON, J. R.; ALBRIGHT, LEWIS E.; AND SMITH, WALLACE J. "Normative Data Information Exchange, Nos. 12-1, 12-2." *Personnel Psychol* 12:143–4 sp '59. *
23. RICH, JOSEPH MCELROY. *Individual Empathy in Relation to Certain Aspects of Group Functioning.* Doctor's thesis, Temple University (Philadelphia, Pa.), 1959. (*DA* 20:742)
24. GIBLETTE, JOHN FRANKLIN. *Differences Among Above Average, Average, and Below Average Secondary School Counselors.* Doctor's thesis, University of Pennsylvania (Philadelphia, Pa.), 1960. (*DA* 21:812)
25. STRUNK, ORLO, JR., AND REED, KENNETH E. "The Learning of Empathy: A Pilot Study." *J Pastoral Care* 14:44–8 sp '60. *
26. SMITH, WILLIAM REED. "Empathy and Writing Ability." *Percept & Motor Skills* 13:315–8 D '61. *
27. DIGHTMAN, CAMERON R., AND FAHRION, STEVEN L. "An Experimental Approach to the Study of Empathy." *Proc Mont Acad Sci* 21:124–31 '62. * (*PA* 37:3144)
28. PATTERSON, C. H. "A Note on the Construct Validity of the Concept of Empathy." *Personnel & Guid J* 40:803–6 My '62. * (*PA* 37:3448)
29. PATTERSON, C. H. "Test Characteristics of Rehabilitation Counselor Trainees." *J Rehabil* 28:15–6 S–O '62. * (*PA* 37:6953)

WALLACE B. HALL, *Assistant Research Psychologist, Institute of Personality Assessment and Research, University of California, Berkeley, California.*

Each form of this test contains three sections: (*a*) a list of 14 common types of music to be ranked in order of popularity; (*b*) 15 names of magazines to be ranked according to paid circulation; and (*c*) 10 common annoying experiences to be ranked from most to least annoying. One total score is obtained, the sum of the differences in ranks assigned by the subject from those in the normative group used in making up the scoring key.

There is generally some disagreement on just what defines empathy. The test measures, according to the manual, "the subject's ability to 'anticipate' certain typical reactions of defined normative persons." English and English[1] define empathy as an "apprehension of the state of mind of another person without feeling (as in sympathy) what the other feels," and the "attitude in empathy is one of acceptance and understanding, of an implicit 'I see how you feel.'" In this test, the defined normative groups which the examinee is asked to "place yourself in the position of" range from "non-office factory workers of the United States" to "persons over age 40"; in the case of the magazine circulation section the implication is that he must isolate subscribers as a group from the entire American population. Such an extension would seem rather distant from the usual person-to-person interaction which is of presumed interest in this test.

Although Form A was copyrighted in 1947, the key indicates that a substitution was made in part 2 for one of the magazines which has ceased publication. Form B was revised in 1961, the revision consisting of the substitution of four magazine names from the 1957 list. No references since 1954 are cited, and more recent and critical studies such as that of Patterson (*28*) are ignored. The printing of the test, manual, and scoring key is carelessly done, and errors in the copy are uncor-

1 ENGLISH, HORACE B., AND ENGLISH, AVA CHAMPNEY. *A Comprehensive Dictionary of Psychological and Psychoanalytical Terms.* New York: Longmans, Green & Co., 1958. Pp. xiv, 594. *

rected or poorly made, so that the entire work presents a rather unprofessional appearance.

The normative data for music preferences were obtained "in a national survey program." The 1962 scoring key shows no change in ranking of preferences from the earlier 1954 scoring key. Normative data for the annoying experiences "are the extensive findings of Hulsey Cason." These findings are neither described nor their source indicated. Some checking of the current appropriateness of all norms would seem to be in order, particularly in the domain of musical taste.

In view of these negative features and the implication that the test is more a measure of general information and prediction of opinions than of interpersonal empathy, there appears little to recommend this test for the purposes stated by its authors.

For a review by Robert L. Thorndike, see 5:50.

[92]

★**[Environment Indexes.]** Grades 9–13, 13–16, adults, employees; 1957–63; environmental press (see 180 for a related test of personal needs covering the same areas); 41 scores for each index: 30 press scores (abasement-assurance, achievement, adaptability-defensiveness, affiliation-rejection, aggression-blame avoidance, change-sameness, conjunctivity-disjunctivity, counteraction-inferiority avoidance, deference-restiveness, dominance-tolerance, ego achievement, emotionality-placidity, energy-passivity, exhibitionism-inferiority avoidance, fantasied achievement, harm avoidance-risk taking, humanities and social science, impulsiveness-deliberation, narcissism, nurturance-rejection, objectivity-projectivity, order-disorder, play-work, practicalness-impracticalness, reflectiveness, science, sensuality-puritanism, sexuality-prudishness, supplication-autonomy, understanding) and 11 factor scores based on combinations of the press scores (aspiration level, intellectual climate, student dignity, academic climate, academic achievement, self-expression, group life, academic organization, social form, play-work, vocational climate); NCS; 4 levels; combined scoring and college norms manual ('63, 30 pages plus sample copies of each of these indexes and the *Stern Activities Index*) for *b* below and the *Stern Activities Index;* no data on reliability and validity; no norms for *a* or *c-d;* separate answer sheets must be used; 25¢ per test; $3.25 per 50 NCS answer sheets; $6 per set of hand scoring stencils (machine scoring by the distributor only); $3.50 per scoring and norms manual; postpaid; scoring and profiling fees: 75¢ to 95¢ per answer sheet, depending on quantity; (20–90) minutes; distributed by National Computer Systems. *

a) HIGH SCHOOL CHARACTERISTICS INDEX. Grades 9–13; 1960; experimental form; no norms; Form 960 ('60, 7 pages); George G. Stern.

b) COLLEGE CHARACTERISTICS INDEX. Grades 13–16; 1957–63; Form 1158 ('58, 7 pages); press score profile ('63, 1 page); factor score profile ('63, 1 page); George G. Stern and C. Robert Pace.

c) EVENING COLLEGE CHARACTERISTICS INDEX. Adults; 1961; experimental form; no norms; Form 161 ('61, 7 pages); George G. Stern, Clifford L. Winters, Jr., N. Sidney Archer, and Donald L. Meyer.

d) ORGANIZATIONAL CLIMATE INDEX. Employees; 1958–63; experimental forms; no norms; Form 1163 ('63, c1958–63, 7 pages); George G. Stern and Carl R. Steinhoff.

REFERENCES

1. PACE, C. ROBERT, AND STERN, GEORGE G. "An Approach to the Measurement of Psychological Characteristics of College Environments." *J Ed Psychol* 49:269–77 O '58. * (*PA* 36:2KA69P)

2. MCFEE, ANNE. *The Relation of Selected Factors to Students' Perception of a College Environment.* Master's thesis, Syracuse University (Syracuse, N.Y.), 1959.

3. THISTLETHWAITE, DONALD L. "College Press and Student Achievement." *J Ed Psychol* 50:183–91 O '59. * (*PA* 35:3964)

4. PACE, C. ROBERT. "Five College Environments." *Col Board R* 41:24–8 sp '60. * (*PA* 35:7056)

5. STERN, GEORGE G. "Congruence and Dissonance in the Ecology of College Students." *Student Med* 8:304–39 Ap '60. *

6. STERN, GEORGE G. "Student Values and Their Relationship to the College Environment," pp. 67–104. In *Research on College Students: Institute Lectures Considering Recent Research on College Student's Motivation, Values and Attitudes, and Campus Cultures.* Edited by Hall T. Sprague. Boulder, Colo.: Western Interstate Commission for Higher Education, 1960. Pp. iv, 188. *

7. HUTCHINS, EDWIN B. "The 1960 Medical School Graduate: His Perception of His Faculty, Peers, and Environment." *J Med Ed* 36:322–9 Ap '61. *

8. MCFEE, ANNE. "The Relation of Students' Needs to Their Perceptions of a College Environment." *J Ed Psychol* 52:25–9 F '61. * (*PA* 36:2KD25M)

9. PACE, WALTER THOMAS. *Profiles of Personal Needs and College Press of Negro Teacher Trainees.* Doctor's thesis, Wayne State University (Detroit, Mich.), 1961. (*DA* 22:3748)

10. STERN, GEORGE G. "Recent Research on Institutional Climates: 1, Continuity and Contrast in the Transition From High School to College," pp. 33–58. In *Orientation to College Learning—A Reappraisal: Report of a Conference on Introduction of Entering Students to the Intellectual Life of the College.* Edited by Nicholas C. Brown. Washington, D.C.: American Council on Education, 1961. Pp. xi, 143. *

11. BEST, SHEILA ANNE. *The Relationship Between the College Characteristics Index and Other Measures of the College Environment.* Master's thesis, Syracuse University (Syracuse, N.Y.), 1962.

12. PACE, C. ROBERT. "Implications of Differences in Campus Atmosphere for Evaluation and Planning of College Programs," pp. 43–61. (*PA* 37:5613) In *Personality Factors on the College Campus: Review of a Symposium.* Edited by Robert L. Sutherland, Wayne H. Holtzman, Earl A. Koile, and Bert Kruger Smith. Austin, Tex.: Hogg Foundation for Mental Health, 1962. Pp. xii, 242. * (*PA* 37:5621)

13. SAGEN, HARRY BRADLEY. *The Relationship of Certain Personality and Environmental Variables to the Satisfaction With Present Position of Faculty in Selected Liberal Arts Colleges.* Doctor's thesis, University of Minnesota (Minneapolis, Minn.), 1962. (*DA* 23:3241)

14. STERN, GEORGE G. Chap. 3, "The Measurement of Psychological Characteristics of Students and Learning Environments," pp. 27–68. In *Measurement in Personality and Cognition.* Edited by Samuel Messick and John Ross. New York: John Wiley & Sons, Inc., 1962. Pp. xi, 334. * (*PA* 38:2638)

15. STERN, GEORGE G. Chap. 21, "Environments for Learning," pp. 690–730. In *The American College: A Psychological and Social Interpretation of the Higher Learning.* Edited by Nevitt Sanford. New York: John Wiley & Sons, Inc., 1962. Pp. xvi, 1084. * (*PA* 36:5KA84S)

16. NUNNALLY, JUM C.; THISTLETHWAITE, DONALD L.; AND WOLFE, SHARON. "Factored Scales for Measuring Characteristics of College Environments." *Ed & Psychol Meas* 23:239–48 su '63. * (*PA* 38:1370)

17. RAAB, WILLIAM EDWIN. *Congruence and Dissonance Between Need and Press in Determining Satisfaction or Dissatisfaction in the University Environment.* Doctor's research study No. 1, Colorado State University (Fort Collins, Colo.), 1963. (*DA* 24:1923)

18. STERN, GEORGE G. "Characteristics of the Intellectual Climate in College Environments." *Harvard Ed R* 33:5–41 w '63. *

19. THISTLETHWAITE, DONALD L. Chap. 21, "The College Environment as a Determinant of Research Potentiality," pp. 265–77. In *Scientific Creativity: Its Recognition and Development.* Edited by Calvin W. Taylor and Frank Barron. New York: John Wiley & Sons, Inc., 1963. Pp. xxiv, 419. * (*PA* 38:2689)

[93]

★**Eysenck Personality Inventory.** High school and college and adults; 1963; revision of *Maudsley Personality Inventory;* 3 scores: extraversion, neuroticism, lie; Forms A, B (2 pages); preliminary manual (16 pages); no data on reliability of the lie scale; British norms only; no norms for the lie scale; $3 per 25 tests; $1.50 per set of scoring stencils; 50¢ per manual; $1.75 per specimen set; postage extra; [15-20] minutes; H. J. Eysenck and Sybil B. G. Eysenck; Educational and Industrial Testing Service. (British edition: University of London Press Ltd.) *

REFERENCES

1. EYSENCK, SYBIL B. G., AND EYSENCK, HANS J. "An Experimental Investigation of 'Desirability' Response Set in a Personality Questionnaire." *Life Sci* 5:343-55 My '63. * (*PA* 38:2712)

JAMES C. LINGOES, *Associate Professor of Psychology, The University of Michigan, Ann Arbor, Michigan.*

The *Eysenck Personality Inventory* (EPI), like the *Maudsley Personality Inventory* (MPI), is an instrument intended to measure the two most important sources of personality questionnaire variance found by Eysenck in a large number of factor analytic studies, i.e., extraversion-introversion (E) and neuroticism-stability (N). Although the EPI and MPI are differently named, they are the same tests in respect to principal authorship, theoretical motivation, traits measured, and methodological derivation. Indeed some items in the two tests are but rewordings of each other, e.g., "Do other people regard you as a lively individual?" (item 44, MPI); "Do other people think of you as being very lively?" (item 27, Form A, EPI); and, "Are you rather lively?" (item 17, Form B, EPI).

Despite the above similarities, nowhere is it stated in the EPI manual that the EPI is a *revision* of the MPI. Nevertheless, the authors explicitly invoke the similarity in respect to content and the high, but regrettably omitted, correlations between the EPI and MPI to buttress their claims for the theoretical and experimental validity of the newer test. In addition, the authors put forth the EPI manual as a preliminary supplement to the MPI manual, further confirming the relatedness of these two tests. Without belaboring the point much more, it is unfortunate, for whatever reasons, that this particular aspect of the status of the EPI was left unclear.

It is this reviewer's opinion that the EPI is in fact a revision of the MPI and has a number of advantages over the latter, the most important of which are: (*a*) the presence of two parallel forms, thus permitting retesting for experimental purposes or increasing the reliability of the instrument; (*b*) the addition in each form of nine different items adapted from the Lie scale of the MMPI to tap one kind of test taking attitude, i.e., to put oneself in a socially favorable light; and (*c*) a better selection of items to minimize the correlation between the two measures, E and N (although further replication with larger and more diverse samples of psychotics than the reported one of size 90 will be needed to substantiate this particular improvement). For non-psychotic samples orthogonality seems adequate.

In regard to the inclusion of a Lie scale (L), although this is a commendable addition in principle, it is strongly suspected that such a scale will prove neither more nor less effective in this test than it has been in the MMPI, the clinical consensus being that the more sophisticated and intelligent examinee can easily avoid this obvious form of deception and that the L scale is probably more useful as a personality measure than a validity scale. One might have hoped for a better set of items or an improved psychometric approach to this important problem with our present knowledge of test taking attitudes. Having adopted the Lie scale, however, the authors could have at least provided norms for L and indicated the equivalent forms reliability coefficient, as well as the correlations between L and E and N for both forms.

Although many of the criticisms leveled against the MPI apply equally to the EPI—e.g., the lack of interpretative richness in a two-dimensional approach to personality for clinical purposes—an additional point can be made about the two forms of the EPI relative to the MPI in the form of the following argument.

If the EPI and MPI, in respect to both E and N, correlate as high or higher than both forms within the EPI, then to that extent the MPI can be considered yet another form of the EPI. If one or both forms of the EPI correlate significantly higher with the MPI than is indicated by the equivalent forms coefficient of around .75 for E and .86 for N of the EPI, then if there are to be only two forms, the MPI should be one of them. On the other hand, if the MPI correlates much less with either form than the forms do with one another, then it is difficult to see how anyone could entertain the hypothesis, especially in reference to E, that univocal scales for these two important dimensions have been constructed. Furthermore, the authors' appeal to the large amount of experimental findings based upon the MPI could not suffice to carry or support EPI validity.

Until the relationships between the MPI and the EPI have been clarified or EPI's superiority has been established, administration of both tests is recommended, or, if only one is practicable, the MPI is to be preferred, since more is known about it. If the EPI is used, however, it will be necessary to establish norms other than the British norms provided in the manual.

[94]

★FIRO-B: [Fundamental Interpersonal Relations Orientation—Behavior]. High school and adults; 1957–61; 6 scores: expressed inclusion, wanted inclusion, expressed control, wanted control, expressed affection, wanted affection; 1 form ('57, 2 pages); no specific manual (technical data are presented in Chapter 4 of *2* below); hectographed norms ['61, 1 page]; no high school norms; 8¢ per test; $1 per scoring template; $6.50 per text ('58, 275 pages, published by Holt, Rinehart & Winston, Inc.); postage extra; (8–15) minutes; William C. Schutz; the Author. *

REFERENCES

1. BENNIS, WARREN; BURKE, RICHARD; CUTTER, HENRY; HARRINGTON, HERBERT; AND HOFFMAN, JOYCE. "A Note on Some Problems of Measurement and Prediction in a Training Group." *Group Psychother* 10:328–41 D '57. * (*PA* 33:5971)

2. SCHUTZ, WILLIAM C. *FIRO: A Three-Dimensional Theory of Interpersonal Behavior.* New York: Holt, Rinehart & Winston, Inc., 1958. Pp. xiii, 267. * (*PA* 33:2479)

3. GROSS, RICHARD LOUIE. *Therapy Group Composition: Personal-Interpersonal Variable.* Doctor's thesis, University of Utah (Salt Lake City, Utah), 1959. (*DA* 20:3377)

4. SCHUTZ, WILLIAM C., AND GROSS, EUGENE F. "The FIRO Theory of Interpersonal Behavior: Empirical Tests and Applications to Business Administration," pp. 161–72. In *Contributions to Scientific Research in Management.* The Proceedings of the Scientific Program Following the Dedication of the Western Data Processing Center, Graduate School of Business Administration, January 29–30, 1959. [Los Angeles, Calif.: the Center, 1959.] Pp. xi, 172. *

5. BORG, WALTER R. "Prediction of Small Group Role Behavior From Personality Variables." *J Abn & Social Psychol* 60:112–6 Ja '60. * (*PA* 34:7528)

6. FISKE, DONALD W. "Variability Among Peer Ratings in Different Situations." *Ed & Psychol Meas* 20:283–92 su '60. * (*PA* 35:6337)

7. HAINES, LEWIS EDGAR. *An Evaluation of the FIRO-B and the EPPS for Predicting College Roommate Compatibility.* Doctor's thesis, Washington State University (Pullman, Wash.), 1960. (*DA* 21:2173)

8. GARD, JOHN GRIFFIN. *Fundamental Interpersonal Relations Orientations in Clinical Groups.* Doctor's thesis, University of Pittsburgh (Pittsburgh, Pa.), 1961. (*DA* 22:4080)

9. SCHUTZ, WILLIAM C. Chap. 4, "The Ego, FIRO Theory and the Leader as Completer," pp. 48–65. In *Leadership and Interpersonal Behavior.* Edited by Luigi Petrullo and Bernard M. Bass. New York: Holt, Rinehart & Winston, Inc., 1961. Pp. xxxiv, 382. * (*PA* 36:1GF82P)

10. SCHUTZ, WILLIAM C. "On Group Composition." *J Abn & Social Psychol* 62:275–81 Mr '61. * (*PA* 36:4GE75S)

11. VODACEK, JOHN, JR. *A Study of the Relationship of FIRO-B Measures of Compatibility to Teacher Satisfaction and Congruence of Role Expectations for the Principal.* Doctor's thesis, University of Wisconsin (Madison, Wis.), 1961. (*DA* 22:1895)

12. CONNERS, C. KEITH. "Birth Order and Needs for Affiliation." *J Personality* 31:408–16 S '63. *

13. LORR, MAURICE, AND MCNAIR, DOUGLAS M. "An Interpersonal Behavior Circle." *J Abn & Social Psychol* 67:68–75 Jl '63. * (*PA* 38:765)

14. SCHUTZ, WILLIAM C. Chap. 10, "The FIRO Theory of Interpersonal Behavior," pp. 141–63. In *Educational Research: New Perspectives.* Edited by Jack A. Culbertson and Stephen P. Hensley. Danville, Ill.: Interstate Printers & Publishers, Inc., 1963. Pp. ix, 374. *

15. SMITH, PETER B. "Differentiation Between Sociometric Rankings: A Test of Four Theories." *Human Relations* 16:335–50 N '63. * (*PA* 38:5901)

For excerpts from related reviews, see B432.

[95]

Family Adjustment Test. Ages 12 and over; 1952–54; title on test is *Elias Family Opinion Survey;* 11 scores: attitudes toward mother, attitudes toward father, father-mother attitude quotient, oedipal, struggle for independence, parent-child friction-harmony, interparental friction-harmony, family inferiority-superiority, rejection of child, parental qualities, total; 1 form ('52, 6 pages); manual ('54, 4 pages); $4 per 25 tests; $1 per specimen set (must be purchased to obtain manual and key); cash orders postpaid; (35–45) minutes; Gabriel Elias; Psychometric Affiliates. *

REFERENCES

1–6. See 5:53.

JOHN ELDERKIN BELL, *Program Director, National Institute of Mental Health, United States Public Health Service, San Francisco, California.*

The critical issue with this well developed test is to identify precisely what it measures. The instructions ask the subject to respond to 114 statements through giving "opinions only about the general family life that existed in your neighborhood when you were a child." It is assumed that this leads to an expression of feelings directly related to the current adjustment of the subject and his family. More particularly, the test is "designed to measure feelings of intrafamily homeyness—homelessness."

Efforts to determine validity have shown the test to differentiate sharply (almost no overlap) between institutionalized juvenile delinquents and matched youths identified by club leaders as from families "as homey as the most homey quarter of New York State families." The homelessness scores are related to age, increasing from ages 10 to 19, then tapering off to a constant level; to sex, male scores being higher than female at all ages; and to extreme poverty as found in city slum or rural shanty economic levels. In contrast, when age, sex, and extreme poverty were held constant, no significant differences were found among racial groups (white, colored, Indian, and yellow); religious groups (Catholic, Hebrew, Mohammedan, and Protestant, as well as among various Protestant subgroups); residents of New York City and towns, cities, and farms of Arkansas. Nor were homelessness scores found to be related to size of family, birth order, mother's occupation, regularity of testee's church attendance, his birthplace or that of his parents, and his nationality descent. Thus, the author claims that the test "appears to be largely culture-free; and differences in race, religion, residence, nationality, and intelligence can be disregarded in its interpretation."

But can they be? Are these factors operative but masked because of the test items and instructions? The family is an open system very much influenced by the community and culture of which it is a part. Family solidarity is only one of the characteristics of the family responsive to these broad influences. A test of "homeyness" that does not reflect cultural variation may not be a test of this variable at all, but of some other which would be worth measuring only if we knew what it is that we are measuring.

Does the test measure feelings of family solidarity? How are we to know? And, if so, are we measuring a generalization based on years of family living or feelings associated with a single or relatively few concrete instances remembered from the distant past or the present moment?

Do we perhaps measure a different approach to the test as we give it to children of varying ages, and thus gain information less about feelings towards the family than about age-level responses to test instructions?

Or does the test measure a prevailing mood, called into expression by the emotionally toned words and phrases of the test items? Are we collecting data on a general positive or negative orientation to the immediate life circumstances in which the subject's mood is being engendered, rather than to his family?

Or does his test performance represent a sincere aim to subsume the community experiences at a historical period when he was a child? Obviously, history is modified by the personal characteristics of the historian, and by his own family experiences, but it may have more rather than less relationship to community data than to his own family.

These are only a few possible hypotheses about what the test measures; until such suggestions and others that might be even more pertinent are tested out, we shall need extreme caution in attributing the results to "homeyness."

For a review by Albert Ellis, see 5:53.

[96]

★Famous Sayings. Grades 9–16 and business and industry; 1958, c1957–58; 4 scores: conventional mores, hostility, fear of failure, social acquiescence; Form 1 ('58, c1957–58, 4 pages); manual ('58, 19 pages, reprint of *6* below); $4.50 per set of test materials; $4 per 50 tests; $1.50 per manual; cash orders postpaid; specimen set not available; (15–30) minutes; Bernard M. Bass; Psychological Test Specialists. *

REFERENCES

1. Bass, Bernard M. "Development and Evaluation of a Scale for Measuring Social Acquiescence." *J Abn & Social Psychol* 53:296–9 N '56. * (*PA* 32:4058)
2. Bass, Bernard M. "Development of a Structured Disguised Personality Test." *J Appl Psychol* 40:393–7 D '56. * (*PA* 32:1350)
3. Kim, K. S. *The Use of the ACE and the Revised Famous Sayings Test in the Prediction of Academic Achievement.* Master's thesis, Louisiana State University (Baton Rouge, La.), 1956.
4. Palmer, George J., Jr. *Discrimination of Psychopaths, Normal Prisoners and Non-Prisoners With a Disguised Structured Technique.* Master's thesis, Louisiana State University (Baton Rouge, La.), 1956.
5. Bass, Bernard. "Validity Studies of a Proverbs Personality Test." *J Appl Psychol* 41:158–60 Je '57. * (*PA* 33:2352)
6. Bass, Bernard M. "Famous Sayings Test: General Manual." *Psychol Rep* 4:479–97 S '58. * (*PA* 33:5073)
7. Gaier, Eugene L., and Bass, Bernard M. "Regional Differences in Interrelations Among Authoritarianism, Acquiescence, and Ethnocentrism." *J Social Psychol* 49:47–51 F '59. * (*PA* 35:4782)
8. Couch, Arthur, and Keniston, Kenneth. "Yeasayers and Naysayers: Agreeing Response Set as a Personality Variable." *J Abn & Social Psychol* 60:151–74 Mr '60. * (*PA* 34:7376)
9. Vidulich, Robert N., and Bass, Bernard M. "Relation of Selected Personality and Attitude Scales to the Famous Sayings Test." *Psychol Rep* 7:259–60 O '60. * (*PA* 35:2215)
10. Husek, T. R. "Acquiescence as a Response Set and as a Personality Characteristic." *Ed & Psychol Meas* 21:295–307 su '61. * (*PA* 36:2HE95H)
11. Murstein, Bernard I. "The Relation of the Famous Sayings Test to Self- and Ideal-Self-Adjustment." Abstract. *J Consult Psychol* 25:368 Ag '61. * (*PA* 37:1312)
12. Shaw, Marvin E. "Some Correlates of Social Acquiescence." *J Social Psychol* 55:133–41 O '61. * (*PA* 36:4HE33S)
13. Shumsky, Walter; Konick, Andrew; and Ward, George, II. "A Note Concerning Extreme Position Response Sets and the California F Scale." *Proc W Va Acad Sci* 34:194–5 N '62. *
14. *Normative Information: Manager and Executive Testing.* New York: Richardson, Bellows, Henry & Co., Inc., May 1963. Pp. 45. *
15. Braun, John R., and Dube, C. S., II. "Note on a Faking Study With the Famous Sayings Test." *Psychol Rep* 13:878 D '63. * (*PA* 38:8403)
16. Coppinger, Neil W.; Bortner, Rayman W.; and Saucer, Rayford T. "A Factor Analysis of Psychological Deficit." *J Genetic Psychol* 103:23–43 S '63. * (*PA* 39:174)
17. Frye, Roland L., and Bass, Bernard M. "Behavior in a Group Related to Tested Social Acquiescence." *J Social Psychol* 61:263–6 D '63. *

Wesley C. Becker, *Professor of Psychology, University of Illinois, Urbana, Illinois.*

Famous Sayings is a relatively new personality test devised with the hope of providing measures which are less transparent to the test taker than those found in the typical personality inventory. The test consists of 130 sayings or proverbs with which the testee is to indicate his agreement or disagreement. The initial item pool for the test was formed by selecting, *a priori,* 20 sayings which might be relevant to each of 13 needs from Murray's system of classification. Factor analysis of the 13 preliminary scales revealed 3 content factors which were labeled Conventional Mores (CM),

Hostility (HO), and Fear of Failure (FF). An item analysis on a new sample was carried out to determine the scoring system. After examining reliabilities, 10 new items were written for the FF scale. For college sophomores, the corrected split-half reliabilities for the 30-item scales are: CM, .73; HO, .69; and FF, .75. These reliabilities are too low to consider using the test for making decisions in individual cases. Intercorrelations among the scales approach an average of .50 for a heterogeneous sample. Homogeneous samples (prisoners and college students) yield lower and conflicting intercorrelations.

A fourth scale, Social Acquiescence (SA), was developed to measure the tendency to accept "a wide variety of generalizations concerning how persons behave or should behave." SA was assumed to be the factor which accounted for the moderate correlations among the first three scales when a heterogeneous population was used. The SA scale consists of 56 items which differentiated persons who agreed with many proverbs from those who agreed with few. Fifteen items in the SA scale overlap with CM, HO, or FF. The author correctly suggests that it may be desirable to remove the overlap for some research purposes. With a sample of West Coast residents and southern college students the corrected split-half reliability of the full SA scale (including the overlapping items) was .92. For 1,491 Louisiana college freshmen the reliability was .81 (KR 21).

Bass has undertaken a number of validity studies and is to be commended for presenting the findings in a straightforward manner. CM, HO, and FF differentiate salesmen from non-salesmen, prison inmates from non-inmates, college students from high school students, and Southerners from non-Southerners in ways consistent with the construct implications of the scales. The magnitude of the differences for salesmen is not sufficient to warrant the test's use as a sole selection device in personnel work, but it might contribute some additional variance as part of a selection battery. The scales have not been found useful in predicting scholastic success, the success of factory supervisors, or the success of grocery products salesmen or sales supervisors. Two studies have related scores from *Famous Sayings* to other self-report measures using college samples (*5, 9*). A number of correlations, usually on the order of .25 to .30, were found with CM and HO. Conventional Mores shows positive correlations with self-report measures of traits labeled sociability, cooperativeness, conservatism, nurturance, affiliation, and conscientiousness, and negative correlations with ethnocentrism and autonomy. Hostility correlates positively with other measures labeled aggression and suspicious-jealous, and negatively with emotional stability, responsibility, and maturity. Fear of Failure to date has failed to relate to other questionnaire trait measures. Social Acquiescence correlates in the .40's with peer nominations of "likes to help" and "thinks well of most," and in the high .20's and low .30's with questionnaire measures of sociability.

The author suggests that the test might best be used as an "industrial and professional screening and classification technique." While the author clearly indicates the test's shortcomings and advises the industrial user to develop his own validity data, the indications from presently available reliability and validity evidence are that *Famous Sayings* is not likely to contribute much to decision making in industry. The Social Acquiescence scale may turn out to have some value in prediction situations, but the reviewer believes it is the responsibility of the test developer to demonstrate this before recommending usage in applied settings. One critical point in judging the potential value of the test over other self-report devices has not yet been examined, namely, the degree to which the test can be faked to make a good impression. The reviewer is not convinced that the test is as unstructured for the subject as the author assumes. Empirical examination of this question is needed.

For the most part, the reviewer's critical reservations about the usefulness of this test reflect the excellent job its author has done in exploring and reporting on the limitations of its construct, concurrent, and predictive validity.

ROBERT L. THORNDIKE, *Professor of Education, and Head, Department of Psychological Foundations, Teachers College, Columbia University, New York, New York.*

In this instrument the author has attempted to devise a structured and objectively scorable, but indirect, measure of three dimensions of personality content which he designates Conventional Mores, Hostility, and Fear of Failure, and one dimension of response style, Social Acquiescence. Unfortunately, though in his discussion the author recognizes the significance of acquiescence as a response set influencing inventory responses, in his instrument he makes no provision for controlling it. In all instances, scoring is based on the "Yes" and "?" responses. Thus, his first three scores are contaminated to an unknown degree by the stylistic factor that his fourth score undertakes to measure. The potential user is left even more in the dark because the manual does not report any correlations between Social Acquiescence and the other three scores. One would like to know what the reliability of the other dimensions would be if the acquiescence factor were balanced out with items keyed both "Yes" and "No," and what would happen to the scale intercorrelations under these circumstances. The reviewer suspects that Hostility would then show fairly substantial negative correlations with Conventional Mores and Fear of Failure.

At least one of the content scores may be a reflection of another stylistic factor. It may be that rather than "hostility" we should speak of "readiness to endorse negatively toned statements." Maybe this is the essence of hostility. The point, however, is that what produces this reaction may be a relatively superficial response set rather than something deep-seated in the personality dynamics of the individual.

The author also seems to be going rather beyond his data in applying the designation "fear of failure" to a group of items that seem to center around the achievement motif. Possibly this *is* the underlying dynamic, but the author presents little to document this conclusion.

As is common with most personality appraisal devices, the evidence on validity is rather unsatisfying. It consists of an assortment of differences in group means, a few modest correlations with scores or ratings on ability and personality tests, and a group of largely nonsignificant correlations with sales success.

Though the reviewer would be willing to accord *Famous Sayings* the status of an instrument suitable for research and exploratory studies, he questions whether in its present form it would repay time spent upon it.

[97]

Fatigue Scales Kit. Adults; 1944–54; 3 scales; hectographed manual ('54, 4 pages); $5 per set of 25 sets of the 3 scales and manual; $3 per 50 copies of any one scale; cash orders postpaid; specimen set not available; [10] minutes; [Willard A. Kerr]; Psychometric Affiliates. *

a) INDUSTRIAL SUBJECTIVE FATIGUE AND EUPHORIA SCALES. Adults; 1944–54; 2 scores: fatigue, unpleasantness; 1 form ('54, 1 page, identical with scale published in 1944).

b) RETROSPECTIVE WORK CURVE FEELINGS FOR NATIONAL RESEARCH PROGRAM ON EMPLOYEE FEELINGS AT WORK. Adults; 1 form ('54, 1 page).

c) STUDY OF DAY [MOTHER'S DAY FATIGUE SCALE]. Housewives; 1 form ('54, 1 page); no data on validity.

REFERENCES

1. GRIFFITH, JOHN W.; KERR, WILLARD A.; MAYO, THOMAS B., JR.; AND TOPAL, JOHN R. "Changes in Subjective Fatigue and Readiness for Work During the Eight-Hour Shift." *J Appl Psychol* 34:163–6 Je '50. * (*PA* 25:4014)

RICHARD S. BARRETT, *Associate Professor of Management Engineering and Psychology, New York University, New York, New York.*

The three Fatigue Scales are each printed on a single sheet of paper, to be used as a tear ballot, that is, the subject is instructed to "answer each of these questions by *TEARING THE PAPER WITH YOUR FINGERS* at the points where you would check your answers if you were using a pencil." Such a format limits the number of questions which can be asked since the scales must be printed on the edge of the paper. In addition to age and sex, the respondents can report the hours when they are most tired, how tired they are at the moment, what kind of activity they find most tiring, etc.

The manual omits essential information such as the name of the author, the conditions under which normative and other data were collected, and the justification behind statements such as the following, quoted in its entirety, regarding the reliability of one Fatigue Scale: "Various sub-samples yield similar subjective fatigue curves. This implies a substantial level of reliability."

Anyone who wishes to obtain ratings of fatigue can develop as valuable a scale in a few minutes.

[98]

★The Forty-Eight Item Counseling Evaluation Test. Adolescents and adults; 1963; 7 problem area scores: anxiety-tension-stress, compulsive-obsessive-rigid behavior, depressive-defeatist thoughts and feelings, friendship-socialization, religious-philosophical goals, inadequacy feelings and behavior, total; 1 form (4 pages); manual (15 pages plus copy of test); no data on reliability of subscores; $8 per examiner's kit of 25 tests, key, and manual; $6.50 per 25 tests; 50¢

per key; $2 per manual; postpaid; (10–20) minutes; Frank B. McMahon; Western Psychological Services. *

[99]

The Freeman Anxiety Neurosis and Psychosomatic Test. Mental patients; 1952–55; title on test is *The Freeman AN and PS Test;* 9 scores: anxiety neurosis, psychosomatic syndrome, and 7 subscores; 1 form ('52, 10 pages); revised manual ('55, 11 pages); revised profile ('55, 1 page); no norms for subscores; $1.75 per 10 tests; $1.25 per manual; postage extra; specimen set not available; administration time not reported; M. J. Freeman; Grune & Stratton, Inc. *

REFERENCES

1–3. See 5:55.
4. Alpert, Richard, and Haber, Ralph Norman. "Anxiety in Academic Achievement Situations." *J Abn & Social Psychol* 61:207–15 S '60. * (*PA* 35:5357)
5. Meyers, William J., and Hohle, Raymond H. "Questionnaire-Anxiety and Social Conformity." *Psychol Rep* 11:436 O '62. *
6. Acker, Charles W. "Personality Concomitants of Autonomic Balance: 2, Inventory Measures." *J Proj Tech* 27:20–2 Mr '63. *
7. Goldstein, Iris Balshan. "A Comparison Between Taylor's and Freeman's Manifest Anxiety Scales." Abstract. *J Consult Psychol* 27:466 O '63. *

Gerald A. Mendelsohn, *Assistant Professor of Psychology, University of California, Berkeley, California.*

This instrument purports to provide a measure of "the nuclear anxiety structure underlying the symptom complex of anxiety neurosis, psychosomatic involvements and the particular neurosis trends of this emotional disorder." It consists of two major parts, the Anxiety Neurosis (or Manifest Anxiety) Test and the Psychosomatic Syndrome Test. In all, nine variables are mentioned in the manual—six diagnostic categories: anxiety neurosis, psychosomatic syndrome, neurasthenia, psychasthenia, conversion hysteria, and hypochondriasis; and three structural types: overconscientious (perfectionistic), comfort (conflict-avoidance), and composite (bi-polar: overconscientious and comfort). In fact, however, the validity data available for the test are relevant only to the anxiety neurosis and psychosomatic syndrome variables.

The items of the test are of two kinds, judgments about the way people in general behave, e.g., "One who often loses his temper feels sorry afterwards. Yes ( ) No ( )," and a checklist of symptoms of both a physical and psychological nature, such as "Headcolds" and "Frequent discouragement." It is claimed that this format and the instructions for the test disguise its intent and "immeasurably" reduce or eliminate faking. Unfortunately, no data whatever are offered to support these assertions, nor is there any provision for assessing the presence of faking in an individual protocol. Thus, two of the "advancements in personality testing" claimed for this instrument are only assumptions.

Kuder-Richardson reliability coefficients for Anxiety Neurosis and Psychosomatic Syndrome are, respectively, .73 and .81, but they are based only on the responses of normal, non-hospitalized male subjects ($n = 100$). While the coefficients indicate a level of internal consistency adequate by present day standards, there is reason to question their generality. Further, there is no information about the stability of scores, since test-retest data are lacking. A considerable amount of additional work would be necessary to obtain an adequate assessment of the reliability of the test.

The criterion group used in validating the Anxiety Neurosis score consisted of hospitalized patients, not necessarily from neuropsychiatric wards, judged by physicians and psychiatrists to display severe manifest anxiety, i.e., "through the behavior of fear and apprehension to an abnormal degree." Their responses to an initial item pool (whose origin is not indicated) were compared to those of hospitalized and non-hospitalized normals and those items which differentiated significantly were combined to produce a total score which was cross validated on new samples. The criterion group seems to have been reasonably well selected, but since the variable of hospitalization makes some difference, it would have been useful to include an unhospitalized manifest anxiety group in developing the test. The means of the criterion and control groups in the cross validation study are significantly different, but using the cutoff score for a diagnosis of manifest anxiety suggested in the manual produces a false positive rate of 30 per cent and a false negative rate of about 40 per cent, both rather high. No data relating the anxiety measure to other test scores are provided in the manual, but an independent study by Ends and Page (*3*) reports pre- and post-therapy correlations of the Freeman and Taylor Manifest Anxiety scores as .06 and .24 and of the Freeman and Pt scale as .14 and .35. These are disappointingly low.

The criterion group used in the validation of the Psychosomatic Syndrome section consisted of hospitalized patients with illnesses for which no organic basis could be found by an examining physician during a (minimum) 30-day observation period. While the criterion group consists of males and females, only males were used for the normal control group. The test author, in an independent paper (*1*), considers this a limitation of the test, but the manual makes no mention of this, nor of the failure to match the criterion and control groups for age. The differentiation of the groups is better for the Psychosomatic Syndrome than for the Anxiety Neurosis part of the test, false positives constituting 30 per cent and false negatives 20 per cent of the cross validation sample. However, in light of the author's statement in the 1950 paper that the test should be administered only after "a medical examination which discloses no organic basis for the physical complaint," it becomes difficult to perceive the utility of the instrument. If the assessment of a psychosomatic syndrome is to be made only after the same assessment has already been made more directly, what purpose does the test serve?

As noted before, validation data are available only for the two basic scores. Scoring of the other diagnostic categories is based on the symptoms checked, but the rationale or evidence for categorizing items as pertaining to one syndrome as opposed to another is not included. Likewise, the system for determining the structural type is based upon a content system which is not explicitly described. The expected test performance of only the comfort type is discussed in the manual, once again with no supporting data. The utility of these additional scores is thus impossible to assess.

The manual supplied with the test is inadequate from a number of standpoints. There is a minimum of validation data, the limitations of the instrument noted elsewhere by the author are omitted, and there is much jargon and unclear writing. Basically, the manual does not provide the test user with the information necessary to apply the instrument sensibly.

In summary, this reviewer finds little utility for the *Freeman Anxiety Neurosis and Psychosomatic Test.* Given the inadequate quantity and quality of the validation and standardization data, other means of assessing anxiety (e.g., MMPI scales, and medical observation and examination) seem preferable.

ROBERT C. NICHOLS, *Program Director, National Merit Scholarship Corporation, Evanston, Illinois.*

This test, constructed for Freeman's doctoral dissertation at Claremont Graduate School, consists of two major groups of items: 141 "anxiety" items in which the subject gives his opinion about the thoughts, feelings, and behavior of "most people" or the "average person," and 98 "psychosomatic" items in which the subject indicates the physical and emotional symptoms or diseases he suffers frequently or constantly. Fifty-six of the "anxiety" items are scored as an "Anxiety Neurosis" (AN) scale and 78 of the "psychosomatic" items are scored as a "Psychosomatic Syndrome" (PS) scale. The remaining items are not used. Forty-two items of the PS scale are categorized, by an unstated method, into four subscales: Neurasthenia, Psychasthenia, Conversion Hysteria, and Hypochondriasis. On the basis of the relationship of the AN and PS scales the profile is classified as one of three structural types: Overconscientious Type (high AN with high PS), Comfort Type (low AN with high PS), and Composite Type (AN and PS about equal).

The subject marks his responses in the 10-page test booklet, and the test is scored by comparing the responses with a key in the manual. The test could be adapted to an answer sheet, however.

The 11-page manual (the cover is counted as one page) is inadequate and misleading so that it is necessary to refer to the two papers by Freeman (*1, 2*) to discover how the test was constructed. Although the manual implies that the scored items survived several item analyses of samples totaling 310 hospitalized patients and 461 "normals," only one item analysis was used actually to select items. Any item which differentiated 150 hospitalized patients diagnosed as showing manifest anxiety from 116 nonhospitalized students was used regardless of its showing on preliminary item analyses. Only 40 of the AN items significantly differentiated these groups, but since this 40 item scale had a reliability (KR 21) of only .49, 16 nonsignificant items were added, raising the reliability to .73. Seventy-one of the PS items significantly differentiated the groups and this scale had a reliability of .81. The last seven items of the PS scale were not included in the item analysis and are stated by the manual to be of "clinical value" only; yet they are included in the scoring key for the scale. The normative data presented in Table 4, however, seem to be based on the 71 item scale.

The recommended cutting scores in the manual are the intersections of percentage frequency distributions of 30 hospitalized anxiety patients and 100 heterogeneous normals. It should be pointed out, in addition to the obvious instability of cutting scores based on such small *n*'s, that these cutting scores are optimal only in groups with equal numbers in the two categories. Even with this ideal base rate the errors of classification would be high.

The manual is almost completely lacking in statistical information about the scales. No correlations with other variables (not even the correlation between AN and PS) are presented. The only validity data is a table which shows that both AN and PS significantly discriminate cross validation groups of normals and hospitalized anxiety patients. The manual reports the sample size for both normal and hospitalized groups as 100, but elsewhere Freeman (*1*) reports the same comparison for the PS scale with identical means, standard deviations, and *t*-ratio, but with the *n* for the hospitalized group indicated as 30.

Other indications that the manual was hastily or carelessly put together are the reporting of the same normative data for the MA scale in both Tables 2 and 4 with the range given as 20 in the former and 29 in the latter; and in the bibliography there are errors in the titles of both of Freeman's articles and in the page reference of the first.

In view of these deficiencies the test cannot be recommended for use. Even the usual recommendation that more research be done does not seem to be called for in regard to this test. Additional tests which differentiate hospitalized mental patients from non-hospitalized normals are not needed and are essentially useless in practice. For the researcher interested in constructing scales to discriminate other groups, much better item pools are available than that represented by this test.

[100]

★**G. C. Personality Development Record.** High school; 1959; ratings by teachers on 9 traits; adapted from a form used in the schools of Newark, N.J.; 1 form ['59, 1 page]; no manual or other accessories; no data on reliability and validity; no norms; 38¢ per pad of 50 records, postage extra; [5] minutes; Guidance Centre. *

[101]

Goldstein-Scheerer Tests of Abstract and Concrete Thinking. Adults; 1941–51; individual; 1 form; 5 tests; manual ('41, 156 pages, see *9* below); supplementary manual ('47, 4 pages) for *a* and *e*; no data on reliability; no norms; $64 per complete set of test materials; $2.25 per manual; postpaid; [30–60] minutes; Kurt Goldstein, Martin Scheerer, and Louis Rosenberg (*c*, record booklet); Psychological Corporation. *

a) GOLDSTEIN-SCHEERER CUBE TEST. 1941–45; separate record booklets ('45, 6 pages) for designs 1–6, 7–12; $5.75 per set of 2 design booklets and supplementary manual; $4.50 per set of Kohs' blocks; $3.50 per 50 copies of either record booklet.

b) GLEB-GOLDSTEIN COLOR SORTING TEST. 1941–51; record booklet ('51, 4 pages); $14.50 per set of wool skeins; $2.80 per 50 record booklets.

c) GOLDSTEIN-SCHEERER OBJECT SORTING TEST. 1941–51; record booklet ('51, 8 pages); supplementary sheet ('51, 1 page) for experiment 3; $16 per set of objects; $4.20 per 50 record booklets; $1 per 50 supplementary sheets.

d) WEIGL-GOLDSTEIN-SCHEERER COLOR FORM SORTING TEST. 1941–45; record booklet ('45, 4 pages); $7.25 per set of blocks; $2.80 per 50 record booklets.

e) GOLDSTEIN-SCHEERER STICK TEST. 1941–45; record booklet ('45, 4 pages); $4.25 per set of sticks and supplementary manual; $2.80 per 50 record booklets.

REFERENCES

1–28. See 3:41.

29–49. See 5:57.

50. LIDZ, THEODORE; GAY, JAMES R.; AND TIETZE, CHRISTOPHER. "Intelligence in Cerebral Deficit States and Schizophrenia Measured by Kohs Block Test." *Arch Neurol & Psychiatry* 48:568–82 O '42. * (*PA* 17:862)

51. SHAPIRO, M. B. "Experimental Studies of a Perceptual Anomaly: 1, Initial Experiments." *J Mental Sci* 97:90–110 Ja '51. * (*PA* 25:6220)

52. MCFIE, J., AND PIERCY, M. F. "Intellectual Impairment With Localized Cerebral Lesions." *Brain* 75:292–311 S '52. * (*PA* 27:7649)

53. LOVIBOND, S. H. "The Object Sorting Test and Conceptual Thinking in Schizophrenia." *Austral J Psychol* 6:52–70 Je '54. * (*PA* 29:6035)

54. YATES, AUBREY J. "The Validity of Some Psychological Tests of Brain Damage." *Psychol B* 51:359–79 Jl '54. *

55. BROWN, IRWIN. "Abstract and Concrete Behavior of Dysphasic Patients and Normal Subjects." *J Speech & Hearing Disorders* 20:35–42 Mr '55. * (*PA* 30:5083)

56. MCGAUGHRAN, LAURENCE S., AND MORAN, LOUIS J. " 'Conceptual Level' vs. 'Conceptual Area' Analysis of Object-Sorting Behaviour of Schizophrenic and Nonpsychiatric Groups." *J Abn & Social Psychol* 52:43–50 Ja '56. * (*PA* 31:3473)

57. HALPIN, VIRGINIA GOULD. "The Performance of Mentally Retarded Children on the Weigl-Goldstein-Scheerer Color Form Sorting Test." *Am J Mental Def* 62:916–9 Mr '58. * (*PA* 33:6537)

58. PAYNE, R. W.; MATTUSSEK, P.; AND GEORGE, E. I. "An Experimental Study of Schizophrenic Thought Disorder." *J Mental Sci* 105:627–52 Jl '59. * (*PA* 34:6384)

59. SEMEONOFF, BORIS. "An Analysis of the Counsellor Personality." *Rorsch Newsl* 4:13–20 Je '59. *

60. WECKOWICZ, T. E., AND BLEWETT, D. B. "Size Constancy and Abstract Thinking in Schizophrenic Patients." *J Mental Sci* 105:909–34 O '59. * (*PA* 34:6402)

61. PAYNE, R. W., AND HEWLETT, J. H. G. Chap. 1, "Thought Disorder in Psychotic Patients," pp. 3–104. In *Experiments in Personality: Vol. 2, Psychodiagnostics and Psychodynamics.* Edited by H. J. Eysenck. London: Routledge & Kegan Paul Ltd., 1960. Pp. viii, 333. *

62. SILVERSTEIN, A. B. "A Cluster Analysis of Object Sorting Behaviour." *J Consult Psychol* 24:98 F '60. * (*PA* 34:7864)

63. SILVERSTEIN, A. B. "Relations Between Intelligence and Conceptual Levels in Active and Passive Concept Formation." *Psychol Rep* 7:202 O '60. * (*PA* 35:1736)

64. KATES, SOLIS L.; KATES, WILLIAM W.; MICHAEL, JAMES; AND WALSH, TERRENCE M. "Categorization and Related Verbalizations in Deaf and Hearing Adolescents." *J Ed Psychol* 52:188–94 Ag '61. * (*PA* 38:2951)

65. NIELSEN, HELLE H. "Visual-Motor Functioning of Cerebral Palsied and Normal Children." *Nordisk Psykologi* 14(2):41–103 '62. * (*PA* 37:3551)

66. PAYNE, R. W., AND FRIEDLANDER, D. "A Short Battery

of Simple Tests for Measuring Overinclusive Thinking." *J Mental Sci* 108:362–7 My '62. * (*PA* 37:3228)
67. SILVERMAN, LLOYD H., AND SILVERMAN, DORIS K. "Ego Impairment in Schizophrenia as Reflected in the Object Sorting Test." *J Abn & Social Psychol* 64:381–5 My '62. * (*PA* 38:1332)
68. SILVERSTEIN, A. B., AND MOHAN, PHILIP J. "Performance of Mentally Retarded Adults on the Color Form Sorting Test." *Am J Mental Def* 67:458–62 N '62. * (*PA* 37:5419)
69. TUTKO, THOMAS A., AND SECHREST, LEE. "Conceptual Performance and Personality Variables." *J Consult Psychol* 26:481 O '62. * (*PA* 39:1766)
70. GOLDMAN, ALFRED E., AND LEVINE, MURRAY. "A Developmental Study of Object Sorting." *Child Develop* 34:649–66 S '63. * (*PA* 38:7924)
71. PAYNE, R. W.; FRIEDLANDER, D.; LAVERTY, S. G.; AND HADEN, P. "Overinclusive Thought Disorder in Chronic Schizophrenics and Its Response to 'Proketazine.'" *Brit J Psychiatry* 109:523–30 Jl '63. *
72. SILVERSTEIN, A. B., AND MOHAN, PHILIP J. "Conceptual Area Analysis of the Test Performance of Mentally Retarded Adults." *J Abn & Social Psychol* 66:255–60 Mr '63. * (*PA* 37:8165)

R. W. PAYNE, *Associate Professor of Psychology, Queen's University, Kingston, Ontario, Canada.*

The authors developed the five tests of abstract thinking which comprise this battery after having had a great deal of experience with brain damaged patients during and following the first world war. They believe that the main effect of brain damage is "concreteness," an impairment of the "abstract attitude," which they define in terms of the following eight characteristics: (*a*) "To detach our ego from the outerworld or from inner experiences." (*b*) "To assume a mental set." (*c*) "To account for acts to oneself; to verbalize the account." (*d*) "To shift reflectively from one aspect of the situation to another." (*e*) "To hold in mind simultaneously various aspects." (*f*) "To grasp the essential of a given whole; to break up a given whole into parts, to isolate and to synthesize them." (*g*) "To abstract common properties reflectively; to form hierarchic concepts." (*h*) "To plan ahead ideationally; to assume an attitude towards the 'mere possible' and to think or perform symbolically."

It is difficult, after reading this extensive definition, to say precisely how the ability to adopt the abstract attitude differs from general intelligence. If the operational definition in terms of the five Goldstein tests is accepted, the distinction becomes even more difficult, because variations of these five tests have nearly all been used in the past as measures of general intelligence.

At least one study suggests that it may not be possible to distinguish between "g" and abstract ability as defined by Goldstein's tests. Payne and Hewlett (*61*) assembled a large battery of tests thought to measure "psychoticism," general intelligence, psychomotor retardation, overinclusive thinking, and concreteness. These were given to carefully matched groups of 20 normals, 20 neurotics, 20 depressives, and 20 schizophrenics. The tests were intercorrelated for all 80 subjects, and a factor analysis carried out. Two relatively independent factors of thought disorder, "retardation," and "over-inclusive thinking" could be defined according to several criteria. A third independent factor of "general intelligence" was obtained, defined by such standard tests as the *Mill Hill Vocabulary Scale,* the *Nufferno Level Test,* and the *Wechsler-Bellevue Intelligence Scale.* Ratings of concreteness were obtained from the Goldstein-Scheerer color form and object sorting tests, by objectifying and quantifying the main levels of performance set out in some detail in Goldstein and Scheerer's monograph (*9*). The Goldstein-Scheerer test ratings proved to be just as good measures of this intelligence factor as any of the other measures, and, like the other intelligence measures, were unrelated to the two specific factors of thought disorder obtained.

These findings do not, of course, invalidate the proposition that brain damaged subjects tend to do poorly on the Goldstein-Scheerer tests. There is some evidence that tests of general intelligence *can* be used to differentiate between brain damaged subjects and a matched control group (*28*). Intelligence tests seem to differentiate best if they are as little as possible influenced by old learning.[1] Thus, for instance, vocabulary tests differentiate poorly.

Unfortunately, as intelligence tests (or as tests of the abstract attitude) the Goldstein-Scheerer tests have several serious disadvantages. First of all, while a relatively standard method of administration is described in the monograph (and even here, there are serious ambiguities), no standard system of scoring is suggested for any of the tests. The psychologist is left to assess the patient's performance subjectively. For these reasons, Goldstein and Scheerer are unable to give objective standardization data of any sort for their battery, nor are measures of reliability available. Indeed, they seem to make the naive assumption that all normal people will be able to perform all the tests perfectly. In view of the

1 MEYER, V. Chap. 14, "Psychological Effects of Brain Damage," pp. 529–65. In *Handbook of Abnormal Psychology: An Experimental Approach.* Edited by H. J. Eysenck. New York: Basic Books, Inc., 1961. Pp. xvi, 816. * (*PA* 35:6719)

considerable amount of precise verbal explanation expected in some of the tests, this assumption seems to be completely unwarranted. This objection alone would be sufficient for most clinical psychologists to prefer a test battery with a scoring system which has been standardized on the various groups (normals, functionals, and brain damaged) which they are likely to encounter in their practical experience.

The Goldstein-Scheerer tests have been used fairly widely in measuring "concreteness" in both brain damaged and schizophrenic patients. The fact that both groups are thought by some investigators to show this deficit, further emphasizes the need for accurate norms, if the tests are ever to be useful in differential diagnosis.

In addition to the general criteria for various levels of abstract performance on these tests, Goldstein and Scheerer describe in detail a large number of specific anomalies of test performance. There seems to be little doubt that these detailed descriptions are the result of years of careful clinical observation. However, it has never been demonstrated that these anomalies are related in any way, nor that they are all, in fact, associated with concreteness, as the authors assume. Indeed, it has never been demonstrated that the overall ratings of concreteness for each test are significantly correlated.

WEIGL-GOLDSTEIN-SCHEERER COLOR FORM SORTING TEST. This test consists of four small plastic squares, four triangles, and four circles, each reproduced in one of four colors. The subject is asked to sort them into groups (form a concept, e.g., color) and then to resort them in a different way (form a second concept, e.g., form). For those who fail, various relatively standard prompting procedures are adopted.

Bolles and Goldstein (*3*) studying 18 schizophrenic patients, and Hanfmann (*7*) studying a single case, report that schizophrenics are "concrete" on this test. However these studies can be dismissed, as no control group of any sort was tested. Payne, Matussek, and George (*58*) and Payne and Hewlett (*61*), developing their own standard scoring system, failed to find significant differences between schizophrenics, normals, and neurotics on this test.

McFie and Piercy (*52*), merely scoring the test "pass" or "fail," found that a sizeable proportion of brain damaged patients "passed" the test, and Tooth (*29*) found the test able to differentiate significantly between brain damaged and normal cases, but not between brain damaged and neurotic patients. This literature seems to suggest that the range of brain damaged performance is so variable on this simple test that it is probably not useful diagnostically because a substantial proportion of all types of cases can complete the test perfectly.

GOLDSTEIN-SCHEERER OBJECT SORTING TEST. The object sorting test consists of a number of everyday objects which must be sorted into groups according to as many different principles as possible.

Some writers, on the basis of earlier studies (*3, 7, 20*), report schizophrenics to be concrete on this test. However these studies cannot be assessed, as no standard scoring system or control group was used. McGaughran [2] (*47*) and McGaughran and Moran (*56*) have developed a scoring system in which behaviour is assessed along two separate dimensions, "open-closed" (conceptual freedom or concreteness) assessed by the number of objects the concept covers, and an unrelated "public-private" dimension, which is the extent to which the concept is usual, or generally accepted. When scored in this way, there is no evidence,[3] (*27, 53, 58, 61*) that schizophrenic patients are abnormally concrete. However, they do tend to produce significantly more "private" sortings. Payne [4] has suggested that this is the result of overinclusive thinking. Lovibond (*53*), who formulated a similar hypothesis, has developed a standard method of rating overinclusive thinking from this test. Payne and others (*61, 66, 71*) have also suggested that a simple measure of overinclusive thinking can be derived from the "handing over" section of this test, which is merely the average number of objects selected as belonging together (a high score indicates overinclusion). Payne and Hewlett (*61*) and Payne and Friedlander (*66*) have published norms for normals, neurotics, depressives, and schizophrenics (but not brain damaged patients) for this score and have provided evidence, both factorial and in terms of its ability

2 McGaughran, Laurence S. "Predicting Language Behaviour From Object Sorting." *J Abn & Social Psychol* 49: 183–95 Ap '54. *

3 McConaghy, N. "The Use of an Object Sorting Test in Elucidating the Hereditary Factor in Schizophrenia." *J Neurol Neurosurg & Psychiatry* 22:243–6 Ag '59. *

4 Payne, R. W. Chap. 6, "Cognitive Abnormalities," pp. 193–261. In *Handbook of Abnormal Psychology: An Experimental Approach.* Edited by H. J. Eysenck. New York: Basic Books, Inc., 1961. Pp. xvi, 816. * (*PA* 35:6719)

to differentiate groups, of its validity. Overinclusive thinking as assessed by this measure seems to be confined to schizophrenic patients.

There is some evidence that, unlike schizophrenics, brain damaged patients, as Goldstein initially suggested, are concrete on this test. McGaughran (*47*) found that, using his scoring system, brain damaged patients produced more "closed" (concrete) sortings. Other research,[5] using a very similar test, suggests that frontal lobe damage in particular may produce inability to perform this test. Unfortunately, there are still far too few norms using some such standard scoring system as McGaughran's for different groups of normals and functional patients, to make this test of practical value in detecting brain damage. At present it would seem therefore to be more useful in detecting overinclusive thinking, using either Payne's or Lovibond's techniques.

GELB-GOLDSTEIN COLOR SORTING TEST. The third sorting test in the Goldstein-Scheerer battery consists of a large number of skeins of wool of varying hue, brightness, and saturation. The subjects are required to sort the skeins into groups according to two different principles, "hue" and "brightness" (although the manual suggests that the authors themselves may not be clear about the difference between brightness and saturation; they do not seem to expect subjects ever to produce this third category). No objective scoring system has ever been devised, and this test appears neither to have been used or modified by other workers. This is perhaps because of the extreme difficulty in getting any subjects, normal or abnormal, to behave in the "abstract" ways specified in this rather obscure section of the manual.

GOLDSTEIN-SCHEERER CUBE TEST. The fourth test is quite unlike the three sorting tests so far discussed. It is merely a modified version of the Kohs *Block Design Test*. The modification consists of a standard set of aids, given to subjects who cannot complete the design (e.g., copying from a life-size picture, from a picture divided up, from a model, etc.). It is amazing in view of the objective nature of this test that no standard scoring system was suggested by the authors, although other workers (*28, 30*) have devised their own systems.

The studies which have been done using this test (*28, 29, 30, 50*) suggest that, like other nonverbal intelligence tests, the *Block Design Test* tends to differentiate between brain damaged subjects and other groups. However the overlap is extremely large, and the range of brain damaged performance is very wide, since it probably is largely a function of pre-illness intellectual level. This makes the test of very little practical value at the moment, as nearly all scores must be ambiguous. However, it does suggest that, if very extensive normative data were collected using, for instance, Boyd's (*30*) scoring system, for individuals of differing pre-illness IQ levels (as measured perhaps by vocabulary), a useful test for brain damage might ultimately emerge.

It is worth pointing out that one particular anomaly described by Goldstein and Scheerer, the "rotation" of constructed block patterns out of their proper orientation, has been subjected to a model of careful experimental analysis by Shapiro and has resulted in a new objective test which appears to be capable of detecting brain damage of a relatively specific type (associated with visual field and "oculomotor" defects).[6]

GOLDSTEIN-SCHEERER STICK TEST. This test requires the subject to copy patterns with small plastic sticks, and to reproduce them from memory. Again, no scoring system is suggested, so that no norms can be given. A number of characteristic anomalies shown by brain damaged patients are described, but no evidence is offered to support the author's contention that

5 RYLANDER, GÖSTA. *Personality Changes After Operations on the Frontal Lobes: A Clinical Study of 32 Cases.* Acta Psychiatrica et Neurologica Supplementum 20. Copenhagen: Ejnar Munksgaard, 1939. Pp. 327. *
HALSTEAD, WARD C. "Preliminary Analysis of Grouping Behaviour in Patients With Cerebral Injury by the Method of Equivalent and Non-equivalent Stimuli." *Am J Psychiatry* 96:1263–94 My '40. *

6 SHAPIRO, M. B. "Experimental Studies of a Perceptual Anomaly: 1, Initial Experiments." *J Mental Sci* 97:90–110 Ja '51. *
SHAPIRO, M. B. "Experimental Studies of a Perceptual Anomaly: 2, Confirmatory and Explanatory Experiments." *J Mental Sci* 98:605–17 O '52. *
SHAPIRO, M. B. "Experimental Studies of a Perceptual Anomaly: 3, The Testing of an Explanatory Theory." *J Mental Sci* 99:394–409 Jl '53. *
SHAPIRO, M. B., AND TIZARD, BARBARA. "Experimental Studies of a Perceptual Anomaly: 6, The Application of the 'Peephole' Analogy to the Perception of 'Organic' Psychiatric Patients." *J Mental Sci* 104:792–800 Jl '58. *
SHAPIRO, M. B.; BRIERLEY, J.; SLATER, P.; AND BEECH, H. R. "Experimental Studies of a Perceptual Anomaly: 7, A New Explanation." *J Mental Sci* 108:655–68 S '62. * (*PA* 38:2989)
WILLIAMS, HAROLD L.; LUBIN, ARDIE; GIESEKING, CHARLES; AND RUBENSTEIN, IRVIN. "The Relation of Brain Injury and Visual Perception to Block Design Rotation." *J Consult Psychol* 20:275–80 Ag '56. * (*PA* 31:7983)
YATES, A. J. "Experimental Studies of a Perceptual Anomaly: 4, The Effect of Monocular Vision on Rotation." *J Mental Sci* 100:975–9 O '54. *
YATES, AUBREY J. "Experimental Studies of a Perceptual Anomaly: 5, Some Factors Influencing the Appearance of the Block Design Rotation Effect in Normal Subjects." *J Mental Sci* 102:761–71 O '56. *

these are also due to concreteness. It may be the case that, like block design rotation, these abnormalities are perceptual in nature, and they may be related to very specific cortical or subcortical lesions. However, until the necessary research has been done, this test material cannot be put to any practical use. Unlike the other Goldstein tests, the stick test so far seems to have inspired little research to date.

The Goldstein-Scheerer test battery is at present of very limited practical value. Although it was intended to assess brain damage, it cannot be used for this purpose because of the lack of a standardized scoring system and the lack of any norms. However, one of the subtests in this battery, the Object Sorting Test, has been standardized by Lovibond (*53*) and by Payne and Hewlett (*61*) as a test of overinclusive thought disorder, which has been found to characterize only schizophrenic patients. Payne and Hewlett have published norms for small groups of normals, neurotics, depressives, and schizophrenics. There are at present, however, no data on the reliability of this test as a measure of schizophrenic thought disorder.

For reviews by Kate Levine Kogan, C. R. Strother (with Ludwig Immergluck), and O. L. Zangwill, see 3:41; for an excerpt from a related book review, see 3:42.

[102]

***Gordon Personal Inventory.** Grades 8–16 and adults; 1956–63, c1955–63; 4 scores: cautiousness, original thinking, personal relations, vigor; 1 form ('63, c1955–56, identical with 1956 form except for format and wording changes in directions); 2 editions: hand scored (3 pages), machine scorable (2 pages); revised manual ('63, c1956–63, 20 pages); mimeographed notes on the scoring system ['63, 5 pages] available upon request; tentative norms for high school students; $3.15 per 35 tests of hand scored edition; $2.90 per 35 IBM test-answer sheets for machine scorable edition; 80¢ per set of scoring stencils for machine scorable edition; 60¢ per specimen set including the complementary *Gordon Personal Profile;* postage extra; (15–20) minutes; Leonard V. Gordon; Harcourt, Brace & World, Inc. *

REFERENCES

1. BASS, BERNARD M. "Normative Data Information Exchange, No. 11-5." *Personnel Psychol* 11:269–70 su '58. *
2. MCKINNEY, EVA DORIS. *The Relationships Between Certain Factors of Personality and Selected Components of Physical Fitness of College Freshmen Women.* Doctor's thesis, Boston University (Boston, Mass.), 1958. (*DA* 19:1287)
3. COCHRAN, WILLIAM MORGAN, JR. "A Correlation Comparison Between the Minnesota Multiphasic Personality Inventory and the Combined Gordon Personal Profile and Personal Inventory (Abstract)." *Proc W Va Acad Sci* 30:189 My '59. * (*PA* 34:2359, title only)
4. MAGAW, DAVID CURLEE. *Criminal Antisocial and Inadequate Personalities—A Clinical and Psychometric Comparison.* Doctor's thesis, Wayne State University (Detroit, Mich.), 1959. (*DA* 20:2144)
5. BRAUN, JOHN R. "Correlates of Ghiselli Self-Description Inventory Scores." *Psychol Rep* 9:727–8 D '61. *
6. BRAUN, JOHN R.; ALEXANDER, SUNYA; AND WEISS, RICHARD. "Relationship Between the Gordon Personal Inventory and Consensus of Peer Ratings." *Psychol Rep* 9:455 O '61. *
7. DUGAN, ROBERT D. "Validity Information Exchange, No. 14-01: D.O.T. Code 0-98.07, Manager, Insurance Office." *Personnel Psychol* 14:213–6 su '61. *
8. KRIEDT, PHILIP H., AND DAWSON, ROBERT I. "Response Set and the Prediction of Clerical Job Performance." *J Appl Psychol* 45:175–8 Je '61. * (*PA* 36:4HF75K)
9. RIED, BLANCHE ROSE. *The Development of a Prognostic Device for Job Success of the Medical Assistant Through the Correlation of In-School Evaluations With Employer Evaluation.* Doctor's thesis, New York University (New York, N.Y.), 1961. (*DA* 23:557)
10. BRAUN, JOHN R. "Effects of a Top Management Faking Set on the Gordon Personal Inventory." *Psychol Rep* 10:611–4 Je '62. * (*PA* 37:5006)
11. BRAUN, JOHN R. "Stereotypes of the Scientist as Seen With the Gordon Personal Profile and Gordon Personal Inventory." *J Psychol* 53:453–5 Ap '62. * (*PA* 37:107)
12. BRAUN, JOHN R. "Fakability of the Gordon Personal Inventory: Replication and Extension." *J Psychol* 55:441–4 Ap '63. * (*PA* 38:991)
13. WILLINGHAM, WARREN W., AND AMBLER, ROSALIE K. "The Relation of the Gordon Personal Inventory to Several External Criteria." Abstract. *J Consult Psychol* 27:460 O '63. *

CHARLES F. DICKEN, *Assistant Professor of Psychology, San Diego State College, San Diego, California.*

This inventory follows a rationale and format similar to those of the *Gordon Personal Profile.* The four traits measured, based on factor studies, and typical items are: cautiousness (C), "doesn't care much for excitement," "does not act on the spur of the moment"; original thinking (O), "a very original thinker," "likes to work primarily with ideas"; personal relations (P), "speaks nothing but the best about other people," "believes that all people are basically honest"; and vigor (V), "a very energetic worker," "full of vigor and vitality." As the items indicate, trait P is a matter of trustingness and patience with others rather than of outgoing sociability.

The items are arranged in tetrads of two favorable and two unfavorable items as in the Profile. The time required is 10 to 15 minutes. The scoring scheme of the latest revision is altered to eliminate negative scores but there is no change in the content or structure of the test.

Factor analysis of items, internal consistency analysis, and judgments of item social desirability were used in building the test. Empirical item selection was apparently not used. Intercorrelations among the scales are generally lower than for the Profile, though there is a moderate correlation ($r = .37$) between C and P in student samples. Correlations of the inventory with the Profile are low to moderate. None of the correlations exceeds .47.

The manual is conscientiously prepared. The

reliabilities of the scales are satisfactory, ranging from .77 to .84. There are a variety of norms. Validity studies in several different settings are cited. Validity data are not quite as extensive as for the Profile, and the external validity of the inventory does not seem as well established by the data available. Omission of empirical item selection in constructing the test may have limited its external validity. Most of the validity correlations do not rise above the .30's. There are some high negative correlations with external criteria. Sales criteria were correlated substantially and negatively with C in one sample, and with P in another.

No illustrative individual cases are provided for the inventory. The question of distortion is dealt with in the same manner as for the Profile, and there are data indicating only small changes under differing motivational conditions, although not as much data as for the Profile. Item transparency seems somewhat more of a problem than with the Profile, and again the reviewer would suggest use of a validity scale.

In summary, the *Gordon Personal Inventory* measures four normal personality traits by a method very similar to that devised for the *Gordon Personal Profile*. There is considerable evidence of validity, although it is somewhat less satisfactory than for the Profile. Empirical item selection was apparently not used in the inventory. The manual is of high quality. The inventory seems generally as satisfactory a measure of traits of this type as other self-report devices which are available, although the external validities reported are frequently quite modest.

Alfred B. Heilbrun, Jr., *Associate Professor of Psychology, State University of Iowa, Iowa City, Iowa.*

The *Gordon Personal Inventory* (GPI) is a brief, largely self-administered questionnaire which provides measures of four personality traits, namely, cautiousness-impulsivity (C), original thinking-noninquisitiveness (O), personal relations (trust in and tolerance of people versus lack of trust in, and criticality of others) (P), and vigor (high versus low vitality) (V). The GPI is a replica of the *Gordon Personal Profile* in its derivation and format, and the manual recommends that the two tests be used in combination when there is interest in extending the breadth of personality assessment.

Gordon considers the GPI to have two principle attributes: (*a*) it was developed via a factor analytic approach, and (*b*) it presents its 20 items in a modified forced-choice format which requires the person to select one of four statements "most" like him and one "least" like him. Each of the four personality scales receives a score for each item with a weight of two assigned for a pair of responses which includes the most socially desirable response for the scale, a zero for a pair of responses which includes the least socially desirable response, and otherwise a one. Gordon suggests that this item format is less susceptible to faking for those individuals motivated to make a good impression. Evidence presented in the manual to support this contention is less cogent than that provided for the companion *Gordon Personal Profile*. In both cases it is assumed that job applicants are more likely to portray themselves favorably whereas counseling clients are more likely to be frank. However, the *Gordon Personal Profile* scores of job applicants were directly compared with employees, whereas GPI comparisons were made only between job applicants and counseling clients (real and simulated). Accordingly, the effects of possible motivation to make a good impression were not separated from group differences in level of adjustment for the GPI.

The percentile norms provided for the inventory are stable and fairly representative, separate norms being provided for males and females at the high school and college level and several occupational groups. Although Gordon recommends the development of local norms for specific testing populations, it would be useful if a "general population" type norm had been provided in the manual for those who wish to use the GPI with samples who are not young, highly educated, or selected from specific industrial work levels.

Reliability is reported in terms of split-half or internal consistency coefficients and is reasonably good (around .80) for all scales. Test-retest stability is not reported, but if the stability of the Profile scales can be assumed, the GPI should also be reasonably reliable over time.

Correlations among the GPI scales tend to be low (.45 or less) and, with the exception of scale O, correlations with measures of intelligence are negligible. Scale O shows a low positive relationship (.26 or less) to both verbal and quantitative tests of ability and a correlation of .31 with total ACE score.

Based upon the validity evidence presented in the manual, the GPI is open to the same criticism as the Profile, probably more so. Not only is there less evidence presented for the validity of the GPI (e.g., no correlations with peer and counselor ratings of the test variables), but the rather dubious procedure was repeated of assuming *any* significant relationship with a performance criterion represents scale validation. For example, the manual gives as validity evidence the finding that scales O and P correlate negatively with rated success as a salesman, whereas in another reported study validity was assumed because the same scales correlate positively with success in an underwater demolition training program. Unless there is some independent evidence or theory which would predict these relationships, the term validity must be treated skeptically. At least, however, the evidence presented in the manual suggests that the GPI scales do allow for group discriminations on certain industrial and training performance criteria.

Summarily, the GPI falls somewhat short of the Profile with respect to what has been accomplished in its development. In many respects a solid beginning has been made in establishing its usefulness as a brief personality measure, but in other respects (commented upon in this review) questions remain which demand further empirical investigation before the test user should employ the instrument without more than the usual caution.

For reviews by Benno G. Fricke and John A. Radcliffe, see 5:58 (2 excerpts).

[103]

***Gordon Personal Profie.** Grades 9–16 and adults; 1953–63, c1951–63; 4 scores: ascendancy, responsibility, emotional stability, sociability; 1 form ('63, c1951–53, identical with 1953 form except for format and wording changes in directions); 2 editions: hand scored (3 pages), machine scorable (2 pages); revised manual ('63, c1953–63, 27 pages); mimeographed notes on the scoring system ['63, 5 pages] available upon request; $3.15 per 35 tests of hand scored edition; $2.90 per 35 IBM test-answer sheets for machine scorable edition; 80¢ per set of scoring stencils for machine scorable edition; 60¢ per specimen set including the complementary *Gordon Personal Inventory;* postage extra; (15–20) minutes; Leonard V. Gordon; Harcourt, Brace & World, Inc. *

REFERENCES

1–16. See 5:59.

17. MUDGE, BERTRAM R. *A Study of the Relationship Between the Gordon Personal Profile and Academic Achievement in College.* Master's thesis, Boston University (Boston, Mass.), 1956.

18. DUFFICY, EDWARD C. *The Relationship Between Scores on the Otis Gamma Quick Scoring Mental Ability Test, the Gordon Personal Profile, and Success in Latin in a Minor Seminary.* Master's thesis, De Paul University (Chicago, Ill.), 1957.

19. WARNE, EARL KEITH. *A Study to Determine Whether the Gordon Personal Profile Will Tend to Measure the Success of Cadet Teachers.* Doctor's research study No. 1, Colorado State College (Greeley, Colo.), 1957.

20. ARBUCKLE, DUGALD S. "Self-Ratings and Test Scores on Two Standardized Personality Inventories." *Personnel & Guid J* 37:292–3 D '58. * (*PA* 36:2HE92A)

21. MCKINNEY, EVA DORIS. *The Relationships Between Certain Factors of Personality and Selected Components of Physical Fitness of College Freshmen Women.* Doctor's thesis, Boston University (Boston, Mass.), 1958. (*DA* 19:1287)

22. VAN BUSKIRK, WILLIAM L. "Normative Data Information Exchange, No. 11-16." *Personnel Psychol* 11:445–6 au '58. *

23. COCHRAN, WILLIAM MORGAN, JR. "A Correlation Comparison Between the Minnesota Multiphasic Personality Inventory and the Combined Gordon Personal Profile and Personal Inventory (Abstract)." *Proc W Va Acad Sci* 30:189 My '59. * (*PA* 34:2359, title only)

24. LOHMANN, KAJ; ZENGER, JOHN H.; AND WESCHLER, IRVING R. "Some Perceptual Changes During Sensitivity Training." *J Ed Res* 53:28–31 S '59. * (*PA* 34:5628)

25. MCCONAGHY, N. "The Use of an Object Sorting Test in Elucidating the Hereditary Factor in Schizophrenia." *J Neurol Neurosurg & Psychiatry* 22:243–6 Ag '59. * (*PA* 34:8166)

26. OAKES, FREDERICK, JR. *The Contribution of Certain Variables to the Academic Achievement of Gifted Seventh Grade Students in an Accelerated General Science Curriculum.* Doctor's thesis, New York University (New York, N.Y.), 1959. (*DA* 20:4002)

27. SMITH, D. D. "Traits and College Achievement." *Can J Psychol* 13:93–101 Je '59. * (*PA* 34:4780)

28. United States Naval Personnel Research Field Activity. "Normative Data Information Exchange, No. 12-4." *Personnel Psychol* 12:146–7 sp '59. *

29. ASH, PHILIP. "Validity Information Exchange, No. 13-05: D.O.T. Code 1-86.12, Salesman, Typewriters." *Personnel Psychol* 13:454 w '60. *

30. BROWN, ALAN W., AND LANDSBERGER, HENRY A. "The Sense of Responsibility Among Young Workers: Part 1, Definition and Measurement." *Occup Psychol* 34:1–14 Ja '60. * (*PA* 35:7236)

31. CAMPBELL, JOEL T.; PRIEN, ERICH P.; AND BRAILEY, LESTER B. "Predicting Performance Evaluations." *Personnel Psychol* 13:435–40 w '60. * (*PA* 36:1LD35C)

32. COSGROVE, AZARIAS MICHAEL. *A Comparison of Personality Patterns as Measured by the Gordon Personal Profile and the Figure Drawing Test.* Master's thesis, Manhattan College (New York, N.Y.), 1960.

33. HUGHES, J. L. "Comparison of the Validities of Trait and Profile Methods of Scoring a Personality Test for Salesmen." *Eng & Ind Psychol* 2:1–7 sp '60. *

34. BRAUN, JOHN R. "Correlates of Ghiselli Self-Description Inventory Scores." *Psychol Rep* 9:727–8 D '61. *

35. HUGHES, J. L., AND DODD, W. E. "Validity Versus Stereotype: Predicting Sales Performance by Ipsative Scoring of a Personality Test." *Personnel Psychol* 14:343–55 w '61. * (*PA* 37:5910)

36. RIED, BLANCHE ROSE. *The Development of a Prognostic Device for Job Success of the Medical Assistant Through the Correlation of In-School Evaluations With Employer Evaluation.* Doctor's thesis, New York University (New York, N.Y.), 1961. (*DA* 23:557)

37. TUCKER, W. T., AND PAINTER, JOHN J. "Personality and Product Use." *J Appl Psychol* 45:325–9 O '61. * (*PA* 36:5LO25T)

38. BRAUN, JOHN R. "Stereotypes of the Scientist as Seen With the Gordon Personal Profile and Gordon Personal Inventory." *J Psychol* 53:453–5 Ap '62. * (*PA* 37:107)

39. APPLEY, MORTIMER H., AND MOELLER, GEORGE. "Conforming Behavior and Personality Variables in College Women." *J Abn & Social Psychol* 66:284–90 Mr '63. * (*PA* 37:8237)

40. GREENBERG, HERBERT; GUERINO, ROSEMARIE; LASHEN, MARILYN; MAYER, DAVID; AND PISKOWSKI, DOROTHY. "Order of Birth as a Determinant of Personality and Attitudinal Characteristics." *J Social Psychol* 60:221–30 Ag '63. * (*PA* 38:4337)

41. MAHER, HOWARD. "Validity Information Exchange, No. 16-01: D.O.T. Code 0-06.71, Feature Writer; 0-06.73, Columnist; 0-06.92, Copyreader (Rewrite Man)." *Personnel Psychol* 16:71–3 sp '63. *

CHARLES F. DICKEN, *Assistant Professor of Psychology, San Diego State College, San Diego, California.*

The Profile was designed to measure four

personality traits, shown with typical high-loading items: ascendancy (A), "takes the lead in group discussions," "able to make important decisions without help"; responsibility (R), "sees a job through despite difficulties," "thorough in any work undertaken"; emotional stability (E), "calm and easygoing in manner," "free from worry or care"; and sociability (S), "enjoys having lots of people around," "a good mixer socially."

The items are arranged in tetrads of two favorably worded and two unfavorably worded items. The examinee selects one most descriptive and one least descriptive item from each tetrad. The reviewer found the format somewhat annoying since identical items occur repeatedly; however the time required to complete the test is refreshingly brief, less than 15 minutes.

The Profile was constructed on the basis of an extensive series of investigations. Traits were initially selected on the basis of personality factors obtained by Cattell and Mosier. Items devised for the traits were factored to derive scales. Item social desirability values were established by ratings in a large subject pool and used to determine the pairings in the tetrads. Peer rating criteria were used to further refine the items, as was internal consistency analysis. There were five revisions in all. The scoring system in the 1963 version has been revised to eliminate negative scores, but there is no change in the content or structure of the Profile itself or in the item weights. As in the earlier edition, no item response is keyed for more than one trait, although the mechanics of arranging the revised stencils give the initial impression that all items are scored on all keys.

Although the four traits were selected as theoretically independent dimensions, scales A and S and scales E and R intercorrelate fairly substantially in most samples. Peer ratings show the same correspondencies, however, suggesting that the overlap may be in the traits themselves rather than the result of an avoidable problem of measurement method.

The manual maintains a high standard. Pertinent data are presented in detail. The discussion of interpretation is conservative, limitations and cautions being specifically pointed out. There are percentile norms for a good variety of groups, including students, low and middle level employees, managers, salesmen, and foremen. Means and sigmas are furnished for 27 different groups.

Reliability estimates based on several populations and computed by several standard methods are satisfactorily high. The validity of the scores in predicting external criteria in more than 20 studies is cited, and low or zero correlations are included as well as higher ones. These data are extensive enough to give the potential user a fair approximation of what he might expect in his own population. Validity correlations with peer ratings of college students are especially impressive, ranging from .47 to .73, but these subjects appear to be the same on which the item analyses were based. Three of the four scores correlate more than .50, however, with counselors' trait ratings in an independent study. How much of the validity in these studies is due to common "halo" or overall-merit variance and how much is due to specific validity of the separate scales for separate ratings is not determinable.

Validities obtained in various employment and military settings are typically lower, but the criteria (mostly supervisory ratings or administrative decisions) are probably not as good as peer nominations. The validities suggest that the A and R scores are probably most valuable in employment applications. Except for the peer data, external validities rarely exceed .30 or .35, although there are some outstanding exceptions. This level of validity is probably typical of the better inventories of normal personality traits, with the criteria available.

Illustrative individual cases are provided which give profile scores and independently obtained personality data. A wider variety of these cases would enhance the value of the manual as an aid in interpretation.

The problem of distortion or "faking" is discussed in a sophisticated manner. The author's basic argument is that the forced-choice format compels the examinee to choose between two favorable (or unfavorable) items and that he will tend to choose the item he feels is most complimentary, which will turn out to be the item actually like him. The author also states that the utility of the test must rest on its validity in operational situations, not on its resistance to distortion.

The evidence presented seems mainly to support this reasoning. Gordon found forced-choice versions of his items more valid than true-false items in constructing the Profile. Several comparisons of scores obtained under differing motivational conditions, including application, guidance, post-employment, and simulated employment-seeking, show only small increases in the scores of subjects presumably motivated to make a favorable impression.

There is, however, some degree of face validity apparent in the items keyed for the various traits. The data do not resolve the problem of role-playing by subjects who are informed or sophisticated as to the traits desired in a given context. The test lacks an explicit control for the total number of favorable items checked, a factor which tends to penalize the candid subject, since endorsement of favorable items increases scores on all scales. It seems possible that at least some items which are valid for the traits, although socially less favorable, could have been found, although this is admittedly difficult. The earlier published version included norms for a total (T) score and a suggestion that extreme values be interpreted as questioning the validity of the record. This is now omitted, unfortunately in the opinion of the reviewer, although a percentile value based on the earlier norms can be obtained through a short series of calculations. The reviewer raised his own A score 58 centile units on the male executive norm by adopting a "leadership" set after first responding with a "candid" set. His T score rose above the 99th percentile, however, which would easily have unmasked the deception.

In summary, the Profile is a brief, forced-choice inventory for four normal personality traits. The inventory was carefully constructed and standardized, and a variety of norms are furnished. Validity data are thoroughly and conscientiously presented. The problem of distortion is considered in detail, and evidence is presented which indicates it is minimal in typical operational settings. However, a validity scale could and probably should be used as a check for distortion. Generally, the validity of the *Gordon Personal Profile* seems as good as usually found in the better inventories of this type.

Alfred B. Heilbrun, Jr., *Associate Professor of Psychology, State University of Iowa, Iowa City, Iowa.*

The *Gordon Personal Profile* (GPP) is a brief 18-item questionnaire, essentially self-administering, and applicable to individuals ranging in age from about 15 years through adulthood. It is proposed as a measure of four significant personality dimensions: (*a*) ascendancy-passivity (A), (*b*) responsibility-irresponsibility (R), (*c*) emotional stability-instability (E), and (*d*) sociability-social introversiveness (S). The statements included in each scale were selected by factor analytic means and underwent a series of revisions which were aimed at sharpening scale prediction and determining which combination elicited an acceptable number of endorsements for each statement of the four in a given item.

The GPP provides a modified forced-choice format which the manual proposes as a control for favorability in self-description. In each of the 18 items, four statements representing the four personality dimensions are grouped so that two are high preference and two are low preference. The individual is asked to select the statement "most" and "least" like himself from each item tetrad. Gordon presents evidence which suggests that faking on the test does not markedly influence group scale score means if it is assumed that application for employment systematically elicits more favorable self-descriptions from job candidates.

Generally speaking, the 1963 revised manual is a commendable product. The empirical groundwork necessary to satisfy the basic requirements of a published test has been satisfactorily completed and presented in the manual in a clear, orderly fashion. Stable and fairly representative college and high school percentile norms are provided as well as several sets of specific norms which might be of interest to those working within a business setting. No "general population" type norm is provided which may limit the effectiveness of the test's use with samples which are not young, highly educated, or selected from one of a few industrial levels. Reliability figures suggest that the GPP scales are both internally consistent and stable over time.

Although the scales are only slightly correlated with measures of intelligence, there are some surprisingly high intercorrelations between some of the scales considering that the traits were derived from a factor analysis. Scales showing the greatest intercorrelation are A and S (r = .64 to .71) and R and E (r = .51 to .61). The fact that the GPP measures but four traits and a moderate correlation exists between some of these would indicate a rather restricted range of inferences which the test user can make from the test. This restriction can be alleviated to some extent by presenting the *Gordon Personal Inventory* in tandem with the GPP, thereby adding four more personality dimensions and increasing testing time by only somewhere between 15 and 30 minutes. In fact, one is led to wonder why the two tests are not published as a single test instrument since their formats are identical.

The validity data bear testimony to the usefulness of the GPP scales. Moderate correlations between them and both counselor and peer ratings of behavior have been demonstrated. The manual also presents numerous correlations between the GPP and indices of performance adequacy in industrial and training situations. These tend to be low but significant, highlighting the fact that the GPP has little power for individual prediction of nontest behavior, which is not surprising since no other objective personality instrument has either. The one feature of the validity findings which leaves the reviewer uneasy is that *any* significant relationship between a scale and a performance rating is regarded as an indicant of validity. For example, it is not specified why ascendancy should relate to one criterion and emotional stability to another.

In summary, if there is interest in a short, convenient measure of a limited number of salient personality traits, the GPP is about as good as you can do. It is carefully conceived, reliable, adequately normed, and has received at least suggestive validation.

For reviews by Benno G. Fricke and John A. Radcliffe, see 5:59 (1 excerpt).

[104]

Group Cohesiveness: A Study of Group Morale. Adults; 1958, c1957–58; title on test is *A Study of Group Morale;* 5 scores: satisfaction of individual motives, satisfaction of interpersonal relations, homogeneity of attitude, satisfaction with leadership, total; 1 form ('57, 1 page); manual ('58, 4 pages); no data on reliability of subscores; $3 per 30 tests; $1 per specimen set; cash orders postpaid; (10–15) minutes; Bernard Goldman; Psychometric Affiliates. *

REFERENCES

1. GOLDMAN, BERNARD. *A Scale for the Measurement of Group Cohesiveness.* Doctor's thesis, University of Buffalo (Buffalo, N.Y.), 1952. (*DA* 12:554)

ERIC F. GARDNER, *Professor of Education and Psychology, and Chairman, Department of Psychology, Syracuse University, Syracuse, New York.*

Group morale is considered by the author to be comparable to group cohesiveness as described by T. R. Newcomb. Four criteria posited as indicators of group cohesiveness and adapted by the author as his definition of morale were used as the basis for item construction. Items, each of which was related to one of the four criteria of morale, were constructed as measures of the four subtest scores presented. The 20 best items, selected by editing and by use of phi coefficients to differentiate between high and low scoring groups, were retained for the test. Each item is scored using a Likert type scale (strongly agree to strongly disagree) and the score of each subtest is obtained by summing the responses where "4" represents the highest degree of cohesiveness.

Although the general procedure is reasonable, the reviewer has serious doubts about certain aspects of its implementation. The selection of the most appropriate items was dependent upon the adequacy of the two criterion groups used. As a criterion, the total responses of the top and bottom 50 scores among 184 nurses leaves much to be desired. An inspection of the final items does nothing to allay one's concern about their adequacy. Many of the statements appear to be rather extreme and not especially adaptable for indicating variability among respondents. For example, the inclusion of the word "all" in the item "I believe that all my associates in this group hold beliefs that are unreasonable" causes the respondent some difficulty in deciding upon the degree of his agreement.

A reliability coefficient of .94 is reported for the total test. The score on the first 10 items was correlated with scores on the second 10 items for a sample of 209 subjects and the result corrected by the Spearman-Brown prophecy formula. Such an index is not very meaningful without more information about the group utilized, especially its variability. No reliability coefficients are reported for the four subtest scores. Since these scores contain from 4 to 7 items each, the reliability coefficients are probably low for use in measuring individual differences.

A table of norms based upon the mean performance of 14 groups for each subtest and the total score is presented. Since there are 20 categories of percentile rank and only 14 observations, the reviewer is unable to understand what operation the author has performed or what he has in mind.

Attempts at the establishment of validity were made by comparing the responses of various groups where cohesiveness or noncohesiveness was presumed to be known. Mean differences which are shown to be statistically significant are presented between (*a*) Great Book study groups ranging from a beginner's group to a leader's group, (*b*) organized dramatic groups compared with informal groups, and (*c*) classrooms using seminar methods contrasted with a group who had been taught by the lecture method. Small mean differences in the direction hypothesized were obtained. These small differences are not too surprising, especially since there is little evidence that the groups labeled high morale groups really had better morale than did the groups labeled low in morale.

The topic is important and a beginning has been made to develop useful measures. It seems to the reviewer that the test is being presented prematurely. Much work needs to be done, including additional item analysis, reliability studies for appropriate specific groups, and validation studies.

CECIL A. GIBB, *Professor of Psychology, The Australian National University, Canberra City, Australia.*

Much as the psychologist concerned with work groups and groups in other settings would welcome an instrument to measure cohesiveness, the approach to this scale will be very cautious indeed. The very equation of "morale" and "cohesiveness," in which Goldman has followed Newcomb, leads to difficulties; for example, rejection of the statement "I believe that the work I do now keeps me in a rut" contributes positively to the "cohesiveness" score and also, in some peculiar way, to a score called "homogeneity of attitude."

Nor will the data given by Goldman dispel many doubts. Development procedures seem to have been standard and a corrected split-half reliability of .94 is claimed, certainly "adequate" for a 20-item scale. Some validity also is demonstrated in terms of scale differentiation between selected criterion groups. However, detailed presentation of means and standard deviations for these groups indicates a rather less happy situation than that suggested by the analysis of variance data offered in the "Validity" discussion.

Goldman claims, "The four criteria of cohesiveness adopted for the purpose of constructing the scale are probably valid measures, in part, of group cohesiveness." This conclusion was arrived at on the sole evidence of part-whole correlation coefficients ranging from .67 to .47—not a very impressive array of data when any part constitutes at least 20 per cent of the whole and in one case as much as 35 per cent. Confidence is further strained when in the next paragraph it is claimed: "The four criteria of cohesiveness are relatively independent of one another as shown by the low intercorrelations among them," and this on the basis of correlations ranging between .49 and .28 with no overlap of items. Other difficulties will certainly face users of this scale, which is presented as being intended for use with groups in general although many of the questions relate only to work and work situations. Much more seriously, the instructions never call for the respondent to identify a group. He is asked to respond, anonymously, to statements about "this group," "my associates," and "the leader of this group" without any attempt at establishing which of the many groups he belongs to is intended, what nature of relationship defines an "associate," and which of many possible "leaders" is to be kept in mind.

It is difficult to see that *Group Cohesiveness: A Study of Group Morale* can make any positive contribution to any of the objectives claimed for it.

[105]

★Group Dimensions Descriptions Questionnaire. College and adult groups; 1956; for research use only; 13 group dimensions scores: autonomy, control, flexibility, hedonic tone, homogeneity, intimacy, participation, permeability, polarization, potency, stability, stratification, viscidity; IBM; Form ERG (8 pages); manual (75 pages, see *4* below); tentative norms; separate answer-profile sheets must be used; $3.50 per 25 tests; 30¢ per single copy; $2 per 25 IBM answer sheets; scoring stencils must be prepared locally; $2.50 per manual; postage extra; [45-60] minutes; John K. Hemphill and Charles M. Westie; distributed by Educational Testing Service. *

REFERENCES

1. HEMPHILL, JOHN K., AND WESTIE, CHARLES M. "The Measurement of Group Dimensions." *J Psychol* 29:325-42 Ap '50. * (*PA* 24:5789)

2. HEMPHILL, JOHN K. "Description of Group Characteristics." *Proc Inv Conf Testing Probl* 1954:85-90; discussion, 91-5 '55. * (*PA* 30:826)

3. BORGATTA, EDGAR F.; COTTRELL, LEONARD S., JR.; AND MEYER, HENRY J. "On the Dimensions of Group Behavior." *Sociometry* 19:223-40 Mr '56. * (*PA* 32:1440)

4. HEMPHILL, JOHN K. *Group Dimensions: A Manual for Their Measurement.* Ohio State University Bureau of Business

Research, Research Monograph No. 87. Columbus, Ohio: the Bureau, 1956. Pp. xi, 66. * (*PA* 31:7657)
5. HILL, THOMAS BARLOW, JR. *The Relationships Between Teacher Morale and the Ability to Establish Rapport With Pupils and Other Selected Variables.* Doctor's thesis, North Texas State College (Denton, Tex.), 1961. (*DA* 22:789)

For an excerpt from a review of the manual, see 5:B203.

[106]

★Guidance Inventory. High school; 1960; identification of problems related to underachievement and need for counseling; 1 form (2 pages); manual (21 pages); no data on reliability; $20 per 200 tests and manual; $1.75 per manual purchased separately; 50¢ per specimen set; postpaid; (50) minutes; Ralph Gallagher; the Author. *

JOHN W. M. ROTHNEY, *Professor of Education, University of Wisconsin, Madison, Wisconsin.*

The 130 items which constitute this inventory are printed on both sides of a cardboard sheet. The student answers by circling a NO or YES for each question. The questions vary from the usual "Do you feel 'low' much of the time?" type of question to such specifics as "Do your teeth need dental attention?" Ninety New Jersey high school principals and superintendents helped the author to decide upon the items that are in the final form. In order to overcome the tendency of students to give favorable answers and cover up difficulties, the author says that the inventory has "carefully inter-related responses, and emotionally charged items have been kept at a minimum."

It is difficult to assess this inventory because the data and the methods of reporting do not follow the usual patterns. There are no reliability coefficients and no evidence of validity of the usual kind. It is said that identification of elements, other than the usual intellectual or academic factors, that are different for pupils doing good and poor work in school is based on "nearly 5,000,000 responses by equal numbers of pupils doing good and poor work in nearly 300 american [spelled with a small a] high schools in 1960." No further identification of populations is given.

A report is given about each of the 130 items. On the fifth item, for example, "Do you often lose your temper?," it is reported that "frequent loss of tempers were reported by over 1/3 of good students. They were reported 1½ times as often by poor students." This is followed by two queries that the counselor might make as to why the pupils lose their tempers and whether or not the pupil is acquainted with the loss of efficiency that accompanies temper outbursts. The counselor is then referred to answers to other items on the inventory such as item 14, "Are you as popular as you would like to be?" Supporting data offered indicates that 43 per cent of all pupils answered YES to item 5 and that from 24 to 60 per cent of pupils in different schools did so. Percentages of girls and boys doing good and poor work who answered YES to the item are given. On the front cover of the manual it is indicated that the percentages are based on 18,668 pupils doing good work and 18,298 pupils doing poor work. No definition of good and poor work is given and there is no further description of the populations or the schools from which they came.

All of the usual objections to such devices can be raised against this one. When one adds lack of evidence of reliability, validity, norms, lack of adequate editing of the manual, and general vagueness one must conclude that counselors could get along without this instrument.

[107]

★Guilford-Holley L Inventory. Adults; 1953–63; leadership behavior; 5 scores: benevolence, ambition, meticulousness, discipline, aggressiveness; IBM; 1 form ('53, 4 pages); manual ('63, 6 pages); separate answer sheets must be used; $3.50 per 25 tests; 4¢ per IBM answer sheet; $1.25 per scoring stencil; 4¢ per profile; 35¢ per manual; 65¢ per specimen set; postage extra; (25) minutes; J. P. Guilford and J. W. Holley; Sheridan Supply Co. *

[108]

The Guilford-Martin Inventory of Factors GAMIN, Abridged Edition. Grades 12–16 and adults; 1943–48; 5 scores: general activity, ascendance-submission, masculinity-femininity, inferiority feelings, nervousness; IBM; 1 form ('43, 4 pages); revised manual ['48, 3 pages]; college norms only; $3.50 per 25 tests; 20¢ per single copy; $1 per scoring key; separate answer sheets may be used; 4¢ per IBM answer sheet; $2.50 per set of either hand or machine scoring stencils; 25¢ per manual; postage extra; (30) minutes; [J. P. Guilford and H. G. Martin]; Sheridan Supply Co. *

REFERENCES

1–7. See 3:43.
8–25. See 4:47.
26–58. See 5:63.
59. TSUJIOKA, BIEN; SONOHARA, TARO; AND YATABE, TATSURO. "A Factorial Study of the Temperament of Japanese College Male Students by the Yatabe-Guilford Personality Inventory." *Psychologia* 1:110–9 D '57. * (*PA* 35:4899)
60. BUDD, WILLIAM C., AND BLAKELY, LYNDA S. "The Relationship Between Ascendancy and Response Choice on the Minnesota Teacher Attitude Inventory." *J Ed Res* 52:73–4 O '58. * (*PA* 34:2027)
61. RISS, ERIC. *Originality and Personality: An Exploratory Investigation to Study the Relationship of Originality to Certain Personality Variables in Art Students.* Doctor's thesis, New York University (New York, N.Y.), 1958. (*DA* 20:743)
62. THOMAS, EDWIN RUSSELL. *The Relationship Between the Strong Vocational Interest Blank and the Guilford-Martin Personality Inventory Among Salesmen.* Doctor's thesis, Syracuse University (Syracuse, N.Y.), 1958. (*DA* 19:2139)

63. GUILFORD, J. P. *Personality.* New York: McGraw-Hill Book Co., Inc., 1959. Pp. xiii, 562. *
64. KELLY, E. LOWELL, AND GOLDBERG, LEWIS R. "Correlates of Later Performance and Specialization in Psychology: A Follow-Up Study of the Trainees Assessed in the VA Selection Research Project." *Psychol Monogr* 73(12):1–32 '59. * (*PA* 34:7952)
65. CARRIGAN, PATRICIA M. "Extraversion-Introversion as a Dimension of Personality: A Reappraisal." *Psychol B* 57:329–60 S '60. * (*PA* 35:4976)
66. CURRAN, ANN MARIE. *Non-Intellective Characteristics of Freshman Underachievers, Normal Achievers, and Overachievers at the College Level.* Doctor's thesis, University of Connecticut (Storrs, Conn.), 1960. (*DA* 21:2584)
67. MITCHELL, LONNIE E., AND ZAX, MELVIN. "Psychological Response to Chlorpromazine in a Group of Psychiatric Patients." *J Clin Psychol* 16:440–2 O '60. * (*PA* 37:3341)
68. BESSENT, EDGAR WAILAND. *The Predictability of Selected Elementary School Principals' Administrative Behavior.* Doctor's thesis, University of Texas (Austin, Tex.), 1961. (*DA* 22:3479)
69. NICHOLS, ROBERT C. "Subtle, Obvious and Stereotype Measures of Masculinity-Femininity." *Ed & Psychol Meas* 22:449–61 au '62. * (*PA* 37:5014)

For a review by Hubert E. Brogden, see 4:47; for a review by H. J. Eysenck, see 3:43; for a related review, see 3:45.

[109]

The Guilford-Martin Personnel Inventory. Adults; 1943–46; 3 scores: objectivity, agreeableness, cooperativeness; IBM; 1 form ('43, 4 pages); manual ['43, 2 pages]; mimeographed supplement ('46, 5 pages); $3.50 per 25 tests; 20¢ per single copy; $1 per scoring key; separate answer sheets may be used; 4¢ per IBM answer sheet; $2.50 per set of either hand or machine scoring stencils; 25¢ per manual; postage extra; (30) minutes; [J. P. Guilford and H. G. Martin]; Sheridan Supply Co. *

REFERENCES

1–7. See 3:44.
8–27. See 4:48.
28–54. See 5:64.
55. TSUJIOKA, BIEN; SONOHARA, TARO; AND YATABE, TATSURO. "A Factorial Study of the Temperament of Japanese College Male Students by the Yatabe-Guilford Personality Inventory." *Psychologia* 1:110–9 D '57. * (*PA* 35:4899)
56. THOMAS, EDWIN RUSSELL. *The Relationship Between the Strong Vocational Interest Blank and the Guilford-Martin Personality Inventory Among Salesmen.* Doctor's thesis, Syracuse University (Syracuse, N.Y.), 1958. (*DA* 19:2139)
57. GUILFORD, J. P. *Personality.* New York: McGraw-Hill Book Co., Inc., 1959. Pp. xiii, 562. *
58. KELLY, E. LOWELL, AND GOLDBERG, LEWIS R. "Correlates of Later Performance and Specialization in Psychology: A Follow-Up Study of the Trainees Assessed in the VA Selection Research Project." *Psychol Monogr* 73(12):1–32 '59. * (*PA* 34:7952)
59. United States Naval Personnel Research Field Activity. "Normative Data Information Exchange, No. 12-3." *Personnel Psychol* 12:145 sp '59. *
60. CARRIGAN, PATRICIA M. "Extraversion-Introversion as a Dimension of Personality: A Reappraisal." *Psychol B* 57:329–60 S '60. * (*PA* 35:4976)
61. MACKINNEY, ARTHUR C., AND WOLINS, LEROY. "Validity Information Exchange, No. 13-01, Foreman II, Home Appliance Manufacturing." *Personnel Psychol* 13:443–7 w '60. *
62. BESSENT, EDGAR WAILAND. *The Predictability of Selected Elementary School Principals' Administrative Behavior.* Doctor's thesis, University of Texas (Austin, Tex.), 1961. (*DA* 22:3479)
63. BUEL, WILLIAM D., AND BACHNER, VIRGINIA M. "The Assessment of Creativity in a Research Setting." *J Appl Psychol* 45:353–8 D '61. * (*PA* 37:1211)

For a review by Neil Van Steenberg, see 4:48; for a review by Benjamin Shimberg, see 3:44; for a related review, see 3:45.

[110]

The Guilford-Zimmerman Temperament Survey. Grades 12–16 and adults; 1949–55; revision and condensation of *Inventory of Factors STDCR, Guilford-Martin Inventory of Factors GAMIN,* and *Guilford-Martin Personnel Inventory;* 10 scores: general activity, restraint, ascendance, sociability, emotional stability, objectivity, friendliness, thoughtfulness, personal relations, masculinity; IBM; 1 form ('49, 8 pages); manual ('49, 12 pages); norms ('55); profile ('55, 1 page); 3 *Falsification Scales* (gross-falsification, subtle falsification, carelessness-deviancy) and manual ('55, 3 pages) by Alfred Jacobs and Allan Schlaff; *G-Z Temperament Map* ('52, 2 pages) by Philip C. Perry; separate answer sheets must be used; $4 per 25 tests; 25¢ per single copy; 5¢ per IBM answer sheet; $2.50 per set of either hand or machine scoring stencils; 4¢ per profile; 35¢ per manual; $4.25 per set of scoring stencils and manual for falsification scales; 4¢ per copy of temperament map; postage extra; (50) minutes; J. P. Guilford and Wayne S. Zimmerman; Sheridan Supply Co. *

REFERENCES

1–5. See 4:49.
6–53. See 5:65.
54. FERGUSON, JOHN L., JR. *A Factorial Study of the Minnesota Teacher Attitude Inventory.* Doctor's thesis, University of Missouri (Columbia, Mo.), 1953. (*DA* 13:1087)
55. BARBER, THEODORE XENOPHON. "A Note on 'Hypnotizability' and Personality Traits." *J Clin & Exp Hypnosis* 4:109–14 Jl '56. * (*PA* 32:3288)
56. BERKOWITZ, LEONARD. "Personality and Group Position." *Sociometry* 19:210–22 Mr '56. * (*PA* 32:1435)
57. HOLMEN, MILTON G.; KATTER, ROBERT V.; JONES, ANNE M.; AND RICHARDSON, IRVING F. "An Assessment Program for OCS Applicants." *HumRRO Tech Rep* 26:1–50 F '56. * (*PA* 31:8957)
58. KEMPE, JAMES EDWIN. *An Experimental Investigation of the Relationship Between Certain Personality Characteristics and Physiological Responses to Stress in a Normal Population.* Doctor's thesis, Michigan State University (East Lansing, Mich.), 1956. (*DA* 19:3383)
59. CRIST, ROBERT L. *A Study of Mean Differences in the R, S, and T Traits of the Guilford-Zimmerman Temperament Survey for Upper and Lower Quarter Students on the Minnesota Teacher Attitude Inventory.* Master's thesis, Purdue University (Lafayette, Ind.), 1957.
60. GOWAN, J. C. "A Summary of the Intensive Study of Twenty Highly Selected Elementary Women Teachers." *J Exp Ed* 26:115–24 D '57. * (*PA* 33:4731)
61. MURRAY, JOHN B. *Training for the Priesthood and Personality Interest Test Manifestations.* Doctor's thesis, Fordham University (New York, N.Y.), 1957.
62. SCHOLL, CHARLES ELMER, JR. *The Development and Evaluation of Methods for Isolating Factors That Differentiate Between Successful and Unsuccessful Executive Trainees in a Large, Multibranch Bank.* Doctor's thesis, University of Michigan (Ann Arbor, Mich.), 1957. (*DA* 18:2034)
63. STARR, HAROLD. *Personality Correlates of Time Estimation.* Doctor's thesis, Purdue University (Lafayette, Ind.), 1957. (*DA* 18:2217)
64. COULSON, ROGER WAYNE. *Relationships Among Personality Traits, Ability and Academic Efficiency of College Seniors.* Doctor's thesis, State University of Iowa (Iowa City, Iowa), 1958. (*DA* 19:1647)
65. HALL, OLIVE A. "Factors Related to Achievement of Home Economics Majors in Chemistry." *J Home Econ* 50:767–8 D '58. *
66. LINDEN, JAMES D. *The Development and Comparative Analysis of Two Forced-Choice Forms of the Guilford-Zimmerman Temperament Survey.* Doctor's thesis, Purdue University (Lafayette, Ind.), 1958. (*DA* 18:2199)
67. MCKINNEY, EVA DORIS. *The Relationships Between Certain Factors of Personality and Selected Components of Physical Fitness of College Freshmen Women.* Doctor's thesis, Boston University (Boston, Mass.), 1958. (*DA* 19:1287)
68. SHAW, MERVILLE C., AND GRUBB, JAMES. "Hostility and Able High School Underachievers." *J Counsel Psychol* 5:263–6 w '58. * (*PA* 34:3413)
69. SINGER, STANLEY L.; STEFFLRE, BUFORD; AND THOMPSON, FRED W. "Temperament Scores and Socio-economic Status." *J Counsel Psychol* 5:281–4 w '58. * (*PA* 34:2791)
70. WEBB, SAM C., AND GOODLING, RICHARD A. "Test Validity in a Methodist Theology School." *Ed & Psychol Meas* 18:859–66 w '58. * (*PA* 34:2123)
71. WEITZENHOFFER, ANDRÉ M., AND WEITZENHOFFER, GENEVA B. "Personality and Hypnotic Susceptibility." *Am J Clin Hypnosis* 1:79–82 O '58. * (*PA* 34:4414)
72. BENDIG, A. W. "The Relationship of Scales of Extraversion-Introversion and Emotionality to Guilford's O, F, and P Scales." *J Psychol Studies* 11:49–51 N–D '59. * (*PA* 34:5597)
73. GAY, JAMES D. "A Comparison of Certain Aspects of

Personality of College Fraternity and Nonfraternity Men." *Proc W Va Acad Sci* 29:87–90 My '59. * (*PA* 34:2764)
74. GRUBER, JOSEPH JOHN, JR. *A Comparative Study of Employed Male Physical Education Graduates and Physical Education Undergraduate Students on Selected Instruments.* Doctor's thesis, Purdue University (Lafayette, Ind.), 1959. (*DA* 20:2676)
75. GUILFORD, J. P. *Personality,* pp. 184–7. New York: McGraw-Hill Book Co., Inc., 1959. Pp. xiii, 562. *
76. JACOBS, ALFRED, AND SCHLAFF, ALLAN. "Falsification on the Guilford-Zimmerman Temperament Survey." *Psychol Newsl* 10:138–45 Ja–F '59. * (*PA* 34:1024)
77. KENNEY, RAYMOND CARROLL. *An Analysis of Self Perceptions in Counselor Trainees.* Doctor's thesis, University of Texas (Austin, Tex.), 1959. (*DA* 20:2677)
78. KHAN, LILIAN. *Factor Analysis of Certain Aptitude and Personality Variables.* Doctor's thesis, University of Southern California (Los Angeles, Calif.), 1959. (*DA* 20:2889)
79. KLUGH, HENRY E., AND BENDIG, A. W. "The Guilford-Zimmerman Temperament Survey and Intelligence." *Psychol Newsl* 10:96–7 Ja–F '59. * (*PA* 34:1033)
80. LINDEN, JAMES D., AND OLSON, KAY W. "A Comparative Analysis of Selected Guilford-Zimmerman Temperament Survey Scales With the Taylor Manifest Anxiety Scale." *J Clin Psychol* 15:295–8 Jl '59. * (*PA* 35:3457)
81. MANHEIM, HENRY L. "Personality Differences of Members of Two Political Parties." *J Social Psychol* 50:261–8 N '59. * (*PA* 35:4833)
82. MANN, RICHARD D. "A Review of the Relationships Between Personality and Performance in Small Groups." *Psychol B* 56:241–70 Jl '59. * (*PA* 34:4194)
83. PALACIOS, JOHN RAYMOND. *A Validation Study of Selected Tests for Possible Use in Admission to Professional Education Sequences at Purdue University.* Doctor's thesis, Purdue University (Lafayette, Ind.), 1959. (*DA* 20:2679)
84. PATTERSON, HOWARD ROSCOE. *The Relationship Between Personality Traits and Preferences for Instructional Methods.* Doctor's thesis, North Texas State College (Denton, Tex.), 1959. (*DA* 20:2906)
85. ROBINSON, TED R. *Guilford-Zimmerman Temperament Profiles of Iowa Vocational Agriculture Instructors.* Master's thesis, Iowa State University (Ames, Iowa), 1959.
86. THRASH, PATRICIA ANN. *Women Student Leaders at Northwestern University: Their Characteristics, Self-Concepts, and Attitudes Toward the University.* Doctor's thesis, Northwestern University (Evanston, Ill.), 1959. (*DA* 20:3638)
87. TUCKER, WOODIE L. *The Relationship Between Personality Traits and Basic Skill in Typewriting.* Doctor's thesis, University of Pittsburgh (Pittsburgh, Pa.), 1959. (*DA* 20:1694)
88. VINEYARD, EDWIN E. "A Study of the Independence of Choice of Science or Non-Science Major and Measures of Personality Traits." *Sci Ed* 43:130–3 Mr '59. *
89. WAGNER, EDWIN ERIC. *Predicting Success for Young Executives From Objective Test Scores and Personal Data.* Doctor's thesis, Temple University (Philadelphia, Pa.), 1959. (*DA* 20:3371)
90. WILSON, JOHN E. "Evaluating a Four Year Sales Selection Program." *Personnel Psychol* 12:97–104 sp '59. * (*PA* 34:3533)
91. WITHERSPOON, PAUL, AND MELBERG, M. E. "Relationship Between Grade-Point Averages and Sectional Scores of the Guilford-Zimmerman Temperament Survey." *Ed & Psychol Meas* 19:673–4 w '59. * (*PA* 34:6577)
92. BALDWIN, THOMAS SANDERSON. *The Relationships Among Personality, Cognitive, and Job Performance Variables.* Doctor's thesis, Ohio State University (Columbus, Ohio), 1960. (*DA* 21:3171)
93. BARROWS, GORDON A., AND ZUCKERMAN, MARVIN. "Construct Validity of Three Masculinity-Femininity Tests." *J Consult Psychol* 24:441–5 O '60. * (*PA* 35:4891)
94. BENDIG, A. W. "Age Differences in the Interscale Factor Structure of the Guilford-Zimmerman Temperament Survey." *J Consult Psychol* 24:134–8 Ap '60. * (*PA* 34:7365)
95. BENDIG, A. W. "Item Analyses of Guilford's GZTS Objectivity, Friendliness, and Personal Relations Scales." *J Psychol Studies* 11:215–20 My–Je '60. *
96. BROWN, DONALD JAMES. *An Investigation of the Relationships Between Certain Personal Characteristics of Guidance Counselors and Performance in Supervised Counseling Interviews.* Doctor's thesis, Ohio State University (Columbus, Ohio), 1960. (*DA* 21:810)
97. CARRIGAN, PATRICIA M. "Extraversion-Introversion as a Dimension of Personality: A Reappraisal." *Psychol B* 57:329–60 S '60. * (*PA* 35:4976)
98. CLARK, CHARLES MARVIN. *Changes in Response Patterns of Counseling Institute Trainees.* Doctor's thesis, Ohio State University (Columbus, Ohio), 1960. (*DA* 21:811)
99. EVANS, GLORIA CAREY. "Validity of Ascendance Measurements in Group Interaction." *Psychol Rep* 7:114 Ag '60. * (*PA* 35:3374)
100. GOWAN, J. C. "A Teaching Prognosis Scale for the Guilford-Zimmerman Temperament Survey." *J Ed Res* 53:345–8 My '60. *
101. GOWAN, JOHN C. "Intercorrelations of the California Psychological Inventory and the Guilford-Zimmerman Temperament Survey With Intelligence as Measured by the ACE." *Calif J Ed Res* 11:213–5 N '60. * (*PA* 35:4856)
102. GRUBER, JOSEPH JOHN. "Personality Traits and Teaching Attitudes." *Res Q* 31:434–9 O '60. *
103. JAMES, ALICE M. *A Study of the Relationship Between the Guilford-Zimmerman Temperament Traits and the Clinical Practice Grade for Physical Therapy Students.* Master's thesis, Boston University (Boston, Mass.), 1960.
104. KIMBELL, FONTELLA THOMPSON. *The Use of Selected Standardized Tests as Predictors of Academic Success at Oklahoma College for Women.* Doctor's thesis, University of Oklahoma (Norman, Okla.), 1960. (*DA* 20:4335)
105. MACKINNEY, ARTHUR C., AND WOLINS, LEROY. "Validity Information Exchange, No. 13-01, Foreman II, Home Appliance Manufacturing." *Personnel Psychol* 13:443–7 w '60. *
106. MARMORALE, ANN M. *The Interrelationships of Measures of Sensory Variability, Scores on Selected Performance Tests, and the Guilford-Zimmerman Temperament Survey.* Doctor's thesis, Fordham University (New York, N. Y.), 1960.
107. PEARSON, WAYNE ORLANDO. *The Relationship Between Item Difficulty and Interitem Correlation in the Minnesota Multiphasic Personality Inventory and the Guilford-Zimmerman Temperament Survey.* Doctor's thesis, Cornell University (Ithaca, N.Y.), 1960. (*DA* 20:4177)
108. SHIRLEY, JACK HAROLD. *A Comparative Study of the Academic Achievements, Interests, and Personality Traits of Athletes and Non-Athletes.* Doctor's thesis, University of Oklahoma (Norman, Okla.), 1960. (*DA* 20:4005)
109. WAGNER, EDWIN E. "Differences Between Old and Young Executives on Objective Psychological Test Variables." *J Gerontol* 15:296–9 Jl '60. * (*PA* 35:1328)
110. BAKER, ROBERT L., AND SCHUTZ, RICHARD E. "A Criterion Factor Analysis of the Case of Mickey Murphy." *Personnel & Guid J* 40:282–5 N '61. * (*PA* 36:4KD82B)
111. BENDIG, A. W. "Improving the Factorial Purity of Guilford's Restraint and Thoughtfulness Scales." Abstract. *J Consult Psychol* 25:462 O '61. * (*PA* 37:3136)
112. BENDIG, A. W., AND EIGENBRODE, CHARLES R. "A Factor Analytic Investigation of Personality Variables and Reminiscence in Motor Learning." *J Abn & Social Psychol* 62:698–700 My '61. * (*PA* 36:4CF98B)
113. BORGATTA, EDGAR F. "Mood, Personality, and Interaction." *J General Psychol* 64:105–37 Ja '61. * (*PA* 35:6415)
114. BORGATTA, EDGAR F.; IN COLLABORATION WITH HENRY J. MEYER. "Make A Sentence Test: An Approach to Objective Scoring of Sentence Completions." *Genetic Psychol Monogr* 63:3–65 F '61. * (*PA* 35:6435)
115. COOK, DESMOND L.; LINDEN, JAMES D.; AND MCKAY, HARRISON E. "A Factor Analysis of Teacher Trainee Responses to Selected Personality Inventories." *Ed & Psychol Meas* 21:865–72 w '61. * (*PA* 36:5HF65C)
116. FOX, AUGUSTA MEREDITH. *Relationships Between Personality and Leader Behavior of Elementary School Principals.* Doctor's thesis, North Texas State College (Denton, Tex.), 1961. (*DA* 22:2263)
117. HAND, JACK, AND REYNOLDS, HERBERT H. "Suppressing Distortion in Temperament Inventories." *J Consult Psychol* 25:180–1 Ap '61. * (*PA* 36:4HF80H)
118. HOWARD, MAURICE LLOYD. *A Study of Under-Achieving College Students With High Academic Ability From the Phenomenological Frame of Reference.* Doctor's thesis, University of Colorado (Boulder, Colo.), 1961. (*DA* 22:3040)
119. HUBERT, WILLIS JONES. *Personality Differences and Similarities Between Offender and Non-Offender Air Force Motor Vehicle Operators.* Doctor's thesis, New York University (New York, N.Y.), 1961. (*DA* 22:156)
120. JACKSON, JAY M. "The Stability of Guilford-Zimmerman Personality Measures." *J Appl Psychol* 45:431–4 D '61. * (*PA* 37:1257)
121. KAESS, WALTER A.; WITRYOL, SAM L.; AND NOLAN, RICHARD E. "Reliability, Sex Differences, and Validity in the Leaderless Group Discussion Technique." *J Appl Psychol* 45:345–50 O '61. * (*PA* 36:5GF45K)
122. KRUG, ROBERT E., AND MOYER, K. E. "An Analysis of the F Scale: 2, Relationship to Standardized Personality Inventories." *J Social Psychol* 53:293–301 Ap '61. * (*PA* 36:1HC93K)
123. MCKENNA, HELEN VERONICA. "Religious Attitudes and Personality Traits." *J Social Psychol* 54:379–88 Ag '61. * (*PA* 36:3GD79M)
124. MARKS, ALVIN; MICHAEL, WILLIAM B.; AND KAISER, HENRY F. "Dimensions of Creativity and Temperament in Officer Evaluation." *Psychol Rep* 9:635–8 D '61. *
125. MARKS, ALVIN; MICHAEL, WILLIAM B.; AND KAISER, HENRY F. "Sources of Noncognitive Variance in 21 Measures of Creativity." *Psychol Rep* 9:287–90 O '61. *
126. REES, MARJORIE E., AND GOLDMAN, MORTON. "Some Relationships Between Creativity and Personality." *J General Psychol* 65:145–61 Jl '61. * (*PA* 36:2HD45R)
127. SUTTER, CYRIL ROBERT. *A Comparative Study of the Interest and Personality Patterns of Major Seminarians.* Doctor's thesis, Fordham University (New York, N.Y.), 1961. (*DA* 22:328)
128. VAN WAGENEN, DONALD RICHARD. *The Relation of Selected Non-Intellectual Factors to Academic Achievement in*

Several College Groups. Doctor's thesis, Syracuse University (Syracuse, N.Y.), 1961. (*DA* 23:539)
129. WATLEY, DONIVAN JASON. *Prediction of Academic Success in a College of Business Administration.* Doctor's thesis, University of Denver (Denver, Colo.), 1961. (*DA* 22:3527)
130. WITHERSPOON, ROBERT PAUL. *A Comparison of the Temperament Trait, Interest, Achievement, and Scholastic Aptitude Test Score Patterns of College Seniors Majoring in Different Fields at the Arkansas State Teachers College.* Doctor's thesis, University of Arkansas (Fayetteville, Ark.), 1961. (*DA* 22:1091)
131. BALSHAN, IRIS D. "Muscle Tension and Personality in Women." *Arch Gen Psychiatry* 7:436–48 D '62. * (*PA* 38:2771)
132. BENDIG, A. W. "Factor Analyses of the Guilford Zimmerman Temperament Survey and the Maudsley Personality Inventory." *J General Psychol* 67:21–6 Jl '62. * (*PA* 37:3169)
133. BENDIG, A. W. "The Factorial Validity of the Guilford Zimmerman Temperament Survey." *J General Psychol* 67:309–17 O '62. * (*PA* 37:8008)
134. BORGATTA, EDGAR F. "The Coincidence of Subtests in Four Personality Inventories." *J Social Psychol* 56:227–44 Ap '62. * (*PA* 37:1247)
135. BORGATTA, EDGAR F. "A Systematic Study of Interaction Process Scores, Peer and Self-Assessments, Personality and Other Variables." *Genetic Psychol Monogr* 65:219–91 My '62. * (*PA* 37:3030)
136. CAMPBELL, JOEL T.; OTIS, JAY L.; LISKE, RALPH E.; AND PRIEN, ERICH P. "Assessments of Higher-Level Personnel: II, Validity of the Over-All Assessment Process." *Personnel Psychol* 15:63–74 sp '62. * (*PA* 37:3908)
137. CAMPBELL, ROBERT E. "Counselor Personality and Background and His Interview Subrole Behavior." *J Counsel Psychol* 9:329–34 w '62. * (*PA* 39:2294)
138. COOK, DESMOND L. "A Note on the Relationships Between MTAI and GZTS Scores for Three Levels of Teacher Experience." *J Ed Res* 55:363–7 My '62. * (*PA* 37:5678)
139. GUPTA, G. C. "Guilford-Zimmerman Temperament Survey and Nursing Profession: A Validational Study." *Manas* 9:51–4 '62. * (*PA* 38:4309)
140. HICKS, JOHN A., AND STONE, JOICS B. "The Identification of Traits Related to Managerial Success." *J Appl Psychol* 46:428–32 D '62. * (*PA* 37:5714)
141. HOGUE, J. PIERRE; OTIS, JAY L.; AND PRIEN, ERICH P. "Assessments of Higher-Level Personnel: VI, Validity of Predictions Based on Projective Techniques." *Personnel Psychol* 15:335–44 au '62. * (*PA* 37:7249)
142. KHAN, LILIAN. "Factor Analysis of Certain Aptitude and Personality Variables." *Indian J Psychol* 37:27–38 Mr '62. * (*PA* 37:6716)
143. LANNA, MATTHEW GEORGE. *Vocational Interests in Relation to Some Aspects of Personality and Adjustment.* Doctor's thesis, Columbia University (New York, N.Y.), 1962. (*DA* 23:4421)
144. MILES, JAMES B. "Aesthetic Learning Through Experiences in a Correlated Program of Instruction in Art, Music and Modern Dance." *Studies Art Ed* 4:34–45 f '62. *
145. ROBINSON, WILLIS. *A Validity Study of the Testing Program for the Selection of Students for Teacher Education.* Doctor's thesis, Purdue University (Lafayette, Ind.), 1962. (*DA* 23:2812)
146. RUPIPER, OMER JOHN. "A Psychometric Evaluation of Experienced Teachers." *J Ed Res* 55:368–71 My '62. *
147. SKLAR, MAURICE, AND EDWARDS, ALLAN E. "Presbycusis: A Factor Analysis of Hearing and Psychological Characteristics of Men Over 65 Years Old." *J Auditory Res* 2:194–207 Jl '62. *
148. STAATS, A. W.; STAATS, C. K.; HEARD, W. G.; AND FINLEY, J. R. "Operant Conditioning of Factor Analytic Personality Traits." *J General Psychol* 66:101–14 Ja '62. * (*PA* 36:3CJ01S)
149. STAGNER, ROSS. "Personality Variables in Union-Management Relations." *J Appl Psychol* 46:350–7 O '62. * (*PA* 37:5811)
150. THOM, WILLIAM T., 3RD. *A Validation of Children's Behavioral Categories Based on Fear, Against the Guilford-Zimmerman Temperament Survey.* Doctor's thesis, Pennsylvania State University (University Park, Pa.), 1962. (*DA* 23:1090)
151. WATLEY, DONIVAN J., AND MARTIN, H. T. "Prediction of Academic Success in a College of Business Administration." *Personnel & Guid J* 41:147–54 O '62. * (*PA* 37:5656)
152. WILLIAMS, DONALD EARL. *The Interrelatedness of Student Teachers' Temperament Traits, Their Attitudes Toward Youth, and Their Teacher-Pupil Interpersonal Problems.* Doctor's thesis, North Texas State University (Denton, Tex.), 1962. (*DA* 23:3255)
153. *Normative Information: Manager and Executive Testing.* New York: Richardson, Bellows, Henry & Co., Inc., May 1963. Pp. 45. *
154. BAGGALEY, ANDREW R. "Comparison of Temperament Scores of Jewish and Gentile Male Students." *Psychol Rep* 13:598 O '63. * (*PA* 38:8232)
155. BENDIG, A. W., AND MARTIN, ANN M. "The Factor Structure of Temperament Traits and Needs." *J General Psychol* 69:27–36 Jl '63. * (*PA* 38:4297)
156. BENDIG, A. W., AND MEYER, WILLIAM J. "The Factorial Structure of the Scales of the Primary Mental Abilities, Guilford Zimmerman Temperament Survey, and Kuder Preference Record." *J General Psychol* 68:195–201 Ap '63. * (*PA* 38:53)
157. BRITTON, JOSEPH H. "Dimensions of Adjustment of Older Adults." *J Gerontol* 18:60–5 Ja '63. * (*PA* 38:4098)
158. COOK, DESMOND L.; LEBOLD, WILLIAM; AND LINDEN, JAMES D. "A Comparison of Factor Analyses of Education and Engineering Responses to Selected Personality Inventories." *J Teach Ed* 14:137–41 Je '63. *
159. COOLEY, WILLIAM W. "Predicting Choice of a Career in Scientific Research." *Personnel & Guid J* 42:21–8 S '63. *
160. DASS, S. L. "Selection of Situations for a Personality Test Based on Movie Pictures." *J Psychol Res* 7:10–5 Ja '63. * (*PA* 38:2691)
161. GOLDSTEIN, IRIS BALSHAN. "A Comparison Between Taylor's and Freeman's Manifest Anxiety Scales." Abstract. *J Consult Psychol* 27:466 O '63. *
162. HUGHES, BILLIE EDWARD. *Predicting Achievement in a Graduate School of Education.* Doctor's thesis, North Texas State University (Denton, Tex.), 1963. (*DA* 24:1448)
163. KASSARJIAN, HAROLD H. "Success, Failure, and Personality." *Psychol Rep* 13:567–74 O '63. * (*PA* 38:8591)
164. KJELDERGAARD, PAUL M., AND CARROLL, JOHN B. "Two Measures of Free Association Response and Their Relations to Scores on Selected Personality and Verbal Ability Tests." *Psychol Rep* 12:667–70 Je '63. * (*PA* 38:6021)
165. LEE, EUGENE C. "Career Development of Science Teachers." *J Res Sci Teach* 1:54–63 Mr '63. *
166. LEVITT, EUGENE E.; BRADY, JOHN PAUL; AND LUBIN, BERNARD. "Correlates of Hypnotizability in Young Women: Anxiety and Dependency." *J Personality* 31:52–7 Mr '63. *
167. MARWELL, GERALD. "Visibility in Small Groups." *J Social Psychol* 61:311–25 D '63. * (*PA* 38:8309)
168. MURRAY, JOHN B., AND GALVIN, JOSEPH. "Correlational Study of the MMPI and GZTS." *J General Psychol* 69:267–73 O '63. * (*PA* 39:1751)
169. SINGER, JEROME L., AND ANTROBUS, JOHN S. "A Factor-Analytic Study of Daydreaming and Conceptually-Related Cognitive and Personality Variables." *Percept & Motor Skills* 17:187–209 Ag '63. * (*PA* 38:7418)
170. WANSER, BYRON ROTHWELL. *The Effect of Loss of Father Upon the Development of Certain Personality Traits.* Doctor's thesis, University of Denver (Denver, Colo.), 1963. (*DA* 24:1484)
171. WIMSATT, WILLIAM R., AND VESTRE, NORRIS D. "Extra-experimental Effects in Verbal Conditioning." *J Consult Psychol* 27:400–4 O '63. * (*PA* 38:4429)
172. WINFREE, PAGE, AND MEYER, MERLE. "Sociability and the Conditioning of Pronouns 'I' and 'We.'" *Psychol Rep* 13:781–2 D '63. * (*PA* 38:8325)
173. ZACHAREWICZ, MARY MISAELA. *Relations Between Teaching Attitudes of Prospective Teachers and Their Self Descriptions.* Doctor's thesis, Fordham University (New York, N.Y.), 1963. (*DA* 24:876)

For a review by David R. Saunders, see 5:65; for reviews by William Stephenson and Neil Van Steenberg, see 4:49 (1 excerpt).

[111]

★**The Handicap Problems Inventory.** Ages 16 and over with physical disabilities; 1960; 4 scores: personal, family, social, vocational; 1 form (4 pages); manual (14 pages); $3 per 25 tests, postage extra; $1 per specimen set, postpaid; (30-35) minutes; George N. Wright and H. H. Remmers; [University Book Store]. *

DOROTHY M. CLENDENEN, *Assistant Director, Test Division, The Psychological Corporation, New York, New York.*

This checklist of 280 items was developed for use with the physically handicapped, and is designed to provide "an estimate of the impact of disability as the client sees it and is able to verbalize it." The manual notes that, for the present at least, the HPI should not be used for screening purposes, since correlational studies using outside criteria have not been made.

Statements obtained from 2,870 responses to 70 sentence completion items which had been administered to a random sample of 100 disabled persons were edited to eliminate duplicate problems and problems applicable only to a specific impairment. Editorial changes were kept to a minimum, except to insure that all words used are at or easier than the fifth grade level. Illustrative items include "Try to forget about being handicapped," "Worry because handicap works a hardship on family," "Lack a well-rounded social life," "Find it hard to make a living."

Those items selected were randomized and submitted to 27 psychologists for assignment to one of four "context" categories, resulting in the following classification: 96 personal items, 68 family items, 54 social items, 62 vocational items. A tryout with another sample of 100 disabled individuals, including interviews with 35, provided evidence of clarity of instructions and items, and of comprehensiveness of the list. The normative sample of 1,027 was randomly selected from those eligible for services of a state department of vocational rehabilitation. Other kinds of agencies are urged to study the composition of the sample prior to assuming that their client group is comparable. Percentile norms are presented for each subtest; although "total test" norms are reported, their use is not recommended.

All administrations of the inventory, including that of the final form for which normative and reliability data were obtained, were by mail. The per cent of return exceeded 86, and "this, and statistically derived information of a technical nature, leads to the conclusion that no important bias resulted from the nonparticipating group." This statistical information should have been clearly presented in the manual.

The inventory is well designed for ease of both administration and hand scoring. A single template for each of the four areas is used on all four pages of the test. Although the manual states that the inventory is machine scorable, such scoring keys must be prepared locally (or by the publisher, at additional cost). The answer sheet has been designed for the IBM 805 test scoring machine, but it was not printed by IBM and inspection indicates the probability that the registration may not be sufficiently exact for accurate and trouble-free machine scoring.

Reliability estimates, computed by Kuder-Richardson formula 20, range from .91 to .95 for the subtests, which suggests sufficiently high internal consistency for use in individual counseling. Means and sigmas are not given. No test-retest coefficients are reported, although these would provide useful evidence of stability, a fact which is noted in the manual under needed research. One also wonders why intercorrelation among the subtests has not been reported, since such information would be of value both from a statistical and from a psychological point of view.

Instructions to the examinee include the sentence "Skip over, do not mark, those problems which you do not have or which you feel have nothing to do with being handicapped." This may mean that some of the problems felt by a disabled person but not, in his thinking, related to his disability will not be checked; these will have to be sought by other instruments or through the interview. The manual, in discussing interpretation, points out that "Area scores indicate which life situations bear the brunt of the greatest impact of the disablement." It cautions the counselor to note that low scores may mean a tendency to minimize one's handicap, or to cover up serious problems. Commendably, it is stated that "Avoidance of known problems....suggests the possibility of intense emotional feelings which must be handled with great caution. Only counselors well trained in clinical psychology should attempt to probe into such defenses."

Frequency of choice for each item by various disability groups is reported; also comparison of means for each subtest by such personal background variables as age, education, years disabled. These data are useful in enabling the counselor to compare an individual's scores with the average of appropriate subgroups. Since statistically significant differences are found on several of these demographic variables, and since the *n*'s are sizable, one wonders why norms are presented only for the total sample.

So far as this reviewer is aware, the manual is accurate in stating that the HPI is "the only instrument of its kind especially constructed for the disabled population." The developmental work has been carefully done, and the manual is modest in its claims. The publisher's interest in cooperative research is made explicit and a list of 12 areas for further research is given, including studies of the relationship of area scores to the individual's actual personality adjustment; studies of predictive validity in reference to outcome of rehabilitation counseling; test-retest studies not only over a short term (for stability), but for comparison of retest scores after application of various rehabilitation services. Despite the reviewer's belief that such research is imperative if the inventory is to achieve maximum usefulness, and a belief that at least some of the above mentioned research should have been done prior to general publication, the HPI may well be used as an aid to the interview and to assist the counselor in understanding the problems of a disabled client.

[112]

★Harvard Group Scale of Hypnotic Susceptibility. College and adults; 1959–62; adaptation of Form A of the *Stanford Hypnotic Susceptibility Scale* for group administration; Form A ('62, 8 pages); manual ('62, 22 pages); no data on reliability; $6.50 per 25 tests; $1.25 per manual; $1.50 per specimen set; postage extra; (50–70) minutes; Ronald E. Shor and Emily Carota Orne; Consulting Psychologists Press, Inc. *

REFERENCES

1. BENTLER, P. M., AND HILGARD, ERNEST R. "A Comparison of Group and Individual Induction of Hypnosis With Self-Scoring and Observer-Scoring." *Int J Clin & Exp Hypnosis* 11:49–54 Ja '63. * (*PA* 37:8085)
1a. BENTLER, P. M., AND ROBERTS, MARY R. "Hypnotic Susceptibility Assessed in Large Groups." *Int J Clin & Exp Hypnosis* 11:93–7 Ap '63. * (*PA* 38:4430)
2. ROSENHAN, DAVID, AND LONDON, PERRY. "Hypnosis: Expectation, Susceptibility, and Performance." *J Abn & Social Psychol* 66:77–81 Ja '63. * (*PA* 37:5238)
3. SHOR, RONALD E., AND ORNE, EMILY CAROTA. "Norms on the Harvard Group Scale of Hypnotic Susceptibility, Form A." *Int J Clin & Exp Hypnosis* 11:39–47 Ja '63. * (*PA* 37:8102)

SEYMOUR FISHER, *Research Professor of Psychology, and Director, Psychopharmacology Laboratory, Boston University School of Medicine, Boston, Massachusetts.*

The *Harvard Group Scale of Hypnotic Susceptibility* provides a quantitative approach to the selection of subjects for participation in hypnotic studies. It is thus particularly aimed at the researcher who requires relatively large numbers of a certain kind of hypnotic subject (e.g., very poor, or excellent) but is seeking some way to avoid individual evaluations of hypnotic susceptibility. Although group induction of hypnosis has long been utilized by researchers for preliminary screening and selection, the Harvard Group Scale permits a more systematic approach than heretofore available.

This approach is based upon self-report scoring by each subject at the termination of a standardized induction procedure. Available data indicate good concordance between a subject's self-report and observer ratings, suggesting that (under these conditions) "*S*s who have been relieved of amnesia following hypnotic induction are able, retrospectively, to report their performance under hypnotic suggestion with a high degree of accuracy" (*1*).

The Group Scale itself is modeled after Form A of the *Stanford Hypnotic Susceptibility Scale,* and yields a single score (from 0 to 12) of susceptibility. The score obtained in a group session correlates .74 with an observer's score in a subsequent individual session (*1*). Individual scores can be predicted from the group score with a standard error of estimate of 1.8.

Availability of the Group Scale should be of immense practical value to the hypnotic researcher as a rapid assessment, screening, and selection device. Other uses of the Group Scale will undoubtedly be suggested with continued use. For certain kinds of studies (e.g., attempts to modify susceptibility), where retesting on an individual basis would seem desirable, it is likely that additional precision may be obtained by including an individual pretest—that is, use the Group Scale as a preliminary means of excluding subjects, and then utilize individual evaluations for those subjects who will participate in the research.

[113]

Heston Personal Adjustment Inventory. Grades 9–16 and adults; 1949; 6 scores: analytical thinking, sociability, emotional stability, confidence, personal relations, home satisfaction; IBM; 1 form (16 pages); manual (39 pages); no non-college adult norms; $5 per 35 tests; separate answer sheets may be used; $1.85 per 35 IBM answer sheets; 40¢ per set of machine scoring stencils; 45¢ per manual; 60¢ per specimen set; postage extra; (40–55) minutes; Joseph C. Heston; [Harcourt, Brace & World, Inc.]. *

REFERENCES

1–2. See 4:50.
3–13. See 5:66.
14. DOTSON, ELSIE JENOISE. *A Study of the Agreement of Introversion-Extroversion Factors as Defined by Various Factor Analysts.* Doctor's thesis, University of Kentucky (Lexington, Ky.), 1951. (*DA* 18:1095)
15. ARBUCKLE, DUGALD S. "Self-Ratings and Test Scores on Two Standardized Personality Inventories." *Personnel & Guid J* 37:292–3 D '58. * (*PA* 36:2HE92A)
16. HOLMES, JACK A. *Personality and Spelling Ability.* University of California Publications in Education, Vol. 12, No. 4. Berkeley, Calif.: University of California Press, 1959. Pp. vii, 213–91. *
17. WRIGHT, JOHN C. "Personal Adjustment and Its Relationship to Religious Attitudes and Certainty." *Relig Ed* 54:521–3 N–D '59. *
18. MCDANIEL, ERNEST D., AND STEPHENSON, HOWARD W. "Prediction of Scholastic Achievement in Pharmacy at the University of Kentucky." *Am J Pharm Ed* 24:162–9 sp '60. *
19. MAGNUSSEN, M. H., AND MAGNUSSEN, M. G. "The Relationship Between University Dispensary Visits, Academic Ability, and Personality Factors." *J Psychol Studies* 11:221–3 My–Je '60. *
20. WELNA, CECILIA THERESA. *A Study of Reasons for Success or Failure in College Mathematics Courses.* Doctor's

thesis, University of Connecticut (Storrs, Conn.), 1960. (*DA* 21:1811)
21. HOSFORD, PRENTISS McINTYRE. *Characteristics of Science-Talented and Language-Talented Secondary School Students.* Doctor's thesis, University of Georgia (Athens, Ga.), 1961. (*DA* 22:2687)
22. KIESSLING, RALPH J., AND KALISH, RICHARD A. "Correlates of Success in Leaderless Group Discussion." *J Social Psychol* 54:359–65 Ag '61. * (*PA* 36:3GE59K)
23. KINGSTON, ALBERT J. "The Relationship of Heston Personal Adjustment Inventory Scores to Other Measures Commonly Employed in Counseling." *J Ed Res* 55:83–6 O '61. *
24. CRANE, WILLIAM J. "Screening Devices for Occupational Therapy Majors." *Am J Occup Ther* 16:131–2 My–Je '62. * (*PA* 37:4078)
25. NICHOLS, ROBERT C. "Subtle, Obvious and Stereotype Measures of Masculinity-Femininity." *Ed & Psychol Meas* 22:449–61 au '62. * (*PA* 37:5014)
26. DURFLINGER, GLENN W. "Academic and Personality Differences Between Women Students Who Do Complete the Elementary Teaching Credential Program and Those Who Do Not." *Ed & Psychol Meas* 23:775–83 w '63. *
27. DURFLINGER, GLENN W. "Personality Correlates of Success in Student-Teaching." *Ed & Psychol Meas* 23:383–90 su '63. * (*PA* 38:1427)

For reviews by Albert Ellis, Hans J. Eysenck, and E. Lowell Kelly, see 4:50 (1 excerpt).

[114]

★The Hoffer-Osmond Diagnostic Test (HOD). Mental patients; 1961; also called *H.O.D. Test;* card sorting test for the diagnosis of schizophrenia; 3 scores: paranoid, perceptual, total; individual; 1 form ['61, 145 cards]; instructions-norms ['61, 6 cards]; record sheet ['61, 1 page]; $22.50 per set of cards, instructions, 100 record sheets, and copy of journal containing reference *2* below; postpaid; [15–20 minutes]; A. Hoffer and H. Osmond; Gilbert & Co. *

REFERENCES

1. HOFFER, A., AND MAHON, M. "The Presence of Unidentified Substances in the Urine of Psychiatric Patients." *J Neuropsychiatry* 2:331–62 Jl–Ag '61. *
2. HOFFER, A., AND OSMOND, H. "A Card Sorting Test Helpful in Making Psychiatric Diagnosis." *J Neuropsychiatry* 2:306–30 Jl–Ag '61. *
3. HOFFER, A., AND OSMOND, H. "The Relationship Between an Unknown Factor ('US') in Urine of Subjects and HOD Test Results." *J Neuropsychiatry* 2:363–70 Jl–Ag '61. *
3a. HOFFER, A., AND OSMOND, H. "The Association Between Schizophrenia and Two Objective Tests." *Can Med Assn J* 87:641–6 S 22 '62. *
4. HOFFER, A., AND OSMOND, H. "A Card Sorting Test Helpful in Establishing Prognosis." *Am J Psychiatry* 118:840–1 Mr '62. *
5. STEWART, CHARLES N., AND MAHOOD, MARGARET C. "A Multiple Group Comparison of Scores on the Hoffer-Osmond Diagnostic Test." *Can Psychiatric Assn J* 8:133–7 Ap '63. *

MAURICE LORR, *Chief, Outpatient Psychiatric Research Laboratory, Veterans Benefits Office; and Lecturer in Psychology, Catholic University of America; Washington, D.C.*

The HOD is a card sorting test designed to differentiate schizophrenics from other diagnostic groups and normal people. The test consists of 145 statements printed on 3 by 5 cards which are to be sorted by the examinee, after shuffling, into two boxes marked True and False. Card responses may be recorded on a separate answer sheet.

The HOD items are concerned with aberrations in perception, thought, and feeling. One group of items resembling WAIS similarity problems measures the way the subject classifies objects; that is, it tests whether he uses a visual or functional classification. The total score is defined as the number of statements sorted True. A paranoid score is based on 15 statements while the perceptual score derives from responses to 53 statements.

The norm sample consisted of patients and normals tested by psychiatric nurses in two Saskatchewan hospitals, one a provincial and the other a university hospital. Patients in the university hospital were tested soon after admission and before active treatment. The chronic schizophrenics from the provincial hospital consisted of patients already hospitalized. Included in the norm sample were 121 non-schizophrenic patients, 100 normals, 158 schizophrenics, and 13 patients with organic psychoses. The non-schizophrenics are grouped by diagnosis, but the schizophrenics are separated only on the basis of duration of illness.

Conventional estimates of reliability are not given nor is it possible to compute these as no measures of score dispersion are provided. Reliability is defined as the experimental ratio of different to similar responses divided by the ratio expected by chance. Since the retest data are confined to repetitions just before patient discharge, their value is questionable.

What evidence is there in support of the validity of HOD? The tables indicate (*a*) scores increase with duration of hospitalization for schizophrenia; (*b*) schizophrenic subjects score significantly higher than neurotics; (*c*) after treatment, clinically improved schizophrenics have lowered scores. Only a few tests of significance are reported, and basic data such as standard deviations are not provided. However, from the frequency distributions of the perceptual and the total scores, it is possible to determine that if a total score of 30 or less is used as a cutting point, 71 per cent of hospitalized schizophrenics may be identified. The perceptual score does better since a cutting score of three or less identifies correctly 79 per cent of schizophrenics and 72 per cent of the non-schizophrenics. However, as no base rates for the various diagnostic groupings are given, the advantage of test identification over base rate prediction cannot be assessed. Structural aspects of the test items and of the subtests, such as their popularity or intercorrelations, are not reported. Only the correlation between paranoid and total scores is given.

The HOD test must thus be viewed as an interesting, partly validated research device in an early stage of development and in need of further statistical analysis. Especially lacking are data characterizing the norm sample and base rates on diagnostic groups. Since intelligence and education may well play an important role in response, evidence concerning these variables should be supplied.

William Schofield, *Professor of Psychology, University of Minnesota, Minneapolis, Minnesota.*

This is an objectively scored card sorting test designed primarily to differentiate schizophrenic from other psychiatric conditions. Format of both the test materials and scoring sheets is attractive and convenient. The 145 items appear singly in large, black type on 8.7 × 6.1 cm. plastic cards. Instructions for administration, recording, and scoring, and norms are reproduced on similar cards, and all are enclosed in a small telescoping box which separates into cover and box proper, labeled, respectively, in large print, "FALSE" and "TRUE"; these provide convenient containers into which the subject sorts the test items to indicate his response. The test can be easily administered by nonprofessional hospital or clinic personnel and is claimed to be applicable to "over 90%" of patients. Scoring is simple, objective, and should be completely reliable within the limits of clerical error.

The 145 symptomatic items represent perceptual distortion in the areas of vision, audition, touch, taste, smell, and time perception; thought disturbances and feelings are also tapped. A check on consistency of response, and presumably on the care with which all items are answered, is afforded by a subset of 20 items adapted from the Similarities subtest of the Wechsler scales. These items permit a response indicative of either a visual or functional classification; by repeating the same content with reverse format, consistency of response is tapped (e.g., "An axe is like a saw because they have handles, rather than because they are tools" and "An axe is like a saw because they are tools, rather than because they have handles").

Items are scored only when answered "True." Weighted scores (either 1, 2, or 5 points) for each card are based solely upon the frequency of a "True" response in a sample of "about 150 normal and non-schizophrenic subjects." Cards seldom (never or once) sorted as "True" by this sample are given 5 points; examples: "There are some people trying to do me harm" and "People look as if they were dead now." Examples of 1-point cards are: "People are often envious of me" and "My body odor is much more unpleasant now." Three scores are obtained: total score, paranoid score, and perceptual score. In a sample of 162 schizophrenics, the paranoid scores and total score correlate .82, while the comparable statistic is .69 for a sample of 125 nonschizophrenic patients.

Test-retest reliability as computed by any of the standard methods is not reported for either psychiatric or normal samples. Cumbersome and ambiguous ratios of the number of true responses constant from test to retest are reported for samples of normals and patients as evidence of reliability. It is probable that orthodox reliability coefficients would be satisfactory.

Failure to use customary analytic techniques in item selection coupled with the grossness of item content results in an instrument of limited diagnostic utility. There is sizeable overlap in the score distributions for schizophrenic and nonschizophrenic patients. Applied in an outpatient setting where borderline pathology and subtlety of symptoms make diagnosis difficult, this test would yield a high rate of false negatives. The authors report that one third of the lowest scores (least pathology) they have observed were obtained by diagnosed schizophrenics.

In a psychiatric hospital population of severely ill patients, the test would probably prove less useful for differentiation of schizophrenia than for measurement of levels of perceptual pathology and especially, by retest, for checking on the effectiveness of therapeutic programs.

[115]

★Holland Vocational Preference Inventory, Research Edition, Third Revision. College and adults; 1953–59; 12 or 13 scores: omitted items, infrequency, acquiescence, physical activity (males only), intellectuality, social responsibility, conformity, verbal activity, emotionality, control, aggressiveness, masculinity-femininity, status; separate forms ('53, 2 pages) for men and women; mimeographed preliminary manual ('59, 36 pages); profile [no date, 2 pages] of temporary norms for college students; no data on reliability for omitted items; tentative norms; $2.25 per 25 tests; $1 per set of keys; $1 per 25 profiles; $1 per manual; $1.50 per specimen set; postage extra; (30-

45) minutes; John L. Holland; Consulting Psychologists Press, Inc. *

REFERENCES

1. WALSH, R. P. *Vocational Interest, Their Stability and Personality Correlates in Hospitalized Tuberculosis Patients.* Master's thesis, University of Maryland (College Park, Md.), 1956.
2. HOLLAND, JOHN L. "A Personality Inventory Employing Occupational Titles." *J Appl Psychol* 42:336–42 O '58. * (*PA* 33:9955)
3. HOLLAND, JOHN L. "Some Limitations of Teacher Ratings as Predictors of Creativity." *J Ed Psychol* 50:219–23 O '59. * (*PA* 36:1KH19H)
4. HOLLAND, JOHN L. "The Prediction of College Grades From Personality and Aptitude Variables." *J Ed Psychol* 51:245–54 O '60. * (*PA* 36:1KL45H)
5. HOLLAND, JOHN L. "The Relation of the Vocational Preference Inventory to the Sixteen Personality Factor Questionnaire." *J Appl Psychol* 44:291–6 Ag '60. * (*PA* 35:4015)
6. FORSYTH, RALPH P., AND FAIRWEATHER, GEORGE W. "Psychotherapeutic and Other Hospital Treatment Criteria: The Dilemma." *J Abn & Social Psychol* 62:598–604 My '61. * (*PA* 36:4IE98F)
7. HOLLAND, JOHN L. "Creative and Academic Performance Among Talented Adolescents." *J Ed Psychol* 52:136–47 Je '61. * (*PA* 38:3201)
8. HOLLAND, JOHN L. "Some Explorations With Occupational Titles." Comment by Henry Borow. *J Counsel Psychol* 8:82–7 sp '61. * (*PA* 36:3LB82H)
9. HOLLAND, JOHN L. "Some Explorations of Theory of Vocational Choice: 1, One- and Two-Year Longitudinal Studies." *Psychol Monogr* 76(26):1–49 '62. * (*PA* 38:9340)
10. HOLLAND, JOHN L., AND ASTIN, ALEXANDER W. "The Prediction of the Academic, Artistic, Scientific, and Social Achievement of Undergraduates of Superior Scholastic Aptitude." *J Ed Psychol* 53:132–43 Je '62. * (*PA* 37:2010)
11. HOLLAND, JOHN L. "Explorations of a Theory of Vocational Choice: Part 1, Vocational Images and Choice." *Voc Guid Q* 11:232–9 su '63. * (*PA* 38:4746)
12. HOLLAND, JOHN L. "Explorations of a Theory of Vocational Choice: Part 2, Self-Descriptions and Vocational Preferences; Part 3, Coping Behavior, Competencies, and Vocational Preferences." *Voc Guid Q* 12:17–24 au '63. * (*PA* 38:6694)
13. HOLLAND, JOHN L. "Explorations of a Theory of Vocational Choice: Part 4, Vocational Daydreams." *Voc Guid Q* 12:93–7 w '63–64. * (*PA* 38:9339)

ROBERT L. FRENCH, *Vice President for Research and Testing, Science Research Associates, Inc., Chicago, Illinois.*

This is a "Research Edition" of a personality instrument designed for use with people of college age or beyond. In form it is a vocational interest checklist involving 300 occupational titles, to each of which a subject responds by indicating interest or lack of interest in the occupation, or, by leaving it unmarked, indecision. The instrument rests on the reasonable assumption that such preferences reflect the operation of significant personality variables. At the same time a unique advantage of the approach appears to be that subjects can provide this information without feeling that it is particularly self-revelatory.

A score can be obtained on each of 13 scales (12 in the case of the woman's form). These reflect an essentially pragmatic rather than a systematic, theoretical orientation. Potentially fruitful scoring dimensions were defined in the first instance after a review of the literature on personality factors in interest and vocational choice. Eight of the scales were then established by assigning items (occupational titles) which appeared intuitively to epitomize a scale definition. These were subsequently revised several times on the basis of analysis of internal consistency data and scale intercorrelations. Of the other five scales, three—Omitted Items, Infrequency, and Acquiescence—are response set scales. The Status scale items are derived from previous studies of occupational status rankings; Masculinity-Femininity items, from analysis of actual sex differences in item response.

Although some of the original scales were eliminated as a result of a cluster analysis and a useful degree of independence was achieved among those remaining, some of the reported intercorrelations are high enough to suggest that further reduction might be possible and desirable. Thus, of the 66 intercorrelations obtained for 12 scales on a sample of 100 male college freshmen, 38 are significant at the .05 level of confidence ($r = .30$) and 8 exceed a value of .65. It should be noted that there is some item overlap between scales; for example, a count of overlaps by pairs of scales for men reveals approximately 60 items in which the same response is scored in a pair of scales, and approximately 40 items in which opposite responses contribute to two scales. This condition does not necessarily reduce the value of the scales, but for simplicity of interpretation it would be desirable either to eliminate all item overlap or to provide in the manual a picture of the extent to which intercorrelations among scales are affected by this factor.

Most of the scales have acceptable levels of reliability. Corrected split-half reliabilities based on 100 male college freshmen range from .72 to .95 on various scales, with a median of .85. For 100 females, they range from .68 to .90, with a median of .79. Test-retest data for 38 tuberculosis patients yielded correlations over a period of about four months which ranged from .58 to .87, with a median of .74.

Various studies, mostly on a fairly small scale, have been reported bearing on the validity of the instrument. Statistically significant and meaningful differences are found, for example, between psychiatric patients and normal controls, and between these groups and samples of tuberculosis patients and criminal psychopaths. Likewise, meaningful differences in profiles have been reported for freshman students in the different colleges of a large university.

It is worth noting that certain scales contribute to the prediction of college achievement among students of superior academic aptitude. Significant correlations have also been obtained between certain scales and selected scales from the MMPI, *Gordon Personal Profile, Strong Vocational Interest Blank, Kuder Preference Record,* and Cattell's 16 PF test. Correlations with intelligence are negligible. Some significant correlations are found with age, most of these, interestingly, being negative.

The manual contains an interesting, useful, and conservatively stated section on interpretation, which summarizes for each scale the empirical correlates thus far established, outlines a clinical interpretation of the scale variable, and offers an heuristic, conceptual definition of the variable. Several actual cases are presented in conclusion, a development which hopefully might be expanded in a future edition of the manual. Tentative normative data are available from the studies of the various populations already noted. These are most extensive for the college student samples, which provide the basis for a profile chart furnished with the test.

In format the test blank, manual, profiles, and scoring keys are appropriate—possibly too appropriate—to a "Research Edition." Administration presents no particular problems, though it would seem that necessary time could be reduced by elimination of the last 40 items, only a few of which are used, and these in the "Infrequency" scale. The test is awkward to score, and it may be hoped that further development will produce a more convenient mechanical scoring procedure.

In summary, the Holland inventory is an ingenious empirical approach to personality measurement which is in a relatively early stage of development. At this stage the author recommends it only for experimental use by students of adult personality, a recommendation which this reviewer can endorse with warmth. Further work with the instrument should help to improve its efficiency and to identify more clearly important areas of application.

H. BRADLEY SAGEN, *Assistant Professor of Education, University of Iowa, Iowa City, Iowa.*

The HVPI is essentially a personality inventory based upon attitudes toward various occupations. The inventory consists of 300 occupational titles to which the respondent replies like or dislike. The items are grouped into 13 scales, including 10 personality scales and 3 response set scales which also serve as check scores. There is virtually no information about the female HVPI and all references will be to the male form.

Although the development of the HVPI is of a generally high order, several points can be raised regarding the resultant characteristics of the scales. The personality scales are not at all independent of the response sets. Six of the 10 scales correlate .54 or above with Acquiescence and 4 correlate .54 or above with Infrequency; i.e., "unpopular" responses. The reason for the high correlations with Acquiescence is obvious, since 7 of the 10 scales are composed entirely of "like" responses. Because an instrument may still be valid or invalid regardless of the extent to which response sets are controlled, the foregoing remarks do not necessarily constitute a major criticism of the HVPI. Nevertheless, the failure to control these additional sources of variance must be considered in any interpretation of the scales.

The relationships of the scale intercorrelations to the respective scale descriptions, although generally consistent, do indicate a few contradictions. The term "passive" is applied to high scores on the Responsibility scale and to low scores on the Aggressive scale, yet the relationship between the two scales is positive ($r = .41$). Similarly, persons with low Infrequency scores and those with high Conformity scores are described as culturally conforming, even though the correlation is again positive ($r = .25$). The most striking example is that in the suggestions for profile interpretation, Holland states: "For example, a subject who has the Responsibility scale as one of the high points would be expected to have the Mf scale low." The actual correlation between the two scales, however, is positive ($r = .41$).

Several of the scale distributions are quite positively skewed and thus are less than satisfactory for assessing differences among individuals at the lower end of the group. For example, on three of the scales 30 per cent of the respondents have raw scores of less than 3. Other examples of susceptibility to chance variation are also found; e.g., a person at the 50th percentile on the Mf scale may shift 20 percentile ranks up or down by the addition or deletion of two responses. (It should be pointed out, however, that the actual scale reliabilities are generally adequate. Only two have a split-half reliability of less than .80.)

The validity data are, for the most part, unimpressive. The majority of the HVPI scales significantly differentiate "normal adults" from psychiatric patients, but the difference is seldom more than one half a standard deviation, and hence the inventory would be of little use for screening purposes. Correlations with several other inventories are also reported, but few of these are substantial enough to be regarded as evidence of construct validity.

Several aspects of the validity data raise questions as to scale interpretation. Persons scoring high on Intellectuality are described as having literary and aesthetic interests, yet there is no empirical evidence to substantiate this point and, on the contrary, the scale fails to correlate significantly with either the Artistic or Literary scales of the Kuder. Secondly, the correlation between the Welsh A scale and Emotionality is nonsignificant, even though both scales are described as indicators of anxiety. Finally, the Intellectuality scale would be expected to differentiate the norm groups of college freshmen and normal adults, described as having the intelligence of semiskilled factory workers. The difference, although not tested by Holland, is obviously nonsignificant.

It is somewhat early to draw any definitive conclusions about the HVPI. Due to the almost total absence of adequate validity data, the inventory is not recommended for individual assessment or for routine use with groups. Furthermore, to this reviewer the failure to control for response sets, the inconsistencies in the intercorrelations, and the sometimes skewed or restricted scale distributions suggest the need for further revision. On the other hand, the attention given to the HVPI's initial development entitles the inventory to serious investigation before any final statement is made regarding its worth.

[116]

★The Hooper Visual Organization Test. Ages 14 and over; 1957–58; organic brain pathology; 1 form ('57, 4 pages); manual ('58, 13 pages); $18 per set of testing materials including manual, 25 tests for group administration, card material for individual administration, and 25 scoring forms; postpaid; specimen set not available; (15–20) minutes; H. Elston Hooper; Western Psychological Services. *

REFERENCES

1. HOOPER, H. ELSTON. *A Study in the Construction and Preliminary Standardization of a Visual Organization Test for Use in the Measurement of Organic Deterioration.* Master's thesis, University of Southern California (Los Angeles, Calif.), 1948.
2. HOOPER, H. ELSTON. "Use of the Hooper Visual Organization Test in the Differentiation of Organic Brain Pathology From Normal, Psychoneurotic, and Schizophrenic Reactions." Abstract. *Am Psychologist* 7:350 Jl '52. *
3. WALKER, ROBERT G. "The Revised Hooper Visual Organization Test as a Measure of Brain Damage." *J Clin Psychol* 12:387–8 O '56. * (*PA* 32:4482)
4. WALKER, ROBERT G. "Schizophrenia and Cortical Involvement." *J Nerv & Mental Dis* 125:226–8 Ap–Je '57. * (*PA* 33:4404)

RALPH M. REITAN, *Professor of Psychology (Neurology), and Director, Section of Neuropsychology, Indiana University Medical Center, Indianapolis, Indiana.*

The *Hooper Visual Organization Test* consists of 30 drawings of common objects, each of which is cut into two or more parts. The subject's task is to name the object. No time limit is set for the subject's response, but he is encouraged to guess after one minute. The score is the number of correct responses, half credit being given on certain responses to 11 of the items.

The manual describes the purpose of the test as being to differentiate subjects with and without brain damage. Some data are presented regarding validity, reliability, and the effects of age, education, and intelligence, but the references are to unpublished studies. While the manual summarizes these studies in some detail, desirable points of information are sometimes omitted. For example, in the only study referred to in which diagnoses were carefully established (normal, psychoneurotic, schizophrenic reactions, and brain damage), no direct comparisons of the groups were made with respect to age, education, or socioeconomic status. The brain damaged group performed significantly more poorly than the other groups and the distributions of scores formed the basis for a recommended cutoff score. However, it is difficult to assess the value and specificity of this finding without specific information regarding the extent to which the groups may or may not have been comparable on other variables. A second unpublished study, cited to indicate the validity of the test as a screening instrument for brain damage, used groups in which the diagnoses were admittedly insecure. Again, the subjects with presumed brain damage performed more poorly than groups with personality disturbances. However, they were also 6.2 to 8.8 years older than the other groups and had

1.2 to 3.3 years less education than the other groups (probability levels not given). Even though additional unpublished data showed a low correlation ($r = .27$) between education and Hooper VOT score and similar findings occurred in studying age, the possible influence of these variables deserves specific assessment in each study. Reliability data was based upon scores of college students and psychoneurotics rather than brain damaged samples, yielding coefficients of .82 and .78, respectively. Two published studies using the Hooper VOT have appeared. In one of these (*4*), evidence was derived to indicate that the scores were related to prognosis in chronic schizophrenia. The other study (*3*) compared "control" patients with patients suspected of having cerebral cortical involvement. The groups did not differ significantly in terms of the usual scoring procedures, but when a special scoring procedure was applied, the intergroup differences were significant.

In summary, there is not yet sufficient evidence to recommend the Hooper VOT as an instrument with special promise for detecting the psychological effects of brain lesions. Some of the preliminary results are of promise and suggest the need for further research. The effects of brain disease or damage are sufficiently diversified and complex that it would be naive to expect a single test to provide a very complete answer. It seems entirely possible that the Hooper VOT might eventually be shown to provide valuable information in the assessment of brain lesions if used as part of a psychological test battery.

Otfried Spreen, *Assistant Research Professor of Neurology, State University of Iowa, Iowa City, Iowa.*

Thirty objects, cut into several parts and arranged randomly on the stimulus cards, have to be named in this test. It utilizes the deficit of visual organization or "Gestalt function" in a similar manner as Rybakoff's geometric designs, Gottschaldt's imbedded figures, fragmented figures, and similar tests which have been used for the detection of brain damage. Since these tests are not available in standardized form, Hooper's test supplements effectively the available tests of drawing, object arrangement, immediate memory, and other tests of organicity by a predominantly perceptual task excluding motor and memory functions.

The manual is rather slim and poorly organized; there is no reason why the two available validation studies should be reported in journal style rather than integrated into the rest of the manual. From the first of these studies it can be inferred that a surprisingly high number of 79 per cent of the brain damaged patients were correctly classified with no misclassification in the normal group. In the second study, this percentage dropped to a more reasonable, but still respectable 64 per cent. The validative value of such percentages depends, of course, on the type and severity of impairment in the brain damaged groups and can successfully be compared with those of other tests only when all tests are given to the same patients. Furthermore, interpretation of the sample differences reported in the manual is difficult because no matching of brain damaged and control groups is reported. Misclassification for other than brain damaged diagnostic groups is described as very low for neurotics and relatively low for two chronic schizophrenic groups (22 and 33 per cent) in the manual, whereas another study (*4*) used the test expressly and successfully for the differentiation and prognosis of chronic and reactive schizophrenia with the chronic schizophrenia group achieving "brain-damaged" scores on the test. This obvious contradiction of Hooper's findings warrants further investigation.

The manual reports split-half reliability coefficients of .82 and .78.

No adjustment of test scores for intelligence and age has been made. From the data presented a moderate to low correlation between test scores and educational level and intelligence in normals and a fairly high correlation with intelligence in retarded subjects can be expected. The age correlation is reported to be insignificant in several normal and clinical groups up to the age of 60, but relatively high in aged subjects. In a second study with five younger adult clinical groups, the manual states that "the absence of significant correlations between the VOT and age and education as well as intelligence....imply that the differences are not due to such factors." It appears that an adjustment for age in older subjects is necessary and that the contradictory results in regard to intelligence need clarification; the results with other tests of this type suggest that adjusted scores for different intelligence levels may be necessary.

Qualitative features have been mentioned as significant aspects for interpretation. For example, neologistic, bizarre, perseverative, or "isolate" responses may be noted in a patient's response. No data are reported as to frequency of occurrence, significance, etc. It appears doubtful whether this aspect of a test with a small number of items, only a few of which are failed by most subjects, will be amenable to systematic use, scoring, and standardization.

The manual claims that "language functions are not important in the test." This statement is rather challenging in view of the fact that the test requires naming or writing of names and is designed for the detection of brain damage. A look at the brain damaged groups, divided into right and left hemisphere lesions might have been sufficient to convince the author that the influence of language functions cannot be avoided in the present form of the test although the vocabulary level of the items is low. The whole question of locus of lesion in relation to test scores remains untouched in this first edition.

The test appears to be a promising addition to the neuropsychological laboratory. For use as a single indicator of brain damage in a screening battery, other more established tests might be preferred until comparative studies with such tests have been made. The test might be more useful if supplemented with alternate administrations avoiding the use of language (e.g., picture multiple choice). It would seem necessary to investigate further the role of locus of lesion in test performance and to adjust the scoring for the influence of intelligence and age.

[117]

Hospital Adjustment Scale. Mental patients; 1951–53; 4 ratings: communication and interpersonal relations, self-care and social responsibility, work and recreation, total; 1 form ('53, 4 pages); manual ('53, 12 pages); $3 per 25 tests; 25¢ per set of scoring key and manual; 50¢ per specimen set; postage extra; (10–20) minutes; James T. Ferguson, Paul McReynolds, and Egerton L. Ballachey (test); [Consulting Psychologists Press, Inc.]. *

REFERENCES

1–5. See 5:67.
6. GERTZ, BORIS; STILSON, DONALD W.; AND GYNTHER, MALCOLM D. "Reliability of the HAS as a Function of Length of Observation and Level of Adjustment." *J Clin Psychol* 15:36–9 Ja '59. * (*PA* 34:3267)
7. MCREYNOLDS, PAUL, AND WEIDE, MARIAN. "Psychological Measures as Used to Predict Psychiatric Improvement and to Assess Behavioural Changes Following Prefrontal Lobotomy." *J Mental Sci* 106:256–73 Ja '60. * (*PA* 35:6530)
8. URMER, ALBERT H.; MALEK, ZENA; AND WENDLAND, LEONARD V. "A Hospital Adjustment Scale for Chronic Disease Patients." *J Clin Psychol* 16:397–8 O '60. * (*PA* 37:3425)

WILSON H. GUERTIN, *Associate Professor of Education and Psychology, University of Florida, Gainesville, Florida.*

The *Hospital Adjustment Scale* (HAS) is an instrument for rating the behavior of psychiatric patients. It has been adequately described in Lorr's review in the previous *Mental Measurements Yearbook.*

The scale's 90 items are marked as "True," "Not True," or "Doesn't Apply" by a psychiatric attendant or nurse familiar with the patient's everyday behavior. Three subscores are computed: (*a*) Communication and interpersonal relations; (*b*) Care of self and social responsibility; and (*c*) Work, activities, and recreation. Total score is derived by combining the subscale scores.

The chief criticism of the HAS relates to its weakness in reflecting multiple aspects of a psychiatric patient's adjustment. The subscales correlate with one another in the .70's. Subscale (*a*) items appear to sample in a rather haphazard fashion, but subscales (*b*) and (*c*) seem to sample important realms of behavior (*4*).

The HAS was the first published scale for rating hospitalized psychotics on the basis of behavior only. This worthy pioneer effort served to demonstrate the feasibility of constructing such a scale but it in turn has been made obsolete by the appearance of the *MACC Behavioral Adjustment Scale* and the even more recent *Psychotic Reaction Profile.* Lorr's *Psychotic Reaction Profile* seems superior to the other two in most respects.

For a review by Maurice Lorr, see 5:67.

[118]

★How Well Do You Know Yourself? High school, college, office and factory workers; 1959–61; 19 scores: irritability, practicality, punctuality, novelty-loving, vocational assurance, cooperativeness, ambitiousness, hypercriticalness, dejection, general morale, persistence, nervousness, seriousness, submissiveness, impulsiveness, dynamism, emotional control, consistency, test objectivity; Form NE-21 ('61, 6 pages, identical with test copyrighted in 1959 except for two interchanges of items); 3 editions (identical except for profiles): secondary school, college, personnel; manual ('59, 28 pages); supplement ('61, 2 pages); $7.50 per 30 tests; $2.50 per specimen set; postage extra; (20) minutes; Thomas N. Jenkins, John H. Coleman (manual), and Harold T. Fagin (manual); Executive Analysis Corporation. *

REFERENCES

1. JENKINS, THOMAS N. "The Problem of Individual Appraisal of Personality With Large Test Batteries." *J Psychol Studies* 12:261–71 N '61 [issued Ap '63]. *
2. JENKINS, THOMAS N. "The Second Order Components of Human Personality." *J Psychol Studies* 12:237–60 N '61 [issued Ap '63]. *

LEE J. CRONBACH, *Professor of Education and Psychology, Stanford University, Stanford, California.*

HWDYKY is an anachronism, harking back to that innocent prewar period when every psychologist interested in measurement had his own list of trait names and a companion "personality test." Unlike those instruments, however, it grows out of a long program of research. The late Professor T. N. Jenkins embarked on a mapping of the domain of self-description about 1940, and for some twenty years elaborated his factor analysis until he had identified no less than 139 "primary traits" ranging from the old standbys "General Morale" and "Conscientiousness" to such oddities as "Naso-Buccal Epicureanism," "Auditory Orexis for Non-Musical Sounds," and (!) "Sexorexia." His interest was principally in basic investigation and secondarily in the development of a "global" instrument of 720 items, selected from a 7,000-item pool, which he proposed to score on all 139 dimensions. Though the outcome of this most solemn of all attempts to factor-analyze personality is a reductio ad absurdum, the work was scholarly and informed. Unfortunately, Professor Jenkins' caution led him to postpone publication until shortly before his death, and his findings are now available only in a few rather incomplete papers and manuscripts.

The present short test, which extracts a mere 17 factorial scores from 120 items, is no more than a casual by-product of the research. The traits included were selected from the list of 139, but they are not in any significant way derived from the factor analysis. Traits with much the same names and meanings were present in the pre-1940 instruments of Guilford and others. The 17 traits appear to have been selected in the interest of practical appeal, because common-sense interpretations of them are available and because counselors and industrial personnel men are likely to consider them important. HWDYKY has been placed on the market essentially without validation, except as one can extrapolate from fragmentary observations reported incidental to Jenkins' other research.

Items are transparent, and items within a scale are often redundant. The "Irritability" scale consists of six items in which the subject confesses that he is cross or loses his temper when people criticize him, or when he is ill, or when things go wrong. Items were allegedly chosen to have high stability on retest and to have high loadings on the factors for which they are scored. Jenkins calls for responses on a six-point scale ranging from "Always" to "Never." This is likely to be less ambiguous than the response scales of other instruments, though not all the items lend themselves to this type of response. Since the scoring system allows from 0 to 5 points per response and each trait is based upon six items, trait scores range from 0 to 30. The person's score is markedly affected by any response set to use, or not use, extreme response positions; saying "Almost always" in preference to "Always" can have a substantial effect on his percentile standing. There are two control scores. One examines consistency on certain repeated items. The other, measuring "Test Objectivity," was constructed empirically and its significance is far from apparent; one way to earn a high score is to stick with the noncommittal responses "Sometimes" and "Often."

One criticism of score reporting in HWDYKY applies to almost every personality inventory. Testers ought to abandon the practice of plotting a profile along a percentile scale. In this instrument, a student falls at the 80th percentile for Irritability, and at the 15th percentile for Punctuality, if he earns 15 points out of a possible 30 on each scale. Even granting that a profile of raw scores is much affected by the wording of items, it is probably more nearly accurate to say that this boy is about as punctual as he is irritable, than to say that he is exceedingly irritable and exceedingly unpunctual. A profile plotted in raw score (or percentage) form, would emphasize the person's salient traits rather than his salient differences from other persons. Percentiles could be superimposed as supplementary information. In measuring personality and interests and attitudes, describing the individual is a more basic concern than comparing him with others.

Although the manual presents its information honestly, it is distinctly unsatisfactory. There are rambling discussions of certain points such as the implications of a low "Objectivity" score. There are unnecessarily technical remarks on factor analysis that the typical consumer cannot possibly follow. A multiple correlation of each score with the "factor score" it represents is given; this value of .90 or above is grossly misleading, being inflated by the fact that the items used in the multiple correlation also contribute to the factor score. A similar inflation vitiates interpretation of the factor loadings for items on which the claim for validity rests. (The manual provides a prime exhibit of the reasons for never using the phrase "factorial validity.") The vitally necessary score intercorrelations are not reported. While retest reliabilities are given, there are no internal-consistency analyses from which we can decide how well the items in a score represent the larger collection of behaviors implied by the trait designation. The description of the norm groups (e.g., "100 twelfth-grade boys") is damnably inadequate, and no doubt the selection of the groups is equally indefensible. Professor Jenkins' research program was extensive, but this test was so far from his center of interest that almost none of the calculations required to make it useful were carried out.

What can we say about the usefulness of the test? A median stability over several weeks of .75 and an estimated standard error of 2 points are not bad for a 20-minute test yielding 17 trait scores. A well trained interpreter will know that the instrument offers no more than a sketchy self-description. Unfortunately, the test is reportedly being sold to counselors and personnel men who have had just one graduate course in tests and measurements; HWDYKY is not at all suited for interpretation by such persons. Even if the manual were ideally clear, few users are able to make the intuitive corrections for differences in "Objectivity" that the authors call for.

HWDYKY is a reasonably well-edited and well-grouped collection of items. It is completely unvalidated with respect to practical decisions. Any subject who wants to falsify his report will have no difficulty in doing so. Its use should be restricted to well qualified counselors who employ a multiscore profile from a brief test as a starting point for an interview.

Harrison G. Gough, *Professor of Psychology, University of California, Berkeley, California.*

The current (1961) version of this questionnaire contains 120 items and yields 19 scores. Seventeen of the scales were factorially derived, and two (consistency and objectivity) were developed by nonfactorial methods. The 17 factorial variables were selected by Jenkins from the full set of 131 identified in his studies of personality structure.

The reasons for choosing the particular set of 17 traits are summarized in the manual (p. 1) in this way:

> The seventeen trait scores provided by this inventory are primary factors. They represent trait estimates of personality characteristics which have been found, from general experience in guidance and personnel functions, to be important for a wide range of the work, career, and interpersonal activities in which normal individuals are commonly involved.

The appeal, that is to say, is to the practical utility of the variables scaled in personnel and guidance work with normal individuals. These objectives are legitimate, but evidence, of course, is necessary to demonstrate that the variables in this test do have this practical relevance.

Unfortunately, very little such evidence is offered in the manual. Only three validational studies are mentioned, and these refer to differentiations between specialists and nonspecialists in the Air Force, between students who sought and who avoided counseling, and to correlations between the scales and the degree of disruption of speech under varying intensities of audiogenic stress. Perhaps a later edition of the manual will bring together a larger number of studies, and studies of more relevance to the uses for which the inventory is recommended.

In light of this lack of evidence, it is rather disturbing to find the section on case interpretations making many statements for which no validational bases have been established. For example, in the case of "Rhoda," a high school girl of modest ability who recently decided to seek a career in nursing, low scores on the scales for practicality and seriousness are said to cast doubt on the authenticity of her decision, and a high score on impulsiveness is seen as strengthening this doubt. Would a dependable research study of the stability of vocational choices among high school girls show the practicality, seriousness, and impulsiveness scales to have such diagnostic value? At least some evidence should be obtained before test users are encouraged to make inferences of this type.

In the case of "Dorothea," a stenographer being considered for assignment as a secretary to a major officer, a high score on the scale titled submissiveness is seen as a favorable quality. Should not scores on the scale for submissiveness be studied as predictors of job performance *before* such interpretation is recommended? An occasional "clinical interpretation" of this type would pose no problem, and indeed would serve to raise some interesting hypotheses. The difficulty in the manual is that gratuitous interpretations of this kind are made repeatedly, with no apparent recognition of the need for evidence and research documentation.

Another problem in the manual is its unsatisfactory handling of reliability. The 17 factorial scales contain only six items each; the attainment of an adequate level of reliability with scales as short as this would be extremely difficult. The manual offers test-retest coefficients (which range from .32 to .96, median of .76), mean item loadings on the factor represented by each scale, and the estimated multiple correlations between each set of six items and its factor. However, no measures of internal consistency for the 19 scales, as they are presented and scored in this inventory, are offered.

The manual attempts to justify this omission by saying, "current methods of measuring reliability can be highly misleading when applied to short tests." This disclaimer does not seem acceptable in a test developed factorially and whose principal appeal is to the unidimensionality and homogeneity of the items in its scales. Internal consistency data on reliability should be given along with the test-retest figures.

A third problem, and as surprising to encounter as the absence of internal consistency reliability data in a factorially-developed instrument, is the lack of any information on intercorrelations among the scales. The manual asserts in several places that the scales are independent and that they do not "influence" each other; yet no data are offered in support of this claim. An intercorrelation matrix among the 19 measures contained in this test is a necessity. Claims concerning absence of correlation between and among scales should be supported by empirical data.

A fourth problem is the contention in the manual that "almost all presently available personality questionnaires....view the subject's personality in terms of the presence or absence of behavior pathology," and that the present test is therefore an "important departure from ....tradition" which offers a "new and hitherto unavailable type of personality assessment." These assertions are highly dubious, as users of questionnaires such as the *Study of Values*, the *Sixteen Personality Factor Questionnaire*, the *Edwards Personal Preference Schedule*, and many others could testify. *How Well Do You Know Yourself?* is not unique in its concern with the normal individual functioning in a normal context. It might also be observed, parenthetically, that four of its scales (dejection, general morale, nervousness, and emotional control) would be hard to distinguish from the psychiatrically oriented devices with which it is contrasted.

A fifth problem is that the psychological implications of the scales are derived almost entirely from a study of the items each one contains. The danger in this procedure is that it provides no check on the common circumstance in which people who talk one way behave another. Are people who say that they (*a*) "always" or "almost always" find that others like to work with them, (*b*) like teamwork, and (*c*) see to it that others do their share of the work, properly described as "cooperative"? The way to find out is to study these people directly in their social behavior, to see if their behavior can properly be characterized as cooperative. The acceptance of inventory responses at face value can lead to rather serious errors in the forecasting of interpersonal and other non-test behavior.

This leads to a final criticism, which is that no data on dissimulation are presented. The test is recommended for practical use, and in some settings, clearly, respondents will be seeking to "fake" certain kinds of desirable outcomes. What would happen to scores on this test if an applicant for a job as a bank clerk, e.g., would try to describe himself as highly honest, punctual, and constructively ambitious, free from any rebellious or self-assertive tendencies? Could such dissembling alter the pattern of scores, and if so, could the fact that simulation had occurred be detected? A manual for a test proposed for use in personnel and industrial settings should consider such topics and offer specific evidence.

In summary, this test offers an interesting set of variables for measurement; its manual is well organized and clearly written, and the case studies point the way toward the kind of individualized interpretation which should be the aim of every test. However, these commendable features are opposed by a number of negative factors. Essential information on reliability, validity, and scale intercorrelations is lacking, unwarranted claims to uniqueness are prominently advanced, and personological data pertaining to the implications of high and low scores on the scales are entirely absent. Interpretations of an arm-chair, speculative nature are the rule rather than the exception, and no attention is paid to problems of dissimulation and self-deception or to the general issue of incongruity between manifest self-description and social behavior. At the present time, therefore, this test should be used only by skilled psychologists, whose personal insight and experience can compensate for the deficiencies of the manual.

J Consult Psychol 23:564 D '59. Edward S. Bordin. This 120-item inventory yields 17 trait scores, e.g., Irritability, Novelty Loving, Vocational Assurance, Submissiveness, Impulsiveness, and two scores regarding test taking attitudes, Consistency and Objectivity. The trait scores are founded on factor analyses. Consistency is simply the tendency to give the same answer to the same item at two different times. The test objectivity items are a refinement of a set empirically derived by differentiating two groups of subjects who, on the basis of interviews, were judged to differ in the realism of their conceptions of themselves. The general format of the test and manual leave something to be desired. The test booklet incorporates a profile and answer sheet and, thus, is expendable, which naturally increases the cost of using this instrument. The manual is written in a pedantic, sometimes opaque style. This test may prove equal or superior to other personality inventories, but the case is not proved by the data summarized in the manual. Although satisfactorily high multiple correlations are reported for the six items of each factor with that factor, the test-retest correlations, not unexpectedly, are low in too many instances. Norms for secondary school, college undergraduate, and office and factory populations of both sexes are based on small inadequately defined samples. While there is evidence of considerable internal analysis of the test, external validation is limited to three studies, all doctoral theses, only one of which has been reported in the general literature. Much more needs to be done.

J Counsel Psychol 6:248–9 f '59. Laurence Siegel. * The test-retest correlational values leave something to be desired, particularly in view of the paucity of validity data presently available for this inventory. The least reliable subscale is the one purporting to measure Consistency. The Consistency measure is so inconsistent as to lead to test-retest coefficients ranging only between .32 and .46. The authors maintain, "This, however, does not decrease the importance of the *Consistency* score as an individual index of consistency in answering test items." This statement is predicated upon the questionable assumption that it is better to measure unreliably with a brief (nine-item) factorially complex scale than not to measure at all. * the validity....is assumed from three validation studies performed upon the global battery which served as an intermediate criterion in the development of this instrument * This is slim evidence indeed for the validity of an inventory for which the authors make some extravagant claims. * The percentile norms.... are exceedingly weak. * These norms are deficient on two counts. First, the norms groups are pitifully small, ranging in size from 100 cases for secondary school males to 276 cases for female office and factory workers. Secondly, the constituency of the norms groups with respect to representativeness of the samples is not discussed in the manual. * authors ....have published an inventory with an item format that may prove irritating to the respondent, a set of scales that are not particularly reliable (from a test-retest standpoint), claims for utility which are predicated upon intuition rather than upon demonstrated validity and percentile conversion tables based upon inadequate samples. It is unfortunate that what seems like a good idea is so poorly implemented.

[119]

***Human Relations Inventory.** Grades 9–16 and adults; 1954–59; social conformity; Form A ('54, 4 pages); manual ('59, 4 pages, identical with manual published in 1954 except for format and supplementary validity data and references); no data on reliability; $2 per 20 tests; $1 per specimen set (must be purchased to obtain manual); cash orders postpaid; (20)

minutes; Raymond E. Bernberg; Psychometric Affiliates. *

REFERENCES

1. BERNBERG, RAYMOND E. "The Direction of Perception Technique of Attitude Measurement." *Int J Opin & Attitude Res* 5:397-406 f '51. * (*PA* 27:336)
2. BERNBERG, RAYMOND E. "Personality Correlates of Social Conformity." *J Appl Psychol* 38:148-9 Je '54. * (*PA* 29:3664)
3. BERNBERG, RAYMOND E. "A Measure of Social Conformity." *J Psychol* 39:89-96 Ja '55. * (*PA* 29:8529)
4. BERNBERG, RAYMOND E. "Personality Correlates of Social Conformity: II." *J Social Psychol* 43:309-12 My '56. * (*PA* 33:3492)
5. ADAMS, ANDREW A. "Identifying Socially Maladjusted School Children." *Genetic Psychol Monogr* 61:3-36 F '60. * (*PA* 34:7515)
6. GORFEIN, DAVID S., AND ANDERSON, LARRY M. "A Note on the Validity of the Bernberg Human Relations Inventory." *J Psychol* 54:65-8 Jl '62. * (*PA* 37:3008)

For reviews by Raymond C. Norris and John A. Radcliffe, see 5:68.

[120]

***The Humm-Wadsworth Temperament Scale.** Adults; 1934-60; 47 scores: normal (4 subscores), hysteroid (6 subscores), manic (4 subscores), depressive (5 subscores), autistic (5 subscores), paranoid (3 subscores), epileptoid (4 subscores), response bias (2 subscores), self mastery (6 component control subscores plus integration index); 1 form ('34, 8 pages); mimeographed manual, 1954-55 revision ('55, 126 pages, with addendum copyrighted in 1960); profile-work sheet ('54, 1 page); qualitative analysis tables ('56, 8 pages); nomogram ('54), with response-bias corrector ('50) overleaf; distribution restricted; service fees for business organizations retaining publisher as consultant: $1,350 for first year (includes 3-week training course for 1-5 persons and consultation service), $10 per month thereafter; no service fees for psychologists; test materials rented to licensees only; $25 for the use of 25 tests and accessories for first year, $5 per year thereafter; separate answer sheets must be used; $2.50 per 25 additional tests; 25¢ per answer sheet; specimen set not available; postage extra; (45-90) minutes; Doncaster G. Humm and Kathryn A. Humm; Humm Personnel Consultants. *

REFERENCES

1-13. See 40:1223.
14-44. See 3:48.
45-64. See 5:69.
65. ELLIS, ALBERT, AND CONRAD, HERBERT S. "The Validity of Personality Inventories in Military Practice." *Psychol B* 45:385-426 S '48. * (*PA* 23:1287)
66. SMITH, GUDMUND, AND MARKE, SVEN. "An Economical Design for the Control of Commercial Screening Tests." *Acta Psychologica* 14(2):144-51 '58. * (*PA* 33:9102)
67. GUILFORD, J. P. *Personality*, pp. 175-8. New York: McGraw-Hill Book Co., Inc., 1959. Pp. xiii, 562. *

JAMES R. GLENNON, *Director, Employee Relations Research, Standard Oil Company (Indiana), Chicago, Illinois.*

Those experienced in selection for industrial jobs should be convinced that temperament or personality is an important determinant of subsequent job performance. Those so experienced, whether as industrial psychologists or as practitioners with other background, would further recognize, in this reviewer's opinion, that the first difficulty would be in defining components of temperament and degrees of personality integration and determining which of these has vital meaning in the performance of most jobs. Assuming resolution of problems of definition, difficulties of measurement would surely constitute the next series of obstacles. Underlying the foregoing challenges would be the knowledge, contended by the Humm-Wadsworth authors, that temperament alone won't guarantee successful job performance even though inadequacies in this area can be highly correlated with failure.

The Humm-Wadsworth scale was designed for use in industry principally for application with job candidates. It has also had clinical applications and has been included in vocational counseling batteries.

The scale asks 318 yes-no questions designed, to quote the manual, "to elicit the patterns of attitudes, social reactions, and emotional tone of the respondent by comparing his answers with the answers of subjects of known temperamental characteristics." Slightly more than one half of the questions, 164 of 318, were found to be significant three decades ago in distinguishing differences in temperament among validation groups consisting of a large number of employed persons and a smaller number of institutional cases. The scored answers produce a primary profile of 7 temperamental components and a further breakdown into 31 subcomponents. Plotted on a two-chart worksheet, these provide the administrator or interpreter with a compact visual summary. Profiles can be interpreted by comparison with patterns presented by the authors (in the extensive manual or, more importantly, under the authors' personal instruction during the training course), or by those combinations based on the test user's experience with the instrument. Industrial norms are provided for interpretation and guidance with both component and subcomponent profiles.

The scale also yields measures of response bias (the number of "no" answers indicating defensiveness or suggestibility) and self mastery. The latter development came from the authors' research on a population of 1,000 permanent employees.

Original definitions of the temperament components came largely from the psychiatric theory of Aaron Rosanoff. Thirty years of industrial use and literally millions of applications have been distilled into observations of temperamental behavior, these descriptions being offered through the manual and through the authors' consulting services.

The seven temperament components measured by the scale are these: normal, hysteriod, manic, depressive, autistic, paranoid, and epileptoid. While these terms carry psychopathological connotations the scoring and interpretation yields plus, minus, or borderline measurements of the characteristics. The operational theory is that these components will be encountered in the general population and are, when in certain balance and control, effective constituents of normal, productive behavior. The user would recognize measures of self mastery and control as of obvious relevance in industrial positions. The weight given to control of these temperamental factors makes this scale, in many respects, a much more realistic approach to such measurement than is true of personality measurement instruments which give unique readings of temperamental qualities without any integral weighting of the dynamic interrelationships.

Early literature claims validity correlations in the .90's between inventory scores and case history assessments. A later report (*57*) correlated scale appraisals with success or failure as a member of the Los Angeles Police Force (the success criterion was attainment of staff membership and dismissal was the failure criterion) and had validities averaging .72.

This reviewer finds such validity claims beyond anything in his own experience. But this is of little matter, since he would advise all potential users (of any selection instrument or technique) to assure themselves of the contribution that would be added to their own present selection practices, rather than make the risky assumption that validity experienced elsewhere is anything more than suggestive.

Reliability of the scale, or, better still, consistency of the components, has been seriously questioned, in this reviewer's mind, by the work of Smith and Marke (*64*). These researchers claim that only three of the components (manic, autistic, and depressive) "tend to hang together." Reliability is not mentioned in the H-W manual. A personal check with a major user of the scale did reveal that reliability and "fakability" had been studied in their organization and found to be acceptable. Again, this reviewer would caution that the potential user plan local studies to be sure of these points.

The authors contend the scale should be used in conjunction with other tests, interviews, and other evidence of candidate qualities rather than being used as the only selection instrument. This contention is consistent with reasonable belief that job success or failure cannot be determined by temperamental or other factors acting alone, but rather behavior will be determined by many causations acting in concert.

The H-W scale is not a "shelf" item that can be purchased by mail order as can most psychological tests. The industrial user must, at considerable expense, receive personal training from the authors and enter a contractual agreement governing conditions of continuing use. Furthermore, the user must submit samples of his applications, from time to time, for the authors' review. While less restrictive agreements are possible for clinicians or professional psychological consultants, the authors contend this initial training and periodic follow-up are essential to successful use of the scale.

The scale can be administered to a large group at one time with individuals completing the test in from 45 to 90 minutes. The authors' accumulated experience shows 70 per cent finishing in one hour or less. Scoring by someone well trained can be accomplished in less than 10 minutes.

The manual gives detailed explanation of the history of the instrument and of the rather involved scoring and interpretation procedures incumbent in its use.

This reviewer would not recommend H-W for use in industrial selection where the number of candidates totals fewer than several hundred a year. This is so because the reviewer would insist on local validation and, secondarily, because the expense of using the scale could be justified only in large-scale application. These conditions being met, the scale deserves consideration for inclusion in a selection battery where it is expected a temperament or personality test could make a contribution to improved selection.

FLOYD L. RUCH, *President, Psychological Services, Inc., Los Angeles, California.*

In the 15 years that have elapsed since the *Humm-Wadsworth Temperament Scale* was reviewed in generally favorable terms by H. J. Eysenck, H. Meltzer, and Lorenz Misbach in the *Third Mental Measurements Yearbook,* some 20 articles concerning it have appeared in the literature available to this reviewer.

Only seven authors report attempts to measure the test's concurrent or predictive validity. In only two of these studies is it clear that all possibility of criterion contamination (advance knowledge of the predictor scores and/or profiles by the judges who rated performance) was ruled out (*46, 61*). In these two studies also there was no predictor contamination. That is to say, each Humm-Wadsworth variable was treated separately and not with knowledge of aptitude or other predictor scores.

Cerf's report (*46*) covers five separate studies, each study based on approximately 200 pilots in primary training. In three of these studies biserial validity coefficients on a pass-fail criterion ranged from 0 to .22. In one of the studies all of the validity coefficients were nonsignificant, ranging from .01 to .16. In each of the two other studies statistically significant validity coefficients were found for both the hysteroid and the epileptoid scales. In each instance, however, the maximum coefficient compared very unfavorably to aptitude test scores and added so little predictive power to aptitude scores that the Humm-Wadsworth was not included in the operational battery.

In one study reported by Cerf, case summaries made by Humm from the cadets' responses to the inventory were compared with training course success or failure. Nonsignificant chi-squares of 1.05 and 4.82 for 4 degrees of freedom were obtained. According to Cerf: "More than 90 per cent of chance deviations would have been as great." In another study based on 195 Air Force pilots, case summaries of temperamental integration made by Humm from the responses to the inventory were compared with the pass-fail criterion. In this study nonsignificant chi-squares of .11 and .34 for 2 degrees of freedom led the author to conclude: "More than 60 per cent of chance deviations would have been as great." This worker concluded that pilot success could not be predicted to an operationally useful degree from Humm's analysis of temperamental integration nor from his case summaries.

A study by Caine (*50*) of aviation cadets ($n = 400$) reports failure to obtain a useful degree of predictive validity. This reviewer found a tetrachoric correlation of .25 between the normal component and success, using the data presented by Caine. The other components were less related, as shown by the chi-square tests reported by Caine. These two studies agree that the various components do not have practical validity when analyzed by conventional statistical techniques.

A study (*57*) of 506 police officers appointed during the war emergency and 115 civil service appointed police officers in Los Angeles is subject to a number of statistical and design flaws which render it uninterpretable. A Humm-trained technician rated each officer into one of seven categories, from very good to very poor. The criterion was whether the officer was retained or dismissed on the basis of his job performance. Predictor contamination was present from knowledge on the part of the technician of intelligence test and other scores, but its influence was discounted by the authors, who state:

> The predictions were based upon test results; but, inasmuch as all officers already had been subjected to selection procedures which would narrow their range of aptitudes and abilities, and inasmuch as temperamental qualifications are among the most difficult to appraise by civil service procedures, it is the consensus of those participating in the collection and analysis of these data that the predictions were influenced powerfully by the findings of the Humm-Wadsworth Temperament Scale. They are, therefore, treated in this paper as predictions based on the Temperament Scale alone. It is probable that, if partial correlation had been used to rule out the effect of intelligence, aptitude, educational preparation, interest, and physical fitness, the effectiveness of the predictions would appear higher than it does here.

For some reason not clear to this reviewer, such partial correlations were not reported. The degree to which an officer's superiors were influenced by their knowledge of the predictor rating in their decision to retain or discharge is not known. If the Humm-Wadsworth ratings were routinely kept in each officer's personnel file and the file was available to each officer's superiors, it is probable that contamination was present.

Glaring as the flaws in the design of the study may be, they are overshadowed by the almost inconceivable misapplication of statistical techniques in the analysis of results. Rather than reporting validity in terms of the correlation between predictor and criterion, the authors divide one sample of 506 police officers into three criterion groups—discharged, resigned, and remaining—and then somewhat mysteriously report a validity coefficient (Sheppard's method of unlike signs) for the discharged group considered alone. This coefficient of .96 is reported as describing the relationship between predictions and this *single* criterion group, without regard to the rest of the sample! Similarly computed correlations on other samples range as low as .54, which is purported to describe the validity of the predictions for a sample of 48 staff members upon which no criterion was available, other than the fact that they were all "successful police workers."

A study of the predictive validity of the Humm-Wadsworth in the selection of salesmen was reported by Harrell (*53*). From the writeup of this study it is not clear whether or not there was predictor contamination. If the practice of the Humm-trained technician was to evaluate the profile and make his prediction with prior knowledge of intelligence test scores as was the case in the Los Angeles police study, there could have been an unknown amount of predictor contamination. If the Humm-Wadsworth ratings went into the employee's file and were available to his superiors, there could have been criterion contamination.

In the Harrell study salesmen ($n = 168$) were rated independently by three supervisors. All three supervisors agreed that 97 of the salesmen were successful and that 39 were unsuccessful. The remainder of 32 were thought to be successful by one supervisor and unsuccessful by another and were omitted from comparison with the test results. Eighty-five of the 136 salesmen who were unanimously rated as either successful or unsuccessful were also evaluated by the Humm-Wadsworth technician as being definitely a good prospect or definitely a poor prospect. Among the 60 prospects recommended on the basis of the Humm-Wadsworth 50, or 83 per cent, proved successful on the job. The corresponding figure for all 85 salesmen was 62, or 73 per cent successful. Because of the lack of knowledge as to the degree of predictor or criterion contamination, it is impossible to determine whether or not the indicated relationship is of practical value.

It is interesting to note that when the mean component scores of the successful and the unsuccessful groups were compared, no statistically or practically significant differences were found. This discrepancy can be explained on the basis that the global profile interpretations advocated by Humm (*54*) can get predictive power out of elements which, taken by themselves, are valueless. Such an interpretation could be accepted only on the assumption that criterion contamination, as well as predictor contamination, has been ruled out.

A follow-up study by Gilliland and Newman (*61*) of 405 "white collar" employees was made 10 years after they had been tested with the Humm-Wadsworth. Of these, 191 were still employed and were performing satisfactorily at the time of the study, another 139 had terminated but without any unfavorable service record, while another 75 had been dismissed or had resigned while still on probation. Of the still-employed group 9.4 per cent had very good profile ratings. Of the 139 no longer employed but with no evidence of success while employed, the corresponding figure was 12.2 per cent. Of the 75 who were dismissed for cause or withdrew during probation, 12.0 per cent were given very good ratings. This study has been criticized by Humm and Humm (*62*) on the basis that Gilliland and Newman did not understand how to rate profiles.

Several studies have reported relationships between Humm-Wadsworth scores and profiles and criteria other than success or failure in training or job performance. In a study of 30 academic underachievers and 31 overachievers, no significant differences were found by Fortune (*52*). A study (*47*) of 106 hospitalized alcoholics compared with a control group of 179 showed the controls to be significantly higher (1 per cent level) on the normal component, and the alcoholics to be significantly higher (9 per cent level) on the hysteroid component. The control group had nearly two more years of schooling. In a study of 56 college students, Greenberg and Gilliland (*60*) found the Humm-Wadsworth component correlating highest with basal metabolic rate was autistic ($r = -.27$, significant at the 5 per cent level). Two studies (*56, 59*) agree in finding that essentially zero correlation exists between the similarly named components of the Humm-Wadsworth and the MMPI. A recent study by Smith and Marke (*64*) sheds light on the lack of correlation between the similarly defined components of the Humm-Wadsworth and MMPI "scales." These workers, using a method of scale analysis developed by Likert, discovered that the Humm-Wadsworth components are so lacking in internal consistency as to fail to meet quite lenient demands for one-dimensionality.

CONCLUSION. Taken as a whole, the reported evidence suggests that the *Humm-Wadsworth Temperament Scale,* despite its some thirty years of age, be regarded as an experimental device and not a promising one at that.

For reviews by H. J. Eysenck, H. Meltzer, and Lorenz Misbach of the 1940 edition, see 3:48; for reviews by Forrest A. Kingsbury and P. E. Vernon, see 40:1223; for a review by Daniel A. Prescott of an earlier edition, see 38:920.

[121]

***The IPAT Anxiety Scale Questionnaire.** Ages 14 and over; 1957–63; also called *IPAT Anxiety Scale;* title on test is *IPAT Self Analysis Form;* 6 scores: self sentiment development, ego strength, protension of paranoid trend, guilt proneness, ergic tension, total anxiety; 1 form ('57, 4 pages); manual, second edition ('63, 16 pages); $3 per 25 tests; 50¢ per scoring key; $1.80 per manual; $2.40 per specimen set; cash orders postpaid; (5–10) minutes; Raymond B. Cattell and I. H. Scheier (manual); Institute for Personality and Ability Testing. *

REFERENCES

1. CATTELL, RAYMOND B. "The Conceptual and Test Distinction of Neuroticism and Anxiety." *J Clin Psychol* 13:221–33 Jl '57. * (*PA* 32:5484)
2. CATTELL, RAYMOND B., AND SCHEIER, IVAN H. "Clinical Validities by Analyzing the Psychiatrist Exemplified in Relation to Anxiety Diagnoses." *Am J Orthopsychiatry* 28:699–713 O '58. * (*PA* 33:10313)
3. RAWN, MOSS L. "The Overt-Covert Anxiety Index and Hostility." *J Clin Psychol* 14:279–80 Jl '58. * (*PA* 33:8387)
4. BENDIG, A. W. "College Norms for and Concurrent Validity of Cattell's IPAT Anxiety Scale." *Psychol Newsl* 10:263–7 My–Je '59. * (*PA* 34:1338)
5. BENDIG, A. W. "'Social Desirability' and 'Anxiety' Variables in the IPAT Anxiety Scale." Abstract. *J Consult Psychol* 23:377 Ag '59. * (*PA* 34:4369)
6. CATTELL, RAYMOND B., AND SCHEIER, IVAN H. "Extension of Meaning of Objective Test Personality Factors: Especially Into Anxiety, Neuroticism, Questionnaire, and Physical Factors." *J General Psychol* 61:287–315 O '59. * (*PA* 35:785)
7. WOHL, JULIAN, AND HYMAN, MARVIN. "Relationship Between Measures of Anxiety and Constriction." *J Clin Psychol* 15:54–5 Ja '59. * (*PA* 34:2797)
8. BENDIG, A. W. "Age Related Changes in Covert and Overt Anxiety." *J General Psychol* 62:159–63 Ap '60. * (*PA* 34:8022)
9. BENDIG, A. W. "Factor Analyses of 'Anxiety' and 'Neuroticism' Inventories." *J Consult Psychol* 24:161–8 Ap '60. * (*PA* 34:8195)
10. BENDIG, A. W. "The Factorial Validity of Items on the IPAT Anxiety Scale." Abstract. *J Consult Psychol* 24:374 Ag '60. *
11. MOSS, C. SCOTT, AND WATERS, THOMAS J. "Intensive Longitudinal Investigation of Anxiety in Hospitalized Juvenile Patients." *Psychol Rep* 7:379–80 O '60. * (*PA* 35:2278)
12. BENDIG, A. W. "A Factor Analysis of Scales of Emotionality and Hostility." *J Clin Psychol* 17:189–92 Ap '61. * (*PA* 38:1034)
13. CATTELL, RAYMOND B., AND SCHEIER, IVAN H. *The Meaning and Measurement of Neuroticism and Anxiety.* New York: Ronald Press Co., 1961. Pp. ix, 535. * (*PA* 36:1HK27C)
14. WAGNER, EDWIN E. "The Interaction of Aggressive Movement Responses and Anatomy Responses on the Rorschach in Producing Anxiety." *J Proj Tech* 25:212–5 Je '61. * (*PA* 36:2HG12W)
15. BENDIG, A. W. "The Reliability and Factorial Validity of the IPAT Anxiety Scale." *J General Psychol* 67:27–33 Jl '62. * (*PA* 37:3276)
16. CATTELL, RAYMOND B. "Psychological Measurement of Anxiety and Depression: A Quantitative Approach." Discussion, pp. S24–8. *Can Psychiatric Assn J* 7(sup):S11–28 '62. *
17. LEVITT, EUGENE E., AND PERSKY, HAROLD. "Experimental Evidence for the Validity of the IPAT Anxiety Scale." *J Clin Psychol* 18:458–61 O '62. * (*PA* 39:5076)
18. PHILIPPUS, MARION JOHN, AND FLEIGLER, LOUIS. "A Study of Personality, Value and Interest Patterns of Student Teachers in the Areas of Elementary, Secondary, and Special Education." *Sci Ed* 46:247–52 Ap '62. *
19. SINGER, JEROME L., AND ROWE, RICHARD. "An Experimental Study of Some Relationships Between Daydreaming and Anxiety." *J Consult Psychol* 26:446–54 O '62. *
20. BENDIG, A. W. "Comparative Reliability of Cattell's 'Covert' and 'Overt' Items as Measures of the Anxiety Factor." *J General Psychol* 69:175–9 O '63. * (*PA* 39:1910)
21. FISHER, GARY M., AND KRAMER, RICHARD A. "The Relation of the Marlow-Crowne Social Desirability Scale to the Cattell Anxiety Scale." *J Clin Psychol* 19:204–5 Ap '63. *
22. LEVITT, EUGENE E.; BRADY, JOHN PAUL; AND LUBIN, BERNARD. "Correlates of Hypnotizability in Young Women: Anxiety and Dependency." *J Personality* 31:52–7 Mr '63. *
23. MANHOLD, J. H.; SHATIN, LEO; AND MANHOLD, BEVERLY S. "Comparison of Interests, Needs, and Selected Personality Factors of Dental and Medical Students." *J Am Dental Assn* 67:601–5 O '63. *

JACOB COHEN, *Professor of Psychology, New York University, New York, New York.*

This is a brief, rapidly stencil-scored, objective, self-administrable questionnaire for the assessment of general free anxiety level as distinct from general neurosis or psychosis. It is offered both for mass screening and individual clinical use with functionally literate adolescents and adults.

It is not difficult to write a respectable anxiety (or "neuroticism," or "adjustment") questionnaire which has some validity. Indeed, it may be difficult *not* to. What is notable about this test is that it is a mature fruit of a third of a century of both methodologically and clinically sophisticated large scale factor-analytic research. This point is made not merely as testimony to the quality of the product, but to advise the test user that the manual, although adequate by the standards of the Technical Recommendations, can provide only an overview of, and entry into, the research and theoretical background on which the test and its interpretation are based.

Raw scores are converted by table into sten and percentile scores. Separate and combined sex norms are provided for adults ($n = 935$), college students ($n = 1{,}392$), and teenagers ($n = 525$). Apart from age, no demographic data are given for the norm samples, a deficiency for some purposes particularly in the case of general adult norms.

The test is an immediate outgrowth of a series of 14 replicated researches with the longer IPAT 16 PF test. The largest of four second-order factors of the correlations of these 16 primaries is interpreted as general or free anxiety and contains loadings for five of the primaries ranging from .45 to .67. The 40 items of the present anxiety scale were selected from these five scales of the 16 PF so as to provide approximate optimal weighting in the total score of the five components.

In addition, the 40 items are also divided so as to yield separate "covert" and "overt" anxiety scores, whose ratio or difference is offered for interpretation. Unlike the five component subscores, the overt-covert distinction receives no warrant from the extensive factor-analytic studies.

Reliability coefficients for the total anxiety score, depending on type and the nature of the group, range from .80 to .93, an adequate level for most purposes. The same cannot be said for the homogeneity reliabilities of the five component scores (based on 4–12 items), which range from .26 to .60. No reliabilities are given in the manual for combinations of overt and covert anxiety scores, but a reference (*7*) gives .24 for the reliability of their difference. The authors warn about the low reliabilities of the various part scores yet suggest that they might be used as "suggestive 'leads.'" However, what is suggested by a score whose reliability is in the twenties will mislead almost as often as it leads. Adequate measurement of these components demands the use of combined Forms A and B of the parent 16 PF scales.

Evidence for the test's validity is varied and impressive. It rests first on the foundation of replicated factor-analytic researches involving not only questionnaire items but objective test and physiological measures, which established and cross-matched the anxiety factor. From these, "construct" validity coefficients in the range .85 to .90 are claimed. These are multiple correlation functions of factor loadings and are therefore probably somewhat overstated. Nevertheless, they are high enough. As for external validity, many lines of evidence converge: (*a*) Correlation with a relatively unreliable psychiatric consensus is .30 to .40 (.60 to .70 when the criterion is attenuation-corrected). (*b*) The mean of 174 anxiety neurotics differs sharply from the population average (by 1.3 standard deviations), which, expressed as a point-biserial *r*, yields .65 (reviewer's computation, assuming equal numbers of anxiety neurotics and general population adults are being discriminated so as to give a maximum correlation). (*c*) The means of 23 groups of clinical interest order them in a clinically compelling way. (*d*) Other data (on occupations, nations, volunteers for experiment, drug effects, etc.) presented or referred to further enrich the background for interpretation and thereby enhance validity.

The test correlates (about −.60) with the Edwards Social Desirability scale (*4*), but SD-like variables have been shown to load importantly in objective-test measured anxiety; thus, SD is conceptually part of the anxiety construct, rather than a response set which must be partialled out.

The *IPAT Anxiety Scale's* impressive systematic research background commends it for use as an overall measure. No competing test can compete in this crucial regard. For a quick measure of anxiety level in literate adolescents and adults for screening purposes, it has no peer. For individual clinical use, where accurate measurement of the five constituent components is likely to be more important than speed, the parent instrument, the IPAT 16 PF, would be clearly preferable.

For reviews by J. P. Guilford and E. Lowell Kelly, see 5:70 (1 excerpt).

[122]

★IPAT Children's Personality Questionnaire. Ages 8–12; 1959–63; title on test is *What You Do and What You Think;* 14 scores: reserved vs. outgoing (A), less intelligent vs. more intelligent (B), affected by feelings vs. emotionally stable (C), phlegmatic vs. excitable (D), obedient vs. assertive (E), sober vs. happy-go-lucky (F), disregards rules vs. conscientious (G), shy vs. venturesome (H), tough-minded vs. tender-minded (I), vigorous vs. doubting (J), forthright vs. shrewd (N), self-assured vs. apprehensive (O), casual vs. controlled (Q3), relaxed vs. tense (Q4); 2 editions; profile ('63, 1 page); $1.90 per pad of 50 profiles; cash orders postpaid; R. B. Porter and R. B. Cattell; Institute for Personality and Ability Testing. *

a) [1959 EDITION.] Forms A, B, ('59, 4 pages); manual ('60, 54 pages); norms for Forms A and B combined also presented; $2.20 per 25 tests; 75¢ per set of keys; $1.80 per manual; $2.70 per specimen set; (50–60) minutes.

b) 1963 EDITION. Forms A, B, ('63, c1959–63, 8 pages); no manual (1959 edition manual used as an interim manual); no data on reliability; no norms; $4 per 25 tests; separate answer sheets may be used; $2.20 per pad of 50 answer sheets; $1.80 per set of scoring stencils; $2.80 per specimen set; (60–120) minutes.

REFERENCES

1. PURCELL, KENNETH; TURNBULL, JOHN W.; AND BERNSTEIN, LEWIS. "Distinctions Between Subgroups of Asthmatic Children: Psychological Test and Behavior Rating Comparisons." *J Psychosom Res* 6:283–91 O–D '62. * (*PA* 37:8210)
2. CATTELL, RAYMOND B. "Teachers' Personality Description of Six-Year-Olds: A Check on Structure." *Brit J Ed Psychol* 33:219–35 N '63. * (*PA* 38:8071)

ANNE ANASTASI, *Professor of Psychology, Fordham University, New York, New York.*

As one of a series of coordinated personality inventories extending from the preschool to the adult level, the *IPAT Children's Personality Questionnaire* (CPQ) should be considered within the framework of the other inventories constructed by Cattell and his associates and of the factorial research on personality traits that led to their development. To facilitate continuity of interpretation, the 14 traits covered by this questionnaire are designated by the same letters and names as the corresponding traits in the earlier *Sixteen Personality Factor Questionnaire* and *IPAT High School Personality Questionnaire*. Each of the two forms of the CPQ consists of 70 two- or three-option items, including five items for each of the 14 traits. As in the case of the earlier inventories in the series, users are urged to administer both forms and obtain a single score based on 10 items for each trait. A 1963 edition, just published at the time of this review, contains twice as many items (140 in Form A_1-A_2 and 140 in Form B_1-B_2). Since the currently available manual covers only the shorter 1959 edition, however, this review will necessarily be limited to that edition.

The CPQ is designed for group administration, answers being marked on the test booklet. The problem of reading difficulty is handled by instructing subjects to ask the examiner for help with words they do not understand. In special cases, entire items or even the whole test may be read to the subject. The manual reports that each factor was balanced for "response sets" by having the same number of "Yes" and "No" answers contributing positively to each trait. This procedure controls only the acquiescence set, not the social desirability set; and there is evidence that the latter materially affects scores, at least in some of the CPQ traits.

Scoring is facilitated by well-designed cardboard stencils. Raw scores are converted to "staves," or 5-point standard scores with a mean of 3 and an SD of 1. Norms are reported for each sex separately, but age differences (which are only significant in three traits) are handled by the use of correction terms. The normative samples comprise 735 boys and 741 girls aged 8 to 12, not otherwise described.

Several types of reliability are reported, of which the most meaningful are probably parallel form correlations and an 18-day retest. When Forms A and B are combined to yield single trait scores, parallel form reliabilities for the 14 traits range from .32 to .67, and retest reliabilities range from .52 to .83. These coefficients were obtained in a group of 260 nine-year-old boys and girls in elementary schools. It is anticipated, of course, that reliabilities will be higher for the longer 1963 forms.

Intercorrelations of the 14 scores indicate little overlap among them. About half of these correlations fall below .20 and none reaches .50. Validity is discussed largely in terms of factorial analysis of items, based primarily on a group of 200 boys and girls not otherwise described. The manual contains detailed interpretations of the 14 traits, much of this discussion apparently drawing upon earlier research with older groups. Utilization of data external to the test is meager and the original studies to which reference is made are not readily accessible to test users. For instance, there are repeated references to unpublished dissertations and to an ONR research report. Many references are to Cattell's *Personality and Motivation Structure and Measurement* (see B119) in which studies pertaining to the age level 8 to 14 receive only brief and general mention because they were still in progress when that book was published. The test authors recommend the computation of an index of profile similarity between an individual's profile and the mean profile of various groups (e.g., delinquents, creative artists), as well as specification equations for predicting criterion performance (e.g., academic achievement); but the data required for these purposes are still largely unavailable.

In summary, it is difficult to evaluate the contribution that the CPQ can make because of inadequacy and vague reporting of validation data and insufficient description of normative samples. Comparative studies of the performance of this instrument in relation to other available instruments would also be desirable, as would direct studies of the longer 1963 forms.

WILBUR L. LAYTON, *Professor of Psychology and Head of the Department, Iowa State University, Ames, Iowa.*

This was this reviewer's first excursion to the wonderful world of perspicacious Professor R. B. Cattell. This man is creative and a prodigious producer of things psychometric. He has a great talent for neologizing and has generated some fascinating labels for the personality factors he has defined. Consider such factor labels as Harria, Parmia, Premsia, and

Zeppia. I can visualize a counselor saying to a student, "Threctia will get you if you don't watch out." After reading the handbook for the *IPAT Children's Personality Questionnaire* (CPQ) and many of Cattell's writings, I was driven to coin the label "Statisticophrenetic" to describe Professor Cattell's professional activities. He has done a tremendous amount of psychologizing about personality traits. Unfortunately, to date, most of his psychologizing has been supported only by factor analysis of items and tests and he has accumulated little evidence (in the nomological net sense) to support the definition of his personality traits. No doubt, further nomological evidence will accumulate.

It is perhaps not worthwhile to review the 1959 edition of the CPQ because it is being lengthened and renormed. However, the revision does not represent a change in the scales and according to Cattell (personal communication) it is aimed primarily at increasing the reliability of the scales. Therefore this review shall discuss information from the handbook (manual for the 1959 edition) and from Cattell, with emphasis on the present edition but with reference to the 1963 edition whenever possible.

The CPQ was planned for use with children in the age range 8 to 12 years. It overlaps by one year both with the as yet unpublished Elementary School Personality Questionnaire (ages 6 to 8) and the *IPAT High School Personality Questionnaire* (ages 12 to high school level). Vocabulary level, according to the test authors, is somewhat difficult for below average third graders and retarded readers. It is permissible to help children with words they don't know. The 1959 edition has two forms, A and B. In each form are 70 items presumably measuring the 14 factors (5 items per factor) considered by Cattell to be the same as those defined at the high school and adult levels. The test authors advocate using both A and B forms so there are a total of 10 items for each factor scale. Administration time for each booklet is approximately 50 minutes. The 1963 edition has two booklets, each containing two 70-item forms, A_1 and A_2 and B_1 and B_2. The authors recommend using all four forms so that one will have 20 items per factor. Separate answer sheets are available for the revised edition.

In the 1959 edition scores are converted to staves (5-point standard score scales with mean 3 and standard deviation 1). In the 1963 edition stens will be used (standard scales of 10-point units, mean 5.5) to align the CPQ with the HSPQ immediately above it and 16 PF for adults.

NORMS. The norms for the 1959 edition are based on 1,476 cases, 735 boys and 741 girls in age range from 8 years through 12 years but centering on 10 years. There is no information given in the handbook to indicate how this sample of children was obtained. There is no further information about the normative sample in the handbook. Profile sheets are available.

RELIABILITY. The handbook presents four types of reliability coefficients (stability, dependability, consistency, and equivalence) for each of the 14 factors for Forms A and B (1959 edition) combined and three types (all but consistency) for the separate forms. The reliability coefficients are based on "260 boys and girls of nine years of age in U.S. elementary schools." Stability coefficients are based on a two-week interval. The coefficients of stability for Forms A and B combined range from .52 to .83 with a median of approximately .70. The dependability coefficients represent test-retest (same form) coefficients without a time interval. These coefficients range from .63 to .87 for the two forms combined, with a median of approximately .75. The coefficients of equivalence estimated for the combination of A and B forms range from .32 to .67 with a median of approximately .55. The coefficients of homogeneity (split-half coefficients based on a mean of three splits) range from .30 to .64 with a median of .54. These reliabilities are reasonably good considering they are based on only 10 items but are not high enough to permit use of factor scores with individuals. The authors, of course, are now lengthening the scales so a total of 20 items can enter each factor score. This is in line with the recommendation of Cattell:[1] "it can be shown statistically that a scale meeting reasonable practical demands for validity and reliability requires, over this range, 0.3 to 0.5 loading per item in any required factor ten to thirty items as a minimum."

VALIDITY. "The essential *validity* of a factor scale is determined by the extent to which the

1 CATTELL, RAYMOND B. *Personality and Motivation Structure and Measurement*, p. 171. Yonkers, N.Y.: World Book Co., 1957. Pp. xxv, 948. *

scale score correlates with the pure factor which it claims to measure. This value is its 'construct'—or, as we prefer—its *concept* validity" (handbook, p. 12). Cattell calculates concept validity in three ways: (*a*) By the multiple correlation of the 10 items in each factor with the pure factor; (*b*) from the equivalence reliability coefficient "assuming that, by reason of suppressor action, the two halves of the test have nothing in common except the common factor they set out to measure"; and (*c*) a circumstantial or indirect validity which is the pattern of relationships between the factor of interest and the other personality and general ability factors defined by the questionnaire.

Theoretically, the use of suppressor action by items is a good one. Thus, Cattell advocates combining in a scale pairs of items, scored in opposite directions, which measure both a wanted factor and an unwanted factor to enable the items to suppress the unwanted factor in each other and to produce on the final scale only variance attributable to the wanted factor. However, the well known unreliability of item responses and instability of coefficients of correlation between pairs of items combine to make the suppressor approach empirically difficult. It is unlikely, even with item suppressor action, that a scale's communality is as great as its reliability. Thus the reliability coefficient is not an adequate estimate of the proportion of common factor variance in the items.

In deriving the coefficient of validity from the coefficient of equivalence Cattell takes the square root. The resulting coefficient is the index of reliability, in Guilford's terms the index of intrinsic validity. This coefficient, of course, is also what Tryon has labeled behavior domain validity. It may be considered to be the correlation between a sample of a trait and its perfect criterion measure. If this index is very high, one knows that the examinees are ranked by observed scores close to their ranking in a perfectly reliable measure of the trait as operationally defined by the items. Cattell might better use the square root of the communality as an index of what Guilford calls relevant validity, the upper limit of the test's validity coefficients.

The range of the indices of validity computed from the coefficients of equivalence range from .56 to .82 for Forms A and B combined, with a median value of approximately .74. The lowest value is for Zeppia vs. Coasthenia (vigorous vs. internally restrained) and the largest for Harria vs. Premsia (tough-minded vs. tender-minded). The data are based on relatively small samples and have not been cross validated. The coefficients of validity presented are based on the first edition (evidently a pre-1959 edition) of the test. They must be regarded as tentative and cross validation is a must before the CPQ can be used in making inferences about individuals.

Since Cattell believes he has discovered 14 or more pure factors in the personality domain, he feels free to discuss the behavioral meaning of these factors at all age levels from 8 to 80. He states:

> Finally, it should be noted that throughout these discussions, *young adult and adult* associations (occupation, adjustment, group behavior) are brought in to enrich the meaning of most of the factor-dimensions. These additional associations are a permissible part of the discussion because it has been established that each of the CPQ personality dimensions continues in essentially similar form as applicable to all later ages. Moreover, adult associations of a dimension are *useful* as well as merely permissible, since they point up the adult occupational, mental health, and other expectations for a child in terms of his present profile on the factors.

This statement is not documented in the handbook by longitudinal evidence, factor analytic or other, and if we look at the coefficients of stability given in the manual, the quoted statement is nonsensical.

If one assumes that the factors defined by Cattell through his measurement procedures are well defined operationally, one still must question whether or not he has established meaning for these factors separate from his factor analytic procedures. He has accumulated very little evidence that the factors identified in the CPQ bear a relationship to behavior outside of the test situation. Consequently, the bulk of the material discussed in the section under "Psychological Interpretation of the Fourteen Primary Personality Traits" is pure speculation. Now, all is not lost. Cattell has demonstrated he is a generator of good hypotheses so the handbook is a gold mine of hypotheses which can be tested by him and his colleagues and by interested researchers. However, the evidence for practical validity is inadequate.

CONCLUSION. It is this reviewer's opinion that the 1959 edition of the *IPAT Children's Personality Questionnaire,* because of its low reliability and insufficient evidence for validity, must be considered a research tool which should *not* be used in counseling or otherwise dealing with individual children. It may be possible for the revised questionnaire to be used to make inferences if it is more reliable than the 1959 edition and if there is substantial evidence that the factor scores allow inferences to be made about children's behavior. Lacking such evidence, the new instrument also should be used solely for research purposes.

ROBERT D. WIRT, *Professor of Psychology, Child Development, and Psychiatry, University of Minnesota, Minneapolis, Minnesota.*

The *IPAT Children's Personality Questionnaire* (CPQ) is an extension downward, to the age range from 8 to 12 years, of the *IPAT High School Personality Questionnaire* (HSPQ) and the *Sixteen Personality Factor Questionnaire* (16 PF). A further extension to years 6 through 8, the Early School Personality Questionnaire (ESPQ), is promised for early publication. The series of tests, with one year overlap between tests, will give continuity from early childhood through adulthood along what are purported to be the same dimensions of personality.

The test consists of two forms, A and B. The authors advise using both forms which gives for a single administration a scale of 10 items for each scale. Most test users will appreciate having alternate forms of the test but will be somewhat dubious of the stability of even a 10-item scale based upon the use of both forms.

The format of the booklets is practical for use by children. The questions are clearly stated and most questions require an either-or response which is to be indicated directly on the test booklet. The scoring is quite straightforward and easily accomplished in a few minutes; the test yields raw scores which can be plotted on a profile in staves (normalized scores ranging from 1 to 5). The handbook gives tables for converting raw scores to staves for boys and for girls separately, for conversion of staves to stens (normalized scores ranging from 0 to 10) and for the properties of staves as standard scores. Significant sex and age differences exist on a large number of the 14 scales.

The language used in defining the dimensions of the CPQ will be bothersome to those not familiar with the 16 PF. However, test users well acquainted with the now considerable literature on factored scales will be pleased that this new addition to the series, as the authors point out, makes possible some kinds of longitudinal studies of personality not before available. It is certainly true, as the authors state in the opening sentence of their handbook, that there is "a great need for trustworthy personality measures of children." That the CPQ is such a trustworthy measure is not established by the data now available.

The publication of the test was premature. There are repeated cautions in the handbook which warn the reader and potential test user that numerous additional research investigations are underway to clarify one point or another, to establish the meaning of certain factors, to improve upon the reliability of scales, and so forth. It is true, of course, that continuing research and refinement are desirable in the upgrading of all aspects of mental measurement and that an author need not wait upon perfection before publishing his work; but still he probably should not publish work designated as a useful practical measuring device and at the same time indicate that much study is yet required before the instrument can be safely used. Perhaps the authors of this instrument should be commended, however, for the care they have taken in indicating the areas of weakness which do exist in the CPQ.

The handbook is unusually well written in parts and quite worth reading for its clear explication of several important problems of test construction. There are sections on various meanings of reliability and validity and on the clinical use of test data that are elegant examples of careful reasoning and statistical sophistication. But when it comes to the specifics of the particular standardization of the CPQ one looks in vain for equal clarity. The numbers given tell the reader that certain correlations are based on "260 boys and girls of nine years of age in U.S. elementary schools" or that some other figures are derived from a study of 200 subjects, and still other data are reported to be based on 1,476 children. Nowhere are there data which *describe* the norm groups. For this reason it is, of course, impossible to know with what standard a test user is to compare results of his subjects.

The writing style of the handbook is often in poor taste, in that the virtues of the approach to testing used by these authors and the validity of the CPQ are over-sold. The reader is urged to believe that *all* of the fundamental dimensions of personality of children are reflected in the CPQ. The authors quite blandly assure the test user that the test is equally valid given individually or in groups, whether the items are read by the subjects or read aloud by the examiner, but they do not give data to support these contentions. Perhaps most distressing is the section on reliability and validity. The discussion of these issues relative to general considerations of test purpose is brilliant, but the relationship of these concepts to the CPQ is absent. The reader is given skimpy secondary data on validity and is referred to other sources for further detail. The references cited for this purpose relate almost exclusively to general texts on the subject of test construction and the measurement and theories of personality having nothing whatever to do with the particular standardization of the CPQ.

In summary, it may be said that the CPQ is a hopeful beginning for careful assessment of personality in children, but until further study is made this instrument should be used for research only.

[123]

IPAT Contact Personality Factor Test. High school and adults; 1954–56; title on test is C.P.F.; 2 scores: extroversion-introversion, distortion; Forms A, B, ('54, 3 pages); mimeographed bits ['54–56, 21 pages] serving as manual; adult norms only; 20¢ per test; $2 per complete specimen set (must be purchased to obtain manual and key); cash orders postpaid; Form A also published, under the title *Employee Attitude Series: C.P.F.*, by Industrial Psychology, Inc.; (10) minutes; Raymond B. Cattell, Joseph E. King, and A. K. Schuettler; Institute for Personality and Ability Testing. *

REFERENCES

1. CATTELL, RAYMOND B. *Personality and Motivation Structure and Measurement.* Yonkers, N.Y.: World Book Co., 1957. Pp. xxv, 948. * (*PA* 32:3918)
2. CLARIDGE, GORDON. Chap. 2, "The Excitation-Inhibition Balance in Neurotics," pp. 107–54. In *Experiments in Personality: Vol. 2, Psychodiagnostics and Psychodynamics.* Edited by H. J. Eysenck. London: Routledge & Kegan Paul Ltd., 1960. Pp. viii, 333. *
3. EYSENCK, H. J. Chap. 5, "A Factor Analysis of Selected Tests," pp. 234–44. In his *Experiments in Personality: Vol. 2, Psychodiagnostics and Psychodynamics.* London: Routledge & Kegan Paul Ltd., 1960. Pp. viii, 333. *
4. HOLLAND, H. C. Chap. 4, "Measures of Perceptual Functions," pp. 193–233. In *Experiments in Personality: Vol. 2, Psychodiagnostics and Psychodynamics.* Edited by H. J. Eysenck. London: Routledge & Kegan Paul Ltd., 1960. Pp. viii, 333. *
5. WILLETT, R. A. Chap. 3, "Measures of Learning and Conditioning," pp. 157–92. In *Experiments in Personality: Vol. 2, Psychodiagnostics and Psychodynamics.* Edited by H. J. Eysenck. London: Routledge & Kegan Paul Ltd., 1960. Pp. viii, 333. *
6. FIELD, J. G., AND BRENGELMANN, J. C. "Eyelid Conditioning and Three Personality Parameters." *J Abn & Social Psychol* 63:517–23 N '61. * (*PA* 37:369)

For reviews by Cecil D. Johnson and S. B. Sells, see 5:71.

[124]

★IPAT 8-Parallel-Form Anxiety Battery. Ages 14 or 15 and over; 1960–62; tests and answer sheets labeled *8-Form* and *8-Parallel-Form Battery*, respectively; Forms A, B, C, D, E, F, G, H, ('60, 7 subtests, each on a separate sheet); manual ('60, 6 pages); supplement ('62, 4 pages); $1.75 per 25 copies of any one subtest of any one form; $8.40 per 25 sets of all subtests of any one form; separate answer sheets may be used; $2.20 per pad of 50 answer sheets; 35¢ per set of manual and supplement; $8 per test kit consisting of single-booklet combination of manual and keyed copies of all subtests of all forms (must be purchased to obtain keys for certain subtests); price of test kit includes permission to reproduce up to 500 copies of each subtest; cash orders postpaid; (10–15) minutes; Ivan H. Scheier and Raymond B. Cattell; Institute for Personality and Ability Testing. *

REFERENCES

1. CATTELL, RAYMOND B., AND SCHEIER, IVAN H. *The Meaning and Measurement of Neuroticism and Anxiety.* New York: Ronald Press Co., 1961. Pp. ix, 535. * (*PA* 36:1HK27C)
2. BENDIG, A. W., AND BRUDER, GAIL. "The Effect of Repeated Testing on Anxiety Scale Scores." Abstract. *J Consult Psychol* 26:392 Ag '62. *
3. CATTELL, RAYMOND B. "Advances in the Measurement of Neuroticism and Anxiety in a Conceptual Framework of Unitary-Trait Theory." *Ann N Y Acad Sci* 93:815–39 O 10 '62. * (*PA* 37:6779)
4. SCHEIER, IVAN H. "Experimental Results to Date From the Viewpoint of the Clinician." *Ann N Y Acad Sci* 93:840–50 O 10 '62. * (*PA* 37:6782)

JACOB COHEN, *Professor of Psychology, New York University, New York, New York.*

Like the other tests coming from Cattell's laboratory, the *IPAT 8-Parallel-Form Anxiety Battery* is not the product of a single ad hoc test construction effort, but is based on a long range research program involving hundreds of variables of diverse kinds applied to thousands of subjects of varying age, clinical status, and background. This program is the consequence of, and feeds back into, a detailed theory of the origins, development, and structure of personality and motivation. The factor-analytically derived IPAT tests are simultaneously the products of this research program and its tools. A consequence of this is that truly effective use of these tests requires considerable familiarity with the Cattellian system such as is provided by the two most recent books: Cattell's 1957 *Personality and Motivation Structure and Measurement* (see B119), which describes the system as a whole, and Cattell and Scheier's 1961 *The Meaning and Measurement of Neuroticism and Anxiety* (*1*), which updates the system and applies it to the segment of the clinical area thus far explored.

The immediate background of the test under review is a series of replicated researches which (*a*) established anxiety as a second-order factor in questionnaire items, (*b*) established anxiety as a first-order factor in objective tests, and (*c*) matched these factors as being the same and found them related to the consensus of clinical ratings of anxiety. From the thousands of items studied, it was then possible to select enough to make up eight equivalent forms, each of 50 items, with inconsequential overlap. The items in each form are divided into seven subtests of from 4–10 items each, selected to tap the following: questionnaire anxiety, susceptibility to annoyance, lack of confidence in untried skills, readiness to confess common faults, the emotionality of chosen reaction to "newspaper items," anxiety-tension symptom self-checklist, and susceptibility to embarrassment. Scoring is objective, and requires the computation of means of attempted items. The term "battery" is somewhat misleading, since the separate subtests in each form are necessarily highly unreliable, and are not recommended by the authors for separate interpretation.

The manual (1960) is headed "For Research and Experimental Purposes Only," and although Supplement #1 (1962) is not so labeled, it should be. Although the impressive research background of the test suggests that it will prove valuable for a variety of uses, the sketchiness of the norms and the ambiguity and incompleteness of the available reliability information permit its use in clinical situations in only the most tentative way.

Preliminary sten and percentile norms are provided for the eight forms for *n*'s varying from 142 to 235 cases. This norm group is not well described, and includes a large (but unspecified) proportion of "abnormal" cases, whose influence was mitigated by a procedure whose details are not given. Furthermore, for any given form about one sixth of the cases represent second administrations for the subject. Finally, the time intervals between forms range from a half day to a week. Given the sophistication of the test's authors, the resultant norms are probably not far from the mark, but confident use of the test requires a tidier norming, which is undoubtedly forthcoming.

The general construct validity provided by the background of the test is supplemented by correlations of each form with a 600-item anxiety estimate for 94 college undergraduates ranging from .50 to .68. Where fewer than eight forms are needed, these values can be raised by the combination of forms.

Some ambiguity attaches to the reliability of the separate forms. The manual gives for the 94 undergraduates, who took all eight forms in a single sitting, interform correlations ranging from .36 to .67, with means per form ranging from .41 to .57. These values are rather low. The supplement provides new determinations ranging from .60 to .85 for subjects taking the forms at two- and seven-day intervals. The authors speculate that this discrepancy may be due to curtailed variance in the single-sitting situation. This is not very convincing, and the easily computed variances are not presented. One would expect the reverse of these findings: equivalence reliabilities on a single occasion should be larger than over an interval of time. The anomaly most likely lies in the difference in composition of the groups or the circumstances of the testing.

The test is offered for the obvious purpose of studying changes in anxiety level over time. For such use, high correlation between forms given on *different* occasions is *not* desirable. What is wanted is that such correlations be low relative to correlations between forms on the *same* occasion, i.e., true equivalence reliabilities. No evidence along these lines (both kinds of correlations on a single defined group, or reliabilities of change scores) is presented, and it must be if the test is to realize its purpose.

In summary, this test comes with a most impressive heritage, although not enough normative and reliability data are yet available to make possible a confident recommendation for routine clinical use. It can, indeed *should*, be used in research which would contribute not only to the understanding of anxiety but to the illumination of its own properties. It is the only available means for objectively studying anxiety fluctuation, and there is probably nothing wrong with it which more data (which are constantly being gathered) will not cure.

Paul M. Kjeldergaard, *Assistant Professor of Education, Harvard University, Cambridge, Massachusetts.*

This test, as its name implies, consists of eight equivalent forms of a paper and pencil, multiple choice, anxiety questionnaire developed from a large factor analytic study. Each form consists of seven subtests: (*a*) questionnaire items (10 items)—the usual personality inventory type item with trichotomous choices, e.g. true, false, or in between; (*b*) susceptibility to annoyance (7 items)—a list of events to be rated on a three-point scale as to how irritating the respondent would find them; (*c*) lack of confidence in untried skills (7 items)—the respondent first rates the frequency with which he has had certain types of experiences and then judges his competence to handle such situations, only those situations with which he has had little experience being scored; (*d*) readiness to confess common faults (7 items)—dichotomous responses to a list of "human frailties"; (*e*) emotionality of comment (4 items)—trichotomous choice responses to "news items"; (*f*) anxiety-tension symptom self-checklist (8 items)—respondents utilize a three-point scale to rate themselves in comparison to others as to the degree to which they possess certain behavioral characteristics, e.g., conceit, or the frequency of certain somatic symptoms, e.g. rapid pulse; and (*g*) susceptibility to embarrassment (7 items)—respondents rate situations on a three-point scale as to the degree of embarrassment the situation would arouse. A total of 350 items were selected from 900 anxiety measure items (60 tests) included in a large factor analytic study. These items were then allocated to the eight forms randomly. Since each form contains 50 items, some item overlap was necessary, although this is minimal.

RELIABILITY. Only equivalent form reliabilities are reported, and then, only the average correlation of each form with all other forms is given.[1] The authors do cite the range of coefficients (.36 to .67) but insofar as the forms involved are not identified this provides minimal information. Subsequent research by another investigator reported somewhat higher interform coefficients (.60 to .85). These discrepancies are explained by differences in procedure and intervals between administrations; the latter results are thought to be more appropriate for the usual application of these instruments.

VALIDITY. The validity coefficients, based upon the correlation of the test with an anxiety factor (a pool of 600 anxiety measure items) range from .50 to .68 with a median coefficient of .54. Although technically these are part-whole correlations, the proportion of test items included in the criterion measure was so small that this is not a serious limitation.

NORMS. Norms, in terms of stens (standard tens) and percentiles based upon 142 to 235 cases, both normal and abnormal, per form are available for each of the eight forms. A complex and undescribed weighting procedure was used for combining the scores of the normals and abnormals into the normative tables. A high (unspecified) proportion of abnormals were tested and their scores were adjusted and weighted such that they contributed proportionately less to the norms than the normals. In addition, for any given form, all observations are not independent; approximately 15 per cent of the observations represent repeated measurement based upon the same individual.

SUMMARY. On the one hand, this test appears to be the product of careful research by competent investigators who have utilized the digital computer to develop an instrument that two decades ago would not have been possible. It is a unique contribution opening new vistas of research opportunities in the field of anxiety related behavior. On the other hand, one cannot help being negatively impressed by the penurious manner in which the manual and norms supplement were written. Although basic information is presented, in many cases it is minimal or inadequate. One instance of this is the reporting of the interform reliabilities discussed above. Other examples are the use of the term "average correlation" with no indication as to whether this is the median coefficient, the mean coefficient after appropriate transformation, or some other possible measure, and an inadequate description of the normative samples and the statistical procedures used in "weighting" the scores used in the norm table.

The above criticisms are relevant where the test is to be used to make judgments about an individual on a specific occasion. These factors would be of relatively little concern to the researcher making group predictions or in correlational studies where raw scores would suffice. The basic development of the instrument appears sound and was based upon a sufficient number of observations to justify confidence in it as a potentially fruitful research instrument.

1 An 8 x 8 matrix requires so little space that one finds it difficult to comprehend why all coefficients are not reported.

[125]

***IPAT Music Preference Test of Personality.** "Adults and young adults"; 1952–63; 11 scores of which the following 8 are profiled: adjustment vs. frustrated emotionality, hypomanic self-centeredness vs. self-distrust and doubt, tough sociability vs. tenderminded individuality, introspectiveness vs. social contact, anxiety and concern vs. paranoid imperiousness, complex eccentricity vs. stability-normality, resilience vs. withdrawn schizothymia, schizothyme tenacity vs. relaxed cyclothymia; Forms A, B, ['60, on one 12-inch, 33⅓ rpm record]; mimeographed manual ('60, c1954–60, 24 pages, identical with manual published in 1952 except for cover page); mimeographed supplement ('63, 4 pages); answer sheet-profile ('59, 1 page); separate answer sheets must be used; $13.50 per set of record, 100 answer sheets, scoring stencil, and manual; $2.25 per 50 answer sheets; $1.80 per specimen set without record; cash orders postpaid; (25–30) minutes; Raymond B. Cattell and Herbert W. Eber; Institute for Personality and Ability Testing. *

REFERENCES

1–4. See 5:73.
5. WILLIAMS, RAYMOND EDMUND. *The Measurement and Prediction of Cooperating Teacher Effectiveness in Music Teacher Education.* Doctor's thesis, University of Illinois (Urbana, Ill.), 1958. (*DA* 19:1023)
6. CHARLES, LOUIS. *A Study of the Power of the IPAT Music Preference Test of Personality to Discriminate Between Normal and Abnormal Groups.* Master's thesis, Kent State University (Kent, Ohio), 1959.
7. CATTELL, RAYMOND B., AND MCMICHAEL, ROBERT E. "Clinical Diagnosis by the IPAT Music Preference Test." *J Consult Psychol* 24:333–41 Ag '60. * (*PA* 35:2237)
8. DUDA, WALTER BOLESLAV. *The Prediction of Three Major Dimensions of Teacher Behavior for Student Teachers in Music Education.* Doctor's thesis, University of Illinois (Urbana, Ill.), 1961. (*DA* 22:1518)
9. MAYESKE, GEORGE W. *Some Associations of Musical Preference Dimensions of Personality.* Doctor's thesis, University of Illinois (Urbana, Ill.), 1962. (*DA* 23:3468)
10. SCHULTZ, CAROL. *The Reliability of Music Preference Under Varying Mood Conditions.* Master's thesis, Fairleigh Dickinson University (Rutherford, N.J.), 1962.
11. SCHULTZ, CAROL, AND LANG, GERHARD. "The Reliability of Music Preferences Under Varying Mood Conditions." *J Clin Psychol* 19:506 O '63. *

KENNETH L. BEAN, *Clinical Psychologist, Veterans Administration Hospital, Knoxville, Iowa.*

This unique approach to a number of aspects of personality has 50 items (brief musical excerpts) in each form. The style of music varies all the way from Bach to boogie-woogie. Some of the phrases are simple in melodic and harmonic structure, with very pronounced rhythm. Others are quite harmonically sophisticated with less definite rhythm and a rather conspicuous absence of any definite melody. Still others have several simultaneous melodic lines. Length of phrases played is held rather constant. The subject is asked to mark his reaction to each selection as "L" (like), "I" (indifferent), or "D" (dislike), and is persuaded to aim at an approximately equal number of responses in each of these three categories, though he is not held rigidly to conformity on this point. Indecision is discouraged, and a rather quick, immediate judgment is requested.

Likes and dislikes have been treated statistically by means of factor analysis, though not all of the 11 factors which emerged were regarded as important. Thorough statistical work has been done with the preferences of an adequate number of adult subjects. A convenient profile quantifies the results in a manner facilitating interpretation, and correlations with personality tests consisting of a different sort of items appear to support validity. Likes and dislikes for the different styles of music included are said to be rather consistent for any one individual, and a preference for each style is said to be associated with a different tendency in personality.

A distortion in the true feelings of some listeners might result from the instructions to approach equal numbers of L, I, and D responses—a suggestion made at the beginning of the recording but immediately partially withdrawn by cautioning the subject not to give too much consideration to this matter. Clearly, it is often demonstrated that one individual may habitually experience slight annoyance in response to nearly all music, while another may be predominantly indifferent, and still another typically favorable toward most kinds of music. Any instruction which would be likely to obscure most such individual differences could result in failure to observe such phenomena as irritability or slight flattening of affect.

Furthermore, the affective response to music is far from free of cultural influences. Chinese music, to give an example not in this test, contains intervals strange and frustrating to American ears. The dissonant harmonic structure of some test items may be disliked by those lacking experience with modern idioms. To a listener hunting for a single melodic line accompanied by chords, the polyphonic structure of Bach can hardly fail to sound confused and impossible to follow as a total pattern. Overworked idioms of simple structure in music can hardly be expected to arouse interest or enthusiasm in the musically sophisticated who would regard them as uninteresting or too simple. To the naive, however, the same selections could prove to be satisfyingly within their capacity to comprehend.

With the wide individual variation known to exist in the listening and performing experiences of people, musical phrases could hardly be expected to be even as appropriate as verbal expressions for stimuli supposed to serve as a means of making a rather pure evaluation of personality. Doubt as to the appropriateness of stimuli selected for this test is further strengthened by the obvious familiarity of many of the selections to most listeners. The inclusion of the hymn "Joy to the World," "Blue Danube Waltz," the violin concerto of Mendelssohn, second movement, and a few popular tunes of the day would seem to invite to enter the evaluation a number of unknown variables which would best be omitted by selecting similar styles and structures totally unfamiliar to most or all subjects. The influence of familiarity, sophistication, and deviations in listening experience has been insufficiently investigated so far by the authors. They should probably clarify the importance of such matters further before assuming that for most people a measure of personality variables can be largely independent of these factors.

Finally, quality of reproduction leaves much to be desired, even if the vast majority of subjects are less aware of distortions and distractions on the disc than is the reviewer. An experienced editor of music tapes could have erased many unwanted sounds from between the desired notes of the music before the disc was cut. Tone quality varies from good to very poor, doubtless affecting some preferences. Critical attitudes regarding what may have been intended as "sloppy" performance of some of the popular selections might be responsible for dislikes by analytical listeners, but no question is raised by the authors regarding the influence of this approach, which is habitual with some individuals. Probably many listeners could disregard performance and tone quality variations and judge only the music itself if instructions were expanded to clarify this point.

As a whole the test is interesting and impressive regarding the thoroughness of quantitative treatment of data, yet the reviewer questions validity for habitual concert goers or musical performers. Refinement by perfection of the recording, choice of unfamiliar examples, and more thorough tryout on populations of musically sophisticated persons might well make the test a more valuable contribution to personality measurement, a contribution whose validity could be more adequately defended.

PAUL R. FARNSWORTH, *Professor of Psychology, Stanford University, Stanford, California.*

The Van Steenberg review of this test in *The Fifth Mental Measurements Yearbook* could well be reprinted almost verbatim in the current volume, for the situation regarding this measure has changed little since 1959. The test items are still piano-rendered snatches of music which often end awkwardly and appear on a double disc recording which would win no prizes for pianistic or engineering excellence. In fact, many of the items, particularly those taken from contemporary music, are so poorly played and recorded that the more musically sophisticated listeners often rebel at continuing with the test. And, if they are persuaded to listen further, they may complain that they cannot follow the test's suggestion to give "indifference" votes to approximately a third of the items. Their tendency is either to like or dislike an item. They react to the item's musical structure, the manner in which it is played, and the way in which it is recorded—sometimes to one and sometimes to another of these variables. However, one worries about the musical aspects of the test items only when the test is regarded as a measure of musical preferences. Whenever the test is to be used solely to distinguish between normal and the several abnormal groups, one frets less about the exact nature of the items. Other musical, art, or quite different sorts of items could most probably have served the same ends almost as well. This reviewer would like the test much better if it made no attempt to uncover the musical preferences of either normals or abnormals. It has a sufficiently worthwhile task within the area of personality testing.

For a review by Neil J. Van Steenberg, see 5:73.

[126]

★Inpatient Multidimensional Psychiatric Scale (IMPS). Hospitalized mental patients; 1953-62; revision of *Multidimensional Scale for Rating Psychiatric Patients, Hospital Form* ('53-54) by Maurice Lorr, R. L. Jenkins, and J. Q. Holsopple, which was a revision of the *Northport Record* by Maurice Lorr, M. Singer, and H. Zobel; 10 scores based on ratings following an interview: excitement, hostile belligerence, paranoid projection, grandiose expansiveness, perceptual distortion, anxious intropunitiveness, retardation and apathy, disorientation, motor disturbance, conceptual disorganization; question booklet ['62, 8 pages]; answer-profile sheet ['62, 4 pages]; manual ('62, 45 pages, including copy of question booklet and answer-profile sheet); separate answer-profile sheets must be used; $5 per 25 question booklets; $3 per 25 answer-profile sheets; $2 per manual; $2 per specimen set; postage extra; (10-15) minutes; Maurice Lorr, James Klett, Douglas M. McNair, and Julian J. Lasky; Consulting Psychologists Press, Inc. *

REFERENCES

1. LORR, MAURICE. *Multidimensional Scale for Rating Psychiatric Patients, Hospital Form.* Veterans Administration

Technical Bulletin, TB 10-507. Washington, D.C.: Veterans Administration, November 16, 1953. Pp. 44. *
2. LORR, MAURICE; RUBINSTEIN, ELI A.; AND REIDY, MARY E. "A Factor Analysis of a Scale for Rating Psychiatric Outpatients." Abstract. *Am Psychol* 8:391–2 Ag '53. *
3. LORR, MAURICE; SCHAEFER, EARL; RUBINSTEIN, ELI A.; AND JENKINS, RICHARD L. "An Analysis of an Outpatient Rating Scale." *J Clin Psychol* 9:296–9 Jl '53. * (*PA* 28:2741)
4. LORR, MAURICE; HOLSOPPLE, JAMES Q.; AND TURK, ELIZABETH. "Development of a Measure of Severity of Mental Illness." Abstract. *Am Psychol* 9:421 Ag '54. *
5. LORR, MAURICE; JENKINS, RICHARD L.; AND HOLSOPPLE, JAMES Q. "Factors Descriptive of Chronic Schizophrenics Selected for the Operation of Prefrontal Lobotomy." *J Consult Psychol* 18:293–6 Ag '54. * (*PA* 29:4429)
6. SCHAEFER, EARL S. "Personality Structure of Alcoholics in Outpatient Psychotherapy." *Q J Studies Alcohol* 15:304–19 Je '54. * (*PA* 29:2709)
7. LORR, MAURICE, AND RUBINSTEIN, ELI A. "Personality Patterns of Neurotic Adults in Psychotherapy." *J Consult Psychol* 20:257–63 Ag '56. * (*PA* 31:8534)
8. LORR, MAURICE; HOLSOPPLE, JAMES Q.; AND TURK, ELIZABETH. "A Measure of Severity of Illness." *J Clin Psychol* 12:384–6 O '56. *
9. LORR, MAURICE; O'CONNOR, JAMES P.; AND STAFFORD, JOHN W. "Confirmation of Nine Psychotic Symptom Patterns." *J Clin Psychol* 13:252–7 Jl '57. *
10. STILSON, DONALD W.; MASON, DONALD J.; GYNTHER, MALCOLM D.; AND GERTZ, BORIS. "An Evaluation of the Comparability and Reliabilities of Two Behavior Rating Scales for Mental Patients." *J Consult Psychol* 22:213–6 Je '58. * (*PA* 35:4887)
11. ELLSWORTH, ROBERT B., AND CLAYTON, WILLIAM H. "Measurement of Improvement in 'Mental Illness.'" *J Consult Psychol* 23:15–20 F '59. * (*PA* 34:1353)
12. KLETT, C. JAMES, AND LASKY, JULIAN J. "Agreement Among Raters on the Multidimensional Scale for Rating Psychiatric Patients." Abstract. *J Consult Psychol* 23:281 Je '59. * (*PA* 34:4387)
13. CASEY, JESSE F.; HOLLISTER, LEO E.; KLETT, C. JAMES; LASKY, JULIAN J.; AND CAFFEY, EUGENE M. "Combined Drug Therapy of Chronic Schizophrenics." *Am J Psychiatry* 117:997–1003 My '61. *
14. JENKINS, RICHARD L. "Quantitative Aspects of Sentence Completion in the Study of the Improvement of Schizophrenic Patients." *J Proj Tech* 25:303–11 S '61. * (*PA* 36:3HI03J)
15. PASAMANICK, BENJAMIN, AND RISTINE, LEONARD. "Differential Assessment of Posthospital Psychological Functioning: Evaluation by Psychiatrists and Relatives." *Am J Psychiatry* 118:40–6 Jl '61. *
16. CERBUS, GEORGE, AND NICHOLS, ROBERT C. "Personality Correlates of Picture Preferences." *J Abn & Social Psychol* 64:75–8 Ja '62. * (*PA* 37:3139)
17. LASKY, JULIAN J.; KLETT, C. JAMES; CAFFEY, EUGENE M., JR.; BENNETT, J. LAMAR; ROSENBLUM, MARCUS P.; AND HOLLISTER, LEO E. "Drug Treatment of Schizophrenic Patients: A Comparative Evaluation of Chlorpromazine, Chlorprothixene, Fluphenazine, Reserpine, Thioridazine and Triflupromazine." *Dis Nerv System* 23:698–706 D '62. *
18. LORR, MAURICE. "Measurement of the Major Psychotic Syndromes." *Ann N Y Acad Sci* 93:851–6 O 10 '62. * (*PA* 37:6761)
19. LORR, MAURICE; MCNAIR, DOUGLAS M.; KLETT, C. JAMES; AND LASKY, JULIAN J. "Evidence of Ten Psychotic Syndromes." *J Consult Psychol* 26:185–9 Ap '62. * (*PA* 37:5468)
20. DURELL, J., AND POLLIN, W. "A Trial on Chronic Schizophrenic Patients of Oxypertine, a Psychotropic Drug With an Indole Ring." *Brit J Psychiatry* 109:687–91 S '63. *
21. EYSENCK, H. J. "Psychoticism or Ten Psychotic Syndromes?" *J Consult Psychol* 27:179–80 Ap '63. * Criticism of 19.
22. LEWINSOHN, PETER M.; NICHOLS, ROBERT C.; PULOS, LEE; LOMONT, JAMES F.; NICKEL, HERBERT J.; AND SISKIND, GEORGE. "The Reliability and Validity of Quantified Judgments From Psychological Tests." *J Clin Psychol* 19:64–73 Ja '63. * (*PA* 39:1893)
23. LORR, MAURICE; MCNAIR, DOUGLAS M.; KLETT, C. JAMES; AND LASKY, JULIAN J. "Canonical Variates and Second-Order Factors: A Reply." *J Consult Psychol* 27:180–1 Ap '63. * A reply to *21*.
24. MICHAUX, MARY HELEN; OTA, KAY Y.; HANLON, THOMAS E.; AND KURLAND, ALBERT A. "Rater Perseveration in Measurement of Patient Change." *Ed & Psychol Meas* 23:171–84 sp '63. * (*PA* 38:2731)
25. MOSELEY, EDWARD C.; DUFFEY, ROBERT F.; AND SHERMAN, LEWIS J. "An Extension of the Construct Validity of the Holtzman Inkblot Technique." *J Clin Psychol* 19:186–92 Ap '63. * (*PA* 39:5083)
26. RASKIN, ALLEN, AND CLYDE, DEAN J. "Factors of Psychopathology in the Ward Behavior of Acute Schizophrenics." *J Consult Psychol* 27:420–5 O '63. * (*PA* 38:4616)

[127]

Interpersonal Check List. Adults; 1955–56; part of the *Interpersonal Diagnosis of Personality;* 1 form ['55, 3 pages]; battery manual ('56, 114 pages, see 2 below); $4 per 20 tests; $2 per scoring template; (15–45) minutes depending on number of persons rated; Timothy Leary, Rolfe LaForge (test), Robert Suczek (test), and others (manual); Psychological Consultation Service. *

REFERENCES

1. LAFORGE, ROLFE, AND SUCZEK, ROBERT F. "The Interpersonal Dimension of Personality: 3, An Interpersonal Check List." *J Personality* 24:94–112 S '55. * (*PA* 30:5990)
2. LEARY, TIMOTHY; WITH THE COLLABORATION OF HELEN LANE, ANNE APFELBAUM, MARY DELLA CIOPPA, AND CHARLOTTE KAUFMANN. *Multilevel Measurement of Interpersonal Behavior: A Manual for the Use of the Interpersonal System of Personality.* Berkeley, Calif.: Psychological Consultation Service, 1956. Pp. vii, 110. *
3. ARMSTRONG, RENATE GERBOTH. *Personality Structure in Alcoholism.* Doctor's thesis, University of Colorado (Boulder, Colo.), 1957. (*DA* 18:1851)
4. EDWARDS, ALLEN L. "Social Desirability and Probability of Endorsement of Items in the Interpersonal Check List." *J Abn & Social Psychol* 55:394–6 N '57. * (Abstract: *Am Psychol* 11:378)
5. LEARY, TIMOTHY. *Interpersonal Diagnosis of Personality: A Functional Theory and Methodology for Personality Evaluation.* New York: Ronald Press Co., 1957. Pp. xix, 518. * (*PA* 31:2556)
6. ARMSTRONG, RENATE GERBOTH. "The Leary Impersonal Check List: A Reliability Study." *J Clin Psychol* 14:393–4 O '58. * (*PA* 34:2983)
7. ARMSTRONG, RENATE GERBOTH, AND WERTHEIMER, MICHAEL. "Personality Structure in Alcoholism." *Psychol Newsl* 10:341–9 Jl–Ag '59. * (*PA* 34:3189)
8. DINITZ, SIMON; MANGUS, A. R.; AND PASAMANICK, BENJAMIN. "Integration and Conflict in Self-Other Conceptions as Factors in Mental Illness." *Sociometry* 22:44–55 Mr '59. * (*PA* 34:1623)
9. KRONENBERGER, E. J. *An Investigation of Interpersonal Aspects of Industrial Accident and Non-Accident Men.* Doctor's thesis, University of Ottawa (Ottawa, Ont., Canada), 1959. (Abstract: *Can Psychologist* 1:115)
10. ALTROCCHI, JOHN; PARSONS, OSCAR A.; AND DICKOFF, HILDA. "Changes in Self-Ideal Discrepancy in Repressors and Sensitizers." *J Abn & Social Psychol* 61:67–72 Jl '60. * (*PA* 35:2253)
11. KRONENBERGER, EARL J. "Interpersonal Aspects of Industrial Accident and Non-Accident Employees." *Eng & Ind Psychol* 2:57–62 su '60. * (*PA* 37:2168)
12. LUCKEY, ELEANORE B. "Implications for Marriage Counseling of Self Perceptions and Spouse Perceptions." *J Counsel Psychol* 7:3–9 sp '60. * (*PA* 35:2440)
13. LUCKEY, ELEANORE BRAUN. "Marital Satisfaction and Congruent Self-Spouse Concepts." Abstract. *Social Forces* 39:153–7 D '60. * (*PA* 35:3680)
14. LUCKEY, ELEANORE BRAUN. "Marital Satisfaction and Its Association With Congruence of Perception." *Marriage & Family Living* 22:49–54 F '60. * (*PA* 36:2IQ49L)
15. LUCKEY, ELEANORE BRAUN. "Marital Satisfaction and Parent Concepts." *J Consult Psychol* 24:195–204 Je '60. * (*PA* 35:6686)
16. ALTROCCHI, JOHN. "Interpersonal Perceptions of Repressors and Sensitizers and Component Analysis of Assumed Dissimilarity Scores." *J Abn & Social Psychol* 62:528–34 My '61. * (*PA* 36:4HL28A)
17. BIERI, JAMES, AND LOBECK, ROBIN. "Self-Concept Differences in Relation to Identification, Religion, and Social Class." *J Abn & Social Psychol* 62:94–8 Ja '61. * (*PA* 36:3GC94B)
18. FOA, URIEL G. "Convergences in the Analysis of the Structure of Interpersonal Behavior." *Psychol R* 68:341–53 S '61. *
19. KLOPFER, WALTER G. "A Cross-Validation of Leary's 'Public' Communication Level." *J Clin Psychol* 17:321–2 Jl '61. * (*PA* 38:8426)
20. TERRILL, JAMES MCGUFFIN. *The Relationships Between Level II and Level III in the Interpersonal System of Personality Diagnosis.* Doctor's thesis, Stanford University (Stanford, Calif.), 1961. (*DA* 21:3529)
21. WEINBERG, NORRIS; MENDELSON, MYER; AND STUNKARD, ALBERT. "A Failure to Find Distinctive Personality Features in a Group of Obese Men." *Am J Psychiatry* 117:1035–7 My '61. *
22. WIGGINS, NANCY A. *Structural Aspects of the Interpersonal System of Personality Diagnosis, Level II.* Master's thesis, Stanford University (Stanford, Calif.), 1961.
23. ZUCKERMAN, MARVIN; LEVITT, EUGENE E.; AND LUBIN, BERNARD. "Concurrent and Construct Validity of Direct and Indirect Measures of Dependency." *J Consult Psychol* 25:316–23 Ag '61. * (*PA* 37:1326)
24. CAIRNS, ROBERT B., AND LEWIS, MICHAEL. "Dependency and the Reinforcement Value of a Verbal Stimulus." *J Consult Psychol* 26:1–8 F '62. * (*PA* 37:4976)
25. DAVIS, J.; MORRILL, R.; FAWCETT, J.; UPTON, V.; BONDY, P. K.; AND SPIRO, H. M. "Apprehension and Elevated

Serum Cortisol Levels." *J Psychosom Res* 6:83–6 Ap–Je '62. * (*PA* 37:5108)
26. GYNTHER, MALCOLM D. "Degree of Agreement Among Three 'Interpersonal System' Measures." Abstract. *J Consult Psychol* 26:107 F '62. * (*PA* 37:4982)
27. GYNTHER, MALCOLM D., AND KEMPSON, J. OBERT. "Seminarians and Clinical Pastoral Training: A Follow-Up Study." *J Social Psychol* 56:9–14 F '62. * (*PA* 36:5GD09G)
28. GYNTHER, MALCOLM D.; MILLER, FRANCIS T.; AND DAVIS, HUGH T. "Relations Between Needs and Behavior as Measured by the Edwards PPS and Inter-Personal Check List." *J Social Psychol* 57:445–51 Ag '62. * (*PA* 37:5063)
29. LOCKWOOD, DORIS H., AND GUERNEY, BERNARD, JR. "Identification and Empathy in Relation to Self-Dissatisfaction and Adjustment." *J Abn & Social Psychol* 65:343–7 N '62. *
30. MCDONALD, ROBERT L. "Intrafamilial Conflict and Emotional Disturbance." *J Genetic Psychol* 101:201–8 D '62. * (*PA* 37:6492)
31. MCDONALD, ROBERT L. "Personality Characteristics of Freshman Medical Students as Depicted by the Leary System." *J Genetic Psychol* 100:313–23 Je '62. * (*PA* 37:3838)
32. SMITH, DONALD C. *Personal and Social Adjustment of Gifted Adolescents.* CEC Research Monograph, Series A, No. 4. Washington, D.C.: Council for Exceptional Children, 1962. Pp. iv, 65. *
33. SPERBER, ZANWIL, AND SPANNER, MARVIN. "Social Desirability, Psychopathology, and Item Endorsement." *J General Psychol* 67:105–12 Jl '62. * (*PA* 37:3238)
34. BENTLER, P. M. "Interpersonal Orientation in Relation to Hypnotic Susceptibility." *J Consult Psychol* 27:426–31 O '63. * (*PA* 38:4226)
35. BRIAR, SCOTT, AND BIERI, JAMES. "A Factor Analytic and Trait Inference Study of the Leary Interpersonal Checklist." *J Clin Psychol* 19:193–8 Ap '63. * (*PA* 39:5040)
36. FROST, BARRY P. "Some Personality Characteristics of Education Students." *Alberta J Ed Res* 9:132–9 S '63. *
37. GUERNEY, BERNARD, JR., AND BURTON, JEAN L. "Relationships Among Anxiety and Self, Typical Peer, and Ideal Percepts in College Women." *J Social Psychol* 61:335–44 D '63. * (*PA* 38:8601)
38. KOGAN, KATE L., AND JACKSON, JOAN K. "Conventional Sex Role Stereotypes and Actual Perceptions." *Psychol Rep* 13:27–30 Ag '63. * (*PA* 38:5865)
39. MCDONALD, ROBERT L., AND GYNTHER, MALCOLM D. "Nonintellectual Factors Associated With Performance in Medical School." *J Genetic Psychol* 103:185–94 S '63. *
See also references for test 233.

P. M. BENTLER, *United States Public Health Service Fellow, Department of Psychology, Stanford University, Stanford, California.*

The *Interpersonal Check List* (ICL) is a self-rating adjective check list specially devised by LaForge and Suczek to measure personality variables of the *Interpersonal Diagnosis of Personality* (see 223). The ICL was subjected to several revisions before the final version, Form 4, was published in 1955. By agreement of the authors and collaborators, the ICL was not copyrighted. It is seen mainly as a research instrument, and although copies of the ICL are available the authors indicate the ICL may be used for any legitimate social science application by merely duplicating the list of items as found in (*1*) or (*5*) in roughly alphabetical order.[1]

The ICL can be used to measure persons' conscious descriptions of themselves or others; frequently, mother, father, spouse, or ideal self are the objects of description. The descriptions of various persons or objects can be compared in terms of resulting profiles or summary scores (explained below). The format of the ICL requires the examinee to check all phrases applying to one person before proceeding on to descriptions of others. Eight interpersonal traits are represented in the 128 items of the ICL: (*a*) Managerial-Autocratic, (*b*) Competitive-Narcissistic, (*c*) Aggressive-Sadistic, (*d*) Rebellious-Distrustful, (*e*) Self-effacing-Masochistic, (*f*) Docile-Dependent, (*g*) Cooperative-Overconventional, and (*h*) Responsible-Hypernormal. These eight interpersonal traits are considered to be present in each person to some extent; however, extreme amounts of any of the traits are considered to be undesirable. While each of the eight variables was subdivided into two components as indicated by the hyphenated phrases above, the eight trait system has been most accepted.

Potential words or phrases entering into the ICL had to meet the criteria of the trait theory outlined above. For each item, psychologists had to agree on the trait to which a phrase belonged, the "intensity" of the phrase, and its expected, hypothesized value in the patient culture for whom the ICL was originally devised. The intensity of an item referred to the amount of the trait; low intensity items referred to trait manifestations in necessary and moderate amounts, while high intensity items referred to trait manifestations in inappropriate and extreme amounts. Intensity referred, in addition, to endorsement frequency of the items: the final four rated intensity levels corresponded approximately to 90, 67, 33, and 10 per cent of examinees agreeing with the phrases as being self-descriptive. Item selection continued on the basis of the following sources of data in addition to the ratings mentioned above: frequencies with which the intensity levels were checked, average test scores, tallies of words not understood by patients, summaries of verbal complaints obtained from interviews, trait intercorrelations, and item intercorrelations.

In addition to the phrase and interpersonal trait measurement levels of the ICL, a higher-order unity is hypothesized to be represented by the variables. The eight personality traits are circularly arranged along the circumference of a circle which is marked with the two bipolar dimensions Dominance-submission (Dom) and Love-hate (Lov). A scoring scheme utilizing several variables allows one to plot a person's Dom and Lov scores within this circle.

The importance of the ICL is seen in its

1 LAFORGE, R. "Research Use of the ICL." Unpublished manuscript, Oregon Research Institute, 1963.

measurement of replicable dimensions of interpersonal behavior (*18*). It can be administered quickly. The ability to assess the examinee's evaluation of persons other than himself on the same dimensions used for describing the self, thus allowing the ICL to be used sociometrically (*26*), is a great achievement in view of evidence indicating the lack of agreement between a variety of tests and scales presumably measuring the same constructs.[2] Although scoring systems have not yet been devised for projective tests which are succesfully related to ICL dimensions (*20*), this possibility still exists and warrants further investigation (see 223, Wiggins' review of the *Interpersonal Diagnosis of Personality*). The ICL has been used in a variety of situations (e.g., *5, 17, 24, 28, 35*), and these situations provide some validation for the hypothesized dimensions of the ICL.

The Dom and Lov dimensions of the ICL have recently been confirmed by factor analysis by Foa (*18*) and Wiggins and the reviewer (in press). However, this dimensionality exists only when persons' differential tendency to agree with adjectives irrespective of content is taken into account. Thus, it is imperative for the test user to compute the average intensity of the items checked if he uses the ICL within an interpersonal framework.[3] Fortunately, the Dom and Lov summary scores take this checking tendency into account. These scores have a very low intercorrelation (e.g., *17*).

While this reviewer clearly recommends the use of the ICL in practical situations, he urges focus on further test development research. Average endorsement frequencies are unequal for the traits[4] (*1, 22*); average social desirability values for the traits are unequal,[5] being 5.3, 4.7, 4.4, 3.2, 4.1, 4.7, 5.9, and 5.7 on a nine-point scale for college students and neuropsychiatric patients combined (the ratings were similar for both groups); further, correlations between a social desirability criterion score and endorsement frequency varies with the trait (*20*). These problems are particularly important since the ICL construction aimed at equating these characteristics. This reviewer recommends that an interested researcher take charge of compiling standardization data and making it publicly available.[6] Since so many of the ICL manuscripts are now difficult to obtain, such a procedure would be highly desirable. At the very least such data could be filed with the American Documentation Institute. This reviewer urges gathering of certain fundamental data on the ICL which is currently unavailable: the stability of summary scores and the stability of Dom-Lov difference scores and a variety of related difference scores so that these may be evaluated.

2 For example: CARTWRIGHT, DESMOND S.; KIRTNER, WILLIAM L.; AND FISKE, DONALD W. "Method Factors in Changes Associated With Psychotherapy." *J Abn & Social Psychol* 66:164–75 F '63. *

3 LAFORGE, *op. cit.*

4 LAFORGE, R., AND SUCZEK, R. F. "Supplementary Information on the Research Use of the Interpersonal Checklist." Unpublished manuscript, University of Illinois Library, 1958.

5 Allen L. Edwards and William S. Kogan kindly made data available. The data were scaled as described by Edwards (*4*).

For excerpts from related book reviews, see 5:B261.

[128]

An Inventory of Factors STDCR. Grades 9–16 and adults; 1934–45; 5 scores: social introversion-extraversion, thinking introversion-extraversion, depression, cycloid disposition, rhathymia; IBM; 1 form ('40, 4 pages); revised manual ['45, 2 pages]: $3.50 per 25 tests; 20¢ per single copy; $1 per scoring key; separate answer sheets may be used; 4¢ per IBM answer sheet; $2.50 per set of either hand or machine scoring stencils; 25¢ per manual; postage extra; (30) minutes; J. P. Guilford; Sheridan Supply Co. *

REFERENCES

1–10. See 3:55.
11–27. See 4:59.
28–55. See 5:78.
56. DOTSON, ELSIE JENOISE. *A Study of the Agreement of Introversion-Extroversion Factors as Defined by Various Factor Analysts.* Doctor's thesis, University of Kentucky (Lexington, Ky.), 1951. (*DA* 18:1095)
57. BOOTH, MARY D. "A Study of the Relationship Between Certain Personality Factors and Success in Clinical Training of Occupational Therapy Students." *Am J Occup Ther* 11:93–6+ Mr–Ap '57. * (*PA* 32:4585)
58. TSUJIOKA, BIEN; SONOHARA, TARO; AND YATABE, TATSURO. "A Factorial Study of the Temperament of Japanese College Male Students by the Yatabe-Guilford Personality Inventory." *Psychologia* 1:110–9 D '57. * (*PA* 35:4899)
59. DUNN, SANDRA; BLISS, JOAN; AND SIIPOLA, ELSA. "Effects of Impulsivity, Introversion, and Individual Values Upon Association Under Free Conditions." *J Personality* 26:61–76 Mr '58. * (*PA* 33:5742)
60. JENKIN, NOËL. "Size Constancy as a Function of Personal Adjustment and Disposition." *J Abn & Social Psychol* 57:334–8 N '58. * (*PA* 33:10816)
61. THOMAS, EDWIN RUSSELL. *The Relationship Between the Strong Vocational Interest Blank and the Guilford-Martin Personality Inventory Among Salesmen.* Doctor's thesis, Syracuse University (Syracuse, N.Y.), 1958. (*DA* 19:2139)
62. CARON, ALBERT J., AND WALLACH, MICHAEL A. "Personality Determinants of Repressive and Obsessive Reactions to Failure-Stress." *J Abn & Social Psychol* 59:236–45 S '59. * (*PA* 34:3310)
63. GUILFORD, J. P. *Personality.* New York: McGraw-Hill Book Co., Inc., 1959. Pp. xiii, 562. *
64. KELLY, E. LOWELL, AND GOLDBERG, LEWIS R. "Correlates of Later Performance and Specialization in Psychology: A Follow-Up Study of the Trainees Assessed in the VA Selection Research Project." *Psychol Monogr* 73(12):1–32 '59. * (*PA* 34:7952)
65. KELTY, EDWARD JOHN. *Normal Electrocortical Activity in Relation to Personality Factors.* Doctor's thesis, Duke University (Durham, N.C.), 1959. (*DA* 20:756)
66. BEACH, LESLIE R. "Sociability and Academic Achievement in Various Types of Learning Situations." *J Ed Psychol* 51:208–12 Ag '60. * (*PA* 35:3977)
67. BORG, WALTER R. "Prediction of Small Group Role

6 Rolfe LaForge of the Oregon Research Institute is carrying out basic ICL research; his ideas greatly aided the preparation of this review.

Behavior From Personality Variables." *J Abn & Social Psychol* 60:112–6 Ja '60. * (*PA* 34:7528)
68. CARRIGAN, PATRICIA M. "Extraversion-Introversion as a Dimension of Personality: A Reappraisal." *Psychol B* 57:329–60 S '60. * (*PA* 35:4976)
69. FRANKS, C. M.; SOUIEFF, M. I.; AND MAXWELL, A. E. "A Factorial Study of Certain Scales From the MMPI and the STDCR." *Acta Psychologica* 17(5):407–16 '60. * (*PA* 35:3428)
70. BESSENT, EDGAR WAILAND. *The Predictability of Selected Elementary School Principals' Administrative Behavior.* Doctor's thesis, University of Texas (Austin, Tex.), 1961. (*DA* 22:3479)
71. KREITMAN, NORMAN. "Psychiatric Orientation: A Study of Attitudes Among Psychiatrists." *J Mental Sci* 108:317–28 My '62. * (*PA* 37:3400)
72. PANEK, RICHARD E., AND HANNUM, THOMAS E. "Relation Between Autokinesis and Introversion-Extraversion." Abstract. *J Consult Psychol* 26:477 O '62. *

For a review by Hubert E. Brogden, see 4:59; for a review by H. J. Eysenck, see 3:55; for a related review, see 3:45.

[129]

★**It Scale for Children.** Ages 5–6; 1956; for research use only; sex role preference; 1 form (37 cards); manual (20 pages, see *2* below); $15 per set of cards and manual, cash orders postpaid; (7–8) minutes; Daniel G. Brown; Psychological Test Specialists. *

REFERENCES

1. BROWN, DANIEL G. "Masculinity-Femininity Development in Children." Abstract. *Am Psychol* 11:415 Ag '56. *
2. BROWN, DANIEL G. "Sex-Role Preference in Young Children." *Psychol Monogr* 70(14):1–19 '56. * (*PA* 31:5815)
3. BROWN, DANIEL G. "The Development of Sex-Role Inversion and Homosexuality." *J Pediatrics* 50:613–9 My '57. * (*PA* 33:4196)
4. BROWN, DANIEL G. "Masculinity-Femininity Development in Children." *J Consult Psychol* 21:197–202 Je '57. *
5. BROWN, DANIEL G. "Sex-Role Development in a Changing Culture." *Psychol B* 55:232–42 Jl '58. * (*PA* 33:8147)
6. KOBASIGAWA, AKIRA. "Sex-Role Preference in Okinawan Pre-school Children." *Psychologia* 2:124–7 Je '59. * (*PA* 35:3236)
7. MUSSEN, PAUL, AND DISTLER, LUTHER. "Masculinity, Identification, and Father-Son Relationships." *J Abn & Social Psychol* 59:350–6 N '59. * (*PA* 34:5673)
8. RICHARDSON, D. H. "Sex-Role Preference in Children." *Ont Hosp Psychol B* 5:10–5 Ap '59. *
9. HARTUP, WILLARD W., AND ZOOK, ELSIE A. "Sex-Role Preferences in Three- and Four-Year-Old Children." *J Consult Psychol* 24:420–6 O '60. * (*PA* 35:4719)
10. BORSTELMANN, L. J. "Sex of Experimenter and Sex-Typed Behavior of Young Children." *Child Develop* 32:519–24 S '61. * (*PA* 36:4FF19B)
11. BROWN, DANIEL G. "Sex-Role Preference in Children: Methodological Problems." *Psychol Rep* 11:477–8 O '62. * (*PA* 37:7881)
12. HARTUP, WILLARD W. "Some Correlates of Parental Imitation in Young Children." *Child Develop* 33:85–96 Mr '62. * (*PA* 37:917)
13. CLARK, EDWARD T. "Sex Role Preference in Mentally Retarded Children." *Am J Mental Def* 67:606–10 Ja '63. * (*PA* 37:7009)
14. CLARK, EDWARD T. "Sex-Role Preference in Mentally Retarded Females." *Am J Mental Def* 68:433–9 N '63. * (*PA* 38:8956)
15. EPSTEIN, RALPH, AND LIVERANT, SHEPHARD. "Verbal Conditioning and Sex-Role Identification in Children." *Child Develop* 34:99–106 Mr '63. * (*PA* 38:5765)
16. HARTUP, WILLARD W.; MOORE, SHIRLEY G.; AND SAGER, GLEN. "Avoidance of Inappropriate Sex-Typing by Young Children." *J Consult Psychol* 27:467–73 D '63. *
17. MUSSEN, PAUL, AND RUTHERFORD, ELDRED. "Parent-Child Relations and Parental Personality in Relation to Young Children's Sex-Role Preferences." *Child Develop* 34:589–607 S '63. * (*PA* 38:8097)
18. NICKERSON, RAYMOND S., AND BROWN, CHARLES R. "A Stimulus Ordering Technique for Controlled Lag Recognition Memory Experiments." *Psychol Rep* 13:319–22 O '63. * (*PA* 38:8006)

PHILIP L. HARRIMAN, *Professor of Psychology, Bucknell University, Lewisburg, Pennsylvania.*

In their monumental inquiry into the masculinity-femininity continuum, Terman and Miles [1] pointed out the need for an adequate measure of sex-role preferences of young children. Except for their research reported in 1936 and their measure of the M-F interest pattern (see 61), objective tests, with scores expressed in statistics of variables, have been lacking. Expository and argumentative discussions, illuminated oftentimes by case histories, attested to the *Sprachgefühl* of their proponents but added little to empirical knowledge.

The ITSC ranks among the first empirical measures of sex-role preferences of middle class, urban American children who are about 5 or 6 years of age. In fact, the children used in standardizing this measure ranged from 5-4 to 6-4, with a median age of 5-10. Whereas in the Terman-Miles M-F measure there are more than 400 items in each form of the test and a wide variety of test patterns, the ITSC includes only 36 picture cards, 3 by 4 inches. Word associations (which for small children might be given orally), inkblots, or items dealing with opinions, ethical attitudes, and emotional situations (which would lend themselves to pictorial adaptation), do not appear in the ITSC. Perhaps one reason why the Terman-Miles precedent was not adapted for small children is that Brown wished to make a simple measure which would not strain the attention span of children, which would be given in just one testing session, and which would not necessitate the laborious statistical analyses used in the Terman-Miles to validate each single item.

ITSC may be illustrated by one example. "It" is a figure drawing of indeterminate sex. Then (Set 2, Group 1) the child chooses the toys that "It" would like to play with, each toy being a stereotype of a masculine or a feminine object. Choice of a toy locomotive, obviously, is taken to indicate a masculine sex-role preference, whereas a doll represents a feminine choice. The scale yields a quantified rating of sex-role preference, with a range from 0 (F) through 84 (M). Marked deviations, plus or minus, from 42 are interpreted as indicative of M or F, respectively.

This reviewer tried out the ITSC with 12 small children in the kindergarten class of a daily vacation church school. After a half day

1 TERMAN, LEWIS M., AND MILES, CATHERINE COX. *Sex and Personality: Studies in Masculinity and Femininity.* New York: McGraw-Hill Book Co., Inc., 1936. Pp. xii, 600. * (*PA* 10:5879)

of testing this reviewer concluded that (*a*) small children seem to enjoy the test, (*b*) administration is easy and pleasant, (*c*) the scale might profitably be extended, (*d*) a more thorough inquiry into sex-role preferences may be desirable using two or three sessions, and (*e*) the present scale points the way to many rewarding pieces of very minor research by students in an undergraduate class in child psychology.

The disquieting issue, however, is the vagueness of definition regarding the M-F continuum. Social class structures involve different types of social learning, even in early childhood. Sex roles, apart from the subculture in America, are subtle, elusive, and intangible to define. Whether it is possible to avoid turgid arguments about the M-F continuum is doubtful. Brown has resolved the difficulty by taking a benignly dogmatic position in this scale. Choices of some of the cards as preferred by "It" indicate M; of other cards, F. *Ipse dixit.* At least, the ITSC merits commendation as a pioneer quantification of a facet of personality. Whether it actually exists as anything more than a hypostatization of an omnibus abstruse concept is still an unanswered question.

BOYD R. MCCANDLESS, *Professor of Education and Psychology; Director, University School Clinic Complex; and Chairman, Department of Special Education; Indiana University, Bloomington, Indiana.*

The basic rationale of the It Scale is based on theories of sex-typing and sex-role identification. The roots of Brown's thinking are, of course, Freudian, but his approach to measurement has been substantially modified by such neo-analytic-learning theorists as Mowrer and such sociologists as Parsons. In other words, one can think of him as an "eclectic yet dynamic" theorist, with a certain flair for translating theory (and cloudy much of the theory in this area is!) into a surprisingly clear and sensible complex of operations which results in a masculinity-femininity score. Furthermore, this score has been shown to improve certain of our predictions, particularly about behavior and reputed environment of kindergarten and first grade males from a Western culture.

THE MANUAL. Brown (*2*) describes his test in a noncommercial, American Psychological Association monograph which serves as the manual, and gave It its maiden airing at professional psychological meetings. Instructions for administering and scoring are adequate and simple, although the rather small sample (for a normative study) is not fully described: we learn only that there are 78 male and 68 female kindergartners from Denver, aged 5-4 to 6-4 years, who came predominantly from the middle class. He reports more extensive data later (*4*). Reliability (test-retest, interval approximately one month) is reasonably satisfactory: $r = .71$ for boys, .84 for girls.

The "hero" or "protagonist" of the test is "It," a presumably sexless stick figure drawing. Hypothetically, the testee identifies with It, and it is It rather than the child who "takes the test." In other words, the test is a "structured projective."

The most feminine possible score It can earn is zero, the most masculine 84. This score is based on three subtests: (*a*) 8 points for choosing all masculine toys from 16 pictured toys, 8 of which are masculine and 8 feminine (zero is scored for 8 feminine toy choices); (*b*) 64 points for totally masculine choices for 8 pairs of pictures: which would It rather be (for example), a male or a female Indian?; and (*c*) 12 points (completely masculine) if It's preference is for the picture of a boyish boy over the pictures of a girlish boy, a boyish girl, and a girlish girl (again, zero is scored if the choice is for a girlish girl and intermediate weights are assigned to the other two possible choices).

Brown's manual gives some report on item validity, but neglects statistical workup on the power and attractiveness (aside from their differential sex pull) of items or subsections, and does not report the adequacy of the assignment of subtest and subsection weights. The latter is probably a serious flaw in view of the recent and repeated demonstrations of the effectiveness of toy choices in discriminating between the sexes. This flaw, of course, would not be difficult to correct.

THE TEST. The test is conveniently put together in a small plastic box; envelopes containing the items are clearly labeled; administration is simple; and the drawings are generally adequate, although not all are as clear as one would like. The reviewer and a former colleague (Iqbal Dar) found in an unpublished study that, with a little redrawing, the test appears to be as suitable for an Eastern (West Pakistan) culture as for a Western one.

RELATED LITERATURE. The space allotted for this review permits only a selection of findings. Findings suggest that progression with age is clear for boys, "full masculinity" apparently having been "gained" by early school ages. This conclusion is based on several United States populations and one Pakistani population ranging in age from two well on into elementary school. Findings are less clear for United States girls, the theory adduced being that in our culture the feminine role is both less desirable and less clearly modeled, and thus later and more reluctantly assumed. The logical flaw here is that there seems to be a tendency for United States girls, even at very early ages, to identify It as a boy and thus, presumably, to respond in terms of cultural expectations rather than projectively. This is a serious drawback in using the test with girls, although this difficulty was not found with a four- to seven-year-old sample of 50 Pakistani girls where, it should be added, the feminine role is exaggeratedly clear.

Other research suggests that children will change It's choices according to logical dynamic predictions when It is labeled as a boy or a girl or is actually assigned the subject's name, and that high masculine boys condition more effectively than low masculine boys for a male than a female examiner. A combination of paternal warmth and power in child rearing practices (judged from projectives and interviews) seems more characteristic of high than low masculine scoring boys, with tentative results following a similar sex-appropriate pattern for girls. Social class differences have not been adequately investigated, although Brown, in a subanalysis within his rather homogeneous original sample, found no such differences. Hartup and Zook (*9*), studying preschool youngsters, also failed to reveal social class differences. However, they worked with a rather special set of nursery school attending lower class youngsters, most of whom were from mother-only homes. Hartup, Moore, and Sager (*16*) did not find approach-avoidance tendencies toward sex-appropriate toys, which were otherwise age-progressive and sex-differential, to be related to It scores for either sex.

EVALUATIVE SUMMARY. This is an ingenious, simple test, related rather sensibly to theory. At present, the It Scale can be recommended as a potentially profitable research tool, particularly for boys; and, with further careful research, it may develop into something useful for clinical practice.

[130]

Johnson Temperament Analysis. Grades 12–16 and adults; 1941–45; 9 scores: nervous-composed, depressive–gay-hearted, active-quiet, cordial-cold, sympathetic–hard-boiled, subjective-objective, aggressive–submissive, critical-appreciative, self-mastery–impulsive; IBM; Form A ('41, 7 pages); manual ('44, 16 pages); revised profile ('45, 1 page); separate answer sheets must be used; $3.50 per 35 tests; 5¢ per IBM answer sheet; $1.05 per set of hand and machine scoring stencils for unweighted scoring; $1.75 per set of hand scoring stencils for weighted scoring; 2¢ per profile; postage extra; 50¢ per specimen set, postpaid; (40–60) minutes; Roswell H. Johnson; California Test Bureau. *

REFERENCES

1–6. See 4:62.
7. HINKELMAN, EMMET ARTHUR. "Relation of Certain Personality Variables to High-School Achievement." *Sch R* 60:532–4 D '52. *
8. TOMEDY, FRANCIS J. "The Relationship of Personality Characteristics to Measured Vocational Interests in High School Women Teachers of English, Social Science, Mathematics, and Physical Science." Abstract. *Am Psychol* 7:384 Jl '52. *
9. TOMEDY, FRANCIS JOSEPH. *The Relationship of Personality Characteristics to Measured Interests of Women Teachers of English, Social Science, Mathematics, and Physical Science in Certain Senior High Schools.* Doctor's thesis, New York University (New York, N.Y.), 1952. (*DA* 12:540)
10. WARD, WILLIAM DAVID. *An Investigation of the Predictability of Academic Success of the A.C.E. and Certain Factors Measured by the Johnson Temperament Analysis.* Doctor's thesis, Bradley University (Peoria, Ill.), 1953. (*DA* 13:518)
11. HOLMES, JACK A. "Factors Underlying Major Reading Disabilities at the College Level." *Genetic Psychol Monogr* 49:3–95 F '54. * (*PA* 28:8982)
12. TYLER, FRED T. *The Prediction of Student-Teaching Success From Personality Inventories.* University of California, Publications in Education, Vol. 11, No. 4. Berkeley, Calif.: University of California Press, 1954. Pp. 233–313. * (*PA* 29:4709)
13. HOLMES, JACK A. "Personality and Spelling Ability." Abstract. *Am Psychol* 10:353–4 Ag '55. *
14. THURSTON, DONALD REID. *An Investigation of the Possibilities of Parole Prediction Through the Use of Five Personality Inventories.* Doctor's thesis, Michigan State University (East Lansing, Mich.), 1955. (*DA* 15:1206)
15. HOLMES, JACK A. *Personality and Spelling Ability.* University of California Publications in Education, Vol. 12, No. 4. Berkeley, Calif.: University of California Press, 1959. Pp. vii, 213–91. *
16. ROZEHNAL, BOHUSLAV JAN. *A Study of the Relationship of Certain Temperament Scale Scores to Persistence in College.* Doctor's thesis, University of Minnesota (Minneapolis, Minn.), 1960. (*DA* 21:814)

For a review by Albert Ellis, see 4:62; for a review by H. Meltzer, see 3:57.

[131]

***Jr.-Sr. High School Personality Questionnaire.** Ages 12–18; 1953–64; 14 scores: reserved vs. outgoing (A), less intelligent vs. more intelligent (B), affected by feelings vs. emotionally stable (C), phlegmatic vs. excitable (D), obedient vs. assertive (E), sober vs. happy-go-lucky (F), disregards rules vs. conscientious (G), shy vs. venturesome (H), tough-minded vs. tender-minded (I), vigorous vs. doubting (J), self-assured vs. apprehensive (O), group dependent vs. self-sufficient (Q2), casual vs. controlled (Q3), relaxed vs. tense (Q4); 3 editions; separate answer sheets must be used; (40–50) minutes; Raymond B. Cattell and Halla Beloff.

a) [IPAT EDITIONS.] 1953–64; 2 editions; manual, second edition ('62, 26 pages) used with both editions; profile ('63, 1 page) for both editions; $4 per 25 tests;

$2.25 per pad of 50 answer sheets; $1.90 per scoring key; $1.90 per pad of 50 profiles; $2.20 per manual; $4 per specimen set; cash orders postpaid; Institute for Personality and Ability Testing. *

1) *IPAT High School Personality Questionnaire, [1958 Edition]*. Formerly called *The Junior Personality Quiz;* title on test is H.S.P.Q.; revised edition listed below; Forms A, B, ('58, 8 pages); norms supplement ('60, 4 pages); norms for combination of Forms A and B also presented.

2) *Jr.-Sr. High School Personality Questionnaire, 1963 Edition.* A 3-alternative response adaptation of the 1958 edition; title on test is Jr.-Sr. H.S.P.Q.; Forms A, B, second edition ('63, c1958-63, 8 pages); mimeographed norms supplement ('64, 4 pages); no data on reliability.

b) JR.-SR. HIGH SCHOOL PERSONALITY QUESTIONNAIRE, [BOBBS-MERRILL EDITION]. 1958-60; title on test is Jr.-Sr. H.S.P.Q.; Forms A, B, ('60, 8 pages, identical with 1958 IPAT edition except for format, title, and directions); manual ('60, c1958-60, 24 pages); norms supplement ('60, c1958-60, 4 pages, identical with IPAT edition except for format and title); profile ('60, 1 page); $4.95 per 35 tests; $1.50 per 35 answer sheets; 40¢ per scoring key; $1.50 per 35 profiles; 75¢ per manual and norms supplement; $1 per specimen set (includes norms supplement but not manual); Bobbs-Merrill Co., Inc. *

REFERENCES

1-4. See 5:72.
5. CATTELL, RAYMOND B.; COAN, RICHARD W.; AND BELOFF, HALLA. "A Re-examination of Personality Structure in Late Childhood, and Development of the High School Personality Questionnaire." *J Exp Ed* 27:73-88 D '58. * (*PA* 34:2819)
6. CATTELL, RAYMOND B. "Anxiety, Extraversion, and Other Second-Order Personality Factors in Children." *J Personality* 27:464-76 D '59. *
7. REID, JACKSON B.; KING, F. J.; AND WICKWIRE, PAT. "Cognitive and Other Personality Characteristics of Creative Children." *Psychol Rep* 5:729-37 D '59. * (*PA* 34:5632)
8. CLEMENTS, SAM D. *The Predictive Utility of Three Delinquency Proneness Measures.* Doctor's thesis, University of Houston (Houston, Tex.), 1960. (*DA* 20:3827)
9. GIBB, CECIL A. "A Note on the I.P.A.T. High School Personality Questionnaire." *Austral J Psychol* 13:77-86 Je '61. *
10. GUINOUARD, DONALD EDGAR. *Personality Traits and Mental Health Habits of Sociometrically Popular and Unpopular Sixth and Eighth Grade Students.* Doctor's thesis, Washington State University (Pullman, Wash.), 1961. (*DA* 22:1085)
11. KOCHNOWER, WILLIAM. "Personality Factors and Success in Mathematics." *High Points* 43:65-72 Ap '61. *
12. MCGUIRE, CARSON. "The Prediction of Talented Behavior in the Junior High School." *Proc Inv Conf Testing Probl* 1960:46-67 '61. *
13. GOTTESMAN, IRVING I. "Differential Inheritance of the Psychoneuroses." *Eug Q* 9:223-7 D '62. * (*PA* 37:7729)
14. GUINOUARD, DONALD E., AND RYCHLAK, JOSEPH F. "Personality Correlates of Sociometric Popularity in Elementary School Children." *Personnel & Guid J* 40:438-42 Ja '62. * (*PA* 36:5KD38G)
15. PURCELL, KENNETH; TURNBULL, JOHN W.; AND BERNSTEIN, LEWIS. "Distinctions Between Subgroups of Asthmatic Children: Psychological Test and Behavior Rating Comparisons." *J Psychosom Res* 6:283-91 O-D '62. * (*PA* 37:8210)
16. BUTCHER, H. J.; AINSWORTH, M.; AND NESBITT, J. E. "Personality Factors and School Achievement: A Comparison of British and American Children." *Brit J Ed Psychol* 33:276-85 N '63. * (*PA* 38:7961)
17. CATTELL, RAYMOND B. "Theory of Fluid and Crystallized Intelligence: A Critical Experiment." *J Ed Psychol* 54:1-22 F '63. * (*PA* 37:7991)
18. GOTTESMAN, IRVING I. "Heritability of Personality: A Demonstration." *Psychol Monogr* 77(9):1-21 '63. * (*PA* 38:423)
19. PIERSON, GEORGE R., AND KELLY, ROBERT F. "Anxiety, Extraversion, and Personality Idiosyncrasy in Delinquency." *J Psychol* 56:441-5 O '63. * (*PA* 38:4582)
20. PIERSON, GEORGE R., AND KELLY, ROBERT F. "HSPQ Norms on a State-Wide Delinquent Population." *J Psychol* 56:185-92 Jl '63. * (*PA* 38:4584)
21. SCHAIE, K. WARNER. "Scaling the Scales: Use of Expert Judgment in Improving the Validity of Questionnaire Scales." *J Consult Psychol* 27:350-7 Ag '63. * (*PA* 38:2713)

C. J. ADCOCK, *Associate Professor of Psychology, Victoria University of Wellington, Wellington, New Zealand.* [Review of the 1958 IPAT and 1960 Bobbs-Merrill Editions.]

This is a junior version of the *Sixteen Personality Factor Questionnaire* but is based upon separate research with adolescents. The number of factors is reduced from 16 to 14 but of these, 2 (D and J) are newcomers. The four missing factors are L, M, N, and Q1. It is quite understandable that paranoid tendencies (L) and sophistication (N) should not have had time to develop as consistent behavioural patterns in children and that radicalism (Q1) would be difficult to measure anyway, but the absence of M (autism) is more surprising. Two new factors appear: D (phlegmatic, stodgy versus excitable, unrestrained) and J (vigorous, group acting versus doubting, individualistic).

Subject to these changes the factor schema has all the strengths and weaknesses of the 16 PF. It is based on careful factor studies, covers a wide range of traits, and is constructed according to the best statistical requirements. Correspondingly it shares some of the weaknesses of the 16 PF. The reviewer has already discussed the meaning of the factors involved in the 16 PF in *The Fifth Mental Measurements Yearbook* (see 5:112) and will not repeat that here. He would like to draw attention, however, to a distinction he would make between what he would call *ego-system components* and what he would describe as simple *traits*. The latter are broad behavioural tendencies resulting from the conditioning of basic drives but the former are functional units in a system which determines choice behaviour. H (shy versus adventurous) and O (confident adequacy versus guilt proneness) are examples of simple traits while G (ego strength) and Q3 (self-sentiment strength) would be examples of ego-system components. Both C and D would be included with the latter but herein is one of the problems with regard to the test. In the 16 PF, Factor C is regarded as a factor of emotional stability and has much in common with Q3 (including a high correlation) and in the HSPQ the actual designation "ego strength" is applied to both C and G while Q3 is again described in terms which have much in common. To complicate the position, D is also presented as an aspect of control (stodgy versus unrestrained, or phlegmatic versus excitable). It seems evident that the control aspects of behaviour have not been well differentiated.

It might be suggested that manifest emotional control involves two major aspects: the degree of braking function manifested and the degree of emotion to be controlled. Unstable behaviour can result from either high emotional charge which accentuates the motivation or poor capacity to inhibit. It is one thing to control emotion and quite another to lack emotion which needs control. Q3 seems to have a definite claim to be regarded as a form of positive control ("will power") while G is concerned with degree of acceptance of moral standards and so another dimension of positive control. C on the other hand, in its negative aspect, involves emotional instability which could just as well come from undue emotion as from poor control. The truth seems to be that the concept of emotionality has never been properly recognised in the preparation of the test items. An inspection of the items scored for Q3 (Form A) shows that they uniformly involve positive control aspects while the C items involve both emotionality, as in the question about being able to take a big meal before an examination, and control, as in making an effort to speak to a new teacher. The D factor also involves many items which indicate emotional sensitivity and it becomes difficult to decide whether C or D might best be regarded as a measure of emotionality. It would appear that D presents a definite problem. It was not included in the 16 PF, although some adult analyses indicated it, but it is included in the junior version. There seems room to doubt whether the actual difference between age groups is sufficient to justify this procedure.

At first sight Factor J seems to be very like Q2 since their low-score aspects are described as "goes readily with group" and "a 'joiner' and sound follower," respectively. The actual correlation between the factor scores, however, is only .12. The distinction probably lies in the fact that the person with high Q2 goes his own way because of strength of character (inner-directed?) while the person with high J avoids the group rather because of weakness. He is a Hamlet rather than a Caesar. But again the problem arises: why is this factor in children but not in adults?

It is gratifying to find that provision has been made for the scoring of two second-order factors. These are the well established anxiety and introversion-extraversion. Two such factors have now turned up in a number of investigations but the naming of the first one is not universally accepted; some would prefer the term "emotionality." The second factor is well agreed upon but there is a complication with regard to the test. According to the matrix of intercorrelations presented, the items which define this extraversion factor do not constitute a consistent cluster. Of the six intercorrelations involved, only one exceeds .07 and one has a negative sign (−.14). An analysis of these data indicates a second factor rather different from the usual introversion-extraversion factor.

Considerable space has been devoted to the question of the nature of the factors because there seems to be no point in considering the validity of measurements unless one knows what they are and whether they are what one wants.

The validity of the factor scores from the full test (Forms A and B combined) ranges from .73 (J and Q3) to .88 (O) on the basis of multiple correlation and from .65 (Q3) to .83 (C and H) when derived from equivalence coefficients. The policy of incorporating "suppressor" items in the test to neutralize effects not required means that the usual consistency coefficients are no longer suitable measures of reliability but one is rather disturbed by the low equivalence correlations (A and B forms) as compared with the validity figures. One cannot help wondering whether the latter do not exaggerate the practical value. The fact that the intercorrelations of the factor scores are appreciably lower than with the 16 PF may be further indication of the lower reliability of the junior version.

The general impression with which one is left is that the HSPQ has rather lower reliability and validity than the 16 PF. This is no reflection on the test construction. The section in the manual dealing with "Construction of the Test" is admirable. The truth seems to be that questionnaire tests are not so satisfactory with children and need to be used with caution. It seems desirable that some further work should be done on the factorial basis of the test but for adequate measurement of child personality hope seems to lie rather in the work being done by Cattell's laboratory on objective forms of test. The ego system components, however, may not all prove amenable to objective measurement. In that case an improved form of the present test may have a very important role to play. To this reviewer it seems the most hopeful of this type yet offered.

PHILIP E. VERNON, *Professor of Educational Psychology, Institute of Education, University of London, London, England.* [Review of the 1958 IPAT and 1960 Bobbs-Merrill Editions.]

Cattell's *Sixteen Personality Factor Questionnaire* and its derivation are too well known to require description. The *Jr.-Sr. High School Questionnaire* aims to measure 12 of the same factors (plus 2 new factors) by items more suitable for adolescents. It also overlaps with the *IPAT Children's Personality Questionnaire* (CPQ) at the bottom end of its intended age range so as to allow repeated assessment from ages 7 or 8 to mature adulthood.

Each of the two forms contains 10 two-choice items referring to each factor, and takes about 40 minutes to answer. The answer sheet is ingeniously arranged so that a single hand scoring stencil yields all 14 scores in one or two minutes. Raw scores are converted to a 10-point scale of stens (mean 5.5, SD 1), or to deciles. The stens may be plotted on a profile sheet labeled with simplified descriptions of the factors. The manual provides ample material on the presumed significance of the factors to aid the school counselor in interpretation. Sex differences are allowed for in the norms; age differences, except perhaps on Factors B and Q3, are negligible.

Cattell's aim is to cover all the major dimensions or source traits of personality as fully as can be done in a short time. One wonders, however, whether counselors will not find it difficult to handle so many rather indistinct and unfamiliar traits simultaneously, and might not prefer a smaller number of more conventional variables. Some grouping of traits is possible; second order factor scores for extraversion-introversion and anxiety may be obtained. Also, a simple regression equation for predicting academic achievement is provided which is claimed to add considerably to predictions from ability measures only. (It might have been better to exclude Factor B, intelligence, from this equation, so as to avoid giving the highest weight to a 10-item intelligence test.) The user could, of course, work out further such equations against other important criteria.

Some will query how far any personality inventory can be said to measure source traits—for Cattell would not agree to accept the scores as merely delineating the subject's self-concepts. He admits the possibility of faking, but states that no systematic changes have been found when the test is answered anonymously, and he hopes to eliminate acquiescence response sets by arranging for roughly equal numbers of "Yes" and "No" responses for each factor. That the social desirability effect is not large is suggested by the rather low intercorrelations between factor scores, despite some intentional obliquity of the factors. The mean of the absolute values of r is .13, though this figure might well be considerably larger if the separate scores were more reliable.

The generally low reliabilities constitute a serious drawback. Even when, as the author suggests, both forms are given, the coefficients fall below conventional standards for individual diagnosis. For one form, the mean retest coefficient after two weeks is .59, the mean split-half coefficient is .32, and the correlation of Form A with Form B is .38. This is to be expected when each response to a single item normally brings about a change of one half a standard deviation in the sten score. Cattell suggests that only sten scores of 7 or higher and 4 or lower (out of 10) be regarded as "definitely departing from the average." Though he agrees, eventually, that adolescent responses are inherently somewhat less reliable than those of adults, especially when the test is not given under the most favourable possible conditions, he argues that reliability is less important than good factorial validity; indeed high reliability is apt to show that the items are too narrowly specific instead of giving a broad sampling of the content of a factor. He is able to show that the factorial validities are satisfactory, but these, of course, refer to a purely internal criterion. Users would be more interested to receive fuller evidence of correlations with external criteria. Cattell claims good agreement with ratings, with other questionnaires such as the 16 PF, and with various real life criteria. But the only evidence presented in the manual consists of profiles for several pairs of contrasted groups, which are not very impressive. For example, the largest differences between delinquents and boy scouts are 2.2 stens on Factor B (intelligence) and 1.0 on G (super ego strength), though a few other smaller differences also appear meaningful.

One fears that there might be considerable danger of over-interpretation if the HSPQ were applied by such persons as teachers and psychology students. Fortunately, sales are restricted; and trained counselors and educational and clinical psychologists should be well aware of the limitations of personality questionnaires in general and they should often find this workmanlike and ambitious instrument suggestive of personality trends in their clients.

[132]

***Kuder Preference Record—Personal.** Grades 9–16 and adults; 1948–60; 6 scores: group activity, stable situations, working with ideas, avoiding conflict, directing others, verification; IBM; 1 form ('48); 2 editions; profile sheets: children ('49), adults ('52), (2 pages); profile leaflets for comparing vocational (see 1063) and personal scores: children ('53), adults ('54), (4 pages); manual, fifth edition ('60, 16 pages, identical with 1953 manual except for bibliography); separate answer pads or answer sheets must be used; $11 per 20 tests; 70¢ per 20 profile sheets; 90¢ per 20 profile leaflets; 75¢ per specimen set of either edition; postage extra; (40–45) minutes; G. Frederic Kuder; Science Research Associates, Inc. *

a) [HAND SCORING EDITION.] Form AH ('48, 16 pages); $2.60 per 20 answer pads.

b) [MACHINE SCORING EDITION.] IBM; Form AM ('48, 19 pages); $5 per 100 IBM answer sheets; $4 per set of scoring stencils.

REFERENCES

1–4. See 4:65.

5–9. See 5:80.

10. FLOWERS, J. F. *Some Aspects of the Kuder Preference Record—Personal as an Instrument for Prediction and Guidance in Ontario Secondary Schools.* Master's thesis, University of Toronto (Toronto, Ont., Canada), 1957.

11. SCHOLL, CHARLES ELMER, JR. *The Development and Evaluation of Methods for Isolating Factors That Differentiate Between Successful and Unsuccessful Executive Trainees in a Large, Multibranch Bank.* Doctor's thesis, University of Michigan (Ann Arbor, Mich.), 1957. (*DA* 18:2034)

12. SMITH, D. D. "Abilities and Interests: 2, Validation of Factors." *Can J Psychol* 12:253–8 D '58. * (*PA* 33:9347)

13. WARD, PAUL LEWIS. *A Study of the Relationship of Evaluative Attitudes to Scholastic Ability and Academic Achievement.* Doctor's thesis, Ohio State University (Columbus, Ohio), 1959. (*DA* 20:3639)

14. ASH, PHILIP. "Validity Information Exchange, No. 13-05: D.O.T. Code 1-86.12, Salesman, Typewriters." *Personnel Psychol* 13:454 w '60. *

15. COSTELLO, CHARLES G., AND ANDERSON, MARIAN E. "The Vocational and Personal Preferences of Psychiatric and General Nurses." *Nursing Res* 9:155–6 su '60. *

16. WAGNER, EDWIN E. "Differences Between Old and Young Executives on Objective Psychological Test Variables." *J Gerontol* 15:296–9 Jl '60. * (*PA* 35:1328)

17. FLOWERS, JOHN F. *An Evaluation of the Kuder Preference Record—Personal for Use in Ontario.* Atkinson Study of Utilization of Student Resources, Supplementary Report No. 4. Toronto, Canada: Department of Educational Research, Ontario College of Education, 1961. Pp. viii, 31. *

18. MCGUIRE, FREDERICK L. "The Kuder Preference Record—Personal as a Measure of Personal Adjustment." *J Clin Psychol* 17:41–2 Ja '61. * (*PA* 37:3262)

19. SUPER, DONALD E., AND CRITES, JOHN O. *Appraising Vocational Fitness by Means of Psychological Tests, Revised Edition,* pp. 555–60. New York: Harper & Brothers, 1962. Pp. xv, 688. * (*PA* 37:2038)

20. BLOCHER, DONALD H. "A Multiple Regression Approach to Predicting Success in a Counselor Education Program." *Counselor Ed & Sup* 3:19–22 f '63. *

DOROTHY M. CLENDENEN, *Assistant Director, Test Division, The Psychological Corporation, New York, New York.*

The *Kuder Preference Record—Personal* was published in 1948, and since then it has had wide use. The 1953 (fourth) edition of the manual stated that since publication scores had been obtained for over 14,000 adults and high school students. This manual also reported (*a*) validity based on relation between preference scores and job satisfaction, and between preference scores and behavior ratings of dominance, (*b*) mean profiles of more than three thousand men and women who like their work, and (*c*) profiles of satisfied and dissatisfied adults in eight occupations. Norms have been published based on samples of 3,650 boys, 3,924 girls, 1,000 men, and 532 women. New data have not been added in the 1960 (fifth) edition of the manual, which differs from the 1953 edition only in its list of references.

The test has 168 items of the forced choice, triad type in which the examinee selects the activity most liked and the one least liked. Personal or social activities are described in terms of behavior by such items[1] as "Be the editor of a magazine," "Change the subject if you find a person doesn't agree with you," and "Get what you want with no effort." With the publication of the 1953 manual, the earlier one-word scale titles were changed to be more descriptive: preference for being active in groups (A), preference for familiar and stable situations (B), preference for working with ideas (C), preference for avoiding conflict (D), and preference for directing or influencing others (E). There is also a sixth scale, verification, developed to check on the "value" of an individual's responses. A scale to identify the "faker" is reported as still in an experimental stage.

Since it was found that two scales (B and D) are positively correlated with age, correction tables have, since 1952, been included on the adult profile sheet to make scores comparable from one age to another.

Items for the Kuder Personal were selected after several tryouts and revisions designed to form relatively independent, homogeneous scales. Two scales appearing in the experimental form were dropped when they did not meet these requirements. Intercorrelations among

[1] Examples are not from the same triad.

the remaining scales (shown for the 1,000 men in the norms group and for samples of college men and college women) support the claim of independence, the highest reported coefficient being .384 between Scales A and E. Reliability estimates, computed by the Kuder-Richardson formula 21, range from .76 to .89. These reliability coefficients are based on the adult norms groups, and on samples of the student groups; the latter are not, however, the same groups as those used for the intercorrelations. No test-retest coefficients are reported, although these would give useful indications of stability. Results from retesting after a considerable lapse of time would be especially useful in a test of this kind.

Means and standard deviations are not given either with the table of intercorrelations or with the reliability data. In another portion of the manual one finds this information for the adult norm groups for each scale. Since a later section on the use of Fisher's discriminant function seems to assume that users of the manual are relatively sophisticated in statistical methodology, it is difficult to understand why such basic supporting statistics as means and standard deviations have not been included throughout.

According to the manual, adult norms represent a 20 per cent response from "a mailing to telephone subscribers....chosen at random from a representative set of telephone directories." One can object that such a group does not constitute a representative sample of adults, recalling that a number of years ago a national magazine which subsequently ceased publication predicted the outcome of a national election quite erroneously, using a similar selection procedure. Occupational composition of the norms groups is shown; professional and managerial workers make up 44 per cent of the men and 51 per cent of the women, an excessive proportion to be representative of the population as a whole. Means and standard deviations on the scales are not given by occupation.

Validity for the Kuder Personal is presented for one criterion: expressed job satisfaction. Three tables showing means for "satisfied workers" in various groups (39 occupations for men and 12 for women) are presented. Although in these tables significant differences from the base group are indicated, the standard deviations for the subgroups are not given so one does not know how homogeneous the individuals in the group were. Of the 51 occupational groups, 28 have 35 or fewer cases, probably not enough to ensure representativeness and stability.

It should be noted that a high score on a scale indicates greater *preference* than most people express for a specific kind of activity; degree of *participation* in that activity is not measured by the scale, nor is skill. The manual calls attention to the fact that "low scores on some scales predict job satisfaction in certain occupations." Table 1, in which jobs are classified according to the interest areas of the *Kuder Preference Record—Vocational,* indicates the Kuder Personal scales on which people in various occupational groups score high or low. The manual states, "For many occupations listed there are *empirical* data that reveal how the people in that occupation tend to score on the *Personal.* These data are indicated by heavy type. * *Personal* scales that appear in light type refer to probable scores. Although empirical data have not yet been obtained from these groups, evidence from related occupations suggests that they *would probably* score in the manner indicated in the table." This reviewer found it difficult, because of the typeface used in printing this table, to distinguish readily the boldface denoting empirical evidence. Actually, only about 40 out of 292 entries (counting combinations as 1 entry) are in boldface; in other words, over 85 per cent of the list is based on armchair speculation, not on data. The reviewer's primary objection here is not that suggestive estimates are offered, but that typefaces were chosen which would minimize rather than emphasize the difference between empirical and speculative entries.

A table showing correlation with other measures has been included in the manual, but since an early experimental form with seven scales was used for the statistics reported, application of the data to the present edition is moot. In the bibliography of the manual, one study is cited which indicates little relationship between Kuder Personal scales and scales of the *Study of Values* having comparable "titles." It would be useful to a counselor interpreting scores to have further evidence to show how similarly named scales on various instruments relate to one another.

In summary, it is the feeling of this reviewer that the Kuder Personal has been carefully developed and could fulfill a need for an instrument which is neither a vocational interest inventory nor a personality inventory, but which is related to both. However, in spite of 15 years of use the test still has limited validity data reported. And although a great deal of statistical work has obviously been done, some essential data have been omitted from the manual. The amount of emphasis on various topics and the assumptions regarding the kinds of knowledge had by the user seem to indicate confusion or ambivalence on the part of the manual writer concerning his audience, so that the user is not given effective aid in understanding the test.

WILBUR L. LAYTON, *Professor of Psychology and Head of the Department, Iowa State University, Ames, Iowa.*

The *Kuder Preference Record—Personal* (KPR-P) was developed to define (measure) interest and personality factors not already covered by the *Kuder Preference Record—Vocational* (KPR-V). Items presented in forced-choice preference triads to adults and high school pupils were selected to yield five scales having high internal consistency and low intercorrelations with each other and with the KPR-V scales.

The five scales were designed to yield information helpful to a person in deciding the interpersonal relationships situation in which he prefers to work. The five scales are titled: (*a*) preference for being active in groups; (*b*) preference for familiar and stable situations; (*c*) preference for working with ideas; (*d*) preference for avoiding conflict; (*e*) preference for directing or influencing others. In addition to these five preference scales there is a verification scale.

The verification (V) score reflects the degree to which the examinee expresses conforming or "popular" responses. Atypical V-scores cast doubt on the meaning of preference scores and may indicate carelessness or ignorance of the examinee in completing the Record. They may also indicate truly unusual preferences which cannot be adequately evaluated by the KPR-P. The acceptable range of scores on the scale was established empirically.

The five preference scales of KPR-P represent an attempt to define constructs useful in counseling. One might have argued with Kuder about the need in counseling for the five constructs he chose to define. However, if we accept his choices, we can only examine critically the measurement operations used by Kuder to determine if they satisfactorily define the chosen constructs.

There is meager evidence supporting the statistical definition of constructs *a* through *e*. Reliability was estimated by Kuder-Richardson formula 21. The resulting internal consistency coefficients range from .76 to .89 over the five scales for six groups: adult men, and women; college men, and women; high school boys, and girls. Considering the item selection procedure employed, there is still considerably more error variance in the scales than one might expect. Furthermore, no evidence of stability of scores or profiles is available. The scale intercorrelations are quite low and are about equally distributed among positive and negative values as one expects from a forced-choice incomplete ipsative procedure. Thus, the constructs defined by the scales have some internal consistency and are relatively well differentiated from each other.

Unfortunately, Kuder has attempted to combine an incomplete ipsative procedure with the normative approach to measurement. Katz [1] and Bauernfeind [2] have criticized the *Kuder Preference Record—Vocational* on this basis. In a complete forced-choice format the scores are experimentally dependent. The scales have the same number of items and every scale is compared equally with every other scale. For every examinee the total number of responses is identical and these responses are divided among the several scales as a closed system. If raw scores on some scales are high, others must be low and one can infer with confidence the examinee's relative preferences. But in the Kuder approach raw score comparisons are not meaningful because the scales vary in total number of items and the frequency with which the items (scales) are combined in triads. Because of this incomplete ipsativity one cannot make meaningful statements about the relative preferences of an examinee such as "your greatest preference is for being active in groups and your lowest preference is for working with ideas." Since many users of KPR-P will make or want to make statements exactly like

1 KATZ, MARTIN. "Interpreting Kuder Preference Record Scores: Ipsative or Normative." *Voc Guid Q* 10:96–100 w '62. * (*PA* 37:1972)

2 BAUERNFEIND, ROBERT H. *Building a School Testing Program*, pp. 213–31. Boston: Houghton-Mifflin Co., 1963. Pp. xvii, 343. *

this anyway, this is a severe defect in the instrument.

Assuming ipsative scores result from KPR-P, one could and should investigate the meaning of *profiles* rather than the meaning of scores on a particular scale. This is equivalent to investigating personality types as defined by the KPR-P. One could determine the frequency of personality types in various groups and investigate important behavior differences among the types. Kuder, on the other hand, assumes normative scores and has established norms and made limited validity studies of scales considered independently.

It is meaningless to use norms with the KPR-P. If it were meaningful, Kuder must be criticized for the norms produced. The adult norms presented in the manual resulted from about a 20 per cent response to mailing to telephone subscribers whose names were drawn from a "representative set of telephone directories for cities, towns, and villages spread out over the United States." The norms for high school pupils are based on 3,650 boys and 3,924 girls from high schools distributed over the country. No data are given in the manual to show the extent to which the norms represent the preferences of adults and high school pupils. However, the occupational distribution of persons in the adult norm groups clearly indicates an over-representation of professional, managerial, sales, and clerical occupations when compared to U.S. census data. Sixty seven per cent of the male norm group and 92 per cent of the female norm group were classified in these upper-level occupational groups!

Even so, in an attempt to give meaning to the preference scores Kuder used the norm groups as reference groups against which to compare scores of men and women in various professional and managerial groups. Consequently, he should be gratified he found some significant differentiation.

Tables 3 and 4 in the manual present means of various occupational groups of men and women compared with the means of the adult norm groups. These data are interesting but for the user of the KPR-P represent the data from the standpoint of the wrong regression line. The user needs to predict occupational placement from test profiles not the reverse.

The manual also reports a study of the relationship of KPR-P scores to job satisfaction. The basic data were taken from the responses of the adult norm groups to the KPR-P and to a question which asked the subject to indicate whether, if given free choice, he would prefer: (*a*) the job he has now; (*b*) the same kind of work but some changes in working conditions or fellow employees; or (*c*) a different kind of work entirely. Those who checked (*c*) were considered dissatisfied and the remainder satisfied workers. Response to a single question of this sort is obviously an unreliable measure of job satisfaction. Mean scores of "satisfied" and "dissatisfied" workers on the five KPR-P scales were compared, and these data are interesting to someone concerned with studying job satisfaction. However, the data yield little information about the predictive validity of the KPR-P scales.

Thus, the KPR-P manual presents only meager evidence supporting the definition of five preference constructs. But the great deficiency of the Kuder procedure is the ill-considered attempt to combine ipsative and normative approaches to psychological measurement. Consequently, the KPR-P in its present form cannot be recommended for use even on an experimental basis.

For a review by Dwight L. Arnold, see 5:80; see also 4:65 (1 excerpt).

[133]

★The Leadership Ability Evaluation. Grades 9–16 and adults; 1961; social climate created in influencing others; 5 scores: laissez faire, democratic-cooperative, autocratic-submissive, autocratic-aggressive, decision pattern; 1 form (8 pages); manual (18 pages); $10 per set of 25 tests and manual; $3 per manual; postpaid; specimen set not available; [30] minutes; Russell N. Cassel and Edward J. Stancik (test); Western Psychological Services. *

REFERENCES

1. CASSEL, RUSSELL N., AND HADDOX, GENEVIEVE. "Comparative Study of Leadership Test Scores for Gifted and Typical High School Students." *Psychol Rep* 5:713–7 D '59. * (*PA* 34:5701)

2. CASSEL, RUSSELL N. "A Construct Validity Study on a Leadership and a Social Insight Tests for 200 College Freshmen Students." *J Genetic Psychol* 99:165–70 S '61. * (*PA* 36:3GF65C)

3. CASSEL, RUSSELL N., AND SANDERS, RICHARD A. "A Comparative Analysis of Scores From Two Leadership Tests for Apache Indian and Anglo American Youth." *J Ed Res* 55:19–23 S '61. * (*PA* 36:4GB19C)

4. CASSEL, RUSSELL, AND CHILDERS, RICHARD. "A Study of Certain Attributes of 45 High-School Varsity Football Team Members by Use of Psychological Test Scores." *J Ed Res* 57:64–7 O '63. *

JOHN D. BLACK, *Director, Counseling and Testing Center, and Consulting Associate Professor of Psychology, Stanford University, Stanford; and President, Consulting Psychologists Press, Inc.; Palo Alto, California.*

This test, printed in an attractive eight-page

expendable booklet containing a profile, confronts the subject with four alternative choices for handling each of fifty "leadership situations." Each alternative is scored on one of the four subscales, three of which are then differentially weighted and combined into a total score called the "Decision Pattern."

Study of item content immediately raises the question of whether the authors' definition of leadership situations may be too broad. Typical questions ask what to do if "your mother shows favoritism to your brother or sister," if your wife opens a charge account against your wishes, if you're a pilot whose plane develops engine trouble, if you see a classmate cheating on an examination. Indeed, the items are very similar—in several cases almost identical—to those in the senior author's *Test of Social Insight,* but the scales have different names.

No information on methods of item selection is given nor is it clear how the subscales were built. The manual asserts that "six research psychologists evaluated the social climate structures used in the four part scores of the LAE; *without exception* there was agreement that the leadership patterns were incorporated in the structure of the LAE" (italics added). Despite such unanimity, the reviewer was puzzled by some of the scaling. For example, on an item about what a teacher should do with a girl who "comes to school in an extremely low-cut dress," the alternative "Send her home" is scored Autocratic-Submissive (AS); "Do nothing" is scored Autocratic-Aggressive (AA); and "Discuss this with the dean of girls" is scored Laissez Faire (LF). The pilot with engine trouble receives a point for LF if he decides to make an emergency landing and a point for AA if he decides to abandon ship.

Corrected split-half reliabilities for the five scores are rather variable, ranging from .91 to .29 in different groups. The total score is most reliable with a median r of .82, the AS least reliable with a median of .46. No test-retest reliability is reported, nor are any validity data given for the subscales. Intercorrelations range from .05 to $-.72$ and are generally low enough to justify use of all scales.

Whatever their limitations, the subscales do represent meaningful ways of conceptualizing leadership behavior and it seems unfortunate that the authors have not made more use of them. Instead, most attention is given to the total score which is computed from the subscales. The authors assert: *"The characteristic decision making pattern* is provided by the *total score* of an individual" (italics theirs). How a single score compounded of three entirely different approaches to leadership situations can constitute a *pattern* is difficult to comprehend.

The total score is obtained by adding 7 times LF and 4 times AS to DC (Democratic-Cooperative), then dividing the sum by 10. Low scores indicate greater leadership ability. AA is excluded from the formula, and the confounding effect of this omission is that one will decrease (i.e., improve) his total score the more Autocratic-Aggressive alternatives he selects. The formula was developed by maximizing discrimination between a group of 100 "leaders" and 200 "typical subjects" (neither group described further). From a study of the table containing the regression weights, it is not entirely clear to the reviewer why AA was omitted and it appears that DC is utilized as a suppressor variable, a confusing situation at best.

One reported cross validation study shows that by using a cutoff score of 10, the LAE total score correctly identifies 60 per cent of a group of 500 "outstanding leaders" of both sexes at the expense of classifying 23 per cent of 500 ninth graders as effective leaders. No doubt the separation would be even less impressive if ordinary adults were substituted for the students. Nevertheless, the manual flatly states that "Total scores of 10 and lower are indicative of effective leaders, while total scores above 10 are indicative of ineffective leaders."

The test authors seem to feel that construct validity of a test is established by reporting a number of miscellaneous correlations with other tests. In this case the data reveal that leadership ability as measured by the LAE is negatively correlated with IQ, reading ability, and a number of other intellectual aptitudes.

Norms provided in the profile for easy conversion of raw to T-scores are based on 2,000 "typical individuals" and 400 "outstanding leaders" (neither identified further). For LF, DC, and total score, the means are reported for a peculiar assortment of groups, many of which have little relevance for a test purporting to measure leadership ability (e.g., "below average typical youth," "delinquent youth," "guidance counselors," "USAF chaplains").

There is a need for a good test of leadership ability; unfortunately, tests of the calibre of this one can only serve to disillusion prospective users. The LAE suffers these principal defects: The item content does not deal primarily with relevant leadership situations. Many of the alternatives representing the four modes of leadership need refinement. Validity has been inadequately studied among groups whose primary function is leadership. The cumbersome formula for total score is inadequately based on a single study and its use as a rigid cutoff score for leadership ability, as recommended by the authors, is entirely unjustified and professionally reprehensible. Finally, the total score, derived as it is, is absolutely devoid of any psychological meaning. It seems likely that the search for a single score to measure leadership ability is futile, and that attention might better be focused on studying patterns of leadership skills required in different situations. In its present form the LAE will not further such useful research.

Cecil A. Gibb, *Professor of Psychology, The Australian National University, Canberra City, Australia.*

General leadership literature suggests that there are many who would be attracted by a test offering assessment of four patterns of leadership described as Laissez Faire, Democratic-Cooperative, Autocratic-Submissive, and Autocratic-Aggressive, though why this should be so is not at all certain.

Even such persons will, however, have misgivings about Cassel's LAE because—if for no other reason—the test form itself rather signals the interpretation to the subject unless he be extraordinarily naive. Four-choice answers are so arranged that the choice letters A, B, C, D are "randomised" to give a particular pattern response always in the same position, and the positions carry the headings AA, AS, DC, and LF in the same order on all six pages of the test. Cassel claims that "face validity" of the test is evident to those taking the LAE and to specialists in test construction. Perhaps this should disqualify the present reviewer.

The 50 items of the LAE are said to "encompass the life activities of an individual in western culture," under the headings of home and family life, work and vocational pursuits, play and avocational pursuits, school and educational pursuits, and community life. There can be little argument but that some of the items are quite inappropriate to any given individual. Cassel apparently believes in a "lowest common denominator" approach to patterns of leader behavior and evidence of situational determinants of such behavior has not impressed him at all.

Instructions for administration and scoring are adequate and reliability and validity statistics given in the manual seem numerous but often defy interpretation, e.g., on the Democratic-Cooperative dimension Cassel says, "Scores above 35 suggest excessive cooperation by the leader; scores below 20 suggest too little cooperation"; but about one third of the group he designates "outstanding leaders" present scores outside these limits. It is also difficult to understand what a total score on this test can mean, yet it is claimed to be "the most important single indicator of acceptable or unacceptable leadership pattern."

[134]

★The Leadership Q-Sort Test (A Test of Leadership Values). Adults; 1958; 7 scores: personal integrity, consideration of others, mental health, technical information, decision making, teaching and communication, total; 1 form (4 pages); manual (56 pages); no data on reliability of subscores; $9 per examiner's kit of 25 tests, 25 item sheets (must be cut up into sorting slips), set of keys, sorting board, and manual; $3 per 25 tests; $1 per set of keys; $2 per 25 item sheets; $1 per sorting board; $3 per manual; cash orders postpaid; (40-50) minutes; Russell N. Cassel; Psychometric Affiliates. *

REFERENCES

1. Carp, Abraham, and Cassel, Russell. "Development and Preliminary Analysis of a New Q Sort Type of Leadership Test." Abstract. *Am Psychologist* 12:464 Jl '57. *

2. Cassel, Russell N., and Carp, Abraham. "Combining Criterion Measures From R and Q Methodologies for Purpose of Validating Tests Related to Leadership." Abstract. *Am Psychologist* 12:408-9 Jl '57. *

3. Cassel, Russell N., and Harriman, B. Lynn. "Comparing Pre- and Post-Training Leadership Test Scores for Colonels and Federal Prisoners and With Other Test Scores." Abstract. *Am Psychologist* 13:370 Jl '58. *

4. Cassel, Russell N., and Haddox, Genevieve. "Comparative Study of Leadership Test Scores for Gifted and Typical High School Students." *Psychol Rep* 5:713-7 D '59. * (*PA* 34:5701)

5. Cassel, Russell N., and Haddox, Genevieve. "Leadership Testing." *Voc Guid Q* 7:189-92 sp '59. *

6. Cassel, Russell N., and Sanders, Richard A. "A Comparative Analysis of Scores From Two Leadership Tests for Apache Indian and Anglo American Youth." *J Ed Res* 55:19-23 S '61. * (*PA* 36:4GB19C)

Joel T. Campbell, *Research Psychologist, Educational Testing Service, Princeton, New Jersey.*

This test is, to quote the author, "concerned with assessing an individual's values with respect to the leadership role. The 60 items which are contained in the test have all been identified by well qualified leaders as being important to the leadership function. Multiple groups of outstanding leaders (and others) have provided ratings on these items which are used as the test norms. By comparing an individual's ratings on the test items with the appropriate test norms a meaningful evaluation is obtained of his leadership values and notions."

The person taking the test is required to sort the 60 items into 11 steps on a scale. The high end of the scale has the description, "Statements most important to good or effective leadership" and the low end, "Statements least important to good or effective leadership." The number of items permitted in each step is controlled so that a normal distribution is forced.

The scoring appears to the reviewer to be a little cumbersome. A two-page form is provided. First, the item numbers are recorded in blocks along the rating scale, so that a check can be made that the proper number of items has been assigned to each step. Then, for each item, the score or step value given by the rater is recorded. (Up to this point, the operations can be performed by the person taking the test.) At this point, a cutout scoring key is applied and, for each item, the *difference* between the score recorded and the keyed value is recorded. These differences are squared, summed, divided by 620, and the quotient subtracted from 1 to obtain a correlation between the Q-sort ratings assigned by the subject and those contained in the norms. By means of a separate table, this is converted to a Fisher's *z* for comparison with various norm groups. Quite likely this is easier to do after one or two trials than it is to describe, but nonetheless it appears quite a cumbersome procedure.

In addition to an overall or total "Leadership Values" score, keys are provided for six subscores. These are labeled Personal Integrity, Consideration, Mental Health, Technical Information, Decision Making, and Teaching and Communication. The 60 items were distributed into these six subtests by the consensual judgment of seven psychologists. The reviewer's experience in comparing factor analysis results with judgment results leads him to question the adequacy of this method of developing subtests.

Normative data are reported for total and part scores for 540 typical youth (mixed sex), 150 USAF colonels, 31 USAF chaplains, and 200 federal reformatory prisoners. Also given are the mean values for each item for these same groups and for 31 research psychologists. These norms probably will not be relevant for an industrial concern, for example, and the reviewer doubts that they are adequate for use in most educational or counseling situations. A potential user would need to provide his own local norms.

Split-half reliabilities are reported as .83 and .84 for the total score. Measurement of reliability was also approached by correlating three pairs of items which were highly similar in content for six groups of individuals. The resulting 18 correlation coefficients range from .008 to .673, with 12 coefficients significant at the .01 level. No other information is given on the reliability of the test, either for total scores or the part scores. Since two of the subtests have only five items each, an estimate of reliability would seem to be particularly important here. Test-retest coefficients should be obtained and reported.

The author has provided several kinds of validity estimates. One study compared Q-sort total scores with other measures for a sample of 100 preflight cadets. The other measures included leadership instructor ratings, mean academic grades, peer status ratings, and peer affiliate ratings. Peer status ratings were defined as "Cadet peer status ratings as to leadership competency given by all Cadets in group" and peer affiliate ratings were defined as "Cadet peer affiliate ratings, or evaluations given by each Cadet to other members of his group as to their leadership competency." Total Q-sort scores correlated .23 with peer status ratings and .39 with leadership instructor ratings. The correlation with peer affiliate rating was zero and with academic grades .04. No explanation is given of the lack of correlation with peer affiliate rating, nor of the −.22 correlation reported between peer status rating and peer affiliate rating.

Another table gives correlations based on a sample of 200, apparently also preflight cadets, for these variables plus several other test scores. Here the correlation of total Q-sort scores with peer status rating was .15 and with peer affiliate rating, −.12. The author summarizes results from this table as, "there is significant relationship with peer and instructor ratings relative to leadership competency, social insight, personality tension and needs, class standing, other leadership test scores, and the like. There is little or no relationship with academic grades, chronological age, ego strength, and the like." Since several of the significant relationships are negative, the reviewer feels that some further explanation is in order.

A second estimate of validity was comparison of total and part scores before and after a leadership training course for 200 preflight cadets. The total score changed in the direction of greater agreement with the norm group of USAF full colonels, "who are presumed to have greater leadership competency than the Cadets." The part scores changed in the direction of assigning greater importance to Personal Integrity, Technical Information, and Teaching and Communication, and less importance to Consideration of Others, Mental Health, and Decision Making.

A third approach to validity estimation was the comparison of mean total scores for various groups. Full colonels had the highest mean score, followed by research psychologists, preflight cadets after leadership training, USAF chaplains, and so on down to basic airmen. It is interesting that federal prisoners have approximately the same mean score as USAF NCO's!

An additional study reported is an inverse factor analysis of four individuals from each of five groups—chaplains, preflight cadets, colonels, research psychologists, and federal prisoners. Five factors were identified: chaplain leadership pattern, military leadership pattern, in-prison leadership pattern, psychologists' leadership pattern, and general leadership pattern. The reviewer would question the naming of at least the first factor, since two of the four psychologists had higher loadings than any of the chaplains, and two of the chaplains have negative loadings!

Before this test is used in business or education, its validity in such situations should be established. It is at least conceivable that the aspects of leadership considered most important in an institutional setting, such as the Air Force or a federal reformatory, will not be so considered in a less rigidly structured environment, such as a small business, a large business, a college, or a political organization.

The language level of the test directions is quite difficult, and the manual is particularly difficult to read. There are a number of minor irritations, such as a grammatical error in item 1 of the test, and the use in the manual of E rather than the conventional capital sigma to indicate summation.

The basic idea of this test seems well worthwhile—namely, that what a person considers to be important to leadership will be reflected in his competency as a leader. The author deserves credit for doing more research on this test than is done on many tests before they are marketed. The research does have the limitation of having been done almost exclusively in institutional settings, rather than with the kind of population with which most users will need to deal.

Cecil A. Gibb, *Professor of Psychology, The Australian National University, Canberra City, Australia.*

On the face of it the *Leadership Q-Sort Test* (LQT) looks promising. The materials are neatly and satisfactorily designed and the compact manual has such section headings as Theory Underlying the LQT, Ipsative Scores, Q-Methodology, Test Development and Validation, Instructions for Administering, Instructions for Scoring, Interpretation of Scores. It also contains many norm tables. Unfortunately, however, this impeccable framework is clothed in a good deal of unsatisfactory discussion and inadequate quantitative detail.

Probably the most disconcerting feature of the LQT manual is Cassel's insistence upon using popular terms, but using them in his own way. For example, in the introduction he uses the heading Theory Underlying the LQT but offers no theory. He claims to "define" leadership but cannot decide whether he wishes to do this as role or behavior. He offers "dimensions" of leadership which are quite unlike those of any empirical research and yet when he offers categories of related characteristics of an effective leader, he approaches much more nearly known dimensions of leader behavior. Similar difficulties exist with description of ipsative scores, Q-methodology, and the forced-choice technique of which Cassel says: "Since the subject is unable to speculate what ratings will prove of vantage for the various items, the test is said to employ a 'forced choice' technique."

Even the critical characteristics technique employed probably suffers a little from the choice of preflight cadets as respondents rather than men with greater and broader experience of leadership in a variety of situations. However, this technique does give results which accord well with other research. Four hundred cadets produced 3,667 statements which, after being edited for redundancy, were subjectively grouped in seven categories labeled: Personal Integrity, Consideration for Others, Mental Health, Technical Information, Decision Making, Teaching and Communication, and Positive and Favorable Attitude. From this wealth of statements 60 items were then selected (again subjectively) in such a way as to keep the number of items in the 60 roughly proportional to the number within the category; thus Personal Integrity has 17 items while Decision Making has 5. Seven research psychologists then assigned one category label to each of the 60 chosen items. The positive attitude category proved to be infrequently used and most of the items belonging to it were assigned to the mental health category; accordingly all items of these two categories were combined under the heading of mental health.

Validity is approached in a number of ways. Internal validity is alleged on the basis of three pairs of items having somewhat similar meanings. Correlations between pair members for a number of groups vary between .008 and .673. Face validity is claimed because unidentified items given to graduate students in psychology classes were judged to be related to management, supervision, or leadership functions. Status validity is assessed by correlating LQT scores (based upon USAF colonels as models) with peer status ratings, leadership competency ratings, academic grades, and peer affiliate ratings of preflight cadets. LQT scores are found to be significantly correlated with peer status ratings (.23) and leadership competency ratings (.39) but to have zero correlations with the other two criteria. It is shown, however, that as a result of a 44 hour leadership training course, the scores of cadets do show a significant shift in the direction of the colonel model. Many other "validation" data are offered but these seem to do nothing to increase confidence in, or understanding of, the test.

To achieve a general purpose scoring key for the LQT, the mean ranking of items for four groups is used. These were 540 typical youths of mixed sex, 150 USAF colonels, 31 USAF chaplains, and some research psychologists. For a reason, not quite clear, data from 200 federal reformatory prisoners were excluded. Separate norms are also given for each of these groups, except the psychologists.

Instructions for administration and scoring are adequate. Seven scores are available, a total score and one for each part corresponding to each of the original six categories. The total score takes the form of a rank correlation coefficient calculated between the ranking made and that of the scoring key. This Cassel calls a Pearson r which is then converted to a Fisher z which, in turn, may be referred to norm tables for interpretation. Part scores are obtained directly. Cutout keys identify the items for each scale and ratings assigned are simply summed and the norm tables entered directly with these sums to obtain T scores.

Just what interpretation of such scores may be obtained is a matter of considerable conjecture. Cassel says, "where the total score on the LQT in terms of a Fisher z' score is .400 or above, the individual has values in the area of leadership which are in significant agreement with similar values by demonstrated effective leaders." But, if he has been understood correctly, this is not so, for the scoring key is derived from a very mixed group and certainly not from "demonstrated effective leaders," unless all psychologists, all chaplains, and all youths fall into this category. Interpretation of the part scores would perhaps be more meaningful if one were not continually aware of the unsatisfactory item selection and validation procedures which give rise to them.

For the research worker in this area of measuring leadership potential there will be food for thought in the *Leadership Q-Sort Test,* but one could not confidently recommend it for routine application in any setting.

WILLIAM STEPHENSON, *Professor of Psychology, University of Missouri, Columbia, Missouri.*

This is an ingenious use of Q-technique, but not of Q-methodology. Statements validated for leadership attributes in R-methodology are provided as a Q-sample with which subjects perform a Q-sort to express how important each is for effective leadership of a person. The Q-sort array is then scored in relation to R-methodological norms. No validation of the Q-scores so provided is reported. One need have no objection to the technique as such, so used, provided it can indicate valid measurements.

But the method is not Q-methodological. This is at once clear when one observes that the measurements provided by the technique are dimensions of so called leadership, its values, insight, ego strength, and anxiety. Q-method does not provide measures of such attributes, but, instead, gives evidence for different *types* of persons. Thus, one might have as an outcome of Q a *cautious* type of leader, a *romantic* type, an *impulsive* type, or whatever. Such are the end products of Q-methodology: not even a semblance of the kind issues from this test.

It should not be necessary, as the manual does, to define Q as concerned with "many tests....administered to few persons," whereas R is "few tests....administered to many persons." The statements of a Q-sample are not tests in the sense of the word in R-method. They are, instead, merely synthetic statements, involving "excess meanings," which can be ego-involving (self-referent) for the person. Nor, in any properly constructed Q-sample, can any person "often desire to give all of [the statements] a top rating": on the contrary, the Q-sample is hinged about a *neutral* point (at the mean score) where statements are not ego-involving (i.e., they do not matter to the person providing the Q-sort) and then disperse in positive and negative directions. That is, there are always, in a Q-sample, some statements which the person cannot agree with or which he *dis*likes and some which he agrees with or likes. It is never possible for him to like them all; it is always the case, in a well constructed Q-sample, that the individual will find that most of the statements don't matter to him.

There ought, therefore, to be a rider in any republication of the leadership test to the effect that it involves Q-technique, not Q-methodology in the proper sense of the word.

Having said this, the ingenuity of the Cassel procedure deserves comment. It is difficult to provide norms for a genuine use of Q-methodology since type descriptions are at issue. Each person's Q-sort would have to be correlated with the Q-arrays defining the types, and this requires sophistication for the necessary calculations. Cassel's method, whilst it doesn't touch on genuine Q-factors, does suggest that *scoring for type* might be sufficiently indicated if a few statements of the Q-sample, strongly indicative of a factor, were scored accordingly. The normative data would then be somewhat as follows: "if statements *x, y, z*....gain scores +5 or +4 (on an 11-point scale from +5 to −5), the individual is likely to be of type A"; similarly, a few high-scoring statements could be used to define each type of item.

Again, however, what *use* one could make of such typifications is another matter. This is ordinarily what one means by validity data, and this would be as necessary for proper normative use of Q as it is of Cassel's so called ipsative methodology.

[135]

***The MACC Behavioral Adjustment Scale: An Objective Approach to the Evaluation of Behavioral Adjustments of Psychiatric Patients.** Psychotic mental patients; 1957–62; Forms 1, 2, (4 pages); Form 2 is a revision of Form 1 rather than a parallel form; $4 per 25 copies of the *Behavior Charting Record* ('59, 2 pages, cumulative record for use with Form 1) by F. Harold Giedt; $8.50 per 25 scales, postpaid; specimen set not available; [5–15] minutes; Robert B. Ellsworth; Western Psychological Services. *

a) FORM 1. 1957; 5 ratings: affect, cooperation, communication, total adjustment, motility; mimeographed manual (10 pages).

b) FORM 2. 1962; 5 ratings: mood, cooperation, communication, social contact, total adjustment; mimeographed manual (17 pages).

REFERENCES

1. ELLSWORTH, ROBERT B., AND CLAYTON, WILLIAM H. "Measurement of Improvement in 'Mental Illness.'" *J Consult Psychol* 23:15–20 F '59. * (*PA* 34:1353)
2. MARKS, JOHN; STAUFFACHER, JAMES C.; AND LYLE, CURTIS. "Predicting Outcome in Schizophrenia." *J Abn & Social Psychol* 66:117–27 F '63. * (*PA* 37:7076)

WILSON H. GUERTIN, *Associate Professor of Education and Psychology, University of Florida, Gainesville, Florida.*

The MACC is named for the four subscales of Form 1: Motility, Affect, Cooperation, and Communication. It is unique among scales for rating behavior of psychotic patients because instead of an omnibus sampling of behavior, Ellsworth preselected items which differentiated between drug-improved and drug-nonimproved patients.

Form 1 employs 14, and Form 2, 16 scales with descriptive statements of behavior to correspond to each of the five scale points. Items were selected and assigned to subscales on the basis of cluster analyses. When the instrument was revised in 1962, the Motility subscale was dropped; a new item was added to the Affect subscale, the name of which was changed to Mood; and a new four-item subscale, Social Contact, was added.

Form 2 modifications do not reflect criticisms set forth in the previous *Mental Meas-*

urements Yearbook review by Lorr (see 5:82). All norms for Form 2 are from male veterans at one hospital. Such norms are worse than none because they may be misleading. The author should merely state that no norms are required for studies evaluating change after treatment.

The revised manual reports only two validity studies employing Form 2. One found that all subscales significantly differentiated between closed and open ward patients, and another that length of subsequent hospitalization was related to MACC total scores obtained shortly after admission.

Although the reasonable criticisms made by Lorr are not obviated by the revised form, we must applaud any effort to improve existing instruments. But it is difficult to see how Form 2 constitutes an improvement. Whereas Form 1 items were preselected to discriminate between improved and nonimproved patients, Form 2 adds four items seemingly not selected on this basis. Moreover, how much of a change has really been effected when the author reports a correlation of .93 between total scores of Form 1 and 2?

The newer *Psychotic Reaction Profile* (see 167) by Lorr can and should replace the MACC for rating behavior of psychotic patients.

For a review by Maurice Lorr of a, *see 5:82.*

[136]

★M-B History Record. Psychiatric patients; 1957–61; interview questionnaire for use with family informants; separate forms ('57) for men (17 pages), women (18 pages); manual ['60, 7 pages]; mimeographed norms ['61] for form for men; no data on reliability; no norms for form for women; 20 or more records, 15¢ each; $1 per specimen set of both forms (must be purchased to obtain manual and norms); postpaid; [60–90] minutes; Peter F. Briggs; the Author. *

REFERENCES

1. Briggs, Peter Farkasch. *Preliminary Validation of a Standard Personal History for Psychiatric Diagnosis.* Doctor's thesis, University of Minnesota (Minneapolis, Minn.), 1955. (*DA* 15:1113)
2. Briggs, Peter F. "Eight Item Clusters for Use With the M-B History Record." *J Clin Psychol* 15:22–8 Ja '59. * (*PA* 34:3262)

[137]

The Manson Evaluation. Adults; 1948; identification of alcoholics, potential alcoholics, and severely maladjusted adults; 8 scores: anxiety, depressive fluctuations, emotional sensitivity, resentfulness, incompleteness, aloneness, interpersonal relations, total; 1 form (4 pages); manual (2 pages); no data on reliability of subscores; $6.50 per 25 tests, postpaid; specimen set not available; (5–15) minutes; Morse P. Manson; Western Psychological Services. *

REFERENCES

1–4. See 4:68.
5. Murphy, Donal G. *The Validity and Reliability of the Manson Evaluation and the Alcadd Test in the Identification of Female Alcoholics.* Master's thesis, Fordham University (New York, N.Y.), 1955.
6. Murphy, Donal G. "The Revalidation of Diagnostic Tests for Alcohol Addiction." *J Consult Psychol* 20:301–4 Ag '56. * (*PA* 31:8340)
7. Clark, James Ward. *Personality Syndromes in Chronic Alcoholism: A Factorial Study.* Doctor's thesis, Queen's University (Kingston, Ont., Canada), 1958. (Abstract: *Can Psychologist* 1:116–7.)
8. Gibbins, Robert J.; Smart, Reginald G.; and Seeley, John R. "A Critique of the Manson Evaluation Test." *Q J Studies Alcohol* 20:357–61 Je '59. * (*PA* 34:6018)
9. Stotsky, Bernard A. "Accuracy of Configurational and Item Analytic Techniques Based on the Manson Evaluation in Diagnostic Classifications." *J Psychol Studies* 12:68–74 Mr '61. *

Dugal Campbell, *Assistant Professor of Psychology, Queen's University, Kingston, Ontario, Canada.*

The Manson Evaluation is intended for use as a screening device (*a*) to detect individuals who were formerly alcoholics, (*b*) to detect nonalcoholics who have personality characteristics similar to alcoholics, and (*c*) to obtain information about psychological processes involved in alcoholic or potential alcoholic personalities. The rationale is that alcoholics have distinctive personality characteristics which can be measured, so that an individual's likelihood of becoming an alcoholic under stress (or his likelihood of being an alcoholic at the moment) can be predicted. Questions designed to measure seven traits (three concerning psychoneuroticism and four concerning psychopathy) are used. In the original investigation, misclassification of alcoholics and nonalcoholics, and vice versa, was in the range 16–21 per cent. Murphy (*5, 6*) tried the test on groups of active alcoholics, Alcoholics Anonymous members, social drinkers, and abstainers. All the critical ratios between the groups were significant.

The test has been severely criticised by Gibbins, Smart, and Seeley (*8*), who point out that the groups used in the standardisation were not comparable and that the critical score used by Manson is based on an estimate of the prevalence of alcoholism which is very much higher than that actually found in the general population. They conclude: "This seems to eliminate most of the situations in which the use of the test for diagnostic purposes would make any sense."

The questions raised by the original reviewers remain unanswered: (*a*) What will happen when genuine job seekers are motivated to fake their answers? (*b*) Do the results vary when the test is used in different circumstances? (For example, when neither group of subjects consists of admitted alcoholics under treatment.) (*c*) Will the arrangement of the questions into seven groups stand up to an objective analysis? (*d*) Will the arrangement be repeated with other subjects? More generally the notion that alcoholics have distinctive personality patterns which are markedly different from those of other groups (both normal and abnormal) has come under fire. Reviews of work based on the idea that alcoholism is associated with particular personality patterns [1] suggest that nothing of this sort has so far been sufficiently clearly demonstrated to provide a practical basis for test construction. Consequently one cannot readily see how the test may be used in either clinical practice or research.

For reviews by Charles H. Honzik and Albert L. Hunsicker, see 4:68.

[138]

★**Maudsley Personality Inventory.** College and adults; 1959–62; 2 scores: neuroticism, extraversion; H. J. Eysenck. *

a) BRITISH EDITION. 1959; 1 form (2 pages); manual (8 pages); may be administered as a short scale; 6*s.* 9*d.* per 25 tests; 4*d.* per single copy; 2*s.* per set of keys; 2*s.* 6*d.* per manual; postage and purchase tax extra; [5] minutes for short scale, [15] minutes for full scale; University of London Press Ltd.

b) UNITED STATES EDITION. 1962; 1 form ('62, c1959–62, 2 pages, items identical with British edition); manual (21 pages); $3 per 25 tests; $1 per set of test booklet hand scoring stencils; separate answer cards may be used; $5 per 100 IBM port-a-punch cards; $1.25 per manual; $1.75 per specimen set; postage extra; (10–15) minutes; manual by Robert R. Knapp; Educational & Industrial Testing Service.

REFERENCES

1. BENDIG, A. W. "Extraversion, Neuroticism, and Manifest Anxiety." Abstract. *J Consult Psychol* 21:398 O '57. *
2. BENDIG, A. W. "Extraversion, Neuroticism, and Verbal Ability Measures." *J Consult Psychol* 22:464 D '58. * (*PA* 33:9928)
3. BENDIG, A. W. "Identification of Item Factor Patterns Within the Manifest Anxiety Scale." Abstract. *J Consult Psychol* 22:158 Ap '58. * (*PA* 35:3448)
4. EYSENCK, H. J. "Hysterics and Dysthymics as Criterion Groups in the Study of Introversion-Extraversion: A Reply." *J Abn & Social Psychol* 57:250–4 S '58. * (*PA* 33:10806)
5. EYSENCK, H. J. "A Short Questionnaire for the Measurement of Two Dimensions of Personality." *J Appl Psychol* 42:14–7 F '58. *
6. JENSEN, ARTHUR R. "The Maudsley Personality Inventory." *Acta Psychologica* 14(4):314–25 '58. * (*PA* 33:9958)
7. SIGAL, JOHN J.; STAR, KOLMAN H.; AND FRANKS, CYRIL M. "Hysterics and Dysthymics as Criterion Groups in the Measure of Introversion-Extraversion: A Rejoinder to Eysenck's Reply." *J Abn & Social Psychol* 57:381–2 N '58. * (*PA* 33:10825)
8. SIGAL, JOHN J.; STAR, KOLMAN H.; AND FRANKS, CYRIL M. "Hysterics and Dysthymics as Criterion Groups in the Study of Introversion-Extraversion." *J Abn & Social Psychol* 57:143–8 S '58. * (*PA* 33:10826)
9. STORMS, LOWELL H., AND SIGAL, JOHN J. "Eysenck's Personality Theory With Special Reference to 'The Dynamics of Anxiety and Hysteria.'" *Brit J Med Psychol* 31:228–46 pts 3 & 4 '58. *
10. BARTHOLOMEW, ALLEN A. "Extraversion-Introversion and Neuroticism in First Offenders and Recidivists." *Brit J Delinq* 10:120–9 O '59. *
11. BARTHOLOMEW, ALLEN A., AND MARLEY, EDWARD. "Susceptibility to Methylpentynol: Personality and Other Variables." *J Mental Sci* 105:957–70 O '59. *
12. BARTHOLOMEW, ALLEN A., AND MARLEY, EDWARD. "The Temporal Reliability of the Maudsley Personality Inventory." *J Mental Sci* 105:238–40 Ja '59. * (*PA* 34:1000)
13. BENDIG, A. W. "College Norms for and Concurrent Validity of the Pittsburgh Revisions of the Maudsley Personality Inventory." *J Psychol Studies* 11:12–7 S–O '59. * (*PA* 34:4053)
14. BENDIG, A. W. "The Relationship of Scales of Extraversion-Introversion and Emotionality to Guilford's O, F, and P Scales." *J Psychol Studies* 11:49–51 N–D '59. * (*PA* 34:5597)
15. BENDIG, A. W. "Score Reliability of Dichotomous and Trichotomous Item Responses on the Maudsley Personality Inventory." Abstract. *J Consult Psychol* 23:181 Ap '59. * (*PA* 34:1339, title only)
16. BENDIG, A. W., AND VAUGHAN, CHARLES J. "Extraversion, Neuroticism, and Motor Learning." *J Abn & Social Psychol* 59:399–403 N '59. * (*PA* 34:6003)
17. BRENGELMANN, J. C. "Differences in Questionnaire Responses Between English and German Nationals." *Acta Psychologica* 16(5):339–55 '59. * (*PA* 34:5788)
18. EYSENCK, H. J. "The Differentiation Between Normal and Various Neurotic Groups on the Maudsley Personality Inventory." *Brit J Psychol* 50:176–7 My '59. * (*PA* 34:2991)
19. EYSENCK, H. J. "Personality and the Estimation of Time." *Percept & Motor Skills* 9:405–6 D '59. * (*PA* 34:5610)
20. FRANKS, C. M., AND LEIGH, D. "The Theoretical and Experimental Application of a Conditioning Model to a Consideration of Bronchial Asthma in Man." *J Psychosom Res* 4:88–98 D '59. * (*PA* 34:8218)
21. KELTY, EDWARD JOHN. *Normal Electrocortical Activity in Relation to Personality Factors.* Doctor's thesis, Duke University (Durham, N.C.), 1959. (*DA* 20:756)
22. LYNN, R. "Two Personality Characteristics Related to Academic Achievement." *Brit J Ed Psychol* 29:213–6 N '59. *
23. RAY, OAKLEY S. "Personality Factors in Motor Learning and Reminiscence." *J Abn & Social Psychol* 59:199–203 S '59. * (*PA* 34:2691)
24. SMITH, C. M., AND HAMILTON, J. "Psychological Factors in the Narcolepsy-Cataplexy Syndrome." *Psychosom Med* 21:40–9 Ja–F '59. * (*PA* 34:1858)
25. VALENTINE, MAX. "Psychometric Testing in Iran." *J Mental Sci* 105:93–107 Ja '59. * (*PA* 34:1065)
26. BENDIG, A. W. "Extraversion, Neuroticism, and Student Achievement in Introductory Psychology." *J Ed Res* 53:263–7 Mr '60. *
27. BENDIG, A. W. "Factor Analyses of 'Anxiety' and 'Neuroticism' Inventories." *J Consult Psychol* 24:161–8 Ap '60. * (*PA* 34:8195)
28. BENDIG, A. W. "Item Factor Analyses of the Scales of the Maudsley Personality Inventory." *J Psychol Studies* 11:104–7 Ja–F '60. * (*PA* 34:7366)
29. BRENGELMANN, J. C.; HAHN, H.; PEDLEY, J. C.; AND AMATO, J. G. "Learning and Personality: 1, A Pilot Experiment." *Acta Psychologica* 17(2):113–8 '60. * (*PA* 35:784)
30. BRONZAFT, A.; HAYES, R.; WELCH, L.; AND KOLTUV, M. "Relationships Between Extraversion, Neuroticism, and Ascendance." *J Psychol* 50:279–85 O '60. * (*PA* 35:6475)
31. BRONZAFT, ARLINE; HAYES, ROSLYN; WELCH, LIVINGSTON; AND KOLTUV, MYRON. "Relationship Between PGR and Measures of Extraversion, Ascendance, and Neuroticism." *J Psychol* 50:193–5 O '60. * (*PA* 35:6522)
32. CARRIGAN, PATRICIA M. "Extraversion-Introversion as a Dimension of Personality: A Reappraisal." *Psychol B* 57:329–60 S '60. * (*PA* 35:4976)
33. CLARIDGE, GORDON. Chap. 2, "The Excitation-Inhibition Balance in Neurotics," pp. 107–54. In *Experiments in Personality: Vol. 2, Psychodiagnostics and Psychodynamics.* Edited by H. J. Eysenck. London: Routledge & Kegan Paul Ltd., 1960. Pp. viii, 333. *
34. EYSENCK, H. J. Chap. 5, "A Factor Analysis of Selected Tests," pp. 234–44. In his *Experiments in Personality: Vol. 2, Psychodiagnostics and Psychodynamics.* London: Routledge & Kegan Paul Ltd., 1960. Pp. viii, 333. *
35. EYSENCK, H. J. "Reminiscence, Extraversion and Neuroticism." *Percept & Motor Skills* 11:21–2 Ag '60. * (*PA* 35:3499)
36. EYSENCK, H. J. *The Structure of Human Personality, Second Edition.* London: Methuen & Co. Ltd., 1960. Pp. xix, 448. *
37. EYSENCK, H. J.; TARRANT, MOLLIE; WOOLF, MYRA; AND ENGLAND, L. "Smoking and Personality." *Brit Med J* (5184):1456–60 My 14 '60. *
38. EYSENCK, S. B. G. "Social Class, Sex, and Response to a Five-Part Personality Inventory." *Ed & Psychol Meas* 20:47–54 sp '60. * (*PA* 34:7381)
39. HOLLAND, H. C. Chap. 4, "Measures of Perceptual Functions," pp. 193–233. In *Experiments in Personality: Vol. 2, Psychodiagnostics and Psychodynamics.* Edited by H. J. Eysenck. London: Routledge & Kegan Paul Ltd., 1960. Pp. viii, 333. *
40. KNOWLES, JOHN. "Maudsley Personality Inventory." *Psychometric Res B* (6):[22–5] su '60. *

1 SYME, LEONARD. "Personality Characteristics and the Alcoholic: A Critique of Current Studies." *Q J Stud Alcohol* 18:288–302 Je '57. *

41. KNOWLES, JOHN B. "The Temporal Stability of MPI Scores in Normal and Psychiatric Populations." Abstract. *J Consult Psychol* 24:278 Je '60. *
42. SAINSBURY, P. "Psychosomatic Disorders and Neurosis in Out-Patients Attending a General Hospital." *J Psychosom Res* 4:261–73 Jl '60. * (*PA* 36:1JU61S)
43. VINSON, D. B., AND ROBBINS, L. R. "Objectivity in the Assessment of the Thyrotoxic Patient." *J Psychosom Res* 4:236–43 Mr '60. * (*PA* 36:1IB36V)
44. VOGEL, MURIEL D. "The Relation of Personality Factors to GSR Conditioning of Alcoholics: An Exploratory Study." *Can J Psychol* 14:275–80 D '60. * (*PA* 35:5200)
45. WILLETT, R. A. Chap. 3, "Measures of Learning and Conditioning," pp. 157–92. In *Experiments in Personality: Vol. 2, Psychodiagnostics and Psychodynamics.* Edited by H. J. Eysenck. London: Routledge & Kegan Paul Ltd., 1960. Pp. viii, 333. *
46. BENDIG, A. W. "A Factor Analysis of Scales of Emotionality and Hostility." *J Clin Psychol* 17:189–92 Ap '61. * (*PA* 38:1034)
46a. COWIE, VALERIE. "The Incidence of Neurosis in the Children of Psychotics." *Acta Psychiatrica Scandinavica* 37(1):37–71 '61. * (*PA* 36:4JV37C)
47. DAS, GITA. "Standardisation of Maudsley Personality Inventory (M.P.I.) on an Indian Population." *J Psychol Res* 5:7–9 Ja '61. * (*PA* 35:5540)
48. FIELD, J. G. "An Interpersonal Validation of the MPI." *Acta Psychologica* 18(5):351–3 '61. * (*PA* 37:1202)
49. FIELD, J. G., AND BRENGELMANN, J. C. "Eyelid Conditioning and Three Personality Parameters." *J Abn & Social Psychol* 63:517–23 N '61. * (*PA* 37:369)
50. FOULDS, G. A. "The Logical Impossibility of Using Hysterics and Dysthymics as Criterion Groups in the Study of Introversion and Extraversion." *Brit J Psychol* 52:385–7 N '61. * (*PA* 36:4HI85F) Comments by H. J. Eysenck and J. G. Ingham and reply by G. A. Foulds. *Brit J Psychol* 53:455–9 N '62. *
51. FRANKS, C. M.; HOLDEN, E. A.; AND PHILLIPS, M. "Eysenck's 'Stratification' Theory and the Questionnaire Method of Measuring Personality." *J Clin Psychol* 17:248–53 Jl '61. * (*PA* 38:8489)
52. FURNEAUX, W. D. "Neuroticism, Extraversion, Drive, and Suggestibility." *J Clin & Exp Hypnosis* 9:195–214 O '61. * (*PA* 36:4II95F)
53. FURNEAUX, W. D., AND GIBSON, H. B. "The Maudsley Personality Inventory as a Predictor of Susceptibility to Hypnosis." *J Clin & Exp Hypnosis* 9:167–77 Jl '61. * (*PA* 36:3II67F)
54. KEEHN, J. D. "Response Sets and the Maudsley Personality Inventory." *J Social Psychol* 54:141–6 Je '61. * (*PA* 36:2HF41K)
55. LIPMAN, RONALD S., AND SPITZ, HERMAN H. "Cortical Conductivity and Vocabulary." *J Abn & Social Psychol* 63:459–60 S '61. * (*PA* 37:200)
56. LUCAS, C. J. "Personality of Students With Acne Vulgaris." *Brit Med J* 2(5248):354–6 Ag 5 '61. *
57. LYNN, R., AND GORDON, I. E. "The Relation of Neuroticism and Extraversion to Intelligence and Educational Attainment." *Brit J Ed Psychol* 31:194–203 Je '61. * (*PA* 36:3HD94L)
58. RIM, Y. "Dimensions of Job Incentives and Personality." *Acta Psychologica* 18(5):332–6 '61. * (*PA* 37:2113)
59. SHANMUGAM, T. E. "Voluntary Inhibition and Disinhibition in Relation to Personality Traits." *Psychol Studies* 6:36–40 Ja '61. * (*PA* 37:1319)
60. SINGH, S. D.; SHARMA, N. R.; AND VIMAL, KUMARI. "Personality Differences in Fluctuation of Attention." *Psychol Studies* 6:55–60 Ja '61. * (*PA* 37:1320)
61. VOGEL, MURIEL D. "GSR Conditioning and Personality Factors in Alcoholics and Normals." *J Abn & Social Psychol* 63:417–21 S '61. * (*PA* 37:1725)
62. BENDIG, A. W. "Factor Analyses of the Guilford Zimmerman Temperament Survey and the Maudsley Personality Inventory." *J General Psychol* 67:21–6 Jl '62. * (*PA* 37:3169)
63. BENDIG, A. W. "A Factor Analysis of Personality Scales Including the Buss-Durkee Hostility Inventory." *J General Psychol* 66:179–83 Ap '62. * (*PA* 37:1246)
64. BIGGS, J. B. "The Relation of Neuroticism and Extraversion to Intelligence and Educational Attainment." *Brit J Ed Psychol* 32:188–95 Je '62. * (*PA* 37:3123)
65. BONIER, RICHARD JOSEPH. *Relationships of Psychosomatic States to Emotional Disturbance and Diffuse Autonomic Activity.* Doctor's thesis, Michigan State University (East Lansing, Mich.), 1962. (*DA* 23:1417)
66. EYSENCK, H. J. "Response Set, Authoritarianism and Personality Questionnaires." *Brit J Social & Clin Psychol* 1:20–4 F '62. * (*PA* 37:1252)
67. EYSENCK, H. J., AND CLARIDGE, G. "The Position of Hysterics and Dysthymics in a Two-Dimensional Framework of Personality Description." *J Abn & Social Psychol* 64:46–55 Ja '62. * (*PA* 37:1281)
68. EYSENCK, S. B. G. "The Validity of a Personality Questionnaire as Determined by the Method of Nominated Groups." *Life Sci* 1:13–8 Ja '62. * (*PA* 37:1253)
69. EYSENCK, S. B. G., AND EYSENCK, H. J. "Rigidity as a Function of Introversion and Neuroticism: A Study of Unmarried Mothers." *Int J Social Psychiatry* 8:180–4 su '62. * (*PA* 37:6932)
70. FITCH, J. H. "Two Personality Variables and Their Distribution in a Criminal Population: An Empirical Study." *Brit J Social & Clin Psychol* 1:161–7 O '62. * (*PA* 37:5449)
71. GIBSON, H. B. "The Lie Scale of the Maudsley Personality Inventory." *Acta Psychologica* 20(1):18–23 '62. * (*PA* 37:3173)
72. HOLLAND, H. C. "A Note on Differences in the Duration of the Spiral After-Effect Following Continuous and Intermittant Stimulation." *Acta Psychologica* 20(4):304–7 '62. * (*PA* 38:3539)
73. HOLLAND, H. C. "The Spiral After-Effect and Extraversion." *Acta Psychologica* 20(1):29–35 '62. * (*PA* 37:2296)
74. JENSEN, ARTHUR R. "Extraversion, Neuroticism, and Serial Learning." *Acta Psychologica* 20(2):69–77 '62. * (*PA* 37:6773)
75. KEEHN, J. D. "Neurotic Questionnaire Responses as Simulated by Normal Individuals." *Austral J Psychol* 14:65–8 Ap '62. * (*PA* 38:6086)
76. KISSEN, DAVID M., AND EYSENCK, H. J. "Personality in Male Lung Cancer Patients." *J Psychosom Res* 6:123–7 Ap–Je '62. * (*PA* 37:5531)
77. LANG, PETER J., AND LAZOVIK, A. DAVID. "Personality and Hypnotic Susceptibility." *J Consult Psychol* 26:317–22 Ag '62. * (*PA* 38:4433)
78. MCGUIRE, RALPH J. "A Study of the M.P.I. Used With Psychiatric In-Patients." Abstract. *B Brit Psychol Soc* 47:56–7 Ap '62. *
79. PAPALOIZOS, ANTOINE. "Personality and Success of Training in Human Relations." *Personnel Psychol* 15:423–8 w '62. * (*PA* 38:1462)
80. SAVAGE, R. D. "Three Experiments Using the Junior Maudsley Personality Inventory: 2, Personality Factors and Academic Performance." *Brit J Ed Psychol* 32:251–3 N '62. * (*PA* 37:8275)
81. STAR, KOLMAN H. "Ideal-Self Response Set and Maudsley Personality Inventory Scores." *Psychol Rep* 11:708 D '62. * (*PA* 38:1003)
82. WALTON, D., AND MATHER, M. D. "Differential Response to Questionnaire Items of Neuroticism by 'Defensive' and 'Non-Defensive' Subjects." *J Mental Sci* 108:501–4 Jl '62. * (*PA* 37:3243)
83. BARTHOLOMEW, A. A. "Some Comparative Australian Data for the Maudsley Personality Inventory." *Austral J Psychol* 15:46–51 Ap '63. *
84. BEECH, H. R., AND ADLER, F. "Some Aspects of Verbal Conditioning in Psychiatric Patients." *Behav Res Ther* 1:273–82 D '63. *
85. BENDIG, A. W. "A Note on Cattell's Radicalism (Q1) Scale." *J Social Psychol* 60:107–13 Je '63. * (*PA* 38:4173)
86. BENDIG, A. W. "The Relation of Temperament Traits of Social Extraversion and Emotionality to Vocational Interests." *J General Psychol* 69:311–8 O '63. * (*PA* 39:1800)
87. BENDIG, A. W., AND MARTIN, ANN M. "The Factor Structure of Temperament Traits and Needs." *J General Psychol* 69:27–36 Jl '63. * (*PA* 38:4297)
88. BERG, PAUL SAUL DAVID. *Neurotic and Psychopathic Criminals: Some Measures of Ego Syntonicity, Impulse Socialization and Perceptual Consistency.* Doctor's thesis, Michigan State University (East Lansing, Mich.), 1963. (*DA* 24:2559)
89. CHOPPY, MARYSE, AND EYSENCK, H. J. "Brain Damage and Depressant Drugs: An Experimental Study of Interaction," pp. 313–23. In *Experiments With Drugs: Studies in the Relation Between Personality, Learning Theory and Drug Action.* Edited by H. J. Eysenck. New York: Macmillan Co., 1963. Pp. xii, 421. * (*PA* 38:5527)
90. CLARIDGE, G. S., AND HERRINGTON, R. N. Chap. 5, "Excitation-Inhibition and the Theory of Neurosis: A Study of the Sedation Threshold," pp. 131–68. In *Experiments With Drugs: Studies in the Relation Between Personality, Learning Theory and Drug Action.* Edited by H. J. Eysenck. New York: Macmillan Co., 1963. Pp. xii, 421. * (*PA* 38:5527)
91. CLARIDGE, G. S., AND HERRINGTON, R. N. "An EEG Correlate of the Archimedes Spiral After-Effect and Its Relationship With Personality." *Behav Res Ther* 1:217–29 D '63. *
92. COPPEN, ALEC, AND KESSEL, NEIL. "Menstruation and Personality." *Brit J Psychiatry* 109:711–21 N '63. * (*PA* 38:8347)
93. COSTELLO, C. G., AND SMITH, C. M. "The Relationships Between Personality, Sleep and the Effects of Sedatives." *Brit J Psychiatry* 109:568–71 Jl '63. * (*PA* 38:4487)
94. CROOKES, T. G., AND HUTT, S. J. "Scores of Psychotic Patients on the Maudsley Personality Inventory." *J Consult Psychol* 27:243–7 Je '63. * (*PA* 38:994)
95. DAVIES, M. H.; CLARIDGE, G. S.; AND WAWMAN, R. J. "Sedation Threshold, Autonomic Lability and the Excitation-Inhibition Theory of Personality: 3, The Blood Pressure Response to an Adrenaline Antagonist as a Measure of Autonomic Lability." *Brit J Psychiatry* 109:558–67 Jl '63. * (*PA* 38:3795)
95a. EVANS, FREDERICK J. "The Maudsley Personality Inventory, Suggestibility, and Hypnosis." *Int J Clin & Exp Hypnosis* 11:187–200 Jl '63. * (*PA* 38:6273)
96. EYSENCK, S. B. G., AND EYSENCK, H. J. "Acquiescent Response Set in Personality Questionnaires." *Life Sci* 2:144–7 F '63. * (*PA* 38:995)

97. EYSENCK, S. B. G., AND EYSENCK, H. J. "On the Dual Nature of Extraversion." *Brit J Social & Clin Psychol* 2:46–55 F '63. * (*PA* 38:916)
98. EYSENCK, SYBIL B. G., AND EYSENCK, H. J. "The Validity of Questionnaire and Rating Assessments of Extraversion and Neuroticism, and Their Factorial Stability." *Brit J Psychol* 54:51–62 F '63. * (*PA* 37:8009)
99. FORREST, D. W. "Relationship Between Sharpening and Extraversion." *Psychol Rep* 13:564 O '63. * (*PA* 38:8488)
99a. FURNEAUX, W. D. "Neuroticism, Extraversion, and Suggestibility: A Comment." *Int J Clin & Exp Hypnosis* 11:201–2 Jl '63. *
100. FURNEAUX, W. D., AND LINDAHL, L. E. H. "How Valid Are Questionnaire Validity Studies?" Abstract. *B Brit Psychol Soc* 16:19A Ap '63. *
101. HESELTINE, G. F. "The Site of Onset of Eczema and Personality Trait Differences: An Exploratory Study." *J Psychosom Res* 7:241–6 D '63. * (*PA* 38:8360)
102. HILGARD, ERNEST R., AND BENTLER, P. M. "Predicting Hypnotizability From the Maudsley Personality Inventory." *Brit J Psychol* 54:63–9 F '63. * (*PA* 37:8091)
103. HOWARTH, E. "Some Laboratory Measures of Extraversion-Introversion." *Percept & Motor Skills* 17:55–60 Ag '63. * (*PA* 38:7242)
104. KISSEN, DAVID M. "Personality Characteristics in Males Conducive to Lung Cancer." *Brit J Med Psychol* 36(1):27–36 '63. * (*PA* 38:921)
105. LITTLE, ALAN. "Professor Eysenck's Theory of Crime: An Empirical Test on Adolescent Offenders." Comments by H. J. Eysenck. *Brit J Criminol* 4:152–63 O '63. * (*PA* 38:6477)
106. LOVIBOND, S. H. "Conceptual Thinking, Personality and Conditioning." *Brit J Social & Clin Psychol* 2:100–11 Je '63. * (*PA* 38:3654)
107. MCGUIRE, R. J.; MOWBRAY, R. M.; AND VALLANCE, R. C. "The Maudsley Personality Inventory Used With Psychiatric Inpatients." *Brit J Psychol* 54:157–66 My '63. * (*PA* 38:1032)
108. MANNE, SIGMUND H.; KANDEL, ARTHUR; AND ROSENTHAL, DAVID. "The Relationship Between Performance Minus Verbal Scores and Extraversion in a Severely Sociopathic Population." *J Clin Psychol* 19:96–7 Ja '63. * (*PA* 39:1676)
109. MEZEY, A. G.; COHEN, SAMUEL I.; AND KNIGHT, E. J. "Personality Assessment Under Varying Physiological and Psychological Conditions." *J Psychosom Res* 7:237–40 D '63. * (*PA* 38:8527)
110. RATH, R., AND MISRA, S. K. "Change of Attitudes as a Function of Some Personality Factors." *J Social Psychol* 60:311–7 Ag '63. * (*PA* 38:4182)
111. ROBINSON, J. O. "A Study of Neuroticism and Casual Arterial Blood Pressure." *Brit J Social & Clin Psychol* 2:56–64 F '63. * (*PA* 38:1347)
112. RUTTIGER, KATHERINE FORD. "Individual Differences in Reaction to Meprobamate: A Study in Visual Perception." *J Abn & Social Psychol* 67:37–43 Jl '63. * (*PA* 38:419)
113. SINGER, JEROME L., AND ANTROBUS, JOHN S. "A Factor-Analytic Study of Daydreaming and Conceptually-Related Cognitive and Personality Variables." *Percept & Motor Skills* 17:187–209 Ag '63. * (*PA* 38:7418)
114. SINGH, S. D. "Extraversion, Neuroticism, and Conformity Behaviour." *J Psychol Res* 7:66–71 My '63. * (*PA* 38:4253)
115. STANLEY, GORDON. "Personality and Attitude Characteristics of Fundamentalist Theological Students." *Austral J Psychol* 15:121–3 Ag '63. * (*PA* 38:6037)
116. TAUSS, W. "A Note on Stability and Equivalence of Long and Short Forms of the M.P.I." *Austral J Psychol* 15:118–20 Ag '63. *
117. VENABLES, ETHEL. "Personality Scores and Achievement Among Technical College Students." Abstract. *B Brit Psychol Soc* 16:58–9 Jl '63. *

ARTHUR R. JENSEN, *Associate Professor of Educational Psychology, and Associate Research Psychologist, Institute of Human Learning, University of California, Berkeley, California.*

By all criteria of excellence in test development the MPI is an impressive achievement. It has grown out of years of intensive research on the dimensional analysis of personality. A great amount of evidence (*36*) has shown that two relatively independent superfactors, identified by Eysenck as neuroticism and extraversion-introversion, represent most of the variance in the personality domain. While it is possible to slice the variance in this domain into many different ways of making up "scales" consisting of various combinations of many kinds of personality inventory items, these scales are almost always highly intercorrelated, despite their widely differing labels. When they are factor analyzed, either at the scale level or at the item level, the first two or three independent factors almost invariably account for all the appreciable common factor variance in the lot. The MPI has been developed to measure two of the most comprehensive factors, Neuroticism (N) and Extraversion (E). Neuroticism refers to general emotional instability, emotional overresponsiveness, and predisposition to neurotic breakdown under stress. Extraversion refers to outgoing, uninhibited, impulsive, and sociable inclinations. The method of developing the inventory was factor analytic and is adequately described in both the British and American editions of the manual.

The MPI consists of 48 items, of which 24 are keyed to N and 24 to E. Unlike some personality inventories (e.g., the MMPI), none of the items could be construed as socially objectionable; thus the inventory can be used with adolescents or adults in almost any setting. Though the MPI takes only about 10 or 15 minutes, there is also a short form—described in the British manual and by Jensen (*6*)—consisting of six items from each scale. The short form has satisfactory reliability and high correlations with the total scales and can be useful when time is very limited.

The MPI derives much of its importance from its theoretical underpinnings. Probably no other psychological test—certainly no other personality inventory—rivals it in psychological rationale. This is particularly true of the E dimension, which has been the subject of intensive experimental research in Eysenck's laboratory for more than a decade. A review of this research is, of course, impossible here. The manual prepared by Robert Knapp for the American edition has a bibliography of 112 items of the most relevant literature, and the manual itself summarizes much of the published findings. Factor-analytically sophisticated readers are also referred to Carrigan's (*32*) critical appraisal of E as a dimension of personality.

NORMS. A great deal of normative data are presented, both for English and American subjects. The American manual presents American college norms (percentiles and stanines based on 1,064 university undergraduates). Means and standard deviations are presented for 32 different groups, including various psychiatric, prison, and industrial populations, totaling over 7,000 subjects (including the American norms group of 1,064 and the English norms group of 1,800). Bartholomew (*83*) has published some Australian norms, which differ little from the English, except that the Australians seem to be slightly more extraverted, as are the Americans.

There are slight sex and social class differences on both the N and E scales; these are fully discussed in the manual. The scales are not correlated with intelligence.

RELIABILITY AND VALIDITY. Split-half and Kuder-Richardson estimates of item intercorrelations for each scale are between .75 and .90 in various samples. N consistently has slightly higher internal consistency than E. Test-retest reliabilities range from .70 to .90. In short, the reliability of the MPI is among the highest to be found for personality inventories. The MPI has also been studied for effects of various types of "response set." These seem to be negligible.

Assessment of the validity of the MPI is a complex matter. There can be little question of its factorial validity. That is to say, the N and E scales invariably have high loadings on factors that are also heavily represented in other measures considered to be indicative of neuroticism or extraversion, and there is little factorial overlap between the scales. Though they were intended to be completely independent measures, it has been found that they are correlated about −.15—slightly more or less depending upon the population sampled. The negative correlation is somewhat higher (usually about −.30) in psychiatric and college populations. Data on correlations with other personality inventories are presented in the manuals. Note, for example, that the N scale correlates almost as highly (.76) with the Taylor Manifest Anxiety Scale as reliability would allow. There is, however, a slightly greater negative correlation between the Taylor scale and the E scale than between the N and E scales.

Descriptive validity of the MPI has been adequately established by the method of nominated groups. Judges rated people on the basis of observable characteristics in terms of neuroticism and extraversion. These ratings show highly significant correlations with the relevant dimensions measured by the MPI.

Most important, but also the most difficult to evaluate, is the "construct validity" of the MPI, that is, the elaborate network of theory, predictions, and experimental findings concerning the N and E dimensions. Adequate discussion of this topic must presuppose the reader's knowledge of Eysenck's theory of personality which relates neuroticism to autonomic lability and extraversion to cortical inhibition.[1] Since an exposition of the theory and the related research is beyond the scope of this review, the reviewer can only give his overall impression of this vast body of work as it relates to the MPI. First, there is no doubt that both N and E scales have shown significant and replicable correlations with experimental phenomena in the fields of perception, motor learning, verbal learning, pain tolerance, and attitudes. Some of these relationships are predictable from Eysenck's and others' theories. All of the research, of course, has not unequivocally supported Eysenck's theoretical deductions and there is a large fringe of ambiguity on the growing edge of the theory which is perhaps somewhat underemphasized in the MPI manuals. It is this area of far reaching, but as yet inadequately substantiated, implications of the theory that has provided Eysenck's critics with an easy target for their often premature unfavorable evaluations. But if one reviews the research of the Maudsley group over the years, it is clear that the theory of personality associated with the MPI is sensitive to experimental findings and is constantly undergoing careful modification and development. It seems to be Eysenck's personal style, more than the facts of the matter, which stimulates criticism and a counsel of caution, since Eysenck tends to stride each step of the way with a rather bold assurance. All in all, it seems safe to say that no other personality test is based upon a body of psychological theory so far reaching and so diligently and ably researched as is the MPI. The chief reason for this is that the MPI is one of the few personality measures that has grown out of a theory concerned with basic psychological

1 EYSENCK, H. J. *The Dynamics of Anxiety and Hysteria: An Experimental Application of Modern Learning Theory to Psychiatry*. London: Routledge & Kegan Paul Ltd., 1957. Pp. xiv, 311. *

processes rather than out of purely empirical attempts to predict certain currently practical criteria.

USES OF THE MPI. The MPI has been little used in clinical diagnosis. It is not listed in Sundberg's [2] survey of the 62 most widely used tests in clinical practice in the United States. The reasons are not hard to find: Clinicians generally want more detailed information than is provided by a subject's scores on two broad dimensions of personality; the MPI dimensions do not correspond at all well to the presently used diagnostic categories (nor are they intended to), and the psychological theory associated with N and E has not been generally incorporated in diagnostic or therapeutic practice. Those who wish to see how the theory underlying the MPI is related to psychiatric diagnosis and therapy are referred to a discussion by Eysenck.[3] As yet this reviewer has not seen evidence of the practical use of the MPI in clinical settings. Certainly it is not of any value for conventional psychiatric diagnosis. McGuire and others (*107*) gave the MPI to an unselected group of psychiatric patients and found that the N scale differentiated all diagnostic groups from the nonpsychiatric controls, but neither the N nor the E scale differentiated significantly among the diagnostic groups. Other studies have shown significant differences among various diagnostic categories, but these differences have not been sufficiently reliable to support the use of the MPI for individual diagnosis. Since in the McGuire study all psychiatric groups averaged 10–15 points higher on the N scale than the normal controls, it is suggested that the MPI might be valuable as a psychiatric screening device.

Also, for screening and group prediction in educational and industrial settings, the MPI shows promise based on research. College examination failure rate and academic achievement, for example, have been shown to be related to N and E in ways predictable from Eysenck's theory. Persistence in menial and monotonous tasks also is related to the MPI dimensions.

The present reviewer has had most experience with the MPI as an adjunct to laboratory research in the field of human learning. The MPI can be used by experimentalists who believe personality factors may play a part in the psychological phenomena under investigation and who wish to account for more of the "between subjects" variance as a means of increasing the precision of experiments. The relevance of anxiety in learning and conditioning experiments, for example, has been amply demonstrated with research using Taylor's Manifest Anxiety Scale. The N scale of the MPI can serve the same purpose as the MAS, with the added advantage that it is shorter, more reliable, and has a greater body of psychological research behind it. It has been found that the importance of the neuroticism factor increases as task complexity becomes greater (*74*). We have also found in our own work that subjects with high N scores are less apt to stand up well throughout an arduous laboratory experiment and are less able to follow complex directions in an experiment, even though they may have high intelligence. The relevance of E to experimental variables, though called for by Eysenck's theory, is not so clearly established at present and must await further investigation. But it is in the realm of experimental psychology, as a covariate in studies of perception, conditioning, learning, persistence, attention, concept attainment, and the like, that this reviewer sees the most immediate potential usefulness of the MPI. The American manual also discusses the uses of the MPI in market research and in vocational selection and counseling.

A word about the British and American editions of the manuals. Both cover the essentials expected of any test manual, but the American edition is more up-to-date and therefore more complete in its coverage of relevant research. Indeed, it is an exemplary model of what a test manual should be.

In summary, the MPI is a brief and highly reliable measure of two relatively independent broad factors of personality—neuroticism and extraversion-introversion. Much sophisticated research has gone into its construction, and the large body of normative data, plus the psychological theory and experimentation associated with the MPI, make it one of the most important of all personality inventories, and certainly the preferred measures of neuroticism (or anxiety) and extraversion.

2 SUNDBERG, NORMAN D. "The Practice of Psychological Testing in Clinical Services in the United States." *Am Psychol* 16:79–83 F '61. *

3 EYSENCK, H. J. Chap. 3, "A Rational System of Diagnosis and Therapy in Mental Illness." In *Progress in Clinical Psychology,* Vol. 4. Edited by Lawrence E. Abt and Bernard F. Riess. New York: Grune & Stratton, Inc., 1960. Pp. ix, 181. *

The American edition of a new version of the MPI, called the *Eysenck Personality Inventory* (EPI), has been published by the American publisher of the MPI. The EPI is described in a preliminary edition of the manual (August, 1963) as an attempt to make the MPI scales more useful for certain purposes. The EPI measures the same two factors as the MPI, but the slight correlation that exists between N and E in the MPI scales has been removed entirely, by adding, subtracting, and rewriting items and subjecting them to repeated factor analyses. Also, many of the items have been reworded in such a way as to increase their reliability when used with subjects of low intelligence or little education. There are two equivalent forms of the EPI. The EPI also contains a "lie" scale (borrowed from the MMPI), a worthwhile addition if the inventory is to be used for screening or selection purposes where subjects might be inclined to "fake good." For experimental work the "lie" scale is usually superfluous, however. The reliability of the EPI scales is slightly higher than for the MPI and the normative data for the English population are quite adequate. American users will have to develop their own norms until such data become available. For experimental use with college subjects the EPI does not seem to offer many substantial advantages over the MPI (unless one insists on eliminating the slight correlation between N and E or wishes to do a retest on an equivalent form) and it has the slight disadvantage of being more time consuming, since it contains 9 more items than the MPI. Further research should make possible more valid and detailed comparisons between the MPI and EPI. Potential users should, of course, examine specimen sets of both the MPI and the EPI to decide which inventory might best suit their purposes in terms of the available norms, etc.

JAMES C. LINGOES, *Associate Professor of Psychology, The University of Michigan, Ann Arbor, Michigan.*

The *Maudsley Personality Inventory* (MPI) is a theoretically based instrument designed to measure the two rather pervasive and relatively independent personality dimensions of extraversion-introversion (E) and neuroticism-stability (N) found by Eysenck and others in a large number of factor analytic studies. The 24 items for each trait were selected on the basis of both item and factor analyses as being the purest questionnaire measures to date of Eysenck's factors.

The MPI is an easily administered, quick, reliable, and fairly simply scored test. With the following exceptions, the manual to the United States edition is commendably successful in meeting the various criteria of technical excellence stipulated in the APA Technical Recommendations. Some minor criticisms of the manual are: (*a*) that the professional qualifications necessary to administer and interpret the test are omitted, and (*b*) that false-positive and false-negative rates are missing in the discussion of validity by nominated groups. Significant mean differences are insufficient to assess properly the value of such studies. More serious deficiencies in the manual are: (*a*) the omission of tables of item intercorrelations and factor loadings as well as other item statistics, essential ingredients for factor based scales; and (*b*) the very inadequate delineation of the N factor as a descriptive or clinical concept to aid the user interpretatively in the individual case, one of the important recommended uses of this test. The user should satisfy himself on the above points by referring to the relevant literature listed in the 112-item bibliography of the manual.

Of more crucial concern to the prospective user are the following observations regarding the test itself and its relationships with other tests purporting to measure the same traits or factors.

First, the MPI is not a general personality test, even though the traits it assesses account for most of the variance in personality inventories. One should not confuse statistical significance with clinical importance, as Eysenck himself would acknowledge. Consequently, if one is looking for a more complete personality profile on a subject, other tests would be more pertinent, e.g., the *Guilford-Zimmerman Temperament Survey* or Cattell's 16PF, being logical choices among factor based tests, or the MMPI, being the best among clinical personality instruments. As a clinical tool the MPI would serve best in an ancillary role, supplementing data from other tests. A two-dimensional approach to personality is insufficient to encompass all the functions and purposes typical of the average clinical setting, no matter how pervasive or important the factors may be.

Second, it has not been established that even for the traits that the MPI measures, it measures them better than comparable instruments. It should be noted that E is only one of several kinds of extraversion, i.e., social, and a number of studies reported in the manual indicate that this trait is measured at least as well by other tests as it is by the MPI if one takes the internal consistency data as a yardstick. Thus, E correlates to the extent of .81 with social extraversion from the *Minnesota T-S-E Inventory* and −.80 with Heron's introversion scale. These validity coefficients lie within the range of Kuder-Richardson and split-half reliability coefficients for E, i.e., between .75 and .85 with the majority above .80, and they are certainly higher than the equivalent forms coefficients (.75) reported for the *Eysenck Personality Inventory.* Furthermore, based upon the original sample of 400 cases used in the item analysis of the MPI, E correlated .79 with the rhathymia scale of the *Inventory of Factors STDCR* and N correlated .92 with the cycloid disposition scale, the latter coefficient being *higher* than the split-half or K-R reliability coefficients reported for N.

Admittedly, other factors must be considered in a consumer's decision to use one test as opposed to others, e.g., cost, ease of administration, ease of distortion or deception, professional time spent in interpretation, the purposes to be served by testing, readability of the items, appeal to the examinees, etc., and while some of the foregoing would favor the MPI, comprehensiveness may well determine the choice in the final analysis given equally good data on reliability and validity.

In conclusion, the present evidence on the MPI would suggest that there was little reason to omit in the American manual the caution expressed in the original British manual, i.e., "In all its applications, the M.P.I. should primarily be regarded as a *research instrument.*" Within Eysenck's theoretical system, the MPI and its revision, the *Eysenck Personality Inventory,* may well indeed be the tests of choice, but more evidence is needed on superior reliability and validity to warrant their supplanting other comparable and better established tests.

William Stephenson, *Professor of Psychology, University of Missouri, Columbia, Missouri.*

The MPI is excellently produced. The American manual is especially informative and comprehensive, listing 112 references up to the end of 1962. The American norms are for 1,064 university and college students. Validation is with respect to *mean differences* for groups of subjects (sample sizes range from as few as 8 to as many as 1,800 and total some 7,200) variously described as Australian prisoners, psychopaths, industrial apprentices, psychosomatics, hysterics, English normals, recidivist prisoners, neurotics, dysthymics, etc., mostly in Britain.

It would not be difficult, in the present reviewer's judgment, to find other compilations of personality statements which, when subjected to such gross validation procedures, would fare no better or no worse than the set of 48 put together for the MPI. It is possible that they may be useful in experimental studies using samples of the order 100 to 1,000 persons. What is not so certain is the credibility of the data the test provides. The public is warned in this respect. But there is an issue which, it seems to the reviewer, requires consideration as psychology grows professionally. After a very careful review of Eysenck's major work,[1] Storms and Sigal (9) have to conclude that the attributes of extraverts and introverts listed by Eysenck in certain studies have not, in fact, been unequivocally demonstrated. Doubt was raised about the validation of the E continuum.

The reviewer would raise again the improbability that a scale based on R-methodological grounds can ever really indicate dynamic conditions such as Eysenck has persistently proposed to examine. Davis,[2] for example, reminded us, and Eysenck in particular, that following a traumatic situation immediate reactions to the situation were apt to be ones of overactivity, or of psychological withdrawal; subsequently, recovery from the shock was attended by preoccupation and fixation of memories, with the establishment of defenses, with the abandonment of defenses, and with a phase of working through the memories.

1 Eysenck, H. J. *The Dynamics of Anxiety and Hysteria: An Experimental Application of Modern Learning Theory to Psychiatry.* London: Routledge & Kegan Paul Ltd., 1957. Pp. xiv, 311. *

2 Davis, D. Russell. "Clinical Problems and Experimental Researches." *Brit J Med Psychol* 31:74–82 pt 2 '58. *

These, it seems to the reviewer, are typical of human reactions: to imagine for a moment that either E or N in general have anything to contribute to such a flow of phenomena seems to the reviewer to be clutching at feathers in the wind. Moreover, there is a simple way to show that dynamic factors can in fact be brought to light, using Eysenck's 48 statements but in the form of a Q-sample so that each person can use the statements relative to one another to display fixations, defenses, etc. The E and N scales never do anything of the kind because they are by definition measurements of behavior *in a general context*. The proof of the matter, that at least one factor common to Q couldn't possibly appear in data derived from R (and vice versa), is there for Eysenck to note. It is astonishing that so diligent a worker has not looked to see what that one factor, at least, could mean for his studies.

PHILIP E. VERNON, *Professor of Educational Psychology, Institute of Education, University of London, London, England.*

Despite the enormous number of available personality inventories, Eysenck's test could well meet a need for a short, simple instrument for use in mental hospitals, in student counseling, and in a variety of experimental researches where it is desired to control major personality differences among the subjects. Only 48 items are included, selected on a factorial basis to give highly saturated measures of extraversion-introversion and neuroticism-stability or anxiety. Reasonable Kuder-Richardson and repeat reliability coefficients ranging from .75 to .85 for Extraversion and from .85 to .90 for Neuroticism are obtained in 10–15 minutes' testing time, and the two scores are virtually uncorrelated except in certain selected groups. The scoring of the American edition can be done by punched card or, in less than a minute per blank, by stencils; the British edition is scored by transparent stencil.

Since his first book in 1947, Eysenck has stressed the pervasiveness of these two personality factors, and in *The Structure of Human Personality* (*36*) he makes a strong case for reducing most of the manifold factors that have been claimed in questionnaire data, ratings, and objective personality tests, to these same dimensions. Much as Spearman, Burt, and the present writer prefer to cover as much variance as possible in abilities by means of *g* and major group factors, and to regard Thurstone's, Guilford's, and other multiple factors as minor subdivisions—so Eysenck considers personality as hierarchically organized, with these two factors as the most inclusive. Moreover, during the ensuing 16 years, he has linked these with a nomological network based on Hullian learning theory, and collected a considerable amount of experimental evidence to support his theoretical deductions covering extraversion and neuroticism, albeit many of these theories and experimental results are open to dispute. He can reasonably claim, therefore, that scores on this inventory possess a good deal of construct validity derived from positive experimental findings in the field of conditioning and the effects of drugs, from factor loadings, from differentiation between such pathological groups as psychopaths and dysthymic neurotics on the one hand and neurotics and normals on the other, and from correlations with other well known tests of related constructs.

Some comment is called for on the extraversion measure. In many of his writings Eysenck has criticized the American conception of extraversion as consisting largely of sociability, and the consequent tendency for extraversion tests to give rather high negative correlations with neuroticism or emotional instability. He favours, rather, Guilford's notion of rhathymia, or uninhibited carefreeness, as being orthogonal to neuroticism and closer to Jung's original description. However, the definition in the manuals of the present test, together with many of the test items, clearly involves the social aspect of extraversion; the highest correlation of the extraversion scale with another test is .81 with the social introversion–extraversion scale of the *Minnesota T-S-E Inventory*. Indeed the fairly good reliability for so short a scale may be largely due to the reiteration of questions about social mixing. The content of the neuroticism items is, however, more varied.

In the American manual, percentile norms for American college students (one college only) and tables of group means and standard deviations are given. The latter reveal interesting differences. Thus on Extraversion, psychopaths average 31 (out of a possible 48), American women students 29, English students and normal adults around 25, hysterics 24, and dysthymics and neurotics 19. On Neuroticism, the means of psychopaths and neurotics mostly fall in the 32–38 range, English students 23–27, American students 20–21, and English normal population 18–20. Negligible relations are reported with sex, social class, and intelligence, except that men are slightly more extraverted than women and women are slightly more neurotic than men. Among English college students both introversion and neuroticism correlate appreciably with academic achievement. One would have thought that this could be more simply explained in terms of the weaker gregarious interests and greater introspectiveness of the serious student than by means of learning theory constructs.

Responses indicative of extraversion may be either Yes or No, but all neurotic responses are Yes. The author of the American manual draws attention to the possibility of acquiescent response set affecting the latter, but dismisses it. No mention is made of the effects of social desirability. The American manual is well designed, with due attention to the APA Committee's suggestions. But the manual to the original British edition, published in 1959, is much more brief and should be brought up to date.

In general the test should be of some use in educational guidance and personality counseling as a quickly obtained index of two important personality trends. It could be given in mental hospitals by nurses as a preliminary aid in psychological assessment, or included in a battery of tests for surveying a population, for example, in market research or, as already indicated, in experimental researches with normal adult subjects.

Brit J Psychol 51:185–6 My '60. A. Bursill. [Review of the British manual.] This Manual reports up-to-date information available on this Yes, No, ?-type questionnaire (*MPI*) comprising two scales of 24 items each, one purporting to measure neuroticism (*N*), the other introversion-extraversion (*I-E*). * The scales can be conveniently adapted to form an even shorter questionnaire (*SMPI*) comprising six items each for *N* and *I-E,* simply by utilizing the first page of the printed form only. * The two scales *N* and *I-E* intended to be orthogonal, have a low correlation (−0.15 for the *MPI,* and −0.05 for the *SMPI*) for normal samples —the correlation increases to the rather unsatisfactory dimension of −0.3 to −0.4 in neurotic groups. Eysenck assigns these anomalies to the non-linearity of the regression lines. The argument is supplemented by a graph of regression lines for 1,200 normal subjects which does not show a serious state of affairs except *I*-scores below about 10. But the explanation as it stands is hardly sufficient to give rise to such large negative correlations between *N* and *I-E* in neurotic groups, whose mean scores lie well within the distributions given for the whole range of the population. This needs investigating in more detail. Meanwhile, when attempting to assess the effects of varying degrees of extraversion in any experiment, Eysenck suggests matching criterion groups of *I* and *E* for *N*. A table containing the size of samples, mean scores and S.D.'s for the different standardization groups is given—but the reader is left to work out the significance of the differences. Unfortunately, the original sources of much of the data are omitted, or are still not available, so that the procedures whereby subjects were selected cannot be ascertained in detail. Two methods of validation are presented: (i) comparison of the standardization groups on *N* and *I-E;* (ii) construct validity—i.e. a set of interlocking predictions forming a theory confirmed by experiment. In a strict sense, neither method can yet be said to have reached satisfactory standards in empirical confirmation. * unusual answers to some two to three items are sufficient to place an individual amongst the most extreme group of dysthymics on *I,* whereas some ten unusual answers are required to place an individual amongst dysthymics on *N*. At the very least there is some reason for attempting—in subsequent versions of the test—to stretch the *I-E* dimension somewhat. But the reviewer is not certain whether the data cannot be taken as undermining one of Eysenck's basic tenets, which is not merely that hysterics are more extraverted than dysthymics but that they are also more extraverted than normals. In view of Hildebrand's similar findings with objective tests (*Brit. J. Psychol.* 1958, 49, 1–11), there is an increasing likelihood that the position of these various abnormal groups is a true feature of this *I-E* dimension, and not some distortion in its scale units—particularly at the *E* end. In fact, Eysenck hints at this situation in the Manual and elsewhere, without explicitly recognizing that it contravenes his and Jung's theoretical position. A factor to be taken into consideration, however, is that presumably this scale measures sociability rather than the other facets of extraversion emphasized by Jung—since *I-E* correlates highly with the "social" scale and lowly with the "thinking" and "emotional" scale of the Minnesota *TSE*. Another feature worth noting is the limited range of items, many of which closely overlap in content. There might here be a tendency to sacrifice validity for reliability. Possibly a source of distortion on the *N*-scale, on the other hand, resides in the fact that in all items neurotic responses are scored in the affirmative (yes). Space does not permit an appraisal of Eysenck's attempt to demonstrate "construct validity" in his *Dynamics of Anxiety and Hysteria,* as claimed in the Manual. However worthy this attempt was, there has been a growing tide of criticism (e.g. by Storms and Sigal, Vernon Hamilton, D. E. Broadbent, R. L. Reid, Taylor and Rechtsscaffer, Spivac and Levine) of the evidence presented for the various components of the theory in this monograph. Eysenck's adroit defences do not altogether dispel these criticisms. Consequently, the reader may have to exercise caution in accepting the construct validity as indeed valid. Generally, Prof. Eysenck is to be congratulated on obtaining such an unusual amount of data on one personality test. It is to be hoped that a more detailed Manual will soon make its appearance; some of the original work is published in rather inaccessible foreign journals. * There is the danger that subjects selected on an *N* and *I-E* basis alone will unduly bias and filter the human material and cause much of importance to the clinician to be omitted. *

J Consult Psychol 23:563 D '59. Edward S. Bordin. [Review of the British Edition.] This brief questionnaire of 48 items and its even briefer short form (12 items) have played an integral part in the author's well known research on personality. Many instruments have been launched for full scale use with much less behind them. The manual represents the height of English diffidence. Only the briefest summary is given of a few of the salient results of research and the reader is referred to the relevant publications. He is told that "the M.P.I. should be regarded as a *research instrument.* Different firms, organizations, hospitals, universities, and other bodies have different problems, deal with different samples of the population, and aim at different solutions of their problems. Only applied research can determine whether instruments such as the M.P.I. can be successfully used by them, and just what form such use can best take." No high powered American merchandising here!

J Psychosom Res 5:66 S '60. G. A. Foulds. [Review of the British Edition.] * The standardization data call for some comment. Neurotics were diagnosed by experienced psychiatrists, or else had their case-papers carefully scrutinized by three experienced clinical psychologists, who arrived at a unanimous diagnosis independently. In his reply (*J. abnorm. soc. Psychol.* 1958, 57, 2) to the paper by Sigal, Starr and Franks (*ibid*) Eysenck rather deplores the latter method. It is unfortunate that their somewhat conflicting results were not available for the Manual, since the claim that "successive samples from different hospitals showed great stability in means and variances" might have required some modification. Eysenck believes that the results obtained on the M.P.I. "in a sense....serve as validation of the scales." This, unfortunately, can only be in an illogical sense. It is not possible to validate the theory and the inventory at the same time. It would be palpably absurd to claim—and certainly Jung did not—that Hysteria and Extraversion are one and the same thing. What Jung said, in effect, was most neurotic extraverts have the characteristics of Hysteria; most neurotic introverts have the characteristics of Dysthymia. A demonstration of differences between Hysteria and Dysthymia does not necessarily tell us anything at all about extraversion:introversion. The differences in the particular instance may be due to quite other characteristics. The M.P.I. has, of course, considerable face-validity for at least some aspects, particularly social, of that elusive concept extraversion. It is doubtful whether reliance on "construct validity" is of any value when there is a large logical hole in the nomological network. In respect of the extraversion:introversion continuum, the position of the recidivist prisoners and the psychosomatic cases is close to the hysterics, a finding which to Eysenck is not unexpected. The reviewer would have expected recidivist prisoners to be closer to hospital psychopaths than to hysterics. With regard to the psychosomatic group, at least one large sub-group consists of people whose intense affective disturbance has resulted in physiological changes such as are rare in hysteria. If Stanley Cobb's two broad categories are correct, one might expect to find the psycho-somatics somewhere between hysterics and dysthymics with a standard deviation larger than either. The Neuroticism scale seems to be of much more certain value.

[139]

★Maxfield-Buchholz Scale of Social Maturity for Use With Preschool Blind Children. Infancy–6 years; 1958; revision of *Maxfield-Fjeld Adaptation of the Vineland Social Maturity Scale;* manual title is *A Social Maturity Scale for Blind Preschool Children;* individual; 1 form ['58]; manual ['58, 46 pages]; record form ['58, 7 pages]; no data on reliability; 75¢ per manual; 10¢ per record form; postpaid; Kathryn E. Maxfield and Sandra Buchholz; American Foundation for the Blind, Inc. *

REFERENCES

1. NORRIS, MIRIAM; SPAULDING, PATRICIA J.; AND BRODIE, FERN H. *Blindness in Children.* Chicago, Ill.: University of Chicago Press, 1957. Pp. xv, 173. * (*PA* 32:824)

2. MAXFIELD, KATHRYN E., AND BUCHHOLZ, SANDRA. *A Social Maturity Scale for Blind Children: A Guide to Its Use.* New York: American Foundation for the Blind, Inc., [1958]. Pp. iv, 43. *

[140]

***Memory-For-Designs Test.** Ages 8.5 and over; 1946–60; brain damage; individual; 1 form ('60, 15 cards, identical with cards distributed by the authors in 1946); revised manual ('60, 43 pages, reprinted from *12* below); norms-scoring examples booklet (12 pages, reprinted from manual); $8.50 per set of test materials including manual; $2.50 per manual; cash orders postpaid; (5–10) minutes; Frances K. Graham and Barbara S. Kendall; Psychological Test Specialists. *

REFERENCES

1–5. See 4:69.

6. ARMSTRONG, RENATE GERBOTH. "The Consistency of Longitudinal Performance on the Graham-Kendall Memory-for-Designs Test." *J Clin Psychol* 8:411–2 O '52. * (*PA* 27:6017)

7. HUNT, HOWARD F. Chap. 7, "Testing for Psychological Deficit," pp. 91–107. In *Progress in Clinical Psychology, Vol. 1.* Edited by Daniel Brower and Lawrence E. Abt. New York: Grune & Stratton, Inc., 1952. Pp. xi, 328. * (*PA* 27:3529)

8. RAPPAPORT, SHELDON R. "Intellectual Deficit in Organics and Schizophrenics." *J Consult Psychol* 17:389–95 O '53. * (*PA* 28:6365)

9. HOWARD, ALVIN R., AND SHOEMAKER, DONALD J. "An Evaluation of the Memory-for-Designs Test." Abstract. *J Consult Psychol* 18:266 Ag '54. * (*PA* 29:4063, title only)

10. GARRETT, EPHRAIM S.; PRICE, A. COOPER; AND DEABLER, HERDIS L. "Diagnostic Testing for Cortical Brain Impairment." *A.M.A. Arch Neurol & Psychiatry* 77:223–5 F '57. * (*PA* 32:1926)

11. BURDUS, J. A., AND GILLILAND, J. "Memory for Designs Test." *Psychometric Res B* (4):[21–3] Ag '59. *

12. GRAHAM, FRANCES K., AND KENDALL, BARBARA S. "Memory-for-Designs Test: Revised General Manual." *Percept & Motor Skills* 11:147–88 O '60. * (*PA* 35:2185)

13. HOVEY, H. BIRNET. "An Analysis of Figure Rotations." *J Consult Psychol* 25:21–3 F '61. * (*PA* 36:3HI21H)

14. WALTERS, C. ETTA. "Reading Ability and Visual-Motor Function in Second Grade Children." *Percept & Motor Skills* 13:370 D '61. *

15. FLYNN, PAUL SPENCER. *Correlation of Form Memory and Academic Achievement at the Fifth Grade Level.* Doctor's thesis, University of Virginia (Charlottesville, Va.), 1962. (*DA* 23:4222)

16. KENDALL, BARBARA S. "Memory-for-Designs Performance in the Seventh and Eighth Decades of Life." *Percept & Motor Skills* 14:399–405 Je '62. * (*PA* 37:2954)

17. LETON, DONALD A. "Visual-Motor Capacities and Ocular Efficiency in Reading." *Percept & Motor Skills* 15:407–32 O '62. * (*PA* 37:8253)

18. TAYLOR, FREDERICK RICHARD. *Two New Psychological Tests for Diagnosing Organic Brain Damage.* Doctor's thesis, University of Utah (Salt Lake City, Utah), 1962. (*DA* 22:4414)

19. BRILLIANT, PATRICIA J., AND GYNTHER, MALCOLM D. "Relationships Between Performance on Three Tests for Organicity and Selected Patient Variables." *J Consult Psychol* 27:474–9 D '63. * (*PA* 38:8404)

20. CRADDICK, RAY A., AND STERN, MICHAEL R. "Effect of Pre- and Post-Stress Upon Height of Drawings in a Perceptual-Motor Task." *Percept & Motor Skills* 17:283–5 Ag '63. * (*PA* 38:7219)

21. FRIEDMAN, ELLEN C., AND BARCLAY, ALLAN. "The Discriminative Validity of Certain Psychological Tests as Indices of Brain Damage in the Mentally Retarded." *Mental Retardation* 1:291–3 O '63. * (*PA* 38:8935)

22. KORMAN, MAURICE, AND BLUMBERG, STANLEY. "Comparative Efficiency of Some Tests of Cerebral Damage." *J Consult Psychol* 27:303–9 Ag '63. * (*PA* 38:2985)

23. TORTORELLA, WILLIAM M. *A Study of the Performance of Normal Children and Feebleminded Adults of Similar Mental Ages on the Graham-Kendall Memory-for-Designs Test.* Master's thesis, Fordham University (New York, N.Y.), 1963.

OTFRIED SPREEN, *Assistant Research Professor of Neurology, State University of Iowa, Iowa City, Iowa.*

In this immediate memory test the subject is required to draw each of 15 geometric designs after it has been shown for five seconds. The test is comparable to other visual memory tests, such as the drawing of figures in the *Wechsler Memory Scale* and the *Benton Visual Retention Test,* and supplements such nonvisual memory tests as the digit span, sentence repetition, and similar techniques, all of which have been shown to be sensitive to brain pathology.

Since its first publication in 1946, the MFD has been considerably refined in scoring technique and a sizable amount of data has been published. The correlation with age and intelligence to be expected in a test of this kind has been accounted for by the presentation of expected score tables for adults and children (age range 8-6 to 60 years) although one subsequent study (*22*) claimed that such a correction was unnecessary for their groups, and another (*19*) found a significant age correlation even after their data had been adjusted on the basis of the expected score tables. Adequate scoring samples are provided in the new manual. An attempt has been made to add a copying of designs administration to the test, but the difficulty level of the test items was found too low for such a procedure.

The original validation was supplemented by two cross validation samples of brain damaged patients and controls (including neurotics and psychotics). With a cutoff point set at a level which would give 4 per cent false positives in the control groups, the correct identification of brain damaged patients varied between 42 and 50 per cent. It should be noted that in these validation studies diagnostic criteria were relatively strict so that a higher proportion of severely brain damaged patients was likely to be included in the brain damaged group. Five other studies (*7, 9, 10, 19, 22*) report correct classifications of 63, 67.5, 43, 57.1, and 90 per cent of their brain damaged patients, respectively. It appears that the validity demonstrated in these studies varies widely with the type of sample used and the group discrimination which was attempted. It should be noted, that in two studies reporting high true-positives (*7, 10*) the brain damaged group included subjects who were considerably older (age ranging up to 84 years) than their normal controls. Whereas all other studies used the "conservative" cutoff point suggested by the test authors, Korman and Blumberg (*22*) use an "optimal" cutting score for their groups with 10 per cent misclassification of non-organics; with Graham and Kendall's cutoff point their hit-rate would have dropped to 32.5 per cent.

Immediate retest reliabilities are reported in the range of .72 to .90. Retesting after 10-day intervals indicated that patients with cortical damage show a higher practice effect than schizophrenics (*6*).

Several special problems have been investigated. Psychotics and neurotics without evidence of mental deterioration achieve scores in the normal range as reported by the test authors. It appears that some independence of test performance from acute motivational and emotional disorders has been established although such independence could not be demonstrated for "chronic psychotic" and "chronic organic psychotic" groups (*6, 9*). Ideopathic epileptics with psychosis and without evidence of brain damage were found to have scores which did not differ significantly from normal groups. Attempts to relate test performance to locus of lesion have so far been unsuccessful. Korman and Blumberg (*22*) report that patients with bilateral brain lesions tend to have higher scores than patients with either right or left hemisphere damage.

An investigation of old subjects (*16*) showed that the mild linear increase of test scores with age turns into a more geometric increase after the age of 60; adjusted scoring tables have not been published so far. Whereas an older study (*3*) did not find a relation between MFD scores and reading ability, more recently (*14*) reading retardation in second grade children was shown to be strongly related. Hovey (*13*) found a highly significant incidence of rotations in a group of brain damaged subjects with evidence of episodic EEG disturbances as compared to those with general EEG abnormalities only. In addition to rotations, several other qualitative features of performance are reported in the manual to be significantly higher in brain damaged as compared to controls; the presented figures are, however, hard to interpret since no adjustment has been made for the overall difference in error score between the two groups. In the general scoring of the test, qualitative features are not routinely evaluated.

The present scoring system as a rule allows two errors in the reproduction of a design without penalty, although rotations are somewhat more heavily penalized. It would seem that this lenient scoring unduly lowers the ceiling of the test and makes it too easy for a considerable proportion of subjects. Considering the results of the validation studies, the information contained in the first two errors on a given design could be utilized to improve the validity of the test as well as to gain information on particular types of errors, some of which have been shown to have considerable diagnostic validity.

Three comparative studies of the MFD and other tests for organicity are available. One study (*19*) found the predictive validity of all three tests investigated (*Bender-Gestalt Test, Benton Visual Retention Test,* MFD) significant at the .001 level in a comparison of severely brain damaged subjects with psychotic, psychopathic, and neurotic groups. A second study (*22*) found the discriminative power of the MFD to rank before the *Spiral Aftereffect Test,* the Trail Making Test, and the *Bender-Gestalt Test* in a comparison of matched groups of severely brain damaged and psychotic, neurotic, psychopathic, and normal subjects. The third study [1] compared the Bender-Gestalt, the Visual Retention Test, the Wechsler Block Design, and the MFD in matched groups of mildly brain damaged and normal hospitalized patients and found the MFD to have the poorest discriminative power with a contribution of the MFD in a multiple validity formula not significantly different from zero. It appears from these studies that the value of the MFD in the diagnosis of severely brain damaged cases is more clearly established than in the mildly im-

1 KEREKJARTO, M. V. "Untersuchung über die Diskriminierungskraft dreier Tests zur Erfassung zerebraler Schäden," pp. 186–7. In *Bericht ueber den 23 Kongress der Deutschen Gesellschaft fuer Psychologie.* Edited by G. Lienert. Göttingen: Hogrefe, 1962.

paired patient. The suggested improvement in scoring may recover the predictive value of the MFD for this diagnostically important group. A reevaluation of the necessity for age corrections and the possible refinement of the scoring of qualitative errors in relation to locus of lesion may further increase the usefulness of this valuable instrument.

[141]

***Mental Health Analysis, 1959 Revision.** Grades 4-8, 7-9, 9-16, adults; 1946-59; 13 scores: close personal relationships, inter-personal skills, social participation, satisfying work and recreation, adequate outlook and goals, total assets, behavioral immaturity, emotional instability, feelings of inadequacy, physical defects, nervous manifestations, total liabilities, total; IBM; 1 form ('59, 11 pages, identical with 1946 form except for format and wording changes); 4 levels; manual ('59, 24 pages); $3.15 per 35 tests; separate answer sheets may be used; 5¢ per IBM answer sheet; 40¢ per set of either hand or machine scoring stencils; postage extra; 50¢ per specimen set of any one level, postpaid; (45-50) minutes; Louis P. Thorpe and Willis W. Clark; California Test Bureau. *

REFERENCES

1. Bledsoe, Joseph C. "Sex Differences in Mental Health Analysis Scores of Elementary Pupils." *J Consult Psychol* 25:364-5 Ag '61. * (*PA* 37:876)
2. Clarke, H. Harrison, and Clarke, David H. "Social Status and Mental Health of Boys as Related to Their Maturity, Structural, and Strength Characteristics." *Res Q* 32:326-34 O '61. *
3. Guinouard, Donald Edgar. *Personality Traits and Mental Health Habits of Sociometrically Popular and Unpopular Sixth and Eighth Grade Students.* Doctor's thesis, Washington State University (Pullman, Wash.), 1961. (*DA* 22:1085)
4. Buckalew, Robert J. *An Investigation of the Interrelationships Among Measures of Interests, Intelligence, and Personality for a Sample of One Hundred Sixty-Two Eighth Grade Boys.* Doctor's thesis, Temple University (Philadelphia, Pa.), 1962. (*DA* 23:3232)
5. McGreevey, James C. "Interlevel Disparity and Predictive Efficiency." *J Proj Tech* 26:80-7 Mr '62. * (*PA* 37:3152)
6. Warner, Bernard E. "Relationships Between Health and Socio-Moral Behavior Pertinent to Health Guidance." *J Sch Health* 32:368-71 N '62. *
7. Bledsoe, Joseph C. "The Relation of Mental Health Analysis Scores to Teacher Ratings of Mental Health Status of Elementary Pupils." *J Ed Res* 56:488-91 My-Je '63. *
8. Nickols, John E., Jr. "Changes in Self-Awareness During the High School Years: A Study of Mental Health Using Paper-and-Pencil Tests." *J Ed Res* 56:403-9 Ap '63. * (*PA* 38:9222)

J. Robert Williams, *Director, Child Study Clinic, and School Psychologist, Public Schools, Kankakee, Illinois.*

This revision of the *Mental Health Analysis* (MHA) involves no basic change in purpose or procedure. The instrument is again offered as a means of providing a picture of mental health status, analyzed broadly in terms of the categories of "assets" and "liabilities" and further defined by 5 "components" within each category. As before, 200 questions make up the MHA, with 20 questions keyed to each component and "designed to sample the individual's adjustment" in the areas designated. By use of percentile norms the 10 component, 2 subtotal, and total scores can be translated into a profile. In the 1959 revision the categories have been transposed to promote a more positive approach to the use of the results. As a consequence, mental health is conceived to be "a combination of freedom from liabilities and the possession of assets."

The authors appear to have been only partially successful in eliminating the main shortcomings listed in the reviews of the 1946 version. Reliability results are now provided for each component score as well as for the assets, liabilities, and total scores. However, the two sets of results are not altogether comparable. Both standard errors of measurement and reliability coefficients are given for the assets, liabilities, and total scores, the coefficients having been computed by Kuder-Richardson formula 21. Only coefficients of reliability are given for component scores and are "expressed as the estimated correlation between a subject's 'obtained score' and his 'true score'....where the component scores are reported in the five percentile intervals drawn on the profile." The coefficients listed for the categories range from .87 to .93 and those for the components from .79 to .87.

The reviews of the former version reported a lack of validity, some being especially critical of the way fundamental problems of validity had been lightly regarded. In the manual of the revision the authors have at least approached these issues with more system and thoroughness, even though the reported results are not yet convincing. The new manual treats both content and concurrent validity. Under content validity the relevance, discriminatory capacity, and disguised nature of the items are discussed. As to relevance, the reader is given little specific information about procedures used to determine the item pool. Generally complete and accurate information is presented to show the discriminating power of items, but the prospective user likely would have welcomed a simpler explanation in addition to the "phi coefficient" value which was used. In spite of the reported attempts to "minimize the inaccuracy of self-judgments" by framing questions in "indirect" form, an examination of the items reveals several questions not so framed.

Five studies are given lengthy treatment as the main basis for evaluating concurrent validity. None of these are recent, although all have occurred since the first publication. Generally, they have to do with comparison of the MHA scores of two oppositely characterized groups—"normal" and "delinquent," "accepted" and "rejected," "successful" and "unsuccessful"—determined in advance by conventional criteria. The reported results of these studies are highly favorable on test-of-significance grounds. However, the adequacy of the criterion in each case remains in doubt, since no data on its reliability are given. Even if reliability is assumed, the nature of validity furnished by such studies is "retrospective" rather than "predictive." The case for validity would be greatly strengthened if individual classifications, predicted on the basis of MHA scores, could then be shown to be significantly related to reliable, independent criteria of such groups.

The question of relationships among categories, components, and total scores has been answered, but only for 100 cases at the adult level. The data show all intercorrelations among the scores to be positive. The *r*'s between components within each category are somewhat larger than those between components of different categories, as one would expect.

Despite some limitations of a fundamental nature, the reviewer is of the opinion that the revised MHA is a definite improvement over the original. The practical considerations related to the everyday use of the analysis appear to have been raised considerably by the refinements. The new manual (combining all 4 levels) simplifies administration, scoring, and some aspects of interpretation. The "completely re-designed" profile sheet facilitates both the determination and location of individual strengths and weaknesses. There is at least a fair amount of logical and consistent material to serve as a guide in interpretation. Claims for the test's diagnostic power are modest, since the manual clearly states that it is "offered as an aid" and that it "does not provide a diagnosis-in-depth of adjustment problems." Justifiable caution has been given for the inexperienced or unwary user.

Confined to the role of a *screening* device or used as a means of getting a *first approximation* to an individual's adjustment in the areas covered, the MHA would seem to be of some usefulness. The specific nature of the questions should aid in giving clues to the direction of further diagnostic work and to a suitable starting point for counseling interviews. If there were two forms and less overlap of meanings among components, its worth would be considerably enhanced. In this respect it is inferior to the factor-based questionnaires of Cattell and associates (CPQ, HSPQ, and 16 PF) covering somewhat the same age levels.

For reviews by William E. Coffman, Henry E. Garrett, C. M. Louttit, James Maxwell, and Douglas Spencer of the original edition, see 3:59 (1 excerpt).

[142]

Minnesota Counseling Inventory. High school; 1953–57; based on *Minnesota Multiphasic Personality Inventory* and *Minnesota Personality Scale;* 9 scores: family relationships, social relationships, emotional stability, conformity, adjustment to reality, mood, leadership, validity, question; IBM; 1 form ('53, 10 pages); profile ('57, 2 pages); manual ('57, 27 pages); no data on reliability of question score; separate answer sheets must be used; $3.50 per 25 tests; $3.75 per 50 IBM answer sheets; 60¢ per set of hand scoring stencils and manual; 90¢ per set of machine scoring stencils and manual; 75¢ per specimen set; postpaid; (50) minutes; Ralph F. Berdie and Wilbur L. Layton; Psychological Corporation. *

REFERENCES

1. Dimmick, Kenneth D. *An Exploratory Study of the Minnesota Counseling Inventory as an Index of Oral Communication Ability.* Master's thesis, Ohio University (Athens, Ohio), 1957.
2. Brown, Frederick Gramm. *Measured Personality Characteristics of Liberal Arts College Freshmen.* Doctor's thesis, University of Minnesota (Minneapolis, Minn.), 1958. (*DA* 19:3009)
3. White, Robert Marshall. *The Predictive Relationship of Selected Variables to the Vocational Interest Stability of High School Students.* Doctor's thesis, University of Minnesota (Minneapolis, Minn.), 1958. (*DA* 19:2141)
4. Berdie, Ralph F., and Layton, Wilbur L. "Research on the Minnesota Counseling Inventory." *J Counsel Psychol* 7:218–24 f '60. * (*PA* 36:1HC18B)
5. Brown, Frederick G. "Identifying College Dropouts With the Minnesota Counseling Inventory." *Personnel & Guid J* 39:280–2 D '60. * (*PA* 35:3923)
6. Brown, Frederick G. "The Validity of the Minnesota Counseling Inventory in a College Population." *J Appl Psychol* 44:132–6 Ap '60. * (*PA* 35:3449)
7. Canty, James J., Jr. *Use of the Minnesota Counseling Inventory in Identifying Male Adolescent "Nonconformists."* Master's thesis, Fordham University (New York, N.Y.), 1962.
8. Fallon, Justin M. *An Adaptation of the Minnesota Counseling Inventory for Use With Religious Counseling.* Master's thesis, De Paul University (Chicago, Ill.), 1962.
9. Leton, Donald A., and Walter, Sidney. "A Factor Analysis of the California Psychological Inventory and Minnesota Counseling Inventory." *Calif J Ed Res* 13:126–33 My '62. * (*PA* 37:3446)
10. Kjeldergaard, Paul M., and Carroll, John B. "Two Measures of Free Association Response and Their Relations to Scores on Selected Personality and Verbal Ability Tests." *Psychol Rep* 12:667–70 Je '63. * (*PA* 38:6021)

Norman Frederiksen, *Director of Research, Educational Testing Service, Princeton, New Jersey.*

The *Minnesota Counseling Inventory* is intended for use in counseling high school students. It consists of 355 statements that are to be answered true or false and was constructed by selecting scales and revising items from two earlier inventories, the *Minnesota Personality Scale* and the *Minnesota Multiphasic Person-*

ality Inventory. The editing was intended to make the items more readable by high school students and acceptable to teachers and parents.

The inventory yields nine scores, one of which is merely the number of items omitted (the Question score). Three scales, Social Relationships, Family Relationships, and Emotional Stability, were derived from the *Minnesota Personality Scale* and are supposed to identify "areas in which students may be adjusting particularly well or poorly." Four scales from the MMPI, Conformity, Adjustment to Reality, Mood, and Leadership, are said to provide information about "methods students employ in making adjustments." The MMPI scales from which they were derived are, respectively, Psychopathic Deviate, Schizophrenia, Depression, and Social Introversion. A fifth MMPI-derived scale is the Validity scale, which comes from the Lie scale.

The number of items contributing to each score varies from 14 for the Validity scale to 61 for Social Relationships. Next to the Validity scale, the smallest number of items is 35. There is a small amount of item overlap, the greatest involving six items common to the Mood and Adjustment to Reality scales. Interestingly enough, two Validity (Lie scale) items contribute to scores on other scales.

The most reliable scales are Family Relationships, Social Relationships, Emotional Stability, and Adjustment to Reality, with odd-even coefficients all above .80 and ranging as high as .95. But the Conformity and Mood reliabilities are rather low for use in a counseling situation; the median of the reported reliability coefficients, is about .63. The "average" test-retest reliability of the Validity scale is said to be about .65, but no details are given.

The correlation between Social Relationships (an "area" of adjustment) and Leadership (a "method") is more than .80, higher than the reliability of the Leadership scale. Such relationships indicate the desirability of reducing the number of scores. The correlations of the Validity scale with other scales are not reported.

Evidence for validity was obtained by asking teachers to nominate students who best conformed to personality descriptions that correspond to extremes of the scales. Each nominated group was compared with its contrasting group when possible and with a random sample of students, with respect to mean score on the relevant scale. Differences and critical ratios are reported. The poorest validities, as judged by the critical ratios, are for Emotional Stability, Adjustment to Reality, and Mood. These are the scales that purport to measure traits that are most private in nature and hence least apparent to an observer. For other scales the critical ratios predominantly show significance. The evidence for validity, however, is based only on a comparison of means, and there is considerable overlapping of score distributions, even for contrasting groups. The authors suggest that the scales may be more valid than the criteria, and they may be right, since the criterion problem is especially difficult in the case of personality measures. Although the authors' conclusion that the scales have "reasonably acceptable" validity is fairly cautious, even this statement is too strong in the light of the evidence presented for one or two of the scales.

Recent studies have shown that a good deal of the variance in MMPI scores can be attributed to response sets, particularly sets toward acquiescence and toward giving socially desirable responses. Since the *Minnesota Counseling Inventory* is a direct descendant of the MMPI, the possibility of response bias in the new inventory must be considered. The effects of acquiescence can be controlled by balancing the items with respect to the proportion keyed true and false for each scale. None of the MCI scales is perfectly balanced, and for some the imbalance is extreme. All 14 items of the Validity scale are keyed false, and all 43 items of the Emotional Stability scale are keyed true. Thus a high score on Emotional Stability might be due in part to acquiescence, a tendency to agree to propositions presented. The number of items keyed true and false, respectively, for the remaining scales is as follows: Family Relations, 26-10; Social Relations, 33-28; Conformity, 21-14; Adjustment to Reality, 47-8; Mood, 18-28; and Leadership, 19-16.

Bias toward giving socially desirable responses is less easily controlled. The solution in this case was to include the Validity scale, which is interpreted as revealing an attempt on the part of the examinee to "look good." A raw score of 8 or higher on this scale is said to invalidate the other scores; this cutting score would eliminate about two per cent of the answer sheets. The basis for selecting this criterion is not stated, and no evidence is presented on the effectiveness of the Validity scale. A more reliable validity scale that is less susceptible to acquiescence would certainly be desirable.

Counselors may find the *Minnesota Counseling Inventory* to be useful. But from a technical point of view there seems little reason to prefer it to some of the older inventories. It does not constitute a significant advance in the development of questionnaires for personality assessment.

JOHN W. M. ROTHNEY, *Professor of Education, University of Wisconsin, Madison, Wisconsin.*

The inventory consists of 355 statements to which students with not less than eighth grade reading levels respond by marking a T if they think the statement is true or mostly true, and an F if it is not usually true as applied to them. The statements such as "I get excited easily," "I like to flirt," "I usually feel that life is worthwhile," "No one seems to understand me" are the kind that commonly appear on the many instruments that are labeled as personality tests.

If a student omits 26 to 50 items, which means that his question score is 25 or above, it is suggested that it is best to discuss the situation with him and to "retest" at a later date. Fourteen items are used to arrive at a validity score. If he makes a score of 6 one suspects the validity of the profile, and scores of 8 or higher invalidate the meaning of the other scales because, it is suggested, "It is more likely that such a score reflects a naïve attempt on the part of the student to 'look good' on the inventory." The scores on the question and validity scales are quite different from the other 7 scores named in the description above. The latter are said to provide "means whereby teachers, counselors, and others working with high school age youth can acquire information about the personality dynamics, personality structure, and personality problems of young people." A large order for any instrument!

The authors offer a word of caution in their very candid statement that no evidence is available concerning the validity of combinations of scores on the inventory. In view of this statement and the varying degrees of reliability of the scales one wonders why profile sheets are offered and their use encouraged.

Twenty-eight odd-even reliability coefficients are reported for the 7 scales. Of these, 6 range from .90 to .95, 11 from .80 to .89, 4 from .70 to .79, 5 lie between .60 and .69, and 2 are less than .60. Twenty-eight test-retest coefficients (1 to 3 month intervals) are reported. Of these only one is above .90, 12 are in the .80 to .89 range, 14 are in the .70's, and one was as low as .56. These coefficients do not suggest high enough stability for use in certain situations as in counseling when one is concerned with one subject at a time. Reliability coefficients for the Mood scale are consistently low. The authors were wise in making the statement that "students' attitudes toward taking the inventory may vary considerably from time to time." Can it then be *really* useful in counseling?

The authors attempted to validate the scales by securing behavior descriptions of students who exhibited unusual negative or positive behavior and comparing their inventory scores with those of samples of subjects for whom no such descriptions were offered by teachers, principals, and other school personnel. There is some evidence of mean differentiation of scores (but "extensive overlapping is found among groups when the distributions themselves are compared") which suggests that the inventory scores sometimes elaborate what was already obvious to teachers and principals. It is suggested that the inventory scores *may* be more valid than the criteria but no evidence is offered. Appropriately enough there is a statement in the validity section about the need for refinement and measurement of suitable criteria for personality scales. In any case the authors suggest that the scales have "reasonably acceptable validity."

Much is made of the point that scores have been obtained from students in 9 or 10 states. The composition of the norm groups that are offered for use is, however, local. Of the 19 schools in Iowa which provided normative data, 13 are in Des Moines, and of the 6 in Minnesota, 5 are in the Minneapolis-St. Paul area. Some earlier studies had indicated that the differences between the data for the norm groups and the data based on samples which included students from other states were very small. Much use is made of data obtained from giving the inventory to the entire population of Phoenix, Arizona, high schools.

No attempt has been made to show how the inventory may be used in counseling. It appears that if counselors *in cities* want to spot those students whose teachers and principals have already recognized as unusual, the inventory may *sometimes* help in that process. In view of the authors' highly commendable critique of their own product, however, one must question seriously whether the test will provide dependable evidence of the "personality dynamics, personality structure, and personality problems of young people."

For an excerpt from a review, see 5:85.

[143]

Minnesota Multiphasic Personality Inventory, Revised Edition. Ages 16 and over; 1942–51; 14 scores: hypochondriasis (Hs, '43), depression (D, '43), hysteria (Hy, '43), psychopathic deviate (Pd, '43), masculinity and femininity (Mf, '43), paranoia (Pa, '43), psychasthenia (Pt, '43), schizophrenia (Sc, '43), hypomania (Ma, '43), social (Si, '51), question (?), lie (L), validity (F, '43), test taking attitude (K, '46); IBM, NCS, and Hankes; 1 form ('43); 2 editions (individual and group); manual ('51, 30 pages); $1.50 per manual; postpaid; (30–90) minutes; Starke R. Hathaway and J. Charnley McKinley; Psychological Corporation. *

a) INDIVIDUAL FORM ("THE CARD SET"). 1942–51; 550 cards plus sorting guides ('43); record blank ('48, 2 pages); $25.50 per set of testing materials including 50 record blanks; $3.75 per 50 record blanks; $8.50 per set of manual and scoring stencils.

b) GROUP FORM ("THE BOOKLET FORM"). 1943–51; IBM, NCS, and Hankes; test ('43, 15 pages); profile ('48, 2 pages); separate answer sheets must be used; $5.50 per 25 tests; $4 per 50 sets of IBM answer sheets and profiles; $2 per 50 Hankes answer sheets (scored by Testscor only, see 667); $3.25 per 50 NCS answer sheets (scored by National Computer Systems only, see 671); $4.50 per set of manual and hand scoring stencils; $4.65 per set of manual and machine scoring stencils; $1.75 per specimen set without scoring stencils.

REFERENCES

1–72. See 3:60.
73–283. See 4:71.
284–779. See 5:86.
780. MONACHESI, ELIO D. "Some Personality Characteristics of Delinquents and Non-Delinquents." *J Crim Law & Criminol* 38:487–500 Ja–F '48. * (*PA* 22:3459)
781. THOMAS, RICHARD WALLACE. *An Investigation of the Psychoanalytic Theory of Homosexuality.* Doctor's thesis, University of Kentucky (Lexington, Ky.), 1951. (*DA* 20:3847)
782. REID, L. LEON. "Comparison of Staff Diagnosis and M.M.P.I. Diagnosis." *Proc W Va Acad Sci* 24:152–3 Je '53. *
783. BLUMBERG, EUGENE M. "Results of Psychological Testing of Cancer Patients," pp. 30–61; discussion by Bruno Klopfer and J. F. T. Bugental, pp. 62–71. In *The Psychological Variables in Human Cancer.* Edited by Joseph A. Gengerelli and Frank J. Kirkner. Berkeley, Calif.: University of California Press, 1954. Pp. vi, 135. *
784. ELLIS, F. W., AND BLUMBERG, E. M. "Comparative Case Summaries With Psychological Profiles in Representative Rapidly and Slowly Progressive Neoplastic Diseases," pp. 72–83; discussion by Eugene Ziskind, Solon D. Samuels, Philip M. West, and Bruno Klopfer, pp. 84–94. In *The Psychological Variables in Human Cancer.* Edited by Joseph A. Gengerelli and Frank J. Kirkner. Berkeley, Calif.: University of California Press, 1954. Pp. vi, 135. *
785. HUNT, J. McV.; EWING, THOMAS N.; LAFORGE, ROLFE; AND GILBERT, WILLIAM M. "An Integrated Approach to Research on Therapeutic Counseling With Samples of Results." *J Counsel Psychol* 6:46–54 sp '54. * (*PA* 34:5955)
786. WEBSTER, A. STANLEY. "Personality and Intelligence of Convicts in West Virginia." *J Crim Law & Criminol* 45:176–9 Jl–Ag '54. * (*PA* 29:6017)
787. BARRON, FRANK. "The Disposition Toward Originality." *J Abn & Social Psychol* 51:478–85 N '55. * (*PA* 31:2533)
788. CORRIGAN, SHIRLEY M. *Psychological Correlates of the Physiological Response to Mecholyl in Psychiatric Outpatients.* Doctor's thesis, University of Minnesota (Minneapolis, Minn.), 1955. (*DA* 15:1650)
789. IMIG, CHARLES. *Personality Differences in Curriculum as Measured by the Minnesota Multiphasic Personality Inventory.* Master's thesis, Illinois Normal University (Normal, Ill.), 1955.
790. FURST, EDWARD J., AND FRICKE, BENNO G. "Development and Applications of Structured Tests of Personality." *R Ed Res* 26:26–55 F '56. * (*PA* 31:6081)
790a. KENDIG, ISABELLE V.; CHAREN, SOL; AND LEPINE, LOUIS T. "Psychological Side Effects Induced by Cycloserine in the Treatment of Pulmonary Tuberculosis." *Am R Tuberc* 73:438–41 Mr '56. *
791. LEARY, TIMOTHY; WITH THE COLLABORATION OF HELEN LANE, ANNE APFELBAUM, MARY DELLA CIOPPA, AND CHARLOTTE KAUFMANN. *Multilevel Measurement of Interpersonal Behavior: A Manual for the Use of the Interpersonal System of Personality.* Berkeley, Calif.: Psychological Consultation Service, 1956. Pp. vii, 110. *
792. SHNEIDMAN, EDWIN S. Chap. 17, "Some Relationships Between the Rorschach Technique and Other Psychodiagnostic Tests," pp. 595–642. In *Developments in the Rorschach Technique: Volume 2, Fields of Application.* By Bruno Klopfer and others. Yonkers, N.Y.: World Book Co., 1956. Pp. xx, 828. * (*PA* 30:7202)
793. STANTON, JOHN M. "Group Personality Profile Related to Aspects of Antisocial Behavior." *J Crim Law & Criminol* 47:340–9 S–O '56. * (*PA* 31:8441)
794. TRUMM, OLIVE. *A Critical Investigation of the Personality Scores of the Tuberculosis Patient by the Use of the Minnesota Multiphasic Inventory.* Master's thesis, Marquette University (Milwaukee, Wis.), 1956.
795. WAUCK, LE ROY. *An Investigation of the Usefulness of Psychological Tests in the Selection of Candidates for the Diocesan Priesthood.* Doctor's thesis, Loyola University (Chicago, Ill.), 1956.
796. WEBSTER, HAROLD. "Some Quantitative Results." *J Social Issues* 12(4):29–41 '56. *
797. BOOTH, E. G., JR. *Personality Traits of Athletes.* Doctor's thesis, State University of Iowa (Iowa City, Iowa), 1957. (*DA* 18:925)
798. BRISKIN, GERALD J., AND STENNIS, JAMES W. "Improving Predictability of Minnesota Multiphasic Personality Inventory." *U S Armed Forces Med J* 8:539–43 Ap '57. * (*PA* 33:3819)
799. CONGER, JOHN J.; GASKILL, HERBERT S.; GLAD, DONALD D.; RAINEY, ROBERT V.; SAWREY, WILLIAM L.; AND TURRELL, EUGENE S. "Personal and Interpersonal Factors in Motor Vehicle Accidents." *Am J Psychiatry* 113:1069–74 Je '57. * (*PA* 32:6071)
800. EDWARDS, ALLEN L. *The Social Desirability Variable in Personality Assessment and Research.* New York: Dryden Press, Inc., 1957. Pp. xv, 108. * (*PA* 32:464)
801. GEIST, HAROLD. "Emotional Aspects of Dermatitis." *J Clin & Exp Psychopathol* 18:87–93 Mr '57. * (*PA* 32:4433)
802. HATHAWAY, STARKE R., AND MONACHESI, ELIO D. "The Personalities of Predelinquent Boys." *J Crim Law & Criminol* 48:149–63 Jl–Ag '57. * (*PA* 33:1764)
803. KILDAHL, JOHN P. *Personality Correlates of Sudden Religious Converts Contrasted With Persons of Gradual Religious Development.* Doctor's thesis, New York University (New York, N.Y.), 1957. (*DA* 18:2210)
804. LEWIS, ROY D. *Some Factors Associated With Perseverence in the Field of Education as Measured by the Minnesota Multiphasic Personality Inventory.* Master's thesis, University of Utah (Salt Lake City, Utah), 1957.
805. LINDE, THOMAS FRANK. *Personality Elements of Thirty-Three Adults With Cerebral Palsy as Measured on the Minnesota Multiphasic Personality Inventory.* Master's thesis, University of Illinois (Urbana, Ill.), 1957.
806. MCNEIL, ELTON B., AND COHLER, J. ROBERT, JR. "The Effect of Personal Needs on Counselors' Perception and Behavior." *Papers Mich Acad Sci Arts & Letters* 42:281–8 pt 2 '57. * (*PA* 37:6924)
807. MURRAY, JOHN B. *Training for the Priesthood and Personality Interest Test Manifestations.* Doctor's thesis, Fordham University (New York, N.Y.), 1957.
808. POLLOCK, EDMUND. *An Investigation Into Certain Personality Characteristics of Unmarried Mothers.* Doctor's thesis, New York University (New York, N.Y.), 1957. (*DA* 18:2215)
809. SANFORD, NEVITT; WEBSTER, HAROLD; AND FREEDMAN, MERVIN. "Impulse Expression as a Variable of Personality." *Psychol Monogr* 71(11):1–21 '57. * (*PA* 33:3336)
810. SMATHERS, SANDRA. *An Analysis of the Responses of Mild and Severe Stutters to Items on the Minnesota Multiphasic Personality Inventory.* Master's thesis, Pennsylvania State University (University Park, Pa.), 1957.
811. STEININGER, EDWARD HENRY. *Changes in the MMPI Profiles of First Prison Offenders During Their First Year of Imprisonment.* Doctor's thesis, Michigan State University (East Lansing, Mich.), 1957. (*DA* 19:3394)
812. TAKALA, MARTTI; PIHKANEN, TOIVO A.; AND MARKKANEN, TOUKO. *The Effects of Distilled and Brewed Beverages: A Physiological, Neurological, and Psychological Study.* The Finnish Foundation for Alcoholic Studies, No. 4. Stock-

holm, Sweden: Almqvist & Wiksell, 1957. Pp. 195. * (*PA* 31:4890)

813. Abe, Steven Kiyoshi. *Nisei Personality Characteristics as Measured by the Edwards Personal Preference Schedule and Minnesota Multiphasic Personality Inventory.* Doctor's thesis, University of Utah (Salt Lake City, Utah), 1958. (*DA* 19:2648)

814. Altus, William D. "The Broken Home and Factors of Adjustment." *Psychol Rep* 4:477 S '58. * (*PA* 33:6053)

815. Buer, Carl Frederick. *An MMPI Configural Index for Determination of Somatization.* Doctor's thesis, University of Minnesota (Minneapolis, Minn.), 1958. (*DA* 19:1443)

816. Cabanski, Stanley J. *A Comparison of Psychogalvanic Responses With Certain Categories of the MMPI.* Master's thesis, Loyola University (Chicago, Ill.), 1958.

817. Chance, June Elizabeth. "Adjustment and Prediction of Others' Behavior." *J Consult Psychol* 22:191–4 Je '58. * (*PA* 35:4977)

818. Clark, James Ward. *Personality Syndromes in Chronic Alcoholism: A Factorial Study.* Doctor's thesis, Queen's University (Kingston, Ont., Canada), 1958. (Abstract: *Can Psychologist* 1:116–7)

819. Comrey, Andrew L., and Levonian, Edward. "A Comparison of Three Point Coefficients in Factor Analyses of MMPI Items." *Ed & Psychol Meas* 18:739–55 w '58. * (*PA* 34:107)

820. Coulson, Roger Wayne. *Relationships Among Personality Traits, Ability and Academic Efficiency of College Seniors.* Doctor's thesis, State University of Iowa (Iowa City, Iowa), 1958. (*DA* 19:1647)

821. Donat, Gertrude McAdam. *Factors Related to Measured Masculinity Among Students Majoring in Secondary Education.* Doctor's thesis, University of Minnesota (Minneapolis, Minn.), 1958. (*DA* 19:1834)

822. Drasgow, James, and Race, Ralph. "The College Success of Psychologically Disturbed and Normal Personalities." *J Higher Ed* 29:444–9 N '58. *

823. Duker, Jan. *The Utility of the MMPI Atlas in the Derivation of Personality Descriptions.* Doctor's thesis, University of Minnesota (Minneapolis, Minn.), 1958. (*DA* 19:3021)

824. Faw, Volney, and Wilcox, Warren W. "Personality Characteristics of Susceptible and Unsusceptible Hypnotic Subjects." *J Clin & Exp Hypnosis* 6:83–94 Ap '58. *

825. Fields, Sidney J. "Personality Inventory Profiles During and After Real Life Stress." *J Med Ed* 33:221–4 Mr '58. * (*PA* 34:2264)

826. Gallese, Arthur James, Jr. *Personality Characteristics and Academic Achievement in School of Engineering Students.* Doctor's thesis, University of Minnesota (Minneapolis, Minn.), 1958. (*DA* 19:3022)

827. Gullion, Mary Elizabeth, and Pierce-Jones, John. "MMPI in Relation to Elementary Teachers' Adjustments to Teaching." *Psychol Rep* 4:619–22 D '58. * (*PA* 34:2133)

828. Hogan, Joe. *Configural Analysis of MMPI Scores With Special Reference to Student Teachers in Nursing Education.* Doctor's thesis, University of Minnesota (Minneapolis, Minn.), 1958. (*DA* 19:2851)

829. Ironside, W. "Medical Students and the M.M.P.I." Abstract. *J Am Med Assn* 168:433 S 27 '58. *

830. Jorgensen, C. "A Short Form of the MMPI." *Austral J Psychol* 10:341–50 D '58. * (*PA* 34:2769)

831. Kelly, E. Lowell; Miller, James G.; Marquis, Donald G.; Gerard, R. W.; and Uhr, Leonard. "Personality Differences and Continued Meprobamate and Proclorperazine Administration." *A.M.A. Arch Neurol & Psychiatry* 80:241–6 Ag '58. * (*PA* 33:10420)

832. Kleinmuntz, Benjamin. *An Investigation of the Verbal Behavior of Paranoid Psychotic Patients and Normals.* Doctor's thesis, University of Minnesota (Minneapolis, Minn.), 1958. (*DA* 19:1444)

833. Knowles, Rex Hanna. *Differential Characteristics of Successful and Unsuccessful Seminary Students.* Doctor's thesis, University of Nebraska (Lincoln, Neb.), 1958. (*DA* 19:1655)

834. Korn, Harold Allen. *Guessing Behavior Modified by Schedules of Reinforcement of Individuals With Selected MMPI Profiles.* Doctor's thesis, University of Minnesota (Minneapolis, Minn.), 1958. (*DA* 19:1445)

835. Martin, James Winston. *The Development and Validation of a Scale for the Minnesota Multiphasic Personality Inventory to Differentiate Presidents from Non-Presidents of College Student Organizations.* Doctor's thesis, University of Missouri (Columbia, Mo.), 1958. (*DA* 19:2003)

836. Mathews, Anne, and Wertheimer, Michael. "A 'Pure' Measure of Perceptual Defense Uncontaminated by Response Suppression." *J Abn & Social Psychol* 57:373–6 N '58. * (*PA* 33:9974)

837. Purdom, Glen A., Jr. *Comparison of Performance of Competent and Incompetent Readers in a State Training School for Delinquent Boys on the WAIS and the Rosenzweig P-F Study.* Doctor's thesis, University of Oregon (Eugene, Ore.), 1958. (*DA* 19:1016)

838. Rand, Martin E. *Face Validity of the Minnesota Multiphasic Personality Inventory.* Master's thesis, Kent State University (Kent, Ohio), 1958.

839. Rapaport, Gerald M. "'Ideal Self' Instructions, MMPI Profile Changes, and the Prediction of Clinical Improvement." *J Consult Psychol* 22:459–63 D '58. * (*PA* 33:10761)

840. Rheinstrom, Diana. *The Minnesota Multiphasic Personality Inventory as Predictor of Subsequent Emotional Problems.* Master's thesis, University of Utah (Salt Lake City, Utah), 1958.

841. Rice, Patrick J. *An MMPI Study of Religious Seminarians.* Master's thesis, Loyola University (Chicago, Ill.), 1958.

842. Rommel, Robert Charles Sherwood. *Personality Characteristics, Attitudes, and Peer Group Relationships of Accident-Free Youths and Accident-Repeating Youths.* Doctor's thesis, Pennsylvania State University (University Park, Pa.), 1958. (*DA* 19:3046)

843. Rosen, Albert. "Differentiation of Diagnostic Groups by Individual MMPI Scales." *J Consult Psychol* 22:453–7 D '58. * (*PA* 33:10358)

844. Shaw, Merville C., and Grubb, James. "Hostility and Able High School Underachievers." *J Counsel Psychol* 5:263–6 w '58. * (*PA* 34:3413)

845. Simon, Werner, and Gilberstadt, Harold. "Analysis of the Personality Structure of 26 Actual Suicides." *J Nerv & Mental Dis* 127:555–7 D '58. *

846. Singer, Margaret Thaler, and Schein, Edgar H. "Projective Test Responses of Prisoners of War Following Repatriation." *Psychiatry* 21:375–85 N '58. * (*PA* 33:10113)

847. Steimel, Raymond J. *A Study of the Relationship of Recalled Childhood Identification and Association to Masculinity-Femininity of Interest Scores on the MMPI and SVIB Among Scholarship Finalists.* Doctor's thesis, University of Kansas (Lawrence, Kan.), 1958.

848. Swenson, W. M., and Grimes, B. P. "Characteristics of Sex Offenders Admitted to a Minnesota State Hospital for Pre-Sentence Psychiatric Investigation." *Psychiatric Q Sup* 32(1):110–23 '58. * (*PA* 34:3250)

849. Truelove, James Wilson. *A Study of Patterns in Motivation Among Entering College Freshmen and of the Relationships Between Motivation and Certain Personality Factors.* Doctor's thesis, University of Alabama (University, Ala.), 1958. (*DA* 19:2857)

850. Voldseth, Edward Victor. *The Development of an Empirically Constructed Scale From the Minnesota Multiphasic Personality Inventory for Identifying Students Likely to Be Elected to Positions of Leadership in College Extra-Curricular Activities.* Doctor's thesis, State University of Iowa (Iowa City, Iowa), 1958. (*DA* 19:2858)

851. Walter, Paul Browning. *A Study of Anxiety Among Elementary and Secondary Education Majors in the School of Education of the University of North Carolina.* Doctor's thesis, University of North Carolina (Chapel Hill, N.C.), 1958. (*DA* 19:2542)

852. Webb, Sam C., and Goodling, Richard A. "Test Validity in a Methodist Theology School." *Ed & Psychol Meas* 18:859–66 w '58. * (*PA* 34:2123)

853. Aalto, Ensio Emil. *Psychological Factors Associated With Appropriateness and Inappropriateness of Vocational Choices.* Doctor's thesis, University of Minnesota (Minneapolis, Minn.), 1959. (*DA* 20:1262)

854. Aaronson, Bernard S. "A Comparison of Two MMPI Measures of Masculinity-Femininity." *J Clin Psychol* 15:48–50 Ja '59. * (*PA* 34:2744)

855. Aaronson, Bernard S. "Hypochondriasis and Somatic Seizure Auras." *J Clin Psychol* 15:450–1 O '59. * (*PA* 36:1JU50A)

856. Anastasio, Mary M. *The Relationship of Selected Personality Characteristics to the Chronology of the Menstrual Cycle in Women.* Doctor's thesis, New York University (New York, N.Y.), 1959. (*DA* 20:3823)

857. Astin, Alexander W. "A Factor Study of the MMPI Psychopathic Deviate Scale." *J Consult Psychol* 23:550–4 D '59. * (*PA* 34:6224)

858. Bairdain, Ernest Frederick. *Psychological Characteristics of Adolescents Who Have Had Imaginary Companions.* Doctor's thesis, Columbia University (New York, N.Y.), 1959. (*DA* 20:747)

859. Ballard, Robert G. "The Interaction Between Marital Conflict and Alcoholism as Seen Through MMPI's of Marriage Partners: The Interrelatedness of Alcoholism and Marital Conflict: Symposium 1958." *Am J Orthopsychiatry* 29:528–46 Jl '59. * (*PA* 34:4600)

860. Bendig, A. W. "An Inter-Item Factor Analysis of Two 'Lie' Scales." *Psychol Newsl* 10:299–303 My–Je '59. * (*PA* 34:94)

861. Bruce, Martin M. "Normative Data Information Exchange, Nos. 12-13, 12-14." *Personnel Psychol* 12:329–30 su '59. *

862. Caditz, Sylvan B. "Effect of a Training School Experience on the Personality of Delinquent Boys." *J Consult Psychol* 23:501–9 D '59. * (*PA* 34:6312)

863. Calden, George, and Hokanson, Jack E. "The Influence of Age on MMPI Responses." *J Clin Psychol* 15:194–5 Ap '59. * (*PA* 35:4739)

864. Caldwell, Morris G. "Personality Trends in the Youthful Male Offender." *J Crim Law & Criminol* 49:405–16 Ja–F '59. * (*PA* 33:10641)

865. Cassius, Joseph. *The Effects of Self-Defense Training*

on Morale, Social Adjustment and Emotionality in Male High School Students: An Evaluation and Analysis of Personality Changes Due to Training in Methods of Self-Defense Known as Judo. Doctor's thesis, Yeshiva University (New York, N.Y.), 1959.

866. COCHRAN, WILLIAM MORGAN, JR. "A Correlation Comparison Between the Minnesota Multiphasic Personality Inventory and the Combined Gordon Personal Profile and Personal Inventory (Abstract)." *Proc W Va Acad Sci* 30:189 My '59. * (*PA* 34:2359, title only)

867. COLEMAN, WILLIAM, AND COLLETT, DOROTHY MANLEY. "Development and Applications of Structured Tests of Personality." *R Ed Res* 29:57–72 F '59. * (*PA* 34:5604)

868. COMREY, ANDREW L. "Comparison of Two Analytic Rotation Procedures." *Psychol Rep* 5:201–9 Je '59. * (*PA* 34:2467)

869. CURTIS, QUIN F.; BENDALL, JOHN W.; AND WILFONG, HARRY D., JR. "Some Problems in the Prediction of Supervisory Success." *Proc W Va Acad Sci* 30:186–8 My '59. * (*PA* 34:3495)

870. CUTTER, FRED. "Psychological Changes in Sexual Psychopaths." *Psychol Newsl* 10:322–9 My–Je '59. * (*PA* 34:1699)

871. DANA, RICHARD H., AND CHRISTIANSEN, KENNETH. "Repression and Psychopathology." *J Proj Tech* 23:412–6 D '59. * (*PA* 35:4981)

872. DESOTO, CLINTON B., AND KUETHE, JAMES L. "The Set to Claim Undesirable Symptoms in Personality Inventories." *J Consult Psychol* 23:496–500 D '59. * (*PA* 34:5605)

873. DRAKE, L. E., AND OETTING, E. R. *An MMPI Codebook for Counselors.* Minneapolis, Minn.: University of Minnesota Press, 1959. Pp. vii, 140. * (*PA* 34:6013)

874. EICHMAN, WILLIAM J. "Discrimination of Female Schizophrenics With Configural Analysis of the MMPI Profile." *J Consult Psychol* 23:442–7 O '59. * (*PA* 34:6351)

875. ENRIGHT, JOHN BURKE. *Profile Types and Prediction From the Minnesota Multiphasic Personality Inventory.* Doctor's thesis, University of California (Berkeley, Calif.), 1959.

876. ESCHENBACH, ARTHUR E., AND DUPREE, LOUIS. "The Influence of Stress on MMPI Scale Scores." *J Clin Psychol* 15:42–5 Ja '59. * (*PA* 34:2757)

877. FILLENBAUM, SAMUEL. "Some Stylistic Aspects of Categorizing Behavior." *J Personality* 27:187–95 Je '59. * (*PA* 34:4063)

878. FINE, BERNARD J., AND GAYDOS, HENRY F. "Relationship Between Individual Personality Variables and Body Temperature Response Patterns in the Cold." *Psychol Rep* 5:71–8 Mr '59. * (*PA* 34:424)

879. FITZELLE, GEORGE T. "Personality Factors and Certain Attitudes Toward Child Rearing Among Parents of Asthmatic Children." *Psychosom Med* 21:208–17 My–Je '59. * (*PA* 34:4731)

880. FOULDS, G. A. "The Relative Stability of Personality Measures Compared With Diagnostic Measures." *J Mental Sci* 105:783–7 Jl '59. * (*PA* 34:6016)

881. FOULDS, G. A., AND CAINE, T. M. "The Assessment of Some Symptoms and Signs of Depression in Women." *J Mental Sci* 105:182–9 Ja '59. * (*PA* 34:1359)

882. FOULDS, G. A., AND CAINE, T. M. "Symptom Clusters and Personality Types Among Psychoneurotic Men Compared With Women." *J Mental Sci* 105:469–75 Ap '59. * (*PA* 34:4715)

883. FULKERSON, SAMUEL C. "Individual Differences in Response Validity." *J Clin Psychol* 15:169–73 Ap '59. * (*PA* 35:4876)

884. GARFIELD, SOL L., AND SINEPS, JON. "An Appraisal of Taulbee and Sisson's 'Configurational Analysis of MMPI Profiles of Psychiatric Groups.'" *J Consult Psychol* 23:333–5 Ag '59. * (*PA* 34:4381)

885. GROSS, LEONARD R. "MMPI L-F-K Relationships With Criteria of Behavioral Disturbance and Social Adjustment in a Schizophrenic Population." *J Consult Psychol* 23:319–23 Ag '59. * (*PA* 34:4678)

886. GUILFORD, J. P. *Personality,* pp. 178–83. New York: McGraw-Hill Book Co., Inc., 1959. Pp. xiii, 562. *

887. HAERTZEN, CHARLES A., AND HILL, HARRIS E. "Effects of Morphine and Pentobarbital on Differential MMPI Profiles." *J Clin Psychol* 15:434–7 O '59. * (*PA* 36:1IC34H)

888. HANVIK, LEO J., AND BYRUM, MILDRED. "MMPI Profiles of Parents of Child Psychiatric Patients." *J Clin Psychol* 15:427–31 O '59. * (*PA* 36:1HF27H)

889. HARDER, DONALD F. "Differentiation of Curricular Groups Based Upon Responses to Unique Items of the MMPI." *J Counsel Psychol* 6:28–34 sp '59. * (*PA* 34:6554)

890. HATHAWAY, STARKE R.; MONACHESI, ELIO D.; AND YOUNG, LAWRENCE A. "Rural-Urban Adolescent Personality." *Rural Sociol* 24:331–46 D '59. * (*PA* 34:7639)

891. HOLMES, JACK A. *Personality and Spelling Ability.* University of California Publications in Education, Vol. 12, No. 4. Berkeley, Calif.: University of California Press, 1959. Pp. vii, 213–91. *

892. HOVEY, H. BIRNET; KOOI, KENNETH A.; AND THOMAS, MADISON H. "MMPI Profiles of Epileptics." *J Consult Psychol* 23:155–9 Ap '59. * (*PA* 34:1849)

893. KASSEBAUM, GENE G.; COUCH, ARTHUR S.; AND SLATER, PHILIP E. "The Factorial Dimensions of the MMPI." *J Consult Psychol* 23:226–36 Je '59. * (*PA* 34:4074)

894. KELLY, E. LOWELL, AND GOLDBERG, LEWIS R. "Correlates of Later Performance and Specialization in Psychology: A Follow-Up Study of the Trainees Assessed in the VA Selection Research Project." *Psychol Monogr* 73(12):1–32 '59. * (*PA* 34:7952)

895. KELTY, EDWARD JOHN. *Normal Electrocortical Activity in Relation to Personality Factors.* Doctor's thesis, Duke University (Durham, N.C.), 1959. (*DA* 20:756)

896. KING, GERALD F., AND SCHILLER, MARVIN. "A Research Note on the K Scale of the MMPI and 'Defensiveness.'" *J Clin Psychol* 15:305–6 Jl '59. * (*PA* 35:3455)

897. KING, PAUL; NORRELL, GWEN; AND ERLANDSON, F. L. "The Prediction of Academic Success in a Police Administration Curriculum." *Ed & Psychol Meas* 19:649–51 w '59. * (*PA* 34:6166)

897a. KLERMAN, GERALD L.; DIMASCIO, ALBERTO; GREENBLATT, MILTON; AND RINKEL, MAX. Chap. 18, "The Influence of Specific Personality Patterns on the Reactions to Phrenotropic Agents," pp. 224–38; discussion by Anthony Sainz and G. J. Sarwer-Foner, pp. 239–42. In *Biological Psychiatry.* Proceedings of the Scientific Sessions of the Society of Biological Psychiatry, San Francisco, May 1958. Edited by Jules H. Masserman. New York: Grune & Stratton, Inc., 1959. Pp. xv, 338. * (*PA* 35:2326)

898. KNEHR, CHARLES A., AND KOHL, RICHARD N. "MMPI Screening of Entering Medical Students." *J Psychol* 47:297–304 Ap '59. * (*PA* 34:5907)

899. KRASNOFF, ALAN. "Psychological Variables and Human Cancer: A Cross-Validation Study." *Psychosom Med* 21:291–5 Jl–Ag '59. * (*PA* 34:4736)

900. LEARMONTH, GEORGE J.; ACKERLY, WILLIAM; AND KAPLAN, MIKE. "Relationships Between Palmar Skin Potential During Stress and Personality Variables." *Psychosom Med* 21:150–7 Mr–Ap '59. * (*PA* 34:1384)

901. LEVITAN, SEYMOUR; GOLDFARB, JACK H.; AND JACOBS, ALFRED. "The Relationship Between an Actuarial and a Clinical Analysis of MMPI Profiles." *Psychol Newsl* 10:295–8 My–Je '59. * (*PA* 34:142)

902. LITTLE, KENNETH B., AND SHNEIDMAN, EDWIN S. "Congruencies Among Interpretations of Psychological Test and Anamnestic Data." *Psychol Monogr* 73(6):1–42 '59. * (*PA* 34:3010)

903. LIVERANT, SHEPHARD. "MMPI Differences Between Parents of Disturbed and Nondisturbed Children." *J Consult Psychol* 23:256–60 Je '59. * (*PA* 34:4393)

904. LOY, DONALD L. "The Validity of the Taulbee-Sisson MMPI Scale Pairs in Female Psychiatric Groups." *J Clin Psychol* 15:306–7 Jl '59. * (*PA* 35:3458)

905. MACHOVER, SOLOMON; PUZZO, FRANK S.; MACHOVER, KAREN; AND PLUMEAU, FRANCIS. "Clinical and Objective Studies of Personality Variables in Alcoholism: III, An Objective Study of Homosexuality in Alcoholism." *Q J Studies Alcohol* 20:528–42 S '59. * (*PA* 34:6254)

906. MAGAW, DAVID CURLEE. *Criminal Antisocial and Inadequate Personalities—A Clinical and Psychometric Comparison.* Doctor's thesis, Wayne State University (Detroit, Mich.), 1959. (*DA* 20:2144)

907. MARKS, PHILIP ANDRE. *The Validity of the Diagnostic Process in a Child Guidance Setting: A Multidisciplinary Approach.* Doctor's thesis, University of Minnesota (Minneapolis, Minn.), 1959. (*DA* 20:2387)

908. MAYO, GEORGE DOUGLAS, AND GUTTMAN, ISAIAH. "Faking in a Vocational Classification Situation." *J Appl Psychol* 43:117–21 Ap '59. * (*PA* 34:2776)

909. MEEHL, PAUL E. "A Comparison of Clinicians With Five Statistical Methods of Identifying Psychotic MMPI Profiles." *J Counsel Psychol* 6:102–9 su '59. * (*PA* 34:4396)

910. MEES, HAYDEN LEROY. *Preliminary Steps in the Construction of Factor Scales for the MMPI.* Doctor's thesis, University of Washington (Seattle, Wash.), 1959. (*DA* 20:2905)

911. MICHAEL, WILLIAM B.; JONES, ROBERT A.; AND HANEY, RUSSELL. "The Development and Validation of a Test Battery for Selection of Student Nurses." *Ed & Psychol Meas* 19:641–3 w '59. * (*PA* 34:6171)

912. NIELSON, LESTER J., JR. *Minnesota Multiphasic Personality Inventory Profiles of Persons Applying for Licenses to Operate Nursing and Convalescent Homes.* Master's thesis, University of Utah (Salt Lake City, Utah), 1959.

913. O'CONNOR, JAMES P., AND STEFIC, EDWARD C. "Some Patterns of Hypochondriasis." *Ed & Psychol Meas* 19:363–71 au '59. * (*PA* 34:6040)

914. PANTON, JAMES H. "The Response of Prison Inmates to MMPI Subscales." *J Social Ther* 5(3):233–7 '59. * (*PA* 34:6195)

915. PANTON, JAMES H. "The Response of Prison Inmates to Seven New MMPI Scales." *J Clin Psychol* 15:196–7 Ap '59. * (*PA* 35:5216)

916. PEEK, ROLAND M., AND OLSON, GORDON W. *Organization and Internal Structure of the MMPI, Second Edition.* St. Paul, Minn.: Department of Public Welfare, State of Minnesota, 1959. Pp. vi, 66. * (*PA* 35:793)

917. PETERSON, MARTHA ELIZABETH. *An Evaluation of Relationships Between Test Data and Success as a Residence Hall Counselor.* Doctor's thesis, University of Kansas (Lawrence, Kan.), 1959. (*DA* 21:3364)

918. RIECK, ELMER CHRISTIAN. *A Comparison of Teachers'*

Response Patterns on the Minnesota Multiphasic Personality Inventory With Response Patterns of Selected Non-Teacher Groups. Doctor's thesis, University of Wisconsin (Madison, Wis.), 1959. (*DA* 20:594)
919. Rogers, Arthur H., and Walsh, Terrence M. "Defensiveness and Unwitting Self-Evaluation." *J Clin Psychol* 15:302–4 Jl '59. * (*PA* 35:3510)
920. Rogge, Harold John. *A Study of the Relationships of Reading Achievement to Certain Other Factors in a Population of Delinquent Boys.* Doctor's thesis, University of Minnesota (Minneapolis, Minn.), 1959. (*DA* 20:4037)
921. Rosen, Albert. "Punched-Card Methods for Item Analysis in the Development of Structured Personality Scales." *J General Psychol* 61:127–35 Jl '59. * (*PA* 35:3441)
922. Sauté, George DeWitt. *Accuracy of Psychomotor Performance as a Function of Instructions, Expression-Repression, and Anxiety.* Doctor's thesis, University of North Carolina (Chapel Hill, N.C.), 1959. (*DA* 20:2908)
923. Schubert, Daniel S. P. "Personality Implications of Cigarette Smoking Among College Students." Abstract. *J Consult Psychol* 23:376 Ag '59. * (*PA* 34:4088)
924. Sheldon, M. Stephen. "Conditions Affecting the Fakability of Teacher-Selection Inventories." *Ed & Psychol Meas* 19:207–19 su '59. * (*PA* 34:4093)
925. Sheldon, M. Stephen; Coale, Jack M.; and Copple, Rockne. "Concurrent Validity of the 'Warm Teacher Scale.'" *J Ed Psychol* 50:37–40 F '59. * (*PA* 35:2810)
926. Sines, Lloyd K. "The Relative Contribution of Four Kinds of Data to Accuracy in Personality Assessment." *J Consult Psychol* 23:483–92 D '59. * (*PA* 34:6046)
927. Smith, C. M., and Hamilton, J. "Psychological Factors in the Narcolepsy-Cataplexy Syndrome." *Psychosom Med* 21:40–9 Ja–F '59. * (*PA* 34:1858)
928. Smith, Ewart E. "Defensiveness, Insight, and the *K* Scale." *J Consult Psychol* 23:275–7 Je '59. * (*PA* 34:4411)
929. Stanek, Richard J. "A Note on the Presumed Measures of Masculinity-Femininity." *Personnel & Guid J* 37:439–40 F '59. *
930. Sulzer, Edward Stanton. *The Psychological Effects of Promazine on Chronic Psychiatric Patients.* Doctor's thesis, Columbia University (New York, N.Y.), 1959. (*DA* 20:1075)
931. Tamkin, Arthur S. "An MMPI Scale Measuring Severity of Psychopathology." *J Clin Psychol* 15:56 Ja '59. * (*PA* 34:3223)
932. Taylor, James Bentley. "Social Desirability and MMPI Performance: The Individual Case." *J Consult Psychol* 23:514–7 D '59. * (*PA* 34:6398)
933. Toobert, Saul; Bartelme, Kenwood F.; and Jones, Eugene S. "Some Factors Related to Pedophilia." *Int J Social Psychiatry* 4:272–9 sp '59. * (*PA* 34:6281)
934. Walton, Donald; Mather, Marica; and Black, D. A. "The Validity of the Meehl M.M.P.I. Psychotic Scale in the Diagnosis of Schizophrenia." *J Mental Sci* 105:869–71 Jl '59. * (*PA* 34:6056)
935. Ward, John. *An Investigation of the Minnesota Multiphasic Personality Inventory in Selecting for the Advanced Air Force Reserve Officer Corps at Purdue University.* Doctor's thesis, Purdue University (Lafayette, Ind.), 1959. (*DA* 20:1647)
936. Wiggins, Jerry S. "Interrelationships Among MMPI Measures of Dissimulation Under Standard and Social Desirability Instructions." *J Consult Psychol* 23:419–27 O '59. * (*PA* 34:5643)
937. Wiggins, Jerry S., and Rumrill, Clark. "Social Desirability in the MMPI and Welsh's Factor Scales *A* and *R*." *J Consult Psychol* 23:100–6 Ap '59. * (*PA* 34:1434)
938. Wiggins, Jerry S., and Vollmar, Judith. "The Content of the MMPI." *J Clin Psychol* 15:45–7 Ja '59. * (*PA* 34:2795)
939. Wirt, Robert D., and Briggs, Peter F. "Personality and Environmental Factors in the Development of Delinquency." *Psychol Monogr* 73(15):1–47 '59. * (*PA* 35:5219)
940. Wirt, Robert D., and Simon, Werner. *Differential Treatment and Prognosis in Schizophrenia.* Springfield, Ill.: Charles C Thomas, Publisher, 1959. Pp. xii, 198. *
941. Wohl, Julian, and Hyman, Marvin. "Relationship Between Measures of Anxiety and Constriction." *J Clin Psychol* 15:54–5 Ja '59. * (*PA* 34:2797)
942. Zuckerman, Marvin, and Oltean, Mary. "Some Relationships Between Maternal Attitude Factors and Authoritarianism, Personality Needs, Psychopathology, and Self-Acceptance." *Child Develop* 30:27–36 Mr '59. * (*PA* 34:3176)
943. Aaronson, Bernard S. "A Dimension of Personality Change With Aging." *J Clin Psychol* 16:63–5 Ja '60. * (*PA* 36:1HE63A)
944. Affleck, D. C., and Garfield, Sol L. "The Prediction of Psychosis With the MMPI." *J Clin Psychol* 16:24–6 Ja '60. * (*PA* 36:1HI24A)
945. Altrocchi, John; Parsons, Oscar A.; and Dickoff, Hilda. "Changes in Self-Ideal Discrepancy in Repressors and Sensitizers." *J Abn & Social Psychol* 61:67–72 Jl '60. * (*PA* 35:2253)
946. Baldwin, Thomas Sanderson. *The Relationships Among Personality, Cognitive, and Job Performance Variables.* Doctor's thesis, Ohio State University (Columbus, Ohio), 1960. (*DA* 21:3171)
947. Ball, John C. "Comparison of MMPI Profile Differences Among Negro-White Adolescents." *J Clin Psychol* 16:304–7 Jl '60. * (*PA* 36:2HF04B)
948. Ball, John C., and Carroll, Donna. "Analysis of MMPI Cannot Say Scores in an Adolescent Population." *J Clin Psychol* 16:30–1 Ja '60. * (*PA* 36:1HF30B)
949. Barrows, Gordon A., and Zuckerman, Marvin. "Construct Validity of Three Masculinity-Femininity Tests." *J Consult Psychol* 24:441–5 O '60. * (*PA* 35:4891)
950. Bendig, A. W. "Factor Analyses of 'Anxiety' and 'Neuroticism' Inventories." *J Consult Psychol* 24:161–8 Ap '60. * (*PA* 34:8195)
951. Brown, Donald James. *An Investigation of the Relationships Between Certain Personal Characteristics of Guidance Counselors and Performance in Supervised Counseling Interviews.* Doctor's thesis, Ohio State University (Columbus, Ohio), 1960. (*DA* 21:810)
952. Brown, Paul L., and Berdie, Ralph F. "Driver Behavior and Scores on the MMPI." *J Appl Psychol* 44:18–21 F '60. * (*PA* 34:8467)
953. Caine, T. M. "The Expression of Hostility and Guilt in Melancholic and Paranoid Women." *J Consult Psychol* 24:18–22 F '60. * (*PA* 34:7967)
954. Calden, George; Dupertuis, C. Wesley; Hokanson, Jack E.; and Lewis, William C. "Psychosomatic Factors in the Rate of Recovery From Tuberculosis." *Psychosom Med* 22:345–55 S–O '60. * (*PA* 35:5280)
955. Canter, Arthur. "The Efficacy of a Short Form of the MMPI to Evaluate Depression and Morale Loss." *J Consult Psychol* 24:14–7 F '60. * (*PA* 34:7837)
956. Carrigan, Patricia M. "Extraversion-Introversion as a Dimension of Personality: A Reappraisal." *Psychol B* 57:329–60 S '60. * (*PA* 35:4976)
957. Chance, June Elizabeth. "Personality Differences and Level of Aspiration." *J Consult Psychol* 24:111–5 Ap '60. * (*PA* 34:7138)
958. Christensen, Clifford M., and Macdonald, John. "Directed Cognition and Personality Change." *Alberta J Ed Res* 6:211–7 D '60. * (*PA* 36:2HJ11C)
959. Claridge, Gordon. Chap. 2, "The Excitation-Inhibition Balance in Neurotics," pp. 107–54. In *Experiments in Personality: Vol. 2, Psychodiagnostics and Psychodynamics.* Edited by H. J. Eysenck. London: Routledge & Kegan Paul Ltd., 1960. Pp. viii, 333. *
960. Clark, Charles Marvin. *Changes in Response Patterns of Counseling Institute Trainees.* Doctor's thesis, Ohio State University (Columbus, Ohio), 1960. (*DA* 21:811)
961. Comrey, Andrew L. "Comparison of Certain Personality Variables in American and Italian Groups." *Ed & Psychol Meas* 20:541–50 au '60. * (*PA* 35:3450)
962. Comrey, Andrew L., and Soufi, Alladin. "Further Investigation of Some Factors Found in MMPI Items." *Ed & Psychol Meas* 20:777–86 w '60. * (*PA* 35:3390)
963. Corlis, Rahe Bassett. *Personality Factors Related to Underachievement in College Freshmen of High Intellectual Ability.* Doctor's thesis, University of Florida (Gainesville, Fla.), 1960. (*DA* 24:832)
964. Couch, Arthur, and Keniston, Kenneth. "Yeasayers and Naysayers: Agreeing Response Set as a Personality Variable." *J Abn & Social Psychol* 60:151–74 Mr '60. * (*PA* 34:7376)
965. Crites, John O. "Ego-Strength in Relation to Vocational Interest Development." *J Counsel Psychol* 7:137–43 su '60. * (*PA* 35:4012)
966. Crowne, Douglas P., and Marlowe, David. "A New Scale of Social Desirability Independent of Psychopathology." *J Consult Psychol* 24:349–54 Ag '60. * (*PA* 35:2183)
967. Crumpton, Evelyn; Cantor, Joel M.; and Batiste, Curt. "A Factor Analytic Study of Barron's Ego Strength Scale." *J Clin Psychol* 16:283–91 Jl '60. * (*PA* 36:2HF83C)
968. Dahlstrom, W. Grant, and Prange, Arthur J., Jr. "Characteristics of Depressive and Paranoid Schizophrenic Reactions on the Minnesota Multiphasic Personality Inventory." *J Nerv & Mental Dis* 131:513–22 D '60. * (*PA* 35:5225)
969. Dahlstrom, W. Grant, and Welsh, George Schlager. *An MMPI Handbook: A Guide to Use in Clinical Practice and Research.* Minneapolis, Minn.: University of Minnesota Press, 1960. Pp. xx, 559. * (*PA* 35:2217)
970. Doehring, Donald G., and Reitan, Ralph M. "MMPI Performance of Aphasic and Nonaphasic Brain-Damaged Patients." *J Clin Psychol* 16:307–9 Jl '60. * (*PA* 36:2HI07D)
971. Doidge, William T., and Holtzman, Wayne H. "Implications of Homosexuality Among Air Force Trainees." *J Consult Psychol* 24:9–13 F '60. * (*PA* 34:8034)
972. Edwards, Allen L.; Heathers, Louise B.; and Fordyce, Wilbert E. "Correlations of New MMPI Scales With Edwards SD Scale." *J Clin Psychol* 16:26–9 Ja '60. * (*PA* 36:1HF26E)
973. Eysenck, H. J. Chap. 5, "A Factor Analysis of Selected Tests," pp. 234–44. In his *Experiments in Personality: Vol. 2, Psychodiagnostics and Psychodynamics.* London: Routledge & Kegan Paul Ltd., 1960. Pp. viii, 333. *
974. Flanagan, Carroll Edward. *A Study of the Relationship of Scores on the Minnesota Multiphasic Personality Inventory to Success in Teaching as Indicated by Supervisory*

Ratings. Doctor's thesis, University of Wisconsin (Madison, Wis.), 1960. (*DA* 21:546)

975. Forsyth, Ralph Patterson, Jr. *MMPI and Demographic Correlates of Post-Hospital Adjustment in Neuropsychiatric Patients.* Doctor's thesis, University of North Carolina (Chapel Hill, N.C.), 1960. (*DA* 21:2783)

976. Foulds, G. A.; Caine, T. M.; and Creasy, M. A. "Aspects of Extra- and Intro-Punitive Expression in Mental Illness." *J Mental Sci* 106:599–610 Ap '60. * (*PA* 35:6429)

977. Franks, C. M.; Souieff, M. I.; and Maxwell, A. E. "A Factorial Study of Certain Scales From the MMPI and the STDCR." *Acta Psychologica* 17(5):407–16 '60. * (*PA* 35:3428)

978. Fulkerson, Samuel C. "Individual Differences in Reaction to Failure-Induced Stress." *J Abn & Social Psychol* 60:136–9 Ja '60. * (*PA* 34:7385)

979. Gilberstadt, Harold, and Duker, Jan. "Case History Correlates of Three MMPI Profile Types." *J Consult Psychol* 24:361–7 Ag '60. * (*PA* 35:2219)

980. Gocka, Edward F. "The Introversion-Extraversion Factor and Social Desirability." *J Clin Psychol* 16:380–3 O '60. * (*PA* 37:3174)

981. Gocka, Edward F., and Mees, Hayden L. "The Representation of MMPI Scales by MMPI Factor Scales." *J Clin Psychol* 16:291–5 Jl '60. * (*PA* 36:2HF91G)

982. Goodstein, Leonard D. "MMPI Differences Between Parents of Children With Cleft Palates and Parents of Physically Normal Children." *J Speech & Hearing Res* 3:31–8 Mr '60. * (*PA* 35:6785)

983. Goodstein, Leonard D. "Personality Test Differences in Parents of Children With Cleft Palates." *J Speech & Hearing Res* 3:39–43 Mr '60. * (*PA* 35:6786)

984. Gottesman, Irving Isadore. *The Psychogenetics of Personality.* Doctor's thesis, University of Minnesota (Minneapolis, Minn.), 1960. (*DA* 21:957)

985. Graves, Bernice Courtney. *Interrelationships Between Some Personality and Decision-Making Variables.* Doctor's thesis, University of Texas (Austin, Tex.), 1960. (*DA* 20:4729)

986. Griffith, Albert V., and Fowler, Raymond D. "Psychasthenic and Hypomanic Scales of the MMPI and Reaction to Authority." *J Counsel Psychol* 7:146–7 su '60. * (*PA* 35:3429)

987. Hackett, Herbert R. "Use of M.M.P.I. Items to Predict College Achievement." *Personnel & Guid J* 39:215–7 N '60. * (*PA* 35:3955)

988. Haney, Russell; Michael, William B.; Jones, Robert A.; and Gaddis, L. Wesley. "Cognitive and Non-Cognitive Predictors of Achievement in Student Nursing." *Ed & Psychol Meas* 20:387–9 su '60. * (*PA* 35:7120)

989. Hathaway, Starke R.; Monachesi, Elio D.; and Erickson, Mary Lee. "Relationship of College Attendance to Personality Characteristics and Early Delinquent Behavior." *Sociol Q* 1:97–106 Ap '60. * (*PA* 36:3JO97H)

990. Hathaway, Starke R.; Monachesi, Elio D.; and Young, Lawrence A. "Delinquency Rates and Personality." *J Crim Law & Criminol* 50:433–40 Ja–F '60. *

991. Hill, Harris E.; Haertzen, Charles A.; and Glaser, Robert. "Personality Characteristics of Narcotic Addicts as Indicated by the *MMPI*." *J General Psychol* 62:127–39 Ja '60. * (*PA* 34:8044)

992. Hokanson, Jack E., and Calden, George. "Negro-White Differences on the MMPI." *J Clin Psychol* 16:32–3 Ja '60. * (*PA* 36:1HF32H)

993. Holland, H. C. Chap. 4, "Measures of Perceptual Functions," pp. 193–233. In *Experiments in Personality: Vol. 2, Psychodiagnostics and Psychodynamics.* Edited by H. J. Eysenck. London: Routledge & Kegan Paul Ltd., 1960. Pp. viii, 333. *

994. Judson, Abe J., and MacCasland, Barbara W. "The Effects of Chlorpromazine on Psychological Test Scores." Abstract. *J Consult Psychol* 24:192 Ap '60. * (*PA* 34:7888)

995. Kanun, Clara, and Monachesi, Elio D. "Delinquency and the Validating Scales of the Minnesota Multiphasic Personality Inventory." *J Crim Law & Criminol* 50:525–34 Mr–Ap '60. * (*PA* 35:6897)

996. Kelsey, Clyde Eastman, Jr. *A Factor Analysis of the MMPI and the Mirror-Tracing Task.* Doctor's thesis, University of Denver (Denver, Colo.), 1960.

997. Kennedy, Wallace A.; Nelson, Willard; Lindner, Ron; Turner, Jack; and Moon, Harold. "Psychological Measurements of Future Scientists." *Psychol Rep* 7:515–7 D '60. * (*PA* 35:1522)

998. Keogh, Jack. "Comments on the Selection of Data for Presentation." Letter. *Res Q* 31:240 My '60. * (Criticism of *733*)

999. Kingsley, Leonard. "MMPI Profiles of Psychopaths and Prisoners." *J Clin Psychol* 16:302–4 Jl '60. * (*PA* 36:2HF02K)

1000. Kleinmuntz, Benjamin. "An Extension of the Construct Validity of the Ego Strength Scale." *J Consult Psychol* 24:463–4 O '60. * (*PA* 35:4892)

1001. Kleinmuntz, Benjamin. "Identification of Maladjusted College Students." *J Counsel Psychol* 7:209–11 f '60. * (*PA* 36:1KD09K) Comment by Clyde A. Parker: 8:88–9 sp '61. * Reply by Benjamin Kleinmuntz: 8:279–80 f '61. *

1002. Kleinmuntz, Benjamin. "Two Types of Paranoid Schizophrenia." *J Clin Psychol* 16:310–2 Jl '60. * (*PA* 36:2JQ10K)

1003. Knapp, Robert H., and Green, Samuel. "Preferences for Styles of Abstract Art and Their Personality Correlates." *J Proj Tech* 24:396–402 D '60. * (*PA* 35:4841)

1004. Knapp, Robert R. "A Reevaluation of the Validity of MMPI Scales of Dominance and Social Responsibility." *Ed & Psychol Meas* 20:381–6 su '60. * (*PA* 35:6431)

1005. Kodman, Frank, Jr., and McDaniel, Ernest. "Further Investigation of the Reliability of an MMPI Scale for Auditory Malingerers." *J Clin Psychol* 16:451 O '60. * (*PA* 37:3110)

1006. Kodman, Frank, Jr.; Sedlacek, Gordon; and McDaniel, Ernest. "Performance of Suspected Auditory Malingerers on the Subtle-Obvious Keys of the MMPI." *J Clin Psychol* 16:193–5 Ap '60. * (*PA* 36:2HF93K)

1007. Korman, Maurice. "Ego Strength and Conflict Discrimination: An Experimental Construct Validation of the Ego Strength Scale." *J Consult Psychol* 24:294–8 Ag '60. * (*PA* 35:2220)

1008. Korman, Maurice. "Two MMPI Scales for Alcoholism: What Do They Measure?" *J Clin Psychol* 16:296–8 Jl '60. * (*PA* 36:2HC96K)

1009. Kuethe, James L., and Hulse, Stewart H. "Pessimism as a Determinant of the Tendency to Claim Undesirable Symptoms on Personality Inventories." *Psychol Rep* 7:435–8 D '60. * (*PA* 35:2221)

1010. L'Abate, Luciano. "The Effect of Paternal Failure to Participate During the Referral of Child Psychiatric Patients." *J Clin Psychol* 16:407–8 O '60. * (*PA* 37:3259)

1011. Laver, A. B. "Testing in Canada: Report No. 2." *Can Psychologist* 1:31–3 Ja '60. *

1012. Lebovits, Binyamin Z.; Visotsky, Harold M.; and Ostfeld, Adrian M. "LSD and JB 318: A Comparison of Two Hallucinogens." *A.M.A. Arch Gen Psychiatry* 2:390–407 Ap '60. * (*PA* 35:5948)

1013. Leventhal, Allen M. "Character Disorders, Disciplinary Offenders, and the MMPI." *U S Armed Forces Med J* 11:660–4 Je '60. *

1014. Lingoes, James C. "MMPI Factors of the Harris and the Wiener Subscales." *J Consult Psychol* 24:74–83 F '60. * (*PA* 34:7402)

1015. Lundin, Robert W., and Kuhn, Jerald P. "The Relationship Between Scholarship Achievement and Changes in Personality Adjustment in Men After Four Years of College Attendance." *J General Psychol* 63:35–42 Jl '60. * (*PA* 35:6432)

1016. Markwardt, Frederick Charles, Jr. *Pattern Analysis Techniques in the Prediction of College Success.* Doctor's thesis, University of Minnesota (Minneapolis, Minn.), 1960. (*DA* 21:2990)

1017. Meehl, Paul E., and Dahlstrom, W. Grant. "Objective Configural Rules for Discriminating Psychotic From Neurotic MMPI Profiles." *J Consult Psychol* 24:375–87 O '60. * (*PA* 35:4962)

1018. Mehlman, Benjamin, and Rand, Martin E. "Face Validity of the *MMPI*." *J General Psychol* 63:171–8 O '60. * (*PA* 35:3459)

1019. Miller, Sutherland, Jr. *The Relationship of Personality to Occupation, Setting and Function.* Doctor's thesis, Columbia University (New York, N.Y.), 1960. (*DA* 21:3518)

1020. Moss, C. Scott, and Waters, Thomas J. "Intensive Longitudinal Investigation of Anxiety in Hospitalized Juvenile Patients." *Psychol Rep* 7:379–80 O '60. * (*PA* 35:2278)

1021. Nakamura, Charles Y. "Validity of K Scale (MMPI) in College Counseling." *J Counsel Psychol* 7:108–15 su '60. * (*PA* 35:3435)

1022. Oakes, William F., and Droge, Arnold E. "Operant Conditioning of Responses to Social Introversion Scale Items on the MMPI." *Psychol Rep* 6:223–5 Ap '60. * (*PA* 35:6433)

1023. Panton, James H. "*MMPI* Code Configurations as Related to Measures of Intelligence Among a State Prison Population." *J Social Psychol* 51:403–7 My '60. * (*PA* 34:8116)

1024. Panton, James H. "A New MMPI Scale for the Identification of Homosexuality." *J Clin Psychol* 16:17–21 Ja '60. * (*PA* 36:1HF17P)

1025. Pearson, Wayne Orlando. *The Relationship Between Item Difficulty and Interitem Correlation in the Minnesota Multiphasic Personality Inventory and the Guilford-Zimmerman Temperament Survey.* Doctor's thesis, Cornell University (Ithaca, N.Y.), 1960. (*DA* 20:4177)

1026. Purcell, Kenneth; Modrick, John A.; and Yamahiro, Roy. "Item vs. Trait Accuracy in Interpersonal Perception." *J General Psychol* 62:285–92 Ap '60. * (*PA* 34:7596)

1027. Rasch, Philip J.; Hunt, M. Briggs; and Robertson, Port C. "The Booth Scale as a Predictor of Competitive Behavior of College Wrestlers." *Res Q* 31:117–8 Mr '60. *

1028. Rempel, Peter P. "Analysis of MMPI Data for Classification Purposes by Multivariate Statistical Techniques." *J Exp Ed* 28:219–28 Mr '60. *

1029. Rippy, Mark Leo, Jr. *Certain Relationships Between Classroom Behavior and Attitude and Personality Characteristics of Selected Elementary Teachers.* Doctor's thesis, George Peabody College for Teachers (Nashville, Tenn.), 1960. (*DA* 21:814)

1030. ROBINOWITZ, RALPH. "A Shortened Schizophrenic Scale: Application to Confined Groups." *J Clin Psychol* 16:301–2 Jl '60. * (*PA* 36:2HI01R)

1031. ROSEN, ALEXANDER C. "A Comparative Study of Alcoholic and Psychiatric Patients With the MMPI." *Q J Studies Alcohol* 21:253–66 Je '60. * (*PA* 35:1087)

1032. SARASON, SEYMOUR B.; DAVIDSON, KENNETH S.; LIGHTHALL, FREDERICK K.; WAITE, RICHARD R.; AND RUEBUSH, BRITTON K. *Anxiety in Elementary School Children: A Report of Research*, pp. 102–8. New York: John Wiley & Sons, Inc., 1960. Pp. viii, 351. * (*PA* 34:7494)

1033. SHIRLEY, JACK HAROLD. *A Comparative Study of the Academic Achievements, Interests, and Personality Traits of Athletes and Non-Athletes.* Doctor's thesis, University of Oklahoma (Norman, Okla.), 1960. (*DA* 20:4005)

1034. SHULTZ, LYLE BRITTON. "Personality and Physical Variables as Related to Refractive Errors." *Am J Optom* 37:551–71 N '60. * (*PA* 36:3HN51S)

1035. SILVER, REUBEN J., AND SINES, LLOYD K. "MMPI High Point Code Frequencies in a State Hospital Population." *J Clin Psychol* 16:298–300 Jl '60. * (*PA* 36:2HF98S)

1036. SINES, LLOYD K., AND SILVER, REUBEN J. "MMPI Correlates of Ward Placement Among State Hospital Patients." *J Clin Psychol* 16:404–6 O '60. * (*PA* 37:3423)

1037. SIVANICH, GEORGE. *Test-Retest Changes During the Course of Hospitalization Among Some Frequently Occurring MMPI Profiles.* Doctor's thesis, University of Minnesota (Minneapolis, Minn.), 1960. (*DA* 21:2787)

1038. STEIMEL, RAYMOND J. "Childhood Experiences and Masculinity-Femininity Scores." *J Counsel Psychol* 7:212–7 f '60. * (*PA* 36:1HF12S)

1039. STEINER, IVAN D. "Sex Differences in the Resolution of A-B-X Conflicts." *J Personality* 28:118–28 Mr '60. * (*PA* 36:3GE18S)

1040. URMER, ALBERT H.; BLACK, HORACE O.; AND WENDLAND, LEONARD V. "A Comparison of Taped and Booklet Forms of the Minnesota Multiphasic Personality Inventory." *J Clin Psychol* 16:33–4 Ja '60. * (*PA* 36:1HF33U)

1041. WALLACH, MICHAEL A., AND GAHM, RUTHELLEN C. "Effects of Anxiety Level and Extraversion-Introversion on Probability Learning." *Psychol Rep* 7:387–98 D '60. * (*PA* 35:1682)

1042. WHITMORE, ELVERN LYLE. *The Use of the Minnesota Multiphasic Personality Inventory for Identifying College Freshmen Men With Potential Personal and Social Adjustment Difficulties.* Doctor's research study No. 1, Colorado State College (Greeley, Colo.), 1960.

1043. WIENER, DANIEL N. "Personality Correlates of Type of Outpatient Psychotherapy Chosen." *Am J Orthopsychiatry* 30:819–26 O '60. * (*PA* 35:6470)

1044. WILLETT, R. A. Chap. 3, "Measures of Learning and Conditioning," pp. 157–92. In *Experiments in Personality: Vol. 2, Psychodiagnostics and Psychodynamics.* Edited by H. J. Eysenck. London: Routledge & Kegan Paul Ltd., 1960. Pp. viii, 333. *

1045. YAMAHIRO, ROY S., AND GRIFFITH, RICHARD M. "Validity of Two Indices of Sexual Deviancy." *J Clin Psychol* 16:21–4 Ja '60. * (*PA* 36:1HE21Y)

1046. ZILLER, ROBERT C., AND BRANCA, ALBERT A. "Personality Correlates of Preferred Reality Testing Schedule." *Psychol Rep* 7:251–2 O '60. * (*PA* 35:2784)

1047. ZIMET, CARL N., AND BERGER, ALLAN S. "Emotional Factors in Primary Glaucoma: An Evaluation of Psychological Test Data." *Psychosom Med* 22:391–9 S–O '60. * (*PA* 35:5300)

1048. ZUCKERMAN, MARVIN, AND BUSS, ARNOLD. "Perceptual Defense and 'Prerecognition Responsivity' in Relation to Hostility, Anxiety and Impulsivity." *J Clin Psychol* 16:45–50 Ja '60. * (*PA* 36:1HL45Z)

1049. AARONSON, BERNARD S., AND GRUMPELT, HOWARD R. "Homosexuality and Some MMPI Measures of Masculinity-Femininity." *J Clin Psychol* 17:245–7 Jl '61. * (*PA* 38:8473)

1050. ALTROCCHI, JOHN. "Interpersonal Perceptions of Repressors and Sensitizers and Component Analysis of Assumed Dissimilarity Scores." *J Abn & Social Psychol* 62:528–34 My '61. * (*PA* 36:4HL28A)

1051. ANASTASI, ANNE. *Psychological Testing, Second Edition*, pp. 498–507. New York: Macmillan Co., 1961. Pp. xiii, 657. * (*PA* 36:1HA57A)

1052. ANDERSON, THELMA HILL. *Dimensions of the Characteristics Related to the High- and Low-Achievement of a Selected Group of Negro College Students.* Doctor's thesis, University of Oklahoma (Norman, Okla.), 1961. (*DA* 22:1082)

1053. ANKER, JAMES M. "Chronicity of Neuropsychiatric Hospitalization: A Predictive Scale." *J Consult Psychol* 25:425–32 O '61. * (*PA* 37:3210)

1054. ARCHIBALD, HERBERT C.; BELL, DOROTHY; MILLER, CHRISTINE; AND THOMPSON, CLARE W. "Psychosomatic V." *J Psychol* 52:281–5 O '61. * (*PA* 36:3JU81A)

1055. ASTIN, ALEXANDER W. "A Note on the MMPI Psychopathic Deviate Scale." *Ed & Psychol Meas* 21:895–7 w '61. * (*PA* 36:5HF95A)

1056. BANNISTER, D., AND BEECH, H. R. "An Evaluation of the Feldman Prognosis Scale for Shock Therapy." *J Mental Sci* 107:503–8 My '61. * (*PA* 36:3ID03B)

1057. BARGER, PATRICIA M., AND SECHREST, LEE. "Convergent and Discriminant Validity of Four Holtzman Inkblot Test Variables." *J Psychol Studies* 12:227–36 N '61 [issued Ap '63]. *

1058. BECKER, WESLEY C. "A Comparison of the Factor Structure and Other Properties of the 16 PF and the Guilford-Martin Personality Inventories." *Ed & Psychol Meas* 21:393–404 su '61. * (*PA* 36:2HF93B)

1059. BEIER, ERNST G.; ROSSI, ASCANIO M.; AND GARFIELD, REED L. "Similarity Plus Dissimilarity of Personality: Basis for Friendship?" *Psychol Rep* 8:3–8 F '61. * (*PA* 36:1GE08B)

1060. BENDIG, A. W. "A Factor Analysis of Scales of Emotionality and Hostility." *J Clin Psychol* 17:189–92 Ap '61. * (*PA* 38:1034)

1061. BINDER, ARNOLD, AND SALOP, PHYLLIS. "Reinforcement and Personality Factors in Verbal Conditioning." *J Psychol* 52:379–402 O '61. * (*PA* 36:3CI79B)

1062. BLOOM, BERNARD L., AND ARKOFF, ABE. "Role Playing in Acute and Chronic Schizophrenia." *J Consult Psychol* 25:24–8 F '61. * (*PA* 36:3JQ24B)

1063. BOOTH, E. G., JR. "Personality Traits of Athletes as Measured by the MMPI: A Rebuttal." *Res Q* 32:421–3 O '61. * (*PA* 36:4HF21B)

1064. BRANCA, ALBERT A., AND PODOLNICK, EDWARD E. "Normal, Hypnotically Induced, and Feigned Anxiety as Reflected in and Detected by the MMPI." *J Consult Psychol* 25:165–70 Ap '61. * (*PA* 36:4II65B)

1065. BRIGGS, PETER F.; WIRT, ROBERT D.; AND JOHNSON, ROCHELLE. "An Application of Prediction Tables to the Study of Delinquency." *J Consult Psychol* 25:46–50 F '61. * (*PA* 36:3JO46B)

1066. BROTHERS, WILBUR L. "Some Correlates With the Minnesota Multiphasic Personality Inventory." *J Ed Res* 55:36–8 S '61. *

1067. BYRNE, DONN. "The Repression-Sensitization Scale: Rationale, Reliability, and Validity." *J Personality* 29:334–49 S '61. * (*PA* 37:3290)

1068. CABEEN, CHARLES W., AND COLEMAN, JAMES C. "Group Therapy With Sex Offenders: Description and Evaluation of Group Therapy Program in an Institutional Setting." *J Clin Psychol* 17:122–9 Ap '61. * (*PA* 38:1107)

1069. CADITZ, SYLVAN B. "Effects of a Forestry Camp Experience on the Personality of Delinquent Boys." *J Clin Psychol* 17:78–81 Ja '61. * (*PA* 37:3630)

1070. CARKHUFF, ROBERT R. *The MMPI: An Outline for General Clinical and Counseling Use.* Lexington, Ky.: the Author, University of Kentucky, 1961. Pp. vi, 60. * (*PA* 37:6811)

1071. CHRISTENSEN, C. M. "Use of Design, Texture, and Color Preferences in Assessment of Personality Characteristics." *Percept & Motor Skills* 12:143–50 Ap '61. * (*PA* 36:1HB43C)

1072. CHYATTE, CONRAD, AND GOLDMAN, IRWIN J. "The Willingness of Actors to Admit to Socially Undesirable Behavior on the MMPI." *J Clin Psychol* 17:44 Ja '61. * (*PA* 37:3170)

1073. CLAGETT, ARTHUR F. "Hathaway vs. Welsh on Coding the MMPI and a Method Proposed to Reconcile Differences of Viewpoint." *J Clin Psychol* 17:154–6 Ap '61. * (*PA* 38:993)

1074. COATS, J. E.; WITH THE ASSISTANCE OF R. G. GARNER. *A Study of the Nature of the Chemical Operator's Occupation and the Personal Qualities That Contribute to Successful Operator Performance.* Midland, Mich.: Dow Chemical Co., March 1961. Pp. iv, 112. *

1075. COLE, DAVID L. "The Prediction of Teaching Performance." *J Ed Res* 54:345–8 My '61. * (*PA* 36:3KM45C)

1076. COMREY, ANDREW L., AND NENCINI, RODOLFO. "Factors in MMPI Responses of Italian Students." *Ed & Psychol Meas* 21:657–62 au '61. * (*PA* 36:4HF57C)

1077. COOK, DESMOND L.; LINDEN, JAMES D.; AND MCKAY, HARRISON E. "A Factor Analysis of Teacher Trainee Responses to Selected Personality Inventories." *Ed & Psychol Meas* 21:865–72 w '61. * (*PA* 36:5HF65C)

1078. COUCH, ARTHUR, AND KENISTON, KENNETH. "Agreeing Response Set and Social Desirability." *J Abn & Social Psychol* 62:175–9 Ja '61. * (*PA* 36:3HF75C)

1079. DENBERG, M. L.; PHILLIPS, R. L.; AND SPERRAZZO, G. "The Relationship Between M.M.P.I. and Prison Disciplinary Reports." *Proc 91st Annual Congr Am Corr Assn* 1961:233–6 '61. *

1080. DUDA, WALTER BOLESLAV. *The Prediction of Three Major Dimensions of Teacher Behavior for Student Teachers in Music Education.* Doctor's thesis, University of Illinois (Urbana, Ill.), 1961. (*DA* 22:1518)

1081. DYER, DOROTHY TUNELL, AND LUCKEY, ELEANORE BRAUN. "Religious Affiliation and Selected Personality Scores as They Relate to Marital Happiness of a Minnesota College Sample." *Marriage & Family Living* 23:46–7 F '61. * (*PA* 36:3IQ46D)

1082. EDWARDS, ALLEN L. "Social Desirability of Acquiescence in the MMPI? A Case Study With the SD Scale." *J Abn & Social Psychol* 63:351–9 S '61. * (*PA* 37:1249)

1083. EDWARDS, ALLEN L., AND WALKER, JERALD N. "A Note on the Couch and Keniston Measure of Agreement Response Set." *J Abn & Social Psychol* 62:173–4 Ja '61. * (*PA* 36:3HF73E)

1084. EDWARDS, ALLEN L., AND WALKER, JERALD N. "A

Short Form of the MMPI: The SD Scale." *Psychol Rep* 8: 485–6 Je '61. * (*PA* 36:2HF85E)
1085. Edwards, Allen L., and Walker, Jerald N. "Social Desirability and Agreement Response Set." *J Abn & Social Psychol* 62:180–3 Ja '61. * (*PA* 36:3HF80E)
1086. Eichman, William J. "Replicated Factors on the MMPI With Female NP Patients." *J Consult Psychol* 25: 55–60 F '61. * (*PA* 36:3HF55E)
1087. Field, J. G., and Brengelmann, J. C. "Eyelid Conditioning and Three Personality Parameters." *J Abn & Social Psychol* 63:517–23 N '61. * (*PA* 37:369)
1088. Fillenbaum, Samuel, and Jackman, Arnold. "Dogmatism and Anxiety in Relation to Problem Solving: An Extension of Rokeach's Results." *J Abn & Social Psychol* 63:212–4 Jl '61. * (*PA* 36:4HK12F)
1089. Fine, Bernard J. "Welsh's Internalization Ratio as a Behavioral Index." *J Appl Psychol* 45:117–9 Ap '61. * (*PA* 36:3LD17F)
1090. Finney, Joseph C. "The MMPI as a Measure of Character Structure as Revealed by Factor Analysis." *J Consult Psychol* 25:327–36 Ag '61. * (*PA* 37:1254)
1091. Flanagan, Carroll Edward. "A Study of the Relationship of Scores on the MMPI to Success in Teaching as Indicated by Supervisory Ratings." *J Exp Ed* 29:330–54 Je '61. *
1092. Florido, Herminia A. *Personality Patterns of 141 Unmarried Mothers on the MMPI.* Master's thesis, Immaculate Heart College (Los Angeles, Calif.), 1961.
1093. Forsyth, Ralph P., and Fairweather, George W. "Psychotherapeutic and Other Hospital Treatment Criteria: The Dilemma." *J Abn & Social Psychol* 62:598–604 My '61. * (*PA* 36:4IE98F)
1094. Fort, Gerald Marshall. *An Actuarial Identification of Characteristics Which Discriminate Among Certain Specified Student Subgroups Enrolled in a Midwestern Land Grant College During a Recent Six Year Period.* Doctor's thesis, University of Minnesota (Minneapolis, Minn.), 1961. (*DA* 22:2683)
1095. Giedt, F. Harold, and Downing, Les. "An Extraversion Scale for the MMPI." *J Clin Psychol* 17:156–9 Ap '61. * (*PA* 38:996)
1096. Gilberstadt, Harold, and Farkas, Edwin. "Another Look at MMPI Profile Types in Multiple Sclerosis." *J Consult Psychol* 25:440–4 O '61. * (*PA* 37:3218)
1097. Gocka, Edward F., and Marks, John B. "Second-Order Factors in the 16 PF Test and MMPI Inventory." *J Clin Psychol* 17:32–5 Ja '61. * (*PA* 37:3175)
1098. Good, Patricia King-Ellison, and Brantner, John P. *The Physician's Guide to the MMPI.* Minneapolis, Minn.: University of Minnesota Press, 1961. Pp. 69. *
1099. Goodstein, Leonard D., and Kirk, Barbara A. "A Six-Year Follow-Up Study of Graduate Students in Public Health Education." *J Appl Psychol* 45:240–3 Ag '61. * (*PA* 36:4LB40B)
1100. Goodstein, Leonard D., and Rowley, Vinton N. "A Further Study of MMPI Differences Between Parents of Disturbed and Nondisturbed Children." Abstract. *J Consult Psychol* 25:460 O '61. * (*PA* 37:2919)
1101. Gorman, John R. *A Study of Adjustment and Interests for Fourth Year Minor Seminarians Studying for the Diocesan Priesthood.* Master's thesis, Loyola University (Chicago, Ill.), 1961.
1102. Gouws, David J. "Prediction of Relapse for Psychiatric Patients." *J Consult Psychol* 25:142–5 Ap '61. * (*PA* 36:4IB42G)
1103. Gynther, Malcolm D. "The Clinical Utility of 'Invalid' MMPI *F* Scores." *J Consult Psychol* 25:540–2 D '61. * (*PA* 37:5039)
1104. Gynther, Malcolm D., and McDonald, Robert L. "Personality Characteristics of Prisoners, Psychiatric Patients, and Student Nurses as Depicted by the Leary System." *J General Psychol* 64:387–95 Ap '61. * (*PA* 36:1HF87G)
1105. Hanley, Charles. "Social Desirability and Response Bias in the MMPI." *J Consult Psychol* 25:13–20 F '61. * (*PA* 36:3HF13H)
1106. Hathaway, Starke R., and Monachesi, Elio D. *An Atlas of Juvenile MMPI Profiles.* Minneapolis, Minn.: University of Minnesota Press, 1961. Pp. xviii, 402. * (*PA* 36:2HF02H)
1107. Heilbrun, Alfred B., Jr. "The Psychological Significance of the MMPI *K* Scale in a Normal Population." *J Consult Psychol* 25:486–91 D '61. * (*PA* 37:5010)
1108. Henry, Phyllis Mellor. *The Relationship Between Empathic Behavior and Personality Variables Among Teachers.* Doctor's thesis, University of Buffalo (Buffalo, N.Y.), 1961. (*DA* 22:2705)
1109. Jackson, Douglas N., and Messick, Samuel. "Acquiescence and Desirability as Response Determinants on the MMPI." *Ed & Psychol Meas* 21:771–90 w '61. * (*PA* 36: 5HF71M)
1110. Karmel, Louis Joseph. *An Analysis of the Personality Patterns, and Academic and Social Backgrounds of Persons Employed as Full-Time Counselors in Selected Secondary Schools in the State of North Carolina.* Doctor's thesis, University of North Carolina (Chapel Hill, N.C.), 1961. (*DA* 23:531)
1111. Kiesler, Charles A., and King, Gerald F. "Individual Differences in Making Perceptual Inferences." *Percept & Motor Skills* 13:3–6 Ag '61. *
1112. Kiresuk, Thomas Jack. *The Effect of Test Sophistication on the Diagnostic Validity of the Minnesota Multiphasic Personality Inventory and the Rorschach With Paranoid Schizophrenics.* Doctor's thesis, University of Minnesota (Minneapolis, Minn.), 1961. (*DA* 22:2875)
1113. Kleinmuntz, Benjamin. "The College Maladjustment Scale (MT): Norms and Predictive Validity." *Ed & Psychol Meas* 21:1029–33 w '61. *
1114. Klopfer, Walter G. "A Cross-Validation of Leary's 'Public' Communication Level." *J Clin Psychol* 17:321–2 Jl '61. * (*PA* 38:8426)
1115. Kuethe, James L. "The Interaction of Personality and Muscle Tension in Producing Agreement on Commonality of Verbal Associations." *J Abn & Social Psychol* 62:696–7 My '61. * (*PA* 36:4HJ96K)
1116. LaForge, Rolfe. "Objective Estimates of Clinical Judgments." *J Consult Psychol* 25:360–1 Ag '61. * (*PA* 37:1288)
1117. Lauterbach, Carl; London, Perry; and Bryan, James. "MMPI's of Parents of Child Guidance Cases." *J Clin Psychol* 17:151–4 Ap '61. * (*PA* 38:700)
1118. Lewis, John W., and Caldwell, Willard E. "A Psycholinguistic Investigation of Verbal Psychological Tests." *J General Psychol* 65:137–44 Jl '61. * (*PA* 36:2HF31L)
1119. Lichtenstein, Edward; Quinn, Robert P.; and Hover, Gerald L. "Dogmatism and Acquiescent Response Set." *J Abn & Social Psychol* 63:636–8 N '61. * (*PA* 37:1231)
1120. Lowe, James Douglas. *The MMPI and Prognosis in Alcoholism.* Master's thesis, University of Alabama (University, Ala.), 1961.
1121. Lutzker, Daniel R. "A Validity Study of Tamkin's 'MMPI Scale Measuring Severity of Psychopathology.'" *J Clin Psychol* 17:289–90 Jl '61. * (*PA* 38:8525)
1121a. McCall, Clarence M.; Szmyd, Lucian; and Ritter, Richard M. "Personality Characteristics in Patients With Temporomandibular Joint Symptoms." *J Am Dental Assn* 62:694–8 Je '61. *
1122. McDonagh, Andrew J. *A Study of Adjustments and Interests of First-Year College Seminarians for the Diocesan Priesthood.* Master's thesis, Loyola University (Chicago, Ill.), 1961.
1123. McKenzie, James Donald, Jr. *An Attempt to Develop Minnesota Multiphasic Personality Inventory Scales Predictive of Academic Over- and Underachievement.* Doctor's thesis, University of Buffalo (Buffalo, N.Y.), 1961. (*DA* 22:632)
1124. MacKinnon, Donald W. "Fostering Creativity in Students of Engineering." *J Eng Ed* 52:129–42 D '61. * (*PA* 36:4HD29M)
1125. Madden, James E. "Semantic Differential Rating of Self and of Self-Reported Personal Characteristics." Abstract. *J Consult Psychol* 25:183 Ap '61. * (*PA* 36:4HF83M)
1126. Marks, Philip A. "An Assessment of the Diagnostic Process in a Child Guidance Setting." *Psychol Monogr* 75(3): 1–41 '61. * (*PA* 36:3IQ41M)
1127. Meier, Manfred J. "Interrelationships Among Personality Variables, Kinesthetic Figural Aftereffect, and Reminiscence in Motor Learning." *J Abn & Social Psychol* 63:87–94 Jl '61. * (*PA* 36:4HJ87M)
1128. Messick, Samuel, and Jackson, Douglas N. "Acquiescence and the Factorial Interpretation of the MMPI." *Psychol B* 58:299–304 Jl '61. * (*PA* 36:3HF99M)
1129. Messick, Samuel, and Jackson, Douglas N. "Desirability Scale Values and Dispersions for MMPI Items." *Psychol Rep* 8:409–14 Je '61. * (*PA* 36:2HF09M)
1130. Miller, Christine; Wertz, Clara; and Counts, Sarah. "Racial Differences on the MMPI." *J Clin Psychol* 17:159–61 Ap '61. * (*PA* 38:998)
1131. Olson, Gordon W. "The Influence of Context on the Depression Scale of the MMPI in a Psychotic Population." *J Consult Psychol* 25:178–9 Ap '61. * (*PA* 36:4HF78O)
1132. Oskamp, Stuart Willard. *The Relationship of Clinical Experience and Training Methods to Several Criteria of Clinical Prediction.* Doctor's thesis, Stanford University (Stanford, Calif.), 1961. (*DA* 21:3527)
1133. Palola, Ernest G.; Jackson, Joan K.; and Kelleher, Daniel. "Defensiveness in Alcoholics: Measures Based on the Minnesota Multiphasic Personality Inventory." *J Health & Human Behav* 2:185–9 f '61. * (*PA* 37:1724)
1134. Parker, Clyde A. "The Predictive Use of the MMPI in a College Counseling Center." *J Counsel Psychol* 8:154–8 su '61. * (*PA* 36:3KI54P)
1135. Pearson, Dean N. *An MMPI Syndrome of Scales Pd, Mf, and Pa, With Counseled University Women.* Master's thesis, Brigham Young University (Provo, Utah), 1961.
1136. Philippus, Marion John. *A Study of Personality, Value and Interest Patterns of Student Teachers in the Areas of Elementary, Secondary and Special Education.* Doctor's thesis, University of Denver (Denver, Colo.), 1961. (*DA* 22:3926)
1137. Randolph, Mary H.; Richardson, Harold; and Johnson, Ronald C. "A Comparison of Social and Solitary Male Delinquents." *J Consult Psychol* 25:293–5 Ag '61. * (*PA* 37:1752)

1138. Rees, Marjorie E., and Goldman, Morton. "Some Relationships Between Creativity and Personality." *J General Psychol* 65:145–61 Jl '61. * (*PA* 36:2HD45R)
1139. Rhudick, Paul J., and Dibner, Andrew S. "Age, Personality, and Health Correlates of Death Concerns in Normal Aged Individuals." *J Gerontol* 16:44–9 Ja '61. * (*PA* 35:6241)
1140. Richardson, Charles E. "Health Education or Hypochondriasis." *Am J Pub Health* 51:1561–71 O '61. *
1141. Rieck, Elmer Christian. "A Comparison of Teachers' Response Patterns on the MMPI With Response Patterns of Selected Non-Teacher Groups." *J Exp Ed* 29:355–72 Je '61. *
1142. Rigney, Francis J., and Smith, L. Douglas. *The Real Bohemia: A Sociological and Psychological Study of the "Beats."* New York: Basic Books, Inc., 1961. Pp. xxi, 250. * (*PA* 36:1GB50R)
1143. Rosen, Ephraim, and Mink, Shirley Holt. "Desirability of Personality Traits as Perceived by Prisoners." *J Clin Psychol* 17:147–51 Ap '61. * (*PA* 38:1000)
1144. Rosen, Ephraim, and Rizzo, Giovanni B. "Preliminary Standardization of the MMPI for Use in Italy: A Case Study in Inter-Cultural and Intra-Cultural Differences." *Ed & Psychol Meas* 21:629–36 au '61. * (*PA* 36:4HF29R)
1145. Sechrest, Lee. "Social Intelligence and Accuracy of Interpersonal Predictions." *J Personality* 29:167–82 Je '61. * (*PA* 36:4HA67S)
1146. Secter, Irving I. "Personality Factors of the MMPI and Hypnotizability." *Am J Clin Hypnosis* 3:185–8 Ja '61. * (*PA* 36:1II85S)
1146a. Secter, Irving I., and Tremaine, Donahue L. "Hypnosis and the Personality of the Operator." *J Am Dental Assn* 63:106–8 Jl '61. *
1147. Silver, Reuben J., and Sines, Lloyd K. "MMPI Characteristics of a State Hospital Population." *J Clin Psychol* 17:142–6 Ap '61. * (*PA* 38:1002)
1148. Singer, Jerome L., and Schonbar, Rosalea A. "Correlates of Daydreaming: A Dimension of Self-Awareness." *J Consult Psychol* 25:1–6 F '61. *
1149. Sinnett, E. Robert. "The Prediction of Irregular Discharge Among Alcoholic Patients." *J Social Psychol* 55:231–5 D '61. * (*PA* 36:3JK31S)
1150. Sprunger, James A. "The Ability of the Individual to Contribute to His Group." *Personnel Psychol* 14:317–30 au '61. * (*PA* 37:5729)
1151. Stiavelli, Richard E. *A Minnesota Multiphasic Personality Inventory Study of College Freshmen.* Master's thesis, Fresno State College (Fresno, Calif.), 1961.
1152. Stricker, George. "A Comparison of Two MMPI Prejudice Scales." *J Clin Psychol* 17:43 Ja '61. * (*PA* 37:3181)
1153. Strommen, Ellen, and Ammons, Robert Bruce. "Relationship of Value Placed on Intellectual Activity to Social Desirability of Attitude, Theoretical Orientation, and Interest in Problem-Solving." *Proc Mont Acad Sci* 20:78–84 '61. * (*PA* 36:1GD78S)
1153a. Sulzer, Edward S. "The Effects of Promazine on MMPI: Performance in the Chronic Psychiatric Patient." *Psychopharmacologia* 2(2):137–40 '61. *
1154. Swenson, Wendell M. "Structured Personality Testing in the Aged: An MMPI Study of the Gerontic Population." *J Clin Psychol* 17:302–4 Jl '61. * (*PA* 38:8534)
1155. Swickard, Don L., and Spilka, Bernard. "Hostility Expression Among Delinquents of Minority and Majority Groups." *J Consult Psychol* 25:216–20 Je '61. *
1156. Taft, Ronald. "A Psychological Assessment of Professional Actors and Related Professions." *Genetic Psychol Monogr* 64:309–83 N '61. * (*PA* 36:3LC09T)
1157. Tamkin, Arthur S. "Effect of Psychopathology Upon Mirror Drawing Performance." *Percept & Motor Skills* 13:82 Ag '61. *
1158. Taulbee, Earl S. "The Relationship Between Rorschach Flexor and Extensor M Responses and the MMPI and Psychotherapy." *J Proj Tech* 25:477–9 D '61. *
1159. Thurston, John R.; Brunclik, Helen L.; and Finn, Patricia A. "The Relationship of MMPI Scores to Personality and Achievement Levels of Student Nurses." *J Psychol Studies* 12:75–86 Mr '61. *
1160. Toms, Esther C. "A Comparative Study of Selected Tranquilizers in the Treatment of Psychiatric Patients." *J Nerv & Mental Dis* 132:425–31 My '61. *
1161. Vertein, Lester Dale. "A Study of the Personal-Social and Intellectual Characteristics of a Group of State College Students Preparing to Teach." *J Exp Ed* 30:159–92 D '61. *
1162. Wagner, Rudolph F., and Williams, John E. "An Analysis of Speech Behavior in Groups Differing in Achievement Imagery and Defensiveness." *J Personality* 29:1–9 Mr '61. * (*PA* 36:1HE01W)
1163. Wahler, H. J. "Response Styles in Clinical and Nonclinical Groups." *J Consult Psychol* 25:533–9 D '61. * (*PA* 37:5020)
1164. Walker, Jerald Neil. *An Examination of the Role of the Experimentally Determined Response Set in Evaluating Edwards' Social Desirability Scale.* Doctor's thesis, University of Washington (Seattle, Wash.), 1961. (*DA* 22:1712)
1165. Weitzenhoffer, Andre M., and Sjoberg, Bernard M. "Suggestibility With and Without 'Induction of Hypnosis.'" *J Nerv & Mental Dis* 132:204–20 Mr '61. * (*PA* 36:1II04W)
1166. Wiener, Daniel N. "Evaluation of Selection Procedures for a Management Development Program." *J Counsel Psychol* 8:121–8 su '61. * (*PA* 36:3LD21W)
1167. Zuckerman, Marvin; Levitt, Eugene E.; and Lubin, Bernard. "Concurrent and Construct Validity of Direct and Indirect Measures of Dependency." *J Consult Psychol* 25:316–23 Ag '61. * (*PA* 37:1326)
1168. Acker, Charles W., and Nakamura, Charles Y. "Performance of Chronic Schizophrenics on Inventory Measures of Over-Controlled and Under-Controlled Behavior." *J Clin Psychol* 18:488–90 O '62. * (*PA* 39:5739)
1169. Adams, Henry B., and Cooper, G. David. "Three Measures of Ego Strength and Prognosis for Psychotherapy." *J Clin Psychol* 18:490–4 O '62. * (*PA* 39:5142)
1170. Ball, John C. *Social Deviancy and Adolescent Personality: An Analytical Study With the MMPI.* Lexington, Ky.: University of Kentucky Press, 1962. Pp. xv, 119. * (*PA* 37:8176)
1171. Bendig, A. W. "A Factor Analysis of 'Social Desirability,' 'Defensiveness,' 'Lie,' and 'Acquiescence' Scales." *J General Psychol* 66:129–36 Ja '62. * (*PA* 36:3HF29B)
1172. Bernard, John L. "Manipulation of Verbal Behavior Without Reinforcement." *Psychol Rep* 11:390 O '62. * (*PA* 37:7960)
1173. Brady, John Paul; Pappas, Nicholas; Tausig, Theodore N.; and Thornton, Douglas R. "MMPI Correlates of Operant Behavior." *J Clin Psychol* 18:67–70 Ja '62. * (*PA* 38:8512)
1174. Brecher, Harold. *An Investigation of the Relationship Between Repression-Sensitization and Perception.* Doctor's thesis, Temple University (Philadelphia, Pa.), 1962. (*DA* 23:699)
1175. Briggs, Peter F.; Johnson, Rochelle; and Wirt, Robert D. "Achievement Among Delinquency-Prone Adolescents." *J Clin Psychol* 18:305–9 Jl '62. * (*PA* 39:1886)
1176. Brown, Robert A., and Goodstein, Leonard D. "Adjective Check List Correlates of Extreme Scores on the MMPI Depression Scale." *J Clin Psychol* 18:477–81 O '62. *
1177. Butterfield, Earl C., and Warren, Sue Allen. "The Use of the MMPI in the Selection of Hospital Aides." *J Appl Psychol* 46:34–40 F '62. * (*PA* 36:5LD34B)
1178. Canter, Arthur; Day, Charles W.; Imboden, John B.; and Cluff, Leighton E. "The Influence of Age and Health Status on the MMPI Scores of a Normal Population." *J Clin Psychol* 18:71–3 Ja '62. * (*PA* 38:8514)
1179. Centi, Paul. "Personality Factors Related to College Success." *J Ed Res* 55:187–8 D–Ja '62. *
1180. Cerbus, George, and Nichols, Robert C. "Personality Correlates of Picture Preferences." *J Abn & Social Psychol* 64:75–8 Ja '62. * (*PA* 37:3139)
1181. Christensen, C. M. "Dimensions and Correlates of Texture Preferences." *J Consult Psychol* 26:498–504 D '62. *
1182. Clegg, Herman D., and Decker, Robert L. "The Evaluation of a Psychological Test Battery as a Selective Device for Foremen in the Mining Industry." *Proc W Va Acad Sci* 34:178–82 N '62. *
1183. Corotto, Loren V., and Curnutt, Robert H. "Ego Strength: A Function of the Measuring Instrument." *J Proj Tech* 26:228–30 Je '62. *
1184. Craft, Michael; Fabisch, Walter; Stephenson, Geoffry; Burnand, Gordon; and Kerridge, David. "100 Admissions to a Psychopathic Unit." *J Mental Sci* 108:564–83 S '62. * (*PA* 38:2138)
1185. Dahlstrom, W. Grant. Chap. 9, "Commentary: The Roles of Social Desirability and Acquiescence in Responses to the MMPI," pp. 157–68. In *Measurement in Personality and Cognition.* Edited by Samuel Messick and John Ross. New York: John Wiley & Sons, Inc., 1962. Pp. xi, 334. * (*PA* 38:2638)
1186. Donoghue, John R. "A Consideration of Taulbee and Sisson's 'Configurational Analysis of MMPI Profiles of Psychiatric Groups.'" *J Clin Psychol* 18:309–12 Jl '62. *
1187. Drake, L. E. "MMPI Patterns Predictive of Underachievement." *J Counsel Psychol* 9:164–7 su '62. * (*PA* 37:7186)
1188. Eaddy, Morris Lee. *An Investigation of the Cannot Say Scale of the Group Minnesota Multiphasic Personality Inventory.* Doctor's thesis, University of Florida (Gainesville, Fla.), 1962. (*DA* 23:1070)
1189. Edwards, Allen L. Chap. 6, "The Social Desirability Hypothesis: Theoretical Implications for Personality Measurement," pp. 91–108. In *Measurement in Personality and Cognition.* Edited by Samuel Messick and John Ross. New York: John Wiley & Sons, Inc., 1962. Pp. xi, 334. * (*PA* 38:2638)
1190. Edwards, Allen L. "Social Desirability and Expected Means on MMPI Scales." *Ed & Psychol Meas* 22:71–6 sp '62. * (*PA* 37:1250)
1191. Edwards, Allen L., and Diers, Carol J. "Social Desirability and the Factorial Interpretation of the MMPI." *Ed & Psychol Meas* 22:501–9 au '62. * (*PA* 37:5008)
1192. Edwards, Allen L., and Heathers, Louise B. "The First Factor of the MMPI: Social Desirability or Ego Strength?" *J Consult Psychol* 26:99–100 F '62. * (*PA* 37:5007)

1193. EDWARDS, ALLEN L.; DIERS, CAROL J.; AND WALKER, JERALD N. "Response Sets and Factor Loadings on Sixty-One Personality Scales." *J Appl Psychol* 46:220–5 Je '62. * (*PA* 37:1226)

1194. EICHMAN, WILLIAM J. "Factored Scales for the MMPI: A Clinical and Statistical Manual." *J Clin Psychol* 18:363–95 O '62. * (*PA* 39:5173)

1195. ENGEL, ILONA MARIA. *A Factor Analytic Study of Items From Five Masculinity-Femininity Tests.* Doctor's thesis, University of Michigan (Ann Arbor, Mich.), 1962. (*DA* 23:307)

1196. EYSENCK, H. J. "Response Set, Authoritarianism and Personality Questionnaires." *Brit J Social & Clin Psychol* 1:20–4 F '62. * (*PA* 37:1252)

1197. FEINGOLD, BEN F.; GORMAN, FRANK J.; SINGER, MARGARET THALER; AND SCHLESINGER, KURT. "Psychological Studies of Allergic Women: The Relation Between Skin Reactivity and Personality." *Psychosom Med* 24:195–202 Mr–Ap '62. * (*PA* 37:3757)

1198. FIGURA, C. JOHN. *Validity of the Beall-Panton MMPI Index of "Escapism" in a State Training School Population.* Master's thesis, Loyola University (Chicago, Ill.), 1962.

1199. FISHER, GARY M., AND PARSONS, THOMAS H. "The Performance of Male Prisoners on the Marlowe-Crowne Social Desirability Scale." *J Clin Psychol* 18:140–1 Ap '62. * (*PA* 38:8487)

1199a. GARETZ, FLOYD K., AND TIERNEY, ROBERT W. "Personality Variables in Army Officer Candidates." *Mil Med* 127:669–72 Ag '62. *

1200. GAURON, EUGENE; SEVERSON, ROGER; AND ENGELHART, ROLAND. "MMPI *F* Scores and Psychiatric Diagnosis." Abstract. *J Consult Psychol* 26:488 O '62. *

1201. GILBERSTADT, HAROLD. "A Modal MMPI Profile Type in Neurodermatitis." *Psychosom Med* 24:471–6 S–O '62. * (*PA* 37:5525)

1201a. GILLER, DONALD W. "Some Psychological Correlates of Recovery From Surgery." *Tex Rep Biol & Med* 20:366–73 f '62. *

1202. GOCKA, EDWARD F. "Scoring Direction and Social Desirability Effects." *J Psychol Studies* 13:31–4 Mr '62 [issued N '63]. *

1203. GOCKA, EDWARD F., AND HOLLOWAY, HILDEGUND. "A Composite MMPI Introversion-Extraversion Scale." *J Clin Psychol* 18:474–7 O '62. * (*PA* 39:5176)

1204. GOLDEN, JULES; MANDEL, NATHAN; GLUECK, BERNARD C., JR.; AND FEDER, ZETTA. "A Summary Description of Fifty 'Normal' White Males." *Am J Psychiatry* 119:48–56 Jl '62. * (*PA* 37:5009)

1205. GOLDFRIED, MARVIN R. "Rorschach Developmental Level and the MMPI as Measures of Severity of Psychological Disturbance." *J Proj Tech* 26:187–92 Je '62. * (*PA* 37:3219)

1206. GOLDMAN, IRWIN J. "Social Desirability, Manifest Anxiety, and Schizophrenic Response." *Psychol Rep* 11:637–8 D '62. * (*PA* 38:2694)

1207. GOLDMAN, IRWIN J. *The Willingness of Music and Visual Art Students to Admit to Socially Undesirable and Psychopathological Characteristics.* Doctor's thesis, Columbia University (New York, N.Y.), 1962. (*DA* 23:732)

1208. GOLDSTEIN, ROBERT H., AND SALZMAN, LEONARD F. "Correlates of Clinical Judgment in Psychiatry." *J Med Ed* 37:1101–4 O '62. *

1209. GOTTESMAN, IRVING I. "Differential Inheritance of the Psychoneuroses." *Eug Q* 9:223–7 D '62. * (*PA* 37:7729)

1210. GYNTHER, MALCOLM D. "Crime and Psychopathology." *J Abn & Social Psychol* 64:378–80 My '62. * (*PA* 38:1295)

1211. GYNTHER, MALCOLM D. "Degree of Agreement Among Three 'Interpersonal System' Measures." Abstract. *J Consult Psychol* 26:107 F '62. * (*PA* 37:4982)

1212. HANEY, RUSSELL; MICHAEL, WILLIAM B.; AND GERSHON, ARTHUR. "Achievement, Aptitude, and Personality Measures as Predictors of Success in Nursing Training." *Ed & Psychol Meas* 22:389–92 su '62. * (*PA* 37:3869)

1213. HANLEY, CHARLES. "The 'Difficulty' of a Personality Inventory Item." *Ed & Psychol Meas* 22:577–84 au '62. * (*PA* 37:4934)

1214. HARTLEY, RAYMOND E., AND ALLEN, ROBERT M. "The Minnesota Multiphasic Personality Inventory (MMPI) and the Edwards Personal Preference Schedule (EPPS): A Factor Analytic Study." *J Social Psychol* 58:153–62 O '62. * (*PA* 37:6733)

1215. HATHAWAY, STARKE R. "Problems of Personality Assessment," pp. 144–60. (*PA* 37:5040) In *Personality Research.* Proceedings of the XIV International Congress of Applied Psychology, Vol. 2. Copenhagen, Denmark: Munksgaard, Ltd., 1962. Pp. 229. *

1216. HETRICK, W. ROBERT, AND HAAS, KURT. "Some Personality Correlates of Verbal Conditioning." *J Psychol* 53:409–15 Ap '62. * (*PA* 37:371)

1217. HEWITT, JOHN H., AND ROSENBERG, LEON A. "The MMPI as a Screening Device in an Academic Setting." *Ed & Psychol Meas* 22:129–37 sp '62. * (*PA* 37:1991)

1218. HILL, HARRIS E.; HAERTZEN, CHARLES A.; AND DAVIS, HOWARD. "An MMPI Factor Analytic Study of Alcoholics, Narcotic Addicts, and Criminals." *Q J Studies Alcohol* 23:411–31 S '62. *

1219. HISPANICUS, PETREOLUS. "Selecting Seminarians," pp. 65–105. In *Screening Candidates for the Priesthood and Religious Life.* By Magda B. Arnold and others. Chicago, Ill.: Loyola University Press, 1962. Pp. x, 205. *

1220. HOENE, EDWARD. *PGR Ratio and the MMPI: An Experimental Approach as to How a Person Handles Emotions.* Master's thesis, Loyola University (Chicago, Ill.), 1962.

1221. HOOKE, JAMES F., AND MARKS, PHILIP A. "MMPI Characteristics of Pregnancy." *J Clin Psychol* 18:316–7 Jl '62. * (*PA* 39:1836)

1222. HULL, J., AND ZUBEK, JOHN P. "Personality Characteristics of Successful and Unsuccessful Sensory Isolation Subjects." *Percept & Motor Skills* 14:231–40 Ap '62. * (*PA* 37:312)

1223. JACKSON, DOUGLAS N., AND MESSICK, SAMUEL. Chap. 8, "Response Styles and the Assessment of Psychopathology," pp. 129–55. In *Measurement in Personality and Cognition.* Edited by Samuel Messick and John Ross. New York: John Wiley & Sons, Inc., 1962. Pp. xi, 334. * (*PA* 38:2638)

1224. JACKSON, DOUGLAS N., AND MESSICK, SAMUEL. "Response Styles on the MMPI: Comparison of Clinical and Normal Samples." *J Abn & Social Psychol* 65:285–99 N '62. *

1225. JENKINS, THOMAS N. "Efficiency of the Jenkins Global Personality Inventory." *J Psychol Studies* 13:11–20 Mr '62 [issued N '63]. *

1226. JOHANNSEN, WALTER J.; FRIEDMAN, SAMUEL H. FELDMAN, EDWARD I.; AND NEGRETE, ABELARDO. "A Reexamination of the Hippuric Acid-Anxiety Relationship." *Psychosom Med* 24:569–78 N–D '62. * (*PA* 37:8046)

1226a. KALIS, BETTY L.; TOCCHINI, JOHN J.; AND THOMASSEN, PAUL R. "Correlation Study Between Personality Tests and Dental Student Performance." *J Am Dental Assn* 64:656–70 My '62. *

1227. KANFER, FREDERICK H., AND MARSTON, ALBERT R. "The Relationship Between Personality Variables and Verbal Response Characteristics." *J Clin Psychol* 18:426–8 O '62. *

1228. KATZELL, RAYMOND A., AND KATZELL, MILDRED E. "Development and Application of Structured Tests of Personality." *R Ed Res* 32:51–63 F '62. * (*PA* 37:1197)

1229. KENNEDY, WALLACE A. "MMPI Profiles of Gifted Adolescents." *J Clin Psychol* 18:148–9 Ap '62. * (*PA* 38:9248)

1230. KENNEDY, WALLACE A., AND SMITH, ALVIN H. "A High Performance MMPI Scale for Adolescents." *Psychol Rep* 11:494 O '62. * (*PA* 37:8257)

1231. KERR, MARILYN; MAKI, BOBBIN; AND AMMONS, R. B. "Personality, Values, and 'Intellectualism.'" *Proc Mont Acad Sci* 21:132–6 '62. * (*PA* 37:3149)

1232. KIRK, BARBARA A.; CUMMINGS, ROGER W.; AND GOODSTEIN, LEONARD D. "Predicting Student Success in Graduate Business Courses." *Calif Mgmt R* 5:63–6 f '62. *

1233. KLEINMUNTZ, BENJAMIN. "Annotated Bibliography of MMPI Research Among College Populations." *J Counsel Psychol* 9:373–96 w '62. *

1234. KLEINMUNTZ, BENJAMIN, AND ALEXANDER, L. BARTON. "Computer Program for the Meehl-Dahlstrom MMPI Profile Rules." *Ed & Psychol Meas* 22:193–9 sp '62. * (*PA* 37:72)

1235. KLØVE, HALLGRIM, AND DOEHRING, DONALD G. "MMPI in Epileptic Groups With Differential Etiology." *J Clin Psychol* 18:149–53 Ap '62. * (*PA* 38:8521)

1236. KNAPP, ROBERT H.; GEWIRTZ, HERBERT; AND HOLZBERG, JULES D. "Some Personality Correlates of Styles of Interpersonal Thought." *J Proj Tech* 26:398–403 D '62. * (*PA* 37:6717)

1237. KODMAN, FRANK, JR., AND SEDLACEK, GORDON. "MMPI Changes Following a Course in Mental Hygiene." *Mental Hyg* 46:95–7 Ja '62. *

1238. KREITMAN, NORMAN. "Psychiatric Orientation: A Study of Attitudes Among Psychiatrists." *J Mental Sci* 108:317–28 My '62. * (*PA* 37:3400)

1239. L'ABATE, LUCIANO. "MMPI Scatter as a Single Index of Maladjustment." *J Clin Psychol* 18:142–3 Ap '62. * (*PA* 38:8523)

1240. L'ABATE, LUCIANO. "The Relationship Between WAIS-Derived Indices of Maladjustment and MMPI in Deviant Groups." *J Consult Psychol* 26:441–5 O '62. *

1241. LADOU, JOSEPH; ELLMAN, GEORGE L.; CALLAWAY, ENOCH, III; EDMINSTER, IVAN F.; AND CHRISTENSEN, ROBERT L. "Correlates of Manifest Anxiety." *J Psychosom Res* 6:41–7 Ja–Mr '62. * (*PA* 37:3323)

1242. LAFORGE, ROLFE. "A Correlational Study of Two Personality Tests: The MMPI and Cattell 16 PF." *J Consult Psychol* 26:402–11 O '62. * (*PA* 39:1743)

1243. LAIR, CHARLES V., AND TRAPP, E. PHILIP. "The Differential Diagnostic Value of MMPI With Somatically Disturbed Patients." *J Clin Psychol* 18:146–7 Ap '62. * (*PA* 38:8524)

1244. LANG, PETER J., AND LAZOVIK, A. DAVID. "Personality and Hypnotic Susceptibility." *J Consult Psychol* 26:317–22 Ag '62. * (*PA* 38:4433)

1245. LAUTERBACH, CARL G.; VOGEL, WILLIAM; AND HART, JOHN. "Comparison of the MMPI's of Male Problem Adolescents and Their Parents." *J Clin Psychol* 18:485–7 O '62. *

1246. LEVINE, DAVID, AND COHEN, JACOB. "Symptoms and Ego Strength Measures as Predictors of the Outcome of Hospitalization in Functional Psychoses." *J Consult Psychol* 26:246–50 Je '62. * (*PA* 38:1304)

1247. LEVINSON, BORIS M. "The MMPI in a Jewish Traditional Setting." *J Genetic Psychol* 101:25–42 S '62. * (*PA* 38:4278)

1248. LIPSHER, DAVID HAROLD. *Consistency of Clinicians' Judgments Based on MMPI, Rorschach and TAT Protocols.* Doctor's thesis, Stanford University (Stanford, Calif.), 1962. (*DA* 22:4409)

1249. MCDONALD, ROBERT L. "Personality Characteristics of Freshman Medical Students as Depicted by the Leary System." *J Genetic Psychol* 100:313–23 Je '62. * (*PA* 37:3838)

1250. MCDONALD, ROBERT L., AND GYNTHER, MALCOLM D. "MMPI Norms for Southern Adolescent Negroes." *J Social Psychol* 58:277–82 D '62. * (*PA* 37:6692)

1251. MACKINNON, DONALD W. "The Personality Correlates of Creativity: A Study of American Architects," pp. 11–39. (*PA* 37:4958) In *Personality Research.* Proceedings of the XIV International Congress of Applied Psychology, Vol. 2. Copenhagen, Denmark: Munksgaard, Ltd., 1962. Pp. 229. *

1252. MARKS, PHILIP A., AND SEEMAN, WILLIAM. "Addendum to 'An Assessment of the Diagnostic Process in a Child Guidance Setting.'" Abstract. *J Consult Psychol* 26:485 O '62. *

1253. MARKWELL, EARL D., JR. "Autonomic Nervous System Measures and Factor Correlates With Personality Indices in a Tuberculous Population." Abstract. *J Consult Psychol* 26:194 Ap '62. * (*PA* 37:5533)

1254. MARTIN, CAROL, AND NICHOLS, ROBERT C. "Personality and Religious Belief." *J Social Psychol* 56:3–8 F '62. * (*PA* 36:5GD03M)

1255. MEGARGEE, EDWIN I., AND MENDELSOHN, GERALD A. "A Cross-Validation of Twelve MMPI Indices of Hostility and Control." *J Abn & Social Psychol* 65:431–8 D '62. *

1256. MOOS, RUDOLF H. "Effects of Training on Students' Test Interpretations." *J Proj Tech* 26:310–7 S '62. * (*PA* 37:3201)

1257. MORSE, PAUL KENNETH. *The Strong Vocational Interest Blank and Minnesota Multiphasic Personality Inventory as Measures of Persistence Toward the Ministry as a Vocational Goal.* Doctor's thesis, University of Michigan (Ann Arbor, Mich.), 1962. (*DA* 23:3239)

1258. MURPHREE, HENRY B.; KARABELAS, MICHAEL J.; AND BRYAN, LAURENCE L. "Scores of Inmates of a Federal Penitentiary on Two Scales of the MMPI." *J Clin Psychol* 18:137–9 Ap '62. * (*PA* 38:8528)

1259. MURPHY, LEONARD. *Changes in the MMPI Scores of Three Groups of Seminarians Retested After One, Two, and Three Years.* Master's thesis, Fordham University (New York, N.Y.), 1962.

1260. NICHOLS, ROBERT C. "Subtle, Obvious and Stereotype Measures of Masculinity-Femininity." *Ed & Psychol Meas* 22:449–61 au '62. * (*PA* 37:5014)

1261. OSKAMP, STUART. "The Relationship of Clinical Experience and Training Methods to Several Criteria of Clinical Prediction." *Psychol Monogr* 76(28):1–27 '62. * (*PA* 38:8654)

1262. PANTON, JAMES H. "The Identification of Habitual Criminalism With the MMPI." *J Clin Psychol* 18:133–6 Ap '62. * (*PA* 38:8529)

1263. PANTON, JAMES H. "The Identification of Predispositional Factors in Self-Mutilation Within a State Prison Population." *J Clin Psychol* 18:63–7 Ja '62. * (*PA* 38:8502)

1264. PANTON, JAMES H. "Use of the MMPI as an Index to Successful Parole." *J Crim Law & Criminol* 53:484–8 D '62. * (*PA* 37:8181)

1265. PATTERSON, C. H. "A Note on the Construct Validity of the Concept of Empathy." *Personnel & Guid J* 40:803–6 My '62. * (*PA* 37:3448)

1266. PATTERSON, C. H. "Test Characteristics of Rehabilitation Counselor Trainees." *J Rehabil* 28:15–6 S–O '62. * (*PA* 37:6953)

1267. PERKINS, JULIA ELLEN. *Contextual Effects on the MMPI.* Doctor's thesis, University of Oregon (Eugene, Ore.), 1962. (*DA* 23:3981)

1268. PRUITT, WALTER A., AND VAN DE CASTLE, R. L. "Dependency Measures and Welfare Chronicity." *J Consult Psychol* 26:559–60 D '62. * (*PA* 39:1896)

1269. RAPAPORT, GERALD M., AND MARSHALL, ROBERT J. "The Prediction of Rehabilitative Potential of Stockade Prisoners Using Clinical Psychological Tests." *J Clin Psychol* 18:444–6 O '62. * (*PA* 39:5087)

1270. ROSEN, ALBERT. "Development of the MMPI Scales Based on a Reference Group of Psychiatric Patients." *Psychol Monogr* 76(8):1–25 '62. * (*PA* 37:3098)

1271. ROWLEY, VINTON N., AND STONE, F. BETH. "MMPI Differences Between Emotionally Disturbed and Delinquent Adolescents." *J Clin Psychol* 18:481–4 O '62. * (*PA* 39:5181)

1272. SECHREST, LEE, AND JACKSON, DOUGLAS N. "The Generality of Deviant Response Tendencies." *J Consult Psychol* 26:395–401 O '62. * (*PA* 39:1822)

1273. SHIPE, DOROTHY; DINGMAN, HARVEY F.; WINDLE, CHARLES; AND MOTICHA, KATHERINE. "Validity of a Measure of Escape Proneness." *Am J Mental Def* 66:872–7 My '62. * (*PA* 37:1708)

1274. SILVER, REUBEN J., AND SINES, LLOYD K. "Diagnostic Efficiency of the MMPI With and Without the K Correction." *J Clin Psychol* 18:312–4 Jl '62. * (*PA* 39:1846)

1275. SINNETT, E. ROBERT. "The Relationship Between the Ego Strength Scale and Rated In-Hospital Improvement." *J Clin Psychol* 18:46–7 Ja '62. * (*PA* 38:8702)

1276. SLATER, PHILIP E. "Parental Behavior and the Personality of the Child." *J Genetic Psychol* 101:53–68 S '62. * (*PA* 38:4090)

1276a. SMALL, JOYCE G.; MILSTEIN, VICTOR; AND STEVENS, JANICE R. "Are Psychomotor Epileptics Different? A Controlled Study." *Arch Neurol* 7:187–94 S '62. * (PA 37:3521)

1277. SMITH, RONALD E. "A Minnesota Multiphasic Personality Inventory Profile of Allergy." *Psychosom Med* 24:203–9 Mr–Ap '62. * (*PA* 37:3770)

1278. SMITH, RONALD E. "A Minnesota Multiphasic Personality Inventory Profile of Allergy: II, Conscious Conflict." *Psychosom Med* 24:543–53 N–D '62. * (*PA* 37:8211)

1279. SMITH, THOMAS E., AND BOYCE, ERNEST M. "The Relationship of the Trail Making Test to Psychiatric Symptomatology." *J Clin Psychol* 18:450–4 O '62. * (*PA* 39:5096)

1280. SPIELBERGER, CHARLES D.; WEITZ, HENRY; AND DENNY, J. PETER. "Group Counseling and the Academic Performance of Anxious College Freshmen." *J Counsel Psychol* 9:195–204 f '62. * (*PA* 38:3184)

1281. STEWART, HORACE F., JR. *A Study of the Relationship Between Certain Personality Measures and Hallucinoidal Visual Imagery.* Doctor's thesis, University of Florida (Gainesville, Fla.), 1962. (*DA* 24:827)

1282. SULZER, EDWARD S., AND SCHIELE, BURTRUM C. "The Prediction of Response to Tranylcypromine Plus Trifluoperazine by the MMPI." *Am J Psychiatry* 119:69–70 Jl '62. *

1283. SUPER, DONALD E., AND CRITES, JOHN O. *Appraising Vocational Fitness by Means of Psychological Tests, Revised Edition,* pp. 520–37. New York: Harper & Brothers, 1962. Pp. xv, 688. * (*PA* 37:2038)

1284. TART, CHARLES T. "Frequency of Dream Recall and Some Personality Measures." *J Consult Psychol* 26:467–70 O '62. * (*PA* 39:2213)

1285. ULLMANN, LEONARD P. "An Empirically Derived MMPI Scale Which Measures Facilitation-Inhibition of Recognition of Threatening Stimuli." *J Clin Psychol* 18:127–32 Ap '62. * (*PA* 38:8535)

1286. VOGEL, WILLIAM. "Some Effects of Brain Lesions on MMPI Profiles." *J Consult Psychol* 26:412–5 O '62. *

1287. WALKER, JERALD N. "An Examination of the Role of the Experimentally Determined Response Set in Evaluating Edwards' Social Desirability Scale." *J Consult Psychol* 26:162–6 Ap '62. * (*PA* 37:5021)

1288. WEISGERBER, CHARLES A. "Survey of a Psychological Screening Program in a Clerical Order," pp. 107–48. In *Screening Candidates for the Priesthood and Religious Life.* By Magda B. Arnold and others. Chicago, Ill.: Loyola University Press, 1962. Pp. x, 205. *

1289. WIGGINS, JERRY S. Chap. 7, "Definitions of Social Desirability and Acquiescence in Personality Inventories," pp. 109–27. In *Measurement in Personality and Cognition.* Edited by Samuel Messick and John Ross. New York: John Wiley & Sons, Inc., 1962. Pp. xi, 334. * (*PA* 38:2638)

1290. WIGGINS, JERRY S. "Strategic, Method, and Stylistic Variance in the MMPI." *Psychol B* 59:224–42 My '62. * (*PA* 37:3183)

1290a. WITTON, KURT, AND ELLSWORTH, ROBERT B. "Social and Psychological (MMPI) Changes 5–10 Years After Lobotomy." *Dis Nerv System* 23:440–4 Ag '62. *

1291. ADAMS, HENRY B.; COOPER, G. DAVID; AND CARRERA, RICHARD N. "The Rorschach and the MMPI: A Concurrent Validity Study." *J Proj Tech* 27:23–34 Mr '63. * (*PA* 38:976)

1292. ANDERSEN, L. BRYCE, AND SPENCER, PATRICIA A. "Personal Adjustment and Academic Predictability Among College Freshmen." *J Appl Psychol* 47:97–100 Ap '63. * (*PA* 37:8281)

1293. ANKER, JAMES M.; TOWNSEND, JOHN C.; AND O'CONNOR, JAMES P. "A Multivariate Analysis of Decision Making and Related Measures." *J Psychol* 55:211–21 Ja '63. * (*PA* 37:6186)

1294. BECKER, ANTHONY J. "A Study of the Personality Traits of Successful Religious Women of Teaching Orders." *Yearb Nat Council Meas Ed* 20:124–5 '63. * (*PA* 38:9287)

1295. BENDIG, A. W., AND MARTIN, ANN M. "The Factor Structure of Temperament Traits and Needs." *J General Psychol* 69:27–36 Jl '63. * (*PA* 38:4297)

1296. BUTTERFIELD, EARL C., AND WARREN, SUE A. "Prediction of Attendant Tenure." *J Appl Psychol* 47:101–3 Ap '63. * (*PA* 37:8112)

1297. BYRNE, DONN; BARRY, JAMES; AND NELSON, DON. "Relation of the Revised Repression-Sensitization Scale to Measures of Self-Description." *Psychol Rep* 13:323–34 O '63. * (*PA* 38:8478)

1298. CARTWRIGHT, DESMOND S.; KIRTNER, WILLIAM L.; AND FISKE, DONALD W. "Method Factors in Changes Associated With Psychotherapy." *J Abn & Social Psychol* 66:164–75 F '63. * (*PA* 37:6833)

1299. COPPINGER, NEIL W.; BORTNER, RAYMAN W.; AND SAUCER, RAYFORD T. "A Factor Analysis of Psychological Deficit." *J Genetic Psychol* 103:23–43 S '63. * (*PA* 39:174)

1300. COSTA, LOUIS D.; LONDON, PERRY; AND LEVITA, ERIC.

"A Modification of the F Scale of the MMPI." *Psychol Rep* 12:427–33 Ap '63. * (*PA* 38:4308)
1301. CRADDICK, RAY A. "MMPI Scatter of Psychopathic and Non-Psychopathic Prisoners." *Psychol Rep* 12:238 F '63. * (*PA* 38:2708)
1302. CRADDICK, RAY A., AND STERN, MICHAEL R. "Note on the Reliability of the MMPI Scatter Index." *Psychol Rep* 13:380 O '63. * (*PA* 38:8407)
1303. DANA, RICHARD H., AND CONDRY, JOHN C., JR. "MMPI Retest Results: Context, Order, Practice, and Test-Taking Anxiety." *Psychol Rep* 12:147–52 F '63. * (*PA* 38:2709)
1304. DANIELS, ROBERT S.; MARGOLIS, PHILIP M.; AND CARSON, ROBERT C. "Hospital Discharges Against Medical Advice." *Arch Gen Psychiatry* 8:120–30 F '63. * (*PA* 38:2881)
1305. DEMPSEY, PAUL. "The Dimensionality of the MMPI Clinical Scales Among Normal Subjects." *J Consult Psychol* 27:492–7 D '63. * (*PA* 38:8515)
1306. DRAGUNS, JURIS G. "Response Sets on the MMPI and in Structuring Ambiguous Stimuli." *Psychol Rep* 13:823–8 D '63. * (*PA* 38:8484)
1307. EDWARDS, ALLEN L., AND WALSH, JAMES A. "The Relationship Between the Intensity of the Social Desirability Keying of a Scale and the Correlation of the Scale With Edwards' SD Scale and the First Factor Loading of the Scale." *J Clin Psychol* 19:200–3 Ap '63. * (*PA* 39:5054)
1308. EDWARDS, ALLEN L.; WALSH, JAMES A.; AND DIERS, CAROL J. "The Relationship Between Social Desirability and Internal Consistency of Personality Scales." *J Appl Psychol* 47:255–9 Ag '63. * (*PA* 38:2693)
1309. ELVEKROG, MAURICE O., AND VESTRE, NORRIS D. "The Edwards Social Desirability Scale as a Short Form of the MMPI." *J Consult Psychol* 27:503–7 D '63. * (*PA* 38:8518)
1310. ENDICOTT, NOBLE A., AND ENDICOTT, JEAN. " 'Improvement' in Untreated Psychiatric Patients." *Arch Gen Psychiatry* 9:575–85 D '63. * (*PA* 38:8643)
1311. ENDICOTT, NOBLE A., AND ENDICOTT, JEAN. "Objective Measures of Somatic Preoccupation." *J Nerv & Mental Dis* 137:427–37 N '63. * (*PA* 38:6356)
1312. EXNER, JOHN E., JR.; MCDOWELL, EUGENE; PABST, JOAN; STACKMAN, WILLIAM; AND KIRK, LYNN. "On the Detection of Willful Falsifications in the MMPI." *J Consult Psychol* 27:91–4 F '63. *
1313. GETZELS, J. W., AND JACKSON, P. W. "Minnesota Multiphasic Personality Inventory," pp. 534–45. In *Handbook of Research on Teaching.* Edited by N. L. Gage. Chicago, Ill.: Rand McNally Co., 1963. Pp. xiii, 1218. * (*PA* 38:9132)
1314. GOCKA, EDWARD F., AND BURK, HAROLD W. "MMPI Test Taking Time and Social Desirability." *J Clin Psychol* 19:111–3 Ja '63. * (*PA* 39:1833)
1314a. GONIK, URI, AND BLUMBERG, STANLEY. "Psychophysical Correlates of Personality Test Variables and Some Properties of Auditory Stimuli." *Tex Rep Biol & Med* 21:198–206 su '63. * (*PA* 38:8636)
1315. GOODSTEIN, LEONARD D.; CRITES, JOHN O.; AND HEILBRUN, ALFRED B., JR. "Personality Correlates of Academic Adjustment." *Psychol Rep* 12:175–96 F '63. * (*PA* 38:3150)
1316. GOTTESMAN, IRVING I. "Heritability of Personality: A Demonstration." *Psychol Monogr* 77(9):1–21 '63. * (*PA* 38:423)
1317. GUTHRIE, GEORGE M., AND MCKENDRY, MARGARET S. "Interest Patterns of Peace Corps Volunteers in a Teaching Project." *J Ed Psychol* 54:261–7 O '63. * (*PA* 38:4126)
1318. GYNTHER, MALCOLM D. "A Note on the Meehl-Dahlstrom Rules for Discriminating Psychotic From Neurotic MMPI Profiles." *J Clin Psychol* 19:226 Ap '63. *
1319. HAERTZEN, CHARLES A., AND HILL, HARRIS E. "Assessing Subjective Effects of Drugs: An Index of Carelessness and Confusion for Use With the Addiction Research Center Inventory (ARCI)." *J Clin Psychol* 19:407–12 O '63. *
1320. HAMERLYNCK, LEO AUGUST. *Personality, Academic Aptitude, and Attitudes of Inexperienced Teachers of Retarded Children.* Doctor's thesis, University of Oregon (Eugene, Ore.), 1963. (*DA* 24:624)
1321. HATHAWAY, STARKE R., AND MONACHESI, ELIO D. *Adolescent Personality and Behavior: MMPI Patterns of Normal, Delinquent, Dropout, and Other Outcomes.* Minneapolis, Minn.: University of Minnesota Press, 1963. Pp. xiii, 193. * (*PA* 38:8110)
1322. HEILBRUN, ALFRED B., JR. "Revision of the MMPI *K* Correction Procedure for Improved Detection of Maladjustment in a Normal College Population." *J Consult Psychol* 27:161–5 Ap '63. * (*PA* 37:7976)
1323. HEILBRUN, ALFRED B., JR. "Social Value-Social Behavior Inconsistency and Early Signs of Psychopathology in Adolescence." *Child Develop* 34:187–94 Mr '63. * (*PA* 38:5808)
1324. HENRICHS, THEODORE. "The Effects of Brief Sensory Reduction on Objective Test Scores." *J Clin Psychol* 19:172–6 Ap '63. * (*PA* 39:5151)
1325. HOOD, ALBERT B. "A Study of the Relationship Between Physique and Personality Variables Measured by the MMPI." *J Personality* 31:97–107 Mr '63. *
1326. JENKINS, THOMAS N. "The Primary Trait Anatomy of the MMPI." *J Psychol* 55:49–61 Ja '63. * (*PA* 37:6739)
1327. JORDAN, EDWARD J., JR. "MMPI Profiles of Epileptics: A Further Evaluation." *J Consult Psychol* 27:267–9 Je '63. * (*PA* 38:1233)
1328. JURJEVICH, R. M. "Interrelationships of Anxiety Indices of Wechsler Intelligence Scales and MMPI Scales." *J General Psychol* 69:135–42 Jl '63. * (*PA* 38:4305)
1329. JURJEVICH, R. M. "Normative Data for the Clinical and Additional MMPI Scales for a Population of Delinquent Girls." *J General Psychol* 69:143–6 Jl '63. * (*PA* 38:4312)
1330. JURJEVICH, R. M. "Relationships Among the MMPI and HGI Hostility Scales." *J General Psychol* 69:131–3 Jl '63. * (*PA* 38:4304)
1331. KLEINMUNTZ, BENJAMIN. "MMPI Decision Rules for the Identification of College Maladjustment: A Digital Computer Approach." *Psychol Monogr* 77(14):1–22 '63. * (*PA* 38:8520)
1332. KLEINMUNTZ, BENJAMIN. "Personality Test Interpretation by Digital Computer." *Sci* 139:416–8 F 1 '63. * (*PA* 38:2696)
1333. KLEINMUNTZ, BENJAMIN. "Profile Analysis Revisited: A Heuristic Approach." Comment by Allen Newell. *J Counsel Psychol* 10:315–24 w '63. * (*PA* 38:8648)
1334. KNOWLES, J. B. "Acquiescence Response Set and the Questionnaire Measurement of Personality." *Brit J Social & Clin Psychol* 2:131–7 Je '63. * (*PA* 38:4306)
1335. KOGAN, KATE L.; FORDYCE, WILBERT E.; AND JACKSON, JOAN K. "Personality Disturbance in Wives of Alcoholics." *Q J Studies Alcohol* 24:227–38 Je '63. *
1336. LAKIN, FRANK PIERCE. *Factors Relative to a Grade Point Average Increase for a Select Group of Students After Matriculation to Oregon State University.* Doctor's thesis, Oregon State University (Corvallis, Ore.), 1963. (*DA* 24:627)
1337. LAVER, A. B. "Testing in Canada." *Can Psychologist* 4:22–3 Ja '63. *
1338. LAWTON, M. POWELL. "Deliberate Faking on the Psychopathic Deviate Scale of the MMPI." *J Clin Psychol* 19:327–30 Jl '63. *
1339. LEVEE, JOHN RICHARD. *A Pilot Investigation Into the Effects of an Interpersonal Therapy Approach Upon Mental Patients in a General Hospital Short-Term Psychiatric Setting.* Doctor's thesis, Michigan State University (East Lansing, Mich.), 1963. (*DA* 24:1245)
1340. LUNDIN, ROBERT W., AND LATHROP, WILLIAM. "The Relationship Between Field of Major Concentration and Personality Adjustment in College Males." *J General Psychol* 69:193–6 O '63. * (*PA* 39:2871)
1341. LYTLE, MILFORD BURTON, JR. *A Recidivism Scale for Adult Male Probationers From the Minnesota Multiphasic Personality Inventory.* Doctor's thesis, University of Minnesota (Minneapolis, Minn.), 1963. (*DA* 24:1077)
1342. MACANDREW, CRAIG, AND GEERTSMA, ROBERT H. "An Analysis of Responses of Alcoholics to Scale 4 of the MMPI." *Q J Studies Alcohol* 24:23–38 Mr '63. *
1343. MCDONALD, ROBERT L., AND GYNTHER, MALCOLM D. "MMPI Differences Associated With Sex, Race, and Class in Two Adolescent Samples." *J Consult Psychol* 27:112–6 Ap '63. * (*PA* 37:8011)
1344. MCHUGH, RICHARD B., AND SIVANICH, GEORGE. "Assessing the Temporal Stability of Profile Groups in a Comparative Experiment or Survey." *Psychol Rep* 13:145–6 Ag '63. * (*PA* 38:4859)
1345. MARKS, JOHN; STAUFFACHER, JAMES C.; AND LYLE, CURTIS. "Predicting Outcome in Schizophrenia." *J Abn & Social Psychol* 66:117–27 F '63. * (*PA* 37:7076)
1346. MARKS, PHILIP A., AND SEEMAN, WILLIAM. *The Actuarial Description of Personality: An Atlas for Use With the MMPI.* Baltimore, Md.: Williams & Wilkins Co., 1963. Pp. xxv, 331. *
1347. MARTIN, D. V., AND CAINE, T. M. "Personality Change in the Treatment of Chronic Neurosis in a Therapeutic Community." *Brit J Psychiatry* 109:267–72 Mr '63. * (*PA* 38:2812)
1348. MICHAEL, WILLIAM B.; HANEY, RUSSELL; AND GERSHON, ARTHUR. "Intellective and Non-Intellective Predictors of Success in Nursing Training." *Ed & Psychol Meas* 23:817–21 w '63. *
1349. MILLER, WILLIAM G., AND HANNUM, THOMAS E. "Characteristics of Homosexually Involved Incarcerated Females." Abstract. *J Consult Psychol* 27:277 Je '63. * (*PA* 38:1288, title only)
1350. MOSELEY, EDWARD C.; DUFFEY, ROBERT F.; AND SHERMAN, LEWIS J. "An Extension of the Construct Validity of the Holtzman Inkblot Technique." *J Clin Psychol* 19:186–92 Ap '63. * (*PA* 39:5083)
1351. MURRAY, JOHN B. "The MF Scale of the MMPI for College Students." *J Clin Psychol* 19:113–5 Ja '63. *
1352. MURRAY, JOHN B., AND GALVIN, JOSEPH. "Correlational Study of the MMPI and GZTS." *J General Psychol* 69:267–73 O '63. * (*PA* 39:1751)
1353. NEALE, CHARLES RUSSELL, JR. *An Investigation of Perception of Visual Space Among Alcoholics.* Doctor's thesis, University of Utah (Salt Lake City, Utah), 1963. (*DA* 24:1702)
1354. NELSON, THOMAS D. *Judgmental Diagnoses Versus*

Actuarial Diagnoses. Doctor's thesis, University of Denver (Denver, Colo.), 1963. (*DA* 24:2126)
1355. NUNNALLY, JUM C., AND FLAUGHER, RONALD L. "Correlates of Semantic Habits." *J Personality* 31:192–202 Je '63. *
1356. PODELL, HARRIETT A. "Note on Successive Dimensional Analysis Applied to Affective, Cognitive, and Personality Traits." *Psychol Rep* 13:813–4 D '63. * (*PA* 38:8503)
1357. POMERANZ, DAVID M. *The Repression-Sensitization Dimension and Reactions to Stress.* Doctor's thesis, University of Rochester (Rochester, N.Y.), 1963. (*DA* 24:2605)
1358. POPPLESTONE, JOHN A. "A Scale to Assess Hyperchondriasis: The Converse of Hypochondriasis." *Psychol Rec* 13:32–8 Ja '63. * (*PA* 38:1050)
1359. REGAL, LOUIS HARVEY. *Personality Patterns in Narcotic Addiction.* Doctor's thesis, University of California (Los Angeles, Calif.), 1963. (*DA* 23:3982)
1360. RORER, LEONARD GEORGE. *The Function of Item Content in MMPI Responses.* Doctor's thesis, University of Minnesota (Minneapolis, Minn.), 1963. (*DA* 24:2566)
1361. ROSEN, ALBERT. "Diagnostic Differentiation as a Construct Validity Indicator for the MMPI Ego-Strength Scale." *J General Psychol* 69:293–7 O '63. * (*PA* 39:1845)
1362. ROSEN, EPHRAIM; SIEGELMAN, ELLEN; AND TEETER, BARBARA. "A Dimension of Cognitive Motivation: Need to Know the Known vs the Unknown." *Psychol Rep* 13:703–6 D '63. * (*PA* 38:7236)
1363. SCHULMAN, ROBERT E., AND LONDON, PERRY. "Hypnotic Susceptibility and MMPI Profiles." *J Consult Psychol* 27:157–60 Ap '63. * (*PA* 37:8101)
1364. SHAFFER, JOHN W. "A New Acquiescence Scale for the MMPI." *J Clin Psychol* 19:412–5 O '63. *
1365. SHARPE, D. TRUDY. *A Study of Response Set as a Personality Variable.* Doctor's thesis, New York University (New York, N.Y.), 1963. (*DA* 24:1077)
1366. SHIPMAN, WILLIAM G., AND MARQUETTE, CARL H. "The Manifest Hostility Scale: A Validation Study." *J Clin Psychol* 19:104–6 Ja '63. * (*PA* 39:1823)
1367. SHUPE, DONALD R., AND BRAMWELL, PAUL F. "Prediction of Escape From MMPI Data." *J Clin Psychol* 19:223–6 Ap '63. * (*PA* 39:5091)
1368. SILLER, JEROME, AND CHIPMAN, ABRAM. "Response Set Paralysis: Implications for Measurement and Control." *J Consult Psychol* 27:432–8 O '63. * (*PA* 38:4284)
1369. SILVER, ALBERT W. "TAT and MMPI Psychopath Deviant Scale Differences Between Delinquent and Nondelinquent Adolescents." Abstract. *J Consult Psychol* 27:370 Ag '63. * (*PA* 38:3032)
1370. SILVERMAN, JEROME. "The Validity of the Barron Ego Strength Scale in an Individual Form." *J Consult Psychol* 27:532–3 D '63. * (*PA* 38:8531)
1371. SILVERMAN, PAUL L. "Some Personality Correlates of Attributive Projection." *Percept & Motor Skills* 17:947–53 D '63. * (*PA* 38:6131)
1372. SINES, L. K., AND SILVER, R. J. "An Index of Psychopathology (Ip) Derived From Clinicians' Judgments of MMPI Profiles." *J Clin Psychol* 19:324–6 Jl '63. *
1373. SMITH, EWART E., AND GOODCHILDS, JACQUELINE D. "Some Personality and Behavioral Factors Related to Birth Order." *J Appl Psychol* 47:300–3 O '63. * (*PA* 38:4254)
1374. SMITH, JAMES REX. *Personality and Interpersonal Factors Associated With the Duration of Marriage Counseling.* Doctor's thesis, University of Southern California (Los Angeles, Calif.), 1963. (*DA* 24:886)
1375. SPREEN, OTFRIED, AND SPREEN, GEORGIA. "The MMPI in a German Speaking Population: Standardization Report and Methodological Problems of Cross-Cultural Interpretations." *Acta Psychologica* 21(3):265–73 '63. * (*PA* 38:8532)
1376. STIEPER, DONALD R., AND LOPER, RODNEY G. "Some Personality Correlates of Blood Protein Bound Iodine." *J Clin Psychol* 19:45–8 Ja '63. * (*PA* 39:2013)
1377. STONE, F. BETH, AND ROWLEY, VINTON N. "MMPI Differences Between Emotionally Disturbed and Delinquent Adolescent Girls." *J Clin Psychol* 19:227–30 Ap '63. *
1378. STRAITS, BRUCE C., AND SECHREST, LEE. "Further Support of Some Findings About the Characteristics of Smokers and Nonsmokers." *J Consult Psychol* 27:282 Je '63. * (*PA* 38:935, title only)
1379. TAYLOR, A. J. W., AND MCLACHLAN, D. G. "MMPI Profiles of Six Transvestites." *J Clin Psychol* 19:330–2 Jl '63. *
1380. ULLMANN, LEONARD P.; KRASNER, LEONARD; AND GELFAND, DONNA M. "Changed Content Within a Reinforced Response Class." *Psychol Rep* 12:819–29 Je '63. * (*PA* 38:5263)
1381. VAN EVRA, JUDY PAGE, AND ROSENBERG, B. G. "Ego Strength and Ego Disjunction in Primary and Secondary Psychopaths." *J Clin Psychol* 19:61–3 Ja '63. * (*PA* 39:2409)
1382. VAUGHAN, JAMES A., JR., AND KNAPP, ROBERT H. "A Study in Pessimism." *J Social Psychol* 59:77–92 F '63. * (*PA* 38:859)
1383. VAUGHAN, RICHARD P. "The Effect of Stress on the MMPI Scales K and D." *J Clin Psychol* 19:432 O '63. *
1384. VAUGHAN, RICHARD P. "A Psychological Assessment Program for Candidates to the Religious Life: Validation Study." *Cath Psychol Rec* 1:65–70 sp '63. * (*PA* 38:6715)
1385. VOGEL, JOHN L. "Failure to Validate the *Cr* and *Sm* Scales of the MMPI." *J Consult Psychol* 27:367 Ag '63. * (*PA* 38:2714)
1386. VOGEL, WILLIAM, AND LAUTERBACH, CARL G. "Relationships Between Normal and Disturbed Sons' Percepts of Their Parents' Behavior, and Personality Attributes of the Parents and Sons." *J Clin Psychol* 19:52–6 Ja '63. *
1387. WALLACH, MARTIN S. "Dream Report and Some Psychological Concomitants." Abstract. *J Consult Psychol* 27:549 D '63. *
1388. WATTRON, JOHN B. "A Prison Maladjustment Scale for the MMPI." *J Clin Psychol* 19:109–10 Ja '63. *
1389. WIGGINS, JERRY S. "Social Desirability Under Role Playing Instructions: A Reply to Walker." *J Consult Psychol* 27:107–11 Ap '63. * (*PA* 37:8014)
1390. WIMSATT, WILLIAM R., AND VESTRE, NORRIS D. "Extraexperimental Effects in Verbal Conditioning." *J Consult Psychol* 27:400–4 O '63. * (*PA* 38:4429)
1391. WINTER, WILLIAM D., AND STORTROEN, MARCUS. "A Comparison of Several MMPI Indices to Differentiate Psychotics From Normals." *J Clin Psychol* 19:220–3 Ap '63. *
1392. WITTENBORN, J. R., AND PLANTE, MARC. "Patterns of Response to Placebo, Iproniazid and Electroconvulsive Therapy Among Young Depressed Females." *J Nerv & Mental Dis* 137:155–61 Ag '63. *
1393. WRIGHT, MORGAN W.; SISLER, GEORGE C.; AND CHYLINSKI, JOANNE. "Personality Factors in the Selection of Civilians for Isolated Northern Stations." *J Appl Psychol* 47:24–9 F '63. * (*PA* 37:8319)
1394. YOUNG, RHODES CHARLES. *Some Parameters of Personality Description With the MMPI in a State Hospital Population.* Doctor's thesis, University of Minnesota (Minneapolis, Minn.), 1963. (*DA* 24:2129)

C. J. ADCOCK, *Associate Professor of Psychology, Victoria University of Wellington, Wellington, New Zealand.*

The major criterion for any test is its validity but this is not the simple concept that it was. Validity is always relative to some end and we have to ask what the test measures before we concern ourselves with how well it measures. In the personality area this question of what dimensions are involved is especially important. There is as yet no agreed schema of fundamental personality dimensions so for any given test it is highly important to consider what the test aims at measuring.

With regard to what they try to measure, personality tests fall into two broad categories: those which make an attempt to span the whole personality area in a systematic way and those which are concerned with some *ad hoc* objective. The former type are usually based upon factorial studies and cannot be validated by any simple correlation procedure. The latter type may be restricted to a single measure, which further simplifies the problem of validity, but the essential point is that there is an available criterion to control the choice of test items and to measure the validity of the test.

The MMPI falls into the second group. It does not pretend to provide basic personality dimensions but to predict the currently accepted psychiatric categories. These may be basic in their own right but this is beside the point. They have empirical validity in that they are the basis of actual treatment. At the present stage of psychiatry these are the categories which are most meaningful from a diagnostic point of view and the problem of measurement is simplified by the possibility of definite, if not perfectly reliable, criteria. The problem of what is to be measured is therefore a simple one for the MMPI.

The implications of this for the user, however, have not always been understood. Because the test is one of the few multidimensional tests, some people have thought of it as a useful test for a general survey of personality. For this it was not designed. It may draw attention to possibly disabling degrees of mental disorder and indicate the form of such disorder, but whether the pattern of disorder tendencies has any significance when none of the scores falls outside the normal range is another matter altogether. Despite the extensive literature which has developed around this test, there is a paucity of evidence on this point.

It is this fact which has probably inspired the development of a variety of new scales. Only one of these is currently described in the manual although reference is made to others. This social introversion scale (Si), although not strictly a clinical scale, is probably of more clinical significance than most other new scales. It is also one of the two major general personality dimensions and the interest shown in it inclines one to the opinion that, if scores on a set of basic personality dimensions were available from the test, it would both add to the value of the test and combat the tendency to make use of the psychiatric scales outside the psychiatric area. The vast number of items in the test makes it likely that they would yield a fairly wide range of such general measures but, by the same token, the appropriate procedures for deriving such measures become more difficult to apply. The obvious requirement is a factorial analysis of the items, but, although numerous analyses have been made, these have been of individual scales or of the scale scores.

Analysis of the scale scores indicates that they involve the usual second-order factors found in personality material. Kassebaum, Couch, and Slater (*893*) who analysed 32 scales derived from the MMPI found three factors of which the first two appeared to be very obviously ego strength and introversion-extroversion, corresponding to the major factors found by Eysenck [1] and the second-order factors of Cattell.[2] There is general agreement about the existence of these two factors but not about the nature of the first of them. Eysenck calls it emotionality, Cattell talks of anxiety, and Kassebaum, Couch, and Slater speak of ego strength. In treating a patient a correct choice among these interpretations might be of some consequence. It may be that each interpretation is quite correct for the test material used but one strongly suspects that the real difficulty is a failure to properly appreciate the complex interrelationships of emotional response. When one test battery provides us with an appropriate differentiation of ego strength, emotionality, and anxiety we shall have more ground for confidence.

In view of the lack of adequate agreement as to the nature of basic personality dimensions it may be argued that it is safer to stick to the strictly empirical approach of the MMPI without playing around with new fangled scales. But this could be no justification for using the psychiatric scales as substitutes for the required basic personality scales and moreover one can raise some awkward questions as to the adequacy of the original scales themselves. Psychasthenia and schizophrenia are regarded as distinct entities but the two scales turn out to be highly correlated. No figures are given in the manual but Kassebaum and others (*893*) find a correlation of .83. Inspection of the reliability figures suggests that the specific variance in these two scales might well be negligible. The high correlation of the F (validity) and K (correction) scales with Pt and Sc raises some further queries and makes one long for some statistical data to throw light on the psychiatric concepts involved. Do the scales present the best survey of clinical symptoms?

An important event in this respect is Rosen's (*1270*) report on an attempt to develop five new psychiatric scales. The choice of items is based upon the efficiency in differentiating the particular category of abnormals from a normal population rather than from other abnormals. This is an important point if the test is to be used for screening purposes with a random population sample. A comparison of the new with the old scales is most interesting.

The conversion reaction scale (Cr) replaces

1 EYSENCK, H. J. *The Structure of Human Personality.* London: Methuen & Co. Ltd., 1953. Pp. xix, 348. *

2 CATTELL, RAYMOND B. *Personality: A Systematic Theoretical and Factual Study.* New York: McGraw-Hill Book Co., Inc., 1950. Pp. xii, 689. * (*PA* 25:4420)

the old Hy scale but has a correlation of −.24 with it! This is explained by the common factor of abnormality, it is argued, but the research does not involve any factor analysis which might make these relationships a little clearer. At this stage we can only take warning that items which differentiate hysterics from other abnormals in the old scale may have to be reversed in sign if one wishes to distinguish hysterics from normals. This is another indication of the danger which may be involved in using the test for any purpose other than that for which it was strictly designed.

Rosen's somatization scale (Sm) correlates highly with the Cr scale (slightly higher than either reliability coefficient!) and also has a negative, though insignificant, correlation with Hy. Paranoid schizophrenia (Pz) correlates slightly better with the old Sc (.81) than it does with itself (.79) but the depressive reaction (Dr) scale has no significant correlation with the old D scale. For the anxiety reaction (Ar) scale there is no equivalent among the old scales.

It is perhaps unfortunate that Rosen should have chosen new psychiatric categories at the same time that he used a normal group as a measure of differentiation efficiency. One would very much like to know what would happen if the original psychiatric groups were retained but the scales validated along Rosen lines. It seems rather as though we may have two problems: the choice of scales and the method of item validation.

VALIDITY. The question of validity for a test of this kind (like the manual we omit reference to the new scales at the moment) is relatively simple. It can be expressed simply as a set of correlation coefficients. Somewhat strangely the authors choose not to do this but instead to provide figures as to the success of the scales in predicting the diagnosis of new psychiatric admissions where 60 per cent success is claimed. This reviewer is disturbed by two points in this connection. In the first place one is uncertain as to the degree to which the psychiatric diagnosis has been influenced by the test results. If two psychiatric categories are closely related (for example, Pt and Sc), the test classification could play a major role and give the appearance of success far beyond what might occur with independent assessment.

In the second place it has to be noted that the population to whom the test is applied is already selected as in need of psychiatric treatment and the test is merely called upon to classify. It is quite in order to report the success of the test in doing this but unfortunately it is only too easy for people who quote the validity figures to lose sight of the qualifying circumstances. The authors warn that in an average population more of the deviant profiles may relate to normal persons than to persons requiring treatment, but this is not always remembered by the casual test user who has in mind a 60 per cent hit evaluation. It would be most interesting to know just how many correct hits would be made in application of the test to a random sample of the general population. This information is vitally necessary if the test is to be used for general screening purposes as it often, in fact, is used. The manual might well provide this information. Rosen's work, reported above, emphasises the need for studies in this area.

Another point raised by the authors justifies comment. It is the fact that persons classified under a certain category may not necessarily have the highest scores for the category; for example, a schizophrenic may show a higher score for depression than for schizophrenia. This is quite understandable but provides another trap for the unskilled user of the test. Furthermore, it raises some further queries about the principles of psychiatric classification and specifically raises the question as to whether the MMPI does not make the mistake of lumping together a number of psychiatric terms without adequate consideration of their logical status. One suspects that masculinity-femininity or depression has rather a different status than that of schizophrenia.

There is a special sense in which validity has to be considered in connection with this test. There are internal measures of testee validity built into it. A recent study of these by Exner and others (*1312*) showed that a group of subjects who were asked to deliberately fake abnormal, but not sufficiently abnormal for institutionalization, raised all their scores significantly *except the lie score!* Attempts to fake good were less successful, the major differences (statistically significant) being in the L, F, K, and Pd scales, in that order. The range of scores for these categories, however, showed too much overlap between honest and fake efforts for any useful individual discrimination. Further doubt about the use of the validity scales is aroused by considering some of the intercorrelations from Rosen's study. In that study F had a correlation of .82 with Pz, and K a correlation of .72 with Cr. In view of the probable reliabilities of these measures one has grave doubts about the amount of their variance related to the correction function.

There is still a steady stream of research reports relating to this test but most of these assume rather than indicate the validity of the test. Some of the comparisons with other tests are of interest. In particular it is worth noting that the MMPI, Guilford-Zimmerman, and Strong measures of masculinity-femininity do not correlate (*949*) and possibly represent different concepts. Incidentally it is probable that class differences may operate strongly in this connection. Taylor and McLachlan (*1379*) found that the MMPI Mf scale successfully differentiated in a group of transvestites between those who were practising homosexuals and those not, and may therefore be psychiatrically significant but they have no data on the applicability of other M-F measures to this group.

All this points up the fact that, while the MMPI is an excellent tool for the skilled psychiatrist who has mastered its intricacies and has a due appreciation of the relevant statistical concepts, it can be highly dangerous in the hands of the casual user who has seized upon it as one of the most reputable of personality tests and one free of the problem of subjective scoring.

JAMES C. LINGOES, *Associate Professor of Psychology, The University of Michigan, Ann Arbor, Michigan.*

Since the appearance of *The Fifth Mental Measurements Yearbook* additional valuable material has been published on the widely used MMPI. Expanding the range of cases covered in the Atlas (*263*) there are now similar books devoted to juvenile MMPI profiles (*1106*) and to college students seen in a counseling service (*873*). Most noteworthy, however, is the publication of Dahlstrom and Welsh's *An MMPI Handbook* (*969*), which complements their earlier publication (*669*) and serves along with it as an indispensable reference work for both the clinician and researcher. The Handbook provides adequate documentation and an objective appraisal of the uses and limitations of the MMPI, more than compensating for the deficiencies of the manual. Nevertheless, a revision of the manual is long overdue. In such a revision one should expect to find an up-to-date summarization of the relevant literature on the topics of reliability and validity, for example, as well as suitable references to the basic texts and pertinent journal articles to guide the prospective user in the proper uses of the inventory. In addition, cognizance should be given to methods of interpretation consonant with the recommendations contained in both the Atlas and the Handbook.

To date there are over 1,000 references on the MMPI, a formidable amount of material covering almost every conceivable aspect of test construction, reliability, validity, and use. The proliferation of scales (over 200 in the last two decades) purportedly measuring or differentiating important classes of behavior, has, if nothing else, fulfilled the wildest dreams of the authors of the MMPI when they chose to qualify the inventory as "multiphasic." The validities of many of these scales remain in doubt, but those that have held up in cross validation (for example, Barron's ego strength scale, Feldman's prognosis for electroshock treatment scale, Welsh's factor scales A and R) have added considerably to the power of this test and, if not entirely fulfilling the aim of the authors in yielding scores on *all* important phases of personality, at least have gone some small way toward it.

If one had to summarize the research on the perennial question of the diagnostic validity of this test the summary would be somewhat as follows. The MMPI can differentiate quite well between those who do and do not have emotional and adjustmental problems in a wide variety of settings and can thus serve as an excellent screening device. The use of this instrument for such purposes, however, requires many complex decisions regarding such things as costs, strategies, base rates, and utilities, and, as a consequence, the potential user should become familiar with these vital issues as they relate to his problem in his agency. It may well be that for highly specific problems simpler devices may suffice, such as the *Cornell Index.* While there is no gainsaying the value of the MMPI in differentiating among individuals coming from normal and abnormal populations, there is much conflicting evidence as to the test's sensitivity in discriminating within the abnormal group itself.

Neurotics, character disorders, psychotics, and possibly some psychosomatic conditions, as broad diagnostic groupings, can be reliably separated, if not among each and all of the several categories at least among selected subsets. Finer distinctions within any one of these nosological groups, however, have been in the main unproductive. Typical of the better studies in the area of differential diagnosis is that of Meehl and Dahlstrom (*1017*) using a multistage sequential decision rule for classifying profiles as neurotic, psychotic, or indeterminate. In a cross validation study of 988 cases selected from eight settings, an overall hit rate of 76 per cent was achieved among the 70 per cent considered determinate.

Although there is no other instrument of its kind that has been so thoroughly researched, as a general test of personality the MMPI has a number of weaknesses, not the least of which is its saturation with pathological items to the exclusion or deemphasis of some variables considered important in present day personality theories. Unfortunately, other tests that might be considered competitive have equal or more serious shortcomings. As a clinical instrument used in conjunction with other tests and media of inference, the MMPI has a definite contribution to make and is unequaled. For assessing personality within the normal range of adjustment, however, it will be found wanting.

For reviews by Albert Ellis and Warren T. Norman, see 5:86; for a review by Arthur L. Benton, see 4:71; for reviews by Arthur L. Benton, H. J. Eysenck, L. S. Penrose, and Julian B. Rotter, see 3:60 (1 excerpt); for excerpts from related book reviews, see B64, B113, B146, B159, B206, B241, B414, see 5:B199, 5:B200, 5:B467, and 4:72.

[144]

***Minnesota T-S-E Inventory.** Grades 13–16 and adults; 1942–57; for research use only; 3 introversion-extroversion scores: thinking, social, emotional; IBM; Experimental Form FETX ('42, 7 pages); revised manual ('57, 24 pages); separate answer sheets must be used; $3.50 per 25 tests; 30¢ per single copy; $1 per 25 IBM scorable answer sheets; $1.50 per set of scoring stencils; $1 per manual; cash orders postpaid; (25–35) minutes; Catharine Evans and T. R. McConnell; distributed by Educational Testing Service. *

REFERENCES

1–6. See 3:62.
7. Chalmers, J. W. "Intelligence and Personality Characteristics of Correspondence Teachers." *Can J Psychol* 2:28–34 Mr '48. * (*PA* 22:4633)
8. Evans, M. Catharine. "Differentiation of Home Economics Students According to Major Emphasis." *Occupations* 27:120–5 N '48. * (*PA* 23:4410)
9. Tyler, F. T. "Personality Tests and Teaching Ability." *Can J Psychol* 3:30–7 Mr '49. * (*PA* 23:4443)
10. Hartshorn, Elizabeth. "A Comparison of Certain Aspects of Student Leadership and Non-Leadership: Significant Differences on Four Psychometric Tests." *J Ed Res* 49:515–22 Mr '56. * (*PA* 31:5098)
11. Straight, Glenn H. *Identifiable Personality Characteristics Resulting From Membership in a Conspicuous Religious Minority in Public High Schools.* Doctor's thesis, University of Nebraska (Lincoln, Neb.), 1956. (*DA* 17:810)

For reviews by Philip Eisenberg and John W. French, see 3:62.

[145]

Mooney Problem Check List, 1950 Revision. Grades 7–9, 9–12, 13–16, adults; 1941–50; IBM for grades 7–16; 4 levels; separate manuals ('50) for grades 7–16 (15 pages), adults (4 pages); no data on reliability for scores of individuals; no norms (authors recommend use of local norms); separate answer sheets must be used with machine scorable forms; $1.90 per 25 tests of hand scored forms; $2.40 per 25 tests of machine scorable forms; $2 per 50 IBM answer sheets; 90¢ per specimen set of hand scored forms, $1 per specimen set of machine scorable forms, 50¢ per specimen set of hand scored form of any one level; postpaid; (20–50) minutes; Ross L. Mooney and Leonard V. Gordon (*c* and *d*); Psychological Corporation. *

a) junior high school form. Grades 7–9; 1942–50; 7 scores: health and physical development, school, home and family, money-work-the future, boy and girl relations, relations to people in general, self-centered concerns; 2 editions ('50): hand scored Form J (6 pages), machine scorable Form JM (4 pages).

b) high school form. Grades 9–12; 1941–50; 11 scores: health and physical development, finances-living conditions-employment, social and recreational activities, social-psychological relations, personal-psychological relations, courtship-sex-marriage, home and family, morals and religion, adjustment to school work, the future—vocational and educational, curriculum and teaching procedures; 2 editions ('50): hand scored Form H (6 pages), machine scorable Form HM (4 pages).

c) college form. Grades 13–16; 1941–50; 11 scores: same as for High School Form; 2 editions ('50): hand scored Form C (6 pages), machine scorable Form CM (4 pages).

d) adult form. Adults; 1950; 9 scores: health, economic security, self-improvement, personality, home and family, courtship, sex, religion, occupation; Form A (6 pages).

REFERENCES

1–17. See 3:67.
18–30. See 4:73.
31–56. See 5:89.
57. Bennett, Bruce L. "Improving College Health Teaching." *J Health Phys Ed & Rec* 23:24–6 D '52. *
58. Hassler, William H. *Use of the Mooney Problem Check List to Determine Potential Drop Outs in the First Two Years of College.* Master's thesis, Pennsylvania State University (University Park, Pa.), 1957.
59. Formica, Louis Anthony. *A Comparative Study of Selected Factors in the Vocational Development of Intellectually Superior College Girls From the Working and Upper-Class Levels.* Doctor's thesis, University of Connecticut (Storrs, Conn.), 1958. (*DA* 19:1012)
60. Jones, Worth R. "Affective Tolerance and Typical Problems of Married and Unmarried College Students." *Personnel & Guid J* 37:126–8 O '58. * (*PA* 36:2KD26J)
61. Smith, Paul Milton, Jr. *Personality Characteristics of Rural and Urban Southern Negro Children.* Doctor's thesis, Indiana University (Bloomington, Ind.), 1958. (*DA* 19:1019)
62. Barnett, Charles D., and Tarver, William N. "Self-Rated Problems of Institutionalized Delinquent vs. Non-Delinquent Girls." *Psychol Rep* 5:333–6 Je '59. * (*PA* 34:3235)
63. Hammes, John A. "Relation of Manifest Anxiety to

Specific Problem Areas." *J Clin Psychol* 15:298–300 Jl '59. * (*PA* 35:3453)

64. MOORE, PHELMA NEWTON. *A Survey of the Orientation Problems Common to Entering Freshmen in Pan American College for the First Semester of the 1958–1959 School Year.* Doctor's thesis, University of Houston (Houston, Tex.), 1959. (*DA* 20:2103)

65. STEFFLRE, BUFORD. "Concurrent Validity of the Vocational Values Inventory." *J Ed Res* 52:339–41 My '59. * (*PA* 34:4211)

66. AMOS, ROBERT T., AND WASHINGTON, REGINALD M. "A Comparison of Pupil and Teacher Perceptions of Pupil Problems." *J Ed Psychol* 51:255–8 O '60. * (*PA* 36:1KM55A)

67. BULLOCH, SARAH I. *A Study of the Impact of Guidance Services on Twelfth Grade Students as Measured by the Mooney Problem Check List.* Master's thesis, University of Tennessee (Knoxville, Tenn.), 1960.

68. RICH, RUTH. "Health Education Needs of High School Students in a Large Diversified Metropolitan Area." *Res Q* 31:631–7 D '60. *

69. WITHERSPOON, PAUL. "A Comparison of the Problems of Certain Anglo- and Latin-American Junior High School Students." *J Ed Res* 53:295–9 Ap '60. *

70. GORMAN, JOHN R. *A Study of Adjustment and Interests for Fourth Year Minor Seminarians Studying for the Diocesan Priesthood.* Master's thesis, Loyola University (Chicago, Ill.), 1961.

71. JERRY, DONALD H. *References and Problems of Thirty High School Football Players and Thirty Non-Football Players.* Master's thesis, Ohio State University (Columbus, Ohio), 1961.

72. MCDONAGH, ANDREW J. *A Study of Adjustments and Interests of First-Year College Seminarians for the Diocesan Priesthood.* Master's thesis, Loyola University (Chicago, Ill.), 1961.

73. MILLER, ROBERT CARL. *The Relationship Between Academic Success and Stated Problems of Selected High School Pupils.* Doctor's thesis, University of Pittsburgh (Pittsburgh, Pa.), 1961. (*DA* 22:3895)

74. SMITH, PAUL M., JR. "Problems of Rural and Urban Southern Negro Children." *Personnel & Guid J* 39:599–600 Mr '61. * (*PA* 35:6309)

75. CRUMBAUGH, JAMES C.; SHAPIRO, DAVID S.; MAHOLICK, LEONARD T.; AND OAKEY, RUTH C. "The Bradley Center Mental Health Assessment Kit: An Analysis of Use in Group Testing." *J Clin Psychol* 18:431–6 O '62. * (*PA* 39:5047)

76. ESPER, GEORGE H. *A Study of Certain Characteristic Differences in Junior High School Students Who May or May Not Seek Counseling.* Doctor's research study No. 1, Colorado State College (Greeley, Colo.), 1962. (*DA* 23:3773)

77. ZUNICH, MICHAEL. "The Relation Between Junior High-School Students' Problems and Parental Attitudes Toward Child Rearing and Family Life." *J Ed Res* 56:134–8 N '62. *

78. BERNOFSKY, SHIRLEY. *Problems of Junior High School Students as Expressed Through the Mooney Problem Check List.* Master's thesis, University of Kansas (Lawrence, Kan.), 1963.

79. CHENEY, TRUMAN M., AND VAN LYDEGRAF, MARY ELLEN. "Establishing Counseling Priorities." *Voc Guid Q* 11:297–300 su '63. * (*PA* 38:4676)

80. DENTON, L. R. "A Survey of Personal Problems of Young People in Public School and University." *B Maritime Psychol Assn* 12:1–27 sp '63. * (*PA* 38:4678)

81. WILLNER, ERIC. *The Adjustment of Jewish All-Day School Pupils Compared to That of Public School Pupils Attending Afternoon Hebrew Schools: as Determined by the Mooney Problem Check List, a Check List of "Problems Related to Religion," and an Adaptation of the Maslow S-I Inventory.* Doctor's thesis, New York University (New York, N.Y.), 1963. (*DA* 24:2794)

THOMAS C. BURGESS, *Associate Professor, Counseling Center, Portland State College, Portland, Oregon.*

The *Mooney Problem Check List* does not pretend to be a measuring device. "Rather, the *Problem Check List* is a form of simple communication between the counselee and counselor designed to accelerate the process of understanding the student and his real problems." The forms are composed simply of lists of common problems, and the student is asked to mark those problems he has, to indicate those which are of most concern to him, and to write a statement about his problems in his own words. On the junior high school, high school, and college forms he is also asked if he would like to discuss his problems with someone, and, on the high school and college forms, to indicate, if he wishes, with whom he would like to talk. There is no mystery here, only a straightforward list of problems and an obvious approach which leaves the counselee free to communicate to the extent of his readiness to do so.

The lists have been compiled carefully by referring to student statements of their problems, case studies, published literature on student problems, and the counseling experience of the authors. Published research reports indicate that students check an average of 20 to 30 problems which suggests that the lists contain a fairly good coverage of problems that students are willing to acknowledge.

Reliability assessment is a problem with this kind of procedure and no reliability figures are given. The manual points out that internal consistency methods are clearly inappropriate, and that retest estimates are subject to error due to rapid changes in the nature of the individual's problems and in the way he perceives them. It is also pointed out in the manual that the way a student perceives his problems may be changed by the process of going through the checklist (which should caution all users to have a control group when using the checklist as recommended by the authors to show the effect of remedial programs on the number of student problems). In spite of the merit in these arguments the reliability should be assessed and reported. The authors do report data indicating considerable stability of pooled results for groups.

To show the validity of the checklist would seem to require the demonstration that actual problems correspond to the problems reported. The obvious, but expensive, method of comparing reported problems with problems established through intensive case studies has apparently not been used. The manual reports the results of one study which contrasted the responses of two groups, a remedial study skills class and a mental hygiene class, and found differences appropriate to the two classes. A number of other studies have been reported in the research literature which also show that problem frequencies differ in appropriate ways when the responses of different groups are compared. For example, intelligent students and honor students check fewer problems than do less intelligent or probation students in the area "Adjustment to (College) School Work." Veterans who check more problems in the area "Occupation" less frequently achieved success in selecting a vocational objective. Results such as these appear to indicate considerable concurrent validity. It would be helpful to have a revised manual incorporating more of this kind of information.

It seems likely, as indicated also by the testimony of students who have taken it, that filling out the checklist gives the student a review of his problems which helps to place them in perspective. It may thus be useful to the students as well as to the counselor, teacher, or researcher who uses it to obtain information about student problems. The authors also recommend its use by school counselors to facilitate the development of the counselor's understanding of the individual case. The suggestions given for its use in counseling seem reasonable but there has been no experimental demonstration of how its use would actually affect the process or results of counseling, or of what circumstances would be most appropriate for the use of such counselor aids.

No norms are given; the authors suggest that local norms would be most appropriate, and that significance does not depend on the number of problems reported. Although this argument is probably correct it would be helpful to have additional information on the relative frequency of the different problems in various groups.

In summary, the information available from all sources suggests that the popularity of the *Mooney Problem Check List* is well deserved, and that it may be used appropriately in the ways suggested by the authors. The authors should be commended for their professionally responsible presentation in the manual, and especially for their repeated warnings about the various ways in which the information from the checklist could be misinterpreted. The user should observe these cautions carefully.

For reviews by Harold E. Jones and Morris Krugman, see 4:73; for reviews by Ralph C. Bedell and Theodore F. Lentz, see 3:67.

[146]

★The Mother-Child Relationship Evaluation. Mothers; 1961; experimental form; 5 scores: 4 direct scores (acceptance, overprotection, overindulgence, rejection) and 1 derived score (confusion-dominance); 1 form (4 pages); mimeographed manual (12 pages); $7 per set of 25 tests and manual; $6.50 per 25 tests; $2.50 per manual; postpaid; specimen set not available; (15-30) minutes; Robert M. Roth; Western Psychological Services. *

JOHN ELDERKIN BELL, *Program Director, National Institute of Mental Health, United States Public Health Service, San Francisco, California.*

Using the definitions of rejection, overindulgence, overprotection, and acceptance developed by Symonds,[1] the author of the test has prepared and selected a series of 48 assertions assumed to reflect these respective attitudes (12 per attitude). By indicating extent of agreement or disagreement with the statements on a five-point scale, the subject provides data for "an objective estimate of a mother's relationship to her child." In addition, a fifth scale seeks to measure the extent to which the relationship between a mother and her child is dominated by an attitude, a combination of attitudes, or confusion. This score is derived from the number of scores on the first four scales that reach the 75th percentile and higher.

The research on which the evaluation of the instrument is based appears modest and the details of the study provided in the manual leave major information gaps. For example, the scores used for developing split-half reliability measures, scale intercorrelations, and percentile norms were secured from 80 middle class mothers, 25 to 35 years of age, living in the same community. No data are supplied regarding marital history, number and ages of children, personality characteristics of the children, and means by which access to the population was secured.

While the instructions and scoring are simple, making for ease in administration, no advice regarding method of interpretation is offered except by indirection through three case illustrations. If the clinical interpretations offered for these cases are meant to suggest uses to which investigators might put the test, only the most radical limitations on the statements generated will protect mothers and children from libel or slander. To state that the test is "primarily an exploratory and experimental one, rather than a refined clinical measurement"

1 SYMONDS, PERCIVAL M. *The Dynamics of Parent-Child Relationships.* New York: Bureau of Publications, Teachers College, Columbia University, 1949. Pp. xvii, 197. *

perhaps means that the author himself is aware of the dangers of its use with individuals.

By far the most dangerous feature of the test is the lack of precision in the definitions of the abstract attitude categories it proposes to measure. Without precise operational definition of the categories or studies to specify behavioral correlates of the test scores, we shall promote unvalidated conclusions from test scores which are assumed but not shown to have a relationship to vaguely-defined global attitudes lacking identified application to a mother's behavior towards her child.

DALE B. HARRIS, *Professor of Psychology and Head of the Department, The Pennsylvania State University, University Park, Pennsylvania.*

Most "tests" of parental attitudes have been designed for specific research projects. In this one, the directions to the parent who responds to the items state: "Keep in mind the child for whom you are seeking help." Thus, despite the disclaimer in the manual, refined clinical measurement is ultimately intended, and the instrument must be judged on this basis.

This scale is global, evaluating the broad dimension of the mother-child relationship identified as acceptance—nonacceptance in the work of P. M. Symonds and his student, Marian Fitz-Simons. The items are general attitude-type, valuative affirmations about "a child," "children," "mothers," "a mother." There are a few items that specifically refer to "my child" or "I." Some of the items obviously tap attitudes rather deeply rooted in middle class folklore and practices of child rearing; others are "iffy," subject to situational contingencies which came to mind at once, and thus are probably not so embedded in strongly held values. The items are Likert-type, permitting five degrees of agreement-disagreement.

The author prepared a pool of 100 items having apparent relevance to one of four dimensions—acceptance, overprotection, overindulgence, and rejection, the latter three being specific expressions of a broader nonacceptance dimension. The 48 items selected for the final scale (12 for each dimension) yielded phi values from .30 to .67, based on the top and bottom 26 per cent of scores made by a homogeneous sample of 80 middle class women on the scales contained in the original pool (unpublished phi values obtained from communication with author). These 80 cases were then rescored to furnish all the standardization data, including percentile norms, supplied in the manual. Pearson product-moment correlations applied to first-half versus second-half scale scores (12-item scales) yielded results from .41 to .57. Intercorrelations of the scales were of about the same order of magnitude. The acceptance scale correlated negatively (−.45 to −.68) with each of the other three, which intercorrelated positively (.28 to .56) among themselves.

The derived score, confusion-dominance, takes a value from one to four and is based on the number of the four scale scores which fall into the highest quarter of the norms, a score of "one" presumably indicating high dominance and a score of "four" indicating high confusion.

Thus far in his work the author rests his case entirely on construct validity as set forth only briefly in the manual. In unpublished studies (personal communication) Roth found zero-order correspondence between mothers' responses to the instrument, and their college-age children's perceptions of how the mothers would respond to the instrument. On the acceptance scale (but not the others) 25 mothers who had been to college scored higher than 25 mothers who had not been to college. These two studies do not greatly strengthen the case for empirical validity.

Unlike Schaefer and Bell's Parental Attitude Research Instrument, this test has the merit of using nonthreatening items, none of which morally condemn the respondent whether he agrees or disagrees. Obviously it needs much more careful and complete standardization if it is to be used clinically. Clinical prediction requires highly stable measurement; such is scarcely possible with 12-item opinion scales subject to the known vicissitudes of semantics, momentary "set," situational and other sources of qualification.

[146a]

★**Motivation Analysis Test.** Ages 17 and over; 1959–64; test booklet title is MAT; 45 scores: 4 motivation scores (integrated, unintegrated, total, conflict) for each of 5 drives (mating, assertiveness, fear, narcism-comfort, pugnacity-sadism) and each of 5 sentiment structures (superego, self-sentiment, career, home-parental, sweetheart-spouse), plus 5 optional scores (total integration, total personal interest, total conflict, autism-optimism, information-intelligence); Form A ('64, c1961–64, 17 pages); manual ('64, c1959–64, 53 pages); profile ('64, c1961–64, 1 page);

reliability data for total motivation scores only; separate answer sheets must be used; $15 per 25 tests; $6 per 50 answer sheets; $3 per set of scoring stencils; $4 per pad of 50 profiles; $2 per manual; $4 per specimen set; cash orders postpaid; (55–65) minutes; Raymond B. Cattell and John L. Horn with the assistance of Arthur B. Sweney and John A. Radcliffe; Institute for Personality and Ability Testing. *

[147]

★Myers-Briggs Type Indicator. Grades 9–16 and adults; 1943–62; 4 scores: extraversion vs. introversion, sensation vs. intuition, thinking vs. feeling, judgment vs. perception; IBM; 2 editions (identical except for directions): Forms F ('57, c1943–57, 12 pages, scored locally), Fs ('62, c1943–62, 12 pages, scored by the publisher); manual ('62, 157 pages); separate answer sheets must be used; $6 per 20 tests; $1 per 25 IBM scorable answer sheets for Form F; $7.50 per set of scoring stencils for Form F; 60¢ per Scribe answer sheet and scoring service for Form Fs; postage extra; $3 per specimen set, postpaid (must be purchased to obtain manual); (50–55) minutes; Katharine C. Briggs (test) and Isabel Briggs Myers; Educational Testing Service. *

REFERENCES

1. MacKinnon, Donald W. "Fostering Creativity in Students of Engineering." *J Eng Ed* 52:129–42 D '61. * (*PA* 36:4HD29M)
2. Knapp, Robert H.; Gewirtz, Herbert; and Holzberg, Jules D. "Some Personality Correlates of Styles of Interpersonal Thought." *J Proj Tech* 26:398–403 D '62. * (*PA* 37:6717)
3. MacKinnon, Donald W. "The Personality Correlates of Creativity: A Study of American Architects," pp. 11–39. (*PA* 37:4958) In *Personality Research.* Proceedings of the XIV International Congress of Applied Psychology, Vol. 2. Copenhagen, Denmark: Munksgaard, Ltd., 1962. Pp. 229. *
4. Mendelsohn, Gerald A., and Kirk, Barbara A. "Personality Differences Between Students Who Do and Do Not Use a Counseling Facility." *J Counsel Psychol* 9:341–6 w '62. * (*PA* 39:1812)
5. Ross, John. Chap. 4, "Factor Analysis and Levels of Measurement in Psychology," pp. 69–81. In *Measurement in Personality and Cognition.* Edited by Samuel Messick and John Ross. New York: John Wiley & Sons, Inc., 1962. Pp. xi, 334. * (*PA* 38:2638)
6. Mendelsohn, Gerald A., and Geller, Marvin H. "Effects of Counselor-Client Similarity on the Outcome of Counseling." *J Counsel Psychol* 10:71–7 sp '63. *
7. Stricker, Lawrence J., and Ross, John. "Intercorrelations and Reliability of the Myers-Briggs Type Indicator Scales." *Psychol Rep* 12:287–93 F '63. * (*PA* 38:2677)
8. Vaughan, James A., Jr., and Knapp, Robert H. "A Study in Pessimism." *J Social Psychol* 59:77–92 F '63. * (*PA* 38:859)
9. Stricker, Lawrence J., and Ross, John. "An Assessment of Some Structural Properties of the Jungian Personality Typology." *J Abn & Social Psychol* 68:62–71 Ja '64. *
10. Stricker, Lawrence J., and Ross, John. "Some Correlates of a Jungian Personality Inventory." *Psychol Rep* 14:623–43 Ap '64. * (*PA* 39:1848)

Gerald A. Mendelsohn, *Assistant Professor of Psychology, University of California, Berkeley, California.*

The *Myers-Briggs Type Indicator* (MBTI), a forced choice, self-report inventory designed for use with normal subjects, is based upon a modification of the Jungian theory of type. Since it was originally developed more than 20 years ago and has undergone several revisions, an unusually large body of reliability and validity data is available for the instrument. A substantial part of these data and a detailed presentation of the underlying theory are included in the test manual.

The four dimensions of the test purport to measure the following dichotomous preferences: Judgment-Perception (JP), coming to a conclusion about something or becoming aware of something; Thinking-Feeling (TF), arriving at judgments by impersonal and logical or by subjective processes; Sensation-Intuition (SN), perceiving directly through the five senses or indirectly by way of the unconscious; and Extraversion-Introversion (EI), orienting toward the outer world of people and things or the inner world of concepts and ideas. The TF, SN, and EI scales are independent, but JP is consistently correlated with SN and less consistently with TF. Internal consistency reliabilities for the scales range in general from .75 to .85, with a low coefficient of .44 appearing for TF. There are little data on the stability of the scores; in the one reported study addressed to this point, 14-month, test-retest correlations of approximately .70 were obtained for EI, SN, and JP, and .48 for TF (*10*). In general, the reliabilities of the test are like those of similar self-report inventories, TF appearing least stable.

Since the construction and successive revisions of the MBTI were guided by an explicit theoretical system, it is necessary to assess the extent to which it embodies the assumptions of that system. Specifically, the following properties are claimed: (*a*) the scales are bipolar and discontinuous, the zero point representing a true dividing point of psychological significance, i.e., the dimensions are dichotomous; and (*b*) the four scales interact in a complex manner in relating to behavior. The evidence for both assertions is not convincing. With respect to the former, there is no evidence of bimodality in the score distributions. Moreover, given the reliabilities of the scales, it seems risky to infer basic personality differences when the omission or change of a single item could alter a subject's classification. The primary evidence offered in support of the claimed dichotomous character of the scales, however, is based on the nature of the regression of independent variables on Indicator scores. The regressions shown in the manual change slope or are discontinuous in the area of the zero point. There are weaknesses in this method of demonstrating a dichotomy though. No statistics are offered to indicate that these are other than chance effects, the decision as to whether the regression line changes at the zero point is highly subjective and easily influenced by the form of data presentation (*10*), and, most important, there is no *a priori* rationale given for selecting the particular independent variables included. Thus while there is some evidence for a change in the regression line for some variables and some scales in the zero region, this does not seem sufficient to support the claimed bipolarity and dichotomy.

There is little data bearing on the assumption of interaction of the scales. Considerable theoretical point is made of this, however, involving the idea of the dominant and auxiliary functions and the effect of the EI setting on the interaction of score patterns. Results of studies in which all four dimensions were used to classify subjects seem most simply explained as additive effects. In an analysis of variance undertaken to investigate this question directly, no interactions of any order were significant (*10*). While more data on this point are needed, at present interpretations involving interaction seem unjustified.

In attempting to assess what these scales measure, it is informative to consider their item content as well as their patterns of relationship to independent variables. The EI scale seems to measure extraversion-introversion in the popular senses rather than in the Jungian sense. The items have to do primarily with ease in and liking for interpersonal contact, the factor of interest in the inner world of ideas being unrepresented. This interpretation is supported by a pattern of correlations with such variables as social introversion, gregariousness, and talkativeness, and the lack of correlation with variables related to thinking introversion and theoretical orientation. The items of the SN scale seem to refer to a practical, conventional, realistic attitude as opposed to one more idea and theory oriented, stressing originality, autonomy, and complexity. This interpretation gains strength from loadings on intellectualism factors and strong correlations with groups 1 and 8 on the Strong.[1] It is consistent also with the finding that highly creative individuals are overwhelmingly intuition types. TF items seem to reflect a legalistic, rationalistic versus humanistic, sympathetic approach. Correlations with independent measures are less clear for this scale but it is related to the theoretical and social values of *Study of Values* and nurturance and affiliation on the *Edwards Personal Preference Schedule.* Finally, JP items refer to a preference for order and planning as opposed to spontaneity and novelty. Correlations resemble those of SN but include also a high correlation with order on the EPPS and it is consistently related to behavior ratings of reliability and dependability. In general, then, it appears that the scales measure only limited aspects of their underlying constructs and that the data support the argument that interpretations based on item content are more accurate and parsimonious.

While the weight of the evidence does not support several basic assertions about the MBTI, the reviewer nevertheless considers the instrument of considerable potential utility. This conclusion is based on the findings which indicate that type scores relate meaningfully to a wide range of variables including personality, ability, interest, value, aptitude and performance measures, academic choice, and behavior ratings. (Some of these relationships are indicated in the previous paragraph.) Although there are better predictors available for particular tasks, few instruments appear to provide as much information as can be derived efficiently from the MBTI. It would seem useful, then, for personality research and, given its relationships to measures of interest, value, aptitude, and achievement, for academic counseling.

In summary, a consideration of the available data suggests that the MBTI does not represent a successful operationalization of Jungian concepts. Nevertheless, it does appear to have potential utility for research and counseling if scores are interpreted in the light of their empirical relationships rather than their assumed theoretical significance.

NORMAN D. SUNDBERG, *Professor of Psychology, University of Oregon, Eugene, Oregon.*

The *Myers-Briggs Type Indicator* will undoubtedly arouse much interest among psychologists for the following reasons: (*a*) it is easy to administer and score; (*b*) it provides scores on variables which are important according to both theory and common sense; (*c*) there is evidence of its relationship to some matters of great practical concern in the 1960's, e.g., creativity, achievement, and success at certain jobs. The Indicator consists of 166 forced

1 STRICKER, LAWRENCE J., AND ROSS, JOHN. "A Description and Evaluation of the Myers-Briggs Type Indicator." Unpublished research bulletin, Educational Testing Service, Princeton, N.J., Mr '62. Pp. 180. *

choice items which can easily be answered within 50 minutes. Item content would usually not be seen as threatening. An example in the instructions is the following: "Are your interests (A) few and lasting, (B) varied." The middle part is somewhat different, rather ambiguously requiring the subject to choose which of two words is more appealing, e.g., "(A) literal," or "(B) figurative." The forced choice format sometimes presents a challenge to the test administrator in establishing test taking motivation as will be discussed later. Scoring of the special answer sheets can be done either by hand or machine and scores are conveniently recorded directly on the answer sheet.

The resulting scores are taken to indicate the subject's preference for four different modes of thinking postulated by Carl Jung's theory of personality types: extraversion-introversion (EI), whether the person prefers to direct his mental activities toward the external world of people and things or toward the inner world of concepts and ideas; sensing-intuition (SN), whether the subject prefers to perceive his world in a factual, realistic way or to perceive inherent, imaginative possibilities; thinking-feeling (TF), whether the person prefers to arrive at decisions by logical analysis or by appreciating personal and interpersonal subjective values; and judgment-perception (JP), whether the subject prefers to take a judgmental attitude or an understanding, perceptive attitude toward his environment. Jungian theory and the exposition in Myers' manual prefer to treat these indexes as alternative choices showing the person's dominant type rather than as scores on a trait continuum. However, it is possible to convert the indexes into continuous scores. The direction of the subject's four preferences are recorded by letter so that he can conveniently be called, for example, an ESTJ type, an INFP type, or an ENFJ type.

Myers' unusually long manual (157 pages) provides an extensive introduction to the theory and interpretation of the results and to related research. She also outlines the history of the inventory starting in 1942 when she and Katharine Briggs tried out items on acquaintances who seemed to represent clear type preferences. The development in recent years turned to extensive norming and revising by internal consistency methods under the aegis of the Educational Testing Service, which published the test in 1962. There is a great deal of appeal to a theoretically developed instrument like this with its logical clarity and scope and its language which fits easily into a personality system. A test interpreter must have an organized system for simplifying results and for grouping individuals. The Jungian types, though not in common usage, could be very helpful in this regard. Unlike the authors of many theoretically derived tests, the workers on MBTI have also endeavored to develop a thorough empirical base.

The Indicator has been answered by several thousands of high school and college students and by certain professional and industrial groups. Reliability studies, which in the manual are limited surprisingly to only internal consistency (split-half) measures, show correlations mostly in the .70 and .80 range for continuous scores. These figures are comparable to those of leading personality inventories. Younger and less capable groups (e.g., underachieving eighth grade boys) tend to obtain somewhat lower reliabilities, and the TF index is less reliable than the others. Since type categories are employed for much of the interpretive theory, it is important to ascertain the reliability of the types as well as continuous scores. Here there is some problem over the appropriate statistic. Stricker and Ross (*7*) using Guttman's lower bound reliability estimate find correlation figures mostly in the .40's and .50's. However, Myers points out that this statistic is appropriate only where scores were originally dichotomous. Using tetrachoric *r*'s and applying the Spearman-Brown prophecy formula, she reports median *r*'s of .83, a figure almost identical with that obtained from continuous scores. Stricker and Ross (*9*) report 14-month retest reliability figures on continuous scores for 41 college students: .48 for TF, .69 for SN and JP, and .73 for EI.

Intercorrelations between scales are low except for JP's relation to SN which ranges from .26 to .47. Obviously, more studies for different subjects and periods of time are needed, and a parallel form of the MBTI would be helpful. For individual counseling it would seem advisable to be cautious about interpreting scores near the border between types.

At this point it would be well to note that in the area of test taking attitude the Indicator leaves much to be desired. I asked a class of 39 graduate students in psychology and education to write their reactions after taking the MBTI and to guess at the purposes of the test. Over half of them found fault with the forced choice format. Some went so far as to say that they felt less motivated to be careful because of the unrealistic choices they were asked to make. They also frequently mentioned that the test seemed obvious and easy to manipulate and questioned the correspondence between preferences and personality. When guessing at the test's purposes, over a fourth specified introversion and extraversion and another fourth thought it had something to do with how organized and flexible a person is. The purposes were partially but not wholly transparent to these students, it would seem. The MBTI does not have any direct indicators of test taking attitude, such as the MMPI validity scales. (There has been some experimentation with an unpublished scale of uncommon responses.) Although there is special weighting to take care of differences in popularity between the choices on items, a direct test of social desirability needs to be done. There is also one very interesting item which test interpreters might use to get at an individual's attitude; the last item asks the testee, "Would you have liked to argue the meaning of (A) a lot of these questions, (B) only a few." In my class three fourths said they would have liked to argue a lot of the questions. In this contentious class there were also positive feelings about the test but these were outweighted by the complaints of difficulty and dislike. This experience certainly suggests the importance of carefully establishing a positive involvement with the test. Certainly more empirical work also needs to be done to improve detection of unusual test taking attitudes, particularly for group usage. The distribution between subtle and obvious items needs to be explored. As it stands, I believe the test would be of dubious value for selection, where conscious faking would be a problem. As the author admits, the Indicator, like any self-report, is subject to dissimulation.

The manual's reports on validity rest mainly on concurrent studies—expected relationship to other tests and to ratings and differences between groups. Relationships to a large number of scales on tests of interest, values, and personality are mostly in the expected directions. For example, *Strong Vocational Interest Blank* interest in sales correlates significantly with extraversion; interest in psychology with intuition; and *Edwards Personal Preference Scale* scores for need for nurturance correlate with a feeling preference. In industrial studies there are scattered reports of useful findings, such as excessive turnover in sales jobs among thinking types and the eventual predominance of extraverted feeling types in such jobs. Creative groups, such as leading architects and writers studied by MacKinnon and others at the Institute of Personality Assessment and Research, have shown distinct preferences for intuition over the sensory approach, which is much more commonly preferred in the general population and less creative groups. Peavy [1] extended the evidence for greater creative activity among intuitive than sensing types to high school seniors. (So far, however, I know of no study doing an item analysis separating the obvious self-report items showing preference for creative and imaginative pursuits from the subtle items; perhaps creative people just say they are interested in being creative and there are no deeper implications regarding personality.) On several samples preferences for the intuitive mode, and to some extent introversion, have low but significant relations to measures of intelligence and school achievement. Also within given aptitude levels judging types achieved higher grades in a large study of Pennsylvania college preparatory schools. Anyone interested in the research should study the extensive material in the manual and in the Educational Testing Service reports.

The question of construct validity is always a complex one: Do these indexes really measure the underlying personality types postulated by Jung's theory? Stricker and Ross (*10*) conclude on the basis of analysis of content of the scales and their correlations with a wide variety of tests that the SN and TF scales may reflect the dimensions they were theorized to represent but that EI and JP are more questionable. A theory attempting to separate people into types requires evidence of separate categories and a cutting point on the measuring scales. Myers recognizes that simple bimodality of distributions does not exist. This finding is in line with the less sophisticated studies of a few decades back showing that instead of being introverts or extraverts most people

1 PEAVY, R. VANCE. *A Study of C. G. Jung's Concept of Intuitive Perception and the Intuitive Type.* Doctor's thesis, University of Oregon (Eugene, Ore.), 1963.

were "ambiverts." The search for answers to the question of dichotomous types has turned to the study of differences in regression lines of the two opposite scales plotted against dependent variables such as grade averages or IQ's. The manual shows that the two regression lines often show a discontinuity or a difference in slope. In contrast Stricker and Ross conclude there is little support for any of the structural properties attributed to the typology, finding with students only a few U-shaped regression lines or discontinuities; TF shows the most likelihood. Apparently we have a controversy here in which methodology and interpretation of type theory are still to be clarified. It may be that sharper distinctions between types could be found with older people than the adolescents mostly studied so far. In any case notions about personality types seem to be enjoying a resurgence in psychology these days, and methodologies are being developed for determining them. Even if one does not accept the structural implications of Jungian theory or even the theory itself, the empirical relations of the inventory's scales can be studied. Purely as a potential research procedure for getting at individual differences in cognitive preferences, it would seem the Indicator would merit a great deal of attention from cognitive theorists.

In regard to application of the MBTI, the manual speaks mostly about vocational counseling in schools and industrial placement. Although there is considerable discussion relating to type requirements of various jobs, there are unfortunately only a few case examples. Little mention is made of clinical applications, although one report in press points to relationships with certain scales on the MMPI, particularly the validity scales. The Jungian hypothesis that lack of clear type preferences is associated with ineffectiveness and maladjustment was not confirmed by Stricker and Ross (*9*). Mendelsohn and Kirk (*4*) have shown that students seeking counseling as compared with nonapplicants have greater preferences for intuitive and perceptive modes of thinking. In my beginning counseling use of the MBTI I have found it very easy and interesting to explain to clients; the person is able to see and understand his own preferences. Counseling usage is aided by the manual's pervasive spirit of respect for the different preferences and types; these are seen as positive choices and not lacks. The suggested interpretations of various types are easy to use but strongly need evidence that they are valid—and not "universally valid"—that is, they need evidence that the descriptions differentiate and individualize persons. An intriguing possibility for use of the Indicator is with groups such as married couples, families, or work groups. Mendelsohn and Geller (*6*) have shown that similarity of type between counselor and client is related to continuation in counseling and probably to greater ability to communicate with each other. It would seem that similarity of types would be related to compatibility, but for certain tasks to be accomplished it would be necessary to have different types represented.

The course and development of the MBTI will be intriguing to watch. There is much about it that suggests great possibilities, but its limits and its areas of need for supportive combination with other tests are not yet clear. The inventory needs to be tried, in many different contexts, maintaining, as Myers puts it, "a constant search for separate verification and new meanings."

J Counsel Psychol 10:307–8 f '63. Laurence Siegel. * The Indicator may be viewed from three perspectives. First, it contains four scales yielding continuous scores which the user can empirically validate. This treatment of the Indicator is contrary to the theory underlying its development. Nevertheless it is precisely this treatment that was used to estimate the reliabilities and certain of the validities offered in support of the instrument. However, normative data for the four scales continuously scored are not presented. An alternative is to treat the Indicator as yielding eight continuous scores—one for each aspect of the dichotomy embodied within each index. Although limited percentile norms are provided for these eight scores, reliability data are not presented for them. Since these scales are only half as long as those for which reliability *was* estimated, there is some serious question about the utility of these percentile conversions for individual guidance. Finally, the importance of Indicator scores can be minimized in favor of giving primary consideration to the type designations derived from these scores. The Manual states that this interpretation is the most legitimate one. The promise of the Indicator so interpreted would seem to depend more heavily upon clinical or intuitive validation than upon the more usual kind of psychometric validation.

[148]

★The Neuroticism Scale Questionnaire. Ages 16 and over; 1961; title on test is *NSQ;* the *IPAT Neurotic Personality Factor Test* (see 5:74), which is still available, is "an earlier version" of this test; 5 scores: depressiveness, submissiveness, overprotection, anxiety, total; 1 form (4 pages); manual (31 pages); $3.10 per 25 tests; 50¢ per key; $1.70 per manual; $2.30 per specimen set; cash orders postpaid; (10–15) minutes; Ivan H. Scheier and Raymond B. Cattell; Institute for Personality and Ability Testing. *

REFERENCES

1. Cattell, Raymond B., and Scheier, Ivan H. *The Meaning and Measurement of Neuroticism and Anxiety.* New York: Ronald Press Co., 1961. Pp. ix, 535. * (*PA* 36: 1HK27C)

E. Lowell Kelly, *Professor of Psychology, The University of Michigan, Ann Arbor, Michigan.*

This is a brief inventory designed to assess "the degree of neurosis in a wide range of situations." According to a footnote in the manual, it is a new "version" of the earlier *IPAT Neurotic Personality Factor Test.* The NSQ is another short inventory derived from the 16 PF but unlike the *IPAT Anxiety Scale* published separately to assess those dimensions constituting a second order personality factor, the NSQ is designed to measure the admittedly impure real life criterion "degree of neuroticism" or "neurotic trend."

Research by the authors (*1*) showed that six of the 16 PF scores differentiate normal persons and those diagnosed neurotic in several different clinical settings. However, since three of the six differentiating scores turned out to be three of the five 16 PF scores constituting the second order anxiety factor, the decision was made to group these three into a single component labeled Anxiety. The other three components are "primary factors" of the 16 PF: I, overprotection, tendermindedness, or sensitivity at the positive pole; F, depressiveness, overseriousness; and E, submissiveness, dependence. Each of the four scales consists of 10 three-response items, scored 0, 1, or 2, with a possible score range of 0 to 20. The neuroticism score is simply the sum of the four part scores. Norm tables (sten values) based on nonclinical subjects (675 men and 393 women) are provided for both component and total scores.

Reliabilities (corrected split-half) based on 300 normal subjects are reported as .55, .57, .47, and .70 for the four component scales and .67 for the total score. The four component scales are relatively independent, the intercorrelations ranging from .08 to .28 for a group of 113 normals.

Two types of validity claims are made in the manual: concept (or construct) and concrete (or concurrent). After making the dubious assumption that the component scores are each pure measures of a single factor, it is argued that the concept validity of each is equal to the square root of its reliability, i.e., the extent to which the score would correlate with a perfect measure of the factor. This logic and method results in reporting highly respectable validity coefficients ranging from .69 to .84 for the four component scores, but precludes a comparable estimate of concept validity for the total score, since it is admittedly not a unitary factor.

Concrete validity is defined in the manual as "the correlation of the test with life performances and categories." Unfortunately, however, the manual does not report any kind of correlation of either total or component scores with any performance or category! The total score of 102 clinically judged neurotics is reported to be significantly higher (at the .0005 level) than the scores of 1,068 normals, but regretfully there is no indication of the amount of overlap of the two distributions. However, the manual reports a mean sten total score of 7.1 for another group of 315 neurotics and, since a sten score of 7 corresponds to a percentile range of 69 to 84 for the norm group, it would appear that nearly 30 per cent of normals score as more neurotic than does the average clinically diagnosed neurotic! Perhaps neuroticism is as widespread in the normal population as these results seem to indicate; alternatively, it is equally possible that the NSQ is such a crude measure of neuroticism that it fails to yield more differentiated distributions of scores for criterion groups. Unfortunately, the evidence for concurrent validity provided in the manual does not enable the reader to decide between these two conclusions. The authors base their argument for concurrent validity largely on the fact that the corresponding 16 PF scores yield statistically significant differences not only between normals and neurotics but also between normals and other clinical groups, e.g., alcoholics, narcotics users, and male homosexuals. Are these groups also to some degree "neurotic" or is the NSQ measuring something other than neuroticism?

Frankly, this reviewer finds it difficult to understand the authors' decision to publish these items as a separate test. If one wishes only to identify persons who will be labeled as neurotic by clinicians, it would appear that the anxiety component score alone would yield higher concurrent validities than the total score. At least the manual shows the 315 neurotics received a sten score of 8.1 on the anxiety component as contrasted with a score of only 7.1 on total neurotic level! One is forced to conclude that the authors hope to find a better or different market for an instrument purporting to assess "Neuroticism" than for the 16 PF or for the Anxiety Scale, either of which would appear to be more useful in simply identifying neurotics. While it is of interest that their research shows clinically diagnosed neurotics to differ from normals on dimensions other than anxiety, the value of constructing a test which combines these several components into a single mixed score is not obvious. Doing so may, in fact, tend to perpetuate the tendency to lump together under a single diagnostic label, individuals who might better be perceived and treated differently.

The manual includes a number of very dubious statements. For example: "Measurement is now recognized as a precondition for dealing with neurosis socially or individually. * The [NSQ] is designed to implement this fundamental measurement precondition." After insisting that the NSQ is designed to give a properly weighted score on neuroticism (p. 4) we read, "Research....shows that about half the differences between neurotics and normals can be accounted for as differences in anxiety level." Yet, a few sentences later, we are told, "the anxiety contribution in the NSQ is weighted at only approximately a fourth of the total neuroticism score." The reason for this weighting is that "anxiety can be measured separately in the IPAT Anxiety Scale." The result of this logic and maneuvering is that the NSQ and Anxiety Scale scores correlate only .36! Using the reported reliabilities of .67 and .84 for these two scales, this value corrected for attenuation becomes .48. Just how does this fit with the earlier claim of "a properly weighted" score?

While admitting that because of the low reliabilities of the several scores the NSQ should be "used cautiously" in diagnosing the individual case, this caution tends to be forgotten in that part of the manual dealing with interpretations where it is suggested that the profile of component scores for an individual can appropriately serve as a basis for deciding on the type of therapy to be used! This and similar expressions of excessive confidence on the part of the authors is almost frightening. For example: "The NSQ can be re-administered to the same persons at intervals of as little as two weeks, e.g., to determine fluctuations in neuroticism level over time and/or in response to therapy or other conditions." Certainly it can be readministered but how much of a change in an individual's score might be expected solely on the basis of errors of measurement?

Whereas this reviewer welcomed the issuance of the separate *IPAT Anxiety Scale* for the assessment of anxiety as a second order personality factor (see 5:70) he feels that there is little if any value to be derived from the use of this particular set of the 16 PF scales which have been found to differentiate persons broadly labeled neurotic by clinicians. Clearly if one wishes to screen for neurotic tendency, the Anxiety Scale is as good and perhaps better than this new scale. If he wishes to use an objective personality measure for individual diagnosis, then surely the testing time required for the total 16 PF or for the MMPI is justified. Incidentally, the manual does not report the relationship between NSQ scores and any other previously published and widely used device for assessing neuroticism. This reviewer finds unconscionable such omissions on the part of those who would sell a new and presumably better instrument for the same purpose.

JEROME D. PAUKER, *Assistant Professor of Clinical Psychology, Medical School, University of Minnesota, Minneapolis, Minnesota.*

The handbook for the NSQ describes the test as being a "brief, accurate, valid, and nonstressful measurement of neurotic trends in the normal or abnormal adult or young adult." In form it is neat, clear, and easily handled by both examiner and subject. There is some question, however, about how well it measures what it sets out to measure.

The NSQ is a more recent version of the *IPAT Neurotic Personality Factor Test* (NPF). It is comprised of 40 questionnaire items, selected from a pool of 200 neuroticism-associated items, which relate to six statistically derived personality dimensions which, according to the research of Cattell and his associates, are the factors that define neuroticism. The term "neuroticism" as used by the authors "is essentially synonymous with 'neurosis' but is intended to convey the recognition that neurosis can vary in degree among normals as well as abnormals."

The test is administered in the form of a four-page booklet, the center two pages containing the 40 questionnaire items in large, dark, easily read letters on an eye-relaxing, light green background. The front page gives instructions and examples, and the back page serves as a record sheet for charting scores and making notes.

The handbook is about as excellent a manual as can be found, with descriptions, administration, scoring, reliability and validity data, tables of norms, interpretations, and so forth all presented in clearly separated and readable form. Scoring is quickly and easily done with the aid of a scoring template, and the results are recorded in the form of standard scores on a ten-unit scale. An explanation of this "sten" system, along with percentile equivalents, is presented in the handbook.

The first three test factors, which are given separate scores, are said to relate, respectively, to overprotected, tenderminded sensitivity, depressive overseriousness, and submissiveness. The final three factors are combined to form one score for anxiety. Fuller descriptions of these factors and how they were derived are given in the handbook and also in Cattell and Scheier's *The Meaning and Measurement of Neuroticism and Anxiety* (*1*). The four component scores are described as being "statistically virtually independent of one another," and are intended to provide a more detailed delineation of the general neuroticism present. Although the handbook lists "profiles" of the four scores for a variety of diagnostic categories, the authors emphasize the greater stability of a fifth score which consists of the sum of the other four scores and they point to the determination of this "total" neuroticism level as being the primary purpose of the test.

Internal consistency is indicated in the form of split-half correlations. Coefficients for the four components are .55, .57, .47, and .70. The coefficient for the total score is .67. These are not of a very encouraging order. There is no measure of stability in the form of test-retest.

The validity section is the weakest in the manual. In the first place, while mention is made of the "very high level of statistical confidence (beyond the .0005 level)" with which the total score differentiates 102 clinically-judged neurotics from 1,068 normals, there is no presentation of cutoff scores for making the differentiation nor is there any discussion of the results in terms of the number of the neurotic group who received "normal" scores and the number of normals who scored as high as the neurotic group did (false negatives and false positives). This information is of particular importance if the test is to be used for individual evaluation. Secondly, data are not presented to support the contention that the test "discriminates sharply, not only between normals and neurotics (or other abnormals), but also, continuously between degrees of neurotic trend running throughout the 'normal' population" (issue No. 16 of the "IPAT News"). A third weakness comes out of the fact that some of the validity data "are less direct in the sense that they did not arise directly from the present NSQ, but rather from that portion of the more comprehensive 16 PF TEST to which the NSQ corresponds." This use of indirect data is justified by the authors on the basis that the same components are being measured in both instances. This logic falters in view of the fact that the indirect data are based on a larger number of items than that in the NSQ, and so are likely to be more reliable. The authors promise that more direct and more extensive validity data will soon become available.

A section on "Interpreting the Test Scores" provides descriptions of behavior presumed to be associated with each of the NSQ components and with the total score. These descriptions run to about a page in length for each part, and this despite the fact that the "minimally acceptable reliability" of each component is stressed. Much of this descriptive section, too, is based on indirect data.

In summary, despite the background of extensive factor analytic work out of which this test was derived, and despite the presence of adequate normative data, there does not as yet seem to be sufficient direct evidence to recommend this test for use in individual evaluation. The total score may be of value for discriminating groups, but even here it should be used cautiously and not as a sole criterion.

This is not a test to be dismissed out-of-hand. It holds promise of being a useful screening device, but until further direct demonstration of its usefulness is forthcoming the promise should be regarded as unfulfilled.

J Counsel Psychol 8:373–4 w '61. John O. Crites. * A brief (5 to 10 minutes) 40 item inventory developed from an analysis of over 4,000 items, the *NSQ* yields part scores on Tender-Mindedness, Depression, Submissiveness, and Anxiety as well as a total Neuroticism score. The sub-scales, which were derived from factor analyses of item intercorrelations, are largely independent of each other, the highest *r* being .28 for Tender-Mindedness and Depression. The rationale for these sub-scales is that "neurotics do not differ from normals on one dimension only, as some have supposed, but on many personality dimensions at once" (Manual, p. 4). The total *NSQ* score is computed because it reflects the over-all neurotic trend of "the statistically relatively rare person who happens to be high on all components at once" (Manual, p. 4). The logic here seems strained, however, since the concept of neuroticism is either multi-dimensional or it is not. If it is the former, then there is no justification for adding the part scores, which represent different *kinds* of behavior, to obtain a composite score, which expresses different *degrees* of behavior. If it is the latter, then one scale is sufficient to measure neuroticism, not four scales. Actually, the validity data reported in the Manual on the four sub-scales of the *NSQ* suggest that "neuroticism" as measured by this inventory is essentially unidimensional. The only scale which consistently differentiates the clinically diagnosed groups of neurotics, psychotics, homosexuals, alcoholics, drug addicts, and psychopaths used in the initial standardization of the *NSQ* is the Anxiety scale. The other scales produce some group differences, but they appear practically insignificant and fit no discernible pattern. Unfortunately, the test authors cite no data on the standard deviations of the groups, correlations between scale scores and group membership, percentages of overlap between groups, misclassification rates (false positives and negatives), etc. Furthermore, they fail to substantiate their assertion that "NSQ scores discriminate not only between neurotics and normals, but also between varying degrees of slighter neurotic trend in persons usually classed as normal" (Manual, p. 4). Finally, they make inferences about the validity of the *NSQ* from data on scales with similar names in the *16 Personality Factor* test which have *different* items! One reason for the low validity of the Tender-Mindedness, Depression, and Submissiveness scales as compared with the Anxiety scale is that they have extremely low reliabilities, even for personality measures. Their respective split-half coefficients, corrected by Spearman-Brown, are .55, .57, and .47, whereas the estimate for Anxiety is .70. The internal consistency coefficient for the total score, based upon the correlation between composites of halves of the sub-scales, is .67. The test authors remark that "Any attempt to augment this reliability by making items in the scale more homogeneous with each other and with the total scale (less different, as between components) would fly in the face of reality—the reality that neuroticism is *not* a single homogeneous thing" (Manual, p. 11). Again, their reasoning reveals the inconsistency between their assumption that "neuroticism" is a multi-dimensional concept and research evidence which indicates the contrary. There are other shortcomings of the *NSQ,* such as its complex scoring key, poorly described norm groups, and unfamiliar trait names, but its major drawbacks are conceptual and empirical. The Manual makes an unconvincing case for the multi-dimensional nature of neuroticism and presents only minimal data on the reliability and validity of the *NSQ*. For the counselor's use in the evaluation of a client's adjustment, the *NSQ* appears to have little demonstrated value. The Anxiety scale may give a rough index of adjustment level, but what the other scales measure with respect to modes of adjustment is unknown, and normative data on adjustment in different areas of life activity are not reported.

J Counsel Psychol 9:280–1 f '62. Ivan H. Scheier. "A Reply to Crites' Review of the Neuroticism Scale Questionnaire (The NSQ)." * Logic aside,....[Crites] claims a failure to demonstrate empirically that neuroticism is multidimensional, since the Anxiety Scale component of the test is (Crites, 1961) "The only scale which consistently differentiates the clinically diagnosed groups of neurotics, psychotics, homosexuals, alcoholics, drug addicts, and psychopaths." Now, the

NSQ *Manual* (top, p. 12) states clearly and unequivocally the (rather obvious, anyhow) point that, primarily, a neurosis test must give different scores for *neurotics* vs. normals; *not* psychotics, homosexuals, etc. vs. normals. If the reviewer had grasped that this neurosis test is validated on neurotics, he would have seen immediately that, not just anxiety, but all four NSQ components tend to deviate significantly from normal over the neurotic groups (*Manual,* Table 5); hence all four are needed to describe the typical neurotic. Neurosis is thereby presented as multidimensional. These are major, emphasized points in the Manual and background literature (Cattell & Scheier, 1961). Homogeneity reliability is +.67 for total NSQ score. The reviewer criticizes this as low, then cites one of the *Manual's* answers to this criticism: that neuroticism is a *heterogeneous* thing (four distinct components), hence, cannot realistically be measured by completely homogeneous items. Here the reviewer argues that neuroticism is homogeneous, but the above two paragraphs just considered have refuted this argument, so the heterogeneity-reducing-reliability point remains. The reviewer might have noted that the *Manual* (p. 11) describes a straightforward way to raise reliability of each NSQ component: add items from comparable scales in the longer 16 PF Test (Cattell & Stice, 1957). The reviewer is actually challenging this well known and accepted comparability principle when he deplores "inferences about the validity of the NSQ from data on scales with similar names in the *16 Personality Factor* test which have different items!" Why so shocked? In an internally consistent set of items measuring, say, anxiety, physical separation of the first and last 50 items doesn't suddenly make them *different* from anxiety and from each other! Just so, certain groups of "different" 16 PF items (Cattell & Stice, 1957) compose "scales with similar names," not coincidentally, but because they actually are comparable forms to the NSQ subscales. Moving now from the test authors' concepts to the reviewer's, 25 per cent of the review considers the concepts of "mode," "area," and "general level" of adjustment. I'm thinking of offering a reward to anyone finding these concepts in the NSQ Manual or background references (Cattell & Scheier, 1961). I can't. "Conceptual coexistence," perhaps, but "conceptual aggression" (attempts to *evaluate and criticize* the NSQ in terms of the reviewer's concepts), no! Example: the NSQ "focuses more upon level than mode or area" and what some of its components "measure with respect to modes of adjustment is unknown." It is "unknown," mainly because the test authors exercised the right to conceptualize their data in their own way. True, an author can't insist on being judged entirely within his own conceptual framework, but whoever imposes a radically different one should identify it as different, even attempt some "translation." The reviewer does neither. * The NSQ key is very simple, requiring only the ability to count and add 1's and 2's for marks showing up through a punched-hole key. Average, or nongenious scoring clerks—I've watched and timed them—need perhaps 2 or 3 minutes to understand instructions, and a minute or so per case after that, for total score. * In all tables and textual references, the NSQ *Manual* uses the basic trait names: "Tender-Mindedness," "Depression," "Submissiveness," "Anxiety," "Neuroticism" or "neurosis," or well-known synonyms for these (e.g., "dependence" for "Submissiveness"). * I am astonished that any psychologist considers terms like "anxiety" and "depression" unfamiliar. I am even more astonished that by the time the reviewer gets around to calling them "unfamiliar," he has already used them himself several times in the review without explaining them to anyone. *

[149]

★Objective-Analytic (O-A) Anxiety Battery. Ages 14 and over; 1955–62; revision of anxiety-to-achieve battery (U.I. 24) of *Objective-Analytic Personality Test Batteries* (see 5:90); individual in part (tests 246-I and 2410-I); 1 form ('60); 10 tests from which user may select those appropriate to his needs: 241-G (susceptibility to annoyance, 4 pages), 242-G (honesty in admitting common frailties, 2 pages), 243-G (modesty in assuming skill in untried performance, 7 pages), 244-G (critical severity vs. indulgent standards, 3 pages), 245-G (number of friends recalled, 2 pages), 246-I (increase or recovery of pulse rate), 247-G (emotionality of comment, 4 pages), 248-G (acceptance of good aphorisms, 1 page), 249-G (susceptibility to embarrassment, 5 pages), 2410-I (systolic blood pressure); manual ('60, 15 pages); norms supplement ('62, 4 pages); no data on reliability of 246-I and 2410-I; norms for college students only; no norms for 246-I, 247-G, 248-G, and 2410-I; prices per 25 tests (up to 500 copies of each may be reproduced locally from the test kit): $4 for 241-G and 247-G, $2.40 for 242-G and 245-G, $5.60 for 243-G, $3.30 for 244-G, $1.25 for 248-G, $4.60 for 249-G; separate answer sheets may be used; $2.70 per pad of 50 answer sheets; no scoring stencils for answer sheets; $6 per test kit consisting of one copy of each test and administration and scoring instructions for each; $1.25 per manual; $7 per specimen set consisting of test kit and manual; cash orders postpaid; additional apparatus necessary for tests 246-I and 2410-I; (25-50) minutes for the complete battery; Raymond B. Cattell and Ivan H. Scheier; Institute for Personality and Ability Testing. *

REFERENCES

1. CATTELL, RAYMOND B., AND SCHEIER, IVAN H. "The Nature of Anxiety: A Review of Thirteen Multivariate Analyses Comprising 814 Variables." *Psychol Rep* 4:351–88 Je '58. * (*PA* 33:5738)
2. CATTELL, RAYMOND B., AND SCHEIER, IVAN H. "The Objective Test Measurement of Neuroticism, U.I. 23 (—)." *Indian J Psychol* 33:217–36 pt 4 '58. *
3. SCHEIER, IVAN H., AND CATTELL, RAYMOND B. "Confirmation of Objective Test Factors and Assessment of Their Relation to Questionnaire Factors: A Factor Analysis of 113 Rating, Questionnaire, and Objective Test Measurements of Personality." *J Mental Sci* 104:608–24 Jl '58. * (*PA* 33:9345)
4. MOSHIN, S. M. "Plea for a Scientific Aptitude Test and a Preliminary Report of the Development of Such Test." *Indian J Psychol* 34:36–42 pt 1 '59. *
5. CATTELL, RAYMOND B., AND SCHEIER, IVAN H. *The Meaning and Measurement of Neuroticism and Anxiety.* New York: Ronald Press Co., 1961. Pp. ix, 535. * (*PA* 36:1HK27C)

HAROLD BORKO, *Human Factors Scientist, Advanced Technology and Research Directorate, System Development Corporation, Santa Monica, California.*

In Cattell's factor indexing system, anxiety is labeled U.I. 24, and it has been the subject of over 20 research studies involving literally thousands of subjects and hundreds of tests. From these earlier researches, the 10 best tests were selected for inclusion in the *Objective-Analytic (O-A) Anxiety Battery.*

The battery is designed to measure the clinical concept of "free anxiety" as characterized by "tension and emotionality, guilt and self-depreciation, irritability, susceptibility to embarrassment, loneliness and 'separation,' high expressed sex drive, and some suspicion and hostility." Ten separate tests are combined to make up the battery. Of these 10, 8 are paper and pencil tests which can be administered to a group, while two tests—246 and 2410—are physiological measurements and require individual administration. Test 246 deals with the increase and recovery of pulse rate following the firing of a .22 blank starting gun three feet behind the subject's head or the immersing of the subject's hand in ice water for exactly 30 seconds. This is a rather awkward test to administer and, while Cattell claims that the test has a loading of .65 with the anxiety factor, no figures are available on the reliability of the test and so one can only wonder whether it is worth administering at all. The other individual test, 2410, is entitled Systolic Blood Pressure. Although the manual states that, "in general, it seems clear that high systolic blood pressure reflects the sheer tension aspects of anxiety," the correlation with the anxiety factor is only .36 and again reliability figures are not available.

The remaining eight tests are paper and pencil, require no special apparatus, and are designed for group administration. The split-half corrected reliability of these eight tests ranges from .56 to .90. The factor validity, which is the multiple correlation of all 10 tests with the factor dimension "is estimated conservatively as .80–.85." The clinical validity of the battery which is its correlation with a "consensus of clinical judgment" of anxiety level is estimated as .35 to .50 with a maximum attainable value, due to the unreliability of clinical judgments, estimated as .70. In essence, these figures indicate that the test battery is reasonably reliable and valid.

One serious difficulty in using this test battery is that norms are available on only 6 of the 10 tests. Furthermore, the standardizing population consists of from 94 to 280 college undergraduates, mostly males. For only three tests were approximately 50 college undergraduate females used and their scores were combined in the norm tables with those of the males. The complete lack of clinical or general population norms, and the inadequacy of the existing norms, necessitates that the prospective user of the battery be very cautious in interpreting any obtained scores. As presently constituted, the *Objective-Analytic (O-A) Anxiety Battery* will be more useful in a research than in a clinical setting.

J Counsel Psychol 7:311 w '60. Gordon V. Anderson. * In contrast to the IPAT Anxiety Scale, which arrives at an anxiety score directly by questionnaire responses indicating the subject's degree of discomfort, apprehensions and related feelings, the new measure assesses the level of anxiety by inferences from a battery of attitude measures. * These objective tests are considered superior because they are not easily "faked." This is a doubtful advantage for counselors, however, to whom clients come for help, not for adulation. The research advantages may justify this approach, however, since such questions as the degree to which anxiety reduces the efficiency of performance, differences in anxiety level among various occupational groups, and effective measures for reducing anxiety, cannot be answered without some attention to this aspect of test taking attitude. * Although this battery is presented for operational use by the publishers, and a lucid, well written manual describes the materials, explains the concepts, and makes suggestions for its application, it is not now possible to give it any meaning in the counselor-client situation. To quote the manual, "Standardization tables will be published and distributed to battery users within about a year." This battery clearly needs much more research. In addition to standardization work, studies need to be made of the stability of O-A Anxiety over time; of its relation to other personality and behavior characteristics. It looks promising, however, and it might help us in problems of motivation and those of translating potential and aspiration into achievement.

[150]

★Omnibus Personality Inventory. College; 1959–63; test booklet title is *Attitude Inventory;* more than four fifths of the items are drawn from other published or unpublished tests, over two thirds of them from *Minnesota Multiphasic Personality Inventory, VC Attitude Inventory, Minnesota T-S-E Inventory,* and *California Psychological Inventory;* for research use only; 16 (Form C) or 12 (Form D) scores: thinking introversion (TI), theoretical orientation (TO), estheticism (Es), complexity (Co), autonomy (Au), developmental status (DS, Form C only), impulse expression (IE), schizoid functioning (SF), social introversion (SI), religious liberalism (RL), social maturity (SM, Form C only), masculinity-femininity (MF), repression and suppression (RS, Form C only), nonauthoritarianism (NA, Form C only, not profiled), lack of anxiety (LA, not profiled for Form C), response set (CK, Form C only, not profiled), response bias (RB, Form D only); IBM and NCS; Forms C ('59, 15 pages), D ('63, 9 pages); Form D is a short form rather than a parallel form; research manual ('62, 81 pages); mimeographed supplement ('63, 4 pages) for Form D; profile ('62, 2 pages) for Form C; separate answer sheets must be used; $3.75 per 25 tests; 20¢ per single copy; $10 per set of stencils for hand scoring IBM answer sheets for Form C; $6.50 per set of stencils for hand scoring NCS answer sheets for Form D; 2¢ per profile for Form C (Form D profiles available only from National Computer Systems); $1.50 per set of manual and supplement; postpaid; specimen set (without manual) free; IBM answer sheets must be purchased elsewhere; see 671 for NCS scoring service accessories and prices; (90–120) minutes for Form C, [50–70] minutes for Form D; OPI Research Program, Center for the Study of Higher Education. *

REFERENCES

1. HEIST, PAUL, AND WEBSTER, HAROLD. "A Research Orientation to Selection, Admission and Differential Education," pp. 21–40. In *Research on College Students: Institute Lectures Considering Recent Research on College Student's Motivation, Values and Attitudes, and Campus Cultures.* Edited by Hall T. Sprague. Boulder, Colo.: Western Interstate Commission for Higher Education, 1960. Pp. iv, 188. *

2. WARREN, JONATHAN R., AND HEIST, PAUL A. "Personality Attributes of Gifted College Students." *Sci* 132:330–7 Ag 5 '60. * (*PA* 35:2214)

3. HEIST, PAUL; MCCONNELL, T. R.; MATZLER, FRANK; AND WILLIAMS, PHOEBE. "Personality and Scholarship." *Sci* 133:362–7 F 10 '61. * (*PA* 36:2KD62H)

4. HEIST, PAUL A., AND WILLIAMS, PHOEBE A. "Variation in Achievement Within a Select and Homogeneous Student Body." *J Col Student Personnel* 3:50–9 D '61. *

5. FARWELL, ELWIN D.; WARREN, JONATHAN R.; AND MCCONNELL, T. R. "Student Personality Characteristics Associated With Groups of Colleges and Fields of Study." *Col & Univ* 37:229–41 sp '62. *

6. HOLLAND, JOHN L., AND ASTIN, ALEXANDER W. "The Prediction of the Academic, Artistic, Scientific, and Social Achievement of Undergraduates of Superior Scholastic Aptitude." *J Ed Psychol* 53:132–43 Je '62. * (*PA* 37:2010)

7. LAKIE, WILLIAM L. "Personality Characteristics of Certain Groups of Intercollegiate Athletes." *Res Q* 33:566–73 D '62. * (*PA* 38:3155)

8. CANON, HARRY JAMES. *The Counseling Relationship as a Function of Certain Personality Variables.* Doctor's thesis, University of Nebraska (Lincoln, Neb.), 1963. (*DA* 24:3414)

9. CAPRETTA, PATRICK J.; JONES, REGINALD L.; SIEGEL, LAURENCE; AND SIEGEL, LILA C. "Some Noncognitive Characteristics of Honors Program Candidates." *J Ed Psychol* 54:268–76 O '63. * (*PA* 38:4674)

10. MCCONNELL, T. R. "Approaches to the Measurement of Intellectual Disposition." *Proc Inv Conf Testing Probl* 1962: 74–88 '63. * (*PA* 38:2637)

11. SHERRY, NANCY MARIE. *Inconsistency Between Measured Interest and Choice of College Major.* Doctor's thesis, University of California (Berkeley, Calif.), 1963. (*DA* 24:2368)

PAUL M. KJELDERGAARD, *Assistant Professor of Education, Harvard University, Cambridge, Massachusetts.*

The OPI, a multiscale, true-false, self-administering personality inventory, was developed to assess the personality characteristics of normal, especially the intellectually superior, college students. Utilizing the techniques of item analysis and criterion keying, appropriate scales from previous inventories, or attitude measures, were refined, or new scales were generated from the available item pool. The original 733 items and 18 scales of the experimental versions, Forms A and B, were pared to 585 items yielding 16 scales (Form C).

The scales can perhaps be best described in terms of the factor analysis (principle components) presented in the manual. Most, though not all, scales appear, after rotation, to be relatively pure so that they may be described as measuring one of the five emergent factors. The five factors (the names presented differ somewhat from those proposed by the test authors) and the relevant scales (in parentheses) follow: (*a*) autonomy-independence (Autonomy, Developmental Status, Nonauthoritarianism, and Religious Liberalism); (*b*) adjustment-maladjustment (Impulse Expression, Lack of Anxiety, Repression and Suppression, and Response Set); (*c*) intellectualism (Complexity, Estheticism, Masculinity-Femininity, Theoretical Orientation, and Thinking Introversion); (*d*) masculinity-femininity (Masculinity-Femininity; Estheticism also has a relatively high negative loading on this factor); and (*e*) social introversion (Social Introversion).

RELIABILITY. The reliability coefficients of the various scales, Kuder-Richardson 21 estimates, vary from .71 (Complexity) to .93 (Regression-Suppression), with a medium coefficient of .84. Inasmuch as these calculations are based upon responses by more than 2,000 subjects, these reliability estimates must be viewed as extremely stable.

The stability of the scales has been measured only by comparing the scores of a small sample ($n = 33$), all females, who took the test on two occasions separated by four weeks. The correlation coefficients for the scales ranged from .68 (Autonomy) to .94 (Thinking Introversion), with a median coefficient of .83. Although other sample characteristics are not described, it is apparent that at least some of the correlations would be based upon a restricted range of scores (e.g., MF) and thus would be spuriously low. Although more evidence is needed, it would appear that most scales are sufficiently stable to permit their use where one is interested in intraindividual comparisons over time.

There are several sources of validity evidence for most of the scales. The manual is well documented with respect to each of the scales, presenting the relevant data. Although space does not permit a detailed consideration of each of the scales separately, some general comments about the types of validity evidence would be in order.

CONTENT VALIDITY. Any scale which has been adopted, more or less intact, from a previous inventory or aptitude scale must be considered to have content validity to the extent that the previous measure has been shown to measure a given trait for some other population in some other context. Such a statement must be qualified, however, insofar as virtually every adopted scale was modified in terms of item content or item format. Further, it is possible that a new context may significantly alter the item response pattern and thus change the measured behavior. Over and above these considerations, the items for the SF scale were first screened such that they were considered by psychiatrists to be descriptive of the ideation or behavior of schizophrenics and they were responded to in the appropriate direction by a high proportion of schizophrenic patients.

All the new scales were criterion keyed, i.e., items were included only if they were differentially responded to by pre-specified groups. Although it is unclear whether any attempt was made to cross validate these scales, this would be important only if no other evidence of validity were offered; this is not the case.

CONCURRENT VALIDITY. Much, though not all, of the external validity evidence is in the form of correlations with appropriate scales from other personality and attitude measures. In particular, OPI scales are correlated with appropriate scales from the *Study of Values, California Psychological Inventory, Myers-Briggs Type Indicator, Stern Activities Index,* and *Strong Vocational Interest Blank.* Since all correlations are based upon samples of 50 or more, they may be considered to have reasonable stability. The emergent correlation pattern is generally what would be predicted on the basis of the scale description, thus offering positive validity evidence.

CONSTRUCT VALIDITY. Several studies utilizing the preliminary form of the instrument have shown that certain scales, particularly Thinking Introversion, Complexity, Originality (an earlier scale), and Nonauthoritarianism would differentiate various subsets of college students in terms of their chosen major or type of institution attended. The magnitude of the differences was generally small and the relative variability large; the instrument would therefore be of little value as a selection device.

NORMS. The norms, reported in terms of raw to standard score conversions, are based upon 2,390 incoming freshmen at the University of California and San Francisco State College. A reported comparison with separate norms generated at UCLA produced only minor differences.

OPI FORM D. Recently (August 1963) a revised, shorter form of the OPI—consisting of 385 items, 10 unmodified Form C scales, and one new and one modified scale—was released. The new scale, Response Bias (28 items), was empirically keyed from a faking experiment where *S*s were told to fake their scores to make a favorable impression. As additional validity evidence, it has been shown that the test would differentiate between already selected school interns and Peace Corps applicants who presumably would be trying to make a favorable impression. It should be pointed out that the K-R reliability coefficient for this scale is rather low, .55 for the original norm group.

In addition to the new scale, the MF scale of Form C has been modified and considerably abridged. The Form D MF scale compares favorably with the earlier version in terms of its reliability and its ability to discriminate between sexes, but correlations with the earlier scale are low and indicate that this scale may be measuring somewhat different aspects of masculinity. The profile sheet for Form D includes the LA scale, which is not on the Form C profile. The scale itself, however, remains unchanged from the earlier form.

SUMMARY. Through cross validation and item analyses, certain of the OPI scales, particularly those dealing with intellectual functions, are unquestionably superior to their predecessors. The clinical scales, though constructed with equal care, appear to be more sensitive to contextual factors and thus may not be measuring the same traits as the instruments from which they were drawn. Witness, for example, the apparent changes that accompanied the truncating of the MF scale from Form C to Form D.

This instrument would be most useful in research on group differences involving relatively normal subjects. As indicated earlier, studies of group differences with various scales have uniformly indicated a degree of distribution overlap that suggests the scales would be of little value for selection or classification in most situations.

NORMAN E. WALLEN, *Associate Professor of Educational Psychology, University of Utah, Salt Lake City, Utah.*

The *Omnibus Personality Inventory* is appropriately named. It is a true-false questionnaire which has neither the alleged theoretical basis of the *Edwards Personal Preference Schedule* nor the avowedly empirical approach of the *California Psychological Inventory.* Rather, it is a collection of items scored for 13 scales plus an additional 3 which are optional. These scales have been gleaned from various sources. The major contributor was the MMPI, though scales and items have also been taken from several other sources. The stated purpose of the inventory is to pull together and refine a number of scales assessing important psychological dimensions appropriate to college students.

Norms for the scales are based on a total of 2,390 entering freshmen at the University of California and San Francisco State College. The manual states that the distribution of scores subsequently obtained at UCLA is essentially the same. No attempt appears to have been made to provide separate norms for males and females, an omission which, in the light of demonstrated sex differences on similar scales in the past, seems rather serious.

With respect to reliability, the Kuder-Richardson 21 coefficients range from .71 to .93 ($n = 2{,}390$). Test-retest reliabilities across a four-week period provide correlations of about the same magnitude; unfortunately the sample size is only 33.

In the various stages of development of this test the authors have struggled with the problem of developing reliable but independent scales. They discovered, as would be expected, that adding items increased reliability but also increased correlations among scales, a result due at least in part to scoring the same item for several scales. Subsequent shortening increased the independence of the scales at the expense of lower reliability. At present 23 per cent of the intercorrelations are .50 or larger. An attempt to construct new items scored for only one scale would seem to be in order.

One of the more unusual features of Form C of this inventory (upon which this review is based) is the great discrepancy in number of items in various scales. The Estheticism scale, for example, contains only 24 items, whereas the Social Maturity scale contains 144 items. A more recent form (D) is available which omits the DS, SM, RS, NA, and CK scales, has a shortened MF scale and a new Response Bias scale, and profiles the LA scale. The recommended testing time of two hours is presumably reduced by about one third.

The scales have been subjected to factor analysis. With unrotated factors a very impressive general factor emerges which accounts for 31 per cent of the total variance. One is tempted to describe this as a social desirability factor, except for the finding that the two scales which are intended to get at social desirability and which correlate with the Edwards social desirability measure do not load particularly high on this factor. The remaining three factors are described as inhibition, femininity, and introversion. Rotated factors are described as tolerance and autonomy, suppression and repression, scholarly orientation, masculine role, and social introversion. In total, the factor analyses suggest that the principal variables measured are a general intellectual attitude, masculinity-femininity, and social introversion. These factors account for about 75 per cent of the variance on each scale.

A point of possible criticism of the scales pertains to some of the labels used for the measures. Although most of the names utilized appear to be fairly objective descriptions of psychological variables, several are not. In particular, the scales entitled Developmental Status and Social Maturity appear to involve the value judgment that nonauthoritarianism, skepticism, and rebellion are characteristic of greater maturity or higher status.

Validity data consist primarily of correlations with other tests and with ratings and comparison of academic groups. There is fair correspondence between the scales of the OPI and the scales on other instruments bearing similar names, but with exceptions. As an example, the Estheticism scale correlates significantly with Kuder scores in literary and music areas but not artistic. One of the difficulties in evaluating validities of personality inventories is nicely illustrated in a study in which the scales are related to dichotomous judgments made by instructors of 40 graduate students where, among others, judgments were made on the trait described as "originality, self-reliance, freedom of thought." The first question we may ask is what OPI scales would be expected to correlate significantly with such a judgment. Description of the scale traits leads this reviewer to expect significant correlations with Thinking Introversion, Theoretical Orientation, Estheticism, Complexity, Autonomy, Developmental Status, Impulse Expression, Religious Liberalism, Social Maturity, and Repression and Suppression, the latter in a negative direction. Thus, based on the descriptions, one would expect significant correlations between the judgments and almost all of the scales. In fact, only the correlation with Complexity is significant.

To summarize, although the authors do not advocate the clinical use of this instrument, the reliability and validity data are about as impressive (or unimpressive) as for any existing inventories. For the purpose of describing and comparing college groups, the norms based on a defined college group are an attractive feature. Since there is little basis in construct validity for choosing among such questionnaires, workers will probably continue to choose the one containing scales whose names attract them. The OPI certainly deserves further study. Whether it will prove more valuable than other inventories for particular purposes remains to be seen.

J Counsel Psychol 10:99–100 sp '63. Laurence Siegel. * Two features of the OPI are abundantly clear. *First, it was intended and is distributed for research purposes only.* The underlying rationale is not one of aiding selection, placement or counseling procedures. This orientation made it possible to focus scale development upon variables potentially significant for hypothesis verification, and away from vocationally-linked objectives. Second, in spite of its multi-scale nature, OPI is most appropriately to be regarded as *an arsenal of research weapons each of which can be independently fired.* Some researchers may be tempted to fire them all simultaneously to "see what happens." This would be unfortunate since in salvos even poorly aimed or inappropriate weapons sometimes chance to strike the target.

[151]

★Opinion, Attitude and Interest Survey. College-bound high school seniors and entering college freshmen; 1962–64, c1955–64; also called OAIS; tests administered at any time at individual high schools (national program only) and colleges (national or institutional program); factors related to academic interest and success; 14 scores: 3 response bias scores (set for true, infrequent response, social undesirability), 6 personality scores (achiever personality, intellectual quality, creative personality, social adjustment, emotional adjustment, masculine orientation), and 5 interest scores (business, humanities, social science, physical science, biological science); 1 form; 2 editions (identical except for format): MRC-scored edition ('64, 15 pages), NCS-scored edition ('63, c1955–63, 19 pages); a third edition, previously scored by Educational Testing Service and also identical except for format, is no longer available; handbook, preliminary edition ('63, 288 pages); separate answer sheets must be used; $5 per 25 tests of either edition; $4 per handbook; $5 per specimen set of either edition; postage extra; (40–60) minutes; Benno G. Fricke; OAIS Testing Program. *

a) INSTITUTIONAL PROGRAM. College freshmen; MRC and NCS; colleges purchase test materials and pay scoring service fees; scores reported to the student's college only (with an extra copy of the report for the student); $2.50 per 50 answer sheets of either type, postage extra; scoring service fees: 50¢ per student, postage extra, for MRC (fee includes punched card report of percentile ranks and raw scores), 75¢ per student, postpaid, for NCS (fee includes punched card and profile report of percentile ranks and standard scores).

b) NATIONAL PROGRAM. High school seniors and college freshmen; MRC; test materials supplied free; scoring service fee (paid by student): $1.50 per student, postpaid; fee includes report of percentile ranks and raw scores to the student's high school and 1–3 colleges designated at time of testing; scoring by Measurement Research Center only (on 17 specified dates between October and April).

REFERENCES

1. FRICKE, BENNO G. *The Development of an Empirically Validated Personality Test Employing Configural Analysis for the Prediction of Academic Achievement.* Doctor's thesis, University of Minnesota (Minneapolis, Minn.), 1954. (*DA* 14:2118)

2. FRICKE, BENNO G. "A Configural-Content-Intensity Item for Personality Measurement." *Ed & Psychol Meas* 16:54–62 sp '56. * (*PA* 31:5787)

3. FRICKE, BENNO G. "Response Set as a Suppressor Variable in the OAIS and MMPI." *J Consult Psychol* 20:161–9 Je '56. * (*PA* 31:6080)

4. FRICKE, BENNO G. "Student Reactions to a Personality Inventory." Comments by Jane Loevinger. *Personnel & Guid J* 35:171–4 N '56. *

JOHN O. CRITES, *Associate Professor of Psychology, University of Iowa, Iowa City, Iowa.*

The *Opinion, Attitude and Interest Survey* (OAIS) represents an attempt to provide empirically derived measures of fairly comprehensive aspects of the normal personality. Designed to be used primarily with college-bound high school seniors and college freshmen, the OAIS is a multidimensional inventory which yields a total of 14 scores from true-false responses to 396 self-descriptive and general attitudinal items, examples of which are: "I prefer dark to light woodwork in a house" and "Men have a better life than women." No explicit theoretical frame of reference, such as Murray's definitions of needs which were followed by Edwards in the construction of the *Edwards Personal Preference Schedule,* was used in writing items for the OAIS. Rather, an initial pool of 700 items was formed from behavioral observations made by the test's author; statements found in the literature on response sets, academic achievement, social and emotional adjustment, and vocational-educational interests; and experience with the behavior of relatively normal adolescents. The items are well written, being brief in length and reasonably clear in meaning, but they have little or no theoretical relevance. They are "subtle" or phenotypic items which bear no apparent relationships to the variables or genotypic factors they supposedly measure. As a result, the OAIS has restricted heuristic value for the study of the normal personality through research and also limited usefulness for its appraisal and evaluation through counseling and selection activities.

The theoretical barrenness of the OAIS is accentuated by the empirical approach which was taken in constructing its various scales and scoring keys. For each of the 14 scales, criterion groups were constituted for the selection of items much as in the development of the MMPI and SVIB, the critical difference being that it is not clear theoretically why most of the groups for the OAIS were chosen. The Intellectual Quality (Int Q) scale, for example, was constructed from items which differentiated between the top and bottom 30 per cent of freshmen at Michigan and Minnesota who had taken the ACE and the OSUPT or *Cooperative Vocabulary Test.* In other words, this scale amounts to a nonintellective measure of scholastic aptitude, which, according to the validity data reported on it, predicts GPA ($r = .23$ for men, .24 for women at Michigan) less well than the tests used in its initial standardization. Why was the scale constructed in the first place, and what is its unique utility in the measurement of academic promise? Similar questions can be asked about several of the other OAIS scales. The Masculine Orientation scale is simply another in a long line of masculinity-femininity measures derived from the differential responses of males and females which correlates with few variables except sex; the Emotional Adjustment scale provides an index of general adjustment status based upon combined clinical judgments and MMPI scores but has unknown nontest behavioral correlates; and, the interest scales for the five areas of Business, Humanities, Social Science, Physical Science, and Biological Science need further study before their validity is established, since they correlate as expected with some variables but not with others.

Probably the most promising scales of the OAIS from a theoretical standpoint, and the ones for which the empirical evidence is least equivocal, are the Achiever Personality (Ach P) and Creative Personality (Cre P) scales. The Ach P key was developed by comparing the responses of students who were classified as "achievers" or "nonachievers" on the basis of discrepancies between their tested scholastic aptitude and actual academic performance (GPA). In other words, the objective was to construct a scale which would measure the factors in scholastic success not assessed by ability tests, and at least tentatively, it can be concluded that the desired goal was reached. In the Michigan sample, Ach P correlated negligibly with the ACE and Cooperative tests but moderate positively ($r = .39$ for men, .36 for women) with GPA, and it increased the multiple correlations with GPA when combined with the ability tests. The manual states that "for most groups Ach P improves predictive efficiency not only significantly (in the statistical sense) but appreciably, averaging about 17 per cent improvement in percentage of variance accounted for." The Cre P scale was constructed from the items which were answered differently by students who had been nominated as "creative" by their instructors and those who had not been nominated, with ability and achievement controlled as much as possible. Correlations of the scale with the ACE and GPA indicate that it is essentially unrelated to these variables, and other data reveal that it is related to creative behavior as rated by teachers, as recognized in awards for original pieces of writing, and as evaluated by the citation indexes of psychologists.

Other features of the OAIS scales which should be noted are the following:

a) Considerable effort was expended to purify the scales so that they would be statistically independent and would be free of response biases. The results may or may not be advantageous, however, since it may be that the purification of the scales has distorted what their interrelationships to other variables actually are. Several of the scales, for example, correlated with the Social Undesirability (Soc U) scale, which was constructed to detect the tendency to give a good impression in taking the OAIS. Revisions in these scales were made, so that their correlations with Soc U were appreciably reduced. Some behaviors, however, particularly those in making good social adjustments, necessitate creating a good impression, and if they are "purified" out of a social adjustment scale, the scale necessarily loses some of its validity. Similarly, the use of "suppressor variables" to eliminate the correlations between scales which are otherwise related may result in an artifactual representation of the relationships which actually exist among the nontest criterion variables for the scales. Only if scale purifications produce interscale correlations which are isomorphic to the intercriteria relationships are they justified, and there is no evidence in the OAIS manual that such is the case.

b) Two types of reliability data, internal consistency and stability estimates, are reported in the manual, and it is clear from the results that neither is really satisfactory. The internal consistency coefficients range from a high of .64 for Emotional Adjustment to a low of .41 for Infrequent Response, with a majority of the r's in the high 40's and low 50's, and the test-retest ($n = 69$, 2 year interval) coefficients range from a high of .76 for Masculine Orientation to a low of .46 for Social Adjustment, with most of the r's in the 50's and 60's. The author argues that the reliability of the OAIS is not an important consideration, if the inventory can be shown to be valid. He recognizes the ceiling which reliability places upon the validity of a test but ignores the effects of the relatively inadequate reliability of the OAIS upon its validity. Unless it can be shown that the low test-retest reliabilities of the OAIS scales are attributable to developmental changes in the variables which it supposedly measures, and which can be accounted for by introducing an age factor into the regression equations for the inventory, it is doubtful that the scales will have much predictive efficiency. Also, unless the internal consistency of the scales can be increased to an acceptable level, the OAIS will be like an unwieldly shotgun which hits all around a target but seldom on it. To illustrate, consider the best of the OAIS scales, Ach P, which has an internal consistency of .45 and a validity of .39 for GPA: its standard error of measurement is 4.88, its standard error of estimate is 6.07, and its coefficient of alienation is .917, the latter indicating only an 8 per cent improvement in prediction over chance.

c) Most of the data on the OAIS are reported in its lengthy, and frequently discursive, manual which should be carefully and critically read by any user of the inventory. The manual is replete with tables of findings on the OAIS, which are interpreted in the accompanying text, but not one statistical test is reported or significance level cited which allows the reader to evaluate the validity and reliability results according to accepted standards. Rationalizations of contradictory findings can be found throughout the manual, as can unsubstantiated criticisms of other tests in the same area of measurement, in particular the SVIB. Inaccurate interpretations of psychometric concepts are presented, such as the confusion of construct with predictive validity, and the literature on interest and personality measurement is used selectively to support the test author's arguments, the logic of which is often untenable as in his discussions of the unimportance of reliability and the assumed inadequacy of the SVIB. At best the manual can be considered to be a vehicle for the presentation of the test author's biases and opinions; at worst it must be judged as a frequently erroneous and misleading treatment of the data on the OAIS.

Despite the many years of research which have gone into the construction and development of the OAIS, it must be concluded that, with the possible exceptions of the Ach P and Cre P scales, the inventory does not fulfill the claims which are made for it, and it is not ready for use in either vocational-educational counseling or academic selection. It has scant theoretical significance; it has only minimal reliability; and it measures neither variables nor constructs with acceptable validity.

Harold Webster, *Associate Research Psychologist, Center for the Study of Higher Education, University of California, Berkeley, California.*

The OAIS handbook contains both the author's philosophy of measurement and some results of a research project of rather heroic proportions. The attitude toward mental measurement is pragmatic and empirical. The presentation in Chapter 2 is oriented toward answering some objections to personality tests. The empirical data, although extensive, are not adequate for answering still other questions often raised by other investigators about the usefulness of tests such as the OAIS. Some case material is presented, but the report lacks a general theory of student functioning that might be supported by these data. Although this last criticism applies to many a published mental test, it seems especially serious when the test focuses upon immediate empirical objectives such as the prediction of school grades or adjustment ratings.

The presentation of the means and standard deviations of untransformed raw scores is inadequate. The manual contains some means and standard deviations for a few small or atypical samples (e.g., pp. 114, 178, 210). The best sample for norms seems to be the one referred to in Table 11, where the means and standard deviations are intended for comparison with random response data. In this sample of 1,101 freshmen the K-R 21 reliabilities are .54 for Achiever Personality, .54 for Intellectual Quality and .51 for Creative Personality. Although the author thinks reliability is not important, these results show that a random replication of a testing session would very likely reorder the persons quite differently on any scale, that is, with too little precision to warrant use of the scales at the individual level. The attributes measured may indeed be significant, but the measurement is not precise, and the comparison of any two persons on a given scale is therefore hazardous unless their scores happen to be widely separated.

Having dismissed reliability except as it accrues directly from validity, the author presents a large number of validity coefficients. These must of course be interpreted according to the aims of the test development, and with the idea that each coefficient would be inflated by some amount if it could actually be corrected for attenuation.

Apparently the author has isolated some variance shared with freshman grades that is not accounted for by conventional predictors; the uncorrected validity coefficients of .39 for men and .36 for women for the Ach P scale may seem more impressive when we find that this scale has also been adjusted in order to reduce its correlations with several other scales, including response bias scales. Similarly, the second scale, Intellectual Quality, "predicts scores on ability tests about as well as the ability tests predict each other." The latter correlations include .24 with ACE quantitative aptitude, .55 with ACE linguistic aptitude, .48 with English achievement, and .26 with mathematics achievement. With the exception of the masculinity-femininity scale, the Int Q scale appears to have the most satisfactory validity. The strongest correlation for the third scale, Creative Personality, is .31, the correlation for 124 students with their instructors' creativity ratings. The other scales, including two that measure social and emotional adjustment, also have low validity coefficients.

There seems to be a tendency among psychologists generally to assume that correlations around .70 or .80 are unconscionably large, although for many purposes a correlation of .90 is clearly not large enough (for example, in comparing linear composites). For example, the author of this test notes that "three ability tests correlate very highly with each other, about .67." This reviewer would insist that .67 is not a *very* high correlation, even when encountered in the field of mental testing. The author does not hesitate to interpret correlations in the range ±.30 with considerable confidence. It is true that many influences can be envisioned (including unreliability) that might have reduced a validity coefficient from .85 to .35. One problem of mental testing is, however, to mitigate such influences so that scores become more useful and interpretable. It may happen that the validity coefficients near .35 reported in the OAIS handbook will fluctuate somewhat in new samples of students attending other institutions, which is a central problem for future research.

The author presents several factor analyses of OAIS scores, together with other variables. His fear of redundancy does not lie at the factor level, however, but at the scale level; the effort to avoid "contaminating" scales with items that might also measure something else has resulted in weaker scales than might otherwise have been obtained. The OAIS seems to be another test where the desire to measure many subtleties well was not initially supported by enough appropriate experimental items, with the result that some failure of scale independence would normally be expected, due to item overlap, if individual scales were built up to full strength.

Perhaps the most serious criticism is that the scale scoring is not available in the manual. This makes it impossible to study scale content in order to formulate hypotheses about why the scales work as well as they do. At this stage in our understanding of college students, some knowledge of their attitudes, as expressed at the item level, could be valuable.

In brief, the OAIS represents a good beginning in the study of the expressed attitudes of college students, but will require considerably more work before it does more than contribute a small increment of predictability to a few criteria that are presently not well understood.

[152]

★**Organic Integrity Test.** Mental patients; 1960; brain damage or dysfunction shown as chromaphilia (loss of form-perception with increased color-perception); individual; 1 form (15 cards); manual (reprint of *1* below); directions for administering (2 pages); diagnostic chart (1 page); $21.50 per set of cards and directions for administering, postpaid; [4–5] minutes; H. C. Tien; the Author. *

REFERENCES

1. TIEN, H. C. "Organic Integrity Test (O.I.T.): A Quick Diagnostic Aid to Rule in Organic Brain Diseases." *Arch Gen Psychiatry* 3:43–52 Jl '60. *

[153]

★**The Orientation Inventory.** College and industry; 1962; kinds of satisfactions and rewards sought in jobs; 3 scores: self-orientation, interaction-orientation, task-orientation; 1 form (4 pages); mimeographed manual, research edition (21 pages); preliminary norms; $3 per 25 tests; $1 per set of manual and key; $1 per specimen set; postage extra; (20–25) minutes; Bernard M. Bass; Consulting Psychologists Press, Inc. *

REFERENCES

1. BASS, BERNARD M.; DUNTEMAN, GEORGE; FRYE, ROLAND; VIDULICH, ROBERT; AND WAMBACH, HELEN. "Self, Interaction, and Task Orientation Inventory Scores Associated With Overt Behavior and Personal Factors." *Ed & Psychol Meas* 23:101–16 sp '63. * (*PA* 38:2706)

2. DUNTEMAN, GEORGE, AND BASS, BERNARD M. "Supervisory and Engineering Success Associated With Self, Interaction, and Task Orientation Scores." *Personnel Psychol* 16:13–21 sp '63. * (*PA* 38:3318)

RICHARD S. BARRETT, *Associate Professor of Management Engineering and Psychology, New York University, New York, New York.*

The *Orientation Inventory* is conceived by the author as a broadly useful instrument which may contribute to such diverse objectives as counseling of students, predicting success on work requiring persistence, and studying self-actualization, social interrelationships, and marital compatibility. It consists of 27 statements of opinions and attitudes. For each statement the subject indicates which of three alternatives is most true or most preferred or most important, and also which alternative is least true or preferred. The set of alternatives for each item contains one alternative of each of the three orientations tapped by the inventory, self-, interaction-, and task-orientation, defined in the manual as follows:

self-orientation: reflects the extent a person describes himself as expecting direct rewards to himself regardless of the job he is doing or the effects of what he does upon others working with him * A person with a high score in self-orientation is more likely to be rejected by others, to be introspective, to be dominating and to be unresponsive to the needs of the others around him. He is concerned mainly with himself, not co-workers' needs or the job to be done.

interaction-orientation: reflects the extent of concern with maintaining happy, harmonious relationships in a superficial sort of way, often making it difficult to contribute to the task at hand or to be of real help to others. Interest in group activities is high, but not ordinarily conducive to the progress of the group in completing tasks.

task-orientation: reflects the extent to which a person is concerned about completing a job, solving problems, working persistently and doing the best job possible. In groups, despite his concern with the task, the task-oriented member tends to work hard within the group to make it productive as possible. If he is interested in what the group is doing, he will fight hard for what he regards as right.

Compared with what would be expected of a commercial test manual, the manual (a research edition) contains more research results, and less normative data (although preliminary norms on 908 college students are presented). Test-retest reliability ranges between .73 and .76 for the three scales. Concurrent validity studies among supervisors show the more successful people to be task-oriented, and the less successful to be self-oriented. The inventory has shown differences between groups based on their training, line of work, and status. The differences, even where significant, are generally small.

The basic lack in the manual is a clear statement of the degree of overlap among the scales. Using the standard that to be classified in one of the orientations a subject's score had to be in the top 25 per cent on that orientation and in the bottom 50 per cent on each of the others, 84 college students were classified into the three orientations, or if they failed to meet these standards, they were placed in a residual category. On reclassification a week later, from 66.6 to 70.6 per cent of those originally classified in one of the three orientations were classified again into the same category. There were many shifts into and out of the residual category. Unfortunately, the data are not clear because they are presented in percentages. When the probable frequencies are reconstructed from the percentages, the residual category is seen to be the largest.

One study reported in the manual seems to confirm the suspicion that the scales are not independent. An unspecified number of salaried management personnel of a large oil refinery participating in a discussion group rated every other participant after a total of 10 two-hour meetings. They used 27 (or 28, the manual is inconsistent) items of behavior to indicate how much the person rated exhibited each of the behaviors. The manual reports the highest correlations between the scale scores of the Ori (as the authors abbreviate it) and the ratings, presumably using .20 in absolute value as the cutoff score. The seven correlations between the behavior ratings and the Self-Orientation scores are independent of the other two, but the Interaction- and Task-Orientations show a pattern which suggests that they are not independent.

Sixteen correlations involving Interaction-Orientation, and 20 involving Task-Orientation are listed; of these, 15 appear in both lists, always with a reversal of signs. The average difference between the 15 pairs of correlations is .91, indicating that the patterns of correlation of the two scales are virtually mirror images of each other. It follows that there must be a high and negative correlation between interaction- and task-orientation as measured by the Ori. The manual would be more useful if data on intercorrelations among the Ori scales were made available.

The Ori is presented primarily as a research instrument with potential in any field where a person's orientation toward himself, his coworkers, or his work is important. Like most self-reports, its usefulness as a selection instrument is limited by its fakability. The usual kind of research on this problem, in which college students are asked first to be honest and then to "fake good" showed that they could manipulate their scores toward Task- and Interaction-Orientation and consequently away from Self-Orientation. Although its usefulness in selection may be limited for this reason, the Ori has promise, some of which has already been fulfilled, as a means of deepening our understanding of how people work. However, it appears that the Ori does not measure three independent orientations as the manual implies, but only two, a self-orientation and a bipolar task-interaction orientation.

H. Bradley Sagen, *Assistant Professor of Education, University of Iowa, Iowa City, Iowa.*

The *Orientation Inventory* (Ori) is a brief forced-choice instrument designed to assess the kinds of rewards and satisfactions sought from interpersonal situations, particularly those situations organized around the solution of problems or the completion of tasks. Possible uses suggested by the author include research in social interrelationships, vocational and educational counseling, and selection in business and industry.

The author's description of the scale format and development raises at least three important issues. (*a*) Although the content of the scales seems generally consistent with the underlying dimensions outlined in the manual, the lack of information about scale development and internal consistency somewhat precludes a clear interpretation of what the Ori is actually measuring. (*b*) There is no evidence that the alternative responses in each triad were equated for social desirability. (*c*) The manual neglects to point out that the three scales are ipsative; i.e., a person's score on one scale is dependent upon his scores on the other scales. Among their other properties, ipsative scales impose negative correlations among the scores and force all subjects' profiles to the same mean. These properties do not necessarily detract from the utility of the Ori, but their relationship to the specific assessment problem should be determined before seriously considering the inventory.

As the author quite rightly notes, test-retest reliabilities of .73, .76, and .75 for the three scales respectively (college students over a one-week period) are somewhat inadequate for purposes of individual diagnosis.

The validity data can best be described as inconclusive. Several of the studies, particularly the correlations with peer ratings and some imaginative demonstrations of the relationship of Ori scores to behavior in prestructured situations, yield results which are consistent with the scale descriptions. On the other hand, the correlations with ratings of experts and with other personality instruments (unfortunately based upon an earlier version of the Ori), are usually barely significant or are nonsignificant. For example, 36 of the 40 "significant" correlations with other instruments are less than .30 and the other 4 are less than .35.

The primary defect in the validity data, however, is that many of the studies are either so lacking in quality or are reported in such haphazard fashion that little can be gained from examining them. A number of the studies reported are based upon small and ill-defined samples. For example, tentative conclusions regarding the effects of maturity are drawn from an analysis of cross-sectional samples consisting of as few as 25 subjects. In other studies the criterion is vague, e.g., "best" versus "less than best" supervisors. In a few cases, the level of significance is not specified and in still others inferences are drawn from nonsignificant results. Finally, a description of the variances is lacking in many of the comparisons so that although the differences may be significant, it is impossible to calculate the amount of overlap between the groups.

An additional point related to validity is that resistance to faking is highly important if the Ori is to be utilized for selection. However, when the mean score changes of college students asked to "fake good" were compared with the mean differences between high and low rated groups in the two studies of job performance, the changes due to faking were greater in all but one comparison.

At present, the greatest potential for the Ori would seem to be as a research instrument. Concepts such as "task orientation," "achievement orientation," etc., abound in the psychological and sociological literature, but little has been accomplished by way of scaling these dimensions. Although the evidence for the Ori is inconclusive, the importance of the dimensions to behavioral research would perhaps justify the time and effort involved in additional validity studies by interested investigators. If such studies are undertaken, the reviewer would suggest the possibility of utilizing the scales normatively as well as in the present ipsative arrangement.

The conclusions are equally uncertain regarding the utility of the Ori for purposes of selection in business and industry. Given adequate validation procedures with respect to specific criteria, and a favorable selection ratio, many of the present criticisms would be reduced in importance. On the other hand, lack of adequate evidence of resistance to faking makes the Ori somewhat suspect as a selection device and in the absence of such evidence this reviewer does not recommend its use where faking is likely to be a possibility.

In view of the somewhat low reliability coefficients and the scarcity of adequate validity data, the Ori is definitely not recommended for individual assessment.

[154]

Personal Adjustment Inventory. Ages 9–13; 1931–61; formerly called *Test of Personality Adjustment;* title on test booklet is *P.A. Inventory;* 5 scores: personal inferiority, social maladjustment, family maladjustment, daydreaming, total; separate forms ('61, 8 pages, identical with tests copyrighted in 1931 except for four wording changes) for boys and girls; manual ('61, 17 pages, identical with 1931 manual except for introduction and minor revisions); $2.50 per 25 tests; 75¢ per specimen set; postage extra; (40–50) minutes; Carl R. Rogers; Association Press. *

REFERENCES

1–19. See 5:117.
20. Burchinal, Lee G. "Parents' Attitudes and Adjustment of Children." *J Genetic Psychol* 92:69–79 Mr '58. * (*PA* 36:1FG69B)
21. Dorfman, Elaine. "Personality Outcomes of Client-

Centered Child Therapy." *Psychol Monogr* 72(3):1–22 '58. * (*PA* 33:8602)
22. OXFORD, LAKE C. *A Study of Personal and Social Adjustment of Seventh Grade Boys and Girls as Influenced by Physical Size, Athletic Ability, Acceptance by Peers, and Acceptance of Peers.* Doctor's thesis, University of Maryland (College Park, Md.), 1958. (*DA* 20:3634)
23. CLEMENTS, SAM D. *The Predictive Utility of Three Delinquency Proneness Measures.* Doctor's thesis, University of Houston (Houston, Tex.), 1960. (*DA* 20:3827)
24. L'ABATE, LUCIANO. "The Effect of Paternal Failure to Participate During the Referral of Child Psychiatric Patients." *J Clin Psychol* 16:407–8 O '60. * (*PA* 37:3259)
25. L'ABATE, LUCIANO. "Personality Correlates of Manifest Anxiety in Children." *J Consult Psychol* 24:342–8 Ag '60. * (*PA* 35:1997)

NORMAN D. SUNDBERG, *Professor of Psychology, University of Oregon, Eugene, Oregon.*

If psychologists and educators have a need to assess the personalities of children, as they undoubtedly do, it is most unfortunate that they do not show the interest and persistence needed for the careful research and development of assessment devices. Carl Rogers' inventory is a curious and sad example of how some seminal ideas frozen into a published test have failed to receive the nurturance needed for growth. First published in 1931, under the title *Test of Personality Adjustment,* the same inadequate norms, scoring methods, and validity and reliability data are still being promulgated in the test and manual only slightly revised and reissued in 1961. What a rueful commentary on the influence of earlier *Mental Measurements Yearbook* reviews!

Undoubtedly there is a need for such an instrument as this. The publishers are still selling copies, but they seem unwilling to take on the responsibilities a real revision would demand. The author's interests have swung away from clinical work with children to adult psychotherapy and personality theory. The work of at least collecting simple normative and reliability data would not have been extremely onerous. How one wishes that Rogers or one of his students could have found the time and interest to apply Rogers' great theoretical insights and clinical wisdom to this important task.

Unfortunately the 1961 manual does not even make use of what research has already been done on the inventory, and somehow no one took the trouble to append a bibliography to the manual. Anyone who uses the test should be directed at least to two pieces of research. One study by Burchinal, Gardner and Hawkes (*18*) suggests a revision of the norms for the four subtests (Personal Inferiority, Social Maladjustment, Family Maladjustment, and Daydreaming) on the basis of results with 256 normal fifth graders in rural areas of the Midwest. Rather surprisingly, the investigators found no need to revise the classifications based on the total score—surprising since the original norms came many years earlier from a mixture of 136 normal and problem children in New York City.

The second major reference is Louis Smith's excellent monograph (*19*) on the concurrent validity of six personality tests for children. The six include Rogers' *Personal Adjustment Inventory, California Test of Personality, Rosenzweig Picture-Frustration Study* and three unpublished tests. Using approximately 245 sixth grade boys separated into poorly adjusted, average adjusted, and well adjusted on the basis of a dual criterion of teacher's and peer's nominations, Smith demonstrated significant validity for differentiating the means of these groups using any of the three published children's tests. These leading group tests showed low degrees of correlation with each other. Interestingly, the subtests of the Rogers' inventory showed very low intercorrelations, suggesting that they are really measuring different aspects of personality. At the present stage, Smith wisely warns that the overlap of the distributions of the three adjustment groups was large and that none of the tests would be good for screening of groups when base rates of maladjustment are low.

Summarizing the psychometric characteristics, one can politely say they leave much to be desired. Norms are for small, unusual samples. They do not cover developmental differences within the 9 to 13 age group for which the test is intended. Reliability figures are scanty. Rogers reports one-month retest correlations for subtests ranging from .65 to .72 and for the total, .72. Though these are not far from reliability figures of most personality inventories, there is obvious need for studies with other subjects and different periods of time and for studies of internal consistency and subtest characteristics. An equivalent form would be helpful. Validity figures are far too limited to generate much confidence, although the few reported suggest some promise. The manual in an inadequately reported study states subtest scores' correlations with clinicians' ratings range from .38 for Family Maladjustment to .48 for Daydreaming. These results point to much caution with individual cases and need for further corroboration of findings.

Many questions arise, such as relation to intelligence, influence of test taking attitudes, and effects of psychotherapy. Certainly the cumbersome scoring could be improved. An examination of the scoring on items reveals two interesting facets: (*a*) sophisticated patterning concepts, e.g., if the child has siblings and answers this way, then give him so many points; and (*b*) hypotheses about the nature of maladjustment that are suggestive of further research. The inventory is not satisfactory as a psychometric instrument now, but as a potential stimulator of research and as a model for incorporating clinical hypotheses, it is worthy of attention by psychologists.

Evaluating the Rogers inventory from a clinical, as distinguished from a psychometric, standpoint, one finds some appealing features. As Louttit and Gough have noted in previous *Yearbook* reviews, the items are clinically insightful, appropriate, and naturally interesting to children—items asking the child his wishes, interests, comparisons with other children, feelings about his family. The items have some variety, including open-ended ways of answering—such as naming the three people the child would take to a desert island with him. The inventory could readily be used as a structured supplement to an interview with a child. The modern clinician would also want to provide himself with other summarizing language more related to personality theory and to clinical decisions than the terms the four subtests suggest. The manual, unlike too many test manuals, pays attention to the needs of the clinician using the test for individual assessment; four well done case illustrations are presented. It is the clinical use of the inventory which Rogers emphasizes, saying, "the numerical scores, taken by themselves, are not highly accurate, and might be misleading in the case of an individual child." He urges the user to examine individual responses to get at the inner world of the child.

As Rogers' inventory stands, psychologists cannot put much confidence in it as a psychometric device. It can profitably be employed (*a*) for research purposes and (*b*) as part of a clinical exploration of adjustment supplemented by other approaches. It is to be hoped that future reviewers will find this inventory supplanted by forms much more carefully cultivated.

Robert D. Wirt, *Professor of Psychology, Child Development, and Psychiatry, University of Minnesota, Minneapolis, Minnesota.*

History, it has been said, is a great teacher. There is much to learn from a study of this instrument and its manual. There was a time when psychologists and educators were willing to place considerable confidence in the generality of conclusions based upon the careful study of a single case or a few cases. Nowadays we tend to disparage such research and insist upon large sample statistics and experimental control or matching of many variables. The writing in this instrument represents some of the best available published documentation of sophisticated, sensitive, and clinically useful methods of examiner behavior and interpretation of subject response; it also represents some of the most flagrant disregard for scientific rigor and contemporary test construction methodology in print.

The test was first published in 1931 under the title *Test of Personality Adjustment.* It was reissued, but *not* revised under the new title in 1961. Both Adler and Gough emphasized the need for revision of the test in their reviews in *The Fifth Yearbook.* The failure to meet the need for revision is unsatisfactorily explained in an introduction to the 1961 edition: "The author regrets that no empirical re-study of the instrument has been made. His own interests have moved into other areas and no one else has taken on the task." It would seem to this reviewer that if the publishers could not find someone else to take on the task, the instrument should have been withdrawn, as Adler recommended (5:117), rather than reissued quite unchanged except for a new title. The publisher does not explain the reason for altering the title. It may, of course, mislead some test users into supposing that the well-known author has standardized a new test. In view of Rogers' widely quoted viewpoint regarding the inadvisability of engaging in diagnostic assessment in clinical practice, that would be a remarkable event indeed.

There is much practical material in both the manual and the separate inventories for girls and for boys. The items range over a number of important areas of a child's attitudes toward himself, his family, and his peers. They are worded in clear language and are sensitively geared to the developmental level for which they are designed. The manual is well written where it deals with instructions for giving the test and with interpretation of results. If the instrument were issued as a guide for interviewing children, it could be highly recommended. It is not a useful *test,* however, despite the claim to that status given in the series title, "Series of Character and Personality Tests."

The instrument was developed on a very small sample: 52 "problem" children and 84 "normal" children. Although the author says "no apology is offered for these small numbers," this reviewer wonders why the publishers failed to take Gough's advice (5:117) to use the very extensive data which must in the past 30 years have been collected in child guidance clinics throughout the country. The reliability and validity of the instrument are both unsatisfactory and even the author cautions against using test scores in making predictions. The scoring system is needlessly complicated.

In summary, it may be said that the *Personal Adjustment Inventory* contains material which still has clinical utility and certainly has historical interest and which may be useful as an interview guide with young children. It is not properly a test and it should not be scored and used as a test. It is a great disappointment that in reissuing this instrument neither the author nor the publisher has taken any advantage of the advances in test construction which have occurred in the past thirty years or of the substantial data which would have been readily available.

For reviews by Dan L. Adler and Harrison G. Gough, see 5:117; for a review by C. M. Louttit, see 40:1258.

[155]

★Personal Qualities Inventory. Business and industry; 1956–63; 1 form ('56, 3 pages); manual ['63, 6 unnumbered pages]; directions for administering and scoring (no date, 2 pages); norms for males only; $3 per 25 tests; 10¢ per key; 75¢ per manual; postage extra; $1 per specimen set, postpaid; (15–20) minutes; Richardson, Bellows, Henry & Co., Inc. *

REFERENCES

1. KIRKPATRICK, JAMES J. "Validation of a Test Battery for the Selection and Placement of Engineers." *Personnel Psychol* 9:211–27 su '56. * (*PA* 31:8964)

[156]

***Personality and Interest Inventory: Elementary Form, Revised.** Grades 4–8; 1935–59; 1 form ('59, 2 pages); directions ('36, 1 page); no data on reliability; no norms; $1.50 per 35 tests; 50¢ per specimen set; postpaid; (30–35) minutes; Gertrude Hildreth; Bureau of Publications. *

REFERENCES

1–3. See 40:1238.

For a review by Stephen M. Corey, see 40:1238; for a review by Jack W. Dunlap, see 38:924.

[157]

The Personality Inventory. Grades 9–16 and adults; 1931–38; 6 scores: neurotic tendency, self-sufficiency, introversion-extroversion, dominance-submission, confidence, sociability; IBM; 1 form ('35, 4 pages); manual ('35, 7 pages); profile (no date, 1 page); tentative norms ('38, 2 pages); $3.25 per 25 tests; $1.25 per 50 profiles; 25¢ per manual; separate answer sheets may be used; $2.20 per 50 IBM answer sheets; $1.50 per 50 Hankes answer sheets (scored by Testscor only, see 667); $1 per set of hand scoring stencils; $5 per set of IBM scoring stencils; 50¢ per specimen set; postage extra; (25) minutes; Robert G. Bernreuter; [Consulting Psychologists Press, Inc.]. *

REFERENCES

1–71. See 40:1239.
72–259. See 4:77.
260–299. See 5:95.
300. FOX, VERNON. "The Influence of Personality on Social Non-Conformity." *J Crim Law & Criminol* 42:746–54 Mr–Ap '52. * (*PA* 28:6298)
301. SCHOLL, GERALDINE. "Some Notes on the Use of Two Personality Tests With Visually Handicapped Students." *New Outlook Blind* 47:287–95 D '53. *
302. GREENBERG, HERBERT M.; ALLISON, LOUISE; FEWELL, MILDRED; AND RICH, CHARLES. "The Personality of Junior High and High School Students Attending a Residential School for the Blind." *J Ed Psychol* 48:406–10 N '57. * (*PA* 33:817)
303. KNOWLES, REX HANNA. *Differential Characteristics of Successful and Unsuccessful Seminary Students.* Doctor's thesis, University of Nebraska (Lincoln, Neb.), 1958. (*DA* 19:1655)
304. TAFT, RONALD. "Is the Tolerant Personality Type the Opposite of the Intolerants?" *J Social Psychol* 47:397–405 My '58. * (*PA* 33:8186)
305. BALL, LEE. *Personality Traits of Varsity Gymnasts as Measured by the Bernreuter Personality Invoice.* Master's thesis, Mankato State College (Mankato, Minn.), 1959.
306. GUILFORD, J. P. *Personality,* pp. 173–5. New York: McGraw-Hill Book Co., Inc., 1959. Pp. xiii, 562. *
307. BOYKIN, LEANDER L. "The Adjustment of 729 Negro College Students as Revealed by the Bernreuter Personality Inventory." *Negro Ed R* 11:43–7 Ja '60. *
308. GAYEN, A. K.; SAHA, R. P.; AND MATHUR, R. K. "Factors in the Study of Personality: Part 2, A Scoring Key for a Short Personality Test." *Indian J Psychol* 35:1–8 pt 1 '60. * (*PA* 36:4HF01G)
309. HARRELL, THOMAS W. "The Relation of Test Scores to Sales Criteria." *Personnel Psychol* 13:65–9 sp '60. * (*PA* 35:7192)
310. MACKINNEY, ARTHUR C., AND WOLINS, LEROY. "Validity Information Exchange, No. 13-01, Foreman II, Home Appliance Manufacturing." *Personnel Psychol* 13:443–7 w '60. *
311. SAHA, GOPI BALLAV. "An Investigation Into the School Maturity of High School Students." *Indian J Psychol* 35:47–54 pt 2 '60. * (*PA* 36:4KD47S)
312. BURGART, HERBERT J. "Art in Higher Education: The Relationship of Art Experience to Personality, General Creativity, and Aesthetic Performance." *Studies Art Ed* 2:14–35 sp '61. *
313. COOLEY, JOHN C. "A Study of the Relation Between Certain Mental and Personality Traits and Ratings of Musical Abilities." *J Res Music Ed* 9:108–17 f '61. *
314. INGENOHL, INGO. "The Significance of the No-Count on the Bernreuter Personality Inventory." *J Social Psychol* 54:127–40 Je '61. * (*PA* 36:2HF27I)
315. MIDDLETON, RUSSELL, AND PUTNEY, SNELL. "A Note on the Validity of the Bernreuter Personality Inventory Measure of Dominance-Submission." *J Social Psychol* 53:325–30 Ap '61. * (*PA* 36:1HF25M)
316. ROBBINS, JAMES E., AND KING, DONALD C. "Validity Information Exchange, No. 14-02: D.O.T. Code 0-97.61, Manager, Sales." *Personnel Psychol* 14:217–9 su '61. *
317. CASH, W. L., JR. "Relationship of Personality Traits and Scholastic Aptitude to Academic Achievement in Theological Studies." *J Psychol Studies* 13:105–10 Je '62 [issued F '64]. *
318. LAUDANO, FRANK S. *A Comparative Study of Various Personality Traits of Teachers and Non-Teachers as Measured by the Bernreuter Personality Inventory.* Master's thesis, Southern Connecticut State College (New Haven, Conn.), 1962.

319. SHAW, MARVIN E. "The Effectiveness of Whyte's Rules: 'How to Cheat on Personality Tests.'" *J Appl Psychol* 46:21-5 F '62. * (*PA* 36:5HF21S)
320. DE SENA, PAUL AMBROSE. *Identification of Non-Intellectual Characteristics of Consistent Over-, Under-, and Normal-Achievers Enrolled in Science Curriculums at the Pennsylvania State University.* Doctor's thesis, Pennsylvania State University (University Park, Pa.), 1963. (*DA* 24:3144)
321. HERBERT, N., AND TURNBULL, G. H. "Personality Factors and Effective Progress in Teaching." *Ed R* 16:24-31 N '63. *

WESLEY C. BECKER, *Professor of Psychology, University of Illinois, Urbana, Illinois.*

Since this test was last reviewed in *The Fourth Yearbook* there have been no changes in its structure, format, manual, or in the implications of the research evidence. Previous reviewers have been quite skeptical about the value of the *Personality Inventory*. The best that Mosier could say for it was that it offered a checklist of symptoms which might be useful in the hands of a trained clinical psychologist. Mosier also suggested that it might be a useful device for screening some kinds of emotional problems, especially the confidence scale (emotional stability), but that "good" scores on the confidence scale did not necessarily imply good adjustment. Newcomb was willing in 1940 to wait and see if Flanagan's two independent factors might not yet correlate with significant human behaviors, but otherwise could find nothing in the 71 studies completed at that time which would lead him to recommend its use. In her 1953 review, Tyler had available more than 250 research papers on this test. She indicated that it was used fairly successfully as a screening technique in the armed forces programs, probably because men in service were more willing to admit their maladjustments in order to avoid unpleasant duties. Tyler also noted that the Bernreuter has had some success in showing group differences between salesmen and nonsalesmen, campus leaders and nonleaders, etc., but that in no case were validity indicators strong enough to support decisions in individual cases. But most important in Tyler's review was the conclusion that the Bernreuter is of doubtful value in selection programs, since it is quite easy to fake desirable scores. This conclusion obviously covers most industrial applications of the Bernreuter. The research conducted since Tyler's review serves only to reinforce this conclusion. The test is easily faked to give an emotionally stable, somewhat outgoing profile (*282, 319*), and while successful and unsuccessful employees of various sorts are occasionally differentiated (*280, 283*), the differences are so small as to preclude their usefulness in making decisions about individuals.

In view of all this, it is indeed surprising to find the following statement in the publisher's catalog: "One of the most famous of all personality inventories, the test of Dr. Bernreuter is very widely used, particularly in business and industry." We have no reason to question the veracity of this statement. Whyte[1] indicates that in 1953, Stanford University Press sold over 1,000,000 copies of the test. Our surprise arises from the apparent failure of research evidence to have an impact on test usage. Whyte's somewhat high-handed critique of psychological testing in industry and the Bernreuter in particular, is not entirely undeserved.

The Bernreuter can also be criticised on other grounds besides its failure to do any job well enough to justify its existence. The publishers and author have made no attempt to improve the test throughout the 32 years of its existence. Its cumbersome scoring system remains, its six scores are still retained when two would do, and its current manual contains no information which was not available in 1935, although over 300 studies have been undertaken using the test. The consumer seeking a personality inventory would be well advised to look elsewhere.

DONALD J. VELDMAN, *Associate Professor of Educational Psychology, University of Texas, Austin, Texas.*

The first sentence of the manual for this instrument indicates the extent to which it is representative of another era in test construction: "*The Personality Inventory* represents a new departure in the measurement of personality in that it measures several different aspects at one time." Considering that the normative data provided with the manual are dated 1938 and that the most recent attempt at scale revision included in the manual is a 1935 factor analysis of the original four scales, this inventory might be expected to be no more now than a landmark in the development of personality assessment techniques. Consulting Psychologists Press, however, claims that it is "very widely used, particularly in business and industry," and even as recently as 1953 a million copies of the test were reported sold. It is

1 WHYTE, WILLIAM H., JR. *The Organization Man*, p. 209. New York: Doubleday & Co., Inc., 1956. Pp. vi, 471. *

difficult to imagine why, when so many more carefully constructed, more adequately standardized, and more thoroughly validated personality inventories are currently available.

SCALE CONSTRUCTION. To determine item weights for the instrument's first four scales (neurotic tendency, self-sufficiency, introversion-extroversion, and dominance-submission), four tests were used to isolate high and low scoring subjects: (*a*) Thurstone's *Personality Schedule,* (*b*) Bernreuter's Self-Sufficiency Test, (*c*) Laird's C2 Introversion Test, and (*d*) the Allports' *A-S Reaction Study.* The latter also served as the source for the items of the dominance scale. The last two scales (confidence, sociability) are the result of a factor analysis of the original four scales. Intercorrelations of the first four scales are reported in the manual, but the fact that all items are weighted for all of the scales makes the interpretation of this table, and hence the factor analysis results, rather difficult. Nevertheless, the .95 correlation between the first and third scales, and the −.80 correlation between scales one and four strongly suggest that little more than a single construct is actually being measured. The fact that 78 per cent of the total extracted variance of the original scales is accounted for by the first factor confirms this conclusion. To what extent these variables might be "untied" through separation of item sets remains an unanswered question. Although attempts have been made to factor items from the instrument (*273*), and various authors have advocated simplified weighting systems (*51, 175*), no extensive attempts to reorganize the scoring of the item pool have appeared in the last ten years. In view of the wealth of multitrait personality inventories now available, such as Cattell's *Sixteen Personality Factor Questionnaire,* there would indeed seem to be little justification for such an investment of research resources.

RELIABILITY. Split-half coefficients ranging from .85 to .92 based on samples of college students are reported in the manual, and coefficients of .86 and .78 obtained from a sample of high school boys are given for the two factor scales. Reports of test-retest reliability, not included in the manual, have been considerably lower, between .52 and .69 (*201*).

NORMATIVE DATA. Percentile equivalents dated 1938 are provided for high school boys and girls, college men and women, and adult men and women. The extent to which cultural changes have made these norms inappropriate is unknown. From another point of view, Hoffman and Abbizu-Miranda (*292*), after demonstrating higher neurotic tendency scale scores for lower class subjects, claimed to find "middle-class bias" in the third of the items which accounted for the differences between lower class subjects' scores and the norms.

VALIDITY. Although the scale structure of the instrument is open to serious criticism, the ultimate criterion for any instrument is its predictive validity. The only "validity" evidence included in the manual is a table of correlations between the four original tests and the marker scales from which the weighting system was derived. The literature all the way back to Super's 1942 review (*156*) of the research has been heavily laden with essentially negative findings. A review of recent investigations, although subject to the bias resulting from editorial policies which inhibit reports of negative findings, still reveals a disquieting number of failures of the instrument to accomplish its intended purposes. Middleton and Putney (*315*), for instance, attempted to predict dominance-submission in husband-wife dyads from the dominance scale and failed; in fact, the predictions were *less* accurate when only extremely dissimilar couples were compared. Bruce found correlations ranging from −.07 to .20 with ratings of the effectiveness of 107 foremen (*283*), and from −.08 to .15 with ratings of 73 salesmen (*298*). With 17 sales managers, however, his coefficients ranged upward to .54 (*287*). Burgess (*295*) failed to find relationships with over- and under-achievement in engineering students. Poe and Berg (*280*) found borderline significance in predicting performance of steel industry production supervisors, and Gowan (*291*) found no correlations exceeding .11 with leadership ratings. Young and Gaier (*285*) could not demonstrate significant correlations with measures of suggestibility.

Many critics have attacked the apparent ease with which the scale scores may be shifted by intentional bias on the part of the respondent (*282*), although some writers defend the use of the instrument in business settings by claiming greater present-day sophistication for personnel specialists (*319*). Perhaps with unconscious cynicism, Powell (*228*) treated the scale scores from the instrument as "self-ratings," and was rather sharply criticized by Brown (*274*). In view of the repeated demonstrations of the ability of subjects to consciously manipulate their scores, this would not appear to be an unreasonable way of interpreting the test results.

Although the implications for the validity of the scales of the *Personality Inventory* are far from clear, Taft (*304*) found that subjects in the center of a distribution of "tolerance" scores were *less* emotionally stable than subjects at the extremes, as measured by the scales of the Bernreuter.

RESCALING OF THE ITEMS. Richardson and Hanawalt (*281*) were able to differentiate adult women who held offices in social organizations from those who did not, using the dominance and confidence scales, but found that a specially constructed scale for "office-holding" was more successful in a cross validation sample. Gehman (*290*) selected 32 items which most effectively differentiated scholastic probationers and obtained a correlation of .29 ($n = 65$) on cross validation.

SUMMARY. The research evidence and the opinions of various reviewers seem to weigh most heavily *against* the use of the *Personality Inventory* in precisely those applications for which it is now most extensively employed—namely, in determining the behavior tendencies of individuals in testing situations which might be expected to arouse defensive improvement of self-characterization. Considering the wide range of more adequate devices of this type now available, there appears to be little rational justification for its continued use in business and industrial settings. Because of the lack of recent normative data and the dearth of successful validity studies, there would seem to be little reason for the choice of this instrument even in settings where biased self-characterization would not be expected.

For a review by Leona E. Tyler, see 4:77; for reviews by Charles I. Mosier and Theodore Newcomb, see 40:1239; for excerpts from related book reviews, see 38:B358 and 36:B108.

[158]

***Personality Rating Scale.** Grades 4–12; 1944–62; test identical with *Child Personality Scale* ('51) except for format; originally called *22-Trait Personality Rating Scale;* modification for use with children of E. Lowell Kelly's *36-Trait Personality Rating Scale* (see *19* below); ratings by classmates and teachers or self-ratings; 22 ratings: pep, intelligence, sociability, nervousness-calmness, popularity, religiousness, punctuality, courtesy, cooperation, generosity, persistence, honesty, neatness, patience, interests, disposition, good sport, boisterous-quiet, entertaining, thoughtfulness, sense of humor, dependability; 1 form ('62, 7 pages); manual ('62, 25 pages); profile ['62, 1 page]; separate answer sheets must be used; $3.50 per 35 tests; 50¢ per specimen set; postpaid; (30–40) minutes for rating 10–15 classmates; S. Mary Amatora; Educators'-Employers' Tests & Services Associates. *

REFERENCES

1–18. See 5:41.
19. KELLY, E. LOWELL. "A 36-Trait Personality Rating Scale." *J Psychol* 9:97–102 Ja '40. * (*PA* 14:3598)
20. TSCHECHTELIN, M. AMATORA. "Children's Ratings of Associates." *J Exp Ed* 13:20–2 S '44. * (*PA* 19:1608)
21. AMATORA, MARY. "The Education Factor in Personality Appraisal." *J Exp Ed* 21:271–5 Mr '53. * (*PA* 28:1583)
22. TSCHECHTELIN, M. AMATORA. "As Teacher Sees Teacher: A Study in Personality." *J Social Psychol* 38:121–5 Ag '53. * (*PA* 28:6610)

LAURANCE F. SHAFFER, *Professor of Psychology and Education, Teachers College, Columbia University, New York, New York.*

Phenomenology and sociometry, while not always congenial bedfellows, are both currently popular constructs for the study of personality. An effective measure of how a person sees himself, comparable to a measure of how others see him, would be a boon to many worthwhile investigations. The *Personality Rating Scale,* which is a little-altered version of the previously reviewed *Child Personality Scale* (1951, see 5:41), attempts to be such an instrument, and its author deserves credit for ingenious inventiveness.

The examinee's booklet contains 22 separate 10-point scales, each worded so as to be within the comprehension of children above the middle of the elementary school. For example, the scale designated as "co-operation" asks, "How well does he work with others?" and the 10 points range from "never joins in" to "always helps the group." In the use of the instrument, each respondent rates five or more designated boys in his class, five or more designated girls, and himself by entering scale numbers on a separate answer sheet. All are rated on one question before proceeding to the next. Scores for the 22 scales are entered on a profile sheet which displays how an examinee is perceived by boys, by girls, by himself, and, optionally, by his teacher or teachers.

Although interesting in conception, the rating scale does not achieve its best potentialities. Some shortcomings are merely mechanical and could be overcome easily. One trivial vexation arises from the scoring instructions to separate the answer sheet elaborately along "perforations," when there are in fact no perforations but only printed broken lines which successfully resist tearing. A little more fundamental is the author's nonchalance about transferring numbers from the scale booklet to the answer sheet, probably a difficult clerical feat for the lower grades. There should be data, too, on the accuracy of the primitive scoring method of adding and averaging; clerks will not always do such a task without error, much less the upper-grade pupils for whom self-scoring is recommended.

More seriously, the instrument suffers from a lack of sophistication in psychometric concepts that is exceptional even in the rarified field of personality measurement. The issue of reliability is presented only in terms of inter-rater agreement, obtained by correlating one child's ratings with those by one other child and then correcting by the Spearman-Brown formula for four raters. Such data are presented for two independent samples each of 100 boys and 100 girls. But one sample is of unspecified composition, and the other was randomly drawn from children in grades 4–8, permitting a possible inflation due to the presumably greater range of scores. While inter-rater reliability is of real interest (and is not too bad, with a median correlation of .80 for the mean ratings of four judges) other reliabilities are needed, too. The vast accumulation of 797,396 ratings to which the author refers might also have provided information on retest stabilities over varying intervals of time.

The norms are as frustrating as the reliabilities. They consist only of mean ratings, on very large numbers of cases, by boys, by girls, by both sexes, and by teachers, and of self-ratings by boys and by girls. All of these means lie close to the rational scale midpoint of 5.5 and are uninformative. There are no variabilities, no tables showing the ratings by ages or grades, and no attention is paid to discrepancy scores between self-ratings and ratings by others. These omissions are seen as serious in view of the use of raw scores in the profiles. Is a raw score of 7 on one scale always higher than one of 5 on another? Not if the variability of the former is half that of the latter, a likelihood hinted by some of the otherwise not too useful standard errors of means.

The reviewer must express sympathy for the author's struggles with the knotty problem of validity. Conventional concurrent or predictive validities probably have limited applicability to these 22 separate and essentially descriptive scales. The median correlations between self-ratings and others' ratings are reported as about .20 for boys and .38 for girls. These are interesting, but they are not "validities." A factor analysis was performed routinely, reported perfunctorily, and put to no use. As descriptive statistics, the matrix of intercorrelations given in a paper by the author would have been more informative than the rotated factor loadings. Perhaps some construct validities based on group comparisons would be revealing. Many interesting and unanswered questions propose themselves: Do the children rated as punctual, cooperative, persistent, neat, and dependable receive higher marks? Are the nervous, angry, or sad ones referred to guidance agencies? Are the sociable, popular, and "good sport" children elected to office by their peers? In such questions lie more useful concepts of construct validities.

As it now stands, the *Personality Rating Scale* is a good base upon which to build a rewarding instrument for research and perhaps for some limited applications. But it needs quite a bit of building.

For reviews by Robert H. Bauernfeind and Dale B. Harris, see 5:41.

[159]

Personality Schedule, 1929 Edition. Grades 13–16 and adults; 1928–30; neurotic tendencies; 1 form ('29, 4 pages); manual ('30, 4 pages); norms for college freshmen only; $2 per 25 tests; 5¢ per manual; 25¢ per specimen set; postpaid; (30–40) minutes; L. L. Thurstone and Thelma Gwinn Thurstone; University of Chicago Press. *

REFERENCES

1–28. See 40:1243.

29. Thurstone, L. L., and Thurstone, Thelma Gwinn. "A Neurotic Inventory." *J Social Psychol* 1:3–30 F '30. * (*PA* 4:1430)

30. Willoughby, Raymond R. "The Personal Equation in Ethical Judgment." *J Social Psychol* 1:424–9 Ag '30. * (*PA* 5:629)

31. Davis, Lawrence W., and Husband, Richard W. "A Study of Hypnotic Susceptibility in Relation to Personality Traits." *J Abn & Social Psychol* 26:175–82 Jl–S '31. * (*PA* 6:648)

32. Pintner, R. "Neurotic Tendency and Its Relation to Some Other Mental Traits." *Sch & Soc* 36:765–7 D 10 '32. * (*PA* 7:1375)

33. Willoughby, Raymond R. "Some Properties of the Thurstone Personality Schedule and a Suggested Revision." *J Social Psychol* 3:401–24 N '32. * (*PA* 7:1645)

34. Habbe, Stephen. "The Selection of Student Nurses." *J Appl Psychol* 17:564–80 O '33. * (*PA* 8:2727)

35. Stagner, Ross. "Improved Norms for Four Personality Tests." *Am J Psychol* 45:303–7 Ap '33. * (*PA* 9:2344)

36. Stagner, Ross. "The Relation of Personality to Academic Aptitude and Achievement." *J Ed Res* 26:648–60 My '33. * (*PA* 7:4857)

37. Lyon, Verne Wesley. "The Use of Vocational and Personality Tests With Deaf." *J Appl Psychol* 18:224–30 Ap '34. * (*PA* 8:5094)

38. Willoughby, Raymond Royce. "Norms for the Clark-Thurstone Inventory." *J Social Psychol* 5:91–7 F '34. * (*PA* 8:4167)

39. HESLER, ALICE RACHEL. *An Examination of Items in the Thurstone Personality Schedule for Diagnostic Patterns of Response.* Master's thesis, University of Oregon (Eugene, Ore.), 1935.
40. KUZNETS, G., AND TRYON, R. C. "A Study of the Incidence in Six Populations of Neurotic Responses to Items of the Thurstone Personality Schedule." Abstract. *Psychol B* 32:539-40 O '35. * (*PA* 10:473, title only)
41. MALLETT, DONALD ROGER. *A Study of the Validity at the College Level of Certain Measures of Personality Adjustment.* Doctor's thesis, University of Iowa (Iowa City, Iowa), 1936.
42. PECK, LEIGH. "A Study of the Adjustment Difficulties of a Group of Women Teachers." *J Ed Psychol* 27:401-16 S '36. * (*PA* 11:475)
43. ROOT, A. R. "College Achievement." *J Higher Ed* 7:387-8 O '36. * (*PA* 11:477)
44. BROOKS, ESTHER. "The Value of Psychological Testing." *Am J Nursing* 37:885-90 Ag '37. *
45. CHOU, SIEGEN K., AND MI, CHING-YUAN. "Relative Neurotic Tendency of Chinese and American Students." *J Social Psychol* 8:155-84 My '37. * (*PA* 11:5174)
46. MCKINNEY, FRED. "Concomitants of Adjustment and Maladjustment in College Students." *J Abn & Social Psychol* 31:435-57 Ja-Mr '37. * (*PA* 11:3784)
47. ROSENBAUM, BETTY B. "Neurotic Tendencies in Crippled Girls." *J Abn & Social Psychol* 31:423-9 Ja-Mr '37. * (*PA* 11:3785)
48. CROOK, MASON N. "A Further Note on Self-Judgments of Constancy in Neuroticism Scores." *J Social Psychol* 9:485-7 N '38. * (*PA* 13:1518)
49. ENGLE, T. L. "The Use of a Short Personality Schedule in High School Personnel Work." *J Appl Psychol* 22:534-8 O '38. * (*PA* 13:2699)
50. BROWN, PAUL A. "Responses of Blind and Seeing Adolescents to a Neurotic Inventory." *J Psychol* 7:211-21 Ap '39. * (*PA* 13:4726)
51. PINTNER, R., AND FORLANO, G. "Dominant Interests and Personality Characteristics." *J General Psychol* 21:251-60 O '39. * (*PA* 14:384)
52. CHILD, IRVIN L. "The Relation Between Measures of Infantile Amnesia and Neuroticism." *J Abn & Social Psychol* 35:453-6 Jl '40. * (*PA* 14:5517)
53. PAYNE, BRYAN. "Personality Patterns in Reformatory Inmates." *J Genetic Psychol* 56:13-9 Mr '40. * (*PA* 14:4216)
54. CROOK, MASON N. "Retest Correlations in Neuroticism." *J General Psychol* 24:173-82 Ja '41. * (*PA* 15:2260)
55. EISENBERG, PHILIP. "Individual Interpretation of Psychoneurotic Inventory Items." *J General Psychol* 25:19-40 Jl '41. * (*PA* 15:5205)
56. EISENBERG, PHILIP, AND WESMAN, ALEXANDER G. "Consistency in Response and Logical Interpretation of Psychoneurotic Inventory Items." *J Ed Psychol* 32:321-38 My '41. * (*PA* 16:1041)
57. BRUNING, HERBERT. *A Study of Personality Compared With Personal, Family, and Education Factors.* Master's thesis, Kansas State Teachers College (Emporia, Kan.), 1942.
58. SPERLING, ABRAHAM. "A Comparison of the Human Behavior Inventory With Two Other Personality Measures." *Ed & Psychol Meas* 2:291-7 Jl '42. * (*PA* 16:4885)
59. CROOK, MASON N. "A Retest With the Thurstone Personality Schedule After Six and One-Half Years." *J General Psychol* 28:111-20 Ja '43. * (*PA* 17:1236)
60. PINTNER, R., AND FORLANO, G. "Consistency of Response to Personality Tests at Different Age Levels." *J Genetic Psychol* 62:77-83 Mr '43. * (*PA* 17:2393)
61. ZIMMERMAN, MARY A. *A Study of the Changes in Personality During One Year in College as Shown by the Thurstone Personality Schedule.* Master's thesis, Kansas State Teachers College (Emporia, Kan.), 1943.
62. BURGESS, ERNEST W., AND WALLIN, PAUL. "Homogamy in Personality Characteristics." *J Abn & Social Psychol* 39:475-81 O '44. * (*PA* 19:442)
63. SEAGOE, MAY V. "Prognostic Tests and Teaching Success." *J Ed Res* 38:685-90 My '45. * (*PA* 19:3184)
64. BLACK, WINFRED. *A Study of the Thurstone Personality Schedule Given to Entering Freshmen at Alabama College Between the Years 1931-32 and 1938-39.* Master's thesis, University of North Carolina (Chapel Hill, N.C.), 1949.
65. ZAKOLSKI, F. C. "Studies in Delinquency: 1, Personality Structure of Delinquent Boys." *J Genetic Psychol* 74:109-17 Mr '49. * (*PA* 23:4925)
66. HSU, E. H. "The Neurotic Score as a Function of Culture." *J Social Psychol* 34:3-30 Ag '51. * (*PA* 27:222)

For a review by J. P. Guilford, see 40:1243.

[160]

★Polyfactorial Study of Personality. Adults; 1959; 11 scores: hypochondriasis, sexual identification, anxiety, social distance, sociopathy, depression, compulsivity, repression, paranoia, schizophrenia, hyperaffectivity; IBM; 1 form (7 pages); manual (12 pages); separate answer sheets must be used; $6.25 per 25 tests; $2.75 per 25 IBM answer sheets; $2 per set of scoring stencils; $2.75 per 25 profiles; $1.75 per manual; $2.50 per specimen set; cash orders postpaid; (45-50) minutes; Ronald H. Stark; Martin M. Bruce. *

BERTRAM D. COHEN, *Professor of Psychology, and Director of Clinical Training, Rutgers, The State University, New Brunswick, New Jersey.*

The development of the PFSP was prompted by the author's dissatisfaction with existing paper and pencil personality tests. The MMPI is explicitly cited in the manual as being too lengthy, poorly worded, insufficient for personality assessment within the normal range, and based on a rationale that is "purely statistical and empirical, but disregards clinical considerations." In addition to the goal of correcting these alleged faults in other tests, the author states that the purpose of the PFSP is to "offer diagnostic profiles approximating those which would be obtained with projective instruments."

Inspection of the PFSP questionnaire indicates that it is indeed less lengthy than the MMPI (containing 300 items rather than 550), and that the items are worded simply and clearly. Beyond this it is not possible to conclude that the instrument represents as yet any substantive improvement over existing tests of its general type.

Initial criteria for selecting items were their correlations with measures from other established objective and projective personality tests, and from clinical interviews. Included were "the Rorschach, the House-Tree-Person Test, the standard clinical scales of the MMPI, and diagnoses based on interviewing." Items were finally chosen on the basis of (*a*) "purity of factor-analytic relationship with other items in the same nosological category," and (*b*) "degree of correlation with the criteria and absence of correlation with items in the same category." Subjects used in all phases of the work included over 200 hospitalized psychotic patients, over 550 prison inmates, over 300 psychiatric outpatients, and over 2,500 normal "white collar and mid-management employees" and applicants.

The author cites as evidence for the "content [?] validity" of the test the presence of significant intercorrelations between Anxiety, for example, and such other scales as Compulsivity, Hypochondriasis, and Repression.

While these relationships may be psychodynamically reasonable, the contribution of simple *item overlap* between the correlated scales should have been taken into account or at least noted.

It is unclear from the manual just what relationships obtain between the PFSP items or scales and the various projective test and diagnostic criteria. According to the manual, separate publication of portions of the basic factor analytic data is planned. Correlations between MMPI scales and those of the PFSP are reported in tabular form in the manual. The two tests "show a 41% variance communality." That some communality would be found is to be expected, of course, since the MMPI was used as one of the criteria for item selection in the first place.

A set of correlations is reported between PFSP scales and *Wechsler Adult Intelligence Scale* subtest scores. According to the author "these correlations strongly suggest that the more severe the disturbance, the lower the I.Q." This conclusion is based on data from a portion of the prison population ($n = 217$). It is possible that the negative correlations found are mediated by the effects of a defensiveness or social desirability variable that relates positively to intelligence and negatively to many of the nosological scales of the PFSP. No provision is made to assess or correct for test taking attitudes, e.g., defensiveness, acquiescence set. In this respect the PFSP does not compare favorably with either the MMPI or other more recent personality inventories.

A test-retest study, using a one-week intertest interval, indicates acceptable reliability coefficients for the various scales. These range from .699 for Anxiety to .927 for Schizophrenia. The prison population was used for this study ($n = 400$ male inmates).

In summary, the PFSP is an attempt to refine and to enrich the meaning of previous personality inventories used for clinical diagnostic purposes. While items are more simply and clearly written than those of the MMPI, for example, their usefulness remains in doubt. It is difficult, at this stage of its development, to see how the PFSP represents an effective improvement over its major competitor. Also, even if a minor point, the number of spelling errors in the manual may irritate readers and make them less secure about essential tabular information. More careful editorial attention in the preparation of the manual should correct this.

Donald R. Peterson, *Professor of Psychology, and Director, Psychological Clinic, University of Illinois, Urbana, Illinois.*

This review was written without benefit of detailed information about test development which the author promises to provide in a forthcoming monograph. Material in the manual, however, gives ample substance for a number of comments about the *Polyfactorial Study of Personality* (PFSP).

The test is reasonably brief, the items are straightforwardly and inoffensively stated, scoring is objective, an 11-phase profile, with a "clinical" name for each dimension, is easily derived, and reliabilities are adequate. For these reasons, the test will probably appeal to personnel officers, and find considerable use as an aid in employee selection. But therein lie most of the dangers. Before the test can be recommended for general use, a number of questions about its construction will have to be answered.

Work began with the assembly of 700 true-false inventory statements. Items were selected, according to the manual, by reference to (*a*) "purity of factor-analytic relationship with other items in the same nosological category," and (*b*) "degree of correlation with the criteria and absence of correlation with items in the same category." Populations employed in the pre-selection are unspecified, and the exact method by which one can choose items which display both pure factor analytic relationships and an absence of correlation with other items in the same category is unclear to the reviewer.

Criteria were then defined. To accompany clinical diagnoses and MMPI scores, over 200 Rorschach scores were reduced to 86 "validated" indices in the analysis, and 24 "validated" H-T-P indices were likewise selected from 100-plus indices. Cross validation is vital in work of this kind. The author does not state whether additional tests of the projective indices were conducted or not. If not, it is questionable practice to call them "validated." If so, if indeed 86 indices from the Rorschach and 24 from the H-T-P have been found to relate dependably to clinical diagnosis, the author of the PFSP has in his possession the most dramatically positive evidence for the validity of the Rorschach and the H-T-P in the entire literature on projective techniques.

The test was given to 1,081 subjects in 15 clinical groups and to 2,576 "normal" white collar employees and job applicants. But just how many of the subjects were used, in what combinations, to develop which scales, is not clear. Presumably none of the 2,000 normals had been given clinical diagnoses. How many of those, and how many of the others had Rorschachs, H-T-P's, and MMPI's cannot be determined from the manual. Even if all S's took all tests, which is unlikely, there is a troublesome lack of information about the particular scores used to represent the criteria. The PFSP yields a measure of "social distance," for example, and another of "repression," but there are no "socially distant" nor "repressed" groups among the clinical samples. If the pertinent scores were developed from the Rorschach, it would be interesting to know how they were "validated."

Statistical procedures are described by listing the various kinds of correlational indices which were used, noting that Rorschach criteria were given double weight, stating that multiple *r*'s were computed between items and each criterion, and asserting that "the correlations of these matrices were employed in the factor analytic procedures to determine purity of items for each nosological category." There is no comment on the techniques of factor extraction and the decisional processes involved in retaining factors for rotation, and no note on how or whether rotations were performed. Variations in some of these procedures can turn the results of a factor analysis upside down. The author was dealing with upwards of 120 criterion variables and an unidentified subset of 700 questionnaire items. Having struggled for years to make sense of much smaller data masses than this, the reviewer is puzzled about the data reduction techniques employed in developing the PFSP. It is difficult to see how factor analysis could have been used in any conventional way. And if unconventional techniques were employed they should be described in the manual. The author appropriately omits "voluminous tables" which "would defeat the purpose of a manual." But further description of procedure would be most desirable.

Claims of validity are supported mainly by reference to the method of derivation, and by tabular citation of intercorrelations with MMPI scales and the *Association Adjustment Inventory* (AAI). The MMPI scales were apparently among the criteria used in original item selection, so the presence of some fairly high and appropriately patterned correlations is not surprising. The AAI, another "adjustment" questionnaire sold by the same publisher, requires only 10 minutes to give, but yields 13 scores in the areas of "deviant thinking," juvenile ideas, and so forth. It was constructed and standardized on the same population used in developing the PFSP. The author says this in the manual, and properly adds that the correlations are probably maximal values. He then goes on to say that the reasonably high and consistent correlations between PFSP and AAI scores "strongly suggest that the 'factor' underlying these high correlations is indeed the ideational disturbances which they both purport to measure." At best, this statement is stronger than the data warrant. At worst, it is untrue. The most accurate statement to make about these data is that two self-report measures standardized on the same population are almost bound to show some high intercorrelations, and that the measures may or may not have anything to do with ideational disturbances as assessed by different means in other settings.

The comments on interpretation tend to be presumptuous and misleading. Consider, for example, the following *non sequitur:* "Because the Rorschach was the major criterion in deriving these scales, it is expected that PFSP profiles will most closely resemble Rorschach profiles." In fact, PFSP profiles do not look like Rorschach profiles at all. Scale descriptions read very much like those for the MMPI, though they are given in a less guarded way, e.g., "When a high SID [Sexual Identification] and HAF [Hyperaffectivity] score appear in the same record, there is strong indication of the acting out of....homoerotic desires." Anyone who considers using the PFSP in personnel selection should be aware that the adequacy of the test in predicting job success is completely unknown.

Indeed it is difficult to see what purpose the test can serve that is not already served better by an existing instrument. If one wants a questionnaire to reflect clinical diagnostic judgment, the MMPI is already available, complete with validity keys and a large body of research. If one is dissatisfied with the particular dimensions involved in the MMPI, the *California Psychological Inventory* is for sale, with another large body of research behind it. If one wants a test developed by rigorous factor analytic techniques, Guilford's *Inventory of Factors STDCR,* the *Guilford-Martin Inventory of Factors GAMIN,* and Cattell's *Sixteen Personality Factor Questionnaire* represent some highly creditable work. If one really wants the kind of profile he might get from the Rorschach, he had better give a Rorschach.

Like other questionnaires, the PFSP will probably be related to a variety of extra-test variables that matter. It may therefore be of use as a research tool. But this is not the way it is presented in the manual. And this is not the way it is billed in the catalog.

J Consult Psychol 24:100 F '60. Edward S. Bordin. A 300-item inventory reportedly selected on the basis of factor analysis and correlations with unspecified criteria. The general impression is that the major criteria may have been other tests, e.g., Rorschach, MMPI, and the H-T-P test. * Test-retest reliability for a prison population suggests that the scores are reasonably stable. No other validation data are offered, even though reference is made to various possible criterion populations. There are no references to published reports. Why was this test issued after so little developmental analysis?

[161]

★Position Response Form and Response Form. Industry; 1958-59; manual ('58, 9 pages including both forms); no norms; scoring and interpretation by the author only; distribution restricted to clients; test prices included in consulting fee; William F. Reiterman, Jr.; the Author. *

a) POSITION RESPONSE FORM. Management personnel; for recording personality requirements of a job; 1 form ('58, 1 page); no data on reliability and validity; (5-10) minutes.

b) RESPONSE FORM. Job applicants; for self-rating of on-the-job personality characteristics; 4 scores: forward action, people action, staying action, dependent action; 1 form ('59, 2 pages, identical with form copyrighted in 1958 except for minor changes); (10-15) minutes.

[162]

The Power of Influence Test. Grades 2-13; 1958; seating preference sociometric test; 1 form (1 page); manual (4 pages); no data on validity; norms for grades 5-11 only; $4 per examiner's kit of 50 tests, scoring sheets, and manual; 50¢ per manual; cash orders postpaid; specimen set not available; [10-15] minutes; Roy Cochrane and Wesley Roeder; Psychometric Affiliates. *

REFERENCES

1. COCHRANE, ROY. "Testing the Sociometric Test." *Univ Wash Col Ed Rec* 16:49-52 F '50. *

ÅKE BJERSTEDT, *Professor of Education, University of Lund, Lund, Sweden.*

The present device is an extremely simplified version of a sociometric technique. The "test" form is nothing more than a half-page sheet with seven spaces (too narrow for many children's large handwriting) for giving seating preferences (the subject and six other pupils he would like to sit near). The only score considered in the manual is the sum of choices received.

Percentile data are given for seven grade levels, and some retest results are briefly referred to. No clear information as to the number and kind of pupils involved at different grade levels is given, nor are we informed of such important factors as class size and sex distribution within the norm groups used. The score yielded is variously referred to as a measure of "power of influence," "friendship capacity," "leadership capacity," and "future ability in salesmanship." Apparently, in the opinions of the authors, these labels are to some extent synonymous, but no data are given to validate these claims or to show any relationships between this particular sociometric score and any other psychological or educational variable. In a report of a study presented by one of the authors in 1950 (*1*), the lack of validation data is admitted, with the statement that such data "would only be obtained by a ten-year follow-up." No explanation is given of why this would be the only way to validate the measure. Now in the sixties, there is still no indication that the authors have tried their own particular kind of ten-year validation; instead, the same general excuse is repeated in the present manual. It is stated that the *Power of Influence Test* has been used "successfully" by "more than" 250 teachers and counselors, but there is no indication of what kind of success is referred to or how it was measured. No references to the large body of sociometric research literature are presented to the reader.

Of course, sociometric techniques similar to the present simple device *can* be extremely helpful instruments to teachers and psychologists for a study of preferential relations as one aspect of group structure. Meaningful correlations with other psychological variables have often been found and give sociometric data additional importance for specific purposes. Teachers interested in such measures (including many other meaningful scores than choices received) are strongly recommended to read the simple guides published by Jennings,[1] Northway and Weld,[2] or the more detailed book by Gronlund,[3] which would be much more helpful guides to a judicious use of sociometric methods than the present manual.

In sum, the reviewer considers the manual oversimplified in its description of sociometric procedures, quasi-exact in presenting norm data of doubtful value, and vague in its general interpretational suggestions. As for the specific "test form," the teacher could probably just as well use a slip of blank paper.

ERIC F. GARDNER, *Professor of Education and Psychology, and Chairman, Department of Psychology, Syracuse University, Syracuse, New York.*

The *Power of Influence Test* is a rather presumptuous title for a diagrammatic format on which a student is asked to write the names of the six fellow students he "would *like* to have sitting near" him. The score, representing the number of times a pupil has been chosen by his classmates, is converted to a "Social Percentile" which is described as "a standard score showing the Friendship Capacity of the individual, his aptitude for making others like him, and his future ability in salesmanship." Since the only data provided are percentile ranks within grades 5 through 11 for the responses of an unspecified number of students, the reader immediately asks himself a series of questions a few of which are: (*a*) What is friendship capacity? (*b*) How do we know the number of choices a student obtains represents his aptitude for *making* others like him? and (*c*) What evidence do we have that a person's score is related to present ability in salesmanship, not to consider the issue of future sales prowess?

After raising serious qualms, the four-page manual stresses the value of the teacher having sociometric data (a point with which the reviewer would concur) but, unfortunately, continues with the same kind of unsupported claims and recommendations to the teacher implied by the title. For example, it reads, "The high ranking pupils on this test can be assumed to be class leaders....The views and opinions expressed by these leaders are the views and opinions of the class. When a teacher disciplines a leader, he is disciplining the whole class." How can one arrive at these and other similar conclusions which are presented? Obviously, one needs help from a greater Power than the *Power of Influence Test.*

The reviewer is favorable to the desires of the authors to promote the use of sociometric data, but he believes they have done a disservice with their extravagant claims and kinds of recommendations for the interpretation of a score from a simple, sociometric, single-choice situation.

1 JENNINGS, HELEN HALL. *Sociometry in Group Relations: A Manual for Teachers, Second Edition.* Washington, D.C.: American Council on Education, 1959. Pp. xi, 105. *

2 NORTHWAY, MARY L., AND WELD, LINDSAY. *Sociometric Testing: A Guide for Teachers.* Toronto, Canada: University of Toronto Press, 1957. Pp. vii, 72. *

3 GRONLUND, NORMAN E. *Sociometry in the Classroom.* New York: Harper & Row, Publishers, Inc., 1959. Pp. xix, 340. *

[163]

★**The Press Test.** Industrial employees; 1961; ability to work under stress; 5 scores: reading speed, color-naming speed, color-naming speed with distraction, difference between color-naming speed with and without distraction, difference between reading speed and color-naming speed; 1 form (10 pages); manual (25 pages); reliability and validity data based on shorter time limits; norms for males only; $5 per 20 tests, postage extra; $1 per specimen set, postpaid; 4.5(15) minutes; Melany E. Baehr, Raymond J. Corsini, Richard Renck, and Measurement Research Division, Industrial Relations Center, University of Chicago (manual); Education-Industry Service. *

WILLIAM H. HELME, *Supervisory Research Psychologist, United States Army Personnel Research Office, Washington, D.C.*

The *Press Test* is a brief pencil and paper group test designed to measure ability to work under stress. The stress resides in the task itself. The subject has to respond quickly to one aspect of the stimulus without being distracted by a conflicting aspect. According to the manual, the purpose of the test is to measure the person's ability in "coping with more or less unique situations and emergencies as they arise," as contrasted with ability for jobs which "call for a systematized and routinized day." While there is mention of more dangerous emergencies, the validation attempted so far deals with differences among executives, foremen, salesmen, and others, rather than with emergency situations *per se.*

Research on the test is rather modest to date. Reliability of the three basic scores appears adequate, though based on only 58 "industrial personnel"—.72 for reading speed, and .82 and .80 for color-naming speed (simple) and color-naming speed with distraction, respectively. The derived difference scores, however, are of low reliability, as would be expected from differences between highly correlated (.81, .86) reliable scores. Retest scores after a one-week interval show substantial practice effects.

The major question is, of course, the evidence for validity. Does the test really measure ability to cope with unique situations and emergencies? Two kinds of validation are offered. The one of more direct interest to industrial users is a study of five groups of men in different industrial occupations, with samples ranging from 33 to 92. Mean scores for each group on each of the five measures are compared. The results show that, on the three basic scores, the samples of engineers and chemists, executives and middle management, and white collar and junior executives score significantly higher than a sample of foremen. The other occupational group, salesmen, score significantly lower than the first three groups in the distraction situation, but higher than the foremen on all three basic scores. Thus the major finding is that the first three groups do not only better than the foremen on the "stress" measure, but equally better on the simple perception-speed measures. (Although two "significant" differences between salesmen and the engineer and executive groups are reported on the first derived score above, the appropriate variance statistical tests of the whole set of samples made by the reviewer shows these to be questionable.)

The second kind of validation consists of correlations with factor scores from the *Temperament Comparator*. Statistically significant, but still very modest, relationships (.13 to .22) are found between the three basic scores and tendency toward sociability and excitability, as well as away from cautious-seriousness and stability. These findings are in the direction that would be expected if the *Press Test* scores measure a ready responsiveness to varying stimuli, with distraction. But it is a long jump from the data to assume that these same characteristics are found in coping with important unique situations and emergencies.

Norms on a new time limit for the test are given, based on 170 industrial personnel. The mean on the difference score between color-naming with and without distraction appears to be a typographical error, but the norm table itself seems correct.

In summary, the statement in the manual that "the test warrants further study and investigation" appears justified. The "evidence for validity of the *Press Test* scores in the selection of higher level personnel, especially upper and middle management, professional, and sales personnel" is very modest, however. The test is not yet sufficiently validated for the industrial user. For users who are prepared to conduct research in their own organizations and who feel that the measurement of such characteristics is worth the effort, the test might be a promising component of a battery of techniques for experimentation. It has simple instructions, and actual testing time after instruction is less than five minutes.

ALLYN MILES MUNGER, *Associate Director, Personnel and Marketing Research Division, The Psychological Corporation, New York, New York.*

The *Press Test,* according to the manual, is expected to differentiate between those individuals who can work in a stress situation and those who cannot. The stress in the test is that part in which the individual is given, in writing, the name of a color, such as green, printed in an ink of a different color, such as yellow. His task is to identify the color of the ink. The validity of the test rests primarily on two approaches.

The first is validation against another test called the *Temperament Comparator.* On securing the information on that test, readily supplied by the authors, it was found that the *Temperament Comparator* was validated on three bases: a factor analytic study of the test itself, correlations with other tests unidentified except for an earlier version of the same test, and differential profiles for industrial personnel. It can only be assumed that the industrial personnel described are the same groups as those used in a second approach for validating the *Press Test* on five groups of industrial personnel. Therefore, a validity approach comparing it to another test can be assumed to be an interesting but not significant measure for industrial use.

In the second approach to validity, the test's ability to discriminate between various industrial groups, there are significant differences between the means for the different groups.

However, the overlap between the distributions would make any use of the test as a selection device extremely tenuous, except for the foreman group. The means rounded off are 72 for engineers and chemists, 73 for executives and middle management, 72 for white collar workers and junior executives, 66 for salesmen, and 55 for foremen. These results would seem to modify the authors' contention that encouraging results have been obtained in discriminating between various industrial groups, but would certainly support the statement that the test warrants further study and investigation.

It is rather common in industrial groups to find differences between the means for any diverse groups on almost any standard test. This is why norms are provided. The need in industry is for a test that will discriminate between good and poor performance within groups. All other tests mentioned in studies in the references were given to an additional group of labor or blue collar personnel, but no mention is made of the administration of this test except the implication given by the statement "these results present some evidence for the validity of the *Press Test* scores in the selection of higher level personnel, especially upper and middle management, professional and sales personnel."

In the manual and in correspondence, the authors are concerned with the low test-retest reliability for the combined scores derived from the test parts. It would seem quite possible that in three 90-second tests of this type, test-retest is not the best method of measuring reliability, as it is quite possible some individuals may learn ways of taking the test which will increase their scores between tests while others may explore another approach which will, in fact, lower their performance. Various forms of this test have been around for several years and, while creating interest, they have failed to show significant validity against rankings and ratings on performance. In its present state, this is an experimental test and should be labeled as such.

[164]

★A Process for In-School Screening of Children With Emotional Handicaps. Grades kgn-3, 3-6, 7-12; 1961-62; for research use only; 3 ratings: teacher, peer, and self; manual ('61, 49 pages); technical report ('61, 66 pages); pupil record folder ('62, 3 pages); no norms; 10¢ per screening summary form; 15¢ per pupil record folder; $2 per manual; $2.50 per technical report; postage extra; $10 per complete specimen set, postpaid; to be administered "over a period of two or three months"; Nadine M. Lambert and Eli M. Bower; distributor in California: Bureau of Special Education, State Department of Education; distributor in all other states: Educational Testing Service. *

a) BEHAVIOR RATINGS OF PUPILS. Grades kgn-12; ratings by teachers; 1 form ('62, 11 pages); no data on reliability; $1 per form; administration time not reported.

b) [PEER RATINGS.] Grades kgn-3, 3-7, 7-12; 3 levels; teacher's scoring instructions and worksheet ('62, 6 pages) for all 3 levels; 2) and 3) also include self-ratings; $1 per teacher's worksheet.

1) *The Class Pictures.* Grades kgn-3; individual; 1 form ('62, 12 cards); record form (1 page); no data on reliability of current edition; $1 per set of pictures; 35¢ per pad of 30 record forms; (15-20) minutes.

2) *A Class Play.* Grades 3-7; 1 form ('62, 8 pages); 20¢ per test; (35-45) minutes.

3) *Student Survey.* Grades 7-12; 1 form ('62, 8 pages); no data on reliability; 20¢ per test; administration time not reported.

c) [SELF-RATINGS.] Grades kgn-3, 3-7, 7-12; 3 levels.

1) *A Picture Game.* Grades kgn-3; separate forms ('62, 66 cards) for boys and girls; $1.75 per set of cards; 15¢ per class record; (30) minutes.

2) *Thinking About Yourself.* Grades 3-7; Forms A (for boys), B (for girls), ('62, 6 pages); score sheet ('62, 1 page); 20¢ per test; 7¢ per score sheet; 15¢ per class record; administration time not reported.

3) *A Self Test.* Grades 7-12; 1 form ('62, 6 pages); score sheet ('62, 1 page); no data on reliability; 20¢ per test; 7¢ per score sheet; 15¢ per class record; administration time not reported.

REFERENCES

1. BOWER, ELI M. "A Process for Identifying Disturbed Children." *Children* 4:143-7 Jl '57. *

2. WEISBROD, KENNETH CONRAD. *The Identification of Potentially Maladjusted Children in the Middle Elementary Grades.* Doctor's thesis, University of Maryland (College Park, Md.), 1958. (*DA* 20:3640)

3. BOWER, ELI M. *Early Identification of Emotionally Handicapped Children in School.* Springfield, Ill.: Charles C Thomas, Publisher, 1960. Pp. xiii, 120. * (*PA* 35:809)

ALAN O. ROSS, *Chief Psychologist, Pittsburgh Child Guidance Center, Pittsburgh, Pennsylvania.*

Most workers in the field of mental health share the belief that psychological disturbances can be prevented if emotional vulnerability is identified and prophylactic steps are taken in the early years of life. If the assumption is valid, this approach would be most effective if identification could take place in the preschool years but it is not until the child goes to school that we have a social institution within which routine screening for emotional vulnerability could take place. Screening for a variety of sensory and physical handicaps has become an accepted part of the school's responsibility but when it comes to screening for emotional handicaps we lack both the public acceptance of such an approach and the necessary instruments to carry it out. The authors of the material here under discussion address themselves to this twin problem by presenting an approach which keeps the need for public acceptance and the demand for valid screening devices clearly in view. They are, however, the first to admit that neither of these goals has yet been reached and the Technical Report accompanying the material is careful to stress the preliminary nature of the work.

The authors must have had a great many misgivings and reservations when they decided to publish their material in order to make it available to other research workers. They stress, and it is worth repeating, that these materials are published as experimental instruments, "available only to those professional researchers conducting projects in which the identification of emotionally handicapped children is an integral function and who are willing to share their data with the authors." It would be most unfortunate if this restriction were not heeded for both the public acceptance of large-scale psychological screening and the progress of this device would be jeopardized by premature practical application.

The screening process involves a combination of three techniques: behavior rating by the teacher, peer ratings by classmates, and self-ratings. Identification of the "emotionally handicapped child" is based on his scores on these instruments relative to those of the other children in his class. If his are among the highest scores on two of the three instruments, the child is considered "likely to have emotional problems" and "should be referred to a specialist in mental health for diagnosis and prescription."

In the school population used for the initial development of the process, 10 to 15 per cent of the children were identified as possibly handicapped. Since the approach is one of ranking the children in a classroom it involves the assumption that emotionally handicapped children are uniformly distributed among the school population. In a class with a high percentage of emotionally disturbed children the screening device would identify only the most severely disturbed, while in a class with few or no emotionally disturbed children three or four "false positives" would be selected. The authors are aware of the need for a more sophisticated method of scoring and also warn against viewing a child whom their device identifies as "different" as a child who will necessarily have an emotional problem. Screening, they say repeatedly, is not the same as diagnosis or classification, but in the final analysis the use or misuse to which these instruments are put will depend largely on the sophistication of school administrators and teachers.

Much work remains to be done before the process can be considered valid for the identification of emotionally handicapped children. But even once this work is completed the question of the practical value of a screening technique of this nature will remain to plague us. What happens to children who are identified as potentially emotionally handicapped? The authors of these instruments hope that their use will encourage teachers to develop "action commitments on behalf of some of the more vulnerable children." They speak of referrals, consultations, and curriculum adjustments and ideally this would indeed be desirable. But how many school systems and teachers are equipped to engage in such efforts and how many parents are willing to accept the recommendations based on even the most careful clinical evaluation which they themselves did not initiate? The Technical Report states, "The fact that school programs are not available to assist emotionally handicapped pupils make a better adjustment to school should not be a deterrent to identifying them." This reviewer cannot help wonder whether, under presently existing conditions, such identification cannot do more harm than good. One can only hope that public sophistication, the enlightenment of school administrators, the sensitivity and understanding of teachers, and the knowledge of what to do for an emotionally handicapped child will keep pace with the development of valid screening procedures toward which the material here discussed has made a major contribution.

J. Robert Williams, *Director, Child Study Clinic, and School Psychologist, Public Schools, Kankakee, Illinois.*

This instrument was developed as a possible aid to schools who are forced to wrestle with the problem of meeting adequately the needs of increasing numbers of children with varied emotional disabilities. It is still strictly a research device as the authors frequently and emphatically state in both manual and previous publications. Teachers and other professional workers in the schools who use it become active participants in an ongoing research program designed to further test the instrument for its ability to serve such purposes as: (*a*) to identify children with emotional handicaps so that they can receive more careful, individual study; (*b*) to help teachers become aware of and better able to cope with these problems from an educational standpoint; and (*c*) to assist schools in setting up plans to work with groups of children having emotional handicaps.

To these ends, those who use the instrument are given, in the Manual for School Administrators and Teachers, a brief but pointed orientation on the nature of emotional handicap, the meaning of "screening" in the present context, and the purpose and use of each of the screening procedures.

In this frame of reference, emotional handicap is conceived by the authors as an internal state which can be inferred from the degree of limited or restricted functioning an individual shows "in choosing from among alternative kinds of behavior." Five types of such limitations as commonly exhibited in the classroom (thus offering cues for identification of emotional handicap) are described in the manual: (*a*) inability to learn, (*b*) inability to build satisfactory interpersonal relationships, (*c*) inappropriate behavior or feelings under normal conditions, (*d*) pervasive mood of unhappiness, and (*e*) tendency to develop physical symptoms associated with personal or school problems.

Three approaches are used in the measurement of (screening for) susceptibility to emotional handicap as above conceived. These include teacher ratings, peer ratings, and self-ratings. The teacher rating of behavior of pupils is done by means of a 7-step scale in a manner simulating the equal-appearing interval procedure. Given a one-sentence description of pupil behavior, the rater is asked to place each pupil on a scale that extends from " 'most like' the pupil described to 'least like' him." This procedure is continued until all pupils are rated on each of eight descriptive behaviors. Scale values of the ratings run from 1 through 7, the higher values being indicative of greater susceptibility to emotional handicap.

Peer ratings are obtained by one of three methods, depending on the grade and reading level as well as the level of interest or maturity of the child. Each method is sociometric in nature, the idea being that each pupil judges every other pupil (in some cases, himself) in terms of the degree to which he is like a child in a pictured or imagined role or the degree to which his behavior matches that of a verbal, descriptive sample. Both "negative" (maladjusted), "positive," and "neutral" situations are included, and the general rationale is that the greater the tendency for a child to be perceived negatively by his peers (or himself) the greater is the degree of his susceptibility to emotional handicap.

Similarly, self-ratings are obtained by somewhat different methods according to grade- and maturity-level of pupils. At lower levels, the children are asked to sort pictures into piles labeled "happy" and "sad," with greater use of the latter category being indicative of more likelihood of emotional handicap. At the intermediate and upper grade levels, what is sought in self-rating is a measure of the difference between a pupil's perception of self "as he *is*" and "as he would like to be." The pupils read items descriptive of different types of children and are to select on a 4-step scale the degree to which they would (or would not) like to be like the hypothetical examples. On a second section of the exercise or test, they are to judge, in like manner, the degree to which they *are* (or are not) like the same hypothetical examples. Greater degree of emotional handicap is thought to be associated with increased difference between self and ideal.

The actual screening for susceptibility to emotional handicap is done by combining the results of the three types of ratings. By listing those pupils receiving highest susceptibility (negative) ratings on each method, it becomes possible to locate those with "two or more" negative ratings, which is considered a mark of significance in the present procedure.

One cannot properly use standard techniques to evaluate *A Process for In-School Screening of Children With Emotional Handicaps.* It is not offered to schools as a finished product; rather, schools are given the opportunity of using it under the condition that they will become partners in a research program designed to improve it and in the belief that they will, through such participation, become better informed as to the nature of emotional handicap and better able to deal with the complex and trying educational problems it presents.

In addition to the manual, a Technical Report is provided which presents a quite detailed account of the developmental history and present status of each screening instrument. In each case the device now in use is the result of one or more revisions. Reliability studies of most of the peer- and self-rating instruments are given and suggested procedures for more inclusive reliability investigations are made. There is a very thorough account of the research done to date on validity. The results on both reliability and validity are promising. However, the authors would not mislead anyone as the following cautious statement shows: "The authors, far from feeling that the data ....are proof of any virtues in the instruments, hope the little evidence that is offered will be useful to other researchers in ascertaining those things which should be studied next in the procedure."

In summary, the writer is of the opinion that the screening process described here stems from a logically sound, theoretical base and that the experimental procedures used in revising it up to now reflect a high caliber of scientific endeavor. Use of the instrument so far has given encouraging, though admittedly limited, results. More accurate appraisal must await the outcome of further experimentation, by now a byword with the authors.

For excerpts from related book reviews, see B93.

[165]

★**Progress Assessment Chart (P-A-C).** Mentally retarded children, mentally retarded adults; 1962–63; behavior checklist for assessing progress in 4 areas: self-help, communication, socialization, occupation; 2 levels; no data on reliability; 12*s.* 6*d.* per 25 charts, postpaid; H. C. Gunzburg; [National Association for Mental Health]. *

a) PROGRESS ASSESSMENT CHART FOR CHILDREN UNSUITABLE FOR EDUCATION AT SCHOOL. Form 1 ['62, 3 pages]; mimeographed notes for users ('62, 1 page).

b) PROGRESS ASSESSMENT CHART FOR THE MENTALLY HANDICAPPED, AGED 16+. Form 2 ['63, 3 pages]; mimeographed notes for users ('63, 2 pages).

[166]

★**Psychometric Behavior Checklist.** Adults; 1960; also called *Maryland Test Behavior Checklist;* for recording unusual test taking behavior; CC Form 19 ['60, 1 page, mimeographed]; instructions (4 pages, reprint of *1* below); specimen set free (checklist may be reproduced locally), postpaid; administration time varies with task rated; Bernard G. Berenson, Kathryn C. Biersdorf, Thomas M. Magoon, Martha J. Maxwell, Donald K. Pumroy, and Marjorie H. Richey; University Counseling Center. *

REFERENCES

1. BERENSON, BERNARD G.; BIERSDORF, KATHRYN C.; MAGOON, THOMAS M.; MAXWELL, MARTHA J.; PUMROY, DONALD K.; AND RICHEY, MARJORIE H. "A Check-List for Recording Test Taking Behavior." *J Counsel Psychol* 7:116–9 su '60. * (*PA* 35:3659)

[167]

★**The Psychotic Reaction Profile (PRP): An Inventory of Patient Behavior for Use by Hospital Personnel.** Mental patients; 1961; ratings by nurses or psychiatric aides; 4 scores: withdrawal, thinking disorganization, paranoid belligerence, agitated depression; 1 form (4 pages); mimeographed manual (9 pages); $7 per 25 tests, postpaid; specimen set not available; (10–15) minutes; Maurice Lorr, James P. O'Connor (test), and John W. Stafford (test); Western Psychological Services. *

REFERENCES

1. LORR, MAURICE; O'CONNOR, JAMES P.; AND STAFFORD, JOHN W. "The Psychotic Reaction Profile." *J Clin Psychol* 16:241–5 Jl '60. * (*PA* 36:2JP41L)

2. CASEY, JESSE F.; HOLLISTER, LEO E.; KLETT, C. JAMES; LASKY, JULIAN J.; AND CAFFEY, EUGENE M. "Combined Drug Therapy of Chronic Schizophrenics." *Am J Psychiatry* 117:997–1003 My '61. *

3. LASKY, JULIAN J.; KLETT, C. JAMES; CAFFEY, EUGENE M., JR.; BENNETT, J. LAMAR; ROSENBLUM, MARCUS P.; AND HOLLISTER, LEO E. "Drug Treatment of Schizophrenic Patients: A Comparative Evaluation of Chlorpromazine, Chlorprothixene, Fluphenazine, Reserpine, Thioridazine and Triflupromazine." *Dis Nerv System* 23:698–706 D '62. *

4. LORR, MAURICE, AND O'CONNOR, JAMES P. "Psychotic Symptom Patterns in a Behavior Inventory." *Ed & Psychol Meas* 22:139–46 sp '62. * (*PA* 37:1260)

WILSON H. GUERTIN, *Associate Professor of Education and Psychology, University of Florida, Gainesville, Florida.*

The *Psychotic Reaction Profile* (PRP) is the most recent of published scales for rating the behavior of psychotic patients. It is clearly superior to the *Hospital Adjustment Scale* and probably will replace the *MACC Behavioral Adjustment Scale* also. Many years of experience developing multidimensional scales for rating psychiatric patients and intensive application of them as criteria in drug studies lie behind this published scale.

The 85 items are marked as "T" (true) or "NT" (not true) by a psychiatric attendant or nurse, who has observed the patient over a three day period. The manual states that these brief, simple items can be completed in 10 to 15 minutes, and, further, that the items are "particularly useful in rating patients who are relatively inaccessible, withdrawn, or disturbed."

Scores on four relatively independent dimensions are: Withdrawal, Thinking Disorganization, Paranoid Belligerence, and Agitated Depression. The authors point out that the last of these is least reliable because only five items relate to it. While other scales of this kind yield a total score, the authors, quite creditably, reject the unidimensional concept of adjustment.

Percentile norms for each sex are based upon data from 500 males and 250 females in

47 hospitals. Little description of the norming sample is given but the norms are of little importance since most users will be working with change scores after treatment.

Reliability of the scales is .90 or better (Kuder-Richardson formula 20) for the first three scales and only .74 for Agitated Depression. Intraclass correlation reliability for the mean ratings of two raters were estimated to range from .58 for Agitated Depression to .92 for Withdrawal.

Validity is supported by the ability of three of the four scales to differentiate between open and closed ward patients. While claims for the scale are very modest, the statement that the manual or the instrument or both are to be regarded as preliminary forms might have been made explicit.

The final 85 items were selected from a pool of 172 items on the basis of their correlations with several predetermined clusters. Only four clusters survived to identify the final scales. Personal correspondence with Lorr discloses his belief that the four final dimensions correspond to second-order factors and that he is continuing his efforts to develop a scale that will evaluate first-order factors.

The PRP may be regarded as a good interim scale for rating the behavior of psychotic patients. It is clearly superior to the much older *Hospital Adjustment Scale* and probably will be preferred over the MACC by most users. Like these other scales, its chief shortcoming seems to be the somewhat limited sampling of the dimensions of behavioral adjustment.

[168]

*__The Purdue Master Attitude Scales.__ Grades 7–16; 1934–60; series title for the first 8 scales was formerly listed as *Generalized Attitude Scales; a–h* have space for insertion of any 5 attitude variables; Forms A, B, ('60, 1 page, the 17 items of each scale were selected from the 37- to 50-item Forms A and B copyrighted in 1934–36); 9 scales; manual ('60, 7 pages); no data on reliability of current forms; $1 per 25 copies of any one scale, postage extra; 50¢ per specimen set of any one scale; $1 per complete specimen set; postpaid; (5–10) minutes per attitude variable; H. H. Remmers (editor and manual author) and others; University Book Store. *

a) A SCALE TO MEASURE ATTITUDE TOWARD ANY SCHOOL SUBJECT. 1934–60; original forms by Ella B. Silance.

b) A SCALE FOR MEASURING ATTITUDES TOWARD ANY VOCATION. 1934–60; original forms by Harold E. Miller.

c) A SCALE FOR MEASURING ATTITUDE TOWARD ANY INSTITUTION. 1934–60; original forms by Ida B. Kelly.

d) A SCALE FOR MEASURING ATTITUDE TOWARD ANY DEFINED GROUP. 1934–60; revision of *A Scale for Measuring Attitude Toward Races and Nationalities;* original forms by H. H. Grice.

e) A SCALE FOR MEASURING ATTITUDES TOWARD ANY PROPOSED SOCIAL ACTION. 1935–60; original forms by Dorothy M. Thomas.

f) A SCALE FOR MEASURING ATTITUDES TOWARD ANY PRACTICE. 1934–60; original forms by H. W. Bues.

g) A SCALE FOR MEASURING ATTITUDE TOWARD ANY HOME-MAKING ACTIVITY. 1934–60; original forms by Beatrix Kellar.

h) A SCALE FOR MEASURING INDIVIDUAL AND GROUP "MORALE." 1936–60; original forms by Laurence Whisler.

i) HIGH SCHOOL ATTITUDE SCALE. 1935–60; original forms by F. H. Gillespie.

REFERENCES

1–9. See 40:1202.
10–46. See 4:46.

DONALD T. CAMPBELL, *Professor of Psychology, Northwestern University, Evanston, Illinois.*

The revision from forms earlier reviewed consists of shortening all forms to 17 items. All criticisms made in previous reviews still hold. The manual gives no criterion for selecting the retained items. No correlations between original and short forms are provided. No data on reliability or reproducibility or factorial structure of the new scales are provided. All evidence on validity comes from the older forms of the scales, with most references from 1934–1938, the latest from 1947. The one study cited to justify the shortening is actually irrelevant, and is misleadingly presented in the manual. As an example of the disregard of research on attitude measurement, in the abbreviation of the scales, neutral items are still retained (e.g., "I have no particular love or hatred for this group"). The revision has provided no basis whatsoever for changing the negative evaluations reported in the previous reviews, nor any basis for recommending the use of these tests.

For reviews by Donald T. Campbell and Kenneth E. Clark of the earlier forms of a–h, *see 4:46; for reviews by W. D. Commins and Theodore Newcomb, see 40:1202; for a review by Stephen M. Corey, see 38:897. For a review by Lee J. Cronbach of the earlier forms of* i, *see 3:46. For excerpts from related book reviews, see 40:B1050, 36:B215, and 36:B216.*

[169]

★**Rutgers Social Attribute Inventory.** Adults; 1959; perception of others (either real persons or generalized classes); 24 trait ratings: good natured-stubborn, intelligent-unintelligent, tense-relaxed, strong-weak, childish-mature, old fashioned-modern, dominating-submissive, thin-fat, adventurous-cautious, lazy-ambitious, optimistic-pessimistic, masculine-feminine, young-old, responsible-irresponsible, crude-refined, tall-short, suspicious-trusting, talkative-quiet, thrifty-wasteful, dependent-self reliant, unsympathetic-sympathetic, good looking-plain, conventional-unconventional, rich-poor; 1 form (1 page); manual (4 pages); no data on reliability; no norms; $2 per 25 tests, postage extra; specimen set not available; (30–60) minutes; William D. Wells; Psychometric Affiliates. *

DAVID B. ORR, *Senior Research Scientist, American Institute for Research; and Director of School and Survey Research, University of Pittsburgh Project Talent Office; Washington, D.C.*

The author states his purpose as "to help raters record their impressions of persons." This is the key to the *Rutgers Social Attribute Inventory*—it is a convenient form for recording impressions, *not* a test in the sense of providing demonstrably accurate measurement. Contrary to the author's statement, however, it is not a standard form, since no standard instructions are provided either on the blank itself or in the manual. Instead the author states that instructions will vary "depending upon details of the study design." Although his discussion of the merits of alternate rating procedures is appropriate, he does not point out the loss of comparability engendered by such nonstandard conditions.

The inventory consists of a one-page set of 24 eight-step trait scales presented "in the general format of the semantic differential (Osgood, Suci, and Tannenbaum, 1957)."[1] Scales are defined by adjectives at the opposing poles and, unlike Osgood's scales, have adverbs of degree printed beneath a line connecting the two pole adjectives. The author has made an appropriate choice of eight categories to increase discrimination, the even number being intended to eliminate the catch-all, middle-of-the-road choice. The adverbial descriptions of the categories (extremely, very, fairly, slightly, slightly, fairly, very, extremely; in that order) leave something to be desired in terms of providing the equal step intervals which would be most desirable. In this respect, however, the inventory does not differ greatly from many other similar rating scales.

In a commendable effort to give his scales more meaning, the author has based them upon the theoretical and factor analytic work of other researchers. Unfortunately, some of the value of this desirable theoretical undergirding appears to have been lost through alterations. The author states, "For the most part, the scales are simplified translations of the basic personality dimensions found in factor analyses of personality ratings and personality inventories (Cattell, 1957; Guilford, 1959)."[2,3] However, other scales have been added and "in many cases, it proved necessary to sacrifice exacting definition [of scales] for simplicity of vocabulary." How much has been lost in such simplification, translation, and addition is not clear.

The blank itself is crowded in appearance. The scales range from traditional traits such as "bossy and dominating"—"submissive; tends to give in easily" through more complex, and hardly undimensional, traits ("responsible & determined"—"irresponsible & quitting") to more observable physical traits such as "thin—fat." Many of these traits are not likely to be truly scalable psychometric dimensions. Though comprehensiveness was an aim, the author admits that field experience limited the inventory to 24 scales. No evidence is presented, however, to show that these 24 scales are the most important or even among the most important social attributes.

Although a brief discussion of possible analyses of the data collected through the use of the inventory is presented, no treatment of reliability and validity is included. Indeed, these essential topics are not even mentioned. No norms of any kind are presented, though several studies are mentioned as having been done.

More than half of the manual is taken up with a discussion of potential uses and applications of the inventory. Categories of uses suggested in the manual include studies of (*a*) "perception of real [specific] persons," such as family members, foremen, labor leaders; (*b*) "perceptions of classes of persons," such as lawyers, Texans, mothers-in-law; (*c*) "the expressive value of specific [personal] characteristics," such as smoking, wearing a beard, having red hair; (*d*) "the expressive value of brands" wherein respondents are asked to rate the typical users of various brand products; (*e*) "the impressions created by advertise-

1 OSGOOD, CHARLES E.; SUCI, GEORGE J.; AND TANNENBAUM, PERCY H. *The Measurement of Meaning.* Urbana, Ill.: University of Illinois Press, 1957. Pp. vii, 342. *

2 CATTELL, RAYMOND B. *Personality and Motivation Structure and Measurement.* Yonkers, N.Y.: World Book Co., 1957. Pp. xxv, 948. *

3 GUILFORD, J. P. *Personality.* New York: McGraw-Hill Book Co., Inc., 1959. Pp. xiii, 562. *

ments" (on prior impressions of brands and brand-users); and (*f*) "the impressions created by other forms of mass communication."

Finally, the manual presents an unbelievably poor appearance. It is crowded, messy, has extremely small type, and is shot through with typographical errors. If the more than a dozen actual misspellings in the manual are indicative of the care with which this inventory was developed then extreme caution in its use is certainly advisable.

In summary, the author shows commendable candor in emphasizing the exploratory nature of his instrument, in calling attention to the probable unequal nature of the scale intervals, and in describing its function in terms of "impressions" rather than "measurements." However, it is this reviewer's impression that a great deal of additional work will be necessary before this inventory takes a place among our more useful psychometric instruments.

JOHN PIERCE-JONES, *Professor of Educational Psychology, The University of Texas, Austin, Texas.*

The *Rutgers Social Attribute Inventory* (RSAI), published in a single form on a single sheet, presents a rater with two dozen 8-point bipolar rating scales (implicitly 9-point scales, zero points having been omitted to force judgments toward one extreme or the other) upon which descriptions of persons, either individually or in classes, may be rendered. The rating form is clearly printed, apparently by multilith; it should be convenient for raters to use and for clerks to handle. Regrettably, the RSAI provides no spaces for recording any of the following important items: (*a*) the identity of the subject rated; (*b*) the identity of the rater; (*c*) the date of making the ratings; (*d*) the purpose of the ratings; (*e*) the degree of the rater's acquaintance with the subject; (*f*) statements of inability to rate a subject on a trait because of insufficient knowledge; (*g*) numerical values to be recorded for various data processing purposes. The manual accompanying the RSAI appears to have been printed by a photo-offset and reduction process; its contents have been so reduced that the booklet may be quite discomfiting to read. The manual deals with such matters as: (*a*) general uses of the RSAI; (*b*) illustrations of the utility of the device in relatively specific researches including studies of person perception, brand images, and the "impressions created by advertisements"; and (*c*) procedures for obtaining, analyzing, and presenting the ratings.

It is extremely unfortunate that the reliability to be expected of RSAI ratings has not been dealt with in the manual. The construct validity of RSAI ratings, which should have been dealt with in detail, appears, from the manual's content, not to have been considered by the instrument's originator and publisher in any serious way. Evidence concerning the predictive validity, broadly conceived, of this device is very scarce, consisting of illustrative profiles from previously unpublished studies (of which no adequate descriptions were found) suggesting that (*a*) "the ideal professor" was rated differently from "the average professor" in four RSAI attributes by 50 Rutgers undergraduates; (*b*) "the average nurse" (and nursing aide) tends to be judged more submissive (less dominating) than "the average doctor" by raters consisting of unspecified numbers of physicians, nurses, and patients of both sexes. The extent to which response set variance affects the validity and reliability of RSAI ratings apparently has not been assayed; it should have been, for it has been shown repeatedly that this influence is usually strong when judgments or self-reports must be registered on the sorts of scales provided by the RSAI.

There now exists among social psychologists and students of personality a substantial, well-founded concern for the development of instruments adequate to assess dimensions of personality and person perception which may be related to "in the world" social behavior. Gough's *California Psychological Inventory,* designed to measure traits such as responsibility and tolerance or factors [1] such as "adjustment by social conformity" and "extraversion," represents one important effort to satisfy this concern with an inventory whose scales are associated with relevant social behavior criteria. Of course, such devices as the CPI are not adapted for obtaining records of the constructions placed by judges on persons individually or in classes. In this connection, the important thing to consider in relation to the RSAI is that structured personality inven-

1 PIERCE-JONES, JOHN; MITCHELL, JAMES V.; AND KING, F. J. "Configurational Invariance in the California Psychological Inventory." *J Exp Ed* 31:65–71 S '62. * (*PA* 37:8012)

tories have generally been examined as predictors of external criteria of the traits purportedly measured, whereas there is little evidence that the RSAI has been so studied. It is surely as important that the validity of rating scales be assessed in relation to independent criteria as it is that more usual scales be so appraised. Moreover, neither the originator nor the publisher of the RSAI should be relieved of clear responsibility for showing (*a*) that ratings elicited by their device are stable, dependable, and reliable, and (*b*) that different, but comparably sophisticated raters (with respect to the attributes rated), can produce relatively comparable ratings of subjects. These responsibilities do not appear to have been met satisfactorily.

There is some merit in Wells' intention to produce scales, similar to the semantic differential, aimed at being coterminous, in the factor analytic sense, with "the basic personality dimensions found in factor analyses of personality ratings and personality inventories" by such workers as Guilford and Cattell. However, this worthy aim is surely not realized simply by setting up two dozen scales with adjectivally labeled poles (e.g., childish-mature, responsible-irresponsible) and the usual adverbial designations of the several degrees of each attribute. We should expect the developer of the RSAI to show by experiment, and we should have expected his publisher to have insisted upon, evidence that data obtained with the instrument do, indeed, bear factorial and construct relevance to the dimensions in which they are presumed to reflect differences. Without the necessary technical information having been made available, the present RSAI is worth little more, in the reviewer's judgment, than the many "home-made" scales investigators often produce for their own purposes.

[170]

***SRA Youth Inventory.** Grades 7–12, 9–12; 1949–60; problems checklist; 9 scores: school, future, myself, people, home, dates and sex, health, general, basic difficulty; IBM; 2 forms; Form S is an extensive revision of Form A rather than a parallel form; (30–45) minutes; H. H. Remmers, Benjamin Shimberg, and Arthur J. Drucker (manual for Form A); Science Research Associates, Inc. *

a) FORM A. Grades 7–12; 1949–53; IBM; 1 form ('49, 14 pages, listed as Forms AH and AM in publisher's catalog); manual, second edition ('53, 22 pages); technical supplement ('53, 23 pages); junior high school profile leaflet ('50, 4 pages); senior high school profile leaflet ('49, 4 pages); separate answer sheets or pads must be used; $10.80 per 20 tests; $5 per 100 IBM answer sheets (scored by the publisher only; fee: 25¢ per student); $2.40 per 20 self-marking answer pads; 50¢ per hand scoring basic difficulty key; $1.20 per 20 profile leaflets; 75¢ per specimen set.

b) FORM S. Grades 9–12; 1955–60; 1 form ('56, 12 pages); manual ('60, 35 pages); profile ('60, 1 page); $2.40 per 20 tests; $1.05 per 20 profiles; 60¢ per manual; 50¢ per specimen set; Spanish edition available.

REFERENCES

1–7. See 4:91.

8–19. See 5:105.

20. NIXON, WARREN WINTERS. *A Comparison of Personality Adjustment Before and After a Series of Discussions Based on Problems Marked on the* Science Research Associates Junior Inventory. Doctor's research study No. 2, Colorado State College (Greeley, Colo.), 1956.

21. BARRAGAN, M. FIDELIS. *A Study of the Problems of a Selected Number of High School Students as Measured by the SRA Youth Inventory.* Master's thesis, Catholic University of America (Washington, D.C.), 1957.

22. BECKWITH, A. VANCE. *A Comparison of Responses of Adjusted and Maladjusted Students to the SRA Youth Inventory.* Master's thesis, Claremont College (Claremont, Calif.), 1957.

23. MUSSELMAN, DAYTON L. *Patterns of Circumstances Related to Problems Expressed by Seventh and Eighth Grade Pupils.* Doctor's thesis, University of Colorado (Boulder, Colo.), 1958. (*DA* 19:2537)

24. RICE, DAVID LEE. *A Comparative Study of the Personal Adjustment of High School Students Attending a Reorganized Rural School With High School Students Attending Selected Rural Township Schools.* Doctor's thesis, Purdue University (Lafayette, Ind.), 1958. (*DA* 19:2005)

25. SMITH, LOUIS M., AND HUDGINS, BRYCE B. "The SRA Youth Inventory and Mental Health." *Personnel & Guid J* 37:303–4 D '58. * (*PA* 36:2JO03S)

26. TALIANA, LAWRENCE EDWIN. *Youth's Problems as They See Them: A Statistical Analysis and Restandardization of the SRA Youth Inventory.* Doctor's thesis, Purdue University (Lafayette, Ind.), 1958. (*DA* 19:167)

27. WEISBRODT, JEROME ALAN. *The Effects of Response Set on the SRA Youth Inventory.* Master's thesis, Purdue University (Lafayette, Ind.), 1959.

28. KULKARNI, S. S. *A Marathi Revision of the SRA Youth Inventory.* Doctor's thesis, Purdue University (Lafayette, Ind.), 1961. (*DA* 22:3261)

29. MILBURN, DONNA J. "Defining Units With a Problem-Detecting Inventory." *Marriage & Family Living* 23:52–3 F '61. *

30. REMMERS, H. H. "Cross-Cultural Studies of Teenagers Problems." *J Ed Psychol* 53:254–61 D '62. * (*PA* 37:4767)

31. CLARKE, H. HARRISON, AND GREENE, WALTER H. "Relationships Between Personal-Social Measures Applied to 10-Year-Old Boys." *Res Q* 34:288–98 O '63. *

FORREST L. VANCE, *Administrative Officer, American Psychological Association, Washington, D.C.*

The examiner's manual for Form A of this inventory indicates that the instrument's value lies in helping school people identify quickly the self-acknowledged problems of students in grades 7 through 12. This is achieved for a particular student by having him respond to 298 problem statements drawn from autobiographical essays obtained from some 15,000 teenagers throughout the United States. In this form of the inventory, the subject checks each item that applies to himself and makes no response to the remaining problem statements. The results are scored in terms of the eight content headings under which the items are printed in the test booklet. These categories include labels such as, "My School," "About Myself," "Getting Along With Others," and so on. These eight judgmentally determined content areas are then treated as scales, and extensive normative data are provided to translate raw scores for each area into percentile ranks.

The stated mission of the instrument is nicely accomplished. One might quibble about the use of content categories as scales, but there is no question that the inventory provides a rapid survey of a wide variety of possible problems to which a cooperative student can respond, indicating his own concerns. Also, the method of item selection and the normative data (derived from a carefully stratified sample of 2,500 students) are commendable in both concept and execution.

However, the generally good impression up to this point is seriously marred by a gratuitous attempt to use the inventory to diagnose psychopathology. This effort has produced an unfortunate clinical and psychometric concoction called the Basic Difficulty Scale. This scale was derived by asking seven judges to classify each of the inventory items as either indicative of simple recognition of a problem or as more likely to indicate a basic personality disturbance. These seven judges, described as "experts in the fields of guidance, clinical psychology, and education," agreed unanimously that 47 items represented basic difficulty and identified 54 others by a 6 to 1 majority. By the same criteria, 97 items were classified as indicators of non-basic problem recognition.

This procedure is justified initially by the extraordinary statement, "It appears that the ability of experts in the field of mental hygiene to agree on the possible significance of 198 items is probably a good indication of the validity of the *Inventory*." At a later point evidence is introduced that shows that the Basic Difficulty Scale does significantly differentiate students independently rated by school counselors as well-adjusted from students rated poorly-adjusted. However, two of the eight content scales differentiate these groups better than the Basic Difficulty Scale, and four of the remaining scales also distinguish these groups reliably.

The plain fact is that all of the scales on this instrument are positively intercorrelated. Data for the eight content scales show correlation coefficients ranging between .20 and .67 with a median of .46. No correlational data are provided for the Basic Difficulty Scale in the manual, but this scale has substantial item overlap with each of the content scales except for "Looking Ahead," which deals almost exclusively with vocational development. The remaining seven content scales share 12 per cent (Boy Meets Girl) to 80 per cent (About Myself) of their items with the Basic Difficulty Scale, leaving little doubt that this scale will be substantially correlated with the others.

Aside from the high probability that the Basic Difficulty Scale adds no information to what is given by the rest of the inventory, one may question the wisdom of introducing clinical concepts into an instrument intended for broad use by persons without special training in any of the mental health professions. It is this reviewer's opinion that the Basic Difficulty key is not appropriate for general use by nonspecialists, and that its present stage of development cautions against applications, other than experimental, by anyone.

A new form of this instrument, Form S, was published in 1956, with its accompanying manual issued in 1960. Form S is a thorough revision which includes some item changes and a new format in which responses are made to 296 problem statements on a four-point scale indicating intensity of that problem for the individual subject. Seventh and eighth grade norms are eliminated and a self interpreting report form is provided for the content area scores. A new Basic Difficulty Scale of 100 items was developed for Form S, using eleven clinical psychologists as judges.

As in the case of Form A, the scales of Form S are highly reliable and highly intercorrelated. The pattern of item overlap between content scales and Basic Difficulty is also similar to Form A, and validity data for this construct are provided only for the earlier scale, although the two forms are not identical.

In general, this is a well-constructed inventory with appropriate content and format for secondary school use as a counseling tool. The scales, based on content areas, are carefully constructed and reliable, and excellent normative information is given for them. As earlier reviews have pointed out, these scales are designed to indicate what the subject *thinks* are his problems, and as such are not susceptible to evaluation against objective criteria. An attempt is also made to develop a psychodiagnostic indicator, but the resulting Basic Difficulty Scale, which *is* open to empirical study, needs extensive validating research before it can be considered anything other than an experimental device.

J Counsel Psychol 7:226–7 f '60. Laurence Siegel. * A rather unusual and highly desirable feature of the Manual is its inclusion of a summary of responses to individual items by the standardization sample. These data show the percentages of respondents, by sex and by grade, marking each response alternative. This tabular presentation contains a gold mine of interesting information for use in undergraduate teacher-training classes and for in-service training programs. The primary value of the Youth Inventory....will be derived from examining individual item responses rather than profiles of subscale scores. The use of the Basic Difficulty Scale scores for screening purposes may be justified in a very large school system wherein teachers and counselors are unable otherwise to identify pupils who are rather seriously disturbed.

For reviews by Kenneth E. Clark and Frank S. Freeman of Form A, see 4:91.

[171]

★**A Scale to Measure Attitudes Toward Disabled Persons.** Disabled and nondisabled adults; 1957–60; title on test is *ATDP Scale;* 1 form ('57, 1 page); manual ('60, 16 pages); $2 per 25 scales; $1 per manual; $1.10 per specimen set; postage extra; (10) minutes; Harold E. Yuker, J. R. Block, and William J. Campbell; Human Resources Foundation. *

[172]

★**Self-Interview Inventory.** Adult males; 1958; 10 scores: current complaints, emotional insecurity, guilt feelings, composite neurotic (based on first 3 scores), prepsychotic or psychotic, behavior problems, childhood illness, composite maladjustment (based on previous 3 scores), validation (lack of carefulness, lack of truthfulness); IBM; 1 form (4 pages); manual (4 pages); profile ['58, 1 page]; no data on reliability; separate answer sheets must be used; $3 per 25 tests; $2 per 25 IBM scorable answer sheets; machine scoring stencil must be constructed locally; $2 per 50 profiles; $1 per specimen set (must be purchased to obtain manual and key); cash orders postpaid; administration time not reported; H. Birnet Hovey; Psychometric Affiliates. *

REFERENCES

1. Hovey, H. Birnet. "A Self-Interview Inventory." *J Clin Psychol* 3:191–3 Ap '47. * (*PA* 21:3121)

Andrew R. Baggaley, *Professor of Psychology, Temple University, Philadelphia, Pennsylvania.*

This inventory attempts "to measure maladjustment potentials in terms of what men declare about their past histories and experiences." One hundred thirty-two of its items were included because they significantly differentiated 50 male neuropsychiatric patients from 50 male Veterans Administration workers in two samples. In addition there are 27 items that differentiated particular subsamples of patients, 10 items constituting a carefulness scale, 10 items constituting a truthfulness scale, and 6 unscored, neutral, introductory items. The fact that 137 of the items are keyed so that an answer of "true" is scored in the direction of "sick" means that a low score can indicate illness, "acquiescence," or some combination of these.

All of the items except the 26 validating and introductory items are scored on a "Composite Maladjustment" scale. By cluster analysis these 159 items (except for 24 "current complaint" items) were grouped into these subscales: Emotional Insecurity, Guilt Feelings, Prepsychotic or Psychotic, Behavior Problems, and Childhood Illness. Additionally, a "Composite Neurotic" scale combines the emotional insecurity, guilt feelings, and current complaint items. A graphic device is provided for transforming scores to standardized scores. The manual also contains a rather long list of suggestions for clinical interpretation.

Since the items within the subscales are listed consecutively in the question booklet, only one scoring template is needed. However, the probable development of response sets tends to offset this advantage; e.g., an examinee who answers "yes" to questions 127 through 154 receives a score of only two on the behavior problems scale. In any case, the publisher should have supplied at least one scoring template made of cardboard rather than soft paper. For all but four items, failure to respond is scored in the direction of "sickness"; the stated rationale is that the patients made somewhat more omissions than the controls. Intercorrelations between the subscales are reported. However, no reliability data whatsoever are given, so the test user has no statistical basis for evaluating the reliability of the profile differences on which the suggested clinical interpretations are based.

The publisher's reproduction of the test materials is abominable. The information was typed and then reproduced by the offset process. There is no double spacing, even between paragraphs. The brightness is uneven, and there are misspellings, poor erasures, and even strikeovers.

In summary, the original research on which this inventory is based provides a good foundation, but there are several technical improvements that should be made in future editions before the inventory can be recommended for general use. Furthermore, the publisher should be urged to do a decent job of reproduction. At present, the inventory can be recommended only as a rough screening device to suggest that some sort of maladjustment (or response set) is present in an adult male.

DAVID T. LYKKEN, *Associate Professor of Psychiatry and Psychology, University of Minnesota, Minneapolis, Minnesota.*

This questionnaire contains 185 MMPI-type true-false items and yields a profile of 10 scale scores. The latter include: a 24 item current complaint scale; 2 putative validity scales of 10 items each; 5 scales based on a rough cluster analysis and labeled Emotional Insecurity (21 items), Guilt Feelings (21 items), Prepsychotic or Psychotic (54 items), Behavior Problems (28 items), and Childhood Illness (11 items); a score obtained by adding the Current Complaints, Emotional Insecurity, and Guilt Feelings scores and labeled Composite Neurotic; and a Composite Maladjustment score based on the sum of all but the two validity scales. One hundred eight of the items are said to have differentiated an unspecified mixture of male VA psychiatric patients from non-patient males at the 5 per cent level in two separate samples of 100 subjects each. The cluster analysis was based upon the data from these same 200 subjects and led to the inclusion of an additional 27 items which appeared to differentiate significantly among clusters. Norms are provided, based on the same 100 control subjects, for converting the 10 scale scores to *T* score equivalents. No additional normative, reliability, or validity data are given.

About one page of the four page manual is devoted to "interpretations." Here the author explains which profile characteristics indicate "an essentially neurotic picture" or "present or impending disintegration of control in a psychopathic personality" or "character disorder with pseudo-psychosis," etc. No empirical justification whatever is provided for any of these interpretations which appear to be based entirely upon simpleminded inference from the item content and the names previously given by the author to the several clusters. Additional insight into the level of psychometric sophistication embodied in this instrument can be had by noting that the items are presented to the subject (i.e., listed in the test booklet) serially by scale; for example, the 10 items on which a truthful respondent is supposed to admit to "common human 'weaknesses' " (and which comprise the Lack of Truthfulness scale) are all listed together as items 176 through 185!

This is an inane and incompetent imitation of the MMPI and one finds it difficult to understand the motivation of either its author or publisher. Such a product is an embarrassment to psychology in general and to the field of mental measurement in particular.

[173]

Shipley-Institute of Living Scale for Measuring Intellectual Impairment. Adults; 1939-46; formerly called *Shipley-Hartford Retreat Scale for Measuring Intellectual Impairment;* 4 scores: vocabulary, abstractions, total, conceptual quotient; 1 form ('39, 2 pages); manual ('46, c1940-46, 4 pages, identical with manual copyrighted in 1940 except for title); $2 per 25 tests; 50¢ per specimen set; postpaid; 20(25) minutes; Walter C. Shipley; distributed by Mrs. Walter C. Shipley. *

REFERENCES

1-25. See 3:95.
26-48. See 5:111.
49. YATES, AUBREY J. "The Validity of Some Psychological Tests of Brain Damage." *Psychol B* 51:359-79 Jl '54. *
50. BARTELME, KENWOOD, AND RILEY, GORDON L. "A Study of Psychiatric Technicians on Selected Measures of Intelligence and Personality." Abstract. *Am Psychol* 10:321 Ag '55. *
51. SINES, LLOYD K., AND SIMMONS, HELEN. "The Shipley-Hartford Scale and the Doppelt Short Form as Estimators of WAIS IQ in a State Hospital Population." *J Clin Psychol* 15:452-3 O '59. * (*PA* 36:1HD52S)
52. GARRETT, WILEY S. "Prediction of Academic Success in a School of Nursing." *Personnel & Guid J* 38:500-3 F '60. * (*PA* 35:3954)
53. SUINN, RICHARD M. "The Shipley-Hartford Retreat Scale as a Screening Test of Intelligence." *J Clin Psychol* 16:419 O '60. * (*PA* 37:3241)
54. WIENS, ARTHUR N., AND BANAKA, WILLIAM H. "Estimating WAIS IQ From Shipley-Hartford Scores: A Cross-Validation." *J Clin Psychol* 16:452 O '60. * (*PA* 37:3119)
55. WIENER, DANIEL N. "Evaluation of Selection Procedures for a Management Development Program." *J Counsel Psychol* 8:121-8 su '61. * (*PA* 36:3LD21W)
56. PULOS, LEE; NICHOLS, ROBERT C.; LEWINSOHN, PETER M.; AND KOLDJESKI, THEODORE. "Selection of Psychiatric Aides and Prediction of Performance Through Psychological Testing and Interviews." *Psychol Rep* 10:519-20 Ap '62. * (*PA* 37:3401)
57. SKLAR, MAURICE, AND EDWARDS, ALLAN E. "Presbycusis: A Factor Analysis of Hearing and Psychological Characteristics of Men Over 65 Years Old." *J Auditory Res* 2:194-207 Jl '62. *
58. WAHLER, H. J., AND WATSON, LUKE S. "A Comparison of the Shipley-Hartford as a Power Test With the WAIS Verbal Scale." Abstract. *J Consult Psychol* 26:105 F '62. * (*PA* 37:5001)
59. ELKIND, DAVID; KOEGLER, RONALD R.; AND GO, ELSIE. "Field Independenec and Concept Formation." *Percept & Motor Skills* 17:383-6 O '63. * (*PA* 38:5349)
60. HAERTZEN, CHARLES A., AND HILL, HARRIS E. "Assessing Subjective Effects of Drugs: An Index of Carelessness and Confusion for Use With the Addiction Research Center Inventory (ARCI)." *J Clin Psychol* 19:407-12 O '63. *
61. LEWINSOHN, PETER M. "Use of the Shipley-Hartford Conceptual Quotient as a Measure of Intellectual Impairment." *J Consult Psychol* 27:444-7 O '63. * (*PA* 38:4291)

For reviews by E. J. G. Bradford, William A. Hunt, and Margaret Ives, see 3:95.

[174]

***Sixteen Personality Factor Questionnaire.** Ages 15 or 16 and over; 1949–63; 16 or 17 scores: reserved vs. outgoing (A), less intelligent vs. more intelligent (B), affected by feelings vs. emotionally stable (C), humble vs. assertive (E), sober vs. happy-go-lucky (F), expedient vs. conscientious (G), shy vs. venturesome (H), tough-minded vs. tender-minded (I), trusting vs. suspicious (L), practical vs. imaginative (M), forthright vs. shrewd (N), placid vs. apprehensive (O), conservative vs. experimenting (Q1), group-dependent vs. self-sufficient (Q2), casual vs. controlled (Q3), relaxed vs. tense (Q4), motivational distortion scale (Form C only); NCS for Forms A and B; Forms A ('62, c1956–62, 10 pages), B ('61, c1957–61, 10 pages), C ('56, c1954–56, 8 pages), X ('63, 11 pages); Form C is a short form and is also available, in combination with the *IPAT Culture Fair Intelligence Test,* with tape recorded directions; Form X is a special edition, presented either in booklet form with tape recorded directions for use with semiliterates or entirely on tape for use with illiterates, available either separately or in combination with the *IPAT Culture Fair Intelligence Test;* manual ('57, 56 pages) for Forms A, B, and C; mimeographed norms supplement ('63, 4 pages) for 1961–62 editions of Forms A and B; supplementary manual, second edition ('62, 25 pages) for Form C; manual ('63, 8 pages) for tape administration of Forms C or X; mimeographed supplement ['63, 6 pages] for Form X; profile ('63, 1 page); reliability data for Forms A and B based upon the 1956–57 editions; norms for combination of Forms A and B also presented; no data on reliability for Form X; separate answer sheets must be used; $12.50 per 25 tests of Forms A or B; $10 per 25 tests of Form C (regular booklet edition); $4.50 per pad of 50 hand scoring answer sheets; $5.40 per pad of 50 combined answer sheet-profiles; $2 per set of keys for Forms A or B; $1 per key for Form C; $3.80 per pad of 50 separate profiles; $3.25 per 50 NCS answer sheets for Forms A and B combined (see 671 for scoring service); $2.90 per manual; $1.20 per supplementary manual for Form C; $5 per specimen set of Forms A and B; $4 per specimen set of Form C; $2.40 per abbreviated specimen set of Form C (includes supplementary manual but not manual); $38–$58 per examiner's kit of tape edition of Forms C or X (includes 2 tests, 50 answer sheets, 3¾ ips tape, and manuals); cash orders postpaid; 1956 edition of Form C also published, under the title *Employee Attitude Series: 16 P.F.,* by Industrial Psychology, Inc.; (50–60) minutes for Forms A or B, (30–40) minutes for Form C, (50–70) minutes for Form X; Raymond B. Cattell and Herbert W. Eber; Institute for Personality and Ability Testing. *

REFERENCES

1–8. See 4:87.

9–29. See 5:112.

30. DOTSON, ELSIE JENOISE. *A Study of the Agreement of Introversion-Extroversion Factors as Defined by Various Factor Analysts.* Doctor's thesis, University of Kentucky (Lexington, Ky.), 1951. (*DA* 18:1095)

31. MCCARTHY, THOMAS N. *The Relationship of Vocational Interests to Personality Traits.* Master's thesis, Catholic University of America (Washington, D.C.), 1952.

32. HOLMEN, MILTON G.; KATTER, ROBERT V.; JONES, ANNE M.; AND RICHARDSON, IRVING F. "An Assessment Program for OCS Applicants." *HumRRO Tech Rep* 26:1–50 F '56. * (*PA* 31:8957)

33. KEMPE, JAMES EDWIN. *An Experimental Investigation of the Relationship Between Certain Personality Characteristics and Physiological Responses to Stress in a Normal Population.* Doctor's thesis, Michigan State University (East Lansing, Mich.), 1956. (*DA* 19:3383)

34. BENNIS, WARREN; BURKE, RICHARD; CUTTER, HENRY; HARRINGTON, HERBERT; AND HOFFMAN, JOYCE. "A Note on Some Problems of Measurement and Prediction in a Training Group." *Group Psychother* 10:328–41 D '57. * (*PA* 33:5971)

35. CATTELL, R. B., AND BAGGALEY, A. R. "A Confirmation of Ergic and Engram Structures in Attitudes Objectively Measured." *Austral J Psychol* 10:287–318 D '58. * (*PA* 34:2748)

36. KELLY, E. LOWELL; MILLER, JAMES G.; MARQUIS, DONALD G.; GERARD, R. W.; AND UHR, LEONARD. "Personality Differences and Continued Meprobamate and Proclorperazine Administration." *A.M.A. Arch Neurol & Psychiatry* 80:241–6 Ag '58. * (*PA* 33:10420)

37. MELVIN, GEORGIA-LEE VIRGINIA. *Personality and Group Status in Adolescents.* Doctor's thesis, University of Illinois, (Urbana, Ill.), 1958. (*DA* 19:1134)

38. WEITZENHOFFER, ANDRÉ M., AND WEITZENHOFFER, GENEVA B. "Personality and Hypnotic Susceptibility." *Am J Clin Hypnosis* 1:79–82 O '58. * (*PA* 34:4414)

39. WELLS, HAROLD PARK. *Relationships Between Physical Fitness and Psychological Variables.* Doctor's thesis, University of Illinois (Urbana, Ill.), 1958. (*DA* 19:2531)

40. BYRD, EUGENE. "Measured Anxiety in Old Age." *Psychol Rep* 5:439–40 S '59. *

41. CATTELL, RAYMOND B., AND SCHEIER, IVAN H. "Extension of Meaning of Objective Test Personality Factors: Especially Into Anxiety, Neuroticism, Questionnaire, and Physical Factors." *J General Psychol* 61:287–315 O '59. * (*PA* 35:785)

42. COPPEDGE, ROBERT J. *Personality, as Determined by the Sixteen Personality Factor Test, and Its Relationship to Musical Tastes.* Master's thesis, Indiana State Teachers College (Terre Haute, Ind.), 1959. (Abstract: *Teach Col J* 31:34)

43. HOLLAND, JOHN L. "Some Limitations of Teacher Ratings as Predictors of Creativity." *J Ed Psychol* 50:219–23 O '59. * (*PA* 36:1KH19H)

44. HUNT, J. MCV.; EWING, THOMAS N.; LAFORGE, ROLFE; AND GILBERT, WILLIAM M. "An Integrated Approach to Research on Therapeutic Counseling With Samples of Results." *J Counsel Psychol* 6:46–54 sp '59. * (*PA* 34:5955)

45. KARRAS, EDWARD J. *A Study of the Personality Variables, as Measured by the Cattell 16 Personality Factor Test, Associated With Musical Aptitude, as Measured by the Drake Musical Aptitude Tests.* Master's thesis, Kent State University (Kent, Ohio), 1959.

46. KARSON, SAMUEL. "The Sixteen Personality Factor Test in Clinical Practice." *J Clin Psychol* 15:174–6 Ap '59. * (*PA* 35:4959)

47. MANN, RICHARD D. "A Review of the Relationships Between Personality and Performance in Small Groups." *Psychol B* 56:241–70 Jl '59. * (PA (34:4194)

48. RAYGOR, ALTON L. "College Reading Improvement and Personality Change." *J Counsel Psychol* 6:211–7 f '59. * (*PA* 35:3909)

49. ANDERSON, A. W. "Personality Scores of Western Australian University Students Entering From State and Private Schools." *Austral J Ed* 4:123–5 Jl '60. *

50. ANDERSON, A. W. "Personality Traits of Western Australian University Entrants." *Austral J Psychol* 12:4–9 Je '60. * (*PA* 35:3916)

51. ANDERSON, A. W. "Personality Traits of Western Australian University Freshmen." *J Social Psychol* 51:87–91 F '60. * (*PA* 34:7624)

52. CARRIGAN, PATRICIA M. "Extraversion-Introversion as a Dimension of Personality: A Reappraisal." *Psychol B* 57:329–60 S '60. * (*PA* 35:4976)

53. COUCH, ARTHUR, AND KENISTON, KENNETH. "Yeasayers and Naysayers: Agreeing Response Set as a Personality Variable." *J Abn & Social Psychol* 60:151–74 Mr '60. * (*PA* 34:7376)

54. HOLLAND, JOHN L. "The Prediction of College Grades From Personality and Aptitude Variables." *J Ed Psychol* 51:245–54 O '60. * (*PA* 36:1KL45H)

55. HOLLAND, JOHN L. "The Relation of the Vocational Preference Inventory to the Sixteen Personality Factor Questionnaire." *J Appl Psychol* 44:291–6 Ag '60. * (*PA* 35:4015)

56. KARSON, SAMUEL. "Validating Clinical Judgments With the 16 P.F. Test." *J Clin Psychol* 16:394–7 O '60. * (*PA* 37:3221)

57. SCOFIELD, ROBERT W., AND SUN, CHIN-WAN. "A Comparative Study of the Differential Effect Upon Personality of Chinese and American Child Training Practices." *J Social Psychol* 52:221–4 N '60. * (*PA* 35:5008)

58. THOMAS, SHAILER. *Socio-Economic Status and Personality Factors as Measured by Cattell's Sixteen Personality Factor Test.* Master's thesis, Michigan State University (East Lansing, Mich.), 1960.

59. ANDERSON, A. W. "Personality Traits in Reading Ability of Western Australian University Freshmen." *J Ed Res* 54:234–7 F '61. *

60. BECKER, WESLEY C. "A Comparison of the Factor Structure and Other Properties of the 16 PF and the Guilford-Martin Personality Inventories." *Ed & Psychol Meas* 21:393–404 su '61. * (*PA* 36:2HF93B)

61. BORGATTA, EDGAR F. "Mood, Personality, and Interaction." *J General Psychol* 64:105–37 Ja '61. * (*PA* 35:6415)

62. BORGATTA, EDGAR F., AND GLASS, DAVID C. "Personality Concomitants of Extreme Response Set (ERS)." *J Social Psychol* 55:213–21 D '61. * (*PA* 36:3HE13B)
63. BORGATTA, EDGAR F.; IN COLLABORATION WITH HENRY J. MEYER. "Make a Sentence Test: An Approach to Objective Scoring of Sentence Completions." *Genetic Psychol Monogr* 63:3–65 F '61. * (*PA* 35:6435)
64. CADY, LEE D., JR.; GERTLER, MENARD M.; GOTTSCH, LIDA G.; AND WOODBURY, MAX A. "The Factor Structure of Variables Concerned With Coronary Artery Disease." *Behav Sci* 6:37–41 Ja '61. * (*PA* 36:1JU37C)
65. CATTELL, RAYMOND B., AND GREENE, RONALD R. "Rationale of Norms on an Adult Personality Test, the 16 P.F.—For American Women." *J Ed Res* 54:285–90 Ap '61. *
66. CATTELL, RAYMOND B., AND SCHEIER, IVAN H. *The Meaning and Measurement of Neuroticism and Anxiety.* New York: Ronald Press Co., 1961. Pp. ix, 535. * (*PA* 36:1HK27C)
67. CATTELL, RAYMOND B., AND WARBURTON, FRANK W. "A Cross-Cultural Comparison of Patterns of Extraversion and Anxiety." *Brit J Psychol* 52:3–15 F '61. * (*PA* 36:1GB03C)
68. DAS, RHEA S. "Validity Information Exchange, No. 14-05: D.O.T. Code 2-66.01, Police Lieutenant." *Personnel Psychol* 14:459–61 w '61. *
69. DAVIES, LILLIAN SCHOLLJEGERDES. *Some Relationships Between Attitudes, Personality Characteristics, and Verbal Behavior of Selected Teachers.* Doctor's thesis, University of Minnesota (Minneapolis, Minn.), 1961. (*DA* 22:3943)
70. GOCKA, EDWARD F., AND MARKS, JOHN B. "Second-Order Factors in the 16 PF Test and MMPI Inventory." *J Clin Psychol* 17:32–5 Ja '61. * (*PA* 37:3175)
71. KARSON, SAMUEL. "Second-Order Personality Factors in Positive Mental Health." *J Clin Psychol* 17:14–9 Ja '61. * (*PA* 37:3176)
72. LEVONIAN, EDWARD. "Personality Measurement With Items Selected From the 16 P.F. Questionnaire." *Ed & Psychol Meas* 21:937–46 w '61. * (*PA* 36:5HB37L)
73. LEVONIAN, EDWARD. "A Statistical Analysis of the 16 Personality Factor Questionnaire." *Ed & Psychol Meas* 21:589–96 au '61. * (*PA* 36:4HF89L)
74. MCLEOD, H. N. "My Two-Hour Psychological Test Battery." *O.P.A. Q* 14:85–7 D '61. *
75. MEYER, M. L., AND PARTIPILO, MICHAEL A. "Examiner Personality as an Influence on the Rorschach Test." *Psychol Rep* 9:221–2 O '61. *
76. MICHAEL, WILLIAM B.; BARTH, GEORGE; AND KAISER, HENRY F. "Dimensions of Temperament in Three Groups of Music Teachers." *Psychol Rep* 9:701–4 D '61. *
77. RAO, M. S. SHARADAMBA. "The Schizophrenic Profile on the 16 P.F. Questionnaire." *Indian J Psychol* 36:93–102 Je '61. *
78. SHIPMAN, W. G.; DANOWSKI, T. S.; AND MOSES, D. C., JR. "The Relation of Some Morphological, Physiological, and Genetic Dimensions to the Cattell 16PF and T.A.T. Scales." Abstract. *Acta Psychologica* 19:208–10 '61. *
79. SUHR, VIRTUS W. "Personality and Driving Efficiency." *Percept & Motor Skills* 12:34 F '61. * (*PA* 35:5720)
80. VERNIER, CLAIRE M.; BARRELL, ROBERT P.; CUMMINGS, JONATHAN W.; DICKERSON, JOSEPH H.; AND HOOPER, H. ELSTON. "Psychosocial Study of the Patient With Pulmonary Tuberculosis: A Cooperative Research Approach." *Psychol Monogr* 75(6):1–32 '61. * (*PA* 36:3JU32V)
81. ARMATAS, JAMES P., AND COLLISTER, E. GORDON. "Personality Correlates of SVIB Patterns." *J Counsel Psychol* 9:149–54 su '62. * (*PA* 37:6710)
82. BORGATTA, EDGAR F. "The Coincidence of Subtests in Four Personality Inventories." *J Social Psychol* 56:227–44 Ap '62. * (*PA* 37:1247)
83. BORTNER, RAYMAN W. "Superego Functioning and Institutional Adjustment." *Percept & Motor Skills* 14:375–9 Je '62. * (*PA* 37:3408)
84. BORTNER, RAYMAN W. "Test Differences Attributable to Age, Selection Processes, and Institutional Effects." *J Gerontol* 17:58–60 Ja '62. * (*PA* 36:5FI58B)
85. BURK, KENNETH WINFIELD. *Biographic, Interest, and Personality Characteristics of Purdue Speech and Hearing Graduates.* Doctor's thesis, Purdue University (Lafayette, Ind.), 1962. (*DA* 23:3021)
86. CATTELL, RAYMOND B. "Personality Assessment Based Upon Functionally Unitary Personality Traits, Factor Analytically Demonstrated," pp. 198–219. (*PA* 37:4977) In *Personality Research.* Proceedings of the XIV International Congress of Applied Psychology, Vol. 2. Copenhagen, Denmark: Munksgaard, Ltd., 1962. Pp. 229. *
87. CATTELL, RAYMOND B. "Psychological Measurement of Anxiety and Depression: A Quantitative Approach." Discussion, pp. S24–8. *Can Psychiatric Assn J* 7(sup):S11–28 '62. *
88. CATTELL, RAYMOND B., AND MORONY, JOHN H. "The Use of the 16 PF in Distinguishing Homosexuals, Normals, and General Criminals." *J Consult Psychol* 26:531–40 D '62. *
89. FRANCESCO, E. "A Pervasive Value: Conventional Religiosity." *J Social Psychol* 57:467–70 Ag '62. * (*PA* 37:4855)
90. HALLER, A. O., AND WOLFF, CAROLE ELLIS. "Personality Orientations of Farm, Village, and Urban Boys." *Rural Sociol* 27:275–93 S '62. * (*PA* 37:2989)
91. HALLER, ARCHIBALD O., AND THOMAS, SHAILER. "Personality Correlates of the Socioeconomic Status of Adolescent Males." *Sociometry* 25:398–404 D '62. * (*PA* 38:4094)
92. HEMPHILL, JOHN K.; GRIFFITHS, DANIEL E.; AND FREDERIKSEN, NORMAN; WITH THE ASSISTANCE OF GLEN STICE, LAURENCE IANNACCONE, WILLIAM COFFIELD, AND SYDELL CARLTON. *Administrative Performance and Personality: A Study of the Principal in a Simulated Elementary School.* New York: Bureau of Publications, Teachers College, Columbia University, 1962. Pp. xix, 432. *
93. HENDRICKSON, DONNA. "Personality Variables: Significant Departures of Occupational Therapists From Population Norms." *Am J Occup Ther* 16:127–30 My–Je '62. * (*PA* 37:5203)
94. HOLLAND, JOHN L., AND ASTIN, ALEXANDER W. "The Prediction of the Academic, Artistic, Scientific, and Social Achievement of Undergraduates of Superior Scholastic Aptitude." *J Ed Psychol* 53:132–43 Je '62. * (*PA* 37:2010)
95. LAFORGE, ROLFE. "A Correlational Study of Two Personality Tests: The MMPI and Cattell 16 PF." *J Consult Psychol* 26:402–11 O '62. * (*PA* 39:1743)
96. RUBY, WALTER MCCLINTOCK, JR. *An Investigation of Differentiating Personality Factors Between Achieving and Low Achieving College Students.* Doctor's thesis, University of Tennessee (Knoxville, Tenn.), 1962. (*DA* 23:3785)
97. STEWART, HORACE F., JR. *A Study of the Relationship Between Certain Personality Measures and Hallucinoidal Visual Imagery.* Doctor's thesis, University of Florida (Gainesville, Fla.), 1962. (*DA* 24:827)
98. AIKEN, LEWIS R., JR. "The Relationships of Dress to Selected Measures of Personality in Undergraduate Women." *J Social Psychol* 59:119–28 F '63. * (*PA* 38:910)
99. BENDIG, A. W. "A Note on Cattell's Radicalism (Q1) Scale." *J Social Psychol* 60:107–13 Je '63. * (*PA* 38:4173)
99a. BURDICK, LOIS A. "Analysis of the Sixteen Personality Factor Questionnaire and Elementary Student Teachers at Indiana State College." *Teach Col J* 35:57–9+ N '63. *
100. CATTELL, RAYMOND B. Chap. 9, "The Personality and Motivation of the Researcher From Measurements of Contemporaries and From Biography," pp. 119–31. In *Scientific Creativity: Its Recognition and Development.* Edited by Calvin W. Taylor and Frank Barron. New York: John Wiley & Sons, Inc., 1963. Pp. xxiv, 419. * (*PA* 38:2689)
101. HORN, JOHN. "Second-Order Factors in Questionnaire Data." *Ed & Psychol Meas* 23:117–34 sp '63. * (*PA* 38:2695)
102. ISAACSON, ROBERT L.; MCKEACHIE, WILBERT J.; AND MILHOLLAND, JOHN E. "Correlation of Teacher Personality Variables and Student Ratings." *J Ed Psychol* 54:110–7 Ap '63. * (*PA* 37:8288)
103. KAPOOR, S. D. "A Comparative Study of the Personality Questionnaire Items Presented in the 1st and 2nd Person." *Manas* 10(1):35–44 '63. * (*PA* 38:8496)
104. KELLY, CHARLES M. "Mental Ability and Personality Factors in Listening." *Q J Speech* 49:152–6 Ap '63. *
105. MARKS, JOHN; STAUFFACHER, JAMES C.; AND LYLE, CURTIS. "Predicting Outcome in Schizophrenia." *J Abn & Social Psychol* 66:117–27 F '63. * (*PA* 37:7076)
106. MITCHELL, JAMES V., JR. "A Comparison of the First and Second Order Dimensions of the 16 PF and CPI Inventories." *J Social Psychol* 61:151–66 O '63. * (*PA* 38:8449)
107. NELSON, THOMAS D. *Judgmental Diagnoses Versus Actuarial Diagnoses.* Doctor's thesis, University of Denver (Denver, Colo.), 1963. (*DA* 24:2126)
107a. OSMON, WILLIAM R. "The Personality Patterns of Failing Freshmen, Indiana State College, 1961–62." *Teach Col J* 35:61–5 N '63. *
108. WARBURTON, F. W.; BUTCHER, H. J.; AND FORREST, G. M. "Predicting Student Performance in a University Department of Education." *Brit J Ed Psychol* 33:68–79 F '63. * (*PA* 38:1416)

MAURICE LORR, *Chief, Outpatient Psychiatric Research Laboratory, Veterans Benefits Office; and Lecturer in Psychology, Catholic University of America; Washington, D.C.*

The 16 PF purports to measure all the main dimensions of personality revealed by factor analysis. Forms A and B each consist of 187 items and include 10 to 13 items for each factor. The simplified short Form C consists of 105 items. The majority of statements concern interests and preferences. The remaining statements represent the customary self-reports of behavior. All items are in trichotomous form.

The inventory yields 16 primary factor scores and 2 second order factor scores.

The Handbook has been carefully prepared and offers an unusually wide range of information. Norms for the 1961–62 editions of Forms A and B are given, in the form of stens, in a norms supplement. There are separate norm tables for each form and for Forms A and B combined, for American college students by sex. The Handbook Supplement for Form C presents general population and college student norms (both by sex) for this form. Except for age, characteristics of the norm samples such as occupation, social class, and source are not delineated. This is certainly an elementary requirement.

The corrected split-half reliabilities for the 1956–57 editions of Forms A and B combined range from .93 to .71 and thus from .87 to .54 for single forms. These values suggest that many single form scale internal consistencies are satisfactory for group prediction only. Only a few two-week interval stability indices are offered although such coefficients are of importance for understanding a trait and for prediction. As of January 1964 no reliability data had been published for the 1961–62 editions of Forms A and B. It would also be highly desirable to have intraclass coefficients to represent factor internal consistency. In this connection Levonian (*73*) studied the 16 PF with regard to its intrafactor interitem phi correlations. He reported that of the 1,612 significant interitem correlations (*a*) only 183 were intrafactor correlations; (*b*) of the 183, 10 were in a direction opposite from that intended by test designers; (*c*) nearly 25 per cent of all intrafactor correlations were in a direction opposite that intended by the test designers; (*d*) 30 per cent of the items had no significant intrafactor correlations. Such evidence of substantial within-factor heterogeneity calls for a critical reappraisal of scale homogeneity. A reading of the items defining the factors is supportive of this conclusion. Many of the statements making up a factor are introspectively quite diverse.

The claim is made that each of the questionnaire factors corresponds to a primary factor in behavior situations or in the *Objective-Analytic Personality Test Batteries.* Evidence of such correspondence is not explicitly offered although it should be. A report by Becker (*60*) raises doubts concerning the independence of the 16 factor scales. His factor analysis of all Form A and B 16 PF scores and scores from Guilford-Martin personality inventories showed at best 8 distinguishable factors within the 16 PF and 5 within the 13 Guilford-Martin factors. This does not imply that there may not be more than eight 16 PF factors but rather that, if such exist, they do not emerge as independent sources of variance as revealed by the tests as presently scored.

Data are provided for predictive use in industry, college, and clinic in the form of possible profile matching and criterion estimation. Tables in the Handbook offer a set of 28 representative occupational profiles. A supplement (IPAT Information Bulletin No. 1, 1959) provides factor sten profiles for 9 clinical syndrome groupings. Other Information Bulletins present additional occupational and clinical data. On the other hand, no statistical data are given as to how well the 16 PF scores discriminate among the clinical or the occupational groups. The Handbook suggests the use of the "pattern similarity coefficient" and offers a nomograph for its rapid calculation. Specification or regression equations are given for a variety of criteria such as accident proneness, scholastic performance, and occupational success of salesmen. However, such essential facts as multiple correlation coefficients and number of misclassifications are not given.

The development of the 16 PF represents and, indeed, reflects a high order of technical skill. Although at present it appears to be the best factor-based personality inventory available, it is the reviewer's view that the 16 PF is still primarily a research instrument. Its major shortcomings are those reported by Levonian and by Becker. These investigations suggest that further critical examination of scale structure and the number of factors measurable by 16 PF is needed. It is recognized that the process of construct validation is lengthy, laborious, and never ended. At the same time more specific facts concerning the construct validity of individual factor scales is needed.

For a review by C. J. Adcock, see 5:112; for reviews by Charles M. Harsh, Ardie Lubin, and J. Richard Wittenborn, see 4:87.

[175]

★A Social Competence Inventory for Adults. Adults; 1960; behavior checklist for use with mentally retarded and senile persons; 1 form (4 pages);

manual (8 pages); no data on reliability; $1.25 per 10 tests; 35¢ per specimen set; postage extra; [30] minutes; Katharine M. Banham; Family Life Publications, Inc. *

WILLIAM J. EICHMAN, *Chief, Psychology Service, Veterans Administration Hospital, Salem, Virginia.*

The *Social Competence Inventory for Adults* is described by the author as a checklist and as a standardized interview. It is similar to the *Vineland Social Maturity Scale* in purpose and approach. The trained interviewer must obtain information from a reliable and competent person who is well acquainted with the person involved. The development of the inventory was stimulated by the federal law providing for grants-in-aid to the permanently and totally disabled adult. The author points out that intelligence test results have relatively little relationship to the social adjustment in the moron group with IQ's between 50 and 75. Use of the Vineland scale was considered as an instrument to assess social competency but many of the items appeared to be unsuitable for adults. Many of the items of the present scale "were selected from case records of persons who had proved incapable of taking care of themselves." They are arranged in four groups with relatively homogeneous content. These are (*a*) bodily control, (*b*) sensory or memory deficit, (*c*) care of self, and (*d*) emotional control. The scoring system is a simple point scale with a total of 55 items. Correlations between social competence scores and IQ's on the Stanford-Binet and Wechsler-Bellevue are presented for six groups, ranging in size from 9 to 27, with a median correlation of .51. General interpretive statements are offered for different levels of total score. Validation of the classifications of total score is based upon an analysis of "case histories of more than twenty adults who had a long record of incompetence" but no data are given.

There is a distinct need for an instrument of this type. The inventory has potentiality for meeting this need, but the data provided in the manual do not adequately demonstrate this. The individual items have face validity to a high degree within each category and with regard to "social competence" in general. Nevertheless, studies of item relationship to part score and to total score should be done. Ideally, the item pool should be factor analyzed to support or change the a priori categories which are currently used. Normative studies should be conducted separately for the various levels of intelligence where the social competence inventory has potential utility. In addition, thorough validity studies should be undertaken.

The *Social Competence Inventory* has current utility as a guided interview when there is question of "social competence." It certainly has the validity of the unstandardized interview and subjective judgment which are currently used. It further guarantees that certain crucial areas of daily living will not be overlooked by the interviewer. It should not interfere with interviewing in other potentially crucial areas; it seems quite possible that the items are not all inclusive.

"Social competency" is not a simple criterion, and it seems unlikely that any psychometric approach based on traditional principles can be adequate to the task of measurement. We can expect various configural effects in general terms, and we can expect considerable variability from one social context to another. In addition, the criterion is not a psychological one which is intrinsic to the behavior of the subject. Instead, social competence can be basically defined as the tolerance of the environment toward the subject.

In general, the inventory appears to be a useful first step toward meeting the social need of evaluating "competency." However, it is a primitive beginning and no evidence for validity or reliability is available. At the present time utility seems confined to the area of a guided interview; total and part scores have not been sufficiently studied to be useful.

JEROME D. PAUKER, *Assistant Professor of Clinical Psychology, Medical School, University of Minnesota, Minneapolis, Minnesota.*

This inventory was devised, the author says, "in the absence....of a suitable rating scale of social competence for adults of limited mental ability." She says that the *Vineland Social Maturity Scale,* for example, has many items which are not appropriate for adults. The *Social Competence Inventory for Adults* is not by any means a standardized technique, nor does its author represent it as such. She states in her Examiner's Manual: "A rating scale of this kind could never be considered an exact measuring device. It is merely a means of general classification." It is essentially an aid in interviewing, containing 55 items divided into sections entitled Motor Skills and Control, Perception and Memory, Self-Care and Self-Help, and Social Relationships and Emotional Control. Those items which apply to a person in question are given a score of 1, and the total score is the sum of the applicable items.

The manual presents some guidelines for interpretation of total scores, e.g.: "An individual who scores between 15 and 30 has inadequate social competence for independent living." These are based on the author's experience with the inventory. She provides no research data to back up such conclusions, although she does write, "This scoring system is tentative, pending standardization on a sample cross-section of the population." She presents some very sketchy and inadequate comparisons with Stanford-Binet and Wechsler-Bellevue IQ's; these might better have been omitted from the manual.

This inventory, then, provides a guide for inquiry into a wide range of appropriate, practical aspects of adult social and independent living. Beyond this, the scoring system which the test author presents remains in need of evaluation.

[176]

***Social Intelligence Test: George Washington University Series, Revised Form.** Grades 9–16 and adults; 1930–55; 3 editions; manual ('55, 5 pages); reliability data and norms for total scores only; $3.75 per 25 tests of *a* or *b*; $3.25 per 25 tests of *c*; 75¢ per specimen set of all 3 editions; postage extra; F. A. Moss, Thelma Hunt, K. T. Omwake, and L. G. Woodward (*a* and manual); Center for Psychological Service. *

a) SECOND EDITION. 1930–55; 6 scores: judgment in social situations, recognition of the mental state of the speaker, memory for names and faces, observation of human behavior, sense of humor, total; 1 form ('49, 11 pages); names and faces sheet ('48, 1 page); 49(55) minutes.

b) SHORT EDITION. 1944–55; 5 scores: same as for Second Edition except for omission of memory for names and faces; 1 form ('44, 6 pages); 40(45) minutes.

c) SP (SPECIAL) EDITION. 1947–55; 3 scores: judgment in social situations, observation of human behavior, total; 1 form ('47, 4 pages); 30(35) minutes.

REFERENCES

1–20. See 40:1253.
21–29. See 3:96.
30–36. See 4:89.
37. BRUCE, MARTIN M. "The Prediction of Effectiveness as a Factory Foreman." *Psychol Monogr* 67(12):1–17 '53. * (*PA* 28:5019)
38. BASS, BERNARD M.; KARSTENDIEK, BARBARA; MCCULLOUGH, GERALD; AND PRUITT, RAY C. "Validity Information Exchange, No. 7-024: D.O.T. Code 2-66.01, 2-66.11, 2-66.12, 2-66.23, Policemen and Detectives, Public Service." *Personnel Psychol* 7:159–60 sp '54. *
39. BRUCE, MARTIN M. "Validity Information Exchange, No. 7-004: D.O.T. Code 0-97.61, Manager, Sales." *Personnel Psychol* 7:128–9 sp '54. *
40. BRUCE, MARTIN M. "Validity Information Exchange, No. 7-076: D.O.T. Code 5-91.101, Foreman II." *Personnel Psychol* 7:418–9 au '54. *
41. KAESS, WALTER A., AND WITRYOL, SAM L. "Memory for Names and Faces: A Characteristic of Social Intelligence?" *J Appl Psychol* 39:457–62 D '55. * (*PA* 30:6866)
42. BRUCE, MARTIN M. "Normative Data Information Exchange, No. 26." *Personnel Psychol* 9:533–4 w '56. *
43. BRUCE, MARTIN M. "Normative Data Information Exchange, No. 27." *Personnel Psychol* 9:535–6 w '56. *
44. BRUCE, MARTIN M. "Validity Information Exchange, No. 10-3: D.O.T. Code 1-86.11, Salesmen, Commercial Equipment and Supplies." *Personnel Psychol* 10:77–8 sp '57. *
45. HECHT, ROBERT, AND BRUCE, MARTIN M. "Normative Data Information Exchange, No. 10-38." *Personnel Psychol* 10:529 w '57. *
46. JUERGENSON, ELWOOD M. *The Relationship Between Success in Teaching Vocational Agriculture and Ability to Make Sound Judgments as Measured by Selected Instruments.* Doctor's thesis, Pennsylvania State University (University Park, Pa.), 1958. (*DA* 19:96)
47. ARON, JOEL, AND HECHT, ROBERT. "Normative Data Information Exchange, No. 12-15." *Personnel Psychol* 12:331 su '59. *
48. CRANE, WILLIAM J. "Screening Devices for Occupational Therapy Majors." *Am J Occup Ther* 16:131–2 My–Je '62. * (*PA* 37:4078)
49. *Normative Information: Manager and Executive Testing.* New York: Richardson, Bellows, Henry & Co., Inc., May 1963. Pp. 45. *
50. HERBERT, N., AND TURNBULL, G. H. "Personality Factors and Effective Progress in Teaching." *Ed R* 16:24–31 N '63. *

For reviews by Glen U. Cleeton and Howard R. Taylor, see 3:96; for a review by Robert L. Thorndike, see 40:1253.

[177]

★Spiral Aftereffect Test. Ages 5 and over; 1958; brain damage; individual; 1 form (1 Archimedes spiral); manual (5 pages); supplementary data (8 pages, reprint of *23* below); record form (1 page); $75 per set of spiral, battery operated testing apparatus, record form, manual, and supplementary data; $1.25 per spiral; 75¢ per 50 record forms; $1 per manual and supplementary data; postage extra; [3–10] minutes; Psychological Research & Development Corporation. * [Many variations of the spiral aftereffect procedure are in use. The references and reviews below relate to the procedure in general as well as to the specific test apparatus and accessories described in this entry.]

REFERENCES

1. FREEMAN, ELLIS, AND JOSEY, WILLIAM E. "Quantitative Visual Index to Memory Impairment: A Preliminary Report." *Arch Neurol & Psychiatry* 62:794–7 D '49. * (*PA* 25:4377)
2. STANDLEE, LLOYD S. "The Archimedes Negative Aftereffect as an Indication of Memory Impairment." *J Consult Psychol* 17:317 Ag '53. * (*PA* 28:4325)
3. PRICE, A. COOPER, AND DEABLER, H. L. "Diagnosis of Organicity by Means of Spiral Aftereffects." *J Consult Psychol* 19:299–302 Ag '55. * (*PA* 30:5118)
4. GALLESE, ARTHUR J., JR. "Spiral Aftereffect as a Test of Organic Brain Damage." *J Clin Psychol* 12:254–8 Jl '56. * (*PA* 31:6511)
5. SAUCER, RAYFORD T., AND DEABLER, HERDIS L. "Perception of Apparent Motion in Organics and Schizophrenics." *J Consult Psychol* 20:385–9 O '56. * (*PA* 31:8243)
6. DAVIDS, ANTHONY; GOLDENBERG, LOUIS; AND LAUFER, MAURICE W. "The Relation of the Archimedes Spiral Aftereffect and the Trail Making Test to Brain Damage in Children." *J Consult Psychol* 21:429–33 O '57. * (*PA* 33:1256)
7. EYSENCK, H. J.; HOLLAND, H.; AND TROUTON, D. S. "Drugs and Personality: 3, The Effect of Stimulant and Depressant Drugs on Visual After-Effects." *J Mental Sci* 103:650–5 Jl '57. * (*PA* 32:4940)
8. GARRETT, EPHRAIM S.; PRICE, A. COOPER; AND DEABLER, HERDIS L. "Diagnostic Testing for Cortical Brain Impairment." *A.M.A. Arch Neurol & Psychiatry* 77:223–5 F '57. * (*PA* 32:1926)
9. HARDING, GEORGE F.; GLASSMAN, SIDNEY; AND HELZ, WILLIAM C. "Maturation and the Spiral Aftereffect." *J Abn & Social Psychol* 54:276–7 Mr '57. * (*PA* 33:5281)
10. PAGE, H. A.; RAKITA, G.; KAPLAN, H. K.; AND SMITH, N. B. "Another Application of the Spiral Aftereffect in the Determination of Brain Damage." *J Consult Psychol* 21:89–91 F '57. * (*PA* 32:809)
11. SPIVACK, GEORGE, AND LEVINE, MURRAY. "The Spiral Aftereffect and Reversible Figures as Measures of Brain

Damage and Memory." *J Personality* 25:767–78 D '57. * (*PA* 33:2791)
12. STILSON, DONALD W.; GYNTHER, MALCOLM D.; AND GERTZ, BORIS. "Base Rate and the Archimedes Spiral Illusion." *J Consult Psychol* 21:435–7 O '57. * (*PA* 33:1323)
13. AARONSON, BERNARD S. "Age, Intelligence, Aphasia and the Spiral After-Effect in an Epileptic Population." *J Clin Psychol* 14:18–21 Ja '58. *
14. BERGER, DAVID; EVERSON, RICHARD; RUTLEDGE, LOUIS; AND KASKOFF, YALE DAVID. "The Spiral Aftereffect in a Neurological Setting." *J Consult Psychol* 22:249–55 Ag '58. * (*PA* 34:1867)
15. GILBERSTADT, HAROLD; SCHEIN, JEROME; AND ROSEN, ALBERT. "Further Evaluation of the Archimedes Spiral Aftereffect." *J Consult Psychol* 22:243–8 Ag '58. * (*PA* 34:1870)
16. GOLDBERG, LEWIS R., AND SMITH, PHILIP A. "The Clinical Usefulness of the Archimedes Spiral in the Diagnosis of Organic Brain Damage." *J Consult Psychol* 22:153–7 Ap '58. * (*PA* 35:3484)
17. HOLLAND, H. C., AND BEECH, H. R. "The Spiral Aftereffect as a Test of Brain Damage." *J Mental Sci* 104:466–71 Ap '58. * (*PA* 33:8353)
18. LONDON, PERRY, AND BRYAN, JAMES H. "The Influence of Instructions on Spiral Aftereffect Reports." Abstract. *Am Psychologist* 13:335 Jl '58. *
19. SCHEIN, JEROME DANIEL. *An Experimental Investigation of Some Psychological Functions in Detection of Brain Damage.* Doctor's thesis, University of Minnesota (Minneapolis, Minn.), 1958. (*DA* 19:2151)
20. PHILBRICK, EMILY B. "The Validity of the Spiral Aftereffect as a Clinical Tool for Diagnosis of Organic Brain Pathology." *J Consult Psychol* 23:39–43 F '59. * (*PA* 34:1410)
21. SPIVACK, GEORGE, AND LEVINE, MURRAY. "Spiral Aftereffect and Measures of Satiation in the Brain-Injured and Normal Subjects." *J Personality* 27:211–27 Je '59. * (*PA* 34:3899)
22. TRUSS, CARROLL V., AND ALLEN, ROBERT M. "Duration of the Spiral Aftereffect in Cerebral Palsy: An Exploratory Study." *Percept & Motor Skills* 9:216–8 S '59. * (*PA* 34:6488)
23. BLAU, THEODORE H., AND SCHAFFER, ROBERT E. "The Spiral Aftereffect Test (SAET) as a Predictor of Normal and Abnormal Electroencephalographic Records in Children." *J Consult Psychol* 24:35–42 F '60. * (*PA* 34:8232)
24. DAY, R. H. "The Aftereffect of Seen Movement and Brain Damage." *J Consult Psychol* 24:311–5 Ag '60. * (*PA* 35:2508)
25. EYSENCK, H. J., AND EYSENCK, S. B. G. "Reminiscence on the Spiral Aftereffect as a Function of Length of Rest and Number of Prerest Trials." *Percept & Motor Skills* 10:93–4 Ap '60. * (*PA* 35:5569)
26. EYSENCK, H. J., AND HOLLAND, H. "Length of Spiral Aftereffect as a Function of Drive." *Percept & Motor Skills* 11:129–30 O '60. * (*PA* 35:1559)
27. LONDON, PERRY, AND BRYAN, JAMES H. "Theory and Research on the Clinical Use of the Archimedes Spiral." *J General Psychol* 62:113–25 Ja '60. * (*PA* 34:8258)
28. MCDONOUGH, JOSEPH M. "Critical Flicker Frequency and the Spiral Aftereffect With Process and Reactive Schizophrenics." *J Consult Psychol* 24:150–5 Ap '60. * (*PA* 34:8167)
29. MAYER, EMANUELA, AND COONS, W. H. "Motivation and the Spiral Aftereffect With Schizophrenics and Brain-Damaged Patients." *Can J Psychol* 14:269–74 D '60. * (*PA* 35:4961)
30. SCHEIN, JEROME D. "The Duration of the Archimedes Spiral Afterimage in the Diagnosis of Brain Damage." *J Consult Psychol* 24:299–306 Ag '60. * (*PA* 35:2247)
31. SAPPENFIELD, BERT R., AND RIPKE, ROBERT J. "Validities of Three Visual Tests for Differentiating Organics From Schizophrenics and Normals." *J Clin Psychol* 17:276–8 Jl '61. * (*PA* 38:8892)
32. SINDBERG, RONALD M. "Some Effects of Stimulus Variation on Spiral Aftereffect in Organic and Nonorganic Subjects." *J Consult Psychol* 25:129–36 Ap '61. * (*PA* 36:4JG20S)
33. SOUEIF, M. I., AND METWALLY, A. "Testing for Organicity in Egyptian Psychiatric Patients." *Acta Psychologica* 18(4):285–96 '61. * (*PA* 36:5JG85S)
34. BRYAN, JAMES H., AND LODER, EDWARD. "Anxiety and the Spiral Aftereffect Test." *J Consult Psychol* 26:351–4 Ag '62. * (*PA* 38:3535)
35. FREUD, SHELDON L. *A Study of Physiological Mechanisms Underlying the Spiral After Effect.* Doctor's thesis, University of Connecticut (Storrs, Conn.), 1962. (*PA* 23:1781)
36. LEVINE, MURRAY, AND SPIVACK, GEORGE. "Adaptation to Repeated Exposure to the Spiral Visual Aftereffect in Brain Damaged, Emotionally Disturbed, and Normal Individuals." *Percept & Motor Skills* 14:425–6 Je '62. * (*PA* 37:3539)
37. SCOTT, THOMAS R., AND MEDLIN, RUFUS E. "Psychophysical Measurement of the Spiral Aftereffect: The MMG." *Am J Psychol* 75:319–21 Je '62. * (*PA* 37:4166)
38. WHITMYRE, JOHN W., AND KURTZKE, JOHN F. "The Archimedes Spiral Aftereffect and Impaired Mentation." *J Clin Psychol* 18:118–21 Ap '62. * (*PA* 38:8930)
39. CLARIDGE, G. S., AND HERRINGTON, R. N. "An EEG Correlate of the Archimedes Spiral After-Effect and Its Relationship With Personality." *Behav Res Ther* 1:217–29 D '63. *
40. FREUD, SHELDON L. "Duration as a Measure of the Spiral Aftereffect." *Percept & Motor Skills* 17:643–6 O '63. * (*PA* 38:5073)
41. KORMAN, MAURICE, AND BLUMBERG, STANLEY. "Comparative Efficiency of Some Tests of Cerebral Damage." *J Consult Psychol* 27:303–9 Ag '63. * (*PA* 38:2985)
42. MANN, LESTER; ALVORD, AGNES; AND PRICE, HARRY. "The Spiral Aftereffect Test (SAET) as a Predictor of School Adjustment and Achievement in First Grade Children." *J Clin Psychol* 19:206–8 Ap '63. * (*PA* 39:5078)
43. SCOTT, THOMAS R.; BRAGG, ROBERT A.; AND SMARR, ROY G. "Brain Damage Diagnosis With the MMG." *J Consult Psychol* 27:45–53 F '63. * (*PA* 37:8146)

WILLIAM J. EICHMAN, *Chief, Psychology Service, Veterans Administration Hospital, Salem, Virginia.*

The spiral aftereffect equipment supplied by this company does not represent a test in the accepted sense of the term. Although considerable work has been done with this perceptual phenomenon, techniques and equipment have varied widely from one investigation to another and cannot be considered entirely comparable. Precise norms on large representative samples have not been obtained with any single procedure. This disadvantage is ameliorated by the fact that perception of the after image tends to be an all or none phenomenon; but nevertheless, it remains a problem. The *Spiral Aftereffect Test* equipment is accompanied by a manual, scoring sheets, and a reprint by Blau and Schaffer (*23*). The manual is not at all satisfactory, but the reprint does contain useful data. These will be discussed separately. In addition, there is considerable accumulated literature on the spiral aftereffect task which deserves additional comment.

The equipment is battery-operated and appears to be well constructed. It has clockwise and counterclockwise rotations at a speed of approximately 82 rpm. An Archimedes spiral of 920° is used. The test procedure is simple and objective and should not take over 15 minutes for administration. Only a single page is devoted to interpretation of results, but no data are presented in regard to reliability, validity, or norms. No references to research are given. The phrasing contained in the manual obviously refers to use of the test in a neuropsychiatric setting with adults. Eight trials are given with a score of 1 for each aftereffect which is perceived. The normal or psychiatric patient is expected to achieve the perfect score of 8; performance at the other end of the range is indicative of "intra-cranial pathology." Aside from a few cautionary remarks regarding false positives, this is all that the manual provides. Thus, it is completely inadequate for clinical or experimental use.

The reprint which is included with the equipment must be considered as a supplemental manual, although this is not stated in any explicit manner. The instructions for administration differ slightly from the manual to the reprint. Blau and Schaffer present a brief, but adequate, review of the literature up to 1958. Thirteen of these studies used adults as subjects and dealt with the detection of organic pathology; three dealt with children, but one of these was a normative study exclusively. Blau and Schaffer studied 420 children who were examined at an outpatient psychological clinic. A U-shaped distribution of scores was found for this sample. The majority of children achieved perfect scores, and the second peak in the distribution is at 0. None of these children were thought to have organic pathology. Other tests utilized included the Bender-Gestalt, Draw-A-Person, and selected tests from the WISC. The criterion was EEG records. Thus, these investigators set for themselves the most difficult task of discriminating borderline "organic" children (those with low scores) from a normal group (those with high scores). They report extremely significant results for the SAET and less conspicuous but significant prediction for most of the other tests. They report 100 per cent correct prediction for normal EEG records and 86 per cent prediction for the abnormal records.

This very significant prediction is extremely unusual for studies in the area of organic brain damage. The basic criticism of most tests for organic brain damage is that the criteria are very complex, whereas the test is usually quite a simple and limited sampling of the subject's behavior. Most studies use an "organic" group and compare it with one or more control groups. Although the number and types of brain damage are usually reported, the organic group is still dealt with as a homogeneous category. Inconsistent results from one study to another are usually a result of failures to take into account the nature of the brain damage, the location, the severity, and the chronicity. In addition, most studies, whether validation or cross validation, employ an organic group where diagnosis is clearcut. With such groups, it is seldom necessary for psychological tests to be administered. When the test is later applied to more difficult cases in a clinical setting, the results are often quite disappointing. The Blau and Schaffer study avoids this last criticism since their organic subjects do not show symptomatic signs of organic dysfunction. Their experimental task, however, is extremely simple and limited; and it seems too optimistic to expect such positive results in further replications.

The literature on the spiral aftereffects task has expanded considerably since 1958. Blau and Schaffer's hope that other investigators would use their procedures has not been fulfilled except for a few studies. In terms of discriminating adult organics from adult controls, 15 out of 16 studies reviewed report significant results. Thus, this simple task seems to have considerable potentiality for diagnostic screening.

The expanding literature deals with a number of basic psychological or physiological variables which influence the perception of the spiral aftereffect. Several studies indicate that it is only those organics who have memory deficit or impaired mentation who show poor performance. McDonough (*28*) investigated the process and reactive dimension in schizophrenia and found that these groups do not differ from each other while both can be discriminated from organic subjects. Several studies with normal subjects report that high drive state or anxiety interfere with perception of the after image. Congruent with this, a study by London and Bryan (*18*) and another study by Mayer and Coons (*29*) report that organic subjects are able to report the aftereffect when reassuring instructions are used. It seems quite possible that anxiety is an intervening variable in the failure of organic subjects to perceive the aftereffect. Schein's results (*30*) seem to indicate that the brain damaged patient is more easily confused than the NP patient, that he sees the phenomenon as often as other subjects but fails to report it. Sindberg (*32*) systematically varied exposure time and speed of rotation with normals, NP patients, and organics. He reports extremely good discrimination of groups (92 per cent of controls and 88 per cent of organics) but also reports that the most successful discrimination is with conditions of medium difficulty. These are at slower rotation speeds than possible with the equipment supplied by this test concern. Optimum exposure time is also greater than that which is used in the Blau and Schaffer study. Several studies report that there is no relationship between task performance and age, sex, intelligence, or length of hospitalization. Reliability appears to be adequate.

Recent literature with children is sparse. Mann and others (*42*) find significant prediction of first grade achievement and adjustment. Bryan and Loder (*34*), using normal children, report that anxious subjects report significantly fewer aftereffects.

In summary, it can be concluded that the spiral aftereffect procedure has considerable potential for the detection of organic brain damage in adults. There are fewer studies with children and greater caution is indicated. The administration of the task is simple, objective, and consumes little time. A fact that seems worthy of note is the successful discrimination of organics from schizophrenic patients; most previous tests for the detection of brain damage appear to have less success in this area. Maximal discrimination appears to be related to a number of variables including instructions, motivational state, exposure time, and rotation speed. The most effective procedure remains to be discovered. Before this task can be standardized, more basic research needs to be done; standardization at this time seems premature. At present, it seems best that the clinician or researcher obtain spiral aftereffect equipment which has adjustable rotation speed rather than the fixed speed provided by this apparatus.

Ralph M. Reitan, *Professor of Psychology (Neurology), and Director, Section of Neuropsychology, Indiana University Medical Center, Indianapolis, Indiana.*

The spiral aftereffect has been investigated rather extensively as a behavioral response subserved by underlying physiological mechanisms of vision (*35*), as an indicator of memory impairment (*1, 2*), and as a test of the organic integrity of the brain. The emphasis in this report will be upon findings related to the last of these areas.

The *Spiral Aftereffect Test* utilizes an Archimedes spiral of 920°, mounted usually on a 6 to 8 inch circular disc. The disc is usually rotated at 78 rpm, but various investigators have employed rotation speeds varying from 18 to 100 rpm. The subject views the spiral at distances that have varied from 6 to 8 feet. Varying exposure times have also been used, but a 30-second exposure was characteristic of the original studies. Instructions to the subject require him to fixate his vision on the rotating spiral. Following the determined exposure time, the subject is asked to report his observation of what the spiral is doing. Four to 10 trials have usually been used.

The apparatus described in the test entry above permits a clockwise and counterclockwise rotation of a standard Archimedes spiral (920°) which is imprinted on a heavy cardboard disc 7¼ inches in diameter. The manual indicates that rotation speed is approximately 82 rpm. The apparatus is compact and works well and easily. However, on a series of four forward and four reverse trials, as called for by the test, a range of 77 to 85 rpm was obtained. On additional trials, totaling 10 forward and 10 reverse, the speed of rotation deteriorated to a low of 69 rpm. A one-year guarantee is provided the purchaser with respect to mechanical difficulty due to faulty manufacture. The instructions for administration and scoring of the test are perfectly straightforward and clear. Scores of 3, 2, or 1 are equated with the following interpretation: "Highly Indicative of the Presence of Intra-Cranial Pathology. Refer for Neurologic and Electroencephalographic Evaluation." This kind of advice regarding interpretation of the results does not appear to be properly qualified in consideration of the diversity of research findings described below.

Price and Deabler (*3*) reported nearly perfect differentiation of 120 patients with central nervous system disease or damage from 40 psychiatric patients and 40 hospital employees, the brain damaged subjects nearly always failing to report the aftereffect in contrast to the regular reports of the aftereffect by the other subjects. Garrett and others (*8*) obtained very similar results in a validational study. Another instance of outstanding agreement of SAET with criterion information is represented in the study of Blau and Schaffer (*23*) in which the apparatus described in the above entry was used. In a sample of 420 referrals to an outpatient psychological clinic, 50 children were identified who failed to perceive the aftereffect on 8 trials. Twenty control children were selected, matching the experimental group in age, who had obtained maximal scores in perceiving the aftereffect. An independent review of EEG tracings was made for these 70 children, with classifications of normal and abnormal assigned. The normal children were identically classified by the two procedures; the SAET was 86 per cent accurate in predicting abnormal EEG records. Other standard psychological tests used in this study were significant but less accurate in their correlation with EEG classifications. Blau and Schaffer conclude that the SAET "probably in combination with one or more standard psychological instruments, would seem to be the best available technique" for determining which patients should be referred for neurological study. This conclusion, however, is not justified by the design of the study since the groups were selected to maximize SAET differences rather than differences in performances on the other tests used.

A considerable number of studies, using various aftereffect procedures, have reported less striking findings than those cited above. Gallese (*4*) found that 3 per cent of persons without brain damage were misclassified whereas 66 per cent of persons with cerebral damage (excluding subjects with idiopathic convulsions and brain damage associated with alcoholism) were correctly identified. Page and others (*10*) found that less than half as many brain damaged subjects reported the aftereffect as did a group with personality disturbances. Davids and others (*6*) reported that normal children performed better than either children with psychiatric disturbances or brain lesions, but that the group with brain damage was significantly poorer than either other group. Schein (*30*) found that 37.7 per cent of a brain damaged group failed to report as compared with 8.7 per cent of psychiatric patients and 12.5 per cent of hospitalized normals. Certain of his results suggested, however, that the brain damaged subjects may perceive the aftereffect but are more readily confused than other subjects and fail to report it. Aaronson's results (*13*) indicated that 44 per cent of 65 epileptic patients made two or more errors, and poor performances were associated with lower Wechsler scores, difficulty in naming common objects, and sensory perceptual impairment especially toward the right side of the body. His findings raise a question of the influence on SAET results of inability to verbalize reactions to an ambiguous stimulus situation. The questions raised by Schein and Aaronson are offered support by the results of a study by Whitmyre and Kurtzke (*38*). They composed two groups with brain damage, one having defective mentation as judged from physical neurological examination and the other showing no such apparent defect. The group without mentation defect was comparable to a group with schizophrenic reactions whereas the group with impaired mentation failed to report the aftereffect significantly more frequently than did the other two groups. Spivack and Levine (*21*) found that the presence of aftereffect was statistically less frequent in a brain damaged group than in controls, but that absence of aftereffect was practically inefficient as a diagnostic sign. The duration of aftereffect, however, was greater for brain damaged subjects. In a later study (*36*), these investigators confirmed the finding regarding duration of aftereffect and also found that normals and emotionally disturbed subjects demonstrated an increased failure, as compared to the brain damaged group, to report aftereffect in the later trials of a series. Holland and Beech (*17*), however, found that the duration of aftereffect was reduced in brain damaged subjects as compared to controls, but that both groups were generally able to see the aftereffect. Gilberstadt and others (*15*) obtained results with regard to reported perception of aftereffect that were within the range of studies reported above. However, when base-rate data were applied, there was no improvement in diagnostic efficiency provided by the test scores. Goldberg and Smith (*16*) found that normals reported aftereffect in every instance, but that psychiatric, post-EST, and brain damaged subjects, in respective order, performed with decreasing efficiency. When scores were adjusted for age these latter groups became statistically indistinguishable. Generally, however, insignificant relationships between age and perception of aftereffect have been reported. Berger and others (*14*) found that 28 per cent of patients admitted to a neurological ward were unable to perform satisfactorily on the spiral task. While performances were unrelated to a number of neurological variables, they were significantly related to spinal fluid findings, visual field studies, and global neurological judgments of brain damage. London and Bryan (*27*) and Bryan and Loder (*34*) have reported results suggesting that anxiety provoked by the test requirements or by specially structured situations may inhibit reports or possibly perception of aftereffect. In a detailed study, Sindberg (*32*) found that only 6 of 50 brain damaged subjects reported aftereffect 6 or more times in 10 trials, but that 46 of 50 neuropsychiatric subjects reported aftereffect. College students gave results almost identical to the neuropsychiatric group. He found that exposure time, rotation speed, and direction of rotation had certain significant effects on reporting aftereffect and felt that multiple factors are of influence. Among the studies reviewed, Philbrick (*20*) was the only investigator who failed to find results of any significance.

The above findings certainly substantiate a conclusion that perception of spiral aftereffect has something to do with the condition of the cerebrum. The efficiency of the test as an indicator of brain damage, however, varies greatly from one study to another. This same statement would be true of almost any test in which identical apparatus has not been used, conditions of testing have varied, and especially a great variety of groups with and without cerebral damage have been employed. The range and variety of conditions subsumed under the category of brain damage is so diverse and variable that uniform, consistent, or even completely compatible results for a single test could hardly be expected. Although the *Spiral Aftereffect Test* is of potential importance, its usefulness still remains to be determined by the individual clinician through experience regarding its contribution to his own data in his specific setting.

[178]

★Stanford Hypnotic Susceptibility Scale. College and adults; 1959–62; Forms A ('59), B ('59), C ('62); Form C, which is for research use only, contains more varied items and is not considered a parallel form; manual for Forms A and B ('59, 56 pages, including both forms and sample interrogatory and scoring blanks); manual for Form C ('62, 52 pages, including test and sample scoring booklet); separate scoring blanks ('59, 1 page) for Forms A, B; interrogatory blank ('59, 1 page) for Forms A and B; scoring booklet ('62, 6 pages) for Form C; norms for college students only; 50¢ per pad of 25 scoring blanks; 75¢ per pad of 50 interrogatory blanks; $2.65 per 25 scoring booklets; $3.25 per manual for Forms A and B; $1.50 per manual for Form C; $4.75 per specimen set of all 3 forms; postage extra; (40) minutes; André M. Weitzenhoffer and Ernest R. Hilgard; Consulting Psychologists Press, Inc. *

REFERENCES

1. Hilgard, Ernest R.; Weitzenhoffer, André M.; and Gough, Philip. "Individual Differences in Susceptibility to Hypnosis." *Proc Nat Acad Sci* 44:1255–9 D 15 '58. *
2. Hilgard, Ernest R.; Weitzenhoffer, André M.; Landes, Judah; and Moore, Rosemarie K. "The Distribution of Susceptibility to Hypnosis in a Student Population: A Study Using the Stanford Hypnotic Susceptibility Scale." *Psychol Monogr* 75(8):1–22 '61. * (*PA* 36:3II22H)
3. London, Perry, and Fuhrer, Marcus. "Hypnosis, Motivation, and Performance." *J Personality* 29:321–33 S '61. * (*PA* 37:3386)
4. Weitzenhoffer, André M., and Sjoberg, Bernard M. "Suggestibility With and Without 'Induction of Hypnosis.'" *J Nerv & Mental Dis* 132:204–20 Mr '61. * (*PA* 36:1II04W)
5. Hilgard, Ernest R. "Lawfulness Within Hypnotic Phenomena," pp. 1–29. In *Hypnosis: Current Problems.* Edited by George H. Estabrooks. New York: Harper & Row, Publishers, Inc., 1962. Pp. ix, 285. *
6. Hilgard, Ernest R., and Lauer, Lillian W. "Lack of Correlation Between the California Psychological Inventory and Hypnotic Susceptibility." *J Consult Psychol* 26:331–5 Ag '62. * (*PA* 38:4432)
7. Lang, Peter J., and Lazovik, A. David. "Personality and Hypnotic Susceptibility." *J Consult Psychol* 26:317–22 Ag '62. * (*PA* 38:4433)
8. London, Perry. "Hypnosis in Children: An Experimental Approach." *Int J Clin & Exp Hypnosis* 10:79–91 Ap '62. * (*PA* 37:3385)
9. London, Perry; Cooper, Leslie M.; and Johnson, Harold J. "Subject Characteristics in Hypnosis Research: 2, Attitudes Towards Hypnosis, Volunteer Status, and Personality Measures; 3, Some Correlates of Hypnotic Susceptibility." *Int J Clin & Exp Hypnosis* 10:13–21 Ja '62. * (*PA* 37:1455)
10. Weitzenhoffer, André M. "Estimation of Hypnotic Susceptibility in a Group Situation." *Am J Clin Hypnosis* 5:115–26 O '62. * (*PA* 37:5246)
11. Bentler, P. M. "Interpersonal Orientation in Relation to Hypnotic Susceptibility." *J Consult Psychol* 27:426–31 O '63. * (*PA* 38:4226)
12. Bentler, P. M., and Hilgard, Ernest R. "A Comparison of Group and Individual Induction of Hypnosis With Self-Scoring and Observer-Scoring." *Int J Clin & Exp Hypnosis* 11:49–54 Ja '63. * (*PA* 37:8085)
13. Bentler, P. M., and Roberts, Mary R. "Hypnotic Susceptibility Assessed in Large Groups." *Int J Clin & Exp Hypnosis* 11:93–7 Ap '63. * (*PA* 38:4430)
14. Hilgard, Ernest R., and Bentler, P. M. "Predicting Hypnotizability From the Maudsley Personality Inventory." *Brit J Psychol* 54:63–9 F '63. * (*PA* 37:8091)
15. Schulman, Robert E., and London, Perry. "Hypnotic Susceptibility and MMPI Profiles." *J Consult Psychol* 27:157–60 Ap '63. * (*PA* 37:8101)
16. Shor, Ronald E., and Orne, Emily Carota. "Norms on the Harvard Group Scale of Hypnotic Susceptibility, Form A." *Int J Clin & Exp Hypnosis* 11:39–47 Ja '63. * (*PA* 37:8102)
17. Weitzenhoffer, André M. "The Nature of Hypnosis: Part 1." *Am J Clin Hypnosis* 5:295–321 Ap '63. * (*PA* 37:8104, title only)

Milton V. Kline, *Consulting Psychologist, 345 West 58th Street, New York, New York.*

The Stanford scales, not tests in the usual sense employed by psychologists, were designed to evaluate the general level of susceptibility to hypnosis. Forms A and B are alternate forms of the same scale. Form C, which includes items not found in Forms A and B, provides for the evaluation of more complex hypnotic phenomena such as age regression, hallucinatory experiences, and sensory alterations.

A standardized induction procedure is outlined and a quantitative system for measuring response to this induction approach is well scaled. The scales are well designed for the objective measuring of an experimental subject's response to the verbal induction of hypnosis and his range of hypnotic responses. As such the procedure provides a basis for some comparative evaluations of a group of subjects who may be employed in research studies.

Scoring is very objective and simple. The

Stanford scales are better constructed (standardized) than previously existing clinical scales, but probably more difficult to utilize in a clinical setting than some of the older techniques like the Davis-Husband scale.

While the authors point out the need for careful inquiry after the hypnotic experience and emphasize the significance of subjective reactions with hypnosis, the Stanford scales themselves do not serve as an effective instrument for diagnostic investigation of the meaningfulness or the psychodynamic basis of the subject's reaction to and management of the hypnotic relationship and process.

In the hands of experimental hypnotists, the Stanford scales are useful, well developed instruments for quantifying some aspects of hypnotic response in experimental settings. They would appear to have little value in a clinical setting and the investigator untrained in hypnosis should not attempt to use the scales as a means of learning how to induce hypnosis.

The *Stanford Hypnotic Susceptibility Scale* represents the most recent attempts at measuring responsiveness to the verbal induction of hypnosis. More specifically this scale quantitatively evaluates reactions of a basically college population group to a standardized means of measuring aspects of susceptibility and hypnotizability, the two not necessarily always being the same. In the hands of experienced research investigators, it can be a useful instrument in attempting to compare experimental groups with respect to certain aspects of hypnotic response.

C. SCOTT MOSS, *Mental Health Consultant, National Institute of Mental Health, United States Public Health Service, San Francisco, California.*

This scale is a modification of one developed by Friedlander and Sarbin in 1938,[1] and is an outgrowth of a long term study of individual differences to hypnosis. The authors operationally define "susceptibility" as the number of times the subject acts like a hypnotized person when hypnosis is induced by a standard procedure and measured by standard test items.

Form A tests the susceptibility of those experiencing hypnosis for the first time, and consists of a complete set of instructions for hypnotic induction and for measuring susceptibility to the induction on 12 specific tasks. Form B is an alternate form for follow-up use and differs in minor detail from Form A. The equivalence of the two forms is demonstrated by standardization data on 124 Stanford students. Retest reliability after a one or two day interval resulted in a correlation of .83. Validity is attested to by the demonstration that some of the higher and lower scoring subjects made respectively better and worse hypnotic subjects on a later date, though there were inconsistencies.

A noteworthy limitation is that norms are based on undergraduate college students, hardly a sample representative of the general population. A related criticism is that these were "coerced volunteers," that is, students in an introductory psychology course who chose the hypnotic experiment in preference to other less palatable experiments. Because of volunteer bias, as well as other factors in subject selection, norms based on various populations, carefully selected in defined ways, are needed. It is to the credit of the authors that they have anticipated many of the objections enumerated here and are currently engaged in the effort to provide more satisfactory normative data.

Another important uncontrolled factor is the so called *social demand* characteristics of the experimental situation. This study was conducted in a college setting by psychology professors, a situation which may predispose students to a high proportion of positive responses with or without hypnosis. The unanswered question is how much of a subject's score is attributable to the demand qualities of the situation and how much to hypnosis, or to put it another way, what would have been the response of these same subjects in a different setting and with hypnosis induced by someone other than an important authority figure?

This last question raises an important theoretical issue, namely, the seeming assumption of the authors that hypnotic susceptibility is a relatively stable personality characteristic. A large number of studies have attempted to establish a relationship between personality traits and hypnotic susceptibility with contradictory and negative results. It is possible that situational factors play a much greater role than has been generally recognized. There is also the confounding probability that once in-

1 FRIEDLANDER, J. W., AND SARBIN, T. R. "The Depth of Hypnosis." *J Abn & Social Psychol* 33:453–75 O '38. *

duced, there is a spontaneous fluctuation in "depth" on an almost moment-to-moment basis.

The authors express the hope that professional as well as research persons will find the scale useful. The likelihood is that practitioners will reject the standardized induction technique as mechanical and inadequate and the test items as injurious to the therapeutic relationship. Most hypnotherapists avoid the use of challenges altogether these days, and the fact that the authors have interspersed easy and difficult items only compounds the problem. Rightly or wrongly, many experienced hypnotherapists also believe there is little or no relationship between trance depth and therapeutic success (the authors apparently differentiate between "susceptibility" and "depth" though this distinction is not made clear in the discussion of their scale).

Form C is also recommended for the second or later testing, when alternate forms of induction are used (the induction procedure is optional), when it is desired to have test items in ascending order of difficulty (making possible an abbreviated administration), or when subjects are being selected for their capacity to experience more varied hypnotic phenomena (the content is richer). Because Form C will often be substituted for Form B, six of the 12 items from Form A are retained unchanged. Despite the differences in test content, the score distributions for Forms A, B, and C are very similar, and according to the authors intercorrelations between test items indicate that all forms are highly saturated with a common factor.

Attention is called to the *Harvard Group Scale of Hypnotic Susceptibility*, Form A (see 112), an adaptation for group administration with self-report scoring of Form A of the Stanford scale. Norms based on data secured from 132 volunteer college students (*16*) indicate that the group-administered version yields results congruent with the individually-administered original. Experience with 79 additional subjects led Bentler and Hilgard (*12*) to the conclusion that self-scores are very similar to observer ratings and that the hypnotic susceptibility manifested in the group is very comparable to that obtained in the individual administration of hypnotic susceptibility tests.

In summary, the Stanford scale represents the latest in a rather extended series of efforts to devise an objective measure of hypnotic susceptibility. While its predecessors have not met with general acceptance by authorities in the field, the present investigators promise a serious and concerted effort to develop objective criteria which will aid the experimentalist in developing both measures of susceptibility and the identification of experiential and personality correlates. The authors' obvious conviction that hypnotic behavior must follow the same laws as other psychological phenomena and therefore can be subjected to laboratory study is most laudatory. It is to be hoped that the apparent feasibility of a group form will encourage the widespread reporting of the use of this scale by a variety of competent research investigators working with diverse subject populations in a multiplicity of settings.

[179]

★Stanford Profile Scales of Hypnotic Susceptibility. College and adults; 1963; 25 scores: agnosia and cognitive distortion (4 item scores plus total), positive hallucinations (4 item scores plus total), negative hallucinations (4 item scores plus total), dreams and regressions (4 item scores plus total), amnesia and post-hypnotic compulsions (3 item scores plus total), total susceptibility; one of the item scores for amnesia and post-hypnotic compulsions is derived from Form A of the *Stanford Hypnotic Susceptibility Scale* and provision is also made for profiling 3 additional scores (loss of motor coordination and 2 subscores) from this scale; Forms 1, 2, (49 pages, both forms presented in a single booklet); forms may be used separately but administration of both is recommended and profile is based upon administration of both; manual (83 pages, includes sample copy of scoring booklet for each form and stimulus cards for 2 subtests); scoring booklet (12–15 pages) for each form; $1.50 per booklet of both forms; $7.75 per 25 sets of scoring booklets for both forms; $2.50 per manual; $4.25 per specimen set; postage extra; administration time not reported; various equipment necessary for administration; Ernest R. Hilgard, André M. Weitzenhoffer (test), Lillian W. Lauer (manual), and Arlene H. Morgan (manual); Consulting Psychologists Press, Inc. *

SEYMOUR FISHER, *Research Professor of Psychology, and Director, Psychopharmacology Laboratory, Boston University School of Medicine, Boston, Massachusetts.*

The *Stanford Profile Scales of Hypnotic Susceptibility* are specially constructed instruments which, at present, have no "validity" in the conventional sense, and consequently are primarily of immediate interest only to researchers. In the foreword to the published test, three general uses are proposed: subject selection, correlation with personality variables, and a change measure of hypnotic susceptibility. However, the test manual itself does not contain any section on "validity," although

Hilgard argues for its "construct validity" (personal communication) and for its overall utility (cf. page 34 of manual which discusses the interpretation of subscale profiles).

The development of these scales represents a reasonable step in Hilgard's (and his Stanford team's) systematic approach to the study of hypnotic behavior. The first step resulted in the publication of the *Stanford Hypnotic Susceptibility Scale;* subsequently, it was felt that, despite the presence of a strong common factor of general susceptibility, sufficient unexplained variance existed to justify moving on to the second step—i.e., a "kind of scale was needed, appropriate to higher scoring subjects, that would be diagnostic of the special areas of susceptibility and insusceptibility."

The Profile Scales yield standard scores on six subscales, each of which can be plotted to provide a profile for the individual subject. Items were clustered on the basis of "intended function," thus representing "intuitive" factors. Judging from the table of intercorrelations, considerable overlap exists among the six subscales; although the authors indicate their awareness of this problem, the disturbing thought still persists: is there really adequate evidence to warrant the use of these Profile Scales rather than a single susceptibility score? Close to 40 per cent of subjects have flat profiles, and almost 75 per cent "can be accounted for as either nondeviating or deviating as much as 1 S.D. in only one subscale." However, the notion that two moderately susceptible hypnotic subjects with equal total scores can be meaningfully differentiated on the basis of patterns of *particular* items which were passed and failed is an intriguing one, and will certainly appeal to the clinically-oriented investigator who seeks reliable psychodynamic correlates of hypnotic performance.

The clinician may be less happy at the realization that much of the variation being measured here becomes manifest following a somewhat superficial (albeit standardized) induction of hypnosis. Is it possible that the perceived need for profile scales might be obviated by intensive efforts to deepen the "trance" maximally prior to a full-dress testing for susceptibility? Available evidence does indeed suggest that for the subjects at both extremes of susceptibility, the nature and sequence of suggestions are probably unimportant; it could well be, however, that for the very group of intermediate subjects for whom these scales are designed, such factors might prove extremely relevant.

One additional characteristic of these Profile Scales merits comment. It is obvious that, in common with all factor-analytic approaches, if other kinds of items or scoring dimensions had been included in the scale contents, other "factors" could be constructed intuitively and empirically; e.g., suggestions of anxiety or increased heart rate might result in an "Autonomic Lability" subscale; or an appropriate scoring modification of existing items could yield a subscale of "Activity-Passivity," first suggested by White[1] many years ago. I am not implying that these other "factors" would necessarily be either more or less useful than the specific ones put forward by the Stanford team; I am, however, emphasizing the fact that these subscales are selective, and only empirical attempts to relate them (and similar subscales) to personality characteristics and other variables can tell us about their ultimate utility and validity. One should always bear in mind the sobering thought that certain "profiles" can be so unique that there are as many different profiles as there are individuals—fingerprint classification, for instance.

Use of the Profile Scales requires additional materials and equipment which do not come with the scales. The materials are generally minor in nature and easily obtainable, but the recommended electrical stimulator and a metal box with light (used for analgesia and hallucinatory tests, respectively) call for some instrumentation of questionable necessity. At the risk of being labeled "antiscientific," this reviewer with clear conscience recommends substituting "mild," "moderate," and "strong" jabs (the experimenter's judgment will provide adequate definition) with a sterile needle for testing analgesia, and two simple flashlights (one on, the other off) for testing positive hallucinations. Should it be objected that these alterations might destroy the standardization norms, I can only question whether the basic stability of these particular phenomena is worthy of writing home about.

In summary, the Profile Scales are available for researchers interested in hypnotic phenomena. Basically, the meaning of these scales is

1 WHITE, ROBERT W. "Two Types of Hypnotic Trance and Their Personality Correlates." *J Psychol* 3:279–89 Ja '37. * (*PA* 11:4127)

presently unknown, but they offer the investigator a multivariate criterion of hypnotic susceptibility. The Profile Scales should not be confused with the *Stanford Hypnotic Susceptibility Scale,* the latter providing a single index of overall susceptibility or "depth" of hypnosis. The Profile Scales do not replace or compete with the *Stanford Hypnotic Susceptibility Scale* (total scores from the two measures only correlate about .50). Whether the subscale differences in the Profile Scales are more apparent than real remains to be determined; in the meantime, if one is studying the effects of some treatment (e.g., drugs, social influence) on hypnotic susceptibility, profile scores might be more sensitive to treatment effects than a single total score. Similarly, personality correlates and other organismic variables might be more reliably related to particular profiles than to an overall index of susceptibility. Undoubtedly, these Profile Scales deserve—and will receive—close empirical scrutiny by researchers in coming years. Their clinical application must impatiently await further validity findings.

Eugene E. Levitt, *Professor of Clinical Psychology, Indiana University School of Medicine, Indianapolis, Indiana.*

The *Stanford Profile Scales of Hypnotic Susceptibility* are essentially an extension of the *Stanford Hypnotic Susceptibility Scale,* of which there are three forms. Forms A and B, which appeared in 1959, are heavily weighted with motor tasks. While these scales have probably been more widely used in a short time than any of their several predecessors, their ability to predict the subject's performance on more complex tasks frequently leaves something to be desired. Form C, which was published in 1962, was an attempt to augment the variety of behaviors which might be tapped in determining hypnotic susceptibility. The Profile Scales represent a further extension of hypnotic tasks in the direction of complexity.

Each of the two forms of the Profile Scales is composed of nine sensory, perceptual, or cognitive phenomena. There are no motor behaviors in either form, but hypnosis is induced via a simple motor task in both, so that at least a sample of such behavior is available. Items on Form 1 are not duplicated on Form 2, but most are parallel either categorically (positive versus negative hallucination) or in terms of the sense modality involved (analgesia versus heat hallucination). Performance on each of the items in the Profile Scales is assessed on a 4-point scale, with scores ranging from 0 to 3. The assignment of numerical values to behaviors is on a logical, rather than an empirical, basis, and will require much clinical judgment at times, but it at least permits the scorer to make a stab at taking into account the consensual belief among experienced hypnotists that hypnotic behavior is often not of the all-or-none variety. The standardization data indicate that distributions of scores of a number of items will tend to be bimodal with modes at 0 and 3. Further investigation is needed to assess the empirical utility of the 4-point scoring system.

Both of the scales require equipment which is not furnished with the test itself. However, the materials needed for the administration of Form 2 are easily obtainable, and it is therefore likely that it will be employed more frequently than Form 1.

The standardization sample consisted of 112 students at Stanford University, whose scores on Form A of the *Stanford Hypnotic Susceptibility Scale* were at least 4. The test constructors point out that the sample thus is not random or unselected, not even from among their own volunteer group. However, this does not undermine the purpose of the Profile Scales, which is to have an objective basis for selecting subjects for hypnosis experiments in which various kinds of behaviors will be required. They are also intended to investigate the hypnotic behavior of the individual who is "moderately susceptible" to hypnosis, i.e., the individual who performs well enough to be used in hypnosis research. There would be little point in establishing a profile or in finding out more about the behavior of an individual who is such a poor hypnotic subject that he could not be used experimentally. Thus, the deliberate discarding of low scorers on the Susceptibility Scale from the standardization sample for the Profile Scales is warranted. The test constructors have carefully avoided generalizations from their restricted samples to broader populations and make no claims about hypnotic behavior in general.

The matter of validity is not taken up in the manual, but this is a calculated omission. There is no need to demonstrate empirical validity for an instrument like the Profile Scales, if their use is limited to the experimental applications suggested by the test constructors. They function like an aptitude test which is composed of items which are themselves instances of the behaviors which the test seeks to measure. Face validity suffices. A degree of empirical validity is implied by the correlations between the Profile Scales and Form A of the Susceptibility Scale (.53 for Form 1 and .47 for Form 2). These correlations are doubtlessly attenuated by the elimination of low scorers on Form A and by the limited range of possible scores on the Profile Scales.

The correlation between scores on Forms 1 and 2 is .75, which may be considered as a reliability estimate since the forms are parallel in terms of items. If the forms are used together as a single instrument, the reliability estimate attained by the Spearman-Brown formula is .86. Correlations between parallel items on the two forms range from .29 to .51. It should be remembered that "poor" hypnotic subjects were eliminated from the standardization sample, which undoubtedly attenuates all these coefficients.

The Profile Scales are not unique in the sense that they are structurally similar to earlier scales for the assessment of hypnotic susceptibility. However, currently they stand alone as the only reasonably objective instrument for the selection of subjects for hypnosis experiments requiring complex behaviors. It is clear that they are intended for experimental use rather than for clinical application, and they appear to have many intriguing potential uses in hypnosis research.

[180]

★**Stern Activities Index.** Grades 7–16 and adults; 1950–63; also called *Activities Index;* personal needs (see 92 for related tests of environmental press covering the same areas); 42 scores: 30 need scores (abasement-assurance, achievement, adaptability-defensiveness, affiliation-rejection, aggression-blame avoidance, change-sameness, conjunctivity-disjunctivity, counteraction-inferiority avoidance, deference-restiveness, dominance-tolerance, ego achievement, emotionality-placidity, energy-passivity, exhibitionism-inferiority avoidance, fantasied achievement, harm avoidance-risk taking, humanities and social science, impulsiveness-deliberation, narcissism, nurturance-rejection, objectivity-projectivity, order-disorder, playwork, practicalness-impracticalness, reflectiveness, science, sensuality-puritanism, sexuality-prudishness, supplication-autonomy, understanding) and 12 factor scores based on combinations of the need scores (self-assertion, audacity-timidity, intellectual interests, motivation, applied interests, orderliness, submissiveness, closeness, sensuousness, friendliness, expressiveness-constraint, egoism-diffidence); NCS; Form 1158 ('58, 7 pages); combined scoring and college norms manual ('63, 30 pages plus sample copies of this index and each of the *Environment Indexes*) for this test and the *College Characteristics Index* (see 92); need score profile ('63, 1 page); factor score profile ('63, 1 page); no data on reliability and validity; manual contains college norms only (profile reports based on high school students and adults available on request when scoring service is used); separate answer sheets must be used; 25¢ per test; $3.25 per 50 NCS answer sheets; $6 per set of hand scoring stencils (machine scoring by the distributor only); $3.50 per scoring and norms manual; postpaid; scoring and profiling fees: 75¢ to 95¢ per answer sheet, depending on quantity; see 671 for prices of other services; (20–90) minutes; George G. Stern; distributed by National Computer Systems. *

REFERENCES

1. NAUGLE, FRED W.; STERN, GEORGE G.; AND ESCHENFELDER, WILLIAM. "The Derivation of Quantitative Personality Models for the Assessment and Prediction of Performance." Abstract. *Am Psychologist* 11:356 Ag '56. *

2. STERN, GEORGE G.; STEIN, MORRIS I.; AND BLOOM, BENJAMIN S. *Methods in Personality Assessment: Human Behavior in Complex Social Situations.* Glencoe, Ill.: Free Press, 1956. Pp. 271. * (*PA* 30:6922)

3. BRIGGS, DANIEL A. "A Study of the Use and Application of the Stern Activities Index as a Means of Predicting Acceptable and Nonacceptable Students at the Syracuse University Sagamore Reading Camp." Abstract. *Am Psychologist* 12:373 Jl '57. *

4. NAUGLE, FRED; AGER, JOEL; HARVEY, DORIS; AND STERN, GEORGE G. "Relationships Between Student Self-Descriptions and Faculty-Student Stereotypes of the Ideal Student." Abstract. *Am Psychologist* 12:391 Jl '57. *

5. SIEGELMAN, MARVIN; PECK, ROBERT F.; AND MCGUIRE, CARSON. "Distinctive Personality Patterns in Three Vocational Groups as Measured by the Stern Activity Index." Abstract. *Am Psychologist* 12:467 Jl '57. *

6. STERN, GEORGE G.; SCHULTZ, DUANE; AND NAUGLE, FRED. "Resistance to Faking on the Activities Index." Abstract. *Am Psychologist* 12:430 Jl '57. *

7. TATHAM, DAVID F.; STELLWAGEN, WALTER; AND STERN, GEORGE G. "The Stern Activities Index as a Measure of Differences Among Vocational and Academic Groups." Abstract. *Am Psychologist* 12:457 Jl '57. *

8. BRIGGS, DANIEL A. *The Stern Activities Index as a Means of Predicting Social Acceptability and Improvement in Reading Skills.* Doctor's thesis, Syracuse University (Syracuse, N.Y.), 1958. (*DA* 19:1947)

9. SCANLON, JOHN CIMEON. *The Activities Index: An Inquiry Into Validity.* Doctor's thesis, Syracuse University (Syracuse, N.Y.), 1958. (*DA* 19:2151)

10. STERN, GEORGE G., AND SCANLON, JOHN C. "Pediatric Lions and Gynecological Lambs." *J Med Ed* 33:12–8 O '58. *

11. MCFEE, ANNE. *The Relation of Selected Factors to Students' Perception of a College Environment.* Master's thesis, Syracuse University (Syracuse, N.Y.), 1959.

12. CRIST, ROBERT LAFOLLETTE. *A Study of the Discrimination Effectiveness of the Stern Activities Index With Achievement Groups in Purdue's Freshmen Engineering Program.* Doctor's thesis, Purdue University (Lafayette, Ind.), 1960. (*DA* 21:1843)

13. DIVESTA, FRANCIS J., AND COX, LANDON. "Some Dispositional Correlates of Conformity Behavior." *J Social Psychol* 52:259–68 N '60. * (*PA* 35:4813)

14. SIEGELMAN, MARVIN, AND PECK, ROBERT F. "Personality Patterns Related to Occupational Roles." *Genetic Psychol Monogr* 61:291–349 My '60. * (*PA* 35:7174)

15. STERN, GEORGE G. "Congruence and Dissonance in the Ecology of College Students." *Student Med* 8:304–39 Ap '60. *

16. STERN, GEORGE G. "Student Values and Their Relationship to the College Environment," pp. 67–104. In *Research on College Students: Institute Lectures Considering Recent Research on College Student's Motivation, Values and Attitudes, and Campus Cultures.* Edited by Hall T. Sprague. Boulder, Colo.: Western Interstate Commission for Higher Education, 1960. Pp. iv, 188. *

17. PACE, WALTER THOMAS. *Profiles of Personal Needs and College Press of Negro Teacher Trainees.* Doctor's thesis, Wayne State University (Detroit, Mich.), 1961. (*DA* 22:3748)

18. STERN, GEORGE G. "Recent Research on Institutional Climates: 1, Continuity and Contrast in the Transition From High School to College," pp. 33–58. In *Orientation to College Learning—A Reappraisal: Report of a Conference on Introduction of Entering Students to the Intellectual Life of the College.* Edited by Nicholas C. Brown. Washington, D. C.: American Council on Education, 1961. Pp. xi, 143. *

19. COSBY, BETTY WALLACE. *An Investigation of Homogeneity on Selected Personality Variables in Formal Social Groups,*

and the Effect of Such Homogeneity on the Personality of Group Members. Doctor's thesis, Syracuse University (Syracuse, N.Y.), 1962. (*DA* 23:4767)

20. SAGEN, HARRY BRADLEY. *The Relationship of Certain Personality and Environmental Variables to the Satisfaction With Present Position of Faculty in Selected Liberal Arts Colleges.* Doctor's thesis, University of Minnesota (Minneapolis, Minn.), 1962. (*DA* 23:3241)

21. STERN, GEORGE G. Chap. 3, "The Measurement of Psychological Characteristics of Students and Learning Environments," pp. 27–68. In *Measurement in Personality and Cognition.* Edited by Samuel Messick and John Ross. New York: John Wiley & Sons, Inc., 1962. Pp. xi, 334. * (*PA* 38:2638)

22. STERN, GEORGE G. Chap. 21, "Environments for Learning," pp. 690–730. In *The American College: A Psychological and Social Interpretation of the Higher Learning.* Edited by Nevitt Sanford. New York: John Wiley & Sons, Inc., 1962. Pp. xvi, 1,084. * (*PA* 36:5KA84S)

23. LORR, MAURICE, AND MCNAIR, DOUGLAS M. "An Interpersonal Behavior Circle." *J Abn & Social Psychol* 67:68–75 Jl '63. * (*PA* 38:765)

24. MUELLER, WILLIAM J. "The Prediction of Personality Inventory Responses From Tape Analysis." *Personnel & Guid J* 42:368–72 D '63. * (*PA* 39:1815)

25. RAAB, WILLIAM EDWIN. *Congruence and Dissonance Between Need and Press in Determining Satisfaction or Dissatisfaction in the University Environment.* Doctor's research study No. 1, Colorado State University (Fort Collins, Colo.), 1963. (*DA* 24:1923)

26. STERN, GEORGE G. "Characteristics of the Intellectual Climate in College Environments." *Harvard Ed R* 33:5–41 w '63. *

27. STONE, LEROY A. "Masculinity-Femininity as Reflected by the Stern Activities Index—A Brief." *J Counsel Psychol* 10:87 sp '63. *

[181]

★Straus Rural Attitudes Profile. Adults; 1956–59; 5 scores: innovation proneness, rural life preference, primary group preference, economic motivation, total; separate forms (Forms M2, F2, '56, 1 page) for men and women; manual ('59, 36 pages, see *1* below); supplementary norms ['59, 1 page, hectographed]; tests must be reproduced locally; single copy, manual, norms, and set of keys free to users agreeing to make results available to the author; (12) minutes; Murray A. Straus; Washington State University. *

REFERENCES

1. STRAUS, MURRAY A. *A Technique for Measuring Values in Rural Life.* State College of Washington, Washington Agricultural Experiment Stations, Institute of Agricultural Sciences, Technical Bulletin 29. Pullman, Wash.: the Institute, August 1959. Pp. ii, 34. *

Sociol & Social Res 44:297 Mr–Ap '60. Emory S. Bogardus. In the "forced-choice techniques" described in this document [the manual], the respondent is asked to choose the one phrase out of four descriptive statements "which is most like himself and the one phrase which is least like himself." The answers to twelve sets of "tetrads" are used to form a profile. This technique is somewhat like the paired comparisons technique, although superior in at least one way. The resultant Rural Attitudes Profile as designed shows certain variables, namely, innovation proneness, rural life preference, primary group preference, and economic motivation. As far as the experiments have thus far been conducted, this technique promises well for use in making rural sociological studies.

[182]

***Study of Values: A Scale for Measuring the Dominant Interests in Personality, Third Edition.** Grades 13 and over; 1931–60; 6 scores: theoretical, economic, aesthetic, social, political, religious; 1 form ('60, 12 pages, identical with test copyrighted in 1951); revised manual ('60, 19 pages); $4 per 35 tests; 60¢ per specimen set; postage extra; (20) minutes; Gordon W. Allport, Philip E. Vernon, and Gardner Lindzey; Houghton Mifflin Co. *

REFERENCES

1–61. See 3:99.

62–86. See 4:92.

87–143. See 5:114.

144. RICHARDSON, HELEN M. "Community of Values as a Factor in Friendships of College and Adult Women." *J Social Psychol* 11:303–12 My '40. * (*PA* 14:5132)

145. NEWCOMB, THEODORE M. *Personality and Social Change: Attitude Formation in a Student Community,* pp. 41–4. New York: Dryden Press, 1943. Pp. x, 225. *

146. Coffin, Thomas E. "A Three-Component Theory of Leadership." *J Abn & Social Psychol* 39:63–83 Ja '44. * (*PA* 18:2167)

147. GRAY, SUSAN W. "A Note on the Values of Southern College Women: White and Negro." *J Social Psychol* 25:239–41 My '47. * (*PA* 22:1606)

148. FISHER, SARAH CAROLYN. *Relationships in Attitudes, Opinions, and Values Among Family Members.* University of California Publications in Culture and Society, Vol. 2, No. 2. Berkeley, Calif.: University of California Press, 1948. Pp. iii, 29–99. * (*PA* 23:4628)

149. VANDERPLAS, JAMES M., AND BLAKE, ROBERT R. "Selective Sensitization in Auditory Perception." *J Personality* 18:252–66 D '49. * (*PA* 25:2862)

150. MOHSIN, S. H. "A Study of the Relationship of Evaluative Attitudes to Sex Difference, Intellectual Level, Expressed Occupational Interest and Hobbies." *Indian J Psychol* 25:59–70 pts 1–4 '50. * (*PA* 27:7051)

151. POSTMAN, LEO, AND SCHNEIDER, BERTRAM H. "Personal Values, Visual Recognition, and Recall." *Psychol R* 58:271–84 Jl '51. * (*PA* 26:3258)

152. MAWARDI, BETTY HOSMER. *The Allport-Vernon Study of Values as a Tool in Vocational Guidance With Liberal Arts College Women.* Master's thesis, Wellesley College (Wellesley, Mass.), 1952.

153. BROWN, DONALD R., AND ADAMS, JOE. "Word Frequency and the Measurement of Value Areas." *J Abn & Social Psychol* 49:427–30 Jl '54. * (*PA* 29:3783)

154. MOFFETT, CHARLES R. *Operational Characteristics of Beginning Master's Students in Educational Administration and Supervision.* Doctor's thesis, University of Tennessee (Knoxville, Tenn.), 1954.

155. LUTON, JAMES N. *A Study of the Use of Standardized Tests in the Selection of Potential Educational Administrators.* Doctor's thesis, University of Tennessee (Knoxville, Tenn.), 1955.

156. CRAWFORD, C. DELISLE. *Critical Thinking and Personal Values in a Listening Situation: An Exploratory Investigation Into the Relationships of Three Theoretical Variables in Human Communication, as Indicated by the Relation Between Measurements on the Allport-Vernon-Lindzey Study of Values and the Watson-Glaser Critical Thinking Appraisal, and Similar Measurements of Responses to a Recorded Radio News Commentary.* Doctor's thesis, New York University (New York, N.Y.), 1956. (*DA* 19:1845)

157. GRAY, SUSAN W., AND KLAUS, RUPERT. "The Assessment of Parental Identification." *Genetic Psychol Monogr* 54:87–114 Ag '56. * (*PA* 33:3404)

158. CONGER, JOHN J.; GASKILL, HERBERT S.; GLAD, DONALD D.; RAINEY, ROBERT V.; SAWREY, WILLIAM L.; AND TURRELL, EUGENE S. "Personal and Interpersonal Factors in Motor Vehicle Accidents." *Am J Psychiatry* 113:1069–74 Je '57. * (*PA* 32:6071)

159. GOWAN, J. C. "A Summary of the Intensive Study of Twenty Highly Selected Elementary Women Teachers." *J Exp Ed* 26:115–24 D '57. * (*PA* 33:4731)

160. JACOB, PHILIP E. *Changing Values in College: An Exploratory Study of the Impact of College Teaching.* New York: Harper & Brothers, 1957. Pp. xvii, 174. *

161. NOBECHI, MASAYUKI, AND KIMURA, TEIJI. "'Study of Values' Applied to Japanese Students." *Psychologia* 1:120–2 D '57. * (*PA* 35:5331)

162. SMITH, ANTHONY J. "Similarity of Values and Its Relation to Acceptance and the Projection of Similarity." *J Psychol* 43:251–60 Ap '57. * (*PA* 33:5307)

163. BENDER, IRVING E. "Changes in Religious Interest: A Retest After Fifteen Years." *J Abn & Social Psychol* 57:41–6 Jl '58. * (*PA* 33:8194)

164. BENDER, IRVING E. "Changing Patterns of Religious Interest." *Humanist* 18:139–44 My–Je '58. *

165. DEIGNAN, FRANK J. "Note on the Values of Art Students." *Psychol Rep* 4:566 D '58. * (*PA* 34:2031)

166. DUNN, SANDRA; BLISS, JOAN; AND SIIPOLA, ELSA. "Effects of Impulsivity, Introversion, and Individual Values Upon Association Under Free Conditions." *J Personality* 26:61–76 Mr '58. * (*PA* 33:5742)

167. NIMKOFF, M. F., AND GRIGG, C. M. "Values and Marital Adjustment of Nurses." *Social Forces* 37:67-70 O '58. * (*PA* 33:11235)

168. NIMNICHT, GLENDON PERRIN. *A Study of Successful Superintendents and Their Leadership Ability.* Doctor's thesis, Stanford University (Stanford, Calif.), 1958. (*DA* 19:720)

169. NUNNERY, MICHAEL Y. *A Study in the Use of Psychological Tests in Determining Effectiveness and Ineffectiveness Among Practicing School Administrators.* Doctor's thesis, University of Tennessee (Knoxville, Tenn.), 1958. (*DA* 19:1276)

170. RAY-CHOWDHURY, K. "Allport-Vernon Study of Values (Old Form) in Indian Situation: 1, Religious Group Differences in Values." *Indian Psychol B* 3:55-67 My-S '58. * (*PA* 37:4826)

171. RAY-CHOWDHURY, K. "Comparative Study of American and Indian Weight Scores on Allport's Ascendance-Submission Reaction Study." *Indian Psychol B* 3:45-7 My-Je '58. * (*PA* 37:4991)

172. SCHEIDEL, THOMAS M.; CROWELL, LAURA; AND SHEPHERD, JOHN R. "Personality and Discussion Behavior: A Study of Possible Relationships." *Speech Monogr* 25:261-7 N '58. * (*PA* 33:9990)

173. SMITH, ANTHONY J. "Perceived Similarity and the Projection of Similarity: The Influence of Valence." *J Abn & Social Psychol* 57:376-9 N '58. * (*PA* 33:9992)

174. STRUNK, ORLO. "Empathy: Need for Cognition and Value Schemata." *Psychol Newsl* 9:160-1 Mr-Ap '58. * (*PA* 33:3075)

175. ANDREWS, JOHN H. M., AND BROWN, ALAN F. "Can Principals Exclude Their Own Personality Characteristics When They Rate Their Teachers?" *Ed Adm & Sup* 45:234-42 Jl '59. * (*PA* 34:6579)

176. BADAL, ALDEN WESLEY. *The Relationship of Selected Test Measures to Administrator Success in the Elementary School.* Doctor's thesis, Stanford University (Stanford, Calif.), 1959. (*DA* 20:1263)

177. BELENKY, ROBERT LOUIS. *The Relationship Between Accuracy in Self Perception and the Perception of Others: A Study of Estimates of Performance on a Test of Values and a Test of Aspiration Level.* Doctor's thesis, Columbia University (New York, N.Y.), 1959. (*DA* 20:3825)

178. ENGSTROM, WARREN C., AND POWERS, MARY E. "A Revision of the Study of Values for Use in Magazine Readership Research." *J Appl Psychol* 43:74-8 F '59. * (*PA* 34:4859)

179. FRUEHLING, ROYAL T. *An Experimental Study to Determine the Degree to Which the 1951 Revision of the Study of Values Is Reliable for Use With High School Seniors.* Master's thesis, Northwestern University (Evanston, Ill.), 1959.

180. JONES, EDWARD E., AND DAUGHERTY, BOICE N. "Political Orientation and the Perceptual Effects of an Anticipated Interaction." *J Abn & Social Psychol* 59:340-9 N '59. * (*PA* 34:5623)

181. KELLY, E. LOWELL, AND GOLDBERG, LEWIS R. "Correlates of Later Performance and Specialization in Psychology: A Follow-Up Study of the Trainees Assessed in the VA Selection Research Project." *Psychol Monogr* 73(12):1-32 '59. * (*PA* 34:7952)

182. LUNDY, RICHARD M. "The Relationship of Changes in Assimilative Projection to Accepting and Rejecting Interpersonal Groups and to the Order of the Groups." *J Social Psychol* 50:327-33 N '59. * (*PA* 35:4993)

183. MILLER, ELEANOR O. "Nonacademic Changes in College Students." *Ed Rec* 40:118-22 Ap '59. * (*PA* 34:2047)

184. MUNSON, HOWARD ROGER. *Comparison of Interest and Attitude Patterns of Three Selected Groups of Teacher Candidates.* Doctor's thesis, State College of Washington (Pullman, Wash.), 1959. (*DA* 19:3237)

185. NOLAN, EDWARD GILLIGAN. *Uniqueness in Monozygotic Twins.* Doctor's thesis, Princeton University (Princeton, N.J.), 1959. (*DA* 21:247)

186. NUNNERY, MICHAEL Y. "How Useful Are Standardized Psychological Tests in the Selection of School Administrators." *Ed Adm & Sup* 45:349-56 N '59. * (*PA* 35:7092)

187. RAY-CHOWDHURY, K. "Allport-Vernon Study of Values (1958 Modification) in Indian Situation." *Indian Psychol B* 4:67-74 My-Je '59. * (*PA* 37:1263)

188. RAY-CHOWDHURY, K. "Allport-Vernon Study of Values (Old and New Forms) and Sex Difference in Indian Situation." *Indian Psychol B* 4:52-7 My-S '59. * (*PA* 37:1264)

189. RAY-CHOWDHURY, K. "Allport-Vernon-Lindzey Study of Values (Old Form) in Indian Situation: 2, Reliability and Item-Analysis." *Indian Psychol B* 4:7-15 Ja '59. * (*PA* 37:4947)

190. RAY-CHOWDHURY, K. "Allport-Vernon-Lindzey Study of Values (Old Form) in Indian Situation: 3, Occupational Group Differences and Norms in Values at the College Level." *Indian Psychol B* 4:20-9 Ja '59. * (*PA* 37:4948)

191. RICCIO, ANTHONY CARMINE. *The Relationship of Selected Variables to Attitudes Toward Teaching.* Doctor's thesis, Ohio State University (Columbus, Ohio), 1959. (*DA* 20:2159)

192. RODD, WILLIAM G. "Cross-Cultural Use of 'The Study of Values.'" *Psychologia* 2:157-64 S '59. * (*PA* 35:3440)

193. SCODEL, ALVIN; RATOOSH, PHILBURN; AND MINAS, J. SAYER. "Some Personality Correlates of Decision Making Under Conditions of Risk." *Behav Sci* 4:19-28 Ja '59. * (*PA* 34:1057)

194. SHELDON, M. STEPHEN; COALE, JACK M.; AND COPPLE, ROCKNE. "Concurrent Validity of the 'Warm Teacher Scale.'" *J Ed Psychol* 50:37-40 F '59. * (*PA* 35:2810)

195. THRASH, PATRICIA ANN. *Women Student Leaders at Northwestern University: Their Characteristics, Self-Concepts, and Attitudes Toward the University.* Doctor's thesis, Northwestern University (Evanston, Ill.), 1959. (*DA* 20:3638)

196. TRAXLER, ARTHUR E., AND VECCHIONE, NICHOLAS. "Scores of Seniors in Six Secondary Schools on the Allport-Vernon-Lindzey *Study of Values.*" *Ed Rec B* 74:75-86 Jl '59. * (*PA* 35:1227)

197. WAGGONER, GLEN HASTINGS. *Administrator's Scores on Selected Standardized Tests and His Administrative Performance as Reported by Classroom Teachers.* Doctor's thesis, Stanford University (Stanford, Calif.), 1959. (*DA* 20:3169)

198. WARD, PAUL LEWIS. *A Study of the Relationship of Evaluative Attitudes to Scholastic Ability and Academic Achievement.* Doctor's thesis, Ohio State University (Columbus, Ohio), 1959. (*DA* 20:3639)

199. WEYBREW, BENJAMIN B., AND MOLISH, H. B. "Approaches to the Study of Motivation of Officer Candidates for the Submarine Service." *U S Naval Med Res Lab Rep* 18:1-47 O '59. * (*PA* 34:8530)

200. BALDWIN, THOMAS SANDERSON. *The Relationships Among Personality, Cognitive, and Job Performance Variables.* Doctor's thesis, Ohio State University (Columbus, Ohio), 1960. (*DA* 21:3171)

201. BOGARD, HOWARD M. "Union and Management Trainees—A Comparative Study of Personality and Occupational Choice." *J Appl Psychol* 44:56-63 F '60. * (*PA* 34:7496)

202. BOYCE, RICHARD DUDLEY. *An Empirical Evaluation of Five Tests for Administrator Selection: The Composite Study.* Doctor's thesis, Stanford University (Stanford, Calif.), 1960. (*DA* 21:2546)

203. BURDOCK, E. I.; CHEEK, FRANCES; AND ZUBIN, JOSEPH. "Predicting Success in Psychoanalytic Training," pp. 176-91. In *Current Approaches to Psychoanalysis.* Proceedings of the 48th Annual Meeting of the American Psychopathological Association Held in New York City, February 1958. Edited by Paul H. Hoch and Joseph Zubin. New York: Grune & Stratton, Inc., 1960. Pp. 207. * (*PA* 36:4IE07H)

204. EBERT, FRANCIS JOHN. *An Empirical Evaluation of Five Tests for the Selection of Elementary School Principals.* Doctor's thesis, Stanford University (Stanford, Calif.), 1960. (*DA* 21:2548)

205. HEIST, PAUL. "Personality Characteristics of Dental Students." *Ed Rec* 41:240-52 Jl '60. * (*PA* 35:7081)

206. JAMES, KENNETH RAYMOND. *An Empirical Evaluation of Five Tests for Administrator Selection in a Metropolitan School District.* Doctor's thesis, Stanford University (Stanford, Calif.), 1960. (*DA* 21:2556)

207. JOHNSON, RONALD ENGLE. *A Quantification and Measurement of Three Qualitative Changes in the Recall of Complex Verbal Materials.* Doctor's thesis, Ohio State University (Columbus, Ohio), 1960. (*DA* 21:2358)

208. KNAPP, ROBERT H., AND GREEN, SAMUEL. "Preferences for Styles of Abstract Art and Their Personality Correlates." *J Proj Tech* 24:396-402 D '60. * (*PA* 35:4841)

209. NEWBIGGING, P. L. "Personal Values and Response Strength of Value-Related Words as Measured in a Pseudo-Perceptual Task." *Can J Psychol* 14:38-44 Mr '60. * (*PA* 35:2280)

210. RALEY, COLEMAN LAVAN. *Personality Traits of High-Academic Achievers at Oklahoma Baptist University, 1958-1959.* Doctor's thesis, University of Oklahoma (Norman, Okla.), 1960. (*DA* 20:2680)

211. RAY-CHOWDHURY, K. "The 1958 Indian Modification of Allport-Vernon-Lindzey Study of Values (1951 Edition): 2, Occupational Group Differences and Norms, in Values at the College Level." *Indian Psychol B* 5:51-60 My '60. *

212. RAY-CHOWDHURY, K. "The 1958 Indian Modification of Allport-Vernon-Lindzey Study of Values (1951 Edition): 3, Variation of 'Values' With Age, Birth-Order, Locality and Region, Socio-Economic Status, and Religion." *Indian Psychol B* 5:61-70 S '60. *

213. RICCIO, ANTHONY C., AND PETERS, HERMAN J. "The Study of Values and the Minnesota Teacher Attitude Inventory." *Ed Res B* 39:101-3 Ap '60. *

214. SCODEL, ALVIN; RATOOSH, PHILBURN; AND MINAS, J. SAYER. "Some Personality Correlates of Decision Making Under Conditions of Risk," pp. 37-49. In *Decisions, Values and Groups: Reports From the First Interdisciplinary Conference in the Behavioral Science Division Held at the University of New Mexico, Vol. 1.* Edited by Dorothy Willner. Sponsored by the Air Force Office of Scientific Research. New York: Pergamon Press, 1960. Pp. xxiv, 348. * (*PA* 36:5CP48W)

215. SHIRLEY, JACK HAROLD. *A Comparative Study of the Academic Achievements, Interests, and Personality Traits of Athletes and Non-Athletes.* Doctor's thesis, University of Oklahoma (Norman, Okla.), 1960. (*DA* 20:4005)

216. SMITH, ANTHONY J. "The Attribution of Similarity: The Influence of Success and Failure." *J Abn & Social Psychol* 61:419-23 N '60. * (*PA* 36:2GE19S)

217. WARREN, JONATHAN R., AND HEIST, PAUL A. "Personality Attributes of Gifted College Students." *Sci* 132:330–7 Ag 5 '60. * (*PA* 35:2214)
218. BILLINGSLY, LEON COMMODORE. *Characteristics of Teacher Effectiveness.* Doctor's thesis, University of Arkansas (Fayetteville, Ark.), 1961. (*DA* 22:1082)
219. BUEL, WILLIAM D., AND BACHNER, VIRGINIA M. "The Assessment of Creativity in a Research Setting." *J Appl Psychol* 45:353–8 D '61. * (*PA* 37:1211)
220. DYER, DOROTHY TUNELL, AND LUCKEY, ELEANORE BRAUN. "Religious Affiliation and Selected Personality Scores as They Relate to Marital Happiness of a Minnesota College Sample." *Marriage & Family Living* 23:46–7 F '61. * (*PA* 36:3IQ46D)
221. HEIST, PAUL; MCCONNELL, T. R.; MATZLER, FRANK; AND WILLIAMS, PHOEBE. "Personality and Scholarship." *Sci* 133:362–7 F 10 '61. * (*PA* 36:2KD62H)
222. HOWARD, MAURICE LLOYD. *A Study of Under-Achieving College Students With High Academic Ability From the Phenomenological Frame of Reference.* Doctor's thesis, University of Colorado (Boulder, Colo.), 1961. (*DA* 22:3040)
223. MACKINNON, DONALD W. "Fostering Creativity in Students of Engineering." *J Eng Ed* 52:129–42 D '61. * (*PA* 36:4HD29M)
224. PHILIPPUS, MARION JOHN. *A Study of Personality, Value and Interest Patterns of Student Teachers in the Areas of Elementary, Secondary and Special Education.* Doctor's thesis, University of Denver (Denver, Colo.), 1961. (*DA* 22:3926)
225. PYRON, BERNARD. "Belief Q-Sort, Allport-Vernon Study of Values and Religion." *Psychol Rep* 8:399–400 Je '61. * (*PA* 36:2GD99P)
226. SCODEL, ALVIN. "Value Orientations and Preference for a Minimax Strategy." *J Psychol* 52:55–61 Jl '61. * (*PA* 36:2CN55S)
227. SPOERL, DOROTHY TILDEN. "The Values of Unitarian-Universalist Youth." *J Psychol* 51:421–37 Ap '61. * (*PA* 35:6310)
228. STROMMEN, ELLEN, AND AMMONS, ROBERT BRUCE. "Relationship of Value Placed on Intellectual Activity to Social Desirability of Attitude, Theoretical Orientation, and Interest in Problem-Solving." *Proc Mont Acad Sci* 20:78–84 '61. * (*PA* 36:1GD78S)
229. UDRY, J. RICHARD; NELSON, HAROLD A.; AND NELSON, RUTH. "An Empirical Investigation of Some Widely Held Beliefs About Marital Interaction." *Marriage & Family Living* 23:388–90 N '61. *
230. WATLEY, DONIVAN JASON. *Prediction of Academic Success in a College of Business Administration.* Doctor's thesis, University of Denver (Denver, Colo.), 1961. (*DA* 22:3527)
231. YOUMANS, RAYMOND ELTON. *A Further Validation of the Modified Study of Values for High School Students.* Doctor's thesis, University of Denver (Denver, Colo.), 1961. (*DA* 22:3529)
232. BOWIE, B. LUCILE, AND MORGAN, G. GERTHON. "Personal Values and Verbal Behavior of Teachers." *J Exp Ed* 30:337–45 Je '62. *
233. COUTTS, ROBERT LAROY. *Selected Characteristics of Counselor-Candidates in Relation to Levels and Types of Competency in the Counseling Practicum.* Doctor's thesis, Florida State University (Tallahassee, Fla.), 1962. (*DA* 23:1601)
234. CRANE, WILLIAM J. "Screening Devices for Occupational Therapy Majors." *Am J Occup Ther* 16:131–2 My–Je '62. * (*PA* 37:4078)
235. DENNY, TERRY. "Achievement of Catholic Students in Public High Schools—II." *Cath Ed R* 60:442–69 O '62. *
236. HUTCHINS, EDWIN B. "The Student and His Environment." *J Med Ed* 37:67–82 D '62. *
237. INOUE, ATSUSHI; AGARI, ICHIRO; MURASHIMA, FUSAKO; YAMASHITA, ISAO; AND USUI, KIMIAKI. "A Factorial Study of Psychological Values." *Psychologia* 5:112–4 Je '62. *
238. KERR, MARILYN; MAKI, BOBBIN; AND AMMONS, R. B. "Personality, Values, and 'Intellectualism.'" *Proc Mont Acad Sci* 21:132–6 '62. * (*PA* 37:3149)
239. KNAPP, ROBERT H.; GEWIRTZ, HERBERT; AND HOLZBERG, JULES D. "Some Personality Correlates of Styles of Interpersonal Thought." *J Proj Tech* 26:398–403 D '62. * (*PA* 37:6717)
240. MACKINNON, DONALD W. "The Personality Correlates of Creativity: A Study of American Architects," pp. 11–39. (*PA* 37:4958) In *Personality Research.* Proceedings of the XIV International Congress of Applied Psychology, Vol. 2. Copenhagen, Denmark: Munksgaard, Ltd., 1962. Pp. 229. *
241. MAEHR, MARTIN L., AND STAKE, ROBERT E. "The Value Patterns of Men Who Voluntarily Quit Seminary Training." *Personnel & Guid J* 40:537–40 F '62. * (*PA* 36:5KI37M)
242. PHILIPPUS, MARION JOHN, AND FLEIGLER, LOUIS. "A Study of Personality, Value and Interest Patterns of Student Teachers in the Areas of Elementary, Secondary, and Special Education." *Sci Ed* 46:247–52 Ap '62. *
243. RAULERSON, LEWIS ALBERT. *A Study of the Values of Doctoral Students in Selected Major Subject Fields.* Doctor's thesis, Florida State University (Tallahassee, Fla.), 1962. (*DA* 23:535)
244. RUPIPER, OMER JOHN. "A Psychometric Evaluation of Experienced Teachers." *J Ed Res* 55:368–71 My '62. *
245. SINGH, PARAS NATH; HUANG, SOPHIA CHANG; AND THOMPSON, GEORGE G. "A Comparative Study of Selected Attitudes, Values, and Personality Characteristics of American, Chinese, and Indian Students." *J Social Psychol* 57:123–32 Je '62. * (*PA* 37:3847)
246. SLIFE, WAYNE GORDON. *The Measurement of Identification and Its Relationship to Behavioral Indices of Personality Organization.* Doctor's thesis, University of Houston (Houston, Tex.), 1962. (*DA* 23:3505)
247. SMITH, MADORAH E. "The Values Most Highly Esteemed by Men and Women in Who's Who Suggested as One Reason for the Great Difference in Representation of the Two Sexes in Those Books." *J Social Psychol* 58:339–44 D '62. * (*PA* 37:6726)
248. SOUTHWORTH, HORTON COE. *A Study of Certain Personality and Value Differences in Teacher Education Majors Preferring Early and Later Elementary Teaching Levels.* Doctor's thesis, Michigan State University (East Lansing, Mich.), 1962. (*DA* 23:1284)
249. SUPER, DONALD E., AND CRITES, JOHN O. *Appraising Vocational Fitness by Means of Psychological Tests, Revised Edition,* pp. 492–9. New York: Harper & Brothers, 1962. Pp. xv, 688. * (*PA* 37:2038)
250. TWOMEY, ALFRED EUGENE. *A Study of Values of a Select Group of Undergraduate Students.* Doctor's research study No. 1, Colorado State College (Greeley, Colo.), 1962. (*DA* 23:3700)
251. WATLEY, DONIVAN J., AND MARTIN, H. T. "Prediction of Academic Success in a College of Business Administration." *Personnel & Guid J* 41:147–54 O '62. * (*PA* 37:5656)
252. *Normative Information: Manager and Executive Testing.* New York: Richardson, Bellows, Henry & Co., Inc., May 1963. Pp. 45. *
253. AIKEN, LEWIS R., JR. "The Relationships of Dress to Selected Measures of Personality in Undergraduate Women." *J Social Psychol* 59:119–28 F '63. * (*PA* 38:910)
254. BAUERNFEIND, ROBERT H. *Building a School Testing Program,* pp. 212–31. Boston, Mass.: Houghton Mifflin Co., 1963. Pp. xvii, 343. *
255. CAPRETTA, PATRICK J.; JONES, REGINALD L.; SIEGEL, LAURENCE; AND SIEGEL, LILA C. "Some Noncognitive Characteristics of Honors Program Candidates." *J Ed Psychol* 54:268–76 O '63. * (*PA* 38:4674)
256. COOLEY, WILLIAM W. "Predicting Choice of a Career in Scientific Research." *Personnel & Guid J* 42:21–8 S '63. *
257. DE SENA, PAUL AMBROSE. *Identification of Non-Intellectual Characteristics of Consistent Over-, Under-, and Normal-Achievers Enrolled in Science Curriculums at the Pennsylvania State University.* Doctor's thesis, Pennsylvania State University (University Park, Pa.), 1963. (*DA* 24:3144)
258. DUA, PREM SAKHI. *Identification of Personality Characteristics Differentiating Elected Women Leaders From Non-Leaders in a University Setting.* Doctor's thesis, Pennsylvania State University (University Park, Pa.), 1963. (*DA* 24:3145)
259. GILBERT, JOSEPH. "Vocational Archetypes: A Proposal for Clinical Integration of Interests and Values in Vocational Counseling and Selection." *Psychol Rep* 13:351–6 O '63. *
260. GREENBERG, HERBERT; GUERINO, ROSEMARIE; LASHEN, MARILYN; MAYER, DAVID; AND PISKOWSKI, DOROTHY. "Order of Birth as a Determinant of Personality and Attitudinal Characteristics." *J Social Psychol* 60:221–30 Ag '63. * (*PA* 38:4337)
261. GUTHRIE, GEORGE M., AND MCKENDRY, MARGARET S. "Interest Patterns of Peace Corps Volunteers in a Teaching Project." *J Ed Psychol* 54:261–7 O '63. * (*PA* 38:4126)
262. KELSEY, IAN BRUCE. *A Comparative Study of Values of Students Attending the University of British Columbia in 1963 as Measured by the Allport-Vernon Test for Personal Values.* Doctor's thesis, University of Washington (Seattle, Wash.), 1963. (*DA* 24:2813)
263. KINNANE, JOHN F., AND GAUBINGER, JOSEPH R. "Life Values and Work Values." Comment by Harry Beilin. *J Counsel Psychol* 10:362–7 w '63. * (*PA* 38:8278)
264. LEE, EUGENE C. "Career Development of Science Teachers." *J Res Sci Teach* 1:54–63 Mr '63. *
265. LIND, AMY. "Measured Personality Characteristics of Occupational Therapy Graduates and Undergraduates at the University of North Dakota." *Univ N Dak Col Ed Rec* 48:69–73 F '63. *
266. MCCUE, KEMPER W.; ROTHENBERG, DAVID; ALLEN, ROBERT M.; AND JENNINGS, THEODORE W. "Rorschach Variables in Two 'Study of Values' Types." *J General Psychol* 68:169–72 Ja '63. * (*PA* 38:2742)
267. MAHER, HOWARD. "Validity Information Exchange, No. 16-01: D.O.T. Code 0-06.71, Feature Writer; 0-06.73, Columnist; 0-06.92, Copyreader (Rewrite Man)." *Personnel Psychol* 16:71–3 sp '63. *
268. MAHER, HOWARD. "Validity Information Exchange, No. 16-02: D.O.T. Code 1-87.26, Advertising Space Salesman." *Personnel Psychol* 16:74–7 sp '63. *
269. MANHOLD, J. H.; SHATIN, LEO; AND MANHOLD, BEVERLY S. "Comparison of Interests, Needs, and Selected Personality Factors of Dental and Medical Students." *J Am Dental Assn* 67:601–5 O '63. *

270. NEWSOME, GEORGE L., JR., AND GENTRY, HAROLD W. "Logical Consistency, Values, and Authoritarianism in a Sample of Public School Superintendents." *J Teach Ed* 14:411-6 D '63. *

271. NOLAN, EDWARD G.; BRAM, PAULA; AND TILLMAN, KENNETH. "Attitude Formation in High-School Seniors: A Study of Values and Attitudes." *J Ed Res* 57:185-8 D '63. *

272. NOLL, VICTOR H., AND NOLL, RACHEL P. "The Social Background and Values of Prospective Teachers." *Yearb Nat Council Meas Ed* 20:108-14 '63. * (*PA* 38:9297)

273. PAIVIO, ALLAN, AND STEEVES, RAY. "Personal Values and Selective Perception of Speech." *Percept & Motor Skills* 17:459-64 O '63. * (*PA* 38:5037)

274. RADCLIFFE, J. A. "Some Properties of Ipsative Score Matrices and Their Relevance for Some Current Interest Tests." *Austral J Psychol* 15:1-11 Ap '63. *

275. RAMSAY, RONALD; JENSEN, SVEN; AND SOMMER, ROBERT. "Values in Alcoholics After LSD-25." *Q J Studies Alcohol* 24:443-8 S '63. *

276. SCHUMACHER, CHARLES F. "Interest and Personality Factors as Related to Choice of Medical Career." *J Med Ed* 38:932-42 N '63. *

277. TERWILLIGER, JAMES S. "Dimensions of Occupational Preference." *Ed & Psychol Meas* 23:525-42 au '63. * (*PA* 38:6698)

278. VAUGHAN, G. M., AND MANGAN, G. L. "Conformity to Group Pressure in Relation to the Value of the Task Material." *J Abn & Social Psychol* 66:179-83 F '63. * (*PA* 37:6621)

279. VAUGHAN, JAMES A., JR., AND KNAPP, ROBERT H. "A Study in Pessimism." *J Social Psychol* 59:77-92 F '63. * (*PA* 38:859)

280. WARBURTON, F. W.; BUTCHER, H. J.; AND FORREST, G. M. "Predicting Student Performance in a University Department of Education." *Brit J Ed Psychol* 33:68-79 F '63. * (*PA* 38:1416)

JOHN D. HUNDLEBY, *Research Assistant Professor of Psychology, University of Illinois, Urbana, Illinois.*

The *Study of Values* has been for many years a test of interest to those concerned with the quantitative assessment of values and interests, and, in particular, those who wish to see standard tests more closely tied to psychological theory. The original, 1931, version of the test contained measures of six values based on Spranger's formulations: theoretical, economic, aesthetic, social, political, and religious. The second edition, published in 1951, included more discriminating items, increased reliability, and reflected a redefining of the social value. The third edition, 1960, with which this review is concerned, shows no change in items from the second. The main difference between these last two editions is the provision of additional normative data. Stability of the test over the past decade necessarily means that many of the problems of earlier versions (considered in earlier reviews) remain, and indeed some have become intensified.

Modifications to the manual of the third edition are slight and are concerned with the presentation of more recent norms and changes in scoring. The norms are presented for total populations (e.g., male students) and also for specific colleges or narrow occupational groups. The means, and usually standard deviations, of each population or subgroup are given for each value. Unfortunately, no further information on the shape of the distribution is presented. It is also to be regretted that revised reliability estimates were not reported, for the present coefficients are based upon groups of only 100 (split-half) and 34 and 53 subjects (retest).

Of theoretical rather than practical importance is the continued lack of compelling evidence that Spranger's system, and these six measures associated with it, have much more to offer than can be obtained from other standard measures of interests. This is not to say that the *Study of Values* lacks validity in the realm of values and interests, for there is considerable supportive evidence on the usefulness of the test in a variety of settings—particularly counseling and selection. What *is* in question, however, is the psychological theory upon which the test is based, and here direct evidence remains very scanty. The majority of researchers appears to be far more concerned with such problems as obtaining specific value scores (usually for different occupational or educational groups) or changes in such scores, than with the theoretical problems of Spranger's system of values in the context of contemporary theory and research findings.

Definitive statistical information still appears to be lacking on whether or not the six measures are unidimensional and relatively distinct. Factor analytic results are not yet conclusive and are made more difficult in interpretation by the ipsative nature of the scales. Item-total scale correlations, unless they are very high, are not sufficient evidence, since it is possible for scale items to have a similar factorial structure and the final scale be a composite of several dimensions. Certain item-total scale correlations may indeed be quite low for, though no figures are reported in the manual, every item enjoys a significant ($P < .01$) correlation with the total scale, but with an n of 780 this need only be .09.

This reviewer remains puzzled as to why the ipsative form has persisted with the *Study of Values*. Admittedly, to measure each value separately would involve more time of testing, but ipsative items can also be time consuming, if for no other reason than the often difficult choices that are presented to the subject. The test authors do not comment at length on the implications of ipsative measures for the test user, and perhaps further emphasis on this point would be desirable.

The *Study of Values* continues to be a measure closely associated with the college-going or college graduate population. This is readily evident from the norms, for apart from 8,369 college students, almost all of the information on occupational differences (Southern business men, teachers, school administrators, Air Force officers, personnel workers, scoutmasters, and clergymen) concerns persons likely to have had *some* college experience. For purposes associated with higher education this is, of course, no problem, but it does impose a severe limitation on the generality of findings from the test and, indeed, further suggests that the values concerned may be appropriate only for a limited segment of the population. Attempts have been made, however, to extend measurement to populations of lower educational level and systematic developments along these lines are to be hoped for.

In summary, with college or college graduate populations where concern is with dimensions of interest and value broader than those of, say, the *Strong Vocational Interest Blank* or *Kuder Preference Record,* the *Study of Values* is quite likely to prove a helpful tool. Lack of conclusive evidence as to unidimensionality of the scales, the problems of interpretation imposed by ipsative scoring, and lack of any real generality beyond the college population, remain as unresolved research issues.

John A. Radcliffe, *Senior Lecturer in Psychology, University of Sydney, Sydney, Australia.*

Designed to measure Spranger's six "value types," the *Study of Values* first appeared in 1931. The second edition made changes in the test itself. In the third edition, changes occur only in the score sheet and in parts of the manual.

The test has two parts. In Part 1 (30 items), each value is paired twice (but with different statements) with every other value, and in Part 2 (15 items), each value is compared (again with different statements) with all combinations of three other values. Now consider Part 1, which has the majority of items. Internal consistency reliability of a subject's score on a value will depend on the equivalence of the item statements and the consistency of his judgments. Retest reliability will depend on the consistency of his judgments over time, and this in turn will depend on the stability of his relative values. If retest reliability is higher than internal consistency reliability, then the instability of relative values is less than the nonequivalence of the item statements. That is, greater retest than internal consistency reliability will indicate that internal consistency reliability could be improved by better equivalence of the item statements.

This is the case with the *Study of Values.* The average total test reliabilities for the different subscales are .89 and .88 (one and two month retest) and .82 (split-half). While these correlations are based on small samples only and probably do not differ significantly statistically, it seems likely, at least with Part 1, that they represent a genuine difference deriving from the item selection procedure. Greater attention to and possible improvement of statement equivalence would have been achieved if item selection had been based on item intercorrelations rather than item-total (corresponding value) score correlations.

To illustrate: consider items 1 and 15, which both contrast theoretical and economic values, and items 12 and 21, which both contrast theoretical and political. Equivalence of value statements and consistency of the subjects' judgments would require that item 1 correlate highly with item 15, and that item 12 correlate highly with item 21. But, unless the sample were "biased" to consist predominantly of subjects whose theoretical, economic, and political values were in the same order of relative strength, the expected correlations of items 1 and 15 with items 12 and 21 would be *zero.* Thus the expected pattern of item intercorrelations would be high correlations between items contrasting the same pair of values and near zero correlations otherwise. Item selection via item intercorrelation would enable better detection of the weaker equivalents than would item selection via item-total correlations.

Of course, item-total correlations depend on item intercorrelations. Maximising one will maximise the other. But the aim here would be to maximise some item intercorrelations and to minimise others. Moreover, it is common practice to obtain such low item-total correlations that selection consists of omitting those items with the lowest correlations rather than retaining those with the highest. The test authors merely report that they retained only those items whose item-total correlations were "significant at the .01 level of confidence."

With their large sample ($n = 780$) these could have been so low that not even those between equivalent items were maximised.

However, these are minor points of criticism and pertain only to show how the test might have been made better than it is. As it is, it has satisfactory reliability, both internal consistency and split-half, for group use, as attested by the results it has produced. Moreover, even if it were improved by greater attention to item equivalence, the interest areas measured are so broad that probably it never would have any greater individual use than that suggested by the authors, namely, "to secure an initial impression....and as a basis for subsequent interviews."

Since every subject obtains the same total score over the six values, the scores are ipsative and the interests of a subject are interpreted intraindividually. Interindividual comparisons are facilitated by scaling the scores so that the "average" individual has a constant score (40) on each value. Variation of his values around this base shows how his relative values compare with those of the "average" individual. If further normative comparisons are desired, the manual provides, for males and females separately, the means and standard deviations for the total standardisation group and its university subsamples, and the means for specialist educational and occupational groups. It is worth noting that the authors specifically recognise the ipsative character of the scores and do not recommend their expression in a percentile profile as do the authors of some other ipsatively scored tests (e.g., *Edwards Personal Preference Schedule*). Also, possibly because the authors emphasise the lack of independence involved with ipsative scores, there has been less correlational use of the *Study of Values* than with other ipsatively scored tests (*274*).

The test is self-scoring, but, as Gage (5:114) has suggested, the way in which this is achieved probably increases its "transparency." Designed as it is for use "with college students, or with adults who have had some college (or equivalent) education," the test's vocabulary level is twelfth grade by a Flesch count (*140*). Two less verbally complex versions have been produced (*140, 178*). In Levy's revision, equivalence of the item statements for the theoretical and social scales could be improved.

Validity data in the manual consist mainly of showing that educational and occupational groups have value patterns as might be expected. Some additional data of this character will be summarised here, but more attention will be given to data different from that given in the manual.

The overall Japanese pattern is high aesthetic and low religious, and includes more scatter than the American, but the educational specialities have high and low scores much as with American students; e.g., high aesthetic for letters, political for law, and economic for economics (*161*). Compared with the standardisation group, "gifted" students have higher theoretical and aesthetic values, and their pattern has greater scatter (*124, 217*). National Merit Scholarship holders at educational institutions with "high academic productivity" differ from those at "low productivity" institutions by having higher theoretical and aesthetic and lower religious interests (*221*). Measured values do not appear to be related to the study of dentistry (*205*), nor to being a "warm teacher" (*194*).

"Feminine" males have a value pattern like that of "normal" females, including high aesthetic, social, and religious scores (*123*). Both male and female "leaders" of organisations differ from members and nonmembers by having the "masculine" pattern of high theoretical, economic, and political values, but the fact that the "leaders" consisted only of volunteers for the study may have some relevance here (*126*). The value patterns of submarine officer candidates and Air Force officers have also been studied (*125, 199*).

If "low belief in change" is regarded as synonymous with "conservatism," then conservative Protestants and Catholics have high religious and low aesthetic values, nonconservative Protestants have high theoretical and low economic, while nonconservative Jews have high aesthetic and low religious values (*225*). The "masculine" high theoretical-economic-political pattern and the "feminine" high aesthetic-social-religious pattern have been suggested to be related to "extratensive" and "intratensive" personality characteristics, respectively, and the "extratensive" were found to be faster and more "stimulus bound" in their associative reactions (*166*). This is difficult to reconcile with the two factors involving the *Study of Values* obtained by Gowan from its correlations with a number of ability and personality tests (*139*), and with his finding that the "gifted," who do not have the "extratensive" pattern, are low on "introversion" and high on "dominance" (*124*).

As well as those cited in the manual, some other studies pertaining to the "construct validity" of the *Study of Values* have included changes in values from freshman to senior year (*183*); the role of values in resistance to pressure to conform (*278*); the role of personality similarity and difference in the study of interpersonal relations (*162, 173, 216*); and conditions relevant to pseudoperception (*209*).

There are wide individual differences in the degree of association between expressed and measured values and the degree of association does not appear to be related to age (*141*). The values of Air Force officers are consistent with some of their high interest areas on the *Kuder Preference Record* (*125*), but those of "gifted" students are not obviously so (*124*). The values of students at "high" and "low productive" institutions are consistent with their *Strong Vocational Interest Blank* theoretical-nontechnical and applied-technical interest patterns, respectively (*221*).

Attendance at church correlated .79 with religious values in a group of Dartmouth graduates (*163*). Magazine reading preferences were consistent with results obtained with a less verbally complex version of the test (*178*). Although the actual results are not given, it appears to have been useful in the study of recruitment in the banking industry.[1] That nurses with high "empathy" have high social and low aesthetic interests is consistent with the description of these values given in the manual (*134*).

Although Spranger's value types have an "armchair" rather than an "empirical" basis, and although it may in some instances fail to distinguish between *value* and *interest* (5:114), the *Study of Values* has remained a useful research instrument. As such, and as a "basis for subsequent interviewing" in individual application, it should continue to be widely used, but it is hoped that any future revision might include attention to the points raised above concerning item analysis procedures.

For a review by N. L. Gage of the second edition, see 5:114; for reviews by Harrison G. Gough and William Stephenson, see 4:92 (1 excerpt); for a review by Paul E. Meehl of the original edition, see 3:99.

1 McMurry, Robert N. "Recruitment, Dependency and Morale in the Banking Industry." *Admin Sci Q* 3:87–117 Je '58. * (*PA* 33:9096)

[183]

★Style of Mind Inventory: Trait, Value and Belief Patterns in Greek, Roman and Judeo-Christian Perspectives. College and adults; 1958–61, c1957–61; formerly called *The Fetler Self-Rating Test*; 3 scores (Greek, Roman, Judeo-Christian) in each of 3 areas (traits, values, beliefs); 1 form ('61, 1 page); explanation sheet ['61, 1 page]; no data on reliability and validity; no norms; 1¢ per test; 1¢ per explanation sheet; postage extra; [60] minutes; Daniel Fetler; the Author. *

[184]

★Survey of Interpersonal Values. Grades 9–16 and adults; 1960–63; 6 scores: support, conformity, recognition, independence, benevolence, leadership; 1 form ('60, 3 pages); preliminary manual ('60, 11 pages); mimeographed supplement, revised ('63, 28 pages); $2.40 per 20 tests; 50¢ per key; 50¢ per manual; $1 per specimen set; postage extra; (15) minutes; Leonard V. Gordon; Science Research Associates, Inc. *

REFERENCES

1. Gordon, Leonard V. "Conformity Among the Non-Conformists." *Psychol Rep* 8:383 Je '61. * (*PA* 36:2JO83G)
2. Wyatt, Thomas C. *A Validation Study of the Gordon Survey of Interpersonal Values.* Master's thesis, Drake University (Des Moines, Iowa), 1961.
3. Fleishman, Edwin A., and Peters, David R. "Interpersonal Values, Leadership Attitudes, and Managerial 'Success.'" *Personnel Psychol* 15:127–43 su '62. * (*PA* 37:7321)
4. Gordon, Leonard V., and Mensh, Ivan N. "Values of Medical School Students at Different Levels of Training." *J Ed Psychol* 53:48–51 F '62. * (*PA* 37:1921)
5. Hedberg, Raymond. "More on Forced-Choice Test Fakability." *J Appl Psychol* 46:125–7 Ap '62. *
6. Woodard, Barbara. *An Investigation of Some Interpersonal Values of Freshman and Senior Nursing Students at the Texas Woman's University.* Master's thesis, Texas Woman's University (Denton, Tex.), 1962.
7. Blume, Dorothy M. *Interpersonal Values of Nursing Students in One University Program.* Master's thesis, University of Texas (Austin, Tex.), 1963.
8. Braun, John R. "Effects of Positive and Negative Faking Sets on the Survey of Interpersonal Values." *Psychol Rep* 13:171–3 Ag '63. * (*PA* 38:6082)
9. Garrison, W. A.; Wilson, H. E.; and Warne, E. K. "Interpersonal Values Related to College Achievement." *Proc Mont Acad Sci* 22:127–31 '63. *
10. Knapp, Robert R. "Personality Correlates of Delinquency Rate in a Navy Sample." *J Appl Psychol* 47:68–71 F '63. * (*PA* 37:8179)
11. Morris, Kenneth Turner. *A Comparative Study of Selected Needs, Values, and Motives of Science and Non-Science Teachers.* Doctor's thesis, University of Georgia (Athens, Ga.), 1963. (*DA* 24:2325)
12. Wilson, Helen; Garrison, W.; and Warne, E. "Analysis of the F Scale Through Use of the Survey of Inter-Personal Values Scales." *Proc Mont Acad Sci* 22:124–6 '63. *

Lee J. Cronbach, *Professor of Education and Psychology, Stanford University, Stanford, California.*

This is an unpretentious instrument, competently presented. About 15 items for each of six scales are arranged into 30 triads. In each triad, the person checks the statement most important to him, and that least important to him. A typical item compares "To be selected for a leadership position," "To be treated as a person of some importance," and "To have things pretty much my own way." The directions are so brief that there is some possibility that subjects will interpret the task in rather different ways. Particularly, it is not clear whether the person is to describe what he wants in a job or what he wants in his life as a whole.

The test construction follows appropriate procedures, though the author perhaps tells too little about four hypothesized dimensions that disappeared in the course of factor analysis, discussing only the six that survived. The reliability information is inadequately analyzed and somewhat misleading. With retest reliabilities in the .80's and internal consistencies in the range .71 to .86, it seems most likely that when one generalizes over *both* items and occasions—as would be required in guidance or theoretically-oriented research—the coefficient would be in the low .70's. The standard errors of scores and of differences within the profile are substantial.

Since the items are quite transparent, the survey is open to faking whenever the subject knows what traits will be considered good in a particular job. The research of Longstaff [1] and French [2] shows quite clearly that forced choice scales are not resistant to faking of patterns, and the test manual promises too much in this respect. The survey is of dubious value for industrial selection, though no more so than other typical questionnaires. The author is on safe ground when he says (in a supplement to the manual), "The SIV is to be treated as a research instrument, and for industrial and other applied purposes should be validated in the situation in which it is intended to be used."

One wonders what an inventory with transparent items will contribute in guidance, beyond what is learned from one simple question or self-rating on each trait. Unlike most manuals, the manual for this test provides a correlational study of just this question, finding contingency coefficients of .47 to .73. The manual points to these as evidence of validity. That they are—but placed alongside the reliability data they indicate that the test has very little *incremental* validity. A conceivable argument for using the inventory in guidance is that converting scores to percentiles (which cannot be done satisfactorily with self-ratings) may enhance their meaning. But the norms, either inadequately collected or inadequately presented, are essentially valueless. There are norms based on, for example, 1,075 college males from colleges representing "all major regions of the country." The colleges are listed, but we are told nothing about whether a given college tested all its freshmen, or perhaps only the juniors enrolled in personnel psychology.

The author, in the manual and a supplement, presents a welcome array of correlations of this test with other tests, and abstracts over a dozen diverse studies relating the test to group differences or external criteria. The claims and interpretations made are reasonable, though the author squeezes too much out of some small-sample studies. One dare not conclude, for example, that lack of Sociability is more characteristic of the person high on Independence (sample $r = -.30$ for 144 cases) than is lack of Responsibility (sample $r = -.16$).

The user who for some reason wants scores on six aspects of self-report that can be given a common sense interpretation, in a format that eliminates the social desirability and acquiescence sets from the score, will find the survey suitable. Whether it has any use in personnel selection, future validity studies will show; the studies reported furnish little basis for optimism. As a counseling aid, the survey seems less likely to give the subject or counselor fresh insights than the *Edwards Personal Preference Schedule* with its 15 scores, the *Kuder Preference Record—Personal,* or Gordon's own Personal Profile.

LEONARD D. GOODSTEIN, *Professor of Psychology, and Director, University Counseling Service, University of Iowa, Iowa City, Iowa.*

The *Survey of Interpersonal Values* (SIV) is a 30 item ipsative instrument; each item consists of a triad of statements, each of which presumably reflects some underlying value or motivational pattern affecting the respondent's interpersonal relationships. The respondent is required to select one of the statements or foils within each triad as "most important" and one as "least important," thus rank ordering the three foils. The manual indicates that an effort was made to equate the three foils in each item for social desirability of response but these social desirability values are not actually reported.

The items are answered directly in the question booklet and are hand scored by means of

1 LONGSTAFF, HOWARD P. "Fakability of the Strong Interest Blank and the Kuder Preference Record." *J Appl Psychol* 32:360–9 Ag '48. *

2 FRENCH, ELIZABETH G. "A Note on the Edwards Personal Preference Schedule for Use With Basic Airmen." *Ed & Psychol Meas* 18:109–15 sp '58. *

a punched, overlay stencil. While such hand scoring would inevitably be laborious, the scoring stencil in the specimen set received for review was rather crudely punched making accurate scoring virtually impossible. It is surprising that the publisher did not extend to the SIV the far more convenient pin-punch booklet developed for the *Kuder Preference Record*.

The SIV yields six scores or measures of interpersonal values: (*a*) Support, which involves being treated with understanding, encouragement, and kindness (15 foils); (*b*) Conformity, or doing what is socially correct or acceptable to others (15 foils); (*c*) Recognition, involving being respected or considered important (13 foils); (*d*) Independence, or being free from external controls and regulations (13 foils); (*e*) Benevolence, or helping others less fortunate (15 foils); and (*f*) Leadership, which involves being in charge of others or controlling them (16 foils). Each foil is scored for one of these values (scored 2 if rated as most important, zero if rated least important, and 1 if left unmarked) and no foil is scored for more than a single value.

The basis upon which these particular six values were included in the published version of the SIV is not clearly indicated in the manual. The author started with items tapping 10 such values, presumably rather arbitrarily selected from the literature, which he then subjected to a factor analysis. This analysis yielded eight factors, six of which are included in the SIV. The details of this factor analysis are not presented, nor is any indication given of why two of the factors were eliminated. While the manual presents a table of intercorrelations, it is difficult to decide how independent these six value scores are since the ipsative nature of the test responses produces an indeterminate negative correlation among the scores.

The test-retest reliability coefficients for the six value scores range from .78 to .89 with median *r* .84. The Kuder-Richardson reliability estimates range from .71 to .86 with median *r* .82. Both sets of reliability data suggest adequate reliability, comparable to that reported for other forced choice personality inventories, e.g., *Edwards Personal Preference Schedule*.

Two sets of percentile equivalents for each of the six scores are presented separately by sex: one for college students, based upon 746 females and 1,075 males, and one for high school students, based upon 782 males and 666 females. The collegiate norms were collected at a variety of institutions "selected so as to represent all major regions of the country," while the high school data were all collected in California. The extension of these high school norms to include a more representative sample as well as the development of some nonacademic normative materials would be highly desirable.

The SIV is offered primarily as a research instrument, although the 1963 manual supplement is far more explicit on this point than is the original 1960 manual where there is the suggestion that the SIV can be used directly for vocational guidance and personality counseling. The more recent supplement specifically cautions the potential user to validate the instrument in the specific situation for which use is contemplated and presents illustratively the results of over two dozen studies using the SIV. These include investigations of the SIV as a predictor of job success with such varied samples and criteria as executives in a manufacturing firm and retail sales personnel in a department store and studies of the SIV as a predictor of success in several different military cadet programs. Several studies report upon the changes in SIV scores as a function of educational and other experiences, and there are also a number of highly interesting cross-cultural comparisons of SIV scores. These studies do strongly suggest that the SIV is indeed a useful research tool but the author's caution not to apply these findings directly to new situations without cross validation is very well taken. It is somewhat unfortunate that the supplement rather uncritically includes the reports of a number of studies that were methodologically weak, for example, a study reporting product-moment correlation coefficients based upon small samples of 19 or 25. While the supplement does disclaim any operational usefulness of such findings, reporting of such data does appear to legitimize some questionable procedures.

In summary, the *Survey of Interpersonal Values* appears to be a useful addition to the growing collection of paper and pencil personality tests which attempt to reduce the influence of social desirability response set by a multiple choice format. The major usefulness of the SIV at this time would be for classroom demonstrations and further research. As the body of research evidence grows, however, the usefulness of the SIV for personnel selection, appraisal, and counseling, the other major uses advocated by the author, will certainly increase.

JOHN K. HEMPHILL, *Director, Developmental Research Division, Educational Testing Service, Princeton, New Jersey.*

The *Survey of Interpersonal Values* is the third sibling in the growing family of personality tests issued by Leonard V. Gordon. Like its predecessors, the *Gordon Personal Profile* and the *Gordon Personal Inventory,* it uses a forced choice format and is based upon the results of a factor analysis. The survey consists of 30 groups of 3 statements each. The examinee first responds by selecting the one of the three "which represents what you consider to be most important to you"; he then selects the one he considers to be least important to him, leaving the third statement unmarked. The test yields scores for six values: Support, Conformity, Recognition, Independence, Benevolence, and Leadership.

Norms are available separately for college males (n = 1,075), college females (n = 746), high school boys (n = 782), and high school girls (n = 666). College norms were developed on a sample of students from 12 colleges or universities, well distributed geographically over the country. The high school norms, however, are based on four schools, all within the state of California.

The test manual is filled with pertinent information. Clearly written directions for administration and interpretation of scores are followed by a good account of the development of the scales and by comprehensive descriptive statistics. Estimates of reliability are provided both as test-retest coefficients ranging from .78 to .89, and Kuder-Richardson estimates ranging from .71 to .86. Intercorrelations among the six scale scores and correlations of the scores with measures of intelligence, other tests of personality, and with scores from the *Study of Values* are shown. None of the scores correlates substantially (the highest in absolute value is −.22) with scores from the *College Qualification Test.* Relationships with scores from the *Gordon Personal Inventory* and the *Gordon Personal Profile* are moderate and range from −.30 between "Support" and "Vigor," to .39 between "Leadership" and "Ascendancy." The relationships are regarded as logical and ones to be expected. Relationships between six scores from the *Study of Values* and the six scale scores likewise appear, for the most part, to be logical and consistent. For example, the correlation between "Benevolence" and "Religious" is .52; between "Leadership" and "Political," .30; and between "Conformity" and "Theoretical," −.36. Correlations of .42 between "Leadership" and "Theoretical" or of .46 between "Independence" and "Aesthetic," are less obviously reasonable, but might be rationalized.

A virtue of the manual and the supplement (called "Research Briefs") is the emphasis that Gordon places upon reporting about the validity of his scales. Many major and minor studies using the survey are summarized. The total evidence from these studies lends support to Gordon's moderate claims for application of the *Survey of Interpersonal Values* in selection, vocational guidance, counseling, and research. This instrument promises to become a respectable member of its family, and a useful companion to the well known but perhaps overworked *Study of Values.*

J Counsel Psychol 9:92–3 sp '62. Laurence Siegel. * The forced-choice format of SIV was designed to reduce the susceptibility of the inventory to deliberate attempts at falsification. All statements in the Manual about the effectiveness of forced-choice in this regard are appropriately cautious. * Triads were constructed by grouping items representing different factors but similar in social desirability. Unfortunately, the Manual is not as clear as it should be in discussing the way in which social desirability indices were obtained and the subsequent selection of items on the basis of these indices. * Retest reliability coefficients....and Kuder-Richardson estimates....for college students are presented * For the six scales, the former range between .78 and .89 and the latter between .71 and .86. The Manual states in summarizing these coefficients that they "....are sufficiently high to permit interpretation of SIV scores for individual use." This is a strong statement when applied to scales with the relatively narrow score ranges characteristic of SIV and without supporting evidence in the form of standard errors of measurement. Reliability coefficients for noncollege samples are not presented. Potential industrial users of this inventory are cautioned in the Manual to develop their own norms to compensate for possible response distortion in the industrial setting. This caution could well have been extended to all users of SIV on the grounds not only of possible distortion but of the inadequacy of the samples upon which currently published norms are based. Percentile norms for college students are presented in the Manual. These norms tables are based upon relatively small samples (1,075 males and 746 females) and their designation as "National Norms" is misleading. Although the samples were drawn from schools in various parts of the country, the implication of representativeness characteristic of truly national norms is unsupported. * In spite of the fact that the number and variety of reported validity studies exceeds those accompanying many other published instruments, a certain amount of ambivalence is unavoidable in assessing this inventory. This reviewer, at least, remains unconvinced about the necessity for a test measuring what SIV measures. This highly subjective reservation aside, it would have been desirable for the Manual to contain a more comprehensive description of the development of SIV and a more cautious statement about the interpretation of raw scores. Although the Manual's cover is labeled "Preliminary Edition," this small cautionary note can be too easily overlooked by persons who weight heavily the professional qualifications of the test author and the reputation of the publisher. The Supplement to the Manual contains the following important statement: "The SIV is to be treated as an experimental instrument and should be validated or evaluated in the situation in which it is intended to be used." This excellent statement should have been placed also on the face sheet of the Manual itself. Failing this, it should at least have appeared *somewhere* in the Manual.

[185]

★Survey of Personal Attitude "SPA" (With Pictures): Individual Placement Series (Area III). Adults; 1960; subtest of *Individual Placement Series;* 3 scores: social attitude, personal frankness, aggressiveness; Form A (14 pages); no manual; no data on reliability and validity; no description of normative population; separate answer sheets must be used; $32.50 per 25 tests; $1.10 per 25 answer sheets; $1 per key; $3.50 per specimen set; postpaid; [20–25] minutes; J. H. Norman; the Author. *

[186]

★Syracuse Scales of Social Relations. Grades 5–6, 7–9, 10–12; 1958–59; pupil ratings of need interactions with classmates and others; 1 form ('58, 8 pages); 3 levels; manual ('59, 24 pages) for each level; $5.40 per 35 tests; 40¢ per specimen set of any one level; postage extra; (50–65) minutes in 2 sessions; Eric F. Gardner and George Thompson; [Harcourt, Brace & World, Inc.]. *

a) ELEMENTARY LEVEL. Grades 5–6; 4 scores: ratings made, received for succorrance, achievement-recognition.

b) JUNIOR HIGH LEVEL. Grades 7–9; 4 scores: ratings made, received for succorance, deference.

c) SENIOR HIGH LEVEL. Grades 10–12; 4 scores: ratings made, received for succorance, playmirth.

REFERENCES

1. GARDNER, ERIC F., AND THOMPSON, GEORGE G. *Social Relations and Morale in Small Groups.* New York: Appleton-Century-Crofts, Inc., 1956. Pp. xi, 312. * (*PA* 30:8184)

2. DEJUNG, JOHN E. *The Measurement of Accuracy of Self-Role Perception.* Doctor's thesis, Syracuse University (Syracuse, N.Y.), 1957. (*DA* 20:776)

3. MEYER, WILLIAM J. *Relationships Between Social Need Strivings and the Development of Heterosexual Affiliations.* Doctor's thesis, Syracuse University (Syracuse, N.Y.), 1957. (*DA* 19:2667)

4. ABEL, HAROLD. *The Relationship of Social Class and Sex to Social Need Satisfaction.* Doctor's thesis, Syracuse University (Syracuse, N.Y.), 1958. (*DA* 19:85)

5. DAVOL, STEPHEN H. *Some Determinants of Sociometric Relationships and Group Structure in a Veterans Administration Domiciliary.* Doctor's thesis, University of Rochester (Rochester, N.Y.), 1958.

6. KUNTZ, ALLEN H. *Some Factors of Learning and Their Relationships to Social Stability.* Doctor's thesis, Syracuse University (Syracuse, N.Y.), 1958. (*DA* 19:3214)

7. SCALEA, CARMEN J. *A Study of Relationships Between the Achievement Need Level of Individuals in a Group and Ratings Given to the Members of the Group for the Potential Satisfaction of This Need.* Doctor's thesis, Syracuse University (Syracuse, N.Y.), 1958. (*DA* 19:91)

8. DEJUNG, JOHN E. "Measurement of Accuracy of Self-Role Perception." *Yearb Nat Council Meas Used Ed* 16:111–6 '59. * (*PA* 34:7378)

9. KUNTZ, ALLEN H. "An Index of Social Stability." *Yearb Nat Council Meas Used Ed* 16:105–10 '59. *

10. MEYER, WILLIAM J. "Relationships Between Social Need Strivings and the Development of Heterosexual Affiliations." *Yearb Nat Council Meas Used Ed* 16:95–104 '59. * (*PA* 34:7488)

11. PAUSLEY, BARBARA HEARNE. *Changes in Need Structure as Measured by the Syracuse Scales of Adolescent Girls in an Organized Camp.* Master's thesis, Syracuse University (Syracuse, N.Y.), 1961.

12. REYNOLDS, JAMES H., AND BRAEN, BERNARD B. "Reliability of a Sociometric Technique Adapted for Use With Disturbed Children." *Psychol Rep* 9:591–7 D '61. *

13. DEJUNG, JOHN E., AND GARDNER, ERIC F. "The Accuracy of Self-Role Perception: A Developmental Study." *J Exp Ed* 31:27–41 S '62. * (*PA* 37:8241)

14. DEJUNG, JOHN E., AND KUNTZ, ALLEN H. "Peer Status Indices From Nominational and Rating Procedures in Regular and Homogeneous Ability Grouped Sixth Grade Classes." *Psychol Rep* 11:693–707 D '62. * (*PA* 38:1395)

15. KUNTZ, ALLEN H., AND DEJUNG, JOHN E. "A Comparison of Achievement Status Indices Obtained in Regular 6th Grade Classes Using Peer Nominational and Rating Procedures." *Yearb Nat Council Meas Ed* 19:97–103 '62. *

16. DEJUNG, JOHN E., AND MEYER, WILLIAM J. "Expected Reciprocity: Grade Trends and Correlates." *Child Develop* 34:127–39 Mr '63. * (*PA* 38:5729)

ÅKE BJERSTEDT, *Professor of Education, University of Lund, Lund, Sweden.*

The present instrument has grown out of a comprehensive and ambitious research effort, partly described in the book *Social Relations and Morale in Small Groups* (*1*). It represents a particular kind of sociometric device with several characteristic features, claimed to have these specific advantages: (*a*) *A psychological need definition of the choice situations.* The social choice situations used by most sociometrists are considered to be extremely gross in definition, resulting in individual choices for quite varying reasons and spuriously heightened correlations between various choice situations. A psychological need definition is aimed to increase precision and invariance, and the present scales claim explicitly to deal with "needs of particular importance at the respective stages of development." (*b*) *A personal reference population for each subject.* Most sociometric methods utilize as the only frame of reference the group within which the choices are made. This closed system approach makes certain comparisons between persons and groups difficult. In the present procedure each subject first chooses five persons out of "all persons ever known" to represent dividing points on each need satisfying continuum (from the person being best suited to satisfy the particular need to the person being least suited). The subsequent rating of the group members is done with these five persons as reference points. This procedure is claimed to insure "comparability....from pupil to pupil, group to group, and need to need." (*c*) *All-to-all reactions.* The typical sociometric nomination process, involving only a limited number of preferred or non-preferred companions, is considered to result in a loss of important information. The present scales therefore force each subject to rate *every* other member of the group in terms of each choice situation used.

While the reviewer finds these basic arguments interesting and well worth continued research effort, he considers the authors slightly overconfident about the value and efficiency of these specific characteristics in their present form.

There is no indication in the manual that the specific needs chosen actually are *the* most important ones at the respective stages of development, nor that *two* needs only (as used in these scales) sufficiently cover the important interaction tendencies in these ages, nor that individual differences in terms of need strength are small enough to insure comparable stimulus situations between raters. Further, in order to demonstrate that need-defined ratings actually *are* more precise than more conventionally phrased social choice situations, it would be necessary to show that intercorrelations between need-defined choice situations are consistently lower than intercorrelations between other specific choice situations, *and* that such increased rating specificity is not a verbal artefact, that is, that it leads to better prediction of person-to-person behavior during actual group processes. No such demonstration is reported in the manual.

The comparability reached by using the individual's inclusive frame of reference (all persons ever known) may easily be overestimated. We obtain a certain kind of *intra*personal comparability: we increase our possibilities to compare a single individual's judgments about persons from different groups. But the most basic problem—that of *inter*personal comparability—seems to be still far from a final solution. The fact that two raters consider a third subject to be at the midpoint of their respective personal range of experience as need satisfiers does not seem to insure any more basic identity of attitude strength between these two raters, as long as the need strength and experience range may be considerably different. In other words, there may be *some* kind of cognitive identity (an isomorphic position within two individuals' cognitive space) without identity as to *attitudinal-preferential* strength (as judged from other kinds of behavior). These are admittedly difficult problems, and the reviewer does not criticize the authors for not having found *the* final solution, but only for sometimes acting as if this were the case.

The final specific characteristic mentioned above—the all-to-all reactions—is not as unique within sociometric research as the authors seem to think: complete rank orders, rating, and paired comparisons have often been used (complete rank orders were especially frequent in early European sociometry). However, the general feeling among sociometrists having tried these methods is that the more detailed information obtained should be considered against the disadvantages of (*a*) a more time consuming procedure, (*b*) a less natural and motivating situation for the subjects, and (*c*) a forced reaction situation which forces the group members to statements about phenomena with no psychological salience in their lifespace. A conventional sociometric choice situation is described in a few sentences, and the choices are usually made in 5–10 minutes. The instructions for the present elementary level form take up *six columns* of text in the manual for *one* of the need situations only, and it is easy to imagine that some pupils will have difficulty in following the instructions or in finishing the one-need rating within the 30 minutes estimated. It is usually a simple and natural affair to select a number of companions for a concrete social situation, but it may seem quite strange and artificial for a child to compare to a person like Uncle Joe all his classmates—boys as well as girls—as satisfiers of his need for achievement-recognition in a hypothetical situation.

These doubts as to the finality of the specific solutions characteristic of this particular sociometric device do not mean that it should be without value. On the contrary, among the few commercially available instruments for assessment of social relations that the reviewer knows of, this should be considered outstanding in several respects. The test forms are well constructed; administration and scoring is clearly described; the manual's handling of interpretational and validational aspects is judicious; and information on data from representative classrooms, including reliability information, is presented in a helpful way. It is also obvious that the novel techniques have opened up stimulating new research possibilities. (The only technical aspects that the reviewer should have liked to see handled in another way are the recommendations on how to score ratings received and mutual ratings. Would it not be a simpler and quicker procedure to compute all scores directly from the tally sheet—without the extra clerical work involved in going back to the individual sheets a second time? But this is a minor matter of differing opinion.)

In sum, the present reviewer doubts that the specific characteristics of this device, which distinguish it from other sociometric techniques, represent final solutions to the difficult problems of (*a*) comparability, (*b*) maximal meaningfulness of choice situations, and (*c*) optimal balance between information received and information "cost." For many situations, the more traditional sociometric choice situations (as described in handbooks by Gronlund,[1] Jennings,[2] Northway,[3] and others) should be just as well or better able to handle the mapping of social relations—especially where simplicity and flexibility are important. On the other hand, for the person wanting a tailor-made sociometric procedure, commercially available and with potential usefulness both in general research and diagnostic charting, the present instrument may be the best available today.

1 GRONLUND, NORMAN E. *Sociometry in the Classroom.* New York: Harper & Row, Publishers, Inc., 1959. Pp. xix, 340. *

2 JENNINGS, HELEN HALL. *Sociometry in Group Relations: A Manual for Teachers, Second Edition.* Washington, D.C.: American Council on Education, 1959. Pp. xi, 105. *

3 NORTHWAY, MARY L., AND WELD, LINDSAY. *Sociometric Testing: A Guide for Teachers.* Toronto, Canada: University of Toronto Press, 1957. Pp. vii, 72. *

DONALD T. CAMPBELL, *Professor of Psychology, Northwestern University, Evanston, Illinois.*

The test booklet at each level is an elaborately prepared rating scale for only two topics (psychological needs). Succorance (ratings as a person you'd like to talk over your troubles with) is used at all three age levels. The reasons for varying the second topic are not given. "Achievement-recognition" refers to whom you would choose to help you make something for public exhibition. "Deference" refers to ratings of others on degree admired. "Playmirth" refers to ratings of others as persons with whom one could feel sure one would have a good time and lots of fun. The required setting is one in which members of a group such as a classroom can rate each other. The elaborateness comes in through the careful induction of personal externally-anchored rating scale points prior to the rating of classmates. With the help of a normal curve graph and a detailed example, each rater records, for the particular relation described, the names of persons selected from "everyone you have ever known in your whole life," assigning each name to one of five positions ranging from "least" to "most." Then the classmates are rated in direct comparison with these five reference persons. Because of the elaborateness of this procedure, the booklets are not self administering but require detailed oral instructions which are provided in the manual. Detailed scoring instructions are provided for ratings given and ratings received, and for clique analysis. Norms based upon over 1,000 students per class level are provided. Test-retest reliabilities on scores for midrating made range from .56 to .75. Reliabilities on midrating received range from .61 to .88. The validity data given are indirect and misleadingly emphasize an only partially similar college level study.

The methodological innovation differentiating this from the numerous "guess-who," "sociometric," and other reputational rating devices is the selection of the personal, external reference persons. No evidence is cited showing the superiority of this method over simpler procedures. In regard to the recurrent problems of halo effects or social desirability factors, the methodological precautions would at best affect mean ratings given, and not at all the spuriously high intercorrelation usually found among favorable traits. The intercorrelations between the two ratings are not presented but are probably high. Nor is any other evidence of discriminant validity presented for these measures.

In summary, while these booklets are probably as useful as any two-topic reputational rating device for classroom use, there is no evidence that they are superior to older and simpler procedures.

J Consult Psychol 24:466 O '60. Edward S. Bordin. This sociometric device makes use of two hypothetical situations as a basis for ratings by each student of his classmates. * One of the situations, at all three levels, involves rating others' ability to offer support, comfort, and sympathy, and is intended to reflect need for succorance; the other is specific to the level. At the elementary level achievement-recognition is tapped; at Junior high, deference, at Senior high, playmirth. * Since every pupil is evaluated by every other one, information becomes available on: (*a*) how each pupil views his classmates as being able to satisfy two of his important psychological needs; (*b*) how each pupil is evaluated by his classmates as being able to satisfy their needs. Large samples, unspecified with regard to such relevant factors as intelligence and socioeconomic status, provide a not fully satisfactory normative basis for interpreting the average ratings given and received for each need. An instrument like this one departs from the pattern of the simpler pencil and paper tests. Evaluation of its usefulness becomes an extremely complex process. The authors rely on five years of research, mostly with college students. Test-retest measures of stability over a one-to-two-week period suggest that these measures have only moderate stability (from .62 to .94). The manual is deficient in not warning potential users that such factors as the passage of time or the period in the school year might have considerable effect on a given score. This uncertainty would tend to impair its usefulness for routine diagnostic use. It will not be possible to involve a whole class in the time consuming procedures required every time the need to understand and help a particular pupil is discerned. Its validity is, of course, not susceptible to simple summary. Brief reference is made to studies whose results are suggestive, and the reader is referred to the author's 1956 book and to a number of unpublished doctoral dissertations. There is lacking any comprehensive or coherent framework for interpreting the results. True, it might be argued that providing such a framework requires more space than a manual can provide. Then the potential user ought to be warned that such a gap exists and referred to the proper sources. This reviewer is more impressed with possible usefulness of these scales for research than for everyday clinical or educational work.

[187]

★**Temperament Comparator.** Adults; 1958–61; identical with *Paired Comparison Temperament Schedule* ('58) except for format of presentation; 24 scores: 18 trait scores (calm, cautious, decisive, demonstrative, emotionally stable, energetic, enthusiastic, even-tempered, lively, persevering, prompt starter, quick worker, seeks company, self-confident, serious, socially at ease, steady worker, talkative), 5 factor scores (controlled vs. outgoing, stable vs. unstable, self-reliant vs. dependent, excitable vs. placid, sociable vs. solitary), and consistency; 1 form ('61, 2 pages); manual ('61, 51 pages); profile ('61, 1 page); administered with snap-on trait-pairing disc ('61); reliability data, validity data, and norms based on test in format of the earlier edition; $3 per 20 tests; $1.50 per set of reusable backing folder and disc; $3 per manual; postage extra; $5 per specimen set, postpaid; (15–20) minutes; Melany E. Baehr and R. W. Pranis; Education-Industry Service. *

REFERENCES

1. Baehr, Melany E. "A Factorial Study of Temperament." *Psychometrika* 17:107–26 Mr '52. * (*PA* 27:1834)

Lawrence J. Stricker, *Research Psychologist, Educational Testing Service, Princeton, New Jersey.*

The *Temperament Comparator* is one of a number of forced choice personality inventories which have appeared in the last few years, largely as a reaction to the thorny problems produced by faking and response styles on the traditional true-false personality scales.

This inventory, like the others, is designed to measure variables within the normal range of behavior and is intended for use in applied settings. It consists of 18 descriptive words or phrases, which the manual calls "traits" (e.g., "impulsive," "cheerful," and "socially at ease"), presented in a paired comparison format, the subject choosing the one trait in each of the 153 pairs of traits that best describes him. Each of these 18 traits loaded one of five oblique factors extracted from judges' ratings of others on 22 such traits (*1*). This original pool of 22 traits had been selected to represent an emotionality dimension conceptualized by Heymans and Wiersma and four second-order factors extracted by Baehr from Thurstone's [1] factor analysis of the Guilford personality scales.

Scores are provided for each of the 18 traits, 5 factor scales corresponding to the oblique factors (obtained by summing the appropriate trait scores), and a measure of consistency [2]—the tendency to make responses which do *not* form circular triads, such as choosing A rather than B, B rather than C, but C rather than A.

The meaning of the scores for the traits and the factor scales is open to question. The use of separate trait scores is questionable because the traits were selected, not because they were of intrinsic interest, but simply because they were expected to generate the five dimensions that were at issue. Insofar as the traits successfully produced the five factors, the information they provide is embodied in the factor scales which they form. Even if these particular traits were of interest per se, their meanings would be ambiguous because they are, in reality, one-item scales, whose generality cannot be determined. People may stably discriminate between any one trait and all the others because they are responding to an idiosyncratic quality, clang association, or some other characteristic of the word or phrase that has nothing to do with the psychological variable presumed to underlie the word or phrase. This kind of problem is avoided by most other forced choice scales in which each trait is represented by a homogeneous set of items.

The factor scales are questionable because they were based on factors extracted from ratings of others and, hence, may not be applicable to the self-descriptive responses elicited in the present form of the inventory. The factor structure for the self-description data may be quite different, particularly in view of the massive effect of social desirability response style on self-descriptive responses but not on ratings of others.

The manual fails to mention that the trait scores are ipsative, a property shared by most other forced choice scales and one which may be troublesome if score interpretations and multivariate computational procedures customarily used with normative scales are not appropriately modified. Some of the ways in which ipsative properties of scores complicate score interpretations and appraisals of statistical relationships are described at length in the present author's review of the *Edwards Personal Preference Schedule* (see 87).

Since the intercorrelations of the 18 traits and the intercorrelations of the 5 factor scales are unknown, the usefulness of interpreting the scores separately cannot be gauged. (The manual does report the intercorrelations of four factor scales on an early version of the *Paired Comparison Temperament Schedule,* which evidently is appreciably different from the *Temperament Comparator,* although the final version of the Schedule differs from the *Temperament Comparator* only in the way that the pairs of traits are presented, the latter using a disc arrangement which will be described later.)

The only available information on reliability is the data reported in the manual on retest-reliability, after a one-week interval, for an industrial sample—the median reliability was .79 for the traits and .90 for the factor scales, and the reliability of the consistency score was .80. These data, however, were obtained with the final form of the Schedule and are based on raw scores, not the normalized standard scores recommended in the manual. Consequently, these reliability estimates are not entirely appropriate for use with the current form of the inventory. The absence of data about the internal-consistency reliability of the factor scales precludes an assessment of their homogeneity, which is particularly crucial in view of the strong possibility that the factor structure for the rating data is not applicable to self-description data.

Very little is known about the validity of this inventory. No published studies could be located, and the manual, despite assertions that the Schedule "has been effectively used in the selection and placement of personnel," reports only two validity studies. One study, which is based on a master's thesis [3] and used an early form of the Schedule, consists of the correla-

1 THURSTONE, L. L. "The Dimensions of Temperament." *Psychometrika* 16:11–20 Mr '51. *
2 KENDALL, MAURICE G. *Rank Correlation Methods, Second Edition.* London: Charles Griffin & Co. Ltd., 1955. Pp. vii, 196. *

3 NOTY, C. *Intercorrelation Design for Determining Executive Placement and Effectiveness.* Master's thesis, Illinois Institute of Technology (Chicago, Ill.), 1960.

tions of four of the five factor scales with the scales of the 16 PF test. The results are more or less consistent with the descriptions of the four factors. The other study consists of comparisons of mean scores on the trait and factor scales, and the consistency measure from the final form of the Schedule for six occupational groups—labor, engineering, executive, white collar, foreman, and sales. The results lend some support to the validity of the inventory, though a statistical analysis which indicated the *extent* to which the scores differentiated between the occupational groups would have been more appropriate.

Despite the advantages claimed by the manual for this approach to personality measurement, including greater reliability of the trait scores and reduction of the effects of social desirability response style, no data on any of these issues are available. Even if the manual did not suggest that this inventory would minimize social desirability response style, data on this issue would be essential in view of its importance. In fact, it seems highly unlikely that the *Temperament Comparator* has succeeded in appreciably minimizing this response style because the traits were not explicitly matched on social desirability; the test authors just selected traits that seemed socially desirable to them and later eliminated a few traits whose scores, when obtained with a paired comparison format, had low means and skewed distributions. Research with the *Edwards Personal Preference Schedule* suggests that even a careful attempt to match items closely on social desirability values does not substantially eliminate social desirability response style, for there is still a tendency to choose the more socially desirable item in each pair [4] and its scales are moderately but significantly correlated with Edwards' [5] social desirability response style scale.[6] This unexpected state of affairs evidently stems from the multidimensionality of social desirability judgments [7] and interaction or context effects which may occur when items are paired.

4 KLETT, C. JAMES. "The Stability of the Social Desirability Scale Values in the Edwards Personal Preference Schedule." *J Consult Psychol* 21:183–5 Ap '57. * (*PA* 33:974)

5 EDWARDS, ALLEN L. *The Social Desirability Variable in Personality Assessment and Research.* New York: Dryden Press, Inc., 1957. Pp. xv, 108. * (*PA* 32:464)

6 MERRILL, REED M., AND HEATHERS, LOUISE B. "The Relation of the MMPI to the Edwards Personal Preference Schedule on a College Counseling Center Sample." *J Consult Psychol* 20:310–4 Ag '56. * (*PA* 31:7949)

7 MESSICK, SAMUEL. "Dimensions of Social Desirability." *J Consult Psychol* 24:279–87 Ag '60. * (*PA* 35:2211)

Although this inventory is intended for general use, the norms that are provided are based on the 478 people from the six occupational groups used in the validity study. Note that these data are based on the final form of the Schedule rather than on the *Temperament Comparator*. The aggregation produced by this indiscriminate pooling of the six groups is a long way from the reasonably representative samples from clearly defined populations required for adequate norms.

Finally, the procedure used to obtain the subjects' choices between each pair of traits—rotating a disc which has each of the 18 traits printed on its circumference and then recording the choice by making a pencil mark through a hole in the disc—may facilitate scoring and may even have some novelty value for the subjects, as the manual suggests, but these marginal advantages are outweighed by the errors that are apt to arise when the subject tries to erase and change his response, loses his place in rotating the disc, or fails to position the disc exactly after each rotation.

In view of the casual way that the *Temperament Comparator* was developed, the uncertain meaning of its scores, and the dearth of relevant data available about it, anyone who intends to measure the kinds of variables found in this inventory would be more likely to obtain useful results if he chose any of several other inventories which are better constructed and better understood, such as the *Guilford-Zimmerman Temperament Survey* or the *Sixteen Personality Factor Questionnaire.* If such inventories, which use a traditional true-false or yes-no format, are chosen, it would be desirable to use them in conjunction with a social desirability response style scale so as to be able to measure the effects of the response style on the inventory results.

ROBERT L. THORNDIKE, *Professor of Education, and Head, Department of Psychological Foundations and Services, Teachers College, Columbia University, New York, New York.*

This device consists of a list of 18 adjectives or adjectival phrases and a gadget. The gadget is a cardboard disc and a record sheet which can be thought to facilitate the paired comparison judgment of each adjective with respect to the other 17. Thus, the individual describes himself (or could be described by others) by the number of times he selects a particular trait name as he compares it with each of the others.

What virtue the instrument has stems from the selection of the trait names. These grew out of previous factor analytic studies, first of personality inventories and then of trait names themselves, and the 18 are considered by the authors to represent the principal dimensions of temperament. The results may be expressed in a profile for the 18 traits, or condensed into a profile of 5 factor scores. All of the traits are designated by rather positive and acceptable labels.

Evidence is reported to indicate that individuals are moderately consistent in their self-descriptions. When the time interval is one week, test-retest reliabilities for single trait names range from .65 to .87, and for factor scores from .78 to .90.

As usual, the validity problem is less happily dealt with. Reference is made to the underlying factor analyses. An assortment of modest correlations are reported with scales of the *Sixteen Personality Factor Questionnaire.* Finally, differences in mean profile scores are reported for sales, labor, and various supervisory and managerial categories.

This device provides a quick technique, possibly appealing to the respondent, for generating an ipsative personality profile based on a set of trait names. Whether the rather abstract and generalized trait names serve as well for this purpose as more specific and concrete behavior descriptions is nowhere made clear to the potential user.

[188]

★Test of Basic Assumptions. Adults; 1959, c1957–59; for experimental and research use only; 12 scores: 3 attitude scores (realist, idealist, pragmatist) for each of 4 "life areas" (organization of effort and problem solving, human abilities and the individual, general philosophy of life, economics and business); Form X ('59, 4 pages); manual ('59, 4 pages); score sheet (1 page); reliability data for total attitude scores only; no norms; $3.50 per 25 tests; 75¢ per specimen set; postpaid; (60) minutes; James H. Morrison and Martin Levit (test); James H. Morrison. *

[189]

★Test of Behavioral Rigidity, Research Edition. Ages 21 and over; 1960, c1956–60; test booklet title is *TBR;* 4 scores: motor-cognitive rigidity, personality-perceptual rigidity, psychomotor speed, total; items of one component scale of personality-perceptual rigidity score selected from *California Psychological Inventory;* 1 form ('60, c1956, 8 pages); mimeographed preliminary manual ('60, 24 pages); no data on reliability; $4.75 per 25 tests; $1 per manual; $1.50 per specimen set; postage extra; (30) minutes; K. Warner Schaie; Consulting Psychologists Press, Inc. *

REFERENCES

1. Schaie, K. W. *Measuring Behavioral Rigidity: A Factorial Investigation of Some Tests of Rigid Behavior.* Master's thesis, University of Washington (Seattle, Wash.), 1953.
2. Schaie, K. Warner. "A Test of Behavioral Rigidity." *J Abn & Social Psychol* 51:604–10 N '55. * (*PA* 31:3074)
3. Schaie, K. Warner. *Some Developmental Concomitants of Rigid Behavior.* Doctor's thesis, University of Washington (Seattle, Wash.), 1956. (*DA* 16:2215)
4. Strother, Charles R.; Schaie, K. Warner; and Horst, Paul. "The Relationship Between Advanced Age and Mental Abilities." *J Abn & Social Psychol* 55:166–70 S '57. * (*PA* 33:3294)
5. Schaie, K. Warner. "Differences in Some Personal Characteristics of 'Rigid' and 'Flexible' Individuals." *J Clin Psychol* 14:11–4 Ja '58. * (*PA* 33:5782)
6. Schaie, K. Warner. "Rigidity-Flexibility and Intelligence: A Cross-Sectional Study of the Adult Life Span From 20 to 70 Years." *Psychol Monogr* 72(9):1–26 '58. * (*PA* 33:9923)
7. Konietzko, K. *An Investigation of the Concept of "Behavioral Rigidity" as Applied to a Penal Population.* Doctor's thesis, Temple University (Philadelphia, Pa.), 1959. (*DA* 20:757)
8. Schaie, K. Warner. "The Effect of Age on a Scale of Social Responsibility." *J Social Psychol* 50:221–4 N '59. * (*PA* 35:4895)
9. Shockley, James T. "Behavioral Rigidity in Relation to Student Success in College Physical Science." *Sci Ed* 46:67–70 F '62. *

Douglas P. Crowne, *Associate Professor of Psychology, University of Connecticut, Storrs, Connecticut.*

This test is designed to measure rigidity, which the author defines as, "a tendency to perseverate and resist conceptual change, to resist the acquisition of new patterns of behavior, and to refuse to relinquish old and established patterns." The *Test of Behavioral Rigidity* (TBR) consists of three tests: the Capitals Test (copying a paragraph written half in capital and half in small letters); the Opposites Test (giving opposites to a series of words); and the Questionnaire, a true-false personality inventory. The capitals and opposites tests are repeated with the tasks somewhat altered; this gives a measure of ability to shift or change set. Several scores are derived from these tests.

A replicated factor analysis of these and other rigidity measures resulted in three factors. The motor-cognitive rigidity factor, defined by factor loadings of the capitals and opposites tests, is interpreted as an ability to shift activities from one to another. The questionnaire is the chief component of the second factor, personality-perceptual rigidity; this factor is defined as an ability to perceive and adapt to new situations. Psychomotor speed is defined by loadings of the capitals and opposites tests (essentially speed scores) and is interpreted as a speed of response or efficiency factor. Scores on the TBR are factor scores, and the total or composite rigidity score is simply an additive linear combination of the three factor scores.

TBR norms reported in the manual are based on a sample of 500 subjects drawn by stratified random sampling from the membership of a group medical plan. The normative sample is grouped by 5-year intervals, each group containing 25 males and 25 females, from ages 20 to 70. In both educational level and occupational status, the normative sample is significantly above the general population.

No data on reliability are reported; the manual avers that this is a major lack in the test. Reliability can be crudely estimated from the replication of the factor analysis in that the factor structure of rigidity tests was almost exactly duplicated. This establishes only the fact of a minimum level of consistency, and test-retest reliability data are urgently required.

The appropriate validation for the TBR is construct validity given the range of behavioral predictions which may be deduced. The author's concept of rigidity stresses developmental changes from early maturity to old age: rigidity should increase with age. In a cross-sectional study of adults from 20 to 70 years, Schaie (*6*) found rigidity increasing with age. These changes paralleled intellectual decline, and substantial correlations with the Thurstone PMA were found at every age level. In another study (*5*), highly rigid individuals were found to be significantly lower than "flexible" persons on each of the following: years of education, income, occupational status, self-rated happiness and success, and social responsibility. Prison inmates have a "rigidity quotient" significantly below that of the normative sample (*7*). No evidence on differential predictions from the three factors is reported, and the composite rigidity score appears to discriminate best (*6*). The meaning and usefulness of the three factors is yet to be demonstrated.

While evidence for the validity of the TBR is very limited, there are two other problems of great importance. First, the TBR correlates highly with intelligence, and the predictions so far made with the test could, perhaps, be made equally well with an intelligence measure. Thus, discriminant validity is lacking; there is the very real possibility that the TBR might be reducible to an intelligence test. Second, the definition of rigidity overlaps and fails to discriminate between *defensive rigidity* of the kind seen in compulsive behavior and the perseveration and inability to change associated with aging and other conditions impairing efficiency. These may even be confounded within the test: The questionnaire seems to be face valid as a measure of the former, while the capitals and opposites tests appear to be more like measures of the latter. A more precise definition of the construct of rigidity is needed. If defensive rigidity is included, then validity studies are required.

Summing up, the TBR is currently limited to research use in investigations of rigid behavior; in this regard the manual is commendably labeled "Research Edition." No individual predictions are warranted from this test in the absence of reliability data and further evidence on validity. The definition of rigidity and the interpretation of the three factors must be regarded as heuristic; they await research confirmation. For the time being, this test should be limited to research establishing its validity as a measure of rigidity. On the positive side, it is an interesting approach to behavioral rigidity and probably a more fruitful one than the Water Jar Test. The TBR is comprehensible to subjects, the directions clear, and the scoring straightforward if tedious for a large number of subjects.

BENJAMIN KLEINMUNTZ, *Associate Professor of Psychology, Carnegie Institute of Technology, Pittsburgh, Pennsylvania.*

The TBR is a group test, currently being published in its "research edition," which according to its manual is "designed to measure the ability of the individual to adjust to the stress imposed upon him by constant environmental change." The test is an outgrowth of its author's studies on the interrelationships between rigidity, age, and intelligence; and most of its components have been appropriated from the early literature on rigidity and perseveration. It consists of three parts:

Part 1, the Capitals Test, was adopted from a study by Bernstein on quickness and intelligence and is a performance task which consists of two 150-second writing exercises. The subject is required to copy in writing a 91 word passage. The second part of the Capitals Test requires that the examinee copy the same passage, but this time he is to write a capital letter wherever a small letter appears in the original, and write a small letter wherever a capital letter appears in the original. Part 2, the Opposites Test, suggested by Scheier and

Ferguson's factorial studies of tests of rigidity, consists of three series of writing exercises. In the first series the subject is required to furnish opposites for a list of 40 words. The second and third series of the Opposites Test each require *synonyms* for a list of 40 words, although the third series requires synonyms only when the stimulus word is printed in capital letters and calls for opposites when the stimulus word is printed in small letters. Each of the three parts of the Opposites Test is timed for two minutes. The last section of the TBR, Part 3, called the Questionnaire, consists of 75 true-false items. The R scale, which is comprised of 22 items, was obtained from Gough's *California Psychological Inventory;* 44 "masking" items were borrowed from the CPI Social Responsibility scale, and a 9-item P scale was patterned after some early work done on perseveration by W. Lankes.

The directions for the administration and the scoring procedures for each of the TBR's three parts are reasonably simple and straightforward and are clearly set forth in the accompanying manual. This reviewer did have some difficulty, however, in the scoring of the Opposites Test. The manual instructs the scorer to treat ratio scores as whole numbers; but it does not clarify whether the decimal point is to be dropped before or after performing subsequent arithmetic operations. In this regard the scoring format that is given for the opposites series on page 6 of the test booklet is definitely in error because it punctiliously leads the scorer through the steps of score computation, but omits completely the step where the individual is to multiply by 100. Since the scores resulting from either omission or inclusion of the multiplication process are plausible, the format is misleading and inaccurate.

In addition to a seven category classification scheme, which in the best tradition of early intelligence testing proposes Rigidity Quotients (RQ) ranging from scores of 69 or below ("very rigid") to 130 or above ("very flexible"), an interpretation for each of the three factors is offered. These factors and their interpretations, arrived at by "logical analysis of the experimental operations" are: (*a*) motor cognitive rigidity, which "indicates the individual's ability to shift without difficulty from one activity to another," (*b*) personality-perceptual rigidity, which "seeks to indicate the individual's ability to adjust readily to new surroundings and change in cognitive and environmental patterns," and (*c*) psychomotor speed, which "indicates the individual's rate of emission of familiar cognitive responses."

There are several features, according to the Technical Recommendations, that must be present in a good psychological test, and the TBR has certain essential ones. It is accompanied by a preliminary manual which summarizes the essential information about the test and which appropriately offers cautious interpretations about the meaning of its several scores. The TBR's standardization procedures assure uniformity of administration and scoring, and the test has been administered to a large representative sample of the type of subjects for whom it is presumably designed. Many hours of careful preparation are reflected in the presentation of this material.

There are two elements missing, however, which are undoubtedly the most important characteristics of a psychometric device. Data on the reliability of the various factors and on the complete test are nonexistent, and validity support is flimsy indeed. The test author acknowledges the lack of the former, but he is a bit disingenuous about the validity of his instrument. Instead of the presentation of validity data and the clear specification of what type of validity is being reported, the author fills the validity and reliability section of his manual with a report of two studies which bear questionable relevance to validity. One of the studies is the TBR author's own in which he compared the personal characteristics of "the 10 most flexible and 10 most rigid members of each age group in the normative sample." As may be expected whenever extremes of two groups are compared, statistically significant differences in the predicted directions were found. However, as should not be expected in a test manual, nor in the literature cited in support of a test being described in a manual, data on the extent of the overlap between the extremes of the groups in question were not presented and if the overlap between the groups was considerable, then even a critical ratio significant at the .0001 level is meaningless.

The second study reported in the validity and reliability section is an unpublished doctoral dissertation done at Temple University, in which the investigator studied a sample of 150 prison inmates "and found their average RQ to be significantly below that of the norm population." To extend this intellectual legerdemain one step further, the test author dazzles the reader with evidence of the above doctoral candidate's "correlation analysis" which "showed the TBR factors to be virtually independent with a maximum correlation of .22 between the motor-cognitive rigidity and psychomotor speed factors." In other words, no validating studies have been made, and here as well as in the case of the evidence for reliability, this reviewer would like to emphasize the test author's plea: "Further data are urgently required."

To summarize, this research edition of the TBR is an outgrowth of its author's studies on the relationships between rigidity and such variables as intelligence and age. It is a potpourri of measures, most of which have been borrowed from the literature on rigidity and perseveration, and which the author has painstakingly rearranged into a psychometric device. In many respects, the TBR qualifies as a psychological test, but in view of the lack of evidence for its validity or reliability, its claim to be a measure of anything is premature.

[190]

★**Test of Social Insight.** Grades 6–12, 13–16 and adults; 1959–63; 6 scores: withdrawal, passivity, cooperation, competition, aggression, total; IBM; 1 form ('59, 8 pages); 2 levels (essentially the same except for wording changes): youth edition, adult edition; manual ('63, 19 pages); separate answer sheets must be used; $6.25 per 25 tests; $2.75 per 25 IBM answer sheets; $1 per set of scoring stencils; $2.75 per 25 profiles; $1.75 per manual; $2.50 per specimen set of either level; cash orders postpaid; French edition available; [20–25] minutes; Russell N. Cassel; Martin M. Bruce. *

REFERENCES

1. CASSEL, RUSSELL N. "A Construct Validity Study on a Leadership and a Social Insight Tests for 200 College Freshmen Students." *J Genetic Psychol* 99:165–70 S '61. * (*PA* 36:3GF65C)
2. CASSEL, RUSSELL N., AND HADDOX, GENEVIEVE. "Comparing Reading Competency With Personality and Social Insight Test Scores." *Calif J Ed Res* 12:27–30 Ja '61. * (*PA* 36:1KJ27C)
3. LANGE, MERLE LEROY. *A Comparative Analysis of Achieving and Under-Achieving Twelfth Grade Students of Phoenix Central High School on the Non-Intellectual Factors of the Group Personality Projective Test and the Test of Social Insight.* Doctor's research study No. 1, Colorado State College (Greeley, Colo.), 1962. (*DA* 23:3778)
4. CASSEL, RUSSELL, AND CHILDERS, RICHARD. "A Study of Certain Attributes of 45 High-School Varsity Football Team Members by Use of Psychological Test Scores." *J Ed Res* 57:64–7 O '63. *

JOHN D. BLACK, *Director, Counseling and Testing Center, and Consulting Associate Professor of Psychology, Stanford University, Stanford; and President, Consulting Psychologists Press, Inc., Palo Alto; California.*

At first glance this test looks promising. It consists of 60 rather well written and ingenious items, confronting the subject with a choice among 5 alternative responses to difficult interpersonal situations. It reminds the reviewer of a verbal multiple choice version of the *Rosenzweig Picture-Frustration Study,* using a different theoretical framework. The five subscales seem to represent appropriate categorizations of response tendencies in human interaction and the items cover a suitable range of home, family, work, and social situations. All the test materials are well designed and the attractive 1963 manual contains 10 pages of tables and an extensive treatment of validity. Obviously an enormous amount of work has preceded publication of this test.

It is, therefore, disappointing and a little saddening to be reminded so forcefully upon closer examination that conscientious work is not enough to produce a good test in the absence of clear thinking and methodological sophistication.

The author does not define social insight, but if one takes it to refer to empathic, intuitive, or perceptive capacities for understanding or responding effectively in social situations, then this test has little or nothing to do with it. The Social Insight score is obtained by adding one tenth of the Cooperativeness score and twice the Competitiveness score to the Aggression score, with lower scores indicating greater social insight. (Scores on Withdrawal and Passivity are ignored.) How this computation could add up to social insight, or any meaningful psychological construct for that matter, is difficult to fathom.

This peculiar system of weights was derived from a discriminant function analysis of the 5 subscale scores of 300 high school students and 300 institutionalized delinquents (sex unspecified). Apparently, the reasoning was this: delinquents have less social insight than normals. Therefore, any combination of scores which tends to separate delinquents from normals will constitute a measure of social insight. This fallacious logic is repeated throughout the validity section. For example, since females (including female guidance counselors) obtain better scores than their male counterparts, validity is supported, because everyone knows that women are more socially insightful than men. The same argument is made with respect to age.

A few of the findings give the author difficulty. In one study, it was discovered that pupils with better (i.e., lower) social insight scores had poorer reading ability ($r = .21$), lower academic achievement scores ($r = .26$), more tension and anxiety ($r = .26$), and lower grade averages ($r = .19$). The manual's only comment on these findings is that they "suggest that certain school competence problems should embrace consideration of social and personality phenomenon." To this reviewer they also suggest what was obvious from the methodology; i.e., that the total score on this test is a predictor of delinquency (and not a very powerful one at that—point biserial = .24). To name it a Test of Social Insight is misleading in the extreme: the total score might have been called a delinquency index, or a socialization or rebelliousness score and been closer to the truth.

The discriminant function method is very appropriately applied to selection problems, but it is ridiculous to take a system of weights developed for a specific problem in a particular population (e.g., delinquent versus normal youth) and try to use it to predict another outcome (e.g., the presence of social insight in other populations). Indeed, the manual includes two other regression analyses which reveal that the test would require different weights to separate ninth from twelfth graders depending upon their sex.

The Social Insight score on this test, then, should not be used at all, except as a possible measure of delinquency-proneness among adolescents. There is no occasion which would justify its use in the adult form of the test. Furthermore, published evidence demonstrates that the Pd scale of the *Minnesota Multiphasic Personality Inventory* or the So scale of the *California Psychological Inventory* are much more successful predictors of asocial tendencies.

The five subscales of the TSI probably warrant some study to see whether they might not function as useful measures of various modes of responding to social situations. Unfortunately, the manual provides no information whatever on the criteria for item selection or any comment on the correlations of item alternatives with their respective scale scores. The author acknowledges that reliabilities of the subscales are not impressive. Indeed, of 80 corrected odd-even coefficients reported, only 7 equal or exceed .80, and 31 fall below .50. No test-retest r's are reported, except for total score ($r = .84$).

For the subscales, the author feels that T scores between 40 and 60 are preferable, and low scores on several scales are said to indicate general "social or psycho-social immaturity," but the evidence for these interpretations is not given. One mildly irritating aspect of TSI interpretation is that *low* total scores are supposedly indicative of *greater* social insight, while *high* scores on the subscales indicate more tendency to respond in the indicated fashion. Norm groups are of adequate size for a new test but poorly described (e.g., "adults," "junior high students").

In this reviewer's opinion, the very considerable time, effort, and money that have been invested in this test should have been devoted to perfecting the subscales. It is not a test author's responsibility to develop regression equations for the many possible prediction problems for which his test might be used, and to make one such set of weights a permanent and integral part of a personality measure intended for wide application is not appropriate. Above all, to call this test a measure of social insight is completely misleading and very unfortunate. The thought of an unsuspecting personnel man using the TSI to select socially-insightful employees fills one with horror.

JOHN PIERCE-JONES, *Professor of Educational Psychology, The University of Texas, Austin, Texas.*

The *Test of Social Insight* (TSI), viewed in the terms in which it is presented in the manual, appears to be an interesting and potentially useful personality inventory. Construction of the device apparently occurred as a result of an interest on the part of the test's author in the construct of "social intelligence" as employed by Edward Lee Thorndike in his familiar tripartite analysis of intelligence. Cassel holds that "social insight" is functionally linked to intelligence, and to personality in both its cognitive and affective aspects, by way of the functioning of the ego. Hence, "social insight" may be appraised through sampling the individual's preferences among various possible modes of coping with "social problems" in several realms. This kind of thinking seems relatively straightforward and will have considerable appeal to potential test users who share the relatively widespread contemporary preference among students of personality for ego-centered theories of social-psychological human functioning.

Cassel's TSI, in both its Youth Edition and Adult Edition, is intended to sample an individual's preferences among five modes of resolving problems he encounters in social relationships. These modes—Withdrawal, Passivity, Cooperation, Competition, and Aggression—are adequately defined and are represented in the TSI by the five response alternatives from which an examinee chooses in answering 60 items which cut across four major areas of social intercourse: (*a*) family relations; (*b*) relations with social agencies and authority; (*c*) play and avocations; (*d*) work. The inventory yields subtest scores—one for each of the five modes of social coping—and a total score (using weighted part scores) presumably representing one's level of "social insight." The reusable test booklets are nicely printed, the separate IBM answer sheets are easily scored by means of scoring stencils, a brief but relatively well conceived Examiner's Manual reporting reliability and validity data has been made available recently (1963), and profile sheets with norms are attractive and convenient.

The reliability coefficients reported for both youth and adult forms are generally Spearman-Brown corrected split-halves equivalence correlations, although two stability coefficients, each based on test and retest scores for 100 cases, have also been presented. By and large the stability and equivalence coefficients for the adult form total score ("social insight") range through the middle .70's and .80's, but for the Youth Edition the total score reliabilities tend to be somewhat lower—too low for individual prediction, certainly, but generally satisfactory for distinguishing between groups of examinees. Coefficients of equivalence for the separate subtests tend to be disappointingly low, and subtest intercorrelations are frequently fairly high, albeit their signs suggest sensible relationships. The reliabilities of the subtests and of the test as a whole might well benefit from lengthening, and the norms might be more discriminating. To some extent, however, the relatively low equivalence reliability of the Youth Edition may reflect the consequences of what appear to be only very minor modifications of wording in taking adult form items over into the youth form. It is this reviewer's impression that many of the items which appear well suited to tapping adults' social coping behavior preferences deal with aspects of social relationships which simply lack relevance for upper elementary school and junior high school youngsters even in sophisticated suburbia. It might have been better to develop children's and adolescents' forms independently than to derive them from the Adult Edition as seems to have been done. And, if it should be that social insight is differently organized in childhood than in adulthood (perhaps around different norms and sanctions which serve to define the modes of social coping), then it may be signally important to try to measure "social insight" in the terms of childhood social intercourse.

Evidence concerning the validities of the TSI appears to be accumulating, although it is not yet highly impressive in amount, and even though some of it—that concerning face validity for example—tends to seem specious. Empirically, TSI "social insight" appears to be associated significantly if modestly with (*a*) being female rather than male; (*b*) chronological age; (*c*) status with one's peers within a single school grade; (*d*) being socio-legally "normal" rather than "delinquent"; and various other test and extra-test criteria including IQ (*California Test of Mental Maturity*), tested scholastic achievement, childhood and family impoverishment, and scores from the *Leadership Ability Evaluation.*

In summary, it is this reviewer's opinion that Cassel's TSI is a promising effort to measure variables of obvious interest and importance to research psychologists, personnel workers, counselors, and educators; that the Youth Edition should not be used with individuals below the ninth grade; that a more relevant form should be devised for children and younger adolescents; that interpretations should be confined to differences between groups; and that individual predictions and diagnoses should not be undertaken until the reliability of the present TSI has been improved.

J Consult Psychol 24:100 F '60. Edward S. Bordin. * The odd-even reliabilities, even after Spearman-Brown corrections, are unsatisfactory, none above .88 and, in some populations, as low as .51. Validities based on inadequately reported unpublished data are more reassuring. Caveat Emptor!

[191]

★Test of Work Competency and Stability. Ages 21 and over; 1960–61, c1959–60; for predicting work capacity and identifying persons psychologically incapable of work; individual; 1 form consisting of an interview questionnaire (5 pages, mimeographed, 1 or 2 scores: ego strength and, optionally, occupational stability) and 4 or 6 tests: 2 perceptual tests of intelligence (digits backward, picture arrangement), 2 psychomotor tests (tapping, steadiness), and (optionally) stress test (mirror drawing), digit symbol; manual ('61, c1959, 58 pages, English edition translated from the 1960 French edition which is also available); record booklet ('60, 4 pages); no data on reliability for interview questionnaire, digits backwards, picture arrangement, or digit symbol; $110 per set of test materials including apparatus for tapping, steadiness, and mirror drawing tests, 25 record booklets, 25 questionnaires, 25 mirror tracing records, 25 tapping records, and manual; $3 per 25 questionnaires; $2 per 25 record booklets; $2.50 per manual; prices include purchase tax; postage extra; stopwatch necessary for administration; (30–40) minutes; A. Gaston Leblanc; Institut de Recherches Psychologiques. *

REFERENCES

1. LEBLANC, GASTON A. *Work Adjustment and Its Measurement.* Doctor's thesis, University of Montreal (Montreal, Que., Canada), 1958.
2. WEIL, PAUL G., AND LEBLANC, G. A. "The Assessment and Rehabilitation of the Psychologically Handicapped." *Med Services J Can* 16:765–72 O '60. *

[192]

Thurstone Temperament Schedule. Grades 9–16 and adults; 1949–53; 7 scores: active, vigorous, impulsive, dominant, stable, sociable, reflective; IBM; 2 editions; manual, second edition ('53, 14 pages); separate answer sheets or pads must be used; $10.80 per 20 tests; $1.15 per specimen set; postage extra; (15–25) minutes; L. L. Thurstone; Science Research Associates, Inc. *
a) [HAND SCORED EDITION.] Form AH ('49, 7 pages); $2.40 per 20 answer pads.
b) [MACHINE SCORABLE EDITION.] IBM; Form AM ('49, 7 pages); $5 per 100 IBM answer sheets; $2.50 per set of scoring stencils.

REFERENCES

1–12. See 5:118.
13. CONGER, JOHN J.; GASKILL, HERBERT S.; GLAD, DONALD D.; RAINEY, ROBERT V.; SAWREY, WILLIAM L.; AND TURRELL, EUGENE S. "Personal and Interpersonal Factors in Motor Vehicle Accidents." *Am J Psychiatry* 113:1069–74 Je '57. * (*PA* 32:6071)
14. NUNNERY, MICHAEL Y. *A Study in the Use of Psychological Tests in Determining Effectiveness and Ineffectiveness Among Practicing School Administrators.* Doctor's thesis, University of Tennessee (Knoxville, Tenn.), 1958. (*DA* 19:1276)
15. TALMADGE, MAX. "Expressive Graphic Movements and Their Relationship to Temperament Factors." *Psychol Monogr* 72(16):1–30 '58. * (*PA* 33:9733)
15a. KEISLAR, EVAN R. "The Validity of the Thurstone Temperament Schedule With Adolescents." *Personnel & Guid J* 38:226–8 N '59. * (PA 35:3758)
16. KING, PAUL; NORRELL, GWEN; AND ERLANDSON, F. L. "The Prediction of Academic Success in a Police Administration Curriculum." *Ed & Psychol Meas* 19:649–51 w '59. * (*PA* 34:6166)
17. NUNNERY, MICHAEL Y. "How Useful Are Standardized Psychological Tests in the Selection of School Administrators." *Ed Adm & Sup* 45:349–56 N '59. * (*PA* 35:7092)
18. COUCH, ARTHUR, AND KENISTON, KENNETH. "Yeasayers and Naysayers: Agreeing Response Set as a Personality Variable." *J Abn & Social Psychol* 60:151–74 Mr '60. * (*PA* 34:7376)
19. FISKE, DONALD W. "Variability Among Peer Ratings in Different Situations." *Ed & Psychol Meas* 20:283–92 su '60. * (*PA* 35:6337)
20. GIBLETTE, JOHN FRANKLIN. *Differences Among Above Average, Average, and Below Average Secondary School Counselors.* Doctor's thesis, University of Pennsylvania (Philadelphia, Pa.), 1960. (*DA* 21:812)
21. BORGATTA, EDGAR F. "Mood, Personality, and Interaction." *J General Psychol* 64:105–37 Ja '61. * (*PA* 35:6415)
22. BORGATTA, EDGAR F.; IN COLLABORATION WITH HENRY J. MEYER. "Make a Sentence Test: An Approach to Objective Scoring of Sentence Completions." *Genetic Psychol Monogr* 63:3–65 F '61. * (*PA* 35:6435)
23. BUEL, WILLIAM D., AND BAEHNER, VIRGINIA M. "The Assessment of Creativity in a Research Setting." *J Appl Psychol* 45:353–8 D '61. * (*PA* 37:1211)
24. MICHAEL, WILLIAM B.; BARTH, GEORGE; AND KAISER, HENRY F. "Dimensions of Temperament in Three Groups of Music Teachers." *Psychol Rep* 9:701–4 D '61. *
25. BORGATTA, EDGAR F. "The Coincidence of Subtests in Four Personality Inventories." *J Social Psychol* 56:227–44 Ap '62. * (*PA* 37:1247)
26. HULL, J., AND ZUBEK, JOHN P. "Personality Characteristics of Successful and Unsuccessful Sensory Isolation Subjects." *Percept & Motor Skills* 14:231–40 Ap '62. * (*PA* 37:312)
27. BECKER, ANTHONY J. "A Study of the Personality Traits of Successful Religious Women of Teaching Orders." *Yearb Nat Council Meas Ed* 20:124–5 '63. * (*PA* 38:9287)
28. GORDON, IRA J. "Personality Patterns of Volunteers for an Experimental Professional Education Program." *J Exp Ed* 32:115–21 f '63. *

For a review by Neil J. Van Steenberg, see 5:118; for reviews by Hans J. Eysenck, Charles M. Harsh, and David G. Ryans, see 4:93 (1 excerpt).

[193]

★Triadal Equated Personality Inventory. Adult males; 1960–63; 22 scores: dominance, self confidence, decisiveness, independence, toughness, suspiciousness, conscientiousness, introversion, restlessness, solemnity, foresight, industriousness, warmth, enthusiasm, conformity, inventiveness, persistence, sex drive, recognition drive, cooperativeness, humility-tolerance, self-control; 1 form ('61, 4 pages); administration and technical manual ('63, 4 pages); norms manual ('61, 4 pages); profile ('61, 1 page); separate answer sheets must be used; $10 per 25 tests; $2 per 25 answer sheets; $20 per set of keys; $2 per 25 profiles; $2 per specimen set (must be purchased to obtain manuals); cash orders postpaid; (60–80) minutes; Research Staff, United Consultants; Psychometric Affiliates. *

[194]

Vineland Social Maturity Scale. Birth to maturity; 1935–53; individual; 1 form ('36, 4 pages); condensed manual ('47, 44 pages); manual ('53, see *83*); $1.80 per 25 record blanks; $1.25 per condensed manual; $7.75 per manual; $1.30 per specimen set; postage extra; Edgar A. Doll; Educational Test Bureau. * (Australian edition: Australian Council for Educational Research.)

REFERENCES

1–58. See 3:107.
59–79. See 4:94.
80–94. See 5:120.
95. DOLL, EDGAR A. "Evaluating Social Maturity." *Ed* 77:409–13 Mr '57. *
96. NORRIS, MIRIAM; SPAULDING, PATRICIA J.; AND BRODIE, FERN H. *Blindness in Children.* Chicago, Ill.: University of Chicago Press, 1957. Pp. xv, 173. * (*PA* 32:824)
97. WERNER, EMMY. "Milieu Differences in Social Competence." *J Genetic Psychol* 91:239–49 D '57. * (*PA* 36:1FC39W)
98. ALLEN, ROBERT M. "Suggestions for the Adaptive Administration of Intelligence Tests for Those With Cerebral Palsy: Part 2, Administration of the Vineland Social Maturity Scale, the Gesell Preliminary Behavior Inventory, and the Cattell Infant Intelligence Scales." *Cerebral Palsy R* 19:6–7 Mr–Ap '58. * (*PA* 33:8853)
99. SMITH, LAURENCE C., JR., AND PHILLIPS, LESLIE. "Social Effectiveness and Developmental Level in Adolescence." *J Personality* 27:239–49 Je '59. * (*PA* 34:3898)
100. ZUK, G. H. "Autistic Distortions in Parents of Re-

tarded Children." *J Consult Psychol* 23:171–6 Ap '59. * (*PA* 34:1687)
101. DUNSDON, M. I.; CARTER, C. O.; AND HUNTLEY, R. M. C. "Upper End of Range of Intelligence in Mongolism." *Lancet* 7124:565–8 Mr 12 '60. *
102. FRANCEY, RUTH E. "Psychological Test Changes in Mentally Retarded Children During Training." *Can J Pub Health* 51:69–74 F '60. *
103. ISCOE, IRA. "A Profile for the Vineland Scale and Some Clinical Applications." *J Clin Psychol* 16:14–6 Ja '60. * (*PA* 36:1HC14I)
104. JOHNSON, G. ORVILLE; CAPOBIANCO, RUDOLPH J.; AND BLAKE, KATHRYN A. "An Evaluation of Behavioral Changes in Trainable Mentally Deficient Children." *Am J Mental Def* 64:881–93 Mr '60. *
105. KADELL, MARY BELLE. *A Factor Analysis of the Vineland Social Maturity Scale and the Stanford-Binet Intelligence Scale.* Master's thesis, University of Minnesota (Minneapolis, Minn.), 1960.
106. PRINGLE, M. L. KELLMER. "Social Learning and Its Measurement." *Ed Res* 2:194–206 Je '60. * (*PA* 35:4694)
107. SAHA, GOPI BALLAV. "An Investigation Into the School Maturity of High School Students." *Indian J Psychol* 35:47–54 pt 2 '60. * (*PA* 36:4KD47S)
108. STEER, M. D., AND DREXLER, HAZEL G. "Predicting Later Articulation Ability From Kindergarten Tests." *J Speech & Hearing Disorders* 25:391–7 N '60. * (*PA* 35:3911)
109. LEVINSON, BORIS M. "Parental Achievement Drives for Preschool Children, the Vineland Social Maturity Scale, and the Social Deviation Quotient." *J Genetic Psychol* 99:113–28 S '61. * (*PA* 36:3FF13L) (Abstract: *Acta Psychologica* 19:420–1)
110. SCHERER, ISIDOR W. "The Prediction of Academic Achievement in Brain Injured Children." *Excep Child* 28:103–6 O '61. *
111. HURST, JOHN G. "The Meaning and Use of Difference Scores Obtained Between the Performance on the Stanford-Binet Intelligence Scale and Vineland Social Maturity Scale." *J Clin Psychol* 18:153–60 Ap '62. * (*PA* 38:8422)
112. WOLFENSBERGER, WOLF. "Age Variations in Vineland SQ Scores for the Four Levels of Adaptive Behavior of the 1959 AAMD Behavioral Classification." *Am J Mental Def* 67:452–4 N '62. * (*PA* 37:5424)
113. BARCLAY, A., AND GOULET, L. R. "An Interpretative Profile Technique for Use With the Vineland Social Maturity Scale." *J Clin Psychol* 19:303–4 Jl '63. *
114. GOULET, L. R., AND BARCLAY, A. "The Vineland Social Maturity Scale: Utility in Assessment of Binet MA." *Am J Mental Def* 67:916–21 My '63. * (*PA* 38:1273)

For reviews by William M. Cruickshank and Florence M. Teagarden, see 4:94; for reviews by C. M. Louttit and John W. M. Rothney, see 3:107 (1 excerpt); for reviews by Paul H. Furfey, Elaine F. Kinder, and Anna S. Starr of Experimental Form B, see 38:1143; for excerpts from related book reviews, see 5:B121.

[195]

★The Visual-Verbal Test: A Measure of Conceptual Thinking. Schizophrenic patients; 1959–60; individual; 1 form ['59, 46 cards]; mimeographed manual ('59, 11 pages); record booklet ('60, 4 pages); $15 per set of picture cards, 25 record booklets, and manual; $6.50 per 25 record booklets; $2.50 per manual; postpaid; specimen set not available; (30–130) minutes; Marvin J. Feldman and James Drasgow; Western Psychological Services. *

REFERENCES

1. BECKER, P. H. *A Visio-Verbal Test for Differentiating Organic Brain Damaged Patients From Schizophrenics.* Master's thesis, University of Buffalo (Buffalo, N.Y.), 1950.
2. FELDMAN, MARVIN J., AND DRASGOW, JAMES. "A Visual-Verbal Test for Schizophrenia." *Psychiatric Q Sup* 25:55–64 '51. * (*PA* 26:5748)
3. DRASGOW, JAMES. *Visio-Verbal Test for Schizophrenia.* Doctor's thesis, University of Buffalo (Buffalo, N.Y.), 1952. (*DA* 12:394)
4. SIEGEL, SAUL MARVIN. *A Study of the Visio-Verbal Test in the Discrimination of Mental Defectives From Other Clinical Groups.* Master's thesis, University of Buffalo (Buffalo, N.Y.), 1952.
5. JACOBS, ELEANOR A. *An Investigation of Some Relationships Between Personality Disturbance and Perceptual Reorganization.* Doctor's thesis, University of Buffalo (Buffalo, N.Y.), 1954. (*DA* 15:1118)
6. DRASGOW, JAMES, AND FELDMAN, MARVIN. "Conceptual Processes in Schizophrenia Revealed by the Visual-Verbal Test." *Percept & Motor Skills* 7:251–64 D '57. * (*PA* 33:2828)
7. SIEGEL, SAUL M. "Discrimination Among Mental Defective, Normal, Schizophrenic and Brain Damaged Subjects on the Visual-Verbal, Concept Formation Test." *Am J Mental Def* 62:338–43 S '57. * (*PA* 33:1654)
8. PAYNE, R. W.; MATTUSSEK, P.; AND GEORGE, E. I. "An Experimental Study of Schizophrenic Thought Disorder." *J Mental Sci* 105:627–52 Jl '59. * (*PA* 34:6384)

R. W. PAYNE, *Associate Professor of Psychology, Queen's University, Kingston, Ontario, Canada.*

The Feldman-Drasgow test of concept formation consists of a set of cards, each of which depicts four objects in a row. For example, the first card pictures four lines. Three are horizontal, and one vertical, and one of the horizontal lines is colored red. The subjects are asked to indicate for each card three objects which are alike in one way (e.g., three horizontal lines) and then to indicate three objects which are alike in some other way (e.g., three black lines). Subjects are given a time limit of three minutes per card, and must explain each concept adequately.

The test is designed to assess the ability to form concepts. A "single miss" is defined as missing one of the two concepts on a card, a "double miss" is defined as missing both. The reliability of the scores ranges from .70 to .86 (corrected split-half). Schizophrenic and brain damaged subjects were expected to perform poorly, and the results given in the manual suggest that neurotics do slightly worse than normals, acute schizophrenics significantly worse than neurotics, chronic schizophrenics worse still, and brain damaged patients and mental defectives worst of all. Results for the affective disorders are not given, an omission which would limit the use of the test for some cases of differential diagnosis.

Several carefully controlled studies[1] using other techniques have reported results which are inconsistent with these, in that acute schizophrenics were not found to be significantly concrete. In fact, Payne, Mattussek, and George (*8*) used a test modeled on the Feldman-Drasgow test, and did not find acute schizophrenics to be significantly more concrete than a neurotic control group. Presumably the explanation for such contradictions must lie in the particular samples tested, and here the main inadequacies of the present manual become apparent. The reader is told virtually nothing

1 PAYNE, R. W. Chap. 6, "Cognitive Abnormalities," pp. 193–261. In *Handbook of Abnormal Psychology: An Experimental Approach.* Edited by H. J. Eysenck. New York: Basic Books, Inc., 1961. Pp. xvi, 816. * (*PA* 35:6719)

about the groups tested. The age, the level of intelligence, the socioeconomic level, the sex, the length of hospitalization, and the major symptomatology are all details which are needed if these norms are to be applied to other populations. Unfortunately none of these data are given. The reader is told that "age and education seem unrelated to error scores on the VVT" but no figures are quoted. Even the mean ages of the groups are not reported. Indeed, the *Visual-Verbal Test* scores themselves are inadequately reported. While the mean and standard deviations of the scores are given, the ranges are not. For such data to be of most use to the practising clinician, the entire histogram should be reproduced.

These deficiencies make the test as presently published of limited value.

Donald R. Peterson, *Professor of Psychology, and Director, Psychological Clinic, University of Illinois, Urbana, Illinois.*

Theories relating to schizophrenic thought have been inspiring tests of cognitive deficit for many years. The *Visual-Verbal Test* (VVT) is one of the more recent products, and it appears to be one of the most promising. The theoretical propositions on which the test is based are elementary and familiar: schizophrenics have difficulty (*a*) in forming categorical concepts, and (*b*) in changing to new concepts once primary ideas have been formed. Test materials are innocuous and easy to manipulate. After appropriate demonstrations, 42 cards, each containing 4 printed figures, are displayed. The task is readily comprehensible; subjects are asked to identify three stimulus items which are alike in some way, and then to identify three which are alike in some other way. Scoring is simple and objective. Three error scores are derived, a "double miss" score representing the number of cards on which the subject formed no accurate concepts at all, a "single miss" score representative of failure to develop more than one concept per card, and a "total miss" score obtained by weighting and adding the other two. Interpretation is relatively straightforward, and evidence on discriminatory power is about as convincing as one can expect at this stage in development of the test.

As to reliability, only odd-even consistency indices are reported. These are adequate but unimpressive. The reviewer computed uncorrected *r*'s ranging from .45 for the double miss score with neurotics to .70 for the single miss score with mental defectives. The manual, of course, reports corrected (Spearman-Brown) values, and these only for the total miss score on three groups. Since much of the useful information from the test is derived from separate single miss and double miss scores, reliabilities of these should also be given. No information is provided on the stability of test performance, and the authors neglect to make proper apologies for the omission.

The test has been given to a variety of clinical groups and to five groups of "normal" adults. Selection of the latter always poses a problem in test development, but the authors of this test have met the problem with greater concern, ingenuity, and effort than is typically shown by the inventors of clinical diagnostic techniques. The original sample was composed of 37 volunteers whose cooperation was solicited while they were sitting around in a bus terminal. Of 40 approached, only 3 refused, and the remaining 37 did not differ reliably from schizophrenics in regard to age, IQ, and reported education. Data have also been obtained from non-psychiatric hospital patients, vocational counselees, and applicants for industrial jobs, as well as the usual group of college students.

The most striking evidence for concurrent validity arises from comparison of schizophrenic patients with the normal groups examined. Single miss scores have differentiated schizophrenics from normals with no overlap whatever. Results like these immediately mobilize some critical suspicions. Considering the limited reliability of psychiatric diagnosis, one begins to wonder whether test performance is not determined by the peculiarities of hospitalization, examiner bias, or some other equally irrelevant influence, rather than the conceptual abilities of subjects. In the knowledge of psychometric history, where one promising device after another has collapsed under careful and continued empirical scrutiny, one grows wary of strong enthusiasm. But Feldman and Drasgow have used no tricky weighting schemes to capitalize on chance; they have examined several groups in most of the classes of subjects, and several different examiners have given the tests. While the need for extensive cross validation remains, the authors appear to have met conventional obligations in a rather commendable way.

Differentiation between clinical groups is less clear, though some interesting patterns of findings have emerged. Acute schizophrenics have differed grossly from normals in single miss scores, and by inference in whatever abilities and dispositions are involved in generating two different concepts per card. On the average, however, acute schizophrenics did not exhibit the massive deficit required to accumulate high double miss scores. Chronic schizophrenics tended to score high in double as well as single errors. In fact the pattern of means for chronic schizophrenics bears close resemblance to that for mental defectives and is not vastly different from that for patients with known organic brain damage. This is consistent with the usual theories of cognitive deficit, but it limits the utility of the test in differential diagnosis and raises some questions about describing the device as a test of conceptual ability *in schizophrenia.* One of the neurotic samples, for instance, obtained a single miss mean nearly as high as that for one of the acute schizophrenic groups. Data on other clinical groups, e.g., affective psychotics, are not given. So the specificity of poor test performance to schizophrenia is in some respects unknown, and in other respects demonstrably limited.

Because of the ease with which the test can be given, and because of the encouraging trend of findings so far, the VVT is rather likely to be used by large numbers of spottily trained examiners, some of whom may test, score, and label patients in an indiscriminate way. The manual contains appropriate warnings about the need for caution in interpreting results, but misuse might be reduced more effectively if the manual offered actual score distributions rather than the "legal" but somewhat misleading schematic distributions which appear, if it contained stronger comment about overlap between clinical groups, and if it deemphasized the notion that conceptual failures are unique to schizophrenia.

Construct validity and predictive utility of the test are essentially unestablished. Minor claims which appear in the manual involve very elastic use of the term "construct validity." Relationships with traditional tests of concept formation, with other tests of psychological function, with behavior observations, treatment outcomes and the like, badly need determination.

But all this can be accomplished through further research. Right now, as it stands, the VVT is a brief, easily administered, fairly homogeneous instrument, yielding objective scores which have so far distinguished clearly between schizophrenic and normal subjects, and which have displayed some patterns, among schizophrenic and mentally retarded subjects particularly, of strong theoretical interest. The test should be given wide use as a research tool. Use as a clinical diagnostic instrument is questionable, but it is fair to say that the test is no less valuable in this regard than most other available instruments.

[196]

★**WLW Personal Attitude Inventory.** Business and industry; 1954–60; 6 scores: emotional stability, friendliness, aggressiveness, humility and insight, reliability, leadership; 2 editions: third edition ('55, 3 pages), fifth edition ('60, 4 pages); distribution of fifth edition restricted to clients; mimeographed manual ['56, 13 pages] for third edition; mimeographed supplement ('56, 2 pages); profile ('56, 1 page); norms for men only; $7.50 per 25 tests, postpaid; [20] minutes; R. W. Henderson, W. E. Brown, T. L. Chappell, L. D. Edmonson, W. H. E. Geiger, R. L. Kaiser, L. C. Steckle, and L. E. Saddler; William, Lynde & Williams. *

[197]

★**Welsh Figure Preference Test, Research Edition.** Ages 6 and over; 1959, c1949–59; 27 scores: don't like total, repeat, conformance, *Barron-Welsh Art Scale,* revised art scale, male-female, neuropsychiatric, children, movement, 5 sex symbol scores, and 13 figure-structure preference scores; 1 form ('59, c1949, 53 pages); mimeographed preliminary manual ('59, 35 pages); reliability data, based on earlier forms, for revised art scale and shortened versions of movement and don't like total only; norms below adult level for ages 6–8 only; separate answer sheets must be used; $8.50 per 25 tests; $2.50 per 50 answer sheets; scoring stencils must be constructed locally; $1 per manual; $1.50 per specimen set; postage extra; (50) minutes; George S. Welsh; Consulting Psychologists Press, Inc. *

REFERENCES

1. WELSH, GEORGE S. *A Projective Figure-Preference Test for Diagnosis of Psychopathology: 1, A Preliminary Investigation.* Doctor's thesis, University of Minnesota (Minneapolis, Minn.), 1949.

2. BARRON, FRANK, AND WELSH, GEORGE S. "Artistic Perception as a Possible Factor in Personality Style: Its Measurement by a Figure Preference Test." *J Psychol* 33:199–203 Ap '52. * (*PA* 26:6844)

3. MACKINNON, DONALD W. "The Development of Useful Tests for the Measurement of Non-Intellectual Functions," pp. 73–88. "Discussion of Professor MacKinnon's Paper," pp. 89–96, by John Dollard. General discussion, pp. 108–13. In *Proceedings of the 1951 Invitational Conference on Testing Problems, November 3, 1951.* Princeton, N. J.: Educational Testing Service, 1952. Pp. 119. *

4. BARRON, FRANK. "The Disposition Toward Originality." *J Abn & Social Psychol* 51:478–85 N '55. * (*PA* 31:2533)

5. ROSEN, JOHN C. "The Barron-Welsh Art Scale as a Predictor of Originality and Level of Ability Among Artists." *J Appl Psychol* 39:366–7 O '55. * (*PA* 30:6932)

6. PEPPER, LENNARD JAY. *The Relationship Between Welsh Figure Preference Test Responses and Indices of Anxiety and*

Repression. Master's thesis, University of North Carolina (Chapel Hill, N.C.), 1957.
7. SCHULTZ, K. V., AND KNAPP, W. E. "Perceptual Preferences and Self Descriptions." *Personnel & Guid J* 37:581–4 Ap '59. *
8. EDWARDS, ELISABETH STETSON. *Comparison of Responses of Children, Normal Adults and Schizophrenics on the Perceptual Maturity Scale.* Doctor's thesis, University of Denver (Denver, Colo.), 1961. (*DA* 23:700)
9. GOLANN, STUART EUGENE. *The Creativity Motive.* Doctor's thesis, University of North Carolina (Chapel Hill, N.C.), 1961. (*DA* 23:701)
10. HARRIS, THOMAS LEWIS. *An Analysis of the Responses Made by Adolescents to the Welsh Figure Preference Test and Its Implications for Guidance Purposes.* Doctor's thesis, University of North Carolina (Chapel Hill, N.C.), 1961. (*DA* 22:2687)
11. MACKINNON, DONALD W. "Fostering Creativity in Students of Engineering." *J Eng Ed* 52:129–42 D '61. * (*PA* 36:4HD29M)
12. CARACENA, PHILIP F., AND KING, GERALD F. "Generality of Individual Differences in Complexity." *J Clin Psychol* 18:234–6 Ap '62. * (*PA* 38:8480)
13. GOLANN, STUART E. "The Creativity Motive." *J Personality* 30:588–600 D '62. * (*PA* 39:1777)
14. L'ABATE, LUCIANO; BOELLING, GARY M.; HUTTON, ROBERT D.; AND MATHEWS, DEWEY L., JR. "The Diagnostic Usefulness of Four Potential Tests of Brain Damage." Abstract. *J Consult Psychol* 26:479 O '62. *
15. MACKINNON, DONALD W. "The Personality Correlates of Creativity: A Study of American Architects," pp. 11–39. (*PA* 37:4958) In *Personality Research.* Proceedings of the XIV International Congress of Applied Psychology, Vol. 2. Copenhagen, Denmark: Munksgaard, Ltd., 1962. Pp. 229. *
16. PINE, FRED. "Creativity and Primary Process: Sample Variations." *J Nerv & Mental Dis* 134:506–11 Je '62. * (*PA* 37:3205)
17. SECHREST, LEE, AND JACKSON, DOUGLAS N. "The Generality of Deviant Response Tendencies." *J Consult Psychol* 26:395–401 O '62. * (*PA* 39:1822)
18. VAN DE CASTLE, R. L. "Perceptual Immaturity and Acquiescence Among Various Developmental Levels." *J Consult Psychol* 26:167–71 Ap '62. * (*PA* 37:5019)
19. BARRON, FRANK. "Discovering the Creative Personality," pp. 79–85. In *The Behavioral Sciences and Education.* New York: College Entrance Examination Board, 1963. Pp. vi, 99. *
20. NORMAN, WARREN T. "Relative Importance of Test Item Content." *J Consult Psychol* 27:166–74 Ap '63. * (*PA* 37:7980)

HAROLD BORKO, *Human Factors Scientist, Advanced Technology and Research Directorate, System Development Corporation, Santa Monica, California.*

The *Welsh Figure Preference Test* (WFPT) was designed "to afford non-language stimulus material suitable for a wide range of subjects who could not be tested readily with conventional personality inventories and projective methods." The design of the WFPT was influenced by the *Minnesota Multiphasic Personality Inventory.* This is understandable for Welsh studied at the University of Minnesota, was influenced by the MMPI, and through his own research influenced the development of the MMPI. It will be recalled that a basic tenet of the MMPI is that if the response to an item differentiates between two groups of people, then it is a "good" item. No assumption need be made as to whether the subject has insight into the meaning of the item or into his own dynamics in answering the item. If one adheres to this philosophy, it is a short but significant step to say that the test item can be meaningless, i.e., it can be a picture, as long as it differentiates between two groups. In essence the WFPT is an abstract form, or picture version, of an MMPI-type test. It consists of a booklet (Welsh also experimented with a card form) containing 400 black and white line drawings. The instructions are simple; the subject is asked "to decide whether you like or don't like each of the drawings on the following pages" and to record the answers on a separate sheet. The test takes 50 to 60 minutes to complete, and the results can be scored objectively.

The reliability of the WFPT has not been satisfactorily demonstrated. In the one reported study, a group of 29 undergraduate students in psychology were given the card form of the test and one week later were given the booklet form containing only 144 items. Another group of 35 students were given the same two tests in reversed order. The protocols were scored for only the Revised Art Scale (RA), a portion of the Movement Scale (MV), and a portion of the Don't Like Scale (DL). The reliability of the RA Scale is high (test-retest correlations of .94 and .90) and, in the words of the author, reflects "remarkable consistency." The reliability of the partial MV Scale is lower (.64 and .74) but still consistent, and the reliability coefficients for the DL Scale are, if anything, remarkably inconsistent (.88 and .51 for the total scale and .92 and .51 for the partial scale). Welsh suggests that, "The markedly lower correlations for the second group were due to two extreme individuals." Perhaps so, but this is all the more reason to use a reasonable sample when obtaining reliability figures. The lack of adequate reliability statistics based upon a representative sample of both normal and patient populations and covering all of the test scales is a most serious deficiency in the test as it now stands. Even the standardizing population is relatively small consisting of (*a*) 100 male patients in a Veterans Administration neuropsychiatric hospital, (*b*) 150 normal adults (75 males and 75 females), and (*c*) 82 children ages 6 to 8 (42 boys and 40 girls).

Putting aside the question of reliability, let us examine the validity of the instrument. The manual states that the WFPT can be used when conventional personality inventories are not appropriate. Since the items are pictorial rather than verbal, the subject need not be literate. This is a distinct advantage, for it does make the test usable when other instruments such as the MMPI would not be appropriate. But what aspects of personality does the test measure? Welsh never really answers this question. He stresses the fact that the test is a research instrument and that the scales are to be considered provisional in nature. He claims that, "One of the scales, the Barron-Welsh Art Scale, has been rather extensively used and can be considered to be in final form." This 65-item scale can separate artists from non-artists. The Revised Art Scale correlates highly with the Barron-Welsh scale, but is apparently not yet in final form. Of the other empirical scales, the Male-Female Scale (MF) has not held up in cross validation. The Children's Scale (CN) which purports to differentiate 6- and 8-year-olds from adults has not yet been validated. On the positive side, the Neuropsychiatric Scale (NP) of 40 items designed to distinguish VA patients from people in general has been cross validated, and the author suggests that it may be used in its present form. There are other scales, both empirical and *a priori* in nature, but they are only suggestive and the scores cannot now be interpreted with any degree of confidence. It appears that the test does not measure many of the personality directions and even these are not measured with much confidence.

As a research instrument the WFPT has potential. The 400 items can be administered to various groups—neurotics and psychotics, gifted and normal, overachievers and underachievers, orientals and Caucasians, etc.—with the objective of finding sets of items that distinguish between these groups. Then the research must be continued and the scales shown to be reliable and valid. Until a set of scales have been validated for the *Welsh Figure Preference Test,* the test has little practical value.

J Counsel Psychol 7:310–11 w'60. Gordon V. Anderson. [Review of the earlier card form.] This psychological instrument is a completely nonverbal measure, the ultimate intent of which is to provide an index of emotional adjustment and to identify and quantify personality characteristics. The format of the test and the instructions for response, however, lead to the inference that it is a measure of aesthetic discrimination or judgment. Indeed, the Barron-Welsh Art Scale is incorporated into the test, yielding a score on aesthetic judgment, which has been accepted by many as one component of artistic ability, although there are better tests of this ability already available. * is made up of 400 "cards" presented to the subject, on each of which is a drawing or design, and the simple instruction is to respond as "Like" or "Don't Like" * The simplicity of the test approach makes it usable with almost any age, and there are no language barriers. * There are two empirically derived scales, the B-W Art scale and a Neuro-psychiatric scale which separates disturbed from normal subjects. Besides these empirical scales, the test yields three other scores: a "Repeat" (RP) score, based on the consistency with which the subject responds to twenty items which have been repeated; a "Don't Like" (DL) score which is a simple count of the total number of items the subject has placed in that category, and a "Conformance" (CF) score, based on a series of items upon which there was high agreement among a general population and artist sample. These scores presently have no known clinical significance, except that the RP score may indicate the possibility of scoring errors or failure of the subject's cooperation. The manual, which is still in preliminary form, doesn't give much information about reliability * The standardization samples for this test are quite small, and should be accepted as only tentative. * The principal purpose in calling this test to the attention of counselors is not in its practical value now. This is quite limited. The test represents, however, a novel line of development which has been spurred during the past few years by psychologists interested in trying to bring together the projective and the psychometric approaches. It would be difficult to guess what lies behind a response on this test. But as careful empirical studies are made, it may be that we can make progress toward discovering what the responses mean for future behavior. In practice, this test may give a useful lead on level of adjustment in cases where a verbal test is not feasible; it may also be useful in working with students interested in the field of art. It is, however, *a research test* and before any reliance can be placed on its scores, further validation work is essential. Most of the scales on the test have been related for one group or another to such leading verbal personality instruments as the Adjective Checklist, the MMPI, the California Psychological Inventory, and the Edwards Personal Preference Schedule. The resulting correlation coefficients are not high enough to permit generalizing from one to another, but are large enough to give us the basis for believing that here is another lead in the direction of structured personality measurement. Clients who seek counseling seem to enjoy taking tests. This one is less likely than most to bias the counseling relationship, and some good research leads might be developed. It would also be a gain if similar tests with more appealing items could be developed. The Welsh figures in the main seem so neutral that this reviewer finds it hard to understand how a meaningful affective response can be made to most of them.

[198]

***The Western Personality Inventory.** Adults; 1948–63; a combination in one booklet of *The Alcadd Test* ('49) and *The Manson Evaluation* ('48); identification of alcoholics and potential alcoholics; 1 form ('63, 6 pages); manual ('63, 4 pages, a combination, including identical norms and technical data, of the 1948 and 1949 manuals for the previously cited tests); $8 per 25 tests and manual; $1 per manual; postpaid; specimen set not available; (20–40) minutes; Morse P. Manson; Western Psychological Services. *

For a review by Dugal Campbell of The Alcadd Test, *see 60; for reviews by Charles H. Honzik and Albert L. Hunsicker, see 4:30. For a review by Dugal Campbell of* The Manson Evaluation, *see 137; for reviews by Charles H. Honzik and Albert L. Hunsicker, see 4:68.*

[199]

★William, Lynde & Williams Analysis of Personal Values, Second Edition. Business and industry; 1958–62; 6 scores: theoretical, practical, social, personal power, aesthetic, religious; 1 form ('60, 4 pages); mimeographed combined manual ('62, 8 pages) for this test and test 1074; no data on reliability and validity; $4 per 25 tests, postpaid; [15] minutes; R. W. Henderson; William, Lynde & Williams. *

[Other Tests]

For tests not listed above, see the following entries in *Tests in Print:* 102, 104, 111–2, 114, 116, 119–20, 122, 125, 127, 132, 135, 140–1, 146, 148–9, 151–2, 156, 158, 162, 166–7, 173, 192, 194–6, 198–200, 202, 205–8, 211–4, 225, 233, 235, 235a, 235b, 236, 238–9, 241–2, 244, 247–9, 251–3, 257–8, 260–2, 266, 268, 271, 273, 278–83, 286–7, 292, 295, 298, 303, 310–2, 317–8, 320, and 323–4; out of print: 100, 107, 115, 150, 177, 186, 232, 237, 240, 263, 269–70, 274, 285, 303b, and 322; status unknown: 105, 160, 197, and 245.

PROJECTIVE

[200]

★The African T.A.T. Urban Africans; 1960–61; individual; 1 form ['60, 9 cards]; no manual; interpretive data presented in *1* below; no data on reliability; 60s. per set of cards, postage extra; [180] minutes; J. C. de Ridder; [Industrial Psychological Services.] *

REFERENCES

1. DE RIDDER, J. C. *The Personality of the Urban African in South Africa: A Thematic Apperception Test Study.* London: Routledge & Kegan Paul Ltd., 1961. Pp. xvi, 180. * (*PA* 37:4811)

For excerpts from related book reviews, see B153.

[201]

★Association Adjustment Inventory. Normal and institutionalized adults; 1959; adaptation of *Kent-Rosanoff Free Association Test;* 13 scores: juvenility, psychotic responses, depressed-optimistic, hysteric-nonhysteric, withdrawal-sociable, paranoid-naive, rigid-flexible, schizophrenic-objective, impulsive-restrained, sociopathic-empathetic, psychosomapathic-physical contentment, anxious-relaxed; total; IBM; 1 form (4 pages); 2 editions: consumable, reusable; manual (15 pages); $5 per 25 tests; $4.50 per set of keys; separate answer sheets must be used with reusable edition; $2.75 per 25 IBM answer sheets; $4.50 per set of scoring stencils; $2.75 per 25 profiles; $1.75 per manual; $5 per specimen set; cash orders postpaid; (10–15) minutes; Martin M. Bruce; the Author. *

W. GRANT DAHLSTROM, *Professor of Psychology, University of North Carolina, Chapel Hill, North Carolina.*

The AAI is offered "for use as a screening instrument for maladjustment....and immaturity....and as an aid in diagnosing deviate ideation." The method of derivation of this instrument parallels that of many group tests of intellective ability, namely, the reliance upon pre-existing tests and scales to provide criteria of different personality characteristics. Whereas the 1916 Stanford-Binet proved to be sufficiently dependable to provide criterion information for the group tests being scaled against it, there are no scales with sufficient precision or established validity available for new test construction efforts in the area of personality and maladjustment. Thus, this promising method of scale development appears to be prematurely applied in this instance.

The limitation in test construction described above would not, of course, be necessarily a fatal one were the test constructor to proceed with the rest of the job of test validation and try to match his test findings with nontest data. Even four or five years after the appearance of this instrument, the potential user of the AAI has at his disposal no dependable validational data or other guides as to the test's accuracy, efficiency, or utility in serving its avowed purposes. The Examiner's Manual includes sets of intercorrelations of the component scales, correlations of these scales with the basic scales of the MMPI (against which they were in part derived), and correlations with the scales of the *Polyfactorial Study of Personality,* a companion test developed by Bruce and Stark on the same population of subjects. While many of these values of interscale relationship are suggestive of useful variance, no meaningful assessment of the utility of the AAI can be drawn from sets of correlational values alone. Detailed tabulations of the degree of clinically relevant separations of selected patients and normals must be made available to determine these performances in practical problems.

The rationale for the AAI is in itself a reasonable one and is advanced as an approach based upon long-standing experimental research. Each of the stimulus words in the Kent-Rosanoff (1910) word list for free association study is provided with four response alternatives in a multiple choice format. The subject is to choose the one alternative that he "associates" with the stimulus word and either circle it (booklet form) or mark the number corresponding to it on the answer sheet (in the reusable form). The alternatives were chosen from words reported in free association studies of adult subjects by Kent and Rosanoff and by Woodrow and Lowell [1] in their study of children's associations. The alternatives for each stimulus word consist of one word that is the most frequent adult association, one that appears rarely (two to six times in a thousand), one that appears only once, and finally one that does not appear in the adult tabulations but is present in the juvenile list of associations. Not all stimulus words could be provided with all four kinds of association alternates, and additional departures from this *a priori* construction of the items were dictated by preliminary studies of the discriminations between normals and disturbed subjects. Since the scoring of four of the scales in the AAI is based upon these item-alternate sources, greater effort could have been extended to get more contemporary sets of responses and frequencies of appearance. Thus, the scale for immaturity, Juvenility (J), is apparently a tally of the number of item alternates marked that came from the children's free association list. Jenkins and Russell [2] report data suggesting that systematic shifts have occurred over the last three or four decades, at least in adult frequencies. Even more importantly, there is little concern shown in this *a priori* scoring of four of the AAI scales for the change in psychological processes reflected in the modification of the material from free association to multiple choice formats. Here many different response sets seem to be called forth in a situation provided with maximum opportunity for editing and dissimulation. This seems particularly the case when the test author labels the test blank with the highly charged term "adjustment" and provides no other guide or instruction to the test subject.

The empirically derived scales were constructed against some (unspecified) score composites of Rorschach variables, House-Tree-Person scores, and MMPI scales, together with psychiatric diagnosis. The basic data came from hospitalized psychiatric patients, prison inmates, outpatients in psychiatric therapy, and a mixed group of normals including college and school students, job applicants for white collar positions, and employees already in those positions. These scale derivations may have been sound but it is impossible to tell from the data provided in the manual. Norms are presented in z score form ($+5.00$ to -5.00) on all scales for both a population of normals and a population of institutionalized subjects. The scoring materials and profiles are well made, legible, and internally consistent, except that the profile only runs the z scores to ± 4.00.

This reviewer looked in vain for the designation on this test, "For Research Use Only." It must be so designated. Several publications are promised in the body of the manual and when they appear, the worth of this original test may prove to be as good as the author now claims. Until that time, it should not be employed in contexts in which important decisions must rest upon the data it provides.

BERTRAM R. FORER, *Consulting Psychologist, and Executive Editor, Journal of Projective Techniques and Personality Assessment, Suite 307, 8833 Sunset Boulevard, Los Angeles, California.*

The inventory represents one of the feasible kinds of modification of the word association

1 WOODROW, HERBERT, AND LOWELL, FRANCES. "Children's Association Frequency Tables." *Psychol Monogr* 22(5):1–110 '16. *

2 JENKINS, JAMES J., AND RUSSELL, WALLACE A. "Systematic Changes in Word Association Norms: 1910–52." *J Abn & Social Psychol* 60:293–304 My '60. * (*PA* 35:4958)

method for the more sophisticated requirements of contemporary psychological assessment. One line of adaptation is the sentence completion method which, by amplifying the content and structure of test stimuli, elicits a broader spectrum of responses with rich possibilities for individual clinical diagnostic use. But there is a corresponding lowering of the likelihood of obtaining objective scores and measures of reliability and validity.

The *Association Adjustment Inventory,* by providing multiple choice responses to single-word stimuli, restricts freedom of response, insures greater reliability of item scoring, and increases the likelihood of developing scales that can be standardized. The test, then, is minimally projective and individuality is represented exclusively in the quantitative scales and the overall profile of scale scores.

The test's development and the manual seem better psychometrically than clinically. The author's rationale in terms of personality theory is rather thin. The response choices might have made better psychological sense if they had been based on clinical acumen rather than the apparently unsystematic method that was used. But it is clear that the author has taken seriously APA recommendations for test standards.

He has achieved moderately good coverage of varied deviant groups; this coverage is probably more satisfactory than his sampling of normal adults and children. The sample of adult normals lacks cases in lower occupational levels and the professions. The children's group is not specified as to age and it is dubious that preadolescent children would understand the test instructions. Hence the reported lack of differentiation of children and psychotics (based on the total score on the original form of the test) is not clearly understandable.

To this reviewer it seems that insufficient information is presented about the method of validating the scales. It is not clear both how and why the Rorschach was employed as one of the major criteria in item analysis. The author and a colleague refer to subsequent publications on this and other points. Eventually they ought to be incorporated in a revised manual.

The author has done a good deal of empirical work in attempts to pursue tests of validity. The evidence of high scale reliability is reassuring. The separate norms for general and institutionalized populations provide some basis for large scale screening but require implementation with considerably more evidence of successful discrimination of other samples of deviant populations.

In no way does this inventory seem to provide the kind of data obtained from projective methods for individual assessment. It is impossible to predict whether it will be as useful as the MMPI with an equal amount of research behind it. It appears to be a reliable instrument and is worthy of experimental use and a chance to prove itself.

J Consult Psychol 24:100 F '60. Edward S. Bordin. * Test-retest correlations for one week and one month intervals are satisfactory, but the base for claiming validity is very unsatisfactory. There is evidence of some general relationships with MMPI scales and with a largely unvalidated inventory. Reference is made to unreported results of diagnostic validity studies that are unpublished. It should have been marked "For Experimental Use."

[202]

***The Behavioral Complexity Test: A Test for Use in Research.** Ages 5 and over; 1955–61; revision of *The Adult-Child Interaction Test;* 9 scores: continuum (weighted total of scores for 5 complexity of response categories), symbolization (5 scores), emotional perceptional (positive, negative, total); individual; 1 form ('61, 8 cards, same as cards used with 1956 test); manual ('61, 14 pages plus test cards); record blank ['61, 3 pages]; no norms; *out of print;* [20–25] minutes; Theron Alexander; distributed by Campus Stores. *

REFERENCES

1. ALEXANDER, THERON. *The Prediction of Teacher-Pupil Interactions With a Projective Test.* Doctor's thesis, University of Chicago (Chicago, Ill.), 1949.
2. ALEXANDER, THERON. *The Adult-Child Interaction Test: A Projective Test for Use in Research.* Monographs of the Society for Research in Child Development, Inc., Vol. 27, Serial No. 55, No. 2. Champaign, Ill.: Child Development Publications, the Society, 1955. Pp. v, 40, plus 8 cards. * (*PA* 29:7252)
3. OHLSEN, MERLE M., AND SCHULTZ, RAYMOND E. "Projective Test Response Patterns for Best and Poorest Student Teachers." *Ed & Psychol Meas* 15:18–27 sp '55. *
4. OELKE, MERRITT C. "A Study of Student Teachers' Attitudes Toward Children." *J Ed Psychol* 47:193–8 Ap '56. * (*PA* 32:2154)

JOHN ELDERKIN BELL, *Program Director, National Institute of Mental Health, United States Public Health Service, San Francisco, California.*

The eight basic stimulus cards appear well designed to provide thematic content around which a subject may invent stories. We have many such cards available, however, and the advantage of these over others as stimuli for narratives should not absorb our time. The distinctive feature of this TAT type instrument is the system developed for categorizing various features of the stories and the blank for recording them. If the user chooses, he may also analyze the stories as projections.

Three overall groups of scores may be developed: (*a*) the occurrence and organization of a series of defined story elements such as the events in the story, their causation, and the outcome—the Behavioral Continuum; (*b*) the stimulus elements used or concrete objects added—Symbolization; and (*c*) the positive and negative feelings and actions attributed to the figures in the cards—the Emotional Perception.

The record blank is well designed for its functions of tabulating for each story the scores in the above three categories and arriving at appropriate overall totals.

Unfortunately, the amount of research based on this test remains limited so that measures of scorer and test-retest reliability and validity recorded in the manual can only suggest that, in respect to these properties, the evidence merits continuing use and evaluation of the test. Because of the objective features of the scoring, the test would seem a particularly valuable complement to the increasing range of instruments for studying the development of perception, imagination, language, and conception in children. It helps to bridge the gap between the perceptual-motor tests and the free story-telling techniques—and in this respect compares with the infrequently used but valuable *Four Picture Test* for adults.

[203]

***[Bender-Gestalt Test.]** Ages 4 and over; 1938–64; individual; the original Bender-Gestalt is listed as *a* below; the modifications listed as *b–e* consist primarily of alterations in administration procedure, new scoring systems, or expanded interpretive procedures, rather than changes in the test materials; *b–e* use essentially the same administration procedure as the basic testing procedure; *c* and *d* provide, in addition, for use of the materials as projective stimuli for associations.

a) VISUAL MOTOR GESTALT TEST. Ages 4 and over; 1938–46; 1 form ('46, 9 cards); directions for administering ('46, 8 pages); manual ('38, see *5* below); no data on reliability; $1.25 per set of cards and directions; $5.35 per manual; postpaid; [10] minutes; Lauretta Bender; American Orthopsychiatric Association, Inc. *

b) THE BENDER GESTALT TEST. Ages 4 and over; 1951; utilizes same test cards as *a*; scoring sheet ['51, 1 page]; manual ('51, see *41* below); $2.25 per pad of 50 scoring sheets; $7.75 per manual; postage extra; (10) minutes; Gerald R. Pascal and Barbara J. Suttell; Grune & Stratton, Inc. *

c) *REVISED BENDER-GESTALT TEST. Ages 7 and over; 1944–60; also called *Hutt Adaptation of the Bender-Gestalt Test;* 1 form ('60, 9 cards, same as cards of *a* except for modification in 1 design and in drawing method throughout); record form ('60, 4 pages); manual ('60, see *192* below); no data on reliability of scored factors; $1.25 per set of cards; $2.50 per 25 record forms; $5 per manual; postage extra; [45–60] minutes; Max L. Hutt and Gerald J. Briskin; Grune & Stratton, Inc. *

d) ★THE BENDER VISUAL MOTOR GESTALT TEST FOR CHILDREN. Ages 7–11; 1962; utilizes same test cards as *a*; manual (72 pages); record form (4 pages); no data on reliability and validity; $2.50 per set of cards; $5.50 per 25 record forms; $6 per manual; postpaid; (10) minutes without associations; Aileen Clawson; Western Psychological Services. *

e) ★THE BENDER GESTALT TEST FOR YOUNG CHILDREN. Ages 5–10; 1964; a developmental scoring system; utilizes same test cards as *a*; manual (204 pages, reprint of *259* below); $6.75 per manual, postage extra; administration time not reported; Elizabeth Munsterberg Koppitz; Grune & Stratton, Inc. *

f) ★THE VISUAL MOTOR GESTALT TEST TWO-COPY DRAWING FORM. 1964; 1 form (1 page plus backing sheet); $6.50 per 25 forms; Western Psychological Services. *

REFERENCES

1–8. See 3:108.
9–42. See 4:144.
43–160. See 5:172.
161. SILVER, ARCHIE A. "Diagnostic Value of Three Drawing Tests for Children." *J Pediatrics* 37:129–43 Jl '50. * (*PA* 25:3191)
162. LAKIN, MARTIN. "Clinical Use of the Bender Visual Motor Test in Psychological Assessment of the Aged." *J Am Geriatrics Soc* 4:909–19 S '56. *
163. BATEMAN, WILLIAM J. *The Validity of the Bender-Gestalt Test in Making a Diagnostic Conclusion.* Master's thesis, North Texas State College (Denton, Tex.), 1957.
164. RIBLER, RONALD IRWIN. *The Detection of Brain Damage Through Measurement of Deficit in Behavioral Functions.* Doctor's thesis, Michigan State University (East Lansing, Mich.), 1957. (*DA* 19:1810)
165. SEAGRAVES, MILTON D. *The Bender-Gestalt Test as a Means of Determining School Readiness.* Master's thesis, University of Tennessee (Knoxville, Tenn.), 1957.
166. CHANG, SIAO-CHANG, AND TANG, KUAN-YING. "A Study of Mental Disturbance Among the Retired Servicemen in the Nuan-Nuan Center." *Acta Psychologica Taiwanica* (1):64–84 N '58. * (*PA* 34:3157)
167. LOTHROP, WILLIAM W. "Relationship Between Bender-Gestalt Test Scores and Medical Success With Duodenal Ulcer Patients." *Psychosom Med* 20:30–2 Ja–F '58. * (*PA* 33:6260)
168. SAFIAN, MURRAY Z. *A Study of Certain Psychological Factors in the Rehabilitation of Potentially Employable Home-bound Adults.* Doctor's thesis, New York University (New York, N.Y.), 1958. (*DA* 19:3372)
169. SIMPSON, WILLIAM HAROLD. *A Study of Some Factors in the Bender Gestalt Reproductions of Normal and Disturbed Children.* Doctor's thesis, University of Oklahoma (Norman, Okla.), 1958. (*DA* 19:1120)
170. VERNIER, CLAIRE M.; STAFFORD, JOHN W.; AND KRUGMAN, ARNOLD D. "A Factor Analysis of Indices From Four Projective Techniques Associated With Four Different Types of Physical Pathology." *J Consult Psychol* 22:433–7 D '58. * (*PA* 33:9360)
171. VITANZA, A. A.; GRAHAM, STANLEY R.; RAWN, M. L.; AND BRINITZER, WALTER. "Psychological Judgment of the Bender Gestalt Test Compared With Three Physiological Vectors and Psychiatric Judgment." *Psychol Rep* 4:729–30 D '58. * (*PA* 34:1432)
172. CHOROST, SHERWOOD B.; SPIVACK, GEORGE; AND LEVINE, MURRAY. "Bender-Gestalt Rotations and EEG Abnormalities in Children." Abstract. *J Consult Psychol* 23:559 D '59. * (*PA* 34:6010)
173. CLAWSON, AILEEN. "The Bender Visual Motor Gestalt Test as an Index of Emotional Disturbance in Children." *J Proj Tech* 23:198–206 Je '59. * (*PA* 35:4717)
174. GOLDBERG, LEWIS R. "The Effectiveness of Clinicians' Judgments: The Diagnosis of Organic Brain Damage From the Bender-Gestalt Test." *J Consult Psychol* 23:25–33 F '59. * (*PA* 34:1364)
175. KOPPITZ, ELIZABETH M.; SULLIVAN, JOHN; BLYTH, DAVID D.; AND SHELTON, JOEL. "Prediction of First Grade School Achievement With the Bender Gestalt Test and Human Figure Drawings." *J Clin Psychol* 15:164–8 Ap '59. * (*PA* 35:5372)

176. LIPSCOMB, DAVID M. *A Study of the Response of Children Enrolled in a School for the Deaf to the Bender Visual Motor Gestalt Test.* Master's thesis, University of Redlands (Redlands, Calif.), 1959.
177. MCDANIEL, JAMES W., JR. *Stimulus Values of the Bender Visual Motor Gestalt Test Designs.* Master's thesis, North Texas State College (Denton, Tex.), 1959.
178. NADLER, EUGENE B.; FINK, STEVEN L.; SHONTZ, FRANKLIN C.; AND BRINK, ROBERT W. "Objective Scoring vs. Clinical Evaluation of the Bender-Gestalt." *J Clin Psychol* 15:39–41 Ja '59. * (*PA* 34:2976)
179. PRICE, JOSEPH W. *Signs of Paranoid Schizophrenic Behavior on the Bender-Gestalt Test.* Master's thesis, North Texas State College (Denton, Tex.), 1959.
180. ARMSTRONG, RENATE G., AND HAUCK, PAUL A. "Correlates of the Bender-Gestalt Scores in Children." *J Psychol Studies* 11:153–8 Mr–Ap '60. * (*PA* 34:7830)
181. AZIMA, FERN CRAMER, AND KRAL, V. A. "Effects of Blindfolding on Persons During Psychological Testing: A Psychometric Study of Various Age Groups." *Geriatrics* 15:780–92 N '60. *
182. COROTTO, LOREN V., AND CURNUTT, ROBERT H. "The Effectiveness of the Bender-Gestalt in Differentiating a Flight Group From an Aggressive Group of Adolescents." *J Consult Psychol* 24:368–9 Ag '60. * (*PA* 35:2204)
183. CROSSON, JAMES E. *Relative Discriminative Efficiency of the Bender-Gestalt and the Modified Vigotsky Tests When Used With Organics, Normals, and Schizophrenics.* Master's thesis, Kansas State College of Pittsburg (Pittsburg, Kan.), 1960.
184. CURNUTT, ROBERT H., AND COROTTO, LOREN V. "The Use of Bender Gestalt Cut-Off Scores in Identifying Juvenile Delinquents." *J Proj Tech* 24:353–4 D '60. * (*PA* 35:5208)
185. FULLER, JERRY B. *Factors Influencing Rotation in the Bender-Gestalt Performance of Children.* Doctor's thesis, University of Ottawa (Ottawa, Ont., Canada), 1960.
186. GARVEY, MARGARET J., AND POPPLESTONE, JOHN A. "Influence of Age and Sex on Bender Gestalt Associations." *Percept & Motor Skills* 11:258 D '60. * (*PA* 35:1975)
187. GAVALES, DANIEL, AND MILLON, THEODORE. "Comparison of Reproduction and Recall Size Deviations in the Bender-Gestalt as Measures of Anxiety." *J Clin Psychol* 16:278–80 Jl '60. * (*PA* 36:2HK78G)
188. GRIFFITH, RICHARD M., AND TAYLOR, VIVIAN H. "Incidence of Bender-Gestalt Figure Rotations." *J Consult Psychol* 24:189–90 Ap '60. * (*PA* 34:7845)
189. HIGBEE, DALE S.; CLARKE, JOHN R.; AND HENDERSON, WAYNE E. "The Bender-Gestalt Test as a Predictor of Length of Hospitalization With Mental Patients." *J Clin Psychol* 16:265–6 Jl '60. * (*PA* 36:2HI65H)
190. HIRSCHENFANG, SAMUEL. "A Comparison of Bender Gestalt Reproductions of Right and Left Hemiplegic Patients." *J Clin Psychol* 16:439 O '60. * (*PA* 37:3534)
191. HUTT, MAX L. "The Revised Bender-Gestalt Visual Motor Test," pp. 30–55, 150–65. In *The Prediction of Overt Behavior Through the Use of Projective Techniques.* Edited by Arthur C. Carr. Springfield, Ill.: Charles C Thomas, Publisher, 1960. Pp. xiii, 177. * (*PA* 36:2HG77C)
192. HUTT, MAX L., AND BRISKIN, GERALD J. *The Clinical Use of the Revised Bender-Gestalt Test.* New York: Grune & Stratton, Inc., 1960. Pp. viii, 168. * (*PA* 35:3384)
193. JUDSON, ABE J., AND MACCASLAND, BARBARA W. "The Effects of Chlorpromazine on Psychological Test Scores." Abstract. *J Consult Psychol* 24:192 Ap '60. * (*PA* 34:7888)
194. KIM, IK CHANG. *The Bender-Gestalt Test: An Analysis of Certain Clinical Groups.* Doctor's thesis, University of Arizona (Tucson, Ariz.), 1960. (*DA* 21:959)
195. KOPPITZ, ELIZABETH MUNSTERBERG. "The Bender Gestalt Test for Children: A Normative Study." *J Clin Psychol* 16:432–5 O '60. * (*PA* 37:3111)
196. KOPPITZ, ELIZABETH MUNSTERBERG. "Teacher's Attitude and Children's Performance on the Bender Gestalt Test and Human Figure Drawings." *J Clin Psychol* 16:204–8 Ap '60. * (*PA* 36:2HE04K)
197. LACHMANN, FRANK M. "Perceptual-Motor Development in Children Retarded in Reading Ability." *J Consult Psychol* 24:427–31 O '60. * (*PA* 35:5339)
198. MCGUIRE, FREDERICK L. "A Comparison of the Bender-Gestalt and Flicker Fusion as Indicators of Central Nervous System Involvement." *J Clin Psychol* 16:276–8 Jl '60. * (*PA* 36:2HI76M)
199. MAGNUSSON, DAVID. "Some Personality Tests Applied on Identical Twins." *Scandinavian J Psychol* 1(2):55–61 '60. * (*PA* 35:6424)
200. MATUNAS, MARIAN ISABEL. *Test Performance of Psychotic Children With Organic Brain Pathology: A Study to Determine Whether the Bender-Gestalt Test, the Benton Visual Retention Test, and the Marble Board Test Can Detect the Presence of Organic Brain Pathology in Psychotic Children.* Doctor's thesis, New York University (New York, N.Y.), 1960. (*DA* 21:1257)
201. PRADO, WILLIAM M.; PEYMAN, DOUGLAS A. R.; AND LACEY, OLIVER L. "A Validation Study of Measures of Flattened Affect on the Bender-Gestalt Test." *J Clin Psychol* 16:435–8 O '60. * (*PA* 37:3231)
202. STORY, R. IAN. "The Revised Bender-Gestalt and Male Alcoholics." *J Proj Tech* 24:186–93 Je '60. * (*PA* 35:1088)
203. TOLOR, ALEXANDER. "The 'Meaning' of the Bender-Gestalt Test Designs: A Study in the Use of the Semantic Differential." *J Proj Tech* 24:433–8 D '60. * (*PA* 35:4845)
204. WIENER, GERALD; CRAWFORD, EDWARD E.; AND SNYDER, ROBERT T. "Some Correlates of Overt Anxiety in Mildly Retarded Patients." *Am J Mental Def* 64:735–9 Ja '60. * (*PA* 35:1055)
205. ASCOUGH, J. C. *The Mosaic Test: Validation and Cross-Validation of Objective Scores, Comparison With Clinical Judgment and the Bender Gestalt Test.* Master's thesis, West Virginia University (Morgantown, W. Va.), 1961.
206. GRIFFITH, RICHARD M., AND TAYLOR, VIVIAN H. "Bender-Gestalt Figure Rotations: A Stimulus Factor." *J Consult Psychol* 25:89–90 F '61. * (*PA* 36:3HC89G)
207. HARRISON, DONNA M. *The Effect of Verbal Reward on Schizophrenic Patients' Performance of the Bender-Gestalt Test.* Master's thesis, University of British Columbia (Vancouver, B.C., Canada), 1961.
208. KEOGH, BARBARA K., AND SMITH, CAROL E. "Group Techniques and Proposed Scoring System for the Bender-Gestalt Test With Children." *J Clin Psychol* 17:172–5 Ap '61. * (*PA* 38:957)
209. KO, YUNG-HO. "A Study of Figure Rotation in the Bender-Gestalt Test." *Acta Psychologica Taiwanica* (3):94–105 Mr '61. * (*PA* 38:8000)
210. KOPPITZ, ELIZABETH M.; MARDIS, VERDENA; AND STEPHENS, THOMAS. "A Note on Screening School Beginners With the Bender Gestalt Test." *J Ed Psychol* 52:80–1 Ap '61. * (*PA* 38:3205)
211. LACHMANN, F. M.; BAILEY, M. A.; AND BERRICK, M. E. "The Relationship Between Manifest Anxiety and Clinicians' Evaluations of Projective Test Responses." *J Clin Psychol* 17:11–3 Ja '61. * (*PA* 37:3113)
212. QUAST, WENTWORTH. "The Bender Gestalt: A Clinical Study of Children's Records." *J Consult Psychol* 25:405–8 O '61. * (*PA* 37:3232)
213. REGER, ROGER, AND DAWSON, ANTOINETTE. "The Use of Psychological Tests to Predict Manual Abilities in Mentally Retarded Boys." *Am J Occup Ther* 15:204+ S–O '61. * (*PA* 36:5JI04R)
214. RIKLAN, MANUEL, AND DILLER, LEONARD. "Visual Motor Performance Before and After Chemosurgery of the Basal Ganglia in Parkinsonism." *J Nerv & Mental Dis* 132:307–14 Ap '61. * (*PA* 36:2JF07R)
215. ROSENBERG, B. G., AND LAUBER, JAMES. "Selected Success and Failure Experiences as Factors in Bender Gestalt Performances." *J General Psychol* 64:31–6 Ja '61. * (*PA* 35:6425)
216. SCHULBERG, HERBERT C., AND TOLOR, ALEXANDER. "The Use of the Bender-Gestalt in Clinical Practice." *J Proj Tech* 25:347–51 S '61. * (*PA* 36:3HI47S)
217. SINGH, BALWANT. "Development of Visuo-motor Capacities in Children from 6–11 Years." Abstract of master's thesis. *Brit J Ed Psychol* 31:299–302 N '61. *
218. SOUEIF, M. I., AND METWALLY, A. "Testing for Organicity in Egyptian Psychiatric Patients." *Acta Psychologica* 18(4):285–96 '61. * (*PA* 36:5JG85S)
219. ASCOUGH, JAMES C., AND DANA, RICHARD H. "Concurrent Validities of the Mosaic and Bender Gestalt Tests." *J Consult Psychol* 26:430–4 O '62. * (*PA* 39:1713)
220. AYLAIAN, ARSEN, AND MELTZER, MALCOLM L. "The Bender Gestalt Test and Intelligence." Abstract. *J Consult Psychol* 26:483 O '62. *
221. BRUCK, MORRIS. "A Note on Modified Instructions for Bender-Gestalt Elaborations and Associations." *J Proj Tech* 26:227 Je '62. *
222. CLAWSON, AILEEN. *The Bender Visual Motor Gestalt Test for Children: A Manual.* Beverly Hills, Calif.: Western Psychological Services, 1962. Pp. ii, 29, 43. *
223. CLAWSON, AILEEN. "Relationship of Psychological Tests to Cerebral Disorders in Children: *A Pilot Study.*" *Psychol Rep* 10:187–90 F '62. * (*PA* 37:1655)
224. COROTTO, LOREN V., AND CURNUTT, ROBERT H. "Ego Strength: A Function of the Measuring Instrument." *J Proj Tech* 26:228–30 Je '62. *
225. FULLER, JERRY B., AND CHAGNON, GILLES. "Factors Influencing Rotation in the Bender-Gestalt Performance of Children." *J Proj Tech* 26:36–46 Mr '62. * (*PA* 37:2833)
226. KO, YUNG-HO. "The Discrepancy Between the B-G Score and the Sum of the Object-Assembly and the Block-Design Test Scores as an Indicator of Organicity." *Acta Psychologica Taiwanica* (4):72–7 Mr '62. * (*PA* 38:6367)
227. KOPPITZ, ELIZABETH MUNSTERBERG. "Diagnosing Brain Damage in Young Children With the Bender Gestalt Test." *J Consult Psychol* 26:541–6 D '62. * (*PA* 39:2476)
228. LETON, DONALD A. "Visual-Motor Capacities and Ocular Efficiency in Reading." *Percept & Motor Skills* 15:407–32 O '62. * (*PA* 37:8253)
229. MCLEAN, MARJORIE J. *A Study of the Bender Visual-Motor Gestalt Test in Relation to Reading Difficulties.* Master's thesis, University of Manitoba (Winnipeg, Man., Canada), 1962.
230. MASTEN, IRVING. *Bender Gestalt Responses of Normal and Deaf Children.* Master's thesis, Brooklyn College (Brooklyn, N.Y.), 1962.
231. NIELSEN, HELLE H. *Visual-Motor Functioning of Cerebral Palsied and Normal Children.* Nordisk Psykologi's

Monografiserie Nr. 14. Copenhagen, Denmark: Ejnar Munksgaards Forlag, 1962. Pp. 41–103. * Same: *Nordisk Psykologi* 14(2):41–103 '62. * (*PA* 37:3551)

232. ORME, J. E. "Bender Design Recall and Brain Damage." *Dis Nerv System* 23:329–30 Je '62. *

233. PACELLA, MICHAEL J. "Inter-Examiner Effects on the Bender-Gestalt." *J Clin Psychol* 18:23–6 Ja '62. * (*PA* 38:8501)

234. PARRISH, ROBERT EDWIN. *A Study of Some Factors in the Bender-Gestalt Reproductions of Reader and Non-Reader Children.* Doctor's thesis, University of Oklahoma (Norman, Okla.), 1962. (*DA* 23:928)

235. PEOPLES, CROCKER, AND MOLL, RICHARD P. "Bender-Gestalt Performance as a Function of Drawing Ability, School Performance and Intelligence." *J Clin Psychol* 18:106–7 Ja '62. * (*PA* 38:9274)

236. ROOS, PHILIP. "Performance of Psychiatric Patients on Two Measures of Ego Strength." *J Clin Psychol* 18:48–50 Ja '62. * (*PA* 38:8505)

237. SCHELLENBERG, ERNEST DAVID. *A Study of the Relationship Between Visual-Motor Perception and Reading Disabilities of Third Grade Pupils.* Doctor's thesis, University of Southern California (Los Angeles, Calif.), 1962. (*DA* 23:3785)

238. SCHULBERG, HERBERT C., AND TOLOR, ALEXANDER. "The 'Meaning' of the Bender-Gestalt Test Designs to Psychiatric Patients." *J Proj Tech* 26:455–61 D '62. * (*PA* 37:6725)

239. SEEMAN, WILLIAM, AND MARKS, PHILIP A. "A Study of Some 'Test Dimensions' Conceptions." *J Proj Tech* 26:469–73 D '62. * (*PA* 37:6678)

240. SILVERSTEIN, A. B., AND MOHAN, PHILIP J. "Bender-Gestalt Figure Rotations in the Mentally Retarded." *J Consult Psychol* 26:386–8 Ag '62. * (*PA* 38:4570)

241. SMITH, CAROL E., AND KEOGH, BARBARA K. "The Group Bender-Gestalt as a Reading Readiness Screening Instrument." *Percept & Motor Skills* 15:639–45 D '62. * (*PA* 38:2447)

242. TOLOR, ALEXANDER, AND SCHULBERG, HERBERT C. *An Evaluation of the Bender-Gestalt Test.* Foreword by Lauretta Bender. Springfield, Ill.: Charles C Thomas, Publisher, 1963. Pp. xxiii, 229. * (*PA* 38:967)

243. VIITAMAKI, R. OLAVI. *Psychoses in Children: A Psychological Follow-Up Study.* Annals of the Finnish Academy of Science and Letters, Series B, Vol. 125, Part 2. Helsinki, Finland: Suomalainen Tiedeakatemia, Academia Scientiarum Fennica, 1962. Pp. 52. * (*PA* 39:2650)

244. ALLEN, ROBERT M., AND FRANK, GEORGE H. "Experimental Variation of the Mode of Reproduction of the Bender Gestalt Stimuli." *J Clin Psychol* 19:212–4 Ap '63. *

245. ARMSTRONG, RENATE GERBOTH. "Recall Patterns on the Bender Gestalt: A Re-evaluation." *J Proj Tech & Pers Assess* 27:418–22 D '63. * (*PA* 38:8397)

246. BENDER, LAURETTA. Chap. 5, "The Origin and Evolution of the Gestalt Function, the Body Image, and Delusional Thoughts in Schizophrenia," pp. 38–62. In *Recent Advances in Psychiatry, Vol. 5.* The Proceedings of the Seventeenth Annual Convention and Scientific Program of the Society of Biological Psychiatry, Toronto, Ontario, May 4–6, 1962. Edited by Joseph Wortis. New York: Plenum Press, 1963. Pp. xiii, 380. *

247. BERNSTEIN, IRA H. "A Comparison of Schizophrenics and Nonschizophrenics on Two Methods of Administration of the Bender-Gestalt Test." *Percept & Motor Skills* 16:757–63 Je '63. * (*PA* 38:6105)

248. BILLINGSLEA, FRED Y. "The Bender Gestalt: A Review and a Perspective." *Psychol B* 60:233–51 My '63. *

249. BRILLIANT, PATRICIA J., AND GYNTHER, MALCOLM D. "Relationships Between Performanec on Three Tests for Organicity and Selected Patient Variables." *J Consult Psychol* 27:474–9 D '63. * (*PA* 38:8404)

250. CONDELL, JAMES F. "The Bender Gestalt Test With Mentally Retarded Children Using the Koppitz Revised Scoring System." *J Clin Psychol* 19:430–1 O '63. *

251. EVANS, RAY B., AND MARMORSTON, JESSIE. "Psychological Test Signs of Brain Damage in Cerebral Thrombosis." *Psychol Rep* 12:915–30 Je '63. * (*PA* 38:6413)

252. FULLER, G. B. "A Further Study on Rotation: Cross-Validation." *J Clin Psychol* 19:127–8 Ja '63. * (*PA* 39:1728)

253. GUERTIN, WILSON H., AND DAVIS, HUGH C. "Similarities in Meaning of Elements and Figures of the Bender-Gestalt." *J Proj Tech* 27:68–72 Mr '63. * (*PA* 38:983)

254. KEOGH, BARBARA KOLTS. *The Bender Gestalt as a Predictive and Dianostic Test of Reading Performance.* Doctor's thesis, Claremont Graduate School (Claremont, Calif.), 1963. (*DA* 24:2360)

255. KO, YUNG-HO, AND HUNG, TSU-PEI. "The Localization of Brain Lesions and the Bender-Gestalt Test Figure-Rotation." *Acta Psychologica Taiwanica* (5):31–6 Mr '63. *

256. KORMAN, MAURICE, AND BLUMBERG, STANLEY. "Comparative Efficiency of Some Tests of Cerebral Damage." *J Consult Psychol* 27:303–9 Ag '63. * (*PA* 38:2985)

257. SMITH, CAROL E., AND KEOGH, BARBARA K. "Developmental Changes on the Bender Gestalt Test." *Percept & Motor Skills* 17:465–6 O '63. * (*PA* 38:6070)

258. THWEATT, ROGER C. "Prediction of School Learning Disabilities Through the Use of the Bender Gestalt Test: A Validation Study of Koppitz's Scoring Technique." *J Clin Psychol* 19:216–7 Ap '63. * (*PA* 39:5104)

259. KOPPITZ, ELIZABETH MUNSTERBERG. *The Bender Gestalt Test for Young Children.* New York: Grune & Stratton, Inc., 1964. Pp. xi, 195. * (*PA* 39:1740)

C. B. BLAKEMORE, *Lecturer in Psychology, Institute of Psychiatry, Maudsley Hospital, University of London, London, England.*

According to a recent survey[1] the Bender-Gestalt remains a very popular test with clinical psychologists. This popularity is understandable in view of its simplicity of materials, ease and speed of administration, and the many claims which have been put forward on its behalf as a diagnostic instrument. It is not surprising, therefore, to find that during the past few years it has joined the ranks of other test giants, such as the Wechsler scales, the Rorschach, and TAT, in having whole books devoted to its administration and scoring (*41, 192*) and evaluations of the literature published on its value in a clinical setting (*242*). In the opinion of this reviewer such popularity and respect for the test cannot be justified on the basis of evidence available in its literature.

It is now some fifteen years since Line was quoted in *The Third Mental Measurements Yearbook* (see 3:109) as having said in the *American Journal of Psychiatry* that the test's "validity and practical value.....must await further research." Since then research has been carried out, but from it has emerged little in favour of the test as a valid and useful clinical tool. It is true, of course, that much of this work has concentrated on the development of systems for scoring test performance. These vary in their objectivity and reliability, but a system such as that developed by Pascal and Suttell (*41*), involving analysis of 105 details of performance over the various designs, has many features to commend it. With such a system moderately respectable correlations of around .70 are reported for test-retest performances, while the reliability of scoring between trained examiners can be in the order of .90. It has also been suggested by Pacella (*233*) that differences between examiners, in terms of their "stress" characteristics, may have little effect on the patient's performance when analysed by this method. In view of its apparent reliability it is understandable that the Pascal and Suttell system, together with the more recent modifications for use with

1 SUNDBERG, NORMAN D. "The Practice of Psychological Testing in Clinical Services in the United States." *Am Psychologist* 16:79–83 F '61. *

children introduced by Koppitz (*195, 259*), should have proved to be the most popular. However, the development of more objective and reliable scoring criteria has not improved upon the test's validity and usefulness as a diagnostic instrument, for it has enabled us to appreciate the correlation of performance with such variables as intelligence, educational level, and age—variables all too frequently ignored in validation studies of "diagnostic" tests. When these variables are controlled in studies of the Bender-Gestalt, the differences between patient groups, and between patients and non-patient controls, dwindle and the ranges of scores show considerable overlap. Many of these validation studies have found statistically significant mean differences in copying performance on this test between, for example, psychotics versus nonpsychotics or brain damaged versus non-brain damaged patients. From the standpoint of clinical usefulness, however, the overlap of scores is usually so great that the correct prediction of an individual's group membership is little better than chance.

This apparent lack of clinical value as a diagnostic test is not altogether surprising. We have in the Bender-Gestalt what would appear to be a simple copying task, with, in some cases, the added information derived from asking for a recall of the test material after initial performance. The assumption underlying most of the validation studies is that patients suffering from different neurological or psychiatric conditions will perform this task differently. We might ask if one or several performance variables are to be held responsible for these group differences. As yet there is no answer to such a question, but the factor analytic studies of the performance of psychiatric patients carried out by Guertin (*58, 83–5*) suggest that the answer may not be a simple one. Before we can accept the assumption that the apparent group differences on the test are related to neurological or psychiatric diagnosis, we must satisfy ourselves that stimulus variables and the conditions of testing are not responsible for the observed differences. It is in the investigation of such problems that research on the Bender-Gestalt has been particularly weak, and where research has been carried out the findings have usually been revealing. Let us examine, as an example, the claim that rotation of the drawings during copying performance is indicative of brain pathology. A number of studies have investigated such rotations and have reliably demonstrated that they may be due largely to stimulus variables (*150, 206*). Indeed, Fuller and Laird,[2] using two of the Wertheimer designs also used by Bender, have made use of this information in their attempts to develop a more valid test of brain damage. We might find eventually that stimulus variables, such as the orientation to the patient of the design to be copied, have particular relevance only for patients suffering from certain conditions, just as Shapiro and others [3] have demonstrated that rotation of Kohs' blocks is dependent to some extent on the presence of visual field defects. But before we can begin to investigate such relationships we must know what are the appropriate stimulus variables, and this is very relevant when one remembers that there is no standard set of Bender-Gestalt figures—a fact which has been stressed by both Billingslea (*14, 248*) and Popplestone (*126*).

In summary, then, it would seem that although reliable scoring methods can be developed for this test, the mean differences in performance between diagnostic groups so far revealed are of little practical value to the clinical psychologist. In addition, we are still short of information regarding the many variables which might determine performance. We *still* await the research which will demonstrate the test's validity and usefulness.

Psychol B 60:233–51 My '63. Fred Y. Billingslea. "The Bender Gestalt: A Review and a Perspective." * Although there are surprisingly few generalizations that can be made about the BG Test as a result of reviewing the published experiences with it over the past decade, the following seem justified in the light of the preceding discussion: (1) The test continues to be popular with clinicians and deserves to remain as an additional tool in his repertoire. (2) It is in great need of universally accepted standard set of designs. (3) The P&S scoring system has proven useful on adult protocols as has Koppitz' modification of it on children's protocols. (4) Reasonably valid MAs can be obtained with it for chil-

2 Fuller, Gerald B., and Laird, James T. "The Minnesota Percepto-Diagnostic Test." *J Clin Psychol* 19:3–34 Ja '63. * (Also published as a separate Monograph Supplement No. 16.)
3 Shapiro, M. B.; Brierley, J.; Slater, P.; and Beech, H. R. "Experimental Studies of a Perceptual Anomaly: 7, A New Explanation." *J Mental Sci* 108:655–68 S '62. * (*PA* 38:2989)

dren 4–12 years and adults with equivalent MAs, but not adolescents and adults with higher MAs. (5) It can be employed as an additional tool in a battery of tests administered to an individual when clues for the possible presence of organic brain pathology are sought. (6) Whether evaluated with objective scores or with some systematic inspection procedure the results tend to discriminate the psychotic from the nonpsychotic and nonpsychiatric subject provided their MAs are 13 or above. It does not detect effectively nonpsychotic emotionally disturbed children, however. (7) When the protocols are interpreted symbolically, the clinician must rely almost completely on the validity of his own subjective professional knowledge. (8) The test has not been standardized sufficiently to permit its use as a norm against which to judge other variables. (9) More research is needed on the perceptual contributions of each design and the effects on such perceptions of their sequential appearance in the protocol.

For reviews by Arthur L. Benton and Howard R. White of a, *see 4:144; for excerpts from related book reviews, see B268, B297, B487, 5:B330, 4:145, 3:109, and 40:B843.*

[204]

***The Blacky Pictures: A Technique for the Exploration of Personality Dynamics.** Ages 5 and over; 1950–62; psychosexual development; individual; 1 form ('50, 12 cards); manual ('50, 24 pages); research guide ('62, 27 pages, reprint of 74 below); inquiry cards ('50, 42 cards, separate sets for boys and girls); record blank ('50, 12 pages); no data on reliability and validity; no norms; $12 per set of test materials and 25 record blanks; $1.25 per research guide; $3.50 per 25 record blanks; postpaid; (35–55) minutes; Gerald S. Blum; Psychological Corporation. *

REFERENCES

1–7. See 4:102.

8–45. See 5:125.

46. SWANSON, G. E. "Some Effects of Member Object-Relationships on Small Groups." *Human Relations* 4(4):355–80 '51. * (*PA* 26:5486)

47. THOMAS, RICHARD WALLACE. *An Investigation of the Psychoanalytic Theory of Homosexuality.* Doctor's thesis, University of Kentucky (Lexington, Ky.), 1951. (*DA* 20:3847)

48. MARQUIS, DOROTHY P.; SINNETT, E. ROBERT; AND WINTER, WILLIAM D. "A Psychological Study of Peptic Ulcer Patients." *J Clin Psychol* 8:266–72 Jl '52. * (*PA* 27:6072)

49. MOLISH, HERMAN B.; LYON, BLANCHARD; AND BRIGGS, DENNIE L. "Character Structure of Adjusted and Maladjusted Naval Recruits as Measured by the Blacky Pictures." *Am J Orthopsychiatry* 24:164–74 Ja '54. * (*PA* 29:3141)

50. STREITFIELD, HAL S. "Specificity of Peptic Ulcer to Intense Oral Conflicts." *Psychosom Med* 16:315–26 Jl–Ag '54. * (*PA* 29:4533)

51. BURNHAM, RHODA K. *The Relationship of Personality to Oral Conditions in Children: An Evaluation by Means of the Rorschach and the Blacky Test.* Doctor's thesis, New York University (New York, N.Y.), 1957. (*DA* 18:1488)

52. ADELSON, JOSEPH, AND REDMOND, JOAN. "Personality Differences in the Capacity for Verbal Recall." *J Abn & Social Psychol* 57:244–8 S '58. * (*PA* 33:9771)

53. LEICHTY, MARY M. *The Absence of the Father During Early Childhood and Its Effect Upon the Oedipal Situation as Reflected in Young Adults.* Doctor's thesis, Michigan State University (East Lansing, Mich.), 1958. (*DA* 19:1821)

54. MARTIN, JAMES O. *A Psychological Investigation of Convicted Incest Offenders by Means of Two Projective Techniques.* Doctor's thesis, Michigan State University (East Lansing, Mich.), 1958. (*DA* 21:241)

55. NEUMAN, GERARD G., AND SALVATORE, JOSEPH C. "The Blacky Test and Psychoanalytic Theory: A Factor-Analytic Approach to Validity." *J Proj Tech* 22:427–31 D '58. * (*PA* 34:1405)

56. ANSBACHER, H. L. "Can Backy Blacken Testing?" Letter. *Am Psychologist* 14:654 O '59. *

57. BERGER, LESLIE. "Crossvalidation of 'Primary' and 'Reactive' Personality Patterns With Non-Ulcer Surgical Patients." *J Proj Tech* 23:8–11 Mr '59. * (*PA* 34:6004)

58. CHRISTIANSEN, BJØRN. *Attitudes Towards Foreign Affairs as a Function of Personality,* pp. 148–87. Oslo, Norway: Oslo University Press, 1959. Pp. 283. * (*PA* 35:3340)

59. DEAN, SIDNEY I. "A Note on Female Blacky Protocols." *J Proj Tech* 23:417 D '59. * (*PA* 35:4907)

60. LASKY, JULIAN J., AND BERGER, LESLIE. "Blacky Test Scores Before and After Genito-Urinary Surgery." *J Proj Tech* 23:57–8 Mr '59. *

61. MACHOVER, SOLOMON, AND PUZZO, FRANK S. "Clinical and Objective Studies of Personality Variabes in Alcoholism: 1, Clinical Investigation of the 'Alcoholic Personality.'" *Q J Studies Alcohol* 20:505–19 S '59. * (*PA* 34:6253)

62. MACHOVER, SOLOMON, AND PUZZO, FRANK S. "Clinical and Objective Studies of Personality Variables in Alcoholism: 2, Clinical Study of Personality Correlates of Remission From Active Alcoholism." *Q J Studies Alcohol* 20:520–7 S '59. * (*PA* 34:6253)

63. MAGNUSSEN, MAX G. "The Blacky Pictures as Personality Measures for Undergraduate Areas of Specialization." *J Proj Tech* 23:351–3 S '59. * (*PA* 35:4931)

64. MARGOLIS, MARVIN O. *A Psychological Study of Mothers of Asthmatic Children.* Doctor's thesis, Michigan State University (East Lansing, Mich.), 1959. (*DA* 23:311)

65. BLUM, GERALD S. Chap. 5, "The Blacky Pictures With Children," pp. 95–104. In *Projective Techniques With Children.* Edited by Albert I. Rabin and Mary R. Haworth. New York: Grune & Stratton, Inc., 1960. Pp. xiii, 392. * (*PA* 35:2229)

66. EASTMAN, DONALD FRANCIS. *An Exploratory Investigation of the Psychoanalytic Theory of Stuttering by Means of the Blacky Pictures Test.* Doctor's thesis, University of Nebraska (Lincoln, Neb.), 1960. (*DA* 21:1629)

67. PERLOE, SIDNEY I. "Inhibition as a Determinant of Perceptual Defense." *Percept & Motor Skills* 11:59–66 Ag '60. * (*PA* 35:3509)

68. VROOM, ANN LOUISE WORKMAN. *A Validation Study of the Blacky Analogies Test.* Doctor's thesis, University of Michigan (Ann Arbor, Mich.), 1960. (*DA* 21:364)

69. BLUM, GERALD S.; IN COLLABORATION WITH JUSTIN L. WEISS, ABRAM MINKOWICH, ANN L. VROOM, GERALD A. MENDELSOHN, SIDNEY I. PERLOE, IRVING W. WOLF, AND ROBERT H. GOLDSTEIN. *A Model of the Mind: Explored by Hypnotically Controlled Experiments and Examined for Its Psychodynamic Implications.* New York: John Wiley & Sons, Inc., 1961. Pp. xi, 229. * (*PA* 36:5II29B)

70. COHEN, SANFORD L.; SILVERMAN, ALBERT J.; WADDELL, WILLIAM; AND ZUIDEMA, GEORGE D. "Urinary Catechol Amine Levels, Gastric Secretion and Specific Psychological Factors in Ulcer and Non-Ulcer Patients." *J Psychosom Res* 5:90–115 F '61. * (*PA* 36:3JH90C)

71. DAVIDS, ANTHONY, AND LAWTON, MARCIA J. "Self-Concept, Mother Concept, and Food Aversions in Emotionally Disturbed and Normal Children." *J Abn & Social Psychol* 62:309–14 Mr '61. * (*PA* 36:4FF09D)

72. ROSSI, ASCANIO M., AND SOLOMON, PHILIP. "A Further Note on Female Blacky Protocols." *J Proj Tech* 25:339–40 S '61. *

73. BERGER, LESLIE, AND EVERSTINE, LOUIS. "Test-Retest Reliability of the Blacky Pictures Test." *J Proj Tech* 26:225–6 Je '62. * (*PA* 37:3185)

74. BLUM, GERALD S. "A Guide for Research Use of the Blacky Pictures." *J Proj Tech* 26:3–29 Mr '62. * (*PA* 37:3188)

75. CARP, FRANCES M. "Psychosexual Development of Stutterers." *J Proj Tech* 26:388–91 D '62. * (*PA* 37:6979)

76. GEIST, HAROLD. *The Etiology of Idiopathic Epilepsy,* pp. 192–201, 278–86. New York: Exposition Press, 1962. Pp. 297. *

77. IRWIN, THOMAS C. *A Contribution to the Construct Validation of the Oral Scales of the Blacky Pictures Test.* Doctor's thesis, University of Rochester (Rochester, N.Y.), 1963. (*DA* 24:2123)

78. STRICKER, GEORGE. "Stimulus Properties of the Blacky Pictures Test." *J Proj Tech & Pers Assess* 27:244–7 Je '63. * (*PA* 38:2727)

79. TIMMONS, EDWIN O., AND NOBLIN, CHARLES D. "The Differential Performance of Orals and Anals in a Verbal Conditioning Paradigm." *J Consult Psychol* 27:383–6 O '63. *

BERT R. SAPPENFIELD, *Professor of Psychology, Montana State University, Missoula, Montana.*

The *Blacky Pictures* were designed as stimuli for "a modified projective technique" to be used in a research study of the psychoanalytic theory of psychosexual development (*2*). They were subsequently published in 1950 as stimuli for "a technique for the exploration of personality dynamics." Since their publication, the *Blacky Pictures* have been widely utilized in research investigations and in clinical practice.

THE TEST STIMULI. The *Blacky Pictures* represent events in the life of a family of dogs. Each of the pictures, or "cartoons," depicts an ungainly dog, named "Blacky," who is expected to be perceived as the hero or the character with whom the subject identifies. Male subjects are told that Blacky is the son, and females that Blacky is the daughter. The other members of Blacky's family are named "Papa," "Mama," and "Tippy." In addition to the first picture, which is used merely to introduce the characters, there is a sequence of 11 pictures, each of which is "designed to depict either a stage of psychosexual development or a type of object relationship." Each picture is presented to the subject with an introductory statement calling attention to Blacky and pointing out, with varying degrees of structuredness, what he is doing or experiencing.

The cartoons, and their introductory comments, may be described as follows: (1) Oral Eroticism: "Here is Blacky with Mama." Blacky appears to be taking nourishment from Mama's udders. (2) Oral Sadism: "Here is Blacky with Mama's collar." Blacky appears to be biting a collar with "Mama" inscribed on it. (3) Anal Sadism: "Here Blacky is relieving himself (herself)." Blacky appears to be digging between dog houses marked "Papa" and "Mama," in a row of houses including smaller ones marked "Tippy" and "Blacky." (4) Oedipal Intensity: "Here Blacky is watching Mama and Papa." Blacky covertly observes Mama and Papa, who are showing affection for each other. (5) Masturbation Guilt: "Here Blacky is discovering sex." Blacky is shown in the act of licking his genital-anal zone. (6) Castration Anxiety, for males, or Penis Envy, for females: "Here Blacky is watching Tippy." Blacky observes blindfolded Tippy, whose tail is on a block, apparently about to be chopped off by a descending knife. (7) Positive Identification: "Here is Blacky with a toy dog." Blacky appears to be instructing, ordering, or dominating a miniature dog on wheels. (8) Sibling Rivalry: "Here Blacky is watching the rest of the family." Blacky is off to one side, observing Papa and Mama, who are showing affection for Tippy. (9) Guilt Feelings: "Here Blacky is very upset." Blacky appears to be cringing before a dog-like "angel" or "conscience" figure, who appears to be expressing hostility toward Blacky. (10) Positive Ego Ideal, for males, or Love-Object, for females: "Here Blacky is having a dream." Blacky, asleep, is having a dream-image of a big black male dog. (11) Positive Ego Ideal, for females, or Love-Object, for males: "Here Blacky is having another dream." Blacky is having a dream-image of a big black female dog.

TEST PROCEDURE. Standard procedure for administering the *Blacky Pictures* requires the subject (*a*) to tell a spontaneous story similar to that required by the TAT and other storytelling projective tests, (*b*) to answer a series of inquiry questions, mostly of the multiple choice type, and (*c*) to sort the pictures into liked and disliked categories, and then to choose the one picture liked most and the one picture disliked most. When used with children, the Blacky instructions are presented in a simplified version and the inquiry questions are, for the most part, asked in open-ended form.

The manual recommends scoring a protocol in terms of four "sources" (spontaneous stories, answers to inquiry questions, cartoon preferences, and related comments on other cartoons), on 13 separate dimensions: (*a*) oral eroticism, (*b*) oral sadism, (*c*) anal expulsiveness, (*d*) anal retentiveness, (*e*) oedipal intensity, (*f*) masturbation guilt, (*g*) castration anxiety (males) or penis envy (females), (*h*) positive identification, (*i*) sibling rivalry, (*j*) guilt feelings, (*k*) positive ego ideal, (*l*) narcissistic love-object, and (*m*) anaclitic love-object.

Two scoring manuals are available for research use of the Blacky technique. The first of these[1] has been utilized for scoring the standard Blacky dimensions in most of the research studies reported to date. The second

[1] BLUM, GERALD S. *Revised Scoring System for Research Use of the Blacky Pictures.* Unpublished mimeographed reports, 1951. Male form, 20 pages; female form, 6 pages.

of these (*74*) is based on results of a factor analysis of Blacky variables and various criterion variables, and permits scoring on 30 separate factors; this 1962 research scoring manual is represented by the author as rendering "obsolete" much of the research previously done with the Blacky technique.

RELIABILITY FINDINGS. Reliability investigations have, for the most part, demonstrated that, although the Blacky dimension scores have statistically significant reliabilities, these reliabilities are not usually high enough to commend the dimension scores for use in diagnosing individual personalities.

Charen (*37*) reported test-retest reliabilities, based on inquiry items only, to be "low or negative," except for the castration anxiety score (Cartoon 4), whose fourfold point correlation was .519. Blum (*34*) criticized Charen's findings because they were based on inquiry items alone, and because test-retest reliability involves "an unknown mixture of changes in set, familiarity with items, and....personality changes."

Granick and Scheflen (*44*) investigated several different aspects of the Blacky's reliability; they reported (*a*) that when 10 judges scored 40 sets of spontaneous stories, scoring each story as "strong" or "weak" on a given dimension, the percentages of agreement varied from 68 to 95 on all but the two dimensions (oral sadism and guilt feelings) on which the agreement was not statistically significant at or beyond the .05 level; (*b*) that 5 of 8 judges were able to match the test and retest protocols, when presented in sets produced by 6 or 7 subjects, with from 72 to 100 per cent accuracy; (*c*) that two judges rating thematic content as similar or dissimilar on 20 sets of three stories to each cartoon (two stories from test and retest of the same subjects and one story from a matched subject), agreed in 68 to 88 per cent of their judgments for each of 8 cartoons (excepting 4, 7, and 9); (*d*) that, however, even though thematic content was judged to be similar on test and retest protocols of the same subjects with significantly greater frequency than on matched but different subjects' protocols, "the amount of consistency in thematic productions by the individual S is not very high"; (*e*) that test and retest cartoon preferences were significantly consistent (70 to 95 per cent) for each cartoon for a group of 20 subjects; (*f*) that odd-even reliability was .92 for verbal fluency (words per story); and (*g*) that odd-even reliability of "structured" versus "unstructured" story responses (utilizing or not utilizing the central theme of the cartoon) was .67, based on scoring by two judges, who showed 100 per cent agreement in their judgments. Except for the last two findings, the study of Granick and Scheflen dealt either with some aspect of interscorer agreement (objectivity rather than reliability) or with some aspect of test-retest reliability (the relevance of which Blum himself has criticized); only the last-mentioned finding, concerning "structured" versus "unstructured" story content, dealt with the internal consistency of one of the Blacky "sources" of scoring (related comments on other cartoons).

A study by Berger and Everstine (*73*) also dealt with test-retest reliability rather than with internal consistency; reliability coefficients varying from .20 to .54 on the separate dimension scores were reported for a group of 50 male college students who had been retested after four weeks.

Although Ellis (*20*) reported high interrater agreements (objectivity) on a single patient's Blacky protocol, no research appears to have been done concerning the split-test or test-retest reliabilities of clinical inferences based primarily on spontaneous stories and related comments, which are likely to be the main sources of interpretation in clinical practice. This research void is, of course, not unique to the Blacky technique, but is shared by many other projective devices.

VALIDITY FINDINGS. As a research instrument, the Blacky technique has been put to many and varied uses. The original revised scoring system is a model of explicit definition and has provided an unusually adequate basis for objective scoring. It is laudable for its built-in provision that each of the sources (spontaneous story, inquiry, related comments, and cartoon preferences) is given approximately equal relative weight in determining the score for each dimension. This scoring system, however, provides only for trichotomous scores (very strong, fairly strong, and weak or absent), and many of the research studies have made use of dichotomous scoring (very strong, and fairly strong, weak, or absent).

A large number of studies which bear, directly or indirectly, on the question of the

Blacky technique's validity have been reported. The research study for which the *Blacky Pictures* were devised (*2*) has been criticized, on methodological grounds, by Seward (*5*). Even though Blum did not originally consider that study to be a validation of the Blacky technique itself, Blum and Hunt (*11*) later reported data from Blum's 1949 report as supporting the test's validity. Subsequent studies have, with few exceptions, been based on the assumption of the Blacky technique's validity for purposes of testing hypotheses derivable from psychoanalytic theory. It is the reviewer's position that studies reported to confirm, in some degree, hypotheses based on the assumption of validity, are themselves to some extent interpretable as validation studies. Brief abstracts of several such studies will be given below.

Michal-Smith, Hammer, and Spitz (*7*) reported a single case in which oral sadism against the mother was expressed in five stories following the one in response to the "mama's collar" cartoon, and in which oedipal content was expressed in four stories subsequent to the "oedipal intensity" cartoon. They reported these "related comments to other cartoons" to be consistent with the clinical findings concerning the subject's adjustment problems.

Blum and Miller (*13*), using a group of 18 third grade boys and girls, investigated, among other problems, the relationship between rankings on oral passivity based on Blacky protocols and several criterion variables thought to be diagnostic of orality. Several significant, though generally low, validity coefficients were found.

Ellis (*20*), after giving the Blacky to a patient who had been in psychoanalysis with him for about 200 hours, submitted the protocol to 22 clinical psychologists and psychological interns, to Blum, to himself, and to the patient, for evaluation in terms of ratings on 38 questions more or less related to the Blacky dimensions, and in terms of a clinical summary. Results showed about 60 per cent agreement by Blum and the psychologists and interns with the criterion (patient and therapist) on the 38 ratings, and 90 agreements as compared with 117 disagreements on statements in the clinical summaries.

Neuman and Salvatore (*55*) factor analyzed the intercorrelations, for males and females separately, which had been reported to occur among the Blacky dimension scores in Blum's investigation (*2*). With data for the male group, six factors interpreted to be consistent with psychoanalytic theory emerged. But, since contradictory and inconsistent findings occurred with the female group data, the question was raised whether the Blacky technique should be used with females.

Several studies have been concerned with testing hypotheses (particularly those of Alexander) relating to the dynamics of peptic ulcer. Blum and Kaufman (*12*) compared a group of 14 male adult ulcer patients with three nonulcer control groups (paranoid schizophrenics, non-paranoid schizophrenics, and normals), on stories to Cartoon 1 (oral eroticism), and found that all scorable stories of the ulcer patients (11 subjects) showed strong disturbance on this dimension, while only half of the control group did so. This finding was consistent with prediction from theory. Further exploration of the data seemed to indicate that the ulcer group could be divided, on the basis of inquiry responses, into "primary" and "reactive" subgroups, the "primary" subgroup accepting oral implications and the "reactive" subgroup evading or rejecting such implications. Marquis, Sinnett, and Winter (*48*) used the Blacky technique with another small group of ulcer patients and found it possible, again, to distinguish between "primary" and "reactive" subgroups. The results were interpreted as being consistent with Alexander's theory that ulcer patients fall into two groups, one of which accepts and acts upon oral needs and the other of which denies and represses these needs. Bernstein and Chase (*30*) applied the Blacky in a study of 20 ulcer patients, 20 psychosomatic non-ulcer patients, and 20 nonpsychiatric patients. Although significant differences occurred on some dimensions for each of the intergroup comparisons, there was no significant difference on the oral eroticism dimension; but the ulcer patients, whether high or low on the oral eroticism dimension, did split into "primary" and "reactive" subgroups. Winter (*32*) devised objectively scorable "primary" and "reactive" scales, based on responses to the Blacky as a whole, and applied these in a study of 68 duodenal ulcer patients; he concluded that "two different patterns are found in people with ulcers, and these can be validly measured by the Blacky scales developed in this investigation." Berger (*57*), however, in a study of 30 non-ulcer patients, as a control for Winter's ulcer group, failed to find positive cross validating evidence for Winter's revised scales since neither differentiated significantly between the ulcer and non-ulcer samples. Despite some contradictory findings, the body of evidence seems to indicate that the Blacky technique can be a useful instrument for further studies of peptic ulcer dynamics.

Smith and Powell (*39*), using Cartoons 1, 4, 10, and 11, without asking for spontaneous stories, found that 6 of 19 inquiry items differentiated significantly between pre-menarcheal and post-menarcheal girls, although cartoon preferences failed to discriminate. Lasky and Berger (*60*), who compared responses of male urological patients before and after genitourinary surgery, concluded that "seven of 13 individual Blacky dimensions were considerably affected" by the surgery. Lindner (*21*) compared male sexual deviates with a control group individually matched on 9 variables, and found that 9 Blacky dimensions "showed a significant difference between the sexually deviant group and the non-sexually-deviant controls." The three preceding studies have in common the fact that they indicate sensitivity of the Blacky test to peculiarities of sexual experience.

McNeil and Blum (*16*) found a number of significant relationships between handwriting variables and Blacky scores; anal retentiveness was the one dimension that was related to the greatest number of handwriting variables, and which, according to psychoanalytic theory, should most clearly be expected to show such relationships.

Aronson (*19*) tested predictions from the psychoanalytic theory of paranoia by comparing paranoids, non-paranoid psychotics, and normals on a large number of Blacky variables; an impressively large number of findings (chiefly, but not wholly, involving responses to inquiry items) conformed to theoretical predictions.

Molish, Lyon, and Briggs (*49*), using only the multiple choice inquiry items of the Blacky, compared the responses of 1,847 "normal" naval recruits with responses of 390 recruits discharged as "unsuitable" and found only 5 items on which the modal responses of "normals" did not conform to "neutral" expectations, but found 11 items on which a significant difference occurred between the "normal" and "unsuitable" groups. This strictly empirical study is, of course, in need of cross validation.

Teevan (*28*) reported that five Blacky dimensions discriminated significantly between undergraduate groups majoring in humanities, social sciences, and natural sciences, respectively. The humanities group showed highest disturbance on oral eroticism; the social science group showed highest disturbance on oral sadism, oedipal intensity, guilt feelings, and anaclitic love-object; the natural science group showed lowest disturbance on all of these dimensions, except oral eroticism. Magnussen (*63*) attempted to replicate Teevan's study and found essentially similar results, except that two of the dimensions (oedipal intensity and anaclitic love-object) showed no significant intergroup differences.

Swanson (*46*) predicted Blacky dimension relationships with variables having to do with participation in a small problem solving group, and found the predictions to be confirmed with respect to five of eight participation variables. Rabin (*45*), using only the multiple choice inquiry items of the Blacky, in a comparison of Kibbutz with non-Kibbutz Israeli boys, found some significant differences in the predicted direction and no significant differences opposite to his predictions. These studies indicate that the Blacky technique shows promise as a research instrument for dealing with problems in social psychology.

About the only reported investigation which has failed to yield some evidence in favor of the validity of the Blacky technique was that of Charen (*36*), in which recovered tubercular patients showed changes in a regressive direction as compared with their pre-recovery responses; however, in this study several other tests were used and none of these yielded significant differences between active tubercular patients and the control groups with which they were compared.

Almost all of the research studies having some bearing on validity have provided some indications in favor of the Blacky technique's validity; typically, in each study some of the predictions from theory have been confirmed and some have failed to be confirmed by statistically significant findings, but only occasionally have statistically significant findings contradicted predictions. In general, then, there appears to be far more evidence for the Blacky's validity than for its lack of validity. Several studies, however, have made use only of responses to the multiple choice inquiry questions, and several other studies have shown responses to the inquiry questions (when "sources" were treated separately) to have relatively great weight in yielding results confirmatory of hypotheses. This relative emphasis on the validity of inquiry responses may imply either that investigators have not been able to score the other "sources" with sufficient objectivity or that, even with adequately objective scoring, the range of individual differences occurring with respect to the other "sources" has not been sufficiently great to yield either significant differences between groups or significant relationships with other variables. Unfortunately, too little data have been reported on the actual distributions of different "source" scores to make it possible to evaluate these possibilities. The fact, however, that responses to these multiple choice questions have yielded impressive validity findings suggests that wider use might be made of combining projective stimuli with multiple choice questions, so as to provide the self-inventory with a distancing device which would make the subject less self-consciously defensive than in the usual case when he must answer questions that are frankly about himself.

Blum's latest "Guide for Research Use of the Blacky Pictures" (*74*) provides scoring instructions for 30 separate factors. On all but five of these factors (those for which "related comments" could conceivably contribute several points to the score) the responses to inquiry items make disproportionately high contributions to total scores. It would appear that Blum is prepared to think of the Blacky technique, when used as a research instrument, as no longer having the function of a deeply probing projective test, since he has conceived of the inquiry as evoking responses "at or close to the conscious level." No normative information is given for the 30 factor scores, although it should have been possible to publish distributions of these scores for the research sample (210 male undergraduates). Nevertheless, the practicing clinical psychologist should be able to glean from the Guide many useful insights to enrich his interpretations of Blacky protocols. For this reason, it might be well for the author to incorporate some of this new material in the manual, either as a supplement to, or as a substitute for, the interpretative material presently included.

THE BLACKY TECHNIQUE AS A CLINICAL INSTRUMENT. Possibly because of the fact that research scoring has typically given much weight to inquiry items and cartoon preferences, there is very little published evidence concerning the value of the Blacky technique as a clinical procedure. The reviewer suspects (without evidence) that many other clinicians are like himself in preferring to use the *Blacky Pictures* mainly for obtaining spontaneous stories, to be followed up by a minimum of non-suggestive questions to induce the subject to make his stories complete. Interpretation, in such a case, would utilize what is understood about principles of interpreting stories obtained with other picture-stimulated story-telling tests, such as the TAT or the CAT.

A number of problems arise in connection with the adequacy of the *Blacky Pictures* (or cartoons) as stimuli for a story-telling projective technique. Some of these problems have been the subject of research, but others have not been mentioned in the growing research literature.

Blacky, a dog, is assumed to take the role of "hero" in every picture and, consequently, in every spontaneous story. Although the dog is, among all animals, traditionally supposed to be "man's best friend," and although dogs have been cast in "human" form in Disney cartoons, it is still an unknown to us to what extent human subjects are able to identify with dogs, as compared with their ability to identify with other animals. It is reasonable to assume, in the absence of research evidence to the contrary, that ability to identify with any given animal should be amenable to extensive individual differences. If this should be true, then requiring subjects to respond to the same animal character throughout the sequence of pictures may result in limited projective yield for those subjects who fail to identify strongly with dogs. Some subjects may tell "good" stories merely because they have knowledge of canine behavior rather than because of strong identification with Blacky. Moreover, research evidence is not yet available to resolve the issue whether a story-telling test is more productive when the same character is used throughout or when many different characters are available for identification in the test stimuli. The Bellak CAT, which uses different animals in different pictures, might rewardingly be compared with the *Blacky Pictures* in an investigation to aid in resolving this issue.

A second problem relates to the use of the name "Blacky" for the hero of the sequence. Blum (*2*), on the basis of an informal study of the problem, concluded that males tend to think of "Blacky" as a male and that females tend to think of "Blacky" as a female. However, more recent studies (*41, 72*) have demonstrated that "Blacky" tends to be perceived by both males and females as a male, and other reports (*55, 59*) have suggested that the *Blacky Pictures* may be more successful in inducing male subjects than in inducing female subjects to identify with "Blacky." Neuman and Salvatore (*55*) have recommended that a "cat family" sequence of pictures be devised for use with females. Another possible implication of the name "Blacky" relates to racial issues (*7*); dark-skinned subjects may find it relatively easy to identify with Blacky, while light-skinned subjects may avoid identification on the basis of prejudice. Finally, the name "Blacky" may have symbolic values for some subjects, so that he (she) is perceived as a representative of darkness or evil and therefore difficult to identify with, except in terms of the subject's less acceptable impulses. In such cases "Tippy" may be perceived, not as a sibling, but as a representative of the subject's more socialized and acceptable personality components. It would be reasonable, then, at times, to regard stories as expressions of intrapersonal conflicts rather than as expressions of interpersonal attitudes.

The structured content of the Blacky cartoons, such that each is intended to represent a given stage of psychosexual development or a given object relationship, brings into focus the importance of norms (which are not to be found in the manual of instructions or in any other published source). It is generally accepted that the more ambiguous or unstructured the stimulus material is, the more confidence can be felt in interpreting a response as stemming from "inner determinants." Responses to the blank card of the TAT, or dreams, or waking hallucinations, are regarded as highly diagnostic of personality, since they are minimally determined by external stimuli; identification of a simple geometrical figure, on the other hand, would have little diagnostic value, since this response is maximally determined by the external stimulus. The Blacky cartoons lie somewhere between these two extremes of structuredness, and, in the absence of norms, it is difficult to determine to what extent responses represent interpretable individual differences in disturbance, conflict, attitudes, object relationships, and the like. The manual, of course, recommends that interpretation be based on latent rather than manifest content of stories; this recommendation is based on the assumption that subjects "know" what the pictures represent and that their denial of this "knowledge" has an interpretable meaning. If this is a fact, then norms should be available to support it. The manual itself, however, contradicts to some extent the principle that interpretation should emphasize latent content, for many examples of "strong" and "not strong" stories appear to emphasize manifest content rather than latent content. Users of the test need to know how to interpret responses, but they are provided with insufficient normative information for this purpose. This criticism is applicable to other story-telling projective techniques, of course, and it can be said of the Blacky, as well as of the others, that clinical experience will provide some normative information, and that any sort of over-emphasis in stories, occurring in response to pictures not demanding such an emphasis, gains significance for interpretation of individual differences. For this reason, the "related comments" source of scoring on the Blacky test should perhaps be given more interpretive importance than it has been given in the manual, since it represents the operation of strong personal trends that overreach the stimulus demands of a given picture.

Still another issue which has remained untouched by the research literature is that related to the sequence of situations as presented to a given subject. The recommended sequence corresponds roughly to the developmental sequence as conceived by Freud's theory of psychosexual development. Apparently no research has been focused on the problem whether the opposite sequence, a gradually regressive sequence, would be more suitable than one which requires a sudden regression by the subject to the infantile attitude of oral erotism. It is true, of course, that using the terms "Papa" and "Mama" to refer to the parents may indeed facilitate the expected regressive attitude; but, on the other hand, continued reference to "Papa" and "Mama" (particularly in the inquiry questions) may function to fixate this regressive attitude in the subject, so that his responses will be unlikely to "mature" along with the developmental sequence of pictured situations.

SUMMARY EVALUATION. In spite of the many questions arising in connection with the Blacky technique as a clinical instrument, it is fair to say that the manual in its present form is one of the most complete and most explicit to be found for projective tests of the picture-story variety, and that the reviewer, and reportedly many other users, have found the Blacky test to provide a rich source of material for clinical evaluation. When used with children, especially boys, having mental ages of about 5 to 10 years, the *Blacky Pictures* often provide adequate material for interpretations concerning problem areas, attitudes toward siblings and parents, characteristic defensive reactions, self-perceptions, and the like. Yet it is the reviewer's impression that, with children of both sexes, aged from about 8 to about 12 years, Bellak's CAT is likely to have a higher interpretive yield than the Blacky. With subjects beyond early adolescence, the reviewer, in most cases, would consider the TAT, rather than the Blacky, to be the instrument of choice. These preferences are based on the various points mentioned above concerning the relative structuredness of the Blacky, the single hero figure available for identification, and various possible objections to the name "Blacky" itself.

It is also the reviewer's judgment that, after 13 years of use, the manual should be thoroughly revised as a guide to clinical interpretation. It appears that dimensional scoring, even though it may have value for research use, should no longer be emphasized for clinical application of the Blacky technique. Although the author has argued against "seeking....to adorn patients with diagnostic labels of an outmoded nosology," the use of dimensional scoring substitutes another nosology, emphasis on which may lead to neglect of significant nuances of personality dynamics. For clinical interpretation, it should be more useful to determine specifically how a subject responds to each of the situations, what defensive maneuvers he characteristically employs, and with what degree of regularity he expresses particular attitudes toward himself, toward his problems, and toward significant others, than to determine in which of the psychosexual areas he manifests greatest "disturbance."

Revision of the manual should also involve, as mentioned above, the inclusion of normative information concerning typical and atypical ways of perceiving the individual cartoons, concerning the relative frequencies of various story plots in response to each of the cartoons, and concerning any other characteristics of responses to the Blacky which would aid in determining whether, and in what ways, an individual protocol deviates from the typical.

For a review by Kenneth R. Newton, see 5:125 (1 excerpt); for a review by Albert Ellis, see 4:102 (3 excerpts).

[205]

★Buttons: A Projective Test for Pre-Adolescent and Adolescent Boys and Girls. Grades 7–9; maladjustment; 1963; 1 form (7 pages); manual (36 pages plus sample copy of test and scoring booklet); scoring booklet (4 pages); no data on reliability of scores; $18 per examiner's kit of 25 tests, 25 scoring booklets, and manual; $4 per manual; postpaid; (45) minutes; Esther P. Rothman and Pearl H. Berkowitz; Western Psychological Services. *

[206]

***Children's Apperception Test.** Ages 3–10; 1949–61; individual; 1 form; 2 editions; short form record booklet ('55, 5 pages) for this test and test 245; no data on reliability and validity; $7.50 per set of cards and manual of either edition; $3 per 25 record booklets; postage extra; [15–50] minutes; Leopold Bellak and Sonya Sorel Bellak; C.P.S. Inc. *

a) CHILDREN'S APPERCEPTION TEST. 1949–61; 1 form ('59, c1949, 10 cards, same as cards published in 1949 and 1951 except for finish); revised manual, fourth edition ('61, c1949, 16 pages, identical with 1959 third edition except for expanded bibliography).

b) CHILDREN'S APPERCEPTION TEST—SUPPLEMENT. 1952–55; 1 form ('52, 10 cards); manual ('52, 8 pages).

REFERENCES

1–2. See 4:103.
3–17. See 5:126.
18. ARMSTRONG, MARY ANN SMITH. "Children's Responses to Animal and Human Figures in Thematic Pictures." *J Consult Psychol* 18:67–70 F '54. * (*PA* 28:8710)
19. LYLES, WILLIAM KARYLE. *The Effects of Examiner Attitudes on the Projective Test Responses of Children: A Study of the Significance of the Interpersonal Relationship in the Projective Testing of Children.* Doctor's thesis, New York University (New York, N.Y.), 1958. (*DA* 19:3024)
20. ROSENBLATT, MARVIN S. *The Development of Norms for the Children's Apperception Test.* Doctor's thesis, Florida State University (Tallahassee, Fla.), 1958. (*DA* 19:2150)
21. LEHMANN, IRVIN J. "Responses of Kindergarten Children to the Children's Apperception Test." *J Clin Psychol* 15:60–3 Ja '59. * (*PA* 34:2828)
22. NOLAN, ROBERT DALE. *A Longitudinal Comparison of Motives in Children's Fantasy Stories as Revealed by the Children's Apperception Test.* Doctor's thesis, Florida State University (Tallahassee, Fla.), 1959. (*DA* 20:3387)
23. WALTON, D. "A Children's Apperception Test—An Investigation of Its Validity as a Test of Neuroticism." *J Mental Sci* 105:359–70 Ap '59. * (*PA* 34:4412)
24. BELLAK, LEOPOLD, AND ADELMAN, CRUSA. Chap. 4, "The Children's Apperception Test (CAT)," pp. 62–94. In *Projective Techniques With Children.* Edited by Albert I. Rabin and Mary R. Haworth. New York: Grune & Stratton, Inc., 1960. Pp. xiii, 392. * (*PA* 35:2229)
25. BUDOFF, MILTON. "The Relative Utility of Animal and Human Figures in a Picture-Story Test for Young Children." *J Proj Tech* 24:347–52 D '60. * (*PA* 35:4716)

26. GOLIAS, GEORGE A. *The C.A.T. as a Measure of Therapeutic Change in Children, Age 6-12.* Master's thesis, Kent State University (Kent, Ohio), 1960.
27. MAGNUSSON, DAVID. "Some Personality Tests Applied on Identical Twins." *Scandinavian J Psychol* 1(2):55-61 '60. * (*PA* 35:6424)
28. REDDY, P. V. *A Study of the Reliability and Validity of the Children's Apperception Test.* Doctor's thesis, University of London (London, England), 1960. (Abstract: *Brit J Ed Psychol* 30:182-4)
29. BUTLER, R. L. "Responses of Institutionalized Mentally Retarded Children to Human and to Animal Pictures." *Am J Mental Def* 65:620-2 Mr '61. * (*PA* 36:1JI20B)
30. CAIN, ALBERT C. "A Supplementary Dream Technique With the Children's Apperception Test." *J Clin Psychol* 17:181-3 Ap '61. * (*PA* 38:1006)
31. WILLIAMS, JESSIE M. "Children Who Break Down in Foster Homes: A Psychological Study of Patterns of Personality Growth in Grossly Deprived Children." *J Child Psychol & Psychiatry* 2:5-20 Je '61. * (*PA* 36:2FF05W)
32. HAWORTH, MARY R. "Responses of Children to a Group Projective Film and to the Rorschach, CAT, Despert Fables and D-A-P." *J Proj Tech* 26:47-60 Mr '62. * (*PA* 37:2893)
33. WEISSKOPF-JOELSON, EDITH, AND FOSTER, HELEN C. "An Experimental Study of the Effect of Stimulus Variation Upon Projection." *J Proj Tech* 26:366-70 S '62. * (*PA* 37:3208)
34. BUDOFF, MILTON. "Animal vs. Human Figures in a Picture Story Test for Young, Mentally Backward Children." *Am J Mental Def* 68:245-50 S '63. * (*PA* 38:5726)
35. GROSS, SEYMOUR Z. "Critique: Children Who Break Down in Foster Homes: A Psychological Study of Patterns of Personality Growth in Grossly Deprived Children." *J Child Psychol & Psychiatry* 4:61-6 Ap '63. *
36. HAWORTH, MARY R. "A Schedule for the Analysis of CAT Responses." *J Proj Tech & Pers Assess* 27:181-4 Je '63. * (*PA* 38:2716)

BERNARD I. MURSTEIN, *Associate Professor of Psychology, Connecticut College, New London, Connecticut.*

The genesis of the CAT stemmed from a discussion between Leopold Bellak and Ernst Kris in which the latter "pointed out how we could expect children to identify themselves much more readily with animals than with persons, a *fact* we have known ever since Freud wrote his story of little Hans in 'The Phobia of a Five Year Old' " (italics mine). Certainly the widespread use of animals with human characteristics in movie cartoons, comic strips, and television would seem to support this "fact." The only contrary note is that a considerable amount of research has been done comparing both the TAT (which contains clearly discernible humans for the most part) and specially created human analogues of the CAT (which were like the CAT cards in every way except for the use of humans rather than animals) with the CAT. Not a single study clearly supports the alleged supremacy of the CAT over pictures with humans. The results of some studies are indecisive or ambiguous [1,2,3] (*6*), but the majority show a clear superiority for figures employing humans [4] (*11-2, 16, 18, 25*). Among the findings supporting the supremacy of pictures with humans were clinicians' ratings of clinical usefulness (*12*); percentage of stories containing expressions of feeling, containing significant conflict, having definite outcome (*16*); more feelings, different kinds of feelings, conflicts, number and kinds of outcomes, number and kinds of themes, and number of figures (*11*); significantly higher Transcendence Index (more nondescriptive statements) (*18*); more involvement in human cards; [5] longer stories, more rapid verbalization, quicker reaction time, more themes; [6] higher word count, story level, Transcendence Index (*25*).

Evidence in favor of the CAT stems from the finding of Boyd and Mandler that most of their subjects preferred the animal stories and gave more emotional material to them, although more involved in the human series.

The other studies either found no difference or are equivocal because of confounded designs. The data have been discussed by the reviewer in greater detail elsewhere.[7]

Bellak and Adelman in a recent review (*24*) have objected to a few of these studies on the grounds that the human analogues were more structured than the CAT and, further, that the age of the children tested was in the upper half of the 3 to 10 year range suitable for the CAT. The first objection seems unjustified on two counts. First, the humanized analogues are essentially equivalent in many of the studies. It is extremely doubtful that this factor *per se* could account for the overwhelming superiority of the human pictures. Second, Bellak believes that the use of structured stimuli violates the basic principles of projective testing. Elsewhere,[8] this reviewer has tried to show that many of these principles do not agree with the findings of most projective studies. To give but one example, ambiguity and projection are not linearly related but rather show a curvilinear relationship. It is possible to weaken the ability of a card to elicit projection by making it too ambiguous and not allow-

1 BILLS, ROBERT E. "Animal Pictures for Obtaining Children's Projections." *J Clin Psychol* 6:291-3 Jl '50. * (*PA* 25:1784)
2 BILLS, ROBERT E.; LEIMAN, CHARLES J.; AND THOMAS, RICHARD W. "A Study of the Validity of the TAT and a Set of Animal Pictures." *J Clin Psychol* 6:293-5 Jl '50. * (*PA* 25:1785)
3 BOYD, NANCY A., AND MANDLER, GEORGE. "Children's Responses to Human and Animal Stories and Pictures." *J Consult Psychol* 19:367-71 '55. *
4 SIMSON, EDUARD. Vergleich von CAT und einer inhaltsanslogen Mensch-Bilderserie. *Diagnostica* 5:54-66 '59. (*PA* 36:1FF54S)
5 BOYD AND MANDLER, *op. cit.*
6 SIMSON, *op. cit.*
7 MURSTEIN, BERNARD I. *Theory and Research in Projective Techniques (Emphasizing the TAT).* New York: John Wiley & Sons, Inc., 1963. Pp. xiii, 385. *
8 *Ibid.*

ing the subject to identify with any of the characters.

Bellak's objection to the lack of studies with young children does not seem to take cognizance of the difficulties experienced by very young children in verbalizing. Budoff (*25*) working with four-year-olds whose minimum IQ was greater than 120 concluded that the stories were not too meaningful because of the immaturity of the children, though the few significant differences reported favored the human analogue of the CAT.

It is also noteworthy that the current manual, published in 1961 and containing 46 references, does not contain a single one reporting any of the negative results cited above. Why?

It is possible but still untested that the CAT is better than the TAT or TAT-type cards for such specific problems, for example, as sibling rivalry, oral fixation, and the Oedipal theme. Also, only one study has used disturbed children (*12*). It is possible (though there is no particular reason to believe so) that the CAT may be more successful here. Last, this reviewer would like to see more meaningful variables tackled than word count, length of stories, and quickness of reaction time.

In sum, the research strongly contradicts the belief that children project more readily to pictures of animals than of humans. Accordingly, as a broad-band instrument, the CAT cannot be recommended at this time as being likely to provide as much clinical utility as the TAT or other pictures with human figures. With regard to specific psychoanalytic hypotheses for which the test was primarily designed, there is no evidence favoring or contradicting the use of the instrument.

ROBERT D. WIRT, *Professor of Psychology, Child Development, and Psychiatry, University of Minnesota, Minneapolis, Minnesota.*

The *Children's Apperception Test* (CAT) continues to be difficult to evaluate. As with other projective techniques, the kind of data one gets using the CAT is not easily translated into statistical, measurement language. While Bellak's book (*9*) is certainly a useful guide for interpretation, the categories are variable and quite dependent upon both the user's theoretical orientation and the nature of his clinical experience. Over the years there have been indications that norms were in process of being established, but to date satisfactory data of this sort do not exist. There is also some question, based on the reviewer's experience, that children actually construe the stimulus material as was hoped by the authors. There was reason to suppose that children might more readily respond to pictures of animals in various situations than to material depicting people. However, it is not at all clear that the CAT succeeds in eliciting stories of such varied thematic properties as, for example, do the children's cards of the TAT. Perhaps this is because the situations shown in the CAT cards are more structured, leading to "popular" responses, and also because the CAT does not really have characters represented (such as young children) with whom a child can immediately identify and upon whom he can project his own self concept. With very young children (under age six) the CAT may be useful in getting at some stereotypy of interpersonal perception in individual cases. But such material is generally fairly evident from other sources, such as the history or free play observation. Perhaps the most useful cards of the CAT are those of the Supplement (the CAT-S) which are designed for assessment of particular problem areas, especially when used as a play technique, as Bellak suggests.

Bellak's book (*9*) is an instructive and necessary companion for the less experienced clinician interested in using the CAT. It is even more useful as an introduction to the TAT. For the CAT it gives an approach to interpretation by employing case material which gives perspective and structure for students in the analysis of children's stories.

The story telling technique has much appeal to children and has been popular with psychologists and psychiatrists for a long time. Nearly all clinical child psychologists would believe that the method has considerable value, but its value comes more from the sensitivity and experience of the clinician than from the particular stimulus material used. Thus far the CAT cannot be said to be any better than any number of other techniques which require a child to tell a story. In fact, the reviewer believes that it is less helpful than using structured doll situations. Until reliable scoring techniques and criteria of interpretation can be standardized the CAT and similar techniques will continue to be of value proportionate to the skill of the interpreter.

For reviews by Douglas T. Kenny and Albert I. Rabin, see 5:126; for reviews by John E. Bell and L. Joseph Stone, see 4:103 (5 excerpts); for excerpts from related book reviews, see 5:B63.

[207]

Controlled Projection for Children, Second Edition. Ages 6–13; 1945–51; individual; 1 form ('51); manual ('51, 178 pages); no data on reliability and validity; 25*s.* per manual, postage and purchase tax extra within U.K.; [20] minutes; John C. Raven; H. K. Lewis & Co. Ltd. * (United States distributor: Psychological Corporation.)

REFERENCES

1–8. See 5:127.

JOHN LIGGETT, *Senior Lecturer in Psychology, University College of South Wales and Monmouthshire, University of Wales, Cardiff, Wales.*

The author's declared aim in the 1944 foreword to the first edition was "to present, not a technique of testing ready for applied psychology, but simply a method of enquiry suitable for experimental work." A good deal of such work has since been undertaken and *Controlled Projection for Children* can now be regarded both as a useful tool and as a model for such enquiries for the future. In refreshing contrast to many megalomanic clinical panaceas the objective here is a carefully limited one: the uncovering—in a reasonably brief testing time, usually about a quarter hour—of some specific aspects of the fantasies and domestic preoccupations of children between the ages of 6 and 13.

The test materials required are of the greatest simplicity: coloured pencils, paper, and a list of 11 questions. The child is asked to draw "anything that comes into your head" and simultaneously to relate a simple story about an imaginary boy or girl. The framework of the story is provided by the psychologist, the detail by the child in response to 11 standard questions about the likes and dislikes, preferred playmates, fears, dreams, parental attitudes and interactions, and other feelings of the imaginary child.

In the manual the author clearly tabulates typical responses made by 150 normal children and 80 clinic cases subdivided into three age groups (6½, 9½, and 12½ years). He gives individual response frequencies and sufficient information to allow the calculation of a "coefficient of conformity" which expresses the extent to which a child's verbal responses are characteristic of his age group. Several children's records are presented in detail with appropriate computations and clinical inferences explicitly presented.

Conclusions derived from the drawings are much more tentative but a useful analytical scheme is presented. The manual is well produced and contains some excellent colour reproductions of children's drawings. The author's arguments are modest and persuasive and, as a record of empirical work in a difficult field, his manual is praiseworthy. There is more than a touch, however, of tedious pedantry in some of his introductory discussion. We should not need to be told (at least in this context) what is meant by "a critical judgement," nor should we need half a page to explain the word "analogy."

Over 12 years of more or less regular use this reviewer has found *Controlled Projection for Children* a powerful yet sensitive clinical aid, a fruitful source of hypotheses about individual cases, and a valuable vehicle for case discussions with psychiatric colleagues. Often, too, with difficult, disturbed cases resistant to interview, it has provided the *only* available route to the inner world of the child.

See 5:127 (3 excerpts); for reviews by Arthur L. Benton and Percival M. Symonds of the original edition, see 3:29 (5 excerpts).

[208]

Curtis Completion Form. Grades 11–16 and adults; 1950–53; emotional maturity and adjustment; Form A ('50, 4 pages); manual ('53, 7 pages); $2 per 20 tests; 25¢ per manual; 25¢ per specimen set; postage extra; (30–35) minutes; James W. Curtis; Science Research Associates, Inc. *

REFERENCES

1. WATSON, WALTER S. "The Validity of the Curtis Completion Form as a Predictor of College Student Personality Deviates." *Yearb Nat Council Meas Used Ed* 12:82–5 pt 2 '55. *

2. FITZSIMMONS, S. J., AND MARCUSE, F. L. "Adjustment in Leaders and Non-Leaders as Measured by the Sentence Completion Projective Technique." *J Clin Psychol* 17:380–1 O '61. * (*PA* 38:8549)

IRWIN G. SARASON, *Associate Professor of Psychology, University of Washington, Seattle, Washington.*

This is a sentence completion test which consists of 52 items. It may be scored objectively by means of a content analysis scoring system described in the manual. The scores may be interpreted by means of a chart which indicates the probabilities with which normal, neurotic, and psychotic behavior would be expected from subjects with varying adjustment scores. The manual describes the test as being of value in any situation in which an evaluation of emotional adjustment is required.

The test appears to be an interesting approach to the sentence completion method and might prove useful in personality research. However, in terms of practical clinical, industrial, and educational work, it is inadequate in several respects. The development of the test was far from thorough. No set of standardized instructions are provided. The sample on which data are provided in the manual involved only 335 subjects, and the description of the subject types is sketchy. The 335 subjects included 199 vocational rehabilitation clients, 87 psychiatric patients who had been referred to one clinical psychologist for testing, and 49 employed adults seeking vocational or personal counseling. Out of this assortment of people, normal, neurotic, and psychotic are differentiated in the manual. This categorization was based on the judgments of clinical workers.

The test's scoring system seems to possess adequate interscorer reliability. However, only four scorers were used in the reliability study reported. The only validity data cited are in terms of the sentence completion adjustment scores obtained by subjects who had been judged by raters to be normal, neurotic, or psychotic. While this finding, if replicated, could be of value, it seems clear that, on the basis of the data presented, the claims for the test are extravagant. For the test to be useful further studies would be required involving better sampling procedures and more validity evidence. If this test is valid, and it may be, it is difficult, with the data available, to say precisely in what way.

Laurance F. Shaffer, *Professor of Psychology and Education, Teachers College, Columbia University, New York, New York.*

This sentence completion test is apparently unchanged, in test form or manual, since it was published in 1950 to 1953, and since it was last reviewed in this series. It consists of 52 completion stems, 50 of the usual sort and 2 partly structured, with a space for the examinee's further remarks. The manual states that it is a measure of "emotional maturity and adjustment"—rather vague concepts whose definition is not elaborated.

In its clarity and objectivity, the scoring method has considerable merit. Each response showing a "Group A factor"—antagonism, suspicion, jealousy, self-pity and pessimism, insecurity, social inadequacy, environmental deprivation, or severe conflict—receives two points. "Group B factors" of avoidance responses and ambiguous and incomplete responses, and "Group C factors" of erasures, cross-outs, or emphatic punctuation each receive one point. Each type of scorable response is well defined and is illustrated by brief but adequate examples. The reported interscorer correlations of from .89 to .95 seem consistent with the clarity of the scoring method.

At first glance, the manual seems a model of adherence to good professional standards in spite of its six-page brevity. Odd-even reliabilities are reported, and the form's validity receives multiple presentation in terms of means and standard deviations, biserial correlations, and an expectancy table which show the discrimination between groups described as normal, neurotic, and psychotic. The reported validity seems good. In fact, on further cogitation, it seems quite too good to be true. It may be doubted that any assessment method whatsoever has a biserial validity of .97 for the discrimination between normal and neurotic, of .98 between normal and all non-normal, and of .73 between neurotic and psychotic. If these coefficients were sound, the *Curtis Completion Form* would have received international acclaim as the ultimate solution of a hitherto elusive diagnostic problem.

What's the trouble? The application of only a little psychometric sophistication reveals three serious sources of error. First, the biserial correlation coefficient was misused. The validation was based on 335 cases, of which 175 are described as normal, 60 as neurotic, and 100 as psychotic. Thus 48 per cent of the cases were non-normal, in comparison to an incidence that probably does not exceed 10 per cent in an unselected sample. Because biserial correlations are affected by the base rate, the reported coefficients are surely somewhat inflated statistically.

Second, all of the 335 subjects used to establish the validities were clients or patients who were seeking help of some kind, drawn from clients of a rehabilitation service, employed adults seeking vocational or personal counseling, and "psychiatric patients referred to one clinical psychologist for testing." Such persons, as much experience and some data show, tend to label themselves. The well-integrated clients are normally matter-of-fact or defensive; the disturbed ones pour out their woes to document their pleas for help. Therefore the validation data are relevant only if the test were to be used solely for voluntary clients, and show no evidence justifying its use for industrial selection or educational counseling as the manual recommends.

Third, and most seriously, the manual gives no evidence that the criterion classifications and the test scores were independent. The distinction between normal, neurotic, and psychotic examinees was based on "ratings....made by skilled professional personnel—clinical psychologists or psychiatrists," who could have had access to the Completion Form as well as to other evidence. The human nature, even of psychologists, being what it is, it is likely that few subjects showing disturbance on the sentence completions were called "normal." In the absence of clear evidence to the contrary, there must be at least a suspicion that the test performances contaminated the criteria.

In summary, the *Curtis Completion Form* remains an attractive blank with a nicely developed scoring method. Whether it is an effective instrument depends on more carefully gathered evidence, still unavailable ten years after its publication.

For a review by Alfred B. Heilbrun, Jr., see 5:128.

[209]

★The Draw-A-Person. Ages 5 and over; 1963; 1 form (1 page plus backing sheet to be interleafed with carbon to make a 2-copy drawing form); manual (33 pages plus sample copies of protocol and interpretive booklets); protocol booklet (4 pages); interpretive booklet (4 pages); $20 per examiner's kit of 25 tests, 25 protocol booklets, 25 interpretive booklets, and manual; $6.50 per 25 copies of either test, protocol booklet, or interpretive booklet; $6 per manual; postpaid; [5-10] minutes; William H. Urban; Western Psychological Services. *

[210]

★The Driscoll Play Kit. Ages 2-10; 1952; personality development and adjustment; individual; 1 form (5 dolls and 27 pieces of furniture); manual (6 pages); no scoring or interpretive procedure; $59 per set of materials, postpaid; manual free; administration time not reported; Gertrude P. Driscoll; Psychological Corporation. *

REFERENCES

1. BOOKBINDER, KATHRYN F. *The Relation of Social Status and Punishment as Observed in Stories Obtained With the Driscoll Play-Kit.* Doctor's thesis, Columbia University (New York, N.Y.), 1955. (*DA* 15:1252)

2. MCELVANEY, MURIEL BAKER. *Four Types of Fantasy Aggression in the Response of "Rebellious" and "Submissive" Children to the Driscoll Playkit, Structured by Parental-Demand and Neutral Stimulus Stories.* Doctor's thesis, Columbia University (New York, N.Y.), 1958. (*DA* 19:364)

[211]

The Eight Card Redrawing Test (8CRT). Ages 7 and over; 1950-57; 1 form ('56, 9 pages); manual ('57, see 5 below); directions for administering ('56, 1 page); score sheet ('56, 1 page); no data on reliability; no norms; $6 per set of test materials for 35 administrations; $4 per manual; postpaid; (30-60) minutes; Leopold Caligor; 8CRT. *

REFERENCES

1-6. See 5:131.

Am J Orthopsychiatry 30:213-4 Ja '60. Alfred B. Heilbrun, Jr. * The potential merits of this new projective device have already been mentioned—increased reliability, scoring objectivity, and clinical data—and for these Caligor deserves considerable credit. However, the term "potential" was used to emphasize that none of these innovations can be considered a diagnostic contribution until it is more clearly demonstrated empirically that the human figure drawings obtained on the 8 CRT are related to the behavior of the artist in specifiable ways. It is here that the 8 CRT remains most vulnerable since many suggested test interpretations do not as yet have the solid backing of research validation. It is hoped that the publication of the 8 CRT, with its increased objectivity and reliability, will stimulate such research and more clearly establish the diagnostic utility of the figure drawing technique.

Int J Social Psychiatry 4:73 su '58. * Caligor has invented a scoring system as complicated and meticulous as that of the Rorschach Test. Scoring is expressed in terms of number and constancy of deviations from a statistical norm, the accuracy of which we must take on trust since, although we are told that a population of 7 years to 70 years has been tested to obtain normative data, statistical tables have not yet been provided in the book. Interpretation of this data is admitted by the author to be based upon "extensive clinical experience," not accounted for within the context by any attempt at correlative proof. * Within each measurable dimension lies a complex scale of scoring. It should be emphasized that their value as a reliable measurement of personality depends entirely upon the accuracy of Dr. Caligor's interpretations of each deviation within a category. This is the weakness of a test aiming at objectivity. It is important that we should not be mesmerized by a complexity of figures into believing that a test is therefore necessarily reliable in interpretation. All that is ensured is agreement between the scorers and a measurement of deviation. It is by the accuracy of the original premises that such a test should be judged. Learning how to draw a man, when a child, is so often a matter of copying and of being taught, and carry-over of the learnt pattern so frequent in adult life; that this, with many other cultural and environmental factors, powerful in influencing such a design, is probably all too readily ignored. It is in Dr. Caligor's case illustrations that the extreme subjectivity of this test is revealed. Although there is much with which common sense would agree within them, some will feel that the author strains credulity to breaking-point in his interpretations of minute data.

J Consult Psychol 23:470–1 O '59. Seymour Fisher. * Caligor does refer to three studies which were undertaken for validation purposes, but his descriptions of these studies are extremely brief and it is clear that he did not attempt to test directly the validity of the meanings assigned to the various scoring categories. One can see that his formulations regarding the significance of given variables are based almost entirely on his clinical experiences and that one must accept them on faith. The 8 CRT is presently a collection of hunches that have been formalized by Caligor into a scoring system. Some of his hunches are novel and interesting and may prove eventually to have an enriching effect upon figure drawing analysis. Thus one is particularly impressed with the novelty and potential importance of his emphasis on such factors as spatial directionality (e.g., up vs. down and right vs. left), symmetry, and mode of maintaining continuity from one drawing to another. Overall, though, it must be said that his scoring categories are not bound together by a unifying concept or viewpoint. They seem, on the contrary, to consist of heterogenous "signs" which were assembled in an arbitrary fashion. One must also question the value of Caligor's mode of defining many of the scoring categories. His definitions are often very vague and hazy. Illustratively, he refers to various signs as indicating "anxiety," "conflict," "immaturity," "lowered ability to orient oneself in the environment," "ability to use inner resources," "awareness of objects or other persons in the environment." How much more would one know about a given subject for having acquired such vague bits of information about him? The 8 CRT does indeed present some new ideas about figure drawing analysis, but it lacks the rationale or validation to be considered a formal test.

J Proj Tech 23:472–3 D '59. Emanuel F. Hammer. * a closely-reasoned, soundly-balanced presentation of the newest offspring of the projective drawing family * All in all, if the Eight-Card-Redrawing Test is reserved for subjects who appear to enjoy drawing, a rich yield of data may be expected to be the rule rather than the exception. In my experience, I have not found it often worth the time and effort with subjects who do not like to draw. A task which asks such a subject to draw eight figures, in addition to whatever other drawing techniques have been administered, serves only to irritate and place an undue strain upon rapport. When used with subjects who take to drawing, however, it often proves to be one of the most rewarding diagnostic techniques in the projective drawing battery. Caligor's book does not appear to do full justice to his own technique. The book treats only expressive aspects of drawing (although content is touched upon in the three case studies presented at the end of the book). Thus, what for the reviewer is the real drama of the Eight-Card-Redrawing Technique, the one that lies in the shifts in content as one goes from one drawing to the next, is not given the focus it deserves. The writing style is somewhat academically-toned, and sprinkled with terms like "lowered environmental cognizance" and sentences like: "Long strokes reflect impulsivity-lability in response to anxiety and stimulability-impulsivity to tactile-sensuous needs." In passing, the reviewer might mention that he has been curious, since first learning of the Eight-Card-Redrawing Test procedure, as to why Caligor has formed his technique around eight, rather than five, ten, or some other number of drawings. The answer is not given in the book. An overall impression is that for those who employ drawings in a quantitative way, there is here a ready-made tool for doing research on, or with, drawings—a handy book and kit to have.

For reviews by Cherry Ann Clark and Philip L. Harriman, see 5:131 (1 excerpt).

[212]

★**The Family Relations Indicator: A Projective Technique for Investigating Intra-Family Relationships.** Emotionally disturbed children ages 3–16;

1962; 1 form (33 cards, 13 each for boys and for girls plus 4 for both boys and girls and 3 introductory cards); manual (36 pages); behavior item sheets (2 pages); no data on reliability; 85*s.* per set of cards, 20 behavior item sheets, and manual; 6*s.* per 20 behavior item sheets; 17*s.* per manual; prices include purchase tax; postpaid within U.K.; (20–30) minutes; J. G. Howells and John R. Lickorish; distributed by National Foundation for Educational Research in England and Wales. *

REFERENCES

1. Howells, John G., and Lickorish, John R. "The Family Relations Indicator: A Projective Technique for Investigating Intra-Family Relationships Designed for Use With Emotionally Disturbed Children." *Brit J Ed Psychol* 33:286–96 N '63. * (*PA* 38:8552)

C. B. Blakemore, *Lecturer in Psychology, Institute of Psychiatry, Maudsley Hospital, University of London, London, England.*

The authors of this new projective technique, a psychiatrist and a psychologist working in a child psychiatry unit in England, justify their development of yet another test on the grounds that, unlike the majority of alternative tests of this type, it is free from any marked theoretical or psychoanalytic bias. Their aim is to investigate intrafamily relationships that may be involved in the difficulties experienced by an emotionally disturbed child. The theoretical position they adopt is that the child "will ascribe to the figures in the given pictures such actions, attitudes and sayings as are drawn from his own immediate experience."

The test itself consists of a set of cards on each of which is a drawing showing a simple family scene. Each child is shown 20 of the 33 cards making up the set, the selection depending on the child's sex, and is asked to describe in each case what is happening in the scene. The first 3 cards are "warm-up" presentations and are not scored; the remaining 17 cards depict the following six family situations: child and father, child and mother, child alone, child and baby, siblings together, and parents both alone and in the company of children. The stories produced by the child are scored according to their content of expressed attitudes and actions within the family setting. The scoring sheet enables the examiner to evaluate each of the six basic family relationships in terms of such categories as attitudes, verbalisations, actions, deprivations, delinquency, and guilt feelings.

There are no data available on the reliability of either the child's performance or the examiner's analysis and scoring of the stories. The only validation study so far reported is on 50 emotionally disturbed children between the ages of 6 and 17 years, ranging in IQ from 67 to 136. The findings from this study claim a high degree of agreement between a psychologist's assessment of intrafamily relationships on the basis of the test, and a psychiatrist's assessment of these relationships on the basis of clinical interviews. There is, however, the possibility of criterion contamination here, for the psychiatrist had some knowledge of the test findings before he completed his assessment.

It would seem reasonable to conclude that before we can regard the *Family Relations Indicator* as being of any greater value than other projective techniques of a similar type, more work needs to be done on the collection of normative and standardization data, on the assessment of reliability, and on further validation studies. It would be surprising if the test proved to be any more successful than its predecessors when such information is available.

Walter Katkovsky, *Associate Professor of Psychology, Fordham University, New York, New York.*

Several distinctive features of the FRI are noted by the authors in their manual. These are as follows: (*a*) the pictures were designed specifically to depict a series of family situations familiar to children of school age with typical family members represented; (*b*) they differ from many other popular projective tests, such as the *Symonds Picture-Story Test* and the *Object Relations Technique,* in that they are suitable for young children; (*c*) they are less structured than the pictures of Jackson's *Test of Family Attitudes* and the *Michigan Picture Test;* and (*d*) they are not based on a single personality theory as is the case with the *Blacky Pictures*. Associated with the last point is the fact that the information sought by the FRI consists of "behavioral units" or descriptive categories of behavior which the child attributes to the characters in the pictures. These "information units" are relatively concrete, specific dimensions, and they may prove useful for clinical purposes as well as for investigating hypotheses derived from diverse personality theories. In addition, the specificity of the information sought by the FRI constitutes a less ambitious aim than that of tests which use more abstract dimensions and purport to measure the overall personality of the child. This specificity promises greater hope of obtaining validity data than is true for many projective tests.

Apart from the above positive features, the test's present stage of development leaves much to be desired. The manual indicates the authors' awareness of the importance of specifying the purpose of the test, presenting standardized instructions, describing scoring methods, and providing data on the test's utility. Yet each of these matters goes begging for clarification and more specific information.

The purpose of the test cited by the authors is "to provide a description of the relations between the various members of the patient's family" and "to provide factual information about the family." At the same time, the authors note that information provided by the test reflects the patient's own attitude toward the family, i.e., the family situation as the patient sees it. There is no attempt to deal with the question of differentiating between the "factual" and the attitudinal. The authors pay only cursory attention to the point that use of a projective approach to gain factual material is inconsistent with the typical assumption that projective tests measure phantasy rather than real life experiences, and to the possibility that there may be better methods of obtaining factual data than by asking children to describe pictures. The assumption that the test responses "are drawn from his [the child's] own immediate experience" avoids the question of whether the responses depict actual experiences or reflect the child's wishes, needs, fears, or misperceptions, and promotes the possibility that responses will be interpreted erroneously as actual characteristics of the family situation. The meaning of the responses to the pictures needs clarification in line with empirical data.

While standardized instructions for administration are presented, several suggested practices may introduce variations in the responses obtained by different administrators. The authors state that cards relevant to a figure who is not part of the child's family constellation should be omitted. This practice provides one subject with less opportunity to respond than another subject. Several of the responses in the manual indicate that the child referred to a family figure not depicted in the picture he was shown. Consequently, it seems likely that cards showing figures who are not a part of the child's family may elicit material about actual family members. Would it not be more systematic to present the same number of cards to all subjects and merely ignore responses inapplicable to the subject's family situation than to vary the number of pictures used? Another inconsistency is introduced when a figure depicted in the picture is misperceived. Two instances of this are present in the responses in the manual: a mother was perceived as a "little girl" and a girl was referred to as a boy. Such misperceptions, which are apt to be frequent with young children, subtract from the standardization of the test stimuli. Perhaps they could be minimized if the administrator briefly described the figures as he presented each picture. Still another possible administrative variation may occur in connection with encouraging elaboration of responses. The authors prefer spontaneous responses, but the use of such questions as "What do you think he is saying?" and "Can you tell me any more?" are left to the judgment of the administrator. Lack of systematic questioning, even with such general leads, may result in different administrators obtaining different responses.

No data are presented on interscorer reliability and two points seem likely to operate against agreement. Only one set of responses is presented as scoring examples and these are insufficient to serve as operational definitions of the many scoring categories, most of which are not defined. Such scoring categories as "suspicious," "apathetic," "deceitful" need elaboration. The second criticism pertains to a summary scoring approach in which severity of a reaction of parents to the child is distinguished from the mere presence of that reaction, but no criterion is given for making this distinction.

A final criticism is with the lack of objective data on the FRI. The authors state the unwarranted belief that split-half and test-retest reliability are inapplicable or impractical with respect to the test and that a reliability check must await development of a parallel set of pictures. They report that the test has been given to over 500 children, but data on the responses of this group are not presented. One validity study is cited in which 80 to 90 per cent of the descriptions of parent-child relationships suggested by the tests on 50 children were consistent with a psychiatrist's judgments concerning the parent-child relationships based on his extensive knowledge of the family situation. The significance of these data is weakened, however, because the psychiatrist had knowledge of the test results prior to the time he made his judgments.

In summary, it should be noted that the FRI consists of two things, a new set of pictures and a scoring system. Depending on the examiner's purpose and preference, the pictures may prove to be useful stimuli in assessing a child's attitudes, feelings, phantasies, and experiences relative to his family members. In the absence of norms and reliability and validity data, however, the pictures should be considered adjunctive stimuli to a clinical interview rather than a test. The scoring system proposed by the authors needs elaboration and evidence of interscorer reliability. Nevertheless, categorizing responses into units of behavior is a practice which allows for both specificity and flexibility and has promise for the clinician and researcher using projective stimuli with children.

[213]

***Four Picture Test (1930), Second Edition.** Ages 10 and over; 1948–58; 1 form ('58, 4 cards); manual ('58, 15 pages); no data on reliability and validity; no norms; gld. 38 ($10) per set of cards and manual, postpaid; (30–45) minutes; D. J. van Lennep and R. Houwink (manual); publisher and distributor in Holland and Belgium: Netherlands Institute of Industrial Psychology; distributor in all other countries: Martinus Nijhoff. *

REFERENCES

1–3. See 4:105.
4. SHNEIDMAN, EDWIN S. "The Case of Jay: Psychological Test and Anamnestic Data." *J Proj Tech* 16:297–345 S '52. * (*PA* 28:2676)
5. SHNEIDMAN, EDWIN S., EDITOR. "The TAT Newsletter, Vol. 6, No. 1, Summer 1952." *J Proj Tech* 16:260–5 Je '52. *
6. SPIEGELMAN, MARVIN. "Jungian Theory and the Analysis of Thematic Tests." *J Proj Tech* 19:253–63 S '55. * (*PA* 30:4601)

S. G. LEE, *Professor of Psychology, University of Leicester, Leicester, England.*

The four pictures comprising this test are executed in a fairly subtle wash, browns and greens predominating. They represent *"four fundamental existential situations"*: (*a*) being with one other person (two men in a room, a table between them); (*b*) being personally alone (a bedroom with the possible outline of a head on the pillow); (*c*) being socially alone (a man standing under a street lamp in the rain); and (*d*) being with many others in a group (spectators and players at a tennis court). The subject is required to write a single story incorporating all four situations.

Certain advantages accrue from this "four-in-one" technique. (*a*) The story tends to cover a greater time span in its content than would, say, a TAT protocol. This can be revealing in terms of, e.g., long term solutions of conflict situations envisaged by the subject. (*b*) More measurable formal characteristics are found in the structuring of the one story from the four stimuli and this increases the possibilities of the test as a diagnostic or taxonomic device. (*c*) Story material connecting the pictures is likely to be projective material that is less stimulus bound—"concept-dominated" rather than "picture-dominated." (*d*) Time taken in administration and scoring is relatively short.

The pictures are unaltered in this second edition of the test, but the accompanying manual is greatly changed. Twenty-two pages of illustrative protocols and analyses have been omitted, together with nearly all the theoretical discussion. The emphasis on order of the pictures in the story is missing. All normative data have been left out and the user is left to apply his own methods of analysis or personality theory to whatever results he may obtain. The acquisition of group norms on which to base any theory is recommended and there is, in contrast to the first edition, no special demand for clinical intuition. Compare the 1958 manual's statement, "Only if comparable (matched) group samples are available, significant differences can be studied," with the following from the 1948 manual: "The understanding is effected in a 'hermeneutical circle,' i.e., each separate expression can only be understood from the composite expressions, and the composite only by way of each separate expression. One has to enter the circle somewhere and must continually confront part and whole with each other in order to arrive at a feeling of evidence. Only a trained psychologist with intuition and experience can have good results."

In brief, this is a manual very slight in content, much more conservative and limited than its predecessor. As an example, one of the most valuable emphases in the test, stressed in the first edition, is on the analysis of formal variables. In the 1958 edition the discussion of these is limited to some three hundred words, anything but exhaustive, and no indication is given of the kind of conclusions to be drawn under such headings as "Style variables proper" or "The writer's attitude towards his own story." In many ways this change would seem to be a pity, for, though the original manual was more controversial in many of its statements, it was fertile in ideas and hypotheses.

The cost of cards and manual has been reduced from $16.90 in 1953 to $10 in 1963. This is an improvement, though your reviewer would regard the first edition as the "better buy." But the second edition is still, for the materials and size of the manual, a very expensive test. In a review excerpted in *The Fourth Mental Measurements Yearbook* (see 4:105) from the *TAT Newsletter,* Robert R. Holt states that he had been assured by the author that "the unusual cost of producing exact duplicates of the original watercolor pictures makes it impossible to market the test [the first edition] for less." This does not carry conviction in the light of recent advances in colour reproduction and the statement in the present manual that the test can be used for groups "if a good colored slide is available." Slight colour changes would not appear likely to alter responses significantly.

Your reviewer has used the test for some years and has found that significant intraperson correlations (in terms of rank orders of need scores) can often be obtained between scores on the FPT and on a complete TAT. The test is a useful one for "main needs" in a personality and will often throw considerable light on environmental pressures on the subject. But two disadvantages should be mentioned. In the description of the pictures above I have used the words "men" and "man" for pictures (*a*) and (*c*). While the figures are blurred it has been my experience that practically all subjects see them as male and here doubts may arise as to the comparability of results from male and female subjects. With the latter, "hero" identification is often very awkward. Again, to many adult subjects the pictures carry a definite atmosphere of the 1920's (e.g., in the "tennis" picture the men are wearing long white flannel trousers), and this can on occasion lead to very flippant stories. While this is doubtless of significance it makes the evaluation of some results very difficult.

However, probably the most cheering paragraph in the whole manual is: "For a period of ten years, a great deal of research has been done on the various variables which can be isolated in FPT protocols. In a study of over 4,000 protocols of normal and abnormal subjects, it has been found possible to isolate over 150 different variables, which lend themselves to more or less objective scoring and which were found to have certain diagnostic importance. The results and statistics of this research cannot be given within the framework of this manual but are to be published at a later date in a book on the Four Picture Test."

Such a book may well prove to be a landmark in the history of projective tests. It should, especially when it is available in English, add incalculably to the value of the *Four Picture Test.*

Johann M. Schepers, *Senior Research Officer, National Institute for Personnel Research, Johannesburg, Republic of South Africa.*

The *Four Picture Test* (FPT) belongs to the general class of projective techniques known as "picture-thematic" tests. It consists of four colored plates, representative of the following four "existential situations": (*a*) being with one other person (two people of ambiguous sex conversing in a room); (*b*) being personally alone (a bedroom scene with no human form visible); (*c*) being socially alone (a lone figure standing against a lamppost in the rain); (*d*) being with many others in a group (a tennis match in progress with four spectators in the foreground).

It is doubtful whether anything has been gained by having the plates produced in color. Color might well constitute a handicap for the colorblind, or else exert a differential influence on their responses. Reproduction in color is also much more costly. It is unlikely that the smudgy use of watercolor has contributed much to the claimed polyvalence of the pictures.

The four plates are presented to the testee simultaneously and in some prearranged serial order. After a lapse of one minute the plates are removed and the testee is requested to *write* a single story, incorporating all four plates. The testee is urged to decide on his own serial order and to write a unified story using all four plates if possible. The authors claim that by requesting a single story, the testee is forced to "historialize" the hero over a longer period of time and so give richer projective material. This constitutes a definite advantage. The test is inherently limited, however, by virtue of the fact that it comprises one item only. Other rival themes might be prevented from showing up under this condition of administration. The solution, of course, is to have more pictures.

The test is untimed, but on the average takes from half an hour to three quarters of an hour to administer. Group administration of the test is also possible, but it is not advisable to have more than about 30 subjects in a group.

It is possible to introduce variations in the instructions of the FPT in order to elicit further projective material. For instance, after the subject has written his ordinary story, he can be asked to write another story in which one of the female figures at the tennis court plays the leading role. It is also possible to fix the serial order of the plates and have the subject relate a story which fits that particular order of the plates. The standardized instruction given in the manual might prove too difficult for subjects of low educational achievement and might well be rewritten in basic English. The authors claim that written protocols are richer in content than ones produced orally, but it is doubtful whether this is true of subjects of borderline intelligence or, for that matter, of psychotics.

In a study of more than 4,000 protocols of both normal and abnormal subjects, the authors have isolated more than 150 different variables which "lend themselves to more or less objective scoring." No attempt, however, is made to introduce the test user to the objective scoring system. There is a promise of a book on the FPT to be published at a later date, but this is no justification for omitting the scoring system from the manual. Some information about the interscorer reliability of the test ought to be given.

The variables isolated can be divided into content variables and formal variables. No information regarding the diagnostic value of these variables is given and, except for a few examples, no interpretive hints are given. The 20 pages on interpretation given in the first edition of the manual have been omitted from the second edition. No illustrative protocols are given and no mention is made of the time or space quality of the stories. In short, the present edition is less satisfactory than the first.

It can be reasonably expected of a test author to give the following information in a test manual: a brief rationale of the test, a standard instruction, a scoring system, an interpretive technique, and normative data. Test-retest reliability, and validity coefficients are minimal requirements on the statistical side. To be really useful, norms ought to be stratified in terms of age, level of education, and intelligence. Pathological indications ought to be given at a certain level of confidence. Judged in the light of the above criteria, the FPT falls far short of the ideal. The FPT is a one-item test and can at most serve as a rough screening device. By contrast, the *Tomkins-Horn Picture Arrangement Test* meets most of the above mentioned criteria and is favored by the present reviewer.

For reviews by John E. Bell, E. J. G. Bradford, and Ephraim Rosen of the original edition, see 4:105 (1 excerpt).

[214]

★The Group Personality Projective Test. Ages 12 and over; 1956–61; formerly called *Kahn Stick Figure Personality Test;* 7 scores: tension reduction quotient, nurturance, withdrawal, neuroticism, affiliation, succorance, total; IBM; 1 form ('58, 17 pages); manual ('61, 20 pages, reprint of *4* below); directions for interpretation ('60, 2 pages); separate answer sheets must be used; $13.50 per examiner's kit of 12 tests, 100 IBM answer-profile sheets, set of scoring stencils, and manual; $2 per manual; cash orders postpaid; specimen set not available; (40–45) minutes; Russell N. Cassel and Theodore C. Kahn; Psychological Test Specialists. *

REFERENCES

1. KAHN, THEODORE C., AND CASSEL, RUSSELL N. "Development and Validation of the Group Personality Projective Test." Abstract. *Am Psychologist* 12:389 Jl '57. *

2. CASSEL, RUSSELL N., AND BRAUCHLE, ROBERT P. "An Assessment of the Fakability of Scores on the Group Personality Projective Test." *J Genetic Psychol* 95:239–44 D '59. *

3. CASSEL, RUSSELL N., AND HARRIMAN, B. LYNN. "A Comparative Analysis of Personality and Ego Strength Test Scores for In-Prison, Neuro-Psychiatric and Typical Individuals." *J Ed Res* 53:43–52 O '59. * (*PA* 35:810)

4. CASSEL, R. N., AND KAHN, T. C. "The Group Personality Projective Test (GPPT)." *Psychol Rep* 8:23–41 F '61. * (*PA* 36:1HB23C)

5. CASSEL, RUSSELL N., AND HADDOX, GENEVIEVE. "Comparing Reading Competency With Personality and Social Insight Test Scores." *Calif J Ed Res* 12:27–30 Ja '61. * (*PA* 36:1KJ27C)

6. LANGE, MERLE LEROY. *A Comparative Analysis of Achieving and Under-Achieving Twelfth Grade Students of Phoenix Central High School on the Non-Intellectual Factors of the Group Personality Projective Test and the Test of Social Insight.* Doctor's research study No. 1, Colorado State College (Greeley, Colo.), 1962. (*DA* 23:3778)

7. CASSEL, RUSSELL, AND CHILDERS, RICHARD. "A Study of Certain Attributes of 45 High-School Varsity Football Team Members by Use of Psychological Test Scores." *J Ed Res* 57:64–7 O '63. *

[215]

***H-T-P: House-Tree-Person Projective Technique.** Ages 3 and over; 1946–64; 1 form ['46, 4 pages]; manual ('48, see *6*); supplement ('64, 119 pages, including copies of drawing form, interrogation folders, and scoring folder); interrogation folder: adult form ('50), children's form ('56), (4 pages); scoring folder ('50, 4 pages); two-copy drawing form ('64); adult norms only; $4 per 25 drawing forms; $6.50 per 25 interrogation folders; $6.50 per 25 scoring folders; $6.50 per 25 two-copy drawing forms; $4 per manual; $5 per supplement; postage extra; specimen set not available; (60–90) minutes; John N. Buck and

Isaac Jolles (children's interrogation folder); Western Psychological Services. *

REFERENCES

1–5. See 3:47.
6–19. See 4:107.
20–80. See 5:139.
81. KLINE, MILTON V., AND GUZE, HENRY. "The Use of a Drawing Technique in the Investigation of Hypnotic Age Regression and Progression." *Brit J Med Hypnosis* 3:10–21 w '51. *
82. SCHNECK, JEROME, AND KLINE, MILTON V. "A Control Study Relating to H-T-P Testing and Hypnosis." *Brit J Med Hypnosis* 3:3–11 au '51. *
83. SCHNECK, JEROME, AND KLINE, MILTON V. "The H-T-P and TAT Hypnodiagnostic Studies." *Brit J Med Hypnosis* 5:3–15 au '53. *
84. BERRYMAN, EILEEN. "The Self-Portrait: A Suggested Extension of the HTP." *Percept & Motor Skills* 9:411–4 D '59. * (*PA* 34:5599)
85. BIELIAUSKAS, VYTAUTAS J., AND BRISTOW, ROBIN B. "The Effect of Formal Art Training Upon the Quantitative Scores of the H-T-P." *J Clin Psychol* 15:57–9 Ja '59. * (*PA* 34:2985)
86. HOYT, THOMAS E., AND BARON, MARTIN R. "Anxiety Indices in Same-Sex Drawings of Psychiatric Patients With High and Low MAS Scores." *J Consult Psychol* 23:448–52 O '59. * (*PA* 34:5622)
87. ORGEL, RITA G. "The Relationship of the H-T-P to a Sociometric Evaluation of a Group of Primary Grade School Children in Determining the Degree of Social Acceptance." *J Clin Psychol* 15:222–3 Ap '59. * (*PA* 35:4691)
88. SILVERMAN, LLOYD H. "A Q-Sort Study of the Validity of Evaluations Made From Projective Techniques." *Psychol Monogr* 73(7):1–28 '59. * (*PA* 34:3030)
89. STRUMPFER, DEODANDUS JOHANN WILLHELM. *A Study of Some Communicable Measures for the Evaluation of Human Figure Drawings.* Doctor's thesis, Purdue University (Lafayette, Ind.), 1959. (*DA* 20:2910)
90. BIELIAUSKAS, VYTAUTAS J. "Sexual Identification in Children's Drawings of Human Figure." *J Clin Psychol* 16:42–4 Ja '60. * (*PA* 36:1HE42B)
91. BIELIAUSKAS, VYTAUTAS J., AND HEFFRON, ANN R. "Differences in Performance on the Chromatic vs. Achromatic H-T-P Drawings." *J Clin Psychol* 16:334–5 Jl '60. * (*PA* 36:2HC34B)
92. HAMMER, EMANUEL F. "An Exploratory Investigation of the Personalities of Creative Adolescent Students." Discussion by Margaret Naumberg. *Studies Art Ed* 1:42–72 sp '60. *
93. HAMMER, EMANUEL F. "The House-Tree-Person (H-T-P) Drawings as a Projective Technique With Children," pp. 258–72. In *Projective Techniques With Children.* Edited by Albert I. Rabin and Mary R. Haworth. New York: Grune & Stratton, Inc., 1960. Pp. xiii, 392. * (*PA* 35:2229)
94. JUDSON, ABE J., AND MACCASLAND, BARBARA W. "A Note on the Influence of the Season on Tree Drawings." *J Clin Psychol* 16:171–3 Ap '60. * (*PA* 36:2HE71J)
95. LAIR, CHARLES V., AND TRAPP, E. PHILIP. "Performance Decrement on the H-T-P Test as a Function of Adjustment Level." *J Clin Psychol* 16:431 O '60. * (*PA* 37:3260)
96. P'SIMER, CHRISTINE. "The House-Tree-Person Test: A Case Study." *Personnel & Guid J* 38:574–6 Mr '60. *
97. SANTORUM, ALDO. "A Cross-Validation of the House-Tree-Person Drawing Indices Predicting Hospital Discharge of Tuberculosis Patients." *J Consult Psychol* 24:400–2 O '60. * (*PA* 35:4966)
98. BIELIAUSKAS, VYTAUTAS J., AND MOENS, JOSÉE F. "An Investigation of the Validity of the H-T-P as an Intelligence Test for Children." *J Clin Psychol* 17:178–80 Ap '61. * (*PA* 38:951)
99. DIGIAMMO, JOHN J., AND EBINGER, RONALD D. "The New-Weighted H-T-P Score as a Measure of Abstraction." *J Clin Psychol* 17:55 Ja '61. * (*PA* 37:3125)
100. JOHNSON, ORVAL G., AND WAWRZASZEK, FRANK. "Psychologists' Judgments of Physical Handicap From H-T-P Drawings." *J Consult Psychol* 25:284–7 Ag '61. * (*PA* 37:1598)
101. MEYER, BERNARD C.; BLACHER, RICHARD S.; AND BROWN, FRED. "A Clinical Study of Psychiatric and Psychological Aspects of Mitral Surgery." *Psychosom Med* 23:194–218 My–Je '61. *
102. SAUNDERS, MAUDERIE HANCOCK. *An Analysis of Cultural Differences on Certain Projective Techniques.* Doctor's thesis, University of Oklahoma (Norman, Okla.), 1961. (*DA* 22:490)
103. CASSEL, ROBERT H.; JOHNSON, ANNA P.; AND BURNS, WILLIAM H. "The Order of Tests in the Battery." *J Clin Psychol* 18:464–5 O '62. * (*PA* 39:5042)
104. MOLL, RICHARD P. "Further Evidence of Seasonal Influences on Tree Drawings." *J Clin Psychol* 18:109 Ja '62. * (*PA* 38:8393)
105. WEBSTER, RAYMOND B. "The Effects of Hypnosis on Performance on the H-T-P and MPS." *Int J Clin & Exp Hypnosis* 10:151–3 Jl '62. * (*PA* 37:5245)
106. BARNOUW, VICTOR. Chap. 17, "Drawing Analysis," pp. 276–98. In his *Culture and Personality.* Homewood, Ill.: Dorsey Press, Inc., 1963. Pp. xi, 410. *
107. BIELIAUSKAS, VYTAUTAS J. *The House-Tree-Person (H-T-P) Research Review.* Beverly Hills, Calif.: Western Psychological Services, 1963. Pp. 50. *
108. CALLAN, SHEILA, AND DERRICK, NOEL. "An Investigation of the Effect of Seasonal Changes in the Environment on the Tree Drawings of Hospitalized and Non-Hospitalized Groups." *Ont Hosp Psychol B* 8:1–6 Ag '63. *
109. COPPINGER, NEIL W.; BORTNER, RAYMAN W.; AND SAUCER, RAYFORD T. "A Factor Analysis of Psychological Deficit." *J Genetic Psychol* 103:23–43 S '63. * (*PA* 39:174)
110. MCHUGH, ANN F. "H-T-P Proportion and Perspective in Negro, Puerto Rican, and White Children." *J Clin Psychol* 19:312–3 Jl '63. *
111. STRUMPFER, D. J. W. "The Relation of Draw-A-Person Test Variables to Age and Chronicity in Psychotic Groups." *J Clin Psychol* 19:208–11 Ap '63. * (*DA* 39:5102)
112. WILDMAN, ROBERT W. "The Relationship Between Knee and Arm Joints on Human Figure Drawings and Paranoid Trends." *J Clin Psychol* 19:460–1 O '63. *

MARY R. HAWORTH, *Associate Professor of Medical Psychology, University of Nebraska College of Medicine, Omaha, Nebraska.*

In essence, this projective technique involves asking the subject to draw first a house, then a tree, and finally a person. The drawings are subsequently evaluated and analyzed for dynamic information relative to personality variables and interactions of the subject with his environment. When this procedure was first formalized in 1948 its purpose was two-fold: a measure of intelligence and a projective tool. Through the years the use of this test for estimating intellectual level has probably diminished to the vanishing point. The nine pages of minute scoring criteria (descriptive and diagrammatic) are so detailed, qualified, and ambiguous that the reliability of scoring is questionable, and no data are offered on this aspect. The time spent in such scoring would be better spent in administering a standard intelligence test.

The H-T-P technique undoubtedly finds its greatest use as a projective instrument with the qualitative interpretations derived therefrom being largely dependent on the clinical acumen, experience, and orientation of the examiner. Buck's original manual (*6*) and publications by Hammer (*58*) and Jolles (*25*) offer numerous interpretive hypotheses for the various drawn details and such overall aspects as proportion, perspective, page placement, and line quality. While very little experimental data can be marshaled in support of such interpretations, nevertheless these publications do serve to make explicit many inferences frequently made by clinicians in interpreting the meaning of drawings. The authors do caution against placing undue significance on individual, isolated items or details without consideration of the total constellation of all three drawings.

According to those who have done the most work with this technique, not only should achromatic drawings be obtained but also a second chromatic set. A structured inquiry should also be conducted. Again, it is questionable whether these procedures have found general clinical adoption. The standard inquiry questions (both the adult and child forms) are highly redundant and repetitive, and many of them do not appear to yield really useful clinical data. Others seem to be "loaded" in a definite direction by their very wording, e.g., "Is the tree alive?" which is soon followed by "Is any part of the tree dead?"; or "Is there a wind blowing?" In giving this test to children, this reviewer has found that most of their responses to the inquiry questions have been rather colorless and lacking in meaningful material, although occasionally a child will use one or several questions as a springboard into a world of dynamic fantasy.

The most recent research studies designed to test various hypotheses connected with the H-T-P's rationale have generally reported non-significant findings. This may not so much reflect on any defects in this particular technique but, rather, the usual methodological difficulties encountered when trying to evaluate the reliability and validity of projective instruments. In spite of such unrewarding findings, "clinical" clinicians will continue to use those projective devices which they have found to be most helpful in making personality appraisals.

Variations in the H-T-P are often employed and the test can be blended with the *Machover Draw-A-Person Test* by the additional request to draw a person of the opposite sex after the first human figure. Also there is no reason why one could not, after the usual Machover drawing test, ask for drawings of a house and a tree, if it becomes evident that rich and meaningful material is being elicited in the drawing medium. Certainly drawing techniques generally have been found to serve as a good introduction to testing sessions, reducing anxiety (usually) and facilitating a transition to more verbal tasks. They are also extremely useful for non-verbal subjects, those with speech defects, and the deaf (so long as the instructions can be communicated to the patient). Obviously in such special cases the inquiry must be dispensed with.

Most clinicians would agree that drawings should not be the only projective tool in the test battery, which view is concurred in by those most closely identified with the H-T-P.

In summary, the H-T-P is now, and no doubt will continue to be, used as a rewarding clinical technique in work with both adults and children. The amount of meaningful projective data to be derived from the drawings (and the inquiry, if used) will depend on the experience and orientation of the clinician. The test can serve as a non-threatening "opener" before more formal testing and has usefulness with speech handicapped patients. Too literal interpretation of specific details is to be avoided. Rather, as Buck himself states in the manual, the H-T-P "is intended to be used as a procedure to facilitate the clinician's acquisition of diagnostically significant data."

For a review by Philip L. Harriman, see 5:139; for reviews by Albert Ellis and Ephraim Rosen, see 4:107 (1 excerpt); for reviews by Morris Krugman and Katherine W. Wilcox, see 3:47; for excerpts from related book reviews, see 5:B234.

[216]

★**The Hand Test.** Ages 6 and over; 1959–62; 10 normed scores: interpersonal, environmental, maladjustive, withdrawal, affection-dependence-communication, direction-aggression, total responses, average initial response time, highest minus lowest response time, pathological; 1 form ('59, 10 cards); scoring sheet ['62, 2 pages]; manual ('62, 65 pages); reliability data for pathological score only; $3 per set of cards; $1 per pad of scoring sheets; $3.50 per manual; postage extra; (10) minutes; Edwin E. Wagner; Mark James Co., Publishers. *

REFERENCES

1. WAGNER, EDWIN E. "The Use of Drawings of Hands as a Projective Medium for Differentiating Normals and Schizophrenics." *J Clin Psychol* 17:279–80 Jl '61. * (*PA* 38:8572)
2. BRICKLIN, BARRY; PIOTROWSKI, ZYGMUNT A.; AND WAGNER, EDWIN E. *The Hand Test: A New Projective Test With Special Reference to the Prediction of Overt Behavior.* Springfield, Ill.: Charles C Thomas, Publisher, 1962. Pp. x, 100. * (*PA* 37:1191)
3. WAGNER, EDWIN E. "The Use of Drawings of Hands as a Projective Medium for Differentiating Neurotics and Schizophrenics." *J Clin Psychol* 18:208–9 Ap '62. *
4. WAGNER, EDWIN E. "Hand Test Content Indicators of Overt Psychosexual Maladjustment in Neurotic Males." *J Proj Tech & Pers Assess* 27:357–8 S '63. * (*PA* 38:4333)
5. WAGNER, EDWIN E., AND COPPER, JOHN. "Differentiation of Satisfactory and Unsatisfactory Employees at Goodwill Industries With the Hand Test." *J Proj Tech & Pers Assess* 27:354–6 S '63. * (*PA* 38:4334)
6. WAGNER, EDWIN E., AND MEDVEDEFF, EUGENE. "Differentiation of Aggressive Behavior of Institutionalized Schizophrenics With the Hand Test." *J Proj Tech* 27:111–3 Mr '63. * (*PA* 38:1336)

GOLDINE C. GLESER, *Professor of Psychology, University of Cincinnati Medical School, Cincinnati, Ohio.*

The *Hand Test* is a projective technique in which the subject is shown a series of drawings of a hand in various ambiguous poses and asked what the hand might be doing. The last card is blank, requiring the subject to imagine a hand and describe what it is doing. The test is considered to reveal "significant perceptual-motor tendencies" presently available to the person and readily expressed in his interaction with others and with the environment.

The test has many features similar to the Rorschach in that time to initial response, card turning, and verbatim responses are recorded and the subject is allowed, and to some extent encouraged, to give more than one response to a card. However, it differs from the Rorschach in that each response is categorized into one of 15 categories according to content; the frequency of occurrence of varying combinations of these categories provides the summary quantitative scores. Additional qualitative aspects of the response may also be scored and used in clinical interpretation.

Differences in the categorization of responses and in the treatment of scores may be noted between the monograph (*2*) and the manual. These are to be expected since the test is still in the process of development. However, the description of categories and the scoring examples given in the manual are sufficiently clear and detailed to enable other investigators to use them with reasonable expectation of comparable results. Only one study of scorer agreement is reported in which three persons scored 100 protocols. Perfect agreement between two scorers was obtained on between 78 and 83 per cent of all responses. Correlations between scorers are reported for the pathological score only and range from .86 to .96.

The normative data on 1,020 cases are presented in a form which has little merit for interpretative purposes. Medians and interquartile ranges are given on the major scoring categories for 17 so-called populations, including normal adults, college students, children, neurotics, psychotics, mental retardates, and antisocial personalities. The groups differ in age, education, socio-economic background, and race-sex composition. No attempt has been made to determine the variance associated with these factors, other than to note that children and teenagers tend to produce higher "acting-out ratios" than do adults. A much broader stratified sample of normal children and adults is needed to assess these factors and to provide a basis for determining the normal range of response. At present, the only clue as to what constitutes an abnormal number of responses in any particular category is an occasional remark in the text of the manual or the monograph.

No studies of the stability of response patterns have been reported, although interpretations imply that responses are characteristic of the person's action tendencies over some interval of time in the absence of radical changes in the subject's environment. Only the pathological score has been examined from the standpoint of generalizability over stimuli (split-half reliability).

Validity studies to date consist of comparison of samples from populations hypothesized to differ with respect to aggressive acting-out or psychopathology. The pathological score differentiated custodial and ambulatory schizophrenics from all other groups, but the median score of first admission schizophrenics was approximately the same as that for neurotics, depressives, mental retardates, and prison inmates. The acting-out score differentiated prison inmates and "acting-out" hospitalized psychiatric patients from normal adults, indigents, and non-acting-out psychiatric patients. No systematic validation of individual differences within a population has been reported, nor have the scores been compared with scores on other tests purporting to measure similar constructs.

The *Hand Test* appears to have possibilities for development as a quantitative multidimensional clinical test relevant to the overt behavior of individuals. However, its psychometric characteristics are essentially unknown so that a great deal more developmental work is needed in order to shape the technique into a measuring instrument rather than a springboard for metaphorical interpretations. Several aspects of the format and administration should be examined for possible improvement. First of all, one wonders to what extent certain maladjustive responses are due to the inadequacies of the original sketches, many of which are so poorly inked as to appear distorted or grotesque. Secondly, additional stimuli should be used in order to obtain a reliable sample of an individual's response tendencies with respect to the 15 categories. Permitting more than one response to a card is not an adequate solution to this problem since additional responses tend to depend more on extraneous factors than on the "total stock of psychic tendencies" of the subject. Furthermore, any advantages which may accrue from allowing number of responses to vary are far outweighed by the disadvantages of handling and interpreting scores, as has been amply demonstrated with the Rorschach. The test at present is of use primarily to those who are interested in further research and development of this technique.

J Proj Tech 26:490–1 D '62. Irving R. Stone. * Wagner's test consists of a series of ten cards on nine of which a hand has been drawn. The last card is blank, very much like that of card 16 on the TAT. The cards are presented one at a time and the subject is asked to tell what the hands are doing. For the last card, the subject is asked to imagine a hand and tell what it is doing. Responses are recorded verbatim along with initial response times per card. The responses are then scored and interpreted in accordance with a somewhat formal and a bit involved procedure. The test, to some extent, represents a cross between the Rorschach in its scoring, timing, observation of card turning, and interpretation and the TAT in the form of its responses and the possibility of analysis and interpretation without some of the need for formal scoring. Too, the scoring resembles some factors of those of Murray and Tomkins in that we find scoring compartmentalization into affection, dependence, communication, exhibition, direction, aggression, acquisition, active, passive, tension, crippled, fear, description, bizarre, and failure. The author states that the test can be administered in about ten minutes, scored in about five, that it is completely nonthreatening and can be easily administered to depressed, deteriorated and hostile subjects. Norms, based upon more than 1,000 protocols, from six years of age and up are included. Reliability was based on the independent scoring of three graduate student scorers of 100 protocols and ranged from .86 to .96. The author recognizes that in the development of the protocols for the total 1,020 cases the subjects mostly resided in Ohio at the time of testing, that the N's are low in some categories, and that the seventeen groups of scoring categories are only the major but not the total of those possible. The drawings are fairly clear but some may lend themselves to misinterpretation (possibly pictures of hands would have been clearer), the manual is clear and complete, and the one sheet scoring blank which has on one side space for recording the initial response time, the responses, and the scoring for each card, and on the reverse side the summary sheet containing the name, address, and other identifying information as well as the ratios, qualitative and administrative observations, case history and diagnostic data, and diagnosis appears to be well-developed. Even though administrative and scoring time would have been extended, it might have been useful to have included some additional cards in which two hands were in some form of relationship. It is hoped that the author will experiment with this to determine whether further development of affectional relationships could be elicited. *

For an excerpt from a related book review, see B95.

[217]

***The Holtzman Inkblot Technique.** Ages 5 and over; 1958–61; individual; 22 scores: reaction time, rejections, location, space, form definiteness, form appropriateness, color, shading, movement, pathognomic verbalization, integration, content (human, animal, anatomy, sex, abstract), anxiety, hostility, barrier, penetration, balance, populars; Forms A, B, ('58, 47 cards); manual ('61, 423 pages, see 7 below); administration and scoring guide ('61, c1958–61, 171 pages, reprinted in part from manual); record form ('58, 8 pages) for each form; summary sheet ('58, 2 pages); $26 per set of cards for either form, 25 record forms, and administration and scoring guide; $46 per set of cards and accessories for both forms; $2.75 per 25 record forms and scoring sheets; $3 per administration and scoring guide; $8 per manual; postpaid; (75) minutes; Wayne H. Holtzman, Joseph S. Thorpe (manual), Jon D. Swartz (manual), and E. Wayne Herron (manual); Psychological Corporation. *

REFERENCES

1. HOLTZMAN, WAYNE H. "Development of an Experimental Inkblot Test, a New Departure From the Rorschach." Abstract. *Am Psychologist* 11:400 Ag '56. *

2. SANDERS, ELLA MOYE. *The Relationship Between Verbal-Quantitative Ability and Certain Personality and Metabolic Characteristics.* Doctor's thesis, University of Texas (Austin, Tex.), 1958. (*DA* 19:2540)

3. YOUNG, HARL H. "Relationships Between and Reliability Estimates of New (Holtzman) Ink Blot Variables and Conventional Rorschach Scoring Categories." *Proc Okla Acad Sci* 38: 111–5 D '58. *

4. SANDERS, ELLA M.; MEFFERD, ROY B., JR.; AND BOWN, OLIVER H. "Verbal-Quantitative Ability and Certain Personality and Metabolic Characteristics of Male College Students." *Ed & Psychol Meas* 20:491–503 au '60. * (*PA* 35:3550)

5. SIMKINS, LAWRENCE. "Examiner Reinforcement and Situational Variables in a Projective Testing Situation." *J Consult Psychol* 24:541–7 D '60. * (*PA* 36:1HG41S)

6. BARGER, PATRICIA M., AND SECHREST, LEE. "Convergent and Discriminant Validity of Four Holtzman Inkblot Test Variables." *J Psychol Studies* 12:227–36 N '61 [issued Ap '63]. *

7. HOLTZMAN, WAYNE H.; THORPE, JOSEPH S.; SWARTZ, JON D.; AND HERRON, E. WAYNE. *Inkblot Perception and*

Personality: Holtzman Inkblot Technique. Published for the Hogg Foundation for Mental Health. Austin, Tex.: University of Texas Press, 1961. Pp. xi, 417. * (*PA* 36:5HB17H)
8. STEFFY, RICHARD A., AND BECKER, WESLEY C. "Measurement of the Severity of Disorder in Schizophrenia by Means of the Holtzman Inkblot Test." Abstract. *J Consult Psychol* 25:555 D '61. * (*PA* 37:5505)
9. BIENEN, SANFORD MORTON. *Verbal Conditioning of Inkblot Responses as a Function of Instructions, Social Desirability, and Awareness.* Doctor's thesis, University of Maryland (College Park, Md.), 1962. (*DA* 24:379)
10. BURKE, MARY. *The Control of Response Choice on Projective Techniques.* Doctor's thesis, University of Denver (Denver, Colo.), 1962. (*DA* 24:2119)
11. HERRON, ELMER WAYNE. *Intellectual Achievement-Motivation: A Study in Construct Clarification.* Doctor's thesis, University of Texas (Austin, Tex.), 1962. (*DA* 23:298)
12. MOSELEY, EDWARD CARLETON. *Psychodiagnosis Based on Multivariate Analysis of the Holtzman Inkblot Technique.* Doctor's thesis, University of Texas (Austin, Tex.), 1962. (*DA* 23:313)
13. HERRON, E. WAYNE. "Psychometric Characteristics of a Thirty-Item Version of the Group Method of the Holtzman Inkblot Technique." *J Clin Psychol* 19:450–3 O '63. *
14. HOLTZMAN, WAYNE H. "Inkblot Perception and Personality: The Meaning of Inkblot Variables." *B Menninger Clinic* 27:84–95 Mr '63. *
15. HOLTZMAN, WAYNE H.; MOSELEY, EDWARD C.; REINEHR, ROBERT C.; AND ABBOTT, ELAINE. "Comparison of the Group Method and the Standard Individual Version of the Holtzman Inkblot Technique." *J Clin Psychol* 19:441–9 O '63. *
16. MOSELEY, E. C.; GORHAM, D. R.; AND HILL, EVELYN. "Computer Scoring of Inkblot Perceptions." Abstract. *Percept & Motor Skills* 17:498 O '63. * (*PA* 38:6097)
17. MOSELEY, EDWARD C. "Psychodiagnosis on the Basis of the Holtzman Inkblot Technique." *J Proj Tech* 27:86–91 Mr '63. * (*PA* 38:1020)
18. MOSELEY, EDWARD C.; DUFFEY, ROBERT F.; AND SHERMAN, LEWIS J. "An Extension of the Construct Validity of the Holtzman Inkblot Technique." *J Clin Psychol* 19:186–92 Ap '63. * (*PA* 39:5083)
19. OTTEN, MARK W., AND VAN DE CASTLE, R. L. "A Comparison of Set 'A' of the Holtzman Inkblots With the Rorschach by Means of the Semantic Differential." *J Proj Tech & Pers Assess* 27:452–60 D '63. * (*PA* 38:8562)
20. PALMER, JAMES O. "Alterations in Rorschach's Experience Balance Under Conditions of Food and Sleep Deprivation: A Construct Validation Study." *J Proj Tech & Pers Assess* 27:208–13 Je '63. * (*PA* 38:2723)
21. SWARTZ, JON D., AND HOLTZMAN, WAYNE H. "Group Method of Administration for the Holtzman Inkblot Technique." *J Clin Psychol* 19:433–41 O '63. *
22. THORPE, JOSEPH S., AND SWARTZ, JON D. "The Roles of Intelligence and Social Status in Rejections on the Holtzman Inkblot Technique." *J Proj Tech & Pers Assess* 27:248–51 Je '63. * (*PA* 38:2728)

RICHARD W. COAN, *Professor of Psychology, University of Arizona, Tucson, Arizona.*

Since the *Holtzman Inkblot Technique* is an application of the Rorschach method to a new set of materials, the judgment of any prospective test user must rest first on his evaluation of this method. Projective tests are often constructed in the hope that a broad range of information can be secured through painstaking analysis of a circumscribed kind of behavior. If our ultimate aim is a procedure for comprehensive personality assessment, it is doubtful that this is the best possible strategy. If we are going to invest much time in examining conceptual responses to inkblots, we must assume that Rorschach's choice of a behavioral bit was an unusually fortunate one.

With respect to the mass of theory which has accrued from its use, the Rorschach technique is unique. The applicability of this theory to a different set of inkblots is open to question. Current Rorschach theory is a complex mixture of logical extrapolations from a body of perceptual and personality theories and *ad hoc* explanations of concomitances noted with varying regularity by Rorschach workers. To the extent that Rorschach theory rests on generally valid principles of perceptual dynamics, it should be applicable to responses elicited by a wide variety of stimulus materials. To the extent that it capitalizes on accidental and unrecognized peculiarities of the Rorschach blots, it will not apply to responses obtained with any other stimuli. And one might add, to the extent that it capitalizes on accidents of observation and case sampling, it may not apply even to the Rorschach blots.

Despite the great number of studies that have been done, research evidence for the validity of Rorschach interpretations is notoriously meager. On the other hand, much of the intended evidence is of doubtful relevance to standard interpretive theory. In deciding whether it is worthwhile to pursue the Rorschach technique further, we must decide whether to give greater heed to the research evidence or to the widespread conviction of clinicians that the technique taps subtle aspects of the personality not subject to a more direct kind of measurement.

If we decide in favor of the technique, we still cannot deny the fact that Rorschach's own work combined theoretical brilliance with methodological naïveté. The test which has evolved from his labors displays an alarming variety of psychometric deficiencies. From the responses to ten blots, one derives a complex set of unreliable and highly interdependent scores, displaying predominantly skewed distributions. All the basic scoring categories display a systematic dependence on overall productivity, even when they are expressed in percentage form.

By far the most satisfactory way of eliminating, or at least minimizing, the psychometric shortcomings, while preserving the basic virtues of the method, is to employ a larger number of blots and secure only one response per blot. This is the solution that Holtzman and his colleagues have adopted. They have produced a richly varied series of blots that yields a wide range of scores with respect to many important aspects of inkblot performance.

The one major Rorschach score category

that is lost in the Holtzman test is productivity. The test provides more satisfactory scaling for all other basic categories. Some of the specific variables of conventional scoring systems have been eliminated from the Holtzman scoring system. There are no "interaction" categories combining determinants with content or form definiteness. Furthermore, no distinction is made between color and achromatic color, among different types of shading responses, or between usual and unusual details. These losses are not irretrievable since any user of the test can add his own score categories and collect fresh standardization data. And as the manual suggests, the interaction categories can be recaptured to an extent by configural scoring of the Holtzman summary sheet.

Some of the departures from convention can be justified in terms of a need for separate quantification of logically independent variables. Some, such as the independent scaling of form definiteness, can be supported in terms of previous statistical findings for the Rorschach. It should also be noted that certain rare features of inkblot response, which do not lend themselves conveniently to quantitative treatment, can best be handled through a detailed analysis of the protocol without formal scoring. Thus, a clinician may secure useful information by noting a particular subject's use of achromatic color. The mere number of achromatic color responses is a relatively trivial datum.

To the conventional scoring categories that are retained, some additional variables of demonstrated value have been added. Some interdependence of scores has been introduced deliberately, but this does not constitute the serious problem seen in Rorschach scoring systems. There are a few minor disturbing peculiarities: card rejection contributes to the location score in the same way as the whole response, with the result that the location score expresses perceptual differentiation to a greater extent than it otherwise would.

On the whole, it is probably reasonable to conclude that the Holtzman scores constitute an improvement over the Rorschach scores. There is satisfactory evidence of interscorer reliability for most of the Holtzman scores, and the evidence on group score differences and developmental trends looks promising. It would be difficult to demonstrate a similar value with respect to information not formally scored. The clinician accustomed to subjective analysis may feel that something vital has been lost if he cannot observe a sequence of responses to a single stimulus.

It is debatable whether the Rorschach approach to personality evaluation has proven its worth. With respect to most demonstrated differences, the *Holtzman Inkblot Technique* appears to be superior to other tests employing this approach. With respect to undemonstrated differences, it may or may not be as good. It deserves extensive research and exploratory application as a prospective replacement for the Rorschach test.

H. J. Eysenck, *Institute of Psychiatry, The Maudsley Hospital, London, England.*

The *Holtzman Inkblot Technique* presents an interesting paradox. The authors have set out to use the fundamental conceptions underlying the Rorschach test in the production of a technique which would be capable of standing up to the usual psychometric tests applicable in this field. In this they brilliantly succeeded. There are two sets of 45 newly designed inkblots, carefully prepared and excellently printed, to each of which only one response is required; responses are then scored according to well defined instructions in categories very closely resembling the orthodox ones. Intra- and interscorer consistency are both high and must be accepted as representing probably the best that can be obtained from projective techniques. Split-half reliabilities for the different scoring categories differ widely, of course, being very high for such categories as rejection, location, and form definiteness, and rather low for space, hostility, and balance. However, on the whole, these reliabilities are most encouraging, ranging as they tend to do between .8 and .9 for the majority of categories and groups. Test-retest reliabilities are very much lower even when periods of only a week are in question; after one year they tend to range around .5.

Much information is given on the intercorrelations between categories and it is disturbing to note that "the magnitude of correlation between any two inkblot variables is likely to vary from one sample to the next, even reversing the sign in some instances." However, numerous factor analyses tend to agree in producing three main factors which had also been found previously in similar analyses of orthodox Rorschach scores, to wit, neuroticism, extraversion-introversion, and psychoticism. Several further factors proved difficult to identify. Proponents of the orthodox Rorschach who might look with disfavour upon these changes in the nature and format of their test will be reassured to note that there is considerable agreement between the old and the new; comparisons between the two methods "indicate quite conclusively that the Rorschach and Holtzman systems have a great deal in common as far as the underlying meaning of their respective variables are concerned."

So far so good. Clearly Holtzman and his team have done a first rate job in translating the Rorschach into acceptable psychometric terms without losing the essence of this rather intangible test. Why must their production be considered paradoxical? The answer lies in the disproportionate amount of space devoted to the details of what are essentially reliability studies and the very small amount of space given over to the much more important question of validity. Out of a book of 417 pages, less than 10 deal with validity, and what the results disclose is the usual complete failure of the Rorschach to link up with any form of outside criterion other than gross psychiatric deviation. Here is Holtzman's summing up:

> Clearly, there is little relationship between personality traits measured by the usual paper-and-pencil approaches and inkblot scores. Nor is it likely that peer-ratings of socially observable traits such as manifest anxiety, hostility, shyness, or dominance will have much in common with inkblot scores except in unusual circumstances.

This, one would imagine, would make it unlikely for anyone to wish to master a complicated and time consuming technique, the results of which could not be expected to correlate with observable personality traits. Holtzman defends himself by saying:

> While such results are useful in pointing out certain kinds of inferences about the more superficial aspects of personality that it is unwise to make from inkblot scores, they are largely irrelevant to the broader issues of validity—developmental, cognitive and perceptual aspects of personality—as well as the psychodiagnostic evaluation of individuals with mental or emotional disturbances.

Holtzman does not indicate why these issues are "broader" or why personality traits are dismissed so glibly as being "superficial," nor does he give any evidence to show that, psychodiagnostically, his test would be anything like as good as a simple 10-minute questionnaire. If only the validity studies had come up to the same level of excellence or success as the reliability studies, how welcome would this test have been! As it is it demonstrates pretty conclusively that the underlying notion of the Rorschach test is at fault. No one is likely to do a better job than Holtzman in making the test psychometrically acceptable; if even he did not succeed in making it valid it seems unlikely that anyone ever will.

BERTRAM R. FORER, *Consulting Psychologist, and Executive Editor, Journal of Projective Techniques and Personality Assessment, Suite 307, 8833 Sunset Boulevard, Los Angeles, California.*

Psychometric techniques and clinical sophistication have come a long way since Hermann Rorschach carved new dimensions of perception and personality out of responses to his ten inkblots. Psychometric experts and specialists in projective psychology have been at odds as to whether Rorschach's method was of any value either in diagnosis or in research. There have been extremists on both sides of the argument. Research evidence over the years has pointed to positive value in the method and serious limitations as well. A change was called for. What has been needed is an instrument which elicits basic information about persons that they themselves are unaware of and unable to communicate directly and which at the same time provides objective, mathematically manipulable and psychologically meaningful scales for both clinical and research purposes.

Holtzman and his associates have created a happy liaison between the richness of clinical information available from the Rorschach and modern statistical techniques for describing, defining, and utilizing the information. Starting with two new sets of 45 inkblots designed to maximize differences in perception between mature and disturbed persons, they have developed a group of 22 scales that encompass most of the information commonly obtained from the Rorschach. And they include new dimensions that have grown out of recent Rorschach and personality research, e.g., penetration, barrier, anxiety, hostility, and pathognomic verbalization scores.

To be sure, something may be lost by including different color responses or shading responses in single scores which may conceal differences in the relative role of color and form or shading and form. But the loss is more imagined than real, for three reasons. First, those who wish to utilize conventional Rorschach scores can still do so. Second, the scores that have been developed have demonstrated meaningfulness in terms of both basic Rorschach concepts and detailed validational and intratest correlational research. And third, the item responses and total scales yield repeat and split-half and alternate form reliabilities and interrater agreements greater than those obtained by the Rorschach.

The scores generated by this new method are reproducible and comparable. Systematic control in the design of the blots has insured adequate individual differences in response. Restricting responses to one per card insures comparability of protocols by removing the contaminant of productivity which has been the bugaboo of so much Rorschach research. For every subject this test contains 45 items. The data are in a numerical form that is easily handled statistically and that permits more rigorous tests of validity than the Rorschach does. Hence the research possibilities are enormously enhanced. Scoring samples are abundant and clear and the test manual and record blanks are well set up and complete.

Use of the scales does not preclude conventional (or idiosyncratic) clinical inference. But there is a danger in carrying over Rorschach lore and norms. These are different blots with stimulus properties that differ from those of the Rorschach. Many who wish to use the method will be inclined to take the easy way of avoiding the new scales and scoring criteria and to disregard the book, *Inkblot Perception and Personality,* which describes in great detail the theory, methods, philosophy, and research findings. It is a fat book and full. To avoid it would be a mistake and a loss. The many tables, norms, and intercorrelations are fascinating in themselves and provide a wealth of background material about psychological development and psychopathology.

One limitation of the Rorschach that is most apparent during the formulation of a diagnostic decision is the absence of a dependable supply of normative or reference group data and the consequent reliance of clinicians upon vaguely remembered group data or subjective appraisal of responses. The Holtzman technique provides distributions of all scores for eight adult, child, and diagnostic groups. The latter are too few at present. Eventually a variety of diagnostic groups will be needed and, no doubt, will be forthcoming. The data and some methods are given for demonstrating the degree of similarity of any score or test profile to each reference group, and techniques are suggested for making statistical decisions about diagnosis.

This technique does not and should not replace the contributions of those who deal with the Rorschach as a clinical projective tool; they complement each other. The present set of blots may or may not provide the same amount of clinical content as the Rorschach. That remains to be seen. In any case the clinical lore developed particularly in connection with the Rorschach still has its place in the diagnostic report. The Holtzman method in addition to its superior research possibilities, adds to the clinical Rorschach approach a new kind of profile which can be used clinically. A case study in the book demonstrates the process of making clinical inferences from a systematic study of the 22 scores in connection with normative data.

This reviewer's overall appraisal is that the Holtzman technique is a significant contribution to the field of personality assessment which provides the first real integration of current standards of test construction, past research findings, and clinical projective techniques. Those who like the Rorschach owe it to themselves to try the Holtzman technique, test it, and improve it.

William N. Thetford, *Associate Professor of Medical Psychology, College of Physicians and Surgeons of Columbia University, New York, New York.*

The aim of the Holtzman technique is to develop a new inkblot approach with demonstrated psychometric value, without sacrificing the rich qualitative data yielded by the Rorschach test. The approach represents a serious attempt to overcome many of the Rorschach weaknesses noted by Zubin and others. Holtzman and his co-workers maintain that the numerous psychometric problems encountered in Rorschach evaluation result from the fundamental confusion arising from the "failure to distinguish between the Rorschach as a projective technique in the hands of skilled clinicians, and the Rorschach as a psychometric device." Holtzman believes that by using more than ten inkblots, limiting the number of responses, and avoiding the highly variable inquiry procedure of the Rorschach, most of its psychometric weaknesses can be overcome.

The Holtzman test has two alternate forms, each containing 45 inkblots and two practice cards. The subject is permitted only one response to each inkblot. To compensate for the usual tendency to give whole responses initially, an attempt has been made to choose cards with high "pulling power" by emphasizing details, space, color, and shading. A brief, nonsuggestive, and relatively simple inquiry is administered after each response. Six of the 22 scoring categories—namely, location, color, shading, movement, form definiteness, and form appropriateness—are regarded as primary. A very carefully developed scoring system, in the form of rating scales, has been worked out for these variables.

Six factors, sufficient to account for the correlations obtained between the variables, have been identified by factor analysis, the first three being quite well defined. The first, defined by movement, integration, human, barrier, and popular, was found to account for more of the obtained variance than any of the others. High scores here are thought to be related to well organized ideational activity, good imaginative capacity, well differentiated ego boundaries, and awareness of conventional concepts. The second is a bipolar factor, primarily defined by color and shading. The positive pole is thought to indicate over-reactivity to color, shading, or symmetrical balance, and the negative to be associated with primary concern for form alone. The third factor is defined primarily by pathognomic verbalizations. High scores here are regarded as indicating disordered thought processes and an active but disturbed fantasy life.

Percentile norms have been constructed for eight reference groups, including college students, average adults, seventh graders, elementary school children, five-year-olds, chronic schizophrenics, mental retardates, and depressed patients. In evaluating a particular subject, comparisons can be made with any of the appropriate reference groups. However, since this procedure is limited to one inkblot score at a time, the authors suggest the use of multivariate analytic procedures which can take into account all of the scores simultaneously. Holtzman gives an example of this kind of approach, along with compelling evidence on behalf of multivariate statistic procedures for classification problems. At present, however, we can only look to the future for the availability of large scale data and high powered computers which such procedures necessarily entail.

Several reliability studies for the different groups are reported. In the main, the obtained coefficients are acceptably high and some are even remarkably so, although on some of the variables they are too low to warrant confidence. Validity studies have dealt primarily with group differences and relationships with other techniques. In the developmental, cognitive, and perceptual aspects of personality functioning, concurrent validity seems reasonably satisfactory. For the identification of psychopathology, the variables of rejection, form appropriateness, movement, pathognomic verbalization, integration, human, and popular are especially powerful.

There are strong indications that the approach has much in common with the Rorschach, particularly in connection with the underlying meanings of their respective categories. Although only one study is reported in which both the Rorschach and Holtzman inkblots were given to the same individuals, a group of eleventh grade students, the correlations between the Beck and Holtzman systems for eight selected scores all reached statistical significance, ranging from .30 to .79.

An enormous amount of excellent statistical work has already been done, and much psychometric data is available. There is, however, much still to be done before it can be said that Holtzman's objective has been met. The eight reference groups require considerable supplementation, and validity studies are far from complete. The Holtzman-Rorschach comparisons are essentially limited, and comparisons based on many more groups would be essential for more conclusive evidence regarding the relationships between the two techniques. Also, while Holtzman believes that the loss of the Rorschach productivity score (R) is well compensated for by the expected gains, the test's empirical value is lessened thereby, and the potential for sequential analysis is lost. Further loss may also be entailed in the Holtzman procedure of using color and shading together, thus losing some of the more traditional Rorschach distinctions.

The Holtzman test is comparatively easy to learn and relatively simple to administer and score. It also has the major advantage of providing parallel forms. However, some of the vagueness of the Rorschach inquiry does remain. The Holtzman technique may also contain another Rorschach weakness in that there are 22 scoring categories which are derived from only 45 responses, which may be asking too much from too little. However, the potentialities for the further development of this test are enormous, and a serious attempt, such as this, to overcome some of the vagueness and the subjective interpretation which frequently characterizes projective test procedures without seriously sacrificing their essential richness, is urgently needed.

For excerpts from reviews of the manual, see B264.

[218]

***Horn-Hellersberg Test.** Ages 3 and over; 1945–62; based on drawings adapted from *Horn Art Aptitude Inventory* (see 5:242); "capacity to function or to adapt to a given surrounding"; 1 form ('45, 4 pages); mimeographed manual, third edition ('61, 16 pages, including 1962 instructions for interpreting part of the test as a "scale for determining developmental stages" for ages 3–11); no data on reliability; no data on validity in manual; no description of normative population; $2 per 25 tests; 25¢ per manual; 35¢ per specimen set; postage extra; (30–90) minutes; Elizabeth F. Hellersberg; the Author. *

REFERENCES

1–5. See 4:108.
6. HELLERSBERG, E. F. "The Horn-Hellersberg Test." *Monogr Soc Res Child Develop* 16(53):138–70, 214–316 '53. * (*PA* 28:4077)

For reviews by Philip L. Harriman and T. W. Richards, see 4:108; for excerpts from related book reviews, see 4:109.

[219]

***The Howard Ink Blot Test.** Adults; 1953–60; individual; 1 form ('53, 12 cards); 1953 manual ('53, 47 pages, reprint of *1* below); 1960 manual ('60, 207 pages, see *4* below); no data on reliability; $12.50 per set of cards; $2 per 1953 manual; $5 per 1960 manual; cash orders postpaid; (90–105) minutes; James W. Howard; Journal of Clinical Psychology. *

REFERENCES

1–3. See 5:141.
4. HOWARD, JAMES W. *The Howard Ink Blot Test.* Brandon, Vt.: Journal of Clinical Psychology, 1960. Pp. v, 202. * (*PA* 35:6381)

JESSE G. HARRIS, JR., *Professor of Psychology and Chairman of the Department, University of Kentucky, Lexington, Kentucky.*

The 12-card *Howard Ink Blot Test* was developed in 1953 from an earlier set of 21 blots devised to elicit a broad range of determinants by the method of group administration. It consists of an irregular sequence of 6 achromatic cards, 3 chromatic cards, and 3 cards which are a mixture of achromatic and chromatic inks. Both cards and blots are larger and colors are more saturated than those of the Rorschach. Individual administration, including notation of reaction and response times, rotation of cards, and inquiry, is similar to that of the conventional Rorschach procedure. The author of the *Howard Ink Blot Test* has engaged in the collection of normative data for approximately 21 years, resulting finally in the publication, in 1960, of a book which is an elaboration of the 1953 manual. The book is distinguished primarily by an enlargement of the earlier sample of 229 normal adults of at least high average, Wechsler-tested intelligence, to 510; the addition of what the author calls a "pseudo-normal" group of 173 subjects having problems in school, work, domestic or social life; and the inclusion of eight clinical groups, ranging in size from 31 to 69 hospitalized adult subjects. The seven additional years of thought and accumulation of data have produced some interesting syntheses and variations of hypotheses, but little of a conceptual nature that is fundamentally new, and with the exception of tabulations of number of responses by the Beck scoring system, virtually nothing of a statistical nature. Tables of comparative data on the responses of normal subjects to the Howard and Rorschach blots are not available in either the manual or the book. There is no clear indication in the author's written contributions that the responses of the Howard normative sample have been compared in unpublished studies with responses of a Rorschach sample of subjects of equally high intelligence, or, as an alternative, that responses to both tests have been obtained from a single group of subjects. If such experimental controls have not been exercised, the advertised "heightened sensitivity" of the *Howard Ink Blot Test* may be a function of differences between the two samples in intelligence alone. A similar restriction on interpretation would be imposed on the analysis of differences reported between the eight clinical groups and the normal sample, particularly since the levels of intelligence and education are reported to be lower for the clinical groups. Many of these differences may even be a function of differences in total number of responses. To the reviewer's knowledge, only two empirical researches (*2–3*) have appeared in American journals, and the results of these studies are highly questionable because they involve an improper application of chi-square technique rather than a more suitable utilization of a matched-pairs nonparametric technique. Even in their inappropriate use of the chi-square method, the authors of the articles have made the elementary error of comparing the Rorschach and Howard tests with respect to total number of responses produced by a single group of schizophrenic subjects to whom the two tests had been administered in counterbalanced order, rather than utilizing the *frequency* of subjects producing a given number of responses in a particular category. Although a lone article[1] in an Italian journal has reported data on the two tests which may appear to be mildly favorable to the Howard test as a possible alternate form of the Rorschach for retesting, the size of the sample ($n = 20$) is too small to provide reliable normative data. There is, at present, no empirically determined evidence for personality correlates of test behavior and no indication that such research is being conducted or planned. Although the traditional Rorschach test has itself been under criticism for many years for lack of conclusive evidence on reliability and on empirical and construct validity, one might expect that a newly advertised marketable test instrument would offer some unique feature which conceivably could elevate it, in some respect, above the controversial status of the Rorschach. With the possible, and doubtful, exception of the article in Italian, there is no empirical research literature to support the use of this instrument in preference to the Rorschach test. The reviewer has suggested in one of his own publications on the Rorschach test the desirability of an open-minded approach to new types of inkblot tests; but there is very little, if any, published evidence that this particular test has contributed anything of a conceptual or statistical nature after two decades of research, beyond what has become the usable lore of Rorschach interpretation. Although it seems appropriate, in this instance, to acknowledge the investigator's contribution of an intuitive interpretative nature, and his long years of devotion to a new form of inkblot test, it is more difficult to commend him, also, for having made a presently demonstrable contribution to scientific knowledge.

If one chooses to employ this test in preference to the Rorschach, he should do so with an awareness that the *Howard Ink Blot Test,* as a device for measurement, is subject to all of the limitations of the Rorschach. The user of either instrument in the clinical setting will find it necessary to develop an individual frame of reference based on his cumulative experience; the researcher who wishes to establish on a comparative basis the assets and liabilities of each, will probably conclude that the element of novelty in the Howard inkblots can scarcely outweigh the advantage of a large body of empirical knowledge developed after more than 40 years of intensive research of wide range of quality on the Rorschach blots. The investigator who is interested in a fundamentally different approach to inkblot testing might examine the *Structured-Objective Rorschach Test* or the *Holtzman Inkblot Technique.*

1 FERRACUTI, FRANCO A., AND RIZZO, GIOVANNI B. "Esame Comparativo dei Fattori di Siglatura al Rorschach ed al Test di Howard." ("A Comparison Between Rorschach and Howard Ink Blot Tests.") *Bollettino di Psicologia e Sociologia Applicate* (13–16):135–41 '56. (*PA* 31:7911)

BERNARD I. MURSTEIN, *Associate Professor of Psychology, Connecticut College, New London, Connecticut.*

This inkblot test consists of 12 cards slightly larger than the Rorschach and in the opinion of this reviewer somewhat more dynamic, offering greater possibilities for shading and texture responses than the Rorschach, notwithstanding the fact that many of the cards somewhat resemble Rorschach cards. The administration and scoring are closely related to Beck's system though several minor revisions have occurred. In *The Fifth Yearbook,* the excerpt from Walter Klopfer's withering review essentially concluded that Howard offered no research supporting any of the claims that his test was more sensitive to personality measurement than the Rorschach.

What has happened since then? As far as this reviewer can determine no new research has appeared to supplement the two articles by Scott (*2–3*) showing that the Howard evinced more shading, movement, and color than the Rorschach. The original sample of 229 normals has been extended to 510. Other groups include 173 pseudo-normals, 69 paranoid schizophrenics, 48 "other" schizophrenics, 37 psychopaths, 31 manic-depressives, 62 borderline schizophrenics, 32 obsession compulsives, 39 depressive reaction patients, and 43 anxiety reaction cases. Means, standard deviations, and *t* tests are given for various scores between these groups.

In addition the scoring of *F* is no longer wholly subjective. By some intricate but not statistically meaningful manipulations, *F*+ and *F*− scores are obtained by comparing the normal group with the others. About 12 per cent of scores are still scored subjectively for form accuracy. Last, the 1960 manual has been considerably expanded from 46 to 202 pages with many more scoring examples included.

These changes meet some of Klopfer's criticisms, but unfortunately only the minor ones. Chief among the unmet criticisms is the fact that there is essentially no research to tell us the behavioral or personological correlates of the responses to this test. It would be dangerous simply to transcribe to the Howard test the findings with the Rorschach, whose stimulus structure is considerably different from the Howard set.

The new norms are not very meaningful. No reliability coefficients appear. Further, the ages, sex, education, and other vital statistics of the groups are not given, so that one is by no means sure that the differences reported in the various determinant scores are attributable to behavior influencing the psychiatric classification rather than to more extraneous causes.

Finally, two new inkblot tests have appeared which offer much more to the clinician "ready for a change" than the Howard. The *Holtzman Inkblot Technique* is undoubtedly a great improvement over the Rorschach from a psychometric point of view. The use of 45 cards and limiting the subjects to one response per card greatly improves reliability and allows the examiner to consider the meaning of the various determinants independently of the number of responses given. The method however is still dependent on the standard inquiry method of the Rorschach. This is disadvantageous because one has no confidence that the subject is truly describing the determinants of his perception, either because he does not want to or because he is simply unaware of what they are. The Baughman method[1] largely overcomes this problem by presenting the orthodox card and one of several modifications emphasizing contour, color, etc. If it is desired to inquire about the role of shading in the percept "bat," a silhouette modification is presented and the subject asked if he still sees a bat.

Where then does this leave the *Howard Ink Blot Test?* It has all of the limitations of the Rorschach with few of its virtues. If one wants to stay with a tested inkblot technique, the Rorschach, with more than 3,000 research articles written about it, cannot be surpassed. If he wants a psychometrically more sound instrument or one more likely to educe the true determinants of perception of an inkblot response, there is more justification for turning to the Baughman or Holtzman innovations, respectively, than to the *Howard Ink Blot Test.*

Can Psychologist 1:140 O '60. H. R. Wideman. [Review of the 1960 manual.] * The book and the test material will be welcomed by those who employ ink blot techniques and wish to experiment in the hope of securing richer protocols. Even those who stick to the *Rorschach* will find many intriguing interpretative hypotheses for their consideration. The reader of this volume will miss clear, logical exposition. In part this is a result of the mixture of theoretical viewpoints and dependence upon discrete clinical hunches; most other texts on projectives have the same failing. However, the writing could have been tightened and more effort put into obtaining a readable style.

For a review by C. R. Strother, see 5:141 (1 excerpt).

[220]

★**The IES Test.** Ages 10 and over and latency period girls; 1956–58; 14 scores: 3 scores each for *a–c* (impulses, ego, superego) plus 5 scores listed in *d* below; individual; 4 tests; manual ('58, 44 pages, reprint of *3* below); instructions ('58, 1 card) for each test; record form ('58, 1 page); norms for females based on fifth and sixth graders only; $28.50 per set of test materials including manual; $3 per manual; cash orders postpaid; (30) minutes; Lawrence A. Dombrose and Morton S. Slobin; Psychological Test Specialists. *

a) ARROW-DOT TEST. 1957–58; reaction to goal barriers; 1 form ('57, 5 pages).

b) PICTURE STORY COMPLETION TEST. 1956–58; conception of outside world; 1 form ('56, 71 cards).

1 BAUGHMAN, E. EARL. "A New Method of Rorschach Inquiry." *J Proj Tech* 22:381–9 D '58. * (*PA* 34:1333)

c) PHOTO-ANALYSIS TEST. 1956–58; desired self-gratifications; 1 form ('56, 9 cards).
d) PICTURE TITLE TEST. 1956–58; recognition and acceptance of ego pressures; 5 scores: impulse, ego, superego, defense, superego plus defense; 1 form ('56, 12 cards).

REFERENCES

1. DOMBROSE, LAWRENCE A., AND SLOBIN, MORTON S. *An Approach to the Measurement of Relative Strengths of Impulses, Ego, and Superego, and the Determination of the Effects of Impulses and Superego Upon Ego Functions.* Joint doctor's thesis, Western Reserve University (Cleveland, Ohio), 1951.
2. ALEXANDER, WILLIAM AUSTIN, JR. *A Study of Normal and Psychotic Subjects Who Deviate in Their Performance on the IES Tests.* Doctor's thesis, Western Reserve University (Cleveland, Ohio), 1954.
3. DOMBROSE, LAWRENCE A., AND SLOBIN, MORTON S. "The IES Test." *Percept & Motor Skills* 8:347–89 D '58. * (*PA* 34:80)
4. BORTNER, RAYMAN W. "Superego Functioning and Institutional Adjustment." *Percept & Motor Skills* 14:375–9 Je '62. * (*PA* 37:3408)
5. HERRON, WILLIAM G. "IES Test Patterns of Accepted and Rejected Adolescents." *Percept & Motor Skills* 15:435–8 O '62. * (*PA* 37:8031)
6. NICKOLS, JOHN E., JR. "Intelligence, Insight, and the Arrow-Dot Test." *J Clin Psychol* 18:164–6 Ap '62. *
7. RANKIN, RICHARD J., AND JOHNSTON, JAMES O. "Influences of Age and Sex on the IES Test." *Percept & Motor Skills* 15:775–8 D '62. * (*PA* 38:2703)
8. VERRILL, BERNARD V., AND COSTANZA, VICTOR. "The IES Test and Ward Behavior." *J Clin Psychol* 18:295–7 Jl '62. *
9. ARMSTRONG, RENATE G., AND HOYT, DAVID B. "Personality Structure of Male Alcoholics as Reflected in the IES Test." *Q J Studies Alcohol* 24:239–48 Je '63. *
10. BORTNER, RAYMAN W. "The Relationship Between Age and Measures of Id, Ego and Superego Functioning." *J Gerontol* 18:286–9 Jl '63. * (*PA* 38:4097)
11. BORTNER, RAYMAN W. "Research Cooperation in Older Institutionalized Males." *Percept & Motor Skills* 16:611–2 Ap '63. * (*PA* 38:2921)
12. GILBERT, JEANNE G., AND LEVEE, RAYMOND F. "A Comparison of the Personality Structures of a Group of Young, Married and a Group of Middle Aged, Married Women." *Percept & Motor Skills* 16:773–7 Je '63. * (*PA* 38:6117)
13. PINCKNEY, GEORGE A. "Relative Strengths of Impulse, Ego and Superego in Female College Students." *Percept & Motor Skills* 17:340 O '63. * (*PA* 38:6063)
14. REMPEL, HENRY, AND SIGNORI, EDRO I. "Further Research on the IES Photo-Analysis Subtest With Special Reference to Sex Differences." *Percept & Motor Skills* 17:295–8 Ag '63. * (*PA* 38:8394)
15. REMPEL, HENRY; SIGNORI, EDRO I.; AND SAMPSON, DONALD L. G. "Differences in Attribution of Impulse (Id), Ego and Superego Functions to Male and Female Photographs." *Percept & Motor Skills* 17:663–5 D '63. * (*PA* 38:6066)

DOUGLAS P. CROWNE, *Associate Professor of Psychology, University of Connecticut, Storrs, Connecticut.*

The aim of the *IES Test* is to measure "the relative strengths of impulses, ego and superego" and the complex interrelations of these functions. As a psychoanalytic instrument it is intended for both clinical use in diagnosis and for research to validate psychoanalytic concepts. The test is presumably disguised so that the examinee is unaware of the purpose of testing and the meaning to be given to his test responses. The several subtests which make up the *IES Test* include a behavioral task (Arrow-Dot Test), two multiple choice measures (the Photo-Analysis Test, a questionnaire in which the examinee attributes motives and behavior to photographs; and the Picture Story Completion Test), and a semi-projective test (Picture Title Test). These standardized test tasks provide controlled stimulus situations in which it is assumed that impulses, ego, and superego will be shown in behavior in distinctive and measurable ways. The test indications of these personality forces are as follows. The I (impulses) score is given for responses which reflect sexuality, hostility, freedom from control, and externalization, and for violation of prohibitions. The E (ego) score is awarded for test responses which reflect a reality testing and problem solving orientation and control of presumably unacceptable impulses. The expression of guilt and rigid, moralistic, self-depriving, and overcautious behavior are scored S (superego).

RELIABILITY. Both test-retest and internal consistency coefficients are reported in the manual. Over the four tests the median test-retest reliability coefficient is .60. This was computed on a sample of 30 male psychotherapy outpatients over an interval of 30 to 60 days. The median internal consistency coefficient is .55. The latter is a generous estimate, since correlations below .20 are not reported. Obviously, little confidence can be placed in an individual's score with reliability values as low as these.

VALIDITY. The test authors recognize the requirement of construct validity of the test. They present two sets of validity studies essentially using the method of contrasted groups. Normals, neurotics, and psychotics (paranoid schizophrenics) were contrasted in their scores on the various tests, and the mean differences between the groups were interpreted as confirming theoretical expectations. Ten-year-old boys (theoretically in the latent stage) were contrasted with adolescents and normal adults in an attempt to test predicted differences in psychosexual development. In another study, 11-year-old boys and girls rated by teachers as impulsive, constricted, and well adjusted were compared. Geriatric groups have also been investigated. Essentially, the validity criteria in these investigations were psychiatric diagnosis, age, and sex. In the studies of children, psychosexual status was not really predicted by the test since no psychosexual criteria other than age were employed.

No evidence of discriminant validity is offered. Careful test validation requires evidence that the test is unrelated to constructs with which it is presumed to differ. At the very least, correlations with intelligence and social desirability should be reported. In the latter case, many of the test tasks appear to be highly transparent and susceptible to response distortion; thus, the score is more likely to reflect the examinee's need to appear in a favorable light than the way in which he copes with his impulses. The following examples from the Photo-Analysis Test illustrate this problem.

1. When this man doesn't get enough change from a clerk, does he
   A. ask for the right amount
   or
   B. call the clerk a crook
   or
   C. forget about it
2. Does he look as if he would
   A. commit suicide
   or
   B. commit murder
   or
   C. live a normal life

The literature on response distortion strongly suggests that disguises such as having the subject attribute characteristics to people depicted in pictures do not succeed in disabusing him of the idea that he is himself being evaluated.

NORMS. Norms in the form of mean scores are presented for 10-year-old boys and girls, adolescents, normal adults, neurotics, paranoid schizophrenics, and the aged. Norms for the clinical groups are based on very small samples, and stratified sampling procedures to control for socioeconomic variables of potential influence on the test scores were not used in sample selection. To take one example, differences in sexual and aggressive behavior (methods of impulse control) associated with social class are well known; since the class characteristics of the normative samples are undetermined we have no way of knowing the effect of this variable on the test. The tables presenting the norms do not report standard deviations nor are cutting scores given. Standard deviations are available from tables elsewhere in the manual, but to look them up is cumbersome and should not be demanded of the test user.

The *IES Test* reflects a rather naïve approach to psychoanalytic test construction. Interpretation of the various test scores appears to be based on the assumption of a direct relationship between behavior and the mediating processes of impulses and impulse control. On the Arrow-Dot Test, for example, crossing forbidden barriers is interpreted as an indication of uncontrolled impulsivity, and circuitous cautiousness is assumed to reflect the oversevere demands of the superego. The assumption of such a 1:1 theoretical correspondence is superficial. The role of defensive processes (e.g., the effects of repression) is essential to the psychoanalytic understanding of behavior control. Also, the meaning of the test tasks to the examinee needs more careful consideration, and a check on defensive or socially desirable response bias should be incorporated in the test.

SUMMARY. *The IES Test cannot be recommended for individual diagnosis* in view of grossly inadequate reliability and limited evidence of validity. Further, the diagnostic rules by which personality interpretations are to be constructed from the relative values of test scores are not specified, although a sample diagnostic interpretation is offered. For the prediction of psychiatric diagnosis or expected psychiatric classification, the MMPI is infinitely preferable. For the prediction of age and sex there are obviously simpler and more reliable variables. In the prediction of psychosexual conflicts and problems, one might as well use the Blacky test. The use of the *IES Test* is limited to research investigations of its validity as a measure of psychoanalytic constructs, and in this its utility is limited by its superficiality.

WALTER KATKOVSKY, *Associate Professor of Psychology, Fordham University, New York, New York.*

The four tests of the IES utilize testing procedures familiar to diagnosticians; viz., selecting pathways to a target, choosing a picture to complete a story sequence, describing faces, and giving titles to pictures. The test materials and tasks are likely to arouse the interest and motivation of most persons within a broad age range.

More distinctive and significant than the test materials and procedures is the purpose of the test. The authors are interested in working within a psychoanalytic framework and they have constructed the tests to measure three variables in this theory, the strengths of impulses, ego, and superego. They have clearly presented the rationale of each test, indicating the ways in which they believe responses will reflect the variables they wish to measure, and they have worked out a clear scoring system based on their *a priori* ideas as to how impulse, ego, and superego forces will be expressed on the tests. Their ideas generally appear to have face validity and consistency with psychoanalytic theory. Clear instructions for standardized administration and scoring are presented in the manual. Scoring agreement of 91 per cent is reported between two independent scorers.

Despite the authors' deliberate efforts to construct an instrument which measures strength of impulses, ego, and superego, three issues which must be considered raise doubts as to whether they have in fact accomplished their aim. These issues are the validity of the tests, their reliability, and the ease of making interpretations of individual scores and records. The topics of validity and interpretation are particularly complex because of the claim that each test measures a different aspect of impulse, ego, and superego strength. For example, the E scores on the various tests are thought to measure the degree of reality-oriented functioning (Arrow-Dot Test), the objectivity of perceptions of the external world (Picture Story Completion Test), the realism and conventionality of wishes and fantasies (Photo-Analysis Test), and the recognition and acceptance of objective judgment as a determinant of functioning (Picture Title Test). The complexity of the interpretations is increased by the fact that very high E scores on the Arrow-Dot and Picture Title Tests are in some cases described as indicative of a strong superego and denial of conflict and pain rather than as realistic ego functioning.

In discussing the validity of their instrument, the authors refer to several studies which have tested theoretical hypotheses contrasting different groups of subjects. They report that more predictions were supported with the IES than would be expected by chance, and while they cite the need for further research, they state that the tests "have a degree of validity to justify their use." Unfortunately, the authors do not make explicit the hypotheses that were and were not supported and refer the reader to original sources, all of which are relatively difficult to obtain since they are unpublished doctoral dissertations. Since publication of the IES in 1958, several additional studies using the tests have been published. Some of these studies obtained results which support the utility of the instrument and some did not. Herron (*5*) found that rejected adolescents placed in a residence for neglected children obtained higher I and lower E scores on the Picture Story Completion Test, and lower E scores on the Picture Title Test, than children never separated from their families. This finding is consistent with an explanation of ego deficiency and externalization of impulses in the rejected group. Rankin and Johnston (*7*) reported several age and sex differences in the scores of college students, and Bortner (*11*) noted differences between the scores of hospitalized patients who showed up for a research appointment and "no shows." Bortner (*4*) also found significant F ratios on three of five superego measures obtained from the IES using groups of non-institutionalized men and groups of men well adjusted and poorly adjusted to institutionalized life. His data are difficult to interpret because of lack of controls, but one possible finding is that his subjects with poor institutional adjustment, in comparison with other groups, overinterpreted environmental restrictions placed on them. Two studies using the IES failed to confirm predictions. Verrill and Costanza (*8*) found no significant correlations between ratings of patients by a psychiatric nurse on impulse, ego, and superego characteristics and corresponding scores on the IES. Gilbert and Levee (*12*), predicting weaker egos and greater superego-id conflict in women in the menopausal age range than in young women, failed to find any differences between young and middle-aged married women.

It is this reviewer's belief that the reported research on the IES is too limited in scope and significance to warrant use of this instrument for purposes other than research. Controlled investigations of the predictive and construct validity of the individual tests are badly needed. The specific interpretations proposed for test scores should be examined by predicting from the scores to criterion measures, where possible, or to behavior consistent with the interpretations.

Even if the validity of the tests is assumed, problems exist with the interpretation of scores. The test manual presents mean scores for various age and pathological groups, but these are based on small samples and the differences between mean scores are small. Consequently, they provide little guidance in the interpretation of an individual record lacking extreme scores. A sample interpretation of a record can be found in the manual as an example of how scoring interpretations are integrated for the individual case. Interpretation of this record, however, is relatively easy because of extreme scores on two of the tests. Interpreting a record with less deviant scores is likely to be a more difficult and subjective task. A second point pertaining to test interpretation is the question of what variables other than impulse, ego, and superego strength may be related to test performance? For example, intelligence may be significantly correlated with E scores on the Arrow-Dot and Picture Story Completion Tests inasmuch as similar procedures are used to measure intelligence on other tests (e.g., Mazes and Picture Arrangement on the *Wechsler Intelligence Scale for Children*). Interpretations of ego strength may well be confounded with intellectual functioning. Research determining relations between IES scores and other variables would aid interpretation of scores.

The stability of the IES is better than the internal consistency of the tests. Test-retest reliabilities after 30 to 60 days on 30 males receiving outpatient psychotherapy range from .35 to .83. The internal consistency of each of the tests, determined by the Kuder-Richardson formula 20 and reported in the test manual and by Rankin and Johnston (7), tends to be low, particularly on the Picture Title and Photo-Analysis Tests. The Arrow-Dot Test, on the other hand, has satisfactory internal consistency.

The advertisement recommending use of this instrument for individual clinical evaluation "in such areas as ego strength, superego rigidity, and 'acting out' behavior" seems unwarranted. Despite the attractiveness of the materials and the ease of administration, sufficient problems exist in the reliability and validity of scores to discourage their use in making interpretations and decisions about individuals in clinical situations. Some of the tests and interpretations of them do appear to warrant further research.

J Counsel Psychol 9:369–72 w '62. John O. Crites. * The four tests of the IES are well-conceived, following an explicit test rationale, and some are ingenious, in particular the PhA and AD tests. In administering the tests to both children and adults, the reviewer found a high level of interest and involvement in their content, which to the test expert has obvious face validity but which to examinees is not obvious, since they typically inquire about what the tests measure after having taken them. Furthermore, the tests are comprehensive, in that they assess a variety of processes from perception and imagination to problem-solving and social conformity, and they can be scored to yield measures not only of id, ego, and superego functioning but of other constructs which are defined by the interrelationships of these variables. * About the only drawback to the administration of the IES is that it can be given to just one person at a time. * Estimates of the homogeneity of the tests, as determined by Kuder-Richardson Formula 20, were generally low, ranging from .20 to .72 in groups of normals, neurotics, and paranoids for all tests except AD, which had considerably higher coefficients * the reliabilities of the tests are disappointingly low, perhaps not so much because they are intrinsically inaccurate measures but more because the test authors did not fairly evaluate their reliability. Not only is a sample as small as 30 inadequate for the computation of reliability estimates, but the *S*s were tested over varying periods of time, instead of at the same time, and they were in psychotherapy, the effects of which, if there were any, are inextricably confounded with the passage of time between test and retest. It is surprising, therefore, not that the data showed the tests to be reliable at all but that they were as reliable as the coefficients indicated. With more adequate data from larger samples, it would seem reasonable to expect that the reliabilities of the IES tests would be considerably higher and within the range generally required for individual appraisal and prediction. * The construct validity studies of the IES are generally favorable and support the promise of the test, but they should be interpreted cautiously for two reasons. First, in the group comparisons it is possible that the differences were due to variables other than those measured by the tests. Only if the groups were comparable on variables which are related to IES performance would it be justifiable to conclude that the test constructs had been validated. * It might be reasonable to expect....that intelligence would be related to the IES ego scores and consequently to the differences between groups on them. Second,....some of the IES tests may be more valid than others and consequently the over-all correct prediction rate should not be generalized to all of the tests without evidence on each one. * it would be extremely helpful to perform a factor analysis on their intercorrelations. It may be that some tests are measuring the same functions or that the id, ego, and superego scores are highly related and define one general factor rather than three relatively independent ones. The IES test has many possibilities for both counseling procedures and research endeavors. Conceptually, it is one of the soundest personality tests which has appeared in some time, dealing as it does with constructs from an explicit theoretical system which has direct relevance for the explanation of counseling and vocational phenomena. Structurally, it is well-designed, conveniently administered, and easily scored, and it captures the interest and motivation of examinees. Empirically, it is based upon some research findings which are encouraging, but a considerable amount of further work is needed before confidence can be had in its reliability and validity. In particular, there should be studies of its factorial structure and its relationships to other test and nontest variables. Until appropriate data are available, the IES should be used with caution and qualification, but it *should* be used. Its potential as a meaningful and useful instrument outweighs its present limitations and commends it to counselors and researchers who are interested in the analysis of cognitive processes and their relationships to adjustment and decision-making.

[221]

***An Incomplete Sentence Test.** Employees, college; 1949–53; Forms M (for men), W (for women), (4 pages); 2 editions; no data on reliability; no norms; 15¢ per test; 25¢ per manual for *a*; 50¢ per specimen set; postpaid; (15–25) minutes; George Spache; [Reading Laboratory and Clinic]. *

a) AN INCOMPLETE SENTENCE TEST FOR INDUSTRIAL USE. Employees; 1949; 2 forms ('49); manual ['49, 8 pages].

b) AN INCOMPLETE SENTENCE TEST [COLLEGE EDITION]. College; 1953; 2 mimeographed forms ['53]; no manual; no data on validity.

For a review by Benjamin Balinsky of a, *see 5:142.*

[222]

★The Industrial Sentence Completion Form. Employee applicants; 1963; experimental form; 1 form (4 pages); no manual; no data on reliability and validity; no norms; [20–30] minutes; $5 per 25 tests, postage extra; specimen set not available; Martin M. Bruce; the Author. *

[223]

Interpersonal Diagnosis of Personality. Adults; 1955–58; a combination of assessment procedures consisting of the *Minnesota Multiphastic Personality Inventory,* the *Interpersonal Check List,* and the *Thematic Apperception Test* or the *Interpersonal Fantasy Test* (see *e* below); manual ('56, 114 pages, see *12* below); $5.50 per manual; specimen set (without manual) of *a–d* free; cash orders postpaid; Timothy Leary, Rolfe LaForge (*a*), Robert Suczek (*a*), and others (manual); Psychological Consultation Service. *

a) INTERPERSONAL CHECK LIST. 1 form ['55, 3 pages]; $4 per 20 tests; $2 per scoring template; (15–45) minutes depending on number of persons rated.

b) RECORD BOOKLET FOR INTERPERSONAL DIAGNOSIS OF PERSONALITY. 1 form ('57, 4 pages); $5 per 20 booklets.

c) RECORD BOOKLET FOR INTERPERSONAL ANALYSIS OF GROUP DYNAMICS. 1 form ['56, 4 pages]; $5 per 20 booklets.

d) RECORD BOOKLET FOR INTERPERSONAL DIAGNOSIS OF FAMILY DYNAMICS. 1 form ['56, 6 pages]; $5 per 20 booklets.

e) INTERPERSONAL FANTASY TEST. 1957–58; 1 form ['57, 26 cards]; no data on reliability or validity; typewritten manual ('58); $15 per set of cards.

REFERENCES

1–11. See 5:144.

12. LEARY, TIMOTHY; WITH THE COLLABORATION OF HELEN LANE, ANNE APFELBAUM, MARY DELLA CIOPPA, AND CHARLOTTE KAUFMANN. *Multilevel Measurement of Interpersonal Behavior: A Manual for the Use of the Interpersonal System of Personality.* Berkeley, Calif.: Psychological Consultation Service, 1956. Pp. vii, 110. *

13. GYNTHER, MALCOLM D.; PRESHER, CHARLES H.; AND McDONALD, ROBERT L. "Personal and Interpersonal Factors Associated With Alcoholism." *Q J Studies Alcohol* 20:321–33 Je '59. * (*PA* 34:6241)

14. BAUMRIND, DIANA. "An Analysis of Some Aspects of the 'Interpersonal System.'" *Psychiatry* 23:395–402 N '60. * (*PA* 36:5IF95B)

15. ROMANO, ROBERT L. "The Use of the Interpersonal System of Diagnosis in Marital Counseling." Comment by T. Leary. *J Counsel Psychol* 7:10–9 sp '60. * (*PA* 35:2441)

16. GYNTHER, MALCOLM D., AND McDONALD, ROBERT L. "Personality Characteristics of Prisoners, Psychiatric Patients, and Student Nurses as Depicted by the Leary System." *J General Psychol* 64:387–95 Ap '61. * (*PA* 36:1HF87G)

17. CHENAULT, JOANN, AND SEEGARS, JAMES E., JR. "The Interpersonal Diagnosis of Principals and Counselors." *Personnel & Guid J* 41:118–22 O '62. * (*PA* 37:5285)

18. DAVID, CHARLOTTE. "Interpersonal Measurement of Two Occupational Interest Groups." *J Proj Tech* 26:276–82 S '62. * (*PA* 37:3895)

19. GAZA, CAESAR THOMAS. *The Prediction of Success in Nursing Training: The Use of the Interpersonal System of Multilevel Personality Diagnosis as an Adjunct to the Selection Program of a Hospital School of Nursing.* Doctor's thesis, New York University (New York, N.Y.), 1963. (*DA* 24:1684)

20. LORR, MAURICE, AND McNAIR, DOUGLAS M. "An Interpersonal Behavior Circle." *J Abn & Social Psychol* 67:68–75 Jl '63. * (*PA* 38:765)

21. MITCHELL, HOWARD E. "Application of the Kaiser Method to Marital Pairs." *Family Process* 2:265–79 S '63. *

See also references for 127.

JERRY S. WIGGINS, *Associate Professor of Psychology, University of Illinois, Urbana, Illinois.*

The *Interpersonal Diagnosis of Personality* provides an intricate theoretical framework for viewing an individual's behavior with respect to himself and significant others at several levels of personality functioning. The Interpersonal battery employs three tests which together are presumed to tap four levels of interpersonal behavior in terms of a common system of 16 variables whose intercorrelations form a circular pattern which has recently been dubbed a "circumplex." [1] The manual provides detailed instructions for scoring each test in terms of a reduced set of interpersonal variables (eight octants) by two basic procedures. (*a*) Graphic scoring involves the pictorial representation of raw (or in one instance standard) scores on the eight variables on a circular profile which serves a supplementary diagnostic function. (*b*) The primary interpersonal diagnosis is made for each of the four levels by a linear combination of raw scores which yield "vector means" on the two principal coordinates of the system, dominance (Dom) and affiliation (Lov). Dom and Lov vector means are converted to standard scores and plotted as a single point in two dimensional space represented by a circular diagnostic grid. The grid is sectioned into eight equal pie-shaped octants which correspond to the eight interpersonal variables. The octant in which an individual's score falls determines his interpersonal diagnosis and his distance from the center of the circle determines the appropriateness of his behavior. Dom and Lov scores of 800 psychiatric outpatients serve as "norms" for diagnoses made at each of the four levels. Test scores which fall close to the mean of this group are classified as "adaptive" while more extreme scores (one sigma above) are considered "maladaptive." False negative diagnostic decisions would seem likely to occur when an individual is judged to be "well off" by reference to a norm based on psychiatric patients. Such a frame of reference also fails to provide an appropriate baseline for the evaluation of improvement which is one of the avowed purposes of the system (*14*).

LEVEL I, PUBLIC INTERPERSONAL BEHAVIOR (MMPI). In principle, the social stimulus value of a patient could be assessed by pooling ratings made by significant others. In practice, a highly questionable use is made of selected MMPI clinical and special scales which are presumed to be "predictive" of such sociometric ratings. Eight MMPI scales were selected to represent the eight interpersonal octants on the basis of the correlations of these scales with sociometric ratings (*3*). The quite meager and often inconsistent nature of these original correlations would not lead one to expect much success in forecasting one set of measurements from the other. Subsequent studies of the relation between MMPI predictive indices of Dom and Lov and sociometric ratings of the corresponding dimensions [2] fail to provide any additional justification for this procedure. Although the view of an MMPI profile as a communication between the patient and significant others has much to recommend it, there is little evidence that the Interpersonal System scoring procedures represent an improvement upon more conventional diagnostic applications of the MMPI.[3]

LEVEL II, VIEW OF SELF AND OTHERS (ICL). The *Interpersonal Check List* (ICL) was carefully and imaginatively designed as a "flexible observational device for personality research" (*4*) which reflects the structural properties of the 16 variable circumplex system. Since the ICL is the subject of a separate review (see 127) it will not be described here. It should be noted that the ICL is the only instrument under discussion that was specifically developed for use in the system and it is therefore not surprising that its psychometric properties are vastly superior to those of the other instruments that were later adapted to the requirements of the system.

LEVEL III, FANTASY (TAT). "Preconscious" aspects of the eight interpersonal variables are assessed by application of an objective and apparently reliable method of content analysis to TAT protocols. Although clinicians are encouraged to attend to more qualitative aspects of TAT protocols, the recommended instructions to the subject (write 3 or 4 sentences) are unlikely to yield protocols of sufficient richness for the more traditional kinds of interpretations.[4] Although no rationale is given for the choice of the 10 TAT cards employed, it seems unlikely that these particular cards will generate distributions of interpersonal themes which have the circular ordering required by the system. Available evidence on the intercorrelations among Level III variables [5] suggests that their intercorrelations are predominantly

1 SCHAEFER, EARL S. "A Circumplex Model for Maternal Behavior." *J Abn & Social Psychol* 59:226–35 S '59. *
FOA, U. G. "Convergences in the Analysis of the Structure of Interpersonal Behavior." *Psychol R* 68:341–53 S '61. *

2 GYNTHER, MALCOLM D. "Degree of Agreement Among Three 'Interpersonal System' Measures." Abstract. *J Consult Psychol* 26:107 F '62. * (*PA* 37:4982)

3 MARKS, PHILIP A., AND SEEMAN, WILLIAM. *The Actuarial Description of Personality: An Atlas for Use With the MMPI.* Baltimore, Md.: Williams & Wilkins Co., 1963. Pp. xxv, 331. *

4 STEIN, MORRIS I. *The Thematic Apperception Test: An Introductory Manual for Its Clinical Use With Adult Males.* Foreword by James G. Miller. Cambridge, Mass.: Addison-Wesley Press, Inc., 1948. Pp. vii, 95. * (*PA* 22:4959)

5 TERRILL, JAMES MCGUFFIN. *The Relationships Between Level II and Level III in the Interpersonal System of Personality Diagnosis.* Doctor's thesis, Stanford University (Stanford, Calif.), 1961. (*DA* 21:3529)

zero which mitigates against further analysis of their dimensionality. The mapping of the TAT variables on the circular grid seems therefore to be an act of faith.

In the "basic validation study" which provides the rationale for use of the TAT (*10*), hypothesized trends occurred primarily in the control group rather than in the therapy group. This study would thus seem to serve equally well as an argument for abandoning this use of the TAT. Unfortunately, the inappropriate application of the chi-square statistic in this study is not untypical of other studies presenting validating evidence (*14*). As an alternative to the TAT, the *Interpersonal Fantasy Test* (IFT) was designed to give broader coverage of the variables required by the system. There is, as yet, no published information available on the characteristics of this instrument.

LEVEL V, CONSCIOUS IDEAL (ICL). At the same time that the subject fills out the ICL for self and others, he is asked to rate his ideal self. Distributions of such ideal ratings tend to cluster in the high dominance-high affiliation octants. Although the vector scoring method compensates for this, graphic profiles of Level V variables will tend to be stereotyped. The ICL self-ideal discrepancy measures have had interesting personality research applications [6] but the diagnostic utility of self-ideal and self-other discrepancies in a hospital population has been seriously questioned.[7]

INTERLEVEL DISCREPANCIES. Since scoring procedures at all levels yield separate diagnoses based on what are presumed to be the same eight interpersonal variables, interlevel discrepancy scores may be calculated and interpreted as defense mechanisms reflecting the structure of personality organization. The standards whereby one would evaluate the extent to which the *same* variables are involved at *different* levels are not specified so that one is uncertain as to whether convergent or discriminant validation [8] would be assessed in cross-level correlations. A system of weighted discrepancy scores is proposed which preserves the circular properties of the system, but this seems arbitrary in light of the non-circular properties of the variables on levels other than Level II.[9] LaForge [10] has proposed that the various tests be viewed as sampling behavioral domains rather than levels and has suggested more realistic methods of multivariate analysis.

Despite the attractiveness of the theoretical framework of the Interpersonal System and the considerable ingenuity exercised in the construction and adaptation of instruments, the battery described in the manual is not considered sufficiently validated to recommend its routine application to problems of clinical diagnosis. With the notable exception of the *Interpersonal Check List,* the recommended modifications of the tests do not seem to represent improvements over more conventional diagnostic applications of the same instruments. Considerable additional test development is required before the Interpersonal System can realize its aim of becoming a functional diagnostic system. Because of the complexities of the psychometric shortcomings of the current system, it would be folly for the practicing clinician to attempt to "compensate" intuitively for them in his test interpretations.

For excerpts from related book reviews, see 5:B261. For a review of the Interpersonal Check List, *see 127.*

6 ALTROCCHI, JOHN; PARSONS, OSCAR A.; AND DICKOFF, HILDA. "Changes in Self-Ideal Discrepancy in Repressors and Sensitizers." *J Abn & Social Psychol* 61:67–72 Jl '60. * (*PA* 35:2253)

7 DINITZ, SIMON; MANGUS, A. R.; AND PASAMANICK, BENJAMIN. "Integration and Conflict in Self-Other Conceptions as Factors in Mental Illness." *Sociometry* 22:44–55 Mr '59. * (*PA* 34:1623)

8 CAMPBELL, DONALD T., AND FISKE, DONALD W. "Convergent and Discriminant Validation by the Multitrait-Multimethod Matrix." *Psychol B* 56:81–105 Mr '59. *

9 TERRILL, *op. cit.*

10 LAFORGE, ROLFE. *Research Use of the ICL.* ORI Technical Report, Vol. 3, No. 4. Eugene, Ore.: Oregon Research Institute, October 1963. Pp. i, 49. *

[224]

***Kahn Test of Symbol Arrangement.** Ages 6 and over; 1949–60; individual; 1 form (16 plastic objects); record blank ('56, c1949–56, 4 pages); administrative manual ('56, 37 pages, reprint of *11*); clinical manual ('57, 75 pages, reprint of *14*); auxiliary evaluation guide ('60, 10 pages); $25 per complete set of test materials; $7.50 per 50 record blanks; $2 per administrative manual; $3 per clinical manual; cash orders postpaid; (15–30) minutes; Theodore C. Kahn; Psychological Test Specialists. *

REFERENCES

1–2. See 4:110.
3–18. See 5:145.
19. FINK, HOWARD H., AND KAHN, THEODORE C. "A Comparison of Normal and Emotionally Ill Children on the Kahn Test of Symbol Arrangement." *J Ed Res* 53:35–6 S '59. * (*PA* 34:5615)
20. BATES, JULIA B. *Use of the Kahn Test of Symbol Arrangement With Adolescents.* Master's thesis, Illinois State Normal University (Normal, Ill.), 1960.
21. GIFFEN, MARTIN B.; KENNY, JAMES A.; AND KAHN, THEODORE C. "Psychic Ingredients of Various Personality Types." *Am J Psychiatry* 117:211–4 S '60. * (*PA* 35:2241)
22. MCLEOD, H. N. "My Two-Hour Psychological Test Battery." *O.P.A. Q* 14:85–7 D '61. *
23. MCLEOD, HUGH N. "The Use of the Kahn Test of Symbol Arrangement as an Aid to Diagnosis With Psychiatric Patients." *Ont Hosp Psychol B* 7:10–20 D '61. *
24. L'ABATE, LUCIANO; BOELLING, GARY M.; HUTTON, ROBERT D.; AND MATHEWS, DEWEY L., JR. "The Diagnostic Usefulness of Four Potential Tests of Brain Damage." Abstract. *J Consult Psychol* 26:479 O '62. *

25. THEINER, ERIC C.; HILL, LARRY K.; LATHAM, WILLIAM R.; AND MCCARTY, WILBUR D. "Validation Study of the Kahn Test of Symbol Arrangement." *J Clin Psychol* 18:454–7 O '62. * (*PA* 39:5103)
26. CRADDICK, RAY A., AND STERN, MICHAEL R. "Relation Between the WAIS and the Kahn Test of Symbol Arrangement." *Percept & Motor Skills* 17:583–5 O '63. * (*PA* 38:6052)
27. HILL, LARRY K.; LATHAM, WILLIAM R.; AND THEINER, ERIC C. "Diagnostic Agreement of Variously Trained Psychologists Using the KTSA." *J Clin Psychol* 19:74–7 Ja '63. *
28. L'ABATE, LUCIANO; FRIEDMAN, WILLIAM H.; VOGLER, ROGER E.; AND CHUSED, THOMAS M. "The Diagnostic Usefulness of Two Tests of Brain-Damage." *J Clin Psychol* 19:87–91 Ja '63. * (*PA* 39:2477)

For reviews by Cherry Ann Clark and Richard Jessor, see 5:145 (1 excerpt); for a review by Edward Joseph Shoben, Jr., see 4:110.

[225]

★The Kell-Hoeflin Incomplete Sentence Blank: Youth-Parent Relations. College, adults; 1959; 2 editions (1 page, identical except for wording changes in 7 items): youth form, parent form; manual (63 pages, see *1* below, includes copies of both editions); no data on reliability of scores for parent form; $2.25 per manual, postpaid; [20] minutes; Ruth Hoeflin and Leone Kell; Child Development Publications, Society for Research in Child Development, Inc. * (Test blanks, available from Leone Kell, $1.25 per 100, postpaid.)

REFERENCES

1. HOEFLIN, RUTH, AND KELL, LEONE. *The Kell-Hoeflin Incomplete Sentence Blank: Youth-Parent Relations.* Monographs of the Society for Research in Child Development, Vol. 24, No. 3, Serial No. 72. Lafayette, Ind.: Child Development Publications, Purdue University, 1959. Pp. 64. * (*PA* 35:767)
2. KENNEDY, WALLACE A., AND WILLCUTT, HERMAN. "Youth-Parent Relations of Mathematically-Gifted Adolescents." *J Clin Psychol* 19:400–2 O '63. *

[226]

Kent-Rosanoff Free Association Test. Ages 4 and over; 1910; for an adaptation, see 201; 1 form ['10, 2 pages]; hectographed manual ['10, 5 pages, reprinted from *Manual of Psychiatry*—seventh edition '38, original edition '05—formerly published by John Wiley & Sons, Inc. and now out of print]; no data on reliability; $3.75 per 50 tests, postage extra; specimen set not available; administration time not reported; G. H. Kent and A. J. Rosanoff; C. H. Stoelting Co. *

REFERENCES

1. KENT, GRACE HELEN, AND ROSANOFF, A. J. "A Study of Association in Insanity." *Am J Insanity* 67:37–96, 317–90 Jl, O '10. *
2. WELLS, FREDERIC LYMAN. "A Preliminary Note on the Categories of Association Reactions." *Psychol R* 18:229–33 Jl '11. *
3. WOODWORTH, R. S., AND WELLS, FREDERIC LYMAN. "Association Tests." *Psychol Monogr* 13(6):73–9 D '11. *
4. EASTMAN, FREDERIC C., AND ROSANOFF, A. J. "Association in Feeble-Minded and Delinquent Children." *Am J Insanity* 69:125–41 Jl '12. *
5. WELLS, FREDERIC LYMAN. "The Question of Association Types." *Psychol R* 19:253–70 Jl '12. *
6. ROSANOFF, ISABEL R., AND ROSANOFF, A. J. "A Study of Association in Children." *Psychol R* 20:43–89 Ja '13. *
7. STRONG, EDWARD K., JR. "A Comparison Between Experimental Data and Clinical Results in Manic-Depressive Insanity." *Am J Psychol* 24:66–98 Ja '13. *
8. OTIS, MARGARET. "A Study of Association in Defectives." *J Ed Psychol* 6:271–88 My '15. *
9. WHIPPLE, GUY MONTROSE. *Manual of Mental and Physical Tests: Part 2, Complex Processes, Second Edition,* pp. 53–71. Baltimore, Md.: Warwick & York, Inc., 1915. Pp. v, 336. *
10. WOODROW, HERBERT, AND LOWELL, FRANCES. "Children's Association Frequency Tables." *Psychol Monogr* 22(5):1–97 '16. *
11. HORN, JOHN LEWIS. "A Case of Pathological Day Dreaming." *Psychol Clinic* 12:89–101 My '18. *
12. OSCHRIN, ELSIE. "Vocational Tests for Retail Saleswomen." *J Appl Psychol* 2:148–55 Je '18. *
13. MITCHELL, IDA; ROSANOFF, ISABEL R.; AND ROSANOFF, A. J. "A Study of Association in Negro Children." *Psychol R* 26:354–9 S '19. *
14. MATEER, FLORENCE. "The Future of Clinical Psychology." *J Delinq* 6:283–93 Ja '21. *
15. MURPHY, GARDNER M. "A Comparison of Manic-Depressive and Dementia Praecox Cases by the Free-Association Method." *Am J Insanity* 77:545–58 Ap '21. *
16. MURPHY, GARDNER M. "Types of Word-Association in Dementia Praecox, Manic-Depressives and Normal Persons." *Am J Psychiatry* 2:539–71 Ap '23. *
17. HUBBARD, LUCILLE M. "Complex Signs in Diagnostic Free Association." *J Exp Psychol* 7:342–57 O '24. *
18. CASON, HULSEY, AND CASON, ELOISE BOEKER. "Association Tendencies and Learning Ability." *J Exp Psychol* 8:167–89 Je '25. *
19. ROSANOFF, AARON J. Chap. 7, "Free Association Test (Kent-Rosanoff)," pp. 546–620. In his *Manual of Psychiatry, Sixth Edition.* New York: John Wiley & Sons, Inc., 1927. Pp. xvii, 697. *
20. WELLS, F. L. Chap. 9, "The Free Association Experiment," pp. 192–231. In his *Mental Tests in Clinical Practice.* Yonkers, N.Y.: World Book Co., 1927. Pp. x, 315. *
21. ELONEN, ANNA S., AND WOODROW, HERBERT. "Group Tests of Psychopathic Tendencies in Children." *J Abn & Social Psychol* 23:315–27 O–D '28. * (*PA* 3:1942)
22. O'CONNOR, JOHNSON. Chap. 2, "Personality," pp. 37–47; and Appendix C, "Responses Given by Two Thousand People in the Free Association Experiment," pp. 225–310. In his *Born That Way.* Baltimore, Md.: Williams & Wilkins Co., 1928. Pp. 323. *
23. MCFADDEN, JOHN HOLMAN. *Differential Responses of Normal and Feebleminded Subjects of Equal Mental Age, on the Kent-Rosanoff Free Association Test and the Stanford Revision of the Binet-Simon Intelligence Test.* Doctor's thesis, University of North Carolina (Chapel Hill, N.C.), 1930.
24. SCHELLENBERG, PETER E. *A Group Free-Association Test for College Students.* Doctor's thesis, University of Minnesota (Minneapolis, Minn.), 1930.
25. MCFADDEN, JOHN HOLMAN. *Differential Responses of Normal and Feebleminded Subjects of Equal Mental Age, on the Kent-Rosanoff Free Association Test and the Stanford Revision of the Binet-Simon Intelligence Test.* Mental Measurement Monographs No. 7. Baltimore, Md.: Williams & Wilkins Co., 1931. Pp. 85. * (*PA* 5:2589)
26. SYMONDS, PERCIVAL M. Chap. 10, "The Free Association Method," pp. 361–99. In his *Diagnosing Personality and Conduct.* New York: Century Co., 1931. Pp. xvi, 602. *
27. THORNDIKE, EDWARD L. "The Significance of Responses in the Free Association Test." *J Appl Psychol* 16:247–53 Je '32. * (*PA* 7:4323)
28. TENDLER, A. D. "Associative Tendencies in Psychoneurotics." *Psychol Clinic* 22:108–16 Je–Ag '33. *
29. LASLETT, H. R., AND BENNETT, ELIZABETH. "A Comparison of Scores on Two Measures of Personality." *J Abn & Social Psychol* 28:459–61 Ja–Mr '34. * (*PA* 8:4158)
30. SHLAUDEMAN, KARL WHITMAN. *A Correlational Analysis of Idiosyncrasy of Response to Tests of Association, Interest, and Personality.* Doctor's thesis, Stanford University (Stanford, Calif.), 1936.
31. KEPHART, NEWELL C., AND HOUTCHENS, H. MAX. "The Effect of the Stimulus Word Used Upon Scores in the Association-Motor Test." *Am J Psychiatry* 94:393–9 S '37. * (*PA* 12:1222)
32. WHITE, RALPH KIRBY. *A Factor Analysis of Tests Designed to Measure Fluency, Atypicality, and Intellectual Curiosity.* Doctor's thesis, Stanford University (Stanford, Calif.), 1937.
33. MEYERS, RUSSELL, AND BRECHER, SYLVIA. "The So-Called Epileptic Personality as Investigated by the Kent-Rosanoff Test." *J Abn & Social Psychol* 36:413–22 Jl '41. * (*PA* 15:5165)
34. KORCHIN, SHELDON JEROME. *A Comparative Study of Three Projective Techniques in the Measurement of Frustration-Reaction Types.* Master's thesis, Clark University (Worcester, Mass.), 1943.
35. SPOERL, DOROTHY TILDEN. "Bilinguality and Emotional Adjustment." *J Abn & Social Psychol* 38:37–57 Ja '43. * (*PA* 17:3837)
36. ROSEN, HJALMAR. *Correlations Between the Schellenberg Free Association Test and the Minnesota Multiphasic Personality Inventory.* Master's thesis, University of Minnesota (Minneapolis, Minn.), 1944.
37. SCHNACK, GEORGE F.; SHAKOW, DAVID; AND LIVELY, MARY L. "Studies in Insulin and Metrazol Therapy: 1, The Differential Prognostic Value of Some Psychological Tests." *J Personality* 14:106–24 D '45. * (*PA* 20:3669)
38. SCHNACK, GEORGE F.; SHAKOW, DAVID; AND LIVELY, MARY L. "Studies in Insulin and Metrazol Therapy: 2, Differential Effects on Some Psychological Functions." *J Personality* 14:125–49 D '45. * (*PA* 20:3669)
39. TENDLER, ALEXANDER D. "Significant Features of Disturbance in Free Association." *J Psychol* 20:65–89 Jl '45. * (*PA* 19:3392)
40. FRENCH, VERA V. "The Structure of Sentiments: 2, A Preliminary Study of Sentiments." *J Personality* 16:78–108 S '47. * (*PA* 22:2512)
41. MUENCH, GEORGE A. *An Evaluation of Non-Directive*

Psychotherapy by Means of the Rorschach and Other Indices. Applied Psychology Monographs of the American Psychological Association, No. 13. Stanford University, Calif.: Stanford University Press, 1947. Pp. 163. * (*PA* 22:320)

42. LEVI, MARIO. *An Analysis of the Influence of Two Different Cultures on Responses to the Rosanoff Free Association Test.* Master's thesis, University of Chicago (Chicago, Ill.), 1949.

43. SMITH, HENRY CLAY. "Psychometric Checks on Hypotheses Derived From Sheldon's Work on Physique and Temperament." *J Personality* 17:310–20 Mr '49. * (*PA* 25:2916)

44. KEENE, CHARLES M. *Commonality of Response on a Word-Association Test: A Study of Standardization Procedures and an Attempt to Forecast Moderate Emotional Maladjustment.* Doctor's thesis, Stanford University (Stanford, Calif.), 1951.

45. TRESSELT, M. E., AND LEEDS, D. S. "The Frequencies of Responses by 124 Males and Females (Ages 22–25) for Each of the 100 Kent-Rosanoff Stimulus Words." *Psychol Newsl* 5:39–74 N–D '53. *

46. TRESSELT, M. E., AND LEEDS, DON S. "The Responses and Frequencies of Responses for Males and Females (18–21) to the Kent-Rosanoff Word List." *Psychol Newsl* 5:1–36 S–O '53. * (*PA* 28:7557)

47. RUSSELL, WALLACE A., AND JENKINS, JAMES J. *The Complete Minnesota Norms for Responses to 100 Words From the Kent-Rosanoff Word Association Test.* Studies on the Role of Language in Behavior, Technical Report No. 11. Contract No. N8-ONR-66216, University of Minnesota (Minneapolis, Minn.), August 1954. Pp. 42. *

48. TRESSELT, M. E., AND LEEDS, DONALD S. "The Responses and Frequencies of Responses for Males and Females (26–29) to the Kent-Rosanoff Word List." *Psychol Newsl* 5:144–77 Jl–Ag '54. *

49. TRESSELT, M. E., AND LEEDS, DONALD S. "The Kent-Rosanoff Word Association: 1, New Frequencies for Ages 18–21 and a Comparison With Kent-Rosanoff Frequencies." *J Genetic Psychol* 87:145–8 S '55. * (*PA* 30:7230)

50. TRESSELT, M. E., AND LEEDS, DONALD S. "The Responses and Frequencies of Responses for Males and Females (Ages 30–33 Years) to the Kent-Rosanoff Word List." *Psychol Newsl* 6:95–127 My–Je '55. * (*PA* 30:4606)

51. TRESSELT, M. E.; LEEDS, DONALD S.; AND MAYZNER, MARK S., JR. "The Kent-Rosanoff Word Association: 2, A Comparison of Sex Differences in Response Frequencies." *J Genetic Psychol* 87:149–53 S '55. * (*PA* 30:7231)

52. BECHER, BARBARA ANN. *The Effect of Education and Intelligence on Community of Responses in the Kent-Rosanoff Free Association Test.* Master's thesis, Fordham University (New York, N.Y.), 1956.

53. HERR, VINCENT V. "The Loyola Language Study." *J Clin Psychol* 13:258–62 Jl '57. * (*PA* 32:5501)

54. PETERSON, MARJORIE SCHAEFER, AND JENKINS, JAMES J. *Word Association Phenomena at the Individual Level: A Pair of Case Studies.* Studies on the Role of Language in Behavior, Technical Report No. 16. Contract No. N8-ONR-66216, University of Minnesota (Minneapolis, Minn.), April 1957. Pp. 49.

55. BOYER, ROSCOE A., AND ELTON, CHARLES F. "Effect of Instructions on Free Association." *J Ed Psychol* 49:304–8 D '58. * (*PA* 36:2CI04B)

56. COFER, CHARLES N. "Comparison of Word Associations Obtained by the Methods of Discrete Single Word and Continued Association." *Psychol Rep* 4:507–10 S '58. * (*PA* 33:5564)

57. TRESSELT, M. E. "The Kent-Rosanoff Word Association List and Geographical Location." *Psychol Newsl* 10:22–6 S–O '58. * (*PA* 33:3597)

58. JENKINS, JAMES J. "Effects on Word-Association of the Set to Give Popular Responses." *Psychol Rep* 5:94 Mr '59. * (*PA* 34:917)

59. SARASON, IRWIN G. "Relationships of Measures of Anxiety and Experimental Instructions to Word Association Test Performance." *J Abn & Social Psychol* 59:37–42 Jl '59. * (*PA* 34:4621)

60. TRESSELT, M. E. "The Responses and Frequencies of Responses for 108 Subjects (Ages 34–41 Years) to the Kent-Rosanoff Word List." *Psychol Newsl* 10:176–212 Mr–Ap '59. * (*PA* 34:1431)

61. BECHER, BARBARA ANN. "A Cross-Sectional and Longitudinal Study of the Effect of Education on Free Association Responses." *J Genetic Psychol* 97:23–8 S '60. * (*PA* 35:6979)

62. BLOCK, JACK. "Commonality in Word Association and Personality." *Psychol Rep* 7:332 O '60. * (*PA* 35:2202)

63. JENKINS, JAMES J. "Commonality of Association as an Indicator of More General Patterns of Verbal Behavior," pp. 307–29. In *Style in Language.* Edited by Thomas A. Sebeok. New York: John Wiley & Sons, Inc., 1960. Pp. xvii, 470. * (*PA* 35:288)

64. JENKINS, JAMES J., AND RUSSELL, WALLACE A. "Systematic Changes in Word Association Norms: 1910–1952." *J Abn & Social Psychol* 60:293–304 My '60. * (*PA* 35:4958)

65. KANFER, FREDERICK H. "Word Association and the Drive Hypothesis of Anxiety." *J Clin Psychol* 16:200–4 Ap '60. * (*PA* 36:2HK00K)

66. SOMMER, ROBERT, AND OSMOND, HUMPHRY. "Association Methods in Anthropology." *Am Anthrop* 62:1051–3 D '60. *

67. SOMMER, ROBERT; DEWAR, ROBERT; AND OSMOND, HUMPHRY. "Is There a Schizophrenic Language?" *Arch Gen Psychiatry* 3:665–73 D '60. * (*PA* 35:3846)

68. TRESSELT, M. E. "The Responses and Frequencies of Responses for 122 Subjects (Ages 42–54 Years) to the Kent-Rosanoff Word List." *J Psychol Studies* 11:118–46 Ja–F '60. * (*PA* 34:7613)

69. ROSENZWEIG, MARK R. "Comparisons Among Word-Association Responses in English, French, German, and Italian." *Am J Psychol* 74:347–60 S '61. * (*PA* 36:3HI47R)

70. ROTHKOPF, ERNST Z., AND COKE, ESTHER U. "Intralist Association Data for 99 Words of the Kent-Rosanoff Word List." *Psychol Rep* 8:463–74 Je '61. * (*PA* 36:2HC63R)

71. ROTHKOPF, ERNST Z., AND COKE, ESTHER U. "The Prediction of Free Recall From Word Association Measures." *J Exp Psychol* 62:433–8 N '61. * (*PA* 37:450)

72. CARROLL, JOHN B.; KJELDERGAARD, PAUL M.; AND CARTON, AARON S. "Number of Opposites Versus Number of Primaries as a Response Measure in Free-Association Tests." *J Verbal Learning & Verbal Behav* 1:22–30 Jl '62. * (*PA* 37:6107)

73. KJELDERGAARD, PAUL M. "Commonality Scores Under Instructions to Give Opposites." Reply by Ray A. Craddick. *Psychol Rep* 11:219–20, reply 238 Ag '62. * (*PA* 37:4983, 4953)

74. PALERMO, DAVID S., AND JENKINS, JAMES J. "Superordinates, 'Maturity' and Logical Analyses of Language." *Psychol Rep* 10:437–8 Ap '62. * (*PA* 37:2843)

75. EICHLER, HERBERT. *Word Association: Commonality and Popularity.* Doctor's thesis, University of Rochester (Rochester, N.Y.), 1963. (*DA* 24:2556)

76. HORTON, DAVID L.; MARLOWE, DAVID; AND CROWNE, DOUGLAS P. "The Effect of Instructional Set and Need for Social Approval on Commonality of Word Association Responses." *J Abn & Social Psychol* 66:67–72 Ja '63. * (*PA* 37:4905)

77. HORVATH, WILLIAM J. "A Stochastic Model for Word Association Tests." *Psychol R* 70:361–4 Jl '63. * (*PA* 38:2626)

78. KJELDERGAARD, PAUL M., AND CARROLL, JOHN B. "Two Measures of Free Association Response and Their Relations to Scores on Selected Personality and Verbal Ability Tests." *Psychol Rep* 12:667–70 Je '63. * (*PA* 38:6021)

79. PALERMO, DAVID S. "Word Associations and Children's Verbal Behavior," pp. 31–68. In *Advances in Child Development and Behavior, Vol. 1.* Edited by Lewis P. Lipsitt and Charles C. Spiker. New York: Academic Press, Inc., 1963. Pp. xiii, 387. *

80. PALERMO, DAVID S., AND JENKINS, JAMES J. "Frequency of Superordinate Responses to a Word Association Test as a Function of Age." *J Verbal Learning & Verbal Behav* 1:378–83 F '63. *

81. TRESSELT, M. E., AND MAYZNER, M. S. "The Kent-Rosanoff Word Association: Word Association Norms as a Function of Age." *Psychon Sci* 1:65–6 Ap '64. *

82. WYNNE, RONALD D. "Are Normal Word Association Norms Suitable for Schizophrenics?" *Psychol Rep* 14:121–2 F '64. * (*PA* 39:2734)

JERRY S. WIGGINS, *Associate Professor of Psychology, University of Illinois, Urbana, Illinois.*

The *Kent-Rosanoff Free Association Test* is the oldest of tests to be reviewed in this issue of the MMY. The test itself is more than a half-century old at this writing, and the technique is as old as scientific psychology. In 1879 Francis Galton [1] wrote a variety of single words on separate pieces of paper and tucked them under a book for future reference. At monthly intervals, he presented the words to himself singly and timed the interval between stimulus presentation and the occurrence of two different ideas. Following the occurrence of ideas, Galton attempted to determine their origin in his own experience by introspection.

1 GALTON, FRANCIS. "Psychometric Experiments." *Brain* 2:149–62 Jl '79. *
GALTON, FRANCIS. "Psychometric Facts." *Nineteenth Century* 5:425–33 Mr '79.*

He felt that collection of normative data on associations would be of interest and clearly anticipated the possibilities of the technique for individual diagnosis: "They lay bare the foundations of a man's thoughts with a curious distinctness, and exhibit his mental anatomy with more vividness and truth than he would probably care to publish to the world."

Galton's technique was modified in Wundt's laboratory by Trautscholdt [2] who presented words to observers and recorded their reaction time. More precise measures of reaction time were obtained by Cattell [3] by use of lip and voice keys. Cattell and Bryant [4] seem to have been the first to employ a list of stimulus words which were presented visually to the subject. Wundt's student Emil Kraepelin [5] was among the first to recognize the application of the technique to the study of psychopathological conditions. In addition to practice effects, his students studied the effects of drugs, fatigue and hunger on free associations. Both Jung [6] and Wertheimer [7] claimed to have originated the method of individual diagnosis of pathological states on the basis of association records.

Interest in the association experiment was so widespread at the turn of the century that a full account would be almost indistinguishable from a general treatise on the psychology of that era. Several historical reviews of the association technique are available.[8] The approach of Kent and Rosanoff was based on the work of Sommer,[9] who felt that types of mental disorder were reflected in specific forms of word association and that the test could be employed in differential diagnosis. The principal contribution of Kent and Rosanoff was their attempted *standardization* of associations to 100 stimulus words (66 of which were from Sommer's list) by reference to frequency tables based on 1,000 normal adults. That this, in itself, was considered no minor achievement for that day is indicated by the report of the APA Committee on Standardizing Procedure in Experimental Tests: "None of the 'mental tests' possesses this quality [standardization] to a degree comparable with the free association experiment, within the limits of the English language. This is mainly due to the work of Kent and Rosanoff which established a definite standard of normality for a specific association material" (*3*, p. 73).

In his pioneering investigations of the diagnostic possibilities of free association, Jung had all but abandoned logical and grammatical analysis of the relations between stimuli and associations in psychiatric groups in favor of such measures as reaction time (under speed instructions) and recall of original associations ("reproduction") as indices of individual complexes. Kent and Rosanoff (*1*, *19*) chose to ignore both the reaction time and reproduction aspects of the procedure because of their interest in logical and grammatical analysis and the statistical differentiation of diagnostic groups. The different emphases of Jung and Kent-Rosanoff procedures parallel the differences between the dynamic (Freud) and descriptive (Kraepelin) psychiatries of that day.[10] Whipple (*9*) suggested that the K-R associations be timed and it has now become fairly standard procedure to obtain measures of both reaction time and reproduction with the K-R list.

NORMS. The original normative material for the K-R test was based on the associations of 1,000 "mixed adults" who varied widely in age, occupation, mental capacity, education and regional location (*1*). Later normative studies were based on 1,000 adult male factory workers (*22*), 925 entering students at the University of Minnesota (*24*), 500 Stanford stu-

2 TRAUTSCHOLDT, MARTIN. "Experimentelle Untersuchungen über die Association der Vorstellungen." *Philosophische Studien* 1:213–50 '83. *

3 CATTELL, JAMES MCKEEN. "Experiments on the Association of Ideas." *Mind* 12:68–74 Ja '87. *

4 CATTELL, J. MCK., AND BRYANT, SOPHIE. "Mental Association Investigated by Experiment." Comments by G. F. Stout, F. Y. Edgeworth, E. P. Hughes, C. E. Collet, and S. Bryant. *Mind* 14:230–50 Ap '89. *

5 KRAEPELIN, EMIL. "Der Psychologische Versuch in der Psychiatrie." *Psychologische Arbeiten* 1:1–91 '96. *
KRAEPELIN, EMIL. *Uber die Beeinflussung Einfacher Psychischer Vorgange Durch Einige Arzneimittel.* Jena, Germany: Gustave Fisher Verlag, 1892. Pp. viii, 258.

6 JUNG, C. G., AND OTHERS. *Studies in Word Association: Experiments in the Diagnosis of Psychopathological Conditions Carried Out at the Psychiatric Clinic of the University of Zurich.* Translated by M. D. Eder. London: William Heinemann (Medical Books) Ltd., 1918. Pp. ix, 575. *

7 WERTHEIMER, MAX. "Experimentelle Untersuchungen zur Tatbestandsdiagnostik." *Archiv für die Gesamte Psychologie* 6:59–131 Ag '05. *
WERTHEIMER, MAX, AND KLEIN, J. "Psychologische Tatbestandsdiagnostik." *Archiv für Kriminal-Anthropologie* 15:72–113 '04.

8 CLAPAREDE, EDOUARD. *L'Association des Idées.* Paris: Octave Doin, Editeur, 1903. Pp. 427. *
JUNG *et al.*, *op. cit.*
KOHS, SAMUEL C. "The Association Method in Its Relation to the Complex and Complex Indicators." *Am J Psychol* 25:544–94 O '14. *
RAPAPORT, DAVID. *Emotions and Memory.* Menninger Clinic Monograph Series, No. 2. Baltimore, Md.: Williams & Wilkins Co., 1942. Pp. ix, 282. *
WARREN, HOWARD C. *A History of the Association Psychology.* New York: Charles Scribner's Sons, 1921. Pp. ix, 328. *
WOODWORTH, ROBERT S. Chap. 15, "Association," pp. 340–67. In *Experimental Psychology.* New York: Henry Holt & Co., Inc., 1938. Pp. xi, 889. *

9 SOMMER, ROBERT. *Lehrbuch der Psychopathologischen Untersuchungsmethoden.* Berlin, Germany: Urban & Schwarzenberg, 1899. Pp. vi, 399.

10 RAPAPORT, *op. cit.*

dents (*44*), and 1,008 students of introductory psychology at the University of Minnesota (*47*). In recent years the latter norms of Russell and Jenkins (*47*) seem to have become the most widely used. A comparison of these several normative studies and especially the 1930 and 1954 norms for Minnesota students has been made by Jenkins and Russell (*64*). Although the normative groups are not directly comparable in terms of sampling characteristics, method of administration and method of recording response, some secular trends were noted (*64*). The most popular associations to stimuli ("primaries") appear to be highly stable and to be increasing in their popularity over time. A decrease in the popularity of superordinate responses was also detected.

Norms have been collected for the associations of normal children (*6, 10, 13*) and for mentally defective children (*4, 8*). Normative data from subjects representing a variety of ages, occupations and geographical locations have been collected by Tresselt and Leeds (*45–6, 48–51, 57, 60, 68*). German,[11] French,[12] and Italian (*42*) translations have also appeared and have been studied in their native groups. As one would expect, differences have been reported in the association patterns of these diverse groups, although the uniformities are perhaps more impressive. In directly comparing associations given to English, French, German and Italian versions of the K-R list, Rosenzweig (*69*) found considerable agreement in the meaning of primaries given in each language. Opposite responses and adjective-adjective responses likewise were in agreement among the different forms.

SCORING PROCEDURES. Kent and Rosanoff classified associations as *common* (appearing in the normative tables), *doubtful* (grammatical variants of common words) and *individual.* The latter category was in turn divided into *normal* (on the basis of a set of rules) and *pathological* reactions. Pathological reactions are further classified into categories reflecting perseverative, neologistic, vague and peculiar linguistic habits. Variants of the K-R scoring procedure (of which there are many) tend to emphasize *grammatical* (noun-adjective), *logical* (contrast), *disturbance* (long reaction time), or *content* categories although the last is employed sparingly even by psychoanalytic writers.[13] Classification systems have been, for the most part, derivatives of the highly elaborate scheme of Jung. Wells (*2*) introduced a modified version of Jung's system which was later further reduced (*20*). Woodworth[14] reviews early classification systems and offers one of his own. Aside from their general unwieldiness, elaborate classification systems suffer from intrinsic unreliability due to arbitrary decisions and frequent category overlap. The number of categories employed in recent years has tended to be smaller and more reliable[15] (*39*).

COMMONALITY. By reference to the K-R tables it is possible to obtain for a subject a commonality score which summarizes that subject's normalcy or typicality with reference to the standardization group. A crude index of commonality may be obtained by tabulating the number of associations per 100 words which appear (irrespective of frequency) in the K-R tables. A more precise index is obtained by calculating the median value of associations based on the actual percentage of occurrence of the associations in the K-R tables.[16] An index which has recently come back into favor (*63*) is provided by counting the number of "primary" (highest frequency) associations given per 100 words.

Commonality of response appears to be related to scores on the Taylor Manifest Anxiety Scale,[17] especially under ego-involving instructions (*59*), but this relationship cannot always be expected to obtain (*65*). Although the *California Psychological Inventory* has a "communality scale," there is a surprising lack of relationship between K-R commonality and all the items of this inventory (*62*). The most systematic investigation of the commonality dimension is found in the work of Jenkins and his associates (*63*). The basic strategy here is

11 RUSSELL, WALLACE A., AND MESECK, OSKAR R. "Der Einfluss der Assoziation auf das Erinnern von Worten in der Deutschen, Französischen und Englischen Sprache." *Zeitschrift für Experimentelle und Angewandte Psychologie* 6(2):191–211 '59. * (*PA* 34:3982)

12 ROSENZWEIG, MARK R. "Études sur L'Association des Mots." *L'Année Psychologique* 57(1):23–32 '57. * (*PA* 33:1163)

13 RAPAPORT, DAVID; GILL, MERTON; AND SCHAFER, ROY. Chap. 2, "The Word Association Test," pp. 13–84. In *Diagnostic Psychological Testing: Vol. 2, The Theory, Statistical Evaluation, and Diagnostic Application of a Battery of Tests.* Chicago: Year Book Publishers, Inc., 1946. Pp. xi, 516. *

14 WOODWORTH, *op. cit.*

15 SIIPOLA, ELSA; WALKER, NANNETTE W.; AND KOLB, DOROTHY. "Task Attitudes in Word Association, Projective and Nonprojective." *J Personality* 23:441–59 Je '55. * (*PA* 30:2922)

16 WOODWORTH, *op. cit.*

17 BUCHWALD, ALEXANDER M. "Manifest Anxiety-Level, Verbal Response-Strength and Paired-Associate Learning." *Am J Psychol* 72:89–93 Mr '59. * (*PA* 34:763)

to separate subjects into high and low commonality groups on the basis of associations to the K-R and contrast the performance of such groups in biographical reports, personality and value inventory responses, learning tasks and a variety of verbal and nonverbal situations. In accord with previous suggestive evidence (*54*) commonality emerged as an important variable in situations involving a wide variety of intraverbal connections. High commonality generalizes to other word association tasks, is associated with a tendency to make "substitution" responses and is a definite asset in learning high (but not low) strength stimulus-response pairs.

Aside from the evidence presented for the centrality of commonality as an intraverbal stylistic index, Jenkins' (*63*) findings with respect to personological correlates are not encouraging. Biographical information, reported social activities, desire for social participation and conformity were essentially unrelated to high and low commonality status. Scores on the *Study of Values* were likewise unrelated to commonality status. In accord with other investigators (*36, 78*), *low* negative correlations were obtained between adjustment scores (in this case MMPI) and commonality. MMPI profiles of low commonality subjects were also found to be somewhat less stable over time. Jenkins' excellent formulation of the measurement model underlying the construct of commonality should provide ample discouragement for those who seek simple linear relations between commonality and personality traits (*63*). Elsewhere, the unitary nature of the commonality score itself has been challenged (*78*).

DIFFERENTIAL DIAGNOSIS. The classic and frequently cited main result of Kent and Rosanoff's work may be summarized as follows: when *all* of the associations of a heterogeneous group of psychiatric patients are pooled, 27 per cent of these associations are not to be found in the tables for normal adults. This manner of presenting data, which was characteristic of early workers, does not allow for an evaluation of the discriminatory efficiency of the test. It is not clear whether we should expect the *average* patient to give 27 per cent individual reactions or 27 per cent of patients to give exclusively individual reactions and the remaining patients all common reactions. Some indication of overlap may be gained from a table (*1*, p. 330) comparing a group of 53 normals, who gave more than 15 individual reactions, with several unselected clinical groups. This group of untypical normals gave a *higher* proportion of individual reactions than were found in paranoids, manic-depressives and general paretics. Subsequent research, based primarily on schizophrenics, has suggested that although psychiatric patients tend to give fewer primary responses, their basic patterns of response hierarchies are the same as normals (*82*) and there appear to be no *uniquely* schizophrenic associations (*67*).

Early and comprehensive investigations by Murphy (*15–6*) evaluated the diagnostic efficiency of some thirteen logical classifications of association in discriminating among normals, schizophrenics, and manic-depressives. His carefully conducted study "shows in every case overlapping of the groups, and in most cases no significant differences in central tendencies" (*16*). Overlapping and reversals in signs among normal, manic and depressed subjects had been noted earlier by Strong (*7*). A critical review of the diagnostic research of the first two decades of the K-R list led Symonds to conclude: "The method, therefore, is presumptive or indicative only and cannot in its present stage safely be used alone in the diagnosis of insanity" (*26*). As representative of more recently published negative findings, we may cite a failure to distinguish epileptics from non-epileptics (*33*) and a failure to distinguish brain-damaged patients from normals.[18]

On the basis of the literature to date and his own work with neurotics, Tendler (*28, 39*) concluded that individual reactions, recall disturbances, slow reaction time and adjective-noun reactions were of the greatest value for differential diagnosis. Accordingly, the percentage of each of these categories was tabulated for all K-R stimuli in 60 adult clinic cases. The mean percentage of these four categories served as an index of "stimulus potency," which was used to select a subset of 25 K-R stimuli with the greatest potential for eliciting such categories. This revised list was administered to a sample of 120 psychiatric in- and out-patients and the four categories, plus contrast, scored. Corrected odd-even reliabilities

18 APPELBAUM, STEPHEN A. "Automatic and Selective Processes in the Word Associations of Brain-Damaged and Normal Subjects." *J Personality* 28:64–72 Mr '60. * (*PA* 36:3JF64A)

of the five categories ranged from .80 to .95. On the basis of category intercorrelations, partial correlations, and enthusiastic extrapolations, Tendler (*39*) concluded that contrast responses are characteristic of normals, adjective-noun responses of neurotics and individual responses of psychotics. Percentile scores were determined from a psychiatric population and median splits on contrast, adjective-noun and individual responses employed for a type of profile analysis (e.g., high C, low A-N, high I). The frequency of various profile types in a hospital and a clinic sample offers partial support for this approach, as do the 12 individual cases presented. Aside from minor technical considerations such as the comparability of some of the samples contrasted, the data presented by Tendler do not allow for adequate estimates of the amount of overlap involved when categories are compared among normal, neurotic, and psychotic groups. Although the trends are clear, their utility for diagnostic work is difficult to assess.

INDIVIDUAL COMPLEXES. In addition to demonstrating the applicability of the association method to the detection of individual conflicts, Jung and his associates [19] performed pioneering work in experimental psychopathology by demonstrating the modifiability of associations under distraction conditions and establishing the relation of physiological indices, such as GSR and respiration, to other indices of associative disturbance. Since an individual "complex" is more of a construct than a criterion, early American investigations emphasized the consistency of such indices rather than their diagnostic efficiency. Wells (*5*) reports consistencies in reaction times on two occasions, as well as a "definite fidelity to type" with respect to logical categories of association. The intercorrelations among nine complex signs were studied by Hull and Lugoff [20] under the reasoning that signs which exhibit the greatest covariation with other signs are the most "reliable" diagnostic indices. Repetition and misunderstanding of the stimulus were the most reliable by this criterion, while long reaction time and defective reproduction shared somewhat less common variance with the other signs than was expected. Hull and Lugoff found later repetition of an association to be of doubtful significance and Hubbard (*17*) likewise failed to find evidence of a perseverative tendency in subsequent reaction times.

Pathological associations are only slightly correlated with neuroticism on the Woodworth Inventory (*21*) and not at all with neuroticism on the Bernreuter (*29*). However, pathological associations are related ($r = .57$) to the rated adjustment of children (*21*). Individual associations are correlated with sales success (*12*) and may be slightly related to psychiatric prognosis (*37–8*), but they are unrelated to body type (*43*). Associative reaction time does not appear to be related to psychometric introversion-extraversion,[21] although such a relationship might be anticipated (*22*). Under relaxed instructions, reaction time and contrast responses appear related to impulsivity and Allport-Vernon-Lindzey values.[22] Reaction time, contrast, and adjective-noun responses are correlated with the Depression Scale of the MMPI.[23]

Aside from their possible reflection of underlying complexes, the Jungian diagnostic signs are highly sensitive to procedural modification or situational pressures. Conditions of distraction,[24] satiation,[25] ego-involvement (*59*), time pressure [26] (*76*), practice,[27] or instructional sets [28] will produce differences in such indices. Alternative (although not incompatible) interpretations of the significance of such complex indicators as long reaction time and reproduction disturbances have been made [29] by appeal to the well established principles that associative reaction time is inversely related to the frequency with which the stimulus ap-

19 JUNG *et al., op. cit.*
20 HULL, CLARK L., AND LUGOFF, L. S. "Complex Signs in Diagnostic Free Association." *J Exp Psychol* 4:111–36 Ap '21. *

21 DUNN, SANDRA; BLISS, JOAN; AND SIIPOLA, ELSA. "Effects of Impulsivity, Introversion, and Individual Values Upon Association Under Free Conditions." *J Personality* 26:61–76 Mr '58. * (*PA* 33:5742)
22 DUNN *et al., op. cit.*
23 MACHOVER, SOLOMON, AND SCHWARTZ, ANITA. "A Homeostatic Effect of Mood on Associative Abstractness and Reaction Time." *J Personality* 21:59–67 S '52. * (*PA* 27:5697)
24 JUNG *et al., op. cit.*
25 SMITH, DONALD E. P., AND RAYGOR, ALTON L. "Verbal Satiation and Personality." *J Abn & Social Psychol* 52:323–6 My '56. * (*PA* 31:4368)
26 FLAVELL, JOHN H.; DRAGUNS, JURIS; FEINBERG, LEONARD D.; AND BUDIN, WILLIAM. "A Microgenetic Approach to Word Association." *J Abn & Social Psychol* 57:1–7 Jl '58. * (*PA* 33:8338)
SIIPOLA *et al., op. cit.*
27 WELLS, FREDERIC LYMAN. "Practice Effects in Free Association." *Am J Psychol* 22:1–13 Ja '11. *
28 HULL AND LUGOFF, *op. cit.*
MARSTON, WILLIAM M. "Reaction-Time Symptoms of Deception." *J Exp Psychol* 3:72–87 F '20. *
MILGRAM, NORMAN, AND GOODGLASS, HAROLD. "Role Style Versus Cognitive Maturation in Word Associations of Adults and Children." *J Personality* 29:81–93 Mr '61. *
29 LAFFAL, JULIUS. "Response Faults in Word Association as a Function of Response Entropy." *J Abn & Social Psychol* 50:265–70 Mr '55. * (*PA* 30:486)

pears in the language[30] (*18*) and positively related to the number of alternative associations which exist for the stimulus.[31]

The modifiability of complex indicators under experimental manipulations and the interpretation of such effects within the broad context of verbal learning (*27*) have, no doubt, contributed to the central position which the word association task occupies in contemporary experimental personality. A considerable literature exists which attests to the fruitfulness of the association test as a laboratory technique for the study of defense mechanisms, emphasizing particularly the modern concepts of "sensitization" and "repression."[32]

SUMMARY. The *Kent-Rosanoff Free Association Test* has enjoyed widespread use in both laboratory and clinic for more than half a century. Unlike many other "mental tests" it has retained its position as a standard laboratory technique because of its lawful relations to other kinds of verbal behavior of interest to verbal learning specialists and because of its utility in the laboratory as an objective measure of certain "defense mechanisms." For these reasons the K-R test occupies a singular position among current psychological tests in that we seem to know more about the mechanisms which underlie responses to this test than we do about the correlates of these responses. This is not to deny that many isolated studies of the personological and adjustmental correlates of response to this test have yielded "promising" or "suggestive" results. Rather, it is to emphasize the fact that no systematic large scale efforts have been made to develop the instrument as a "personality test," in the current usage of these words, since its inception in 1910. Since the test was judged by the critics of 20 and 30 years ago to be unacceptable as a routine device for individual or differential diagnosis, it is not surprising that, in its present unchanged form, it fails to meet our current standards as an acceptable instrument for these purposes.

30 SCHLOSBERG, HAROLD, AND HEINEMAN, CHARLES. "The Relationship Between Two Measures of Response Strength." *J Exp Psychol* 40:235–47 Ap '50. * (*PA* 24:6245)
THUMB, ALBERT, AND MARBE, KARL. *Experimentelle Untersuchungen uber die Psychologischen Grundlagen der Sprachlichen Analogiebildung.* Leipzig, Germany: Englemann, 1901. Pp. 87.
31 LAFFAL, *op. cit.*
WIGGINS, JERRY S. "Two Determinants of Associative Reaction Time." *J Exp Psychol* 54:144–7 Ag '57. * (*PA* 33:755)
32 CARLSON, V. R. "Individual Differences in Recall of Word-Association-Test Words." *J Personality* 23:77–87 S '54. * (*PA* 28:6717)
LEVINGER, GEORGE, AND CLARK, JAMES. "Emotional Factors in the Forgetting of Word Associations." *J Abn & Social Psychol* 62:99–105 Ja '61. * (*PA* 36:3CL99L)
MERRILL, REED M "The Effect of Pre-Experimental and Experimental Anxie... on Recall Efficiency." *J Exp Psychol* 48:167–72 S '54. * (*PA* 29:5250)

[227]

The Lowenfeld Kaleidoblocs. Ages 2.5 and over; 1958; individual; 1 form ['58]; 2 mimeographed manuals ['58]: adults (12 pages), children (9 pages); no data on reliability and validity; no norms; 52*s.* 6*d.* ($11) per set of testing materials, postage extra; specimen set not available; (60) minutes; Margaret Lowenfeld; Badger Tests Co., Ltd. *

REFERENCES

1. AMES, LOUISE BATES, AND LEARNED, JANET. "Developmental Trends in Child Kaleidoblock Responses." *J Genetic Psychol* 84:237–70 Je '54. * (*PA* 29:4023)
2. AMES, LOUISE BATES, AND LEARNED, JANET. "Individual Differences in Child Kaleidoblock Responses." *J Genetic Psychol* 85:3–38 S '54. * (*PA* 29:5686)
3. LOWENFELD, MARGARET. "Concerning Unrealized Factors in International Attitudes and Their Bearing on International Health." *Int Mental Health Res Newsl* 4(3–4):5–7 f-w '62. *

T. R. MILES, *Professor of Psychology, University College of North Wales, Bangor, Wales.*

The material for this test comprises 26 painted pieces of wood—cubes, half cubes, triangular and rectangular blocks, and three special shapes with flat bases and curved tops. The adult test has four sections. In the first, the subject is invited to use the blocks to construct whatever he pleases; sections 2–4 consist of problems of varying kinds, e.g., building the blocks into familiar objects, reconstructing a particular arrangement, etc. The children's test has a similar first section, together with a second section of somewhat easier problems.

Work on this test is still only in the initial stages and there has so far been no systematic standardisation and follow-up. Its great merits, however, in the opinion of the reviewer, are first that, within the framework of certain standardised conditions, it allows for the study of *spontaneous* behaviour, and secondly that it includes a genuine attempt to study *imaginative* ability. Psychometrics has given us plenty of statistics, but all too often these statistics relate to performance at fatuous and uninspired test items in highly artificial conditions. No doubt much in the present test depends on the clinical skill of the tester, and, for the first section in particular, worthwhile standardisation may turn out to be difficult, as in the Rorschach test; but Lowenfeld has at least offered a clear challenge to the more orthodox proponents of so-called "intelligence" and "personality" tests.

Plenty of questions remain on the theoretical side. In the introductory section of the instructions we are told: "The task of psychology, in the detailed study of human personality, is to invent methods of estimating the component elements and their structure in any given individual." Lowenfeld is not the first thinker who has wanted to explain the characteristics of big things in terms of the behaviour of smaller or more "elemental" ones. If she is right in trying to do so, then the breakthrough will come when the appropriate smaller things have been *named* (as, for instance, in the case of oxygen). However, in view of the variety of responses which human nervous systems make possible, one wonders whether this approach (which, incidentally, is not very different from that of the factor analysts) is feasible for psychologists studying personality. Indeed, it is not clear that Lowenfeld is doing more than paying lip-service to it, since there is no obvious logical connexion between her reference to "elements" and the actual test items which follow. One wonders if a link-up with the theories of Melanie Klein might in fact turn out to be more promising; if this is right, more could possibly have been done to study the subjects' responses to *people,* e.g., by the introduction of shapes having a greater resemblance to parts of the human body. This, however, is perhaps to ask for a different kind of test.

In the reviewer's opinion the *Lowenfeld Kaleidoblocs* have considerable potentialities. Those who use them, however, will need both flexibility and imagination—and perhaps a mentality similar to that of Lowenfeld herself.

George Westby, *Professor of Psychology, University College of South Wales and Monmouthshire, University of Wales, Cardiff, Wales.*

This is a fascinating test though manifestly still in an experimental stage of development. The *Lowenfeld Kaleidoblocs* are clearly inspired by a commendable respect for the child's right not only to play his way to the development of his personality but to learn his cognitive alphabets as far as possible by spontaneous experiment and with accompanying fun. It is clear that, in the hands of an enthusiast, such a set of brightly coloured wooden blocks embodying basic mathematical relationships will be an aid to exploring the natural resources of ability in the perception and manipulation of forms in space and will be a help in developing insight into basic mathematical relationships. It is not easy to see much use for the blocks in, as the author claims, "professional guidance" and "personnel management" where prediction is involved. No evidence of such value is presented in the present cyclostyled manuals. There is also a footnote to the effect that no standardization data are as yet available and a further warning that "all the statements made about it [the test]....are tentative and based upon preliminary findings" (presumably at the Institute of Child Psychology Ltd. and at the Gesell Institute of Child Development where the test has been used).

There is no published evidence known to the reviewer of the test's use in the form recommended for adults, which is in four separate sections. The task in the first is similar to mosaic building, the instruction being simply, "Make whatever you like with these blocks." The second section consists of nine "problems" of a type similar to many which have been used to test perceptual and spatial ability. They have differing time limits. The following is typical of a five-minute task. Four large triangular blocks are presented and put together as a single solid block as a demonstration. The instruction is as follows. "This you see is a symmetrical solid block with smooth edges. It can be placed with the broader or narrower side downwards. I want you to see in how many different symmetrical smooth-edged blocks you can arrange these four triangles." There are 21 possible arrangements. The third section consists of a variety of tasks again of varied time limits. They include the making of a person and a common object such as a table or chair from the blocks. In section four all the blocks have to be used as in a jigsaw to make a solid rectangular block.

The children's form uses the same blocks but is in two sections only. The first consists of free building and the second of much simpler problems than in the adult form including, as in Kohs' blocks, the copying of geometrical and colour arrangements.

This group of tasks may well be considered as tools for research in the field of spatial, mathematical attainment, but little criticism can usefully be offered until, by properly designed experimental investigation, they have been compared with alternative methods of achieving similar ends.

[228]

Lowenfeld Mosaic Test. Ages 2 and over; 1930–58; individual; 1 form ['30]; 2 sets: standard (456 pieces), minor (228 pieces); directions for administering ['58, 9 pages, directions printed in English,

French, German, and Spanish in same booklet]; manual ('54, see 39); revised record booklet ['54, c1951, 4 pages]; no data on reliability; 205*s.* ($55) per standard set; 110*s.* ($35) per minor set; 21*s.* ($3) per tray; 52*s.* 6*d.* ($3.25) per 25 record booklets; 50*s.* ($8.50) per manual; postage extra; (20–40) minutes; Margaret Lowenfeld; Badger Tests Co., Ltd. *

REFERENCES

1–13. See 4:115.
14–56. See 5:147.
57. WERTHAM, FREDERIC. "A New Sign of Organic Brain Disease." Abstract. *Trans Am Neurol Assn* 65:197 '39. *
58. LISTER, ROBERT CARL. *The Use of the Lowenfeld Mosaic Test and the Mooney Closure Test With Seventy-Two Cerebral Palsied Children.* Master's thesis, University of Texas (Austin, Tex.), 1956.
59. MCCORMICK, ANNE, AND LIGHT, BERNARD H. "The Lowenfeld Mosaic Test: A Critique." *Proc W Va Acad Sci* 27:108–11 Je '56. *
60. CHASE, J. A. *A Developmental Study of the Lowenfeld Mosaic Test: Ages 6, 7, 8.* Master's thesis, University of Maine (Orono, Me.), 1957.
61. COLMAN, JAMES A. *Projective Test for Children (Modified Mosaic).* Master's thesis, Claremont College (Claremont, Calif.), 1957.
62. ZUCKER, LUISE J. *Ego Structure in Paranoid Schizophrenia.* Springfield, Ill.: Charles C Thomas, Publisher, 1958. Pp. x, 186. * (*PA* 33:1916)
63. ROBINSON, MARY EVANS. *An Investigation of the Performance of Brain-Injured Children on Certain Perceptual Tasks.* Doctor's thesis, Purdue University (Lafayette, Ind.), 1959. (*DA* 20:1870)
64. ABEL, THEODORA M. "Differential Responses to Projective Testing in a Negro Peasant Community: Montserrat, B.W.I." *Int J Social Psychiatry* 6:218–24 au '60. *
65. GLADSTON, ELAINE R., AND AMADO-HAGUENAUER, GINETTE. "Fluidity in the Limits of the Self." *Int J Social Psychiatry* 6:260–8 au '60. *
66. HORNE, E. P., AND BOVA, L. W., JR. "The Effect of Color on Pattern Stability in Mosaic Productions." *J General Psychol* 63:229–32 O '60. * (*PA* 35:3469)
67. HORNE, E. P., AND LANE, W. P. "Constancy or Creativity in Patterning Mosaic Test Performance." *J General Psychol* 63:165–70 O '60. * (*PA* 35:3408)
68. ASCOUGH, J. C. *The Mosaic Test: Validation and Cross-Validation of Objective Scores, Comparison With Clinical Judgment and the Bender Gestalt Test.* Master's thesis, West Virginia University (Morgantown, W. Va.), 1961.
69. METZ, J. RICHARD. "A Method for Measuring Aspects of Ego Strength." *J Proj Tech* 25:457–70 D '61. *
70. PELZ, KURT S.; AMES, LOUISE B.; AND PIKE, FRANCES. "Measurement of Psychologic Function in Geriatric Patients." *J Am Geriatrics Soc* 9:740–54 S '61. *
71. AMES, LOUISE BATES, AND ILG, FRANCES L. *Mosaic Patterns of American Children.* New York: Hoeber Medical Division, Harper & Row, Publishers, Inc., 1962. Pp. xii, 297. *
72. ASCOUGH, JAMES C., AND DANA, RICHARD H. "Concurrent Validities of the Mosaic and Bender Gestalt Tests." *J Consult Psychol* 26:430–4 O '62. * (*PA* 39:1713)
73. LOWENFELD, MARGARET. "Concerning Unrealized Factors in International Attitudes and Their Bearing on International Health." *Int Mental Health Res Newsl* 4(3–4):5–7 f–w '62. *
74. PELZ, KURT; PIKE, FRANCES; AND AMES, LOUISE B. "A Proposed Battery of Childhood Tests for Discriminating Between Different Levels of Intactness of Function in Elderly Subjects." *J Genetic Psychol* 100:23–40 Mr '62. * (*PA* 37:975)
75. ZUCKER, LUISE J. "Evaluating Psychopathology of the Self." *Ann N Y Acad Sci* 96:844–52 Ja 27 '62. * (*PA* 37:6769)
76. AMES, LOUISE BATES. "Usefulness of the Lowenfeld Mosaic Test in Predicting School Readiness in Kindergarten and Primary School Pupils." *J Genetic Psychol* 103:75–91 S '63. * (*PA* 39:1711)

T. R. MILES, *Professor of Psychology, University College of North Wales, Bangor, Wales.*

The material for the LMT comprises 456 small coloured pieces—squares, half squares, diamonds, and equilateral and scalene triangles. Six different colours are used (red, green, blue, yellow, white, and black) and each shape is available in all six colours. The subject is instructed simply to "do something" with this material, with no restriction as to the choice of pieces. The test has been used *inter alia* for assessment of neurotic and psychotic patients of all ages, for detection of brain damage, for industrial selection, for marriage guidance, in the anthropological field, for developmental studies in children, and indeed for much else. The relevant literature is now extensive, though attempts at statistical validation have yielded somewhat inconclusive results (*4*).

The LMT, in the reviewer's opinion, is comparable in stature to the Rorschach test. Moreover by its very nature it is liable to give rise to the same sort of controversy. Confusion exists in the case of tests of this kind as to the criteria by means of which one assesses their value. On the one hand it might be argued that if the test provides its users with relevant information in clinical and other contexts no further justification is needed. On the other hand it could be said that unless one takes seriously the possibility of statistical check one is simply being unscientific and obscurantist. In the reviewer's opinion the concept of "scientific validation" raises more problems than is commonly realised. Grounds for believing something may have all degrees of adequacy. Thus if on the basis of the LMT a user recommends an industrial firm to appoint X rather than Y, then ideally from the point of view of validation one ought to place X in the job for a given length of time, then "put the clock back" and place Y in identical conditions, and compare the results. (One subject in the experimental group and one subject in the control group are in theory all that is needed.) Now it need not be irrational to believe the hypothetical proposition that if per impossible this were done X would receive greater commendation from his employers than Y; and even a casual report from the firm to the effect that X is "doing all right," with no evidence at all about Y, gives some justification, albeit of a flimsy kind, for believing this hypothetical proposition to be true. The choice is not between cast-iron statistical validation on the one hand and sheer irrationality on the other; there is such a thing as a "good bet" and even such a thing as a "bad bet."

The LMT, in the reviewer's opinion, comes into the "good bet" category. It is clear from her book that the author has the flair for breaking new ground. Thus she tells us that it was her observations of different types of embroidery at festivals of peasants in central Europe which first gave her the idea of this kind of test. Again, one's confidence in the test is increased by the variety of different situations in which it can be given. So long as users of the test appreciate that they are exploring, not just following out a routine procedure such as taking someone's temperature, their investigations should certainly be encouraged.

George Westby, *Professor of Psychology, University College of South Wales and Monmouthshire, University of Wales, Cardiff, Wales.*

To the experienced clinical psychologist, the well made and attractively presented Mosaic Test of Margaret Lowenfeld needs little introduction, especially in circles where a holistic or "psychodynamic" approach to personality is paramount. Perhaps the newest recommendation to the more experimentally minded psychologist of this now more widely used technique of personality study is the conclusion of that well known Keeper of the Ark of the Scientific Convenant, Professor Eysenck, namely, that there is a statistically significant correlation between the personality descriptions made by experienced users of the test from subjects' mosaic designs, on the one hand, and the reports of psychiatrists on the other.

The present reviewer, having used the test experimentally without the benefit of norms or data on reliability, well remembers looking forward to reading the full account of the author and her collaborators at the Institute of Child Psychology, London, which she published in 1954 in the form of a definitive manual-text (*39*). One hoped to be able to decide whether the test offered advantages over other projective techniques of enquiry into personality structure, most of which are time consuming and uncertain to the point of frustration in the busy clinic context. The data given in the manual, however, lead one to wonder whether the problems of objectivity of scoring, communicability of results, validation, adequate norms, and reliability yield any more easily to satisfactory solution in the case of the LMT than in the Rorschach, the TAT, or other projective techniques such as free painting.

The claim made by the author is a large one. With these highly structured materials studied "in an exceptionally wide range of subjects" for 25 years, "the response made by the subject," it is stated, "though entirely spontaneous, nevertheless inescapably registers facts, not only about the subject's personality, but also about his power to perceive and manipulate accurately objects of defined shape. The test is capable, therefore, of providing exact information as to the stage of development or the degree of disturbance of perceptual powers in cases of amentia, severe neurosis or cerebral disease." The data so far available do suggest that some of these claims are true, but no less a claim is made for other well known techniques and with their more extensive published evidence they will naturally appeal more to the worker in the applied field. The LMT is attractive to children and as one would expect elicits an immediate and natural "play" response, a principle central to Lowenfeld's approach. But others offer this appeal also and it is doubtful if the LMT is more economical of time.

The crucial comparative judgments, however, must be made in respect of the "problem" criteria enumerated above.

The *Lowenfeld Mosaic Test* has certainly achieved a high degree of success in respect of the first of the desiderata of a good test—exact description and analysis of test products. The author's highly developed score sheet of four quarto pages requires entries under 23 main divisions of up to 220 defining characteristics, some of which are esoteric (e.g., "Kite reaction," "Fox reaction," "Rhinoceros reaction"), but most of which are in useful terms of commonly accepted and easily agreed geometrical and colour criteria and Gestalt configurative qualities. A careful reference to the 144 coloured plates of designs (which come with the manual in a special box) in the reading of the chapters on classification gives a considerable confidence in the thoroughness of this analysis and of the fitness of the scheme and its reliability for the recording and effectual communication of the common qualities and individuality of the designs produced. But, like many other promising research instruments in the field of personality, these descriptive categories have few, if any, equally impressive behavioural "dimensions" of the abiding personality with which to assess the predictive power of the test in respect of any general "erlebnistyp" (to use Rorschach's term). It is, however, a merit of the test as a research tool that it has not been constructed (like *The Blacky Pictures* for instance) on prematurely dogmatic theoretical foundations. Were it not that the few main syndromes of psychopathology are very firmly based on pre-theoretical empirical observation, the subsequent explanatory underpinning of these by often contradictory but "elastic" (though dogmatic!) theories would have no plausibility whatever. With an empirical (though *not* anti-theoretical) approach in clinical psychology and psychiatry, Lowenfeld's test seems to come to practical agreement. The test data are reality-anchored in observables and describables. Her recent statement of theories she is developing on the basis of her experience with the test is highly cautious. She explicitly states in the manual that she has deliberately eschewed in her description of the test and its uses, "the question of the relation between the forms of pattern produced, and possible psycho-analytic interpretations of such elements of design." She stresses the obvious dangers with such a flexible instrument of "falling into the trap of subjective intuitive interpretation." In the absence of exact analysis, she notes, "it is a dangerous instrument that can easily lead into the bog of superficial analogies that have no real basis." Explicitly in her "Theory of E" she refuses to dogmatize the test descriptions, e.g., in respect of aggressive behaviour as being necessarily due to an aggressive "instinct." "Explanations put forward by different schools," she says, "do not necessarily exclude one another"—a refreshingly scientific sentiment for a projective theorist. Nor does Lowenfeld belong to the cookbook school of colour interpretation. Red must not, she warns, lead one to an interpretation of hidden anger or destructiveness, for only in conversation with the subject can we be certain that the colour has not been used simply because it pleases him. Exclusive use of black and white may, likewise, "be expressive of aesthetic values or of retreat from emotional experience or expression." "Colours," she rightly says, "mean so many different things to different people" that a list of colour associations common in the "area" of the tester should be drawn up before attempting interpretation! And then presumably, even assuming a proper sampling, allowance must be made for individual differences of cultural conditionability and only very tentative suggestions in this field are possible. One cannot be surprised that interpretation is a difficult art.

The author's caution, however, is not so much in evidence outside her own clinical field. In the chapter, "The Use of the L.M.T. in the Study of Cultural Problems," the generalising of cultural attitudes into "Am-type" and "Eu-type," corresponding to the American and European civilisation, seems quite unsupported by any adequate sampling. The hypothesis indeed seems jejune in itself, possibly conceivable in an earlier climate of thought in social anthropology and sociology, but surely greatly weakened by the careful empirical studies of recent decades which have unveiled a bewildering variety of cultures and sub-cultures with complicating internal inconsistencies which render far more doubtful any generalisations about personality differences between "the" American and "the" European.

What of the test's claim to provide a communicable psychogram or diagnostic category? Sadly we must conclude that only insofar as a clinical group-language is shared will this be possible in theoretical terms. Among clinical workers generally, precious few validated and theoretically-anchored "dimensions" of personality continue to exist across the frontiers of the different research groups and analytical schools. As to the diagnostic and prognostic value of the test, insufficient evidence has emerged as yet of a scientifically acceptable kind. Larger groups fully statistically analysed are required and perhaps such research may be forthcoming with the increasing interest of American research workers in the test. Indeed, many of its less promising rivals, earlier and better known by the accident of history, have had much greater efforts lavished upon them. Scientifically precise instruments based on a sufficiency of varied experimental evidence no doubt will eventually be forged for the study of personality and for decision making in the applied fields. To this end the enthusiastic work of Lowenfeld is wholly admirable. But the clinical psychologist hoping to find such an instrument already available must be disappointed. Nevertheless, it is no small thing to be able to say that the LMT has the legitimate character and practical value of a clinical craftsman's "knack" as opposed to a clinical "gimmick." It is as a tool for continuing research, however, that the immediate future of the test, so far unjustifiably neglected, probably most properly lies.

For a review by C. J. Adcock, see 5:147; for excerpts from related book reviews, see B51 and 5:B274.

[229]

Machover Draw-A-Person Test. Ages 2 and over; 1949; also called *Machover Figure Drawing Test*; manual (192 pages, see 5 below); no accessories; $5.50 per manual, cash orders postpaid; (5-60) minutes without associations, (20-90) minutes with associations; Karen Machover; Charles C Thomas, Publisher. *

REFERENCES

1-13. See 4:111
14-52. See 5:148.
53. FATERSON, HANNA. "The Figure Drawing Test as an Adjunct in the Selection of Medical Students." *J Med Ed* 31:323-7 My '56. * (*PA* 31:1749)
54. BROWN, DANIEL G., AND TOLOR, ALEXANDER. "Human Figure Drawings as Indicators of Sexual Identification and Inversion." *Percept & Motor Skills* 7:199-211 S '57. * (*PA* 32:4167)
55. GEIST, HAROLD. "Emotional Aspects of Dermatitis." *J Clin & Exp Psychopathol* 18:87-93 Mr '57. * (*PA* 32:4433)
56. HENRICHS, THEODORE F. *Somatic Preoccupation and the Draw-A-Person Test: A Validation Study.* Master's thesis, Ohio University (Athens, Ohio), 1957.
57. HICKS, DAVID J. *Personality Factors Found in Institutionalized Deaf Adolescents as Compared to Non-Deafened Adolescents as Measured by the Draw-A-Person Test.* Master's thesis, University of Redlands (Redlands, Calif.), 1957.
58. HONIGMANN, JOHN J., AND CARRERA, RICHARD N. "Cross-Cultural Use of Machover's Figure Drawing Test." *Am Anthrop* 59:650-4 Ag '57. * (*PA* 33:3621)
59. SWENSEN, CLIFFORD H., JR. "Empirical Evaluations of Human Figure Drawings." *Psychol B* 54:431-66 N '57. * (*PA* 33:3807)
60. WIGGENHORN, ALLAN HAROLD. "An Investigation of Changes in Human Figure Drawings as a Function of Changes in the 'Self-Concept.'" *Provo Papers* 1:15-41 O '57. * (*PA* 35:2301)
61. COPELAND, LYNN P. "Draw A Person." *Psychometric Res B* (1):[6-8] My '58. *
62. DIAMOND, FLORENCE. *Style and Content in Personality Rigidity.* Doctor's thesis, Claremont Graduate School (Claremont, Calif.), 1958. (*DA* 20:2901)
63. DWINELL, ALICE J. *An Investigation of the Machover Personality Projection Test as an Approach to Locating Personality Problems at the First Grade Level.* Master's thesis, Boston University (Boston, Mass.), 1958.
64. FISHER, RHODA LEE. "The Effect of a Disturbing Situation Upon the Stability of Various Projective Tests." *Psychol Monogr* 72:1-23 '58. * (*PA* 34:1357)
65. ROSENFELD, IRWIN JOSEPH. *Mathematical Ability as a Function of Perceptual Field-Dependency and Certain Personality Variables.* Doctor's thesis, University of Oklahoma (Norman, Okla.), 1958. (*DA* 19:880)
66. VERNIER, CLAIRE M.; STAFFORD, JOHN W.; AND KRUGMAN, ARNOLD D. "A Factor Analysis of Indices From Four Projective Techniques Associated With Four Different Types of Physical Pathology." *J Consult Psychol* 22:433-7 D '58. * (*PA* 33:9360)
67. ARBIT, JACK; LAKIN, MARTIN; AND MATHIS, ANDREW G. "Clinical Psychologists' Diagnostic Utilization of Human Figure Drawings." *J Clin Psychol* 15:325-7 Jl '59. * (*PA* 35:3479)
68. BOLOTIN, MAX. *The Use of Human Figure Drawings in Evaluating Children and Adolescents of Special Educational and Cultural Background: An Examination of the Effectiveness of Current Diagnostic Criteria With the Draw-A-Person Test as Applied to Puerto Rican Children and Adolescents.* Doctor's thesis, New York University (New York, N.Y.), 1959. (*DA* 20:4030)
69. BUTLER, R. L., AND MARCUSE, F. L. "Sex Identification at Different Ages Using the Draw-A-Person Test." *J Proj Tech* 23:299-302 S '59. * (*PA* 35:4871)
70. CLEVELAND, SIDNEY E. "Personality Dynamics in Torticollis." *J Nerv & Mental Dis* 129:150-61 Ag '59. * (*PA* 34:6407)
71. COLTHARP, FRANCES C. *A Validation Study of the Draw-A-Person Test.* Master's thesis, Southern Methodist University (Dallas, Tex.), 1959.
72. EPSTEIN, LAWRENCE, AND HARTFORD, HUNTINGTON. "Some Relationships of Beginning Strokes in Handwriting to the Human Figure Drawing Test." *Percept & Motor Skills* 9:55-62 Mr '59. * (*PA* 34:1354)
73. FISHER, GARY M. "Comment on Starr and Marcuse's 'Reliability in the Draw A Person Test.'" *Percept & Motor Skills* 9:302 S '59. * (*PA* 34:7842)
74. FISHER, GARY M. "Relationship Between Diagnosis of Neuropsychiatric Disorder, Sexual Deviation, and the Sex of the First-Drawn Figure." *Percept & Motor Skills* 9:47-50 Mr '59. * (*PA* 34:1356)
75. GRIFFITH, ALBERT V., AND PEYMAN, D. A. R. "Eye-Ear Emphasis in the DAP as Indicating Ideas of Reference." Abstract. *J Consult Psychol* 23:560 D '59. * (*PA* 34:6020)
76. HOYT, THOMAS E., AND BARON, MARTIN R. "Anxiety Indices in Same-Sex Drawings of Psychiatric Patients With High and Low MAS Scores." *J Consult Psychol* 23:448-52 O '59. * (*PA* 34:5622)
77. LEPPEL, LEON. *The Stability of Performance of Schizophrenics on the Draw-A-Person Test.* Doctor's thesis, Temple University (Philadelphia, Pa.), 1959. (*DA* 20:375)
78. LEVITT, EUGENE E., AND GROSZ, HANUS J. "A Note on Sex Sequence in the Draw-A-Person Test." *Psychol Newsl* 10:213-4 Mr-Ap '59. * (*PA* 34:1387)
79. LUBIN, BERNARD. "Differentiation of Overtly Stable and Unstable Psychiatric Aides by Means of the DAP Test." *Psychol Rep* 5:26 Mr '59. * (*PA* 34:1388)
80. MACHOVER, SOLOMON, AND PUZZO, FRANK S. "Clinical and Objective Studies of Personality Variables in Alcoholism: 1, Clinical Investigation of the 'Alcoholic Personality.'" *Q J Studies Alcohol* 20:505-19 S '59. * (*PA* 34:6253)
81. MACHOVER, SOLOMON, AND PUZZO, FRANK S. "Clinical and Objective Studies of Personality Variables in Alcoholism: 2, Clinical Study of Personality Correlates of Remission From Active Alcoholism." *Q J Studies Alcohol* 20:520-7 S '59. * (*PA* 34:6253)
82. MACHOVER, SOLOMON; PUZZO, FRANK S.; MACHOVER, KAREN; AND PLUMEAU, FRANCIS. "Clinical and Objective Studies of Personality Variables in Alcoholism: 3, An Objective Study of Homosexuality in Alcoholism." *Q J Studies Alcohol* 20:528-42 S '59. * (*PA* 34:6254)
83. ORME, J. E. "Human Figure Drawings of Schizophrenic and Depressed Patients." *Psychiatria et Neurologia* 138:364-8 '59. *
84. RABIN, A. I., AND LIMUACO, JOSEFINA A. "Sexual Differentiation of American and Filipino Children as Reflected in the Draw-A-Person Test." *J Social Psychol* 50:207-11 N '59. * (*PA* 35:4765)
85. SCHMIDT, LYLE D., AND MCGOWAN, JOHN F. "The Differentiation of Human Figure Drawings." *J Consult Psychol* 23:129-33 Ap '59. * (*PA* 34:1418)
86. SPOCK, ANNE INGERSOLL. *An Investigation of the Relationship Between Confusion in Sex-Role Identification and Social Maladjustment in Childhood.* Doctor's thesis, American University (Washington, D.C.), 1959. (*DA* 20:2893)
87. STARR, S., AND MARCUSE, F. L. "Reliability in the 'Draw-A-Person' Test." *J Proj Tech* 23:83-6 Mr '59. *
88. BICKLEY, BENJAMIN R. *A Validity Study of Machover's Homosexual Signs in the Draw-A-Person Test.* Master's thesis, Fresno State College (Fresno, Calif.), 1960.
89. BLIZZARD, B. THEODORE. *Projective Limitations in the Use of the Draw-A-Person With Mentally Retarded Adolescents.* Master's thesis, Kansas State College of Pittsburg (Pittsburg, Kan.), 1960.
90. BODWIN, RAYMOND F., AND BRUCK, MAX. "The Adaptation and Validation of the Draw-A-Person Test as a Measure of Self Concept." *J Clin Psychol* 16:427-9 O '60. * (*PA* 37:3104)
91. DAVIDS, ANTHONY, AND DEVAULT, SPENCER. "Use of the TAT and Human Figure Drawings in Research on Personality, Pregnancy, and Perception." *J Proj Tech* 24:362-5 D '60. * (*PA* 35:4872)
92. FISHER, SEYMOUR. "Right-Left Gradients in Body Image, Body Reactivity, and Perception." *Genetic Psychol Monogr* 61:197-228 My '60. * (*PA* 35:6478)
93. HAGGERTY, ARTHUR D. "Cautions Required in the Interpretation of Projective Tests With Applicants to a School of Professional Nursing." *J General Psychol* 63:57-62 Jl '60. * (*PA* 35:7080)
94. HUNT, RAYMOND G., AND FELDMAN, MARVIN J. "Body Image and Ratings of Adjustment on Human Figure Drawings." *J Clin Psychol* 16:35-8 Ja '60. * (*PA* 36:1HE35H)
95. MACHOVER, KAREN. Chap. 13, "Sex Differences in the Developmental Pattern of Children as Seen in Human Figure Drawings," pp. 238-57. In *Projective Techniques With Children.* Edited by Albert I. Rabin and Mary R. Haworth. New York: Grune & Stratton, Inc., 1960. Pp. xiii, 392. * (*PA* 35:2229)
96. MACHOVER, KAREN, AND LIEBERT, ROBERT. "Human Figure Drawings of Schizophrenic and Normal Adults: Changes Following Administration of Lysergic Acid." *Arch Gen Psychiatry* 3:139-52 Ag '60. *
97. SPOTTS, JAMES V., JR. *A Test of Machover's Hypothesis Regarding the Social Significance of the Head and Face in Children's Human Figure Drawings.* Master's thesis, University of Kansas (Lawrence, Kan.), 1960.
98. ARMSTRONG, RENATE G., AND HAUCK, PAUL A. "Sexual Identification and the First Figure Drawn." *J Consult Psychol* 25:51-4 F '61. * (*PA* 36:3HE51A)
99. COHEN, SANFORD L.; SILVERMAN, ALBERT J.; WADDELL, WILLIAM; AND ZUIDEMA, GEORGE D. "Urinary Catechol Amine Levels, Gastric Secretion and Specific Psychological Factors in Ulcer and Non-Ulcer Patients." *J Psychosom Res* 5:90-115 F '61. * (*PA* 36:3JH90C)
100. FISHER, GARY M. "Nudity in Human Figure Drawings." *J Clin Psychol* 17:307-8 Jl '61. * (*PA* 38:8548)
101. HAWORTH, MARY R., AND NORMINGTON, CHERYL J. "A Sexual Differentiation Scale for the D-A-P Test (for Use With Children)." *J Proj Tech* 25:441-50 D '61. *
102. JONES, LEONA W., AND THOMAS, CAROLINE B. "Studies on Figure Drawings." *Psychiatric Q Sup* 35:212-61 pt 2 '61. * (*PA* 37:5041)

103. LACHMANN, F. M.; BAILEY, M. A.; AND BERRICK, M. E. "The Relationship Between Manifest Anxiety and Clinicians' Evaluations of Projective Test Responses." *J Clin Psychol* 17:11–3 Ja '61. * (*PA* 37:3113)
104. MCGUIRL, DONALD. *Communication in Drawings: An Indirect Validation Study of the "Draw-A-Person" Test Through the Cartoons of William Steig.* Master's thesis, University of Kansas (Lawrence, Kan.), 1961.
105. NIELSEN, HELLE H. "Human Figure Drawings by Normal and Physically Handicapped Children: Draw-A-Person Test." *Scandinavian J Psychol* 2(3):129–38 '61. *
106. SAUNDERS, MAUDERIE HANCOCK. *An Analysis of Cultural Differences on Certain Projective Techniques.* Doctor's thesis, University of Oklahoma (Norman, Okla.), 1961. (*DA* 22:490)
107. STOLTZ, ROBERT E., AND COLTHARP, FRANCES C. "Clinical Judgments and the Draw-A-Person Test." *J Consult Psychol* 25:43–5 F '61. * (*PA* 36:3HI43S)
108. WHITAKER, LEIGHTON, JR. "The Use of an Extended Draw-A-Person Test to Identify Homosexual and Effeminate Men." *J Consult Psychol* 25:482–5 D '61. * (*PA* 37:5051)
109. BAUGH, VERNER S., AND CARPENTER, B. L. "A Comparison of Delinquents and Nondelinquents." *J Social Psychol* 56:73–8 F '62. * (*PA* 36:5JO73B)
110. BRUCK, MAX, AND BODWIN, RAYMOND F. "The Relationship Between Self-Concept and the Presence and Absence of Scholastic Underachievement." *J Clin Psychol* 18:181–2 Ap '62. * (*PA* 38:9278)
111. CRADDICK, RAY A. "Draw-A-Person Characteristics of Psychopathic Prisoners and College Students." *Percept & Motor Skills* 15:11–3 Ag '62. * (*PA* 37:5446)
112. CRADDICK, RAY A.; LEIPOLD, WILLIAM D.; AND CACAVAS, PETER D. "The Relationship of Shading on the Draw-A-Person Test to Manifest Anxiety Scores." *J Consult Psychol* 26:193 Ap '62. * (*PA* 37:5080)
113. CROVITZ, HERBERT F. "On Direction in Drawing A Person." Abstract. *J Consult Psychol* 26:196 Ap '62. * (*PA* 37:4978)
114. DALY, WILLIAM, AND HUBER, WILLIAM. "A Note on 'Sexual Identification in Mentally Subnormal Females' by Fisher." *Am J Mental Def* 66:782–3 Mr '62. * (*PA* 37:1683, title only)
115. EXNER, JOHN E., JR. "A Comparison of the Human Figure Drawings of Psychoneurotics, Character Disturbances, Normals, and Subjects Experiencing Experimentally-Induced Fear." *J Proj Tech* 26:392–7 D '62. * (*PA* 37:6754)
116. FISHER, GARY M. "A Note on 'Sexual Identification in Mentally Subnormal Females' by Fisher: Reply to Daly and Huber." *Am J Mental Def* 66:784 Mr '62. * (*PA* 37:1689, title only)
117. HAWORTH, MARY R. "Responses of Children to a Group Projective Film and to the Rorschach, CAT, Despert Fables and D-A-P." *J Proj Tech* 26:47–60 Mr '62. * (*PA* 37:2893)
118. LAIRD, JAMES T. "A Comparison of Male Normals, Psychiatric Patients and Alcoholics for Sex Drawn First." *J Clin Psychol* 18:302 Jl '62. * (*PA* 39:1861)
119. MCGUIRL, DONALD, AND MOSS, C. SCOTT. "An Indirect Validation Study of the Draw-A-Person Test Through the Cartoons of William Steig." *J Proj Tech* 26:88–95 Mr '62. * (*PA* 37:3115)
120. MOGAR, ROBERT E. "Anxiety Indices in Human Figure Drawings: A Replication and Extension." Abstract. *J Consult Psychol* 26:108 F '62. * (*PA* 37:4989)
121. NICHOLS, ROBERT C., AND STRÜMPFER, DEODANDUS J. W. "A Factor Analysis of Draw-A-Person Test Scores." *J Consult Psychol* 26:156–61 Ap '62. * (*PA* 37:4990)
122. NICKOLS, JOHN. "Size Judgment and the Draw-A-Person Test." *J Psychol Studies* 13:117–9 Je '62 [issued F '64]. *
123. PEDRINI, DUILIO T., AND PEDRINI, LURA NANCY. "Hearing Efficiency–Inefficiency and Personal-Social Ease–Dis-ease, 2." *Psychiatric Q* 36:428–54 Ja '62. *
124. SHANAN, JOEL. "Intraindividual Response Variability in Figure Drawing Tasks." *J Proj Tech* 26:105–11 Mr '62. * (*PA* 37:3161)
125. STRÜMPFER, DEODANDUS J. W., AND NICHOLS, ROBERT C. "A Study of Some Communicable Measures for the Evaluation of Human Figure Drawings." *J Proj Tech* 26:342–53 S '62. * (*PA* 37:3240)
126. ZUK, G. H. "Relation of Mental Age to Size of Figure on the Draw-A-Person Test." *Percept & Motor Skills* 14:410 Je '62. * (*PA* 37:3325)
127. BARNOUW, VICTOR. Chap. 17, "Drawing Analysis," pp. 276–98. In his *Culture and Personality.* Homewood, Ill.: Dorsey Press, Inc., 1963. Pp. xi, 410. *
128. BRUCK, MAX, AND BODWIN, RAYMOND F. "Age Differences Between SCS-DAP Test Results and GPA." *J Clin Psychol* 19:315–6 Jl '63. *
129. CRADDICK, RAY A. "The Self-Image in the Draw-A-Person Test and Self-Portrait Drawings." *J Proj Tech & Pers Assess* 27:288–91 S '63. * (*PA* 38:4298)
130. ENDICOTT, NOBLE A., AND ENDICOTT, JEAN. " 'Improvement' in Untreated Psychiatric Patients." *Arch Gen Psychiatry* 9:575–85 D '63. * (*PA* 38:8643)
131. EVANS, RAY B., AND MARMORSTON, JESSIE. "Psychological Test Signs of Brain Damage in Cerebral Thrombosis." *Psychol Rep* 12:915–30 Je '63. * (*PA* 38:6413)
132. HEBERLEIN, MARJORIE, AND MARCUSE, F. L. "Personality Variables in the DAP." Abstract. *J Consult Psychol* 27:461 O '63. *
133. KARP, STEPHEN A.; POSTER, DOROTHY C.; AND GOODMAN, ALAN. "Differentiation in Alcoholic Women." *J Personality* 31:386–93 S '63. *
134. MCHUGH, ANN F. "Sexual Identification, Size, and Associations in Children's Figure Drawings." *J Clin Psychol* 19:381–2 Jl '63. *
135. WEST, J. V.; BAUGH, V. S.; AND BAUGH, ANNIE P. "Rorschach and Draw-A-Person Responses of Hypnotized and Nonhypnotized Subjects." *Psychiatric Q* 37:123–7 Ja '63. *
136. WOLFSON, WILLIAM. "Profile Drawings and Procrastination." *Percept & Motor Skills* 17:570 O '63. * (*PA* 38:6112)

PHILIP M. KITAY, *Professor of Psychology, Adelphi University, Garden City, New York.*

This projective technique, second only to the Rorschach in popularity according to Sundberg,[1] has gained a large following probably because it appears to be easy to administer and interpret, economical of time, and interesting. Herein lies a danger. Machover (*12*) admits that the test is vulnerable to misuse because there are no special materials needed, no complicated directions, scoring, and coding to be mastered. She wisely advises that it is best used in combination with other techniques, both in diagnosis and research.

As is typical for projective techniques, the value of the yield from human figure drawings depends upon the clinical skills of the examiner, his knowledge of psychodynamics, and experience with the technique. It is important for the examiner to be well versed on body symbolism, interpretation of expressive movements, and graphomotor functioning.

More skill is required of the examiner in administering the test than is implied in Machover's (*12*) statement that it may be administered to groups of any size since actual administration requires only partial attention of the examiner. In the case of group administration, interpretation based on sequence in drawing body parts, time spent on each, questions asked of the examiner, spontaneous comments, and number of repeated erasures is not possible. The value of the optional associations or post-drawing inquiry depends upon the examiner's skill in handling it. More research is needed upon this aspect of the test.

Insufficient consideration has been given to the possible influences upon the drawings of such variables as the setting and the examinee's perception of the purpose of the examination. Effort and seriousness of approach may be different for individuals participating in a re-

1 SUNDBERG, NORMAN D. "The Practice of Psychological Testing in Clinical Services in the United States." *Am Psychologist* 16:79–83 F '61. *

search group administration of the test and for those being privately examined for clinical diagnosis. One would like to know whether the perception of the test as a measurement of creative ability, of intelligence, of artistic aptitude, or of emotional stability has an influence upon the kind of drawing produced. Research studies fail to emphasize sufficiently whether group or individual administration was employed, with the unwarranted implication that it is an unimportant variable.

The Machover manual (*5*) is most inadequate in its coverage of theoretical bases and procedures for interpretation, reliability, and validity. It is deficient in regard to number of illustrative drawings, exactness of description of drawing items to be interpreted, and rationale and empirical evidence for interpretations offered. Statistical normative data are not presented. A similar omission of statistical data is found in a recent large scale empirical study by Machover (*95*) of sex differences in drawings of children. There is need for a comprehensive manual providing detailed consideration of administration, description and interpretation of items along a scale, large number of illustrative plates for item and global interpretation, normative data by age, sex, and other population variables, and summary of research studies on reliability and validity.

The examiner may find helpful in overcoming some of the above shortcomings: (*a*) Vernier's [2] large collection of drawings grouped by psychiatric diagnosis of testees and Gurvitz's appendix (*10*) of drawings by seventeen patients and (*b*) "Short Scale of Figure Drawing Items" in Appendix A of *Personality Through Perception* by Witkin and others (*30*) for exact description of some drawing items. For evaluation of voluminous research on human figure drawing, the review by Swensen (*59*) of an eight year period and one by Jones and Thomas (*102*) of a decade are most useful. Swensen concludes that more research evidence contradicts Machover's hypotheses on interpretation than supports them. He urges more research on reliability and validity of patterns of signs rather than of individual signs. Jones and Thomas recommend further research on validity and reliability due to the present unclear picture in regard to them. They find encouraging the reliability of scoring and satisfactory correlations with other personality assessments demonstrated in the study by Witkin and others (*30*). In both reviews (*59, 102*) the sound advice is given that for clinical diagnosis the test be used as part of a battery and that by itself it be used only as a screening device. The reviewer agrees with this position.

Zimmer's [3] complaint that research on validity has employed criteria of adjustment-maladjustment instead of indicators of personality dynamics seems worthy of consideration by researchers. Brown's (*17*) opinion that many sets of successive drawings, as in the Caligor [4] modification of human figure drawing technique, may be more revealing than a single set should spur more investigation into this approach. An important warning is given by both Brown (*17*) and Buck [5] that the Draw-A-Person technique is very sensitive to psychopathology. There is danger that the diagnostician may therefore overestimate the degree of pathology present in the personality evaluated.

This reviewer believes that a most promising approach to an increased understanding of the meaning of drawings is to be found in studies of the effects of experimental manipulation of subjects upon their drawings. For example, clinical improvement in patients after regressive electric shock treatment was paralleled in improvement in successive drawings; [6] lowered self-concept resulting from artificially created stress was reflected in before-after drawings (*60*); and increased use of shading, an anxiety indicator, appeared following experimentally induced fear (*115*).

In spite of Machover's (*5, 28, 95*) repeated observations on the differences between males and females in their drawings of the human figure, she fails to provide systematized and separate guides for the interpretation of drawings by males and females. She reported (*28*)

2 VERNIER, CLAIRE MYERS. *Projective Test Productions: I, Projective Drawings.* New York: Grune and Stratton, Inc., 1952. Pp. vii, 168. *

3 ZIMMER, HERBERT. Chap. 4, "Validity of Sentence Completion Tests and Human Figure Drawings," pp. 58–75. (*PA* 30:7239) In *Progress in Clinical Psychology, Volume II.* Edited by Daniel Brower and Lawrence E. Abt. New York: Grune and Stratton, Inc., 1956. Pp. viii, 364. *

4 CALIGOR, LEOPOLD. "The Determination of the Individual's Unconscious Conception of His Own Masculinity-Femininity Identification." *J Proj Tech* 15:494–509 D '51. *

5 BUCK, JOHN N., EDITOR. *Administration and Interpretation of the H-T-P Test: Proceedings of the H-T-P Workshop Held at Veterans Administration Hospital, Richmond 19, Virginia, March 31, April 1, 2, 1950.* [Beverly Hills, Calif.: Western Psychological Services, 1950.] Pp. 67. Paper, mimeographed. *

6 GLUECK, BERNARD C., JR.; KRASNER, JACK D.; AND PARRES, RAMON. Chap. 13, "The Use of Serial Testing in Regressive Electroshock Treatment," pp. 244–57. In *Relation of Psychological Tests to Psychiatry.* Edited by Paul H. Hoch and Joseph Zubin. New York: Grune & Stratton, Inc., 1952. Pp. viii, 301. *

that body projection as reflected in the D-A-P was more closely related to personality in men than in women. With self-portraits drawn from the mirror by adolescents, Stewart [7] found that girls' portraits were more stereotyped than those done by boys and that the same stylistic graphic variables had very different relationships to personality traits in boys and girls. He noted that the opposite poles on some drawing items were indicators of a similar personality makeup and that the distributions of stylistic variables in the population were of unusual types for which most of the popular tests of statistical significance might be inappropriate. Do these findings on self-portrait apply to the Machover technique? If it is found to be so, approaches to its validation will need modification. There is an urgency for published data on distributions of population samples on graphic variables on the D-A-P.

Since the D-A-P technique is so frequently included in diagnostic test batteries in spite of uncertainty about its reliability and validity, clinicians appear to be impressed by the extent and congruency of its contribution to the evaluation of personality. In the hands of experienced clinicians with their checking on internal consistency and weighting of evidence from various tests in the battery, there is little danger of naïve reliance upon the D-A-P. The many negative findings in the literature should make clinicians more concerned about avoiding a mechanical or reflex type of application of Machover's hypotheses to the interpretation of drawings. The user of the D-A-P test may gain greater exactness and precision in approach by following some of the recommendations made by Buck [8] in his rather overlaborious and highly quantitative approach for his House-Tree-Person test. Inexactness in the description of graphic signs, looseness in exposition of principles of interpretation, and absence of published normative data are the most formidable obstacles to placing the D-A-P technique on the firm foundation that it deserves.

For reviews by Philip L. Harriman and Naomi Stewart, see 4:111; for excerpts from related book reviews, see 4:112.

7 Stewart, Louis H. "The Expression of Personality in Drawings and Paintings." *Genet Psychol Monogr* 51:45–103 F '55. (*PA* 30:628)
8 Buck, *op. cit.*

[230]

Make A Picture Story. Ages 6 and over; 1947–52; individual; 1 form ('47, 22 background pictures and 67 figure cutouts); figure location sheet ('48, 4 pages); manual ('52, 96 pages, see *27* below); no data on reliability and validity; $17 per set of test materials, 25 figure location sheets, and manual; $2 per 25 figure location sheets; $2.50 per manual; $16.50 per theater (optional); postpaid; (45–90) minutes; Edwin S. Shneidman; Psychological Corporation. *

REFERENCES

1–19. See 4:113.
20–38. See 5:149.
39. Shneidman, Edwin S. Chap. 17, "Some Relationships Between the Rorschach Technique and Other Psychodiagnostic Tests," pp. 595–642. In *Developments in the Rorschach Technique: Volume 2, Fields of Application.* By Bruno Klopfer and others. Yonkers, N.Y.: World Book Co., 1956. Pp. xx, 828. * (*PA* 30:7202)
40. Feffer, Melvin H. "The Cognitive Implications of Role Taking Behavior." *J Personality* 27:152–68 Je '59. * (*PA* 34:4380)
41. Little, Kenneth B., and Shneidman, Edwin S. "Congruencies Among Interpretations of Psychological Test and Anamnestic Data." *Psychol Monogr* 73(6):1–42 '59. * (*PA* 34:3010)
42. Hess, D. Wilson. *The Evaluation of Personality and Adjustment in Deaf and Hearing Children Using Nonverbal Modification of the Make A Picture Story (MAPS) Test.* Doctor's thesis, University of Rochester (Rochester, N.Y.), 1960.
43. Shneidman, Edwin S. Chap. 7, "The MAPS Test With Children," pp. 130–48. In *Projective Techniques With Children.* Edited by Albert I. Rabin and Mary R. Haworth. New York: Grune & Stratton, Inc., 1960. Pp. xiii, 392. * (*PA* 35:2229)
44. Fine, Reuben. "The Case of El: The MAPS Test." *J Proj Tech* 25:383–9 D '61. *
45. Forer, Bertram R. "The Case of El: Vocational Choice." *J Proj Tech* 25:371–4 D '61. *
46. Murray, Henry A. "Commentary on the Case of El." *J Proj Tech* 25:404–11 D '61. *
47. Rashap, Bernard Leonard. *An Exploratory Study of Mediational Processes in Verbal Behavior: An Investigation of Verbal Mediator Interaction Reflected by Changes in a Form of the Semantic Differential as Applied to a Thematic Projective Technique.* Doctor's thesis, New York University (New York, N.Y.), 1961. (*DA* 22:653)
48. Shneidman, Edwin S. "The Logic of El: A Psychological Approach to the Analysis of Test Data." *J Proj Tech* 25:390–403 D '61. *

Arthur R. Jensen, *Associate Professor of Educational Psychology, and Associate Research Psychologist, Institute of Human Learning, University of California, Berkeley, California.*

The MAPS test is a thematic apperception test—a kind of do-it-yourself TAT—in which the subject makes up his own pictures and then tells stories about the pictures. The test materials consist of 22 pictorial backgrounds, including a blank card, of varying degrees of structure (a living room, a bedroom, a bathroom, a cave, a schoolroom, etc.). These pictures (8½ by 11 inches in size) are held upright in a wooden frame. The dramatis personae are 67 cutout cardboard figures—male and female adults, nudes, children, minority figures such as Negroes, Mexicans, and Orientals, animal figures, legendary and fictitious characters (e.g., Santa Claus), silhouettes, and figures with blank faces. The figures are held upright by insertion into a wooden base. The examiner places a background picture before the subject and asks him to select any figures he wishes to put into the scene and to make up a story about it in much the same manner as subjects are instructed to do for the TAT. Usually not more than 10 of the scenes are used. Even then, the test is very time consuming, usually requiring from 45 to 90 minutes. A study (*35*) of the clinical use of the test with 64 children from ages 3½ to 16 indicates that 12 clinicians used on the average 8 scenes, with a range from 2 to 12. The average number of figures used by the subjects was 3.9 per card.

The MAPS protocol can be subjected to various elaborate formal scoring schemes (*18, 27, 35*)[1] which require a great deal of the examiner's time. In clinical practice, however, the protocol is most often interpreted in a holistic, impressionistic manner in much the same way as the TAT is approached. Detailed examples of how the test is interpreted by experts may be found in the book edited by Shneidman (*18*), the inventor of the MAPS.

Because the MAPS is much more cumbersome to use than the TAT and does not seem to yield anything substantially different from the kinds of psychological insights gained through the TAT, it has not gained widespread popularity as a clinical instrument. Clinicians who have acquired subjective "norms" through extensive use of the TAT are reluctant to take the time required to develop a "feel" for the MAPS. A nationwide survey[2] on the use of psychological tests in clinical practice showed that among 62 tests the MAPS ranks 26th in frequency of usage.

The MAPS has inspired comparatively little research. There are no satisfactory normative data (*35*), and, indeed, norms would be extremely difficult to establish because of the tremendous variability in the stimulus situation for every subject. Even if norms did exist, it is doubtful that they would serve any practical purpose. Normative data on the TAT, for example, are rarely referred to in clinical practice. The aim of these unstructured tests is to yield protocols that can act as projective materials for the play of the clinician's own intuitions. The clinician's written report of the interpretation, in turn, might be regarded as projective material for the psychiatrist to whom it is addressed. The question is, how much does it really add to anyone's knowledge of the patient?

RELIABILITY AND VALIDITY. The best study of the reliability and validity of MAPS interpretation is provided by Little and Shneidman (*41*), who had 12 experts in the use of the MAPS perform a number of interpretive tasks on the protocols of 12 patients equally divided among the categories of psychiatrically normal, psychotic, neurotic, and psychosomatic. (Experts of the Rorschach, TAT, and MMPI performed the same tasks for comparative purposes.) The same interpretive tasks were carried out by 23 psychiatrists and one clinical psychologist on the basis of very thorough anamnestic data.

The reliability was assessed in terms of the agreement among the MAPS judges and the agreement of each judge with himself when performing the same interpretive tasks on the same protocols 10 days later. In the assignment of diagnostic labels there was no greater than chance agreement among the judges. (This was true also for the TAT.) On a set of 117 true-false personality items typical of the statements in psychological reports, the correlations between the MAPS judges and the anamnestic judges ranged from −.19 to .67, with a mean of .33. The same interpretive task performed 10 days later by the MAPS judges produced correlations with their original interpretations ranging from .48 to .94, with a mean of .77. On a set of 100 true-false factual items from the patients' case histories, the MAPS judges produced correlations ranging from −.22 to .50, with a mean of .16. Correlations between interpretations performed 10 days apart ranged from .38 to .91, with a mean of .77. The judges also performed Q-sorts of 76 items typical of interpretive statements found in psychological reports. The correlations among the Q-sorts of the MAPS judges ranged from .07 to .71, with a mean of .35. The correlations of each judge with himself 10 days later ranged from .19 to .94, with a mean of .60. Correlations between Q-sorts of the MAPS judges and of the anamnestic judges ranged from −.39 to .53, with a mean of .13. There was an average correlation of .22 among the Q-sorts of different patients rated by the same judge, indicating that the judges tend to make their in-

1 FINE, REUBEN. "A Scoring Scheme for the TAT and Other Projective Techniques." *J Proj Tech* 19:306–9 S '55. * (*PA* 30:4571)

2 SUNDBERG, NORMAN D. "The Practice of Psychological Testing in Clinical Services in the United States." *Am Psychologist* 16:79–83 F '61. *

terpretations in a stereotyped manner more or less independent of the subject.

SUMMARY. The MAPS is a highly unstructured projective technique similar in purpose and product to the TAT. The inter-judge reliability of interpretations based on the MAPS is in the region of .30 to .40 for experts. The validity of interpretation is represented by correlations in the range of .10 to .20 for experts. Validity such as this, of course, is useless for individual assessment. At present there is no basis for recommending the MAPS for any practical use.

For reviews by Albert I. Rabin and Charles R. Strother, see 4:113; for excerpts from related book reviews, see 4:114.

[230a]

★Miner Sentence Completion Scale. Adults, particularly managers and management trainees; 1961–64; 1 form ('61, 4 pages); scoring guide ('64, 64 pages); scoring sheet ('61, 1 page); no data on reliability and validity; $8.50 per set of 50 scales and 50 scoring sheets; $2.75 per scoring guide; postpaid; specimen set not available; [30] minutes; John B. Miner; Springer Publishing Co., Inc. *

REFERENCES

1. MINER, JOHN B. "The Effect of a Course in Psychology on the Attitudes of Research and Development Supervisors." *J Appl Psychol* 44:224–32 Je '60. * (*PA* 35:4094)
2. MINER, JOHN B. "Occupational Differences in the Desire to Exercise Power." *Psychol Rep* 13:18 Ag '63. *

[231]

★Minnesota Percepto-Diagnostic Test. Ages 8–15, 18–65; 1962–63; brain damage and emotional disturbances; individual; 1 form ('62, 6 cards and protractor); manual ('63, 33 pages, reprint of *1* below); separate profiles ('62, 1 page) for children, adults; $3.50 per set of testing materials; $2.50 per 50 profiles; $2.50 per manual; postpaid; administration time not reported; G. B. Fuller and J. T. Laird; Journal of Clinical Psychology. *

REFERENCES

1. FULLER, GERALD B., AND LAIRD, JAMES T. "The Minnesota Percepto-Diagnostic Test." *J Clin Psychol* 19:3–34 Ja '63. * (Also published as a separate Monograph Supplement No. 16.) (*PA* 39:1696)
2. UYENO, ENSLEY. "Differentiating Psychotics From Organics on the Minnesota Percepto-Diagnostic Test." Abstract. *J Consult Psychol* 27:462 O '63. *

RICHARD W. COAN, *Professor of Psychology, University of Arizona, Tucson, Arizona.*

The *Minnesota Percepto-Diagnostic Test* (MPD) utilizes two of Wertheimer's well known designs. Since each of these appears in three different orientations, the test contains a total of six stimulus figures. The subject is asked to copy the figures, as in Bender's *Visual Motor Gestalt Test,* and his reproductions are scored for amount of rotation.

The test rests on a theoretical rationale like that underlying Bender's test, but its aim is the more limited one of differentiating such broad diagnostic classes as organic brain damage, functional disturbance, and clinical normality. To further this aim, the authors have focused on the score variable which offers greatest promise and, in the course of systematic research, have selected the figures yielding best discrimination in terms of this variable. Obvious virtues of the test are a well standardized procedure, simplicity and brevity of administration, and an objective scoring system.

The manual does not purport to provide research findings in detail, but the details it does provide are sometimes misleading. In places, impressive significance levels are cited without the information on statistical procedures, specific comparisons made, and subgroup sample sizes that the reader would need to attach a clear meaning to the probabilities. In the summaries of two preliminary studies, critical scores devised for differential prediction are presented, without proper designation, in lieu of the data from which they are derived. The reader is thereby given the false impression that, without exception, "organics rotated 60 degrees or more, those with a personality disturbance both psychotic and neurotic, rotated from 21 to 59 degrees, and normals rotated under 21 degrees." The critical scores themselves may be appropriate, depending on what errors of diagnostic classification one seeks to minimize, but the manual would have been strengthened by a separate section dealing with the rationale and procedures employed in their derivation. A questionable bit of statistical logic appears in the discussion of a table presumably consisting of correlations (the statistic itself not being explicitly identified). Here the authors suggest that a high and significant relationship between rotation and IQ may be an artifact attributable to the narrow range of intelligence in the sample.

The usefulness of the manual as a whole could have been increased by more careful editing. Here and there, communication is hampered by oddities of grammar and expression. ("Correlations in terms of one score being compared to a retest score lowers the statistical relationship" and "The protractor placed on the base line would have the line extend through degree 90.") Both in the body of the text and in a table, a *positive* value of .40 is reported for the correlation between rotation and IQ in a normal sample. Yet it is stated that "the higher the IQ in a normal group, the less the rotation evidenced." In the scoring example for card 2, an unrotated figure is shown; the line allegedly representing the central axis of the figure is drawn in an incorrect position, and a rotation of 6° is recorded.

Despite these deficiencies, it must be granted that Fuller and Laird have succeeded in devising an instrument that discriminates well between normals and functionally disturbed individuals and between the latter and the organically brain damaged. At least in comparison with other instruments that serve this purpose, the MPD displays quite satisfactory validity. In practical applications, of course, it is not likely to display the same level of efficiency found in research. For one thing, expectancies for different types of disorders in any clinical setting will differ from those in a research employing predetermined numbers of brain damage cases, schizophrenics, etc. The likelihood of correctly diagnosing a case that is actually organic may not be affected by this difference, but the likelihood of interpreting a given score correctly will be affected. In a clinical population with very few organic cases, for example, most cases diagnosed by the test as organic will be false positives. Furthermore, the clinician must often evaluate patients whose symptoms are less clear-cut than those of research cases, and it is questionable whether mild brain damage can be reliably distinguished from, say, schizophrenia on the basis of a single index of rotation. For both of these reasons, it could be argued that the sort of differential diagnosis sought with the MPD can be accomplished best through the use of score patterns (not necessarily those now in use), rather than single indices. It should be noted that Fuller and Laird themselves stress the need for caution in interpreting MPD scores, in view of the fact that the amount of rotation may be affected by intelligence, personality variables (such as perfectionism), and the type and location of brain pathology.

In the present stage of test development, the MPD has much to recommend it. It is a convenient and economical clinical instrument whose most appropriate application is the diagnosis of organic brain damage. In comparison with comparable tests, it displays substantial validity for this purpose. While it may not provide the ultimate solution to a difficult psychodiagnostic problem, it merits inclusion in batteries designed for cases of suspected organicity. It should provide a useful supplement to the information yielded by other kinds of tests.

Eugene E. Levitt, *Professor of Clinical Psychology, Indiana University School of Medicine, Indianapolis, Indiana.*

This instrument is based on the view that Bender-Gestalt reproductions of psychiatric patients tend to be rotated from the axis of presentation, the tendency being greater among organics than among those with functional disturbances. In various experimental studies, rotation has been arbitrarily defined as a deviation of at least 30°, or 45°, etc. The MPD is one of the first attempts to derive a continuous, quantitative rotation score.

The test consists of six test figures, Figures A and 3 of the Bender-Gestalt, each presented in three ways: conventionally; on a diamond-shaped card with the figure rotated 90° from the usual presentation; and conventionally on a diamond-shaped card. The subject is not allowed to move the stimulus or the response sheet, and is then required to draw each of the figures. The measure derived is the amount of rotation in degrees from the vertical or horizontal axis, measured with a protractor and ruler. Scores of more than 25° are scored as 25°, so that there is an imposed ceiling of 150° on the subject's test score.

Distributions of scores for fairly large samples show little overlap between normals (mean of 16), those with various emotional disturbances (mean of 38), and a sample with chronic brain syndromes (mean of 77). Using cutoff points based on distributions, more than 80 per cent of the standardization samples were correctly categorized. Within the standardization groups, there are no correlations between test scores and IQ, age, and educational level, except for a correlation of .40 for IQ in the normal sample. However, descriptive sample characteristics suggest the possibility of inter-sample correlations which may have confounded results. Mean intelligence, age, and educational level are clearly related to diagnostic category. The normals are 15 IQ points higher than the emotionally disturbed group, which is 14 points higher than the organics; the normals are youngest and best educated, and so forth. Similar trends are found for IQ and educational level in the standardization sample for children. It cannot be stated definitely that actual confounding has occurred, but it certainly appears that one might predict the diagnostic category as well from IQ, age, and educational level as from test scores.

Discounting for the moment the possibility of confounding in the standardization data, the test does at least as well in discriminating organics as other instruments for this purpose which are easily administered and scored. Using the provided cutoff points, there would be 11 per cent false positives among the normals and 18 per cent false negatives among the organics. This compares favorably with the Trail Making Test, for example, which yields about 15 per cent incorrect identifications in each group.

The MPD has the advantage of not being a speed test and hence is likely to be less affected by functional overlays such as depression. There is a problem in scoring distorted reproductions. Of course, these are likely to be themselves manifestations of organicity to such an extent that the scoring of rotation is gratuitous. In the standardization sample, it appears that a maximum score of 25 was assigned to such figures. One wonders about the possible effect on the standardization group means.

Again ignoring the possibility of confounding factors, the test appears clinically useful in the diagnosis of organicity. That is, it has demonstrated considerable ability to discriminate between persons without brain damage and those who have all sorts of "manifest symptomatology" indicative of brain damage, i.e., severe cases. However, the hospital psychologist is rarely called upon to apply his clinical tests to cases in which the diagnosis of a brain syndrome is so evident. The standardization data do not permit the inference that the test would be clinically successful in diagnosing cases with minimal or even moderate organicity, the sort of questionable case which is often referred to the psychologist for differential diagnosis.

The ability of the test to discriminate between normals and those with emotional disturbances suggests some intriguing possibilities for research, but it does not indicate any important clinical use. Unfortunately, psychotics, neurotics, and character disturbances are lumped together in the standardization data, and there is no way of determining whether the test could discriminate among them, a feat which would, of course, render it clinically useful.

The MPD is new and all the available work with it thus far has been done by the senior test constructor and his collaborators. It is invariably prudent to await additional research findings by disinterested individuals before attempting to make a definite statement about the instrument's utility. Certainly the possibility of confounding of the standardization data by personal factors of the subjects requires further investigation.

[232]

★Myokinetic Psychodiagnosis (MKP). Ages 10 and over; 1951–58; expressive movement technique; individual; 1 form ('58, c1951–58, 8 pages); manual ('58, c1951–58, see *8* below); norms based upon South American subjects; $5 per 25 tests; $6.75 per manual; cash orders postpaid; table of prescribed dimensions, stopwatch, and other accessories required for administration; [20–30] minutes in 2 sessions 1 week apart; English edition ('58, translated from the French edition, '51, by Mrs. Jacques Dubois); Emilio Mira y Lopez; Hoeber Medical Division, Harper & Row, Publishers, Inc. *

REFERENCES

1. MIRA, EMILIO. "Myokinetic Psychodiagnosis: A New Technique of Exploring the Conative Trends of Personality." *Proc Royal Soc Med* 33:173–94 F '40. * (*PA* 14:4645)

2. MIRA, EMILIO. Appendix, "Technique and Interpretation of the Myokinetic Psychodiagnosis (M.P.D.)," pp. 159–96, passim. In his *Psychiatry in War.* New York: W. W. Norton & Co., Inc., 1943. Pp. 206. *

3. BELL, JOHN ELDERKIN. Chap. 15, "Mira Myokinetic Psychodiagnosis," pp. 328–40. In his *Projective Techniques: A Dynamic Approach to the Study of Personality.* New York: Longmans, Green & Co., Inc., 1948. Pp. xvi, 533. * (*PA* 23:1284)

4. BELL, JOHN ELDERKIN. "The Case of Gregor: Psychological Test Data." *Rorsch Res Exch & J Proj Tech* 13(2):155–205 '49. * (*PA* 24:2589)

5. LOPEZ, E. M. "Recent Development of the Myokinetic Psychodiagnosis," p. 88. Abstract. In *Proceedings and Papers of the Twelfth International Congress of Psychology Held at the University of Edinburgh, July 23rd to 29th, 1948.* Edinburgh, Scotland: Oliver and Boyd Ltd., 1950. Pp. xxviii, 152. *

6. WILSON, ROBERT G. *A Study of Expressive Movements in Three Groups of Adolescent Boys, Stutterers, Non-Stutterers Maladjusted and Normals, by Means of Three Measures of Personality, Mira's Myokinetic Psychodiagnosis, the Bender-Gestalt, and Figure Drawing.* Doctor's thesis, Western Reserve University (Cleveland, Ohio), 1950.

7. TAKALA, MARTTI. "Analysis of the Mira Test," pp. 67–112, passim. In his *Studies of Psychomotor Personality Tests I.* Annals of the Finnish Academy of Science and Letters, Series B, No. 81, Part 2. Helsinki, Finland: Suomalainen Tiedeakatemia, Academia Scientiarum Fennica, 1953. Pp. 130. * (*PA* 28:6055)

8. MIRA Y LOPEZ, EMILIO. *M.K.P.: Myokinetic Psychodiagnosis.* Translated by Mrs. Jacques Dubois from the 1951 French Edition. New York: [Hoeber Medical Division, Harper & Row, Publishers, Inc.], 1958. Pp. xx, 186. * (*PA* 33:7261)

9. TALMADGE, MAX. "Expressive Graphic Movements and Their Relationship to Temperament Factors. *Psychol Monogr* 72(16):1–30 '58. * (*PA* 33:9733)

10. HAKKINEN, SAULI, AND TOIVAINEN, YRJO. "Psychological Factors Causing Labour Turnover Among Underground Workers." *Occup Psychol* 34:15–30 Ja '60. * (*PA* 35:7162)

PHILIP L. HARRIMAN, *Professor of Psychology, Bucknell University, Lewisburg, Pennsylvania.*

A small weight attached to the end of a

string held in the outstretched hand of a blindfolded person moves in an interesting fashion as the holder imagines a particular type of movement. The direction of the swingings, commented upon by Chevreuil as long ago as 1828, was interpreted as one more bit of evidence that motor activities result from ideas. In 1874, William B. Carpenter, the English physiologist, coined the term *ideomotor action* to describe the elicitation of motor response by the presence of strong ideas. Conversely, many informed persons once accepted without question the view that certain patterns of motor activity furnish evidence regarding the ideas unexpressed in writing, speech, or other forms of intentional behavior. To one accepting the interactionist solution of the body-mind problem, what could be more obvious?

The possibilities in analyses of expressive activities, therefore, are said to be well nigh limitless, particularly if the person under scrutiny be unaware of what he is doing, be "caught off guard," or be distracted by some projective technique. Expressive drawings or finger paintings, manipulations of objects, or unimpeded outflows of words may be construed either as "royal roads" to the unconscious or as types of ideomotor actions, depending upon the modernity of their advocate. If Margaret F. Washburn be correct, consciousness itself is, indeed, motor activity—a likelihood that William James almost postulated. Hence, to explore a person's motor activities is to acquire valid knowledge of his innermost mind.

The *Myokinetic Psychodiagnosis* (MKP) is an expressive technique requiring the person merely to draw lines of various types. Administration is simple; materials consist of nothing but pencils, a low table, a chair, a screen to be interposed between the subject's eyes, the paper upon which the lines are drawn, and a manual giving simple, easily comprehended directions. Two sessions are necessary to complete the drawings. The observer takes notes on comments made, alterations in posture, special difficulties encountered, and other types of behavior of the subject. Thus, at the end of the second testing period, preferably a week after the first, there is a booklet filled with the prescribed drawings—half drawn with the right and half with the left hand—and some notes recorded during the sessions. The procedure is simple to administer and easy to carry out by the subject, although some arm fatigue is often reported, a requirement being that the elbow must at all times be raised above the table.

The MKP technique was first popularly known back in 1943, when Emilio Mira y Lopez, at one time professor of psychiatry at Barcelona and then of the faculty at Buenos Aires, published in English his challenging book entitled *Psychiatry in War*. The appendix (*2*) is devoted to an exposition of his novel diagnostic technique, its method of administration, and the types of subjects upon whom he standardized it. A year before—in the Salmon Lecture before the New York Academy of Medicine—he interested a very small group in the diagnostic possibilities of his technique. Mira y Lopez may now gain a wide hearing among psychoclinicians, for a new translation (*8*), this time from French into English, appeared in 1958. Previously, Harold H. Anderson [1] and J. E. Bell (*3*) had devoted some space to the MKP in their well-known expositions of projective techniques. Obviously, therefore, a serious student of psychological tests and measures and of diagnostic techniques ought to be familiar with Mira's contribution. For even though more than 95 per cent of the articles discussing it heretofore have appeared only in Spanish or Portuguese, it may be predicted that research articles will begin appearing in scientific journals in English-speaking countries.

This reviewer believes that quantitative evaluations, following the explicit instructions given by Mira, are relatively easy to make. Further use of the MKP will clear up ambiguities in objective ways of measuring the shiftings of the lines, particularly those which are relative. The temporal aspects of subtests must be examined closely. Objective scorings for disparities between right and left hand drawings await investigation. Qualitative evaluations of MKP test booklets are still in the realm of impressionistic conjectures and intuitive opinions. All that may be safely inferred at this time is that the line drawings of depressed individuals are markedly different from those of hypomanics. The possibilities for research seem to be great. If the promised book by Michael Finn does not give the last

1 ANDERSON, HAROLD H., AND ANDERSON, GLADYS L. *An Introduction to Projective Techniques and Other Devices for Understanding the Dynamics of Human Behavior.* New York: Prentice-Hall, Inc., 1951. Pp. xxv, 720. *

word on the Mira technique, MKP will serve the needs of many a candidate for the master's or the doctor's degree in clinical psychology. As for using the technique to influence judgments in cases involving human welfare, a psychoclinician must be advised to wait at least a decade for nomothetic and idiographic research pertaining to its validity. The reviewer, in a temerarious mood, predicts that the MKP will soon be forgotten.

IRWIN G. SARASON, *Associate Professor of Psychology, University of Washington, Seattle, Washington.*

Mira's book contains a manual for administration of the MKP test, together with normative data and his rationale for construction of the test. The rationale, stated most generally, is that the analysis of expressive movements can provide valuable data relevant to personality diagnosis. On the basis of quantitative and qualitative analysis of expressive movements, Mira believes that valid statements can be made concerning aggressiveness, conflict, degree of psychopathology, emotionality, and other characteristics. In addition, the author believes that inferences concerning intelligence can also be made.

The manual provides a careful description of the materials and procedures required for administration. The MKP test consists of a series of simple motor tasks. The task for the subject is to draw with each hand (and, for one task, with both hands simultaneously) simple geometric figures such as straight and zigzag lines. These drawings are made by the subject under conditions in which the stimulus to be reproduced is in full view and also under conditions in which the subject cannot see the stimulus. The manual states that the test should be administered twice to each subject with a one week time interval. It is further recommended that another pair of protocols be obtained one month following initial testing.

The manual adequately describes the procedure for quantitative scoring of the test. The scoring is in terms of deviations of lines and figures drawn by subjects from the standard stimuli contained in the test booklet. In all, the manual describes 79 measurements of aspects of subjects' drawings which are required for test interpretation. The complexities presented by so many scoring categories, together with the readministration of the test recommended in the manual, make it an impractical tool. It seems likely that shorter versions of the test could be constructed after appropriate factor analytic and other psychometric studies have been carried out. Test-retest reliabilities for the various drawing tasks are reported as ranging from .53 to .71 with a one week interval and .20 to .76 with a one year interval. Tables of norms (means and standard deviations for a variety of measures of expressive behavior) are provided for normal adults, children and adolescents, primitive people, and criminals. While some quantitative comparisons are reported among these groups, many of Mira's interpretations appear to be based on clinical inference rather than statistical findings. However, the data provided could be used to make such comparisons.

The test is highly original in conception. The manual represents the culmination of over 20 years of work with MKP. Unfortunately, little besides the manual is available in English. Since the test does not call for verbal behavior, cultural factors are probably less pronounced than would be the case for most personality tests. Nonetheless, use in countries other than the South American ones where most of the work on MKP was conducted clearly requires independent normative studies. For this reason MKP, at the present time, must be regarded as a research instrument rather than a well established clinical one. While one might have great sympathy with Mira's emphasis on expressive behavior as a path to understanding personality, it is still necessary to evaluate empirically the various interpretations of expressive behavior contained in the manual.

In conclusion, then, MKP is a test which seems to tap a dimension—that of expressive behavior in the form of subjects' drawings—which has not received much attention by American students of personality. MKP provides a research tool with which this aspect of expressive behavior might profitably be studied. However, the test is neither a very practical nor economical (in terms of time) test for wide clinical usage.

For excerpts from reviews of the manual, see B343.

[233]

The Object Relations Technique. Ages 11 and over; 1955; individual; 1 form ['55, 13 cards]; manual ('55, 232 pages, see *3*); no data on reliability; 63*s.* per set of cards and manual; postage extra; (90) minutes; Herbert Phillipson; Tavistock Publications. *

REFERENCES

1–6. See 5:151.
7. O'Kelly, E. "The Object Relations Test—Some Quantitative Findings Relating to Early Separation From the Mother." *B Brit Psychol Soc* 29:24 My '56. *
8. Phillipson, H. "The Use of Cognitive and Projective Tests as an Approach to the Therapy of a Student Teacher Who Has Serious Spelling Difficulties." *Rorsch Newsl* 3:24–31 D '58. *
9. Orme, J. E. "O.R.T. Performance in Schizophrenia." *J Mental Sci* 105:1119–22 O '59. * (*PA* 34:6381)
10. Gladston, Elaine R., and Amado-Haguenauer, Ginette. "Fluidity in the Limits of the Self." *Int J Social Psychiatry* 6:260–8 au '60. *
11. Haskell, Royal J., Jr. "Relationship Between Aggressive Behavior and Psychological Tests." *J Proj Tech* 25:431–40 D '61. *
12. Vernon, M. D. "The Relation of Perception to Personality Factors." *Brit J Psychol* 52:205–17 Ag '61. * (*PA* 36:3HG05V)
13. Viitamaki, R. Olavi. *Psychoses in Children: A Psychological Follow-Up Study.* Annals of the Finnish Academy of Science and Letters, Series B, Vol. 125, Part 2. Helsinki, Finland: Suomalainen Tiedeakatemia, Academia Scientiarum Fennica, 1962. Pp. 52. * (*PA* 39:2650)

H. R. Beech, *Lecturer in Psychology, The Institute of Psychiatry, Maudsley Hospital, London, England.*

Information concerning the application and usefulness of this technique has been slow in accumulating. To some extent this may be attributed to satisfaction with better established projective techniques, and those potential users who have considered this test may well feel that Phillipson has not made out a convincing case for a change to be made to the ORT. The technique purports to offer some of the advantages of both the *Thematic Apperception Test* and the Rorschach, this being largely accomplished by having the pictorial representations somewhat more ambiguous than in the TAT, but less so than in the Rorschach. In other particulars the test appears to have some degree of uniqueness, but it is not clear what advantages actually do accrue to, for example, subtle differences in administration and instruction over and above those used in other projective tests.

It seems likely from the published records of patients' responses to the ORT that, thus far, only persons with a specialized knowledge of psychoanalytic theory and a particular kind of experience would be in a position to duplicate the interpretations offered, in which case one might argue that the usefulness of the ORT depends upon the limitations both of the examiner and of psychoanalytic theory.

Whether one accepts or rejects the theoretical orientation common to projective techniques, and the special theoretical position underlying the ORT, appears to be a matter of personal preference, opinion, and training rather than of fact. This is not to say that certain facts are not available, for evidence concerning the reliability and validity of projective tests has accumulated to the point where one can say that, in these respects, such techniques leave much to be desired. In the case of the ORT the course of the development of the technique is not entirely clear, although it appears that the test has been used fairly extensively (presumably by Phillipson and his colleagues) both in the clinic and in a commercial application, and there is no doubt that some individuals have acquired a great deal of personal experience in the use of this test. However, the ORT will prove something of a disappointment for those looking for some evidence concerning the reliability and validity of the tests and techniques they use.

The reliability of the technique is still unknown and, it should be said, would be difficult to establish in view of the kind of material dealt with. No satisfactory evidence is yet available respecting validity which rests almost entirely upon the author's report that he and his colleagues have found the technique suitable and useful for subjects of 14 years and upward, and that comparisons between ORT findings and psychiatric interview reports have been made. This information concerning validity must be taken on trust and no information is provided which would enable one to evaluate these claims and implications. The sparse evidence of the kind which is usually found more acceptable (e.g., *9, 11*) does not inspire a great deal of confidence in the technique.

Phillipson seems to be susceptible to two kinds of pressure: that which stems from a psychodynamic theoretical orientation and traditional emphasis upon qualitative global analysis, and that from "scientific" considerations which urge piecemeal assessment and quantification. He has responded, not hopefully, to the latter pressure by providing data respecting the frequency of certain classes of response to ORT cards. These data, obtained from 50 young psychiatric outpatients (almost all with IQ's of 120 or above) and 40 normal adolescent girls, are clearly limited in scope and are not significantly enhanced in this respect by the addition of O'Kelly's (*6*) quantification of the ORT responses of two groups of delinquent adolescent girls.

It is apparent that the ORT does not differ in any fundamental from currently available projective techniques and that it may even be at some disadvantage in view of its comparatively brief history. Fortunately the gaps created by the exclusion of projective devices show signs of being bridged by techniques characterized by greater emphasis upon the basic attributes of tests which are most usually thought desirable. The most promising of these seems to be the Repertory Grid technique [1] which is extremely flexible and has considerable potential for clinical use both in revealing unique characteristics and relationships of the individual construing system [2] and in its adaptation for diagnostic purposes, on a group basis.[3] To a lesser extent and with some qualifications, the Osgood Semantic Differential,[4] the Q-sort,[5] and the Personal Questionnaire [6] could be adapted to serve some of those functions most often reserved for projective techniques. These techniques could contribute a precision and objectivity characteristically absent in projective tests, and it is a point to be appreciated that they are not wedded to any particular theoretical standpoint.

In summary it might be said that the ORT is a projective technique with a largely unknown development, without information respecting its reliability, and not having any very acceptable evidence concerning its validity. The claims made for the technique have yet to be substantiated and users of projective techniques may well feel that the ORT has no obvious advantages over the available alternatives.

Int J Group Psychother 8:481–2 O '58. Leopold Bellak. * The test pictures are well chosen and nicely executed. There are a number of case studies, one done in detail, which demonstrates that the test elicits very useful material (some indications of exhibitionism-voyeurism seem to have been overlooked in the test material of the first case). The normative data—based on fifty patients of an outpatient clinic and forty adolescent girls—are not better or worse than those of most projective tests and not of primary importance as far as the content is concerned. Such normative data are of more relevance with regard to the effect of the shading nuances, which seem altogether not systematically enough investigated. There is, in fact, ground for reasonable doubt that the special features of the test, in form of object content *or* shading, add significant dimensions of responses. * this is an interesting test, originated and described by a competent psychoanalytic psychologist. It will take a great deal of future empirical evidence, however, to establish whether the Object Relations Test adds anything basically new or better to our armamentarium for diagnosing object relations.

1 KELLY, GEORGE A. *The Psychology of Personal Constructs: Vol. 1, A Theory of Personality; Vol. 2, Clinical Diagnosis and Psychotherapy.* New York: W. W. Norton & Co., Inc., 1955. Pp. xviii, 1–556; x, 559–1218. *

2 BEECH, H. R. "Some Theoretical and Technical Difficulties in the Application of Behaviour Therapy." *B Brit Psychol Soc* 16:25–33 Jl '63. *

3 BANNISTER, D. "Conceptual Structure in Thought Disordered Schizophrenics." *J Mental Sci* 106:1230–49 O '60. *

4 OSGOOD, CHARLES E.; SUCI, GEORGE J.; AND TANNENBAUM, PERCY H. *The Measurement of Meaning.* Urbana, Ill.: University of Illinois Press, 1957. Pp. vii, 342. *

5 STEPHENSON, WILLIAM. *The Study of Behavior: Q-Technique and Its Methodology.* Chicago, Ill.: University of Chicago Press, 1953. Pp. ix, 376. * (With reservations set out by Lee J. Cronbach and Goldine C. Gleser in their review in *Psychometrika* 19:327–30 D '54. See 5:B408 for an excerpt from this review.)

6 SHAPIRO, M. B. "A Method of Measuring Psychological Changes Specific to the Individual Psychiatric Patient." *Brit J Med Psychol* 34:151–5 pt 2 '61. *

For a review by George Westby, see 5:151; for excerpts from reviews of the manual, see 5:B338.

[234]

★Pickford Projective Pictures. Ages 5–15; 1963; 1 form (120 cards); manual (130 pages, see 5 below); no data on reliability; 25*s.* ($5) per set of cards; 30*s.* ($4) per manual; 50*s.* per set of cards and manual; postage extra; to be administered about 6 pictures at a time over about 20 therapy sessions; R. W. Pickford with the assistance of Ruth Bowyer and John Struthers; Tavistock Publications Ltd. (United States publisher: Springer Publishing Co., Inc.) *

REFERENCES

1. PICKFORD, R. W. "Personality and the Interpretation of Pictures: A New Projection Technique." *J Personality* 17:210–20 D '48. * (*PA* 25:3177)

2. PICKFORD, R. W. "New Projection Material for Child Therapy." *B Brit Psychol Soc* 1:358–63 Jl '50. * (*PA* 27:5202)

3. PICKFORD, R. W. "Pictures for Child Psychotherapy." *Scottish Med J* 5:530–6 D '60. *

4. PICKFORD, R. W. "Picture Projection Material for Child Psychotherapy." Abstract. *Acta Psychologica* 19:860–1 '61. *

5. PICKFORD, R. W.; WITH THE ASSISTANCE OF RUTH BOWYER AND JOHN STRUTHERS. *Pickford Projective Pictures.* London: Tavistock Publications Ltd., 1963. Pp. xi, 122. *

STANLEY J. SEGAL, *Associate Professor of Psychology, and Director, Student Counseling Center, State University of New York at Buffalo, Buffalo, New York.*

The suggested use of these pictures is as a basis for therapeutic interaction with children from 5–15. It is recommended that the 120 ambiguous line drawings of people in a variety of situations be presented over a series of interviews and form the basis for the therapeutic interaction. The manual suggests five approaches that have been followed, from using the pictures as a cathartic experience for the child to using the responses as a basis for psychoanalytic therapy.

Although there are statements that the pictures have diagnostic value, there is little clear indication of this use of the pictures outside of the context of psychotherapy.

The manual clearly indicates the authors' concern for the need for the accumulation of additional data and the firmer establishment of diagnostic and therapeutic validity for the pictures. The data presented are based on the experiences with 129 children seen in a number of child guidance clinics in and around Glasgow, Scotland. Not all children were given the entire series.

The authors correctly point out that one unique advantage of this instrument is the large number of items available, widening its use. They offer tabulation of responses for each of the pictures typically indicating, separately for boys and girls, frequency of sex identification of the pictured figures, identification of other objects presented, and actions, interactions, or outcomes. There is also a listing of each picture with the most frequent story themes, a descriptive list of the pictures, and a categorization according to the pictured themes using such categories as "relationship of one child to both parent figures," "sexual curiosity," "situations involving tensions over food." These listings can be helpful to users if they plan to use only part of the series for some specific purpose.

The statistical analysis of 129 records uses as a validity criterion clinician's estimate of value, diagnostically, therapeutically, or both. This is a tabulation of clinicians' statements broken down in terms of presenting symptoms, but is not dealt with to produce the usual validity coefficient. The test may be used over the IQ range from 80 and upward with its estimated value being equal for low and high intelligence quotients. As expected, children with high IQ's tend to give longer and more elaborate stories. The data reported suggest that the pictures are equally valuable for boys and girls and for younger and older children, with some comment that older children tend to be more comfortable with this task than with play materials.

This test differs markedly in approach from most others in that the emphasis is on the direct utilization of the materials in therapeutic work with children, and in this respect it is similar to Lowenfeld's World Material. The length of the series, the authors' attempts to get as many complete records as possible, and the use of the stories as a vehicle of change suggests that the problem of reliability is a difficult one and this may be attested by the lack of such data in the manual. The illustrative cases, which are carefully presented, complete with many stories on each child, gave this reviewer the impression that the themes from story to story were similar enough for different pictures that some attempt at a split-half reliability based on the authors' categorization of pictures might be usefully carried out and presented.

A strength of Pickford's presentation is his insistence that the protocols need not be used within a single theoretical framework. He gives illustrations in a chapter by L. R. Bowyer of a Rogerian approach, while his own illustrative examples are quite clearly within a psychoanalytic framework.

All data are on a British sample, but from the stories presented it would be surprising if American children reacted in a markedly different manner. Only three or four of the pictures present figures that are so typically British that American children would sense the cultural difference.

I would feel that this set of pictures can be a valuable aid to the clinician working with children. Its adequacy as a diagnostic tool is unclear from the data available, and one can only second the authors' comments that a great deal of additional work is needed. There does seem great utility in the series as a focus of therapeutic interaction with a child. The brief comments about its use in helping children with school learning problems are intriguing and exciting. This is an area where great value may well emerge if the few cases discussed prove to be fairly typical of the kind of progress one can expect.

I would encourage child guidance workers and school psychologists to evaluate the manual and the pictures in order to judge whether the *Pickford Projective Pictures* may not represent a valuable addition to the approaches they presently use in working with children.

Brit J Ed Psychol 33:335 N '63. R. Hetherington. Those who have tried the various available forms of picture projective tests with young children, will have noticed the gap that exists between the T.A.T. or Symond's Picture Story Test for older children, and the rather childish and off-putting C.A.T. Professor Pickford's new set of pictures may help to fill this gap. The unwillingness of young children to tell lengthy stories, makes it desirable to have a large number of pictures yielding many short stories in which recurrent themes may be discerned. The Pickford Projective Pictures consist of 120 simple line-drawings which "cover a very wide range of stimulus content" varying from relationships with father figures and authority, and relationships with mother figures including sibling jealousy; to play and conflict between children, and death and ghosts. There are some twenty distinctive themes represented. Professor Pickford suggests that the pictures should be used about six at a time, so that the material will last for about twenty therapeutic sessions. However, for diagnostic use, a larger number of pictures each yielding a short story might well reveal highly significant recurrent themes reflecting some of the child's pre-occupations and worries. The book accompanying the test material contains some very useful data for responses given to the pictures by fairly large groups of children in Glasgow child guidance clinics. Data of this sort are too rarely available for projective tests. The book also contains a chapter on the use of the pictures in analytic treatment which must not be allowed to antagonise people who are allergic to Freudian interpretations of innocent comments by children. For example, the comment, "This little boy stole apples from a rough farmer's orchard" is interpreted as a wish to rob the father of his sexuality. This interpretation goes on, for good measure, to interpret the tummy-ache the boy is said to have after eating the apples as a phantasy of incestuous pregnancy, on the part of the girl telling the story! With or without interpretations of this kind, the pictures seem to have been used successfully in clinics in Glasgow, and should help to fill a gap in our techniques for persuading children to talk in a revealing way about themselves.

Percept & Motor Skills 17:647 O '63. * While standardization of the test does not even approach the official APA standards for test construction, the stimuli and preliminary data indicate that further work is reasonable and likely to be profitable.

Scottish Ed J 46:711 S 20 '63. * The first advantage of this material lies in the number and variety of cards available. The next advantage lies in the fact that freedom of presentation is allowed to the person administering it to the child. Anyone using this material would probably be psychoanalytically inclined, yet it is not essential to subscribe to this school. * Psychologists will find this a useful addition to their equipment but it is doubtful if it could be used by teachers in school who had not a solid background of training in psychology.

[235]

★**Psychiatric Attitudes Battery.** Adults; 1955–61; attitudes toward mental hospitals, psychiatrists, and psychiatric treatment; 5 parts; directions for administration and scoring presented in *2* below; no data on reliability of scores; no data on validity; no norms; $2 per set of cards for *a*; $1 per manual for *b*; postpaid; reprint of *2* below free; test forms may be reproduced locally; Marvin Reznikoff, John Paul Brady, William W. Zeller, and Omneya Souelem (*d*); Institute of Living. *

a) PICTURE ATTITUDES TEST. 1 form ['59, 3 cards, separate cards for men and women and a general card]; [15] minutes.

b) SENTENCE COMPLETION ATTITUDES TEST. 4 attitude scores: psychiatrists, hospitals, treatment, outcome; 1 form ['59, 1 hectographed page]; revised scoring manual ('61, 17 hectographed pages); [10] minutes.

c) MULTIPLE CHOICE ATTITUDES QUESTIONNAIRE. 1 form ['59, 2 hectographed pages]; [5] minutes.

d) SOUELEM ATTITUDES SCALE. Forms A, B, ['55, 2 hectographed pages]; [10] minutes.

e) DEGREE OF IMPROVEMENT RATING SCALE. Ratings by psychiatrists; 1 form ['59, 1 hectographed page]; "a minute or two."

REFERENCES

1. BRADY, JOHN PAUL; ZELLER, WILLIAM W.; AND REZNIKOFF, MARVIN. "Attitudinal Factors Influencing Outcome of Treatment of Hospitalized Psychiatric Patients." *J Clin & Exp Psychopathol* 20:326–34 D '59. * (*PA* 34:6073)

2. REZNIKOFF, MARVIN; BRADY, JOHN PAUL; AND ZELLER, WILLIAM W. "The Psychiatric Attitudes Battery: A Procedure for Assessing Attitudes Toward Psychiatric Treatment and Hospitals." *J Clin Psychol* 15:260–6 Jl '59. * (*PA* 35:3644)

3. BRADY, JOHN PAUL; REZNIKOFF, MARVIN; AND ZELLER, WILLIAM W. "The Relationship of Expectation of Improvement to Actual Improvement of Hospitalized Psychiatric Patients." *J Nerv & Mental Dis* 130:41–4 Ja '60. * (*PA* 35:6649)

4. REZNIKOFF, MARVIN; BRADY, JOHN PAUL; ZELLER, WILLIAM W.; AND TOOMEY, LAURA C. "Attitudinal Change in Hospitalized Psychiatric Patients." *J Clin & Exp Psychopathol* 21:309–14 D '60. * (*PA* 35:5118)

5. TOOMEY, LAURA C.; REZNIKOFF, MARVIN; BRADY, JOHN PAUL; AND SCHUMANN, DWIGHT W. "Attitudes of Nursing Students Toward Psychiatric Treatment and Hospitals." *Mental Hyg* 45:589–602 O '61. *

6. TOOMEY, LAURA C.; REZNIKOFF, MARVIN; BRADY, JOHN PAUL; AND SCHUMANN, W. DWIGHT. "Some Relationships Between the Attitudes of Nursing Students Toward Psychiatry and Success in Psychiatric Affiliation." *Nursing Res* 10:165–9 su '61. *

7. IMRE, PAUL D. "Attitudes of Volunteers Toward Mental Hospitals Compared to Patients and Personnel." *J Clin Psychol* 18:516 O '62. * (*PA* 39:4807)

8. IMRE, PAUL, AND WOLF, SIDNEY. "Attitudes of Patients and Personnel Toward Mental Hospitals." *J Clin Psychol* 18:232–4 Ap '62. * (*PA* 38:8795)

9. GYNTHER, MALCOLM D.; REZNIKOFF, MARVIN; AND FISHMAN, MELBA. "Attitudes of Psychiatric Patients Toward Treatment, Psychiatrists and Mental Hospitals." *J Nerv & Mental Dis* 136:68–71 Ja '63. *

10. REZNIKOFF, MARVIN. "Attitudes of Psychiatric Nurses and Aides Toward Psychiatric Treatment and Hospitals." *Mental Hyg* 47:360–4 Jl '63. *

[236]

★Rock-A-Bye, Baby: A Group Projective Test for Children. Groups of 9–16 aged 5–10; 1959, c1951–56; sibling rivalry; 6 scores: self concept, jealousy index, aggression to parents, guilt index, anxiety index, index of obsessive trends; stimulus material presented by 35-minute 16 mm. sound film ('56, script previously published in 1951); 1 form ['59]; mimeographed manual ['59, 33 pages, containing record form and analysis sheet which must be reproduced locally]; no data on reliability of scores; no norms for self concept and aggression to parents; film may be rented ($10 per week) or purchased ($157); $1 per manual; monograph (see *1* below) free with manual; postage extra; (60) minutes; Mary R. Haworth and Adolf G. Woltmann; distributed by Psychological Cinema Register. *

REFERENCES

1. HAWORTH, MARY ROBBINS. "The Use of a Filmed Puppet Show as a Group Projective Technique for Children." *Genetic Psychol Monogr* 56:257–96 N '57. * (*PA* 33:10332)
2. HAWORTH, MARY R. Chap. 9, "Films as a Group Technique," pp. 177–90. In *Projective Techniques With Children.* Edited by Albert I. Rabin and Mary R. Haworth. New York: Grune & Stratton, Inc., 1960. Pp. xiii, 392. * (*PA* 35:2229)
3. HAWORTH, MARY R. "Repeat Study With a Projective Film for Children." *J Consult Psychol* 25:78–83 F '61. * (*PA* 36:3HG78H)
4. HAWORTH, MARY R. "Responses of Children to a Group Projective Film and to the Rorschach, CAT, Despert Fables and D-A-P." *J Proj Tech* 26:47–60 Mr '62. * (*PA* 37:2893)

[237]

***Rorschach.** Ages 3 and over; 1921–60; variously referred to by such titles as Rorschach Method, Rorschach Test, Rorschach Ink Blot Test, Rorschach Psychodiagnostics; many variations and modifications are in use with no one method of scoring and interpreting generally accepted; unless otherwise indicated, the word Rorschach may be interpreted as referring to the use of the Psychodiagnostic Plates listed as *f* below.

a) BEHN-RORSCHACH TEST. 1941–56; a parallel set of inkblots; also called *The Bero-Test;* 1 form ('41, 10 cards); manual ('56, 198 pages, see *2156* below, translation of the German edition published in 1941); record blank ('51, 1 page); Fr. 19 ($11) per set of cards; Fr. 9 ($3) per pad of 100 record blanks; Fr. 25 ($8) per manual; postage extra; Hans Zulliger; Hans Huber. (United States distributor: Grune & Stratton, Inc.) *

b) THE BUHLER-LEFEVER RORSCHACH DIAGNOSTIC SIGN LIST AND RECORD OF THE RORSCHACH STANDARDIZATION STUDIES FOR THE DETERMINATION AND EVALUATION OF THE BASIC RORSCHACH SCORE. 1954; 1 form (4 pages); $6.50 per 25 booklets, postpaid; Charlotte Buhler, Karl Buhler, and D. Welty Lefever; Western Psychological Services. *

c) HARROWER'S GROUP RORSCHACH. Ages 12 and over; 1941–45; $12.50 per set of the original Rorschach inkblots on slides for standard projector; $4.70 per set of 25 record blanks; postpaid; (70–90) minutes; distributed by Psychological Corporation.

d) HARROWER'S MULTIPLE CHOICE TEST. Ages 12 and over; 1943–45; for use with either cards or slides; $3 per 25 record blanks, postage extra; M. R. Harrower; distributed by Psychological Corporation. *

e) *PSYCHODIAGNOSTIC INKBLOTS. 1945–60; a parallel set of inkblots; manual uses the title *Harrower Inkblots;* 1 form ('45, 10 cards); revised manual ('60, 70 pages); $6.50 per set of cards; $3.50 per manual; postage extra; M. R. Harrower and M. E. Steiner; distributed by Grune & Stratton, Inc. * (Administration instructions are written in terms of an expendable set of the inkblots, which is available at $2 per set from the author, M. R. Harrower.)

f) PSYCHODIAGNOSTIC PLATES, FIFTH EDITION. 1921–54; 1 form ('54, 10 cards, identical with original edition copyrighted in 1921); manual, fifth edition ('51, 263 pages, translation of the 1942 German edition with the addition of a bibliography); record blank ('47, 1 page); Fr. 27 ($12.50) per set of cards; Fr. 8.50 ($3.50) per pad of 100 record blanks; Fr. 23 ($7) per manual; postage extra; Hermann Rorschach; Hans Huber. (United States distributor: Grune & Stratton, Inc.) *

g) RORSCHACH COMBINED LOCATION AND RECORD FORM. 1957; 1 form (12 pages); $2.75 per 25 booklets; 30¢ per specimen set; postpaid; Nicholas De Palma; the Author. *

h) THE RORSCHACH EVALOGRAPH. 1954; 1 form (28 pages); $5 per 10 booklets, postpaid; Morse P. Manson and George A. Ulett; Western Psychological Services. *

i) RORSCHACH LOCATION CHARTS (BECK'S SCORING AREAS). 1951–54; 1 form ('54, 12 cards, identical with set copyrighted in 1951); Fr. 9.50 ($3.25) per set of cards, postage extra; Julian C. Davis; Hans Huber. (United States distributor: Grune & Stratton, Inc.) *

j)*RORSCHACH METHOD OF PERSONALITY DIAGNOSIS, REVISED EDITION. 1939–60; 1 form ('60, 4 pages); directions ('60, 4 pages); $3.10 per 35 blanks, postage extra; Bruno Klopfer and Helen H. Davidson; [Harcourt, Brace & World, Inc.]. *

k) THE RORSCHACH MINIATURE INKBLOTS: A LOCATION CHART. 1955; $5.50 per pad of 100 sheets, postpaid; Morse P. Manson; Western Psychological Services. *

l) STRUCTURED-OBJECTIVE RORSCHACH TEST: PRELIMINARY EDITION. See 242.

REFERENCES

1–147. See 40:1246.
148–598. See 3:73.
599–1219. See 4:117.
1220–2297. See 5:154.
2298. COFFIN, THOMAS E. "Some Conditions of Suggestions and Suggestibility: A Study of Certain Attitudinal and Situational Factors Influencing the Process of Suggestion," pp. 47–64. *Psychol Monogr* 53(4):1–125 '41. * (*PA* 16:2662)
2299. SHAW, BARRIE. *Sex Populars in the Rorschach.* Doctor's thesis, University of Kentucky (Lexington, Ky.), 1949. (*DA* 20:4178)
2300. ZUBIN, JOSEPH. Chap. 21, "Rorschach Test," pp. 283–95. In *Selective Partial Ablations of the Frontal Cortex: A Correlative Study of Its Effects on Human Psychotic Subjects, Vol. 1.* Edited by Fred A. Mettler. New York: Paul B. Hoeber, Inc., 1949. Pp. xiv, 517. *
2301. "Brief Report on the First International Rorschach Meeting." *Rorschachiana* (3):110–3 '50. *
2302. SKIFF, STANLEY CUBE. *A Study of Some Relationships Between Personality Traits and Learning Ability.* Doctor's thesis, University of Kentucky (Lexington, Ky.), 1950. (*DA* 20:3861)
2303. FISHER, SEYMOUR, AND HINDS, EDITH. "The Organization of Hostility Controls in Various Personality Structures." *Genetic Psychol Monogr* 44:3–68 Ag '51. * (*PA* 26:2889)
2304. JERNIGAN, AUSTIN JACK. *A Rorschach Study of Normal and Psychotic Subjects in a Situation of Stress.* Doctor's thesis, University of Kentucky (Lexington, Ky.), 1951. (*DA* 20:3833)
2305. MARTIN, HARRY. *A Rorschach Study of Suicide.* Doctor's thesis, University of Kentucky (Lexington, Ky.), 1951. (*DA* 20:3837)
2306. PECK, CECIL P. *An Investigation of Association-Provoking Properties and Meanings Attributed to the Rorschach Inkblots.* Doctor's thesis, University of Kentucky (Lexington, Ky.), 1951. (*DA* 20:3841)
2307. HAIMOWITZ, NATALIE READER, AND HAIMOWITZ, MORRIS L. Chap. 3, "Personality Changes in Client-Centered Therapy," pp. 63–93. (*PA* 27:7822) In *Success in Psychotherapy.* Edited by Werner Wolff and Joseph A. Precker. New York: Grune & Stratton, Inc., 1952. Pp. viii, 196. *
2308. HAMLIN, ROY M.; BERGER, BENJAMIN; AND CUMMINGS, S. THOMAS. Chap. 4, "Changes in Adjustment Following Psychotherapy as Reflected in Rorschach Signs," pp. 94–111. (*PA* 27:7823) In *Success in Psychotherapy.* Edited by Werner Wolff and Joseph A. Precker. New York: Grune & Stratton, Inc., 1952. Pp. viii, 196. *

2309. RIZZO, CARLO. "The Rorschach Method in Italy." *Rorschachiana* 1(4):306–20 '53. * (*PA* 28:7543)
2310. THALER, MARGARET B. *An Application of Three Theories of Personality to the Rorschach Records of Seventy-Five Aged Subjects.* Doctor's thesis, University of Denver (Denver, Colo.), 1953.
2311. ALLEN, ROBERT M., AND DORSEY, ROBERT N. "The Effect of Suggestion on Human Movement Productivity in Rorschach's Test." *Zeitschrift für Diagnostische Psychologie und Persönlichkeitsforschung* 2(2):137–42 '54. * (*PA* 29:4021)
2312. BLUMBERG, EUGENE M. "Results of Psychological Testing of Cancer Patients," pp. 30–61; discussion by Bruno Klopfer and J. F. T. Bugental, pp. 62–71. In *The Psychological Variables in Human Cancer.* Edited by Joseph A. Gengerelli and Frank J. Kirkner. Berkeley, Calif.: University of California Press, 1954. Pp. vi, 135. *
2313. ERON, LEONARD D. "Use of the Rorschach Method in Medical Student Selection." *J Med Ed* 29:35–9 My '54. * (*PA* 29:4686)
2314. GARDEBRING, OLOV G. "High P% in the Rorschach Test." *Zeitschrift für Diagnostische Psychologie und Persönlichkeitsforschung* 2(2):142–3 '54. * (*PA* 29:4054)
2315. KELLY, JOSEPH. "The Influence of Mescaline on Rorschach Responses." *Psychologische Forschung* 24(6):542–56 '54. *
2316. KLOPFER, B., AND DAVIDSON, HELEN H. "Explanation of Rorschach-Scoring Symbols." *Zeitschrift für Diagnostische Psychologie und Persönlichkeitsforschung* 2(4):371–5 '54. *
2317. MOFFETT, CHARLES R. *Operational Characteristics of Beginning Master's Students in Educational Administration and Supervision.* Doctor's thesis, University of Tennessee (Knoxville, Tenn.), 1954.
2318. MORGENTHALER, W. "The Battle for Publication of the 'Psychodiagnostics': For Hermann Rorschach's 70th Birthday (November 8, 1954)." *Zeitschrift für Diagnostische Psychologie und Persönlichkeitsforschung* 2(4):355–62 '54. * (*PA* 29:5783)
2319. RICHARDS, T. W. Chap. 4, "The Chinese in Hawaii: A Rorschach Report," pp. 67–89. Discussion by Richard P. Wang. In *Aspects of Culture and Personality: A Symposium.* Edited by Francis L. K. Hsu. New York: Abelard-Schuman, Inc., 1954. Pp. xiii, 305. *
2320. SIEGEL, MAX. "The Personality Structure of Children With Reading Disabilities as Compared With Children Presenting Other Clinical Problems." *Nerv Child* 10(3–4):409–14 '54. * (*PA* 29:2983)
2321. STREITFIELD, HAL S. "Specificity of Peptic Ulcer to Intense Oral Conflicts." *Psychosom Med* 16:315–26 Jl–Ag '54. * (*PA* 29:4533)
2322. YATES, AUBREY J. "The Validity of Some Psychological Tests of Brain Damage." *Psychol B* 51:359–79 Jl '54. *
2323. BAGH, D. "Use of Rorschach's Ink Blot Test Among School Adolescents." *Indian J Psychol* 30:61–4 Jl–D '55. * (*PA* 31:1606)
2324. BARRON, FRANK. "The Disposition Toward Originality." *J Abn & Social Psychol* 51:478–85 N '55. * (*PA* 31:2533)
2325. EWING, RUSSELL M., AND VINCENT, MARGARET STEVENSON. "Study of Patients' Choices of 'Father Card' and 'Mother Card' on the Rorschach Test." *B Maritime Psychol Assn* 4:16–20 D '55. * (*PA* 30:8288)
2326. KENNA, J. C. "The Effects of Lysergic Acid on the Rorschach." Abstract. *B Brit Psychol Soc* 25:27 Ja '55. *
2327. LUTON, JAMES N. *A Study of the Use of Standardized Tests in the Selection of Potential Educational Administrators.* Doctor's thesis, University of Tennessee (Knoxville, Tenn.), 1955.
2328. MONS, W. R. "Normative Study of Children's Rorschachs." Abstract. *B Brit Psychol Soc* 25:26 Ja '55. *
2329. NEWMAN, R. E. "The Application of the Rorschach Technique to a Primitive Group." *Zeitschrift für Diagnostische Psychologie und Persönlichkeitsforschung* 3(3):187–222 '55. * (*PA* 30:5897)
2330. NORGARB, BRIAN N. "Psychodiagnostic Testing and Hypnosis." *J Clin & Exp Hypnosis* 3:44–8 Ja '55. * (*PA* 29:8624)
2331. POWERS, WILLIAM THOMAS. *A Comparative Analysis of Deviant Rorschach Response Characteristics.* Doctor's thesis, University of Pittsburgh (Pittsburgh, Pa.), 1955. (*DA* 16:159)
2332. RAY, P. C. "The Tensional Feelings Among the Abors and Gallongs as Indicated by the Rorschach Technique." *Indian J Psychol* 30:95–103 Mr–Je '55. * (*PA* 31:2788)
2333. RICKERS-OVSIANKINA, MARIA A. "Prognostic Rorschach Indices in Schizophrenia." *Zeitschrift für Diagnostische Psychologie und Persönlichkeitsforschung* 3(3):246–54 '55. * (*PA* 30:6184)
2334. SPINDLER, GEORGE D. *Sociocultural and Psychological Processes in Menomini Acculturation.* University of California Publications in Culture and Society, Vol. 5. Berkeley, Calif.: University of California Press, 1955. Pp. viii, 271. * (*PA* 29:8556)
2335. WHEELER, W. M. "The Psychoanalytic Theory of Object Relations and the Rorschach Technique." Abstract. *B Brit Psychol Soc* 25:25–6 Ja '55. *
2336. WILKENS, WALTER L., AND ADAMS, AUSTIN J. "The Use of the Rorschach Test Under Hypnosis and Under Sodium Amytal in Military Psychiatry." *Brit J Med Hypnosis* 6:22–8 sp '55. *
2337. "The Rorschach Record of a Case of Aphasia." *Rorsch Newsl* 1:29–35 My '56. *
2338. ANDERSON, DOROTHY V., AND HIGHAM, EILEEN. Chap. 6, "The Use of the Rorschach Technique in Child Guidance Clinics," pp. 177–94. In *Developments in the Rorschach Technique: Volume 2, Fields of Application.* By Bruno Klopfer and others. Yonkers, N.Y.: World Book Co., 1956. Pp. xx, 828. * (*PA* 30:7202)
2339. BAKER, GERTRUDE. Chap. 11, "Diagnosis of Organic Brain Damage in the Adult," pp. 318–75. In *Developments in the Rorschach Technique: Volume 2, Fields of Application.* By Bruno Klopfer and others. Yonkers, N.Y.: World Book Co., 1956. Pp. xx, 828. * (*PA* 30:7202)
2340. BAKER, GERTRUDE. Chap. 12. "Diagnostic Case Studies of Male Adults Having Organic Brain Damage," pp. 376–428. In *Developments in the Rorschach Technique: Volume 2, Fields of Application.* By Bruno Klopfer and others. Yonkers, N.Y.: World Book Co., 1956. Pp. xx, 828. * (*PA* 30:7202)
2341. BOLGAR, HEDDA. Chap. 18, "A Re-evaluation of Projective Theory," pp. 643–57. In *Developments in the Rorschach Technique: Volume 2, Fields of Application.* By Bruno Klopfer and others. Yonkers, N.Y.: World Book Co., 1956. Pp. xx, 828. * (*PA* 30:7202)
2342. CAUDILL, WILLIAM, AND DE VOS, GEORGE. "Achievement, Culture and Personality: The Case of the Japanese Americans." *Am Anthrop* 58:1102–26 D '56. *
2343. FOX, JACK. Chap. 4. "The Psychological Significance of Age Patterns in the Rorschach Records of Children," pp. 88–103. In *Developments in the Rorschach Technique: Volume 2, Fields of Application.* By Bruno Klopfer and others. Yonkers, N.Y.: World Book Co., 1956. Pp. xx, 828. * (*PA* 30:7202)
2344. FRIEDEMANN, A. "Inequalities in the Reproduction of the Plates for the Rorschach Form Interpretation Experiment." *Zeitschrift für Diagnostische Psychologie und Persönlichkeitsforschung* 4(1):104–7 '56. *
2345. GEORGE, CLAY E., AND BONNEY, WARREN C. "Rorschach's Affect-Color Hypothesis and Adaptation-Level Theory." *Psychol R* 63:294–8 S '56. * (*PA* 31:6819)
2346. HALLOWELL, A. IRVING. Chap. 14, "The Rorschach Technique in Personality and Culture Studies," pp. 458–544. In *Developments in the Rorschach Technique: Volume 2, Fields of Application.* By Bruno Klopfer and others. Yonkers, N.Y.: World Book Co., 1956. Pp. xx, 828. * (*PA* 30:7202)
2347. HARRIS, RILDA. *A Comparative Study of Two Groups of Boys, Delinquent and Non-Delinquent, on the Basis of Their Wechsler and Rorschach Test Performances.* Master's thesis, Dalhousie University (Halifax, N.S., Canada), 1956.
2348. KENDIG, ISABELLE V.; CHAREN, SOL; AND LEPINE, LOUIS T. "Psychological Side Effects Induced by Cycloserine in the Treatment of Pulmonary Tuberculosis." *Am R Tuberc* 73:438–41 Mr '56. *
2349. KLOPFER, BRUNO. Chap. 8, "The Clinical Situation," pp. 215–66. In *Developments in the Rorschach Technique: Volume 2, Fields of Application.* By Bruno Klopfer and others. Yonkers, N.Y.: World Book Co., 1956. Pp. xx, 828. * (*PA* 30:7202)
2350. KLOPFER, BRUNO, AND SPIEGELMAN, MARVIN. Chap. 9, "Methodological Research Problems," pp. 267–80. In *Developments in the Rorschach Technique: Volume 2, Fields of Application.* By Bruno Klopfer and others. Yonkers, N.Y.: World Book Co., 1956. Pp. xx, 828. * (*PA* 30:7202)
2351. KLOPFER, BRUNO, AND SPIEGELMAN, MARVIN. Chap. 10, "Differential Diagnosis," pp. 281–317. In *Developments in the Rorschach Technique: Volume 2, Fields of Application.* By Bruno Klopfer and others. Yonkers, N.Y.: World Book Co., 1956. Pp. xx, 828. * (*PA* 30:7202)
2352. KLOPFER, BRUNO; FOX, JACK; AND TROUP, EVELYN. Chap. 1, "Problems in the Use of the Rorschach Technique With Children," pp. 3–21. In *Developments in the Rorschach Technique: Volume 2, Fields of Application.* By Bruno Klopfer and others. Yonkers, N.Y.: World Book Co., 1956. Pp. xx, 828. * (*PA* 30:7202)
2353. KLOPFER, BRUNO; SPIEGELMAN, MARVIN; AND FOX, JACK. Chap. 2, "The Interpretation of Children's Records," pp. 22–44. In *Developments in the Rorschach Technique: Volume 2, Fields of Application.* By Bruno Klopfer and others. Yonkers, N.Y.: World Book Co., 1956. Pp. xx, 828. * (*PA* 30:7202)
2354. KLOPFER, WALTER G. Chap. 7, "The Application of the Rorschach Technique to Geriatrics," pp. 195–212. In *Developments in the Rorschach Technique: Volume 2, Fields of Application.* By Bruno Klopfer and others. Yonkers, N.Y.: World Book Co., 1956. Pp. xx, 828. * (*PA* 30:7202)
2355. KUMAR, MYRA. "Rorschach Patterns of a Group of Normal Adults." *Indian J Psychol* 31:153–8 Jl–D '56. *
2356. MEILI-DWORETZKI, GERTRUDE. Chap. 5, "The Development of Perception in the Rorschach," pp. 104–76. In *Developments in the Rorschach Technique: Volume 2, Fields of Application.* By Bruno Klopfer and others. Yonkers, N.Y.: World Book Co., 1956. Pp. xx, 828. * (*PA* 30:7202)
2357. MONS, W. E. R., AND BARKER, G. B. "Scoring Problems." *Rorsch Newsl* 1:20–2 D '56. *

2358. MOYLAN, JOSEPH J. *The Role of Stimulus Generalization in Projective Test (Rorschach) Behavior.* Doctor's thesis, University of Massachusetts (Amherst, Mass.), 1956.
2359. ROTHNEY, JOHN W. M., AND HEIMANN, ROBERT A. "Development and Applications of Projective Technics." *R Ed Res* 26:56–71 F '56. * (*PA* 31:6127)
2360. SHANKER, UDAY. "Rorschach Responses of a Group of Juvenile Thieves." *Indian J Psychol* 31:125–30 Jl–D '56. * (*PA* 35:3823)
2361. SHNEIDMAN, EDWIN S. Chap. 17, "Some Relationships Between the Rorschach Technique and Other Psychodiagnostic Tests," pp. 595–642. In *Developments in the Rorschach Technique: Volume 2, Fields of Application.* By Bruno Klopfer and others. Yonkers, N.Y.: World Book Co., 1956. Pp. xx, 828. * (*PA* 30:7202)
2362. SIEGEL, SAUL M. "The Relationship of Hostility to Authoritarianism." *J Abn & Social Psychol* 52:368–72 My '56. * (*PA* 31:4494)
2363. SNOWDEN, ROBERT F. Chap. 16, "Top Management and the Rorschach Technique," pp. 582–92. In *Developments in the Rorschach Technique: Volume 2, Fields of Application.* By Bruno Klopfer and others. Yonkers, N.Y.: World Book Co., 1956. Pp. xx, 828. * (*PA* 30:7202)
2364. SPIEGELMAN, MARVIN. Chap. 13, "The Rorschach Technique in Social Psychology," pp. 431–57. In *Developments in the Rorschach Technique: Volume 2, Fields of Application.* By Bruno Klopfer and others. Yonkers, N.Y.: World Book Co., 1956. Pp. xx, 828. * (*PA* 30:7202)
2365. SPIEGELMAN, MARVIN, AND KLOPFER, BRUNO. Chap. 3, "Rorschach Reactions and Child Therapy: A Case Study," pp. 45–87. In *Developments in the Rorschach Technique: Volume 2, Fields of Application.* By Bruno Klopfer and others. Yonkers, N.Y.: World Book Co., 1956. Pp. xx, 828. * (*PA* 30:7202)
2366. WAUCK, LE ROY. *An Investigation of the Usefulness of Psychological Tests in the Selection of Candidates for the Diocesan Priesthood.* Doctor's thesis, Loyola University (Chicago, Ill.), 1956.
2367. WEBB, EUGENE J. *Statistical Selection of Individuals Forming Groups Using Rorschach Test Scores.* Doctor's thesis, University of Chicago (Chicago, Ill.), 1956.
2368. WHITE, J. M.; JONES, A. M.; AND INGHAM, J. G. "A Rorschach Study of the Neurodermatoses." *J Psychosom Res* 1:84–93 F '56. *
2369. WHITEMAN, DORIT B. *An Experimental Study of the Rorschach Apperceptive Type.* Doctor's thesis, New York University (New York, N.Y.), 1956. (*DA* 19:3376)
2370. WILLIAMS, GERTHA, AND KELLMAN, SAMUEL. Chap. 15, "The Rorschach Technique in Industrial Psychology," pp. 545–81. In *Developments in the Rorschach Technique: Volume 2, Fields of Application.* By Bruno Klopfer and others. Yonkers, N.Y.: World Book Co., 1956. Pp. xx, 828. * (*PA* 30:7202)
2371. WYSOCKI, BOLESLAW A. "Rorschach Card Preferences as a Diagnostic Aid." *Psychol Monogr* 70(6):1–16 '56. * (*PA* 31:6151)
2372. ZUK, GERALD H. "The Influence of Social Context on Impulse and Control Tendencies in Preadolescence." *Genetic Psychol Monogr* 54:117–66 N '56. * (*PA* 33:3464)
2373. ALLEN, ROBERT M. "A Longitudinal Rorschach Analysis." *Tohoku Psychologica Folia* 15(3–4):23–9 '57. * (*PA* 32:5475)
2374. BECK, S. J. "Rorschach Scoring Symbols." *Zeitschrift für Diagnostische Psychologie und Persönlichkeitsforschung* 5(1):62–3 '57. *
2375. BECK, SAMUEL J. "The Light-Dark Determinant: A Survey of the Problems," pp. 179–93. In *Rorschachiana V: Proceedings of the III International Rorschach Congress, Rome, September 13–16, 1956.* Beiheft zur Schweizerischen Zeitschrift für Psychologie und ihre Anwendungen, No. 34. Bern, Switzerland: Hans Huber, [1957?]. Pp. 445. *
2376. BERGER, STANLEY I. *Similarities of Rorschach Records Obtained Through Re-testing Procedures as Indicated by the Ability of Judges to Match Protocols.* Doctor's thesis, University of Kansas (Lawrence, Kan.), 1957.
2377. BOREHAM, J. L. "A Form of Reporting Projective Test Findings." *Rorsch Newsl* 2:7–12 D '57. *
2378. BURNHAM, RHODA K. *The Relationship of Personality to Oral Conditions in Children: An Evaluation by Means of the Rorschach and the Blacky Test.* Doctor's thesis, New York University (New York, N.Y.), 1957. (*DA* 18:1488)
2379. GEIST, HAROLD. "Emotional Aspects of Dermatitis." *J Clin & Exp Psychopathol* 18:87–93 Mr '57. * (*PA* 32:4433)
2380. HARRIS, RILDA. "A Comparative Study of Two Groups of Boys, Delinquent and Non-Delinquent, on the Basis of Their Wechsler and Rorschach Test Performances." *B Maritime Psychol Assn* 6:21–8 sp '57. * (*PA* 33:4295)
2381. HERMAN, JACK L. *Ideational and Motor Correlates of the Rorschach Experience Type.* Doctor's thesis, New York University (New York, N.Y.), 1957. (*DA* 20:3831)
2382. KALDEGG, A. "A Rorschach Re-test of a Schizophrenic Under Promazine (HCL)." *Rorsch Newsl* 2:3–4 D '57. *
2383. LOW, NATALIE S. *A Rorschach Study of the Parents of Children With Childhood Schizophrenia.* Doctor's thesis, New York University (New York, N.Y.), 1957. (*DA* 21:240)
2384. MOORE, EARL LEE. *The Concept of "Distanciation" Applied to the Rorschach and Draw-A-Person Techniques.* Doctor's thesis, University of Denver (Denver, Colo.), 1957.
2385. PENNINGTON, HARRY, III. *An Experimental Investigation of Several Card-Concepts, Using the Rorschach Ink Blots as Stimuli.* Master's thesis, University of Texas (Austin, Tex.), 1957.
2386. SAMIS, FRANCIS W. *A Study of the Characteristics of a Group of Mentally Competent Offenders as Revealed by the Rorschach Test.* Master's thesis, University of Alberta (Edmonton, Alta., Canada), 1957.
2387. STERNBERG, ULRICH; SPITZ, HERMAN; AND GOYNE, JAMES B. "Evaluation of Chlorpromazine and Reserpine Therapy With Follow-Up Study." *J Clin & Exp Psychopathol* 18:258–68 S '57. * (*PA* 33:1504)
2388. TAKALA, MARTTI; PIHKANEN, TOIVO A.; AND MARKKANEN, TOUKO. *The Effects of Distilled and Brewed Beverages: A Physiological, Neurological, and Psychological Study.* The Finnish Foundation for Alcoholic Studies, No. 4. Stockholm, Sweden: Almqvist & Wiksell, 1957. Pp. 195. * (*PA* 31:4890)
2389. TRAISMAN, ROBERT NEIL. *A Study of Rorschach Characteristics of Asthmatic Children.* Doctor's thesis, Loyola University (Chicago, Ill.), 1957.
2390. ZEEUW, JOH. DE. "The Administration and Interpretation of the Rorschach Test in Three Phases." *Zeitschrift für Diagnostische Psychologie und Persönlichkeitsforschung* 5(1):5–19 '57. *
2391. ADCOCK, CYRIL J., AND RITCHIE, JAMES E. "Intercultural Use of Rorschach." *Am Anthrop* 60:881–92 O '58. * (*PA* 33:10152)
2392. ALLEN, ROBERT M., AND GROMAN, WILLIAM. "A Note on Rorschach Test Age Norms." *Zeitschrift für Diagnostische Psychologie und Persönlichkeitsforschung* 6(2):178–80 '58. * (*PA* 33:10308)
2393. BAGH, D. "An Experimental Study of Rorschach Characteristics of Different Cultural Groups of Rural Bengal." *Indian J Psychol* 33:55–66 Ja–Mr '58. * (*PA* 35:3320)
2394. BAUGHMAN, E. EARL. "A New Method of Rorschach Inquiry." *J Proj Tech* 22:381–9 D '58. * (*PA* 34:1333)
2395. BENE, EVA. "A Rorschach Investigation Into the Mothers of Autistic Children." *Brit J Med Psychol* 31:226–7 pt 3 & 4 '58. * (*PA* 34:1340)
2396. BONDEL, GERTRUDE. *An Investigation Into the Relationship Between the Rorschach Test and the First Dream in Therapy.* Doctor's thesis, New York University (New York, N.Y.), 1958. (*DA* 19:3018)
2397. BOVA, LOUIS WILLIAM, JR. *Perceptual Rigidity: An Experiment With the Rorschach Test and the Autokinetic Effect.* Doctor's thesis, University of Florida (Gainesville, Fla.), 1958. (*DA* 19:1112)
2398. CANTER, ARTHUR. "The Effect of Unshaded Bright Colors in the Rorschach Upon the Form-Color Response Balance of Psychotic Patients." *J Proj Tech* 22:390–3 D '58. * (*PA* 34:1343)
2399. CARR, ARTHUR C. Chap. 4, "The Psychodiagnostic Test Battery: Rationale and Methodology," pp. 28–39. In *Progress in Clinical Psychology, Vol. 3.* Edited by Daniel Brower and Lawrence E. Abt. New York: Grune & Stratton, Inc., 1958. Pp. vi, 249. * (*PA* 33:8255)
2400. CASTRO, PERLA N. *A Cross Cultural Study of Popular Responses in the Rorschach Test.* Master's thesis, University of Kansas (Lawrence, Kan.), 1958.
2401. CHARNY, ISRAEL W. *Rorschach Areas Designated as "Sex Populars."* Doctor's thesis, University of Rochester (Rochester, N.Y.), 1958.
2402. CURTIS, JEAN MCCALLEY. *The Use of the Rorschach Prognostic Rating Scale With Children.* Doctor's thesis, University of California (Los Angeles, Calif.), 1958.
2403. DELAY, J.; PICHOT, P.; LEMPÉRIÈRE, J.; AND PERSE, J. *The Rorschach and the Epileptic Personality.* New York: Logos Press, Inc., 1958. Pp. xx, 265. * (*PA* 33:8866)
2404. DIAMOND, FLORENCE. *Style and Content in Personality Rigidity.* Doctor's thesis, Claremont Graduate School (Claremont, Calif.), 1958. (*DA* 20:2901)
2405. EDMONSTON, WILLIAM E., AND GRIFFITH, RICHARD M. "Rorschach Content and Ink Blot Structure." *J Proj Tech* 22:394–7 D '58. * (*PA* 34:1350)
2406. EIDUSON, BERNICE T. "Artist and Nonartist: A Comparative Study." *J Personality* 26:13–28 Mr '58. * (*PA* 33:5807)
2407. FA-YU, CHENG; CHU-CHANG, CHEN; AND HSIEN, RIN. "A Personality Analysis of the Ami and Its Three Subgroups by Rorschach Test." *Acta Psychologica Taiwanica* (1):131–43 N '58. *
2408. FISHER, RHODA LEE. "The Effect of a Disturbing Situation Upon the Stability of Various Projective Tests." *Psychol Monogr* 72(14):1–23 '58. * (*PA* 34:1357)
2409. FISHER, SEYMOUR, AND CLEVELAND, SIDNEY E. *Body Images and Personality.* Princeton, N.J.: D. Van Nostrand Co., Inc., 1958. Pp. xi, 420. * (*PA* 32:3926)
2410. FOX, JACK. "A Note on Klopfer's Hypothesis About Shading Responses." *J Proj Tech* 22:398 D '58. * (*PA* 34:1360)
2411. GOLDBERGER, L. *Individual Differences in Effects of Perceptual Isolation as Related to Rorschach Manifestations*

of the Primary Process. Doctor's thesis, New York University (New York, N.Y.), 1958. (*DA* 19:1816)

2412. GOLDSTONE, MARTIN H. *The Relationship Between Certain Rorschach Indicators and the Magnitude of Kinesthetic After-Effect.* Doctor's thesis, Yeshiva University (New York, N.Y.), 1958. (*DA* 21:1254)

2413. GOODALL, BEBE J. *Investigation of Rorschach Personality Factors Related to Educational Progress in the Educable Mentally Handicapped Adolescent.* Master's thesis, De Paul University (Chicago, Ill.), 1958.

2414. GRUEN, ARNO. "A New Level of Aspiration Test and an Application of It." *J General Psychol* 59:73-7 Jl '58. * (*PA* 36:2HB73G)

2415. GRUEN, ARNO. "Psychological Testing With the Older Client: A Case of Paresis." *J Proj Tech* 22:26-32 Mr '58. * (*PA* 33:6232)

2416. HABER, WILLIAM B. "Reactions to Loss of Limb: Physiological and Psychological Aspects." *Ann N Y Acad Sci* 74:14-24 S 30 '58. * (*PA* 34:3359)

2417. HAFNER, A. JACK. "Rorschach Test Behavior and Related Variables." *Psychol Rec* 8:7-12 Ja '58. * (*PA* 33:7602)

2418. HAMBY, RONALD. *The Trailmaking Test and Immediately Successive Administrations of the Rorschach Psychodiagnostic Test in the Differentiation and Study of the Effects of Brain Damage.* Master's thesis, University of Kansas (Lawrence, Kan.), 1958.

2419. HAWARD, L. R. C. "Rorschach." *Psychometric Res B* (2):[31-3] Ag '58. *

2420. HEATH, DOUGLAS. "Projective Tests as Measures of Defensive Activity." *J Proj Tech* 22:284-92 S '58. * (*PA* 33:10333)

2421. HOLT, ROBERT R., AND LUBORSKY, LESTER; WITH THE COLLABORATION OF WILLIAM R. MORROW, DAVID RAPAPORT, AND SIBYLLE K. ESCALONA. *Personality Patterns of Psychiatrists: A Study of Methods for Selecting Residents, Vol. 1.* New York: Basic Books, Inc., 1958. Pp. xiv, 386. * (*PA* 33:5751)

2422. HOWIE, MARGARET M. "The Rorschach Test Applied to a Group of Scottish Children." *Rorsch Newsl* 3:14-5 Je '58. *

2423. KADEN, S. *A Formal-Comparative Analysis of the Relationships Between the Structuring of Marital Interaction and Rorschach Blot Stimuli.* Doctor's thesis, Clark University (Worcester, Mass.), 1958. (*DA* 19:1820)

2424. KANTER, V. B., AND WILLIAMS, CELIA. "The Interaction of Emotional and Organic Factors in the Rorschach and T.A.T. Records of a Male Alcoholic Aged 60." *Rorsch Newsl* 3:22-3 D '58. *

2425. KING, GERALD F. "A Theoretical and Experimental Consideration of the Rorschach Human Movement Response." *Psychol Monogr* 72(5):1-23 '58. * (*PA* 33:10338)

2426. LEIDING, WALDEMAR C. *A Comparison of the Content and Sign Approaches in Evaluating a Projective Test Battery and Its Component Tests.* Doctor's thesis, University of Houston (Houston, Tex.), 1958. (*DA* 19:1822)

2427. LEVINE, ABRAHAM. "A Comparative Evaluation of Latent Schizophrenic and Overt Schizophrenic Patients With Respect to Certain Personality Variables." *J Hillside Hosp* 7:131-52 Jl-O '58. * (*PA* 34:3280)

2428. LEVINSON, BORIS M. "Some Aspects of the Personality of the Native-Born White Homeless Man as Revealed by the Rorschach." *Psychiatric Q Sup* 32:278-86 pt 2 '58. * (*PA* 34:3213)

2429. MANUS, GERALD IRWIN. *A Study of the Relationship of Certain Rorschach Content Factors to Successful and Unsuccessful Extra-Mural Adjustment of Hospitalized Schizophrenic Patients.* Doctor's thesis, New York University (New York, N.Y.), 1958. (*DA* 19:2149)

2430. MARKHAM, SYLVIA. "The Dynamics of Post-Partum Pathological Reactions as Revealed in Psychological Tests." *J Hillside Hosp* 7:178-89 Jl-O '58. * (*PA* 34:3011)

2431. MARSZALEK, K. S. "Munroe Check List." *Psychometric Res B* (1):[3-5] My '58. *

2432. MONS, W. E. R. "The Development of the Personality as Seen in the Rorschach." *Rorsch Newsl* 3:32-8 D '58. *

2433. MONS, W. E. R. "The Function of Extreme Types of Personality in Neurosis and Hysteria, and Some Psychoses." *Rorsch Newsl* 3:9-13 Je '58. *

2434. NEWMAN, R. E. "Personality Development in a Primitive 'Adolescent' Group (as Revealed by the Rorschach Technique)." *Zeitschrift für Diagnostische Psychologie und Persönlichkeitsforschung* 6(3):241-53 '58. * (*PA* 34:2779)

2435. PAREIS, EGBERT NELSON. *Inkblot Perception and Personality: An Experimental Departure From the Rorschach Test.* Doctor's thesis, University of Texas (Austin, Tex.), 1958. (*DA* 19:1118)

2436. PERLMAN, STANFORD EUGENE. *Some Correlates of Social Awareness.* Doctor's thesis, Columbia University (New York, N.Y.), 1958. (*DA* 21:242)

2437. PIOTROWSKI, ZYGMUNT A. Chap. 8, "The Psychodiagnostic Test Battery: Clinical Application," pp. 72-85. In *Progress in Clinical Psychology, Vol. 3.* Edited by Daniel Brower and Lawrence E. Abt. New York: Grune & Stratton, Inc., 1958. Pp. vi, 249. * (*PA* 33:8255)

2438. PIOTROWSKI, ZYGMUNT A., AND BRICKLIN, BARRY. "A Long-Term Prognostic Criterion for Schizophrenics Based on Rorschach Data." *Psychiatric Q Sup* 32:315-29 pt 2 '58. * (*PA* 34:3293)

2439. PRENSKY, SAMUEL J. *An Investigation of Some Personality Characteristics of Epileptic and Psychosomatic Patients: An Evaluation of Certain Personality Measures and Reactions to Frustration in Idiopathic Epileptic, Symptomatic Epileptic, and Peptic Ulcer Patients.* Doctor's thesis, New York University (New York, N.Y.), 1958. (*DA* 19:3025)

2440. RIESSMAN, FRANK, AND MILLER, S. M. "Social Class and Projective Tests." *J Proj Tech* 22:432-9 D '58. * (*PA* 34:1268)

2441. ROTHSTEIN, CHARLES, AND COHEN, IRA S. "Hostility and Dependency Conflicts in Peptic Ulcer Patients." *Psychol Rep* 4:555-8 D '58. * (*PA* 34:1856)

2442. RYAN, WILLIAM. *Capacity for Mutual Dependence and Involvement in Group Psychotherapy.* Doctor's thesis, Boston University (Boston, Mass.), 1958. (*DA* 19:1119)

2443. SAFIAN, MURRAY Z. *A Study of Certain Psychological Factors in the Rehabilitation of Potentially Employable Homebound Adults.* Doctor's thesis, New York University (New York, N.Y.), 1958. (*DA* 19:3372)

2444. SCHAFER, ROY. "On the Psychoanalytic Study of Retest Results." *J Proj Tech* 22:102-9 Mr '58. * (*PA* 33:6286)

2445. SCHON, MARTHA, AND BARD, MORTON. "The Effect of Hypophysectomy on Personality in Women With Metastatic Breast Cancer as Revealed by the Rorschach Test." *J Proj Tech* 22:440-5 D '58. * (*PA* 34:1419)

2446. SCOTT, EDWARD M. "A Case of Folie à Deux and Projective Techniques." *J Consult Psychol* 22:90 Ap '58. * (*PA* 35:3636, title only)

2447. SELIG, KALMAN. *Personality Structure as Revealed by the Rorschach Technique of a Group of Children Who Test at or Above 170 I.Q. on the 1937 Revision of the Stanford-Binet Scale (Volumes I-V).* Doctor's thesis, New York University (New York, N.Y.), 1958. (*DA* 19:3373)

2448. SHEEHAN, JOSEPH G. "Projective Studies of Stuttering." *J Speech & Hearing Disorders* 23:18-25 F '58. *

2449. SHERMAN, RUTH LAUBGROSS. *A Study With Projective Techniques of Sociometrically High and Sociometrically Low Children.* Doctor's thesis, University of Maryland (College Park, Md.), 1958. (*DA* 20:767)

2450. SINGER, MARGARET THALER, AND SCHEIN, EDGAR H. "Projective Test Responses of Prisoners of War Following Repatriation." *Psychiatry* 21:375-85 N '58. * (*PA* 33:10113)

2451. SPIVACK, GEORGE; LEVINE, MURRAY; AND SPRIGLE, HERBERT. "Barron M Threshold Values in Emotionally Disturbed Adolescents." *J Proj Tech* 22:446-9 D '58. * (*PA* 34:1423)

2452. STAFFORD-CLARK, D. "Projective Tests and Clinical Judgment." *Rorsch Newsl* 3:4 Je '58. *

2453. STAMPFL, THOMAS G. *Rorschach Prognostic Rating Scale Assessment of Ego Structure in the Children of Psychotic Parents.* Doctor's thesis, Loyola University (Chicago, Ill.), 1958.

2454. STEIN, HARRY. "Age, Physical Disability and Responsivity in Relation to Spontaneous Rotation of Rorschach Cards." *J Proj Tech* 22:450-2 D '58. * (*PA* 34:1424)

2455. SU, HSIANG-YU; CHANG, SIN-HWA; CHANG, SOPHIA; AND HSIAO, SHIH-LANG. "A Study of 'Goitrous Personality' From the Rorschach Responses." English abstract. *Acta Psychologica Taiwanica* (1):103 N '58. * (*PA* 34:3034)

2456. SWENSON, W. M., AND GRIMES, B. P. "Characteristics of Sex Offenders Admitted to a Minnesota State Hospital for Pre-Sentence Psychiatric Investigation." *Psychiatric Q Sup* 32(1):110-23 '58. * (*PA* 34:3250)

2457. TAMKIN, ARTHUR S. "Rorschach Card Rejection by Psychiatric Patients." *J Consult Psychol* 22:441-4 D '58. * (*PA* 33:10784)

2458. TANIGUCHI, MAYUMI; DE VOS, GEORGE; AND MURAKAMI, EIJI. "Identification of Mother and Father Cards on the Rorschach by Japanese Normal and Delinquent Adolescents." *J Proj Tech* 22:453-60 D '58. * (*PA* 34:1428)

2459. TAYLOR, JAMES BENTLEY. *Social Desirability and the MMPI Performance of Schizophrenics.* Doctor's thesis, University of Washington (Seattle, Wash.), 1958. (*DA* 19:1828)

2460. VERNIER, CLAIRE M.; STAFFORD, JOHN W.; AND KRUGMAN, ARNOLD D. "A Factor Analysis of Indices From Four Projective Techniques Associated With Four Different Types of Physical Pathology." *J Consult Psychol* 22:433-7 D '58. * (*PA* 33:9360)

2461. VERRILL, BERNARD VICTOR. *An Investigation of the Concept of Impulsivity.* Doctor's thesis, University of Houston (Houston, Tex.), 1958. (*DA* 19:183)

2462. WENAR, CHARLES. "The Degree of Psychological Disturbance in Handicapped Youth." *Excep Child* 25:7-10+ S '58. * (*PA* 33:10380)

2463. WILLIAMS, JESSIE M. "The Use of the Rorschach in the Study of Personality Development of Cerebral-Palsied Children." *Rorsch Newsl* 3:3-21 D '58. *

2464. WINDER, C. L., AND KANTOR, ROBERT E. "Rorschach Maturity Scores of the Mothers of Schizophrenics." *J Consult Psychol* 22:438-40 D '58. * (*PA* 33:10381)

2465. YOUNG, HARL H. "Relationships Between and Reliability Estimates of New (Holtzman) Ink Blot Variables and

Conventional Rorschach Scoring Categories." *Proc Okla Acad Sci* 38:111–5 D '58. *
2466. ZUCKER, LUISE J. *Ego Structure in Paranoid Schizophrenia.* Springfield, Ill.: Charles C Thomas, Publisher, 1958. Pp. x, 186. * (*PA* 33:1916)
2467. "An Organic-Looking Rorschach Obtained From a Depressed Patient." *Rorsch Newsl* 4:25–7 Je '59. *
2468. ABEL, THEODORA M., AND METRAUX, RHODA. "Sex Differences in a Negro Peasant Community: Montserrat, B.W.I." *J Proj Tech* 23:127–33 Je '59. * (*PA* 35:4755)
2469. ADCOCK, C. J., AND RITCHIE, JAMES E. "Intercultural Use of Rorschach: Rejoinder to Clifton." Letter. *Am Anthrop* 61:1090–2 D '59. *
2470. ADCOCK, C. J., AND RITCHIE, JAMES E. "Rejoinder to Edgerton and Polk." Letter. *Am Anthrop* 61:1093–4 D '59. *
2471. AFFLECK, D. CRAIG, AND MEDNICK, SARNOFF A. "The Use of the Rorschach Test in the Prediction of the Abrupt Terminator in Individual Psychotherapy." *J Consult Psychol* 23:125–8 Ap '59. * (*PA* 34:1328)
2472. AINSWORTH, MARY D., AND KUETHE, JAMES L. "Texture Responses in the Rorschach and in a Sorting Test." *J Proj Tech* 23:391–402 D '59. * (*PA* 35:4900)
2473. ALCOCK, THEODORA, AND TUSTIN, FRANCES. "Personality Disturbance Impairing Educational Ability: The Case of Derek B." *Rorsch Newsl* 4:7–18 D '59. *
2474. AMES, LOUISE BATES. "Further Check on the Diagnostic Validity of the Ames Danger Signals." *J Proj Tech* 23:291–8 S '59. * (*PA* 35:4949)
2475. AMES, LOUISE BATES; MÉTRAUX, RUTH W.; AND WALKER, RICHARD N. *Adolescent Rorschach Responses: Developmental Trends From Ten to Sixteen Years.* New York: Hoeber Medical Division, Harper & Row, Publishers, Inc., 1959. Pp. xiii, 313. * (*PA* 34:1329)
2476. APPELBAUM, STEPHEN. "The Effect of Altered Psychological Atmosphere on Rorschach Responses: A New Supplementary Procedure." *B Menninger Clinic* 23:179–89 S '59. * (*PA* 35:794)
2477. ARNAUD, SARA H. "Some Psychological Characteristics of Children of Multiple Sclerotics." *Psychosom Med* 21:8–22 Ja–F '59. * (*PA* 34:1863)
2478. ARNAUD, SARA H. "A System for Deriving Quantitative Rorschach Measures of Certain Psychological Variables, for Group Comparisons." *J Proj Tech* 23:403–11 D '59. * (*PA* 35:4901)
2479. BARKER, G. B. "Diagnostic Study of a Young Woman, Using Rorschach Tests and Paintings." *Rorsch Newsl* 4:19–26 D '59. *
2480. BASIT, ABDUL. *A Comparative Study of Personality Development in Identical and Fraternal Twins by Means of the Rorschach Method.* Master's thesis, University of Kansas (Lawrence, Kan.), 1959.
2481. BATHURST, G. C. "Some Tentative Inferences From the Rorschach Records of 100 Alcoholics." *Rorsch Newsl* 4:11–2 Je '59. *
2482. BATHURST, G. C., AND GLATT, M. M. "Some Psychological Reflections on Vulnerability to Alcoholism." *Psychiatria et Neurologia* 138:27–46 '59. *
2483. BAUGHMAN, E. EARL. "The Effect of Inquiry Method on Rorschach Color and Shading Scores." *J Proj Tech* 23:3–7 Mr '59. * (*PA* 34:6002)
2484. BAUGHMAN, E. EARL. "An Experimental Analysis of the Relationship Between Stimulus Structure and Behavior on the Rorschach." *J Proj Tech* 23:134–83 Je '59. * (*PA* 35:4902)
2485. BEACH, LEE. "Rorschach Variables and Vocational Choice." *B Maritime Psychol Assn* 8:28–33 Ap '59. *
2486. BERGER, LESLIE. "Crossvalidation of 'Primary' and 'Reactive' Personality Patterns With Non-Ulcer Surgical Patients." *J Proj Tech* 23:8–11 Mr '59. * (*PA* 34:6004)
2487. BIRCH, HERBERT G., AND DILLER, LEONARD. "Rorschach Signs of 'Organicity': A Physiological Basis for Perceptual Disturbances." *J Proj Tech* 23:184–97 Je '59. * (*PA* 35:4903)
2488. BLECKNER, JANET E. "The Responses of Average and Gifted Students on the Group Rorschach Test." *Calif J Ed Res* 10:200–6 N '59. * (*PA* 34:7831)
2489. BOHM, EWALD. *A Textbook in Rorschach Test Diagnosis for Psychologists, Physicians, and Teachers.* Translated by Anne G. Beck and Samuel J. Beck. New York: Grune & Stratton, Inc., 1959. Pp. xiii, 322. * (*PA* 33:6211)
2490. BOLIN, B. J. "An Investigation of Relationship Between Birth-Duration and Childhood Anxieties." *J Mental Sci* 105:1045–52 O '59. * (*PA* 34:6227)
2491. BOLLE, A. M. *The Personality Structure of Thyroid Patients on the Rorschach Test.* Doctor's thesis, University of Ottawa (Ottawa, Ont., Canada), 1959. (Abstract: *Can Psychologist* 1:112–3)
2492. BRICKLIN, BARRY. *The Prediction of Long Term Follow Up Conditions of Schizophrenic Patients by Means of the Rorschach Test.* Doctor's thesis, Temple University (Philadelphia, Pa.), 1959. (*DA* 20:3373)
2493. BROWN, D. G. "Psychosomatic Correlates in Contact Dermatitis: A Pilot Study." *J Psychosom Res* 4:132–9 D '59. * (*PA* 34:8214)
2494. CAMPBELL, FRANCES A., AND FIDDLEMAN, PAUL B. "The Effect of Examiner Status Upon Rorschach Performance." *J Proj Tech* 23:303–6 S '59. * (*PA* 35:4904)
2495. CHARNY, ISRAEL W. "A Normative Study of Rorschach 'Sex Populars' for Males." *J Proj Tech* 23:12–23 Mr '59. * (*PA* 34:6008)
2496. CLEVELAND, SIDNEY E. "Personality Dynamics in Torticollis." *J Nerv & Mental Dis* 129:150–61 Ag '59. * (*PA* 34:6407)
2497. CLIFTON, JAMES A. "On the Intercultural Use of the Rorschach." Letter. *Am Anthrop* 61:1087–90 D '59. *
2498. COAN, RICHARD W. "Perceptual Aspects of Attributed Movement." *Genetic Psychol Monogr* 59:45–100 F '59. * (PA 34:1346)
2499. DANA, RICHARD H. "American Culture and Chinese Personality." *Psychol Newsl* 10:314–21 My–Je '59. * (*PA* 34:1213)
2500. DAVIS, HANNAH SUSAN. *Judgments of Intellectual Level From Various Features of the Rorschach Including Vocabulary.* Doctor's thesis, Columbia University (New York, N.Y.), 1959. (*DA* 20:1436)
2501. EDGERTON, ROBERT B., AND POLK, KENNETH. "Statistical Problems in the Intercultural Use of Rorschach." Letter. *Am Anthrop* 61:1092–3 D '59. *
2502. EISDÖRFER, CARL. *The Effect of Sensory Decrement Upon Rorschach Performance in a Senescent Population.* Doctor's thesis, New York University (New York, N.Y.), 1959.
2503. ENGEL, CYNTHIA. "The Relationship Between Rorschach Responses and Attitudes Toward Parents." *J Proj Tech* 23:311–4 S '59. * (*PA* 35:4910)
2504. EXNER, JOHN E., JR. "The Influence of Chromatic and Achromatic Color in the Rorschach." *J Proj Tech* 23:418–25 D '59. * (*PA* 35:4911)
2505. EXNER, JOHN ERNEST, JR. *The Influence of Color in Projective Testing.* Doctor's thesis, Cornell University (Ithaca, N.Y.), 1959. (*DA* 20:754)
2506. EYSENCK, H. J. "Personality Tests: 1950–55," pp. 118–59. In *Recent Progress in Psychiatry, Vol. 3.* Edited by G. W. T. H. Fleming and A. Walk. London: J. & A. Churchill Ltd., 1959. Pp. iv, 397. *
2507. FARBEROW, NORMAN L. "Validity and Methodology in Projective Tests." *J Proj Tech* 23:282–6 S '59. * (*PA* 35:4912)
2508. FEFFER, MELVIN H. "The Cognitive Implications of Role Taking Behavior." *J Personality* 27:152–68 Je '59. * (*PA* 34:4380)
2509. FISHER, SEYMOUR; BOYD, INA; WALKER, DONALD; AND SHEER, DIANNE. "Parents of Schizophrenics, Neurotics, and Normals." *A.M.A. Arch Gen Psychiatry* 1:149–66 Ag '59. * (*PA* 34:6184)
2510. FOLLETT, GEORGE C., JR. *The Comparison of Rorschach Responses Between Superior, Average, and Retarded Children.* Master's thesis, Kent State University (Kent, Ohio), 1959.
2511. FORSYTH, RALPH P. "The Influences of Color, Shading, and Welsh Anxiety Level on Elizur Rorschach Content Test Analyses of Anxiety and Hostility." *J Proj Tech* 23:207–13 Je '59. * (*PA* 35:4915)
2512. GARDNER, RILEY W.; HOLZMAN, PHILIP S.; KLEIN, GEORGE S.; LINTON, HARRIET B.; AND SPENCE, DONALD P. "Cognitive Control: A Study of Individual Consistencies in Cognitive Behavior." *Psychol Issues* 1(4):1–186 '59. * (*PA* 35:2266)
2513. GLADSTON, ELAINE R., AND HAGUENAUER, GINETTE. "Somatic Preoccupation in a Paranoid Schizophrenic: Mlle. V." *Rorsch Newsl* 4:27–33 D '59. *
2514. GLICKSTEIN, MITCHELL. "A Note on Wittenborn's Factor Analysis of Rorschach Scoring Categories." *J Consult Psychol* 23:69–75 F '59. * (*PA* 34:125)
2515. GORDON, JESSE E. "Rorschach Responses as Verbal Behavior." *J Proj Tech* 23:426–8 D '59. * (*PA* 35:4916)
2516. GROSS, LEONARD R. "Effects of Verbal and Nonverbal Reinforcement in the Rorschach." *J Consult Psychol* 23:66–8 F '59. * (*PA* 34:1368)
2517. GRUEN, WALTER. "Behavioral Correlates of Some Dimensions of the Cognitive Field." *J Personality* 27:169–86 Je '59. * (*PA* 34:3882)
2518. GUILFORD, J. P. *Personality,* pp. 288–98, 309–14. New York: McGraw-Hill Book Co., Inc., 1959. Pp. xiii, 562. *
2519. HEIMAN, N., AND COOPER, S. "An Experiment in Clinical Integration." *J Hillside Hosp* 8:290–7 O '59. * (*PA* 35:4919)
2520. HEIMANN, ROBERT A., AND ROTHNEY, JOHN W. M. "Development and Applications of Projective Techniques." *R Ed Res* 29:73–83 F '59. * (*PA* 34:6021)
2521. HELME, WILLIAM HURD. *A Study of Relationships Between the Rorschach Method and Objective Tests of Interests and Values by Means of Factor Analysis.* Doctor's thesis, New School for Social Research (New York, N.Y.), 1959.
2522. HERTZ, MARGUERITE R. "The Use and Misuse of the Rorschach Method: 1, Variations in Rorschach Procedure." *J Proj Tech* 23:33–48 Mr '59. * (*PA* 34:6022)
2523. JACKSON, PHILIP W., AND GETZELS, JACOB W. "Psychological Health and Classroom Functioning: A Study of Dissatisfaction With School Among Adolescents." *J Ed Psychol* 50:295–300 D '59. * (*PA* 34:8368, 36:1FH95J)
2524. JENSEN, ARTHUR R. "The Reliability of Projective Techniques: Review of the Literature." *Acta Psychologica* 16(1):108–36 '59. * (*PA* 34:5956)
2525. KAHN, MARVIN W. "A Comparison of Personality,

Intelligence, and Social History of Two Criminal Groups." *J Social Psychol* 49:33–40 F '59. * (*PA* 35:5214)

2526. KATAGUCHI, YASUFUMI. "Rorschach Schizophrenic Score (RSS)." *J Proj Tech* 23:214–22 Je '59. * (*PA* 35:4960)

2527. KOENIG, FRANCES G. *A Study of Anxiety in Children With Rheumatic Fever: The Relationship Between Recurrences of Rheumatic Fever and Rorschach Indices of Anxiety in Children.* Doctor's thesis, New York University (New York, N.Y.), 1959. (*DA* 20:1438)

2528. KRASNOFF, ALAN. "Psychological Variables and Human Cancer: A Cross-Validation Study." *Psychosom Med* 21:291–5 Jl–Ag '59. * (*PA* 34:4736)

2529. LANGE, HERBERT. *An Investigation of the Validity of the Rorschach Technique in Predicting Sociability.* Doctor's thesis, Purdue University (Lafayette, Ind.), 1959. (*DA* 20:2920)

2530. LEARMONTH, GEORGE J.; ACKERLY, WILLIAM; AND KAPLAN, MIKE. "Relationships Between Palmar Skin Potential During Stress and Personality Variables." *Psychosom Med* 21:150–7 Mr–Ap '59. * (*PA* 34:1384)

2531. LEDWITH, NETTIE H. *Rorschach Responses of Elementary School Children: A Normative Study.* Pittsburgh, Pa.: University of Pittsburgh Press, 1959. Pp. xi, 185. * (*PA* 34:1385)

2532. LEVINE, DAVID. "Rorschach Genetic-Level and Mental Disorder." *J Proj Tech* 23:436–9 D '59. * (*PA* 35:4925)

2533. LEVINE, MURRAY; SPIVACK, GEORGE; AND WIGHT, BYRON. "The Inhibition Process, Rorschach Human Movement Responses, and Intelligence: Some Further Data." *J Consult Psychol* 23:306–12 Ag '59. * (*PA* 34:4390)

2534. LEVY, LEON H., AND ORR, THOMAS B. "The Social Psychology of Rorschach Validity Research." *J Abn & Social Psychol* 58:79–83 Ja '59. * (*PA* 34:1388)

2535. LINTON, HARRIET, AND GRAHAM, ELAINE. Chap. 4, "Personality Correlates of Persuasibility," pp. 69–101. (*PA* 34:7403) In *Personality and Persuasibility.* Edited by Carl I. Hovland and Irving L. Janis. New Haven, Conn.: Yale University Press, 1959. Pp. xiv, 333. *

2536. LITTLE, KENNETH B. "Connotations of the Rorschach Inkblots." *J Personality* 27:397–406 S '59. * (*PA* 34:6032)

2537. LITTLE, KENNETH B., AND SHNEIDMAN, EDWIN S. "Congruencies Among Interpretations of Psychological Test and Anamnestic Data." *Psychol Monogr* 73(6):1–42 '59. * (*PA* 34:3010)

2538. LOVELAND, NATHENE TURK, AND SINGER, MARGARET THALER. "Projective Test Assessment of the Effects of Sleep Deprivation." *J Proj Tech* 23:323–34 S '59. * (*PA* 35:4928)

2539. LYNN, DAVID B. "Ambiguity and Projection." *Psychol Newsl* 10:289–94 My–Je '59. * (*PA* 34:1393)

2540. MACHOVER, SOLOMON, AND PUZZO, FRANK S. "Clinical and Objective Studies of Personality Variables in Alcoholism: 1, Clinical Investigation of the 'Alcoholic Personality.'" *Q J Studies Alcohol* 20:505–19 S '59. * (*PA* 34:6253)

2541. MACHOVER, SOLOMON, AND PUZZO, FRANK S. "Clinical and Objective Studies of Personality Variables in Alcoholism: 2, Clinical Study of Personality Correlates of Remission From Active Alcoholism." *Q J Studies Alcohol* 20:520–7 S '59. * (*PA* 34:6253)

2542. MACHOVER, SOLOMON; PUZZO, FRANK S.; MACHOVER, KAREN; AND PLUMEAU, FRANCIS. "Clinical and Objective Studies of Personality Variables in Alcoholism: 3, An Objective Study of Homosexuality in Alcoholism." *Q J Studies Alcohol* 20:528–42 S '59. * (*PA* 34:6254)

2543. MCKEEVER, WALTER F., AND GERSTEIN, ALVIN I. "Base Rate Data on Rorschach Card Rejection." *J Clin Psychol* 15:425–7 O '59. * (*PA* 36:1HI25M)

2544. MCREYNOLDS, PAUL, AND WEIDE, MARIAN. "The Prediction and Assessment of Psychological Changes Following Prefrontal Lobotomy." *J Mental Sci* 105:971–8 O '59. * (*PA* 34:6471)

2545. MARKS, JOHN B. "Rorschach Water Responses in Alcoholics: Levels of Content Analysis and Consensual Validation." *J Proj Tech* 23:69–71 Mr '59. * (*PA* 34:6035)

2546. MARTIN, HARRY JEROME, JR. *A Comparison of Sign and Clinical Approaches in Predicting Psychiatric Diagnosis.* Doctor's thesis, University of Houston (Houston, Tex.), 1959. (*DA* 20:3837)

2547. MONS, W. E. R., AND KANTER, V. B. "Use of a 'Blind' Analysis of the Rorschach in the Investigation of an Insurance Compensation Case." *Rorsch Newsl* 4:2–10 Je '59. *

2548. MOYLAN, JOSEPH J. "Stimulus Generalization in Projective Test (Rorschach) Behavior." *J Personality* 27:18–37 Mr '59. * (*PA* 34:3966)

2549. MURSTEIN, BERNARD I., AND WHEELER, JOHN I., JR. "The Projection of Hostility on the Rorschach and Thematic Stories Test." *J Clin Psychol* 15:316–9 Jl '59. * (*PA* 35:3474)

2550. MYDEN, WALTER. "Interpretation and Evaluation of Certain Personality Characteristics Involved in Creative Production." *Percept & Motor Skills* 9:139–58 Je '59. *

2551. NEIGER, STEPHEN. "Frequent Rorschach Responses in the Toronto Area and Their Comparison With Responses From Other Areas." *Ont Hosp Psychol B* 5:10–24 D '59. *

2552. NELSON, MARVEN O.; WOLFSON, WILLIAM; AND LOCASCIO, RALPH. "Sexual Identification in Responses to Rorschach Card III." *J Proj Tech* 23:354–6 S '59. * (*PA* 35:4934)

2553. NIKELLY, A. G. *The Bruner-Postman Hypothesis Theory and Perceptual Responses to Inkblots.* Doctor's thesis, University of Ottawa (Ottawa, Ont., Canada), 1959. (Abstract: *Can Psychologist* 1:115–6)

2554. NUNNERY, MICHAEL Y. "How Useful Are Standardized Psychological Tests in the Selection of School Administrators." *Ed Adm & Sup* 45:349–56 N '59. * (*PA* 35:7092)

2555. OGDON, DONALD P., AND ALLEE, RUTH. "Rorschach Relationships With Intelligence Among Familial Mental Defectives." *Am J Mental Def* 63:889–96 Mr '59. * (*PA* 34:1675)

2556. OTIS, LEON S. "What Does the Rorschach *Z* Score Reflect?" *J Consult Psychol* 23:373–4 Ag '59. * (*PA* 34:4399)

2557. PARKER, ROLLAND S. *An Investigation of the Content of the Rorschach Human Movement Response Utilizing the Subjects' Associations to Their Own M.* Doctor's thesis, New York University (New York, N.Y.), 1959. (*DA* 20:384)

2558. PENA, CESAREO D. "Influence of Social Desirability Upon Rorschach Content." *J Clin Psychol* 15:313–6 Jl '59. * (*PA* 35:3436)

2559. PEPINSKY, HAROLD B. "A Note on the Rorschach Prognostic Rating Scale." *J Counsel Psychol* 6:160–2 su '59. *

2560. PHILLIPS, LESLIE; KADEN, STANLEY; AND WALDMAN, MARVIN. "Rorschach Indices of Developmental Level." *J Genetic Psychol* 94:267–85 Je '59. *

2561. PIOTROWSKI, ZYGMUNT A. "Test Indication and Contraindications for Adult Therapy: Indications and Contraindications for Adult Therapy: Workshop, 1958." *Am J Orthopsychiatry* 29:60–8 Ja '59. * (*PA* 34:3062)

2562. PIOTROWSKI, ZYGMUNT A., AND LEVINE, DAVID. "A Case Illustrating the Concept of the Alpha Schizophrenic." *J Proj Tech* 23:223–36 Je '59. * (*PA* 35:5256)

2563. PODELL, JEROME E., AND PHILLIPS, LESLIE. "A Developmental Analysis of Cognition as Observed in Dimensions of Rorschach and Objective Test Performance." *J Personality* 27:439–63 D '59. *

2564. PORT, YALE I. *An Investigation of the Effect of Optimal Symptom Alleviation of Parkinson's Disease Upon Certain Aspects of the Personality as Reflected in the Rorschach.* Doctor's thesis, Yeshiva University (New York, N.Y.), 1959.

2565. RABIN, A. I. "A Contribution to the 'Meaning' of Rorschach's Inkblots via the Semantic Differential." *J Consult Psychol* 23:368–72 Ag '59. * (*PA* 34:4403)

2566. RIOCH, MARGARET J., AND LUBIN, ARDIE. "Prognosis of Social Adjustment for Mental Hospital Patients Under Psychotherapy." *J Consult Psychol* 23:313–8 Ag '59. * (*PA* 34:4404)

2567. ROSEN, ALEXANDER C. "A Clinical Evaluation of Eysenck's 'Objective Rorschach.'" *J Clin Psychol* 15:320–1 Jl '59. * (*PA* 35:3477)

2568. RYCHLAK, JOSEPH F. "Forced Associations, Symbolism, and Rorschach Constructs." *J Consult Psychol* 23:455–60 O '59. * (*PA* 34:5978)

2569. SANDLER, JOSEPH. "The Rorschach and the Feeling of Safety." *Rorsch Newsl* 4:2–6 D '59. *

2570. SASLOW, HARRY LEWIS. *Longitudinal Stability of Rorschach Factorial Structure of School-Age Children.* Doctor's thesis, University of Pittsburgh (Pittsburgh, Pa.), 1959. (*DA* 20:3391)

2571. SCHMEIDLER, GERTRUDE RAFFEL; NELSON, MARJORY J.; AND BRISTOL, MARJORIE. "Freshman Rorschachs and College Performance." *Genetic Psychol Monogr* 59:3–43 F '59. * (*PA* 34:1972)

2572. SHANMUGAM, A. V. "A Rorschach Study of Stars and Isolates Among High School Students." *Psychol Studies* 4:35–49 Ja '59. *

2573. SHAPIRO, DAVID. "The Integration of Determinants and Content in Rorschach Interpretation." *J Proj Tech* 23:365–73 S '59. * (*PA* 35:4938)

2574. SHRIFTE, MIRIAM HARRIET. *An Investigation of Relationship Between Underlying Unpleasant Feeling Tensions and Cancer Growth: A Comparative Study of Two Groups of Cancer Patients Differentiated on the Basis of Cancer Course.* Doctor's thesis, New York University (New York, N.Y.), 1959. (*DA* 20:4179)

2575. SILVERMAN, LLOYD H. "A Q-Sort Study of the Validity of Evaluations Made From Projective Techniques." *Psychol Monogr* 73(7):1–28 '59. * (*PA* 34:3030)

2576. SINES, LLOYD K. "The Relative Contribution of Four Kinds of Data to Accuracy in Personality Assessment." *J Consult Psychol* 23:483–92 D '59. * (*PA* 34:6046)

2577. SJOSTEDT, ELSIE MARIE, AND HURWITZ, IRVING. "A Developmental Study of Sexual Functioning by Means of a Cognitive Analysis." *J Proj Tech* 23:237–46 Je '59. * (*PA* 35:5205)

2578. SMITH, C. M., AND HAMILTON, J. "Psychological Factors in the Narcolepsy-Cataplexy Syndrome." *Psychosom Med* 21:40–9 Ja–F '59. * (*PA* 34:1858)

2579. SMITH, LAURENCE C., JR., AND PHILLIPS, LESLIE. "Social Effectiveness and Developmental Level in Adolescence." *J Personality* 27:239–49 Je '59. * (*PA* 34:3898)

2580. SOSKIN, WILLIAM F. "Influence of Four Types of Data on Diagnostic Conceptualization in Psychological Testing." *J Abn & Social Psychol* 58:69–78 Ja '59. * (*PA* 34:1422)

2581. SPIVACK, GEORGE; LEVINE, MURRAY; AND SPRIGLE, HERBERT. "Intelligence Test Performances and the Delay

Functions of the Ego." *J Consult Psychol* 23:428–31 O '59. * (*PA* 34:6049)
2582. SPIVACK, GEORGE; LEVINE, MURRAY; FUSCHILLO, JEAN; AND TRAVERNIER, ANN. "Rorschach Movement Responses and Inhibition Processes in Adolescents." *J Proj Tech* 23: 462–6 D '59. * (*PA* 35:4939)
2583. STONE, JOHN TRUMAN. *An Experimental Investigation of the Effect of Mode of Color Stimulation on Inkblot Response Items.* Doctor's thesis, University of Pittsburgh (Pittsburgh, Pa.), 1959. (*DA* 20:2391)
2584. TABOR, ANTHONY B. *Process Analysis of Rorschach Interpretation.* Doctor's thesis, Loyola University (Chicago, Ill.), 1959.
2585. TAMKIN, ARTHUR S. "Intelligence as a Determinant of Rorschach Card Rejection." *J Clin Psychol* 15:63–4 Ja '59. * (*PA* 34:2740)
2586. TOWBIN, ALAN P. "Hostility in Rorschach Content and Overt Aggressive Behavior." *J Abn & Social Psychol* 58: 312–6 My '59. * (*PA* 34:6052)
2587. TYCKO, MILICENT. "Rorschach Responses at Four Exposure Levels." *Percept & Motor Skills* 9:167–80 Je '59. * (*PA* 38:4331)
2588. VALENTINE, MAX. "Psychometric Testing in Iran." *J Mental Sci* 105:93–107 Ja '59. * (*PA* 34:1065)
2589. WALLER, PATRICIA FOSSUM. *Correlates of Rorschach Shading Scores Obtained With Two Methods of Inquiry.* Doctor's thesis, University of North Carolina (Chapel Hill, N.C.), 1959. (*DA* 20:2912)
2590. WILENSKY, HAROLD. "Rorschach Developmental Level and Social Participation of Chronic Schizophrenics." *J Proj Tech* 23:87–92 Mr '59. * (*PA* 34:6058)
2591. WISHNER, JULIUS. "Factor Analyses of Rorschach Scoring Categories and First Response Times in Normals." *J Consult Psychol* 23:406–13 O '59. * (*PA* 34:5999)
2592. WITTENBORN, J. R. "Some Comments on Confounded Correlations Among Rorschach Scores." *J Consult Psychol* 23:75–7 F '59. * (*PA* 34:187)
2593. WOLF, MARTIN G. *The Rorschach as an Indicator of Intelligence in Seventh Grade Children.* Master's thesis, North Texas State College (Denton, Tex.), 1959.
2594. WOLPIN, MILTON, AND HAMLIN, ROY M. "Effect of Form-Color Incongruity on Responses to Inkblots." *J Clin Psychol* 15:151–5 Ap '59. * (*PA* 35:4947)
2595. ABEL, THEODORA M. "Differential Responses to Projective Testing in a Negro Peasant Community: Montserrat, B.W.I." *Int J Social Psychiatry* 6:218–24 au '60. *
2596. ALCOCK, THEODORA. "Some Personality Characteristics of Asthmatic Children." *Brit J Med Psychol* 33:133–41 pt 2 '60. * (*PA* 35:2671)
2597. ALLEN, ROBERT M., AND LICHTENSTEIN, DON. "The Rorschach and Intelligence: A Note of Caution." *J Genetic Psychol* 97:169–71 S '60. * (*PA* 35:6434)
2598. AMES, LOUISE B.; WITH THE ASSISTANCE OF MARJEAN KREMER. "Longitudinal Survey of Child Rorschach Responses: Older Subjects Ages 10 to 16 Years." *Genetic Psychol Monogr* 62:185–229 Ag '60. * (*PA* 35:6200)
2599. AMES, LOUISE BATES. "Age Changes in the Rorschach Responses of a Group of Elderly Individuals." *J Genetic Psychol* 97:257–85 D '60. * (*PA* 35:6220)
2600. AMES, LOUISE BATES. "Age Changes in the Rorschach Responses of Individual Elderly Subjects." *J Genetic Psychol* 97:287–315 D '60. * (*PA* 35:6221)
2601. AMES, LOUISE BATES. "Constancy of Content in Rorschach Responses." *J Genetic Psychol* 96:145–64 Mr '60. * (*PA* 34:7829)
2602. AMES, LOUISE BATES. "Longitudinal Survey of Child Rorschach Responses: Younger Subjects Two to 10 Years." *Genetic Psychol Monogr* 61:229–89 My '60. *
2603. AMMONS, CAROL H., AND AMMONS, R. B. "Rorschach Responses of Individuals Sensitive to Stress Induced by Extreme Perceptual-Motor Conflict." *Psychologia* 3:246–53 D '60.*
2604. ARMON, VIRGINIA. "Some Personality Variables in Overt Female Homosexuality." *J Proj Tech* 24:292–309 S '60. * (*PA* 35:818)
2605. AZIMA, FERN CRAMER, AND KRAL, V. A. "Effects of Blindfolding on Persons During Psychological Testing: A Psychometric Study of Various Age Groups." *Geriatrics* 15: 780–92 N '60. *
2606. BECK, SAMUEL J. *The Rorschach Experiment: Ventures in Blind Diagnosis.* New York: Grune & Stratton, Inc., 1960. Pp. viii, 256. * (*PA* 34:7753)
2607. BOHM, EWALD. Chap. 8, "The Binder Chiaroscuro System and Its Theoretical Basis," pp. 202–22. In *Rorschach Psychology.* Edited by Maria A. Rickers-Ovsiankina. New York: John Wiley & Sons, Inc., 1960. Pp. xvi, 483. * (*PA* 35:2231)
2608. BORELLI, GEORGE LOUIS. *A Study of the Meanings of Rorschach Cards Through Use of the Semantic Differential Technique.* Doctor's thesis, Ohio State University (Columbus, Ohio), 1960. (*DA* 21:3161)
2609. BOWER, PHILIP A.; TESTIN, ROBERT; AND ROBERTS, ALAN. "Rorschach Diagnosis by a Systematic Combining of Content, Thought Process, and Determinant Scales." *Genetic Psychol Monogr* 62:105–83 Ag '60. * (*PA* 35:6203)
2610. BURNAND, G. "A Scale for Assessing Psychosis From the Rorschach." *Psychometric Res B* (6):[5–10] su '60. *
2611. BURNAND, G. "A Scale for Psychosis." *Rorsch Newsl* 5:27–8 Je '60. *
2612. CARRIGAN, PATRICIA M. "Extraversion-Introversion as a Dimension of Personality: A Reappraisal." *Psychol B* 57: 329–60 S '60. * (*PA* 35:4976)
2613. CARSTAIRS, G. M.; PAYNE, R. W.; AND WHITTAKER, S. "Rorschach Responses of Hindus and Bhils." *J Social Psychol* 51:217–27 My '60. * (*PA* 34:7762)
2614. COHEN, IRWIN H. *Adaptive Regression, Dogmatism, and Creativity.* Doctor's thesis, Michigan State University (East Lansing, Mich.), 1960. (*DA* 21:3522)
2615. CROOKES, T. G., AND KELLER, ANNA J. "Rorschach Card Rejection and IQ." *J Clin Psychol* 16:424–6 O '60. * (*PA* 37:3140)
2616. DASTON, PAUL G., AND SAKHEIM, GEORGE A. "Prediction of Successful Suicide From the Rorschach Test, Using a Sign Approach." *J Proj Tech* 24:355–61 D '60. * (*PA* 35: 4952)
2617. DAVIS, A. D. "Some Physiological Correlates of Rorschach Body Image Productions." *J Abn & Social Psychol* 60:432–6 My '60. * (*PA* 35:5035)
2618. DELANY, LLOYD T. *A Comparison of the Individual Rorschach Method and the Group Discussion Rorschach Method as a Diagnostic Device With Delinquent Adolescent Boys: A Study of Certain Personality Characteristics of Delinquent Adolescent Boys as Revealed by Their Responses to the Individual and the Group Discussion Rorschach Method.* Doctor's thesis, New York University (New York, N.Y.), 1960. (*DA* 20:4715)
2619. DINOFF, MICHAEL. "Subject Awareness of Examiner Influence in a Testing Situation." Abstract. *J Consult Psychol* 24:465 O '60. * (*PA* 35:4909)
2620. DRECHSLER, ROBERT J. "Affect-Stimulating Effects of Colors." *J Abn & Social Psychol* 61:323–8 N '60. * (*PA* 36: 2HG23D)
2621. DREGER, RALPH MASON. "The Relation Between Rorschach *M* and TAT Content Categories as Measures of Creative Productivity in a Representative High-Level Intelligence Population." *J General Psychol* 63:29–33 Jl '60. * (*PA* 35: 6437)
2622. DUDEK, STEPHANIE (ZUPERKO). *Creativity and the Rorschach Human Movement Response.* Doctor's thesis, New York University (New York, N.Y.), 1960.
2623. EIGENBRODE, CHARLES R., AND SCHIPMAN, WILLIAM G. "The Body Image Barrier Concept." *J Abn & Social Psychol* 60:450–2 My '60. * (*PA* 35:5282)
2624. EISDORFER, CARL. "Developmental Level and Sensory Impairment in the Aged." *J Proj Tech* 24:129–32 Je '60. * (*PA* 35:4740)
2625. EISDORFER, CARL. "Rorschach Rigidity and Sensory Decrement in a Senescent Population." *J Gerontol* 15:188–90 Ap '60. * (*PA* 35:6230)
2626. ELSTEIN, ARTHUR. *Behavioral Correlates of the Rorschach Shading Response.* Doctor's thesis, University of Chicago (Chicago, Ill.), 1960.
2627. EYSENCK, H. J. Chap. 7, "The Analysis of Projective Techniques," pp. 271–85. In his *The Structure of Human Personality, Second Edition.* London: Methuen & Co. Ltd., 1960. Pp. xix, 448. *
2628. FAGER, ROBERT E. "Relation of Rorschach Movement and Color Responses to Cognitive Inhibition." Abstract. *J Consult Psychol* 24:276 Je '60. *
2629. FISHER, SEYMOUR. "Right-Left Gradients in Body Image, Body Reactivity, and Perception." *Genetic Psychol Monogr* 61:197–228 My '60. * (*PA* 35:6478)
2630. FONDA, CHARLES P. Chap. 4, "The White-Space Response," pp. 80–105. In *Rorschach Psychology.* Edited by Maria A. Rickers-Ovsiankina. New York: John Wiley & Sons, Inc., 1960. Pp. xvi, 483. * (*PA* 35:2231)
2631. FRIEDMAN, HOWARD. "A Note on the Revised Rorschach Development Scoring System." *J Clin Psychol* 16:52–4 Ja '60. * (*PA* 36:1HC52F)
2632. GILBERT, M. M., AND MARADIE, L. J. "The Differential Diagnosis Between Postconcussion Syndrome and Neuroses by Use of Rorschach Content Analysis." *J Neuropsychiatry* 1:210–2 Mr–Ap '60. *
2633. GOLDMAN, ROSALINE. "Changes in Rorschach Performance and Clinical Improvement in Schizophrenia." *J Consult Psychol* 24:403–7 O '60. * (*PA* 35:4596)
2634. GOTTLIEB, ANN LODGE, AND PARSONS, OSCAR A. "A Coaction Compass Evaluation of Rorschach Determinants in Brain Damaged Individuals." *J Consult Psychol* 24:54–60 F '60. * (*PA* 34:8243)
2635. HAFNER, A. JACK, AND KAPLAN, ARTHUR M. "Hostility Content Analysis of the Rorschach and TAT." *J Proj Tech* 24:137–43 Je '60. * (*PA* 35:4918)
2636. HALPERN, FLORENCE. Chap. 2, "The Rorschach Test With Children," pp. 14–28. In *Projective Techniques With Children.* Edited by Albert I. Rabin and Mary R. Haworth. New York: Grune & Stratton, Inc., 1960. Pp. xiii, 392. * (*PA* 35:2229)
2637. HAMMER, EMANUEL F. "An Exploratory Investigation of the Personalities of Creative Adolescent Students." Discussion by Margaret Naumberg. *Studies Art Ed* 1:42–72 sp '60. *
2638. HARRIS, JESSE G., JR. Chap. 14, "Validity: The Search for a Constant in a Universe of Variables," pp. 380–

439. In *Rorschach Psychology*. Edited by Maria A. Rickers-Ovsiankina. New York: John Wiley & Sons, Inc., 1960. Pp. xvi, 483. * (*PA* 35:2231)

2639. HEMMENDINGER, LAURENCE. Chap. 3, "Developmental Theory and the Rorschach Method," pp. 58–79. In *Rorschach Psychology*. Edited by Maria A. Rickers-Ovsiankina. New York: John Wiley & Sons, Inc., 1960. Pp. xvi, 483. * (*PA* 35:2231)

2640. HERTZ, MARGUERITE R. Chap. 2, "The Organization Activity," pp. 25–57. In *Rorschach Psychology*. Edited by Maria A. Rickers-Ovsiankina. New York: John Wiley & Sons, Inc., 1960. Pp. xvi, 483. * (*PA* 35:2231)

2641. HERTZ, MARGUERITE R. Chap. 3, "The Rorschach in Adolescence," pp. 29–60. In *Projective Techniques With Children*. Edited by Albert I. Rabin and Mary R. Haworth. New York: Grune & Stratton, Inc., 1960. Pp. xiii, 392. * (*PA* 35:2229)

2642. HERTZ, MARGUERITE R., AND PAOLINO, ALBERT F. "Rorschach Indices of Perceptual and Conceptual Disorganization." *J Proj Tech* 24:370–88 D '60. * (*PA* 35:4957)

2643. HILKEVITCH, RHEA R. "Social Interactional Processes: A Quantitative Study." *Psychol Rep* 7:195–201 O '60. * (*PA* 35:2114)

2644. HOLT, ROBERT R. "Cognitive Controls and Primary Processes." *J Psychol Res* 4:105–12 S '60. * (*PA* 35:4921)

2645. HOLT, ROBERT R., AND HAVEL, JOAN. Chap. 10, "A Method for Assessing Primary and Secondary Process in the Rorschach," pp. 263–315. In *Rorschach Psychology*. Edited by Maria A. Rickers-Ovsiankina. New York: John Wiley & Sons, Inc., 1960. Pp. xvi, 483. * (*PA* 35:2231) [Revision of reference 2051.]

2646. HOLZBERG, JULES D. Chap. 13, "Reliability Re-examined," pp. 361–79. In *Rorschach Psychology*. Edited by Maria A. Rickers-Ovsiankina. New York: John Wiley & Sons, Inc., 1960. Pp. xvi, 483. * (*PA* 35:2231)

2647. HOOKER, EVELYN. "The Fable." *J Proj Tech* 24:240–5 S '60. * (*PA* 35:10)

2648. JUDSON, ABE J., AND MACCASLAND, BARBARA W. "The Effects of Chlorpromazine on Psychological Test Scores." Abstract. *J Consult Psychol* 24:192 Ap '60. * (*PA* 34:7888)

2649. KADEN, STANLEY E., AND LIPTON, HERBERT. "Rorschach Developmental Scores and Post-Hospital Adjustment of Married Male Schizophrenics." *J Proj Tech* 24:144–7 Je '60. * (*PA* 35:1136)

2650. KAGAN, JEROME. "The Long Term Stability of Selected Rorschach Responses." *J Consult Psychol* 24:67–73 F '60. * (*PA* 34:7851)

2651. KAGAN, JEROME; MOSS, HOWARD A.; AND SIGEL, IRVING E. "Conceptual Style and the Use of Affect Labels." *Merrill-Palmer Q* 6:261–78 Jl '60. *

2652. KAHN, MARVIN W. "Psychological Test Study of a Mass Murderer." *J Proj Tech* 24:148–60 Je '60. * (*PA* 35:5213)

2653. KAHN, ROBERT L., AND FINK, MAX. "Prognostic Value of Rorschach Criteria in Clinical Response to Convulsive Therapy." *J Neuropsychiatry* 1:242–5 My–Je '60. *

2654. KALDEGG, A. "A Note on Tabulating Scores." *Rorsch Newsl* 5:25 D '60. *

2655. KAMANO, DENNIS K. "Symbolic Significance of Rorschach Cards IV and VII." *J Clin Psychol* 16:50–2 Ja '60. * (*PA* 36:1HG50K)

2656. KANTER, V. B. "Body Image and Psychosomatic Illness." *Rorsch Newsl* 5:2–14 D '60. *

2657. KAPLAN, DONALD MARTIN. *Differences in Attitudes and Personality of "Subject-Oriented" and "Pupil-Oriented" Secondary School Teachers: A Comparative Analysis of Two Groups of Secondary School Teachers With the Minnesota Teacher Attitude Inventory and the Rorschach*. Doctor's thesis, New York University (New York, N.Y.), 1960. (*DA* 21:2988)

2658. KING, GERALD F. "An Interpersonal Conception of Rorschach Human Movement and Delusional Content." *J Proj Tech* 24:161–3 Je '60. * (*PA* 35:5248)

2659. KLOPFER, WALTER G.; ALLEN, BERNADENE V.; AND ETTER, DAVID. "Content Diversity on the Rorschach and 'Range of Interests.'" *J Proj Tech* 24:290–1 S '60. * (*PA* 35:801)

2660. KORCHIN, SHELDON J. Chap. 5, "Form Perception and Ego Functioning," pp. 109–29. In *Rorschach Psychology*. Edited by Maria A. Rickers-Ovsiankina. New York: John Wiley & Sons, Inc., 1960. Pp. xvi, 483. * (*PA* 35:2231)

2661. KRIMSKY, MARTIN LOUIS. *The Rebirth Fantasy in Catatonic Schizophrenia and Its Implications*. Doctor's thesis, University of Oklahoma (Norman, Okla.), 1960. (*DA* 21:367)

2662. KUHN, ROLAND. Chap. 11, "Some Problems Concerning the Psychological Implications of Rorschach's Form Interpretation Test," pp. 319–40. In *Rorschach Psychology*. Edited by Maria A. Rickers-Ovsiankina. New York: John Wiley & Sons, Inc., 1960. Pp. xvi, 483. * (*PA* 35:2231)

2663. KUMAR, PRAMOD. "The Rorschach Test in Manic and Normal Groups." *Indian J Psychol* 35:35–8 pt 1 '60. *

2664. LAPKIN, B. *The Relation of Primary Process Thinking to the Recovery of Subliminal Material*. Doctor's thesis, New York University (New York, N.Y.), 1960. (*DA* 21:3165)

2665. LEBO, DELL; TOAL, ROBERT; AND BRICK, HARRY. "Rorschach Performance in the Amelioration and Continuation of Observable Anxiety." *J General Psychol* 63:75–80 Jl '60. * (*PA* 35:6529)

2666. LEBOVITS, BINYAMIN Z.; VISOTSKY, HAROLD M.; AND OSTFELD, ADRIAN M. "Lysergic Acid Diethylamide (LSD) and JB 318: A Comparison of Two Hallucinogens: 2, An Exploratory Study." *Arch Gen Psychiatry* 3:176-87 Ag '60. *

2667. LEDWITH, NETTIE H. *A Rorschach Study of Child Development*. Pittsburgh, Pa.: University of Pittsburgh Press, 1960. Pp. ix, 336. * (*PA* 35:1998)

2668. LESLEY, EUGENIA LUKAS. *Selected Rorschach Responses of First-Year Students of Dentistry, Engineering, and Law*. Doctor's thesis, University of Denver (Denver, Colo.), 1960.

2669. LESSING, ELISE ELKINS. "Prognostic Value of the Rorschach in a Child Guidance Clinic." *J Proj Tech* 24:310–21 S '60. * (*PA* 35:965)

2670. LEVINE, ABRAHAM. "Appraising Ego Strength From the Projective Test Battery." *J Hillside Hosp* 9:228–40 Jl '60. *

2671. LEVINE, DAVID. "Rorschach Genetic Level and Psychotic Symptomatology." *J Clin Psychol* 16:164–7 Ap '60. * (*PA* 36:2HG64L)

2672. LEVITT, EUGENE E., AND GROSZ, HANUS J. "A Comparison of Quantifiable Rorschach Anxiety Indicators in Hypnotically Induced Anxiety and Normal States." *J Consult Psychol* 24:31–4 F '60. * (*PA* 34:7855)

2673. LEVITT, EUGENE E., AND PERSKY, HAROLD. "Relation of Rorschach Factors and Plasma Hydrocortisone Level in Hypnotically Induced Anxiety." *Psychosom Med* 22:218–23 My–Je '60. * (*PA* 35:5038)

2674. LEZAK, MURIEL DEUTSCH. *The Conscious Control of Rorschach Responses*. Doctor's thesis, University of Portland (Portland, Ore.), 1960.

2675. MCREYNOLDS, PAUL, AND WEIDE, MARIAN. "Psychological Measures as Used to Predict Psychiatric Improvement and to Assess Behavioural Changes Following Prefrontal Lobotomy." *J Mental Sci* 106:256–73 Ja '60. * (*PA* 35:6530)

2676. MAGNUSSEN, M. G. "Verbal and Nonverbal Reinforcers in the Rorschach Situation." *J Psychol Studies* 11:203–5 My–Je '60. * Slightly condensed reprinting in *J Clin Psychol* 16:167–9 Ap '60. * (*PA* 36:2HG67M)

2677. MAGNUSSON, DAVID. "Some Personality Tests Applied on Identical Twins." *Scandinavian J Psychol* 1(2):55–61 '60. * (*PA* 35:6424)

2678. MARSH, LOYAL FRANCIS. *The Meaning of Rorschach Cards IV and VII*. Doctor's thesis, University of Portland (Portland, Ore.), 1960.

2679. MASLING, JOSEPH. "The Influence of Situational and Interpersonal Variables in Projective Testing." *Psychol B* 57:65–85 Ja '60. * (*PA* 34:7788)

2680. MINER, HORACE M., AND DE VOS, GEORGE. *Oasis and Casbah: Algerian Culture and Personality in Change*. University of Michigan, Museum of Anthropology, Anthropological Papers, No. 15. Ann Arbor, Mich.: the Museum, 1960. Pp. v, 236. *

2681. MOGENSEN, ALAN; FENGER, GJERTRUD; AND LANGE, BENT. *Rorschach on 122 Ten-Year Old Danish Children: A Standardizational and Structural Study: A, The Normative Results*. Psychological Research Report 2A. Risskov, Denmark; Institute of Psychiatry, State Mental Hospital, [1960]. Pp. 54. * (*PA* 36:4HG49M)

2682. MOLLER, HELLA. *Stuttering, Predelinquent, and Adjusted Boys: A Comparative Analysis of Personality Characteristics as Measured by the WISC and the Rorschach Test*. Doctor's thesis, Boston University (Boston, Mass.), 1960. (*DA* 21:1461)

2683. MONS, W. E. R. "Group Signs and the Dynamics of the Personality." *Rorsch Newsl* 5:5–7 Je '60. *

2684. MOYLAN, JOSEPH H.; SHAW, JULIE; AND APPLEMAN, WAYNE. "Passive and Aggressive Responses to the Rorschach by Passive-Aggressive Personalities and Paranoid Schizophrenics." *J Proj Tech* 24:17–20 Mr '60. *

2685. MUMMERY, WILLIAM JAMES. *An Investigation of Conformity as It Relates to Ways of Handling Hostility*. Doctor's thesis, University of Oklahoma (Norman, Okla.), 1960. (*DA* 21:241)

2686. MURPHY, LOIS, AND MURPHY, GARDNER. Chap. 12, "Hermann Rorschach and Personality Research," pp. 341–57. In *Rorschach Psychology*. Edited by Maria A. Rickers-Ovsiankina. New York: John Wiley & Sons, Inc., 1960. Pp. xvi, 483. * (*PA* 35:2231)

2687. MURSTEIN, BERNARD I. "Factor Analyses of the Rorschach." *J Consult Psychol* 24:262–75 Je '60. * (*PA* 35:6446)

2688. NEEL, ANN FILINGER. "Inhibition and Perception of Movement on the Rorschach." *J Consult Psychol* 24:224–30 Je '60. * (*PA* 35:6447)

2689. O'REILLY, P. O., AND HARRISON, K. "Experimentation With an Objective Test Battery." *Can Psychiatric Assn J* 5:108–23 Ap '60. *

2690. PERDUE, WILLIAM CARROLL. *A Comparison of the Rorschach Responses of Two Groups of Murderers Confined in Prison*. Master's thesis, College of William and Mary (Williamsburg, Va.), 1960.

2691. PHARES, E. JERRY; STEWART, LAWRENCE M.; AND FOSTER, JAMES M. "Instruction Variation and Rorschach Performance." *J Proj Tech* 24:28–31 Mr '60. * (*PA* 35:803)

2692. PINE, FRED, AND HOLT, ROBERT R. "Creativity and Primary Process: A Study of Adaptive Regression." *J Abn & Social Psychol* 61:370–9 N '60. * (*PA* 36:2HD70P)

2693. PIOTROWSKI, ZYGMUNT A. Chap. 6, "The Movement Score," pp. 130–53. In *Rorschach Psychology.* Edited by Maria A. Rickers-Ovsiankina. New York: John Wiley & Sons, Inc., 1960. Pp. xvi, 483. * (*PA* 35:2231)

2694. PIOTROWSKI, ZYGMUNT A. "The Rorschach Test," pp. 56–67, 116–49. In *The Prediction of Overt Behavior Through the Use of Projective Techniques.* Edited by Arthur C. Carr. Springfield, Ill.: Charles C Thomas, Publisher, 1960. Pp. xiii, 177. * (*PA* 36:2HG77C)

2695. RADER, GORDON E. "Rorschach Productivity and Participation in Group Psychotherapy." *J Clin Psychol* 16:422–4 O '60. * (*PA* 37:3369)

2696. REISMAN, JOHN M. "Types of Movement in Children's Rorschachs." *J Proj Tech* 24:46–8 Mr '60. * (*PA* 35:806)

2697. RICHARDS, THOMAS W. "Personality of Subjects Who Volunteer for Research on a Drug (Mescaline)." *J Proj Tech* 24:424–8 D '60. * (*PA* 35:4554)

2698. RICKERS-OVSIANKINA, MARIA A. Chap. 1, "Synopsis of Psychological Premises Underlying the Rorschach," pp. 3–22. In her *Rorschach Psychology.* New York: John Wiley & Sons, Inc., 1960. Pp. xvi, 483. * (*PA* 35:2231)

2699. RICKERS-OVSIANKINA, MARIA A., Editor. *Rorschach Psychology.* New York: John Wiley & Sons, Inc., 1960. Pp. xvi, 483. * (*PA* 35:2231)

2700. RIKLAN, MANUEL; DILLER, LEONARD; AND WEINER, HERMAN. "Psychological Studies on the Effects of Chemosurgery of the Basal Ganglia in Parkinsonism: 2, Aspects of Personality." *Arch Gen Psychiatry* 3:267–75 S '60. *

2701. ROE, ANNE, AND MIERZWA, JOHN. "The Use of the Rorschach in the Study of Personality and Occupations." *J Proj Tech* 24:282–9 S '60. * (*PA* 35:1301)

2702. ROSEN, EPHRAIM. "Connotative Meanings of Rorschach Inkblots, Responses, and Determinants." *J Personality* 28:413–26 D '60. * (*PA* 35:4936)

2703. ROSNER, STANLEY. "Inquiry: Partial or Total." *J Proj Tech* 24:49–51 Mr '60. * (*PA* 35:807)

2704. RYCHLAK, JOSEPH F., AND GUINOUARD, DONALD. "Rorschach Content, Personality, and Popularity." *J Proj Tech* 24:322–32 S '60. * (*PA* 35:686)

2705. SCHAFER, ROY. "Bodies in Schizophrenic Rorschach Responses." *J Proj Tech* 24:267–81 S '60. * (*PA* 35:1142)

2706. SCHAFER, ROY. "Representations of Perceiving and Acting in Psychological Test Responses," pp. 291–312. (*PA* 35:850) In *Festschrift for Gardner Murphy.* Edited by John G. Peatman and Eugene L. Hartley. New York: Harper & Brothers, 1960. Pp. xi, 411. *

2707. SCHLEIFER, MAXWELL J., AND HIRE, A. WILLIAM. "Stimulus Value of Rorschach Inkblots Expressed as Trait and Affective Characteristics." *J Proj Tech* 24:164–70 Je '60. * (*PA* 35:4937)

2708. SCHMEIDLER, GERTRUDE RAFFEL. "Changing Field Relations of an ESP Experiment," pp. 94–105. (*PA* 35:398) In *Festschrift for Gardner Murphy.* Edited by John G. Peatman and Eugene L. Hartley. New York: Harper & Brothers, 1960. Pp. xi, 411. *

2709. SCHMEIDLER, GERTRUDE RAFFEL. *ESP in Relation to Rorschach Test Evaluation.* Parapsychology Monographs, No. 2. New York: Parapsychology Foundation, Inc., 1960. Pp. iii, 89. *

2710. SCOTT, EDWARD M. "Psychological Examination of Quadruplets." *Psychol Rep* 6:281–2 Ap '60. * (*PA* 35:5080)

2711. SEIDEL, CLAUDENE. "The Relationship Between Klopfer's Rorschach Prognostic Rating Scale and Phillips' Case History Prognostic Rating Scale." *J Consult Psychol* 24:46–9 F '60. * (*PA* 34:-862)

2712. SEMEONOFF, BORIS. "Rorschach Concomitants of Self-Description Variables." *Rorsch Newsl* 5:26–34 D '60. *

2713. SHAPIRO, DAVID. Chap. 7, "A Perceptual Understanding of Color Response," pp. 154–201. In *Rorschach Psychology.* Edited by Maria A. Rickers-Ovsiankina. New York: John Wiley & Sons, Inc., 1960. Pp. xvi, 483. * (*PA* 35:2231)

2714. SILVERMAN, LLOYD H., AND SILVERMAN, DORIS K. "Womb Fantasies in Heroin Addiction: A Rorschach Study." *J Proj Tech* 24:52–63 Mr '60. * (*PA* 35:1094)

2715. SINES, J. O. "An Approach to the Study of the Stimulus Significance of the Rorschach Ink Blots." *J Proj Tech* 24:64–6 Mr '60. *

2716. SINGER, JEROME L. Chap. 9, "The Experience Type: Some Behavioral Correlates and Theoretical Implications," pp. 223–59. In *Rorschach Psychology.* Edited by Maria A. Rickers-Ovsiankina. New York: John Wiley & Sons, Inc., 1960. Pp. xvi, 483. * (*PA* 35:2231)

2717. STARER, EMANUEL, AND ROSENBERG, SELIG. "A Multiple Choice Rorschach Technique for Increasing Test Productivity in Chronic Schizophrenics." *J Proj Tech* 24:429–32 D '60. * (*PA* 35:4940)

2718. STEIN, HARRY. "Rotation and Reliability of the Rorschach." *J Proj Tech* 24:171–81 Je '60. * (*PA* 35:4941)

2719. STONE, HERBERT K., AND DELLIS, NICHOLAS P. "An Exploratory Investigation Into the Levels Hypothesis." *J Proj Tech* 24:333–40 S '60. * (*PA* 35:791)

2720. THOMAS, CAROLINE BEDELL. "Characteristics of Smokers Compared With Nonsmokers in a Population of Healthy Young Adults, Including Observations on Family History, Blood Pressure, Heart Rate, Body Weight, Cholesterol and Certain Psychologic Traits." *Ann Internal Med* 53:697–718 O '60. *

2721. TOBIAS, S. *Effects of Reinforcement of Verbal Behavior on Response Changes in a Nonreinforced Situation.* Doctor's thesis, Columbia University (New York, N.Y.), 1960. (*DA* 21:964)

2722. TOLOR, ALEXANDER; GLASS, HARVEY L.; AND MERMELSTEIN, MATTHEW D. "Rorschach Card Rejection as a Correlate of Intelligence in Children." *J Proj Tech* 24:71–4 Mr '60. * (*PA* 35:2250)

2723. TONG, J. E., AND MURPHY, I. C. "Rorschach Indices and Autonomic Stress Reactivity." *J Clin Psychol* 16:324–8 Jl '60. * (*PA* 36:2HN24T)

2724. TOOMEY, LAURA C., AND RICKERS-OVSIANKINA, MARIA A. "Tabular Comparison of Scoring Systems," pp. 441–65. In *Rorschach Psychology.* Edited by Maria A. Rickers-Ovsiankina. New York: John Wiley & Sons, Inc., 1960. Pp. xvi, 483. * (*PA* 35:2231)

2725. VAN DE CASTLE, R. L. "Perceptual Defense in a Binocular-Rivalry Situation." *J Personality* 28:448–62 D '60. * (*PA* 35:5010)

2726. VINSON, DAVID B. "Responses to the Rorschach Test That Identify Schizophrenic Thinking, Feeling, and Behavior." *J Clin & Exp Psychopathol* 21:34–40 Ja–Mr '60. * (*PA* 34:4703)

2727. VON HOLT, HENRY W., JR.; SENGSTAKE, CORD B.; SONODA, BEVERLY C.; AND DRAPER, WILLIAM A. "Orality, Image Fusions and Concept-Formation." *J Proj Tech* 24:194–8 Je '60. * (*PA* 35:4943)

2728. VORHAUS, PAULINE G. "The Hibernating Syndrome." *J Proj Tech* 24:199–210 Je '60. * (*PA* 35:4944)

2729. WALLER, PATRICIA F. "A Comparison of Shading Responses Obtained With Two Rorschach Methodologies From Psychiatric and Nonpsychiatric Subjects." *J Consult Psychol* 24:43–5 F '60. * (*PA* 34:8188)

2730. WALLER, PATRICIA F. "The Relationship Between the Rorschach Shading Response and Other Indices of Anxiety." *J Proj Tech* 24:211–7 Je '60. * (*PA* 35:4945)

2731. WILKINSON, NORMAN W. "A Rorschach Study of 'Olga': A Schizoid Adolescent Girl." *Rorsch Newsl* 5:15–22 D '60. *

2732. WILSON, V. W. "The Use of the Rorschach Method With Asian People." *Austral J Psychol* 12:199–202 D '60. *

2733. WYSOCKI, BOLESLAW A. "A Factorial Study of Rorschach Protocols." *Percept & Motor Skills* 10:105–6 Ap '60. * (*PA* 35:6451)

2734. YAMAHIRO, ROY S., AND GRIFFITH, RICHARD M. "Validity of Two Indices of Sexual Deviancy." *J Clin Psychol* 16:21–4 Ja '60. * (*PA* 36:1HE21Y)

2735. ZAMANSKY, HAROLD S., AND GOLDMAN, ALFRED E. "A Comparison of Two Methods of Analyzing Rorschach Data in Assessing Therapeutic Change." *J Proj Tech* 24:75–82 Mr '60. * (*PA* 35:2234)

2736. ZAX, MELVIN, AND LOISELLE, ROBERT H. "The Influence of Card Order on the Stimulus Value of the Rorschach Inkblots." *J Proj Tech* 24:218–21 Je '60. *

2737. ZAX, MELVIN, AND LOISELLE, ROBERT H. "Stimulus Value of Rorschach Inkblots as Measured by the Semantic Differential." *J Clin Psychol* 16:160–3 Ap '60. * (*PA* 36:2HG60Z)

2738. ZAX, MELVIN, AND STRICKER, GEORGE. "The Effect of a Structured Inquiry on Rorschach Scores." *J Consult Psychol* 24:328–32 Ag '60. * (*PA* 35:2235)

2739. ZAX, MELVIN; LOISELLE, ROBERT H.; AND KARRAS, ATHAN. "Stimulus Characteristics of Rorschach Inkblots as Perceived by a Schizophrenic Sample." *J Proj Tech* 24:439–43 D '60. * (*PA* 35:4948)

2740. ZAX, MELVIN; STRICKER, GEORGE; AND WEISS, JONATHAN H. "Some Effects of Non-Personality Factors on Rorschach Performance." *J Proj Tech* 24:83–93 Mr '60. * (*PA* 35:2236)

2741. ABRAMS, STANLEY. *The Relationship of Repression, Projection and Preference in the Realm of Hostility.* Doctor's thesis, Temple University (Philadelphia, Pa.), 1961. (*DA* 22:635)

2742. ADAMS, HENRY B., AND COOPER, G. DAVID. "Rorschach Response Productivity and Overt Psychiatric Symptomatology." *J Clin Psychol* 17:355–7 O '61. * (*PA* 38:8538)

2743. ALCOCK, THEODORA. "The Reality Basis of Rorschach Interpretation." *Rorsch Newsl* 6:6–11 D '61. *

2744. ANASTASI, ANNE. *Psychological Testing, Second Edition,* pp. 568–73. New York: Macmillan Co., 1961. Pp. xiii, 657. * (*PA* 36:1HA57A)

2745. APPELBAUM, STEPHEN A. "The End of the Test as a Determinant of Response." *B Menninger Clinic* 25:120–8 My '61. * (*PA* 36:4HE20A)

2746. BARCLAY, A., AND HILDEN, ARNOLD H. "Variables Related to Duration of Individual Psychotherapy." *J Proj Tech* 25:268–71 S '61. * (*PA* 36:3IE68B)

2747. BARENDREGT, J. T.; ARIS-DIJKSTRA, M.; DIERCKS, L. M. J.; AND WILDE, G. J. S. Chap. 3, "The Rorschach Test as a Means of Testing the Hypothesis of Psychosomatic Specificity: A Cross Validation Study," pp. 33–52. In *Research in Psychodiagnostics.* Edited by J. T. Barendregt. The Hague, Holland: Mouton & Co., 1961. Pp. vii, 221. *

2748. BEARDSLEY, KATHARINE. "Analysis of Psychological

Tests of Persons Diagnosed Sociopathic Personality Disturbance." *Arch Crim Psychodynam* 4:389–411 su '61. *
2749. BECK, SAMUEL J.; BECK, ANNE G.; LEVITT, EUGENE E.; AND MOLISH, HERMAN B. *Rorschach's Test: 1, Basic Processes, Third Edition.* New York: Grune & Stratton, Inc., 1961. Pp. x, 237. * (*PA* 36:1HG37B)
2750. BENE, EVA. "Anxiety and Emotional Impoverishment in Men Under Stress." *Brit J Med Psychol* 34:281–9 pt 3 & 4 '61. * (*PA* 37:1297)
2751. BERRYMAN, EILEEN. "Poets' Responses to the Rorschach." *J General Psychol* 64:349–58 Ap '61. * (*PA* 36:1HG49B)
2752. BIRCH, HERBERT G., AND BELMONT, IRA. "Functional Levels of Disturbance Manifested by Brain-Damaged (Hemiplegic) Patients as Revealed in Rorschach Responses." *J Nerv & Mental Dis* 132:410–6 My '61. * (*PA* 36:2JF10B)
2753. BLATT, SIDNEY J.; ENGEL, MARY; AND MIRMOW, ESTHER LEE. "When Inquiry Fails." *J Proj Tech* 25:32–7 Mr '61. * (*PA* 36:1HG32B)
2754. BLOOM, BERNARD L., AND ARKOFF, ABE. "Role Playing in Acute and Chronic Schizophrenia." *J Consult Psychol* 25:24–8 F '61. * (*PA* 36:3JQ24B)
2755. BOSGANG, IRWIN. *A Construct Validation Study of the Leveling-Sharpening Cognitive Control by Means of Rorschach Response Behavior.* Doctor's thesis, New York University (New York, N.Y.), 1961. (*DA* 23:698)
2756. BOWYER, RUTH. "A Case of Over-Identification in Childhood Schizophrenia." *Rorsch Newsl* 6:30–2 Je '61. *
2757. BRAMS, JEROME M. "Counselor Characteristics and Effective Communication in Counseling." *J Counsel Psychol* 8:25–30 sp '61. * (*PA* 36:3KI25B)
2758. BRICKLIN, BARRY. "Clinical Use of the n Affiliation Score." *J Proj Tech* 25:277–81 S '61. * (*PA* 36:3HG77B)
2759. BRICKLIN, BARRY, AND GOTTLIEB, SOPHIE G. "The Prediction of Some Aspects of Marital Compatibility by Means of the Rorschach Test." *Psychiatric Q Sup* 35:281–303 pt 2 '61. * (*PA* 37:5297)
2760. BROWN, FRED; CHASE, JANET; AND WINSON, JUDITH. "Studies in Infant Feeding Choices of Primiparae: 2, Comparison of Rorschach Determinants of Accepters and Rejecters of Breast Feeding." *J Proj Tech* 25:412–21 D '61. *
2761. BROWN, THELMA E. "Factors Relating to Turnover Among Veterans Administration Nursing Assistants." *J Clin & Exp Psychopathol* 22:226–34 D '61. *
2762. BURNAND, GORDON. "Further Work on a Scale for Assessing Psychosis From the Rorschach." *Rorsch Newsl* 6:27–9 Je '61. *
2763. BURSTEIN, ALVIN G. "A Note on Time of First Responses in Rorschach Protocols." *J Consult Psychol* 25:549–50 D '61. * (*PA* 37:5023)
2764. CHUNG, BOM MO. "A Factorial Study of Rorschach Protocols." Abstract. *Acta Psychologica* 19:123–4 '61. *
2765. CLIFTON, JAMES A., AND LEVINE, DAVID. *Klamath Personalities: Ten Rorschach Case Studies.* [Lawrence, Kan.: James A. Clifton, University of Kansas], 1961. Pp. iv, 80. *
2766. COBRINIK, LEONARD, AND POPPER, LILY. "Developmental Aspects of Thought Disturbance in Schizophrenic Children: A Rorschach Study." *Am J Orthopsychiatry* 31:170–80 Ja '61. * (*PA* 36:1JQ70C)
2767. COHEN, SYDNEY. *An Experimental Investigation of the Validity of Universal Symbolic Significance as Employed in the Content Analysis of the Rorschach Ink Blot Test.* Doctor's thesis, New York University (New York, N.Y.), 1961. (*DA* 23:305)
2768. COLE, DAVID L. "The Prediction of Teaching Performance." *J Ed Res* 54:345–8 My '61. * (*PA* 36:3KM45C)
2769. DAVIS, HANNAH S. "Judgments of Intellectual Level From Various Features of the Rorschach Including Vocabulary." *J Proj Tech* 25:155–7 Je '61. * (*PA* 36:2HG55D)
2770. DAVIS, HAROLD BERNARD. *Some Symbolic Meanings of the Rorschach Inkblots.* Doctor's thesis, Michigan State University (East Lansing, Mich.), 1961. (*DA* 22:4405)
2771. DREIER, JACOB LEON. *An Inverted Factor Analysis of Rorschach Protocols of Neurotic Parents in a Child Guidance Clinic.* Doctor's thesis, Adelphi College (Garden City, N.Y.), 1961.
2772. ECKHARDT, WILLIAM. "Piotrowski's Signs: Organic or Functional?" *J Clin Psychol* 17:36–8 Ja '61. * (*PA* 37:3172)
2773. EXNER, JOHN E., JR. "Achromatic Color in Cards IV and VI of the Rorschach." *J Proj Tech* 25:38–40 Mr '61. * (*PA* 36:1HG38E)
2774. FREED, GRIFFITH OSLER. *A Projective Test Study of Creativity in College Students in Visual Arts.* Doctor's thesis, University of Michigan (Ann Arbor, Mich.), 1961. (*DA* 22:640)
2775. GEISER, ROBERT LEE. *The Psychodiagnostic Efficiency of WAIS and Rorschach Scores: A Discriminant Function Study.* Doctor's thesis, Boston University (Boston, Mass.), 1961. (*DA* 22:915)
2776. GILBERT, MICHAEL M., AND MARADIE, LOUIS J. "The Incidence of Psycopathy in a Group of Prisoners Referred for Psychiatric Evaluation." *Arch Crim Psychodynam* 4:480–8 su '61. * (*PA* 36:2JO80G)
2777. GILL, HARWANT SINGH. *Delay of Response in Problem Solving and Color Response to Rorschach Stimuli.* Doctor's thesis, Boston University (Boston, Mass.), 1961. (*DA* 22:1252)
2778. GLADSTON, ELAINE R., AND AMADO-HAGUENAUER, GINETTE. "Distanciation in Space and Time: A Study in Unstable Hypo-Manic Denial." *Rorsch Newsl* 6:16–26 Je '61. *
2779. GOLDBERGER, LEO. "Reactions to Perceptual Isolation and Rorschach Manifestations of the Primary Process." *J Proj Tech* 25:287–302 S '61. * (*PA* 36:3HJ87G)
2780. GOLDFARB, ALLAN. "Performance Under Stress in Relation to Intellectual Control and Self-Acceptance." *J Consult Psychol* 25:7–12 F '61. * (*PA* 36:3HJ07G)
2781. GOLDMAN, ALFRED E., AND HERMAN, JACK L. "Studies in Vicariousness: The Effect of Immobilization on Rorschach Movement Responses." *J Proj Tech* 25:164–5 Je '61. * (*PA* 36:2HG64G)
2782. GRIB, THOMAS F. *Pattern Analysis of Movement Responses and Location Choices on the Rorschach.* Doctor's thesis, Loyola University (Chicago, Ill.), 1961.
2783. GRIFFITH, RICHARD M. "Rorschach Water Percepts: A Study in Conflicting Results." *Am Psychologist* 16:307–11 Je '61. * (*PA* 36:2JK07G)
2784. HAFNER, A. JACK. "Rorschach Card Stimulus Values for Children." *J Proj Tech* 25:166–9 Je '61. * (*PA* 36:2HG66H)
2785. HAMMER, EMANUEL F. "Emotional Instability and Creativity." *Percept & Motor Skills* 12:102 F '61. * (*PA* 35:6439)
2786–7. HASKELL, ROYAL J., JR. "Relationship Between Aggressive Behavior and Psychological Tests." *J Proj Tech* 25:431–40 D '61. *
2788. HAZARI, ANANDI, AND SINHA, S. N. "Rorschach Ranking Conformity Test: A Revision and an Evaluation." *J Psychol Res* 5:77–9 My '61. * (*PA* 38:8550)
2789. HERTZ, MARGUERITE R. *Frequency Tables for Scoring Rorschach Responses, Fourth Edition.* Cleveland, Ohio: Western Reserve University Press, 1961. Pp. ii, 253. *
2790. HORIUCHI, HARUOY. "A Study of Perceptual Process of Rorschach Cards by Tachistoscopic Method on Movement and Shading Responses." *J Proj Tech* 25:44–53 Mr '61. * (*PA* 36:1HG44H)
2791. JOURARD, SIDNEY M. "Self-Disclosure and Rorschach Productivity." *Percept & Motor Skills* 13:232 O '61. *
2792. KALDEGG, A. "The Case of an Alcoholic—Prognosis and Follow-Up." *Rorsch Newsl* 6:12–9 D '61. *
2793. KIKUCHI, TETSUHIKO. "Rorschach Response and Epileptic Personality." *Tohoku Psychologica Folia* 19(3–4):93–102 '61. *
2794. KIKUCHI, TETSUHIKO; KITAMURA, SEIRŌ; AND ŌYAMA, MASAHIRO. "Rorschach Performance in Alcoholic Intoxication." *Tohoku Psychologica Folia* 20(1–2):45–71 '61. * (*PA* 36:5DK45K)
2795. KIRESUK, THOMAS JACK. *The Effect of Test Sophistication on the Diagnostic Validity of the Minnesota Multiphasic Personality Inventory and the Rorschach With Paranoid Schizophrenics.* Doctor's thesis, University of Minnesota (Minneapolis, Minn.), 1961. (*DA* 22:2875)
2796. KLOPFER, BRUNO, AND BOYER, L. BRYCE. "Notes on the Personality Structure of a North American Indian Shaman: Rorschach Interpretation." *J Proj Tech* 25:170–8 Je '61. * (*PA* 36:2HG70K)
2797. KODMAN, FRANK, JR., AND WATERS, JERRY E. "Rorschach Responses of Children Exhibiting Psychogenic Auditory Symptoms." *J Clin Psychol* 17:305–6 Jl '61. * (*PA* 38:8554)
2798. KUMAR, PRAMOD. "The Rorschach Test in Psychoneurotic and Normal Groups." *Indian J Psychol* 36:169–72 D '61. * (*PA* 37:6741)
2799. KUMAR, PRAMOD. "The Rorschach Test in Some Mental Disorders—Schizophrenic Group." *Psychologia* 4:36–40 Mr '61. *
2800. KUTSCHE, RUDOLPH PAUL, JR. *A Rorschach Comparison of Adult Male Personality in Big Cove, Cherokee, North Carolina, and "Henry's Branch," Kentucky.* Doctor's thesis, University of Pennsylvania (Philadelphia, Pa.), 1961. (*DA* 22:969)
2801. LEAGUE, BETTY JO, AND JACKSON, DOUGLAS N. "Activity and Passivity as Correlates of Field-Independence." *Percept & Motor Skills* 12:291–8 Je '61. * (*PA* 36:2HJ91L)
2802. LEBEL, RICHARD AIMÉ. *A Study to Measure the Stimulus Value of Color as an Indicator of an Individual's Emotional Relationship to the Environment.* Doctor's thesis, Boston University (Boston, Mass.), 1961. (*DA* 23:152)
2803. LENOUE, DALE; SPILKA, BERNARD; VAN DE CASTLE, ROBERT; AND PRINCE, ALBERT. "Social Desirability and the Group Rorschach." *J Clin Psychol* 17:175–7 Ap '61. * (*PA* 38:1016)
2804. LESSER, ERWIN. "Popularity of Rorschach Training in the United States." *J Proj Tech* 25:179–83 Je '61. * (*PA* 36:2HG79L)
2805. LINDZEY, GARDNER. *Projective Techniques and Cross-Cultural Research.* New York: Appleton-Century-Crofts, Inc., 1961. Pp. xi, 339. * (*PA* 37:3199)
2806. LIPSHUTZ, DANIEL M. "Some Dynamic Factors in the Problem of Aggression." *Psychiatric Q* 35:78–87 Ja '61. * (*PA* 36:2IF78L)
2807. LOVELAND, NATHENE TURK. "Epileptic Personality and Cognitive Functioning." *J Proj Tech* 25:54–68 Mr '61. * (*PA* 36:1HG54L)
2808. LUCAS, WINAFRED B. "The Effects of Frustration on

the Rorschach Responses of Nine Year Old Children." *J Proj Tech* 25:199–204 Je '61. * (*PA* 36:2FF99L)

2809. MacCasland, Barbara Whittredge. *The Relation of Aggressive Fantasy to Aggressive Behavior in Children.* Doctor's thesis, Syracuse University (Syracuse, N.Y.), 1961. (*DA* 23:300)

2810. McConnell, R. A. "The Discontinuity in Schmeidler's ESP-Rorschach Data." *J Psychol* 52:87–97 Jl '61. * (*PA* 36:2BP87M)

2811. McCully, Robert S. "Human Movement in the Rorschach Materials of a Group of Pre-Adolescent Boys Suffering From Progressive Muscular Loss." *J Proj Tech* 25:205–11 Je '61. * (*PA* 36:2HG05M)

2812. Malmivaara, Katri, and Kolho, Pirkko. "Retesting of Primary School Children With Sceno and Rorschach Tests." *Annales Paediatriae Fenniae* 7(4):251–8 '61. *

2813. Malmivaara, Katri, and Kolho, Pirkko. "Use of the Sceno and the Rorschach Tests in the Study of Personality in Children of Kindergarten Age." *Annales Paediatriae Fenniae* 7(1):44–61 '61. *

2814. Mandler, George; Mandler, Jean M.; Kremen, Irwin; and Sholiton, Robert D. "The Response to Threat: Relations Among Verbal and Physiological Indices." *Psychol Monogr* 75(9):1–22 '61. * (*PA* 36:3HN22M)

2815. Markham, Sylvia. "A Comparative Evaluation of Psychotic and Nonpsychotic Reactions to Childbirth." *Am J Orthopsychiatry* 31:565–78 Jl '61. * (*PA* 36:4JP65M)

2816. Marks, Philip A. "Effects of Texture and Form on the Popular Response to Card VI of the Rorschach." *J Clin Psychol* 17:38–41 Ja '61. * (*PA* 37:3200)

2817. Marsh, Loyal F. "Parental Attitudes as the Basis for Attributing Meaning to Rorschach Cards IV and VII." *J Proj Tech* 25:69–74 Mr '61. * (*PA* 36:1HE69M)

2818. Mayer, Joseph, and Binz, Elizabeth. "Stimulus Values of Rorschach Cards." *J Clin Psychol* 17:186–7 Ap '61. * (*PA* 38:1019)

2819. Meyer, M. L., and Partipilo, Michael A. "Examiner Personality as an Influence on the Rorschach Test." *Psychol Rep* 9:221–2 O '61. *

2820. Meyer, Mortimer M. "The Case of El: Blind Analysis of the Tests of an Unknown Patient." *J Proj Tech* 25:375–82 D '61. *

2821. Nikelly, Arthur G. " 'Hypothesis' Theory and Perceptual Responses to Inkblots." *J Proj Tech* 25:75–80 Mr '61. * (*PA* 36:1HG75N)

2822. Pelz, Kurt S.; Ames, Louise B.; and Pike, Frances. "Measurement of Psychologic Function in Geriatric Patients." *J Am Geriatrics Soc* 9:740–54 S '61. *

2823. Perdue, William C. "A Study of the Rorschach Records of Forty-Seven Murderers." *J Social Ther* 7(3):158–67 '61. * (*PA* 36:4JO58P)

2824. Piotrowski, Zygmunt A. "Prediction of Overt Behavior From Projective Test Data." Abstract. *Acta Psychologica* 19:111–4 '61. *

2825. Piotrowski, Zygmunt A., and Bricklin, Barry. "A Second Validation of a Long-Term Rorschach Prognostic Index for Schizophrenic Patients." *J Consult Psychol* 25:123–8 Ap '61. * (*PA* 36:4JQ23P)

2826. Ramer, John Carl. *The Rorschach Barrier Score and Social Behavior.* Doctor's thesis, University of Washington (Seattle, Wash.), 1961. (*DA* 22:4086)

2827. Reisman, John M. "An Interpretation of *m*." Abstract. *J Consult Psychol* 25:367 Ag '61. * (*PA* 37:1273)

2828. Richardson, Charles E. "Health Education or Hypochondriasis." *Am J Pub Health* 51:1561–71 O '61. *

2829. Rigney, Francis J., and Smith, L. Douglas. *The Real Bohemia: A Sociological and Psychological Study of the "Beats."* New York: Basic Books, Inc., 1961. Pp. xxi, 250. * (*PA* 36:1GB50R)

2830. Rossi, Ascanio M., and Neuman, Gerard G. "A Comparative Study of Rorschach Norms: Medical Students." *J Proj Tech* 25:334–8 S '61. * (*PA* 36:3HC34R)

2831. Rychlak, Joseph F., and Guinouard, Donald E. "Symbolic Interpretation of Rorschach Content." Abstract. *J Consult Psychol* 25:370 Ag '61. * (*PA* 37:1275)

2832. Sappenfield, Bert R. "Perception of Masculinity-Femininity in Rorschach Blots and Responses." *J Clin Psychol* 17:373–6 O '61. * (*PA* 38:8569)

2833. Sherman, Murray H., Editor. *A Rorschach Reader.* New York: International Universities Press, Inc., 1961. Pp. xvi, 440. * (*PA* 36:4HG40S)

2834. Speisman, Joseph C., and Singer, Margaret Thaler. "Rorschach Content Correlates in Five Groups With Organic Pathology." *J Proj Tech* 25:356–9 S '61. * (*PA* 36:3HI56S)

2835. Stein, Harry. "An Evaluation of Rorschach Reliability Through the Alternate-Response Method." *J Clin Psychol* 17:241–5 Jl '61. * (*PA* 38:8438)

2836. Symonds, Percival M.; with Arthur R. Jensen. *From Adolescent to Adult*, pp. 119–75, 213–402. New York: Columbia University Press, 1961. Pp. x, 413. * (*PA* 35:2021)

2837. Taulbee, Earl S. "The Relationship Between Rorschach Flexor and Extensor M Responses and the MMPI and Psychotherapy." *J Proj Tech* 25:477–9 D '61. *

2838. Van Pelt, Warren Palmer. *Perceptual-Cognitive Development as Reflected by Rorschach Test Content.* Doctor's thesis, Syracuse University (Syracuse, N.Y.), 1961. (*DA* 23:316)

2839. Wagner, Edwin E. "The Interaction of Aggressive Movement Responses and Anatomy Responses on the Rorschach in Producing Anxiety." *J Proj Tech* 25:212–5 Je '61. * (*PA* 36:2HG12W)

2840. Weiner, Irving B. "Cross-Validation of a Rorschach Checklist Associated With Suicidal Tendencies." *J Consult Psychol* 25:312–5 Ag '61. * (*PA* 37:1734)

2841. Weiner, Irving B. "Three Rorschach Scores Indicative of Schizophrenia." *J Consult Psychol* 25:436–9 O '61. * (*PA* 37:3717)

2842. Wells, St. "The Relationships Between Real and Apparent Movement and Rorschach Form Perception." Abstract. *Acta Psychologica* 19:823–4 '61. *

2843. Williams, Celia, and Boreham, John. "Test and Re-test—Mr. John: Changes in the Rorschach Following Short-Term Psychoanalytically Orientated Psychotherapy." *Rorsch Newsl* 6:3–15 Je '61. *

2844. Williams, Jessie M. "Children Who Break Down in Foster Homes: A Psychological Study of Patterns of Personality Growth in Grossly Deprived Children." *J Child Psychol & Psychiatry* 2:5–20 Je '61. * (*PA* 36:2FF05W)

2845. Zax, Melvin, and Benham, Frank G. "The Stimulus Value of the Rorschach Inkblots as Perceived by Children." *J Proj Tech* 25:233–7 Je '61. * (*PA* 36:2HG33Z)

2846. Zuckerman, Marvin; Levitt, Eugene E.; and Lubin, Bernard. "Concurrent and Construct Validity of Direct and Indirect Measures of Dependency." *J Consult Psychol* 25:316–23 Ag '61. *

2847. Zukowsky, Eugene. *Measuring Primary and Secondary Process Thinking in Schizophrenics and Normals by Means of the Rorschach.* Doctor's thesis, Michigan State University (East Lansing, Mich.), 1961. (*DA* 23:316)

2848. Adams, Henry B., and Cooper, G. David. "Three Measures of Ego Strength and Prognosis for Psychotherapy." *J Clin Psychol* 18:490–4 O '62. * (*PA* 39:5142)

2849. Alimena, Benjamin. "An Experimental Investigation of the Affective Qualities of Rorschach Color, Form and Shading." *J Clin Psychol* 18:107–9 Ja '62. * (*PA* 38:8539)

2850. Appelbaum, Stephen A., and Holzman, Philip S. "The Color-Shading Response and Suicide." *J Proj Tech* 26:155–61 Je '62. * (*PA* 37:3622)

2851. Arnholter, Ethelwyne G. "The Validity of Fisher's Maladjustment and Rigidity Scales as an Indicator of Rehabilitation." *Personnel & Guid J* 40:634–7 Mr '62. * (*PA* 37:1544)

2852. Baldwin, Joan Carroll. *Rorschach Personality Pattern Differences Between Overachievers, Normals and Underachievers at the Fifth Grade Level.* Doctor's thesis, Loyola University (Chicago, Ill.), 1962.

2853. Belmont, Ira, and Birch, Herbert G. " 'Productivity' and Mode of Function in the Rorschach Responses of Brain-Damaged Patients." *J Nerv & Mental Dis* 134:456–62 My '62. * (*PA* 37:1652)

2854. Block, William E. "Psychometric Aspects of the Rorschach Technique." *J Proj Tech* 26:162–72 Je '62. * (*PA* 37:3186)

2855. Bloom, Bernard L. "The Rorschach Popular Response Among Hawaiian Schizophrenics." *J Proj Tech* 26:173–81 Je '62. * (*PA* 37:3187)

2856. Brawer, Florence Blum. *The Introversive-Extratensive Dimensions of the Rorschach Technique and Their Relationships to Jungian Typology.* Master's thesis, University of California (Los Angeles, Calif.), 1962.

2857. Bricklin, Barry. "Comment on Adcock and Ritchie's 'Intercultural Use of Rorschach.' " *Am Anthrop* 64:1296–9 D '62. *

2858. Burgemeister, Bessie B. *Psychological Techniques in Neurological Diagnosis.* New York: Hoeber Medical Division, Harper & Row, Publishers, Inc., 1962. Pp. viii, 248. *

2859. Burke, Mary. *The Control of Response Choice on Projective Techniques.* Doctor's thesis, University of Denver (Denver, Colo.), 1962. (*DA* 24:2119)

2860. Burnand, Gordon. "Note on the Main Changes in the 1962 Revision of the Severe Disturbance Scale." *Rorsch Newsl* 7:20 D '62. *

2861. Buss, Arnold H.; Fischer, Herbert; and Simmons, Alvin J. "Aggression and Hostility in Psychiatric Patients." *J Consult Psychol* 26:84–9 F '62. * (*PA* 37:5055)

2862. Caracena, Philip F., and King, Gerald F. "Generality of Individual Differences in Complexity." *J Clin Psychol* 18:234–6 Ap '62. * (*PA* 38:8480)

2863. Caspari, Irene E. "A Rorschach Record of an Adolescent With Severe Reading Difficulties and Some Notes on His Remedial Teaching." *Rorsch Newsl* 7:3–14 Je '62. *

2864. Cleveland, Sidney E., and Johnson, Dale L. "Personality Patterns in Young Males With Coronary Disease." *Psychosom Med* 24:600–10 N–D '62. * (*PA* 37:8204)

2865. Coates, Stephen. "Homosexuality and the Rorschach Test." *Brit J Med Psychol* 35:177–90 pt 2 '62. * (*PA* 37:3612)

2866. Cooper, George David. *Changes in Ego Strength Following Brief Social and Perceptual Deprivation.* Doctor's thesis, Duke University (Durham, N.C.), 1962. (*DA* 23:4742)

2867. Coopersmith, Stanley. "Resources and Strength in Child Personality: Clinical Explorations of Self Esteem," pp. 61–78. (*PA* 37:4730) In *Child and Education.* Proceedings of the XIV International Congress of Applied Psychology, Vol. 3. Copenhagen, Denmark: Munksgaard, Ltd., 1962. Pp. 197. *

2868. CRAFT, MICHAEL; FABISCH, WALTER; STEPHENSON, GEOFFRY; BURNAND, GORDON; AND KERRIDGE, DAVID. "100 Admissions to a Psychopathic Unit." *J Mental Sci* 108:564–83 S '62. * (*PA* 38:2138)
2869. CRUMPTON, EVELYN. "Projective Case Study of a True Hermaphrodite." *J Proj Tech* 26:266–75 S '62. * (*PA* 37:3396)
2870. DANA, RICHARD H. "The Validation of Projective Tests." *J Proj Tech* 26:182–6 Je '62. * (*PA* 37:3189)
2871. DASTON, PAUL G., AND MCCONNELL, OWEN L. "Stability of Rorschach Penetration and Barrier Scores Over Time." Abstract. *J Consult Psychol* 26:104 F '62. * (*PA* 37:5024)
2872. DUBRIN, ANDREW J. "The Rorschach 'Eyes' Hypothesis and Paranoid Schizophrenia." *J Clin Psychol* 18:468–71 O '62. * (*PA* 39:5197)
2873. EIDUSON, BERNICE T. *Scientists: Their Psychological World.* New York: Basic Books, Inc., 1962. Pp. xvi, 299. * (*PA* 37:111)
2874. EISDORFER, CARL. "Changes in Cognitive Functioning in Relation to Intellectual Level in Senescence," pp. 888–96. In *Social and Psychological Aspects of Aging.* Proceedings of the Fifth Congress of the International Association of Gerontology. Edited by Clark Tibbitts and Wilma Donahue. New York: Columbia University Press, 1962. Pp. xviii, 952. *
2875. EPSTEIN, SEYMOUR; LUNDBORG, ELIZABETH; AND KAPLAN, BERT. "Allocation of Energy and Rorschach Responsivity." *J Clin Psychol* 18:236–8 Ap '62. * (*PA* 38:8547)
2876. EXNER, JOHN E., JR. "The Effect of Color on Productivity in Cards VIII, IX, X of the Rorschach." *J Proj Tech* 26:30–3 Mr '62. * (*PA* 37:3191)
2877. FISHER, SEYMOUR. "Relationship of Rorschach Human Percepts to Projective Descriptions With Self Reference." *J Proj Tech* 26:231–3 Je '62. * (*PA* 37:3193)
2878. FREEMAN, FRANK S. *Theory and Practice of Psychological Testing, Third Edition,* pp. 614–38. New York: Holt, Rinehart & Winston, Inc., 1962. Pp. xix, 697. *
2879. GEERTSMA, ROBERT H. "Factor Analysis of Rorschach Scoring Categories for a Population of Normal Subjects." *J Consult Psychol* 26:20–5 F '62. * (*PA* 37:5026)
2880. GEIST, HAROLD. *The Etiology of Idiopathic Epilepsy,* pp. 116–53, 234–55. New York: Exposition Press, 1962. Pp. 297. *
2881. GLYMOUR, CLARK; AMMONS, C. H.; AND AMMONS, R. B. "Projective Test Protocols of Students Placing Extreme (High or Low) Value on Intellectual Activity." *Proc Mont Acad Sci* 21:105–12 '62. * (*PA* 37:3195)
2882. GOLDFRIED, MARVIN R. "Rorschach Developmental Level and the MMPI as Measures of Severity of Psychological Disturbance." *J Proj Tech* 26:187–92 Je '62. * (*PA* 37:3219)
2883. GOLDFRIED, MARVIN R. "Some Normative Data on Rorschach Developmental Level 'Card Pull' in a Psychiatric Population." *J Proj Tech* 26:283–7 S '62. * (*PA* 37:3196)
2884. GORDON, ROSEMARY. "Fear and Attraction to Death as Shown by Rorschach Material." *Rorsch Newsl* 7:25–34 Je '62. *
2885. GRIMM, ELAINE R. "Psychological Investigation of Habitual Abortion." *Psychosom Med* 24:369–78 Jl–Ag '62. * (*PA* 37:5427)
2886. HAUSER, RUSSELL JEROME. *The Validity of the Formal and Linguistic Aspects of the Rorschach in Predicting Intelligence.* Doctor's thesis, New York University (New York, N.Y.), 1962. (*DA* 24:833)
2887. HAWORTH, MARY R. "Responses of Children to a Group Projective Film and to the Rorschach, CAT, Despert Fables and D-A-P." *J Proj Tech* 26:47–60 Mr '62. * (*PA* 37:2893)
2888. HERSCH, CHARLES. "The Cognitive Functioning of the Creative Person: A Development Analysis." *J Proj Tech* 26:193–200 Je '62. * (*PA* 37:3129)
2889. HERZBERG, IRENE. "The Pre-Psychotic Patient: How Can the Rorschach Test Help in Assessing Whether the Pre-Psychotic Patient Is Likely to Break Down in Treatment?" *Rorsch Newsl* 7:21–40 D '62. *
2890. HIRT, MICHAEL, EDITOR. *Rorschach Science: Readings in Theory and Method.* New York: Free Press of Glencoe, 1962. Pp. ix, 438. * (*PA* 37:6737)
2891. HOWARD, KENNETH I. "The Convergent and Discriminant Validation of Ipsative Ratings From Three Projective Instruments." *J Clin Psychol* 18:183–8 Ap '62. * (*PA* 38:8551)
2892. HUZIOKA, YOSINARU. "Rorschach Test in Farming Villages of North Thailand," pp. 139–273. In *Nature and Life in Southeast Asia, Vol. 2.* Edited by Tatuo Kira and Tadao Umesao. Kyoto, Japan: Fauna and Flora Research Society, 1962. Pp. vii, 276. *
2893. KETTELL, MARJORIE E. "Rorschach Indicators of Senility in Geriatric Patients," pp. 639–43. In *Social and Psychological Aspects of Aging.* Proceedings of the Fifth Congress of the International Association of Gerontology. Edited by Clark Tibbitts and Wilma Donahue. New York: Columbia University Press, 1962. Pp. xviii, 952. *
2894. KIKUCHI, TETSUHIKO; KITAMURA, SEIRO; AND ŌYAMA, MASAHIRO. "Rorschach Performance in Alcoholic Intoxication, 2." *Tohoku Psychologica Folia* 21(1–3):19–46 '62–63. * (*PA* 37:7711)
2895. KLOPFER, BRUNO, AND DAVIDSON, HELEN H. *The Rorschach Technique: An Introductory Manual.* New York: Harcourt, Brace & World, Inc., 1962. Pp. viii, 245. *
2896. KNOBLOCK, PETER. *An Investigation of Essential Elements of the Reading Process by Means of Standard and Experimental Administrations of the Rorschach Inkblot Test.* Doctor's thesis, University of Michigan (Ann Arbor, Mich.), 1962. (*DA* 23:532)
2897. KORNER, IJA N.; ALLISON, ROGER B., JR.; AND ZWANZIGER, MAX D. "Stimulus Size and Rorschach Responses." *J Psychol* 54:491–4 O '62. * (*PA* 37:6740)
2898. KOTTENHOFF, HEINRICH. "Metric Determination of Schizophrenic Dementia." *Psychol Rep* 11:646 D '62. * (*PA* 38:3058)
2899. KUMAR, PRAMOD. "Popular Responses in the Rorschach Test." *Psychologia* 5:161–9 S '62. * (*PA* 38:2717)
2900. KUMAR, PRAMOD. "The Rorschach Test in Depressive and Normal Groups." *Indian J Psychol* 37:89–92 Ja '62. * (*PA* 37:6760)
2901. LEVIN, RACHEL BABIN. *The Psychology of Women: An Empirical Test of a Psychoanalytic Construct.* Doctor's thesis, Syracuse University (Syracuse, N.Y.), 1962. (*DA* 24:837)
2902. LEVINE, DAVID, AND COHEN, JACOB. "Symptoms and Ego Strength Measures as Predictors of the Outcome of Hospitalization in Functional Psychoses." *J Consult Psychol* 26:246–50 Je '62. * (*PA* 38:1304)
2903. LEVINE, MURRAY, AND SPIVACK, GEORGE. "Human Movement Responses and Verbal Expression in the Rorschach Test." *J Proj Tech* 26:299–304 S '62. * (*PA* 37:3197)
2904. LEVITT, EUGENE E.; LUBIN, BERNARD; AND ZUCKERMAN, MARVIN. "A Simplified Method of Scoring Rorschach Content for Dependency." *J Proj Tech* 26:234–6 Je '62. * (*PA* 37:3198)
2905. LIPSHER, DAVID HAROLD. *Consistency of Clinicians' Judgments Based on MMPI, Rorschach and TAT Protocols.* Doctor's thesis, Stanford University (Stanford, Calif.), 1962. (*DA* 22:4409)
2906. LUCAS, CAROL. "Frustration and the Perception of Aggressive Animals." *J Consult Psychol* 26:287 Je '62. * (*PA* 38:926)
2907. MCCULLY, ROBERT S. "Certain Theoretical Considerations in Relation to Borderline Schizophrenia and the Rorschach." *J Proj Tech* 26:404–18 D '62. * (*PA* 37:6742)
2908. MAJUMDAR, ALOK KUMAR, AND ROY, ARUNANGSU BIKASH. "Latent Personality Content of Juvenile Delinquents." *J Psychol Res* 6:4–8 Ja '62. * (*PA* 37:3643)
2909. MALMIVAARA, KATRI, AND KOLHO, PIRKKO. "The Personality of 5- to 7-Year-Old Enuretics in the Light of the Sceno and Rorschach Tests." *Annales Paediatriae Fenniae* 8(3):166–72 '62. *
2910. MALMIVAARA, KATRI, AND KOLHO, PIRKKO. "The Personality of Stuttering Children at the Age of 5–7 Years in the Light of the Sceno and Rorschach Tests." *Annales Paediatriae Fenniae* 8(1):17–23 '62. *
2911. MEKETON, BETTY W.; GRIFFITH, RICHARD M.; TAYLOR, VIVIAN H.; AND WIEDEMAN, JANE S. "Rorschach Homosexual Signs in Paranoid Schizophrenics." *J Abn & Social Psychol* 65:280–4 O '62. *
2912. MOGAR, ROBERT E. "Anxiety Indices in Human Figure Drawings: A Replication and Extension." Abstract. *J Consult Psychol* 26:108 F '62. * (*PA* 37:4989)
2913. MOOS, RUDOLF H. "Effects of Training on Students' Test Interpretations." *J Proj Tech* 26:310–7 S '62. * (*PA* 37:3201)
2914. MOSKOWITZ, SAMUEL. *Concrete and Formal Thought in Personification and Causal Responses in the Rorschach Test.* Doctor's thesis, New York University (New York, N.Y.), 1962. (*DA* 24:2125)
2915. MUELLER, A. D. "Pain Study of Paraplegic Patients: The Rorschach Test as an Aid in Predicting Pain Relief by Means of Chordotomy." *Arch Neurol* 7:355–8 O '62. * (*PA* 37:5367)
2916. NEIGER, STEPHEN; SLEMON, ALAN G.; AND QUIRK, DOUGLAS A. "The Performance of 'Chronic Schizophrenic' Patients on Piotrowski's Rorschach Sign List for Organic CNS Pathology." *J Proj Tech* 26:419–28 D '62. * (*PA* 37:6763)
2917. NEURINGER, CHARLES. "Manifestations of Anxiety on the Rorschach Test." *J Proj Tech* 26:318–26 S '62. * (*PA* 37:3203)
2918. ORME, J. E. "Rorschach Sex Response in a Psychiatric Population." *J Clin Psychol* 18:303 Jl '62. * (*PA* 39:1867)
2919. PALMER, JAMES O., AND LUSTGARTEN, BILLIE J. "The Prediction of TAT Structure as a Test of Rorschach's Experience-Balance." *J Proj Tech* 26:212–20 Je '62. * (*PA* 37:3204)
2920. PAUKER, JEROME D. "Base Rates in the Prediction of Suicide: A Note on Appelbaum's and Holzman's 'The Color-Shading Response and Suicide.'" Reply by Stephen A. Appelbaum and Philip S. Holzman. *J Proj Tech* 26:429–30 D '62. *
2921. PELZ, KURT; PIKE, FRANCES; AND AMES, LOUISE B. "A Proposed Battery of Childhood Tests for Discriminating Between Different Levels of Intactness of Function in Elderly Subjects." *J Genetic Psychol* 100:23–40 Mr '62. * (*PA* 37:975)
2922. PETERSEN, PAUL A. *A Correlational Investigation Between Rorschach Indices and Independent Ratings of Empathy and Over-Control vs Over-Lability of Feelings.* Master's thesis, De Paul University (Chicago, Ill.), 1962.
2923. PETTIFOR, R. E. "Personality Studies in Ulcer and Alcoholic Patients." *Med Services J Can* 18:187–90 Mr '62. *
2924. PHELAN, J. G. "Projective Techniques in the Selection

of Management Personnel." *J Proj Tech* 26:102–4 Mr '62. * (*PA* 37:3915)
2925. Pine, Fred. "Creativity and Primary Process: Sample Variations." *J Nerv & Mental Dis* 134:506–11 Je '62. * (*PA* 37:3205)
2926. Price, A. Cooper. "A Rorschach Study of the Development of Personality Structure in White and Negro Children in a Southeastern Community." *Genetic Psychol Monogr* 65: 3–52 F '62. *
2927. Purcell, Kenneth; Turnbull, John W.; and Bernstein, Lewis. "Distinctions Between Subgroups of Asthmatic Children: Psychological Test and Behavior Rating Comparisons." *J Psychosom Res* 6:283–91 O–D '62. * (*PA* 37:8210)
2928. Quirk, Douglas A.; Quarrington, Mary; Neiger, Stephen; and Slemon, Alan G. "The Performance of Acute Psychotic Patients on the Index of Pathological Thinking and on Selected Signs of Idiosyncrasy on the Rorschach." *J Proj Tech* 26:431–41 D '62. * (*PA* 37:6745)
2929. Ricciuti, Henry. "Development and Application of Projective Techniques of Personality." *R Ed Res* 32:64–77 F '62. * (*PA* 37:1274)
2930. Rosenthal, Melvin. "Some Behavioral Correlates of the Rorschach Experience-Balance." *J Proj Tech* 26:442–6 D '62. * (*PA* 37:6747)
2931. Sato, Isao; Ōyama, Masahiro; Kitamura, Seiro; and Kikuchi, Tetsuhiko. "Rorschach Performance Under Ravona Dosage." *Tohoku Psychologica Folia* 21(1–3):1–17 '62–63. * (*PA* 37:7715)
2932. Seeman, William, and Marks, Philip A. "A Study of Some 'Test Dimensions' Conceptions." *J Proj Tech* 26: 469–73 D '62. * (*PA* 37:6678)
2933. Semeonoff, Boris. "Self-Description as an Instrument in Personality Assessment." *Brit J Med Psychol* 35:165–75 pt 2 '62. * (*PA* 37:3236)
2934. Silverman, Lloyd H.; Lapkin, Benjamin; and Rosenbaum, Ira S. "Manifestations of Primary Process Thinking in Schizophrenia." *J Proj Tech* 26:117–27 Mr '62. * (*PA* 37:3712)
2935. Smith, Thomas E. "The Relationship Between Depressive Personality Characteristics and Rorschach Card Preference." *J Consult Psychol* 26:286 Je '62. * (*PA* 38:934)
2936. Stark, Stanley. "A Note on Time, Intelligence, and Rorschach Movement Responses." *Percept & Motor Skills* 15: 267–72 O '62. * (*PA* 37:7997)
2937. Stein, Harry. "An Analysis of Two Components Entering Into Rorschach Reliability Values." *J Proj Tech* 26: 474–7 D '62. * (*PA* 37:6748)
2938. Super, Donald E., and Crites, John O. *Appraising Vocational Fitness by Means of Psychological Tests, Revised Edition*, pp. 560–75. New York: Harper & Brothers, 1962. Pp. xv, 688. * (*PA* 37:2038)
2939. Thomas, Caroline Bedell, and Kendrick, Mildred A. "Psychobiological Studies: 1, The Relationship of Intellectual Productivity as Measured by the Rorschach Test to Body Weight." *Ann Internal Med* 56:440–7 Mr '62. *
2940. Tizard, Barbara. "The Personality of Epileptics: A Discussion of the Evidence." *Psychol B* 59:196–210 My '62. * (*PA* 37:3522)
2941. Viitamaki, R. Olavi. *Psychoses in Children: A Psychological Follow-Up Study.* Annals of the Finnish Academy of Science and Letters, Series B, Vol. 125, Part 2. Helsinki, Finland: Suomalainen Tiedeakatemia, Academia Scientiarum Fennica, 1962. Pp. 52. * (*PA* 39:2650)
2942. Vinson, David B., and Gaitz, Charles M. "The Objective Measurement of Psychobiologic Decline: A Preliminary Report," pp. 578–82. In *Social and Psychological Aspects of Aging.* Proceedings of the Fifth Congress of the International Association of Gerontology. Edited by Clark Tibbitts and Wilma Donahue. New York: Columbia University Press, 1962. Pp. xviii, 952. *
2943. Weiner, Irving B. "Rorschach Tempo as a Schizophrenic Indicator." *Percept & Motor Skills* 15:139–41 Ag '62. * (*PA* 37:5050)
2944. Wiseman, Richard John. *The Rorschach as a Stimulus for Hypnotic Dreams: A Study of Unconscious Processes.* Doctor's thesis, Michigan State University (East Lansing, Mich.), 1962. (*DA* 23:3996)
2945. Wolfensberger, Wolf P.; Miller, Martin B.; Foshee, James G.; and Cromwell, Rue L. "Rorschach Correlates of Activity Level in High School Children." *J Consult Psychol* 26:269–72 Je '62. * (*PA* 38:711)
2946. Zucker, Luise J. "Evaluating Psychopathology of the Self." *Ann N Y Acad Sci* 96:844–52 Ja 27 '62. * (*PA* 37:6769)
2947. Acker, Charles W. "Personality Concomitants of Autonomic Balance: 1, Rorschach Measures." *J Proj Tech* 27:12–9 Mr '63. * (*PA* 38:1064)
2948. Acker, Charles W. "Personality Concomitants of Autonomic Balance: 2, Inventory Measures." *J Proj Tech* 27:20–2 Mr '63. * (*PA* 38:1064)
2949. Adams, Henry B.; Cooper, G. David; and Carrera, Richard N. "The Rorschach and the MMPI: A Concurrent Validity Study." *J Proj Tech* 27:23–34 Mr '63. * (*PA* 38: 976)
2950. Alcock, Theodora. *The Rorschach in Practice.* London: Tavistock Publications (1959) Ltd., 1963. Pp. xii, 252. *
2951. Alcock, Theodora. "The Vulnerable Personality." *Rorsch Newsl* 8:2 D '63. *
2952. Apperson, Louise; Goldstein, Arnold D.; and Williams, W. W. "Rorschach Form Level as an Indicator of Potential in Mentally Retarded Children." *J Clin Psychol* 19:320–2 Jl '63. *
2953. Barnouw, Victor. Chap. 15, "The Rorschach Test," pp. 239–59. In his *Culture and Personality.* Homewood, Ill.: Dorsey Press, Inc., 1963. Pp. xi, 410. *
2954. Barron, Frank. Chap. 11, "The Disposition Toward Originality," pp. 139–52. In *Scientific Creativity: Its Recognition and Development.* Edited by Calvin W. Taylor and Frank Barron. New York: John Wiley & Sons, Inc., 1963. Pp. xxiv, 419. * (*PA* 38:2689)
2955. Blatt, Sidney J., and Allison, Joel. "Methodological Considerations in Rorschach Research: The W Response as an Expression of Abstractive and Integrative Strivings." *J Proj Tech & Pers Assess* 27:269–78 S '63. * (*PA* 38:4316)
2956. Block, William E. "Sequential Effects in the Presentation of Rorschach Inkblots." *J Clin Psychol* 19:462 O '63. *
2957. Boyd, Richard W. "Cross-Validation of an Objective Rorschach." *J Clin Psychol* 19:322–3 Jl '63. *
2958. Bricklin, Barry, and Zeleznik, Carter. "A Psychological Investigation of Selected Ethiopian Adolescents by Means of the Rorschach and Other Projective Tests." *Hum Org* 22:291–303 w '63–64. *
2959. Burnand, Gordon. "Relative Difficulty of Rorschach Cards and Diagnosis, Personality Defects and Symptoms, Part 1." *Rorsch Newsl* 8:24–30 Je '63. *
2960. Burnand, Gordon. "Relative Difficulty of Rorschach Cards and Diagnosis, Personality Defects and Symptoms, Part 2." *Rorsch Newl* 8:27–33 D '63. * (*PA* 38:8544)
2961. Cerbus, George, and Nichols, Robert C. "Personality Variables and Response to Color." *Psychol B* 60:566–75 N '63. * (*PA* 38:4228)
2962. Clemes, Stanley; Tanous, James C.; and Kantor, Robert E. "Level of Perceptual Development and Psychosomatic Illness." *J Proj Tech & Pers Assess* 27:279–87 S '63. * (*PA* 38:4317)
2963. Cooley, William W. "Predicting Choice of a Career in Scientific Research." *Personnel & Guid J* 42:21–8 S '63. *
2964. Davids, Anthony, and Talmadge, Max. "A Study of Rorschach Signs of Adjustment in Mothers of Institutionalized Emotionally Disturbed Children." *J Proj Tech & Pers Assess* 27:292–6 S '63. * (*PA* 38:4318)
2965. Davids, Anthony, and Talmadge, Max. "Utility of the Rorschach in Predicting Movement in Psychiatric Casework." *Am J Orthopsychiatry* 33:290–1 Mr '63. *
2966. Eble, Selma J.; Fernald, L. Dodge, Jr.; and Graziano, Anthony M. "The Comparability of Quantitative Rorschach and Z-Test Data." *J Proj Tech & Pers Assess* 27:166–70 Je '63. * (*PA* 38:2692)
2967. Eiduson, Bernice T.; Meyer, Mortimer M.; and Lucas, Winafred B. "Contribution of Psychological Testing of Parents to the Understanding of the Child." *J Proj Tech & Pers Assess* 27:387–417 D '63. * (*PA* 38:8088)
2968. Eisdorfer, Carl. "Rorschach Performance and Intellectual Functioning in the Aged." *J Gerontol* 18:358–63 O '63. * (*PA* 38:5822)
2969. Eisner, Betty Grover. "Some Psychological Differences Beween Fertile and Infertile Women." *J Clin Psychol* 19:391–5 O '63. *
2970. Endicott, Noble A., and Endicott, Jean. "'Improvement' in Untreated Psychiatric Patients." *Arch Gen Psychiatry* 9:575–85 D '63. * (*PA* 38:8643)
2971. Endicott, Noble A., and Endicott, Jean. "Objective Measures of Somatic Preoccupation." *J Nerv & Mental Dis* 137:427–37 N '63. * (*PA* 38:6356)
2972. Engel, Mary. "Psychological Testing of Borderline Psychotic Children." *Arch Gen Psychiatry* 8:426–34 My '63. * (*PA* 38:2451)
2973. Evans, Ray B., and Marmorston, Jessie. "Psychological Test Signs of Brain Damage in Cerebral Thrombosis." *Psychol Rep* 12:915–30 Je '63. * (*PA* 38:6413)
2974. Gleser, Goldine C. "Projective Methodologies." *Annual R Psychol* 14:391–422 '63. *
2975. Goff, Regina M. "Trait Identification as a Means of Predicting Academic Goal Attainment." *J Exp Ed* 31:297–302 Mr '63. *
2976. Goldfried, Marvin R. "The Connotative Meaning of Some Animal Symbols for College Students." *J Proj Tech* 27: 60–7 Mr '63. * (*PA* 38:1010)
2977. Grebstein, Lawrence C. "Relative Accuracy of Actuarial Prediction, Experienced Clinicians, and Graduate Students in a Clinical Judgment Task." *J Consult Psychol* 27: 127–32 Ap '63. * (*PA* 37:8023)
2978. Gross, Seymour Z. "Critique: Children Who Break Down in Foster Homes: A Psychological Study of Patterns of Personality Growth in Grossly Deprived Children." *J Child Psychol & Psychiatry* 4:61–6 Ap '63. *
2979. Howard, Kenneth I. "Ratings of Projective Test Protocols as a Function of Degree of Inference." *Ed & Psychol Meas* 23:267–75 su '63. * (*PA* 38:1013)
2980. Kikuchi, Tetsuhiko; Sato, Isao; and Ōyama, Masahiro. "Types of Alcoholic Alteration of Rorschach Test Performance: A Case Study." *Tohoku Psychologica Folia* 21(4):97–105 '63. * (*PA* 38:4322)
2981. Kiviluoto, H. "Trends of Development in Ror-

schach Responses 1962." *Rorsch Newsl* 8:9–16 D '63. * (*PA* 38:8553)
2982. KURZ, RONALD B. "Relationship Between Time Imagery and Rorschach Human Movement Responses." *J Consult Psychol* 27:273–6 Je '63. * (PA 38:1015)
2983. LAUNER, PHILIP T. *The Relationship of Given Interest-Patterns to Certain Aspects of Personality.* Doctor's thesis, New York University (New York, N.Y.), 1963. (*DA* 24:2564)
2984. LEBOWITZ, ANNE. "Patterns of Perceptual and Motor Organization." *J Proj Tech & Pers Assess* 27:302–8 S '63. * (*PA* 38:4502)
2985. LEVINE, MURRAY, AND SPIVACK, GEORGE. "The Rorschach Index of Ideational Repression: Application to Quantitative Sequence Analysis." *J Proj Tech* 27:73–8 Mr '63. * (*PA* 38:1017)
2986. LEVITT, EUGENE E.; BRADY, JOHN PAUL; AND LUBIN, BERNARD. "Correlates of Hypnotizability in Young Women: Anxiety and Dependency." *J Personality* 31:52–7 Mr '63. *
2987. LOISELLE, ROBERT H., AND KLEINSCHMIDT, ANN. "A Comparison of the Stimulus Value of Rorschach Inkblots and Their Percepts." *J Proj Tech & Pers Assess* 27:191–4 Je '63. * (*PA* 38:2719)
2988. LOVELAND, NATHENE T.; WYNNE, LYMAN C.; AND SINGER, MARGARET T. "The Family Rorschach: A New Method for Studying Family Interaction." *Family Process* 2:187–215 S '63. * (*PA* 38:8558)
2989. MCCUE, KEMPER W.; ROTHENBERG, DAVID; ALLEN, ROBERT M.; AND JENNINGS, THEODORE W. "Rorschach Variables in Two 'Study of Values' Types." *J General Psychol* 68:169–72 Ja '63. * (*PA* 38:2742)
2990. MCCULLY, ROBERT S. "An Interpretation of Projective Findings in a Case of Female Transsexualism." *J Proj Tech & Pers Assess* 27:436–46 D '63. * (*PA* 38:8766)
2991. MATHUR, SHANTA, AND PAIS, CLARA M. "Extratensive and Introversive Experience Balances as Tested by the Rorschach Test and the Sacks Completion Test." *Manas* 10(1):1–13 '63. * (*PA* 38:8559)
2992. MONS, W. E. R. "Nail-Biters and Card-Rejectors." *Rorsch Newsl* 8:11–4 Je '63. *
2993. NEIGER, STEPHEN, AND PAPASTERGIOU, CHRISTOS. "The Relationship Between Depressive Personality Characteristics and Rorschach Card Preference: A Reply to T. E. Smith." Abstract. *J Consult Psychol* 27:463 O '63. *
2994. NICKOLS, JOHN. "Rorschach Z Scores on Disturbed Subjects." *J Consult Psychol* 27:544–5 D '63. * (*PA* 38:8561)
2995. ORME, J. E. "Rorschach Alphabetical and Geometrical Responses." *J Clin Psychol* 19:459–60 O '63. *
2996. OSBORNE, ELSIE L. "Some Problems Associated With School Phobia as Illustrated in the Rorschach Record of a 6 Yr. Old Girl." *Rorsch Newsl* 8:3–10 Je '63. *
2997. OTTEN, MARK W., AND VAN DE CASTLE, R. L. "A Comparison of Set 'A' of the Holtzman Inkblots With the Rorschach by Means of the Semantic Differential." *J Proj Tech & Pers Assess* 27:452–60 D '63. * (*PA* 38:8562)
2998. PALMER, JAMES O. "Alterations in Rorschach's Experience Balance Under Conditions of Food and Sleep Deprivation: A Construct Validation Study." *J Proj Tech & Pers Assess* 27:208–13 Je '63. * (*PA* 38:2723)
2999. PARKER, ROLLAND S. "The Perceiver's Identification of the Figure in the Rorschach Human Movement Response." *J Proj Tech & Pers Assess* 27:214–9 Je '63. * (*PA* 38:2724)
3000. PAUKER, JEROME D. "Relationship of Rorschach Content Categories to Intelligence." *J Proj Tech & Pers Assess* 27:220–1 Je '63. * (*PA* 38:2725)
3001. PIOTROWSKI, ZYGMUNT A. "Use of the Rorschach Test as a Diagnostic Criterion." Letter. *Am Psychologist* 18:621–2 S '63. *
3002. PIOTROWSKI, ZYGMUNT A., AND ROCK, MILTON R.; WITH THE ASSISTANCE OF JOHN J. GRELA. *The Perceptanalytic Executive Scale: A Tool for the Selection of Top Managers.* New York: Grune & Stratton, Inc., 1963. Pp. iv, 220. * (*PA* 38:9357)
3003. POPE, BENJAMIN, AND BARE, CAROLE E. "Rorschach Percepts and Personal Concepts as Semantically Equivalent Members." *Percept & Motor Skills* 17:15–22 Ag '63. * (*PA* 38:8563)
3004. RAMER, JOHN. "The Rorschach Barrier Score and Social Behavior." *J Consult Psychol* 27:525–31 D '63. * (*PA* 38:8564)
3005. RAY, JOSEPH B. "The Meaning of Rorschach White Space Responses." *J Proj Tech & Pers Assess* 27:315–23 S '63. * (*PA* 38:4325)
3006. RICHARDSON, HELEN. "Rorschachs of Adolescent Approved School Girls, Compared With Ames' Normal Adolescents." *Rorsch Newsl* 8:3–8 D '63. * (*PA* 38:8566)
3007. RICKERS-OVSIANKINA, MARIA A.; KNAPP, ROBERT H.; AND MCINTIRE, DONALD W. "Factors Affecting the Psychodiagnostic Significance of Color Perception." *J Proj Tech & Pers Assess* 27:461–6 D '63. * (*PA* 38:8567)
3008. ROSS, W. D.; ADSETT, NANCY; GLESER, GOLDINE; JOYCE, C. R. B.; KAPLAN, S. M.; AND TIEGER, M. E. "A Trial of Psychopharmacologic Measurement With Projective Techniques." *J Proj Tech & Pers Assess* 27:222–5 Je '63. *
3009. SAPOLSKY, ALLAN. "An Indicator of Suicidal Ideation on the Rorschach Test." *J Proj Tech & Pers Assess* 27:332–5 S '63. * (*PA* 38:4328)
3010. SCHULMAN, R. E. "Use of the Rorschach Prognostic Rating Scale in Predicting Movement in Counseling." *J Counsel Psychol* 10:198–9 su '63. *
3011. SEMEONOFF, BORIS. "An Application of Inter-Person Analysis in Personality Assessment." *Brit J Psychol* 54:71–81 F '63. * (*PA* 37:8004)
3012. SILVER, ALBERT W., AND DERR, JOHN. "The Effect of Oral Gratification on Children's Rorschach Scores and Differences Between Examiners." *J Clin Psychol* 19:310–1 Jl '63. *
3013. SILVERMAN, LLOYD H. "On the Relationship Between Aggressive Imagery and Thought Disturbance in Rorschach Responses." *J Proj Tech & Pers Assess* 27:336–44 S '63. * (*PA* 38:4329)
3014. SINGER, MARGARET THALER, AND WYNNE, LYMAN C. "Differentiating Characteristics of Parents of Childhood Schizophrenics, Childhood Neurotics, and Young Adult Schizophrenics." *Am J Psychiatry* 120:234–43 S '63. *
3015. STOKVIS, BERTHOLD, AND BOLTEN, MART P. "Statistical Data on Personality Alterations in Chronic Illness." *Psychol Rep* 13:829 D '63. * (*PA* 38:9114)
3016. TAKAHASHI, S. "Statistical Analysis of Scoring Assumption Employed in the Psychodiagnosis via Group Method of the Rorschach Test." English abstract. *Jap J Psychol* 34:82–3 Je '63. *
3017. TESTIN, ROBERT FRANCIS. *Ego Strength Scale Differences Between Psychotic and Nonpsychotic Inpatients.* Doctor's thesis, Fordham University (New York, N.Y.), 1963. (*DA* 24:839)
3018. THOMAS, CAROLINE BEDELL, AND ROSS, DONALD CLARE. "A New Approach to the Rorschach Test as a Research Tool: 1, Preliminary Note." *B Johns Hopkins Hosp* 112:312–7 Je '63. *
3019. THOMAS, E. LLEWELLYN. "Eye Movements and Fixations During Initial Viewing of Rorschach Cards." *J Proj Tech & Pers Assess* 27:345–53 S '63. * (*PA* 38:4330)
3020. VORHAUS, PAULINE G. "The Ego-Asserting; Ego-Deflating Syndrome." *J Proj Tech & Pers Assess* 27:379–86 D '63. *
3021. VOTH, HAROLD M., AND MAYMAN, MARTIN. "A Dimension of Personality Organization: An Experimental Study of Ego-Closeness–Ego-Distance." *Arch Gen Psychiatry* 8:366–80 Ap '63. * (*PA* 38:2651)
3022. WAGONER, ROBERT A. "The Rorschach Test: A Perceptual or a Grammatical Device?" *Percept & Motor Skills* 17:419–22 O '63. * (*PA* 38:6102)
3023. WALLACE, JOHN, AND SECHREST, LEE. "Frequency Hypothesis and Content Analysis of Projective Techniques." *J Consult Psychol* 27:387–93 O '63. * (*PA* 38:4335)
3024. WEINGOLD, HAROLD P.; WEBSTER, RONALD L.; AND DAWSON, JOSEPH G. "Reinforcing Properties of Selected Rorschach Cards: A Methodological Study." *Percept & Motor Skills* 17:655–8 D '63. * (*PA* 38:5316)
3025. WEST, J. V.; BAUGH, V. S.; AND BAUGH, ANNIE P. "Rorschach and Draw-A-Person Responses of Hypnotized and Nonhypnotized Subjects." *Psychiatric Q* 37:123–7 Ja '63. *
3026. YANG, KUO-SHU; TZUO, HUAN-YUAN; AND WU, CHING-YI. "Rorschach Responses of Normal Chinese Adults: 2, The Popular Responses." *J Social Psychol* 60:175–86 Ag '63. * (*PA* 38:4336)
3027. YEN, YI-SHIU. "The Diagnostic Indicators of Simple Schizophrenia in the Rorschach Test." *Acta Psychologica Taiwanica* (5):52–6 Mr '63. * (*PA* 38:8573)
3028. ZAX, MELVIN; COWEN, EMORY L.; AND PETER, MARY. "A Comparative Study of Novice Nuns and College Females Using the Response Set Approach." *J Abn & Social Psychol* 66:369–75 Ap '63. * (*PA* 37:8005)
3029. ZELIN, MARTIN, AND SECHREST, LEE. "The Validity of the 'Mother' and 'Father' Cards of the Rorschach." *J Proj Tech* 27:114–21 Mr '63. * (*PA* 38:1027)
3030. LEVINE, MURRAY, AND SPIVACK, GEORGE. *The Rorschach Index of Repressive Style.* Springfield, Ill.: Charles C Thomas, Publisher, 1964. Pp. xvi, 164. * (*PA* 39:1747)

RICHARD H. DANA, *Professor of Psychology, University of South Florida, Tampa, Florida.*

In a previous review Shaffer suggested that the Rorschach is no longer a "promising" measuring instrument (see 5:154). More evidence has appeared in specific area reviews of anxiety scores (*2917*), factor analytic studies (*2687*), set and examiner (*2740*), situational and interpersonal variables (*2679*), and the stimulus (*2251*). Psychometric aspects of the Rorschach have been rigorously reexamined (*2854*).

This review will not duplicate specific area reviews and is based on 315 articles, including some dissertations where available, which appeared from 1958 through summer 1963. The literature for even this period is incomplete. However, classification should represent interests: general discussions (6 per cent), validation (40 per cent), stimulus (11 per cent), norms (9 per cent), and modified tests (7 per cent). Since 11 per cent of the studies were not relevant, this leaves a scant 16 per cent for administration, reliability, subject, examiner, and scoring variables, not to mention case studies. Clearly, the emphasis is still on applied research with the exception of sustained concern with stimulus properties of the blots.

When the validity studies are tallied, a similar result is noted. Criterion-oriented or concurrent, predictive, and congruent designs account for 32, 17, and 20 per cent, respectively. Construct validation has been employed in 18 per cent and the remainder are general discussions. A few years ago it would have made sense to tally positive and negative results for each kind of validation. The lack of replication, systematic or otherwise, or of consensus in definition of variables, and the capricious dilettantism of some investigators, renders such scrutiny empty and mechanical.

No one now doubts that the early research history combined misplaced conviction and methodological naïveté. However, these attitudes are gradually being replaced by a more uniform competence: recent studies are sophisticated methodologically and prone to ask meaningful questions. We still experience the clinician's trust in procedural evidence while psychological science demands empirical justification for the continued daily use of the Rorschach. Nonetheless, in the attempt to provide a factual basis for practice, we invest our methodologies with our preconceptions and our labors are rewarded in the same coin.

Levy and Orr (*2534*) randomly and reliably selected 40 Rorschach studies and classified them in terms of the researcher's institution, academic or nonacademic, type of validity, criterion or construct, and outcome, favorable or unfavorable. The probability of positive results varies from 70 to 50 per cent for construct validity, and from 34 to 59 per cent for criterion-oriented validity as a function of academic or nonacademic settings, respectively. Where we work tends to focus our biases and dictates not only the research preoccupation but affects the probability of obtaining particular results.

Two blatant discrepancies between methodology and practice continue to be relevant. First, the methodology used to examine the Rorschach asks questions which differ from those asked of the test in clinical practice. The clinician uses scores and nonquantifiable data in combination, common interpretations are abstracted, and finally these interpretations are rationally ordered or contrived in terms of the Rorschacher's frame of reference. Reports are rich in meaning and in testable hypotheses to the extent that the clinician is able to maximize his use of these available cues in the context of a wealth of theoretical data and past experience. And finally the technical skill in putting the report on paper is related to the usefulness of the hypotheses contained therein. In this process there are no unqualified interpretative hypotheses for particular scores or combinations of scores. It has been shown repeatedly that the kind of data is irrelevant in the conceptual diagnostic task (*2580*).

Our research subculture has stereotyped the kinds of questions which may be legitimately asked. We attempt to relate specific Rorschach variables to external criteria which are about as unreliable as the test scores themselves. The psychologist in a clinical position is often concerned with concurrent validity, typically the prediction of clinical diagnosis. While this effort may be relevant to institutional practice, it rests upon acknowledged disagreement among experts as to the criterion diagnoses. Similarly, predictive validity is often concerned with outcome of psychotherapy. Again there is no acceptable criterion for therapy outcome. Congruent validity asks the question of relationship to another test of either questionable reliability or dubious validity, or both. There is no rational reason to expect successful prediction of an external criterion, except by accident or a combination of situation-determined variables which render cross validation unlikely. Construct validation is also hazardous. One attempts to construct theory with a relatively constricted methodology and in terms of quasi-reliable measures. The result is a plethora of tenuous relationships. For example, even the relatively well established relationships between M, human movement, and inhibition appear to have limited generality (*2688*).

Further complications result from the now well documented belief that the Rorschach measures a level of personality which is somewhat below the surface behavior (2719). No systematic attempt has been made to assess the aspect of validation neglected by Levy and Orr (2534), the expectation of differential results when the test is used for different measurement purposes. Additionally, while the preeminence of examiner influence is recognized, such awareness is not reflected in systematic examination of clinician impact upon Rorschach performance, scoring, or interpretation. For example, the examiner and not the specific instructional set is responsible for response differences (2691). It is noteworthy that only a very few studies were found in this area.

The second clinical versus research usage discrepancy is that the traditional and formal scores (e.g., Beck and Klopfer) are not genuine psychometric scores but a clinical shorthand (2687). This notation is dependent upon the subject's verbal skills which are inhibited or facilitated by social class bias (2440). Examiner judgment assesses the "goodness of fit" between a stimulus and a response mediated by verbal behavior (2854). Since the examiner's own behavior has directed and reinforced these responses (2516, 2619, 2676), the confounding in scores is apparent. The use of these nominal scale products as ordinal or ratio scales has further confused the validity issue. The presence of formal scores has endowed us with a convenient set of ready made variables which are often used instead of psychological thinking. Such scores are often isolated from theory and may not even be representative of the processes being studied (2444, 2955).

The purpose of these remarks is to outline a dilemma. We expose faith in the Rorschach and in our own clinical skills by continuing to use it in the face of strong professional admonitions to the contrary. We recognize that adequate use of the test is dependent upon the clinician; a function of training, experience, and unknown personality variables. Simultaneously, there is continual pressure to demonstrate that the test meets the usual psychometric criteria of objectivity, reliability, validity, additivity, scaling procedures, etc., which in fact it does not.

There is a recent and novel tendency to think about the meaning of the Rorschach task, to ask questions and find tentative answers within the context of theory (e.g., 2753). The vehicles are content categories and composite variables derived as deductions from theory or presented as ways of testing clinical hypotheses. Several kinds of modified scoring variables merit discussion.

Werner is responsible for general developmental theory which has stimulated Rorschach scores (2639). Distribution-free measures provide quantification for the genetic level of perceptual behavior and comparisons between normal and deviant patterns of perceptual activity. These scores are of known and adequate reliability (2560). These developmental indices are related to personality and behavior variables in a variety of studies (2255, 2274, 2590). While there remains doubt as to the diagnostic validity of these scores (2631), the meaning of particular responses (e.g., 2582 for M and 2955 for W), and of personality processes (e.g., cognitive function, 2888) has been enriched.

An elaborate and psychoanalytically derived method of scoring for primary and secondary process analysis has been developed as a research tool (2645). The emphasis is on primary process analysis of content in relatively sophisticated adults. Although reliability assessment is difficult, gross estimates of nominal and ordinal variables obtained with trained scorers are satisfactory. Goldberger (2779) has explored validation aspects of combined scores for adaptive and maladaptive regression. Cohen (2614) has studied artistic creativity in terms of primary process. Pine and Holt (2692) have evidence that expression and control of primary processes are independent. Sample differences appear to be relevant (2925). While the body of research using this system is still meager, the wealth of conceptually related data available in Rorschach records scored on these variables suggests that classical scoring variables are expendable.

Examples of highly specific scores occur in the work of McReynolds and Weide (2544, 2675) and Birch and Belmont (2752, 2853). The McReynolds J score from the Concept Evaluation Technique results from the number of agreements with suggested concepts for 50 blot areas. The J score apparently reflects rigor in habits of conceptualization and a low score is related to post lobotomy improvement. Levels of functioning in the response, inquiry, and testing-the-limits, may be distinguished (2752). Comparison of traditional and functional level scoring resulted in new information about the consequences of brain injury in left hemiplegic patients. Heath (*2420*) has made a plea for more highly structured stimuli and replication as antidote for the confounding of stimulus characteristics and the assumed manifest or latent stimulus meanings. His own Phrase Association Test for measuring defensive behavior is an example. These studies were selected to represent three degrees of alteration in administration, sources of scoring variables, or a substitute stimulus.

Personality study is stimulated by new scores developed from theory. Each new score gives us something else and not necessarily something new upon which to focus our awareness. As such these are exercises in sensitization similar to those offered by Zubin 25 years ago. The parameters of human complexity and human inventiveness provide wide limits for development of new scores. While the new scores lend hope that the Rorschach dilemma is resolvable, they are test-oriented solutions.

Somewhere in our hasty hope that nomothetic science would provide the empirical basis for Rorschach practice, we have overlooked the obvious. It is clinician and not test which enables personality study. In spite of our persistent attempts to convert the Rorschach into a psychometric instrument, we have failed. At best the test can provide an approximation of another person's reality, a framework for giving our hypotheses the possibility of being tested, and a consistent stimulus to minimize our own biases.

Indeed we have come to the end of an era: preoccupation with the Rorschach as a test. Perhaps the salient issue has been a wish to endow the Rorschach with respectability and a place of honor in psychometrica. This necessarily implies precedence of empirical over procedural evidence, a substitution of academic social sanctions for an understanding that requires neither replication nor statistics. We are limited in our tools for exploring man *qua* man; we do tend to rely on instruments less ambiguous and prone to folly and blind choice than ourselves. The Rorschachiana, empirical and otherwise, has confirmed some antique wisdom and provoked discard of legend about humanness. However, this has been a byproduct, largely of the construct validity studies, the most sustained systematic replication that the technique has undergone (*2870*).

The Rorschach is being replaced for three sensible reasons: (*a*) limited tests for particular measurement purposes can be given more than a semblance of psychometric purity; (*b*) the Holtzman inkblots have been constructed in such a manner that many of the psychometric cavils are met for more generalized personality study; (*c*) the aura of magic surrounding an unknown and miraculous instrument has been dispelled by empirical studies. In Masling's choice words (*2679*), the x-ray did become a mirror in which we confused our own image with those of test and subject. While there is no ready tranquilizer for our test-oriented anxiety, there is still hope for self-understanding among clinicians. Moreover, for the psychologist who accepts his own inner resources as the instrument for putting together the pieces of someone else's experience, the Rorschach will continue to be a convenient touchstone.

Leonard D. Eron, *Professor of Psychology, State University of Iowa, Iowa City, Iowa.*

This reviewer will not attempt to survey the voluminous Rorschach literature to date. Previous editions of the yearbook have contained such reviews and the monotonous overall conclusions have been that there is little evidence to support the claims made for the technique by its proponents. The results of research published subsequent to the last edition of the yearbook have not perceptibly altered this grim picture of the reliability and validity of the Rorschach procedure. Yet its use in clinical and educational settings continues unabated. Although it has been suggested that this persistence is nothing more than a demonstration of functional autonomy, it is this reviewer's opinion that the use of the Rorschach method persists because it is a useful tool in personality assessment and often can contribute to an understanding of the individual. At the very least, it is right more often than it is wrong. However, when it is right, it probably is so for the wrong reasons. Although this is unfortunate for those who have been trying to validate the traditional scoring systems, it very likely explains why the Rorschach method works in the clinic but not in research. There is no evidence, e.g., that color and shading responses *per se* have the significance for personality functioning traditionally assigned to them, and location of response has been consistently related to nothing. There is some slight evidence that human movement responses are an index to cognitive inhibition (*2196*) and the ability to inhibit motility (*1444*), although even these minimal claims have not uniformly been replicated (*2688*), and that indefiniteness and inaccuracy of form are indications of impulsivity and poor reality testing (*1257*). However, it is the content of the responses, devaluated by Rorschach himself and long neglected by his followers, that stands up as the lone aspect of the responses that has any stability and relates consistently to outside criteria. In this regard, whatever validity the human movement response and form accuracy have is very likely a function of content.

Rorschach and most of those who have come after him have regarded his procedure as a perceptual task. However, there is little reason to believe that telling an examiner what inkblots look like is a task essentially perceptual in nature. Even if it were, there is certainly no agreement among those doing research in perception that perception is indeed a function of personality. Thus, the so called perceptual determinants of the responses are largely irrelevant and it is as a conceptual task, with content taking its rightful place, that the Rorschach method should reasonably be evaluated. When it is so regarded, attempts at validation have been more successful, as will be noted in the following discussion.

It has been suggested by Zubin (*1826*) that the Rorschach is nothing more or less than a standard interview and should be treated as such by a systematic analysis of the content. In a forthcoming volume,[1] Zubin, Eron, and Schumer present a series of standard scales by which Rorschach responses can be evaluated. Previously, Zubin, Eron, and Sultan (*2155*), utilizing these scales, rated the records of 43 superior individuals and obtained very high interscorer reliability. However, they were also concerned with another kind of reliability which has to do with the subject's consistency of performance. It would be expected that if an individual perceives in Rorschach space the same way he perceives in real life space, then these characteristic habits of perception would consistently mark his performance. Thus, some degree of agreement should emerge when ratings on one half of an individual's responses are compared with ratings on the other half. Alternative responses were used to divide each of the protocols in half. The authors found that those scales which measured so called perceptual habits, e.g., use of color, form, texture, shading, etc., produced reliabilities so low as to indicate they revealed little that was consistently characteristic of the subjects. However, those scales which measured content factors and ways of thinking had such high reliabilities that they were obviously reflecting consistent trends in the subjects.

The superiority of content scoring in terms of various kinds of reliability has been corroborated by a number of other studies which have used both content and so called perceptual scoring. Ramzy and Pickard (*853*) obtained very high interscorer agreement on Beck's content categories but not on any other scores. Holzberg and Wexler (*966*), using 20 schizophrenic subjects, studied temporal reliability over a three-week period and found correlations for scores at the two different times ranging from −.17 to .95, with reliabilities for content categories, M, and F clustering around .70 and color and shading clustering around .30. Kagan (*2650*), reporting on the long term stability of Rorschach responses (subjects were 37 males and 38 females tested at ages 10, 13, 16, and finally at 35), found only number of responses, human movement, and content showing statistically significant stability.

Since perceptual scoring reveals little that is consistently characteristic of individuals, while content scoring does, it can be concluded that the content of the protocols and not the so called perceptual factors is the basis for whatever success the Rorschach has achieved. However, more is meant by content scoring than Rorschach's simple classification of responses into animal, human, object, etc. Emphasis has often been laid on the dynamic or psychoanalytic aspects of the response and its symbolic referent (*981, 1787, 2051, 2645*). For example, Schafer's volume (*1787*) is devoted mostly to an examination of the total Rorschach situation from a psychoanalytic point of view. The

1 ZUBIN, JOSEPH; ERON, LEONARD D.; AND SCHUMER, FLORENCE. *An Experimental Approach to Projective Techniques.* New York: John Wiley & Sons, Inc. Scheduled for publication in 1965.

principles, rules of thumb, and skills presented here are based largely on insightful, undoubtedly wise but not necessarily public procedures, since they are derived almost entirely from the author's own clinical experience. In his chapter on thematic analyses, Schafer illustrates his psychoanalytic method of thematic (content) analysis. He cautions the clinician that it is important not to be too "wild" with interpretations which always should be corroborated by turning to other tests to see if the themes recur. The general methods of content analysis which Schafer proposes may be extremely helpful clinically, but they await validation through more advanced methodological and theoretical developments than are now available. Fisher and Cleveland (*2409*) have developed a content scoring system from a different theoretical point of view, based on constructs relating to body image. Responses may have vulnerable boundaries (scored P-penetration) or nonvulnerable boundaries (scored B-barriers) and this dichotomy is purportedly related to attitudes and feelings the subject has about his own body. These attitudes in turn, it is claimed, reflect personality and diagnostic groupings.

However, in analyzing Rorschach responses in terms of nonperceptual factors, it is not necessary to delve into the symbolic significance of each utterance in order to derive meaningful material for personality description. The subject's verbal productions can be placed into such categories as compulsive thinking, disorganized thinking, or creative thinking; poverty of ideas or fluency; confabulation or clarity; rigidity or flexibility; perplexity or straightforwardness; rejection or compliance. The scales noted above which have been developed by Zubin and his students cover many aspects of the response which are not regarded as perceptual in nature but which tap the quality of the subject's verbalizations and interpretive attitudes. If the Rorschach situation is conceived of as an interview in which the subject is presented with a novel, but standardized, problem solving task, it can be seen that there are many facets of his behavior which can be assessed in a meaningful way for personality interpretation. For example, reliable scales have been developed to assess attitudinal factors (dominance, evaluative attitude, mood, self reference, dehumanization) and thinking processes (perseveration, elaboration, congruity, communality, definiteness of concept, distance in time and space). It is these attitudes and characteristics of thought which indicate, for example, whether the subject is schizophrenic or normal, just in the same way that the clinical interview might reveal these factors. The advantage of the Rorschach inheres in the fact that it is a standard interview providing a systematic framework for eliciting psychopathological trends. Furthermore, it may elicit these trends in patients who are otherwise not communicative. The inclusive quality of the scales which have been mentioned, in addition to the fact that their reliability and validity are open to public inspection and use, contrast this approach to that utilized by psychoanalytically oriented workers who are concerned with what they claim to be more clinically meaningful and provocative schemes.

Validity studies using content-oriented scoring schemes have met with more success than the standard Rorschach study. McCall (*1152*), using the Zubin scales, found that psychometrically weighted nonperceptual categories having to do with verbalization of content and thought process related significantly to outcome in psychosurgery, either pre or post operatively or both. The ascendance-submission scale was the most sensitive, although no rationale was provided to explain why those destined for eventual improvement showed a consistent tendency to see more submissive human figures in the Rorschach cards. In the same evaluation of psychosurgery (*2300*), researchers utilizing these scales found quantitative relationships with anxiety, e.g., the number of movement responses rose and fell with anxiety level (as judged both by a psychiatrist and on the basis of psychological interviewing using anchored scaling devices). The degree of tentativeness or insecurity in giving responses also correlated positively with these ratings of anxiety.

Sen (*1030*) administered the Rorschach to 100 Indian students who had been living together in England for two years and who also evaluated each other's personalities. The correlations between these evaluations and Beck's scores were nonsignificant. However, when scored for content the correlations ranged from .57 to .66. Sandler and Ackner (*1184*) factor analyzed the content scores of 50 psychiatric patients. Four factors were obtained whose psychological meaningfulness was ascertained by correlating them with personality evaluations on the basis of psychiatric interview and case history methods. The productivity factor (R) was related to previous productivity in life, to chronicity of symptoms, and to a schizo-affective picture at the time of hospitalization. The anatomy factor was related to an insecure, withdrawn, "previous" personality picture, bad physical health, and an emotional deluded state for the present symptoms. The remaining factors were analyzed in similar fashion.

Watkins and Staufacher (*1461*) provided a series of quantitative indices of deviant verbalizations based on the content of protocols (derived from Rapaport's 13 types of deviant Rorschach responses), and found that such indicators had a reliability of .77 between two raters and that these indices distinguished normals from neurotics and the latter from schizophrenics. Powers and Hamlin (*2283*) replicated this work and further refined Rapaport's deviant response types into four large classes: intellectual disorganization, inappropriate increase or loss of distance, deviant content, and affective response. All four classes could be reliably scored but the first two proved to be the most differentiating. Bower, Testin, and Roberts (*2609*) have developed an extensive series of scales which tap content and thought processes as reflected in Rorschach protocols. These scales were empirically weighted to result in maximum discriminatory power. Although some promising trends were found, further refinement of the scales and cross validation on a new population must be awaited before any overall evaluation of this research can be made.

Elizur (*799*) found that an analysis of content in relation to anxiety and hostility yielded significant interscorer and split-half reliabilities and also related significantly to self ratings as well as ratings made by three judges on the basis of observation of a 45-minute semistructured interview. On the whole, evidence for the validity of Elizur's RCT, obtained in studies by other investigators, has been positive when applied to the records of undergraduates (*1639*), NP patients (*1883*), and adolescents (*1348*), but not so successful when used with children (*2808*).

Rader's (*2214*) results in trying to predict overt aggressive verbal behavior from Rorschach content, analyzed by an expanded version of the Elizur method, were more equivocal. His subjects were 38 state prison inmates and his criterion was behavior in therapeutic discussion groups. He found that aggressive content, especially mutilation, was significantly, positively related to aggressive behavior (primarily verbal) although the correlations were not high enough to be used in individual prediction. Towbin (*2586*) also found a significant, positive correlation between assaultive behavior on a VA neuropsychiatric ward and two measures of aggression based on the content of the Rorschach record, one having to do with aggressive comments directed toward the card and one with the actual concepts seen.

Although anxiety and aggression are the primary variables for which content scoring systems have been developed, other variables have also been the object of this type of analysis. DeVos (*1330*) developed a system of scoring Rorschach content for dependency which has been somewhat simplified by Levitt, Lubin, and Zuckerman (*2904*). The latter scheme proved quite reliable even when the scoring was done by non-expert judges and some evidence for construct validity was derived from two replications of a study which showed that dependency scores for volunteers for a hypnosis experiment were significantly greater than for non-volunteers. However, a concurrent measure of validity, relationship of dependency scores to peer ratings of dependency, was less successful (*2846*). Rychlak and Guinouard (*2704*) confirmed their hypothesis, using the Harrower Group Rorschach, that certain limited measures of content (whether human, animal, kind of interaction, or extent of tension indicated) would be related to independent measures of personality (*IPAT High School Personality Questionnaire*) and popularity (sociometric choice). The results of these studies dealing with content and description of thought process are impressive when viewed against the uniformly negative research findings with determinant scores.

In general, Rorschach validation has been directed toward relating either the individual scores or global impressions and holistic configurations to outside criteria. As indicated above, attempts at validating the so called perceptual scores have been almost wholly unsuccessful while correlation of overall impressions of the Rorschach records with ratings, case histories, and behavioral criteria has by and large met with more success. Zamansky and Goldman (*2735*), for example, have shown that global Rorschach evaluations were much better indicators of actual changes in ward social adjustment (ratings made after completion of various ancillary therapies with a group of male and female hospitalized psychotics) than were 11 quantitative Rorschach indices. Crumpton (*2032*), in a study of signs of color shock, has shown that although statistical use of the usual signs failed to discriminate records based on an achromatic and a chromatic (standard) Rorschach series in which the judges did not know on which series the records were based, the use of clinical, global ratings of the protocols did result in a statistically significant, valid differentiation of the records.

Corsini, Severson, Tunney, and Uehling (*1858*) explored the relative validity of a Rorschach checklist (*928*), and judgments of clinicians in separating "normal" and "abnormal" Rorschach protocols. The normal records were obtained from 50 prison guards, and the abnormal records were obtained from a group of 50 prisoners who had not only committed serious felonies, but had been referred for testing because of a possibility of having "serious personality deviations." All identifying data had been removed from the Rorschach protocols, and prisoners and guards were matched, as far as possible, for age. Inmates of average intelligence and lower middle class status only were used. Subjects were all white. Four psychologists were asked to rank all protocols, from 1 to 100, in terms of adjustment of the subject. Reliability of rankings (interjudge comparisons) was of a relatively low order. But comparison of number of normal protocols placed in the top half of the rankings by the Davidson Rorschach Adjustment Scale and by each of the judges, yielded the finding that global judgments were more accurate. Time spent in the judging process was shown to be positively related to the accuracy of the ranking, it might be noted. The findings do indeed suggest that global, clinical methods are more successful than mechanical checklists, in terms of "separation capacity," but a question should be raised as to whether or not either of these methods could have effectively separated a more meaningful, better matched group—prisoners with and without "serious personality deviations." Language, content, and general approach to the Rorschach situation might well differ sufficiently between guards and prisoners to yield definite clues, independent of Rorschach scoring itself, as to which subject is likely to come from which group.

Although the relative superiority of global impressions of the Rorschach record over the use of individual scores lends support to the notion that the Rorschach is best evaluated as an interview, it should be pointed out that the record of success even with global evaluations is not totally encouraging and until we find out the basis on which the global evaluations are made, we are no further ahead scientifically or in the ability to teach the technique to others.

Another indication that the Rorschach method is best considered a more or less standardized interview is the accumulated information concerning the examiner-subject interaction (*1786, 2740*). The quantity and quality of responses elicited by the inkblots are affected to a measurable degree by the individual characteristics and overt behavior of the administrator. The effect of the examiner is further complicated by the purpose of the subject in taking the test. Is he there by order of the court? Is he trying to get a discharge from the army or compensation for injuries? Is he an applicant to a medical school or a junior executive looking for a promotion? Is he an introductory psychology student picking up extra credits by being a subject for a graduate student's experiment? What are the reasons given to the subject by the examiner for taking the test; what are the subject's preconceptions about the procedure and what is his cover story?

Early studies were directed toward showing that when large samples of protocols obtained by different examiners from similar populations were compared, many more differences in scoring categories than could reasonably be expected by chance were found among the examiners even though the same scoring system was used by all (*1079, 1224, 1525*). Some examiners consistently had more of one kind of response than others. It was apparent that it was necessary to look at the examiners' behavior to determine what accounted for these consistent differences. Later studies indicated that the differences could be explained by variations in instructions given by the examiner (*968, 1111, 2311*); by the sets with which the subjects were provided, whether deliberately or not (*916, 1067, 2050, 2070, 2298, 2619*); by the specific but often subtle reinforcing behaviors of the examiner (*2145, 2516, 2676*); by whether he and the subjects were male or female (*1096, 1767, 1871*); by the difference between them in social class and ethnic group (*2440*); and by the examiner's warmth and friendliness or lack thereof (*1567*). It has been demonstrated that despite instructions to the examiner that he behave otherwise, his basic personality, as judged by others, whether warm and permissive or cold and authoritarian, comes through and affects the response (*982*). Overt and covert hostility and anxiety of the examiner, as independently rated by others, are also related to specific patterns of scores obtained by the subjects (1606).

Of all parts of the Rorschach it would seem that it is in the inquiry that the examiner can most directly influence the ultimate scoring of the response. A number of investigators have been concerned about the lack of standard procedure in the inquiry and have demonstrated its effect on the scoring of the responses (*1344, 2483, 2738*). Baughman (*2394*) has suggested a method which he claims achieves more precision and standardization in the inquiry. Essentially it is a paired comparison technique in which the subject is asked to contrast the standard card with six types of modified cards, identical in form to the Rorschach, but systematically varying in color, shading, figure-ground contrast, and complexity of form. By use of a series of standard questions the examiner can determine precisely the influence and relevance of color, shading, etc.

Although his technique has been criticized for being unwieldy and time consuming, the modifications Baughman has introduced seem to represent considerable improvement over standard inquiry procedure. The question of the validity of the scores themselves, however, remains pertinent, with or without the use of Baughman's method. As a case in point, Baughman has indicated that the paired comparison technique should produce significantly more shading responses when the standard and modified inquiries are compared, suggesting the technique affords greater opportunity for more valid, as well as more reliable, indicators of determinants to emerge. However, Waller (*2730*) found that, although the number of shading responses did indeed increase with the modified inquiry, there was no improvement in prediction to three independent measures of anxiety. It would seem that no matter how refined and reliable the measures of shading become, relations to outside criteria won't improve because, as mentioned before, it's neither shading nor texture nor achromatic color but the content that is the most likely aspect of the response that is significant for personality.

The majority of studies cited here present unmistakable evidence of the fact that situational and interpersonal variables influence responses to the Rorschach procedure, thus reinforcing the view that the Rorschach best be analyzed as an interview situation in which the test response and the accompanying behavior of both the examiner and the subject must always be interpreted in the light of the total situation. Because the Rorschach response is susceptible to these influences and is not the foolproof x-ray it was once claimed to be, does not mean it has no value in assessment. These influences are not always sources of error; they can indicate the way the subject—as well as the examiner—approaches a novel problem solving task and how he adapts to it. These behaviors, along with the content produced in the record, are subject to the most rigorous scrutiny. The Zubin scales provide a framework for such an evaluation of the Rorschach. The recommended approach requires a shift in emphasis from the perceptual to the thought content aspects of the Rorschach. It is indeed true that Hermann Rorschach himself turned away from the content of the subject's responses and advocated a perceptual analysis. He stated that the content of the responses yielded little insight into the content of the personality; but he may have been wrong. Or he may have defined content too narrowly. If content is defined as an essential element of the protocol, including verbalization of thought processes and problem solving behavior, and the Rorschach record is treated like any other interview material, the mystery surrounding the expert's interpretation may yet yield to scientific scrutiny, since it is a moot question whether Rorschach experts do not indeed derive most of their insights into personality from a direct or indirect analysis of content and the interaction of the subject with the examiner.

ARTHUR R. JENSEN, *Associate Professor of Educational Psychology, and Associate Research Psychologist, Institute of Human Learning, University of California, Berkeley, California.*

In the 43 years since Hermann Rorschach published the *Psychodiagnostik,* his set of ten carefully chosen inkblots has become the most popular of all psychological tests. A recent survey [1] of hospitals, clinics, guidance centers, and the like, indicates that the Rorschach clearly outstrips all its competitors, both in the number of institutions using the test and in the amount of usage. Furthermore, the curve depicting the increase in popularity of the Rorschach over the past decade is positively accelerated. On the basis of Sundberg's survey we can safely estimate that, at the very least, the Rorschach is administered to a million persons a year in the United States; it consumes on the average approximately five million clinical man-hours (which is 571 years), at a total cost to the clients of approximately 25 million dollars. Thus, in terms of usage the Rorschach is easily the Number One psychological instrument. It has become as closely identified with the clinical psychologist as the stethoscope is with the physician.

The amount of research and publication on the Rorschach is even more impressive. On this count no other test equals it. Over the past decade it has inspired on the average not fewer than three publications per week in the United States alone. The rate of Rorschach publication, also, is positively accelerated. The Rorschach bibliography has already passed 3000.

Of course, it is too much to expect any one person to review and assess in its totality any phenomenon of such fabulous proportions as the Rorschach. *The Fifth Mental Measurements Yearbook* presented very thorough and comprehensive reviews of the most important Rorschach research up to that time, and the conclusions arrived at by these reviewers are highly representative of the assessments made of the Rorschach in psychological textbooks reviewing much the same material. Put frankly, the consensus of qualified judgment is that the Rorschach is a very poor test and has no practical worth for any of the purposes for which it is recommended by its devotees.

To make his task manageable, the present reviewer has decided to focus attention on the Rorschach literature appearing since *The Fifth Mental Measurements Yearbook,* to determine the degree to which recent research has turned up anything that might in some way alter the negative judgments arrived at by earlier reviewers. Much of the early research on the Rorschach has often been criticized for methodological and statistical inadequacy, but this fortunately can no longer be said of the recent research published in the leading psychological journals. There are now a number of methodologically and statistically sound and sophisticated studies. Even more important, in terms of doing full justice to the Rorschach, is that the good research is now being done by the Rorschachers and projective test experts themselves, often with the full cooperation of their clinical colleagues who are highly experienced in the use of projective techniques. No longer can it be claimed that negative findings are the result of bluenose methodologists of statistics and experimental psychology applying inappropriate criteria to an instrument for which they have no sympathy, no clinical experience, no intuitive feeling, and no talent.

Detailed reviews of recent Rorschach research have been made by Heiman and Rothney (*2520*) and by Ricciuti (*2929*). A book edited by Rickers-Ovsiankina (*2699*) is probably the most important publication in the field in the past several years and contains excellent discussions of Rorschach research by a number of prominent psychologists in the fields of projective techniques, clinical psychology, and personality research. The reader is also referred to the *Annual Review of Psychology* for coverage of the most important contributions; the review by Gleser (*2974*) is especially worthwhile.

RORSCHACH TRAINING. The Rorschach is not just another test which the clinician can learn to use by reading a manual. It is a whole culture, the full acquisition of which depends upon intensive tutorial training, a great deal

1 SUNDBERG, NORMAN D. "The Practice of Psychological Testing in Clinical Services in the United States." *Am Psychologist* 16:79–83 F '61. *

of clinical experience with projective materials, a certain degree of dedicated discipleship, and, perhaps most difficult of all, acclimatization to an atmosphere that is philosophically quite alien to the orientation of modern psychology as it is now taught in the leading American and British universities. In addition, the would-be Rorschacher, if he is to hold his own among the experts, must possess a kind of gift similar to the literary talent of a novelist or biographer, combining a perceptive and intuitive sensitivity to human qualities and the power to express these perceptions in subtle, varied, and complex ways. The Rorschach report of an expert is, if nothing else, a literary work of art. This is the chief criterion of expertness with the Rorschach, for the research has not revealed any significant differences in reliability or validity between beginners in the Rorschach technique and acknowledged masters.

Qualified Rorschachers generally have had at least three semesters, the equivalent of a year and a half, of intensive training in the use of the Rorschach. The first semester is usually devoted merely to learning how to score the test, while the second and third semesters are devoted to interpretation. As is typical of most textbooks on the Rorschach, there is little or no reference to the research literature in most traditional Rorschach courses. At least 100 tests must be administered, scored, and interpreted under the close supervision of an expert before the novice is considered sufficiently qualified to be left on his own. Unfortunately, many clinicians, and especially school psychologists, who use the Rorschach in their daily clinical practice are inadequately trained, with the consequence that their reports have a stereotyped, cookbook quality which can add nothing of clinical value to the understanding of the patient and can often be injudiciously misleading or even harmful. It is the reviewer's impression from reading many psychological reports based on the Rorschach that the acknowledged experts are usually more cautious and wise in their use of the instrument than are clinicians who have had relatively meager training or who are self-taught.

USES OF THE RORSCHACH. The technique has been used with all age levels in clinics, guidance centers, hospitals, schools, and in industry, to assess, diagnose, and describe every aspect of the human personality—cognitive, emotional, and motivational—in both normal and psychiatric subjects. In tabulating the types of interpretive statements made from a single Rorschach protocol (analyzed by Klopfer), Shneidman (*2361*) concluded that the Rorschach concentrates on the areas of affect, diagnosis, quality of perception, ego capacity, personality mechanisms, sexual thought, and psychosexual level. One is impressed after reading a large number of Rorschach reports that no facet of the human psyche and no aspect of human feeling or behavior is inaccessible to the Rorschach. Certainly it excels all other psychological tests in permitting a richness of personality description that comprehends the entire lexicon of human characteristics. It has even been used to attempt to differentiate children with defective hearing from those with normal hearing (*2520*). Its chief use, however, remains that of aiding in the formulation of psychiatric diagnosis and prognosis.

The Rorschach has also been used, with questionable success, as a research tool in the investigation of personality and in anthropological and cross-cultural studies. Its contributions in the personality realm have been evaluated by Gardner and Lois Murphy (*2686*), and Lindzey (*2805*) has written a comprehensive review of its use in cross-cultural research. Neither the Murphys nor Lindzey credits the Rorschach with substantial contributions to research in these fields.

ADMINISTRATION AND SCORING. The test materials have not changed in 43 years; they are the same 10, bilaterally symmetrical blots originated by Rorschach. The Rorschach culture apparently has assumed that these 10 blots cannot be improved upon and that they alone are a sufficient foundation for building a science of personality diagnosis. The great orthodoxy and appeal to authority in the Rorschach culture is reflected also in the scoring procedures which have changed in only minor details from the method originally laid down by Rorschach.

Incidentally, if the color in the five chromatic blots plays as important a role as the Rorschachers claim for it, then note should be taken of the fact that different editions of the blots differ in color, some being more vivid and others more pastel.

The test takes approximately 45 to 60 minutes to administer, depending upon the productivity of the subject and the thoroughness of the examiner's inquiry and testing of the limits. The procedures are described in detail in all the Rorschach textbooks and are matters on which authorities differ very little.

The scoring of the subject's responses, which generally number between 10 and 30, is a highly technical procedure requiring many hours of practice before it becomes an easy task. The several different scoring systems currently in use are all basically much alike, and once having learned one it is easy to adopt another. The systems of Rorschach and Binder, Rapaport and Schafer, Beck, Piotrowski, Hertz, and Klopfer have been systematically compared in the last chapter of the volume edited by Rickers-Ovsiankina (*2724*).

RORSCHACH INTERPRETATION. Many elements enter into interpretation. First there are the formal scores, which are generally interpreted in terms of configurations or combinations with other Rorschach scores. Textbooks on interpretation are seldom explicit or precise concerning the quantitative aspects of the Rorschach scores and indices, although the language of the discussion clearly implies quantitative considerations. Reference is made to "a lot of shading responses," "a high M per cent," "long reaction time," "many CF responses," and so on. The exact quantity is rarely specified. Examiners must have had experience with at least 100 protocols before developing some subjective notion of the "norms" of the various scores. There are, however, published norms (e.g., *1300, 1651, 2475*), but these are seldom referred to by clinicians, and the leading textbooks on Rorschach interpretation make no use of them. Almost every page of the long-awaited and important book on Rorschach interpretation by Piotrowski (*2211*) contains typical examples of the interpretations connected with various scores. For example: "There is something uncompromising, inflexible, and daring about those subjects who give *c'*R (dark shading responses). By contrast, the individual with many *c*R (light shading responses) prefers to sacrifice....his important goals of external achievement in order to appear less competitive and assertive to the world. If necessary, he surrenders part of his personality rather than antagonize others." These elaborate and subtle interpretations of Rorschach scores are totally unsupported by any kind of research evidence.

But much more than the formal scores enters into the interpretation. The subject's language, the content of his responses, the particular sequence of his responses, his reaction time to each card, the way he handles the cards and turns the cards, every aspect of his behavior during the testing—all are grist for the interpretive mill which grinds extremely fine. The full flavor of this art can be savoured from a number of published Rorschach reports by masters of the technique. The thinking that enters into the interpretation is clearly delineated by Schafer in his excellent text (*1787*) and in the detailed case analysis presented in the textbook by Phillips and Smith (*1588*). A highly professional report by Stephanie Dudek, typical of the productions of the most skilled Rorschachers, is to be found in Appendix A of the book by Symonds and Jensen (*2836*). It is evident that nothing in the Rorschach protocol or in the subject's behavior during the testing is regarded as "noise" in the system—everything is considered significant and interpretable. And the final report of an expert, in its wealth of detail, its subtlety of personality description, breadth of comprehension, and depth of penetration, can often rival the most elaborate characterizations of Marcel Proust or Henry James.

Aside from considerations of reliability and validity, a question must be asked concerning the semantics of the Rorschach report itself. How unambiguously meaningful is the interpretation to a number of different persons reading the final report? Little is factually known about this. It could well be that the Rorschach report is itself projective material for the person to whom the report is referred, serving mainly to bolster his confidence in his own interpretations derived from other sources. The real question is, how much can the report *add* to the psychiatrist's understanding of his patient gained through other means, even assuming it is valid? This we do not know, but the question becomes wholly academic when we take account of the known reliability and validity of Rorschach interpretation.

RELIABILITY. Few other tests provide so many opportunities for the multiplication of error variance as does the Rorschach. We must consider separately the reliability of scoring and of interpretation, the stability of these in time, the internal consistency of scores, and the effect of the interaction of examiners and subjects.

First, it must be pointed out that most of the traditional Rorschach scores have two strikes against them from a psychometric standpoint. In the typical protocol, most of the scoring categories are used relatively infrequently so that their reliability is practically indeterminate. For example, the average frequencies of various Rorschach scores in a sample of 28 nonpsychiatric subjects (*2836*) is Dd = 1.0, S = 0.3, M = 2.9, k = 0.2, K = 0.1, FK = 0.6, FC = 0.9, C = 0.2. The only really large frequencies are R (number of responses) = 22.1, D (large detail) = 12.1, W (whole responses) = 8.0, and F (form) = 7.5. The distributions of these scores are generally very skewed, and the small amount of variation that occurs among the majority of subjects easily falls within the standard error of measurement for most of the scores. By all criteria R (number of responses) has the highest reliability of any of the scores, and by virtue of this it spuriously inflates the reliability of the various index scores into which it enters, such as M%, F%, W%, etc. Most of the combinational scores from the Rorschach, consisting of ratios and differences among the various primary scores, are, of course, even more unsusceptible to a satisfactory demonstration of reliability than are the primary scores.

Another question that is seldom asked is whether the scoring categories themselves have any particular meaning or uniqueness in a psychological sense. That is, are the various movement responses, shading responses, color responses, texture responses, or content of the responses measuring some common factor more or less peculiar to these particular classes of determinants? Factor analyses of the scores indicate that the underlying factors do not coincide at all well with the traditional scoring categories (e.g., *1058*). Correlations between the various movement responses (M, FM, m) on the Rorschach, Behn-Rorschach, and Levy Movement Cards are in the range from .12 to .41 (*2281*), so that if the tendency to perceive movement in ambiguous figures is an important and stable characteristic of individuals, as Rorschach theory would have us believe, it is apparent that the Rorschach is unable to demonstrate reliable individual differences in this trait. That is to say, various M responses seem to be highly stimulus-specific. The various color scoring categories have been brought even more seriously into question by experiments using totally achromatic reproductions of the Rorschach blots. In a review of this research Baughman concluded that "color has little or no effect upon a subject's behavior to the extent that his behavior is represented by the psychogram or similar scoring scales" (*2251*). The 25 studies of this type reviewed by Baughman lead to the conclusion that "the form or shape of the blot is the only relevant dimension. Certainly color does not appear to affect behavior very much, and if color is ineffective shading seems even less likely to be a significant variable." In view of this, how meaningful is an index such as the very important M:sum C ratio, which is said to indicate the subject's "experience-type" measured along the dimension of "introversive-extratensive"? The literature on experience-type is reviewed by Singer (*2716*), who concludes that after 40 years of the Rorschach nothing yet is known concerning the psychometric or statistical characteristics of the very central experience balance ratio of M:sum C.

A word of caution concerning improper estimates of Rorschach reliability: these often consist of reporting the *percentage of agreement* between two or more judges. It should be clear that percentage agreement is not a legitimate measure of reliability and tells us none of the things we want to know when we ask about the reliability of a test. What we want to know is the proportion of variance in the scores that is not error variance. The reliability coefficient tells us this; the percentage agreement does not. The latter measure can often be misleading and should always be discounted as an index of reliability unless other crucial information is also provided. Take the following fictitious example, in which two judges independently sort a sample of 500 protocols in terms of the presence or absence of indicators of a particular syndrome. The judges agree on presence in 491 protocols and on absence in one protocol. The eight on which they disagree are evenly divided into agree-disagree and disagree-agree categories. This percentage agreement is 98 per cent—impressively high. When reliability is obtained in the proper way, however, by determining the correlation between the two judges, the reliability coefficient turns out to be only .19.

The present reviewer has presented a detailed discussion of the reliability of Rorschach scores elsewhere (*2524*), and a more recent consideration of the whole reliability problem has been presented by Holzberg (*2646*). Some of the conclusions may be summarized briefly:

Scoring reliability per se has been determined very seldom. The few instances reported in the literature constitute the highest reliabilities to be found for any aspect of the Rorschach. Reliability of scoring depends to a large extent upon the degree of similarity of the training of the scorers and has been reported as ranging from .64 to .91.

Split-half reliability has always been frowned upon by Rorschachers as inappropriate. Nevertheless, split-half estimates have yielded comparatively high reliabilities, ranging in one study (*16, 17*) from .33 (F+%) to .91 (R), with an average reliability coefficient of .54 (corrected by the Spearman-Brown formula). In another study (*21*) an odd-even split of the cards for 100 subjects yielded an average reliability for 20 Rorschach scores of .83, with a range from .67 to .97.

Test-retest reliability ranges from about .10 to about .90, depending largely upon the test-retest interval and the particular score. For a two-weeks interval the reliabilities of various scores range between .60 and .80 (*2254*). The most extensive determination of retest reliability is that of Epstein and others (*2179*), who gave the Rorschach to 16 college students a total of 10 times over a period of five weeks. The average reliabilities for various response categories ranged from .20 to .56.

Parallel forms reliability has been determined by use of the Behn-Rorschach, a set of similar blots which seem to meet all the psychometric criteria for qualifying as an equivalent form of the Rorschach. For 35 scoring categories the means and standard deviations of the Behn and the Rorschach do not differ significantly in normal and psychiatric populations and the two forms seem to correlate as highly with each other as each correlates with itself. The correlations for various scores range from about zero to .86, with a mean around .60.

Examiner and situational influences have been increasingly recognized in recent research as significant contributors to the variance of Rorschach scores (e.g., *982, 1079, 1525, 1606, 2050*). The subject-examiner interaction is certainly one of the most important aspects of the test. The effect of the setting in which the test is taken and the fact that different examiners consistently elicit different amounts of various scored determinants from subjects should make it imperative that future Rorschach studies be based upon a representative sampling of examiners as well as of subjects.

Reliability of interpretation is, of course, the most important matter of all. It may be stated as a general principle that the most crucial reliability is that of the end product of the test, which, in the case of the Rorschach, usually consists of a verbal description of personality characteristics based on a global evaluation of all aspects of the subject's protocol. Contrary to the usual claim of Rorschachers that this global interpretation is more reliable or more valid than any of the elements on which it is based, such as the scores and the various derived combinations and indices, a systematic search of the literature has not turned up a single instance where the overall interpretation was more reliable than the separate elements entering into it. Rorschach textbooks have not presented any evidence of satisfactory reliability of the final product of the test and the reviewer has not been able to find any such evidence in the research literature.

Here are some typical examples of what has been found. Lisanksy (*2074*) had six highly qualified Rorschachers rate 40 subjects on 10 personality items which they agreed could be confidently assessed from the Rorschach protocol. To make the experiment similar to clinical conditions the Rorschachers were provided also with an abstract of each patient's history. The degree of agreement between the judges was measured by the phi coefficient, which averaged .33. Six other clinicians rated the same traits on the basis of the case history abstracts alone, with an average phi of .31, which is not significantly different from the reliability of the clinicians who were aided by the Rorschach. The interesting point is that the 10 rated personality items were specially selected as being the kinds of questions which the Rorschach, and not particularly the case history, is supposed to be able to answer.

Korner and Westwood (*1913*) had three clinical psychologists, qualified in the use of the Rorschach, sort the protocols of 96 college freshmen into three categories for level of personality adjustment. The average correlation among the three judges was .31.

Datel and Gengerelli (*1863*) found that when 27 Rorschachers were required to match personality interpretations written by each other on the basis of the protocols of six subjects (presented for matching in sets of six), there were more mismatchings than correct matchings. Of the total of 324 discrete matchings, 148 were correct and 176 incorrect. Despite the fact that the subjects from whom the protocols were obtained differed greatly from one another in nosology, etc., the average reliability for the individual clinicians was not significantly greater than zero.

The most careful and methodologically sophisticated study of Rorschach reliability and validity has been carried out by two leading projective test experts, Little and Shneidman (*2537*). The editors of the *Journal of Projective Techniques* chose 12 distinguished Rorschach experts—all eminent teachers and writers in this field—to participate in the study. Rorschach protocols were obtained from 12 patients, three each from the psychotic, neurotic, psychosomatic, and psychiatrically normal diagnostic categories. The Rorschach judges were each provided with one protocol from each of the four categories and asked to perform the following interpretive tasks: assign diagnostic labels, rate the subject for personality adjustment (on a scale from 0 to 8), answer 100 true-false factual items taken from the case histories of the subjects, answer 117 true-false personality items typical of those contained in psychological reports, and perform a Q-sort of 76 items typical of the kinds of statements made in Rorschach interpretations. The reliability estimate of the diagnostic labeling consisted of having four other judges rate degree of similarity of diagnosis among pairs of the Rorschach judges on a 6-point scale (0–5). The mean rating among all the Rorschach judges was 2.50, which led the authors to conclude that "diagnostic labels based upon blind analyses of protocols may be quite wide of the mark and the present analysis indicates that the judges may not be even shooting at the same target." The method of treating the ratings of maladjustment makes it difficult to obtain an estimate of interrater reliability, but it is interesting that the nonpsychiatric patients were rated as considerably more pathological on the basis of their Rorschachs (as well as on three other clinical tests of personality) than when they were rated solely on the basis of anamnestic data. This tendency for Rorschach interpretations to be excessively biased toward the pathological has been well known from earlier studies; a good illustration of the tendency may be found in the Rorschach analyses of 28 nonpsychiatric subjects reported in great detail by Symonds and Jensen (*2836*). The true-false factual and personality items were correlated with outside criteria and therefore will be discussed in the section on validity. The Q-sort yielded the most easily interpretable index of inter-judge reliability. The correlations between the judges' Q-sorts for the 12 patients range from −.13 to .64, with a mean of .31. It is instructive to note that when the Q-sorts of each set of four subjects rated by the same judge are intercorrelated, the mean correlation is .27, which is not significantly different from the *inter*-judge reliability of .31. In other words, at least as much of the variance in Rorschach interpretations is attributable to differences among the interpreters as to differences among the subjects. Little and Shneidman concluded, "Test interpreters tend to make their interpretations in a stereotyped manner independent of the subject."

How well did each interpreter agree with himself? To find out, the investigators had the judges perform the same interpretive tasks on the same protocols just 10 days later and intercorrelated the ratings of the first occasion with those of the second. Only those results which can be reported in terms of a correlation coefficient are reported here. For the factual true-false items the average correlation is .74; for the personality true-false items the mean correlation is .77; for the Q-sorts the correlations range from .26 to .81, with a mean of .61.

Silverman (*2575*) carried out a somewhat more detailed study of Rorschach reliability and validity, using the Q-sort. The judges were selected in terms of amount of training and clinical experience with projective techniques, including the Rorschach. There were 10 noted projective test experts, 10 clinicians with 5 to 8 years of experience in projective testing, and 10 clinicians with fewer than three years of experience in projective testing. The Rorschach, TAT, H-T-P, and the Most Unpleasant Concept test were obtained from 10 adult males undergoing psychotherapy. There were six separate Q-sorts for different areas of interpretation. The 180 Q-sort items were typical of the statements found in Rorschach and projective reports. The reliabilities, as estimated from the correlations among the Q-sorts, were: defenses = .27, motivating needs and affects = .25, character traits = .44, diagnosis and symptoms = .44, interpersonal behavior = .21. The overall reliability was .34. The degree of reliability was unrelated to the amount of experience of the judges: there was no higher agreement among the most experienced clinicians than among the least experienced.

One recent study (*2891*) strongly stacked the cards in favor of maximizing the reliability by selecting seven clinicians who had very similar orientations toward the use and interpretation of psychological tests and 10 subjects who were very heterogeneous in pathology. The clinicians' task was to rank 10 psychological needs as to their relative importance for each of the 10 subjects. The interrater reliability was .12. (When the same task was performed with the TAT and a sentence completion test, the reliabilities were .14 and .30, respectively.)

VALIDITY. Considering the reliability of the Rorschach, its poor validity would seem to be a foregone conclusion. However, though it is axiomatic in psychometric theory that the validity of a test cannot be higher than the square root of its reliability, it has often been claimed that the Rorschach (as well as other projective tests) is exempt from this general rule. Therefore a study of the evidence for the validity of the Rorschach might be worthwhile.

Guilford (*2518*) succinctly reviewed the status of Rorschach validity up to 1959 and came to the following conclusions:

> In spite of the widespread popularity and use of the Rorschach ink blots, the reliabilities of scores tend to be relatively low, and validities, although quite varied, are generally near zero. This statement regarding validity applies to use of the instrument in discriminating pathological from normal individuals, for diagnosis of more particular pathologies such as anxiety, for indicating degree of maladjustment in the general population, and for predicting academic and vocational success.

The most recent comprehensive review and discussion of Rorschach validity is by Harris (*2638*). It is the most thoughtful and objective article on this subject the present reviewer has encountered. From his extensive survey, Harris concluded: "By the canons of test analysis, the Rorschach technique as a whole has been shown at present to have neither satisfactory validity nor invalidity." Predicting the future of Rorschach research, Harris states, "There is very little concrete basis for making an optimistic prediction that a review of studies of validity, in which the ten Rorschach cards have served as the sole instrument of investigation, will be any different 25 years from now than they were when reviewed in 1954 by Ainsworth [in *1730*]."

What, specifically, have the most recent studies found?

First, a distinction must be made between experimental and clinical types of validation studies. In experimental studies, particular Rorschach scores (often scores that have been specially derived for the particular study) are in some way tested for their correlation with some non-Rorschach criterion. The criterion may or may not be of clinical relevance. Clinical validation studies, on the other hand, involve a more global use of the Rorschach protocol, typical of its use in clinical practice, with the aim of testing the correlation of the Rorschach with various clinically relevant criteria. Older reviews of Rorschach validity are based predominantly on the experimental type of study. Recent research has concentrated more on the clinical validity of the instrument as it is typically used by clinical psychologists. Many of the experimental type studies have been reviewed by Zubin (*1826*). The fact that some of these studies have reported validity coefficients which, when significant at all, are generally in the range of .20 to .40, cannot be interpreted as supporting the clinical usefulness of the test. Aside from the fact that validity in this range is practically useless for individual assessment, the validated "scores" are often not those used by the clinician or they are used in a different way. Even when the scores do happen to be those that enter into the clinical interpretation of the protocol, such as the M per cent, clinicians seldom heed the experimental findings. It is easy to find statements in current clinical reports that a subject is "creative" on the basis of a high M per cent in his protocol, despite the well known failure of this relationship to be borne out in studies which are seemingly ideal for capturing it (e.g., *539*).

Beck's *z* and *g* scores, characterized as an "organizational factor," are derived scores which have gained popularity in clinical use. These scores are a systematic weighted combination of Rorschach attributes claimed to be indicative of intelligence and efficiency of intellectual functioning. The *g* score does have some validity, showing correlations with psychometrically measured intelligence in the range of .20 to .25 (*2640*).

Another special scoring method has been devised by Holt and Havel (*2645*) to measure degree of adaptive versus maladaptive regressive tendencies. When this index was correlated with 55 items of various behavioral and personality test criteria, 20 of the correlations were significant beyond the .10 level. The mean of the correlations significant beyond the .10 level was .59. Cross validation of such studies generally loses many of the formerly significant correlations, and no such correlations should be accepted without evidence of cross validation. For example, Holt and Havel (*2645*) state concerning the validity of the regression score,

> The correlation coefficients are not impressively large, for the most part not even being highly significant, but they are in the right directions. A word of caution, however: Incomplete but largely negative preliminary results from a group of college girls of the same age [as the college men on whom the original correlations were obtained] suggest that these correlations may not hold up in different samples, but may, in some as yet unknown way, be specific to unknown parameters of the present group of college boys.

It seems safe to conclude that experimental studies of particular Rorschach attributes have been able to show statistically significant correlations with other psychological criteria. These correlations have been generally rather low (i.e., between .20 and .40), only rarely exceeding .50, and most such correlations have not stood the test of cross validation.

How valid is the Rorschach when it is used as a clinical instrument by acknowledged experts? Three recent studies, which have taken care to avoid the criticism that the obtained validity coefficients do not represent the validity of the Rorschach when used by experts, are instructive.

The study by Little and Shneidman (*2537*), which has already been described in the section on reliability, used 12 Rorschach experts who were selected by the editors of the *Journal of Projective Techniques* and whose names are given in the appendix of the published monograph. The Rorschach protocols were obtained from 12 patients equally divided among the psychiatrically normal, neurotic, psychosomatic, and psychotic categories. The various criteria against which validation was attempted were obtained from the pooled judgments of 23 psychiatrists and one psychologist on the basis of a comprehensive psychiatric case history on each patient, obtained by one psychiatrist in 4 to 8 interviews of 1 to 3 hours duration. On a true-false questionnaire of 117 personality items typical of those in Rorschach reports, the correlation between the Rorschach judges and the anamnestic judges ranged from −.20 to .74, with a mean of .37. With a true-false questionnaire of 100 factual items which could be verified from the case history, the Rorschach correlations ranged from −.12 to .42, with a mean of .14. The correlations between a Q-sort of personality items obtained from the Rorschach judges and from the anamnestic judges ranged from −.10 to .47, with a mean of .17. This validity coefficient becomes .21 when corrected for attenuation of the criterion. But as compared with the other psychological tests used in the Little and Shneidman study (*Make A Picture Story, Thematic Apperception Test,* and *Minnesota Multiphasic Personality Inventory*), the Rorschach is not much worse. The MMPI, for example, which made a consistently better showing than any of the projective techniques, had an overall Q-sort validity of .33 (corrected for attenuation).

The study by Silverman (*2575*) described in the section on reliability compared Q-sorts of projective test experts with Q-sorts performed by the therapists of 10 adult males after 35 hours of psychotherapy. There were six Q-sorts made up of typical Rorschach report items covering the areas of defenses, motivating needs and affects, character traits, diagnosis and symptoms, interpersonal behavior, and infancy and childhood perceptions of parental figures. The validity coefficients for these areas range from .12 to .50, with a mean of .29.

On the basis of a preliminary study (*1983*) in which the Rorschach protocol of a patient in psychotherapy was sent to 12 Rorschach experts for independent interpretations, the one expert with the largest percentage of "hits" in agreement with the psychotherapist's knowledge of the patient was selected to perform Rorschach analyses of 28 nonpsychiatric subjects who were also assessed by interviews and other tests. A detailed account of the Rorschach analyses is presented by Symonds and Jensen (*2836*). The Rorschach expert was asked to rank the subjects for overall personality adjustment on the basis of her analysis of the Rorschach protocols. As the criterion two psychologists performed the same task from anamnestic data and from direct impressions gained in several hours of interview with each subject. The correlation between the Rorschach ratings and the criterion, corrected for attenuation, was .34. One could argue that the criterion itself had little validity, but this points up one of the crucial problems of Rorschach interpretation: are the test interpreter and the person to whom the interpretation is addressed both speaking the same language? If not, of what value is the Rorschach report? Most psychiatrists receiving psychological reports based in whole or in part on the Rorschach, it should be remembered, have not been trained in Rorschach interpretation.

The use of the Rorschach in vocational psychology has been reviewed by Super and Crites (*2938*), who conclude that "too little is now known to justify its use in practical counseling or personnel work." Similarly, Ricciuti (*2929*) has concluded a recent review of this subject as follows: "The practical usefulness of projective techniques in predicting educational or industrial criteria continues to be small."

SUMMARY. Research on the Rorschach published since the *Fifth Mental Measurements Yearbook* has not brought forth any substantial evidence that would alter the conclusions of the reviewers in that volume. If anything, recent studies add support to the conclusion that the Rorschach as a clinical instrument has too inadequate reliability and too meagre validity, even in the hands of the most expert, to justify any claims for its practical usefulness. The strong bias toward pathology in Rorschach reports on nonpsychiatric subjects can lead to harmful consequences in nonpsychiatric settings, such as in schools and in industry. Even in cases where harm might not result, one must weigh the scant validity of the test against the fact that of all psychological assessment techniques it is the most time consuming and requires the most extensive training of its practitioners. Many psychologists who have looked into the matter are agreed that the 40 years of massive effort which has been lavished on the Rorschach technique has proven unfruitful, at least so far as the development of a useful psychological test is concerned.

Until proponents of the Rorschach can produce evidence which substantially contradicts this verdict—and thus far such evidence is conspicuously lacking in the Rorschach textbooks—it seems not unreasonable to recommend that the Rorschach be altogether abandoned in clinical practice and that students of clinical psychology not be required to waste their time learning the technique.

The question of why the Rorschach still has so many devotees and continues to be so widely used is quite another problem and is beyond the scope of this review. A satisfactory explanation of the whole amazing phenomenon is a task for future historians of psychology and will probably have to wait upon greater knowledge of the psychology of credulity than we now possess. Meanwhile, the rate of scientific progress in clinical psychology might well be measured by the speed and thoroughness with which it gets over the Rorschach.

For reviews by Samuel J. Beck, H. J. Eysenck, Raymond J. McCall, and Laurance F. Shaffer, see 5:154; for a review by Helen Sargent, see 4:117; for reviews by Morris Krugman and J. R. Wittenborn, see 3:73; for excerpts from related book reviews, see B40, B52, B72–3, B91, B129, B152, B260, B295, B306–7, B344, B398, B409, B452, B526, 5:B32, 5:B34, 5:B40–1, 5:B60, 5:B73, 5:B79, 5:B190, 5:B247–8, 5:B337, 5:B369, 5:B372, 5:B402, 4:118–28, and 3:74–91.

[238]

***Rosenzweig Picture-Frustration Study.** Ages 4–13, 14 and over; 1944–60; also called *Rosenzweig P-F Study;* 15 scores: direction of aggression (extrapunitive, intropunitive, impunitive), type of aggression (obstacle-dominance, ego-defense, need-persistence), 9 combinations of the preceding categories; 2 levels; record blank ('48, 1 page) for each level; $5 per 25 tests; $1.25 per 25 record blanks; postage extra; specimen set not available; [15–20] minutes; Saul Rosenzweig; the Author. *

a) FORM FOR CHILDREN. Ages 4–13; 1948–60; 1 form ('48, 7 pages); manual ('48, 53 pages, reprint of *21* below); supplementary data ('60, 29 pages, reprint of

222 below); tentative norms; $1.25 per manual and supplementary data.

b) REVISED FORM FOR ADULTS. Ages 14 and over; 1944–49; 1 form ('48, 7 pages); manual ('47, 48 pages, reprint of *15* below; includes 1949 revised norms); no data on reliability and validity; norms for ages 20–29 only; $1.25 per manual.

REFERENCES

1–77. See 4:129.

78–186. See 5:155.

187. FISHER, SEYMOUR, AND HINDS, EDITH. "The Organization of Hostility Controls in Various Personality Structures." *Genetic Psychol Monogr* 44:3–68 Ag '51. * (*PA* 26:2889)

188. REID, L. LEON. "An Evaluation of the Rosenzweig Picture-Frustration Test." *Proc W Va Acad Sci* 23:170–2 Ap '52. *

189. ANGELINO, HENRY, AND SHEDD, CHARLES L. "Reactions to 'Frustration' of Mentally Retarded Children as Measured by the Rosenzweig P-F Test." Abstract. *Proc Okla Acad Sci* 36:104–5 D '55. *

190. ZUK, GERALD H. "The Influence of Social Context on Impulse and Control Tendencies in Preadolescence." *Genetic Psychol Monogr* 54:117–66 N '56. * (*PA* 33:3464)

191. COONS, MARGERY OLSTEAD. "Rosenzweig Differences in Reaction to Frustration in Children of High, Low, and Middle Sociometric Status." *Group Psychother* 10:60–3 Mr '57. * (*PA* 33:3393)

192. TAKALA, ANNIKA, AND TAKALA, MARTTI. "Finnish Children's Reactions to Frustration in the Rosenzweig Test: An Ethnic and Cultural Comparison." *Nordisk Psykologi* 9(1):43–50 '57. * Also in *Acta Psychologica* 13(1):43–50 '57. * (*PA* 33:1326)

193. TAKALA, MARTTI; PIHKANEN, TOIVO A.; AND MARKKANEN, TOUKO. *The Effects of Distilled and Brewed Beverages: A Physiological, Neurological, and Psychological Study.* The Finnish Foundation for Alcoholic Studies, No. 4. Stockholm, Sweden: Almqvist & Wiksell, 1957. Pp. 195. * (*PA* 31:4890)

194. FRIEDMAN, BERT. *A Study of the Szondi Assumptions of Identification and Counteridentification Utilizing Modified Versions of the Rosenzweig P-F Study on Criminal Groups.* Doctor's thesis, Fordham University (New York, N.Y.), 1958.

195. NORMAN, RALPH D., AND KLEINFELD, GERALD J. "Rosenzweig Picture-Frustration Study Results With Minority Group Juvenile Delinquents." *J Genetic Psychol* 92:61–7 Mr '58. * (*PA* 36:1JO61N)

196. PAREEK, UDAI. "Some Preliminary Data About the Indian Adaptation of Rosenzweig P-F Study (Children's Form)." *Ed & Psychol* 5:105–13 Je '58. * (*PA* 34:1407)

197. PAREEK, UDAI. "Studying Cultural Differences in Personality Development With the Help of Rosenzweig P-F Study." *J All-India Inst Mental Health* 1:113–23 Jl '58. * (*PA* 35:720)

198. PRENSKY, SAMUEL J. *An Investigation of Some Personality Characteristics of Epileptic and Psychosomatic Patients: An Evaluation of Certain Personality Measures and Reactions to Frustration in Idiopathic Epileptic, Symptomatic Epileptic, and Peptic Ulcer Patients.* Doctor's thesis, New York University (New York, N.Y.), 1958. (*DA* 19:3025)

199. PURDOM, GLEN A., JR. *Comparison of Performance of Competent and Incompetent Readers in a State Training School for Delinquent Boys on the WAIS and the Rosenzweig P-F Study.* Doctor's thesis, University of Oregon (Eugene, Ore.), 1958. (*DA* 19:1016)

200. SHEEHAN, JOSEPH G. "Projective Studies of Stuttering." *J Speech & Hearing Disorders* 23:18–25 F '58. *

201. SMITH, MARSHALL L. *Some Effects of Socio-Economic, Age, and Sex Factors on Children's Responses in Adult-Child and Child-Child Situations in the Rosenzweig Picture-Frustration Study.* Master's thesis, Southern Methodist University (Dallas, Tex.), 1958.

202. TAFT, RONALD. "Is the Tolerant Personality Type the Opposite of the Intolerants?" *J Social Psychol* 47:397–405 My '58. * (*PA* 33:8186)

203. BATHURST, G. C., AND GLATT, M. M. "Some Psychological Reflections on Vulnerability to Alcoholism." *Psychiatria et Neurologia* 138:27–46 '59. *

204. HAYASHI, KATSUZO; SUMITA, KATSUMI; AND ICHITANI, TSUYOSHI. "A Factorial Study of the Rosenzweig Picture-Frustration Study." *Jap Psychol Res* 1:20–6 N '59. *

205. LANGE, PATRICIA. "Frustration Reactions of Physically Handicapped Children." *Excep Child* 25:355–7 Ap '59. * (*PA* 35:2493)

206. LIPMAN, RONALD S. "Some Test Correlates of Behavioral Aggression in Institutionalized Retardates With Particular Reference to the Rosenzweig Picture-Frustration Study." *Am J Mental Def* 63:1038–45 My '59. * (*PA* 34:4587)

207. MCQUEEN, ROBERT, AND PEARSON, WAYNE O. "Stimulus-Word Changes in Picture-Frustration Situations." *Percept & Motor Skills* 9:407–10 D '59. * (*PA* 34:5629)

208. PAREEK, UDAI. "Rosenzweig Picture-Frustration Study —A Review." *Psychol Newsl* 10:98–114 Ja–F '59. * (*PA* 34:1047)

209. PAREEK, UDAI, AND ROSENZWEIG, SAUL. *Manual of the Indian Adaptation of Rosenzweig Picture-Frustration Study (Children's Form).* Delhi, India: Mānasāyan, 1959. Pp. iv, 71. *

210. ROGERS, ARTHUR H., AND PAUL, COLEMAN. "Impunitiveness and Unwitting Self-Evaluation." *J Proj Tech* 23:459–61 D '59. * (*PA* 35:5005)

211. STOLTZ, ROBERT E., AND SMITH, MARSHALL D. "Some Effects of Socio-Economic, Age and Sex Factors on Children's Responses to the Rosenzweig Picture-Frustration Study." *J Clin Psychol* 15:200–3 Ap '59. * (*PA* 35:4725)

212. TRAPP, E. PHILIP. "Threat and Direction of Aggression." *J Clin Psychol* 15:308–10 Jl '59. * (*PA* 35:3513)

213. VINACKE, W. EDGAR. "A Comparison of the Rosenzweig P-F Study and the Brown Interracial Version: Hawaii." *J Social Psychol* 49:161–75 My '59. * (*PA* 34:4232)

214. WILSON, MILTON E., JR. *The Rosenzweig Picture-Frustration Study: An Appraisal of Methodology and Underlying Assumptions.* Master's thesis, Kent State University (Kent, Ohio), 1959.

215. BENNETT, LAWRENCE A., AND RUDOFF, ALVIN. "Changes in Direction of Hostility Related to Incarceration and Treatment." *J Clin Psychol* 16:408–10 O '60. * (*PA* 37:3269)

216. DAVIDS, ANTHONY, AND OLIVER, GERALDINE R. "Fantasy Aggression and Learning in Emotionally Disturbed and Normal Children." *J Proj Tech* 24:124–8 Je '60. * (*PA* 35:1069)

217. GABRIEL, JOHN, AND HERD, JEAN. "Culturally Expected Responses and the Rosenzweig P-F Test, Children's Form." *Austral J Psychol* 12:178–88 D '60. *

218. GOLD, LEO. *Reaction of Male Adolescent Addicts to Frustration as Compared to Two Adolescent Non-Addicted Groups.* Doctor's thesis, New York University (New York, N.Y.), 1960. (*DA* 20:4716)

219. KASWAN, J.; WASMAN, M.; AND FREEDMAN, LAWRENCE ZELIC. "Aggression and the Picture-Frustration Study." *J Consult Psychol* 24:446–52 O '60. * (*PA* 35:4923)

220. PAREEK, UDAI. "Developmental Patterns of Rosenzweig P-F Study Variables in Indian Children." *Manas* 7:19–35 '60. * (*PA* 37:890)

221. PAREEK, UDAI. "An Investigation of the Validity of the Indian Adaptation of the Rosenzweig Picture-Frustration Study (Children's Form)." *Indian J Psychol* 35:71–88 pt 2 '60. * (*PA* 36:4HG71P)

222. ROSENZWEIG, SAUL. Chap. 8, "The Rosenzweig Picture-Frustration Study, Children's Form," pp. 149–76. In *Projective Techniques With Children.* Edited by Albert I. Rabin and Mary R. Haworth. New York: Grune & Stratton, Inc., 1960. Pp. xiii, 392. * (*PA* 35:2229)

223. SHAW, MERVILLE C., AND BLACK, MICHAEL DORIS. "The Reaction to Frustration of Bright High School Underachievers." *Calif J Ed Res* 11:120–4 My '60. * (*PA* 35:7025)

224. SMITH, STANLEY KECK, JR. *A Factor Analytic Study of the Rosenzweig Picture-Frustration Study as a Predictor of Academic Achievement.* Doctor's thesis, Temple University (Philadelphia, Pa.), 1960. (*DA* 22:647)

225. CORKE, PATRICIA PERRY. *A Comparison of Frustration-Aggression Patterns of Negro and White Southern Males and Females.* Doctor's thesis, University of Houston (Houston, Tex.), 1961. (*DA* 22:2870)

226. HARRIGAN, JOHN E.; DOLE, ARTHUR A.; AND VINACKE, W. EDGAR. "A Study of Indignation-Bigotry and Extrapunitiveness in Hawaii." *J Social Psychol* 55:105–12 O '61. * (*PA* 36:4GD05H)

227. MASKIT, MAE LEE. *Management of Aggression in Preadolescent Girls: Its Effects on Certain Aspects of Ego Functioning.* Doctor's thesis, University of Michigan (Ann Arbor, Mich.), 1961. (*DA* 22:917)

228. MAUSNER, BERNARD. "Situational Effects on a Projective Test." *J Appl Psychol* 45:186–92 Je '61. * (*PA* 36:4HG86M)

229. SWICKARD, DON L., AND SPILKA, BERNARD. "Hostility Expression Among Delinquents of Minority and Majority Groups." *J Consult Psychol* 25:216–20 Je '61. *

230. TRENTINI, G. "A New Method of Validation Applied to Reaffirm the Validity of the Rosenzweig P.F.S." Abstract. *Acta Psychologica* 19(2):121–2 '61. *

231. BREWER, JETTA J. A. *A Comparison of Slightly and Severely Orthopedically Disabled Adults on Rosenzweig's Picture-Frustration Study.* Master's thesis, University of Utah (Salt Lake City, Utah), 1962.

232. CESA-BIANCHI, MARCELLO, AND TRENTINI, GIANCARIO. "A Further Contribution to the Study of Adjustment in Old Age," pp. 623–7. In *Social and Psychological Aspects of Aging.* Proceedings of the Fifth Congress of the International Association of Gerontology. Edited by Clark Tibbitts and Wilma Donahue. New York: Columbia University Press, 1962. Pp. xviii, 952. *

233. CHOROST, SHERWOOD BRUCE. "Parental Child-Rearing Attitudes and Their Correlates in Adolescent Hostility." *Genetic Psychol Monogr* 66:49–90 Ag '62. * (*PA* 37:4743)

234. FOREMAN, MILTON E. "Predicting Behavioral Problems Among Institutionalized Mental Retardates." *Am J Mental Def* 66:580–8 Ja '62. * (*PA* 36:4JI80F)

235. HARVEY, O. J. "Personality Factors in Resolution of Conceptual Incongruities." *Sociometry* 25:336–52 D '62. *

236. KIRSCHNER, R.; McCARY, J. L.; AND MOORE, C. W. "A Comparison of Differences Among Several Religious Groups of Children on Various Measures of the Rosenzweig Picture-Frustration Study." *J Clin Psychol* 18:352–3 Jl '62. * (*PA* 39:1575)
237. MERCER, MARGARET, AND KYRIAZIS, CHRIST. "Results of the Rosenzweig Picture-Frustration Study for Physically Assaultive Prisoner Mental Patients." Abstract. *J Consult Psychol* 26:490 O '62. *
238. MUTHAYYA, B. C. "An Experimental Validation of the Madras Picture-Frustration Study." *Psychol Studies* 7: 10–5 Ja '62. * (*PA* 37:1206)
239. RAPAPORT, GERALD M., AND MARSHALL, ROBERT J. "The Prediction of Rehabilitative Potential of Stockade Prisoners Using Clinical Psychological Tests." *J Clin Psychol* 18: 444–6 O '62. * (*PA* 39:5087)
240. HERBERT, N., AND TURNBULL, G. H. "Personality Factors and Effective Progress in Teaching." *Ed R* 16:24–31 N '63. *
241. MOORE, MARY E., AND SCHWARTZ, MILTON M. "The Effect of the Sex of the Frustrated Figure on Responses to the Rosenzweig P-F Study." *J Proj Tech & Pers Assess* 27:195–9 Je '63. * (*PA* 38:2720)
242. NATHAN, PETER E. "Conceptual Ability and Indices of Frustration Tolerance on the Rosenzweig Picture-Frustration Study." *J Proj Tech & Pers Assess* 27:200–7 Je '63. * (*PA* 38:2639)
243. ROSENZWEIG, SAUL. "Validity of the Rosenzweig Picture-Frustration Study with Felons and Delinquents." *J Consult Psychol* 27:535–6 D '63. *
244. ROSS, W. D.; ADSETT, NANCY; GLESER, GOLDINE; JOYCE, C. R. B.; KAPLAN, S. M.; AND TIEGER, M. E. "A Trial of Psychopharmacologic Measurement With Projective Techniques." *J Proj Tech & Pers Assess* 27:222–5 Je '63. *
245. SUMITA, K.; HAYASHI, K.; ICHITANI, T.; AND YAMAGUCHI, H. "Personality Types as Revealed by the Factorial Pattern of the Rosenzweig Picture-Frustration Study." *Manas* 10(1):25–34 '63. * (*PA* 38:8508)
246. WEINSTEIN, A. D.; MOORE, C. W.; AND McCARY, J. L. "A Note on Comparison of Differences Between Several Religious Groups of Adults on Various Measures of the Rosenzweig Picture-Frustration Study." *J Clin Psychol* 19:219 Ap '63. * (*PA* 39:5220)
247. WITTENBORN, J. R., AND PLANTE, MARC. "Patterns of Response to Placebo, Iproniazid and Electroconvulsive Therapy Among Young Depressed Females." *J Nerv & Mental Dis* 137:155–61 Ag '63. *

ÅKE BJERSTEDT, *Professor of Education, University of Lund, Lund, Sweden.*

The purpose of the *Rosenzweig P-F Study* is to enable the investigator to study typical reaction patterns in potentially frustrating situations. Representing an attempt to translate a theory of frustration into operational terms, the instrument has been used (*a*) as a research tool in testing various general theories on frustration tolerance, directions of "aggression," etc. as related to other biosocial variables, and (*b*) for individual diagnostic assessment of frustration-related behavior tendencies.

The P-F Study has certainly not remained unnoticed. About 275 published references were known to the test author in 1962, and considering its widespread international use, there is probably an additional number of articles in more remote sources and in less well-known languages.

In view of this abundance of material it is obviously impossible in this review to give more than scattered attention to the work done. Inasmuch as the manuals now distributed with the test forms present much too little of what is known about the tests, there is a great need for integrative surveys. The best single source written by the test author is a chapter in a book on projective techniques (*222*), but this covers only the children's version. Among the best general sources by other authors is a 132-page report by Christiansen,[1] but this is written in Norwegian and now somewhat dated.

BASIC THEORY AND TERMINOLOGY. As is well known, subject's responses to cartoon-like drawings of frustrating situations are categorized in a three-by-three system which cross-classifies "types" and "directions" of "aggression." In some earlier texts Rosenzweig used the more neutral term "type of reaction," but in 1960 he explicitly recommended the use of the term "aggression." "Need-persistence" is considered in terms of "constructive aggression" and "ego-defense" in terms of "destructive aggression," while "obstacle-dominance" is described as a type of aggression in which the response is curtailed before either of the other modes can be actuated. The reviewer cannot help finding this overall use of the term "aggression" (already overused in psychology) unnecessarily confusing. Would not more neutral phrases like "direction of activity" (instead of "direction of aggression") and "attention dominance" (instead of "type of aggression") be less misleading?

The test author has apparently had a feeling that the punitive overtones were somewhat too strong in the terminology, for in 1960 he recommended that the term "extrapunitive," earlier used for all outward-oriented reactions, should now refer only to the ego-defensive type of outward-reaction, whereas the obstacle-dominant type should be called "extrapeditive," and the need-persistent type, "extrapersistive." Similar innovations were recommended for the inward reactions ("intropeditive," "intropunitive," and "intropersistive") and the passivity reactions ("impeditive," "impunitive," and "impersistive"). These neologisms seem useful, but no new terms were presented for the more comprehensive concepts earlier called "extrapunitive," "intropunitive," and "impunitive." In a personal communication, however, Rosenzweig has informed the reviewer that he has been using the notations "extra-directed," "intro-directed," and "im-directed" in his oral teaching to refer to the more inclusive categories. Recently these terms have also found

1 CHRISTIANSEN, BJØRN. *Rosenzweigs billed-frustrasjonstest: en diskusjon av dens anvendbarhet belyst ved andres og egne undersøkelser.* Nordisk Psykologi's Monografiserie No. 7. Copenhagen: Einar Munksgaard, 1955. Pp. 132. *

their way into print (*242*). The last mentioned term may be somewhat awkward linguistically in its attempt to retain the "m" from "impunitive," but on the whole this set of words represents a less loaded terminology. In a way, questions of terminology like these are unimportant, as long as operational definitions are clear. On the other hand, surplus meanings evoked by everyday usage or well-known etymology are difficult to get rid of and tend to make interpretational discussions less rigorous than desirable.

Some behavior categories derived by Rosenzweig from the cross-classification tend to be less natural than others. "Obstacle-dominance" apparently was a latecomer in Rosenzweig's theory [2] and seems to fit in best with outward-reaction ("extrapersistive") as long as frustrations are imposed from outside. Finding illustrations of "intropeditive" reactions is, consequently, difficult. No examples of this category are given for 15 out of the 24 situations in the scoring samples from about 500 American child records or in the scoring samples from 1,000 Indian child records for 17 of the situations. Such unevenness makes interpretations and comparisons between the categories more difficult and tends to make the low frequency categories less useful and reliable. It is not quite clear whether this unevenness is a logical or psychological necessity, or if it could be corrected for by another sample of stimulus situations.

Rosenzweig (*53, 243*) is well aware of the problem of level of response, but his awareness has not been followed by any solution to the problem. We do not know whether the subject's reactions mirror (*a*) his overt everyday behavior as observed by others, (*b*) his behavior experienced subjectively but consciously by himself, (*c*) his covert needs, or (*d*) his opinions on how he ought to behave. The only solutions offered are the advice to assume if no other clues are at hand that the overt level has been tapped, and the recommendation to make non-leading inquiry. Neither suggestion is very helpful. The assumption mentioned might be tenable as a gross probability statement in some groups, but it is of very little value for handling of a single case; as to the inquiry, Rosenzweig himself admits that rationalizations may be even more frequent in this phase than in the original testing.

This problem pops up again and again in interpretational discussions. To take only one example: The Group Conformity Rating, derived by comparing each item score with modal responses in the norm group, is usually interpreted as a rough measure of social adjustment. Some empirical data tend to verify this interpretation (*186*). To two investigators (*133*) it was an unexpected finding that delinquents had high conformity scores, depressed extrapunitive scores, and elevated intropunitive scores. In discussing these findings, Rosenzweig points to several possibilities: (*a*) that delinquent subjects in the situation used might have been motivated to put up a good face on their responses (ideal-level response); or (*b*) that their delinquency was of the conformity type (gang conformity, overt response); or (*c*) that their delinquency was inspired by an unconscious sense of guilt (the intropunitive scores reflecting a covert need symptom). Any or all of these hypotheses—covering three different "levels" of behavior—may be correct, but the need for such rationalizations or guesswork *after* testing and without support for any of the alternatives leaves the reader unsatisfied.

For certain general categories of interaction tendencies, Leary [3] has shown that a testing strategy utilizing different methodological approaches at the same time for the mapping of the same categories of behavior may clarify the problem of levels and help for individual diagnosis. Could not such a strategy be a solution also to the problem of levels in the P-F Study? For example, same-category behavior on different methodological levels may indicate behavioral stability over time, whereas different-category behavior on various levels may signal intrapersonal conflict with subsequent changes on the overt level. That different personality types have different degrees of interlevel similarity would then not be a methodological weakness, but, when established by the test battery, a diagnostic indication of importance (*187*). Apparently, Rosenzweig started out long ago with a multi-method instrument but later singled out the more absorbing projective-method part for separate study (*222*). Would it not be good to take up again the more

2 ROSENZWEIG, SAUL. "An Experimental Study of 'Repression' With Special Reference to Need-Persistence and Ego-Defensive Reactions to Frustration." *J Exp Psychol* 32:64–74 Ja '43. *

3 LEARY, TIMOTHY. *Interpersonal Diagnosis of Personality: A Functional Theory and Methodology for Personality Evaluation.* New York: Ronald Press Co., 1957. Pp. xix, 518. *

inclusive approach once envisioned, at least for the purpose of further research? Such a multilevel frustration test, where the P-F type of approach was only one of various approaches, might have been a better guide in the decisions on alternative interpretations in several studies. It might also be a better guide in decisions on whether or not a subject has succeeded in putting up a good face in a personally important test situation. Some investigators (*179, 228*) have seen such situational effects whereas one investigator [4] found the present test fairly resistive to faking.

TEST STIMULI. Each form consists of 24 frustration situations involving two persons. One says something which frustrates the other or helps to describe his frustration. The subject gives the verbal reaction of the other person (the identification figure). Facial features are vague to facilitate projective structuring. There is some indication of low item homogeneity. Few items yield responses in all nine possible categories, and some very one-sidedly attract responses in a particular category. Lack of homogeneity should not be considered too serious in itself in this device (unless it leads to *excessive* lack of differentiation). More important are "situational representativeness" and "subject-category fairness." The situations sampled should be representative of the frustrating situations characteristic of the target population. The author leaves us without information on his exact procedures to ensure such representativeness. Further, various potential subgroups, such as male and female subjects, ought to be given parallel treatment. This is not done for the present instrument. It may be a disproportion representative of the American scene that in the child form a boy has to answer a female adult in a frustrating situation in seven cases whereas only in one case must a girl answer a male adult. Such a disproportion may be acceptable, but it is not acceptable that a girl subject has only 8 same-sex identification figures, whereas a boy has 16 same-sex identification figures. In a similar way the adult form is best adapted to male subjects: there are 16 males as against 6 female identification figures (while 2 cases are somewhat ambiguous). In no case in the adult form does a woman have to answer a man. In sum, it might be of value to try to construct for research purposes a parallel P-F form with more explicit selection procedures, with more fair sex treatment, and with more strict criteria on response differentiation. Such an instrument might well be more reliable and valid and thus more useful for its intended purpose than the present one.

TEST SITUATION. The test situation was not the same for various age groups in the norm population: the youngest children responded orally, older children wrote their answers and then read them aloud, and adults only wrote their answers. This variation may make for some difficult-to-interpret differences between various groups and be a source of error in developmental studies. Oral responses may increase censorship for some kinds of children, decrease it for others. In a way, oral responses should be the most sensitive indicators of response nature since intonation can give the same word various meanings. This argument would favor using an oral response procedure in all cases. On the other hand, group testing procedures could not then be used. In addition to being more economical, group testing with written answers has the advantage of minimizing influence of the specific investigator-subject relationship which may otherwise be a source of variation not to be overlooked in a situation leaning so heavily on interactional statements, especially where the investigator himself also *reads* the frustrating statements to the subject. More studies of the importance of various ways of presentation would be desirable and should include attempts to use oral stimulus and oral response in a nonpersonal and nonvarying setting, for instance, with the aid of tape recording equipment of the language laboratory type. In such a setting, group testing with identical stimulus situations could be arranged while still maintaining oral responses. In addition, permanent records for more reliable scoring of intonational overtones would be obtained. At present the user has to choose either desirable auditive discrimination together with undesirable interactional variations and undesirable administration costs or desirable minimal interaction variation and desirable time economy together with undesirable lack of spontaneous auditive information. Most users seem to prefer the latter alternative.

Total time is recorded, but no important use seems to be made of this variable. Differential time information, especially stimulus-response

4 TRENTINI, GIANCARIO. *Contributo sperimentale alla validazione del test di Rosenzweig.* Contributi dell' Istituto di Psicologia, Serie 25. Milan, Italy: Società Editrice Vita e Pensiero, 1961. Pp. 20.

interval for specific pictures, might be more interesting (*108*). The tape recording situation recommended above might be a good instrument for studying this possibility further.

Little information is given on how to keep the recommended inquiry free from leading suggestions and after-rationalizations. A certain number of unscorable answers might be better than answers scored from two different interactional situations. (Some answers, easily scored directly from the written text, are not inquired about, while others are scored on the basis of questions in a specific investigator-subject interaction.) The few references to techniques of inquiry in empirical studies lead us to believe that inquiry is usually not used. The reviewer has not been able to locate definite studies on the value of inquiry.

SCORING. Scoring is—at least compared to several other projective techniques—fairly easy and is facilitated by extensive and good scoring samples. These scoring samples would have been still better, however, if the authors had indicated the frequency of various answer categories (the German manual gives better information than the American in this respect) and if the authors had indicated on what kind of answers they considered inquiry essential. It is not clear from the samples if the position of some answers with seemingly strange placement is due to additional information obtained through inquiry. Trend scoring is especially interesting and contributes to one type of operational definition of "frustration tolerance" (*52*). However, a longer series of stimuli, with forced-tempo reactions and with scoring over more than two phases, would perhaps yield more valid data on individual process characteristics. So far most studies have been mainly interested in the sum scores within classification categories, but to this reviewer an extended process analysis is an area of potential importance for future research.

Could other types of scores, not usually used, be of some value? Attempts to assess intensity of reaction would be one possibility, since some categories contain a great variety of reaction intensities not mirrored in the scores. (Cf. Zuk's attempts to derive an "impulsivity" score, *190*.) Scoring over separate stimulus categories would be another possibility: ego-blocking versus superego-blocking, child-adult versus child-child, male-frustrator versus female-frustrator, etc. Some studies (e.g., *171*) indicate that such subdivisions may be meaningful for certain purposes and that item homogeneity is increased when studied by such a "regional analysis." A third possibility includes inter-role comparisons. Scores expressing discrepancies between various perceived roles, as well as scores expressing discrepancies or similarities between ego role and the perceived roles of others, carry a potential interest (and would start out from separate administrations with the instruction to guess the reactions of specified others).

NORM DATA. As published in the two manuals, norm data are somewhat limited in value and should be considered tentative only. The reviewer does not regret too much that representative national norms were not established; the cost of such samples may outweigh their possible contributions in devices of this type. But more comprehensive and better defined groups would be desirable. The adult sample is limited to ages 20–29 and seems overrepresentative of people with above-average education. The child norms are established on fairly small groups per age level, the lower levels coming from private schools, the higher levels from public schools. No controlling subdivisions for social class, occupation, or intelligence are reported. That intelligence influences situation perception, and hence responses, is indicated in some studies (e.g., *121*). No attempts are made to base conclusions about developmental trends on longitudinal studies. Of course, the fairly limited norm data in the manual are considerably extended in other published reports. Normative information is available for other American groups and for non-American groups, such as French, German, Indian, Italian, and Japanese children. Unfortunately, the scattered normative data have not been integrated and incorporated in the general manuals. If this were done (with additional information on relevant comparative variables) it could mean a better frame of reference for interpretation and, in addition, a starting point for interesting hypotheses on intercultural variations in basic interaction patterns. Tentative work in this direction has been reported from various corners of the world (e.g., *192*).

RELIABILITY. The P-F Study has one foot in the projective-test camp, with its underlying theory of projections on identification figures, and one foot in the psychometric camp, with a scoring technique that emphasizes the quantitative approach. This commendable attempt has the disadvantage to attract criticisms from two frontiers. Some clinically oriented psychologists see the test as too restricted in aim and too simple in interpretational background. On the other hand, psychometrists are sometimes quick to point out flaws in measurement precision in terms of reliability. Interscorer consistency is fairly high according to several studies (e.g., *13*), but could probably be further improved by stimulus revisions, since some items tend to attract far more inconsistencies than others. Internal consistency, on the other hand, is very often found to be low (*115*). If other test utility indicators are high, this one need not be taken too seriously, however. (There is no reason why, for instance, first-half scores should be identical with second-half scores. On the contrary, the analysis of trend, especially, uses score discrepancies between phases for diagnostic purposes.) Parallel test consistency has not attracted much attention, although some study of the interchangeability of the adult and children forms has been made. Retest reliability is more important for the interpretational possibilities than internal consistency, for even though we do not expect interaction tendencies to be free from change, too much change from one time to another will make the test worthless for predictional purposes. Studies of retest data do show the reliability of some scores (such as GCR) to be rather low for individual diagnosis, whereas others are as reliable as could be expected for data of this kind (*25, 111*).

VALIDITY. The question of empirical validity is not given much attention in the manuals, but many studies have contributed to the field. Good surveys of earlier studies are given by Mirmow (*108*) and Rosenzweig (*222*). The evidence is somewhat ambiguous. It would, apparently, seldom be fair to demand a one-to-one correspondence between scores from a test of this type and specific outside criteria. We do not consider this test a short-cut measure of something we have a reliable, but time consuming, measure of somewhere else, which we could use as a prototype in validation studies. Neither is a test of this type a one-purpose prediction tool, for which non-ambiguous data on prediction success could be collected. Instead, it is an instrument based on a theory of individual differentiation in the frustration reaction field and on a number of relevant subhypotheses. If this instrument could be shown to "behave" according to theoretical expectations, so that we obtain patterns of meaningful correlations and group differences, we would feel that it works. Hence, while not demanding one-to-one correspondences, we desire relational fertility in terms of meaningful result patterns. A large body of data now shows increasing evidence of this type. Interesting findings are reported by Christiansen,[5] Davids and Oliver (*216*), Duhm,[6] Farberow (*43*), French (*44*), Kaswan, Wasman, and Freedman (*219*), Levitt and Lyle (*150*), Rosenzweig and Rosenzweig (*110*), and others. Among the methods used are experiments with artificially induced frustration, which, for example, significantly increased O-D and E scores (*209*). Original approaches for studying validity are presented by Rogers and Paul (*210*) and by Schwartz (*177*). But among many supportive findings, unexpected inconsistencies occur. Obviously, the question of relational fertility is intimately connected with the basic difficulties in terms of level of response and, to some extent perhaps, the problems of stimulus sampling, both discussed above. If these problems could be solved better than they are now, we would have reason to expect a higher degree of consistency in the validity studies.

RECOMMENDATIONS ON CHANGES AND RESEARCH. Summarizing some of the points made above, a list of *desiderata* for future work would include (*a*) revised manuals, incorporating and integrating the now scattered information on norms, reliability, and validity; (*b*) an attempt to construct a parallel instrument including more systematic and sex-fair test stimuli and using a sorting-out process for situations with low differentiating value; (*c*) research on various administration strategies, including oral-nonpersonal presentation; (*d*) studies of whether or not inquiry increases validity of information; and (*e*) research on the basic problem of response level, especially with attempts to construct a multilevel instrument.

RECOMMENDATIONS ON USES. As stated earlier, two main uses have been made of this test: (*a*) individual diagnosis of frustration-related behavior tendencies, and (*b*) research in testing various general theories on frustration

5 CHRISTIANSEN, *op. cit.*
6 DUHM, ERNA. "Die Reaktionen von Problemkindern im Rosenzweig-Picture-Frustration-Test." *Psychologische Rundschau* 10:283–91 O '59. *

tolerance, directions of "aggression," etc., as related to other biosocial variables. What conclusions should be drawn from the comments made above? Apparently, the P-F Study has many features that may evoke criticism, especially from more tough-minded psychometrists. The test stimuli could have been chosen according to a more explicit empirical procedure. The test situation involves uncertainties as to the best strategy. Norms as presented in the manuals should be considered tentative only. Retest reliability is low for some scoring categories. Basic theoretical problems, such as the question of response level, have not been solved.

Especially the last two facts mentioned would lead us to conclude that it should not be used in its present form for individual clinical decisions without intra-case validation from other sources. While the advanced clinician who is keenly aware of its limitations and knows how to supplement its information may sometimes find it of interest in clinical work, this test cannot be generally recommended for routine use or for immediate practical decisions by school psychologists, guidance workers, or teachers. It might be added that this characteristic is shared by most of today's personality devices and that to the reviewer's knowledge there is no competing test designed to study the same specific patterns of behavior that could claim any better standing in this respect.

A fairly specific use might be mentioned in passing. With its attempt to combine projective and psychometric features, it has often been a stimulating starting point for discussions in advanced personality assessment courses. In such a use, some of its difficulties are educationally very fruitful, tending quickly to involve students in basic methodological debate.

The main use of the P-F Study, however, has been and will be for basic research for testing theories on inter-variable relationships in frustration. In addition, it seems to be a good starting point for the further penetration of the theoretical and methodological questions on behavior levels. If successful, attempts to construct a multilevel instrument as recommended above may in time lead us toward a revolution in personality assessment strategy, so that one-level, one-shot instruments are replaced by multilevel approaches. If so, the P-F Study will have the merit of being one of the first instruments that made this problem—implicit in so much personality testing—explicit and acute. Whatever specific changes the test may undergo in the future, however, the basic methodology—unique as it is—will continue to attract the interest of research workers and clinicians alike. At present, it is without doubt one of the most interesting and research-generating projective devices we have.

For reviews by Richard H. Dana and Bert R. Sappenfield, see 5:155; for reviews by Robert C. Challman and Percival M. Symonds, see 4:129.

[239]

The Rotter Incomplete Sentences Blank. Grades 9–12, 13–16, adults; 1950; 1 form (2 pages); 3 levels; manual (86 pages); manual and standardization data based on college level only; $1.25 per 25 tests; $1.90 per manual; postpaid; specimen set not available; (20–40) minutes; Julian B. Rotter and Janet E. Rafferty (manual); Psychological Corporation. *

REFERENCES

1–6. See 4:130.
7–24. See 5:156.
25. FITZGERALD, BERNARD JOSEPH. *The Relationship of Two Projective Measures to a Sociometric Measure of Dependent Behavior.* Doctor's thesis, Ohio State University (Columbus, Ohio), 1954. (*DA* 20:2380)
26. LENT, ADA. "A Survey of the Problems of Adolescent High School Girls Fourteen to Eighteen Years of Age." *Alberta J Ed Res* 3:127–37 S '57. * (*PA* 33:3415)
27. SCHMITT, JOHN A. *Identifying Maladjusted Youth in a Rural High School—an Investigation of the Usefulness of Rotter's Incomplete Sentences Blank.* Master's thesis, Cornell University (Ithaca, N.Y.), 1957.
28. YOSHPE, SELINA R. *A Validation Study of the Rotter Incomplete Sentences Blank: High School Form.* Master's thesis, Sacramento State College (Sacramento, Calif.), 1957.
29. CHANCE, JUNE ELIZABETH. "Adjustment and Prediction of Others' Behavior." *J Consult Psychol* 22:191–4 Je '58. * (*PA* 35:4977)
30. GUERTIN, WILSON H. "An Analysis of Gross Errors on a Sentence Completion Test." *J Clin Psychol* 15:415–6 O '59. * (*PA* 36:1HC14G)
31. HALE, PETER P. "The Rotter: A Vocational Counselor's Goldmine." *Voc Guid Q* 9:119–20 w '60. *
32. STEPHENS, MARK W. "The Incomplete Sentences Blank: Sources of Variance in Retest Reliability." *J Clin Psychol* 16:331–3 Jl '60. * (*PA* 36:2HC31S)
33. PRENTICE, NORMAN M. "Ethnic Attitudes, Neuroticism, and Culture." *J Social Psychol* 54:75–82 Je '61. * (*PA* 36:2HF75P)
34. BILLARD, RICHARD G. "Comparison of Teacher Ratings of Personality With Results of an Incomplete Sentences Blank." *Personnel & Guid J* 41:58–9 S '62. *
35. DOYLE, FLORENCE ESTHER. *An Analysis of Intercorrelations Among Adjustment Scores Attained by Delinquents on Independent and Experimental Measures Based on the Luker Index.* Doctor's research study No. 1, Colorado State College (Greeley, Colo.), 1962. (*DA* 23:1271)
36. NEWTON, DARWIN RUSSELL. *An Analysis of Intercorrelations Between the Rotter ISB and Other Measures of Adjustment Based on the Luker Index.* Doctor's research study No. 1, Colorado State College (Greeley, Colo.), 1962. (*DA* 22:4272)
37. RENNER, K. EDWARD; MAHER, BRENDAN A.; AND CAMPBELL, DONALD T. "The Validity of a Method for Scoring Sentence-Completion Responses for Anxiety, Dependency, and Hostility." *J Appl Psychol* 46:285–90 Ag '62. * (*PA* 37:3155)
38. THEINER, ERIC C. "The Magnitude of Four Experimental Needs as Expressed by Two Projective Techniques." *J Proj Tech* 26:354–65 S '62. * (*PA* 37:3163)
39. JESSOR, RICHARD; LIVERANT, SHEPHARD; AND OPOCHINSKY, SEYMOUR. "Imbalance in Need Structure and Maladjustment." *J Abn & Social Psychol* 66:271–5 Mr '63. * (*PA* 37:8032)
40. KENNEDY, WALLACE A.; COTTRELL, TED; AND SMITH, AL. "Norms of Gifted Adolescents on the Rotter Incomplete Sentence Blank." *J Clin Psychol* 19:314–5 Jl '63. *
41. WALLACE, JOHN, AND SECHREST, LEE. "Frequency Hypothesis and Content Analysis of Projective Techniques." *J Consult Psychol* 27:387–93 O '63. * (*PA* 38:4335)

For reviews by Charles N. Cofer and William Schofield, see 4:130.

[240]

★The South African Picture Analysis Test. Ages 5–13; 1960, c1959; 8 interpretive categories: condition of hero, environmental pressure, needs, reactions, characteristics of stories (4 categories); individual; 1 form (12 cards, 8 for boys or girls and 2 for boys only and 2 for girls only); manual ('60, c1959, 71 pages); no data on reliability; gld. 24,50 ($6.75) per set of cards and manual; gld. 7,90 ($2.25) per manual purchased separately; postage extra; (60) minutes; B. F. Nel and A. J. K. Pelser; Swets & Zeitlinger. *

S. G. Lee, *Professor of Psychology, University of Leicester, Leicester, England.*

The pictures of this test have been specifically designed to elicit projections from primary school children aged 5–13. The intention is to fill a presumed age gap between the TAT, the *Symonds Picture-Story Test,* and the CAT. The final version adopted to reduce the time taken in administration and scoring consists of 12 pictures.

Before considering the test material and its administration and interpretation in more detail it is informative to consider the theoretical and moral biases of the authors. For, from the statement, "there is a vast difference between the philosophy of life of the American and that of the Continental psychologist, i.e., a pragmatic philosophy of life as against an idealistic rationalistic philosophy of life," we are led on to the "continental" idea of the "person," a "moral being" whose personality is far from representing "the external manifestations of traits or qualities, which develop from the animalistic layers [*sic*] of the human organism"—this last being the view of "American psychology." The authors in fact identify themselves with the "continental" view: "Under personality is understood the external manifestation of this original and inherent spiritual core of the human existence. It may be pointed out that this conception of personality acquires a more comprehensive and more profound meaning when the human being is also considered as a Creation of God. Owing to the fact that this Creation has a spiritual core and is therefore a 'person,' he does not only build up relations with his fellow man but also and especially with God, his Creator." Again we have: "Man cannot be understood from within himself, but only in his complete existential relation, i.e., in his contact, in his dialogue with the things and human beings around him and with God." In similar vein, and closer to the purposes of the test, we are told that real projection can only take place in an "existential" situation. A protocol produced by the testee in a projective test should be "a story in which no attention is given to its essence but which is the direct emanation of his whole existence. Existence is identical to freedom; freedom to choose the ways and means of self-realization." As a result of all this we are told, later in the text of the manual, "In other words all the characters in the story feel, think and act as the testee does."

If all this means anything useful, and the reviewer does not feel himself metaphysically capable of evaluating it in other than the terms of basic English and scientific enquiry, this test should be literally a marvellous one. The authors state, "Suffice it to say that according to the experience of the authors the SAPAT has the qualities of a suitable projection test." Throughout the manual, minimal empirical support for this statement is adduced by Nel and Pelser. As Mark Twain might have said: "It don't suffice me."

In the devising of the test, "five hundred odd pupils of both sexes" [*sic*] were asked what their preferences in stories were from a limited list of stories, possibly appropriate, set before them by the authors. Themes ranging from fairy stories to Tarzan stories emerged as preferred. Boys of eight and above were no longer interested in fairy stories. If this is a useful criterion to use in the choice of stimulus pictures it seems odd that in this test for children up to 13, seven of the final twelve stimulus pictures are of pixies, fairies, and similar "wee folk," two are of mice dressed in human clothes, and three are of ordinary human beings. By the authors' own criteria three quarters of the pictures could be more or less inappropriate for the older child. The pictures are crudely drawn and "slanted" in content, in terms of the preconceptions of the authors, e.g., picture 2, which the authors describe as follows: "Mickey Mouse is standing in a room and talking seriously to a little mouse. Behind and against a wall are hanging a sjambok [rhinoceros hide whip—reviewer's translation], a hunting knife and a mounted buck's head. In the background a mother mouse sits knitting, and on the table lies a pair of scissors. * The symbols of punishment (the sjambok), and of castration (the scissors and the knife) might evoke further projections."

Indeed, the authors' analysis of protocols is largely that of *verstehende* psychology, mostly Freudian, with the occasional touch of Jung. They acknowledge that their scheme of interpretation is, in many respects, "based on work previously done by Murray, Rotter, Tomkins, Rapaport, Rosenzweig, Van Lennep, and others." With the possible exception of the last-named, all these would presumably be regarded by the authors as "pragmatic psychologists" interested only in the products of the "animalistic layers" of the human organism. Their following of these is astonishing in that the underlying philosophy of the authors is essentially the existentialism of Jean-Paul Sartre.

It seems to me that there is precious little that is new or useful in this test but much that is bad. Some analysis is given of 63 specimen protocols, three complete records among them. Specimen analysis sheets are given. The easy identification of the "hero" and of the subject's motives is assumed throughout. Some stories are dismissed as "insignificant," others contain "numerous significant projections." In another case, "The stories are unnatural and the pictures are often misunderstood and misinterpreted." No norms are quoted and it is impossible for this reviewer to see how these certainties were arrived at. The authors seem to be ignorant or heedless of the great body of controlled and experimental investigation into the mechanism of projection that has been accumulated in the West over the last 20 years. Instead: "It is presumed that the analyst has a thorough knowledge of the basical [*sic*] theories underlying projection tests."

One additional comment must be made. I can feel nothing but pity for children attending any child guidance clinic whose personalities are assessed in these subjective and biased terms. I wish that there were space in this review to cite the whole of the last complete record given in the manual. Perhaps the beginning and end of this "analysis" will give some idea of the type of judgments arrived at throughout the examples given:

> The child is well cared for, mostly happy and feels herself quite adequate. She is full of confidence and able to take care of herself. She is however restless, due to internal stresses of a sexual nature. She is pre-occupied with "sexual" adventures: going to parties, dances, for a walk with a friend, etc. Her needs are therefore those for affiliation, play or exhibitionism, always however with a sexual connotation. She is independent, practical and generally happy. Her attitude towards, and intense interest in sexual matters is however of such a cold-blooded nature that there seems to be real danger that she might try experimenting in this direction. * Her exaggerated interest in sexual matters, which is probably accompanied by masturbation, explains the tics as well as her desire to be the centre of attraction.

The authors give no clue as to how they arrived at these "conclusions" from the stories cited. To this reviewer and to other psychologists consulted, few or no sexual themes are discoverable in the stories told by the nine-year-old girl in question, and it might be appropriate to rechristen the SAPAT as "The South African Psychomantic Analysis Test." The *analyses* do, I think, demonstrate clearly the validity of the concept of projection.

JOHANN M. SCHEPERS, *Senior Research Officer, National Institute for Personnel Research, Johannesburg, Republic of South Africa.*

Working at the Child Guidance Clinic of the Faculty of Education, University of Pretoria, the authors felt the need for a projective test of the TAT type, specially suited for use with children in the age range 5–13 years. The *South African Picture Analysis Test* (SAPAT) is their answer to this need.

The construction of the SAPAT raises many important questions and merits our serious consideration.

Every attempt at projective test construction is hampered by the fact that several questions of fundamental importance concerning the construction of the stimulus material have remained unanswered. More often than not some *ad hoc* approach to the matter is followed, with the result that very little is learned in the process. Issues such as the following need to be settled before we can confidently embark on the task of projective test construction: What types of stories will appeal most to children of various age levels? How stable are these preferences when viewed cross-nationally or cross-culturally? What features of the stimulus material facilitate the production of projective responses? Is identification with some central figure necessary for projection? Will the level of projection co-vary with the degree of identification with some central figure? What would happen if the figures depicted in projective material represent an ethnic type dissimilar to that of the testee? Will children readily identify with animal characters? How will children's projections be influenced by bedtime stories about animals if animal characters are used? What is the optimal degree of structuredness of stimulus material for use with children? Should one vary the style of the pictures by having more than one artist? Should one introduce color into the pictures?

The authors have given a detailed account of the various considerations they had in mind when constructing the SAPAT. A commendable feature of their research is the fact that they first tried to establish what types of stories would appeal most to the primary school child. A study involving 500 odd cases showed a wide divergence in the choice of stories, with the result that the authors had to use as wide a range of figures as possible in order to cover the spectrum of interests.

Twenty themes were selected and the pictures drawn by a commercial artist. After an initial investigation using 40 primary school children, eight of the pictures were discarded as relatively unsuitable. Eight pictures were found to be equally suitable for both boys and girls, two were found to be specially suitable for boys and two for girls. Ten pictures were accordingly selected for use with boys and 10 for girls. The authors decided not to reduce the number of pictures to less than 10 because they have found "that there is a definite positive relation between the number of stories analysed and the validity of the interpretation."

The authors claim that in each of the pictures there is one person or figure with whom a child can readily identify. The 12 pictures finally selected are composed as follows: (*a*) Two pictures where the hero is alone. (*b*) Two pictures where the hero is with one other person. (*c*) Three pictures where the hero is in the company of two other people or figures. (*d*) Four pictures where the hero is in the company of more than two people. (*e*) Two pictures where the home situation is depicted. (*f*) One picture where the school situation is represented. (*g*) One picture where the playground situation is depicted. (*h*) Three pictures with a sexual connotation. (*i*) One picture concerning achievement, competition, and exhibitionism.

The authors purposely tried to make the pictures more structured than the usual TAT pictures, because they had found that children tend to lose interest if the themes are vague. They tried to achieve this by having the facial expressions of the characters clearly defined whilst keeping the background fairly neutral. At the same time the authors state that their pictures are polyvalent. It is very difficult to judge this claim because no distribution of themes over the 12 pictures is shown.

The usual TAT instruction is given, but in simpler language. The stories which are produced orally are recorded by the examiner. The test requires less than one hour to administer.

A detailed scheme for the analysis of the protocols is given in the 74-page manual. Eight interpretive categories are presented, four of which relate to the content of the protocols and four to the formal characteristics of the stories. The authors make it clear that the interpretation remains a matter of "verstehen" and that they offer the scheme to compel "the analyst to judge more objectively." Their scheme is comprehensive and might well be used with TAT's generally.

The manual contains numerous illustrative protocols and case histories, together with brief analyses of these protocols. However, no normative material is presented, and one is left with the impression that the test has not yet been extensively applied. No information regarding scorer reliability, test-retest reliability, or validity is given. The psychology of "verstehen" is offered as an apology for this omission.

The authors are at pains to eschew the American approach to personality and projection, and to espouse the Continental approach. American readers might well find the vague metaphysical language of existentialism disturbing. Paradoxically, however, the authors find it necessary to draw heavily on the work of Murray, Tomkins, Rapaport, and others.

The SAPAT is unique in the sense that it is specially suitable for use with primary school children, and as such should fulfil a real need. The dwarf and fairylike characters resemble "real" boys and girls fairly closely and might therefore be of general appeal cross-nationally.

J Proj Tech 24:446 D '60. Wilson H. Guertin. * a constructive contribution * The authors seem to have accomplished their goal of filling the gap between the Childrens Apperception Test (CAT) (animal pictures) and the Symonds Picture Story Test (adolescents). Interest should be optimum for children from about five to twelve years of age. None of the pictures depicts anything culturally unique to Africa and all children are White. Like the CAT each picture is distinctly drawn. It would appear that the clarity of the structure of the stimulus material would decrease the range of different needs that might be projected into a given picture. Thus, ambivalence would probably not be as clearly expressed in responses to the SAPAT cards as to the Symonds or TAT pictures. The manual's introduction concerning differences between European and American conceptions of personality and projection may interest some. However, the final analysis of a protocol by the authors differs in no significant way from American analysis of TAT pictures. The semiobjective scheme for analysis appears to be an eclectic American approach. * Some examples of stories and interpretations are given in the manual. However, the neophyte should not expect to find a scoring and interpretation scheme that dispenses with the intuitive skills of the clinician. The reviewer must admit that the stimuli appear to meet the need for TAT type material for the grade-school child. A sound, objectively-scored projective test would have made a greater methodological contribution, but the clinical value of the TAT method is such that it deserves to be extended to all populations.

[241]

★**Structured Doll Play Test.** Ages 2–6; 1959–60; family and peer relationships; individual; 2 forms; 3 editions (identical except for test figures): Caucasian, Negroid, Oriental; no data on reliability and validity; $14 per set of all 3 editions including 10 record forms, general manual, and manual of instructions; $10 per Caucasian-figures edition including preceding accessories; $3.50 per 25 record forms; $1 per general manual; $3.50 per manual of instructions; postpaid; (30–45) minutes; David B. Lynn; Test Developments. *

a) [SERIES 1.] 1959; 1 form ['59, 12 cardboard figures and objects and 4 background cards]; manual of instructions ('59, 18 pages); general manual ('59, 25 pages); record form ('59, 10 pages).

b) [SERIES 2.] 1959–60; for research use only; 1 form ['60, 10 cardboard figures and objects and 3 background cards]; manual of instructions ('60, 15 pages); general manual ('60, 4 pages); record form ('59, 8 pages); no norms.

REFERENCES

1. LYNN, DAVID B. "Development and Validation of a Structural Doll Play Test for Children." *Q B Indiana Univ, Med Center* 17:16–7 Ja '55. *
2. LYNN, DAVID B. *An Investigation of Hypotheses Basic to a Concept of Relative Intensity of Interaction as Applied to Structural Doll Play Test Responses.* Doctor's thesis, Purdue University (Lafayette, Ind.), 1955. (*DA* 15:869)
3. LYNN, ROSALIE. *A Study of the Responses of Four and Six Year Olds to a Structured Doll Play Test.* Master's thesis, Purdue University (Lafayette, Ind.), 1955.
4. LYNN, DAVID B. "A Relative Measure of Interaction." *J Psychol Studies* 11:52–61 N–D '59. * (*PA* 34:5774)
5. LYNN, DAVID B., AND LYNN, ROSALIE. "The Structured Doll Play Test as a Projective Technique for Use With Children." *J Proj Tech* 23:335–44 S '59. * (*PA* 35:4929)
6. LYNN, ROSALIE. *Sex Role Preference and Mother-Daughter Fantasies in Young Girls.* Doctor's thesis, University of Denver (Denver, Colo.), 1961. (*DA* 22:4084)

TERENCE MOORE, *Research Psychologist and Lecturer, Centre for the Study of Human Development, University of London Institute of Education, London, England.*

It is well known that young children readily project their feelings and fantasies about close personal relationships onto dolls, and there are obvious attractions in the idea of exploring these aspects of their personality through a systematically structured technique. Such systematic exploration is clearly indicated for research purposes, and has advantages also in a clinical setting wherever the aim is not, as in free doll play, to ventilate whatever fantasies are uppermost in the child's mind at the moment, but rather to survey in a single interview a wide range of areas in which conflicts commonly arise, or to map out the parts played by father and mother in the child's mental schema of family life. Although not so defined by the author, these appear to be the main functions of Lynn's *Structured Doll Play Test.*

The 18 situations of Series 1 cover most aspects of the everyday life of a typical preschool child, while Series 2 takes him on to school, to the doctor's, and introduces a "bad animal," thus inviting rather more symbolic fantasy. In nearly every scene the child is first asked to make a choice (either a choice between a more and a less mature object, e.g., a glass and a baby's bottle for the ego doll, or else a choice between the parents) and then encouraged by more open questions to extend his fantasy as he will. The choices are used as a basis for scoring, while the freer fantasy is of more general clinical interest. In order not to limit the fantasy to the chosen parent, each scene is followed by another in which the examiner introduces the non-chosen parent in a somewhat similar role, and asks the subject what will happen. This is ingenious, but is fairly often defeated by a strong-minded child who demands the parent of his own choice in the second scene as well, while some children are anxious to include both parents, suggesting that they place a high valuation on family harmony—an attitude that can easily get obscured by uncritical acceptance of the underlying assumption that a child should choose (and in choosing, prefer or identify with) *either* father *or* mother. Moreover, since the roles (nurturant, authoritarian, depriving, etc.) allotted to father or mother dolls vary fundamentally from scene to scene and from subject to subject, one may wonder how useful it is to add them up. A better case could be made for adding responses indicative of maturity-immaturity, which is at least generally thought of as unidimensional; but are four items an adequate measure of it?

Norms (in the form of percentages of each age-sex group from 2 to 6 years making either possible choice in each item, and summed over items) are presented in a layout that makes comparison of ages and sexes unnecessarily difficult, and Lynn records his impression that his standardization sample of 240 private school children (30 per age-sex group) came from a higher than average socio-economic level and included a disproportionate number of children from broken homes. He claims "construct validity" on the grounds that the scores do differentiate age, sex, and educational groups, and to some extent between children whose fathers are at home and away. This in itself would not seem to bear closely on the value of the scores for individual diagnosis. For this purpose the free material produced in response to the open questions would seem much more useful; and in the reviewer's experience such material is produced in diagnostically useful quantities mainly by older, brighter, and less inhibited children.

The author originally designed the test for children aged 2 to 6, and now finds that it is acceptable with slight verbal modifications for children up to 11. Lower school children will indeed often use dolls for expressing their fantasies quite readily if they are presented in the right way. As regards the lower age limit, while it is possible that choices might be elicited from bright children of 2+, fantasy is rarely articulate enough to provide very rich clinical material much below 4. Nevertheless, this technique does offer the younger child an acceptable and easily comprehended medium through which to express whatever he can and will, either in words or action or both. Given dolls to handle and a few questions to stimulate fantasy, many children are able to respond much more fruitfully than they can to a test such as the CAT, which requires the ability both to construct and to verbalize a story from pictures alone.

The dolls used in this test are of die-cut cardboard and any necessary furniture is printed on cardboard sheets. Besides making for cheapness and portability as compared with more realistic toys, this design is said to reduce tangential manipulation without reducing fantasy content. Although children do seem to identify with these not very attractive cardboard objects, and to express fantasy through them, it is a question whether they are not limited by the rigidity of the board figures and derive less pleasure from handling them than they would from the conventional wire dolls. Having tried both, the reviewer still prefers three-dimensional apparatus. The envelopes supplied as containers, opening at the ends, are not very satisfactory, as they lead to a good deal of fumbling and hunting; or if the contents are emptied out, the child sees more than he is intended to have. A flat box divided into shallow compartments with hinged lids would serve better.

The recording sheet is well drawn up, with small diagrams which remind the examiner of the positions of the dolls and properties for each item and also facilitate recording of the choices made. An improvement found useful by this reviewer in similar work is a list of abbreviations of the commoner types of overt affect, which can be printed for each item and circled as the child's expressions are observed, to capture something of the emotional flavour of each response.

If an adequate picture of the child's outlook on life is required, full account must be taken of the affect expressed around each situation, and to this end, refusals, avoidances, tangential conversation, and spontaneous extension of the play situations are at least as important as the responses proper. But no directions for recording these occur in the manual. Nor is any attempt made to discuss interpretation. One caution should perhaps be issued: since fantasy functions at different levels of realism from child to child, and even from moment to moment in the same child, we must beware of the fallacy of attributing behaviour or attitudes depicted in the play too glibly to the real child and his parents. One interaction of the dolls may represent a wish fulfilment, the next a feared event, a third the reflection of a real life relationship. All will have their significance, but other evidence may well be needed in deciding between the possible interpretations.

In summary, then, this technique does provide a useful projective screen for eliciting fantasy material from young children; it has the advantage over pictorial tests in that it does not require the child to be especially creative or able to order his fantasy in verbal terms; its structure is such that it taps many of the crucial conflict areas, and its combination of choices and open questions gives satisfactory scope for most children. Like all projective techniques, it must be interpreted with tact and caution, and the value of its scoring system still remains to be demonstrated.

ALAN O. ROSS, *Chief Psychologist, Pittsburgh Child Guidance Center, Pittsburgh, Pennsylvania.*

This instrument represents a cross between the *Make A Picture Story* with its cut-out figures and variable background scenes, the Duess-Despert Fables [1] with their structured situational questions, and the little-known but ingenious Miniature Situation Test [2] with its binary choices. This discussion is based primarily on the first of the two forms, i.e., Series 1.

The *Structured Doll Play Test,* which its author describes as a "clinically useful doll play projective technique," presents the child with a cardboard doll in 18 family or peer situations. Each situation is verbally structured and pictorially represented and the child is asked to resolve the situation and to play the story out with the cardboard dolls and props. In 12 of the situations the child is asked to make a choice between two alternatives—e.g., between crib and bed, bottle and glass, father and mother, toilet and potty. The remaining 6 situations require the child to say what is taking place or will happen in the scene structured by the examiner.

The following will serve as an example of the test items: A picture of a crib and a bed is placed before the child who is handed a cardboard doll representing his sex with the instructions, "Take the little boy (girl) in your hand. This is the baby crib and this is the bed. Let's pretend that this little boy can sleep in either the baby crib or the bed. You put him to sleep. Lay him down on either the bed or the baby crib." After the child has made the choice he is asked, "Why is it he sleeps in the bed (baby crib) and not in the baby crib (bed)?" Immediately following this the parent dolls are presented and the child is told, "Now let's pretend the little boy (girl) is in bed and mommy or daddy comes in. Which one comes in, mommy or daddy?" The child is handed the chosen parent and instructed, "Now take mommy (daddy) in your hand and show me and tell me what happens."

The immature wording of many of the questions can be modified when the test is used with older children but even then some of the situations, such as the child being taken to the toilet by one of his parents, would be more suitable for children under six despite the fact that the manual states that the test is "equally useful with children from seven through eleven."

The normative data included in the manual show the percentage of various choices made by 240 children between the ages of 2 and 6. The data presented show an increase in the "maturity" of choices when younger children are compared with older children. The easily checked test-retest reliability of these choices is not reported and it is impossible to determine whether an "immature" choice actually reflects immaturity or, for example, a more active and accessible fantasy life on the part of the younger children. The meaning of any particular response is left to the clinician to interpret, for the author feels that it is premature to publish interpretive guides at the present stage of this test's development, though he promises to publish interpretive hypotheses representing a blend of research and clinical knowledge at a later time.

For research purposes the author offers a mimeographed preliminary scoring manual providing for quantification of 163 response categories. This system is admittedly far too complex for everyday clinical use and the author again promises a brief modification for clinical purposes for some later date. If such a scoring manual could indeed be produced it would represent a true contribution to the field of thematic testing.

In one of the publications describing this test (5) the author makes the observation that "Fortunately, the period in Clinical Psychology is virtually ended when a psychologist can originate a test and place it on the market without supporting research. Some research has been

1 MOSSE, HILDE L. "The Duess Test." *Am J Psychother* 8:251–64 Ap '54. *
2 SANTOSTEFANO, SEBASTIAN. "Miniature Situation Tests as a Way of Interviewing Children." *Merrill-Palmer Q* 8:261–9 O '62. *

completed with the SDP and more is currently under way." There have indeed been a few studies, mostly with earlier or modified forms of the test, but when the manual speaks of "norms and research findings which will be published in the future" it raises the question whether publication of this instrument as a clinically useful projective technique might not have been premature.

The SDP is a cleverly designed device which can facilitate the study of young children in a manner which has more structure and objectivity than the usual thematic picture test, but whether it elicits more or better information than available projective techniques, including the informal and spontaneous doll play interview, remains to be demonstrated.

[242]

Structured-Objective Rorschach Test: Preliminary Edition. Adults; 1958; also called *S-O Rorschach Test;* 15 scores (for deriving 26 traits): whole-blot (W), major details (D), minor details (Dd), white space (S), form resemblance (F), poor form resemblance (F–), human movement (M), animal movement (FM), color and form resemblance (FC), color and poor form resemblance (CF), shading (Fch), animal figure (A), human figure (H), modal responses (P), rare responses (O); IBM; 1 form; 2 editions; preliminary manual (28 pages); separate answer sheets must be used; 10¢ per IBM answer sheet; $1.50 per set of hand scoring stencils; postage extra; scoring service available; (30–50) minutes; Joics B. Stone; California Test Bureau. *

a) ILLUSTRATED EDITION. 1 form (12 pages); $7.50 per test.

b) NON-ILLUSTRATED EDITION. 1 form (23 pages); to be used with slides or cards; $5 per 10 tests; $13 per set of inkblot cards; $12.50 per set of kodaslides; $1 per specimen set without slides or cards, postpaid.

REFERENCES

1. KHAN, LILIAN. *Factor Analysis of Certain Aptitude and Personality Variables.* Doctor's thesis, University of Southern California (Los Angeles, Calif.), 1959. (*DA* 20:2889)
2. ANGELINO, HENRY, AND HALL, RICHARD L. "Temperament Factors in High- and Low-Achieving High School Seniors." *Psychol Rep* 7:518 D '60. * (*PA* 35:2005)
3. HAMPTON, PETER J. "Use of Rorschach Test in Selecting Factory Supervisors." *Personnel J* 39:46–8 Je '60. * (*PA* 35:7190)
4. HOSFORD, PRENTISS MCINTYRE. *Characteristics of Science-Talented and Language-Talented Secondary School Students.* Doctor's thesis, University of Georgia (Athens, Ga.), 1961. (*DA* 22:2687)
5. MINK, OSCAR GORTON. *A Study of Certain Cognitive and Conative Factors Affecting Academic Progress in Chemical and Metallurgical Engineering at Cornell University.* Doctor's thesis, Cornell University (Ithaca, N.Y.), 1961. (*DA* 22:2695)
6. HAMMES, JOHN A., AND OSBORNE, R. TRAVIS. "Discrimination of Manifest Anxiety by the Structured-Objective Rorschach Test." *Percept & Motor Skills* 15:59–62 Ag '62. * (*PA* 37:5083)
7. HICKS, JOHN A., AND STONE, JOICS B. "The Identification of Traits Related to Managerial Success." *J Appl Psychol* 46:428–32 D '62. * (*PA* 37:5714)
8. KHAN, LILIAN. "Factor Analysis of Certain Aptitude and Personality Variables." *Indian J Psychol* 37:27–38 Mr '62. * (*PA* 37:6716)
9. LANGER, PHILIP. "Compulsivity and Response Set on the Structured Objective Rorschach Test." *J Clin Psychol* 18:299–302 Jl '62. * (*PA* 39:1862)
10. LANGER, PHILIP. "Social Desirability and Acquiescence on the SORT." *Psychol Rep* 11:531–4 O '62. * (*PA* 37:8018)
11. LAW, DAVID H., AND NORTON, JOSEPH L. "The SORT as a Differentiator Between High and Low Achievers." *J Counsel Psychol* 9:184 su '62. *
12. LITTLE, ELDON LEROY. *SORT Evaluation of Midshipmen in the First Year Naval Reserve Officers' Training Corps Program.* Doctor's thesis, University of Oklahoma (Norman, Okla.), 1962. (*DA* 23:2012)
13. VINSON, DAVID B. "Objectivity in the Assessment of Psychobiologic Decline." *Vita Hum* 4(3):134–42 '62. *
14. LANGER, PHILIP; CARLISLE, ALMA L.; AND HAYES, WILLIAM G. "The Effects of Anxiety and Conformity on the Structured-Objective Rorschach Test (SORT)." *J Clin Psychol* 19:317–9 Jl '63. *
15. LANGER, PHILIP; HAYES, WILLIAM G.; AND SHARP, HEBER C. "Effect of Anxiety and Induced Stress on the Structured-Objective Rorschach Test." *Percept & Motor Skills* 16:573–80 Ap '63. * (*PA* 38:2718)
16. PERRY, MARIAN LOUISE. *The Relationship of Selected Variables to the Success of Camp Counselors.* Doctor's thesis, University of Southern California (Los Angeles, Calif.), 1963. (*DA* 24:613)

JESSE G. HARRIS, JR., *Professor of Psychology and Chairman of the Department, University of Kentucky, Lexington, Kentucky.*

The *Structured-Objective Rorschach Test* is a multiple choice instrument which uses the 10 original inkblots in either an illustrated or non-illustrated booklet form, the latter of which must be accompanied by either the 10 cards or slides for a projector. The SORT requires neither free association nor inquiry, is suitable for individual or group administration, and is objectively scored by means of templates or IBM test scoring machine. The subject is required, by forced choice procedure, to select from each of 10 sets of triads for each card the response which is *"most clearly represented by* the blot or *by some part* of the blot." The concrete, abstract, and mythological noun responses are, in some items, qualified by descriptive adjectives. Each response alternative provides at least two scores and, in some instances, additional scores for content and for statistically determined populars and originals. The scoring format is apparently an eclectic synthesis of several well known scoring systems, including the Beck, Klopfer and Kelley, Schafer, and Harrower-Erickson. The 15 basic raw scores are converted to normalized *T* scores and, for subsequent interpretation of personality attributes, are read as ratings of "high," "above average," "average," "below average," or "low," from tables of single variables or from the diagonal bands of two-dimensional abacs, when multiple determinants are involved.

The method of analysis is an approximation to the "cookbook" approach for inexperienced technicians, a methodology for which Rorschach enthusiasts, ironically, have long expressed a profound distaste. Although the details of method of derivation and sequential arrangement of response choices are not described clearly either in the manual or in the research literature, the procedure has involved use of Beck's location charts, Harrower-Erickson's tables of frequency of occurrence of responses, and a judgmental arrangement of response combinations. Both tester and researcher must assume a high probability of correspondence between the subject's actual percept and the area of the blot for which the structured response was intended by the author. Mutual contamination of verbal and perceptual free associations is inevitable in this, as in any other, type of multiple choice inkblot test, regardless of the seemingly structured nature of the response alternatives. The manual states that the SORT provides an assessment of temperament patterns for educational-vocational guidance work and for personnel selection, and that it is not intended for clinical use, apparently because it lacks the free associational characteristics of the more commonly used projective techniques.

The instrument seems to possess properties which are usually regarded as highly desirable for a research tool designed for large scale investigation. Although it suffers the usual lack of a suitable alternate form for studies of reliability, the SORT has test-retest reliability coefficients at least equivalent to, and possibly higher than, those of similar tests (medians of 15 scoring variables for two groups reported in the Preliminary Manual of the order, $r = .75$, with a minimum value of $r = .62$). Concurrent validity coefficients are reported for 1,616 telephone company employees as correlations between Rorschach variables and job classification, and for 2,600 college freshmen as correlations between Rorschach variables and grade point average. Tables of mean number of responses are presented for several different occupational groups. Information on construct validity of the instrument is provided in the Preliminary Manual in the form of measures of correspondence between supervisors' ratings and Rorschach ratings.

The SORT has also generated research by other investigators concerned with construct validity, as is reflected in the accompanying list of titles of research articles. Some of the hypotheses in these studies have been sound, and others which have produced negative results may or may not reflect inadequacy of the test instrument. Only further research can determine whether the SORT describes or predicts behavior as accurately as, or more accurately than, conventional personality inventories. Khan (*8*) has reported, in a factor analytic study, a relative independence of variables on the SORT from those of the *Guilford-Zimmerman Temperament Survey* and of the *Multiple Aptitude Tests,* devised by Segel and Raskin. Although the SORT has now made its formal appearance among the storm-swept islands of Rorschach literature and, of necessity, will be required to generate some impressive research data on validity if it is to advance the cause of inkblot testing, it does seem to possess a set of structural attributes which should permit a rigorous evaluation, on a large scale basis, of fundamental Rorschach hypotheses.

The SORT has the same physical limitations which are inherent in the original set of Rorschach inkblots, but the techniques of collecting, scoring, and interpreting data are sufficiently economical and objective to encourage further research with the instrument, not only in the areas of personnel selection and counseling, but also in more basic studies of perception. With regard to construction of response alternatives and statistical properties of the instrument as a whole, the SORT may prove to have an advantage over the multiple choice Rorschach test, developed by Harrower and Steiner, which is similar in purpose and in application. From the point of view of construction of stimulus materials, however, the SORT may have less to recommend it than the *Holtzman Inkblot Technique,* which employs free association and inquiry and is highly developed statistically. The SORT deserves further exploration at the level of collection and analysis of raw data in a variety of settings. Interpretation of data need not be restricted to a reading of the author's abacs or to an adoption of his first order derivatives of conventional Rorschach hypotheses. Economy of method, it would seem, is sufficient justification for further research with this test on a large scale basis by persons who have convictions about the merits of the inkblot approach to the study of the normal or abnormal personality. One might hope, also, that the author of the SORT would plan and develop a manual to supersede the preliminary edition, reporting all findings, both positive and negative, which have been obtained on samples of large size. Such a request should seem reasonable, if the author is himself convinced of the fundamental worth of the test as an instrument of science.

BORIS SEMEONOFF, *Reader in Psychology, University of Edinburgh, Edinburgh, Scotland.*

Introducing the *Structured-Objective Rorschach Test* (SORT), the author claims that it "combines the subtle features of the widely respected and highly developed Rorschach inkblot projective methodology with the practical group methodology of the objective test." The second of these requirements has certainly been met: the SORT has been admirably produced; instructions, layout, recording and scoring devices, etc. could hardly be bettered. Nevertheless, whether the test can truly be described as "objective" is open to doubt, and its claim to possess the "subtle features" of Rorschach could not be upheld by any but the most naïve user of the original technique.

The test is constructed on the forced-choice principle. The stimuli are the 10 original Rorschach blots, for each of which 10 triads of responses are offered; the instruction is "select the *one* response from each group of three items that you think is *best represented* by the blot or some part of the blot." Every protocol will thus consist of 100 responses, which are analysed to yield 15 "scores." Expressed in Rorschach symbols these are: W, D, Dd, S, F, F–, M, FM, FC, CF, Fch, A, H, P, O. These are mostly self-explanatory, but the following divergences from normal Rorschach practice should be noted: (*a*) All S (space) responses are also scored as W, D, or Dd. (*b*) CF responses are defined as those "involving color and poorly resembling the form of the stimulus." (*c*) Fch covers all responses "involving textural density of gray or shading." (*d*) P indicates "modal" responses, i.e., the responses most commonly chosen from each and every triad. (*e*) O covers many responses which will be recognised by the experienced Rorschach user as not even "rare," let alone *original* in the orthodox sense.

Raw scores are converted to *T*-scores, and these in turn to ratings, on a five-point scale, on each of 26 attributes, either direct from a single "factor," or by means of "abacs" based on a combination of scores on two or more factors. The 26 attributes (in actual fact 30, since one has 5 subvarieties) are grouped under four broad heads: mental functioning (9 items); interests (2); responsiveness (2); and temperament (13).

The rationale for these attributes is said to rely on "basic Rorschach interpretation." In most cases this claim is justified (assuming, at any rate, that the techniques are equivalent), but there are some curious exceptions. Thus, Concentration (a "Mental functioning" variable) and Impulsiveness (a "Temperament" variable) are both derived from a combination of F and F– ; examination of the respective abacs indeed reveals that one is the exact inverse of the other. There are also some oddities in terminology, the chief example being Aggressiveness (derived, incidentally, from F and M), which is defined as "the aspiration toward goals by means of well-accepted and morally developed procedures; willingness and desire to work; sense of a mature self-control with social conformity."

The points of criticism so far noted are of course of a minor nature, and it must be added that the manual for the SORT presents reasonably satisfactory reliability and validity data. On construct validity the data may be summed up by saying that in two studies of correspondence between trait ratings of employees by supervisors and on the basis of SORT, a good measure of agreement was obtained in roughly 70 per cent of cases. The author is also careful to state that the SORT is "not intended for clinical use" but is "designed to appraise and analyze vocationally significant temperament traits." In fact, he leans over backward in recommending caution and "the exercise of suspended judgement." In view of all these facts is it unfair to extend criticism on the basis of one or two unusually surprising results?

Probably not, if examination of the underlying causes calls attention to fundamental weaknesses in test construction. To take but a single case: A highly qualified psychologist received a rating of "Low" (actual *T*-score 27, or almost into the lowest 1 per cent *of the general population*) on the attribute Theoretical, defined as "facility for generalizing, capacity for abstraction"—in other words, as near as one can get to Spearman's "g." This rating is derived direct from the W score, and the palpable "incorrectness" of the rating prompted the writer to find out what are, in fact, the available W responses. Scrutiny showed that of the 62 possible W responses, no less than 25 come into categories such as "modernistic painting," "coat of arms," "squashed bug," and others which would almost certainly be regarded as in some way "unfavourable" by users of normal Rorschach. Further examination showed that to achieve a rating of "High" on Theoretical one would have to have used *at least four* of these "unfavourable" responses.

Clearly something is specifically wrong here, but more important is the wider implication that a forced choice technique which assumes that a given response can always be scored in the same way is basically fallacious. To take one further example: the response "X-ray of bony structure" to Card 1 is scored W; the subject quoted above chose this response, but referred it to a D area—which suggests that his W score (and his Theoretical rating) should really have been still further reduced! What the SORT therefore may be doing is not scoring a subject's response objectively, but guessing at what the subject meant and scoring that guess.

Can the SORT, then, be said to be "objective"? Or in more general terms, is a test objective if it is not clear to what question a particular answer has been given? Even if it were possible to frame test items in such a way as to circumvent this difficulty, a still more fundamental objection to equating SORT with Rorschach remains. Reference to Rorschach's original text shows that the object of his "experiment" was to arrive at an understanding of personality through analysis of perception, the subject's spontaneous perception and the ways in which he organizes it—not, as in the case of SORT, the way in which he handles someone else's perceptions. Stone, although conceding that a subject may experience difficulty in choosing between three interpretations all of which seem inappropriate to him, claims that something similar is done in "limits-testing." But normal Rorschach practice keeps spontaneous and forced responses quite separate, whereas in SORT the distinction is irretrievably lost. Again, SORT gives no information about creativity, *genuine* originality, nor any of the truly "subtle features" of the full Rorschach protocol. This surely is throwing the baby out with the bath water. Yet again one must recognize that Stone is aware of this; SORT, he says, "defers to the individual protocol which....permits greater usefulness in diagnosis of deviant emotional syndromes." Unfortunately, a previous application of SORT is almost certain to contaminate one's response to normal Rorschach, and it seems a pity to run this risk when other, unrelated means of vocational assessment are available.

J Consult Psychol 23:471–2 O '59. Edward S. Bordin. * The validity of the test seems to rest mainly on two bases: first, its supposed relationship to Rorschach phenomena; second, two empirical studies. Without considerable empirical evidence, there is great room for doubt that responses to the SORT are mainly tapping perceptual phenomena analogous to its prototype. The method of test administration contains no procedures that ensure that the subject has seen the percept that he chooses nor for that matter that he has even looked at the blot. Response sets of various sorts, particularly social desirability stereotypes, are probably greatly enhanced under such circumstances. The manual gives a brief report of two unpublished validity studies. In one, the SORT increased the correlation of high school grade point average with first year grades from .59 to .68, using the best 2 of 15 scores. No cross-validation data are offered. In the other, the SORT variables are correlated with supervisors' ratings in 29 occupational groups. A suggestive but not impressive array of correlations was obtained. Again no cross-validation. This all sums up to the fact that we have here an interesting new experiment in adapting Rorschach testing techniques to the need for large scale testing and objective scoring and interpretation. But it is still *experimental,* and every effort should be made to warn against adopting it for operational use. I do not believe the "Preliminary Edition" in the title or the caution section in the manual, largely irrelevant to this issue, represent sufficient effort to emphasize the fact that this instrument is not ready for operational use.

J Counsel Psychol 6:72–3 sp '59. Laurence Siegel. * The development of an objectively scorable form of the Rorschach test specifically designed for vocational applications will be welcomed in many quarters. The S-O *Rorschach Test* is well-conceived and excellently executed. The manual is a model of clarity and organization. It is likely that the test will be extensively used for executive appraisal in industry, for vocational guidance in schools and for research purposes in countless settings wherein the personnel director, counselor or researcher wants Rorschach-type data for some non-clinical purpose. The attractiveness of the SORT format does, however, necessitate consideration of a problem that may eventually prove to be of some consequence. The fact that this test makes it possible for persons who otherwise would never have considered themselves sufficiently qualified to administer a Rorschach now to do so, means that we may anticipate increased exposure to the Rorschach blots. Persons who have taken the SORT are no longer naive with respect to the specific Rorschach content. Their resultant sophistication may be of import at some future time when they may be required to respond to the Rorschach as an aid to clinical diagnosis. Perhaps an even more serious consideration is the fact that the SORT exposes respondents not only to the Rorschach ink-blot, but also to 30 possible responses to each of these blots. How many (if indeed any) and what kinds of these responses may subsequently be parroted by the previously SORT-tested clinical respondent is a problem that merits additional research.

[243]

***Szondi Test.** Ages 4 and over; 1937–61; 8 factors, 4 vectors (each vector is a total of 2 factors): homosexual, sadistic, sexual vector, epileptic, hysteric, paroxysmal vector, catatonic, paranoic, schizophrenic vector, depressive, manic, contact vector; 1 form; 2 editions: individual, group; no data on reliability; postage extra; Lipot Szondi; Hans Huber. * (United States publisher of English-language manual and distributor of the individual test: Grune & Stratton, Inc.; United States distributor of the group test: Intercontinental Medical Book Corporation.)

a) [INDIVIDUAL] SZONDI TEST. 1937–52; 1 form ('47, 48 pictures); manual ('52, 264 pages, translated by Gertrude All, see *87* below); 10-profile form ('49, 1 page, labeled Form B); table of tendency tension ('49, 1 page, labeled Form C); record folder ('49, 3 pages, labeled Form A, a combination of Forms B and C); computing form ('47, 1 page, labeled Form D); sexual-social index form ('47, 1 page); Fr. 34 per set of pictures, 20 copies of Form B, and 10 copies of Form A; $11 per set of pictures; Fr. 8 ($3.25) per 50 copies of Form A; Fr. 8 ($3.25) per 100 copies of Form B; Fr. 2.50 per 100 copies of Form D (Grune & Stratton, Inc. sells, at $2 per 50 copies, an IBM answer sheet, labeled Form D, designed by H. P. David, but there are no scoring stencils and no instructions for using the separate answer sheet); Fr. 12 per 100 sexual-social index forms (not available in the U.S.); $14 per manual; must be administered "at least six, preferably ten, times with at least one day intervals between administrations"; (10–15) minutes per administration.

b) THE GROUP SZONDI TEST. 1961; 1 form (12 slides, pictures identical with the 1947 pictures in the individual form); directions for administration (26 pages, containing instructions in English, French, and German); 10-profile form (1 page, labeled Form 2, identical with 1949 individual Form B); tendency tension quotient computing form (1 page, called form 6); record folder (3 pages, called form 1, identical with 1949 individual Form A); test behavior record (1 page, called form 5); computing form (1 page, called form 7); separate answer sheets (called form 3) must be used; Fr. 48 ($12) per set of 10 copies of form 1, 20 copies of Form 2, 100 copies of form 3, 100 copies of form 5, 100 copies of form 6, 10 copies of form 7, scoring templates, and directions; Fr. 52 ($13) per set of slides; 8–10 administrations are recommended with 2 administrations per day suggested; [15–30] minutes per administration; adapted for group administration by A. Friedemann.

REFERENCES

1–64. See 4:134.
65–138. See 5:162.
139. SCOTT, E. *The Szondi Test as a Diagnostic Instrument in Predicting Delinquency.* Doctor's thesis, University of Portland (Portland, Ore.), 1953.
140. ABEL, THEODORA M., AND METRAUX, RHODA. "Sex Differences in a Negro Peasant Community: Montserrat, B.W.I." *J Proj Tech* 23:127–33 Je '59. * (*PA* 35:4755)
141. BLAZSANYIK, J. "Psychological Impotency: A Case Analysis." *Austral J Psychol Res* 1:49–54 O '59. *
142. COULTER, WALTER M. "The Szondi Test and the Prediction of Antisocial Behavior." *J Proj Tech* 23:24–9 Mr '59. * (*PA* 34:6011)
143. HAMILTON, J. T. "A Study of Incidental Stimulus Values in the Szondi Test." *J Clin Psychol* 15:322–4 Jl '59. * (*PA* 35:3468)
144. NOLAN, EDWARD GILLIGAN. *Uniqueness in Monozygotic Twins.* Doctor's thesis, Princeton University (Princeton, N.J.), 1959. (*DA* 21:247)
145. SZONDI, LIPOT; MOSER, ULRICH; AND WEBB, MARVIN W. *The Szondi Test: Its Diagnosis, Prognosis and Treatment.* Philadelphia, Pa.: J. B. Lippincott Co., 1959. Pp. xv, 309. * (*PA* 33:10370)
146. WALDER, HANS. *Drive Structure and Criminality: Criminobiologic Investigations, Revised Edition.* Translated by Marvin W. Webb. Springfield, Ill.: Charles C Thomas, Publisher, 1959. Pp. xvii, 174. *
147. WALDER, HANS. "Crime and Destiny." *Austral J Psychol Res* 2:13–24 sp '60. *
148. BARATZ, STEPHEN S. *A Semantic Analysis of the Szondi Test.* Master's thesis, University of Kansas (Lawrence, Kan.), 1961.
149. BEARDSLEY, KATHARINE. "Analysis of Psychological Tests of Persons Diagnosed Sociopathic Personality Disturbance." *Arch Crim Psychodynam* 4:389–411 su '61. *
150. BEELI, ARMIN. "Some Psychological Aspects of Religious Formation." *Austral J Psychol Res* 2:66–79 au '61. *
151. BLAZSANYIK, J. "Separation Anxiety, Despair and Detachment During Puberty." *Austral J Psychol Res* 2:112–20 au '61. *
152. CONWAY, RONALD. "The Szondi Test: An Elementary Discussion." *Austral J Psychol Res* 2:121–4 au '61. *
153. HOLMQVIST, S. "The Reliability of the Szonditest." Abstract. *Acta Psychologica* 19:120 '61. *
154. LOGAN, JAMES C. "Szondi Profile Changes From Sorrow Arousal." *J Proj Tech* 25:184–92 Je '61. * (*PA* 36:2HE84L)
155. MOGENSEN, ALAN, AND JUEL-NIELSEN, NIELS. "Factors Influencing the Selection and Rejection of Szondi's Pictures: A Study of Uniovular Twins Brought Up Apart." *Acta Psychiatrica Scandinavica* 37(1):32–6 '61. * (*PA* 36:4HG32M)
156. NOLAN, EDWARD G. "Szondi Test Protocols of Monozygotic and Dizygotic Twin Populations." *J Proj Tech* 25:471–6 D '61. *
157. RAMFALK, CARL W., AND RUDHE, LENNART. "A Contradicted Hypothesis Related to Szondi's Theory: The Szondi Test as Used on Alcoholics." *Scandinavian J Psychol* 2(2):100–4 '61. * (*PA* 36:2HI00R)
158. FANCHER, EDWIN C. "A Comparative Study of American and Hungarian Developmental Trends With the Szondi Test." *J Genetic Psychol* 101:229–53 D '62. * (*PA* 37:6467)
159. SEEMAN, WILLIAM, AND MARKS, PHILIP A. "A Study of Some 'Test Dimensions' Conceptions." *J Proj Tech* 26:469–73 D '62. * (*PA* 37:6678)

For reviews by Ardie Lubin and Albert I. Rabin, see 4:134; for a review by Susan K.

Deri, see 3:100; for excerpts from related book reviews, see B474, B501, 5:B418, and 4:135.

[244]

★Ten Silhouettes. Ages 5 and over; 1959-60; individual; 1 form ['60, 10 cards]; directions for administering ['60, 2 pages]; no data on reliability and validity; no norms; 63s. per set of testing materials, postpaid; [45] minutes; B. E. Dockar-Drysdale; the Author. *

REFERENCES

1. DRYSDALE, B. E. DOCKAR. "Notes on the History of the Development of a Projection Technique 'The Silhouettes.'" *Acta Psychologica* 16(3):157-64 '59. * (*PA* 34:5935)
2. RUDOLPH, RIGMOR. "The Silhouette Test." *Acta Psychologica* 16(1):25-43 '59. * (*PA* 34:3023)
3. RUDOLPH, RIGMOR. "The Silhouette Test." *Nordisk Psykologi* 11(1):25-44 '59. * (*PA* 34:1415)
4. SMITH, B. BABINGTON. "Ten Silhouettes: An Account of Perceptual and Procedural Problems Encountered in the Development of a Fresh Projective Technique." *Acta Psychologica* 16(3):165-77 '59. * (*PA* 34:5983)

[245]

Thematic Apperception Test. Ages 4 and over; 1936-43; commonly known as TAT; individual; 1 form ('43, 20 cards); manual ('43, 20 pages); no data on reliability; $6 per set of testing materials; 50¢ per manual; cash orders postpaid; 100(120) minutes in 2 sessions 1 day apart; Henry A. Murray; Harvard University Press. * (*Bellak TAT Blank.* 1947-51; 1 form ('47, 6 pages); analysis sheet ('47, 2 pages); manual ('51, 10 pages); $1.25 per 10 blanks; $1.75 per 100 analysis sheets; 35¢ per manual; 60¢ per specimen set of 1 blank, 10 analysis sheets, and manual; postpaid; Leopold Bellak; Psychological Corporation. *)

REFERENCES

1-101. See 3:103.
102-299. See 4:136.
300-610. See 5:164.
611. GUREL, L. *Quantitative Differences in Responses to Twenty Stimulus Cards of the Thematic Apperception Test.* Master's thesis, Purdue University (Lafayette, Ind.), 1950.
612. FISHER, SEYMOUR, AND HINDS, EDITH. "The Organization of Hostility Controls in Various Personality Structures." *Genetic Psychol Monogr* 44:3-68 Ag '51. * (*PA* 26:2889)
613. RAPAPORT, DAVID. "Projective Techniques and the Theory of Thinking." *J Proj Tech* 16:269-75 S '52. * (*PA* 28:2254)
614. SHANMUGAM, T. E. "Characteristics of Adolescent Girls Fantasy." *J Madras Univ* 22(1):119-28 '52. *
615. SCHNECK, JEROME, AND KLINE, MILTON V. "The H-T-P and TAT Hypnodiagnostic Studies." *Brit J Med Hypnosis* 5:3-15 au '53. *
616. FITZGERALD, BERNARD JOSEPH. *The Relationship of Two Projective Measures to a Sociometric Measure of Dependent Behavior.* Doctor's thesis, Ohio State University (Columbus, Ohio), 1954. (DA 20:2380)
617. HENRY, WILLIAM E. "Trukese T.A.T.'s." Letter. *Am Anthrop* 56:889 O '54. *
618. BARRON, FRANK. "The Disposition Toward Originality." *J Abn & Social Psychol* 51:478-85 N '55. * (*PA* 31:2533)
619. NORGARB, BRIAN N. "Psychodiagnostic Testing and Hypnosis." *J Clin & Exp Hypnosis* 3:44-8 Ja '55. * (*PA* 29:8624)
620. BOLTON, RITA J. *A Comparison of the T.A.T. and the Michigan Picture Test With Adolescents.* Master's thesis, Cornell University (Ithaca, N.Y.), 1956.
621. CARTWRIGHT, ROSALIND DYMOND; SEEMAN, JULIUS; AND GRUMMON, DONALD L. "Patterns of Perceived Interpersonal Relations." *Sociometry* 19:166-77 Mr '56. * (*PA* 31:8009)
622. CAUDILL, WILLIAM, AND DE VOS, GEORGE. "Achievement, Culture and Personality: The Case of the Japanese Americans." *Am Anthrop* 58:1102-26 D '56. *
623. LEARY, TIMOTHY; WITH THE COLLABORATION OF HELEN LANE, ANNE APFELBAUM, MARY DELLA CIOPPA, AND CHARLOTTE KAUFMANN. *Multilevel Measurement of Interpersonal Behavior: A Manual for the Use of the Interpersonal System of Personality.* Berkeley, Calif.: Psychological Consultation Service, 1956. Pp. vii, 110. *
624. ROTHNEY, JOHN W. M., AND HEIMANN, ROBERT A. "Development and Applications of Projective Technics." *R Ed Res* 26:56-71 F '56. * (*PA* 31:6127)
625. SHNEIDMAN, EDWIN S. Chap. 17, "Some Relationships Between the Rorschach Technique and Other Psychodiagnostic Tests," pp. 595-642. In *Developments in the Rorschach Technique: Volume 2, Fields of Application.* By Bruno Klopfer and others. Yonkers, N.Y.: World Book Co., 1956. Pp. xx, 828. * (*PA* 30:7202)
626. VENTUR, PIERRE; KRANSDORFF, MORRIS; AND KLINE, MILTON V. "A Differential Study of Emotional Attitudes Toward Hypnosis With Card 12M of the Thematic Apperception Test." *Brit J Med Hypnosis* 8:5-16 w '56-57. *
627. ZUK, GERALD H. "The Influence of Social Context on Impulse and Control Tendencies in Preadolescence." *Genetic Psychol Monogr* 54:117-66 N '56. * (*PA* 33:3464)
628. GUNDLACH, RALPH. "Research With Projective Techniques." *J Proj Tech* 21:350-4 D '57. *
629. MCNEIL, ELTON B., AND COHLER, J. ROBERT, JR. "The Effect of Personal Needs on Counselors' Perception and Behavior." *Papers Mich Acad Sci Arts & Letters* 42:281-8 pt 2 '57. * (*PA* 37:6924)
630. TAKALA, MARTTI; PIHKANEN, TOIVO A.; AND MARKKANEN, TOUKO. *The Effects of Distilled and Brewed Beverages: A Physiological, Neurological, and Psychological Study.* The Finnish Foundation for Alcoholic Studies, No. 4. Stockholm, Sweden: Almqvist & Wiksell, 1957. Pp. 195. * (*PA* 31:4890)
631. "The Personality of Duodenal Ulcer Patients: A Note on Mr. V. B. Kanter's Investigation of T.A.T. Material." *Rorsch Newsl* 3:8 Je '58. *
632. ABEGGLEN, JAMES C. "Personality Factors in Social Mobility: A Study of Occupationally Mobile Businessmen." *Genetic Psychol Monogr* 58:101-59 Ag '58. * (*PA* 34:990)
633. ANDERSON, DARRELL EDWARD. *Personality Variables and Verbal Conditioning.* Doctor's thesis, University of Nebraska (Lincoln, Neb.), 1958. (*DA* 19:1811)
634. ATKINSON, JOHN W., EDITOR. *Motives in Fantasy, Action, and Society: A Method of Assessment and Study.* Princeton, N.J.: D. Van Nostrand Co., Inc., 1958. Pp. xv, 873. * (*PA* 33:758)
635. CALOGERAS, ROY C. "Some Relationships Between Fantasy and Self-Report Behavior." *Genetic Psychol Monogr* 58:273-325 N '58. * (*PA* 34:2028)
636. CARR, ARTHUR C. Chap. 4, "The Psychodiagnostic Test Battery: Rationale and Methodology," pp. 28-39. In *Progress in Clinical Psychology, Vol. 3.* Edited by Daniel Brower and Lawrence E. Abt. New York: Grune & Stratton, Inc., 1958. Pp. vi, 249. * (*PA* 33:8255)
637. CLIFFORD, PAUL I. "Emotional Contacts With the External World Manifested by a Selected Group of Highly Creative Chemists and Mathematicians." *Percept & Motor Skills* 8:3-26 Mr '58. * (*PA* 33:3039)
638. DAVIDS, ANTHONY, AND PILDNER, HENRY, JR. "Comparison of Direct and Projective Methods of Personality Assessment Under Different Conditions of Motivation." *Psychol Monogr* 72(11):1-30 '58. * (*PA* 33:9937)
639. DILWORTH, TOM, IV. "A Comparison of the Edwards PPS Variables With Some Aspects of the TAT." Abstract. *J Consult Psychol* 22:486 D '58. * (*PA* 33:10321)
640. DILWORTH, TOM, IV. *A Comparison of the Edwards Personal Preference Schedule Variables With Some Aspects of the Thematic Apperception Test.* Master's thesis, Southern Methodist University (Dallas, Tex.), 1958.
641. EIDUSON, BERNICE T. "Artist and Nonartist: A Comparative Study." *J Personality* 26:13-28 Mr '58. * (*PA* 33:5807)
642. FISHER, RHODA LEE. "The Effect of a Disturbing Situation Upon the Stability of Various Projective Tests." *Psychol Monogr* 72(14):1-23 '58. * (*PA* 34:1357)
643. FISHER, SEYMOUR, AND CLEVELAND, SIDNEY E. *Body Images and Personality.* Princeton, N.J.: D. Van Nostrand Co., Inc., 1958. Pp. xi, 420. * (*PA* 32:3926)
644. GUREL, LEE, AND ULLMANN, LEONARD P. "Quantitative Differences in Response to TAT Cards: The Relationship Between Transcendence Score and Number of Emotional Words." *J Proj Tech* 22:399-401 D '58. * (*PA* 34:1369)
645. HEATH, DOUGLAS. "Projective Tests as Measures of Defensive Activity." *J Proj Tech* 22:284-92 S '58. * (*PA* 33:10333)
646. HOKANSON, JACK E., AND GORDON, JESSE E. "The Expression and Inhibition of Hostility in Imaginative and Overt Behavior." *J Abn & Social Psychol* 57:327-33 N '58. * (*PA* 33:10523)
647. HOLT, ROBERT R., AND LUBORSKY, LESTER; WITH THE COLLABORATION OF WILLIAM R. MORROW, DAVID RAPAPORT, AND SIBYLLE K. ESCALONA. *Personality Patterns of Psychiatrists: A Study of Methods for Selecting Residents, Vol. 1.* New York: Basic Books, Inc., 1958. Pp. xiv, 386. * (*PA* 33:5751)
648. KANTER, V. B., AND WILLIAMS, CELIA. "The Interaction of Emotional and Organic Factors in the Rorschach and T.A.T. Records of a Male Alcoholic Aged 60." *Rorsch Newsl* 3:22-3 D '58. *
649. LEICHTY, MARY M. *The Absence of the Father During Early Childhood and Its Effect Upon the Oedipal Situation as Reflected in Young Adults.* Doctor's thesis, Michigan State University (East Lansing, Mich.), 1958. (*DA* 19:1821)
650. LUBIN, BERNARD. *Some Effects of Set and Stimulus Properties on Thematic Apperception Test Stories and on Resulting Clinical Judgment.* Doctor's thesis, Pennsylvania State University (University Park, Pa.), 1958. (*DA* 19:181)
651. LYLE, J. G., AND GILCHRIST, A. A. "Problems of T.A.T.

Interpretation and the Diagnosis of Delinquent Trends." *Brit J Med Psychol* 31:51–9 pt 1 '58. * (*PA* 33:8371)
652. McCandlish, Leo Alexander. *An Investigation of a New Method of T.A.T. Analysis.* Doctor's thesis, Loyola University (Chicago, Ill.), 1958.
653. Markham, Sylvia. "The Dynamics of Post-Partum Pathological Reactions as Revealed in Psychological Tests." *J Hillside Hosp* 7:178–89 Jl–O '58. * (*PA* 34:3011)
654. Neugarten, Bernice L., and Gutmann, David L. "Age-Sex Roles and Personality in Middle Age: A Thematic Apperception Study." *Psychol Monogr* 72(17):1–33 '58. * (*PA* 33:10103)
655. Rosenfeld, Irwin Joseph. *Mathematical Ability as a Function of Perceptual Field-Dependency and Certain Personality Variables.* Doctor's thesis, University of Oklahoma (Norman, Okla.), 1958. (*DA* 19:880)
656. Safian, Murray Z. *A Study of Certain Psychological Factors in the Rehabilitation of Potentially Employable Homebound Adults.* Doctor's thesis, New York University (New York, N.Y.), 1958. (*DA* 19:3372)
657. Sano, Katsuo, and Makita, Hitoshi. "Fundamental Requirements for the Construction of TAT." *Jap Psychol Res* 1:22–34 Jl '58. *
658. Shanmugam, T. E. "Sex Delinquent Women and Their Fantasies." *J Psychol Res* 2(2):77–82 '58. * (*PA* 33:6591)
659. Sheehan, Joseph G. "Projective Studies of Stuttering." *J Speech & Hearing Disorders* 23:18–25 F '58. *
660. Singer, Margaret Thaler, and Schein, Edgar H. "Projective Test Responses of Prisoners of War Following Repatriation." *Psychiatry* 21:375–85 N '58. * (*PA* 33:10113)
661. Zuckerman, Marvin, and Grosz, Hanus J. "Suggestibility and Dependency." Abstract. *J Consult Psychol* 22:328 O '58. * (*PA* 34:1435)
662. Budnoff, Christine K. *Awareness of Identification as a Factor on the TAT: A Proposed Modification of the Administration of the TAT.* Master's thesis, City College of New York (New York, N.Y.), 1959.
663. Cleveland, Sidney E. "Personality Dynamics in Torticollis." *J Nerv & Mental Dis* 129:150–61 Ag '59. * (*PA* 34:6407)
664. Dana, Richard H. "American Culture and Chinese Personality." *Psychol Newsl* 10:314–21 My–Je '59. * (*PA* 34:1213)
665. Dana, Richard H. "The Perceptual Organization TAT Score: Number, Order, and Frequency of Components." *J Proj Tech* 23:307–10 S '59. * (*PA* 35:4906)
666. Dana, Richard H. "Proposal for Objective Scoring of the TAT." *Percept & Motor Skills* 9:27–43 Mr '59. * (*PA* 34:1347)
667. Dana, Richard H., and Christiansen, Kenneth. "Repression and Psychopathology." *J Proj Tech* 23:412–6 D '59. * (*PA* 35:4981)
668. Easton, Judith C. "Some Personality Traits of Underachieving and Achieving High School Students of Superior Ability." *B Maritime Psychol Assn* 8:34–9 Ap '59. * (*PA* 34:4786)
669. Fisher, Seymour; Boyd, Ina; Walker, Donald; and Sheer, Dianne. "Parents of Schizophrenics, Neurotics, and Normals." *A.M.A. Arch Gen Psychiatry* 1:149–66 Ag '59. * (*PA* 34:6184)
670. Foulds, G. A. "The Relative Stability of Personality Measures Compared With Diagnostic Measures." *J Mental Sci* 105:783–7 Jl '59. * (*PA* 34:6016)
671. Greenwald, Alan F. "Affective Complexity and Psychotherapy." *J Proj Tech* 23:429–35 D '59. * (*PA* 35:5070)
672. Guilford, J. P. *Personality,* pp. 299–303. New York: McGraw-Hill Book Co., Inc., 1959. Pp. xiii, 562. *
673. Hartman, A. A. "Personality Factors in Perceptual Distortion." *J General Psychol* 61:181–8 Jl '59. * (*PA* 35:798)
674. Heimann, Robert A., and Rothney, John W. M. "Development and Applications of Projective Techniques." *R Ed Res* 29:73–83 F '59. * (*PA* 34:6021)
675. Henry, William E., and Farley, Jane. "A Study in Validation of the Thematic Apperception Test." *J Proj Tech* 23:273–7 S '59. * (*PA* 35:4920)
676. Henry, William E., and Farley, Jane. "The Validity of the Thematic Apperception Test in the Study of Adolescent Personality." *Psychol Monogr* 73(17):1–40 '59. * (*PA* 35:694)
677. Jensen, Arthur R. "The Reliability of Projective Techniques: Review of the Literature." *Acta Psychologica* 16(1):108–36 '59. * (*PA* 34:5956)
678. Kagan, Jerome. "The Stability of TAT Fantasy and Stimulus Ambiguity." *J Consult Psychol* 23:266–71 Je '59. * (*PA* 34:4385)
679. Kagan, Jerome, and Moss, Howard A. "Stability and Validity of Achievement Fantasy." *J Abn & Social Psychol* 58:357–64 My '59. * (*PA* 34:6027)
680. Koenig, Kathryn, and McKeachie, W. J. "Personality and Independent Study." *J Ed Psychol* 50:132–4 Je '59. * (*PA* 35:1201)
681. Lebo, Dell. "An Empirical Approach to Problems Concerning the Diagnostic Value of a Pictureless TAT." *J Proj Tech* 23:107 Mr '59. *
682. Lebo, Dell, and Sherry, P. James. "Visual and Vocal Presentation of TAT Descriptions." *J Proj Tech* 23:59–63 Mr '59. *
683. Lindzey, Gardner, and Silverman, Morton. "Thematic Apperception Test: Techniques of Group Administration, Sex Differences, and the Role of Verbal Productivity." *J Personality* 27:311–23 S '59. * (*PA* 34:6031)
684. Lindzey, Gardner; Bradford, Jean; Tejessy, Charlotte; and Davids, Anthony. *The Thematic Apperception Test: An Interpretive Lexicon for Clinician and Investigator.* Journal of Clinical Psychology Monograph Supplement No. 12. Brandon, Vt.: Journal of Clinical Psychology, April 1959. Pp. 98. *
685. Little, Kenneth B., and Shneidman, Edwin S. "Congruencies Among Interpretations of Psychological Test and Anamnestic Data." *Psychol Monogr* 73(6):1–42 '59. * (*PA* 34:3010)
686. Lynn, David B. "Ambiguity and Projection." *Psychol Newsl* 10:289–94 My–Je '59. * (*PA* 34:1393)
687. MacBrayer, Caroline Taylor. "Relationship Between Story Length and Situational Validity of the TAT." *J Proj Tech* 23:345–50 S '59. * (*PA* 35:4930)
688. Machover, Solomon, and Puzzo, Frank S. "Clinical and Objective Studies of Personality Variables in Alcoholism: 2, Clinical Study of Personality Correlates of Remission From Active Alcoholism." *Q J Studies Alcohol* 20:520–7 S '59. * (*PA* 34:6253)
689. Maddox, George L., and Jennings, Audrey M. "An Analysis of Fantasy: An Exploratory Study of Social Definitions of Alcohol and Its Use by Means of a Projective Technique." *Q J Studies Alcohol* 20:334–45 Je '59. * (*PA* 34:5852)
690. Magnusson, David. *A Study of Ratings Based on TAT.* Swedish Council for Personnel Administration, Report No. 22. Stockholm, Sweden: Almqvist & Wiksell, 1959. Pp. 176. * (*PA* 34:1394)
691. Motto, Joseph J. "The TAT in the Counseling Process." *Voc Guid Q* 8:29–37 au '59. *
692. Murstein, Bernard I., and Wheeler, John I., Jr. "The Projection of Hostility on the Rorschach and Thematic Stories Test." *J Clin Psychol* 15:316–9 Jl '59. * (*PA* 35:3474)
693. Nolan, Edward Gilligan. *Uniqueness in Monozygotic Twins.* Doctor's thesis, Princeton University (Princeton, N.J.), 1959. (*DA* 21:247)
694. Peck, Robert F. "Measuring the Mental Health of Normal Adults." *Genetic Psychol Monogr* 60:197–255 N '59. * (*PA* 34:5913)
695. Petrauskas, Francis Bernard. *A TAT and Picture-Frustration Study of Naval Offenders and Nonoffenders.* Doctor's thesis, Loyola University (Chicago, Ill.), 1959.
696. Phares, E. Jerry. "The Relationship Between TAT Responses and Leaving-the-Field Behavior." *J Clin Psychol* 15:328–30 Jl '59. * (*PA* 35:3475)
697. Pile, Everett; Mischel, Walter; and Bernstein, Lewis. "A Note on Remoteness of TAT Figures as an Interpretive Concept." *J Consult Psychol* 23:252–5 Je '59. * (*PA* 34:4402)
698. Pine, Fred. "Thematic Drive Content and Creativity." *J Personality* 27:136–51 Je '59. * (*PA* 34:4026)
699. Scodel, Alvin; Ratoosh, Philburn; and Minas, J. Sayer. "Some Personality Correlates of Decision Making Under Conditions of Risk." *Behav Sci* 4:19–28 Ja '59. * (*PA* 34:1057)
700. Semeonoff, Boris. "An Analysis of the Counsellor Personality." *Rorsch Newsl* 4:13–20 Je '59. *
701. Sheldon, M. Stephen; Coale, Jack M.; and Copple, Rockne. "Concurrent Validity of the 'Warm Teacher Scale.'" *J Ed Psychol* 50:37–40 F '59. * (*PA* 35:2810)
702. Shelley, Ernest L. V. *The Effect of an Organized Counseling Program on the Anti-Social Themes Elicited by the Thematic Apperception Test From Youthful Prison Inmates.* Doctor's thesis, Michigan State University (East Lansing, Mich.), 1959. (*DA* 21:3528)
703. Silverman, Lloyd H. "A Q-Sort Study of the Validity of Evaluations Made From Projective Techniques." *Psychol Monogr* 73(7):1–28 '59. * (*PA* 34:3030)
704. Silverstein, A. B. "Identification With Same-Sex and Opposite-Sex Figures in Thematic Apperception." *J Proj Tech* 23:73–5 Mr '59. *
705. Solkoff, Norman. "Effects of a Variation in Instructions and Pictorial Stimuli on Responses to TAT-Like Cards." *J Proj Tech* 23:76–82 Mr '59. *
706. Trice, Harrison M. "The Affiliation Motive and Readiness to Join Alcoholics Anonymous." *Q J Studies Alcohol* 20:313–20 Je '59. * (*PA* 34:6283)
707. Viitamaki, R. Olavi. *Psychometric Analysis of the Thematic Apperception Test: With Reference to Personality Structure and School Success in Adolescence.* Annals of the Finnish Academy of Science and Letters, Series B, Vol. 115, Part 2. Helsinki, Finland: Suomalainen Tiedeakatemia, Academiae Scientiarum Fennicae, 1959. Pp. 61. * (*PA* 38:4332)
708. Caine, T. M. "The Expression of Hostility and Guilt in Melancholic and Paranoid Women." *J Consult Psychol* 24:18–22 F '60. * (*PA* 34:7967)
709. Chowdhury, Uma. "An Indian Modification of the Thematic Apperception Test." *J Social Psychol* 51:245–63 My '60. * (*PA* 34:7764)
710. Dana, Richard H. "Objective TAT Scores and Personality Characteristics: Perceptual Organization (PO)." *Percept & Motor Skills* 10:154 Ap '60. * (*PA* 35:6436)
711. Dana, Richard H., and Goocher, Buell. "Pessimism Reaffirmed: A Reply to Witkin." *Percept & Motor Skills* 11:243–4 D '60. * (*PA* 35:2206)

712. DAVIDS, ANTHONY, AND DEVAULT, SPENCER. "Use of the TAT and Human Figure Drawings in Research on Personality, Pregnancy, and Perception." *J Proj Tech* 24:362-5 D '60. * (*PA* 35:4872)

713. DE VOS, GEORGE. "The Relation of Guilt Toward Parents to Achievement and Arranged Marriage Among the Japanese." *Psychiatry* 23:287-301 Ag '60. * (*PA* 36:4GB87D)

714. DOLLIN, ADELAIDE POLIZZOTTO. *The Effect of Order of Presentation on Perception of TAT Pictures.* Doctor's thesis, University of Connecticut (Storrs, Conn.), 1960. (*DA* 21:1999)

715. DREGER, RALPH MASON. "The Relation Between Rorschach *M* and TAT Content Categories as Measures of Creative Productivity in a Representative High-Level Intelligence Population." *J General Psychol* 63:29-33 Jl '60. * (*PA* 35:6437)

716. FAETH, HAROLD WILLIAM, JR. *The Discrepancy Between Self-Ideal Self Concepts as Needs Projected to Thematic Apperception Test Pictures.* Doctor's thesis, Purdue University (Lafayette, Ind.), 1960. (*DA* 21:1999)

717. FISHER, SEYMOUR, AND FISHER, RHODA LEE. "A Projective Test Analysis of Ethnic Subculture Themes in Families." *J Proj Tech* 24: 366-9 D '60. * (*PA* 35:4760)

718. GARCIA-PALMIERI, RAFAEL A. *Autonomic Response Specificity and Anxiety.* Doctor's thesis, Louisiana State University (Baton Rouge, La.), 1960. (*DA* 21:2364)

719. GOLDSTEIN, MICHAEL J., AND BARTHOL, RICHARD P. "Fantasy Responses to Subliminal Stimuli." *J Abn & Social Psychol* 60:22-6 Ja '60. * (*PA* 34:6932)

720. HAFNER, A. JACK, AND KAPLAN, ARTHUR M. "Hostility Content Analysis of the Rorschach and TAT." *J Proj Tech* 24:137-43 Je '60. * (*PA* 35:4918)

721. HAMMER, EMANUEL F. "An Exploratory Investigation of the Personalities of Creative Adolescent Students." Discussion by Margaret Naumberg. *Studies Art Ed* 1:42-72 sp '60. *

722. HENRY, WILLIAM E. "The Thematic Apperception Test," pp. 18-29, 106-15. In *The Prediction of Overt Behavior Through the Use of Projective Techniques.* Edited by Arthur C. Carr. Springfield, Ill.: Charles C Thomas, Publisher, 1960. Pp. xiii, 177. * (*PA* 36:2HG77C)

723. JOHN, LAVERD. *The Relationship of the Achievement Motives as Projected Into Thematic Apperception Stories to Children's School Achievement.* Doctor's thesis, Utah State University (Logan, Utah), 1960. (*DA* 21:2985)

724. KAGAN, JEROME. Chap. 6, "Thematic Apperceptive Techniques With Children," pp. 105-29. In *Projective Techniques With Children.* Edited by Albert I. Rabin and Mary R. Haworth. New York: Grune & Stratton, Inc., 1960. Pp. xiii, 392. * (*PA* 35:2229)

725. KAGAN, JEROME; MOSS, HOWARD A.; AND SIGEL, IRVING E. "Conceptual Style and the Use of Affect Labels." *Merrill-Palmer Q* 6:261-78 Jl '60. *

726. KAHN, MARVIN W. "Psychological Test Study of a Mass Murderer." *J Proj Tech* 24:148-60 Je '60. * (*PA* 35:5213)

727. KOHN, HUGH. "Some Personality Variables Associated With Binocular Rivalry." *Psychol Rec* 10:9-13 Ja '60. * (*PA* 34:7853)

728. KRUMBEIN, ELIEZER. *Reliability of Techniques for Scoring T.A.T. Responses and Rating Predicted Executive Behavior: A Study of Advertising Agency Executives.* Doctor's thesis, Northwestern University (Evanston, Ill.), 1960. (*DA* 21:1256)

729. LEBO, DELL. "The Development and Employment of VTAT's or Pictureless TAT's." *J Psychol* 50:197-204 O '60. * (*PA* 35:6443)

730. LUBIN, BERNARD. "Some Effects of Set and Stimulus Properties on TAT Stories." *J Proj Tech* 24:11-6 Mr '60. * (*PA* 35:802)

731. MARUI, FUMIO. "A Normative Study on TAT: Chiefly on Emotional Tone, Outcome and Shift." English abstract. *Jap J Psychol* 31:93-4 Jl '60. *

732. MASLING, JOSEPH. "The Influence of Situational and Interpersonal Variables in Projective Testing." *Psychol B* 57:65-85 Ja '60. * (*PA* 34:7788)

733. MUMMERY, WILLIAM JAMES. *An Investigation of Conformity as It Relates to Ways of Handling Hostility.* Doctor's thesis, University of Oklahoma (Norman, Okla.), 1960. (*DA* 21:241)

734. MURSTEIN, BERNARD I. "The Effect of Long-Term Illness of Children on the Emotional Adjustment of Parents." *Child Develop* 31:157-71 Mr '60. *

735. MURSTEIN, BERNARD I. "The Measurement of Ambiguity for Thematic Cards." *J Proj Tech* 24:419-23 D '60. * (*PA* 35:4933)

736. NI, LIAN. "Study on the Concealment of Subjects in Telling Stories on TAT Pictures." *Acta Psychologica Taiwanica* (2):1-6 Mr '60. * (*PA* 38:8560)

737. O'CONNOR, PATRICIA ANN CLAIRE. *The Representation of the Motive to Avoid Failure in Thematic Apperception.* Doctor's thesis, University of Michigan (Ann Arbor, Mich.), 1960. (*DA* 20:4708)

738. PECK, ROBERT F. "Personality Factors in Adjustment to Aging." *Geriatrics* 15:124-30 F '60. * (*PA* 35:4747)

739. PERRY, C. W. "Some Properties of T.A.T. Influencing Response." Abstract. *Austral J Psychol* 12:237-8 D '60. *

740. PINE, FRED. "A Manual for Rating Drive Content in the Thematic Apperception Test." *J Proj Tech* 24:32-45 Mr '60. * (*PA* 35:804)

741. PINE, FRED, AND HOLT, ROBERT R. "Creativity and Primary Process: A Study of Adaptive Regression." *J Abn & Social Psychol* 61:370-9 N '60. * (*PA* 36:2HD70P)

742. RICHARDS, THOMAS W. "Personality of Subjects Who Volunteer for Research on a Drug (Mescaline)." *J Proj Tech* 24:424-8 D '60. * (*PA* 35:4554)

743. ROSEN, JACQUELINE L., AND NEUGARTEN, BERNICE L. "Ego Functions in the Middle and Later Years: A Thematic Apperception Study of Normal Adults." *J Gerontol* 15:62-7 Ja '60. * (*PA* 35:6242)

744. ROSENBLATT, DANIEL. "Responses of Former Soviet Citizens to Selected *TAT* Cards." *J General Psychol* 62:273-84 Ap '60. * (*PA* 34:7657)

745. SCHAFER, ROY. "Representations of Perceiving and Acting in Psychological Test Responses," pp. 291-312. (*PA* 35:850) In *Festschrift for Gardner Murphy.* Edited by John G. Peatman and Eugene L. Hartley. New York: Harper & Brothers, 1960. Pp. xi, 411. *

746. SCODEL, ALVIN; RATOOSH, PHILBURN; AND MINAS, J. SAYER. "Some Personality Correlates of Decision Making Under Conditions of Risk," pp. 37-49. In *Decisions, Values and Groups: Reports From the First Interdisciplinary Conference in the Behavioral Science Division Held at the University of New Mexico, Vol. 1.* Edited by Dorothy Willner. Sponsored by the Air Force Office of Scientific Research. New York: Pergamon Press, 1960. Pp. xxix, 348. * (*PA* 36:5CP48W)

747. SCOTT, EDWARD M. "Psychological Examination of Quadruplets." *Psychol Rep* 6:281-2 Ap '60. * (*PA* 35:5980)

748. SOLKOFF, NORMAN. "Effects of a Variation in Instructions on Responses to TAT Cards." *J Proj Tech* 24:67-70 Mr '60. * (*PA* 35:808)

749. STARR, SHELDON. *The Relationship Between Hostility-Ambiguity of the TAT Cards, Hostile Fantasy, and Hostile Behavior.* Doctor's thesis, Washington State University (Pullman, Wash.), 1960. (*DA* 21:2372)

750. ANASTASI, ANNE. *Psychological Testing, Second Edition,* pp. 573-8. New York: Macmillan Co., 1961. Pp. xiii, 657. * (*PA* 36:1HA57A)

751. BELLAK, LEOPOLD; SALK, LEE; AND ROSENHAN, DAVID. "A Process Study of the Effects of Deprol on Depression: Exemplification of a Method of Psychodynamic Process Study of Psychotropic Drugs." *J Nerv & Mental Dis* 132:531-8 Je '61. *

752. BLENDSTRUP, UFFE, AND NIELSEN, GERHARD S. "Transcendence in the TAT." *Scandinavian J Psychol* 2(2):105-12 '61. * (*PA* 36:2HG05B)

753. BRAYER, RICHARD; CRAIG, GRACE; AND TEICHNER, WARREN. "Scaling Difficulty Values of TAT Cards." *J Proj Tech* 25:272-6 S '61. * (*PA* 36:3HG72B)

754. BRENNER, MARLIN SYDNEY. *The Relationship Between TAT Hostility and Overt Hostile Behavior as a Function of Self Reported Anxiety.* Doctor's thesis, Columbia University (New York, N.Y.), 1961. (*DA* 22:637)

755. CLEVELAND, SIDNEY E. "Personality Patterns Associated With the Professions of Dietitian and Nurse." *J Health & Human Behav* 2:113-24 su '61. * (*PA* 36:3AK13C)

756. CONRAD, WALTER KARR. *Prediction of TAT Imagery From Measures of Arousal.* Doctor's thesis, University of California (Berkeley, Calif.), 1961.

757. CUMMING, ELAINE, AND HENRY, WILLIAM E. *Growing Old: The Process of Disengagement.* New York: Basic Books, Inc., 1961. Pp. xvi, 293. *

758. DANA, RICHARD H., AND MUELLER, DONALD J. "Congruent Validation of a TAT Score: Perceptual Organization." *J Psychol Studies* 12:150-7 Jl '61 [issued Mr '63]. *

759. DAVIDS, ANTHONY; DEVAULT, SPENCER; AND TALMADGE, MAX. "Psychological Study of Emotional Factors in Pregnancy: A Preliminary Report." *Psychosom Med* 23:93-103 Mr-Ap '61. * (*PA* 36:3JU93D)

760. DOLLIN, ADELAIDE, AND REZNIKOFF, MARVIN. "TAT Stories and the Social Desirability Variable." *Percept & Motor Skills* 13:281-2 D '61. *

761. EWALD, HATTIE HOFF. *The Relationship of Scores on the Differential Aptitude Tests to Scholarship in High School and College.* Doctor's thesis, State University of South Dakota (Vermillion, S.D.), 1961. (*DA* 22:800)

762. FESHBACH, SEYMOUR. "The Influence of Drive Arousal and Conflict Upon Fantasy Behavior," pp. 119-40. Discussion by Kenneth Purcell and others, pp. 141-52. In *Contemporary Issues in Thematic Apperceptive Methods.* Edited by Jerome Kagan and Gerald S. Lesser. Springfield, Ill.: Charles C Thomas, Publisher, 1961. Pp. xiv, 328. * (*PA* 36:1HG28K)

763. FINE, REUBEN. "The Case of El: The MAPS Test." *J Proj Tech* 25:383-9 D '61. *

764. FISHER, GARY M., AND SHOTWELL, ANNA M. "Preference Rankings of the Thematic Apperception Test Cards by Adolescent Normals, Delinquents and Mental Retardates." *J Proj Tech* 25:41-3 Mr '61. * (*PA* 36:1HG41F)

765. FORER, BERTRAM R. "The Case of El: Vocational Choice." *J Proj Tech* 25:371-4 D '61. *

766. FORSYTH, RALPH P., AND FAIRWEATHER, GEORGE W. "Psychotherapeutic and Other Hospital Treatment Criteria: The Dilemma." *J Abn & Social Psychol* 62:598-604 My '61. * (*PA* 36:4IE98F)

767. FREED, GRIFFITH OSLER. *A Projective Test Study of*

Creativity in College Students in Visual Arts. Doctor's thesis, University of Michigan (Ann Arbor, Mich.), 1961. (*DA* 22: 640)

768. HAMMER, EMANUEL F. "Emotional Instability and Creativity." *Percept & Motor Skills* 12:102 F '61. * (*PA* 35: 6439)

769. HASKELL, ROYAL J., JR. "Relationship Between Aggressive Behavior and Psychological Tests." *J Proj Tech* 25: 431-40 D '61. *

770. HOLT, ROBERT R. "The Nature of TAT Stories as Cognitive Products: A Psychoanalytic Approach," pp. 3-43. Discussion by Silvan S. Tomkins and others, pp. 44-50. In *Contemporary Issues in Thematic Apperceptive Methods.* Edited by Jerome Kagan and Gerald S. Lesser. Springfield, Ill.: Charles C Thomas, Publisher, 1961. Pp. xiv, 328. * (*PA* 36:1HG28K)

771. KAGAN, JEROME. "Stylistic Variables in Fantasy Behavior: The Ascription of Affect States to Social Stimuli," pp. 196-220. Discussion by Irving E. Sigel and others, pp. 221-8. In *Contemporary Issues in Thematic Apperceptive Methods.* Edited by Jerome Kagan and Gerald S. Lesser. Springfield, Ill.: Charles C Thomas, Publisher, 1961. Pp. xiv, 328. * (*PA* 36:1HG28K)

772. KAGAN, JEROME, AND LESSER, GERALD S., EDITORS. *Contemporary Issues in Thematic Apperceptive Methods.* Springfield, Ill.: Charles C Thomas, Publisher, 1961. Pp. xiv, 328. * (*PA* 36:1HG28K)

773. KAGAN, JEROME, AND MOSS, HOWARD A. "The Availability of Conflictful Ideas: A Neglected Parameter in Assessing Projective Test Responses." *J Personality* 29:217-34 Je '61. * (*PA* 36:4HG17K)

774. KENNY, DOUGLAS T. "A Theoretical and Research Reappraisal of Stimulus Factors in the TAT," pp. 288-310. Discussion by Paul H. Mussen and others, pp. 311-4. In *Contemporary Issues in Thematic Apperceptive Methods.* Edited by Jerome Kagan and Gerald S. Lesser. Springfield, Ill.: Charles C Thomas, Publisher, 1961. Pp. xiv, 328. * (*PA* 36: 1HG28K)

775. LAZARUS, RICHARD S. "A Substitutive-Defensive Conception of Apperceptive Fantasy," pp. 51-71. Discussion by John W. Atkinson and others, pp. 72-82. In *Contemporary Issues in Thematic Apperceptive Methods.* Edited by Jerome Kagan and Gerald S. Lesser. Springfield, Ill.: Charles C Thomas, Publisher, 1961. Pp. xiv, 328. * (*PA* 36:1HG28K)

776. LEIMAN, ALAN HOWARD. *Relationship of TAT Sexual Drive, Sexual Guilt and Sexual Conflict.* Doctor's thesis, University of Massachusetts (Amherst, Mass.), 1961.

777. LINDZEY, GARDNER. *Projective Techniques and Cross-Cultural Research.* New York: Appleton-Century-Crofts, Inc., 1961. Pp. xi, 339. * (*PA* 37:3199)

778. LUBIN, BERNARD. "Judgments of Adjustment From TAT Stories as a Function of Experimentally Altered Sets." *J Consult Psychol* 25:249-52 Je '61. *

779. MACCASLAND, BARBARA WHITTREDGE. *The Relation of Aggressive Fantasy to Aggressive Behavior in Children.* Doctor's thesis, Syracuse University (Syracuse, N.Y.), 1961. (*DA* 23:300)

780. MARKHAM, SYLVIA. "A Comparative Evaluation of Psychotic and Nonpsychotic Reactions to Childbirth." *Am J Orthopsychiatry* 31:565-78 Jl '61. * (*PA* 36:4JP65M)

781. MARQUIS, JOHN NEIL. *Fantasy Measures of Aggressive Behavior.* Doctor's thesis, University of Michigan (Ann Arbor, Mich.), 1961. (*DA* 21:3854)

782. MASKIT, MAE LEE. *Management of Aggression in Preadolescent Girls: Its Effect on Certain Aspects of Ego Functioning.* Doctor's thesis, University of Michigan (Ann Arbor, Mich.), 1961. (*DA* 22:917)

783. MOSS, HOWARD A. "The Influences of Personality and Situational Cautiousness on Conceptual Behavior." *J Abn & Social Psychol* 63:629-35 N '61. * (*PA* 37:1310)

784. MOSS, HOWARD A., AND KAGAN, JEROME. "Stability of Achievement and Recognition Seeking Behaviors From Early Childhood Through Adulthood." *J Abn & Social Psychol* 62: 504-13 My '61. * (*PA* 36:4HJ04M)

785. MULLEN, F. A. "An Inductive Method for Determining Significant Aspects of the Responses of Mentally Handicapped Children to the Thematic Apperception Test and the Michigan Picture Test." Abstract. *Acta Psychologica* 19:861-2 '61. *

786. MURRAY, HENRY A. "Commentary on the Case of El." *J Proj Tech* 25:404-11 D '61. *

787. MURSTEIN, BERNARD I. "The Role of the Stimulus in the Manifestation of Fantasy," pp. 229-73. Discussion by Gerald S. Lesser and others, pp. 274-87. In *Contemporary Issues in Thematic Apperceptive Methods.* Edited by Jerome Kagan and Gerald S. Lesser. Springfield, Ill.: Charles C Thomas, Publisher, 1961. Pp. xiv, 328. * (*PA* 36:1HG28K)

788. MURSTEIN, BERNARD I.; DAVID, CHARLOTTE; FISHER, DAVID; AND FURTH, HANS G. "The Scaling of the TAT for Hostility by a Variety of Scaling Methods." *J Consult Psychol* 25:497-504 D '61. * (*PA* 37:5029)

789. MUSSEN, PAUL. "Some Antecedents and Consequents of Masculine Sex-Typing in Adolescent Boys." *Psychol Monogr* 75(2):1-24 '61. * (*PA* 36:3FH24M)

790. NAWAS, MUNIR MIKE. *A Longitudinal Study of the Changes in Ego Sufficiency and Complexity From Adolescence to Young Adulthood as Reflected in the TAT.* Doctor's thesis, University of Chicago (Chicago, Ill.), 1961.

791. OLTMAN, RUTH MARIE. *Personality Differences Between Orthopedically Handicapped and Non-Handicapped Persons as Measured by the Thematic Apperception Test.* Doctor's thesis, Western Reserve University (Cleveland, Ohio), 1961.

792. PHARES, E. JERRY. "TAT Performance as a Function of Anxiety and Coping-Avoiding Behavior." *J Consult Psychol* 25:257-9 Je '61. *

793. PIOTROWSKI, ZYGMUNT A. "Prediction of Overt Behavior From Projective Test Data." Abstract. *Acta Psychologica* 19:111-4 '61. *

794. REITMAN, E. EDWARD, AND WILLIAMS, CARL D. "Relationships Between Hope of Success and Fear of Failure, Anxiety, and Need for Achievement." *J Abn & Social Psychol* 62:465-7 Mr '61. * (*PA* 36:4HJ65R)

795. REYHER, JOSEPH, AND SHOEMAKER, DONALD. "A Comparison Between Hypnotically Induced Age Regressions and Waking Stories to TAT Cards: A Preliminary Report." *J Consult Psychol* 25:409-13 O '61. * (*PA* 37:3388)

796. REZNIKOFF, MARVIN. "Social Desirability in TAT Themes." *J Proj Tech* 25:87-9 Mr '61. * (*PA* 36:1HG87R)

797. REZNIKOFF, MARVIN, AND DOLLIN, ADELAIDE. "Social Desirability and the Type of Hostility Expressed on the TAT." *J Clin Psychol* 17:315-7 Jl '61. * (*PA* 38:8565)

798. RHUDICK, PAUL J., AND DIBNER, ANDREW S. "Age, Personality, and Health Correlates of Death Concerns in Normal Aged Individuals." *J Gerontol* 16:44-9 Ja '61. * (*PA* 35:6241)

799. RIGNEY, FRANCIS J., AND SMITH, L. DOUGLAS. *The Real Bohemia: A Sociological and Psychological Study of the "Beats."* New York: Basic Books, Inc., 1961. Pp. xxi, 250. * (*PA* 36:1GB50R)

800. ROSENBAUM, MILTON E., AND STANNERS, ROBERT F. "Self-Esteem, Manifest Hostility, and Expression of Hostility." *J Abn & Social Psychol* 63:646-9 N '61. * (*PA* 37: 1317)

801. SECTER, IRVING I. "T.A.T. Card 12M as a Predictor of Hypnotizability." *Am J Clin Hypnosis* 3:179-84 Ja '61. * (*PA* 36:1II79S)

802. SHIPMAN, W. G.; DANOWSKI, T. S.; AND MOSES, D. C., JR. "The Relation of Some Morphological, Physiological, and Genetic Dimensions to the Cattell 16PF and T.A.T. Scales." Abstract. *Acta Psychologica* 19:208-10 '61. *

803. SHNEIDMAN, EDWIN S. "The Logic of El: A Psychological Approach to the Analysis of Test Data." *J Proj Tech* 25:390-403 D '61. *

804. SHNEIDMAN, EDWIN S. "Psycho-logic: A Personality Approach to Patterns of Thinking," pp. 153-90. Discussion by Julian D. Rotter and others, pp. 191-5. In *Contemporary Issues in Thematic Apperceptive Methods.* Edited by Jerome Kagan and Gerald S. Lesser. Springfield, Ill.: Charles C Thomas, Publisher, 1961. Pp. xiv, 328. * (*PA* 36:1HG28K)

805. STRAUSS, F. H. "Analytic Implications of the Test Situation." *Brit J Med Psychol* 34:65-72 pt 1 '61. * (*PA* 36: 2HE65S)

806. TERRILL, JAMES MCGUFFIN. *The Relationships Between Level II and Level III in the Interpersonal System of Personality Diagnosis.* Doctor's thesis, Stanford University (Stanford, Calif.), 1961. (*DA* 21:3529)

807. VEROFF, JOSEPH. "Thematic Apperception in a Nationwide Sample Survey," pp. 83-111. Discussion by William E. Henry and others, pp. 112-8. In *Contemporary Issues in Thematic Apperceptive Methods.* Edited by Jerome Kagan and Gerald S. Lesser. Springfield, Ill.: Charles C Thomas, Publisher, 1961. Pp. xiv, 328. * (*PA* 36:1HG28K)

808. WEISSKOPF-JOELSON, EDITH, AND WICH, RICHARD. "An Experiment Concerning the Value of a 'Pictureless TAT.'" *J Proj Tech* 25:360-2 S '61. *

809. WELCH, BRIAN; SCHAFER, ROY; AND DEMBER, CYNTHIA FOX. "TAT Stories of Hypomanic and Depressed Patients." *J Proj Tech* 25:221-32 Je '61. * (*PA* 36:2HI21W)

810. ZUCKERMAN, MARVIN; LEVITT, EUGENE E.; AND LUBIN, BERNARD. "Concurrent and Construct Validity of Direct and Indirect Measures of Dependency." *J Consult Psychol* 25:316-23 Ag '61. *

811. ARNOLD, MAGDA B. "A Screening Test for Candidates for Religious Orders," pp. 1-63. In *Screening Candidates for the Priesthood and Religious Life.* By Magda B. Arnold and others. Chicago, Ill.: Loyola University Press, 1962. Pp. x, 205. *

812. ARNOLD, MAGDA B. *Story Sequence Analysis: A New Method of Measuring Motivation and Predicting Achievement.* New York: Columbia University Press, 1962. Pp. ix, 287. *

813. AVILA, DONALD L., AND LAWSON, JOHN R. "The Thematic Apperception Test as a Diagnostic Tool With Retarded Adults." *Percept & Motor Skills* 15:323-5 O '62. * (*PA* 37: 8015)

814. BURKARD, M. INNOCENTIA. "Discernment of Teacher Characteristics by TAT Sequence Analysis." *J Ed Psychol* 53:279-87 D '62. * (*PA* 37:5677)

815. CLEVELAND, SIDNEY E., AND JOHNSON, DALE L. "Personality Patterns in Young Males With Coronary Disease." *Psychosom Med* 24:600-10 N-D '62. * (*PA* 37:8204)

816. COX, F. N. "An Assessment of Children's Attitudes Towards Parent Figures." *Child Develop* 33:821-30 D '62. * (*PA* 37:6484)

817. COX, F. N. "An Assessment of the Achievement Be-

havior System in Children." *Child Develop* 33:907–16 D '62. * (*PA* 37:6465)
818. Crumpton, Evelyn. "Projective Case Study of a True Hermaphrodite." *J Proj Tech* 26:266–75 S '62. * (*PA* 37:3396)
819. Dollin, Adelaide, and Sakoda, James M. "The Effect of Order of Presentation on Perception of TAT Pictures." *J Consult Psychol* 26:340–4 Ag '62. * (*PA* 38:4320)
820. Eiduson, Bernice T. *Scientists: Their Psychological World.* New York: Basic Books, Inc., 1962. Pp. xvi, 299. * (*PA* 37:111)
821. Field, P. B.; Maldonado-Sierra, E. D.; Wallace, S. E.; Bodarky, C. J.; and Coelho, G. V. "An Other-Directed Fantasy in a Puerto Rican." *J Social Psychol* 58:43–60 O '62. * (*PA* 37:6883)
822. Filmer-Bennett, Gordon, and Klopfer, Walter G. "Levels of Awareness in Projective Tests." *J Proj Tech* 26:34–5 Mr '62. * (*PA* 37:3192)
823. Freeman, Frank S. *Theory and Practice of Psychological Testing, Third Edition,* pp. 638–49. New York: Holt, Rinehart & Winston, Inc., 1962. Pp. xix, 697. *
824. Geist, Harold. *The Etiology of Idiopathic Epilepsy,* pp. 153–92, 256–77. New York: Exposition Press, 1962. Pp. 297. *
825. Glymour, Clark; Ammons, C. H.; and Ammons, R. B. "Projective Test Protocols of Students Placing Extreme (High or Low) Value on Intellectual Activity." *Proc Mont Acad Sci* 21:105–12 '62. * (*PA* 37:3195)
826. Grimm, Elaine R. "Psychological Investigation of Habitual Abortion." *Psychosom Med* 24:369–78 Jl–Ag '62. * (*PA* 37:5427)
827. Hogue, J. Pierre; Otis, Jay L.; and Prien, Erich P. "Assessments of Higher-Level Personnel: 6, Validity of Predictions Based on Projective Techniques." *Personnel Psychol* 15:335–44 au '62. * (*PA* 37:7249)
828. Howard, Kenneth I. "The Convergent and Discriminant Validation of Ipsative Ratings From Three Projective Instruments." *J Clin Psychol* 18:183–8 Ap '62. * (*PA* 38:8551)
829. Ismir, Awad A. "The Effects of Prior Knowledge of the Thematic Apperception Test on Test Performance." *Psychol Rec* 12:157–64 Ap '62. * (*PA* 37:6738)
830. Kramer, Harvey J. *Stimulus Variables in Auditory Projective Testing: 1, An Information Theory Method for Measuring Psychological Ambiguity; 2, Effects of Varying Ambiguity and Type of Content Upon Projection With Blind and Sighted.* AFB Publications, Research Series No. 9. New York: American Foundation for the Blind, Inc., 1962. Pp. 81. * (*PA* 37:5028)
831. Levitt, Eugene E.; Lubin, Bernard; and Brady, John Paul. "On the Use of TAT Card 12M as an Indicator of Attitude Toward Hypnosis." *Int J Clin & Exp Hypnosis* 10:145–50 Jl '62. * (*PA* 37:5233)
832. Lipsher, David Harold. *Consistency of Clinicians' Judgments Based on MMPI, Rorschach and TAT Protocols.* Doctor's thesis, Stanford University (Stanford, Calif.), 1962. (*DA* 22:4409)
833. McGreevey, James C. "Interlevel Disparity and Predictive Efficiency." *J Proj Tech* 26:80–7 Mr '62. * (*PA* 37:3152)
834. McNeil, Elton B. "Aggression in Fantasy and Behavior." *J Consult Psychol* 26:232–40 Je '62. * (*PA* 38:1018)
835. Murstein, Bernard I., and Collier, Herbert L. "The Role of the TAT in the Measurement of Achievement as a Function of Expectancy." *J Proj Tech* 26:96–101 Mr '62. * (*PA* 37:3202)
836. Palmer, James O., and Lustgarten, Billie J. "The Prediction of TAT Structure as a Test of Rorschach's Experience-Balance." *J Proj Tech* 26:212–20 Je '62. * (*PA* 37:3204)
837. Partridge, Cloyd Ronald. *The Use of Biographical and Projective Data in Predicting Productivity of Business Machine Salesmen.* Doctor's thesis, Purdue University (Lafayette, Ind.), 1962. (*DA* 23:3980)
838. Phelan, J. G. "Projective Techniques in the Selection of Management Personnel." *J Proj Tech* 26:102–4 Mr '62. * (*PA* 37:3915)
839. Pine, Fred. "Creativity and Primary Process: Sample Variations." *J Nerv & Mental Dis* 134:506–11 Je '62. * (*PA* 37:3205)
840. Pishkin, Vladimir, and Wolfgang, Aaron. "Relationship of Empathy to Job Performance in a Psychiatric Setting." *J Clin Psychol* 18:494–7 O '62. * (*PA* 39:5482)
841. Ricciuti, Henry. "Development and Application of Projective Techniques of Personality." *R Ed Res* 32:64–77 F '62. * (*PA* 37:1274)
842. Rothaus, Paul. "Problems in the Measurement of Aggression-Anxiety." *J Proj Tech* 26:327–31 S '62. * (*PA* 37:3301)
843. Ruby, Walter McClintock, Jr. *An Investigation of Differentiating Personality Factors Between Achieving and Low Achieving College Students.* Doctor's thesis, University of Tennessee (Knoxville, Tenn.), 1962. (*DA* 23:3785)
844. Schaefer, Judith Blake. *Stability and Change in Thematic Apperception Test Response From Adolescence to Adulthood.* Doctor's thesis, University of Chicago (Chicago, Ill.), 1962.
845. Seeman, William, and Marks, Philip A. "A Study of Some 'Test Dimensions' Conceptions." *J Proj Tech* 26:469–73 D '62. * (*PA* 37:6678)
846. Semeonoff, Boris. "Self-Description as an Instrument in Personality Assessment." *Brit J Med Psychol* 35:165–75 pt 2 '62. * (*PA* 37:3236)
847. Simmons, William L., and Christy, Edward G. "Verbal Reinforcement of a TAT Theme." *J Proj Tech* 26:337–41 S '62. * (*PA* 37:2455)
848. Singer, Margaret Thaler. "A Conceptual Model for Rating Projective Test Responses From Aged Subjects: Relationships Between Test Ratings, Health Status, and Certain Behavioral Features," pp. 644–9. In *Social and Psychological Aspects of Aging.* Proceedings of the Fifth Congress of the International Association of Gerontology. Edited by Clark Tibbitts and Wilma Donahue. New York: Columbia University Press, 1962. Pp. xviii, 952. *
849. Smith, Donald C. *Personal and Social Adjustment of Gifted Adolescents.* CEC Research Monograph, Series A, No. 4. Washington, D.C.: Council for Exceptional Children, 1962. Pp. iv, 65. *
850. Stricker, George. "The Construction and Partial Validation of an Objectively Scorable Apperception Test." *J Personality* 30:51–62 Mr '62. * (*PA* 38:8507)
851. Tedeschi, James T., and Kian, Mohamed. "Cross-Cultural Study of the TAT Assessment for Achievement Motivation: Americans and Persians." *J Social Psychol* 58:227–34 D '62. * (*PA* 37:6551)
852. Theiner, Eric C. "The Magnitude of Four Experimental Needs as Expressed by Two Projective Techniques." *J Proj Tech* 26:354–65 S '62. * (*PA* 37:3163)
853. Turner, George C., and Coleman, James C. "Examiner Influence on Thematic Apperception Test Responses." *J Proj Tech* 26:478–86 D '62. * (*PA* 37:6749)
854. Vassiliou, Vasso. *Motivational Patterns of Two Clinical Groups as Revealed by TAT Sequence Analysis.* Doctor's thesis, Loyola University (Chicago, Ill.), 1962.
855. Weatherley, Donald. "Maternal Permissiveness Toward Aggression and Subsequent TAT Aggression." *J Abn & Social Psychol* 65:1–5 Jl '62. * (*PA* 38:4092)
856. Weiss, Peter, and Emmerich, Walter. "Dependency Fantasy and Group Conformity in Ulcer Patients." *J Consult Psychol* 26:61–4 F '62. * (*PA* 37:5540)
857. Abramson, Leonard S. "A Comparison of an Auditory and a Visual Projective Technique." *J Proj Tech* 27:3–11 Mr '63. * (*PA* 38:1005)
858. Barnouw, Victor. Chap. 16, "The Thematic Apperception Test," pp. 260–75. In his *Culture and Personality.* Homewood, Ill.: Dorsey Press, Inc., 1963. Pp. xi, 410. *
859. Barron, Frank. Chap. 11, "The Disposition Toward Originality," pp. 139–52. In *Scientific Creativity: Its Recognition and Development.* Edited by Calvin W. Taylor and Frank Barron. New York: John Wiley & Sons, Inc., 1963. Pp. xxiv, 419. * (*PA* 38:2689)
860. Berg, Paul Saul David. *Neurotic and Psychopathic Criminals: Some Measures of Ego Syntonicity, Impulse Socialization and Perceptual Consistency.* Doctor's thesis, Michigan State University (East Lansing, Mich.), 1963. (*DA* 24:2559)
861. Bernstein, Lewis, and Dana, Richard H. "Effect of Order of Presentation of TAT Cards." *J Consult Psychol* 27:533–5 D '63. * (*PA* 38:8540)
862. Bramel, Dana. "Selection of a Target for Defensive Projection." *J Abn & Social Psychol* 66:318–24 Ap '63. * (*PA* 37:8038)
863. Breger, Louis. "Conformity as a Function of the Ability to Express Hostility." *J Personality* 31:247–57 Je '63. *
864. Britton, Joseph H. "Dimensions of Adjustment of Older Adults." *J Gerontol* 18:60–5 Ja '63. * (*PA* 38:4098)
865. Brown, L. B., and Hetzel, B. S. "Stress, Personality and Thyroid Disease." *J Psychosom Res* 7:223–8 D '63. * (*PA* 38:8584)
866. Cartwright, Desmond S.; Kirtner, William L.; and Fiske, Donald W. "Method Factors in Changes Associated With Psychotherapy." *J Abn & Social Psychol* 66:164–75 F '63. * (*PA* 37:6833)
867. Cleveland, Sidney E. "Personality Characteristics of Dietitians and Nurses." *J Am Dietetic Assn* 43:104–9 Ag '63. *
868. Conners, C. Keith. "Birth Order and Needs for Affiliation." *J Personality* 31:408–16 S '63. *
869. Cooley, William W. "Predicting Choice of a Career in Scientific Research." *Personnel & Guid J* 42:21–8 S '63. *
870. Endicott, Noble A., and Endicott, Jean. "'Improvement' in Untreated Psychiatric Patients." *Arch Gen Psychiatry* 9:575–85 D '63. * (*PA* 38:8643)
871. Endicott, Noble A., and Endicott, Jean. "Objective Measures of Somatic Preoccupation." *J Nerv & Mental Dis* 137:427–37 N '63. * (*PA* 38:6356)
872. Engel, Mary. "Psychological Testing of Borderline Psychotic Children." *Arch Gen Psychiatry* 8:426–34 My '63. * (*PA* 38:2451)
873. Epley, David, and Ricks, David R. "Foresight and Hindsight in the TAT." *J Proj Tech* 27:51–9 Mr '63. * (*PA* 38:1008)
874. Fisher, Seymour, and Seidner, Richard. "Body Experiences of Schizophrenic, Neurotic and Normal Women." *J Nerv & Mental Dis* 137:252–7 S '63. * (*PA* 38:6358)

875. GILL, WAYNE S. "Interpersonal Affect and Conformity Behavior in Schizophrenics." *J Abn & Social Psychol* 67:502–5 N '63. * (*PA* 38:4602)
876. GLESER, GOLDINE C. "Projective Methodologies." *Annual R Psychol* 14:391–422 '63. *
877. HEDVIG, ELEANOR B. "Stability of Early Recollections and Thematic Apperception Stories." *J Indiv Psychol* 19:49–54 My '63. * (*PA* 38:1011)
878. HOWARD, KENNETH I. "Ratings of Projective Test Protocols as a Function of Degree of Inference." *Ed & Psychol Meas* 23:267–75 su '63. * (*PA* 38:1013)
879. KENNY, DOUGLAS T., AND CHAPPELL, MARGUERITE C. "Anxiety Effects in Thematic Apperception Induced by Homogeneous Visual Stimulation." *J Proj Tech & Pers Assess* 27:297–301 S '63. *
880. LEVITT, EUGENE E., AND LUBIN, BERNARD. "TAT Card '12 MF' and Hypnosis Themes in Females." *Int J Clin & Exp Hypnosis* 11:241–4 O '63. * (*PA* 38:8556)
881. LITTIG, LAWRENCE W. "Effects of Motivation on Probability Preferences." *J Personality* 31:417–27 S '63. *
882. MCEVOY, THEODORE LEE. *A Comparison of Suicidal and Nonsuicidal Patients by Means of the Thematic Apperception Test.* Doctor's thesis, University of California (Los Angeles, Calif.), 1963. (*DA* 24:1248)
883. MITCHELL, HOWARD E. "Application of the Kaiser Method to Marital Pairs." *Family Process* 2:265–79 S '63. *
884. MURSTEIN, BERNARD I. "The Relationship of Expectancy of Reward to Achievement Performance on an Arithmetic and Thematic Test." *J Consult Psychol* 27:394–9 O '63. * (*PA* 38:4144)
885. MURSTEIN, BERNARD I. "TAT Hostility and the Buss Hostility Scale." *Percept & Motor Skills* 16:520 Ap '63. * (*PA* 38:2699)
886. MURSTEIN, BERNARD I. *Theory and Research in Projective Techniques (Emphasizing the TAT).* New York: John Wiley & Sons, Inc., 1963. Pp. xiii, 385. * (*PA* 38:6098)
887. MURSTEIN, BERNARD I., AND WIENS, ARTHUR N. "A Factor Analysis of Various Hostility Measures on a Psychiatric Population." *J Proj Tech & Pers Assess* 27:447–51 D '63. * (*PA* 38:8594)
888. NORMAN, RUSSELL P. "Need for Social Approval as Reflected on the TAT." Abstract. *J Consult Psychol* 27:464 O '63. *
889. POSER, ERNEST G., AND LEE, S. GILLMORE. "Thematic Content Associated With Two Gastrointestinal Disorders." *Psychosom Med* 25:162–73 Mr–Ap '63. * (*PA* 38:4505)
890. RYCHLAK, JOSEPH F. "Personality Correlates of Leadership Among First Level Managers." *Psychol Rep* 12:43–52 F '63. * (*PA* 38:2600)
891. SALTZ, GEORGE, AND EPSTEIN, SEYMOUR. "Thematic Hostility and Guilt Responses as Related to Self-Reported Hostility, Guilt, and Conflict." *J Abn & Social Psychol* 67:469–79 N '63. * (*PA* 38:4327)
892. SEMEONOFF, BORIS. "An Application of Inter-Person Analysis in Personality Assessment." *Brit J Psychol* 54:71–81 F '63. * (*PA* 37:8004)
893. SILVER, ALBERT W. "TAT and MMPI Psychopath Deviant Scale Differences Between Delinquent and Nondelinquent Adolescents." Abstract. *J Consult Psychol* 27:370 Ag '63. * (*PA* 38:3032)
894. SINGER, MARGARET THALER, AND WYNNE, LYMAN C. "Differentiating Characteristics of Parents of Childhood Schizophrenics, Childhood Neurotics, and Young Adult Schizophrenics." *Am J Psychiatry* 120:234–43 S '63. *
895. TESTIN, ROBERT FRANCIS. *Ego Strength Scale Differences Between Psychotic and Nonpsychotic Inpatients.* Doctor's thesis, Fordham University (New York, N.Y.), 1963. (*DA* 24:839)
896. WALLACE, JOHN, AND SECHREST, LEE. "Frequency Hypothesis and Content Analysis of Projective Techniques." *J Consult Psychol* 27:387–93 O '63. * (*PA* 38:4335)
897. WYLIE, RUTH C.; SISSON, BOYD D.; AND TAULBEE, EARL. "Intraindividual Consistency in 'Creative' and 'Memory' Stories Written for TAT Pictures." *J Consult Psychol* 27:145–51 Ap '63. * (*PA* 37:8022)

C. J. ADCOCK, *Associate Professor of Psychology, Victoria University of Wellington, Wellington, New Zealand.*

Writing a review of a test like the TAT is rather like the task of the journalist who has to write about Christmas. It has been done so many times before that one feels everything of consequence must have been said and yet the status of the test is not very different from when the last *Mental Measurements Yearbook* was published. The number of papers grows apace but there is still a lack of reassuring validative studies. There are still numerous research projects which have used the test with degrees of success impossible to estimate. There are still enthusiastic clinicians and doubting statisticians. Since there are few important developments in its literature we may usefully discuss some basic issues in a systematic way.

THE RATIONALE OF THE TEST. The basic assumption of the test is that, when called upon to tell a story about a picture, one necessarily gives expression to one's own motives, interests, and anxieties, and provides evidence of one's experiences. That this is true to some extent seems reasonable enough but there remains much doubt as to the degree to which it holds in any particular instance. A character may be described as interested in astronomy, not because the testee has any interest in this subject but because he read a story about such a person recently. Similarly, the testee may provide details of lurid upbringing because he has recently seen an account of this kind of thing and contrasts it with his own sheltered life.

The degree of projection involved in story telling must always be problematical and must be assessed in the light of internal and external evidence. The clinician who has repeatedly met his patient is thus in a much stronger position to interpret the TAT record. He just has more evidence and in particular is in a position to distinguish between behavioural tendencies and compensatory fantasy. Bold deeds and aggressive responses may figure largely in the protocol of a timid introvert and must not be confused with the real life tendencies of an uninhibited extravert.

Such considerations constitute a warning against any mere counting of needs, presses, and the like. This may have good significance when we are concerned with group averages but may be grossly misleading with regard to John Smith. It may, of course, be useful to score Smith's protocol in this way but only as one way of classifying the evidence for further study. No useful conclusion can be arrived at without the insight which develops from long acquaintance with the complexity of determination which enters into story telling of this kind.

The fundamental fact which we have to face with regard to a test of this type is that it is subject to a much wider range of distorting factors than operate with regard to questionnaire tests or even some other projective tests. It is not a matter of individual items being unreliable yet the sum tending to average out the errors but rather the possibility of the test as a whole being distorted to an unknown degree. This fact seems to require that the test be restricted to two major uses: (*a*) a clinical tool which can be supplemented and validated by other clinical procedures; and (*b*) a research tool for the investigation of group differences. Such indeed appears to be the general tendency in practice.

WHAT DOES IT MEASURE? The range of a projective test is determined by the degree of structure of the stimuli. In this case the variety of pictures and the range of responses which can be made to each ensure that there will be a broad coverage. There seems no reason why all the more basic personality factors should not be represented but there is no guarantee that they will and even less certainty that they will be present to a degree to make reliable measurement possible. If you wish to assess a student's knowledge of psychology it may be sufficient to ask him to write an essay on a psychological topic of his own choice but this approach may also fail to give information about many aspects. If you require specific information you must ask specific questions.

An important point about the TAT is that it can provide information about the particular content of the subject's cognitive and affective reference frames. It is one thing to decide that a patient has a severe superego and quite another to be able to say what are the particular requirements laid down by his superego. This is the type of knowledge which this test can often provide as few other tests can. Some would claim that it is a useful instrument to measure the relative strengths of various types of motivation but there is room to doubt its suitability for this purpose. Specially designed instruments of the same type may be useful but the shotgun approach is too unreliable for this purpose. This breadth and lack of specificity, on the other hand, may make it an ideal instrument for picking up specific sources of disturbance in the subject's life. Like King Charles' head these will intrude themselves into the protocol.

We shall take the position that as an indicator of general interests, important current sources of motivation, areas of emotional disturbance, and clues for clinical discussion the test has excellent possibilities, but it is not suitable for providing a profile of personality traits or a reliable measurement of any one trait.

WHAT IS ITS RELIABILITY? This is a thorny problem. Some have sought to measure reliability in terms of interscorer agreement. Apart from the fact that this reliability may be negatively correlated with validity (simply counting words may ensure perfect interscorer agreement but useless scores), it is obvious that the level of reliability will vary according to the system involved. These are legion and no coefficient can be considered except in relation to the particular system concerned. Jensen, in his review of this test in *The Fifth Mental Measurements Yearbook* (5:164) reported 15 estimates of scoring reliability ranging from .54 to .91. The succeeding years have not changed this position. It is obvious that under optimum conditions this is not a serious source of unreliability and that even the lower estimates indicate enough agreement for many research purposes.

But we are concerned not merely with the reliability of the scorer. The test data themselves may lack reliability. This would be indicated either by lack of internal agreement or low retest reliability. On this point too there is little to add to Jensen's report. Only three of the studies listed in *Psychological Abstracts* during the last three years concern themselves with reliability and these deal with specific aspects. The average internal consistency reliability of .13 reported by Jensen seems to call for no revision and indicates a grave need for caution. It is sometimes argued that with a test of this kind internal reliability is not a fair measure, but insofar as summed scores are resorted to, it must be justified by such a criterion.

Retest reliability is seriously contaminated by a tendency to remember and repeat the same stories. To have any significance, different stories must be required and under these circumstances many attempted measures appear to be of doubtful significance. The evidence would seem to indicate that to expect to get reliable measures of more than half a dozen personality aspects would be very optimistic and that to expect such reliability to be greater than would justify group differentiation would be even more optimistic.

HOW VALID IS IT? The data available on reliability do not raise any high expectations with regard to validity. So far as statistical data are concerned, there has been little advance in the last few years. Takahashi [1] found no significant relationship between hostile content of TAT stories and overt aggression. His Hostile Sentence Completion Test, however, scored high with both extreme aggressors and extreme nonaggressors and low with moderates. Possibly a similar ambivalent effect was operating with the TAT but in a less systematic way so that the two opposing tendencies simply cancelled out. Hafner and Kaplan (*720*) found no significant relationship between the TAT overt and covert scales and Rorschach results. Dreger (*715*) found no relation between productivity as measured by the Rorschach and TAT. Dana (*666*) has suggested a new objective scoring system and presents evidence from which he concludes that it is satisfactory for clinical use. In a study of two identical twins, Henry (*722*) succeeded in identifying the disturbed one but formulated no clear principles for this purpose.

CONCLUSIONS. The aim of a review such as this is largely to inform those unfamiliar with the test so that they can decide about the desirability of using it. For such a person the answer seems plain enough in this case: if you need to consult the review you had better not use the test. It is definitely a test for the sophisticated. For research purposes it may sometimes be the best approach available but it would be wise to look for other suitable tests first. For the clinical psychologist no advice is necessary. He will recognise the test as another vehicle for his use of clinical insight but he may well be warned against developing false confidence based on his subjective impression of reliability. Because one draws the same conclusion from two sources of evidence it may be easy to decide that both are valid.

For reviews by Leonard D. Eron and Arthur R. Jensen, see 5:164; for a review by Arthur L. Benton, see 4:136; for reviews by Arthur L. Benton, Julian B. Rotter, and J. R. Wittenborn, see 3:103 (1 excerpt); for excerpts from related book reviews, see B60, B326, 5:B63, 5:B204, 5:B395, 4:139–41, 3:104, and 3:104a.

1 TAKAHASHI, SHIGEO. "Toei kensa ni yoru jidō no kōgekiteki kōdō no kenkyū." *Jap J Ed Psychol* 8:85–91 '60. (*PA* 35:2232) Original article not seen; citation based upon the English abstract in *Psychological Abstracts*.

For an excerpt from a review of the Bellak TAT Blank, *see 4:137. For excerpts from reviews of the* Thompson Modification, *see 4:138.*

[246]

***The Tomkins-Horn Picture Arrangement Test.** Ages 10 and over; 1942–59; 1 form ('44, 30 pages); manual ('57, 399 pages, see 5 below); interpretation manual ('59, 191 pages, see 7 below); scoring materials ['57, 63 cards, 100 sheets, punch, board, and instructions, 8 pages, reprinted from manual]; profile ('58, 4 pages); $15 per 50 tests; $25 per set of scoring materials; $4.50 per 100 scoring sheets; $17.50 per 100 profiles; $10 per manual; $5.50 per interpretive manual; postage extra; (30–60) minutes; Silvan S. Tomkins, Daniel Horn, and John B. Miner (manuals); Springer Publishing Co., Inc. *

REFERENCES

1–6. See 5:167.

7. TOMKINS, SILVAN S., AND MINER, JOHN B. *PAT Interpretation: Scope and Technique.* New York: Springer Publishing Co., Inc., 1959. Pp. vii, 184. * (*PA* 34:1430)

8. MINER, JOHN B. "The Concurrent Validity of the PAT in the Selection of Tabulating Machine Operators." *J Proj Tech* 24:409–18 D '60. * (*PA* 35:5391)

9. MCCARTER, ROBERT E.; SCHIFFMAN, HAROLD M.; AND TOMKINS, SILVAN S. "Early Recollections as Predictors of Tomkins-Horn Picture Arrangement Test Performance." *J Indiv Psychol* 17:177–80 N '61. *

10. MINER, JOHN B. "The Validity of the PAT in the Selection of Tabulating Machine Operators: An Analysis of Predictive Power." *J Proj Tech* 25:330–3 S '61. * (*PA* 36:3LD30M)

11. PATE, KENTON DONESE. *The Picture Arrangement Test as Related to Occupational Choice Values.* Doctor's thesis, University of Houston (Houston, Tex.), 1961. (*DA* 21:3856)

12. MINER, JOHN B. "Personality and Ability Factors in Sales Performance." *J Appl Psychol* 46:6–13 F '62. * (*PA* 36:5LD06M)

13. HIGASHIMACHI, WILFRED H. "The Construct Validity of the Progressive Matrices as a Measure of Superego Strength in Juvenile Delinquents." *J Consult Psychol* 27:415–9 O '63. * (*PA* 38:4302)

ROBERT C. NICHOLS, *Program Director, National Merit Scholarship Corporation, Evanston, Illinois.*

The novel method of obtaining objectively recorded projective responses, the extensive standardization, and the elaborate scoring procedure of the *Tomkins-Horn Picture Arrangement Test* (PAT) have been described by previous reviewers (5:167). The test consists of 25 plates, each with three pictures which the subject arranges in one of six possible orders to tell a story. The arrangements are scored for 651 scales which are made manageable by screening out a few extreme scores for interpretation and ignoring the rest.

The PAT scales (called "patterns" or "keys") consist of several arrangements with some common feature. The arrangements to be counted for a given key were selected according to two criteria: content, and frequency of occurrence in a normative group ($n = 1500$). The 156 content areas represented by keys are grouped into 32 general areas of personality (e.g., social restlessness, optimism, superego, etc.). Each of the 156 content scales is scored for from one to six subscales, determined by the frequency with which the scored arrangements were given by the normative group. In addition to the content scales a group of 96 "Conformity" keys were constructed solely on the basis of response frequency. Arrangements falling in eight frequency categories were grouped into keys separately for 12 subgroups of the normative sample based on age, education, and intelligence.

The content keys are quite short; some consist of only two arrangements, and the average is about four per key. Item overlap among the keys is great and some keys are identical with others.

In the suggested interpretation of the various keys it is assumed that personality is expressed quite literally by picture arrangements. For example, the "High General Sociophilia" key (arrangements ending with the hero in the company of other people) is interpreted as "a preference for, or expectation of, being with people rather than being alone when a choice is possible." In a case study in the interpretive manual, a major reason for diagnosing a subject's vocational maladjustment as due to limited opportunities for interpersonal contact on the job was a very high "High General Sociophilia" score. No evidence is offered for the validity of these suggested interpretations, and the experienced clinician may legitimately wonder if in the personality area anything this self-evident can really be true.

The manual reports those keys on which certain diagnostic groups of mental patients obtain extremely high scores more frequently than normals. (Those on which normals obtain higher scores are not reported.) The performance of these diagnostic groups on the various keys does not increase confidence in the proposed interpretations. For example, high scores on the "High General Sociophilia" key are obtained more frequently by paranoid schizophrenics, schizophrenics, and character disorders than by the normative group, and high scores on the "High General Self-confidence" key are obtained more frequently by paranoid schizophrenics, schizophrenics, and manic-depressives than by normals. One wishes that the test authors had presented fewer scales and more evidence bearing on the interpretation of the scales.

The limitations of *a priori* scales have long been recognized by users of personality inventories, yet *a priori* content scales, even without internal consistency analysis, seem to be accepted uncritically by many projective testers, including the authors of the PAT. Scales superior to the present *a priori* keys could probably be constructed for the PAT by criterion keying or other scale construction procedures.

According to the manual, the meaning of a given response is often ambiguous because the response may be given for different reasons by different subjects. It is assumed that infrequently occurring responses have fewer possible causes and are thus more clearly interpretable. For this reason only responses which occur rarely (in less than 5 per cent of normative subjects) are used in the usual interpretation of the PAT. The rare responses considered for interpretation include "pattern rares" (extreme scores on the various keys) and "plate rares" (unusual single arrangements).

No empirical evidence is offered in support of the thesis that rare responses and extreme scores are less ambiguous than more common responses or scores. Evidence is presented, however, which suggests that the rare responses are less reliable in a test-retest situation than more common ones.

In view of the shortage of evidence supporting the assumptions on which the test is constructed and interpreted, one would like to have available a number of studies dealing with the usefulness of the test in a practical assessment situation. This requirement is only minimally satisfied by the PAT. Miner has reported on the use of the PAT in the selection of tabulating machine operators (*8*) and petroleum dealer salesmen (*12*). Essentially the same procedure was used in both of these studies. The PAT's and criterion performance (sales records of the salesmen and supervisor's ratings of the machine operators) for a small sample of subjects were studied intensively to derive a single predictive PAT score which was cross validated on the remaining cases (*n*'s of 44 salesmen and 31 machine operators). Validity coefficients for the overall criterion were .57 for salesmen and .72 for machine operators. (The latter correlation is a biserial coefficient which is not appropriate for the essentially dichotomous PAT prediction. Corrected to the more appropriate point-biserial, the validity coefficient is .58.) Both of these studies were concurrent, but in a further study of the tabulating machine operators Miner (*10*) showed that the PAT index predicted performance ratings over an average of seven months with a validity of .61. (The corresponding point-biserial is .45.)

These findings are indeed impressive. Regardless of what one may think of its rationale and method of development, if the PAT can continue to produce such results in other situations and for investigators other than the test authors, it should rightfully take its place among our most valuable assessment devices. However, in view of the theoretical questions raised above, the uncritical acceptance of the PAT is not recommended before these further validation studies are completed.

J Proj Tech 23:474–5 D '59. Leonard P. Ullmann. [Review of the interpretive manual.] The rationale....assumes that the most useful information about a person deals with that individual's distinctive behaviors. The logic of test interpretation thus rests upon the response which is rare or improbable when one compares one subject with all others but which is very frequent for the person under investigation. * With consistency and scientific honesty ....[the earlier book-manual for the test; see 5:167] presents the reasoning and decisions made when constructing a test in which this rationale was followed and in which explicitly no contemporary theory of personality was felt to be powerful enough to determine the test content or interpretation. The result is a stimulating case history in science. While the reader might well disagree with many of the authors' decisions, in supporting his disagreements the reader would have to do some thinking and come to greater understanding of his own position. In view of this background, *PAT Interpretation,* a book of interpretations of PAT protocols, is somewhat disappointing. Some of the reasons for this may be traced to the derivation of the test. With no particular theory of personality, the test has no particular focus or purpose. Any number of scales might have been derived, and indeed a great number of keys are presented. The areas covered by these keys—social orientation, optimism-pessimism, and level of functioning—were, in the authors' words, selected by "prejudice and hunch, both personal and professional." The difficulties in PAT scoring are not reduced by the presence of three sets of norms: age, I.Q., and education. Since an individual falls into all of these categories, the authors suggest averaging across the three norms to establish the probabilities of the occurrence of a response for an individual. Having isolated the relevant (rare) responses, interpretation becomes the crucial problem. Assuming the validity of the statistical procedures used to designate relevant material, all the examiner knows is that a behavior is rare. At this point the authors assume a commonality of the perception of the stimuli and an equivalence of psychological meaning of identical stimulus orderings. The basis on which interpretation is made therefore is face validity. The strength of the use of protocols presented in *PAT Interpretation* lies in the public specification of how the material to be used was selected and in explicit statement of the probability levels from which inferences were made. That is, a part of the clinician's work, normally done implicitly, is made explicit. However, because of the lack of theory, the write-ups seem, at least to this reviewer, to validate antecedent descriptions of the subjects and to add little to enrich or extend knowledge of these people, or even, at times, to help to describe them as unique individuals. The result is essentially a summation of "signs" of dubious value and arbitrary selection. In summary, *PAT Interpretation* is the fruit of the consistent application of a methodological view point. Following through the sample cases for scoring and interpretation, the clinician will learn something about the most fascinating client he will ever have, himself. In terms of clinical application, an interesting set of stimuli has been added to the tester's armamentarium. While the work done by the authors is more than sufficient to merit a fair trial in the clinic, when dealing with the individual case the amount of time required for scoring, the tenuous validity of the instrument, and the fragmentary nature of the interpretations will probably lead to limited acceptance and use of the PAT.

Occupational Psychol 34:149–50 Ap '60. H. Phillipson. [Review of the manual.] * While the development of the test as described in this volume is clearly a monumental piece of work, admirable in its thinking, design and execution, the psychologist who is experienced in the uses of such techniques as Rorschach and T.A.T. will feel a sense of disappointment at the end product. The individual personality picture that emerges from the quantitative data is too general and too lacking in dynamic and causal information, and one is thrown back on the verbal material, which though valuable is not likely to be more useful than the more traditional projective test responses. For the present reviewer it is the lack of theoretical rationale for the choice of test material and the interpretation of the responses that brings the main feelings of dissatisfaction. For without this we cannot postulate why the subject behaves as he does with the test material, nor what his behaviour means in terms of his personality functioning as a whole.

Personnel & Guid J 38:240–2 N '59. Sidney E. Cleveland. [Review of the interpretive manual.] * The thoroughness and detail with which the authors describe the scoring procedure, tabulation of scores, and reference to the normative tables make for rather tedious and uninteresting reading. No doubt this is inevitable in a technical manual of this nature. However, the reader tends to lose sight of the person whose test responses are being analyzed while pursuing the intricacies of the mechanics of interpretation. It is interesting to note that despite all of the attention paid by the authors to a careful statistical analysis of the frequency of the various picture arrangement sequences, a wealth of dynamic material is gained from simply a clinical appraisal of the subject's free written responses to each sorting. * The PAT is an ingenious device which combines the clinical insights offered in a projective technique with the efficiency of scoring found in a psychometric instrument. For this reason, if no other, the test should have considerable promise in research projects involving the testing of large groups. The modification of projective tests to suit large scale testing is a promising development and one being applied to an increasing number of testing devices (for example, The Holtzman Ink Blot Test, University of Texas). One can foresee the possibility of administering a battery of group projective tests, including a measure such as the PAT, and emerging with test data as rewarding as if individual TAT's and Rorschachs had been obtained. In summary, the volume *PAT Interpretation* represents a thorough guidebook for those uninitiated but interested in the application of a relatively new addition to the assessment of human motives and behavior.

For reviews by Donald W. Fiske, John W. Gittinger, and Wayne H. Holtzman, see 5:167 (1 excerpt).

[247]

★**Visual Apperception Test '60.** Ages 12 and over; 1960–62; prevalent mood and clinical diagnosis; 1 form ('60, 14 pages); manual, third edition ('62, 30 pages); $10 per 15 tests and manual; 50¢ per single copy; $2.50 per manual; postpaid; set of crayons necessary for administration; [35] minutes; Rafi Z. Khan; Midwest Psychological Services. *

BERT R. SAPPENFIELD, *Professor of Psychology, Montana State University, Missoula, Montana.*

The inventor of the VAT '60 makes several laudatory statements about his test, which, if eventually confirmed by research and clinical experience, would place the VAT '60 among the top ranking clinical instruments of all time. The test is said to be "a highly sensitive instrument capable of multilevel functioning * [It] can guide us into the labyrinths of the deep psyche, step by step, without groping in the dark * [It] provides a great insight into the personality stratification which is of immense help in the psychotherapeutic planning."

The stimuli for the VAT '60 are 12 "plates consisting of lines randomly drawn under controlled conditions." Each of these plates (with one exception) has the appearance of a doodle produced by drawing a continuous line, with much overlapping and crossing of itself, until the final product takes on a more or less circular or elliptical shape, containing within itself many other delineated forms; the twelfth plate differs from the others in that it has been produced by making fairly square turns and in that the final gestalt has a more or less rectangular appearance.

The subject is provided with eight crayons (red, orange, blue, green, yellow, purple, brown, and black) and told to "color whatever design, pattern or object" he sees in each plate. He is permitted to choose the color or colors to be used in each drawing, and is asked to give a name to whatever he draws.

The nature of the subject's drawings is purported to be a valid basis for clinical diagnosis. The manual describes, and gives examples of, the types of patterns said to be characteristic of each of 12 different nosological categories (including normals, neurotics, psychopaths, and three types of schizophrenics). The validity information is, at best, extremely ambiguous. The author lists the number of patients in each of eight clinical categories (total n = 149) and states that the patients were compared with 87 "normal" subjects. He immediately concludes, without further description of his procedure, that "the validity coefficient for the above clinical types is .89." Since no operational definition of this "validity coefficient" is provided, the reader comes away with the equivalent of no validity information whatever.

The manual's treatment of retest reliability is also ambiguous; the procedure appears to have involved diagnosis "by three persons specially trained in the interpretation of responses on VAT '60," and a comparison of "diagnoses" of individual patients on the test and retest. In any case, the retest reliability (reported to be .79 for an n of 359) may not be, for a test of this kind, as appropriate as some form of split-half technique.

The names given by the subject to his drawings are purported to have value for thematic interpretation, although the author considers this type of analysis to be at an experimental stage. He gives some examples of this approach, one of which involves the case of a "woman with an unhappy marital relationship [who] perceived [her drawing as] her husband being clubbed by somebody."

What Khan calls "mood measurement" is based on the subject's choice of colors. Khan believes that he has evidence that blue and green indicate cheerful moods, that yellow indicates anxiety, that black and brown indicate depression, that red and orange indicate aggression, and that purple indicates self-control and psychotherapeutic resistance. On the basis of an elaborate tabulation of color choices, the subject's inferred "moods" can be ordered into a hierarchy, which purportedly corresponds to an "emotional stratification"; the predominant "mood" is said to be most manifest in behavior, while the less predominant "moods" are said to be less available for expression. The manual gives one example of this "emotional stratification" and its utilization in psychotherapy, and also describes briefly and incompletely two studies which led Khan to believe in the emotional significance of color choices.

Any critical reader of Khan's manual is likely to be either awed or doubt-ridden by the alleged virtues of the VAT '60. The test would turn out to be a truly remarkable instrument if it should prove to accomplish what it is stated to accomplish in the way of clinical diagnosis and "mood measurement." The reviewer is inclined to believe that the VAT '60 should not be ignored, that it may eventually be demonstrated to have some, though probably limited, value for personality diagnosis. However, at present, it is likely that the VAT '60 should be used, if at all, only with cautious skepticism.

STANLEY J. SEGAL, *Associate Professor of Psychology, and Director, Student Counseling Center, State University of New York at Buffalo, Buffalo, New York.*

The foreword by Silvano Arieti in the VAT '60 manual forewarns by its tentative endorsement, "Even if we do not accept the early conclusions of the author, concerning his first results and his classification of mental disorders, we must admit that the test is offering a new and valuable approach."

The VAT '60, presenting the subject with 12 plates of lines randomly drawn and asking that he *color* "whatever design, pattern, or object" he sees, is yet another new projective technique, rushed into publication with promises of things to come, but with very little evidence that what is already presented has been carefully constructed, standardized, and evaluated.

Prevalent mood is measured by standardized scoring of the incidence of use of eight colors in the drawings. The manual offers little explanation of: (*a*) The basis for relating particular colors to particular moods. ("Initial studies revealed that the choice of colors by the patients in spontaneous drawing reflected their moods." No studies are described and no bibliographic references are listed.) (*b*) The rationale of the scoring system where the extent of use of a color, that is if it is the only one used, or dominates, or is secondary, is weighted on a 3, 2, 1 basis.

Clinical diagnosis is based on a standardization group of "149 patients of distinct clinical types in whose case the diagnosis was 'finally and firmly' established." The eight groups listed include from 10 to 39 patients and do not include manics, depressives, or organics with the possible exception of "structural epileptics with an IQ range of 37–59." Yet some of the diagnostic illustrations given offer typical patterns of organics. In this area, as with prevalent mood, discussion of interpretation is *not* offered in terms of normative data but rather seems offhand, clinical, intuitive, and frequently overgeneralized. In some instances, a specific case is given with some brief discussion while in others a more general group, for example, "emotionally immature adults," is discussed.

Although there is discussion of testing of children, no age range is mentioned in the manual and there are no data offered about children's reactions to the test. (This is one of the promises for later.)

The author indicates that individuals with an IQ of 34 and up complete the test. There is, however, no analysis offered on the standardization group as to whether IQ affects performance. In those examples given where IQ is noted, the reviewer felt that this might be a significant variable.

Other specific criticism can be raised, but it would seem unnecessary, for the author's report of high correlations with the MMPI suggests that the Multiphasic measures these same variables and offers the test user a more meaningful basis for interpretation. It seems unlikely that there is a good basis for the claim in the manual that the *Visual Apperception Test* differentiates types of schizophrenia since only 23 psychotics classified as simple schizophrenics or delusional psychoses with a limited IQ range are included in the standardization group. Therefore, this claim used as evidence of an advantage of the VAT '60 over the MMPI seems untenable.

For the moment this new projective would seem poorly constructed with limited normative data available and with many questions as to the basis of interpretations offered. Until the author can offer some of the promised data and can approach the task of validation in a more careful and exacting manner, the VAT '60 would seem to offer little of value to the diagnostician.

The publication of this test at its present stage of development is another sad example of clinically oriented people prejudicing the case for the use of projective techniques by adding to the already existing number rather than devoting themselves to testing and improving those presently in wide use. Perhaps a moratorium on the publication of new projectives is needed until the wheat is separated from the chaff of those already in print.

[Other Tests]

For tests not listed above, see the following entries in *Tests in Print:* 325, 333–4, 337–40, 342, 344, 346–7, 359, 364–5, 368–70, 376, 378, 380, 383–4, 391–2, and 394–7; out of print: 343, 354, 386, and 390; status unknown: 330 and 377.

ENGLISH

REVIEWS BY *J. Douglas Ayers, Hillel Black, M. Alan Brimer, Miriam M. Bryan, Henry Chauncey, William E. Coffman, Charlotte Croon Davis, Clarence Derrick, Leonard S. Feldt, J. Raymond Gerberich, Marvin D. Glock, Albert N. Hieronymus, Stephen Hunka, Margaret F. Lorimer, William H. Lucio, T. R. Miles, Stanley Nisbet, Victor H. Noll, Osmond E. Palmer, A. E. G. Pilliner, Gus P. Plessas, Robert C. Pooley, Roger A. Richards, Holland Roberts, Benjamin Rosner, H. J. Sants, Richard E. Schutz, John C. Sherwood, George D. Spache, Bernard Spolsky, Robert E. Stake, John M. Stalnaker, and George P. Winship, Jr.*

[248]

***American School Achievement Tests: Part 3, Language and Spelling.** Grades 4–6, 7–9; 1941–63; subtest of *American School Achievement Tests;* 2 scores: language, spelling; 4 forms (2 sheets); Forms D, E, and F are identical with Forms A, B, and C copyrighted 14 years earlier except for format; 2 levels; $3 per 35 self-marking tests; 50¢ per specimen set of either level; postage extra; Willis E. Pratt, Robert V. Young, and Clara E. Cockerille (manuals); Bobbs-Merrill Co., Inc. *

a) INTERMEDIATE BATTERY. Grades 4–6; Forms D ('55), E ('56), F ('57), G ('58); battery manual ('61, 17 pages); 32(45) minutes.

b) ADVANCED BATTERY. Grades 7–9; Forms D ('56), E ('56), F ('57), G ('58); battery manual ('63, 17 pages); 37(50) minutes.

REFERENCES

1. GROFF, PATRICK J. "Parts of Speech in Standardized English Tests." *Sch R* 69:457–60 w '61. *

For reviews by M. A. Brimer and Clarence Derrick, see 5:174. For reviews of the complete battery, see 2, 5:1, 4:1, and 3:1.

[249]

***Analytical Survey Test in English Fundamentals.** Grades 9–13; 1932–57; formerly called *Diagnostic Survey Test in English Fundamentals;* 8 scores: spelling, capitalization, punctuation, sentence organization, sentence structure, grammatical usage, grammatical terminology, total; Forms 3 ['57], 4 ('57), (8 pages); mimeographed manual ('57, 10 pages); no data on reliability of current forms; tentative norms; $3.50 per 35 tests; 50¢ per specimen set; postage extra; 33(45) minutes; J. Helen Campbell and Walter Scribner Guiler; Bobbs-Merrill Co., Inc. *

REFERENCES

1. GUILER, WALTER SCRIBNER. "Capitalization Disabilities of College Freshmen." *J Am Assn Col Reg* 22:317–27 Ap '47. *

2. GUILER, WALTER SCRIBNER. "Punctuation Disabilities of College Freshmen." *J Am Assn Col Reg* 22:183–91 Ja '47. *

LEONARD S. FELDT, *Professor of Education, State University of Iowa, Iowa City, Iowa.*

The main purpose of this test, as stated in the mimeographed manual, is "to discover the particular phases of the mechanics of English usage in which individual students (or the class as a whole) need further training." To perform this diagnostic function the authors have included 20 items on spelling, 16 on capitalization, 16 on punctuation, 8 on sentence organization, 16 on sentence structure, 16 on grammatical usage, and 8 on grammatical terminology. The reader who doubts that such short subtests could yield scores which are sufficiently reliable for diagnostic purposes will find no data in the manual to allay these fears. He will find other inadequacies as well.

Content validity is obviously a crucial characteristic of an instrument of this kind, but the manual presents practically no evidence on which to base judgment. The authors state that curriculum validity was insured by including "only those usages that have high functional value and that thereby constitute legitimate educational objectives. The criterion used in judging functional value was whether or not violation of the usage constitutes a flagrant language error." There is no indication, however, that the authors have referred to the research on the incidence of various errors, to the curriculum publications of the National Council of Teachers of English, or to studies bearing on the acceptability of many usages encountered in formal and informal writing. Thus the case must rest on the potential user's personal evaluation of the test content.

Throughout the manual the authors state that they are concerned with skills of functional value. Yet in Part 2, Sentence Structure, the student may lose eight points if he cannot identify the principles which have been violated in a series of poorly constructed sentences. It is not enough that he recognize a sentence is faulty, but he must know which of seven principles account for the fault. In Part 7, Grammatical Terminology, the examinee may lose eight points if he cannot identify the technical names of parts of sentences. These may be functional skills in learning about the structure of the English language, but they hardly seem functional skills in the use of language. One might also argue that a number of the items fail to represent examples of flagrant errors. For example, the Sentence Structure subtest includes the following item: "One reason that camels are used on the desert is because their ....feet do not sink in the sand." According to the key, this sentence is unacceptable, since a clause beginning with *because* cannot be used as a predicate noun. Many teachers of English may agree. Leonard and others,[1] however, in their survey of linguists and teachers, conclude, "The opinions of the judges in this instance leave little doubt that the expression is acceptable colloquially." Other usages scattered through the test fall into the category which Marckwardt and Walcott [2] call "disputable"—constructions upon which linguists and teachers evidence substantial difference of opinion. Clearly, the reaction of a potential user to this test will be conditioned by the degree to which his definition of flagrant error is consistent with that of the authors.

One final bit of evidence bearing on validity concerns the correlation of scores on an earlier edition with first semester English grades. A coefficient of .65 is reported in the manual, but no details are offered as to the institution involved, the nature of the examinee population, or the skills represented in this grade criterion. The obtained coefficient is therefore relatively meaningless.

Despite the absence of concrete evidence of validity in the manual, individual teachers might react favorably to the test content. Other aspects of the test more surely deserve criticism. Though separate scores are to be obtained on individual parts and the presence of specific

1 LEONARD, STERLING ANDRUS. *Current English Usage,* p. 145. National Council of Teachers of English, English Monographs, No. 1. Chicago, Ill.: the Council, 1932. Pp. xxii, 232. *

2 MARCKWARDT, ALBERT H., AND WALCOTT, FRED C. *Facts About Current English Usage,* p. 112. National Council of Teachers of English, English Monographs, No. 7. New York: D. Appleton-Century Co., Inc., 1938. Pp. 144.

weaknesses is to be inferred from these scores, no reliability data are reported for the subtests. Only one reliability coefficient is presented in the manual; it pertains to the total score for an undescribed group of college freshmen. No reliability information at all is available for grades 9 through 12. Minimum standards of excellence in test development have advanced quite far beyond the point where such meager evidence can be regarded as sufficient.

Were the aforementioned weaknesses not enough to cause potential users to look elsewhere for a test of language skills, the faulty standardization of this test would surely constitute sufficient grounds for its rejection. The norms consist solely of median scores on each part and total for groups that are not described in any respect. Test users have rightfully come to expect more complete tables of norms and relatively comprehensive descriptions of the samples on which the norms are based. Since the present manual contains no information whatever about the norms groups, even the scant data that are provided are practically useless.

In summary, the faults of this test appear to outweigh its virtues by a wide margin. If a potential user is attracted to the particular sets of items in each subtest, he should realize that he is getting little more for his money than a collection of pre-tried exercises. He should be prepared to investigate reliability extensively before using the test for diagnostic purposes and to develop his own norms. While most standardized tests of language facility have not been favorably reviewed in the past, other tests, such as the *Cooperative English Tests [1960 Revision]*, will probably have greater appeal for the majority of English teachers.

Roger A. Richards, *Assistant Professor of English, Jersey City State College, Jersey City, New Jersey.*

The manual accompanying this test states, in a sentence of curious structure, that "The revised edition has the further advantage over the earlier edition in that [*sic*] it can be administered in less time, 33 minutes instead of 38." This statement illustrates one of the many ways in which the attempt to make a test administratively attractive can rob it of its validity. The stated purpose of the test is sufficiently ambitious in itself to give rise to mild suspicion: "The main purpose....is to discover the particular phases of the mechanics of English usage in which individual students (or the class as a whole) need further training. It is also designed to measure general achievement in the mechanics of English usage." To claim that such a noble purpose can be served by only 33 minutes of testing time seems incredible.

The seven parts of the test reflect varying degrees of inadequacy. Time limits for individual subtests range from three to six minutes. None of the parts contains more than 20 items, and two, covering the broad fields of "Sentence Organization" and "Grammatical Terminology," consist of only eight. The rest are tests of 16 questions. It is especially inconceivable that the 20-word subtest can adequately appraise overall spelling ability of students in the range from ninth grade through first year of college.

Statistical data concerning the test are grossly inadequate. No information concerning validity or reliability of the various parts is given. We are told only (*a*) that for 350 college freshmen, scores on the earlier forms of this test correlated .65 and .62 with first semester English grades and total first semester average, respectively, and (*b*) that the reliability of scores "made by more than 300 college freshmen on the two test forms [the earlier Forms 1 and 2]" was .90. A single set of norms for both of the current forms is presented solely in terms of median part scores and total scores for students at each grade level from 9 through 13. No information is given concerning the origin of the norms. For all the test user knows, they might be based on nothing more than speculation. What relevance they could possibly have to the present-day performance of students is not clear. If they are based on some sort of evidence, we are in grave trouble. Consider, for example, the spelling section. Each item presents three alternative spellings of some commonly used word. Many of the distractors seem invented just to furnish multiple responses. We have, among others, these: "decidedly, decidedaly, decidedely," "satisfactorily, satisfactorely, satisfactorally," "curosity, curiosity, curiosety," "courtesies, curtesies, curtisies." Confronted with such choices, the median college freshman, according to the norms, makes a score of only 14 out of 20!

Some of the scoring procedures seem inappropriate. In Parts 2 (Capitalization) and

3 (Punctuation), the score is determined by the number of sentences right; the result is that on the Form 4 capitalization subtest, item 1, containing a single capital letter, and items 8 and 12, requiring no capitals, are weighted the same as item 2, which requires 10 capitals! It is doubtful that Part 4 measures skill in "Sentence Organization," though this reviewer must confess that he has no idea of what language skill is referred to by the term or how, if it exists, the skill differs from "Sentence Structure" covered by Part 5. Whatever is involved, the key is inadequate. It makes no provision for giving credit to a student who rearranges "disconnected groups of words" to form interrogative sentences. And a student with keen insight into language would have difficulty accepting the "right" reconstruction of item 2 of Form 3: "(1) made to carry (2) with folding blades (3) in the pocket (4) is a knife (5) a pocket knife." According to the key this sentence should read "A pocket knife is a knife with folding blades made to carry in the pocket." The misplaced modifying phrase "made to carry" is not likely to cause any breakdown in communication, but its appearance seems unforgivable in a test designed to measure a student's ability in "Sentence Organization."

In addition to the multitude of similar measurement crudities, the approach to language reflected by the test will be objectionable to the more enlightened English teachers in today's schools. Many parts of the test confront the student with tasks that he will never meet except on such exercises as these. Moreover, no awareness of such vital linguistic considerations as levels of usage, the importance of appropriateness, or the constant change in language shows through.

These tests ought to be withdrawn from the market. If they are permitted to continue in circulation, however, they should not be used except as the basis of class discussions. Even then, they will probably appeal only to teachers of an extremely traditional orientation.

[250]

***Barrett-Ryan English Test.** Grades 7–13; 1926–61; IBM; Forms 1 ('56), 2 ('56), 3 ('58), (4 pages, revisions of tests copyrighted in 1929), 6 ('44), 1948, 1954 ['55], (4 pages); revised manual ('58, 6 pages); supplementary norms: Forms 1 and 2 ['57], Form 3 ('61), Forms 1948 and 1954 ['48, same as norms originally issued for Form 1948 alone]; $1.40 per 25 tests; separate answer sheets may be used; 85¢ per 25 IBM answer sheets; 30¢ per scoring stencil; postage extra; 50¢ per specimen set, postpaid; 50(55) minutes; E. R. Barrett, Teresa M. Ryan, M. W. Sanders (1, 2, 3), H. E. Schrammel (1948, 1954, manual), and E. R. Wood (manual); Bureau of Educational Measurements. *

REFERENCES

1. ANDERSON, MARY R., AND STEGMAN, ERWIN J. "Predictors of Freshman Achievement at Fort Hays Kansas State College." *Ed & Psychol Meas* 14:722–3 w '54. * (*PA* 29:7952)
2. GROFF, PATRICK J. "Parts of Speech in Standardized English Tests." *Sch R* 69:457–60 w '61. *

CLARENCE DERRICK, *Professor of English, and Chairman, Humanities Department, University of Florida, Gainesville, Florida.*

Wines and cheeses improve with age; objective English tests do not. The *Barrett-Ryan English Test* was first published in 1926, and the revised forms suffer from the influence of the earlier editions. Even more important, in the confusion of form designations, the unwary purchaser may fail to recognize that Form 6 (1944), Form 1948, and Form 1954 differ significantly from revised Form 3 (1958). If one has to use the Barrett-Ryan test, he will be better off using the 1956–1958 revisions. This review will concentrate on these later forms with only passing reference to the earlier editions.

In Part 1, Punctuation, 30 items test the use of the colon, comma, question mark, semicolon, apostrophe, hyphen, double quotation marks, simple quotation marks. The principal difficulty is that the item type used reduces most of the items to two, or at best, three-choice items although they are apparently five-choice items. For example, the student is asked to select for an indicated spot in a sentence the appropriate mark from a key list containing these possibilities—colon, comma, question mark, semicolon, no punctuation. The first sentence in Form 1 is, "Omaha, Nebraska ( ) is known as a cattle market." It doesn't take much knowledge to eliminate the question mark, the colon, and the semicolon as possibilities. The 10 capitalization items in Part 2 are presented in the same manner as true-false items. The student has a fifty-fifty chance of getting these items correct by guessing. Part 3, The Sentence, tests sentence structure, diction, and recognition of the complete sentence. This 45-item section also calls for a true-false type of response. The subtest on recognition of the complete sentence uses an informal letter as the text, a poor choice since there is a freedom in the informal letter which is not present in more formal writing. Part 4, Verb Usage, contains 15 more true-false type items of verb forms frequently confused. Part 5, Grammar, has 50 paired true-false items. In the first item of a pair, the student indicates whether or not an error is present; and in the second item of the pair, he indicates whether or not a stated reason is applicable to that error. The aroma of the traditional textbook hangs heavy over this part of the test. Considerable emphasis is given to who-whom, whoever-whomever problems. One correct sentence is this rhetorical gem: "The class elected me, who am the youngest, as president." (Whoever-whomever) permitted this sentence to stand as "correct" has a tin ear.

Only the barest minimum of information on reliability and validity is reported in the manual. Similarly, the norms for the test are based on populations described as midyear high school students and beginning-of-the-year college freshmen. What high school students? What college freshmen?

Other inadequacies of the *Barrett-Ryan English Test* could be discussed; but enough limitations have been suggested to lead to the conclusion that there are other tests which are much more useful in providing the teacher with information about a student's proficiency in punctuation, capitalization, the sentence, verb usage, and grammar.

For a review by J. Raymond Gerberich, see 5:175.

[251]

***California Language Test, 1957 Edition With 1963 Norms.** Grades 1–2, 2.5–4.5, 4–6, 7–9, 9–14; 1933–63; subtest of *California Achievement Tests;* 4 scores: mechanics of English, spelling, total, handwriting; IBM and Grade-O-Mat for grades 4–14; 2–4 forms ('63 printings, c1957–63, are identical with tests copyrighted in 1957 except for profile); 5 levels; battery manual ('63, c1957–63, 53–70 pages) for each level; battery technical report ('57, 48 pages) on 1957 edition with 1957 norms; battery individual profile ('63, 2 pages) for each level; no norms for grades 13–14; separate answer sheets or cards may be used in grades 4–14; 5¢ per IBM answer sheet; 9¢ per Scoreze answer sheet; 3¢ per set of Cal-Cards; 4¢ per set of Grade-O-Mat scorable punch-out cards; 20¢ per either IBM answer sheet or Cal-Card hand scoring stencil; 20¢ per either IBM answer sheet or Grade-O-Mat machine scoring stencil; 2¢ per profile; postage extra; technical report free; 75¢ per specimen set of *a* or *b,* $1 per specimen set of *c, d,* or *e;* postpaid; Ernest W. Tiegs and Willis W. Clark; California Test Bureau. *

a) LOWER PRIMARY. Grades 1–2; Forms W ('63), X ('57), (8 pages); $2.45 per 35 tests; 27(40) minutes.
b) UPPER PRIMARY. Grades 2.5–4.5; Forms W ('63), X ('57), (6 pages); $2.80 per 35 tests; 30(40) minutes.
c) ELEMENTARY. Grades 4–6; IBM and Grade-O-Mat; Forms W ('63), X ('57), Y ('63), Z ('57), (10 pages); $3.15 per 35 tests; 40(50) minutes.
d) JUNIOR HIGH LEVEL. Grades 7–9; IBM and Grade-O-Mat; Forms W ('63), X ('57), Y ('57), Z ('57), (10 pages); $3.15 per 35 tests; 32(40) minutes.
e) ADVANCED. Grades 9–14; IBM and Grade-O-Mat; Forms W ('63), X ('57), Y ('57), (14 pages); $3.15 per 35 tests; 38(48) minutes.

REFERENCES

1–3. See 5:177.
4. GROFF, PATRICK J. "Parts of Speech in Standardized English Tests." *Sch R* 69:457–60 w '61. *

RICHARD E. SCHUTZ, *Professor of Education, and Director, Testing Service, Arizona State University, Tempe, Arizona.*

Although no changes have been made in item content, the 1957 edition of the *California Language Test* has been restandardized and now appears with 1963 norms. The manual gives three reasons for renorming the test: (*a*) to maintain the proper relationship with the 1963 revision of the *California Test of Mental Maturity,* which was normed at the same time, (*b*) to utilize newly determined age-grade relationships, (*c*) to update the norms in line with curriculum changes since 1957.

The dominant reason for the renorming appears to be the 1963 revision of the CTMM series. The age-grade relationships were derived directly from the CTMM standardization program. And if curriculum change was indeed an important consideration, this should have required a complete revision of the test content in line with the modified curriculum rather than simply an updating of norms for outmoded test content.

How do the new norms compare with the old? A comparison of the 1963 and 1957 age-grade relationships shows students in 1963 consistently 2–3 months older at each grade level. This appears to indicate a reversal of the declining age-in-grade trend observed between the early 1920's and the mid-1950's. It is difficult to account for such a consistent reversal throughout the grades from elementary school through college in the brief period between 1957 and 1963. The manual makes no attempt to explain the changes or their determinants.

The changes in the test norms are less regular. At the primary level the 1963 derived normative scores run consistently lower than the 1957 norms in both mechanics of English and spelling. For example, a raw score of 35 yields a grade placement of 1.9 on the 1963 norms and 2.3 on the 1957 norms. A raw score of 10 on the spelling test yields a 1963 grade placement of 2.7 versus 3.9 in 1957, a difference greater than one full grade. Disregarding sampling errors, this difference indicates that language instruction has improved considerably in the lower grades. With differences of this magnitude, the new norms may come as a shock to primary teachers when they compare their class results with those obtained in previous years with 1957 norms. "Falling back" six months to a year in terms of grade placement may be regarded by the individual teacher as a slap in the face for present efforts rather than as a pat on the back for past efforts in upgrading language instruction generally. It is hoped that a knowledgeable person will be on hand to help interpret the comparison, since the manual does not anticipate the need for this kind of help.

At the elementary level, the mechanics of English norms are uniformly 3 to 5 grade placement scores lower at the fourth through sixth grade range for which the test is designed. Differences in the spelling norms at the elementary level are complicated. At grade placement 4.0 there is a 2 point difference with the 1963 norms lower. At 6.0 there is a 6 point difference with the 1963 norm again lower. These differences are difficult to account for other than in terms of sampling error.

At the junior high school and advanced levels, differences between the 1957 and 1963 mechanics of English norms are slight and not in any consistent direction. The 1963 spelling norms, on the other hand, are uniformly higher than the 1957, with differences of 1–4 points from the ninth through twelfth grade range. This difference suggests that the terminal spelling achievement of current high school graduates may be somewhat below the accomplishment of their 1957 counterparts, which leaves a rather unpleasant taste following the pleasant swallow of improvement in the early grades.

Unfortunately, it is impossible to separate sampling error from true variability in assessing any of the normative differences. In fact, the entire 1963 standardization program is so ill-defined in the manuals that the sample's representativeness of any population rests on little more than faith. It is clear, however, that the 1963 standardization strategy represents a radical departure from that utilized in 1957. In 1957 about 70,000 students from 341 schools in 48 states were involved in the standardization. In 1963, only 15,351 students were involved, with the number of schools and states not reported. The 1957 manuals describe in considerable detail the sampling criteria used in selecting the standardization participants. The 1963 revised manuals state only that the sample was obtained from two phases: "(1) independent class units from seven geographic regions representing forty-nine states, and (2) complete school systems, including all students in Grades 1 through 12 from five school systems located in the northeastern, eastern, central, and western areas of the United States." Test data from the two phases were combined in generating the norms.

The 1963 tables of norms are much more conveniently presented in the manuals than were the 1957 tables. All of the grade placement norms for the reading, arithmetic, and language tests are grouped on single pages rather than separated by test. Percentile ranks are presented for separate grades and in terms of raw scores, rather than across grades and in terms of grade placement scores as in 1957. In addition, stanine intervals and *T* scores are included with the percentile ranks. Anticipated grade achievement norms are tabled rather than graphed. These layout modifications will save users much time and reduce clerical errors in manually performed conversions.

There may be some administrative confusion in transferring from the 1957 to the 1963 norms. The 1957 answer sheet with its diagnostic profile in terms of grade placement is still usable for responses. The 1963 answer sheet includes a profile based on the revised norms. The diagnostic profile included on the answer sheet is of importance, since it contains grade placements for the subscores of capitalization, punctuation, and word usage available from no other source. Since no reliability data are reported for these subscores, however, extreme caution should be exercised in their use.

The only other innovation in the 1963 revision is the availability of specially devised mark-sense and porta-punch cards as response recording modes at the elementary levels and above. Although no evidence is given concerning the comparability of results obtained via these various response modes, they may prove of interest to school systems which have data processing equipment readily available.

The basic content and organization of the *California Language Test* have changed little from the days of the *Progressive Achievement*

Tests. This stability can be defended without great difficulty in the areas of capitalization, punctuation, and spelling. A defense of the word usage subsection is more difficult in light of present knowledge in descriptive and structural linguistics. However, the lag between scientific advances and classroom instruction is probably sufficient to maintain the curricular validity of "usage" items for the majority of classrooms for some time to come. Even so, many would regard the generality of the title "Language Test" to be inappropriate without consideration of such topics as dialect differences, structural patterns, and verbal expression.

For reviews by Constance M. McCullough and Winifred L. Post, see 5:177; for reviews by Gerald V. Lannholm and Robert C. Pooley of the 1950 edition, see 4:151; for reviews by Harry A. Greene and J. Paul Leonard of an earlier edition, see 40:1292. For reviews of the complete battery, see 3, 5:2, 4:2, 3:15, 40:1193, and 38:876.

[252]

★Canadian Achievement Test in English (CATE). Grade 10; 1961–63; this test and tests 5, 365, 565, and 566 make up the *Canadian Test Battery,* grade 10. 1 form ('61, 11 pages); 2 editions of manual (for use also with test 365): hand scoring ('63, 7 pages), machine scoring ('63, 8 pages); supplementary data ('63, 6 pages) for the battery; separate answer sheets or cards must be used; $1.25 per 25 tests; $1 per set of 50 hand scoring answer sheets and hand scoring manual; 20¢ per hand scoring stencil; 20¢ per 15 battery profiles; 50¢ per set of 25 IBM answer cards (machine scoring through the Department of Educational Research only); 10¢ per machine scoring manual; 50¢ per specimen set; $2.15 per battery specimen set; postage extra; 60(70–75) minutes; Department of Educational Research, Ontario College of Education, University of Toronto; distributed by Guidance Centre (machine scoring manual and answer cards must be purchased from the Department of Educational Research). *

REFERENCES

1. D'Oyley, Vincent R. *Technical Manual for the Canadian Tests: Statistical Data on the Carnegie Study Tests of Academic Aptitude and Achievement in Grades 8, 9, and 10 in Ontario Schools and Grades 7 and 8 in Toronto Schools.* Carnegie Study of Identification and Utilization of Talent in High School and College, Bulletin No. 4. Toronto, Canada: Department of Educational Research, Ontario College of Education, University of Toronto, 1964. Pp. viii, 50. *

2. D'Oyley, Vincent R. *Testing: The First Two Years of the Carnegie Study 1959 to 1961: Analysis of Scores by Course, Sex, and Size of Municipality.* Carnegie Study of Identification and Utilization of Talent in High School and College, Bulletin No. 6. Toronto, Canada: Department of Educational Research, Ontario College of Education, University of Toronto, 1964. Pp. ix, 53. *

Bernard Spolsky, *Assistant Professor of Education, McGill University, Montreal, Quebec, Canada.*

This test was "developed for use in the Carnegie Study of Identification and Utilization of Talent in High School and College, a longitudinal study of approximately 90,000 Grade 9 students enrolled in Ontario schools in September, 1959"; the norms supplied are based on a total population of approximately 60,600 students in grade 10 in Ontario schools in 1960–61. The test is available in 1963 in both machine and hand scoring editions, each edition being accompanied by full and clear directions for administration.

Lacking a statement on the part of the authors as to what specific abilities the test is aimed to measure or as to what achievement in English is held to mean, one is forced to draw inferences from the test itself. Work in grade 10 in English includes the development of abilities in reading and expression; the former includes comprehension and appreciation, and the latter both the mechanics (spelling, punctuation, acceptable usage) and the effectiveness of expression. One would expect then that a test of achievement in English would give some sort of attention to each of these areas. But this test falls far short of the ideal: it omits effectiveness of expression entirely, pays only lip service to comprehension and appreciation, and concentrates on those aspects of mechanics which are most susceptible of objective testing. This becomes evident when one considers the type of item used: of 110 items, 43 test what might be called elementary editorial ability by calling on the student to mark incorrect forms and another 21 call for the application of traditional grammatical terminology.

This failure of the test to reflect the aims of English teaching is also made clear when one looks at the content of the various sections. The section headed "Comprehension and Appreciation," for instance, seems to be concerned not with these abilities but with the student's ability to apply critical labels. The three questions on a prose passage do not test understanding of the passage but call for the selection of responses dealing with intention and means: the student has to decide the application of such vague expressions as "building to a climax," "creating atmosphere," and "producing contrast," and to decide whether atmosphere was created by "vivid verbal constructions" or "vague adverbs." Questions asked about a ten-line extract from a poem are similarly unsuitable: in one item, the question refers to "the poem," with the result that a student who knew the whole poem would be led to an incorrect response to two items; three items are concerned with terminology; one asks for identification of the line in which the poet makes "most effective use of repetition of words and sounds to make the picture more forceful" (the response given as correct ignores the frequent use of alliteration throughout the extract and chooses the line with the greatest number of repeated words, the least effective line in the whole extract); and two ask for identification of metaphors. The last three items of this section call for selection of expressions that will "contribute *most* towards the effectiveness" of given sentences; the answers required involve rather the selection of the most usual word or expression for the context; in other words, this is a test of vocabulary, or, more precisely, of ability to use clichés. The section as a whole does not test comprehension and even reflects a considerable lack of appreciation of language.

The test must be considered, therefore, as measuring certain areas of the mechanics of English. Even these items are not well chosen. The punctuation section includes two items where decisions are not covered by hard-and-fast rules but are matters of stylistic variation, and one where something that is clearly direct speech is to have two punctuation marks added but is to be left without quotation marks. The vocabulary section consists of five items requiring completion of sentences with the best of five words and nine requiring choice of a synonym. Unfortunately, the sentences do not fully control the choice of words (for instance, one is as likely to have second helpings of food because of its succulence, pleasantness, or refreshing nature as because of its palatability). And the various synonyms offered are at times equally satisfactory (the *Shorter Oxford Dictionary,* for instance, gives for the word *contraction:* "shrinking, narrowing;....the action of contracting or establishing by contract," but the test demands that the student choose between "an agreement," "a shrinking," and "a narrowing"). The major part of the grammar and usage section calls for the student to mark incorrect forms. I referred to this above as elementary editorial ability; actually, it is less than this. The errors are embedded in sentences that have been constructed to contain at least three crucial usages, each of which is underlined; it is thus not a measure of the student's ability to select errors himself. The sentences produced read very strangely. Many of them are most unlikely to have any existence outside a grammar book, e.g., "Your friends may approve of *your* going, but I, who *am* your mother, *forbids* it." What seems to be called for in many of the items is ability to recognise that certain words are out of place in the extremely formal style set up by the other usages, or, alternatively, ability to recognise the items that might be marked wrong by cautious teachers. Generally, the test does not call for any normally accepted forms to be marked incorrect, but many of the correct forms represent a preciousness of usage that is old fashioned.

Satisfactory split-half reliability coefficients are provided. On the other hand, validity data showing intercorrelations of the test with two other tests in the battery (*Canadian Achievement Test in Mathematics and Canadian Achievement Test in French*) and with school marks (based on a random sample population of 1,000) indicate that the test is not so much a measure of English achievement as a reflection of some more general ability in school work: one notes that it is about as good as a predictor of the grade 10 French mark (correlation of .56) and of marks for the other two tests (.53, .54) as it is in predicting the grade 10 English mark (.58).

Taking all these factors into consideration, one feels that, whatever its use may have been in the study for which it was prepared, the CATE has little to recommend it as a test of achievement in grade 10 English.

[253]

★**Canadian English Achievement Test (CEAT).** Grades 8.5–9.0; 1959–63; this test and tests 445 and 567 make up the *Canadian Test Battery,* grades 8–9; 3 or 4 scores: reading comprehension, effectiveness of expression, and (grade 9 only) mechanics of expression, or (grade 8 only) punctuation-capitalization, grammatical usage; 1 form; separate parts 1 ('59, reading comprehension), 2 ('59, mechanics of expression), 3 ('59, effectiveness of expression; items selected from earlier forms of *Cooperative English Test: Lower and Higher Levels*), (6 pages); 2 editions of battery manual: hand scoring ('63, 11 pages), machine scoring ('63, 13 pages); supplementary data ('63, 6 pages) for the battery; battery profile ('63, 2 pages); no data on reliability of part 1; separate answer sheets or cards must be used; $1.25 per 25 tests; $1 per set of 50 hand scoring answer sheets and hand scoring manual; 20¢ per hand scoring stencil; 20¢ per 15 battery profiles; 50¢ per 25 IBM answer cards (machine scoring through the Department of Educational Research only); 10¢ per machine scoring manual; 50¢ per specimen set; $2.75 per battery specimen set;

postage extra; 30(40–45) minutes per part; Department of Educational Research, Ontario College of Education, University of Toronto; distributed by Guidance Centre (machine scoring manual and answer cards must be purchased from the Department of Educational Research). *

REFERENCES

1. D'Oyley, Vincent R. *Technical Manual for the Canadian Tests: Statistical Data on the Carnegie Study Tests of Academic Aptitude and Achievement in Grades 8, 9, and 10 in Ontario Schools and Grades 7 and 8 in Toronto Schools.* Carnegie Study of Identification and Utilization of Talent in High School and College, Bulletin No. 4. Toronto, Canada: Department of Educational Research, Ontario College of Education, University of Toronto, 1964. Pp. viii, 50. *

2. D'Oyley, Vincent R. *Testing: The First Two Years of the Carnegie Study 1959 to 1961: Analysis of Scores by Course, Sex, and Size of Municipality.* Carnegie Study of Identification and Utilization of Talent in High School and College, Bulletin No. 6. Toronto, Canada: Department of Educational Research, Ontario College of Education, University of Toronto, 1964. Pp. ix, 53. *

J. Douglas Ayers, *Associate Professor of Educational Psychology, University of Alberta, Edmonton, Alberta, Canada.*

The *Canadian English Achievement Test* is one of several tests "developed for use in the Carnegie Study of Identification and Utilization of Talent in High School and College, a longitudinal study of approximately 90,000 Grade 9 students enrolled in Ontario schools in September, 1959." The test has three subtests: Reading Comprehension, Mechanics of Expression, and Effectiveness of Expression.

The directions for administration have certain flaws, one of which is crucial. Both the directions for administration and the test booklets for Reading Comprehension and Effectiveness of Expression fail to inform the students whether they should "guess" or not. This is a very serious oversight as testwiseness and willingness to guess are affected by previous experience with both standardized and teacher made tests. Consequently variation in testing conditions is introduced by lack of standard directions on guessing and the effect on the reported norms is unknown. Certainly, the individual teacher can make no interpretation about the relative standing of the students in her class. The directions for Mechanics of Expression, on the other hand, caution against wild guessing. Then in scoring for grade 9 the wrongs are subtracted from the rights whether there are two or three alternatives, but there is no correction for guessing for grade 8. There is also a minor flaw. The manual states that the Mechanics of Expression subtest "is considered as having two parts for Grade 8." Some teachers, therefore, may allow 30 minutes for each part. Such confusion could be avoided easily by saying that the test has two subscores within one time limit.

Reading Comprehension is undoubtedly the poorest of the subtests. It involves only three aspects of comprehension (main idea, suitable title, and simple deduction) and does not involve such important aspects as inference, implication, purpose of passage, and relevant versus irrelevant detail. The 10 short simple paragraphs are all of approximately the same length. Such selections do not allow for development of ideas within a passage and for selecting and synthesizing several ideas to obtain the main idea. In fact, the main idea in short paragraphs becomes the topic sentence. In several instances the conclusion is not from the paragraph as a whole but from an isolated statement within it. Flexibility of approach is limited because the passages are nearly all description and precluded because the questions for each paragraph are posed in identical form.

The punctuation section of Mechanics of Expression has a uniform three-alternative format which prevents the use of some seductive misleads, for example, a comma in item 14. Item 13 has no correct answer due either to a misprint or lack of item analysis. The capitalization section has 35 questions in 98 words, and 75 per cent of the text is geographical. Five of the capitals occur at the beginning of sentences. In each of the items in the grammatical usage section the testee has only to choose from two options. This type of item has almost disappeared from modern tests as it should.

While the individual items in Effectiveness of Expression were borrowed from earlier editions of the *Cooperative English Test,* the format, time limit, and proportion of items of various types has been changed. In addition, the directions for Sections D, E, and F have been made unnecessarily complicated and repetitive and the items space consuming.

The norms for grade 9 are based on virtually all students in Ontario in November 1959, but as was pointed out above, the lack of standard directions has an unknown effect on the reported percentile norms. The grade 8 norms are based on a representative sample of approximately 6,500 Ontario students tested in May 1962. On the subtests that can be compared, means for grade 8 are one point higher than for grade 9. The reasons for such a difference are not indicated. In any case, if this test is to be used over several grades it should have progressively higher means over successive grades.

The manual contains no data on item analysis, reliability, or validity, but recently some data have become available on reliability and validity. The split-half reliability of Mechanics of Expression for 200 cases in grade 8 is quoted as .93, and at grade 9 it is .92; for Effectiveness of Expression, the reliabilities are .80 and .86. For Reading Comprehension, K-R reliabilities of .63 and .61 are reported.

It should be noted that the *Canadian English Achievement Test* is not "Canadian" nor has it been standardized on a Canadian population. Also, because of variations in grade structure between provinces, Ontario norms are unlikely to be appropriate outside that province. It would seem that this test was hurriedly thrown together before its original use in 1959 and that it has now been published without any further study or analysis.

BERNARD SPOLSKY, *Assistant Professor of Education, McGill University, Montreal, Quebec, Canada.*

Norms are provided for grades 8 and 9, the former being based on what is called in the manual "a representative sample" of approximately 6,500, the latter on a total population of 85,000. The grade 8 norms for Parts 1 and 3 (the only parts comparable, for there is a different system for marking Part 2 for each grade) are higher than those of grade 9. This may be explained by the different time of year at which the test was administered to each grade, but it does suggest that the norms must be used with very considerable care, and serves to cast doubt on the validity of the test as a whole.

Part 1, Reading Comprehension, presents 10 passages that range in difficulty from a school textbook to J. S. Mill and asks each time for the choice of best title, main idea, and a conclusion. Generally, this is well done, although the rigidity of the structure leads to some questions that are not as good as they might be: some items are ambiguous (in one, for example, the student is expected to conclude that the main idea of a passage mentioning air mileage and air freight has to do with air travel) and some of the selections of titles involve an ability apart from comprehension.

Part 2, Mechanics of Expression, is less satisfactory. In the punctuation section the student is asked to choose which of three possibilities (two alternatives and a "no punctuation") should be placed at a numbered point. Ability to do this is not necessarily the same as ability to punctuate an unpunctuated selection or to use punctuation in one's own writing. One item offers as the correct answer the wrong pair of quotation marks (" instead of " to open a quotation). The section on capitalization follows the same system, except that only two alternatives are used. The remainder of the test is on usage, the student being required to choose which of two forms is "correct" in the sentence given. In grade 9 Mechanics of Expression is treated as one test, with incorrect responses being deducted from the total correct; in grade 8, the test is considered as having two parts, the score being the total correct. No explanation is given for the change in system. As so often seems to happen in an objective test of usage, the items call for standard schoolroom usage, completely ignoring all questions of levels and functional varieties. In other words, while the test may show how much the student has learned about "correct" forms, or, more likely, something about his social and economic background, it will not show whether or not he appreciates what is implied by appropriateness of usage. This is clear from the instruction ("decide which of the two forms given is correct"). The student with understanding of usage is not the one who will say that *it is I* is correct (and one is surprised to find this form called for when *it is me* has been shown to be sanctified not merely by the usage of the majority of educated speakers but also by the historical development of the language) but the one who realises that while *busted* is normal and acceptable in many levels of conversation, *burst* is preferred in formal situations. Its blurred conception of usage will vitiate the test for anyone who is aware of current scholarship and attitudes in this field.

Part 3, Effectiveness of Expression, contains items from earlier forms of the *Cooperative English Test.* It is an interesting attempt to measure objectively a subjective ability. Eleven items involve choosing the best way of expressing an idea, ten are concerned with choice of the best word to complete a sentence, two sections call for the ordering of sentences and paragraph headings, and the last asks that certain pieces of information be classified according to which of several parts of a composition they would fit. Clearly, this section does measure some of the abilities involved in effective expression, but just as clearly it will provide only a very limited picture of the student's ability to write.

Taking all this into consideration, one feels that the test requires considerable revision before it will be ready for more than experimental use.

[254]

***College Entrance Examination Board Advanced Placement Examination: English.** High school students desiring credit for college level courses or admission to advanced courses; 1954–63; replaces the separate tests in literature and English composition which were formerly part of the program; for more complete information, see 761; 180(200) minutes; program administered for the College Entrance Examination Board by Educational Testing Service. *

For a review by Robert C. Pooley of an earlier form of the English composition test, see 5:205; for a review by John S. Diekhoff of an earlier form of the literature test, see 5:211.

[255]

***Cooperative English Test: Usage, Spelling, and Vocabulary.** Grades 7–16; 1932–51; 4 scores: usage, spelling, vocabulary, total; IBM; Forms OM ('38, 14 pages), PM ('39, 15 pages); manual ('51, 4 pages); norms booklet ['38, 8 pages]; separate answer sheets must be used; $4 per 25 tests; $1 per 25 IBM answer sheets; 50¢ per set of scoring stencils; postage extra; $1 per specimen set of this test and three other English tests, cash orders postpaid; 70(80) minutes; M. F. Carpenter, E. F. Lindquist, W. W. Cook, D. G. Paterson, F. S. Beers, and Geraldine Spaulding; Cooperative Test Division. *

REFERENCES

1–11. See 40:1271.
12. Stucky, Milo O., and Anderson, Kenneth E. *A Study of Persistence in College Attendance in Relation to Placement-Test Scores and Grade-Point Averages.* University of Kansas, School of Education, Kansas Studies in Education, Vol. 9, No. 2. Lawrence, Kan.: the School, April 1959. Pp. 58. *
13. Stucky, Milo O., and Anderson, Kenneth E. "A Study of the Relationship Between Entrance-Test Scores and Grade-Point Averages and Length of Stay in College." *Yearb Nat Council Meas Used Ed* 16:164–70 '59. *
14. McKey, Eleanor F. "The Standardized Test—Are Improvements Needed?" *Engl J* 49:35–7 Ja '60. *
15. Barnhart, E. L., and Anderson, Kenneth E. *A Study of the Relationships Between Grade-Point Averages, Placement-Test Scores, Semester Hours Earned, and Area of Major Interest for the Group Who Entered the University of Kansas in the Fall of 1954.* University of Kansas, School of Education, Kansas Studies in Education, Vol. 11, No. 1. Lawrence, Kan.: the School, January 1961. Pp. 36. *
16. Taulbee, George C., Sr. *Construction and Validation of a Scale for Predicting Graduation From a College of Optometry.* Doctor's thesis, University of Houston (Houston, Tex.), 1963. (*DA* 24:387)

Margaret F. Lorimer, *Associate Professor, Office of Institutional Research, Michigan State University, East Lansing, Michigan.*

The *Cooperative English Test,* widely used for many years in high schools and colleges, is designed to measure achievement in three areas: usage, spelling, and vocabulary. Scores for each of the three areas and the total score have been translated into percentile ranks for secondary students in public schools in the South, in public schools in the East, West, and North, and in private schools, and for entering freshmen in preprofessional colleges, in liberal arts colleges, and in junior colleges and teachers colleges. Since the norms were established many years ago (1938), they are possibly outdated by now.

The usage test is divided into four parts, each separately timed: a 75-item (60 items in Form PM) grammar and diction test, a 60-item punctuation test, a 30-item capitalization test, and a 15-item sentence structure test. The first three of these ask the student to choose the best from two to five choices for insertion at a given point. The fourth part offers four versions of the same sentence and asks the student to choose the best of the four.

The spelling test of 45 items lists five words for each item, any or none of which may be wrong. The most seasoned writer and reader soon finds any confidence in his spelling ability shaken as he works through the lists of words, many of which are taken from collections of words most often misspelled.

The vocabulary test of 100 items offers five synonyms for each word. Many of the words might be expected to be in the reading vocabularies of advanced high school and college students, but few of them would be in their speaking vocabularies.

The division of the battery into six distinct tests helps the teacher in diagnosing the student's errors, but it removes from the student the responsibility of spotting errors and leaves him only the responsibility of choosing the best of several alternatives.

The test may be useful in measuring the degree to which a student has mastered the basic rules of grammar and punctuation, and to some extent useful in measuring the extent of his reading vocabulary and his ability to proofread for spelling errors. It does not test ability to write or to speak effectively. It resembles tests which might be found at the end of a workbook of English exercises.

JOHN M. STALNAKER, *President, National Merit Scholarship Corporation, Evanston, Illinois.*

That this test enjoys enough annual usage to justify the publisher's continuing to reprint it suggests that some users find it of value in comparison with the newer tests now available in this area. The test covers usage, spelling, and vocabulary. The usage section is divided into four parts: grammar and diction, punctuation, capitalization, and sentence structure, each separately timed for a total of 40 minutes. Spelling is allowed 10 minutes, and vocabulary 20 minutes.

In the usage test, one of two or more alternate words or phrases is to be checked as the most appropriate for the sentence. In the punctuation section, some 60 places are numbered in an essay and the student is asked to choose for each the appropriate punctuation mark from several given on an answer sheet. In the capitalization exercise, the student indicates whether or not each of 30 marked words should start with a capital letter. Not all errors, however, are marked. Thus, even the corrected sentence may be a poor one containing errors. In the sentence structure section, a sentence is presented in four ways; in each group the sentence which is better than any of the others is to be checked.

In the spelling test, groups of four different words are presented, with the student marking which, if any, is incorrectly spelled. Finally, the vocabulary test asks for the selection of one of five words which most nearly corresponds in meaning to a stimulus word.

The answer sheet gives a table for changing raw scores into scale scores. The norm booklet, undated, gives percentile ranks for several groups and grades within groups, e.g., end of tenth grade, public secondary schools of the South. A manual of directions describes the administrative regulations and the scoring, which is based on corrections for guessing. The booklet "Introduction to the Norms," dated 1938 and referred to in the norms booklet, is out of print.

The chief limitation of this test is the one common to all objective tests in English. It does not measure directly what the teacher means by the ability to write clearly and accurately. However, the scores relate to writing ability measured in other ways, although no evidence of this type is presented.

As long as there is a demand, one might wish that such tests and norms were revised periodically, and a discussion of the validity and significance of the test given. However, the limited number of users, one assumes, have developed their own norms. The publisher has covered the same major content in the 1960 revision of the *Cooperative English Tests* (see 256), for which 1960 norms are given. For most users, the 1960 revision will be preferable to this test.

For reviews by Carleton C. Jones, Jeanette McPherrin, Louis C. Zahner, Henry D. Rinsland, and L. K. Shumaker of Form PM and earlier forms, see 40:1271; for reviews by John M. Stalnaker, Charles S. Thomas, and John H. Thompson, see 38:961.

[256]

***Cooperative English Tests, [1960 Revision].** Grades 9–12, 13–14; 1940–60; revision of *Cooperative English Test: Lower and Higher Levels;* 6 scores: vocabulary, reading comprehension (level, speed, total), English expression, total; IBM; Forms A, B, C, ('60); 2 levels (tests labeled, say, for grades 13–14, Form 1A; for grades 9–12, Form 2A); 2 tests (reading comprehension, English expression) available in separate booklets (7–11 pages) or a single booklet (16–18 pages); directions for administering ('60, 16 pages); manual for interpreting ('60, 42 pages); technical report ('60, 35 pages); distribution of Form 1C restricted to colleges; separate answer sheets must be used; $4 per 20 copies of either test; $6 per 20 tests (single booklet); $1 per 20 IBM scorable answer sheets for both tests; 25¢ per scoring stencil for either test; $1 per 20 Scribe answer sheets for both tests (scored by the publisher only); $1 per manual for interpreting; $1 per technical report; postage extra; $2 per specimen set, cash orders postpaid; 40(45) minutes per test; revision by Clarence Derrick, David P. Harris, and Biron Walker; Cooperative Test Division. *

REFERENCES

1–2. See 40:1276.
3–31. See 3:120.
32–84. See 4:155.
85–142. See 5:179.
143. MOFFETT, CHARLES R. *Operational Characteristics of Beginning Master's Students in Educational Administration and Supervision.* Doctor's thesis, University of Tennessee (Knoxville, Tenn.), 1954.
144. JONES, WILLIAM ALTEN. *The Adequacy of Certain Measures Used in the Selection of Freshman State and Merit Scholarship Recipients at Indiana University.* Doctor's thesis, Indiana University (Bloomington, Ind.), 1955. (*DA* 15:1553)
145. LUTON, JAMES N. *A Study of the Use of Standardized Tests in the Selection of Potential Educational Administrators.* Doctor's thesis, University of Tennessee (Knoxville, Tenn.), 1955.
146. JEX, FRANK B. *University of Utah Studies in the Prediction of Academic Success.* University of Utah Research Monographs in Education, Vol. 1, No. 1. Salt Lake City, Utah: the University, July 1957. Pp. ix, 51. *
147. PETRO, PETER K. *Student Aptitudes and Abilities Correlated With Achievement in First Semester High School Bookkeeping.* Master's thesis, Iowa State Teachers College (Cedar Falls, Iowa), 1957.
148. BELAI, LOUISA. "A Comparative Study of the Results of Standardized Tests and Achievement at a Liberal Arts College for Women." *J Ed Res* 52:94–100 N '58. * (*PA* 33:11014)
149. METZGER, STANLEY MILES. *A Study of Selected Characteristics of the Male Graduates and Scholastic Drop-Outs of*

the 1951 Freshman Class Entering State University of New York Teachers College at Cortland. Doctor's thesis, Syracuse University (Syracuse, N.Y.), 1958. (*DA* 19:2020)
150. NUNNERY, MICHAEL Y. *A Study in the Use of Psychological Tests in Determining Effectiveness and Ineffectiveness Among Practicing School Administrators.* Doctor's thesis, University of Tennessee (Knoxville, Tenn.), 1958. (*DA* 19:1276)
151. SAVAGE, H. W. *An Evaluation of the Cooperative English Test of Effectiveness of Expression for Use in Ontario.* Atkinson Study of Utilization of Student Resources, Supplementary Report No. 1. Toronto, Canada: Department of Educational Research, Ontario College of Education, University of Toronto, 1958. Pp. vi, 39. *
152. WEBB, SAM C., AND GOODLING, RICHARD A. "Test Validity in a Methodist Theology School." *Ed & Psychol Meas* 18:859–66 w '58. * (*PA* 34:2123)
153. WIGGINS, NEWTON W. *The Predictive Ability of the Total and Partial Raw Scores of the A.C.E. Psychological Examination, the Cooperative English Tests, and High School Marks in Determining the Scholastic Success of Prospective Freshmen at Western Illinois University.* Master's thesis, Western Illinois University (Macomb, Ill.), 1958.
154. AKAMINE, TOSHIO. *A Study of High School Students' Records and Certain Test Scores as Predictors of Academic Achievement at the State College of Washington.* Doctor's thesis, State College of Washington (Pullman, Wash.), 1959. (*DA* 20:955)
155. BLACK, D. B. "A Comparison of the Performance on Selected Standardized Tests to That on the Alberta Grade XII Departmental Examination of a Select Group of University of Alberta Freshmen." *Alberta J Ed Res* 5:180–90 S '59. * (*PA* 34:6559)
156. EINSPAHR, MARTIN HARLEY. *The Construction and Validation of Scales for Predicting Academic Success in College.* Doctor's thesis, University of Houston (Houston, Tex.), 1959. (*DA* 20:3366)
157. GUTEKUNST, JOSEF GRANT. *The Prediction of Art Achievement of Art Education Students by Means of Standardized Tests.* Doctor's thesis, Temple University (Philadelphia, Pa.), 1959. (*DA* 20:3202)
158. HENDERSON, HAROLD L., AND MASTEN, SHERMAN H. "Six Predictors of College Achievement." *J Genetic Psychol* 94:143–6 Mr '59. * (*PA* 36:4KL43H)
159. LEAHY, DOROTHY M. "Reading Ability of College Home Economics Students." *Calif J Ed Res* 10:42–8 Ja '59. * (*PA* 34:2106)
160. NUNNERY, MICHAEL Y. "How Useful Are Standardized Psychological Tests in the Selection of School Administrators." *Ed Adm & Sup* 45:349–56 N '59. * (*PA* 35:7092)
161. STACK, SHIRLEY ELLEN. *A Study of the Relationships Between Prospective Teachers' Scores on the Chicago Certification Examination and on Standardized Ability and Achievement Tests.* Doctor's thesis, Northwestern University (Evanston, Ill.), 1959. (*DA* 20:2160)
162. STINSON, PAIRLEE J., AND MORRISON, MILDRED M. "Sex Differences Among High School Seniors." *J Ed Res* 53:103–8 N '59. *
163. ALOIA, ALEX D., AND SALINDA, JUAN F. "A Correlation Study Between Grades in English and Cooperative English Test Scores of College Freshmen." *Calif J Ed Res* 11:7–13 Ja '60. * (*PA* 34:8393)
164. BLACK, DONALD B. "The Prediction of Freshman Success in the University of Alberta From Grade XII Departmental Results." *Alberta J Ed Res* 6:38–53 Mr '60. *
165. KIMBELL, FONTELLA THOMPSON. *The Use of Selected Standardized Tests as Predictors of Academic Success at Oklahoma College for Women.* Doctor's thesis, University of Oklahoma (Norman, Okla.), 1960. (*DA* 20:4335)
166. VINEYARD, EDWIN E., AND BAILEY, ROBERT B. "Interrelationships of Reading Ability, Listening Skill, Intelligence, and Scholastic Achievement." *J Develop Read* 3:174–8 sp '60. * (*PA* 35:1274)
167. ZABEL, RONALD L. *The Determination of the Ability of the Total Score of the Cooperative School and College Ability Test, the Total Reading Comprehension Score of the Cooperative English Test, and High School Rank to Predict Scholastic Success of Freshmen at Western Illinois University.* Master's thesis, Western Illinois University (Macomb, Ill.), 1960.
168. BESSENT, EDGAR WAILAND. *The Predictability of Selected Elementary School Principals' Administrative Behavior.* Doctor's thesis, University of Texas (Austin, Tex.), 1961. (*DA* 22:3479)
169. CENTI, PAUL. "Intellective and Language Factors Related to College Success." *Cath Ed R* 59:319–22 My '61. *
170. COPEMAN, JAMES; PASCOE, ROBERT; AND WARD, GEORGE, II. "The Edwards Personal Preference Schedule and Revised Cooperative English Test as Predictors of Academic Achievement." *Proc W Va Acad Sci* 33:124–6 '61. * (*PA* 36:5KL24C)
171. EELLS, KENNETH. "How Effective Is Differential Prediction in Three Types of College Curricula?" *Ed & Psychol Meas* 21:459–71 su '61. * (*PA* 36:2KJ59E)
172. GREENBERG, BRADLEY S. "Predicting Journalism Student Ability." *Journalism Ed* 16:60–5 su '61. *
173. GROFF, PATRICK J. "Parts of Speech in Standardized English Tests." *Sch R* 69:457-60 w '61. *
174. SWANSON, EDWARD O., AND BERDIE, RALPH F. "Predictive Validities in an Institute of Technology." *Ed & Psychol Meas* 21:1001–8 w '61. Errata: 22:258 su '62. *
175. SWEENEY, MARY ROSE. *A Study of the Relationship of the Quantity of High School English to College Performance in English.* Doctor's thesis, University of Kansas (Lawrence, Kan.), 1961. (*DA* 22:2640)
176. WOLINS, LEROY; MACKINNEY, A. C.; AND STEPHANS, PAUL. "Factor Analyses of High School Science Achievement Measures." *J Ed Res* 54:173–7 Ja '61. * (*PA* 35:7129)
177. BERDIE, RALPH F.; LAYTON, WILBUR L.; HAGENAH, THEDA; AND SWANSON, EDWARD O. *Who Goes to College? Comparison of Minnesota College Freshman, 1930–1960.* Minneapolis, Minn.: University of Minnesota Press, 1962. Pp. vii, 56. *
178. CASH, W. L., JR. "Predictive Efficiency of Freshman Entrance Tests." *J Psychol Studies* 13:111–6 Je '62 [issued F '64]. *
179. GILLESPIE, HORACE FORD. *The Construction and Validation of Scales for Predicting Academic Success in College in Specified Subject Matter Areas.* Doctor's thesis, University of Houston (Houston, Tex.), 1962. (*DA* 23:1576)
180. JONES, REGINALD L., AND SIEGEL, LAURENCE. "The Individual High School as a Predictor of College Academic Performance." *Ed & Psychol Meas* 22:785–9 w '62. * (*PA* 37:7189)
181. JUNGEBLUT, ANN. "Some Results of the 1960 Revision of the Cooperative English Tests in a Small Group of Independent Schools." *Ed Rec B* 80:49–55 F '62. *
182. LEWIS, JOHN W. "Utilizing the Stepwise Multiple Regression Procedure in Selecting Predictor Variables by Sex Group." *Ed & Psychol Meas* 22:401–4 su '62. * (*PA* 37:3871)
183. REID, JOHN W.; JOHNSON, A. PEMBERTON; ENTWISLE, FRANK N.; AND ANGERS, WILLIAM P. "A Four-Year Study of the Characteristics of Engineering Students." *Personnel & Guid J* 41:38–43 S '62. * (*PA* 37:5655)
184. RUDD, JOHN PAUL. *A Study of the Validity of Selected Predictors for Placement in Three-Rail Curricula.* Doctor's research study No. 1, Colorado State College (Greeley, Colo.), 1962. (*DA* 24:184)
185. VICK, MARY CATHARINE, AND HORNADAY, JOHN A. "Predicting Grade Point Average at a Small Southern College." *Ed & Psychol Meas* 22:795–9 w '62. * (*PA* 37:7205)
186. BOWMAN, ALDEN E.; COBERLY, R. L.; LUCAS, DONALD; AND WHALEY, EARL R. "Selection and Performance of Scholarship Hall Award Winners." *J Col Student Personnel* 4:220–6+ Je '63. *
187. HUGHES, BILLIE EDWARD. *Predicting Achievement in a Graduate School of Education.* Doctor's thesis, North Texas State University (Denton, Tex.), 1963. (*DA* 24:1448)
188. KING, DONALD THOMAS. *A Comparison of a College Generation of Rural and Nonrural Students in Selected Colleges of Arkansas With Respect to Academic Success and Number of Semesters of Undergraduate Study Completed.* Doctor's thesis, University of Arkansas (Fayetteville, Ark.), 1963. (*DA* 24:626)
189. MACK, LAURENCE L. "Examining the Efficiency of Predictors Presently Being Used at the University of Alberta." *Alberta J Ed Res* 9:100–10 Je '63. *
190. MORICE, HERBERT OSCAR. *The Predictive Value of the High School Grade Point Average and a Select Group of Standardized Tests for Junior College Achievement.* Doctor's thesis, University of Houston (Houston, Tex.), 1963. (*DA* 24:1482)
191. NORTH, ROBERT D. "Results of the ERB Public School Norms Project, 1962–63." *Ed Rec B* 84:72–4 Jl '63. *
192. SASSENRATH, JULIUS M., AND FATTU, NICHOLAS A. *Relationships Among Factors Obtained for Elementary and Secondary Student Teachers.* Bulletin of the School of Education, Indiana University, Vol. 39, No. 5. Bloomington, Ind.: Bureau of Educational Studies and Testing, the School, September 1963. Pp. vii, 34. * (*PA* 38:6666)
193. WILLIAMS, JOHN E., AND JOHNSTON, ROBERT A. "The Area Tests of the Graduate Record Examination as a Partial Criterion of Academic Success." *J Exp Ed* 32:95–100 f '63. *
194. ZIMMERER, ANN MORGAN. *A Study of Selected Variables for Predicting Success in a College of Engineering.* Doctor's thesis, University of Houston (Houston, Tex.), 1963. (*DA* 24:842)

LEONARD S. FELDT, *Professor of Education, State University of Iowa, Iowa City, Iowa.*

The *Cooperative English Tests* measure achievement in two general areas: written expression and reading. It seems appropriate to consider each area separately and then to return to issues relevant to the entire battery.

ENGLISH EXPRESSION TEST. The validity of multiple choice English tests as a substitute for more tedious evaluation procedures based on student themes has long been challenged by teachers of composition. In the test manual the authors seek to reassure the user on this point, claiming that "evidence suggests that ability to do well on this kind of test is related to ability to write well in an 'essay' situation." Those who can accept this proposition will find many virtues in the English effectiveness portion of this test. The content is based on at least one authoritative study of student errors and was checked by a competent panel of composition teachers. The specific error situations covered by the exercises are itemized in detail, permitting the potential user to make an informed judgment concerning the adequacy of test coverage. Counterbalancing this generally favorable impression of content validity is the absence of items bearing on the broader aspects of writing quality. The test does not assess the student's ability to select a phraseology more appropriate to one kind of writing than another, to organize ideas effectively, or to break a composition into meaningful paragraphs. None of the items force the student to consider appropriateness of content, the logical ordering of ideas, or the adequacy of an introduction or conclusion. Teachers who are primarily concerned with measuring these abilities might well follow the publisher's advice and consider the use of the STEP essay and writing tests.

READING COMPREHENSION TEST. The reading subtest is less likely to evoke the misgivings which many teachers harbor about multiple choice tests of writing ability. The selections are varied in content and in length, and pose a variety of comprehension problems. Some of the reading material is humorously anecdotal, some is predominantly factual, and some emphasizes subtleties of mood or feeling. The questions based on literary excerpts frequently call for judgment of those elements which contribute to the effectiveness of the selection. The questions over natural science or social studies materials, on the other hand, often tend to dwell on factual details. There are no questions, for example, that call for the recognition of implicit assumptions by the writer, the deduction of conclusions or generalizations from presented data, or the differentiation of fact from opinion. Thus the skills emphasized in the test are probably more representative of the reading skills of concern to teachers of English than to teachers of the sciences or social studies.

The test yields one comprehension score which is largely unaffected by rate and a second comprehension score that is very much affected by rate. No pure rate measure, in terms of words per minute, is obtained. At the high school and college levels remedial reading efforts are largely concerned with the improvement of rate. If this test were to be used to identify potential candidates for a rate improvement class, selection would have to be made by comparing the power score with the score which reflects both power and speed. One might wonder whether a scoring scheme which yields operationally independent measures of these two aspects of reading might not be more useful, diagnostically, in this classification problem.

TECHNICAL DATA. The two manuals which accompany these tests provide a wealth of technical data on validity, reliability, scaling, and norming. In addition to information bearing on content validity, the manual includes a summary of the results of about twenty predictive validity studies primarily against grade criteria. All but one of these involve earlier forms of the reading comprehension test. The median coefficient is in the .40–.45 range, a value quite consistent with other research in this field. Reliability data are reported for grades 10 and 12 only, a deficiency to be lamented. Since the standard error of measurement plays an important role in the interpretive techniques suggested by the publisher, one might wonder how the standard error values were arrived at for grades 9, 11, and 13.

The national norming studies for this edition were carefully planned and executed, though that ever-present difficulty—the non-cooperating school—was encountered to a significant degree. The publisher provides spring percentile rank norms for grades 9–12 and college sophomores, fall norms for college freshmen. For groups tested at other times of the year, the publisher recommends the most nearly appropriate norms table and warns that standings will be slightly under or overestimated. Since this warning appears to constitute an invitation to the user to adjust or interpolate within the tabled ranks, it probably would have been wiser for the publication agency itself to have provided a more complete set of norms, even if these could be derived only by interpolation.

INTERPRETIVE TECHNIQUES. In this test, as in other recent CTD publications, a strong emphasis is placed on percentile rank bands, rather than on single-valued estimates of a student's rank. While cautious interpretation of test results is certainly desirable, this reviewer feels that the mandatory use of a confidence interval is not the best means to insure caution. In practice, the use of an interval appears to lead to the same types of "inappropriate" statements about a student's performance that were formerly made from a single-valued estimate of his rank. For example, one manual example involves a boy whose percentile rank band extends from 75 to 90. The user is told that this means "about 10% of freshmen in the norms group score higher and about 75% score lower." This is a regrettable corruption of the notion of a 68 per cent confidence interval.

On a quite different point, the publishers surely deserve criticism. In the interpretation of class performance, they suggest that teachers conduct an informal item analysis via a show of hands to determine per cent of error for each item. These data are then to be referred to the classifications of item content to determine where additional teaching emphasis should be laid. Such interpretations, based as they are on clusters of two or three items, are extremely untrustworthy, and measurement authorities have consistently warned against this practice. It seems incongruous that the publisher be so concerned about unreliability of the total scores of individual students and so unconcerned about the unreliability of class performance on individual items. Does a high percentage of error on *one* specific exercise necessarily suggest a class weakness on *all* such situations?

SUMMARY. Despite the reservations noted above, this reviewer has no hesitancy in strongly recommending these tests. They are well constructed, efficient instruments and should prove extremely useful to every teacher who recognizes and accepts their basic limitations.

MARGARET F. LORIMER, *Associate Professor, Office of Institutional Research, Michigan State University, East Lansing, Michigan.*

The *Cooperative English Tests* are intended to measure the achievement of high school and college students in two areas: reading and written expression. The two tests are available in separate booklets or in a single booklet and can be administered separately if desired. Since the general directions and time limits are the same for both tests and for all forms at each level, more than one test or more than one form can be administered simultaneously.

Scores may be used for academic advisement, placement, and evaluation. Adequate directions for their use and a helpful student profile are provided.

College norms seem to be based on a very limited sample of students; high school norms, though based on greater numbers of students, are hardly representative of the various regions or of the general population. High schools in the sample are located for the most part in small towns in rural areas. Interpretation of scores on the basis of these norms should take these facts into consideration.

The 1960 edition incorporates a number of revisions, all apparently based on sound reasons: choices for each item have been reduced to four; the number of reading items has been reduced from 90 to 60; the mechanics and effectiveness items have been combined into one test; and a new type of mechanics item has been introduced which places on the student responsibility not only of correcting the error but of finding it.

The reading comprehension test has two parts: a vocabulary test and a reading test of 60 items each. Each vocabulary item consists of a word out of context and four choices of synonym. Most words included are in fairly common use. For the student who is at all familiar with the word, the choice is simple. One wonders, however, whether such words as "divagation," "concatenation," and "encomium" are valid choices for any vocabulary test.

The reading test consists of passages varying from 60 to 300 words and covering a wide range of subjects and types of materials. Most are sufficiently relevant and interesting to engage students of the age for which the test is intended. Most are appropriate; those which fall short are those which demand some specific previous knowledge or experience, as for example knowledge of the meaning of "aperture" in the selection and use of a camera or of "quadrant" in the passage dealing with the area around the South Pole. Also of questionable appropriateness are those fragments the meaning of which depends heavily on what has come before. Some, as in Form 2C, 55–57 and Form 1B, 39–42, leave the reader without sufficient orientation; others, as in Form 1B, 21–25, could easily have been clarified if the editors had inserted a few words. It is doubtful if the skill of figuring out what went before, who is who, or who is on whose side is a reading skill or even worth one's time.

The items imply that "reading" encompasses many skills ranging from those which demand no more than spotting information without regard for its importance, to those which demand considerable depth of understanding. How much validity one is willing to concede to the test depends on his acceptance of the range of the skills included. To the teacher who holds high the value of getting students to read for main ideas, to think critically about the ideas involved, and to draw inferences, it is irksome for a test to require and therefore place value on the ability to go back and count the number of kinds of thrushes mentioned in a long passage about thrushes found in the United States. On the other hand it is gratifying to see the many passages which do ask the student to interpret and make judgments.

The way any set of test items is keyed is sure to raise some controversy. Most indefensible to students (and the manual suggests that the tests be followed up by class review of the test) are the keys to the items which ask what a good title for the selection would be. The "correct" answer is often puzzling, and it is doubtful if these items add much to the test since a really valid judgment must rest on much more of a passage than the fragment presented. Also indefensible are the keys to items involving a judgment based on one's point of view or attitude. One's understanding or interpretation of what he reads is necessarily filtered through his values; hence the passage about the student who believed it important to "work for his college" by playing football is comprehended differently by the one who shares the student's view and the one who shares the views of the English teacher who keyed the item. In such a case the "good" reader is one who is perceptive enough to anticipate the view of English teachers who make and key such items.

Students also point out—with justification—that the keys do not take into consideration that people differ in what they find amusing. When a man is so unimaginative as to be amusing, it is hardly fair to ask the student to choose between "amusing" and "unimaginative" to describe the man.

The expression test is divided into two parts: an effectiveness test of 30 items which supplies four words or phrases to be inserted into or used to complete a sentence, and a mechanics test of 60 items, each a sentence printed on three lines, one of which or none of which may contain an error.

The effectiveness items appear to be an improvement over the jumbled sentences used in the earlier edition. They probably come as close as possible to measuring the precision with which a student chooses his words; however the ability to choose the best word from a list of four is a different task indeed from thinking of the right word or recognizing the word one chooses as a solecism as one composes a theme. The test undoubtedly serves some use in measuring a student's ability to criticize writing, but the only adequate test of effectiveness is to give the student a subject, a blank sheet of paper, and a pen, and ask him to write.

The mechanics test is basically an exercise in proofreading. Controversial usage and rules for punctuation have for the most part been avoided. It is unfortunate that errors in spelling are included with those in usage and punctuation. Such a combination lessens the diagnostic value of the test and consumes time which might better be devoted to other tasks. In essence, the test asks the student to check the spelling of hundreds of words. Some of the usage errors seem far too obvious, especially on the college forms. To be sure, "he don't," "you was," and "his mother learned him" are errors found in the speech patterns of students, and on that basis can be justifiably included; but one wonders just what such items measure—perhaps nothing more than a student's ability to recognize those expressions which displease English teachers. Again the real test of a student's mechanics is his speech and writing, his creative faculty, not his critical faculty.

One final criticism stems from the experience of the writer in administering this battery to hundreds of students in successive sessions. When the single booklet was used, but only the reading test administered, we could never be sure that the students previously using the books had closed them with the reading test on top since both covers are the same color and have the same general appearance. It would be an invaluable aid if the cover of the expression test could be a different color from that of the reading test.

This battery of tests has undoubted merit and is probably among the best on the market. It is not without its shortcomings which have been pointed out here chiefly to emphasize what all of us know but wish we did not have to admit—that the measurement, if not the formal teaching, of language skills is so complex and so evasive as to be almost impossible.

J Counsel Psychol 7:225–6 f '60. Laurence Siegel. Every once in a while a reviewer is privileged to consider a test that is truly outstanding. The new battery of *Cooperative English Tests* afforded such an opportunity. The techniques utilized for test development and standardization set a high standard for test constructors; the Technical Report is written with unusual care and lucidity; the testing materials themselves are highly attractive; and the ancillary materials provided for teachers, counselor and pupils are well designed. * It is impossible, in a review of this type, to do justice to the ingenious sampling procedures employed for various aspects of the standardization process. * The student of test construction procedures will find that a careful reading of the Technical Report proves to be enlightening and, at times, almost inspiring. The presentation made in the Report is so carefully done that this reviewer found that it anticipated every one of his procedural objections or questions. * The only weakness evident in the manual is in the reported predictive validity. Although a sizable number of prediction studies with earlier forms of the Reading Comprehension subtest are summarized in tabular form, no such studies are reported for the 1960 revision. * There is little doubt that the revision of the battery will prove to have reasonably high predictive validity against the usual criteria of scholastic success. *

For reviews by John C. Sherwood and John M. Stalnaker of the expression test, see 258; for a review by Chester W. Harris of the mechanics and expression tests of the earlier edition, see 4:155; for reviews by J. Paul Leonard, Edward S. Noyes, and Robert C. Pooley, see 3:120. For reviews by W. V. Clemans and W. G. Fleming of the reading test, see 806; for reviews by Robert Murray Bear and J. B. Stroud of the earlier edition, see 3:497.

[257]

English: Every Pupil Scholarship Test. Grades 2–4, 5–6, 7–8, 9–12; 1926–64; new form (4 pages) usually issued each January and April; forms from previous testing programs also available; 4 levels; general directions sheet ['63, 2 pages]; no data on reliability; norms for new forms available following testing program; 4¢ per test; 4¢ per key; postage extra; 40(45) minutes for grades 2–8, 50(55) minutes for grades 9–12; Bureau of Educational Measurements. *

REFERENCES

1. Groff, Patrick J. "Parts of Speech in Standardized English Tests." *Sch R* 69:457–60 w '61. *

[258]

English Expression: Cooperative English Tests [1960 Revision]. Grades 9–12, 13–14; 1940–60; separate booklet edition of expression subtest of *Cooperative English Tests [1960 Revision]*; revision of *Mechanics of Expression: Cooperative English Test: Lower and Higher Levels, Test A* and *Effectiveness of Expression: Cooperative English Test: Lower and Higher Levels, Tests B1 and B2*; IBM; Forms A, B, C, ('60, 7 pages); 2 levels (tests labeled, say, for grades 13–14, Form 1A; for grades 9–12, Form 2A); battery directions for administering ('60, 16 pages); battery manual for interpreting ('60, 42 pages); battery technical report ('60, 35 pages); distribution of Form 1C restricted to colleges; separate answer sheets must be used; $4 per 20 tests; $1 per 20 IBM scorable answer sheets for the battery; 25¢ per scoring stencil; $1 per 20 Scribe answer sheets for the battery (scored by the publisher only); $1 per manual for interpreting; $1 per technical report; postage extra; $2 per specimen set of the battery, cash orders postpaid; 40(45) minutes; revision by Clarence Derrick, David P. Harris, and Biron Walker; Cooperative Test Division. *

John C. Sherwood, *Professor of English, University of Oregon, Eugene, Oregon.*

If testmaking in composition had never become "scientific," if statisticians and psychologists had never concerned themselves with the process, a reviewer of the *Cooperative English Tests* would have a comparatively easy task. If he considered merely the tests as they stand, without any reference to the process by which they were prepared or the results which they produce in practice, he could simply enumerate certain seeming advantages and mention a few not very urgent objections. Unhappily, we know that test evaluation is no such simple process. But let us begin with the test.

The most obvious merit of the test is its efficiency—a combination of relative brevity (testing time is 40 minutes) and relatively good coverage of the different aspects of "expression," of the details of composition—sentence structure, diction, and the like—as distinguished from such broader aspects as unity and organization. (A distinction is made between "mechanics" and "effectiveness" in the arrangement of the test.) One is impressed with the generally high quality of the items. The accusation is sometimes made that the student taking an objective test is compelled not so much to *produce* a correct answer as to try to *guess* what answer will suit the testmaker, and the problem could well be troublesome in the area of style, where personal prejudice and current taste inevitably enter in. But assuming the values generally held by college teachers today, it is usually easy to spot the answer expected by the testers—though one form falls down somewhat in this respect, as will be noted later.

No "objective" test measures the ability to write; it tests certain critical powers which are related to the ability to write. In one way the mechanics section of this test comes nearer to the actual writing of themes than some tests, including its own ancestors. It does simulate one part of the writing process, the period of proofreading and revision. Any teacher of remedial English knows that some students can become quite proficient in spotting errors in workbook exercises, where they know what they are looking for, without being able to detect the same errors in their own themes. The mechanics section differs from a workbook exercise and resembles a set of sentences in a theme at least to the extent that a given item may contain any one of the standard errors or none at all. If the Cooperative test cannot test the actual ability to write, it does at least test the ability to evaluate what has been written.

In this connection we should note that on this test the student is required to do no more than spot errors or choose between more and less effective constructions; some other tests would require him to cite specific rules and know a specific terminology. The approach used by the Cooperative test would seem preferable in an age of competing grammars and terminologies. In most other respects the test is rather conservative. The gerund still takes the possessive, and even the innocently colloquial use of *most* for *almost* could cost the student a point. The liberal grammarian would doubtless find the test usable, but not exactly to his taste.

Against these virtues—assuming that conservatism is a virtue—we may set a few apparent objections. Although the coverage of "expression" is relatively thorough, one form (1A) shows a lack of balance in the "effectiveness" section, where 20 out of 30 items are concerned with exact word choice, leaving only 10 for all other stylistic problems put together. In this same form are several diction items where more than one answer could be considered correct—or to be more exact, in which several of the four choices would yield perfectly plausible English sentences; the sentences would indeed differ slightly in meaning, but there is no clear basis in the context for preferring one to the other. Did "we" (in item 23) eat the food because it was "nutritive" or "palatable" or "refreshing"? It might well have been all three, and our motive for eating it would have depended on the state of our appetites at the time. To make a rational choice between two words the student must have a clear picture of the situation to which the sentence refers; otherwise he might distinguish the words precisely and yet not know which to use.

To stop with a simple examination of the test would be most unjust to both testers and users; we cannot ignore the formidable effort that went into preparing both the test and the technical apparatus that goes with it. One hesitates to cast doubts on a particular item, for instance, when it might very well be that this item has proved in practice to be one which the better students answer in accord with expectation. A test heavily weighted toward diction may be objectionable or it may not; possibly discrimination in this area is symptomatic of general verbal competence, so that such a test might in fact be as sound as one seemingly better balanced. At the same time we must understand what soundness means in this context. It means well-established norms, consistency from form to form and in repeated testings, and other things susceptible of precise statistical measurement. It even means that a careful user of the test will know when *not* to expect absolute precision—he will know that "converted scores" which look significantly different may lose that significance when translated into "percentile bands." What soundness in a test of this kind does not mean, unfortunately, is more than a rough prediction as to how well a student will actually write.

"It is not a direct measure of writing ability, but evidence suggests that ability to do well on this kind of test is related to ability to write well in an 'essay' situation." An experiment at the University of Florida produced a correlation of .54 between one form and essay examinations. Precisely what this means is hard to say, however, since essay grading is itself such a variable and subjective process.

These final doubts apply to objective tests in general, and not merely to the Cooperative; in fact, as already indicated, the Cooperative test more closely approximates the ordinary writing process than some. The test is compact and efficient; it has been carefully done and is provided with all the technical apparatus one could expect. At a time when grammarians are in conflict, it will probably suit all but the very liberal. As long as objective tests remain a necessity in the administration of composition courses, the *Cooperative English Tests* should remain in favor.

JOHN M. STALNAKER, *President, National Merit Scholarship Corporation, Evanston, Illinois.*

A promotional brochure issued by the publisher states: "The 1960 revision of the Cooperative English Tests is a distinctive contribution to the testing world, representing, as it does, a combination of measurement characteristics which have worked in thousands of practical situations over many years and the latest developments in the tests-and-measurements art."

In each of three forms at each level, the first 15 minutes are used for measuring effectiveness, which "refers to the choice of the written expression which precisely conveys the meaning intended." Mechanics (25 minutes) "refers to usage, spelling, punctuation, and capitalization." The student is given a series of three-line sentences, and asked to identify in each sentence the line in which any mechanics error occurs, or to indicate that the sentence contains no such error. The kinds of errors used have been taken from a list of errors compiled from a group of about 20,000 actual themes gathered from various sections of the country.

No grade designations appear on the test booklets, but two levels of the test are available. Form 1 is for college freshmen and sophomores. Form 2 is for students in grades 9–12. Each level has three forms of the test. Some advanced tenth grade students, for example, could take Form 1A (for college freshmen or sophomores) though most would take Form 2A (for grades 9–12). Scores on Form 1 and Form 2 are said to be "directly comparable," i.e., reported on the same scale. A technical report describes sketchily the development of the test, the converted score scales, the norming, and the standard characteristics, including reliability and a brief consideration of validity. The tests are said to be valid because well-qualified people have constructed them. In one study, the predictive validity of the test was measured by correlating test scores with scores on a composite of all regular English tests given in the first semester; the correlation obtained was .67.

The test appears to have been competently developed, although it would be difficult to justify the claim quoted at the beginning of this review. The manual for interpreting the scores is helpfully arranged. The norms (1960) and the conversion procedures are clearly explained. A classification of the mechanical error items in each form will help the teacher check the coverage. The technical manual adds certain facts for those interested in the techniques which have been followed.

Such a test, obviously, has limited value. As stated in the manual, such tests should "never discourage teachers from setting as many free-writing exercises for their students as possible," and neither should they be taken as measuring all of the necessary skills which are required for effective writing. However, when properly interpreted, these tests have the values described in the manual and can serve the classroom teacher well.

For reviews of the complete battery, see 256; for reviews of the earlier edition of the complete battery, see 4:155 and 3:120.

[259]

***English Language and Literature: National Teacher Examinations.** College seniors and teachers; 1940–62; for more complete information, see 700; 80(90) minutes; Educational Testing Service. *

HOLLAND ROBERTS, *Director, Academic Freedom Committee, P.O. Box 5503, San Francisco, California.* [Review of Form KNT.]

Secondary school supervisors of English, administrators, teacher education institutions, and organizations concerned with modern trends in the preparation and selection of high school teachers of English will find a unique, useful testing tool in this 1962 edition of the English Language and Literature test of the National Teacher Examinations. It is part of the program initiated by the American Council on Education in 1940 and since 1950 administered annually by Educational Testing Service in many centers throughout the United States.

Form KNT is an objective type examination of 105 items each offering five possible answers from which the examinee is asked to choose the one he thinks best. The testmakers have made an effort "to get at the quality of the test-taker's thinking and judgment—e.g., his ability to interpret, analyze, synthesize, evaluate," and to write items requiring "reasoning and application of principles rather than the recollection of specific facts." They have designed a systematic approach to the examination of *theoretical* preparation for the teaching of high school English as it is commonly practiced in the United States today, emphasizing in the main some of the newer progressive thinking of leaders in the National Council of Teachers of English. The test presents a variety of the problems that every English teacher faces in the classroom and in school staff meetings.

All the major areas of secondary English teaching are represented: poetry, prose, oral and written composition—including creative writing and listening—language usage and grammar, and film, but it would be interesting to know how the testmakers arrived at the emphases they have given to the various divisions. More than three fourths of the items deal with literature, with prose outweighing poetry. Written composition, oral composition, reading, and usage follow in this order. What are the assumptions and rationale back of these proportions? No authority is given and no studies are cited.

One of the special values of the test is the effective way in which modern thinking in current English usage and composition is brought into sharp focus in contrast with conventional and unscholarly procedures which center attention on formal grammar and rules. Everyday classroom situations in literature are presented, such as a class consideration of a poem by Robert Frost. The test taker is asked to choose one of five meanings, e.g., the main theme, the mood, or prevailing emotion. Of course, a thoughtful teacher or student will not often find what he wants to say in the alternatives which even the best of objective tests impose. Those who refuse to accept a rigid mechanical framework are penalized and their thinking cannot be properly evaluated without some opportunity for commentary. No such opportunity is offered. There is the further serious limitation that the classroom situations described are presented scantily. The most capable, talented teacher could not tell from the brief descriptions given what to do without experience with the class or student. It is much like asking a physician to prescribe without seeing the patient. Medical ethics do not allow physicians to prescribe *in absentia,* and teachers should not be asked to make snap judgments about the education of students they know nothing about.

There is little indication that the testmakers are aware of the great social currents which are sweeping through America and over the mountains and plains of every continent. The new horizons are not visible here. There is a single reference to Chekhov and almost no other mention of the wide range of world literature. Latin America, Asia, Africa, and continental Europe are blank areas, with no hint of their literary heritage. Even the rich fields ploughed by English and American authors are poorly represented. There is no indication of the socially significant creative work of Mark Twain, Thoreau, Melville, Emerson, Jack London, and Whitman. Negro writers are conspicuously lacking. Apparently the American Revolution, the continuing struggle for the freedom of the Negro people from the Civil War down to the present, and the rising, urgent campaign for world peace are out of bounds in the English classroom as here conceived. There is no recognition of the principle that living content of major significance for our times is the core of literature and all communication. It is a central failure of this test as of many English classrooms that the subject matter is shallow and offers little challenging guidance to the student's and teacher's concern with language and literature in the swirling current of life outside the classroom doors. The form is here. The essence of the teaching of English—the unity of form and nascent content—is not grasped. There is a modernity in method but the principle that growth in ability to speak and write and know significant literature depends upon grappling with the basic and creative problems of the students' lives is lacking.

In short, in its basic conception this test falls short in covering the content with which American teachers of English must deal if they are to prepare their students to understand the meaning and uses of literature and composition in the era of the expanding world of the space ship. There is no evidence that the narrowly conceived content of this test reflects our richest literature or the new world currents which are deepening and widening the teaching of English. The authors of the coming revision have a major opportunity to enlarge the conception of what an English teacher can be.

Those who use the present examination form will be aware that it is far too brief to evaluate sufficiently the theoretical grasp of those who take it and that such a pencil and paper objective test makes no attempt to discover what the person who takes it would *do* in the English classroom. As a supplementary device it has its uses if the results are evaluated in relationship to more thorough efforts to plumb the qualities needed in the English classroom. The search for talent and creativity in the theory of the teaching of English and for applied knowledge as it functions in the schoolroom lie beyond it.

For reviews of the testing program, see 700, 5:538, and 4:802.

[260]

English Language and Literature: Teacher Education Examination Program. College seniors preparing to teach secondary school; 1957; inactive form of *English Language and Literature: National Teacher Examinations;* for more complete information, see 709; IBM; 80(95) minutes; Educational Testing Service. *

For a review of the testing program, see 5:543. For reviews of the National Teacher Examinations, *see 700, 5:538, and 4:802.*

[261]

***English Progress Tests.** Various ages 7.5–14; 1952–63; 11 levels; 8*s.* per 12 tests; 9*d.* per single copy; 1*s.* per manual for any one level except *b, h, j,* and *k;* prices include purchase tax; postage extra; A. F. Watts (*a, e, g, i, k*), M. A. Brimer (*c, g, i*), S. M. Unwin (*j*), Betsy Barnard (*b*), Valerie Land (*f*), and Jennifer Henchman (*h*); published for the National Foundation for Educational Research in England and Wales; Newnes Educational Publishing Co. Ltd. *

a) ENGLISH PROGRESS TEST A. Ages 8.0–9.0; 1952–60; 1 form ['52, 6 pages]; manual ['60, 8 pages]; 39(45) minutes.

b) ENGLISH PROGRESS TEST A2. Ages 7.5–9.0; 1962; 1 form ['62, 8 pages]; mimeographed directions ['63, 5 pages]; no data on reliability; no norms; directions free on special request from the National Foundation; (40–45) minutes.

c) ENGLISH PROGRESS TEST B. Ages 9.0–10.0; 1956–62; 1 form ['56, 7 pages]; manual ['62, 7 pages, identical with 1957 manual except for additional norms]; (40–45) minutes.

d) ENGLISH PROGRESS TEST B2. Ages 8.5–10.0; 1959–60; 1 form ['59, 7 pages]; manual ['60, 7 pages]; (40–45) minutes.

e) ENGLISH PROGRESS TEST C. Ages 10.0–11.0; 1952–60; formerly called *English Grading Test 3;* 1 form ['52, 8 pages]; revised manual ('60, 7 pages); (50–55) minutes.

f) ENGLISH PROGRESS TEST C2. Ages 9.5–11.0; 1961; 1 form ['61, 8 pages]; manual ['61, 7 pages]; (40–45) minutes.

g) ENGLISH PROGRESS TEST D. Ages 11.0–12.0; 1956; 1 form ['56, 7 pages]; manual ['56, 8 pages]; provisional norms; (40–45) minutes.

h) ENGLISH PROGRESS TEST D2. Ages 10.0–11.0; 1963; 1 form ['63, 8 pages]; mimeographed directions ['63, 6 pages]; no data on reliability; no norms; directions free on special request from the National Foundation; 45(50) minutes.

i) ENGLISH PROGRESS TEST E. Ages 12.0–13.0; 1956; 1 form ['56, 8 pages]; manual ['56, 8 pages]; provisional norms; (40–45) minutes.

j) ENGLISH PROGRESS TEST E2. Ages 11.0–13.0; 1962–63; 1 form ['62, 8 pages]; mimeographed directions ['63, 6 pages]; no data on reliability; no norms; directions free on special request from the National Foundation; 45(50) minutes.

k) ENGLISH PROGRESS TEST F. Ages 13.0–14.0; 1953; 1 form ['53, 8 pages]; manual ['53, 10 pages]; no data on reliability; 1*s.* 3*d.* per manual; (50–55) minutes.

For reviews by Neil Gourlay and Stanley Nisbet, see 5:187.

[262]

***English Test (Adv.).** Ages 12-0 to 13-11; 1954–60; 4 tests; distribution restricted to directors of education; 10*s.* per 12 tests; 1*s.* per single copy; 1*s.* 3*d.* per manual for any one test; prices include purchase tax; postage extra; 50(55) minutes; G. A. V. Morgan (*a*); published for the National Foundation for Educational Research in England and Wales; Newnes Educational Publishing Co. Ltd. *

a) ENGLISH TEST (ADV.) 1. 1954–55; 1 form ['54, 11 pages]; manual ['55, 11 pages].

b) ENGLISH TEST (ADV.) 2. 1957; 1 form ['57, 12 pages]; manual ('57, 12 pages).

c) ENGLISH TEST (ADV.) 3. 1958; 1 form ['58, 12 pages]; manual ('58, 9 pages).

d) ENGLISH TEST (ADV.) 4. 1960; 1 form ['60, 12 pages]; manual ('60, 10 pages).

A. E. G. PILLINER, *Senior Lecturer in Education, University of Edinburgh, Edinburgh, Scotland.*

The authors give no specific indication of the purpose of these tests. From the title, the age range in the norms, and the description of the standardisation groups, the tests are apparently intended to discriminate levels of English attainment of children of age 12 to 14.

In all cases the time allowance is 50 minutes. There are 120 items in the first test, and 100 in each of the others. The measures obtained are standardised scores, normally distributed with mean 100 and standard deviation 15.

The norms for the first three tests are based on the performances of 1,500 to 2,000 children "in a chosen area." It is a pity that the test constructors do not give more information. If the "chosen area" is (as seems probable) a single Local Education Authority, the norms will be appropriate for the group of children tested on that occasion in that authority. The manuals do not tell us, however, how closely performance in that authority conforms to performance in a national sample.

A more serious matter is the manner in which reliability data are presented. The only coefficient reported is a KR-20 for each test based on a random sample of around 200 scripts. In the manual for Test 2, for example, it is stated that "the value was found to be .979. This leads to the value of 2.2 for the standard error (S.E.) of the tests. The Kuder-Richardson formula is accepted for comparison of tests, being associated with (although distinct from) the test-retest correlation." This statement is gravely misleading. Who accepts KR-20 for comparison of tests? What does it mean to say that KR-20 is "associated with (although distinct from) the test-retest correlation"? KR-20 does have its legitimate uses. It is a valuable measure of the internal consistency of a test. As Cronbach has illuminatingly shown, it is the mean of the boosted split-half coefficients obtained from every possible split of the test into halves. It is the lower bound of the coefficient of equivalence of the test. All these are valid and informative uses of KR-20. But to quote the numerical value of the standard error derived from KR-20 as "being associated with (although distinct from) the test-retest correlation" is, at best, vague, and, at worst, invalid and erroneous. Specifically, a standard error of 2.2 (based on KR-20 = .979) is the inferred upper bound to the variability of a child's standardised score from one test to another, when it is reasonable to assume that the content of each test is a stratified sample from a complex universe of items, and when the occasions of testing are identical; or (which amounts to the same thing) when one test, constructed according to this specification, is substituted for another, similarly constructed, on a single occasion of testing. However, the assumptions underlying the precise statement made in the previous sentence are not met in the actual testing situation. Firstly, inspection shows that the tests are *not* parallel in the sense defined above. Secondly, grounds of convenience, which fixed the date of testing, might have fixed another date; and it cannot be assumed that the actual occasion of testing, and the alternative occasion which *might* have been chosen, are identical in the sense demanded by the specification on which alone the precise interpretation of KR-20 and the corresponding standard error of measurement are valid estimates.

Apart from these statistical defects, the manuals are well done. The instructions for administration and directions for marking are clear and unambiguous; the tables of norms are easy to read; and the answers in the marking key are aligned with the questions in the test—a useful procedure increasingly employed by the better test agencies producing hand scored tests.

Judging by the norms, the tests are of appropriate difficulty and the raw score dispersion is adequate (the latter is reported specifically for the first test only). On all four tests the mean raw score of the girls in the reference groups was, as usual, significantly superior to that of the boys. The reported increases in score with age show no consistent pattern. For Test 2 the increase is reported, without comment, as equivalent (for boys) to 1.049 points of standardised score, and (for girls) to .048, the difference being highly significant. Accordingly, separate sets of norms have been constructed for the two sexes, and it must be admitted that those for girls present a surprising appearance. Can these figures be truly representative?

The forms of the items in the tests include multiple choice, open-ended with forced responses, and open-ended with unforced responses (the testee, in the latter, being required to complete a sentence of which part is presented, the marker having discretion to accept or reject). The printing of the tests is admirable, and the overall effect pleasing to the eye. The test material, however, is uneven in quality; some parts of each test fall below the generally high standard. There are two main points of criticism. Firstly, insufficient care has gone into the editing of the tests; and secondly, the final versions appear to have escaped scrutiny by a critical subject expert.

Of all tests, those of English attainment in particular should be impeccable in style and should display a sensitive awareness of how precise statement is dependent on the flexibility of language. Judged by these criteria, the tests fall short in some measure. Nevertheless, as one would expect with tests bearing the imprimatur of the National Foundation for Educational Research, they are competently constructed and basically well founded. Statistically, the tests are patently sound, and a not extensive though critical revision would transform them into models that others would do well to follow. Following such revision this reviewer would not hesitate to commend them to the most critical user.

[263]

★English Test (Four-Year Course): Affiliation Testing Program for Catholic Secondary Schools. Grade 12 and students who are candidates for the high school diploma issued by the Catholic University of America; 1949–63; administered annually in May at individual schools; IBM; new form issued annually; Form Z ('63, 15 pages) used in 1963 program; separate answer sheets must be used; 50¢ per test and IBM answer sheet; postpaid; specimen set of the complete battery free; fee includes purchase of test booklets, scoring, and other services; for more complete information, see 758; 90(100) minutes; Program of Affiliation, Catholic University of America. *

HENRY CHAUNCEY, *President, Educational Testing Service, Princeton, New Jersey.* [Review of Forms Y and Z.]

We are informed in the interpretive materials that the number of items used in each area of testing is proportioned to an index of emphasis in instruction. Consequently, we can conclude that the four-year course, for which the test serves as an achievement measure, is to be outlined somewhat as follows: spelling (10–13 per cent), grammar and usage (9–12), punctuation (9–10), capitalization (5), vocabulary (13), paragraph analysis (6–7), literary history (24–27), literary forms (7), identification of literary works (6), and analysis of a poem (5–7). The test is to be regarded as an objective or indirect measure of accomplishment in studies that have been described as follows:

> The objectives of the four-year course in English are to provide the student with skill in the communicative arts of reading, writing, and speaking, and to lead him through close contact with masterpieces of literary art to a sense of artistic form and to some development of his own literary powers of concentration, interpretation, and discrimination.

The problem of the reviewer is to decide whether the test is adequate as a measure of these objectives. Since "skill" in the communicative arts and a "sense" of literary form, as well as some development of "literary powers," are major objectives, one would expect, at a minimum, a reading test on unfamiliar literary, or other, materials to put these skills to work. The outline of test content, however, runs heavily to rules and forms, and to facts and types and literary information.

An examination of test items confirms the preliminary judgment, for the emphasis is strongly upon "what have you been taught about ______?" rather than "what have you learned about ______, and what can you do with it?" The grammar and usage items are not applicatory but analytical (identifying "nominatives of address," for example), requiring knowledge of the term rather than careful use, or distinction in use, of the thing itself. (In Form Y, the illustration of this type, item 43, is itself an example of poor use and inadequate or improper punctuation.) In paragraph analysis, questions do not pertain to judgment of what is said, as content, or the effectiveness of the saying, but only to the formalized "topic sentence, means of transition, type of development" kind of analysis. Pages of the test are devoted to literature, but none to its comprehension or judgment—merely to its recall as type and identity, where memory is everything and "skill" or "sense of" are not even hinted. A careful student might, one should judge, do exceptionally well on the literature items without having read any of the works mentioned.

The problem of the reviewer has, therefore, changed focus: Is the test inadequate for the objectives stated, or are the objectives so colored, or even twisted, by a pedagogical concept that this kind of test is a faithful mirror of the instruction? There is some internal evidence that the latter is the case. We are informed that the test is validated against grades in English courses, and the figures[1] are high:

1 The publisher reports validity coefficients corrected for attenuation. The validity coefficients presented in this review were computed from data presented in the manual.

Form Y, .55; Form Z, .69. The conclusion would seem to be that the test is measuring the outcomes of instruction and, on its own terms, therefore, it is an excellent test. That it is testing outcomes of English instruction of what must be the most dismally traditional sort is beside the point. The kind of instruction is a matter of curriculum and pedagogical emphasis, beyond the scope of a test review.

For a review of the complete program, see 758.

[264]

***English Tests 1, 3–13.** Ages 10 to 11–11; 1951–62; 12 tests (12 pages except for *c–e*); distribution restricted to directors of education; 10*s*. per 12 tests; 1*s*. per single copy; manual for any one test: 1*s*. for *a* and *c*, 1*s*. 3*d*. for *b*, *d–l*; prices include purchase tax; postage extra; 50(55) minutes except for *a* and *c*; G. A. V. Morgan (*a–d*), M. A. Brimer (*e*), and A. E. Davies (*h*); published for the National Foundation for Educational Research in England and Wales; Newnes Educational Publishing Co. Ltd. *

a) ENGLISH TEST 1. 1951–58; 1 form ['51]; manual ['58, 8 pages]; 45(50) minutes.

b) ENGLISH TEST 3. 1952–53; 1 form ['52]; manual ['53, 10 pages].

c) ENGLISH TEST 4. 1953–57; 1 form ['53, 10 pages]; manual ('57, 8 pages); 40(45) minutes.

d) ENGLISH TEST 5. 1954–55; 1 form ['54, 10 pages]; manual ('55, 10 pages); no norms for ages 11–6 to 11–11.

e) ENGLISH TEST 6. 1955–56; 1 form ['55, 11 pages]; manual ('56, 12 pages); no norms for ages 11–10 to 11–11.

f) ENGLISH TEST 7. 1956–59; 1 form ['56]; manual ('59, 12 pages, identical with 1957 manual).

g) ENGLISH TEST 8. 1957–58; 1 form ['57]; manual ('58, 12 pages).

h) ENGLISH TEST 9. 1958–59; 1 form ['58]; manual ('59, 12 pages).

i) ENGLISH TEST 10. 1959–60; 1 form ['59]; manual ('60, 12 pages).

j) ENGLISH TEST 11. 1960–61; 1 form ['60]; manual ('61, 12 pages); Welsh edition ['61] available.

k) ENGLISH TEST 12. 1961–62; 1 form ['61]; manual ('62, 11 pages).

l) ENGLISH TEST 13. 1962–63; forms 13A, 13B, ['62]; manual ('63, 12 pages) for each form.

REFERENCES

1. MORETON, C. ANNE, AND BUTCHER, H. J. "Are Rural Children Handicapped by the Use of Speeded Tests in Selection Procedures?" *Brit J Ed Psychol* 33:22–30 F '63. * (*PA* 38:684)

STANLEY NISBET, *Professor of Education, University of Glasgow, Glasgow, Scotland.*

These "closed" tests, obtainable only by directors of education, have been used extensively in England during the past 10 years, and are still used as part of the assessment batteries whereby pupils are allocated to types of secondary school. Since the main purpose of such batteries is to discriminate between the able minority (fit for a grammar school) and the rest, the tests are rather too difficult for the less able children in the age group, but they give plenty of headroom for the brightest.

The following comments are based on a study of the tests and manuals themselves, without supplementary data.

a) There are a few items in each test in which, if the marking key is strictly followed, injustice would seem to be done to some pupils (for example, items 10, 88, and 92 in Test 1; items 7, 12, and 110–113 in Test 3; and item 40 in Test 6).

b) There are numerous items to which exception could be taken on grounds of layout, correctness, or clarity (for example, items 13, 14, 23, 24 ff., 46, 65 ff., 73, and 78 in Test 1; and items 6 and 20 in Test 6).

c) The number of questionable items decreases as the series goes on. It is clear that lessons learned from the application of the earlier tests were applied in the construction of the later ones.

d) As the series proceeded, a deliberate policy was adopted of decreasing the number of totally objective items (for example, multiple choice) and increasing the number of "controlled completion" and "creative response" items. This is a defensible policy (the reviewer would go further and say it is desirable), but no evidence is given of the *amount* of objectivity actually achieved in these open-response items. The Kuder-Richardson reliability coefficient would appear to show merely the general interitem correlation when each script is marked by a single person: it offers no information about agreement between independent markers. If this is so, it is strange to read in some of the manuals, after the Kuder-Richardson coefficient has been quoted, that "the reliability of this test is very high despite the deliberate inclusion of some items requiring an element of subjectivity in the marking." [1]

e) Since this is a test of English it is perhaps surprising that so many items call for mental gymnastics of the type normally associated with intelligence tests and relatively fewer items call for the straightforward comprehension of English passages.

f) Much ingenuity has been shown in de-

[1] Since writing the above the reviewer has seen the next tests in this series (13A and 13B). Some of the criticisms made of the earlier tests no longer apply, and in particular the manuals give experimental evidence of agreement between different markers.

vising new types of items, especially those allowing a measure of freedom in the response. Some of these appear quite promising.

SUMMARY. In the light of these comments, it would be difficult to recommend the tests, though it is possible that some of the misgivings might be allayed by further data, especially on item analysis.

H. J. SANTS, *Lecturer in Education, University College of North Wales, Bangor, Wales.*

The manuals, with details about construction, standardisation, sex differences, reliability, and administration, conspicuously avoid comment about what the tests may be measuring. However, insofar as standardised objective tests of English and arithmetic are used together with intelligence tests in selection procedures at the end of primary schooling, it can be assumed that the items have been based on the common elements of the English syllabi in use in primary schools. In order to cope successfully with these tests a child would not in fact necessarily need to have had a formal teaching in English grammar, although this would probably be an advantage, but he would need a familiarity with the written word and some interest in the structure of language. For example, Test 12 begins with items requiring the child to substitute pronouns for proper names. This could be tackled intuitively from background reading or it could be negotiated from a conscious knowledge of syntax comparable to the test deviser's.

Considerable use is made throughout the series of the sentence completion test. Completing a sentence appears to call for some particular kind of verbal reasoning, and thus these English tests are not merely tests of attainment in the sense of being tests of knowledge about ways of classifying parts of language. Indeed, explicit mention is made in the series from 1956 onwards of a policy of increasing the number of controlled completion items and creative response items generally at the expense of selective response questions requiring a tick or underlining. The trend away from the testing of attainment based on the school syllabus towards a testing of the ability to use the basic constructions of primary school English in a general way has, perhaps, been responsible for the decrease in the number of items drawn from school subjects, like history and geography. In Test 1 there are references to Napoleon and his battles and to summers in Australia in November, whereas in Test 12 topics are much more akin to the topics of basic school reading books with reference to John at the football match and Mary and her holidays.

The subject matter of any book or document that a 10- or 11-year-old child reads is surely in part responsible for his attitudes towards the material; but there is not a word of explanation about choice of topics in the manuals. Nor indeed is there any evidence that the matter has been given much thought. Items for girls are sprinkled tentatively. Some alarming topics, such as disaster at sea, are used repeatedly throughout the series. The themes of objective tests have a monotonous oddity which may well be one of the many unfortunate consequences of the close familiarity which test designers have with the work of their predecessors.

In terms of currently accepted notions about test construction this series of tests has undoubtedly improved over the years with the backing of research carried out by the National Foundation's own workers as well as others. Great care has been taken over standardisation of administration, but just because of this the teachers and children using the tests must inevitably feel a great sense of their taking part in a very important occasion. The use of tests as a sole means of selecting children for secondary education is on the decrease in Great Britain. One of the widespread objections to using test results is that a child's ability is being sampled on a single decisive occasion with resultant anxiety. In considering the tests under review it is surprising that very little thought appears to have been given to reducing test situation strain by considering the impression that a child would get from the appearance of these publications. Publishers of other school material for children have been giving increasing care and skill to the improvement of layout.

The 1951 test booklet has the words ENGLISH TEST 1 in enormous block capitals with the Foundation's name boldly across the top. There are large underlined warnings about not wasting time and working carefully. The general impression is that of a government form. By 1961 the booklet is much improved in this respect, but even here the instructions to the child are presented like a public notice, numbered from 1 to 6, and end with the rigorous command ASK NO QUESTIONS AT ALL ONCE THE TEST HAS BEGUN. Greater efforts could surely be made to present tests to children in a manner more in keeping with normal classroom procedure without losing the necessary standard control of administration.

Emphasis has been given in this review to neglect of the child's view because this continued neglect in the field of group testing is in striking contrast to a prevailing child-centered approach to education. Nevertheless this series of standardised attainment tests in English has been thoughtfully improved from year to year and the tests under review are about as efficient as tests of their kind are likely to be within the framework of current test theory. The danger is that in so efficiently meeting the demands of selecting by examination, the skills which have been found to be the easiest to test will become those which will dominate both primers and teachers.

[265]

English Usage: Every Pupil Test. Grades 3–4, 5–6, 7–9, 10–12; 1929–64; new form (4 pages) usually issued each December and April; forms from previous testing programs also available; 4 levels; general directions sheet ('63, 2 pages); no data on reliability; Ohio norms for new forms available following testing program; 5¢ per test; 3¢ per key; postpaid; 40(45) minutes; Ohio Scholarship Tests. *

REFERENCES

1. Edminston, R. W., and Gingerich, C. N. "The Relation of Factors of English Usage to Composition." *J Ed Res* 36:269–71 D '42. * (*PA* 17:2169)
2. Groff, Patrick J. "Parts of Speech in Standardized English Tests." *Sch R* 69:457–60 w '61. *

For a review by J. R. Gerberich of the 1946 forms, see 3:127.

[266]

Essentials of English Tests, Revised Edition. Grades 7–13; 1939–61; 6 scores: spelling, grammatical usage, word usage, sentence structure, punctuation and capitalization, total; Forms A, B, ('61, 8 pages, identical with forms copyrighted in 1939 and 1940 except for revisions in 12 items); manual ['61, 6 pages, essentially the same as 1944 manual except for wording changes]; no norms for grade 13; reliability data and norms the same as published in 1939–44; $2.50 per 25 tests, postage extra; 75¢ per specimen set of both forms, postpaid; 45(50) minutes; original edition by Dora V. Smith and Constance M. McCullough, revision by Carolyne Green; American Guidance Service, Inc. *

J. Raymond Gerberich, *Visiting Professor of Education, University of Maryland, College Park, Maryland.*

The *Essentials of English Tests* include parts on spelling, grammatical usage, word usage, sentence structure, and punctuation and capitalization. Supplementary materials consist of a six-page manual; of a folder including norms, a score tabulation form, and a class record; of strip scoring keys, plus optional transparent overlays for Part 5; and of four-page forms for use in analyzing errors. The test booklets carry both 1940 and 1961 copyright dates but neither a copyright date nor a printing date appears on the manual or any of the other materials.

In Parts 1, 2, and 3, the pupil is asked to discriminate between what is correct and what is incorrect in: (*a*) spellings of 25 words appearing in list form, (*b*) grammatical usages of 44 italicized words and phrases appearing in context in an essay of some 450 words, and (*c*) word usages in unspecified portions of 15 rather short sentences. Two patterns of pupil responses are asked for in these completion-type parts—a "C" for each item judged to be correct and a word or phrase designed to correct errors in all other items. In Part 3, the pupil is also asked to underline the word he judges to be incorrect in each "wrong" sentence.

Part 4 is composed of 20 four-option multiple choice items in each of which the same idea is expressed in four different ways. The pupil is asked to mark the sentence structure that best expresses the idea. Part 5 consists of a short narrative setting and a dependent business letter in which 57 underlined and numbered positions indicate points where errors in capitalization, errors or omissions in punctuation, or even combinations of a capitalization and punctuation error may exist. If the pupil thinks there is a mistake or an omission at any underlined point in the passage, he is asked to make an appropriate insertion. He is not asked to respond in any way, however, to those underlined positions where he thinks the usage is correct.

Although the format of the booklets and accompanying materials is in general quite good, several discrepancies that careful editing would have eliminated detract from the test in minor degree.

A more important consideration is that portions of Part 4, on sentence structure, seem not to come up to modern standards of item writing. For example, several items fail to include the same details in all four options (A-8; A-13; B-13) and others employ two sentences or sentence fragments in some options instead of the implied if not promised one sentence (A-1; A-9; B-1). Again, one item presents one good and three incredibly bad options (B-1), whereas another (B-4), to be more specific, offers three grammatically acceptable versions of opposition to drinking—one to drinking in general (option *a*) and two to drinking in the assembly (options *b* and *c*). Since face validity and empirical validity are not often contradictory for achievement test items, it is difficult to harmonize the structural limitations of these items, and perhaps of others, with desirable degrees of discriminative power.

Scoring problems may well arise for Part 3, on word usage, and Part 5, on capitalization and punctuation. The intent in Part 3 is apparently to provide for a maximum score of 15 by counting one point for each correct underlining and one point for each correct completion and dividing the total by two. However, there is no mention in the scoring key of how responses to the errorless sentences are to be scored or how the fractional values that will inevitably result when the total is divided by two are to be handled. Even more serious problems are likely to occur in Part 5, where points are awarded in such an array of patterns that scoring is unlikely to be handled objectively by most classroom teachers. One point is variously supposed to be awarded, for example, for no response, for one simple response, for two separate and separated responses, for a compound two-step response, for a simple triple response, and for a complex three-step response.

Three of the most important characteristics of a test—validity, reliability, and comparability of results—receive very sketchy attention in the manual and tables of norms. Validity is based, according to the manual, on studies of usage and of errors, content of English placement tests for college freshmen, opinions of English specialists, and "item experimentation" involving 1,416 high school pupils and 400 college students. Only the last of these four sources receives more than passing attention. Statements about reliability are even more deficient in comprehension of the technical problems involved, as evidenced by failure to mention range of talent or to present other important background information. In fact, the sole quantitative observation is that "the correlation of score between comparable forms ran about as usual (.87 to .89)."

The tables of norms, designated as "Grade Profiles," show what the authors term "percentile readings" (the 5th, 25th, 50th, 75th, and 95th percentiles within grades) for the five part scores and total scores based on 36,480 pupils in grades 7 to 12 representing "all sections of the country." Separate tables appear for Forms A and B as well as for grades 7 to 12. No norms are given for grade 13, even though the booklets specify that the test is designed for use with college freshmen. It is true that the manual suggests at one point that major values occur when the teacher analyzes the errors of individual pupils on the special form provided and uses the results in remedial teaching. Elsewhere, however, the values of "percentile distributions" for making "intra-school comparisons" are stressed.

A comparison of the 1961 revision with the 1939–40 first edition discloses very few differences. About a dozen items in the two comparable Forms A and B vary in great or small degree. The revision is somewhat improved in printing and paper quality over the original, but the formats are almost identical. The accessory materials differ slightly in their organization and format but hardly at all in their content. The parallelism extends even to the percentile norms, identical in the two editions, which means that they must be based on the 36,480 pupils in grades 7 to 12 who were tested prior to 1940. The new manual, too, differs from its predecessor primarily in unimportant details of wording.

A revision of an achievement test, especially one that appears as much as two decades after its predecessor, should reflect improved understanding of the abilities it is designed to measure, refinement in techniques of item writing, progress in methods of establishing validity and reliability, and more insightful assistance to test users through the manual of directions and other supplementary materials.

The preface to the manual of this English test sets the stage for updating the instrument by indicating that a testing program in this area must keep pace with rapid changes in language usages and pedagogical methods as revealed through restudy and research. The disharmony between this modern stage setting and the 1940-style production is portended, however, by a succeeding comment that only "a very limited revision" seemed to be necessary at this time because of the foresight of the original "editors."

Since the 1961 revision and its 1939–40 predecessor differ insignificantly in content, and not at all in accompanying norms or evidence concerning reliability and validity, it must be concluded that the difference of 21 years in copyright dates reflects the chief distinction between the two editions. A book publisher is sometimes criticized for putting out a new "edition" that differs from its predecessor in such minor revisions on a small number of pages that only a careful scrutiny will reveal differences between what are more nearly two printings than two editions. The differences between the two editions under discussion here are so minor that a similar indictment of the *Essentials of English Tests* does not seem to be at all inappropriate.

It is reasonable to expect, moreover, that the 1961 revision of this test should reflect ideas presented in the three reviews of the first edition that appeared in the *Third Mental Measurements Yearbook* in 1949 and the recommendations for authors and publishers of achievement tests that were published in the middle 1950's by two national organizations concerned with measurement and evaluation. However, the preceding portions of this review indicate that the revisions were so minor that at best they can be looked upon as a patch-up job. Moreover, there is no evidence to indicate that the revision took any account of the Technical Recommendations. Of the 43 major recommendations in that source, in fact, most of them listed as essential for a well standardized test, the *Essentials of English Tests* met only five and distinctly failed to meet 25, or 58 per cent, whereas the remaining 13 were classified by this reviewer as doubtful or not applicable to this test. The greatest deficiencies occur for the sections on validity, reliability, and scales and norms, where the English test failed to conform to the recommendations respectively in 11 of 18, 5 of 7, and 4 of 8 instances. An inescapable conclusion is that the first edition was better according to 1940 understandings about the characteristics of good achievement tests than is the 1961 revision in terms of 1961 criteria.

For reviews by Charlotte Croon Davis and Gerald V. Lannholm, see 3:128 (1 excerpt).

[267]

***The Iowa Tests of Educational Development: Test 3, Correctness and Appropriateness of Expression.** Grades 9–12; 1942–61; IBM; Forms X-3S, Y-3S, ('52, 9 pages); battery examiner's manual ('58, c1949–57, 23 pages); battery general manual ('59, 37 pages); student profile leaflet, sixth edition ('61, c1958, 2 pages); see the complete battery entry (14*b*) for other accessories; no data on reliability; separate answer sheets must be used; $2.40 per 20 tests; $5 per 100 IBM answer sheets; 50¢ per scoring stencil; $3 per specimen set of the complete battery; postage extra; 60(70) minutes for full length version, 40(50) minutes for class period version; prepared under the direction of E. F. Lindquist; Science Research Associates, Inc. *

REFERENCES

1. Groff, Patrick J. "Parts of Speech in Standardized English Tests." *Sch R* 69:457–60 w '61. *

For reviews of the complete battery, see 14 and 5:17; for reviews of earlier forms, see 4:17 and 3:12.

[268]

***Language Arts: Minnesota High School Achievement Examinations.** Grades 7, 8, 9, 10, 11, 12; 1955–63; earlier forms called *English IX–XII: Midwest High School Achievement Examinations;* series formerly called *Midwest High School Achievement Examinations;* new form issued each May; norms available in June following release of new form; Form F ('63, 4–8 pages) used in 1963 testing; 6 levels; no specific manual; series manual ('63, 4 pages); series norms ['63, 4 pages]; series cumulative profile ('62, 2 pages); no data on reliability; no description of normative population; 12¢ per test; $2.50 per 100 profiles; postage extra; 20¢ per specimen set, postpaid; 60(65) minutes; American Guidance Service, Inc. *

Marvin D. Glock, *Professor of Educational Psychology, Cornell University, Ithaca, New York.* [Review of Forms E and F.]

The manual states that "this battery of tests is designed primarily for the improvement of instruction." Examples of the use of the Minnesota High School Achievement Examinations to realize this aim are cited in the series manual as follows. (*a*) Each test is divided into a number of units and the number of questions in each unit reflects the relative importance of the unit in the course. Teachers can spot units on which their students did poorly and adjust the teaching program accordingly. (*b*) Teachers can compare performance on local teacher-made tests with performance on the Minnesota test. A discrepancy indicates that an evaluation of local procedures might be needed. (*c*) Similar to the first example, the average achievement levels on the various Minnesota tests can be compared to determine subject matter areas which need greater stress or better teaching methods.

Although the manual states that "the items.... were chosen because they measured the subject matter objectives of the curriculum," it does not state what these objectives are or how they were selected as curriculum objectives. This information is extremely important since the manual recommends close scrutiny of the local curricula when pupils deviate widely from the norms of the tests.

No information is given concerning the reliability of the tests.

Although the manual mentions the use of the tests to detect units which are poorly taught, no norms are supplied for individual units. Norms for the total scores are supplied, but there is no mention of the number of people or the specific schools from which the norms were compiled.

The tests are easy to administer since they can be given to large groups and since each test has a time limit of one hour. If the results of individual units are to be used by schools, it would have been advantageous, however, to have allotted a given amount of time per unit to assure appropriate attention to each unit.

The tests, with 109–150 items per exam, are designed to be hand scored. The entire test is of a multiple choice format and answer sheets which can be machine scored could be used, but are not supplied.

It is difficult to compare the content of the tests at various grade levels for several reasons. The tests are divided into units, but the number varies from 6 to 12 units per test, depending upon the grade level and form. Also, the descriptive title for a given unit is not uniform. For example, the questions in the unit titled "Language Study Skills," grade 7, are almost identical to those classified as the "Library" unit in grade 9.

In addition to the differences in labeling of like units, there are differences in the combinations which make up a unit. Questions similar to those which form the unit, "Sources of Information," grade 12, appear in the "Language Study Skills" and the "Library" units mentioned above, but the latter two units encompass a broader area. Some variability in units also occurs from Form E to Form F at the same grade level.

The reviewer grouped the units in Form F into 6 broad categories after examining the type of question in each unit. The following table shows the amount to which each category is stressed at the various grade levels by giving the percentage of the total questions which deal with each category.

Category	Grade					
	7	8	9	10	11	12
Literature	—	21	24	9	42	28
Spelling	23	10	11	28	18	9
Vocabulary	23	10	11	17	11	21
Grammar	44	59	37	37	24	12
Composition	—	—	7	9	5	21
Library	10	—	10	—	—	9

It is doubtful that each test has "a selected number of questions reflecting the importance of each unit in the course." From the distribution of questions, one would be forced to conclude that knowledge of literature is not one of the "subject matter objectives of the curriculum" in the language arts in grade 7, and that its importance in the curriculum varies greatly from year to year, being of little significance in grade 10, but extremely important in grade 11. The amount of emphasis in each category also varies with the form.

The manual states, in reference to all the tests in the series, "the ratio of concept questions to purely factual questions differs widely by tests because of the nature of the particular subject." Within the same subject area, however, the ratio also varies widely. For example, in the literature category, all of the questions at grade 9 are factual and many of the questions at grade 10 involve interpretation of literature selections.

EVALUATION. The manual gives insufficient information concerning test construction, validation, reliability, and composition of norms. The purpose of the test is to measure the subject matter objectives of the curriculum, but the nonuniform nature of the test content at the six grade levels and across forms, along with the lack of any apparent developmental trends in the stress placed upon subject areas (with the possible exception of a decrease of stress on grammar), introduces doubt as to the realization of the test purpose.

The suggested use of unit scores is not recommended, and the use of total scores should be preceded by a careful examination of the test content at each level. The tests are not recommended as an evaluative guide for school curricula.

For a review by Roger A. Richards of earlier forms, see 5:186.

[269]

★**Language Perception Test.** Business and industry; 1959–63; forms 1, 2, 3, ('59, 2 pages, form designations do not appear on tests); manual ['63, 5 unnumbered pages]; reliability data for 1 form (unspecified) only; norms for males only; $2 per 25 tests; 10¢ per key; $1 per manual; postage extra; $1 per specimen set, postpaid; 5(10) minutes; Richardson, Bellows, Henry & Co., Inc. *

[270]

★**Metropolitan Achievement Tests: High School Language Tests.** Grades 9–12; 1962–64; subtest of *Metropolitan Achievement Tests;* 4 scores: reading, spelling, language, language study skills; IBM and MRC; Forms AM ('62), BM ('63), (12 pages); manual ('64, c1962–64, 28 pages); content outline ['64, 4 pages]; revised interpretive manual for the battery ('64, c1962–64, 16 pages); separate answer sheets must be used; $6 per 35 tests; $2.25 per 35 IBM answer sheets; 40¢ per set of scoring stencils; $4 per 100 sets of Harbor answer cards (machine scoring service, by Measurement Research Center, Inc., may be arranged through the publisher); 40¢ per specimen set; postage extra; 95(112) minutes; Walter N. Durost, William H. Evans, James D. Leake, Howard A. Bowman, Clarke Cosgrove, and John G. Read; Harcourt, Brace & World, Inc. *

For reviews of the complete battery, see 15.

[271]

★**[Moray House English Tests.]** Ages 8.5–10.5, 10–12, 12–14; 1935–63; 3 levels; distribution restricted to education authorities; 56*s.* per 100 tests; 12*d.* per single copy; 1*s.* 9*d.* per manual for any one form of any one test; postpaid; purchase tax extra; 40(50) minutes; Department of Education, University of Edinburgh; University of London Press Ltd. *

a) MORAY HOUSE JUNIOR ENGLISH TEST. Ages 8.5–10.5; 1949–58; 2 forms: *Junior English Test* ['52], *Junior English Test 2* ['58], (11 pages); manual [dates same as for tests, 12 pages] for each form.

b) MORAY HOUSE ENGLISH TEST. Ages 10–12; 1935–63; 1–2 new forms issued annually; 11 forms (12 pages) currently available: forms 23 ['53], 24 ['54], 25 ['55], 27 ['57], 28 ['58], 30 ['59], 31 ['60], 32 ['60], 33 ['61], 34 ['62], 35 ['63]; manual (dates same as for tests, 11 pages) for each form.

c) MORAY HOUSE ENGLISH TEST (ADV.). Ages 12–14; 1947–58; forms 1 ['56], 2 ['58], (12 pages); manual [dates same as for tests, 12 pages] for each form.

REFERENCES

1. LAMBERT, CONSTANCE M. "Symposium on Selection of Pupils for Different Types of Secondary Schools: 7, A Survey of Ability and Interest at the Stage of Transfer." *Brit J Ed Psychol* 19:67–81 Je '49. *

2. PILLINER, A. E. G. "The Position and Size of the Border-Line Group in an Examination." *Brit J Ed Psychol* 20:133–6 Je '50. * (*PA* 25:1281)

3. EMMETT, W. G., AND WILMUT, F. S. "The Prediction of School Certificate Performance in Specific Subjects." *Brit J Ed Psychol* 22:52–62 F '52. * (*PA* 27:667)

4. EMMETT, W. G. "Secondary Modern and Grammar School Performance Predicted by Tests Given in Primary Schools." *Brit J Ed Psychol* 24:91–8 Je '54. * (*PA* 29:3036)

5. PEEL, E. A., AND ARMSTRONG, H. G. "Symposium: The Use of Essays in Selection at 11+; 2, The Predictive Power of the English Composition in the 11+ Examination." *Brit J Ed Psychol* 26:163–71 N '56. * (*PA* 31:8840)

6. MUKHERJEE, L. "An Analysis of the Degree of Relationship Between Comprehension Questions and Mechanical Aspects of English in Moray House English Tests." *Brit J Ed Psychol* 28:79 F '58. * (*PA* 33:6838)

7. NISBET, JOHN, AND BUCHAN, JIM. "The Long-Term Follow-Up of Assessments at Age Eleven." *Brit J Ed Psychol* 29:1–8 F '59. * (*PA* 34:3444)

M. ALAN BRIMER, *Senior Research Fellow in Education, University of Bristol, Bristol, England.*

FORMS 33, 34, AND 35. This test is designed exclusively for use in selective admission to secondary schools in Britain and its distribution is restricted to Directors of Education of Local Education Authorities. Each form is intended to be used as part of a battery, the complementary tests being measures of verbal reasoning and arithmetic. Since forms 33, 34, and 35 are to be used as the terminal tests of a six-year course of primary education, there is also a responsibility for them to produce favourable effects upon primary school syllabuses in the last two years.

The forms under review represent consecutive publications over the years 1961–1963; thus differences in content and presentation may represent progressive adjustments to syllabus. Each form is composed of 120 items grouped according to type of process, there being a cyclical arrangement of groups with progressive increase in difficulty. Throughout, there is a concern for objectivity, only one answer to each question being permissible, and a majority (66 to 75 per cent) of questions demanding selection of response from given alternatives. All three forms have a basically similar pattern; reading comprehension and vocabulary items are dominant features. Language usage, spelling, grammatical control, and punctuation are consistently appearing elements. Form 33 contains five items requiring matching of verse samples and four requiring identification of the style of prose passages which have no parallel in 34 and 35. Form 35 alone tackles the hoary problem of assessing parsing and attempts to avoid reference to formal grammatical categories by asking children to select, from the words in the second sentence of a pair, a word which "does the same work" as the word marked in the first sentence. In most cases this is achieved without ambiguity, but in the first item of the set, the adjective to be matched may be regarded as qualitative and attributive and the answer expected is qualitative and predicative. An alternative choice of answer would be the possessive, attributive adjective, which is not admitted in the scoring key. A similar objection could be lodged against item 94.

Despite occasional items evaluating understanding of metaphor, the emphasis throughout is on word knowledge and verbal reasoning. Since no evidence is presented on construct or content validity, the criteria against which these aspects of the tests are to be judged can only be presumed. It is fair to observe, however, that Moray House maintains a close relationship with the education authorities which cooperate in the standardisation, and receives back data bearing on construction. It may be presumed that care is taken to adjust test content to the syllabuses followed. The way in which such cooperation may act is suggested by the change in treatment of punctuation from form 33 to form 35. Form 33 contains five punctuation items which are the last items of the 120. Under the speeded conditions of testing, it is unlikely that many children will attempt them. In form 34 there is only one punctuation item, the 115th item of the test. This apparent depreciation of punctuation was perhaps unfavourably received, since in form 35 there are five punctuation items in the first quarter of the test.

Administration and scoring of Moray House tests have become standardised over many years and, for British teachers, represent the most familiar system of test handling. Preliminary instructions are read with the children and after testing has begun it is the child's responsibility to interpret the explanations of the various item types. The explanations require considerable reading comprehension in themselves and there is little consistency between forms in supplementing explanations with examples. Answers are often indirect, requiring the number of the correct response to be given, although no penalty is imposed for failure to conform with the required method of recording the answer.

The norms provided are in the form of normalised scores with mean 100 and standard deviation 15, and they incorporate adjustments for each month of age. The standardisation samples are large (between 22,778 and 38,265 children) and have been drawn from education authority areas in such a way as to form representative samples of children of this age in England. Reliabilities calculated by an internal consistency method do not fall below .98 and must be regarded as very high. It would have been helpful to the authorities using the test if standard errors of measurement had been quoted and if these had included the standard error of the age adjustment. Significant sex differences in mean scores in favour of girls are reported for each of the forms but separate norms are not provided.

No evidence of construct, content, or predictive validity is presented. Moray House tests are institutionalised in English education, and there is a temptation to regard this reticence as justified by the long exposure of previous tests in the series to scrupulous examination. However, the limited content of the tests and the restriction of the response by item form casts doubt on the construct and content validity. The independent predictive value of each form within its battery must be limited by its high correlation with the accompanying verbal reasoning test of each series. In each case at least 81 per cent of the variance of the English test is accounted for by verbal reasoning. Even the arithmetic test has over 70 per cent of its variance in common with the English test in each case. There would seem to be a need for more venturesome sampling of English language skills than these forms attempt.

The standard of technical competence in construction represented by the control of mean raw score, by the consistently high standard deviation of raw score, and by high reliability, needs to be matched by an equal concern for the range of functions evaluated. A new form of the *Moray House English Test* appears every year and has its effects upon the primary school English syllabus as well as upon the admission of children to secondary schools. Under these conditions, the responsibility of Moray House is clear; as yet this responsibility does not seem to have been faced with the same readiness to admit change as it has by its competitor, the National Foundation for Educational Research.

ADVANCED FORM 2. This test is designed specifically for use in selecting children for transfer between secondary schools in Great Britain. It is intended to be used in conjunction with a verbal reasoning test and an arithmetic test.

There is little diversity of content and process within the 120 items, which appear to be characterised by a preoccupation with objectivity. Over three quarters of the items require selective responses and no item requires continuous written English. Eighty-one items are devoted to reading comprehension and vocabulary, including 20 in paragraph completion tasks. Spelling and punctuation occupy 17 items; sentence structure and verb forms, 11;

rhymes, 6; and literary knowledge, 6. The heavy weighting in favour of reading and vocabulary skills and the absence of opportunities for the children to use their own words is undoubtedly deliberate. Nevertheless, to teachers of English in secondary schools, the test must seem curiously restricted and biased and even retrogressive in its neglect of fluency and precision of expression.

No account is given of the methods of construction or the principles which guided it. For most users of the test, the reputation of Moray House is sufficient guarantee that care and skill have gone into the preparation, but even the most eminent of test construction agencies has a duty to give to its clients an account of the syllabus considerations that have led to the particular sampling of attainment represented by the test.

Administration and scoring procedures follow a pattern well known to British teachers. No difficulties are likely to arise in applying them. Raw scores are converted to normalised scores with mean 100 and standard deviation 15, with age adjustments at intervals of one month. The normalised scores and age adjustments are based on the performances of a sample of adequate size. However, the sample was drawn from only two education authority areas, two separate year-groups of children in one authority being combined with one from a second area to provide the standardisation data. Both authority areas are small and how representative the sample is of children of this age in England must be questioned. A warning is given in the manual that "norms on an attainment test must always be of a somewhat tentative nature" and that performance "will depend on the school syllabus and on the time devoted in schools to the subject." The manual also warns that the test is difficult and this is borne out in the norms, where mean raw score at median age is given as 44.

Reliability, evaluated by an internal consistency method, is high, but this is not surprising in a test of this length and of such relatively homogeneous content. No evidence of construct, content, or predictive validity is given in the manual and evidence of concomitant variation is restricted to correlations with performances on a verbal reasoning test and an arithmetic test.

Despite all the adverse comments offered above, it must be remembered that this test follows a pattern well tried in England, and that the impoverishment of content and item form is probably explained by an attempt to assess only elements that can be regarded as common to diverse syllabuses. It is perhaps time that the conventions of the past were reexamined in the light of more recently defined syllabus objectives.

[272]

★Nationwide English Grammar Examination. Grades 4–12; 1959–63; new form issued each April; norms available following the testing program; 1 form ('63, 2 pages); no manual; mimeographed norms ('63, 1 page); no data on reliability; 10¢ per test, postage extra; (40–45) minutes; [Donald R. Honz]; Educational Stimuli. *

[273]

***Novelty Grammar Tests, Second Revision.** High school; 1936–61; volume of 74 short-answer tests (1 page each) on specific areas of grammar; 1 form ('61, c1936–61, 170 pages); no data on reliability; no norms; $3 per test booklet (tests may be reproduced without permission), cash orders postpaid; administration time not reported; Clarine Coffin and Frank Connor; J. Weston Walch, Publisher. *

[274]

★The Pribble-Dallmann Diagnostic Tests in Elementary Language Skills. Grades 3–4, 5–6, 7–8; 1948–61; tests for grades 7–8 called *Pribble-Dallmann Diagnostic Tests in Basic English Skills;* 3 levels; all forms and manuals essentially the same as materials copyrighted in 1948–49; reliability data the same as reported in 1948–49; norms the same as those labeled tentative in 1948–49; specimen set not available; postage extra; Evalin Pribble and Martha Dallmann; Lyons & Carnahan. *

a) GRADES 3–4. 1949–61; 5 scores: sentences, punctuation, capitalization, choosing the right words, total; Forms A, B, ('61, 7 pages); manual ['61, 5 pages]; $2.20 per 25 tests; 26(36) minutes for grade 3, 23(33) minutes for grade 4.

b) GRADES 5–6. 1949–61; 6 scores: same as for grades 3–4 plus unnecessary words; Forms A, B, ('61, 8 pages); manual ['61, 5 pages]; $2.20 per 25 tests; 35(45) minutes.

c) GRADES 7–8. 1948–61; 8 scores: sentences, verbs, nouns, pronouns and modifiers, spelling, capitalization, punctuation, total; Forms A, B, ('61, 11 pages); manual ['61, 3 pages]; $3 per 25 tests; 46(51) minutes.

WILLIAM H. LUCIO, *Professor of Education, University of California, Los Angeles, California.*

Each of the three Pribble-Dallmann tests covers a two-grade sequence—3 and 4, 5 and 6, and 7 and 8. There are two forms at each level. The test entry above indicates the subsections and time requirements for the three tests. The test booklets are printed on an acceptable quality of paper with typography appropriately differentiated between the lower and the upper grade tests. Answers to test items are entered in the test booklets. Scores are the number of correct responses. No norms other than medians are provided. The manuals contain relatively clear and simple directions for test administration.

The manuals provide a minimum of information concerning the construction of the tests, the establishment of normative data, and the curriculum validity of the content. With regard to validity, further information concerning the universe of linguistic skills sampled, the explicit curriculum outcomes assessed, the kinds of item analyses performed, and the relationships among the three levels of the test should be provided.

Alternate form reliability coefficients—the decimal points are obviously misplaced—are reported as follows: 98.5 ($n = 26$, grade 4); 94.39 ($n = 27$, grade 6); and 91.6 ($n = 37$, grade 7). Even if the decimals were properly placed, these reliabilities are of little value considering the size and selection of samples and the absence of adequate population description. No information on the reliability of part scores is given—a serious omission in a diagnostic test.

Medians or "norms" are reported for each subsection of the tests by grade level, but no information is provided regarding the determination of these medians. If the medians are based on the same small samples used to calculate the test reliabilities, then little importance can be attached to them. The instructions on the use of the medians do not provide explicit enough directions for analyzing the tests for diagnostic purposes. For example, one section of the grades 7–8 manual states: "A comparison of each pupil's scores with the norms for each part will enable a teacher to discover each pupil's weaknesses in language usage. Such comparisons will materially aid in planning the individual remedial work." However, another section of the manual states: "Finding a pupil's score on a test and comparing it with the median for his grade is, after all, not a very important function of a diagnostic test. More important is the detailed study of a pupil's errors for suggestions in teaching." Users of the tests might be less confused in interpreting these comments if diagnostic indices of performance and explicit information on what is being tested and the significance thereof were presented in the manuals.

Though both forms of all three tests were examined, particular reference will be made to Form A. Most of the comments on Form A are also applicable to Form B. In general, study of the items in the tests revealed shortcomings of both a substantive and mechanical nature.

The test for grades 3–4 appears to test only for certain "common errors" in English usage. As with the other tests in the battery, the ability to understand vocabulary is not tested. The section on sentences contains a total of eight items. To what extent this section tests correct English is debatable. The section on the use of *and* contains no examples of the use of *and* in legitimately joining clauses. The practice examples for the section on punctuation, unlike examples in other sections, do not provide the examinee with the opportunity to demonstrate understanding by means of a written answer; instead, oral instructions and responses are employed. No purpose seems served by deviating from the general pattern of instructions for this particular subtest. The items in the punctuation section require that only one punctuation mark be added to each sentence, with the result that the responses may be too predictable.

The test for grades 5–6 contains a number of questionable items, judged by contemporary test writing standards. The subsection on sentences presents several items in which unrelated ideas are joined by the word *and,* requiring the examinee to determine which part of the total item is a sentence. Several of the sentences which are paired would hardly ever appear in the same paragraph. For children to join such disparate ideas as appear in these sentences by the word *and* would seem unlikely. As in the other tests, punctuation items require only one response to complete the item, so that the presence of one set of marks may signal the need for the other. Several items are unrealistic, e.g., "(Leave, Let) your wraps in the hall." It is doubtful that any child would use *let* in this particular sentence. In some items, keyed for a single correct answer, either choice would be acceptable, e.g., "The (Jones, Joneses) live next door." Some items seem out of place in a particular set.

The test for grades 7–8 reveals shortcomings in item writing similar to those discovered in the other tests. The section on sentences requires the examinee to determine which groups of words make complete sentences. However, of the total of 13 items in this section, at least 5 items lack proper punctuation which, if included, would change the responses entirely. Such items are confusing, since they well could be punctuated as sentences in writing and thus be acceptable. The items in the section on the use of *and, then,* and *so* seem unrealistic. Some of the sentences in this section, even with or without the use of the required insert choice words, would hardly ever follow one another. In the section on nouns several items seem overly simple for the intended grade level. Is it possible that any eighth grade student given the test items "How many (child) are in the group?" and "How many (man) are on the job?" does not know the forms *children* or *men?* The inclusion of nondiscriminating items tends to decrease the value of the test.

Overall, these tests cover a small number of pet items and do not cover them economically. Apparently almost no improvement in certain skills, such as punctuation, is expected over the years covered by the tests. Each test involves the same very limited set of situations. Contemporary English language programs appear to be concerned with an order of linguistic skills differing in degree and kind from those which these tests purport to measure. Because these tests do not reflect a precise application of commonly accepted procedures for test development and standardization, lack adequate data on reliability and validity, display a number of shortcomings in item construction, and do not provide specific diagnostic indices for the user, they do not warrant serious consideration for use as diagnostic tests of English skills.

GEORGE D. SPACHE, *Professor of Education, and Head, Reading Laboratory and Clinic, University of Florida, Gainesville, Florida.*

These tests represent an attempt to provide diagnostic information which would lead directly to differentiated instruction in English mechanics. The tests for grades 3–4 and 5–6 are essentially similar in sampling the pupil's sentence sense, and knowledge of capitalization, punctuation, and usage. (The test for grades 5–6 also has a score for "unnecessary words.") That for grades 7–8 includes similar tests plus a brief spelling scale and separate scores for verbs, nouns, and pronouns and modifiers.

The separate tests have a degree of face validity in that they obviously sample the skills they purport to measure. The question of the adequacy of the sampling of significant skills, or the content validity of the tests, is debatable. The authors suggest that the primary function of each subtest is to indicate the pupil's errors and thus reveal the difficulties that should be given attention in group or individual remedial work. Whether this suggestion can be implemented with the facts supplied by the authors is very doubtful.

No detailed lists of the skills tested in each subtest, nor of those facts which the average pupil should know, are given. The norms simply list the median number of correct answers found in each subtest for groups of what are presumably average pupils. For example, the capitalization test in grades 3–4 includes nine items and samples five types of capitalization. The norms indicate that, on the average, third graders answer three items correctly, while fourth graders achieve five items. There is no indication which three items third graders know, nor which of the five types of capitalization they should know.

Perhaps the authors intend for teachers to assume that the tests sample all significant skills and that remedial instruction should be given to correct any pupil errors. Following this assumption, teachers would provide sufficient instruction on all the types of items in each subtest until the pupils could perform in all types without error. Yet the norms show that such a procedure is impractical and literally impossible, for there is very little gain in the norms for subtest scores from year to year. The tests are also inconsistent in their identification of the fundamental language skills, for the skill of spelling appears only in the test for grades 7–8. Apparently spelling is not a significant language skill prior to this level.

For survey testing, the test-retest reliability coefficients quoted by the authors are certainly adequate. It would have been helpful, both in evaluating the tests and in interpreting class performance, if the authors had supplied some information regarding the size and nature of the normative population, the reliabilities of part scores, and standard errors of measurement for the various scores. Norms expressed in percentiles, stanines, or scaled scores would also have permitted more intelligent interpretation of the scores.

In summary, the tests fail to achieve their primary purpose of supplying diagnostic information to guide instruction by (*a*) not clarifying the true significance of the various skills tested; and (*b*) not indicating the expected performances of pupils in each subskill. At best, the tests can serve only a survey function in sampling pupil progress in the large areas of capitalization, punctuation, and usage.

[275]

★**The Pribble-McCrory Diagnostic Tests in Practical English Grammar.** Grades 9–10, 11–12; 1942–60; 8 scores: sentences, verbs, pronouns, adjectives and adverbs, nouns, redundancy, punctuation, total; Forms A, B, C, ['60, 8 pages]; 2 levels; manual ['60, 4 pages] for each level; all forms and manuals essentially the same as materials copyrighted in 1942–44; norms and reliability data the same as reported in 1942–44; $2 per 25 tests, postage extra; specimen set not available (sample copy of tests free); Evalin E. Pribble and John R. McCrory; Lyons & Carnahan. *
a) TEST 1. Grades 9–10; 1944–60; 44(49) minutes.
b) TEST 2. Grades 11–13; 1942–60; 45(50) minutes.

CLARENCE DERRICK, *Professor of English, and Chairman, Humanities Department, University of Florida, Gainesville, Florida.*

The title of this "test" raises three questions: Is it a test? Is it diagnostic? Is it concerned with "grammar"? This reviewer's answer to all three of these questions is no.

English teachers have available to them workbooks where the student fills in the blanks. This "test" uses the workbook format as illustrated in the following item: "4. (were, was) I heard that you ...... ill." English tests in usage have a limited function, but even this limited function is further reduced when there is no provision for machine scoring. A good standardized objective test permits an evaluation of an individual's performance in comparison with the performance of a carefully selected and described normative population. This "test" gives only median scores for each of the subtests. What do these median scores mean? The three-page "manual" has this significant comment: "The medians given above are based on reports sent in by schools from widely separated parts of the country." One marvels at the unsophistication and ignorance of a test author who would write such a statement as explanation of normative data and procedures.

A good diagnostic test has parts sufficiently long that the part scores have stability. Test 1 in this series has parts with these numbers of items: 20, 77, 22, 16, 20, 12, 10. There is no evidence of the reliabilities of any of these parts and it is extremely doubtful that, even if they had been calculated, the publisher could afford to expose them to the light of day. Most modern English teachers draw a distinction between "grammar" and "usage." Neither in the "test" nor in the "manual" is there evidence of an awareness of this distinction.

Test 1, designed for grades 9 and 10, is similar to, but not identical with, Test 2, designed for grades 11 and 12 and the first year of college. In both forms the subtest "Verbs" has the largest number of items—77 in Test 1 and 68 in Test 2. The medians for Test 1 for the subtest "Verbs" for May testing is 64 in grade 9 and 65 in grade 10. For Form 2, the corresponding medians for grades 11 and 12 are 61 and 61. What do these figures indicate? First, that students in grade 9 do just about as well as those in grade 10 and that students in grade 11 do as well as those in grade 12. Secondly, that these tests are too easy, since the median score for Test 1 is 83 per cent of the total possible score and in Test 2 is 90 per cent of the total possible score.

As classroom exercises these materials would be useful to an English teacher, but to classify them as standardized "tests" is to be guilty of gross mislabeling. The disclaimer in the "manual" that "Comparison of a class or an individual with standards is not an important function of a diagnostic test" cannot be accepted. The *Pribble-McCrory Diagnostic Tests in Practical English Grammar* are not tests, they are not diagnostic, and in many situations they are not practical.

[276]

***The Purdue High School English Test.** Grades 9–12; 1931–62; an abbreviated modification of *New Purdue Placement Test in English* (1931–55, see 5:199) which is also available; all items selected from the earlier test; 6 scores: grammar, punctuation, effective expression, vocabulary, spelling, total; IBM and MRC; Forms 1, 2, ('62, 7 pages); manual ('62, 22 pages); separate answer sheets or cards must be used; $4.20 per 35 tests; $2.49 per set of 35 self-marking answer sheets and manual; $3.15 per 100 IBM answer sheets; 42¢ per set of scoring stencils; $2.55 per 100 MRC answer cards (machine scoring service, by Measurement Research Center, Inc., may be arranged through the publisher); 42¢ per manual; 84¢ per specimen set; postage extra; 36(45) minutes; H. H. Remmers, R. D. Franklin, G. S. Wykoff, and J. H. McKee; Houghton Mifflin Co.*

CHARLOTTE CROON DAVIS, *Test Research Service, Bronxville, New York.*

What conclusion does the reader of this review draw from the following observations about this test?

a) Of the 20 items in Part 1 (Grammar), five in each form hinge on using the proper case of pronoun as the object of a preposition; five others in each form on agreement between subject and verb. To mention some of the omissions: no item in either form tests the distinction between *lie* and *lay, sit* and *set, leave* and *let, its* and *it's, their* and *they're, your* and *you're,* or *between* and *among;* or the common misuse of *real* to modify an adjective or an adverb, of *whom* where *who* is correct, or of an adverb in place of a predicate adjective ("he feels badly"). How *neither* should be construed rates two items in Form 2, but neither form contains an item touching on the singularity of *each* or *every.*

b) Of the 30 items in Part 2 (Punctuation), 12 in Form 1 and 13 in Form 2 concern the semicolon used correctly, or the semicolon used incorrectly, or some other mark used where a semicolon would be correct; only one item in each form deals with the punctuation to be used in a direct quotation; and no item deals with an incorrect use of the colon or of the question mark.

c) Item 4 in Part 4 (Vocabulary) of Form 1 requires the examinee to recognize that *ardent* means *fervent;* item 22 that *fervor* means *ardor.* Items 26 of Form 1 and 24 of Form 2 overlap similarly.

d) Nine of the 90 words covered in Part 5 (Spelling) of Form 1 recur in Form 2. One word, *apparatus,* occurs twice in the same form. One item includes the word *grammer,* despite its appearance, spelled correctly, as the title of a preceding part.

If the reader has concluded that these examples—and more could readily be cited—of duplication of content and inadequacy of coverage indicate that the test authors were careless, he would be mistaken. The manual makes it clear that the items were carefully, systematically chosen. They are the "best two thirds" of those in the corresponding parts of Forms D and E of the *New Purdue Placement Test in English,* published in 1955. "Best" appears to mean those items that turned out to have high discrimination (internal-consistency) indices and be of suitable difficulty when Forms D and E were given to 370 students in grades 9–12, chosen so as to "insure a wide range of knowledge in the areas to be measured by the test." Since the process of item selection also accomplished the equating of Forms 1 and 2 ("items with similar statistics were paired and one item from each pair was assigned to each form"), the authors apparently deemed it wise to let these statistics determine the content. The statistical matching of items to produce parallel forms, however, does not guarantee that raw scores on the forms will exactly correspond. Table 9 in the manual gives a difference of two points in mean total raw score between Forms 1 and 2, which is roughly equivalent to four percentile ranks on the norms tables provided. Nevertheless, the norms are not differentiated by form, though they are by sex.

These illustrations of what can happen when statistics control item selection are stressed for two reasons: to demonstrate that the results are likely to aid and comfort those who make it their business to carp at objective tests and condemn their use; and to urge test authors to regard difficulty and discrimination indices as two considerations among many, and not as overriding determiners, in assembling tests.

Part 3 (Effective Expression) consists of 20 sentences, each of which is to be marked *r* if it is "clear and effective" or *w* if it is "not clear or if it is not effective." Most of those that are keyed *w* are seriously faulty in structure and consequently test the ability to recognize ineffective expression at a rather low level. These items present no problem to the able examinee; but how is he to mark a sentence that is not wrong, not unclear, but not particularly effective?

Consider this sentence: "The wall paper [*sic*] was of a pattern which was old-fashioned but which still pleased most people." Although purists would object to *which* in the restrictive clauses, there is nothing wrong with the sentence by currently accepted standards; and it is perfectly clear. But would it not be somewhat more effective—that is, less wordy and awkward—if expressed in any one of the following ways? (The reviewer prefers the third version.) (*a*) "The pattern of the wallpaper was old-fashioned but still pleasing to most people." (*b*) "Though old-fashioned, the pattern of the wallpaper pleased most people." (*c*) Most people liked the old-fashioned pattern of the wallpaper."

The truly discerning and critical examinee is likely to regard sentences like this one as ineffective and therefore to miss them, since they are keyed *r*. If he thereby obtains, say, a raw score of 14 instead of 19, his percentile rank on this part will be 72 rather than 99.

The trouble lies in using the right-wrong response dichotomy in this area. The examinee doesn't know among what ways of expressing the idea in a sentence the test author made his judgment. A better technique is to present two or more ways of expressing the idea and to ask the examinee to choose the more (or the most) effective.

The items in Parts 1 and 2, also, would be more direct and searching if the examinee had to *select* the right grammatical form and the right punctuation instead of merely marking each sentence "right" or "wrong" as a whole. The latter procedure is one step further away from what the student does when he is actually writing or speaking. Moreover, it is certain that these sentences are occasionally marked *r* or *w* for completely irrelevant reasons; examinees are sometimes unaware of what point a sentence is intended to test.

Now to call attention to some of the praiseworthy features of the test: the format is clear and pleasing; the time limit fits neatly into the average class period; the self-marking answer sheet is convenient to use and easy to score; the norms are based on a nationwide representative sample of students in a randomly selected group of high schools.

Perhaps more useful than the table of percentages of students in the norms group who responded in various ways to "opinion questions" (presented as evidence of "construct validity"), which occupies two pages in the manual, would be percentile tables for each part *by grade*. It would also be informative to have reliability coefficients based on *single-grade* samples (especially since the group on which the coefficients were computed represents the same nationwide range of ability as the norms group), as well as data supporting the statement that "the test is essentially a power test in that most students will have time to attempt all of the items." This statement appears inconsistent with one made earlier in the manual that "an error of a few seconds in the time allowed may mean a difference of several points in a score," which suggests that some parts, at least, are rather highly speeded for some examinees. Whether most examinees do actually have time to consider (not just hastily guess at) all the items is important; because over half of the items are two-choice, guessing (which the examinees are told to do, if necessary, in order to answer all the items) could play a substantial part in the scores of some examinees.

To sum up: the advantages of this test are convenience and economy in administration, scoring, and interpretation of scores; the faults lie in subject matter coverage, item content, and techniques of testing. Since excellence in the latter areas is basic to the construction of *good* achievement tests and no amount of subsequent statistical manipulation of the items or detailed analyses of the norms group can compensate for lacks in the fundamentals, the reviewer cannot recommend this test. In her opinion, it is inferior—in the ways that matter most—to many of the tests available in this field.

BENJAMIN ROSNER, *Director, Test Development Division, Educational Testing Service, Princeton, New Jersey.*

The *Purdue High School English Test* was designed to provide a less time consuming estimate of a student's knowledge of "good English" than the *New Purdue Placement Test in English* from which it was derived. The briefer version, which can be administered within a single class period, yields five subtest scores (Grammar, Punctuation, Effective Expression, Vocabulary, and Spelling) and a total test score. Total group norms are provided for subtest scores and separate sex and grade norms accompany the total test score. As the normative emphasis implies, total test performance is the more significant index. Overall, the total score yields an acceptable measure of what are essentially the mechanics of English usage confounded by a rather inadequate assessment of effective English expression.

From a test administrator's point of view, the manual is satisfactory. Instructions for administering and scoring are clear, although the organization of the test booklet may interfere with rigorous control over the exposure time of the subtests. Because each subtest occupies a single page, pairs of tests are exposed simultaneously. To avoid double exposure it is necessary for the student to fold back the pages of the test booklet. This procedure, however, is likely to reduce the life span of the booklet. An alternate assembly plan, which should not add significantly to production costs, would be to reverse the printing on successive pages.

Traditionally, the validity of achievement tests is supported by evidence of curricular relevance. Unfortunately no such information is available. Evidence of validity is based largely on correlations between total test score and self-reported grades in school. The reported correlation of .60 with English grades and "usual school grades" may indicate appreciable concurrent validity. On the other hand, correlations of similar magnitude are frequently reported for tests of mental ability generally, and verbal aptitude particularly. The same argument would tend to depreciate the reported contingencies between total test performance and a number of student characteristics. Although the total test score appears correlated—and in the expected direction—with student social class, grade level, curriculum track, career plans, study habits, and sex, similar associations are likely to be found with general measures of scholastic aptitude. The somewhat indirect evidence of concurrent and construct validity would be markedly enhanced by direct testimony of content validity.

Although the reliability of the total test score is acceptable (K-R 21 is .91), the reliabilities of several subtests are markedly inadequate. Particularly deficient is the reliability of Effective Expression. The reported K-R 21 estimates of .49 and .55 for Forms 1 and 2, respectively, suggest the need for major revisions or deletion. Similarly inadequate are the reported reliabilities of approximately .70 and .65 for Grammar and Punctuation. Only Vocabulary and Spelling approach respectability with K-R 21's of approximately .80. Moreover, the probable saturation of the entire test with a speed factor makes even these reliability estimates somewhat spurious. The use of subtest scores for diagnostic purposes is emphatically not recommended.

In part, the inadequate reliabilities of the part scores may be attributed to their minimum length (the subtests contain either 20 or 30 items), and, in part, to their item format. Except for Vocabulary and Spelling, the subtests rely on a "right-wrong" item type. Considering the two choice format and the rather restricted test length, the subtests have a markedly curtailed non-chance score range. Adopting a uniform four-option multiple choice format would probably improve test reliability, even though increasing test length would add to testing time. If the subtest scores were ignored, the present instrument would provide a reasonable assessment of student knowledge of "good English." But if the part scores are regarded as desirable or meaningful components of the test, efforts will have to be made to enhance their reliability.

On a more positive note, the distribution of communities participating in the norming operation seems fairly representative of a nationwide secondary school population. Care seems to have been taken to ensure adequate regional, rural-urban, sex, and grade level representation. Although the norm group seems a bit more representative of the Midwest than other areas of the country, the potential distortion is rather minor and should not interfere with the general utility of the percentile and stanine total score norms. Because of the restricted non-chance ranges of the subtest scores, norms for part scores should probably be ignored. On the grammar test, for example, a chance score of 10 has a percentile rank of 45. A score of 12, still within reasonable chance limits, has a percentile rank of 64. Until the reliabilities of the subtest scores are improved, subtest norms might properly be deleted from the manual. Their presence only serves to encourage unwarranted practice.

In summary, the *Purdue High School English Test* may provide an adequate global assessment of a student's familiarity with conventional English usage. Evidence of content validity would increase its general acceptance, and improvement in subtest reliability would increase its general utility.

For reviews by Gerald V. Lannholm and M. J. Wantman of the earlier test, see 5:199.

[277]

***SRA Achievement Series: Language Arts.** Grades 2–4, 4–6, 6–9; 1954–64; subtest of *SRA Achievement Series;* title on tests for grades 2–6 is *How Should We Say This?;* 2 editions; battery teacher's handbook ['64, c1955, 47 pages] for both editions; 50¢ per teacher's handbook; postage extra; Louis P. Thorpe, D. Welty Lefever, and Robert A. Naslund; Science Research Associates, Inc. *

a) FORMS A AND B. Grades 2–4, 4–6, 6–9; 1954–64; 3 scores: capitalization-punctuation, grammatical usage, spelling; IBM for grades 4–9; 3 levels; battery school administrator's manual ('58, c1955–56, 32 pages); battery technical supplement, second edition ('57, 45 pages); battery pupil progress and profile charts ('59, c1955–59, 4 pages); separate answer sheets must be used in grades 4–9; 90¢ per 20 pupil progress and profile charts; 50¢ per school administrator's manual; $1 per technical supplement; $1.50 per specimen set of any one level of the complete battery.

1) *Grades 2–4.* Forms A ('55), B ('57), (14 pages); battery examiner's manual, third edition ('60, c1955–60, 27 pages); $2 per 20 tests; 50¢ per hand scoring stencil; 70(95) minutes in 2 sessions.

2) *Grades 4–6.* IBM; Forms A ('54), B ('56), (16 pages); battery examiner's manual, second edition ('56, c1954–56, revised '60, 39 pages); $2.15 per 20 tests; $5 per 100 IBM scorable answer sheets; $1 per set of machine scoring stencils; 50¢ per hand scoring stencil; 75(90) minutes.

3) *Grades 6–9.* IBM; Forms A ['55], B ('56), (14 pages); battery examiner's manual, second edition ('56, c1955–56, revised '60, 39 pages); $2 per 20 tests; $5 per 100 IBM scorable answer sheets; $1 per set of machine scoring stencils; 50¢ per hand scoring stencil; 60(75) minutes.

b) FORMS C AND D. Grades 2–4; 1955–64; 4 scores: capitalization and punctuation, grammatical usage, spelling, total; Forms C ('55, revised '63), D ('57, revised '63), (18 pages); tests are essentially the same as Forms A and B, published in 1955 and 1957, respectively, except for format; battery examiner's manual ('64, c1955–64, 43 pages) for each form; battery test coordinator's manual ('64, c1961–64, 64 pages); battery pupil progress and profile charts ('64, c1955–64, 4 pages); $2 per 20 tests; 90¢ per 20 pupil progress and profile charts; 50¢ per test coordinator's manual; $2 per specimen set of the complete battery and the complete battery for grades 1–2; 60(85) minutes in 2 sessions.

REFERENCES

1. GROFF, PATRICK J. "Parts of Speech in Standardized English Tests." *Sch R* 69:457–60 w '61. *

MIRIAM M. BRYAN, *Associate Director of Test Development, Educational Testing Service, Princeton, New Jersey.* [Review of Forms A and B.]

These tests were most competently reviewed both as individual tests and as part of the series in *The Fifth Mental Measurements Yearbook* (see 5:200 and 5:21). This review will, therefore, be concerned with the single modification which has been made in the tests since they were reviewed earlier—the addition of a recall-type spelling test to the battery for grades 2–4—and with a few comments regarding content and format not mentioned by previous reviewers.

The spelling test was added to the battery for grades 2–4 to permit the plotting of growth in spelling achievement in all the grades in which it is generally taught. The test was added at the time Form B was developed.

From a list of 100 words assembled from standard word lists for grades 2–4, two 25-word lists of equal difficulty and equal range of difficulty were assembled after pretesting. Grade equivalent and percentile norms were then developed by administering the test system-wide in a single school system in conjunction with the equating of Form B to Form A of the whole battery. The words seem to be quite sensibly chosen. As might be expected, the test is extremely difficult in the first semester of grade 2 and of middle difficulty in the first semester of grade 4.

With regard to the spelling test for grades 4–6, and, to a slightly more limited extent, to the spelling test for grades 6–9, the reviewer has reservations. In these two batteries the spelling items are presented in the context of a continuous narrative, and the pupil is required to indicate the correct spelling by choosing among different spellings presented in multiple choice form. While the presentation of the spelling words in context is to be commended, one wonders whether the use of a narrative of more than 400 words to present a 20-item test in the 4–6 battery is not taxing the time and reading ability of the pupil who has already read through several pages of context in the capitalization-punctuation and grammatical usage sections. Add to the pupil load the fact that limiting the spelling items to 20 results in grade equivalent increases of between one half year and one year and increases of as many as 15 and 20 percentile points for each additional spelling correctly chosen and the evidence is quite convincing that a larger number of spelling words presented in more limited context would be desirable. In the battery for grades 6–9, where 30 spelling words are presented in approximately 350 words of context, the grade equivalent values and percentile ranks are more palatable, but there is still a lot of reading to be done.

In both batteries the work for the pupil would be greatly simplified if in the multiple choices from which he chooses the correct spelling, the word as it appears in the narrative were always in the same position, probably first with the other choices following. As the choices are presented now, the word as it appears in the narrative may be found in any position among the choices.

This same comment applies, by the way, to the arrangement of the choices in the capitalization-punctuation and grammatical usage sections in all the batteries. The reviewer can see no justification for requiring the pupil to hunt for an expression about the correctness of which he has already made his decision in the reading of the context.

The coverage in the capitalization-punctuation and grammatical usage sections of the batteries at all levels is quite complete even though several of the items included in the 2–4 battery seem somewhat sophisticated for pupils of the primary grades. The most serious criticism that the reviewer has of the 2–4 battery is of the lack of precision of the underlining of the items in the narratives. In at least 17 items in the two forms, cutting the underline short where end punctuation is involved results in there being two correct answers that can be claimed by the quibbler, and in one item making the underline too long results in there being no right answer. The lack of precision in underlining is also a problem in the 4–6 and 6–9 batteries, but to a much lesser degree.

In the batteries at all levels there is an occasional inconsistency between the punctuation required in a particular item situation and punctuation used elsewhere in the test. The inconsistencies involve the proper punctuation of nonrestrictive adjective clauses and the separation of an introductory adverbial clause from the rest of the sentence. Yes, even in the 2–4 battery, there is a punctuation item involving an introductory adverbial clause! Among the punctuation items the reviewer would question the validity of items involving the use of the comma before "and" in a series since language experts are not in agreement on this.

The accessory materials supplied with the batteries are quite complete and convenient, both for reference and for use. This reviewer agrees with previous reviewers that the information presented attests to the care with which the tests were constructed and standardized. Just two comments here: In the Pupil Progress and Profile Chart there is some confusion in the use of the word "scores" for "percentile ranks," but the correction of this involves only a minor editorial change. In the Examiner's Manual this reviewer could find no suggestions to either the examiner or the examinees regarding the proper placing and manipulating of the rather complicated answer sheet criticized by a previous reviewer. Such suggestions should be included.

Most of the critical comments of this reviewer are relatively minor when one considers the generally high quality of the tests themselves and the adequacy of the accessory materials insofar as both content and format are concerned. Except for some modification in the presentation of the spelling section in the two higher level batteries, all changes implied by the criticisms could be met with some careful editing when the tests are reprinted. All in all, the reviewer would rank these tests high among existing tests in language arts for the grade levels for which they are designed.

For reviews by Constance M. McCullough and Winifred L. Post of Forms A and B, see 5:200. For reviews of Forms A and B of the complete battery, see 21 and 5:21.

[278]

***Scholastic Achievement Series: English-Spelling.** Grades 2.5–3, 4–6, 7–9; 1954–59; various titles used by publisher; for Catholic schools; subtest of *Scholastic Achievement Series;* 4 scores: punctuation and capitalization, correct usage, English total, spelling; IBM for grades 4–9; 3 levels; $3 per 20 tests; separate answer sheets may be used in grades 4–9; $1 per 20 IBM scorable answer sheets; 24¢ per scoring stencil; 50¢ per specimen set of any one level; postage extra; (40–50) minutes; Oliver F. Anderhalter, R. Stephen Gawkoski, and John O'Brien; Scholastic Testing Service, Inc. *

a) PRIMARY TEST. Grades 2.5–3; Forms A ('54, identical with English-spelling tests of complete battery copyrighted in 1953), B ('55), (6 pages); battery manual ('59, 12 pages).

b) ELEMENTARY TEST. Grades 4–6; IBM; Forms A ('54), B ('55), (12 pages); battery manual ('58, 21 pages, technical data and norms same as in 1955 manual).

c) ADVANCED TEST. Grades 7–9; IBM; Forms A ('54), B ('55), (13 pages); battery manual ('59, 22 pages, technical data and norms same as in 1955 manual).

REFERENCES

1. GROFF, PATRICK J. "Parts of Speech in Standardized English Tests." *Sch R* 69:457–60 w '61. *

For reviews by Geraldine Spaulding and Ruth Strickland, see 5:201. For reviews of the complete battery, see 23 and 5:23.

[279]

***Stanford Achievement Test: Spelling and Language Tests.** Grades 4–5.5, 5.5–6.9, 7–9; 1941–64, c1940–64; same as spelling and language subtests of *Stanford Achievement Test, [1964 Revision]*; 2 scores: spelling, language; IBM and MRC; Form W ('64, 8–9 pages); 3 levels; manual ['64, 8 pages] for each level; supplementary directions ['64, 1 page each] for use with IBM answer sheets, Harbor answer cards; separate answer sheets or cards may be used; $1.75 per 35 IBM answer sheets; 40¢ per set of scoring stencils; $4 per 100 sets of Harbor answer cards (machine scoring service, by Measurement Research Center, Inc., may be arranged through the publisher); 40¢ per specimen set of any one level; postage extra; Truman L. Kelley, Richard Madden, Eric F. Gardner, and Herbert C. Rudman; Harcourt, Brace & World, Inc. *

a) INTERMEDIATE 1. Grades 4–5.5; $6 per 35 tests; 56(65) minutes.

b) INTERMEDIATE 2. Grades 5.5–6.9; $6 per 35 tests; 63(70) minutes.

c) ADVANCED. Grades 7–9; $5 per 35 tests; 61(70) minutes.

For a review of the complete battery, see 26; for a review of the 1953 revision, see 5:25; for reviews of earlier editions, see 4:25 and 3:18.

[280]

★Survey of Language Achievement: California Survey Series. Grades 7–9, 9–12; 1959; all items from *California Language Test, 1957 Edition;* 2 scores: English, spelling; IBM; 2 levels; $2.45 per 35 tests; separate answer sheets may be used; 5¢ per IBM answer sheet; 20¢ per scoring stencil; 10¢ per series class record sheet; 2¢ per series individual

record sheet; postage extra; 50¢ per specimen set of either level, postpaid; Ernest W. Tiegs and Willis W. Clark; California Test Bureau. *
a) JUNIOR HIGH LEVEL. Grades 7–9; Forms 1, 2, (8 pages); no specific manual; combined manual (20 pages) for this test and the junior high levels of tests 638 and 815; 27–28(36) minutes.
b) ADVANCED. Grades 9–12; Forms 1, 2, (9 pages); no specific manual; combined manual (20 pages) for this test, test 591, and the advanced level of test 815; 30–31(36) minutes.

MIRIAM M. BRYAN, *Associate Director of Test Development, Educational Testing Service, Princeton, New Jersey.*

These tests have been adapted from longer tests in the 1957 edition of the *California Achievement Tests,* reviewed both in *The Fifth Mental Measurements Yearbook* and in this Yearbook. Form 1 of each test has been produced from items taken from Forms Y and Z, and Form 2 from items taken from Forms W and X of the parent tests, so that, by proper selection of forms to be used, the shorter survey tests and the longer achievement tests can be administered to the same class without any item duplication.

The survey tests are designed to measure mastery in basic language skills: good English usage; knowledge of tense, person, number, case, and parts of speech; capitalization and punctuation; and spelling. The tests are not recommended for use for diagnostic purposes, such use being reserved for the longer tests.

A manual for each level, designed to accompany the survey tests of reading and arithmetic as well as the tests under review, offers data regarding the reliability and validity of the tests and the equivalence of the two forms; makes suggestions concerning the use of the tests for individual and group appraisal; gives directions for administering and scoring; describes the norms population and the norming procedure; and presents percentile, grade placement, and age norms.

Reliability coefficients, computed by Kuder-Richardson formula 21, are reported for two grades, 8 and 11. These are .95 for English and .90 for spelling for one junior high level form and .88 for English and .74 for spelling for one advanced form. The standard errors of measurement, expressed both in raw score and in grade placement units, are given for the two grades.

The description of the care with which the original selection of items for the parent tests was made and of the procedure which was followed for the selection from the larger pool of items for equivalent forms of the shorter tests is impressive. If the parent tests possess high validity, then the shorter tests should also. (Only the English tests, by the way, are presented in a shorter form; the words in the spelling tests have not been changed.) Convincing data are also presented from experimental testing conducted to ensure that the two forms at each level would be equivalent with regard both to item difficulty and item discrimination.

That the standardization samples were rigorously selected with regard to geographical location, size of community, grade assignment, chronological age, and mental age is borne out by the account of the selection of the samples given in the manuals. Each individual tested also took a mental maturity test. Normative data presented in the manual include for each raw score or set of raw scores at each grade level a standard score, a percentile score, a percentile interval, and a grade placement score, all derived from the standardization data, and chronological age equivalents to grade placement scores, derived from an independent survey. At all grade levels the English tests appear to be of somewhat less than middle difficulty; this is not surprising since a large number of the items present two choices only and there is no correction for guessing. The spelling tests are of approximately middle difficulty for the middle grades for which they are intended.

The tests are of the multiple choice type throughout. The grammar and usage section employs discrete two-choice items, and the capitalization and punctuation section presents four-choice items in continuous context. In the spelling test four different words, any one of which may be misspelled, are presented in each item, making a total of 120 words for the student to review.

This reviewer would question the devotion of such a large proportion of the grammar and usage section to rules or familiarity with grammar terminology, especially in the advanced form where 28 out of 44 items are of the latter type. A previous reviewer of the parent tests listed several important elements of language as not being covered—among them the dangling element, the misplaced word, phrase, or clause, the lack of parallel structure, faulty comparisons, illogical metaphors—and as these elements were missing from the parent tests so they are missing from the shorter tests. The usage items dwell heavily on number, tense, and case forms, the choices ranging from the illiterate to the literate without, however, too much opportunity, because of the small number of items of this type, to measure comprehensively the steady progression in language competence that one would expect from grade to grade.

This reviewer would also question the heavy stress on capitalization. While the student is given an opportunity to show his familiarity with most of the basic rules for capitalization, the attempt to offer three incorrect choices with the correct choice in a single line of context pads the section unnecessarily and frequently results in some rather far-fetched options. Here the number of options could be reduced without any compromise to the contribution of the section to total test score.

In spite of these critical comments regarding content, which should really be directed to the parent tests rather than the tests under review, the reviewer is of the opinion that the survey tests have much to offer the English teacher who wants a measure of basic language competence which can be administered conveniently during a single class period and who understands the limitations of tests of this length. The tests compare favorably with other available language achievement tests of the same type with which the reviewer is familiar.

[281]

***Survey Tests of English Usage.** Grades 9–13; 1947–49; some forms entitled *Achievement Test of English Usage;* Forms E ('47), H ('48), S ('49), (2 pages, for use at the beginning of either semester); Forms G ('47), N ('48), T ('49), (2 pages, for use during the second semester); Forms J, K, ('49, 2 pages) based on the book *Self-Aid in English Usage;* directions sheet (no date, 2 pages) including 1950 normative data; teacher's remedial sheet ('47, 2 pages); no data on reliability; $2.50 per 100 tests of Forms J or K; 90¢ per 30 tests of other forms; 35¢ per specimen set; postage extra; (35–40) minutes; L. J. O'Rourke; Psychological Institute. *

REFERENCES

1. GROFF, PATRICK J. "Parts of Speech in Standardized English Tests." *Sch R* 69:457–60 w '61. *

HOLLAND ROBERTS, *Director, Academic Freedom Committee, P.O. Box 5503, San Francisco, California.*

The pattern proposed in these English usage tests was established in the 1930's and is familiar to all experienced teachers who began their work a generation ago. At the opening of the school year, or any term, an individual written survey test is given each member of the class and is then followed by a parallel achievement test at the end of the year or semester. Each test of 75 short, generally single sentence unrelated items is divided into three parts: (*a*) Essential Points of Usage, (*b*) Points of Secondary Importance, and (*c*) Finer Points. Each test focuses attention on parts of speech, punctuation, capitalization, and sentence structure. In the opinion of the test builder, "The scores will enable teachers to determine their students' mastery in these classifications."

The approach the tests make to the problems of the English classroom shows unawareness of modern conceptions of language usage and many developments of the last decade in English teaching embodied in the publications of the National Council of Teachers of English. The tests concentrate on the mechanics of language and in so doing place student and teacher in an educational strait jacket that inhibits the free flow of thought and feeling basic to growth and significant communication. As Professor Robert C. Pooley wrote more than thirty years ago in the forward to the second printing of a National Council of Teachers of English monograph, Leonard's *Current English Usage:*[1] "Good usage is that form of speech which is appropriate to the purpose of the speaker, true to the language as it is, and comfortable to the speaker and listener. It is the product of custom, neither cramped by rule, nor freed from all restraint; it is never fixed, but changes with the organic life of the language." These usage tests violate the letter and the spirit of this established view of language usage.

A correlative basic limitation in the tests is the confusion resulting from the identification of usage with the mechanics of language. Mechanics as they are conceived here cease to be a means and become an end. As the philologist, Professor Arthur G. Kennedy of Stanford University, wrote in his monograph, *English Usage,*[2] "usage is the art of speaking

1 LEONARD, STERLING A. *Current English Usage.* National Council of Teachers of English, English Monographs, No. 1. Chicago, Ill.: the Council, 1935. Pp. xxii, 232.

2 KENNEDY, ARTHUR G. *English Usage: A Study in Policy and Procedure.* National Council of Teachers of English, English Monographs, No. 15. New York: D. Appleton-Century Co., 1942. Pp. 166.

and writing....[and] is broader than....grammar ....choice of words....punctuation."

There is nothing in these tests or the classroom drills for which they set the teaching pattern that bears any relationship to anything students think or want to say. That they are instead a Procrustean bed for teacher and students alike, a glance at the accompanying Teachers Remedial Sheet will quickly show. Rule 71 postulates that "The pronoun following *to be* is in the objective case when the infinitive *to be* links the pronoun to a noun or another pronoun in the objective case." It requires ingenuity and a tortuous approach to education to so obfuscate and belabor English usage.

Along with such examples of English jargon, numerous awkward and distorted sentences appear. The following un-English sentence is given as an example in the instructions in Form H of the test and marked "correct": "Carl and she went with us." Students are warned not to rewrite this and similar "models" of English usage.

The failure to grasp the meaning of English usage has led the test builder into other central difficulties. Language usage is a creative art. These are proofreading tests and there is no evidence offered that a high score correlates with ability to use customary usage in letters, reports, or imaginative literature, or in conversations or talks to groups. Even as tests of proofreading ability, they are formal classroom exercises with scant resemblance to life situations outside rigid school doors. If there is even any evidence that scores on these tests correlate positively with student ability to proofread their own writing or recognize usage problems and revise the written work of others in daily life situations, there is no hint of it in the test material.

Reference is made in the descriptive literature accompanying the tests to 1930 and 1947–50 studies from which "A new index of mastery of points of usage in each high school year and in college freshman classes was obtained," but there is no description of these studies or references to authoritative work done in the field of English. There is no support given for the statement, "The items are representative of the common types of errors." Whose errors? In what *social* situations?

Certain assumptions on which the tests are based need examination:

a) It is assumed that there is *one* unchanging standard of correct usage for all occasions. There is no distinction made between formal and informal English nor indication of their changing patterns.

b) The three categories into which each test is divided (Essential Points of Usage, Points of Secondary Importance, and Finer Points) have no scholarly or established educational basis and are purely arbitrary divisions that have no existence outside these tests.

c) Each item in the test is assumed to be of equal value and is given equal weight in arriving at a final score. Consortiums of things like cabbages and kings are added and subtracted, but no rationale is offered to give meaning to the total.

d) It is assumed that 75 items are sufficient to test a student's use of the infinite complexities of the English language.

Teachers and school authorities who wish to strengthen their students in the functional command of the English language will do well to look beyond early conventional tests of this character. Instead they should use the informal tests which emphasize constant varied practice in every day language, formal and informal usage. The first and final tests of language usage are to be found in every day speech and writing in social situations that encourage students to say something that has meaning to them. There are no mechanical shortcuts to testing and teaching the complexities of English usage. The Evaluating Scales developed by the National Council of Teachers of English are the most thoughtful and useful aids.

[282]

★T.C. English Test. Teachers college entrants; 1955–58; most items selected or adapted from *Cooperative English Test: Lower and Higher Levels,* Lower Level Tests A and C1; 5 scores: grammatical usage, spelling, punctuation and capitalization, comprehension, total; 1 form ['56, 6 pages]; mimeographed manual ['58, 6 pages]; no data on reliability; no norms for subscores; distribution restricted to teacher training institutions; separate answer sheets must be used; 6*s.* per 10 tests; 2*s.* per 10 answer sheets; 4*s.* per key; 2*s.* 6*d.* per manual; 7*s.* 6*d.* per specimen set; postpaid within Australia; 35(40) minutes; Australian Council for Educational Research. *

[283]

Test of English Usage. High school and college; 1950; 4 scores: mechanics of writing, accurate use of words, building sentences and paragraphs, total; IBM; Forms A, B, (9 pages); manual (15 pages); individual diagnostic record (4 pages); $3.50 per 35 tests; separate answer sheets may be used; 9¢ per Scoreze answer sheet; 5¢ per IBM answer sheet;

$1.05 per set of machine scoring stencils; 20¢ per hand scoring stencil; postage extra; 50¢ per specimen set, postpaid; 100(110) minutes; Henry D. Rinsland, Raymond W. Pence, Betty S. Beck, and Roland L. Beck; California Test Bureau. *

JOHN C. SHERWOOD, *Professor of English, University of Oregon, Eugene, Oregon.*

It would seem advisable at the very beginning to mention two characteristics of the test which might well be crucial in determining whether it would be suitable for a given testing situation. First of all, it should be understood that the test is regarded by its authors as "primarily diagnostic"; it must serve as a tool of instruction as well as for placement, must detect particular strengths and weaknesses in addition to giving a general rating of the student's competence in "usage." The manual makes specific suggestions for the use of the test in detecting and curing the linguistic maladies both of whole classes and of individual students. The choice of items for testing was determined in part by an actual check of the errors in 3,800 high school English papers. The diagnostic emphasis does not, of course, exclude the use of the test for placement purposes: percentile norms for grades 10–13 are provided, based on a reasonably large sampling from schools and colleges of various types in different parts of the country. The test seems somewhat long (100 minutes) to be used solely for placement; if no use is to be made of individual items for diagnosis, a shorter test, such as the 1960 revision of the Cooperative English expression test, would seem to be equally useful and more economical.

A second distinctive characteristic of the test is that the student is required not merely to recognize correct and incorrect forms, as with some tests, but also to make conscious application of specific rules and to know traditional grammatical terminology. In the punctuation section, for instance, a series of rules is printed, followed by a series of sentences to which the rules might be applicable: the student must match sentence to rule. Likewise in the verb forms section the student must name the form of the verb (past tense, past participle, etc.) to be used, and here the difficulty is increased by the use of terms such as "root infinitive" and "gerundive" (for present participle), a knowledge of which cannot be assumed even among students well grounded in traditional grammar. (It is true that they might be able to guess the meaning of the terms from the examples given.) Possibly a student ought to be penalized for ignorance of the theory of grammar, regardless of whether he makes mistakes in practice; if so, we should frankly admit what we are doing and not pretend that we are testing skill in writing. Under present conditions, when various competing grammars (traditional, structural, and transformational) are in use, it seems more equitable to avoid as far as possible the use of terminology in testing students from varying backgrounds.

The terminology used suggests a rather conservative attitude toward grammar, an attitude which is also visible in the choice of items, which tend to distinguish between the correct and incorrect, standard and substandard rather than between degrees of rhetorical effectiveness. In this respect the section titles are somewhat deceptive. The section titled "Words in Action" proves to be concerned not with precise diction but with gross errors in such matters as agreement. "Building Sentences and Paragraphs" sounds rhetorical, but even here about half the sentence items involve the avoidance of error rather than the exercise of skill. It is only in the section on paragraphing that we find something which requires an active exercise of taste and judgment.

This rather interesting section is intended to test unity and coherence, the first by requiring the student to arrange specific details under the proper subheadings in a proposed theme, the second by requiring him to put the scrambled sentences of paragraphs back in their logical order. The exercises, especially the second, are rather cleverly done. This section might well be given special weight in selecting students for honors sections, since the rest of the test is largely concerned with mechanical matters which industrious but mediocre students often handle as well as their betters.

If this final section is the most interesting and artful of the exercises, still the general quality of the items seems very satisfactory—providing, of course, that one accepts the conservative views of the authors. Many constructions which have received the blessing of *College English* (not to mention *Webster's Third New International Dictionary!*) will still cost the student points on this test.

To conclude, this would appear to be a good test for certain situations. It is best suited for diagnostic use, or for diagnosis and placement together; for placement alone it seems unnecessarily long. It would presumably work best with students who have had a rather conservative training and might discriminate against others, however competent they might be in actual composition. For testers who understand its character and want what it has to offer, it should give satisfactory service.

For a review by Charlotte Croon Davis, see 4:175.

[284]

★A Test of English Usage [Manasayan]. English-speaking high school and college students and adults; 1963-64; 1 form ('63, 9 pages); mimeographed manual ['64, 12 pages]; no norms (authors recommend use of local norms); separate answer sheets must be used; Rs. 12.50 per 25 tests; Rs. 2.50 per 25 answer sheets; Rs. 0.50 per set of scoring stencils; Rs. 2.50 per manual; postage extra; 35(45) minutes; A. Edwin Harper, Jr., and Rhea S. Das; Manasayan. *

[285]

★Test of Language Skill. Business and industry; 1949-63; 1 form ('49, 5 pages); manual ['63, 6 unnumbered pages]; $3.50 per 25 tests; 10¢ per key; $1 per manual; postage extra; $1 per specimen set, postpaid; 25(30) minutes; Richardson, Bellows, Henry & Co., Inc. *

[286]

Tressler English Minimum Essentials Tests, Revised Edition. Grades 8-12; 1932-56; 8 scores: grammatical correctness, vocabulary, punctuation and capitalization, the sentence and its parts, sentence sense, inflection and accent, spelling, total; IBM; Forms A ('54, 8 pages, identical with test copyrighted in 1941 except for changes in 4 items), AM ('56, 8 pages, machine scorable edition of Form A), B ('41, 8 pages), C ('41, 8 pages); manual ['55, 5 pages, identical with sheet copyrighted in 1941 except for minor changes]; no data on reliability; separate answer sheets must be used with Form AM; $2.90 per 35 tests; 7¢ per IBM answer sheet; 40¢ per machine scoring stencil; 50¢ per specimen set; postage extra; (40-50) minutes; J. C. Tressler; Bobbs-Merrill Co., Inc. *

REFERENCES

1. Groff, Patrick J. "Parts of Speech in Standardized English Tests." *Sch R* 69:457-60 w '61. *

Osmond E. Palmer, *Professor, Office of Evaluation Services, Michigan State University, East Lansing, Michigan.*

The various forms of this test were worked out rather carefully, except that the answer sheet and the scoring stencil for Form AM—even those recently received from the publisher for review—are mislabeled Form A and the keying of Test 3, items 34-35 in AM, disagrees with that of the same items in Form A, Test 3, sentence 9. The forms are fairly comparable, though not exactly so. Subtest 1, Grammatical Correctness, contains a fairly good range of defensible points to test for, even though it requires the student to choose only between two responses. Subtest 2, Vocabulary, has a wide range of words and is generally well done. So also is subtest 7, Spelling. One would guess that the total score on this test would reflect fairly well students' abilities. But, for the reasons discussed below, the test would not be as useful as others in telling teachers about their students' competence in English essentials.

The data given in the pamphlet Directions for Administering and Scoring are not very adequate. The directions to the student are too brief. He is not warned, for example, that subtest 1 will be scored on the basis of rights minus wrongs. Further, in the spelling subtest of the machine scorable Form AM, the student is told to mark the number of the misspelled word and to spell it correctly in the space provided on the answer sheet. Nowhere, however, in the directions for scoring or on the scoring stencil for this form is there any indication that this part of the test must be hand scored; nor is the scorer told whether he is to give any credit for recognition of the misspelled word if the student does not spell it correctly.

The norms (based on "more than twenty thousand scores") look valid enough, but these are the same norms that were provided in the directions published in 1941. One suspects that, particularly at the upper end, the norms do not reflect too accurately the performance of the current generation of students. Norms are given only by grade and not by sex, but on a test in this area girls regularly perform better than boys. The grade-equivalent scores given for each of the subtests are meaningless because the subtests are short and in some cases ambiguous.

The value of subtest 3, Punctuation and Capitalization, is dubious. In the three hand scored forms, this subtest consists of 10 sentences in which all capitalization and internal and terminal punctuation have been removed. In these forms the student has to insert in the test booklet all necessary capitalization and punctuation, the required number of insertions ranging from 2 to 13 per sentence. He can, however, score only 10 points, one for each sentence which is punctuated exactly as the key demands. There is no ambiguity in the key; nevertheless, a student could make a correct decision in 70 out of 75 cases in Form B and still score very poorly on the subtest. (I had to look very sharply to see whether a final period had been omitted.) Besides this, one can question the significance of asking a student to capitalize George, Chicago, and August; it seems to me that most students by ninth grade capitalize such words automatically. Similarly, one may question the likelihood of error when the terminal punctuation of a sentence is simply a period.

The author seems to have recognized these last two points when he came to make out subtest 3 of Form AM, the machine scorable form. He supplied most of the capitals omitted from Form A and inserted terminal punctuation in all but one of the sentences (8 out of 10) which end in a period. He then put numbers at various points below the sentences to come up with a total of 40 items (compared to the 55 corrections required in the 10 sentences in Form A and the 75 required in Form B). To keep the same number of points for punctuation (10) in all forms of the test, he decided that the score for this section in Form AM would be one fourth of the number of right responses. The validity of requiring students to make several correct judgments in order to earn one point on the hand scored forms is dubious.

Subtests 1–3 and 7 simply require the student to recognize or supply an acceptable grammatical form, mark of punctuation, or correct spelling. The other three subtests, however, expect him to understand grammatical terminology and to apply it. The terminology is not very extensive or complicated, but so few items are involved that one would not be able to be sure whether the student did not have the information asked for or whether he simply did not understand the term involved. Three items ask the student to identify a sentence as simple, complex, or compound. Four ask him to identify the "subject word" and the "verb" in a sentence. In three others he is asked to supply the correct form of a verb, such as, "past perfect active of *bite*," "past passive of *tear*."

More indefensible yet are the four items in each form devoted to pronunciation. Not only is this an inadequate sample and its relationship to minimum essentials dubious, but in most cases the words chosen are those with an unusual, and consequently ambiguous, accent. For three of the four words in Form C—"orchestra," "municipal," and "hospitable"—*Webster's Third New International Dictionary* shows two more or less acceptable pronunciations. One may quarrel with Merriam-Webster, but their book is recent and their pronunciations are based upon transcripts of the current speech practices of educated people.

There are also a few items in each form which are not well done. One would prefer another synonym for "frankly" than "freely" (Form A), and something other than "mistaken" for "fallacious" (Form C). One can also object to the range of style in the tests. Some sentences, taken, apparently, from student papers, are barely acceptable; others are highly literary and formal. The range is from extremely colloquial sentences (for examples, "The boy who was called on to recite said that uriah's hair which was red was cropped close to his head" in Form A, "In reply to your advertisement in the Sunday *Journal* for a nurse with hospital training I am applying for the place" in Form C, and "Lord Bridgewater's family took part in the play his sister taking the part of a lady" in Form C) to extremely literary ones (for examples, "Of thy unspoken word thou art master; thy spoken word is master of thee" in Form B and "The applause of listening senates to command.... [and three more lines of suspension before the main part of the sentence] Their lot forbade" in Form C).

This test would not do as good a job for the teacher as the SRA *Writing Skills Test*, which is much more recent, has, consequently, more meaningful norms, covers much of the same ground, and is not open to the objections raised against various parts of this test.

ROGER A. RICHARDS, *Assistant Professor of English, Jersey City State College, Jersey City, New Jersey.*

Among many English teachers, the name of Tressler is nearly a charmed word. Even those who are not enthusiasts of the Tressler series of textbooks regard the author with respect. It is to be hoped that the confidence inspired by the Tressler name will not be automatically transferred to this test. There is no reason to believe that the tests are in any way correlated, in content or in quality, with the textbook series.

Despite the changes in the teaching of English over the past quarter century, the tests currently marketed are substantially the same as those produced in 1941. The only real revision, in fact, involved the adaptation of Form A to machine scorable format. In the testing of capitalization and punctuation, the modification increased validity, though in other sections the new (1956) Form AM appears less valid than its counterpart of the old fashioned variety.

It is almost a mistake to consider these as standardized tests; they might more accurately be regarded as simply printed exercises available nationally. Instructions for administration are indefinite, the following excerpt being typical: "Give every pupil time to complete the tests. If necessary, hurry along the especially slow ones."

There is no information concerning reliability or validity, nor does the author state what the purposes of the test are. Although there is a table of norms, these appear not to be very trustworthy. On Test 1, for example, a chance score (10 right out of 20 items) corresponds to a grade placement of 10.9. An eighth grader on a lucky day might very possibly earn a grade equivalent of 11.7 on this section even if he couldn't read English.

The content of the tests is not good enough to make one want to overlook the deficiencies of standardization. Sampling of the various skills and content areas covered by the test is so meager as to make the subscores meaningless. In many places the items are ambiguous. Consider, for example, the test on "Punctuation and Capitalization" in Forms A, B, and C, in which the student is told, "Do not divide one good sentence into two sentences." There is room for much legitimate debate over what constitutes a "good sentence," especially among students who understand how to use a semicolon. The same difficulty arises in Test 5, "Sentence Sense," in which the student must indicate "the number of complete sentences in each of the following." Moreover, the lack of context makes a few items unanswerable, notably those involving decisions concerning restrictive or non-restrictive clauses.

In short, one wonders how these tests could ever have been of substantial value. If they were, they long ago ceased to be. They should, therefore, be replaced by materials which are more sophisticated in measurement technique and which are in content more compatible with modern thinking concerning the nature of language and the determination of acceptable usage.

[Other Tests]

For tests not listed above, see the following entries in *Tests in Print:* 398, 403–4, 407–8, 410–1, 417–9, 420a, 421–2, 425–8, 432–3, 435–6, 440, 442, 444–6, 448, 455, 457, 459, 461–4, 467–8, 471–2, 475, 477, and 479–80; out of print: 399, 412, 415–6, 420, 430, 439, 441, 443, and 452–4.

COMPOSITION

[287]

***College Entrance Examination Board Achievement Test: English Composition.** Candidates for college entrance; 1943–64; for more complete information, see 760; 60(80) minutes; program administered for the College Entrance Examination Board by Educational Testing Service. *

REFERENCES

1–6. See 4:178.
7–20. See 5:204.
21. Black, D. B. "A Comparison of the Performance on Selected Standardized Tests to That on the Alberta Grade XII Departmental Examination of a Select Group of University of Alberta Freshmen." *Alberta J Ed Res* 5:180–90 S '59. * (*PA* 34:6559)
22. Palmer, Orville. "Sense or Nonsense? The Objective Testing of English Composition." *Engl J* 50:314–20 My '61. *
23. Farmer, Paul. "Literature, Reading, and the College Board Exams." *Engl J* 51:9–13 Ja '62. *
24. French, John W. "The Creativity Dimension in Student Writing." *West Reg Conf Testing Probl* 11:45–57 ['62]. *
25. *Manual of Freshman Class Profiles, 1963 Edition.* Princeton, N.J.: College Entrance Examination Board, 1963. Pp. 642. *
26. Noyes, Edward S. "Essay and Objective Tests in English." *Col Board R* 49:7–11 w '63. *

Charlotte Croon Davis, *Test Research Service, Bronxville, New York.* [Review of Forms FBE1, KBE, and KBO3.]

Each of the forms sent for review consists of three parts, or subtests. In one form (KBE), internal time limits are enforced; in the other two forms, the amount of time to be spent on each part is merely suggested. The nine subtests represented by these three forms include seven different types of exercise, as follows: (*a*) recognizing which underlined part of a sentence, if any, contains an error in usage; (*b*) recognizing both the existence of an error and, if it exists, the best way to correct it; (*c*) recognizing whether a sentence is erroneous and, if so, identifying the error as poor diction, wordiness, use of clichés, or faulty grammar; (*d*) recognizing which one of four lines appropriately completes a stanza of poetry and deciding in what way each of the other three lines is inappropriate—whether in meaning, rhythm, or style; (*e*) rephrasing a sentence to accord with a given change in its structure (although in format this is a recognition exercise—and therefore objectively scorable—the examinee has actually to reconstruct the sentence in his mind); (*f*) arranging the sentences of a paragraph in logical order; and (*g*) correcting a badly written theme by adding or omitting words, shifting their position, or by rewriting whole phrases, clauses, or sentences.

Exercise type *g*, called the "interlinear," comes fairly close to free writing and is not objectively scorable. The CEEB examiners in English, all of whom have served as readers of the interlinear, are "convinced of its value" but concerned about its scoring cost. To find out how it compares with the objective types of exercise listed above as a measure of writing skill, the CEEB has conducted an interesting and important study.[1] Each of the (nearly) 650 participating students wrote five essays on assigned topics, each of which was rated by five different readers; the sum of these 25 ratings (by 25 different readers) became the criterion score, which appears to be about as pure a measure of writing ability as can be secured in an experimental setup and which turned out to have the high reliability coefficient of .92. This type of criterion, though troublesome and expensive to obtain, is certainly much better than the often used one of grades in English composition courses, which are influenced by many extraneous factors.

The correlations between the eight subtests (there were two interlinears—one dealing with a narrative, the other with exposition) and the criterion ranged from .71 (for type *a*) to .46 (type *f*); the interlinear coefficients were .67 and .64. When various combinations of three subtests were correlated with the criterion, the coefficients ranged from .78 to .72. The highest ones occurred when the combination included an interlinear, but the differences among the correlations, though statistically significant, are so small that whether this exercise is worth its extra cost is still debatable. (In the reviewer's opinion, another factor to be considered is the time required for each type of exercise; 30 minutes is allotted to, or suggested for, the interlinear whereas the examinee is expected to do each of the objective subtests in 15 or 20 minutes. Perhaps some combination of *four* 15-minute objective subtests would predict the criterion better than any combination of *three* tests. The question of predictive efficiency per unit of time is not discussed in either of the brief preliminary reports of the study available to the reviewer.)

On the basis of this evidence, Edward S. Noyes, a CEEB vice-president and in years past a skeptical and severe critic of attempts to measure writing ability objectively,[2] concluded that "it seems impossible to justify any longer the criticism that the ECT—*whether it consists of objective items only* or includes an interlinear exercise—is not a sound measurement of the ability to write" [reviewer's italics].

After systematic inspection of the objective subtests included in these forms, the reviewer believes that their substantial correlations with the criterion are due partly to their high quality. The various testing techniques are well worked out and, with the possible exception of type *d*, suited to their purpose; some show ingenuity and originality. The range of usage errors covered is wide and the selection sensible. On the whole, the items seem natural and uncontrived (though doubtless they are not); many are thought provoking and even searching. In only a very few cases did the reviewer wonder what an item was driving at or think that an unkeyed response might be defensible. One minor objection is to penalizing the student who has been taught—perhaps by an old-fashioned, finicky parent (like the reviewer)—to prefer *that* to *which* in a restrictive clause. It would be better not to raise this issue at all.

The descriptive booklet furnished to prospective examinees is excellent. The instructions regarding whether and when to guess are explicit and fair, and the fact that the objective subtests are scored with a correction for chance success[3] should reduce the influence of certain personality factors and a certain kind of coaching. The illustrative ECT items in the booklet are well chosen, and enough of

1 Type *d* was not included in the study; instead an analogous prose exercise was used in which the examinee recognizes which one of four sentences appropriately completes a paragraph and classifies each of the other three sentences as lacking in sense, improper in tone or diction, or grammatically faulty. The latter exercise has more face validity since most students will need to express themselves far more often in prose than in verse. Type *d* seems more apropriate to a test of literary comprehension or appreciation.

2 In an earlier MMY (3:120), Noyes said that "'effectiveness of expression'....can only be discovered by giving the student a blank page and a pencil and setting him to write."

3 The need for this correction is shown by the fact that only 44 per cent of the students who took Form KBO3 in May 1962 finished the third subtest. Obviously this form at least (percentages finishing were not given for the other forms) is speeded for most examinees.

them are unkeyed to provide a bona fide work sample. A key to these items is supplied at the end of the section on the ECT so that the student can score his responses, perhaps discover the source of any mistakes, and, most important, make sure that he understands exactly what he is to do in each type of exercise. Counselors and teachers should insist that all students who are to take the ECT follow this procedure since the examinee who is unacquainted with the various exercises may be handicapped.

Although the writer does not recall the specific content of the ECT forms reviewed in a previous MMY (4:178), it is her considered opinion that certain of the testing techniques in the present forms, the instructions about guessing, and the method of scoring the objective subtests are significantly better than those used by the CEEB thirteen years ago.

ROBERT C. POOLEY, *Professor of English, University of Wisconsin, Madison, Wisconsin.* [Review of Forms FBE1 and KBE.]

This test, designed to measure indirectly writing ability, is to be administered in 60 minutes. Two parts of each form are objective, with multiple choice answers recorded on an answer sheet for machine scoring. The third part is a free response exercise answered by interlinear changes and corrections on the test booklet.

FORM FBE1. Section 1 is designed to measure objectively the ability to organize written paragraphs and a poem. The student reads a paragraph as separate sentences out of order. He then indicates his rearrangement of the material by responding to such questions as "Which sentence did you put first?" and "Which sentence did you put after (a)?" In the poem the stanzas are disarranged units. There are four of these exercises.

Section 2 measures taste and sensitivity. The materials offered deal with figurative language, meaning, and tone in prose and poetry, and also rhythm in poetry. The student responds by using a four-letter key to indicate whether he considers each of four suggested completions for a missing line in a poem: appropriate, inappropriate in rhythm or meter, inappropriate in style or tone, or inappropriate in meaning. There are four of these exercises.

Section 3, the free response section, presents a poorly written passage to be revised. The student is instructed to locate anything he thinks defective and correct it, by changing the position of words, adding or deleting words, or rewriting whole clauses or sentences. He is cautioned not to attempt to rewrite the entire piece. Ordinary correction procedures are sanctioned as in marking proof. The authorized changes are furnished in an answer key which the examiner compares with the students' markings. Provision is made for alternate acceptable changes. This exercise presents about 50 items for correction, including punctuation, capitalization, word choice, word order, numbers agreement, and tense agreement.

This test is notable for its omission of the oft-repeated usage items: no "who-whom" situations, no "reason is....because," no "everybody brought their books." It is indeed gratifying to note that composition ability can be measured without resort to these chestnuts. Confusions of number and tense and other problems of concord are dealt with in Part 3.

FORM KBE. Closely parallel to Form FBE1, this test is printed in two separate booklets to permit the interlinear exercise to be scored separately from the machine scored portion. In this form Section 1 is the interlinear exercise, clearly printed and widely spaced for effective correction. The text of the exercise contains infelicities and awkwardnesses of expression, together with specific faults of number of agreement, tense sequence, and mechanics. This is a proofreading exercise at its best, affording every opportunity to the student to reveal his sensitivity to concord and apt phrasing. Thirty minutes' time is allowed.

Section 2 comprises sentences with underlined lettered words and phrases some of which present errors in word choice, usage, grammar, and idiom. Some of the underlined items are correct. The student marks a separate answer sheet to indicate his judgment on each sentence. This section contains such usage items as "couldn't hardly," "who-whom," "lay-laid," "one" followed by "they," "our," etc., "data were," and many others. There are 30 of these sentences to be dealt with in 15 minutes.

Section 3 contains 60 sentences representing examples of poor diction, verbosity and redundancy, clichés and abused metaphors, and faulty grammar and sentence structure. Not more than one such error occurs in a sentence, and some are without error. The student uses a key to indicate which, if any, of these errors is present in each sentence. Fifteen minutes' time is allowed.

While the interlinear portion of this form is very good indeed, the two following sections are weak in presenting too much of the same thing in both parts, and in relying too heavily upon infelicities of usage.

CONCLUSION. One may ask, "this is all very interesting, but does the test measure the ability to write expository prose?" Can a test that requires no writing measure the ability to write? The answer, based upon an exhaustive study recently completed (*26*), seems a convincing affirmative. Six hundred and fifty students from eleventh and twelfth grades of 24 different schools each wrote five essays, each of which was read and evaluated by five trained readers. The total of the five readers' ratings of the five essays was used as the criterion of writing ability. Each of the students also took eight subtests (two interlinear exercises and eight objective sections) from forms of the ECT. The correlations between theme ratings and various combinations of the subtests are high ranging from .72 to .78. It appears that the ECT measures quality of writing at least as well as five readers of five compositions by the same subject; since most themes are read by one reader only, it may be assumed that the reliability of ECT is greater than the reliability of any one reader.

The great advance of Form FBE1 over previous tests is its avoidance of details of usage and its emphasis upon organization of thought and the felicitous flow of good prose. Evidence is not available as to which of these forms is more highly predictive of success in college composition, but intuition at least would favor the form which seems to strike closer to the foundations of good writing. Sensitivity to usage is undoubtedly a factor in the prediction of writing success, but it should not become, as it does in Form KBE, the principal criterion. Form FBE1 might be improved by a little more attention to the more subtle aspects of usage. Form KBE could profit from the addition of tests of organization and the flow of prose.

HOLLAND ROBERTS, *Director, Academic Freedom Committee, P.O. Box 5503, San Francisco, California.* [Review of Forms FBE1, KBE, and KBO3.]

The rapid nationwide increase in the use of the College Board entrance examinations centers attention on the English composition test. It is administered to at least 70 per cent more students than the number taking any of the 14 other CEEB achievement tests. Like the others, it is "developed to reflect, as far as possible, what is being taught in secondary schools, and at the same time, to show whether students are prepared for the work they will be expected to do as freshmen in college." Within this broad area the ECT is specifically designed "to measure, however indirectly, only the ability to write" (*26*). The testmakers assert, "it is abundantly clear that, although the English Composition Test is not a direct measure of writing ability, it does measure the underlying abilities which are necessary to good writing * correctness and effectiveness of expression, organizational ability, and taste and sensitivity in the use of language." The time allowed to reach these sweeping objectives is one hour and the instrument generally has been an objective multiple choice group test which includes six types of items: (*a*) sentence structure correction; (*b*) recognition of faulty usage—grammar, diction, and minimal attention to basic structure and mechanics; (*c*) correcting sentence errors such as mistakes in grammar, diction, verbosity, clichés, and bad metaphors; (*d*) reorganizing sentences in a scrambled paragraph; (*e*) filling in a missing sentence in a paragraph from four choices in which the selection tests the student's knowledge of grammar, diction, construction, and good sense; and (*f*) shifting the parts of a sentence to improve construction.

Form KBO3 is made up of 100 items based in the main upon the correction and rephrasing of single sentences or the rearrangement of scrambled paragraphs. Form FBE1 offers 41 scrambled sentences and poetry completion items and a purposely poorly written brief prose passage to be revised; the 1962 Form KBE consists of a 275–300 word prose passage arranged for interlinear correction and 60 objective items. Maximum time allowed for consideration of the 60 individual items averages one half minute. The basic assumption appears to be that ability in English composition can be measured by testing the mechanics of writing.

How well do these composition tests accomplish their purpose? Can they predict academic success in college? Speaking of all tests in the Admissions Testing Program, the testmakers indicate that the findings of studies provide evidence that a combination of the test scores with high school records will "provide greater accuracy of prediction of college grades than is provided by high school records alone." However, "the College Board recommends that colleges planning to require the tests for admission conduct validity studies designed to evaluate the efficacy of the tests for their own local groups and conditions." For the composition test a Kuder-Richardson formula 20 reliability of .85 and a standard error of measurement of 39 is reported, indicating satisfactory discrimination among the members of the test group.

But do these hour long tests measure writing ability? Here the question is still moot. It is difficult to say what the tests measure. The publishers have given no definition of this complex of thought and personal and social action called "writing ability," nor of the underlying abilities they state the test measures: "correctness and effectiveness of expression, organizational ability, and taste and sensitivity in the use of the language." They report that in their search for a "pure" criterion they studied eleventh and twelfth grade students in 24 varied College Board secondary schools from all major geographic regions. They asked each student to write five essays on five given topics, two of 40 minutes with an expository-argumentative topic and three of 20 minutes each—one expository, one descriptive, and one narrative. When the research workers found agreement among the essay readers on each piece of student writing and a positive correlation between the scores on each subtest and the total essay scores, they concluded that "the ECT objective items do an amazingly effective job of ranking students' writing ability in the same way that a trained group of readers would rank them on a sizeable sample of their actual writing."

Can we now conclude with the *College Board Review* (*26*) that the test is a sound measure of the ability to write? However interesting and useful these studies may be, they have not yet grappled with the problem outside the limited bounds of the restricted schoolroom situation in which students are working against the pressure of time on set imposed topics. For those teachers who think that writing ability is the capacity to communicate in a normal life situation, convincing evidence on the value of what these tests measure is not yet in. To evaluate a piece of writing we need to know to whom it was addressed, why it was created, and under what conditions. What purpose did it serve for writer and recipient? If a high school student has nothing he wants to say on a topic imposed on him, can we then judge his ability to write by what he produces in brief, rigid periods under compulsion? Writing worth reading comes out of a person who has something he wants to communicate. The conditions set up should help him do it.

The College Board's Committee on Examinations apparently is concerned to overcome weaknesses in these objective, machine scored composition tests, as it has now authorized the examiners in English to use a theme as one of the subtests. This is an important step toward reality and away from the pedagogical stereotype that fritters away millions of valuable student hours by concentrating as these tests have upon form and skill to the exclusion of content. Perhaps the next move will be to insure that the writing is communication under normal life conditions.

This key question of subject matter applies to all sections of the tests in their present form—to both the single sentence items and the paragraphs and verses to which the student is asked to respond. From the fragments of which the test sentences, paragraphs, and verses are made, a student cannot know much about what the authors wanted to say. The first part of many of the test items is a puzzle in guessing at the meaning. When the student is formulating or revising his own written work he *knows* what he wants to say. That is the test of sanity and a basic principle in composition teaching which many testmakers, and some teachers, have yet to bring into their work. Form and content are a unity in viable composition as in all rational thought and daily activity. There can be no divorcement. The danger in using tests such as these is that teachers will organize the work of the English classroom so that their students can pass them and so distort the curriculum.

In the 1962 Guide for Admissions Officers, the College Board, in commenting on the error of measurement, recognizes two other omnipresent test problems: "All tests are limited by the number of questions they can ask and the time available to answer them. Thus, even the best test can do no more than provide an incomplete sampling of the student's capabilities. It follows that a series of tests, even if made as comparable as possible and taken by the same student, will yield varying scores." Further, the *College Board Review* (*26*) cautions that "there will always be students whose performances in class belie their test scores." It is useful to keep these balanced statements in mind in using tests and in working on the improvement of composition tests in English in the days ahead.

For a review by Charlotte Croon Davis of earlier forms, see 4:178. For reviews of the testing program, see 760.

[288]

★College Entrance Examination Board Placement Tests: English Composition Test. Entering college freshmen; 1962–63, c1958–63; tests are reprints of inactive forms of *College Entrance Examination Board Achievement Test: English Composition;* IBM; Forms KPL1, KPL2, in a single booklet (c1958–62, 30 pages); for more complete information, see 759; 60(70) minutes; program administered for the College Entrance Examination Board by Educational Testing Service. *

For reviews of the College Entrance Examination Board Achievement Test: English Composition, *see 287 and 4:178.*

[289]

★College Entrance Examination Board Writing Sample. Candidates for college entrance; 1960–63; tests are not scored but are sent ungraded to the student's secondary school and 1–3 colleges or scholarship programs designated at time of application; for more complete information, see 760; 60(75) minutes; program administered for the College Entrance Examination Board by Educational Testing Service. *

REFERENCES

1. Blau, Harold. *How to Write the College Entrance Examination "Writing Sample."* Philadelphia, Pa.: Chilton Co., 1961. Pp. xi, 100. *
2. Valentine, John A. "The First Year of the Writing Sample." *Col Board R* 46:22–6 w '62. *

Robert C. Pooley, *Professor of English, University of Wisconsin, Madison, Wisconsin.* [Review of Forms KWS3 and LWS1 through LWS6.]

This test, designed to be used alone or to supplement the *College Entrance Examination Board Achievement Test: English Composition,* is on one sheet printed on both sides. The face contains the instructions, including information to the student that he is writing an original and four carbons at the same time. Fifteen minutes time is allowed to read the instructions, to supply necessary information on the forms, and to plan the essay. When the supervisor gives the instruction *Begin Work* the student has a full hour for the writing and correcting of his essay.

The reverse of the sheet is labeled "Assignment Sheet" and contains a brief statement or quotation, ranging from two to nine lines in length, which the student is to use for his subject. He is asked to write a well planned essay of from 300 to 500 words, arranged into several paragraphs. When the essay is completed, the student is instructed to underline the sentence which he thinks comes closest to summarizing his central idea.

The Writing Sample is not scored by the CEEB but only by the institution receiving it. Although it is not a standardized test, it is in wide use, 126,280 students having written Samples in 1961–1962. The reasons given for its use are (*a*) to provide samples of a student's writing under controlled conditions, and (*b*) to emphasize the significance of written compositions to encourage schools to lay more stress on writing. There is no evidence to date concerning the effectiveness of this second reason.

Most schools using the Writing Sample employ it as a supplement to the English composition test (ECT). The topics for writing were chosen by a panel of college English teachers, who sponsored a trial run of 10 topics. From this trial run the best four were chosen for the four different forms of the Writing Sample in its first year of use. The results of the trial run have set criteria for the continuing selection of topics.

For so subjective a test the evaluation must necessarily be subjective. To begin with, the device of a quotation is probably as fair and challenging a motivation of writing as any can be. While the difficulty of the quotation itself may vary from year to year, as indeed it does vary in length, every student who writes from a certain quotation is compared only with other students using the same stimulus, and furthermore is judged only in his own institution by the same judges. Judges may be influenced by memories of previous years to consider one set of papers superior to another, but the relative standing of any particular student in any one year is not jeopardized. The quotation as the source of an essay is obviously superior in fairness to any list of specific subjects, no matter how wisely chosen. It is inconceivable that a national test of essay writing could be based on one specific subject only.

In a broader sense, the true evaluation of the Writing Sample lies in the demand for it. All present evidence points to it as currently filling a need or meeting an objective of value to admissions officers and committees. If the opinion often expressed is true, that a person writes from what he is as a result of the totality of his experience, then the composition written as an honest reaction to a thought provoking quotation comes as close as anything can to revealing the kind of person who is applying for admission to the college. The wide use of the Writing Sample would seem to be evidence that many college officials believe that the free essay reveals information of value in the appraisal of applicants beyond what objective tests can furnish. While this belief has not yet been incontrovertibly established, it appears valid enough to justify the expenditure of money and professional time in acting on it. As a device for securing non-objective data about college entrance candidates, the Writing Sample is convenient, efficient, and apparently rewarding.

For reviews of the testing program, see 760.

[290]

★Nationwide English Composition Examination. Grades 4-12; 1959-63; new form issued each April; norms available following the testing program; 1 form ('63, 2 pages); no manual; mimeographed norms ('63, 1 page); no data on reliability; 10¢ per test, postage extra; (40-45) minutes; [Donald R. Honz]; Educational Stimuli. *

[291]

***Sequential Tests of Educational Progress: Essay Test.** Grades 4-6, 7-9, 10-12, 13-14; 1957-62; Forms A, B, C, D, ('57, 7 pages); 4 levels; handbook ('57, 34 pages) for each level; battery technical report ('57, 58 pages); 1958 SCAT-STEP supplement ('58, 32 pages); 1962 SCAT-STEP supplement ('62, 49 pages); battery profile ('57, 1 page); battery student report ('58, 4 pages); $1 per 20 tests; 50¢ per 20 profiles; 50¢ per 20 student reports; $1 per handbook; $1 per technical report and supplement; postage extra; $1.25 per specimen set (includes sample handbook but not technical report; $1 per supplement); cash orders postpaid; 35(40) minutes; Cooperative Test Division. *

a) LEVEL 4. Grades 4-6; Forms 4A, 4B, 4C, 4D.
b) LEVEL 3. Grades 7-9; Forms 3A, 3B, 3C, 3D.
c) LEVEL 2. Grades 10-12; Forms 2A, 2B, 2C, 2D.
d) LEVEL 1. Grades 13-14; Forms 1A, 1B, 1C, 1D.

REFERENCES

1. BLACK, DONALD B. "A Note on the Use in Alberta of the Sequential Tests of Educational Progress: Essay Test." *Alberta J Ed Res* 4:172-80 S '58. *
2. ANDERSON, C. C. "The New Step Essay Test as a Measure of Composition Ability." *Ed & Psychol Meas* 20:95-102 sp '60. * (*PA* 34:8329)
3. FINDLEY, WARREN G. "Improvement of Writing Ability in the Elementary Grades." *Yearb Nat Council Meas Ed* 20:149-52 '63. * (*PA* 38:9260)

For reviews by John S. Diekhoff, John M. Stalnaker, and Louis C. Zahner, see 5:206. For reviews of the complete battery, see 25 and 5:24.

[292]

***Sequential Tests of Educational Progress: Writing.** Grades 4-6, 7-9, 10-12, 13-14; 1956-63; IBM and Grade-O-Mat; Forms A, B, ('57, c1956-57, 11-20 pages); 4 levels; battery directions ('57, 12 pages); interpretive manual ('57, 32 pages); battery technical report ('57, 58 pages); 1958 SCAT-STEP supplement ('58, 32 pages); 1962 SCAT-STEP supplement ('62, 49 pages); 1963 SCAT-STEP supplement of urban norms ('63, 16 pages); battery teacher's guide ('59, 85 pages); battery profile ('57, 1 page); battery student report ('58, 4 pages); no data on reliability of Form B; separate answer sheets must be used; $4 per 20 tests; $1 per 20 IBM scorable answer sheets; 25¢ per scoring stencil; see 666 for prices of Grade-O-Mat cards; $1 per 20 profiles; $1 per 20 student reports; $1 per interpretive manual; $1 per technical report; $1 per supplement; $1 per teacher's guide; postage extra; $2 per specimen set, cash orders postpaid; 70(90-100) minutes; Cooperative Test Division. *

a) LEVEL 4. Grades 4-6; Forms 4A, 4B.
b) LEVEL 3. Grades 7-9; Forms 3A, 3B.
c) LEVEL 2. Grades 10-12; Forms 2A, 2B.
d) LEVEL 1. Grades 12-13; Forms 1A, 1B.

REFERENCES

1. GROFF, PATRICK J. "Parts of Speech in Standardized English Tests." *Sch R* 69:457-60 w '61. *
2. ENDLER, NORMAN S., AND STEINBERG, DANNY. "Prediction of Academic Achievement at the University Level." *Personnel & Guid J* 41:694-9 Ap '63. * (*PA* 39:2888)
3. MICHAEL, WILLIAM B.; CATHCART, ROBERT; ZIMMERMAN, WAYNE S.; AND MILFS, MILO. "Gains in Various Measures of Communication Skills Relative to Three Curricular Patterns in College." *Ed & Psychol Meas* 23:365-74 su '63. * (*PA* 38:1384)

HILLEL BLACK, *Senior Editor, Saturday Evening Post, New York, New York.*

To anyone concerned with the paucity of good writing among students, the STEP writing tests can only be described as performing a grave disservice to the teaching of English composition. This review will attempt to show why this is so.

STEP Writing, according to the Manual for Interpreting Scores, contains items which fall into five categories. They are: organization, conventions, critical thinking, effectiveness, and appropriateness.

While the aims are inclusive, these tests fail in all but the second category. In this category, they only partially succeed in measuring "conventions" when the mental process is an act of memory involving such mechanical tasks as spelling and punctuation. Let us examine "organization" as an illustration of failure.

It is certainly apparent to every reviewer in the MMY that there are a multiplicity of ways in which he could have ordered his ideas and facts in writing his critique. The choice he eventually makes is an individual choice which cannot be made for him. He must weed out the trivial, discard the irrelevant, and organize his material in such a way that he makes sense effectively. The creation and selection of ideas and the ordering of facts are his. Yet the STEP writing tests leave the student without this choice. What choice he does make consists largely of taking facts and ideas already organized for him and then performing what may be called minor editing, such as rearranging or deleting sentences. The skills required for writing anything are infinitely more difficult and creative than making minor editorial revisions. To equate the two, as the authors do, is misleading and presumptuous. Moreover, it has yet to be shown that creativity can be measured or even identified through the multiple choice format. Yet this in effect is what the STEP writing tests claim they can do.

But let us be more precise. According to one of the authors' selection criteria, "The materials [in the writing tests] should represent *typical writing needs* and desires of the student through careful selection of situations and forms of writing" [italics added]. It is for this reason that the examples on which the questions are based were written by students themselves.

One of the most distressing aspects of the tests is that only rarely does this student material rise to the level of mediocrity. Indeed, it would appear that the "typical writing needs" of our students are so great that we are in imminent danger of seeing the collapse of the English language. To take one example, in Form 1B, eight questions are based on a 248-word student editorial with the heading, "Treat Us Like Adults." This illustrates the kind of material employed to measure college freshmen and sophomores. In introducing the material to the students the authors note, perhaps wryly, "This article, submitted by a freshman applicant for a position on the staff of a college weekly, was returned to the writer for revision." Part of the material follows:

1 It is time this college woke up and started treating we, the students, like grown-ups and not like a bunch of high school kids. **2** Why should there be compulsory class attendance? **3** We graduated high school and now we should be allowed to grow up. **4** We all learned how to study in high school so we should be allowed to do it on our own here. **5** Most of us students would go to class anyway. * **14** Our parents would like us to have these things and they pay the bills. **15** We need to grow in other ways, not just intelectual. **16** Only four years until we are out in the world. **17** That doesnt give us much time in order to be responsible and take care of ourselves. **18** Socializing and recreation are just as worthwhile as much knowledge and high marks later on.

It is not possible to see how such material—and many other examples could be given—can form the basis for measuring four of the five categories which the tests' authors rightly suggest go into making good writing. For instance, item 8 corrects the first sentence to read as follows: "It is time this college woke up and started treating us students like grown-ups...." What is disturbing about this "correct" choice is that it abounds in clichés. Selecting the correctly worded clichés cannot be a test of writing skills. The only sensible alternative, an alternative which is not offered, is to eliminate the sentence and write one that is entirely new and different.

In item 13, the student is asked to select the simplest and most accurate revision of sentence 17. Again recall the problems involved in writing. Certainly a key to good writing is rewriting. But a writer must know what to revise. Once someone else has picked out the sentence or phrase that needs correction, the creative aspect of writing markedly diminishes. In short, this kind of question, which occurs repeatedly, measures only a peripheral aspect of the craft.

Question 15 asks: "Of the following possible weaknesses of this paper as an editorial, which is most serious?" The student is then given the following choices: "A Its misspelled words B Its poorly constructed sentences C Immature phrasing D Its unsupported generalizations."

Let us put aside the question's obvious weakness. While the correct answer is supposedly D, excellent arguments can be made to support C and possibly B. But the most apparent alternative is not even offered and that is the editorial's superficiality of thought, which truly is its essential weakness. In addition to subjecting a student to impoverished ideas atrociously expressed—a dubious educational device—the tests with their inherent limitations prevent him from offering any original concepts composed in an original manner. To contend, as the authors do, that "The STEP Writing tests seek to measure comprehensively the full range of skills involved in the process of good writing" must put a strain on any writer's credulity. Hopefully any educator who wishes to measure "the full range of skills involved in the process of good writing" will resort to writing itself, despite what he has been told about his frailty to make an intelligent, sensitive, and reliable judgment.

ALBERT N. HIERONYMUS, *Professor of Education and Psychology, State University of Iowa, Iowa City, Iowa.*

This is a series of highly ingenious and well constructed tests in an area in which objective measurement has always been extremely difficult. They are excellent tests of what might be termed the power of writing: organization, clarity, effectiveness, and appropriateness of expression. They call for the application of higher level mental processes of reasoning and judgment.

The tests require a relatively advanced level of reading comprehension, not so much in the original passages as in the items. In understanding the passages, considerable emphasis is placed upon ascertaining the meaning of poorly (atrociously!) written materials in order to substitute more precise or elegant versions of the same ideas. Most of the material is interesting and cleverly adapted to the purposes of the tests.

It is not entirely clear whether the skills specifications for the tests were determined before or after the tests were constructed. There is considerable disparity between the statement of relative emphasis in the Manual for Interpreting and the classifications presented in the Teacher's Guide. For example, for the five skills categories (organization, conventions, critical thinking, effectiveness, and appropriateness) at Level 4, the relative emphasis is listed as 30, 20, 15, 20, and 15 per cent, respectively. When the total number of items in the two forms (120) is used as a base, the relative emphasis is 27, 67, 16, 43, and 25 per cent, respectively. When the total number of item classifications (213) is used as a base, the relative emphasis is 15, 38, 9, 24, and 14 per cent. Similar discrepancies are to be found at other levels. There are also marked differences between forms.

As tests of the mechanics of writing, these leave much to be desired; they are inefficient and incomplete. This is largely the result of the general philosophy underlying the whole STEP venture: to achieve continuity of measurement throughout grades 4–14. The fact that the commonly accepted objectives of the writing program differ radically at the extremes of this grade range makes compromise inevitable. These tests appear to be better suited to the objectives at higher grade levels than to those at lower levels. Of the 60 items in Level 4, Form A (grades 4–6), for example, only 1 item is concerned primarily with spelling; 1 with capitalization; 6 with punctuation; and 4 with correctness of word usage. Only two uses of the comma are tested as error situations —one with the salutation and the other with the complimentary close of a friendly letter. This would appear to under-represent the place of mechanics in the language skills program through grade 6.

Apparently it has been necessary to compromise also with the ideal in item difficulty distributions, especially at the lower levels. In grade 4, the median difficulty index (per cent right) was 32 in Form A and 35 in Form B. Seventeen items in Form A and 11 items in Form B were at or below chance (25 per cent). In Level 4, the raw score medians were 35, 46, and 57 per cent of the total number of items for grades 4, 5, and 6, respectively, instead of the 62.5 per cent which was stated as a goal. In Level 3, these were 43, 48, and 57 per cent, respectively, for grades 7, 8, and 9.

A "show-of-hands" method of item analysis is recommended as one of the principal follow-up techniques. Methods of evaluating the statistical significance of differences between class performance and the item analysis norm are provided. Unfortunately, this appears to be such a "scientific" procedure for locating areas in need of concentrated attention that users are likely to forget the differences between norms and standards and the role that sound judgment plays in setting expectation.

Issues relating to SCAT and to the STEP battery as a whole are treated elsewhere. However, on the issue of the use of percentile bands, data on the reliabilities of differences for college freshmen presented in the 1958 SCAT-STEP Supplement reflect upon the uniqueness of the writing test. Of particular interest are the reliabilities of differences between STEP Reading and STEP Writing

(.04), and between STEP Writing and SCAT Verbal (.27). These low reliabilities make the rule-of-thumb procedures for interpreting profile differences for an individual student highly suspect. This is pointed out in the Supplement but one wonders what changes in procedures for profile comparisons would be necessary if similar data were available for Reading, Listening, and Writing for the other levels.

SUMMARY. The tests measure very effectively higher-order writing skills, particularly those of effectiveness and appropriateness which tend to be slighted in other batteries. There is more operational and statistical overlap with reading than is desirable. The tests should be supplemented with better measures of the mechanical writing skills, particularly in the elementary and junior high schools.

Personnel & Guid J 42:298–303 N '63. Dean A. Allen. The Fifth Mental Measurements Yearbook....contains three reviews of the full STEP series of achievement tests and three of STEP-Writing; all six deserve the close attention of test users and test publishers. Many of the present reviewer's observations derive from the discussions in Buros, but in addition to study of the original STEP-W materials, the published literature related to STEP-W has been searched in an effort to bring this evaluation of the test up to date. * The student-written passages that comprise STEP-W are almost unvarying in their poor quality and trivial content. Not only are they shot through with errors, misconstructions, and infelicities of every sort, of which only a few are singled out for revision, but the choice of topics is altogether disappointing. The use of such inferior material not only renders the reading of the tests, as Stalnaker (in Buros, p. 362) puts it, "an ordeal....for the student who is sensitive to the written word," but all too often makes the student's choice of *best answer* hinge on the relative importance he assigns to consistency of style vs. good English. In some items a clearly superior revision is so out of keeping with the rest of the passage that to mark it as *best* or *most effective* means virtually to disregard the context from which it was drawn. There are a few instances (an average of one or two per 30-item part) of items with no acceptable good answer, with two or more equally good answers, or with a clearly wrong answer keyed as correct. For the most part, the keyed answers appear to be defensible; careful editing would have avoided the mistakes noted. * There is evidence that STEP-W has a heavy loading of a general factor. * Comparable data for college freshmen —correlations between STEP-W and the other STEP and SCAT tests (1958, *Supplement*, p. 28)—confirm the impression that, in avoiding subject matter dealt with in specific courses, STEP-W may be measuring general scholastic aptitude rather than writing skills as such. * The use of bands rather than single scores sets an example which other test publishers are urged to consider following. * Surprisingly lacking are correlations between alternate forms, data one would assume to be almost obligatory evidence of careful test construction. * Converted scores are in fact not comparable in terms of percentile ranks. Consider comparisons across fields. A college freshman who earned a converted score of 286 on all Level 1 STEP tests would fall at mid-percentile ranks of 11 in reading, 15 in listening, 25 in writing, 34 in social studies, 57 in science, and 63 in mathematics. Such variations in percentile equivalents would be understandable in the case of raw scores—it would mean only that the tests were not equally difficult—but the concept of "a common continuous score scale" seems to imply a parallelism within the STEP battery which does not exist, at least in terms of percentile equivalents. If we consider scores earned within a single field in successive grades, we find a similar lack of comparability, though the publishers state that converted scores "represent a statistical derivation and are more meaningful (than raw scores) because through their use scores from form to form of STEP-Writing are comparable" * While there is a rough relation between converted scores and median achievement level in that converted scores get higher as one goes up the grades, there is no regular pace or pattern of increments with "growth" or normal progress through the grades. Moreover, these grade-by-grade converted score increments vary from test to test; the median student gains one point on STEP-Writing between grades 6 and 7 but gains 10 points on STEP-Reading. As it turns out, converted scores are never really useful for comparisons between different students' scores on the same test, or between a single student's scores on two tests in different fields or two tests at different levels in the same field. The publishers, while insisting on the use of converted scores, actually make all comparisons between tests, levels, students, and fields on the basis of percentiles (which could as easily be obtained from raw scores), and they instruct test users to do the same. The interpolated operation of translating raw scores to converted scores is apparently unnecessary. * Despite promises in the various STEP materials that additional data would be forthcoming, and despite the critical comment of the reviewers in Buros directed against the lack of appropriate statistical evidence, almost five years after its birth, STEP-W is still without the obvious sorts of reliability information, information which should accompany distribution of a test battery. * The absence of data accompanying publication of STEP-W and the meager evidence at hand five years later make it impossible either to endorse or to discount any statement of the test's validity beyond the original assertion of content validity. The correlations may be simply reflections of the fact that any test of general intellectual aptitude will bear some relationship to school performance. The 1958 *Supplement* reports briefly on one study, and the 1962 *Supplement* on three studies, comparing STEP-W scores with school grades. All are unpublished. This situation caused the author to undertake a further investigation of STEP-W. * Entering freshmen at Bowdoin College were tested on STEP-W in the fall of 1961. The split-half (odd-even) reliability coefficient was found to be 0.43, which corrected by the Spearman-Brown formula, becomes 0.60, obviously too low to afford confidence in the stability of individual students' scores. The poor reliability is partly the result of the homogeneity of Bowdoin students with regard to writing skills, but then, homogeneity greater than that of the nation-wide norming group would characterize almost any single school or college sample. Freshmen at Bowdoin take a required course, English 1–2, in which success is largely dependent on writing skills. The correlation between final grades and STEP-W raw scores was 0.39. The correlation between STEP-W and SAT-V scores was found to be 0.46. Moreover, the r between SAT-V and grades in English 1–2 was 0.49. In spite of the fact that students are admitted to Bowdoin in part on the basis of SAT-V scores, SAT-V appears to be a somewhat better predictor of grades in the freshman writing course than does STEP-Writing. *Conclusions.* No over-all grade can be awarded the STEP publishers for their aims and their accomplishments. Individual test users will have to make the judgment about the worth of STEP-W in their own schools. But some final comments may serve as guidelines. A. STEP-W has been ambitiously conceived, carefully planned, and attractively printed. B. Detailed presentation of technical information regarding development, norming, statistical methods, and the like accompanies the test. C. A very large variety of accessory materials and interpretive literature is available and necessary for full use of STEP-W. D. In their effort to avoid dependence on local course content, the publishers may have produced a measure more of general scholastic aptitude than of writing skills. E. Statistical evidence of validity and reliability is inadequate. F. The test content is largely trivial, tedious, and unnecessarily, though deliberately, fraught with errors; so much so that the intelligent student's task in selecting suitable revisions may come down to pitting his desire to preserve consistency of (poor) style against his feeling for literate writing. G. Presentation of scores as percentile bands rather than as single numbers is a commendably cautious tactic in guarding against the appearance of precision where it does not exist. H. Converted scores, a feature of which the publishers are unaccountably proud, seem to be needless or even misleading. I. Finally, and perhaps most important, is the question of whether STEP-W (or any multiple-choice test, for that matter) can accurately assess writing ability. Although the arguments against the inefficiency, the unreliability of grading, and the limited sampling of content typical of essay tests are persuasive, traditionalists will doubtless persist in their belief that the best way to judge writing skills is to examine specimens of students' writing. They will ask: Does STEP-W really measure what it claims to measure? If we take at face value the publishers' statement that content validity is a criterion by which to judge STEP-W, then Zahner's description seems reasonable: that STEP-W is not a test of writing at all but "somewhere between a test of proofreading and one of editing" (Buros, p. 362). The burden of demonstrating usefulness falls on the publishers. So it is remarkable that, among all the statistics relating to the test, none can be found comparing STEP-W scores with any other measure of writing, including even the companion STEP essay writing test. Five years after publication, STEP-Writing is still an attractive test of uncertain worth.

For reviews by Charlotte Croon Davis, John M. Stalnaker, and Louis C. Zahner, see 5:207. For reviews of the complete battery, see 25 and 5:24.

[293]

★**Writing Skills Test.** Grades 9–12; 1961, c1960–61; IBM; Form A ('61, c1960, 8 pages); manual ('61, 31 pages); separate answer sheets must be used; $3 per 20 tests; $4 per 100 IBM answer sheets; 25¢ per scoring stencil; 75¢ per specimen set; postage extra; 40(50) minutes; Macklin Thomas; Science Research Associates, Inc. *

WILLIAM E. COFFMAN, *Director of Research and Development, College Board Programs Division, Educational Testing Service, Princeton, New Jersey.*

The *Writing Skills Test,* according to the manual, is offered for use "as a measure of English course achievement" in grades 9–12, "in the differential assignment of students to English sections," and "as a teaching aid." The test itself is described as "an easily administered, forty-minute examination of some of the basic skills used in composition."

The potential user will agree with the description. He may wonder, however, at the recommended uses, for of all the sample data presented in the manual, the most appropriate in the reviewer's opinion are based on "college freshmen students attending....a large urban junior college....in Illinois." He may suspect that a test originally constructed for use in the placement of college freshmen has been "adapted" to secondary school use because of the larger market. In such a case, the appropriateness of the "adaptation" becomes of crucial significance.

The test is unusually difficult for unselected students in grades 9–12. There are 70 four-choice and five-choice questions and the score is number of right answers. Thus, the mean chance score is 15.5 and the standard deviation of chance scores is 3.5. From the norms table, it is possible to determine that if a boy in the ninth grade sample had marked his paper at random, he would have had one chance in six of scoring above the 50th percentile for ninth grade boys. A twelfth grade boy adopting the same strategy would have one chance in six of scoring above the 23rd percentile. From the data regarding item difficulty, it can be determined that there are 29 five-choice items which were answered correctly by 62 per cent or fewer of the sample from the twelfth grade norms population and 24 four-choice items which were answered correctly by 60 per cent or fewer of the sample. This means that, if the possibility of correct guesses is taken into account for each item, fewer than half of the samples from the norms population of twelfth graders know the answer to 53 of the 70 questions. Of course, since most students do not mark at random, this difficult test turns out to have validity even for ninth grade groups. However, the user must realize that there is always the danger that in individual cases scores well up in the distribution may represent only random responses. Since similar tests are available which contain easier questions covering essentially the same content, it is difficult to justify the use of this particular test for typical high school groups.

In view of the difficulty of the test for the high school samples, it is surprising to read in the manual, "The test apparently does not possess enough ceiling to discriminate between students at colleges that have selective admissions policies." This statement is based on the fact that at a small liberal arts college and a large private university in Illinois, the mean scores were, respectively, 49.86 and 53.01. But these scores are only 7.11 and 10.26 points above the ideal mean of 42.75; they are fully 20.14 and 16.99 points below the ceiling of 70. In contrast, the mean scores for the national samples of ninth and tenth graders were 23.90 and 28.04. These scores are 18.85 and 14.71 points below the ideal mean and only 8.40 and 12.54 points above the chance score of 15.50. If there is a problem with the test, it is that it has too high a floor for ordinary secondary school classes, not too low a ceiling for classes of college freshmen.

The test will have limited usefulness for measuring English course achievement at any level because there are no parallel forms. The manual contains data indicating high stability in measurement over an academic year (test-retest correlations range from .87 to .91) but there is no information regarding how much of the mean difference is due to growth and how much is due to practice effect. Certainly, if the teacher adopts the advice in the manual to use the test as a basis for class discussion, its usefulness as a measuring instrument will be destroyed for the students in that class. With only one form available, one may doubt the usefulness of class discussion of results. The sample of 70 questions is quite small in comparison with the hundreds of exercises to be found in the typical textbook. As a method of demonstrating the need for concentrated effort in preparation for taking a parallel test, class discussion of results might have some value; as a means of teaching basic principles of writing, it is of doubtful value.

The recommendation that the test be used in combination with essay ratings to place students in sections needs to be examined critically. It is proposed in the manual that high scoring students and low scoring students be placed on the basis of the test score alone and that essay papers be read for those scoring in the middle of the distribution. Such a plan is highly attractive because it reduces the number of essays to be read; however, it has the effect of basing the final decision on the less reliable measure—a procedure exactly the opposite of what is desirable.

Research studies have demonstrated that a combination of essay rating and objective test scores provides the optimum measurement of composition skill per unit of testing time; on the other hand, the combination does not result in "greatly improved" accuracy as claimed by the author of the *Writing Skills Test*. The improvement is only slight when all essays are rated and included in the combination; if essay scores are used as a second stage in a sequence, the results may actually be less accurate. Unreliable essay scores are a poor basis for deciding the fate of borderline cases; in combination with scores from good objective tests, they can be expected to increase validity a little.

The *Writing Skills Test* appears to be appropriate for use in differential assignment of college freshmen or students in above average classes in grades 9–12. The national norms data provided in the manual are appropriate primarily for showing how inadequate is the preparation of the typical secondary school student for a test of this sort. Without parallel forms, the test is of limited value in evaluating learning. While considerable ingenuity has been exercised in developing the questions for the test, the item pool from which the questions were chosen appears to have been limited; otherwise there would be no excuse for publishing a single form only and including in it such extremely difficult items. The prospective user would do well to examine the test booklet carefully and arrive at his own conclusions regarding the adequacy of the sampling for purposes other than differential assignment.

Osmond E. Palmer, *Professor, Office of Evaluation Services, Michigan State University, East Lansing, Michigan.*

This test is nearly a model, so far as it goes, of what a good objective test can be. It is carefully worked out. There is a 31-page manual giving directions for administering the test and for using the test results, showing the difficulty of each item at each grade level, and giving a lengthy discussion of the norming of the test and correlation data with grades in English, with other English tests, and with reading and psychological tests. In addition, the sections on grammar and punctuation contain a statement of the rule involved for each item and how that rule applies specifically.

The front of the answer sheet shows percentile norms at each grade level for boys and girls combined; the back gives percentiles for boys and girls separately. Since there is a mean difference of approximately five points in favor of girls this distinction is well worth making.

The test itself is attractively printed and each section is preceded by a statement of purpose and by directions as extensive as necessary. For instance, the spelling section which uses a common set of responses for all items reprints the set in abbreviated form for each item. And the last section, Sentence Building, which contains a type of item the student probably has never seen, is preceded by two examples.

The test consists of six parts. In the vocabulary section a single word is followed by four foils. In Sentence Recognition a group of unpunctuated sentences is written as a block and the student is to decide how many sentences there are in each block (none to four or more). In the grammar part, one continuous sentence is split into five responses in one of which an error has been introduced. In Punctuation and Mechanics an error has been made at one of five lettered points in a sentence. Each spelling item consists of seven words one of which is misspelled. The student is to find that word and then decide whether he would correct it by changing one letter to another, by taking out one or more letters, by putting in one or more letters, or by switching letters around. One cannot tell from this whether the correction a student selects is meant to apply to the misspelled word or to some other word which he thinks is misspelled.

Sentence Building, the last section, contains an ingenious type of item. The attempt is to see how well a student can handle the structure of the language by giving him a good sentence and then asking him to rewrite it (mentally) with a different construction involved. For instance, given the sentence, "He is compelled by circumstances to earn his own living," the student has to decide which of five words or expressions would appear in the sentence if it were recast to begin with "Circumstances." The options are "made," "he," "him," "compelled," and "compelling." This type of item has two virtues. It moves from a good English sentence to a good English sentence and does not require the student to recognize an error which possibly he does not make; and, it is hoped, it gives some measure of the student's ability to handle a variety of sentence patterns in his own writing.

One finds little to quarrel with in the test. The vocabulary words are well chosen and the answer marked right is clearly best. The spelling section has a judicious selection of words illustrating the rules and the spelling demons. The section on grammar avoids testing for tricky points, and cleverly introduces a couple of simple who-whom situations in the foils but does not directly test for them. When, however, there are only 10 items on grammar one wishes that 2 of them had not been devoted to the omission of "d" in "he is suppose to" and to the use of the possessive with a gerund. Some of the sentences in the grammar section were selected, seemingly, from student papers and strike one as being a bit too colloquial. A student might be tempted to mark as an error "I really grew hot [angry]."

The main question one has to raise about the test, and the author is aware of it, is how does it relate to English as taught? One can well ask whether in a writing skills test one can justify devoting 23 of 70 items to vocabulary. This reviewer would like to see more items devoted to grammar and punctuation; he would like to see some items on capitalization (proper adjectives, words like "the North," use of capitals in titles); he would like to see some attempt to measure a student's sense of organization and his ability to choose in a specific context the word that best fits that context.

This test, however, may be used with a great deal of confidence to measure reliably what it does measure.

[Other Tests]

For tests not listed above, see the following entry in *Tests in Print:* 484 (out of print).

LITERATURE

[294]

***American Literature: Every Pupil Test.** High school; 1934–64; new form (4 pages) usually issued each April; forms from previous testing programs also available; general directions sheet ('63, 2 pages); no data on reliability; Ohio norms for new forms available following testing program; 5¢ per test; 3¢ per key; postpaid; 40(45) minutes; Ohio Scholarship Tests. *

[295]

★Book Review Tests. High school; 1950–63; 1 form; 195 tests (4 pages) on specific books: *Abe Lincoln in Illinois* ['60], *Abe Lincoln Grows Up* ['57], Drinkwater's *Abraham Lincoln* ['60], *Adam Bede* ['58], *Age of Innocence* ['63], *Aku Aku* ['63], *Alice Adams* ['58], *All the King's Men* ['59], *An American Tragedy* ['63], *Animal Farm* ['60], *Anna and the King of Siam* ['61], *Anna Karenina* ['63], *Anne Frank: The Diary of a Young Girl* ['59], *Around the World in Eighty Days* ['63], *Arms and the Man* ['63], *The Autobiography of Benjamin Franklin* ['57], *Autocrat of the Breakfast Table* ['63], *Babbitt* ['58], *The Babe Ruth Story* ['57], *The Barretts of Wimpole Street* ['59], *Beau Geste* ['58], *Bell for Adano* ['62], *Ben Hur* ['58], *Beowulf* ['59], *The Black Arrow* ['53], *Black Beauty* ['63], *The Black Rose* ['63], *Brave New World* ['61], *Brideshead Revisited* ['63], *The Bridge of San Luis Rey* ['58], *Brothers Karamazov* ['59], *The Caine Mutiny* ['58], *The Call of the Wild* ['53], *The Canterbury Tales* ['53], *Captains Courageous* ['57], *The Child Buyer* ['63], *A Christmas Carol* ['53], *The Citadel* ['50], *The Count of Monte Cristo* ['58], *The Courtship of Miles Standish* ['58], *The Covered Wagon* ['57], *The Cricket on the Hearth* ['63], *The Crisis* ['58], *Cry, the Beloved Country* ['60], *Cyrano de Bergerac* ['58], *Day of Infamy* ['63], *Death Be Not Proud* ['61], *The Deerslayer* ['58], *A Descent Into the Maelstrom* ['59], *The Devil and Daniel Webster* ['63], *Dragon Seed* ['58], *Dr. Jekyll and Mr. Hyde* ['59], *Drums* ['59], *Drums Along the Mohawk* ['59], *The Egg and I* ['63], *The Enemy Within* ['63], *Enoch Arden* ['57, identical—except for title and format—with the out of print 1947 form of the test on this book in the series *Objective Tests in English*], *George Washington Carver* ['63], *Giants in the Earth* ['58], *Gone With the Wind* ['58], *Goodbye, Mr. Chips* ['59], *The Good Earth* ['53], *Good Morning, Miss Dove* ['58], *The Grapes of Wrath* ['61], *The Great Stone Face* ['59], *Green Mansions* ['59], *Green Pastures* ['62], *Gulliver's*

Travels ['58], *Heidi* ['59], *Hie to the Hunters* ['62], *The History of Henry Esmond* ['60], *Hiroshima* ['60], *The Hoosier Schoolmaster* ['58], *The Hound of the Baskervilles* ['63], *How Green Was My Valley* ['58], *The Hurricane* ['63], *The Iliad* ['58], *The Innocents Abroad* ['63], *Intruder in the Dust* ['63], *Jane Eyre* ['58], *John Brown's Body* ['60], *Jude the Obscure* ['63], *The Jungle* ['63], *The Jungle Books* ['63], *The Keys of the Kingdom* ['63], *Kon Tiki* ['59], *A Lantern in Her Hand* ['53], *The Last of the Mohicans* ['58], *The Last of the Plainsmen* ['57], *The Late George Apley* ['63], *Leaves of Grass* ['63], *The Legend of Sleepy Hollow* ['59], *Les Miserables* ['58], *Let the Hurricane Roar* ['63], *Life on the Mississippi* ['63], *Life With Father* ['63], *The Light in the Forest* ['62], *The Light That Failed* ['58], *The Little Foxes* ['62], *The Little Minister* ['58], *Little Women* ['57], *The Lively Lady* ['61], *Lord Jim* ['58], *Lord of the Flies* ['63], *Lorna Doone* ['58], *Lost Horizon* ['60], *Love Is Eternal* ['60], *The Loved One* ['63], *Madame Curie* ['63], *The Magnificent Ambersons* ['53], *Magnificent Obsession* ['60], *Main Street* ['58], *Maria Chapdelaine* ['58], *The Master of Ballantrae* ['58], *Masters of Deceit* ['63], *The Mayor of Casterbridge* ['57], *Men Against the Sea* ['63], *Men of Iron* ['58], *The Mill on the Floss* ['58], *Milton* ['60], *Monsieur Beaucaire* ['58], *The Moonstone* ['63], *Mutiny on the Bounty* ['58], *My Antonia* ['57], *My Friend Flicka* ['59], *My Name Is Aram* ['60], *A Nation of Sheep* ['63], *The Night They Burned the Mountain* ['63], *Northwest Passage* ['60], *O Pioneers!* ['60], *The Old Man and the Sea* ['58], *Old Yeller* ['63], *On the Beach* ['63], *The Oregon Trail* ['57], *Our Town* ['53], *The Ox Bow Incident* ['60], *Paradise Lost* ['53], *The Pathfinder* ['63], *The Pearl* ['62], *The Pearl Lagoon* ['58], *Penrod* ['60], *The Perfect Tribute* ['59], *The Pilgrim's Progress* ['53], *Pitcairn's Island* ['63], *Point of No Return* ['63], *Pride and Prejudice* ['58], *The Prince and the Pauper* ['57], *The Prisoner of Chillon* ['60], *Profiles in Courage* ['63], *Pygmalion* ['62], *Quentin Durward* ['58], *Quo Vadis* ['62], *Ramona* ['58], *Random Harvest* ['63], *The Red Badge of Courage* ['53], *The Red Pony* ['61], *Richard Carvel* ['63], *Rip Van Winkle* ['59], *The Robe* ['60], *Robinson Crusoe* ['53], *Saratoga Trunk* ['60], *Scaramouche* ['62], *School for Scandal* ['61], *Sea Wolf* ['59], *The Secret Garden* ['63], *A Separate Peace* ['61], *Seventeen* ['59], *Show Boat* ['60], *A Single Pebble* ['63], *Sink the Bismarck* ['63], *The Story of My Life* ['62], *Swiss Family Robinson* ['63], *Tales From Shakespeare* ['60], *Tess of the D'Urbervilles* ['58], *The Three Musketeers* ['63], *To Have and to Hold* ['58], *To Kill a Mockingbird* ['61], *Tom Sawyer* ['53], *The Turn of the Screw* ['63], *Twice Told Tales* ['63], *Two Years Before the Mast* ['62], *Uncle Tom's Cabin* ['59], *The Unknown Lincoln* ['57], *Up From Slavery* ['60], *Vanity Fair* ['53], *Victory* ['62], *The Virginian* ['57], *The Voice of Bugle Ann* ['63], *The Wall* ['63], *Washington Square* ['63], *The Way West* ['57], *Witness* ['63], *Wuthering Heights* ['57], *Yankee From Olympus* ['63], *You Can't Go Home Again* ['63]; no manual; no data on reliability; no norms; 1–4 copies of any one test, 15¢ each; 5 or more copies, 10¢ each; $14.95 per complete set; cash orders postpaid; [25–30] minutes per test; Joseph Bamberger (5 tests), F. S. Belcher, Jr. (25 tests), Frances Chastain (4 tests), M. Dorothy (27 tests), Nellie F. Falk (47 tests), Eugene W. Graham (4 tests), Robert J. Jones (31 tests), Carl H. Larson (20 tests), Margaret Leeney (1 test), Donald Racky, Jr. (24 tests), and Robert Ruby (5 tests); Perfection Form Co.*

[296]

★Catholic Book Tests. Grades 7–10, 10–12, 1954; 2 levels; at each level, 2 series of 30 tests (1 page) on specific Catholic literary works; directions (2 sheets); no data on reliability; no norms; $1.25 per series, postage extra; (3–5) minutes per test; teachers and librarians of the U.S. Province Brothers of Holy Cross; Bruce Publishing Co.*

a) FIRST SERIES. Grades 10–12; 30 tests: *And Spare Me Not in the Making, The Art of Courageous Living, Burnt Out Incense, The Deer Cry, Fire in the Rain, God Goes to Murderer's Row, God's Underground, The Great Mantle, I Had to Know, Karen, Late Have I Loved Thee, A Life of Mary, Co-Redemptrix, The Mark, Miracle at Carville, More Murder in a Nunnery, Murder at St. Dennis, Mystic in Motley, And Nora Said "Yes," Nun in Red China, Our Lady of Light, Our Lady's Fool, Pacific Hopscotch, St. Angela of the Ursulines, Saints Westward, Shepherd's Tartan, The Story of Therese Neumann, Tar Heel Apostle, Tomorrow's Memories, Where There Is Love, Yankee Priest.*

b) SECOND SERIES. Grades 10–12; 30 tests: *At the End of the Santa Fe Trail, Brother Andre of Mount Royal, Brother Petroc's Return, Calvary in China, Cardinal Mindszenty, Chaminade: Apostle of Mary, The Chosen, Color Ebony, Damien the Leper, The Early Days of Maryknoll, Father Paul of Graymoor, Gates of Dannemora, Giant in the Wilderness, The Happiness of Father Happé, The House on Humility Street, The Mass of Brother Michel, The Mouse Hunter, My Hay Ain't In, My Russian Yesterdays, The Next Thing, The Quiet Light, Reproachfully Yours, The Road to Damascus, St. John Baptist de La Salle, Six O'Clock Mass, Springs of Silence, Star Inn, The Stranger, Tumbleweed, The Vatican.*

c) THIRD SERIES. Grades 7–10; 30 tests: *Accent on Laughter, The Boy Jesus, Captain Johnny Ford, City on a Mountain, Dark Was the Wilderness, The Glowing Lily, The Good Bad Boy, Larger Than the Sky, Louis Braille, The Man Who Sold Christmas, Mangled Hands, The Maryknoll Story, Mississippi Blackrobe, Nothing Ever Happens to Me!, Pattern for Tomorrow, The Pirate's Prisoner, Polish Folk Tales, Queen of Heaven, The Red Flame of Sound, Roman Collar Detective, Royal Banners Fly, Running Waters, Saint Maria Goretti, Save Us a Seat, Timmy, A Shepherd and a King, Strong Men South, That Boy!, These Two Hands, Three Cheers for Tomorrow, Tom Playfair.*

d) FOURTH SERIES. Grades 7–10: 30 tests; *The Adventures of Ramon of Bolivia, Arrows of Iron, Blood on the Mountain, Children of Fatima, The Children of La Salette, Eskimo Parish, Flying Priest Over the Arctic, God and the General's Daughter, Hero of the Hills, Little Queen, Man of Molokai, Master of Mischief Makers, The Medal, Mickey O'Brien, Ned Haskins, Nicholas the Boy King, The Oldest Story, The Parish Priest of Ars, Patrick O'Neal: Dona Maria, Paul of St. Peter's, Pennies for Pauline, Plot at Nicaragua, Pope Pius XII, Quest of Don Bosco, Scott and His Men, Sketch Me, Berta Hummel!, Spirit of Joques Prep, The Story of Mary, The Mother of Jesus, The Yang Brothers, A Year to Grow.*

[297]

***Davis-Roahen-Schrammel American Literature Test.** High school and college; 1938–58: Forms A Revised ('58), B ('39), (4 pages); manual ('38, 4 pages); Form A Revised norms ['58]; no data on reliability of Form A Revised; $1.20 per 25 tests, postage extra; 25¢ per specimen set, postpaid; 60(65) minutes; V. A. Davis, R. L. Roahen, and H. E. Schrammel; Bureau of Educational Measurements. *

For reviews by Paul B. Diederich and Violet Hughes, see 40:1300.

[298]

***English Literature: Every Pupil Test.** High school; 1934–64; new form (4 pages) usually issued each April; forms from previous testing programs also available; general directions sheet ('63, 2 pages); no data on reliability; Ohio norms for new forms available following testing program; 5¢ per test; 3¢ per key; postpaid; 40(45) minutes; Ohio Scholarship Tests. *

[299]

***The Graduate Record Examinations Advanced Tests: Literature.** Grades 16–17; 1939–63; for more complete information, see 762; 180(200) minutes; Educational Testing Service. *

For a review by Robert C. Pooley of an earlier form, see 5:215. For a review of the testing program, see 5:601.

[300]

***The Iowa Tests of Educational Development: Test 7, Ability to Interpret Literary Materials.** Grades 9–12; 1942–61; IBM; Forms X-3S, Y-3S, ('52, 7 pages); battery examiner's manual ('58, c1949–57, 23 pages); battery general manual ('59, 37 pages); student profile leaflet, sixth edition ('61, c1958, 2 pages); see the complete battery entry (14*b*) for other accessories; no data on reliability; separate answer sheets must be used; $2.40 per 20 tests; $5 per 100 IBM answer sheets; 50¢ per scoring stencil; $3 per specimen set of the complete battery; postage extra; 50(60) minutes for full length version, 40(50) minutes for class period version; prepared under the direction of E. F. Lindquist; Science Research Associates, Inc. *

REFERENCES

1. TRELA, THADDEUS MICHAEL. *A Comparison of Ninth Grade Achievement on Selected Measures of General Reading Comprehension, Critical Thinking, and General Educational Development.* Doctor's thesis, University of Missouri (Columbia, Mo.), 1962. (*DA* 23:2382)

For reviews of the complete battery, see 5:17; for reviews of earlier forms, see 4:17 and 3:12.

[301]

***Literature: Every Pupil Scholarship Test.** Grades 7–8, 9–12; 1928–64; some test booklet titles for grades 7–8 are *Elementary Literature;* new form (4 pages) usually issued each January and April; forms from previous testing programs also available; 2 levels; general directions sheet ['63, 2 pages]; no data on reliability; norms for new forms available following testing program; 4¢ per test; 4¢ per key; postage extra; 40(45) minutes; Bureau of Educational Measurements. *

[302]

★Objective Tests in American Anthology. High school; 1959–61; 1 form; 6 tests: 5 tests ('59, 4 pages) on specific periods and a final examination ('61, 6 pages); no manual; no data on reliability; no norms; 5 or more tests with answer sheet, 10¢ each; 15¢ per key (free with 24 or more copies of any one test); $1.55 per specimen set; cash orders postpaid; [60] minutes per test; Carl H. Larson; Perfection Form Co. *

[303]

★Objective Tests in English Anthology. High school; 1959; 1 form; 8 tests: 7 tests (4 pages) on specific periods and a final examination (6 pages); no manual; no data on reliability; no norms; 5 or more tests with answer sheet, 10¢ each; 15¢ per key (free with 24 or more copies of any one test); $2.15 per specimen set; cash orders postpaid; [60] minutes per test; Carl H. Larson; Perfection Form Co. *

[304]

***Objective Tests in English.** High school; 1929–63; 1 form (except where otherwise indicated); 102 tests (4 pages unless otherwise indicated) on specific books: *Abe Lincoln Grows Up* ('61), *Anthony and Cleopatra* ('52), *Arrowsmith* ('55), *As You Like It* ('47), *Bleak House* ('63), *The Bridge of San Luis Rey* ('63), *The Call of the Wild* ('57), *A Christmas Carol* ('56), *Cimarron* ('57), *Come Rack! Come Rope!* ('54), *A Connecticut Yankee in King Arthur's Court* ('54), *Crime and Punishment* ('60, 5 pages), *The Crisis* ('54), *David Copperfield* ('31–48), *Death Comes for the Archbishop* ('54), *Doctor Zhivago* ['61], *Dombey and Son* ('63), *Don Quixote* ('54), *Enoch Arden* ('47–57), *Ethan Frome* ('55), *Evangeline* ('29–57), *Giants in the Earth* ('54), *Gods, Heroes and Men of Ancient Greece* ('63), *Great Expectations* ('53), *The Great Gatsby* ('63), *Hamlet* ('31–48), *Henry IV* ('63, in 2 parts), *Henry V* ('31), *The House of Seven Gables* ('47–56), *Huckleberry Finn* ('50), *The Human Comedy* ('56, 3 pages), *The Idylls of the King* ('29–47), *Ivanhoe* ('48), *Jane Eyre* ('54), *Johnny Tremain* ('50), *Julius Caesar* (2 forms: '48, '57), *Kenilworth* ('32), *Kidnapped* ('48), *Kim* ('57), *King Lear* ('29), *King Richard II* ('63), *King Richard III* ('63), *The Lady of the Lake* ('29–48), *The Last of the Mohicans* ('56), *Les Miserables* ('63), *Little Dorrit* ('63), *Lorna Doone* ('52), *Lost Endeavor* ('56), *Macbeth* (2 forms: '48, '57), *The Man Without a Country* ('32), *Martin Chuzzlewit* ('63), *The Merchant of Venice* ('29–49), *A Midsummer Night's Dream* ('31–48), *The Mill on the Floss* ('56), *Moby Dick* ('49), *Much Ado About Nothing* ('60), *Nicholas Nickleby* ('63), *The Odyssey* ('55), *Of Human Bondage* ('59), *The Old Curiosity Shop* ('63), *The Old Man and the Sea* ('63), *Oliver Twist* ('50), *Othello* ('29, 3 pages), *Our Town* ('56, 3 pages), *Pickwick Papers* ('60), *Prester John* ('55), *Pride and Prejudice* ('54), *The Red Badge of Courage* ('56), *The Return of the Native* ('51), *The Rime of the Ancient Mariner* (2 forms: '47, 3 pages; '63), *The Rise of Silas Lapham* ('52), *Romeo and Juliet* ('29–49), *Ruggles of Red Gap* ('57), *The Scarlet Letter* ('32), *The Scarlet Pimpernel* ('54), *Shadows on the Rock* ('54, 3 pages), *She Stoops to Conquer* ('49), *Silas Marner* (2 forms: '48, 3 pages; '57), *Sir Roger de Coverlay Papers* ('31), *The Sketch Book* ('37), *Snow-Bound* ('31–48), *So Big* ('57), *Sohrab and Rustum* ('29–57), *The Spy* ('31), *A Tale of Two Cities* (2 forms: '48, '57), *The Talisman* ('54), *The Taming of the Shrew* ('59), *The Tempest* ('48), *The Thread That Runs So True* ('63), *To Have and to Hold* ('57), *Treasure Island* ('47), *The Turmoil* ('56), *Twelfth Night* ('50), *Twenty Thousand Leagues Under the Sea* ('56), *The Vicar of Wakefield* ('47), *The Virginian* ('54), *The Vision of Sir Launfal* ('48), *War and Peace* ('63), *The White Company* ('60), *White Fang* ('58),

Wuthering Heights ('56), *The Yearling* ('50); no manual; no data on reliability; no norms; 1-4 copies of any one test with key, 30¢ each; 5 or more copies, 10¢ each; 15¢ per key (free with 24 or more copies of any one test); $19.95 per complete set; cash orders postpaid; (20-40) minutes per test; F. S. Belcher, Jr. (25 tests), Frances Chastain (6 tests), Alpha Hobbs Darlington (7 tests), Sarah E. Dorn (3 tests), M. Dorothy (2 tests), Nellie F. Falk (26 tests), Robert J. Jones (2 tests), Alta H. Kibler (1 test), Carl H. Larson (1 test), Margaret Leeney (1 test), Dorothy A. Mason (1 test), Claude E. Stephenson (4 tests), Garland Miller Taylor (15 tests), M. Teresa (5 tests), Augusta Kibler Turpin (2 tests), Hannah Van Nostrand (1 test), Paul E. White (1 test), Maye Alexander Wilson (2 tests), and LaDuskie Wood (2 tests); Perfection Form Co. *

[305]

★Outside Reading Tests for Freshmen and Sophomores. Grades 9-10; 1956; volume of short tests on 500 specific books; 1 form (165 pages); key booklet (19 pages); no data on reliability; no norms; $2.50 per set of test book and key booklet (tests may be reproduced without permission), cash orders postpaid; [10] minutes per test; Christobel M. Cordell; J. Weston Walch, Publisher. *

[306]

★Outside Reading Tests for Juniors and Seniors, Third Edition. Grades 11-12; 1950-63; volume of short tests on 600 specific books; 1 form ('63, c1958-63, 228 pages); key booklet ('63, c1958-63, 35 pages); no data on reliability; no norms; $3 per set of test book and key booklet (tests may be reproduced without permission), cash orders postpaid; [10] minutes per test; Christobel M. Cordell; J. Weston Walch, Publisher. *

[307]

★Outside Reading Tests for Junior High Schools. Grades 7-9; 1959; volume of short tests on 350 specific books; 1 form (164 pages); key booklet ['59, 29 pages]; no data on reliability; no norms; $2.50 per set of test book and key booklet (tests may be reproduced without permission), cash orders postpaid; [10] minutes per test; Christobel M. Cordell; J. Weston Walch, Publisher. *

[Other Tests]

For tests not listed above, see the following entries in *Tests in Print:* 487, 495-6, 501, 505, 507, 509, 512-3, 515, 517-9, and 521; out of print: 485, 488, 490, 492-3, and 520.

SPEECH

[307a]

★The Arizona Articulation Proficiency Scale. Mental ages 2-14; 1963; individual; 1 form (67 cards); may also be administered as a short form using only 44 cards; manual (11 pages plus sample copies of record booklet and survey test form); record booklet (4 pages); survey test form (1 page); no data on reliability; no description of normative population; $20 per set of cards, 25 record booklets, 25 survey test forms, and manual; $6.50 per 25 record booklets; $3.50 per 25 survey test forms; $3.50 per manual; postpaid; [20-30] minutes; Janet Barker; Western Psychological Services. *

REFERENCES

1. Barker, Janet O. "A Numerical Measure of Articulation." *J Speech & Hearing Disorders* 25:79-88 F '60. (*PA* 35:264)
2. Barker, Janet, and England, Gene. "A Numerical Measure of Articulation: Further Developments." *J Speech & Hearing Disorders* 27:23-7 F '62. * (*PA* 36:5GH23B)

[308]

★Forms From Diagnostic Methods in Speech Pathology. Children and adults with speech problems; 1952-63; 20 forms consisting of coordination forms, rating scales, attitude surveys, and biographical questionnaires (1-6 pages, each reprinted separately from *1* below); manual (see *1* below); no data on reliability; 5¢ per copy of Forms 1-2, 9-14, 17-20; 8¢ per copy of Forms 3-4, 6-8, 16; 10¢ per copy of Forms 5, 15; $7.50 per manual (available from publisher, Harper & Row, Publishers, Inc.); postage extra; Wendell Johnson, Frederic L. Darley, and D. C. Spriestersbach; Interstate Printers and Publishers, Inc. *

a) FORM 1, CHART OF SIGNIFICANT VARIATIONS IN SEVERITY OF THE STUTTERING PROBLEM SINCE ONSET.
b) FORM 2, GENERAL SPEECH BEHAVIOR RATING.
c) FORM 3, ARTICULATION TEST. Special printing of combined record and analysis sheets of *Templin-Darley Screening and Diagnostic Tests of Articulation.*
d) FORM 4, SPEECH MECHANISM EXAMINATION.
e) FORM 5, GENERAL VOICE QUALITY EXAMINATION.
f) FORM 6, SUPPLEMENTARY EXAMINATION FOR BREATHINESS.
g) FORM 7, SUPPLEMENTARY EXAMINATION FOR HARSHNESS.
h) FORM 8, SUPPLEMENTARY EXAMINATION FOR NASALITY.
i) FORM 9, MEASURES OF SPEECH AND LANGUAGE DEVELOPMENT.
j) FORM 10, MEASURES OF RATE OF SPEAKING AND ORAL READING.
k) FORM 11, MEASURES OF DISFLUENCY OF SPEAKING AND ORAL READING.
l) FORM 12, SPEAKING-TIME LOG.
m) FORM 13, CHECK LIST OF STUTTERING REACTIONS.
n) FORM 14, SCALE FOR RATING SEVERITY OF STUTTERING.
o) FORM 15, IOWA SCALE OF ATTITUDE TOWARD STUTTERING.
p) FORM 16, STUTTERER'S SELF-RATINGS OF REACTIONS TO SPEECH SITUATIONS.
q) FORM 17, MEASURES OF ADAPTATION OF STUTTERING AND ORAL READING RATE.
r) FORM 18, MEASURES OF STUTTERING CONSISTENCY.
s) FORM 19, IOWA UNIMANUAL HAND USAGE QUESTIONNAIRE.
t) FORM 20, IOWA PERFORMANCE TEST OF SELECTED MANUAL ACTIVITIES.

REFERENCES

1. Johnson, Wendell; Darley, Frederic L.; and Spriestersbach, D. C. *Diagnostic Methods in Speech Pathology.* New York: Harper & Row, Publishers, Inc., 1963. Pp. xvii, 347. *

For excerpts from reviews of the manual, see B281.

[309]

The Graduate Record Examinations Advanced Tests: Speech. Grades 16-17; 1953; available only in the Institutional Testing Program; for more complete information, see 762; 180(200) minutes; Educational Testing Service. *

REFERENCES

1. CROCKER, LIONEL. "The Graduate Record Examination and the Small College." *Speech Teach* 8:246–50 S '59. *

For a review of the testing program, see 5:601.

[310]

★The Houston Test for Language Development. Ages 6 months to 3 years, 3–6 years; 1958–63; individual; 1 form; 2 levels; $20 per complete kit of both levels; postpaid; (30) minutes; Margaret Crabtree; Houston Test Co. *

a) [PART 1.] Ages 6 months to 3 years; 1958; mimeographed manual ('58, 26 pages); scoring sheet ['58, 2 pages]; $7.50 per examiner's kit of manual, set of 20 vocabulary cards, and 25 scoring sheets; $3.50 per manual.

b) PART 2. Ages 3–6; 1963; manual ('63, 38 pages); record form ('63, 4 pages); no data on reliability; $15 per examiner's kit of manual, set of 38 vocabulary cards (20 of which are the same as those used with part 1), set of test objects, and 20 record forms; $3 per manual.

REFERENCES

1. CRABTREE, MARGARET COOPER. *The Construction and Trial Study of a Language Development Test for Children Up to Three Years of Age.* Doctor's thesis, University of Houston (Houston, Tex.), 1957. (*DA* 17:1713)

[311]

★An Integrated Articulation Test for Use With Children With Cerebral Palsy. Ages 3–16; 1961; individual; orally administered; 2 forms; manual (24 pages, including copies of 5 record sheets for each form); 50¢ per manual, postpaid; [75–100] minutes in 2 sessions; Orvis C. Irwin; Cerebral Palsy Review. *

REFERENCES

1. IRWIN, ORVIS C. "A Short Test for Use With Cerebral Palsy Children." *J Speech & Hearing Disorders* 21:446–9 S '56. * (*PA* 31:5028)
2. IRWIN, ORVIS C. "A Second Short Test for Use With Children Who Have Cerebral Palsy." *Cerebral Palsy R* 18:18–9 Jl–Ag '57. * (*PA* 33:1990)
3. IRWIN, ORVIS C. "Validation of Short Consonant Articulation Tests for Use With Children Who Have Cerebral Palsy." *Cerebral Palsy R* 18:12 Mr–Ap '57. * (*PA* 32:5806)
4. IRWIN, ORVIS C. "A Fourth Short Consonant Test for Use With Children With Cerebral Palsy." *Cerebral Palsy R* 19:12–4 Mr–Ap '58. * (*PA* 33:8881)
5. IRWIN, ORVIS C. "A Third Short Consonant Test for Use With Children With Cerebral Palsy." *Cerebral Palsy R* 19:8–10 Ja–F '58. * (*PA* 33:6597)
6. IRWIN, ORVIS C. "A Short Vowel Test for Use With Children With Cerebral Palsy." *Cerebral Palsy R* 21:3–4 Jl–Ag '60. * (*PA* 35:2516)
7. IRWIN, ORVIS C. "A Manual of Articulation Testing for Use With Children With Cerebral Palsy." *Cerebral Palsy R* 22:1–24 My–Je '61. * (*PA* 36:2JH01I)
8. IRWIN, ORVIS C. "Verification of Results Obtained With an Integrated Articulation Test for Use With Children With Cerebral Palsy." *Cerebral Palsy R* 22:8–13 S–O '61. * (*PA* 36:4JH08I)
9. IRWIN, ORVIS C. "The Applicability of an Articulation Test With Mentally Retarded Children." *Cerebral Palsy R* 24:3–8 Ja–F '63. * (*PA* 37:8158)

[312]

★Language Modalities Test for Aphasia. Adults; 1961; individual; Forms 1, 2, (26 pages); manual (91 pages); instruction manual (15 pages, reprinted from manual); record booklet (21 pages) for each form; medical history-scoring summary (4 pages); $35 per examiner's kit of 20 response booklets, 10 record booklets for each form, filmstrip for each form, 20 medical history-scoring summary forms, manual, and 4 instruction manuals; $3 per 10 response booklets; $4 per 10 record booklets; $7 per filmstrip; $3.50 per 10 medical history-scoring summary forms; $3 per manual; $1 per 4 instruction manuals; postage extra; 35 mm. filmstrip viewer or projector necessary for administration; a filmstrip viewer (DuKane Corporation Model 576-48A) may also be purchased through the publisher: $74.50 plus postage; (60–90) minutes in 1–3 sessions; Joseph M. Wepman and Lyle V. Jones; Education-Industry Service. *

REFERENCES

1. JONES, LYLE V., AND WEPMAN, JOSEPH M. "Dimensions of Language Performance in Aphasia." *J Speech & Hearing Res* 4:220–32 S '61. * (*PA* 36:2JE20J) Comments by Hildred Schuell and James J. Jenkins. 4:295–9 S '61. *

T. R. MILES, *Professor of Psychology, University College of North Wales, Bangor, Wales.*

This test is the result of collaboration between a psychometric laboratory and a speech and language clinic. Its purpose is to make possible the collection of meaningful information about aphasic patients in a standardised form, with a view to both therapy and research. Both visual and auditory stimuli are used, and the subject is set many varieties of tasks, such as naming pictures, repeating words, copying geometric forms, matching them from a choice of visually presented alternatives, and so on.

A theoretical distinction is drawn between aphasia in the strict sense on the one hand—a failure to comprehend verbal symbols—and agnosia and apraxia on the other. Aphasia is regarded as a disorder of integration, agnosia and apraxia as disorders of transmission. The former involves failure to match incoming stimuli to existing concepts; the latter two involve failure of the motor or "output" processes. In earlier work, according to the authors, this distinction is not made as clear as it should have been.

The authors, in the reviewer's opinion, have done an excellent job. Their theoretical approach seems promising and is backed by careful and well documented evidence; the test items are well chosen, and the instructions are clearly set out. In addition they have shown how effective inter-disciplinary collaboration can sometimes be; indeed it is one of the interesting things about the study of aphasia that a large number of different disciplines can all contribute to our understanding of it.

There are a few minor points of criticism. The statement in the manual that "Unimpaired children about ten years of age are known to be able to respond to every item without difficulty" is put forward without supporting evidence; and in the section on research findings it is somewhat tantalising to be given the conclusions and even the level of statistical significance without being given the statistics! Also, since the authors' classification of aphasias includes "semantic" and "syntactical," which are terms also used in Head's somewhat different classification, some comparison between the authors' views and those of Head would perhaps have been interesting. Finally, there may be potential users for whom expense is a highly relevant consideration. It is not entirely clear what is gained by the use of filmstrip in place of printed cards for the presentation of visual material, and one must point out that the subjects' response booklet, though admittedly inexpensive, consists for the most part of almost blank sheets! Possibly the publishers could consider putting a cheaper version of the test on the market.

These, however, are only minor criticisms; the whole publication is an important addition to the literature on aphasia, of interest not only to psychologists working in the clinical field but also to those who are concerned with more theoretical issues.

[313]

★Nationwide Speech Examination. Grades 4–12; 1959–63; new form issued each April; norms available following the testing program; 1 form ('63, 2 pages); no manual; mimeographed norms ('63, 1 page); no data on reliability; 10¢ per test, postage extra; (40–45) minutes; [Donald R. Honz]; Educational Stimuli. *

[313a]

★The Orzeck Aphasia Evaluation. Mental and brain damaged patients; 1964; individual; 1 form; manual (9 pages plus sample copy of record booklet); record booklet (4 pages); no data on reliability and validity; no norms; $8 per set of 25 record booklets and manual; $6.50 per 25 record booklets; $2 per manual; postpaid; (30–40) minutes; Arthur Z. Orzeck; Western Psychological Services. *

[314]

★Speech Articulation Test for Young Children (Revised Edition). Ages 3.5–8.5; 1955; individual; 1 form; manual (30 pages, including test materials and record form); no data on reliability; $1.10 per manual, postage extra; [30] minutes; Merlin J. Mecham; [University Press, Brigham Young University]. *

[315]

★Templin-Darley Screening and Diagnostic Tests of Articulation. Ages 3–8; 1960; individual; 1 form (4 pages); 2 tests: screening test, total diagnostic test; manual (157 pages); no data on reliability of diagnostic test; $1.50 per manual including test materials; 75¢ per 25 record forms; postage extra; $1.70 per specimen set, postpaid; [10–20] minutes for screening test, [30–60] minutes for total diagnostic test; Mildred C. Templin and Frederic L. Darley; Bureau of Educational Research and Service. *

REFERENCES

1. TEMPLIN, MILDRED C. "A Non-Diagnostic Articulation Test." *J Speech Disorders* 12:392–6 D '47. * (*PA* 22:4206)
2. TEMPLIN, MILDRED C. "Spontaneous Versus Imitated Verbalization in Testing Articulation in Preschool Children." *J Speech Disorders* 12:293–300 S '47. *
3. TEMPLIN, MILDRED C. "Norms on a Screening Test of Articulation for Ages Three Through Eight." *J Speech & Hearing Disorders* 18:323–31 D '53. * (*PA* 28:6284)
4. SPRIESTERSBACH, DUANE C.; DARLEY, FREDERIC L.; AND ROUSE, VERNA. "Articulation of a Group of Children With Cleft Lips and Palates." *J Speech & Hearing Disorders* 21:436–45 S '56. * (*PA* 31:4910)
5. TEMPLIN, MILDRED C. *Certain Language Skills in Children.* University of Minnesota, Institute of Child Welfare Monograph Series, No. 26. Minneapolis, Minn.: University of Minnesota Press, 1957. Pp. xviii, 183. * (*PA* 31:7556)
6. JORDAN, EVAN P. "Articulation Test Measures and Listener Ratings of Articulation Defectiveness." *J Speech & Hearing Res* 3:303–19 D '60. * (*PA* 35:2534)
7. MORRIS, HUGHLETT L.; SPRIESTERSBACH, D. C.; AND DARLEY, FREDERIC L. "An Articulation Test for Assessing Competency of Velopharyngeal Closure." *J Speech & Hearing Res* 4:48–55 Mr '61. * (*PA* 35:6795)
8. SIEGEL, GERALD M. "Experienced and Inexperienced Articulation Examiners." *J Speech & Hearing Disorders* 27:28–35 F '62. * (*PA* 36:5GH28S)
9. BETTS, CARL EUGENE. *Communication Skills of Mentally Retarded Children Aged 7, 9, and 11.* Doctor's thesis, State University of Iowa (Iowa City, Iowa), 1963. (*DA* 24:888)

J Speech & Hearing Disorders 28:97–8 F '63. Harry Hollien. * Happily, the authors have been very precise and thorough in developing these tests; regrettably, such thoroughness is often lacking for test construction in the area of speech pathology and audiology. Moreover, they have demonstrated not only the ability to carry out the basic research necessary for the development of a sound test, but also the ability to keep clearly in mind the very real needs of the speech clinician and client while doing so. In addition, the clear, precise presentation of both the research results and administration procedures allows the user to gather the necessary information concerning articulation skills while remaining cognizant of the interrelationships of clients' performance with the provided normative data. The Templin-Darley manual provides the clinician with a complete articulation testing kit which consists of (1) a diagnostic test of articulation with associated descriptions, (2) similar materials for a shorter screening test of articulation, (3) sentences for testing older subjects, (4) a set of 57 black and white test cards to stimulate spontaneous speech of young children, and (5) a copy of the test form. All materials, except the test forms, are bound into a single volume of modest size. * The speech clinician may encounter some difficulty with client fatigue when the diagnostic test is administered. The number of items (176) included would seem excessive and might lead to this problem especially when the test is given to young children. * this difficulty may be circumvented....by administering parts of the test at successive meetings. * The

Templin-Darley screening test of articulation consists of 50 items which are drawn from the larger diagnostic test. * Included in the manual are a set of 57 cards containing 176 black and white drawings. These cards are arranged in such a way that the first 16 constitute the 50-item screening test and the total set, the diagnostic test. * the 176 drawings are not among the strong features of these tests. The quality of the drawings is somewhat uneven—some are small, others ambiguous, and yet others suffer from lack of skill of the artist. On the other hand, they present reasonably and simply the appropriate stimuli and, with the assistance of the starter phrases, it should be easy to elicit the desired responses. Having the picture articulation cards bound into the manual would seem to be a real advantage in the testing situation and clinicians report that this feature allows smooth test administration. * designed basically to test those individuals who exhibit inadequate articulation of speech sounds as a primary problem. Undoubtedly, the tests also can be used to assess the articulation of individuals whose speech problem is secondary, such as those with cleft palate or cerebral palsy. Better yet, the Templin-Darley tests could be used as the basic tool supplemented by special articulation tests, such as O. C. Irwin's articulation test for children with cerebral palsy. In any event, the Templin-Darley tests are a very welcome addition to the available tools in speech pathology. * they should be included among every speech clinician's materials.

Speech Teach 11:175 Mr '62. Al Knox. * This test requires skill in speech science, phonetics, and speech pathology, and sophistication in testing. It should not be attempted by anyone other than a qualified speech pathologist. The manual....should be studied by every student of speech pathology.

[316]

★Verbal Language Development Scale. Birth to age 15; 1958–59; extension of the communication section of *Vineland Social Maturity Scale* (see 5:120); behavior checklist for use in interviewing adult informants; 1 form ('59, 4 pages); manual ('58, 10 pages); no data on reliability; $1.30 per 25 score sheets; 50¢ per manual; postage extra; 55¢ per specimen set, postpaid; [30] minutes; Merlin J. Mecham; Educational Test Bureau. *

REFERENCES

1. MECHAM, MERLIN J. "The Development and Application of Procedures for Measuring Speech Improvement in Mentally Defective Children." *Am J Mental Def* 60:301–6 O '55. * (*PA* 30:6096)

2. MECHAM, MERLIN J. "A Scale for Screening Level of Verbal Communication Behavior in Cerebral Palsy." *Cerebral Palsy R* 18:22–3 Jl–Ag '57. * (*PA* 33:1994)

3. WILLIAMS, W. G. *An Appraisal of the Adequacy and Usefulness of an Objective Language Scale When Administered to Elementary School Children.* Master's thesis, Brigham Young University (Provo, Utah), 1958.

4. BARNARD, L. W. *The Validation of a Scale for Measuring Level of Verbal Communication Behavior in Children.* Master's thesis, Brigham Young University (Provo, Utah), 1959.

5. MECHAM, MERLIN J. "Measurement of Verbal Language Development in Cerebral Palsy." *Cerebral Palsy R* 21:3–4 My–Je '60. * (*PA* 35:2520)

6. WILLIAMS, WILLIAM G. "The Adequacy and Usefulness of an Objective Language Scale When Administered to Elementary School Children." *J Ed Res* 54:30–3 S '60. *

7. BOWN, JESSE CLINTON, JR., AND MECHAM, MERLIN J. "The Assessment of Verbal Language Development in Deaf Children." *Volta R* 63:228–30 My '61. *

[Other Tests]

For tests not listed above, see the following entries in *Tests in Print:* 526–8 and 530; out of print: 522.

SPELLING

[317]

Ayer Standardized Spelling Test. Grades 9–12; 1950; Forms 1, 2, ('50, 1 page); directions ('50, 4 pages) for each form; no data on reliability; $1 per 40 tests; 25¢ per specimen set; cash orders postpaid; (30) minutes; Fred C. Ayer; Steck Co. *

GUS P. PLESSAS, *Associate Professor of Education, Sacramento State College, Sacramento, California.*

The *Ayer Standardized Spelling Test* is designed to measure general spelling achievement among students in high school. The test includes two comparable forms having 30 test words each.

The procedures for administering the test are simple and easy. Each test word is pronounced, read in a prepared sentence, and pronounced again; thus, the meaning of each word to be spelled is illustrated adequately. The students, in turn, write the spelling words in blanks in the test sentences printed on individual test sheets. Sufficient space is provided in each sentence to allow for writing in the blanks.

Technical sources and procedures for selecting the test words are not stated in the manual, nor is the validity of the test reported. However, in a separately published bulletin,[1] Ayer implies that these words are usually taught in elementary school and are commonly found in the writings of high school students. A careful analysis of these words does indicate that the test has a measure of curricular validity, even though the selection of words is questionable in some respects on the basis of utility. For

[1] AYER, FRED C. *The Evaluation and Measurement of High School Spelling.* Austin, Tex.: Steck Co., 1950. Pp. 6. *

instance, 27 per cent of the words in Form 1 and 43 per cent of the words in Form 2 are not included among the most frequently written words by children and adults in Fitzgerald's *A Basic Life Spelling Vocabulary.*[2]

The standardization of the test is based on scores of 35,000 high school students in 48 states. Unfortunately, however, reliability data are not presented in the manual. Since the spelling test includes only 30 words, reliability information concerning the instrument assumes greater importance, and, undoubtedly, 10 or 20 additional words would insure a higher degree of reliability.

The normative data include the standard scores for each word in terms of per cent correct in grades 9 through 12 in addition to average per cent scores for the total test at each high school grade. Since the test was published in 1950, recent evidence suggests that the standardized scores need revision in order to provide a basis for comparison against current standards. For example, according to the *New Iowa Spelling Scale,* at the eighth grade level, the per cent correct is higher than the per cent indicated in the manual at the ninth grade level in spelling four words in Form 1 and six words in Form 2, or 17 per cent of the total words.

The individual test sheets or summary forms that accompany the test facilitate the comparison of the spelling status of an individual, class, or school with national norms in such a way that above average, average, or below average performances are identified. The test, however, does not adequately satisfy the claims advanced by its author. First, it does not have sufficient level of difficulty to satisfactorily discriminate spelling ability among average or above average groups of high school students, particularly those in the junior or senior year. The mean per cent of correct spelling of the Form 2 words, for instance, is 81 and 85 for grades 11 and 12, respectively, for the average high school. Second, the test does not reveal specific strengths or weaknesses, because it does not have any diagnostic features to determine a student's strong and weak areas in spelling. Third, the test does not point out a specific level—such as a grade level score or percentile rank—at which an individual performs in spelling. Fourth, in no way will the results of this test indicate specific approaches in teaching spelling, since the knowledge of individual errors is not sufficient to reveal detailed weakness other than a general level of high, average, or low spelling performance. At best, this instrument serves as a general measure of spelling ability among high school students, particularly at the freshman level.

2 FITZGERALD, JAMES A. *A Basic Life Spelling Vocabulary.* Milwaukee, Wis.: Bruce Publishing Co., 1951. Pp. 161. *

For a review by Harold H. Bixler, see 4:198.

[318]

*__Gates-Russell Spelling Diagnostic Tests.__ Grades 2–6; 1937–40; 9 scores: spelling words orally, word pronunciation, giving letters for letter sounds, spelling one syllable, spelling two syllables, word reversals, spelling attack, auditory discrimination, visual-auditory-kinaesthetic and combined study methods; individual; 1 form ('37, 4 pages); revised manual ('40, 53 pages); no description of normative population; $2.25 per 35 tests; $1 per specimen set (must be purchased to obtain manual); postpaid; Arthur I. Gates and David H. Russell; Bureau of Publications. *

For a review by George Spache, see 4:200; for reviews by John C. Almack and Thomas G. Foran, see 38:1159.

[319]

★**Group Diagnostic Spelling Test.** Grades 9–13; 1958; Forms A, B, ['58, 3 mimeographed pages]; hectographed manual ['58, 7 pages]; separate answer sheets must be used; 5¢ per test; 1¢ per mimeographed answer sheet; 25¢ per manual; 35¢ per specimen set; postpaid; (20–30) minutes; Thomas G. Kemp; Reading Laboratory and Clinic. *

[320]

*__Lincoln Diagnostic Spelling Tests.__ Grades 2–4 or 2–5, 4–8 or 5–8, 8–12 or 9–12; 1941–62; 2 editions; A. L. Lincoln.

a) [EDUCATIONAL RECORDS BUREAU EDITION.] Grades 2–4 or 2–5, 4–8, 8–12; 1941–62; 3 levels; norms for independent school students only; 8¢ per test, postage extra; Educational Records Bureau. *

1) *Lincoln Primary Spelling Test.* Grades 2–4 in independent schools or 2–5 in public schools; 1960–62; Forms W and X for fall testing, Y and Z for spring testing; response booklet ('60, 4 pages) for all forms; dictation lists (6 pages): Forms W ['61], X ['60], Y ['61], Z ['62]; mimeographed manual ('60, 7 pages); norms (1 page): Forms W ('61), X ('60), Y ('62), Z ('62); no data on reliability; norms for grades 2 and 3 only; [60] minutes.

2) *Lincoln Intermediate Spelling Test.* Grades 4–8; 1941–62; Forms A, B, C, ('49, 4 pages, identical with tests published in 1947 and 1948), D ('49, 4 pages); Forms A and C for fall testing, B and D for spring testing; dictation list (1 page) for each form; combined manual ('51, 10 pages) for this test and 3) below; revised norms (1 page): Forms A ('61), B ('62), C ('60), D ('61); (30–40) minutes.

3) *Lincoln Diagnostic Spelling Test [Advanced].* Grades 8–12; 1941–62; Forms 1 ('49, identical with test copyrighted in 1941), 2 ['42], 3 ['43], 4 ['44], (4 pages); dictation list (1 page) for each form; combined manual ('51, 10 pages) for this test and 2) above; revised fall norms (1 page): Forms 1

('62), 2 ('61), 3 ('59), 4 ('57); revised spring norms (1 page): Forms 1 ('58), 2 ('60), 3 ('62), 4 ('61); (30-40) minutes.

b) [BOBBS-MERRILL COMPANY EDITION.] Grades 5-8, 9-12; 1949-56; Forms A (for fall testing), B (for spring testing); 2 levels; manual ('56, 16 pages); tentative norms; $3.15 per 35 tests; 50¢ per specimen set; postage extra; (30-40) minutes; Bobbs-Merrill Co., Inc. *

1) *Intermediate.* Grades 5-8; Forms A, B, ('56, 4 pages, same as Forms A, B of the *Lincoln Intermediate Spelling Test* published in 1947 and 1948).

2) *Advanced.* Grades 9-12; Forms A, B, ('56, 4 pages, same as Forms 1, 2 of *Lincoln Diagnostic Spelling Test* published in 1941 and 1942).

REFERENCES

1. TOWNSEND, AGATHA. "A Study of the Lincoln Diagnostic Spelling Test." *Ed Rec B* 38:49-53 Je '43. *

2. TOWNSEND, AGATHA. "A Report on the Use of the Lincoln Intermediate Spelling Test." *Ed Rec B* 49:40-8 F '48. * (*PA* 22:3648)

3. LUNTZ, LESTER. "A Comparison of Results Obtained With Dictation and Multiple-Choice Spelling Tests." *Ed Rec B* 65:76-84 F '55. * (*PA* 29:7866)

4. WALDMAN, JOHN, AND TRIGGS, FRANCES ORALIND. "Measurement of Word Attack Skills." *El Engl* 35:450-63 N '58. *

5. TRAXLER, ARTHUR E. "Some Data on the Difficulty, Reliability, and Validity of a New Spelling Test for the Primary Grades." *Ed Rec B* 77:67-73 Jl '60. *

6. VECCHIONE, NICHOLAS. "Sex Differences in Spelling Skills of Independent Secondary School Pupils." *Ed Rec B* 76:65-8 F '60. *

GUS P. PLESSAS, *Associate Professor of Education, Sacramento State College, Sacramento, California.* [Review of the Educational Records Bureau Edition.]

PRIMARY TEST. The *Lincoln Primary Spelling Test* is constructed to include three distinct but overlapping levels of spelling words so that the same test with different words can be used with children of independent schools (in grades 2-4) and those (in grades 3-5) of public schools.

The spelling words, selected from Gates' *A List of Spelling Difficulties in 3876 Words,* total 144, only 72 of which are used in any one testing situation. Since the appropriate words are identified according to grade level, type of school, and time of testing (fall or spring), the starting and stopping points are different for each grade level and for the independent and public schools.

According to the manual, the words are arranged in ascending order of difficulty, covering a grade placement of from 1.1 to 7.1. Included is the median grade placement value of each level of spelling words. Although not stating so explicitly in the manual, the author apparently assigned a grade value to each word on the basis of its average grade placement as reported by Gates. These reported grade placement values can be misleading if they are equated with difficulty levels. For instance, the author advances the notion that the words to be spelled are ranked according to their spelling difficulty. Perhaps the words are in the order of difficulty, but this arrangement cannot be defended solely on the basis of their grade placement, particularly as identified by Gates. In the first place, grade placement of spelling words is determined mainly by their frequency of use, permanent value, and difficulty. In the second place, Gates' work, which began in 1928 and was published in 1937, included the average grade placement of words in various textbooks and courses of study that are now at least 30 years old. As a consequence, for example, Gates' placement of the spelling word *rolled* is 2.55, but according to the *New Iowa Spelling Scale,* only 28 per cent of third grade children can correctly spell it. In contrast, Gates' average grade placement for the word *maybe* is 4.55, but 49 per cent of children in third grade classes can spell this word correctly. Therefore, to say that the words in the test are arranged according to their difficulty is not entirely accurate.

In the manual, the author states, "The Primary Level of the Lincoln Spelling Test series is designed to pinpoint a selected number of strengths and weaknesses in word attack or phonics." Although the test is organized to provide diagnostic information in terms of the pupils' spelling performances, no evidence or validity studies are presented to support the major aim of the test. This point is discussed in more detail in the next section of this review (*Lincoln Intermediate Spelling Test*).

Percentile ratings and grade score equivalents accompany the test. The percentile norms, however, are based on grossly inadequate numbers. Illustrative of the situation is Form X, for which percentile ranks are based on 98 pupils in grade 2 and 92 pupils in grade 3. Furthermore, the percentile scale was extended only to grades 2 and 3. In addition, there is no evidence to indicate the basis upon which the grade score equivalents were determined. It seems that the grade scores were arbitrarily derived by statistical extrapolation.

Satisfactory directions for administering and scoring the test are provided in the manual. The pupils write the spelling words in a specially prepared booklet which has adequate space for writing the words and which is also organized to facilitate correcting.

Perhaps the best use of this spelling test is as a general measure of spelling achievement among children in the primary grades, despite the fact that no data concerning validity and reliability are provided.

INTERMEDIATE TEST. The *Lincoln Intermediate Spelling Test,* for grades 5–8, is designed to measure spelling achievement with particular attention to the evaluation of specific disabilities. It includes four reasonably equivalent forms, each consisting of 100 words arranged generally in ascending order of difficulty as indicated by their average grade placement according to Gates, Betts, and the New York State List, which are the sources of the words.

The words are also arranged so that words representing a common phonetic element or a particular spelling generalization bear a common final digit. Each word can easily be identified by category to facilitate the diagnosis of spelling performances when spelling errors are recorded by categories, which include erroneous pronunciation in terms of number of syllables, the *ie-ei* rule, the *y* to *i* rule, final *e* before a suffix, double consonant, spelling demons, prefixes and suffixes, erroneous pronunciation in terms of quality of syllables, homonyms, and possessives and contractions.

Students write the words in a thoughtfully prepared booklet. Beside each blank is an illustrative sentence with the spelling word omitted so that the students can check the meaning of the word as it is pronounced. Thus, since the examiner does not need to use the words in sentences, the time for testing is reduced to approximately 40 minutes. Most sentences which illustrate the meanings of the words are carefully written.

Despite a reported total score correlation of .90 between performances of seventh graders on the *Lincoln Intermediate Spelling Test* and on the spelling section of the *Stanford Achievement Test,* there is serious question regarding the validity of the diagnostic features and of the part scores. The fact that a student misspells several words that have been classified in the same way does not necessarily indicate a related weakness. For example, in spelling words having affixes a pupil can easily misspell the base word rather than the affix, in which case his problem may be unrelated to the spelling of suffixes. Similarly, what does it mean when a student misspells demons among other misspelled words? Is this a case of general or specific disability? Furthermore, since each category is represented by only 10 words, the usefulness of the diagnostic aspects of the test is sharply limited, especially since the words are listed in ascending order of difficulty and many students will not spell correctly many words at the upper levels of the test. It seems important to stress, therefore, that the diagnosis of spelling disabilities is an individual matter and that the use of this test for such a purpose involves much more than simply categorizing misspelled words; it involves the judicious interpretation of each misspelled word.

Reliabilities for the total test and for the part scores of the intermediate test are reported to have a median coefficient of .93 for the five grades from 4 through 8.

Median and quartile scores and percentile ratings for independent schools accompany the test. Norms for public schools are available only upon request from the publisher.

In short, this test is perhaps best used as a measure of general spelling achievement of students in grades 4 through 8 in independent schools.

ADVANCED TEST. The chief purpose of the *Lincoln Diagnostic Spelling Test* is to evaluate certain areas in the spelling performances of students in grades 8–12. This test purports to examine the effect of pronunciation, enunciation, and use of rules on spelling.

The words in the test are not arranged in order of difficulty, but follow the classification system outlined above for the intermediate test, except that at this level the erroneous pronunciation (quality of syllables) category is replaced by one dealing with Latin endings. The criticism of the lower level is equally applicable to this test. Similarly the method of administration is identical.

Validity and reliability studies are cited in the manual. As evidence for statistical validity, Townsend (*1*) reports a .93 correlation with Mechanics of Expression of the *Cooperative English Test,* Form T, which included a spelling section. Correlation of .85 was found by Spaulding[1] in a comparison of the Lincoln test and the *Progressive Achievement Tests.* This finding perhaps indicates the validity of the test as a measure of spelling achievement; however, its curricular validity as a diagnostic instrument is questionable, particularly in light of some areas purportedly tested in spelling.

1 SPAULDING, GERALDINE. "The Use of the Progressive Achievement Test at the Ninth-Grade Level in Independent Schools." *Ed Rec B* 56:73–7 Ja '51. *

Townsend and Spaulding also reported total score reliability coefficients (Spearman-Brown) of .93 and .89, respectively; however, the Spearman-Brown reliabilities of the part scores were considerably lower. Among 118 independent school pupils in grade 10, Townsend found a range of .47 to .80 with a median of .69.

As a standardized test for national use, this test has normative data in terms of percentile ranks for independent schools, but the number of cases used to standardize the measure is low for certain grades and forms. For example, the standardization of Form 1, fall 1962, involved only 514 students at Grade 8.

In summary, the *Lincoln Diagnostic Spelling Test* is best used as a general measure of spelling performance with some analytical features to assess deficiencies in the use of certain spelling rules among students at the high school level of independent schools.

For reviews by Walter Scribner Guiler and George Spache of the intermediate and advanced tests, see 4:202–3.

[321]

★**Nationwide Spelling Examination.** Grades 4–12; 1959–63; new form issued each April; norms available following the testing program; 1 form ('63, 2 pages); no manual; mimeographed norms ('63, 1 page); no data on reliability; 10¢ per test, postage extra; (40–45) minutes; [Donald R. Honz]; Educational Stimuli. *

[322]

★**The New Iowa Spelling Scale.** Grades 2–8; 1954; master word list with difficulty values by grades from which teacher may compile tests; manual ('54, 180 pages including word list); no data on reliability; 65¢ per manual, postage extra; Harry A. Greene; Bureau of Educational Research and Service. *

REFERENCES

1. GROFF, PATRICK J. "The New Iowa Spelling Scale: How Phonetic Is It?" *El Sch J* 62:46–9 O '61. *

[323]

***Spelling and Vocabulary: Every Pupil Test.** Grades 3–4, 5–6, 7–9, 10–12; 1948–64; new form (4 pages) usually issued each December and April; forms from previous testing programs also available; 4 levels; general directions sheet ('63, 2 pages); no data on reliability; Ohio norms for new forms available following testing program; 5¢ per test; 3¢ per key; postpaid; 40(45) minutes; Ohio Scholarship Tests. *

[324]

★**[Spelling and Word Meaning Tests.]** Business and industry; 1957–62; 1 form ('57, 5 pages); 2 tests in a single booklet; manual ['63, 9 unnumbered pages]; no data on reliability; $3.50 per 25 tests; 10¢ per key; 75¢ per manual; postage extra; $1 per specimen set, postpaid; 10(20) minutes; Richardson, Bellows, Henry & Co., Inc. *

[325]

***Spelling: Every Pupil Scholarship Test.** Grades 3, 4–6, 7–8, 9–12; 1928–64; new form (2 pages) usually issued each January and April; forms from previous testing programs also available; 4 levels; general directions sheet ['63, 2 pages]; no data on reliability; norms for new forms available following testing program; 4¢ per test; 4¢ per key; postage extra; 15(20) minutes for grades 3–8, 30(35) minutes for grades 9–12; Bureau of Educational Measurements. *

[326]

Traxler High School Spelling Test. Grades 9–12; 1937–55; Forms 1, 2, 3, ('55, 2 pages, same as tests published in 1937–40); manual ('55, 4 pages); no data on reliability of Form 3; norms based upon testing in private schools in 1937–40; $2.80 per 35 tests; 50¢ per specimen set; postage extra; administration time not reported; Arthur E. Traxler; Bobbs-Merrill Co., Inc. *

GUS P. PLESSAS, *Associate Professor of Education, Sacramento State College, Sacramento, California.*

Although the purpose is not stated, the *Traxler High School Spelling Test* appears designed to measure general spelling ability among students in grades 9 through 12.

Unlike typical test procedures for presenting words to be spelled by saying the word, using it in a sentence, and repeating it, the procedures for presenting the spelling words in this test are simplified. The test words are pronounced by the examiner and the students write them on the form provided. For each word there is a sentence in which the dictated word is replaced by dots. Illustrative sentences, without the spelling words, are printed beside the appropriate blanks that are at the right side of the page. Consequently, this organization has the favorable result of reducing the testing time and of facilitating the correction of the test.

According to the directions, the illustrative sentences are given to help the student understand the spelling words; however, a careful examination of these sentences suggests that many are inadequate to illustrate satisfactorily the meanings of the words to be spelled. Consider the following examples. In Form 1, *miscellaneous* is illustrated by the sentence "That is a....group," and *sovereign* is represented by "He is the....of the entire nation." Likewise, in Form 2, *occurrence* is illustrated by the sentence "This is a rare....in our city," and *appropriate* is demonstrated by "This is the....page." Obviously, students who are unfamiliar with *miscellaneous, occurrence, sovereign,* and *appropriate* are not particularly aided by these illustrative sentences in trying to infer the meanings of these spelling words.

This spelling test has three 50-word forms, of which Forms 1 and 2 are judged equivalent. The test words in these two forms were selected from the *Buckingham Extension of the Ayers Spelling Scale* and checked against Horn's *A Basic Writing Vocabulary.* Although selected on the same basis, the spelling words in Form 3 are more difficult in order that a higher level of spelling achievement can be measured, particularly among exceptional students. Thus, Form 3 is not comparable to Forms 1 and 2, and it should not be used as an equated form to measure spelling progress.

The test manual reports that no statistical study was conducted to determine the validity of the spelling instrument but states that the test has face validity because the words to be spelled represent a sample of high school students' active spelling vocabulary, since most of the words are found in the more common 5,000 words of the Horn list. However, according to Fitzgerald's list of 2,650 most commonly written words by children and adults, Forms 1, 2, and 3 have 32, 24, and 2 per cents, respectively, of their words among the most common. This finding suggests that there is a higher degree of curricular validity for Forms 1 and 2 than for Form 3 and that many spelling words in Form 3 are questionable on the basis of utility. For example, such spelling words as *hippopotamus, maneuver, chandelier,* and *distillery* are not likely to be part of the "active" writing vocabulary of high school students.

Reliability coefficients are reported above .90 for correlations between scores on Form 1 and scores on Form 2 made by students in one public high school. Unfortunately, however, the number of cases upon which the reliability data were determined seems indeed small and inadequate for a standardized instrument that is for high school use in all states; moreover, no information is given regarding the reliability of Form 3. Similarly, percentile norms are based on scores of less than 500 students for any particular test form at a specific grade with a range from 191 to 471. A typical example is the standardization data of Form 2 at the ninth grade, in which the percentile norms are based on only 388 pupils. This unsatisfactory number has certainly weakened the dependability of the test, especially the norms.

For a review by Henry D. Rinsland, see 4:212.

[Other Tests]

For tests not listed above, see the following entries in *Tests in Print:* 531–2, 534, 538–40, 542, 545, 547, 552, 555–7, and 559; out of print: 535–6, 541, 550, and 554.

VOCABULARY

[327]

***A.C.E.R. Word Knowledge Test—Adult Form B.** Ages 18 and over; 1933–60; Form B ['54, 4 pages, identical with part 1 of *A.C.E.R. Silent Reading Tests,* Form B for grades 3–8 except for directions]; mimeographed manual ('60, 11 pages); 3*s.* 6*d.* per 10 tests; 3*s.* per key; 3*s.* per manual; 6*s.* 6*d.* per specimen set; postpaid within Australia; 8(10) minutes; T. M. Whitford (manual) and the Australian Council for Educational Research; the Council. *

REFERENCES

1. Bucklow, Maxine, and Doughty, Patricia. "The Use of Aptitude Tests in Clerical Employment: The Selection of Accounting Machinists." *Personnel Pract B* 13:35–44 S '57. * (*PA* 33:2256)

For a review by Fred J. Schonell of the reading test, see 5:616.

[328]

★American Literacy Test. Adults; 1962; vocabulary; 1 form (3 pages); manual (2 pages); norms for "university seniors," "technical trade candidates," and "illiterates"; normative groups not otherwise described; $3 per 25 tests; $1 per specimen set of 5 tests (must be purchased to obtain manual); cash orders postpaid; 4(10) minutes; John J. McCarty; Psychometric Affiliates. *

Victor H. Noll, *Professor of Education, Michigan State University, East Lansing, Michigan.*

This test consists of 50 four-response multiple choice vocabulary items which require the subject to select the choice which "means the same or about the same" as the stimulus word. Answers are marked on the test blank, although standard machine scorable answer sheets could be used with a slight modification in directions. The time allowed is four minutes. Test-retest reliability based on 59 subjects, six weeks intervening, is reported as .82. Scores on the test for 43 students in English at Southern Illinois University yielded a correlation of .49 with scores on a test of English fundamentals. A point biserial coefficient contrasting the performance on the test of 263 associate degree candidates with that of 102 senior engineers was found to be .82. Scores of 16 illiterates were all below 10, which is below a chance score for anyone attempting all items. Percentile norms are given for university seniors, technical trade candidates, and illiterates. Since these norms are not otherwise described, one may infer that they are based on the 102 engineers, 263 associate degree candidates, and 16 illiterates mentioned above.

The test purports to be a "highly useful test of literacy," "economical of time, efficient in design and reliability of construction, and well-spiralled or graduated in item difficulty so as to yield reliable spread of respondents according to degree of literacy." It also purports to "bear some reasonable relation to knowledge of the grammar and mechanics of the English language."

The test seems misnamed in the generally accepted use of the term literacy, that is, the ability to read and write. It is not a test of reading (except in the very limited sense that many reading tests contain tests of word knowledge as part of the total) and it is obviously not a test of ability to write. The claim that it is economical of time is substantiated by the fact that it requires only four minutes of working time plus possibly five minutes for instructions. If being printed on a four page folder and having one page left over means "efficient in design" the claim is justified. Since the reviewer does not know what is meant by the latter part of the statement that a highly useful test of literacy should be "efficient in design and *reliability of construction,"* and since no information on this point is given, no judgment as to how well this purpose was achieved can be rendered. No information is provided on the basis for selection of words to be included or on results of item analysis. That items vary in percentage of correct responses between 20 and 92 for 300 adults hardly constitutes an adequate criterion for selection for the final form.

Information on reliability and validity is difficult to interpret because of (*a*) small numbers of subjects involved in most instances, (*b*) lack of information regarding the nature of these subjects, and (*c*) questionable statistical technique.

Lacking information as noted, the test must be regarded as simply a collection of 50 vocabulary items little different from, or better than, what any teacher might put together over a quiet weekend. It appears to have no unusual qualities or superior merit though the implications of the statements by the author and publisher lead one to expect them. Few of the recommendations of the committees on test standards appear to have been met. At 12¢ per copy it seems like no bargain at all.

[329]

★**Bruce Vocabulary Inventory.** Business and industry; 1959; IBM; 1 form (4 pages); manual (4 pages); $5 per 25 tests; 25¢ per hand scoring key; separate answer sheets may be used; $2.75 per 25 IBM answer sheets; 50¢ per set of scoring stencils; 75¢ per manual; $1 per specimen set; cash orders postpaid; (15–25) minutes; Martin M. Bruce; the Author. *

[330]

Durost-Center Word Mastery Test: Evaluation and Adjustment Series. Grades 9–13; 1951–52, c1950–52; 3 scores: vocabulary, vocabulary in context, use of context; IBM; Form AM ('51, 7 pages); manual ('52, 15 pages); separate answer sheets must be used; $4.70 per 35 tests; $1.75 per 35 IBM answer sheets; 40¢ per specimen set; postage extra; 60(80) minutes in 2 sessions 2–7 days apart; Walter N. Durost and Stella S. Center; [Harcourt, Brace & World, Inc.]. *

GEORGE P. WINSHIP, JR., *Professor of English, King College, Bristol, Tennessee.*

The distinctive feature of the *Durost-Center Word Mastery Test* is the score representing the use of context in determining the meaning of a word. The student is examined twice on the same 100 words, once in a conventional multiple response test presenting the basic word alone with four choices, and a second time including a sentence using each word in a meaningful way. If the two parts of the test are administered several days apart, there should be a marked improvement when the words are encountered the second time in context. This improvement is held to be a measure of the student's ability to make use of contextual clues as a means of building his own vocabulary: a score representing the difference is expressed as a percentile rank; separate scores on the two parts may also be expressed as percentile ranks.

No information is given in the manual about the effect of giving the first part of the test (the isolated words) twice to the same students. It would seem that for certain students, at least, there might be a measurable improvement after a week even without context.

In many vocabulary tests employing context, the sentences are by intention sometimes ambiguous; they give no help. The authors of this test have tried to make the sentences meaningful. The range of helpfulness may be indicated by these examples: "The law says we should not molest that which belongs to others. To *molest* means to: (1) desire, (2) copy, (3) harm, (4) alter." Here each of the suggested synonyms fits fairly well in the sentence. The context gives little aid. This is an unusual example; more characteristic is this: "A child resents being scolded for something which he did not do. To *resent* is to: (1) store up, (2) deny, (3) feel angry, (4) admit." Here the context is helpful. Although the third alternative should be "feel angry at," a person totally unfamiliar with the word *resent* can still solve the item by a very careful examination of the context. From the inspection of Form AM, I should judge that no contexts are misleading, that nearly half of them give substantial help (narrowing the choice to about two alternatives), and about half of the contexts give the tested word away entirely. That is, they would do so to a very intelligent student entirely unacquainted with the word. This student is somewhat imaginary. Those who are skilful in determining meanings from context have already learned most of the words, which are well distributed through the first 20,000 words in frequency in the Thorndike-Lorge lists. Those who are unfamiliar with such words obviously lack skills in reading. The most obvious exceptions would be those whose native tongue is not English.

Certainly the skill tested is one of the most important to any student interested in reading more effectively. The Use of Context score would seem to tell the teacher very little she would not already know from other sources. But it might tell the student a good deal. His failures, and particularly his successes, in determining the meaning of a word from its use in a sentence on this test will tell him more about how to read than a great deal of exhortation.

The Durost-Center test seems best adapted to the lower secondary grades or to classes not above average in reading ability. For teachers working with students who lack skill in determining meanings from context, it can be a valuable tool.

For a review by A. N. Hieronymus, see 5:233.

[331]

★Gulick Vocabulary Survey. College and superior high school seniors; 1961, c1954–61; IBM; Forms A1, A2, B1, B2, ('61, c1954–57, 6 pages); manual ('61, c1957–61, 17 pages); student report ('61, c1957–61, 1 page); data card ('61, c1957–61, 1 page); norms for college freshmen only; separate answer sheets must be used; 15¢ per test; 50¢ per set of scoring stencils (available only with 25 or more tests); 3¢ per student report; 3¢ per data card; 50¢ per manual (free with 25 or more tests); postage extra; specimen set free; IBM answer sheets must be purchased elsewhere; (35–40) minutes; Sidney L. Gulick and Darrell Holmes (manual); Chandler Publishing Co. *

REFERENCES

1. GULICK, SIDNEY L., AND HOLMES, DARRELL. "A Vocabulary Tool for the English Teacher." *Col Engl* 19:214–7 F '58. *

GEORGE P. WINSHIP, JR., *Professor of English, King College, Bristol, Tennessee.*

The four forms of the *Gulick Vocabulary Survey* are multiple choice tests of 100 items each. In Forms A1 and A2 the words to be identified appear alone; in Forms B1 and B2 they are given in short phrases of context which sometimes identify the general area of meaning; in other instances they give no information but possibly build confidence in the student. Occasionally the context serves only to confuse: consider *"Intersperse* your answer with examples." This should, of course, have been *"Intersperse* examples in your answer," and if it had been so phrased, an able student could have selected *scatter,* the "correct" answer. As it stands, a student sensitive to English will be drawn toward two wrong answers, *enliven* and *fill up.* "Scatter your answer with examples" is clearly impossible.

This item raises a question of fundamental importance, that of what kind of skill in diction is being examined. To be sure, most of the 400 items offer clear cut choices to students familiar with the words. So do numerous other carefully constructed vocabulary tests now on the market. What is distinctive about this Survey? Each form comprises a random selection from the Thorndike-Lorge list of 30,000 words (omitting the most frequent 10,000); thus each word correctly identified on one of the tests should indicate a probable "knowledge" of 200 words from among the 20,000 most important for a high school or college student to study. Or such is the assumption expressed in the manual and implied on the tests themselves and in the accompanying report form. For example, a raw score of 60 out of the 100 items is said to mean that the student knows 60 times 200 or 12,000 words, in addition to nearly all of the 10,000 commonest words in printed English, or a total of 22,000 words. Such a score would place him at the 80th percentile of college freshmen. A total of 24,000, or about 10 more right answers, is a basis for prediction of success in graduate school. A total vocabulary of 18,000 or less presages grave difficulty in college.

These observations are of great interest and, if true, of great importance to guidance counselors and teachers. The test may be used, of course, for the placement or comparative rating of students whether or not it accurately estimates the size of their total vocabularies. But the total estimate is the special feature of the Gulick Survey. It is for this reason that the author has adhered strictly to a sampling procedure to select his words. Many of these which he has been obliged to use are easy and obvious, even though they fall beyond the first 10,000 of the Thorndike-Lorge list. There seems to be little point in testing the knowledge of tomcat, overgrown, brainless, and snow-white. But since these words have to be in the test, the test writer is impelled to construct reasonably difficult items by searching out obscure synonyms or distractors, and not infrequently the item is as tricky as the casket scene in *The Merchant of Venice*.

Apparently no clear definition exists of a student's "knowledge" of a word. In our schools we define this knowledge as the student's ability to match a word with one of four other words, which may vary widely in their familiarity and their ability to confuse him. He may recognize the word in one context or several but not in the sense selected for the test. To take a simple example, on this test a city boy must show he knows *newt* (and 199 other words) by matching it with *salamander*. He has never seen the little lizard, but he has met "eye of newt" in *Macbeth* and supposes it to be some small animal, probably disgusting. To him, however, a salamander is an oil heater used by builders to dry plaster in wet weather, or possibly a mythical being in *The Rape of the Lock*. He can't match it with *newt*. There go his 200 words, though he is reasonably knowledgeable. On the other hand, he may "correctly" identify *devourer* as *glutton* without recognizing the difference in connotation and even denotation between the words. He may identify *unfelt* as *being not aware of* without recognizing that these expressions are grammatically opposite and cannot possibly be interchanged.

The claim is made that the four forms are "comparable" and that "a student taking two forms of the test usually obtains scores within five points of equality." A very small scale test by the reviewer indicates that A1 is considerably more difficult than the others and B2 considerably easier. However strict the mathematical procedure for the random selection of words, there apparently is no uniformity of difficulty of the distractors.

In short, the four forms of the *Gulick Vocabulary Survey* are fairly well constructed multiple choice tests of a conventional sort. The special feature, which is the estimate of the total size of the student's vocabulary, is of doubtful value since no clear concept of "knowledge" of a word is implied. As a teaching tool, these tests are somewhat inefficient since so many of the words present no important difficulty.

[332]

***The Iowa Tests of Educational Development: Test 8, General Vocabulary.** Grades 9–12; 1942–61; IBM; Forms X-3S, Y-3S, ('52, 3 pages); battery examiner's manual ('58, c1949–57, 23 pages); battery general manual ('59, 37 pages); student profile leaflet, sixth edition ('61, c1958, 2 pages); see the complete battery entry (14*b*) for other accessories; no data on reliability; separate answer sheets must be used; $2.40 per 20 tests; $5 per 100 IBM answer sheets; 50¢ per scoring stencil; $3 per specimen set of the complete battery; postage extra; 22(30) minutes; prepared under the direction of E. F. Lindquist; Science Research Associates, Inc. *

For reviews of the complete battery, see 14 and 5:17; for reviews of earlier forms, see 4:17 and 3:12.

[333]

***Johnson O'Connor English Vocabulary Worksamples.** Ages 9–14, 15 and over, "high vocabulary students and adults"; 1934–62; 3 levels; mimeographed manual ('60, 37 pages); no data on reliability; $5 per set of manual and any 2 forms, postpaid; specimen set not available; [30] minutes; Johnson O'Connor and others; Human Engineering Laboratory Inc. *

a) INTERMEDIATE FORM WORKSAMPLE 176. Ages 9–14; form AD ('56, c1944–56, 4 pages); also available on tape for use with ages 7–10 and persons with reading difficulty.

b) WORKSAMPLE 95. Ages 15 and over; all but 3–7 items of Forms AD, BC, and CC are revisions of items from *The Inglis Tests of English Vocabulary* (see 5:234); Forms AD ('39), BC ('41), CC ('41), DB ('36), EB ('41), IA ('47), JB ('62), (4 pages except Form IA, 10 mimeographed pages); Form JB, titled *Intermediate Worksample 95*, is an easier form and may also be used with ages 9–14; Form

IA is a more difficult form; norms for Form JB based on an earlier edition.
c) ADVANCED FORM WORKSAMPLE 180. "High vocabulary students and adults"; Form 180 AD ('55, c1949–55, 4 pages).

REFERENCES

1. O'CONNOR, JOHNSON, AND FILLEY, MARY E. "A Junior English Vocabulary Test." *Personnel J* 12:204–12 D '33. * (*PA* 8:2783)
2. ACHARD, F. H., AND CLARKE, FLORENCE H. "You *Can* Measure the Probability of Success as a Supervisor." *Personnel* 21:353–73 My '45. *
3. GELMAN, BABETTE. *A Preliminary Comparison of Vocabulary Levels With Choice of Reading Material.* Human Engineering Laboratory, Inc., Technical Report No. 176. Boston, Mass.: the Laboratory, October 1945. Pp. 24. *
4. FISHER, FRANCES. *Scenario on Word Straggled 95 A D Word Number 83.* Human Engineering Laboratory, Inc., Technical Report No. 208. Boston, Mass.: the Laboratory, January 1946. Pp. 4. *
5. UHRBROCK, RICHARD STEPHEN. "Construction of a Selection Test for College Graduates." *J General Psychol* 41:153–93 O '49. * (*PA* 24:4874)

[334]

★Johnson O'Connor Vocabulary Tests. Professionals; 1937–58; 6 tests; no manual; no data on reliability; no norms; $1 per test, postpaid; [10–30] minutes; [Johnson O'Connor and staff]; Human Engineering Laboratory Inc. *
a) JOHNSON O'CONNOR VOCABULARY OF MATHEMATICS. 1945–56; Forms 280 AA, 280 BB, 280 CB, ('56, 4 pages).
b) JOHNSON O'CONNOR VOCABULARY OF ARCHITECTURE. 1946–56; Form 250 AB ('56, 4 pages).
c) JOHNSON O'CONNOR VOCABULARY OF MUSIC. 1945–56; Form 295 AC ('56, 4 pages).
d) JOHNSON O'CONNOR VOCABULARY OF PHYSICS. 1937–58; Forms 181 CC ('56), 181 DC ('56), 181 EB ('58), (4 pages).
e) JOHNSON O'CONNOR VOCABULARY OF RADIO AND PHYSICS. 1952–56; Form 370 AC ('56, 4 pages).
f) JOHNSON O'CONNOR VOCABULARY OF SPORTS. 1953–56; Form 375 AD ('56, 4 pages).

[335]

★Nationwide English Vocabulary Examination. Grades 4–12; 1959–63; new form issued each April; norms available following the testing program; 1 form ('63, 2 pages); no manual; mimeographed norms ('63, 1 page); no data on reliability; 10¢ per test, postage extra; (40–45) minutes; [Donald R. Honz]; Educational Stimuli. *

[336]

***New Standard Vocabulary Test.** Grades 7–12; 1955–63; reprinted from the Educational Edition of *Reader's Digest;* IBM; Forms A ('61), C ('62), and E ('63) for fall testing, B ('62), D ('63), and F ('61) for spring testing, (12 pages, Forms A, B, and C identical with tests copyrighted 1955, 1956, and 1956, respectively, except for slight modification in 1 sentence of directions; Forms D, E, and F identical with tests copyrighted 1957, 1957, and 1958, respectively); manual ('59, 23 pages); $2.50 per 35 tests; separate answer sheets may be used; $3 per 100 IBM answer sheets; postpaid; answer sheet scoring stencils must be constructed locally; 30(35) minutes; Miriam M. Bryan, Janet G. Afflerbach, and Herbert A. Landry; Educational Division, Reader's Digest Services, Inc. *

For reviews by Richard A. Meade and Osmond E. Palmer, see 5:236.

[337]

Quick-Scoring Vocabulary Test: Dominion Tests. Grades 9–13; 1958; Forms A, B, (2 pages); preliminary manual (4 pages); $1 per 25 test-answer sheets; 20¢ per scoring stencil; 75¢ per specimen set; postage extra; 20(30) minutes; Department of Educational Research, Ontario College of Education, University of Toronto; distributed by Guidance Centre. *

STEPHEN HUNKA, *Assistant Professor of Educational Psychology, University of Alberta, Edmonton, Alberta, Canada.*

The *Quick-Scoring Vocabulary Test* consists of two forms, each containing 90 multiple choice items. Each item presents the stimulus word followed by five words, one of which the student is to select as being the same or nearly the same as the stimulus word. Each question is contained within an enclosed rectangle and responses are marked directly within this area, by blackening a small rectangular space. Plastic scoring stencils are supplied. The scoring sheet appears similar to an IBM sheet, but the manual makes no reference to the possibility of electronic scoring. A single raw score is obtained for each paper and conversion of this score to a percentile is recommended.

Although the manual appears adequate with respect to the details of test administration and scoring, it leaves much to be desired when recommendations of the American Psychological Association are considered. Parallel form reliability coefficients are given for each of five grade levels, and tend to vary between .90 and .93. However, evidence that in fact Forms A and B are comparable is lacking. No means or standard deviations based upon both forms are reported. No measures of item difficulty or internal consistency are reported.

Estimates of the validity of the tests, either predictive, content, or construct, are also lacking; in fact, the user is given no indication as to the type of decisions for which the test may be helpful. The percentile norms are based upon sample sizes ranging from 1,133 to 2,639 at each grade level selected in Ontario during 1956. Characteristics of the norming group other than grade level are lacking, thus making it difficult to determine whether a user's sample is similar to the norming population. No emphasis has been placed upon collection of local norms.

The universe of content from which the words were selected is not defined. An analysis of the frequency of occurrence of stimulus and answer words was made by the reviewer using Thorndike and Lorge's *Teacher's Word Book of 30,000 Words.* In Form A 70 per cent and in Form B 80 per cent of the stimulus words fall into the category 1 to 8 per million. In most instances the correct word in the alternatives appears with considerably greater frequency than the stimulus word.

The most serious deficiency in the test rests in the failure of the authors to describe adequately: (*a*) the universe of content, (*b*) the characteristics of the norming group, and (*c*) how the test score can assist the user in making better decisions about the testee. For the present time it is recommended that the *Durost-Center Word Mastery Test* be used. Although this test may be considered deficient to some extent according to criteria *b* and *c*, the psychometric characteristics have been much more carefully explored and reported.

[338]

★A Test of Active Vocabulary. Grades 9-12; 1961; Forms A, B, (8 pages); no manual; no data on reliability; no norms; 2 or more tests, 15¢ each; 20¢ per single copy; postpaid; 30(35) minutes; Paul W. Lehmann; Educational Publications. *

[339]

***Vocabulary: Every Pupil Scholarship Test.** High school; 1935-64; new form (2 pages) usually issued each January and April; forms from previous testing programs also available; general directions sheet ['63, 2 pages]; no data on reliability; norms for new forms available following testing program; 4¢ per test; 4¢ per key; postage extra; 40(45) minutes; Bureau of Educational Measurements. *

[340]

★Vocabulary Test [Management Service Co.]. Employee applicants; 1949; 1 form (1 page); mimeographed instructions (1 page); no data on reliability; no description of normative population; $3 per 10 tests, cash orders postpaid; specimen set not available; (10) minutes; Eugene J. Benge; [Management Service Co.]. *

[341]

★Vocabulary Test [Richardson, Bellows, Henry & Co.]. Applicants for clerical and stenographic positions; 1948-63; 1 form ('48, 2 pages); manual ['63, 7 unnumbered pages]; no data on reliability; $2 per 25 tests; 10¢ per key; 75¢ per manual; postage extra; 75¢ per specimen set, postpaid; 5(10) minutes; Richardson, Bellows, Henry & Co., Inc. *

[342]

★Vocabulary Test—GT. Ages 21 and over; 1957-60; based on items standardized for *I.E.R. Intelligence Scale CAVD;* Forms 1 ('57), 2 ('57), 3 ('58), 4 ('58), 5 ('60), (1 page); mimeographed directions-norms ('60, 6 pages); no data on reliability; 5¢ per test; $1 per specimen set of all forms (must be purchased to obtain directions-norms); postpaid; (5-10) minutes; Robert L. Thorndike (1,2) and Irving Lorge (3,4,5); Institute of Psychological Research. *

REFERENCES

1. Thorndike, Robert L. "Two Screening Tests of Verbal Intelligence." *J Appl Psychol* 26:128-35 Ap '42. * (*PA* 16:4205)
2. Thorndike, Robert L., and Gallup, George H. "Verbal Intelligence of the American Adult." *J General Psychol* 30:75-85 Ja '44. * (*PA* 18:2290)
3. Thorndike, Robert L. "An Evaluation of the Adult Intellectual Status of Terman's Gifted Children." *J Genetic Psychol* 72:17-27 Mr '48. * (*PA* 22:4836)
4. Miner, John B. *Intelligence in the United States.* New York: Springer Publishing Co., Inc., 1957. Pp. xii, 180. * (*PA* 32:1344)
5. Miner, John B. "On the Use of a Short Vocabulary Test to Measure General Intelligence." *J Ed Psychol* 52:157-60 Je '61. *
6. Granick, Samuel. "Comparative Analysis of Psychotic Depressives With Matched Normals on Some Untimed Verbal Intelligence Tests." *J Consult Psychol* 27:439-43 O '63. * (*PA* 38:4628)

Robert E. Stake, *Associate Director, Office of Educational Testing, University of Illinois, Urbana, Illinois.*

Intelligence is not simply verbal ability. A vocabulary test exposes but one facet of intellect. Furthermore, not enough behavior can be sampled in a five-minute testing period (in this decade) to provide a valid index of any important intellectual trait. Yet we find continuing efforts to develop a quick vocabulary test for the measurement of intelligence. A person interested in describing individual human beings should ignore these efforts. But a person interested in comparisons, even crude comparisons, of groups of human beings may find these efforts useful.

Verbal ability is an important dimension of intellect, and vocabulary items have gained general acceptance for the estimation of verbal ability. For these reasons, and because vocabulary items are easily and quickly administered, the vocabulary test continues to be utilized to measure intellect by those persons who are investigating something other than intellect.

With the *Vocabulary Test—GT,* the authors have provided such investigators with five "equivalent" forms of a 20-item, multiple choice, verbal ability test. The items can be completed by most adults in less than 10 minutes. One can infer from the manual that just about any directions that suit the investigator will do. Thorndike and Gallup (*2*), for example, told respondents that the words were being screened for a quiz show; Miner (*4*) administered the items orally when it seemed that the respondent had difficulty reading them.

The vocabulary words were selected by E. L. Thorndike before 1925. No basis of selection, either of words or of alternative responses, has been indicated in the manual or literature. (An examinee cramming for this test would be wise to study words beginning with a, b, and c because over half of these vocabulary words do.) An updated study of word usage would probably eliminate such archaisms as *flying machine* and *beshrew* and locate words more indicative of intellectual effectiveness than *bray, chirrup,* and *abattoir.*

Some alternative responses appear to be more difficult words than the stem word. Many distractors are synonyms of approximate homonyms, such as *tool* with *AWE.* Some pairs of distractors are related, probably leading naïve examinees to guess between them. With such deliberate distraction less than 20 per cent will respond correctly to some of the difficult items, and discrimination thereby is enhanced.

Although test reliability is not reported in the manual, R. L. Thorndike (*1*) estimated it at .83 for parallel forms used with an adult population. This is commendable reliability for five minutes of testing. The manual includes approximate score equivalences with the *Otis Self-Administering Tests of Mental Ability, American Council on Education Psychological Examination,* and *Army General Classification Test.* Norms are based on large and reasonably well defined groups.

Much of the vocabulary used in this test is over four hundred years old, and many of the items are over forty years old. Still, the test is a new one, needing more refinement and revision if it is to be even an auxiliary tool for the educator, sociologist, and industrial psychologist. Because it is a five-minute test, it is relatively unreliable. It is easy to administer, but the chances of examinees misinterpreting instructions are relatively high. Because the investigator usually doesn't worry much about administering such a simple test, the chances are higher that he will forget that intelligence is not simply verbal ability. As a final word of caution, perhaps neither the *Vocabulary Test—GT* nor any other five-minute vocabulary test should be used by anyone not capable of building a better test himself.

[342a]

★Vocabulary Test for High School Students and College Freshmen. Grades 9–13; 1964; IBM; Forms A, B, (2 pages); manual (9 pages); provisional norms; $3.30 per 35 IBM 1230 test-answer sheets; 25¢ per scoring stencil; 50¢ per specimen set; postage extra; 15(20) minutes; Arthur E. Traxler; Bobbs-Merrill Co., Inc. *

[343]

★Word Clue Test. Grades 5 and over; 1962; functional vocabulary; Forms A, B, AA, (15 pages); test booklet title of Form AA is *Word Clue Appraisal;* manual (6 pages); no data on reliability; no norms; distribution of Forms A and B restricted to schools; separate answer sheets must be used; 25¢ per test; $2 per 100 answer sheets; 20¢ per scoring stencil; 60¢ per specimen set of Forms A and B; postage extra; (40–45) minutes; Stanford E. Taylor, Helen Frackenpohl, and Arthur S. McDonald; Educational Developmental Laboratories, Inc. *

[Other Tests]

For tests not listed above, see the following entries in *Tests in Print:* 562–3, 566–7, 570–2, 574, 578, and 582–3; out of print: 565 and 576–7; status unknown: 584.

FINE ARTS

REVIEWS BY *Kenneth L. Bean, Paul R. Farnsworth, William S. Larson, Robert W. Lundin, Harold A. Schultz, and Herbert D. Wing.*

[344]

★Oberlin Test of Music and Art. College; 1960; experimental form for evaluating college music and art programs; 2 scores: music, art; IBM; Forms A Revised, B Revised, D Revised, ['60, 10 pages], C Revised ['60, 13 pages]; administration of all 4 forms is recommended; supervisor's manual ['60, 17 pages]; no data on reliability; no norms; separate answer sheets must be used; $2 per 25 tests; $1.10 per 100 IBM answer sheets; $35 per set of eight 7½ rpm tape recordings (2 for each form), ten 35 mm. color slides (2–4 for each form), 2 tests of each form, set of scoring stencils, and manual (this set may also be rented for $10); postage extra; specimen set loaned free except for $3 postage and handling charge; tape recorder and 2 slide projectors necessary for administration; (60) minutes per form; Oberlin College; distributed by Educational Testing Service. *

ART

[345]

★Art Education: National Teacher Examinations. College seniors and teachers; 1961–63; for more complete information, see 700; 80(90) minutes; Educational Testing Service. *

Harold A. Schultz, *Professor of Art Education, University of Illinois, Champaign, Illinois.* [Review of Forms JNT and LNT.]

This is one of 13 Optional Examinations in special teaching fields which supplement and which are offered, together with the Common Examinations, under the general heading of the National Teacher Examinations. While the Common Examinations are designed to measure some of the knowledge and abilities expected of all teachers, the Optional Examinations are planned to assist in judging the candidate's "preparation to teach in his chosen field."

Art Education is new, having been designed and first administered in 1961. Its purpose is to measure the prospective teacher's knowledge about art and how it is taught. The examination does not attempt to measure directly such qualities as personality, ability to stimulate learning, interest in children, and other characteristics so essential to successful teaching.

The examination contains 105 objective questions to be answered within a time limit of 80 minutes. For each question asked or problem posed, five plausible answers are given from which the candidate must select the one he believes best. Most of the test items place emphasis upon reasoning and the application of principles rather than the mere recollection of facts. What is asked for is clearly stated and the vocabulary and the phrasing used are common to the profession of art education.

The examination is carefully constructed and covers a diversity of topics including evaluation, objectives, motivation, art processes, research, theory, literature on art education, the crafts, and characteristics of child art. It is obvious that with such a range of content no one aspect can be measured in depth. However, the number of items in most of the categories is sufficient to indicate the candidate's knowledge and understanding and the extent of his ability to apply principles.

The examination can be used to serve a number of purposes. Colleges and universities can use it to advantage to evaluate the effectiveness of their teacher education programs in art and as a means to determine student admission to graduate study. It may also be useful, from a personal point of view, to individuals desiring a measure of their professional development. However, the examination is primarily intended to aid the public schools in the selective recruitment of teachers. For this purpose a complete transcript of the scores is sent not only to the examinee but to any school system or employing agency he designates.

It is important for those who use the results to realize the limits of the examination and not to assume that the test will permit a judgment of qualities which it was not intended to measure. The test does not measure the candidate's ability to establish harmonious relationships with students, his ability to motivate learning, or his own personal adjustment. Thus it is conceivable for an individual to score high on the examination and not become a very successful art teacher. On the other hand, a candidate may have an average score and, because of qualities not measured by the examination, have a bright future as a teacher of art. In view of such possibilities it is imperative, in evaluating an applicant's qualifications for a teaching position, that the test score be supplemented with information of a subjective kind obtained through interviews and perhaps other types of examinations.

In published information supplied to the candidates and to school officials, Art Education is listed among the Optional Examinations to be taken by those who intend to teach the subject in the secondary school. Actually Art Education includes items related to teaching in the primary, elementary, and junior high school as well as the senior high school. Although there are considerably fewer questions on art education at the junior high school level, it is evident that the examination was designed for specialists in art who may teach in either the elementary or secondary school or may supervise education at all levels.

The examination has been carefully constructed following the thorough procedures used in designing all tests in this series. Consistent with the Educational Testing Service policy of frequently reviewing tests, the 1962 edition of Art Education was revised on the basis of a very careful statistical analysis of the results. Apparently a number of items were found to be unsatisfactory for one reason or another and newly constructed items were designed and substituted for these in the 1963 edition.

The teaching of art is a highly personal process varying in emphasis, intent, and method among teachers and schools. It is possible that competent people in the profession may take exception to the correct answers to some of the questions. This may be particularly true for those items describing a classroom situation and asking the candidate to select a reply which best illustrates what he would do under such circumstances. This reviewer found a number of items for which an answer other than the correct one seemed more plausible under certain school and art room conditions.

But this is a minor matter in what is, on the whole, an excellent examination. Every encouragement is given to its use as one important measure of the qualifications of a teacher of art. The directions for taking the examination are brief and precise. Consistent with all other National Teacher Examinations it is administered only under highly controlled conditions. The test analysis is impressive in its thoroughness and there is nothing statistically reported that would cause undue concern in such matters as skewness, reliability, standard deviation, and mean item difficulty.

No other examination of its kind is available and what is particularly encouraging is that, as the examination is used, it will continue to be reviewed and revised by ETS in the light of progress in research and changes in emphasis in the teaching of art.

For reviews of the testing program, see 700, 5:538, and 4:802.

[346]

***The Meier Art Tests.** Grades 7–16 and adults, 9–16 and adults; 1929–63; 2 tests; Norman Charles Meier; Bureau of Educational Research and Service. *

a) THE MEIER ART TESTS: I, ART JUDGMENT. Grades 7–16 and adults; 1929–42; revision of *Meier-Seashore Art Judgment Test;* IBM; 1 form ('40, 101 pages); manual ('42, 24 pages); separate answer sheets must be used; 5–24 tests, $1.10 each; 5¢ per IBM answer sheet; 30¢ per set of machine scoring stencils; 5¢ per hand scoring record sheet; 12¢ per key for record sheet; 30¢ per manual; postage extra; $1.60 per specimen set, postpaid; (45–60) minutes.

b) THE MEIER ART TESTS: 2, AESTHETIC PERCEPTION. Grades 9–16 and adults; 1963; 1 form (53 pages); preliminary manual (4 pages); no data on reliability; tentative norms; separate record sheets must be used; 5-24 tests, $1.40 each; 5¢ per record sheet; postage extra; $1.70 per specimen set, postpaid; administration time not reported.

REFERENCES

1–15. See 40:1326.
16–19. See 3:172.
20–28. See 4:224.
29. CRANNELL, C. W. "The Validity of Certain Measures of Art Appreciation in Relation to a Drawing Task." *J Psychol* 35:131–42 Ja '53. * (*PA* 27:6436)
30. BOLTON, EURI BELLE. "Brief Evaluation of Two Tests of Aesthetic Judgment." *Peabody J Ed* 32:211–23 Ja '55. * (*PA* 29:6947)
31. GOWAN, J. C., AND SEAGOE, MAY. "The Relation Between Interest and Aptitude Tests in Art and Music." *Calif J Ed Res* 8:43–5 Ja '57. * (*PA* 32:296)
32. GUTEKUNST, JOSEF GRANT. *The Prediction of Art Achievement of Art Education Students by Means of Standardized Tests.* Doctor's thesis, Temple University (Philadelphia, Pa.), 1959. (*DA* 20:3202)
33. NOLAN, EDWARD GILLIGAN. *Uniqueness in Monozygotic Twins.* Doctor's thesis, Princeton University (Princeton, N.J.), 1959. (*DA* 21:247)
34. UNSER, M. CARLENE. *The Relationship Between Art Judgment as Measured by the Meier Art Judgment Test and Manipulative Dexterity in Art as Evidenced by a Specific Example of Free Association and Creative Drawing.* Master's thesis, Marquette University (Milwaukee, Wis.), 1959.
35. BROWN, ROBERT LEWIS. *A Study of the Relationship Between Ability Ratings of Art and Architecture Students, Intelligence, and Scores on Two Art Aptitude Tests.* Doctor's thesis, University of Arkansas (Fayetteville, Ark.), 1962. (*DA* 23:528)
36. SUPER, DONALD E., AND CRITES, JOHN O. *Appraising Vocational Fitness by Means of Psychological Tests, Revised Edition,* pp. 305–10. New York: Harper & Brothers, 1962. Pp. xv, 688. * (*PA* 37:2038)

HAROLD A. SCHULTZ, *Professor of Art Education, University of Illinois, Champaign, Illinois.* [Review of test 2.]

This new test is the second in a series of three on aesthetic judgment and sensitivity. The first on art judgment was published in 1930 and revised in 1940. The third test on creative imagination is in the process of construction and is scheduled for completion in two or three years. The three are to constitute a battery of tests which, when used together, will attempt to get at a basic measure of different facets of aesthetic sensitivity.

Test 2, Aesthetic Perception, contains 50 test items selected, with few exceptions, from a total of 70 items contained in the original experimental form of the test. On each page a test item is presented in four versions, with each version varied slightly in ways in which a sculptor, designer, or painter might have done them before selecting the solution which was best. Of the four versions, one is the original work of art. The other three are constructions made to resemble the original in total concept, but varying in either form, design, or light and dark pattern, or a combination of these qualities. The degree of variation in some items is pronounced, while in others the changes are quite subtle.

The subject taking the test is expected to study the compositional organization of the object, noting how the versions differ in unity, proportion, form, and design, or how they vary as satisfying wholes. A ranking procedure is called for; the subject must perceive and record which of the four choices is the best aesthetically, the second best, the third best, and the poorest.

The 50 items cover a sampling of world art from ancient to contemporary in a wide range and variety of forms. The emphasis is on examples in painting, sculpture, and abstract composition and design. Of particular note in the selection is the avoidance of popularly known works of art which might be easily recognized by the subject taking the test. Thus previous knowledge is largely eliminated as a possible influence. The use of a number of examples of nonobjective art has the advantage of isolating the choices to more purely aesthetic qualities. In examples using recognizable forms such as humans and natural phenomena, there is the possibility that an adverse judgment would be made simply on the basis that the form is unpleasantly distorted.

The test contains a number of three dimensional works, including sculpture. Some of these are presented against a background tone, limited by a border outline. The result is that one is apt to make a value judgment of the object as it relates to confined space, much as an evaluation of a painting whose elements are organized within a framework is made. Examples numbered 101 and 128 are without such backgrounds, as the sculptor intended, and allow the individual to make choices solely on the basis of his perception of sculptural form.

On the whole, the painting and design items, each with four versions, successfully convey the impression that they are reproductions of paint, paper, crayon, and other media as the artist uses them. Most of the sculpture items, on the other hand, appear to be drawings of sculpture which, of course, they really are. While fully recognizing the technical problems involved in constructing the items, there might be some advantage to building the altered versions in clay, wood, or other appropriate material and then photographing these to arrive at test items having a more faithful three dimensional effect.

The directions on the record sheet are clear and concise and the test is easy to score. An informative preliminary manual presumably will be replaced by one in final form when additional information is accumulated from more extensive use of the test. The scoring key is temporary, and tentative norms have been established on the basis of test results from approximately 350 high school students taking art and 350 college-adult subjects.

The construction of a test measuring the special qualities that make up ability in art is a time consuming and arduous task. What is to be measured is rather elusive; because there are no absolutes in art it is difficult to establish precise yardsticks against which qualities can be rated.

In spite of the inherent difficulties in building a test of this kind, Aesthetic Perception represents an advance in measurement. Its use is recommended not only because of what it is in its present form, but because improvement in measuring the entire art ability complex comes with the widespread use of the best tests available. It is only through the results so accumulated that those concerned with test construction can move in the direction of perfecting an instrument designed to measure artistic qualities.

For a review by Harold A. Schultz of test 1, see 4:224; for a review by Edwin Ziegfeld, see 3:172; for reviews by Paul R. Farnsworth and Aulus Ward Saunders of the original edition of test 1, see 40:1326.

[Other Tests]

For tests not listed above, see the following entries in *Tests in Print:* 588–92 and 594; out of print: 587.

MUSIC

[347]

***[Aliferis-Stecklein Music Achievement Tests.]** Music students; 1954–62, c1947–62; may be administered using piano, but tape recording is recommended; 2 levels; $3 per 20 tests; 50¢ per key; $9.50 per tape recording (7½ ips); $3 per manual; $3.75 per specimen set of either level; postage extra; James Aliferis and John E. Stecklein (*b*); University of Minnesota Press. *

a) ALIFERIS MUSIC ACHIEVEMENT TEST: COLLEGE ENTRANCE LEVEL. Entering freshman music students; 1954, c1947–54; 4 scores: melody, harmony, rhythm, total; 1 form ('54, c1947–54, 8 pages); manual ('54, c1947–54, 28 pages); (40–45) minutes.

b) ALIFERIS-STECKLEIN MUSIC ACHIEVEMENT TEST: COLLEGE MIDPOINT LEVEL. Music students at end of grade 14 or beginning of grade 15; 1962, c1952–62; subtitle is *A Measure of Auditory-Visual Discrimination;* 4 scores: melodic interval, chord, rhythm, total; 1 form ('62, c1952–62, 8 pages); manual ('62, c1952–62, 36 pages); (45–50) minutes.

REFERENCES

1–5. See 5:243.
6. COLEWELL, RICHARD. *An Investigation of Achievement in Music in the Public Schools of Sioux Falls, South Dakota.* Doctor's thesis, University of Illinois (Urbana, Ill.), 1961. (*DA* 22:1653)
7. DUDA, WALTER BOLESLAV. *The Prediction of Three Major Dimensions of Teacher Behavior for Student Teachers in Music Education.* Doctor's thesis, University of Illinois (Urbana, Ill.), 1961. (*DA* 22:1518)
8. WHITE, ADOLPH. "The Aliferis Music Achievement Test as a Predictor of Success in Music Theory at St. Olaf College." *J Ed Res* 54:315–7 Ap '61. *
9. ROBY, A. RICHARD. "A Study in the Correlation of

Music Theory Grades With the *Seashore Measures of Musical Talents* and the *Aliferis Music Achievement Test.*" *J Res Music Ed* 10:137–42 f '62. * (*PA* 37:7200)
10. COLEWELL, RICHARD. "An Investigation of Musical Achievement Among Vocal Students, Vocal-Instrumental Students, and Instrumental Students." *J Res Music Ed* 11:123–30 f '63. * (*PA* 38:6655)

PAUL R. FARNSWORTH, *Professor of Psychology, Stanford University, Stanford, California.* [Review of College Midpoint Level.]

The *Aliferis Music Achievement Test: College Entrance Level,* first copyrighted in 1947, proved so successful that a measure of somewhat similar construction has now been devised for music students at the college midpoint level. The authors of the new level have felt that the end of the second college year or the beginning of the third should be an appropriate time (*a*) to reexamine the auditory-visual discriminations of those students selected two years earlier for concentrations in the field of music, and (*b*) to find how well college achievement in music can be measured by an advanced test of the same sort as the very successful earlier measure.

It is rare indeed to find a test so carefully standardized as this 45-minute music achievement measure. Starting in 1950, follow up studies were undertaken, item analyses were made, and the help of member schools of the National Association of Schools of Music was obtained to insure a proper American sample for the midpoint level test. As a result, the present norms are national in scope and are based on almost 2,500 music students. Separate norms are offered for each of several geographical regions, for type of instrument studied (it would have been better to have eliminated the percussion norms since these are based on only 23 persons), and for type of school. Separate norms for each of the three parts of the test are also provided. It is a little odd that separate norms for the two sexes were not compiled, for surely sex differences of some magnitude must exist. While it will come as no surprise that the students from conservatories associated with academic institutions made the highest mean score, it may come as a shock to some that the 135 students from independent conservatories made up the third lowest group. Mean scores of piano and string students were found to be considerably higher than those of students specializing in woodwind, brass, percussion, or voice. This difference, however, may be due to the fact that the two highest scoring groups had by far the most years of private music study.

As was true of the earlier test, the college midpoint level taps auditory-visual discrimination in the areas of melody, harmony, and rhythm. Whereas the entrance level test employed both elements and idioms in each of its three parts, the present measure makes use only of harmonic (chord) elements and of melodic (interval) and rhythmic idioms.

The first two sections intercorrelate .78 and each is quite reliable (.90 and .84). The rhythm section is more independent of the other two. Like most other rhythm tests now on the market it is not very reliable (.69) and, hence, should not be employed as a separate test. One can forecast, however, that the typical music tester will bother little with the college midpoint level's subtests. Happily, the Aliferis-Stecklein test, taken as a unit, is quite reliable (.92).

The test correlated .41 with honor point ratios of music education majors in music courses and .51 with honor point ratios of applied music majors in music courses. Interestingly enough, the relationship to grades in all courses is virtually as high. The authors do not mention the probability that the addition of a good intelligence test would appreciably increase the size of the *r*'s with music grades and would greatly raise the correlations with total grades. While the *r*'s reported in the manual are of a size any tester might expect to find, the authors are certainly not justified in calling them "high." Perhaps a better justification for the forecasting worth of this test could have been made had its relation to the academic failures been carefully studied. Presumably, the reliability and validity data have been obtained by giving the test via prerecorded tape. It is likely that the reliability and validity figures would have been lower had the items been presented by piano.

The manual makes clear that the possession of absolute pitch is not a prerequisite for high scoring and that the harmony (chord) portion of the test is not as difficult as it may at first appear to be. There is no suggestion in this manual, as there was in the earlier one, that the test be taken along with the *Seashore Measures of Musical Talent.* This is probably just as well since both the English music tester, H. D. Wing, and the present reviewer have found that the addition of the Seashore tests does not improve the validity of the college entrance form. The manual announces that this series of music achievement tests will eventually contain a graduate test with norms for those entering at the master's or at the doctoral level.

A danger inherent in any achievement test is that the teacher or supervisor may come to assume that an average score not only shows what the typical person in the normative group *has* achieved but what he *should* score. The danger is perhaps more acute when the testing is in the area of music or some other of the arts than it is in a "required" subject area since, historically, there seems to have been less agreement on what constitutes growth in the arts. Room must be kept for the periodic changes in educational philosophies which in turn lead to curriculum changes. But if the authors issue new norms from time to time and have an occasional overhaul of their test items, particularly those of the graduate level test, there will be little likelihood that their tests will act as a brake on progress in music education. Indeed, these measures cannot help but make the music educator's task easier, since, without well standardized tests of the Aliferis-Stecklein sort, there could well be a return to the day of variable standards when a graduate of one conservatory might be little better than a second year student in some other institution. A test series which reflects so well the philosophy of the National Association of Schools of Music will help stabilize standards and, hence, should be warmly received.

HERBERT D. WING, *Principal, City of Sheffield Training College, Sheffield, England.* [Review of the College Midpoint Level.]

This test consists of 79 items of piano music played on either a 7½ ips tape or a piano (tape is recommended). The items are to be compared with the given melody, rhythm, or harmony notation. The item numbers are not announced on the tape and, as experience has shown, the students can easily have their attention distracted and lose their place when comparing the sounds with the notation. Why 79 was chosen for the number of items is not clear and it certainly does not make for ease in calculating statistical data. As there is a choice of four alternatives in each item the guessing total should be 19.75. I chose the fourth alternative as my guess and actually scored a guessing total of 23, i.e., the dice are weighted in favour of the last of the alternatives.

Whether or not the effect of the guessing total has been allowed for in the statistics is not clear. If it has, then it is a little difficult to understand the claim in the manual that a table of item difficulty indices "shows that.... the test was of average difficulty." Certainly the students who were given the test reported it difficult. As mentioned, I secured a guessing total of 23 by choosing the last alternative. If this be taken as the zero point of the scale and we add the midpoint of the remainder of the scale (27.5) this gives the midpoint of the whole test as a score of 50.5. If we now take the norms for colleges (which by definition is what the test is intended for) we find that this midpoint student has a percentile rank of 88 compared with state college students, 78 compared with private college students, and 87 compared with teachers college students. This would certainly indicate to me that the test needs a greater number of easier items. As the next 10 percentiles (20 for private colleges) take the whole of the remaining marks, it would further seem to me that some more difficult items are also required. In short, according to this, the test would seem to be too homogeneous. Certainly, in the limited application which I have been able to give the test, the results were very disappointing in their separating power as compared with Aliferis' college entrance level test.

A study of the manual gave me the impression that the statistics are honest enough but their interpretation into words is, to say the least, generous and at the worst, misleading. It is claimed that "the discrimination levels of the items in the interval and chord sections were excellent." In fact, 15 of the 26 discrimination indices for chord items are in the interval .30 to .39. Also, mention is made of "the high correlation of test scores with all music courses." These figures are actually .51, .41, and .44, and represent a forecasting efficiency of only 14 per cent, 9 per cent, and 10 per cent, respectively. Concerning another table of correlations between test scores and course grades it is stated that the "evidence of validity is impressive"; the correlations referred to are .40, .44, and .42, representing forecasting efficiencies of 8½ per cent, 10 per cent, and 9 per cent! Such results can hardly be described as "impressive" nor do they support the claim made that "In general, the predictive validity of the College Midpoint Test was found to be very good."

It should be noted that these criticisms are not of the musical content of the test. Nor are they of the nature of the test, which would appear to the reviewer to be quite satisfactory within the sphere of achievement in auditory-visual discrimination. This is a quality likely to be of considerable importance to a professional conductor or composer. The ability as tested is not, of necessity, vital to a performer. The reviewer would therefore consider that the test is safer if used as a positive test rather than as a screen test, i.e., that the musician who is highly successful at the test possesses qualities which are likely to be of great value to him if he is going to become a conductor, but it would be unjust to condemn a performer if his score on the test was only mediocre.

Compared with the college entrance level test, the reviewer was disappointed. He would like to see more work done on the midpoint level to discover the effect of including some easier items and some more difficult ones; above all he would like a reassessment of the terms used in describing the statistics lest the user be misled concerning the validity and reliability of his results.

For a review by Herbert D. Wing of the College Entrance Level, *see 5:243.*

[348]

The Graduate Record Examinations Advanced Tests: Music. Grades 16–17; 1951; available only in the Institutional Testing Program; for more complete information, see 762; 105(125) minutes; Educational Testing Service. *

For a review by William S. Larson, see 5:247. For a review of the testing program see 5:601.

[349]

★Jones Music Recognition Test. Grades 4–8, 9–16; 1949; 1 form (3 pages); 2 levels; no data on reliability; no norms; $1.50 per 30 tests; $1.25 per teacher's manual; postage extra; piano necessary for administration; Archie N. Jones; Carl Fischer, Inc. *
a) PART 1—FOR ELEMENTARY AND JUNIOR HIGH SCHOOLS. Grades 4–8; [45] minutes.
b) PART 2—FOR SENIOR HIGH SCHOOLS AND COLLEGES. Grades 9–16; [60] minutes.

HERBERT D. WING, *Principal, City of Sheffield Training College, Sheffield, England.*

The *Jones Music Recognition Test* consists of 180 well known musical excerpts which are played on the piano in batches of 10. As each excerpt is played, the student is asked to select the correct title from a group of 12. The first 80 items are for children in grades 4–8, the last 100 items are for students in grades 9–16. In the latter case students are asked to add composers' names to the given titles. For the first part no indications of required speed are given; for the second part the usual musical names for the tempi are given, but there are no exact metronome times. However, most musicians will no doubt play the selections within reasonably narrow limits of speed.

For purposes of this review, it was felt highly desirable to record the test (on tape at 7½ ips) before applying it to 154 second year students (mean age 20 years) at the City of Sheffield Training College. One or two slips in the printing of the music or answers were noticed during the recording. The whole test took some hours to record and about two and a half hours to play back under test conditions.

Although this reviewer thinks that a test which claims to assess musical aptitude in a few minutes is a psychological abomination, the Jones test as it stands does seem to go towards the opposite extreme. Each half of each part, however, may justifiably be regarded as an alternative form. The testing of Sheffield students was, therefore, limited to 50 items which were nicely covered in 50 minutes. Scoring and interpretation were difficult because scoring stencils, age norms, and other statistical data are not provided with the test.

Not a great deal is claimed for the test beyond what is implied by its title. Still, the proof of the pudding is in the eating, and the students certainly found the dish prepared by Jones to be a very palatable one. The selections are highly musical and follow on quite easily without any violence to any musical mood. In itself the test is a musical experience worth having.

The split-half reliability for the group tested was .76. The correlations between the 50-item Jones test and the *Musical Aptitude Test* and the *Wing Standardised Tests of Musical Intelligence* were .54 and .60, respectively. All such correlations are, of course, a function of the group as well as of the test.

The procedure of correlating the Jones test against two other tests of general musical aptitude is implicitly based on the assumption that there is a general factor for musical aptitude, and that any specialised musical test must measure general musical aptitude to some extent. The results obtained do show that the Jones test will measure general musical aptitude with a fair measure of success.

Undoubtedly this test deserves a greater measure of attention than it appears to have received, both as a research instrument in the particular field it is intended to deal with, and in the more general sphere of the measurement of general musical aptitude. If full use is to be made of the possibilities of this test, however, it would need to be developed by using the resources of statistics. Perhaps for this purpose the musician author might team up with an equally efficient statistical psychologist? The result of such exercises as, for example, an item analysis would mean an improved test by putting the easier items early in the test; by sorting out the more efficient items from the less efficient ones; in adjusting the uniformity of the test to various ages, etc. Such work would improve the reliability and validity, and make the test into a valuable instrument for research.

[350]

***Music Education: National Teacher Examinations.** College seniors and teachers; 1957–63; for more complete information, see 700; 80(90) minutes; Educational Testing Service. *

WILLIAM S. LARSON, *Professor of Music Education and Chairman of the Department, The Eastman School of Music, The University of Rochester, Rochester, New York.* [Review of Forms INT and LNT.]

The examination in music education is one of the 13 Optional Examinations of the National Teacher Examinations which are "designed to aid in evaluating the teacher's preparation to teach in his chosen field." Like the other Optional Examinations, Music Education is ordinarily given in addition to the Common Examinations which are "designed to measure certain knowledge and abilities expected of every teacher." In some instances, however, schools may request candidates to submit only an Optional Examination score. Hence, it is possible to take the Optional Examination in music education without having the Common Examinations precede it, although a teacher or prospective teacher of music making application for a music position with an NTE score requirement would very possibly be expected to take both of them. The Common Examinations, given in the forenoon, require 190 minutes of testing time; Optional Examinations, given in the afternoon, require 80 minutes each.

The two forms presented for review (Form INT copyrighted in 1959, and Form LNT copyrighted in 1963) are two of the five editions published since the original was presented in 1957. The original form was prepared by a panel of five recognized music educators. In each new edition a varying number of new items were substituted for a corresponding number of old ones. These new items were written by music education specialists recommended by former members of the panel.

This reviewer will consider only Forms INT and LNT, as previously indicated, but with more attention given to the latter because of its more recent use. Both forms present 105 questions, each having five multiple choice, "plausible" answers. From these five answers the candidate is instructed to choose the one he considers to be the best answer, except in the last section constituting approximately one seventh of the test, all answers but one are considered desirable and he is asked to choose the least plausible of the five choices. About 10 per cent of the questions in Forms INT and LNT are the same. The Educational Testing Service states in a letter to the reviewer that over 50 per cent of the items in the LNT form were completely new, i.e., not used in any of the older forms. These changes are in keeping with ETS's plan of having new editions contain varying proportions of new items; in the case of Form LNT the new item proportion seems to be very high. The substitutions may have been due to a statistical analysis of items in former editions; also, they may have been made for the purpose of maintaining test security.

Form INT was administered in February 1960 to 229 candidates, of whom 182 indicated that music education was the field in which they were best prepared to teach. Of the 578 candidates who took Form LNT in February 1963, 551 gave music as their field of best preparation. Even considering the increase in candidates taking Form LNT it is evident that only a small per cent of those taking the National Teacher Examinations—administered in February 1963 to about 28,000 seniors in teachers colleges and candidates for teaching positions—elected to take the Optional Examination in music education either as a first option or otherwise.

The test analysis reports made available to the reviewer cover a variety of statistical procedures normally done by a statistical analysis department of a testing organization. From these reports, from the Handbook for School and College Officials, and from special mimeographed data and correspondence, the reviewer has selected some of the more pertinent statistics on the two forms of the music education test under consideration.

Allowance is made for guessing by subtracting one fourth of the number of incorrect answers from the number of correct answers; the resulting scores are then converted to scaled scores with a mean of 60 and a standard deviation of 10. The range of the raw scores for both forms and also their means indicate that these tests generally may be considered demanding even for candidates who choose Music Education as a first option; the 1963 edition seems to be somewhat more difficult than the former edition. The reliabilities of both the 1959 and 1963 forms are quite satisfactory: .90 and .84, respectively. It is interesting to note, particularly in the light of later discussion, that in 1958, the year for which statistics in this area are available, the correlation between the Common Examinations (weighted total score) and the Optional Examination in music education was a high .78.

But it is in the vital area of validity that this kind of test must finally be weighed so as to show whether it may be helpful in determining competency in music education and thereby be of prognostic value in selecting successful music teachers. A number of points need to be considered. The handbook states that the NTE tests "do not purport to measure directly such significant factors as personal and social characteristics, interests, attitudes, and ability to motivate learning." These factors, however, are of decided significance in teaching, and especially so in the field of music education where so much of a music teacher's success depends on his having those personal and musical traits which enhance his ability to secure and maintain suitable and varied opportunities for students to gain desirable musical experience either through performing or listening to music. Musical talent must be recognized as basically a special capacity with little or no correlation with the general intellectual competencies which the National Teacher Examinations generally stress. The optional tests are designed to "aid in assessing the teacher's understanding of subject matter and methods in his field of specialization." But, as applied to the music education test, this is essentially an intellectual, not a musical, demand. Moreover, the handbook states that "the validity of the NTE is more appropriately judged on the basis of proximate criteria than on ultimate success in teaching" because of the lack of "universally acceptable criteria of teaching effectiveness." This conclusion can hardly justify the position of some city school boards which may either require or suggest that a candidate submit a score on this test when filing an application for a teaching position, or a situation in which some state education departments may consider the examination results as a partial basis for certification, thereby requiring or suggesting that prospective teachers take tests of this nature. Certainly, this is a dubious practice to introduce and maintain in music education, as a brief review of the Optional Examination in music education will indicate.

A perusal of the 105 items in this test shows that about 70 to 75 per cent may be roughly classified as devoted predominantly to either factual or judgment items, these being about equal in number. Another 20 to 25 per cent of the items depend rather equally on both facts and judgment, leaving less than 5 per cent (a very few) of the questions requiring a strictly *musical* response through musical imagery. This lack of a strictly musical demand indeed is and always has been the danger and difficulty in developing a nonaural objective test in music. Items of fact and judgment are better adapted to this type of test, but in it the intelligent but nonmusical student has an advantage over the fairly intelligent but highly musical student. However, that is not the order of advantage found in educational situations which require successful music teaching in both appreciation and performance aspects. The teacher first of all must be musical if he is to gain the most effective musical responses from children. Because of different kinds of demands and emphases in music instruction in our schools, however, successful music teaching in most instances depends on a happy combination of musical talent, intelligence, and personal traits.

The test items may be questioned in other ways. One observes that they can be roughly classified as dealing with background courses in history of music, nonaural theory of music, pedagogy in both general and special areas, definition of musical terms, and technical knowledge of specialized subjects, such as choral conducting, instrumental conducting, choral literature, instrumental literature, instrumentation, and elementary school vocal music. There is a growing belief on the part of many music educators that, because of the multiple requirements of developing a fine musician and teacher with an added breadth of background not only in associated musical areas but also in academic subjects and professional courses in education and music education, it is advisable or even necessary to prepare college music education students for either vocal or instrumental teaching in the public schools, not both—when the college has a large enough music faculty and adequate facilities to provide both types of instruction. A recent survey of the 29 colleges in New York State having music teacher training curricula indicated that about half of them favored two separate courses of study: one for preparation for vocal teaching, the other for preparation for instrumental teaching. A student so trained would be better equipped to teach in his special area; however, he would be at a disadvantage in the NTE music education test in that many of the questions are highly technical or complex either in the instrumental or vocal areas. Furthermore, despite the fact that the handbook explains, "each of the....Optional Examinations is designed primarily to measure the candidate's understanding of the principles, objectives, and methods of teaching the subject at the *secondary* school level [italics mine] and his mastery of subject matter," a large number of the questions pertain solely to some other level or to some specific area of music education for which the specialist in vocal music or instrumental music would not be well equipped. As an example, the instrumental specialist would not be very well prepared for questions pertaining to teaching vocal music, either in elementary school or high school, and the student specially prepared for teaching some level or branch of vocal music would be handicapped in answering complex questions about band or orchestral methods, procedures, or scoring. This diversity in the preparation of candidates likely accounts in part for many of the low raw scores on this general music education test.

This reviewer also questions a number of the judgment items, for it seems doubtful whether there is always one answer in the five possible choices that would be accepted as the best answer by most music educators. Equally competent music educators might not agree on the designated "best" single answer in some of the questions because of fundamental differences in music educational philosophy, because they belong to different schools of pedagogy, or because they have different orientations or conditions in mind when answering the question. It is true that a panel of recognized music educators decided on which answer was the "best" answer, but individuals on the particular panel that came to this reviewer's attention are known as specialists in particular areas of music education—instrumental teaching or conducting, the teaching and supervision of elementary vocal music, music administration, and the like. Under this circumstance, in deciding upon the best of the five plausible answers there could well be deference shown to the peculiar philosophical, pedagogical, or theoretical views of the specialist who presented the question or represented the particular area of the question.

The examination in music education is well constructed and presented and is sponsored by a highly recognized testing service. It undoubtedly is demanding and encompassing for the type of test that it represents. The danger lies in a possible misinterpretation of the test results by those either selecting or certifying music teachers, for they may not realize from the test's title and the nature of its promotion that no matter how effective it may be in its general approach to the factual, general informational, and judgment aspects of music education, it does not cover an area of prime importance for successful music teaching, the inherent musicality of the music teacher. This limitation in inclusiveness and the high correlation (.78) between the test and the Common Examinations seem to indicate that ultimately the two tests may be measuring much the same basic factors. And since the purpose of the National Teacher Examinations is said to be "to provide objective examinations of measureable *intellectual* competencies [italics mine] which are commonly considered basic to effective classroom teaching," the high relationship between the Common Examinations and the music education examination may well depend on general intellectual capacity and on the near exclusion from the music education test of the important variable of musical talent. Therefore, it would seem that the Common Examinations might favorably serve for both, thereby obviating the danger involved when those who very possibly may not realize the significance of the restricted scope of this music education examination attempt to interpret scores from it.

For reviews of the testing program, see 700, 5:538, and 4:802.

[351]

★Music Education: Teacher Education Examination Program. College seniors preparing to teach secondary school; 1958; an inactive form of *Music Education: National Teacher Examinations;* for more complete information, see 709; IBM; 80(95) minutes; Educational Testing Service. *

For a review of the testing program, see 5:543. For reviews of the National Teacher Examinations, *see 700, 5:538, and 4:802.*

[352]

Musical Aptitude Test: Series A. Grades 4–10; 1950; 4 scores: rhythm, pitch, melody, total; IBM; 1 form; manual ('50, 24 pages, including test materials); separate answer sheets must be used; 5¢ per IBM answer sheet; 20¢ per either hand or machine scoring stencil; $3 per manual; postage extra; piano necessary for administration; (40–50) minutes; Harvey S. Whistler and Louis P. Thorpe; California Test Bureau. *

REFERENCES

1. WHISTLER, HARVEY S., AND THORPE, LOUIS P. "Testing for Musical Talent." *Ed Music Mag* 31:16–7+. Mr–Ap '52. *
2. BENTLEY, RICHARD R. *A Critical Comparison of Certain Music Aptitude Tests.* Doctor's thesis, University of Southern California (Los Angeles, Calif.), 1955. (Abstract: *Calif J Ed Res* 7:139)

HERBERT D. WING, *Principal, City of Sheffield Training College, Sheffield, England.*

The Whistler-Thorpe test is one which is played from the piano, an advantage to the music teacher in that it is cheap and permits the musical material to be studied at leisure. In Parts 1 and 5 the candidate states whether some rhythms are the same or different; in Part 3 whether two melodies are the same or different. In Part 2 the candidate must judge how often a played tone occurs in a melody and, in Part 4, whether a second chord is higher or lower than the first.

For purposes of this review, the music was recorded on tape at 7½ ips, using timing which seemed appropriate but which might differ somewhat from tester to tester. If comparable statistics are to be obtained from different groups tested at different times the music must be recorded. When recorded, the whole test took about 50 minutes, which is regarded as a reasonable testing time. The items were somewhat dull and the effect of the chord progressions was uncomfortably jerky.

The test was applied to 154 students (74 men and 80 women), approximately 20 years of age, who were in their second year at the City of Sheffield Training College. It was soon discovered by some of the brighter students that there were very few items with "S" (same) as the correct alternative, so that a good score could be achieved by continuously writing "D" (different). One student stated afterwards that he had used this scheme to get a good score, even though he was not musically talented. Since there are 40 "D" items and only 10 "S" items out of the 75 items in the test, the student's success in obtaining a good score can easily be appreciated. A test which does not observe the statistical niceties of balancing the alternatives must result in lower validity. Likewise, one which does not clearly state whether the student is to guess, or to guess when not sure, will tend to have lower reliability. This reviewer estimated the split-half reliability of the total score as .68 for the 154 students tested. The manual gives .87 as the reliability, estimated from an unspecified Kuder-Richardson formula.

If, as this reviewer believes, there is a strong general factor in musical aptitude, this test, which measures three aspects of music (rhythm, pitch, and melody), may well cover a sufficiently wide aspect of musical aptitude to give valid results for testing children. In fact, the correlations of this test with the *Wing Standardised Tests of Musical Intelligence* and the *Jones Music Recognition Test* were found by the reviewer to be .68 and .54, respectively. Whether, in fact, the test has enough coverage to be used for a choice of musical career, as the manual claims it does, is questionable. As it is, the test may be taken as sufficiently valid and reliable for ordinary school purposes with students of a wide range of talent and ability, using a general broad classification on a five-point scale. To give percentile ranks for the separate tests may, however, be misleading in implying a degree of accuracy which is not inherent in the separate tests as they stand.

For a review by Robert W. Lundin, see 5:250; for a review by William S. Larson, see 4:228.

[353]

***Seashore Measures of Musical Talents, Revised Edition.** Grades 4–16 and adults; 1919–60; 6 scores: pitch, loudness, rhythm, time, timbre, tonal memory; IBM; 1 form: Series A ('57, 1 33⅓ rpm record, essentially the same as 1939 revision except for record size and modifications in directions); manual, second revision ('60, 10 pages); no adult norms; $12 per set of record, 50 IBM answer sheets, scoring key, and manual; $2.30 per 50 IBM answer sheets; 60¢ per set of manual and scoring key; postpaid; (60) minutes; Carl E. Seashore, Don Lewis, and Joseph G. Saetveit; Psychological Corporation. *

REFERENCES

1–55. See 40:1338.
56–101. See 3:177.
102–117. See 4:229.
118–126. See 5:251.
127. Goldstein, Hyman. "Will Your Students Succeed in Music?" *Etude* 68:16–7 O '50. *
128. Fleishman, Edwin A. "Predicting Code Proficiency of Radio-Telegraphers by Means of Aural Tests." *J Appl Psychol* 39:150–5 Je '55. * (*PA* 30:3561)
129. Parthasarathy, K. "Musical Aptitude and Appreciation Among High School Students." *J Psychol Res* 1:49–59 My '57. * (*PA* 33:4710)
130. Smith, Olin W. "Relationship of Rhythm Discrimination to Motor Rhythm Performance." *J Appl Psychol* 41: 365–9 D '57. * (*PA* 33:4844)
131. Forman, Hortense. "An Experiment in Group Use of the Seashore Measures of Musical Talent." *Int J Ed Blind* 8:41–5 D '58. *
132. Lundin, Robert W. "What Next in the Psychology of Musical Measurement?" *Psychol Rec* 8:1–6 Ja '58. * (*PA* 33:7960)
133. Lease, Gus C. *A Study of the Musicality, Intelligence, and Music Achievement of Vocalists and Instrumentalists in Selected High Schools.* Doctor's thesis, State University of South Dakota (Vermillion, S.D.), 1959. (*DA* 19:3631)
134. Cooley, John C. "A Study of the Relation Between Certain Mental and Personality Traits and Ratings of Musical Abilities." *J Res Music Ed* 9:108–17 f '61. *
135. French, Elizabeth I. *A Study of the Relationship of Scores Obtained on the Gaston Test of Musicality and the Seashore Measures of Musical Talents to Responses to Four Thematic Apperception Test Pictures.* Master's thesis, University of Tennessee (Knoxville, Tenn.), 1962.
136. Rankin, Richard J. "Auditory Discrimination and Anxiety." *Psychol Rep* 11:391–4 O '62. * (*PA* 37:7511)
137. Roby, A. Richard. "A Study in the Correlation of Music Theory Grades With the *Seashore Measures of Musical Talents* and the *Aliferis Music Achievement Test.*" *J Res Music Ed* 10:137–42 f '62. * (*PA* 37:7200)
138. Rohrs, Dennis Kerlin. *Predicting Academic Success in a Liberal Arts College Music Education Program.* Doctor's thesis, State University of Iowa (Iowa City, Iowa), 1962. (*DA* 23:2937)
139. Super, Donald E., and Crites, John O. *Appraising Vocational Fitness by Means of Psychological Tests, Revised Edition,* pp. 316–26. New York: Harper & Brothers, 1962. Pp. xv, 688. * (*PA* 37:2038)

Kenneth L. Bean, *Clinical Psychologist, Veterans Administration Hospital, Knoxville, Iowa.*

These tests, which had their origin long ago, have improved over the years as a result in part of refinements in recording technique and also as a consequence of the accumulation of information regarding the validity and practical importance of each subtest. The present battery—which is slightly modified in format for the purposes of achieving greater interest value, especially to children, and increasing validity—is much like that originated by Carl E. Seashore. This re-evaluation points out improvements made and limitations which still remain.

Several improvements may be noted on the new record. The examiner now tells subjects when to begin each new column of answers. This is helpful in preventing much of the falling behind and recording of answers in the wrong spaces which accompanied the use of the old record. Slight modifications of the stimuli on the time test now make comprehension of instructions easier to grasp; there are now two tones to compare in length rather than two lengths of silence between clicks as on the original record. The use of a 33⅓ LP disc of high quality reproduction and rather free from the annoying surface noise present on the older 78's creates less distraction than did the older records.

Seashore may well have been right in asserting that the elements we commonly refer to together as musical talent are so numerous that it is best to measure only the few basic ones. However, much disagreement has occurred among investigators as to which measures are essential. More measures than those included in the present battery (such as some measures of motor aspects) may be needed to make predictions more adequate, or, as some users of the battery have pointed out, there may be some duplication of effort in the inclusion of as many as now exist. Longer subtests with more trials at each level of difficulty could reduce chance factors. Limitations of the frequency range and of evenness of response of the average phonograph may be such as to prevent or distort accurate measures of timbre if upper overtones are varied; therefore, description or choice of quality on the timbre test of the Seashore record relies only upon lower partials which are more easily reproduced accurately. This restriction of quality differences to lower partials may perhaps limit the scope of this subtest too much. Lack of provision for some aspects of emotional response to music, usually regarded as very essential, may be a serious deficiency if the best is to be achieved by the student. If the end product is to be spontaneous and original, imagery for a composer must of necessity have a vivid and accurate quality seldom found. These are aspects of musical talent unexplored by the Seashore battery. While the tests appear to be the most nearly pure measures known and while they may be recognized as of considerable predictive value before training even starts, if a comprehensive evaluation of potential for a career in music is wanted some expansion of the tests to include more complex aspects of timbre, aesthetic judgment, and possibly creativity may be desirable.

This reviewer has observed that some subjects miss easy trials but answer correctly all later, more difficult ones of similar type. This suggests that such subjects wander off mentally too quickly and frequently. Implications for teaching are obvious. The Seashore manual could be improved by discussion of interpretation of lapses of attention.

Since investigators have presented conflicting results regarding which of the subtests are valid, which overlap others to the extent that omission of one or more would be desirable, and whether or not such abilities as pitch discrimination can be improved materially with practice, more research to clarify these issues seems very desirable. No better battery than the Seashore is known to this reviewer, but it is likely that Seashore's tests could make better predictions of success in extensive professional training in music if supplemented by more complex measures of some other aspects of what we usually call musical talent. The present limited stage of our knowledge of the best predictors permits only a tentative suggestion, to be applied and interpreted with caution. This reviewer prefers to try a battery consisting of Seashore's pitch, time, tonal memory, and rhythm measures along with an evaluation of a little more complex aspects such as could be obtained, for instance, from Gaston's *Test of Musicality* (see 5:253). Defense of the suggested battery as the most economical of time with a broad enough scope to be practical in counseling music students would be very tentative at present until thorough tryout of it in comparison with several possible alternatives has been completed.

The procedure in the Seashore battery represents good laboratory controls in the measurement of very basic aspects of musical behavior. It appears unlikely that a radical departure from these tests will ever prove superior to a defensible selection of the best subtests and their supplementation with evaluations of some more complex functions prepared by other investigators and sufficiently well standardized.

ROBERT W. LUNDIN, *Professor of Psychology, The University of the South, Sewanee, Tennessee.*

This is basically the same test battery that first appeared in its revised form in 1939. Reviews have appeared in the third and fourth editions of *The Mental Measurements Yearbook* (see 3:177 and 4:229) and the test is listed with some additional references in the fifth edition (see 5:251). In 1960 the Psychological Corporation published a second revised manual (first revision in 1956) at about the time the original items were transferred from three 78 rpm discs to one 33⅓ LP record. This revised manual contains three sets of norms based on percentile ranks for three educational levels (grades 4–5, grades 6–8, and grades 9–16). The norms are the same as those appearing in the 1956 manual. No adult norms are given since the authors have always maintained that the discriminations measured by the tests do not change appreciably with age.

The second revision of the manual can hardly be called a revision since the only changes since the 1956 manual appear to be slight alterations in directions and a longer list of bibliographical references. A recent innovation refers to the addition of some oral directions on the record before each test. "This is the ______ test. Ready now for Column A." Such an addition is intended to reduce the chances of a subject's losing his place. The announcer also says, "Column B," "Column C," etc. at appropriate places in the test. Prior to this innovation the columns were separated only by a lengthened time interval between sets of items. Unfortunately, this reviewer has found the addition quite aversive at least for older subjects. The voice is loud in comparison to the tonal presentation and the articulation is very stilted. Some of our subjects have found it quite comical.

The same old statements of reliability and validity still appear. Seashore is quoted as maintaining the tests are valid because they measure exactly what they purport to measure: pitch, loudness, time, rhythm, timbre discriminations, and tonal memory. Of course, the real question as to what these sensory discriminations have to do with musical talent in a more general sense is never made very clear.

A couple of decades ago a very lively controversy raged between the "omnibus" theorists and the "specificity" theorists who supported the Seashore tests. Anyone interested in reviewing this controversy can find it in Lundin (*123*). Despite the authors' feeling against an "omnibus" kind of validation technique, studies have been done and are summarized in Bienstock (*95*), Lundin (*132*), and Farnum (*119*). Generally, it appears that when the test is validated against some general external criterion of musical performance, the tests of pitch, rhythm, and tonal memory come out best. Today the controversy is not so lively and alternate tests have been devised which attempt to measure musical talent in a more general fashion. These include the *Wing Standardised Tests of Musical Intelligence* and the *Drake Musical Aptitude Tests* which have become more prominent and report successful predictability.

The reliabilities reported earlier are basically unchanged. They are not what they ought to be considering the authors' and publisher's suggestion of employing the specificity theory, namely that the tests measure separate talents and results must be considered individually. Norms are never presented for total scores. K-R 21 reliabilities for grades 9-16 range from .64 for the time test to .84 for the pitch test. In these days of more rigorous standards for test construction such reliabilities are substandard.

Despite the barrage of attacks against this test, many musicians still seem to like and use it. Although no exact data are available, one has the strong feeling that this is still one of the most widely used measures even though newer tests have been developed. Regardless of what any individual's personal opinions may be, he must admit this oldest of all musical aptitude tests has "stood the test of time."

For reviews by John McLeish and Herbert D. Wing of the 1939 revision, see 4:229; for reviews by Paul R. Farnsworth, William S. Larson, and James L. Mursell, see 3:177.

[354]

***Wing Standardised Tests of Musical Intelligence.** Ages 8 and over; 1939–61; 8 scores: chord analysis, pitch change, memory, rhythmic accent, harmony, intensity, phrasing, total; IBM; 1 form ['60] consisting of 7½ ips standard tape recording; manual ('60, 11 pages); answer booklet ('61, 4 pages); norms for total score and for total of first 3 scores only; separate answer sheets may be used; 92*s*. per set of tape recording, answer booklet, scoring stencil, 20 IBM answer sheets, and manual; 22*s*. per set of 100 IBM answer sheets and scoring stencil; 9*s*. per manual; prices include purchase tax; postpaid within U.K.; German and French editions available; edition for the blind available; (25–35) minutes for shortened version (first 3 scores), (50–60) minutes for complete test; H. D. Wing; distributed by National Foundation for Educational Research in England and Wales. *

REFERENCES

1–6. See 4:230.
7–10. See 5:254.
11. CAIN, MARTHA LEE. *A Comparison of the* Wing Standardized Tests of Musical Intelligence *with a* Test of Musicality *by Gaston and the* Drake Musical Aptitude Tests. Master's thesis, University of Kansas (Lawrence, Kan.), 1960.
11a. WING, HERBERT D. "A Revision of the Wing Musical Aptitude Test." *J Res Music Ed* 10:39–46 sp '61. * (*PA* 37:3085)
12. HELLER, JACK JOSEPH. *The Effects of Formal Music Training on the Wing Musical Intelligence Scores.* Doctor's thesis, State University of Iowa (Iowa City, Iowa), 1962. (*DA* 23:2936)
13. WING, HERBERT D. "A Revision of the Wing Musical Aptitude Test." *J Res Music Ed* 10:39–46 sp '62. *
14. HEIM, KENNETH E. *Musical Aptitude of Senior High School Students in Residential Schools for the Blind as Measured by the* Wing Standardized Tests of Musical Intelligence. Master's thesis, University of Kansas (Lawrence, Kan.), 1963.
15. WERTZ, CHARLES BRADLEY. *Relation of Changes in Musical Preference to Scores on the* Wing Standardized Tests of Musical Ability and Appreciation. Master's thesis, University of Kansas (Lawrence, Kan.), 1963.

WILLIAM S. LARSON, *Professor of Music Education and Chairman of the Department, The Eastman School of Music, The University of Rochester, Rochester, New York.*

The present battery of tests, the culmination of Wing's interest and study in the field of music testing during the past 30 years, emerged into its present form through the selection of the most promising of a large number of tests tried in his early years of study. Since that time, Wing has constantly reviewed the items and has improved his methods of testing and scoring.

Wing considers his tests to be a measure of "both acuity of musical hearing and a sensitivity to performance" (*13*). Perhaps the first three tests of the battery, Chord Analysis, Pitch Change, and Memory, may be roughly placed in the "acuity" class; the last four, Rhythmic Accent, Harmony, Intensity, and Phrasing, in the realm of "sensitivity to performance."

SCORING AND NORMS. The battery has a four-page answer sheet which can be corrected by placing it inside the scoring key, the correct answers appearing in the punched boxes thereof. Also available for use in the United States is an IBM form of answer sheet which, however, does not have the advantage of a printed explanation at the beginning of each of the seven tests as does the answer sheet regularly offered with the tests. The instructions for the first three tests are also given on the tape, along with several trial examples which, aided by the commentary on the tape, provide the students with a chance to practice doing these tests by recording their answers for the trial examples and then checking them. The practice items may be repeated, if necessary.

Wing gives two tables of norms, one covering only the first three tests of the battery, the other for all of the seven tests. Both tables have a letter-grade score evaluation for each age from 8 to 17 (or adult). In addition, an "approximate musical age" may be obtained.

The reason for the option of using only the first three tests seems to be two-fold: (*a*) it provides a shorter test for those who consider the battery of seven tests too long for group testing; (*b*) it obviates the fatigue element for younger children and for those of a *musical age* below about 10 years, for whom Wing considers the last four tests rather advanced and "largely a waste of time." However, for the more musically talented, Wing states that the first three tests serve only as the first stage of testing.

RELIABILITY AND VALIDITY. Wing reports that "reliability coefficients for older children have been of the order of .9 and above, but for younger children they drop to .7." He summarizes (*13*) several unpublished studies by others to indicate the validity of his tests. The most important such study seems to be one carried out in 1959 at the Royal Marines School of Music in which the Wing test was given to 223 junior musicians under training. Wing reports that this investigator found "a positive and significant correlation" between test results and gradings given by instructors of average, above average, and below average, and concluded that (in Wing's words) "if only those candidates had been selected who scored above a certain mark....the failure rate could have been considerably reduced." Wing also mentions a thesis study in which a substantial agreement between test results and the year's class marks in music was found and another thesis study in which the test results were found to agree well with specialist teachers' estimates of aptitude and very little with the estimates of nonspecialists. Various studies such as the three mentioned above have led Wing to conclude that "figures from investigations so far tend to indicate that children of high aptitude can be selected so that they can start training on a musical instrument with a good probability of success." One could wish for more evidence of validity. But Wing, although a well trained psychologist, is a college administrator, a musician but not a music teacher, and so, like some other leading test builders, has had to depend in large part on others in favorable music teaching situations for reports on validity. And it is difficult for most music teachers who may lack time, interest or background to provide data on validity for this involves not only administering the talent tests but also establishing and maintaining control conditions in the process of musical training, partialing out such student traits as personality and industry, and making allowance for varying pedagogical aims and procedures in teaching music. Because of these conditions, Wing has been conservative when reviewing reports of music teachers who have used his tests and has moderately stated (*13*), "evidence is not wanting to show that as a consequence of testing, many children who might otherwise have remained neglected, have been discovered and given opportunities to develop their talent for music."

CONCLUSIONS. The *Wing Standardised Tests of Musical Intelligence* make demands on musicality and are a measure of musical sensitivity. While students who have had more musical experience may have an advantage, particularly in the interpretative demands of the last four tests, the fundamental and determining requirements underlying all the tests in the battery are musical in nature, not factual. Hence, as they should be in musical talent tests, inherent musical traits are of greater importance in discrimination in the Wing tests than are the intellectual traits. The tests are well constructed and clearly presented; they have an acceptable theoretical approach to measuring musicality; and they deserve greater consideration for study and acceptance in this country. It is hoped that further studies will be made with them and that their use will prove to be of real practical value to music educators in the selection of students for special instruction.

ROBERT W. LUNDIN, *Professor of Psychology, The University of the South, Sewanee, Tennessee.*

The *Wing Standardised Tests of Musical Intelligence* probably have not received the attention in this country that they justly deserve. However, with the recent 1960 revision we have a significant contribution to the field of musical measurement. Although norms are available for ages ranging from 8 years to adult, the tests are particularly designed to discover musically bright children at an age when they would ordinarily begin the study of a musical instrument. The test battery attempts to measure both hearing acuity (tests 1–3) and sensitivity for musical appreciation (tests 4–7). Norms are available for the total of the first three tests as well as for total scores for the entire battery. Because of the difficulty of some of the later tests and the overall length of the entire series, the author feels it quite justifiable to use only the first three in selecting fairly young children at least on a first grading.

Although both reliabilities and validities are reported to differ for various age groups, for older children and adults the split-half reliabilities are very good—in the low .90's. For the younger age groups the test-retest reliabilities are reported to be in the low .70's. On validity, when scores of younger children of 11 years, for example, are compared with teachers' estimates of ability, the resulting coefficient is reported to be .60. A factor analysis of an earlier edition of the test battery indicates that there is a rather general factor of musical ability common to all subtests which accounts for 40 per cent of the variance (*3*). Other more specific factors are also isolated.

It would seem, therefore, that the general rationale of the tests supports an "omnibus" kind of theory of musical talent rather than one of "specificity."

One of the greatest difficulties with the test series is its length if the full series is given. Boredom and fatigue are often reported. In order to overcome this difficulty the author has suggested that the testing may be done over two testing periods. Also, for younger subjects, a shorter form, which consists of only the first three tests, may be used.

This revised version has been standardized on a large population (over 8,000) divided over the age ranges from eight years to adulthood. Separate age norms are quite appropriate since the author has found that scores do improve with age up to about 17 years (*7*). The presentation of the tonal stimuli using a piano is now on tape instead of separate phonograph records previously used. This has produced a marked improvement in recording quality. For the first three tests the instructions are presented on the tape prior to the start of each test. These can be readily followed by younger subjects. No taped instructions are presented for the last four tests although they appear on the answer blanks.

The current edition is the result of many years of careful revision and standardization. With the revised version available on tape, along with standardized answer forms, a vastly simplified scoring procedure, and norms for various age groups, test users in this country ought to become acquainted with this series of measures which appears to be potentially a considerable asset to the field of musical aptitude testing.

For a review by John McLeish of an earlier edition, see 4:230; for excerpts from related book reviews, see 4:231.

[Other Tests]

For tests not listed above, see the following entries in *Tests in Print:* 596–9, 603–6, and 610–2; out of print: 602.

FOREIGN LANGUAGES

REVIEWS BY *Nelson Brooks, John B. Carroll, Henry Chauncey, Harold B. Dunkel, Wayne D. Fisher, Walter V. Kaulfers, Gilbert C. Kettelkamp, Bertram B. Masia, Theodor F. Naumann, Paul Pimsleur, James H. Ricks, Jr., Herbert Schueler, Mariette Schwarz, Marion F. Shaycoft, Jack M. Stein, Mary E. Turnbull, and Clarence E. Turner.*

[355]

***Foreign Language Prognosis Test.** Grades 8–9; 1930–59; 2 tests labeled Forms A ('59, c1930–59), B ('58, c1930–58), (8 pages, identical with tests copyrighted in 1930 except for cover page), either or both of which may be administered; manual ('59, c1930–59, 6 pages); $4 per 35 tests; 50¢ per specimen set of both tests (must be purchased to obtain manual); postpaid; 44(60) minutes; Percival M. Symonds; Bureau of Publications. *

a) FORM A. 5 scores: English inflection, word translation-English to Esperanto, sentence translation-Esperanto to English, related words, total.

b) FORM B. 5 scores: word translation-Esperanto to English, artificial language, sentence translation-English to Esperanto, formation of parts of speech in English, total.

REFERENCES

1–6. See 40:1340.
7. VEON, DOROTHY HELENE. *The Relationship of Learning Factors Found in Certain Modern Foreign-Language Aptitude Tests to the Prediction of Shorthand Achievement in College.* Stillwater, Okla.: Division of Commerce, Oklahoma Agricultural and Mechanical College, 1950. Pp. 74. *

WAYNE D. FISHER, *Assistant Professor of Education in Russian; and* BERTRAM B. MASIA, *Assistant Professor of Education; The University of Chicago, Chicago, Illinois.*

The *Foreign Language Prognosis Test,* which bears a first copyright date of 1930 and whose contents seem not to have been changed at the time of the 1959 copyright, has been outmoded by the application of principles of linguistics to the teaching of foreign languages. This relatively recent development conceives of language learning as based upon analytical contrastive studies of the signaling systems of the native and target languages. Instruction, therefore, focuses almost exclusively upon the problems indicated by the contrastive studies. The implications of this development for prognostic testing are clear. Such tests must be able to indicate the outcome of the encounter of the student with these linguistic problems. Whether the prognostic tests will have to vary with the particular native and target languages remains to be seen.

The usefulness of the *Foreign Language Prognosis Test* is therefore limited to those teachers whose instruction has little relation to the nature of language behavior. If the foreign language instruction emphasizes encoding and decoding, and looks upon language learning as essentially the acquisition of a large vocabulary, then success in such a course could be predicted fairly well with such a test. However, it is quite likely that this success can be predicted just as well with a shorter and more straightforward test of general verbal ability.

An inspection of test item types reveals both the author's conception of foreign language learning as being intellectual rather than behavioral, and the test's being at least a first cousin to tests of verbal fluency *in English.* Test 1 of Form A is a case in point. In this test the student is required to change a word in a sentence as indicated. For example, for the sentence, "Are you reading an interesting book?" he is directed to change the verb to the future perfect tense. This type of test item confuses (*a*) knowledge of terminology about language with (*b*) knowledge of language. It measures the first and presupposes that the first is necessary for the achievement of the second. Such an assumption is unwarranted. In the item cited a person might not be able to perform the task, yet could produce the future perfect structure whenever needed. In a deeper sense this type of task is no more than an intellectual exercise in manipulating rules of English grammar.

Test 2 of Form A reveals another fundamental weakness in the *Foreign Language Prognosis Test.* The student is presented with a story in Esperanto followed by its English translation. Then he is given a set of multiple choice items in which the task is to indicate one of five Esperanto words as being the equivalent of the English word presented. He makes his choice of the correct alternative by comparing the Esperanto and English renderings of the story. Here are two languages with similar signaling systems. At best this test could be useful in predicting performance in a language with an origin and an alphabet common to English. But it would not give any significant information concerning mastery of a language with different symbols such as Russian, Hebrew, and Chinese. What we have here essentially is a problem solving exercise which requires the use of mental processes whose relation to language as behavior is not clear.

A final example is from Test 4. Here the student is confronted with a series of sentences in Esperanto, each one containing an italicized word. His task is to translate the italicized word into English. Again we have a highly intellectualized exercise which possibly has face validity for knowledge about language but not for the acquisition of skills in the use of language. Performance on this type of test may be negatively correlated with success in a course which truly emphasizes the acquisition of language behavioral skills.

All eight subtests in the two noncomparable forms of the *Foreign Language Prognosis Test* are open to the same criticism. Since this appears to be nothing more than a test of verbal ability, nothing would be lost to evaluation of foreign language instruction if it were withdrawn from circulation.

For a review by William B. Michael, see 4:232; for a review by Walter V. Kaulfers, see 40:1340.

[356]

★The Graduate School Foreign Language Testing Program. Graduate level degree candidates required to demonstrate foreign language reading proficiency; 1963–64; tests administered 4 times annually (January, April, August, October) at participating graduate schools; departments must agree to test "all students deemed ready to meet reading proficiency requirements" in the languages; Forms K-LFG1, K-LFG2 ('63, 33–44 pages); 3 tests: French, German, Russian; for part of each test, examinees elect the 1 section out of 4 (biological sciences, humanities, physical sciences, social sciences) which contains materials related to their major field; handbook for deans and examiners ('63, 10 pages); bulletin of information for students ('63, 11 pages); guide for interpretation ('64, 21 pages); score interpretation leaflet for students ['64, 4 pages]; supervisor's handbook for administering the publisher's testing programs ('63, 24 pages); no data on reliability of section 2 of the Russian test; separate Scribe answer sheets must be used; examination fee: $6 per student tested, postage extra; fee includes scoring service and report of scores to the graduate school (extra copies of individual score reports are included for examinees); 80(100) minutes; Educational Testing Service. *

For a review of the French test, see 377; for a review of the German test, see 391.

[357]

★Modern Language Aptitude Test. Grades 9–16 and adults; 1959, c1955–58; earlier experimental form called *Psi-Lambda Foreign Language Aptitude Battery;* 4–6 scores: number learning (long form only), phonetic script (long form only), spelling clues, words in sentences, paired associates, total; IBM; Form A ('59, c1955–58) consists of 2 parts: test-answer sheet (2 pages) for parts 1 and 2, and test booklet (12 pages) for parts 3, 4, and 5; parts 3–5 may be administered as a short form; practice sheet ('59, c1955–58, 1 page); manual ('59, 27 pages); no norms for grades 12 and 14–16; separate answer sheets must be used; $3.50 per 25 tests; $3.60 per 50 IBM answer sheets and 50 practice sheets; 60¢ per set of stencils and manual; 75¢ per specimen set; $7.50 per 3¾ ips tape recording (essential for long form, optional for short form); postpaid; (30) minutes for short form, (60–70) minutes for long form; John B. Carroll and Stanley M. Sapon; Psychological Corporation. *

REFERENCES

1. CARROLL, JOHN B. "The Harvard Foreign Language Aptitude Tests." *Yearb Nat Council Meas Used Ed* 12:9–11 pt 2 '55. *

2. CARROLL, JOHN B. "A Factor Analysis of Two Foreign Language Aptitude Batteries." *J General Psychol* 59:3–19 Jl '58. * (*PA* 36:2KK03C)

3. CARROLL, JOHN B. "Use of the *Modern Language Aptitude Test* in Secondary Schools." *Yearb Nat Council Meas Used Ed* 16:155–9 '59. *

4. MARQUARDT, WILLIAM F. "Can Foreign Student Selection Be Based on Aptitude for Learning English?" *News B Inst Int Ed* 36:2–8 Ap '61. *

5. KJELDERGAARD, PAUL M. "Predicting Paired-Associate Learning Speed." *Psychol Rep* 11:353–4 O '62. * (*PA* 37:7587)

6. PIMSLEUR, PAUL; STOCKWELL, ROBERT P.; AND COMREY, ANDREW L. "Foreign Language Learning Ability." *J Ed Psychol* 53:15–26 F '62. * (*PA* 37:2003)

7. CIEUTAT, VICTOR J. "Predicting Speed of Serial and Paired-Associate Learning." *Psychol Rep* 13:786 D '63. *

8. KURLANDER, EDWIN D. "The Modern Language Aptitude Test as a Guidance Tool." *Sch Counselor* 10:129–31 Mr '63. *

9. MUELLER, KLAUS A., AND WIERSMA, WILLIAM, JR. "Correlation of Foreign Language Speaking Competency and Grades in Ten Midwestern Liberal Arts Colleges." *Mod Lang J* 47:353–5 D '63. *

10. WEAVER, WENDELL W., AND KINGSTON, ALBERT J. "A Factor Analysis of the Cloze Procedure and Other Measures of Reading and Language Ability." *J Commun* 13:252–61 D '63. * (*PA* 39:188)

WAYNE D. FISHER, *Assistant Professor of Education in Russian; and* BERTRAM B. MASIA, *Assistant Professor of Education; The University of Chicago, Chicago, Illinois.*

Tests designed to predict achievement in the study of a foreign language invariably reflect two rather serious weaknesses: (*a*) they are not rooted in psychological studies of language and language behavior, and (*b*) they do not indicate the specific language learning outcomes or instructional objectives the test is designed to predict.

The first weakness has given rise to validity coefficients between predictor and criterion variables which are not significantly higher than coefficients obtained when general scholastic ability tests are used as predictors. What appear as a result of cursory inspection to be measures of language abilities, turn out in statistical analysis to be nothing more than measures of general abilities.

The second weakness gives rise to a range of predictive validity coefficients when the prognostic instrument is used with foreign language classrooms of different teachers and in different schools. Since error and bias in the criterion variable, particularly when it is represented by teacher grades, is most likely random across teachers and schools, variability in predictive validity coefficients may in large measure be associated with variations in instructional objectives.

It is clear that the search for what might be termed "primary language abilities" which are operative for all goals of language instruction is as fruitless as the medieval search for the philosopher's stone. We do not mean to imply that there are no specific language learning abilities. But we do contend that such abilities are inextricably tied to purposes and goals of instruction, to the teacher's conception of the nature of foreign language behavior and how it is acquired. Thus aptitude must be viewed in terms of classroom implementation of foreign language instructional goals rather than in terms of language and language behavior *per se*. Often overlooked is the fact that a person has demonstrated his aptitude for learning a second language by having acquired skill in using his native language for his own purposes. An American student studying a foreign language has already gained practical, though perhaps not stylistic, proficiency in English. He is able to carry on a conversation, although he may not be able to do it with the skill of an Alexander Woollcott. He certainly can write, often not with any appreciable degree of precision, no less elegance. Yet in his proficiency in English, no matter what his level, he has demonstrated his linguistic aptitude. It is therefore unreasonable to expect the student of a second language to be more proficient in the basic language skills (e.g., speaking, listening, etc.) in the second language than he is in his native language. What is reasonable to expect is that the student of a foreign language should approximate the level of behavior of his counterpart in the cultural speech community of which the language is representative.

In terms of these two weaknesses of foreign language aptitude tests, to what extent does Carroll and Sapon's *Modern Language Aptitude Test* succeed in overcoming them? Predictive validities are generally .20 higher than those obtained for general ability and intelligence tests. But it is difficult to determine whether this overall increment in prediction is traceable to systematic psychological- and linguistic-oriented studies made by Carroll's Harvard Language Aptitude Project or to the more accidental effect of the test constructors' ingenuity in devising test models which are empirically more efficient for reasons which are not very clear. Since the MLAT manual does not provide a theoretical rationale for the instrument and does not claim that the parts of the test correspond with those cognitive ability factors reported elsewhere by the senior test author (*3*), we must accept the latter explanation for the reported overall increment in prediction.

Does the MLAT predict some types of instructional outcomes better than others? The manual states: "it was originally planned to study comparative validities of the MLAT in 'traditional' as opposed to 'new-type' courses, and efforts were made to collect data in both types of courses. It soon appeared, however, that there was no systematic fluctuation of validity dependent on teacher methodology. High validities were obtained for intensive courses, all of which laid much stress on oral work, but there were also some institutions stressing written work where reasonably high validities were obtained."

One problem is that the difference in methodology—the implementation of the teacher's views regarding the nature of language and how it is learned—between the so-called "traditional" course and the "new type" course is not as great in most cases as the literature would have us believe. More important than whether the course is labeled "traditional" or "new type" is whether the intention is to learn the new language in terms of its own linguistic elements or in terms of its restatement in the student's mother tongue. Our observations of both traditional and new type courses support the contention that courses of both types never relinquish the mother tongue. In Brooks' words, "language symbols are 'decoded' from one system to another, and comprehension, meaning, and value are all in terms of the student's first language."[1]

When a second language is learned as an alternate system of behavior, however, the ultimate goal must be the control of the linguistic elements (phonology, morphology, syntax, intonation, stress, graphic symbolization, and vocabulary) as the native speaker controls them. It is only further evidence in support of our criticism above that both teaching and testing in foreign languages place heavy emphasis on the acquisition of vocabulary. This one linguistic element not only is heavily stressed, it interferes with learning and testing of all the other linguistic elements. Language learning involves the acquisition of an alternate communication system which develops different signals, different sounds, different structures, and different structuring of reality from that of the native language.

In the MLAT the "target" language of the test is a restatement of American English. In every aspect of the test the similarities between English and a "target" language are emphasized, whereas in language learning it is precisely in these areas that transfer readily occurs and minimal difficulties are encountered by the student (unless language is taught as academic discipline, rather than as behavior). Language learning difficulties arise, to any significant degree, only at those points in the phonological system, the morphological system, the syntactical system, the rhythmical and intonational system which are *contrastive* to the native language.[2]

Our own consideration of the test content suggests that it measures the student's ability to recode English. The sound system used throughout the test is the English sound system. The structures used throughout the test are English structures. Even with vocabulary, nonsense words are here substituted for English words, thus giving the erroneous impression that language learning is in large measure a matter of the substitution of one set of words for another.

If the MLAT reveals, through "nonsense-substitute" vocabulary, the learner's knowledge of English sounds and structure, it is likely that the student's academic record in English classes would be as valid a predictor of success as the MLAT. Also, if our assertion of the pronounced English orientation of this test is a valid one, then the test should be a better predictor of English grades than of grades in a foreign language course.

In this connection our recommendation for improving the MLAT is the inclusion of non-English sounds in the taped portion, and the use of non-English linguistic characteristics in all other parts of the test. There should also be some non-Roman symbolization.

1 Brooks, Nelson. *Language and Language Learning: Theory and Practice,* p. 104. New York: Harcourt, Brace & World, Inc., 1960. Pp. xv, 238. *

2 Lado, Robert. *Linguistics Across Cultures: Applied Linguistics for Language Teachers.* Ann Arbor, Mich.: University of Michigan Press, 1957. Pp. ix, 141. *

Marion F. Shaycoft, *Senior Research Scientist, American Institute for Research; and Director of Measurement Research, University of Pittsburgh Project Talent Office; Pittsburgh, Pennsylvania.*

The purpose of the *Modern Language Aptitude Test* is broader than its name implies, since the test is designed to measure aptitude for learning *any* foreign language—not just modern ones. It is suitable for high school and college students, and for adults.

The first two of the five parts involve oral presentation of the test material, via a prerecorded magnetic tape. The Short Form, which consists of the last three parts, is intended for use where available testing time is limited or where it is not feasible to use tape recorder playback equipment.

The test material itself is quite novel in character and represents an ingenious attack on the problem of getting a better measure of aptitude for learning a foreign language quickly and well than is yielded by IQ.

Part 1, Number Learning, is reported to have a fairly large specific variance, hypothesized to represent auditory alertness. Part 2, Phonetic Script, measures the ability to learn orthographic symbols corresponding to specific sounds. The authors suggest that it may also measure memory for speech sounds, and that it is correlated with ability to mimic these sounds. Part 3, Spelling Clues, the only highly speeded section of the test, also measures sound-symbol association to some extent but, unlike Part 2, is dependent in addition on size of the student's vocabulary. Part 4, Words in Sentences, is intended to measure sensitivity to grammatical structure. The item type, an ingenious one, yields scores that are not dependent on specific memory for grammatical terminology. Part 5, Paired Associates, measures the rote memory aspect of learning a foreign language.

The test as a whole and the individual items that compose it are carefully constructed. The administrative procedures are well planned and easy to carry out, particularly if the tape is used. The directions might be improved slightly, however, by clarifying the instructions on guessing. Although the scores are not corrected for chance guessing, the students are neither explicitly instructed to attempt every item nor told that the score is number right. This lack could reduce the test's validity a little.

The manual is an exceptionally good one; it is clear and sound and contains suitable words of caution and explanation throughout, to keep the user from misinterpreting or misusing the results. It describes the test, contains instructions for administration and scoring, presents normative data, reliability coefficients, validity coefficients, expectancy tables, and auxiliary statistics, and discusses suggested uses of the test.

Percentile norms are presented for both the total test and the Short Form, for beginning language students (boys and girls separately) in grades 9, 10, and 11, and in the freshman year of college, and also for military and civilian personnel assigned to intensive foreign language training. Most of the norms groups are relatively small, however, consisting of only a few hundred cases each, and probably not comparable from grade to grade (if one may judge from the fact that the grade 10 boys' mean is somewhat lower than that for grade 9 boys, and from selection factors affecting the grade at which high school students embark on foreign language study). Thus the norms probably should be regarded as only suggestive, rather than definitive.

The validity coefficients (against course grades and proficiency test scores) are high enough, when criterion limitations are considered, to provide evidence that the test fulfills its basic purpose successfully.

Neither norms nor validity coefficients are presented for the part scores. Such data might be helpful in view of the fact that the intercorrelations among the parts are low enough to suggest that the part scores measure somewhat different aspects of foreign language aptitude. It appears to the reviewer that the neglect of part scores may be partly responsible for the finding, reported in the manual, that the test does not have differential validity for different languages. Using the total score could easily wipe out any differential validity the parts have. The manual does suggest the use of part scores for predicting particular kinds of learning difficulties. Several of the parts are reliable enough to justify such use, although interpretations would have to be cautious.

Split-half reliability coefficients for scores on the total test and Short Form are excellent, most of them exceeding .90 and several exceeding .95.

One statistic that this reviewer hunted for in vain was the correlation between Short Form and total test scores. Potential users of the Short Form would probably be interested in this coefficient.

SUMMARY. The *Modern Language Aptitude Test* is ingeniously constructed, carefully developed, and a generally excellent instrument for measuring the ability to learn foreign languages. Its few weaknesses (such as the paucity of data presented on part scores) are very minor ones, vastly outweighed by its numerous and substantial merits.

French R 33:634–5 My '60. Harold B. Dunkel. At all educational levels both the cost and the mortality rate of language instruction are relatively high. Any device which enables us to counsel into language programs students able to profit from them and to keep out of these classes students likely to fail is more than merely useful. The long search for prognostic tests has, however, encountered a variety of fundamental problems. Because of the correlation between almost all educational tests, whether of academic achievement or intelligence (with most of the correlations being low positive ones of the order of .20–.50), nearly any test is to some degree a predictor of linguistic achievement. Of these general measures, the experience of most of us indicates that the tests of "verbal intelligence" (such as the L-score of the ACE Psychological Examination) usually give the best results, correlations in the neighborhood of .50 or a little better. Unfortunately, this degree of correlation between the predictor and the criterion of actual performance does not permit confident counseling in individual cases, precisely the situation in which prediction is most wanted. Earlier tests built specifically for language prognosis often do a little better, but usually not enough better to justify the additional testing time and money, since decisions in individual situations were still fairly precarious statistically. Finally, an inherent difficulty has been the diverse nature of foreign-language programs. It has seemed unlikely to many of us that a single instrument could predict later achievement in such varied courses as are suggested by the labels: "intensive aural-oral," "grammar-translation," "culture and civilization," "extensive reading," and the varied mixtures and compounds of all these and other emphases. It is against this background of past experience that we must consider the present effort. * The test has many good features, and in the manual the authors have presented users with a generous array of information about the test and its scores. Norms are based on about 1900 high-school students, 1200 college students and 1000 students in special language schools. The reliabilities of the parts and of the whole are good (usually in the .90's), and the parts show fairly low intercorrelations. The important question is, of course, how well it predicts later achievement. As might be expected, the answer here is complicated. The correlations between scores on the test and the various criteria (course grades, final exam grades, etc.) swing over a wide range, from .13 to .83, with the majority of them falling between .40 and .60. The kind of course involved, the validity and reliability of the criterion, and other familiar complications are all involved. In sum, this is a well planned and carefully developed test, but it is far from a magic bullet in slaying the problems of language prognosis. As the authors point out, teachers and programs will have to develop their own experience with it. For some it may prove a waste of time and money; for others, it may be a means of improving their present ability to predict student achievement in language courses.

J Consult Psychol 24:99–100 F '60. Edward S. Bordin. * Sufficient data bearing on reliability and validity are presented to warrant issuing the test and to establish confidence in its usefulness as a diagnostic device. The normative data, particularly for high school and adult norms, are weak.

J Counsel Psychol 6:319 w '59. Laurence Siegel. * appears to be a highly successful venture. It does what its authors claim it will do, and does it well. It is a more valid predictor of success in learning foreign languages than are various intelligence tests. There are undoubtedly many situations wherein this kind of predictor may be used advantageously.

Personnel & Guid J 38:582–4 Mr '60. Herschel T. Manuel. * The *Manual* of the MLAT has a wealth of information in addition to the detailed directions for administering and scoring the test. * Reported reliability coefficients are generally good * the *Manual,* which is excellent in many respects, could be improved by interpreting reliability in terms of its practical bearing upon the scores of individuals. Even the cautious language, such as "tend to mean," in the discussion of the use of the parts of the test in diagnosis does not seem to cover this need adequately. Validity coefficients.... are of the magnitude often found in correlating general scholastic aptitude with total college marks at the end of the first semester and are high enough to indicate that the test may be used effectively. * The authors have given education a new measuring instrument which promises to be useful in a field in which measurement is needed. Since it is so new, no complete evaluation can be made. It must be tried by others in various situations. The reviewer expresses the hope that the authors will continue their study of basic problems and especially the nature of aptitude for language. The MLAT is offered modestly as an instrument for predicting for a student "how rapidly he can acquire the basic knowledge of the foreign language which will enable him to speak, understand, read, or write, depending upon the training he is given in these aspects of performance." The authors have presented evidence that the test is related to achievement in these areas. Will they not now go forward with further analyses? Perhaps the reviewer may use this occasion to suggest the need for an integrated approach to the discovery of differences in ability to learn a foreign language. Instead of suggesting a test such as the MLAT as a *better* test than an intelligence test, for example, we should try to see how various tests fit together to give us the information which we need. Nor should we be satisfied by prediction coefficients, which express only the relation between a pretest and a measure of actual performance. We need also to explore what students *can* do, what abilities they have for language learning. This is not at all the same as predicting what they *will* accomplish. It might even be better in prediction to start with measures already in common use, such as tests of verbal ability, and ask what additional information special aptitude tests will provide. It would please the reviewer to have the emphasis shift from prediction to an analysis and measurement of the abilities which constitute aptitude for a foreign language—or perhaps better for any language. In such a shift of attention from prediction to abilities, from *will* to *can,* we must be prepared for longer measuring instruments and more time for using them. Measurement must not rob the student of time to learn, to be sure, but the analysis which we need will take more time than the 30 or even 70 minutes which "practical" considerations are forcing upon testing. There is a long history of attempts to discover the nature of aptitude for foreign language and to construct useful measures. The MLAT and the research out of which it grew are a significant contribution to the solution of this problem. The reviewer commends both to the careful attention of those who need a measuring instrument and of those who are interested in the general problem.

[Other Tests]

For tests not listed above, see the following entries in *Tests in Print:* 615 and 616.

ENGLISH

[358]

***English Usage Test for Non-Native Speakers of English.** Non-native speakers of English; 1955–62; Forms A ['55, 8 pages], B ['57, 11 pages], C ['58, 11 pages], D ['60, 11 pages], E ['61, 7 pages], F ('62, 8 pages); directions sheets (2 pages): Forms A ['55], B–D ['60], E ['61], F ('62); reliability data for Form D only; distribution of Forms B–F restricted to the Agency for International Development or the Bureau of Educational and Cultural Affairs of the U.S. Department of State; distribution of Form A restricted to the Department of State; separate self-scoring answer sheets must be used; 60(65) minutes for Forms A, E, and F, 75(80) minutes for Forms B–D; A. L. Davis (A–C), Kenneth Croft (A–C), Harry Freeman (C), David P. Harris (D–F), Winifred E. Jones (D), and Leslie A. Palmer (F); American Language Institute. *

[359]

★Listening Test for Students of English as a Second Language. Non-native speakers of English; 1961–62; administered orally or by tape recording; Forms A ('61), B ('62), (7 pages); examiner's booklets: Forms A ('61), B ('62), (10 pages); distribution restricted to the Agency for International Development or the Bureau of Educational and Cultural Affairs of the U.S. Department of State; separate self-scoring answer sheets must be used; [25] minutes; David P. Harris and Leslie A. Palmer; American Language Institute. *

[360]

★Michigan Test of English Language Proficiency. Applicants from non-English language countries for admission to American colleges; 1961–62; Form A ('61, 15 pages); manual ('62, 15 pages); separate answer sheets must be used; $9 per 20 tests, 100 answer sheets, key, and manual; $2 per specimen set; postpaid; 75(90) minutes; test by John Upshur, Leslie Palmer, John Harris, and Geraldine May; manual by Division of Testing and Certification, English Language Institute, University of Michigan; distributed for the Institute by Follett's Michigan Book Store, Inc. *

JOHN B. CARROLL, *Professor of Educational Psychology, Harvard University, Cambridge, Massachusetts.*

The test under review is only a part of a larger battery designed to estimate "whether a student whose native language is not English is able to pursue academic study in an English language college or university, and how much study he might be able to undertake at his present level of proficiency in English." The larger battery "includes an impromptu 30 minute written composition test" and either a test of aural comprehension or an oral interview rating. What validity data are given in the manual for this test pertain more to the larger battery than to this test specifically; it is thus difficult to appraise the *Michigan Test of English Language Proficiency* separately from the battery of which it is a part. Further, there is no indication in the manual as to how the results of this test are to be used in conjunction with the other tests of the battery.

The test contains 100 objective four-choice items in three sections: 40 items on grammar, 40 items on vocabulary, and 20 items for reading comprehension. The examinee is allowed 75 minutes to complete these 100 items; the sections are not separately timed, and the manual gives no clear statement on whether the test is intended as a power or a speed test, except that it is suggested that students who adopt a wrong approach (e.g., "parsing" in the grammar section) will generally not have sufficient time for the entire test. I judge, however, that highly proficient students should be able to complete the test easily within 75 minutes. On the other hand, it is unfortunate that what may be fairly time consuming for slower students, the reading comprehension test, is put at the end of the test; some slower students may never reach it and thus never be tested for reading comprehension as such. Separate timing of sections might have yielded more meaningful scores. The authors were probably wise in not providing for separate scores on the sections since these sections are too short to be sufficiently reliable.

The items seem to have been well selected and constructed to test difficulties that non-native speakers have with English. The items in the grammar and vocabulary sections were drawn from pools of items tried out in pretests so as to give "maximal valid discrimination"—of what, we are not told, though it was probably the total score on the pretest.

The leads in the grammar items present snatches of conversation to provide a suitable context for the filling in of a missing word or phrase from the four alternatives given: a well prepared student can in many cases immediately produce the desired response without even looking for it among the alternatives, thus saving time. One infers from the manual that the authors carefully decided upon an outline for the grammar section that would specify 16 items on verb forms, 11 on "function words" excluding verb auxiliaries, 8 on nominal structures, and 5 on modification structures. The function word items actually test what some would call vocabulary, e.g., the meaning of the word *otherwise,* and one suspects also a component of general reasoning ability in many of these items. For example, a kind of reasoning may be involved in deciding whether to fill in *otherwise* or *anyway* in the following context: "We have been waiting for you for over an hour." "The traffic was very heavy; ______ I would have been here 50 minutes sooner."

The vocabulary items are of two kinds: (*a*) a "selection" type where the examinee chooses one of four alternatives to fill in a blank in a sentence; and (*b*) a "substitution type" in which the examinee selects a synonym or substitute for an underlined word. The manual states that 30 of the 40 items test words in the range of the 4,000 to 6,000 most common words of the Thorndike-Lorge general word count. Some of the words appear to be rather literary, or specialized in application, e.g., *spouse, fettered, prune* (trees), but in view of the broad range of disciplines to which university students are exposed perhaps this catholicity is necessary. The fact is that it is difficult to test vocabulary at all adequately with a test of only 40 items.

The reading comprehension section contains four paragraphs of 139 to 217 words in length, each followed by five items. The items require rather close reading and careful interpretation of the passages, more or less on the style of the reading comprehension sections of the CEEB *Scholastic Aptitude Test* except that these passages are shorter. Here again, intellectual verbal ability is probably measured fully as much as proficiency in English; this is excusable only on the supposition that foreign students would be all of high intelligence if tested in their native language. A virtue of these items, however, is that they cannot be answered on the basis of general information or reasoning: answering them requires one to read the passages.

The test is well printed and contains no typographical errors. The special answer sheet seemed to me a bit crowded, however, and I could imagine some foreign students making merely clerical errors in indicating answers. On the other hand, provisions have been made to permit induction of the student into the process of test taking: the manual presents a sample test and answer sheet which the user may reproduce and give to students in advance. Template scoring of the answer sheets is about as easy and efficient as hand scoring can be.

The normative data are not as complete as one might expect. For example, even though the test is reported to have been administered to 284 foreign students at two midwest universities, the only data on this norming consist of a table for translating the test scores to scores on the *Test of Aural Comprehension* (see 5:261), Form A, also given to these students. Thus, no frequency distribution or table of percentiles is presented in the manual. In another section of the manual, under the heading of reliability, we are told that for a group of 300 students with 10 "unrelated" language backgrounds and constituting a random selection of applicants to 150 American universities, the mean raw score was 75.35 (maximum = 100, chance-level score = 25) with a standard deviation of 12.77. Split-half reliability for this group is reported as .965 (no indication is given as to whether it was "stepped up" in the usual way), with a resulting standard error of measurement of 3.35. A standard error of measurement of 3.54 was reported for another, somewhat more homogeneous group. Reliability of the test thus appears to be up to usual standards, although the standard error of measurement is actually a bit too large to inspire confidence in placements based on the test.

This latter statement is made in the light of the suggestions offered in the manual regarding the interpretations of the scores after they have been transformed into scores equated to the aural comprehension test. For example, depending upon which of the following score ranges the equated score lies in—96–100, 90–95, 85–89, 80–84, 70–79, or 69 and below—different recommendations are made with regard to the kind of academic load the student can bear and the further English language training the student should take. For example, if the student is to be an undergraduate in liberal arts or education and makes an equated score between 85 and 89, he "may take up to ¾ the normal academic load plus a special course (4 hrs. per week) in English as a foreign language." The fact that such a score band is not much greater than *one* standard error of measurement raises a question as to the appropriateness of such precise recommendations in individual cases, even if these recommendations were backed up by sound validity data. The authors report that at the University of Michigan, the recommendations of the English Language Institute, based presumably not only on the test under review, but also on other parts of the proficiency battery, have been regularly followed in selecting and placing students. They report further that "there have been too few cases in which recommendations have been waived to allow a meaningful determination of the efficiency of the test as a predictor of academic success." This is not an adequate excuse for failing to report some kind of follow-up data on the actual academic success of students placed in the various categories of recommendation. For example, how many students placed in the highest category ("Can compete with native speakers of English on equal or nearly equal terms—no restrictions need be placed on elections") did in fact appear to be able to compete with native speakers of English? Instead, the only predictive validity data reported in the manual are a series of correlations between *battery* scores and academic success (average grades) in six different programs of the university, obtained at a time when student placement was not based upon English Language Institute recommendations. These correlations, ranging from .26 to .77, are uninterpretable because no means and standard deviations are given; i.e., one cannot judge the degree to which the various groups may have been selected. Also, there is no way of separating the validity of the test as a measure of *English proficiency* from its validity as a predictor of *academic success.* Of course, it can be argued that a battery whose purpose is described in such ambiguous terms as that of "estimating whether a student whose native language is not English is able to pursue academic study in an English language college or university" perhaps needs to contain both elements specifically valid for measuring English language proficiency and elements specifically valid for predicting academic success. If so, the test under review can be indicted both on the count that it fails to differentiate these two aspects of validity and on the count that it appears to emphasize the measurement of English proficiency over the prediction of academic success.

Despite the fact that the research underpinnings for recommendations based on the test are somewhat weak, this is a generally well constructed test and if the user acquires experience in interpreting scores it could help in selecting and placing non-English speaking foreign students. It must be recognized that the test under review is solely a written test; an assiduous student of English grammar books could easily get a high score on it even though he lacked the degree of facility in speaking and understanding English that would be prerequisite for succeeding in an English-speaking college or university. It would be dangerous to use this test as a sole predictor.

[361]

★Oral Rating Form for Rating Language Proficiency in Speaking and Understanding English. Non-native speakers of English; 1959–62; also called *AULC Interview Rating Form;* 6 ratings by interviewers: comprehension, pronunciation, grammar and word-order, vocabulary, general speed of speech and sentence length, total; individual; 1 form ('62, 2 pages, identical with form published in 1959 except for title and some wording changes); manual ('60, 11 pages); no data on reliability; distribution restricted to the Agency for International Development and the Bureau of Educational and Cultural Affairs of the U.S. Department of State; (15–30) minutes; [David P. Harris]; American Language Institute. *

[362]

★Test of Aural Perception in English for Japanese Students. Japanese students in American colleges; 1950; for research use only; orally administered; 1 form; manual (18 pages, including examiner's script); no data on reliability; no norms; separate answer sheets must be used; $4 per 100 answer sheets; $1.50 per set of manual and scoring stencil; postpaid; [30] minutes; Robert Lado and R. D. Andrade; distributed for English Language Institute, University of Michigan by Follett's Michigan Book Store, Inc. *

[363]

★A Vocabulary and Reading Test for Students of English as a Second Language, Revised Edition. Non-native speakers of English; 1960–62; Forms A ('61), VR-B ('62), (11 pages); directions sheets: Form A ['60, 2 pages], Form VR-B ('62, 2 pages); no data on reliability of revised edition; distribution restricted to the Agency for International Development and the Bureau of Educational and Cultural Affairs of the U.S. Department of State; separate answer sheets must be used; 60(65) minutes; David P. Harris and Leslie A. Palmer (VR-B); American Language Institute. *

[Other Tests]

For tests not listed above, see the following entries in *Tests in Print:* 619–22, 624, 626, and 628.

FRENCH

[364]

★Baltimore County French Test. 1 year high school; 1962; 2 scores: parts A, B; administered orally or by tape recording in part; IBM; 1 form (10 pages); manual (9 pages); no data on reliability; separate answer sheets must be used; $3.75 per 35 tests; $1.75 per 35 IBM answer sheets; 25¢ per scoring stencil; 50¢ per specimen set; $7.50 per 3¾ ips tape recording; postage extra; 80(90) minutes in 2 sessions; Baltimore County French Language Committee; Bobbs-Merrill Co., Inc. *

REFERENCES

1. JUNGEBLUT, ANN. "Experimentation With Baltimore County French Test in Independent Schools." *Ed Rec B* 84:67–71 Jl '63. *

NELSON BROOKS, *Associate Professor of French, Yale University, New Haven, Connecticut.*

This test is designed for use at the end of the first year's study of French in junior and senior high schools. It was planned, the authors say, to satisfy a new need resulting from a shift from a reading approach to a listening and speaking approach.

It is divided into two parts, Part A with 90 items and Part B with 50 items. Each part can be given in a single class period not less than 43 minutes long. In Part A, the first 60 items are done entirely with paper and pencil while the last 30 items involve a spoken stimulus only (these are true-false items, and no reading of response is necessary). In Part B a spoken stimulus is involved in every item, the response being printed and also read aloud. All the spoken parts have been recorded on one continuous tape prepared to accompany the test. A complete script is also provided in case the teacher wishes not to use tape but to give the spoken stimuli by live voice.

About a test with this new orientation we must ask certain key questions: What is the role of the different skills? What is the role of English? What is the role of translation? What is the relative emphasis placed upon structure and upon vocabulary? In this test only the receptive skills are brought into play; nothing is either said or written by the student. What we have, then, is a test of reading and listening. The reading of French is involved in 95 items. Listening comprehension is involved, more or less importantly, in 80 of them. English is an integral part of about a third of the items in Part A (15 items on culture are entirely in English). There is no English in the items of Part B. At no point is the candidate asked to translate, but there are 15 grammar items in which English sentences are translated into French except for a word or expression. In less than 20 per cent of the items is the focus upon problems of structure; in all the others it is a matter of vocabulary, idiom, and overall comprehension.

The items in which certain parts are spoken present a complicated pattern of listening alone and listening-plus-reading. In the 30 true-false items in Part A, there is merely the hearing of a statement, repeated once, on the basis of which it is deemed true or false. In Part B, in the first 42 items, the stimulus is heard but not seen, while the response is both heard and seen. For the final 8 items of Part B, the passage and the alternative answers to the questions are both heard and seen, while the questions are heard but not seen. Throughout the test, everything that is spoken is repeated, with the exception of the text of the brief story at the end of Part B, which is heard only once.

The tape that accompanies the test uses an American voice for English instructions and native speakers for the parts that are in French. The French voices are of good quality and are recorded clearly. The directing of the recording of these voices, however, was faulty. The speed of speech is not satisfactory, being almost uniformly too slow—so much so that at times the language is actually deformed. Sometimes the French voices say English words, with quaint results. The word "number" is repeated over and over again, through dozens of items, to no purpose. With respect to speed, the American voice reading the instructions in English presents a good example of what should have been done in French.

Forty items in the test involve a true-false choice. This is regrettable because of the limited value of true-false items unless their number is considerably greater than it is here. One must admit that a candidate may know nothing whatever about a subject and still score 50 per cent when multiple-choice provides only two possible answers and, as in the case of this test, there is no correction for guessing. Though useful as a class exercise, the true-false technique has not proved satisfactory for the formal measurement of language learning.

In the overemphasis upon meaning and the lack of emphasis upon control of structure we find the most disappointing aspect of this test, an aspect which reveals the strong influence of the popular fallacy that a language is its vocabulary. The heart of a language is its sound system and its systems of order and form; these are what should receive major emphasis during the first levels of learning. In this test the student needs to know a few verb forms, a little about the forms of adjectives, and some uses of the partitive. But there is no reference at all to matters of pronoun substitution, to forms of negation and interrogation, or to comparison—to say nothing of face-to-face exchange between speaker and hearer as reflected in utterance and rejoinder. All these should be introduced very early in any basic course, and all lend themselves very readily to testing.

The authors have shown imagination and initiative in presenting an interesting variety of item types. It would be equally welcome if the content of the language referred more often than it does to something beyond the horizons of the classroom and the childlike preoccupations of the elementary school.

All will admit the extreme difficulty of preparing a standardized test for use at the end of the first year of work at the secondary level, for the patent reason that there is no widespread professional agreement on appropriate materials. The idea of the test attempted here is excellent; it is almost doomed to failure from the start because of the variety of curricular content appearing in various schools. If, as the authors imply on page 4 of the Teacher's Manual, the prospective user's students have been learning what the students in Baltimore County have been learning, the test will measure reasonably well.

Mary E. Turnbull, *Formerly Head of Test Production, Educational Testing Service, Princeton, New Jersey.*

The *Baltimore County French Test* is a good achievement test which should be particularly useful at the end of a first-year French course or at the beginning of a second-year course, when its use could show the teacher the strengths and weaknesses of the class.

The test consists of Part A and Part B, each designed as a 40-minute test. Part A, the more varied, is divided into Part 1, Vocabulary (7 minutes), Part 2, Reading (6 minutes), Part 3, Culture (5 minutes), Part 4, Grammar (7 minutes), and Part 5, Aural Comprehension (15 minutes). This is not a speed test and, except for Part 5, students may go on to each part before time for the previous part has been called. Part B is an aural test, which students accustomed to a reading approach to French will probably find very difficult. Like Part 5 of Part A, it is recorded on a tape; alternatively, the examiner's voice may be substituted for the taped voices. Part B consists of three sections—30 French questions or incomplete sentences, 12 short French paragraphs, each describing an object that must be identified, and 8 French questions based on a short story that is read to the student and is also printed in the test book. Each of the 50 items of Part B has three given choices that are read to the student and are also printed in the test book.

The vocabulary section is made up of easy English-to-French items and French sentence completions. Mainly nouns and verbs are tested. Item 9, which includes "Sur *sa* tête," exposes the student to somewhat poor French.

The reading section has 10 true-false French

statements and two interesting short French paragraphs that are followed by questions based on them. One (item 26) of the questions could be answered without regard to the paragraph.

The culture section has 15 five-choice items in English; here the emphasis is mainly on points of interest in Paris and on French geography. To answer six of the questions the student must refer to a map of France in his test book. The map is well done except for a slight flaw—the letter C on the map could easily be mistaken for a G and C is the correct answer to item 42. If the order of the letter choices in this section had been alphabetical, selection of the desired answer might have been easier.

The grammar section tests mainly verb forms, although there are some questions on agreement of adjectives. In each item an incomplete French translation of a given English sentence is to be completed. Item 51 might be better placed in the vocabulary part and although choice 4 is given as the correct answer for item 52, a good argument could be made for choice 3.

The aural comprehension section is composed of 30 true-false French statements. On the tape these are read slowly and clearly; each statement is read twice, there are well timed pauses between each, and the item numbers are clearly indicated so that the student should have no difficulty recording his answers beside the correct item numbers.

Part B has good variety in the kinds of questions asked and should prove interesting to the student. The recording is excellent and shows much care in preparation and delivery. Again the student is exposed to rather awkward French in a couple of items (25 and 33), but, in general, this part is of high quality. For those who do not use the tape, the statements, questions and answers, and short story and its questions and answers are printed in the Teacher's Manual and are to be read by the examiner. Having more choice 2's as correct answers would give a better balance in correct answer-choice distribution in this part.

The printing and proofreading of the test book and of the Teacher's Manual have been very carefully done, except for the misplacement of two lines in column 2 of the first page of the manual.

One answer sheet can be used for both Parts A and B; however, it may be difficult to use only one for both parts if they are administered at different times. In the directions for scoring the test the scorer is told to record the score "in the box on the answer sheet after 'Total,'" but there is no "Total" box on the answer sheet.

The purpose of the test is clearly stated in the manual and a concise description of it is also given there. No attempt has been made at oral testing. The test's validity has not been measured nor are there any data on reliability. Phi coefficients have been computed for all the test items and a distribution of these is given in the manual. Separate percentile tables for Part A and Part B are given, based on 4,078 first-year French students in Baltimore County in 1960 and 1961.

One of the great assets of the *Baltimore County French Test* is the tape recording which is used for the last section of Part A and for the whole of Part B. This is particularly well done and should be very useful in schools where a listening and speaking approach to French is stressed.

[365]

★Canadian Achievement Test in French (CATF). Grade 10; 1961–63; this test and tests 5, 252, 565, and 566 make up the *Canadian Test Battery*, grade 10; 1 form ('61, 8 pages); 2 editions of manual (for use also with test 252): hand scoring ('63, 7 pages), machine scoring ('63, 8 pages); supplementary data ('63, 6 pages) for the battery; battery profile ('63, 1 page); separate answer sheets or cards must be used; $1.25 per 25 tests; $1 per set of 50 hand scoring answer sheets and hand scoring manual; 20¢ per hand scoring stencil; 20¢ per 15 battery profiles; 50¢ per set of 25 IBM answer cards (machine scoring through the Department of Educational Research only); 10¢ per machine scoring manual; 50¢ per specimen set; $2.15 per battery specimen set; postage extra; 60(70–75) minutes; Department of Educational Research, Ontario College of Education, University of Toronto; distributed by Guidance Centre (machine scoring manual and answer cards must be purchased from the Department of Educational Research). *

REFERENCES

1. D'OYLEY, VINCENT R. *Technical Manual for the Canadian Tests: Statistical Data on the Carnegie Study Tests of Academic Aptitude and Achievement in Grades 8, 9, and 10 in Ontario Schools and Grades 7 and 8 in Toronto Schools.* Carnegie Study of Identification and Utilization of Talent in High School and College, Bulletin No. 4. Toronto, Canada: Department of Educational Research, Ontario College of Education, University of Toronto, 1964. Pp. viii, 50. *

2. D'OYLEY, VINCENT R. *Testing: The First Two Years of the Carnegie Study 1959 to 1961: Analysis of Scores by Course, Sex, and Size of Municipality.* Carnegie Study of Identification and Utilization of Talent in High School and College, Bulletin No. 6. Toronto, Canada: Department of Educational Research, Ontario College of Education, University of Toronto, 1964. Pp. ix, 53. *

MARY E. TURNBULL, *Formerly Head of Test Production, Educational Testing Service, Princeton, New Jersey.*

The *Canadian Achievement Test in French* is a very good one-hour test for grade 10 students, consisting of four parts, not separately timed: 1, Vocabulary (35 items); 2, Grammar (45 items); 3, Comprehension (10 items); and 4, Pronunciation (12 items).

The test is accurately and attractively printed, the directions are clear, and it contains a good variety of questions. In almost all cases, the given choices are excellent, with many logical distractors included.

The first three parts are broken down into a number of short groups of questions—English to French, French to English, French sentence completion, French synonyms, French antonyms, etc.—a nice selection of slightly differing problems which should hold the students' interest and avoid monotony. Within the groups the questions seem usually to be in ascending order of difficulty.

Part 1, Vocabulary, concentrates mainly on nouns, verbs, and adjectives, whereas Part 2, Grammar, tests a good selection of verb forms, pronouns, adjectives, and prepositions. Part 3, Comprehension, contains three short and interesting paragraphs, each of which is followed by two good multiple choice questions. Part 4, Pronunciation, briefly tests words with the same pronunciation, underlined sounds, pronounced final consonants, silent consonants, and nasal vowels. No attempt has been made at aural testing.

In three groups of items where the sentences to be completed follow the given choices, having the sentences printed before the choices would probably assist the test taker. Two items (45 and 48) in the grammar part seem more appropriately classified as tests of vocabulary. The last group in the grammar part contains only two items, one of which (80) tests the same form of the same verb that has already been tested in item 43. The alert student will find the answer to item 54 given in item 33, and item 50 will tell him the answer to item 3, while item 81, in turn, will give him the answer to item 50.

The manuals tell of the development of the test, give clear and concise directions for administration, and include an answer key and percentile rank norms based on 42,264 grade 10 French students. A profile norm chart is available for the six tests in the *Canadian Test Battery* for grade 10, of which this test is one. An item analysis of this test and computation of validity coefficients between the grade 10 school French mark and the *Canadian Achievement Test in French* are in process of completion and reports on the findings will be available soon.[1]

This is an excellent French test covering a wide range of the different aspects of the mastery of the French language. It deserves widespread use and most students should almost enjoy taking it.

[366]

***College Entrance Examination Board Achievement Test: French.** Candidates for college entrance with 2–4 years high school French; 1901–64; for more complete information, see 760; 60(80) minutes; program administered for the College Entrance Examination Board by Educational Testing Service. *

REFERENCES

1–7. See 4:237.
8–9. See 5:263.
10. BLACK, D. B. "A Comparison of the Performance on Selected Standardized Tests to That on the Alberta Grade XII Departmental Examination of a Select Group of University of Alberta Freshmen." *Alberta J Ed Res* 5:180–90 S '59. * (*PA* 34:6559)
11. CABAT, LOUIS, AND GODIN, JACOB D. *How to Prepare for College Board Achievement Tests in French.* Great Neck, N.Y.: Barron's Educational Series, Inc., 1960. Pp. vi, 110. *
12. BRÉE, GERMAINE. "College Board French Tests." *French R* 36:119–24 D '62. *
13. SCHEIDER, ROSE M. "Evolution of the Listening Comprehension Tests." *Col Board R* 48:24–8 f '62. *

For a review by Walter V. Kaulfers of earlier forms, see 4:237. For reviews of the testing program, see 760.

[367]

★College Entrance Examination Board Achievement Test: French Listening Comprehension. Candidates for college entrance with 2–4 years high school French; 1960–63; tests administered at the local secondary school on a specified date in February; candidates must also be registered to take one or more achievement tests in one of the regular program administrations; for more complete information, see 760; (30–40) minutes; program administered for the College Entrance Examination Board by Educational Testing Service. *

For reviews of the testing program, see 760.

[368]

***College Entrance Examination Board Advanced Placement Examination: French.** High school students desiring credit for college level courses or admission to advanced courses; 1954–63; for more complete information, see 761; 180(200) minutes; program administered for the College Entrance Examination Board by Educational Testing Service. *

REFERENCES

1. VALLEY, JOHN R. "College Actions on CEEB Advanced Placement Language Examination Candidates." *Mod Lang J* 43:261–3 O '59. *

[1] The supplementary data referred to in the entry above became available after this review was completed.—Editor.

2. NIESS, ROBERT J. "The Advanced Placement Program in French." *French R* 35:311–8 Ja '62. *
3. NELSON, ROBERT J. "The Relation of Language to Literature in the Advanced Placement Program." *French R* 36:617–28 My '63. *

[369]

★College Entrance Examination Board Placement Tests: French Listening Comprehension Test. Entering college freshmen; 1962–63, c1955–61; IBM; Forms DLC1, DLC2 in a single booklet ('55), KPL1, KPL2 in a single booklet (c1960–61, 11 pages, a reprint of inactive forms of *College Entrance Examination Board Achievement Test: French Listening Comprehension*); test administered by 7½ ips tape recording; for more complete information, see 759; 30(40) minutes; program administered for the College Entrance Examination Board by Educational Testing Service. *

[370]

★College Entrance Examination Board Placement Tests: French Reading Test. Entering college freshmen; 1962–63, c1955–63; IBM; Forms KPL1, KPL2 in a single booklet (c1955–57, 22 pages, a reprint of inactive forms of *College Entrance Examination Board Achievement Test: French*); for more complete information, see 759; 60(70) minutes; program administered for the College Entrance Examination Board by Educational Testing Service. *

For a review of the College Entrance Examination Board Achievement Test: French, *see 4:237.*

[371]

★Common Concepts Foreign Language Test: French [Research Edition]. "Students [in any grade] who have had enough foreign language instruction to place them at the Level 1 stage in their achievement"; 1962–64; aural comprehension; may be administered using live voice but tape recording is recommended; IBM; Forms 1, 2; a single booklet ('62, 31 pages) presents response options for both forms of this test and the German and Spanish tests of the series; mimeographed preliminary manual ('64, 24 pages); interim norms (grades 7–12 only); separate answer sheets or cards must be used; 75¢ per test; $5.95 per 3¾ ips tape recording; 5¢ per IBM answer sheet; 20¢ per scoring stencil; 2¢ per Cal-Card; 20¢ per hand scoring stencil; 15¢ per manual; postage extra; $1 per specimen set without tape; $6.95 per specimen set with tape; postpaid; scoring service available; (40–45) minutes; Bela H. Banathy, Miles V. Zintz, W. James Popham, Joseph M. Sadnavitch, Rena Krichbaum, Fred B. Gannon, Valdemar Hempel, and Klaus A. Mueller; California Test Bureau. *

[372]

★Ford-Hicks French Grammar Completion Tests. High school; 1944; variously titled; Forms A, B, C, D, ['44, 4 pages]; manual ['44, 4 pages]; $1 per 12 tests; 10¢ per single copy; $1 per set of key and manual; postpaid; 35(40) minutes; H. E. Ford and R. K. Hicks; J. M. Dent & Sons (Canada) Ltd. *

[373]

***French I and II: Minnesota High School Achievement Examinations.** 1 or 2 years high school; 1953–63; series formerly called *Midwest High School Achievement Examinations;* new norms issued each June; Form F ('60, 6 pages, originally called Form C) used in 1963 testing; no specific manual; series manual ('63, 4 pages); series norms ['63, 4 pages]; series cumulative profile ('62, 2 pages); no data on reliability; no description of normative population; 12¢ per test; $2.50 per 100 profiles; postage extra; 20¢ per specimen set, postpaid; 60(65) minutes; American Guidance Service, Inc. *

For a review by Mary E. Turnbull of earlier forms, see 5:268.

[374]

French: Teacher Education Examination Program. College seniors preparing to teach secondary school; 1957; for more complete information, see 709; IBM; 80(95) minutes; Educational Testing Service. *

For a review of the testing program, see 5:543.

[375]

★French Test (Two-Year Course): Affiliation Testing Program for Catholic Secondary Schools. Grades 10–12 and students who are candidates for the high school diploma issued by the Catholic University of America; 1949–63; administered annually in May at individual schools; IBM; new form issued annually; Form Z ('63, 13 pages) used in 1963 program; separate answer sheets must be used; 50¢ per test and IBM answer sheet, postpaid; specimen set of the complete battery free; fee includes purchase of test booklets, scoring, and other services; for more complete information, see 758; 90(100) minutes; Program of Affiliation, Catholic University of America. *

HENRY CHAUNCEY, *President, Educational Testing Service, Princeton, New Jersey.* [Review of Forms Y and Z.]

The French test of the Affiliation Testing Program appears to be well suited for the two years of French it is designed to test.

Those areas of foreign language learning that can be tested by multiple choice questions (listening comprehension, reading comprehension, vocabulary, structure, and cultural background) are all covered by easy to difficult questions appropriate to two-year programs. However, the practice of having the proctor read the listening comprehension passages and questions hardly provides for standardized administration of this part of the test. In this age of widespread use of tape recorders, it would seem that a tape might well be used to provide more uniform testing conditions and thereby achieve greater reliability.

Instructions for taking the test are quite clear and understandable. The practice of using an English translation of the stem of sample items in describing the best answer for each sample question in Form Z is questionable.

This technique leads to statements such as: "The opposite of 'large' is *petit*." Actually, of course, the opposite of large is small; petit is the opposite of grand. If it is felt necessary to indicate the English meaning of the stem, it might be preferable to say: "The opposite of 'grand' (large) is *petit*."

Students should be able to finish the test in the allotted time, provided the proctor does not use more than the time specified for the listening comprehension part. The approximate time is indicated for the listening test, but no specific time is indicated for the remainder of the test; time allotments should be indicated for both these sections of the test, so that they will not vary from administration to administration. This, incidentally, is another reason why it might be wiser to tape the listening comprehension portion of the test.

The items are generally well written. Occasionally a nonexistent form is given as a distractor, for example, Form Y, item 53 (option 1); Form Z, items 22 (option 3), 23 (options 2, 3, 4), and 29 (option 2). This practice is questionable.

The test as a whole is well organized, well written, and well presented. A good balance of items in the various areas tested is provided. The avoidance of the use of English as a testing device is commendable.

For a review of the complete program, see 758.

[376]

***The Graduate Record Examinations Advanced Tests: French.** Grades 16–17; 1939–63; for more complete information, see 762; 180(200) minutes; Educational Testing Service. *

NELSON BROOKS, *Associate Professor of French, Yale University, New Haven, Connecticut.* [Review of Form K-GGR.]

The preparation of a multiple choice test to estimate a student's fitness for advanced work in cultural and literary studies in the field of French is no mean task. These are times in which successful candidates are likely to pursue their studies under the direction of faculty members, many of whom are made queasy at the very thought of measurement and selection by multiple choice tests, and one cannot deny that these test authors faced a serious challenge. Yet they have met this challenge with resourcefulness and aplomb, and have produced an instrument that does what it sets out to do with thoroughness and distinction. Apart from a few flaws—only one of them serious—this test could well stand as an eloquent rebuttal to those who look upon this kind of measurement as intellectual heresy. From beginning to end, it requires just the kind of perception, knowledge, and range of acquaintance that the candidate had better be in possession of if he hopes to flourish in graduate school courses in this field.

The test is composed of 200 items, each with five proposed choices. There are in all nine separate (but continuously timed) sections of the test, each with its own set of directions. These directions are in English. There is no English in any of the items themselves. In three sections there are quoted passages of some length, each with a sequence of statements or questions based upon it. Five other sections ask for knowledge of general cultural and historical background, of literary vocabulary, of titles and characters famous in literature, of wide-ranging and detailed knowledge of literary history from medieval to modern. One section asks for the interpretation of a number of brief unidentified quotations. These nine sections are arranged in such a way as to vary the candidate's task from time to time, interspersing groups of self-contained items with other groups dealing with given texts. A few of the self-contained items deal with short quotations, but most of them refer only to knowledge the candidate is expected to possess. Some items deal with morphology, stylistics, and poetics, others with literary schools and salons. Still others present questions concerning the overall comprehension of quoted passages, the precise meaning of words and lines, and language change. The substance of the items differs widely, from acquaintance with the notions of important philosophies to the present day use of a written accent; all are germane to problems the student is sure to encounter in advanced studies.

The items themselves are of three varieties: (*a*) a question plus five answers, (*b*) a stem plus five completions, and (*c*) a word matched with one of five other words. In three sections of the test, only the last named variety appears. In the remaining sections the first two are intermixed at random.

In four of the nine sections the directions are adequate to describe the task that is set, in five sections they are not. The point at issue is the terminology "questions and answers" used to apply to items that are not question-and-answer but stem-and-completion. In one section this problem is handled with wording that is fully satisfactory; the same could easily have been true of the others. To mention this minor detail in the giving of directions may seem close to quibbling, yet a test of this kind sets up a situation in which the candidate must sensitize himself to preciseness and minute discrimination, and it is disturbing to him when laxness and inadequacy are apparent in the English that is telling him what to do. A test that is so well written, so important, and so widely used deserves better editing and printing. Not only should the directions be more accurately related to the nature of the items, but the page layout could be greatly improved, especially in the separation of one item from another. In some of the self-contained items that are preceded by a short quotation it looks at first, because of the way in which the item numbers are printed, as if this quotation belonged to the preceding item. Furthermore, the sections themselves are not clearly marked off. For psychological reasons, it would be better to make the candidate fully aware of the various phases and the change of pace in the questioning to which he is being subjected.

The wrongness of the wrong choice (in some cases the right one) is a basic problem in all tests of this kind. For the most part, the authors have handled this difficult matter in a fully commendable way, and it is regrettable that they did not do so all the way through. In most of the items the candidate is asked to *accept* one choice out of five, but in some cases he is to *reject* one out of five. It is in some of these last that the authors have left themselves open to criticism on this score. When wrongness is the result of a beginning and ending not fitting together, or of a statement, correct in itself, not being attributed to the appropriate author, we are within legitimate bounds. But when the wrongness of what is suggested appears only in the completion proper and results in the printing of statements that are incorrect or untrue, we have crossed a frontier that is of extreme importance in multiple choice testing. We are then in very deep water, and are involved with the philosophical distinction between term and proposition, with problems of learning psychology, and above all with matters of professional principles. It is well known that the multiple choice technique has been shamefully cheapened in foreign language tests by offering in the printed choices examples of incorrect spelling, incorrect agreements, incorrect word order, and faulty meaning—the wrongness not being the result of appropriate terms wrongly fitted together into unsatisfactory propositions, but being an integral part of terms that are themselves spurious. In this test there are eight items in which the wrongness is exclusively in the completion. Seven of these present definitions or attributions rather loosely related, and, though suspect, they can be said to do little more than reflect the internal processes of fitting and matching that characterize this kind of test—though the inner processes of language behavior and the actuality of printing are of vastly different levels of reality. But one item contains in one of its completions a full-fledged sentence that is flatly inexact (it is, of course, the right answer). To have presented these eight items, and especially this last, is a regrettable lapse in what is otherwise an exemplary series of multiple choice items. The presence of these dubious items is not likely to affect the performance of the test as a discriminating instrument; statistical accuracy is not jeopardized. But *noblesse oblige*. Many of those who take this graduate school test will themselves be making tests for students, and before very long. And in their inexperienced and less capable hands, items containing the wrongness of the sort concerning us here can easily lead to poor measurement and to the further compromise of a test technique that is already in hazard. The introduction into such tests of completion elements that are *in themselves* wrong is tantamount to the intrusion into a jigsaw puzzle of pieces that do not fit into the puzzle in question, nor, for that matter, into any other. Professional scruples would appear to demand that problems of this degree of falsity be eschewed.

The student who takes this test is asked to deal with a total field of impressive proportions. He must be able to envisage vast areas in perspective, he must have a wide acquaintance with important persons and ideas, with literary history and with literary works in different forms, with significant cultural, historical, and geographical facts, and with memorable characters in fiction. He must time and again look closely at examples of literary art and report with accuracy on what he reads in the lines themselves and between the lines. And, happily, he is asked not only to display a knowledge acquired before presenting himself for the test, but also to call upon his command of language, his acquaintance with literature, and his own perceptive sensibilities to carry on constructive processes and arrive at conclusions that to him are new. This opportunity for synthesis during the test leads not only to fully satisfactory discrimination among competing candidates, but also provides a sense of intellectual accomplishment for the candidate himself. This is testing at its best.

For a review by Walter V. Kaulfers, see 5:270. For a review of the testing program, see 5:601.

[377]

★Graduate School Foreign Language Test: French. Graduate level degree candidates required to demonstrate reading proficiency in French; 1963–64; Forms K-LFG1, K-LFG2, ('63, 33 pages); for more complete information, see 356; 80(100) minutes; Educational Testing Service. *

CLARENCE E. TURNER, *Professor of Romance Languages, Rutgers, the State University, New Brunswick, New Jersey.* [Review of Form K-LFG2.]

The test at hand is in response to a long felt need. Graduate faculties, in order that their candidates may control research material published all over the world, are accustomed to require a reading knowledge usually of two foreign languages, one of which is nearly always French. A sound standardized test in this area would permit each year on a university campus the saving (depending on the testing methods now practiced) of up to 200 faculty man-hours. It would open up the prospect of reciprocity among faculties, today usually denied. The impersonality of the procedure would probably have a good effect on graduate student morale.

The operational realities must always be borne in mind. At least half of these graduate students, and among scientists the proportion is still higher, have had little or no French in school or college. To meet the requirement, they have learned French either on their own or through a special course adapted to their case. To this they can normally devote part of a year in addition to their full program in the courses and laboratories of their discipline. Typically, they attend one French session per week, whose oral-aural element is of necessity greatly reduced or omitted altogether. The accurate translation into English of specialized material is likely to be the one language skill in which they have been well trained, and at this they are often extremely good.

Section 1 of the present test seems not to be aimed at the persons just described. On the sound premise that knowledge of the structure of French is a relevant skill, Section 1 begins with 25 discrete items which would be wholly admirable to test students with two or more years of French in a modern secondary or college classroom. These items assume ear-training, experience in the construction of French sentences, the ability to think in French, and a sense of what "is French" and what is "not French." These things are all desirable and feasible in themselves, but all are denied to many, probably most, graduate students seeking to establish a research tool. Now there are frequently recurring aspects of structure which are vital to correct translation, and here was an opportunity to test them: for example, relative *qui* and *que,* telling noun from adjective by position, *ne....que,* the force of tenses, indefinite adjectives, or connectives like *il n'en est pas ainsi* and *quoi qu'il en soit.* In short, the structure items of Section 1 in their present form lack face validity for the population, and it is not surprising to read in the accompanying test analysis booklet that Section 1 proved "quite difficult." For graduate students as I have observed them, I should think Section 1 would be bewildering and demoralizing as well.

Section 2 offers each candidate four paragraphs of French with multiple choice questions in English. The material is generally well selected and ingeniously arranged in a system permitting each student to read in his own or a closely related field. Here, where vocabulary and concepts should be familiar, was the opportunity to construct a fairly rigorous test of accurate comprehension of details. Comparatively few items, however, pinpoint a specific problem of French. More typically, the problem lies in following the tentacles of the author's speculative thought and coming up with an opinion as to the author's purpose, or as to the main drift or general idea of a passage.

Not uncommonly the correct answer is obvious independently of the text. My suspicions aroused by student comment after administration of this test, I decided to pose as a graduate student in the social sciences and take *without reading a word of French text* those portions of Section 2 that such a candidate would answer, as well as those portions of Section 1 that are based on a text. I have assured myself in this fashion of a comfortable position at the 63rd percentile. A bright graduate student with advanced training in the subject matter could, of course, have done much better, still without reading a single word of any French text.

It should be mentioned that the test is speeded. On no section did 75 per cent of the students complete the test, and on some sections barely over half completed it. Since reasonable speed of reading is by definition part of the concept of a research tool, this is not out of line with the purpose of the test except when combined with the above-mentioned emphasis on skimming for the general idea.

It would be naïve to expect a test like this to yield a direct pass or fail score, yet of course this is just the kind of conversion that a graduate dean must ultimately make. To aid him in this, the accompanying Guide to Interpretation of Scores offers scaled scores and percentile norms based on administration of the test to 1,744 subjects in 37 institutions, 243 electing the biological sciences option, 560 the humanities, and the other groups falling between those extremes. Parallel testing by some other method is recommended, and demonstration is made with imaginary statistics of how this might be useful. Whatever circumstances may have prevented the inclusion of real data from cooperating institutions, the results of such experiments would have been most welcome here, and it is to be hoped that they will be forthcoming.

To conclude, I could recommend this test to a graduate dean for his purposes only after revision of Section 1 to bring it into line with graduate students' training and experience; revision of Section 2 to bring greater emphasis to accuracy of detail and less to the general idea; and study of experimental data from parallel testing in my own institution, but hopefully also in others.

[378]

★MLA-Cooperative Foreign Language Tests: French. 1 or 2 years high school or 2 semesters college, 3 or 4 years high school or 4 semesters college; 1963–64; 4 tests in a single booklet: listening, speaking, reading, writing; IBM in part; 2 levels; directions for administering and scoring ['64, 39 pages] for this and the German, Italian, Russian, and Spanish tests of the series; no data on reliability; no norms; $5 per 10 tests; separate answer sheets may be used for listening and reading tests; $1 per 20 IBM scorable answer sheets; $1 per 10 scoring stencils (answer pattern must be punched out locally); $7 per 3¾ ips tape for listening test; $7 per 3¾ ips tape for speaking test (blank tapes or discs for recording student responses must be obtained locally); postage extra; $2 per specimen set, cash orders postpaid; (25–35) minutes for listening, (10–20) minutes for speaking, 35(40) minutes for reading, 35(40) minutes for writing; prepared in cooperation with the Modern Language Association of America; Cooperative Test Division. *

a) [LOWER LEVEL.] 1 or 2 years high school or 2 semesters college; form LA ('63, 23 pages).

b) [HIGHER LEVEL.] 3 or 4 years high school or 4 semesters college; form MA ('63, 25 pages).

[379]

★MLA Foreign Language Proficiency Tests for Teachers and Advanced Students: French. Grades 15–17 and foreign language teachers; 1961–64; IBM in part; 7 tests; 2 forms ('61): Form JML1 (also called Form A, available for institutional programs), Form JML2 (also called Form B, restricted to state and local teacher certification programs); series supervisor's manual ['62, 34 pages]; series norms leaflet ('64, 4 pages); series interpretive leaflet ('64, 4 pages); examination fees: $15 per battery of 7 tests, $12.50 per battery of 4 skill tests (listening, speaking, reading, writing); fees include rental of test materials and scoring and reporting service; postage extra; fee for 30-day examination, $3.70 per battery; Modern Language Association of America and Educational Testing Service; program administered by Educational Testing Service. *

a) LISTENING COMPREHENSION TEST: FRENCH. IBM; 2 forms ('61, 6–7 pages, containing response options only); stimulus material presented on 3¾ or 7½ ips tape; $1.50 per examinee; (20–30) minutes.

b) SPEAKING TEST: FRENCH. 2 forms ('61, 9 pages, containing scripts for all languages in the series plus a section on 3¾ or 7½ ips tape); responses recorded on tapes or records supplied by the publisher; $6.75 per examinee; (15–30) minutes.

c) READING TEST: FRENCH. IBM; 2 forms ('61, 12 pages); $1.25 per examinee; 40(50) minutes.

d) WRITING TEST: FRENCH. IBM in part; 2 forms ('61, 8 pages); $3.50 per examinee; 45(55) minutes.

e) APPLIED LINGUISTICS TEST: FRENCH. IBM; 2 forms ('61, 10 pages); $1.25 per examinee; 40(50) minutes.

f) CIVILIZATION AND CULTURE TEST: FRENCH. IBM; 2 forms ('61, 10 pages); $1.25 per examinee; 30(40) minutes.

g) PROFESSIONAL PREPARATION TEST. IBM; 2 forms ('61, 10 pages) common to all languages in the series; $1.25 per examinee; 45(55) minutes.

REFERENCES

1. STARR, WILMARTH H. "Competency First: New Tests in Foreign Languages." *Proc Inv Conf Testing Probl* 1960: 97–110 '61. *

2. STARR, WILMARTH H. "Proficiency Tests in Modern Foreign Languages." *PMLA* 76:7–11 My '61. *

3. STARR, WILMARTH H. "MLA Foreign Language Proficiency Tests for Teachers and Advanced Students." *PMLA* 77:31–42 S '62. *

PAUL PIMSLEUR, *Director, The Listening Center, The Ohio State University, Columbus, Ohio.*

The publication of this series of tests is a major event for the foreign language teaching profession. This is the first time that this subject field—perhaps any subject field—has provided a reliable standard for evaluating prospective teachers on a nationwide scale. The tests are gradually being accepted by states as a basis for certification of teacher candidates, and by teacher training institutions as a means of assessing the preparation of their graduates. By holding up the present unevenness of teacher preparation to public scrutiny, they will no doubt have a beneficial effect on the quality of foreign language teacher preparation throughout the country.

The tests were prepared by committees of foreign language teachers and so represent, in a sense, an effort of the foreign language teaching profession to test itself. The French is correct, authentic, and representative of various social levels of discourse, from colloquial to literary. The item types are, on the whole, well chosen, and the items themselves are well constructed. Within the framework of this generally favorable evaluation, a certain number of criticisms, mostly minor, may be offered:

The Reading Test intends to measure both vocabulary (15 items) and reading comprehension (35 items). However, many of the comprehension items are really vocabulary items in another form, so that in all at least 25 of the 50 items are on vocabulary. Moreover, the item writers have succumbed occasionally to the easy way out of testing oddball vocabulary (e.g., "mettre le grappin dessus"). The test could be revised to weight comprehension more heavily and to eliminate a few comprehension items which can be answered without referring to the passage at all. This test, like several others in the series, is perhaps overly long in time; it takes 40 minutes for only 50 items.

The Writing Test is a compromise with feasibility. It confines itself to such technical matters as correct use of prepositions and subject-verb agreement, making no attempt to judge spelling and punctuation, much less choice of words, variety of expression, or originality of style. On the whole, the compromise is a reasonable one, and the testmakers are to be complimented on their willingness to forsake machine scorability for the sake of validity. The 45-minute time limit seems too generous for this 60-item test.

The Listening Comprehension Test, containing 36 items, is shorter than all the rest (except Speaking, which has to be short to limit scoring time). Part 3 is probably inefficient, taking three minutes to tell a story about which only eight true-false questions are asked, four of which may be right by chance. Either this test, which takes 20 minutes, is too short, or the others, which take twice that time, are too long. Probably the latter is the case, since the publisher indicates high reliability (.91–.92) for this test. It would be desirable to shorten the tests, since it now takes over five hours to administer the whole battery. As concerns the recording, the speech is too deliberate in speed and at times is unnatural (e.g., the liaison in "demander une").

The Speaking Test is an attempt to achieve objective measurement of the speaking skill—apparently a successful one, judging by the high interscorer reliability. However, all the scoring must be done by trained judges at the company's headquarters, which raises the cost as well as the reliability. In Part B, the examinee is instructed to read aloud in "natural colloquial style, treating liaison in accord with this style of speech"; this instruction is at variance with the speech style used in the Listening Comprehension Test. In Part C, the pictures which the examinee is to describe have been badly chosen. They depend too much on his knowing a single word, or on his "getting" a rather lame visual gag. This part of the test should be revised without delay.

The Professional Preparation Test is easily the most controversial of the battery, dealing, as it does, with methodology, about which teachers heartily disagree with each other. The test reflects a "new key" orientation toward language teaching. In the best sense, it will be an incentive to language teachers to learn (and to administrators to insist that they learn) of recent developments in methodology, including the contributions of structural linguistics and educational psychology. In the worst sense, this test shows what happens when creative attempts to develop effective teaching methods evolve into matters of dogma. It measures principally whether the examinee has attended an NDEA Institute or otherwise been exposed to this set of doctrines about methodology. Users should be aware that, despite its title, this test does not measure a teacher's classroom effectiveness. Data on 1,007 participants in 1962 Spanish Institutes yielded a correlation of only .29 between scores on the Professional Preparation Test and instructor evaluations of the individuals' professional preparation. Corresponding validity figures for the other six tests were considerably higher.

The Civilization and Culture Test will be rough going for any teacher without graduate training and residence in France. It calls for considerable familiarity with the history of France, ancient and modern, its painters, its architecture, its political organization, and its literature. This reviewer finds it overloaded with literature, politics, and fine arts, and lacking in items about contemporary French life. School administrators may find it difficult to see how a knowledge of façades of buildings and backs of chairs makes a better French teacher.

The Applied Linguistics Test, like the Professional Preparation Test and the Civilization and Culture Test, has a didactic as well as a testing function; it is meant to upgrade the foreign language teaching field and hence represents what the foreign language teacher of the future *should* know, rather than what today's teacher *does* know. These three tests are visionary, and this is good, for they will lead to improved preparation of teachers. But the user has a right to know this fact so that, for example, a principal will not think his teachers are the only ones who did badly in the tests.

The publishers are gradually gathering and presenting information on the validity of the tests and the interpretation of scores. However, the user needs much more guidance than is yet available to help him interpret what a certain score—or set of scores—means, and what predictions he can make about a candidate's probable effectiveness as a teacher. More information of this kind will no doubt be forthcoming as experience accrues with this battery. In any event, and despite whatever shortcomings they may have, the publication of this set of tests is an important milestone in the efforts of the U.S. Office of Education to assist the foreign language teaching profession in upgrading the teaching of foreign languages throughout the country and at all educational levels.

JAMES H. RICKS, JR., *Assistant Director, Test Division, The Psychological Corporation, New York, New York.*[1]

This ambitious and, on the whole, well realized testing program is at the time of this review (spring 1964) about to pass from experimental and special-situation use to the broader practical uses which were the goal of its construction. The preliminary and developmental research shows that the tests do what the battery title claims: provide useful and reliable information on the examinee's mastery of spoken and written French. The test constructors have done their work well; what remains to be seen is whether users of the test results will manifest equal skill.

For while "advanced students" appears in the title of the battery, the project will certainly have been a failure if these tests are not widely used as a basis for certifying teachers. In fact, at least one state already accepts scores on the tests as a basis for excusing teachers who are French natives from the usual academic requirements in the language itself, and James B. Conant, in *The Education of American Teachers,*[2] after certain reservations (pp. 181–2) says, "I am ready to recommend enthusiastically to all colleges and universities training foreign language teachers that they use this proficiency test to determine who is to be certified as a teacher." There can be little doubt that the battery constitutes a genuine advance over the kind of measurement represented by the Optional Examinations in various subjects that are part of the National Teacher Examinations.

The seven tests fall into three categories. There are four tests of proficiency in the language: Listening Comprehension Test, Speaking Test, Reading Test, and Writing Test. None of these involves translation from French to English or from English to French. Two tests, the Applied Linguistics Test and the Civilization and Culture Test, are peculiar to French but are made up of questions in English designed to sample mastery of the knowledge their titles indicate. One test, the Profes-

1 In reviewing test *content*, the writer gratefully acknowledges the assistance of Professor Daniel P. Girard of Teachers College, Columbia University.

2 CONANT, JAMES B. *The Education of American Teachers.* New York: McGraw-Hill Book Co., Inc., 1963. Pp. 275.

sional Preparation Test, is common to all of the languages included in the program (Spanish, Italian, German, Russian, and French). This review will consider the seven tests together as to technical and psychometric aspects, separately as to content.

MECHANICS. The first two tests, the Listening Comprehension Test and the Speaking Test, are administered by means of tape recordings, and for the Speaking Test the examinee's responses also must be recorded (on tape or disc). With these exceptions, the entire battery consists of paper and pencil procedures.

The Speaking Test is scored in Princeton by trained scorers. Interscorer reliability (language of the test studied is not specified) is reported as .89, and considerable care has been devoted to minimizing an observed tendency for scorers to raise their standards as they gain familiarity with the material. The Writing Test consists of completion items and an interlinear editing task; interscorer reliability (again, language unspecified) for these are reported as .99 and .95, respectively. (An essay section which appeared in experimental forms was finally discarded because of unsatisfactory interscorer reliability.) The remaining tests all are multiple choice, with entirely objective scoring. Scores are converted to an arbitrary scale based on the addition of 20 points to raw score on Form JML1.

Accompanying accessory materials and directions show appropriate care for high standards of examining, as evidenced by such details as provision for reporting of irregularities that may affect performance.

STATISTICS. An inconvenience to users and prospective users arises from the fact that data are spread through a number of separate leaflets and reports. A well organized manual bringing together the scattered data should have been prepared before the tests were offered for general use. Except for a pilot study of graduating foreign language majors in a Pennsylvania state program, all data are from NDEA Institutes.

Reliability. Kuder-Richardson formula 20 coefficients are .91 or higher for three of the skill tests: reading, writing, and listening. No such coefficient was computed for the Speaking Test because there was no way to estimate the degree of halo effect resulting from the rating of every item on a response tape by a single rater; as reported above, the interscorer coefficient obtained was .89 (even when the three parts are rated by three different scorers). The K-R 20 values for the other three tests are in the upper .80's. For the Applied Linguistics Test, which definitely is speeded, test-retest coefficients are needed but were not computed; they would be of interest also for the Reading Test and the Civilization and Culture Test which are somewhat speeded. There may be some element of speed in scores on the paced or self-timed tests, listening and speaking, but it is not possible to estimate its magnitude and not reasonable to think that it is very important. It is stated that the Writing Test is "generously timed" and this is the reviewer's impression also, but the statistics on the per cent of examinees filling the last blanks in Part A and attempting corrections in the last sentence of Part B are not reported as they are for all the other tests except listening.

Intercorrelations. Among the four skill tests, intercorrelation coefficients range from .73 (reading with speaking) to .87 (reading with writing). The other three tests are less highly correlated with each other and with the skill tests, coefficients ranging from .20 to .67, mostly between .50 and .60. For each of the four skill tests, the multiple correlation was computed to determine how well the score on each could be estimated from the scores on the other three; the resulting coefficients were .83, .85, .89, and .89.

When an examinee scores high on the Speaking Test, might not at least a reasonable competence in listening comprehension be assumed without testing? If the Writing Test score is fairly high, is the level of reading comprehension for the same examinee ever really low? These questions, which may be important for situations where limited testing time is available, are not answered or even discussed in the test analysis reports. Simple expectancy (or experience) tables could present this information usefully.

In any event, all four of the skill tests should remain in the battery, whether or not their overlap is greater than the most efficient statistical design might dictate. The specification of these areas of competence by the MLA Steering Committee will lead to use of the battery in situations where obtaining high scores on these tests will become one of the goals of language study. This places upon the battery a demand for a kind of balance and coverage that seems well met by the present design, whatever the intercorrelations. (For the three knowledge tests, this is less certain.)

Validity. Of criteria presently available for evaluating competence in a foreign language, probably none is superior to the four skill tests in this battery, even when allowance is made for continuing argument about the choice of specific items of content. As compared with the content validity of the skill tests, the content, construct, and predictive validities of the three other tests are much harder to estimate. In the end, nothing will serve as a satisfactory criterion but some yet to be developed means of measuring the performance of good and poor teachers. The teaming up of ETS and MLA for the present project offers some hope that we may be moving nearer to such an instrument or procedure. (The concurrent validation of the test scores against faculty ratings reported in one of the studies affords only the expected reassurance that the nature and goals of the tests are well accepted by the kind of people who helped make them up.)

Norms. Percentile norms for both the pretesting and the posttesting of graduate students enrolled in NDEA Foreign Language Institutes in 1961–1963—some 4,500–4,700 examinees—are the present basis of interpretation of the French test results. These are supplemented by norms based on about 160 French majors in a number of Pennsylvania colleges tested in the fall of their senior year. The seniors are more homogeneous than the institute enrollees and score about as high as the latter do at the beginning of the institutes. It may be surmised that both groups are somewhat superior to the general run of French teachers currently at work, but no data are available on this point.

States or institutions that may consider introducing the battery as a step in their certification procedures face a number of interesting questions: how high to set the requirements, whether to establish minima on all or several of the scores, whether to apply the tests in some sort of successive-hurdles fashion, and whether to use some single-number total, for example. Material accompanying the battery is silent on these problems, and their solution will presumably be empirical (and not necessarily the same in different states). With regard to the possible use of a single total score, simple summation would result in weighting the speaking score more than twice as heavily and the reading and writing scores almost one and one half times as heavily as the listening comprehension, applied linguistics, civilization and culture, and professional preparation scores; to the reviewer, this seems a quite appropriate weighting for teacher selection purposes.

Other data. Data on skewness of presently available distributions and on frequency of below chance scores, and a summary of item analysis statistics are available to those to whom they may be of interest.

CONTENT. While the tests are not entirely free from flaws, the reviewer would like to say at once that participants in test construction selected by MLA and ETS clearly were both competent and conscientious and have done, on the whole, an excellent job.

Listening Comprehension Test. The examinee listens to a French question, or to a monologue or conversation followed by questions, and chooses the appropriate answer from among four printed (in French) in a booklet but not spoken (28 items); for the last 8 of the 36 items, a spoken response (not printed) is to be marked true or false on the answer sheet. The voices are good; both sexes and a variety of accents, tones, speeds, and contexts are represented. In only one of the 36 questions did it seem to the reviewer that the speaker perhaps contributed more difficulty to the item than the testmakers may have intended.

The composition and choice of distractors, perhaps more difficult here than for most multiple choice tests, reflect a nice blend of the testmaker's and the linguist's arts. Inevitably, however, the content at times becomes that which might be used to measure mental ability (as in a comprehension question on one of the Wechsler scales) or memory. In fact, at a lower level than college or graduate school, the test might function as an intelligence test for natives of France. One is required to assume that for its stated purposes, the test is freed from influence of this factor by the self-selection or circumstantial selection of those examined. If the test is used with French students or teachers currently at work in some situations, this assumption may not be justified. But it has to be accepted—at least the reviewer cannot imagine any way of surely getting around it.

Since the instructions are given entirely in French, one wonders why for the last eight questions an examinee who has been told to indicate whether the statement is *"Vraie ou fausse"* is then expected to mark T or F instead of V or F on the answer sheet (in the literature surrounding the tests, the statement is made frequently and with appropriate pride that the tests do not require translation at any point). The conversation or *"scène dramatique"* which, according to the instructions on the tape, is to be about three minutes long, actually runs for just two minutes.

Speaking Test. The examinee (after instructions given in English, unlike the preceding test) first repeats sentences spoken in French, then reads aloud a printed passage (involving dialogue), and lastly responds to pictured situations with a description, a story, and role playing. The first task is one of mimicry—exact reproduction of the sound as spoken is required—while in the second and third, the speech of an educated native regardless of regional accent is the standard of acceptability. As noted above, great care has been given to the scoring of these performances and a high degree of scorer reliability and interscorer equivalence has been achieved.

Unavoidably in such a test there is room for disagreement as to what should be credited and what counted wrong. At certain points (especially in the first part), the examinee may be counted wrong for speaking in a way that a great many native French *do* speak, but this cannot be helped and the necessary choices in such cases seem to have been made on the side of the angels. The scoring guide is not explicit in some instances—for example, as to whether in the case of an initial *r*, either the uvular Parisian or the trilled provincial *r* or both may be accepted. The usefulness of the test as a whole, however, is impaired very little by flaws of this kind.

Reading Comprehension Test. Fifteen French sentences each omit a word or two for which the examinee chooses among four French alternatives. Then vocabulary questions (French-French, not French-English) and questions of understanding or interpretation (in French) are asked about several prose passages. Finally there are five questions requiring the interpretation of poetry. The test seems to be moderately speeded but this may be partly a reflection of the change in item content for the later questions. Otherwise it seems unexceptionable—a good, workmanlike instrument.

Writing Test. First, 30 blanks in two paragraphs are to be filled in, each by a single word or contraction. Both knowledge of what word is correct and knowledge of proper form, gender, tense, and spelling are measured by this part. Second, interlinear editing of two poorly written passages is required. Missing an error or a mistake in correcting it loses a point of score, but there is no penalty for "correcting" a word or expression that does not need correction—even if the "correction" contains an error. Vocabulary, grammar, and perhaps some rhetoric are involved. Alternative correct responses are indicated for some items in the scoring manual; the expert scorers (including some natives of France) are permitted, with the majority approval of the scoring group, to credit correct responses that do not appear in the manual. This test represents the best way the reviewer knows of approaching the goal of a measure of writing ability in the present state of the psychometric art; diehards who would insist on an essay or nothing ought to read the story of the essay test efforts in the address by Miriam M. Bryan, Director of the MLA Testing Programs at ETS, before the Conference on Teacher Education in Foreign Languages at the University of Minnesota in February 1963.[3]

Applied Linguistics Test. The five parts of this test include Pronunciation and Phonetics (12 items), The Writing System: Spelling and Pronunciation (10 items), Grammar: Morphology and Syntax (23 items), General Linguistics (7 items), and Historical Grammar (3 items). As the test analysis report duly notes, less than half the NDEA Institute examinees complete the test (even in the posttest use) and 10 per cent of examinees leave a quarter of the test unattempted, so either speed is a more important component of scores than it should be or (less likely) the last two sections of the test strike examinees as peculiarly difficult or threatening. With total working time for the battery already nearly four hours and practical administration time nearer to five, it might be profitable to allow 50 minutes instead of 40 for this test.

The almost impeccable editing and proofreading which characterize the four skill tests

3 This address, available from ETS on request, is enlightening reading for all prospective users of the tests.

seem less evident in this and the two tests which follow. For example, in one item on this test either the key is wrong or the question stem must be rewritten, while in another a careless accent mark turns a verb into a preposition. In a third, choice of one wrong (according to the key) answer probably reflects lack of clarity in the definition contained in the stem more often than a mistake by the examinee in applying the definition. The apology contained in the overlengthy instructions preceding the last three items (historical grammar) will reinforce the convictions of those who think these questions have no necessary or useful place in the test anyway. On balance, however, the test is neither bad nor unfair and does seem to the reviewer worthy of inclusion in the battery. Like the Professional Preparation Test, the Applied Linguistics Test may or may not predict relative effectiveness of teaching among average and better teachers; it should help, though, to identify the pretender who knows French well but knows little about the teaching of it.

Civilization and Culture Test. The 60 multiple choice questions comprised in this test sample knowledge of French geography, history, economics, politics, art, literature, and ways. An adequate measure of no one of these, it seems to the reviewer to serve its general purpose well. It might easily have been made too hard or too easy, but on evidence of the data it seems pitched at about the right (rather stiff) level of difficulty, with plenty of room left under the ceiling.

It is marred by several specific flaws or errors. One question may have had a correct answer among the choices when it was written but no longer does because of changes in French election law. Several similar items could easily become out of date, as could some based on current information of other than legal nature. Still other items are questions of logic or explanation in no way dependent on acquaintance with the affairs of France. There is reflection of the profession's difficulty (remarked on by the program director in the address referred to above) in agreeing on the proper proportion of *c*ulture to *C*ulture.

Professional Preparation Test. These 65 questions on teaching practices are not prepared especially for students or teachers of French; they are the same for all languages in the program. This test will certainly draw the heaviest critical fire, especially while there continues to be honest disagreement between proponents of the traditional and the audio-lingual methods. And of all seven tests, this is in fact the one about which there may be the greatest reasonable doubt that it contributes much in the settings in which the battery is to be used.

Some of the items are arguable (the instructions prudently ask for the "best" rather than the "correct" answer), and some are unarguably trivial. At least one item will be answered wrong if the examinee remembers the Writing Test he took earlier in the battery and assumes it to be an example of good foreign language test construction. The test as a whole is wordy, and some questions seem as appropriate to a reading comprehension (in English) measure as to one of professional knowledge and understanding.

Yet perhaps it cannot be otherwise. Professional preparation was specified as the seventh essential competence by the MLA Steering Committee; of the seven, it probably was the area that the testmakers felt least at peace with. Most likely, those who include this test and those who use only the first six will not hire or certify very different teachers.

SUMMARY. In the French version, the *MLA Foreign Language Proficiency Tests for Teachers and Advanced Students* are tests of good quality. Their flaws are not great and are, for the most part, correctible. The needed information that is not now available (e.g., better evidence of the all-around equivalence of alternate forms, norms on other than NDEA Institute samples) probably will become available in time. Very badly needed is a well organized manual to place in more coherent form and in better perspective the information already reported; it simply is not reasonable to expect prospective users to dig through the welter of current reports, and it is insulting to suggest the alternative that they take the tests on faith.

As noted in the test analysis report, "On the average, the tests are of greater than middle difficulty for these teachers." And teachers enrolling in NDEA Foreign Language Institutes may well be abler, on the average, than French teachers at large. With less able groups, there is a possibility that the tests' discriminating power may weaken as scores approach the chance level (especially on the three nonskill tests). Undoubtedly, however, it was wise to build the tests with room at the top for measurement of the superior teachers that new emphases, new techniques, and new money may develop.

The—*how* do people working regularly with the battery make an easy mouthful of that title? The *flipttas,* perhaps?—the tests almost certainly are better than most procedures previously available for deciding who should be certified and who should be hired. They may well provide a model for similar examinations in other teaching areas. They deserve wide use.

[380]

A Standardised French Grammar Test. Ages 11–17 with 1–5 years of French; 1951; Forms A, B, ['51, 4 pages]; manual ['51, 12 pages]; 3*s.* per 12 tests of Form A; 2*s.* 6*d.* per 12 tests of Form B; 4*d.* per single copy of Form A; 3*d.* per single copy of Form B; 2*s.* 6*d.* per manual; postage and purchase tax extra; 25(30) minutes; T. S. Percival; University of London Press Ltd. *

REFERENCES

1. PERCIVAL, THOMAS STURDY. *Achievement Tests in French Grammar and Vocabulary.* Master's thesis, University of Durham (Durham, England), 1950. (Abstract: *Brit J Ed Psychol* 21:156)

For reviews by Nelson Brooks and Donald G. Burns, see 4:242.

[381]

A Standardised French Vocabulary Test. Ages 11–17 with 1–5 years of French; 1951; Forms A, B, ['51, 4 pages]; manual ['51, 12 pages]; 3*s.* per 12 tests of Form A; 2*s.* 6*d.* per 12 tests of Form B; 4*d.* per single copy of Form A; 3*d.* per single copy of Form B; 2*s.* 6*d.* per manual; postage and purchase tax extra; 35(40) minutes; T. S. Percival; University of London Press Ltd. *

REFERENCES

1. PERCIVAL, THOMAS STURDY. *Achievement Tests in French Grammar and Vocabulary.* Master's thesis, University of Durham (Durham, England), 1950. (Abstract: *Brit J Ed Psychol* 21:156)

For reviews by Nelson Brooks and Donald G. Burns, see 4:243.

[Other Tests]

For tests not listed above, see the following entries in *Tests in Print:* 631, 635, 638–41, 643, 646, and 649–50; out of print: 630, 636, and 647.

GERMAN

[382]

★AATG German Test. 2 years high school or 1 year college, 4 years high school or 2 years college; 1960–63; IBM; 1 form ['60, 10–11 mimeographed pages]; 2 levels: lower level, higher level; mimeographed instructions for administration ['60, 1 page]; mimeographed interpretive data ['63, 4 pages]; separate answer sheets must be used; $1.25 per 5 tests with IBM scorable answer sheets; 10¢ per 5 IBM scorable answer sheets; 50¢ per scoring stencil; postpaid; 45(50) minutes; Harry Steinhauer and others; American Association of Teachers of German. *

GILBERT C. KETTELKAMP, *Professor of Education, University of Illinois, Urbana, Illinois.*

This test evaluates three aspects of German foreign language learning: reading comprehension, knowledge of correct language usage, and a combination of reading comprehension and correct language usage. It is set up to measure at two levels of student achievement. The Lower Level is constructed to evaluate achievement at the completion of two years of German study in high school or one year in college. The Higher Level is structured to evaluate four years of high school study or two years of work in college.

The lower level test is divided into three parts. Part 1 is in German and is structured to test vocabulary knowledge of the language. Part 2 employs a translation approach from English to evaluate the usage of correct German. Both parts are relatively free of ambiguous items. Part 3 evaluates reading comprehension by providing five selected passages in German. The student is then asked to select from multiple choice items in German the correct responses to statements or questions concerning these passages. The reading selections are varied enough in content to provide a reasonably broad sampling of vocabulary words.

The lower level test, as its name implies, has been constructed to evaluate student language achievement during the early period of study. The test contains only a limited number of samplings to evaluate correct language usage, but contains a much larger number of samplings to evaluate vocabulary knowledge. Possibly there is little need to evaluate in detail correct usage based on structural knowledge during this early period of study, but if there is, then more valid testing instruments will have to be utilized.

The time required to administer the lower level test is 45 minutes, hence it is well adapted for use during the average length class period. The instructions for administering the test are clear and concise. It can be scored by machine, hence is economical in time. The cost is generally well in line with the cost of test materials of this type.

In general, the higher level test is similar

in structure to the lower level test. Part 1 evaluates vocabulary knowledge. In a few instances as, for example, in items 7, 12, and 20, the multiple choice items are of such a nature as to make more than one answer acceptable. However, in general the items are free of this characteristic. In Part 2, English statements are used to test student ability to complete equivalent German statements. In this section there is a variety of content as well as an extended range of difficulty. Part 3, constructed to test reading comprehension, contains a wide range of material; the selection of multiple choice items is excellent. The cost and administrative characteristics of this test are the same as those for the lower level test.

The higher level test contains a broader sampling of correct language usage material than does the lower level test; this, of course, is to be expected of material of a more advanced nature. Both tests are relatively free of multiple choice answers which are not readily identifiable. The few such items that do occur in the higher level test are certainly not of such a critical nature as to affect the validity of the test.

In summary, the dual AATG test, constructed to evaluate at two levels of learning, is a valuable instrument for measuring achievement in correct usage of German and achievement in reading comprehension in German. However, it is not intended to evaluate audio-lingual achievement in the language. Since this goal is at present a major objective in modern language learning, other instruments of measurement must be used for this aspect of learning. The test is concise in form, reasonable in cost, and easily administered. This instrument is a valuable addition to the standardized tests now being made available to evaluate instruction and learning in present day classrooms.

THEODOR F. NAUMANN, *Associate Professor of Psychology, Central Washington State College, Ellensburg, Washington.*

The Lower Level of this German test is for students who had German for two years in high school or for one year in college, while the Higher Level is for those who had four years of high school or two years of college German. Each level consists of three parts to assess German vocabulary, grammar, and reading comprehension. There are 78 multiple choice items in the Lower Level and 80 in the Higher Level. Each form has 30 vocabulary items. The grammar parts have 25 items (Lower Level) and 20 items (Higher Level), and the comprehension parts have 23 and 30 items, respectively.

The content of both tests appears adequate. There are no unusual or outstanding characteristics. On the whole the tests are well written. (In the higher level form the surname of the physicist Hertz is consistently misspelled.)

Basic statistics are given for each form. The high school and college norm groups included 1,602 and 1,265 students, respectively, for the Lower Level, and 132 and 450 students, correspondingly, for the Higher Level. Percentile ranks are given for each of the four norm groups. Reliabilities are .88 and .84 for the Lower Level and .90 and .84 for the Higher Level (Kuder-Richardson 21), which may be considered fair for an achievement test.

It seems somewhat strange that a new test in this area fully follows traditional form and fails to reflect the language study approach based on modern linguistics. Oral-aural skills are not assessed by the tests, and no indication is given that any efforts to do so are being made in any supplementary tests. The absence of information about the representativeness of the norm groups reduces the value of the statistics provided. The reason for the time limit is not explained. These limitations indicate that the tests should in their present form be labeled "for research only" with the understanding that at best they may become good instruments for assessing the traditional type of German instruction.

[383]

***College Entrance Examination Board Achievement Test: German.** Candidates for college entrance with 2–4 years high school German; 1901–64; for more complete information, see 760; 60(80) minutes; program administered for the College Entrance Examination Board by Educational Testing Service. *

REFERENCES

1–3. See 4:244.
4–6. See 5:272.

GILBERT C. KETTELKAMP, *Professor of Education, University of Illinois, Urbana, Illinois.* [Review of Forms KAC and LAC1.]

The recent forms, KAC and LAC1 of this German test are constructed to evaluate language reading comprehension and knowledge of language structure and usage. The levels of achievement tested are broad enough in scope to include most of the possibilities that will arise in testing situations in the subject. The estimated reliability for Form KAC ranges from .90 for candidates with three semesters of German to .95 for candidates with three, five, and seven semesters of training combined. There are also data on the standard error of measurement. No statistical data are as yet available for Form LAC1.

Form KAC consists of five parts or sections. Part A, made up of 18 items, requires that the student select from among four multiple choice statements the one that is most likely to be made in the situation described in the key statement. All statements and choices are in German. The testing is at a reasonably low level of ability.

Part B contains three passages varying in length from 17 to 29 lines. For each item the student is to complete a statement by selecting the best completion from among four suggested possibilities. There are 15 items in the section. The testing here is not only at a somewhat higher level of ability but also provides a somewhat different approach to evaluating reading comprehension than is used in Part A.

In Part C there are 25 items in which the item stems are all in English. This section requires that the student select the German expression that correctly completes the translation of the English sentence. The testing here is again mainly for reading comprehension, but for the student to select the correct answer it is necessary for him to have some knowledge of correct language usage.

The 22 items of Part D consist of German sentences from which specific words or phrases have been omitted. The student is to select the expression which, when inserted in the sentence, best fits in with the meaning of the sentence as a whole. This section tests the student's knowledge of shades of meaning in words that have similarities in meaning or in spelling. The range of difficulty of the material is reasonably extensive.

Part E contains two 25- to 30-line passages in which certain words or expressions are underlined. From English expressions the student is to select the most appropriate translation of each underscored item. The section also contains a number of incomplete German statements which relate to the content of the passages. The student is to select the best completion for each item. This material is at a fairly advanced level, hence is appropriate for testing student ability at a comparable level.

Form KAC is a well constructed test. It evaluates reading comprehension as well as correct language usage. The ability level range is broad. It is generally free from ambiguity in its multiple choice items. In this respect it is an improvement over earlier Form FAC in which it was not always possible to identify distinctly one correct answer from among the given multiple choice alternatives.

Form LAC1 is divided into five parts containing a total of 95 items. Part A is made up of 15 statements, each of which describes, in German, a situation or condition. From four multiple choices given, again in German, for each statement, the student is to select the remark most likely to be made in the situation described. It is obvious that this part of the test has been constructed to evaluate reading comprehension and association. All items are clear and concise with the possible exception of number 4 where either of the first two answers might be considered acceptable. The range of difficulty of the 15 selections is excellent.

Part B is structured to test ability to select the correct language form to complete the translation of a given English statement or question. Indirectly it evaluates the students' knowledge of grammar.

Part C contains three groups of four-choice items, each group based on a passage. The passage describes three dramatic situations in reasonable detail as a basis for the items. This part of the test is characterized by variety of content material, as well as appropriate range of difficulty.

Part D is a test of vocabulary knowledge. Each given statement is to be completed with the selection of an appropriate word. Here, as in Part C, there is variety along with reasonable range of difficulty.

Part E appears to be a valid measure of high level reading ability. The two descriptive passages which serve as sources for the questions are advanced in difficulty, yet the questions themselves are relatively simple in form.

Forms KAC and LAC1 have been constructed to evaluate achievement in German language usage and reading comprehension. For these purposes the forms appear to be valid instruments of measurement. Although they do not measure grammatical knowledge as such, a background knowledge of language structure is helpful to the student in selecting correct verb forms from among the listed choices. The test certainly measures ability to use the language correctly, regardless of the means by which the ability has been acquired.

It is encouraging to German teachers to find that the gap which has existed over the years in testing the listening phase of foreign language instruction is now being filled. The publication of the *College Entrance Examination Board Achievement Test: German Listening Comprehension* now makes available an instrument to cover that phase of instruction. As a result, the College Board's offerings in German now include tests to measure the three major objectives of listening, reading, and comprehension. Improvements on these tests will, of course, be made in the future, but for the present there are available instruments of measurement which were only dreamed of a few years ago.

For a review by Harold B. Dunkel of an earlier form, see 5:272; for a review by Herbert Schueler see 4:244. For reviews of the testing program, see 760.

[384]

★College Entrance Examination Board Achievement Test: German Listening Comprehension. Candidates for college entrance with 2–4 years high school German; 1960–63; tests administered at the local secondary school on a specified date in February; candidates must also be registered to take one or more achievement tests in one of the regular program administrations; for more complete information, see 760; (30–40) minutes; program administered for the College Entrance Examination Board by Educational Testing Service. *

REFERENCES

1. SCHEIDER, ROSE M. "Evolution of the Listening Comprehension Tests." *Col Board R* 48:24–8 f '62. *

HAROLD B. DUNKEL, *Professor of Education, The University of Chicago, Chicago, Illinois.* [Review of Forms IBA and KBA.]

Both of these forms follow the same general pattern in their four parts and have a total of 50 and 57 items, respectively. The first parts contain 15 or so two-sentence conversations, and the student is asked to judge whether or not the second sentence is coherent with the first. (The reviewer is not enthusiastic about this type of exercise since it seems particularly liable to the familiar difficulty of having the item actually hinge on a single word.) The second parts contain another set of 10 or so two-sentence conversations, with the student asked to indicate the probable locale of the conversation. The third part again involves two-sentence conversations, but this time of a do-it-yourself sort, with the student required to select the proper second sentence from among four offered. In the fourth part, multiple choice questions test the student's comprehension of longer dialogues and readings.

In spite of the variety in the type of exercise, the test does not seem fragmented, but rather seems merely to reflect the different settings in which one does hear a foreign language (conversations, plays, lectures, and the rest). Moreover, dislike or distrust of any one sort of exercise does not ruin the entire test for any student, teacher, or critic since that part is merely one among several.

The reliabilities of both forms for groups with two years and with three years of training are .82 to .85 or better. In view of the variety of milieu and equipment used in administering aural tests, the smallness of the groups available for three-year norms, and other familiar factors, figures of this sort are not to be taken too seriously, but the present ones certainly suggest the adequate reliability of the two tests.

One can always think, of course, that reliability would be better if some of the weaker items had been removed. For example, in Form IBA a case can be made for the wrong answer to item 11 and the literal-minded student is likely to make it; in item 34 the keyed response is certainly the only possible one among those offered, but it doesn't seem quite the response which the student who has understood the item will be looking for as a right answer and this twist may cause confusion under pressure of time. But these and similar minor infelicities inevitably dog tests. Instead of worrying about them we should be happy that the CEEB has given us an examination which has all the earmarks of a valid and reliable test of the ability to understand spoken German.

HERBERT SCHUELER, *Director of Teacher Education, Hunter College of the City University of New York, New York, New York.* [Review of Forms IBA and LBA.]

These 30-minute listening comprehension tests are of extremely high quality in both conception and execution. They present tape recorded stimuli of ascending difficulty of four types: (*a*) 15 or 16 brief conversations between two people that are to be judged as either logical or illogical; (*b*) 10 additional conversations for each of which the student is to choose one of four locations as the most likely setting; (*c*) 10–13 questions for which one of four alternatives is to be chosen; and (*d*) three sustained passages (one an anecdote, the second a dialogue, and the third an excerpt from a speech) followed by 5–6 aural four-choice questions each.

Obviously, the quality of the aural stimulus material is crucial in a recorded listening comprehension test. The student has no recourse to repetition once the material is heard. For a listening comprehension test to be a true measure of the skill it purports to measure, it must provide recorded voices speaking the standard version of the language without distracting regionalisms, at a colloquial pace and manner, and with exemplary clarity. This is achieved to an admirable and consistent degree by both male and female voices on these tapes. Whatever faults these tests may have, therefore, are not due to the quality of the recordings. The language content itself is colloquial, appropriate, and generally free from the artificialities of some foreign language textbook material. Here and there, however, this reviewer feels that more careful editing, particularly in the sustained listening passages, might have removed some irrelevant bars to comprehension that may indeed detract from a valid measure of listening comprehension. The use in one passage, for example, of a highly unusual family name (when Schultz or Schmidt would have done as well) possibly introduces an unnecessary difficulty. Similarly, when a person is reported as saying something with a strong American accent and then says it instead in perfect native German, or when a piano selection, heard in the background and obviously played in a professional manner, is said to sound as if played by a child without notes, the material itself is in danger of introducing factors that may possibly skew the attention and the responses of the student. In addition, there is an occasional ambiguity in possible choices in earlier sections of each of the forms, but not enough to impair seriously the validity of the tests as a whole.

Analysis of the scores of 632 candidates on Form IBA and 2,213 on Form LBA reveals the two forms to be generally appropriate for students with three years of the language in secondary school, being pitched at the middle difficulty for the three-year sample, very difficult for the two-year sample, and quite easy for the four-year sample. In the main, these tests are quite satisfactory in appropriateness of content, and superior in recording quality and in test reliability. More careful editing of the linguistic material will make future forms even better.

For reviews of the testing program, see 760.

[385]

***College Entrance Examination Board Advanced Placement Examination: German.** High school students desiring credit for college level courses or admission to advanced courses; 1954–63; 2 levels; for more complete information, see 761; 180(200) minutes; program administered for the College Entrance Examination Board by Educational Testing Service. *

a) INTERMEDIATE GERMAN. 3 years high school, including the equivalent of an intermediate college level course; discontinued during 1964.

b) ADVANCED GERMAN: INTRODUCTION TO GERMAN LITERATURE. 4 years high school, including the equivalent of a college level German literature course.

REFERENCES

1. PRESEL, ROSE. "German and the German Examination in the 'School and College Study for Admission With Advanced Standing.'" *German Q* 28:85–8 Ja '55. *

2. REICHARD, JOSEPH R. "The College Board and Advanced Placement in German." *German Q* 29:220–4 N '56. *

3. VALLEY, JOHN R. "College Actions on CEEB Advanced Placement Language Examination Candidates." *Mod Lang J* 43:261–3 O '59. *

4. REICHARD, JOSEPH R. "German Advanced Placement Under the College Board: Promising Signs." *German Q* 33:153–8 Mr '60. *

5. NEWMARK, MAXIM, AND SCHERER, PHILIP. *How to Prepare for College Board Achievement Tests: German.* Great Neck, N.Y.: Barron's Educational Series, Inc., 1962. Pp. viii, 134. *

For a review by Herbert Schueler of an earlier form, see 5:273.

[386]

★College Entrance Examination Board Placement Tests: German Listening Comprehension Test. Entering college freshmen; 1962–63, c1955–63; IBM; Forms DLC1, DLC2 in a single booklet ('55), KPL1, KPL2 in a single booklet (c1960–61, 12 pages, a reprint of inactive forms of *College Entrance Examination Board Achievement Test: German Listening Comprehension*); test administered by 7½ ips tape recording; for more complete information, see 759; 30(40) minutes; program administered for the College Entrance Examination Board by Educational Testing Service. *

For reviews of the College Entrance Examination Board Achievement Test: German Listening Comprehension, *see 384.*

[387]

★College Entrance Examination Board Placement Tests: German Reading Test. Entering college freshmen; 1962–63, c1957–63; test is a reprint, with 15 items omitted, of an inactive form of *College Entrance Examination Board Achievement Test: German;* IBM; Form KPL1 (c1957, 12 pages); for more complete information, see 759; program administered for the College Entrance Examination Board by Educational Testing Service. *

For reviews of the College Entrance Examination Board Achievement Test: German, *see 383, 5:272, and 4:244.*

[388]

★**Common Concepts Foreign Language Test: German [Research Edition].** "Students [in any grade] who have had enough foreign language instruction to place them at the Level 1 stage in their achievement"; 1962–64; aural comprehension; may be administered using live voice but tape recording is recommended; IBM; Forms 1, 2; a single booklet ('62, 31 pages) presents response options for both forms of this test and the French and Spanish tests of the series; mimeographed preliminary manual ('64, 24 pages); interim norms (grades 7–12 only); separate answer sheets or cards must be used; 75¢ per test; $5.95 per 3¾ ips tape recording; 5¢ per IBM answer sheet; 20¢ per scoring stencil; 2¢ per Cal-Card; 20¢ per hand scoring stencil; 15¢ per manual; postage extra; $1 per specimen set without tape; $6.95 per specimen set with tape; postpaid; scoring service available; (40–45) minutes; Bela H. Banathy, Miles V. Zintz, W. James Popham, Joseph M. Sadnavitch, Rena Krichbaum, Fred B. Gannon, Valdemar Hempel, and Klaus A. Mueller; California Test Bureau. *

[389]

★**German: Every Pupil Test.** 1 or 2 years high school; 1962–64; test booklet titles vary; new form (4 pages) usually issued each April; forms from previous testing programs also available; general directions sheet ('63, 2 pages); no data on reliability; Ohio norms for new forms available following testing program; 5¢ per test; 3¢ per key; postpaid; 40(45) minutes; Ohio Scholarship Tests. *

[390]

***German I and II: Minnesota High School Achievement Examinations.** 1 or 2 years high school; 1953–63; series formerly called *Midwest High School Achievement Examinations;* new norms issued each June; Form F ('51, 5 pages, formerly called Form I & D) used in 1963 testing; no specific manual; series manual ('63, 4 pages); series norms ['63, 4 pages]; series cumulative profile ('62, 2 pages); no data on reliability; no description of normative population; 12¢ per test; $2.50 per 100 profiles; postage extra; 20¢ per specimen set, postpaid; 60(65) minutes; American Guidance Service, Inc. *

For a review by Harold B. Dunkel, see 5:276.

[391]

★**Graduate School Foreign Language Test: German.** Graduate level degree candidates required to demonstrate reading proficiency in German; 1963–64; Forms K-LFG1, K-LFG2, ('63, 34 pages); for more complete information, see 356; 80(100) minutes; Educational Testing Service. *

JACK M. STEIN, *Professor of German, Harvard University, Cambridge, Massachusetts.* [Review of Form K-LFG2.]

The existence of this test is cause for hope that order, continuity, and reliability in testing the German competence of Ph.D. candidates in all fields will replace the inadequacy, unreliability, and general chaos of testing procedures used up to now for this purpose. Such procedures vary incredibly from department to department and from university to university, but there is general agreement that they share one chief characteristic: they are all unsatisfactory. The present test, though it is not without defects, to be discussed below, is unquestionably an enormous improvement over that which it is designed to replace. Developed by Educational Testing Service under a contract between the United States Office of Education and Cornell University after a preliminary study conference to determine acceptable specifications for standardized foreign language reading proficiency tests for graduate students, which was attended by representatives of 18 graduate schools, it has been extensively pretested at 37 cooperating institutions. A wide variety of explanatory material has wisely been prepared, since in the great majority of instances the persons in charge of testing at this level are not testing experts and are largely unfamiliar with the characteristics of machine scored multiple choice tests. This supplementary material gives clear and useful information, not only on the test itself, but on various methods of deriving local norms and determining local passing scores.

All examinees, from whatever department, take Section 1 (40 minutes, two parts). Part A consists of 25 items, brief sentences with words, phrases, or clauses underlined. The examinee is asked to choose that one of four alternative German expressions which is the equivalent of what is underlined. Both vocabulary and syntax are thus tested. Part 2 of Section 1 contains three passages, roughly 600 words in all, each passage followed by five items in German, with four alternatives each. The examinee is to choose the alternative which best matches the passage. The level of difficulty of this section is moderate and the passages are like those typically found in a magazine or newspaper. The vocabulary and subject matter is of a general nature, such as it is reasonable to assume could be readily grasped by anyone with a command of German sufficient to cope with the demands of a more specific and scholarly nature made in Section 2. Thus Section 1 serves admirably as a uniform base upon which the separate subdivisions of Section 2 are superimposed.

Section 2 is the really critical part of the examination. It is divided into four major subject matter areas (Biological Sciences, Humanities, Physical Sciences, Social Sciences), the examinee selecting that area in which his field of specialization lies. In this section (40 minutes) he is confronted with five or six passages totaling roughly 1,500 words, each passage followed by items to a total in the entire section of 30. These multiple choice statements, each with four alternatives, are in English, rather than in German as they were in Section 1. This change into English has presumably the effect of reducing the barrier of specialized vocabulary, since most, if not all, of the passages with which each examinee is dealing fall more or less outside his own area of specialization.

This, indeed, is the major dilemma of the examination. Of six faculty members (in as many large graduate departments) whom I consulted, only one was willing to go along with the necessarily broad coverage represented in the respective second sections. Thus a history man pointed out that only one of the social science passages was in history; and a social relations professor showed me that not one of the behavioral sciences (psychology, anthropology, sociology) was represented on the test at all. For better or worse, there was the feeling that an examination at this stage of the examinee's career which does not test in the immediate field of specialization, or at least very close to it, necessarily has a dilettantish flavor. Only one of the six men, I am pleased to report, objected to the absence of translation.

A more serious defect, indeed it would seem an inexcusable one, was pointed out in the physical sciences section. Here many of the distractors could be eliminated without reference to the passage because they consisted of scientific nonsense. Often two of the three distractors, and in some cases all three of them, in an item were thus nonfunctional, so that the correct answer could be selected entirely without reference to the German! Most of the items were carefully phrased "The author of this passage" etc., but obviously no selection would have been chosen which argues palpable error. This does not seem to be the case with the other sections, though the reviewer cannot guarantee it except in the humanities, which is his own field.

Two bad misprints were found (*praussisch* for *preussisch* and *berufen, worden* for *berufen worden*), the latter being far more critical for the examinee than it may look. There was also inconsistency within the same passage in the use of the nineteenth century spelling *th* and its twentieth century equivalent *t*, and inconsistent use of the digraph ß.

Lest these deficiencies seem too grave, the reader should bear in mind three important points. First, the only alternatives to this test, with all its faults, are the grossly, sometimes grotesquely, inadequate present practices of graduate departments. Measured against these, rather than against some hypothetical ideal, the test is a major breakthrough. Second, this is a pioneer attempt in a testing area at once so diffuse and so highly compartmentalized that great vigilance (apparently more than was exercised) is necessary to avoid error. Third, and most important, the existence of this test establishes for the first time a professional framework to which improvements derived from cumulative experience can be annually adapted. It offers the happy prospect that nationwide respectability and uniformity can at last be achieved in what has been up to now the shoddiest testing area in our entire educational system.

[392]

★MLA-Cooperative Foreign Language Tests: German. 1 or 2 years high school or 2 semesters college, 3 or 4 years high school or 4 semesters college; 1963–64; 4 tests in a single booklet: listening, speaking, reading, writing; IBM in part; 2 levels; directions for administering and scoring ['64, 39 pages] for this and the French, Italian, Russian, and Spanish tests of the series; no data on reliability; no norms; $5 per 10 tests; separate answer sheets may be used for listening and reading tests; $1 per 20 IBM scorable answer sheets; $1 per 10 scoring stencils (answer pattern must be punched out locally); $7 per 3¾ ips tape for listening test; $7 per 3¾ ips tape for speaking test (blank tapes or discs for recording student responses must be obtained locally); postage extra; $2 per specimen set, cash orders postpaid; (25–35) minutes for listening, (10–20) minutes for speaking, 35(40) minutes for reading, 35(40) minutes for writing; prepared in cooperation with the Modern Language Association of America; Cooperative Test Division. *

a) [LOWER LEVEL.] 1 or 2 years high school or 2 semesters college; form LA ('63, 23 pages).

b) [HIGHER LEVEL.] 3 or 4 years high school or 4 semesters college; form MA ('63, 24 pages).

[393]

★MLA Foreign Language Proficiency Tests for Teachers and Advanced Students: German. Grades 15–17 and foreign language teachers; 1961–64; IBM in part; 7 tests; 2 forms ('61): Form JML1 (also called Form A, available for institutional programs), Form JML2 (also called Form B, restricted to state and local teacher certification programs); series supervisor's manual ['62, 34 pages]; series norms leaflet ('64, 4 pages); series interpretive leaflet ('64, 4 pages); examination fees: $15 per battery of 7 tests, $12.50 per battery of 4 skill tests (listening, speaking, reading, writing); fees include rental of test materials and scoring and reporting service; postage extra; fee for 30-day examination, $3.70 per battery; Modern Language Association of America and Educational Testing Service; program administered by Educational Testing Service. *

a) LISTENING COMPREHENSION TEST: GERMAN. IBM; 2 forms ('61, 7 pages, containing response options only); stimulus material presented on 3¾ or 7½ ips tape; $1.50 per examinee; (20–30) minutes.

b) SPEAKING TEST: GERMAN. 2 forms ('61, 9 pages, containing scripts for all languages in the series plus a section on 3¾ or 7½ ips tape); responses recorded on tapes or records supplied by the publisher; $6.75 per examinee; (15–30) minutes.

c) READING TEST: GERMAN. IBM; 2 forms ('61, 12 pages); $1.25 per examinee; 40(50) minutes.

d) WRITING TEST: GERMAN. IBM in part; 2 forms ('61, 7–8 pages); $3.50 per examinee; 45(55) minutes.

e) APPLIED LINGUISTICS TEST: GERMAN. IBM; 2 forms ('61, 9 pages); $1.25 per examinee; 40(50) minutes.

f) CIVILIZATION AND CULTURE TEST: GERMAN. IBM; 2 forms ('61, 9–10 pages); $1.25 per examinee; 30(40) minutes.

g) PROFESSIONAL PREPARATION TEST. IBM; 2 forms ('61, 10 pages) common to all languages in the series; $1.25 per examinee; 45(55) minutes.

REFERENCES

1. STARR, WILMARTH H. "Competency First: New Tests in Foreign Languages." *Proc Inv Conf Testing Probl* 1960: 97–110 '61. *
2. STARR, WILMARTH H. "Proficiency Tests in Modern Foreign Languages." *PMLA* 76:7–11 My '61. *
3. STARR, WILMARTH H. "MLA Foreign Language Proficiency Tests for Teachers and Advanced Students." *PMLA* 77:31–42 S '62. *

HAROLD B. DUNKEL, *Professor of Education, The University of Chicago, Chicago, Illinois.*

Since three tests in this battery are efforts in areas relatively new to standardized testing (applied linguistics, civilization and culture, and professional preparation) while the four tests of the language skills (speaking, listening, reading, and writing) cover more familiar objectives, the limited space here will be devoted primarily to the three new varieties.

For obvious reasons of test security, reviewers are asked not to quote items. In some respects this limitation is unimportant; the Educational Testing Service usually does too competent a job to make quibbles about individual items profitable or even possible. The only unfortunate consequence is that comments on larger issues must appear somewhat vague and *ex cathedra* since the supporting evidence cannot be cited.

The selection of "Professional Preparation" as the title for the one test is most interesting since the only aspect of professional preparation covered is knowledge of the theory of language teaching. If one wonders why the examination was not so named, one immediately realizes that this label would have highlighted the major inherent difficulty. Most of us think we know a good bit about language teaching and the right way of doing it, but whether our knowledge is of the sort that permits right and wrong answers is another matter. We should ask ourselves whether our theory has the comprehensiveness, coherence, and demonstrability possessed by those things called "theory" in other fields. In fact, a most stimulating seminar on language teaching could be conducted simply by having the group work through this test, item by item, and asking precisely what evidence there is, both in quality and quantity, for each correct response. Though most of us might agree with most of the items, our evidence for a good many points is tenuous. As a result, the test actually measures current received opinion. That most of us, or even all of us, receive these opinions makes little difference. Some danger exists, consequently, that this test may become a catechism on the doctrine of the language teaching establishment. The reviewer is old enough to belong to the generations which were worried by tests of orthodoxy.

As one who has grumbled for many years, both in previous *Mental Measurements Yearbooks* and elsewhere, that there is no point in talking about "Culture and Civilization" unless we test for knowledge of them and grade students on the results, the reviewer welcomes that part of the battery which is an objective and reliable test of these matters. But many of us will wonder as we read through these bits and pieces of geography, literature, history, and fine arts whether these snippets of knowledge are what we mean by culture and civilization. Probably to some extent they are. The person who knows a country, its culture, and its civilization does know its main rivers and mountains, its chief writers and what they wrote, important epochs in the country's history, and all the rest. The fact that the items are jumbled (probably in the order of empirical difficulty as observed in tryout forms) makes the test seem somewhat more of a hodgepodge than it probably is. Grouping the items by topics, as is done in the Applied Linguistics Test, would at least give this examination a more coherent appearance and might remind the testmaker as well as the test taker of the problem of some intelligible sampling of the major areas. The reviewer has no serious quarrel with the test as far as it goes; but most of us, including no doubt its constructors, probably hope that later versions will go further. A fruitful direction is indicated by the last item, which asks the student to explain why a joke is funny. What a culture sees as funny, honorific, disgraceful, unquestionable, and the like are important keys to that culture, and the person who understands the culture understands these viewpoints while the person strange to the culture finds them perplexing and absurd. Admittedly, items of this kind are extremely difficult to write, but is not this sort of insight the target at which we aim—particularly for advanced students and teachers? Possibly satire (from the standup comedian through the musical play to the satiric novel) would be a fruitful source of such items. To poke fun at the culture, the satirist must know where the chinks in a particular cultural armor are, and we might do well to follow the lead of these experts in detecting specific points of attack.

The Applied Linguistics Test is particularly interesting because of the long directions which inform the student why the questions are asked. Although the reviewer belongs to the school which believes that tests can and should constitute learning experiences and not just hurdles for the student, he is not certain that this learning should stem from the reading of test directions which are primarily justifications for the items rather than instructions for marking them. Considerations of testing aside, the test serves as an extensional definition of what is meant by the application of descriptive linguistics to foreign language teaching, with the directions giving the rationale and the items exemplifying the points. The items, covering pronunciation, phonetics, grammar, orthography, general linguistics, and historical and comparative philology, are familiar to takers and makers of advanced German tests.

Of the four tests of skills, the Reading Test seems weak in two of its parts. One group of items asks the students to supply a missing word in a sentence; a second set asks them to replace an underlined word by a synonym (which does not always seem easier or more familiar than the original word). Though exercises of this sort are related to reading, they are not reading; they patently demand a more active command of the language than mere reading requires. One can only hope that the prevailing doctrine of the priority of speech is not forcing us into reading tests thrown into the form of "what should I say next?" rather than "what is the author saying?"

The other three tests can briefly be noted as good. The Speaking Test, in its first part, measures the ability to read aloud, with the grade based on the correct pronunciation of certain phonemes appearing in the selection; the last part involves response to picture stimuli. The Listening Comprehension Test and the Writing Test involve familiar and well tested procedures. (In the first part of the listening test the continuous change of speakers for each brief isolated item is probably more troublesome for the student than valuable for measurement.) In general, all tests of the battery attain high reliabilities of .90 or better.

Though the reviewer is not a True Believer in all the current dogma, he applauds the appearance of a test which does take that doctrine seriously and which measures on a broad front the skills and knowledge stressed by the doctrine. As is usual with competent examinations, these tests make clearer than any number of more abstract statements the viewpoint on which they are based. Those who find the viewpoint acceptable will have here adequate and reliable tests.

HERBERT SCHUELER, *Director of Teacher Education, Hunter College of the City University of New York, New York, New York.*

The Modern Language Association proficiency tests for teachers and advanced students represent the culmination of a monumental effort on the part of the profession of foreign language teachers to establish national standards of linguistic and professional competence designed to help in the improvement of foreign language teaching in this country. Two major events provided the basis for these tests. The first was the promulgation in 1955 by a committee of the Modern Language Association of a statement of "Qualifications for Secondary School Teachers of Modern Foreign

Languages." This statement, subsequently endorsed by all the major regional and national professional organizations concerned with the teaching of modern foreign languages, established levels of proficiency for seven areas of language teaching competence: aural understanding, speaking, reading, writing, language analysis, culture, and professional preparation. The second was the establishment of Foreign Language Institutes, with the support of the National Defense Education Act, to provide the necessary upgrading in foreign language competence and in teaching methodology for the profession. The first event provided the necessary standards and the second the means, need, and initial population for the development of standardized tests in all aspects of foreign language competence for teachers. The tests resulting are therefore landmarks of wide professional involvement combining the resources of a representative cross section of foreign language scholars and teachers with test experts. The two forms of seven tests now available represent the end result of experimental tryouts with enrollees in the summer 1960, 1961, and 1962 Foreign Language Institutes. In addition, experimental forms were tested with graduating college seniors and applicants for study in foreign languages.

The Form JML1 versions of these tests are available for institutional programs; the Form JML2 equivalent versions are restricted to state and local teacher certification programs. While the seven tests are available separately, they divide themselves naturally into a battery of four skill tests (listening, speaking, reading, writing) and three tests particularly applicable to teachers (applied linguistics, civilization and culture, and professional preparation).

LISTENING COMPREHENSION TEST. This 20- to 30-minute test presents its stimulus material on 3¾ or 7½ ips tape, and requires candidates to react either to four response or true-false options. In the first part, the candidate hears a series of remarks or questions and must choose one response from four printed responses. In the second he hears a series of sustained dialogues or expositions to which he responds to a series of four-response descriptive options. In the third, he hears a protracted dialogue and must respond to a series of aural descriptive statements in the form of true or false options. The tapes are uniformly clear and the several voices, while speaking standard German, do exhibit regional differences in pronunciation, a feature deliberately built into the tapes and most appropriate for advanced measures of aural comprehension.

This test appears to be quite difficult, an opinion substantiated by results of available pre- and post-Institute test analysis made on the basis of testing during the summer of 1961. The extent to which the test is made more difficult by presenting single playings of each aural stimulus, particularly those of extended length, is undetermined. It might be interesting to ascertain changes in scores when the test provides repetitions of stimuli. In addition, the test provides further examples for speculation on the relationship between linguistic aural competence and general intelligence. It is this reviewer's contention that several of the items are more a measure of the respondent's intelligence than his aural command of the language. Perhaps the administration of this test to groups of native speakers of German of demonstrable variation on standard measures of intelligence might provide some interesting clues to the validity of this test as a measure of aural comprehension per se.

SPEAKING TEST. The MLA speaking tests represent the first widely available tests of speaking ability. While the United States Armed Forces Institute pioneered in experimenting with foreign language speaking tests during and immediately after World War II, unfortunately none of the many significant attempts of that time has been made available for subsequent civilian administration and study. The MLA tests must therefore be judged without reference to these earlier tests, nor have they had the benefit of these earlier experiments. The tests of 20–30 minutes duration are in three parts: (*a*) imitation exercises in which the candidate reproduces on his own tape or disc stimuli representing critical sounds and intonations usually difficult for the American student of a foreign language to master; (*b*) reading exercises in which the candidate reads orally, written material presented in the test booklet; (*c*) free oral responses stimulated by pictorial stimuli. It is obvious that in a speaking test the crucial problem is not so much the stimuli as the standards and uniformity of rating, particularly in the section testing the candidate's free speech. The achievement of a high degree of scorer consistency is a product of rigorous training of, and imposition of controls on, expert raters. The reported gains in interscorer reliability and in individual scorer consistency achieved by training sessions organized by the Educational Testing Service in 1961 and 1962 are impressive; interscorer reliabilities of .89 and better are almost too good to be true, and augur well for the usability of these tests.[1] The reliability (pre- and post-NDEA Institute testing) of the German Speaking Test is reported as .81 (*3*). The test requires painstaking attention to the details of administration; without proper facilities for recording students' responses on tape or disc, it should not be attempted. Without optimum conditions, candidates cannot fail to be handicapped.

READING TEST. This 40-minute test consists of three parts: (*a*) a completion test in which the candidates choose from among four alternatives to complete missing elements in a series of 15 sentences; (*b*) three extended reading passages followed by two types of items, (1) choices from four synonyms to substitute for underlined words in the passage, and (2) choices from four statements to complete a series of statements based on the passages; (*c*) short excerpts from poetry followed by four alternative interpretive statements. This is a challenging test, most suitable to advanced levels of reading competence. While conventional in form, it is nevertheless of demonstrated high reliability and presumed validity for testing advanced students and teachers of the language.

WRITING TEST. This test is in two parts: (*a*) a completion test requiring the student to insert missing words in two extended passages, and (*b*) a composition replete with errors which the candidate is required to correct as if he were the teacher. This test is interesting not so much for what it includes as for what is conspicuously missing. Unlike the speaking test, the written test provides no opportunity for free production of the language. The original specifications for the MLA testing program called for the inclusion of free writing stimuli, but frustrating experiences in seeking interscorer reliability resulted in their abandonment. While it was possible to achieve interscorer reliability of close to .90 in the rating of the free speaking items, the best that could be achieved for the experimental free writing items was .62. It was wisely decided, therefore, to defer the inclusion of free writing items for the time being. As a result, this test gives an impression of incompleteness, however well conceived its two parts may be.

APPLIED LINGUISTICS TEST. This 40-minute test presents multiple choice items in six areas: English and German Pronunciation, Phonetics, Grammar, The Writing System, General Linguistics, and Historical and Comparative Philology. The test presents a fitting complement to the Professional Preparation Test (below) in providing a measure of the candidate's command of comparative linguistic analysis of his language with English and of both the basic terminology and applications to German of modern structural linguistics. While the candidate not versed in modern structural linguistics might do better in the historical and the writing system sections, he would be at a loss in the technical terminology of the others. This test, then, is, as is the Professional Preparation Test, firmly grounded in the so-called audio-lingual language teaching movement and its foundation in modern structural linguistics.

CIVILIZATION AND CULTURE TEST. This 60-item, multiple choice test presents a wide sampling of geographical, political, historical, literary, and artistic material, ranging from earliest times to the present. Fully half the questions present combinations of answers rather than calling for choice of single responses. Thus, in a four alternative item, the candidate is frequently expected to choose from among such combinations as I and II only; I and III only; I and IV only; and III and IV only. This device undoubtedly broadens the scope of any given item, makes possible the injection of subtleties of interpretation, and provides a greater range of difficulty. It may, however, introduce some mechanical difficulties unrelated to what is being tested, requiring as it does constant referral to numerical labels. The selection of but 60 items from among the broad sweep of German culture and civilization is a formidable task at best, and the test succeeds as well as any this reviewer has seen.

PROFESSIONAL PREPARATION TEST. This 65-item, 45-minute, multiple choice test is, as is the Applied Linguistics Test, thoroughly grounded in the so-called audio-lingual method of teaching foreign languages. This reviewer

[1] It is not indicated whether the studies which yielded these figures included the speaking tests in all languages and, if not, on which language test or tests the figures are based.

knows many foreign language teachers who would quarrel, sometimes even violently, with some of the items, and particularly with the scoring key. An analysis of particular items here would, however, violate the security of the tests and thus cannot be attempted in this review. It must be understood, particularly if certification authorities will make use of this test, that it is an expression of a particular foreign language teaching doctrine, and valid only if teachers are to be tested for their knowledge of, and commitment to, this movement. As a test of professional preparation within the scope, material, and method of the audio-lingual movement, it is admirable. Its use for teacher certification, therefore, will depend on the acceptance of this methodology and its precept as a requirement for the preparation and evaluation of foreign language teachers.

[Other Tests]

For tests not listed above, see the following entries in *Tests in Print:* 654–5; out of print: 657.

GREEK

[394]

*__College Entrance Examination Board Achievement Test: Greek.__ Candidates for college entrance with 2–3 years high school Greek; 1901–63; tests administered at the local secondary school on a specified date in February; candidates must also be registered to take one or more achievement tests in one of the regular program administrations; for more complete information, see 760; 3 parts (candidate takes only one): Attic prose, Homeric poetry, Attic prose and Homeric poetry; 90(100) minutes; program administered for the College Entrance Examination Board by Educational Testing Service. *

For a review by Konrad Gries of an earlier form, see 5:277. For reviews of the testing program, see 760.

[395]

★**College Entrance Examination Board Placement Tests: Greek Test.** Entering college freshmen; 1962–63, c1957–63; test is a reprint of an inactive form of *College Entrance Examination Board Achievement Test: Greek;* IBM; Form KPL1 (c1957, 17 pages) in a single booklet with the Italian test of the series; 2 parts (student generally takes only one): Attic prose, Homer and Attic prose; for more complete information, see 759; 60(70) minutes per part; program administered for the College Entrance Examination Board by Educational Testing Service. *

For a review of the College Entrance Examination Board Achievement Test: Greek, *see 5:277.*

HEBREW

[396]

★**College Entrance Examination Board Achievement Test: Hebrew.** Candidates for college entrance with 2–4 years high school Hebrew; 1961–64; available only in January testing program; for more complete information, see 760; 60(80) minutes; program administered for the College Entrance Examination Board by Educational Testing Service. *

For reviews of the testing program, see 760.

[397]

★**Test on the Fundamentals of Hebrew.** Grades 2–5, 3–6, 4–7; 1955–59; 4–5 scores: sentences (grades 3–6 and 4–7 only), vocabulary, stories, grammar, total; 1 form; 3 levels: lower ('55, 5 pages), intermediate ('58, 7 pages), upper ('55, 7 pages); mimeographed manual ('59, 19 pages); no data on reliability; tentative norms; no norms for part scores; separate answer sheets must be used; 10¢ per test; $1 per 100 mimeographed answer sheets; $3 per 100 self-marking answer sheets; 35¢ per manual; 75¢ per specimen set; postpaid; (30–45) minutes; Committee on Tests of the American Association for Jewish Education; the Association. *

ITALIAN

[398]

★**College Entrance Examination Board Achievement Test: Italian Listening Comprehension.** Candidates for college entrance with 2–4 years high school Italian; 1961–63; tests administered at the local secondary school on a specified date in February; candidates must also be registered to take one or more achievement tests in one of the regular program administrations; for more complete information, see 760; (30–40) minutes; program administered for the College Entrance Examination Board by Educational Testing Service. *

For reviews of the testing program, see 760.

[399]

*__College Entrance Examination Board Achievement Test: Italian Reading and Essay.__ Candidates for college entrance with 2–4 years high school Italian; 1924–63; tests administered at the local secondary school on a specified date in February; candidates must also be registered to take one or more achievement tests in one of the regular program administrations; for more complete information, see 760; 90(100) minutes; program administered for the College Entrance Examination Board by Educational Testing Service. *

For reviews of the testing program, see 760.

[400]

★**College Entrance Examination Board Placement Tests: Italian Listening Comprehension.** Entering college freshmen; 1962–63; IBM; Form KBA ('62, 5 pages, an inactive form of *College Entrance Examination Board Achievement Test: Italian Listening Comprehension*); test administered by 7½ ips tape recording; for more complete information, see 759; 30(40) minutes; program administered for the College Entrance Examination Board by Educational Testing Service. *

[401]

★College Entrance Examination Board Placement Tests: Italian Test. Entering college freshmen; 1962–63, c1957–63; test is a reprint of an inactive form of *College Entrance Examination Board Achievement Test: Italian Reading and Essay;* IBM; Form KPL1 (c1957, 12 pages) in a single booklet with the Greek test of the series; for more complete information, see 759; 60(70) minutes; program administered for the College Entrance Examination Board by Educational Testing Service. *

[402]

★MLA-Cooperative Foreign Language Tests: Italian. 1 or 2 years high school or 2 semesters college, 3 or 4 years high school or 4 semesters college; 1963–64; 4 tests in a single booklet: listening, speaking, reading, writing; IBM in part; 2 levels; directions for administering and scoring ['64, 39 pages] for this and the German, French, Russian, and Spanish tests of the series; no data on reliability; no norms; $5 per 10 tests; separate answer sheets may be used for listening and reading tests; $1 per 20 IBM scorable answer sheets; $1 per 10 scoring stencils (answer pattern must be punched out locally); $7 per 3¾ ips tape for listening test; $7 per 3¾ ips tape for speaking test (blank tapes or discs for recording student responses must be obtained locally); postage extra; $2 per specimen set, cash orders postpaid; (25–35) minutes for listening, (10–20) minutes for speaking, 35(40) minutes for reading, 35(40) minutes for writing; prepared in cooperation with the Modern Language Association of America; Cooperative Test Division. *

a) [LOWER LEVEL.] 1 or 2 years high school or 2 semesters college; form LA ('63, 25 pages).
b) [HIGHER LEVEL.] 3 or 4 years high school or 4 semesters college; form MA ('63, 24 pages).

[403]

★MLA Foreign Language Proficiency Tests for Teachers and Advanced Students: Italian. Grades 15–17 and foreign language teachers; 1961–64; IBM in part; 7 tests; 2 forms ('61): Form JML1 (also called Form A, available for institutional programs), Form JML2 (also called Form B, restricted to state and local teacher certification programs); series supervisor's manual ['62, 34 pages]; series norms leaflet ('64, 4 pages); series interpretive leaflet ('64, 4 pages); tentative norms; examination fees: $15 per battery of 7 tests, $12.50 per battery of 4 skill tests (listening, speaking, reading, writing); fees include rental of test materials and scoring and reporting service; postage extra; fee for 30-day examination, $3.70 per battery; Modern Language Association of America and Educational Testing Service; program administered by Educational Testing Service. *

a) LISTENING COMPREHENSION TEST: ITALIAN. IBM; 2 forms ('61, 6–7 pages, containing response options only); stimulus material presented on 3¾ or 7½ ips tape; $1.50 per examinee; (20–30) minutes.
b) SPEAKING TEST: ITALIAN. 2 forms ('61, 9 pages, containing scripts for all languages in the series plus a section on 3¾ or 7½ ips tape); responses recorded on tapes or records supplied by the publisher; $6.75 per examinee; (15–30) minutes.
c) READING TEST: ITALIAN. IBM; 2 forms ('61, 12 pages); $1.25 per examinee; 40(50) minutes.
d) WRITING TEST: ITALIAN. IBM in part; 2 forms ('61, 8 pages); $3.50 per examinee; 45(55) minutes.
e) APPLIED LINGUISTICS TEST: ITALIAN. IBM; 2 forms ('61, 8–9 pages); $1.25 per examinee; 40(50) minutes.
f) CIVILIZATION AND CULTURE TEST: ITALIAN. IBM; 2 forms ('61, 9 pages); $1.25 per examinee; 30(40) minutes.
g) PROFESSIONAL PREPARATION TEST. IBM; 2 forms ('61, 10 pages) common to all languages in the series; $1.25 per examinee; 45(55) minutes.

REFERENCES

1. STARR, WILMARTH H. "Competency First: New Tests in Foreign Languages." *Proc Inv Conf Testing Probl* 1960: 97–110 '61. *
2. STARR, WILMARTH H. "Proficiency Tests in Modern Foreign Languages." *PMLA* 76:7–11 My '61. *
3. STARR, WILMARTH H. "MLA Foreign Language Proficiency Tests for Teachers and Advanced Students." *PMLA* 77:31–42 S '62. *

LATIN

[404]

***College Entrance Examination Board Achievement Test: Latin.** Candidates for college entrance with 2–4 years high school Latin; 1901–64; for more complete information, see 760; 60(80) minutes; program administered for the College Entrance Examination Board by Educational Testing Service. *

REFERENCES

1–2. See 4:250.
3. See 5:280.

For a review by Konrad Gries of an earlier form, see 5:280; for a review by Harold B. Dunkel, see 4:250. For reviews of the testing program, see 760.

[405]

***College Entrance Examination Board Advanced Placement Examination: Latin.** High School students desiring credit for college level courses or admission to advanced courses; 1954–63; for more complete information, see 761; 2 levels in 1 booklet: Latin 4 (candidates who present the advanced Vergil course), Latin 5 (candidates who have studied 2 of the following fields: prose, lyric poetry, comedy); 180(200) minutes; program administered for the College Entrance Examination Board by Educational Testing Service. *

[406]

★College Entrance Examination Board Placement Tests: Latin Reading Test. Candidates for college entrance; 1962–63, c1955–63; tests are reprints of inactive forms of *College Entrance Examination Board Achievement Test: Latin;* IBM; Forms KPL1, KPL2 in a single booklet (c1955–56, 22 pages); for more complete information, see 759; 60(70) minutes; program administered for the College Entrance Examination Board by Educational Testing Service. *

For reviews of the College Entrance Examination Board Achievement Test: Latin, *see 5:280 and 4:250.*

[407]

***First- and Second-Year Latin: Every Pupil Test.** 1 or 2 years high school; 1929–64; new form

(4 pages) usually issued each December and April; forms from previous testing programs also available; general directions sheet ('63, 2 pages); no data on reliability; Ohio norms for new forms available following testing program; 5¢ per test; 3¢ per key; postpaid; 40(45) minutes; Ohio Scholarship Tests. *

[408]

***First Year Latin: Every Pupil Scholarship Test.** 1 year high school; 1926–64; new form (2 pages) usually issued each January and April; forms from previous testing programs also available; general directions sheet ['63, 2 pages]; no data on reliability; norms for new forms available following testing program; 4¢ per test; 4¢ per key; postage extra; 40(45) minutes; Bureau of Educational Measurements. *

[409]

***Latin I and II: Minnesota High School Achievement Examinations.** 1 or 2 years high school; 1953–63; series formerly called *Midwest High School Achievement Examinations;* new norms issued each June; Form F ('53, 3 pages, formerly called Form II, B, D and originally published as Form 2 of *Latin I and II: Achievement Examinations for Secondary Schools*) used in 1963 testing; no specific manual; series manual ('63, 4 pages); series norms ['63, 4 pages]; series cumulative profile ('62, 2 pages); no data on reliability; no description of normative population; 12¢ per test; $2.50 per 100 profiles; postage extra; 20¢ per specimen set, postpaid; 90(95) minutes; American Guidance Service, Inc. *

[410]

★Latin Test (Two-Year Course): Affiliation Testing Program for Catholic Secondary Schools. Grades 10–12 and students who are candidates for the high school diploma issued by the Catholic University of America; 1949–63; administered annually in May at individual schools; IBM; new form issued annually; Form Z ('63, 11 pages) used in 1963 program; separate answer sheets must be used; 50¢ per test and IBM answer sheet, postpaid; specimen set of the complete battery free; fee includes purchase of test booklets, scoring, and other services; for more complete information, see 758; 90(100) minutes; Program of Affiliation, Catholic University of America. *

HENRY CHAUNCEY, *President, Educational Testing Service, Princeton, New Jersey.* [Review of Forms Y and Z.]

These two forms are probably not too difficult for a candidate who has studied Latin for two years. Whether they are sufficiently demanding seems more questionable. Most of the objectives which the Program of Affiliation suggests the Latin course should cover, particularly those pertaining to a knowledge of the Latin language and to the ability to read it, are sampled. Gains in the understanding of the English language, which are also desired, are measured only indirectly.

The instructions for taking the test are clear, although the fact that four, not five, answer positions are used throughout could be pointed out in connection with the example on the cover, as well as each time a new item type is introduced.

The exercises in vocabulary in Part 1 probably have single answers for the two-year Latin student. There are, however, occasional questions (for example, Form Z, item 15, options 2 and 3) which have two possible answers. In others (for example, Form Z, item 16) the meaning given as correct is not the most common one. Thus the candidate who knows more than the average, or more than he has been taught in a particular class, may be at a disadvantage.

The questions testing knowledge of grammar are not of equal difficulty in the two forms. In Form Y, Part 2, the candidate is given Latin sentences containing English words or phrases for which he is to select the correct Latin replacement. This jumble of languages is not good, and the exercise is easier than the comparable one in Form Z, where the sentence contains a blank rather than an English word. In both exercises options can be eliminated because the forms offered are nonexistent in Latin (for example, Form Y, item 25, option 2, and item 45, option 4; Form Z, item 42, options 1 and 2). Thus these questions do not always fully test the kind of grammatical knowledge they purport to test.

In both forms the passages used to test the candidate's reading comprehension are extremely easy, and at least one question (Form Z, item 85) can be answered without reference to the passage. It is to be regretted that the passages are used only to test reading comprehension, and that knowledge of vocabulary, grammar, and syntax, and the ability to translate idiomatic Latin, are not tested by questions based on the passages, as well as by discrete items. A real understanding of Latin involves the ability to use it in the translation of the literature, not merely in fabricated exercises.

For a review of the complete program, see 758.

[411]

***Second Year Latin: Every Pupil Scholarship Test.** 2 years high school; 1939–64; new form (2 pages) usually issued each January and April; forms from previous testing programs also available; general directions sheet ['63, 2 pages]; no data on reliability; norms for new forms available following testing program; 4¢ per test; 4¢ per key; postage extra; 40(45) minutes; Bureau of Educational Measurements. *

[Other Tests]

For tests not listed above, see the following entries in *Tests in Print:* 665, 668, 670–3, 675–6, 678–80, and 683–4; out of print: 681.

RUSSIAN

[412]

★**College Entrance Examination Board Achievement Test: Russian.** Candidates for college entrance with 2–4 years high school Russian; 1961–64; available only in January testing program; for more complete information, see 760; 60(80) minutes; program administered for the College Entrance Examination Board by Educational Testing Service. *

For reviews of the testing program, see 760.

[413]

★**College Entrance Examination Board Achievement Test: Russian Listening Comprehension.** Candidates for college entrance with 2–4 years high school Russian; 1963; tests administered at the local secondary school on a specified date in February; candidates must also be registered to take one or more achievement tests in one of the regular program administrations; for more complete information, see 760; (30–40) minutes; program administered for the College Entrance Examination Board by Educational Testing Service. *

For reviews of the testing program, see 760.

[414]

★**College Entrance Examination Board Placement Tests: Russian Listening Comprehension Test.** Entering college freshmen; 1962–63; IBM; Form LPL ('62, 8 pages, a reprint of an inactive form of *College Entrance Examination Board Achievement Test: Russian Listening Comprehension*); test administered by 7½ ips tape recording; for more complete information, see 759; 30(40) minutes; program administered for the College Entrance Examination Board by Educational Testing Service. *

[415]

★**Graduate School Foreign Language Test: Russian.** Graduate level degree candidates required to demonstrate reading proficiency in Russian; 1963–64; Forms K-LFG1, K-LFG2, ('63, 44 pages); for more complete information, see 356; 80(100) minutes; Educational Testing Service. *

[416]

★**MLA-Cooperative Foreign Language Tests: Russian.** 1 or 2 years high school or 2 semesters college, 3 or 4 years high school or 4 semesters college; 1963–64; 4 tests in a single booklet: listening, speaking, reading, writing; IBM in part; 2 levels; directions for administering and scoring ['64, 39 pages] for this and the German, Italian, French, and Spanish tests of the series; no data on reliability; no norms; $5 per 10 tests; separate answer sheets may be used for listening and reading tests; $1 per 20 IBM scorable answer sheets; $1 per 10 scoring stencils (answer pattern must be punched out locally); $7 per 3¾ ips tape for listening test; $7 per 3¾ ips tape for speaking test (blank tapes or discs for recording student responses must be obtained locally); postage extra; $2 per specimen set, cash orders postpaid; (25–35) minutes for listening, (10–20) minutes for speaking, 35(40) minutes for reading, 35(40) minutes for writing; prepared in cooperation with the Modern Language Association of America; Cooperative Test Division. *

a) [LOWER LEVEL.] 1 or 2 years high school or 2 semesters college; form LA ('63, 24 pages).

b) [HIGHER LEVEL.] 3 or 4 years high school or 4 semesters college; form MA ('63, 25 pages).

[417]

★**MLA Foreign Language Proficiency Tests for Teachers and Advanced Students: Russian.** Grades 15–17 and foreign language teachers; 1961–64; IBM in part; 7 tests; 2 forms ('61): Form JML1 (also called Form A, available for institutional programs), Form JML2 (also called Form B, restricted to state and local teacher certification programs); series supervisor's manual ['62, 34 pages]; series norms leaflet ('64, 4 pages); series interpretive leaflet ('64, 4 pages); examination fees: $15 per battery of 7 tests, $12.50 per battery of 4 skill tests (listening, speaking, reading, writing); fees include rental of test materials and scoring and reporting service; postage extra; fee for 30-day examination, $3.70 per battery; Modern Language Association of America and Educational Testing Service; program administered by Educational Testing Service. *

a) LISTENING COMPREHENSION TEST: RUSSIAN. IBM; 2 forms ('61, 6 pages, containing response options only); stimulus material presented on 3¾ or 7½ ips tape; $1.50 per examinee; (20–30) minutes.

b) SPEAKING TEST: RUSSIAN. 2 forms ('61, 9 pages, containing scripts for all languages in the series plus a section on 3¾ or 7½ ips tape); responses recorded on tapes or records supplied by the publisher; $6.75 per examinee; (15–30) minutes.

c) READING TEST: RUSSIAN. IBM; 2 forms ('61, 14–15 pages); $1.25 per examinee; 40(50) minutes.

d) WRITING TEST: RUSSIAN. IBM in part; 2 forms ('61, 7 pages); $3.50 per examinee; 45(55) minutes.

e) APPLIED LINGUISTICS TEST: RUSSIAN. IBM; 2 forms ('61, 8 pages); $1.25 per examinee; 40(50) minutes.

f) CIVILIZATION AND CULTURE TEST: RUSSIAN. IBM; 2 forms ('61, 9 pages); $1.25 per examinee; 30(40) minutes.

g) PROFESSIONAL PREPARATION TEST. IBM; 2 forms ('61, 10 pages) common to all languages in the series; $1.25 per examinee; 45(55) minutes.

REFERENCES

1. STARR, WILMARTH H. "Competency First: New Tests in Foreign Languages." *Proc Inv Conf Testing Probl* 1960: 97–110 '61. *

2. STARR, WILMARTH H. "Proficiency Tests in Modern Foreign Languages." *PMLA* 76:7–11 My '61. *

3. STARR, WILMARTH H. "MLA Foreign Language Proficiency Tests for Teachers and Advanced Students." *PMLA* 77:31–42 S '62. *

WAYNE D. FISHER, *Assistant Professor of Education in Russian, and Associate Coordinator of the Master of Arts in Teaching Program in Russian, The University of Chicago, Chicago, Illinois.*

The general impression I have of this battery is that it represents a most significant milestone along the path toward thoroughly reliable and valid tests which will yield specific information about language abilities. The battery does not represent the ideal, but not on that account should there be any hesitancy to make use of it. However, the limitations of the instruments should be kept in mind when making decisions about language abilities of examinees.

Developed by the Modern Language Association and the Educational Testing Service under contract with the United States Office of Education, the preparation of the tests in five languages has involved some 200 persons representing all teaching levels in many different institutions throughout the country. At least 25 teachers were directly involved in the Russian tests alone. The tests are designed to measure proficiency in seven areas: listening comprehension, speaking, reading, writing, applied linguistics, civilization and culture, and professional preparation. There are two parallel forms of each test, one available for institutional testing and the other for certification programs.

The Listening Comprehension Test is received from master tapes, and the examinee's responses are recorded on answer sheets. The Speaking Test is also received from master tapes, but the examinee's responses are recorded on tapes or discs. The Writing Test includes completion and interlinear exercises for which the examinee writes responses. The other four tests are of the written, multiple choice type. The Reading Test is presented in Russian; the Applied Linguistics Test, Civilization and Culture Test, and Professional Preparation Test are in English.

The reported K-R 20 reliability coefficients on all but the Speaking Test range from .82 to .96. That the Educational Testing Service was not able to overcome the difficulties associated with computing the statistical reliability of scores on the Speaking Test is a major shortcoming of the battery. The correlation between pre- and post-Institute scores (with training at summer 1961 NDEA Foreign Language Institutes intervening) is reported as .79.

As with most existing foreign language tests, the tests in this battery are so constructed that the single linguistic element of vocabulary has a controlling influence on the measurement of the examinee's grasp of all other elements. Thus the validity of the various tests as measures of proficiency in areas other than vocabulary remains open to serious doubt. It is unlikely that standardized tests in foreign languages will ever be valid as instruments for measuring general language proficiency until vocabulary is controlled, for testing purposes. One simple way of accomplishing this would be for the testmakers to publish a list of the vocabulary used in their tests and to distribute it in advance to examinees. When we think we are measuring the examinee's "ability to reproduce critical sounds and intonations usually difficult for the American student" of the language, we should indeed be doing so, rather than measuring his control of vocabulary. When we think we are measuring the examinee's ability to comprehend spoken language, we should be certain that this is what we are doing, rather than measuring his control of vocabulary. When we think we are measuring the examinee's control of grammatical structure, we must be certain that we are not instead measuring his control of vocabulary. When we think we are measuring the examinee's ability to speak in response to picture stimuli, we should be certain that the stimuli are so broad and panoramic that any examinee would find something in them about which he might speak, in accordance with his own vocabulary experience and training. Testmakers must give this vocabulary problem closer attention, for language learning is much more than simply acquiring vocabulary.

Some questions concerning validity have to be raised in the parts of the Speaking Test where reading Russian print aloud is the testing situation; reading obviously enters as a factor affecting validity. Scoring of the Speaking Test is likely to be impressionistic rather than objective. Extraneous factors which are nonlanguage factors, such as the examinee's introversion-extroversion and creativity in story telling, are likely to influence the scorer's impression.

I suspect the Listening Comprehension Test is more of a clue-response measure of intellectual sleuthing ability than a measure of listening comprehension as normal language behavior. Examinees may be able to catch a word here and there, look at the printed Russian multiple choice answers, and draw upon their general knowledge of the Russian scene to fill in the gaps so that intelligence, memory, and general knowledge, as well as comprehension, are affecting performance on the test. The validity of this test must be further challenged because of the fact that the examinee is required to read the choice of answers in Russian, which, again, unnecessarily introduces the reading factor.

A very important use of the Applied Linguistics Test and the Professional Preparation Test would be for administration to native speakers who are being considered for teaching positions. A native speaker of Russian is not qualified, by virtue of that fact alone, to teach the language in American schools. On the college level, the effects of poor teaching may be overcome, occasionally, by the ingenuity of the students; but on the precollegiate levels the performance of a native speaker who is not also an effective teacher usually leads to disastrous results, or at best makes it possible for only the most talented students to succeed in the Russian classroom. American-educated teachers should also be given these two tests to determine if they are reasonably well informed on current linguistic and pedagogical practices.

Institutions engaged in teacher education might find it useful to administer the full battery of tests in pre- and post-training situations to ascertain the progress of their students and to help evaluate the effectiveness of their programs.

The four skill tests in this battery do represent the greatest advance in foreign language testing to date. They are infinitely better than teacher-made tests which, by their very nature, must interfere with learning. These professionally made tests hold out great promise that wholly valid and reliable tests can be constructed which do in fact measure what we want them to.

SPANISH

[418]

★Baltimore County Spanish Test. 1 year high school; 1962; 2 scores: parts A, B; administered orally or by tape recording in part; IBM; 1 form (10 pages); manual (9 pages); no data on reliability; separate answer sheets must be used; $3.75 per 35 tests; $1.75 per 35 IBM answer sheets; 25¢ per scoring stencil; 50¢ per specimen set; $7.50 per 3¾ ips tape recording; postage extra; 80(90) minutes in 2 sessions; Baltimore County Spanish Language Committee; Bobbs-Merrill Co., Inc. *

MARIETTE SCHWARZ, *Associate in Foreign Languages, Educational Testing Service, Princeton, New Jersey.*

This test was designed to satisfy a need resulting from the changing emphasis in foreign language teaching from a traditional reading approach to the aural-oral approach. The main purpose of the test is to measure achievement in the mastery of Spanish for students who have completed one year of high school study of the language. It also purports to serve three other purposes: to predict performance in a second-year course; to aid in appraising effectiveness of curriculum materials and methods of instruction; to aid in establishing objective standards for placement in second-year courses.

The test consists of two parts, each to be completed in 40 minutes of testing time. Part A contains 90 multiple choice and true-false items and measures the candidate's proficiency in vocabulary, reading, grammar, culture, and aural comprehension. Fifty of the questions have five choices and 40 are of the true-false type.

Part B contains 55 three-choice items and is intended to measure entirely aural comprehension. For all items in Part B all the choices are printed in the test booklet; for 10 of the items, not only the choices but even the short stories on which the items are based are printed in the booklet. For these items, selecting the correct answers does not necessarily prove listening skill; the candidate could arrive at them on the basis of reading skill.

Part 1 of Part A consists of 15 items testing vocabulary. In five items the student must choose the correct translation into Spanish from an English word or words. In light of present-day teaching methods, it would seem preferable to construct these similarly to the other 10 items which test vocabulary within the context of a Spanish sentence. A wide range of vocabulary with a considerable degree of interest is presented throughout the test, a feat which is often difficult when selection must be restricted to vocabulary within the competence of students with only one year of high school training in Spanish.

Part 2 consists of 15 items measuring reading comprehension. Individual statements which must be answered as true or false provide 10 scorable units which do not require much testing time. The others are multiple choice items based on a preceding paragraph. The questions, which are entirely in Spanish, are well chosen; they cannot be answered without the understanding of the passage.

Part 3 consists of 15 items testing both Spanish and Latin American culture. This part is written in English with some Spanish words interspersed and could be regarded as a contribution to the variety of approaches within the test.

Part 4, a grammar test, consists of 15 items. Each contains an English sentence followed by the Spanish translation with a word or phrase missing. The student must select the word or phrase which best completes the Spanish translation. Ten of the 15 items can be answered without referring to the English sentence, making the English sentences useless. The other five items could easily be revised so as not to necessitate the use of English in this part. Furthermore, two questions have more than one possible correct answer. One question presents a nonexistent word as a choice. It is likely that by the use of English, testing time is being wasted; in view of the trends of present-day language teaching the skill of translation might well be eliminated.

Part 5 tests aural comprehension. It can be administered either by tape or by the examiner reading the script, which is printed in the teacher's manual. This alternate choice of methods for administration, which also applies for all of Part B, suggests that the test cannot be considered completely standardized. Lack of standardization is further substantiated by the fact that there are approximately a dozen discrepancies between the tape and the script, although some of them are minor. In Part B, item number 23 as presented in the script is not the same item as presented on the tape, and the candidate will find no correct answer in his test booklet.

A rerecording of the tape would improve the test considerably. The English voice is pleasant and clear. However, the Spanish voice, which is not that of a native speaker of Spanish, commits serious errors in stress and pronunciation, as well as in basic grammar, by deviating from the script. This comment is made with the realization of the fact that regional differences do exist. For example, in question 35 of Part B, the stress is placed incorrectly on the word "país." No incorrect Spanish should be presented to students in a testing situation. Furthermore, the Spanish voice reads the question numbers in English with a strong German accent. It would be preferable to use an English voice for all of the English and a carefully chosen native speaker of Spanish for the Spanish voice. Also, speed of the tape is unnatural to the extent of producing continuous open junctures and errors in pronunciation.

The fact that all the directions for the test are in English is to be commended especially at this level of language learning since it does not penalize students for their lack of comprehension of the directions. It might also have been helpful to the student to be presented, wherever possible, with an example for each different type of question. The directions for the second section of Part B need further editing. The student is told to identify objects which have been described. Some of the answers required are not names of objects. It would undoubtedly be of value in Part B to insert additional directions on the tape as an explanation and a warning to anticipate lengthy pauses.

The test is intended to be a power test and, although no data are given on speededness, it does not appear that the test is speeded.

In the section of the manual entitled "Validity and reliability," only data on item discrimination are given. Even these, however, are misleading because they consist of phi coefficients calculated on the basis of extreme groups. Furthermore, while no direct comparison can be made with data of other tests, it has been the reviewer's experience that more discriminating items can be constructed for tests of this type.

The only norms available are the Baltimore County norms (n = 2,020). There is no indication whether the norming administration was performed on a sample to which the aural comprehension parts were administered by means of the tape or by readings of the teacher or by a combination of both. No information is given regarding the correlation between Part A and Part B; neither are means and standard deviations given.

From the point of view of item construction, some improvements would be desirable mainly with regard to stems, but also to the choices, which lack consistency in the use or omission of articles.

This test is designed presumably for use with several types of foreign language curricula —those using a moderate oral-aural approach, those with a reading approach, and those with a strong oral-aural approach. This reviewer believes that it may be most satisfactory for the first type of curriculum. Part A cannot be compared to other tests due to the diversity of types of skills and knowledge measured. With regard to Part B, neither from the viewpoint of quality of Spanish nor of test construction does it compare favorably with the lower level listening test of the *MLA-Cooperative Foreign Language Tests: Spanish.* However, some capability is shown for testing the basic elements of elementary Spanish. Despite the shortcomings cited, there might be situations in which a teacher would find this test applicable.

[419]

***College Entrance Examination Board Achievement Test: Spanish.** Candidates for college entrance with 2–4 years high school Spanish; 1902–64; for more complete information, see 760; 60(80) minutes; program administered for the College Entrance Examination Board by Educational Testing Service. *

REFERENCES

1–3. See 4:259.
4. See 5:287.
5. CABAT, LOUIS, AND GODIN, JACOB D. *Spanish: How to Prepare for College Board Achievement Tests in Spanish.* Great Neck, N.Y.: Barron's Educational Series, Inc., 1960. Pp. vi, 107. *

For reviews of the testing program, see 760.

[420]

★College Entrance Examination Board Achievement Test: Spanish Listening Comprehension. Candidates for college entrance with 2–4 years high school Spanish; 1960–63; tests administered at the local secondary school on a specified date in February; candidates must also be registered to take one or more achievement tests in one of the regular program administrations; for more complete information, see 760; (30–40) minutes; program administered for the College Entrance Examination Board by Educational Testing Service. *

For reviews of the testing program, see 760.

[421]

***College Entrance Examination Board Advanced Placement Examination: Spanish.** High school students desiring credit for college level courses or admission to advanced courses; 1954–63; for more complete information, see 761; 180(200) minutes; program administered for the College Entrance Examination Board by Educational Testing Service. *

REFERENCES

1. VALLEY, JOHN R. "College Actions on CEEB Advanced Placement Language Examination Candidates." *Mod Lang J* 43:261–3 O '59. *

[422]

★College Entrance Examination Board Placement Tests: Spanish Listening Comprehension Test. Entering college freshmen; 1962–63, c1955–63; IBM; Forms DLC1, DLC2 in a single booklet (c1955), Forms JPL, KPL1 in a single booklet (c1960–61, 20 pages, a reprint of inactive forms of *College Entrance Examination Board Achievement Test: Spanish Listening Comprehension*); test administered by 7½ ips tape recording; for more complete information, see 759; 30(40) minutes; program administered for the College Entrance Examination Board by Educational Testing Service. *

REFERENCES

1. SCHEIDER, ROSE M. "Evolution of the Listening Comprehension Tests." *Col Board R* 48:24–8 f '62. *

[423]

★College Entrance Examination Board Placement Tests: Spanish Reading Test. Entering college freshmen; 1962–63, c1955–63; tests are reprints of inactive forms of *College Entrance Examination Board Achievement Test: Spanish;* IBM; Forms KPL1, KPL2 in a single booklet (c1955–57, 22 pages); for more complete information, see 759; 60(70) minutes; program administered for the College Entrance Examination Board by Educational Testing Service. *

[424]

★Common Concepts Foreign Language Test: Spanish [Research Edition]. "Students [in any grade] who have had enough foreign language instruction to place them at the Level 1 stage in their achievement"; 1962–64; aural comprehension; may be administered using live voice but tape recording is recommended; IBM; Forms 1, 2; a single booklet ('62, 31 pages) presents response options for both forms of this test and the French and German tests of the series; mimeographed preliminary manual ('64, 24 pages); interim norms (grades 7–12 only); separate answer sheets or cards must be used; 75¢ per test; $5.95 per 3¾ ips tape recording; 5¢ per IBM answer sheet; 20¢ per scoring stencil; 2¢ per Cal-Card; 20¢ per hand scoring stencil; 15¢ per manual; postage extra; $1 per specimen set without tape; $6.95 per specimen set with tape; postpaid; scoring service available; (40–45) minutes; Bela H. Banathy, Miles V. Zintz, W. James Popham, Joseph M. Sadnavitch, Rena Krichbaum, Fred B. Gannon, Valdemar Hempel, and Klaus A. Mueller; California Test Bureau. *

[425]

The Graduate Record Examinations Advanced Tests: Spanish. Grades 16–17; 1946–58; for more complete information, see 762; 180(200) minutes; Educational Testing Service. *

For a review of the testing program, see 5:601.

[426]

★MLA-Cooperative Foreign Language Tests: Spanish. 1 or 2 years high school or 2 semesters college, 3 or 4 years high school or 4 semesters college; 1963–64; 4 tests in a single booklet: listening, speaking, reading, writing; IBM in part; 2 levels; directions for administering and scoring ['64, 39 pages] for this and the German, Italian, Russian, and French tests of the series; no data on reliability; no norms; $5 per 10 tests; separate answer sheets may be used for listening and reading tests; $1 per 20 IBM scorable answer sheets; $1 per 10 scoring stencils (answer pattern must be punched out locally); $7 per 3¾ ips tape for listening test; $7 per 3¾ ips tape for speaking test (blank tapes or discs for recording student responses must be obtained locally); postage extra; $2 per specimen set, cash orders postpaid; (25–35) minutes for listening, (10–20) minutes for speaking, 35(40) minutes for reading, 35(40) minutes for writing; prepared in cooperation with the Modern Language Association of America; Cooperative Test Division. *

a) [LOWER LEVEL.] 1 or 2 years high school or 2 semesters college; form LA ('63, 24 pages).
b) [HIGHER LEVEL.] 3 or 4 years high school or 4 semesters college; form MA ('63, 24 pages).

[427]

★MLA Foreign Language Proficiency Tests for Teachers and Advanced Students: Spanish. Grades 15–17 and foreign language teachers; 1961–64; IBM in part; 7 tests; 2 forms ('61): Form JML1 (also called Form A, available for institutional programs), Form JML2 (also called Form B, restricted to state and local teacher certification programs); series supervisor's manual ['62, 34 pages]; series norms leaflet ('64, 4 pages); series interpretive leaflet ('64, 4 pages); examination fees: $15 per battery of 7 tests, $12.50 per battery of 4 skill tests (listening, speaking, reading, writing); fees include rental of test materials and scoring and reporting service; postage extra; fee for 30-day examination, $3.70 per battery; Modern Language Association of America and Educational Testing Service; program administered by Educational Testing Service. *
a) LISTENING COMPREHENSION TEST: SPANISH. IBM; 2 forms ('61, 6 pages, containing response options only); stimulus material presented on 3¾ or 7½ ips tape; $1.50 per examinee; (20–30) minutes.
b) SPEAKING TEST: SPANISH. 2 forms ('61, 9 pages, containing scripts for all languages in the series plus a section on 3¾ or 7½ ips tape); responses recorded on tapes or records supplied by the publisher; $6.75 per examinee; (15–30) minutes.
c) READING TEST: SPANISH. IBM; 2 forms ('61, 12 pages); $1.25 per examinee; 40(50) minutes.
d) WRITING TEST: SPANISH. IBM in part; 2 forms ('61, 8 pages); $3.50 per examinee; 45(55) minutes.
e) APPLIED LINGUISTICS TEST: SPANISH. IBM; 2 forms ('61, 9 pages); $1.25 per examinee; 40(50) minutes.
f) CIVILIZATION AND CULTURE TEST: SPANISH. IBM; 2 forms ('61, 9 pages); $1.25 per examinee; 30(40) minutes.
g) PROFESSIONAL PREPARATION TEST. IBM; 2 forms ('61, 10 pages) common to all languages in the series; $1.25 per examinee; 45(55) minutes.

REFERENCES

1. STARR, WILMARTH H. "Competency First: New Tests in Foreign Languages." *Proc Inv Conf Testing Probl* 1960:97–110 '61. *
2. STARR, WILMARTH H. "Proficiency Tests in Modern Foreign Languages." *PMLA* 76:7–11 My '61. *
3. STARR, WILMARTH H. "MLA Foreign Language Proficiency Tests for Teachers and Advanced Students." *PMLA* 77:31–42 S '62. *

WALTER V. KAULFERS, *Professor of Education, University of Illinois, Urbana, Illinois.*

This battery of seven tests represents a promising attempt to measure "three general levels of proficiency (Minimal, Good, and Superior) for seven areas of language teaching competencies: 1) aural understanding, 2) speaking, 3) reading, 4) writing, 5) language analysis, 6) culture, 7) professional preparation" (*3*). Administration of the battery in one sitting is impractical, not just because of its length (over four hours) but also because of the special equipment required for the Listening Comprehension Test and the Speaking Test. Fortunately, the examinations can be given independently of each other, and in almost any order desired.

Percentile norms are available based on the converted scores of some 4,400 participants in the Spanish sections of the National Defense Education Act Foreign Language Institutes of 1961, 1962, and 1963. These, however, should be used only by evaluators competent to make allowances for the limitations governing the validity and reliability of the tests. The relationship between ratings given to the examinees by the faculties of the Institutes and the actual scores made by the participants on the tests is at times rather low—e.g., Professional Preparation Test scores versus ratings in all test areas including professional preparation. Percentile norms for a limited sampling (33–138 cases) of Pennsylvania college seniors are also available. The number of cases involved, however, is at present too limited for the norms to be useful as criteria of evaluation.

Inasmuch as a "Superior" level of competence in reading, writing, aural comprehension, and speaking was defined by the Steering Committee of the Foreign Language Program of the Modern Language Association of America as proficiency approximating that of an educated native, it is regrettable that the tests of the aforementioned abilities could not have been administered to a representative sampling of educated natives of Spanish-speaking countries. This would have provided scores with some point of reference or anchorage in reality. It might then be possible to tell, at least within reasonable limits, whether an examinee's performance approximates that of a native, whether it is about half as good, or nearly two thirds as good, etc. In the absence of such validation the reviewer would prefer some of the tests prepared for the College Entrance Examination Board as measures of proficiency in Spanish proper.

The unique features of the battery are the Applied Linguistics Test, the Speaking Test, and the Professional Preparation Test. These are probably the first tests in these fields published for widespread professional use. Unfortunately each falls somewhat short of the reliability commonly expected of examinations designed to differentiate between individuals. Although the battery has already been revised to reduce its original length by nearly two hours, some of the standard errors of measurement are still a little high for tests consisting of only 36 to 65 items. The reviewer has been assured that further revisions are already under way.

The Listening Comprehension Test attempts to measure ability to understand spoken Spanish by means of 36 tape recorded multiple choice questions divided into three parts. As throughout most of the battery, the Spanish of the test, whether printed or recorded on tape, is idiomatic, well edited, and generally above criticism. The use of both male and female voices is well advised. So, too, is the use of acceptable regional variations in the speech of educated natives of Spain and the Spanish-speaking Americas. Only Part 3, however, is strictly an aural comprehension test. The preceding two sections require the examinee to read and choose among four possible answers involving a total of from 8 to 37 words. In fact, some of the items in Parts 1 and 2 of the Listening Comprehension Test actually involve more "reading" than is required in Part 1 of the Reading Test proper. For this reason the validity of the test—namely, the exact meaning of the scores obtained from it—is open to question. In Part 2 the length of some of the comprehension items also suggests that they may measure memory as much as understanding. The examinee is constantly distracted by the necessity of choosing the correct response from among four possible answers printed in Spanish.

The reliability of .91 as measured by Kuder-Richardson formula 20 is satisfactory. That this is an unnecessarily difficult test for many people, however, is confirmed by the fact that while "the mean number of unanswered items is less than one * the score distributions show substantial numbers of scores not only below the dashed lines [99th percentile of the theoretical chance score distribution] but also below the expected mean chance score of 11.00." It is the reviewer's opinion that not a small part of the trouble lies not in the difficulty of the spoken Spanish which the examinees are expected to comprehend, but in the involved printed statements from among which they are so often expected to make a choice. While selecting an answer the examinee can easily forget some of what he heard on tape.

The Speaking Test is administered entirely on tape from directions given in English. The examinee records his responses for evaluation by scorers trained by the Educational Testing Service. Part 1 has him repeat verbatim short spoken sentences and questions. Part 2 requires him to read aloud a printed passage of Spanish dialogue. Part 3 requests him to describe in Spanish what he sees in a series of situation drawings. Since Parts 1 and 2 are essentially tests of pronunciation, intonation, and ability in oral reading, only Part 3 is actually a "speaking" test in the everyday sense of the word. To score the latter the evaluator is obliged to keep in mind simultaneously a rating scale embracing 20 different levels of performance—5 each for vocabulary, pronunciation, structure, and fluency!

The fact that even with scoring done by specially trained evaluators interscorer reliabilities in the .80's are difficult to obtain shows that this is not an examination to be scored or interpreted by amateurs. As one of the first tests of speaking ability in Spanish to be produced for widespread professional use since the days of the Army Student Training Program, however, it is an additional milestone in foreign language achievement testing.

The three parts of the 40-minute Reading Test are designed to afford a measure of comprehension in silent reading. Since an educated native of Spain or Spanish America would be able to complete the examination in much less time than the 40 minutes allowed, it is essentially a power test. It will not always discriminate between fast and slow readers—between those who can actually "read" Spanish and those who can do little more than "decode" it. Although Part A is well constructed and apparently scaled in ascending order of difficulty, some of the items actually require less "reading" than is involved in the Listening Comprehension Test.

Part B consists of four passages of from approximately 130 to 250 words each. The reviewer found it possible to choose the correct answers to several questions here without reading the selection itself. Items 16 through 21 of Form JML1 are more tests of vocabulary than of reading comprehension. Part C consists of five passages of poetry. The abstract symbolism of some of the verses will present a challenge even to able readers.

Although the Kuder-Richardson reliability coefficients of .91 and .90 for the two forms appear satisfactory, the validity of the examination is limited by the fact that it provides no measure of ability to comprehend material presented in a conversational or dialogue context, as is often the case in plays, novels, and short stories.

The Writing Test consists of two parts. In the two printed passages of Part A each numbered line replaces a word that has been omitted. Since some of the 30 blanks permit more than one acceptable answer, scoring the test objectively is not an easy matter. The scorer is permitted to use personal judgment in the case of dubious or far-fetched responses —a seeming throwback to the infancy of foreign language achievement testing a generation ago. Space 28 (in Form JML1), for example, suggested five acceptable alternatives to the reviewer who made no attempt to exhaust the possibilities. Applied to Part A the title, "Writing Test," is a misnomer since this part involves far more reading than writing. Little more writing is involved here than was frequently required in tests of "active vocabulary" a generation ago.

Part B confronts the examinee with two poorly written passages. He is to treat them as though they were student compositions and to revise them so that they conform to standard Spanish. This part is highly functional in that it affords an indication of the examinee's ability to correct student compositions, written exercises, board work, etc. However, by its very nature it is more a measure of "proofreading" ability than of proficiency in original composition.

The reliability coefficients of .94 and .95 for the two forms show that satisfactory reliability can be achieved even for tests which are not entirely objective, provided the scorers are agreed from previous orientation sessions regarding just how they will evaluate such things as minor slips in the omission of accent marks, minor misspellings, or cases of borderline legibility.

The Applied Linguistics Test is divided into four parts. Part A covers phonetics, pronunciation, and orthography. Part B covers morphology and syntax with a view to testing the examinee's "knowledge of some of the differences and similarities among Spanish grammatical patterns on the one hand, and between Spanish and English on the other." Part C tests the examinee's understanding of some of the terms of phonetics and descriptive linguistics, and more importantly his "ability to identify Spanish illustrations of the concepts represented by these terms." The last part consists of only three items dealing with historical linguistics.

Inasmuch as the Applied Linguistics Test is probably the first objective examination in this field to be published for widespread professional use it is unfortunate that neither form has a reliability of more than .85—a little short of the reliability of .90 commonly considered desirable if a test is to differentiate between individuals. Scaling the items in ascending order of difficulty (of which there is little evidence in the examination) should help here, as would recasting the multiple choice items to reduce the word length of the four responses. In general, the greater the word length of the multiple choice answers the more time consuming and "difficult" taking the test becomes regardless of the examinee's knowledge of the subject. Moreover, there are other types of machine scorable test items that could have been employed to advantage here as in other parts of the battery.

The Civilization and Culture Test covers mainly the geography, history, and literature of Spain and Spanish America, with passing attention to art, music, and politico-economic conditions. Items 1, 2, 15, 17, 22, and 45 in Form JML1, as well as all items of this type in Form JML2, should be cast in another form. Selecting the correct response here is exasperatingly time consuming because of the amount of "decoding" involved. The sequence of items without any apparent attempt either to scale them in ascending order of difficulty or to group them according to topic (as in the linguistics test) is unfortunate. The omnibus scores provided by the test prevent it from affording ready suggestions concerning the specific aspects of Spanish or Spanish-American civilization and culture in which an examinee may be strong or weak. A reconstruction of the test to meet these objections should enhance its utility and also increase its present reliability of .89 so as to make it even more dependable in differentiating between individuals.

The 45-minute, 65-item multiple choice Professional Preparation Test is primarily an attempt to measure an examinee's acquaintance with objectives, methods, and resource materials approved by exponents of the audio-lingual ("linguistic") approach in foreign language teaching. Several items relate to the teaching of foreign languages in the elementary grades. Knowledge of the ways and means for accommodating students of different abilities, however—viz., gifted as compared with very slow learners, stammerers, etc.—is apparently beyond the purview of this examination. Moreover, even a perfect score will provide no assurance that the teacher can give intelligent counsel to parents asking, for example, if their five-year-old son is too immature to begin learning a second language.

The reliability coefficients of .86 and .87 for Forms JML1 and JML2 barely approximate the reliability generally expected of tests designed to differentiate between individuals. A grouping of items by topic into three or more parts should help raise the test's reliability by reducing the number of shifts in mindset which the present unscaled, unorganized sequence requires. Recasting items 34 and 35 in Form JML1 should also help. As presently framed they are unnecessarily time consuming because of the "decoding" involved and hence probably more difficult to answer than the subject justifies. Grouping the items by topics into three or more parts might also increase both the validity and the utility of the examinations by affording a diagnosis of the respects in which an examinee's professional preparation is adequate or deficient. As probably the first test of this kind to be published for widespread professional use it is an important first step in the right direction. In its present form, however, it should be regarded as tentative and experimental. Fortunately, this test has been under almost continuous revision since its first printing.

In summary, the *MLA Foreign Language Proficiency Tests for Teachers and Advanced Students: Spanish* are designed to serve an important need which to date they barely succeed in meeting satisfactorily. The excellent statistical analyses of the tests, however, indicate that they have enough promise to warrant further revision. In their present state they should be used only by examiners thoroughly acquainted with the nature of the subject matter tested, aware of the limitations of the individual tests, and willing to give borderline examinees either a supplementary test or the benefit of any doubt.

[428]

★National Spanish Examination. 2, 3, 4 years high school; 1957–63; new form issued annually for administration in April at local secondary schools or centers established by local chapters of the AATSP; 4 scores: aural, usage, reading, total; 3 levels; Forms G2S, G3S, G4S, ['63, 4 pages] used in 1963 program; no manual; no directions for administration; no data on reliability; summary of results (based on locally scored papers returned to the test development committee) is published in *Hispania* in September following the testing program; 10¢ per test; $5.50 per 7½ ips tape recording for aural subtest; postpaid; copies of previous year's tests and tapes available at the same prices; (105–115) minutes; [Test Development Committee, American Association of Teachers of Spanish and Portuguese]; the Association (distributed by local chapter treasurers and the national chairman). *

REFERENCES

1. SAPORTA, SOL, AND CHARLY, H. T. "Report on the 1957 National Spanish Examinations." *Hispania* 40:333–5 S '57. *
2. POWELL, JAMES D. "Second Report on the 1958 National Spanish Examinations." *Hispania* 41:499–501 D '58. *
3. POWELL, JAMES D., AND CHARLY, HARRY T. "Preliminary Report on the 1958 National Spanish Examinations." *Hispania* 41:336–7 S '58. *
4. POWELL, JAMES D.; HARTSOOK, JOHN H.; AND CHARLY, HARRY T. "Report on the 1959 National Spanish Examinations." *Hispania* 42:356–7 S '59. *
5. HARTSOOK, JOHN H., AND CHARLY, HARRY T. "Report on the 1960 National Spanish Examinations." *Hispania* 43:422–4 S '60. *
6. CHARLY, HARRY T., AND HARTSOOK, JOHN H. "Report on the 1961 National Spanish Examinations." *Hispania* 44:499–500 S '61. *
7. CHARLY, HARRY T. "Report on the 1962 National Spanish Examinations." *Hispania* 45:498–500 S '62. *
8. BOYER, MILDRED V., AND CHARLY, HARRY T. "Report on the 1963 National Spanish Examinations." *Hispania* 46:587–90 S '63. *

[429]

***Spanish I and II: Minnesota High School Achievement Examinations.** 1 or 2 years high school; 1951–63; series formerly called *Midwest High School Achievement Examinations;* new norms issued each June; Form F ('53, 5 pages, formerly called Form II, B, D and originally published as Form 2 of *Spanish I and II: Achievement Examinations for Secondary Schools*) used in 1963 testing; no specific manual; series manual ('63, 4 pages); series norms ['63, 4 pages]; series cumulative profile ('62, 2 pages); no data on reliability; no description of normative population; 12¢ per test; $2.50 per 100 profiles; postage extra; 20¢ per specimen set, postpaid; 90(95) minutes; American Guidance Service, Inc. *

[430]

Spanish: Teacher Education Examination Program. College seniors preparing to teach secondary school; 1957; for more complete information, see 709; IBM; 80(95) minutes; Educational Testing Service. *

For a review of the testing program, see 5:543.

[431]

★Spanish Test (Two-Year Course): Affiliation Testing Program for Catholic Secondary Schools. Grades 10–12 and students who are candidates for the high school diploma issued by the Catholic University of America; 1949–63; administered annually in May at individual schools; IBM; Form Y ['62, 12 pages] used in 1963 program; tests loaned only; separate answer sheets must be used; 50¢ per test and IBM answer sheet, postpaid; specimen set of the complete battery free; fee includes scoring and other services; for more complete information, see

758; 90(100) minutes; Program of Affiliation, Catholic University of America. *

HENRY CHAUNCEY, *President, Educational Testing Service, Princeton, New Jersey.* [Review of Form Y.]

According to the data for interpretation, as well as personal judgment, the test in its entirety is of average difficulty for students having had a two-year sequence of Spanish study in high school. Although Part 2, which purports to measure reading comprehension, borders on the easy side with a mean per cent of right answers of 60, and Part 5, measuring cultural background, is a difficult part with 32 per cent of right answers, the test appears to be well suited for its educational level, and it is not speeded.

It is questionable, however, that the test really measures all four language skills—listening, speaking, reading, and writing—as implied on page 51 of the booklet Program of Affiliation. This booklet states, "Oral and written expression can be tested only indirectly by an objective test, especially by questions on grammar and syntax." However, questions on grammar and syntax can hardly be said, even indirectly, to provide a measure of speaking and writing, at least not now with the absence of any correlation studies to prove the contrary. Furthermore, Part 2 of the test does not represent a true measure of reading comprehension. Although a paragraph is presented, it appears to be there mainly for face validity. Following the first paragraph, for example, 18 out of the 20 questions can be answered without ever having read the passage. The candidate merely chooses the English translation of a word or group of words. At best, this could be called the testing of vocabulary in context, providing that the candidate is helped by referring to the paragraph. Each of the two remaining questions has only one attractive distractor. In other words, it is necessary to read the passage only in order to choose between two of the options.

In terms of the syllabus, the area of the content tested is broad and still realistic, although the vocabulary of the test is based upon a designated word list. In certain respects, both the Spanish course outline and the test seem to retain features of the traditional grammar-translation approach, while also incorporating some characteristics of audio-lingual language teaching and testing. It appears that, in light of the syllabus, translation of vocabulary and testing of grammar partially through translation are justified. It is commendable that nowhere are incorrect structures presented to the candidate. However, in light of the changing emphasis of present-day foreign language curricula, perhaps some of the course objectives, as well as the resulting test specifications, might be reexamined and item types modified or new ones employed.

For a review of the complete program, see 758.

[Other Tests]

For tests not listed above, see the following entries in *Tests in Print:* 691–2, 694–6, 699–701, and 703; out of print: 690, 697, and 704.

INTELLIGENCE

REVIEWS BY *J. Stanley Ahmann, Lewis E. Albright, James M. Anderson, Mary C. Austin, Andrew R. Baggaley, Ralph F. Berdie, L. B. Birch, Donald B. Black, Morton Bortner, John E. Bowers, Alvin G. Burstein, W. V. Clemans, Paul C. Davis, Jerome E. Doppelt, N. M. Downie, S. S. Dunn, Marvin D. Dunnette, Walter N. Durost, Dorothy Eichorn, George A. Ferguson, Warren G. Findley, Elizabeth D. Fraser, Robert L. French, Gustav J. Froehlich, James R. Glennon, Goldine C. Gleser, Bert A. Goldman, Russel F. Green, Mary R. Haworth, A. W. Heim, John R. Hills, C. B. Hindley, Marshall S. Hiskey, Marjorie P. Honzik, John E. Horrocks, Lloyd G. Humphreys, John D. Hundleby, Frank B. Jex, H. Gwynne Jones, J. A. Keats, James E. Kennedy, J. S. Lawes, D. Welty Lefever, Philip M. Levy, John Liggett, Howard B. Lyman, Boyd R. McCandless, Melvin R. Marks, William B. Michael, T. R. Miles, John E. Milholland, T. Ernest Newland, John Nisbet, Stanley Nisbet, David A. Payne, Douglas A. Pidgeon, Ellen V. Piers, A. E. G. Pilliner, S. Rachman, Benjamin Rosner, Arthur B. Royse, David G. Ryans, H. J. Sants, William B. Schrader, Richard E. Schutz, Julian C. Stanley, Naomi Stewart, Abraham J. Tannenbaum, Erwin K. Taylor, Albert S. Thompson, Leona E. Tyler, Wimburn L. Wallace, Norman E. Wallen, Emmy E. Werner, Warren W. Willingham, Leroy Wolins, Frank B. Womer, and Wayne S. Zimmerman.*

GROUP

[432]

*__A.C.E.R. Higher Tests.__ Ages 13 and over; 1944–59; formerly called *A.C.E.R. General Ability Test: Advanced M;* 3 scores: linguistic, quantitative, total; 2 forms; 2 parts; mimeographed manual ('59, 36 pages); 3*s*. 6*d*. per 10 tests of either part; 1*s*. 6*d*. per key; 6*s*. 6*d*. per manual; 8*s*. 6*d*. per specimen set of either part; postpaid within Australia; D. Spearritt (original manual), M. L. Clark (revised manual), and B. Christeson (form W); Australian Council for Educational Research. *

a) FORMS ML AND WL [LINGUISTIC]. 2 forms: ML ['48], WL ['59], (4 pages); 15(25) minutes.
b) FORMS MQ AND WQ [QUANTITATIVE]. 2 forms: MQ ['48], WQ ['59], (4 pages); 20(30) minutes.

REFERENCES

1. MASON, P. L., AND CASEY, D. L. "The Use of Psychological Tests for Selecting Tabulating Machine Operators." *Personnel Prac B* 16:39–41 S '60. * (*PA* 35:4063)

For a review by C. Sanders, see 5:297.

[433]

*__A.C.E.R. Intermediate Test A.__ Ages 10–0 to 14–0; 1938–61; test essentially the same as *A.C.E.R. General Test A* ['38]; 1 form ['61, 4 pages]; mimeographed manual ['61, 23 pages]; no description of normative population; 3*s*. 6*d*. per 10 tests; 1*s*. 6*d*. per key; 6*s*. 6*d*. per manual; 8*s*. 6*d*. per specimen set; postpaid within Australia; 30(50) minutes; Australian Council for Educational Research. *

For excerpts from related book reviews, see 3:1110 and 40:B1005.

[434]

*__A.C.E.R. Junior A Test.__ Ages 8.5–12.0; 1946–58; formerly called *General Test T;* 1 form ['46, 8 pages]; mimeographed manual ['58, 18 pages]; 6*s*. per 10 tests; 3*s*. per key; 7*s*. 6*d*. per manual; 11*s*. 3*d*. per specimen set; postpaid within Australia; 30(40) minutes; Australian Council for Educational Research. *

For a review by R. Winterbourn, see 5:299.

[435]

*__A.C.E.R. Junior B Test.__ Ages 8.5–12.0; 1948–58; 1 form ['48, 8 pages]; manual ('58, 29 pages); not available to government schools; 6*s*. per 10 tests; 6*d*. per key; 9*s*. 6*d*. per manual; 10*s*. 9*d*. per specimen set; postpaid within Australia; 35(60) minutes; Australian Council for Educational Research. *

REFERENCES

1. DUNN, S., AND SPEARRITT, D. "A Comparative Study of the Reliability of Some Verbal and Non-Verbal Intelligence Tests." *Austral J Psychol* 7:169–74 D '55. * (*PA* 31:1030)

For a review by R. Winterbourn, see 5:300.

[436]

★**A.C.E.R. Test W.N.V.** Ages 13–6 to 16–11; 1960; for research use only; pictorial general ability test; 1 form ['60, 4 pages]; mimeographed manual ['60, 9 pages]; tentative norms; 9*s*. per 10 tests; 1*s*. 6*d*. per key; 2*s*. 6*d*. per manual; 5*s*. per specimen set; postpaid within Australia; 15(25) minutes; Australian Council for Educational Research. *

[437]

★**Academic Alertness "AA": Individual Placement Series (Area I).** Adults; 1957–59; 7 scores: general knowledge, arithmetic, vocabulary, reasoning ability, logical sequence, accuracy, total; Forms A, B, ('57, 6 pages); preliminary manual ('59, 15 pages); no data on reliability; no description of normative population; separate answer sheets must be used; $20 per 25 tests; $1 per 25 answer sheets; 50¢ per key; $2.50 per specimen set; postpaid; 20(25) minutes; J. H. Norman; the Author. *

[438]

American Council on Education Psychological Examination for College Freshmen. Grade 13; 1924–54; 3 scores: quantitative, linguistic, total; IBM; Editions 1949, 1952, 1954, (14 pages); manual ('50, 7 pages); norms booklet (27–32 pages) for each edition: 1949 Edition ('50), 1952 Edition ('53), 1954 Edition ('55); separate answer sheets must be used; $4 per 25 tests; $1 per 25 IBM answer sheets; 25¢

per set of scoring stencils; postage extra; $1 per specimen set, cash orders postpaid; 38(65) minutes; 1947 and earlier editions by L. L. Thurstone and Thelma Gwinn Thurstone; later editions prepared by publisher from materials developed by the Thurstones; Cooperative Test Division. * (Withdrawn November 1964.)

REFERENCES

1–48. See 40:1377.
49–143. See 3:217.
144–276. See 4:277.
277–439. See 5:308.
440. SPANEY, EMMA. "Personality Tests and the Selection of Nurses." *Nursing Res* 1:4–26 F '53. *
441. JONES, WILLIAM ALTEN. *The Adequacy of Certain Measures Used in the Selection of Freshman State and Merit Scholarship Recipients at Indiana University.* Doctor's thesis, Indiana University (Bloomington, Ind.), 1955. (*DA* 15:1553)
442. JEX, FRANK B. *University of Utah Studies in the Prediction of Academic Success.* University of Utah Research Monographs in Education, Vol. 1, No. 1. Salt Lake City, Utah: the University, July 1957. Pp. ix, 51. *
443. SALTZGAVER, L. DUANE. *An Investigation of the A.C.E. Psychological Examination Percentile Rankings Made by Freshmen Students Who Have Entered the College of Education at the University of Maryland in Alternate Years From 1947 to 1955.* Master's thesis, University of Maryland (College Park, Md.), 1957.
444. SCARF, ROBERT C. "Differential Scores and Unstable Personality." *J Ed Psychol* 48:268–72 My '57. * (*PA* 33:2190)
445. WILLIAMS, CECIL L. *A Study of the Relative Effectiveness of the ACE Psychological Examination and the School and College Ability Test in Predicting First Semester Grade Point Averages.* Master's thesis, University of Kansas (Lawrence, Kan.), 1957.
446. BELAI, LOUISA. "A Comparative Study of the Results of Standardized Tests and Achievement at a Liberal Arts College for Women." *J Ed Res* 52:94–100 N '58. * (*PA* 33:11014)
447. GREHL, PAUL F. *Relative Predictive Value of ACE Psychological Examination for Freshmen, Science-Mathematics Students at Niagara University for the Years 1948, 1949, and 1950.* Master's thesis, Niagara University (Niagara University, N.Y.), 1958.
448. HVISTENDAHL, J. K. "Language Ability as a Factor in 'Cloze' Scores." *Journalism Q* 35:353–4 su '58. *
449. METZGER, STANLEY MILES. *A Study of Selected Characteristics of the Male Graduates and Scholastic Drop-Outs of the 1951 Freshman Class Entering State University of New York Teachers College at Cortland.* Doctor's thesis, Syracuse University (Syracuse, N.Y.), 1958. (*DA* 19:2020)
450. RILEY, ROBERT C. "Comparison of Results of AIA Achievement Test and ACE Psychological Examination." *Acctg R* 33:128–30 Ja '58. *
451. RILEY, ROBERT C., AND LOVE, JEAN O. "The Predictive Value of College Test Scores." *J Higher Ed* 29:393–5+ O '58. *
452. SPIELBERGER, CHARLES D. "On the Relationship Between Manifest Anxiety and Intelligence." *J Consult Psychol* 22:220–4 Je '58. * (*PA* 35:4898)
453. SPILKA, BERNARD. "Numerical-Verbal Ability Differentials: A Theory and Research Program." *Psychol Newsl* 10:48–55 N–D '58. * (*PA* 33:9351)
454. STINSON, PAIRLEE J. "A Method for Counseling Engineering Students." *Personnel & Guid J* 37:294–5 D '58. * (*PA* 36:2KI94S)
455. WEBBER, VIVIENNE L., AND LEAHY, DOROTHY M. "Home Economics Majors Compared With Other Majors in Education on A.C.E. Test." *Calif J Ed Res* 9:74–9 Mr '58. * (*PA* 33:9053)
456. WIGGINS, NEWTON W. *The Predictive Ability of the Total and Partial Raw Scores of the A.C.E. Psychological Examination, the Cooperative English Tests, and High School Marks in Determining the Scholastic Success of Prospective Freshmen at Western Illinois University.* Master's thesis, Western Illinois University (Macomb, Ill.), 1958.
457. AKAMINE, TOSHIO. *A Study of High School Students' Records and Certain Test Scores as Predictors of Academic Achievement at the State College of Washington.* Doctor's thesis, State College of Washington (Pullman, Wash.), 1959. (*DA* 20:955)
458. BLACK, D. B. "A Comparison of the Performance on Selected Standardized Tests to That on the Alberta Grade XII Departmental Examination of a Select Group of University of Alberta Freshmen." *Alberta J Ed Res* 5:180–90 S '59. * (*PA* 34:6559)
459. BROAD, ELMER J. *An Investigation of the Relative Effectiveness of the American Council on Education Psychological Examination and the School and College Ability Test in Predicting College Grade Point Averages.* Master's thesis, San Francisco State College (San Francisco, Calif.), 1959.
460. BURKETT, BILLIE. *The ACE Psychological Examination as a Predictor of Academic Success.* Master's thesis, Howard Payne College (Brownwood, Tex.), 1959.
461. CHARLES, DON C., AND PRITCHARD, SALLY ANN. "Differential Development of Intelligence in the College Years." *J Genetic Psychol* 95:41–4 S '59. *
462. DEIGNAN, FRANK J. "Two-Year Changes on the ACE by Students in a College of Art and Architecture." *J Psychol* 47:223–30 Ap '59. * (*PA* 34:6565)
463. EINSPAHR, MARTIN HARLEY. *The Construction and Validation of Scales for Predicting Academic Success in College.* Doctor's thesis, University of Houston (Houston, Tex.), 1959. (*DA* 20:3366)
464. GUTEKUNST, JOSEF GRANT. *The Prediction of Art Achievement of Art Education Students by Means of Standardized Tests.* Doctor's thesis, Temple University (Philadelphia, Pa.), 1959. (*DA* 20:3202)
465. HENDERSON, HAROLD L., AND MASTEN, SHERMAN H. "Six Predictors of College Achievement." *J Genetic Psychol* 94:143–6 Mr '59. * (*PA* 36:4KL43H)
466. HENDERSON, NORMAN B., AND MALUEG, EVELYN. "The Predictive Value of the American Council on Education Psychological Examination for College Freshmen." *Calif J Ed Res* 10:157–66 S '59. * (*PA* 34:8400)
467. KING, PAUL; NORRELL, GWEN; AND ERLANDSON, F. L. "The Prediction of Academic Success in a Police Administration Curriculum." *Ed & Psychol Meas* 19:649–51 w '59. * (*PA* 34:6166)
468. LEAHY, DOROTHY M. "Reading Ability of College Home Economics Students." *Calif J Ed Res* 10:42–8 Ja '59. * (*PA* 34:2106)
469. LEPLEY, WILLIAM M. "Predicting Success in Nurses Training." *J Psychol* 48:121–4 Jl '59. * (*PA* 34:6169)
470. MEYER, BURTON. "An Analysis of the Results of Pre-Nursing and Guidance, Achievement, and State Board Test Pool Examinations." *Nursing Outlook* 7:538–41 S '59. *
471. OBST, FRANCES. "A Study of Selected Psychometric Characteristics of Home Economics and Non-Home Economics Women at the University of California, Los Angeles." *Calif J Ed Res* 10:180–4+ S '59. * (*PA* 34:7957)
472. PETERSON, MARTHA ELIZABETH. *An Evaluation of Relationships Between Test Data and Success as a Residence Hall Counselor.* Doctor's thesis, University of Kansas (Lawrence, Kan.), 1959. (*DA* 21:3364)
473. STACK, SHIRLEY ELLEN. *A Study of the Relationships Between Prospective Teachers' Scores on the Chicago Certification Examination and on Standardized Ability and Achievement Tests.* Doctor's thesis, Northwestern University (Evanston, Ill.), 1959. (*DA* 20:2160)
474. STUCKY, MILO O., AND ANDERSON, KENNETH E. *A Study of Persistence in College Attendance in Relation to Placement-Test Scores and Grade-Point Averages.* University of Kansas, School of Education, Kansas Studies in Education, Vol. 9, No. 2. Lawrence, Kan.: the School, April 1959. Pp. 58. *
475. STUCKY, MILO O., AND ANDERSON, KENNETH E. "A Study of the Relationship Between Entrance-Test Scores and Grade-Point Averages and Length of Stay in College." *Yearb Nat Council Meas Used Ed* 16:164–70 '59. *
476. WEEKS, JAMES S. "The Predictive Validity of A.C.E. and S.C.A.T." *Personnel & Guid J* 38:52–4 S '59. *
477. BLACK, DONALD B. "The Prediction of Freshman Success in the University of Alberta From Grade XII Departmental Results." *Alberta J Ed Res* 6:38–53 Mr '60. *
478. DANSKIN, DAVID G., AND HOYT, DONALD P. "A Study of Some Potential Selective Admissions Criteria." *Col & Univ* 36:68–78 f '60. *
479. DARBES, ALEX. "Relationships Among College Students Scores on ACE, Otis, and WAIS Tests." *Proc W Va Acad Sci* 32:214–6 D '60. * (*PA* 36:3KK14D)
480. GOWAN, J. C. "Intercorrelations of the American Council Psychological Examination With Other Types of Tests." *J Ed Res* 54:157–9 D '60. *
481. GOWAN, JOHN C. "Intercorrelations of the California Psychological Inventory and the Guilford-Zimmerman Temperament Survey With Intelligence as Measured by the ACE." *Calif J Ed Res* 11:213–5 N '60. * (*PA* 35:4856)
482. JUOLA, ARVO E. "Predictive Validity of Five College-Level Academic Aptitude Tests at One Institution." *Personnel & Guid J* 38:637–41 Ap '60. * (*PA* 35:2791)
483. LANG, MARY JANE. *The Relationship Between Certain Psychological Tests and Shorthand Achievement at Three Instructional Levels.* Doctor's thesis, University of Missouri (Columbia, Mo.), 1960. (*DA* 21:2632)
484. MARCHES, JOSEPH R. "An Empirical Study of Performance in Mathematics and Performance on Selected Entrance Examinations." *J Ed Res* 53:181–7 Ja '60. * (*PA* 35:7087)
485. MARKWARDT, FREDERICK CHARLES, JR. *Pattern Analysis Techniques in the Prediction of College Success.* Doctor's thesis, University of Minnesota (Minneapolis, Minn.), 1960. (*DA* 21:2990)
486. MAXWELL, MARTHA JANE. *An Analysis of the California Psychological Inventory and the American Council on Education Psychological Test as Predictors of Success in Different College Curricula.* Doctor's thesis, University of Maryland (College Park, Md.), 1960. (*DA* 21:549)
487. MILLER, ROBERT E. "Selection of Engineering Students for an Abbreviated Mathematics Sequence." *Personnel & Guid J* 39:224–5 N '60. *

488. VINEYARD, EDWIN E., AND BAILEY, ROBERT B. "Interrelationships of Reading Ability, Listening Skill, Intelligence, and Scholastic Achievement." *J Develop Read* 3:174-8 sp '60. * (*PA* 35:1274)

489. WELNA, CECILIA THERESA. *A Study of Reasons for Success or Failure in College Mathematics Courses.* Doctor's thesis, University of Connecticut (Storrs, Conn.), 1960. (*DA* 21:1811)

490. WOLPIN, MILTON, AND GARFIELD, SOL L. "Continuance in Medical School as Related to ACE Scores." *J Med Ed* 35:999-1002 N '60. *

491. BARNHART, E. L., AND ANDERSON, KENNETH E. *A Study of the Relationships Between Grade-Point Averages, Placement-Test Scores, Semester Hours Earned, and Area of Major Interest for the Group Who Entered the University of Kansas in the Fall of 1954.* University of Kansas, School of Education, Kansas Studies in Education, Vol. 11, No. 1. Lawrence, Kan.: the School, January 1961. Pp. 36. *

492. CLYDE, ROBERT BURDETTE. *An Empirical Comparison of the School and College Ability Tests and the American Council on Education Psychological Examination.* Doctor's thesis, University of Southern California (Los Angeles, Calif.), 1961. (*DA* 22:151)

493. COOLEY, JOHN C. "A Study of the Relation Between Certain Mental and Personality Traits and Ratings of Musical Abilities." *J Res Music Ed* 9:108-17 f '61. *

494. IVANOFF, JOHN M. "The Use of Discriminant Analysis for Predicting Freshman Probationary Students at One Midwestern University." *Ed & Psychol Meas* 21:975-86 w '61. *

495. MCADAMS, HENRY EDWARD. *The Prediction of General and Differential Achievement in Two Samples of Junior College Students.* Doctor's thesis, University of Southern California (Los Angeles, Calif.), 1961. (*DA* 22:3524)

496. OMMEN, DUANE F. *A Statistical Study of the Relationship of the American Council on Education Psychological Examination Scores and High School Rank to Future College Success.* Master's thesis, South Dakota State College (Brookings, S.D.), 1961.

497. ROTH, ROBERT M., AND GILBERT, JEAN. "AF: A New Approach to the Concept of Achievement." *J Ed Res* 55:90-2 O '61. *

498. THOMSEN, STEPHEN J. "Academic Achievement and Institutional Testing Program Scores: A Longitudinal Study of One Class at a Liberal Arts College." *Proc W Va Acad Sci* 33:120-3 N '61. * (*PA* 36:5KL20T)

499. WITHERSPOON, ROBERT PAUL. *A Comparison of the Temperament Trait, Interest, Achievement, and Scholastic Aptitude Test Score Patterns of College Seniors Majoring in Different Fields at the Arkansas State Teachers College.* Doctor's thesis, University of Arkansas (Fayetteville, Ark.), 1961. (*DA* 22:1091)

500. ZUCKOWSKY, LEO MARK. *The Efficiency of SCAT and Other Selected Variables in Predicting Success in the Various Lower Division College Curricula.* Doctor's thesis, University of Notre Dame (Notre Dame, Ind.), 1961. (*DA* 22:2297)

501. ATKINSON, JOHN ALLEN. *Factors Related to the Prediction of Academic Success for Disabled Veterans in a Four Year College Engineering Program.* Doctor's thesis, University of Denver (Denver, Colo.), 1962. (*DA* 23:2786)

502. BERDIE, RALPH F.; LAYTON, WILBUR L.; HAGENAH, THEDA; AND SWANSON, EDWARD O. *Who Goes to College? Comparison of Minnesota College Freshman, 1930-1960.* Minneapolis, Minn.: University of Minnesota Press, 1962. Pp. vii, 56. *

503. CAMPBELL, JOEL T.; OTIS, JAY L.; LISKE, RALPH E.; AND PRIEN, ERICH P. "Assessments of Higher-Level Personnel: 2, Validity of the Over-All Assessment Process." *Personnel Psychol* 15:63-74 sp '62. * (*PA* 37:3908)

504. CASH, W. L., JR. "Predictive Efficiency of Freshman Entrance Tests." *J Psychol Studies* 13:111-6 Je '62 [issued F '64]. *

505. CRISTANTIELLO, PHILIP D. "Attitude Toward Mathematics and the Predictive Validity of a Measure of Quantitative Aptitude." *J Ed Res* 55:184-6 D-Ja '62. *

506. DARLEY, JOHN G. *Promise and Performance: A Study of Ability and Achievement in Higher Education.* Berkeley, Calif.: Center for Study of Higher Education, University of California, 1962. Pp. vii, 191. *

507. GILLESPIE, HORACE FORD. *The Construction and Validation of Scales for Predicting Academic Success in College in Specified Subject Matter Areas.* Doctor's thesis, University of Houston (Houston, Tex.), 1962. (*DA* 23:1576)

508. GREENWOOD, ROBERT LEROY. *The Prediction of Academic Success in the Technical Curricula of Community Colleges: An Investigation of the Prediction of Academic Success in the Chemical, Electrical, and Mechanical Curricula of Three Community Colleges in New York State.* Doctor's thesis, New York University (New York, N.Y.), 1962. (*DA* 23:898)

509. JONES, REGINALD L., AND SIEGEL, LAURENCE. "The Individual High School as a Predictor of College Academic Performance." *Ed & Psychol Meas* 22:785-9 w '62. * (*PA* 37:7189)

510. LONGENECKER, E. D. "Perceptual Recognition as a Function of Anxiety, Motivation, and the Testing Situation." *J Abn & Social Psychol* 64:215-21 Mr '62. * (*PA* 38:1723)

511. RALSTON, NANCY C. "The Advanced Placement Program in the Cincinnati Public Schools." *Personnel & Guid J* 40:557-60 F '62. * (*PA* 36:5KB57R)

512. ROHRS, DENNIS KERLIN. *Predicting Academic Success in a Liberal Arts College Music Education Program.* Doctor's thesis, State University of Iowa (Iowa City, Iowa), 1962. (*DA* 23:2937)

513. SUPER, DONALD E., AND CRITES, JOHN O. *Appraising Vocational Fitness by Means of Psychological Tests, Revised Edition,* pp. 109-18. New York: Harper & Brothers, 1962. Pp. xv, 688. * (*PA* 37:2038)

514. WHITESIDE, OSCAR R. *The Cooperative Algebra Test and the ACE Psychological Quantitative Test as Predictors of Mathematical Success for Engineering Success for Engineering Majors at Arlington State College.* Master's thesis, Texas Christian University (Ft. Worth, Tex.), 1962.

515. ANGOFF, WILLIAM H. "Can Useful General-Purpose Equivalency Tables Be Prepared for Different College Admission Tests?" *Personnel & Guid J* 41:792-7 My '63. *

516. ANGOFF, WILLIAM H. "Can Useful General-Purpose Equivalency Tables Be Prepared for Different College Admissions Tests." *Proc Inv Conf Testing Probl* 1962:57-73 '63. * (*PA* 38:3187)

517. BOWMAN, ALDEN E.; COBERLY, R. L.; LUCAS, DONALD; AND WHALEY, EARL R. "Selection and Performance of Scholarship Hall Award Winners." *J Col Student Personnel* 4:220-6+ Je '63. *

518. COROTTO, LOREN V. "The Prediction of Success in Initial College Mathematics Courses." *J Ed Res* 56:268-71 Ja '63. *

519. DURFLINGER, GLENN W. "Academic and Personality Differences Between Women Students Who Do Complete the Elementary Teaching Credential Program and Those Who Do Not." *Ed & Psychol Meas* 23:775-83 w '63. *

520. DURFLINGER, GLENN W. "Personality Correlates of Success in Student-Teaching." *Ed & Psychol Meas* 23:383-90 su '63. * (*PA* 38:1427)

521. EYDE, LORRAINE D., AND WALDROP, ROBERT S. "Predictors of Scores on an Employment Counselor Selection Battery." *Ed & Psychol Meas* 23:799-805 w '63. *

522. GIANNELL, A. STEVEN, AND FREEBURNE, CECIL M. "The Comparative Validity of the WAIS and the Stanford-Binet With College Freshmen." *Ed & Psychol Meas* 23:557-67 au '63. * (*PA* 38:6057)

523. JONES, KENNETH J. "Predicting Achievement in Chemistry: A Model." *J Res Sci Teach* 1:226-31 S '63. *

524. KAMMANN, RICHARD A. "Aptitude, Study Habits, and Reading Improvement." *J Develop Read* 6:77-86 w '63. *

525. KING, DONALD THOMAS. *A Comparison of a College Generation of Rural and Nonrural Students in Selected Colleges of Arkansas With Respect to Academic Success and Number of Semesters of Undergraduate Study Completed.* Doctor's thesis, University of Arkansas (Fayetteville, Ark.), 1963. (*DA* 24:626)

526. MACK, LAURENCE L. "Examining the Efficiency of Predictors Presently Being Used at the University of Alberta." *Alberta J Ed Res* 9:100-10 Je '63. *

527. MORICE, HERBERT OSCAR. *The Predictive Value of the High School Grade Point Average and a Select Group of Standardized Tests for Junior College Achievement.* Doctor's thesis, University of Houston (Houston, Tex.), 1963. (*DA* 24:1482)

528. MORRISON, JACK. "The Comparative Effectiveness of Intellective and Non-Intellective Measures in the Prediction of the Completion of a Major in Theater Arts." *Ed & Psychol Meas* 23:827-30 w '63. *

529. NORTH, ROBERT D. "Results of the ERB Public School Norms Project, 1962-63." *Ed Rec B* 84:72-4 Jl '63. *

530. OSBORN, LYNN R. "An Analysis of the Relationship Between Speech Performance and Performance on Written Examinations of Course Content in a Beginning College Speech Course as Reflected in Assigned Grades." *Univ Kans B Ed* 17:68-71 F '63. *

531. POWERS, GLENN F., AND WITHERSPOON, PAUL. "ACE Scores as a Possible Means of Predicting Success in General College Physics Courses." *Sci Ed* 47:416 O '63. *

532. SASSENRATH, JULIUS M., AND FATTU, NICHOLAS A. *Relationships Among Factors Obtained for Elementary and Secondary Student Teachers.* Bulletin of the School of Education, Indiana University, Vol. 39, No. 5. Bloomington, Ind.: Bureau of Educational Studies and Testing, the School, September 1963. Pp. vii, 34. * (*PA* 38:6666)

533. TAULBEE, GEORGE C., SR. *Construction and Validation of a Scale for Predicting Graduation From a College of Optometry.* Doctor's thesis, University of Houston (Houston, Tex.), 1963. (*DA* 24:387)

534. WILLIAMS, JOHN E., AND JOHNSTON, ROBERT A. "The Area Tests of the Graduate Record Examination as a Partial Criterion of Academic Success." *J Exp Ed* 32:95-100 f '63. *

535. ZIMMERER, ANN MORGAN. *A Study of Selected Variables for Predicting Success in a College of Engineering.* Doctor's thesis, University of Houston (Houston, Tex.), 1963. (*DA* 24:842)

For reviews by Hanford M. Fowler and William B. Michael, see 5:308; for reviews by

W. D. Commins and J. P. Guilford of the 1946 Edition, see 3:217; for reviews by Jack W. Dunlap and Robert L. Thorndike of the 1939 Edition, see 40:1377; for reviews by Anne Anastasi and David Segel of the 1937 Edition, see 38:1037.

[439]

★**American School Intelligence Test.** Grades kgn–3, 4–6, 7–9, 10–12; 1961–63; tests for grades 4–12 "developed from the *Illinois General Intelligence Scale*" (1920–26) which was designed for grades 3–8; IBM for grades 4–12; 4 levels; 2 editions (self-marking, machine scorable) for grades 4–12; separate answer sheets must be used with machine scorable edition; $3.20 per 35 tests for grades kgn–3, 4–6, or 7–9; $3.60 per 35 tests for grades 10–12; $1.75 per 35 IBM answer sheets; 25¢ per scoring stencil for answer sheets; 50¢ per specimen set of any one level; postage extra; (55–65) minutes; Willis E. Pratt, M. R. Trabue, Rutherford B. Porter, and George A. W. Stouffer, Jr.; Bobbs-Merrill Co., Inc. *

a) PRIMARY BATTERY. Grades kgn–3; self-marking Forms D, E, ('63, 8 pages); manual ('63, 25 pages).

b) INTERMEDIATE BATTERY. Grades 4–6; self-marking Forms D, E, ('61, 4 pages); machine scorable Forms DM, EM, ('61, 4 pages); separate manuals (identical except for directions) for self-marking edition (18 pages) and machine scorable edition (16 pages) of this level and advanced level below.

c) ADVANCED BATTERY. Grades 7–9; details same as for intermediate level.

d) HIGH SCHOOL BATTERY. Grades 10–12; self-marking Forms D, E, ('63, 4 pages); machine scorable Forms DM, EM, ('63, 4 pages); manual ('63, 15 pages) for both editions.

REFERENCES

1. HOFFORTH, ROGER A. *An Investigation of the Validity of the American School Intelligence Tests.* Master's thesis, Indiana State College (Terre Haute, Ind.), 1961. (Abstract: *Teach Col J* 33:45)

DAVID A. PAYNE, *Assistant Professor of Education, Syracuse University, Syracuse, New York.*[1]

These tests, available at four levels with two forms each, are designed to cover the range of mental ability from kindergarten through grade 12.

The tests for grades 4–12 "have been developed from the *Illinois General Intelligence Scale,* published in 1926," which was designed for use in grades 3 through 8. They are intended to include "samplings....of the types of mental abilities" commonly possessed by American students. For the three upper levels these abilities, called "factors," are: analogies, arithmetic problems, sentence vocabulary, nonverbal analogies, "sentence ingenuity," "arithmetic ingenuity," and synonyms and antonyms. Each of the three upper level tests is composed of 110 five-choice items apparently arranged in order of difficulty without regard to the exact character of the items. Tables are provided for conversion of single raw scores to MA's, IQ's, and percentile ranks. No attempt is made to obtain or use part scores representing differential abilities. No theoretical or empirical rationale for the selection of these "factors," which are the same rubrics included in the older test of 38 years ago, is presented. The statement, "a survey was first made of all the currently used intelligence tests to determine which of these factors were measured in such tests," is the only justification offered for the item content and type utilized in the tests. The reviewer believes the use of the word "factor" is somewhat inappropriate since apparently no factor analysis has been made of the ASIT.

At the primary level the abilities sampled are grouped in the test according to the following categories: comprehension, similarities, picture completion, series completion, "form" (object completion), arithmetic, discrimination, and opposites. These tests, which are composed of 77 items, again yield only a single score for conversion to MA, IQ, or percentile rank.

Some statistical data regarding the tests are furnished in the manuals. Alternate form reliability coefficients range between .85 and .92 for samples of from 120 to 222 pupils. Of interest is the fact that the high school and the primary level tests, which were reportedly administered within a single grade, give higher reliability coefficients than do the intermediate and advanced tests for which testing was done in a three-grade span. Some confusion exists about the nature of the sample used to study the equivalence reliability for the primary level test. The coefficient is reported for 145 first grade students, with standard deviations of 18 and 20 for Forms D and E, respectively. Other within-grades data indicate SD's half as large for the same level groups. The equivalent forms reliability estimate was probably based on a grades kindergarten–3 sample. Since one would expect greater variability across grades, the intermediate and advanced level reliability estimates are probably spuriously high. The coefficients for the intermediate and advanced tests would have been lower if they had been computed within a single grade. Even so, these coefficients are relatively high for alternate form reliabilities. Odd-even reliabilities, which are given for the primary and high school tests, run higher of course. The

1 The reviewer wishes to acknowledge with thanks the assistance of Dr. Eric F. Gardner in the preparation of this review.

authors should be commended for presenting with each reliability coefficient, standard errors of measurement along with appropriate descriptive statistics.

The validity of an intelligence test, as is well recognized, is more difficult to evaluate and demonstrate than its reliability. No attempt is made in the manuals to present a discussion of what is sometimes called "rational" validity as was done so well in the Lorge-Thorndike manual. Only the statement that the items "were developed and pretested with great care" is offered. However, some information about concurrent validity—erroneously called by the authors construct or congruent (?) validity—is reported. Correlations, obtained from small samples, between the various batteries of the *American School Intelligence Test* and other intelligence tests such as the Stanford-Binet, WISC, WAIS, CTMM, and PMA are presented. These correlations are amazingly high, being in many instances as high as one of the reliability coefficients. Estimates of validity were made also by comparing test scores with school success. Correlations between ASIT IQ's obtained from the primary, intermediate, and advanced tests and scores on the *American School Achievement Tests* are reported as .92, .82, and .84, respectively for samples of 64–215 cases. Correlations between each of the batteries and school grades are .81, .75, .65, and .76, respectively. Although these coefficients are relatively high, they were obtained from rather small samples ($n = 45$ to 215) in specific situations over a period of years.

Test norms are presented in terms of mental age, IQ, percentile ranks, and stanines. Percentile ranks and stanines are presented for each form by age, but mental age is tabled without respect to form. No within-grade normative data are provided. Special emphasis is given to the use of the MA and "ratio" IQ for interpretative purposes despite the increasing amounts of research data which bear upon the variable rate of mental ability development as it interacts with psychometric scale characteristics. Such practice appears to be inconsistent with present knowledge. Detailed, but in a few instances somewhat inexact, descriptions of these norms are provided. Considering the studies which had been done relating the achievement test batteries and the intelligence test batteries, it is surprising to the reviewer that no expectancy tables are provided. These would have greatly facilitated the interpretation of resulting scores. Efforts were made to obtain a representative sample of the children attending school in the United States. It is reported that the children were selected on a randomized basis and stratified with respect to geographical location, size of community, school enrollment, and grade assignment. Efforts were made also to take into account socio-economic status, race, and other factors of cultural significance. Although the impossibility of obtaining a truly representative sample is well known, the concern of the authors to take into account variables known to be related to intelligence is commendable. In the selection of a normative sample, research has shown that the number of pupils included is secondary to the number of classrooms represented. Over 300 classrooms, over 10,000 pupils, and schools in more than 70 school systems were used at each of the four levels. Over 35 states are represented. The participating communities are listed in the manuals.

Numerous interpretive problems are associated with ASIT scores. Although reasonable guidelines are provided for interpreting relative position of examinees with respect to the norms (percentile ranks and stanines), no attempt is made to show how scores can be used in actual educational settings. Answers to such questions as, "What can I say about the nature of the intelligence indicated by scores on this test," are not offered. Nine potential uses of the ASIT are listed in the manuals under the heading "Nature and Purposes of Intelligence Tests." Nowhere in the manuals are methods described whereby the uses can be made operational. Furthermore, the user is given little help in understanding the technical data. Coefficients of all types abound, but the user is left to his own devices to determine their significance. Occasionally misleading statements bearing upon interpretation are found, e.g., the standard error of measurement "is a more significant predictor of reliability than the correlation coefficients."

In conclusion, the *American School Intelligence Test* represents the adaptation and modification of earlier efforts to devise an omnibus single score measure of "academic brightness" which was undertaken initially at the time this concept was so popular. In providing such a measure it compares reasonably well with other group intelligence tests. It does not, however, provide separate verbal and quantitative measures as do many others, nor do the authors take advantage of their opportunity to provide concurrent standardization of intelligence and achievement scores. Obviously, it has little value for differential academic prediction, where multiscore measures of general academic ability might better be used. In spite of the reviewer's generally favorable impression of the care taken in developing this test he is unable to note any unique contribution. The tests do look promising as single score tests, but, even here, more data are needed before recommendations for use can be made. Information bearing upon construct and predictive validity, equivalence-stability reliability, and within-grades normative data, together with detailed examples of specific applications of test data, are requested.

FRANK B. WOMER, *Associate Professor of Education, and Test Consultant, Bureau of School Services, The University of Michigan, Ann Arbor, Michigan.* [Review of Intermediate and Advanced Batteries.]

The *American School Intelligence Test* (ASIT), new in 1961, is based upon the *Illinois General Intelligence Scale,* published in 1926. The tests show their ancestry in purpose, design, and items. They are spiral omnibus tests, and are designed for ease of use in securing a single "global" IQ.

The tests are designed to sample "the types of mental abilities involved in learning most of the materials commonly taught in American schools." An inspection of test items supports this assertion. The inspection, however, does not lend support to the authors' assertion that these tests are measuring "seven factors" of intelligence. The claim of measuring seven factors is made because seven item types are utilized. Item types such as analogies, arithmetic problems, sentence vocabulary, nonverbal analogies, sentence ingenuity, arithmetic ingenuity, and synonyms and antonyms may be defended in a "global" intelligence test, but should not be labeled "factors."

EDITING. The tests represent the poorest job of editing this reviewer has seen. The following examples are taken from the teacher's manuals for the edition utilizing carbon-type test-answer sheets. (*a*) In the table of contents every chapter except one is wrong in its pagination, and all tables are paged incorrectly. For example, Chapter 7, "Technical Data," is listed as beginning on page 27; the manual has 18 pages. These errors have been corrected in the manual for the IBM answer sheet edition. (*b*) In the tables of contents of both manuals, each chapter and table is identified by a Roman numeral. In the manuals each is identified by an Arabic number. (*c*) The directions for administration state that "approximately 55 minutes" of actual testing time is "suggested." At no place is an exact time limit stated. (*d*) Directions for administration end with the examiner asking pupils if they have any questions. There are no directions to "Begin Work" and no directions to "Stop Working." (*e*) Mental and chronological ages are printed in six-month intervals in the table of IQ's. No mention is ever made of whether to interpolate or use the nearest six month age. (*f*) A cover sheet for each specimen set says that the tests "were standardized among students in each of the 50 states." In the manual it is stated that "thirty-five states....were represented in the sample." If one counts the states as they are listed, 35 are named but a footnote for 3 of them says "Scores not tabulated."

RELIABILITY. Alternate-form reliabilities of .846 and .862 are claimed. These certainly are satisfactory. However, a claimed standard error of 1.087 for Form D intermediate level raw scores, when the standard deviation is 16.196 and the reliability .846, is a little difficult to fathom. This must be an error in computation. In the reliability tables all four reported standard errors of raw scores are 1.21 or less with SD's 16, 17, 14, and 14, and *r*'s .864 and .862. Standard errors of IQ's also are reported in the validity tables. They run from 1.63 to 5.33 (for a situation in which 35.77 is the standard deviation). They obviously are in error.

VALIDITY. The principal claims of validity are made on the basis of concurrent evidence. Relationships between the ASIT and other intelligence tests are about .72 and .70 with *SRA Primary Mental Abilities,* .84 and .82 with the *California Short-Form Test of Mental Maturity,* and .67 with WISC. These indices are as high as one would expect to find generally. However, group mean IQ's vary by +2.5, −8.5, −6.3, +9, and +21 points in the five possible comparisons. More disturbing than the mean differences are the comparative SD's. For the five comparisons the differences in SD run +17.36 (PMA), +4.11 (CTMM-S), +4.73 (CTMM-S), +22.36 (WISC), and +12.17 (PMA). An intelligence test yielding standard deviations running 22 points higher than the WISC and 12 or 17 points higher than the PMA, or even 4 points higher than the CTMM-S (in a situation suggesting a homogeneous group) is subject to serious question.

Two comparisons are made with the *American School Achievement Tests* (*r*'s of .82 and .84). Again, the standard deviations of IQ's are high (29.52 and 27.81). Two comparisons are made with school grades (*r*'s of .75 and .65) and the IQ standard deviations are 32.12 and 28.21. Whatever the IQ scale is for the ASIT, it is not the conventional one with mean 100 and standard deviation 16. In connection with the latter point, it is interesting to note that the ASIT uses the ratio IQ rather than the deviation IQ. All major intelligence tests have shifted to the deviation IQ.

STANDARDIZATION. The ASIT were standardized in 1961 along with the *American School Achievement Tests,* the intermediate and advanced levels of which were restandardized. It is claimed that this conforms to "a general trend or pattern." Presumably a test user can use both the intelligence test and the achievement tests and then make some judgment as to whether a pupil is working up to capacity. It is true that this same procedure is used by other authors and publishers, but before a test user decides to make such comparisons he should look carefully at the correlations between the tests. The ASIT and ASAT correlate .82 and .84 whereas the ASIT's reliabilities are given as .85 and .86. This suggests that the ASAT are so closely related to the ASIT that they could reasonably be considered alternate forms. Under such circumstances, comparisons for assessing under- or over-achievement are highly suspect.

The manuals state that "the same national sampling yielded normative data for both tests." Yet an inspection of the names of communities participating in the ASIT sample yields the names of 14 cities (excluding those with "scores not tabulated") that do not appear in the norm group for the intermediate level ASAT. (Four of the 14 names do appear in the norm group for the advanced level.) Whether this is another case of poor editing or whether the two tests, in actuality, were normed on different samples cannot be determined from the manuals.

CONCLUSION. This reviewer cannot imagine a situation in which he would care to use the *American School Intelligence Test.* Many of the statistics presented in the manuals are either incorrect or misleading, and the editorial work on the manuals is the poorest seen by the reviewer. It is a shame that a test with reasonably good face validity should have been treated so poorly. The test user seeking an easily administered intelligence test yielding a single IQ should look to the *Henmon-Nelson Tests of Mental Ability* or the *Otis Quick-Scoring Mental Ability Tests.*

[440]

★**Analysis of Relationships.** Grades 12–16 and industry; 1960; manual subtitle is *A Test of Mental Ability;* 1 form (4 pages); mimeographed preliminary manual (6 pages); tentative norms; $2.75 per 25 tests; $1 per manual and key; $1.25 per specimen set; postage extra; (30–60) minutes; Edwin E. Ghiselli; Consulting Psychologists Press, Inc. *

REFERENCES

1. GHISELLI, EDWIN E. "The Relationship Between Intelligence and Age Among Superior Adults." *J Genetic Psychol* 90:131–42 Je '57. *
2. GHISELLI, EDWIN E. "Intelligence and Managerial Success." *Psychol Rep* 12:898 Je '63. * (*PA* 38:6759)

GUSTAV J. FROEHLICH, *Director, Bureau of Institutional Research, University of Illinois, Urbana, Illinois.*

The *Analysis of Relationships* purports to measure "the same type of general intellectual abilities that are ordinarily measured by intelligence tests"; but the author makes no attempt to define or explain the term "general intellectual abilities." As a matter of fact, this reviewer, after studying the materials available to him, has the very strong impression that this test project is far from finished—that whatever unique merit there might be in the use of items involving a response based on ability to analyze an implied relationship among sets of terms, statements, and numbers, has not been demonstrated.

The test, consisting of 40 multiple choice questions, is a conglomerate arrangement of items involving number series, vocabulary, proverbs, and arithmetic. These 40 items were selected, according to the author, from an original pool of 120 such items on the basis of (*a*) "the best distribution of responses among the incorrect alternatives," (*b*) "the highest correlations with total test score," (*c*) "the highest correlations with college grades and with scores on the *Otis Self-Administering Test of Mental Ability*," and (*d*) their ability to discriminate among individuals, "even at the higher occupational and educational levels." This reviewer can only guess at the degree to which these criteria are operative. Adequate evidence, both statistical and descriptive, is lacking in the published materials available.

Evidence of the validity of the total test score is limited to three simple tables. The first table gives seven different correlations with school grades, ranging from .65 for the average of four years of high school work (the same correlation was also found for the first two years of college work) to .25 for first semester college freshman grades. This low correlation, however, is based on a sample of only 37 cases.

The second table of validity coefficients consists of nine coefficients showing "occupational validity." All those with a numerical value of better than .60 are based on samples of less than 40. The other coefficients range from .31 to .22, all except one again being based on very small samples.

The third set of validity coefficients are correlations with other tests. They range from .78 for the *Otis Self-Administering Tests of Mental Ability* (based on 127 cases) to .35 with an unidentified vocabulary test (based on 36 cases).

Evidence of the reliability of the total test score is limited to a single table of 12 odd-even coefficients, ranging from .90 (for 123 high school seniors) to .70 (for 30 clerical workers).

The table of percentile norms attempts to differentiate among lower division, upper division, and graduate college students, as well as among management personnel, salesmen, line supervisors, clerical workers, and skilled workers. These norms are not too meaningful on a nation-wide basis. All cases for the university student classifications are based on students from only one institution—the University of California at Berkeley. The other categories are based on very small samples.

The test booklet is a four-page expendable booklet, clearly printed with clearly stated and adequate directions. Hand scoring must be used; but the arrangement of the items in the booklet and the available scoring key make this a relatively simple task.

At best the *Analysis of Relationships* is a short, easily administered, untimed, group intelligence test. It may be useful when a gross measure of mental ability must be obtained quickly. It should not, however, be used routinely for guidance purposes.

WIMBURN L. WALLACE, *Director, Professional Examinations Division, The Psychological Corporation, New York, New York.*

The only description of the test provided in the manual is that it is "designed to measure the same type of general intellectual abilities that are ordinarily measured by intelligence tests....[and to] yield finer discriminations at the higher levels of ability." The manual goes on to say that the test has been used successfully with students and industrial personnel but fails to say for what purpose. No suggestions on the interpretation of scores are offered. Evaluation of the test is difficult in the absence of statements concerning its intended use and purpose and comments concerning the meaning of results.

The *Analysis of Relationships* is a short omnibus test. Its 40 items are divided more or less equally among the following five types: proverbs, analogies, arithmetic problems, number series, and word knowledge.

Reliability estimates are reported on 12 groups of students and employed personnel. Odd-even, split-half coefficients, adjusted by the Spearman-Brown formula, range from .70 to .90 with a median of .82. These values are rather low, especially for discriminations among individuals. The lack of a second form of the test eliminates the possibility of any alternate form reliability estimates.

As evidence of validity, three sets of correlation coefficients between scores on the test and external criteria are presented: (*a*) seven correlations between scores and average grades in high school or college range from .25 to .65, and are all concurrent validities; (*b*) nine correlations between scores and job or rating criteria in industry range from .22 to .76, but all the groups in which job proficiency ratings were used as the criterion measure comprised fewer than 40 individuals; hence, they were rather small for stable evidence; (*c*) six correlations between scores on this and other tests included highs of .70 with the *California Test of Mental Maturity* and .78 with the *Otis Self-Administering Tests of Mental Ability;* however, the remaining correlations indicate relatively low relationships which cannot be interpreted because the other tests were identified only as "arithmetic," "vocabulary," etc. For none of the correlation coefficients is the mean or standard deviation for either variable provided. This serious omission frustrates meaningful interpretation of the coefficients reported. It should also be noted that no predictive validation is described.

Mention of sex differences on the test is based on four small groups of students and employed persons in which the men tended to score about .6 point higher than the women. Although means and standard deviations are again lacking for these groups, it is very dubious that this small difference warrants the general conclusion that "the scores of males are slightly superior to those of females." At any rate, no separate norms are provided for the two sexes.

Similarly, statements about age differences in scores are insufficiently supported by data. Average scores of students and employed persons in different age brackets are compared, but groups of 50, 31, 11, and 6 persons in the four age ranges above 39 are much too small for even tentative indications about age differences in test performance.

Tables of norms are provided for three levels of college students and five categories of employed personnel. The collegiate norms were based solely on students at the Berkeley campus of the University of California. At least some of the employed groups are atypical, such as those of foremen and skilled workers which contained over half with some college education. Four of the five industrial norm groups comprise fewer than 100 persons. The 32 line supervisors in the smallest group hardly constitute an adequate number for even preliminary norms tables. Estimates for general population norms are derived from equivalencies with Otis and CTMM scores. They appear rather unrealistic in comparison with the other norms, in that the medians for all the student, managerial, sales, and clerical groups fall above the 90th percentile of the general population norms. No mean or standard deviation is provided for any norm group, but some indication of the restricted dispersion of scores can be inferred from the fact that the semi-interquartile range is only about three points in each of the seven norm groups.

SUMMARY. The *Analysis of Relationships* is a short test of mental ability containing an assortment of five general types of items. Lack of alternate forms is unfortunate. Reliability of the test borders on the inadequate, especially for individual discriminations. Evidence of validity is sketchy and erratic and is as yet insufficient in extent or description to provide a basis for evaluating the effectiveness of the test. No means or standard deviations are supplied with any of the coefficients or norms tables in the manual. The norms, based on university student groups and some personnel in employed categories, should be considered highly tentative in view of the questionable sampling and atypical composition of those groups. Statements on the purpose and uses of the test, as well as aids in interpretation of scores documented with relevant data, are needed in subsequent editions of the manual. Until these deficiencies are remedied, the test should be considered only for experimental use. Future assessment of potential utility will depend on the development and availability of the needed information about the test.

[441]

***Army General Classification Test, First Civilian Edition.** Grades 9–16 and adults; 1940–60; also called AGCT; IBM; 1 form ('47, identical with the 1940 Form 1a of the Army edition); 2 editions; revised manual ('60, 19 pages); technical report ('60, 31 pages); separate answer pads or sheets must be used; $10.80 per 20 tests; 60¢ per technical report; 75¢ per specimen set of either edition; postage extra; 40(50) minutes; test by Personnel Research Section, the Adjutant General's Office, War Department; Science Research Associates, Inc. *

a) [HAND SCORING EDITION.] 1947–60; Form AH ('47, 19 pages); $2.40 per 20 answer pads.

b) [MACHINE SCORING EDITION.] 1947–60; IBM; Form AM ('47, 12 pages); $5 per 100 IBM answer sheets; $1 per set of scoring stencils.

REFERENCES

1–14. See 3:219.
15–29. See 4:280.
30–46. See 5:310.
47. LESHAN, LAWRENCE; MARVIN, SIDNEY; AND LYERLY, OLGA. "Some Evidence of a Relationship Between Hodgkin's Disease and Intelligence." *A.M.A. Arch Gen Psychiatry* 1:477–9 N '59. * (*PA* 34:5584)
48. DARLEY, JOHN G. "The Basis for Equivalent Scores on the Annual Editions of the American Council on Education Psychological Examination (ACE), 1941 to 1954," pp. 170–83. In his *Promise and Performance: A Study of Ability and Achievement in Higher Education.* Berkeley, Calif.: Center for Study of Higher Education, University of California, 1962. Pp. vii, 191. *
49. GRIFFITH, RICHARD M.; ESTES, BETSY WORTH; AND ZEROF, SELWYN A. "Intellectual Impairment in Schizophrenia." *J Consult Psychol* 26:336–9 Ag '62. * (*PA* 38:4604)
50. SUPER, DONALD E., AND CRITES, JOHN O. *Appraising Vocational Fitness by Means of Psychological Tests, Revised Edition,* pp. 120–8. New York: Harper & Brothers, 1962. Pp. xv, 688. * (*PA* 37:2038)
51. KENT, ERIC G.; PRICE, A. COOPER; AND ANDERSON, RICHARD J. "The Performance of Patients With Organic Brain Impairment and Unimpaired Patients on the Army General Classification Block Counting Test." *J Gerontol* 18:180–1 Ap '63. * (*PA* 38:4547)

Bert A. Goldman, *Associate Professor of Education, and Associate, Counseling Service, State University of New York at Albany, Albany, New York.*

The 1960 revised manual and technical report contain data which suggest the early version of the AGCT, released for civilian consumption in 1947, may be used as a test of general mental ability, scholastic aptitude (high school, college, and graduate school), trade school success, success in industrial training programs, and perhaps to a limited extent in the identification of mental illness, as well as an indicator of cultural background. A test of such extensive applicability would truly be a psychometric Goliath! However, John T. Dailey came to a much different conclusion in the *Fourth Mental Measurements Yearbook:* "it would appear that the early version of the AGCT released to the public domain would have little to recommend it to the civilian user in preference to many of the similar commercial tests now on the market." The following review supports Dailey's 1953 appraisal by strongly suggesting that there is little, if any, evidence in the revised manual or technical report to justify a more favorable conclusion.

Nothing is provided in the way of new reliability studies. Though the reliability coefficients are commendable, the majority falling in the .90's, they appear to be the same correlations based upon studies of military personnel reported in the old manual. In addition, a single test-retest study over a one-year interval showing the average gain in raw score to be 4.42 is gleaned from a small, select group—75 per cent of an original group of 59 war veterans in one trade school.

Norms for two of the four high school grades are derived by interpolation, instead of being collected by actually administering the AGCT. Norms for college graduates are based upon converted academic aptitude test scores (names not mentioned), rather than on actual AGCT scores. The two sets of norms for university freshmen were collected from very select groups and show wide discrepancies—a raw score of 90, for example, equaling the 20th percentile in one set and the 60th percentile in the other. Trade school norms are included, but no mention is made of the curriculum of the one school upon which they are based.

Adult male norms appear to be identical to those provided in the 1948 manual, with the exception that in the latest listing the raw scores are grouped in intervals. Each interval is presented with the middle standard score and percentile for the interval instead of separately listing each raw score with its corresponding standard score and percentile as is true of the 1948 presentation.

Nothing new is presented in the way of occupational norms. The same classical chart devised by Stewart almost 20 years ago appears in both the manual and technical report. How well do these norms apply to today's general civilian population when 20 years ago there was concern that Stewart's sample was not representative of the population because it did not include women, non-whites, officers, or those who did not take the AGCT because of deferment, rejection, and discharge? Then too, how well represented are those occupations with relatively few subjects who may or may not have been successful men in the civilian job they *claimed* they held before induction?

At first glance, the 10 pages of validity data contained in the technical report appear impressive. Upon closer scrutiny the data seem to be a catch-as-catch-can collection of correlations derived from a study by SRA's professional staff, old military studies, unpublished dissertations, published articles, and in addition what is referred to as personal communication. Such a conglomeration offers little in the way of a detailed, systematic effort to validate the many uses claimed for the AGCT.

The technical report contains four pages of studies involving a multitude of ratings for various military trainee courses of World War II fame. This research offers little, if any, value to present-day civilian consumers of the AGCT. Such data merely pad the pages!

The technical report asserts that each part of the test measures specific factors. No data are presented to show that such assertions are founded upon statistical analysis. On the contrary, two part score intercorrelation studies included in the technical report strongly suggest that the three types of items are far from measuring separate factors.

AGCT standard scores based upon a mean of 100 and a standard deviation of 20, when used as intelligence test results, may mislead naïve individuals to believe they are dealing with IQ's.

Included in the technical report is an informative table, compiled by the Army Personnel Research Section during World War II, containing indices of difficulty and discrimination for each item in Form 1A of the AGCT. Although the item analysis published almost two decades ago suggests that many arithmetic items are too easy for the general population, no changes have been made in the test. Also, five block counting items, along with eight vocabulary items, appear to be poor discriminators. It would also be helpful to know whether biserial or point biserial coefficients were used to determine discrimination indices, since the former are usually larger.

Apart from the statistical analysis, cursory reading of the items indicates that changes are in order for dated expressions, such as 2 packs of cigarettes for 25 cents, milk selling for 9 cents per quart, and 5½ pounds of meat costing 10 cents per pound. Also, the answer to block counting item 120 is given as 10. Where is the tenth block hidden?

In sum, this reviewer recommends that the publishers conduct a complete set of validity and reliability studies of the AGCT. New and complete norms are needed, in addition to a revision of several of the items. Until systematic and comprehensive data are provided, this reviewer would prefer to use those instruments which are supported by such data.

Howard B. Lyman, *Associate Professor of Psychology, University of Cincinnati, Cincinnati, Ohio.*

This is still the same test reviewed critically by John T. Dailey in the *Fourth Mental Measurements Yearbook*. His comments are still pertinent, in spite of a new technical report and a new examiner's manual, both published in 1960.

The new manual contains little beyond directions for administering and scoring. Less than seven pages are devoted to norms, uses, validity, reliability, and the like. Of these, two pages are used in presenting Stewart's classic study of AGCT scores by previous civilian occupations of World War II white enlisted men; however, Stewart's name is mentioned nowhere in the manual, nor is any date given for her study of nearly 20 years ago. One could easily assume that these scores had been obtained recently and, except for a parenthetical statement in small type, that they had been obtained from civilians.

Percentile norms are given for ninth, tenth, eleventh, and twelfth grade boys and girls, and for adult males; no further description of these groups is given in the manual.

The technical report (of 31 pages) is a little better. Some effort is made to state the number of subjects involved, type of statistic used, etc.; however, even here the publisher uses many vague phrases, such as "at various intervals" (this phrase describing a test-retest reliability coefficient). In a table, "The AGCT as a Predictor of High School Achievement," SRA fails to mention the time lag between testing and collection of criterion data (to assure us that these are coefficients of *predictive,* rather than *concurrent,* validity).

The report suggests that "meaningful data may be gleaned from an analysis of these [part] scores," but gives little supportive evidence; there are no part score norms, no consideration of part score reliabilities, etc.

Neither the manual nor the report cautions the test user to guard against overgeneralization of Stewart's World War II occupations study; nor does either source mention that most World War II soldiers were tested on forms other than Form 1a (which became the First Civilian Edition). Previous editions of the MMY contained these criticisms.

It is surprising that such an old test has not been more adequately reported. SRA does little to warn the unsophisticated test user against possible misuse or overinterpretation. The large number of omitted or vague statements does much to argue against the use of the AGCT. Either the publishers did not realize that the points should have been made more clear, or they deliberately left the points unclear; in either instance, most test users probably will want to consider selecting a test which comes closer to meeting the APA Technical Recommendations.

For a review by John T. Dailey, see 4:280; see also 3:219 (1 excerpt).

[442]

California Analogies and Reasoning Test. Grades 10–13; 1958; IBM; Forms A, B, (10 pages); manual (16 pages); $4.20 per 35 tests; separate answer sheets may be used; 5¢ per IBM answer sheet; 20¢ per scoring stencil; postage extra; 50¢ per specimen set, postpaid; 40(50) minutes; Claude Mitchell; California Test Bureau. *

JOHN R. HILLS, *Director, Testing and Guidance, The University System of Georgia, Atlanta, Georgia.*

The *California Analogies and Reasoning Test* (CART) is described by the publisher as a scholastic aptitude test, for grades 10 to 13, whose nature and difficulty make it particularly effective with the more able students. The publisher claims that the analogies items, based on content in natural science, mathematics, social science, English, and literature, call upon reasoning power, knowledge of terms, recognition of relationships, and analytical skill. Since the various subject matters appear in random order, the publisher claims that the score reflects adaptability as well as breadth and accuracy of knowledge.

This analogies test surely does use content from the named subjects, and in about equal amounts, but the reviewer could find no substantiation for claims that reasoning power, analytical skill, or adaptability influence the scores. It appears to the writer that the test measures primarily diffuse knowledge of miscellaneous information and terms. Few items could be "figured out" if at least one of the specific terms in the analogy was not known or recognized. Often knowledge about one term was sufficient to determine the correct answer. Such content may, however, be a sound basis from which to make predictions about school grades, i.e., to measure scholastic aptitude.

Is the test particularly effective with more able students? They may enjoy taking it, but the resulting measures will not be very good. The test doesn't have enough top except at the tenth grade. Both the limited set of norms provided and the table of item difficulties (a very commendable feature in a test manual!) reveal the preponderance of items which are answered correctly by the bulk of twelfth grade students. If a tenth grader gets fewer than 20 of the 101 items correct, he is below the first percentile.

The test should be easy to use. The score is the number right with no correction for guessing. The same key is used for both forms, which appear to be sound alternates in content, difficulty, etc. The items are not tricky. Only one error was found, that being an equating of "alliteration" and "rhyming."

As to technical details, reliabilities quoted for Form A appear adequate, ranging from .88 to .94; none are given for Form B. While correlations are reported between CART scores and scores from several other aptitude tests (for example, the *California Short-Form Test of Mental Maturity,* the *American Council on Education Psychological Examination,* and the *Miller Analogies Test*), the school user will be most interested in the validity of the CART scores for predicting school and college grades. Here the data are not as "extensive" as one might be led to believe from the publisher's catalog. They are based on students from five different secondary schools and one college of undesignated type or location. There is no indication of the proportions of male and female students in the groups; apparently the data were not treated separately by sex. The largest group on which prediction of grades was studied was 168. However, from these limited data it appears that validities for school grade prediction in the .50's can be expected, which is about the usual validity for scholastic aptitude tests.

The norms, as mentioned above, are limited. The manual gives a brief description of some procedure by which the CART norms were supposed to be made representative of a national sample by giving both the CART and the *California Short-Form Test of Mental Maturity* to about 800 students. That description was not at all clear to the reviewer after several readings. In fact, he was left wondering why he should not choose the *California Short-Form Test of Mental Maturity* in the first place for whatever purpose he had in mind in considering CART. Even if further inquiry revealed that the CART norms truly represented unselected national groups at the designated grade levels, it is severely handicapping that males and females are not presented separately. Table 3 in the manual leads one to believe that this test generally favors males. This is very unusual for a test so heavily loaded with verbal material. Certainly separate norms for the sexes are necessary. Other tests for similar purposes often give far more extensive norms and validity information, as for example, the *College Qualification Tests* or the *Cooperative School and College Ability Tests.* While these two tests take longer to administer and thus may not directly compete with CART, there is no justification for the shorter test having available so much less adequate interpretive material.

In summary, the *California Analogies and*

Reasoning Test may not be a bad choice as a predictor of school grades. As with any such tests, local specific validity studies provide the answer to this question. The best the publisher can do is provide data indicating that the local validities are likely to be of useful magnitude. The CART has good alternate forms (neither of them is "secure"), is easy to use, and simple to score. Its most serious weaknesses are that it is too easy for able students and its normative data are minimal. Potential users should consider such tests as the *Otis Quick-Scoring Mental Ability Tests* and the *California Short-Form Test of Mental Maturity* as likely alternate choices for predicting academic grades from about the same amount of testing time.

WIMBURN L. WALLACE, *Director, Professional Examinations Division, The Psychological Corporation, New York, New York.*

The *California Analogies and Reasoning Test* (CART) is a general mental ability test intended for use in grades 10–13. Each of the two forms of the test contains 101 items in the form of analogies, the first half in the stem and the second half in the options. Content is drawn from science, social studies, mathematics, and English. Since most of the items depend on specific factual knowledge, claims in the manual that the test involves reasoning power and a number of primary verbal abilities are not substantiated.

The reliability of CART is probably satisfactory, but the estimates of it reported in the manual are insufficient evidence. Coefficients computed by the Kuder-Richardson formula 21 range from .88 to .94 for Form A, but this method is inappropriate with timed tests. One retest coefficient of .93 is reported for a group of 64 twelfth grade students, but the sample is so small and isolated that it can hardly be considered sufficient. In the "validity" section of the manual, an alternate-form coefficient of .82 is reported based on 307 twelfth grade students tested on Forms A and B with a one-week interval between the testings. This would appear to be a more meaningful reliability coefficient than the others reported.

Validity data are extremely meager. Students in five high schools were tested during their senior year and their CART scores were correlated with overall grade averages for their last one, two, three, or four years. One group of 85 college freshmen (which obtained a mean CART score lower than the means of two of the five high school groups), was tested during the freshman year and their scores were correlated with first semester grade averages. These concurrent validity coefficients against academic criteria ranged from .30 to .59. Some correlations with other tests are reported. The tables include a gratuitous list of coefficients corrected for range of the other test and for attenuation on both tests. For four groups of students in grades 10, 11, and 13, coefficients of correlation between scores on CART and scores on scholastic aptitude tests range from .51 with ACE to .76 with SCAT. For two small groups of students in grades 12 and 13, correlations with parts of the Cooperative English and General Achievement tests tended to run higher than those with academic ability tests. Although these two samples of 49 and 59 students do not provide adequate basis for generalizations, a closer relationship of CART with achievement tests than with aptitude tests would not be surprising in view of the content of CART.

A table of percentile and standard score norms for each grade 10–13 appears in the manual. The explanation of the derivation of these norms is so beclouded that it would be meaningless to most users. Number of cases, distribution by sex, mean score, and standard deviation are not given for any of the four norm groups. There is a surprisingly large jump in the scores from grades 10 to 11, then only small increases from grades 11 to 12 to 13. No mention is made of sex differences in performance on the CART nor of justification for providing only combined sex norms.

The section of the manual entitled "Uses of Test Results" is rather pretentious in view of the limited research on the efficacy of the test. In the suggested applications to counseling and selection situations, there are repeated references to prediction of later performance in spite of the fact that there is no evidence at all contained in the manual on the predictive validity of the test. Such statements as the following are hardly sophisticated aids to the interpretation of test results:

> The greatest values will be realized from the percentiles or standard scores developed from local distributions of scores, either for high school or college groups. The real purpose and value of such a percentile or standard score is in helping students understand their potentialities with reference to a specific situation. This is particularly true if constructively presented to those whose abilities to succeed are seem-

ingly precluded or to those who tend to under-estimate their abilities. In either case, the expectancy concept inherent in the data is a positive approach that can reduce feelings of frustration and failure in some and can build up confidence in others.

SUMMARY. CART is a 101-item test designed to assess general scholastic ability. The items are in the form of analogies and appear to depend on specific information in science, social studies, mathematics, and English rather than on reasoning ability. Although the manual suggests that CART is usable for educational counseling in grades 10–13, evidence of validity for this purpose is as yet too meager to justify such application. Either more extensive standardization or clarification of the derivation and adequacy of the present norms is needed. At least until these deficiencies in validity and normative data are remedied, the CART cannot be recommended over other readily available tests which are designed for the same purpose and have much superior documentation of their essential characteristics and function.

J Consult Psychol 23:471 O '59. Edward S. Bordin. * The studies offered to support its predictive validity are less than adequate because they are based on samples tested either concurrently with the collection of criterion data (academic grades) or where the grades had already been earned. Thus, there is evidence to support the test's value for concurrent validity or for postdiction, but none for prediction.

J Counsel Psychol 7:53–4 su '60. Gordon V. Anderson. * According to its title, this is an analogies and reasoning test; it would be hard to prove or disprove the correctness of this. It is the feeling of the present reviewer, however, that very few of the items require the kind of reasoning ability usually considered necessary for solving analogies. * Altogether, more than two-thirds of the items are simple matching exercises, and most of them are so constructed that a correct answer will result from knowledge of only one of the two pairs. The analogies form of question is usually expected to require the testee to make use of information which he possesses. It is not normally used to merely check the presence or absence of that information. When a test has been constructed to do a particular job, perhaps to quibble over face validity is picayune. The CART is offered as a test of scholastic ability, so it should be judged on the basis of its predictive validity. Unfortunately, up to the present time no data are available for such a judgment. * Whether the CART measures aptitude or achievement, the score pattern is clearly related to educational level. Careful study of the test and of the statistical data reported in the manual lead to the conclusion here that it is a rough measure of general culture or educational development. There are no data to support its use for prediction purposes. On the plus side, it can be said that the test is well printed, it is easy to administer and interesting to take. The manual is well prepared, but the erroneous bias that it has proven usefulness as a prediction instrument could mislead naive counselors and is likely to irritate the more sophisticated ones.

[443]

***California Short-Form Test of Mental Maturity, 1963 Revision.** Grades kgn–1.5, 1–3, 3–4, 4–6, 6–7, 7–9, 9–12, 12–16 and adults; 1938–64; 7 scores: logical reasoning, numerical reasoning, verbal concepts, memory, language total, nonlanguage total, total; IBM, NCS, and Grade-O-Mat for grades 4 and over; 8 levels; profile (date same as for test, 1 page) for each level; series guide to interpretation ('64, 38 pages) for this and test 444; $4.20 per 35 tests for Levels 0–1H; 10¢ per scoring key; $4.90 per 35 tests for Levels 2–5; separate answer sheets or cards may be used at Levels 2–5; 5¢ per IBM answer sheet; 20¢ per hand scoring stencil; 80¢ per set of machine scoring stencils; 9¢ per Scoreze answer sheet; 3¢ per Cal-Card; 20¢ per hand scoring stencil for Cal-Cards; 4¢ per set of Grade-O-Mat scorable punch-out cards; 6¢ per stylus; 6¢ per backing pad; 2¢ per profile; see 671 for prices of NCS answer sheets; 50¢ per guide to interpretation; tape recorded directions for administration of Levels 2–5 available at $5.95; postage extra; $1 per specimen set of any one level; $6.95 per specimen set of any one level (Levels 2–5) with tape; postpaid; Elizabeth T. Sullivan, Willis W. Clark, and Ernest W. Tiegs; California Test Bureau. *

a) LEVEL 0. Grades kgn–1.5; 1 form ('62, 11 pages); manual ('63, 49 pages); 34(39) minutes.
b) LEVEL 1. Grades 1–3; 1 form ('62, 12 pages); manual ('63, 52 pages); 41(46) minutes.
c) LEVEL 1H. Grades 3–4; 1 form ('62, 10 pages); manual ('64, 55 pages); 42(47) minutes.
d) LEVEL 2. Grades 4–6; 1 form ('61, 11 pages); manual ('63, 59 pages); 43(48) minutes.
e) LEVEL 2H. Grades 6–7; 1 form ('61, 11 pages); manual ('63, 60 pages); 41(46) minutes.
f) LEVEL 3. Grades 7–9; 1 form ('61, 11 pages); manual ('63, 57 pages); 41(46) minutes.
g) LEVEL 4. Grades 9–12; 1 form ('61, 11 pages); manual ('63, 53 pages); 39(45) minutes.
h) LEVEL 5. Grades 12–16 and adults; 1 form ('61, 11 pages); manual ('63, 47 pages); 39(45) minutes.

REFERENCES

1–15. See 5:313.
16. STACK, SHIRLEY ELLEN. *A Study of the Relationships Between Prospective Teachers' Scores on the Chicago Certification Examination and on Standardized Ability and Achievement Tests.* Doctor's thesis, Northwestern University (Evanston, Ill.), 1959. (*DA* 20:2160)

17. GUNDERSEN, RICHARD O., AND FELDT, LEONARD S. "The Relationship of Differences Between Verbal and Nonverbal Intelligence Scores to Achievement." *J Ed Psychol* 51:115–21 Je '60. * (*PA* 35:3981)
18. KOO, GLADYS Y. *A Study of the Stability of Test-Retest IQ Scores Derived From the California Short Form Tests of Mental Maturity.* Master's thesis, University of Hawaii (Honolulu, Hawaii), 1960.
19. MACARTHUR, R. S. "The Coloured Progressive Matrices as a Measure of General Intellectual Ability for Edmonton Grade III Boys." *Alberta J Ed Res* 6:67–75 Je '60. * (*PA* 36:2HD67M)
20. WARREN, PHYLLIS A. "A Mental Maturity Test as One Criterion for Admission to an American School Abroad." *Personnel & Guid J* 39:197–202 N '60. * (*PA* 35:3966)
21. WOLINS, LEROY; MACKINNEY, A. C.; AND STEPHANS, PAUL. "Factor Analyses of High School Science Achievement Measures." *J Ed Res* 54:173–7 Ja '61. * (*PA* 35:7129)
22. CLEGG, HERMAN D., AND DECKER, ROBERT L. "The Evaluation of a Psychological Test Battery as a Selective Device for Foremen in the Mining Industry." *Proc W Va Acad Sci* 34:178–82 N '62. *
23. DREW, ALFRED STANISLAUS. *The Relationship of General Reading Ability and Other Factors to School and Job Performance of Machinist Apprentices.* Doctor's thesis, University of Wisconsin (Madison, Wis.), 1962. (*DA* 23:1261)
24. MCDONNELL, M. W. "The Prediction of Academic Achievement of Superior Grade Three Pupils." *Alberta J Ed Res* 8:111–8 Je '62. * (*PA* 37:3886)
25. MACARTHUR, R. S., AND ELLEY, W. B. "The Reduction of Socioeconomic Bias in Intelligence Testing." *Brit J Ed Psychol* 33:107–19 Je '63. * (*PA* 38:4271)
26. NELSON, MARVEN O., AND EDELSTEIN, GERALD. "Raven Progressive Matrices, Non-Language Multi-Mental Test, and California Test of Mental Maturity: Intercorrelations." *Psychol Rep* 13:46 Ag '63. * (*PA* 38:6061)

JULIAN C. STANLEY, *Professor of Educational Psychology, and Director, Laboratory of Experimental Design, University of Wisconsin, Madison, Wisconsin.*

At the time this review was prepared (late March 1964), the Guide to Interpretation and Technical Report were not available to the reviewer, though the Examiner's Manuals for all but Level 1H were. Thus most technical questions can only be asked, not answered. A discussion of the norms must also await the appearance of these two accessories.

This 1963 revision (the tests themselves were copyrighted in 1961 or 1962) requires about 40 minutes of actual test-marking time, including several minutes for the tester to read a story to the examinees, compared with about 50 minutes for all but the lowest level of the previous version. This reduction in testing time in an attempt to fit the Short Form within a single school period was effected partly by reducing the number of items (e.g., from 145 to 120 in the highest level) and partly by reducing the time per item (14 per cent increase in speededness for the highest level, from 2.8 items per minute to 3.1).

Of the seven subtests, one (Delayed Recall) is completely new, whereas "Tests 1 through 6 include from 40 to 60 per cent new items [at Level 5; the percentage of new items ranges from 16 to 73 for subtests at other levels]. The 'core items' are those selected as the most efficient from the 1957 Edition." No criterion of efficiency is mentioned, though presumably it will be discussed in the Technical Report.

The eight levels, from preprimary to advanced, differ considerably in content but far less in format. In order to cover them all carefully, the reviewer sought the help of several persons well versed in teaching, testing, and measurement.[1] From his study of their critiques and the forms, he will note certain pervasive aspects and some specificities.

The most general observation is that the tests are intended primarily for students tested by their teachers. Directions for administering the various levels are for the most part clear, simple, and detailed. It seems likely that a conscientious teacher with little or no formal training in measurement can administer the CTMM S-Form adequately. He will of course need some training in order to interpret the results, however; the profile on the back of the test booklet bombards him with 12 raw scores from this one test. Some of these scores are expressible as percentile ranks, two kinds of standard scores, standard score IQ's, MA's, and an ISI (Intellectual Status Index, which "reflects the examinee's performance in relation to a national norm population for his *grade* placement").

The materials come separately designed for the various grade levels in reasonably convenient form. Failure to include even the simplest statistical evidence of reliability and validity in the Examiner's Manuals seems unfortunate, however. The less-than-one-page "Interpretation and Use of Results" part of the manuals, where the significance of intra-individual differences is considered, provides criteria for guarding against overinterpreting small and moderate differences between factor scores or section scores for the same person, but if material this complex can be presented in the Examiner's Manuals, then more basic aspects of reliability could have been included also.

This leads us to consider the statements in the Examiner's Manual that:

> Factor analysis by the Thurstone centroid method produced four discrete factors, which form major interpretive units of the 1963 *Short-Form.* The composition of Factor 1, Logical Reasoning, has been considerably revised in the new *Short-Form.* For-

[1] He thanks the following persons for their assistance: Ronald D. Anderson, Patricia M. Davis, Frank H. Fox, William E. Hauck, Nora Hubbard, Yakub R. Namek, Louis A. Pingel, Andrew C. Porter, Robert M. Pruzek, Yoshiyuki Matsuura, D. G. Woolpert, and Patricia A. Woolpert.

merly, this factor consisted of two tests, Similarities and Inferences. In the 1963 Revision, the Inferences test has been removed and the Analogies and Opposites tests have been added to the factor.

Other changes were made, too, and new factor analyses were done to justify changes made in the subtests whose scores are summed to yield factor scores.

The two greatest weaknesses of the 1963 S-Form appear to be lack of care in editing items and poor quality of the art work. Nearly all of my collaborators pointed out defective items. For example, at the higher grade levels the sample item for Test 1, Opposites, consists of five drawings of men's hats. The stem is a drawing of a new light colored banded felt "city" hat with creased crown. Four options are given for its "opposite": an old appearing dark banded (straw?) city hat with creased crown; a new light colored unbanded felt "ten-gallon" hat with creased crown; a battered (old?) dirty looking banded felt city hat with creased crown; and a new light colored banded felt city hat with uncreased crown. Directions that the teacher reads to pupils for this *sample* item are:

Look at the pictures of hats in the first row....The first picture shows a man's new hat. Look at the other pictures of hats in the same row. Find the picture that is the *opposite* of the first picture—the one with a difference. * The old hat is the correct answer because it is the opposite of the new hat.

Perhaps examinees unerringly perceive that of the six (at least) dichotomous concepts embodied in this sample item, which can generate 64 options, the relevant concept is oldness versus newness, but surely a less complex example could easily have been constructed.

Certain items of Test 1, Opposites, were mentioned by several of my collaborators as being defective conceptually and artistically. This subtest's quality varies somewhat from level to level, so the prospective user should study the particular level in which he is interested. At the highest level (Level 5), for example, he will want to scrutinize items 4, 5, 6, 11, and 15 (of 15 items) carefully for keying and ready intelligibility of drawings.

Test 2, Similarities, depends heavily on drawings, 7 for each of the 15 items at the five upper levels, 5 for each of 8–13 items at the three lowest levels. Some of these are easily interpreted, whereas others are indistinct, partly because of excessive blackness and lack of contrast in the printing.

Test 3, Analogies, also consists entirely of pictures, to which the same cautions apply.

Test 4, Numerical Values, involves counting of pictured objects at the lower grade levels (Levels 0 and 1), number series at Level 1H, and making change at the higher grade levels. The format for the latter is ingenious, but it results at Level 4 (grades 9–12) in 18 of the 60 distractors' being virtually ineffective because they can be eliminated quickly by noting that they do not contain the specified number of coins (e.g., an item calling for use of 7 coins to make 15 cents has two options that include only 6 coins, thereby making the question essentially a two-option item). Apparently, the constructors were trying to make this type of item easy enough for Level 4, because at Level 5 (grades 12 through adult) only two items (48 and 55) have options that can be eliminated in this way.

Test 5, Number Problems, features the familiar CTMM arithmetical reasoning items at the higher grade levels, but only 10 of them. Some of these would have benefited by editing. At Level 5, for example, the pilot flying the airmail and carrying 50 gallons of gasoline as fuel (item 65) is outdated. In items 61 and 69 the social context causes a logical fallacy; for example, "Jim *says* his age is one-fourth of his uncle's, and that their ages together total 40 years. How many years difference *is* there between Jim's and his uncle's age?" (Italics mine.) Isn't it time that we dropped from the stems of test items this groping at dialogue, especially at the higher grade levels? The same point is covered, without distraction, by "Jim is one fourth as old as his uncle, and their ages together total 40 years."

In Test 6 verbal comprehension is tested by the typical one-word stem, four-option (three-option at Level 1H) vocabulary item at Levels 1H and up. Directions are "Mark the number of the word that means the same or about the same as the first word." The 25 items at Level 5 are illustrative of the need for more careful selection and editing. Two of them are military terms, "bivouac" and "trajectory." One of the distractors for "bivouac" is the difficult word "coloratura," whereas the other options are the relatively simple nouns "party," "revision," and "encampment." Likewise, item 73, "predicament," has as one of its distractors "mantua"! It would be helpful to see an item analysis of these items and others in the CTMM S-Form.

The first item on the Level 5 vocabulary test has as its stem "inefficient" and as the keyed option "incompetent," the only one of the four options having the prefix "in." Also, how nearly synonymous are these two words?

Item 76, "whimsical," has as the keyed response "fanciful," with distractors "accurate," "weighty," and "fashionable." It seems likely that the structural similarity between stem and key will make this item too easy and perhaps less discriminating than it would be with a different answer or with distractors more like the stem.

Use of "issue" in item 92 to mean "offspring" seems rather quaint in 1963, this being the twelfth meaning of "issue" in the *American College Dictionary* and probably more familiar to our grandparents than to our children.

Some of the distractors are not the same part of speech as the stem—for example, "digit" (which also occurs as a distractor in item 82) for "vex," "hangman" for "vigilant," and "sorry" for "articulation." For item 81 the stem is "tangent," which may be either a noun or an adjective; one must search the options "blend," "agent," "sensing," and "touching" to decide which part of speech is intended. The authors may have had an explicit rationale for varying the part of speech, but again it would be helpful to study item analyses and to try the items with options homogeneous with respect to part of speech.

The seventh and final test is Delayed Recall. A short story is read to the examinees before they begin Test 1, and they are asked questions about it after they complete Test 6. It is of course difficult to keep the stimulus, the reading of the story, constant from class to class. Also, it is not easy to find stories containing material so novel for the examinee that he cannot answer some of the questions without having heard the story. Furthermore, answering the questions at all but the two lowest levels requires considerable reading, so sheer memory is not all that is tested.

The reviewer administered the 25 items of Test 7 of Level 5 to a bright adult and an above average 15-year-old girl, *without* reading the story to them. They scored 17 and 13, respectively, the 69th and 46th percentiles for their age groups. Both 17 and 13 are significantly greater than the chance expected value of $25/4 = 6\frac{1}{4}$.

Of the four factor scores three (numerical reasoning, verbal concepts, and memory) are based on only 25 items each at the higher five levels and 8–25 items each at the lower three levels. The other (logical reasoning) is based on 45 at the higher levels and 23–41 at the lower levels. In the absence of the Technical Report, the California Test Bureau has provided a "Reliability Report" and an apparently subsequent technical memo to show various characteristics of the four factor scores. The two reports have quite different statistics, generally much more favorable in the memo. For example, at Level 2 the factor score Kuder-Richardson formula 21 coefficients of equivalence change from .80, .84, .87, and .82 in the report to .87, .88, .91, and .81 in the memo, thereby making the language, nonlanguage, and total score K-R 21 coefficients rise from .90, .84, and .93 to .94, .89, and .95. The memo contains no explanation of these changes, nor does it refer to the reliability report. It is not clear from the memo just how heterogeneous the groups on whom the K-R 21's were computed were. It seems unlikely, however, that in a typical school the K-R 21 coefficients would be nearly as high as above. We cannot determine, either, to what extent the coefficients are inflated by speededness of the tests. Because there are no comparable forms of any of the S-Form levels, coefficients of equivalence and stability (i.e., comparable form reliability coefficients) cannot be computed. However, in its Technical Memo No. 5, the CTB staff compares scores from the 1957 and 1963 S-Forms at four levels. The correlations between total score IQ's for these two versions are .81, .76, .74, and .72. The time interval between the two testings is not specified.

A comment about the test booklets themselves: Words in them are readily legible, but (as noted above) figures do not always reproduce well. The format is in general attractive and effective, except at the lower grade levels where some pictures are too small and indistinct. The booklet cover seems unduly flimsy, tending to tear and shred easily.

EVALUATION. Overall, the reviewer feels that the CTMM S-Form is most useful at kindergarten through about the third grade (Levels 0 and 1) and progressively less useful in the higher grades. Its emphasis on nonverbal material, perhaps appropriate for children learning to read, is disproportionate at the higher levels. A simpler rationale, such as verbal versus quantitative as in the SCAT, SAT, and the GRE Aptitude Test, seems preferable from grade 4 upward. At the junior and senior high school levels one also has carefully prepared verbal tests such as the Terman-McNemar and multi-factor tests such as the APT and DAT to consider. Variety in testing throughout the school life of pupils is probably more important than attempted continuity via different levels of a given publisher's tests. Local norms within a school system can make comparisons from one test to another feasible. By the tenth or eleventh grade "external" programs (e.g., PSAT, NMSQT, CEEB, and ACT) have taken the majority of the *scholastic* aptitude and achievement testing load off the schools.

For a review by Cyril Burt of the 1957 edition, see 5:313; see also 4:282 (1 excerpt); for reviews of the regular edition, see 5:314, 3:223, 40:1384, and 38:1042.

[444]

***California Test of Mental Maturity, 1963 Revision.** Grades 4–6, 7–9, 9–12, 12–16 and adults; 1936–64; 1957 edition (see 5:314) still available; 8 scores: logical reasoning, spatial relationships, numerical reasoning, verbal concepts, memory, language total, non-language total, total; IBM; 1 form ('61, 19 pages); 4 levels; manual ('64, 53–66 pages) for each level; series guide to interpretation ('64, 38 pages) for this and test 443; profile ('61, 1 page) for each level (also contained on back of test booklet and back of answer sheet); no data on reliability and validity of revised long form; $7 per 35 tests; separate answer sheets may be used; 10¢ per set of IBM answer sheet-profiles; 40¢ per set of hand scoring stencils; 80¢ per set of machine scoring stencils; 18¢ per set of Scoreze answer sheets; 50¢ per guide to interpretation; postage extra; $1 per specimen set of any one level, postpaid; Elizabeth T. Sullivan, Willis W. Clark, and Ernest W. Tiegs; California Test Bureau. *

a) LEVEL 2. Grades 4–6; 83(93) minutes.
b) LEVEL 3. Grades 7–9; 83(93) minutes.
c) LEVEL 4. Grades 9–12; 81(91) minutes.
d) LEVEL 5. Grades 12–16 and adults; 81(91) minutes.

REFERENCES

1–5. See 40:1384.
6–15. See 3:223.
16–39. See 4:282.
40–73. See 5:314.
74. KREBS, STEPHEN O. *A Study of the I.Q. Consistency, Internal Consistency and Correlations With Certain Academic Grades of the California Test of Mental Maturity (Short Form).* Master's thesis, Michigan State University (East Lansing, Mich.), 1957.
75. BARRY, CHARLES A., AND JONES, ARLYNNE L. "A Study of the Performance of Certain Freshman Students." *J Ed Res* 52:163–6 Ja '59. * (*PA* 34:2088)
76. CHAMBERS, JACK A. "Preliminary Screening Methods in the Identification of Intellectually Superior Children." *Excep Child* 26:145–50 N '59. * (*PA* 35:3249)
77. KING, PAUL; NORRELL, GWEN; AND ERLANDSON, F. L. "The Prediction of Academic Success in a Police Administration Curriculum." *Ed & Psychol Meas* 19:649–51 w '59. * (*PA* 34:6166)
78. KORTMEYER, HOWARD A. *A Statistical Study of the Relationship of the California Test of Mental Maturity Scores of South Dakota High School Freshmen to Future Academic Success.* Master's thesis, South Dakota State College (Brookings, S.D.), 1959.
79. CASSEL, RUSSELL N., AND STANCIK, EDWARD J. "Factorial Content of the Iowa Tests of Educational Development and Other Tests." *J Exp Ed* 29:193–6 D '60. *
80. CLYMER, THEODORE, AND BRENDEMUEHL, FRANK L. "A Study of the Validity of the California Test of Mental Maturity, Elementary, Non-Language Section." *Yearb Nat Council Meas Used Ed* 17:123–9 '60. *
81. JACOBS, RONALD E. "A Comparison of Tests: The Primary Mental Abilities: The Pintner Mental Abilities: The California Test of Mental Abilities." *Sch Counselor* 8:12–8 O '60. *
82. OSBORNE, R. T. "Racial Differences in Mental Growth and School Achievement: A Longitudinal Study." *Psychol Rep* 7:233–9 O '60. * (*PA* 35:2782)
83. RAMSEY, WALLACE. "An Analysis of Variables Predictive of Reading Growth." *J Develop Read* 3:158–64 sp '60. *
84. STAKE, ROBERT E., AND MEHRENS, WILLIAM A. "Reading Retardation and Group Intelligence Test Performance." *Except Child* 26:497–501 My '60. * (*PA* 35:539)
85. WELNA, CECILIA THERESA. *A Study of Reasons for Success or Failure in College Mathematics Courses.* Doctor's thesis, University of Connecticut (Storrs, Conn.), 1960. (*DA* 21:1811)
86. ANDERSON, HARRY E., JR. "The Prediction of Reading and Language From the California Tests." *Ed & Psychol Meas* 21:1035–6 w '61. *
87. ANDERSON, HARRY E., Jr. "A Study of Language and Nonlanguage Achievement." *Ed & Psychol Meas* 21:1037–8 w '61. *
88. CASSEL, RUSSELL N., AND STANCIK, EDWARD J. "California Test of Mental Maturity by Weights for Predicting a Composite Score on the Iowa Tests of Educational Development." *J Genetic Psychol* 98:119–26 Mr '61. * (*PA* 35:7074)
89. CENTI, PAUL. "Intellective and Language Factors Related to College Success." *Cath Ed R* 59:319–22 My '61. *
90. CLYMER, THEODORE. "A Study of the Validity of the California Test of Mental Maturity Elementary, Language Section." *Yearb Nat Council Meas Ed* 18:125–35 '61. *
91. FRENCH, JOSEPH L. "A Predictive Test Battery." *Nursing Res* 10:104–5 sp '61. *
92. LUCIER, OMER, AND BURNETTE, RICHARD. "The Lowry Reasoning Test Combination With Younger Adolescents." *J Social Psychol* 55:113–24 O '61. * (*PA* 36:4HD13L)
93. MCGUIRE, CARSON. "The Prediction of Talented Behavior in the Junior High School." *Proc Inv Conf Testing Probl* 1960:46–67 '61. *
94. BALDWIN, JOSEPH W. "The Relationship Between Teacher-Judged Giftedness, a Group Intelligence Test and an Individual Intelligence Test With Possible Gifted Kindergarten Pupils." *Gifted Child Q* 6:153–6 w '62. * (*PA* 37:8255)
95. CARNEY, RICHARD E., AND TROWBRIDGE, NORMA. "Intelligence Test Performance of Indian Children as a Function of Type of Test and Age." *Percept & Motor Skills* 14:511–4 Je '62. * (*PA* 37:2830)
96. CLARK, WILLIS W. "Item Selection Techniques for a Long-Range Continuous Mental Age Scale." *Yearb Nat Council Meas Ed* 19:72–7 '62. *
97. COBB, BART B. "Problems in Air Traffic Management: 2, Prediction of Success in Air Traffic Controller School." *Aerospace Med* 33:702–13 Je '62. *
98. NORMAN, RALPH D.; CLARK, BETTY P.; AND BESSEMER, DAVID W. "Age, Sex, IQ, and Achievement Patterns in Achieving and Nonachieving Gifted Children." *Excep Child* 29:116–23 N '62. * (*PA* 37:7159)
99. BALDAUF, ROBERT J. "Predicting Success in Eighth Grade Algebra." *Psychol Rep* 12:810 Je '63. * (*PA* 38:6580)
100. BOBBE, CAROL; CAMPBELL, WILLIAM; LAMBERTI, ELAINE; AND SHEPPARD, CHARLES. "A Correlation Analysis in Testing." *Ed* 83:375–8 F '63. *
101. CLINE, VICTOR B.; RICHARDS, JAMES M., JR.; AND NEEDHAM, WALTER E. "Creativity Tests and Achievement in High School Science." *J Appl Psychol* 47:184–9 Je '63. * (*PA* 37:8223)
102. CLYMER, THEODORE. "A Study of the Influence of Reading Ability on the Validity of Group Intelligence Tests." *Slow Learnng Child* 10:76–84 N '63. *
103. MACARTHUR, R. S., AND ELLEY, W. B. "The Reduction of Socioeconomic Bias in Intelligence Testing." *Brit J Ed Psychol* 33:107–19 Je '63. * (*PA* 38:4271)

For reviews by Frank S. Freeman and John E. Milholland of the 1957 edition, see 5:314; see also 4:282 (1 excerpt); for a review by Henry E. Garrett of an earlier edition, see 3:233 (2 excerpts); for reviews by Raymond B. Cattell and F. Kuhlmann, see 40:1384 (1 excerpt); for reviews by W. D. Commins,

Rudolf Pintner, and Arthur E. Traxler, see 38:1042 (1 excerpt). For reviews of the short form, see 443, 5:313, and 4:282.

[445]

★Canadian Academic Aptitude Test (CAAT). Grades 8.5–9.0; 1959–63; this test and tests 253 and 567 make up the *Canadian Test Battery,* grades 8–9; 3 scores: verbal, mathematical, non-verbal; 1 form; separate parts 1 ('62, verbal reasoning), 2 ('62, mathematical reasoning), 3 ('59, non-verbal reasoning), (4 pages); 2 editions of battery manual: hand scoring ('63, 11 pages), machine scoring ('63, 13 pages); supplementary data ('63, 6 pages) for the battery; battery profile ('63, 2 pages); separate answer sheets or cards must be used; $1.25 per 25 tests; $1 per set of 50 answer sheets and hand scoring manual; 20¢ per hand scoring stencil; 20¢ per 15 battery profiles; 50¢ per 25 IBM answer cards (machine scoring through the Department of Educational Research only); 10¢ per machine scoring manual; 50¢ per specimen set; $2.75 per battery specimen set; postage extra; 30 (40–45) minutes per part; Department of Educational Research, Ontario College of Education, University of Toronto; distributed by Guidance Centre (machine scoring manual and answer cards must be purchased from the Department of Educational Research). *

REFERENCES

1. D'Oyley, Vincent R. *Technical Manual for the Canadian Tests: Statistical Data on the Carnegie Study Tests of Academic Aptitude and Achievement in Grades 8, 9, and 10 in Ontario Schools and Grades 7 and 8 in Toronto Schools.* Carnegie Study of Identification and Utilization of Talent in High School and College, Bulletin No. 4. Toronto, Canada: Department of Educational Research, Ontario College of Education, University of Toronto, 1964. Pp. viii, 50. *

2. D'Oyley, Vincent R. *Testing: The First Two Years of the Carnegie Study 1959 to 1961: Analysis of Scores by Course, Sex, and Size of Municipality.* Carnegie Study of Identification and Utilization of Talent in High School and College, Bulletin No. 6. Toronto, Canada: Department of Educational Research, Ontario College of Education, University of Toronto, 1964. Pp. ix, 53. *

Donald B. Black, *Professor of Education, University of Alberta, Edmonton, Alberta, Canada.*

This test consisting of three subtests, each of 30 minutes' length, can best be viewed as an experimental instrument. No alternate forms are available and by admission in the manual, no item analyses have been completed. This is not to suggest that the items are entirely new. Many items in the verbal reasoning subtest may be found in the intermediate and advanced levels of the *Group Test of Learning Capacity: Dominion Tests.* Unlike the Dominion Tests, however, the test format and item form is much improved. However, a serious defect that occurs in the test directions and which is common to all tests in the Canadian Test Battery for grades 8–9, is that no indication is given as to whether the student is to guess or that there will be a correction for guessing. This is considered important, particularly so since part of one of the tests (*Canadian English Achievement Test*) in the battery corrects for guessing at the grade 9 level.

The test, as part of the Carnegie Study of Identification and Utilization of Talent in High School and College, was administered to every grade 9 student in the province of Ontario in October and November 1959. The grade 9 percentile norms are based on this population which is in excess of 85,000 cases. No subnorms by type of school or community are given. The grade 8 norms are based on a "representative" sample of about 6,500 Ontario grade 8 students tested in May 1962. These latter norms are reported as percentiles correct to one place of decimal. No evidence is given as to the basis upon which these norms can be considered representative. It is interesting to note that for the verbal and nonverbal reasoning subtests, the mean and median scores for the grade 8 norms are higher in each case than those reported for grade 9. No mean and median are reported for the mathematical reasoning subtest for grade 9, but examination of the appropriate percentile norms would strongly suggest that the same pattern holds true for the median, at least. Just how reliable these differences are is not known since variability data are not provided, but the consistent trend shown would suggest that possibly the grade 8 norms are not as representative as they claim to be.

The publishers provide profile charts for each grade for interpreting the scores on the total battery. The grade 9 chart has minor inaccuracies. These could serve to magnify, in certain instances, misinterpretation of the battery results. The most serious defect is that nowhere in the manual nor on the charts is mention made of the standard error of measurement or its implications for interpreting scores. The absence of any variability and reliability data in the manual makes calculation of the standard errors of measurement impossible. A further disconcerting suggestion for interpreting scores is the suggestion in the manual that the percentile scores on the tests may be averaged to give class and student average performance.

A statistical supplement (October 31, 1963) containing reliability and validity data on the CAAT has been recently forwarded to the reviewer. Split-half reliabilities between .85 and .90 are reported for a sample of 200 grade 8 students and between .81 and .91 for a sample of 200 cases at the grade 9 level. Because of the nature of the item content in each subtest, the reviewer would much prefer K-R 20 reliability coefficients but, in the absence of item analysis and variability data noted above, the publisher obviously had little recourse than to use the split-half method.

The supplementary technical data sheets also include battery intercorrelation data and validity data for grade 9 average marks and year-end marks in English and mathematics based on a random sample of 1,000 cases. These data plus other data from the Carnegie Study and available in other reports, represent the most desirable aspect of this battery to the test user in Ontario schools. Intercorrelations of the subtests reveal coefficients of between .68 (Verbal Reasoning and Mathematical Reasoning) and .56 (Verbal Reasoning and Non-Verbal Reasoning). Considering the type of items, this is about what would be expected in light of similar correlations of other batteries of this type, and it suggests a high general intelligence factor. The validity data show correlations of .53 and .51 between Verbal Reasoning and grade 9 English grades and average grades, respectively. This, too, could be anticipated due to the heavy weighting of vocabulary-type items in the verbal reasoning test. Mathematical Reasoning correlates .40 with grade 9 English marks, .49 with mathematics marks, and .47 with average marks, and again this would be expected from the intercorrelation matrix. The nonverbal reasoning test, which contains conventional figure analogy items and a heavy weighting of "domino" items (15 of 40), correlates between .34 and .39 with the criterion scores. It is hoped that in subsequent editions the publisher, with the classroom teacher in mind, will devote some serious attention to the proper interpretation of these data and data from other studies for academic guidance purposes.

In summary, this is an excellent example of an experimental instrument being pushed into publication, presumably by demands from the schools for continued use of the test, before it was properly prepared. Why item analysis based even on pretesting data was not done, or why alternate forms were not prepared, or why complete statistical data were not reported before publication, is difficult to understand. It is difficult to accept the lack of sophistication of the manual and particularly the suggestions for the interpretation of test scores, for it has long been established that the test publisher owes the test consumer some concern for leadership in this regard. When these matters are attended to, and only when these are done, will the tests fully realize their potential for school use. Certainly, the provision of validity data, if only for Ontario schools, marks an excellent beginning in a most desirable direction.

George A. Ferguson, *Professor of Psychology, McGill University, Montreal, Canada.*

The *Canadian Academic Aptitude Test* is part of a test battery developed for use in a Carnegie sponsored longitudinal study on the identification and utilization of talent in the high schools and colleges of Ontario. The test is restricted in use to the end of grade 8 and the beginning of grade 9. It consists of three subtests, Verbal Reasoning, Mathematical Reasoning, and Non-Verbal Reasoning. The verbal reasoning subtest contains items of the usual type, analogies, opposites, vocabulary, and classification. The mathematical reasoning subtest is composed of simple arithmetic and number series problems. The nonverbal reasoning subtest is constructed of figure analogy items, and a matrix-type item using dominoes.

Percentile rank norms are available for each subtest for grade 8 and grade 9. The grade 8 norms are based on a sample of 6,500 students in Ontario schools tested in 1962 near the end of the eighth grade year. The grade 9 norms are based on a complete, or almost complete, population of 85,000 grade 9 students tested in 1959 early in their ninth grade year. The standardization of tests on precisely defined complete populations is uncommon in North America, although in Britain the Moray House Tests, originally developed by Godfrey Thomson, have for many years been standardized on complete populations. A surprising feature of the standardization is that scores for grade 8 appear in general to be higher than for grade 9. For example, on the verbal reasoning subtest a score of 28 has a percentile rank of 49 for grade 8, whereas for grade 9 the same score has a percentile rank of 56. The test authors provide no explanation for this, although a variety of possible explanations come readily to mind, e.g., bias in the 1962 sample, dropout of superior students between grades 8 and 9, or some overall improvement in aptitude between the years 1959 and 1962.

No reliability or validity information are provided by the authors.[1] Much is known, however, about the reliability of this type of test material, and, assuming that conventional test construction methods have been used, we may assume that reliability coefficients of .90 or greater can be obtained for the subtests.[2] With regard to validity, detailed information on the relation between test scores and grade averages should shortly be available. Much is known, of course, about the validity of tests of this type in other contexts.

On the negative side the reviewer notes that this test contains no new or novel features either in content or construction. Tests of this kind have existed for many years. No arguments of a technical or scientific nature are advanced to justify their replication. It may well be that the authors wished to achieve a high degree of discrimination for a specific group, namely ending grade 8 and beginning grade 9 students, although this point is not discussed. A further negative point is that the three subtests are comprised of types of test material which are known to correlate highly. The minimum total time for administration is two hours. It seems probable that a shorter test might effectively accomplish about the same results.

Because the present test was developed for use in a comprehensive longitudinal study, the reviewer anticipates that the authors will in due course provide a body of substantive validity data which will enhance the test's usefulness.

[446]

★Cardall-Miles Test of Mental Alertness. Adults in business and industry; 1960–61; 1 form ('60, 3 pages); directions for administering ['61, 2 pages]; no data on reliability and validity; typewritten norms ('61, 1 page); norms also included in manual for *Cardall Test of Practical Judgment;* $8.50 per 100 tests; $1 per specimen set; postage extra; 15(20) minutes; Alfred J. Cardall and Gerald E. Miles; Cardall Associates. *

[447]

★The Carlton Picture Intelligence Test. Ages 6–3 to 7–9; 1962; Forms A, B, (16 pages); manual (16 pages); 22*s.* 6*d.* per 25 tests; 1*s.* per single copy; 2*s.* 6*d.* per manual; postage and purchase tax extra; 32(70) minutes in 2 sessions; W. K. Carlton; University of London Press Ltd. *

1 This review was completed before the supplementary data referred to in the test entry preceding the review became available.—Editor.

2 Obtained corrected odd-even coefficients were later reported as .88 and .91 for verbal, .81 and .85 for mathematical, and .88 and .90 for nonverbal.—Editor.

ELIZABETH D. FRASER, *Professor of Psychology, University of Aberdeen, Aberdeen, Scotland.*

This test is designed for children passing from the infant to the primary school, a transfer which normally takes place between the ages of 6 years 6 months and 7 years 6 months. The test in fact provides norms for the ages 6 years 3 months to 7 years 9 months.

There are two forms of the test, each consisting of eight sections with eight items in each section. The test is entirely pictorial; no writing is required of the child who simply marks the chosen answer with a cross; and detailed instructions are read out by the teacher or other person administering the test.

The tasks required of the child include picking out from a group of five pictures the one which has something silly in it; picking the one object in a group which is different from the rest; finding the missing part in a picture; completing pictorial analogies; choosing two things which a given object always has; ordering sets of four pictures into a time sequence; selecting from five objects the one which has something in common with a given set of three objects; and completing a series of symbols such as XOXOX______. Each section of eight items is preceded by three sample items illustrating the type of problem. Many of the items are ingenious and most, though perhaps not all, should be within the range of experience of an average seven year old.

The test appears to have had a thorough tryout. The 128 items now used in Forms A and B are those which survived item analysis from the original test which consisted of 11 sections and of 330 items. The item analysis was carried out section by section on samples of 200 children of the appropriate age group.

Norms were based on a complete age group of Glasgow children, Forms A and B being given in two successive years to 29,863 and 29,950 children, respectively. The norms are presented in easily read tables with one-month age intervals on one axis, raw score on the other, and IQ appearing in the body of the table.

A great deal of care has obviously gone into the test, and the cooperation of the teaching profession has clearly been extremely valuable, especially in the standardisation process. The major criticism to be leveled against the test is that the drawings are occasionally difficult to identify, and this is true not only for adults. Part of the trouble is that since the drawings for each item appear in a strip across the page, scale has had to be sacrificed; thus, for example, an eye is the same size as a house, a nib is as large as an ink bottle, and so on. This is particularly noticeable in the sections where the child has to find the missing part and where he has to pick out two things an object always has. In both of these, identification without any clues to scale may be a matter of chance.

In other items, identification is difficult because of bad drawings: to the reviewer, at least, the car engine in section 4, item 4, Form A, looked like the remains of a car after a particularly bad smash, and the item had to be solved by guesswork.

In spite of these criticisms, the test can claim high reliability; by the Kuder-Richardson formula 20 it is .97 for Form A and .96 for Form B. The intercorrelation between the two forms is also high, .94 on a sample of 8,846 children, and the correlations with Terman-Merrill on a sample of 120 children were .86 for Form A and .85 for Form B.

Designed for a very specific age range, this test has something to offer. It is intrinsically interesting to the child, and it is pleasant to report on a test which, in spite of some drawbacks, has at least gone through the necessary trial stages before being placed on the market.

S. Rachman, *Lecturer in Psychology, Institute of Psychiatry, University of London, London, England.*

This new group intelligence test for children has been prepared for use in a limited age range—75 to 93 months. The two parallel forms, A and B, which are administered, scored, and interpreted in the same manner, each consist of eight sections. Apart from the tester's instructions and the examples which precede each section, the test takes 32 minutes to administer. The author states that it is essential to separate the first and second four sections with a 15 minute interval. The duration and timing of the rest interval appear to have been arbitrarily chosen and there is no information about the possible effects of varying this procedure. In the absence of such information, users are advised to adhere to Carlton's procedure.

The instructions for testers are concise and explicit and are unlikely to give rise to difficulties even if the test is administered by people without specialised training. The scoring of the tests is also explained in a lucid manner. The instructions which must be read to the children, however, are very detailed and sometimes rather involved. The test material is entirely pictorial and is all contained in a single booklet. While the great majority of the drawings are admirably simple and clear, three of those contained in section 7 of Form A appeared to the reviewer to be ambiguous (the eighth drawing in sample item A, the third drawing in item 7, and the sixth drawing in item 8).

The test was standardised on an impressively large sample—Form A was given to 29,863 children and Form B to 29,950 children. Unfortunately, the author provides no details of the methods used in the standardisation procedure beyond referring to an unpublished paper by Talman. It would be a valuable addition to the working manual if he included this information, perhaps as a technical appendix. The data which Carlton provides on the reliability and validity of the test are encouraging but not sufficiently comprehensive; these gaps will undoubtedly be filled in the future. The reliability coefficients of the two forms as calculated by the Kuder-Richardson formula 20 were .97 for Form A and .96 for Form B. These coefficients are extremely satisfactory but unfortunately the sample size was omitted. The two forms of the test were found to be highly correlated (.94) and there appears to be a negligible practice effect if Form A is administered first. Although this information is not entirely clear, it appears that the 8,846 children who participated in this study were given Form A followed by Form B five months later. In order to rule out the possibility of practice effect, a replication of this study should be conducted with Form B preceding Form A. Both forms of the test were found to correlate positively with Terman-Merrill IQ's (Form A, .86 and Form B, .85). Even allowing for the relative smallness of this sample (n = 120), these results are satisfactory.

Although the samples used by Carlton in ascertaining the reliability and stability of the test are of a salutary size, he unfortunately omitted details of the composition of the groups of children concerned. In the initial standardisation of the test he used "complete year groups of children" in two successive years. No further information about the social and geographical background of the children is given; one must assume, however, that they were all British schoolchildren. Neither the 8,846 children who participated in the test-retest study nor the 120 children in the validity study are described. For this reason, the possibility of sample bias cannot be effectively rejected.

The advantages of the Carlton test are those of any satisfactory group test. It is short and comparatively easy to administer and score. In addition, the available data on reliability and validity are encouraging as far as they go. The test promises to be of value as a screening instrument and should arouse reasonably wide interest, particularly if the age range is extended.

[448]

***Classification Test 40-A.** Job applicants; 1957–59; 1 form ('57, 14 pages plus fold-out answer sheet); preliminary mimeographed manual ('57, 11 pages); general PPA mimeographed directions ['57, 7 pages]; norms ('59, 2 pages); no data on reliability; 10–49 tests, 68¢ each; $2 per specimen set; postpaid; 50(60) minutes; Public Personnel Association. *

N. M. DOWNIE, *Professor of Psychology, Purdue University, Lafayette, Indiana.*

As stated by the authors, the chief purpose of this test is "to assist in the selection of applicants for a wide variety of jobs where information about the applicant's general capacity to learn to do the job will be useful." They also note that the test will be of assistance in the placement, training, and promotion of employees.

The test is made up of 60 multiple choice items, equally divided among vocabulary, arithmetic reasoning, and picture classification varieties, the latter being reasoning items. The arithmetic reasoning items consist of the usual type of problems. The picture classification items are composed of sets of four pictures, three of which are in some way related. The vocabulary items are made up of short definitions of words. The examinee is to think of a word that fits the definition and begins with one of the four pairs of letters presented. The items are arranged in groups of five of a kind and these groups are in an ascending order of difficulty throughout the test.

Each copy of the test contains a fold-in answer sheet on which the responses are to be marked as on the usual IBM answer sheet, which may also be used. The answers are so arranged that verbal, numerical, and reasoning subscores may be obtained. An individual's score is the number correct.

Although part scores may be obtained, the authors recommend that they not be used in prediction because of their probable low reliability. It is suggested that these part scores may be used as an aid in placement or in understanding the strengths and weaknesses of a job applicant.

Page 1 consists of practice problems for which five minutes are allotted. Fifty minutes are allowed for the completion of the test. The authors state that the test is a power test. This is undoubtedly true as 50 minutes seems adequate for any examinee to answer about as many items as he ever would be able to.

According to the manual the test was developed on about 1,000 applicants or present employees of 12 public personnel agencies located "throughout the United States and Canada" and representing "a wide variety of occupational fields....including one sample of high school seniors." Apparently a 90-item form was first developed and this was subsequently shortened to the current 60-item form which is said to yield an almost perfect correlation with the longer form and to represent "the minimum number of items consistent with the required degree of reliability." It is interesting to note that this is the only mention of the reliability of the test in the 11-page manual.

Correlations between part and total scores are reported to range from .61 to .85. Intercorrelations among scores on the three parts of the test are said to fall between −.10 and .37. No details are given for the specific relationships.

In the manual itself no norms are presented. There is a general discussion of "absolute" and "flexible" passing points or percentages. Passing points, the authors note, must be determined locally, but they recommend that a score of 30 per cent correct be regarded as representing "minimum competence" and that passing points not be set below this point.

In a separate Test Service Memo, frequency distributions of scores are presented for a collection of 17 occupations based upon present employees and job applicants, the *n*'s varying from a low of 8 to a high of 280 with a median of 19.

It is interesting to note that not a single mention of validity is made in any of the materials accompanying this test.

In the Test Service Memo it is stated that

more than 100 agencies have purchased over 6,000 copies of the test. Since it is possible to use homemade answer sheets, probably many more individuals have been given this test by personnel managers of varying degrees of skill, competence, and training using a totally inadequate manual. The test seems well made and to have at least face validity. But there its goodness seems to stop. The test was published in 1957 with no reliability coefficients reported, no indication of the validity of the instrument for use in any specific type of personnel work, and no adequate or usable norms. An evaluation of the materials which the buyer gets with the test shows that practically nothing has been added in these three areas since the original publication.

The test seems to have some potential in that it differs from the typical test used in industry by being a power test rather than a heavily speeded one. For many types of positions, it seems to this reviewer that a power test would be a much more appropriate instrument than the 12 or 15 minute speed test. The authors could make this test acceptable. However, until they remedy the points discussed above, the test should be considered as unsatisfactory for the uses stated. Despite the claims made and the uses suggested by the authors, personnel managers should continue to use our more established tests such as the *Wonderlic Personnel Test* or the *Adaptability Test* in employee selection.

DAVID G. RYANS, *Director, Bureau of Educational Research, University of Hawaii, Honolulu, Hawaii.*

This test is intended to reflect "general capacity to learn" in job situations "which do not demand any special abilities." It is intended to be a power test and consists of 20 vocabulary, 20 arithmetic reasoning, and 20 picture classification items alternately presented in groups of 5 items of each type and arranged in order of difficulty. Working time (50 minutes) is for the test as a whole. A single score is obtained, the total number of correct responses to the 60 items. (Part scores may be obtained, but the potential user is warned that reliabilities of part scores are low.) No reliability data, either for part or for total scores, are provided.

Development of the test proceeded through several revisions, leading to production of a 90-item tryout form from which the present 60 items were selected after administration to 1,000 applicants and employees by 12 public personnel agencies. Part scores on the vocabulary, arithmetic reasoning, and picture classification items are reported to correlate .61 to .85 with total score, whereas intercorrelations between the part scores are given as from −.10 to .37.

A Test Service Memo dated April 1959 provides distributions (*n*'s ranging from 8 to 280 per distribution; total $n = 776$) of raw scores of public service employees and candidates for public service jobs. Suggestions are offered by the manual for determining "absolute" and "flexible" passing points (adapted to agency policies) with regard to the raw score earned on the test.

No validity data are reported for the test. The items appear to be of standard quality, but little information is available about the test other than general statements relating to development procedures. Due to lack of technical information, use of the test cannot be recommended. Its usefulness as a predictor of a "general capacity to learn" in various job situations has not been demonstrated.

[449]

***College Entrance Examination Board Scholastic Aptitude Test.** Candidates for college entrance; 1926–63; for more complete information, see 760; 2 scores: verbal, mathematical; 180(210) minutes; program administered for the College Entrance Examination Board by Educational Testing Service. *

REFERENCES

1–22. See 4:285.
23–42. See 5:318.
43. DYER, HENRY S. *College Board Scores.* New York: College Entrance Examination Board, [1953]. Pp. xxiii, 70. * (*PA* 28:4936)
44. DYER, HENRY S., AND KING, RICHARD G. *College Board Scores: Their Use and Interpretation, No. 2.* New York: College Entrance Examination Board, 1955. Pp. viii, 192. * (*PA* 30:1616)
45. FISHMAN, JOSHUA A. *1957 Supplement to College Board Scores No. 2.* New York: College Entrance Examination Board, 1957. Pp. vi, 206. *
46. FLEMING, W. G. *Aptitude and Achievement Scores Related to Immediate Educational and Occupational Choices of Ontario Grade 13 Students.* Atkinson Study of Utilization of Student Resources, Report No. 3. Toronto, Canada: Department of Educational Research, Ontario College of Education, University of Toronto, 1958. Pp. xix, 380. *
47. FLEMING, W. G. *Ontario Grade 13 Students: Their Aptitude, Achievement, and Immediate Destination.* Atkinson Study of Student Resources, Report No. 4. Toronto, Canada: Department of Educational Research, Ontario College of Education, University of Toronto, 1958. Pp. ix, 55. *
48. FRANZ, GRETCHEN; DAVIS, JUNIUS A.; AND GARCIA, DOLORES. "Prediction of Grades From Pre-Admissions Indices in Georgia Tax-Supported Colleges." *Ed & Psychol Meas* 18:841–4 w '58. * (*PA* 34:2097)
49. GARDNER, FRANK E. *A Study to Determine the Relationship Between High School Preparation, the College Entrance Examination Board Scholastic Aptitude Tests, and the First Semester College Grades.* Master's thesis, Whittier College (Whittier, Calif.), 1958.
50. HOLLAND, JOHN L. "Prediction of Scholastic Success for a High Aptitude Sample." *Sch & Soc* 86:290–3 Je 21 '58. *
51. ALTUS, WILLIAM D. "Personality Correlates of Verbal-

Quantitative Discrepancy Scores on the Scholastic Aptitude Test." *J Psychol* 48:219–25 O '59. * (*PA* 35:4868)

52. BLACK, D. B. "A Comparison of the Performance on Selected Standardized Tests to That on the Alberta Grade XII Departmental Examination of a Select Group of University of Alberta Freshmen." *Alberta J Ed Res* 5:180–90 S '59. * (*PA* 34:6559)

53. DUGGAN, JOHN M. "Puzzles and Powers in Junior SAT Scores." *Col Board R* 37:37–40 w '59. *

54. FLEMING, W. G. *Personal and Academic Factors as Predictors of First Year Success in Ontario Universities.* Atkinson Study of Utilization of Student Resources, Report No. 5. Toronto, Canada: Department of Educational Research, Ontario College of Education, University of Toronto, 1959. Pp. xi, 137. *

55. FRENCH, JOHN W., AND DEAR, ROBERT E. "Effect of Coaching on an Aptitude Test." *Ed & Psychol Meas* 19:319–30 au '59. * (*PA* 34:6568)

56. GILBERT, ARTHUR C. F. "The Efficiency of Certain Variables in Predicting Survival in an Engineering School." *Psychol Newsl* 10:311–3 My–Je '59. * (*PA* 34:1992)

57. GILBERT, ARTHUR C. F. "Prediction of Achievement in Chemistry." *Psychol Newsl* 10:135–7 Ja–F '59. * (*PA* 34:2099)

58. HILLS, JOHN R.; FRANZ, GRETCHEN; AND EMORY, LINDA B. *Counselor's Guide to Georgia Colleges.* Atlanta, Ga.: Office of Testing and Guidance, Regents of the University System of Georgia, December 1959. Pp. 32. *

59. HOLLAND, JOHN L. "The Prediction of College Grades From the California Psychological Inventory and the Scholastic Aptitude Test." *J Ed Psychol* 50:135–42 Ag '59. * (*PA* 35:2796)

60. SPAULDING, HELEN. "The Prediction of First-Year Grade Averages in a Private Junior College." *Ed & Psychol Meas* 19:627–8 w '59. * (*PA* 34:6574)

61. BLACK, DONALD B. "The Prediction of Freshman Success in the University of Alberta From Grade XII Departmental Results." *Alberta J Ed Res* 6:38–53 Mr '60. *

62. FRANKEL, EDWARD. "Effects of Growth, Practice and Coaching on Scholastic Aptitude Test Scores." *High Points* 42:34–45 Ja '60. *

63. FRANKEL, EDWARD. "Effects of Growth, Practice, and Coaching on Scholastic Aptitude Test Scores." *Personnel & Guid J* 38:713–9 My '60. * (*PA* 35:2790)

64. GILBERT, ARTHUR C. F. "Predicting Graduation From an Engineering School." *J Psychol Studies* 11:229–31 Jl–Ag '60. * (*PA* 35:7045)

65. HILLS, JOHN R.; EMORY, LINDA B.; AND FRANZ, GRETCHEN. *Freshman Norms for the University System of Georgia, 1958–59.* Atlanta, Ga.: Office of Testing and Guidance, Regents of the University System of Georgia, March 1960. Pp. ix, 91. *

66. HOLLAND, JOHN L. "The Prediction of College Grades From Personality and Aptitude Variables." *J Ed Psychol* 51:245–54 O '60. * (*PA* 36:1KL45H)

67. HURWITZ, HOWARD L. "Reflections on SAT Coaching and College Board Scores." *High Points* 42:48–9 O '60. *

68. JUOLA, ARVO E. "Predictive Validity of Five College-Level Academic Aptitude Tests at One Institution." *Personnel & Guid J* 38:637–41 Ap '60. * (*PA* 35:2791)

69. KETCHAM, HERBERT E., (MRS.) "Reading Tests and College Performance," pp. 63–6. In *Research and Evaluation in College Reading.* Ninth Yearbook of the National Reading Conference for College and Adults. Fort Worth, Tex.: Texas Christian University Press, 1960. Pp. 137. *

70. LORET, PETER G. *A History of the Content of the Scholastic Aptitude Test.* College Entrance Examination Board, Research and Development Reports, Test Development Memorandum TDM-60-1. [New York: the Board], October 1960. Pp. ii, 132. *

71. PIPHER, J. A. "An Appraisal of the Use of the Dominion Group Test of Learning Capacity (Advanced) in the Atkinson Study of Utilization of Student Resources." *Ont J Ed Res* 3:17–23 O '60. *

72. ROSEN, NED A. *A Validation Study of the College Entrance Examination Board Examinations and Other Predictors at Purdue University.* Purdue University, Division of Educational Reference, Studies in Higher Education, No. 90. Lafayette, Ind.: the Division, August 1960. Pp. 26. * (*PA* 35:2788)

73. WEXLER, AMELIA H. "Coaching and the SAT Tests." *High Points* 42:46–50 Ja '60. *

74. ALLEN, ROSCOE JACKSON. *An Analysis of the Relationship Between Selected Prognostic Measures and Achievement in the Freshman Program for Secretarial Majors at the Woman's College of the University of North Carolina.* Doctor's thesis, Pennsylvania State University (University Park, Pa.), 1961. (*DA* 23:122)

75. ALTUS, WILLIAM D. "Correlative Data for First-Semester Grade Averages at the University of California, Santa Barbara." *J Genetic Psychol* 98:303–5 Je '61. * (*PA* 36:2KJ03A)

76. ANGERS, WILLIAM P. "Pre-Engineering Characteristics of Entering Freshmen." *Voc Guid Q* 9:189–91 sp '61. * (*PA* 36:1KI89A)

77. HILLS, JOHN R.; EMORY, LINDA B.; AND MASTERS, PAULINE B. *Freshman Norms for the University System of Georgia, 1959–60.* Atlanta, Ga.: Office of Testing and Guidance, Regents of the University System of Georgia, September 1961. Pp. vii, 65. *

78. HILLS, JOHN R.; EMORY, LINDA B.; FRANZ, GRETCHEN; AND CROWDER, DOLORES GARCIA. "Admissions and Guidance Research in the University System of Georgia." *Personnel & Guid J* 39:452–7 F '61. * (*PA* 35:7102)

79. HILLS, JOHN R.; MASTERS, PAULINE B.; AND EMORY, LINDA B. *Supplement Counselor's Guide to Georgia Colleges.* Atlanta, Ga.: Office of Testing and Guidance, Regents of the University System of Georgia, 1961. Pp. ix, 35. *

80. HOLLAND, JOHN L. "Creative and Academic Performance Among Talented Adolescents." *J Ed Psychol* 52:136–47 Je '61. * (*PA* 38:3201)

81. MANN, M. JACINTA. "The Prediction of Achievement in a Liberal Arts College." *Ed & Psychol Meas* 21:481–3 su '61. * (*PA* 36:2KL81M)

82. MOCK, WILLIAM LINDSEY. *Selected Personality, Intellective, and Community Characteristics as Related to Academic Success of University of Georgia Students.* Doctor's thesis, University of Georgia (Athens, Ga.), 1961. (*DA* 22:1087)

83. PALLONE, NATHANIEL J. "Effects of Short- and Long-Term Developmental Reading Courses Upon S.A.T. Verbal Scores." *Personnel & Guid J* 39:654–7 Ap '61. * (*PA* 36:1KK54P)

84. SWANSON, EDWARD O., AND BERDIE, RALPH F. "Predictive Validities in an Institute of Technology." *Ed & Psychol Meas* 21:1001–8 w '61. Errata: 22:258 su '62. *

85. WATLEY, DONIVAN JASON. *Prediction of Academic Success in a College of Business Administration.* Doctor's thesis, University of Denver (Denver, Colo.), 1961. (*DA* 22:3527)

86. ANDERSON, SCARVIA B. *Letters to the Editor: SCAT and SAT.* Princeton, N.J.: Cooperative Test Division, 1962. Pp. 29. *

87. CHAUNCEY, HENRY. *Educational Testing Service Annual Report, 1961–62,* pp. 9–46. Princeton, N.J.: Educational Testing Service, 1962. Pp. 132. *

88. DARLEY, JOHN G. "The Basis for Equivalent Scores on the Annual Editions of the American Council on Education Psychological Examination (ACE), 1941 to 1954," pp. 170–83. In his *Promise and Performance: A Study of Ability and Achievement in Higher Education.* Berkeley, Calif.: Center for Study of Higher Education, University of California, 1962. Pp. vii, 191. *

89. ESSER, BARBARA F. "A Preliminary Factor Analysis of the Scholastic Aptitude Test Mathematics Section." *Yearb Nat Council Meas Ed* 19:83–93 '62. *

90. FLEMING, W. G. *The Use of Predictive Factors for the Improvement of University Admission Requirements.* Atkinson Study of Utilization of Student Resources, Report No. 9. Toronto, Canada: Department of Educational Research, Ontario College of Education, University of Toronto, 1962. Pp xi, 76. *

91. FOULKES, DAVID, AND HEAXT, SUSAN. "Concept Attainment and Self Concept." *Psychol Rep* 11:399–402 O '62. * (*PA* 37:7625)

92. FRENCH, JOHN W. "Effect of Anxiety on Verbal and Mathematical Examination Scores." *Ed & Psychol Meas* 22:553–64 au '62. * (*PA* 37:5082)

93. HILLS, JOHN R.; EMORY, LINDA B.; AND MASTERS, PAULINE B. *Freshman Norms for the University System of Georgia, 1960–61.* Atlanta, Ga.: Office of Testing and Guidance, Regents of the University System of Georgia, January 1962. Pp. xi, 65. *

94. JEFFREYS, LEONARD CHARLES, JR. *The Relationship of Selected Background Factors to the Academic Performance of Students of the Newark College of Arts and Sciences.* Doctor's thesis, Rutgers University (New Brunswick, N.J.), 1962. (*DA* 23:4224)

95. MASTEN, SHERMAN HASBROUCK. *The Value of Entrance Tests and Nine High School Variables in the Selection of Freshmen at Hofstra College: A Study in Differential Prediction.* Doctor's thesis, New York University (New York, N.Y.), 1962. (*DA* 23:886)

96. MICHAEL, WILLIAM B.; JONES, ROBERT A.; COX, ANNA; GERSHON, ARTHUR; HOOVER, MARVIN; KATZ, KENNETH; AND SMITH, DENNIS. "High School Record and College Board Scores as Predictors of Success in a Liberal Arts Program During the Freshman Year of College." *Ed & Psychol Meas* 22:399–400 su '62. * (*PA* 37:3872)

97. OLIVER, R. A. C. "The Selection of University Students: A 'Scholastic Aptitude Test'?" *Univ Q* 16:264–73 Je '62. *

98. REID, JOHN W.; JOHNSON, A. PEMBERTON; ENTWISLE, FRANK N.; AND ANGERS, WILLIAM P. "A Four-Year Study of the Characteristics of Engineering Students." *Personnel & Guid J* 41:38–43 S '62. * (*PA* 37:5655)

99. SHAW, HUBERT S. "Let's Simplify the Aptitude Test Schedule." *Col Board R* 47:20–2 sp '62. *

100. VICK, MARY CATHARINE, AND HORNADAY, JOHN A. "Predicting Grade Point Average at a Small Southern College." *Ed & Psychol Meas* 22:795–9 w '62. * (*PA* 37:7205)

101. WATLEY, DONIVAN J., AND MARTIN, H. T. "Prediction of Academic Success in a College of Business Administration." *Personnel & Guid J* 41:147–54 O '62. * (*PA* 37:5656)

102. WHITLA, DEAN K. "Effect of Tutoring on Scholastic

Aptitude Test Scores." *Personnel & Guid J* 41:32–7 S '62. * (*PA* 37:5660)
103. WILLINGHAM, WARREN W., AND STRICKLAND, JAMES A. "Conversion Tables for Otis Gamma and Scholastic Aptitude Test." *Personnel & Guid J* 41:356–8 D '62. * (*PA* 37:7183)
104. *Manual of Freshman Class Profiles, 1963 Edition.* Princeton, N.J.: College Entrance Examination Board, 1963. Pp. 642. *
105. AIKEN, LEWIS R., JR. "College Dropouts and Difference Scores." *Psychol Rep* 13:905–6 D '63. * (*PA* 38:9255)
106. AIKEN, LEWIS R., JR. "The Grading Behavior of a College Faculty." *Ed & Psychol Meas* 23:319–22 su '63. * (*PA* 38:1425)
107. ANGOFF, WILLIAM H. "Can Useful General-Purpose Equivalency Tables Be Prepared for Different College Admission Tests?" *Personnel & Guid J* 41:792–7 My '63. *
108. ANGOFF, WILLIAM H. "Can Useful General-Purpose Equivalency Tables Be Prepared for Different College Admissions Tests." *Proc Inv Conf Testing Probl* 1962:57–73 '63. * (*PA* 38:3187)
109. BURNS, RICHARD LEO. *An Investigation of the Value of the American College Testing Program, the Scholastic Aptitude Test and the Purdue Placement Tests as Predictors of Academic Success of Purdue University Freshmen.* Doctor's thesis, Purdue University (Lafayette, Ind.), 1963. (*DA* 24:1477)
110. COFFMAN, WILLIAM E. *The Scholastic Aptitude Test—1926–1962.* College Entrance Examination Board, Research and Development Reports, Test Development Report TDR-63-2. [New York: the Board], June 1963. Pp. i, 26. *
111. College Entrance Examination Board. *A Description of the College Board Scholastic Aptitude Test.* Princeton, N.J.: the Board, 1963. Pp. 53. * (Earlier editions published in 1960 and 1962.)
112. FUNKENSTEIN, DANIEL H. "Mathematics, Quantitative Aptitudes and the Masculine Role." *Dis Nerv System* 24(Sect 2):140–6 Ap '63. *
113. GRUBER, EDWARD C. *Practice for Scholastic Aptitude Tests: Complete Preparation.* New York: ARC Books, Inc., 1963. Pp. vi, 277. *
114. HILLS, JOHN R.; KLOCK, JOSEPH A.; AND LEWIS, SANDRA C. *Freshman Norms for the University System of Georgia, 1961–62.* Atlanta, Ga.: Office of Testing and Guidance, Regents of the University System of Georgia, June 1963. Pp. xi, 65. *
115. JACOBS, PAUL I. *A Study of Large Score Changes on the Scholastic Aptitude Test.* College Entrance Examination Board, Research and Development Reports, Research Bulletin RB-63-20. [New York: the Board], June 1963. Pp. iii, 47. *
116. JUOLA, ARVO E. "SAT Validities as Two-Variable Expectancy Tables." *Personnel & Guid J* 42:269–73 N '63. *
117. LEVINE, HAROLD G., AND LYONS, WILLIAM A. "Comparability of Scores on Three Examinations Sponsored by External Agencies in Secondary Schools in New York State." *Personnel & Guid J* 41:596–601 Mr '63. *
118. MICHAEL, WILLIAM B., AND JONES, ROBERT A. "Stability of Predictive Validities of High School Grades and of Scores on the Scholastic Aptitude Test of the College Entrance Examination Board for Liberal Arts Students." *Ed & Psychol Meas* 23:375–8 su '63. * (*PA* 38:1424)
119. MUELLER, KLAUS A., AND WIERSMA, WILLIAM, JR. "Correlation of Foreign Language Speaking Competency and Grades in Ten Midwestern Liberal Arts Colleges." *Mod Lang J* 47:353–5 D '63. *
120. SPAULDING, GERALDINE. "Relations Between the NAIS Junior Scholastic Aptitude Test and the CEEB Scholastic Aptitude Tests." *Ed Rec B* 84:55–62 Jl '63. *
121. WILLINGHAM, WARREN W. "Erroneous Assumptions in Predicting College Grades." Comment by Donald P. Hoyt. *J Counsel Psychol* 10:389–94 w '63. * (*PA* 38:9168)

JOHN E. BOWERS, *Director of Testing, Office of Admissions and Records, University of Illinois, Urbana, Illinois.* [Review of Form KSA45.]

The *College Entrance Examination Board Scholastic Aptitude Test* (SAT), introduced in 1926, has become one of the more familiar test instruments used by college and university personnel for predicting the scholastic achievement of college freshmen. Since an appraisal of the SAT should not ignore the reporting services associated with the admissions program of the College Entrance Examination Board, this reviewer will first describe the characteristics of the SAT and, secondly, comment upon aspects of the referral services.

Form KSA45 consists of five sections, beginning with a 30-minute section and followed by alternating 45-minute and 30-minute sections for a total of 180 minutes of testing time. Respondents are cautioned to guess prudently.

Two scores, verbal (based upon antonyms, sentence completion, analogies, and reading comprehension items) and mathematical (based upon word problems and data sufficiency items), are reported, each as a number on a scale between 200 and 800. Prior to 1941, both scores were scaled each year with a mean of 500 and a standard deviation of 100. The April 1941 national test administration results became the basis for equating all subsequent scales (*44*). At the present time, scaled scores for new forms introduced in each year are independently equated through a "double part-score equating" procedure [1] to two earlier reference forms.

Test-retest reliability coefficients of .89 for the verbal scale and .85 for the mathematical scale were found for time intervals up to 10 months. Reliability coefficients (K-R 20's modified by Dressel's procedure for use when there is a correction for guessing) for both scales for 14 1959–1962 SAT forms consistently approximate .90; standard errors of measurement for both scaled scores for these 14 forms vary, in general, between 30 and 35 points. Internal consistency reliability estimates appear not to contain a speed component.

The mean correlation between verbal and mathematical scores for the 14 forms introduced during the period 1959–1962 is .64. This is compared to the mean intercorrelation of .54 for six forms introduced during the period 1950–1953, .56 for six 1953–1956 forms, and .62 for nine 1956–1959 forms.

Percentile ranks of scaled scores are tabled separately by sex for secondary school seniors and for seniors who later entered college in College Board Score Reports: A Guide for Counselors and College Board Score Reports: A Guide for Admissions Officers. Norms for seniors were developed from scores on the *Preliminary Scholastic Aptitude Test* administered nation-wide in the fall of 1960, which were then converted to the SAT scale (multiplying

1 ANGOFF, WILLIAM H., AND WAITE, ANNETTE C. *A Study of Double Part-Score Equating for the Scholastic Aptitude Test.* Unpublished statistical report, Educational Testing Service, Princeton, N.J., August 1959. Pp. 12. *

by 10) and adjusted for ability growth between the fall and winter of 1960. College-attending senior norms are based upon a fall 1961 follow-up study of the senior norm group. The publishers correctly point out that local norms, specific to the individual college, are perhaps of greater value to the high school and college counselor.

On each scale, coaching results in average gains of less than the associated standard errors of measurement (*55*). Practice resulting from the first administration of the SAT effects an increase of approximately 10 scaled score points on both sections for both sexes. Two administrations effect a gain of approximately 20 points on both sections for both boys and girls. Ability growth from May of the junior year in high school to January of the senior year in high school is reflected in an average gain of about 20 points on the verbal scale for both sexes; a 15-point average gain for boys and a 5-point average gain for girls is observed for the mathematical scale. Score changes resulting from practice on the mathematical sections also reflect the amount of mathematics taken in the senior year.[2]

Much validity data for a variety of colleges is summarized in *College Board Scores No. 2* (*44*). In general, the verbal scale has been found to predict freshman grades better than the mathematical scale in liberal arts colleges, while the mathematical scale has been more valid for engineering colleges.

A review of the SAT naturally invites comparison with its major competitor, the *American College Testing Program Examination*. The ACT and the SAT are administered throughout the nation at several Saturday test dates during the year. Each program also schedules Sunday test dates for respondents who, because of religious reasons, prefer not to be tested on Saturday. At the present time, the ACT and the SAT respondent may refer his score results to three institutions. Individual score results will be forwarded to additional institutions or agencies for a small fee. Both the ACT and the SAT reporting services are prompt, reliable, and provide punched-card information which may be immediately entered into local mechanized research systems.

2 LEVINE, RICHARD S., AND ANGOFF, WILLIAM H. *The Effects of Practice and Growth on Scores on the Scholastic Aptitude Test.* Unpublished research report, Educational Testing Service, Princeton, N.J., February 1958. Pp. 22. *

In the reviewer's opinion, the advantages, at the present time, of the SAT program are: (*a*) SAT test forms are available for the handicapped; (*b*) there are overseas SAT administration centers; and (*c*) a list of the SAT respondents who select an institution as first, second, or third choice at each national test administration date is sent immediately to the institution.

The advantage of the ACT program is that the institutional "consumer" may assemble data which the ACT Research Service will summarize, tabulate, and analyze. For many institutions, these kinds of validity analyses might otherwise not be accomplished.

The choice of either instrument for use in situations involving subjects with fairly wide ranges of ability is probably a function of scale familiarity rather than discriminable utility. It would be a matter of empirical test to determine, for homogeneous ability level groupings, which instrument functions more validly. The unfortunate aspect for the prospective college student, undecided about his choice of college, is that he is often required to take both tests as "insurance" in order to meet different institutional entrance test requirements. This reviewer hopes that the evidence which might be accumulated from present duplicate testings will be collected in order to determine whether equivalencies between the ACT and the SAT are justified for some admissions purposes.

WAYNE S. ZIMMERMAN, *Test Officer, Los Angeles State College, Los Angeles, California.* [Review of Form KSA45.]

The SAT is a college entrance examination designed to measure general verbal and mathematical comprehension, the two abilities which the accumulation of statistical evidence argues are the most important cognitive traits contributing to success in academic work. The test was developed as an instrument to be administered to students who aspire to attend college. Its primary purpose is to provide information to college officials who are interested in selecting the most promising students from among those who apply for admission. The scores can be utilized also by high school counselors or other authorized officials to help guide a student either to an appropriate college or to consider an alternative pursuit, although the *Preliminary Scholastic Aptitude Test* has recently been designed specifically to serve this purpose.

The publishers expect that SAT scores will be used as a supplement to such information as previous school performance, biographical data, and scores from noncognitive inventories and questionnaires, plus scores on tests of other cognitive abilities.

Form KSA45 is similar in format to previous forms. The test is divided into five separately timed sections. Scores on two sections are combined to produce the total verbal score, scores on two sections are combined to produce the total mathematics score, and the fifth section is included for the purpose of obtaining data on new items which can be used later in the construction of additional alternative forms.

Items in the verbal sections are presented in four formats. In all instances the examinee is instructed to select the one correct answer from among five alternatives and to mark his choice on a separate machine scorable answer sheet. One verbal format requires a word to be selected which will correctly fill in a blank in a sentence. Another format requires an antonym to be selected for a given stimulus word. A third requires the examinee to select from the alternatives the second half of a verbal analogy, the first half being presented as a stimulus. The fourth presents questions based upon comprehension of content of written passages. Classically the first format would be recognized as a vocabulary test, the second as an antonym test, the third as a verbal analogies test, and the fourth a test of reading comprehension. In the theoretical framework of Guilford's structure of intellect, a vocabulary test might measure "cognition of semantic units," an antonym test, "cognition of semantic classes," a verbal analogies test, "cognition of semantic relations," and a reading comprehension test, "cognition of semantic systems" and cognition of semantic implications. Thus, there would appear to be a potentially good coverage of the Guilford factors of semantic cognition. In the analysis of similar tests, however, Guilford and his associates have found that where the vocabulary level is as high as it is throughout SAT "cognition of semantic units" predominates. This finding would appear to account for the very high correlations usually obtained among these potentially different measures and the fact that a well designed vocabulary test will substitute so well for the more comprehensive set of measures.

The mathematical sections begin with common arithmetical operations and, with difficulty increasing as the test progresses, move on to higher level reasoning type problems involving algebraic and elementary geometric concepts. Although some items are quite difficult, this difficulty is achieved through the level of reasoning required rather than through use of material which would be covered in more advanced mathematics courses. Theoretically, a student who has a grasp of first year high school algebra should be equipped to work all of the kinds of problems that are presented. The symbolic factors in Guilford's structure of intellect are not yet well determined. Consequently, only some very tentative conclusions can be drawn. SAT mathematical problems would be expected to cut across the realms of both symbolic-cognitive and symbolic-convergent production. Possibly one memory factor, "memory for symbolic implications," and one divergent production factor, "divergent production of symbolic relations" are present in some degree. The difficult word problems undoubtedly add some semantic variance, which would help to account for the moderate correlations between the SAT verbal and mathematical sections. Possibly the major portion of the SAT mathematics variance is in "cognition of symbolic systems."

Fourteen recent SAT forms are discussed in an ETS bulletin, covering the period from August 1959 to May 1961. Kuder-Richardson formula 20 reliability coefficients are listed for all forms. The reported verbal test reliabilities range from .88 to .91, while mathematics test reliabilities range from .87 to .91. The reliabilities of Form KSA45 are .92 for verbal and .93 for mathematical scores.

The selected validity coefficients reported for predicting success of male liberal arts students as measured by freshman average grades are modest. They range from .16 to .61 with a median of .35 for the verbal scores, and from .15 to .53 with a median of .33 for mathematics scores. Corresponding selected validity coefficients for female subjects cover approximately the same range with median values of .36 and .26 for verbal and mathematics scores, respectively. Validity coefficients are corrected for restriction in range, while multiple correlations are adjusted for shrinkage. One of the studies from which these data were selected[1] reports multiple correlations of the verbal and mathematics scores with first term grade averages ranging from .22 to .63 before correction and from .18 to .62 after correction for shrinkage. These corrected figures, however, cannot be relied upon as an indication of how well the reported multiple correlations would hold up in cross validation.

SAT has a number of major strengths which should be noted. In the first place, the test is very carefully constructed and it is thoroughly analyzed by appropriate methodology before being presented for use in the selection of students. Its range is sufficiently wide to differentiate among both the lowest and highest levels in the college bound or freshman samples. No other competing test publisher prepares so many alternate forms in which items are so carefully matched for content and difficulty and scores are so painstakingly equated. It is safe also to conclude that no other competing test publisher maintains as high a level of security. Trained security officers are available to be called to the scene immediately should a booklet be reported missing. In the few instances where booklets have been taken, the officers have a remarkably fine record of tracing and recovering them. No other test presents a greater abundance of normative data nor such a vast amount of detailed information concerning the test. Users who have time to read all of the reports are kept up to date by frequent bulletins and reports of new developments. It is not surprising, therefore, that the SAT continues to be the leading test for selection of college students throughout the nation, despite the fact that some inroads have been made. In the eastern states SAT is used almost exclusively. It is also the most frequently used test in the West. It is only in the Midwest and South where competing tests may be used more frequently.

If any adverse criticism were to be made of the SAT in this review, it would have to be aimed at the question of how much time is actually needed to measure two academic abilities. There is little question but what the SAT predicts academic achievement at the college level as well as or better than any competitive test, or at least that it adds more unique variance if it is used in conjunction with an evaluation of high school marks. The question is simply whether it is necessary and appropriate for a student to invest a half day of his time in order for school officials to obtain adequate measures of these two abilities. It seems reasonable to expect, in the light of more recent developments, that shorter factor analytically refined measures of the several verbal and numerical dimensions could be administered in considerably less time without a significant loss in predictive validity. The time saved in administering a shorter test could be utilized either in sampling other abilities and attributes, or for administering placement tests in at least the two areas that are particularly critical—college freshman English and mathematics. In this reviewer's opinion a one half day test composed of four sections designed to yield separate scores for verbal aptitude, quantitative aptitude, English proficiency, and mathematics proficiency would yield more useful information per unit of testing time.

In conclusion, where high school and college officials are satisfied to devote one half a day to the measurement of two abilities, there is probably no better test available to estimate the entering student's college level verbal and mathematical comprehension.

1 Olsen, Marjorie. *Summary of Main Findings on the Validity of the CEEB Tests of Developed Ability as Predictors of College Grades.* Unpublished statistical report, Educational Testing Service, Princeton, N.J., October 1957. Pp. 59. *

For a review by John T. Dailey of an earlier form, see 5:318; for a review by Frederick B. Davis of earlier forms, see 4:285.

[450]

***College Qualification Tests.** Candidates for college entrance; 1955–61; 6 scores: verbal, numerical, science information, social studies information, total information, total; IBM; Forms A ('56), B ('56), C ('59); 2 editions; revised manual ('61, 61 pages); distribution of Forms B and C restricted to colleges and universities; separate answer sheets must be used; postpaid; George K. Bennett, Marjorie G. Bennett, Wimburn L. Wallace, and Alexander G. Wesman; Psychological Corporation. *

a) COMBINED BOOKLET EDITION. (14 pages); $5 per 25 tests; $3.50 per 50 IBM answer sheets; 75¢ per specimen set; 80(105) minutes.

b) SEPARATE BOOKLET EDITION. $2.50 per 25 tests; $2 per 50 IBM answer sheets; 90¢ per specimen set.

1) *Test V* [*Verbal*]. (5 pages); 15(25) minutes.

2) *Test N* [*Numerical*]. (6 pages); 35(45) minutes.

3) *Test I* [*Information*]. (6 pages); 3 scores: science information, social science information, total; 30(40) minutes.

REFERENCES

1. Kirk, Barbara A. "Comparison of Transfer Students by Source of Origin With Entering Students on the College Qualification Test." *Jun Col J* 29:218–21 D '58. *

2. Seashore, Harold. "Academic Abilities of Junior College Students." *Jun Col J* 29:74–80 O '58. *

3. SPAULDING, HELEN. "The Prediction of First-Year Grade Averages in a Private Junior College." *Ed & Psychol Meas* 19:627–8 w '59. * (*PA* 34:6574)

4. WESMAN, ALEXANDER G., AND BENNETT, GEORGE K. "Multiple Regression vs. Simple Addition of Scores in Prediction of College Grades." *Ed & Psychol Meas* 19:243–6 su '59. * (*PA* 34:4820)

5. JUOLA, ARVO E. "Predictive Validity of Five College-Level Academic Aptitude Tests at One Institution." *Personnel & Guid J* 38:637–41 Ap '60. * (*PA* 35:2791)

6. JUOLA, ARVO E. "The Differential Validity of the College Qualification Tests for Diverse Curricular Groups." *Personnel & Guid J* 39:721–4 My '61. * (*PA* 36:1KJ21J)

7. JUOLA, ARVO E. "Multi-Variable Grade Expectancy Tables: An Aid to Test Interpretation." *Yearb Nat Council Meas Ed* 18:91–9 '61. *

8. DARLEY, JOHN G. "The Basis for Equivalent Scores on the Annual Editions of the American Council on Education Psychological Examination (ACE), 1941 to 1954," pp. 170–83. In his *Promise and Performance: A Study of Ability and Achievement in Higher Education.* Berkeley, Calif.: Center for Study of Higher Education, University of California, 1962. Pp. vii, 191. *

9. RAO, S. NARAYANA. "Predicting Academic Achievement of Students in Science and Arts Colleges." *Psychol Studies* 7:16–9 Jl '62. * (*PA* 37:5669)

10. KIRK, BARBARA A.; CUMMINGS, ROGER W.; AND GOODSTEIN, LEONARD D. "The College Qualification Tests and Differential Guidance With University Freshmen." *Personnel & Guid J* 42:47–51 S '63. *

11. RAO, S. NARAYANA. "Prediction of Academic Achievement of Students in an Engineering College." *J Psychol Res* 7:114–7 S '63. *

RALPH F. BERDIE, *Professor of Psychology, and Director, Student Counseling Bureau, University of Minnesota, Minneapolis, Minnesota.*

When Educational Testing Service discontinued publishing new forms of the *American Council on Education Psychological Examinations* the authors of the *College Qualification Tests* assumed, and apparently correctly in light of the wide use of the CQT, that a brief, convenient, and relatively valid college aptitude test providing somewhat the same information as the old ACE was still worthwhile. Whereas some other college predicting tests have tended to include items more typical of the traditional academic achievement test, this test continues in the tradition of the old Army Alpha, the early Otis test, and the ACE.

The items in the vocabulary section of the tests require the student to select from four words the one that means the same as or the opposite of a fifth word. Since the early 1920's such vocabulary tests have proved to be among the best predictors of college success.

The numerical items consist of simple problems in mathematics covering fractions, decimals, square root, elementary algebra, and simple geometry.

The information test consists of items dealing with (*a*) physics, chemistry, and biology, and (*b*) history, government, economics, and geography. The items call for knowledge of facts and terminology and, as the title of the subtest implies, are designed to measure how much information the student has at his command rather than how he can use or interpret this information to solve problems. The information items can be scored to provide a science score and a social studies score as well as a total information score. The manual states that the test can be used for placement of students, but the items included in the information subtests do not resemble the items constructed by college teachers for inclusion in tests they use for classifying students in mathematics or social studies and no evidence is presented in the manual concerning the validity of the test for classification or placement purposes.

The manual has unusually complete information on reliability and standard errors of measurement. Reliability of the tests appears satisfactory. The coefficients for the verbal test vary between .84 and .95 with most of them being above .90. Those for the numerical test range between .77 and .93, with most being in or above the high .80's. The reliability coefficients for the total score on the information test range between .79 and .89, somewhat lower than those for either the verbal or numerical tests. The individual science and social studies scores have reliabilities in the .70's and low .80's. The manual does not present information concerning the reliability of the combined verbal and numerical scores, omitting the information section, but the inference appears justified that the reliability of this combined score would usually be in the low to mid .90's; these test scores would provide reliable information concerning college aptitude.

Validity data are presented in three tables, one containing data from publicly controlled four-year institutions, one data from privately controlled institutions, and one data from junior colleges. The institutions are identified only by geographical regions, within institutions data being classified by sex. Correlations are presented between the criterion (always college grades) and each of the six CQT scores.

In general, the size of the validity coefficient depends on the college being studied. Among the four-year publicly controlled institutions the correlation coefficients between verbal scores and grades range from .19 to .63; and the correlations between grades and total score range from .34 to .73. For the 47 correlations reported between total score and grades for the four-year institutions, the median correlation is .57. This is somewhat higher than the figure of .50 that for years people have used to describe the typical correlation between college aptitude test scores and freshman college grades. Somewhat discouraging, however, is the fact that good college aptitude tests available today still do not provide correlation coefficients consistently above the mid-fifties.

One considering using these tests for prediction purposes would wish to know the relative effectiveness of the verbal and numerical scores combined compared to the total CQT score. The manual does not provide this information, but some data from the Arts College of the University of Minnesota suggest the two scores combined provide as effective prediction as does the total score. In predicting first quarter grade-point average in 1962 the verbal test had a correlation with grades for men of .37, for women of .45. The numerical test had correlations of .39 and .45. The combined verbal and numerical scores provided correlations for the men of .49 and for the women of .57. Correlations between grades and total CQT scores were, for the men, .51 and for the women, .59, in each case only .02 higher than the correlations obtained from the combined verbal and numerical scores.

At Minnesota the multiple correlation coefficient between grades and scores predicted from the verbal and numerical scores was identical with the zero order correlations between grades and the totals of the verbal and numerical scores. The same thing was found when the verbal, numerical, science information, and social science information scores were combined in a multiple correlation coefficient and compared to the zero order correlation for the total test score. These results agree with the study by Wesman and Bennett (*4*) who found that the simple addition of three CQT scores predicted first-term college grades about as well as multiple regression equations. The use of the total test score provides the optimal weighting and adding the two information scores does not significantly increase the predictive efficiency of the test, particularly at the University of Minnesota.

Little information concerning the validity of the tests has been published other than that contained in the manual. One study (*5*) compared the predictive validities of five college aptitude tests and found that they differed only slightly in validity.

The normative information presented in the manual is superior to similar information presented in manuals for most aptitude tests. Norms are presented separately for men and women, and in light of known sex differences, it is surprising that so many test manuals fail to make this distinction. Not only are general norms for college freshmen presented, but norms also are presented for freshmen in state universities, in privately controlled universities, and for groups of college freshmen who are candidates for A.B. degrees, for B.S. degrees, and degrees in business, education, engineering, technical courses, and nursing. Geographical norms are also provided with separate norms for college freshmen in southern institutions, for freshmen in junior colleges, and for junior college freshmen registered in transfer and in terminal curricula. Finally norms are provided for high school students in grades 11 and 12.

Scores are reported as equivalent on Forms A and B and the same norm tables are presented for these forms. Separate norm tables are presented for Form C.

The three available forms of the test provide a significant advantage. Form A is available to high schools and colleges. Forms B and C are available only to colleges and colleges making use of these forms can be assured that candidates have not had experience with the forms being employed.

In summary, the *College Qualification Tests* are as good as but no better than the best of the other college aptitude tests. The tests have many advantages and no disadvantages that are not inherent in tests of this type. They are well constructed, edited, and printed. They have satisfactory reliability and are as valid as other tests available for these purposes; they are easy to administer and to score. The CQT is as adequate for identifying, admitting, classifying, and counseling college students as any other college aptitude test.

WARREN G. FINDLEY, *Professor of Education, and Coordinator of Educational Research, University of Georgia, Athens, Georgia.*

Two elements have been added since these tests were reviewed by three specialists as a new offering in the preceding issue of this yearbook. Form C, issued in 1960, constitutes a second restricted form for use in colleges and universities, but not in high schools. Also, the manual was revised in 1961 to incorporate the results of further validity and reliability studies.

Since the tests are offered as instruments for use in selective admissions, placement, and counseling, and since there were differing degrees of consensus among the previous reviewers regarding suitability of the tests for these various purposes, it will be well to organize this review along the line of suitability for the three purposes, respectively. The new data and argument will fall into place under these headings.

SUITABILITY FOR SELECTIVE ADMISSIONS. There was unanimous agreement among the previous reviewers on suitability of the tests for selective admissions purposes. The availability of a second restricted form and the promise of successive biennial forms for restricted use strengthen this use operationally. The fact that a Form D was not issued on schedule in 1962, or in 1963, suggests only that the need has not been as pressing as originally anticipated.

In addition to reporting an increased number of validity and reliability coefficients accumulated since the 1957 manual was published, the present manual includes illustrative expectancy tables for two institutions. These present graphically in parallel 100 per cent bars the proportions of freshmen attaining grade-point averages below 2.0, between 2.0 and 2.9, and between 3.0 and 4.0, for successive intervals of 10 percentile points on the CQT total score. These serve not only to underline the importance of local institutional norms, but also to provide a model form for their presentation and use.

Of course, the predictive power diminishes as one moves from the total score to the part scores and finally to the subpart scores. The medians of 65 correlations with college grade-point average for each of the scores are .51 for total score, .45 for Information, .44 for Numerical, .43 for Verbal, .39 for Science Information, and .38 for Social Studies Information. This is largely a function of the reliability of these part scores. It is interesting to note, however, that the medians of 12 reliability coefficients for each of the scores are .96 for total score, .93 for V, .89 for N, .86 for I, .79 for social studies, and .77 for science. It may be worth pondering that information scores prove quite as predictive of college GPA as either verbal or numerical scores despite their appreciably lower reliability. It is also noticeable that the reliability coefficients for boys run higher than those for girls for five of the six scores, while the reverse is true of the validity coefficients.

Failure of the verbal test to show higher predictive validity may be due partially to the item types used. This reviewer found it quite awkward to shift from seeking synonyms to seeking opposites and back again. In the opposites section he became frustrated at times at inability to find a synonym, only to realize suddenly that opposites were to be sought. It may also be questioned whether the verbal score should reflect only what a vocabulary test can measure. Most competing test offerings use reading comprehension in some form in arriving at the verbal measure.

The numerical test is a power test of problem solving ability based on fundamental concepts and operations of arithmetic, algebra, and geometry. Its somewhat lower reliability is shared by mathematics scores in other batteries. The fact that its median predictive validity is comparable to that of other parts involves a sex difference in college courses chosen. For boys the numerical score tends to be relatively more predictive, while for girls it tends to be relatively less predictive, than the verbal and information scores.

Inclusion of an information test gives this battery an advantage over most competing measures of scholastic aptitude. Some may wish to quarrel with the highly factual nature of the content on grounds not only of its face validity, but also of its influence on instruction in preparatory institutions. The first criticism is met directly by the validity coefficients, showing this test, if anything, slightly more predictive of GPA than the verbal and numerical tests are.

The criticism of unfavorable impact on instruction is more serious. For years this has deterred the College Entrance Examination Board from considering the introduction of such a section in its Scholastic Aptitude Test despite the probability that the predictive power of that measure would be enhanced thereby. Such criticism on a policy level is not to be met by statistical evidence. It is met in the American College Testing Program and related offerings by inclusion of reading comprehension tests in the subject fields; these tests contain small segments of items based on general knowledge of each area not involved in the content of the reading passages. The policy choice made for the *College Qualifica-*

tion Tests is to supplement the factorially based verbal and numerical sections found in so many academic aptitude batteries with this distinct element.

It should be noted in regard to this issue that scholastic aptitude measures which lack an information section are also subject to criticism on two counts, predictive and instructional. The predictive criticism, *supported by validity coefficients,* is that structured knowledge of useful factual information is quite as basic a characteristic of a vigorous mind as are the "basic skills" of verbal comprehension and quantitative reasoning. A proper sample of as many as 75 items of *significant* information from science and social studies can represent this area of substantive knowledge in the scholastic aptitude battery in much the same relative proportion to verbal comprehension and quantitative reasoning as prevails in the high school curriculum. It may be that some students will have had better instruction than others in these substantive areas, but that is equally true of mathematics and reading. To the degree that this reviewer is correct in the supposition that the predictiveness of reading comprehension and quantitative reasoning tests is attributable to the fact that rudimentary instruction in both areas has been generally available to those who have completed high school and that excellence on these tests reflects one's motivation and ability to learn these "basic" skills, a well constructed test of information may likewise be said to achieve its predictiveness by reflecting students' motivation and ability to learn equally "basic" substantive knowledge. Moreover, such a test need be no more coachable than tests of verbal and numerical skill. A good general education would be the best preparation. And those who sought to add to their knowledge and to structure it for effective recall would be strengthening their intellectual competence quite as intrinsically as those who now review their basic arithmetic and put it into more usable form.

The scholastic aptitude battery that lacks an information test may be criticized for favoring those with basic skills who have not put their skills to use in mastering substantive knowledge, over students with somewhat lesser basic skills who have put their skills to good use in acquiring structured knowledge. Many have viewed with concern the apparent emphasis put on scores from the *College Entrance Examination Board Scholastic Aptitude Test* in determination of scholarship awards, for example. It is an excellent test for prediction of college achievement and has the added virtue of being a common measure, taken by all competitors, which is relatively uninfluenced by special preparation or superior teaching. As of the date of writing this review, that test has not incorporated in it any measure of substantive knowledge. Some would argue that achievement tests, specifically those of the College Board, should be used for this purpose. It must be remembered, however, that such achievement tests measure advanced work much influenced by availability and by quality of advanced instruction. What is called for is a test of substantive knowledge with the characteristics already cited as characterizing the verbal and mathematics sections of the SAT.

The resolution of the issue would thus appear to depend on development of a *general* test of *significant* structured knowledge in a form least likely to be considered by students and their parents and teachers as a test requiring or favoring rote memorization of encyclopedic information.

Regarding the usefulness of this battery in admissions programs, one further question arises. The College Entrance Examination Board and the American College Testing Program offer their tests under secure administrative procedures that do not require the individual college to handle this considerable chore, fraught as it is with possibilities of loss of security when operated under ordinary circumstances. These programs also make provision, through multiple test administration (four or five times a year) and special arrangements, to achieve the local flexibility that is achievable through use of the *College Qualification Tests.* These two secure programs are rapidly gaining acceptance nationwide over such offerings as the *College Qualification Tests.* It would appear, then, that the future of the CQT as an instrument of college admissions must lie in extending to it the secure administration and scoring service the publishers now offer for testing of prospective graduate students, executives, and research and management personnel.

SUITABILITY FOR ACADEMIC PLACEMENT. To the extent that placement in curriculums, courses, and sections within courses is viewed simply as an extension of selective admission *to* college to selective admission *within* college, the same validity coefficients that establish the suitability of these tests for college admission also establish their suitability for placement purposes. There are several points to be borne in mind, however. First, since assignment within college generally deals with a narrower range of competence on each test than does selection for admission, a heavier strain is placed on validity and reliability. Second, assignment to curriculums and courses requires evidence of differential prediction. Norms for national groups specializing in different college curriculums are only suggestive and are not directly interpretable. The offer of the publishers to cooperate in local norms studies becomes important here. Also, the user will want to pay greater attention to high school grades and/or placement tests of prerequisite study for both course assignment and sectioning. The CQT would help in general sectioning and, in cases of extremely high or low scores in the verbal and numerical tests, in curriculum assignment. The total information score would play its part primarily as a contributor to total CQT score. The part scores for science and social studies information are not sufficiently reliable for differential use. Differences between them and differences from other scores would be useful only as they confirm or are confirmed by other evidence, such as differences in reported high school grades. Class sectioning needs to be done subject by subject, as is widely recommended for high school and college and has been done in a number of colleges for many years. And it is at least as important that provision be made for reassignment to the most appropriate section at an early evaluation point in each course as for proper initial assignment. Viewed in this light, initial sectioning must be considered tentative. Initial assignment should be made as valid as possible by taking into account as much relevant information about students as possible, but always with the expectation that some individuals will prove to have been incorrectly assigned and to require reassignment.

SUITABILITY FOR HIGH SCHOOL AND COLLEGE COUNSELING. College counseling may be considered a still further extension of selective admissions, beyond selective placement. Counseling implies less directive action by the institution, however, and more joint planning with the student or simply advisement of the student. Once in the college, the student can be properly advised only in terms of expectancy tables or charts showing him probabilities of attaining given averages in each of several curriculums in that college in the light of his tested aptitude and previous academic achievement. Counseling regarding advanced professional training during upperclass years would require similar expectancy tables for success in graduate work in particular fields within particular institutions.

High school counseling regarding college choice can be considerably helped by results of the *College Qualification Tests.* Again, this reviewer would strongly recommend use of expectancy tables of the sort provided in the *Counselor's Guide to Georgia Colleges,* prepared and distributed by the Office of Testing and Guidance of the Regents of the University System of Georgia. This publication and its supplements present in separate tables for each institution, and for each curriculum within each institution, separately by sex, the probability of attaining a grade average of C or better, B or better, or A, for high school students with particular values of predictive composites based on high school grades and, in this publication, College Board SAT scores. The CQT would do better to take advantage of high school grade averages as a supplement in such prediction rather than offer to supplant such grade averages. The practical value of a test for high school counseling is to be judged not in terms of its own unaided predictive power, but in terms of the extent to which it improves the predictive power of automatically available data like high school grade averages. The long and creditable history of predictive power which these averages have, makes it especially appropriate to evaluate tests as supplementary measures.

For counseling to be most effective, individual profiles of scores should be provided as accessories. It would be particularly helpful if such profiles incorporated the percentile band device of the Cooperative Test Division's STEP and SCAT series, or the difference device used in the CQT publisher's own *Differential Aptitude Tests,* to indicate when differences between an individual's scores on the separate tests warrant notice and differential prediction.

The value of the tables of special norms provided so generously in the CQT manual is real, but limited. State universities differ among themselves, as do privately controlled institutions (and their subdivisions that lead to different degrees and specializations), southern universities, and junior colleges and their subgroups of students in terminal and transfer programs. The norms of the samples just mentioned, calculated separately for the two sexes, reveal a number of significant general relations that provide a useful background for counseling. However, consider the norms for education majors and arts and sciences majors. These favor arts and sciences generally, more for boys than for girls. But research has shown that for many years students in teachers colleges in certain states have compared favorably with the national norms for arts and sciences majors, and even more favorably with arts and sciences majors from certain individual institutions or groups of institutions. The sample of privately controlled institutions is notably unrepresentative, while the sample of southern institutions is so varied as to make the norms not truly representative of any of them. The high school norms are more extensive, but not certainly representative. In fairness to the tests' authors, it should be noted that they argue for local norms and provide the model already cited for their calculation and presentation in the form of expectancy charts. However, these recommendations and strictures on interpretation, so carefully stated, are often overlooked or forgotten in preoccupation with seemingly appropriate special norms. This discussion should be viewed as an attempt to reinforce the authors' thoroughly professional presentation, rather than to criticize it.

SUMMARY. The *College Qualification Tests* are well conceived, show excellence in item construction, are supported by varied and substantial data on reliability, validity, and norms, which are in turn reported with professional rigor and contain a significant emphasis on substantive knowledge which is unique for a scholastic aptitude battery. They are appropriate for selective admissions but must compete with complete admissions testing services. They can serve academic placement and counseling uses as presently constituted but might be strengthened in ways indicated in this review. Users may rely on this instrument as sound and in some ways unique. Competing offerings abound and present a variety of important decisions to make.

For reviews by Gustav J. Froehlich, A. E. G. Pilliner, and David V. Tiedeman, see 5:320.

[451]

Concept Mastery Test. Grades 15–16 and graduate students and applicants for executive and research positions; 1956, c1950; IBM; Form T ('56, 4 pages); manual ('56, 9 pages); separate answer sheets must be used; $3.50 per 25 tests; $2 per 50 IBM answer sheets; 40¢ per set of manual and scoring key; 50¢ per specimen set; postpaid; (35–45) minutes; Lewis M. Terman; Psychological Corporation. *

REFERENCES

1–4. See 5:321.
5. McNemar, Quinn. Chap. 12, "Intellectual Status of the Gifted Subjects as Adults," pp. 140–6. In *The Gifted Child Grows Up: Twenty-Five Years' Follow-Up of a Superior Group.* By Lewis M. Terman and others. Genetic Studies of Genius, Vol. 4. Stanford, Calif.: Stanford University Press, 1947. Pp. xiv, 448. * (*PA* 22:2080)
6. Terman, Lewis M., and Oden, Melita H.; in association with Nancy Bayley, Helen Marshall, Quinn McNemar, and Ellen B. Sullivan. Chap. 11, "Intelligence Tests of 1940," pp. 125–39. In their *The Gifted Child Grows Up: Twenty-Five Years' Follow-Up of a Superior Group.* Genetic Studies of Genius, Vol. 4. Stanford, Calif.: Stanford University Press, 1947. Pp. xiv, 448. * (*PA* 22:2080)
7. Terman, Lewis M., and Oden, Melita H. Chap. 5, "Intellectual Status at Mid-Life," pp. 52–63. In their *The Gifted Group at Midlife: Thirty-Five Years' Follow-Up of the Superior Child.* Genetic Studies of Genius, Vol. 5. Stanford, Calif.: Stanford University Press, 1959. Pp. xv, 187. * (*PA* 33:7905)
8. MacKinnon, Donald W. "Fostering Creativity in Students of Engineering." *J Eng Ed* 52:129–42 D '61. * (*PA* 36:4HD29M)
9. Camp, William L., and Rothney, John W. M. "Use of the Concept Mastery Test in Study of Superior High School Seniors." *Voc Guid Q* 10:223–5 su '62. * (*PA* 37:7181)
10. Curtis, H. A., and Kropp, R. P. "Standard and Visual Administrations of the Concept Mastery Test." *Audiovis Commun R* 10:38–42 Ja–F '62. * (*PA* 37:1193)
11. Kennedy, Wallace A., and Smith, Alvin H. "Norms for Mathematically Gifted Adolescents on the Concept Mastery Test." *Percept & Motor Skills* 17:698 D '63. * (*PA* 38:6059)
12. Taylor, Donald W. Chap. 19, "Variables Related to Creativity and Productivity Among Men in Two Research Laboratories," pp. 228–50. In *Scientific Creativity: Its Recognition and Development.* Edited by Calvin W. Taylor and Frank Barron. New York: John Wiley & Sons, Inc., 1963. Pp. xxiv, 419. * (*PA* 38:2689)

For reviews by J. A. Keats and Calvin W. Taylor, see 5:321.

[452]

***Cooperative School and College Ability Tests.** Grades 4–6, 6–8, 8–10, 10–12, 12–14, 15–16; 1955–63; also called SCAT; 3 scores: verbal, quantitative, total; IBM, NCS, and Grade-O-Mat; 6 levels; STEP-SCAT student report ('58, 4 pages); STEP-SCAT profile ('57, 2 pages); accessories for levels 1–5: directions for administering ('57, 11 pages), manual for interpreting ['57, 49 pages], technical report ['57, 43 pages], 1958 SCAT-STEP supplement ('58, 32 pages), 1962 SCAT-STEP supplement ('62, 48 pages), 1963 SCAT-STEP supplement of urban norms ('63, 16 pages), letters to the editor—SCAT and SAT ('62, 29 pages); manual for upper level ('63, 24 pages); separate answer sheets must be used; $4 per 20 tests; $1 per 20 IBM scorable answer sheets; $1 per 10 scoring stencils (answer pattern must be punched out locally); $1 per 20 Scribe answer sheets (see 763 for scoring service); see 666 for prices of Grade-O-Mat cards; see 671 for prices of NCS answer sheets; $1 per 20 student reports; $1 per 20 profiles; $1 per manual for interpreting; $1 per technical report; $1 per supplement; $1 per manual for upper level; postage extra; $1.25 per combined specimen set of levels 1–5; $1 per specimen set of upper level; cash orders postpaid; 70(95) minutes; Cooperative Test Division. *

a) SCHOOL ABILITY TEST. Grades 4–6, 6–8, 8–10, 10–12; 1955–63; 2 forms (12–14 pages); 4 levels.

1) [*Level 5.*] Grades 4–6; Forms 5A, 5B, ('56).
2) [*Level 4.*] Grades 6–8; Forms 4A, 4B, ('56).
3) [*Level 3.*] Grades 8–10; Forms 3A, 3B, ('56).
4) [*Level 2.*] Grades 10–12; Forms 2A, 2B, ('55).

b) COLLEGE ABILITY TEST. Grades 12–14, 15–16; 1955–63; 2 levels.

1) [*Level 1.*] Grades 12–14; Forms 1A, 1B, 1C, 1D, ('55, 12 pages); Forms 1C and 1D available only by special arrangement for use with students in college.
2) *Level U.* Grades 15–16; Forms UA, UB, ('61, 16 pages); Form UB available only by special arrangement.

REFERENCES

1–7. See 5:322.

8. WILLIAMS, CECIL L. *A Study of the Relative Effectiveness of the ACE Psychological Examination and the School and College Ability Test in Predicting First Semester Grade Point Averages.* Master's thesis, University of Kansas (Lawrence, Kan.), 1957.

9. BLACK, D. B. "A Study of the Relationship of the Grade IX Principal's Rating to Performance on the Alberta Grade IX Departmental Examinations." *Alberta J Ed Res* 4:227–36 D '58. * (*PA* 34:2089)

10. FLEMING, W. G. *Aptitude and Achievement Scores Related to Immediate Educational and Occupational Choices of Ontario Grade 13 Students.* Atkinson Study of Utilization of Student Resources, Report No. 3. Toronto, Canada: Department of Educational Research, Ontario College of Education, University of Toronto, 1958. Pp. xix, 380. *

11. FLEMING, W. G. *Ontario Grade 13 Students: Their Aptitude, Achievement, and Immediate Destination.* Atkinson Study of Utilization of Student Resources, Report No. 4. Toronto, Canada: Department of Educational Research, Ontario College of Education, University of Toronto, 1958. Pp. ix, 55. *

12. KENNEDY, PHYLLIS E. "The Validity of the School and College Ability Test for Prediction of College Achievement." *Calif J Ed Res* 9:67–71 Mr '58. * (*PA* 33:9044)

13. MAYER, ROBERT W. "A Study of the STEP Reading, SCAT and WISC Tests, and School Grades." *Reading Teach* 12:117+ D '58. * (*PA* 34:3441)

14. BLACK, D. B. "A Comparison of the Performance on Selected Standardized Tests to That on the Alberta Grade XII Departmental Examination of a Select Group of University of Alberta Freshmen." *Alberta J Ed Res* 5:180–90 S '59. * (*PA* 34:6559)

15. BROAD, ELMER J. *An Investigation of the Relative Effectiveness of the American Council on Education Psychological Examination and the School and College Ability Test in Predicting College Grade Point Averages.* Master's thesis, San Francisco State College (San Francisco, Calif.), 1959.

16. ENGELHART, MAX D. "Obtaining Comparable Scores on Two or More Tests." *Ed & Psychol Meas* 19:55–64 sp '59. * (*PA* 34:114)

17. FLEMING, W. G. *Personal and Academic Factors as Predictors of First Year Success in Ontario Universities.* Atkinson Study of Utilization of Student Resources, Report No. 5. Toronto, Canada: Department of Educational Research, Ontario College of Education, University of Toronto, 1959. Pp. xi, 137. *

18. KLUGH, HENRY E., AND BIERLEY, ROBERT. "The School and College Ability Test and High School Grades as Predictors of College Achievement." *Ed & Psychol Meas* 19:625–6 w '59. * (*PA* 34:6569)

19. LEASE, GUS C. *A Study of the Musicality, Intelligence, and Music Achievement of Vocalists and Instrumentalists in Selected High Schools.* Doctor's thesis, State University of South Dakota (Vermillion, S.D.), 1959. (*DA* 19:3631)

20. MOTT, DONALD D. *An Actuarial Study of Scores Received by High School Seniors on the Cooperative School and College Ability Test and These Students' Grades Received During the First Year of Attendance in South Dakota Colleges.* Master's thesis, South Dakota State College (Brookings, S.D.), 1959.

21. WEEKS, JAMES S. "The Predictive Validity of A.C.E. and S.C.A.T." *Personnel & Guid J* 38:52–4 S '59. *

22. WHITE, ARDEN JUNIOR. *A Comparison of the Flanagan Aptitude Classification Tests With the Wechsler Adult Intelligence Scale, the School and College Ability Test, and Three Other Measures of Mental Variables at the High School Level.* Doctor's research study No. 1, Colorado State College (Greeley, Colo.), 1959.

23. BARTLETT, CLAUDE J., AND BAUMEISTER, ALFRED A. "Prediction of Classroom Discipline Problems." *Excep Child* 27:216–8+ D '60. * (*PA* 36:4JO16B)

24. BERRY, CHARLES A., AND JONES, ARLYNNE L. "A Further Note on the Predictive Value of the National Freshman Testing Program." *Negro Ed R* 11:120–5 Jl '60. *

25. BLACK, DONALD B. "The Prediction of Freshman Success in the University of Alberta From Grade XII Departmental Results." *Alberta J Ed Res* 6:38–53 Mr '60. *

26. BUEGEL, HERMANN F. "Comparison of SCAT Scores of High School Juniors in Parochial and Public Schools." *Psychol Rep* 7:497–8 D '60. * (*PA* 35:2789)

27. CASSEL, RUSSELL N. "Expected Achievement Beta Weights on SCAT (Form 1A) for College Freshmen." *Psychol Rep* 6:401–2 Je '60. * (*PA* 35:7100)

28. DEWEES, JOSEPH P. *Predicting College Success for Freshmen at the College of the Pacific From Scores Made on the SCAT Test.* Master's thesis, College of the Pacific (Stockton, Calif.), 1960.

29. JONES, ARLYNNE LAKE. *An Investigation of the Response Patterns Which Differentiate the Performance of Selected Negro and White Freshmen on SCAT.* Doctor's thesis, University of Colorado (Boulder, Colo.), 1960. (*DA* 21:2986)

30. JUOLA, ARVO E. "Predictive Validity of Five College-Level Academic Aptitude Tests at One Institution." *Personnel & Guid J* 38:637–41 Ap '60. * (*PA* 35:2791)

31. KIMBELL, FONTELLA THOMPSON. *The Use of Selected Standardized Tests as Predictors of Academic Success at Oklahoma College for Women.* Doctor's thesis, University of Oklahoma (Norman, Okla.), 1960. (*DA* 20:4335)

32. LONG, JOHN MARSHALL. *The Prediction of College Success From a Battery of Tests and From High School Achievement.* Doctor's thesis, University of Virginia (Charlottesville, Va.), 1960. (*DA* 21:1100)

33. MILAM, OTIS H., JR., AND WARD, GEORGE, II. "The 1961–62 State College Selective Admissions Policy: Some Data." *Proc W Va Acad Sci* 32:209–13 D '60. * (*PA* 36:3KA09M, title only)

34. O'SHAUGHNESSY, MARY MICHAEL. *Some Effects of Praise and Reproof on Test Performances on School Ability and Reading Achievement Tests.* Catholic University of America, Educational Research Monograph, Vol. 24, No. 2. Washington, D.C.: Catholic University of America Press, December 2, 1960. Pp. x, 114. *

35. PIPHER, J. A. "An Appraisal of the Use of the Dominion Group Test of Learning Capacity (Advanced) in the Atkinson Study of Utilization of Student Resources." *Ont J Ed Res* 3:17–23 O '60. *

36. TEMPERO, HOWARD E., AND IVANOFF, JOHN M. "The Cooperative School and College Ability Test as a Predictor of Achievement in Selected High School Subjects." *Ed & Psychol Meas* 20:835–8 w '60. * (*PA* 35:3976)

37. TRAXLER, ARTHUR E. "Some Independent School Results on the Cooperative School and College Ability Tests, Levels 2–5." *Ed Rec B* 76:57–64 F '60. *

38. ZABEL, RONALD L. *The Determination of the Ability of the Total Score of the Cooperative School and College Ability Test, the Total Reading Comprehension Score of the Cooperative English Test, and High School Rank to Predict Scholastic Success of Freshmen at Western Illinois University.* Master's thesis, Western Illinois University (Macomb, Ill.), 1960.

39. CLYDE, ROBERT BURDETTE. *An Empirical Comparison of the School and College Ability Tests and the American Council on Education Psychological Examination.* Doctor's thesis, University of Southern California (Los Angeles, Calif.), 1961. (*DA* 22:151)

40. CURTIS, H. A., AND KROPP, R. P. "A Comparison of Scores Obtained by Administering a Test Normally and Visually." *J Exp Ed* 29:249–60 Mr '61. *

41. EELLS, KENNETH. "How Effective Is Differential Prediction in Three Types of College Curricula?" *Ed & Psychol Meas* 21:459–71 su '61. * (*PA* 36:2KJ59E)

42. GUSTAFSON, MONTY C. "Relationships Between Scholastic Aptitude Scores and Achievement of Junior College Freshmen." *Jun Col J* 32:147–50 N '61. *

43. KENNEDY, PHYLLIS E. "The Predictive Value of the College Ability Test for a Group of College Freshmen." *Calif J Ed Res* 12:174–7 S '61. *

44. LUCIER, OMER, AND FARLEY, JOHN. "The Lowry Reasoning Test Combination as a Status Free Technique." *J Social Psychol* 55:125–31 O '61. * (*PA* 36:4HB25L)

45. MANN, M. JACINTA. "The Prediction of Achievement in a Liberal Arts College." *Ed & Psychol Meas* 21:481–3 su '61. * (*PA* 36:2KL81M)

46. WAICHES, VINCENT CASIMIR. *Intellectual and Personality Changes in College Students as Measured by the Cooperative College Ability Test and the Personal Judgment Scale.* Doctor's thesis, University of Texas (Austin, Tex.), 1961. (*DA* 21:3706)

47. ZUCKOWSKY, LEO MARK. *The Efficiency of SCAT and Other Selected Variables in Predicting Success in the Various Lower Division College Curricula.* Doctor's thesis, University of Notre Dame (Notre Dame, Ind.), 1961. (*DA* 22:2297)

48. ANDERSON, SCARVIA B. *Letters to the Editor: SCAT and SAT.* Princeton, N.J.: Cooperative Test Division, 1962. Pp. 29. *

49. DARLEY, JOHN G. "The Basis for Equivalent Scores on the Annual Editions of the American Council on Education Psychological Examination (ACE), 1941 to 1954," pp. 170–83. In his *Promise and Performance: A Study of Ability and Achievement in Higher Education.* Berkeley, Calif.: Center

for Study of Higher Education, University of California, 1962. Pp. vii, 191. *
50. JOHNSON, ELMIRA LAYAGUE. *The Performance of Filipino College Freshmen on the School and College Ability Test.* Doctor's thesis, University of Wisconsin (Madison, Wis.), 1962. (*DA* 22:3922)
51. KIRK, BARBARA A.; CUMMINGS, ROGER W.; AND GOODSTEIN, LEONARD D. "The Differential Validity of the College Ability Test for Transfer Students in Six Curricular Fields." *Jun Col J* 33:131–40 O '62. *
52. LEWIS, JOHN W. "Comparing Zero-Order Correlation From SCAT Total and Multiple Correlation From SCAT Q and V at Southern Illinois University." *Ed & Psychol Meas* 22:397–8 su '62. * (*PA* 37:3870)
53. LEWIS, JOHN W. "Utilizing the Stepwise Multiple Regression Procedure in Selecting Predictor Variables by Sex Group." *Ed & Psychol Meas* 22:401–4 su '62. * (*PA* 37:3871)
54. PEARSON, MARGARET ADELLE. *The Establishment of School and College Ability Test Norms for Blind Children in Grades 4, 5, and 6.* Doctor's thesis, University of Oklahoma (Norman, Okla.), 1962. (*DA* 23:890)
55. REID, JOHN W.; JOHNSON, A. PEMBERTON; ENTWISLE, FRANK N.; AND ANGERS, WILLIAM P. "A Four-Year Study of the Characteristics of Engineering Students." *Personnel & Guid J* 41:38–43 S '62. * (*PA* 37:5655)
56. RUDD, JOHN PAUL. *A Study of the Validity of Selected Predictors for Placement in Three-Rail Curricula.* Doctor's research study No. 1, Colorado State College (Greeley, Colo.), 1962. (*DA* 24:184)
57. VICK, MARY CATHARINE, AND HORNADAY, JOHN A. "Predicting Grade Point Average at a Small Southern College." *Ed & Psychol Meas* 22:795–9 w '62. * (*PA* 37:7205)
58. CHEERS, ARLYNNE LAKE, AND SHERMAN, DOROTHY M. "Response Pattern Differences of Selected Negro and White Subjects on S.C.A.T." *Personnel & Guid J* 41:582–9 Mr '63. * (*PA* 39:1482)
59. DOLEYS, ERNEST J., AND RENZAGLIA, GUY A. "Accuracy of Student Prediction of College Grades." *Personnel & Guid J* 41:528–30 F '63. *
60. ENDLER, NORMAN S., AND STEINBERG, DANNY. "Prediction of Academic Achievement at the University Level." *Personnel & Guid J* 41:694–9 Ap '63. * (*PA* 39:2888)
61. FORTNA, RICHARD O. "A Factor-Analytic Study of the Cooperative School and College Ability Tests and Sequential Tests of Educational Progress." *J Exp Ed* 32:187–90 w '63. *
62. GOLDMAN, BERT A. "SCAT Versus WAIS: An Enigma." *J Ed Res* 57:51–3 S '63. *
63. LIGGITT, WILLIAM A. "An Evaluation of General Education in Elementary Teacher Preparation." *J Ed Res* 57:156–9 N '63. *
64. OSBORN, LYNN R. "An Analysis of the Relationship Between Speech Performance and Performance on Written Examinations of Course Content in a Beginning College Speech Course as Reflected in Assigned Grades." *Univ Kans B Ed* 17:68–71 F '63. *
65. PEARSON, MARGARET ADELLE. "The Establishment of School and College Ability Test Norms for Blind Children in Grades 4, 5, and 6." *Int J Ed Blind* 12:110–2 My '63. * (*PA* 38:1213)
66. PEMBERTON, W. A. *Ability, Values, and College Achievement.* University of Delaware Studies in Higher Education, No. 1. Newark, Del.: the University, 1963. Pp. xii, 77. * (*PA* 38:6573)
67. SARASON, IRWIN G. "Test Anxiety and Intellectual Performance." *J Abn & Social Psychol* 66:73–5 Ja '63. * (*PA* 37:5672)
68. SMITH, W. N. "Differential Prediction of Two Test Batteries." *J Ed Res* 57:39–42 S '63. *
69. SOMMERFELD, ROY E., AND TRACY, NEAL H. "A Study of Selected Predictors of Success in Second-Year Algebra in High School." *H Sch J* 46:234–40 Ap '63. *
70. TERWILLIGER, JAMES S. "Dimensions of Occupational Preference." *Ed & Psychol Meas* 23:525–42 au '63. * (*PA* 38:6698)
71. WELLCK, A. A. "Statewide Tests and Academic Success at the University of New Mexico." *Personnel & Guid J* 42:403–5 D '63. *

RUSSEL F. GREEN, *Associate Professor of Psychology, The University of Rochester, Rochester, New York.*

The SCAT series of six tests, covering grades 4 through 16, can best and most directly be described as academic aptitude tests. They were constructed specifically to "aid in estimating the capacity of a student to undertake the academic work of the next higher level of schooling." Their standardization is probably equal to that of any of their competitors and may be about as good as one can expect in a very large and relatively free society.

ETS has published some 260 pages of text and tables in nine manuals that describe SCAT's development, interpretation, uses, and statistical characteristics. Probably because ETS is attempting to write for both specialists and non-specialists, their literature is, in its entirety, somewhat confusing and in places even somewhat misleading. This confusion centers in statements of purposes, descriptions of what is measured, and, to some extent, the interpretation of test results.

In various descriptions of the purpose or function of the tests such phrases as measuring academic aptitude, estimating the capacity for academic work, predicting end-of-year grades, and "serving a function in guidance at four transitional periods" are used. Whatever phrase one chooses, he *can* use the tests to *help* make predictions about a student's probable academic performance, at least for the following two years. The validity of the tests as aids for such predictions, at least from grade 5 up, has been well demonstrated by a considerable number of research projects. Correlations between SCAT scores and either grade-point averages (GPA) or specific courses appear to be highest at about grade 7, ranging in the .70's and up for prediction of seventh grade math and English grades, and GPA. Prediction of college freshman GPA appears to range from about .4 to .6. These validities compare quite favorably with those obtained with other tests. However, two trends should be noted. The first is that the SCAT scores appear to predict academic achievement somewhat better among women than they do among men. The second is that the SCAT total score usually predicts English grades better than they are predicted by the verbal score. The quantitative score tends to predict math grades better than the SCAT total but the difference is often small and even reversed. This means that the best use of all three scores for prediction and guidance probably involves more complexity than is presented in the manuals. If it were not for trying to make more refined inferences from the "profile" than one can make from the total score, one would have no reason to get the verbal score at all. How much predictive efficiency is gained from including the verbal score in a "profile" has not been formally investigated; hence, one includes it primarily as an act of faith.

The publisher has, in various manuals, described SCAT as measuring: two kinds of school-related abilities (Q and V); four kinds of abilities (verbal comprehension, manipulating numbers and applying number concepts, comprehending the sense of a sentence read, and quantitative problems); and, finally, " 'school learned abilities' directly, rather than psychological characteristics....which afford indirect measurement of *capacity* for school learning" [italics added]. Confusion over what is measured and for what purpose stems from trying to avoid talking about specific abilities or dimensions of intellect.

ETS obtained samples of behavior on four kinds of tasks and reduced these to two subscores, Q and V. Clearly, each must be regarded as arising from a complex set of abilities. These two subscores are combined into a single score which can confidently be interpreted as a measure of "general intelligence." (General intelligence scores can probably be most clearly described as one of the important elements in the measurement of scholastic aptitude.) This point is supported by the following observations. SCAT total correlates with the *Wechsler Adult Intelligence Scale* total at about .84 and with WAIS verbal at about .88. Both of these correlations were obtained on 84 eleventh and twelfth grade boys, and, therefore, from a somewhat restricted range of ability. In large samples tested in a junior college, the correlations of SCAT with the *Otis Quick-Scoring Mental Ability Tests* were .77 and .81. Clearly there is good evidence for concurrent validity with general intelligence.

The "school learned" abilities which are measured by the various levels of the tests are not clearly and directly related to content of specific course work beyond grammar school. This is especially true of the arithmetic sections. Very little algebra appears at any level and no mathematics higher than algebra is used; in fact at level U (for grades 15 and 16) well over half the problems do not require calculations on paper. (One can presume that this last point was intentional and it clearly is desirable.) The implied proposition that advanced math courses contribute to scoring ability has to be taken on faith, since no direct evidence is presented.

The principal device used by ETS for interpreting test scores is to transform raw scores into percentile bands. The use of percentile bands is an excellent device for avoiding the tendency to regard a number as representing something exactly or precisely determined. There are difficulties, however, which the publisher has not solved as satisfactorily as one might wish. These difficulties start with one of the two statistics on which the width of the band depends, the reliability coefficient. They also involve the difficulty level of the tests and the proper use of percentile bands.

The reliability of SCAT, while probably substantial, is not known. The authors report internal consistency reliability for the total test of about .95 for each level. Since, however, the tests are speeded to an unknown extent, this estimate is high to an unknown extent. The test authors hold that the speeding that occurs is probably relatively unimportant because "all but the slowest students can complete [the tests] in the time limits allowed." However, these "slowest students" turn out to include up to 35 per cent on sentence completion, up to 20 per cent on vocabulary, up to 52 per cent on computation, and up to 40 per cent on arithmetic reasoning. How much of the failure to finish is due to time and how much due to difficulty is undetermined. Most observers would conclude that speeding could be important and should have been allowed for in the method of estimating reliability used. The estimate of the reliability affects the size of the band widths. Due to the fact that the tests are to some extent speeded, the band widths probably should be somewhat wider.

For the careful reader, the interpretations by ETS of the band widths will cause some confusion and perhaps some error, even though the kind of error involved may not be of practical importance. The difficulty comes from inconsistency in the use of bands. For a person whose band width is 82–89, it is stated in the manual that he scored lower than 11 per cent of the cases. It is also stated that students are not to be considered different unless their percentile bands do not overlap. *Less* than 11 per cent of the *bands* of other students will fail to include the 89th percentile. The 11 per cent figure comes from reverting to the counting of other students' scores as percentile *points*. Perhaps a three class interpretation would be suitable: (*a*) percentage of higher non-overlapping bands; (*b*) percentage of overlapping bands;

and (*c*) percentage of lower nonoverlapping bands. Lacking such interpretation one might better just use the simple percentile scores.

A final word about difficulty seems needed. In spite of the confusion between speed and difficulty, most of the tests may be reasonable in difficulty. However, 24 per cent of the quantitative scores of fourth graders fall in the chance range. Hence, if one wants discrimination at the low level, the test should not be used for this grade.

SUMMARY. The SCAT series, then, can be confidently regarded as a set of very good scholastic aptitude tests which probably is in most ways the equal of any of its competitors. In most ways, also, it is a good model of how such a series should be planned, developed, standardized, and validated. The most disturbing lack is that throughout all its voluminous and sometimes contradictory literature one is never given any real insight into the philosophy of measurement which guided the developers—if there really was one. We are never satisfactorily told why four "kinds" of tasks were used (even though it is apparent that three would have produced somewhat better results) to produce two scores which are associated with two "abilities"—verbal and numerical—which are, in turn, combined into a single total score which the authors seem reluctant to defend as representative of anything definite even though it is clearly defensible as an important component in "scholastic aptitude."

The nature and extent of use to which SCAT can be put will depend on the objectives that are sought through a testing program. If one is concerned with diagnosis of scholastic difficulties, the "profile" obtained from the three SCAT scores is certainly of limited, if not dubious, value. Other tests, such as SAT, will be preferred.

If, however, one is primarily concerned with prediction of general overall levels of future performance, SCAT can clearly be recommended for use from grades 5 through 16. Or if one wishes to install a system which will focus on academic aptitude while at the same time avoiding the use of IQ labels with all the potential for mischief that such labels carry, then SCAT appears to be ready made for him. It is a good general IQ test from which one cannot legitimately calculate IQ's. This may be a real virtue. We probably would be wise to deemphasize the IQ concept and, through the use of a test series such as SCAT, to emphasize instead statements of relative likelihood of success in specific situations.

For reviews by Frederick B. Davis, Hanford M. Fowler, and Julian C. Stanley of the tests for grades 4–14, see 5:322.

[453]

*__Culture Fair Intelligence Test.__ Ages 4–8 and mentally defective adults, 8–13 and average adults, grades 10–16 and superior adults; 1933–63; formerly called *Culture Free Intelligence Test;* 2 editions; Raymond B. Cattell and A. K. S. Cattell (Scales 2 and 3).

a) IPAT CULTURE FAIR INTELLIGENCE TEST. 1933–63; title on test is *Test of g: Culture Fair;* 3 levels; cash orders postpaid; Institute for Personality and Ability Testing. *

1) *Scale 1.* Ages 4–8 and mentally defective adults; 1933–62; identical with *Cattell Intelligence Tests, Scale 0: Dartington Scale;* individual in part; 1 form ('50, 12 pages); manual ('62, 14 pages, identical with manual copyrighted in 1960 except for format and one word change in text); no data on reliability; $3.50 per 25 tests; $3 per set of cards for classification test; 50¢ per scoring key; 75¢ per manual; $1.35 per specimen set; materials for following directions test must be assembled locally; (22–60) minutes.

2) *Scale 2.* Ages 8–13 and average adults; 1949–63; Forms A ('57, c1949–57), B ('61 edition, c1949–60, essentially the same as test copyrighted in 1956 except for some item and option order changes and revision in 8 items), (8 pages); Form A also available, either separately or in combination with the *Sixteen Personality Factor Questionnaire,* in a special edition ('63, 8 pages) for use with tape recorded directions; manual ('58, 35 pages); supplementary directions sheet ('60); manual ('63, 8 pages) for tape administration of Form A; $3.30 per 25 tests; separate answer sheets may be used; $2.25 per 50 answer sheets; 50¢ per either booklet or answer sheet hand scoring key; $1.60 per manual; $2.20 per specimen set; $30–$58 per examiner's kit of tape edition of Form A (includes 2 tests, 50 answer sheets, 3¾ ips tape, and manuals); 12.5(30) minutes.

3) *Scale 3.* Grades 10–16 and superior adults; 1950–63; Forms A ('63, c1950–63, identical with 1959 second edition except for printing and redrawing of some figures), B ('61, c1950–61), (8 pages); manual, 1961 edition (c1959, 51 pages); $3.30 per 25 tests; separate answer sheets may be used; $2.25 per 50 answer sheets; 50¢ per either booklet or answer sheet hand scoring key; $1.90 per manual; $2.45 per specimen set; 12.5(30) minutes.

b) CATTELL CULTURE FAIR INTELLIGENCE TEST. 1960–61; IBM; 1 form (16 pages, a single-booklet printing—labeled parts 1 and 2—of the current IPAT Forms A and B of each level); parts 1 or 2 may be administered alone although use of both parts is recommended; 2 levels; $5.75 per 35 tests; separate answer sheets may be used; 7¢ per IBM scorable answer sheet; 40¢ per scoring stencil; 75¢ per specimen set of either level; postage extra; Bobbs-Merrill Co., Inc. *

1) *Scale 2.* Ages 8–14 and average adults; 1 form ('60, c1949–60, 16 pages); manual ('60, c1949–60, 23 pages, a modification—with additional norms—for school use of the 1958 IPAT manual); 25(50) minutes for the full test.

2) *Scale 3.* Grades 9–16 and superior adults; 1 form ('61, c1950–61, 16 pages); manual ('60, c1959–60,

23 pages, a modification for school use of the 1961 IPAT manual); 25(30-60) minutes for the full test.

REFERENCES

1-2. See 4:300.
3-13. See 5:343.
14. XYDIAS, NELLY. "R. B. Cattell's Intelligence Test," pp. 333-44. In *Social Implications of Industrialization and Urbanization in Africa South of the Sahara.* Prepared under the auspices of Unesco by the International African Institute. Paris: Unesco, 1956. Pp. 743. *
15. BUSS, F. HOWARD. *The Effect of Socio-Economic Factors Upon a Culture-Bound Test and the Cattell Culture Free Test.* Master's thesis, Kent State University (Kent, Ohio), 1959.
16. CHAMBERS, JACK A. "Preliminary Screening Methods in the Identification of Intellectually Superior Children." *Excep Child* 26:145-50 N '59. * (*PA* 35:3249)
17. RODD, WILLIAM G. "A Cross-Cultural Study of Taiwan's Schools." *J Social Psychol* 50:3-36 Ag '59. * (*PA* 35:3960)
18. KIDD, ALINE HALSTEAD. *A Factor and Item Analysis of the Test of G; Culture-Free and the Stanford-Binet, Form L.* Doctor's thesis, University of Arizona (Tucson, Ariz.), 1960. (*DA* 21:366)
19. KNAPP, ROBERT R. "The Effects of Time Limits on the Intelligence Test Performance of Mexican and American Subjects." *J Ed Psychol* 51:14-20 F '60. * (*PA* 34:7395; 35:2197)
20. FARRANT, ROLAND HARVARD. *A Factor Analytic Study of the Intellective Abilities of Deaf and Hard of Hearing Children Compared With Normal Hearing Children.* Doctor's thesis, Northwestern University (Evanston, Ill.), 1961. (*DA* 22:2870)
21. BARRATT, ERNEST S.; CLARK, MARJORIE; AND LIPTON, JAMES. "Critical Flicker Frequency in Relation to Cattell's Culture Fair Intelligence Score." *Am J Psychol* 75:324-5 Je '62. * (*PA* 37:4952)
22. COOPER, JAMES G. "The Culture-Free Intelligence Test in a College of the Western Pacific." *Personnel & Guid J* 41:123-5 O '62. * (*PA* 37:5659)
23. KIDD, ALINE H. "The Culture-Fair Aspects of Cattell's Test of g: Culture-Free." *J Genetic Psychol* 101:343-62 D '62. * (*PA* 37:6702)
24. MEYERS, E.; ORPET, R. E.; ATTWELL, A. A.; AND DINGMAN, H. F. *Primary Abilities at Mental Age Six.* Monographs of the Society for Research in Child Development, Vol. 27, No. 1, Serial No. 82. Lafayette, Ind.: Child Development Publications, 1962. Pp. 40. * (*PA* 38:8462)
25. ALVI, SABIR ALI. *Traditional and "Culture Fair" Aptitude Test Performance of College Students From Different Academic and Cultural Backgrounds.* Doctor's thesis, Indiana University (Bloomington, Ind.), 1963. (*DA* 24:2775)
26. CATTELL, RAYMOND B. "Theory of Fluid and Crystallized Intelligence: A Critical Experiment." *J Ed Psychol* 54:1-22 F '63. * (*PA* 37:7991)
27. JORDHEIM, G. D., AND OLSEN, INGER A. "The Use of a Non-Verbal Intelligence Test of Intelligence in the Trust Territory of the Pacific." *Am Anthrop* 65:1122-5 O '63. *
28. MACARTHUR, R. S., AND ELLEY, W. B. "The Reduction of Socioeconomic Bias in Intelligence Testing." *Brit J Ed Psychol* 33:107-19 Je '63. * (*PA* 38:4271)

JOHN E. MILHOLLAND, *Professor of Psychology, The University of Michigan, Ann Arbor, Michigan.*

The two major claims made for these scales are that they have high saturation on general ability, *g,* and that they are relatively independent of school achievement, social advantages, and various other environmental influences. In Scale 1, however, only four of the eight subtests are represented as being fully culture free. All tests are paper and pencil tests, except Test 5 of Scale 1 which requires that the examiner have various specific objects.

The four subtests of Scale 1 which Cattell considers to be culture fair are symbol copying, classification of pictures, mazes, and identification of similar drawings. The other four tests involve selecting familiar objects when named, following directions, identifying what is wrong with pictures of familiar objects, and riddles. The room in which Scale 1 is administered should have at least one oblong table low enough for a child easily to survey the top, two additional chairs, and a door which a child can open and shut.

Scale 1 is identical with Scale 0 (Dartington Scale) of the *Cattell Intelligence Tests* and thus shares Scale 0's research basis which, according to the manual, is reported in a paper by Cattell and Bristol.[1] Scores on 18 tests, each composed of only one item type, were intercorrelated in a sample of 100 six-year-olds. Thirteen of the tests were drawn from tests in common use; the other five were devised especially for this study. The eight tests with highest mean correlations with the others were used to form the Dartington Scale. The distribution of tetrad differences for the correlation matrix had a mean of approximately zero and a quartile deviation of .04, and these data were taken as sufficient to indicate that the tests were measuring just one factor, presumably *g.* The tests now constitute Scale 1 of the culture fair tests.

The standardization for this scale was based on "more than 400 cases combining American and British samples." A table of mental age equivalents of raw scores and one for converting raw scores to IQ's are provided. A table for converting IQ's to percentile ranks is based on an IQ standard deviation of 20 points. Cattell thinks the correct standard deviation for ratio IQ's is about 25, arguing that the reduced scatter in traditional intelligence tests is due to contamination of intelligence with achievement.

Scales 2 and 3 have four subtests: Series, which requires that the examinee complete a sequence of four drawings by choosing one from among five options; Classifications, which requires that he pick out one of a set of five drawings that is different from the rest; Matrices, requiring the selection of a drawing to complete a matrix; and Conditions, which requires that the examinee select from among five drawings of overlapping geometric figures the one in which one or two dots could be placed to fit the specifications of a model. These two scales each have a Form A and a Form B (called Parts 1 and 2 in the Bobbs-Merrill single booklet edition) which are par-

1 CATTELL, RAYMOND B., AND BRISTOL, HILDA. "Intelligence Tests for Mental Ages of Four to Eight Years." *Brit J Ed Psychol* 3:142-69 Je '33.

allel in form, and if time presses only one part may be given. The authors advise against this.

The manual for Scale 2 of the Bobbs-Merrill edition recommends that users of the test construct their own norms, but nonetheless provides six tables of normative data. The only information about the standardization group is that it consisted of 4,328 boys and girls, "sampled from varied regions" of the United States and Britain. Percentile and normalized standard score IQ equivalents of raw scores for the two parts of the scale, separately and combined, are given, as well as a table of special norms (based on 14- and 15-year-olds only) for administration under unspeeded conditions and a table for converting IQ's to percentile ranks.

The norms tables for Scale 3 that appear in the Bobbs-Merrill manual are not entirely the same as those given in the 1961 IPAT Handbook. The "Usual, Routine Norm Table" in the IPAT Handbook is the same as the Bobbs-Merrill table for converting raw scores directly into IQ's, except that the former is reported to be based on 3,140 "American High School students....and young adults in a stratified job sample," while the latter is based on 3,140 high school students with no mention of the employed young adults. Both manuals contain a table for converting IQ's to standard scores and percentiles for the general adult population ($n = 1{,}788$), but the row of the IPAT table geared to an IQ standard deviation of 24 is omitted from the Bobbs-Merrill table. In both these tables there are different norms for Part 1 scores, depending on whether the examinee has had experience with the test before. A third table in each manual provides a conversion of raw scores to standard scores and percentile ranks for college students, and is based on a sample of 1,097 undergraduates, mainly sophomores, from two north central state universities, one southern university, and a medium sized private college. Finally, there is in each manual a table of age corrections after early adulthood, to be applied only to speeded administrations. The IPAT Handbook gives one additional table which does not appear in the Bobbs-Merrill manual: a "Research Norm Table" based on a sample of 3,140 high school students and young adults (presumably the same sample as the sample for the "Usual, Routine Norm Table"). The research table, however, is geared to an IQ standard deviation of 24 points, the other to one of 16 points.

The underlying rationale that it would be good to have a test as independent of circumstantial factors and as near to measuring innate ability as possible, is certainly a sound one. There are two facets to the problem: the measurement of what we think of as general intelligence, and the avoidance of cultural influences. The attainment of one objective without the other may be considerably easier than accomplishing both together. As one of the manuals states, "pictorial tests still involve cultural influence, while performance tests often avoid intelligence in avoiding culture!"

A sound rationale, however, is no guarantee of successful execution. No one yet has produced a satisfactory culture fair test, and we need to see the evidence bearing on the extent to which the Cattell test meets its goals of providing a test of *g* that is minimally susceptible to cultural influences. The manuals are woefully inadequate in meeting this requirement. The most convincing exhibit would be some factor matrices which would enable the reader to see for himself the basis for claims made. Instead, there appear only some isolated factor loadings, purporting to come from the list of references (numbering 62 in the 1961 edition of the IPAT Handbook for Scale 3). One who tries to check these data, however, is in for a frustrating experience. I was unable to locate a number of the references, and the ones I did find did not provide the information cited. For example, one paragraph which appears in the section titled "Proof of Validity, and the Correct Technical Definition of Intelligence" in both the IPAT and Bobbs-Merrill manuals for Scales 2 and 3 cites seven references as containing data in support of the correlation with *g* of the four subtests. I was able to examine five of these references and in none of them did I find any evidence of the *g* saturation of the tests. (One of the cited references, in fact, is I. Macfarlane Smith's review in the Fifth Yearbook and the only data cited in it are from the test manual. This kind of research referencing seems a bit circular.)

The foregoing indicates that one must not be overwhelmed by the array of references cited in the text of the manuals. The necessity (and sometimes, the impossibility) of tracking down each citation also makes it hard on the conscientious reviewer. This reviewer strongly urges that diligent editing be applied to these manuals.

The picture is not completely dark, however. Cattell (*26*) has recently published a factor analytic study to test his hypothesis that *g* may be separated into "fluid" and "crystallized" intelligence. He believes that fluid intelligence is closer to unadulterated *g* and that the culture fair test should load on it. Included in the test battery in this study were two forms of the *SRA Primary Mental Abilities* (verbal, spatial, number, reasoning, fluency) and two forms of the *IPAT High School Personality Questionnaire* with 14 scores on each form. Subjects were 277 seventh and eighth graders. Two second-order factors were interpreted as fluid and crystallized intelligence. The loadings for the culture fair subtests on the fluid factor were: Series, .35; Classification, .63; Matrices, .50; and Conditions, .51. The only other substantial loading on this factor was .32 for the PMA spatial subtest. The PMA V, R, and N and the culture fair Series subtest also loaded on crystallized intelligence. These results are consonant with Cattell's hypothesis, but hardly enough to convince a skeptic that the factor underlying the culture fair test is *g*.

It must be acknowledged that the demonstration of freedom from culture bias is very tricky. The manuals have cited a few cross cultural studies, but most of them are not readily available in the literature. Again, one must be prepared to be unimpressed by the citations of references. For example, the following statement appears in the IPAT manual for Scale 3: "In the originally reported research....the CF test was administered to foreign language immigrants to the USA at the time of entry and again after some degree of acclimation." In the study cited, the immigrants were tested after living approximately 14 months in this country and then retested after 77 more days. After the estimated gain attributable to practice effects with the test was taken out, the following standard score gains were recorded: Binet, .45; Culture Fair, .17; Arthur, .09; ACE, .13; and Ferguson formboards, −.14. These results hardly seem to furnish definitive evidence of the outstanding freedom from culture effects of the culture fair test.

The manuals are deficient in other respects, being long on theoretical discussion and short on precise and definite information about the tests themselves. It seems a shame that a test that has been in published form for so long should still be criticized for lack of satisfactory manuals, but the necessary research to support the claims made for the Cattell tests either has not been done or has not been thoroughly and clearly presented in the manuals.

Culture fair tests would seem to have possibilities for great usefulness on the current scene, now that we are getting more and more concerned about culturally deprived segments of our population. Not only would it be eminently desirable to locate persons of high intelligence who did not show up well on our conventional tests, but it would be a good thing to have a fair assessment of everyone's potential regardless of the level at which he could eventually function. I would need to see some real longitudinal validity data before I could become convinced that the Cattell culture fair tests are suitable for this job. On the other hand, it seems to me they show promise, and I would like to see the research undertaken that would evaluate them.

ABRAHAM J. TANNENBAUM, *Associate Dean, Graduate School of Education, Yeshiva University, New York, New York.*

The IPAT is offered as a culture fair test of intelligence, a tool that enables psychometrists to depart from allegedly antiquated practices in mental measurement. Its design is based on Cattell's (*26*) theory of fluid general ability in contrast to the traditional concepts of crystallized intelligence. The two characterizations of mental activity differ in a variety of ways:

a) Crystallized intelligence (g_c) is reflected in cognitive performance that has become patterned through earlier learning experiences. Fluid ability (g_f), on the other hand, manifests itself through adaptive mental behavior in situations so unfamiliar that previously learned skills can be of no help in guiding such behavior.

b) Diversity in cultural interests and opportunities produces more individual differences in g_c than in g_f, even before biological maturity (age 15–25) has been reached.

c) Both types of ability reach their growth peaks at different ages, g_f leveling off sometime in early adolescence, while g_c may continue to grow in late adolescence and early adulthood, depending on the length of participation in cultural pursuits.

d) Standardized tests measuring g_c show a much smaller sigma than does a test like IPAT, measuring g_f. The reason is that in a given subculture the previous learning experiences which strongly influence g_c scores are so circumscribed that they tend to reduce the variance at a given age level. One example of the restrictive nature of learning activity may be found in the typical classroom where a wide range of potential is funneled into narrow-range performance as bright pupils are restrained from moving ahead and dull pupils are pushed to achieve more than they can.

e) With g_f rooted relatively more in heredity and physiology and g_c based relatively more on environment and experience, the latter type of measure will show greater fluctuation in test norms over the years.

In order to achieve cultural fairness, the IPAT tests were constructed to include mostly nonsense material, universally unfamiliar, and some commonplace material, universally familiar. The effects of special previous training could, therefore, not be transferred to the problems posed in these instruments, and the supposedly contaminating effects of social class, ethnicity, and even nationality on test results are said to be filtered out.

Scale 1 was restandardized after 1960 on a sample of under 500 cases drawn from America and Great Britain. Although larger than previous standardizing samples, the current group is still quite small, and there is no information provided on the size of the various age subgroups. It is interesting to note, however, that no difference was found between the American and British subsamples at any age level. Also, the age plots from 3½ to 12 years reportedly "show internal consistency and smooth progression," although no statistical evidence is presented to support these observations. Nor does the 1962 Handbook include data relating to the vital matters of reliability and validity. It is therefore difficult to assess the value of Scale 1 until the Handbook's assurance that "a more extensive standardization is in progress" results in a detailed report.

Scale 2 was standardized on 4,328 subjects from various parts of Great Britain and the U.S.A. No breakdown by age is noted. Scale 3 was standardized on 3,140 American youth divided equally among high school freshmen, sophomores, juniors, and seniors, and "young adults in a stratified job sample."

Evidence of validity is impressive, as far as it goes. Subtest correlations with Spearman's *g* (general mental capacity) range from .53 to .99 on American samples and from .78 to .83 on French samples. Full test correlations are reported on the order of .59 with the ACE, .84 with the Wechsler-Bellevue, anywhere from .56 to .85 with the Stanford-Binet, and an average of .73 with the Otis group test.

Evidence on the validity of the test in predicting scholastic achievement is not impressive. One study reports a correlation of .36 with the *Stanford Achievement Test* as against a Stanford-Binet correlation of .25 with the same measure. However, the sample was not only small in size ($n = 28$) but restricted in ability range, the group consisting of pupils in summer school, half of whom were making up academic deficiencies. Additional evidence taken from small samples shows that the IPAT tends to predict achievement test scores better than does the Otis. Other than these scant bits of information the only comment in the manuals on predictive validity is a speculative one to the effect that a culture fair test might have done a better job than conventional IQ measures in forecasting future accomplishment for such "late bloomers" as Darwin, Winston Churchill, and the Wright brothers.

Both Scales 2 and 3 show moderate internal consistency. Split-half and test-retest coefficients exceeded .80 in most samples tested. The author, however, urges the use of both forms in order to obtain more valid and reliable results.

Since the IPAT is designed to be culture fair, one basic question is whether it succeeds in eliminating the so-called contaminating effects of culture. At best, one can only answer that the success is partial. On the credit side, the manuals refer to studies showing that test norms for Taiwan and France did not differ from our own. On the other hand, mention is made of findings that detect norm differences between Indian and British-American populations; between Belgian Congo and American groups; and between Puerto Rican immigrants to America and native born Americans. Moreover, there is reference to data revealing a positive correlation between IPAT scores and socioeconomic status in this country.

In essence, then, it must be admitted that the long-pursued goal of demonstrating equality among national and international subpopulations on some measure of general ability has not been reached by this test. Is it, indeed, a goal worth pursuing? Even if it were possible to devise a test so antiseptic as to clean out inequality not only among subcultures but also among other groups showing differences in test intelligence, such as those classified by sex, age, education, geographic origin, body type, physical health, personality structure, and family unity—what kind of instrument would we then have? Since such a test must perforce be so thoroughly doctored as to omit tasks that reveal these group differences, or substitute others that show "no difference," what could it possibly measure? What could it predict? Covering up group differences in this way does not erase test bias. Rather, it delimits drastically the kinds of information one can gather about problem solving strengths and weaknesses associated with groups as well as individuals.[1]

It might be argued that the effort to eliminate cultural bias in the IPAT is only derivative of an attempt to assess latent potential rather than learned skills. This is, after all, a test designed to measure fluid, not crystallized, intelligence, and the assumption is that although there may be *individual* differences in fluid intelligence, *group* differences are unthinkable except to a racist. It should be borne in mind, however, that the concept of fluid intelligence is predicated on the belief that ability is fixed and its growth predetermined. It assumes that nature and nurture are *additive* components contributing to human behavior. Recent commentary on the subject, however, marshals considerable evidence to suggest that the two elements may be *interactive* instead.[2] A valuable encounter with environment enriches mental functioning just as proper nutrients contribute to physical development. It is quite possible that heredity and environment *affect each other* in setting the growth limits in both instances. There is even reason to believe that experiential impoverishment early in life inhibits intellectual growth regardless of how much compensatory experience may be supplemented in later years. It is therefore by no means certain that any test of latent potential can obtain a score that is free of cultural "contamination" if the very essence it purports to measure may itself be so "contaminated."

In the last analysis, a test of intelligence must provide practical insights. The emphasis in the IPAT is on the location of "hidden potential" or "real capacity." If such exists in the fixed, pure sense as assumed by the test authors, it should be possible to forecast accomplishment by combining test data with an analysis of the learning environment. Or, it could have predictive validity in circumstances where it is possible to control human experience and opportunity. This has yet to be tested. Until such an evaluation is made, one is forced to suspend endorsement of the IPAT and of its underlying theory of fluid ability.

1 Lorge, Irving. "Difference or Bias in Tests of Intelligence." *Proc Inv Conf Testing Probl* 1952:76–83 '53. *
2 Hunt, J. McV. *Intelligence and Experience.* New York: Ronald Press Co., 1961. Pp. ix, 416. * (*PA* 36:4AD16H)

For a review by I. Macfarlane Smith of the IPAT edition, see 5:343; for reviews by Raleigh M. Drake and Gladys C. Schwesinger, see 4:300.

[454]

★**The D48 Test.** Grades 5 and over; 1963, c1961–63; translation of the French edition published in 1948; for research use only; 1 form ('61, 10 pages); preliminary manual ['63, 12 pages]; American norms for grades 5–6 only; separate answer sheets must be used; $5.25 per 25 tests; $2.20 per 50 answer sheets; $1.50 per set of hand scoring stencils and manual; postage extra; specimen set not available; 25(35) minutes; translation and American manual by John D. Black; Consulting Psychologists Press, Inc. *

REFERENCES

1. Keehn, J. D., and Prothro, E. Terry. "Non-Verbal Tests as Predictors of Academic Success in Lebanon." *Ed & Psychol Meas* 15:495–8 w '55. * (*PA* 30:7765)
2. Cronholm, Borje, and Schalling, Daisy. "Intellectual Deterioration After Focal Brain Injury." *Arch Surgery* 86:670–87 Ap '63. *
3. Gough, Harrison G., and Domino, George. "The D 48 Test as a Measure of General Ability Among Grade School Children." *J Consult Psychol* 27:344–9 Ag '63. * (*PA* 38:2667)

Paul C. Davis, *Dean and Professor of Psychology, Los Angeles Pacific College, Los Angeles, California.*

The *D48 Test* consists of pictured arrangements containing from 4 to 14 dominoes. The examinee's task is to determine the numbers of dots that should be in the blank domino in each arrangement in order for it to fit correctly into the set or series shown. The examinee is provided with an answer sheet showing the arrangement of dominoes for each item but without dots. He writes the correct numbers in the two halves of the domino shown in dotted outline. Time for the test, after instructions and sample items, is 25 minutes.

The test is simple in format, easy to administer and score, and is apparently homogeneous in content, although one who is multiple-factor oriented may suspect the presence of much more complexity than Vernon found in his bifactor analysis (loading of .87 in *g*).

Gough and Domino (*3*) emphasize the familiarity of many cultures with dominoes and identify the D48 as an approach to culture free testing involving general *familiarity* rather than *unfamiliarity* with the medium. In this same connection the test is recommended as "almost entirely non-verbal." In view of the extensive verbal directions and the importance of the testee's *understanding* the samples and requirements of the test, it is the reviewer's attitude that more than opinion is needed before the nonverbal characterization can be accepted.

The test's validity as an instrument for estimating intellectual level or predicting achievement has been explored. Gough and Domino summarized the results of French, Belgian, Italian, and American studies involving testing of a total of some 3,000 persons from about age 10 to adulthood. This summary indicates that (*a*) for the same age and educational level, mean scores tend to be similar in different countries; (*b*) there tends to be a steady upward progression in mean scores with age and educational level; (*c*) overall results show no consistent sex difference in mean score; and (*d*) studies of fifth and sixth grade American students ($n = 86$) showed that the test predicted total GPA well; in fact, approximately as well as does previous year GPA.

According to the test manual two studies of reliability have been reported. Odd-even reliability of .89 was obtained while a test-retest reliability study yielded a correlation of .69. Item difficulty has also been studied by Gough and Domino. They found the items generally to be in ascending order of difficulty, but report some apparent misplacements of items; e.g., item 22 is one of the most difficult while item 33 is passed by more than half of the group. They also found that difficulties are similar among the different populations reported.

SUMMARY. The *D48 Test* is a simple instrument that offers encouraging possibilities. Foreign administration plus administration to limited groups of American children suggests that the test may be a good predictor of academic achievement. It appears to be adequately reliable and mean scores appear to increase methodically with age and educational level. While percentile norms for various age groups based on data from French studies are given in the manual, the D48 is, for American users, essentially an experimental instrument. It is hoped that norms for American populations may soon be forthcoming.

S. S. DUNN, *Assistant Director, Australian Council for Educational Research, Hawthorn, Victoria, Australia.*

The manual for the *D48 Test* contains the following notice: "This test is for experimental use only: adequate normative and validity data on United States populations are *not* available."

The test was developed by the staff of the Centre de Psychologie Appliquée in France, based on the British Army Dominoes Test prepared by Anstey. The manual contains some information of French origin as well as "one study based on fifth and sixth graders in a California school and one report of means and sigmas on a group of American college students." The comments which follow are based on the material given in the American manual which has been adapted from the French.

The directions for administration allow great freedom to the examiner. He is told that it is his responsibility to see that the testee understands all four examples. For those who prefer to use them, verbatim instructions are included. In the opinion of the reviewer, understanding by testees is more likely to come from a carefully prepared standard set of directions than from allowing too great freedom to examiners.

The answer sheet repeats the pattern of the domino boxes with a domino space for the answer outlined in broken lines. This may help people of limited ability, but no reason is given for using this layout, which requires two pages and a more complicated scoring key, rather than a one-page answer sheet giving the answer space only.

The section on development gives some background history. It also contains a paragraph beginning "Research has demonstrated that:" followed by three statements. For the first statement no research evidence is given, the second finishes with a sentence beginning "Experience has shown that," and the third has nothing to do with research, but is merely a statement that the D48, being an open-ended test, is not subject to guessing answers by chance.

The evidence of difficulty in Table 1, based on California children, suggests that before the test is distributed in the United States, further testing is warranted to check the order of difficulty of questions. Several items (17, 18, 22, 24, and 25) seem badly misplaced.

The data on reliability show a satisfactory split-half reliability ($r = .89$), but a relatively low test-retest figure ($r = .69$) after a time interval of two months. The standard deviations of this group do not appear unduly restricted.

The validity data given are mostly of French

origin and not of a kind likely to be useful to an American user. A reference is made to the use of the test in the measurement of mental deterioration. Two references in French are given to deterioration studies.

Until the publishers produce evidence that this test is equal or superior to the many nonverbal tests published in the United States, it has little to commend it for use in guidance situations. The fact that it is a test of a single item type may make it useful for certain factor analytic studies.

[455]

★Deeside Non-Verbal Reasoning Test: English-Welsh Bilingual Version. Ages 10–12; 1961–63; 2 forms: test 1 ('61), test 2 ('63), (16 pages); separate mimeographed manuals for test 1 ['61, 17 pages], test 2 ['63, 19 pages]; distribution restricted to directors of education; 25*s.* per 25 tests; 7*s.* 6*d.* per manual; postage and purchase tax extra; 37–38(60) minutes; W. G. Emmett; George G. Harrap & Co. Ltd. *

[456]

***Doppelt Mathematical Reasoning Test.** Grades 16–17 and employees; 1954–63; IBM; Form A ('54, 4 pages); manual ('58, 10 pages); bulletin of information ('63, 36 pages); revised procedures for testing center operation ('63, 8 pages); distribution restricted and test administered at specified licensed university centers; scoring and reporting handled by the local center; examination fee to centers: $1 per examinee; fees to examinees are determined locally and include reporting of scores to the examinee and to 3 institutions or companies designated at the time of testing; additional score reports may be secured from the publisher at a fee of $1 each; 50(60) minutes; Jerome E. Doppelt; Psychological Corporation. *

REFERENCES

1. SCHWARTZ, MILTON M., AND CLARK, F. EUGENE. "Prediction of Success in Graduate School at Rutgers University." *J Ed Res* 53:109–11 N '59. * (*PA* 35:1223)
2. ROEMMICH, HERMAN. "The Doppelt Mathematical Reasoning Test as a Selection Device for Graduate Engineering Students." *Ed & Psychol Meas* 21:1009–10 w '61. *

W. V. CLEMANS, *Director, Test Department, Science Research Associates, Inc., Chicago, Illinois.*

The *Doppelt Mathematical Reasoning Test* contains 50 problems that differ from the usual pattern for multiple choice questions in that there are no stems. The task facing the examinee is defined once for the entire set in the directions which state:

> Each problem in this test consists of five mathematical figures or expressions. Four of these have something in common which is not shared by the remaining one. You are to choose the *one* figure or expression which does *not* belong with the other four and mark the letter corresponding to your choice in the proper place on the answer sheet.

None of the problems involves mathematics beyond the usual secondary school level. The test can be easily administered to large groups or to individuals.

The manual states that the test "was designed primarily as an aid in the selection of students for graduate work" and that it "may also be useful in the classification and assignment of college graduates applying for positions in industry which require mathematical reasoning."

Correlations of the DMRT with faculty ratings or grades for three groups of 41, 57, and 109 graduate students taking mathematics suggest that the test may have some value for selecting graduate students. The coefficients obtained were .52, .71, and .43, respectively. Similar coefficients are reported for 28 graduate students in chemistry and 26 undergraduates in a psychometrics course, but a coefficient of only .32 was found for 29 medical students. This latter finding is hardly significant, but is the only coefficient reported for a criterion group whose course work is not primarily quantitative. The Psychological Corporation supplies summaries of five studies reported by independent investigators that tend to corroborate the claim that the test relates to measures of success in graduate study in mathematics or statistics. Apparently no systematic approach has been made to determining how valuable the test is for graduate students in other areas. Validity data for industrial criteria have not yet been supplied.

In the norms section of the manual percentile equivalents are given for five small student samples ranging in size from 102 to 145 students selected from 15 colleges and universities. The groups consisted of senior psychology students, medical students, psychology majors, education majors, and graduate students taking courses in statistics. Percentile equivalents are also given for a group of 388 engineers from one industrial organization.

Reliability coefficients were computed for each of the six groups using the odd-even approach and the Spearman-Brown formula. The coefficients range from .78 to .85. The author points out that the lowest values were found for the most homogeneous groups. He fails to point out, however, that the three groups yielding the highest reliability coefficients (all .85) not only had the largest standard deviations but also the lowest means. This phenomenon suggests to this reviewer that the higher values may have been due to speededness. The author claims that the time limit is adequate for most examinees to finish, but no data are supplied to indicate what is meant by "most" or how the different "norm" groups fared in this regard.

Several correlation coefficients obtained between the DMRT and other tests are given. Nine coefficients are given for the DMRT and the *Miller Analogies Test.* The median value is .34. Only one study is reported correlating the DMRT with the *Minnesota Engineering Analogies Test.* The coefficient is .71 and was obtained on 132 employed engineers. This value is exceptionally high considering the fact that the reliability for the DMRT obtained on a similar group of employed engineers is only .78.

In summary, five points should be stressed. First, claims are made for the test which could produce misleading impressions. Second, considering its reliability, the test is very highly related to the *Minnesota Engineering Analogies Test.* Third, norms are limited. Fourth, quantitative information on speededness for reliability samples is not given. Finally, no validity data are given for one suggested use of the test (classification in industry). It must be concluded that if this test is a gem, it is an unpolished one.

[457]

***Figure Reasoning Test: A Non-Verbal Intelligence Test, Second Edition.** Ages 10 and over; 1949–62; 1 form ('62, 55 pages, identical with 1949 edition except for format); manual ('62, 15 pages, 1949 norms remain unchanged); separate answer sheets must be used; 4*s.* 6*d.* per test; 1*s.* 6*d.* per manual (free with 20 tests); postage extra; answer sheets must be duplicated and scoring stencils constructed locally; 30(40) minutes; John C. Daniels; Crosby Lockwood & Son, Ltd. *

A. W. HEIM, *Medical Research Council, The Psychological Laboratory, University of Cambridge, Cambridge, England.*

This test is described, on its cover and in its manual, as "a non-verbal intelligence test." As with other tests so designated, this signifies a test with a strong visual (diagrammatic) bias. It consists of 45 test items and 6 preliminary examples, every one of which is of the same form. In the top half of the page is a large square containing two rows of three diagrams and one row of two diagrams; in the lower half of the page are two rows of three diagrams, one and only one of which correctly completes the third row in the top half of the page. The subject's task is to select the appropriate one of these six diagrams.

The test is distinguishable from the *Progressive Matrices* in three respects: (*a*) the test booklet is much smaller; (*b*) the subject is required to make his selection always from six alternatives (Sets C to E in *Progressive Matrices* offer eight alternative solutions); and (*c*) preliminary examples are given. Apart from these differences the two tests are remarkably similar both in the drawing of the diagrams and the principles employed. These principles include addition, subtraction, deletion, superimposition, and progressions of various kinds.

For the reviewer, these intelligence tests whose questions all have the same bias and whose questions, moreover, all take identical form, have "face-monotony." The manual suggests, however, that the *Figure Reasoning Test* has good validity (reaching .93, not surprisingly, when correlated with *Progressive Matrices,* and only slightly lower coefficients when compared with other well known tests such as the WISC) and high consistency—whether the criterion chosen be split-half (.96) or test-retest with an interval of one year (.89). The test author writes also of the "information that has been gathered on the *Figure Reasoning Test's* predictive efficiency when used for specific educational purposes." But having thus whetted our curiosity he does nothing further in the manual to allay it.

It seems to the reviewer that Daniels makes a bid, on two occasions in the manual, to have things both ways. First, he describes the test as "a measure of 'non-verbal' intelligence" (p. 12)—and, indeed, there is not one word in the test itself. Yet, later (p. 14) he writes that subjects "have to solve these problems by the use of fairly complex language skills" and that they "will be required to undertake fairly complex, theoretical, and therefore to a degree, verbal tasks." It is, of course, perfectly possible to engage in "complex, theoretical" problem solving without the use of words: examples of this may be found in mathematics, for instance. Secondly, he gives a table for converting test scores into standard scores with mean 100 and standard deviation 15, which "to all intents and purposes, we can treat....as if they were IQ's." It is as though Daniels wishes to claim the benefit of the IQ umbrella whilst disclaiming responsibility for the holes in the fabric which he and others have observed.

The manual gives the impression of having

been got out rather on the cheap: no frequency distribution curves are shown and no headings are given for the second page of the conversion table—which renders it slow to read. The text has not been carefully checked: for example, the second "C" on page 10 should read "E"; the answer to the fifth preliminary example is not given; and the fact that the phrase "Modern views" on page 14 is followed by a singular rather than a plural verb adds to the considerable confusion of the long sentence in question. The actual printing in the test occasionally leaves something to be desired, notably for items 11, 30, 32, and 43.

It is not possible for a 17-year-old (or older) to gain an IQ on this test of more than 128, even if he gets right all 45 items; nor is it possible for a 10-year-old to gain an IQ of less than 66, even if his score be zero. A score of 8, i.e., around chance, gained by a 10-year-old who tackles every question gives him an IQ of 81. The time limit is described by Daniels as generous.

Despite these objections, the test may well be useful in certain circumstances. The booklet is exceptionally small, lightweight, and neat; the actual testing time is only 30 minutes; the question of item order has been carefully considered, and the cogency of most of the items is beyond reproach. As stated above, the test fulfils the necessary conditions of consistency and of validity based on other standard tests and also on factorial analysis criteria. This is more than can be said for many of the current paper and pencil tests of intelligence.

For reviews by E. J. G. Bradford and James Maxwell, see 4:291 (1 excerpt).

[458]

***General Verbal Practice Tests.** Ages 10 to 11-11; 1954-61; to be given at least 3 weeks before administering a verbal intelligence test in order to equalize coaching effects; keys are not provided since scoring of the test is not recommended; 3 forms; distribution restricted to directors of education; 8*d.* per manual for any one test; prices include purchase tax; postage extra; published for the National Foundation for Educational Research in England and Wales; Newnes Educational Publishing Co. Ltd. *

a) GENERAL VERBAL PRACTICE TEST G1. 1954; test (8 pages); manual (4 pages); 8*s.* per 12 tests; 9*d.* per single copy; 45(50) minutes.

b) GENERAL VERBAL PRACTICE TEST G2. 1959; test (4 pages); manual (4 pages); 5*s.* per 12 tests; 6*d.* per single copy; 25(30) minutes.

c) GENERAL VERBAL PRACTICE TEST G3. 1961; test (6 pages); manual (4 pages); 8*s.* per 12 tests; 9*d.* per single copy; 30(35) minutes.

[459]

★Gestalt Continuation Test. Illiterate and semi-literate Bantu industrial workers; 1960-63; experimental form; administered orally or in pantomime; Forms A ('62), B ('63), C ('63), (1 page); manual ('63, 11 pages); no norms; R5.00 per 100 tests; R.40 per specimen set of all 3 forms; postage extra; a demonstration sheet for group administration is also available; [5-10] minutes; H. Hector; National Institute for Personnel Research. *

REFERENCES

1. HECTOR, H. "Results From a Simple Gestalt Continuation Test Applied to Illiterate Black Mineworkers." *J Nat Inst Personnel Res* 8:145-7 D '60. * (*PA* 35:4858)
2. TEKANE, I. "A New and Objective Scoring Method for the Gestalt Continuation Test." *J Nat Inst Personnel Res* 8:148-50 D '60. * (*PA* 35:4864)
3. MUNDY-CASTLE, A. C., AND NELSON, G. K. "A Neuropsychological Study of the Knysna Forest Workers." *Psychologia Africana* 9:240-72 '62. * (*PA* 37:4822)

[460]

***Goodenough-Harris Drawing Test.** Ages 3-15; 1926-63; revision and extension of the *Goodenough Intelligence Test;* 1 form ('63, 4 pages); manual ('63, 80 pages, reprinted from *135* below); quality scale cards ('63, 24 cards); $3 per 35 tests; $2.50 per set of quality scale cards; $1 per manual; postage extra; (15-20) minutes; Florence L. Goodenough and Dale B. Harris; Harcourt, Brace & World, Inc. *

REFERENCES

1-60. See 4:292.
61-94. See 5:335.
95. SILVER, ARCHIE A. "Diagnostic Value of Three Drawing Tests for Children." *J Pediatrics* 37:129-43 Jl '50. * (*PA* 25:3191)
96. UTSUGI, ETSUKO, AND OHTSUKI, KATSUKO. "A Study on the Human Figure Drawing of Children." *Tohoku Psychologica Folia* 14:131-45 '54-55. * (*PA* 30:1067)
97. EISEN, VIRGINIA W. *Comparison of Human Figure Drawings by Behavior Problem and Normal Control Boys.* Doctor's thesis, Fordham University (New York, N.Y.), 1956.
98. PHATAK, PRAMILA. "Draw-A-Man Test: Survey of Investigations." *Indian J Psychol* 31:31-40 Ja-Je '56. * (*PA* 32:5522)
99. GROSS, DEAN G. *An Experiment With the Columbia Mental Maturity Scale and the Goodenough Draw-A-Man Test to Determine Their Utility as Testing Devices for the Severely Mentally Retarded as Compared to the Stanford-Binet.* Master's thesis, San Francisco State College (San Francisco, Calif.), 1958.
100. COLEMAN, J. M.; ISCOE, IRA; AND BRODSKY, MARVIN. "The 'Draw-A-Man' Test as a Predictor of School Readiness and as an Index of Emotional and Physical Maturity." *Pediatrics* 24:275-81 Ag '59. *
101. HARRIS, DALE B. "A Note on Some Ability Correlates of the Raven Progressive Matrices (1947) in the Kindergarten." *J Ed Psychol* 50:228-9 O '59. * (*PA* 36:1FE28H)
102. HENDERSON, KENT. "Objective Evaluation of a Remotivation Project on a Deteriorated Ward of Mental Hospital Patients." *Ont Hosp Psychol B* 5:4-9 D '59. *
103. LEVINSON, BORIS M. "A Comparison of the Performance of Bilingual and Monolingual Native Born Jewish Preschool Children of Traditional Parentage on Four Intelligence Tests." *J Clin Psychol* 15:74-6 Ja '59. * (*PA* 34:2729)
104. MITCHELL, ANNA CARR. "A New Maximum CA for the Draw-A-Man Test." *J Consult Psychol* 23:555-7 D '59. * (*PA* 34:5586)
105. PHATAK, PRAMILA. "Application of Phatak's Draw-A-Man Scale for Indian Children of Gujarat." *Psychol Studies* 4:45-54 Jl '59. *
106. POPPLESTONE, JOHN A. "Clinical Status and the Draw-A-Man Test: Congruence and Divergence." *Percept & Motor Skills* 9:131-3 Je '59. * (*PA* 38:4281)
107. RICHEY, MARJORIE H., AND SPOTTS, JAMES V. "The Relationship of Popularity to Performance on the Goodenough Draw-A-Man Test." *J Consult Psychol* 23:147-50 Ap '59. * (*PA* 34:1414)
108. ARMON, VIRGINIA. "Some Personality Variables in Overt Female Homosexuality." *J Proj Tech* 24:292-309 S '60. * (*PA* 35:818)
109. DENNIS, WAYNE. "The Human Figure Drawings of Bedouins." *J Social Psychol* 52:209-19 N '60. * (*PA* 35:4758)
110. KOPPITZ, ELIZABETH MUNSTERBERG. "Teacher's Attitude and Children's Performance on the Bender Gestalt Test and Human Figure Drawings." *J Clin Psychol* 16:204-8 Ap '60. * (*PA* 36:2HE04K)
111. MAGNUSSON, DAVID. "Some Personality Tests Applied

on Identical Twins." *Scandinavian J Psychol* 1(2):55–61 '60. * (*PA* 35:6424)
112. STEER, M. D., AND DREXLER, HAZEL G. "Predicting Later Articulation Ability From Kindergarten Tests." *J Speech & Hearing Disorders* 25:391–7 N '60. * (*PA* 35:3911)
113. TOBIAS, JACK, AND GORELICK, JACK. "The Utility of the Goodenough Scale in the Appraisal of Retarded Adults." *Am J Mental Def* 65:64–8 Jl '60. * (*PA* 35:3792)
114. WARREN, SUE ALLEN, AND COLLIER, HERBERT L. "Suitability of the Columbia Mental Maturity Scale for Mentally Retarded Institutionalized Females." *Am J Mental Def* 64:916–20 Mr '60. * (*PA* 35:6846)
115. WEST, JOHN HAMILTON. "Correlates of the Draw-A-Scene Test." *J Clin Psychol* 16:44–5 Ja '60. * (*PA* 36:1HB44W)
116. ESTES, BETSY WORTH; CURTIN, MARY ELLEN; DEBURGER, ROBERT A.; AND DENNY, CHARLOTTE. "Relationships Between 1960 Stanford-Binet, 1937 Stanford-Binet, WISC, Raven, and Draw-A-Man." *J Consult Psychol* 25:388–91 O '61. *
117. HANNA, RALPH; COLEMAN, JAMES M.; ISCOE, IRA; KELTON, W. W.; PRICE, P. CLIFT; SEDBERRY, MILES E.; AND WEIR, MORTON W. "'Draw-A-Man' Test." *Tex State J Med* 57:707–11 Ag '61. *
118. HIRSCHENFANG, SAMUEL. "A Comparison of the Revised Columbia Mental Maturity Scale (CMMS) and Goodenough Draw-A-Man Test in Children With Speech Disorders." *J Clin Psychol* 17:381–2 O '61. * (*PA* 38:8918)
119. ISARD, ELEANORE S., AND LASKY, DAVID I. "A Discrepancy Score Method in Predicting Scholastic Achievement of College Freshmen Counseled During Probation." *Personnel & Guid J* 39:725–8 My '61. * (*PA* 36:1KL25I)
120. LESSING, ELISE ELKINS. "A Note on the Significance of Discrepancies Between Goodenough and Binet IQ Scores." *J Consult Psychol* 25:456–7 O '61. * (*PA* 37:3130)
121. NIELSEN, HELLE H. "Human Figure Drawings by Normal and Physically Handicapped Children: Draw-A-Person Test." *Scandinavian J Psychol* 2(3):129–38 '61. *
122. PHATAK, P. "Comparative Study of Revised Draw-A-Man Scale (Harris) and Phatak Draw-A-Man Scale for Indian Children." *Psychol Studies* 6:12–7 Jl '61. * (*PA* 38:2674)
123. SINGH, BALWANT. "Development of Visuo-Motor Capacities in Children from 6–11 Years." Abstract of master's thesis. *Brit J Ed Psychol* 31:299–302 N '61. *
124. THOMAS, R. MURRAY, AND SJAH, ANWAR. "The Draw-A-Man Test in Indonesia." *J Ed Psychol* 52:232–5 O '61. * (*PA* 38:2678)
125. CARKHUFF, ROBERT R. "The Goodenough Draw-A-Man Test as a Measure of Intelligence in Noninstitutionalized Subnormal Adults." Abstract. *J Consult Psychol* 26:476 O '62. *
126. CARNEY, RICHARD E., AND TROWBRIDGE, NORMA. "Intelligence Test Performance of Indian Children as a Function of Type of Test and Age." *Percept & Motor Skills* 14:511–4 Je '62. * (*PA* 37:2830)
127. CLAWSON, AILEEN. "Relationship of Psychological Tests to Cerebral Disorders in Children: A Pilot Study." *Psychol Rep* 10:187–90 F '62. * (*PA* 37:1655)
128. GILBERT, JEANNE G., AND HALL, MARION R. "Changes With Age in Human Figure Drawing." *J Gerontol* 17:397–404 O '62. * (*PA* 37:4775)
129. LINDNER, RONALD S. *The Goodenough Draw-A-Man Test: Its Relationship to Intelligence, Achievement, and Cultural Variables of Negro Elementary School Children in the Southeast United States.* Doctor's thesis, Florida State University (Tallahassee, Fla.), 1962. (*DA* 23:703)
130. ROHRS, FREDERICK W., AND HAWORTH, MARY R. "The 1960 Stanford-Binet, WISC, and Goodenough Tests With Mentally Retarded Children." *Am J Mental Def* 66:853–9 My '62. * (*PA* 37:1704)
131. VANE, JULIA R., AND EISEN, VIRGINIA W. "The Goodenough Draw-A-Man Test and Signs of Maladjustment in Kindergarten Children." *J Clin Psychol* 18:276–9 Jl '62. * (*PA* 39:1874)
132. ALEXANDER, THERON. "The Effect of Psychopathology in Children's Drawing of the Human Figure." *J Psychol* 56:273–82 O '63. *
133. CHODORKOFF, JOAN, AND WHITTEN, CHARLES F. "Intellectual Status of Children With Sickle Cell Anemia." *J Pediatrics* 63:29–35 Jl '63. *
134. GRANICK, SAMUEL. "Comparative Performance of Normal and Psychoneurotic Children on the Draw-A-Person Test." *J Germantown Hosp* 4:17–22 F '63. * (*PA* 38:2623)
135. HARRIS, DALE B. *Children's Drawing as Measures of Intellectual Maturity: A Revision and Extension of the Goodenough Draw-A-Man Test.* New York: Harcourt, Brace & World, Inc., 1963. Pp. xv, 367. * (*PA* 39:1697)
136. PRINGLE, M. L. KELLMER, AND PICKUP, K. T. "The Reliability and Validity of the Goodenough Draw-A-Man Test: A Pilot Longitudinal Study." *Brit J Ed Psychol* 33:297–306 N '63. * (*PA* 38:8424)
137. THOMPSON, JACK M., AND FINLEY, CARMEN J. "The Relationship Between the Goodenough Draw-A-Man Test and the Stanford-Binet Form L-M in Children Referred for School Guidance Services." *Calif J Ed Res* 14:19–22 Ja '63. * (*PA* 37:7875)

For a review by Naomi Stewart of the original edition, see 4:292.

[461]

***The Graduate Record Examinations Aptitude Test.** Grades 16–17; 1949–63; for more complete information, see 762; 2 scores: verbal, quantitative; 150(170) minutes; Educational Testing Service. *

REFERENCES

1–2. See 4:293.
3–9. See 5:336.
10. CONWAY, MADONNA THERESE. *The Relationship of the Graduate Record Examination Results to Achievement in the Graduate School at the University of Detroit.* Master's thesis, University of Detroit (Detroit, Mich.), 1955.
11. RUPIPER, OMER JOHN. "An Analysis of the Graduate Record Examinations for Doctoral Majors in Education." *Peabody J Ed* 36:279–85 Mr '59. *
12. WILLIAMS, OLIVER HOYT. *Criteria for Admission to the Graduate School of the University of Texas in Relation to the Aptitude Test of the Graduate Record Examinations.* Doctor's thesis, University of Texas (Austin, Tex.), 1959. (*DA* 20:2685)
13. BESCO, ROBERT ORIN. *The Measurement and Prediction of Success in Graduate School.* Doctor's thesis, Purdue University (Lafayette, Ind.), 1960. (*DA* 21:1994)
14. KING, DONALD C., AND BESCO, ROBERT O. "The Graduate Record Examination as a Selection Device for Graduate Research Fellows." *Ed & Psychol Meas* 20:853–8 w '60. * (*PA* 35:3972)
15. LAW, ALEXANDER. "The Prediction of Ratings of Students in a Doctoral Training Program." *Ed & Psychol Meas* 20:847–51 w '60. * (*PA* 35:3973)
16. MICHAEL, WILLIAM B.; JONES, ROBERT A.; AND GIBBONS, BILLIE D. "The Prediction of Success in Graduate Work in Chemistry From Scores on the Graduate Record Examination." *Ed & Psychol Meas* 20:859–61 w '60. * (*PA* 35:3957)
17. ROBERTSON, MALCOLM, AND NIELSEN, WINNIFRED. "The Graduate Record Examination and Selection of Graduate Students." *Am Psychologist* 16:648–50 O '61. * (*PA* 36:4KJ48R)
18. SLEEPER, MILDRED L. "Relationship of Scores on the Graduate Record Examination to Grade Point Averages of Graduate Students in Occupational Therapy." *Ed & Psychol Meas* 21:1039–40 w '61. *
19. THOMSEN, STEPHEN J. "Academic Achievement and Institutional Testing Program Scores: A Longitudinal Study of One Class at a Liberal Arts College." *Proc W Va Acad Sci* 33:120–3 N '61. * (*PA* 36:5KL20T)
20. HOWARD, JANICE S. *A Study of the Graduate Record Examination Aptitude Tests and Other Selected Factors in Predicting Graduate School Success at Rhode Island College.* Master's thesis, Rhode Island College (Providence, R.I.), 1962.
21. JOHNSON, JANET WILDMAN. *An Investigation of Relationships Between College and Senior Student Characteristics and Performance on the Aptitude and Area Tests of the Graduate Record Examination at the George Washington University.* Doctor's thesis, George Washington University (Washington, D.C.), 1962.
22. MABERLY, NORMAN CHARLES. *The Validity of the Graduate Record Examinations as Used With English-Speaking Foreign Students.* Doctor's thesis, University of Southern California (Los Angeles, Calif.), 1962. (*DA* 23:2424)
23. TULLY, G. EMERSON. "Screening Applicants for Graduate Study With the Aptitude Test of the Graduate Record Examinations." *Col & Univ* 38:51–60 f '62. *
24. BORG, WALTER R. "GRE Aptitude Scores as Predictors of GPA for Graduate Students in Education." *Ed & Psychol Meas* 23:379–82 su '63. * (*PA* 38:1419)
25. MABERLY, NORMAN C. "The Validity of the Graduate Record Examinations as Used With English-Speaking Foreign Students." *Ed & Psychol Meas* 23:785–8 w '63. *
26. RUDMAN, JACK. *Graduate Record Examination: How to Pass Aptitude Test: Questions and Answers.* Brooklyn, N.Y.: College Publishing Corporation, 1963. Pp. v, 294. *

ROBERT L. FRENCH, *Vice President for Research and Testing, Science Research Associates, Inc., Chicago, Illinois.* [Review of Forms GGR and LGR1.]

The first forms of this test of scholastic aptitude, XGR and YGR, were published in the period 1949–51 and reviewed in *The Fourth Mental Measurements Yearbook.* Since that time several new forms have been produced.

Form EGR was reviewed in *The Fifth Mental Measurements Yearbook*. The most recent form available for review, LGR1, appears to differ in no substantial way from Form EGR. The test continues in its successive forms to be a well constructed, suitably difficult, and otherwise conventional test of general scholastic potential. Reliability remains satisfactory, normative data extensive, validity data sparse. Administrative literature pertinent to the test is quite complete, but the score interpretation booklet does not adequately bring together all of the information required for technical evaluation (e.g., item data), nor identify the specific forms with which particular sets of data were obtained.

The paucity of validity information is especially unfortunate. In the present atmosphere, critics of testing are bound to ask whether an aptitude test is appropriate or necessary for applicants who have recorded 16 or so years of school achievement and taken a number of similar tests in the process. Other and more sympathetic critics may well wonder at the lack of continuing exploration and appraisal of a variety of factors in graduate performance, some of which they might suspect of being both more accessible and more important than scholastic aptitude for differentiating applicants. Intelligent responses cannot be made to either set of critics without data from studies of criteria and the relative predictive value of various measures. It may be hoped that the publisher of the GRE will attack this problem more vigorously in the future than in the past, despite the obvious difficulties involved.

WARREN W. WILLINGHAM, *Director of Evaluation Studies, Georgia Institute of Technology, Atlanta, Georgia.* [Review of Forms GGR and LGR1.]

The Graduate Record Examinations include the Aptitude Test (verbal and quantitative), 3 Area Tests (social science, natural science, and humanities), and 20 Advanced Tests in specialized curriculum areas. This review is concerned only with the Aptitude Test, but since all of the GRE tests are designed to complement one another, the prospective user might well examine the reviews of the achievement tests also.

The Aptitude Test is similar in format to the familiar *College Entrance Examination Board Scholastic Aptitude Test* but pitched at a higher level of difficulty. The verbal score is based upon verbal reasoning and reading comprehension items. The quantitative section includes computation, reasoning, and data interpretation. These items presuppose no more than high school mathematics but a college senior's quantitative score would undoubtedly suffer had he taken no mathematics in college.

The verbal and quantitative scores have satisfactory K-R 20 reliabilities (.91 for Form GGR verbal, .90 for GGR quantitative, and .92 for each score on LGR1). No alternate form reliability estimates, long term retest reliability estimates, or reliability estimates based upon subgroups with a restricted range are reported. The score interpretation booklet, Scores for Basic Reference Groups, does provide a useful table showing the probability that selected score differences do not represent real differences.

This booklet does not contain any information pertaining to the predictive validity of the Aptitude Test. In the reviewer's opinion, this is an unfortunate omission. Available research (*11, 14–8, 23–4*) indicates that correlations between the Aptitude Test and graduate grade-point average range from moderately high to zero. The validity coefficients tend to become smaller when any criterion less prosaic than the point average is used. Since the criterion of graduate success varies widely among institutions and among disciplines, it would seem all the more necessary to document the predictive validity as extensively as possible.

The score interpretation booklet and other reports available from the publisher contain a very large amount of normative material for the Aptitude Test and its associated GRE tests. These include Aptitude Test norms for students in different curricula. There are signs here and there of the extreme difficulty of obtaining representative norms for different graduate populations, but this problem is mitigated to some extent by accurate descriptions of the norm groups included. The publisher has recently introduced a novel and promising solution to the norms problem. For a modest fee an institution can obtain norms based upon any 10 or more institutions selected from a longer list. At present this service is offered through the Institutional Testing Program and is somewhat limited in terms of the norm groups available. If the service expands it could prove quite useful, particularly in conjunction with institutional evaluation.

Typical for the publisher, the Aptitude Test has well designed supplementary materials. Directions for administering are complete; instructions to candidates are informative; brochures are attractive and professional. The score interpretation booklet should be very helpful to the non-specialist. As noted above, however, it does not contain several types of technical information normally considered essential.

The chief competitor of the Aptitude Test is the *Miller Analogies Test.* Both are well constructed tests which have their individual appeals.

In summary, the Aptitude Test is recommended as a good measure of high level verbal and quantitative ability. With its related tests and extensive system of norms, it should be useful in institutional evaluation. Many schools will find the test useful in selecting graduate students, but local validity studies are strongly recommended.

For a review by John T. Dailey of an earlier form, see 5:336; for reviews by J. P. Guilford and Carl I. Hovland of earlier forms, see 4:293. For a review of the testing program, see 5:601.

[462]

***The Henmon-Nelson Tests of Mental Ability, Revised Edition.** Grades 3-6, 6-9, 9-12, 13-17; 1931-61; previous edition (see 4:299) still available; IBM and MRC; 4 levels; $2.55 per 100 MRC answer cards (machine scoring service, by Measurement Research Center, Inc., may be arranged through the publisher); postage extra; Tom A. Lamke, M. J. Nelson, and Paul C. Kelso (*d*); Houghton Mifflin Co. *

a) GRADES 3-6. 1931-60; 2 editions: consumable, reusable; Forms A (consumable edition, '57, 4 pages; reusable edition, '60, 7 pages), B (consumable edition, '58, 4 pages; reusable edition, '60, 7 pages); manual ('57, 24 pages) for both editions; separate answer sheets must be used with reusable edition; $3.60 per 35 tests; $1.38 per 35 IBM answer sheets; 21¢ per scoring stencil; $2.25 per specimen set including *b* and *c* below; 30(35) minutes.

b) GRADES 6-9. 1931-60; forms, prices, and time same as for grades 3-6.

c) GRADES 9-12. 1931-60; forms, prices, and time same as for grades 3-6.

d) GRADES 13-17. 1931-61; 3 scores: quantitative, verbal, total; Forms A, B, ('61, 7 pages); manual ('61, 19 pages); norms for college freshmen only; separate answer sheets must be used; $3.60 per 35 tests; $2.52 per 35 self-marking answer sheets; $2.91 per 100 IBM answer sheets; 64¢ per set of scoring stencils; $1 per specimen set; 40(45) minutes.

REFERENCES

1-25. See 4:299.
26-39. See 5:342.
40. KACZKOWSKI, HENRY R. "Using Expectancy Tables to Validate Test Procedures in High School." *Ed & Psychol Meas* 19:675-7 w '59. * (*PA* 34:6536)
41. KNIGHT, R., AND STENNETT, R. G. "Intelligence and Academic Success: Preliminary Report." *Ont Hosp Psychol B* 5:2-3 D '59. *
42. LAVER, A. B. "Testing in Canada: Report No. 1." *Can Psychologist* 8:102-3 O '59. *
43. BARRETT, HARRY O. "The Predictive Efficiency of Grade 8 Objective Tests in Terms of Grade 9 Achievement." *Ont J Ed Res* 2:101-7 Ap '60. *
44. CONDELL, JAMES F. "Comparison of Henmon-Nelson and Jastak Scores of Seventh Graders." *Psychol Rep* 9:622 D '61. *
45. KIRK, BARBARA A.; CUMMINGS, ROGER W.; AND GOODSTEIN, LEONARD D. "Predicting Student Success in Graduate Business Courses." *Calif Mgmt R* 5:63-6 f '62. *
46. SAX, GILBERT, AND CARR, ALBERT. "An Investigation of Response Sets on Altered Parallel Forms." *Ed & Psychol Meas* 22:371-6 su '62. * (*PA* 37:3267)
47. BLOSSER, GEORGE H. "Group Intelligence Tests as Screening Devices in Locating Gifted and Superior Students in the Ninth Grade." *Except Child* 29:282-6 F '63. * (*PA* 38:2434)
48. JURJEVICH, RATIBOR. "An Evaluation of the Henmon-Nelson Group *IQ* Test With Delinquent Girls." *J General Psychol* 69:227-33 O '63. * (*PA* 39:1778)
49. SCHROEDER, WAYNE LEE. *Factors Related to the Academic Success of Male College Students From Five Selected Wisconsin Counties.* Doctor's thesis, University of Wisconsin (Madison, Wis.), 1963. (*DA* 23:4207)
50. WEINER, MAX, AND TOBIAS, SIGMUND. "Chance Factors in the Interpretation of Group Administered Multiple-Choice Tests." *Personnel & Guid J* 41:435-7 Ja '63. * (*PA* 39:1771)

NORMAN E. WALLEN, *Associate Professor of Educational Psychology, University of Utah, Salt Lake City, Utah.* [Review of the college level.]

This review is restricted to the college level of this test which appeared on the market in 1961. The format is much the same as for the lower levels of the test although the number of items is increased from 90 to 100. With respect to item content, format, and general adequacy of the manual, this level conforms to the high standard demonstrated in the lower levels. One interesting departure, however, is the provision of separate verbal and quantitative scores in addition to the overall score. The manual is still pessimistic about the value of these separate scores and gives the impression that they have been included primarily as a result of social pressure. Although the test is intended for use from the freshman through the first year of graduate school the norms provided are based only on beginning college freshmen. The authors report that their attempts "to obtain cluster sampling stratified by size, location, and type of institution" were unsuccessful and hence they resorted to a random sample "stratified by location, size, and type of institution." For these variables the distribution of cases conforms quite closely to national data. Approximately one hundred colleges and universities are represented in the normative group which totals 1,002.

Only percentile norms are provided. It is difficult to understand why some form of standard score is not provided for the measures, particularly since one may certainly expect that differences between Q and V will be examined and the difficulties inherent in comparing differences in raw scores or in percentile ranks are well known.

The odd-even reliabilities, based on 100 cases, are .92 and .89 for Q, .92 and .93 for V, and .95 and .94 for total score on Forms A and B, respectively. Alternate forms testing with an interval of approximately 35 days provided reliabilities of .84 for the quantitative, .88 for the verbal, and .89 for the total score. A slight practice effect amounting to four raw score points, due almost entirely to the quantitative items, was noted. The standard error of measurement is reported for all three scores. Considerable effort has, it is stated, resulted in the two forms being very closely parallel but data to this effect should be reported.

With respect to validity, the first argument offered is in terms of the internal consistency of the scores resulting from a considerable amount of statistical tryout to assure homogeneity of items. Regarding congruent and predictive validity a few correlations with other tests and grades are presented. Correlations with freshman first semester grade point, based on a sample of 95 college freshmen, are of the expected magnitude, ranging from .46 to .54 across the three scores. Correlations between 120 preliminary items and ACE scores show correlations of .55 between the corresponding quantitative and total scores and .75 with the verbal scores.

One of the interesting features of this test has to do with the item types to be found. Of the total of 100 items, 47 were classified by this reviewer as straight vocabulary definition, 22 as number series, 17 as arithmetic reasoning, 12 as verbal analogies. Of the remaining two, one is a sentence arrangement item and the other is a combination of verbal reasoning and arithmetic skills. This is in contrast, at least, to the next lower level of the test, intended for grades 9 to 12, which comes much closer to approximating an omnibus type test containing a greater number of different type items, although the largest number of items is still vocabulary. This difference in item content may to some extent be responsible for the relatively low stability data reported by comparing the college level scores with scores obtained on the level 9 to 12 test with time interval ranging from 4 to 18 months. Based on 88 cases, this correlation for the total college level test is .79. It may also be, of course, that the correlations simply reflect changes in the individuals made possible by a longer time interval.

Of the competing tests, SCAT, CQT, and OSUPE seem to be more heavily dependent on prior school learning and hence are likely to be better predictors of academic success. If, however, one wants an index of intellectual skills which is less a function of schooling and individual testing is not feasible, this test has considerable appeal, especially in view of the short time required.

J Counsel Psychol 10:201–3 su '63. John O. Crites. [Review of college level.] * The authors....have made a commendable attempt to take into consideration some of the criticisms which were made of earlier editions and have been successful in large part in overcoming the more serious defects of the older forms. * Unlike its predecessors, the present edition.... yields Verbal and Quantitative part scores as well as a Total score. The V scale consists of 60 items, whereas the Q scale is comprised of only 40 items, which may be undesirable for several reasons. Not only is the reliability of the Q score adversely affected....but the test is more heavily weighted with the V factor. Also, a count of the items keyed to the two scales in each succeeding fifth of the test reveals that there is a disproportionate number of Q items in the last section of the test. Thus, for the slower examinee who fails to complete the test, the total score is based upon a higher ratio of V to Q items than for the examinee who finishes within the time limit. * One obvious omission in the description of the normative sample is the percentages of males and females included in it. The Manual states only that the Ss were college freshmen, which in itself is a somewhat disappointing if not misleading fact, since the test is advertised as applicable to students at all levels from the first year of college to the first year of graduate school. The test's authors suggest that local norms are more useful than national norms for graduate students, which is not only a debatable observation but one which tells nothing about the value of the test for the selection and guidance of advanced students. It is unfortunate that the nature of the national normative data restricts the applicability of the test to college freshmen. * It would appear that the test is very difficult for even the brightest college freshmen. Perhaps this is a desirable characteristic for a test which is supposed to be as wide-ranging as the Henmon-Nelson, but it may reduce the test's predictive validity at the lower levels by restricting its effective range, which would be the effect of a steep difficulty gradient. * Forms A and B were constituted from....200 items, which were matched on each of the item indices. The actual data on the latter, however, are not reported in the Manual, so that it is not possible to gain an explicit impression of the comparability of the "equivalent forms" or of the nature of the item difficulty gradients. Since the two forms were combined to develop norms for the test, it is important to know how similar they are. * It would be interesting and informative, however....to determine the correlations of the test with a factorial battery, such as the PMA or DAT. * the 1961 revision....rather closely approximates the ideal for measures of its kind. It is relatively short, easily administered, quickly scored, acceptably reliable, and reasonably valid. It would be extremely valuable to have norms for students at the higher college and beginning graduate school levels which are national in scope but hopefully these will be made available through the efforts of the test's authors and their cooperating colleges and universities. Also, it would be very useful to have data on the relationships of Henmon-Nelson test scores to eventual occupational membership and attainment for purposes of vocational counseling. At present, the test is primarily useful for educational rather than vocational guidance. As a final observation on the rationale for the revision, it would seem that the Henmon-Nelson Test has retained its usefulness as a predictor of academic success despite the recent emphasis upon multi-factor aptitude batteries and the test authors' acquiescence to this *Zeitgeist* as manifested in their development of the Q and V scales. It still remains to be demonstrated that the factorial batteries are supplements, and not merely complements, for a good measure of general scholastic aptitude.

For reviews by D. Welty Lefever and Leona E. Tyler of a-c, *see 5:342 (1 excerpt); for a review by H. M. Fowler of the previous edition, see 4:299; for reviews by Anne Anastasi, August Dvorak, Howard Easley, and J. P. Guilford, see 40:1398 (1 excerpt).*

[463]

★Inventory No. 2. Ages 16 and over; 1956; "a mental ability test"; 1 form ['56, 4 pages]; manual (3 pages); $3 per 25 tests; $1 per set of manual and key; postage extra; specimen set not available; 15(20) minutes; Stevens, Thurow & Associates Inc. *

[464]

***Junior Scholastic Aptitude Test, Revised Edition.** Grades 7-9; 1935-60; tests copyrighted 1959-60 identical with those copyrighted 1957 except for cover page directions; for independent schools; 2 scores: verbal, numerical; IBM; Forms A ('59), B ('59), C ('60), (14 pages); directions ['59, 4 pages]; technical data and independent school norms presented in various issues of *Ed Rec B;* separate answer sheets must be used; tests rented only; examination fee: $1 per student, postage extra; fee includes scoring service; 60(80) minutes in 1 or 2 sessions; Secondary Education Board (original edition); [Geraldine Spaulding] (revised edition); distributed for the National Association of Independent Schools by Educational Records Bureau. *

REFERENCES

1-3. See 3:233.
4-10. See 5:345.
11. SPAULDING, GERALDINE. "Some Observations on the Results of the Revised Junior Scholastic Aptitude Test." *Ed Rec B* 76:53-6 F '60. *
12. SPAULDING, GERALDINE. "Some Data on the Relation Between the Junior Scholastic Aptitude Test and the General School Ability Test Used in the Secondary School Admission Test Program." *Ed Rec B* 79:62-4 Jl '61. *
13. VECCHIONE, NICHOLAS. "Summary of Results of the Revised Forms of the Junior Scholastic Aptitude Test in the Fall and Spring Testing Programs for Independent School Pupils in Grades 7, 8, and 9." *Ed Rec B* 80:66-9 F '62. *
14. JUNGEBLUT, ANN. "Stability of Results on the Junior Scholastic Aptitude Test." *Ed Rec B* 83:61-6 F '63. *
15. SPAULDING, GERALDINE. "Relations Between the NAIS Junior Scholastic Aptitude Test and the CEEB Scholastic Aptitude Tests." *Ed Rec B* 84:55-62 Jl '63. *

JEROME E. DOPPELT, *Assistant Director, Test Division, The Psychological Corporation, New York, New York.*

The earliest edition of the *Junior Scholastic Aptitude Test* (JSAT) was developed in the latter 1930's by the Bureau of Research of the Secondary Education Board to measure the verbal and numerical aptitudes of pupils in grades 7, 8, and 9. Three forms of the JSAT were prepared and after slight revision these became known as Forms DR, ER, and FR. The tests were turned over to the Educational Records Bureau for distribution, with the understanding that the test would be handled on a controlled basis with required scoring at the Bureau. Since 1939, the JSAT has been included in testing programs conducted by the Educational Records Bureau in independent (private) schools. Each of Forms DR, ER, and FR consisted of eight subtests from which a verbal score and a numerical score were obtained. A considerable amount of time was needed to administer one of these forms. In addition to 76 minutes of actual working time, a rather lengthy practice booklet was administered before the regular testing session.

In 1957 and 1958, the staff of the Educational Records Bureau undertook a revision of the JSAT intended primarily to shorten working time for the test and to incorporate the practice material into the administration of the test. Some items in the old forms were replaced or rewritten but items considered to be functioning well were retained. After experimental tryout in 1958, the revised forms were produced and designated as Forms A, B, and C.

Each revised form contains five parts and the entire test can be administered in about 80 minutes. A verbal score is obtained from 90 items in three parts which include paired opposites (selection of the two words that have opposite meanings), double definitions (selection of two missing words to complete a definition), and verbal analogies. The numerical score is based on 50 items in two parts which include number series and arithmetic reasoning. The verbal and numerical raw scores are translated into converted scores for which 500 represents the average performance of independent school pupils in the spring of grade 8 and 100 is the standard deviation of this group. Percentile norms corresponding to converted scores are available for each form and grade. The norms are based on the performance of independent school pupils and the tables are revised as additional data for a particular form become available.

The test items reflect good craftsmanship and are clearly presented with adequate directions. The test booklets are sealed and numbered in keeping with the concept of control of materials. Instructions to the examiner are also presented clearly in a four-page leaflet. The lack of a single manual containing technical data is an inconvenience. These data are given in different Bulletins of the Educational Records Bureau. Although it may be assumed that schools using the JSAT receive the Bulletins of the Bureau, it would be desirable to have the relevant information in one document.

The reliability coefficients reported for the verbal and numerical scores range from .93 to .95 for verbal, and from .91 to .95 for numerical. These are odd-even reliability coefficients which are not appropriate for speeded tests. Since the directions on the cover page of the test booklet acknowledge the effects of speed by the statement, "It is expected that many pupils will not have time to answer all the items," one must assume that the coefficients overestimate reliability. Correlations are reported between scores on Forms A and B administered, with an average time interval of about six months, to two groups: 344 students tested first in grade 7 and then in grade 8; 100 students tested first in grade 8 and then in grade 9. These correlations, which may be regarded as stability coefficients, were .88 and .84 for verbal; for numerical, the coefficients were .80 and .88, in the two groups respectively. Reliability coefficients based on immediate retesting with an alternate form would probably be somewhat higher than the stability coefficients. It would be helpful to have means and standard deviations for the reliability samples as well as for the norms groups but these are not presented. There is, indeed, a conspicuous absence of means and standard deviations in the statistical reports. This prevents the user from determining whether or not the groups for which reliability and other data are reported are similar to his own groups.

Correlations were computed between scores on the JSAT and scores on various achievement tests, when all tests were given in the same testing program. These correlations tend to be high where one would expect them to be high; however, exception may be taken to the conclusion that "correlations with various achievement measures indicate that the Verbal Score may be considered a good predictor of achievement in school subjects that are chiefly verbal in nature, and that the Numerical Score should provide a good prediction of achievement in mathematical subjects." The conclusion may well be true but it is not supported by evidence based on tests administered in the same program since there is no true prediction involved. A time interval between the predictors and the criteria is necessary.

Data were obtained on the relationship between the JSAT and the *Secondary School Admissions Tests: General School Ability and Reading Test*. The latter battery is taken by students who plan to enter an independent secondary school. On the basis of these data a table of equivalent percentiles on the two tests was prepared. The July 1963 Educational Records Bureau Bulletin includes tables of equivalence between grade 9 JSAT scores and scores on the PSAT in grade 11 and on the SAT in grade 12. These should provide useful information to counselors in the independent schools but it is to be hoped that they will evaluate the accuracy of the predictions for their own students.

In a study of the correlations between fall 1957 scores on one of the older forms and spring 1958 scores on the revised forms, the coefficients between verbal scores on the old and the new editions varied between .81 and .90; the coefficients for the numerical scores were between .75 and .82. There is obviously considerable similarity between the old and new tests but it would be desirable to collect and report validity data for the revised edition. It is reasonable to suppose such studies will be undertaken by the Educational Records Bureau.

The revised forms of the JSAT, like the earlier editions of that test, were developed for independent schools. Other published tests are probably equally suitable for measuring verbal and numerical aptitudes but independent schools may prefer a controlled test intended primarily for their use. The new forms are well constructed measures but additional supporting data would be desirable. More detailed reporting of results and evidence on the prediction of success in school would permit better evaluation of the revised JSAT as a functioning instrument.

[465]

***The Kingston Test of Intelligence.** Ages 10-0 to 12-11; 1953-63; Forms A ('53), B ('62), (8 pages); practice sheet ['53, 2 pages]; manual ('63, 20 pages, identical with 1954 manual except for wording changes and addition of Form B norms); no data on reliability of Form B; no data on validity; 12*s.* 6*d.* per 25 tests of Form A; 15*s.* per 25 tests of Form B; 8*d.* per single copy; 3*s.* per manual; postage and purchase tax extra; 33(78) minutes; M. E. Hebron; George G. Harrap & Co. Ltd. *

H. J. SANTS, *Lecturer in Education, University College of North Wales, Bangor, Wales.*

Upon opening these compact test booklets and manual both teacher and pupil are likely to get the impression that they have an intelligence test which they can manage: the manual is concerned with administration rather than construction; the test booklets have instructions which are brief, with words to be underlined or small spaces to be filled as the test response required. But this apparent concern to put both manual and booklet into the language of the classroom has created some unsatisfactory features.

The children work for 33 minutes on the test proper, having first worked 15 minutes on a practice test and spent 10 to 15 minutes in discussion. The inclusion of standardised coaching is to be commended but testers will surely have difficulties in "following verbatim the standardized method." What the tester has to say, although admirably phrased for putting children at their ease, is so lengthy that a teacher would need either a better than average memory, or a special skill at reading as though talking spontaneously. With these long passages administration is unlikely to remain standard in the strictest sense, especially as the words to be used by the tester are not clearly separated from the remainder of the instructions. In the 1963 manual, the same instructions are used for both forms.

From the child's point of view the content of these tests is a good deal more inviting than that of many objective tests. The items are simple but not dull, e.g., "Linoleum is to Carpet as Mackintosh is to (Coat, Hat, Gloves, Rug)." Besides the verbal analogies section there are four other sections in each test: number series, diagrammatic analogies (occupying three and a half pages of the total eight), classification, and arranging words in order of size and intensity. Heim criticised the logic of the classification test in *The Fifth Mental Measurements Yearbook* and this section in Form B is again curiously constructed. Having been asked to "underline the word which may be *sometimes* true but *not always* so," the child is given such sentences, "All Clocks are essential, reliable, purchasable, mechanical." The correct answer listed for this example is "reliable." In choosing *reliable* rather than *essential* the child is having to choose the answer he thinks the teacher would prefer. This calls for conformity as well as intelligence. A child may be intellectually capable of deciding which answer the tester would favour but be emotionally incapable of giving it to him.

In addition, the Note on the Construction and Standardization of the Tests is no more satisfactory in the 1963 manual than in the earlier one. Its brevity can only irritate the expert and mislead the layman. The note should either be expanded technically with more data or replaced by a general cautionary note.

These criticisms have been made from inspection, and in the same way the attraction of using the test in the classroom can also be seen. A teacher meeting a new class might find results from these tests a useful addition to scholastic results obtained from school records, thus getting closer to an assessment of the intellectual potential of his pupils.

For a review by A. W. Heim, see 5:347.

[466]

***Kuhlmann-Anderson Intelligence Tests, Seventh Edition.** Grades kgn, 1, 2, 3–4, 4–5, 5–7, 7–9, 9–12; 1927–63; sixth edition (see 5:348) still available; 3 scores for grades 7–12: verbal, quantitative, total; IBM for grades 4–12; 8 levels (labeled Booklets K, A, B, CD, D, EF, G, and H); *Booklets K, A, B, and CD* (grades kgn, 1, 2, 3–4): 1 form ('63, 9–10 pages), administration and norms manual ('63, 36–51 pages) for each level, technical manual ('63, 31 pages) for all levels; *Booklets D and EF* (grades 4–5, 5–7): 1 form ('60, c1927–60, 10 pages), manual for administering ('61, 23 pages) for each level, norms manual ('61, 20 pages) for both levels, technical manual ('62, 26 pages) for both levels; *Booklets G and H* (grades 7–9, 9–12): 1 form ('60, c1927–60, 9 pages), manual for administering ('60, c1927–60, 22 pages) for each level, revised norms manual ('63, c1960–62, 34 pages) for both levels, revised technical manual ('63, c1960–62, 49 pages) for both levels, student's interpretive report form ('63, 1 page); supplementary norms manual ('63, 23 pages) for Booklets D–H; separate answer sheets must be used with Booklets D–H; $3 per 25 tests; $2.40 per 50 IBM answer sheets; 25¢ per set of scoring stencils; $1.10 per 50 student's interpretive report forms; 25¢ per norms manual; 50¢ per technical report; 50¢ per supplementary norms manual; $1 per specimen set of Booklets A and CD, D and EF, or G and H; postpaid; 22(45) minutes for Booklets K and A, 20(40–45) minutes for Booklet B, 26(45) minutes for Booklet CD, 30(60) minutes for Booklets D and EF, 23(50) minutes for Booklets G and H; F. Kuhlmann (fourth and earlier editions) and Rose G. Anderson; Personnel Press, Inc. *

REFERENCES

1–15. See 40:1404.
16–40. See 3:236.
41–50. See 4:302.
51–65. See 5:348.
66. Holsopple, Ila G. *Factorial Analysis of the Kuhlmann-Anderson Intelligence Tests and the Stanford Achievement Tests at Fourth and Eighth Grade Levels.* Doctor's thesis, Pennsylvania State College (State College, Pa.), 1948.
67. Lloyd, Claude J. *The Relationship Between the Scores Made by Pupils on the Primary Mental Abilities Test, the Metropolitan Achievement Reading Test, and the Kuhlmann-Anderson Intelligence Test.* Master's thesis, University of Southern California (Los Angeles, Calif.), 1958.
68. Cabanski, Carolyn L. *The Predictive Value of the Kuhlmann-Anderson Subtests Regarding Reading Improvement.* Master's thesis, Loyola University (Chicago, Ill.), 1959.
69. Chambers, Jack A. "Preliminary Screening Methods in the Identification of Intellectually Superior Children." *Excep Child* 26:145–50 N '59. * (*PA* 35:3249)
70. Knight, Robert. "Intelligence Test Data From One Public and Two High Schools." *Ont Hosp Psychol B* 5:6–8 Ag '59. *
71. Racky, Donald J. "Predictions of Ninth Grade Woodshop Performance From Aptitude and Interest Measures." *Ed & Psychol Meas* 19:629–36 w '59. * (*PA* 34:6572)
72. Vecchione, Nicholas. "Stability of Kuhlmann-Anderson IQ's of Independent School Pupils in Elementary Grades Covering Six Testings Over a Five-Year Period." *Ed Rec B* 79:65–72 Jl '61. *
73. North, Robert D. "Results of the Seventh Edition Kuhlmann-Anderson Test for Independent School Pupils in Grades 7–12." *Ed Rec B* 80:56–65 F '62. *
74. North, Robert D. "A Further Analysis of the Kuhlmann-Anderson Seventh Edition Test." *Ed Rec B* 83:53–60 F '63. * (*PA* 38:962)
75. Schena, Richard A. "A Search for Talented Pupils." *J Exp Ed* 32:27–41 f '63. *
76. Sniffen, Allan Mead. *A Correlation Study of Group Intelligence Tests With Achievement in Reading and Arithmetic in Grade Four: An Investigation of the Effectiveness of Using Group Intelligence Test Scores for Evaluating Academic Achievement in the Tool Subject Areas of Reading and Arithmetic in Public Elementary Schools.* Doctor's thesis, New York University (New York, N.Y.), 1963. (*DA* 24:826)

William B. Michael, *Professor of Education and Psychology, University of California, Santa Barbara, California.*

That the same excellent standards of workmanship as those associated with previous editions of the Kuhlmann-Anderson tests have been perpetuated in the series of eight coordinated tests of the new seventh edition is unmistakably evident from an examination of the carefully constructed items in the various forms, from exploration of the lucid norms manuals in which explicit directions are given concerning problems of scoring and interpretation, from inspection of the readily applied manuals for administration, and from detailed study of the three comprehensive and competently prepared technical manuals. Although the sixth edition is still available, the seventh edition introduces several new features that are in agreement with a great deal of modern thinking about the assessment of intelligence. Moreover nearly 40 per cent of the content of the seventh edition is new.

For Booklets K, A, B, and CD, which are intended for use in kindergarten, grade 1, grade 2, and grades 3 and 4, respectively, 8 tests instead of the former 10 are used, although the number of items in each test has been augmented. Another change is the introduction of grade percentile ranks for total scores on the A, B, and CD booklets. In place of the IQ's based on the ratio of mental age to chronological age, deviation IQ's for total scores are presented corresponding to intervals of three months in chronological age.

Similarly for Booklets D and EF, which are planned to be administered in grades 4 and 5 and in grades 5, 6, and 7, respectively, the same types of modifications have been effected. In addition both a verbal (V) score and a quantitative (Q) score may be derived for use in research studies, although the admonition has been set forth that the scores are not sufficiently independent for purposes of analysis of differential aptitudes. In contrast to the previous edition, the test booklets may be reused, and IBM answer sheets may be scored mechanically.

For the third sequence of booklets, G and H, which are appropriate for grades 7, 8, and 9 and for grades 9, 10, 11, and 12, respectively, the same kinds of revisions were undertaken. However, grade percentile ranks are provided for both V and Q scores (as well as for T scores) in view of the existence of a sufficient degree of independence and reliability of each of these part scores for differential use.

Several other praiseworthy improvements in the seventh edition should be briefly cited. In the current forms for the earlier grade levels, as compared with the corresponding forms of the sixth edition, the ceiling limitation has been obviated. Moreover, through use of the deviation IQ the standard deviations of scores from one grade level to the next have been shown in empirical studies to be not only wider, but also more nearly constant than in the instance of the forms of the sixth edition in which ratio IQ's were derived. Hence improved discrimination among pupils has been realized, particularly among those within either the higher or lower segments of the range of ability. In addition—apparently in view of the widespread use of standard scores by several school systems—the author has furnished stanine equivalents for the deviation IQ scores.

Another commendable effort in the presentation of normative data has been the introduction of percentile bands for a realistic interpretation of V, Q, and T scores for Booklets G and H. To enable the examinee in junior or senior high school to understand the meaning of percentile bands for each of his three scores, a Student's Interpretive Report Form has been developed. Although a conscientious attempt has been made to explain the significance of test bands upon the MAP (Measure of Academic Potential) profile, the reviewer has serious reservations regarding whether most high school students will be able to grasp the import of the discussion. A graphically portrayed example would be helpful.

Great care has been exercised in the development of representative norms, in the acquisition of data furnishing indices of both predictive and concurrent validity, and in the presentation of standard errors of measurement and of various types of reliability estimates.

On both a relative and absolute basis the seventh edition of the Kuhlmann-Anderson tests compares favorably with any other competitive instrument measuring general intelligence. The various manuals are noteworthy not only for their comprehensive and discerning exposition about the test forms but also for their cautious and modest statements. Finding little to criticize either concerning the construction and standardization of the test or regarding the adequacy of the interpretative data furnished, the reviewer can only hope that the teachers, counselors, principals, and other responsible persons will take pains to study and to apply the wealth of information to be found in the general and technical manuals. Both the author (Rose G. Anderson) and the publisher have attained a standard of excellence of which both the psychometric specialist and practitioner in the schools can be most appreciative.

DOUGLAS A. PIDGEON, *Deputy Director, National Foundation for Educational Research in England and Wales, Slough, Bucks, England.*

The changes made in the seventh edition of these well known tests, while probably more drastic than any made hitherto, are such as to retain most of the character of the original tests, and yet at the same time to bring them more in line with modern practices. As with previous editions, the tests appear in separate booklets, but the overlapping between adjacent booklets has been somewhat reduced. Also the correspondence of grade to booklet has been changed slightly from the sixth edition, and now a choice of booklet is available for pupils in grades 4, 5, 7, and 9. The number of tests in each booklet has been reduced from 10 to 8, but the number of items in each test has been increased, resulting in larger standard deviations and thus affording better discrimination among high and low scorers.

About 40 per cent of the content of this edition is new. The new items were tried out with the sixth edition and item analyses performed using the median mental age on the sixth edition as a criterion. This procedure was presumably adopted in order to ensure continuity of item content, and, as the technical manuals state, "The validity of the Sixth Edition was built into the Seventh Edition tests." It is to be noted, however, that the correlations quoted between the sixth and seventh edition booklets are no higher, and indeed tend to be lower, than those quoted between adjacent booklets of the seventh edition despite a somewhat smaller proportion of common items in the latter. Booklets D and EF, for example, correlate together about .86, but only .80 and .77 with the corresponding sixth edition Booklets D and E.

In general no a priori justification is made for the inclusion of any particular item type. From Booklet D onwards certain subtests have been added, however, so that separate verbal and quantitative scores could be obtained, although the user is warned against employing those derived from Booklets D and EF except for research purposes since, in the few empirical studies quoted, no sizable differences occur at these levels among the correlations of V and Q scores and grades in verbal and quantitative subjects. The inclusion of a perceptual test among the other quantitative tests at these levels is questionable.

It can be argued that, unlike achievement tests, nationally representative norms are of paramount importance for intelligence tests. This certainly appears to be the view held by the test authors, yet, while the difficulties involved in carrying out this task appear to have been fully appreciated, the steps taken to obtain a representative sample fall far short of ideal. Despite uneasiness, however, about the methods employed to select schools, a remarkably close agreement was found in one study with a group of fourth graders, between the means and standard deviations for IQ's derived from these tests (123.0 and 19.2) and from Stanford-Binet Form L-M (123.6 and 18.5). A comparison with WAIS IQ's for a group of twelfth graders did not produce such agreement.

Perhaps the greatest change in this edition is in the reporting of scores, and the author is to be congratulated on the clarity with which different methods of doing this are presented. Grade percentile ranks are provided for each booklet for the beginning, middle, and end of the school year, and users are gently encouraged to employ them. Tables of deviation IQ's, with a mean of 100 and a standard deviation of 16, are also provided, and for those who find difficulty in weaning themselves from the concept, instructions are given for estimating mental ages. Finally, apparently again to encourage broader grouping of scores, there are tables for converting IQ's into stanine equivalents.

Data on reliability are extensively and well reported in the manuals, and the coefficients quoted are generally satisfactory if not high. Test-retest coefficients, with as much as two grades between testings, range from .83 to .92; while testing with adjacent forms produces correlations from .77 to .89. For Booklets K to CD split-half coefficients range from .93 to .95, and in Booklets D, EF, G, and H, factor analyses of subtests were carried out, from which estimates of the reliability for the total score were made ranging from .85 to .95. The reliabilities of the V and Q scores from Booklets G and H estimated from the same data were much lower, and the reliability of the V-Q difference, lower still. Users, however, are clearly warned against any rash interpretations of such differences.

As was stated above, it is claimed that the validity of the sixth edition was "built into the Seventh" by the method of item analysis employed. However, despite a proportion of common content, the range of correlations reported between similar level booklets in the two editions is little different from what might be obtained between separate measures of, say, arithmetic and English, and hence constitutes no valid argument for supposing that the tests of the two editions are in fact measuring the same thing. Nor is this reviewer really impressed with the numerous (more than 150) correlations reported between these tests and other tests of intelligence and measures of achievement. These range, over all booklets, from the high .40's to the high .80's; but a good vocabulary test would also yield correlations of this order. The fact is that no evidence of concurrent validity will ever *prove* that these tests are measuring "intelligence" or "academic potential."

That these tests are measuring academic potential is certainly more assumed than proved. The manuals give no evidence, for example, to show that, given appropriate remedial treatment, pupils of low achievement but apparently high potential according to the tests are more likely to show improvement in school subjects than pupils of similar achievement levels who are apparently already working up to their potential.

An obvious point that is worth stressing yet again is that intelligence tests should only be used if satisfactory empirical evidence is available to show that the tests are valid for the purposes intended, be it grouping, predicting academic success, diagnosing underachievement, or whatever. Furthermore, such evidence should be based on groups as similar as possible to those to whom the tests are to be given. Unfortunately, while some quite satisfactory evidence is given in the manuals concerning the predictive validity of these tests, insufficient descriptive data (means, SD's, etc.) are given to enable a user to judge its relevance for his own group.

In summary it can be said that the reputation of these Kuhlmann-Anderson tests should be distinctly enhanced by the seventh edition, which now incorporates most of the desirable features that the user of modern tests requires. It is to be hoped that further validatory evidence, relevant to the actual use to which these tests will be put, will be published shortly.

Personnel & Guid J 40:481–4 Ja '62. Frederick B. Davis. [Review of Booklets G and H.] * attractively printed * An excellent *Manual of Directions for Administering and Scoring the Test* and a comprehensive *Technical Manual* are ....provided. * The seventh edition yields verbal, quantitative, and total raw scores, percentile ranks for each of these scores in each of grades seven through twelve (based on beginning-of-the-year testing), and deviation IQ scores corresponding to the total raw scores. IQ scores are not provided for the verbal and quantitative scores separately. * the verbal and quantitative scores are highly correlated * No convenient way of evaluating the difference between an individual's verbal and quantitative score is provided. The V and Q scores are not directly comparable so the method for evaluating their statistical significance given on page 27 of the *Technical Manual* cannot properly be used in the manner illustrated. * The reliability coefficients of the V, Q, and Total scores and of the IQ's derived from the Total scores are very satisfactory for tests of this type that take only 45 minutes to administer. * Some counselors and psychologists have been worried by the fact that most pupils do not have a chance to try all of the items in the parts of the Kuhlmann-Anderson tests. Scores, therefore, are greatly influenced by the rate at which pupils try the items. Data provided in the *Technical Manual* show this to be a fact. Pupils at the same level in capacity to understand concepts, to remember and use word meanings correctly, and to make arithmetic computations accurately work at different rates of speed. Habit, predisposition, and motivation greatly affect speed of mental operation. Counselors and psychologists who prefer to measure level of performance separately from speed of performance will not find the seventh edition of these tests any more to their liking than previous editions. In the *Technical Manual,* Dr. Anderson indicates a belief that intelligence tests should measure speed of mental functioning. Data are presented that show that doubling the time limits for the parts of the Kuhlmann-Anderson tests increases only slightly the correlations of V and Q scores with various achievement-test scores and with academic grades. It seems reasonable to conclude that these tests measure ability to succeed in school as well as any tests of their type. A commendable effort was made to obtain norm groups representative of all American school children in the grades for which the tests are appropriate for use. * Inspection of the items reveals them to be in generally good shape. The brightest pupils may be a bit troubled by some of the items in Test 2 of Booklet G. The procedure for getting the keyed response to items in this test consists sometimes of dropping out one number to leave a rule-following set of four numbers (as in Sample X) and sometimes of changing a number to create a rule-following set of five numbers (as in Sample Y). If the examinee creates a rule-following set of five numbers by changing, say 4, 6, 8, 9, 10 to 4, 6, 8, 10, 12, he will get no credit for the item if he marks both changes (9 to 10 and 10 to 12) or if he marks only the change of 10 to 12. In item 19 of this test, a rule-following series of five numbers can be created by changing choice E (17) to 15. But the response keyed as correct assumes the creation of a rule-following series of four numbers by dropping out choice B (10). * Since correction for chance is not employed, the answer sheets must be carefully inspected prior to scoring for excess marks per item. More than one mark is proper for some items so this inspection is more of a chore than usual. Then the excess marks must be erased (for machine scoring) or crossed out (for hand scoring). Since the tests were constructed to be administered with time limits so short that very few examinees would reach items near the end of any part, correction for chance success would be of maximum usefulness in scoring them. As they are scored, examinees who disregard the directions to "avoid careless guessing" and proceed to mark a response to every item (guessing when necessary) will tend to have an advantage over conscientious examinees who try to follow instructions to the letter. Finally, it should be pointed out that a large amount of very interesting and useful information about the development and uses of the test is given in the *Norms Manual* and the *Technical Manual*. The author and publisher are to be congratulated.

For reviews by Henry E. Garrett and David Segel of the sixth edition, see 4:302; for reviews by W. G. Emmett and Stanley S. Marzolf of an earlier edition, see 3:236; for a review by Henry E. Garrett, see 40:1404; for reviews by Psyche Cattell, S. A. Courtis, and Austin H. Turney, see 38:1049.

[467]

***The Lorge-Thorndike Intelligence Tests.** Grades kgn–1, 2–3, 4–6, 7–9, 10–12; 1954–62; IBM and MRC for grades 4–12; Forms A, B, ('54, 6–11 pages); 5 levels; 2 tests (nonverbal, verbal) and 2 editions (consumable, reusable) of each test for levels 3–5; manual ('57, 20–32 pages) for each level (1–5); MRC manual ('59, 32 pages) for each level (3–5); revised technical manual ('62, 24 pages); *Levels 1–2:* $3.45 per 35 tests; *Levels 3–5:* $2.70 per 35 copies of either test of consumable edition, separate answer sheets must be used with reusable edition, $3 per 35 copies of either test of reusable edition, $1.44 per 35 IBM answer sheets for either test, 24¢ per scoring stencil, $7.50 per 100 MRC answer sheets for both tests, 45¢ per MRC stencil for hand scoring (machine scoring service, by Measurement Research Center, Inc., may be arranged through the publisher), 45¢ per MRC manual; 45¢ per technical manual; 45¢ per combined specimen set of levels 1–2; 45¢ per specimen set of any one of levels 3–5; $2.25 per complete specimen set; postage extra; Spanish directions available for nonverbal batteries; Irving Lorge and Robert L. Thorndike; Houghton Mifflin Co. *

a) LEVEL 1, NONVERBAL BATTERY. Grades kgn–1; (35) minutes in 2 or 3 sessions.

b) LEVEL 2, NONVERBAL BATTERY. Grades 2–3; (35) minutes.

c) LEVEL 3. Grades 4–6; IBM and MRC.
1) *Verbal Battery.* 34(44–49) minutes.
2) *Nonverbal Battery.* 27(37–39) minutes.

d) LEVEL 4. Grades 7–9; IBM and MRC.
1) *Verbal Battery.* 34(44–49) minutes.
2) *Nonverbal Battery.* 27(37–39) minutes.

e) LEVEL 5. Grades 10–12; IBM and MRC.
1) *Verbal Battery.* 34(44–49) minutes.
2) *Nonverbal Battery.* 27(37–39) minutes.

REFERENCES

1–6. See 5:350.
7. HAGE, DEAN SILVERS. *The Effect of Reading Proficiency on Intelligence Scores.* Doctor's thesis, State University of Iowa (Iowa City, Iowa), 1957. (*DA* 18:930)
8. HAGE, DEAN S., AND STROUD, JAMES B. "Reading Proficiency and Intelligence Scores, Verbal and Nonverbal." *J Ed Res* 52:258–62 Mr '59. * (*PA* 34:4813)
9. KNIEF, LOTUS M., AND STROUD, JAMES B. "Intercorrelations Among Various Intelligence, Achievement, and Social Class Scores." *J Ed Psychol* 50:117–20 Je '59. * (*PA* 35:779)
10. GNAUCK, JOHANNA, AND KACZKOWSKI, HENRY. "Prediction of Junior High School Performance." *Ed & Psychol Meas* 21:485–8 su '61. * (*PA* 36:2KL85G)
11. ANDERSON, WILLIAM F. "Relation of Lorge-Thorndike Intelligence Test Scores of Public School Pupils to the Socio-Economic Status of Their Parents." *J Exp Ed* 31:73–6 S '62. * (*PA* 37:7990)
12. BROMER, JOHN A.; JOHNSON, J. MYRON; AND SEVRANSKY, PAUL. "Validity Information Exchange, No. 15-02: D.O.T. Code 4-97.010, 4-75.120, 4-85.040, Craft Foremen Correspond to Foremen I; 5-91.275, 5-91.088, 5-91.091, 5-91.831, 5-91.812, Process, Production, and Warehouse Foremen Correspond to Foremen II." *Personnel Psychol* 15:107–9 sp '62. *
13. DOHERTY, VICTOR W., AND INGEBO, GEORGE S. "The Development of a School Ability Measure Based on the Lorge-Thorndike Intelligence Test." *Yearb Nat Council Meas Ed* 19:67–71 '62. *
14. KILGORE, LEONARD LOUIS, JR. *Relationships Between Socioeconomic Levels and Changes in Measured Intelligence.* Doctor's thesis, George Peabody College for Teachers (Nashville, Tenn.), 1962. (*DA* 23:2009)
15. WOMER, FRANK B. "BJMP Test Project Establishes Local Norms." *Mich Ed J* 39:522–3+ Ap '62. *
16. CAPLAN, STANLEY W.; RUBLE, RONALD A.; AND SEGEL, DAVID. "A Theory of Educational and Vocational Choice in Junior High School." *Personnel & Guid J* 42:129–35 O '63. *
17. MACARTHUR, R. S., AND ELLEY, W. B. "The Reduction of Socioeconomic Bias in Intelligence Testing." *Brit J Ed Psychol* 33:107–19 Je '63. * (*PA* 38:4271)

For reviews by Frank S. Freeman, John E. Milholland, and D. A. Pidgeon, see 5:350.

[468]

★Lowry-Lucier Reasoning Test Combination. Grades 5–16 and adults; 1956–59; 3 scores: total and 2 scores listed below; 2 tests; manual ('59, 15 pages); no data on reliability; tentative norms; $3.50 per 25 copies of either test; $6.50 per 25 sets of both tests; $1 per key; 50¢ per manual; postage extra; specimen set not available; Ellsworth Lowry (test) and Omer Lucier; distributed by Rowland & Co. *

a) TEST A. Sequential relations; 1 form ('56, 3 pages); 15(20) minutes.

b) TEST B. Spatial relations; 1 form ('56, 3 pages); 20(25) minutes.

REFERENCES

1. LUCIER, OMER, AND BURNETTE, RICHARD. "The Lowry Reasoning Test Combination With Younger Adolescents." Abstract. *Am Psychologist* 12:373 Jl '57. *
2. BURNETT, ELIZABETH LEE. *A Study of the Validity and Reliability of the Lowry Reasoning Test Combination in Grades Five, Six, and Seven.* Master's thesis, University of Richmond (Richmond, Va.), 1958.
3. LEBO, DELL; ANDREWS, ROBERT S.; AND LUCIER, OMER. "The Lowry Test: A Simple Status-Free Measure of Intellectual Ability." *J Appl Psychol* 43:411–2 D '59. * (*PA* 34:7352)
4. ANDREWS, ROBERT S.; LEBO, DELL; AND LUCIER, OMER. "A Pragmatic Validation of a Simple, Status Free Measure of Intellectual Ability." *J Social Psychol* 54:273–82 Ag '61. * (*PA* 36:3LD73A)
5. LUCIER, OMER, AND BURNETTE, RICHARD. "The Lowry Reasoning Test Combination With Younger Adolescents." *J Social Psychol* 55:113–24 O '61. * (*PA* 36:4HD13L)
6. LUCIER, OMER, AND FARLEY, JOHN. "The Lowry Reasoning Test Combination as a Status Free Technique." *J Social Psychol* 55:125–31 O '61. * (*PA* 36:4HB25L)

ANDREW R. BAGGALEY, *Professor of Psychology, Temple University, Philadelphia, Pennsylvania.*

These two tests represent an attempt to develop a short measure of reasoning ability that is relatively uninfluenced by cultural experiences. Test A contains questions concerning serial relationships among days of the week, and Test B contains problems involving the elimination of match sticks from rectangular designs to obtain specified results. Both tests are quite steeply graded in difficulty. The homogeneous nature of the items probably justifies the temporary absence of measures of internal consistency, but it would be highly desirable for the test manual to report retest reliabilities. The instructions for administration are appropriately detailed, especially for examinees under 15 years of age.

Recently published research indicates that the *Lowry-Lucier Reasoning Test Combination* is less correlated with measures of social status than each of three commonly used intelligence tests. In one of these studies, the correlation was lower within the groups of middle and low status examinees than within the high status examinees. Yet the Lowry-Lucier test gave somewhat higher validities for predicting criterion performance of soldiers and school children. The test manual reports the means and standard deviations of test scores for pupils in the fifth, sixth, and seventh grades, college freshmen, and soldiers.

The authors suggest that their test may be particularly valuable in "the selection of college freshmen from rural areas and lower class homes." In view of the data that have been reported so far, such research seems to be well worth undertaking.

RUSSEL F. GREEN, *Associate Professor of Psychology, The University of Rochester, Rochester, New York.*

Information concerning the properties of this test is as yet too sketchy to permit its recommendation for any specific situation except one: it can be used as a research instrument if it appears appropriate to one's needs. However, it might also prove useful as a measure of scholastic aptitude which is freer than usual of bias from formal education and social class, *providing* the user is willing to develop his own norms, to carry out his own validation and reliability studies, and probably also even to perform his own item analyses.

The authors stress the idea that the test is essentially free of class bias. It probably is not entirely free of such bias but one can agree that it is more so than the usual IQ test. This is achieved by using more familiar materials to construct problems than is normally done.

The test is divided into two parts and involves the use of two rather novel kinds of materials. Subtest A uses manipulations of time relationships defined in terms of the days of the week. Subtest B uses a series of match stick problems. Contrary to the expectations of the authors, experience on both subtests is not really constant since similar ideas have occurred as parlor games and puzzles.

The authors state that the test "estimates" reasoning abilities: part A, verbal reasoning interacting with immediate memory; part B, spatial visualization. No validation for these claims is offered. Apparently the test correlates with measures of "general intelligence" somewhere in the range of .5 to .7, so that while it overlaps up to half of the variance of IQ tests, it is no substitute for them. It has, however, predicted proficiency ratings of a small group of servicemen at least as well as one general intelligence measure (.45 versus .34), and it has predicted grade-point averages of a seventh grade class as well as another such measure (.59 versus .57). If on further analysis validities such as these continue to be found, then it might be that greater utility could be achieved with this test than with most intelligence tests since it is briefer than most of them.

Anyone interested in trying to use the test should look closely at the possibility that the later items in subtest B might not correlate well with the earlier items of the subtest. For some of these items the solutions can be found only by correctly inferring that additional instructions are contained in the solutions to immediately preceding items. The subject is not warned of this. This procedure is rather unusual and may well have undesirable effects. If it does, then improvements in the instructions might yield improved results.

In summary, the test contains an interesting idea which may prove quite useful if and when it is adequately standardized and validated.

[469]

★**Maddox Verbal Reasoning Test.** Ages 9.5–10.5; 1960; 1 form (12 pages); manual (14 pages); 5*d.* per test; 1*s.* 9*d.* per manual; postage and purchase tax extra; 45(60) minutes; H. Maddox; Oliver & Boyd Ltd. *

T. R. MILES, *Professor of Psychology, University College of North Wales, Bangor, Wales.*

"Assuming that a child has had an ordinary schooling and the usual educational opportunities," says Maddox, "verbal tests of this type are the best available predictors of school performance." This claim may well be true, but it is unfortunate that no references are given in support. Despite this criticism, however, the test can certainly be commended; it is clearly the work of a skilled educationalist who has taken considerable trouble over standardisation and related matters.

There is little to criticise on the practical side. However, in question 50 ("We painted the chair....not the table") the only correct word for filling the blank is given as "but," whereas there are surely contexts where "and" is as good (e.g., if we did not have time to paint both or misunderstood which of the two we were supposed to paint). Also (question 60) it is false that a game always has player*s* (in the plural); patience has only one player. As regards unfair items, however, this test seems to the reviewer to compare very favourably with others of the same kind.

On the theoretical side one is far less happy. The test is said to provide "a measure of verbal intelligence for children between the ages of 9½ and 10½"; but in the very next paragraph the author states, "It should be regarded as measuring scholastic aptitude rather than pure intelligence," while two paragraphs later one reads, "It should not be assumed, however, that a low score on the test necessarily indicates lack of intelligence." Finally, the manual tells how to convert the scores into IQ's; but unless "IQ" is being redefined out of all recognition this surely means that the test *is* measuring intelligence after all. Thus in four sentences one is apparently told twice that the test does measure intelligence and twice that it does not! If Maddox had limited himself to saying "This is a test that will be useful in helping to 'stream' children in the junior school" and had added the proviso that one should be cautious in interpreting a low score, he could have omitted the controversial references to "intelligence" and "IQ" altogether. In the reviewer's opinion the concept of "IQ" is one of the biggest disasters in the history of psychology; because of its connexion with the word "intelligence" it is ambiguous, and in addition it implies a false view as to what can be done to *improve* children's intelligence.

Of its kind this is undoubtedly a good test; but it cannot be too much emphasised that the justification for using such tests is pragmatic and is not based on universally agreed theoretical premises.

A. E. G. Pilliner, *Senior Lecturer in Education, University of Edinburgh, Edinburgh, Scotland.*

In his description of this "omnibus" test the author points out that it is intended to measure scholastic aptitude rather than pure intelligence. Unfortunately it is probably necessary still to issue such a warning with tests of this sort.

The test proper, occupying 45 minutes without pauses, is preceded by a practice test lasting 15 minutes. In the latter most (but not all) of the item types included in the test proper are exemplified and worked by the children under the guidance of the teacher who (though this is insufficiently stressed) is expected to adhere exactly to the text presented.

The items employed in the test are conventional in type: alphabet items, similarities (several forms), opposites, "doesn't belong," missing words, "always has," order, series, and problems. The author is perhaps wise to limit himself to these well tried types which, however, have now been employed so extensively that other constructors will find many old friends amongst the items in this test. This is not a serious defect, provided the items are well constructed, which, in the main, they are. However, few tests are perfect in this respect, and the Maddox test is not one of them. Thus item 4 ("Which is the last letter of the alphabet that appears in DESERT but not in DANGER?") might be more intelligible to the testees if it read "Which is the letter latest in the alphabet that appears...." Also the notorious difficulty of avoiding ambiguity in classification items is exemplified here. Are a crab and a lobster "more alike," because they are crustaceans, than a herring and an eel, which are fish? Are fish and meat, both fleshy foods, "more alike" than peas and apples, both spherical? Again, items in which missing words are to be inserted sometimes present difficulties. The gap in "We painted the chair ______ not the table" is filled better by "but" than by "and"; but the latter (which is not credited) conforms to the requirement of being "sensible and right." So, too, in circumstances not too difficult to conceive, is "told" (not credited) used to fill the gap in "He ______ me what I was doing," though certainly it would be less usual than the required response "asked." Finally, the familiar "cyclic" difficulty again crops up. Which are the extremes in May,

July, January, September, March? It all depends on where one starts. Is the child who starts at May and finishes at March to be penalised for his unconventionality?

There are a few further points which can be easily dealt with in later editions. One item refers to ten men and 5 days. In another, the answer £1 is given credit, but not, apparently, 20 shillings, which seems hard. Yet another, in which different breeds of dog are to be assigned to their owners—a good item, this—is overdetermined.

The test norms presented in the manual are of the type now conventional. They relate testees' total raw scores and ages to standardised scores normally distributed with a standard deviation of 15 about a mean of 100. Standardisation is based on a representative sample of 4,518 children in Birmingham and Staffordshire, but the method of selecting the sample is not reported. The only reliability coefficient presented in the manual is K-R 20 = .95, a somewhat low result which, however, cannot be properly evaluated since no information is given about the nature of the sample from which it was obtained. Information is lacking also about the sample of 108 children, all from one school, for whom the correlation between scores on this test and scores on Schonell's *Essential Intelligence Test* was .86. The reviewer suggests that subsequent editions of the manual should report the Maddox test mean and standard deviation for the group so that interpretation of this validity coefficient is made possible. It would be useful also if the author were to report the procedure used in particularly designing the test "to give reliable scores in the I.Q. (standardised score) range 100 to 120," and to present evidence of the success achieved.

Finally, this reviewer cannot agree with the statement made in the manual that "at this age (9½–10½) it first becomes possible to obtain reliable test scores by the group test method." Evidence of group test-retest correlations at 7+ of nearly .9, and at 9+ of .95, is available.

To sum up: the criticisms made of the test are generally of a minor character. On the whole it is sound, though it displays few original features. The manual would benefit by a fuller reporting of the nature of the standardisation sample and of reliability and validity data. It remains to add that the publishers are to be congratulated on the excellent appearance of the test.

This reviewer agrees with the author that the test "should prove useful as an internal school examination and assist in allocating children to classes within the junior school."

Brit J Ed Psychol 30:289–90 N '60. Almost all group intelligence tests for children below 10½ use the Mental Age method of scoring, thus this new one will be a welcome addition for testing third-year juniors. It closely resembles a Moray House Verbal Reasoning test with deviation-quotient norms, though in fact, it does not register below I.Q. 78 at 9½ years. It was standardised on some 4,500 children in the Midlands. The one-hundred items are of conventional type, and 45 minutes are allowed. It is preceded by a practice sheet taking about 15 minutes, but thereafter, the children have to read the instructions and items for themselves. The author admits its dependence on reading, and prefers to regard it as a measure of "scholastic aptitude" rather than "intelligence."

[470]

***Manchester General Ability Test (Senior).** Ages 12-10 to 14-6, 13-6 to 15-2; 1952–59; 2 levels; no data on validity; postage and purchase tax extra; Stephen Wiseman; University of London Press Ltd. *
a) MANCHESTER GENERAL ABILITY TEST (SEN.) 1. Ages 12-10 to 14-6; 1 form ['52, 8 pages]; manual ['52, 11 pages]; practice test ['52, 1 page]; 5*s.* 6*d.* per 12 tests; 7*d.* per single copy; 1*s.* per 12 practice tests; 1*d.* per single copy; 9*d.* per manual; 10(15) minutes for practice test, 45(50) minutes for test.
b) MANCHESTER GENERAL ABILITY TEST (SEN.) 2. Ages 13-6 to 15-2; 1 form ('59, 8 pages); manual ('59, 8 pages); 5*s.* 6*d.* per 12 tests; 7*d.* per single copy; 1*s.* 6*d.* per manual; 60(65) minutes.

REFERENCES

1. WRIGLEY, JACK. "The Factorial Nature of Ability in Elementary Mathematics." *Brit J Ed Psychol* 28:61–78 F '58. * (*PA* 33:6845)

A. W. HEIM, *Medical Research Council, The Psychological Laboratory, University of Cambridge, Cambridge, England.*

These two group tests are fun to do. They comprise a wide variety of verbal and numerical problems, some of which have original and entertaining features. The verbal items include analogies, series, sames-opposites, "scrambled" words, and classification questions; the numerical items include the supplying of omitted digits in multiplication and division calculations and the completion of ingenious tables such as a table of school cricket scores with "some of the scores....omitted owing to the carelessness of our scorer, Blenkinsop." There are no diagrammatic or pictorial items. Wiseman states that these tests "are designed to measure 'general ability' or what is usually known as 'verbal intelligence.'" The reviewer considers the equating of these two concepts to be controversial and, in view of the substantial minority of numerically biased items, questions the exclusively verbal nature of what is tested here.

There is, however, little doubt that the 13- to 15-year-olds for whom the tests are intended will enjoy doing them and this important condition for successful testing seems often to be forgotten. The original features include among other things: the instruction in the sames-opposites sections to "choose the numbered word which means nearly the same *or* nearly the opposite of the first word"; the requirement in analogy items of choice from three words in each of two parts of the analogy; and, in the classification questions, the precautionary measure, "In these questions you have to find the word in the second line [six words] which is most like the three words in capitals [first line] and is different from the rest."

Despite this precaution, some of the classifications—as seems almost inevitable with such items—appear to the reviewer to lack cogency. For example, in the question, "BUT IF OR 1. go 2. and 3. man 4. yes 5. perhaps 6. when," the correct answer, according to the manual, is 2. Surely an equally good case could be made for 6.

Similar objections apply to some of the sames-opposites—which do, of course, require particular care in view of their instruction to choose a word which means nearly the same *or* nearly the opposite. For instance, in the question, "*PERMIT:* 1. JUDGE 2. FORGIVE 3. BLAME 4. ALLOW 5. ADMIT 6. DENY," 4 and 6 are equally defensible. It seems especially unfortunate that this should be the first item in one of the tests. And in view of current butcher terminology, in the following question, 4 seems as apt as 5! "*PIG* is to PORK as 1. *BEEF* 2. *VEAL* 3. *SHEEP* is to 4. LAMB 5. MUTTON 6. CALF."

These doubtful questions are rare, however; they occur more frequently in classifications than in any other type of item; and, not unnaturally, they are more frequent in the harder than in the easier questions. A more serious criticism is the lack of a preliminary test for Sen. 2 for the subjects to work through on their own, and the inadequacy of the preliminary examples which are provided in the practice test for Sen. 1. These latter examples (*a*) offer only four alternatives from which to choose, as opposed to the six offered in the test itself, and (*b*) are, apart from this, intrinsically easier problems than occur on the whole in the test proper. In addition, the tester is specifically told, in the manual, that whether the subjects "are getting the right answers or not does not matter—what is important is that they are not *writing* an answer if a *number* is required." Thus some of the most vital reasons for having preliminary examples for the subject to work through are explicitly ignored.

There are some minor objections to the layout. For instance, in the supply-digits calculations where alignment is important there is occasional misalignment, and the presentation of question numbers which are printed on a level with the answer numbers and are identical with these in shape and size, is apt to be confusing, especially as this occurs at the very beginning of the test.

The manuals are satisfactory apart from the points already made about preliminary practice and what the tests are designed to measure. On the latter point, it is worth mentioning that absolutely no reference to validation is made in either manual. The reliability is over .90 both on split-half (Spearman-Brown formula correction) and on an unspecified Kuder-Richardson formula. Test-retest reliability is not mentioned. The test instructions are simple and clear; the directions to scorers are exceptionally careful and detailed; and the notes on the interpretation of scores might with benefit be added to every test manual.

For Sen. 1 the standardisation is based on the scores of 4,175 children, aged 13-1 to 14-0 years but conversion tables are given covering the ages 12-10 to 14-6. Instructions are given for converting the test scores of children aged 14-7 to 15-0, inclusive, by means of extrapolation. For Sen. 2 the standardisation is based on the scores of 13,442 children, aged 14-1 to 15-0 years and conversion tables are given covering the ages 13-6 to 15-2. For this test, neither extrapolation nor IQ is mentioned under the conversion tables but for both tests the standard scores are said to be "comparable with 'I.Q.s' from other group tests of intelligence, *provided that* the constructors of such other tests have used a standard deviation of 15 in compiling their conversion tables."

The reviewer is disquieted by the following combination of facts: (*a*) Sen. 1 is ostensibly for subjects aged 12-10 to 14-6 whilst Sen. 2 is ostensibly for ages 13-6 to 15-2, but (*b*) the two tests, each comprising 100 items, are described as "parallel" although one has a time limit of 45 minutes and the other has a time limit of an hour, yet (*c*) a score of, for example, 10 points gained by a 14½-year-old yields an IQ of 80 on Sen. 1 and of 84 on Sen. 2—the latter test having *the longer time limit.* Such anomalies occur also at the top end of the scale (though not around IQ's of 100). They are due to the fact that Sen. 2, having the same number of items as Sen. 1 but a longer time limit, produces a considerably wider range of scores.

The variety of questions and their subject matter, however, is likely to achieve good motivation and to render the tests more "general" than are the exclusively diagrammatic type of intelligence test. They might well prove a useful pair of tests for the somewhat neglected age groups for which they cater, if satisfactory validation data were adduced.

ARTHUR B. ROYSE, *Lecturer in Psychology, The University of Hull, Hull, England.*

These tests are parallel group verbal tests of conventional type, designed to extend the existing range of tests used for academic selection in English schools to include the neglected ages of 13 to 14 (Sen. 1) and 14 to 15 (Sen. 2). According to the manual, they are thus "more appropriately to be used in the secondary grammar school and the upper ability levels of the secondary modern school." But no indication is given of specific purposes for which they can validly be used. Indeed, no validation data of any kind are given. The author contents himself with the statement that the test provides "a measure of general ability in the verbal and academic field."

This claim appears to be based on nothing stronger than the assumption that because most of the items are of conventional type—sames and opposites, series, analogies, classifications, insertion of missing numbers in sums, etc.—the test must be highly correlated with any similar test for which validation is available.

The same preference for face validity over statistical decision is apparent in the choice of test items. No statistical evidence was collected to justify the inclusion of individual items nor to determine their order of presentation in the tests. Despite this, however, internal consistency is moderately good, "boosted" split-half reliability coefficients of .95 (Sen. 1) and .96 (Sen. 2) and Kuder-Richardson coefficients of .93 (Sen. 1) and .95 (Sen. 2) being obtained. Unfortunately, however, no test-retest reliability coefficients are reported.

The layout and typography of the tests is excellent and the instructions for administration and scoring are lucid and comprehensive. Scoring is simple, each item being scored 0 or 1, and, in the interests of accuracy, the marking instructions are rigid. No credit is allowed for a "correct" answer unless it is indicated in the authorised manner. The provision of a practice test provides an opportunity for the child to learn these rigid requirements while supervisors "make sure all the children are doing the questions in the correct *way.*"

Standardisation was thorough, 4,175 children aged 13-1 to 14 being used for Sen. 1 and 13,442 children aged 14-1 to 15 being used for Sen. 2. In both cases, the group was a virtually complete age group in the area selected. Raw scores are converted to give standardised "quotients" with a mean of 100 and a standard deviation of 15. The conversion tables include extrapolations to cover ages 12-1 to 14-6 for Sen. 1 and 13-6 to 15-2 for Sen. 2, but the basis and justification for these extrapolations is not given. No information is given concerning possible sex differences and no sex differentiation is given in the tables.

The tables indicate that the conventional aim of such tests—that of providing a skewed distribution of raw scores to ensure a wide range of scores in the critical area of decision—was achieved. For the median age group of Sen. 1 the raw scores at the 15th, 50th, 84th, and 95th percentiles are approximately 10, 23, 40, and 53, respectively; for the median age group for Sen. 2 the comparable raw scores are 11, 28, 56, and 74. These data suggest that both tests, but particularly Sen. 1, are rather difficult.

The manual claims that the standardised quotients, although not comparable with IQ's derived from mental age, are comparable with quotients from other group verbal tests having the same standard deviation. The warning against confusion with Binet-type quotients is to be applauded but the claim to comparability with other tests is misleading. If it is meant only to indicate that the MGAT shares with other tests a common method of conversion of raw scores, then the statement is trivial. If, however, it is meant to imply that MGAT quotients are interchangeable with others for purposes of selection, prediction, etc., then it is inaccurate. The claim would be justified only if the two quotients were obtained from tests which (*a*) have been standardised on the same age group, (*b*) are highly correlated, and (*c*) have been converted to the same standard deviation by identical conversion formulae.

Quotients from the two MGAT forms are comparable, however, with each other. Although not standardised on the same age group, both tests were given to the second standardisation group. A correlation of .934 is quoted but despite its computation to three places of decimals, its value is limited because (*a*) it is based only on scores for the 14-1 to 15-0 group and no evidence is given to justify extrapolation to the other groups, (*b*) no evidence is given to justify the assumption of linearity of regression, and (*c*) no indication is given of whether the figure includes corrections for attenuation or for restriction of sample.

On the whole, the MGAT is a good example of the type of verbal test used for academic selection in English schools. Its limitations are shared with many such tests and there is nothing to suggest that it is better than the best of them or worse than the worst of them. The lack of competing tests in the age range covered should ensure its use among those testers who share the compiler's faith in its face validity. But for those testers who believe that intuitive judgment is a poor substitute for statistical decision in selection, and who demand indices of forecasting efficiency for use with specified external criteria in clearly defined situations, the test has little to offer.

For a review by A. E. G. Pilliner of a, *see 5:351.*

[471]

***Mill Hill Vocabulary Scale.** Ages 4 and over, 11–14, 14 and over; 1943–58; 2 editions; manual ('58, 66 pages); 15*s.* per 50 tests; 20*s.* per key; 5*s.* 6*d.* per manual; 25*s.* per specimen set including 5 copies of each form and a specimen set of the complementary *Standard Progressive Matrices;* postage and purchase tax extra; (15–20) minutes; John C. Raven; H. K. Lewis & Co. Ltd. *

a) ORAL DEFINITIONS FORM. Ages 4 and over; consists of all words from both forms of the junior and senior levels below; individual; 1 form ('48, 4 pages).

b) WRITTEN TEST. Ages 11–14, 14 and over; Forms 1, 2, ('48, 4 pages); 2 levels: junior, senior. (Australian edition of senior level: Australian Council for Educational Research.)

REFERENCES

1–3. See 3:239.
4–10. See 4:303.
11. PINKERTON, PHILIP, AND KELLEY, JOSEPH. "An Attempted Correlation Between Clinical and Psychometric Findings in Senile-Arteriosclerotic Dementia." *J Mental Sci* 98:244–55 Ap '52. * (*PA* 27:585)
12. DUNSDON, M. I. "The Application of Vocabulary Tests to a Large Sample of Children." Abstract. *B Brit Psychol Soc* 26:22 inset My '55. *
13. DUNSDON, M. I., AND ROBERTS, J. A. FRASER. "A Study of the Performance of 2,000 Children on Four Vocabulary Tests: 1, Growth Curves and Sex Differences." *Brit J Stat Psychol* 8:3–15 My '55. * (*PA* 30:3363)
14. DUNSDON, M. I., AND ROBERTS, J. A. FRASER. "A Study of the Performance of 2,000 Children on Four Vocabulary Tests: 2, Norms, With Some Observations on the Relative Variability of Boys and Girls." *Brit J Stat Psychol* 10:1–16 My '57. * (*PA* 33:2155)
15. ORME, J. E. "Non-Verbal and Verbal Performance in Normal Old Age, Senile Dementia, and Elderly Depression." *J Gerontol* 12:408–13 O '57. *
16. FOULDS, G. A. "The Relative Stability of Personality Measures Compared With Diagnostic Measures." *J Mental Sci* 105:783–7 Jl '59. * (*PA* 34:6016)
17. DESAI, MAHESH M. "Intelligence and Verbal Knowledge in Relation to Epstein's Overinclusion Test." *J Clin Psychol* 16:417–9 O '60. * (*PA* 37:3226)
18. DUNSDON, M. I., AND ROBERTS, J. A. FRASER. Chap. 3, "A Study of the Performance of 2000 Children on Four Vocabulary Tests," pp. 41–76. In *Stoke Park Studies: Mental Subnormality (Second Series): World Mental Health Year Memorial Volume.* Edited by J. Jancar. Bristol, England: John Wright & Sons Ltd., 1961. Pp. x, 135. *
19. LYNN, R., AND GORDON, I. E. "The Relation of Neuroticism and Extraversion to Intelligence and Educational Attainment." *Brit J Ed Psychol* 31:194–203 Je '61. * (*PA* 36:3HD94L)
20. VENABLES, ETHEL C. "Placement Problems Among Engineering Apprentices in Part-Time Technical College Courses: Part 2, Level of Ability Needed for Success in National Certificate Courses." *Brit J Ed Psychol* 31:56–8 F '61. * (*PA* 36:1KJ56V)
21. COSTA, LOUIS D., AND VAUGHAN, HERBERT G., JR. "Performance of Patients With Lateralized Cerebral Lesions: 1, Verbal and Perceptual Tests." *J Nerv & Mental Dis* 134:162–8 F '62. *
22. FOULDS, G. A., AND DIXON, PENELOPE. "The Nature of Intellectual Deficit in Schizophrenia: Part 1, A Comparison of Schizophrenics and Neurotics." *Brit J Social & Clin Psychol* 1:7–19 F '62. * (*PA* 37:1788)
23. FOULDS, G. A., AND DIXON, PENELOPE. "The Nature of Intellectual Deficit in Schizophrenia: Part 3, A Longitudinal Study of the Sub-Groups." *Brit J Social & Clin Psychol* 1:199–207 O '62. * (*PA* 37:5488)
24. FOULDS, G. A.; DIXON, PENELOPE; MCCLELLAND, MARILYN; AND MCCLELLAND, W. J. "The Nature of Intellectual Deficit in Schizophrenia: Part 2, A Cross-Sectional Study of Paranoid, Catatonic, Hebephrenic and Simple Schizophrenics." *Brit J Social & Clin Psychol* 1:141–9 Je '62. * (*PA* 37:3685)
25. GRAHAM, CONRAD. "Differential Marking of Two Vocabulary Tests." *Psychol Rep* 12:421 Ap '63. * (*PA* 38:4275)
26. HAMILTON, VERNON. "I.Q. Changes in Chronic Schizophrenia." *Brit J Psychiatry* 109:642–8 S '63. * (*PA* 38:6506)

MORTON BORTNER, *Chief Psychologist, Department of Physical Medicine and Rehabilitation, New York Medical College, New York, New York.*

The author recommends that this test be used in conjunction with his *Progressive Matrices.* This vocabulary test consists of two sets (A and B) of 44 words of graduated difficulty.

There are three variations of this basic set of words. The first version is individually administered and consists of the examiner reading the words from both Sets A and B to the testee and writing down the responses. In the manual this is called the Standard Scale and is also referred to as the Oral Definitions Test. On the test form it is called the Definitions Form, and the normative data for this test are under the heading Oral Test. This kind of presentation of information is likely to lead to some confusion.

The second version, called the Written Test, consists of the first 33 words of each set; it is administered as follows: the testee writes his definitions to Set A and chooses from multiple choice items on Set B. This method makes the test feasible for group testing and also provides one with two comparison scores which the author believes to be clinically useful. A more difficult third version, the senior level of the Written Test, consists of the last 33 words of the original 44 and is administered in the same way as described for the second version.

Retest reliability figures for the Written Test range from .87 to .98. No reliability data are offered for the Oral Test. No validity coefficients are offered for either test.

It may be difficult to interpret poor performance on that portion of the test which requires the testee to write his answers, for poor spelling ability may lead him to use inappropriate substitute words, or his general expressive ability may be systematically inferior to his actual comprehension as indicated by an oral test. These considerations suggest that this test is measuring more than merely the "acquired information" the author seeks in order to supplement his *Progressive Matrices.*

The suggestion that this test be used together with the *Standard Progressive Matrices* helps to counterbalance the latter's excessively perceptual approach to the measurement of intelligence. It does not go far enough, since it still leaves unmeasured the variety of measureable abilities commonly subsumed under the matrix of intelligence.

All good clinicians are aware of a hierarchy of cognitive levels implied in different vocabulary responses. They also interpret many vocabulary responses in the light of personality psychodynamics. The suggestions by the author dealing with qualitative analyses of these factors are valuable and point the way to a use of the test that goes beyond its resultant scores.

For a review by David Wechsler, see 3:239.

[472]

***Miller Analogies Test.** Candidates for graduate school; 1926-63; IBM; Forms G ('47), H ('50), J ('52), K ('59), (4 pages); use of Form G restricted to special projects approved by the publisher; Form H also published under the title *Advanced Personnel Test* for use in business; revised manual ('60, 23 pages); bulletin of information ('63, 36 pages); revised procedures for testing center operation ('63, 8 pages); distribution restricted and test administered at specified licensed university centers; scoring and reporting handled by the local center; examination fee to centers: $1 per examinee; fees to examinees are determined locally and include reporting of scores to the examinee and to 3 institutions or companies designated at the time of testing; additional score reports may be secured from the publisher at a fee of $1 each; 50(55) minutes: W. S. Miller; Psychological Corporation. *

REFERENCES

1-16. See 4:304.
17-44. See 5:352.
45. MOFFETT, CHARLES R. *Operational Characteristics of Beginning Master's Students in Educational Administration and Supervision.* Doctor's thesis, University of Tennessee (Knoxville, Tenn.), 1954.
46. LUTON, JAMES N. *A Study of the Use of Standardized Tests in the Selection of Potential Educational Administrators.* Doctor's thesis, University of Tennessee (Knoxville, Tenn.), 1955.
47. NUNNERY, MICHAEL Y. *A Study in the Use of Psychological Tests in Determining Effectiveness and Ineffectiveness Among Practicing School Administrators.* Doctor's thesis, University of Tennessee (Knoxville, Tenn.), 1958. (*DA* 19:1276)
48. BADAL, ALDEN WESLEY. *The Relationship of Selected Test Measures to Administrator Success in the Elementary School.* Doctor's thesis, Stanford University (Stanford, Calif.), 1959. (*DA* 20:1263)
49. KELLY, E. LOWELL, AND GOLDBERG, LEWIS R. "Correlates of Later Performance and Specialization in Psychology: A Follow-Up Study of the Trainees Assessed in the VA Selection Research Project." *Psychol Monogr* 73(12):1-32 '59. * (*PA* 34:7952)
50. NUNNERY, MICHAEL Y. "How Useful Are Standardized Psychological Tests in the Selection of School Administrators." *Ed Adm & Sup* 45:349-56 N '59. * (*PA* 35:7092)
51. PLATZ, ARTHUR; MCCLINTOCK, CHARLES; AND KATZ, DANIEL. "Undergraduates Grades and the Miller Analogies Test as Predictors of Graduate Success." *Am Psychologist* 14:285-9 Je '59. * (*PA* 34:4817)
52. SCHWARTZ, MILTON M., AND CLARK, F. EUGENE. "Prediction of Success in Graduate School at Rutgers University." *J Ed Res* 53:109-11 N '59. * (*PA* 35:1223)
53. SPIELBERGER, CHARLES D. "Evidence of a Practice Effect on the Miller Analogies Test." *J Appl Psychol* 43:259-63 Ag '59. * (*PA* 34:6408)
54. WAGGONER, GLEN HASTINGS. *Administrator's Scores on Selected Standardized Tests and His Administrative Performance as Reported by Classroom Teachers.* Doctor's thesis, Stanford University (Stanford, Calif.), 1959. (*DA* 20:3169)
55. BOYCE, RICHARD DUDLEY. *An Empirical Evaluation of Five Tests for Administrator Selection: The Composite Study.* Doctor's thesis, Stanford University (Stanford, Calif.), 1960. (*DA* 21:2546)
56. BURDOCK, E. I.; CHEEK, FRANCES; AND ZUBIN, JOSEPH. "Predicting Success in Psychoanalytic Training," pp. 176-91. In *Current Approaches to Psychoanalysis.* Proceedings of the 48th Annual Meeting of the American Psychopathological Association Held in New York City, February 1958. Edited by Paul H. Hoch and Joseph Zubin. New York: Grune & Stratton, Inc., 1960. Pp. 207. * (*PA* 36:4IE07H)
57. COLADARCI, ARTHUR P. "An Analysis of Miller Analogies Test Score Changes." *Ed & Psychol Meas* 20:817-23 w '60. * (*PA* 35:3405)
58. EBERT, FRANCIS JOHN. *An Empirical Evaluation of Five Tests for the Selection of Elementary School Principals.* Doctor's thesis, Stanford University (Stanford, Calif.), 1960. (*DA* 21:2548)
59. JAMES, KENNETH RAYMOND. *An Empirical Evaluation of Five Tests for Administrator Selection in a Metropolitan School District.* Doctor's thesis, Stanford University (Stanford, Calif.), 1960. (*DA* 21:2556)

60. NELSON, ROBERTA J., AND ENGLAND, GEORGE W. "Graduate Training in Industrial Relations: An Early Look." *Personnel & Guid J* 39:53-7 S '60. * (*PA* 35:4021)
61. BESSENT, EDGAR WAILAND. *The Predictability of Selected Elementary School Principals' Administrative Behavior.* Doctor's thesis, University of Texas (Austin, Tex.), 1961. (*DA* 22:3479)
62. COLVER, ROBERT M., AND SPIELBERGER, CHARLES D. "Further Evidence of a Practice Effect on the Miller Analogies Test." *J Appl Psychol* 45:126-7 Ap '61. * (*PA* 36: 3HD26C)
63. GREENBERG, BRADLEY S. "Predicting Journalism Student Ability." *Journalism Ed* 16:60-5 su '61. *
64. MOORE, ROBERT BURKLAND. *A Comparison of Test Performance and Current Status of Administrative Candidates in Twenty-Four School Districts.* Doctor's thesis, Stanford University (Stanford, Calif.), 1961. (*DA* 22:476)
65. LOCKE, LAWRENCE F. "Performance of Administration Oriented Male Physical Educators on Selected Psychological Tests." *Res Q* 33:418-29 O '62. *
66. SCOTT, C. WINFIELD, AND WEXLER, NORMAN. "Concurrent Validity of the Miller Analogies Test in a Graduate School of Education." *Yearb Nat Council Meas Ed* 19:134-9 '62. *
67. STEFFLRE, BUFORD; KING, PAUL; AND LEAFGREN, FRED. "Characteristics of Counselors Judged Effective by Their Peers." *J Counsel Psychol* 9:335-40 w '62. * (*PA* 39:2312)
68. TULLY, G. EMERSON. "Screening Applicants for Graduate Study With the Aptitude Test of the Graduate Record Examinations." *Col & Univ* 38:51-60 f '62. *
69. *Normative Information: Manager and Executive Testing.* New York: Richardson, Bellows, Henry & Co., Inc., May 1963. Pp. 45. *
70. MEDNICK, MARTHA T. "Research Creativity in Psychology Graduate Students." *J Consult Psychol* 27:265-6 Je '63. * (*PA* 38:958)

LLOYD G. HUMPHREYS, *Professor of Psychology and Head of the Department, University of Illinois, Urbana, Illinois.*

The *Miller Analogies Test* is well known, it has been reviewed earlier by Dailey and others, and there has been little change in recent years other than the publication of a revised manual in 1960. It is a good test, has high reliability in the homogeneous graduate student population, has plenty of top, and has fairly substantial predictive validity for the criterion of graduate school grades. It exists in four alternate forms of which only the earliest (Form G) shows any significant discrepancy from the others in terms of its raw score equivalents. The remaining three forms appear to be about as close to the classical definition of parallel forms as one can find in the psychological literature.

This reviewer's criticisms are directed not so much at the present test as at practices used in its norming and validation, practices that are common to many tests and to many test publishers. The norms, for example, are virtually meaningless. Samples represent in no case any well defined population having general meaning to the test user. For selection purposes this is not critical since norms developed from one's own applicants are most meaningful. The chief competitor of the Miller test, the *Graduate Record Examinations Aptitude Test,* probably has no better norms. The one thing that is certain is that the two sets of norms are based upon quite different groups.

The procedures used in validating the Miller test are deplorable though commonplace. People who have used the test in a particular institution have reported their data in the literature or contributed their data to the author and publisher on a voluntary basis. One wonders, however, how much voluntary suppression of data in which correlations were low has taken place at the local level. The reviewer happens to know of one case in which a negative correlation between the test and graduate grades was not submitted. Research workers, both pure and applied, tend to bury negative findings. The author and publisher have no control over this tendency. It would clearly be better, though more difficult, to obtain in some one year the cooperation of 20 or more large graduate schools, give the test, obtain similar criteria, and report a single coefficient for each criterion (though probably on a within-groups basis).

The present manual reports many validity studies of various kinds, with various criteria, and with many samples. The bewildering array of coefficients presented is difficult to comprehend, though the manual provides some ready-made rationalizations for the range of values provided. Thus, the reader is told that the reliability of course grades varies, the homogeneity of groups varies, some courses are more difficult than others, and some courses require little other than rote memory. The conclusion is: "Each of these conditions would affect the validity coefficients in a specific situation." This reviewer was just a little annoyed with the attitude underlying this section. Each of the propositions is testable, yet none was tested. Furthermore, an even more likely contributor to variance among correlation coefficients, sampling errors associated with small *n*'s, was not mentioned.

It is still probably safe to conclude that this test will make a contribution toward the prediction of academic success in graduate school in most situations. It most nearly parallels the verbal scale of the GRE Aptitude Test, but is not by any means a parallel form of that scale. For reasons of heterogeneity of sources of words used, the reasoning content, or both, it is probably more valid than the GRE verbal scale for appropriate criteria. There is less similarity between the Miller test and the GRE quantitative scale. For criteria for which the latter scale has substantial validity, one would probably not be able to substitute the Miller test. There are no good comparative data, to this reviewer's knowledge, however. This seems surprising considering the very common use of selection tests by departments of psychology, particularly.

WILLIAM B. SCHRADER, *Director of Statistical Analysis, Educational Testing Service, Princeton, New Jersey.*

This well known test has followed faithfully the pattern established by the late W. S. Miller 38 years ago. Initially designed to measure scholastic aptitude at the graduate school level, it has also been found useful in selection for high level positions in business. The difficulty level is well adapted to these uses. Administration is conducted on a decentralized basis with effective procedures for maintaining test security. The test manual, revised in 1960, is attractive and comprehensive.

Empirical validation necessarily plays a prominent role in the interpretation of scores on this test. In all, 95 validity coefficients for the test and tables showing performance of 9 contrasted groups are reported in the manual. These data are accompanied by succinct summaries of the studies in which they were obtained. Users should find this extensive summary helpful.

The manual also includes a general discussion of factors which cause the test to be more effective in one situation than another. The discussion does not mention the fact that correlation coefficients based on small samples have a large sampling error. All but 16 of the 95 validity coefficients are based on samples of less than 100 and 25 are based on samples of less than 50. There is no methodological discussion of the vexing problems of validating tests at the graduate level, so that the reader is not cautioned about the special difficulties that arise when data are pooled across departments in the same university or across universities. Finally, the manual does not state any conclusions about the test on the basis of the data presented. Perhaps no conclusions should be drawn, since the groups and the criteria are exceedingly diverse. However, 11 coefficients from 10 studies related test scores to average grades for graduate students in education, psychology, or both. The median coefficient is .38. This figure should be regarded as reasonably satisfactory when account is taken of the heterogeneity of programs followed by different students, the less than perfect reliability of graduate school grades, and the likelihood that test scores were used in selecting at least some of the groups. The validity evidence as a whole indicates that the test measures abilities which are related to performance in academic and other intellectual fields.

A persistent question about the test is whether or not it measures important abilities over and above verbal ability. That it is predominantly a measure of verbal ability is reasonably clear from the high correlations with verbal tests reported in the manual. (For some reason, the dates for the studies of correlations with other tests have been omitted.) The correlations with verbal tests are undoubtedly lower than the corresponding reliabilities. It appears that a factor study would be needed to clarify the nature of what the test measures.

Norms distributions are given for 18 academic groups and for 5 industrial groups. Means and standard deviations are given for 13 additional industrial groups. Like the validity results, these data suffer from the fact that they are essentially compilations rather than reports of studies conducted by the publisher to answer specific questions. The manual makes no claim that any of the norms groups is representative of anything but itself, but the user is not cautioned that the norms groups may not be representative. For most of the academic groups, the number of students drawn from each academic institution included is specified. Even if it is recognized that local norms should play the chief role in score interpretation, it would seem that efforts to secure data on more nearly representative samples would result in more useful norms.

Beginning in February 1963, scores have been released to the examinees. In spite of the extensive controversy about revealing scores on psychological tests to examinees, the decision to reveal scores to MAT examinees was undoubtedly a wise one. Interestingly enough, this decision raises the norms question discussed in the preceding paragraph in a more acute form. In reporting scores to examinees, condensed normative data for first year graduate students in each of nine major fields are shown. Although the reader of the test manual knows that the norms are not necessarily comparable from field to field, the examinee has no way of knowing this. As a result, the norms data given are of doubtful value and may be misleading. This situation could be remedied by adding to the otherwise excellent statement to the examinee a frank admission that the data presented are probably not representative of all first year graduate students in the various fields.

The reliability coefficients for current forms are satisfactory. Both odd-even and test-retest coefficients are reported. An interesting technical question arises in evaluating the test-retest figures. In computing these coefficients, all cases were used even though half had taken one form first and the other half had taken the other form first. As shown in the manual, the correlation between Form J and Form K was .91 regardless of which form was taken first. When the data for both orders were combined, the coefficient was .87, and this figure is taken as the test-retest reliability of Form J versus Form K. It would seem that this procedure gives undue weight to practice effect, which is small but not negligible, in determining the error variance, and thus underestimates the reliability. One final comment with respect to reliability is that the usefulness of the standard error of measurement in score interpretation is not pointed out. Standard errors of measurement are not reported for the various forms.

The *Miller Analogies Test* is a well constructed, secure, convenient, single-score test of high difficulty level. Excellent aids to score interpretation have been provided for its users.

Warren W. Willingham, *Director of Evaluation Studies, Georgia Institute of Technology, Atlanta, Georgia.*

The *Miller Analogies Test* (MAT) consists of 100 verbal analogy items which cover a broad range of knowledge. The test is quite difficult and was designed to aid in the selection of graduate students and high level personnel. Despite (or perhaps because of) very tight security regulations, the MAT has been used extensively for many years.

Data reported in the manual indicate that the test is quite reliable (.85 to .94) for heterogeneous groups of seniors and graduate students. The manual does not contain reliability estimates based upon more restricted groups which would be encountered commonly in operational use of the test. However, extensive summary statistics are included which indicate how much restriction in ability may be expected in special groups. In one study (57) the retest reliability of the MAT was found to be .82 after a median time lapse of 16 months. Higher retest reliability (.87 to .89) was found in a recent unpublished study conducted by the publisher.

The validity section of the manual is unusually complete in several respects. A large number of prediction studies are reported objectively and in sufficient detail. Mean MAT score is also reported for various groups of employees and successful and unsuccessful students. While the MAT is frequently a good predictor of performance in graduate school, it is evident that wide variations occur from one institution to another. Another important consideration in evaluating the validity of the MAT is the extent to which it adds useful information to the undergraduate grade-point average. The manual contains relatively little information on this question, but it is crucial since virtually all graduate schools refer to the undergraduate record in selecting students. This fact plus the variability among institutions and curricula underscore the necessity for systematic local studies.

The construct validity of the MAT is more difficult to evaluate. On the one hand it is clear that the test measures largely verbal comprehension in the context of general information. On the other hand it has been called a hodgepodge of subject matter which reflects no clear philosophy of graduate education. This criticism may be true; it may also put the cart before the horse. Systematic analyses of what constitutes successful graduate work are largely nonexistent. A hodgepodge predictor may provide the best available answer to an inadequate question. Unless the goals of a graduate department are articulated with considerably more precision than is typical, there does not appear to be any compelling reason to prefer or reject, a priori, the particular content of the MAT.

The usefulness of a test like the MAT is greatly improved by diverse normative data. The manual includes a great deal of normative information from both business and educational institutions, but the shortcomings of incidentally available norms are illustrated in several instances. For example, the norms for psychology graduate students appear to be fairly representative, while those for several other groups are based only upon students at two large midwestern universities. The normative groups are carefully described, however, and this should allow the reader to judge their comparability. It is worth noting at this point that the publisher has recently changed the security regulations which have governed the dissemination of MAT scores. Scores are now available to the candidate plus any three persons he designates, many of whom will not have a manual. In this regard the MAT is now in line with other similar tests.

The MAT manual is a joy. It starts with modest claims and proceeds inexorably to describe, explain, and document. It is brief yet remarkably complete. Few manuals follow more closely the letter and spirit of the technical recommendations of the American Psychological Association.

The chief competitor of the MAT is the *Graduate Record Examinations Aptitude Test.* Even if there were extensive comparative validity studies on the two tests, it is quite doubtful that either could be judged superior for all purposes. Both are well constructed tests which have their individual appeals.

In summary, the *Miller Analogies Test* is a very difficult, well constructed test. It has been subjected to a considerable amount of research and is supported by an excellent manual. The test is recommended as a measure which is likely to be useful in screening high level personnel and graduate students.

For a review by John T. Dailey, see 5:352; for reviews by J. P. Guilford and Carl I. Hovland, see 4:304.

[473]

★**Mitchell Vocabulary Test.** Adults; 1958; 1 form (2 pages); instructions and norms contained in manual for *Diagnostic Performance Tests* (see *1* below); reliability and validity data and norms based on an earlier version (same as present version except for item order and instructions); 14*s.* per pad of 50 tests; 35*s.* per DPT manual; prices include purchase tax; postpaid within U.K.; 15(20) minutes; [A. Mitchell]; distributed by the National Foundation for Educational Research in England and Wales. *

REFERENCES

1. SEMEONOFF, BORIS, AND TRIST, ERIC. Appendix 3, "The Mitchell Vocabulary Test," pp. 135–47. In their *Diagnostic Performance Tests: A Manual for Use With Adults.* London: Tavistock Publications Ltd., 1958. Pp. xvi, 176. *

[474]

*[**Moray House Intelligence Tests.**] Ages 8.5–10.5, 10–12, 10–12 of above average ability, 12–14, 13.5 and over; 1930–63; 5 levels; distribution restricted to education authorities; 37*s.* 6*d.* per 100 tests (except *a,* 56*s.*); 7*d.* per single copy (except *a,* 9*d.*); 11*s.* per 100 practice tests for *b* or *d;* 1*s.* 6*d.* per manual for any one form of any one test (except *c,* 2*s.*); postpaid; purchase tax extra; Department of Education, University of Edinburgh; University of London Press Ltd. *

a) MORAY HOUSE JUNIOR REASONING TEST FOR NINE YEAR OLDS. Ages 8.5–10.5; 1947–58; 2 forms: *Junior Intelligence Test 1a* ['56, 12 pages], *Junior Reasoning Test 2* ['58, 12 pages]; manual [dates same as for tests, 18 pages] for each form; 41.5(91.5) minutes for form 1a, 45(104) minutes for form 2.

b) MORAY HOUSE VERBAL REASONING TEST. Ages 10–12; 1930–63; earlier forms called *Moray House Intelligence Tests;* 2–3 new forms issued annually; 14 forms (8 pages) currently available: forms 60 ['58], 61 ['58], 62 ['59], 63 ['59], 64 ['60], 65 ['60], 66 ['61], 67 ['61], 68 ['61], 69 ['62], 70 ['62], 71 ['63], 72 ['63], 73 ['63]; manual [dates same as for tests, 12 pages] for each form; practice test [dates generally same as for test, 2 pages] for each form; 10(15) minutes for practice test, 45(50) minutes for test.

c) [MORAY HOUSE VERBAL REASONING TEST: VERNIER TEST 2.] Ages 10–12 of above average ability; 1954–57; a "slightly more difficult" test than the tests in *b* above; 1 form ['57, 8 pages]; manual ['57, 12 pages]; 45(50) minutes.

d) MORAY HOUSE VERBAL REASONING TEST (ADV.). Ages 12–14; 1940–56; forms 6 ['49], 8 ['53], 9 ['55], 10 ['56], (8 pages); manual [dates same as for test, 12 pages] for each form; practice tests (2 pages) 5 ['52, for form 6], 6 ['53, for forms 8–9], 7 ['54, for form 10]; 10(15) minutes for practice test, 45(50) minutes for test.

e) MORAY HOUSE ADULT INTELLIGENCE TEST 1. Ages 13.5 and over; 1952; 1 form ['52, 8 pages]; manual ['52, 15 pages]; 45(50) minutes.

REFERENCES

1–2. See 3:241.
3–4. See 5:353.
5. THOMSON, GODFREY H. "The Standardization of Group Tests and the Scatter of Intelligence Quotients: A Contribution to the Theory of Examining." *Brit J Ed Psychol* 2:92–112, 125–38 F, Je '32. * (*PA* 6:3031)
6. THOMSON, GODFREY H. "Following Up Individual Items in a Group Intelligence Test." *Brit J Psychol* 32:310–7 Ap '42. * (*PA* 16:2908)
7. LAMBERT, CONSTANCE M. "Symposium on Selection of Pupils for Different Types of Secondary Schools: 7, A Survey of Ability and Interest at the Stage of Transfer." *Brit J Ed Psychol* 19:67–81 Je '49. *
8. PEEL, E. A. "Symposium on Selection of Pupils for Different Types of Secondary Schools: 6, Evidence of a Practical Factor at the Age of Eleven." *Brit J Ed Psychol* 19:1–15 F '49. *
9. PEEL, E. A. "A Note on Practice Effects in Intelligence Tests." *Brit J Ed Psychol* 21:122–5 Je '51. * (*PA* 26:929)
10. EMMETT, W. G., AND WILMUT, F. S. "The Prediction of School Certificate Performance in Specific Subjects." *Brit J Ed Psychol* 22:52–62 F '52. * (*PA* 27:667)
11. JONES, W. R. "The Language Handicap of Welsh-Speaking Children: A Study of Their Performance in an English Verbal Intelligence Test in Relation to Their Non-Verbal Mental Ability and Their Reading Ability in English." *Brit J Ed Psychol* 22:114–23 Je '52. * (*PA* 27:2197)
12. PEEL, E. A. "Practice Effects Between Three Consecutive Tests of Intelligence." *Brit J Ed Psychol* 22:196–9 N '52. * (*PA* 27:5156)
13. WISEMAN, STEPHEN, AND WRIGLEY, JACK. "The Comparative Effects of Coaching and Practice on the Results of Verbal Intelligence Tests." *Brit J Psychol* 44:83–94 My '53. * (*PA* 28:2261)
14. EMMETT, W. G. "Secondary Modern and Grammar School Performance Predicted by Tests Given in Primary Schools." *Brit J Ed Psychol* 24:91–8 Je '54. * (*PA* 29:3036)
15. PEEL, E. A., AND ARMSTRONG, H. G. "Symposium: The Use of Essays in Selection at 11+; 2, The Predictive Power of the English Composition in the 11+ Examination." *Brit J Ed Psychol* 26:163–71 N '56. * (*PA* 31:8840)
16. NISBET, JOHN, AND BUCHAN, JIM. "The Long-Term Follow-Up of Assessments at Age Eleven." *Brit J Ed Psychol* 29:1–8 F '59. * (*PA* 34:3444)
17. HERBERT, N., AND TURNBULL, G. H. "Personality Factors and Effective Progress in Teaching." *Ed R* 16:24–31 N '63. *

For a review by Patrick Slater of earlier forms, see 3:241.

[475]

*__Moray House Picture Test 2.__ Ages 6.5–8.0; 1944–61; earlier test called *Moray House Picture Intelligence Test 1;* 1 form ('61, 15 pages); manual ('61, 16 pages); no data on validity; distribution restricted to education authorities; 65*s.* per 100 tests; 2*s.* per manual; postpaid; purchase tax extra; 32(75) minutes; Department of Education, University of Edinburgh; University of London Press Ltd. *

REFERENCES

1–5. See 4:306.

For reviews by Gertrude Keir and M. L. Kellmer Pringle of the earlier test, see 4:306.

[476]

★**Multi-Racial Picture Intelligence Tests Suitable for Use in African and Asian Schools.** Ages 10–11.5; 1955; 1 form ['55, 16 pages]; instructions ['55, 4 pages]; no data on validity; no norms; 6*d.* per test; 1*s.* per key; postage and purchase tax extra; 60(90) minutes; Y. K. Lule; A. Wheaton & Co., Ltd. *

[477]

★**[N. B. Group Tests.]** Ages 5–6, 7–8; 1958; 1 form ['58, 8 pages]; 2 levels; mimeographed manual ['58, 35 pages]; no data on validity; R 1.40 per 100 tests, postage extra; manual free; specimen set not available; (65–75) minutes; National Bureau of Educational and Social Research. *

a) N. B. GROUP TEST FOR FIVE AND SIX YEAR OLDS.
b) N. B. GROUP TEST FOR SEVEN AND EIGHT YEAR OLDS.

[478]

★**Non-Verbal Reasoning Test.** Job applicants and industrial employees; 1961; 1 form (7 pages); manual (17 pages); norms for men only; $3 per 20 tests, postage extra; $1 per specimen set, postpaid; (15–30) minutes; Raymond J. Corsini and Measurement Research Division, Industrial Relations Center, University of Chicago (manual); Education-Industry Service. *

JAMES E. KENNEDY, *Associate Professor of Psychology, University of Wisconsin, Madison, Wisconsin.*

The *Non-Verbal Reasoning Test* is described in its manual as a measure of "a person's capacity to think logically through the medium of pictorial problems." A paper and pencil test, it may be administered to groups and requires no writing. The test consists of sets of five pictures. The subject is instructed to look at the first picture and then from the remaining four to pick out the one which "goes best with" the first picture. There are 44 items ordered for difficulty; total score is the number answered correctly. A key for hand scoring is provided.

This test has been revised several times; an earlier and longer form was item analyzed against total score and the poorest items were deleted. The final form was found, for various groups, to have reliabilities, ranging from .61 to .85 as estimated by the K-R 20 and K-R 21 formulae. Split-half reliability (corrected) was reported as .79; test-retest reliability was not judged to be appropriate. In an effort to minimize the effects of cultural factors, the items were shown to a sample of at least 30 individuals of widely different backgrounds and the only items retained were those having elements recognizable to at least 90 per cent of the group. The manual claims that since test performance is "not influenced by facility in language, it is fair to people who have not had much formal education, who are not accustomed to taking tests, or who are not familiar with paper-and-pencil activity." Some, or all, of these claims may be true to some degree, but no evidence is presented to support them.

In the manual "two approaches to validity" are discussed. The first consists in showing that this test correlated in the low .30's with *Verbal Reasoning,* developed by the same author. On the basis of this result, the author concludes only that "the test measures in the general area of mental abilities." The second approach involved reporting that the mean score for a group of "unskilled and semi-skilled employees" was *not* significantly different from the mean score for a group of "foremen, foremen trainees, and leadmen" and that the mean score for this latter group *was* significantly different from that of a group of "salesmen, office staff employees, engineers, middle and top management personnel." No further statement is made to suggest in what way this result might be interpreted as support, or lack of support, of the validity of the test, however validity might be defined. The unwary test user might misinterpret the discussion of these results under the heading of "validity," especially with the emphasis on the occupational characteristics of the groups, and infer that in some way this shows the test to be useful for selection and placement purposes. No correlations are reported between this test and any other psychologically relevant variable, such as other measures of nonverbal reasoning, general intelligence tests, age at time of testing, number of years of schooling, etc.

In summary, this test must be considered as an experimental instrument which measures with moderate reliability a capacity which might quite reasonably be called nonverbal reasoning. Sometime in the future it might conceivably make a contribution to theory or practice. At its present stage of development, its value is extremely limited by the total lack of information about its validity as that term is defined in any conventional manner. There is certainly no evidence to recommend its use for selection and placement in business and industry.

DAVID G. RYANS, *Director, Bureau of Educational Research, University of Hawaii, Honolulu, Hawaii.*

This is a 44-item test, each item consisting of five horizontally displayed pictures of objects, geometric forms, symbols, or configurations of objects, forms, or symbols. The first picture in each row is intended to establish a frame of reference and the testee is directed to draw a diagonal line through one of the remaining four pictures which "goes best with" the first picture. The current test represents a fourth version of an instrument originally called the Picture Test, and the 44 items in the current instrument were selected from a preceding 56-item version in light of analyses of the scores of 371 male industrial employees (same sample for which standard scores and percentiles and reliability and validity data are reported for the current instrument).

The score on the test is the number of the testee's responses corresponding to the scoring key. Normalized standard scores and percentile score equivalents are provided for the sample of 371 males, consisting of three subsamples: group 1, 125 unskilled and semiskilled industrial employees; group 2, 122 foremen, foremen trainees, and leadmen; and group 3, 124 salesmen, office workers, engineers, and management personnel. For this group of 371 males, the score mean was 33.90 and the standard deviation 5.85.

Reliabilities estimated by Kuder-Richardson indices vary among the three subsamples. For K-R 21 and K-R 20, respectively, coefficients are reported as .61 and .72 for group 1, .80 and .85 for group 2, and .67 and .72 for group 3. (Group 3 showed the smallest variance and the highest mean; groups 1 and 2 are similar with respect to mean score, but the standard deviation is higher for group 2.) Differences significant at the .001 level between the mean scores of groups 1 and 3 and groups 2 and 3 are presented as evidence of validity. Correlations of .31, .33, and .61 between the *Non-Verbal Reasoning Test* and another test, *Verbal Reasoning,* based, respectively, on 66 laborers, 71 management personnel, and the combined group "show that the test measures in the general area of mental abilities."

The *Non-Verbal Reasoning Test* may be of limited use for providing gross estimates of general ability when administered to groups. The reliability is too low to make the test useful for individual prediction except possibly for individuals whose scores deviate substantially from the mean.

The manual provides very little useful information. Normative, reliability, and validity data are inadequate, being restricted to the three loosely defined subsamples of male industrial workers. From the data presented it cannot be presumed that the *Non-Verbal Reasoning Test* and *Verbal Reasoning* are equivalent in any sense. No information is provided about the differential predictive effectiveness of the test scores for different purposes. In addition to more extensive data relating to the test use, it also would have been well to have determined the extent to which the *Non-Verbal Reasoning Test* scores correspond to those yielded by well known and widely used instruments purporting to measure general ability; and also how these scores relate to tests of special abilities such as those measured by the *Differential Aptitude Tests.* The test should not be made available and recommended for general use in the absence of a systematic effort to obtain and make available more extensive data. No one possessing even moderate sophistication in behavioral measurement would use this instrument in its present form.

[479]

***Non-Verbal Tests.** Ages 8 to 11-0, 10 to 12-11, 10 to 15, 12 to 13-11; 1947–60; 4 levels; prices include purchase tax; postage extra; published for the National Foundation for Educational Research in England and Wales; Newnes Educational Publishing Co. Ltd. *

a) NON-VERBAL TESTS 1–2. Ages 10 to 12-11; 1947–59; title on test is *A Scale of Non-Verbal Mental Ability;* 2 forms (12 pages); optional practice test ['50, 3 pages]; no data on validity; distribution restricted to directors of education; 10*s.* per 12 tests; 1*s.* per single copy; 5*s.* per 12 practice tests; 6*d.* per single copy; 2*s.* 6*d.* per manual for either form; 10(15) minutes for practice test, 30(35) minutes for test.

1) *Non-Verbal Test 1.* 1947–59; 1 form ['49]; revised manual ('59, 20 pages); no norms for ages 12 to 12-11 for administration with practice test; Welsh edition ['54] available; J. W. Jenkins.

2) *Non-Verbal Test 2.* 1948–51; 1 form ['49]; manual ['51]; supplementary provisional norms ['51, for ages 10-3 to 11-2 only] for administration with practice test; D. M. Lee and J. W. Jenkins.
b) NON-VERBAL TEST 3. Ages 10 to 15; 1953–58; 1 form ['53, 28 pages]; may be administered as a short form for ages 10-6 to 12-0; revised manual ('58, 8 pages); no data on reliability; separate answer sheets must be used; 20*s.* per 12 tests; 2*s.* per single copy; 2*s.* 6*d.* per 12 answer sheets; 1*s.* 6*d.* per manual and stencil; 50(60) minutes for full test, 35(45) minutes for short version; B. Calvert (test) and I. Macfarlane Smith (original manual).
c) NON-VERBAL TEST 4. Ages 12 to 13-11; 1951–60; 1 form ['51, 11 pages]; manual ['60, 8 pages, with 1951 norms]; no data on validity; 10*s.* per 12 tests; 1*s.* per single copy; 1*s.* 3*d.* per manual; 40(50) minutes.
d) NON-VERBAL TEST 5. Ages 8 to 11-0; 1953–58; 1 form ['53, 17 pages]; revised manual ('58, 15 pages); no data on validity; 15*s.* per 12 tests; 1*s.* 6*d.* per single copy; 1*s.* 6*d.* per manual; 20(40) minutes; D. A. Pidgeon.

REFERENCES

1–3. See 4:307.
4. See 5:356.
5. LEWIS, D. G. "Bilingualism and Non-Verbal Intelligence: A Further Study of Test Results." *Brit J Ed Psychol* 29:17–22 F '59. * (*PA* 34:2730)

T. R. MILES, *Professor of Psychology, University College of North Wales, Bangor, Wales.*

Alas! these tests are for the most part merely "the mixture as before." There are a few refinements which were absent from some of the earlier group tests: the "standard error" of each test is calculated (apparently as a function of reliability, though details are not given); the number of children used for standardisation purposes is somewhat larger than previously; and in the manual for Test 5 test users are reminded, sensibly enough, to check their stopwatches beforehand. It is all very painstaking—and utterly unsatisfactory.

The time is ripe, in the reviewer's opinion, for a rethinking of fundamentals. In particular, one would welcome a clear statement of why it is considered desirable to take up the time of young people by making them do tests of this kind. In what ways are these so-called "non-verbal" tests an improvement on tests of English or mathematics? Do they point the way to any new and exciting psychological theory? Is there any good evidence as to their validity (as distinct from reliability) in terms of independent criteria? Are there any new facts emerging which would enable us to pass beyond the old and barren controversies about the existence of "*g*" and such matters? A manual of test instructions is admittedly no place for detailed discussion of theory; but if the above doubts can indeed be answered at all the reader should surely have been told where to look for the answers. The information given is in fact minimal. Thus Test 4 is said to have been designed "to obtain a measure of....non-verbal ability"; but surely no one can claim that "non-verbal ability" is a concept calling for no further justification or elucidation. Even Pidgeon, whose Test 5 impresses perhaps more than the others by its general competence, is constrained to talk of the child's " 'true' score"; but his inverted commas round the word "true" merely underline the basic problem and do not solve it.

From suitably constructed tests of this kind there could well be material for useful research. Thus it would be interesting to do further studies on the growth of the ability to distinguish, e.g., vertical lines with a semicircle on the top left from vertical lines with a semicircle on the top right, on the ability to recognise conventional symbols (e.g., letters of the alphabet or Arabic numerals) as compared with ability to recognise meaningless shapes, on the difference between ability to recognise and ability to reproduce, on the difference between ability to organise in terms of visual space and ability to organise in terms of kinaesthetic space, and on the ability to describe complex patterns verbally; also one would welcome theoretical discussion on the question whether in any important sense these tests are "non-verbal" at all. If only research workers in this field would spend more time considering fundamentals and less time on the proliferation of actual tests—administered, incidentally, in conditions where the child's approach and performance cannot easily be watched in detail—we would all be the gainers. It should be remembered, too, that one inspired idea can often be worth many pages of norms, and that a few original observations on a single child can sometimes be of more value to psychology than the most elaborate and painstaking survey.

JOHN NISBET, *Professor of Education, University of Aberdeen, Aberdeen, Scotland.*

The *Non-Verbal Tests* vary so greatly in content, form, and age range that a separate review could be written for each test. They do not constitute a series of parallel tests but are rather a succession of experiments in group testing by differing methods.

Test 1 suffers from premature publication. Designed for the "11-plus" age group, it was originally used with printed instructions which were read by the children before they attempted the nonverbal problems. A subsequent revised procedure removed this verbal element by substituting a preliminary practice test and oral instructions. Two sets of norms are given, one for each procedure; but the norms for the revised procedure do not cover the whole age range.

Test 3 seems to have had a chequered career. Originally standardised for ages 10-6 to 12-0, it was subsequently used experimentally with those "aged between 14 and 15 years." Norms are now given for ages 10-0 through 15-0. There is also a shortened form for the younger children.

Tests 4 and 5 limit the variety of types of problem and give systematic practice before testing. The age range for Test 5 is 8-0 to 11-0; but the test is too difficult at age 8-0 (median raw score only 20 out of 100) and it is not until age 10 that the full range of scores is used. The cypher subtest in Test 5, with 100 items to be coded in 3½ minutes, is a speed test. Test 4 for ages 12-0 to 13-11 appears to be the best of the series.

Standardisation has been done on substantial numbers, but the manuals give inadequate information on the composition of the standardisation groups. For Test 1 it is merely stated: "The scores of 2700 children were collected." Reliability coefficients are .92 or above, although for Test 3 this information is given in the catalogue and not in the manual.

No attempt is made to control guessing, though there are some multiple choice items with only four possibilities. Norms are given for scores below chance; but we cannot assume that dull children do not realise that they might guess.

It is possible to make many criticisms and to regret that the National Foundation has not set a higher standard in publishing these tests. Nevertheless, we must recognise that these are the best nonverbal group tests in England for restricted age ranges. *Progressive Matrices* is much easier to administer, but its range of difficulty is so extensive that within one age group of children individual differences depend on as few as 12 items, some of the test being much too easy and some much too hard. The *Non-Verbal Tests* give a much wider scatter of raw scores.

These tests should be regarded as experimental tests, exploring the problem of how to present nonverbal material in a form suitable for group testing and yet still relevant to the school situation. Tests 4 and 5 are as good as any other English test of this particular type. They cannot be recommended for general use in educational guidance since there are still many sources of error in the scores they produce and the manuals fail to give adequate data on construction, validity, and relation to other tests.

For a review by Cyril A. Rogers of tests 1–3, see 5:356; for a review by E. A. Peel of the original edition, see 4:307.

[480]

Otis Group Intelligence Scale. Grades kgn–4, 5–16 and adults; 1918–40; 2 levels; no data on reliability; no data on validity presented in manuals; specimen set not available; postage extra; Arthur S. Otis; [Harcourt, Brace & World, Inc.]. * (British edition: George G. Harrap & Co. Ltd.)

a) PRIMARY EXAMINATION. Grades kgn–4; 1920–40; Forms A, B, ('20, 8 pages); revised manual ('40, 10 pages); $3.60 per 35 tests; (40) minutes.

b) ADVANCED EXAMINATION. Grades 5–16 and adults; 1918–29; Forms A, B, ('19, 11 pages); manual ('29, 12 pages); $4.50 per 35 tests; (60) minutes.

REFERENCES

1. OTIS, A. S. "An Absolute Point Scale for the Group Measure of Intelligence." *J Ed Psychol* 9:239–61, 333–48 My, Je '18. *

2. ARMENTROUT, W. D. "Classification of Junior High School Pupils by the Otis Scale." *J Ed Psychol* 11:165–8 Mr '20. *

3. DICKSON, VIRGIL E. "Use of Group Mental Tests in the Guidance of Eighth-Grade and High-School Pupils." *J Ed Res* 2:601–10 O '20. *

4. LOOMIS, A. K. "Some Correlations With the Otis Scale." *J Ed Res* 2:594 S '20. *

5. MONROE, WALTER S. "Some Correlations Between Otis Scale and Rogers Mathematical Tests." *J Ed Res* 2:774–6 N '20. *

6. SMITH, WILLIAM H. "The Otis Group Intelligence Tests and High-School Grades." *Sch & Soc* 12:71–2 Jl 17 '20. *

7. COLVIN, STEPHEN S. "Some Recent Results Obtained From the Otis Group Intelligence Scale." *J Ed Res* 3:1–12 Ja '21. *

8. COXE, WARREN W. "Norms for the Otis Group Intelligence Scale." *J Ed Res* 3:313–4 Ap '21. *

9. COXE, WARREN W. "School Variation in General Intelligence." *J Ed Res* 4:187–94 O '21. *

10. DICKSON, VIRGIL E., AND NORTON, J. K. "The Otis Group Intelligence Scale Applied to the Elementary School Graduating Classes of Oakland, California." *J Ed Res* 3:106–15 F '21. *

11. STENQUIST, JOHN L. "Unreliability of Individual Scores in Mental Measurements." *J Ed Res* 4:347–54 D '21. *

12. WEST, ROSCOE L. "An Experiment With the Otis Group Intelligence Scale in the Needham, Massachusetts, High School." *J Ed Res* 3:261–8 Ap '21. *

13. GARRISON, S. C., AND TIPPETT, JAMES S. "Comparison of the Binet-Simon and Otis Tests." *J Ed Res* 6:42–8 Je '22. *

14. GEYER, DENTON L. "The Reliability of Rankings by Group Intelligence Tests." *J Ed Psychol* 13:43–9 Ja '22. *

15. HOKE, ELMER. "Intelligence Tests and College Success." *J Ed Res* 6:177 S '22. *

16. JOHNSON, O. J. "Group Intelligence Examinations for Primary Pupils." *J Appl Psychol* 6:403–16 D '22. *

17. JORDAN, A. M. "Correlations of Four Intelligence Tests With Grades." *J Ed Psychol* 13:419–29 O '22. *

18. ROOT, W. T. "Correlations Between Binet Tests and Group Tests." *J Ed Psychol* 13:286–92 My '22. *

19. VITELES, MORRIS S. "A Comparison of Three Tests of 'General Intelligence.'" *J Appl Psychol* 6:391–402 D '22. *

20. GATES, ARTHUR I. "The Unreliability of M.A. and I.Q. Based on Group Tests of General Mental Ability." *J Appl Psychol* 7:93–100 Mr '23. *

21. JORDAN, A. M. "The Validation of Intelligence Tests." *J Ed Psychol* 14:348–66, 414–28, S, O '23. *
22. MCGEOCH, JOHN A. "Some Results From Three Group Intelligence Tests." *Sch & Soc* 17:196 F 17 '23. *
23. MORRISON, J. CAYCE; CORNELL, W. B.; AND CORNELL, ETHEL. "A Study of Intelligence Scales for Grades Two and Three." *J Ed Res* 9:46–56 Ja '24. *
24. WILSON, J. H. "Comparison of Certain Intelligence Scales." *Brit J Psychol* 15:44–63 Jl '24. *
25. ACKERSON, LUTON, AND ESTABROOKS, GEORGE H. "On the Correlation of Intelligence Test Scores With Imputed Intelligence." *Brit J Psychol* 18:455–9 Ap '28. *
26. KUHLMANN, F. "The Kuhlmann-Anderson Intelligence Tests Compared With Seven Others." *J Appl Psychol* 12:545–94 D '28. * (*PA* 3:1751)
27. COLE, ROBERT D. "A Conversion Scale for Comparing Scores on Three Secondary School Intelligence Tests." *J Ed Res* 20:190–8 O '29. * (*PA* 4:439)
28. STECKEL, MINNIE L. "The Restandardization of IQ's of Different Tests." *J Ed Psychol* 21:278–83 Ap '30. *
29. CHARLES, C. M. "A Comparison of the Intelligence Quotients of Three Different Mental Tests Applied to a Group of Incarcerated Delinquent Boys." *J Appl Psychol* 17:581–4 O '33. * (*PA* 8:2662)
30. EDDS, JESS H., AND MCCALL, W. MORRISON. "Predicting the Scholastic Success of College Freshmen." *J Ed Res* 27:127–30 O '33. * (*PA* 8:595)
31. MILLER, W. S. "Variation of IQ's Obtained From Group Tests." *J Ed Psychol* 24:468–74 S '33. * (*PA* 8:662)
32. TERRY, PAUL W. "The Prognostic Value of Different Types of Tests in Courses in Educational Psychology." *J Appl Psychol* 18:231–40 Ap '34. * (*PA* 8:5251)
33. ROBERTS, J. A. FRASER; NORMAN, R. M.; AND GRIFFITHS, RUTH. "Studies on a Child Population: 1, Definition of the Sample, Method of Ascertainment, and Analysis of the Results of a Group Intelligence Test." *Ann Eug* 6:319–38 D '35. * (*PA* 10:3766)
34. WILSON, J. H. "The Exactness of '*g*' as Determined by Certain Intelligence Tests." *Brit J Psychol* 26:93–8 Jl '35. *
35. ADKINS, DOROTHY C. "The Effects of Practice on Intelligence Test Scores." *J Ed Psychol* 28:222–31 Mr '37. * (*PA* 11:3629)
36. ROBERTS, J. A. FRASER, AND GRIFFITHS, RUTH. "Studies on a Child Population: 2, Retests on the Advanced Otis and Stanford-Binet Scales, With Notes on the Use of a Shortened Binet Scale." *Ann Eug* 8:15–45 O '37. * (*PA* 12:2179)
37. ROBERTS, J. A. FRASER; NORMAN, R. M.; AND GRIFFITHS, RUTH. "Studies on a Child Population: 3, Intelligence and Family Size." *Ann Eug* 8:178–215 Ja '38. * (*PA* 12:4260)
38. ROBERTS, J. A. FRASER; NORMAN, R. M.; AND GRIFFITHS, RUTH. "Studies on a Child Population: 4, The Form of the Lower End of the Frequency Distribution of Standard-Binet Intelligence Quotients and the Fall of Low Intelligence Quotients With Advancing Age." *Ann Eug* 8:319–36 Ag '38. * (*PA* 13:798)
39. CURETON, EDWARD E. "Note on the IQ Obtained From the Otis Group Intelligence Scale, Advanced Examination." *J Appl Psychol* 23:416–7 Je '39. * (*PA* 13:5938)
40. TIFFIN, JOSEPH, AND GREENLY, R. J. "Employee Selection Tests for Electrical Fixture Assemblers and Radio Assemblers." *J Appl Psychol* 23:240–63 Ap '39. * (*PA* 13:4840)
41. KIRK, HARRY A. *The Relation Between Intelligence Rating and Achievement in Shorthand and Typing.* Master's thesis, Kent State University (Kent, Ohio), 1942.
42. MCRAE, HUGH. "The Inconstancy of Group Test I.Q.'s." *Brit J Ed Psychol* 12:59–70 F '42. * (*PA* 16:2905)
43. MORGAN, C. L., AND STEINMAN, C. C. "An Evaluation of a Testing Program in Educational Psychology." *J Ed Psychol* 34:495–502 N '43. * (*PA* 18:1891)
44. COFER, CHARLES N., AND BIEGEL, MARK M. "A Study of the Kent and Buck Screen Tests of Mental Ability in Relation to Otis and Stanford Achievement Test Scores." *J Consult Psychol* 12:187–9 My–Je '48. * (*PA* 22:4943)

D. WELTY LEFEVER, *Professor of Education, University of Southern California, Los Angeles, California.*

The *Otis Group Intelligence Scale* is one of the oldest standardized tests still listed in the catalogue of a major publishing house in 1963. Although several widely used intelligence tests may be regarded as lineal descendants of the *Otis Group Intelligence Scale,* the test in its present form has remained essentially unchanged since 1920. The Advanced Examination is perhaps the most important pioneer group intelligence test. It was almost completed when the United States entered World War I. Otis' research and experience made an indispensable contribution to the development of the Army Alpha and the subsequent success of group mental tests.

Otis' test received an enthusiastic reception when it was published in 1918. An early brochure about the test stated:

> The success of the Otis Scale has been entirely unprecedented in the history of American schoolbook publishing. After the first edition issued in March it was necessary to put through a second printing in June of a hundred thousand; and in September it was found necessary to print a third of a million more. Plans were then laid for a still larger printing in December in order to supply schools examining pupils at the mid-year.

Lewis M. Terman wrote:

> The *Otis Group Intelligence Scale* was the first scientifically grounded and satisfactory scale for testing subjects in groups, and it probably comes as near testing raw "brain power" as any system of tests yet devised. It is a necessity in schools, industries, armies, or any other institution or situation in which the mental ability of human beings is a factor for consideration.

The publishers of the new test promised enthusiastically:

> The 1929 edition of the *Otis Group Intelligence Scale* is a valid measure of general mental ability. It will enable a teacher or school administrator to measure the native mental ability of pupils in groups rapidly and accurately for the purpose of (1) *classification* in regard to the native capacities to learn; (2) *elimination of the feeble minded* who should be placed in special institutions; (3) *selection of the vocation* in which the degree of mentality indicates the highest possible attainment; and (4) *determination of cases of probable delinquency* or potential delinquency and the proper punishment or remedial action for many criminal acts.

In the introduction to the test manual of the Otis scale dated 1921 Terman prophesied with great clairvoyance:

> Thanks to the use of such [intelligence] tests in the United States Army, their experimental period is a thing of the past. * It would be surprising to find teachers and school principals lacking that open-mindedness toward psychological methods which was so conspicuously present in army officers, and we may confidently look forward to seeing millions of school children classified annually on the basis of intelligence tests.

It is interesting to note the amount of optimism expressed by the psychologists and publishers of 40 years ago regarding the purchase and use of a new and largely untried device. No doubt such a confident outlook was both prompted and basically justified by the tremendous flood of publicity which the administration of the Army Alpha test to nearly two million men in World War I produced.

The test manual makes no direct mention of reliability. For a discussion of reliability and validity of the test the manual refers the test purchaser to two articles (*1*) published in 1918. The reliability coefficient reported is a correlation of .97 between two experimental forms of the scale. The sample studied in this pioneer development was 121 pupils in grades 4, 6, and 8. Such a large interform correlation would be regarded as spuriously high today because of the heterogeneity of a sample which included fourth, sixth, and eighth grade pupils. This reliability coefficient has been quoted in the textbook references to the *Otis Group Intelligence Scale* ever since. As far as this reviewer knows no other reliability data have been provided.

Incidentally, those of us who can recall having administered objective tests in schools that had never seen such an instrument before can appreciate Otis' experiences administering the test to the experimental groups. "Pupils were adjured at the beginning of the testing not to give or receive aid during the taking of any test. On the whole the pupils were orderly and attentive."

The evidence of concurrent validity presented in the journal article includes three correlations between Otis scores and teachers' marks of .80 (43 fourth grade pupils); .41 (40 sixth grade pupils); and .50 (38 eighth grade pupils). Two additional kinds of evidence for test validity are available in the test manual but not so designated. The point scores on the scale were tabulated in relation to the chronological age of the sample. The norm table for the Advanced Examination in the 1921 Manual of Directions is based on some 25,000 cases from grades 4 through 12, and shows a systematic increase of average scores with each advancing age group. A second source of information on validity presented in the 1921 manual, but not labeled as such, is the table of Binet mental age equivalents which indicates a definite relationship between Otis scores and Binet mental age values.

Research involving the scores of 800 pupils on both the Primary Examination and the *Otis Quick-Scoring Mental Ability Tests* reported in 1938, showed that the original norms were too low by more than 50 per cent at the 6 year and 7 year age levels. The differences between 1920 and 1938 norms diminish to less than 2 per cent at the 12 year level. However, since the 1938 norms are the latest reported one wonders whether any additional shifts in norm values would be shown if more recent surveys were conducted.

As we look back to those pioneering times when aptitude tests were new and appeared to possess psychological and statistical magic we may well ask ourselves how much real progress we have made in the past 50 years in the measurement of human intelligence. Have we accomplished any major breakthroughs like those made by Binet, Terman, Otis, et al.?

Certainly in 1963 we honor the *Otis Group Intelligence Scale* as a milestone in the history of aptitude measurement but we wish that it were either thoroughly updated or accorded an honorable retirement from the catalogues of a highly respected publishing house. By today's standards the information furnished the consumer of the *Otis Group Intelligence Scale* is both antiquated and inadequate.

[481]

***Otis Quick-Scoring Mental Ability Tests.** Grades 1.5–4, 4–9, 9–16; 1936–62; IBM and MRC; 3 levels; Forms As of Alpha Test, EM and FM of Beta Test, and EM and FM of Gamma Test are labeled New Edition; pre-1954 forms of Beta and Gamma Tests are revisions of *Otis Self-Administering Tests of Mental Ability* (still available, see 5:363); 40¢ per specimen set of any one level; postage extra; Arthur S. Otis; Harcourt, Brace & World, Inc. *

a) ALPHA TEST. Grades 1.5–4; 1936–54; 2 editions.

1) *Alpha Test* [*Long Form*]. 3 scores: nonverbal, verbal, total (either subtest may be administered alone); Forms A ('36), B ('38), (11 pages); manual ('39, c1936–39, 22 pages); $3.75 per 35 tests; 20(25) minutes for nonverbal subtest, (30) minutes for verbal subtest.

2) *Alpha Short Form*. Form As ('53, c1936–52, 7 pages); the Form Bs listed in the publisher's 1963–64 catalog was withdrawn before publication; manual ('54, c1936–54, 15 pages); $3 per 35 tests; (35) minutes.

b) BETA TEST. Grades 4–9; 1937–62; IBM (Forms CM, DM, EM, FM) and MRC (Forms EM, FM); hand scored Forms A, B, ('37, 6 pages); machine scorable Forms CM ('37), DM ('39), EM ('54), FM ('54), (6 pages); manual ('37, 12 pages) for hand scored forms; manual ('54, c1939–54, 8 pages) for machine scorable forms; IQ tables ['62, 4 pages] for Forms CM and DM; $2.65 per 35 tests of hand scorable forms; $3.10 per 35 tests of machine scorable forms; separate answer sheets or cards may be used with machine scorable forms; $1.40 per 35 IBM answer sheets; 20¢ per scoring stencil; $2 per 100 Harbor answer cards (machine scoring service, by Measurement Research Center, Inc., may be arranged through the publisher); 30(35) minutes.

c) GAMMA TEST. Grades 9–16; 1937–62; IBM (Forms AM, BM, EM, FM) and MRC (Forms EM, FM);

hand scored Forms C, D, ('39, 6 pages); machine scorable Forms AM ('37), BM ('37), EM ('54), FM ('54), (6 pages); manual ('39, 8 pages) for hand scored forms; manual ('54, c1939–54, 6 pages) for machine scorable forms; IQ tables ['62, 4 pages] for all forms; prices same as for Beta Test; 30(35) minutes.

REFERENCES

1–9. See 3:249.
10–42. See 5:362.
43. HOLMES, JACK A. "Factors Underlying Major Reading Disabilities at the College Level." *Genetic Psychol Monogr* 49:3–95 F '54. * (*PA* 28:8982)
44. SHAW, GERALDINE SAX. "Prediction of Success in Elementary Algebra." *Math Teach* 49:173–8 Mr '56. *
45. DUFFICY, EDWARD C. *The Relationship Between Scores on the Otis Gamma Quick Scoring Mental Ability Test, the Gordon Personal Profile, and Success in Latin in a Minor Seminary.* Master's thesis, De Paul University (Chicago, Ill.), 1957.
46. CAMPBELL, ROBERT J. *An Analysis to Determine the Value of Otis I.Q. Test and the Iowa Silent Reading Test in Predicting Final Academic Success of Adams State College Students.* Master's thesis, Adams State College (Alamosa, Colo.), 1958.
47. MCQUEEN, ROBERT, AND WILLIAMS, KENNETH C. "Predicting Success in Beginning High School Algebra." *Psychol Rep* 4:603–6 D '58. * (*PA* 34:2009)
48. CROFT, ELLA JOYCE. "Prediction of Clothing Construction Achievement of High School Girls." *Ed & Psychol Meas* 19:653–5 w '59. * (*PA* 34:6562)
49. ENGELHART, MAX D. "Obtaining Comparable Scores on Two or More Tests." *Ed & Psychol Meas* 19:55–64 sp '59. * (*PA* 34:114)
50. LAVER, A. B. "Testing in Canada: Report No. 1." *Can Psychologist* 8:102–3 O '59. *
51. NORTON, DANIEL P. "The Relationship of Study Habits and Other Measures to Achievement in Ninth-Grade General Science." *J Exp Ed* 27:211–7 Mr '59. * (*PA* 35:1283)
52. CASS, JOHN C., AND TIEDEMAN, DAVID V. "Vocational Development and the Election of a High School Curriculum." *Personnel & Guid J* 38:538–45 Mr '60. *
53. DARBES, ALEX. "Relationships Among College Students Scores on ACE, Otis, and WAIS Tests." *Proc W Va Acad Sci* 32:214–6 D '60. * (*PA* 36:3KK14D)
54. DI BONA, LUCILLE J. "Predicting Success in Shorthand." *J Bus Ed* 35:213–4 F '60. *
55. ROSINSKI, EDWIN F. "Must All Tests Be Multi-Factor Batteries?" *J Exp Ed* 28:235–40 Mr '60. *
56. MARINACCIO, LAWRENCE V. *Relationships Between Work Experience and Intelligence Quotients of Secondary School Pupils.* Doctor's thesis, University of Connecticut (Storrs, Conn.), 1961. (*DA* 22:2693)
57. ROBERTS, HELEN ERSKINE. "Comparison of Otis and Stanford-Binet IQ's." *Calif J Ed Res* 12:8–15 Ja '61. * (*PA* 36:1HD08R)
58. SIEBERT, LAWRENCE A. "Otis IQ Scores of Delinquents." *J Clin Psychol* 18:517 O '62. * (*PA* 39:5720)
59. VON WITTICH, BARBARA. "Prediction of Success in Foreign Language Study." *Mod Lang J* 46:208–12 My '62. *
60. WILLINGHAM, WARREN W., AND STRICKLAND, JAMES A. "Conversion Tables for Otis Gamma and Scholastic Aptitude Test." *Personnel & Guid J* 41:356–8 D '62. * (*PA* 37:7183)
61. ALVI, SABIR ALI. *Traditional and "Culture Fair" Aptitude Test Performance of College Students From Different Academic and Cultural Backgounds.* Doctor's thesis, Indiana University (Bloomington, Ind.), 1963. (*DA* 24:2775)
62. BLOSSER, GEORGE H. "Group Intelligence Tests as Screening Devices in Locating Gifted and Superior Students in the Ninth Grade." *Excep Child* 29:282–6 F '63. * (*PA* 38:2434)
63. CLYMER, THEODORE. "A Study of the Influence of Reading Ability on the Validity of Group Intelligence Tests." *Slow Learning Child* 10:76–84 N '63. *
64. HIGGINS, CONWELL. "Multiple Predictor Score Cut-Offs Versus Multiple-Regression Cut-Offs in Selection of Academically Talented Children in Grade 3." *Yearb Nat Council Meas Ed* 20:153–64 '63. * (*PA* 38:9247)
65. SIEBERT, LAWRENCE A. "Matched Otis and Wechsler IQ Scores of Delinquents." *J Clin Psychol* 19:215–6 Ap '63. *
66. WEINER, MAX, AND TOBIAS, SIGMUND. "Chance Factors in the Interpretation of Group Administered Multiple-Choice Tests." *Personnel & Guid J* 41:435–7 Ja '63. * (*PA* 39:1771)

For reviews by D. Welty Lefever and Alfred Yates of the New Edition forms, see 5:362; for a review by Frederic Kuder of the earlier forms, see 3:249; for reviews by F. Kuhlmann and C. Spearman, see 40:1413; for reviews by Psyche Cattell and R. Pintner, see 38:1053 (2 excerpts).

[482]

★Performance Alertness "PA" (With Pictures): Individual Placement Series (Area I). Adults; 1961; Form C (4 pages); no manual; no data on reliability and validity; no description of normative population; separate answer sheets must be used; $12.50 per 25 tests; $1 per 25 answer sheets; $1 per key; $2.50 per specimen set; postpaid; 12(17) minutes; J. H. Norman; the Author. *

[483]

★Personal Classification Test. Business and industry; 1953–59; Forms H, R, ('53, 3 pages); mimeographed manual ['53, 2 pages] for Form R; no manual for Form H; Form H norms ('59, 1 page); no data on reliability and validity of Form H; $4 per 25 tests, postpaid; 10(15) minutes; W. E. Brown, W. H. E. Geiger, R. W. Henderson, and L. C. Steckle; William, Lynde & Williams. *

[484]

Personnel Research Institute Classification Test. Adults; 1943–54; formerly called *Classification Test for Industrial and Office Personnel;* Forms A ('47, revision of 1943 form), B ('47), (4 pages); revised manual ('54, 4 pages); $3 per 25 tests; 50¢ per specimen set; postage extra; 15(20) minutes; Jay L. Otis, Evelyn Katz (A), Robert W. Henderson (A), Mary Aiken (A), David J. Chesler (B), and Gardner E. Lindzey (B); Personnel Research Institute. *

REFERENCES

1. OTIS, JAY L., AND CHESLER, DAVID J. "A Short Test of Mental Ability." *J Appl Psychol* 33:146–50 Ap '49. * (*PA* 24:16)
2. CAMPBELL, JOEL T. "Validity Information Exchange, No. 16-04: D.O.T. Code 7-36.250, Gas Deliveryman." *Personnel Psychol* 16:181–3 su '63. *

JAMES R. GLENNON, *Director, Employee Relations Research, Standard Oil Company (Indiana), Chicago, Illinois.*

An industrial psychologist concerned with problems of selection from among applicants for almost any job within business or industry will surely include a test or tests of mental ability in his selection battery. Assuming that the hierarchy of jobs applies in his selection situation, he will first be concerned with the more numerous selections to be made for entry level jobs in plant or office. Confronted with the comparatively modest educational achievements and mental ability of the majority of applicants for lower level jobs, he will most likely choose from one or more of the short, easily administered mental ability tests.

The *Personnel Research Institute Classification Test* would appear to fit the foregoing prescription in that it is short (15 minutes) and presents 100 multiple choice items in a simple, easily administered form. The manual describes the purpose in the development of the test as one of meeting "the need for a short, easily administered test for use with office, shop, and sales personnel." The test differs from most mental ability tests in that the items are at the same level of difficulty and that level is by design a relatively low level. This constitutes an advantage, in the authors' eyes, over tests which present items of increasing difficulty, since these more difficult instruments discourage individuals of lesser ability. On the other hand, the test is a speed test with only 4 per cent of a college population able to complete the 100 items in less than the 15-minute time limit. This would be discouraging to many individuals from all levels of ability.

In an article by two of the authors (*1*) the argument is made that the *Classification Test for Industrial and Office Personnel* (the former title of this instrument) would be useful as a screening or pretest instrument for application in industry or in vocational counseling. Performance on this low-powered test would suggest the kind of further testing which might then be indicated. This reviewer would accept that as a feasible use for the Classification Test, but would prefer other short mental ability tests with a broader range of difficulty for use in general selection practices meant to include all or several levels of jobs.

Wider general application is suggested by the change in the name of the test, and the absence in the manual of any suggestion that the test could not serve for general selection. Norm groups shown in the four-page manual include college students, college applicants, and even high level administrative and research personnel. The higher ability groups, as might be expected, appear to knock the practical ceiling out of the instrument, averaging almost 75 per cent correct answers. In view of the avowed low horizon of the test, the classical criticism of the adequacy of the norms can be reversed and the comment made that the instrument is inadequate for some of its norms.

Norm groups reported in the manual total almost 24,000 and include in addition to those noted in the preceding paragraph, more appropriate norm populations, such as service station personnel, transit operators, factory workers, clerical applicants, and the like. Lower groups on the average answer about 50 of the 100 items correctly.

The manual covers construct validity by presenting a table of correlations between the test and several other tests of mental maturity with correlations ranging from .62 to .83. The authors' explanation of these modest correlations is the limited difficulty range of the Classification Test. Of more pertinence to the industrial user is evidence of concurrent validity given in a table of correlations of test results with "Measures of Job Success." Four of these criteria are based on ratings and show correlations in the .30's and .40's. One "hard" criterion, total sales for two years for a group of 45 maintenance salesmen, shows a relationship of .21, which is the lowest relationship reported. The manual does not define "maintenance" salesmen nor explain how ratings were made or by whom.

Reliability between Forms A and B is reported as .86 when the tests were given to groups of high school and college students. Reversing the order to B-A resulted in slightly lower reliability for similar groups.

The Classification Test used in accordance with what presumably was the authors' original intention—as a low-level screening device—could have certain applications in counseling and doubtless some limited use in industry. Weighed against the advantages of other short pencil and paper mental ability tests which do have items of increasing difficulty, this reviewer would prefer the *Adaptability Test* or *Wonderlic Personnel Test* for industrial selection.

MELVIN R. MARKS, *Professor of Business Administration, The University of Rochester, Rochester, New York.*

Each form of this 15-minute test consists of 100 multiple choice items, spiraled in series of five as follows: vocabulary, general information, arithmetic, general information, analogy. A special feature of the test is that all items are claimed to be of relatively constant difficulty.

Item content is typical for a general intelligence test with the following exceptions: there are no spatial items; verbal ability is measured both by vocabulary and analogy items; there are no mechanical items. For some of the items, the "rightness" of the designated correct alternatives lacks rigor. For example, "picture is to frame as stamp is to *envelope*"; "to revise means to overhaul"; "an improbable event is *unlikely*" (in the context where "uncertain" is also an alternative). However, this reviewer's overall evaluation of item content is favorable, especially since no anachronisms appear even though the test was last revised in 1954.

Two kinds of validity data are supplied. First, seven correlations with other intelligence tests are presented, but without information about the means and standard deviations of the groups tested. These coefficients range from .62 for 254 nursing applicants to .83 for 44 junior clerks. Second, correlations between scores and job success are presented for maintenance salesmen, heater salesmen, junior clerks, and semiskilled laborers. The job performance criteria include ratings of sales performance, total sales, "sales ability," "job rating," "progress rating," and "performance rating." The validity coefficients range from .21 to .49. These coefficients offer reasonable prediction of criteria which are certainly not limited to cognitive elements. On the other hand, the included jobs do not involve technical and spatial abilities; this suggests that validity coefficients might be lower for such jobs, since the test has no corresponding predictor.

Reliability data are furnished in terms of alternate form coefficients (appropriate for a speeded test) which range from .80 to .86 on groups varying from 72 to 159 examinees. The data indicate that the forms are almost completely equivalent in difficulty.

Normative data by tenths are furnished for 15 special samples of various classes of students, clerks, salesmen, factory personnel, etc. Sample sizes range from 113 college students to 6,679 undifferentiated factory personnel. Minimum raw score (out of a possible 100) necessary for the 90th percentile ranges from 67 for telephone operators to 90 for college applicants.

There is no explanation as to why the test is called a classification test. This term is usually reserved for batteries from which the scores of parts are combined in different ways to yield differential prediction of various jobs.

In summary, the test is well constructed, with adequate reliability and validity for use in a variety of job situations. Because of the short time required for administration, the test would appear to be very suitable for screening purposes and for vocational counseling, with resulting economy for both employer and applicant. In the absence of validity data for jobs involving mechanical or spatial skills, the test should not be used to make employment decisions on applicants for such jobs.

[485]

Personnel Research Institute Factory Series Test. Applicants for routine industrial positions; 1950–56; Form B ('50, 3 pages); manual ['56, 7 pages]; no data on validity; $3 per 25 tests; 35¢ per specimen set; postage extra; 10(15) or 15(20) minutes; Jay L. Otis and Alfred H. Exton; Personnel Research Institute. *

N. M. Downie, *Professor of Psychology, Purdue University, Lafayette, Indiana.*

This test is another of those short, easily administered tests of mental ability widely used in industry for general employment practices. The test consists of 50 items—measuring general knowledge, ability in arithmetic, and block counting skill—similar to those found on the Otis tests. The items are arranged in a spiral order of difficulty and are mostly of an academic nature.

The test can be administered using either a 10-minute or 15-minute time limit. The examinee puts his answers on the test booklet, where they can be scored by using strip keys. The score is the number correct.

Split-half reliability coefficients of .931 for the 10-minute and .934 for the 15-minute administration lead the authors to state that the test may be employed with confidence using either time limit. Just what one has confidence in is unknown, for the authors have neither determined exactly what the test measures or shown that it selects the most intelligent or most satisfactory workers. A test with a 1950 copyright date and no demonstrated validity is still being distributed 13 years later.

Percentile norms are given for both the 10- and 15-minute time limit. Nothing whatever is said about the number or type of individuals on whom these norms were based.

While this test appears similar to such established industrial tests as the *Wonderlic Personnel Test* and the *Adaptability Test,* there is no reason why the use of these should be abandoned in favor of the test under review. The authors have yet to demonstrate the validity of their test or to establish norms for groups upon whom the test is to be used. The present inadequate manual offers little to help the personnel man, especially the inexperienced one, in using the test.

[486]

***Picture Test 1.** Ages 7 to 8-1; 1955–62; formerly called *Picture Intelligence Test 1;* 1 form ['62, 16 pages, identical with test published in 1955 except for title]; manual ('58, 8 pages, identical with 1955 manual); no data on validity; *12s. 6d.* per 12 tests; *1s. 3d.* per single copy; *1s.* per manual; prices include purchase tax; postage extra; 22(45) minutes; Joan E. Stuart; published for the National Foundation for Educational Research in England and Wales; Newnes Educational Publishing Co. Ltd. *

For reviews by Charlotte E. K. Banks and M. L. Kellmer Pringle, see 5:367.

[487]

★The Preliminary Scholastic Aptitude Test. Grades 11–12; 1959–63; abbreviated adaptation of the *College Entrance Examination Board Scholastic Aptitude Test* for guidance and scholarship testing; administered annually in October at participating secondary schools; 2 scores: verbal, mathematical; supervisor's manual ('63, 18 pages); score report booklet for students ('63, 18 pages); score report booklet for counselors ('63, 40 pages, also covers the Admissions Testing Program, see 760); bulletin of information ('63, 17 pages); examination fee: $1 per student; fee includes reporting of scores to the secondary school (schools may release scores to students at their discretion); 120(140) minutes; program administered for the College Entrance Examination Board by Educational Testing Service. *

REFERENCES

1. COFFMAN, WILLIAM E. "Evidence of Cultural Factors in Responses of African Students to Items in an American Test of Scholastic Aptitude." *Yearb Nat Council Meas Ed* 20:27–37 '63. * (*PA* 38:9272)
2. SEIBEL, DEAN W. "Prediction of College Attendance." *Voc Guid Q* 11:265–72 su '63. * (*PA* 38:4657)

WAYNE S. ZIMMERMAN, *Test Officer, Los Angeles State College, Los Angeles, California.* [Review of Forms HPT2 and KPT.]

The *Preliminary Scholastic Aptitude Test* (PSAT) is a shortened version of the *College Entrance Examination Board Scholastic Aptitude Test* (SAT). It is designed for use in secondary school guidance programs. The scores can be interpreted by high school counselors and other authorized officials in guiding a student either to select an appropriate college or to consider alternative goals.

The PSAT is parallel to the SAT both in form and in content. Items for the PSAT are drawn from the same pool as those for the SAT, or from obsolete forms of the SAT. The PSAT is designed so that it will discriminate best at the eleventh and twelfth year levels. Comparatively easier items are selected, therefore, than those selected for the college level SAT.

Like SAT, the PSAT measures verbal and mathematical comprehension. The test is composed of two sections, each one hour long. The design of the test is dictated by the College Board philosophy that only two cognitive traits contribute significantly to success in academic work. As its name implies the PSAT is intended for use in conjunction with the SAT. In other words, it is a preliminary test to be administered one or two years before the student is eligible to take the SAT. Because of the similarity between the two tests the PSAT is expected to predict how well the student should perform when later he becomes eligible to take the SAT.

Since the PSAT is designed to predict performance on the SAT its effectiveness depends not only on how well it does this but also on how well the SAT predicts college performance. A summary of data gathered between 1959 and 1962 shows correlations between PSAT and SAT verbal scores ranging from .83 to .88, and correlations between PSAT and SAT mathematical scores ranging from .82 to .85. The sizes of these samples range from 337 to 984. The correlations approach the reported reliabilities. The Kuder-Richardson formula 20 reliability estimates available to the reviewer range from .86 to .91 for PSAT verbal scores, and from .88 to .91 for PSAT mathematical scores. These reliabilities compare with reliabilities of .90 to .93 and .88 to .92 reported for the same two scores on SAT. It would appear that the scores on the PSAT are excellent predictors of SAT scores. The interested reader is referred to the review of the SAT (see 449) for a discussion of its effectiveness in predicting college success.

Like all tests produced and administered on a large scale by Educational Testing Service, norming procedures are thorough and as satisfactory as can reasonably be expected. Percentile norms based on a regional stratified national sampling of high schools are given for both eleventh and twelfth grade students.

Because the PSAT is a preliminary and parallel version of the SAT, most of the same criticisms that apply to the SAT apply to it. The major criticism of the SAT raised by this reviewer concerns the amount of time devoted to the measurement of two academic abilities. The PSAT administration time is two hours, compared to the SAT time of four hours. For a discussion of this issue the reader again is referred to the SAT review.

The PSAT has no competing test. It does the job that it was designed to do and does it well.

[488]

★[**Pressey Classification and Verifying Tests.**] Grades 1–2, 3–6, 7–12 and adults; 1922–58; IBM for grades 7–12 and adults; 3 levels; no data on reliability; no description of normative population; 50¢ per specimen set of any one test; postage extra; S. L. Pressey (except *a*) and L. C. Pressey; Bobbs-Merrill Co., Inc. *

a) PRIMARY CLASSIFICATION TEST. Grades 1–2; 1922; Form A (4 pages); manual (4 pages); mimeographed norms (1 page); $2.80 per 35 tests; (30–40) minutes.

b) PRESSEY INTERMEDIATE CLASSIFICATION-VERIFYING TESTS. Grades 3–6; 1922–58; 1 form ('58, 4 pages, same as tests copyrighted in 1922 and 1923 except for format, directions, and minor changes in a few items); 2 tests; publisher recommends administration of *b* a day or so after *a* and use of the higher of the two scores; manual ('58, 4 pages); $3.50 per 35 self-marking tests; 14(25) minutes per test.

1) *Pressey Intermediate Classification Test.*

2) *Pressey Intermediate Verifying Test.*

c) PRESSEY SENIOR CLASSIFICATION-VERIFYING TESTS. Grades 7–12 and adults; 1922–58; 2 tests; publisher recommends administration of *b* a day or so after *a* and use of the higher of the two scores; manual ('58, 4 pages); 16(25) minutes per test.

1) *Pressey Senior Classification Test.* IBM; 1 form; 2 editions (differing in item order and 4 items): self-marking edition ('58, 4 pages, same as test copyrighted in 1922 except for format, directions, and minor changes in a few items), machine scoring edition (1940 edition, c1922, 2 pages); $3.50 per 35 self-marking tests; 15¢ per IBM test-answer sheet; 40¢ per set of machine scoring stencils.

2) *Pressey Senior Verifying Test.* 1 form ('58, 4 pages, same as test copyrighted in 1922 except for format, directions, and minor changes in a few items); $3.50 per 35 self-marking tests.

REFERENCES

1. HENMON, V. A. C., AND STREITZ, RUTH. "A Comparative Study of Four Group Scales for the Primary Grades." *J Ed Res* 5:185–94 Mr '22. *

2. PRESSEY, S. L., AND PRESSEY, L. C. "A Revision of the Pressey Primer and Cross-Out Scales." *J Ed Res* 6:178–9 S '22. *

3. MILLER, W. S. "The Variation and Significance of Intelligence Quotients Obtained From Group Tests." *J Ed Psychol* 15:359–66 S '24. *

4. SANGREN, PAUL V. "Comparative Validity of Primary Intelligence Tests." *J Appl Psychol* 13:394–412 Ag '29. * (*PA* 3:4324)

5. MILLER, W. S. "Variation of IQ's Obtained From Group Tests." *J Ed Psychol* 24:468–74 S '33. * (*PA* 8:662)

6. FINCH, F. H. "Equating Intelligence Quotients From Group Tests." *J Ed Res* 28:589–92 Ap '35. * (*PA* 9:3929)

7. GREEN, HELEN J., AND BERMAN, ISABEL R.; UNDER THE DIRECTION OF DONALD G. PATERSON AND M. R. TRABUE. *A Manual of Selected Occupational Tests for Use in Public Employment Offices,* pp. 8, 23–31. University of Minnesota, Bulletins of the Employment Stabilization Research Institute, Vol. 2, No. 3. Minneapolis, Minn.: University of Minnesota Press, July 1936. Pp. 31. *

8. LORGE, IRVING. "A Table of Percentile Equivalents for Eight Intelligence Tests Frequently Used With Adults." *J Appl Psychol* 20:392–5 Je '36. * (*PA* 10:5552)

9. HACKMAN, RAY CARTER. *The Differential Prediction of Success in Two Contrasting Vocational Areas.* Doctor's thesis, University of Minnesota (Minneapolis, Minn.), 1940.

10. GHISELLI, EDWIN E. "The Use of the Strong Vocational Interest Blank and the Pressey Senior Classification Test in the Selection of Casualty Insurance Agents." *J Appl Psychol* 26:793–9 D '42. * (*PA* 17:2452)

11. BENDER, W. R. G., AND LOVELESS, H. E. "Validation Studies Involving Successive Classes of Trainee Stenographers." *Personnel Psychol* 11:491–508 w '58. * (*PA* 34:2143)

WALTER N. DUROST, *Associate Professor of Education, University of New Hampshire, Durham, New Hampshire.*

The justification for including a review of the *Pressey Classification and Verifying Tests* in this edition of the MMY must come from the opportunity it affords to pay tribute to one of the truly great men in educational psychology and testing. The original tests were copyrighted in the early 20's and although they never obtained the wide currency won by certain other tests such as the *Otis Group Intelligence Test* or the *National Intelligence Test,* the Pressey tests nevertheless represented a pioneer effort in the measurement of intelligence.

The current editions of the intermediate and advanced level tests have a copyright date of 1958 but this copyright date most obviously must have been based upon the inclusion of a very minute amount of new material since by no stretch of the imagination are the present tests representative of the 1958 period of test development. The continued publication of these instruments in their present form is, in fact, inexcusable in this day and age; they should be either withdrawn or revised.

There is a complete lack of any information on reliability and validity, and almost no data whatsoever concerning the nature and extent of the populations upon which the norms for these tests are based. "B scores" are provided, but an examination of a single sheet insert reveals that these "B scores" are nothing but the traditional grade equivalents which have been largely discredited in achievement testing, at least at the professional and technical level, and which certainly have little place in mental ability measurement. They do *not* serve to make the Pressey test results comparable with achievement test grade equivalents.

One has to examine the tests themselves to see the spark of quality that is consistent with the man who devised them. When one recalls that these test items were written in the 1920's, when knowledge of test item writing techniques was almost nonexistent, it is nothing short of astonishing that so many of them stand up under critical scrutiny as still being good items. This is not to deny that the quality of the item writing varies; it does—from poor to excellent—but by far the larger proportion of the items are on the plus side of good.

The self-scoring device invented by Pressey, making use of a carbon deposit underlying the answer spaces, is very useful and its close connection to his interest in teaching machines is obvious.

The idea of a second test to "verify" the results of the first administration, just as worthy now as it was when it was initiated, deserves emulation by others. It is much better than just giving advice to the user to verify by using a second form, advice he rarely takes.

To be more detailed would be to labor the shortcomings of the test as it presently appears and this would be to deny the very purpose of this review. It pleased the writer to be asked to review this test, not for the opportunity it afforded to provide a constructively critical appraisal of a colleague's work, but for the opportunity to pay personal tribute to one of the very few living pioneers in the field of testing.

[489]

*__Primary Verbal Tests.__ Ages 8.0-10.5, 9.0-11.5, 10.0-12.0; 1953-62; 3 levels; 7*s.* 6*d.* per 12 tests; 9*d.* per single copy; 1*s.* per manual for any one level; postage extra; published for the National Foundation for Educational Research in England and Wales; Newnes Educational Publishing Co. Ltd. *

a) PRIMARY VERBAL TEST 1. Ages 8.0-10.5; 1953-58; formerly called *Primary School Verbal Intelligence Test 1;* adaptation of *A.C.E.R. Junior A Test* and *A.C.E.R. Junior B Test;* 1 form ['53, 8 pages]; manual ('58, 7 pages, essentially the same as 1953 manual except for additional validity data); 30(40) minutes; D. A. Pidgeon.

b) PRIMARY VERBAL TEST 2. Ages 9.0-11.5; 1959; 1 form ['59, 8 pages]; manual ['59, 7 pages]; 35(50) minutes; Valerie Land.

c) PRIMARY VERBAL TEST 3. Ages 10.0-12.0; 1962; 1 form ['62, 8 pages]; manual ['62, 12 pages]; (45-50) minutes; Neville Postlethwaite.

REFERENCES

1. MADDOX, H. "Mental Age Scales." *Brit J Ed Psychol* 29:72-3 F '59. * (*PA* 34:2731)

For reviews by John Nisbet and F. W. Warburton of a, *see 5:369.*

[490]

*__Progressive Matrices.__ Ages 5 and over; 1938-63; 3 levels; postage and purchase tax extra (postpaid); J. C. Raven; H. K. Lewis & Co. Ltd. (U.S. distributor: Psychological Corporation.) * (Australian edition of *a* and *c:* Australian Council for Educational Research.)

a) STANDARD PROGRESSIVE MATRICES. Ages 6 and over; 1938-60; manual also uses the title *Progressive Matrices (1938), 1956 Revision;* 1 form ('56, 62 pages, identical with test copyrighted in 1938 except for change in one item and order of items); revised manual ('60, 25 pages, identical with 1956 manual except for bibliography); no norms for individual administration for ages 14 and over; separate record forms or answer sheets must be used; 210*s.* ($14) per 25 (10) tests; 12*s.* 6*d.* ($1.50) per 50 record forms (answer sheets); 30*s.* (75¢) per scoring key (set of scoring key and manual); 3*s.* 6*d.* per manual; 25*s.* per specimen set including 5 copies of the complementary *Mill Hill Vocabulary Scale* ($2.85 per specimen set); (60) minutes.

b) COLOURED PROGRESSIVE MATRICES. Ages 5-11 and mental patients and senescents; 1947-63; individual for ages 5-6; 1 form ('56, 38 pages, subtest Sets A and B same as subtest Sets A and B of the *Standard Progressive Matrices* except for color); revised manual ('63, 43 pages, identical with 1958 and 1960 manuals except for bibliography and revision in norms tables); record booklet (no date); separate record forms or answer sheets must be used for group administration; 210*s.* ($14.50) per 25 (10) tests; 17*s.* 6*d.* ($1.50) per 50 record forms (answer sheets); 5*s.* 6*d.* (80¢) per manual (set of scoring key and manual); 22*s.* 6*d.* per specimen set including 12 copies of the complementary *Crichton Vocabulary Scale* ($3 per specimen set); [30] minutes.

c) ADVANCED PROGRESSIVE MATRICES. Ages 11 and over; 1943-62; 2 editions; manual ('48, 20 pages); 12*s.* 6*d.* per 50 record forms for both editions; 30*s.* per scoring key for both editions.

1) *Progressive Matrices (1947): Set 1.* For use either as a practice test for Set 2 or as a rough screening test; 1 form ('47, 14 pages); 50*s.* per 25 tests; 5*s.* per single copy ($3.30 per specimen set including *Mill Hill Vocabulary Scale* and *Crichton Vocabulary Scale*); (10) minutes.

2) *Advanced Progressive Matrices, Set 2: 1962 Revision.* For use either as "a test of intellectual capacity" when used without a time limit or as "a test of intellectual efficiency" when used with a time limit ("usually of 40 minutes"); 1 form ('62, 38 pages, a revision and abbreviation of the 1947 Set 2); no data on reliability and validity and no norms for revised form; distribution restricted to registered users who after signing an agreement and paying an annual service fee may either borrow the materials for indefinite periods at 150*s.* per set of 25 tests or for 4 weeks at 20*s.* per set of 25 tests, or purchase the materials at 340*s.* per 25 tests or 25*s.* per single copy; specimen set not available; [40] minutes.

REFERENCES

1-8. See 40:1417.
9-21. See 3:258.
22-53. See 4:314.
54-115. See 5:370.
116. BIESHEUVEL, S.; JACOBS, G. F.; AND COWLEY, J. J. "Maladjustments of Military Personnel." *J Nat Inst Personnel Res* 5:138-68 D '53. * (*PA* 29:3119)
117. RATH, R. "Correlation of Progressive Matrices With Verbal Intelligence Tests and Written Tests on Some Other Subjects." *Ed & Psychol* 1(4-5):20-5 '54. * (*PA* 31:3804)
118. ALLEN, ROBERT M., AND COLLINS, MARJORIE G. "Suggestions for the Adaptive Administration of Intelligence Tests for Those With Cerebral Palsy: Part 1, Administration of the Ammons Full-Range Picture Test, Columbia Mental Maturity Test, Raven's Progressive Matrices and Leiter International Performance Scale." *Cerebral Palsy R* 16:11-4+ My-Je '55. * (*PA* 30:3284)
119. WYSOCKI, BOLESLAW A., AND CANKARDAS, AYDIN. "A New Estimate of Polish Intelligence." *J Ed Psychol* 48:525-33 D '57. * (*PA* 33:3298)
120. CATTELL, RAYMOND B., AND SCHEIER, IVAN H. "The Objective Test Measurement of Neuroticism, U.I. 23 (—)." *Indian J Psychol* 33:217-36 pt 4 '58. *
121. FOULDS, G. A., AND CAINE, T. M. "Personality Factors and Performance on Timed Tests of Ability." *Occup Psychol* 32:102-5 Ap '58. *
122. HIGGINS, CONWELL, AND SIVERS, CATHRYNE H. "A Comparison of Stanford-Binet and Colored Raven Progressive Matrices IQs for Children With Low Socioeconomic Status." *J Consult Psychol* 22:465-8 D '58. * (*PA* 33:9919)
123. MUNDY, LYDIA, AND MAXWELL, A. E. "Assessment of the Feeble-minded." *Brit J Med Psychol* 31:201-10 pt 3 & 4 '58. * (*PA* 34:1673)
124. TRACHT, VERNON SLOAN. *A Comparative Study of Cerebral Palsied and Normal Adults on Two Forms of Raven's "Progressive Matrices."* Doctor's thesis, Loyola University (Chicago, Ill.), 1958.
125. VOGGENTHALER, ANN LOUISE. *A Comparison of the Progressive Matrices (1947), Set II, With Certain Group*

Tests Used With High School Students and School Grades. Master's thesis, University of Texas (Austin, Tex.), 1958.
126. COSTELLO, C. G. "Aphasic Cerebral Palsied Children's Wrong Answers on Raven's 'Progressive Matrices.'" *J Clin Psychol* 15:76–7 Ja '59. * (*PA* 34:3342)
127. DASH, S. C., AND KANUNGO, R. "Progressive Matrices and School Success: A Factor Analytical Study." *Psychologia* 2:246–50 D '59. * (*PA* 35:3952)
128. FOULDS, G. A. "The Relative Stability of Personality Measures Compared With Diagnostic Measures." *J Mental Sci* 105:783–7 Jl '59. * (*PA* 34:6016)
129. HARRIS, DALE B. "A Note on Some Ability Correlates of the Raven Progressive Matrices (1947) in the Kindergarten." *J Ed Psychol* 50:228–9 O '59. * (*PA* 36:1FH28H)
130. JENSEN, ARTHUR R. "A Statistical Note on Racial Differences in the Progressive Matrices." *J Consult Psychol* 23:272 Je '59. *
131. JORDAN, THOMAS E. "Formboard Comparability in the Colored Progressive Matrices." *J Clin Psychol* 15:422–3 O '59. * (*PA* 36:1HC22J)
132. JORDAN, THOMAS E., AND DECHARMS, RICHARD. "The Achievement Motive in Normal and Mentally Retarded Children." *Am J Mental Def* 64:457–66 N '59. * (*PA* 34:8011)
133. KNIEF, LOTUS M., AND STROUD, JAMES B. "Intercorrelations Among Various Intelligence, Achievement, and Social Class Scores." *J Ed Psychol* 50:117–20 Je '59. * (*PA* 35:779)
134. KURODA, JITSUO. "Application of the Colored Progressive Matrices Test for the Japanese Kindergarten Children." *Psychologia* 2:173–7 S '59. * (*PA* 35:3253)
135. LEVINSON, BORIS M. "A Comparison of the Coloured Progressive Matrices (CPM) With the Wechsler Adult Intelligence Scale (WAIS) in a Normal Aged White Male Population." *J Clin Psychol* 15:288–91 Jl '59. * (*PA* 35:3299)
136. LEVINSON, BORIS M. "A Comparison of the Performance of Bilingual and Monolingual Native Born Jewish Preschool Children of Traditional Parentage on Four Intelligence Tests." *J Clin Psychol* 15:74–6 Ja '59. * (*PA* 34:2729)
137. LORANGER, ARMAND W., AND MISIAK, HENRYK. "Critical Flicker Frequency and Some Intellectual Functions in Old Age." *J Gerontol* 14:323–7 Jl '59. * (*PA* 34:4153)
138. MEHROTRA, S. N. "An Educational-Vocational Guidance Project for Intermediate Students: A Follow-Up Study." *Indian J Psychol* 34:148–62 pt 3 '59. * (*PA* 36:4KJ48M)
139. MOSHIN, S. M. "Plea for a Scientific Aptitude Test and a Preliminary Report of the Development of Such Test." *Indian J Psychol* 34:36–42 pt 1 '59. *
140. SPERRAZZO, GERALD, AND WILKINS, WALTER L. "Racial Differences on Progressive Matrices." *J Consult Psychol* 23:273–4 Je '59. * (*PA* 34:4266)
141. VALENTINE, MAX. "Psychometric Testing in Iran." *J Mental Sci* 105:93–107 Ja '59. * (*PA* 34:1065)
142. DESAI, MAHESH M. "Intelligence and Verbal Knowledge in Relation to Epstein's Overinclusion Test." *J Clin Psychol* 16:417–9 O '60. * (*PA* 37:3226)
143. DILS, CHARLES W. "The Colored Progressive Matrices as an Indicator of Brain Damage." *J Clin Psychol* 16:414–6 O '60. * (*PA* 37:3530)
144. HAZARI, ANANDI. "The Stability of Raven's Coloured Progressive Matrices Scores for Selected Children." *J Psychol Res* 4:102–4 S '60. * (*PA* 35:5371)
145. LORANGER, ARMAND W., AND MISIAK, HENRYK. "The Performance of Aged Females on Five Non-Language Tests of Intellectual Functions." *J Clin Psychol* 16:189–91 Ap '60. * (*PA* 36:2FI89L)
146. LUNZER, E. A. "Aggressive and Withdrawing Children in the Normal School: 2, Disparity in Attainment." *Brit J Ed Psychol* 30:119–23 Je '60. *
147. MACARTHUR, R. S. "The Coloured Progressive Matrices as a Measure of General Intellectual Ability for Edmonton Grade III Boys." *Alberta J Ed Res* 6:67–75 Je '60. * (*PA* 36:2HD67M)
148. MAHER, BRENDAN A. "Position Errors and Primitive Thinking in the Progressive Matrices Test." *Am J Mental Def* 64:1016–20 My '60. * (*PA* 35:6407)
149. MALPASS, LESLIE F.; BROWN, RONALD; AND HAKE, DONALD. "The Utility of the Progressive Matrices (1956 Edition) With Normal and Retarded Children." *J Clin Psychol* 16:350 Jl '60. * (*PA* 36:2JI50M)
150. MASON, P. L., AND CASEY, D. L. "The Use of Psychological Tests for Selecting Tabulating Machine Operators." *Personnel Prac B* 16:39–41 S '60. * (*PA* 35:4063)
151. NYMAN, G. EBERHARD, AND SMITH, GUDMUND J. W. "Serial Performance Patterns in Raven's Progressive Matrices." *Scandinavian J Psychol* 1(3):103–11 '60. * (*PA* 35:4862)
152. URMER, ALBERT H.; MORRIS, ANN B.; AND WENDLAND, LEONARD V. "The Effect of Brain Damage on Raven's Progressive Matrices." *J Clin Psychol* 16:182–5 Ap '60. * (*PA* 36:2JF82U)
153. WOLF, WILLAVENE SHEETS. *The Contribution of Speed of Response in Mental Measurement.* Doctor's thesis, State University of Iowa (Iowa City, Iowa), 1960. (*DA* 21:1467)
154. CLARK, PHILIP J.; VANDENBERG, STEVEN G.; AND PROCTOR, CHARLES H. "On the Relationship of Scores on Certain Psychological Tests With a Number of Anthropometric Characters and Birth Order in Twins." *Hum Biol* 33:163–80 My '61. * (*PA* 36:3DP63C)
155. CROOKES, T. G., AND FRENCH, J. G. "Intelligence and Wastage of Student Mental Nurses." *Occup Psychol* 35:149–54 Jl '61. * (*PA* 37:2046)
156. ESTES, BETSY WORTH; CURTIN, MARY ELLEN; DEBURGER, ROBERT A.; AND DENNY, CHARLOTTE. "Relationships Between 1960 Stanford-Binet, 1937 Stanford-Binet, WISC, Raven, and Draw-A-Man." *J Consult Psychol* 25:388–91 O '61. * (*PA* 37:3127)
157. FEINBERG, IRWIN, AND GARMAN, EUGENIE M. "Studies of Thought Disorder in Schizophrenia: 2, Plausible and Implausible Errors on a Modification of the Progressive Matrices Test." *Arch Gen Psychiatry* 4:191–201 F '61. * (*PA* 35:6924)
158. HIGDON, BETTINA P. *Raven's Progressive Matrices, Set I, Administered to Even-Aged Students From 6 to 16.* Master's thesis, Alabama College (Montevallo, Ala.), 1961.
159. JAMUAR, K. K. "Personality and Achievement." *Psychol Studies* 6:59–65 Jl '61. * (*PA* 38:3203)
160. LYNN, R., AND GORDON, I. E. "The Relation of Neuroticism and Extraversion to Intelligence and Educational Attainment." *Brit J Ed Psychol* 31:194–203 Je '61. * (*PA* 36:3HD94L)
161. MCLEOD, H. N., AND RUBIN, J. "Correction Between the Raven Matrices (Rev. 1956) and the Wechsler Adult Intelligence Scale (1955)." *Ont Hosp Psychol B* 6:47–9 Mr '61. *
162. ORME, J. E. "The Coloured Progressive Matrices as a Measure of Intellectual Subnormality." *Brit J Med Psychol* 34:291–2 pt 3 & 4 '61. * (*PA* 37:1698)
163. VENABLES, ETHEL C. "Changes in Intelligence Test Scores of Engineering Apprentices Between the First and Third Years of Attendance at College." *Brit J Ed Psychol* 31:257–64 N '61. * (*PA* 36:5KK57V)
164. Venables, Ethel C. "Placement Problems Among Engineering Apprentices in Part-Time Technical College Courses: Part 2, Level of Ability Needed for Success in National Certificate Courses." *Brit J Ed Psychol* 31:56–8 F '61. * (*PA* 36:1KJ56V)
165. WOLF, WILLAVENE, AND STROUD, JAMES B. "The Contribution of Response in Mental Measurement." *J Ed Psychol* 52:249–53 O '61. * (*PA* 38:3192)
166. YATES, AUBREY J. "Item Analysis of Progressive Matrices (1947)." *Brit J Ed Psychol* 31:152–7 Je '61. * (*PA* 36:3HD52Y)
167. BLAZSANYIK, J. "Clinical Diagnostic Use of P.M. 38 and Verbal Tests." *Austral J Psychol Res* 3:5–8 au '62. *
168. ELLEY, W. B., AND MACARTHUR, R. S. "The Standard Progressive Matrices as a Culture-Reduced Measure of General Intellectual Ability." *Alberta J Ed Res* 8:54–65 Mr '62. * (*PA* 37:3126)
169. FOULDS, G. A., AND DIXON, PENELOPE. "The Nature of Intellectual Deficit in Schizophrenia: Part 1, A Comparison of Schizophrenics and Neurotics." *Brit J Social & Clin Psychol* 1:7–19 F '62. * (*PA* 37:1788)
170. FOULDS, G. A., AND DIXON, PENELOPE. "The Nature of Intellectual Deficit in Schizophrenia: Part 3, A Longitudinal Study of the Sub-Groups." *Brit J Social & Clin Psychol* 1:199–207 O '62. * (*PA* 37:5488)
171. FOULDS, G. A.; DIXON, PENELOPE; MCCLELLAND, MARILYN; AND MCCLELLAND, W. J. "The Nature of Intellectual Deficit in Schizophrenia: Part 2, A Cross-Sectional Study of Paranoid, Catatonic, Hebephrenic and Simple Schizophrenics." *Brit J Social & Clin Psychol* 1:141–9 Je '62. * (*PA* 37:3685)
172. JORDAN, THOMAS E. "Normative Data on the Progressive Matrices (1938)." *Psychol Rep* 10:122 F '62. * (*PA* 37:1204)
173. KNEHR, CHARLES A. "Factor Analyses of Schizophrenic and Organic Test Data." *J Psychol* 54:467–71 O '62. * (*PA* 37:6759)
174. LEVINSON, BORIS M. "Positional and Figural Errors Made by the Aged on Raven Coloured Progressive Matrices." *J Genetic Psychol* 100:183–92 Je '62. * (*PA* 37:2955)
175. MCDONNELL, M. W. "The Prediction of Academic Achievement of Superior Grade Three Pupils." *Alberta J Ed Res* 8:111–8 Je '62. * (*PA* 37:3886)
176. MCLEOD, HUGH N., AND RUBIN, JOSEPH. "Correlation Between Raven Progressive Matrices and the WAIS." *J Consult Psychol* 26:190–1 Ap '62. * (*PA* 37:4960)
177. MEYERS, E.; ORPET, R. E.; ATTWELL, A. A.; AND DINGMAN, H. F. *Primary Abilities at Mental Age Six.* Monographs of the Society for Research in Child Development, Vol. 27, No. 1, Serial No. 82. Lafayette, Ind.: Child Development Publications, 1962. Pp. 40. * (*PA* 38:8462)
178. NICKOLS, JOHN E., JR. "Insight, Superior Intelligence, and the Raven Progressive Matrices, Set E." *J Clin Psychol* 18:351 Jl '62. * (*PA* 39:1752)
179. RAO, S. NARAYANA. "Predicting Academic Achievement of Students in Science and Arts Colleges." *Psychol Studies* 7:16–9 Jl '62. * (*PA* 37:5669)
180. SCHEPERS, J. M. "A Components Analysis of a Complex Psychomotor Learning Task." *Psychologia Africana* 9:294–329 '62. * (*PA* 37:4314)
181. YOUNG, HARBEN BOUTOURLINE; TAGIURI, RENATO; TESI, GINO; AND MONTEMAGNI, GABRIELLA. "Influence of Town and

Country Upon Children's Intelligence." *Brit J Ed Psychol* 32:151–8 Je '62. * (*PA* 37:2883)
182. BURNETT, A.; BEACH, H. D.; AND SULLIVAN, A. M. "Intelligence in a Restricted Environment." *Can Psychologist* 4:126–36 O '63. * (*PA* 38:6050)
183. EDWARDS, ALLAN E., AND WINE, DAVID B. "Personality Changes With Age: Their Dependency on Concomitant Intellectual Decline." *J Gerontol* 18:182–4 Ap '63. * (*PA* 38:4099)
184. EVANS, RAY B., AND MARMORSTON, JESSIE. "Psychological Test Signs of Brain Damage in Cerebral Thrombosis." *Psychol Rep* 12:915–30 Je '63. * (*PA* 38:6413)
185. HAMILTON, VERNON. "I.Q. Changes in Chronic Schizophrenia." *Brit J Psychiatry* 109:642–8 S '63. * (*PA* 38:6506)
186. HIGASHIMACHI, WILFRED H. "The Construct Validity of the Progressive Matrices as a Measure of Superego Strength in Juvenile Delinquents." *J Consult Psychol* 27:415–9 O '63. * (*PA* 38:4302)
187. KING, W. H. "The Development of Scientific Concepts in Children." *Brit J Ed Psychol* 33:240–52 N '63. * (*PA* 38:8062)
188. MACARTHUR, R. S., AND ELLEY, W. B. "The Reduction of Socioeconomic Bias in Intelligence Testing." *Brit J Ed Psychol* 33:107–19 Je '63. * (*PA* 38:4271)
189. NELSON, MARVEN O., AND EDELSTEIN, GERALD. "Raven Progressive Matrices, Non-Language Multi-Mental Test, and California Test of Mental Maturity: Intercorrelations." *Psychol Rep* 13:46 Ag '63. * (*PA* 38:6061)
190. RAO, S. NARAYANA. "Prediction of Academic Achievement of Students in an Engineering College." *J Psychol Res* 7:114–7 S '63. *
191. RICH, CHARLES CLIFTON. *The Validity of an Adaptation of Raven's Progressive Matrices Test for Use With Blind Children.* Doctor's thesis, Texas Technological College (Lubbock, Tex.), 1963. (*DA* 24:1714)
192. SIGEL, IRVING E. "How Intelligence Tests Limit Understanding of Intelligence." *Merrill-Palmer Q* 9:39–56 Ja '63. * (*PA* 39:1791)
193. VENABLES, ETHEL C. "Social Differences Among Day-Release Students in Relation to Their Recruitment and Examination Success." *Brit J Social & Clin Psychol* 2:138–52 Je '63. * (*PA* 38:4659)

MORTON BORTNER, *Chief Psychologist, Department of Physical Medicine and Rehabilitation, New York Medical College, New York, New York.*

These tests represent an attempt to measure intellectual functioning within the context of Spearman's concept of *"g."* The tasks or matrices consist of designs which require completion. The testee chooses from multiple choice options the design or design part which best fits. An answer which fits may: (*a*) complete a pattern, (*b*) complete an analogy, (*c*) systematically alter a pattern, (*d*) introduce systematic permutations, or (*e*) systematically resolve figures into parts. The number of items correctly solved is the score which is then translated into a percentile rank. The author recommends that the *Standard Progressive Matrices* be used in conjunction with the *Mill Hill Vocabulary Scale* and that the *Coloured Progressive Matrices* be used in conjunction with the *Crichton Vocabulary Scale* in order to supplement the Matrices' measure of "capacity" with a measure of acquired information.

The accumulating literature dealing with the validity and reliability of these scales is equivocal. Continuing revisions of the tests have dealt with the adequacy of the designs, but have not departed from the original strategy of the test which is to measure *"g"* via various forms of "perceptual reasoning." Although the author breaks the perceptual task down into subcategories of perceptual functioning (enumerated above) their relevance to intellectual functioning in general remains to be documented.

These tests should be quite helpful as screening devices for groups where estimates of levels of intelligence need to be determined. They have already been found helpful in comparing various psychiatric, socioeconomic, and ethnic groups. (See *112* for an extensive review of the literature.) *Progressive Matrices* should also be helpful in estimating general level of intellectual functioning of individuals who have communication disorders as no verbal responses are required. The tests are easy to administer, require little verbal instruction, and are relatively brief. For the above reasons, these tests will probably continue to be justifiably used.

The value of the tests as clinical instruments is limited. The use of perceptual items, however finely the author breaks them down into subcategories, seems to provide a measure of perceptual adequacy rather than of intellectual capacity. The fact that perceptual adequacy and intellectual capacity are highly related in the normal hardly provides a basis for using one as the measure of the other, especially in the abnormal. Unless we are merely interested in a score, the diagnostic value of most tests of intellectual capacity comes from an analysis of the errors made and from observations made of the subject's attempts to deal with the task. Such analyses and observations are not forthcoming from the Matrices, hence nothing is known about what the subject is thinking when he is thinking wrong. For that matter, very little is known about what he is thinking when he is thinking right. That is, what does it signify to be able to break up designs into constituent parts, to find perceptual analogies, to complete a design, etc.? In the absence of developmental data concerning these aspects of perceptual adequacy, and their relation to other factors in intelligence, they remain theoretical constructs which might better serve the cause of perceptual research than psychometric testing.

Special groups such as the deaf, cerebral palsied, and individuals with communication disorders often are not easily tested with the standard procedures, and the Matrices will be helpful in establishing a mental level for them. However, the clinical usefulness of the Matrices as indicators of "process" in thinking is less than that of such tests as the *Leiter International Performance Scale* or the *Arthur Point Scale of Performance Tests,* where the clinician in addition to getting his score has opportunity to observe and make inferences about responses to a wide variety of tasks, many if not all of which have practical significance for life experiences even if they are not factorially pure.

The *Progressive Matrices* (*1947*), titled *Advanced Progressive Matrices* on the test booklet, was constructed with a view to evaluating "people of more than average intellectual capacity." Estimated percentile norms are available for the age range 11–40 for the 1947 Set 2. Reliability coefficients range from .76 to .91. Norms and technical data for the 1962 revision of Set 2 are not yet available. The validity of the 1947 test receives some favorable support from a study incorporated in the manual dealing with a comparison of advantaged and disadvantaged children with the expected differences occurring. The value of this test as a large scale screening device for identifying various levels of superior functioning remains unknown despite its use since 1943 when the original form was drafted for use by the War Officer Selection Boards in Great Britain.

A word about the manuals. The author seems to have combined in his manuals both something more and something less than what a manual should be. Much of the information offered might better be submitted as journal articles. Some of the information might better be offered not at all. Some prospective users might be confused to learn that a "board form" of the *Coloured Progressive Matrices* discussed in much detail is not commercially available, or that the working time for Set 2 of the *Advanced Progressive Matrices* "can be adjusted [from 15 minutes to an hour] to secure the type of score distribution one requires." In addition, as noted above, the manual for Advanced Set 2 does not yet cover the 1962 revision. Revision of the manuals is in order.

For reviews by Charlotte Banks, W. D. Wall, and George Westby, see 4:314; for reviews by Walter C. Shipley and David Wechsler of the 1938 edition, see 3:258; for a review by T. J. Keating, see 40:1417.

[491]

Purdue Non-Language Test. Grades 9–12 and adults; 1957–58; Forms A, B, ('57, 3 pages); preliminary manual ('58, 4 pages); $1.75 per 20 tests; 30¢ per specimen set of both forms; postage extra; 25(30) minutes; Joseph Tiffin, Alan Gruber, and Kay Inaba; Science Research Associates, Inc. *

JOHN D. HUNDLEBY, *Research Assistant Professor of Psychology, University of Illinois, Urbana, Illinois.*

Each item in the *Purdue Non-Language Test* consists of five designs or geometric shapes. The subject's task is to indicate which design is different from the other four. There are two parallel forms, A and B, both consisting of 48 items.

As presented by the publisher's 1963–1964 catalog, the specimen set contains a copy of both Forms A and B and a manual. On inspection, however, the manual is that published in March 1958, and designated at that time as a "preliminary manual." Further, the term "Experimental Form" appears on the specimen set package, but not on the test itself. This ambiguity is likely to be misleading to the user and needs to be corrected. For present purposes the test and manual will be evaluated as judged satisfactory by the authors and publishers for general distribution.

The manual is brief and overly concise. Thus norms for United States and Venezuelan high school students are given separately, while industrial supervisory personnel and civil service laborers are presented without national identification or further detail of group compositions. Another example is in the description of groups upon which reliability estimates were based. Here, two Cuban groups are described as "San Jose, Cuba (applicants), Rural" and "Havana, Cuba (applicants), Urban." "Applicants for what?" one may ask.

The section on norms occupies about one third of one page and is inadequate. To present test users with norms based on 77 cases (as for "U.S. High School"), 89 cases (for "Venezuelan High School"), 184 (for "Industrial Supervisory Personnel"), or 99 cases (for "Civil Service Laborers"), is clearly an overoptimistic use of normative procedures. Particularly is this true when *no information at all* is given on age, sex, grade level, socioeconomic class, or on any of the generally accepted ways in which normative populations are described. No information is presented suggesting the extent to which the normative groups may be regarded as representative of some larger population. Indeed if the U.S. and Venezuelan students came from single high schools without any attempt at sampling, it is impossible to judge the extent to which the reported differences may reflect discrepancies between high schools rather than between U.S. and Venezuelan children.

The *Purdue Non-Language Test* is described as "a 'culture fair' test designed to measure mental ability." It is stated that "since it consists entirely of geometric forms, there is evidence to show that it can be used effectively with persons having markedly different cultural or educational backgrounds." To describe a test as culture fair simply because geometric forms are used is somewhat hazardous, and indeed what little empirical evidence there is—the U.S. versus Venezuela comparison referred to above—is not supportive. Why such national differences should occur in a "culture fair" test is not even commented upon. Correlations with the *Adaptability Test* are reported of .65 for 184 industrial salaried employees and .55 for 99 laborers, and this appears to be the sole evidence that the test is a measure of general ability rather than of any particular specific ability (such as spatial relations) or combination of such abilities. No attempt was made to correlate the test with standard measures of roughly similar intent and no factor-analytic evidence is presented. The latter would appear to be mandatory in validating a general ability test of this type.

Equivalent forms reliabilities of this test range from .78 to .88, and internal consistency (usually odd-even) reliabilities from .90 to .93. These figures would be acceptable if it were not for the apparent assumption that this is a power test. With 48 items to be completed in 25 minutes (a rate of 32 seconds per item) this is questionable. If total score does include speed elements, then the reliability coefficients are likely to be too large, and certain rather undesirable implications appear for the test's validity. Unfortunately, no data are reported that would clear up this matter, and information on item difficulty level appears to be based upon the original pool of items from which both forms of the test were constructed. Presumably this original administration was untimed.

No mention of guessing is made in the manual and it would appear advisable to make appropriate additions to the administrator's instructions, and possibly to utilize appropriate correction formulas. Certainly if, as the reviewer suspects, this test may be speeded at least for groups of low educational background or ability, this problem becomes more acute.

This review, in summary, has been very critical of the *Purdue Non-Language Test*. In many ways the test falls short of generally accepted standards and at present there is not enough supportive evidence for the test user to prefer this over most other nonlanguage or culture fair tests that are available. If this test is to play any part in the future measurement of ability, then more research is necessary and a satisfactory pattern of correlation with other measures must be presented. Finally, a considerably revised and expanded manual with statistical information based upon a substantial normative sample is needed before this test can be recommended for general use.

Benjamin Rosner, *Director, Test Development Division, Educational Testing Service, Princeton, New Jersey.*

Reviewing an experimental test presents major difficulties. Does one evaluate need, promise, or current status? And by what criteria? Present need? Conventional standards of test utility? The promise of further research? Or are experimental forms exempted from rigorous psychometric evaluation and, if so, for how long? When, specifically, are experimental editions no longer experimental? At the publisher's discretion? After some reasonable but arbitrarily imposed time limit? When experimentation ceases?

The case in point, the *Purdue Non-Language Test,* was published in 1958 as an experimental "culture fair" test of mental ability. In 1963, five years later, the review set contained the same preliminary manual and test materials. Is the test still experimental? The publisher apparently thinks so. But if so, where is the evidence of continued experimentation? Surely "experimental" denotes experimentation. Are we not, consequently, to anticipate periodic revision of the test manual? Or are we to regard the presence of unaltered experimental materials five years after initial publication as evidence of publisher disinterest? Or lack of faith? Or is the test to stand on its own?

Had I reviewed the test in 1958 I would have called attention to its gross inadequacies but I would probably have encouraged further research. Initially I would have questioned the need for another "culture fair" test if only because reliance on geometric forms duplicated more fully developed nonverbal instruments of similar constructs. The issue, however, is moot.

Secondly, I would have questioned the reliability data, particularly the odd-even versions, because of the speed factor that seems to permeate the task. Although each test form contains only 48 items, 25 minutes of testing time places a premium on speed for the intended examinee population. Moreover, although the more appropriate alternate form reliabilities of approximately .84 suggest minimally acceptable levels—certainly encouraging for experimental editions—these, too, are somewhat spurious for the data seem to have been derived from the sample providing the initial item statistics. At least this is not clear, for descriptions of the samples are rather fragmentary.

Next I would have underscored the need for predictive validity studies against appropriate academic and vocational criteria. There is some evidence of congruent validity in terms of correlations with the *Adaptability Test.* Since these data are encouraging, why weren't the "situational validity" tests carried out or reported? The manual almost suggests they were forthcoming.

Finally, I would have pointed to the woefully inadequate normative material. Not only are descriptions of the norming samples virtually absent, but the number of cases, ranging from 77 "U.S. High School" students to 184 "Industrial Supervisory Personnel," are obviously substandard.

In every regard, then, the experimental edition cannot stand on its own. It is, obviously, unacceptable for practical usage. If it is still experimental, the publishers must assume their experimental obligations to restore our faith.

[492]

★Quantitative Evaluative Device. Entering graduate students; 1959–62; also called QED; tests administered at college centers established by the author; "potential for quantitative sophistication"; Form D ('59, 8 pages); manual ('62, 4 pages); no data on reliability of present form; separate answer sheets must be used; tests rented only; rental fee: $1 per student, postpaid; IBM answer sheets must be purchased elsewhere; 50(60) minutes; R. E. Stake; [Lincoln Test Service]. *

REFERENCES

1. Stake, Robert E. "A Non-Mathematical Quantitative Aptitude Test for the Graduate Level: The QED." *J Exp Ed* 31:81–3 S '62. * (*PA* 37:8280)

[493]

***Quick-Scoring Group Test of Learning Capacity: Dominion Tests.** Grades 7–9, 10–13 and adults; 1934–63; quick scoring edition of *Group Test of Learning Capacity: Dominion Tests* (see 5:341); Forms A, B; 2 levels; 2 editions; no data on reliability and validity; postage extra; 30(40) minutes; Department of Educational Research, Ontario College of Education, University of Toronto; distributed by Guidance Centre (manual and answer cards for *b* must be purchased from the Department of Educational Research). *

a) [HAND SCORING EDITION.] 1934–58; Forms A, B, ('58, 4 pages); 2 levels; separate answer sheets must be used; $1.75 per 25 tests; 20¢ per scoring key; 75¢ per complete specimen set.

1) *Intermediate.* Grades 7–9; 1958; manual ('58, 4 pages).

2) *Advanced.* Grades 10–13 and adults; 1955–58; manual ('58, 8 pages).

b) MACHINE-SCORING EDITION. 1962–63; Forms A, B, ('62, 6 pages); 2 levels: intermediate, advanced; manual ('63) in 2 parts: Parts 1 (6 pages), 2 (4 pages); separate answer cards must be used; $1.25 per 25 tests; 50¢ per 25 IBM answer cards (machine scoring through the Department of Educational Research only); 10¢ per manual; 20¢ per specimen set.

Donald B. Black, *Professor of Education, University of Alberta, Edmonton, Alberta, Canada.*

The tests under review can best be appreciated by a study of their genealogy. The original test or rather the earliest form available to the reviewer was the 1934 *Group Test of Learning Capacity.* These were revised in 1939 (advanced) and 1950 (intermediate) to give omnibus editions of 75 items each. The 1939 manual was not available to the reviewer but the 1950 manual for the intermediate level gives Hoyt and parallel form reliabilities for this level of .93 based on a sample of urban students. The 1940 manual for the advanced level reports reliabilities of .81–.90. Revised norms for the two levels were produced in 1952 and 1954 for the intermediate and advanced levels, respectively. The 1950 (intermediate) and 1940 (advanced) reliability data are reproduced in the manuals containing these norms. The 1958 Quick-Scoring Edition represents a change from a consumable test booklet form to conventional multiple choice form with a separate answer sheet. This has meant, basically, only the provision of alternates for the mathematical items and a revising of the order of the stem for the number series items for the new edition. The 1963 Machine-Scoring Edition is a shortened version (70 items) of the 1958 editions. All items but three on the one form at one level examined by the reviewer are taken directly from the same form and level of the 1958 edition. In other words, the two tests under review are very similar in content to each other and to the earlier 1939 and 1950 Omnibus Editions.

No reliability data are reported for the current tests. Instead the reader is referred to the earlier manuals for the *Group Test of Learning Capacity* and the 1939 and 1950 data for the omnibus tests. No form to form or edition to edition data are available for the 1958 and 1963 editions. There is no evidence of item analyses. The alternates in the 1958 edition often violate good practice, presumably to ensure a proper distribution of correct responses. The 1963 edition has fewer instances of this and on the whole has a better general format.

The manuals for the 1958 edition note that Ontario pupils in 17 and 30 rural and urban schools were tested using the intermediate and advanced forms, respectively, in February 1957. "It was found that the 1952 [1954 for the advanced level] mental age equivalents were valid also for the Quick-Scoring [1958] Edition," and thus the earlier norms were used. The intermediate manual indicates these earlier (1952) norms were adjusted to give a mean IQ slightly higher than 100 for reasons of selection, a standard deviation of approximately 16, and a reasonably normal distribution. For the 2,500 cases of the 1952 norming sample, the mean IQ was 102.3; the standard deviation, 16.1; and the distribution of IQ's was normal. The advanced level 1954 norms are based on 13,468 students in grades 9 to 13 tested in the fall of 1953. No adult norming groups are defined nor is there any description of the adjustments of IQ's as in the intermediate level. However, a table of CA (months) adjustments is provided presumably to achieve the same end. The February 1957 testing with the 1958 edition contained no adults nor grade 13 students.

The procedure to obtain IQ's is the ratio method. The test scores are converted first to mental ages even though it has been adequately established that the use of this concept for the age ranges covered by these tests is highly suspect.

The 1963 edition norms, on the other hand, are based on a new norming population of a "representative" sample of Ontario students in grades 7–12. No evidence is given as to the basis on which the norming sample could be called representative nor are reliability and comparability of form data given. The norms for this test are reported in percentiles for each grade. It is interesting to note that the cover of the advanced level test booklet suggests the advanced form covers a grades 10 to 13 range. As noted, grade 12 is the highest level of norms provided. (The reader may be confused by the Ontario grade system in which all tests were normed and by grade 13 in particular. The latter could be best considered as college bound high school seniors.)

Several other comments should be directed to the manuals on points of administration. There is nothing to suggest to the student whether to guess or not, or that a correction for guessing will or will not be made, or that the best answer is to be selected. The Machine-Scoring Edition is so called because the manual directs use of a special IBM mark-sensing answer card. The Quick-Scoring Edition uses a special answer sheet which appears to be a conventional IBM mark-sensing answer sheet. However, a hand scoring key is provided. No mention is made of possible use of a scoring machine for these answer sheets. If the answer sheets provided with the specimen sets supplied for review are typical answer sheets, difficulty would be experienced in machine scoring because of poor cutting. It would seem that the publisher should provide answer sheets capable of machine scoring and that these should also be provided as an alternative to the IBM cards for the 1963 edition for those who have local machine scoring facilities and need not rely on the special facilities which are needed for the IBM cards and which are available only in Toronto.

Further, while the test items are generally typical of the type associated with single score or omnibus type IQ tests, there is nothing to suggest that these particular items have virtue for Canadian schools or disadvantage for American schools; there is no evidence that item analysis reflected any national differences from similar items in American tests. With 70 or 75 items to be attempted in 30 minutes, there obviously is a high speed factor in any score reported. No factorial weightings are reported in the manuals.

In summary, it would appear that the publishers could greatly assist the discriminating test consumer by even a cursory adherence to the suggestions of the Technical Recommendations.

GEORGE A. FERGUSON, *Professor of Psychology, McGill University, Montreal, Canada.*

Both tests are adaptations of the *Group Test of Learning Capacity: Dominion Tests.* They are composed of vocabulary, analogies, arithmetic reasoning, number sequence, classification, and related types of items commonly used in group tests of intelligence. The items have been carefully selected from earlier Dominion Tests. The user is assured that from a test construction viewpoint much technical skill has been exercised by the test authors.

The hand-scored Quick-Scoring Edition has essentially the same content as the Machine-Scoring Edition. The only difference of any consequence is that the former contains 75 and the latter 70 items. The Quick-Scoring Edition uses a separate answer sheet with a plastic stencil for hand scoring. The Machine-Scoring Edition uses an answer card with electrographic pencils. The Department of Educational Research, University of Toronto, through its Test Scoring and Item Analysis Section, will score the Machine-Scoring Edition and provide statistical data to the test user. The tests may also be scored locally by hand scoring answer keys provided in the manuals.

Norms for the Quick-Scoring Edition, advanced level, are based on over 13,000 secondary school students tested in Ontario in 1954. The norms provide mental age equivalents which, with chronological ages, may be used in the calculation of IQ's. A two-page nomograph is provided in the manual for converting raw score and chronological age to IQ. This appears to be a clumsy substitute for a very simple arithmetical calculation. Norms for the Quick-Scoring Edition, intermediate level, are the same as the 1952 norms for the Omnibus Edition of the intermediate level *Group Test of Learning Capacity: Dominion Tests.* The Machine-Scoring Edition was separately standardized in 1961–62 and percentile rank norms are based on about 1,000–3,000 Ontario pupils per grade.

No useful purpose is served by a discussion of either the validity or reliability of these tests. Although no data are provided in the manuals for the present tests, relevant data are available in the manuals of earlier editions of the *Group Tests of Learning Capacity.* Tests of this type have been widely used for many years, and their validity and reliability checked in many contexts.

On the whole these are well constructed tests of a conventional kind. No reasons exist to suppose that their usefulness for educational progress has diminished, or that their content has been superceded by some new and superior variety of test material.

[494]

Revised Beta Examination. Ages 16–59; 1931–57; revision of *Army Group Examination Beta* ('20); nonlanguage; 1 form ('35, 14 pages); revised manual ('57, 11 pages); norms for men only; $4.50 per 25 tests; 50¢ per specimen set; postpaid; French edition available; 15(30) minutes; 1946 revision by Robert M. Lindner and Milton Gurvitz; basic revision by C. E. Kellogg and N. W. Morton; Psychological Corporation. *

REFERENCES

1–4. See 40:1419.
5–9. See 3:259.
10–23. See 5:375.
24. ALPER, THELMA G., AND BORING, EDWIN G. "Intelligence-Test Scores of Northern and Southern White and Negro Recruits in 1918." *J Abn & Social Psychol* 39:471–4 O '44. * (*PA* 19:455)
25. GARRETT, HENRY E. "Comparison of Negro and White Recruits on the Army Tests Given in 1917–1918." *Am J Psychol* 58:480–95 O '45. * (*PA* 20:855)
26. MONTAGU, M. F. ASHLEY. "Intelligence of Northern Negroes and Southern Whites in the First World War." *Am J Psychol* 58:161–88 Ap '45. * (*PA* 19:2299)
27. MARCUSE, F. L., AND BITTERMAN, M. E. "Notes on the Results of Army Intelligence Testing in World War I." *Sci* 104:231–2 S 6 '46. * (*PA* 21:204)
28. PASTORE, NICHOLAS. "A Fallacy Underlying Garrett's Use of the Data of the Army Alpha and Beta Tests—A Comment." Letter. *Sci Mo* 69:279–80 O '49. * (*PA* 24:1145)
29. CUOMO, SYLVIA, AND MEYER, HERBERT H. "Validity Information Exchange, No. 8–19: D.O.T. Code 6-78.632, Floor Assembler." *Personnel Psychol* 8:270 su '55. *
30. NI, LIAN, AND HSIAO, SHIH-LANG. "A Study of Mental Declination With Aging Among the Retired Servicemen Tested in Nuan-Nuan Center." *Acta Psychologica Taiwanica* (1):9–47 N '58. * (*PA* 34:2849)
31. COHEN, LEONARD MARLIN. *The Relationship Between Certain Personality Variables and Prior Occupational Stability of Prison Inmates.* Doctor's thesis, Temple University (Philadelphia, Pa.), 1959. (*DA* 20:3375)
32. DOPPELT, JEROME E., AND SEASHORE, HAROLD G. "Psychological Testing in Correctional Institutions." *J Counsel Psychol* 6:81–92 sp '59. * (*PA* 34:6012)
33. PANTON, JAMES H. "Beta-WAIS Comparisons and WAIS Subtest Configurations Within a State Prison Population." *J Clin Psychol* 16:312–7 Jl '60. * (*PA* 36:2HD12P)
34. DURRETT, HAROLD L. "Validity Information Exchange, No. 14-03: D.O.T. Code 5-21.010, Continuous Miner Operator (Bituminous Coal Industry)." *Personnel Psychol* 14:453–5 w '61. *
35. COPPINGER, NEIL W.; BORTNER, RAYMAN W.; AND SAUCER, RAYFORD T. "A Factor Analysis of Psychological Deficit." *J Genetic Psychol* 103:23–43 S '63. * (*PA* 39:174)
36. TWAIN, DAVID C., AND BROOKS, EDWARD M. "A Comparison of Wechsler, Revised Beta and Otis Scores of Delinquents." *Brit J Criminol* 3:288–90 Ja '63. *

BERT A. GOLDMAN, *Associate Professor of Education, and Associate, Counseling Service, State University of New York at Albany, Albany, New York.*

In 1934, Kellogg and Morton published the *Revised Beta Examination* which was a revision of the *Army Group Examination Beta* developed during World War I. Following, in 1943, the authors prepared a revised manual. Three years later, 1946, Lindner and Gurvitz published a manual which described a procedure for converting Beta raw scores into IQ's resembling the scheme in the *Wechsler-Bellevue Intelligence Scale*. The present manual, revised in 1957 by Lindner and Gurvitz, is essentially the same as their 1946 edition and accompanies the original Kellogg and Morton *Revised Beta Examination* now some 30 years old. Apparently, the only major difference between the 1946 manual and the 1957 edition is the omission of the Kellogg-Morton standardization data from the latter. In place of this information a few reliability coefficients and correlations with other instruments have been added.

A paucity of statistical data is presented to support the authors' claim that the test is intended "to serve as a measure of general intellectual ability of persons who are relatively illiterate or who are non-English speaking." With the exception of two correlation coefficients, apparently all data are based upon the performance of white, male, adult prisoners at the U.S. Federal Penitentiary, Lewisburg, Pennsylvania.

The Lindner-Gurvitz standardization sample comprises 1,225 inmates of the Lewisburg penitentiary. Although the authors point out that these men were selected so that their education and socioeconomic status were in proportion to the 1940 census the fact is the sample is devoid of non-whites, females, and non-convicts. How closely does this sample represent the relatively illiterate or non-English speaking populations for whom the test is intended? Further, why was so *selected* a sample used? In lieu of an explanation, this reviewer assumes that such a captive group was used to effect a relatively easy task of standardization; but if this be the case, why should one run the risk of using unrepresentative norms merely for the convenience of the authors?

In an attempt to establish validity, two correlations are provided. One coefficient of .92 based upon 168 prisoners is reported between the *Revised Beta Examination* and the *Wechsler-Bellevue Intelligence Scale*. The second, a coefficient of .71 between the Beta and the *Otis Self-Administering Tests of Mental Ability*, utilized 198 prisoners. While the correlations are quite significant, especially the .92, additional studies involving a less restricted sample of subjects would add greatly to the notion that the test is a measure of general intelligence.

Reliability coefficients of .81 and .75 based, respectively, upon 199 and 104 prisoners are cited. They were obtained by correlating weighted scores on the three odd-numbered subtests with scores on the three even-numbered subtests. No rationale is provided for splitting the test in this fashion; nor is the reader told whether these coefficients embrace the split-half correction. The standard error of measurement was also determined for each of the two groups and found to be 4.8 and 4.3, respectively. The manual contains a third reliability coefficient of .90 which may be of dubious quality in that it was "estimated from intercorrelations of subtests." The authors provide no explanation for determining reliability in this fashion.

Intercorrelations among the six subtests ranging from .51 to .76 suggest that each subtest is far from measuring an independent factor. Correlations of subtests with the total weighted score range from .68 to .86.

Additional correlations reported by Bennett and Wesman in 1947 between the *Revised Beta Examination* and the *Hand-Tool Dexterity Test* (.36) and the *Tests of Mechanical Comprehension* (.56) are included in the manual, but owing to the content of the latter two instruments these correlations afford little if any support for validity of the *Revised Beta Examination* as a measure of intelligence. Likewise, little is added to the test's validity by including a few additional corelations ranging from .51 to .75 between Beta and the *PTI Oral Directions Test* and the verbal score on the *Wesman Personnel Classification Test*. Such correlations appear to do nothing more than pad the manual's dearth of statistical data.

It seems that ample time has passed during which a representative sample could have been secured for the purpose of building satisfactory norms; it is high time an item analysis of the test itself be conducted. Additional validity and reliability studies are equally in order. The statistical section of the present manual appears to contain nothing more than data helpful perhaps to those who would screen white, male adults at the U.S. Federal Penitentiary, Lewisburg, Pennsylvania; and at that, one must consider such data are more than 17 years old.

For reviews by Raleigh M. Drake and Walter C. Shipley, see 3:259; for reviews by S. D. Porteus and David Wechsler, see 40:1419.

[495]

***SRA Tests of Educational Ability, 1962 Edition.** Grades 4-6, 6-9, 9-12; 1957-63; tests identical with those published in 1957 and 1958 except for minor changes in format and directions; 4-5 scores: language, reasoning, quantitative, total, (grades 4-6 only) nonreading total; IBM; 1 form; 3 levels; revised profile ('62, 1 page); technical supplement, third edition ('63, c1957-63, 41 pages); separate answer sheets must be used; $7 per 20 tests; $7 per 100 IBM answer sheets; 50¢ per scoring stencil; $1 per technical supplement; 75¢ per specimen set of any one level; scoring service available; fee: 25¢ per student; test materials may also be rented with either IBM or DocuTran answer sheets and scored by the publisher; fee: 45¢ per student; postage extra; L. L. Thurstone and Thelma Gwinn Thurstone; Science Research Associates, Inc. *

a) GRADES 4-6. 1958-63; 1 form ('62, c1958, 14 pages); revised manual ('62, c1958-62, 33 pages); 26(52) minutes.

b) GRADES 6-9. 1958-63; 1 form ('62, c1958, 13 pages); revised manual ('62, c1958-62, 32 pages); 42(67) minutes.

c) GRADES 9-12. 1957-63; 1 form ('62, c1957, 11 pages); revised manual ('62, c1958-62, 26 pages); 27(45) minutes.

REFERENCES

1. NORTH, ROBERT D. "An Appraisal of the SRA Tests of General Ability Based on Independent School Results." *Ed Rec B* 78:68-76 F '61. *

J. STANLEY AHMANN, *Professor of Psychology and Head of the Department, Colorado State University, Fort Collins, Colorado.*

As in the case of the 1958 edition, the 1962 edition of the *SRA Tests of Educational Ability* (TEA) provides "three aptitude measures for use by the teacher and counselor in judging a student's potentiality for success in school." Language, reasoning, and quantitative scores are available, and are usually combined to obtain a total score which can then be converted to an IQ score or a percentile rank. The scores are available for all three levels of the TEA. In addition, the first level (for grades 4-6) provides a total nonreading score. This score is based entirely on test items containing a picture or a drawing as the item stem.

Accompanying the three levels of the TEA is a technical supplement. This is the third edition of such a supplement and contains highly useful information. In addition, the technical supplement is well written. Teachers and counselors should find it an easy task to obtain the information about validity, reliability, and norms which they wish to have from this supplement.

FORMAT. The format of the tests is extremely well designed. The printing is attractive. In all cases the directions to the test administrator for the process of administration, scoring, and interpretation of scores seem to be as complete as needed.

The most striking feature of the format is the manner in which color is used. Each of the three levels is given a distinctive color, namely, blue for the first level (grades 4-6), green for the second level (grades 6-9), and red for the third level (grades 9-12). The use of the assigned color is completely consistent throughout the manual of directions for the tests of that level, the test itself, the answer sheets, whether IBM or DocuTran, and the keys for hand scoring. In the case of the manual of directions, the edges of important pages which give specific directions for the administration of the test are marked with the appropriate color. In addition, throughout the manual key sentences and headings are printed in the color appropriate for the level. Certainly the consistent use of a single color for a single level should simplify the task of the teacher as he uses that level and should minimize the likelihood of confusing the various materials provided for each level. Multi-level test batteries of all kinds might well profit from the same careful use of color as applied by the publishers of TEA.

VALIDITY AND RELIABILITY. Considerable attention has been given the questions related to the degree of validity and reliability of the TEA. The emphasis of the presentation is changed somewhat since the 1958 edition included normative profiles in its technical supplement. The use of such profiles automatically raised considerations with regard to the intercorrelations between the language, reasoning, and quantitative scores. In addition, the reliability of these scores had to be interpreted in view of this proposed use of the scores. Reviewers of the 1958 edition often felt that the intercorrelations were somewhat high and the reliabilities of the three test scores somewhat low to justify such normative profiles. All mention of normative profiles has been eliminated from the 1962 technical supplement, thereby simplifying the presentation of validity and reliability data since the total score is recommended as the score which is generally most useful.

Correlations between the total score of the TEA and the total scores of other common tests of mental ability are found to be quite high. For example, these correlations with various levels of the Kuhlmann-Anderson range from .69 to .82. In the case of the *California Test of Mental Maturity,* the correlations range from .66 to .79. In the case of the publisher's *Tests of General Ability* they range between .51 and .78.

Predictive validity data were determined on the basis of samples of students from the western, midwestern, and northeastern sections of the United States. Correlation coefficients between the three subtest scores and the total score were found for high school grade-point averages and scores on the *SRA Achievement Series.* The length of time which elapsed between the administration of the TEA and the determination of the criterion value was relatively short. Evidently it did not exceed two months. The correlations are very high. They range from .57 to .72 for the lowest level, from .68 to .84 for the middle level, and from .68 to .80 for the highest level.

Only one study is mentioned in the technical supplement with regard to the use of multiple regression techniques to predict some meaningful criterion on the basis of a number of part scores from the TEA. Multiple correlation coefficients were computed between the three TEA subscores and grade-point averages and composite scores on three achievement batteries. The authors conclude that "a comparison of the multiple coefficients of correlation and the product-moment coefficients of correlation for the unweighted sum of the raw scores indicates that, in general, little would be gained by weighting the subtest scores in accordance with the regression coefficients."

The coefficients of reliability for the total score are quite acceptable. Typically these values exceeded .90. The standard error of measurement for the IQ scores derived from the total score did not exceed four IQ units in any of the determinations. The authors quite properly point out that "this precision compares favorably with that attained in individually administered tests of intelligence." The foregoing findings were derived from samples of students drawn from grades 6 through 12 only. In the case of grades 4 through 6, the reliability is slightly less.

THE STANDARDIZATION SAMPLE. The authors made a serious attempt to draw a suitable standardization sample. Although recognizing that norms for intelligence measures are characteristically age oriented rather than grade oriented, the authors decided to base their sample on those individuals still in public school at the time of the standardization testing. A nationwide sampling for standardization took place in April 1962, and was based on a directory of public secondary schools compiled by the United States Office of Education. Three preliminary sample lists of secondary schools were drawn. These schools were stratified on the basis of regional location and school size. Secondary schools in the initial sample were contacted first. If the school could not participate, its counterpart in the second sample was contacted. If the second secondary school could not participate, then its counterpart in the third sample was contacted. Elementary schools were identified by asking the cooperation of the feeder school closest to the participating secondary school. A total of 20,338 pupils in 64 schools representing 25 school systems participated in the standardization.

For the purpose of drawing the sample, the United States was divided into eight regions. Due to the fact that some secondary schools were unable to cooperate, some regions were under-represented, and others therefore are over-represented. The two regions under-represented to the greatest degree were the mideast (Delaware, District of Columbia, Maryland, New Jersey, New York, and Pennsylvania) and the southwest (Arizona, New Mexico, Oklahoma, and Texas). The three areas over-represented to the greatest degree are the plains (Iowa, Kansas, Minnesota, Missouri, Nebraska, South Dakota, and North Dakota), the Rocky Mountains (Colorado, Idaho, Montana, Utah, and Wyoming), and New England (Connecticut, Maine, Massachusetts, New Hampshire, Rhode Island, and Vermont).

It is not surprising that the standardization sample reveals considerable age variation within each grade level. Also, there is a sharp drop in the number of students tested in the eleventh grade as compared with the tenth grade. The fact that, in most states, school attendance is no longer mandatory in the eleventh grade and thereafter is no doubt the reason for this phenomenon.

Table 12 of the technical supplement shows a careful comparison of the proportions of pupils in the standardization sample within three months of a given birthday for the TEA and within one month of a given birthday for the Stanford-Binet (1937) as distributed by grade. Except for grades 11 and 12 the proportion of older students in each grade is almost identical for both samples. The 1937 Binet sample had a higher proportion of younger children within each grade.

Since it is impossible to obtain an unbiased age sampling through the use of school systems, the authors took steps to adjust for the bias in determining the IQ norms. Based on the reports of four earlier investigations, estimates were made of the expected mean IQ for each of grades 4–12.

SUMMARY. The *SRA Tests of Educational Ability* are carefully designed and described tests of educational ability. The administration of the tests is not difficult, and the time required is relatively short. Considerably more data are available about the reliability, validity, and norms of these tests than was true in the case of the 1958 edition, and one can safely assume that additional data in large quantity will be made available in the future.

Although the normative profiles of TEA are not useful, there is much to recommend these tests provided the need of the individual selecting the tests is for a single score representing scholastic aptitude. This score is then to be used primarily in a predictive validity sense. In other words, anticipations are to be made of future academic success. The tests have a high educational loading and hence correlate very highly with common criterion measures such as grade-point averages and achievement test scores. In summary, these tests should be of value to public school teachers and guidance counselors within the framework of formal education.

JOHN E. HORROCKS, *Professor of Psychology, The Ohio State University, Columbus, Ohio.*

The 1962 standardization of the TEA is based on an April testing of 20,338 students enrolled in 64 schools representing 25 school systems scattered broadly over the United States. Representativeness of the normative sample was achieved by a stratified (regional location and school size) random drawing of schools from the United States Office of Education *Directory of Public Secondary Schools, 1958–59*. The random sample was supplemented by elementary and junior high schools feeding into the selected schools. Standardization subjects for each of the grades 4 through 12 contained in the total normative sample ranged from a low of 1,661 for grade 12 to a high of 3,282 for grade 9. Eight regions of the United States were represented, although unavailability of selected schools in some regions has loaded the sample with some regional inequalities. Regional weighting was not attempted to compensate for such bias since it was felt that weighting would only serve to magnify rather than to reduce the bias. It would appear, however, that the regional bias is not serious and that the TEA 1962 norms, as compared to those of other similar measures, are both reasonably representative and numerically adequate. Obviously no normative sample is perfect and a question could be raised as to the comprehensiveness of norms representing 25 school districts and 20,388 cases even when the selection was made on a stratified random basis. Latest data on the TEA are provided by the third edition of a technical supplement carrying the date 1963. Each of the three levels of the TEA is provided with a well written manual giving explicit administration and scoring directions.

The purpose of the TEA is cited as that of providing measures of "aptitude for schoolwork," which places it directly in the tradition of those tests which approach intelligence through an analysis of an individual's ability to learn as evidenced by his acquisition of the skills and knowledges learned in school. While the TEA is defined by its authors as an academic aptitude test, the possibility of converting the total scores into an IQ makes it necessary to evaluate it as a general line measure of intelligence. The concept of IQ dies hard, but it would appear that elimination of the possibility of deriving IQ ratios would have emphasized the status of the TEA as an academic aptitude measure and would have avoided the possible abuses of interpretation so often accorded the IQ in the public schools and in parents' aspirations. The three subscores, language, reasoning, and quantitative, fall short of the more diagnostically useful factors of the earlier Thurstone tests, but do represent an expansion of the L and Q scores of the old ACE. Actually, TEA, which is an outgrowth of the *SRA Primary Mental Abilities,* really represents nothing new in intelligence testing. Its items taken out of context are typical of the kinds of items perennially appearing on measures of intelligence since the days of the Army Alpha and Beta and the earlier work of the Thurstones. Perhaps the TEA can be thought of as striking a middle ground between a multi-factor or differential analysis and the single score global approach of some of the earlier measures of intelligence following World War I. It is unfortunate that there have been so few innovations in intelligence testing since 1917. Newer tests such as the TEA can only justify their presence and selection over similar existing measures if they offer something new and better—something that the TEA has really failed to do. It is a good test as such tests go and has been well worked up, but it is a fair question to ask why it appeared in the first place. The 1963 manual points to the possibly "unique contribution" of its part scores "when multiple-regression techniques are applied in order to predict some meaningful criterion," but cites only one preliminary study in support of such application.

Validity of the TEA is cited in terms of grade-point average and scores on the *SRA Achievement Series.* Grade-point average correlations with TEA total scores range from .69 to .73 depending on the level, with language scores showing a higher relationship (.67 to .69) than do either reasoning or quantitative scores (.45 to .66). SRA achievement composite scores correlate .72 with TEA 4–6 total scores, .84 with TEA 6–9 total scores and .80 with TEA 9–12 total scores. The part score intercorrelations do not exceed .66 at any level, but do not go lower than .36 in any case. TEA correlations with other intelligence tests range from .51 to .82 for the TEA total score, .59 to .75 for the L score, .42 to .67 for the R score, and .24 to .81 for the Q score.

In general, while TEA represents nothing new in intelligence testing it is a good example of its type and should prove as satisfactory as any other available group measure of general intelligence. More validity information would be helpful, and the technical manual could present its validity, reliability, and background information in a somewhat more coherent style, particularly aimed at teachers who will be the primary consumers of the test.

J Counsel Psychol 6:249 f '59. Laurence Siegel. * Each battery includes only those tests which correlate substantially with school success. Thus TEA is not particularly suitable when the aim of testing is to secure an estimate of ability apart from the influence of formal educational experiences. The series emphasizes power rather than speed, and the difficulty gradient is rather steep. It follows then, that although TEA will identify pupils of unusually low ability, it will not discriminate as well between such pupils as it will at the middle and upper ability levels. Finally, the series does not strive for score stability over a period of time in the sense that IQ measures strive for stability. The referrent in establishing TEA norms was grade level rather than age level. Consequently, this battery is not suitable as a measure of "brightness" relative to the population at large of a given age. The foregoing statements are neither criticism nor deficiencies of TEA. *

For reviews by Joshua A. Fishman, William B. Michael, and E. A. Peel of the 1957–58 edition of c, *see 5:377.*

[496]

★[SRA] Tests of General Ability. Grades kgn–2, 2–4, 4–6, 6–9, 9–12; 1959–60, c1957–60; 3 scores: information, noncultural reasoning, total; IBM for grades 4–12; Form A ('59, except for tests for grades 4–12 which are copyrighted 1957); 5 levels; $1 per technical report ('60, 39 pages); $2.50 per complete specimen set; postage extra; tests for grades 4–12 may be rented; fee (45¢ per student) includes scoring service; Spanish edition available; (35–45) minutes; John C. Flanagan; Science Research Associates, Inc. *

a) GRADES KGN–2. 12 pages; manual ('59, 19 pages); $3.20 per 20 tests; 50¢ per specimen set.

b) GRADES 2–4. Details same as for grades kgn–2.

c) GRADES 4–6. 15 pages; manual ('59, 21 pages); separate answer sheets must be used; $4.25 per 20 tests; $5 per 100 IBM scorable answer sheets; 50¢ per scoring stencil; 75¢ per specimen set.

d) GRADES 6–9. Details same as for grades 4–6 except: manual ('59, 25 pages).

e) GRADES 9–12. Details same as for grades 4–6 except: manual ('59, 19 pages).

JOHN E. HORROCKS, *Professor of Psychology, The Ohio State University, Columbus, Ohio.*

Equating general ability, general intelligence, and "basic ability to learn" as the same thing, the TOGA series provides a scale of equal units for five consecutive grade levels. That intelligence and ability to learn, if not exactly interchangeable concepts, are at least so closely related that an individual's ability to learn offers a good approach to the measurement of his intelligence is nothing new to ability testing. Numerous measures of intelligence have been described by their authors as well as by others as measures of learning ability—their difference consists in the kinds of learning experiences stressed and the kinds of items selected as most likely to offer adequate measures of that learning. TOGA represents a relatively new departure by attempting to eliminate, or at least place less stress upon, school learned skills such as reading, writing, and arithmetic. For that reason TOGA should offer a fairer testing context for those who, for one reason or another, have had limited or atypical opportunities to learn.

All TOGA test items at all levels are multiple choice and are pictorial in form. Two classes of items are represented: those which require reasoning on the part of the examinee and those which require information, vocabulary, and concepts. Information required, particularly at the younger levels, is of the kind ordinarily gained outside of the classroom, and stress is placed upon application rather than upon knowledge accumulation. Eight kinds of information items are included: (*a*) recognition of a pictured object when it is named, (*b*) recognition of an object from its classification, (*c*) recognition of an object on the basis of its similarity to another object, (*d*) recognition of an object's symbolic status, (*e*) selection of a picture as representative of an abstract concept, (*f*) selection of an object which involves a concept determining its use, (*g*) selection of an object as representative of the application of a principle, and (*h*) selection of an object depicting an element basic to an idea or a social institution. Content settings for information items include home, community, nature and recreation, science, and social science. Reasoning items present five line drawings, four of which are constructed on the basis of a specific rule, the fifth being different in that the rule does not apply. Speed has been eliminated in determining information performance and has been minimized for the reasoning section as a *way*, according to the author, of providing "'purer' measures of information depth and reasoning power." The question here is the advisability of de-emphasizing speed as an aspect of intellectual functioning. In life, behavior takes place under time conditions and an individual's effectiveness is often judged in terms of his "alertness" or ability to respond quickly. Insofar as speed is actually an aspect of real life effective functioning it would appear to beg the issue to eliminate it under the excuse of "power" in a measure designed to assess an individual's capacity to function in the cognitive domain.

Preliminary tryouts of TOGA items took place in 22 public and parochial schools in the Pittsburgh area and items included at the various levels in the final forms had to meet three criteria: (*a*) internal consistency as demonstrated by a correlation of "about" .40 or better with other items of the same type at all levels, (*b*) item difficulty figures which showed a trend of increase with respondents' age, and (*c*) a difficulty range between 30 and 70 per cent for the middle grade of the level at which the item was placed. Norms are based on 8,041 students enrolled in 40 schools in 20 school systems located in 12 different states. With the exception of Texas (Austin and Bryan) southern and southwestern states are not included in the normative sample, nor are the states in New England and the northwest. A more complete normative picture is needed if TOGA is to find defensible use as a nationally applicable test, although its normative background is already superior to some measures of intelligence which have been on the market considerably longer.

Since TOGA is a relatively new test (1957) potential users will have to depend upon reliability and validity information supplied by the very adequate technical report provided for users of the test. The report cites 20 reliability studies of TOGA total scores, with coefficients ranging for the various levels from .77 to .90. Correlations cited (19 studies) between TOGA total scores and those of other intelligence tests vary with the level being tested but range from a low of .41 (TOGA 6–9 level and Kuhlmann-Anderson) to a high of .80 (TOGA 6–9 and Kuhlmann-Anderson). Correlations with various measures of achievement tend to cluster between .50 and .60 and range from .38 to .81. Correlations between TOGA part scores (10 studies) ranged from .25 to .67, and part score split-half reliabilities (20 studies) ranged from .69 to .83. Part score correlations with other intelligence and achievement measures present about the same picture as that provided by the total score. In general TOGA Part 1 (information) scores appear to relate most closely to Thurstone's verbal comprehension factor, and Part 2 (reasoning) scores to his reasoning factor.

TOGA is a promising, carefully constructed general measure of verbal intelligence whose author has provided excellent quantitative background information for prospective users. Further and more representative normative data are needed as well as independent data on reliability and validity. The attempt to eliminate school centered information in writing test items is a particularly strong feature, but this reviewer would question the de-emphasis of the speed factor in a general line intelligence test. Such de-emphasis, insofar as it is tenable at all, would appear more appropriate in a school learning centered academic aptitude measure.

RICHARD E. SCHUTZ, *Professor of Education, and Director, Testing Service, Arizona State University, Tempe, Arizona.*

This test is graphic proof that the technology involved in the production of general ability tests has achieved an unprecedented level of sophistication. Major test publishers have facilities at their disposal to produce a complete intelligence test series with minimal effort and expense. These technical procedures can be counted on to produce a new test that will do almost, if not everything, that currently available tests do and will have gimmick appeal for a specified audience. Find a name that has acrostic characteristics with positive evaluative connotations, produce it in an artistic package, and you have an attractive seller. Although these reproductive efforts increase the population of test instruments, the desirability of such a population explosion is questionable.

The *Tests of General Ability* (TOGA) were "designed to provide measures of basic learning ability (general intelligence) without the use of test materials that are explicitly dependent upon school-learned skills such as reading, writing, and arithmetic." This is an accurate descriptive statement. Each form of the five levels of the tests contains two parts. Part 1 is composed of information items. Each item presents five pictured choices. The examinee is required to mark the drawing that best meets the specifications read orally by the examiner. The items sample a wide range of content. They are intended to test "the individual's ability to grasp meanings, recognize relationships, and understand the basic concepts and underlying principles of our natural and social environment." The K–2 and 2–4 levels include 35 items. The upper levels include 45 items.

Part 2 is composed of figure relationship items designed to test the examinee's abstract reasoning skill. Each item presents five line drawings of geometric forms. "Four of the drawings are constructed on the basis of a specific rule. The remaining figure is different; the rule does not apply." The examinee is required to select the figure representing the exception to the rule. The K–2 and 2–4 levels include 28 items; the upper levels, 40 items. The test as a whole requires 35 to 45 minutes.

The claim is made that Part 2 of the test is culture fair: "Part 2 avoids any cultural content * This part of the test presents an equal challenge to all children regardless of their cultural backgrounds." Herein lies the special appeal of the tests. "These tests are designed to provide a relatively fair measure of intelligence for all individuals, even those who have had atypical opportunities to learn."

No data are presented to support this culture fair validity claim. Rather, the validity of the tests is defended on a definition basis: "The validity of the TOGA series rests primarily on its definition of intelligence as basically involving information (including verbal concepts) and reasoning abilities, and its emphasis on test materials that do not require school-learned skills."

It would have been a straightforward task to check the claim that "the following types of students possessing *good general intelligence,* but *poor educational achievement* can be expected to obtain high scores on one or both parts of the *Tests of General Ability*" (italics in original). These groups include "children who may not have had the usual amount of schooling....who come from home environments where there are bilingual or other language problems....who attend schools in which the quality of instruction is clearly deficient....who come from homes where learning opportunities are limited because of parental neglect, parental illness, or other factors." By administering TOGA and some other commonly used test of general intelligence, it could easily have been determined whether any or all of the groups specified actually receive higher scores on TOGA. No such data are presented, however. A suggestive set of descriptive statistics are hidden away in a table of TOGA normative equivalence to other IQ tests. The mean IQ's for "a low-income area public school in New York City" at grade 6 are 80.5 on TOGA and 84.2 on the Otis Beta.

The accessory materials make no reference whatsoever to predictive validity. But the concurrent validity coefficients and other external correlations that are presented in the technical report suggest that TOGA scores function in much the same way as other general intelligence test scores. For example, the correlations of the TOGA total score with 19 other intelligence test scores range from .41 to .80 with a median of .62. The correlations of the TOGA total score with various achievement test scores are of the same order, ranging from .39 to .81 with a median of .58. The correlations with teacher grade averages range from .38 to .65 with a median of .49. These correlations are all in line with what one would anticipate for a conventional group intelligence test.

Neither does the pattern of part score correlations support the overall TOGA rationale. The median correlation of each of the parts with 10 other intelligence test scores is .59 for Part 1 and .55 for Part 2. The correlations with achievement test scores are of the same magnitude, with Part 1 correlating consistently higher than Part 2. The widest discrepancy in the part score correlations is found with the *SRA Reading Record,* where Part 1 has a median correlation of .70 versus .50 for Part 2.

Among the lowest correlations presented for the part scores are those between the part scores themselves at various grade levels. The coefficients range from .25 to .67, with a median of .43. These coefficients indicate that the two parts of the test sample nonoverlapping response classes. In fact, the low magnitude of the correlations calls to question the rationale for deriving a single IQ based on the total number of correct responses to the test as a whole.

By and large, the raw score standard deviations of Part 1 are higher than those of Part 2, indicating that the information items in Part 1 contribute more heavily to the IQ than the figural reasoning items in Part 2. This is particularly true for the high school level of the tests where the standard deviations run 7.5 versus 4.9 at grade 9 and 8.0 versus 5.5 at grade 12.

The steps in the production of TOGA are clearly outlined in the technical report. A blueprint is presented for each part of the test classifying the items in Part 1 by function and content area and those in Part 2 by function. Only summaries are shown for each level, however, so that it is impossible to cross check the classification item by item. On the three independent classifications I made, there were a number of discrepancies between my totals and those shown in the report. Lacking more detailed information from the TOGA report, it is impossible to clarify the reasons for the discrepancies.

A similar superficiality is evident with respect to the description of the item analysis procedures. While the statistical procedures involved in making the analysis are described in good detail, no information is given concerning the size or the characteristics of the examinees involved in the analysis other than that they were "at all levels from kindergarten through the twelfth grade." It is difficult to evaluate the adequacy of the item analysis without further information concerning the representativeness of the population and sample involved.

The IQ norms for the tests were derived by first equating TOGA raw scores to grade equivalents on the *SRA Achievement Series* in grades 1–9 and to the *Iowa Tests of Educational Development* in grades 9–12 using equipercentile procedures. The grade equivalents were then converted to mental age equivalents by adding a constant of 5.2, the average age at entrance to kindergarten. "At the higher levels, extrapolated equivalent mental ages were obtained in accordance with the usual practice." (I assume that this is a euphemistic way of saying someone arbitrarily extended the penciled curve with a deft twist of the wrist.) Ratio IQ's were then computed and are presented in the manual for each level along with the grade equivalents.

The manuals create the erroneous impression that the IQ's and grade expectancies are two independent scores: "The tests provide two scores for each child: an IQ and a grade expectancy score. The grade expectancy score shows the school level of the child's ability." Actually the grade expectancy scores represent nothing more than the IQ numerators. Moreover, the examples given in the manual in connection with the instructions for reading the norms table contain highly misleading statements. For example, a fourth grade pupil, "Linda" is shown to have an IQ of 114 and a "grade expectancy" of 5.2. The manual states: "Although Linda is in the fourth grade the test also shows that she is capable of doing school work as advanced as the first half of the fifth grade." "Joe" is in the sixth grade and has an IQ of 133 with a "grade expectancy" of 9.8. "The *Tests of General Ability* show that Joe has a very superior IQ. Although Joe is in the sixth grade, the test also shows that he is capable of doing school work as advanced as the last half of the ninth grade." An unsophisticated user could do serious damage to a child if he attempted to generalize this interpretation to his own situation.

The entire standardization of the tests involved a very modest total of 8,041 students from 40 schools in 20 school systems. Each of the schools completed a descriptive questionnaire, but no data concerning their responses are presented beyond the statement that "the procedure was found to be effective in providing a group of schools and school systems which yielded a reasonably representative sample of the nation's students." How the completion of a questionnaire could accomplish this highly desirable objective is not specified. No information is given concerning the number of grades or students tested in each school nor the criteria for their selection. Norms interlock studies were conducted in two individual schools. A norms continuity study was conducted in a single school. The equating of adjacent levels was based on samples ranging from 475 to 594 students.

Despite these small and inadequately described samples, TOGA norms appear to be fairly comparable to those of other IQ tests with respect to mean scores. TOGA IQ standard deviations, however, run consistently higher than those of other tests. This greater variability is an important consideration, particularly in testing at the extremes of the IQ scale.

Split-half and Kuder-Richardson 21 reliability coefficients are presented for the total and part scores. Total score split-half reliability ranges from .80 to .90 with a median of .87. K-R reliabilities run .01 to .05 points lower with a median coefficient of .83. The part score reliabilities hold up reasonably well, with median split-half coefficients of .84 for Part 1 and .80 for Part 2 and K-R 21 coefficients of .80 and .77. While not spectacularly high in comparison with other tests, the coefficients are at least minimally respectable.

Turning to practical considerations, the tests are attractively printed. Although some of the pictured objects are rather small, the detail is not emphasized and should be well within the range of the normally sighted child. The directions for administering the tests are clear. However, a good deal is left to the examiner's discretion, particularly in Part 1. "In general, specific instructions are to be read only once, but the examiner must use judgment in following such a rule. It is permissible to repeat instructions if it appears that the pupils have not understood them." Standardizing the timing of the items in Part 1 constitutes a problem. The routine is: read the item, pause 2 seconds, repeat the item, pause 5 seconds. The examiner is instructed to do the timing by counting "slowly to yourself." Even in Part 2, where there is a 15-minute time limit, the instructions to the examiner leave room for variability in interpretation: "Remind the pupils once or twice during the test to work as quickly as they can * It is essential that they do not stop concentrating on the test or become restless." Thus, the examiner load in monitoring the tests is reasonably heavy compared to other group intelligence tests. With the wide availability of tape recorders in the modern school, the publishers might give thought to tape recording the directions. This would not only relieve the teacher of a burdensome chore but would standardize the test conditions.

Separate IBM 805 machine or hand scoring answer sheets are used for the upper levels beginning at 4–6. For K–2 and 2–4 the keyed responses are printed in the manual with the suggestion that "the teacher make a key in a test booklet to help in scoring the tests more quickly." This is not very adequate service. Strip keys could easily be provided which would reduce the probability of error both in the preparation of the keys and their use in scoring and would also save the teacher's time.

Altogether, TOGA appears to be new wine in old bottles. Although the application of modern psychometric brewing processes has yielded a series which has most of the same characteristics as its related ancestors, one should not expect the results of the test to be any more beneficially intoxicating than those of predecessor group intelligence tests.

J Counsel Psychol 8:91–2 sp '61. Laurence Siegel. * Flanagan's TOGA is particularly well-tailored (oops!) to intellectual assessment when opportunities for formal schooling have been deficient. Beyond this, brevity, technical quality, and soundness of rationale appear to commend it for wide use as an all-purpose measure of general intelligence. The utility of TOGA will be further enhanced when two of its current deficiencies are rectified. First, the absence of reported predictive validities, and of any mention of the necessity for such studies, is disappointing in an instrument of otherwise good quality. Second, since alternate forms of the series are not yet available, group administration in cramped quarters and readministration for the purpose of score verification in suspect cases is impeded.

[497]

★Safran Culture Reduced Intelligence Test. Grades 1–6; 1960–62; 1 form ('60, 42 pages); mimeographed manual ('62, 9 pages); mimeographed instructions for group administration ['61, 6 pages]; mimeographed instructions for individual administration ['61, 1 page]; mimeographed tentative norms ['62, 1 page]; separate answer sheets must be used; 43¢ per test; $1.50 per 100 mimeographed answer sheets; postage extra; (30–45) minutes; C. Safran; the Author. *

REFERENCES

1. SAFRAN, C. "An Introduction to the Safran Culture Reduced Intelligence Test and Some Reports on Its Validity From Current Studies." *Alberta J Ed Res* 9:36–44 Mr '63. * (*PA* 37:8274)

[498]

***Schrammel General Ability Test.** Grades 9–17; 1953–59; based in part upon *Army Group Examination Alpha* and revisions; IBM; Forms A ('53), B ('55), C ('56), D ('57), (6 pages); manual ('59, 9 pages); $1.50 per 25 tests; separate answer sheets may be used; 85¢ per 25 IBM answer sheets; 30¢ per set of either hand or machine scoring stencils; postage extra; 35¢ per specimen set, postpaid; 50(60) minutes; H. E. Schrammel; Bureau of Educational Measurements. *

For a review by Henry E. Garrett, see 5:381.

[499]

★Secondary Verbal Tests. Ages 11-0 to 13-6, 13-0 to 15-6; 1960–62; 2 levels; 8*s.* per 12 tests; 9*d.* per single copy; 1*s.* per manual for *a;* prices include purchase tax; postage extra; Valerie Land and Olive Wood (*a*); published for the National Foundation for Educational Research in England and Wales; Newnes Educational Publishing Co. Ltd. *

a) SECONDARY VERBAL TEST 1. Ages 11-0 to 13-6; 1960; 1 form ['60, 8 pages]; manual ['60, 7 pages]; 40(45) minutes.

b) SECONDARY VERBAL TEST 2. Ages 13-0 to 15-6; 1962; 1 form ['62, 8 pages]; no manual; no data on reliability and validity; no norms; 45(50) minutes.

STANLEY NISBET, *Professor of Education, University of Glasgow, Glasgow, Scotland.* [Review of Test 1.]

This is a well composed, clearly printed group intelligence test, designed for use in the first two years of secondary schools in England. The manual claims that the test measures "general scholastic ability" for purposes of classification, but, rather strangely perhaps, insists that it "should not be regarded as providing in any way a measure of capacity for learning." The items seem to be sound, although it is surprising, especially in a test with this title, to find so many which involve juggling with the positions of letters and figures and so few which involve the understanding of straightforward sentences or passages. As for minor flaws or ambiguities, the reviewer thinks items 1, 4, 35, 53, 54, and 76 might possibly be improved.

Although no limitation of use to the upper ranges of ability (e.g., to use in English grammar schools) is suggested in the manual, the table of norms shows clearly that the test discriminates much better at the upper end. The median child in the 11-0 age group scores only 12 points out of 90, and even at the top end of the table the median child in the 13-6 age group scores less than half the total. For use within the prescribed ages, therefore, one would hesitate to recommend the test to English secondary modern or comprehensive schools if good differentiation in the lower reaches was desired.

In short, this is a useful and soundly constructed test, easy to administer and well standardized, but it differentiates better among the abler children than it does among the less able.

[500]

Ship Destination Test. Grades 9 and over; 1955–56; general reasoning; IBM; Form A ('55, 3 pages); manual ('56, 3 pages); separate answer sheets must be used; $2.50 per 25 tests; 15¢ per single copy; 5¢ per IBM answer sheet; $1 per scoring stencil; 35¢ per manual; postage extra; 15(20) minutes; Paul R. Christensen and J. P. Guilford; Sheridan Supply Co. *

REFERENCES

1. BERGER, R. M.; GUILFORD, J. P.; AND CHRISTENSEN, P. R. "A Factor-Analytic Study of Planning Abilities." *Psychol Monogr* 71(6):1–31 '57. * (*PA* 33:6967)
2. HILLS, JOHN R. "Factor-Analyzed Abilities and Success in College Mathematics." *Ed & Psychol Meas* 17:615–22 w '57. * (*PA* 33:4696)
3. HANEY, RUSSELL; MICHAEL, WILLIAM B.; AND JONES, ROBERT A. "Identification of Aptitude and Achievement Factors in the Prediction of the Success of Nursing Trainees." *Ed & Psychol Meas* 19:645–7 w '59. * (*PA* 34:6164)

4. KETTNER, NORMAN W.; GUILFORD, J. P.; AND CHRISTENSEN, PAUL R. "A Factor Analytic Study Across the Domains of Reasoning, Creativity, and Evaluation." *Psychol Monogr* 73(9):1–31 '59. * (*PA* 34:7333)
5. MICHAEL, WILLIAM B.; JONES, ROBERT A.; AND HANEY, RUSSELL. "The Development and Validation of a Test Battery for Selection of Student Nurses." *Ed & Psychol Meas* 19:641–3 w '59. * (*PA* 34:6171)
6. MARKS, ALVIN; MICHAEL, WILLIAM B.; AND KAISER, HENRY F. "Dimensions of Creativity and Temperament in Officer Evaluation." *Psychol Rep* 9:635–8 D '61. *
7. MARKS, ALVIN; MICHAEL, WILLIAM B.; AND KAISER, HENRY F. "Sources of Noncognitive Variance in 21 Measures of Creativity." *Psychol Rep* 9:287–90 O '61. *
8. MERRIFIELD, P. R.; GUILFORD, J. P.; CHRISTENSEN, P. R.; AND FRICK, J. W. "The Role of Intellectual Factors in Problem Solving." *Psychol Monogr* 76(10):1–21 '62. *

WILLIAM B. SCHRADER, *Director of Statistical Analysis, Educational Testing Service, Princeton, New Jersey.*

This interesting test requires the subject to perform a series of easy additions and subtractions for each item. The numbers to be added or subtracted are determined by a set of rules. The specific rules governing the work are different for each set of 3 items, and the complexity of the rules increases with each successive set of 12 items. The task is described to the subject in terms of conditions affecting the progress of a ship from one point to another. No doubt the formulation of the task in those more concrete terms makes the instructions easier to understand and keep in mind. Essentially, however, the problems seem to be artificial and formal.

A series of factor studies conducted in Guilford's laboratory have shown consistently that this test is a good measure of the factor designated as general reasoning and that it is a relatively pure measure of that factor. Thus, it should be useful in further factor research as a reference or "marker" test. Probably of more general interest is the fact that arithmetical reasoning, which is widely used in tests of intelligence and scholastic aptitude, has relatively high loadings on general reasoning and on numerical facility (*1*). This finding raises the interesting question of the relative importance of numerical facility and of general reasoning in making the arithmetical reasoning test effective in prediction. The test manual reports some fairly substantial correlation coefficients for the *Ship Destination Test* with course grades at the Coast Guard Academy and with performance rankings of 20 operations analysts, but notes that another study yielded essentially zero validities for an earlier form of the test with mathematics grades. Further validation work should be decidedly useful, particularly if both the *Ship Destination Test* and a measure of arithmetical reasoning were studied for the same groups.

As a practical instrument, the test has certain limitations which should be pointed out. First, only a single form is available. Second, since the test is somewhat speeded, the lack of a parallel form results in reliability estimates that are not entirely rigorous, as the authors point out. They used Tucker's modification of Kuder-Richardson formula 21, but do not indicate what account was taken of the fact that the test is formula scored in computing the various reliability coefficients reported. Third, no item analysis was done, on the grounds that the content of the items is homogeneous and that the relative difficulty of the items is apparent. Although these considerations are relevant, certain possible weaknesses of the test might have been avoided if an item analysis had been made. Thus, inspection of the norms table for men and women students enrolled in San Diego State College suggests that the test is somewhat too easy for the men, but about right for the women. (The norms tables must be interpreted in the light of the fact that the score is defined as rights plus one fifth omits. However, only about one fourth of the men and about one half of the women are below a score of 30, which is halfway between a chance score and a perfect score.) It is possible that the jump in difficulty from the third to the fourth set of 12 items is greater than it should be. Item analysis might also have shown that some of the more difficult items are ambiguous. Fourth, if this test were to be used widely in selection programs, the possible effect of special practice, using similar materials, on test performance should be investigated.

This test is imaginatively conceived, excellently printed, and psychologically meaningful. The brief, four-page manual provides a substantial amount of relevant data to aid in test use. For research purposes, it should be a very valuable instrument. For purposes of counseling or selection, however, its limitations, particularly with regard to empirical validation, definitely restrict its present usefulness.

For a review by C. J. Adcock, see 5:383.

[501]

The Simplex GNV Intelligence Tests. Ages 11–13.0; 1952–57; titles on tests are, for example for form 1, *The Simplex Intelligence Test GNV 1;* forms 1 ('52), 2 ('54), 3 ('54), 4 ('55), 5 ('56), 6 ('57),

(8 pages); manual for each form (dates as for tests, 7 pages); no data on reliability and validity; 10*s.* 6*d.* per 25 tests; 6*d.* per single copy; 1*s.* per manual; postage and purchase tax extra; 60(70) minutes; C. A. Richardson; George G. Harrap & Co. Ltd. *

REFERENCES

1. SHUTTLEWORTH, CLIFFORD W. "Tests of Technical Aptitude." *Occupational Psychol* 16:175–82 O '42. *
2. NISBET, JOHN D. "Contributions to Intelligence Testing and the Theory of Intelligence: IV, Intelligence and Age: Retesting With Twenty-Four Years' Interval." *Brit J Ed Psychol* 27:190–8 N '57. *

PHILIP M. LEVY, *Lecturer in Psychology, Institute of Education, University of Birmingham, Birmingham, England.*

Aimed primarily at the English "eleven-plus" testing market, these tests neither display nor indeed claim any originality. They appear to be competent productions in the usual "eleven-plus" mould. The items, numbering between 75 and 89 in each test, display the usual range of functions and include verbal analogies, number series, classification tasks, coding, opposites and similarities, syllogisms, and verbal and numerical reasoning tasks. The tests are easy to administer: the children read through the instructions for each item type for themselves.

The manuals tell the user only how to administer and score the tests. No other information is given. Indeed, this is clearly the author's intention, for he titles the manuals "Directions for Setting and Scoring." While no reliability or validity data are available, the publishers report (private communication) that the tests were standardised on "two or three thousand children from urban and rural areas in Great Britain." It appears that the potential user must accept the face validity of the tests or assume that data available from earlier Simplex tests are transferable.

The scoring keys, a list of right answers given in small print within the manuals, must be inconvenient to use and the scorer will be driven to devise his own. The two tables giving conversions to standard scores (mean 100, standard deviation 15) and mental ages provide values only for steps of 5 raw score units. Contrary to the author's statement in the manual, interpolation is not easy: 5 raw score units variously correspond to between 2 and 7 standard points and between 5 and 14 months of mental age. The routine user is again inconvenienced unnecessarily.

The author does not suggest why it might be "sometimes desired to obtain IQ's from mental ages" when he quotes the unnecessary, and surely discredited, age ratio formula. His warning that "Such IQ's will differ from the standard IQ's owing to differences in standard deviation" is only part of the story for there are also likely to be differences in the means. Those who make this outdated calculation may also be puzzled by the small discrepancies between the two tables: the chronological age at which a raw score has the standard score equivalent of 100 sometimes differs by a month or two from the mental age equivalent of the same raw score. No doubt there is a good answer to this admittedly minor point, but why encourage this practice at all?

In summary, these tests are easy to administer and have high face validity; but they are totally unsupported by their manuals, which even fail to give convenient scoring keys and conversion tables. It is doubtful whether these six tests can offer the same overall service as the 70 or so produced by the Moray House organisation or the growing numbers produced by the National Foundation for Educational Research.

[502]

***Sleight Non-Verbal Intelligence Test.** Ages 8–9, 6–10; 1931–63; 2 levels; no data on reliability and validity; tentative norms; postage and purchase tax extra; George F. Sleight and Preston Education Committee (revision of *a*); George G. Harrap & Co. Ltd. *

a) SLEIGHT NON-VERBAL INTELLIGENCE TEST: PRESTON REVISION. Ages 8–9; 1 form ('63, 16 pages); mimeographed manual ['63, 13 pages]; distribution restricted to directors of education; 25*s.* per 25 tests; 1*s.* 3*d.* per single copy; 7*s.* 6*d.* per manual; 27(75) minutes.

b) SLEIGHT NON-VERBAL INTELLIGENCE TEST. Ages 6–10; 1 form ['31, 20 pages]; manual ('31, 31 pages); 17*s.* 6*d.* per 25 tests; 9*d.* per single copy; 1*s.* per manual; 20(75) minutes.

REFERENCES

1. LYTTON, H. "Symposium: Contributions to the Diagnosis and Remedial Treatment of Reading Difficulties: 6, An Experiment in Selection for Remedial Education." *Brit J Ed Psychol* 31:79–95 F '61. * (*PA* 36:1KE79L)

For reviews by John C. Daniels and M. L. Kellmer Pringle of b, *see 5:387.*

[503]

★**Survey of Mental Maturity: California Survey Series.** Grades 7–9, 10–12 and adults; 1959; all items from *California Test of Mental Maturity, 1957 Edition;* 3 scores: language, nonlanguage, total; IBM; Forms 1, 2, (11 pages); 2 levels: junior high, advanced; manual (20 pages) for each level; $2.80 per 35 tests; separate answer sheets may be used; 5¢ per IBM answer sheet; 20¢ per scoring stencil; 10¢ per series class record sheet; 2¢ per series individual record sheet; postage extra; 50¢ per specimen set of either level, postpaid; 30(35) minutes; Willis W. Clark, Elizabeth T. Sullivan, and Ernest W. Tiegs; California Test Bureau. *

Naomi Stewart, *Formerly Staff Associate, Educational Testing Service, Princeton, New Jersey.*

The *Survey of Mental Maturity,* the newest instrument in the *California Test of Mental Maturity* series, is intended for use by teachers and counselors "as a screening device to obtain mental ages and intelligence quotients." The Survey yields language and nonlanguage scores. The nonlanguage section consists of spatial relationship items, pictorial analogies, opposites, similarities, and number series items. The language section includes vocabulary, quantitative reasoning problems, and items requiring syllogistic reasoning. Each section contains 40 items, and the two sections are separately timed, each being allotted 15 minutes.

The manual for each level provides percentile values and standard scores for the language and the nonlanguage scores, separately for each of a large number of age groups. The total score may be converted into a mental age, and thence to an intelligence quotient, or it may be converted into a percentile rank or a standard score for a variety of age groups. Through an elaborate equating procedure which is briefly described in the manual, all of these values for the scores on the *Survey of Mental Maturity* have been articulated into the standardization data for the 1957 edition of the *California Test of Mental Maturity* and the *California Achievement Tests,* so that scores on the *Survey of Mental Maturity* can presumably be interpreted in the context of this large mass of already-available data.

It is apparent that a great deal of effort has gone into the preparation of this test, and it is regrettable that the result is of only fair quality. The major failing seems to lie in the test items themselves, particularly the nonlanguage items, and this is especially ironic inasmuch as the *Survey of Mental Maturity,* according to the manuals, "contains a selection of the most discriminating portions of the *California Test of Mental Maturity.*" For the advanced level, items were taken from the junior high and advanced levels of the CTMM; for the junior high school level, items were taken from the secondary and elementary levels of the parent instrument. In each case, 100 language items and 90 nonlanguage items were tentatively selected, made up into two experimental forms, and administered without time limits to obtain difficulty and discrimination indices. The best 80 language and the best 80 nonlanguage items were retained to form two parallel forms of 80 items each.

The procedure for item selection is not described in sufficient detail to make it possible to judge why it proved inadequate, but it certainly did allow some items of very dubious quality to slip through the screening process. Perhaps the initial pool of items was not large enough. In any event, the nonlanguage items are not very good. Some are absurdly easy and some are very difficult indeed, but for the wrong reasons. Most of the nonlanguage items —all, in fact, but the number series items— involve drawings of various kinds. Unfortunately, the drawings are not always clear enough to convey the meaning that is intended. Many of the items, too, require a very high degree of visual acuity almost as a minimum prerequisite. Time and again, for example, particularly in the spatial visualization items, the choice will narrow down to two alternative figures so nearly identical that differences between them are almost microscopic. (A magnifying glass, come to think of it, would make an ideal "crib" for this test!) Forcing the examinee to detect these minute differences is presumably intentional, though almost certainly ill advised, but many of the drawings, or the reproductions of the drawings, are of such poor quality as to be almost indecipherable.

Nonlanguage items generally, and indecipherable nonlanguage items in particular, are time consuming, yet the examinee is given no more time for the 40 nonlanguage items than for the 40 language items—15 minutes in each case. Although no data on speededness are presented, it would seem that the nonlanguage section is much more highly speeded than the language section. Unfortunately, this element of speededness, coupled with the item deficiencies already noted, operates to exert a systematic downward pull on the nonlanguage scores of the most intelligent examinees. (While increasing error variance generally, an indecipherable illustration does nothing to hurt the score of an examinee who would not be able to answer the item correctly in any event, and an item not reached does nothing to hurt the score of an examinee who would not be able to answer it correctly if he reached it.) Since the total score on the test—the basic measure from which mental ages and intelligence quotients are obtained—is the sum of the raw scores on the language and nonlanguage sections, there is also an artificial lowering of total raw scores for the most intelligent examinees.

The poor quality of the nonlanguage items, then, results in introducing both unreliability and systematic bias into the total score, particularly blunting the precision of discriminations made in the upper part of the intelligence range. For examinees of high intelligence of a scholastic nature, the addition of the nonlanguage score to the language score will result in an under-assessment of ability; this under-assessment is likely to be quite drastic in the case of very bright examinees whose vision is slightly defective. It is necessary therefore to be very cautious in interpreting total scores on the test, and probably unwise to use the test for such purposes as identifying highly superior students.

According to the manual, "these two types of response patterns [language and nonlanguage] are tested and scored separately....so that individual differences in the pattern of language and nonlanguage ability can be studied." Despite this encouragement from the manual, it seems quite inadvisable to make judgments about a student's language ability relative to his nonlanguage ability on the basis of the subscores. To give only one of a number of technical reasons, the errors of measurement associated with the two sets of raw scores are such that a difference of seven or eight raw score points can easily arise through chance alone. Now, to pick an example quite at random, a 13-year-old who got scores of 31 on the language section and 24 on the nonlanguage section of the junior high level test would have percentile ranks of 84 and 34, respectively. For a 14-year-old the same raw scores would yield percentiles of 66 and 18, respectively. The norms for other ages give different figures, but the tenor is the same: except for extreme scores, a 7-point difference in raw scores gives rise to roughly a 50-point difference in percentile scores below the age of 15 and about a 35- to 40-point difference in percentiles above the age of 15.

The suggestion that either the nonlanguage score or the language score may be used by itself to obtain a rough estimate of the examinee's IQ also seems inadvisable. Although the manual does not give mental age or IQ equivalents for the raw scores on the two sections directly, it sketches a procedure whereby IQ equivalents for these scores may be obtained by first converting the raw scores into standard scores and then looking up the IQ equivalent for the particular standard score or percentile. This is a shaky procedure because of the large amount of error introduced by the use of successive conversions or equivalences, each of which is in itself merely an approximation.

The general saturation of the norms tables with conversions and equivalences, and the multiplicity of breakdowns (including, for example, such generally useless and confusing information as that given in the column headed "Intelligence (M.A.) Grade Placement") gives a misleading impression of rigorous exactitude. In point of fact, most of the actual figures in the tables were obtained by equating new data to earlier data, and interpolating and extrapolating as necessary. Even with sizable numbers of cases in the equating population, there are so many breakdowns that the number of experimental observations nailing down any given figure is quite small.

The least objectionable procedure would probably be to use the language score by itself, but to do so twice, i.e., to administer both Form 1 and Form 2 to each student, calculate mental age separately each time, and then average the two. This is not to be taken as a suggested procedure for general use—merely as a reasonably acceptable way of "making do" with this test if one is forced to use it. Overall, the test is not recommended.

[504]

★**Test of Learning Ability.** Business and industry; 1947–63; Forms S, T, ('47, 5 pages), ST ('57, 8 pages); Form ST is a long form combination of Forms S and T; manual for Forms S and T ['63, 24 unnumbered pages]; manual for Form ST ['63, 8 unnumbered pages]; Form ST norms for males only; $3.50 per 25 tests of Form S or T; 10¢ per key; $2 per manual; $5.50 per 25 tests of Form ST; 15¢ per key; $1 per manual; postage extra; $1 per specimen set of Form S or T; $1.25 per specimen set of Form ST; postpaid; 15(20) minutes for Forms S and T, 25(30) minutes for Form ST; Richardson, Bellows, Henry & Co., Inc. *

REFERENCES

1. PERRINE, MERVYN WILLIAM. "The Selection of Drafting Trainees." *J Appl Psychol* 39:57–61 F '55. * (*PA* 30:1725)
2. SPARKS, CHARLES P., AND WAITE, W. DUDLEY. "Normative Data Information Exchange, No. 10-18." *Personnel Psychol* 10:238–40 su '57. *

[505]

★**Test of Non-Verbal Reasoning.** Business and industry; 1948–63; 1 form; 2 editions: long form ('48, 5 pages), short form ('50, 3 pages); manual ['63, 9–10 unnumbered pages] for each edition; $3.50 per 25 tests of long form; $3 per 25 tests of short form; 10¢ per key; $1 per manual for either edition; postage extra; $1 per specimen set, postpaid; Spanish edition of long form and Spanish, French, and Arabic editions of short form available; 10(15) minutes for short form, 15(20) minutes for long form; Richardson, Bellows, Henry & Co., Inc. *

REFERENCES

1. CUOMO, SYLVIA. "Validity Information Exchange, No. 8-17: D.O.T. Code 5-92.601, Foreman II." *Personnel Psychol* 8:268 su '55. *

2. CUOMO, SYLVIA, AND MEYER, HERBERT H. "Validity Information Exchange, No. 8-16: D.O.T. Code 5-92.601, Foreman II." *Personnel Psychol* 8:267 su '55. *

3. KIRCHNER, WAYNE; HANSON, RICHARD; AND BENSON, DALE. "Selecting Foremen With Psychological Tests." *Personnel Adm* 23:27-30 N-D '60. *

[506]

Tests AH4 and AH5. Ages 10 and over, 13 and over; 1955-56; 1 form; 2 levels; separate answer sheets must be used; 5*s.* per 25 answer sheets; postpaid within U.K.; A. W. Heim; distributed by the National Foundation for Educational Research in England and Wales. *

a) TEST AH4: GROUP TEST OF INTELLIGENCE. Ages 10 and over; 1955; 1 form ['55, 8 pages]; manual ['55, 16 pages]; no norms for age 10; 18*s.* per 25 tests; 6*s.* per set of scoring key and manual; 7*s.* per specimen set; 20(30-45) minutes.

b) TEST AH5: GROUP TEST OF HIGH-GRADE INTELLIGENCE. Ages 13 and over; 1956; 1 form ['56, 8 pages); manual ['56, 20 pages]; 19*s.* per 25 tests; 5*s.* per set of scoring key and manual; 8*s.* per specimen set; 40(60-70) minutes.

REFERENCES

1-11. See 5:390.

JOHN LIGGETT, *Senior Lecturer in Psychology, University College of South Wales and Monmouthshire, University of Wales, Cardiff, Wales.*

Tests AH4 and AH5 are group tests of general intelligence employing similar question and answer materials and similar methods of administration and scoring. They are, however, of very different levels of difficulty. AH4 is intended for "a cross section of the adult population," whereas AH5 is designed for use with selected highly intelligent adult subjects ("students and research workers, and potential entrants to the university and the professions"). AH4 allows 20 minutes for questions and the more difficult AH5 allows 40 minutes. Further time is required in each case for initial practice with examples—an aspect of the administration of the test which the author considers particularly important.

The items in both tests are similar in character. In Part 1 of each test there are verbal directions, opposites, analogies, synonyms, numerical series, and numerical computations. Part 2 of each is composed of diagrammatic problems—analogies, sames, subtractions, series, directions, and superimpositions. A novel type of item, "similar relationships," is introduced in Part 1 of AH5. The subject is asked to choose from several given words the one which bears a similar relation to each of another two words. He has, in fact, to find out for himself whether the required relationship is one of sameness or opposition. A further variant of this idea is introduced in Part 2 of AH5 in the diagrammatic items which the author calls "features in common." The subject is shown five diagrams from which he has to select the "odd man out." As a guide he is given two further diagrams, each of which is declared to possess the odd feature. In this way the author has sought to avoid the ambiguity often found in classification test items.

The test booklets, separate answer sheets, and keys are quite conventional. The test score (the number of items correct) is readily convertible to a grade from A to E by reference to the norms representing the percentage distribution 10-20-40-20-10.

Test-retest consistency and validity are carefully considered in the manual. For AH4 the test-retest correlation is .92 (n = 100). For AH5 a test-retest correlation of .84 was obtained with 94 Cambridge undergraduates. Three sorts of validity data are presented for each test: correlations with other tests, comparisons with "real life" criteria such as examination results, and demonstration of the regular rise of test scores with chronological age. On this latter point the author makes the interesting report that the AH5 score may continue to increase even beyond the age of 18.

The manuals are well written in a modest, clear, and honest style, though their almost identical appearance invites confusion between the two tests. The test sheets themselves are poorly printed in a quaint mixture of old type faces and the diagrams are poorly reproduced. This is much less than the tests deserve.

In constructing AH4, Heim was attempting to provide a brief group test of general intelligence with items drawn from a wide field. In AH5 her major concern was to provide an instrument which would effect discrimination between highly intelligent subjects. Both of these aims she has achieved with a good deal to spare and there is little doubt that both AH4 and AH5 will do much valuable work. They are imaginatively based, soundly constructed, and well documented.

For reviews by George A. Ferguson of Test AH4 and J. A. Keats of Test AH5, see 5:390.

[507]

***Tests of General Ability: Cooperative Inter-American Tests.** Grades kgn and first grade entrants, 1–3.5, 4–7, 8–13, 10–13; 1950–63; levels 1 and 5 (*a* and *e* below) called *Test of General Ability: Inter-American Series;* a series of parallel tests and manuals in English and Spanish; IBM for grades 4–13; 5 levels; tentative norms (publisher recommends use of local norms); separate answer sheets must be used for grades 4–13; postage extra; 30¢ per specimen set of any one level, postpaid; prepared under the direction of Herschel T. Manuel; Guidance Testing Associates. *

a) LEVEL 1—PRIMARY. Grade kgn and first grade entrants; 1962–63; 3 scores: verbal and numerical, nonverbal, total; English language Form CE ('62, 9 pages); Spanish language Form CEs ('62, 11 pages); pretest ('62, 4 pages) for use in teaching testing procedures to immature children; directions ['62, 11 pages]; tentative norms ('63, 1 page); $3.50 per 25 tests; 5¢ per pretest (3¢ when purchased with test booklet); 30¢ per specimen set of either English or Spanish edition; 50¢ per combined specimen set; [40–50] minutes in 2 sessions.

b) PRIMARY LEVEL. Grades 1–3.5; 1950; 4 scores: oral vocabulary, classification, association, total; English language Forms AE, BE, ('50, 9 pages); Spanish language Forms AS, BS, ('50, 9 pages); directions ('50, 10 pages); series manual ('50, 18 pages); no data on reliability; no norms for subscores; $3 per 25 tests; 30¢ per set of keys; (30–40) minutes.

c) INTERMEDIATE LEVEL. Grades 4–7; 1950; 3 scores: nonverbal, verbal, total; IBM; English language Forms AE, BE, ('50, 12 pages); Spanish language Forms AS, BS, ('50, 12 pages); combined directions ('50, 7 pages) for this and *d* below; series manual ('50, 18 pages); no data on reliability; no norms for subscores; $3 per 25 tests; 5¢ per IBM answer sheet; 30¢ per set of scoring stencils; 34(50) minutes.

d) ADVANCED LEVEL. Grades 8–13; 1950; 3 scores: nonverbal, verbal, total; IBM; English language Forms AE, BE, ('50, 12 pages); Spanish language Forms AS, BS, ('50, 12 pages); combined directions ('50, 7 pages) for this and *c* above; series manual ('50, 18 pages); no data on reliability; no norms for subscores; prices same as for intermediate level; 34(50) minutes.

e) LEVEL 5—ADVANCED. Grades 10–13; 1962–63; 4 scores: verbal, nonverbal, numerical, total; IBM; English language Form CE ('62, 15 pages); Spanish language Form CEs ('62, 15 pages); directions ['62, 7 pages]; tentative norms and technical data ['63, 7 pages] for this and the level 5 reading test of the series; $4 per 25 tests; 5¢ per IBM answer sheet; 30¢ per set of scoring stencils; 30¢ per specimen set of either English or Spanish edition; 50¢ per combined specimen set; 52(65) minutes.

REFERENCES

1–8. See 4:325.

For reviews by Raleigh M. Drake and Walter N. Durost of b–d, *see 4:325.*

[508]

★The Verbal Power Test of Concept Equivalence. Ages 14 and over; 1959–63; Forms A, B, ('59, 2 pages) on a single sheet; manual ('63, 12 pages); $6 per set of 25 tests, key, and manual; $2 per manual; postpaid; (10–15) minutes; E. Francesco; Western Psychological Services. *

REFERENCES

1. FRANCESCO, E. "The Verbal Power Test of Concept Equivalents (*VPT*)." *J Psychol* 49:213–6 Ap '60. * (*PA* 34:7349)

2. FRANCESCO, E. "Below Chance Performance on a Verbal Test Using Paired Concepts." *J Clin Psychol* 17:312–5 Jl '61. * (*PA* 38:8412)

3. FRANCESCO, E. "Below Chance Performance on a Verbal Test: A Replication." *Psychol Rep* 10:601–2 Ap '62. * (*PA* 37:3868)

[509]

★Verbal Reasoning. Job applicants and industrial employees; 1958–61; 1 form ('58, 3 pages); manual ('61, c1959–61, 20 pages); norms for males only; $3 per 20 tests, postage extra; $1 per specimen set, postpaid; 15(20) minutes; Raymond J. Corsini, Richard Renck, and Measurement Research Division, Industrial Relations Center, University of Chicago (manual); Education-Industry Service. *

JAMES E. KENNEDY, *Associate Professor of Psychology, University of Wisconsin, Madison, Wisconsin.*

Verbal Reasoning is described in the manual as a measure of "a person's capacity to reason logically from written material." The test consists of 12 problems stated in words; each problem gives a verbal description of the activities of four brothers, followed by a three-part question. The answers may be deduced from the information given in the descriptions and the three-part questions. A paper and pencil test, *Verbal Reasoning* is suitable for administration to groups and has a strict time limit of 15 minutes. The items are said to be ordered for difficulty, although the description of the procedure followed is obscure. In its present format the test must be hand scored; the total score, ranging from 0 to 36, is the number of right answers. Only one form of the test is available. The sole estimate of the test's reliability is a test-retest correlation of .69 based on 68 cases.

While the organization and format of the manual are good, information about important features of the test is either missing or vague. Taking the positive features first, the instructions for administering and scoring the test are intelligible and should present no difficulties for the inexperienced. Rationales for percentile scores and normalized standard scores are well presented and procedures for converting raw scores are clear. Norm groups are reasonably large and are described in more detail than in most manuals for tests of this kind, although more information about age and education distributions would have been helpful.

On the negative side, the principal limitation of the manual is the incomplete and ambiguous discussion of validity and related issues. The manual provides no explanation of why, on theoretical grounds, the authors believe this test might be a useful measure of a capacity they call "verbal reasoning," in what ways the test is similar to or different from existing tests of either verbal reasoning in particular or intelligence in general, or why measurement of this capacity has been limited to a single type of item with only minor variations. Nowhere in the manual is there a statement, or an explicit suggestion, as to the purposes for which the test might be used. While these omissions are serious, the reviewer's objections would not be as strong if the manual reported the empirical relationships between performance on this test and performance on a variety of standard, relevant psychological measures. If this had been done the reader might have been able to infer for himself what the test does or does not measure and for what purposes it might be useful.

The validity of the test is said to be approached in two ways. The first consists in showing that low positive correlations (.10 to .55) exist between this test and three other tests: Thelma Thurstone's *Understanding Communication* (*Verbal Comprehension*), Corsini's *Non-Verbal Reasoning Test,* and his *Word Fluency.* (These are newly published, equally untried tests by the same group that developed *Verbal Reasoning.*) On the basis of these results, and with no further elaboration, the authors conclude "the test measures in the area of mental abilities." The second approach consists in showing that mean scores on the test differ, sometimes significantly and sometimes not, for various skill levels of industrial personnel. No interpretation of these results is made. Since this analysis was discussed under the heading "validity," the authors presumably believed the results have some bearing on the test's validity, but they do not say what it might be. While this situation is considerably better than making unfounded claims for validity, it is undesirable in that it might be misinterpreted by the unwary or inexperienced test user as evidence that this test has demonstrated validity for selection or placement purposes. Incidentally, the skill groups among which the test discriminated were widely different in educational levels and possibly differed significantly in age. The authors take no interpretative note of this.

In summary, we can say only that this test may prove in the future to be a useful contribution to theory or practice, but at its present stage of development it must be considered as an experimental test of good face validity, moderate reliability, but of no demonstrated validity of any kind. There is certainly no evidence to indicate it has predictive validity for use in business and industry.

DAVID G. RYANS, *Director, Bureau of Educational Research, University of Hawaii, Honolulu, Hawaii.*

This test is intended to estimate an individual's "capacity to reason logically from written material." It is made up of 12 problems selected by an approximation method of item analysis from "preliminary research forms" administered to small groups of job applicants, and presented in order of difficulty. Directions printed on the cover page of the test read: "This booklet contains problems about four brothers: Art(A), Bill(B), Carl(C), and Dan(D). Each question refers to *one of the four brothers.* For each answer cross out either A-B-C-or-D." A sample problem which follows the directions reads: "On their jobs, Art wears a white coat, Bill a uniform, Carl overalls and Dan a business suit." The examinee must judge from this information which brother is the plumber, which the butcher, and which the policeman. Three responses are required to each problem situation, resulting in a total possible score of 36. (Within a given problem the three responses obviously are not independent.) An individual's score on the test is the number of correct responses. Raw scores may be converted to normalized standard scores and percentile ranks.

Test-retest results, based upon administration of the problems to 68 employed men over intervals of from six to eight weeks, yielded a correlation coefficient of .69, which is presumed to reflect test reliability. Validity is judged by two approaches: (*a*) comparisons of test results with other test data, and (*b*) t-tests between paired means of different groups. Correlation with Corsini's *Non-Verbal Reasoning Test* scores yielded coefficients of .31 for 66 laborers and .33 for 71 management personnel; with Thelma Thurstone's *Understanding Communication* scores coefficients of .52 for 193 unskilled employees and .48 for 45 professional executive employees were found; and with Corsini's *Word Fluency* scores correlations ranged from .10 to .55 with a median of .27. The t-tests between paired means of six different groups showed statistically significant differences between the means of groups of "unskilled and semi-skilled employees" and "foremen," and between means of each of these groups and those of groups of "engineers and chemists," "executives and middle management," "white collar and junior executives," and "salesmen." (The *n* for the unskilled and semiskilled employee group was 244 and for the engineers and chemists, 146; the other group *n*'s ranged from 35 to 59.)

The test-retest reliability coefficient reported is based on too small a sample to provide generalization and the interval between testing leaves doubt about whether the data yield an acceptable test reliability index. If, however, the obtained coefficient is accepted as a reliability index, it would argue against use of the test; it is far too low to be acceptable. Evidence of concurrent validity is not convincing due to the low correlations with other tests. Use should have been made of analysis of variance in comparing differences between mean scores of different groups of employees.

Normalized standard score equivalents are given for raw scores of a group of 1,486 industrial personnel which showed a raw score mean of 16.58 and standard deviation of 7.04. Means and standard deviations are provided for six subgroups: professionals, executives, junior executives, salesmen, foremen, and hourly workers. (Interestingly, the mean for 35 salesmen in the "validity" study was reported to be 22.37; for 150 salesmen in the norms group the mean is 16.36.)

The Test Administration Manual is nontechnical and, indeed, unsophisticated (e.g., "The results shown in Tables 1 and 2 show that the Verbal Reasoning test measures in the general area of mental abilities"). The manual also is confusing and nonspecific in its statements about the test and its interpretation. It would have been desirable to have indicated the extent to which this short test of 12 problems and 36 responses correlates with various "abilities" measured by widely used tests of differential abilities and with factorially pure tests of such factors as deductive reasoning and inductive inference.

The test cannot be recommended for use due to lack of supporting information. If used, it definitely should be considered a trial test that has not been fully developed.

[510]

***Verbal Test (Adv.).** Ages 12 to 13-11; 1954-60; 4 forms; practice test [dates same as for tests, 2 pages] for each test; no data on validity; distribution restricted to directors of education; 10*s.* per 12 tests; 1*s.* per single copy; 2*s.* 6*d.* per 12 practice tests; 4*d.* per single copy; 1*s.* 3*d.* per manual for any one test; prices include purchase tax; postage extra; 10(15) minutes for practice test, 45(55) minutes for test (except for *a*); D. A. Pidgeon (*a*); published for National Foundation for Educational Research in England and Wales; Newnes Educational Publishing Co. Ltd. *

a) VERBAL TEST (ADV.) 1. 1954-55; 1 form ['54, 10 pages]; manual ('55, 10 pages); 50(60) minutes.
b) VERBAL TEST (ADV.) 2. 1957; 1 form ['57, 11 pages]; manual ('57, 11 pages).
c) VERBAL TEST (ADV.) 3. 1958; 1 form ['58, 11 pages]; manual ('58, 9 pages).
d) VERBAL TEST (ADV.) 4. 1960; 1 form ['60, 11 pages]; manual ('60, 9 pages).

J. S. LAWES, *Senior Lecturer in Education, Westminster College, North Hinksey, Oxford, England.*

These four tests are included in the series published by the National Foundation for Educational Research for use by Local Education Authorities, particularly in selection and guidance procedures. Basically the tests contain similar material, the majority of the items being of types common to all four tests although the balance between different types of items varies from test to test. For example, Test 2 and Test 3 contain approximately 25 per cent analogy type questions, Test 1 about 15 per cent, and Test 4 only 5 per cent. Tests 2 and 3 show the greatest degree of similarity containing exactly the same types with only slight variations in the proportions. These examples show that although the tests are similar and designed for similar purposes they are not in fact exact parallel forms. It would be useful to collect information regarding intertest correlation.

The manuals of these tests are evidence of the continued adequacy of the standards of construction demanded by the National Foundation. In addition to complete administration and scoring instructions and conversion tables, full description of the standardisation and reliability procedures is given. The reliability coefficients, obtained by Kuder-Richardson formula 20 on samples of 200 to 300 pupils, are all .97 or a little higher. The manuals for Tests 2, 3, and 4 contain a warning to the effect that, although the reliability is very high, errors attached to a child's score are not inconsiderable and the reliability should be taken into account in any allocation procedure. This warning could well be included in any new edition of the manual for Test 1.

The standardisation of Tests 1, 2, and 3 is good in that it was carried out in each case on a complete population of the appropriate age range, with populations numbering between 1,500 and 2,000, but it is to be noted that each standardisation population was from one area only. Test 4 was not standardised on a complete population but calibrated against Test 3 on "a small but representative group of children"—in fact, 532 children. A direct standardisation on a larger population would be a useful check. The conversion tables provide standardised scores with a mean of 100 and a standard deviation of 15. For Test 2 only, separate conversion tables are provided for boys and girls since the rates of increase in score with age for the two sexes show a highly significant difference. The only other significant sex difference quoted is for raw scores on Test 3, but it is good to find in each manual a recommendation that for any allocation procedure the two sexes should be considered independently.

The one piece of information which is missing from the manuals is that important one, "Validation Data." Unfortunately the Foundation is unable to provide such data, having itself been unable to follow up pupils who have worked the tests. This reviewer can offer the meagre information that when correlating Test 1 scores with school examination marks for small groups of secondary school boys he has obtained significant correlations of the order .50 to .60 with performance in English. If those who have used the tests, especially on a large scale, were able to provide follow-up data the value of the tests would be greatly enhanced.

In conclusion, these tests are soundly constructed and well presented. Some format problems, such as the effort to place all responses on the right hand side of each page in Test 1, an arrangement which can be confusing to some children, have been avoided in the later tests. The manuals are fully informative. Standardisation is in the main adequate but could well be repeated in other geographical areas. The only reservation against full recommendation is the lack of validation data.

JOHN NISBET, *Professor of Education, University of Aberdeen, Aberdeen, Scotland.*

This series of tests is designed for selection in English secondary schools, particularly among pupils at the end of their second year of secondary education. Consequently, the tests discriminate well among the middle two thirds of a fairly restricted age range but are less accurate at the extremes of high and low ability. They have been soundly constructed, using representative samples of over 1,500 cases (except Test 4 which was merely calibrated against Test 3). Reliability coefficients are all at least .97.

But recommendation of the use of these tests depends on the reputation of the National Foundation for Educational Research and personal knowledge of the high standards of their test construction, rather than on any evidence presented in the manuals. Since it is assumed that the tests will be used in a routine official testing programme (sale is restricted to education authorities, though the tests may be made available for research projects) the manuals are little more than marking keys with instructions for teachers administering the tests. Scanty data are given for assessing the adequacy of the standardisation: a single page is devoted to details of construction and much of the information is not precise. The standardisation groups are referred to in terms such as "all children in a chosen area aged between 12-0 and 14-0," without specifying such details as whether the area was urban or mixed rural-urban. No comparison with other tests is reported, and norms are given in one form only, the deviation quotient used in English selection procedures. This makes for economy in cost, but one would have hoped that the National Foundation might set an example to commercial publishers in the information given.

Performance in these tests is heavily dependent on reading skill and speed, since most items have separate instructions and there are 100 items to answer in 45–50 minutes. Below IQ 80 scores cannot be valid, though norms down to 70 are given.

Test 2 is different from the others, being at an easier level and therefore lacking discrimination in the upper range of ability. (Boys aged 13-11 must have over 97 items right out of 100 to score over 120.) Test 2 differs also in that it presents separate norms for boys and for girls. The sex differences are disconcertingly large and cast doubt on the standardisation: at age 12-0, the median raw score is 41 for boys and 65 for girls.

With the exception of Test 2, these are sound tests which can be recommended for use in assessing scholastic aptitude of 12- and 13-year-olds in the middle range of ability. They are very similar to the *Moray House Verbal Reasoning Test (Advanced)*, but the Moray House series is preferable in that it has fewer defects and presents slightly more information in its manuals.

[511]

***Verbal Tests 1–2, 4–13.** Ages 10–12; 1951–63; 12 tests (8–10 pages); new test published annually; practice test (2 pages, dates same as for test except for Test 7) for each test; no data on validity; distribution restricted to directors of education; 8*s.* per 12 tests; 9*d.* per single copy; 2*s.* 6*d.* per 12 practice tests; 4*d.* per single copy; manual for any one test: 1*s.* for Tests 1, 4, 5, 1*s.* 3*d.* for Tests 2, 6–13; prices include purchase tax; postage extra; 10(15) minutes for practice test, 45(50) minutes for test (except for Test 1); I. Macfarlane Smith (*a–d*), M. A. Brimer (*e*), and others; published for the National Foundation for Educational Research in England and Wales; Newnes Educational Publishing Co. Ltd. *

a) VERBAL TEST 1. 1951–53; 1 form ['51]; manual ('53, 8 pages); 50(55) minutes.
b) VERBAL TEST 2. 1952–53; 1 form ['52]; manual ['53, 11 pages]; no norms for ages 11-7 to 11-11.
c) VERBAL TEST 4. 1953–58; 1 form ['53]; manual ('58, 8 pages).
d) VERBAL TEST 5. 1954–55; 1 form ['54]; manual ('55, 8 pages); no norms for ages 11-7 to 11-11.
e) VERBAL TEST 6. 1955–57; 1 form ['55]; manual ('57, 9 pages).
f) VERBAL TEST 7. 1957–59; forms 7A, 7B, ['57]; practice tests: 7A ['59], 7B ['58]; manuals: 7A ('59, 9 pages, identical with 1957 manual), 7B ('57, 9 pages).
g) VERBAL TEST 8. 1957–58; forms 8A ['57], 8B ['58]; manual ('58, 12 pages) for each form.
h) VERBAL TEST 9. 1959; forms 9A, 9B, ['59]; manual ('59, 9 pages) for each form.
i) VERBAL TEST 10. 1959–60; forms 10A, 10B, ['59]; manual ('60, 10 pages) for each form.
j) VERBAL TEST 11. 1960–61; forms 11A, 11B, 11C, ['60]; manual ('61, 11 pages) for each form.
k) VERBAL TEST 12. 1961–62; forms 12A, 12B, ['61]; manual ('62, 11 pages) for each form.
l) VERBAL TEST 13. 1962–63; forms 13A, 13B, ['62]; manual ('63, 11 pages) for each form.

REFERENCES

1. MORETON, C. ANNE, AND BUTCHER, H. J. "Are Rural Children Handicapped by the Use of Speeded Tests in Selection Procedures?" *Brit J Ed Psychol* 33:22–30 F '63. * (*PA* 38:684)

ARTHUR B. ROYSE, *Lecturer in Psychology, The University of Hull, Hull, England.*

These group tests are designed for use in the annual allocation of children to selected English secondary schools. To ensure that no child has had previous experience with the test, a new test (or a new parallel form) is produced for each year and circulation is restricted to directors of education. The several authors deserve congratulation for consistently producing tests of high reliability in the limited time available.

The layout of the tests is good and the instructions for administration and marking are detailed and lucid. A praiseworthy feature is the use of a scoring system which allows the child credit for his intentions, however expressed, but which is sufficiently detailed to ensure consistency of marking by different examiners. Information regarding standardisation groups, sex differences, reliability coefficients, and methods of interpretation of scores is given clearly and concisely.

Unfortunately, no validation data are given. Serious in any test, this omission is especially so for these tests. Because of their eminence, the method of construction has been copied in detail by many other compilers of tests used for the same—and even for different—purposes. The obvious criterion of validity would be the test's ability to predict success in grammar school or, alternatively, a high correlation with an existing test whose predictive ability has been established. Clearly the first could not be obtained, since each new test has to be in use before such evidence can be collected. But failure to collect the second type of evidence appears to be due solely to the authors' belief that such correlation could be assumed without test.

The resultant loss of scientific rigour might be regarded as negligible if each new test involved only minor deviations from the old and, indeed, this is true for the earlier one-author tests. But the earlier procedure was clearly regarded as an unnecessary handicap, for, in a review of previous tests, the manual to Test 7 (1957) states that "there is a danger when one person writes all the items that in successive years he will repeat and restrict the content." From this test on, items were collected from several contributors and a number of new types of item and variations in the format of conventional items appear.

The implicit assumption that the infinite population of possible verbal items, of whatever form or content, is homogeneous with respect to abilities measured and variables predicted becomes explicit in the manual to Test 10 (1960) which claims, "The validity of verbal tests as predictors of success in the Grammar School has been firmly established in the light of empirical evidence obtained from various follow-up studies." Published evidence that *some* verbal tests have been successful in such predictions appears to have been taken as a license to include in subsequent NFER tests any item which could be classified as a verbal item, irrespective of its form or content. From this test on, the differences between earlier and later tests become even more marked, the most significant trend being the decline in the proportion of items requiring the child to educe relations from given data in favour of items requiring him to search his memory store for exemplars of a given rule.

In contrast, standardisation is good, each test being administered to all the children forming the top year group in primary schools in a number of selected areas. The number of children, varying from 4,167 (Test 4) to 19,256 (Test 2) and comprising approximately equal numbers of boys and girls, is given but the basis of selection of areas is not. Raw scores are converted to standardised scores having a mean of 100 and a standard deviation of 15. The difference between mean scores for boys and girls is given and, where the difference is statistically significant, it is wisely recommended that the sexes be considered independently in allocation procedures. But separate conversion tables are not given unless the regression coefficients of score on age also show significant differences. No indication is given of how these regression coefficients are derived and no justification is offered to support the assumption of linearity of regression or the extrapolations to age groups included in the tables but not in the standardisation groups.

Internal consistency coefficients (Kuder-Richardson formula 20) are computed from small random subsamples of around 200 scripts. They are generally high, the majority being around .98 with none lower than .95. Unfortunately, except for a few of the earlier tests, no test-retest reliability coefficients are given; for these earlier tests, values around .94 were obtained from small samples of less than 100 scripts.

Despite their weakness in scientific rigour and statistical refinement, these tests provide an invaluable service to education authorities. They succeed in providing a reliable scale which has a wide range of raw scores in the area critical for selection and can be recommended strongly to those who are prepared to accept as reasonable the compilers' assumptions of validity. Even for those who would prefer a firmer basis for statistical decision these tests can be recommended as being as good as the best in this special field.

[512]

★**The Western Personnel Tests.** College and adults; 1962; Forms A, B, C, D, (3 pages); manual (4 pages); $5.50 per 25 tests, postpaid; specimen set not available; Spanish edition available; 5(10) minutes; Robert L. Gunn and Morse P. Manson; Western Psychological Services. *

LEWIS E. ALBRIGHT, *Assistant Director, Employee Relations Research, Standard Oil Company (Indiana), Chicago, Illinois.*

The *Western Personnel Tests* (W-P-T) are four parallel forms designed as alternate short measures of mental ability. Testing time required is five minutes for any one form, each form containing 24 items arranged in order of difficulty. The content of the items is typical of that of most short mental ability tests, including number series, word meaning, disarranged sentences, and arithmetic reasoning. Three sample items precede the test problems. The format is attractive, with large, readable type throughout.

The manual states that the W-P-T was designed for use in business and industry, and suggests that the tests may also be useful in clinics, schools, hospitals, institutional settings, and government agencies. Unfortunately, the norms provided would be of little help in these other situations. The norms, in fact, are quite inadequate even for industrial settings. There are five "occupational" norm groups and a "general population" group which is the total of the five occupational groups. The five groups are professional workers, college students, clerical workers, skilled workers, and unskilled workers. The number of cases in each group for any one form is very small, ranging from 25 to 72.

No detailed description of the groups' composition is given. The college student group, for example, consists of "first year students through graduate students working for Ph.D.s," with no indication of how many students at each level. Nothing is said regarding the amount of education of the other groups; also unspecified are the age and sex composition of all groups. This latter omission is certainly contrary to accepted practice and runs counter to much evidence of important sex differences on mental ability as well as other types of tests.

When a test is as short as the W-P-T, we

may properly be concerned about its reliability. Here again, the manual is disappointing. Split-half coefficients in the high .80's and low .90's are given for the four forms, but these must be spuriously high precisely because of the speeded nature of the test. Verifying this suspicion is a subsequent table of interform correlations ranging from the low to middle .80's. What one would like to see, of course, are retest reliabilities, but they are not to be found.

The evidence for validity is even less satisfying, consisting merely of correlations of each W-P-T form with Form B of the *Wonderlic Personnel Test.* Although these coefficients are of the same magnitude as the interform correlations cited above, some evidence of the *predictive* or, at least, *concurrent* validity of the W-P-T is needed. One can argue that, because this test is easy to administer and score (as it appears to be) and because it requires only five minutes of testing time, we have a right to expect the authors to conduct validation studies of their instrument against relevant criteria of job success. Until the findings of such research can be presented, it would have been better to delay publication.

Besides its other omissions, the manual contains no reference to the American Psychological Association technical recommendations on test validity and reliability. Similarly, there is no description of the item analysis procedures used in constructing the test. On the subject of administration and scoring of the W-P-T, the novice test administrator would hardly be enriched by this instruction from the manual: "If questions are raised [by those taking the test], they should be answered simply and clearly." How should the administrator deal with a question about guessing, for example? Is he to encourage guessing or discourage it?

In sum, brevity is unquestionably a virtue of tests designed for industrial use and because the W-P-T yields a mental ability score in only five minutes, it may achieve some measure of popularity on this account. Brevity of test manuals is quite another matter, however, and here the W-P-T suffers to the point of incompleteness compared with such tests as the *Wonderlic Personnel Test,* the *Otis Quick-Scoring Mental Ability Tests,* or the *Adaptability Test.* The personnel officer who has accumulated experience with any of these or similar instruments would be well advised to conduct careful studies to determine the effectiveness of the W-P-T before discarding the old standbys just to gain a few minutes of testing time.

ERWIN K. TAYLOR, *President, Personnel Research and Development Corporation, Cleveland, Ohio.*

The three-page manual for this device claims to provide "the essential information about the W-P-T, its construction, normative data, administration, scoring, and interpretation." Primarily designed for use in industry, the W-P-T comes in four forms. The intercorrelations among these (apparently administered on a timed basis) vary from .81 to .87. Each of the four forms consists of a hodgepodge of 24 items of World War I vintage, apparently patterned after the highly speeded Wonderlic and its predecessor the Otis. The conglomerate includes items in vocabulary, arithmetic reasoning, number series, paper formboards, name and number checking, and verbal reasoning.

The four forms are reasonably parallel since in the case of each form the rank order correlation between the item number and its difficulty is to all intents and purposes minus one as is the rank order correlation of the item difficulties among the several forms. That these item difficulties were determined from highly speeded administrations is evidenced by the magnitude of this correlation and by the fact that the same undescribed populations were apparently used in correlating the scores from this instrument with the Wonderlic. These correlations, incidentally, ranging from .81 to .85, are the manual's sole claim to "validity." Under such highly speeded conditions it is safe to assume that the item difficulty values given are more a measure of the proportion of the population that reached the item than a measure of how difficult the item would have been had the test been administered on a power basis. Aside from this table of item difficulties on this undescribed population the manual makes no mention of the source of items, the nature of the test construction and item analysis, or of any other basis—rational or statistical—for including the particular set of questions which constitute the device.

The manual further claims that the W-P-T provides:

1. *Rapid* tests to measure mental ability....
2. *Practical* and *inexpensive* measures of intelligence and *learning ability.*

3. Means for *selecting* and *evaluating* new employees, trainees, and present employees relative to hiring, placement, training, promotion, transfer, reassignment and other personnel purposes.

8. *Rapid measures of intellectual functions* such as the use of language, size of vocabulary, reasoning ability, numerical skills, perceptiveness, general alertness, and scope of background.

9. Tests to *reinforce measurements of non-intellectual* abilities and traits: interests, aptitudes, skills, personality characteristics.

10. Tests which are *reliable* and *valid* measurements of intelligence.

The six examples of the 12 claims made for the test in the manual seem to this reviewer to go far beyond anything supported by the data. As a matter of fact, he wonders if these claims do not border on the unethical.

The "reliability" of this highly speeded form (based on the same populations apparently as the item difficulties) is determined by applying the Spearman-Brown formula to the odd-even item correlations administered under highly speeded conditions. Similarly, the intercorrelations among the four versions of the device, although ranging from .81 to .87, cannot, assuming that they were not administered under power conditions, be considered any more than a measure of the reliability of speed, if that.

There are norms for professional ($n = 27$ to 35), college ($n = 25$ to 47), clerical ($n = 37$ to 45), skilled ($n = 34$ to 72), and unskilled ($n = 39$ to 53) populations.

Perhaps the greatest affront to the intelligence of the reader of the manual is the section entitled "Interpretation of the W-P-T Scores." Here the authors present three hypothetical applicants for a clerical job. Their general population percentile scores (based on an n of 200) are 99, 70, and 35, respectively, while their clerical group percentile scores ($n = 45$) are 95, 65, and 20, respectively. Without reference to the nature or complexity of the job, the manual states with respect to the top scoring candidate, "On the basis of intellectual capacity only, he appears to be an exceptionally strong candidate." The other two applicants are discussed as follows: "Harry H. places at the 70th percentile of the General Population, and at the 65th percentile in the Clerical group; this suggests he is above the average for the General Population and for the Clerical group. He would be a good risk, but not as strong as John W. Robert S. with a raw score of 7 places at the 35th percentile in the General Population, and at the 20th percentile in the Clerical group. He appears to be a poor risk for a clerical job."

The manual pays the usual lip service to the desirability of individual organizations building their own norms and suggests that such data can be useful for many purposes, such as validation, besides selecting and training employees.

Such instruments are grist for the mills of the Grosses, the Hoffmans, and the Whites. Such instruments, available to anyone with access to a business letterhead and sufficient money to make the purchase, unfortunately afford considerable veracity to the contentions of these critics of testing. It is devoutly to be desired that no personnel manager considering the use of tests is so gullible as to install this instrument.

[513]

***Wonderlic Personnel Test.** Adults; 1939–61; Forms D and F are adaptations, for business and industrial use, of *Otis Self-Administering Tests of Mental Ability,* Higher Form; Forms A ('42), B ('42), D ['39], F ['39], 1 ('59), 2 ('59), 4 ('59), 5 ('59), EM ('59), (3 pages); revised manual ('61, 11 pages); norms supplement ('61, 14 pages); distribution of Form EM restricted to employment agencies; $8 per 100 tests and manual; 50¢ per manual; postage extra; norms supplement and 3 other reports free on request; $4 per introductory package of manual, norms supplement, 3 other reports, and 20 copies each of Forms A and B or 1 and 2; postpaid; 12(20) minutes; E. F. Wonderlic; E. F. Wonderlic & Associates. *

REFERENCES

1–2. See 40:1415.
3–9. See 3:269.
10–68. See 5:400.
69. BARTON, GLADYS. *The Personnel Test (Wonderlic) and Its Effectiveness in the Selection of Clerical Workers (Ticket Sorters).* Master's thesis, Temple University (Philadelphia, Pa.), 1958.
70. HUTTNER, LUDWIG, AND STENE, D. MIRIAM. "Foremen Selection in Light of a Theory of Supervision." *Personnel Psychol* 11:403–9 au '58. * (*PA* 33:11090)
71. SKOLNICKI, JOHN. "Normative Data Information Exchange, Nos. 11-17, 11-18." *Personnel Psychol* 11:447–8 au '58. *
72. ALBRIGHT, LEWIS E.; SMITH, WALLACE J.; AND GLENNON, J. R. "A Follow-Up on Some 'Invalid' Tests for Selecting Salesmen." *Personnel Psychol* 12:105–12 sp '59. * (*PA* 34:3463)
73. BUSCH, ALLEN C., AND WOODWARD, RICHARD H. "Normative Data Information Exchange, No. 12-27." *Personnel Psychol* 12:646 w '59. *
74. BUSCH, ALLEN C., AND WOODWARD, RICHARD H. "Validity Information Exchange, No. 12-18: D.O.T. Code 0-18.01, Industrial Engineer." *Personnel Psychol* 12:481 au '59. *
75. KAZMIER, LEONARD J. "Normative Data Information Exchange, No. 12-21." *Personnel Psychol* 12:503 au '59. *
76. KAZMIER, LEONARD J., AND BROWNE, C. G. "Comparability of Wonderlic Test Forms in Industrial Testing." *J Appl Psychol* 43:129–32 Ap '59. * (*PA* 34:3474)
77. MACKINNEY, ARTHUR C., AND WOLINS, LEROY. "Validity Information Exchange, No. 12-19: D.O.T. Code 1-36.05, Coding Clerk; 1-17.02, File Clerk II, Circulation Clerk." *Personnel Psychol* 12:482–3 au '59. *
78. CAMPBELL, JOEL T.; PRIEN, ERICH P.; AND BRAILEY, LESTER B. "Predicting Performance Evaluations." *Personnel Psychol* 13:435–40 w '60. * (*PA* 36:1LD35C)
79. HAWKINS, WILLIAM ANDREW. *Deviant Responses, Response Variability, and Paired-Associate Learning.* Doctor's thesis, Louisiana State University (Baton Rouge, La.), 1960. (*DA* 21:2365)
80. KIRCHNER, WAYNE; HANSON, RICHARD; AND BENSON, DALE. "Selecting Foremen With Psychological Tests." *Personnel Adm* 23:27–30 N–D '60. *
81. NEEL, ROBERT G., AND DUNN, ROBERT E. "Predicting Success in Supervisory Training Programs by the Use of

Psychological Tests." *J Appl Psychol* 44:358-60 O '60. * (*PA* 35:4081)
82. COATS, J. E.; WITH THE ASSISTANCE OF R. G. GARNER. *A Study of the Nature of the Chemical Operator's Occupation and the Personal Qualities That Contribute to Successful Operator Performance.* Midland, Mich.: Dow Chemical Co., March 1961. Pp. iv, 112. *
83. ROBBINS, JAMES E., AND KING, DONALD C. "Validity Information Exchange, No. 14-02: D.O.T. Code 0-97.61, Manager, Sales." *Personnel Psychol* 14:217-9 su '61. *
84. MCNAMARA, WALTER J. "Retraining of Industrial Personnel." *Personnel Psychol* 16:233-47 au '63. * (*PA* 38:6728)
85. SHOTT, GERALD L.; ALBRIGHT, LEWIS E.; AND GLENNON, J. R. "Predicting Turnover in an Automated Office Situation." *Personnel Psychol* 16:213-9 au '63. * (*PA* 38:6714)

N. M. DOWNIE, *Professor of Psychology, Purdue University, Lafayette, Indiana.*

Since the appearance of the last *Mental Measurements Yearbook,* five new forms of this test have appeared, 1, 2, 4, 5, and EM. Each of these, like the earlier forms, is a spiral-omnibus type of intelligence test of 50 items of an academic nature with a 12-minute time limit. The two original forms, D and F, were developed from the Higher Form of the *Otis Self-Administering Tests of Mental Ability.* Wonderlic's purpose was to develop a test for measuring mental ability of adults for hiring and placement in business and industry.

The author suggests that each company employ two forms and rotate their use. He also suggests that when this is done the following combinations be used: A and B, A and 5, 1 and 2, 1 and 4, or 2 and 4. Although the manual covers the 12-minute administration only, Wonderlic suggests that the test may be used as a power test with unlimited time. However, no suggestions are given concerning the interpretation of such scores. He also suggests that, if time is available, each applicant be given two forms to increase reliability.

Scoring with strip keys is rapid and simple; the score is the number right. Normative data are presented on some 50,000 adults in the age range 20–65 for the five newer forms and on about 35,000 adults for the earlier forms. Wonderlic recommends the use of raw scores rather than the IQ's for all practical uses of the instrument.

The new forms, like the earlier ones, have the items arranged from very easy to very difficult. Difficulty values are normally distributed with a mean of about 60 per cent. Correlation between position in the test and item difficulty is said to be above .90.

The reliability of the tests with a 12-minute time limit, one test being immediately followed by another, was found to vary between .82 and .94. Odd-even internal consistency coefficients ranging between .88 and .94 are also reported.

The author states that validity is demonstrated because the number of correct answers "distinguishes between good and poor groups of employees differentiated on work records accumulated over a period of five years."

Tables are presented to aid in interpreting results. Among these is a listing of minimum scores for various occupations. Another table shows the effect of age with suggestions that points be added to the score to compensate for score decrements related to age. For ages 60–69 this is 11 points. Although scores are shown to be related to educational level, as might be expected, there is considerable variance among scores in any one educational level. Finally, tables are provided for sex and last grade in school attended, for age, for applicants for clerical work in a bank, and for male applicants with types of work not specified. Conversion tables are presented for comparing forms and for transforming scores to Otis scores. In the 1961 supplement to the norms, distributions of scores by educational levels, stabilized for age groups, for males and females on each form are also given.

In summary this is an economical, generally adequate, and convenient instrument for measuring mental ability in an industrial situation. However, certain things leave much to be desired. The discussion of validity is inadequate. The validity of the test should be demonstrated for particular jobs, and for showing relationship to success in training for specific jobs. Expectancy charts for various occupations would be useful. Normative data should be presented for workers in different types of work and for variations in any job category. For example, it is not enough to give norms for clerical work; information should be available on bank clerks, time clerks, supply clerks, file clerks, etc. Percentile ranks or some type of standard score would be useful in giving more meaning to the raw scores used by Wonderlic.

MARVIN D. DUNNETTE, *Professor of Psychology, University of Minnesota, Minneapolis, Minnesota.*

The *Wonderlic Personnel Test* is a 50-item, timed (12 minutes), omnibus measure of intelligence. Forms D and F were formed from items contained in the Otis S-A tests and were standardized for industrial use and published in 1938. Forms A and B, consisting of new and more diverse item content, were published in

1942, and Forms 1, 2, 4, 5, and EM were published in 1959. The manual suggests, on the basis of "extremely high" correlations, that Forms 1, 2, 4, and 5 may be substituted, respectively, for Forms A, B, D, and F without requiring a restandardization. Form EM was developed for the exclusive use of fee employment agencies in order to avoid the possible conflict of interest between industrial employment departments and the private agencies. However, there is no evidence that these good intentions are backed up with any administrative device to insure that employment agencies do not also purchase the other forms. The manual, the norms booklet, and most of the reports on the Wonderlic test carry an order blank urging "any personnel executive" to purchase the tests. The easy availability of the *Wonderlic Personnel Tests* must, therefore, be regarded as one of the major disadvantages to their use. It is probably a rare applicant who is not exposed to the Wonderlic test several times during any given job search; the promotional literature on the test claims that over 6,500 organizations are using it for selection and placement procedures.

For such a widely used test, it is surprising and very disappointing to find such a paucity of information about the test in the manual. The manual carries a copyright date of 1961; yet, it contains only 16 references about the test, and many of these are from trade journals such as the *Mellon Bank News* or the *Wall Street Journal*. Furthermore, the references are old—10 dated in the late 30's and 40's and only 6 in the 50's, the most recent being 1958. Citations also are given to some of the classic texts such as Tiffin's *Industrial Psychology* and Yoder's *Personnel Management and Industrial Relations*. Here again, the citations are to the hopelessly out-of-date 1942 editions of these books. The Tiffin volume is now in its fourth edition and the Yoder in its fifth. One wonders what the more recent editions have to say about the *Wonderlic Personnel Test*. Thus, the manual seems *not* to include results of any recent studies by other investigators even though it does present information on a 1960–61 so-called restudy in which over 50,000 adults were tested. Unfortunately, however, the impressive *n* of 50,000 cannot make up for the lack of technical information on reliability and validity.

Reliability has been estimated in two ways. Equivalent form coefficients (one form given *immediately* after another) ranging from .82 to .94 are cited, but no *n*'s are given, and the nature of the samples used is not described. Also, odd-even coefficients ranging from .88 to .94 are cited. Again no information is given about *n*'s, the kinds of samples employed, or the forms to which the coefficients apply. Even more serious is the fact that an odd-even reliability estimate is clearly inappropriate for this highly speeded test.

No evidence of validity is given in the manual, although the flat claim is made that "This test has been shown to be a valid instrument in determining success on a number of different jobs." It is probably true that many studies have shown the Wonderlic test to be a valid indicator of job success; however, the potential user of the test should not have to make his own literature search to find evidence of validity nor should he be required to accept on faith the author's claim that "the test is valid." It is too bad that this up-dated manual was prepared without heeding the 1955 APA Technical Recommendations for the preparation of test manuals. Had they been heeded, a comprehensive and useful summary of the many studies using the test would have been included as well as carefully documented evidence for the content, predictive, concurrent, and construct validities of the Wonderlic tests. As it is, 25 years of research is very nearly ignored in favor of presenting a simplified and innocuous manual seemingly designed for businessmen rather than for psychologists. The only other evidence of validity is given in a supplemental publication titled "Summary of Experiences with the Wonderlic Personnel Test" which consists of a potpourri of anecdotal accounts, average scores obtained by different employees, frequencies with which the test is used, etc., etc.

A complete and careful job of norming (based on 27,366 males and 25,988 females) for the many forms of the test has been done; the norms are presented in a supplemental publication titled "Performance Norms," and separate norms are available by sex and educational level for each of the forms of the test. In addition, a table is provided enabling the user to convert raw scores from one form to equivalent scores on any of the other forms. The manual still suggests that corrections should be made for the effect of age on test scores; however, the correction tables are obviously based on cross-sectional comparisons, and the rationale for making the correction seems questionable.

In summary, the *Wonderlic Personnel Test* is a widely used, convenient, and easily available measure of general intelligence. It is also likely that the tests are adequately reliable and that they are also valid for a variety of jobs and for a variety of situations. It is extremely unfortunate, however, that these tests, in use now for 25 years, are not more rigorously described in the test manual. Instead, the manual and other supplementary materials seem primarily designed to sell tests rather than to inform the user in the appropriate use of the tests. I personally believe that these tests have a good deal of merit for use in industry, but I would hate to try to support such a claim solely on the basis of the *non-evidence* presented by the author and publisher.

For reviews by H. E. Brogden, Charles D. Flory, and Irving Lorge, see 3:269.

[Other Tests]

For tests not listed above, see the following entries in *Tests in Print:* 706–7, 710, 713, 715, 717–21, 726–7, 730, 734–5, 737, 741, 744–6, 748–54, 757–8, 760, 765–8, 770–1, 774–6, 778–81, 783, 785, 796, 801–3, 805–13, 818–9, 824, 826–7, 832, 835, 837–8, 840, 843, 845, 847–9, 854–5, 857, 860, 862, 865–8, and 871–4; out of print: 723, 739, 747, 756, 769, 814, 839, 844, 851, 859, and 861; status unknown: 728 and 786.

INDIVIDUAL

[514]

***Alexander Performance Scale: A Performance Scale for the Measurement of Practical Ability.** Ages 7–19; 1935–58; individual; 1 form; 3 tests; manual ('46, 66 pages); record sheet ('58, 1 page); 162*s.* per set of testing materials, 50 record sheets, and manual; 12*s.* per 50 record sheets; 8*s.* per manual; prices include purchase tax; postpaid within U.K.; (40–50) minutes; W. P. Alexander; distributed by National Foundation for Educational Research in England and Wales. *

a) THE PASSALONG TEST. 1932–37; may be administered alone as a quick measure of practical ability; (15) minutes.

b) KOHS' BLOCK DESIGN TEST. 1919–36; a modification of the original Kohs' *Block-Design Test.*

c) CUBE CONSTRUCTION TEST. 1918–25.

REFERENCES

1–3. See 40:1376.
4. See 3:270.
5–8. See 4:334.
9. SLATER, PATRICK. "Evidence on Selection for Technical Schools." *Occup Psychol* 21:135–40 Jl '47. * (*PA* 22:460)
10. LEFF, BARBARA. *Some Aspects of the Measurement of Technical Aptitude in Boys Aged 12 Years, With Special Reference to Alexander's Performance Scale.* Master's thesis, University of London (London, England), 1949.
11. NELSON, CALVIN CLAYTON. *A Comparison of Retarded and Normal Children With Respect to Alexander's "F" Factor.* Doctor's thesis, University of Oregon (Eugene, Ore.), 1958. (*DA* 19:1015)

H. GWYNNE JONES, *Senior Lecturer in Psychology, St. George's Hospital Medical School, London, England.*

This performance scale was developed in Britain to aid in the allocation of children to different types of secondary education at about the age of 11 years. In particular, it was designed to assess "practical ability," operationally defined as "that ability necessary for success in a technical school." Paper and pencil group tests had proved unsuitable for this purpose.

Each of the three subtests which make up the scale consists of graded series of items involving the solution of spatial problems and the manipulation of coloured wooden blocks. The adaptation of Kohs' well known *Block-Design Test* requires the reproduction of two-dimensional patterns; the *Cube Construction Test* extends this principle into the third dimension, and the *Passalong Test* requires the execution of a planned series of moves from an initial to a final pattern. The test materials are convenient, robust, and attractive, and, although the examiner needs to study the manual carefully and familiarise himself thoroughly with the material to achieve smoothness of administration, the instructions are clear and precise. Scoring is based jointly on level achieved and speed of performance.

Separate norms for boys and girls are provided for the total scale and for the *Passalong Test* alone. These are in the form of mental ages from 7 to 19 years to be converted into *practical ability ratios* equivalent to IQ's. No precise information is given concerning the distribution of these scores, but it is claimed that the norms were arranged so as to approximate to a mean of 100 and a standard deviation of 15. Certainly its standardisation is the weakest aspect of this scale, as indicated by the inclusion in the manual of a request for additional data from users. Evidence from the references quoted suggests that this weakness is least serious within the age range of 10 to 13, for which the norms are based on several hundred scores.

The reliability of the scale is not outstandingly high but is as high as can be expected for a performance scale of this kind and length: the test-retest correlation is of the order of .8.

Allowing for this, the *Kohs' Block Design Test* and the *Passalong Test* are very closely related (corrected correlation .96) but have lower correlations with the *Cube Construction Test* (corrected correlations .63 and .73, respectively). Factor analyses indicate that the scale is a good measure of general intellectual ability, and also of "practical ability," which most contemporary psychologists would identify with spatial ability.

The validity of the scale has been mainly assessed in terms of its predictive power in relation to success in technical school subjects. Whereas a verbal scale is a more efficient predictor of performance in the more academic verbal and science subjects, the performance scale is greatly superior for the more technical subjects, such as machine drawing and lathe work.

At one time the Alexander scale was very frequently used in Britain, in conjunction with the Binet scale, for the all round intellectual assessment of children for various purposes. During the last decade, the WISC has tended to become the popular tool for use with school age children. Whereas the WISC has many advantages over the earlier combination, it is by no means certain that the WISC performance scale is superior to the Alexander. The Block Design and Object Assembly subtest of the WISC are probably measures of the same spatial ability as that assessed by the Alexander scale, but this is not necessarily true of the overall performance IQ, which is also partially determined by various other abilities reflected in the other subtest scores. One definite advantage of the Alexander is the provision of separate sex norms: there is ample clear evidence of appreciable sex differences in spatial ability. In an experimental or other situation for which the adequacy of the initial standardisation data is not of the first importance, the Alexander might well still be the performance scale of choice for the appropriate age group.

[515]

***Cattell Infant Intelligence Scale.** Ages 3–30 months; 1940–60; downward extension of the *Revised Stanford-Binet Intelligence Scale, Second Revision* (see 5:413); individual; 1 form; revised manual ('60, c1940, see *18* below, essentially the same as previous edition); record form ('40, 4 pages); $60 per set of testing materials, carrying case, and 25 record blanks; $1.70 per 25 record blanks; $6 per manual; postpaid; (20–30) minutes; Psyche Cattell; Psychological Corporation. *

REFERENCES

1. CATTELL, PSYCHE. *The Measurement of Intelligence of Infants and Young Children.* New York: Psychological Corporation, 1940. Pp. 274. * (*PA* 15:2397)

2. CATTELL, PSYCHE. "Intelligence of Infants and Its Measurement." *Trans N Y Acad Sci, Series II* 3:162–71 Ap '41. * (*PA* 15:4041)

3. GERSTEIN, REVA APPLEBY. "An Analysis of Infant Behavioural Development." Abstract. *B Can Psychol Assn* 5:73–5 O '45. * (*PA* 20:938, title only)

4. ESCALONA, SIBYLLE. "The Predictive Value of Psychological Tests in Infancy: A Report on Clinical Findings." Abstract. *Am Psychologist* 3:281 Jl '48. * (*PA* 22:5366, title only)

5. ESCALONA, SIBYLLE. "The Use of Infant Tests for Predictive Purposes." *B Menninger Clinic* 14:117–28 Jl '50. * (*PA* 25:5387)

6. HARMS, IRENE E. *A Study of Some Variables Affecting the Reliability of Intelligence Test Scores During Late Infancy.* Doctor's thesis, State University of Iowa (Iowa City, Iowa), 1951.

7. WATSON, ROBERT I. *The Clinical Method in Psychology,* pp. 333–40. New York: Harper & Bros., 1951. Pp. xii, 779. * (*PA* 26:5577)

8. KLATSKIN, ETHELYN HENRY. "Intelligence Test Performance at One Year Among Infants Raised With Flexible Methodology." *J Clin Psychol* 8:230–7 Jl '52. * (*PA* 27:5764)

9. MILLER, ELSA, AND ROSENFELD, GEORGE B. "The Psychologic Evaluation of Children With Cerebral Palsy and Its Implications in Treatment: Preliminary Report." *J Pediatrics* 41:613–21 N '52. * (*PA* 27:6706)

10. CATTELL, PSYCHE. "Infant Intelligence Scale," pp. 507–9. (*PA* 27:7759) In *Contributions Toward Medical Psychology: Theory and Psychodiagnostic Methods, Vol. II.* Edited by Arthur Weider. New York: Ronald Press Co., 1953. Pp. xi, 459–885. *

11. GALLAGHER, JAMES J. "Clinical Judgment and the Cattell Infant Intelligence Scale." *J Consult Psychol* 17:303–5 Ag '53. * (*PA* 28:4353)

12. CAVANAUGH, MAXINE C.; COHEN, IRA; DUNPHY, DONAL; RINGWALL, EGAN A.; AND GOLDBERG, IRVING D. "Prediction From the Cattell Infant Intelligence Scale." *J Consult Psychol* 21:33–7 F '57. * (*PA* 32:266)

13. FROMM, ERIKA; HARTMAN, LENORE DUMAS; AND MARSCHAK, MARIAN. "Children's Intelligence Tests as a Measure of Dynamic Personality Functioning." *Am J Orthopsychiatry* 27:134–44 Ja '57. * (*PA* 32:1621)

14. NORRIS, MIRIAM; SPAULDING, PATRICIA J.; AND BRODIE, FERN H. *Blindness in Children.* Chicago, Ill.: University of Chicago Press, 1957. Pp. xv, 173. * (*PA* 32:824)

15. ALLEN, ROBERT M. "Suggestions for the Adaptive Administration of Intelligence Tests for Those With Cerebral Palsy: Part 2, Administration of the Vineland Social Maturity Scale, the Gesell Preliminary Behavior Inventory, and the Cattell Infant Intelligence Scale." *Cerebral Palsy R* 19:6–7 Mr–Ap '58. * (*PA* 33:8853)

16. HARMS, IRENE E., AND SPIKER, CHARLES C. "Factors Associated With the Performance of Young Children on Intelligence Scales and Tests of Speech Development." *J Genetic Psychol* 94:3–22 Mr '59. * (*PA* 36:4FE03H)

17. KRALOVICH, ANNE MARIE. "A Study of Performance Differences on the Cattell Infant Intelligence Scale Between Matched Groups of Organic and Mongoloid Subjects." *J Clin Psychol* 15:198–9 Ap '59. * (*PA* 35:5178)

18. CATTELL, PSYCHE. *The Measurement of Intelligence of Infants and Young Children, Revised 1960.* New York: Psychological Corporation, 1940 [published 1960]. Pp. 274. * [Although "Revised 1960" appears on the title page, the publisher has informed the MMY that the book is only a reprinting of the original edition (*1*) with corrections of a few typographical errors.]

19. WIGGIN, MARTHA K. *The Use of Certain Items From the Cattell Intelligence Scale for Infants and Young Children With Deaf-Blind Children.* Master's thesis, Boston University (Boston, Mass.), 1960.

20. ESCALONA, SIBYLLE K., AND MORIARTY, ALICE. "Prediction of Schoolage Intelligence From Infant Tests." *Child Develop* 32:597–605 S '61. * (*PA* 36:4FE97E)

21. PEASE, DAMARIS; ROSAUER, JOSEPHINE KEEFE; AND WOLINS, LEROY. "Reliability of Three Infant Developmental Scales Administered During the First Year of Life." *J Genetic Psychol* 98:295–8 Je '61. * (*PA* 36:2FB95P)

22. LONDON, SUSAN KATHERINE. *The Stability of the IQ of Mentally Retarded Pre-School Children.* Doctor's thesis, University of Michigan (Ann Arbor, Mich.), 1962. (*DA* 23:310)

For reviews by Florence M. Teagarden and Beth L. Wellman, see 3:281 (1 excerpt).

[516]

★**Children's Picture Information Test.** Ages 2–6 with motor handicaps; 1959; individual; 1 form (41 pages); instructions for administering (1 page); norms-technical data (7 pages, reprint of 2 below); $10 per set of testing materials, postpaid; [10–25] minutes; Kate L. Kogan and Richard L. Crager; Spastic Aid Council, Inc. *

REFERENCES

1. KOGAN, KATE L. "A Method of Assessing Capacity in Preschool Cerebral Palsied Children." *J Clin Psychol* 13:54–6 Ja '57. *

2. KOGAN, KATE L., AND CRAGER, RICHARD L. "Standardization of the Children's Picture Information Test." *J Clin Psychol* 15:405–11 O '59. * (*PA* 36:1HC05K)

DOROTHY EICHORN, *Associate Research Psychologist, and Administrator, Harold E. Jones Child Study Center, Institute of Human Development, University of California, Berkeley, California.*

This test consists of 40 sets of colored pictures, and the child indicates, by pointing or responding in some other discriminable way, which of four alternatives "goes with" the picture. Instructions for administration are clear and a specimen record form is provided, but examiners must number the pages of the test booklet and supply record forms. The authors emphasize that the test was devised for the "relatively rapid" assessment of young children lacking oral and manipulative skills, and "Under no circumstances would....be preferred if more extensive and varied examination" were possible. They are equally specific in describing the procedures used in establishing norms and estimating reliability and validity.

From a total of 568 normal children aged 2 through 6 years, tested in Seattle, 400 were chosen for the standardization population. Limitations of size and geographic sampling are mitigated by the attention given to selecting for each age interval a sample of 50 balanced for sex, age in months across the six-month range, and conformity of parental occupation to the distribution of the 1950 census. Norms are in the form of normalized *T*-scores and centiles because the raw score distributions were skewed—positively at the younger ages and negatively at the older ages—and of unequal variance. Increases in median score between successive age groups were significant at the one per cent level only from 2½ through 5½ years.

Two subgroups of 50 subjects each, balanced for age distribution from 2 to 6 years and with parental occupations approximating the census groupings, were also selected. The "reliability group" was retested after one to three weeks; the "validity group" received the Stanford-Binet, Form L. Binet and CPIT scores were also available for 59 handicapped children. The product-moment correlations between CPIT score and Binet mental age for the normal and handicapped groups were .89 and .80, respectively. Lower coefficients might be expected with a more restricted age range. The test-retest correlation was .93. Split-half reliability correlations, computed for 4 one-year age intervals of 100 subjects each and corrected by the Spearman-Brown formula, ranged from .85 to .90.

Test construction is only briefly discussed, but apparently was done less carefully than standardization. The pictures are cut from children's books, rather than designed to standard specifications. The authors claim that mounting the pictures of one set on paper of the same color eliminates any possible influence of color preference. However, the pictures differ in hue, brightness, scale relationships, fineness of detail, clarity, figure-ground contrast, and contrast with the mounting paper. Among the cerebral palsied, for whom the test is intended, are individuals whose performance may be particularly affected by such uncontrolled variables. "An effort was made to restrict the content largely to everyday household situations" with which an "immobilized child of confined environment" would be familiar. Some of the pictures do not meet this criterion, e.g., an igloo and a factory, but in the main this objective has been achieved.

Kogan and Crager recognize that factors in addition to "amount of information assimilated" influence performance, but overlook the cognitive processes involved in classifying the correct alternative as "belonging with" the key. A variety of principles of abstraction are required. One of the more frequent is a part-whole strategy, in which the key is a part of the correct alternative, or vice versa. Several sets require functional matching, e.g., a child's overalls and a flatiron. A third basis for matching is conventional proximity, such as ocean water (very indistinct) and a fish. Some sets admit of more than one method of classification, e.g., color matching and another strategy. The two strategies do not always lead to the same response. A frying pan is the correct match for the stove, but a chair is the only other piece of furniture. Such ambiguities may produce nondiscriminating items, either because equal proportions of different ability groups pass, using different conceptual bases of choice, or because incorrect choices are based on higher order abstractions. There is no indication that sets were pretested either to eliminate nondiscriminating items or to insure that the decoys in a set were of equal appeal and difficulty. Structuring the test to include several strategies should, however, strengthen it as a source of information about intellectual function by sampling more widely of cognitive processes—a real advantage when the clinician is asked to assess a child on the basis of relatively little material. Further, if some strategies are more difficult than others, tabulation of passes in terms of classification systems is a potentially powerful tool for item construction and selection.

The skewed distributions and poor discrimination at both ends of the age range indicate that the CPIT lacks "floor" and "ceiling." Items could be added without lengthening testing time if sets were arranged in order of difficulty and testing restricted to a critical range, from basal to ceiling. At present all sets must be given, although the medians at the lower ages are only 25 to 50 per cent of the total, and at the upper ages approximate the ceiling.

Despite the deficiencies in test construction, the standardization data indicate that Kogan and Crager have had considerable success in developing a test to meet a real need. It is easily administered, discriminates between adjacent six-month intervals from 2½ to 5½ years, produces satisfactory reliability coefficients, and correlates reasonably well with a conventional test of intelligence. For immediate use with young handicapped children, many may prefer the *Peabody Picture Vocabulary Test*. It is at least as easy and quick to administer and has the advantages of more "bottom" and "top," demonstration items, an alternate form, MA and IQ norms as well as percentiles, and more carefully constructed pictures. However, the potential which the CPIT offers for assessing aspects of intellectual function beyond sheer accumulation of information is a strong argument for its further use and refinement.

T. ERNEST NEWLAND, *Professor of Educational Psychology, University of Illinois, Urbana, Illinois.*

The test materials consist of a booklet of forty 10 by 11 inch pages on each of which appears a stimulus picture and four possible response pictures, generally 1½ by 2½ inches in size. The subject's attention is called to the stimulus picture and he then is asked to identify which of the possible response pictures "belongs with," or "goes with" the stimulus picture. The subject may be trained to whatever extent the examiner deems desirable, but he receives no score in any items used in training. In all but 5 of the 200 test item elements the figure-ground contrast is sharply delineated. The positional placements of the correct responses are well randomized. All of the 200 figures depicted are in color, 68 per cent of them being on a white background. Colored mats offset the elements from the black pages of the booklet. In terms of the kinds of behavior sampled, 9 items involve the categorization of stimulus and response elements (Hallowe'en pumpkin-witch); 10 items involve the recognition of whole-part or part-whole relationships (desk-telephone; chimney-house); and the remaining items call for the identification of use relationships (object-user; user-object; object-use; and joint use).

On a disabled population of 59 subjects, presumably of varying degrees and kinds of cerebral palsied involvement, and of unspecified age and sex distribution, CPIT scores correlated with "mental age ratings" .80. Test-retest reliability obtained on scores of 50 nondisabled subjects (26 males and 24 females), who presumably were equally distributed over the eight six-month age groups, is reflected in a product-moment coefficient of .93. On the basis of the results obtained on 400 nondisabled subjects, *T*-score equivalents are presented for each possible CPIT raw score for half-year age groups and for full-year age groups. A further table is provided for converting the *T*-score equivalents into centiles.

Children and clinicians being what they are, it is highly likely that the CPIT will make possible a helpful discrimination among children in this age range—certainly in the case of nondisabled youngsters, probably among disabled youngsters, and possibly among the highly heterogenous group of cerebral palsied youngsters. The light which scores on the CPIT will throw on the psychological functioning of cerebral palsied children in the preferred age ranges must be regarded as limited. The authors rightly point out that the CPIT "appears to measure the amount of information the child has assimilated," and, as in the case of so much "intelligence" testing, this is taken as the basis for inferring subsequent capacity to assimilate. Very properly, the authors perceive their device as capable of reflecting only certain "facets of intelligence," and recognize that psychological evaluation beyond the use of the CPIT will be needed. The CPIT is presented as a device developed for the purpose of better obtaining a kind of measurement of the learning aptitude of cerebral palsied children. Yet the only evidence presented to support this intent is a reasonably high correlation between the scores on the CPIT and the mental ages obtained by means of the Stanford-Binet Form L. Since it was because of the limitations of the Binet that a new device was conceived, this type of correlational validation has a highly involutional aspect to it, and actually could be self-defeating.

The authors, like others who have tried to produce devices presumably clinically more appropriate for measuring the "intelligence" (or facets of it) of physically deviant groups, such as the cerebral palsied, the deaf, and the blind, have been caught in a near-unresolvable dilemma. On the one hand, a device is developed, is standardized on a nondeviant population, and is concurrently validated—still on the nondeviant population—against the device which has been criticized. The two devices then are applied to a deviant population and if the resulting correlation is high enough, the appropriateness of the new device for use with the deviant population is taken as established. On the other hand, a newly developed device is standardized entirely on a deviant population and if the content validity appears satisfactory, it is assumed to yield results connoting the same kind of psychological functioning which extant (but criticized) devices yield on nondeviant populations. The authors, who have much company, have pursued the former course. But those who compare results obtained on cerebral palsied populations will need to be quite cautious when they try to rationalize correlations between results obtained by means of the CPIT and those obtained by means of other devices. The fact that so much of the precise statistical work was done on CPIT results obtained on a nondeviant population and so little on a cerebral palsied population will have to be kept clearly in mind.

More specifically, it is most unfortunate that the physical conditions (kinds of cerebral palsy, degrees of involvement, sensory conditions), age distribution, and sex distribution of the cerebral palsied population are not specified. From a test administration standpoint, it is quite possible that if at least the response elements were arranged and presented parallel to the bottom of the page, rather than vertical to it, the pointing responses of young involved subjects might be facilitated. As is so often true in newly developed devices, subjects may give perfectly justifiable responses which are not provided for in the key. Such would appear to be possible on items such as these: electric iron–overalls, as contrasted with iron–bus (both metal); little girl–tricycle (girl–moving van); tree–bird (tree–door, both wood); sleeping girl–bed (girl–toy); and Hallowe'en pumpkin–witch (pumpkin–turkey). Only a systematic analysis of response "errors" can establish the validity or invalidity of such concern.

[517]

***Columbia Mental Maturity Scale, Revised Edition.** Mental ages 3–12; 1954–59; 1 form ('59, 100 cards, same as 1954 edition except for 17 new items and reordering of items); manual ('54, 15 pages); hectographed supplementary data ('59, 3 pages); revised norms ['59, 1 page]; individual record, revised ('59, c1954–59, 1 page); no data on reliability of revised edition; $35 per examiner's kit of cards and manual (owners of earlier edition may purchase revised cards only for $5.50); $1.40 per 35 individual records; $5.75 per carrying case; postage extra; (15–30) minutes; Bessie B. Burgemeister, Lucille Hollander Blum, and Irving Lorge; [Harcourt, Brace & World, Inc.]. *

REFERENCES

1–13. See 5:402.
14. BLUM, LUCILLE H.; BURGEMEISTER, BESSIE B.; AND LORGE, IRVING D. "The Mental-Maturity Scale for the Motor Handicapped." *Sch & Soc* 73:232–3 Ap 14 '51. *
15. BLUM, LUCILLE H.; BURGEMEISTER, BESSIE B.; AND LORGE, IRVING. "Trends in Estimating the Mental Maturity of the Cerebral-Palsied Child." *J Excep Child* 17:174–7 Mr '51. *
16. ALLEN, ROBERT M., AND COLLINS, MARJORIE G. "Suggestions for the Adaptive Administration of Intelligence Tests for Those With Cerebral Palsy: Part 1, Administration of the Ammons Full-Range Picture Test, Columbia Mental Maturity Test, Raven's Progressive Matrices and Leiter International Performance Scale." *Cerebral Palsy R* 16:11–4+ My–Je '55. * (*PA* 30:3284)
17. BERKO, MARTIN J. "The Measurement in Intelligence of Children With Cerebral Palsy: The Columbia Mental Maturity Scale." *J Pediatrics* 47:253–60 Ag '55. * (*PA* 30:5078)
18. GUSLOFF, RICHARD F. *Comparability of Columbia Mental Maturity Scale Quotients.* Master's thesis, Illinois Normal University (Normal, Ill.), 1955.
19. ALLEN, ROBERT M., AND SANDLER, JACK. "Concerning the Variation of Responses on the Columbia Mental Maturity Scale." *Cerebral Palsy R* 17:38+ Mr–Ap '56. * (*PA* 31:4668)
20. FRENCH, JOSEPH, AND WORCESTER, D. A. "A Critical Study of the Columbia Mental Maturity Scale." *Excep Child* 23:111–3+ D '56. * (*PA* 31:7912)
21. GALLAGHER, JAMES J.; BENOIT, E. PAUL; AND BOYD, HERBERT F. "Measures of Intelligence in Brain Damaged Children." *J Clin Psychol* 12:69–72 Ja '56. * (*PA* 30:5093)
22. GALLAGHER, JAMES J. *A Comparison of Brain-Injured and Non-Brain-Injured Mentally Retarded Children on Several Psychological Variables.* Monograph of the Society for Research in Child Development, Vol. 22, No. 2. Lafayette, Ind.: Child Development Publications, 1957. Pp. 79. * (*PA* 33:1632)
23. GROSS, DEAN G. *An Experiment With the Columbia*

Mental Maturity Scale and the Goodenough Draw-A-Man Test to Determine Their Utility as Testing Devices for the Severely Mentally Retarded as Compared to the Stanford-Binet. Master's thesis, San Francisco State College (San Francisco, Calif.), 1958.
24. BLIGH, HAROLD F. "Concurrent Validity Evidence on Two Intelligence Measures for Young Children." *Yearb Nat Council Meas Used Ed* 16:56–66 '59. * (*PA* 34:7345)
25. DUNN, LLOYD M., AND HARLEY, RANDALL K. "Comparability of Peabody, Ammons, Van Alstyne, and Columbia Test Scores With Cerebral Palsied Children." *Excep Child* 26:70–4 O '59. * (*PA* 35:3733)
26. ESTES, BETSY WORTH; KODMAN, FRANK; AND AKEL, MACY. "The Validity of the Columbia Mental Maturity Scale." Abstract. *J Consult Psychol* 23:561 D '59. * (*PA* 34:5578)
27. WITSAMAN, L. R., AND JONES, REGINALD L. "Reliability of the Columbia Mental Maturity Scale With Kindergarten Pupils." *J Clin Psychol* 15:66–8 Ja '59. * (*PA* 34:2740)
28. LEVINSON, BORIS M., AND BLOCK, ZELICK. "Research Note on Columbia Mental Maturity Scale (CMMS) and Revised Stanford Binet (L) in a Preschool Population." *J Clin Psychol* 16:158–9 Ap '60. * (*PA* 36:2HC58L)
29. WARREN, SUE ALLEN, AND COLLIER, HERBERT L. "Suitability of the Columbia Mental Maturity Scale for Mentally Retarded Institutionalized Females." *Am J Mental Def* 64:916–20 Mr '60. * (*PA* 35:6846)
30. HIRSCHENFANG, SAMUEL. "A Comparison of the Revised Columbia Mental Maturity Scale (CMMS) and Goodenough Draw-A-Man Test in Children With Speech Disorders." *J Clin Psychol* 17:381–2 O '61. * (*PA* 38:8918)
31. HIRSCHENFANG, SAMUEL. "Further Studies on the Columbia Mental Maturity Scale (CMMS) and Revised Stanford Binet (L) in Children With Speech Disorders." *J Clin Psychol* 17:171 Ap '61. * (*PA* 38:956)
32. SMITH, BESSIE S. "The Relative Merits of Certain Verbal and Non-Verbal Tests at the Second-Grade Level." *J Clin Psychol* 17:53–4 Ja '61. * (*PA* 37:3595)
33. FLEMING, KATHRYN. *A Comparison of Mental Age Scores on the Revised Columbia Mental Maturity Scale and the Stanford-Binet Intelligence Test, Form L, at the Five Through Eight Year Mental Age Levels.* Master's thesis, Bowling Green State University (Bowling Green, Ohio), 1962.
34. KODMAN, FRANK, JR.; WATERS, JERRY E.; AND WHIPPLE, CLIFFORD I. "Psychometric Appraisal of Deaf Children Using the Columbia Mental Maturity Scale." *J Speech & Hearing Disorders* 27:275–9 Ag '62. * (*PA* 37:3488)
35. MASCIA, GEORGE V. *An Investigation Into the Use of the Revised Columbia Mental Maturity Scale as a Psychometric Instrument Sensitive to Brain Injury.* Master's thesis, University of Kansas (Lawrence, Kan.), 1962.

MARSHALL S. HISKEY, *Professor of Educational Psychology, and Director, Educational Psychological Clinic, University of Nebraska, Lincoln, Nebraska.*

Designed to measure intelligence of handicapped children, this pictorial type classification test "calls for no verbal response and a minimum of motor response." Each of the 100 items has a series of three to five drawings presented on a card which is 6 by 19 inches. The test, an untimed individual type scale, utilizes perceptive discriminations involving color, shape, size, use, number, kind, missing parts, and symbolic material. The subject responds by selecting the picture in each series which is different from, or unrelated to, the others.

In general, children enjoy this test. The pictures are large and clear and the test can be administered in 15 to 20 minutes. The record blank makes recording an easy procedure, and the conversion of the raw score to a mental age is a simple matter.

The present revision (1959) of the original scale (1954) took place after reports of research gave highly conflicting evidence in regard to validity and reliability coefficients, adequacy of norms, item difficulty, and the rationale for responses. The original scale had some items that contained printed words, thus making it necessary for the child to have considerable word recognition ability in order to complete the item successfully. Furthermore, some pictures in the original scale were not clearly discernible.

The replacement of 17 cards with new items and the rearrangement of items in terms of difficulty should alleviate some of the shortcomings of the original scale. Unfortunately, the reporting on the revision is such that one is unable to determine the extent to which it is an improvement over the original issue.

Items have been arranged in a new sequence on the basis of analysis of successive age groups, but no pertinent figures or tables are presented. The revised table of norms provokes some questions regarding item difficulty and the retention of certain items. For example, at the lower end of the scale there are several instances where three successive scores or two successive scores yield the same mental age. By contrast, differences of one point at the upper end of the scores listed result in mental age differences of two to five months each. Putting it another way, scores from 1 to 30 show a mental age difference of only 12 months while scores of 61 to 90 give a range of 90 months. It would seem feasible, on the basis of item analysis, to eliminate a number of items at the lower level and perhaps to add a few additional items at the upper level. Since there is no magic in having 100 items, there is little reason to retain items which add little or nothing to the effectiveness of the scale.

A new manual was not developed for the revised scale. A few pages of hectographed material are provided for insertion in the original manual. It would appear that a test that merits revision also merits a revised manual. The manual (1954) shows that the original scale was standardized on 957 normal children ranging from 3 to 12 years of age whereas the insertion (1959) states that "the revised edition....was administered to selected samples of boys and girls at each age level from 4 to 12."

On the original standardization, all children in the sample were given the Stanford-Binet. The revision makes comparison with the Stanford-Binet at the four- and five-year levels only. Children in grades 1 through 4 were given group tests of intelligence. These results were utilized in the norming process. It is not clear as to what procedure was used with children above the fourth grade. The reader is quite properly advised that the procedure utilized "will tend to perpetuate, in the Columbia norms, any systematic errors present in the norms for the other tests." The new norms for the revised Columbia should result in somewhat lower IQ's for high scoring subjects than did the original norms. No reference is made to the reliability of the revised edition.

Experience with the scale, as well as reports of research, reveal that younger children, retarded children, and deaf children have difficulty comprehending what the examiner wants when he asks them to indicate the one that does *not* belong. The concept of different or not belonging is much more elusive and subtle than is the concept of "same," "alike," or "go together." Perhaps this is why numerous young and/or handicapped children tend to perseverate in their responses. At the lower levels perseveration may be encouraged by the fact that the correct answer tends to appear on the same number consecutively, especially at the lower end of the scale. The tendency to perseverate could give an advantage or penalize the subject. For example, if the subject should by chance make the correct response (the first) on item 1 and should perseverate to the extent of the first 21 items, he would have 11 correct responses. Should he continue such perseveration through the next 13 items he would not have a single correct response.

In summary, the *Columbia Mental Maturity Scale* is a nonverbal test which is enjoyed by most children and one which can be administered in a relatively short time. The test has promise but needs not only further study and statistical analysis, but also an up-to-date manual. In spite of certain limitations, this test can be a useful part of a battery of tests, especially where nonverbal instruments are mandatory. Through observation of the child during the testing, the trained examiner can get quality judgments of the child and his method of attacking problems. The norms to interpret the performance of the child should be utilized with caution, especially at the extremes. The revised CMMS appears to be more satisfactory than the original version.

T. ERNEST NEWLAND, *Professor of Educational Psychology, University of Illinois, Urbana, Illinois.*

The 1959 revision differs from the 1954 edition in three ways: 17 cards have been replaced; the items have been rearranged in order of difficulty; and new norms have been established. The new cards reduce the sampling of acculturation (less reading, less demand on geographic and historical information). Order of difficulty has been determined for successive chronological year levels. The new norms reflect relationships between performances on the revised CMMS and (*a*) 1937 Stanford-Binet mental ages (196 kindergarten children), and (*b*) group test raw scores on children in grades 1–4 inclusive. The numbers of cases in the several group tests range for each grade level from 117 to 201. No criterion test was administered more than a month after the CMMS was given. Order of test administration was not randomized. On the school age children, the results on the different group tests were statistically synthesized by a method of "equipercentiles," the publishers forthrightly recognizing the assumption of the comparability of the group tests and the possibility of the resulting CMMS norms reflecting, or perpetuating, any systematic errors present in the norms of these group tests. No information on sex distribution is given on either the group or individual test populations. The preschool subjects were from the New Haven area and from Florida; the school age children were from New York City.

The new norms yield mental ages from 41 months to 167 months in contrast to the 29 to 195 range for the earlier standardization. From the four-year level upward, the scores yield mental age equivalents discernibly lower than on the 1954 form: 7 months lower at the five-year level; 12 months lower at the six-year level, and up to 34 months lower at the ten-year level. Below the four-year level, mental age equivalents are higher on the 1959 revision than on the 1954 norms. Regardless of the question of the general validity of the particular mental ages, the revision should yield smaller standard deviations than did its precursor. Whether the mental age equivalents will have the generality which is so often presumed will have to be determined by subsequent research. The 1959 CMMS mental ages show no discrimination between grade 3 and grade 4, although those for the group tests did. Just why the publishers present certain of their background normative data in terms of grade levels rather than in terms of the chronological ages of the children in those grades is not clear.

Four published studies have been made on nondisabled populations, in the four- to nine-year age range. The studies on disabled populations are quite diverse, both as to kind of disability and age range: institutionalized mentally retarded women (9 to 30 years of age); residential school deaf pupils (6–22); a mixed speech impaired group (3–15); and a public school, special class group of cerebral palsied children (7–16). Such heterogeneity, further complicated by a multiplicity of tests checked against (10) and by differing methodologies, provides little basis for generalizing about how the revised CMMS is performing. Sigmas on the revision appear to be relatively smaller than those of the 1954 form; they tend either to approximate or somewhat to exceed those for other tests (*25, 28–9, 31–2*). Revised CMMS IQ's correlated .88 with 1937 Binet IQ's on a speech impaired population (*31*); .39 with 1960 Binet IQ's on a nondisabled group of four- and five-year-olds (*28*), whereas correlations of .78 and .62 with 1937 Binet IQ's were found on these year levels, respectively—the latter apparently on the publisher's revision groups (*24*); .61 and .73 with Otis Alpha nonverbal IQ's on a deaf population (*34*); .68 to .70 with IQ's on the Wechsler's on female institutionalized defectives (*29*); .45 and .52, respectively, with WISC verbal and WISC performance IQ's on a nondisabled second grade population (*32*). Revised CMMS MA's correlated in the low .80's with MA's on the *Peabody Picture Vocabulary Test* and on the *Full Range Picture Vocabulary Test* on a cerebral palsied group, as compared with a .87 correlation with the *Van Alstyne Picture Vocabulary Test* (*25*). More significant for the educator is the fact that, in this latter study, the revised CMMS MA's tended to be one half to two years lower than those on the PPVT and on the FRPVT. Observations regarding the 1959 CMMS ranged from "improved" (*25*), to not yielding as good a single IQ measure as the (Norwegian) Binet and the Raven Matrices,[1] to "only partially successful" with six- to eight-year-old deaf children (*34*), to need for further scoring revision (*31*), to skepticism regarding its value below the four-year level (*25*), and to error in level placement of two cards (*28*).

As was true of the 1954 CMMS, the 1959 revision has been standardized only on a nonhandicapped population. Stemming from a desire to develop a psychometric device which could be used with the cerebral palsied (*14*), and later more generally "with subjects having serious verbal and motor impairment," the present revision, whatever its strengths and weaknesses, must be regarded as capable of throwing more light upon the learning aptitude of nondisabled children than on that of disabled children, particularly the cerebral palsied and the acoustically impaired. Any inference drawn regarding the psychologically sound usability of this device with either of these disabled groups has in its favor the fact that psychological processes essential to learning are being tapped. But the extent to which such an inference is valid in the case of the cerebral palsied, or even of the deaf, is yet to be determined. For children of the age for which this device is intended, the problem is not one of ascertaining whether it orders the members of a given age or grade group pretty much in the same manner as does some extant and validated device. Such a correlational approach can throw no light upon whether a CMMS mental age of, say, six should suggest educational expectations for the child earning it—as does, say, a 1960 Binet mental age of six. And this type of need is what is experienced by the teacher or occupational therapist of the cerebral palsied. It would seem that studies purporting to show high correlations between any pair of tests or to show that a level score (MA) on one is similar to a level score on another must be based upon the demonstrated psychological comparability of behavior samplings in the two tests, or upon the fact that the different behaviors sampled by the two devices have a sufficiently large underlying common factor (say, "*g*") to warrant a belief in reasonable interchangeability of the two level scores. The statistical treatment in the revision process and in connection with studies involving the use of

1 LANDMARK, MARGRETE, AND GRINDE, TURID. "Undersøkelse av en gruppe normale barn med forskjellige intelligensprøver." *Nordisk Psykologi* 14(4):171–85 '62. *

the 1959 CMMS has little, if any, bearing upon the concepts presented.

Actually, the studies on this test, as well as the publisher's revision data, throw only limited light upon possible educational or clinical values of the 1959 CMMS. Concurrent validity correlational approaches are highly involutional in nature; they yield one kind of information to the psychometrist but may actually mislead educators. Any inspection of the revision data would make one most cautious to use 1959 CMMS results below the 4-year or above the 10-year levels. The critical user of this test will be aware of the possibility that East Coast norms may not be generally applicable. The complete absence of any direct evidence on the reliability of the revision seems inexcusable. Those who are interested in the psychological processes by which subjects arrive at their responses to tests will have difficulty accepting certain of the publisher's unique correct responses, especially to four of the new ones: items 69, 76, 83, and 97. Those working clinically, rather than psychometrically, with subjects will be tempted to depart from the directions for the use of this test and let the subject give either volunteered verbal or required pointing responses, as mentioned by one user (*28*). The directions in the manual, prepared with speech impaired subjects in mind, could be adapted so that the subject could be helped to employ whatever manner of response would be effective in his communication process, whether it be speaking, pointing, looking, or some clear combination of these. More systematic study and preparation of this device is needed before it can have the clinical and educational (and even psychometric) value which lies largely dormant within it.

[518]

Crichton Vocabulary Scale. Ages 4–11; 1950; individual; 1 form; combined record form (4 pages) for this test and the complementary *Coloured Progressive Matrices;* manual (15 pages); 17*s.* 6*d.* per 50 record forms; 3*s.* 6*d.* per manual; 22*s.* 6*d.* per specimen set including 12 record forms and a specimen set of the *Coloured Progressive Matrices;* postage and purchase tax extra; (15–20) minutes; John C. Raven; H. K. Lewis & Co. Ltd. *

REFERENCES

1. Ravenette, A. T. "An Empirical Approach to the Assessment of Reading Retardation: 7, Vocabulary Level and Reading Attainment." *Brit J Ed Psychol* 31:96–103 F '61. * (*PA* 36:1KF96R)

Morton Bortner, *Chief Psychologist, Department of Physical Medicine and Rehabilitation, New York Medical College, New York, New York.*

This test is recommended by its author for use in conjunction with the *Coloured Progressive Matrices.* Its use is intended to supplement the Matrices with a measure of acquired information. The test consists of two sets of 40 words each, both of which are orally administered. Set one consists of the first 40 words of the *Mill Hill Vocabulary Scale.* Both sets combine to give a raw score which is translated into a percentile rank. The test is addressed to children of defective intelligence or for all children from 4 to 11 years of age.

Retest reliability coefficients are .87, .95, and .98 for three separate age groups. Concurrent validity is suggested by reported correlations of .84 and .79 with the Terman-Merrill scale, for six- and nine-year-olds, respectively.

The directions contain a flexibility of administration which raises some question as to the significance of any particular score. As usual, the child is encouraged to explain in his own words the meaning of each word. As is *not* usual in similar tests, "The person giving the test can say: 'You know what a cap is? What is it? Tell me what a cap is? What is a cap like? What do you do with a cap?' " Such leading questions clearly set up different tasks of varying difficulty and suggest that not merely "acquired information," but various aspects of comprehension, are being measured.

This test was constructed to fill a gap the author felt was left by the *Coloured Progressive Matrices.* The two together now constitute a battery for the measurement of two important aspects of intelligence. It is desirable that they be further supplemented by additional measures of different modes of intellectual functioning. As presently constituted these two tests offer no advantages over the more well known and clinically more useful WISC or Stanford-Binet.

For reviews by Charlotte Banks and W. D. Wall, see 4:337.

[519]

★**Diagnostic Performance Tests.** Adults; 1958; "behavior related to disturbances in cognitive function"; individual; 5 tests; manual (185 pages, see *1*) also presents instructions and norms for *Mitchell Vocabulary Test;* instructions listed below are largely excerpted from the manual; no data on reliability except for *c;* tentative norms; 35*s.* per manual; prices include purchase tax; postpaid within U.K.; Boris

Semeonoff and Eric Trist; distributed by National Foundation for Educational Research in England and Wales. *

a) SEMEONOFF-VIGOTSKY TEST. Adults of average and above average intelligence; adaptation of *Concept Formation Test* (see 4:35); conceptual thinking; 1 form (22 blocks); instructions (6 pages); 59*s.* per set of testing materials and instructions; (40–60) minutes.

b) TRIST-HARGREAVES TEST. Adults of average and below average intelligence; conceptual thinking; 1 form (12 pieces); instructions (4 pages); scoring sheet (1 page); 67*s.* per set of testing materials, instructions, and pad of 50 scoring sheets; [20–30] minutes.

c) TRIST-MISSELBROOK-KOHS TEST. Primarily adults (although age norms down to age 8 are also presented); modification of Kohs' *Block-Design Test;* 1 form (24 blocks); instructions (3 pages); scoring sheet (1 page); norms for immediate retesting of adults also presented; 116*s.* per set of testing materials, instructions, and pad of 50 scoring sheets; (15–20) minutes for test, (30) minutes including retest.

d) CARL HOLLOW SQUARE TEST. Primarily adults (although age norms down to age 8 are also presented); essentially the same as *Carl Hollow Square Scale* except for norms and some modifications in instructions; 1 form (29 blocks, identical with original Carl blocks); instructions (8 pages); scoring sheet (1 page); 182*s.* per set of testing materials, instructions, and pad of 50 scoring sheets; administration time not reported.

e) THE REVISED PASSALONG TEST. Adults; modification, especially in scoring system, of *The Passalong Test;* 1 form (set of blocks and 8 cards); instructions (8 pages); scoring sheet (1 page); 77*s.* per set of testing materials, instructions, and pad of 50 scoring sheets; administration time not reported.

REFERENCES

1. SEMEONOFF, BORIS, AND TRIST, ERIC. *Diagnostic Performance Tests: A Manual for Use With Adults.* London: Tavistock Publications Ltd., 1958. Pp. xvi, 176. *

H. GWYNNE JONES, *Senior Lecturer in Psychology, St. George's Hospital Medical School, London, England.*

This battery of tests is not intended only as an orthodox performance scale for the objective and quantitative assessment of nonverbal intellectual abilities. This function is made subordinate to the qualitative, diagnostic, clinical assessment of abnormalities and other personality traits. Thus each test is regarded as a miniature stress situation, and emphasis is laid on the interpersonal aspects of individual testing, on flexibility of administration procedures, and on the intuitive interpretation of the testee's style and methods of dealing with the material and problems. Deliberate and systematic use is made of prompting techniques akin to those employed by Goldstein and in Rorschach limits testing. The battery was used originally in a clinical situation but was developed and extended in a wartime military selection setting.

Five tests are included in the battery, but it is not intended that all five be administered to all subjects. Two are tests of conceptual thinking of the sorting variety: the Semeonoff-Vigotsky is similar to Haufmann and Kasanin's *Concept Formation Test,* while the *Trist-Hargreaves Test* is an original sorting test intended as an "easier alternative" to the former. Kohs' *Block-Design Test* appears in a greatly modified form designed to facilitate its use as a learning situation. The *Carl Hollow Square* "formboard" test is included in its original form, and Alexander's *Passalong Test* is modified only in terms of the scoring system in order to make it more suitable for adults. The difficulty range of the latter may also be extended by use of an additional item. The test materials are well made and packed in convenient boxes. Brief instructions for the administration of each test are provided as separate leaflets, but an examiner needs to have studied the book-length manual.

Critical evaluation is difficult owing to the multi-purpose nature of the battery. As a straightforward intelligence test it has serious shortcomings. No formal data concerning reliability and validity are given, except for the intercorrelations between the tests in the battery and between these and certain conventional intelligence tests. These correlations are generally low, but they are based on very restricted populations. Factor analyses provide evidence for "general intellectual," "spatial," and "conceptual" factors. Because of the intended flexibility of administration it must be assumed that tester reliability would be relatively low. The standardisation is tentative and, although a table of estimated general population percentile norms is provided, it is based on highly selected military populations.

However, the authors stress that the psychometric aspects of the battery are secondary to its diagnostic value. It is in terms of the latter that these techniques must be assessed, but the reviewer is given little upon which to base his judgment. Isolated examples of tentative interpretations of idiosyncratic behaviour are given; two illustrative cases are described in some detail, and four more in outline. The authors had hoped to carry out a full validation study on the military data, but security considerations prevented this and the only surviving evidence of validity is the general impression of all concerned that a rating based on these techniques had roughly similar status to any other single portion of an elaborate selection procedure.

Clearly, the *Diagnostic Performance Tests* do not provide a ready-made solution for any of the problems of psychological assessment, but this limitation does not imply that they should be dismissed. The work described in the manual is best regarded as a large scale pilot study, the results of which point to various directions in which further work might be fruitful. The basic notion that important aspects of personality are revealed in a person's approach to problems of an intellectual nature is a sound one. Semeonoff and Trist have made a serious and valuable attempt to combine qualitative and quantitative methods of assessment, and flexibility and rigour of approach. Their diagnostic battery could be employed with advantage for further research in this field.

For excerpts from reviews of the manual, see B449.

[520]

★**English Picture Vocabulary Test.** Ages 5-0 to 8-11, 7-0 to 11-11; 1962-63; derived from *Peabody Picture Vocabulary Test;* individual for Test 1; 1 form ('62); 2 levels: Test 1 (44 pages), Test 2 (47 pages); manual ('63, 39 pages); separate answer sheets (for group administration, Test 2 only) or record sheets (for individual administration) must be used; 8*s.* per test; 5*s.* per 25 record sheets; 5*s.* per 50 answer sheets; 6*d.* per scoring stencil for answer sheets; 5*s.* per manual; 13*s.* per specimen set of either level; prices include purchase tax; postpaid within U.K.; [15-45] minutes; M. A. Brimer and Lloyd M. Dunn; distributed by National Foundation for Educational Research in England and Wales. *

L. B. Birch, *Senior Lecturer in Educational Psychology, Institute of Education, University of Sheffield, Sheffield, England.*

These tests are derived from Dunn's *Peabody Picture Vocabulary Test* and make use of the same pictures. They are, however, completely reconstructed and standardised for English children. Their purpose is to assess levels of listening vocabulary independent of the ability to read. Although essentially for use with normal children, they can be used with children with gross motor impairment.

Each test is of 40 items, the task in each being to identify from among four pictures the one which corresponds to a spoken stimulus word. Test 1, for children under 9 years, is an individual test; Test 2 can be administered either individually or to a group and covers ages 7 to 11 years. In either case, administration, scoring, and scaling of results are all very simple and well able to be carried out by class teachers.

The manual is an exemplar which other test-makers could well follow. Instructions for the use of the tests are simple, complete, and unambiguous, the methods of construction and standardisation are clearly given, and conversion tables and norms are easy to read. The norms are expressed as normalised scores with a mean of 100 and standard deviation of 15; these can be converted by a table into percentile ranks. The standardisation sample consisted of some 3,200 children for Test 1 and more than 5,000 for Test 2, taken from some 90 schools selected to represent closely the total population of England and Wales. There was a small sex difference in favour of boys comparable with that found by other investigators, but separate norms are not provided.

The tests seem satisfactorily reliable. Kuder-Richardson estimates range from .87 to .92 for different age groups on Test 1 and from .88 to .96 on Test 2. Estimates of the standard error of measurement are given together with a note explaining its meaning in nonstatistical terms. Evidence for the validity of the tests is, of course, somewhat more limited. A convincing case is made out for the adequacy of their content validity. The construct they claim to represent is that of "listening vocabulary" but, as is fairly pointed out in the manual, performance may depend to some extent upon other cues than the spoken word, e.g., visual perceptual cues. The testmakers were aware of this possible contamination and took appropriate steps to avoid it. Correlation coefficients between scores on Test 2 and three other tests were high; that with Schonell's *Graded Word Reading Test* was .80 and with the WISC vocabulary was .76.

At this stage it is difficult to predict how valuable a knowledge of children's listening vocabulary may be to clinical practice and teaching, but these two new tests may provide very good tools for finding out.

Philip M. Levy, *Lecturer in Psychology, Institute of Education, University of Birmingham, Birmingham, England.*

This test, based on the *Peabody Picture Vocabulary Test,* is "designed to assess levels of listening vocabulary" in a manner which is "functionally independent of reading skill." The tester calls out a word and the child responds by identifying that one of four line drawings to which the word refers. Increase in difficulty, it is claimed, is brought about through the essential word difficulty and not by perceptual difficulty.

The two reusable test booklets are clearly printed and are strongly constructed as is appropriate for materials which are to be handled by young children. The separate answer sheets both for individual administration (Tests 1 and 2) and group administration (Test 2) are neatly designed. By contrast, the manual which serves both test booklets is an uneven product: the print is rather small (being photographically reduced typescript), and the early sequence of headings and subheadings is not as logically arranged as it could be. It does, however, contain adequate instructions for administration by teachers (the "experienced teacher"). The directions for scoring and the tables for score conversion to standardised scores and percentiles are clear and convenient.

The analyses appear to be particularly thorough in several respects: a large initial pool of items was used; distractors were checked for their distraction validity; reliabilities were calculated from samples other than those used for item analysis; most of the standardisation data were obtained by teachers, the potential users, and not by professional testers; and the essential equivalence of individual and group administration was established for Test 2 by a special experiment which took account of the order of testing.

Reliability data are presented in what perhaps is confusing variety: corrected split-half, Kuder-Richardson formula 20, and test-retest coefficients are variously reported for a number of age ranges and different samples. The coefficients do, however, show a high agreement among themselves, a typical value for a single year group being .88 for Test 1 and .92 for Test 2. The "eleven-plus" type of verbal ability and English tests gave correlations of .79 and .82, respectively, with Test 2 for the 11-year-old children. Correlations between the EPVT and other vocabulary tests range from .61 to .80, but these are for the full four-year age range of Test 2.

The test is said to be "diagnostically relevant to the understanding of reading difficulties and other verbal learning handicaps" and to provide "reading-free predictors of future language attainment." It may be too soon to demand experimental evidence to support these claims. Meanwhile, the test users, particularly the teachers, deserve some guidance in the manual about the interpretation and use of the scores so that the EPVT does not become just another test which claims but does not prove "diagnostic relevance" and "predictive value" with reference to reading skills. The test obviously deserves further research to support its use.

In summary then, the EPVT is a well produced and well documented instrument and deserves further research. The manual, however, needs an improved quality of production, a better layout, and some instructions on the use and interpretation of scores.

[521]

Full-Range Picture Vocabulary Test. Ages 2 and over; 1948; individual; Forms A, B, (16 cards, used with both forms); instructions (1 card); mimeographed norms (6 pages); record sheet (1 page) for each form; $7.50 per set of cards, instructions, norms, and sample record sheets; $1.10 per 25 record sheets; postage extra; specimen set not available; (10–15) minutes; Robert B. Ammons and Helen S. Ammons; Psychological Test Specialists. *

REFERENCES

1–10. See 4:340.
11. Katz, Irving Stanley. *A Validation Study of the Full-Range Picture Vocabulary Test at the Lower Grade Levels.* Master's thesis, Pennsylvania State College (State College, Pa.), 1951.
12. Tucker, D. A. *A Study of Adult Male Negroes With the Full-Range Picture Vocabulary Test.* Master's thesis, University of Louisville (Louisville, Ky.), 1951.
13. Coppinger, Neil W., and Ammons, R. B. "The Full-Range Picture Vocabulary Test: 8, A Normative Study of Negro Children." *J Clin Psychol* 8:136–40 Ap '52. * (*PA* 27:1952)
14. Allen, Robert M.; Thornton, Thomas E.; and Stenger, Charles A. "Ammons and Wechsler Test Performances of College and Psychiatric Subjects." *J Clin Psychol* 10:378–81 O '54. * (*PA* 29:4022)
15. Richardson, Elizabeth J., and Kobler, Frank J. "Testing the Cerebral Palsied." *Excep Child* 21:101–3+ D '54. * (*PA* 29:6108)
16. Sloan, William, and Bensberg, Gerard J. "An Exploratory Study of the Full-Range Picture Vocabulary Test With Mental Defectives." *Am J Mental Def* 58:481–5 Ja '54. * (*PA* 28:7700)
17. Smith, Louis M., and Fillmore, Arline R. "The Ammons FRPV Test and the WISC for Remedial Reading Cases." Abstract. *J Consult Psychol* 18:332 O '54. * (*PA* 29:5799, title only)
18. Allen, Robert M., and Collins, Marjorie G. "Suggestions for the Adaptive Administration of Intelligence Tests for Those With Cerebral Palsy: Part 1, Administration of the Ammons Full-Range Picture Test, Columbia Mental Maturity Test, Raven's Progressive Matrices and Leiter International Performance Scale." *Cerebral Palsy R* 16:11–4+ My–Je '55. * (*PA* 30:3284)
19. Allen, Robert M.; Thornton, Thomas E.; and Stenger, Charles A. "A Note on the Ammons Full-Range Picture Vocabulary Test as a Screening Device for College Students." *Psychol Rep* 1:459–60 D '55. * (*PA* 30:6329)
20. Rabin, A. I.; King, G. F.; and Ehrmann, J. C. "Vocabulary Performance of Short-Term and Long-Term Schizophrenics." *J Abn & Social Psychol* 50:255–8 Mr '55. * (*PA* 30:1361)
21. Sanders, Christopher C., Jr. *The Reliability and "Validity" of the Ammons Full-Range Picture Vocabulary Test.* Master's thesis, University of Tennessee (Knoxville, Tenn.), 1955.
22. Allen, Robert M.; Thornton, Thomas E.; and Stenger, Charles A. "The Full-Range Picture Vocabulary

Test Compared With Two Short Forms of the Wechsler Scale." *J Ed Res* 50:133–7 O '56. * (*PA* 32:933)
23. TEMPLIN, MILDRED C. Chap. 6, "Vocabulary," pp. 105–20. In her *Certain Language Skills in Children.* University of Minnesota, Institute of Child Welfare Monograph Series, No. 26. Minneapolis, Minn.: University of Minnesota Press, 1957. Pp. xviii, 183. * (*PA* 31:7556)
24. BLACK, A. D., AND GRINDER, R. E. "Reliability of the Ammons FRPV Test and the Relationship Between Two Measures of Verbal Comprehension for a Japanese-American Sample." *Psychol Rep* 5:261–3 Je '59. * (*PA* 34:2938)
25. BLATT, SIDNEY J. "Recall and Recognition Vocabulary: Implications for Intellectual Deterioration." *A.M.A. Arch Gen Psychiatry* 1:473–6 N '59. * (*PA* 34:6005)
26. CONDELL, JAMES F. "Note on the Use of the Ammons Full-Range Picture Vocabulary Test With Retarded Children." *Psychol Rep* 5:150 Mr '59. * (*PA* 34:1408)
27. DUNN, LLOYD M., AND HARLEY, RANDALL K. "Comparability of Peabody, Ammons, Van Alstyne, and Columbia Test Scores With Cerebral Palsied Children." *Excep Child* 26:70–4 O '59. * (*PA* 35:3733)
28. WINITZ, HARRIS. "Relationships Between Language and Nonlanguage Measures of Kindergarten Children." *J Speech & Hearing Res* 2:387–91 D '59. * (*PA* 34:5896)
29. CARSON, ARNOLD S., AND RABIN, A. I. "Verbal Comprehension and Communication in Negro and White Children." *J Ed Psychol* 51:47–51 Ap '60. * (*PA* 35:2049)
30. FISHER, GARY M.; SHOTWELL, ANNA M.; AND YORK, DOROTHY H. "Comparability of the Ammons Full-Range Picture Vocabulary Test With the WAIS in the Assessment of Intelligence of Mental Retardates." *Am J Mental Def* 64:995–9 My '60. * (*PA* 35:6830)
31. MORGAN, ELMER F., JR. "Efficacy of Two Tests in Differentiating Potentially Low From Average and High First Grade Achievers." *J Ed Res* 53:300–4 Ap '60. *
32. NORMAN, RALPH D., AND MEAD, DONALD F. "Spanish-American Bilingualism and the Ammons Full-Range Picture-Vocabulary Test." *J Social Psychol* 51:319–30 My '60. * (*PA* 34:7650)
33. SCOGGINS, BETTY JOANNE. *A Comparative Study of the Full-Range Picture Vocabulary Test and the Peabody Picture Vocabulary Test.* Master's thesis, Vanderbilt University (Nashville, Tenn.), 1960.
34. STERNE, DAVID M. "Use of the Ammons FRPV With the Long-Term Chronically Ill." *J Clin Psychol* 16:192–3 Ap '60. * (*PA* 36:2HD92S)
35. SMITH, BESSIE S. "The Relative Merits of Certain Verbal and Non-Verbal Tests at the Second-Grade Level." *J Clin Psychol* 17:53–4 Ja '61. * (*PA* 37:3595)
36. MEYERS, E.; ORPET, R. E.; ATTWELL, A. A.; AND DINGMAN, H. F. *Primary Abilities at Mental Age Six.* Monographs of the Society for Research in Child Development, Vol. 27, No. 1, Serial No. 82. Lafayette, Ind.: Child Development Publications, 1962. Pp. 40. * (*PA* 38:8462)
37. SCHUELL, HILDRED; JENKINS, JAMES J.; AND CARROLL, JOHN B. "A Factor Analysis of the Minnesota Test for Differential Diagnosis of Aphasia." *J Speech & Hearing Res* 5:349–69 D '62. * (*PA* 37:5358)
38. HO, DAVID, AND WHITE, DELILAH T. "Use of the Full-Range Picture Vocabulary Test With the Mentally Retarded." *Am J Mental Def* 67:761–4 Mr '63. * (*PA* 38:1275)
39. MOED, GEORGE; WIGHT, BYRON W.; AND JAMES, PATRICIA. "Intertest Correlations of the Wechsler Intelligence Scale for Children and Two Picture Vocabulary Tests." *Ed & Psychol Meas* 23:359–63 su '63. * (*PA* 38:960)
40. SIMKINS, LAWRENCE, AND BURGIN, JUDITH. "A Comparison of Individual and Group Administrations of the Full-Range Picture Vocabulary Test." *J Ed Res* 57:189–92 D '63. *

For reviews by William D. Altus and William M. Cruickshank, see 4:340.

[522]

Gesell Developmental Schedules, 1940 Series. Ages 4 weeks to 6 years; 1925–49; individual; 1 form ('49); manuals: *The First Five Years of Life* ('40, see *20*), *Developmental Diagnosis, Second Edition* ('47, see *31*), and *Infant and Child in the Culture of Today* ('43, see *34*, which is for use with behavior day charts and which contains supplementary normative data); general instructions booklet ('49, 15 pages); 10 record forms: Forms 1A (for ages 4–8 weeks), 1B (for ages 12–20 weeks), 1C (for ages 24–32 weeks), 1D (for ages 36–44 weeks), 1E (for ages 48–56 weeks), 1F (for ages 15–21 months), 1G (for ages 21–30 months), 1H (for ages 30–42 months), 1I (for ages 42–54 months), 1J (for ages 54–72 months), ['40, 1 page]; analytic forms: Forms 2A (postural behavior), 2B (prehensory behavior), 2C (perceptual behavior), 2D (adaptive behavior), 2E (language-social behavior), 2F (analytic scoring sheet), ['40, 1 page]; observation record, Form 3 ['40, 1 page]; interview sheet, Form 4 ['40, 2 pages]; summary sheet, Form 5 ['40, 1 page]; behavior day chart, form 6 ['43, 2 pages]; preliminary behavior inventory, Form 7 ['43, 1 page]; $85 per set of testing materials, carrying case, and record forms; 90¢ per 25 record forms except form 6; $1.50 per 25 behavior day charts (form 6); 90¢ per specimen set of record forms; postpaid; (20–40) minutes; Arnold Gesell and others; Psychological Corporation. *

REFERENCES

1–28. See 3:276.
29–33. See 4:341.
34. GESELL, ARNOLD, AND ILG, FRANCES L.; IN COLLABORATION WITH JANET LEARNED AND LOUISE B. AMES. *Infant and Child in the Culture of Today: The Guidance of Development in Home and Nursery School.* New York: Harper & Brothers, 1943. Pp. xiii, 399. *
35. SILVER, ARCHIE A. "Diagnostic Value of Three Drawing Tests for Children." *J Pediatrics* 37:129–43 Jl '50. * (*PA* 25:3191)
36. GESELL, ARNOLD. "Gesell Developmental Schedules," pp. 485–94. (*PA* 27:7767) In *Contributions Toward Medical Psychology: Theory and Psychodiagnostic Methods, Vol. 2.* Edited by Arthur Weider. New York: Ronald Press Co., 1953. Pp. xi, 459–885. *
37. SIEVERS, DOROTHY J., AND NORMAN, RALPH D. "Some Suggestive Results in Psychometric Testing of the Cerebral Palsied With Gesell, Binet, and Wechsler Scales." *J Genetic Psychol* 82:69–90 Mr '53. * (*PA* 27:7974)
38. MACRAE, JOHN M. "Retests of Children Given Mental Tests as Infants." *J Genetic Psychol* 87:111–9 S '55. * (*PA* 30:6976)
39. SIMON, ABRAHAM J., AND BASS, LIBBY G. "Toward a Validation of Infant Testing." *Am J Orthopsychiatry* 26:340–50 Ap '56. * (*PA* 31:4713)
40. WITTENBORN, J. R.; WITH THE COLLABORATION OF MYRTLE A. ASTRACHAN, MARJORIE W. DEGOOYER, W. WALLACE GRANT, IRMA Z. JANOFF, ROBERT B. KUGEL, BARBARA J. MYERS, ANNALIESE RIESS, AND ELLERY C. RUSSELL. "A Study of Adoptive Children: 2, The Predictive Validity of the Yale Developmental Examination of Infant Behavior." *Psychol Monogr* 70(2):59–92 '56. * (*PA* 31:5860)
41. WOLK, SHIRLEY MAE. *The Gesell Technique as Applied to Twenty-Five Children in a Study Clinic for Mental Retardation.* Master's thesis, Immaculate Heart College (Los Angeles, Calif.), 1957.
42. ALLEN, ROBERT M. "Suggestions for the Adaptive Administration of Intelligence Tests for Those With Cerebral Palsy: Part 2, Administration of the Vineland Social Maturity Scale, the Gesell Preliminary Behavior Inventory, and the Cattell Infant Intelligence Scale." *Cerebral Palsy R* 19:6–7 Mr–Ap '58. * (*PA* 33:8853)
43. GARDENER, D. BRUCE, AND SWIGER, MARYBELLE K. "Developmental Status of Two Groups of Infants Released for Adoption." *Child Develop* 29:521–30 D '58. * (*PA* 34:4120)
44. KNOBLOCH, HILDA; SAYERS, MARTIN P.; AND HOWARD, WILLIAM H. R. "The Relationships Between Findings in Pneumoencephalograms and Clinical Behavior." *Pediatrics* 22:13–9 Jl '58. * See also 46.
45. DRILLIEN, CECIL MARY. "A Longitudinal Study of the Growth and Development of Prematurely and Maturally Born Children: Part 3, Mental Development." *Arch Dis Childh* 34:37–45 F '59. *
46. KUGEL, ROBERT B. "Pneumoencephalograms and Clinical Behavior." Letter. *Pediatrics* 23:174–5 Ja '59. * Criticism of 44 above. Reply by Hilda Knobloch. *Pediatrics* 23:175–8 Ja '59. *
47. RUESS, A. L.; DOLLY, ANNE; AND LIS, EDWARD F. "The Gesell Developmental Schedules and the Physically Handicapped Child." *Am J Occup Ther* 13:117–24+ My–Je '59. * (*PA* 34:4769)
48. ILLINGWORTH, R. S. *The Development of the Infant and the Young Child: Normal and Abnormal.* Edinburgh, Scotland: E. & S. Livingston Ltd., 1960. Pp. viii, 318. *
49. KNOBLOCH, HILDA, AND PASAMANICK, BENJAMIN. "An Evaluation of the Consistency and Predictive Value of the 40 Week Gesell Developmental Schedule," pp. 10–31; discussion, pp. 32–41. (*PA* 36:1FB10K) In *Child Development and Child Psychiatry.* Edited by Charles Shagass and Benjamin Pasamanick. Psychiatric Research Reports 13. Washington, D.C.: American Psychiatric Association, 1960. Pp. ix, 225. *
50. DRILLIEN, CECIL MARY. "A Longitudinal Study of the Growth and Development of Prematurely and Maturally Born Children: Part 7, Mental Development 2–5 Years." *Arch Dis Childh* 36:233–40 Je '61. *
51. ESCALONA, SIBYLLE K., AND MORIARTY, ALICE. "Prediction of Schoolage Intelligence From Infant Tests." *Child Develop* 32:597–605 S '61. * (*PA* 36:4FE97E)
52. ILLINGWORTH, R. S. "The Predictive Value of Developmental Tests in the First Year, With Special Reference

to the Diagnosis of Mental Subnormality." *J Child Psychol & Psychiatry* 2:210–5 N '61. * (*PA* 36:5JI10I)
53. PEASE, DAMARIS; ROSAUER, JOSEPHINE KEEFE; AND WOLINS, LEROY. "Reliability of Three Infant Developmental Scales Administered During the First Year of Life." *J Genetic Psychol* 98:295–8 Je '61. * (*PA* 36:2FB95P)
54. PELZ, KURT S.; AMES, LOUISE B.; AND PIKE, FRANCES. "Measurement of Psychologic Function in Geriatric Patients." *J Am Geriatrics Soc* 9:740–54 S '61. *
55. SHARE, JACK; WEBB, ALLEN; AND KOCH, RICHARD. "A Preliminary Investigation of the Early Developmental Status of Mongoloid Infants." *Am J Mental Def* 66:238–41 S '61. * (*PA* 36:3JI38S)
56. KNOBLOCH, HILDA, AND PASAMANICK, BENJAMIN. "The Developmental Behavioral Approach to the Neurologic Examination in Infancy." *Child Develop* 33:181–98 Mr '62. * (*PA* 37:823)
57. AMES, LOUISE BATES, AND ILG, FRANCES L. "The Gesell Incomplete Man Test as a Measure of Developmental Status." *Genetic Psychol Monogr* 68:247–307 N '63. *
58. KOCH, RICHARD; SHARE, JACK; WEBB, ALLEN; AND GRALIKER, BETTY V. "The Predictability of Gesell Developmental Scales in Mongolism." *J Pediatrics* 62:93–7 Ja '63. *
59. LIDDICOAT, RENÉE, AND KOZA, CONSTANCE. "Language Development in African Infants." *Psychologia Africana* 10:108–16 D '63. * (*PA* 38:8009)
60. WILSON, MIRIAM G. "Gesell Developmental Testing." Editorial. *J Pediatrics* 62:162–4 Ja '63. *

EMMY E. WERNER, *Assistant Professor of Child Development, University of California, Davis, California.*

Since the last review in *The Third Mental Measurements Yearbook,* the *Gesell Developmental Schedules* have been used fairly extensively as a criterion measure in the follow-up of infants with complications at birth or as predictors of intellectual development in the preschool and early school years.

Information on standardization procedures, norms, and instructions for administration and scoring of the Gesell Schedules is scattered in three volumes: standardization data in *The Psychology of Early Growth* (*13*), which is out of print, instructions for the administration and scoring of the Schedules from 1 to 6 years in *The First Five Years of Life* (*20*), and instructions for the Schedules from 4 through 56 weeks in *Developmental Diagnosis* (*31*). It would be extremely helpful if the information considered essential for a test manual according to the APA recommendations could be assembled in one concise volume. This would also help lower the combined cost of test and manuals which now approaches $100.

This reviewer has noticed that the enthusiasm for the merits of the *Gesell Developmental Schedules* has continued to run high in the medical profession, especially among pediatricians and neurologists. Most psychologists, while not discounting the merits of the careful and detailed descriptions of a young child's behavior, have their enthusiasm dampened by the awareness that the Schedules lack many of the qualifications which would be considered *essential* for a psychological test or diagnostic technique.

THE STANDARDIZATION SAMPLE. There is a real need for a restandardization of the Gesell Schedules on a large sample of children representative of United States infants of the 1960's. There is reason to suspect: (*a*) that individual variation within the small groups of children on whom the Schedules were originally standardized may have unduly influenced item placement; (*b*) that over a period of almost two generations there have been changes in the "typical" pattern of infant behavior, probably due to better nutritional status, better pediatric care, and changed child rearing practices (Knobloch and Pasamanick, *49,* find a shift toward earlier "achievement" in both gross motor and personal-social behavior of 39-, 40-, and 41-week-old infants on samples 10 times as large as Gesell's original sample); and (*c*) that there are significant differences in the development of infants drawn from different socioeconomic strata and ethnic stock.

RELIABILITY. Knobloch and Pasamanick report the only reliability data this reviewer has found—correlations between the Developmental Quotients obtained by the examiner and several observers (all trained by the same examiner). Two sets of correlations were computed: one for clinical cases (one third abnormal), the other for normal infants participating in a longitudinal follow-up study. The *r*'s reported vary from .90 to .99 on samples of 40-week-old infants with *n*'s ranging from 12 to 44. These tester-observer reliability coefficients are surprisingly high, considering the vagueness of the scoring method. There is a pressing need for additional reliability studies, both tester-observer and test-retest, at different age levels.

CONCURRENT VALIDITY. Knobloch and Pasamanick report a high correlation between the *Gesell Developmental Schedules* for older children (three years old) and the Stanford-Binet ($r = .87, n = 195$). This is not surprising since a number of items in the Gesell Schedules at the three-year level are taken directly from the Binet.

Less encouraging is a finding by Gardner (*43*) in a study of 128 infants, age 4–92 days (mean 32 days). He obtains a moderately high *negative* correlation (−.64) between the DQ and CA, demonstrating the inadequate discriminative power of the Gesell Schedules during the early weeks of infancy.

PREDICTIVE VALIDITY. Follow-up studies of infants tested below eight months have shown little predictive value. Escalona and Moriarty (*51*) find no relationship between Gesell scores of normal infants tested between 3 weeks and 33 weeks and retested between 6 years and 9 years. Share, Webb, and Koch (*55*) find that the DQ's for mongoloids tested at median age of 7.5 months are not good predictors of later DQ's. In contrast, DQ's of the same 16 mongoloids tested at median age 17.0 months and median age 29.5 months yield a correlation of .86.

Knobloch and Pasamanick report an r of .51 between the Gesell scores of 40-week-old infants and their 3-year Gesell scores (.74 for 48 abnormal infants in this group, .43 for the 147 normal cases). Correlations between 40-week Gesell scores and 3-year Binet are in the same range ($r = .48$, $n = 195$). The same authors report a correlation of .50 between 40-week Gesell scores and 7-year intelligence test scores. Simon and Bass (*39*) obtained what seem essentially similar results by classifying infants' Gesell scores into three categories (dull normal and defective; average; above average and superior). Contingency coefficient correlations vary between .45 and .52 for children tested in infancy on the Gesell and retested after age 5 with the S-B or WISC.

SUMMARY EVALUATION AND RECOMMENDATION. The *Gesell Developmental Schedules* should not be considered as an infant and preschool intelligence test, but as detailed observational schedules for a young child's developmental status. They are in need of an extensive revision on a large and representative sample of present-day infants. In the hands of a carefully trained examiner who is aware of their limitations (including questionable reliability of scoring method) the Gesell Schedules can tell us a certain amount about the *present* position of the child in relation to developmental expectancies. Predictions about *future* development, especially intellectual development, cannot be made with the certainty which Gesell has us believe (see p. 116 in *Developmental Diagnosis*). Contrary to his assumption, evidence accumulated suggests that predictions regarding future developmental status are extremely hazardous in the first half, and not much better in the second half, of the first year. After that a gross classification of the infant's development into categories of below average, average, and above average bears a moderate relationship to preschool and school age intelligence test scores (.40–.60), too low for certainty about an individual case.

Nancy Bayley is presently undertaking a restandardization of her California Scales on a large sample of children of different ethnic stocks, items selected after careful test-retest and tester-observer reliability studies. Until the revised Bayley scale is on the market, this reviewer would prefer to use the *Cattell Infant Intelligence Scale* in the range from birth through two years and the *Stanford-Binet Intelligence Scale,* 1960 edition, thereafter.

For reviews by Nancy Bayley and Florence M. Teagarden, see 3:276. For excerpts from related book reviews, see 3:277–80 and 40:B912–6.

[523]

The Griffiths Mental Development Scale for Testing Babies From Birth to Two Years. 1951–55; 6 scores: locomotor, personal-social, hearing and speech, eye and hand, performance, total; individual; 1 form ('54); manual ('54, see *2*); revised record booklet ('55, 8 pages); test materials sold only to persons taking author's lecture course or a guidance course by correspondence; fee for lecture course, 315*s.*; fee for guidance course, 210*s.*; postpaid; 252*s.* per set of testing materials; 12*s.* per 25 record booklets; 30*s.* per manual; postage extra; [20–40] minutes; Ruth Griffiths; the Author. *

REFERENCES

1–3. See 5:404.
4. WOOLF, L. I.; GRIFFITHS, RUTH; MONCRIEFF, ALAN; COATES, STEPHEN; AND DILLISTONE, F. "Dietary Treatment of Phenylketonuria." *Arch Dis Childh* 33:31–45 F '58. *
5. GRIFFITHS, RUTH. "The Extension of the Griffiths Mental Development Scale to Cover the Years From Two to Seven." Abstract. *B Brit Psychol Soc* 41:44 My '60. *
6. HINDLEY, C. B. "The Griffiths Scale of Infant Development: Scores and Predictions From 3 to 18 Months." *J Child Psychol & Psychiatry* 1:99–112 Je '60. *
7. HINDLEY, C. B. "Social Class Influences on the Development of Ability in the First Five Years," pp. 29–41. (*PA* 37:4717) In *Child and Education.* Proceedings of the XIV International Congress of Applied Psychology, Vol. 3. Copenhagen, Denmark: Munksgaard, Ltd., 1962. Pp. 197. *

C. B. HINDLEY, *Research Psychologist, Centre for the Study of Human Development, Institutes of Education and Child Health, University of London, London, England.*

The author clearly set herself the task of "measuring intelligence" in babies and is hopeful of the possibility of doing so, but she also acknowledges doubts as to whether in fact her test procedure "can claim to measure this innate ability as efficiently as tests for older subjects." Hers is the only infant test standardized on British children.

The Griffiths scale consists of a total of 260

items covering the first two years. Like the Stanford-Binet it is an age scale, with three items for each week of credit in the first year, and two items per week in the second year. As the ceiling of the test is two years of developmental age, brighter children will reach this level from about the age of 18 months. The author suggests in such cases that the Stanford-Binet should be used and mental age credits of both tests combined to obtain an MA. A drawback here is that the standard deviations of the two tests differ. Quotients are obtained from the developmental ages.

The author attaches a great deal of importance to the five subscales: Locomotor, Personal-Social, Hearing and Speech, Eye and Hand, and Performance. The test contains an equal number of items in each subscale for each age period, and therefore it is possible to calculate separate DA's and quotients for the subscales. Although the author is hopeful about the value of profiles and presents some very convincing ones of children with marked deafness, blindness, or other defects, she also recognizes the possibility, suggested by Gesell, that development of normal children may follow a spiral course, with a child centring his interests in one direction at one period, only to be followed by progress in another direction a little later.

The test instructions are full, and the tester is sensibly enjoined to capitalize on the child's interests, rather than following any definite order of presenting the items. While the majority of items are tested for, in quite a number of instances reliance has to be placed on mothers' testimony, e.g., items regarding the number of different sounds the infant makes, whether he enjoys a bath, and whether he listens to music. A good deal of use is made of particular sorts of apparatus, such as formboards in the Performance Scale in the second year, so that a child who is not interested in them is likely to be penalized.

The main criticisms that can be made of the scale apply in greater or lesser degree to other baby tests. The standardization sample, consisting of children from a London borough and largely from infant welfare clinics and day nurseries, can be regarded neither as a random sample nor as a representative sample of any defined population. Samples ranged from 16 to 31 children at each month of age, amounting to a total of 571 children, some of whom were tested twice.

The scale was constructed from a wider number of items, some derived from other infant tests and some resulting from the author's own observations of infants. By a "cut and fit" procedure, items were allocated to appropriate ages in each subscale. A table is presented showing that mean numbers of items passed, both on the global scale and the subscales at each age, conform fairly clearly to the required numbers. After correction of MA's and CA's of eight months or less for "floor effect" (lack of credit for earlier items when testing is begun at the one-month level), the mean GQ ("general quotient") is 99.7 and the standard deviations of GQ's are similar at different ages, being about 12 points.

Unfortunately, no evidence is presented concerning how the various items correlate with the test as a whole, nor is there any evidence, such as a factor analysis might provide, to support the breakdown of the items into the five subscales. It is difficult to see much difference between the Performance and Eye and Hand Scales. Again, certain speech items are to be found in the Hearing and Speech Scale and others in the Personal-Social Scale; the latter seems a mixture of developmental items and others which depend on special training, such as "Bowel control complete" at 19 months. There is no table of standard deviations of the subscales, which makes the significance of any particular partial quotient the more doubtful.

The big question concerning baby tests is, of course, how far they are predictive of later intelligence. Griffiths does not make any great claims here, but she reports the rather astonishing value of $r = .87$ between first and second testing over an interval of an average of 30 weeks (range 7 to 70 weeks) on 60 cases in the standardization sample. This is far higher than other workers have reported with other infant tests, or than figures reported by the reviewer (*6*) for the Griffiths scale, and would be considered eminently satisfactory on such a standard instrument as the Stanford-Binet. As all the tests were given by the author alone, one wonders whether independent testers would have reached such a high level of agreement. Longer term predictions reported by the reviewer (correlations between Griffiths GQ's at ages 6 months or 18 months and Stanford-Binet IQ's at age 5 years) were not sufficiently high for practical purposes (.32 and .40, respectively), though they were somewhat higher than those reported for other tests (7).

It is quite possible that higher levels of prediction could be obtained among subjects with definite defects, such as blindness or spasticity, but this remains to be demonstrated.

The test has an obvious value for British users, despite the rather inadequate information on many points, because it is the only infant test standardized on a British population. For other users it has the advantage of having an unusually large number of items, equal numbers of items for each subscale at each age, and reasonable stability of mean quotients and standard deviations from age to age. As with other tests of infant development it is wise to consider the Griffiths scale as assessing the current level of development, and it would be unwise to rely on it for prediction among normal children. It can also be regarded as a suitable device for picking out cases of gross handicap. Insufficient evidence is given regarding the internal consistency and standard deviations of subscales, so that one must advise that profiles be used only with caution and be regarded as providing pointers to be confirmed by other means.

For a review by Nancy Bayley, see 5:404.

[524]

★**Kahn Intelligence Tests: Experimental Form.** Ages 1 month and over, particularly the verbally or culturally handicapped; 1960; uses same test objects as *Kahn Test of Symbol Arrangement;* main scale plus 6 optional scales: brief scale, concept formation, recall, motor coordination, scale for use with the deaf, scale for use with the blind; individual; 1 form (16 plastic objects); record form (4 pages); manual (34 pages, reprint of *2* below); $26 per set of testing materials including 50 record forms and manual; $2.50 per manual; cash orders postpaid; administration time not reported; Theodore C. Kahn; Psychological Test Specialists. *

REFERENCES

1. Kahn, T. C. "A New 'Culture-Free' Intelligence Test." *Psychol Rep* 6:239–42 Ap '60. * (*PA* 35:6402)

2. Kahn, Theodore C. "Kahn Intelligence Tests: Experimental Form (KIT:EXP)." *Percept & Motor Skills* 10:123–53 Ap '60. * (*PA* 35:6383)

[525]

***The Leiter Adult Intelligence Scale.** Adults; 1949–59; revision of the *Leiter-Partington Adult Performance Scale;* includes *The FR-CR Test, Pathways Test, The Leiter Adaptation of Arthur's Stencil Design Test,* and *The Leiter Adaptation of the Painted Cube Test;* individual; 3 scores: language, nonlanguage, total; 1 form ['56]; mimeographed manual ['56, 55 pages]; revised record booklet ('59, 4 pages); $30.50 per set of testing materials, 100 record booklets, and manual; $5 per 100 record booklets; $2 per manual; postage extra; (40–60) minutes; Russell Graydon Leiter; C. H. Stoelting Co. *

REFERENCES

1–4. See 4:350.

5. International Psychological Service Center. "The FR-CR Test With Quantitative Scores and a Qualitative Check List for Clinical Use in the Evaluation of Brain Injury." *Psychol Service Center J* 1:52–61 S '49. * (*PA* 24:2918)

6. Leiter, Russell Graydon. "The Leiter Adaptation of Arthur's Stencil Design Test." *Psychol Service Center J* 1:62–8+ S '49. * (*PA* 24:2920)

7. Leiter, Russell Graydon. "The Leiter Adaptation of the Painted Cube Test." *Psychol Service Center J* 1:29–45 S '49. * (*PA* 24:2921)

8. Partington, John E. "Detailed Instructions for Administering Partington's Pathways Test." *Psychol Service Center J* 1:46–8 S '49. * (*PA* 24:3215)

9. Partington, John E., and Leiter, Russell Graydon. "Partington's Pathways Test." *Psychol Service Center J* 1:9–20 Mr '49. * (*PA* 23:5528)

10. Watson, Neal. "A Qualitative Check List for the Clinical Use of Partington's Pathways Test in the Evaluation of Brain Injury." *Psychol Service Center J* 1:49–51 S '49. * (*PA* 24:3351)

11. Watson, Neal. "A Qualitative Check List for the Clinical Use of the Leiter Adaptation of Arthur's Stencil Design Test in the Evaluation of Brain Injury." *Psychol Service Center J* 1:69–70 S '49. * (*PA* 24:3350)

12. Cozan, Lee W. "Industrial Use of the Partington Pathways Test." *J Appl Psychol* 35:112–3 Ap '51. * (*PA* 25:8077)

13. Leiter, Russell Graydon. "The Leiter Adult Intelligence Scale." *Psychol Service Center J* 3:1–52 D '51. *

14. Sydow, Donald Wayne. *A Psychometric Differentiation Between Functional Psychotics and Non-Psychotics With Organic Brain Damage.* Doctor's thesis, University of Minnesota (Minneapolis, Minn.), 1953. (*DA* 13:1267)

15. Cozan, Lee W. "Short Mental Ability Test for Industrial Use." *J Personnel Adm & Ind Rel* 1:191–4 '54. * (*PA* 29:8054)

16. Payne, R. W.; Mattussek, P.; and George, E. I. "An Experimental Study of Schizophrenic Thought Disorder." *J Mental Sci* 105:627–52 Jl '59. * (*PA* 34:6384)

17. Payne, R. W., and Hewlett, J. H. G. Chap. 1, "Thought Disorder in Psychotic Patients," pp. 3–104. In *Experiments in Personality: Vol. 2, Psychodiagnostics and Psychodynamics.* Edited by H. J. Eysenck. London: Routledge & Kegan Paul Ltd., 1960. Pp. viii, 333. *

18. Vinson, David B. "Objectivity in the Assessment of Psychobiologic Decline." *Vita Hum* 4(3):134–42 '62. *

19. Vinson, David B., and Gaitz, Charles M. "The Objective Measurement of Psychobiologic Decline: A Preliminary Report," pp. 578–82. In *Social and Psychological Aspects of Aging.* Proceedings of the Fifth Congress of the International Association of Gerontology. Edited by Clark Tibbitts and Wilma Donahue. New York: Columbia University Press, 1962. Pp. xviii, 952. *

Paul C. Davis, *Dean and Professor of Psychology, Los Angeles Pacific College, Los Angeles, California.*

The author states frankly that he revised the original (1949) scale to its present form (1959) because it was criticized for lack of language content. To the Free Recall–Controlled Recall test he has added two more tests, Similarities–Differences and Digits Forward and Backward, to round out a language battery of three tests. The nonlanguage battery consists of the same three tests used in the original scale: Pathways, Stencil Design, and Painted Cubes. As was the original scale, the revised scale is designed only as an individual instrument primarily for clinical use.

Several advantages are likely to recommend the scale to potential users: (*a*) it is relatively easy to administer and simple to score, (*b*) it is economical of time, requiring an average of 40 minutes for administration, and (*c*) the material is varied and arouses considerable inherent interest in adults. The author also lists as a recommending characteristic the fact that one subscale can be administered, if necessary, entirely without verbal directions.

Certain minor technical errors may confuse the first-time user of the scale. In the Painted Cube test, the table for scoring Part 1 appears in the midst of instructions for Part 2. Also, tables for all three parts show minimum credits for up to 119, 239, and 239 seconds while maximum times are 120, 240, and 240. How are the exact maximum times to be scored? The reviewer would suggest revising the terminal limit of the last interval up to the maximum time.

Reliability data (unidentified K-R) are given, based on an *n* of 256. Respectable reliability is indicated for all tests except Digits (.65) and Stencil Design (.67). These latter low reliabilities call into special question the author's providing equivalent IQ's for raw scores on individual tests. Although the author says this is done so the examiner "can have some idea of how the subject is progressing.... and whether....performance on any given test is above average, average, or below average," this purpose could as well be served by converting raw scores to scaled scores with an arbitrary mean and standard deviation, a device employed by many test authors. The sophisticated user will of course be wary of the unreliability of individual test IQ's, but the author does a disservice by including conversion tables without warning to the user.

Using an *n* of 256, the author computed intercorrelations among the subtests, language and nonlanguage subscales, total scale, and the Stanford-Binet. Subtest correlations with the S-B ranged from .57 (Painted Cubes) to .75 (Similarities-Differences), while total language correlated .82, nonlanguage, .78, and total scale, .88, with the same criterion. Although of course the Stanford-Binet is not the ultimate criterion measure of intelligence it has been widely employed as *a* criterion so that the reported correlations give the user considerable confidence that the Leiter scale is a reasonably good measure of intelligence as commonly conceived.

SUMMARY. The new scale is undoubtedly superior to its predecessor in that it contains balanced language and nonlanguage subscales. The scale is easy and economical to administer and score, and is interesting to adults. Reliabilities of subtests are adequate if scores are used only in arriving at language, nonlanguage, and total scores. Providing individual test score IQ equivalents tends to encourage false confidence in the reliability of individual tests. Intercorrelations of tests, scales, and the Stanford-Binet indicate that the *Leiter Adult Intelligence Scale* and the Stanford-Binet measure similar intellectual functions. For those seeking a new or alternative individual measure of intelligence, the Leiter scale offers interesting possibilities. However, much more research and evidence will be required to put the scale in the class, say, of the *Wechsler Adult Intelligence Scale*.

FRANK B. JEX, *Professor of Educational Psychology, University of Utah, Salt Lake City, Utah.*

The *Leiter Adult Intelligence Scale* derives from the Army Individual Test of General Mental Ability (1944) which was standardized on a group of 256 unselected male war veterans between the ages of 19 and 36, about whom the manual provides no further background information.

The three tests comprising the language scale are: (*a*) Similarities-Differences (telling how pairs of words are alike, and how they are different); (*b*) Digits Forwards and Backwards (repeating number series presented orally, as in the Wechsler scales); (*c*) FR-CR (after listening to a lengthy paragraph, first repeating it as a measure of free recall, then responding to a series of related questions as a measure of controlled recall).

The three tests comprising the nonlanguage scale (previously published as the *Leiter-Partington Adult Performance Scale*) are: (*a*) Pathways (first drawing lines from number to number in sequence, and then from numbers to letters alternately); (*b*) Stencil Designs (reproducing designs which resemble military shoulder patches by superimposing circular stencils of colored paper); (*c*) Painted Cube Test (duplicating various designs by arranging one-inch cubes to conform to the stimulus cards).

The scale purports to measure "a sufficient variety of mental functions to indicate the learning capacity of the adult being tested." The author's criterion of learning capacity is score on the 1937 Stanford-Binet, developed for use with children and inappropriate as a criterion of adult intelligence. For the standardization group, Stanford-Binet scores correlate .82 with scores on the language scale, .78 with nonlanguage scores, and .88 with total scores. Kuder-Richardson estimates of the scale's reliability are: language scores, .90, nonlanguage scores, .88, total scale scores, .94.

In 1951, without the benefit of standardization on a more representative adult population, the Army scale was rechristened the *Leiter Adult Intelligence Scale* and made available for civilian use. In the meantime a few relationship and validational studies have begun to appear, but most of them have been confined to the *Psychological Service Center Journal,* founded, edited, and published by Leiter himself.

Since the appearance of the mimeographed manual in 1956, the *Leiter Profile* has been published, employing the individual patterning on the WAIS, the LAIS, and the *Porteus Maze Test* to arrive at a measure of social sufficiency among patients in mental hospitals. This research is not without promise, but the completely inadequate standardization of the LAIS remains to plague the user and to discourage serious research with the scale. Perhaps this inadequacy also explains the relatively limited clinical use of the LAIS, as contrasted to the WAIS, even though the much shorter LAIS is now reported by the publishers to correlate .93 with a Wechsler-Bellevue scale.

The six tests of the LAIS do have an interesting history (although little of this is reflected in the manual), and that they are administered and scored much after the fashion of the WAIS suggests that the two scales might be used as alternate forms for assessing adult intelligence. For purposes of this review both the LAIS and the WAIS were administered to 50 University of Utah students (26 males and 24 females) enrolled in the College of Education. For this sample LAIS language correlated .67 with WAIS verbal, LAIS nonlanguage correlated .52 with WAIS performance, and LAIS total correlated .68 with WAIS total. The LAIS IQ's ranged from 96 through 136 with a mean of 122 and a standard deviation of 9 (published standard deviation of 20). The WAIS IQ's ranged from 103 through 133 with a mean IQ of 119 and a standard deviation of 7 (published standard deviation of 15). Considering the differences in published standard deviations, these average performances are fairly comparable for the two scales. For this restricted range of ability, correlations with cumulative college GPA were: WAIS verbal IQ, .41; LAIS language IQ, .27; WAIS performance IQ, .19; LAIS nonlanguage IQ, .16; WAIS total IQ, .38; LAIS total IQ, .27. While most of these correlations are statistically significant, they are not large enough to be of much help for purposes of selection or prediction, and all appear to be less valid in our situation than scores on the *Henmon-Nelson Tests of Mental Ability,* which correlate .47 with college grades for this same group of students. These data also suggest that academic success is predicted as well by verbal IQ alone as by total IQ on either the WAIS or LAIS. (Indeed, scores on the WAIS vocabulary test alone correlate .38 with college grades for this sample.) The WAIS IQ's for our students are fairly normally distributed. The LAIS IQ's are truncated at the top end, which is largely attributable to the fact that 72 per cent of the group went off the top end of the norms on one or more of the tests in the scale. Clearly the LAIS lacks adequate ceiling for use with college students, while the WAIS is much more adequate in this respect, none of our sample having gone off the norms for any of the WAIS tests.

Administration time for the LAIS ranged from 37 to 63 minutes, with an average time of 49 minutes, which closely approximates the published time limits. On the WAIS, administration time ranged from 60 to 100 minutes, with an average time of 76 minutes, suggesting that the published time for the WAIS may be a considerable underestimate.

Scoring of the 6-test LAIS is obviously less time consuming than the 11-test WAIS, but the LAIS directions are more ambiguous and the criteria for scoring much less adequate. Small scoring discrepancies between the manual and the record booklet for the Pathways and the Painted Cubes constitute a further annoyance in the LAIS. Of greater concern is the weighting for arriving at the full scale IQ, raw scores for all six subtests being simply summed. This practice results in giving some tests two (and in one case nearly three) times as much weight as others, for which the author offers no defensible rationale.

Another serious limitation is evident in both the Painted Cubes and the Pathways, where a single mistake makes the difference between a high and a low score. The Pathways are scored in "all or none" fashion and contain only two scorable tasks. If one of the two is failed and the other passed with the highest possible credit, the Pathways IQ is 91. If both items are passed with the highest possible credit (a feat achieved by 10 per cent of our sample) the Pathways IQ is 149. These examples are merely indicative of the numerous and basic shortcomings of the LAIS as revealed in its use with 50 college students. In short, although more quickly administered and scored than the WAIS, in its present poorly standardized form the LAIS is not a suitable instrument for measuring adult intelligence, and cannot be recommended as an alternate to the WAIS.

J Consult Psychol 21:93 F '57. L(aurance) F. S(haffer). The *Leiter Adult Intelligence Scale* is a brief individual test for adults which requires about 40 minutes of administration time. It seems close kin to the Army Individual Test of World War II, to which the author made considerable contributions. The three language subtests are similarities-differences, digits forward and backward, and a story memory test; the three nonverbal are a pathways test, stencil designs, and painted cubes. * The manual contains sufficient directions for administering and scoring, and tables of adult IQ norms for each subtest, the two subtotals, and the total score. Reliabilities, intercorrelations, sex differences, and correlations with other tests are satisfactorily reported for several groups. There is no statement about the sample used for the derivation of the norms. Implications from previously published studies suggest that the IQ norms were obtained entirely from 256 young male veterans who had also been given the Stanford Binet. Since the reported studies of sex differences concern college women and men only, the extension of the norms to women, and indeed to men in general, seems a bit risky.

For reviews by Harold A. Delp and Herschel Manuel of the original edition, see 4:350 (1 excerpt); for a review by George K. Bennett of the Pathways Test, *see 4:355 (1 excerpt); for additional information regarding the other subtests, see 4:347 (1 excerpt), 4:348 (1 excerpt), and 4:339.*

[526]

Leiter International Performance Scale. Ages 2–18, 3–8; 1936–55; individual; 2 editions; postage extra; Russell Graydon Leiter and Grace Arthur (*b*); C. H. Stoelting Co. *

a) 1948 REVISION. Ages 2–18; 1936–52; 1 form ('48); manual in 2 parts: Parts 1 ['52, 75 pages, also published in 1959 as *45* below], 2 ('50, 85 pages, reprint of *27*); record card ['48, 2 pages]; $187.50 per set of testing materials, 100 record cards, carrying case, and manual; $5 per 100 record cards; specimen set not available; [30–60] minutes.

b) ARTHUR ADAPTATION. Ages 3–8; 1952–55; author recommends use with *Arthur Point Scale of Performance Tests;* administered by pantomime; individual; 1 form ['52]; test materials consist of Trays 1 and 2 of the 1948 revision (*a* above); manual ('52, 78 pages); record card ['55, 2 pages]; $136.50 per set of testing materials, 100 record cards, carrying case, and manual; $5 per 100 record cards; $4 per manual; (30–60) minutes.

REFERENCES

1–25. See 4:349.
26–42. See 5:408.
43. ALLEN, ROBERT M., AND COLLINS, MARJORIE G. "Suggestions for the Adaptive Administration of Intelligence Tests for Those With Cerebral Palsy: Part 1, Administration of the Ammons Full-Range Picture Test, Columbia Mental Maturity Test, Raven's Progressive Matrices and Leiter International Performance Scale." *Cerebral Palsy R* 16:11–4+ My–Je '55. * (*PA* 30:3284)
44. WILSON, BARBARA A. *A Comparison of Intelligence Quotients for Readers and Non-Readers Using the Leiter International Performance Scale and the 1937 Revision of the Stanford-Binet.* Master's thesis, Sacramento State College (Sacramento, Calif.), 1958.
45. LEITER, RUSSELL GRAYDON. "Part I of the Manual for the 1948 Revision of the Leiter International Performance Scale." *Psychol Service Center J* 11:1–72 '59. * [Same as manual, part 1, issued in 1952.]
46. WOLF, WILLAVENE SHEETS. *The Contribution of Speed of Response in Mental Measurement.* Doctor's thesis, State University of Iowa (Iowa City, Iowa), 1960. (*DA* 21:1467)
47. BRENGELMANN, JOHANNES C., AND KENNY, JOSEPH T. "Comparison of Leiter, WAIS and Stanford-Binet IQ's in Retardates." *J Clin Psychol* 17:235–8 Jl '61. * (*PA* 38:8953)
48. HUNT, BETTY M. "Differential Responses of Mentally Retarded Children on the Leiter Scale." *Excep Child* 28:99–102 O '61. * (*PA* 37:1693)
49. WOLF, WILLAVENE, AND STROUD, JAMES B. "The Contribution of Response in Mental Measurement." *J Ed Psychol* 52:249–53 O '61. * (*PA* 38:3192)
50. MAISEL, RICHARD N.; ALLEN, ROBERT M.; AND TALLARICO, ROBERT B. "A Comparison of the Adaptive and Standard Administration of the Leiter International Performance Scale With Normal Children." *Cerebral Palsy R* 23:3–4+ S–O '62. * (*PA* 37:3549)
51. MIRA, MARY P. "The Use of the Arthur Adaptation of the Leiter International Performance Scale and the Nebraska Test of Learning Aptitude With Preschool Deaf Children." *Am Ann Deaf* 107:224–8 Mr '62. * (*PA* 37:1617)
52. BIRCH, JANE R.; STUCKLESS, E. ROSS; AND BIRCH, JACK W. "An Eleven Year Study of Predicting School Achievement in Young Deaf Children." *Am Ann Deaf* 108:236–40 Mr '63. * (*PA* 37:8132)

EMMY E. WERNER, *Assistant Professor of Child Development, University of California, Davis, California.* [Review of the Arthur adaptation.]

The Arthur adaptation of the *Leiter International Performance Scale,* a nonverbal scale for young children, is a point-scale which yields both an MA and an IQ. Arthur stresses the following assets of the adaptation: (*a*) It requires no verbalization on the part of the examiner or the child. This makes it especially useful for the testing of children with speech and hearing difficulties, mental retardates, foreign-born or bilingual children, and shy or withdrawn children. (*b*) It has no time limits. (*c*) It reaches down to lower chronological age levels than other performance scales. (*d*) The tests lowest in the scale are tests of ability to learn rather than tests of acquired skills or materials already learned. (*e*) The materials for the test are interesting to children.

The test contains 60 items, ranging in difficulty level from ages 2 to 12. It is considered most suitable for the testing of children from 3 to 8 years and others whose mental age falls within this range.

The materials consist of a response frame with an adjustable card holder. All tests are administered by attaching the appropriate picture card to the frame. Directions are pantomimed. The child chooses the matching blocks and inserts them into the frame. The types of tasks range from matching of colors and forms to completion of patterns, analogous designs, classification of objects. Most of the items require a good deal of perceptual organization and discrimination.

Some questions may be raised about: (*a*) The seeming unevenness in difficulty level (nowhere could this reviewer find a reference to percentage of passes by item and age level). (*b*) The outdatedness of certain pictures (e.g., items V-1, V-3, VII-4). (*c*) The extent of culture fairness of the scale. Tate (*32*), studying children from extremely heterogenous socioeconomic backgrounds, found as much variability among them on the Leiter as on the Stanford-Binet. Although intended for cross cultural study, there has been no extensive use of the scale with children in cross cultural research. (*d*) The question of content or construct validity. What abilities does the scale measure? There seems to be an abrupt shift in the content of items when one compares those below age eight with those above. Factor-analytical studies of the scale at different age levels might provide an answer. (*e*) The relatively small number of items which represent each year level; on the upper level accidental failure can severely penalize a child. Arthur has worked out a somewhat complicated bonus system to compute the basal age. In spite of it, mean scores on the scale run generally lower than those on the S-B or the WISC. Orgel and Dreger (*35*) find that this tendency is extreme where Binet scores are high.

The 1952 manual contains very little of the information considered essential in the APA Technical Recommendations. In 1952 (the full scale manual) and 1959 (*45*) Leiter published an extensive account of the standardization, reliability, and validity data which had accumulated on the different revisions of the *Leiter International Performance Scale,* including the Arthur adaptation. This material ought also to be incorporated in the manual for the adaptation.

The 289 children who comprise the standardization group for the scale came from a very homogenous (middle class, midwestern, metropolitan background). There were few cases at either extreme of the socioeconomic distribution and apparently few or none of the children for whom the scale was originally designed: i.e., children who would be handicapped on a verbal scale. It might be helpful to expand the norms to cover a more representative sample of children, and to test more adequately the claims of culture fairness which have been made for the scale.

Arthur gives no reliability data in her manual; split-half reliabilities quoted by Anastasi and Freeman in their texts are in the .90's. There is a real need to determine both tester-observer and test-retest reliability, in view of the few items which represent each age range.

A number of studies have been undertaken which establish the concurrent validity of the scale. Correlations between the scale and the S-B, on samples of 4-, 5-, 7-, and 8-year-old public school children, range between .69 and .93 (*28, 30*); correlations based on mentally retarded or brain damaged children run generally a little lower, between .56 and .86 (*29, 39*). The performance scale of the WISC correlates higher with the Arthur (.79–.80) than the verbal scale (.40–.78) and about as high as the total score (.77–.83). This reviewer knows of no study reporting on the predictive validity of the scale.

SUMMARY. It is evident that a lot of work still needs to be done to establish more comprehensive norms, a better scoring system and the predictive value of the Arthur adaptation. Given the fairly high correlations with the two most widely used individual intelligence tests for children which have been demonstrated, there is encouragement to pursue this "clean-up work." Within the limits of what we presently know about the construction of culture fair tests, the Arthur scale is a very promising instrument, and has made possible the testing of many children who could not be properly evaluated by the Stanford-Binet or WISC. Its use in cross cultural research with young children should be more encouraged; for the time being this reviewer recommends the Arthur adaptation for research purposes and as a special diagnostic instrument for the experienced clinician.

For a review by Gwen F. Arnold of a, *see 4:349 (1 excerpt); for excerpts from a related book review, see 40:B989.*

[527]

Merrill-Palmer Scale of Mental Tests. Ages 24–63 months; 1926–31; individual; 1 form; 15 tests: *Stutsman Color-Matching Test, Wallin Peg Boards, Stutsman Buttoning Test, Stick-and-String Test, Stutsman Language Test, Stutsman Picture Formboard, Mare and Foal Formboard*, modification of *Seguin-Goddard Formboard, Manikin Test, Decroly Matching Game, Stutsman Nested Cubes, Action Agent Test* (modification of *Action-Agent Association Test* ['11] by R. S. Woodworth and F. L. Wells), *Copying Test, Pyramid Test,* and *Little Pink Tower Test;* manual ('31, see 5); record blank [no data, 4 pages]; no data on reliability; $75 per set of testing materials, 50 record blanks, and manual (manual may also be purchased separately from the publisher, Harcourt, Brace & World, Inc.); $2.50 per 50 record blanks; postage extra; administration time not reported; Rachel Stutsman; C. H. Stoelting Co. *

REFERENCES

1–13. See 40:1406.
14. Barrett, Helen Elizabeth, and Koch, Helen Lois. "The Effect of Nursery-School Training Upon the Mental-Test Performance of a Group of Orphanage Children." *J Genetic Psychol* 37:102–22 Mr '30. * (*PA* 4:2163)
15. Aldrich, Cecelia G., and Doll, Edgar A. "Comparative Intelligence of Idiots and Normal Infants." *J Genetic Psychol* 39:227–57 Je '31. * (*PA* 6:520)
16. Smitter, Faith Winters. *The Serviceability of the Merrill-Palmer and Stanford-Binet Scales for Ages Three to Six.* Master's thesis, University of Southern California (Los Angeles, Calif.), 1936.
17. Coffey, Hubert Stanley. *A Study of Certain Mental Functions and Their Relation to Changes in the Intelligence of Preschool Children.* Doctor's thesis, University of Iowa (Iowa City, Iowa), 1938.
18. Anderson, L. Dewey. "The Predictive Value of Infancy Tests in Relation to Intelligence at Five Years." *Child Develop* 10:203–12 S '39. * (*PA* 13:6507)
19. De Forest, Ruth. "A Study of the Prognostic Value of the Merrill-Palmer Scale of Mental Tests and the Minnesota Preschool Scale." *J Genetic Psychol* 59:219–23 S '41. * (*PA* 16:1231)
20. Allan, Mary Elizabeth, and Young, Florene M. "The Constancy of the Intelligence Quotient as Indicated by Retests of 130 Children." *J Appl Psychol* 27:41–60 F '43. * (*PA* 17:2631)
21. Ebert, Elizabeth, and Simmons, Katherine. *The Brush Foundation Study of Child Growth and Development: 1, Psychometric Tests.* Monographs of the Society for Research in Child Development, Vol. 8, No. 2, Serial No. 35. Washington, D.C.: the Society, National Research Council, 1943. Pp. xiv, 113. * (*PA* 18:3322)
22. Harris, Dale B. "An Item Analysis and Evaluation of the Merrill-Palmer Scale of Mental Tests for Preschool Children." Abstract. *Am Psychologist* 2:302 Ag '47. *
23. Stutsman, Rachel. *Guide for Administering the Merrill-Palmer Scale of Mental Tests.* A reprint of Part 3 of the author's *Mental Measurement of Preschool Children* published in 1931. Yonkers, N.Y.: World Book Co., 1948. Pp. 139–262. *
24. Haines, Miriam Stearns. *Test Performance of Pre-School Children With and Without Organic Brain Pathology.* Doctor's thesis, Columbia University (New York, N.Y.), 1953. (*DA* 14:1099)
25. Haines, Miriam Stearns. "Test Performance of Preschool Children With and Without Organic Brain Pathology." *J Consult Psychol* 18:371–4 O '54. * (*PA* 29:5707)
26. Walsh, Rosaline. *The Prognostic Value of the Merrill-Palmer Mental Tests and the Nebraska Test of Learning Aptitude for Pre-School Deaf Children.* Master's thesis, University of Buffalo (Buffalo, N.Y.), 1954.
27. Hurst, John G. "A Factor Analysis of the Merrill-Palmer With Reference to Theory and Test Construction." *Ed & Psychol Meas* 20:519–32 au '60. * (*PA* 35:3251)
28. Horton, Carrell P., and Crump, E. Perry. "Growth and Development 11: Descriptive Analysis of the Backgrounds of 76 Negro Children Whose Scores Are Above or Below Average on the Merrill-Palmer Scale of Mental Tests at Three Years of Age." *J Genetic Psychol* 100:255–65 Je '62. * (*PA* 37:2871)
29. Hurst, John G. "Factor Analysis of the Merrill-Palmer at Two Age Levels: Structure and Comparison." *J Genetic Psychol* 102:231–44 Je '63. * (*PA* 38:4074)

Marjorie P. Honzik, *Lecturer in Psychology, and Associate Research Psychologist, Institute of Human Development, University of California, Berkeley, California.*

The *Merrill-Palmer Scale of Mental Tests* was constructed to serve as a substitute for, or supplement to, revisions of the Binet scale. It differs in this respect from a number of other preschool mental tests (e.g., the *California Preschool Mental Scale,* and the *Minnesota Preschool Scale,* as well as the Stanford revisions) which include items from the Binet. The Merrill-Palmer's independence from the Stanford-Binet has made it a highly useful adjunct to the testing program in nursery schools and clinics, as well as in developmental research.

The Merrill-Palmer scale is composed of 3 to 14 test items per six-month age period beginning at 18 months and extending to 6 years. There are 10 or more items at each level except ages 60 to 65 months and 66 to 71 months. The majority of items depend in part on fine motor skill: pegboards, block building, tower building with blocks of varying sizes, drawing, formboards (Seguin), buttoning, and picture puzzles. There are a few verbal items: repetition of or memory for words and groups of words; questions such as "What does a doggie say?" and the Action Agent Test which asks "What sleeps?", "What roars?", etc.

This scale is a delightful one for both the young child and the examiner. It includes few verbal items but those which are included are interesting to young children. Another advantage of this test is the provision it makes for refusals. Rachel Stutsman Ball has given more thoughtful consideration to the problem of resistance in the test situation than have the authors of any other preschool tests. Her listing of the many factors in the test situation which influence the child's cooperation has remained the best available for over 30 years. Refused and omitted items are considered in arriving at a total score which may then be converted into mental age, sigma value, or percentile rank.

The provision for refusals suggests a marked

sensitivity to the characteristics of the preschool child; but an insensitive aspect and major fault of the Merrill-Palmer scale, which causes difficulty when examining the very young child, is the large proportion of timed tests. Not only the pegboards but also the block building, buttoning, and even the puzzle tasks are timed. The slow moving but thoughtful child is severely penalized on this test.

Another difficulty of the scale is the scores which it yields. The standard deviations of the mental ages do not increase in proportion to advancing chronological ages so that IQ's cannot be computed. The author recommends that percentile ranks or standard deviation units be used. Since percentile ranks are not suitable measures to use for computation, and thus research, one is left with the standard scores which, for this scale, are presented in such a way as to cover a wide range of ability. Standard scores are computed to the nearest half standard deviation. This means that almost half of a normal sample would receive a standardized deviation score of −.5, 0, or .5.

The reliability of the scale was not reported by Stutsman in her manual but she states that the test is valid on the basis that it (*a*) is composed of items which differentiated between children judged bright or dull by other criteria; (*b*) yields high correlations with chronological age; (*c*) differentiates between feebleminded and normal children; and (*d*) yields high correlations with Stanford-Binet mental ages for a far too wide spread of chronological ages.

The Merrill-Palmer scale has been widely used at child research centers (e.g., those at the Universities of Minnesota, Iowa, and California), and its predictive value was reported by Ebert and Simmons (*21*) for the Brush Foundation's longitudinal study at Western Reserve. In this study the correlations between the Merrill-Palmer and Stanford-Binet for two-, three-, and four-year-old children were in the .60's. Prediction of later Stanford-Binet IQ's from the Merrill-Palmer given between the ages of 2 and 4 years "fluctuates within the rather narrow range from .39 to .54." In this same study the abilities measured by the Merrill-Palmer were less closely related to the Stanford-Binet IQ's than the performance test scores (*Kent-Shakow Formboard, Kohs' Block-Design Test,* and the *Minnesota Paper Form Board Test*), at least in boys.

In summary, the Merrill-Palmer scale is one which is enjoyed by children, partly because of the large proportion of performance items, has good provisions for handling refused tests, and has played an important role in assessing abilities not tested by Binet-type tests. The disadvantages lie in its restricted age range of usefulness, large proportion of timed test items, and method of presenting scores, and in the fact that it was standardized on a nonrepresentative and relatively small sample at each age level. It is to be hoped that this scale will be revised since its value has been proved in the clinic and as a research tool.

For reviews by Nancy Bayley, B. M. Castner, Florence L. Goodenough, and Florence M. Teagarden, see 40:1406; for excerpts from related book reviews, see 40:B1123.

[528]

Minnesota Preschool Scale. Ages 1.5-6; 1932-40; 3 scores: verbal, nonverbal (ages 3.0-6.0 only), total; individual; Form A ('32); manual ('40, 127 pages); record booklet ('40, 4 pages, same as record booklet copyrighted in 1932); $38 per set of testing materials, 25 record blanks, and manual; $1.60 per 25 record blanks; postage extra; $2.15 per specimen set, postpaid; [10-30] minutes; Florence L. Goodenough, Katherine M. Maurer, and M. J. Van Wagenen; Educational Test Bureau. *

REFERENCES

1-3. See 40:1407.
4-5. See 3:286.
6-7. See 4:351.
8. Lyle, J. G. "The Effect of an Institution Environment Upon the Verbal Development of Imbecile Children: 1, Verbal Intelligence." *J Mental Def Res* 3:122-8 D '59. *
9. Lyle, J. G. "The Effect of an Institution Environment Upon the Verbal Development of Imbecile Children: 2, Speech and Language; 3, The Brooklands Residential Family Unit." *J Mental Def Res* 4:1-23 Je '60. * (*PA* 35:2565-6)
10. Lyle, J. G. "A Comparison of the Verbal Intelligence of Normal and Imbecile Children." *J Genetic Psychol* 99:227-34 D '61. * (*PA* 36:3JI27L)

Marjorie P. Honzik, *Lecturer in Psychology, and Associate Research Psychologist, Institute of Human Development, University of California, Berkeley, California.*

In the manual for the *Minnesota Preschool Scale,* the authors wrote that they felt that there was "a real demand for a series of tests which....accurately reveal the development of mental ability in early childhood." Since the publication of these scales 30 years ago, several longitudinal studies have shown that whereas mental test scores after six years of age are fairly stable, marked changes in relative standing on mental tests are likely to occur during the first five years. Thus there is still need for good preschool mental scales to delineate the changes which take place during these years and the factors which are related to these changes. An important question, then, is why the well standardized *Minnesota Preschool Scale* has been so little used either in developmental research or for diagnostic purposes.

Forms A and B of the scale (Form B is out of print) each contain 26 tests equally divided into verbal and nonverbal items. Verbal tests include language comprehension (points to parts of body and to objects in pictures, follows directions, comprehends problem situations); language facility (names objects, describes pictures, knows colors, vocabulary, opposites, and verbal absurdities); memory for objects, incomplete pictures, and digits. The nonverbal tests involve drawing (both copying and imitating); block building; discrimination, recognition, and tracing of forms; picture puzzles; paper folding; recognition of omitted parts in pictures; and imitating position of clock hands.

These scales were rigorously standardized. The norms are based on the tests of 50 boys and 50 girls examined at half-year levels. Within each age level, the children were selected so as to represent a cross section of the population. The statistical analysis is impeccable and the resulting C scores can be converted into IQ equivalents.

The authors report, for half-year age ranges, reliabilities ranging from .68 to .94 for the verbal scale, and from .67 to .92 for the nonverbal scale, when the scores on alternate forms were correlated. For the combined verbal and nonverbal scores, reliabilities range from .80 to .94.

The test materials are conveniently boxed and the manual of instructions is clearly written. The test materials have not become dated since toys are few and the pictures to be described are reproductions of paintings which would be equally difficult for all children. Although the test materials include a doll, blocks, and puzzles, these scales have less appeal to children than other preschool tests. Form L-M of the Stanford-Binet, for example, has an attractive formboard, small cars, an engine, and other toys which help maintain rapport. In fact, formboards, pegboards, and small toys are found in greater numbers in all other preschool tests: *Gesell Developmental Schedules, California Preschool Mental Scale,* and the *Merrill-Palmer Scale of Mental Tests.* A further difficulty of the Minnesota scale is the requirement that with few exceptions all tests be given to each child and in the prescribed order. This makes for a long test which taxes the patience of the child and the ingenuity of the examiner. Additionally, there is no provision for refusals. Form L-M of the Stanford-Binet has alternate test items which can be given if one is refused or is inappropriate. The Merrill-Palmer and California scales have specific adjustments in scoring when tests are refused or when there is an error in the administration of a test item. If a child does not "cooperate actively" on the Minnesota scale, the examiner is instructed to discontinue the test and allow the child to play with other toys. The authors add that in the case of an unusually shy child, two or three preliminary visits may be advisable. In practice, it is not always possible to have preliminary sessions before the actual test is given.

A further reason why these scales are used so infrequently is the limited age range of usefulness. The Merrill-Palmer is the only other test with such a limited age range. Other scales articulate with either an infant scale or with tests for older children.

In summary, the *Minnesota Preschool Scale* is among the most carefully standardized preschool tests and, although published 30 years ago, the test materials are not unduly dated. The disadvantages of this scale lie in the limited age range of usefulness, and in the lack of appeal to the young child because the test materials are not interesting and the procedures are too inflexible. At the present time, Form L-M of the Stanford-Binet is the test of choice for research and clinic, since it covers the age range 2 to adulthood, is more flexible, includes test materials with more intrinsic appeal to the young child, and has been more widely used. However, it is fortunate that the *Minnesota Preschool Scale* is still available since alternate tests are often needed on research projects and in confirming a diagnosis in the clinic.

For a review by Beth L. Wellman, see 3:286; for reviews by Rachel Stutsman Ball, Nancy Bayley, and Florence M. Teagarden of the original edition, see 40:1407; for excerpts from related book reviews, see 4:352, 3:287, and 3:288.

[529]

*__Non-Verbal Intelligence Tests for Deaf and Hearing Subjects.__ Ages 3–16; 1939–59; title on record booklet is *S.O.N. Snijders-Oomen Non-Verbal*

Intelligence Scale; administered orally or in pantomime; 9 scores: mosaic, picture memory, arrangement, analogies, completion, Knox cubes, drawing, sorting, I.Q.; individual; 2 forms ('58): Scales P (consisting of mosaic, picture memory, arrangement, and analogies subtests), Q (consisting of completion, Knox cubes, drawing, and sorting subtests); Scale Q can be used as parallel form or combined with Scale P for longer test; manual ('59, 140 pages); record booklet ['58, 4 pages]; $85 (600*s.*) per set of testing materials, 100 scoring forms, and manual; $1.50 (11*s.*) per 100 scoring forms; $3.75 (27*s.*) per manual; postage extra; Dutch, German, and French editions available; [45] minutes per scale; J. Th. Snijders and N. Snijders-Oomen; J. B. Wolters. *

REFERENCES

1. SNIJDERS, J. TH., AND SNIJDERS-OOMEN, N. *Non-Verbal Intelligence Tests for Deaf and Hearing Subjects: Snijders-Oomen Non-Verbal Scale, S.O.N.* Groningen, Netherlands: J. B. Wolters, 1959. Pp. 141. *
2. NEUHAUS, MAURY. "Measuring the Nonverbal Intelligence of Gifted Elementary-School Children." *Excep Child* 28:271–3 Ja '62. *

J. S. LAWES, *Senior Lecturer in Education, Westminster College, North Hinksey, Oxford, England.*

This scale, first constructed in 1939–42 for use with deaf children, has now been revised, enlarged, and restandardised on both deaf and hearing subjects. The first form aimed to sample four aspects of intelligence: form, combination, abstraction, and memory. This grouping has been retained. The new version has eight subtests, two for each aspect and thus consists of two parallel subscales P and Q which can be used separately or together.

Within each subtest the principle of construction has been to maintain the same type of material and the same manner of presentation over the whole age range from 3 to 16 years. The Knox cubes test used to assess the "Memory" aspect in Scale Q is an example. Where such continuity has not been possible a change to material of similar but not identical type takes place. For example the "Form" subtest of Scale P consists of simple mosaics with four or five red squares up to age 5-3, more complex mosaics with up to 16 red and white squares from 5-3 up to 8-6, then a modified version of Kohs' *Block-Design Test.* Of such changes the manual says, "the correlation of the adjoining parts has been examined and, when necessary, raised by revision of items," but no details are given. In structure the scale has the advantage over the various Binet revisions that its pattern is the same at all age levels and, like the Wechsler scales, it is a point scale rather than an age scale.

Each subtest forms a separate point scale and tables are provided to convert raw scores to standard scores with a mean of 25 and standard deviation 5. Further tables convert the sum of the standard scores into a deviation IQ of mean 100 and standard deviation 15. For those who desire scores expressed as mental ages, tables are given for converting raw score in each subtest into a mental age, called a subtest age. Mental age is defined as the median of the subtest ages. This scoring system is explained clearly in the manual and there is a good section on interpretation of scores.

The tables are based on a standardisation sample which included Dutch children only. For the "hearing" group 50 children were selected for each half year of age from 3 to 5½ years and 100 children for each year from 6 up to 16. This gives a praiseworthy sample size of 1,400 cases. We are told that "Each age-sample was selected in exactly the same manner. The criteria were: birthday, sex, residence, type of school, social level of parents," but it is not clear whether this means that within each age sample the whole range of "type of school," "social level of parents," etc. was included or simply that the same, restricted, range of types was included at each level. The "deaf" sample included "all pupils of the Dutch schools for the deaf up to age 16." Although this means variation in age group size and some extrapolation, it also means that the conversion tables for deaf children are based on a whole population.

Reliability is reported as split-half coefficients and standard errors of measurement. The split-half coefficients for the whole scale at ages 5 to 5½ years, 10 to 11 years, and 15 years are .94, .91, and .91 for hearing children, .95, .93, and .94 for deaf children. These compare well with WISC performance scale reliabilities. Of the two subscales P shows a reliability similar to that of the whole scale but Q has a slightly lower reliability and, particularly with hearing children, shows a tendency to be less reliable with older subjects, viz. .89, .80, and .76 at the three ages quoted above. Reliability figures for the separate subtests vary from .36 up to .93. The lowest figures are found in the two "memory" subtests and in these also the reliability drops considerably within the middle age range. This raises the question of the desirability of using the individual subtests in isolation or in "profile" analysis; but one notes that the authors do, in the manual, sound a note of caution here.

Linked with this question is that of the validity of the theoretical construct of four aspects of intelligence. No evidence is offered to support this apart from the comment "it has only partly been confirmed by the factorial analysis of the standardisation data." No details are given, nor are we given any data from this factorial analysis to demonstrate the validity of the scale as a whole.

Validity of the scale as a measure of intelligence rests, at present, on correlations with teachers' judgments. For two groups of pupils numbering 300–400 and for two smaller groups of 25 pupils, all groups being hearing children, correlation coefficients range from .38 to .57. A group of 78 deaf pupils was tested in 1952 and again in 1956. Correlations of the two sets of scores with teachers' judgments made in 1956 are .42 and .49, respectively. This hint of test stability is confirmed by the correlation between the IQ's obtained in 1952 and 1956. These are .80 for the whole scale, .81 for P scale, and .63 for Q scale.

This all adds up to a well constructed scale, composed of pleasant and easy to handle material—some familiar, some modified from familiar tests, and some original. The price however seems unduly high, especially when tax and duty for British purchasers are added. The authors' advice that Scale Q should be reserved for retesting or added to Scale P for an extended scale is to be commended. The manual is well translated into English and gives full information for administration and scoring. Given large-scale standardisation in the United States and Britain, this English translation could be a welcome addition to the available range of nonverbal and performance scales.

[530]

★**Peabody Picture Vocabulary Test.** Ages 2.5–18; 1959; individual; Forms A, B, (154-page picture booklet used with both forms); pictures also available in a plastic booklet; manual (29 pages); individual record (2 pages) for each form; $10 per examiner's kit of picture booklet, 25 individual records for each form, and manual ($15 with plastic booklet instead of regular picture booklet); $3 per 50 individual records; postage extra; (10–15) minutes; Lloyd M. Dunn; American Guidance Service, Inc. *

REFERENCES

1. DUNN, LLOYD M., AND HARLEY, RANDALL K. "Comparability of Peabody, Ammons, Van Alstyne, and Columbia Test Scores With Cerebral Palsied Children." *Excep Child* 26:70–4 O '59. * (*PA* 35:3733)
2. GARRETT, JANE. *Comparison of the Peabody Picture Vocabulary Test and Wechsler Intelligence Scale for Children.* Master's thesis, George Peabody College for Teachers (Nashville, Tenn.), 1959.
3. DUNN, LLOYD M., AND BROOKS, SADYE T. "Peabody Picture Vocabulary Test Performance of Educable Mentally Retarded Children." *Training Sch B* 57:35–40 Ag '60. * (*PA* 35:1043)
4. KIMBRELL, DON L. "Comparison of Peabody, WISC, and Academic Achievement Scores Among Educable Mental Defectives." *Psychol Rep* 7:502 D '60. * (*PA* 35:2554)
5. MOSS, JAMES W., AND EDMONDS, PHYLLIS. "The Peabody Vocabulary Test With English Children." *Brit J Ed Psychol* 30:82 F '60. *
6. NORRIS, RAYMOND C.; HOTTEL, JOHN V.; AND BROOKS, SADYE. "Comparability of Peabody Picture Vocabulary Test Scores Under Group and Individual Administration." *J Ed Psychol* 51:87–91 Ap '60. * (*PA* 35:2780)
7. SCOGGINS, BETTY JOANNE. *A Comparative Study of the Full-Range Picture Vocabulary Test and the Peabody Picture Vocabulary Test.* Master's thesis, Vanderbilt University (Nashville, Tenn.), 1960.
8. DUNN, LLOYD M., AND HOTTEL, JOHN V. "Peabody Picture Vocabulary Test Performance of Trainable Mentally Retarded Children." *Am J Mental Def* 65:448–52 Ja '61. * (*PA* 35:6829)
9. TOBIAS, JACK, AND GORELICK, JACK. "The Validity of the Peabody Picture Vocabulary Test as a Measure of Intelligence of Retarded Adults." *Training Sch B* 58:92–8 N '61. * (*PA* 36:4JI92T)
10. HARTMAN, BERNARD-THOMAS. *Comparative Investigation of the Peabody Picture Vocabulary Test With Three Etiologic Groups of Institutionalized Mentally Retarded Students.* Doctor's thesis, Indiana University (Bloomington, Ind.), 1962. (*DA* 23:2008)
11. HIMELSTEIN, PHILIP, AND HERNDON, JAMES D. "Comparison of the WISC and Peabody Picture Vocabulary Test With Emotionally Disturbed Children." *J Clin Psychol* 18:82 Ja '62. * (*PA* 38:8420)
12. MEIN, R. "Use of the Peabody Picture Vocabulary With Severely Subnormal Patients." *Am J Mental Def* 67:269–73 S '62. * (*PA* 37:3582)
13. MUELLER, MAX W. "Effects of Illustration Size on Test Performance of Visually Limited Children." *Excep Child* 29:124–8 N '62. *
14. REGER, ROGER. "Brief Tests of Intelligence and Academic Achievement." *Psychol Rep* 11:82 Ag '62. * (*PA* 37:5654)
15. SHIPE, DOROTHY M. *Discrepancies Between the Peabody Picture Vocabulary Test and the WISC as Related to Emotional Disturbance in Children of Retarded and Normal Intelligence.* Doctor's thesis, George Peabody College for Teachers (Nashville, Tenn.), 1962. (*DA* 23:3984)
16. WOLFENSBERGER, WOLF. "The Correlation Between PPVT and Achievement Scores Among Retardates: A Further Study." *Am J Mental Def* 67:450–1 N '62. * (*PA* 37:5425)
17. BUDOFF, MILTON, AND PURSEGLOVE, ELEANOR MATHIAS. "Peabody Picture Vocabulary Test: Performance of Institutionalized Mentally Retarded Adolescents." *Am J Mental Def* 67:756–60 Mr '63. * (*PA* 38:1259)
18. MATTHEWS, CHARLES G., AND REITAN, RALPH M. "Relationship of Differential Abstraction Ability Levels to Psychological Test Performances in Mentally Retarded Subjects." *Am J Mental Def* 68:235–44 S '63. * (*PA* 38:6430)
19. MOED, GEORGE; WIGHT, BYRON W.; AND JAMES, PATRICIA. "Intertest Correlations of the Wechsler Intelligence Scale for Children and Two Picture Vocabulary Tests." *Ed & Psychol Meas* 23:359–63 su '63. * (*PA* 38:960)
20. TAYLOR, JOHN R. "Screening Intelligence." *J Speech & Hearing Disorders* 28:90–1 F '63. *
21. WEEKS, RICHARD WILLIAM. "Effectiveness of the Peabody Picture Vocabulary Test With College Students." *J Ed Res* 57:109–10 O '63. *

HOWARD B. LYMAN, *Associate Professor of Psychology, University of Cincinnati, Cincinnati, Ohio.*

The PPVT is an untimed individual test, administered in 15 minutes or less, consisting of a booklet with 3 practice and 150 test plates, each with 4 numbered pictures. The same booklet is used for both Form A and Form B, the forms differing only in the stimulus word (and, therefore, the picture which is the correct response) for each of the 150 items. Answer sheets, different for each form, give the stimulus word for each item, the correct response number, and space for recording the subject's response; the reverse side contains space for identifying information and for recording behavioral observations.

The examiner reads the stimulus word, and the subject responds by pointing to, giving the number of, or otherwise indicating the picture best illustrating the word. The manual states that the examiner must not spell, define, or even show the word to the subject.

Items are arranged in ascending order of difficulty, and the subject responds only to the items between his "basal" (eight consecutive correct responses) and his "ceiling" (six failures out of eight consecutive responses). The manual suggests appropriate starting points for different ages. Scoring is rapid and objective. The examiner places a mark over the item number of incorrect responses; these are counted and subtracted from the ceiling score.

This total score can be converted to any of three types of derived score: percentile rank, mental age, or standard score deviation IQ with a mean of 100 and a standard deviation of 15. Present tables include values for raw scores of 5 to 150 for IQ's, 6 to 140 only for percentile ranks, and 5 to 111 only for mental ages. These tables should be expanded to include derived score equivalents for all possible raw scores.

In developing the PPVT, the author had line drawings made for 2,055 illustratable words (from a population of 3,885) found in *Webster's New Collegiate Dictionary, Second Edition* (1956). Level of difficulty and item placement were determined on a sample of 360 subjects ranging in ages from 2 through 18 years. In a second pretest study, 750 subjects were used in selecting the final 300 stimulus words and 150 plates. (Some pictures appear in more than one of the plates.)

Standardization was based entirely on 4,012 white children and youth in and around Nashville, Tennessee. Numbers ranging from a minimum of 92 to a maximum of 354, at 19 different age levels from 2.5 years to 18 years, were tested on both forms. Only younger children (under 9 years of age) were given the test individually. At and above this age, the PPVT was administered as a group test by using photographic slides; justification for this procedure is based on a study of four 15-pupil fifth grade classes, which showed "no significant or appreciable differences" for type of administration.

Apparently norms for both Forms A and B are based on the entire samples of cases rather than on only the approximately one half who took a given form first. It seems likely that all of the norms tables are biased to an indeterminate extent because of this procedure.

The publisher effects an economy in printing the manual by using 6-month (through 5 years) and 12-month chronological age classifications; however, the use of such gross intervals is reflected in big "jumps" in the IQ table. For example, for a raw score of 50, a child of 5-5 would receive an IQ of 101 while a child of 5-6 would receive an IQ of only 89. "Jumps" of as much as 20 IQ points can be found at the extremes for younger children. The Stanford-Binet, tabling CA's in one-month units, has much smaller "jumps" (rarely above 2 IQ points).

Alternate form reliabilities ranging from .67 at the 6-year level to .84 at the 17- and 18-year levels are cited in the manual. Also cited are alternate form reliabilities of .83, .87, and .97 with handicapped and retarded groups; however, these cover such a range in ages as to seem spurious. The .97 reliability coefficient was based on 20 cerebral palsied children ranging in age from 7-1 through 16-2 years.

Although several validity studies are mentioned in the manual, the author states that "all of the statistical validity on the test are limited and preliminary." In one study with 150 seventh grade children, researchers reported correlations of .58 between Form B and the *California Test of Mental Maturity*, and .61 between Form B and the *Henmon-Nelson Tests of Mental Ability*. All other validity coefficients reported appear to be spurious because of the great range in ages.

The test is attractive and should be interesting to most subjects. It is simple to administer and score. No specialized preparation is required of the examiner beyond assuring himself of the proper pronunciation of all stimulus words. No special equipment is needed; the examiner needs only the book of plates (about 7 by 8½ inches), an answer sheet, and a pencil.

In summary, the PPVT is a highly usable test, of moderate reliability, and largely unestablished validity. Considerable caution needs to be used in interpreting the norms, especially in communities other than Nashville.

Ellen V. Piers, *Associate Professor of Psychology, The Pennsylvania State University, University Park, Pennsylvania.*

The PPVT is designed "to provide a well-standardized estimate of a subject's *verbal intelligence* through measuring his hearing vocabulary." As in other picture vocabulary tests, the subject indicates in some fashion which one of four pictures best fits the stimulus word read aloud to him. Besides serving as a quick estimate of intelligence for normal subjects, it was developed for use with special groups for whom the standard intelligence tests are not always appropriate, e.g., persons with reading problems, speech problems, brain damage, cerebral palsy, mental retardation, or emotional withdrawal. The author states that administration of the test requires no special training.

Its purpose, then, is similar to the Ammons *Full-Range Picture Vocabulary Test.* It may have been developed in order to improve on the FRPV, and in many ways it appears to have succeeded. Operating on the principle that different pictures for each stimulus word would provide more interest, the PPVT has 150 plates in the form of a booklet, only a portion of which are used for any one subject. (A plastic version designed to last longer has also been published.) The added interest would appear to outweigh the economy of using 16 or, as in the new Ammons *Quick Test,* only one plate per form, and the simplicity of the first few pages makes it more useful at the lower levels. The format also permits gradually increasing difficulty in the form and nature of the decoys. The pictures are sharply and clearly drawn with little ambiguity even in the more detailed plates. They were selected according to carefully defined criteria from a large pool taken from all illustratable words in *Webster's New Collegiate Dictionary.* Content validity and "item" validity thus seem well established.

The manual is for the most part a model of clarity, and illustrates admirably many of the 1954 APA Technical Recommendations. Part 1 contains directions for administering and scoring and includes tables for deriving mental ages, deviation IQ's, and percentiles. The user may find it inconvenient that scores were carried out to only three standard deviations so that IQ's are limited to the range of 55 to 145. The author states in the manual that age norms are the most useful scores beyond this range, but has reported in a personal communication to the reviewer that work is under way on methods of extrapolating IQ's downward.

Part 2 describes the test construction and standardization. Alternate form reliability is courageously presented for each age level and ranges from .67 to .84 with standard errors of measurement from 6.00 to 8.61 IQ points. Studies with wider age ranges report correspondingly higher reliabilities, ranging from .83 to .97. No test-retest reliability is reported in the manual, but a recent study (*19*) reports a test-retest coefficient of .88 after one year, with 29 physically disabled children. Both coefficients of equivalence and temporal stability appear, therefore, to be adequate for such a short test.

Although the standardization sample consisted of 4,012 white subjects restricted as to geographical area, the author employed an ingenious method of attempting to counteract these limitations. Rather than the frequently used stratified occupational sample, he chose schools where pupils' previous IQ scores provided a composite normal probability curve, or drew a random sample in some schools until the available IQ scores approximated a normal distribution. Group administration was used with upper levels, after it was established that scores would not be affected significantly. This not only provided a larger standardization sample, but appears to permit a wider application of the test.

One might question the author's assumption that recognition vocabulary measures verbal intelligence *in the same way* that verbal definition vocabulary tests are said to measure it, and that the demonstrated predictive value for school success of the latter is thus automatically transferred to a picture vocabulary test.

The section on congruent validity also raises some questions. The author, although he quotes the results of several comparison studies, states that "correlating the PPVT with other intelligence tests probably has limited utility." This reviewer would agree that such correlations may be misleading when done with small samples and restricted IQ ranges and when it is not entirely clear, as in the manual, whether mental ages were correlated in all cases or whether some studies used IQ's. On the other hand, it is essential—certainly until more evidence for predictive validity is in—that users know what a PPVT score means. Most particularly it is important since no special training is required to administer the test and many nonpsychologists will be using it. So far, from studies reported in the manual and others published since, correlations with Stanford-Binet mental ages seem to be on the order of .70's and low .80's, with IQ correlations running lower. With WISC IQ's they seem to be in the high .70's and low .80's. Correlations with three group intelligence tests are reported to be in the .60's, but the PPVT does not seem to correlate as highly with achievement test scores as do some of the group tests, although, as would be expected, coefficients are higher with reading or language than with other areas.

Perhaps the greatest potential danger in the use of this test resides in the same qualities which make it convenient—its shortness, its simplicity, its adaptability to group administration. Picture vocabulary tests can be good substitutes for the standard individual intelligence tests whenever verbal and performance responses cannot be obtained. But the encouraging of judgments of intelligence from such short and restricted samples of behavior by untrained individuals is unwise, unless the user is aware that what Guilford might call the "cognition of figural units" is only one aspect of the very complex domain called intelligence.

In any case, in this reviewer's opinion the PPVT is probably now the best of its kind. It seems to do at least as well as the Ammons FRPV, and has considerably more range than the Van Alstyne. It is too early to make comparisons with the Ammons *Quick Test* but it is almost certainly more discriminating at the lower levels. The plates and format are attractive and the test has a good manual, something still anticipated for the FRPV. A substantial list of references is already available and the test is stimulating current research. The author, according to personal communication, plans soon to revise the reliability and validity sections of the manual to pull together results of research that have accumulated since its publication.

[531]

★**Pictorial Test of Intelligence.** Ages 3–8; 1964; prepublication titles were *North Central Individual Test of Mental Ability* and *Pictorial Intelligence Test;* 7 scores: picture vocabulary, form discrimination, information and comprehension, similarities, size and number, immediate recall, total; individual; 1 form (54 stimulus cards and 137 response cards); may also be administered to 3- and 4-year-olds as a short form; manual (64 pages); record form (4 pages); no data on reliability of subscores; $24 per examiner's kit of test cards, 35 record forms, manual, and metal carrying case; $1.68 per 35 record forms; $3 per manual; postage extra; (45) minutes for full test; Joseph L. French; Houghton Mifflin Co. *

REFERENCES

1. French, Joseph L. *Development of the North Central Individual Test of Mental Ability.* Doctor's thesis, University of Nebraska (Lincoln, Neb.), 1957. (*DA* 17:2498)
2. French, Joseph L. "Intellectual Appraisal of Physically Handicapped Children." *J Genetic Psychol* 94:131–41 Mr '59. * (*PA* 36:4FE31F)

[532]

***The Porteus Maze Test.** Ages 3 and over; 1914–59; individual; 2 scores: quantitative, qualitative; 1 form; 3 editions and 2 supplements; no adult norms; Stanley D. Porteus. *

a) VINELAND REVISION. Ages 3 and over; 1914–24; 1 form ('21); 13 mazes: years 3–12, 14, adult 1, 2; manual ['24, 21 pages]; $11.50 per set of manual and 100 mazes of any one level; $1 per 100 copies of any one maze; postage extra; (15–60) minutes; C. H. Stoelting Co.

b) VINELAND REVISION: NEW SERIES. Ages 3 and over; 1914–59; 1 form ('33); 12 mazes: years 3–12, 14, adult 1; combined manual ('59, 208 pages, see 95 below) for New Series and Extension (*c* below); $13.50 per set of 100 copies of each maze and pad of 100 scoring sheets; $1.50 per 100 mazes of any one level; $5.60 per manual; postpaid; (15–60) minutes; Psychological Corporation.

c) PORTEUS MAZE EXTENSION. Ages 14 and over; 1953–59; for use only as a supplement to the *Vineland Revision: New Series;* 1 form ('53); 8 mazes: years 7–12, 14, adult; combined manual ('59, 208 pages, see 95 below) for Extension and New Series (*b* above); $9.75 per set of 100 copies of each maze and pad of 100 scoring sheets; $1.50 per 100 mazes of any one level; $5.60 per manual; postpaid; (25) minutes; Psychological Corporation.

d) PORTEUS MAZE SUPPLEMENT. Ages 7 and over; 1959; a retesting series; 1 form ('59); 8 mazes: years 7–12, 14, adult; supplementary manual ('59, 12 pages, including copies of all mazes); manual for *b* and *c* above must also be purchased; $8.75 per set of 100 copies of each maze; $1.50 per 100 mazes of any one level; 75¢ per supplementary manual; postpaid; (25) minutes; Psychological Corporation.

e) BRITISH EDITION. Ages 3 and over; 1914–52; 1 form ('52, same as *Vineland Revision: New Series* copyrighted in 1933 except for format); 12 mazes: years 3–12, 14, adult 1; manual ('52, 61 pages); 5*s.* per 100 mazes of any one level; 5*s.* per 100 scoring sheets; 6*s.* per manual; postage and purchase tax extra; [15–60] minutes; George G. Harrap & Co. Ltd.

REFERENCES

1–56. See 4:356.
57–84. See 5:412.
85. Piddington, Marjorie, and Piddington, Ralph. "Report of Field Work in Northwestern Australia." *Oceania* 2:342–58 Mr '32. *
86. Joseph, Alice, and Murray, Veronica F. *Chamorros and Carolinians of Saipan: Personality Studies,* pp. 119–35, 329–36, passim. Cambridge, Mass.: Harvard University Press, 1951. Pp. xviii, 381. * (*PA* 26:3359)
87. Shimota, Helen Emma. *The Relation of Psychomotor Performance to Clinical Status and Improvement in Schizophrenic Patients.* Doctor's thesis, University of Minnesota (Minneapolis, Minn.), 1956. (*DA* 16:2530)
88. Foulds, G. A., and Caine, T. M. "Personality Factors and Performance on Timed Tests of Ability." *Occup Psychol* 32:102–5 Ap '58. *
89. Porteus, S. D. "What Do the Maze Tests Measure?" *Austral J Psychol* 10:245–56 D '58. * (*PA* 34:2780)
90. Verrill, Bernard Victor. *An Investigation of the*

Concept of Impulsivity. Doctor's thesis, University of Houston (Houston, Tex.), 1958. (*DA* 19:183)
91. FOULDS, G. A. "The Relative Stability of Personality Measures Compared With Diagnostic Measures." *J Mental Sci* 105:783-7 Jl '59. * (*PA* 34:6016)
92. FOULDS, G. A., AND CAINE, T. M. "Symptom Clusters and Personality Types Among Psychoneurotic Men Compared With Women." *J Mental Sci* 105:469-75 Ap '59. * (*PA* 34:4715)
93. LORANGER, ARMAND W., AND MISIAK, HENRYK. "Critical Flicker Frequency and Some Intellectual Functions in Old Age." *J Gerontol* 14:323-7 Jl '59. * (*PA* 34:4153)
94. PORTEUS, S. D. "Recent Maze Test Studies." *Brit J Med Psychol* 32:38-43 pt 1 '59. * (*PA* 34:2690)
95. PORTEUS, STANLEY D. *The Maze Test and Clinical Psychology.* Palo Alto, Calif.: Pacific Books, 1959. Pp. vii, 203. * (*PA* 34:3571)
96. ARONSON, H., AND KLEE, G. D. "Effect of Lysergic Acid Diethylamide (LSD-25) on Impulse Control." *J Nerv & Mental Dis* 131:536-9 D '60. *
97. DOCTER, RICHARD F. "Interrelationships Among Porteus Maze Test Qualitative Errors." *J Clin Psychol* 16:336-8 Jl '60. * (*PA* 36:2HE36D)
98. DOCTER, RICHARD F. "Test-Retest Performance of Schizophrenics on Two Forms of the Porteus Mazes." *J Clin Psychol* 16:185-7 Ap '60. * (*PA* 36:2JQ85D)
99. HENKER, BARBARA A. *The Porteus Maze Test and Female Delinquency: A Controlled Comparison of the Qualitative Score Performance of Delinquent and Non-Delinquent Girls.* Master's thesis, Sacramento State College (Sacramento, Calif.), 1960.
100. JUDSON, ABE J. "The Effects of Chlorpromazine on Psychological Test Scores." Abstract. *J Consult Psychol* 24:192 Ap '60. * (*PA* 34:7888)
101. LORANGER, ARMAND W., AND MISIAK, HENRYK. "The Performance of Aged Females on Five Non-Language Tests of Intellectual Functions." *J Clin Psychol* 16:189-91 Ap '60. * (*PA* 36:2FI89L)
102. PORTEUS, S. D., AND KLEMAN, J. P. "A New Anthropometric Approach." *Mankind Q* 1:23-30 Jl '60. *
103. PORTEUS, S. D.; BARCLAY, J. E.; CULVER, H. S.; AND KLEMAN, J. P. "Measurement of Subconscious Memory." *Percept & Motor Skills* 10:215-29 Je '60. * (*PA* 35:6448)
104. SARASON, SEYMOUR B.; DAVIDSON, KENNETH S.; LIGHTHALL, FREDERICK K.; WAITE, RICHARD R.; AND RUEBUSH, BRITTON K. *Anxiety in Elementary School Children: A Report of Research,* pp. 171-88. New York: John Wiley & Sons, Inc., 1960. Pp. viii, 351. * (*PA* 34:7494)
105. SMITH, AARON. "Changes in Porteus Maze Scores of Brain-Operated Schizophrenics After an Eight-Year Interval." *J Mental Sci* 106:967-78 Jl '60. * (*PA* 35:5044)
106. BAREY, JOHN R.; EVERSTINE, LOUIS; AND KLEMAN, JOHN P. "An Abbreviated Qualitative Score for the Porteus Mazes." *J Clin Psychol* 17:291 Jl '61. * (*PA* 38:8398)
107. JENSEN, MILTON B. "The 'Low Level' Airman in Retesting and Basic Training: A Sociopsychological Study." *J Social Psychol* 55:177-90 D '61. * (*PA* 36:3LD77J)
108. PORTEUS, S. D. "Ethnic Group Differences." *Mankind Q* 1:187-200 Ja '61. *
109. ZUBIN, JOSEPH; SUTTON, SAMUEL; SALZINGER, KURT; SALZINGER, SUZANNE; BURDOCK, E. I.; AND PERETZ, DAVID. Chap. 10, "A Biometric Approach to Prognosis in Schizophrenia," pp. 143-203. In *Comparative Epidemiology of the Mental Disorders.* The Proceedings of the Forty-Ninth Annual Meeting of the American Psychopathological Association, Held in New York City, February 1959. Edited by Paul H. Hoch and Joseph Zubin. New York: Grune & Stratton, Inc., 1961. Pp. xvi, 290. * (*PA* 36:2JV90H)
110. CRAFT, MICHAEL; FABISCH, WALTER; STEPHENSON, GEOFFRY; BURNAND, GORDON; AND KERRIDGE, DAVID. "100 Admissions to a Psychopathic Unit." *J Mental Sci* 108:564-83 S '62. * (*PA* 38:2138)
111. DENTLER, ROBERT A., AND MACKLER, BERNARD. "The Porteus Maze Test as a Predictor of Functioning Abilities of Retarded Children." *J Consult Psychol* 26:50-5 F '62. * (*PA* 37:5400)
112. PORTEUS, S. D. "Maze Test Reports." *Percept & Motor Skills* 14:58 F '62. * (*PA* 37:3230)
113. PORTEUS, S. D., AND DIAMOND, A. L. "Porteus Maze Changes After Psychosurgery." *J Mental Sci* 108:53-8 Ja '62. * (*PA* 37:1382)
114. PURCELL, KENNETH; TURNBULL, JOHN W.; AND BERNSTEIN, LEWIS. "Distinctions Between Subgroups of Asthmatic Children: Psychological Test and Behavior Rating Comparisons." *J Psychosom Res* 6:283-91 O-D '62. * (*PA* 37:8210)
115. TOBIAS, JACK, AND GORELICK, JACK. "The Porteus Maze Test and the Appraisal of Retarded Adults." *Am J Mental Def* 66:600-6 Ja '62. * (*PA* 36:4JI00T)
116. AARONSON, BERNARD S. "The Comparative Sensitivity of the Qualitative and Quantitative Porteus Maze Scores to Drug Effects." *J Clin Psychol* 19:184-5 Ap '63. * (*PA* 39:4180)
117. ANTHONY, ARISTOTLE A. "The Relationship Between Neuroticism, Stress, and Qualitative Porteus Maze Performance." *J Consult Psychol* 27:513-9 D '63. * (*PA* 38:9090)
118. ANTHONY, ARISTOTLE ARISTIDES. *The Relationship Between Anxiety and Qualitative Porteus Maze Performance.* Doctor's thesis, Columbia University (New York, N.Y.), 1963. (*DA* 24:2119)
119. BRIGGS, PETER F. "The Validity of the Porteus Maze Test Completed With the Non-Dominant Hand." *J Clin Psychol* 19:427-9 O '63. *
120. GREGOR, A. JAMES, AND MCPHERSON, D. ANGUS. "The Correlation of the Porteus Maze and the Gestalt Continuation as Personnel Selection Tests of Peripheral Peoples." *J Psychol* 56:137-42 Jl '63. * (*PA* 38:4276)
121. PORTEUS, S. D., AND GREGOR, A. JAMES. "Studies in Intercultural Testing." *Percept & Motor Skills* 16:705-24 Je '63. * (*PA* 38:6026)
122. RUEBUSH, BRITTON K.; BYRUM, MILDRED; AND FARNHAM, LOUISE J. "Problem Solving as a Function of Defensiveness and Parental Behavior." *J Abn & Social Psychol* 67:355-62 O '63. * (*PA* 38:4084)

For reviews by C. M. Louttit and Gladys C. Schwesinger, see 4:356; for excerpts from related book reviews, see B400, 4:357, 38:B453, and 36:B210.

[533]

★Quick Screening Scale of Mental Development. Ages 6 months to 10 years; 1963; individual; 6 mental age ratings: body coordination, manual performance, speech and language, listening attention and number, play interests, general mental level (mean of preceding 5 ratings); 1 form (4 pages); manual (6 pages); no data on reliability of subscores; tentative norms; no description of normative population; $10 per examiner's kit of 25 tests and manual (must be purchased to obtain manual); $5 per additional 25 tests; cash orders postpaid; specimen set not available; (30) minutes; Katharine M. Banham; Psychometric Affiliates. *

BOYD R. MCCANDLESS, *Professor of Education and Psychology; Director, University School Clinic Complex; and Chairman, Department of Special Education; Indiana University, Bloomington, Indiana.*

THE TEST. This scale consists of five sections, each of which contains 16 statements "of readily observable behavior." Each statement is keyed "to an age between six months and ten" years. Items are arranged in order of age, one item for each six months' level up to 6 years, and one item for each 12 months' level from 6 to 10 years. According to the author (and from inspection of the items), most items have been taken from already standardized tests of motor ability or general aptitude. Thus, despite the author's failure to indicate reliability either for individual items or for the five categories of the test, notions of the reliability of most individual items can be gained by patient research, and an estimate for the different categories can be formed. The "basal" for each category is passes on two successive items, the "ceiling" failures on two successive items.

Most of the items in Part 1, Bodily Coordination, from age 6 on are postural, and some of the items for the very young seem prematurely placed. In category 2, Manual Performance, all items from age 1-6 are drawing items, and six of them (and all from age 8 on) are draw-a-man items of one form or another. Category 3, Speech and Language, is conventional, although the reviewer believes that too much reliance is placed on parental report for verbalization items at 1-0 and 1-6 years. For category 4, Listening, Attention, and Number, items test attention and imitation through 2-0 years and thereafter are made up entirely of digit span (forward and backward), counting, and simple arithmetic tasks. Factorially, this is probably a rather complex category. Category 5, Play Interests, depends almost entirely on parental report for its scoring, or upon an inordinate amount of time spent in observing. Its first three items overlap with Manual Performance and Listening, Attention, and Number.

A "Mental Level" can be calculated for each of the five categories, although the term "Mental" appears ill suited for category 1, Bodily Coordination. Total mental level is estimated from a composite of scores for all five categories. Again, the inclusion of category 1 seems dubious in view of the essential lack of correlation, described in the literature, between motor-postural behavior and behavior more conventionally described as "mental" or "intellectual."

THE MANUAL. The author's goal—to help busy clinicians—is unexceptionable, although print in the manual is so fine that the busy clinician is likely to have to hunt out his reading glasses unless his eyes are young and strong. The presence of errors and careless reporting is disturbing to this reviewer: In one place, category 4 is referred to as category 3; in another spot, mention is made of "the four categories of behavior" and later of the "five mental levels." "Validity coefficients" (*r*'s) with the Binet L-M and the Cattell—58 and 13 children, respectively, aged 6 months to 12 years—are reported as .89 and .95, respectively. These (chronologically heterogeneous) samples are not described, nor is the sample or its size for the reported test-retest correlation of .93, based on a one-month interval.

The reviewer was not happy with the rationale for the heavy infusion of digit span items: "because of their indicative value as an aid in discovering emotional disturbances."

Banham recommends a fluid testing procedure, gives adequate cautions about testing conditions, provides illustrative indirect questions for eliciting information from adult informants about Play Interests, and provides directions for administering and scoring each item. These strike the reviewer as particularly inadequate for many of the drawing items.

In sum, this is a rough screening instrument, only tentatively standardized, not well supported by its manual, and—the reviewer believes—of only modest usefulness to "busy clinicians" in its present form.

[534]

★The Quick Test. Ages 2 and over; 1958–62; picture vocabulary; individual; Forms 1, 2, 3, ('58, 1 card); provisional manual ('62, 54 pages, reprint of 2 below); instruction cardboard ('62, 1 page); item cardboard ('62, 1 page, includes words for all 3 forms); record-norms sheet ('62, 2 pages); norms for combinations of 2 or 3 forms also presented; $8 per set of testing materials including all 3 forms, 100 record sheets, and manual; $2.50 per manual; cash orders postpaid; specimen set not available (manual illustrates all materials); (3–10) minutes; R. B. Ammons and C. H. Ammons; Psychological Test Specialists. *

REFERENCES

1. BURGESS, THOMAS C. "Form Equivalence of the Ammons Quick Picture Vocabulary Test." *Psychol Rep* 5:276 Je '59. * (*PA* 34:3433)

2. AMMONS, R. B., AND AMMONS, C. H. "The Quick Test (QT): Provisional Manual." *Psychol Rep* 11:111–61 Ag '62. * (*PA* 37:4941)

3. BURGESS, THOMAS C., AND WRIGHT, DOLORES D. "Seventh-Grade Evaluation of the Ammons Quick Test (QT)." *Psychol Rep* 10:791–4 Je '62. * (*PA* 37:5644)

BOYD R. MCCANDLESS, *Professor of Education and Psychology; Director, University School Clinic Complex; and Chairman, Department of Special Education; Indiana University, Bloomington, Indiana.*

For discussion purposes, this test seems to the reviewer to be best approached in much the same way the examiner of any new test approaches it: first, he is curious about the smaller items of the kit, then moves on to its manual and standardization and finally, often with a peek ahead, to the test itself.

INSTRUCTION CARDBOARDS. These are two easily handled sheets, clearly printed, one of which gives suggestions for administration, scoring, and interpretation, while the other lists, in approximate order of difficulty, the 50 items (words) for each of the three forms of the test.

The former gives in admirably brief and simple form two easy sets of instructions for introducing the test to the testee, informs the examiner that, for each of the three forms, the base of the test is six consecutive passes, while its ceiling is six successive failures; gives a rationale about guessing and suggestions for minimizing it; indicates that probing for unusual responses should be carried out and gives suggestions for how to do this; makes a brief introduction to the norms and final scores; and suggests flexible administrative procedures.

PROVISIONAL MANUAL. The Manual is respectably complete, is simply written (even chattily at times), and is frank about the aspirations the authors hold for the test but also realistic about its weaknesses (although they perhaps pass rather lightly over the facts that the sample, first, is not particularly large for a test so ambitiously designed, second, does not extend beyond the age limit of 45 years, and third, is geographically circumscribed).

The test is modeled closely after the authors' *Full-Range Picture Vocabulary Test*. Preliminary work on the present offspring seems sound enough; the sample is rather well balanced from nursery school through grade 12, plus an occupationally stratified adult sample, evenly divided between men and women, of from 24 to 45 years (distribution by age within the sample is not reported). The sample for the school aged subjects is selected by grade rather than by age, and the increasing age heterogeneity as we move into the upper grades is duly noted.

Clear information about percentiles and quotients (mean quotient is about 100, SD about 15) is provided. A number of reliability statistics (conservatively given by restricted age ranges) are reported. The most meaningful reliabilities, perhaps, are the interform reliabilities. These range from .60 to .96, the latter being based on an exception to the narrow age ranges usually employed (it is based on subjects ranging from age 2 through twelfth grade).

Most of the reported validities concern correlations of the QT with the parent instrument. As might be expected, these are high, from the high .60's into the .90's.

There is a chatty and interesting section in the manual on who should use the test, how novices should be trained, and how guessing should be handled, as well as other potentially useful testing tips.

The limits of the upper score ranges (above IQ 135) are discussed frankly and accurately enough, in the reviewer's judgment; the reported gain from age 17 to maturity (at least to age 30) seems sensible enough, and adequate appendices are also provided.

THE TEST. There are three 50-word forms, each form having as its basis a single plate of four complex line drawings. These seem adequate to the reviewer, and could, in his judgment, be used easily in most western or industrial cultures. Terminal scores can be computed for the forms, separately or together.

The record sheets impressed the reviewer favorably. They are clear, handy, and self-contained in providing for recording, scoring, and final establishment of percentile, MA and —for adults—IQ scores, for each form singly, and for the combined forms.

In summary, the QT appears to be worth looking into further as a clinical instrument and as a possibly useful tool around which a nomothetic network may be built.

ELLEN V. PIERS, *Associate Professor of Psychology, The Pennsylvania State University, University Park, Pennsylvania.*

The *Quick Test* is described in the manual as the "little brother" of the *Full-Range Picture Vocabulary Test* (FRPV). It was developed to provide new stimulus materials, additional forms which could be used with the FRPV, and a *very brief* intelligence test. Its purpose is the same as the FRPV—that is, to provide rapid intelligence screening, or to estimate the intelligence of special groups such as the mentally or physically handicapped for whom standard measures cannot be used. For the screening of large groups, the saving of an additional five or so minutes may indeed be valuable. For clinical purposes, however, considering the length of time typically spent on a Rorschach or TAT, 5 or 10 minutes hardly seems worth saving, particularly when reliability suffers. This point is apparently recognized by the authors in that they frequently recommend giving all three forms of the test, or combining the QT with the FRPV.

Plates have been reduced from 16 for the two forms of the FRPV to one plate for each of three forms of the QT. No rationale is given for the choice of the original drawings, the process apparently having been completely empirical. The drawings are designed to elicit responses at all difficulty levels. Though an ingenious idea, it does not seem entirely successful. Not only is there a great deal of detail in many of the pictures, but the drawings themselves are made with such heavy lines as to render many details ambiguous. That this is unnecessary is evident when one looks either at the *Peabody Picture Vocabulary Test* or the *Van Alstyne Picture Vocabulary Test* whose drawings are sharp and clear.

The effect of this ambiguity will probably be most evident at the lower levels. Recently this reviewer observed the testing of a 12-year-old severe retardate without speech. On the Peabody he obtained a mental age of 2 years 2 months but he could not complete a single item on the *Quick Test.* The extrapolated scores presented for ages 2-0 and 1-5 should therefore (as the authors suggest) be used very cautiously until more evidence is available.

Reliability estimates are all alternate form. Mean interform coefficients for one age level or for restricted ranges are seldom above the .60's, although the two- and three-form coefficients predicted from these by the Spearman-Brown formula range from .75 to .92. Wider age ranges show correspondingly higher reliabilities. Standard errors are given only for raw scores and not for IQ's. But by using the standard deviation which was adjusted to 15 IQ points, one could predict standard errors of measurement of over 9 IQ points in some cases for a single form.

Validity data so far consist chiefly of comparisons with the FRPV, some school grades, and some achievement tests. The former comparisons are unfortunately limited to preschoolers or college age and above. Ignoring the corrections for attenuation, they range from .62 to .93. The authors feel that they are high enough so that the QT and FRPV can be used interchangeably, and that since FRPV correlates well with other measures of intelligence one can assume that the QT will also, and therefore has high validity. Although perhaps a reasonable assumption, the reviewer would prefer a little more evidence before accepting it as fact. Certainly the logic for their further deduction that the QT therefore comprises a better measure of intelligence than the Wechsler or Binet is extremely questionable.

Some materials of the QT are a considerable improvement over the FRPV. Answer sheets are printed, and usable for any form. Mental age norms for "458 white children and adults," and IQ's and percentiles for an unspecified number of white adults are on the back. However, IQ's are not reported for children, although it is suggested that one can divide MA's by CA's, particularly when all three forms are given. One wonders, why not deviation IQ's? For adults, IQ values are extrapolated beyond 65 and 135.

At first glance, the standardization sample of 458 cases ranging from 2 years to adulthood (plus 40 supplementary cases) seems woefully inadequate. The authors contend, however, that this was carefully controlled for age, grade placement, own (or husband's) or father's occupation, and sex. On the basis of previous work they felt that geographical control was not important.

In general, any weaknesses of the norms, both for preschoolers and adults, are clearly pointed out, and limitations of use suggested. Another good feature is the spelling out of restrictions concerning use of the test in general. The one-page test description says, "Critical decisions of considerable importance demand supporting data from other tests. Interpretations by non-psychologists should be cautious." Tests which are otherwise good, such as the Peabody, might incorporate some of these cautions.

Finally, the provisional manual is a great improvement after the years of inadequate information concerning the FRPV. But the authors have failed to make a distinction between a manual and a research monograph. A manual should be shorter and more concise. Important material seems buried in their present long narrative. This reviewer spent considerable time trying to find the answers to the usual questions which could be contained in a dozen pages. The rest is valuable but could be published separately.

In spite of the weaknesses of the *Quick Test,* it will probably, like the FRPV, be very useful as a large-scale screening test, particularly when time is at a premium. But it is doubtful, in view of the somewhat questionable standardization, the lack of established, first-hand validity, and the complexity and poor quality of the drawings, whether a clinician would choose it over other available instruments at this point. Final evaluation must await further research.

[535]

★Slosson Intelligence Test (SIT). Ages 1 month and over; 1961–64; based in part upon *Stanford-Binet Intelligence Scale, Third Revision* and *Gesell Developmental Schedules;* individual; 1 form ('63, c1961–63); manual ('63, c1961–63, 43 pages, including test questions, sample score sheet, IQ finder, and other materials); score sheet ('63, 2 pages); IQ classification chart ('64, 2 pages); $3.75 per examiner's kit of manual, pad of 20 score sheets, and pad of 20 copies of the *Slosson Oral Reading Test;* 75¢ per additional pad of 20 score sheets; 75¢ per pad of 20 IQ classification charts; postpaid; (10–30) minutes; Richard L. Slosson; Slosson Educational Publications. *

[536]

***Stanford-Binet Intelligence Scale, Third Revision.** Ages 2 and over; 1916–60; a single-form combination of items selected from Forms L and M ('37) of the Second Revision, which is still available (see 5:413); individual; Form L-M ('60); manual ('60, 374 pages, see *657a* below); record booklet ('60, 15 pages); record form ('60, 5 pages); no data on reliability; $33.20 (160*s.*) per set of test materials including manual; $4.40 (28*s.*) per 35 record booklets; $2.20 (14*s.*) per 35 abbreviated record forms; $4.48 (21*s.*) per manual; postage extra; (30–90) minutes; revised IQ tables by Samuel R. Pinneau; Lewis M. Terman and Maud A. Merrill; Houghton Mifflin Co. * (British edition: George G. Harrap & Co. Ltd.)

REFERENCES

1–134. See 40:1420.
135–351. See 3:292.
352–493. See 4:358.
494–620. See 5:413.
621. MATEER, FLORENCE. "The Future of Clinical Psychology." *J Delinq* 6:283–93 Ja '21. *
622. GARRISON, S. C., AND TIPPETT, JAMES S. "Comparison of the Binet-Simon and Otis Tests." *J Ed Res* 6:42–8 Je '22. *
623. ROOT, W. T. "Correlations Between Binet Tests and Group Tests." *J Ed Psychol* 13:286–92 My '22. *
624. ROSANOFF, AARON J. Chap. 4, "Stanford Revision and Extension of the Binet-Simon Intelligence Scale," pp. 500–38. In his *Manual of Psychiatry, Sixth Edition.* New York: John Wiley & Sons, 1927. Pp. xvii, 697. *
625. ROBERTS, J. A. FRASER; NORMAN, R. M.; AND GRIFFITHS, RUTH. "Studies in a Child Population: 3, Intelligence and Family Size." *Ann Eug* 8:178–215 Ja '38. * (*PA* 12:4260)
626. LIDZ, THEODORE; GAY, JAMES R.; AND TIETZE, CHRISTOPHER. "Intelligence in Cerebral Deficit States and Schizophrenia Measured by Kohs Block Test." *Arch Neurol & Psychiatry* 48:568–82 O '42. * (*PA* 17:862)
627. MCNEMAR, QUINN. Chap. 12, "Intellectual Status of the Gifted Subjects as Adults," pp. 140–6. In *The Gifted Child Grows Up: Twenty-Five Years' Follow-Up of a Superior Group.* By Lewis M. Terman and others. Genetic Studies of Genius, Vol. 4. Stanford, Calif.: Stanford University Press, 1947. Pp. xiv, 448. * (*PA* 22:2080)
628. TERMAN, LEWIS M., AND ODEN, MELITA H.; IN ASSOCIATION WITH NANCY BAYLEY, HELEN MARSHALL, QUINN MCNEMAR, AND ELLEN B. SULLIVAN. Chap. 11, "Intelligence Tests of 1940," pp. 125–39. In their *The Gifted Child Grows Up: Twenty-Five Years' Follow-Up of a Superior Group.* Genetic Studies of Genius, Vol. 4. Stanford, Calif.: Stanford University Press, 1947. Pp. xiv, 448. * (*PA* 22:2080)
629. MCFIE, J., AND PIERCY, M. F. "Intellectual Impairment With Localized Cerebral Lesions." *Brain* 75:292–311 S '52. * (*PA* 27:7649)
630. MILLER, ELSA, AND ROSENFELD, GEORGE B. "The Psychologic Evaluation of Children With Cerebral Palsy and Its Implications in Treatment: Preliminary Report." *J Pediatrics* 41:613–21 N '52. * (*PA* 27:6706)
631. BERKO, MARTIN J. "A Note on 'Psychometric Scatter' as a Factor in the Differentiation of Exogenous and Endogenous Mental Deficiency." *Cerebral Palsy R* 16:20 Ja–F '55. * (*PA* 29:8715)
632. BERKO, MARTIN J. "Psychometric Scatter: Its Application in the Clinical Prediction of Future Mental Development in Cases of Childhood Brain Injury." *Cerebral Palsy R* 16:16–8 Mr–Ap '55. * (*PA* 30:1011)
633. KATZ, ELIAS. "Intelligence Test Performance of 'Athetoid' and 'Spastic' Children With Cerebral Palsy." *Cerebral Palsy R* 16:17–8 My–Je '55. * (*PA* 30:3303)
634. KATZ, ELIAS. "Success on Stanford-Binet Intelligence Scale Test Items of Children With Cerebral Palsy as Compared With Non-Handicapped Children." *Cerebral Palsy R* 16:18–9 Ja–F '55. * (*PA* 29:8855)
635. KATZ, ELIAS. "A Method of Selecting Stanford-Binet Intelligence Scale Test Items for Evaluating the Mental Abilities of Children Severely Handicapped by Cerebral Palsy." *Cerebral Palsy R* 17:13–5 Ja–F '56. * (*PA* 31:1566)
636. FIRNHABER, EDGAR P. *Variations in Performance on the Stanford Binet Figure Completion Test Among Children of Different Mental Ages.* Master's thesis, University of Nebraska (Lincoln, Neb.), 1957.
637. GALLAGHER, JAMES J. *A Comparison of Brain-Injured and Non-Brain-Injured Mentally Retarded Children on Several Psychological Variables.* Monograph of the Society for Research in Child Development, Vol. 22, No. 2. Lafayette, Ind.: Child Development Publications, 1957. Pp. 79. * (*PA* 33:1632)
638. BRADWAY, KATHERINE P.; THOMPSON, CLARE W.; AND CRAVENS, RICHARD B. "Preschool IQs After Twenty-Five Years." *J Ed Psychol* 49:278–81 O '58. * (*PA* 36:2HD78B)
639. HIGGINS, CONWELL, AND SIVERS, CATHRYNE H. "A Comparison of Stanford-Binet and Colored Raven Progressive Matrices IQs for Children With Low Socioeconomic Status." *J Consult Psychol* 22:465–8 D '58. * (*PA* 33:9919)
640. MUNDY, LYDIA, AND MAXWELL, A. E. "Assessment of the Feebleminded." *Brit J Med Psychol* 31:201–10 pt 3 & 4 '58. * (*PA* 34:1673)
641. SCHACHTER, FRANCES FUCHS, AND APGAR, VIRGINIA. "Comparison of Preschool Stanford-Binet and School-Age WISC IQs." *J Ed Psychol* 49:320–3 D '58. * (*PA* 36:2HD20S)
642. WILSON, BARBARA A. *A Comparison of Intelligence Quotients for Readers and Non-Readers Using the Leiter International Performance Scale and the 1937 Revision of the Stanford-Binet.* Master's thesis, Sacramento State College (Sacramento, Calif.), 1958.
643. LEHMANN, IRVIN J. "Rural-Urban Differences in Intelligence." *J Ed Res* 53:62–8 O '59. * (*PA* 35:780)
644. LEVINSON, BORIS M. "A Comparison of the Performance of Bilingual and Monolingual Native Born Jewish Preschool Children of Traditional Parentage on Four Intelligence Tests." *J Clin Psychol* 15:74–6 Ja '59. * (*PA* 34:2729)
645. NALE, STANLEY LEO. *A Factor Analysis of the Stanford-Binet Scores of Mentally Defective Children.* Doctor's thesis, Pennsylvania State University (University Park, Pa.), 1959. (*DA* 20:760)
646. POST, MILDRED. *Differences in Performance on Stanford-Binet Items of Children Who Function Above and Below Grade Level in Word Recognition.* Doctor's thesis, Syracuse University (Syracuse, N.Y.), 1959. (*DA* 20:590)
647. BYRD, ENOLA. *The Equivalence of the Two Forms of the 1937 Revision of the Stanford-Binet Intelligence Scale.* Master's thesis, Atlanta University (Atlanta, Ga.), 1960.
648. DUNSDON, M. I.; CARTER, C. O.; AND HUNTLEY, R. M. C. "Upper End of Range of Intelligence in Mongolism." *Lancet* 7124:565–8 Mr 12 '60. *
649. FRANCEY, RUTH E. "Psychological Test Changes in Mentally Retarded Children During Training." *Can J Pub Health* 51:69–74 F '60. *
650. KADELL, MARY BELLE. *A Factor Analysis of the Vineland Social Maturity Scale and the Stanford-Binet Intelligence Scale.* Master's thesis, University of Minnesota (Minneapolis, Minn.), 1960.
651. KIDD, ALINE HALSTEAD. *A Factor and Item Analysis of the Test of G; Culture-Free and the Stanford-Binet, Form L.* Doctor's thesis, University of Arizona (Tucson, Ariz.), 1960. (*DA* 21:366)
652. KONSTANS, D. JANICE. *Stanford-Binet Responses of Elementary School Children: A Relational Analysis of Range, Intellectual Performance, Race, and Sex.* Master's thesis, University of Chicago (Chicago, Ill.), 1960.
653. LEVINSON, BORIS M. "The Binet Non-Verbal Preschool Scale." *J Clin Psychol* 16:12–3 Ja '60. * (*PA* 36:1HC12L)
654. LEVINSON, BORIS M., AND BLOCK, ZELICK. "Research Note on Columbia Mental Maturity Scale (CMMS) and Revised Stanford Binet (L) in a Preschool Population." *J Clin Psychol* 16:158–9 Ap '60. * (*PA* 36:2HC58L)
655. MAXWELL, JAMES, AND PILLINER, A. E. G. "The Intellectual Resemblance Between Sibs." *Ann Hum Genetics* 24:23–32 Ap '60. * (*PA* 35:2199)
656. STEIN, ZENA, AND SUSSER, MERVYN. "Families of Dull Children: Part 4, Increments in Intelligence." *J Mental Sci* 106:1311–9 O '60. * (*PA* 35:5182)
657. STOTT, D. H. "Observations on Retest Discrepancy in Mentally Sub-Normal Children." *Brit J Ed Psychol* 30:211–9 N '60. *
657a. TERMAN, LEWIS M., AND MERRILL, MAUD A. *Stanford-Binet Intelligence Scale: Manual for the Third Revision, Form L-M.* With revised IQ tables by Samuel R. Pinneau. Boston, Mass.: Houghton-Mifflin Co., 1960. Pp. xi, 363. *
658. WEISE, PHILLIP. "Current Uses of Binet and Wechsler Tests by School Psychologists in California." *Calif J Ed Res* 11:73–8 Mr '60. * (*PA* 35:7098)
659. ZUK, G. H. "Size: Its Significance in the Copied Drawings of Children." *J Clin Psychol* 16:38–42 Ja '60. * (*PA* 36:1HE38Z)
660. ACK, MARVIN; MILLER, IRVING; AND WEIL, WILLIAM B., JR. "Intelligence of Children With Diabetes Mellitus." *Pediatrics* 28:764–70 N '61. *
661. ANASTASI, ANNE. *Psychological Testing, Second Edition,* pp. 189–212. New York: Macmillan Co., 1961. Pp. xiii, 657. * (*PA* 36:1HA57A)
662. BRADWAY, KATHERINE P., AND ROBINSON, NANCY M. "Significant IQ Changes in Twenty-Five Years: A Follow-Up." *J Ed Psychol* 52:74–9 Ap '61. * (*PA* 38:2484)
663. BRENGELMANN, JOHANNES C., AND KENNY, JOSEPH T.

"Comparison of Leiter, WAIS and Stanford-Binet IQ's in Retardates." *J Clin Psychol* 17:235–8 Jl '61. * (*PA* 38:8953)
664. DARBES, ALEX. "A Comparison of Scores Achieved by 55 Subjects Administered the Wechsler and Binet Scales of Intelligence." *Proc W Va Acad Sci* 33:115–9 N '61. * (*PA* 36:5HD15D)
665. DRILLIEN, CECIL MARY. "A Longitudinal Study of the Growth and Development of Prematurely and Maturely Born Children: Part 7, Mental Development 2–5 Years." *Arch Dis Childh* 36:233–40 Je '61. *
666. DUNSDON, M. I., AND ROBERTS, J. A. FRASER. Chap. 3, "A Study of the Performance of 2000 Children on Four Vocabulary Tests," pp. 41–76. In *Stoke Park Studies: Mental Subnormality (Second Series): World Mental Health Year Memorial Volume.* Edited by J. Jancar. Bristol, England: John Wright & Sons Ltd., 1961. Pp. x, 135. *
667. ESTES, BETSY WORTH; CURTIN, MARY ELLEN; DEBURGER, ROBERT A.; AND DENNY, CHARLOTTE. "Relationships Between 1960 Stanford-Binet, 1937 Stanford-Binet, WISC, Raven, and Draw-A-Man." *J Consult Psychol* 25:388–91 O '61. * (*PA* 37:3127)
668. FISHER, GARY M.; KILMAN, BEVERLY A.; AND SHOTWELL, ANNA M. "Comparability of Intelligence Quotients of Mental Defectives on the Wechsler Adult Intelligence Scale and the 1960 Revision of the Stanford-Binet." *J Consult Psychol* 25:192–5 Je '61. *
669. GASKINS, JOHN R. *A Comparison of the Stanford-Binet Form L and Form L-M Results of Educable Mentally Retarded Children.* Master's thesis, Kent State University (Kent, Ohio), 1961.
670. GRAHAM, DORIS D. *Some Relationships Between Early Stanford-Binet Scores and Later Measures of Achievement.* Master's thesis, Claremont College (Claremont, Calif.), 1961.
671. HEATON-WARD, W. A. Chap. 4, "An Interim Report on a Controlled Trial of the Effect of Niamid on the Mental Age and Behaviour of Mongols," pp. 77–80. In *Stoke Park Studies: Mental Subnormality (Second Series): World Mental Health Year Memorial Volume.* Edited by J. Jancar. Bristol, England: John Wright & Sons Ltd., 1961. Pp. x, 135. *
672. HIRSCHENFANG, SAMUEL. "Further Studies on the Columbia Mental Maturity Scale (CMMS) and Revised Stanford Binet (L) in Children With Speech Disorders." *J Clin Psychol* 17:171 Ap '61. * (*PA* 38:956)
673. HUNT, DENNIS. *The Comparative Performance of a Ten-Year-Old Group of Children on the Wechsler Intelligence Scale for Children and the Revised Stanford-Binet Scale of Intelligence, Form L-M.* Master's thesis, University of Saskatchewan (Saskatoon, Sask., Canada), 1961.
674. KENNEDY, WALLACE A.; MOON, HAROLD; NELSON, WILLARD; LINDNER, RONALD; AND TURNER, JACK. "The Ceiling of the New Stanford-Binet." *J Clin Psychol* 17:284–6 Jl '61. * (*PA* 38:8457)
675. LESSING, ELISE ELKINS. "A Note on the Significance of Discrepancies Between Goodenough and Binet IQ Scores." *J Consult Psychol* 25:456–7 O '61. * (*PA* 37:3130)
676. LYTTON, H. "Symposium: Contributions to the Diagnosis and Remedial Treatment of Reading Difficulties: 6, An Experiment in Selection for Remedial Education." *Brit J Ed Psychol* 31:79–95 F '61. * (*PA* 36:1KE79L)
677. MCFIE, JOHN. "The Effect of Education on African Performance on a Group of Intellectual Tests." *Brit J Ed Psychol* 31:232–40 N '61. * (*PA* 36:5HD32M)
678. PARSLEY, K. M., JR., AND POWELL, MARVIN. "Relationships Between the Lee-Clark Reading Readiness Test and the 1937 Revision of the Stanford-Binet Intelligence Test, Form L." *J Ed Res* 54:304–7 Ap '61. *
679. PAYNE, R. W. Chap. 6, "Cognitive Abnormalities," pp. 193–261. In *Handbook of Abnormal Psychology: An Experimental Approach.* Edited by H. J. Eysenck. New York: Basic Books, Inc., 1961. Pp. xvi, 816. * (*PA* 35:6719)
680. PINNEAU, SAMUEL R. *Changes in Intelligence Quotient: Infancy to Maturity: New Insights From the Berkeley Growth Study With Implications for the Stanford-Binet Scales and Applications to Professional Practice.* Boston, Mass.: Houghton Mifflin Co., 1961. Pp. xi, 233. * (*PA* 37:6706)
681. QUERESHI, MOHAMMED Y. "Effects of Various Scoring Cutoffs on Reliability Estimates." *Am J Mental Def* 65:753–60 My '61. * (*PA* 36:1HD53Q)
682. ROBERTS, HELEN ERSKINE. "Comparison of Otis and Stanford-Binet IQ's." *Calif J Ed Res* 12:8–15 Ja '61. * (*PA* 36:1HD08R)
683. SCHERER, ISIDOR W. "The Prediction of Academic Achievement in Brain Injured Children." *Excep Child* 28:103–6 O '61. *
684. SHINE, AILEEN. "Relationship Between Arithmetic Achievement and Item Performance on the Revised Stanford-Binet Scale." *Arith Teach* 9:57–9 F '61. *
685. SHINE, AILEEN ELIZABETH. *Relationship Between Arithmetic Achievement and Item Performance on the Revised Stanford-Binet Scale.* Doctor's thesis, University of Colorado (Boulder, Colo.), 1961. (*DA* 22:3047)
686. SILVERSTEIN, A. B., AND FISHER, GARY M. "An Evaluation of Two Short Forms of the Stanford-Binet, Form L-M, for Use With Mentally Retarded Adults." *Am J Mental Def* 65:486–8 Ja '61. * (*PA* 35:6818)
687. STOTT, D. H. "I.Q. Changes Among Educationally Sub-Normal Children." *Special Ed* 50:11–4 Je '61. *
688. BALDWIN, JOSEPH W. "The Relationship Between Teacher-Judged Giftedness, a Group Intelligence Test and an Individual Intelligence Test With Possible Gifted Kindergarten Pupils." *Gifted Child Q* 6:153–6 w '62. * (*PA* 37:8255)
689. BRADWAY, KATHERINE P., AND THOMPSON, CLARE W. "Intelligence at Adulthood: A Twenty-Five Year Follow-Up." *J Ed Psychol* 53:1–14 F '62. * (*PA* 37:1210)
690. CLELAND, DONALD L., AND TOUSSAINT, ISABELLA H. "The Interrelationships of Reading, Listening, Arithmetic Computation and Intelligence." *Reading Teach* 15:228–31 Ja '62. *
691. FLEMING, KATHRYN. *A Comparison of Mental Age Scores on the Revised Columbia Mental Maturity Scale and the Stanford-Binet Intelligence Test, Form L, at the Five Through Eight Year Mental Age Levels.* Master's thesis, Bowling Green State University (Bowling Green, Ohio), 1962.
692. FREEMAN, FRANK S. *Theory and Practice of Psychological Testing, Third Edition,* pp. 197–240, 323–30. New York: Holt, Rinehart & Winston, Inc., 1962. Pp. xix, 697. *
693. HARTMAN, BERNARD-THOMAS. *Comparative Investigation of the Peabody Picture Vocabulary Test With Three Etiologic Groups of Institutionalized Mentally Retarded Students.* Doctor's thesis, Indiana University (Bloomington, Ind.), 1962. (*DA* 23:2008)
694. HINDLEY, C. B. "Social Class Influences on the Development of Ability in the First Five Years," pp. 29–41. (*PA* 37:4717) In *Child and Education.* Proceedings of the XIV International Congress of Applied Psychology, Vol. 3. Copenhagen, Denmark: Munksgaard, Ltd., 1962. Pp. 197. *
695. HOLOWINSKY, IVAN. "IQ Constancy in a Group of Institutionalized Mental Defectives Over a Period of 3 Decades." *Training Sch B* 59:15–7 My '62. * (*PA* 37:3578)
696. HURST, JOHN G. "The Meaning and Use of Difference Scores Obtained Between the Performance on the Stanford-Binet Intelligence Scale and Vineland Social Maturity Scale." *J Clin Psychol* 18:153–60 Ap '62. * (*PA* 38:8422)
697. JARVIK, LISSY FEINGOLD. "Biological Differences in Intellectual Functioning." *Vita Hum* 5(4):195–203 '62. * (*PA* 38:970)
698. JARVIK, LISSY FEINGOLD; KALLMANN, FRANZ J.; AND FALEK, ARTHUR. "Intellectual Changes in Aged Twins." *J Gerontol* 17:289–94 Jl '62. * (*PA* 37:2952)
699. KIDD, ALINE H. "The Culture-Fair Aspects of Cattell's Test of g: Culture-Free." *J Genetic Psychol* 101:343–62 D '62. * (*PA* 37:6702)
700. MEIN, R. "Use of the Peabody Picture Vocabulary With Severely Subnormal Patients." *Am J Mental Def* 67:269–73 S '62. * (*PA* 37:3582)
701. NELSON, THOMAS M., AND BARTLEY, S. HOWARD. "Various Factors Playing a Role in Children's Responses to Flat Copy." *J Genetic Psychol* 100:289–308 Je '62. * (*PA* 37:2874)
702. ROHRS, FREDERICK W., AND HAWORTH, MARY R. "The 1960 Stanford-Binet, WISC, and Goodenough Tests With Mentally Retarded Children." *Am J Mental Def* 66:853–9 My '62. * (*PA* 37:1704)
703. THWEATT, ROGER C. "A Rapid Technique for Stanford-Binet Test Object Placement." *J Clin Psychol* 18:355 Jl '62. * (*PA* 39:1795)
704. VAN DE RIET, VERNON. *The Standardization of the Third Revision of the Stanford-Binet Intelligence Scale on Negro Elementary-School Children in Grades One, Two, and Three in the Southeastern United States.* Doctor's thesis, Florida State University (Tallahassee, Fla.), 1962. (*DA* 23:3985)
705. WHITE, JAMES C., JR. *The Standardization of the Third Revision of the Stanford-Binet Intelligence Scale on Negro Elementary-School Children in Grades Four, Five, and Six in the Southeastern United States.* Doctor's thesis, Florida State University (Tallahassee, Fla.), 1962. (*DA* 23:3969)
706. WILK, WALTER S. *A Comparative Study of the Wechsler Intelligence Scale for Children and the Revised Form of the Stanford-Binet Intelligence Scale.* Master's thesis, Southern Connecticut State College (New Haven, Conn.), 1962.
707. ZEAMAN, DAVID, AND HOUSE, BETTY J. "Mongoloid MA Is Proportional to Log CA." *Child Develop* 33:481–8 S '62. *
708. BENSON, ROBERT R. "The Binet Vocabulary Score as an Estimate of Intellectual Functioning." *J Clin Psychol* 19:134–5 Ja '63. * (*PA* 39:1715)
709. British Psychological Society, English Division of Professional Psychologists (Educational and Clinical). "Report of the Working Party on Subnormality." Prepared by J. H. F. Castell, A. D. B. Clarke, P. Mittler, and W. M. Woodward. *B Brit Psychol Soc* 16:37–50 O '63. *
710. BUDOFF, MILTON, AND PURSEGLOVE, ELEANOR MATHIAS. "Forms L and LM of the Stanford Binet Compared for an Institutionalized Adolescent Mentally Retarded Population." *J Clin Psychol* 19:214 Ap '63. * (*PA* 39:5041)
711. EDWARDS, ALLEN JACK. "Using Vocabulary as a Measure of General Ability." *Personnel & Guid J* 42:153–4 O '63. *
712. GARFUNKEL, FRANK, AND BLATT, BURTON. "The Standardization of Intelligence Tests on Southern Negro School Children." *Training Sch B* 60:94–9 Ag '63. * (*PA* 38:4274)
713. HIGGINS, CONWELL. "Multiple Predictor Score Cut-Offs Versus Multiple-Regression Cut-Offs in Selection of Academically Talented Children in Grade 3." *Yearb Nat Council Meas Ed* 20:153–64 '63. * (*PA* 38:9247)
714. HO, DAVID, AND WHITE, DELILAH T. "Use of the Full-

Range Picture Vocabulary Test With the Mentally Retarded." *Am J Mental Def* 67:761-4 Mr '63. * (*PA* 38:1275)
715. JARVIK, LISSY F., AND FALEK, ARTHUR. "Intellectual Stability and Survival in the Aged." *J Gerontol* 18:173-6 Ap '63. * (*PA* 38:4103)
715a. KENNEDY, WALLACE; VAN DE RIET, VERNON; AND WHITE, JAMES C., JR. *A Normative Sample of Intelligence and Achievement of Negro Elementary School Children in Southeastern United States.* Monographs of the Society for Research in Child Development, Vol. 28, No. 6. Lafayette, Ind.: Child Development Publications, 1963. Pp. 112. *
716. KENNEDY, WALLACE A.; VAN DE RIET, VERNON; AND WHITE, JAMES C., JR. "Use of the Terman-Merrill Abbreviated Scale on the 1960 Stanford-Binet Form L-M on Negro Elementary School Children of the Southeastern United States." *J Consult Psychol* 27:456-7 O '63. * (*PA* 38:4277)
717. NASH, PAT NEFF. *The Effectiveness of Composite Predictors of Reading Success in the First Grade.* Doctor's thesis, North Texas State University (Denton, Tex.), 1963. (*DA* 24:1482)
718. NEWLAND, T. ERNEST, AND MEEKER, MARY M. "Binet Behavior Samplings and Guilford's Structure of the Intellect." *J Sch Psychol* 2:55-9 w '63-64. *
719. PRINGLE, M. L. KELLMER, AND PICKUP, K. T. "The Reliability and Validity of the Goodenough Draw-A-Man Test: A Pilot Longitudinal Study." *Brit J Ed Psychol* 33:297-306 N '63. * (*PA* 38:8424)
720. RUSHTON, C. S., AND STOCKWIN, A. E. "Changes in Terman-Merrill I.Qs. of Educationally Sub-Normal Boys." *Brit J Ed Psychol* 33:132-42 Je '63. * (*PA* 38:4293)
721. SCHENA, RICHARD A. "A Search for Talented Pupils." *J Exp Ed* 32:27-41 f '63. *
722. SILVERSTEIN, A. B. "An Evaluation of Two Short Forms of the Stanford-Binet, Form L-M, for Use With Mentally Retarded Children." *Am J Mental Def* 67:922-3 My '63. * (*PA* 38:964)
723. SPEARMAN, LEONARD H. O. "A Profile Analysis Technique for Diagnosing Reading Disability." *Yearb Nat Council Meas Ed* 20:75-86 '63. * (*PA* 38:9235)
724. TATHAM, CLIFFORD B., AND DOLE, ARTHUR A. "A Note on the Relationship of CTMM-SF to the Revised Binet, Form L-M." *J Clin Psychol* 19:302 Jl '63. *
725. THOMPSON, JACK M., AND FINLEY, CARMEN J. "The Relationship Between the Goodenough Draw-A-Man Test and the Stanford-Binet Form L-M in Children Referred for School Guidance Services." *Calif J Ed Res* 14:19-22 Ja '63. * (*PA* 37:7875)
726. VALETT, ROBERT E. "A Clinical Profile for the Stanford-Binet." *J Sch Psychol* 2:49-54 w '63-64. *
727. WIENER, GERALD; RIDER, ROWLAND V.; AND OPPEL, WALLACE. "Some Correlates of IQ Changes in Children." *Child Develop* 34:61-7 Mr '63. * (*PA* 38:5777)
728. ZINGLE, HARVEY W., AND LAMBERT, ROLAND A. "Experimental Tests of Two Hypotheses Concerning Normalization of Form Perception." *Alberta J Ed Res* 9:147-56 S '63. *

ELIZABETH D. FRASER, *Professor of Psychology, University of Aberdeen, Aberdeen, Scotland.*

The most obvious feature of the 1960 revision of the *Stanford-Binet Intelligence Scale* is the condensation of the two earlier Forms L and M into one, the new L-M scale. The offspring of these 23-year-old parents inherits much more from the L parent than from M: the ratio of L to M items in the new scale is about 9 to 7.

Apart from this one major change, the test has been brought up to date by eliminating items that are no longer appropriate to the present day, and by reordering items which for some reason have altered in difficulty since 1937. The condensation into one form has allowed the selection of items which best satisfy the criteria of a good item, viz., that with increase in age there should be an increase in the percentage passing the item, and that the item should correlate well with the test as a whole.

In addition, a number of ambiguities in administration and scoring have been cleared up, the layout of the test material and of the test manual, especially the section on scoring standards, has been vastly improved, and the problem of fluctuating standard deviations of IQ's at different ages has at last been tackled.

Many of these changes are welcome, and even the loss of a parallel form is not likely to disturb the great majority of users. Form L was always much more widely used than Form M, and with the WISC now available as a second sound individual test, the need for a parallel form for the Stanford-Binet is less acute than it was in 1937.

The improvement in layout is particularly welcome. The clear differentiation between plus, Q, and minus answers for each item is a great improvement on the old manual. Scoring standards are still tucked away at the back of the book, and inexpert testers who have to check standards frequently will continue to be irritated. An arrangement by which each test item was followed by its scoring standards would inevitably lead to much duplication, but there might be something to be said for having scoring standards in a separate booklet altogether, so that one could have access to both test item and scoring criteria simultaneously.

The provision of conversion tables which automatically correct for differences in standard deviation at different ages, takes care of the old criticism that an IQ of 130 at age 6 did not mean the same as an IQ of 130 at age 8. But there is strong insistence on the fact that the Stanford-Binet is still an age scale making use of age standards of performance, although this begins to lose some of its point when one encounters at the adult levels mental ages of 22 years 11 months.

In all its fundamentals, however, the Stanford-Binet remains very much its old self. Minimal changes have been introduced into the items themselves, and at some ages it is almost exactly the old Form L. Testers experienced in the old version are not likely to find any difficulty in adjusting to the new.

The main criticism likely to be leveled at this revision is that these changes in subtest composition have been introduced without any restandardisation process. The putting together of the items with the greatest internal validity is well worthwhile, but there is no guarantee that the final test, taken as a whole, will give the same result as either the old Form L or Form M. Thus, even if items a + b + c + d + e + f from Form L were equivalent to items m + n + o + p + q + r from Form M, it is not necessarily true that a + b + m + d + q + r will be equivalent to either of the former groupings. This has yet to be shown to be the case.

Comparisons between the Stanford-Binet and the WISC will no doubt continue to be drawn, and the devotees of each test will continue to argue for the test of their choice. Some of the disadvantages of the Stanford-Binet have been eliminated, but it is still rather less convenient to administer than the WISC, and it does not attempt a breakdown analysis of the total score as WISC does. The advantages of the Stanford-Binet remain: better coverage at the lower end of the scale, and more reliable assessment of the extreme ranges of intelligence.

Austral J Ed 6:233–4 O '62. Marie D. Neale. This revision of the Stanford-Binet Intelligence Scale will be widely welcomed. Since its second revision in 1937, the scale has won outstanding recognition by psychologists working in diverse fields. It is not too much to claim that the scale has become a basic tool in psychological equipment for research and clinical diagnostic work. However, since the practical implications of an I.Q. obtained on the scale are extremely important, often affecting an individual's opportunities for schooling or placement within an educational setting, sensitive test users will be relieved to know that this revision addresses itself mainly to the provision of up-to-date content and more reliable norms. * In format, the 1960 revision has some pleasing features. Spiral binding has been used for the printed card material, making it easier for the examiner to locate and present particular test items in the correct sequence. From a limited use of the new scale, the reviewer would suggest that the presentation of the picture vocabulary in this form contributes greatly to the co-operation and interest of young subjects. The manual is well designed with clear, comprehensive directions for administering and scoring the test. The I.Q. tables, in particular, are well set out, attributing to both speed and efficiency in evaluating the results. * In summary, this revision is timely. Its material, manual and equipment are presented in an attractive format, while the changes in content and the revised I.Q. tables will assure it the respect and popularity which the 1937 revision has hitherto enjoyed.

Brit J Ed Psychol 32:214 Je '62. L. B. Birch. [Review of the British edition.] An anglicised version of the 1960 Terman and Merrill Test is now available in this country. * There is no doubt that the material in the new form is more appropriate to present-day conditions. This writer found it pleasant to use and easy to pick up from an intimate knowledge of the 1937 version. As yet, of course, we know nothing of the relevance of the norms for British children or whether corrections like that of Roberts and Mellone will be needed. A report by the Division of Professional Psychologists on field trials of the test will be welcomed.

Brit J Psychol 53:472 N '62. James Maxwell. [Review of the British Edition.] * The administration of the new scales will present no difficulty to users of the 1937 revision, and there seems justification for the claim that the more rigorous selection of items has improved the test. Another welcome improvement is the establishment of a uniform standard deviation of I.Q. for each age, so that an I.Q. of, say, 70 at age 6 means, relatively, the same as I.Q. 70 at age 12. Also, the book itself is well thought out in its presentation, with easy reference to test items and an adequate set of tables for conversions to I.Q. The new revision, however, is not wholly without debit items. The cost of an improved selection of items is the loss of the alternate version, which had its value in testing the Binet-sophisticated child. The cards and material accompanying the tests are well planned but are rather shoddy and somewhat expensive, and there seems also to be an unnecessarily profuse supply of different kinds of record forms. At the present stage, only the administration of the test can be assessed; the validity of the new item selection and the norms for British children is as yet unknown.

Personnel & Guid J 39:155–6 O '60. Benjamin Balinsky. * No basic changes were made in the revision. It is still an age scale and measures the same kind of mental activities as the original scale, mainly falling under the category of general intelligence. The changes are essentially in the subtests and their placement, and in certain improvements in the IQ Tables that eliminate atypical variability and make the IQ's for all ages comparable. The 1960 revision incorporates in a single scale the best of the subtests from the L and M Forms of the 1937 scale. * Much careful work seems to have been done in keeping the best test items and eliminating the worst. This revision is not a complete restandardization. The norms are essentially based on the 1937 standardization with adjustments resulting from the data obtained in the more recent samplings. The removal of obsolete items and the revised placement of certain of the subtests should make for a general improvement of the Scale. There are no validity data specific to the revision. Its validity is based upon the fact that the same type of tests are used as in the 1937 Scale. Because of the great amount of overlap and the careful selection of subtests to be used in the revision, the probability is high that the validity of the revision will be at least equal to if not greater than the 1937 version. * The book should serve its purposes very well. For any user of the revision it is a must. For students of intelligence testing it brings together succinctly the major outlines in the development of age scales and, if studied together with previous works on the subject, provides much important additional material.

Personnel & Guid J 39:226–7 N '60. Julian C. Stanley. * Constructing a well standardized age scale of intelligence is truly a formidable undertaking, and "retreading" an old one (published in 1937) is no chore for the faint-hearted. We are indebted to the late Professor Terman and to his collaborators on the 1937 and 1960 versions—especially Professors Maud Merrill and Quinn McNemar for their great zeal, energy, patience, and skill in combining laboratory standards of exactitude with extensive statistical verification. Along with Pinneau, who constructed the new standard-score IQ tables, they have elevated the "cut and trying" of age scaling to a high art and infused into it considerable science. We must ponder seriously, however, whether it is any longer worthwhile to work this hard preserving the cumulated-months mental age, only to fly to standard-score IQ tables (desired mean at each age level 100, standard deviation 16). Devising point scales seems much more straightforward, and it is possible to supplement standard scores and percentile ranks with grade equivalents and "point mental ages." Practically everyone, including Terman and Merrill, seems to have given up the MA/CA ratio-type IQ, thereby removing one of the chief reasons for having intelligence scales scored on the basis of months of mental age. A large number of psychologists —school and otherwise—will be grateful for this improved version of their favorite standardized interviewing technique, as it might be called. Gone are obsolescent items that puzzled today's children. (But the American flag still has only 48 stars!) Put together in one neat package are the best items from Forms L and M, even more heavily weighted with a general intellectual factor ("manipulation of symbols"?) than before * This reviewer concurs with their "reasonable assurance to test users that the third Revision of the Stanford-Binet Scales can be relied upon to perform even more dependably the functions that have come to be expected of them" (p. v). The revision is by no means a complete restandardization, but it does seem to be a distinct improvement in several respects.

For reviews by Mary R. Haworth and Norman D. Sundberg of the Second Edition, see 5:413; for a review by Boyd R. McCandless, see 4:358; see also 40:1420 (3 excerpts); for reviews by Francis N. Maxfield, J. W. M. Rothney, and F. L. Wells, see 38:1062; for excerpts from related book reviews, see B396, 3:293, 3:294, 40:B1093, and 38:B497.

[537]

***Van Alstyne Picture Vocabulary Test.** Mental ages 2–7; 1929–61; revision of *Van Alstyne Picture Vocabulary Test for Pre-school Children* ('29); individual; 1 form ('60, 61-page picture booklet); manual ('61, 15 pages); record blank ('61, 1 page); $4.80 per examiner's kit of picture booklet, manual, and record blank; $1.50 per 35 record blanks; postage extra; (15) minutes; Dorothy Van Alstyne; Harcourt, Brace & World, Inc. *

REFERENCES

1. VAN ALSTYNE, DOROTHY. *The Environment of Three-Year-Old Children: Factors Related to Intelligence and Vocabulary Tests.* Columbia University, Teachers College, Contributions to Education, No. 366. New York: Bureau of Publications, the College, 1929. Pp. vii, 108. * (*PA* 4:386)

2. MOORE, JOSEPH E. "A Comparison of Negro and White Preschool Children on a Vocabulary Test and Eye-Hand Coordination Test." *Child Develop* 13:247–52 D '42. * (*PA* 17:2079)

3. SCHNEIDERMAN, NORMA. "A Study of the Relationship Between Articulatory Ability and Language Ability." *J Speech & Hearing Disorders* 20:359–64 D '55. * (*PA* 30:7690)

4. BLIGH, HAROLD F. "Concurrent Validity Evidence on Two Intelligence Measures for Young Children." *Yearb Nat Council Meas Used Ed* 16:56–66 '59. * (*PA* 34:7345)

5. DUNN, LLOYD M., AND HARLEY, RANDALL K. "Comparability of Peabody, Ammons, Van Alstyne, and Columbia Test Scores With Cerebral Palsied Children." *Excep Child* 26:70–4 O '59. * (*PA* 35:3733)

6. VECCHIONE, NICHOLAS. "An Appraisal of the Van Alstyne Picture Vocabulary Test for Use in Determining Readiness of Pre-School Children for First Grade." *Ed Rec B* 83:79–84 F '63. *

MARY R. HAWORTH, *Associate Professor of Medical Psychology, University of Nebraska*

College of Medicine, Omaha, Nebraska.

The current test is a revision of the 1929 *Van Alstyne Picture Vocabulary Test for Preschool Children,* which must have been one of the first tests of this type. Its chief competitors at the present time are the Ammons' *Full-Range Picture Vocabulary Test* (1948) and the *Peabody Picture Vocabulary Test* (1959). The manual describes the test as a "quick, individually administered screening test for mental ability" designed for children in the mental age range from two to seven years.

The test consists of a spiral booklet containing 60 plates, all of which are administered to the subject. No verbal response is required; the child is asked to point to the one of four pictures on the page which corresponds to the stimulus word given by the examiner. Administration takes approximately 15 minutes and scoring consists simply of summing correct responses and determining the appropriate mental age from a table listing all possible scores.

The nonverbal aspects of the test make it especially suited to children with delayed speech or speech handicaps and for those with motor impairments.

A commendable feature of the test is the rationale used in selecting the three "incorrect" pictures for each plate. In addition to being of equal order of frequency, the words chosen for representation are either commonly associated with the test word (e.g., thimble—thread, nail—hammer, sleeve—cuff) or have similar initial sounds (e.g., parrot—penguin, picking—peeking, crawl—cry). If errors of either type are made repeatedly, valuable qualitative clues are provided for further exploration of possible aphasic-like tendencies or difficulties in making fine auditory discriminations. The subject must also frequently make rather fine distinctions with respect to functions, activities, or species (e.g., smoke—flame, geese—swan). Perseverative trends can also be observed, especially in brain damaged youngsters, since the same picture may appear on several plates (but only be a correct response on one of them) and will continue to be picked out for its familiarity even though its selection is no longer appropriate for the stimulus word. Unfortunately, the author suggests scoring simply as pass or fail, thus discouraging collection of additional information needed for qualitative evaluations.

The standardization data presented in the manual are sketchy at best. Apparently the scores of fewer than 500 subjects between the ages of four and seven (second grade) served as the basis for the table of mental age equivalents which range from 2 years 1 month through 10 years 5 months. These mental ages were established by comparisons with scores achieved on the Stanford-Binet for the preschool subjects, but from a variety of group intelligence tests for first and second graders.

The only evidence offered for validity consists of correlations between the Van Alstyne and other intelligence tests (in terms of test scores and of IQ's). Since the outside criterion tests were also those used as the basis for arriving at the Van Alstyne mental age equivalents in the first place, one might expect this dubious procedure to yield spuriously high correlations. Instead they range from .49 to .71.

Split-half reliabilities for the four age groups range from .71 to .85 and the standard error of measurement is 2 raw score points at age seven, but close to 3 points for each of the younger age levels. Inspection of the table of mental ages shows that 1 score point generally represents 1 month of mental age up to four years of age; from four to six years of age, 1 score point is equivalent to 1 or 2 months of MA; beyond age six, 1 point represents 3 to 4 months of MA. Consequently, mental ages can be in error by as much as 6 to 8 months.

The manual suggests converting MA's to IQ's in the usual way (MA/CA) and presents a table of percentile ranks based on these IQ's. The author also states that the test provides an "estimate of mental ability....based on the child's vocabulary comprehension," and proceeds to point out that vocabulary items have generally correlated highly with total scores on standard intelligence tests. The assumption is made that the two methods of testing verbal comprehension, namely by pointing to a word named and by defining it in verbal terms, are tapping equivalent cognitive functions. This has yet to be demonstrated experimentally.

Nevertheless, a good case can be made for the test, and picture vocabulary tests in general, if their purpose is specifically stated as the measurement of comprehension of the spoken word without inferring the equivalence to mental ability in general. Consequently scoring might well be kept in terms of age equivalents rather than converting to mental ages and IQ's.

The Van Alstyne test seems superior to the Ammons for the under 10 age range since there are more items per year at the younger levels on the Van Alstyne. The Peabody test is quite similar to the Van Alstyne in format and a correlation of .94 has been reported between the two tests (5). The Van Alstyne appears to have some advantages over the Peabody in terms of the selection of pictures as mentioned above. On the other hand, the Peabody has more test plates at the youngest age levels, extends upwards to 18 years, and was standardized on a much larger sample. Also, two forms of the Peabody can be administered using the same plates.

The Van Alstyne test could be improved with the addition of more items at the younger levels; and also at the upper levels to allow for more ceiling for bright seven-year-olds. Other suggestions of a more mechanical nature include: a larger spiral binding so that the test plates can more readily be turned over and under; and the printing of the stimulus words on the recording blank so that the examiner does not need to refer back and forth to the manual and the blank. Some provision should also be made for easy recording of wrong responses (by numbering the pictures or descriptive words on the test blank) to aid in later qualitative evaluation of patterns of errors. The overall value of the test might also be increased if some number concepts were added, or more adjectival stimuli for discriminations at higher levels, and more items likely to elicit aphasic trends or associations (such as comb—brush, table—chair).

In summary, this test basically has merit if its stated purpose is kept in mind, i.e., as a screening test with minimal emphasis on deriving an IQ from the test scores. Its stature could be improved with additional standardization data. The test has promise of clinical usefulness in testing young normal and older retarded children and those subjects with verbal or motor impairments who cannot be adequately evaluated by the more usual testing procedures.

Ellen V. Piers, *Associate Professor of Psychology, The Pennsylvania State University, University Park, Pennsylvania.*

This is a revision of the 1929 *Van Alstyne Picture Vocabulary Test for Pre-school Children.* While an improvement over the original, it still has its weaknesses. Its stated purpose is to provide an estimate of the mental ability of children in the mental age range from two to seven years, based on vocabulary comprehension. There are now 60 stimulus words presented in two groups of odd-numbered cards and even-numbered cards, each with four pictures. The drawings are good, and the record blank simple. The manual is short and easy to read. Twenty-eight new words were selected from a basic vocabulary list. Decoys were selected which had an equal level of frequency, were associated in life situations, or had a similar initial sound to the test word.

The manual does not make clear the total number of standardization cases but says they were "selected groups of preschool children in New Haven, Connecticut and in several localities in Florida, and in-school groups in New York City." No basis for selection is given. No children were below four years of age or above second grade, so that norms below and above that level are based on deviant children, the number of whom is unknown. Preschool children were given the 1937 Stanford-Binet as well as the Van Alstyne, and school aged children apparently were given one (or more?) of the following: Columbia, Otis Quick-Scoring, Pintner-Cunningham or Pintner-Durost, and Lorge-Thorndike. The mental age of each child was established from these tests, and the percentage of subjects answering each Van Alstyne item correctly at successive mental ages was determined. Increase in percentage passing with increasing mental age was used largely in the choice of 60 items out of an original 70, and equivalent mental age scores for the Van Alstyne were then derived from the other tests. IQ tables are not presented but may be determined in the now out-of-date manner of dividing MA by CA. Percentile ranks are given for a normal distribution of IQ's with a standard deviation of 16, but where the latter was plucked from is not stated.

Having used the same sample for both item selection and standardization, the author proceeds to use it again to establish concurrent validity! In spite of being the source for the establishment of Van Alstyne's mental age norms, correlations of the other tests with the Van Alstyne, both for mental age, raw scores or IQ's, ranged only from .49 to .71.

Split-half reliability of raw scores for ages 4–8 ranged from .71 to .85. No other reliabilities are reported.

In spite of some glaring weaknesses in standardization, this little test may still be useful in its middle range—that is, from 3 or 4 to 6 or 7 years. One study (5) in which it was compared with the Peabody and Ammons picture vocabulary tests with 20 cerebral palsied children reported high intercorrelations, partially one expects because of the wide age range. Mean mental age scores, however, showed the Ammons significantly different from (higher than) the Van Alstyne, and it was felt that the latter had insufficient ceiling.

If the test were worth revising, it seems a pity that a more sophisticated job of revision could not be undertaken. In this reviewer's opinion the better choice of test for preschool children would probably be the *Peabody Picture Vocabulary Test.* More conclusive evaluation of the Van Alstyne will have to await further research.

For a review by Ruth W. Washburn of the original edition, see 3:296.

[538]

Wechsler Adult Intelligence Scale. Ages 16 and over; 1939–55; revision of Form 1 of *Wechsler-Bellevue Intelligence Scale;* also called WAIS; individual; 14 scores: verbal (information, comprehension, arithmetic, similarities, digit span, vocabulary, total), performance (digit symbol, picture completion, block design, picture arrangement, object assembly, total), total; 1 form ['55]; manual ('55, 116 pages); record booklet ('55, 4 pages); supplementary record sheet ('55, 1 page); $24 per set of testing materials, 25 record booklets, and manual; $2.10 per 25 record booklets; 90¢ per 25 supplementary record sheets; $3 per manual; postpaid; (40–60) minutes; David Wechsler; Psychological Corporation. (Australian edition of record form and manual amendment slips: Australian Council for Educational Research; British modification of test questions: National Foundation for Educational Research in England and Wales.) *

REFERENCES

1–42. See 5:414.

43. Neuringer, Charles. *A Statistical Comparison of the Wechsler-Bellevue Intelligence Scale, Form I and the Wechsler Adult Intelligence Scale for a College Population.* Master's thesis, University of Kansas (Lawrence, Kan.), 1956.

44. Bennett, George K. Chap. 11, "Relationship of Age and Mental Test Scores Among Older Persons," pp. 152–7. In *The New Frontiers of Aging.* Edited by Wilma Donahue and Clark Tibbitts. Ann Arbor, Mich.: University of Michigan Press, 1957. Pp. x, 209. * (*PA* 33:927)

45. Evans, LaVon. *A Comparison of Test Scores for the 16–17 Year Age Group of Navaho Indians With Standardized Norms for the Wechsler Adult Intelligence Scale.* Master's thesis, Brigham Young University (Provo, Utah), 1957.

46. Lewis, Lena L. "The Relation of Measured Mental Ability to School Marks and Academic Survival in the Texas School for the Blind." *Int J Ed Blind* 6:56–60 Mr '57. *

47. Ricks, James H., Jr. *Age and Vocabulary Test Performance: A Qualitative Analysis of the Responses of Adults.* Doctor's thesis, Columbia University (New York, N.Y.), 1957. (*DA* 19:182)

48. Heilbrun, Alfred B., Jr. "The Digit Span Test and the Prediction of Cerebral Pathology." *A.M.A. Arch Neurol & Psychiatry* 80:228–31 Ag '58. * (*PA* 33:10334)

49. Howard, William. "A Note on McNemar's 'On Abbreviated Wechsler-Bellevue Scales.'" *J Consult Psychol* 22:414 D '58. * (*PA* 33:9920, title only)

50. Klett, William G. *An Analysis of Item Order in Seven Subtests of the Wechsler Adult Intelligence Scale (WAIS).* Master's thesis, Loyola University (Chicago, Ill.), 1958.

51. Miele, John Anthony. *Sex Differences in Intelligence: The Relationship of Sex to Intelligence as Measured by the Wechsler Adult Intelligence Scale and the Wechsler Intelligence Scale for Children.* Doctor's thesis, New York University (New York, N.Y.), 1958. (*DA* 18:2213)

52. Plant, Walter T. "Mental Ability Scores for Freshmen in a California State College." *Calif J Ed Res* 9:72–3+ Mr '58. * (*PA* 33:9051)

53. Purdom, Glen A., Jr. *Comparison of Performance of Competent and Incompetent Readers in a State Training School for Delinquent Boys on the WAIS and the Rosenzweig P-F Study.* Doctor's thesis, University of Oregon (Eugene, Ore.), 1958. (*DA* 19:1016)

54. Bloom, Bernard L. "Ecologic Factors in the WAIS Picture Completion Test." Abstract. *J Consult Psychol* 23:375 Ag '59. * (*PA* 34:4237)

55. Clayton, Hugh, and Payne, Dan. "Validation of Doppelt's WAIS Short Form With a Clinical Population." Abstract. *J Consult Psychol* 23:467 O '59. * (*PA* 34:5603)

56. Coons, W. H., and Peacock, E. P. "Inter-Examiner Reliability of the Wechsler Adult Intelligence Scale With Mental Hospital Patients." *O.P.A. Q* 12:33–7 Jl '59. *

57. Doppelt, Jerome E., and Seashore, Harold G. "Psychological Testing in Correctional Institutions." *J Counsel Psychol* 6:81–92 sp '59. * (*PA* 34:6012)

58. Eisdorfer, Carl; Busse, Ewald W.; and Cohen, Louis D. "The WAIS Performance of an Aged Sample: The Relationship Between Verbal and Performance IQ's." *J Gerontol* 14:197–201 Ap '59. * (*PA* 34:1136)

59. Fisher, Gary M., and Shotwell, Anna M. "An Evaluation of Doppelt's Abbreviated Form of the WAIS for the Mentally Retarded." *Am J Mental Def* 64:476–81 N '59. * (*PA* 34:8003)

60. Garfield, Sol L. "Problems in the Psychological Evaluation of the Subnormal Individual." *Am J Mental Def* 64:467–71 N '59. * (*PA* 34:8005)

61. Howard, William. "Validities of WAIS Short Forms in a Psychiatric Population." Abstract. *J Consult Psychol* 23:282 Je '59. * (*PA* 34:4384)

62. Jones, Nelson Fredrick, Jr. *Validity of Clinical Judgments of Schizophrenic Pathology Based on Verbal Responses to Intelligence Test Items.* Doctor's thesis, Northwestern University (Evanston, Ill.), 1959. (*DA* 20:2383)

63. Ladd, Clayton E. *An Analysis of the WAIS Performance of Brain Damaged and Neurotic Patients.* Master's thesis, State University of Iowa (Iowa City, Iowa), 1959.

64. Levinson, Boris M. "A Comparison of the Coloured Progressive Matrices (CPM) With the Wechsler Adult Intelligence Scale (WAIS) in a Normal Aged White Male Population." *J Clin Psychol* 15:288–91 Jl '59. * (*PA* 35:3299)

65. Levinson, Boris M. "Traditional Jewish Cultural Values and Performance on the Wechsler Tests." *J Ed Psychol* 50:177–81 Ag '59. * (*PA* 35:2059)

66. Loranger, Armand W., and Misiak, Henryk. "Critical Flicker Frequency and Some Intellectual Functions in Old Age." *J Gerontol* 14:323–7 Jl '59. * (*PA* 34:4153)

67. Plant, Walter T., and Lynd, Celia. "A Validity Study and a College Freshman Norm Group for the Wechsler Adult Intelligence Scale." *Personnel & Guid J* 37:578–80 Ap '59. *

68. Poland, Ronal G. *A Factor Analysis of the WAIS and the EPSAT.* Doctor's thesis, Universty of Denver (Denver, Colo.), 1959.

69. Saunders, David R. "On the Dimensionality of the WAIS Battery for Two Groups of Normal Males." *Psychol Rep* 5:529–41 S '59. * (*PA* 38:4283)

70. Sines, Lloyd K., and Simmons, Helen. "The Shipley-Hartford Scale and the Doppelt Short Form as Estimators of WAIS IQ in a State Hospital Population." *J Clin Psychol* 15:452–3 O '59. * (*PA* 36:1HD52S)

71. Stinson, Pairlee J., and Morrison, Mildred M. "Sex Differences Among High School Seniors." *J Ed Res* 53:103–8 N '59. *

72. Wagner, Edwin Eric. *Predicting Success for Young Executives From Objective Test Scores and Personal Data.* Doctor's thesis, Temple University (Philadelphia, Pa.), 1959. (*DA* 20:3371)

73. Wiens, Arthur N.; Matarazzo, Joseph D.; and Gaver, Kenneth D. "Performance and Verbal IQ in a Group of Sociopaths." *J Clin Psychol* 15:191–3 Ap '59. * (*PA* 35:5102)

74. Borgatta, Edgar F., and Corsini, Raymond J. "The Quick Word Test (QWT) and the WAIS." *Psychol Rep* 6:201 Ap '60. * (*PA* 35:6397)

75. Briggs, Peter F. "The Validity of WAIS Performance Subtests Completed With One Hand." *J Clin Psychol* 16:318–20 Jl '60. * (*PA* 36:2HC18B)

76. Darbes, Alex. "Relationships Among College Students Scores on ACE, Otis, and WAIS Tests." *Proc W Va Acad Sci* 32:214–6 D '60. * (*PA* 36:3KK14D)

77. Field, J. G. "Two Types of Tables for Use With Wechsler's Intelligence Scales." *J Clin Psychol* 16:3–7 Ja '60. * (*PA* 36:1HC03F)

78. Fisher, Gary M. "The Altitude Quotient as an Index of Intellectual Potential: I, WAIS Data for Familial and Undifferentiated Mental Retardates." *Am J Mental Def* 65:252–5 S '60. * (*PA* 35:3779)

79. Fisher, Gary M. "A Corrected Table for Determining the Significance of the Difference Between Verbal and Per-

formance IQ's on the WAIS and the Wechsler-Bellevue." *J Clin Psychol* 16:7-8 Ja '60. * (*PA* 36:1HC07F)
80. FISHER, GARY M. "Differences in WAIS Verbal and Performance IQ's in Various Diagnostic Groups of Mental Retardates." *Am J Mental Def* 65:256-60 S '60. * (*PA* 35: 3780)
81. FISHER, GARY M.; DOOLEY, MILTON D.; AND SILVERSTEIN, ARTHUR B. "Wechsler Adult Intelligence Scale Performance of Familial and Undifferentiated Mental Subnormals." *Psychol Rep* 7:268 O '60. * (*PA* 35:2552)
82. FISHER, GARY M.; SHOTWELL, ANNA M.; AND YORK, DOROTHY H. "Comparability of the Ammons Full-Range Picture Vocabulary Test With the WAIS in the Assessment of Intelligence of Mental Retardates." *Am J Mental Def* 64:995-9 My '60. * (*PA* 35:6830)
83. GARDNER, MARGARET SEYMOUR. *Factors Associated With Success in First Grade Teaching.* Doctor's thesis, Northwestern University (Evanston, Ill.), 1960. (*DA* 21:2609)
84. GOLDMAN, BERT ARTHUR. *Relationships Between Intelligence and Immediate Memory-Reasoning.* Doctor's thesis, University of Virginia (Charlottesville, Va.), 1960. (*DA* 21:2192)
85. HIRSCHENFANG, SAMUEL. "A Comparison of WAIS Scores of Hemiplegic Patients With and Without Aphasia." *J Clin Psychol* 16:351 Jl '60. * (*PA* 36:2JF51H)
86. HUNT, WILLIAM A.; WALKER, RONALD E.; AND JONES, NELSON F. "The Validity of Clinical Ratings for Estimating Severity of Schizophrenia." *J Clin Psychol* 16:391-3 O '60. * (*PA* 37:3220)
87. KALDEGG, A. "A Note on the Application of Doppelt's Short Form of the Wechsler Adult Intelligence Scale to a Clinical Population." *Brit J Med Psychol* 33:221-3 pt 3 '60. *
88. KENNEDY, WALLACE A.; NELSON, WILLARD; LINDNER, RON; TURNER, JACK; AND MOON, HAROLD. "Psychological Measurements of Future Scientists." *Psychol Rep* 7:515-7 D '60. * (*PA* 35:1522)
89. LEVINSON, BORIS M. "A Research Note on Subcultural Differences in WAIS Between Aged Italians and Jews." *J Gerontol* 15:197-8 Ap '60. * (*PA* 35:6403)
90. LEVINSON, BORIS M. "A Research Note on the Knox Cubes as an Intelligence Test for Aged Males." *J Gerontol* 15:85-6 Ja '60. * (*PA* 35:6234)
91. LORANGER, ARMAND W., AND MISIAK, HENRYK. "The Performance of Aged Females on Five Non-Language Tests of Intellectual Functions." *J Clin Psychol* 16:189-91 Ap '60. * (*PA* 36:2FI89L)
92. MAXWELL, A. E. "Obtaining Factor Scores on the Wechsler Adult Intelligence Scale." *J Mental Sci* 106:1060-2 Jl '60. * (*PA* 35:4861)
93. PANTON, JAMES H. "Beta-WAIS Comparisons and WAIS Subtest Configurations Within a State Prison Population." *J Clin Psychol* 16:312-7 Jl '60. * (*PA* 36:2HD12P)
94. PARSONS, OSCAR A., AND KEMP, DAVID E. "Intellectual Functioning in Temporal Lobe Epilepsy." *J Consult Psychol* 24:408-14 O '60. * (*PA* 35:5156)
95. REITAN, RALPH M. "The Significance of Dysphasia for Intelligence and Adaptive Abilities." *J Psychol* 50:355-76 O '60. * (*PA* 35:6767)
96. SAUNDERS, DAVID R. "A Factor Analysis of the Information and Arithmetic Items of the WAIS." *Psychol Rep* 6:367-83 Je '60. * (*PA* 35:6411)
97. SAUNDERS, DAVID R. "A Factor Analysis of the Picture Completion Items of the WAIS." *J Clin Psychol* 16:146-9 Ap '60. * (*PA* 36:2HD46S)
98. SCHAFER, ROY. "Representations of Perceiving and Acting in Psychological Test Responses," pp. 291-312. (*PA* 35: 850) In *Festschrift for Gardner Murphy.* Edited by John G. Peatman and Eugene L. Hartley. New York: Harper & Brothers, 1960. Pp. xi, 411. *
99. SILVERSTEIN, A. B., AND FISHER, GARY M. "Reanalysis of Sex Differences in the Standardization Data of the Wechsler Adult Intelligence Scale." *Psychol Rep* 7:405-6 D '60. * (*PA* 35:2201)
100. SINNETT, KATHLEEN, AND MAYMAN, MARTIN. "The Wechsler Adult Intelligence Scale as a Clinical Diagnostic Tool: A Review." *B Menninger Clinic* 24:80-4 Mr '60. * (*PA* 35:3416)
101. STEIN, ZENA, AND SUSSER, MERVYN. "Families of Dull Children: Part 4, Increments in Intelligence." *J Mental Sci* 106:1311-9 O '60. * (*PA* 35:5182)
102. WAGNER, EDWIN E. "Differences Between Old and Young Executives on Objective Psychological Test Variables." *J Gerontol* 15:296-9 Jl '60. * (*PA* 35:1328)
103. WIENS, ARTHUR N., AND BANAKA, WILLIAM H. "Estimating WAIS IQ From Shipley-Hartford Scores: A Cross-Validation." *J Clin Psychol* 16:452 O '60. * (*PA* 37:3119)
104. WOLFF, B. BERTHOLD. "The Application of the Hewson Ratios to the WAIS as an Aid in the Differential Diagnosis of Cerebral Pathology." *J Nerv & Mental Dis* 131:98-109 Ag '60. *
105. WOLFSON, WILLIAM, AND BACHELIS, LEONARD. "An Abbreviated Form of the WAIS Verbal Scale." *J Clin Psychol* 16:421 O '60. * (*PA* 37:3102)
106. WOLFSON, WILLIAM, AND WELTMAN, ROBERT E. "Implications of Specific WAIS Picture Completion Errors." *J Clin Psychol* 16:9-11 Ja '60. * (*PA* 36:1HI09W)
107. ALIMENA, BENJAMIN. "A Note on Norms for Scatter Analysis on the Wechsler Intelligence Scales." *J Clin Psychol* 17:61 Ja '61. * (*PA* 37:3103)
108. ANASTASI, ANNE. *Psychological Testing, Second Edition,* pp. 303-15, 320-5. New York: Macmillan Co., 1961. Pp. xiii, 657. * (*PA* 36:1HA57A)
109. BEARDSLEY, KATHARINE. "Analysis of Psychological Tests of Persons Diagnosed Sociopathic Personality Disturbance." *Arch Crim Psychodynam* 4:389-411 su '61. *
110. BIRREN, JAMES E. Chap. 12, "Research on the Psychology of Aging: Concepts and Findings," pp. 203-22; discussion by Joseph Zubin, pp. 223-6. In *Psychopathology of Aging.* The Proceedings of the Fiftieth Annual Meeting of the American Psychopathological Association, Held in New York City, February 1960. Edited by Paul H. Hoch and Joseph Zubin. New York: Grune & Stratton, Inc., 1961. Pp. xiv, 321. * (*PA* 36:3FI21H)
111. BIRREN, JAMES E., AND MORRISON, DONALD F. "Analysis of the WAIS Subtests in Relation to Age and Education." *J Gerontol* 16:363-9 O '61. * (*PA* 36:5FI63B)
112. BRADWAY, KATHERINE P., AND ROBINSON, NANCY M. "Significant IQ Changes in Twenty-Five Years: A Follow-Up." *J Ed Psychol* 52:74-9 Ap '61. * (*PA* 38:2484)
113. BRENGELMANN, JOHANNES C., AND KENNY, JOSEPH T. "Comparison of Leiter, WAIS and Stanford-Binet IQ's in Retardates." *J Clin Psychol* 17:235-8 Jl '61. * (*PA* 38:8953)
114. COOK, RICHARD A., AND HIRT, MICHAEL L. "Verbal and Performance IQ Discrepancies on the Wechsler Adult Intelligence Scale and Wechsler-Bellevue, Form 1." *J Clin Psychol* 17:382-3 O '61. * (*PA* 38:8446)
115. DUNCAN, DONN R., AND BARRETT, ALBERT M. "A Longitudinal Comparison of Intelligence Involving the Wechsler-Bellevue 1 and WAIS." *J Clin Psychol* 17:318-9 Jl '61. * (*PA* 38:8453)
116. EISDORFER, CARL, AND COHEN, LOUIS D. "The Generality of the WAIS Standardization for the Aged: A Regional Comparison." *J Abn & Social Psychol* 62:520-7 My '61. * (*PA* 36:4FI20E)
117. FISHER, G. M. "A Comparison of the Performance of Endogenous and Exogenous Mental Retardates on the Wechsler Adult Intelligence Scale." *J Mental Def Res* 5:111-4 D '61. * (*PA* 36:4JI11F)
118. FISHER, GARY M.; KILMAN, BEVERLY A.; AND SHOTWELL, ANNA M. "Comparability of Intelligence Quotients of Mental Defectives on the Wechsler Adult Intelligence Scale and the 1960 Revision of the Stanford-Binet." *J Consult Psychol* 25:192-5 Je '61. *
119. FISHER, GARY M.; RISLEY, TODD R.; AND SILVERSTEIN, ARTHUR B. "Sex Differences in the Performance of Mental Retardates on the Wechsler Adult Intelligence Scale." *J Clin Psychol* 17:170 Ap '61. * (*PA* 38:952)
120. GEISER, ROBERT LEE. *The Psychodiagnostic Efficiency of WAIS and Rorschach Scores: A Discriminant Function Study.* Doctor's thesis, Boston University (Boston, Mass.), 1961. (*DA* 22:915)
121. KEEFE, MARY KAREN. *An Abbreviated WAIS With Bilingual Women.* Master's thesis, Saint Louis University (Saint Louis, Mo.), 1961.
122. LANFELD, EILEEN S., AND SAUNDERS, D. R. "Anxiety as 'Effect of Uncertainty': An Experiment Illuminating the OA Subtest of the WAIS." *J Clin Psychol* 17:238-41 Jl '61. * (*PA* 38:8498)
123. MCCARTHY, DOROTHEA. "Administration of Digit Symbol and Coding Subtests of the WAIS and WISC to Left-Handed Subjects." *Psychol Rep* 8:407-8 Je '61. * (*PA* 36: 2HD07M)
124. MCKEEVER, WALTER F. "The Validity of the Hewson Ratios: A Critique of Wolff's Study." *J Nerv & Mental Dis* 132:417-9 My '61. *
125. MCLEOD, H. N. "My Two-Hour Psychological Test Battery." *O.P.A. Q* 14:85-7 D '61. *
126. MCLEOD, H. N. "The Use of the Information and Block-Design Sub-Tests of the WAIS as a Measure of Intelligence in Psychiatric Hospital Patients." *Ont Hosp Psychol B* 7:5-7 Ag '61. * Supplement, 7:12 Ap '62. *
127. MCLEOD, H. N., AND RUBIN, J. "Correction Between the Raven Matrices (Rev. 1956) and the Wechsler Adult Intelligence Scale (1955)." *Ont Hosp Psychol B* 6:47-9 Mr '61. *
128. MAXFIELD, KATHRYN E., AND PERRY, JAMES D. "The Intelligence Status of Some Vocational Rehabilitation Clients." *New Outlook Blind* 55:19-20 Ja '61. *
129. MAXWELL, A. E. "Trends in Cognitive Ability in the Older Age Ranges." *J Abn & Social Psychol* 63:449-52 S '61. * (*PA* 37:973)
130. MILLER, D. R.; FISHER, G. M.; AND DINGMAN, H. F. "A Note on Differential Utility of WAIS Verbal and Performance IQ's." *Am J Mental Def* 65:482-5 Ja '61. * (*PA* 35:6855)
131. NORMAN, RUSSELL P., AND WILENSKY, HAROLD. "Item Difficulty of the WAIS Information Subtest for a Chronic Schizophrenic Sample." *J Clin Psychol* 17:56-7 Ja '61. * (*PA* 37:3227)
132. SAUNDERS, DAVID R. "Digit Span and Alpha Frequency: A Cross-Validation." *J Clin Psychol* 17:165-7 Ap '61. * (*PA* 38:394)
133. SCHWARTZMAN, A. E.; HUNTER, R. C. A.; AND PRINCE,

R. H. "Intellectual Factors and Academic Performance in Medical Undergraduates." *J Med Ed* 36:353–8 Ap '61. *

134. STOTSKY, BERNARD A. "A Study of Factors in Recovery of Aged Patients From Chronic Physical Illness." *J Psychol Studies* 12:28–34 Ja '61. *

135. WAITE, RICHARD R. "The Intelligence Test as a Psychodiagnostic Instrument." *J Proj Tech* 25:90–102 Mr '61. * (*PA* 36:1HD90W)

136. WARREN, SUE ALLEN, AND KRAUS, MATTHEW J., JR. "WAIS Verbal Minus Performance IQ Comparisons in Mental Retardates." *J Clin Psychol* 17:57–9 Ja '61. * (*PA* 37:3599)

137. WOLFF, B. BERTHOLD. "The Validity of the Hewson Ratios: A Reply to McKeever's Critique." *J Nerv & Mental Dis* 132:420–4 My '61. *

138. WOLFSON, WILLIAM, AND LOCASCIO, RALPH. "Digit Symbol Performance of Nursing School Applicants." *J Clin Psychol* 17:59 Ja '61. * (*PA* 37:3876)

139. ALLEN, ROBERT M. "The Real Question in Digit Span Performance." *Psychol Rep* 11:218 Ag '62. * (*PA* 37:4951)

140. AYLAIAN, ARSEN, AND MELTZER, MALCOLM L. "The Bender Gestalt Test and Intelligence." Abstract. *J Consult Psychol* 26:483 O '62. *

141. BECK, AARON T.; FESHBACH, SEYMOUR; AND LEGG, DONALD. "The Clinical Utility of the Digit Symbol Test." *J Consult Psychol* 26:263–8 Je '62. * (*PA* 38:1177)

142. BIRREN, JAMES E., AND SPIETH, WALTER. "Age, Response Speed, and Cardiovascular Functions." *J Gerontol* 17:390–1 O '62. * (*PA* 37:4772)

143. BLOOM, BERNARD L., AND GOLDMAN, RUTH K. "Sensitivity of the WAIS to Language Handicap in a Psychotic Population." *J Clin Psychol* 18:161–3 Ap '62. * (*PA* 38:8233)

144. BRADWAY, KATHERINE P., AND THOMPSON, CLARE W. "Intelligence at Adulthood: A Twenty-Five Year Follow-Up." *J Ed Psychol* 53:1–14 F '62. * (*PA* 37:1210)

145. BRILL, RICHARD G. "The Relationship of Wechsler IQ's to Academic Achievement Among Deaf Students." *Excep Child* 28:315–21 F '62. * (*PA* 37:1609)

146. COSTA, LOUIS D., AND VAUGHAN, HERBERT G., JR. "Performance of Patients With Lateralized Cerebral Lesions: 1, Verbal and Perceptual Tests." *J Nerv & Mental Dis* 134:162–8 F '62. *

147. CRADDICK, RAY A., AND GROSSMANN, KLAUS. "Effects of Visual Distraction Upon Performance on the WAIS Digit Span." *Psychol Rep* 10:642 Je '62. * (*PA* 37:4954)

148. FISHER, GARY M. "The Efficiency of the Hewson Ratios in Diagnosing Cerebral Pathology." *J Nerv & Mental Dis* 134:80–3 Ja '62. *

149. FISHER, GARY M. "Further Evidence of the Invalidity of the Wechsler Adult Intelligence Scale for the Assessment of Intelligence of Mental Retardates." *J Mental Def Res* 6:41–3 Je '62. (*PA* 37:3571)

150. FISHER, GARY M. "A Note on the Validity of the Wechsler Adult Intelligence Scale for Mental Retardates." *J Consult Psychol* 26:391 Ag '62. * (*PA* 38:4273)

151. FOGEL, MAX L. "The Intelligence Quotient as an Index of Brain Damage." Abstract. *Am J Orthopsychiatry* 32:338–9 Mr '62. *

152. FREEMAN, FRANK S. *Theory and Practice of Psychological Testing, Third Edition,* pp. 241–79, 330–8. New York: Holt, Rinehart & Winston, Inc., 1962. Pp. xix, 697. *

153. GRIFFITH, RICHARD M.; ESTES, BETSY WORTH; AND ZEROF, SELWYN A. "Intellectual Impairment in Schizophrenia." *J Consult Psychol* 26:336–9 Ag '62. * (*PA* 38:4604)

154. GUERTIN, WILSON H.; RABIN, ALBERT I.; FRANK, GEORGE H.; AND LADD, CLAYTON E. "Research With the Wechsler Intelligence Scales for Adults: 1955–60." *Psychol B* 59:1–26 Ja '62. * (*PA* 37:1203)

155. HIRT, MICHAEL L., AND COOK, RICHARD A. "Use of a Multiple Regression Equation to Estimate Organic Impairment From Wechsler Scale Scores." *J Clin Psychol* 18:80–1 Ja '62. * (*PA* 38:8421)

156. HULICKA, IRENE MACKINTOSH. "Verbal WAIS Scores of Elderly Patients." *Psychol Rep* 10:250 F '62. * (*PA* 37:966)

157. HUNT, WILLIAM A., AND WALKER, RONALD E. "A Comparison of Global and Specific Clinical Judgments Across Several Diagnostic Categories." *J Clin Psychol* 18:188–94 Ap '62. * (*PA* 38:8574)

158. JONES, REGINALD L. "Analytically Developed Short Forms of the WAIS." *J Consult Psychol* 26:289 Je '62. * (*PA* 38:943)

159. KO, YUNG-HO. "The Discrepancy Between the B-G Score and the Sum of the Object-Assembly and the Block-Design Test Scores as an Indicator of Organicity." *Acta Psychologica Taiwanica* (4):72–7 Mr '62. * (*PA* 38:6367)

160. L'ABATE, LUCIANO. "The Relationship Between WAIS-Derived Indices of Maladjustment and MMPI in Deviant Groups." *J Consult Psychol* 26:441–5 O '62. * (*PA* 39:1742)

161. LABRECQUE, JEAN M. *The Rationale of the WAIS Block Design Subtest.* Master's thesis, University of Ottawa (Ottawa, Ont., Canada), 1962.

162. LEVINSON, BORIS M. "Jewish Subculture and WAIS Performance Among Jewish Aged." *J Genetic Psychol* 100:55–68 Mr '62. * (*PA* 37:969)

163. MCLEOD, HUGH N., AND RUBIN, JOSEPH. "Correlation Between Raven Progressive Matrices and the WAIS." *J Consult Psychol* 26:190–1 Ap '62. * (*PA* 37:4960)

164. MINER, JOHN B. "Personality and Ability Factors in Sales Performance." *J Appl Psychol* 46:6–13 F '62. * (*PA* 36:5LD06M)

165. NICKOLS, JOHN E., JR. "Brief Forms of the Wechsler Intelligence Scales for Research." *J Clin Psychol* 18:167 Ap '62. * (*PA* 38:8500)

166. O'NEIL, W. M. "The Stability of the Main Pattern of Abilities With Changing Age." *Austral J Psychol* 14:1–8 Ap '62. * (*PA* 38:6025)

167. RAPAPORT, GERALD M., AND MARSHALL, ROBERT J. "The Prediction of Rehabilitative Potential of Stockade Prisoners Using Clinical Psychological Tests." *J Clin Psychol* 18:444–6 O '62. * (*PA* 39:5087)

168. RIEGEL, RUTH M., AND RIEGEL, KLAUS F. "A Comparison and Reinterpretation of Factor Structures of the W-B, the WAIS, and the HAWIE on Aged Persons." *J Consult Psychol* 26:31–7 F '62. * (*PA* 37:4965)

169. SARASON, IRWIN G., AND MINARD, JAMES. "Test Anxiety, Experimental Instructions, and the Wechsler Adult Intelligence Scale." *J Ed Psychol* 53:299–302 D '62. * (*PA* 37:4968)

170. SATZ, PAUL, AND MOGEL, STEVE. "An Abbreviation of the WAIS for Clinical Use." *J Clin Psychol* 18:77–9 Ja '62. * (*PA* 38:8436)

171. SHAFFER, JOHN W. "A Specific Cognitive Deficit Observed in Gonadal Aplasia (Turner's Syndrome)." *J Clin Psychol* 18:403–6 O '62. * (*PA* 39:5565)

172. SILVERSTEIN, A. B. "Length of Hospitalization and Intelligence Test Performance in Mentally Retarded Adults." *Am J Mental Def* 66:618–20 Ja '62. * (*PA* 36:4JI18S)

173. SILVERSTEIN, A. B.; SHOTWELL, ANNA M.; AND FISHER, GARY M. "Cultural Factors in the Intellectual Functioning of the Mentally Retarded." *Am J Mental Def* 67:396–401 N '62. * (*PA* 37:5420)

174. SMALL, JOYCE G.; MILSTEIN, VICTOR; AND STEVENS, JANICE R. "Are Psychomotor Epileptics Different? A Controlled Study." *Arch Neurol* 7:187–94 S '62. * (*PA* 37:3521)

175. WAHLER, H. J., AND WATSON, LUKE S. "A Comparison of the Shipley-Hartford as a Power Test With the WAIS Verbal Scale." Abstract. *J Consult Psychol* 26:105 F '62. * (PA 37:5001)

176. WALL, HARVEY W.; MARKS, EDMOND; FORD, DONALD H.; AND ZEIGLER, MARTIN L. "Estimates of the Concurrent Validity of the W.A.I.S. and Normative Distributions for College Freshmen." *Personnel & Guid J* 40:717–22 Ap '62. * (*PA* 37:1998)

177. *Normative Information: Manager and Executive Testing.* New York: Richardson, Bellows, Henry & Co., Inc., May 1963. Pp. 45. *

178. BENSON, ROBERT R. "The Binet Vocabulary Score as an Estimate of Intellectual Functioning." *J Clin Psychol* 19:134–5 Ja '63. * (*PA* 39:1715)

179. BIRREN, JAMES E. "Research on the Psychologic Aspects of Aging." *Geriatrics* 18:393–403 My '63. * (*PA* 38:8121)

180. British Psychological Society, English Division of Professional Psychologists (Educational and Clinical). "Report of the Working Party on Subnormality." Prepared by J. H. F. Castell, A. D. B. Clarke, P. Mittler, and W. M. Woodward. *B Brit Psychol Soc* 16:3?–50 O '63. *

181. CLORE, GERALD L., JR. "Kent E-G-Y: Differential Scoring and Correlation With the WAIS." Abstract. *J Consult Psychol* 27:372 Ag '63. * (*PA* 38:2665)

182. CRADDICK, RAY A., AND STERN, MICHAEL R. "Relation Between the WAIS and the Kahn Test of Symbol Arrangement." *Percept & Motor Skills* 17:583–5 O '63. * (*PA* 38:6052)

183. EISDORFER, CARL. "Rorschach Performance and Intellectual Functioning in the Aged." *J Gerontol* 18:358–63 O '63. * (*PA* 38:5822)

184. EISDORFER, CARL. "The WAIS Performance of the Aged: A Retest Evaluation." *J Gerontol* 18:169–72 Ap '63. * (*PA* 38:4100)

185. ESTES, BETSY WORTH. "A Note on the Satz-Mogel Abbreviation of the WAIS." *J Clin Psychol* 19:103 Ja '63. * (*PA* 39:1727)

186. EVANS, RAY B., AND MARMORSTON, JESSIE. "Psychological Test Signs of Brain Damage in Cerebral Thrombosis." *Psychol Rep* 12:915–30 Je '63. * (*PA* 38:6413)

187. FRIEDMAN, ELLEN C., AND BARCLAY, ALLAN. "The Discriminative Validity of Certain Psychological Tests as Indices of Brain Damage in the Mentally Retarded." *Mental Retardation* 1:291–3 O '63. * (*PA* 38:8935)

188. GIANNELL, A. STEVEN, AND FREEBURNE, CECIL M. "The Comparative Validity of the WAIS and the Stanford-Binet With College Freshmen." *Ed & Psychol Meas* 23:557–67 au '63. * (*PA* 38:6057)

189. GOLDMAN, BERT A. "Relationships Between Intelligence and Reasoning With Immediately Remembered Discrete Materials." *J Exp Ed* 31:279–84 Mr '63. *

190. GOLDMAN, BERT A. "SCAT Versus WAIS: An Enigma." *J Ed Res* 57:51–3 S '63. *

191. GRANICK, SAMUEL. "Comparative Analysis of Psychotic Depressives With Matched Normals on Some Untimed Verbal

Intelligence Tests." *J Consult Psychol* 27:439–43 O '63. * (*PA* 38:4628)
192. HAMLIN, ROY W., AND JONES, ROBERT E. "Vocabulary Deficit in Improved and Unimproved Schizophrenic Subjects." *J Nerv & Mental Dis* 136:360–4 Ap '63. * (*PA* 38:4605)
193. HARDYCK, CURTIS, AND PETRINOVICH, LEWIS F. "The Patterns of Intellectual Functioning in Parkinson Patients." Abstract. *J Consult Psychol* 27:548 D '63. *
194. IMRE, PAUL D. "A Correlation Study of Verbal IQ and Grade Achievement." *J Clin Psychol* 19:218–9 Ap '63. *
195. JARVIK, LISSY F., AND FALEK, ARTHUR. "Intellectual Stability and Survival in the Aged." *J Gerontol* 18:173–6 Ap '63. * (*PA* 38:4103)
196. JURJEVICH, R. M. "Interrelationships of Anxiety Indices of Wechsler Intelligence Scales and MMPI Scales." *J General Psychol* 69:135–42 Jl '63. * (*PA* 38:4305)
197. JURJEVICH, RATIBOR. "An Analysis of the Altitude *IQ*s of Delinquent Girls." *J General Psychol* 69:221–6 O '63. * (*PA* 39:1779)
198. JURJEVICH, RATIBOR. "An Evaluation of the Henmon-Nelson Group *IQ* Test With Delinquent Girls." *J General Psychol* 69:227–33 O '63. * (*PA* 39:1778)
199. KARP, STEPHEN A. "Field Dependence and Overcoming Embeddedness." *J Consult Psychol* 27:294–302 Ag '63. * (*PA* 38:2629)
200. KARRAS, ATHAN. "Predicting Full Scale WAIS IQs From WAIS Subtests for a Psychiatric Population." *J Clin Psychol* 19:100 Ja '63. * (*PA* 39:1737)
201. KENNEDY, WALLACE A.; WILLCUTT, HERMAN; AND SMITH, ALVIN. "Wechsler Profiles of Mathematically Gifted Adolescents." *Psychol Rep* 12:259–62 F '63. * (*PA* 38:3174)
202. LAVER, A. B. "Testing in Canada." *Can Psychologist* 4:22–3 Ja '63. *
203. LEVINSON, BORIS M. "The WAIS Quotient of Subcultural Deviation." *J Genetic Psychol* 103:123–31 S '63. * (*PA* 39:1810)
204. LEVINSON, BORIS M. "Wechsler M-F Index." *J General Psychol* 69:217–20 O '63. * (*PA* 39:1748)
205. MOGEL, STEVE, AND SATZ, PAUL. "Abbreviation of the WAIS for Clinical Use: An Attempt at Validation." *J Clin Psychol* 19:298–300 Jl '63. *
206. NEURINGER, CHARLES. "The Form Equivalence Between the Wechsler-Bellevue Intelligence Scale, Form I and the Wechsler Adult Intelligence Scale." *Ed & Psychol Meas* 23:755–63 w '63. * (*PA* 38:8427)
207. NICKOLS, JOHN. "Structural Efficiency of WAIS Subtests." *J Clin Psychol* 19:420–3 O '63. *
208. PAUKER, JEROME D. "Relationship of Rorschach Content Categories to Intelligence." *J Proj Tech & Pers Assess* 27:220–1 Je '63. * (*PA* 38:2725)
209. PAUKER, JEROME D. "A Split-Half Abbreviation of the WAIS." *J Clin Psychol* 19:98–100 Ja '63. * (*PA* 39:1755)
210. PIERCE, ROBERT C. "Note on Testing Conditions." *J Consult Psychol* 27:536–7 D '63. *
211. PRENTICE, NORMAN M., AND KELLY, FRANCIS J. "Intelligence and Delinquency: A Reconsideration." *J Social Psychol* 60:327–37 Ag '63. * (*PA* 38:4585)
212. RAFI, A. ABI. "A Note on the Cultural Aspects of the WAIS Vocabulary Subtest in Relation to British Mental Patients." *Brit J Social & Clin Psychol* 2:44–5 F '63. * (*PA* 38:963)
213. REED, HOMER B. C., JR., AND REITAN, RALPH M. "A Comparison of the Effects of the Normal Aging Process With the Effects of Organic Brain-Damage on Adaptive Abilities." *J Gerontol* 18:177–9 Ap '63. * (*PA* 38:4108)
214. ROBERTSON, MALCOLM H., AND WOLTER, DOUGLAS J. "The Effect of Sensory Deprivation Upon Scores on the Wechsler Adult Intelligenec Scale." *J Psychol* 56:213–8 Jl '63. * (*PA* 38:3610)
215. ROSS, D. "A Short-Form of the WAIS for Use in Mental Subnormality." *J Mental Subnorm* 9:91–4 D '63. *
216. ROTH, ROBERT M. "The Comprehension Subtest of the Wechsler Adult Intelligence Scale as an Indicator of Social Awareness." *J Ed Res* 56:387–8 Mr '63. *
217. SIEBERT, LAWRENCE A. "Matched Otis and Wechsler IQ Scores of Delinquents." *J Clin Psychol* 19:215–6 Ap '63. *
218. SILVERSTEIN, A. B. "WISC and WAIS IQs for the Mentally Retarded." *Am J Mental Def* 67:617–8 Ja '63. *
219. SPENCE, JANET TAYLOR. "Patterns of Performance on WAIS Similarities in Schizophrenic, Brain-Damaged and Normal Subjects." *Psychol Rep* 13:431–6 O '63. * (*PA* 38:8381)
220. TWAIN, DAVID C., AND BROOKS, EDWARD M. "A Comparison of Wechsler, Revised Beta and Otis Scores of Delinquent Boys." *Brit J Criminol* 3:288–90 Ja '63. *
221. WEBB, ALLEN P. "A Longitudinal Comparison of the WISC and WAIS With Educable Mentally Retarded Negroes." *J Clin Psychol* 19:101–2 Ja '63. * (*PA* 39:1769)
222. WITTENBORN, J. R., AND PLANTE, MARC. "Patterns of Response to Placebo, Iproniazid and Electroconvulsive Therapy Among Young Depressed Females." *J Nerv & Mental Dis* 137:155–61 Ag '63. *

For reviews by Nancy Bayley and Wilson H. Guertin, see 5:414. For reviews of the Wechsler-Bellevue Scale, see 5:415, 4:361, 3:298, and 40:1429. For excerpts from related book reviews, see B503, 3:299, 3:300, 3:301, and 40: B1121.

[539]

Wechsler-Bellevue Intelligence Scale. Ages 10 and over; 1939–47; individual; 2 forms; record form ('47, 4 pages) for each form; $2.10 per 25 record forms; postpaid; (40–60) minutes; David Wechsler; Psychological Corporation. (South African adaptation: National Institute for Personnel Research; Australian edition of record form and manual supplementary sheet: Australian Council for Educational Research.) *

a) FORM I. 1939–47; out of print except for record form; see 538 for a revision.

b) FORM 2. 1946–47; catalog states that "Form 2 is the retest instrument for the WAIS as well as for Form I"; 14 scores: verbal (general information, general comprehension, digit span, arithmetic, similarities, vocabulary, total), performance (picture arrangement, picture completion, block design, object assembly, digit symbol, total), total; manual ('46, 97 pages); $21 per set of testing materials, 25 record forms, and manual; $2.25 per manual.

REFERENCES

1–2. See 40:1429.
3–121. See 3:298.
122–371. See 4:361.
372–625. See 5:415.
626. MCFIE, J., AND PIERCY, M. F. "Intellectual Impairment With Localized Cerebral Lesions." *Brain* 75:292–311 S '52. * (*PA* 27:7649)
627. DENTON, L. R. "Intelligence Test Performance and Personality Differences in a Group of Visually Handicapped Children." *B Maritime Psychol Assn* 3:47–50 D '54. * (*PA* 29:7786)
628. YATES, AUBREY J. "The Validity of Some Psychological Tests of Brain Damage." *Psychol B* 51:359–79 Jl '54. *
629. HARRIS, RILDA. *A Comparative Study of Two Groups of Boys, Delinquent and Non-Delinquent, on the Basis of Their Wechsler and Rorschach Test Performances.* Master's thesis, Dalhousie University (Halifax, N.S., Canada), 1956.
630. MARSHAK, M. D. *A Study of the Wechsler-Bellevue Intelligence Scale Applied to British School Children.* Doctor's thesis, University of London (London, England), 1956.
631. BROWN, MORONI H., AND BRYAN, G. ELIZABETH. "Sex as a Variable in Intelligence Test Performance." *J Ed Psychol* 48:273–8 My '57. * (*PA* 33:778)
632. MAHRER, ALVIN R. "Potential Intelligence Testing: A Case Study." *U S Armed Forces Med J* 8:684–92 My '57. * (*PA* 33:3286)
633. PARSONS, OSCAR A.; STEWART, KENNETH D.; AND ARENBERG, DAVID. "Impairment of Abstracting Ability in Multiple Sclerosis." *J Nerv & Mental Dis* 125:221–5 Ap–Je '57. * (*PA* 33:4478)
634. SIDDIQUE, HABIBA. *A Translation of the Wechsler-Bellevue Intelligence Scale for Children With Adaptations, Suitable to West Pakistan.* Master's thesis, Claremont College (Claremont, Calif.), 1957.
635. STERNBERG, ULRICH; SPITZ, HERMAN; AND GOYNE, JAMES B. "Evaluation of Chlorpromazine and Reserpine Therapy With Follow-Up Study." *J Clin & Exp Psychopathol* 18:258–68 S '57. * (*PA* 33:1504)
636. KLØVE, HALLGRIM, AND REITAN, RALPH M. "Effect of Dysphasia and Spatial Distortion on Wechsler-Bellevue Results." *A.M.A. Arch Neurol & Psychiatry* 80:708–13 D '58. *
637. GASTON, CHARLES OWEN. *The Predictive Power of Attitudinal and Behavioral Indices Versus Formal Test Scores on the Wechsler-Bellevue Test.* Doctor's thesis, University of Houston (Houston, Tex.), 1958. (*DA* 19:1816)
638. HAWARD, L. R. C. "Wechsler Bellevue Form I." *Psychometric Res B* (2):[34–6] Ag '58. *
639. HEILBRUN, A. B., JR. "The Digit Span Test and the Prediction of Cerebral Pathology." *A.M.A. Arch Neurol & Psychiatry* 80:228–31 Ag '58. * (*PA* 33:10334)
640. HOLT, ROBERT R., AND LUBORSKY, LESTER; WITH THE COLLABORATION OF WILLIAM R. MORROW, DAVID RAPAPORT, AND SIBYLLE K. ESCALONA. *Personality Patterns of Psychiatrists: A Study of Methods for Selecting Residents, Vol. I.* New York: Basic Books, Inc., 1958. Pp. xiv, 386. * (*PA* 33:5751)
641. HOWARD, WILLIAM. "A Note on McNemar's 'On Abbreviated Wechsler-Bellevue Scales.'" *J Consult Psychol* 22:414 D '58. * (*PA* 33:9920, title only)

642. LEIDING, WALDEMAR C. *A Comparison of the Content and Sign Approaches in Evaluating a Projective Test Battery and Its Component Tests.* Doctor's thesis, University of Houston (Houston, Tex.), 1958. (*DA* 19:1822)

643. LEVINE, MURRAY. "'Not Alike' Responses in Wechsler's Similarities Subtest." Abstract. *J Consult Psychol* 22:480 D '58. * (*PA* 33:10742)

644. MUNDY, LYDIA, AND MAXWELL, A. E. "Assessment of the Feebleminded." *Brit J Med Psychol* 31:201-10 pt 3 & 4 '58. * (*PA* 34:1673)

645. PLANT, WALTER T. "Mental Ability Scores for Freshmen in a California State College." *Calif J Ed Res* 9:72-3+ Mr '58. * (*PA* 33:9051)

646. ARMSTRONG, DOLORES MARIE. *The Differential Predictive Value of the Wechsler-Bellevue Scale.* Doctor's thesis, Stanford University (Stanford, Calif.), 1959. (*DA* 20:1262)

647. BIESHEUVEL, S., AND LIDDICOAT, R. "The Effects of Cultural Factors on Intelligence-Test Performance." *J Nat Inst Personnel Res* 8:3-14 S '59. * (*PA* 34:5785)

648. BLATT, SIDNEY J. "Recall and Recognition Vocabulary: Implications for Intellectual Deterioration." *A.M.A. Arch Gen Psychiatry* 1:473-6 N '59. * (*PA* 34:6005)

649. BRIDGES, CECIL. "Nomographs for Computing the 'Validity' of WISC or Wechsler-Bellevue Short Forms." *J Consult Psychol* 23:453-4 O '59. * (*PA* 34:5576)

650. CAMPBELL, J. CHANDLER. *The Relationship Between the Wechsler-Bellevue Scale and High School Achievement.* Doctor's thesis, Indiana University (Bloomington, Ind.), 1959. (*DA* 20:4031)

651. GUERTIN, WILSON H. "Auditory Interference With Digit Span Performance." *J Clin Psychol* 15:349 Jl '59. * (*PA* 35:3407)

652. KAHN, MARVIN W. "A Comparison of Personality, Intelligence, and Social History of Two Criminal Groups." *J Social Psychol* 49:33-40 F '59. * (*PA* 35:5214)

653. KARLE, H. "Wechsler Bellevue." *Psychometric Res B* (4):[26-9] Ag '59. *

654. KLØVE, HALLGRIM. "Relationship of Differential Electroencephalographic Patterns to Distribution of Wechsler-Bellevue Scores." *Neurology* 9:871-6 D '59. * (*PA* 35:1014)

655. KNOWLES, J. B. "Wechsler Bellevue." *Psychometric Res B* (4):[5-7] Ag '59. *

656. LONG, JAMES ALAN. *A Longitudinal Study of Some Factors Influencing the Performance of Adolescents on the Wechsler Bellevue Intelligence Scale 1.* Doctor's thesis, Louisiana State University (Baton Rouge, La.), 1959. (*DA* 19:3368)

657. MARTIN, HARRY JEROME, JR. *A Comparison of Sign and Clinical Approaches in Predicting Psychiatric Diagnosis.* Doctor's thesis, University of Houston (Houston, Tex.), 1959. (*DA* 20:3837)

658. MASLING, JOSEPH. "The Effects of Warm and Cold Interaction on the Administration and Scoring of an Intelligence Test." *J Consult Psychol* 23:336-41 Ag '59. * (*PA* 34:4395)

659. NORMAN, RALPH D., AND DALEY, MARVIN F. "Senescent Changes in Intellectual Ability Among Superior Older Women." *J Gerontol* 14:457-64 O '59. * (*PA* 34:4157)

660. REITAN, RALPH M. "The Comparative Effects of Brain Damage on the Halstead Impairment Index and the Wechsler-Bellevue Scale." *J Clin Psychol* 15:281-5 Jl '59. * (*PA* 35:3739)

661. REITAN, RALPH M. "Correlations Between the Trail Making Test and the Wechsler-Bellevue Scale." *Percept & Motor Skills* 9:127-30 Je '59. * (*PA* 38:4282)

662. RIOCH, MARGARET J., AND LUBIN, ARDIE. "Prognosis of Social Adjustment for Mental Hospital Patients Under Psychotherapy." *J Consult Psychol* 23:313-8 Ag '59. * (*PA* 34:4404)

663. SMITH, JEANNE BAKER. *Abbreviated Wechsler-Bellevue Intelligence Scales With a Select High School Population.* Doctor's thesis, Bradley University (Peoria, Ill.), 1959. (*DA* 20:3637)

664. STRONG, PASCHAL N., JR. "Correlation Between the Ohio Literacy Test, Grade Achieved in School, and Wechsler Bellevue IQ." *J Clin Psychol* 15:71-2 Ja '59. * (*PA* 34:3452)

665. THORP, THOMAS R., AND MAHRER, ALVIN R. "Predicting Potential Intelligence." *J Clin Psychol* 15:286-8 Jl '59. * (*PA* 35:3418)

666. VICTOR, MAURICE; HERMAN, KENNETH; AND WHITE, ELISABETH E. "A Psychological Study of the Wernicke-Korsakoff Syndrome: Results of Wechsler-Bellevue Intelligence Scale and Wechsler Memory Scale Testing at Different Stages in the Disease." *Q J Studies Alcohol* 20:467-79 S '59. * (*PA* 34:6401)

667. AZIMA, FERN CRAMER, AND KRAL, V. A. "Effects of Blindfolding on Persons During Psychological Testing: A Psychometric Study of Various Age Groups." *Geriatrics* 15:780-92 N '60. *

668. BELL, ANNE, AND ZUBEK, JOHN P. "The Effect of Age on the Intellectual Performance of Mental Defectives." *J Gerontol* 15:285-95 Jl '60. * (*PA* 35:1039)

669. BROWN, FRED. "Intelligence Test Patterns of Puerto Rican Psychiatric Patients." *J Social Psychol* 52:225-30 N '60. * (*PA* 35:4855)

670. FIELD, J. G. "The Performance-Verbal IQ Discrepancy in a Group of Sociopaths." *J Clin Psychol* 16:321-2 Jl '60. * (*PA* 36:2HI21F)

671. FISHER, GARY M. "A Corrected Table for Determining the Significance of the Difference Between Verbal and Performance IQ's on the WAIS and the Wechsler-Bellevue." *J Clin Psychol* 16:7-8 Ja '60. * (*PA* 36:1HC07F)

672. GARFIELD, SOL L. "An Appraisal of Object Assembly on the Wechsler-Bellevue and WAIS." *J Clin Psychol* 16:8-9 Ja '60. * (*PA* 36:1HC08G)

673. HEILBRUN, ALFRED B., JR. "Specificity of Immediate Memory Function Associated With Cerebral Cortex Damage." *J Mental Sci* 106:241-5 Ja '60. * (*PA* 35:6745)

674. JUDSON, ABE J. "The Effects of Chlorpromazine on Psychological Test Scores." Abstract. *J Consult Psychol* 24:192 Ap '60. * (*PA* 34:7888)

675. KINGSLEY, LEONARD. "Wechsler-Bellevue Patterns of Psychopaths." Abstract. *J Consult Psychol* 24:373 Ag '60. * (*PA* 35:2244)

676. LANSING, KENNETH M. "Intelligence and Art Ability." *Studies Art Ed* 1:73-84 sp '60. *

677. MCFIE, JOHN. "Psychological Testing in Clinical Neurology." *J Nerv & Mental Dis* 131:383-93 N '60. * (*PA* 35:3736)

678. MORAN, LOUIS J.; GORHAM, DONALD R.; AND HOLTZMAN, WAYNE H. "Vocabulary Knowledge and Usage of Schizophrenic Subjects: A Six-Year Follow-Up." *J Abn & Social Psychol* 61:246-54 S '60. * (*PA* 35:5253)

679. MUNDY-CASTLE, A. C. "Comments on Saunders' 'Further Implications of Mundy-Castle's Correlations Between EEG and Wechsler-Bellevue Variables.'" *J Nat Inst Personnel Res* 8:102-5 D '60. * (*PA* 35:5895)

680. MUNDY-CASTLE, A. C., AND NELSON, G. K. "Intelligence, Personality and Brain Rhythms in a Socially Isolated Community." *Nature* 185:484-5 F 13 '60. *

681. O'REILLY, P. O., AND HARRISON, K. "Experimentation With an Objective Test Battery." *Can Psychiatric Assn J* 5:108-23 Ap '60. *

682. PETERS, JAMES S., III. "A Study of the Wechsler-Bellevue Verbal Scores of Negro and White Males." *J Negro Ed* 29:7-16 w '60. *

683. PLUMEAU, F.; MACHOVER, S.; AND PUZZO, F. "Wechsler-Bellevue Performances of Remitted and Unremitted Alcoholics, and Their Normal Controls." *J Consult Psychol* 24:240-2 Je '60. * (*PA* 35:6871)

684. RIKLAN, MANUEL; DILLER, LEONARD; WEINER, HERMAN; AND COOPER, IRVING S. "Psychological Studies on Effects of Chemosurgery of the Basal Ganglia in Parkinsonism: 1, Intellectual Functioning." *A.M.A. Arch Gen Psychiatry* 2:22-32 Ja '60. * (*PA* 34:8265)

685. SAUNDERS, D. R. "Further Implications of Mundy-Castle's Correlations Between EEG and Wechsler-Bellevue Variables." *J Nat Inst Personnel Res* 8:91-101 D '60. * (*PA* 35:5896)

686. WIGGINS, NEWTON WAYNE. *A Comparative Evaluation of the Wechsler-Bellevue Scale Performance of Selected Brain-Injured and Non-Injured Subjects.* Doctor's thesis, Indiana University (Bloomington, Ind.), 1960. (*DA* 21:2602)

687. BALTHAZAR, EARL E., AND MORRISON, DON H. "The Use of Wechsler Intelligence Scales as Diagnostic Indicators of Predominant Left-Right and Indeterminate Unilateral Brain Damage." *J Clin Psychol* 17:161-5 Ap '61. * (*PA* 38:1236)

688. BALTHAZAR, EARL E.; TODD, RONALD E.; MORRISON, DON H.; AND ZIEBELL, PETER W. "Visuoconstructive and Verbal Responses in Chronic Brain-Damaged Patients and Familial Retardates." *J Clin Psychol* 17:293-6 Jl '61. * (*PA* 38:8932)

689. BONIER, RICHARD J., AND HANLEY, CHARLES. "Handedness and Digit Symbol Performance." *J Clin Psychol* 17:286-9 Jl '61. * (*PA* 38:8444)

690. COOK, RICHARD A., AND HIRT, MICHAEL L. "Verbal and Performance IQ Discrepancies on the Wechsler Adult Intelligence Scale and Wechsler-Bellevue, Form 1." *J Clin Psychol* 17:382-3 O '61. * (*PA* 38:8446)

691. COROTTO, LOREN V. "The Relation of Performance to Verbal IQ in Acting Out Juveniles." *J Psychol Studies* 12:162-6 Jl '61 [issued Mr '63]. *

692. CRADDICK, RAY A. "Wechsler-Bellevue IQ Scores of Psychopathic and Non-Psychopathic Prisoners." *J Psychol Studies* 12:167-72 Jl '61 [issued Mr '63]. *

693. CROOKES, T. G. "Wechsler's Deterioration Ratio in Clinical Practice." *J Consult Psychol* 25:234-8 Je '61. *

694. DARBES, ALEX. "A Comparison of Scores Achieved by 55 Subjects Administered the Wechsler and Binet Scales of Intelligence." *Proc W Va Acad Sci* 33:115-9 N '61. * (*PA* 36:5HD15D)

695. DIBNER, ANDREW S., AND CUMMINS, JAMES F. "Intellectual Functioning in a Group of Normal Octogenarians." *J Consult Psychol* 25:137-41 Ap '61. * (*PA* 36:4FI37D)

696. DOEHRING, DONALD G.; REITAN, RALPH M.; AND KLØVE, HALLGRIM. "Changes in Patterns of Intelligence Test Performance Associated With Homonymous Visual Field Defects." *J Nerv & Mental Dis* 132:227-33 Mr '61. * (*PA* 36:1JF27D)

697. DUNCAN, DONN R., AND BARRETT, ALBERT M. "A Longitudinal Comparison of Intelligence Involving the Wechsler-Bellevue 1 and WAIS." *J Clin Psychol* 17:318-9 Jl '61. * (*PA* 38:8453)

698. FISHER, GARY M. "Discrepancy in Verbal and Per-

formance IQ in Adolescent Sociopaths." *J Clin Psychol* 17:60 Ja '61. * (*PA* 37:3214)

699. FITZHUGH, KATHLEEN B.; FITZHUGH, LOREN C.; AND REITAN, RALPH M. "Psychological Deficits in Relation to Acuteness of Brain Dysfunction." *J Consult Psychol* 25:61-6 F '61. * (*PA* 36:3JF61F)

700. GASTON, CHARLES O., AND DELANGE, WALTER H. "The Relationship Between Wechsler-Bellevue Digit Symbol Performance and Psychosis." *Tex Rep Biol & Med* 19:76-9 sp '61. *

701. GILGASH, CURTIS A. "Thorazine Therapy With Catatonic Schizophrenics in Relation to Wechsler Verbal and Performance Subtest Comparison." *J Clin Psychol* 17:95 Ja '61. * (*PA* 37:3687)

702. HILER, E. WESLEY, AND NESVIG, DAVID. "Changes in Intellectual Functions of Children in a Psychiatric Hospital." *J Consult Psychol* 25:288-92 Ag '61. * (*PA* 37:1495)

703. LIDDICOAT, RENEE. "A Study of Non-Institutionalized Homosexuals." *J Nat Inst Personnel Res* 8:217-49 S '61. * (*PA* 36:4JL17L)

704. McFIE, JOHN. "The Effect of Education on African Performance on a Group of Intellectual Tests." *Brit J Ed Psychol* 31:232-40 N '61. * (*PA* 36:5HD32M)

705. MURSTEIN, BERNARD I., AND LEIPOLD, WILLIAM D. "The Role of Learning and Motor Abilities in the Wechsler-Bellevue Digit Symbol Subtest." *Ed & Psychol Meas* 21:103-12 sp '61. * (*PA* 36:1HE03M)

706. PAYNE, R. W. Chap. 6, "Cognitive Abnormalities," pp. 193-261. In *Handbook of Abnormal Psychology: An Experimental Approach.* Edited by H. J. Eysenck. New York: Basic Books, Inc., 1961. Pp. xvi, 816. * (*PA* 35:6719)

707. SUGARMAN, LOLA. "Alpha Rhythm, Perception and Intelligence." *J Nat Inst Personnel Res* 8:170-9 S '61. * (*PA* 36:4DG70S)

708. CASSEL, ROBERT H.; JOHNSON, ANNA P.; AND BURNS, WILLIAM H. "The Order of Tests in the Battery." *J Clin Psychol* 18:464-5 O '62. * (*PA* 39:5042)

709. COYNE, WILLIAM J. *The Effect of Reading Instruction and Further Education Upon the Intelligence Quotient as Measured by the Wechsler-Bellevue Scale.* Master's thesis, Cardinal Stritch College (Milwaukee, Wis.), 1962.

710. FISHER, GARY M., AND PARSONS, PATRICIA A. "The Effect of Intellectual Level on the Rate of False Positive Organic Diagnoses From the Hewson and Adolescent Ratios." *J Clin Psychol* 18:125-6 Ap '62. * (*PA* 38:8924)

711. FITZHUGH, KATHLEEN B.; FITZHUGH, LOREN C.; AND REITAN, RALPH M. "Relation of Acuteness of Organic Brain Dysfunction to Trail Making Test Performances." *Percept & Motor Skills* 15:399-403 O '62. * (*PA* 37:8142)

712. FITZHUGH, KATHLEEN B.; FITZHUGH, LOREN C.; AND REITAN, RALPH M. "Wechsler-Bellevue Comparisons in Groups With 'Chronic' and 'Current' Lateralized and Diffuse Brain Lesions." *J Consult Psychol* 26:306-10 Ag '62. * (*PA* 38:4544)

713. GUERTIN, WILSON H.; RABIN, ALBERT I.; FRANK, GEORGE H.; AND LADD, CLAYTON E. "Research With the Wechsler Intelligence Scales for Adults: 1955-60." *Psychol B* 59:1-26 Ja '62. * (*PA* 37:1203)

714. HAUSER, RUSSELL JEROME. *The Validity of the Formal and Linguistic Aspects of the Rorschach in Predicting Intelligence.* Doctor's thesis, New York University (New York, N.Y.), 1962. (*DA* 24:833)

715. JARVIK, LISSY F.; KALLMANN, FRANZ J.; LORGE, IRVING; AND FALEK, ARTHUR. "Longitudinal Study of Intellectual Changes in Senescent Twins," pp. 839-59. In *Social and Psychological Aspects of Aging.* Proceedings of the Fifth Congress of the International Association of Gerontology. Edited by Clark Tibbitts and Wilma Donahue. New York: Columbia University Press, 1962. Pp. xviii, 952. *

716. JARVIK, LISSY FEINGOLD. "Biological Differences in Intellectual Functioning." *Vita Hum* 5(4):195-203 '62. * (*PA* 38:970)

717. JARVIK, LISSY FEINGOLD; KALLMANN, FRANZ J.; AND FALEK, ARTHUR. "Intellectual Changes in Aged Twins." *J Gerontol* 17:289-94 Jl '62. * (*PA* 37:2952)

718. KLØVE, HALLGRIM. "The Differential Relationships of Psychological Test Results to Electroencephalographic Criteria in Older and Younger Age Groups," pp. 873-9. In *Social and Psychological Aspects of Aging.* Proceedings of the Fifth Congress of the International Association of Gerontology. Edited by Clark Tibbitts and Wilma Donahue. New York: Columbia University Press, 1962. Pp. xviii, 952. *

719. KLØVE, HALLGRIM, AND FITZHUGH, KATHLEEN B. "The Relationship of Differential EEG Patterns to the Distribution of Wechsler-Bellevue Scores in a Chronic Epileptic Population." *J Clin Psychol* 18:334-7 Jl '62. * (*PA* 39:2475)

720. LASKOWITZ, DAVID. "Wechsler-Bellevue Performance of Adolescent Heroin Addicts." *J Psychol Studies* 13:49-59 Mr '62 [issued N '63]. *

721. LIDDICOAT, RENEE, AND ROBERTS, A. O. H. "Interim Standardization of the South African Version of the Wechsler-Bellevue Adult Intelligence Test." *Psychologia Africana* 9:273-85 '62. * (*PA* 37:4957)

722. McFARLAND, ROBERT L.; NELSON, CHARLES L.; AND ROSSI, ASCANIO M. "Prediction of Participation in Group Psychotherapy From Measures of Intelligence and Verbal Behavior." *Psychol Rep* 11:291-8 Ag '62. * (*PA* 37:5190)

723. MANNE, SIGMUND H.; KANDEL, ARTHUR; AND ROSENTHAL, DAVID. "Differences Between Performance IQ and Verbal IQ in a Severely Sociopathic Population." *J Clin Psychol* 18:73-7 Ja '62. * (*PA* 38:9008)

724. MATTHEWS, CHARLES G.; GUERTIN, WILSON H.; AND REITAN, RALPH M. "Wechsler-Bellevue Subtest Mean Rank Orders in Diverse Diagnostic Groups." *Psychol Rep* 11:3-9 Ag '62. * (*PA* 37:4944)

725. MUNDY-CASTLE, A. C., AND NELSON, G. K. "A Neuropsychological Study of the Knysna Forest Workers." *Psychologia Africana* 9:240-72 '62. * (*PA* 37:4822)

726. NICKOLS, JOHN E., JR. "Brief Forms of the Wechsler Intelligence Scales for Research." *J Clin Psychol* 18:167 Ap '62. * (*PA* 38:8500)

727. REITAN, RALPH M., AND REED, HOMER B. C., JR. "Consistencies in Wechsler-Bellevue Mean Values in Brain-Damaged Groups." *Percept & Motor Skills* 15:119-21 Ag '62. * (*PA* 37:5046)

728. RIEGEL, KLAUS F., AND RIEGEL, RUTH M. "Analysis of Differences in Test and Item Difficulty Between Young and Old Adults." *J Gerontol* 17:97-105 Ja '62. * (*PA* 36:5FI97R)

729. RIEGEL, RUTH M., AND RIEGEL, KLAUS F. "A Comparison and Reinterpretation of Factor Structures of the W-B, the WAIS, and the HAWIE on Aged Persons." *J Consult Psychol* 26:31-7 F '62. * (*PA* 37:4965)

730. SHAPIRO, M. B.; BRIERLEY, J.; SLATER, P.; AND BEECH, H. R. "Experimental Studies of a Perceptual Anomoly: 7, A New Explanation." *J Mental Sci* 108:655-68 S '62. * (*PA* 38:2989)

731. ANGERS, WILLIAM P. "Patterns of Abilities and Capacities in the Epileptic." *J Genetic Psychol* 103:59-66 S '63. *

732. BALTHAZAR, EARL E. "The Alleged Refractory Nature of Verbal Subtest Scores in Brain-Damaged Cases." *Am J Mental Def* 67:871-8 My '63. * (*PA* 38:1235)

733. BALTHAZAR, EARL E. "Cerebral Unilateralization in Chronic Epileptic Cases: The Wechsler Object Assembly Subtest." *J Clin Psychol* 19:169-71 Ap '63. * (*PA* 39:5627)

734. BERKOWITZ, BERNARD, AND GREEN, RUSSEL F. "Changes in Intellect With Age: 1, Longitudinal Study of Wechsler-Bellevue Scores." *J Genetic Psychol* 103:3-21 S '63. *

735. BURNETT, A.; BEACH, H. D.; AND SULLIVAN, A. M. "Intelligence in a Restricted Environment." *Can Psychologist* 4:126-36 O '63. * (*PA* 38:6050)

736. CAPUTO, DANIEL V.; EDMONSTON, WILLIAM E., JR.; L'ABATE, LUCIANO; AND RONDBERG, SAMUEL R. "Type of Brain Damage and Intellectual Functioning in Children." Abstract. *J Consult Psychol* 27:184 Ap '63. *

737. COPPINGER, NEIL W.; BORTNER, RAYMAN W.; AND SAUCER, RAYFORD T. "A Factor Analysis of Psychological Deficit." *J Genetic Psychol* 103:23-43 S '63. *

738. CRONHOLM, BORJE, AND SCHALLING, DAISY. "Intellectual Deterioration After Focal Brain Injury." *Arch Surgery* 86:670-87 Ap '63. *

739. FITZHUGH, KATHLEEN B.; FITZHUGH, LOREN C.; AND REITAN, RALPH M. "Effects of 'Chronic' and 'Current' Lateralized and Non-Lateralized Cerebral Lesions Upon Trail Making Test Performances." *J Nerv & Mental Dis* 137:82-7 Jl '63. * (*PA* 38:3755)

740. GIANNELL, A. STEVEN, AND FREEBURNE, CECIL M. "The Comparative Validity of the WAIS and the Stanford-Binet With College Freshmen." *Ed & Psychol Meas* 23:557-67 au '63. * (*PA* 38:6057)

741. KLØVE, HALLGRIM, AND WHITE, PHILIP T. "The Relationship of Degree of Electroencephalographic Abnormality to the Distribution of Wechsler-Bellevue Scores." *Neurology* 13:423-30 My '63. *

742. MATTHEWS, CHARLES G., AND REITAN, RALPH M. "Relationship of Differential Abstraction Ability Levels to Psychological Test Performances in Mentally Retarded Subjects." *Am J Mental Def* 68:235-44 S '63. * (*PA* 38:6430)

743. NEURINGER, CHARLES. "The Form Equivalence Between the Wechsler-Bellevue Intelligence Scale, Form 1 and the Wechsler Adult Intelligence Scale." *Ed & Psychol Meas* 23:755-63 w '63. * (*PA* 38:8427)

744. PARSONS, OSCAR A.; MORRIS, FREDA; AND DENNY, J. PETER. "Agitation, Anxiety, Brain-Damage and Perceptual-Motor Deficit." *J Clin Psychol* 19:267-71 Jl '63. *

745. PRENTICE, NORMAN M., AND KELLY, FRANCIS J. "Intelligence and Delinquency: A Reconsideration." *J Social Psychol* 60:327-37 Ag '63. * (*PA* 38:4585)

746. REED, HOMER B. C., JR., AND REITAN, R. M. "Intelligence Test Performances of Brain Damaged Subjects With Lateralized Motor Deficits." *J Consult Psychol* 27:102-6 Ap '63. * (*PA* 37:8145)

747. REED, HOMER B. C., JR., AND REITAN, RALPH M. "Changes in Psychological Test Performance Associated With the Normal Aging Process." *J Gerontol* 18:271-4 Jl '63. * (*PA* 38:4109)

748. SILVERSTEIN, A. B.; FISHER, GARY M.; AND OWENS, EARL P. "The Altitude Quotient as an Index of Intellectual Potential: 3, Three Studies of Predictive Validity." *Am J Mental Def* 67:611-6 Ja '63. * (*PA* 37:7026)

For reviews by Murray Aborn and William D. Altus, see 4:361; for a review by Robert I.

Watson, see 3:298; for a review by F. L. Wells, see 40:1429 (2 excerpts); for excerpts from related book reviews, see 5:B332, 4:362, 3:299–301, and 40:B1121.

[540]

Wechsler Intelligence Scale for Children. Ages 5-15; 1949; downward extension of Form 2 of *Wechsler-Bellevue Intelligence Scale;* also called WISC; 15 scores: verbal (information, comprehension, arithmetic, similarities, vocabulary, digit span-optional, total), performance (picture completion, picture arrangement, block design, object assembly, mazes-optional, coding, total), total; individual; 1 form; record booklet (6 pages, revised slightly in 1958 but dated 1949); manual (117 pages); $25 per set of testing materials, 25 record booklets, and manual; $2.50 per 25 record booklets; $1.35 per 25 WISC Maze Tests, an alternate subtest which may be used in place of Coding; $3 per manual; postpaid; Spanish edition available; (40-60) minutes; David Wechsler; Psychological Corporation. * (Australian edition: Australian Council for Educational Research.)

REFERENCES

1-22. See 4:363.
23-133. See 5:416.
134. CHALMERS, JAMES MCNISH. *An Investigation Into the Nature of the Results Obtained on the WISC by Mentally Superior Children.* Master's thesis, University of Alberta (Edmonton, Alta., Canada), 1953.
135. DENTON, L. R. "Intelligence Test Performance and Personality Differences in a Group of Visually Handicapped Children." *B Maritime Psychol Assn* 3:47-50 D '54. * (*PA* 29:7786)
136. HUNTRESS, DAN W. *Wechsler Intelligence Scale for Children and Associative Learning Disability.* Master's thesis, Illinois Normal University (Normal, Ill.), 1955.
137. HARRIS, RILDA. "A Comparative Study of Two Groups of Boys, Delinquent and Non-Delinquent, on the Basis of Their Wechsler and Rorschach Test Performances." *B Maritime Psychol Assn* 6:21-8 sp '57. * (*PA* 33:4295)
138. LEWIS, LENA L. "The Relation of Measured Mental Ability to School Marks and Academic Survival in the Texas School for the Blind." *Int J Ed Blind* 6:56-60 Mr '57. *
139. INDOW, TAROW. "The Mental Growth Curve Defined on the Absolute Scale: Comparison of Japanese and Foreign Data." *Jap Psychol Res* 1:35-48 Jl '58. * (*PA* 34:2725)
140. MAYER, ROBERT W. "A Study of the STEP Reading, SCAT and WISC Tests, and School Grades." *Reading Teach* 12:117+ D '58. * (*PA* 34:3441)
141. MIELE, JOHN ANTHONY. *Sex Differences in Intelligence: The Relationship of Sex to Intelligence as Measured by the Wechsler Adult Intelligence Scale and the Wechsler Intelligence Scale for Children.* Doctor's thesis, New York University (New York, N.Y.), 1958. (*DA* 18:2213)
142. NELSON, CALVIN CLAYTON. *A Comparison of Retarded and Normal Children With Respect to Alexander's "F" Factor.* Doctor's thesis, University of Oregon (Eugene, Ore.), 1958. (*DA* 19:1015)
143. SCHACHTER, FRANCES FUCHS, AND APGAR, VIRGINIA. "Comparison of Preschool Stanford-Binet and School-Age WISC IQs." *J Ed Psychol* 49:320-3 D '58. * (*PA* 36:2HD20S)
144. BAROFF, GEORGE S. "WISC Patterning in Endogenous Mental Deficiency." *Am J Mental Def* 64:482-5 N '59. * (*PA* 34:7995)
145. BENISKOS, JEAN-MARIE. *WISC Patterns and Reading Achievement.* Doctor's thesis, University of Ottawa (Ottawa, Ont., Canada), 1959. (Abstract: *Can Psychologist* 1:112)
146. BRIDGES, CECIL. "Nomographs for Computing the 'Validity' of WISC or Wechsler-Bellevue Short Forms." *J Consult Psychol* 23:453-4 O '59. * (*PA* 34:5576)
147. CHAMBERS, JACK A. "Preliminary Screening Methods in the Identification of Intellectually Superior Children." *Excep Child* 26:145-50 N '59. * (*PA* 35:3249)
148. COHEN, JACOB. "The Factorial Structure of the WISC at Ages 7-6, 10-6, and 13-6." *J Consult Psychol* 23:285-99 Ag '59. *
149. FINLEY, CARMEN, AND THOMPSON, JACK. "Sex Differences in Intelligence of Educable Mentally Retarded Children." *Calif J Ed Res* 10:167-70 S '59. * (*PA* 34:8002)
150. JILLSON, RICHMOND P. *An Investigation of the Clinical Possibilities of Certain Abbreviated Forms of the Wechsler Intelligence Scale for Children.* Master's thesis, Boston University (Boston, Mass.), 1959.
151. JONES, S. *A Statistical Study of the Wechsler Intelligence Scale for Children.* Doctor's thesis, University of London (London, England), 1959.
152. LARR, ALFRED L., AND CAIN, EARL R. "Measurement of Native Learning Abilities of Deaf Children." *Volta R* 61:160-2 Ap '59. *
153. LEVINSON, BORIS M. "A Comparison of the Performance of Bilingual and Monolingual Native Born Jewish Preschool Children of Traditional Parentage on Four Intelligence Tests." *J Clin Psychol* 15:74-6 Ja '59. * (*PA* 34:2729)
154. LEVINSON, BORIS M. "Traditional Jewish Cultural Values and Performance on the Wechsler Tests." *J Ed Psychol* 50:177-81 Ag '59. * (*PA* 35:2059)
155. MAXWELL, A. E. "A Factor Analysis of the Wechsler Intelligence Scale for Children." *Brit J Ed Psychol* 29:237-41 N '59. *
156. MAXWELL, A. E. "Tables to Facilitate the Comparison of Sub-Test Scores on the WISC." *J Clin Psychol* 15:293-5 Jl '59. *
157. ROGGE, HAROLD JOHN. *A Study of the Relationships of Reading Achievement to Certain Other Factors in a Population of Delinquent Boys.* Doctor's thesis, University of Minnesota (Minneapolis, Minn.), 1959. (*DA* 20:4037)
158. SHELDON, M. STEPHEN, AND GARTON, JEANETTE. "A Note on 'A WISC Profile for Retarded Readers.'" *Alberta J Ed Res* 5:264-7 D '59. * (*PA* 35:771)
159. SIMPSON, WILLIAM H., AND BRIDGES, CECIL C., JR. "A Short Form of the Wechsler Intelligence Scale for Children." *J Clin Psychol* 15:424 O '59. * (*PA* 36:1HC25S)
160. STOFFEL, CLARENCE M., JR. *A Study of the Wechsler Intelligence Scale for Children Subtest Scores of Homeless and Wayward Boys.* Master's thesis, Creighton University (Omaha, Neb.), 1959.
161. WHITE, ARDEN JUNIOR. *A Comparison of the Flanagan Aptitude Classification Tests With the Wechsler Adult Intelligence Scale, the School and College Ability Test, and Three Other Measures of Mental Variables at the High School Level.* Doctor's research study No. 1, Colorado State College (Greeley, Colo.), 1959.
162. WINITZ, HARRIS. "Relationships Between Language and Nonlanguage Measures of Kindergarten Children." *J Speech & Hearing Res* 2:387-91 D '59. * (*PA* 34:5896)
163. ALPER, ARTHUR EUGENE. *An Analysis of the Wechsler Intelligence Scale for Children With Institutionalized Mental Defectives.* Doctor's thesis, University of Florida (Tallahassee, Fla.), 1960. (*DA* 20:4711)
164. BURNS, ROBERT C. "Behavioral Differences Between Brain-Injured and Brain-Deficit Children Grouped According to Neuropathological Types." *Am J Mental Def* 65:326-34 N '60. * (*PA* 35:3732)
165. BURT, CYRIL. "The Factor Analysis of the Wechsler Scale." *Brit J Stat Psychol* 13:82-7 My '60. *
166. CARSON, ARNOLD S., AND RABIN, A. I. "Verbal Comprehension and Communication in Negro and White Children." *J Ed Psychol* 51:47-51 Ap '60. * (*PA* 35:2049)
167. DOCKRELL, W. B. "The Use of Wechsler Intelligence Scale for Children in the Diagnosis of Retarded Readers." *Alberta J Ed Res* 6:86-91 Je '60. * (*PA* 36:2KF86D)
168. FIELD, J. G. "Two Types of Tables for Use With Wechsler's Intelligence Scales." *J Clin Psychol* 16:3-7 Ja '60. * (*PA* 36:1HC03F)
169. FISHER, GARY M. "A Cross-Validation of Baroff's WISC Patterning in Endogenous Mental Deficiency." *Am J Mental Def* 65:349-50 N '60. * (*PA* 35:3406)
170. FROST, BARRY P. "An Application of the Method of Extreme Deviations to the Wechsler Intelligence Scale for Children." *J Clin Psychol* 16:420 O '60. * (*PA* 37:3216)
171. HAFNER, A. JACK; POLLIE, DONALD M.; AND WAPNER, IRWIN. "The Relationship Between the CMAS and WISC Functioning." *J Clin Psychol* 16:322-3 Jl '60. * (*PA* 36:2FC22H)
172. HIRST, LYNNE SCHELLBERG. "The Usefulness of a Two-Way Analysis of WISC Subtests in the Diagnosis of Remedial Reading Problems." *J Exp Ed* 29:153-60 D '60. *
173. HOLLAND, WILLIAM R. "Language Barrier as an Educational Problem of Spanish-Speaking Children." *Excep Child* 27:42-50 S '60. *
174. JACKSON, M. A. "The Factor Analysis of the Wechsler Scale." *Brit J Stat Psychol* 13:79-82 My '60. *
175. KILMAN, BEVERLY A., AND FISHER, GARY M. "An Evaluation of the Finley-Thompson Abbreviated Form of the WISC for Undifferentiated, Brain-Damaged and Functional Retardates." *Am J Mental Def* 64:742-6 Ja '60. * (*PA* 35:1030)
176. KIMBRELL, DON L. "Comparison of Peabody, WISC, and Academic Achievement Scores Among Educable Mental Defectives." *Psychol Rep* 7:502 D '60. * (*PA* 35:2554)
177. LEVINSON, BORIS M. "Subcultural Variations in Verbal and Performance Ability at the Elementary School Level." *J Genetic Psychol* 97:149-60 S '60. * (*PA* 35:6404)
178. LITTELL, WILLIAM M. "The Wechsler Intelligence Scale for Children: Review of a Decade of Research." *Psychol B* 57:132-56 Mr '60. * (*PA* 34:7353)
179. LUCITO, LEONARD, AND GALLAGHER, JAMES. "Intellectual Patterns of Highly Gifted Children on the WISC." *Peabody J Ed* 38:131-6 N '60. * (*PA* 35:4860)
180. MAXWELL, A. E. "Discrepancies in the Variances of Test Results for Normal and Neurotic Children." *Brit J Stat Psychol* 13:165-72 N '60. * (*PA* 36:3HD65M)

181. MOLLER, HELLA. *Stuttering, Predelinquent, and Adjusted Boys: A Comparative Analysis of Personality Characteristics as Measured by the WISC and the Rorschach Test.* Doctor's thesis, Boston University (Boston, Mass.), 1960. (*DA* 21:1461)
182. MUKHERJEE, BISHWA NATH. "A Report on the Preliminary Item-Analysis of a Tryout Form of WISC for Gujerati Children." *Psychol Studies* 5:118–26 Jl '60. * (*PA* 38:2672)
183. OGDON, DONALD P. "WISC IQs for the Mentally Retarded." *J Consult Psychol* 24:187–8 Ap '60. * (*PA* 34:8014)
184. ROBECK, MILDRED C. "Subtest Patterning of Problem Readers on WISC." *Calif J Ed Res* 11:110–5 My '60. * (*PA* 35:7034)
185. SALVATI, SAVERIO R. *A Comparison of WISC I.Q.'s and Altitude Scores as Predictors of Learning Ability of Mentally Retarded Subjects.* Doctor's thesis, New York University (New York, N.Y.), 1960. (*DA* 21:2370)
186. SCHWARTZ, LEWIS, AND LEVITT. EUGENE E. "Short-Forms of the Wechsler Intelligence Scale for Children in the Educable, Non-Institutionalized, Mentally Retarded." *J Ed Psychol* 51:187–90 Ag '60. * (*PA* 35:3786)
187. SCOTT, EDWARD M. "Psychological Examination of Quadruplets." *Psychol Rep* 6:281–2 Ap '60. * (*PA* 35:5980)
188. STUMPF, JOHN C. *The Correlation Between the Wechsler Intelligence Scale for Children and Reading Scores From the Stanford Achievement Test.* Master's thesis, University of Utah (Salt Lake City, Utah), 1960.
189. TALBOT, SHELAGH C. *A Cross Validation Study With the Wechsler Intelligence Scale for Children of the Diagnostic Signs for the Syndrome Sociopathy.* Master's thesis, Drake University (Des Moines, Iowa), 1960.
190. WEISE, PHILLIP. "Current Uses of Binet and Wechsler Tests by School Psychologists in California." *Calif J Ed Res* 11:73–8 Mr '60. * (*PA* 35:7098)
191. ALIMENA, BENJAMIN. "A Note on Norms for Scatter Analysis on the Wechsler Intelligence Scales." *J Clin Psychol* 17:61 Ja '61. * (*PA* 37:3103)
192. ANASTASI, ANNE. *Psychological Testing, Second Edition,* p. 315. New York: Macmillan Co., 1961. Pp. xiii, 657. * (*PA* 36:1HA57A)
193. BALTHAZAR, EARL E., AND MORRISON, DON H. "The Use of Wechsler Intelligence Scales as Diagnostic Indicators of Predominant Left-Right and Indeterminate Unilateral Brain Damage." *J Clin Psychol* 17:161–5 Ap '61. * (*PA* 38:1236)
194. BAUMEISTER, ALFRED A. *The Dimensions of Ability for Retardates on the Wechsler Intelligence Scale for Children.* Doctor's thesis, George Peabody College for Teachers (Nashville, Tenn.), 1961.
195. COROTTO, LOREN V. "The Relation of Performance to Verbal IQ in Acting Out Juveniles." *J Psychol Studies* 12:162–6 Jl '61 [issued Mr '63]. *
196. DARLEY, FREDERIC L., AND WINITZ, HARRIS. "Comparison of Male and Female Kindergarten Children on the WISC." *J Genetic Psychol* 99:41–9 S '61. * (*PA* 36:3FE41D)
197. DUNSDON, M. I., AND ROBERTS, J. A. FRASER. Chap. 3, "A Study of the Performance of 2000 Children on Four Vocabulary Tests," pp. 41–76. In *Stoke Park Studies: Mental Subnormality (Second Series): World Mental Health Year Memorial Volume.* Edited by J. Jancar. Bristol, England: John Wright & Sons Ltd., 1961. Pp. x, 135. *
198. ENBURG, RICHARD; ROWLEY, VINTON N.; AND STONE, BETH. "Short Forms of the WISC for Use With Emotionally Disturbed Children." *J Clin Psychol* 17:280–4 Jl '61. * (*PA* 38:8454)
199. ESTES, BETSY WORTH; CURTIN, MARY ELLEN; DEBURGER, ROBERT A.; AND DENNY, CHARLOTTE. "Relationships Between 1960 Stanford-Binet, 1937 Stanford-Binet, WISC, Raven, and Draw-A-Man." *J Consult Psychol* 25:388–91 O '61. * (*PA* 37:3127)
200. FISHER, GARY M. "The Altitude Quotient as an Index of Intellectual Potential: 2, WISC Data for Familial and Undifferentiated Mental Retardates." *J Psychol Studies* 12:126–7 My '61. *
201. GALLAGHER, JAMES J., AND LUCITO, LEONARD J. "Intellectual Patterns of Gifted Compared With Average and Retarded." *Excep Child* 27:479–82 My '61. * (*PA* 36:4KE79G)
202. GOODENOUGH, DONALD R., AND KARP, STEPHEN A. "Field Dependence and Intellectual Functioning." *J Abn & Social Psychol* 63:241–6 S '61. * (*PA* 37:1214)
203. HOPKINS, KENNETH D., AND MICHAEL, WILLIAM B. "The Diagnostic Use of WISC Subtest Patterns." *Calif J Ed Res* 12:116–7+ My '61. * (*PA* 36:3HD16H)
204. HUNT, DENNIS. *The Comparative Performance of a Ten-Year-Old Group of Children on the Wechsler Intelligence Scale for Children and the Revised Stanford-Binet Scale of Intelligence, Form L-M.* Master's thesis, University of Saskatchewan (Saskatoon, Sask., Canada), 1961.
205. KALLOS, GEORGE L.; GRABOW, JOHN M.; AND GUARINO, EUGENE A. "The WISC Profile of Disabled Readers." *Personnel & Guid J* 39:476–8 F '61. * (*PA* 35:7084)
206. LEVINSON, BORIS M. "Subcultural Values and IQ Stability." *J Genetic Psychol* 98:69–82 Mr '61. * (*PA* 35:6405)
207. MCCARTHY, DOROTHEA. "Administration of Digit Symbol and Coding Subtests of the WAIS and WISC to Left-Handed Subjects." *Psychol Rep* 8:407–8 Je '61. * (*PA* 36:2HD07M)
208. MARKS, JOHN B., AND KLAHN, JAMES E. "Verbal and Perceptual Components in WISC Performance and Their Relation to Social Class." Abstract. *J Consult Psychol* 25:273 Je '61. *
209. MAXWELL, A. E. "Discrepancies Between the Pattern of Abilities for Normal and Neurotic Children." *J Mental Sci* 107:300–7 Mr '61. * (*PA* 36:2FF00M)
210. MAXWELL, A. E. "Inadequate Reporting of Normative Test Data." *J Clin Psychol* 17:99–101 Ja '61. * (*PA* 37:3116)
211. NEVILLE, DONALD. "A Comparison of the WISC Patterns of Male Retarded and Non-Retarded Readers." *J Ed Res* 54:195–7 Ja '61. * (*PA* 35:6842)
212. PAVLOS, ANDREW JOHN. "Sex Differences Among Rural Negro Children on the Wechsler Intelligence Scale for Children." *Proc W Va Acad Sci* 33:109–14 N '61. * (*PA* 36:5FE09P)
213. PELZ, KURT S.; AMES, LOUISE B.; AND PIKE, FRANCES. "Measurement of Psychologic Function in Geriatric Patients." *J Am Geriatrics Soc* 9:740–54 S '61. *
214. PINNEAU, SAMUEL R. Chap. 12, "Wechsler Intelligence Scale for Children," pp. 106–11. In his *Changes in Intelligence Quotient: Infancy to Maturity: New Insights From the Berkeley Growth Study With Implications for the Stanford-Binet Scales and Applications to Professional Practice.* Boston, Mass.: Houghton Mifflin Co., 1961. Pp. xi, 233. * (*PA* 37:6706)
215. REGER, ROGER, AND DAWSON, ANTOINETTE. "The Use of Psychological Tests to Predict Manual Abilities in Mentally Retarded Boys." *Am J Occup Ther* 15:204+ S–O '61. * (*PA* 36:5JI04R)
216. ROWLEY, VINTON N. "Analysis of the WISC Performance of Brain Damaged and Emotionally Disturbed Children." Abstract. *J Consult Psychol* 25:553 D '61. * (*PA* 37:5382)
217. SAWA, HIDEHISA. "Interference of Intelligence With Temperament." *Psychologia* 4:235–41 D '61. * (*PA* 38:974)
218. SMITH, BESSIE S. "The Relative Merits of Certain Verbal and Non-Verbal Tests at the Second-Grade Level." *J Clin Psychol* 17:53–4 Ja '61. * (*PA* 37:3595)
219. STOUT, DONALD H. *The Wechsler Intelligence Scale for Children and the Wechsler Adult Intelligence Scale: A Comparison Study.* Master's thesis, Fresno State College (Fresno, Calif.), 1961.
220. WILLIAMS, JESSIE M. "Children Who Break Down in Foster Homes: A Psychological Study of Patterns of Personality Growth in Grossly Deprived Children." *J Child Psychol & Psychiatry* 2:5–20 Je '61. * (*PA* 36:2FF05W)
221. BAUMEISTER, ALFRED, AND BARTLETT, CLAUDE J. "Further Factorial Investigations of WISC Performance of Mental Defectives." *Am J Mental Def* 67:257–61 S '62. * (*PA* 37:3557)
222. BAUMEISTER, ALFRED A., AND BARTLETT, CLAUDE J. "A Comparison of the Factor Structure of Normals and Retardates on the WISC." *Am J Mental Def* 66:641–6 Ja '62. * (*PA* 36:4JI41B)
223. BELLUOMINI, HENRY M. *Wechsler Intelligence Scale for Children: Predicting Success in Corrective Reading.* Master's thesis, Sacramento State College (Sacramento, Calif.), 1962.
224. BORTNER, MORTON, AND BIRCH, HERBERT G. "Perceptual and Perceptual-Motor Dissociation in Cerebral Palsied Children." *J Nerv & Mental Dis* 134:103–8 F '62. * (*PA* 37:1667)
225. BRILL, RICHARD G. "The Relationship of Wechsler IQ's to Academic Achievement Among Deaf Students." *Excep Child* 28:315–21 F '62. * (*PA* 37:1609)
226. CLAWSON, AILEEN. "Relationship of Psychological Tests to Cerebral Disorders in Children: A Pilot Study." *Psychol Rep* 10:187–90 F '62. * (*PA* 37:1655)
227. FREEMAN, FRANK S. *Theory and Practice of Psychological Testing, Third Edition,* pp. 269–79, 330–8. New York: Holt, Rinehart & Winston, Inc., 1962. Pp. xix, 697. *
228. FROST, BARRY P., AND FROST, RUTH. "The Pattern of WISC Scores in a Group of Juvenile Sociopaths." *J Clin Psychol* 18:354–5 Jl '62. * (*PA* 39:2603)
229. GAINER, W. L. "The Ability of the WISC Subtests to Discriminate Between Boys and Girls of Average Intelligence." *Calif J Ed Res* 13:9–16 Ja '62. * (*PA* 36:5HD09G)
230. GAINER, WILLIAM LEE. *An Abbreviated Form of the Wechsler Intelligence Scale for Children.* Doctor's thesis, University of the Pacific (Stockton, Calif.), 1962. (*DA* 23:690)
231. HIMELSTEIN, PHILIP, AND HERNDON, JAMES D. "Comparison of the WISC and Peabody Picture Vocabulary Test With Emotionally Disturbed Children." *J Clin Psychol* 18:82 Ja '62. * (*PA* 38:8420)
232. JOHNSON, OLIVE L. *A Study of Scaled Scores on the Wechsler Intelligence Scale for Children in Relation to Organic Impairment Affecting Language Acquisition.* Master's thesis, Northwestern University (Evanston, Ill.), 1962.
233. JONES, SHEILA. "The Wechsler Intelligence Scale for Children Applied to a Sample of London Primary School Children." *Brit J Ed Psychol* 32:119–32 Je '62. * (*PA* 37:2872)
234. LAVOS, GEORGE. "W.I.S.C. Psychometric Patterns Among Deaf Children." *Volta R* 64:547–52 N '62. *
235. O'NEIL, W. M. "The Stability of the Main Pattern of Abilities With Changing Age." *Austral J Psychol* 14:1–8 Ap '62. * (*PA* 38:6025)
236. OSBORNE, R. TRAVIS, AND ALLEN, JERRY. "Validity of Short Forms of the WISC for Mental Retardates." *Psychol Rep* 11:167–70 Ag '62. * (*PA* 37:4945)

237. PELZ, KURT; PIKE, FRANCES; AND AMES, LOUISE B. "A Proposed Battery of Childhood Tests for Discriminating Between Different Levels of Intactness of Function in Elderly Subjects." *J Genetic Psychol* 100:23–40 Mr '62. * (*PA* 37:975)
238. RAVENETTE, A. T., AND KAHN, J. H. "Intellectual Ability of Disturbed Children in a Working-Class Area." *Brit J Social & Clin Psychol* 1:208–12 O '62. * (*PA* 37:5456)
239. REGER, ROGER. "Repeated Measurements With the WISC." *Psychol Rep* 11:418 O '62. * (*PA* 37:7987)
240. ROBECK, MILDRED C. "Children Who Show Undue Tension When Reading: A Group Diagnosis." *Int Rdg Assn Conf Proc* 7:133–8 '62. *
241. ROHRS, FREDERICK W., AND HAWORTH, MARY R. "The 1960 Stanford-Binet, WISC, and Goodenough Tests With Mentally Retarded Children." *Am J Mental Def* 66:853–9 My '62. * (*PA* 37:1704)
242. SHAFFER, JOHN W. "A Specific Cognitive Deficit Observed in Gonadal Aplasia (Turner's Syndrome)." *J Clin Psychol* 18:403–6 O '62. * (*PA* 39:5565)
243. SHIPE, DOROTHY M. *Discrepancies Between the Peabody Picture Vocabulary Test and the WISC as Related to Emotional Disturbance in Children of Retarded and Normal Intelligence.* Doctor's thesis, George Peabody College for Teachers (Nashville, Tenn.), 1962. (*DA* 23:3984)
244. SHORE, MILTON F. "The Utilization of the Patient-Examiner Relationship in Intelligence Testing of Children." *J Proj Tech* 26:239–43 Je '62. *
245. SIEGMAN, ARON WOLFE. "A Cross-Cultural Investigation of the Relationship Between Religiosity, Ethnic Prejudice and Authoritarianism." *Psychol Rep* 11:419–24 O '62. * (*PA* 37:7936)
246. TEAHAN, JOHN E., AND DREWS, ELIZABETH M. "A Comparison of Northern and Southern Negro Children on the WISC." *J Consult Psychol* 26:292 Je '62. * (*PA* 38:966)
247. THOMPSON, JACK M., AND FINLEY, CARMEN J. "A Further Comparison of the Intellectual Patterns of Gifted and Mentally Retarded Children." *Excep Child* 28:379–81 Mr '62. *
248. THOMPSON, JACK M., AND FINLEY, CARMEN J. "The Validation of an Abbreviated Wechsler Intelligence Scale for Children for Use With the Educable Mentally Retarded." *Ed & Psychol Meas* 22:539–42 au '62. * (*PA* 37:4970)
249. THRONE, FRANCES M.; SCHULMAN, JEROME L.; AND KASPAR, JOSEPH C. "Reliability and Stability of the Wechsler Intelligence Scale for Children for a Group of Mentally Retarded Boys." *Am J Mental Def* 67:455–7 N '62. * (*PA* 37:5421)
250. VIITAMÄKI, R. OLAVI. *Psychoses in Children: A Psychological Follow-Up Study.* Annals of the Finnish Academy of Science and Letters, Series B, Vol. 125, Part 2. Helsinki, Finland: Suomalainen Tiedeakatemia, Academia Scientiarum Fennica, 1962. Pp. 52. * (*PA* 39:2650)
251. WEMPEN, EDITH H. *A Comparative Study of WISC Subtests for Achievers and Underachievers.* Master's thesis, Chico State College (Chico, Calif.), 1962.
252. WIGHT, BYRON W., AND SANDRY, MARTIN. "A Short Form of the Wechsler Intelligence Scale for Children." *J Clin Psychol* 18:166 Ap '62. * (*PA* 38:8511)
253. WILK, WALTER S. *A Comparative Study of the Wechsler Intelligence Scale for Children and the Revised Form of the Stanford-Binet Intelligence Scale.* Master's thesis, Southern Connecticut State College (New Haven, Conn.), 1962.
254. WUNDERLIN, ROBERT J., AND MCPHERSON, MARION WHITE. "Sensitivity to Imbalance in Normal and Anoxic Damaged Children." *J Clin Psychol* 18:410–3 O '62. *
255. BAUMEISTER, ALFRED A.; BARTLETT, CLAUDE J.; AND HAWKINS, WILLIAM F. "Stimulus Trace as a Predictor of Performance." *Am J Mental Def* 67:726–9 Mr '63. * (*PA* 38:1255)
256. BELDOCH, MICHAEL. "Applicability of the Norms of the Wechsler Intelligence Scale for Children to Five-Year-Olds." *J Consult Psychol* 27:263–4 Je '63. * (*PA* 38:950)
257. CAPUTO, DANIEL V.; EDMONSTON, WILLIAM E., JR.; L'ABATE, LUCIANO; AND RONDBERG, SAMUEL R. "Type of Brain Damage and Intellectual Functioning in Children." Abstract. *J Consult Psychol* 27:184 Ap '63. *
258. CHODORKOFF, JOAN, AND WHITTEN, CHARLES F. "Intellectual Status of Children With Sickle Cell Anemia." *J Pediatrics* 63:29–35 Jl '63. *
259. COHEN, THEODORE B. "Prediction of Underachievement in Kindergarten Children." *Arch Gen Psychiatry* 9:444–50 N '63. * (*PA* 38:8040)
260. COLEMAN, JAMES C. "Stability of Intelligence Test Scores in Learning Disorders." *J Clin Psychol* 19:295–8 Jl '63. *
261. COLEMAN, JAMES C., AND RASOF, BEATRICE. "Intellectual Factors in Learning Disorders." *Percept & Motor Skills* 16:139–52 F '63. * (*PA* 38:1377)
262. GRAHAM, CONRAD. "Differential Marking of Two Vocabulary Tests." *Psychol Rep* 12:421–2 Ap '63. * (*PA* 38:4275)
263. JURJEVICH, RATIBOR. "An Analysis of the Altitude *IQ*s of Delinquent Girls." *J General Psychol* 69:221–6 O '63. * (*PA* 39:1779)
264. JURJEVICH, RATIBOR. "An Evaluation of the Henmon-Nelson Group *IQ* Test With Delinquent Girls." *J General Psychol* 69:227–33 O '63. * (*PA* 39:1778)
265. LANDRUM, JACK PORTER. *A Study of the WISC Performance of Under-Achievers in Comparison to Average-Achievers and Over-Achievers.* Doctor's thesis, University of Colorado (Boulder, Colo.), 1963. (*DA* 23:4606)
266. LESSING, ELISE ELKINS, AND LESSING, JOHN CURTIS. "WISC Subtest Variability and Validity of WISC IQ." *J Clin Psychol* 19:92–5 Ja '63. * (*PA* 39:1746)
267. MCHUGH, ANN F. "WISC Performance in Neurotic and Conduct Disturbances." *J Clin Psychol* 19:423–4 O '63. *
268. MAHAN, THOMAS W., JR. "Diagnostic Consistency and Prediction: A Note on Graduate Student Skills." *Personnel & Guid J* 42:364–7 D '63. * (*PA* 39:2880)
269. MOED, GEORGE; WIGHT, BYRON W.; AND JAMES, PATRICIA. "Interest Correlations of the Wechsler Intelligence Scale for Children and Two Picture Vocabulary Tests." *Ed & Psychol Meas* 23:359–63 su '63. * (*PA* 38:960)
270. NICKOLS, JOHN, AND NICKOLS, MARCIA. "Brief Forms of the WISC for Research." *J Clin Psychol* 19:425 O '63. *
271. OSBORNE, R. T. "Factorial Composition of the Wechsler Intelligence Scale for Children at the Pre-school Level." *Psychol Rep* 13:443–8 O '63. * (*PA* 38:6915)
272. PATERRA, MARY ELIZABETH. "A Study of Thirty-Three WISC Scattergrams of Retarded Readers." *El Engl* 40:394–405 Ap '63. *
273. PRENTICE, NORMAN M., AND KELLY, FRANCIS J. "Intelligence and Delinquency: A Reconsideration." *J Social Psychol* 60:327–37 Ag '63. * (*PA* 38:4585)
274. PRINGLE, M. L. KELLMER, AND PICKUP, K. T. "The Reliability and Validity of the Goodenough Draw-A-Man Test: A Pilot Longitudinal Study." *Brit J Ed Psychol* 33:297–306 N '63. * (*PA* 38:8424)
275. REID, WILLIAM RESA. *Psychological Subtest Patterns and Reading Achievement.* Doctor's thesis, State University of Iowa (Iowa City, Iowa), 1963. (*DA* 24:2366)
276. ROWLEY, VINTON N., AND STONE, F. BETH. "A Further Note on the Relationship Between WISC Functioning and the CMAS." *J Clin Psychol* 19:426 O '63. *
277. SHINAGAWA, FUJIRO. "Studies on the Relationship Between Intelligence Structure and Personality Traits: An Analysis of WISC Discrepancy." *Jap Psychol Res* 5:55–62 Jl '63. * (*PA* 38:6033)
278. SIEBERT, LAWRENCE A. "Matched Otis and Wechsler IQ Scores of Delinquents." *J Clin Psychol* 19:215–6 Ap '63. *
279. SILVERSTEIN, A. B. "Effects of Proration on the WISC IQs of Mentally Retarded Children." *Psychol Rep* 12:646 Je '63. * (*PA* 38:6068)
280. SILVERSTEIN, A. B. "WISC and WAIS IQs for the Mentally Retarded." *Am J Mental Def* 67:617–8 Ja '63. *
281. SILVERSTEIN, A. B., AND MOHAN, PHILIP J. "Conceptual Area Analysis of the Test Performance of Mentally Retarded Adults." *J Abn & Social Psychol* 66:255–60 Mr '63. * (*PA* 37:8165)
282. SOLKOFF, NORMAN, AND CHRISIEN, GIL. "Frustration and Perceptual-Motor Performance." *Percept & Motor Skills* 17:282 Ag '63. *
283. SPEARMAN, LEONARD H. O. "A Profile Analysis Technique for Diagnosing Reading Disability." *Yearb Nat Council Meas Ed* 20:75–86 '63. * (*PA* 38:9235)
284. TALERICO, MARGUERITE, AND BROWN, FRED. "Intelligence Test Patterns of Puerto Rican Children Seen in Child Psychiatry." *J Social Psychol* 61:57–66 O '63. * (*PA* 38:8066)
285. THOMPSON, BERTHA BOYA. "A Longitudinal Study of Auditory Discrimination." *J Ed Res* 56:376–8 Mr '63. *
286. THOMPSON, JACK M., AND FINLEY, CARMEN J. "An Abbreviated WISC for Use With Gifted Elementary School Children." *Calif J Ed Res* 14:167–77 S '63. * (*PA* 38:6072)
287. TWAIN, DAVID C., AND BROOKS, EDWARD M. "A Comparison of Wechsler, Revised Beta and Otis Scores of Delinquents." *Brit J Criminol* 3:288–90 Ja '63. *
288. WEBB, ALLEN P. "A Longitudinal Comparison of the WISC and WAIS With Educable Mentally Retarded Negroes." *J Clin Psychol* 19:101–2 Ja '63. * (*PA* 39:1769)

ALVIN G. BURSTEIN, *Associate Professor of Psychology, Neuropsychiatric Institute, University of Illinois College of Medicine, Chicago, Illinois.*

In an era when fads in test construction and test consumption combine to produce rapid obsolescence and turnover, the WISC can be regarded as a highly successful test, if only on the grounds of durability. In the nearly 15 years since its introduction, it has not displaced the older Stanford-Binet, but has certainly come to rival its predecessor as an instrument of choice in the testing of school age children. In fact, the one time infant offspring of the

Wechsler-Bellevue now boasts offspring of its own in the shape of short forms and foreign language versions.

Proliferation of derivative forms might be taken as an index of success, indicating successful negotiation of the gantlet and elevation from the status of experimental test to criterion variable. A second reflection of the WISC's success is its popularity as the subject of journal notes and articles. Interest on this front continues, with more than 150 new articles having appeared in print since WISC was reviewed in *The Fifth Mental Measurements Yearbook*.

The interested reader may wish to refer to the six reviews of WISC in the last two *Mental Measurements Yearbooks* and to Littell's (*178*) more recent review for accounts of the literature prior to 1958; the literature since that time will be the focus of this review.

Overall, any judgment of the WISC on the basis of the current literature must be tempered by the unhappy realization that far too many studies are inadequately conducted or reported. The siren call of the subtest scores appears to lure many a researcher into a helter-skelter atheoretical attempt to dredge up a "significant" correlation with some dependent variable or other and then to rush into print without careful cross validation. Generally, too, little precision is involved in the choice of dependent variables or in the constituency of the sample representing that variable.

The literature which has accumulated on the WISC may be regarded as falling into four major categories. The first of these consists essentially of studies of the instrument in which effort is directed at determining how consistently WISC scores approximate those of earlier administrations of the WISC, or of other tests of intelligence. These reliability and concurrent validity studies, accounting for perhaps a fifth of the recent literature, are quite consistent with earlier work of this sort, characterizing the WISC as a well standardized, stable instrument, correlating well with other tests of intelligence.

The second major category contains those studies which deal with derivatives of the instrument. In this group, one would include accounts dealing with foreign language equivalents of the WISC (French, German, Japanese, and Puerto Rican) and with the development of short forms. Prescriptions for short forms vary somewhat, in part because some are developed for general use, some for use with retarded or brain damaged children. However, the consensus is that correlations in the .80's with full scale scores are possible with abbreviated administrations consisting of five or six subtests from both Verbal and Performance scales. In order of popularity, scales chosen have been Block Design, Information, Picture Completion, Picture Arrangement, and Coding; Arithmetic, Similarities, Vocabulary, and Object Assembly have also been used, though less frequently. The chief reason for abbreviating the test would appear to be time savings; these would appear to be on the order of 30 minutes. In cases where there is a good deal of between-test scatter such a time saving would appear both excessively hazardous and expensive in terms of lost information.

The third basic category of current research on the WISC deals with what might be termed psychopathological applications. Here the WISC or some part of the test is given to some special group in the hope of learning more about the group, in terms of either theory or diagnostic characteristics, or of learning more about the capacities tapped by the various parts of the WISC. Hence, reports are available dealing with special intellectual states (mentally retarded, gifted, brain damaged, school achievement, or inhibition), with socio-cultural effects (sex differences, cross cultural studies, socio-economic status differences), with psychiatric symptomatology (enuresis, interpersonal difficulty, psychopathic personality), and with basic psychic processes (anxiety, perceptual organization). This area of psychopathological investigation is unfortunately most prone to the experimental and theoretical liabilities already mentioned. Therefore, though results are sometimes intriguing, they are never definitive.

The final, and to my mind most important, category consists of those reports in which the nature and purpose of intelligence testing is directly examined. Psychological testing has a highly heterogeneous past; many very different traditions (psycho-physical, psychiatric, educational) make themselves felt in current practice. In general, though, there seems to be a trend for psychological tests, originally developed for special purposes, to become utilized in more and more general ways, generating conclusions about general personality function. Outstanding examples of this tendency are to be seen in the amplified usages of the Bender's *Visual Motor Gestalt Test* and the *Machover Draw-A-Person Test.* There is some evidence that similar changes are occurring in the use of both the WAIS and the WISC in recent articles by Sinnett and Mayman [1] and by Fromm and others [2] and foreshadowed by Rapaport.[3] The general approach is to analyze test protocols not only from the point of view of subscale or subtest scores, but from a much more microscopic analysis of responses to individual items, making inferences not only in terms of intelligence, but also in terms of total personality variables involved. Hence, Fromm outlines some 40 variables, including derivatives of the psychoanalytic model of ego functions of motility, memory, and perception, and including id, superego, and cultural variables as well. Less formally and less structurally, Sinnett and Mayman seem to view the test as a means of eliciting associations to widely varied stimuli, describing the vocabulary subtest of the WAIS as "a tool with which to assess the clarity, conciseness, and subtlety of a subject's thought processes and his facility in communicating thoughts" and suggesting that clues with respect to "capacity for impulse modulation....for empathy; and his capacity to grasp subtle subjective processes in himself and others" may be available.

Clearly such a broadening and diffusion of the test's use will send shudders coursing down the spine of many a psychometrical purist who depends upon criterion clarity. Nevertheless, the effort to integrate intelligence and concepts of general personality with their differing backgrounds is an important effort for general psychology, and the ultimate test of any construction placed upon data is its pragmatic utility. Broad-gauge clinical use of the test should not be prohibited or avoided, only made explicit and pragmatically assessed. Hopefully this will be the direction of future research with the WISC and similar devices.

For reviews by Elizabeth D. Fraser, Gerald R. Patterson, and Albert I. Rabin, see 5:416; for reviews by James M. Anderson, Harold A. Delp, and Boyd R. McCandless, see 4:363 (1 excerpt).

1 Sinnett, Kathleen, and Mayman, Martin. "The Wechsler Adult Intelligence Scale as a Clinical Diagnostic Tool: A Review." *B Menninger Clinic* 24:80–4 Mr '60. * (*PA* 35:3416)
2 Fromm, Erika; Hartman, Lenore Dumas; and Marschak, Marian. "Children's Intelligence Tests as a Measure of Dynamic Personality Functioning." *Am J Orthopsychiatry* 27:134–44 Ja '57. * (*PA* 32:1621)
3 Rapaport, David. "Projective Techniques and the Theory of Thinking." *J Proj Tech* 16:269–75 S '52. *

[541]

★Williams Intelligence Test for Children With Defective Vision. Ages 5–15 (blind and partially sighted); 1956; individual; 1 form ['56, a series of objects, orally presented tasks, and Braille cards]; handbook ('56, 54 pages plus fold-out IQ conversion tables); record form ['56, 4 pages]; no data on reliability and validity; 60*s*. per set of testing material; 2*s*. per 12 record forms; postage extra; 1*s*. per set of card material; 10*s*. per handbook; postpaid; prices include purchase tax; [60] minutes; M. Williams; University of Birmingham Institute of Education. *

REFERENCES

1. Williams, Myfanwy. "An Intelligence Test for Blind and Partially Sighted Children." Abstract. *B Brit Psychol Soc* (30):32 S '56. *
2. Williams, Myfanwy. "Research Into Intelligence Tests for Children With Defective Vision." *Teach Blind* 45:121–5 Jl '57. *

T. Ernest Newland, *Professor of Educational Psychology, University of Illinois, Urbana, Illinois.*

This 100-item test is patterned forthrightly on the *Revised Stanford-Binet Intelligence Scale.* At least 64 of the items have obvious Binet parentage, 45 coming from Form M, 7 from Form L, and 12 common to both forms. Twelve of the items have been adapted to make them usable with visually impaired subjects; three have been modified to provide for greater range in usage; and three have been culturally adapted to British subjects. Other items were taken from Valentine's *Intelligence Tests for Children,* from Burt's Reasoning Tests, and some from group tests. Four items have been included for optional use to arouse or sustain the interest of younger subjects, but they are not scored. The 40-word vocabulary test, the score on which is used only for determining the point of entry into the scale, is adapted from the *Wechsler Intelligence Scale for Children;* four new words have been substituted and a new order of difficulty has been established. No items necessitate the use of Braille.

After a preliminary tryout on 120 subjects, the items were administered to 939 children from age 4 up to 16. Subjects included both the blind and partially sighted. Since separate standardizations indicated no significant differences between performances of the two impaired groups, a single set of norms was established. No reliability or validity data are reported, and *Psychological Abstracts* records no formal publications on the test (through October 1963). Used as a point scale, deviation intelligence quotients are read directly from tables, at the intersections of raw scores and chronological ages (to the nearest month). Score distributions have been normalized so as to yield mean IQ's of 100 and sigmas of 15 for each age group, by month from 3 years 6 months to 16 years 0 months.

In terms of what is known about the value of the Binet in predicting academic learning in sighted children and in view of the nature of the psychological processes and the learning products sampled in this test (referred to by the author as the "Birmingham Scale"), one could assume that results obtained by means of this device should theoretically provide a fair basis for predicting the learning behavior of visually impaired children. However, it is highly likely that predictive validity coefficients obtained on sight impaired populations will tend to run lower than in a parallel case of Binet data on sighted children. Probably contaminating such correlations on visually impaired populations would be factors such as the unique nature of certain of the educational stimuli and responses in the form of Braille, the frequency of intervening emotional conditions, and the institutional practices and expectancies in many schools for the visually impaired—especially in the case of most residential schools. Any assumption that a Birmingham IQ of 100 on, say, a 10-year-old blind child has the same connotation regarding general learning aptitude as does a Binet IQ of 100 on a sighted child will have to be the responsibility of the one making such an assumption. Any assumption beyond that connoting averageness for a specified group (impaired or nonimpaired) will need to be most critically examined.

From an editorial standpoint, the title for item 61 is in error. Some may be curious about time specifications for at least items 80 and 91 (coding), and maybe items 95 and 99 (problem solving). However, the nature of the total testing situation is such that, in practically all instances, the setting of such time limits need not be crucial. From the standpoint of content validity, one could be justly concerned about items 79 and 92 (directions) and wonder how meaningful the terms "north," "south," "east," and "west" are, especially to the born blind. There is also an inconsistency in the ways in which the user is provided with the correct responses to certain items; this condition could be particularly important in the cases of those administering the test who are not well grounded in Binet testing.

In an overall sense the development of this device must be regarded as a potentially worthwhile contribution. Those who are Binet-oriented in their work with school children may miss the direct yielding of mental ages. Such persons can, however, make a reverse use of the tables and ascribe a mental age score to a child by finding the chronological age for which his obtained point score is the median and use that as the child's "mental age." Whether such mental age (or, better, "test age") will have the same implication for educational expectancies for visually impaired children as for nonimpaired children can be shown only by considerable research.

[Other Tests]

For tests not listed above, see the following entries in *Tests in Print:* 877–9, 884–5, 891–2, 894, 900, 903–4, 906, and 908–9; out of print: 889, 902, and 911.

SPECIFIC

[542]

★**Alternate Uses.** Grades 6–16 and adults; 1960; revision of *Unusual Uses;* experimental form; spontaneous flexibility; Form A (4 pages); mimeographed manual, second preliminary edition (7 pages); reliability data based on preliminary form; norms for grades 6, 9, and 13 only; $2 per 25 tests; 15¢ per single copy; 35¢ per manual; postage extra; 12(20) minutes; Paul R. Christensen, J. P. Guilford, Philip R. Merrifield, and Robert C. Wilson; Sheridan Supply Co. *

REFERENCES

1. BARRON, FRANK. "The Disposition Toward Originality." *J Abn & Social Psychol* 51:478–85 N '55. * (*PA* 31:2533)
2. GUILFORD, J. P. *Personality.* New York: McGraw-Hill Book Co., Inc., 1959. Pp. xiii, 562. *
3. BRITTAIN, W. LAMBERT, AND BEITTEL, KENNETH R. "A Study of Some Tests of Creativity to Performances in the Visual Arts." *Studies Art Ed* 2:54–65 sp '61. *
4. MARKS, ALVIN; MICHAEL, WILLIAM B.; AND KAISER, HENRY F. "Dimensions of Creativity and Temperament in Officer Evaluation." *Psychol Rep* 9:635–8 D '61. *
5. MARKS, ALVIN; MICHAEL, WILLIAM B.; AND KAISER, HENRY F. "Sources of Noncognitive Variance in 21 Measures of Creativity." *Psychol Rep* 9:287–90 O '61. *
6. ABDEL-RAZIK, TAHER MOHAMED. *An Investigation of Creative Thinking Among College Students.* Doctor's thesis, Ohio State University (Columbus, Ohio), 1963. (*DA* 24:2775)
7. BARRON, FRANK. Chap. 11, "The Disposition Toward Originality," pp. 139–52. In *Scientific Creativity: Its Recognition and Development.* Edited by Calvin W. Taylor and Frank Barron. New York: John Wiley & Sons, Inc., 1963. Pp. xxiv, 419. * (*PA* 38:2689)

[543]

Benton Visual Retention Test, Revised Edition. Ages 8 and over; 1946–55; title on manual is *Revised Visual Retention Test;* individual; Forms C, D, E, ('55, 10 cards) in a single booklet; manual ('55, 72 pages); record blank ('55, 1 page); $5 per set of cards, 50 record blanks, and manual; $2.30 per manual; postpaid; 5(10) minutes; Arthur L. Benton; distributed by Psychological Corporation. *

REFERENCES

1–3. See 4:360.
4–8. See 5:401.
9. CASTLETON, B. "Benton Visual Recognition." *Psychometric Res B* (4):[13–5] Ag '59. *

10. CROOKES, T. G. "Benton V.R." *Psychometric Res B* (5):[16–9] N '59. *
11. HEILBRUN, ALFRED B., JR. "Specificity of Immediate Memory Function Associated With Cerebral Cortex Damage." *J Mental Sci* 106:241–5 Ja '60. * (*PA* 35:6745)
12. MATUNAS, MARIAN ISABEL. *Test Performance of Psychotic Children With Organic Brain Pathology: A Study to Determine Whether the Bender-Gestalt Test, the Benton Visual Retention Test, and the Marble Board Test Can Detect the Presence of Organic Brain Pathology in Psychotic Children.* Doctor's thesis, New York University (New York, N.Y.), 1960. (*DA* 21:1257)
13. BENTON, ARTHUR L., AND SPREEN, OTFRIED. "Visual Memory Test: The Simulation of Mental Incompetence." *Arch Gen Psychiatry* 4:79–83 Ja '61. * (*PA* 35:6824)
14. ROWLEY, VINTON N., AND BAER, PAUL E. "Visual Retention Test Performance in Emotionally Disturbed and Brain-Damaged Children." *Am J Orthopsychiatry* 31:579–83 Jl '61. * (*PA* 36:4JG79R)
15. SCHNORE, MORRIS M. "Memory-for-Designs Tests in the Diagnosis of Brain Damage." *Ont Hosp Psychol B* 7:2–4 Ag '61. *
16. BENTON, ARTHUR L., AND FOGEL, MAX L. "Three-Dimensional Constructional Praxis: A Clinical Test." *Arch Neurol* 7:347–54 O '62. * (*PA* 37:5373)
17. BENTON, ARTHUR L., AND MCGAVREN, MUSETTA. "Qualitative Aspects of Visual Memory Test Performance in Mental Defectives." *Am J Mental Def* 66:878–83 My '62. * (*PA* 37:1680)
18. L'ABATE, LUCIANO; BOELLING, GARY M.; HUTTON, ROBERT D.; AND MATHEWS, DEWEY L., JR. "The Diagnostic Usefulness of Four Potential Tests of Brain Damage." Abstract. *J Consult Psychol* 26:479 O '62. *
19. LETON, DONALD A. "Visual-Motor Capacities and Ocular Efficiency in Reading." *Percept & Motor Skills* 15:407–32 O '62. * (*PA* 37:8253)
20. RIDDELL, S. A. "The Performance of Elderly Psychiatric Patients on Equivalent Forms of Tests of Memory and Learning." *Brit J Social & Clin Psychol* 1:70–1 F '62. * (*PA* 37:1208)
21. SHAFFER, JOHN W. "A Specific Cognitive Deficit Observed in Gonadal Aplasia (Turner's Syndrome)." *J Clin Psychol* 18:403–6 O '62. * (*PA* 39:5565)
22. SILVERSTEIN, A. B. "Perceptual, Motor, and Memory Functions in the Visual Retention Test." *Am J Mental Def* 66:613–7 Ja '62. * (*PA* 36:4JI13S)
23. BRILLIANT, PATRICIA J., AND GYNTHER, MALCOLM D. "Relationships Between Performance on Three Tests for Organicity and Selected Patient Variables." *J Consult Psychol* 27:474–9 D '63. * (*PA* 38:8404)
24. CANTER, ARTHUR. "A Background Interference Procedure for Graphomotor Tests in the Study of Deficit." *Percept & Motor Skills* 16:914 Je '63. * (*PA* 38:6348)
25. CRONHOLM, BORJE, AND SCHALLING, DAISY. "Intellectual Deterioration After Focal Brain Injury." *Arch Surgery* 86:670–87 Ap '63. *
26. FRIEDMAN, ELLEN C., AND BARCLAY, ALLAN. "The Discriminative Validity of Certain Psychological Tests as Indices of Brain Damage in the Mentally Retarded." *Mental Retardation* 1:291–3 O '63. * (*PA* 38:8935)
27. L'ABATE, LUCIANO; FRIEDMAN, WILLIAM H.; VOGLER, ROGER E.; AND CHUSED, THOMAS M. "The Diagnostic Usefulness of Two Tests of Brain-Damage." *J Clin Psychol* 19:87–91 Ja '63. * (*PA* 39:2477)
28. SILVERSTEIN, A. B. "Qualitative Analysis of Performance on the Visual Retention Test." *Am J Mental Def* 68:109–13 Jl '63. * (*PA* 38:4569)
29. SPREEN, OTFRIED, AND BENTON, ARTHUR L. "Simulation of Mental Deficiency on a Visual Memory Test." *Am J Mental Def* 67:909–13 My '63. * (*PA* 38:1281)
30. STRICKER, GEORGE, AND COOPER, ALLAN. "The Efficacy of the Benton Visual Retention Test at the 'Very Superior' Intelligence Level." *J General Psychol* 68:165–7 Ja '63. * (*PA* 38:2676)

For a review by Nelson G. Hanawalt, see 5:401; for reviews by Ivan Norman Mensh, Joseph Newman, and William Schofield of the original edition, see 4:360; see also 3:297 (1 excerpt).

[544]

★Christensen-Guilford Fluency Tests. Grades 7–16 and adults; 1957–63; 1 form; 4 tests; mimeographed manual, second edition ('59, 8 pages); mimeographed supplementary norms ['63, 2 pages]; $1.55 per complete specimen set; postage extra; Paul R. Christensen and J. P. Guilford; Sheridan Supply Co. *

a) WORD FLUENCY. Form A ('58, 3 pages); $2 per 25 tests; 15¢ per single copy; 4(10) minutes.
b) IDEATIONAL FLUENCY I. Form A ('57, 5 pages); $3.75 per 25 tests; 25¢ per single copy; 12(20) minutes.
c) ASSOCIATIONAL FLUENCY I. Form A ('57, 3 pages); $2 per 25 tests; 15¢ per single copy; 4(10) minutes.
d) EXPRESSIONAL FLUENCY. Form A ('58, 5 pages); $3.75 per 25 tests; 25¢ per single copy; 8(15) minutes.

REFERENCES

1. GUILFORD, J. P. *Personality.* New York: McGraw-Hill Book Co., Inc., 1959. Pp. xiii, 562. *
2. MERRIFIELD, P. R.; GUILFORD, J. P.; CHRISTENSEN, P. R.; AND FRICK, J. W. "The Role of Intellectual Factors in Problem Solving." *Psychol Monogr* 76(10):1–21 '62. *
3. ABDEL-RAZIK, TAHER MOHAMED. *An Investigation of Creative Thinking Among College Students.* Doctor's thesis, Ohio State University (Columbus, Ohio), 1963. (*DA* 24:2775)
4. CHRISTENSEN, PAUL R., AND GUILFORD, J. P. "An Experimental Study of Verbal Fluency Factors." *Brit J Stat Psychol* 16:1–26 My '63. * (*PA* 38:4879)

J. A. KEATS, *Reader in Psychology, University of Queensland, Brisbane, Australia.*

With these tests there is a danger that the intending user will reject them as trivial, particularly if he is not familiar with the extensive research programme conducted by Guilford and his co-workers. To call the number of words containing a specified letter which can be written in two minutes, a measure of "word fluency" seems arbitrary at best. The reasons for specifying one letter rather than two or three or none at all are not obvious. Similar comments might be made on the tests of expressional fluency, associational fluency, and ideational fluency. However these tests have arisen from factor analytic studies of the original verbal fluency factor of Thurstone and the justification for this particular form of the tests is given in Christensen and Guilford (*4*) and earlier studies. These references should be studied by intending users before final decisions are made.

There appears, however, to be one point that is not covered in either the research or the manual of instructions. The subject is not told that he is to respond only in English. Admittedly the instructions are in English as are the examples of acceptable responses, but it seems surprising that the problem has not arisen sufficiently often for this point to be covered either in the instructions to subjects or in the scoring procedures. Apart from the practical problem which may be trivial, this question raises the interesting experimental possibility of administering the tests to bilingual subjects—once in English and once in their other language. Using the careful experimental designs of Guilford and Christensen such a study might indicate clearly which, if any, of these fluency factors transcend the language medium.

From the point of view of practical use for selection or guidance these tests are still at the developmental stage. The reliabilities are of the order of .7 and no validity data are available apart from factorial validity. The tests are stated to cover grades 7–16 and adults, but the only norms based on identified groups are for naval and air force trainees, and then only for three of the four tests.[1] The reliability would have to be improved by adding more parts to the existing tests and, in view of the research findings, the only way to be certain that the extended tests had the desired factor structure would be to carry out a fresh factor study. This study could also include criterion measures so that validity data for the particular situation could be obtained. The four published tests could serve as reference measures in such a study. It is in this area of applied research that the current tests are likely to prove most valuable.

The scoring instructions for the four tests contain the following sentence: "The scorer should note carefully the exact specifications given in each item and should see that they are followed, but he may be *literal* in applying each specification" (reviewer's italics). This is either an awkward use of English or "literal" should be "liberal" and so change the meaning completely. The existing manual needs thorough revision to provide more information and clearer instructions for scoring and administration.

This battery of tests would need considerable developmental work before it could have much practical application. The intending user might well decide to construct his own tests from the published descriptions of test batteries and the factor analytic results. However, in checking his final tests by factor analysis or other methods, he might well find some use for the present battery as reference tests.

1 The supplementary norms referred to in the entry preceding the review present means for 229 boys, 228 girls, and 206 unidentified subjects in a "high-IQ group," and norms for all four tests. The norms group is not identified and the boys, girls, and high-IQ group are not described except for number.—Editor.

ALBERT S. THOMPSON, *Professor of Psychology and Education, Teachers College, Columbia University, New York, New York.*

This battery of tests of four types of fluency with verbal materials is designed to measure certain aspects of creative ability, or divergent thinking, to use the more technical term. All require the testee to produce words as rapidly as possible, in response to the following types of instructions: (*a*) Word Fluency—words containing a specified letter, (*b*) Ideational Fluency—names of things in a certain class such as "objects that move," (*c*) Association Fluency—words similar in meaning to a specified word, and (*d*) Expressional Fluency—four-word sentences beginning with specified letters for each word.

The total working time for the battery is 28 minutes. It can be administered to individuals or groups. Scoring requires judgment as to the acceptability of the response words. The manual presents the rationale and gives extensive examples of acceptable response.

The current manual (Second Edition, 1959) is an 8-page description of the administration and scoring procedures with one page devoted to interpretation of scores. The only norms presented are based on several hundred naval air cadets and naval officer candidates, described merely as typically high school graduates with some college education and with a general intellectual level substantially above average. No norms are presented for Expressional Fluency.[1]

Split-half reliabilities (corrected) range from .63 to .76 for the three tests, based on the Navy sample. No data on scorer agreement are presented.

It is clear that the tests are not yet in the operational stage—in the sense of being useful for individual or group appraisal in a service situation. However, they can be recommended for continued experimental use and for further research on the nature and correlates of creative behavior. Validity to date is of the construct, not predictive type, and is based on a number of factor analysis studies which have identified the existence of verbal fluency as a basic dimension of human ability and which have shed light on the nature of creative thinking.

Since tests of this type by their very nature must be open ended, they are subject to scorer unreliability and to testee variability in the ability to "create" at a specified moment of time. Data on these sources of variation should be made available.

Research referred to in the 12-item bibliography in the manual has certainly demonstrated the existence of verbal fluency and its impor-

1 See footnote 1 to the preceding review.—Editor.

tance in divergent thinking. Most of the studies, however, are directed toward the analytic study of human intellect rather than predictive validity of the instrument. What few prediction studies are found in the literature (but not reported in the manual) suggest relationship with creative performance of students, leadership behavior, and writing skill. Guilford's book *Personality* (*1*) is the basic source of information rather than the manual.

[545]

★**Closure Flexibility (Concealed Figures).** Industrial employees; 1956–63; revision of *Gottschaldt Figures;* formerly called *Concealed Figures: A Test of Flexibility of Closure;* Form A ('56, 8 pages); manual ('63, 20 pages); norms for males only; $5 per 20 tests, postage extra; $1 per specimen set, postpaid; 10(15) minutes; L. L. Thurstone (test), T. E. Jeffrey (test), and Measurement Research Division, Industrial Relations Center, University of Chicago (manual); Education-Industry Service. *

REFERENCES

1. Corter, Harold M. "Factor Analysis of Some Reasoning Tests." *Psychol Monogr* 66(8):1–31 '52. * (*PA* 27:4995)
2. Weckowicz, T. E., and Blewett, D. B. "Size Constancy and Abstract Thinking in Schizophrenic Patients." *J Mental Sci* 105:909–34 O '59. * (*PA* 34:6402)
3. Gordon, Oakley J., and Tikofsky, Ronald S. "Performance of Brain-Damaged Subjects on Gottschaldt's Embedded Figures." *Percept & Motor Skills* 12:179–85 Ap '61. * (*PA* 36:1JG79G)
4. Gordon, Oakley; Brayer, Richard; and Tikofsky, Ronald. "Personality Variables and the Perception of Embedded Figures." *Percept & Motor Skills* 12:195–202 Ap '61. * (*PA* 36:1HJ95G)

Leona E. Tyler, *Professor of Psychology, University of Oregon, Eugene, Oregon.*

One is likely to be a little puzzled by the name of this test, *Closure Flexibility,* unless he is familiar with Thurstone's classic monograph *A Factorial Study of Perception.*[1] One of the perceptual tests included in Thurstone's battery was the set of concealed figures Gottschaldt had used in studying the effects of experience on perception.[2] The present form of the test is a revision based on several research investigations carried out by Thurstone and his associates. The name is the label given the "second closure factor" which showed up repeatedly in these studies. The trait is defined as "the ability to hold a configuration in mind despite distraction."

It is a brief test, requiring only 10 minutes. On each line is a simple geometrical figure followed by four complex ones. The subject places a check mark under the complex figure if it contains the simple one, a zero if it does not. Thus the test is very easily scored. The only reliability data included in the manual are from the research studies mentioned above, a split-half coefficient of .78 reported by Thurstone on an earlier form and a corrected split-half coefficient of .94 reported by Pemberton[3] on the present form. It would obviously be advantageous to have more information about reliability. A split-half coefficient is not appropriate for a time-limited test like this.

The standard score norms provided by the present publishers are based on the test performance of 1,105 industrial employees. This norm group is made up of various numbers of professionals, executives, salesmen, foremen, and hourly workers. It does not constitute a representative sample of any definable population. Thus it is difficult to see just what use one would make of these standard scores.

Though both reliability and norms are inadequate, what the test needs more than anything else is more evidence as to what it measures, that is, what it is valid *for.* The authors of the manual summarize the results of the factor analytic studies by Thurstone and others.[4] These indicate that closure flexibility is related to mechanical aptitude and certain kinds of reasoning. They also summarize the evidence obtained by Pemberton that subjects who score high on this trait are more likely than those who score low to describe themselves on paper and pencil tests as socially retiring, not dependent on social conventions, having theoretical interests, and having a drive for achievement. Thurstone's findings that the test differentiated campus leaders from other students, and more successful public administrators from less successful, are also cited. In addition, the manual presents data on the industrial population used as a norm group. These data show a clear differentiation between most of the subgroups represented. Professional men are highest, hourly workers lowest. But since almost any intelligence test would differentiate these groups at least this well, it is not clear what the results are supposed to

1 Thurstone, L. L. *A Factorial Study of Perception.* Chicago, Ill.: University of Chicago Press, 1944. Pp. vi, 158.

2 Gottschaldt, Kurt. "Über den Einfluss der Erfahrung auf die Wahrnehmung von Figuren: 2, Vergleichende Untersuchungen über die Wirkung figuraler Einprägung und den Einfluss spezifischer Geschehensverläufe auf die Auffassung optischer Komplexe." *Psychologische Forschung* 12:1–87 F '29. *

3 Pemberton, Carol L. *A Study of the Speed and Flexibility of Closure Factors.* Doctor's thesis, University of Chicago (Chicago, Ill.), 1951.

4 Bechtoldt, Harold P. *Factorial Study of Perceptual Speed.* Doctor's thesis, University of Chicago (Chicago, Ill.), 1947.

Botzum, William A. *A Factorial Study of the Reasoning and Closure Factors.* Doctor's thesis, University of Chicago (Chicago, Ill.), 1950.

Yela, Mariano. "Application of the Concept of Simple Structure to Alexander's Data." *Psychometrika* 14:121–35 Je '49. *

show about the particular trait of closure flexibility.

The conclusion follows that *Closure Flexibility* has not reached a stage of development where it is useful for any practical clinical, counseling, or selection purpose. It is to the credit of the publishers that they clearly specify that the test is to be used only under carefully prescribed conditions. What is a little puzzling about the presentation in the manual, however, is the detailed explanation about the meaning of standard scores. If the test is to be released only for research purposes, are such explanations necessary?

Since a much more extensive body of research knowledge has collected around another modification of the Gottschaldt test, the *Embedded Figures Test,* it might well be considered preferable to this one even for research. However, the fact that the Thurstone version is a short group test, easily scored, may constitute an advantage in many situations. Research on flexibility of closure has been suggestive and interesting. If the publication of this test in its present form facilitates more of it, it will have served a worthwhile purpose.

[546]

★Closure Speed (Gestalt Completion). Industrial employees; 1956–63; formerly called *Gestalt Completion: A Test of Speed of Closure;* Form A ('56, 3 pages); manual ('63, 16 pages); reliability data for present form based on college students only; norms for males only; $3 per 20 tests, postage extra; $1 per specimen set, postpaid; 3(8) minutes; L. L. Thurstone (test), T. E. Jeffrey (test), and Measurement Research Division, Industrial Relations Center, University of Chicago (manual); Education-Industry Service. *

REFERENCES

1. BASS, BERNARD M., AND COATES, CHARLES H. "Validity Information Exchange, No. 7-082: R.O.T.C. Cadets." *Personnel Psychol* 7:553–4 w '54. *

2. BASS, BERNARD M.; KARSTENDIEK, BARBARA; MCCULLOUGH, GERALD; AND PRUITT, RAY C. "Validity Information Exchange, No. 7-024: D.O.T. Code 2-66.01, 2-66.11, 2-66.12, 2-66.23, Policemen and Detectives, Public Service." *Personnel Psychol* 7:159–60 sp '54. *

3. MCCARTY, JOHN J. "Normative Data Information Exchange, No. 10-94." *Personnel Psychol* 10:537 w '57. *

LEONA E. TYLER, *Professor of Psychology, University of Oregon, Eugene, Oregon.*

The research L. L. Thurstone reported in 1944 in the monograph *A Factorial Study of Perception* [1] identified two "closure" factors. The first of these, labeled Closure Speed, showed up most clearly on a kind of test adapted from Street's *Gestalt Completion Test,*[2] in which the subject is required to identify a picture from incomplete material. Later studies by Thurstone and his students and associates contributed some information about the way in which this ability to "perceive an apparently disorganized or unrelated group of parts as a meaningful whole" is related to various other indicators of special ability and temperament.

The test is very short (24 items, 3-minute time limit) and its reliability for individual assessment is not really adequate (.68, .70, .67 in three studies), although the authors of the manual say that the reliabilities "are at an acceptable level for test scores." The fact that the first two of the figures cited were obtained by the split-half method, not legitimately used for timed tests, casts further doubt on the conclusion. The standard score norms are not of much value because the norm group of 1,252 male industrial employees does not constitute a representative sample of any intelligible population.

None of the evidence summarized under validity really tells the user very much about what the test is measuring. Most of it comes from Pemberton's dissertation [3] in which she showed that persons scoring above the mean on *Closure Speed* characterized themselves as socially outgoing, confident and optimistic, energetic and impulsive, not logical or theoretical, and possessing strong artistic interests. Pemberton [4] also produced some indications that spatial ability and inductive reasoning were related to Closure Speed, and Thurstone found that it differentiated between subjects high and low in mechanical interest and experience. The Industrial Relations Center, under whose auspices the test is now being published, adds to this factorial type of data some evidence that occupational groups are differentiated by their average scores. There seems to be a large amount of overlapping between groups at the successive levels, however, and it is a well known fact that many measures of ability and interest produce similar differentiations. Thus the contribution these results make to our understanding of the specific validity of the Gestalt completion test is slight.

It is apparent that the technical characteristics of this test are unsatisfactory if one is

1 THURSTONE, L. L. *A Factorial Study of Perception.* Chicago, Ill.: University of Chicago Press, 1944. Pp. vi, 158.

2 STREET, ROY F. *A Gestalt Completion Test: A Study of a Cross Section of Intellect.* Columbia University, Teachers College, Contributions to Education, No. 481. New York: Bureau of Publications, the College, 1931. Pp. vii, 65. *

3 PEMBERTON, CAROL L. *A Study of the Speed and Flexibility of Closure Factors.* Doctor's thesis, University of Chicago (Chicago, Ill.), 1951.

4 PEMBERTON, CAROL. "The Closure Factor Related to Other Cognitive Processes." *Psychometrika* 17:267–88 S '52. *

considering it for any practical purpose. In research studies where no conclusions will be drawn about the meaning of individual scores except on the basis of results actually obtained in the study, the test may have something to contribute. If such research findings accumulate and steps are taken to increase the reliability and improve the norms, the test may someday merit more extensive use.

[547]

★**Consequences.** Grades 9–16 and adults; 1958–62; 2 scores: originality, ideational fluency; 1 form ('58, 11 pages); mimeographed manual, second edition ['62, 24 pages]; $5 per 25 tests; 25¢ per single copy; $1 per manual; postage extra; 20(30) minutes; P. R. Christensen, P. R. Merrifield, and J. P. Guilford; Sheridan Supply Co. *

REFERENCES

1. BARRON, FRANK. "The Disposition Toward Originality." *J Abn & Social Psychol* 51:478–85 N '55. * (*PA* 31:2533)
2. BERGER, R. M.; GUILFORD, J. P.; AND CHRISTENSEN, P. R. "A Factor-Analytic Study of Planning Abilities." *Psychol Monogr* 71(6):1–31 '57. * (*PA* 33:6967)
3. GUILFORD, J. P. *Personality*. New York: McGraw-Hill Book Co., Inc., 1959. Pp. xiii, 562. *
4. KETTNER, NORMAN W.; GUILFORD, J. P.; AND CHRISTENSEN, PAUL R. "A Factor Analytic Study Across the Domains of Reasoning, Creativity, and Evaluation." *Psychol Monogr* 73(9):1–31 '59. * (*PA* 34:7333)
5. BRITTAIN, W. LAMBERT, AND BEITTEL, KENNETH R. "A Study of Some Tests of Creativity to Performances in the Visual Arts." *Studies Art Ed* 2:54–65 sp '61. *
6. MCGUIRE, CARSON. "The Prediction of Talented Behavior in the Junior High School." *Proc Inv Conf Testing Probl* 1960:46–67 '61. *
7. MARKS, ALVIN; MICHAEL, WILLIAM B.; AND KAISER, HENRY F. "Dimensions of Creativity and Temperament in Officer Evaluation." *Psychol Rep* 9:635–8 D '61. *
8. MARKS, ALVIN; MICHAEL, WILLIAM B.; AND KAISER, HENRY F. "Sources of Noncognitive Variance in 21 Measures of Creativity." *Psychol Rep* 9:287–90 O '61. *
9. CLINE, VICTOR B.; RICHARDS, JAMES M., JR.; AND ABE, CLIFFORD. "The Validity of a Battery of Creativity Tests in a High School Sample." *Ed & Psychol Meas* 22:781–4 w '62. * (*PA* 37:7184)
10. ABDEL-RAZIK, TAHER MOHAMED. *An Investigation of Creative Thinking Among College Students*. Doctor's thesis, Ohio State University (Columbus, Ohio), 1963. (*DA* 24:2775)
11. BARRON, FRANK. Chap. 11, "The Disposition Toward Originality," pp. 139–52. In *Scientific Creativity: Its Recognition and Development*. Edited by Calvin W. Taylor and Frank Barron. New York: John Wiley & Sons, Inc., 1963. Pp. xxiv, 419. * (*PA* 38:2689)
12. CLINE, VICTOR B.; RICHARDS, JAMES M., JR.; AND NEEDHAM, WALTER E. "Creativity Tests and Achievement in High School Science." *J Appl Psychol* 47:184–9 Je '63. * (*PA* 37:8223)
13. JACOBSEN, T. L., AND ASHER, J. J. "Validity of the Concept Constancy Measure of Creative Problem Solving." *J General Psychol* 68:9–19 Ja '63. * (*PA* 38:2684)

GOLDINE C. GLESER, *Professor of Psychology, University of Cincinnati Medical School, Cincinnati, Ohio.*

Consequences is one of a large battery of group administered tests which were developed in order to explore systematically the "structure of the intellect" and isolate the factors of creative thinking. The test consists of 10 items each requiring the subject to list what the results might be if some unusual situation came to pass, as for example, "What would be the results if none of us needed food any more in order to live?" Relevant, nonduplicated responses are classified as "obvious" or "remote," the frequency of the former yielding a score of ideational fluency and the latter a score on originality.

This is an interesting and ingenious test in a field where relatively few good tests are available. However, one receives the impression that the authors have reluctantly taken time out from their own factor analytic studies to publish it for use in other research and that they are totally uninterested in developing it as a clinical tool. The samples on which statistics are based are inadequately described. Minimal attention has been given to insuring comparability of results by different scorers. While guidelines and examples are given for differentiating remote and obvious responses, many of the distinctions made are tenuous at best. For example, in response to the item mentioned above, "more neurosis" is scored as remote whereas "more suicides" is scored as obvious. Likewise, the criterion of what constitutes a relevant nonduplicated response is extremely vague. The authors recognize the latter as a source of difficulty in developing norms or comparing scores obtained by different scorers. However, they report no studies investigating scorer reliability or the magnitude of this "leniency bias." Such studies could give an indication of the extent to which effort should be expended in tightening the scoring system.

Estimates of internal consistency reliability are given for the two scores for ninth grade students and young adult males separately. The reliability of the obvious score is estimated at .86 for the 10-item test over all samples. The remote score is less reliable, particularly with ninth graders (.67). This may not reflect any difference between the groups in variability of scores over items but rather may reflect the greater homogeneity (smaller variance) of the ninth graders in the ability tapped by this score. The authors indicate that with adults four or five items may be sufficiently accurate for some research purposes.

The many studies undertaken by Guilford and his associates to verify, modify, and reconfirm the hypotheses on the structure of the intellect also yield much information on the construct validity of this test. The obvious score has an average validity of .62 for the factor DMU (ideational fluency) on the basis of five samples of young adult males each consisting of over 200 cases. In most of these samples only four items of the test were used. A slightly lower average loading (.54) was found for this factor in four samples of ninth graders. Thus, from 29 to 38 per cent of the score variance is attributable to this one factor. Loadings on other intellectual factors, including originality, are negligible with the exception that for the ninth graders an average loading of .33 was found for DMI (elaboration).

The remote score has its largest average loading (.42) on the factor DMT (originality) for young adults. For ninth graders, however, the highest loading (.40) is for DMC (spontaneous flexibility). It is difficult to evaluate the importance of this difference, particularly since the authors indicate that these factors are difficult to separate experimentally. From a practical standpoint factorial purity is not necessarily desirable. A test measuring several aspects of creativity or originality may have more predictive validity than a pure test. Some indication of this fact is given in the one study of practical validity reported in the manual in which it was found that for 80 engineering students the obvious score correlated .17 while the remote score correlated .44 with grade-point average. That the latter correlation is not simply attributable to verbal intelligence is indicated by the fact that the remote score in other studies correlated only .23 with vocabulary and .18 with reading comprehension.

In summary, *Consequences* shows considerable promise as a test of intellectual factors not usually covered in the objectively scored aptitude tests. It is recommended as a research instrument, particularly to explore its usefulness in various decisions where flexibility and originality might be important. However, scorer reliability should be investigated, and efforts should be made to tighten the scoring system and provide ways of reducing scorer bias regarding what constitutes an "acceptable" response. One helpful method might be to provide a set of protocols which a potential user might score and then compare his results with that of the authors to determine and correct bias.

[548]

★**Decorations.** Grades 9–16 and adults; 1963; "divergent production of figural implications" or "ability to add meaningful details"; Form A (5 pages); mimeographed manual (4 pages); norms for ninth graders only; $3.75 per 25 tests; 20¢ per single copy; 25¢ per manual; postage extra; 12(16) minutes; Arthur Gershon, Sheldon Gardner, Philip R. Merrifield, and J. P. Guilford; Sheridan Supply Co. *

REFERENCES

1. GUILFORD, J. P. *Personality.* New York: McGraw-Hill Book Co., Inc., 1959. Pp. xiii, 562. *

[549]

★**Illinois Test of Psycholinguistic Abilities, Experimental Edition.** Ages 2.5–9; 1961–63; based in part upon the unpublished *Differential Language Facilities Test* by Dorothy J. Sievers; 10 scores: auditory-vocal automatic, visual decoding, motor encoding, auditory-vocal association, visual-motor sequencing, vocal encoding, auditory-vocal sequencing, visual-motor association, auditory decoding, total; individual; 1 form ('61, 113-page picture booklet, 21 cards, and a series of objects); manual ('61, 137 pages); selected studies monograph ('63, 101 pages, see *22* below); record form ('61, 4 pages); $32 per examiner's kit of testing materials, 25 record forms, selected studies monograph, and manual; $3.75 per 25 record forms; $2.50 per selected studies monograph; $3.50 per manual; postage extra; (45–60) minutes; James J. McCarthy and Samuel A. Kirk; distributed by University of Illinois Press. *

REFERENCES

1. SIEVERS, DOROTHY JEAN. *Development and Standardization of a Test of Psycholinguistic Growth in Preschool Children.* Doctor's thesis, University of Illinois (Urbana, Ill.), 1955. (*DA* 16:286)
2. GALLAGHER, JAMES J. *A Comparison of Brain-Injured and Non-Brain-Injured Mentally Retarded Children on Several Psychological Variables.* Monograph of the Society for Research in Child Development, Vol. 22, No. 2. Lafayette, Ind.: Child Development Publications, 1957. Pp. 79. * (*PA* 33:1632)
3. McCARTHY, JAMES J. *Qualitative and Quantitative Differences in the Language Abilities of Young Cerebral Palsied Children.* Doctor's thesis, University of Illinois (Urbana, Ill.), 1957. (*DA* 18:499)
4. SIEVERS, DOROTHY J. "A Study to Compare the Performance of Brain-Injured and Non-Brain-Injured Mentally Retarded Children on the Differential Language Facility Test." *Am J Mental Def* 63:839–47 Mr '59. * (*PA* 34:4583)
5. McCARTHY, JAMES J. "A Test for the Identification of Defects in Language Usage Among Young Cerebral Palsied Children." *Cerebral Palsy R* 21:3–5 Ja–F '60. * (*PA* 35:6444)
6. OLSON, JAMES LADD. *A Comparison of Sensory Aphasic, Expressive Aphasic, and Deaf Children on the Illinois Test of Language Ability.* Doctor's thesis, University of Illinois (Urbana, Ill.), 1960. (*DA* 21:2950)
7. SIEVERS, DOROTHY J., AND ROSENBERG, CARL M. "The Differential Language Facility Test and Electroencephalograms of Brain-Injured Mentally Retarded Children." *Am J Mental Def* 65:46–50 Jl '60. * (*PA* 35:3787)
8. KIRK, SAMUEL A., AND McCARTHY, JAMES J. "The Illinois Test of Psycholinguistic Abilities: An Approach to Differential Diagnosis." *Am J Mental Def* 66:399–412 N '61. * (*PA* 36:4HI99K)
9. QUERESHI, MOHAMMED Y. "Effects of Various Scoring Cutoffs on Reliability Estimates." *Am J Mental Def* 65:753–60 My '61. * (*PA* 36:1HD53Q)
10. SIEVERS, DOROTHY J., AND ESSA, SHIRLEY H. "Language Development in Institutionalized and Community Mentally Retarded Children." *Am J Mental Def* 66:413–20 N '61. * (*PA* 36:4JI13S)
11. HERMANN, ANITA LOUISE. *An Experimental Approach to the Educability of Psycholinguistic Functions in Children.* Master's thesis, University of Illinois (Urbana, Ill.), 1962.
12. KIRK, SAMUEL A., AND BATEMAN, BARBARA. "Diagnosis and Remediation of Learning Disabilities." *J Excep Child* 29:73–8 O '62. * (*PA* 37:6758)
13. SIEVERS, DOROTHY J., AND ROSENBERG, CARL M. "The Differential Language Facility Test and Electroencephalograms of Brain-Injured Mentally Retarded Children," pp. 567–72. In *Proceedings of the London Conference on the Scientific Study of Mental Deficiency, 1960, Vol. 2.* Edited by B. W. Richards. Dagenham, England: May & Baker Ltd., 1962. Pp. 353–690. *
14. BATEMAN, BARBARA D. "Reading and Psycholinguistic Process of Partially Seeing Children," pp. 70–86. In *Selected Studies on the Illinois Test of Psycholinguistic Abilities.* By Dorothy J. Sievers and others. [Urbana, Ill.: University of Illinois Press], 1963. Pp. vi, 96. *
15. CENTER, WILLIAM RUSSELL. *A Factor Analysis of Three Language and Communication Batteries.* Doctor's thesis, University of Georgia (Athens, Ga.), 1963. (*DA* 24:1918)
16. JAECKEL, LINDA RUTH. *A Study in the Comparison of Teachers' Ratings and the Illinois Test of Psycholinguistic Abilities in Determining the Language Ability of Deaf and Hard of Hearing Children.* Master's thesis, University of Kansas (Lawrence, Kan.), 1963.
17. KASS, CORRINE E. "Some Psychological Correlates of

Severe Reading Disability (Dyslexia)," pp. 87–96. In *Selected Studies on the Illinois Test of Psycholinguistic Abilities.* By Dorothy J. Sievers and others. [Urbana, Ill.: University of Illinois Press], 1963. Pp. vi, 196. *
18. McCarthy, James J. "Qualitative and Quantitative Differences in the Language Abilities of Young Cerebral Palsied Children," pp. 27–45. In *Selected Studies on the Illinois Test of Psycholinguistic Abilities.* By Dorothy J. Sievers and others. [Urbana, Ill.: University of Illinois Press], 1963. Pp. vi, 96. *
19. Myers, Patricia Irene. *A Comparison of Language Disabilities in Young Spastic and Athetoid Children.* Doctor's thesis, University of Texas (Austin, Tex.), 1963. (*DA* 24:2788)
20. Olson, James L. "A Comparison of Receptive Aphasic, Expressive Aphasic, and Deaf Children on the Illinois Test of Psycholinguistic Abilities," pp. 46–69. In *Selected Studies on the Illinois Test of Psycholinguistic Abilities.* By Dorothy J. Sievers and others. [Urbana, Ill.: University of Illinois Press], 1963. Pp. vi, 96. *
21. Sievers, Dorothy J. "Development and Standardization of a Test of Psycholinguistic Growth in Preschool Children," pp. 1–26. In *Selected Studies on the Illinois Test of Psycholinguistic Abilities.* By Dorothy J. Sievers and others. [Urbana, Ill.: University of Illinois Press], 1963. Pp. vi, 96. *
22. Sievers, Dorothy J., and others. *Selected Studies on the Illinois Test of Psycholinguistic Abilities.* [Urbana, Ill.: University of Illinois Press], 1963. Pp. vi, 96. *

[550]

★**Jensen Alternation Board.** Ages 5 and over; 1959–60; learning age; individual; 2 forms on 1 board ['59]; mimeographed manual ['59, 5 pages]; supplementary data ('60, 15 pages, reprint of *2* below); $59 per board, postage extra; (5–70) minutes; Milton B. Jensen; Lafayette Instrument Co. *

REFERENCES

1. Jensen, Milton B. "A Light-Switch Alternation Apparatus." *Am J Psychol* 71:441–2 Je '58. * (*PA* 33:7238)
2. Jensen, Milton B. "Alternation Learning and Mental Pathology: Test Procedures and Findings." *J Psychol* 50:211–25 O '60. *

[551]

★**Kit of Reference Tests for Cognitive Factors, 1963 Revision.** Various grades 6–16; 1954–63; previously called *Kit of Selected Tests for Reference Aptitude and Achievement Factors;* for factorial research; groups of 3–5 tests which separately define 24 factors (listed below); manual ('63, 126 pages); no data on reliability and validity; no norms; $7.50 per set of manual and 1 copy of each test; cash orders postpaid on ETS orders; postage extra on Sheridan Supply Co. orders; additional copies of Sheridan Supply Co. tests (excluding *m1*, *p1*, *s2*, *w2*, and *x1* below) must be ordered directly from that publisher; all other tests may be reproduced without permission; kit of tests compiled and manual written by John W. French, Ruth B. Ekstrom, and Leighton A. Price; Educational Testing Service. *

a) FACTOR CF: FLEXIBILITY OF CLOSURE. Grades 6–16; 1962; 1 form (3–5 pages); 3 tests.
1) *Hidden Figures Test, Cf-1.* $2.75 per 25 tests; 20(25) minutes.
2) *Hidden Patterns Test, Cf-2.* $2.75 per 25 tests; 4(8) minutes.
3) *Copying Test, Cf-3.* $2 per 25 tests; 6(10) minutes.

b) FACTOR CS: SPEED OF CLOSURE. Grades 6–16; 1962; 1 form (5 pages); 2 tests; $2.75 per 25 tests; 6(10) minutes.
1) *Gestalt Completion Test, Cs-1.*
2) *Concealed Words Test, Cs-2.*

c) FACTOR FA: ASSOCIATIONAL FLUENCY. Grades 6–16; 1957–62; 3 tests.
1) *Controlled Associations Test, Fa-1.* 1962; 1 form (3 pages); $2 per 25 tests; 12(15) minutes.
2) *Associational Fluency 1,* [*Fa-2*]. See 544c; 1957; Form A (3 pages); $2 per 25 tests; 4(10) minutes; Paul R. Christensen and J. P. Guilford; Sheridan Supply Co.
3) *Associations 4, Fa-3.* 1962; 1 form (3 pages); $2 per 25 tests; 14(18) minutes; J. P. Guilford.

d) FACTOR FE: EXPRESSIONAL FLUENCY. Grades 8–16; 1958–62; 3 tests.
1) *Expressional Fluency,* [*Fe-1*]. See 544d; 1958; Form A (5 pages); $3.75 per 25 tests; 8(12) minutes; Paul R. Christensen and J. P. Guilford; Sheridan Supply Co.
2) *Simile Interpretations, Fe-2.* 1962; 1 form (3 pages); $2 per 25 tests; 4(10) minutes; J. P. Guilford.
3) *Word Arrangement, Fe-3.* 1962; 1 form (3 pages); $2 per 25 tests; 8(12) minutes; J. P. Guilford.

e) FACTOR FI: IDEATIONAL FLUENCY. Grades 8–16; 1962; 1 form (3 pages); 3 tests; $2 per 25 tests.
1) *Topics Test, Fi-1.* 8(12) minutes.
2) *Theme Test, Fi-2.* 8(12) minutes.
3) *Thing Categories Test, Fi-3.* 6(10) minutes.

f) FACTOR FW: WORD FLUENCY. Grades 6–16; 1962; 1 form (3 pages); 3 tests; $2 per 25 tests; 6(10) minutes.
1) *Word Endings Test, Fw-1.*
2) *Word Beginnings Test, Fw-2.*
3) *Word Beginnings and Endings Test, Fw-3.*

g) FACTOR I: INDUCTION. Grades 8–16; 1962; 3 tests.
1) *Letter Sets Test, I-1.* 1 form (3 pages); $2 per 25 tests; 14(20) minutes.
2) *Locations Test, I-2.* 1 form (3 pages); $2 per 25 tests; 12(17) minutes.
3) *Figure Classification, I-3.* 1 form (9 pages); $3.75 per 25 tests; 16(20) minutes.

h) FACTOR LE: LENGTH ESTIMATION. Grades 6–16; 1962; 1 form (3 pages); 3 tests; $2 per 25 tests.
1) *Estimation of Length Test, Le-1.* 6(10) minutes.
2) *Shortest Road Test, Le-2.* 4(8) minutes.
3) *Nearer Point Test, Le-3.* 4(8) minutes.

i) FACTOR MA: ASSOCIATIVE (ROTE) MEMORY. Grades 6–16; 1962; 1 form (6 pages); 3 tests; $3.75 per 25 tests.
1) *Picture-Number Test, Ma-1.* 14(20) minutes.
2) *Object-Number Test, Ma-2.* 10(15) minutes.
3) *First and Last Names Test, Ma-3.* 10(15) minutes.

j) FACTOR MK: MECHANICAL KNOWLEDGE. 1962; 1 form (5–7 pages); 3 tests.
1) *Tool Knowledge Test, Mk-1.* Grades 6–16; $2.75 per 25 tests; 10(15) minutes.
2) *Mechanical Information Test, Mk-2.* Grades 8–16; $3.75 per 25 tests; 10(15) minutes.
3) *Electrical Information Test, Mk-3.* Grades 8–16; $3.75 per 25 tests; 12(17) minutes.

k) FACTOR MS: MEMORY SPAN. Grades 6–16; 1962; 1 form (2 pages); 3 tests; $2 per 25 tests; (10) minutes.
1) *Auditory Number Span Test, Ms-1.*
2) *Visual Number Span Test, Ms-2.*
3) *Auditory Letter Span Test, Ms-3.*

l) FACTOR N: NUMBER FACILITY. Grades 6–16; 1962; 1 form (3 pages); 3 tests; $2 per 25 tests; 4(10) minutes.
1) *Addition Test, N-1.*
2) *Division Test, N-2.*
3) *Subtraction and Multiplication Test, N-3.*

m) FACTOR O: ORIGINALITY. Grades 10–16; 1958–62; 3 tests.
1) *Plot Titles, O-1.* 1962; 1 form (3 pages); $2 per 25 tests; 6(10) minutes; Sheridan Supply Co.
2) *Symbol Production, O-2.* 1962; 1 form (5 pages); $2.75 per 25 tests; 10(15) minutes; J. P. Guilford.
3) *Consequences.* See 547; 1958; 1 form (11 pages); $5 per 25 tests; 20(30) minutes; P. R. Christensen, P. R. Merrifield, and J. P. Guilford; Sheridan Supply Co.

n) FACTOR P: PERCEPTUAL SPEED. Grades 6–16; 1962; 3 tests.
1) *Finding A's Test, P-1.* 1 form (11 pages); $5 per 25 tests; 4(10) minutes.
2) *Number Comparison Test, P-2.* 1 form (3 pages); $2 per 25 tests; 3(8) minutes.
3) *Identical Pictures Test, P-3.* 1 form (5 pages); $2.75 per 25 tests; 3(8) minutes.

o) FACTOR R: GENERAL REASONING. 1955–62; 4 tests.
1) *Mathematics Aptitude Test, R-1.* Grades 6–12; 1962; 1 form (7 pages); $3.75 per 25 tests; 20(25) minutes.
2) *Mathematics Aptitude Test, R-2.* Grades 11–16; 1962; 1 form (7 pages); $3.75 per 25 tests; 20(25) minutes.
3) *Ship Destination Test,* [*R-3*]. See 500; 1955; Form A (3 pages); $2.50 per 25 tests; 15(20) minutes; Paul R. Christensen and J. P. Guilford; Sheridan Supply Co.
4) *Necessary Arithmetic Operations Test, R-4.* Grades 6–16; 1962; 1 form (7 pages); $3.75 per 25 tests; 10(15) minutes.

p) FACTOR RE: SEMANTIC REDEFINITION. Grades 10–16; 1962; 1 form (3–4 pages); 3 tests.
1) *Gestalt Transformation, Re-1.* $2 per 25 tests; 10(15) minutes; Sheridan Supply Co.
2) *Object Synthesis, Re-2.* $2 per 25 tests; 10(15) minutes; J. P. Guilford.
3) *Picture Gestalt, Re-3.* $2.75 per 25 tests; 9(15) minutes; J. P. Guilford.

q) FACTOR RS: SYLLOGISTIC REASONING. Grades 11–16; 1955–62; 3 tests.
1) *Nonsense Syllogisms Test, Rs-1.* 1962; 1 form 3 pages); $2 per 25 tests; 8(12) minutes.
2) *Logical Reasoning* [*Rs-2*]. See 5:694; 1955; Form A (7 pages); $4 per 25 tests; 20(25) minutes; Alfred F. Hertza and J. P. Guilford; Sheridan Supply Co.
3) *Inference Test, Rs-3.* 1962; 1 form (7 pages); $3.75 per 25 tests; 12(17) minutes.

r) FACTOR S: SPATIAL ORIENTATION. 1947–62; 3 tests.
1) *Card Rotations Test, S-1.* Grades 8–16; 1962; 1 form (3 pages); $2 per 25 tests; 8(12) minutes.
2) *Cube Comparisons Test, S-2.* Grades 8–16; 1962; 1 form (3 pages); $2 per 25 tests; 6(10) minutes.
3) *Guilford-Zimmerman Aptitude Survey: Part 5, Spatial Orientation,* [*S-3*]. See 772e; 1947; Form A (8 pages); $4 per 25 tests; 10(20) minutes; J. P. Guilford and Wayne S. Zimmerman; Sheridan Supply Co.

s) FACTOR SEP: SENSITIVITY TO PROBLEMS. Grades 8–16; 1962; 1 form (5–7 pages); 3 tests.
1) *Apparatus Test, Sep-1.* $2.75 per 25 tests; 14(20) minutes; J. P. Guilford.
2) *Seeing Problems, Sep-2.* $2.75 per 25 tests; 12(15) minutes; Sheridan Supply Co.
3) *Seeing Deficiencies, Sep-3.* $3.75 per 25 tests; 20(25) minutes; J. P. Guilford.

t) FACTOR SS: SPATIAL SCANNING. Grades 6–16; 1962; 1 form (3–6 pages); 3 tests.
1) *Maze Tracing Speed Test, Ss–1.* $2 per 25 tests; 6(10) minutes.
2) *Choosing a Path, Ss-2.* $3.75 per 25 tests; 14(20) minutes.
3) *Map Planning Test, Ss-3.* $2 per 25 tests; 6(10) minutes.

u) FACTOR V: VERBAL COMPREHENSION. 1962; 1 form (3 pages); 5 tests; $2 per 25 tests.
1) *Vocabulary Test, V-1.* Grades 7–12; 8(12) minutes.
2) *Vocabulary Test, V-2.* Grades 7–12; 8(12) minutes.
3) *Wide Range Vocabulary Test, V-3.* Grades 7–16; 12(17) minutes.
4) *Advanced Vocabulary Test, V-4.* Grades 11–16; 8(12) minutes.
5) *Vocabulary Test, V-5.* Grades 11–16; 8(12) minutes.

v) FACTOR VZ: VISUALIZATION. Grades 9–16; 1962; 1 form (3–5 pages); 3 tests.
1) *Form Board Test, Vz-1.* $2.75 per 25 tests; 16(20) minutes.
2) *Paper Folding Test, Vz-2.* $2 per 25 tests; 6(10) minutes.
3) *Surface Development Test, Vz-3.* $2.75 per 25 tests; 12(15) minutes.

w) FACTOR XA: FIGURAL ADAPTIVE FLEXIBILITY. Grades 11–16; 1962; 3 tests.
1) *Match Problems 2, Xa-1.* 1 form (4 pages); $3.75 per 25 tests; 14(20) minutes; Sheridan Supply Co.
2) *Match Problems 5, Xa-2.* 1 form (3 pages); $2 per 25 tests; 10(15) minutes; Sheridan Supply Co.
3) *Planning Air Maneuvers, Xa-3.* 1 form (7 pages); $3.75 per 25 tests; 16(25) minutes.

x) FACTOR XS: SEMANTIC SPONTANEOUS FLEXIBILITY. Grades 6–16; 1960–62; 3 tests.
1) *Utility Test, Xs-1.* 1962; 1 form (3 pages); $2 per 25 tests; 10(15) minutes; Sheridan Supply Co.
2) *Alternate Uses,* [*Xs-2*]. See 542; 1960; 1 form (4 pages); $2 per 25 tests; 12(17) minutes; J. P. Guilford, Philip R. Merrifield, and Robert C. Wilson; Sheridan Supply Co.
3) *Object Naming, Xs-3.* 1962; 1 form (3 pages); $2 per 25 tests; 4(8) minutes; J. P. Guilford.

[552]

★**Making Objects.** Grades 9–16 and adults; 1963; "divergent production of figural systems" or "figural expressional fluency"; Form A (3 pages); mimeographed manual (4 pages); no data on reliability; norms for ninth graders and adult males only; $2 per 25 tests; 10¢ per single copy; 25¢ per manual; postage extra; [3(10)] minutes; Sheldon Gardner, Arthur Gershon, Philip R. Merrifield, and J. P. Guilford; Sheridan Supply Co. *

REFERENCES

1. GUILFORD, J. P. *Personality.* New York: McGraw-Hill Book Co., Inc., 1959. Pp. xiii, 562. *

[553]

★**Marianne Frostig Developmental Test of Visual Perception, Third Edition.** Ages 3–8; 1961–64; 6 scores: eye-motor coordination, figure-ground discrimination, form constancy, position in space, spatial relations, total, perceptual quotient; 1 form ('63, c1961, 19 pages); demonstration cards ['63, 11 cards]; administration and scoring manual ('64, c1961–64, 37 pages); monograph on 1963 standardization ('64, 38 pages, *Percept & Motor Skills* 19:463–99 O '64); $10.50 per examiner's kit of 10 tests, scoring keys, demonstration cards, monograph, and manual; $5 per specimen set (without demonstration cards); postage extra; (30–45) minutes for individual administration, (40–60) minutes for group administration; Marianne Frostig in collaboration with D. Welty Lefever, John R. B. Whittlesey, and Phyllis Maslow (monograph); Consulting Psychologists Press, Inc. * [The reviews which follow are of the third edition materials which were previously published by the Marianne Frostig School of Educational Therapy and which, except for format, were essentially the same as the materials described in this entry.]

REFERENCES

1. FROSTIG, MARIANNE; LEFEVER, D. WELTY; AND WHITTLESEY, JOHN R. B. "A Developmental Test of Visual Perception for Evaluating Normal and Neurologically Handicapped Children." *Percept & Motor Skills* 12:383–94 Je '61. * (*PA* 36:2JF83F)

2. FROSTIG, MARIANNE. "Visual Perception in the Brain-Damaged Child." Abstract. *Am J Orthopsychiatry* 32:279–80 Mr '62. *
3. FROSTIG, MARIANNE, AND HORNE, DAVID. "Assessment of Visual Perception and Its Importance in Education." *A.A.M.D. Ed Reporter* 2:11–2 Ap '62. *
4. SCHELLENBERG, ERNEST DAVID. *A Study of the Relationship Between Visual-Motor Perception and Reading Disabilities of Third Grade Pupils.* Doctor's thesis, University of Southern California (Los Angeles, Calif.), 1962. (*DA* 23:3785)
5. CORAH, NORMAN L., AND POWELL, BARBARA J. "A Factor Analytic Study of the Frostig Developmental Test of Visual Perception." *Percept & Motor Skills* 16:59–63 F '63. * (*PA* 38:677)
6. FROSTIG, MARIANNE. "Visual Perception in the Brain-Injured Child." *Am J Orthopsychiatry* 33:665–71 Jl '63. * (*PA* 38:7979)
7. FROSTIG, MARIANNE; LEFEVER, WELTY; AND WHITTLESEY, JOHN. "Disturbances in Visual Perception." *J Ed Res* 57:160–2 N '63. *

JAMES M. ANDERSON, *Research Consultant, Institute of Therapeutic Psychology, Santa Ana, California.*

According to the authors, "The test is designed to measure certain operationally defined perceptual functions, and to pinpoint the age at which they normally develop." There are five subtests: Test 1, Eye-Motor Coordination (16 items); Test 2, Figure-Ground (8 items); Test 3, Form Constancy (17 items); Test 4, Position in Space (8 items); and Test 5, Spatial Relations (8 items). Results are reported in terms of age equivalents, scale scores, and perceptual quotients (analogous in appearance, though not in method of derivation, to Wechsler type intelligence quotients).

All of the materials supplied with the specimen set range in aesthetic quality from mediocre to poor. This statement holds for both the quality of the art work and the printing. This seems hardly excusable for a "third" edition.

The directions on the whole are clear and concise. However, lack of time limits or instructions for what to do with the laggards should prove a handicap for some teachers. (I may be presumptuous here since there is no indication of the level of training needed for scoring or interpretation.) The directions for Test 2 could be improved if they were made more consistent. The examiner is told: "It is important to explain 'outline' and to use this word consistently throughout the remainder of the test. The expression 'draw around' is often interpreted literally by the child, and he may draw a circle around the figure." Yet for item 2 of this test the child is instructed to "Find the long box and trace around it." The same directions are employed for items 3 and 4 of this test. (The reviewer is here quoting from a typed second revision of the third edition of the Administration Manual supplied by the senior author and apparently intended to obviate the difficulty encountered in the manual supplied with the specimen set, which contains the instruction to "draw around.") Similarly, on Test 3 the inclusion of the word "mark" in the instructions introduces a confusing element since the scoring standards require outlining within fairly strict limits. Then, for two items in Test 3 the instructions are, "You are to draw around all of the balls (circles)" when outlining is required. Although the test is untimed, in Test 3 the examiner is advised, "If one child takes longer than the rest of the group, stop him and continue the test." From this it would follow that the last child finishing would be interrupted on each item of this test.

Instructions for scoring are straightforward and clear. Good examples illustrate the criteria for scoring each item. The Scoring and Evaluation Booklet should prove most helpful to users of the test. A paradoxical situation, however, prevails in the scoring of Test 1 wherein items 5 and 9, the most difficult items, receive decreased weight. No rationale is presented for this paradox.

Information for evaluating this test is at best incomplete if not haphazardly presented. The latest edition of the Scoring and Evaluation Booklet refers to the "Fourth preliminary standardization....on 2116 unselected school children at the nursery school, kindergarten, first, second and third grade levels." Nowhere in this booklet is there presented a breakdown of the composition of this standardization population. One cannot help but wonder if this increased *n,* increased over any previously published figure, represents a cumulation of cases accumulated under questionable conditions of variation in both test materials and directions.

The authors of this test have such a real contribution to offer to educators and psychologists alike that it is regrettable that they have apparently prematurely offered their test as a finished product. In a prepublication report on the 1962 standardization, this reviewer finds evidence of much thought and careful work as well as an excellent start at standardization. The concepts of perceptual age and perceptual quotient appear most useful and intriguing. Both reliability and validity studies reported in this paper are promising and even exciting though they are done on inadequate samples and on varying age groups.

The primary use of this instrument at this

time would seem to be that of predicting learning success in the primary grades. It contains types of items commonly found in reading readiness tests. The authors have apparently chosen to build a test of low band width (complexity of information) and high fidelity (exactness of information). In this they seem to have succeeded. It is hoped that when a complete manual on the test is presented it will present the authors' theoretical position in the field of perception as well as some attempt at construct validity.

MARY C. AUSTIN, *Professor of Education, Western Reserve University, Cleveland, Ohio.*

Frostig and her co-workers consider vision a developmental process which is directly related to early school success. They have evolved a series of tests for young children to measure their perceptual abilities and "to pinpoint the age at which they normally develop." To the extent that school success depends on these abilities it can, they believe, be predicted from the test. The severity of the perceptual disturbances can be evaluated, regardless of their etiology, and training procedures designed to correct the specific disabilities can be provided.

During the testing period the child attempts carefully graded tasks in five areas of visual perception. In eye-hand coordination, he must draw straight and curved lines between increasingly narrow boundaries or a straight line to a target. In figure-ground perception, he must discriminate between intersecting shapes and find hidden figures. In the form constancy subtest, he must discriminate circles and squares, in different shadings, sizes, and positions, from other shapes on the page. Subtest four, a measure of the perception of position in space, requires the child to differentiate between figures in an identical position and those in a reversed or rotated position. In the final test, one of spatial relationships, the task is to copy patterns by linking dots. Obviously, the tasks are varied, and the use of colored pencils on some of the items should further capture the child's interest. Even so, the time element involved appears lengthy for the attention span of young children.

Directions for administering the test are relatively clear from the examiner's standpoint. The initial directions to children, however, may be somewhat confusing for them, particularly the concept of not lifting the pencil from the paper in the eye-hand coordination test. There is some evidence also of inappropriate vocabulary for young children, i.e., the word "tunnel" which is necessary to the successful completion of the first test item. The test booklet itself may be too bulky for nursery and first grade youngsters to handle. Folding pages back is difficult for children at these ages. The stated optimum number for group testing at the kindergarten level is 6 to 8 (8 to 10 in a typewritten copy of the second revision of the manual for administration), and this size group would make the testing of an entire group too time consuming in most school situations.

Scoring of the Frostig test is for the most part objective and easy to learn. A perceptual quotient as well as a perceptual age can be derived from the score. The perceptual quotient (PQ) shows the developmental level of the child in relation to his chronological age. There may be a tendency, especially for the untrained and inexperienced, to interpret the perceptual quotient as something akin to the intelligence quotient. A thorough explanation of the PQ would have to be undertaken before the results of the test could be used effectively. Some examiners have questioned the practice of giving no credit in the eye-hand coordination subtest for an exercise with lines drawn too short or too long, underdrawing and overdrawing being measured to an eighth of an inch and a half inch, respectively. The scoring standards on subtests 3a and 3b (Form Constancy) are somewhat difficult to interpret and understand.

The test has been standardized on over 1,800 apparently "normal" children, with no tests given by untrained examiners. Sampling appears adequate within the five- to nine-year age range. This is not true at the lower levels, and more subjects at the preschool level should be tested. The authors' proposals for future research include the possibility of gathering additional samples for the purpose of comparing the norms of nursery school children with those in day care centers and those children not attending any nursery school. Hopefully, such comparisons may shed light on the question of differential performance at this age level. In any event, children of lower socioeconomic classes should be included since there are almost none of them in the present standardization group.

Test-retest reliability of the perceptual quotient (n = 35 first and 37 second graders tested two weeks apart) is reported as .80 for the total sample. Subtest scale score test-retest correlations are reported to range from .42 (Figure-Ground) to .80 (Form Constancy). Validity has been investigated through correlations between scaled scores and teacher ratings of classroom adjustment (.44), motor coordination (.50), and intellectual functioning (.50). Correlations between Frostig and Goodenough scores range from .32 to .46. In a study of 25 children the Frostig test "proved to be highly accurate" in identifying children who would not attempt to learn to read when "exposed to reading material but not forced to use it." Low test scores are also reported to be related to the presence of severe learning difficulties.

The Frostig test appears to be a significant one. It has proved useful as a screening tool with groups of nursery school, kindergarten, and first grade children, primarily because it permits identification of those children who need special perceptual training in five important areas of visual perception. It should also be valuable as a clinical tool with children beyond first grade.

[554]

★**Match Problems.** Grades 9–16 and adults; 1963; formerly called *Match Problems 2;* "divergent production of figural transformations" or "originality in dealing with concrete visual material"; Form A (4 pages); mimeographed manual, preliminary edition (3 pages); scoring guide (5 pages); norms for ninth graders on the current form and adults on an earlier form only; $3.75 per 25 tests; 20¢ per single copy; 50¢ per set of manual and scoring guide; postage extra; 14(22) minutes; Raymond M. Berger and J. P. Guilford; Sheridan Supply Co. *

REFERENCES

1. Berger, R. M.; Guilford, J. P.; and Christensen, P. R. "A Factor-Analytic Study of Planning Abilities." *Psychol Monogr* 71(6):1–31 '57. * (*PA* 33:6967)
2. Guilford, J. P. *Personality.* New York: McGraw-Hill Book Co., Inc., 1959. Pp. xiii, 562. *
3. Brittain, W. Lambert, and Beittel, Kenneth R. "A Study of Some Tests of Creativity to Performances in the Visual Arts." *Studies Art Ed* 2:54–65 sp '61. *
4. Marks, Alvin; Michael, William B.; and Kaiser, Henry F. "Dimensions of Creativity and Temperament in Officer Evaluation." *Psychol Rep* 9:635–8 D '61. *
5. Marks, Alvin; Michael, William B.; and Kaiser, Henry F. "Sources of Noncognitive Variance in 21 Measures of Creativity." *Psychol Rep* 9:287–90 O '61. *
6. Cline, Victor B.; Richards, James M., Jr.; and Abe, Clifford. "The Validity of a Battery of Creativity Tests in a High School Sample." *Ed & Psychol Meas* 22:781–4 w '62. * (*PA* 37:7184)
7. Cline, Victor B.; Richards, James M., Jr.; and Needham, Walter E. "Creativity Tests and Achievement in High School Science." *J Appl Psychol* 47:184–9 Je '63. * (*PA* 37:8223)

[555]

*__Nufferno Tests of Speed and Level.__ Mental Ages 11 and over; 1956–62; 5 tests; 6*s.* per 25 tests; postage extra; W. D. Furneaux; distributed by University of London Press Ltd. *

a) NUFFERNO SPEED TESTS. 1956–62; 5 scores: speed (stressed or unstressed), speed-range, speed slope, stress speed-gain, accuracy; 2 tests; manual ['56, 34 pages] plus 18 mimeographed pages ['62] of corrections and revisions; 9*s.* 6*d.* per manual and supplementary pages; 10*s.* per specimen set.
1) *Nufferno Sheet 1: Test GIS/14E.36.* Mental ages 11–15; Forms A(1), A(2), ['56, both forms on 1 sheet]; (15) minutes.
2) *Nufferno Sheet 2: Test GIS/14E.36.* Mental ages 13 and over; Forms A(2), B(1), ['56, both forms on 1 sheet]; (20) minutes.

b) NUFFERNO LEVEL TESTS. 1956; 3 tests; manual ['56, 22 pages]; 6*s.* 6*d.* per manual; 7*s.* 6*d.* per specimen set.
1) *Nufferno Level Test Cards: Test IL/2(AB)36.* Mental ages 11 and over; individual; 2 scores: personal level, situation level; 1 form ['56, 54 cards]; 17*s.* 6*d.* per set of cards; (40) minutes.
2) *Nufferno Sheet 3: Test GL/2C.46.* Adults with IQ's 100 and over; 1 form ['56, 2 pages]; (40) minutes.
3) *Nufferno Sheet 4: Test GL/3A.35.* Mental ages 11 and over; 1 form ['56, 2 pages]; (40) minutes.

REFERENCES

1–3. See 5:357.
4. Payne, R. W.; Mattussek, P.; and George, E. I. "An Experimental Study of Schizophrenic Thought Disorder." *J Mental Sci* 105:627–52 Jl '59. * (*PA* 34:6384)
5. Payne, R. W., and Hewlett, J. H. G. Chap. 1, "Thought Disorder in Psychotic Patients," pp. 3–104. In *Experiments in Personality: Vol. 2, Psychodiagnostics and Psychodynamics.* Edited by H. J. Eysenck. London: Routledge & Kegan Paul Ltd., 1960. Pp. viii, 333. *
6. Brierley, Harry. "The Speed and Accuracy Characteristics of Neurotics." *Brit J Psychol* 52:273–80 Ag '61. * (*PA* 36:3HI73B)
7. Payne, R. W. Chap. 6, "Cognitive Abnormalities," pp. 193–261. In *Handbook of Abnormal Psychology: An Experimental Approach.* Edited by H. J. Eysenck. New York: Basic Books, Inc., 1961. Pp. xvi, 816. * (*PA* 35:6719)

For reviews by John Liggett and E. A. Peel, see 5:357.

[556]

★**Perceptual Speed (Identical Forms).** Grades 9–16 and industrial employees; 1959, c1956–59; 1 form ('56, 8 pages); manual ('59, 13 pages); norms for males only; $4 per 20 tests, postage extra; $1 per specimen set, postpaid; 5(10) minutes; L. L. Thurstone (test), T. E. Jeffrey (test), and Measurement Research Division, Industrial Relations Center, University of Chicago (manual); Education-Industry Service. *

Leroy Wolins, *Associate Professor of Psychology and Statistics, Iowa State University, Ames, Iowa.*

This test is very likely a good measure of the perceptual speed factor, which, in turn, is known to be predictive of performance in certain types of jobs. However, the manual presents only a few validity studies involving small samples and it is not clear whether the reliability data reported are specific to this instrument.

The normative data presented are not useful since the manual does not describe the sample adequately. It merely states that the sample consists of 182 male industrial employees.

More useful normative data are available from the publisher.

In summary, the only acceptable portion of the manual is the instructions for administration and scoring. This reviewer is pleased that this test has been made available and would not discourage its use for those who wish to find out if it is valid in their particular situation.

[557]

★**Pertinent Questions.** Grades 9–16 and adults; 1960; experimental form; conceptual foresight; Form A (3 pages); duplicated manual, preliminary edition (13 pages); no norms for high school; $2 per 25 tests; 15¢ per single copy; 50¢ per manual; postage extra; 12(20) minutes; Raymond M. Berger, J. P. Guilford, and P. R. Merrifield (manual); Sheridan Supply Co. *

REFERENCES

1. Marks, Alvin; Michael, William B.; and Kaiser, Henry F. "Dimensions of Creativity and Temperament in Officer Evaluation." *Psychol Rep* 9:635–8 D '61. *
2. Marks, Alvin; Michael, William B.; and Kaiser, Henry F. "Sources of Noncognitive Variance in 21 Measures of Creativity." *Psychol Rep* 9:287–90 O '61. *
3. Merrifield, P. R.; Guilford, J. P.; Christensen, P. R.; and Frick, J. W. "The Role of Intellectual Factors in Problem Solving." *Psychol Monogr* 76(10):1–21 '62. *

[558]

★**Possible Jobs.** Grades 6–16 and adults; 1963; "divergent production of semantic implications" or "ability to suggest alternative deductions"; Form A (3 pages); mimeographed manual (6 pages); norms based on sixth, ninth, and tenth graders only; $2 per 25 tests; 10¢ per single copy; 35¢ per manual; postage extra; 10(15) minutes; Arthur Gershon and J. P. Guilford; Sheridan Supply Co. *

REFERENCES

1. Guilford, J. P. *Personality.* New York: McGraw-Hill Book Co., Inc., 1959. Pp. xiii, 562. *

[559]

★**The Rutgers Drawing Test.** Ages 4–6, 6–9; 1952–61; 2 levels labeled forms; no data on reliability; $2 per 25 tests; $1 per specimen set of both levels; postpaid; (5–10) minutes; Anna Spiesman Starr; the Author. *

a) [Form A.] Ages 4–6; 1952; test ['52, 1 page]; manual ('52, 21 pages, reprint of *1* below).
b) Form B. Ages 6–9; 1959–61; test ('59, 1 page); manual ('61, 31 pages).

REFERENCES

1. Starr, Anna Spiesman. "The Rutgers Drawing Test." *Training Sch B* 49:45–64 My '52. * (*PA* 27:444)
2. Leton, Donald A. "A Factor Analysis of Readiness Tests." *Percept & Motor Skills* 16:915–9 Je '63. * (*PA* 38:6584)

[560]

★**Subsumed Abilities Test.** Ages 9 and over; 1957–63; subtitle on manual is *A Measure of Learning Efficiency;* 5 scores: recognition, abstraction, conceptualization, total (demonstrated abilities), potential abilities; 1 form ('57, 8 pages); manual ('63, 12 pages); no data on reliability of subscores or potential abilities score; no norms for potential abilities score; $6.25 per 25 tests; $2.75 per 25 scoring key-tabulation sheets; $1.75 per manual; $2.50 per specimen set; cash orders postpaid; 30(40) minutes; Joseph R. Sanders; Martin M. Bruce. *

Naomi Stewart, *Formerly Staff Associate, Educational Testing Service, Princeton, New Jersey.*

This test is made up of 30 items, to each of which the examinee must give not one but two responses. Each item consists of four line drawings; the examinee must identify three that are alike in some way (shape, size, content, position, or whatever) and then, again, three (which may or may not be the same three) that are alike in a different way.

In theory, at least, success on the *Subsumed Abilities Test* depends on three "subsumed" or "hierarchical" perceptual skills: the first, Recognition, is, according to the manual, a prerequisite of the second, Abstraction, which, in turn, is a prerequisite of the third, Conceptualization. Of the 30 items, 10 are supposed on a purely a priori basis to be recognition items, another 10, abstraction items, and the remaining 10, conceptualization items. The three sets of items are loosely matched with respect to general character of the line drawings they comprise—e.g., items 1, 11, and 21, supposedly measuring Recognition, Abstraction, and Conceptualization, respectively, all contain vaguely canoe-shaped figures; items 4, 14, and 24, supposedly measuring Abstraction, Conceptualization, and Recognition, in that order, all contain rectangular figures. One point is given for each correct response. The maximum possible score on each subtest is 20 and the maximum possible total score, called the "Demonstrated Abilities Score," is 60.

Provision is also made for calculating still another score, namely, the "Potential Abilities Score." In this calculation, a correct response to a conceptualization item earns 3 points regardless of whether the companion recognition and abstraction items are correct or incorrect. An incorrect answer to a conceptualization item earns 1 point if the corresponding recognition item is right but the abstraction item is wrong, and 2 points if the abstraction item is right regardless of the response to the recognition item.

This is an exceedingly elaborate structure of scores, subscores, and superscores to base on a total of 30 items, especially when the available reliability figures are thin and fragmentary. No reliability data are given for Recognition, Abstraction, or Conceptualization, or for Potential Abilities. With respect to Demonstrated Abilities (which is simply the total number of correct responses), odd-even reliability figures of .97, .81, and .35, respectively, are reported for 30 hospitalized psychotic veterans, 21 fifth and sixth grade students, and 26 tenth grade students; a split-half reliability of .96 is given for a group of 26 open ward psychotics; and a test-retest reliability of .64 is reported for a group of college students (number of cases not given).

So far as validity data are concerned, the figures are even more fragmentary. Moreover, it is almost impossible to ascertain what the test is intended to measure or what it is actually measuring. There are at least three different, and to some extent mutually incompatible, foci of emphasis or "motifs" running through the various statements in the Examiner's Manual: first, the "subsumed abilities" motif (stressing the idea that the test is supposedly measuring a hierarchy of perceptual skills) for which no empirical support is ever given; secondly, what might be called the "fluidity" motif; and third, the "learning efficiency" motif.

Because an examinee must make more than one response to each item, the test presumably involves an element of fluidity, or ability to make appropriate shifts in perceptual responses. This "fluidity" aspect of the test is given major emphasis in the historical background section of both the original (1958) and the revised (1963) Examiner's Manual. Both manuals trace the relationship and similarity of the test to certain earlier (individually administered) tests requiring flexibility of perceptual response, which successfully differentiated psychotic from normal subjects. But whereas the original manual extends and enlarges upon this general train of thought—stating, e.g., "The purpose of the Subsumed Abilities Test is to measure intellectual abilities in relation to emotional state. It is a measure of a person's ability to perform complex intellectual tasks under varying degrees of stress"—the revised manual soft-pedals this motif outside of the historical background section. It makes no mention of stress or of measuring intellectual abilities in relation to emotional state. Without any qualification it terms the test "a measure of learning efficiency," and talks of its applicability to the junior and senior high school counseling situation, to the personnel hiring situation, to employee placement, and to rehabilitation counseling.

The publisher's catalog, too, omits any reference to stress, the differentiation of psychotics from nonpsychotics, and similar matters, and describes the test as a "non-verbal test measuring ability to handle abstractions and concepts," characterizing it as "a valuable aid in diagnosing the ability to learn." This shift toward an emphasis on the *general* applicability of the *Subsumed Abilities Test* seems most unfortunate, inasmuch as the validity of the test as a general measure of learning ability, or learning efficiency, has in no way been established.[1] Moreover, such data as appear in the manual tend to refute, rather than confirm, the likelihood that the test possesses any useful discriminating power except perhaps in the very special type of circumstances found in a mental hospital.

Of all the various figures given in the manual, only the data for psychotics versus nonpsychotics reveal a difference in demonstrated ability score (DAS) means that is large enough to possess any practical significance: (*a*) 26 open ward psychotics—mean DAS 45.35, SD 7.60; (*b*) 15 closed ward psychotics—mean DAS 36.46, SD 12.98; (*c*) 30 hospitalized psychotic veterans—mean DAS 41.40, SD 9.95; (*d*) "normal" group of college students (very roughly equal in age and education to groups *a* and *b*)—mean DAS 51.88, SD 5.59. Unfortunately, the data are not only based on very small numbers of cases but also are not readily accessible in the original; the figures for group *c* are reported as coming from a personal communication to the test author, and the remaining ones from an unpublished master's thesis.

The lack of general applicability of the test may be seen by examining the demonstrated ability score distributions given in the manual for various "normative" groups. For example, the 193 college psychology students (mean DAS 52.50, SD 8.71) and the 291 salesmanship students (mean DAS 51.68, SD 5.31) perform about on a par with the 45 sixth grade school children (mean DAS 51.63, SD 7.96) and the 21 fifth and sixth grade school children (mean DAS 52.57, SD 4.11), but not

1 The 1958 Examiner's Manual at least was frank in that respect, stating (page 12): "*To what extent does performance on the S.A.T. correspond to one's ability to learn a novel skill or subject?* Copies of the group version of the S.A.T. and this manual are being distributed in order to gather answers to this and related questions." If any answers were gathered they are not given in the 1963 Examiner's Manual, and the question itself has been deleted from the text, which now fails to make explicit what is still perfectly true.

quite so well as the 26 tenth grade children (mean DAS 55.27, SD 2.44). The 74 supervisors—middle management and executive personnel, including such job titles as factory superintendent, chief chemist, personnel director, and vice president for sales—do about as well (mean DAS 49.65, SD 6.41) as the 23 factory workers who were applying for jobs as lappers, grinders, and inspectors in a ball bearing factory (mean DAS 49.70, SD 6.21)!

Presumably to forestall this very type of criticism, the 1963 Examiner's Manual furnishes a disclaimer under Conclusions (page 7):

> These studies suggest that the SAT is a relatively valid and reliable instrument when used as a screening device for separating those who are willing and able to learn or to utilize visual symbol systems from those for whom either an interview or further testing is needed to determine if such willingness and ability are present. It does not appear to be a highly reliable instrument for differentiating among individuals currently demonstrating relatively good ability to learn and to utilize visual symbol systems (e.g., accelerated tenth graders and college students). These findings are consistent with the purpose and rationale of the test, and are reflected in the limits recommended for interpreting scores.

Regrettably, of the three sentences that make up this quotation, the first and last are not substantiated by any data given in the manual, while the disclaimer itself is too well buried in a mass of verbiage to be of much use as a deterrent to anyone contemplating the purchase of the test.

The failure of the demonstrated abilities score to differentiate among the various groups is not really surprising. Even a superficial examination of the items making up the test reveals that in a great many instances it is possible to arrive at a "wrong" answer that is just as good by many standards as the answer keyed as correct. Some of the correct responses, moreover, are so obvious as to be almost insulting, and consequently in many instances the more intelligent examinee is more likely than the less intelligent one to produce a "wrong" answer. This is particularly true of the recognition items, as evidenced by the fact that (*a*) the mean recognition score is above 19 for nine of the ten "normative" groups (18.92 for the tenth), 20 being the maximum possible score, and (*b*) the only individuals who gave as many as 7 incorrect responses to the 10 recognition items were college students, professional, white collar, and secretarial applicants, and supervisors. None of the grade school children or factory workers made this many errors! Some of the abstraction items also appear to be operating in reverse, and this is borne out by examination of the abstraction score distributions. The conceptualization score seems to be least affected by this kind of attenuation. (Parenthetically, one might note in this connection that if the potential abilities score has any useful discriminating power—and there are no data on this point in the manual—it is undoubtedly because the largest contributor to the variance of the potential abilities score is the number of correct conceptualization responses.)

There are a number of additional criticisms that might be made, particularly of the misleading and certainly over-optimistic use in the manual of such terms as "cross-validation group," "content validity studies," and "concurrent validity studies," but there seems no point in belaboring this matter further. If the *Subsumed Abilities Test* is a valid measure of anything at all, this has yet to be demonstrated, and so far as this reviewer is concerned, it is highly questionable whether it should be offered for sale as a testing device.

[561]

***Wechsler Memory Scale.** Adults; 1945–63; individual; Forms 1, 2; record forms for Forms 1 ('62, c1945), 2 ('63, c1948), (2 pages, slight revisions of the forms copyrighted in 1945 and 1948); manual ('62, 21 pages, a combined reprinting of *1* and *2* published in 1945 and 1946); $3.75 per set of 50 record forms and set of cards for visual reproduction subtest; 75¢ per manual; $1 per specimen set of both forms; postpaid; (15) minutes; David Wechsler and Calvin P. Stone (Form 2); Psychological Corporation. *

REFERENCES

1–3. See 3:302.
4–9. See 4:364.
10. Weider, Arthur. "Wechsler Memory Scale," pp. 757–9. (*PA* 27:7806) In *Contributions Toward Medical Psychology: Theory and Psychodiagnostic Methods, Vol. II.* Edited by Arthur Weider. New York: Ronald Press Co., 1953. Pp. xi, 459–885. *
11. Howard, Alvin R. "Further Validation Studies of the Wechsler Memory Scale." *J Clin Psychol* 10:164–7 Ap '54. * (*PA* 29:926)
12. Parker, James W. "The Validity of Some Current Tests for Organicity." *J Consult Psychol* 21:425–8 O '57. * (*PA* 33:1297)
13. Shontz, Franklin C. "Evaluation of Intellectual Potential in Hemiplegic Individuals." *J Clin Psychol* 13:267–9 Jl '57. * (*PA* 32:5816)
14. Strother, Charles R.; Schaie, K. Warner; and Horst, Paul. "The Relationship Between Advanced Age and Mental Abilities." *J Abn & Social Psychol* 55:166–70 S '57. * (*PA* 33:3294)
15. Walton, D. "The Diagnostic and Predictive Accuracy of the Wechsler Memory Scale in Psychiatric Patients Over 65." *J Mental Sci* 104:1111–8 O '58. * (*PA* 33:10793)
16. Bloom, Bernard L. "Comparison of the Alternate Wechsler Memory Scale Forms." *J Clin Psychol* 15:72–4 Ja '59. * (*PA* 34:3261)
17. Victor, Maurice; Herman, Kenneth; and White, Elisabeth E. "A Psychological Study of the Wernicke-Korsakoff Syndrome: Results of Wechsler-Bellevue Intelligence Scale and Wechsler Memory Scale Testing at Different Stages in the Disease." *Q J Studies Alcohol* 20:467–79 S '59. * (*PA* 34:6401)

18. SHAW, JAMES HOWARD. *Memory Processes in Schizophrenics and Normals.* Doctor's thesis, Washington State University (Pullman, Wash.), 1960. (*DA* 21:2371)

For reviews by Ivan Norman Mensh and Joseph Newman, see 4:364; for a review by Kate Levine Kogan, see 3:302.

[562]

★**Word Fluency.** Industrial employees; 1959–61; 1 form ('61, 2 pages); manual ('59, 30 pages); norms for males only; $2 per 20 tests, postage extra; $1 per specimen set, postpaid; 10(15) minutes; Raymond J. Corsini and Measurement Research Division, Industrial Relations Center, University of Chicago; Education-Industry Service. *

JAMES E. KENNEDY, *Associate Professor of Psychology, University of Wisconsin, Madison, Wisconsin.*

Word Fluency attempts to measure "the speed (or quickness) of verbal associations" in such a way that "verbal comprehension and limited vocabulary do not have a significant bearing on the score." The subject is presented with 16 letters of the alphabet and 5 categories: automobiles, flowers, countries, colors, and tools. For each category he must write an example which starts with each of the letters. The test may be administered on a group basis; the time limit is set at 10 minutes; the total score is the number of acceptable responses (spelling is not important). It is reported that the test has been used "principally with male industrial subjects" but the purpose for which it has been used is not stated.

The manual gives adequate instructions for administering and scoring the test, for converting raw scores to standard scores, and for interpreting converted scores. A scoring key provides examples of acceptable responses for each category. The norms provided are based on 1,045 industrial personnel of varied occupation.

In a section headed "Background Research" the manual notes that L. L. Thurstone in his early studies of primary mental abilities identified two relatively distinct verbal factors: word fluency and verbal comprehension. Thurstone's test to measure word fluency, which required the subject to produce three synonyms for each of a list of stimulus words, was found to have "a high correlation with the word fluency factor and a negligible correlation with the verbal-comprehension factor." The manual does not explain why the new Corsini test of word fluency was developed, or in what ways the author believes it to be similar to or different from the Thurstone test. No evidence is provided to indicate how well the new test measures the word fluency factor or how it correlates with the verbal comprehension factor.

Test-retest reliability, based on a sample of 48 subjects, was found to be .78; Kuder-Richardson formula 21 estimates range from .67 to .84 for various occupational groups.

According to the manual, "two approaches to the validity of the test were taken." The first concerned the fact that *Word Fluency* correlated, for various occupational groups, between .10 and .55 with *Verbal Reasoning* and between −.02 and .56 with *Understanding Communication.* The author concludes that these results "indicate [the test] measures in the area of mental abilities"; no further interpretation is made. Correlations between *Word Fluency* and each of six subscale scores of the *Paired Comparison Temperament Schedule,* an earlier edition of the *Temperament Comparator,* were found to range, for six different occupational groups, from −.30 to .52. Two of these 42 correlations are identified as being "of interest" but the reason given for this belief is vague and unconvincing.

The second "approach to validity" consisted of comparing the mean scores of groups of industrial personnel at different skill levels. Some of the comparisons indicated significant differences; others did not. Since these results are presented under the heading of "validity," the author presumably believes they have some relevance for that topic but does not say what it might be.

In summary, this test presumably was designed to measure Thurstone's word fluency factor. No evidence is presented to demonstrate that it does. No evidence is provided to indicate that it is, as the author intended, independent of verbal comprehension and vocabulary factors. Although the test has been used principally with male industrial personnel, nowhere does the manual state for what purpose it has been used or for what purpose it might be used. There is certainly no evidence to indicate it has predictive validity for use in the selection and placement of industrial personnel.

[Other Tests]

For tests not listed above, see the following entries in *Tests in Print:* 918, 922–4, 925, 927–30, 934–5, and 937–8; out of print: 921.

MATHEMATICS

REVIEWS BY *O. F. Anderhalter, Paul Blommers, Henry Chauncey, Stanley Clark, William R. Crawford, Paul L. Dressel, Gerald L. Ericksen, Marvin D. Glock, E. W. Hamilton, Cyril J. Hoyt, Richard T. Johnson, Peter A. Lappan, Jr., Kenneth Lovell, William H. Lucio, Saunders Mac Lane, Kenneth F. McLaughlin, Donald L. Meyer, Arthur Mittman, G. A. V. Morgan, Frances Crook Morrison, Sheldon S. Myers, Stanley Nisbet, Douglas A. Pidgeon, Lynnette B. Plumlee, C. Alan Riedesel, James P. Rizzo, Paul C. Rosenbloom, John Sutherland, Harold C. Trimble, and Willard G. Warrington.*

[563]

★Business Mathematics: Every Pupil Scholarship Test. High school; 1956–63; 1 form ('56, 2 pages); general directions sheet ['63, 2 pages]; no data on reliability; 4¢ per test; 4¢ per key; postage extra; 40(45) minutes; Bureau of Educational Measurements. *

[564]

***California Mathematics Test: 1957 Edition With 1963 Norms.** Grades 9–14; 1933–63; subtest of *California Achievement Tests;* 3 scores: reasoning, fundamentals, total; IBM and Grade-O-Mat; Forms W ('63, c1957–63, identical with test copyrighted in 1957 except for profile), X ('57), Y ('57), (11 pages); battery manual ('63, 70 pages); battery technical report ('57, 48 pages) on 1957 edition with 1957 norms; battery individual profile ('63, 2 pages); no norms for grades 13–14; $3.15 per 35 tests; separate answer sheets or cards may be used; 5¢ per IBM answer sheet; 9¢ per Scoreze answer sheet; 3¢ per set of Cal-Cards; 4¢ per set of Grade-O-Mat scorable punch-out cards; 20¢ per set of either IBM answer sheet or Cal-Card hand scoring stencils; 60¢ per set of machine scoring stencils; postage extra; $1 per specimen set, postpaid; technical report free; Ernest W. Tiegs and Willis W. Clark; California Test Bureau. *

REFERENCES

1. GUILER, W. S. "Computational Weaknesses of College Freshmen." *J Am Assn Col Reg* 20:367–82 Ap '45. * (*PA* 19:2750)

2. BONNER, LEON WILLIAM. *Factors Associated With the Academic Achievement of Freshmen Students at a Southern Agricultural College.* Doctor's thesis, Pennsylvania State University (State College, Pa.), 1956. (*DA* 17:266)

3. HANEY, RUSSELL; MICHAEL, WILLIAM B.; AND JONES, ROBERT A. "Identification of Aptitude and Achievement Factors in the Prediction of the Success of Nursing Trainees." *Ed & Psychol Meas* 19:645–7 w '59. * (*PA* 34:6164)

4. MICHAEL, WILLIAM B.; JONES, ROBERT A.; AND HANEY, RUSSELL. "The Development and Validation of a Test Battery for Selection of Student Nurses." *Ed & Psychol Meas* 19:641–3 w '59. * (*PA* 34:6171)

5. HANEY, RUSSELL; MICHAEL, WILLIAM B.; JONES, ROBERT A.; AND GADDIS, L. WESLEY. "Cognitive and Non-Cognitive Predictors of Achievement in Student Nursing." *Ed & Psychol Meas* 20:387–9 su '60. * (*PA* 35:7120)

6. MICHAEL, WILLIAM B.; JONES, ROBERT A.; GETTINGER, TED, JR.; HODGES, JOHN D., JR.; KOLESNIK, PETER E.; AND SEPPALA, JAMES. "The Prediction of Success in Selected Courses in a Teacher Training Program From Scores in Achievement Tests and From Ratings on a Scale of Directed Teaching Performance." *Ed & Psychol Meas* 21:995–9 w '61. *

7. CANISIA, M. "Mathematical Ability as Related to Reasoning and Use of Symbols." *Ed & Psychol Meas* 22:105–27 sp '62. * (*PA* 37:1212)

8. HANEY, RUSSELL; MICHAEL, WILLIAM B.; AND GERSHON, ARTHUR. "Achievement, Aptitude, and Personality Measures as Predictors of Success in Nursing Training." *Ed & Psychol Meas* 22:389–92 su '62. * (*PA* 37:3869)

9. MICHAEL, WILLIAM B.; HANEY, RUSSELL; AND GERSHON, ARTHUR. "Intellective and Non-Intellective Predictors of Success in Nursing Training." *Ed & Psychol Meas* 23:817–21 w '63. *

For a review by Robert D. North of this test and the California Arithmetic Test, *see 5:468. For reviews of the complete battery, see 3, 5:2, 4:2, 3:15, 40:1193, and 38:876.*

[565]

★Canadian Achievement Test in Mathematics (CATM). Grade 10; 1961–63; this test and tests 5, 252, 365, and 566 make up the *Canadian Test Battery,* grade 10; IBM; 1 form ('61, 8 pages); 2 editions of manual (for use also with test 566): hand scoring ('63, 6 pages), machine scoring ('63, 7 pages); supplementary data ('63, 6 pages) for the battery; battery profile ('63, 1 page); separate answer sheets or cards must be used; $1.25 per 25 tests; $1 per set of 50 hand scoring answer sheets and hand scoring manual; 20¢ per hand scoring stencil; 20¢ per 15 battery profiles; 50¢ per 25 IBM answer cards (machine scoring through the Department of Educational Research only); 10¢ per machine scoring manual; 50¢ per specimen set; $2.15 per battery specimen set; postage extra; 60(70–75) minutes; Department of Educational Research, Ontario College of Education, University of Toronto; distributed by Guidance Centre (machine scoring manual and answer cards must be purchased from the Department of Educational Research). *

REFERENCES

1. D'OYLEY, VINCENT R. *Technical Manual for the Canadian Tests: Statistical Data on the Carnegie Study Tests of Academic Aptitude and Achievement in Grades 8, 9, and 10 in Ontario Schools and Grades 7 and 8 in Toronto Schools.* Carnegie Study of Identification and Utilization of Talent in High School and College, Bulletin No. 4. Toronto, Canada: Department of Educational Research, Ontario College of Education, University of Toronto, 1964. Pp. viii, 50. *

2. D'OYLEY, VINCENT R. *Testing: The First Two Years of the Carnegie Study 1959 to 1961: Analysis of Scores by Course, Sex, and Size of Municipality.* Carnegie Study of Identification and Utilization of Talent in High School and College, Bulletin No. 6. Toronto, Canada: Department of Educational Research, Ontario College of Education, University of Toronto, 1964. Pp. ix, 53. *

FRANCES CROOK MORRISON, *Associate Professor of Education, State University of New York at Albany, Albany, New York.*

The *Canadian Achievement Test in Mathematics* is one of four tests "developed for use in the second year of the Carnegie Study of Identification and Utilization of Talent in High School and College, a longitudinal study of approximately 90,000 Grade 9 students enrolled in Ontario schools in September, 1959." The test consists of 30 items and is divided into three sections, labeled Algebra (15 items), Geometry (12 items), and Mensuration (3 items), but the parts are not separately timed and no part scores are obtained.

The 15 items in the algebra section include two verbal problems; in one case the potentially confusing suggestion is given that the variable in the equation should be the number of dollars in the *first* payment of an installment loan, when the problem is to find the amount of the *last* payment. The remaining items in this section require routine algebraic manipulation within a rather limited range of difficulty; the only item related to the solution of an equation, for example, asks for the result of multiplying both sides of the following equation by 12:

$$\frac{x+1}{3}+2=\frac{4x-2}{4}-\frac{x-3}{2}$$

The five alternative answers given in the item just mentioned can easily be reduced to two or even one by rapid inspection; there is only one option in which the last term on the left side is +24 and the last term on the right is +18. In this and in many other items it was difficult to provide five reasonable alternatives; consequently, some of the options appear unlikely to be effective distractors.

There seems to be no good reason for providing a separate title for the last three items since all of them require the computation of the area of a plane figure and could properly have been included with the geometry items. The 12 items in the geometry section include questions involving numerical computation and statements concerning geometrical relationships, based mainly on the properties of a triangle or of congruent triangles.

This test shows no evidence of the influence of current activity in high school mathematics and of the work of such groups as the School Mathematics Study Group or the more recently formed Ontario Mathematics Commission. Even as a test to be used at the end of a very traditional mathematics course in the second year of high school, the CATM appears to have limited content validity; it may be compared unfavorably with the *Cooperative Mathematics Tests for Grades 7, 8, and 9* or with several of the mathematics tests in the Evaluation and Adjustment Series.

The manual for the CATM, as for the test prepared for the same study at the grade 9 level, is most inadequate except as a means of describing standardized conditions for administering the test. Part 2 of the manual, entitled Interpretation of Results, consists of a single sheet printed on two sides; one side contains a table of percentile norms and the other mainly a description of the norm groups for both the test under review and two other forms prepared for technical and commercial students.

This test, like the others in the battery, is said to be a Canadian achievement test, but there is no indication of its relevance to the mathematics curriculum in the second year of high schools in Ontario or elsewhere in Canada. There is also no discussion in the manual of the problems involved in interpreting profiles prepared on the chart provided; in fact, for a class or for individuals the manual introduces an additional difficulty by referring to comparisons among the six tests in the *Canadian Test Battery* for grade 10 when three of these tests are the various forms of the mathematics achievement test and so would not all be taken by any one student.

It is unfortunate that a test labeled "Canadian" reflects such a limited point of view concerning the high school mathematics curriculum and also such inadequate technical qualities in test construction. There are certainly systems in Canada where mathematics is better taught and tests are better constructed than this sample would indicate. However, those in Ontario and elsewhere who wish to compare their pupils with those in that province with respect to their achievement on a rather limited test may find the *Canadian Achievement Test in Mathematics* of some value.

[566]

★Canadian Achievement Test in Technical and Commercial Mathematics (CATTCM). Grade 10; 1961–63; this test and tests 5, 252, 365, and 565 make up the *Canadian Test Battery*, grade 10; IBM; Forms C ('61, commercial), T ('61, technical), (6 pages, both forms printed in same booklet); 2 editions of manual (for use also with test 565): hand scoring ('63, 6 pages), machine scoring ('63, 7 pages); supplementary data ('63, 6 pages) for the battery; battery profile ('63, 1 page); separate answer sheets or cards must be used; $1.25 per 25 tests; $1 per set of 50 hand scoring answer sheets and hand scoring manual; 20¢ per hand scoring stencil; 20¢ per 15 battery profiles; 50¢ per 25 IBM answer cards (machine scoring through the Department of Educational Research only); 10¢ per machine scoring manual; 50¢ per specimen set; $2.15 per battery specimen set; postage extra; 60(70–75) minutes; Department of Educational Research, Ontario College of Education, University of Toronto; distributed by Guidance Centre (machine scoring manual and answer cards must be purchased from the Department of Educational Research). *

REFERENCES

1. D'OYLEY, VINCENT R. *Technical Manual for the Canadian Tests: Statistical Data on the Carnegie Study Tests of Academic Aptitude and Achievement in Grades 8, 9, and 10 in Ontario Schools and Grades 7 and 8 in Toronto Schools.* Carnegie Study of Identification and Utilization of Talent in High School and College, Bulletin No. 4. Toronto, Canada: Department of Educational Research, Ontario College of Education, University of Toronto, 1964. Pp. viii, 50. *

2. D'OYLEY, VINCENT R. *Testing: The First Two Years of the Carnegie Study 1959 to 1961: Analysis of Scores by Course, Sex, and Size of Municipality.* Carnegie Study of Identification and Utilization of Talent in High School and College, Bulletin No. 6. Toronto, Canada: Department of Educational Research, Ontario College of Education, University of Toronto, 1964. Pp. ix, 53. *

STANLEY CLARK, *Professor of Education, University of Saskatchewan, Saskatoon, Saskatchewan, Canada.*

The *Canadian Achievement Test in Technical and Commercial Mathematics* (CATTCM) was constructed in Ontario, Canada, as a research instrument for use in the Carnegie Study of Identification and Utilization of Talent in High School and College. The research group from the Department of Educational Research at the Ontario College of Education employed the two "forms" (Form C, Commercial, and Form T, Technical) in the second year of the study to survey the extent to which mathematical skills had been developed by students in the commercial or the technical course.

The test booklets have not been appropriately modified for more extensive use. Form C and Form T are printed on opposite pages of the same folder. The general directions in the booklet make reference to the machine scored answer cards and the examiner has to make suitable changes when administering the hand scored edition. Separate booklets are to be made available when the tests are reprinted. Each form contains 30 multiple choice items, 16 of which are common to the two tests. The items are well selected in that each requires a different principle for its solution. Interested examiners must decide for themselves whether these items provide the sampling they look for in a survey test. Anyone satisfied with the coverage afforded might consider reducing the time limits and establishing local norms.

The manuals for the hand scored and machine scored editions contain the instructions for administering and scoring the tests and for interpreting the results. They contain no information about the selection of the test items, content and concurrent validity, and test reliability.

Additional information has been supplied by the Department of Educational Research. (*a*) The order of items in each form was based upon an item analysis made during the trial runs preceding the construction of the CATTCM. (*b*) Validity studies of the two forms have been completed. Correlations of Form C results with the criteria, grade 10 mathematics marks and grade 10 averages, are .55 and .39, respectively. Correlations of Form T scores with similar criteria are .48 and .38, respectively. Whether these coefficients are to be regarded as evidence of concurrent or of predictive validity is not clear. (*c*) Corrected split-halves (odd-even) reliability coefficients have been obtained from samples of 200 commercial course students and 200 technical course students. These are .80 for Form C and .76 for Form T. Such moderately-sized coefficients possibly reflect the relatively short lengths of the two forms.

Directions for scoring are simple and clear; hand scoring of the answer sheets is facilitated by the transparent keys provided. The percentile rank norms are based upon the performance in May 1961 of grade 10 students enrolled in commercial and technical courses in the Ontario secondary schools. The comparability on relevant variables of these students with grade 10 students in general is not discussed.

In summary, these tests are primarily research tools constructed for use at a particular time in the school careers of grade 10 students taking the commercial or technical option in the schools of Ontario. Their usefulness in this role can be assessed only by the research group participating in the Carnegie Study. Conceivably, teachers of the specified mathematics courses in the province might include these tests in their evaluation programs. This is a possible reason for the otherwise rather premature appearance of the CATTCM as a commercially obtainable test. Examiners elsewhere should have access to more detailed information in order to come to some decision about the adequacy of the test.

[567]

★Canadian Mathematics Achievement Test (CMAT). Grades 8.5–9.0; 1959–63; this test and tests 253 and 445 make up the *Canadian Test Battery,* grades 8–9; 3 scores: arithmetic computation, facts-terms-concepts, measurement; IBM; 1 form; separate parts 1 ('62, arithmetic computation), 2 ('59, facts-terms-concepts), 3 ('59, measurement), (4 pages); 2 editions of battery manual: hand scoring ('63, 11 pages), machine scoring ('63, 13 pages); supplementary data ('63, 6 pages) for the battery; battery profile ('63, 2 pages); separate answer sheets or cards must be used; $1.25 per 25 tests of any one part; $1 per set of 50 hand scoring answer sheets and hand scoring manual; 20¢ per hand scoring stencil; 20¢ per 15 battery profiles; 50¢ per 25 IBM answer cards (machine scoring through the Department of Educational Research only); 10¢ per machine scoring manual; 50¢ per specimen set; $2.75 per battery specimen set; postage extra; 30(40–45) minutes per part; Department of Educational Research, Ontario College of Education, University of Toronto; distributed by Guidance Centre (machine scoring manual and answer cards must be purchased from the Department of Educational Research). *

REFERENCES

1. D'Oyley, Vincent R. *Technical Manual for the Canadian Tests: Statistical Data on the Carnegie Study Tests of Academic Aptitude and Achievement in Grades 8, 9, and 10 in Ontario Schools and Grades 7 and 8 in Toronto Schools.* Carnegie Study of Identification and Utilization of Talent in High School and College, Bulletin No. 4. Toronto, Canada: Department of Educational Research, Ontario College of Education, University of Toronto, 1964. Pp. viii, 50. *
2. D'Oyley, Vincent R. *Testing: The First Two Years of the Carnegie Study 1959 to 1961: Analysis of Scores by Course, Sex, and Size of Municipality.* Carnegie Study of Identification and Utilization of Talent in High School and College, Bulletin No. 6. Toronto, Canada: Department of Educational Research, Ontario College of Education, University of Toronto, 1964. Pp. ix, 53. *

Stanley Clark, *Professor of Education, University of Saskatchewan, Saskatoon, Saskatchewan, Canada.*

In the fall of 1959, the Department of Educational Research at the Ontario College of Education entered the first stage of a longitudinal study of over 85,000 grade 9 students in the schools of the province. The three parts of the CMAT were designed to provide measures of initial status in mathematics achievement.

The manuals for the hand scored and machine scored editions comprise Part 1, Directions for Administration, and Part 2, Interpretation of Results. The same manual is used with all three parts or subtests of the CMAT. Directions specific to the administration of each subtest are printed on the relevant test folder. Since the test booklets are intended for use with answer cards, the examiner has to make suitable changes in the wording when administering the hand scored edition. Although expected information about the construction, validity, and reliability of the CMAT has not been included in the manual, the Department of Educational Research has made available the following additional details: (*a*) The order of the items in each part was based upon the results from the preliminary trials of the CMAT. (*b*) A validity study employing a random sample of 1,000 grade 9 students has been completed; whether this was a new sample or a subsample of the 1959 grade 9 population was not stated. Part of the study involved finding the correlations between the scores from the CMAT and two criterion measures, grade 9 mathematics marks and grade 9 averages. For Part 1, the correlations with the criteria are .48 and .46, respectively; for Part 2, they are .49 and .52; for Part 3, they are .50 and .47. These figures are in line with those commonly encountered in studies of predictive validity under similar conditions. (*c*) The intercorrelations between the parts of the CMAT, based upon the same sample, are .41 between Parts 1 and 2, .48 between Parts 1 and 3, and .65 between Parts 2 and 3. The three subtests appear to be measuring to a considerable degree different aspects of mathematical ability. (*d*) Split-half reliability coefficients are .83, .72, and .88 for Parts 1, 2, and 3, respectively, for a sample of 200 grade 8 students. For a sample of like size in grade 9, the corresponding coefficients are .84, .82, and .90.

Different answer sheets or answer cards must be used with each of the three parts. Users of the machine scored edition should obtain the Information Sheet on Test Scoring and Item Analysis Service from the Department of Educational Research.

The test booklets have excellent format. All the items are of the multiple choice type. Part 1, Arithmetic Computation, contains 26 items arranged in blocks according to the operation to be performed. Part 2, Facts, Terms, and Concepts, provides a well selected sample of 40 items designed to test the student's knowledge and understanding. Part 3, Measurement, contains 16 items involving fundamental operations with denominate numbers and 9 short problems. The usefulness of the CMAT will be restricted by the fact that some important topics (e.g., percentage) receive scant treatment.

Percentile rank norms have been provided for the three parts of the CMAT. There is no provision for a composite score in mathematics achievement. Grade 9 norms, based upon the performance of the entire student body participating in the Carnegie Study, were obtained in November 1959. The authors have supplied grade 8 norms also. These resulted from the administration of the CMAT to a representative sample of about 6,500 students in May 1962. Although the latter were superior to the grade 9 students in all the subtests, no explanation is suggested in the manual.

Officials of the Department of Educational Research consider that the *Canadian Mathematics Achievement Test* is still in the experimental stage. After sufficient information has been gathered from the Carnegie Study, examiners might well expect that a revised and more complete manual will be published in order that the technical adequacy of the CMAT might be compared with that of any competing test.

Frances Crook Morrison, *Associate Professor of Education, State University of New York at Albany, Albany, New York.*

This set of three tests is among those developed for use in the Carnegie Study of Identification and Utilization of Talent in High School and College, a longitudinal study of students enrolled in Ontario schools in the fall of 1959.

In Part 1, Arithmetic Computation, 22 out of 26 items involve the four fundamental operations and 10 of these require computation with whole numbers; the remaining four items consist of two requiring conversion of a decimal or common fraction to a per cent and two in which the pupil is to find a per cent of a number, such as 8 per cent of 400. The test is thus severely limited in content, and the norms indicate that the range of difficulty is also limited, since the top quarter of the group had fewer than three errors. The multiple choice form with five options is used, and the distractors sometimes appear to be rather carelessly prepared. "None of these" is used only five times and is the correct choice once, although it could have been used to advantage more frequently. In many of the items it was difficult to find enough reasonable alternative answers, so that some of the distractors probably are not functioning.

In the second test, Facts, Terms, and Concepts, nearly half of the 40 multiple choice items are vocabulary items, while the others involve such problems as interpreting formulas, comparing areas, and stating processes to be used in a given situation. This test, as might be expected, provided a greater range of difficulty than did the first test, the median score being 25 and the upper quartile point about 29.

Part 3, Measurement, contains 25 items; 16 of these involve the four fundamental operations with denominate numbers and the remaining 9 are problems about perimeter, area, volume, and relationships between units of measurement. One of the latter group is such an extraordinarily unrealistic problem involving wallpapering that it deserves to be quoted: "A roll of wallpaper contains 9 sq. yd. How many rolls will be needed to paper one wall of a room which is 27 ft. long and 9 ft. high?" In this "measurement" test there are no items dealing with such matters as rounding, significant figures, and computation with approximate numbers, but it is possible that the emphasis on routine computation with denominate numbers and the omission of such concepts as those mentioned reflects correctly the curricular emphasis in Ontario elementary schools.

The CMAT is accompanied by a very brief manual in two parts. In the first part the Carnegie study is described as "a longitudinal study of approximately 90,000 Grade 9 students enrolled in Ontario schools in September, 1959," while in Part 2 it is stated that the ninth grade norms are based on the total population of about 85,000 students who were enrolled in that grade in October and November of 1959 and who also participated in the opening year of the Carnegie study. The slight discrepancies in dates and numbers in the two parts of the manual are indicative of what may have been hasty preparation of a test for a specific purpose and what certainly is undue haste in presenting the test for general use.

The test manual contains only directions for administering the test, a brief statement concerning the population on which the norms are based, and percentile norms for the end of grade 8 and the beginning of grade 9. A profile chart for the nine tests in the *Canadian Test Battery* is also available, but there is no discussion in the manual of the problems of interpreting profiles. No data concerning validity and reliability are given.[1]

These mathematics achievement tests are labeled "Canadian," but no evidence is given of their relevance to the elementary mathematics curriculum of Canadian schools generally or, indeed, to the Ontario curriculum on which they could more reasonably be supposed to be based. In fact, it seems hard to believe that the tests have adequate content validity for use even in Ontario schools. The overemphasis on routine computation and on computation with denominate numbers has already been mentioned; there is also very little evidence of an attempt to measure the ability to apply computational skills or to understand mathematical principles. The inadequacy of the manual further limits the usefulness of the test. It is likely that the tests were of some value for their original purpose, but it is to be hoped that those who need a valid instrument for measuring general mathematical achievement at the beginning of high school will look elsewhere.

[568]

***College Entrance Examination Board Achievement Test: Advanced Mathematics.** Candidates for college entrance; 1901–64; for more complete information, see 760; 60(80) minutes; program administered for the College Entrance Examination Board by Educational Testing Service. *

REFERENCES

1–4. See 4:367.
5–7. See 5:417.
8. BLACK, D. B. "A Comparison of the Performance on Selected Standardized Tests to That on the Alberta Grade XII Departmental Examination of a Select Group of University of Alberta Freshmen." *Alberta J Ed Res* 5:180–90 S '59. * (*PA* 34:6559)
9. GILBERT, ARTHUR C. F. "The Efficiency of Certain Variables in Predicting Survival in an Engineering School." *Psychol Newsl* 10:311–3 My–Je '59. * (*PA* 34:1992)
10. BLACK, DONALD B. "The Prediction of Freshman Success in the University of Alberta From Grade XII Departmental Results." *Alberta J Ed Res* 6:38–53 Mr '60. *

SAUNDERS MAC LANE, *Max Mason Distinguished Service Professor of Mathematics, The University of Chicago, Chicago, Illinois.* [Review of Forms FAC, KAC, and LAC.]

The advanced mathematics achievement test presents 50 five-response exercises to be done in one hour. Most of these exercises are excellently chosen: they are brief, not hackneyed but imaginative, and often test for ingenuity or ability to combine different techniques. They are well arranged in increasing order of difficulty and end with admirably sharp and hard questions. A number of exercises require that the student consult the listed responses *before* answering; frequently this could have been avoided by providing a more detailed statement of the exercise in the item stem. In the total of 150 exercises on the three forms examined I noticed only one silly one (the examiners tried to combine algebraic manipulations with "rectangular solids") and two with ambiguous answers—one a play with matchsticks, another dealing with the "total" surface area of a hemisphere. In each of these two cases, an ingenious student might be led astray. In all other cases, the answers are clear.

The traditional subjects of algebra, geometry, and trigonometry are well represented. In each of these areas the test (as it must) shows a preference of topics—expressed by way of both the numbers and the interest of the exercises. In algebra, quadratic equations are imaginatively treated, as are inequalities and absolute values (a "modern" topic); for logarithms only the basic definition is tested, and every exercise on complex numbers is dull. In geometry, there are some wonderfully fresh questions touching on spatial perception and on the use of mensuration formulas, while analytic geometry gets a full but less stimulating treatment. The definition and behavior of the basic trigonometric functions are examined thoroughly and very well, though the examiners might have managed without the frequent use of the unimportant functions secant and cosecant. By general agreement, the solution of triangles by logarithms is not tested; these tests push the agreement further to minimize the use of the law of sines and the law of cosines.

Current rapid changes in the mathematics curriculum make the construction of such a uniform test very difficult. The CEEB had an important hand in starting the current reform in mathematical education, with its Commission on Mathematics (1955–1958). The Commission's report, as is appropriate, was cautiously progressive (and influential); subsequent reform groups, as is also appropriate, have been vigorously progressive. These tests treat "modern mathematics" in the cautiously progressive style. Set theory and logic are barely represented; there are a few dull exercises on limits and on the function concept, plus a couple of utterly insignificant questions on "modern algebra." It would have been hard to do much better; for new topics, variously treated in the schools, a uniform examination

1 This review was completed before the supplementary data referred to in the entry above became available.—Editor.

could hardly display the imaginative flexibility displayed on often-tested older topics. But note that the Board gives just *one* advanced test in mathematics. The schools (according to the Board's own data) give a wide variety of new senior year courses. At present the Board reassures the student ("obviously, no one is likely to know the answers to all the questions on a test. However, if you are able to think correctly with what you have been taught, you can expect to make a respectable score on the tests for which you have prepared"). A better reassurance to students taking the advanced mathematics test might be a distinctly labeled choice: Answer these questions if you have studied college algebra, these if you have studied calculus, these if you have studied statistical inference. This would also make for better questions on such topics.

Nowhere in the test is there any evidence that the formulas of algebra or trigonometry can be used in other sciences. Perhaps this point is covered in achievement tests in these sciences. However, the 1962 edition of the Board's pamphlet, *A Description of the College Board Achievement Tests* lists 79 sample questions in the sciences. Included are several on a biological growth curve. The "correct" answer to question 53 involves an incorrect use of the phrase "multiplying geometrically"; the "correct" answer to question 56 is a nearly meaningless comment on asymmetry.

Some topics just don't appear. In the 150 questions making up these three forms there is just one "word problem" in algebra. There is no test of interpolation in tables of functions, nor is there any hint that logarithms can be used for calculation. Some "modern" ideas are similarly absent—for example, the number system and the notion that mathematics contains axioms, theorems, and proofs (even Euclid did!). The Board knows better. In the pamphlet quoted above it appears that college preparatory mathematics is seen as including "Emphasis....upon the principles of deductive reasoning." In the same place, statistical inference is mentioned. Statistical inference does not appear in the tests—there are just a few semistandard questions on elementary probability.

Why the omissions? One can only guess. These topics would be exceedingly difficult to test in interesting and brief five-response exercises. This standard test pattern may well tend to select the topics tested. Given the current pressure for college admission, this selection could presently substantially influence the topics taught. Before this happens, the five-response pattern should be varied to fit the subject matter.

For a review by Paul L. Dressel of earlier forms, see 4:367. For reviews of the testing program, see 760.

[569]

***College Entrance Examination Board Achievement Test: Intermediate Mathematics.** Candidates for college entrance; 1901–64; for more complete information, see 760; 60(80) minutes; program administered for the College Entrance Examination Board by Educational Testing Service. *

REFERENCES

1–2. See 4:368.
3–5. See 5:418.
6. Black, D. B. "A Comparison of the Performance on Selected Standardized Tests to That on the Alberta Grade XII Departmental Examination of a Select Group of University of Alberta Freshmen." *Alberta J Ed Res* 5:180–90 S '59. * (*PA* 34:6559)

Paul L. Dressel, *Director of Institutional Research, Michigan State University, East Lansing, Michigan.* [Review of Forms KAC and LAC1.]

The review of a test must take into account not only the test content, statistics, and adequacy of instructions and suggestions for administration and interpretation, but also the appropriateness of the test to the prevalent curriculum and instructional practice. In appraising the appropriateness of a secondary school mathematics test, confusion reigns, partly due to the emerging new curricula, partly due to the great range of courses offered in various schools, and partly due to the increasing tendency for students to take College Board examinations earlier. Thus it appears that the use of two mathematics tests in the CEEB Admissions Testing Program, the intermediate test here to be reviewed and an advanced test, can no longer fully recognize differing kinds and amounts of preparation in mathematics. Furthermore, the student is faced with a difficult choice as to which test to take. Materials supplied by the Educational Testing Service to aid in this review indicate that there will shortly be a return to a composite test more inclusive than the current intermediate test and less specialized than the current advanced test. Thus this review of the intermediate test may have only historical interest.

The College Board, through its Commission on Mathematics, has had marked influence on trends in the mathematics curriculum. The Committee of Examiners in Mathematics is thoroughly versed in these trends and desirous of abetting them, but recognizes also that its test cannot be used to force abrupt shifts in the curriculum or risk unfairness to students in those curricula which still reflect traditional approaches. Review of Forms KAC and LAC1 of the intermediate test suggests that the committee has found a reasonable compromise.

The tests include a few items involving such unifying ideas as the concept of sets, the structure of the number system, inequalities, coordinate geometry, and logic. Yet the items used are so constructed that the alert student who really *understands* whatever he has learned should be able to reason his way through to the correct answer. Indeed, considerable ingenuity has been exercised in building items which test insight and understanding rather than rote recall or routine problem solving skills. Calculation is minimized by choice of the numbers used in problems and frequently can be even further simplified by insightful application of algebraic or geometric principles.

Although statistical analysis of the most recent form reviewed (Form LAC1) was not yet available, an impressive array of data are available on past forms and the systematic procedures in use insure no worse results in newer ones. Reliability is of the order .85 to .90. A variety of correlations with first term college grades yield a range from .48 to .59. In a program of the scope of CEEB, scaling is a major concern, but long experience and continuing research appear to have yielded adequate procedures to insure comparability of scaled scores from one form to another.

Because of the necessarily restricted nature of the CEEB examinations, users are not able to check test content nor can they have access to current data on tests when new forms are continually being prepared. Users may be confident, however, that the tests are prepared with the strictest quality control measures to a carefully stated set of specifications and—what may be even more important in the current period—with full awareness of the rapidly changing nature of the mathematics curriculum.

For a review by Paul J. Blommers of earlier forms, see 4:368. For reviews of the testing program, see 760.

[570]

***College Entrance Examination Board Advanced Placement Examination: Mathematics.** High school students desiring credit for college level courses or admission to advanced courses; 1954–63; for more complete information, see 761; 180(200) minutes; program administered for the College Entrance Examination Board by Educational Testing Service. *

REFERENCES

1. DOUGLAS, EDWIN C. "The College Entrance Examination Board's Examination for Advanced Placement in Mathematics." *Math Teach* 50:458–61 O '57. *

2. VALLEY, JOHN R. "A Report on CEEB Advanced Placement Mathematics and Natural Sciences Examinations Candidates, May 1958." *Sci Teach* 26:399–402 O '59. *

3. GILBERT, ARTHUR C. F. "Predicting Graduation From an Engineering School." *J Psychol Studies* 11:229–31 Jl–Ag '60. * (*PA* 35:7045)

4. GROSSMAN, GEORGE. "Advanced Placement Mathematics—For Whom?" *Math Teach* 40:560–6 N '62. *

For a review by Paul L. Dressel of an earlier form, see 5:419.

[571]

★College Entrance Examination Board Placement Tests: Advanced Mathematics Test. Entering college freshmen; 1962–63, c1957–63; test is a reprint of an inactive form of *College Entrance Examination Board Achievement Test: Advanced Mathematics;* IBM; Form KPL1 (c1957, 10 pages); for more complete information, see 759; 60(70) minutes; program administered for the College Entrance Examination Board by Educational Testing Service. *

For reviews of the College Entrance Examination Board Achievement Test: Advanced Mathematics, *see 568 and 4:367.*

[572]

★College Entrance Examination Board Placement Tests: Intermediate Mathematics Test. Entering college freshmen; 1962–63, c1956–63; tests are reprints of inactive forms of *College Entrance Examination Board Achievement Test: Intermediate Mathematics;* IBM; Forms KPL1, KPL2 in a single booklet (c1956–57, 20 pages); for more complete information, see 759; 60(70) minutes; program administered for the College Entrance Examination Board by Educational Testing Service. *

For reviews of the College Entrance Examination Board Achievement Test: Intermediate Mathematics, *see 569 and 4:368.*

[573]

Cooperative General Achievement Tests: Test 3, Mathematics. Grades 9–12 and college entrants; 1937–56; formerly called *A Test of General Proficiency in the Field of Mathematics;* IBM; Forms XX ('53, c1947–53, 8 pages, revision of Form X), YZ ('55, c1948–51, 10 pages, revision of Forms Y and Z, identical with test copyrighted in 1951); battery manual ('56, 16 pages); high school norms same as those published in 1938; separate answer sheets must be used; $4 per 25 tests; $1 per 25 IBM answer sheets;

25¢ per scoring stencil; postage extra; 50¢ per specimen set, cash orders postpaid; 40(50) minutes; Paul J. Burke (XX) and [Bernice Orshansky]; Cooperative Test Division. *

REFERENCES

1. DeGooyer, Melvin Henry. *Validation of the Cooperative General Achievement Test in Mathematics at the University of Utah.* Master's thesis, University of Utah (Salt Lake City, Utah), 1948.
2. Bromley, Ann, and Carter, Gerald C. "Predictability of Success in Mathematics." *J Ed Res* 44:148–50 O '50. * (*PA* 25:5630)
3. Jones, Reginald L., and Siegel, Laurence. "The Individual High School as a Predictor of College Academic Performance." *Ed & Psychol Meas* 22:785–9 w '62. * (*PA* 37:7189)
4. Taulbee, George C., Sr. *Construction and Validation of a Scale for Predicting Graduation From a College of Optometry.* Doctor's thesis, University of Houston (Houston, Tex.), 1963. (*DA* 24:387)

For a review by John F. Randolph of earlier forms, see 3:316. For reviews of the complete battery, see 7, 5:6, 4:5, and 3:3.

[574]

★ERB Mathematics Tests, Experimental Form. High school; 1961–62; IBM; 4 tests; directions ['61, 1 page]; tentative norms ('62, 1 page, for independent school students); no data on reliability; separate answer sheets must be used; 10¢ per test; 4¢ per IBM answer sheet; 25¢ per scoring stencil; postage extra; 40(45) minutes; Subcommittee on Mathematics Tests of the Educational Records Bureau; Educational Records Bureau. *

a) TEST 1: ANALYTICAL GEOMETRY TEST. Grade 12; 1 form ('61, 5 pages).
b) TEST 2: SETS, EQUATIONS, INEQUALITIES, AND NUMBER CONCEPTS. Grades 9–12; 1 form ('61, 5 pages).
c) TEST 3: PROBABILITY AND STATISTICS. Grade 12; 1 form ('61, 6 pages).
d) TEST 4: INTRODUCTORY CALCULUS. Grade 12; 1 form ('61, 5 pages).

REFERENCES

1. North, Robert D. "Some Notes on the New ERB Mathematics Tests." *Ed Rec B* 79:57–61 Jl '61. *
2. North, Robert D. "Results of the ERB Mathematics Tests in the 1962 Spring Program." *Ed Rec B* 82:57–60 Jl '62. * (*PA* 37:5666)

[575]

***General Mathematics: Every Pupil Scholarship Test.** High school; 1926–64; new form (2 pages) usually issued each January and April; forms from previous testing programs also available; general directions sheet ['63, 2 pages]; no data on reliability; norms for new forms available following testing program; 4¢ per test; 4¢ per key; postage extra; 40(45) minutes; Bureau of Educational Measurements. *

[576]

★General Mathematics: Every Pupil Test. Grades 9–10; 1963-64; new form (4 pages) usually issued each December and April; 3 scores: computations and concepts, problems, total; general directions sheet (2 pages); no data on reliability; Ohio norms for new forms available following testing program; 5¢ per test, postpaid; 40(45) minutes; Ohio Scholarship Tests. *

[577]

***General Mathematics: Minnesota High School Achievement Examinations.** Grade 9; 1955–63; series formerly called *Midwest High School Achievement Examinations;* new form issued each May; norms available in June following release of new form; Form F ('63, 4 pages) used in 1963 testing; no specific manual; series manual ('63, 4 pages); series norms ['63, 4 pages]; series cumulative profile ('62, 2 pages); no data on reliability; no description of normative population; 12¢ per test; $2.50 per 100 profiles; postage extra; 20¢ per specimen set, postpaid; 60(65) minutes; American Guidance Service, Inc. *

Gerald L. Ericksen, *Assistant Professor of Psychology, St. Olaf College, Northfield, Minnesota.*

The 1963 general mathematics test of the Minnesota High School Achievement Examinations consists of seven problem units: "fundamental processes, numeration, everyday living, measurements and formulas, graphs, rate-ratio-proportion, miscellaneous and algebra." Beyond this information, the potential user is provided with little or no data upon which to base any serious consideration of the test.

A four-page brochure, labeled "Manual," accompanies the test. It consists of broad generalizations concerning the entire range of school subjects but contains no specific information about the general mathematics test. Such statements as "Extreme care and considerable time went into the selection of the present authors" and "this battery of tests is designed primarily for the improvement of instruction" tell nothing about the specific manner of test development. In addition, the implication that the test may also serve as an interest inventory is a misleading simplification of the relationship between student interest and mathematical achievement. In the reviewer's opinion, the sales style of the brochure leaves the test user with essentially no manual of information.

It is relatively easy to construct a general mathematics test with some degree of face validity. While the 65 items of the seven units of this test do include many topics commonly taught in a general mathematics course, there are noticeable omissions. The various number systems, problems of rounding and significance, practical interest formulas, angular relationships, and statistical measures are areas not covered by the test.

The only indication of any item analysis is given in the brochure as follows:

> The authors of many of the tests gave the entire test of selected items experimentally to students locally in order to include only those items in the final edition which seemed to carry a high degree of validity. The editors further eliminated no fewer than 10 per cent of the questions on the basis that these did not carry as high validity as desirable.

Such careless reporting is typical of the statistical development of the test. The practice of keeping normative data up to date and revising items in accordance with curriculum changes is obviously desirable. The development of an adequate examination, however, requires careful statistical analysis rather than the mere formation of a new item pool year after year. The user of this test will be at a complete loss when attempting to find such basic information as the nature of the normative group and evidence of internal consistency or any form of external validity. The editors even go as far as to recommend examination of the local curriculum should a particular school vary greatly from this unknown normative group.

Administration and scoring are straightforward, although the test time could easily have been reduced to a single class period. The median of the normative data is only 5 raw score points above a chance score, yet no consideration is given to a correction for guessing. Moreover, it would be desirable to have a greater score variability than is indicated by the narrow range of the norms.

In summary, it is unfortunate that the same defects present in the Midwest High School Achievement Examinations have been perpetuated under a new name. The shift from "Midwest" to "Minnesota" in the title in no way makes the tests more appropriate for Minnesota educators. In light of the many test defects and availability of other achievement examinations, such as the *Sequential Tests of Educational Progress* and the *Cooperative Mathematics Tests for Grades 7, 8, and 9,* it is the reviewer's recommendation that the general mathematics teacher look elsewhere for a good standardized achievement test.

[578]

***The Graduate Record Examinations Advanced Tests: Mathematics.** Grades 16–17; 1939–64; for more complete information, see 762; 180(200) minutes; Educational Testing Service. *

PAUL C. ROSENBLOOM, *Professor of Mathematics, Institute of Technology, and Director, Minnesota School Mathematics and Science Center, University of Minnesota, Minneapolis, Minnesota.* [Review of Forms FGR, K-JGR2, and MGR.]

Each of these tests consists of 75 multiple choice items. They are, in general, well constructed. The committees in charge of constructing the tests consist of outstanding mathematicians, assisted by very competent personnel from Educational Testing Service.

The changes in test content over the seven year period (1957–64) represented by these forms reflect the influence of the Committee on the Undergraduate Program in Mathematics of the Mathematical Association of America, in which several members of the mathematics test committee are active. The latest form is a compromise between what colleges are actually teaching and the recommendations of CUPM.

Content coverage is indicated by the following table showing the number of items on each of these forms dealing with each of the topics listed.

Table 1
Number of Items Devoted to Various Content Areas on Three Forms of GRE Mathematics

Content Area	Form FGR	Form K-JGR2	Form MGR
College algebra	11	5	5
Elementary calculus [1]	40	37	28
Analytic geometry	8	7	6
Intermediate calculus	3	2	0
Differential equations	3	2	4
Advanced calculus	3	5	9
Probability and statistics	2	2	5
Modern algebra	4	6	10
Complex variables	1	2	1
Number theory	0	2	2
Set theory	0	2	2
Elementary topology	0	3	3

1 By elementary calculus is meant what is covered in a good elementary text such as that by Thomas; by intermediate calculus is meant topics which may be covered in either an elementary or an advanced calculus course.

All the items on set theory and all but one on probability and statistics are on topics covered in a conservative college algebra text published in 1959. The total numbers of items on each form which deal with topics usually taught to freshmen and sophomores are 62, 51, and 43, respectively; this is a very significant sign of progress. Most of the items on modern algebra and topology test for understanding of definitions of concepts, i.e., they test mathematical literacy. The most obvious gap in coverage is geometry at the junior-senior level. This is surprising since the committee includes an outstanding geometer.

I found six defective items on Form FGR, and two on each of the other forms, which may represent progress. One item on Form FGR is incorrect. A few are ambiguous in wording. The answer to one item on K-JGR2 depends on which concept of integral is meant, and a good student may easily be penalized.

These tests do a good job of testing information, routine skills, and understanding of concepts in the subjects covered. For prediction of success in graduate school one would want also to test imagination and creativity. I was able to identify only about a half dozen items of this type on the latest form (MGR).

The technical aspects of the GRE tests were discussed in detail by Gardner and Seashore in *The Fifth Mental Measurements Yearbook* (see 5:427 and 5:601). The interpretive materials routinely distributed with the test provide no information on the subsequent performance in graduate school of students who took the advanced test in mathematics prior to admission. Some data on the predictive validity of various tests in the program are available in the form of special reports which must be requested separately, but the predictive value of the current forms of the mathematics test is unknown. Since the tests are widely used for admission to graduate school and for awarding fellowships, research of this nature should be undertaken and the results incorporated in the interpretive materials.

For a review by Eric F. Gardner of an earlier form, see 5:427. For a review of the testing program, see 5:601.

[579]

***The Iowa Tests of Educational Development: Test 4, Ability to Do Quantitative Thinking.** Grades 9–12; 1942–61; IBM; Forms X-3S, Y-3S, ('52, 7 pages); battery examiner's manual ('58, c1949–57, 23 pages); battery general manual ('59, 37 pages); student profile leaflet, sixth edition ('61, c1958, 2 pages); see the complete battery entry (14*b*) for other accessories; no data on reliability; separate answer sheets must be used; $2.40 per 20 tests; $5 per 100 IBM answer sheets; 50¢ per scoring stencil; $3 per specimen set of the complete battery; postage extra; 65(75) minutes for full length version, 40(50) minutes for class period version; prepared under the direction of E. F. Lindquist; Science Research Associates, Inc. *

PETER A. LAPPAN, JR., *Assistant Professor of Mathematics, Lehigh University, Bethlehem, Pennsylvania.*

The title and purposes of this test require a bit of explanation. According to the information given students, "this test measures your ability to use arithmetic and mathematical principles in the solution of practical problems." As such, the test makes no pretense of being a measure of ability to think abstractly, or of being a test which will pick out students with special aptitudes in mathematics or related fields. On the contrary, the test attempts to measure an ability to function in a world filled with situations which require some knowledge of basic arithmetic. It is how well the test succeeds in attaining this limited goal with which we shall be concerned.

The test, a five-choice multiple choice test, seems to provide an adequate measure of ability to solve verbal arithmetic problems in a variety of settings. The subject matter is taken from the world of simple financial transactions, common measurements, and other areas of practical interest to the nontechnical student. There are only a few questions in either form of the test which a reasonably well prepared student entering high school should not be able to handle without undue difficulty. However, the student will occasionally have to sift through irrelevant data to get to the heart of the problem. In this sense, some of the problems may cause difficulties for the student whose understanding of arithmetic is of a superficial nature, even though the student would be able to handle many of these same problems if the unnecessary data were removed. It is here that this test varies from the kind of test the student is most likely to encounter in the classroom.

Although the test is generally fair to the student, some thought should be given to revision of some of the questions. There are some choices of words which might lead to ambiguity. In these cases, the careful student may have to guess what the testmaker had in mind. These potential ambiguities probably would not seriously affect the scores of most persons, but they do present an undesirable situation.

On each form of the test, the option "not given," meaning that the correct numerical answer to the question is not among the options presented, is used too freely. The reviewer particularly objects to the use of this option as the correct answer as early in the test as it appears. It is possible that the use of this option so early and so often (34 times on Form X-3S and 41 times on Form Y-3S) may have an adverse effect on the confidence of the student taking the test and perhaps adversely affect his score. It should also be noted that the use of such an option so often may indicate that the testmaker did not take the trouble to think of five plausible options, but was content as soon as he thought of four options. A change of this policy by the testmaker would certainly be desirable.

The range of difficulty of the problems appears to be reasonable, and the tests have sufficient variety to maintain the interest of the students. However, on the whole, the test will not challenge the brighter student. The typical problem will require that the student understand the terminology and setting, sort out the essential information from that which is irrelevant, and perform a simple arithmetic calculation.

The test can be administered in two versions: a class period version consisting of 33 questions for a time of 40 minutes, and a full length version consisting of 53 questions for a time of 65 minutes. The full length version of each form consists of 20 questions added to the class period version, but except for the additional length and time required, the full length version seems to add little to what is tested. It should be noted here that three of the questions included in the full length version of Form X-3S do require a knowledge of some simple concepts of trigonometry, and these are the only questions on either form which do so. The main purpose of the longer form would seem to be to increase the test reliability. However, the class period version would seem to be adequate for most purposes.

It should be kept clearly in mind that this test measures a combination of reading ability, cultural and educational backgrounds, and ability to do arithmetic reasoning and calculation, and not just this last item. A poor score may reflect a weakness in any one or several of these areas. Thus a poor score in itself is only an indicator of some deficiency; it would require further testing to pinpoint this deficiency.

Statistical data which are said to apply to a national standardization done in 1957 are supplied. Insufficient information is available to the reviewer to make any judgment as to the value of this information, other than to say that the data supplied seem reasonable. In any case, the user should avoid putting undue importance on such standardization information.

In summation, this test seems to be a reasonable measure of ability to do arithmetic in a practical setting. Although improvements are possible and should be undertaken in any future forms, the test seems to accomplish its advertised purpose. However, no attempt to interpret the test scores apart from this announced purpose seems desirable.

For reviews of the complete battery, see 14 and 5:17; for reviews of earlier forms, see 4:17 and 3:12.

[580]

★**Junior Math Reasoning Test.** Grades 10–12 and adults; 1943–61; formerly published by Science Research Associates, Inc.; Form X ('61, same as test booklet copyrighted 1943), Y ('43), (1 page); mimeographed manual ('43, 2 pages); no adult norms; $6 per 100 tests; 25¢ per key; $1 per specimen set; postage extra; 35(40) minutes; Alfred J. Cardall; Cardall Associates. *

[581]

***Mathematics: Every Pupil Test.** Grades 7, 8; 1930–64; new form (2–4 pages) usually issued each December and April; forms from previous testing programs also available; 2 levels; general directions sheet ('63, 2 pages); no data on reliability; Ohio norms for new forms available following testing program; 5¢ per test; 3¢ per key; postpaid; 40(45) minutes; Ohio Scholarship Tests. *

[582]

★**Mathematics: Minnesota High School Achievement Examinations.** Grades 7, 8; 1962–63; earlier forms called *Arithmetic: Midwest High School Achievement Examinations;* new form issued each May; norms available in June following release of new form; Form F ('63, 4 pages) used in 1963 testing; 2 levels; no specific manual; series manual ('63, 4 pages); series norms ['63, 4 pages]; series cumulative profile ('62, 2 pages); no data on reliability; no description of normative population; 12¢ per test; $2.50 per 100 profiles; postage extra; 20¢ per specimen set, postpaid; 60(65) minutes; American Guidance Service, Inc. *

[583]

***Mathematics: National Teacher Examinations.** College seniors and teachers; 1940–62; for more complete information, see 700; 80(90) minutes; Educational Testing Service. *

PAUL BLOMMERS, *Professor of Education, State University of Iowa, Iowa City, Iowa.* [Review of Forms JNT and KNT.]

The NTE optional mathematics examination is intended for the prospective teacher of secondary school mathematics who has majored in, or at least has had some concentrated training in, undergraduate mathematics including a course in the methods of teaching the subject at the secondary level. Some 10 to 15 per cent of the items deal with matters of teaching secondary school mathematics. The remaining items are intended to provide a measure of mastery of the content of secondary school mathematics. Of the latter items somewhat less than half (40 to 45 per cent) deal with topics treated in the more advanced high school courses, i.e., with such topics from algebra, analytic trigonometry and geometry, differential and integral calculus, and probability and statistics (very few items) as are to be found in the more recent textbooks written primarily for use with eleventh and twelfth grade classes. The test does not provide any check on competency in college level mathematics. If the appropriateness of this approach can be assumed, this distribution of emphasis is probably reasonably sound.

On the whole the items are of good quality, calling considerably more for insight than for memory of facts or manipulative skill. Statistically, the item characteristics are excellent. The item-test correlations (biserials) average .44 for Form JNT and .48 for Form KNT. The J form is somewhat the more difficult of the two but in neither case did the mean number of items correctly solved by the members of a random sample of 300 from among those designating the test as their first option, differ appreciably from half the total possible. The reliabilities of both forms are good (.90 and .92 for the J and K forms, respectively).

The norms (standard scores and percentile ranks) for the various forms of each of the Optional Examinations are based on the performances of those individuals who, in the most recent nationwide administration involving the given form, designated the particular Optional Examination as their first choice. In the case of mathematics this means that the norms for the J and K forms were based on about 400 and 850 examinees, respectively. While *n*'s of this magnitude are clearly quite small for the purpose of establishing norms they do nevertheless involve all the pertinent data available from the first widespread use of the given form.

Examinees may, if they wish, elect to take a second Optional Examination in a minor or related teaching field. While the mathematics test is not a particularly popular second choice it is selected by sufficient numbers (about 140 and 200 for the J and K forms, respectively) to warrant a comparison between the average performance of the groups taking it as a first and as a second choice. The clearcut superiority of the first choice group over the second (the difference between raw score means was 4.24 for the J form and 8.31 for the K form with both differences being highly statistically significant) constitutes a sort of minimal or *sine qua non* type of evidence of the instrument's validity.

Actually the question of the validity of the NTE mathematics examination for what appears to be its principal use, the screening or selection of teacher personnel by school systems, is an extremely complex and difficult one. One would expect to find some data given on the accuracy with which this test, in combination with the Common Examinations and other standard types of information, would predict ultimate success as a teacher of mathematics. However, the Handbook for School and College Officials is not only quick to question the existence of "acceptable criteria of teaching effectiveness," but argues in support of use of "proximate criteria" (e.g., see preceding paragraph) in preference to the criterion of ultimate teaching success and submits the thesis that: "*A priori* evidence of the validity of the content of the NTE is inherent in the manner in which the tests are planned and constructed." The handbook position, it would seem, is that lack of predictive validity data is not only excusable but justifiable (*a*) because no acceptable criterion of teaching effectiveness exists, and (*b*) because even if such a criterion did exist it is inappropriate to validate the NTE against it. Apparently the only admissible statements regarding the validity of this instrument are statements of a judgmental character.

There is no doubt that the criterion problem, which is always a knotty one, is particularly difficult in this instance. On the other hand, there can be no denying that reports of performance on this mathematics test are sold on the grounds that together with similar reports on the Common Examinations they will provide information which when combined with information from other standard sources (college transcripts, letters of recommendation, personal interviews, etc.) will somehow improve the process of screening or selecting teaching personnel. Granting a certain lack of candidate to candidate comparability of college transcripts and other such information, granting also the overall excellence of the individual test items, and assuming, but not necessarily granting, the infinite wisdom of the educational experts who designed the test plan and specifications, it would still be most surprising (but most welcome) to learn that the instrument contributed consequentially to any improvement in this process. In any case, it seems incontrovertible that the buyer has a right, and the seller an obligation, to provide at least some evidence of such improvement, all excuses to the contrary notwithstanding.

For reviews of the testing program, see 700, 5:538, and 4:802.

[584]

Mathematics: Teacher Education Examination Program. College seniors preparing to teach secondary school; 1957; an inactive form of *Mathematics: National Teacher Examinations;* for more complete information, see 709; IBM; 80(95) minutes; Educational Testing Service. *

For a review of the testing program, see 5:543. For reviews of the National Teacher Examinations, *see 700, 5:538, and 4:802. For a review of* Mathematics: National Teacher Examinations, *see 583.*

[585]

***Mathematics Test (Adv.).** Ages 12-0 to 13-11; 1954–60; 4 forms; distribution restricted to directors of education; 10*s.* per 12 tests (except *a,* 8*s.* per 12 tests); 1*s.* per single copy (except *a,* 9*d.* per single copy); 1*s.* 3*d.* per manual for any one form (except *a,* 1*s.* per manual); prices include purchase tax; postage extra; 50(55) minutes; D. A. Pidgeon (*a*); published for the National Foundation for Educational Research in England and Wales; Newnes Educational Publishing Co. Ltd. *

a) ARITHMETIC TEST (ADV.) 1. 1954–57; test ['54, 8 pages]; manual ('57, 8 pages).
b) MATHEMATICS TEST (ADV.) 2. 1957; test ['57, 12 pages]; manual ('57, 12 pages).
c) MATHEMATICS TEST (ADV.) 3. 1958; test ['58, 12 pages]; manual ('58, 9 pages).
d) MATHEMATICS TEST (ADV.) 4. 1960; 1 form ['60, 12 pages]; manual ('60, 9 pages).

KENNETH LOVELL, *Lecturer in Educational Psychology, University of Leeds, Leeds, England.*

Arithmetic Test (Adv.) 1 is an adaptation of an experimental test that was highly successful in differentiating between 12- and 13-year-olds who were capable of tackling an advanced course in mathematics and those who were not. Thus Test 1, together with Tests 2, 3, and 4, is used not only for grading purposes but for the allocation or reallocation of children to different types of secondary education.

Test 1 was standardized on 796 boys and 758 girls drawn from 10 secondary modern and 3 grammar schools. No information is available about the areas in which these schools were situated or the socioeconomic background of the pupils concerned. In the case of Test 2, roughly 1,000 boys and 1,000 girls were used for standardization purposes; the corresponding numbers for Test 3 are some 900 boys and 800 girls. For neither test are there any details given about the schools or the areas from which the children were drawn. The standardization of Test 4 was accomplished by calibrating the performance of a representative sample of 214 boys and 155 girls between the ages of 12-10 and 13-10 against the performance of the same children on Test 3. The first question that potential users will have to ask themselves is whether or not the population used in the standardization procedure was representative of the whole country. The information given in the manuals does not enable the reviewer or likely buyers to make a judgment on this issue.

Tables for converting raw scores to standardized scores were constructed for each test by adapting the method devised by Lawley.[1] For all four tests the mean score for boys exceeds that of girls and it is recommended that in any allocation procedure the two sexes should be considered separately unless sex differences are known to be absent in the sample. The increase of score with age on each test was also determined separately for the sexes. In the case of Test 2, the difference between the two age rates is significant and separate conversion tables for boys and girls are provided.

The reliability of these tests (calculated from Kuder-Richardson formula 20) varies from .956 for Test 4 based on a random sample of 195 scripts, to .988 for Test 3 calculated for a sample of 215 scripts. The manuals of Tests 2, 3, and 4 point out that comparison of children at different ages is affected by sampling errors of estimates of the age allowance. Values for a modified standard error are given for use in comparing children of two ages (12-0 and 13-11) with children of the mean age of the standardization sample. Furthermore, the manuals comment that although test reliabilities are high, errors attached to a child's score can be considerable, and it is recommended that the reliability coefficients be considered in all allocation procedures since the size of the "borderline" group is affected. In all these matters care has been taken in providing statistics which are of help to the user. There are, however, no details given in respect of item analysis.

Instructions for the use of the conversion tables, for administration, and for marking are clear and concise and cover many eventualities.

1 LAWLEY, D. N. "A Method of Standardizing Group-Tests." *Brit J Psychol, Stat Sect* 3:86–9 Je '50. *

In the manuals for Tests 3 and 4 useful hints are also given that will facilitate marking. The layout of the questions in the test booklets is generally satisfactory but the size of print varies from test to test. In the reviewer's opinion that used in Test 4 is the most suitable. The items are mainly of the problem type and there is a good coverage of the mathematics that might be expected in the age range of 12-0 to 13-11 if adequate discrimination between candidates is demanded. These tests bear comparison with other tests available for use with a definite eye to allocating pupils to different types or courses of secondary education.

Summing up it may be said that few data are provided about the populations on which these tests were standardized. Apart from this blemish, statistics relevant to the use of the tests as part of the selection procedure have been carefully prepared. The tests themselves are satisfactory in presentation and the manuals give adequate information about administration and marking. The tests may be recommended; they are comparable with other "closed" tests available for this age group in Great Britain.

[586]

★Metropolitan Achievement Tests: High School Mathematics Tests. Grades 9-12; 1962-64; subtest of *Metropolitan Achievement Tests;* 2 scores: computation and concepts, analysis and problem solving; IBM and MRC; Forms AM ('62), BM ('63), (7 pages); manual ('64, c1962-64, 22 pages); content outline ['64, 4 pages]; revised interpretive manual for the battery ('64, c1962-64, 16 pages); separate answer sheets or cards must be used; $4.50 per 35 tests; $1.80 per 35 IBM answer sheets; 20¢ per scoring stencil; $2 per 100 Harbor answer cards (machine scoring service, by Measurement Research Center, Inc., may be arranged through the publisher); 40¢ per specimen set; postage extra; 72(86) minutes; Walter N. Durost, William H. Evans, James D. Leake, Howard A. Bowman, Clarke Cosgrove, and John G. Read; Harcourt, Brace & World, Inc. *

For reviews of the complete battery, see 15.

[587]

★Minimum Essentials for Modern Mathematics. Grades 6-8; 1963; Forms P, Q, (4 pages); manual (4 pages); norms sheet (2 pages); mimeographed content analysis (2 pages); $3.25 per 30 tests, postage extra; 30¢ per specimen set, postpaid; 40(45) minutes; Ernest Hayes; [Hayes Educational Test Laboratory]. *

GERALD L. ERICKSEN, *Assistant Professor of Psychology, St. Olaf College, Northfield, Minnesota.*

Minimum Essentials for Modern Mathematics has a stated purpose of grouping students, measuring achievement, and diagnosing difficulties of concepts when administered at the end of grades 6, 7, or 8. The normative data indicate that the test discriminates best above the mean for grade 6, facilitating "early identification of mathematical aptitude." The grade 8 discrimination is best below the mean, facilitating "grouping students for grade 9 General Mathematics (the lower 40 to 60 per cent of students entering grade 9)." For this reason, the test is claimed to add "broadening in scope of measurement" to the *Portland Prognostic Tests for Mathematics* (by the same author) which are more difficult tests designed to predict success in algebra for grade 8 and grade 9.

Because the normative data are based entirely on schools in Oregon, Washington, and California, the test user should be cautious in accepting the item content as representative of the material covered in any particular school. Most noticeable among junior high school topics omitted by the test are the techniques of graphing, knowledge of angular relationships, and properties of the circle.

The test user is expected to rely heavily on the effectiveness of the PPTM in assessing the validity of the minimum essentials test. No validation coefficients are reported between student achievement and scores on this test. The manual states that the PPTM has "proven validity (by research)" and reports correlations between the two tests of .82 and .86 for grade 8 Form A and grade 9 Form A, respectively. In this sense, the manual presents inadequate direct evidence of the predictive validity of the minimum essentials test. Satisfactory split-half reliabilities of .95 are reported for each grade level on *Minimum Essentials for Modern Mathematics.*

It is unfortunate that nowhere in the test is the teacher's judgment taken into account when estimating student achievement levels for grades 7, 8, and 9. There is evidence that teacher ratings from the previous grade predict achievement in mathematics as well as does a single test.[1] Simply converting stanine scores into a normal grading curve, as suggested in the manual, ignores this information which is available in most practical school situations. Cutting points based on both test scores and teacher judgments, as are provided with the

1 BARNES, WARD EWING, AND ASHER, JOHN WILLIAM. "Predicting Students' Success in First-Year Algebra." *Math Teach* 55:651-4 D '62. *

PPTM, would better utilize the available information about a student when attempting letter grade predictions.

A separate item analysis content sheet is available which merely describes each item in terms of the mathematical operations required. No supporting data are presented on the item analysis sheet regarding the discriminating power of any of the 55 items. Together these items supposedly are adequate for discriminating between grade levels as well as within a given grade. Some evidence for this claim is found in the normative data. One half of the grade 6 norm group answered less than 35 per cent of the items correctly, one half of the grade 7 group had less than 50 per cent correct, and one half of the grade 8 group had more than 60 per cent correct.

The mechanics of administration and scoring are straightforward with the exception that only a minimum amount of rough work space is provided for each item. In some cases this may limit the diagnostic value of close examination of the student's attempt at a particular problem solution.

In summary, insufficient direct validation data related to student achievement, and failure to include some measure of teacher judgment in establishing cutting scores, are the principal weaknesses of this test. There is also a lack of specific instructions to the test user as to just how to implement both this test and the PPTM in classes of varying ability ranges for grades 7 and 8. Nevertheless, investigators will find *Minimum Essentials for Modern Mathematics* useful in identifying students of superior mathematical aptitude in grade 6 and in discriminating between grade 8 students scheduled to take grade 9 non-college preparatory general mathematics courses.

[588]

★Portland Prognostic Tests for Mathematics. Grades 6.9–8.0, 8.5–9.0; 1960–64; 2 levels; administration and norms manual ('63, 4 pages); statistical manual ('63, 4 pages); $3.25 per 30 tests, postage extra; 30¢ per specimen set of one level, postpaid; 30(35) minutes; Ernest Hayes; [Hayes Educational Test Laboratory]. *

a) GRADES 7–8. Grades 6.9–8.0; Forms A ('60), B ('63), (4 pages); supplementary data ('64, 2 pages) for prognosis for grade 7.

b) GRADE 9. Grades 8.5–9.0; Forms A, B, ('60, 4 pages).

REFERENCES

1. KEARNEY, CHARLES P. *A Comparative Study of the Predictive Efficiency of the Iowa Algebra Aptitude Test and the Portland Prognostic Test.* Master's thesis, University of Portland (Portland, Ore.), 1960.

CYRIL J. HOYT, *Professor of Educational Psychology, University of Minnesota, Minneapolis, Minnesota.*

The manual for the *Portland Prognostic Tests for Mathematics* contains data indicating that this test has relatively high validity for predicting success in first year algebra at both the eighth and ninth grade levels. The validity coefficients of .74 reported for the ninth grade test were corrected for attenuation. Prior to this correction the actual correlations were .68. This latter information does not appear in the manual but is available in a research report available from the publisher on request. The reviewer considers these predictive validity coefficients substantial for prognostic tests. This magnitude of predictive efficiency was obtained in a group of 271 pupils in one school and also in a second group of 148 in a Portland, Oregon school district. The reviewer has also observed a predictive correlation of .68 between PPTM and teacher's grades for 104 pupils in a St. Paul, Minnesota high school.

The manual reports a predictive validity coefficient of .83 for the grades 7–8 Form A. This value, however, is based on one very small sample of pupils (61) from one school in Portland. This sample is more variable (standard deviation of 10.87) than the norm group whose standard deviation is 9.34. When the observed correlation of .83 is adjusted to the value it would have for a group as variable as the norm group, it decreases to .76. The small sample used and the reviewer's data indicate that the reported validity coefficient is an overestimate by approximately .10. The test does, however, have a validity coefficient sufficiently high to be recommended for use.

The manual states that the tests were designed to meet the need "to select with some degree of efficiency those students who can profit by taking college preparatory courses in mathematics as well as placement of students into classes for the gifted." The manual, however, presents no data which indicate how useful the PPTM is for either of these purposes.

The two subtests comprising the test, Number Series and Arithmetic Comprehension, are considered "different aspects of quantitative thinking," though this latter construct is not further defined. The stated intercorrelation between the subtests is .67. This is somewhat (.10) below that found by the reviewer in four samples of pupils who took each form in each grade.

The manual contains normative data based on 3,086 cases for grade 8 from schools in Oregon, Washington, and California (1960) and 5,724 cases for grade 9 from schools in Oregon (1957 and 1958).[1] Two linear transformations of the raw scores are given, "T scores" (mean 50 and standard deviation 10) and "deviation scores" (mean 100 and standard deviation 15). Percentile scores and stanines are given for each grade as well as a crude translation to predicted grades from A to C−. The manual does not report how the grades were predicted nor the amount of data used for this purpose. The statement in the manual is confusing particularly in regard to the percentage distribution of the "T scores" since the inclusion of 68 per cent between scores of 40 and 60 is not necessarily true of linear transformations to mean 50 and standard deviation 10.

Administration and scoring of the tests are made somewhat inefficient by the arrangement of the subtests in the test booklet. If the order of the subtests had been reversed the pupils would have been presented with familiar arithmetic problems first and also would have had the whole subtest open to their view. This arrangement would also have facilitated scoring of the test, which must be done by capable scorers since the test is a free response type.

Data collected by the reviewer substantiated the equivalence of means and variances of Forms A and B at both grade levels. This finding is particularly gratifying since many so-called parallel forms of other tests that have come under the scrutiny of the reviewer do not possess the equivalence shown in this case.

Internal consistency reliability coefficients are reported in the manual as .92 for both the eighth and ninth grade forms. This yields standard errors of measurement of 2.7 and 2.2 raw score points for these respective forms. These are equivalent to .29 and .25 standard deviations, respectively. This is fairly high reliability of measurement though tests of mathematical abilities often show higher reliability than those of other school learnings.

The cutoff norms reported in the manual were revised upward somewhat on the basis of a study of 148 cases in the ninth grade and 61 cases in the eighth grade in the Portland school. These revisions are available from the test publisher. Hence, a prospective user should request copies of the Research Reports 62-1 and 62-2, as well as the test manual, in order to use the cutoff norms provided. It is hoped that a revision of the manual will incorporate the 1962 data soon.

The reviewer recommends the use of the PPTM in situations where uniform grades or teacher recommendations on the advisability of individuals' enrollment are not available. Since the ratings of previous teachers show a correlation of .63 with algebra achievement for grade 9 while the use of this test in conjunction with teachers' recommendations raises the predictive coefficient to .76, there seems some evidence to indicate the test can be useful even when previous teachers' recommendations are available. This particular test cannot be machine scored and hence is not recommended in situations where teacher scoring is not available.

1 The supplementary data for prognosis for grade 7 referred to in the entry preceding the review were published since the review was written.—Editor.

[589]

★The Purdue Mathematics Training Test: Arithmetic and Algebra. Grade 13; 1951–60; IBM; Forms AM, BM, ('51, 11 pages); manual ('60, 6 pages); separate answer sheets must be used; $5 per 25 tests; $1.25 per 25 IBM answer sheets; postage extra; 75¢ per specimen set, postpaid; 60(65) minutes; M. W. Keller, H. F. S. Jonah, H. H. Remmers, and P. C. Baker; University Book Store. * Out of print.

REFERENCES

1. Keller, M. W., and Jonah, H. F. S. "Measures for Predicting Success in a First Course in College Mathematics." *Math Teach* 51:350–5 D '48. *
2. Remmers, H. H., and Gage, N. L. "The Abilities and Interests of Pharmacy Freshmen." *Am J Pharm Ed* 12:1–65 Ja '48. * (*PA* 22:4107)
3. Remmers, H. H., and Gage, N. L. "Student Personnel Studies of the Pharmaceutical Survey." *Am J Pharm Ed* 13:6–126 Ja '49. * (*PA* 23:1004)
4. Remmers, H. H.; Elliott, D. N.; and Gage, N. L. "Curricular Differences in Predicting Scholastic Achievement: Applications to Counseling." *J Ed Psychol* 40:385–94 N '49. * (*PA* 24:3407)
5. Belman, H. S., and Evans, R. N. "Selection of Students for a Trade and Industrial Education Curriculum," pp. 9–14. In *Motives and Aptitudes in Education: Four Studies.* Edited by H. H. Remmers. Purdue University, Division of Educational Reference, Studies in Higher Education, No. 74. Lafayette, Ind.: the Division, December 1950. Pp. iii, 63. * (*PA* 26:3010)
6. Belman, H. S., and Evans, R. N. "Selection of Students for a Trade and Industrial Educational Curriculum." *J Ed Psychol* 42:52–8 Ja '51. * (*PA* 25:6486)
7. Baker, Paul Cleo. *Experiments in Variable Selection for Prediction of Academic Achievement.* Doctor's thesis, Purdue University (Lafayette, Ind.), 1955. (*DA* 15:2565)
8. Palacios, John Raymond. *A Validation Study of Selected Tests for Possible Use in Admission to Professional Education Sequences at Purdue University.* Doctor's thesis, Purdue University (Lafayette, Ind.), 1959. (*DA* 20:2679)

Lynnette B. Plumlee, *Personnel Research and Testing Division, Sandia Corporation, Albuquerque, New Mexico.*

This brief review pertains to Forms AM and

BM. New forms, which are expected to be available by the end of 1965, should eliminate problems with the forms and manual reviewed here.[1]

The test is intended to measure "mastery of the fundamentals of arithmetic and algebra" and appears to be designed primarily for college freshmen. Items are well written and are good formal measures of important concepts covered in a traditional arithmetic and algebra curriculum. The potential user should, however, review the test to determine the appropriateness of the content for his purpose, since certain topics sometimes covered in a traditional algebra course are not included in this test.

The current forms are parallel almost item for item. However, Form BM is to be preferred to Form AM, since there are a few typographical errors in Form AM. Typesetting falls short of desirable standards for easy reading but probably won't cause difficulty for most students.

The manual is relatively brief, but includes large-sample norms data and some validity information. The standard error of measurement of the double-length test appears to be in error, since it is less than that of the single length test and would be expected to be greater.

In summary, the test is generally acceptable in its present form but has limitations in coverage for some uses. The publisher is especially to be commended on his professional attitude in accepting constructive criticism and in taking prompt action to improve the tests he publishes.

[590]

***Sequential Tests of Educational Progress: Mathematics.** Grades 4–6, 7–9, 10–12, 13–14; 1956–63; IBM, NCS, and Grade-O-Mat; Forms A, B, ('57, c1956–57, 10–12 pages); 4 levels; battery directions ('57, 12 pages); interpretive manual ('57, 31 pages); battery technical report ('57, 58 pages); 1958 SCAT-STEP supplement ('58, 32 pages); 1962 SCAT-STEP supplement ('62, 49 pages); 1963 SCAT-STEP supplement of urban norms ('63, 16 pages); battery teacher's guide ('59, 85 pages); battery profile ('57, 1 page); battery student report ('58, 4 pages); no data on reliability of Form B; separate answer sheets or cards must be used; $4 per 20 tests; $1 per 20 IBM scorable answer sheets; 25¢ per scoring stencil; see 671 for prices of NCS answer sheets and scoring services; see 666 for prices of Grade-O-Mat cards; $1 per 20 profiles; $1 per 20 student reports; $1 per interpretive manual; $1 per technical report; $1 per supplement; $1 per teacher's guide; postage extra; $2 per specimen set, cash orders postpaid; 70(90–100) minutes; Cooperative Test Division. *

a) LEVEL 4. Grades 4–6; Forms 4A, 4B.
b) LEVEL 3. Grades 7–9; Forms 3A, 3B.
c) LEVEL 2. Grades 10–12; Forms 2A, 2B.
d) LEVEL 1. Grades 13–14; Forms 1A, 1B.

REFERENCES

1. NORTH, ROBERT D. "The Step Mathematics Test Viewed From Independent School Results." *Ed Rec B* 73:47–56 F '59. *
2. TRAXLER, ARTHUR E. "Correlation of STEP Mathematics Test and Certain Other Measures With Mathematics Marks of Independent School Pupils." *Ed Rec B* 73:57–63 F '59. *
3. KIMBELL, FONTELLA THOMPSON. *The Use of Selected Standardized Tests as Predictors of Academic Success at Oklahoma College for Women.* Doctor's thesis, University of Oklahoma (Norman, Okla.), 1960. (*DA* 20:4335)
4. ENDLER, NORMAN S., AND STEINBERG, DANNY. "Prediction of Academic Achievement at the University Level." *Personnel & Guid J* 41:694–9 Ap '63. * (*PA* 39:2888)
5. LIGGITT, WILLIAM A. "An Evaluation of General Education in Elementary Teacher Preparation." *J Ed Res* 57:156–9 N '63. *

ARTHUR MITTMAN, *Associate Professor of Education, University of Oregon, Eugene, Oregon.*

The tests of the STEP battery were carefully designed to place emphasis on broad understandings and the ability to utilize learned skills in solving new problems rather than merely the ability to handle the facts obtained from the lesson materials. The writers of the mathematics tests have succeeded in complying with this underlying philosophy.

In *The Fifth Mental Measurements Yearbook* (see 5:24) the complete battery was criticized for the following reasons: (*a*) lack of evidence of empirical validity, (*b*) failure to provide an equivalent forms estimate of reliability, (*c*) questionable quality of the national norms as national norms, (*d*) meaninglessness of the converted score scale, and (*e*) failure to provide a chart designating the concepts and abilities measured by the different tests. The mathematics test items were criticized for their tendency towards an excessive amount of reading which in some instances is mere "window dressing." In fairness to the publisher, it should be stated that cognizance was taken in the Technical Manual of the first two criticisms listed above.

During the interim period three SCAT-STEP supplements (1958, 1962, and 1963) and a Teacher's Manual (1959) have been made available. As reflected in these materials, the publisher's response to the above criticisms may be summarized as follows: (*a*) some data on concurrent and predictive validity have been published; (*b*) systematic data on parallel-forms reliability have not been provided; (*c*) the norms have been supplemented but the same questions may be raised concerning the new norms; (*d*) the score scale remains the same; (*e*) item-by-item concept analyses of the tests have been published.

[1] Forms AM and BM were withdrawn since this review was written.—Editor.

Since the tests have not been changed the criticism of the tendency towards a surplus amount of "window dressing" in many items is still applicable. The correlation of STEP mathematics scores with SCAT verbal scores lends credence to this criticism. Particularly at the lower grade levels, this tendency may result in the tests' rewarding reading ability as much as quantitative ability. As a case in point, one item reads, "Mr. Jones says his cows give an average of two gallons of milk per day. Which of the following objects has a capacity closest to *one* gallon? A tea cup B one-pound coffee can C man's shoe box D bath tub." It would appear that the question to which an answer is sought is independent of Mr. Jones' cows and their milk producing ability. Likewise, as in any test, it is possible to detect a few items which may prove to be ambiguous, especially to the brighter student. In spite of these limitations, the nature and significance of the questions asked throughout all forms and levels are commendable.

The three SCAT-STEP supplements are part of the publisher's plan to disseminate results of validity studies and additional norms tables as they become available. The 1958 supplement reports substantial correlation (.65) between STEP mathematics scores and seventh grade arithmetic marks, but this figure is no better than the correlation reported between SCAT-Q and seventh grade mathematics marks (.69). In addition this supplement offers estimated spring norms for college sophomores. The 1962 supplement provides estimated spring norms for twelfth grade, mid-percentile ranks for college sophomores, and an annotated bibliography of validity studies involving the STEP tests. The 1963 supplement supplies urban norms tables for cities over 100,000 in population. These norms had to be established on the basis of the results from those city school systems which were willing to participate and thus are handicapped in much the same manner as the published national norms. It would be helpful if data were supplied which would indicate the estimated effect, if any, of voluntary participation on the STEP national norms. The publisher does provide such data for the SCAT norms in the 1958 supplement. The 1963 urban norms are also handicapped by the fact that, since testing was done only in grades 5, 7, 9, and 11, the spring norms for grades 4, 6, 8, 10, and 12 are estimated rather than based on actual testing.

The Teacher's Guide outlines procedures for using the tests as both diagnostic and learning instruments. In response to earlier criticisms it includes a categorization of mathematics items, but the classification is by concept only and would need to be spelled out in greater detail before the prospective user could determine whether or not the test had content validity for his mathematics program.

A plan for within-class item analysis and class discussion of troublesome items is clearly outlined. The extent to which a teacher would employ these techniques would depend upon the purpose for which the examination was administered and whether it was intended to be used as a teaching device. The detailed analysis suggested in the Teacher's Guide is of questionable merit. Item statistics are quite unstable especially for a small group; it is questionable whether the process of comparing class performance on a single item or group of items with the performance of the national norm group has either statistical or practical significance.

The prospective user of the mathematics test should carefully consider what additional information will be provided if the STEP mathematics tests are administered either to augment an existing testing program or as a replacement. If the interest is primarily in prediction or sectioning, it is questionable whether scores from the STEP mathematics tests will enhance that process. They definitely will not be valid for advanced placement due to their independence of formal mathematics curriculums. They are valid as measures of the student's ability to apply mathematical concepts and they should prove useful for preliminary screening for placement purposes.

As future forms of the tests are prepared (and as yet there is no indication that additional forms are planned), some provision will need to be made for the inclusion of items that are appropriate more specifically to the domain of the new mathematics curriculum. This is especially true if the tests are designed to be of value for counseling and guiding students in schools in which modern mathematics is being taught. Curriculum changes in many areas will demand the careful scrutiny of test publishers.

In summary, these tests are exemplary with respect to the manner in which they were planned and constructed. Except for the effects of heavy reading load at some levels, the items are of good quality and of value for assessing the extent to which quantitative abilities have been developed. The validity evidence to date indicates that STEP mathematics scores do not predict success in mathematics any better than does a good aptitude measure. The supplements and Teacher's Guide are valuable additions to the STEP materials and deserve the careful scrutiny of any prospective user.

DOUGLAS A. PIDGEON, *Deputy Director, National Foundation for Educational Research in England and Wales, Slough, Bucks, England.*

As these tests were extensively reviewed in *The Fifth Yearbook,* attention is mainly given here to the subsequent publications listed above. For the benefit, however, of potential users in Great Britain, it should be noted that these tests cannot be used without considerable alteration. Apart from the obvious changes necessary on all items dealing with money—by no means an easy task—many of the questions are set in a context strange to British children.

Since the initial publication of the STEP series of tests in 1956–57, three supplements to the Technical Report have appeared as well as a Teacher's Guide and a Battery Report Form. The mathematics tests, however, form but a small part of the total SCAT-STEP series, and only a very small part of the supplementary material is of direct relevance to the mathematics tests.

The Teacher's Guide contains a complete classification of the test items according to the concepts they are intended to measure—information that was missing from the original manual. In addition, facility values for each item, estimated from the norms data, are given for each group for which each test is appropriate. The fact that not everyone will agree with the classification matters little. With a guide of this kind, teachers can be encouraged to examine their test results more analytically and then to use them constructively, for the benefit of both their pupils and themselves.

One deficiency in the original manual has not been rectified. Although supposedly equivalent forms of the tests are supplied at each of four levels, alternate form reliability coefficients are still missing. That such coefficients, if calculated, would be somewhat lower than the Kuder-Richardson formula 20 values given originally for Form A, is hardly to be doubted. It is true that the Technical Manual demonstrates equivalence of alternate forms in terms of difficulty, but the difference in the concept classification between forms is quite large. Indeed, until the results of the further correlational analyses promised in 1957 are forthcoming, the scores on alternate forms can hardly be regarded as equivalent. It is also to be noted that the separate reliabilities for Form B still have to be published.

The Technical Report quite rightly stresses the importance of content validity, although it also states that empirical validity studies relating test scores to suitable criteria measures would subsequently be published. Overlooking the important question as to what constitutes a suitable criterion measure for tests of this kind, the supplements since published make reference only to three small studies of doubtful relevance. In a group of 271 seventh grade students, the correlation between STEP mathematics scores (form not stated) and arithmetic grades presumably obtained about the same time was .65, and a follow-up of 118 of the same students to the end of the eighth grade gave a similar correlation of .71. These results are interesting but tell nothing about the validity of the test for the purpose stated—namely, to measure mastery of broad mathematical concepts. The results of the two other studies, both in independent schools, are not even interesting since in one the tests were administered at atypical levels, and in the other the *n*'s "were extremely small."

For the remainder of the supplements, apart from a set of urban norms obtained in 1962, there is nothing of particular relevance to the mathematics tests. It may be asking too much to expect a further supplement devoted specifically to these tests, but it is to be hoped that the further validation studies promised and the necessary data on reliability will still appear.

For reviews by Paul L. Dressel, Gordon Fifer, and Tom A. Lamke, see 5:438. For reviews of the complete battery, see 25 and 5:24.

[591]

★**Survey of Mathematics Achievement: California Survey Series.** Grades 9–12; 1959; all items from *California Mathematics Test, 1957 Edition;* IBM; Forms 1, 2, (8 pages); no specific manual; combined manual (20 pages) for this test and the advanced levels of tests 280 and 815; $2.45 per 35 tests; separate answer sheets may be used; 5¢ per IBM answer sheet;

20¢ per scoring stencil; 10¢ per series class record sheet; 2¢ per series individual record sheet; postage extra; 50¢ per specimen set, postpaid; 38(43) minutes with answer sheets, 35(40) minutes without answer sheets; Ernest W. Tiegs and Willis W. Clark; California Test Bureau. *

WILLIAM R. CRAWFORD, *Office of Research in Medical Education, University of Illinois College of Medicine, Chicago, Illinois.*

The *Survey of Mathematics Achievement* is one of a series of tests in mathematics, English, reading, and spelling. The two forms are composed of items taken from the longer *California Mathematics Test,* part of the *California Achievement Tests, 1957 Edition.* The new tests, unlike the parent instrument, are not designed to yield diagnostic scores but rather to "measure mastery of the basic skills." With respect to type of intellectual function measured, the manual states: "The two phases of achievement in arithmetic—reasoning and skill in the fundamental processes—are both included in the seventy items comprising this test." This reviewer feels that this goal has been achieved, at least in part, since both forms contain some items which require the student to apply mathematical principles to new situations, as well as items which call for simple manipulation (adding, subtracting, dividing) of numbers.

The manual states that since items for the two forms of the *Survey of Mathematics Achievement* were selected from the three forms of the *California Mathematics Test,* item duplication need not occur if both tests are given to the same group. However, an actual comparison of items indicates that complete avoidance of overlap is impossible. Form 1 of the survey test overlaps 8 per cent with Form X of the achievement test, 14 per cent with Form W, and 77 per cent with Form Y; Form 2 overlaps 10 per cent with Form Y, 43 per cent with Form W, and 47 per cent with Form X. Consequently, if both tests are to be used, the best combination will be Form 1 and Form X (8 per cent overlap) or Form 2 and Form Y (10 per cent overlap).

All test items were validated by referring them to curriculum and testing experts when the *California Mathematics Test* was prepared. From a large pool of items only the best were selected, utilizing the criteria of statistical adequacy and curricular relevance. It should, however, be noted that a number of school systems have made radical changes in the mathematics curriculum since the time when these items were selected. A number of schools have all but abandoned the traditional approach to mathematics instruction and have introduced certain advanced topics such as set theory, matrix algebra, and even calculus. The items in the *Survey of Mathematics Achievement* do not reflect these changes in curriculum. Therefore, potential users should be extremely cautious and examine the content closely before deciding to use the test. This admonition is particularly germane to those school systems which may, for whatever reason, be using both types of curriculum structure. Even if one assumes a traditional curriculum structure there is little to recommend the use of these tests above the junior high school level since there are few, if any, items which require more than a rudimentary knowledge of the principles of algebra. Most of the items deal with simple arithmetical operations which this reviewer feels are not adequate for measuring the mathematical competence of high school students. The norms tend to support this hypothesis since in many cases the percentile and standard score levels for adjacent high school grades are separated by only one standard error of measurement or less.

The two survey test forms were carefully matched and their means and standard deviations differ by less than one raw score point in the standardization sample. The reliability of the test (form unspecified) is reported as .90 (Kuder-Richardson formula 21). This coefficient, however, is based only on a sample of students in the eleventh grade, and no information is furnished with respect to reliability at other levels of achievement. There is little reason to believe that the reliability of scores is constant over grade levels, especially since the range of grades for which the test is intended is so wide. It is truly unfortunate that only the reliability for grade 11 was reported since the items seem much too elementary for that level and one would normally expect very stable scores over material which was not especially challenging to the examinees.

The norms provided in the manual permit raw score conversion to grade placements, percentiles, and standard scores. The manual also provides adequate descriptions of how these tables were constructed and how they can best be utilized. In addition to the criticism aimed at the inappropriateness of the norms for high school students in general, a second major objection to these descriptions is that not enough warning is provided against overinterpreting grade placement norms. Warnings of this type are sorely lacking in most manuals for commercially available tests, but they are particularly needed for this instrument since the standard error encompasses almost one full year of achievement.

In general, there is little to recommend the use of this test at the high school level. Upon examining it, school officials might find it appropriate for use in junior high schools or even in upper elementary grades which have been involved in an accelerated traditionally-oriented mathematics program. In examining the test, potential users should always keep in mind that it was not designed for use as a diagnostic tool but rather for giving an estimate of overall present achievement in mathematics. Both the manual and booklet are attractively printed, easy to use, and furnish adequate information with respect to validity and norming procedures. It is felt that a significant step forward in measurement will have been made when all publishers provide manuals and booklets as well done as these are.

ARTHUR MITTMAN, *Associate Professor of Education, University of Oregon, Eugene, Oregon.*

This test is an abbreviated form of the 1957 *California Mathematics Test*. Specifically, most Form 1 items were taken from Form Y and most Form 2 items were taken from Forms W and X of the parent test. Forms 1 and 2 are equivalent both from the standpoint of content and on the basis of the supporting statistical information provided in the manual.

The intent of the publisher was to provide a test that could be easily administered within a class period of 45 minutes and which would provide a "general, but accurate, estimate of the extent to which an individual or group has acquired knowledges and understandings with regard to a specific subject or area of learning." In essence, the test is a mastery test of the four fundamental operations involving integers, fractions, mixed numbers, decimals, and, to a limited extent, literal numbers. Eight items in each form ask the student to apply the operations of arithmetic to consumer situations of a trite nature. A minimum of items is devoted to measurement of reasoning, but the preponderance deal with basic skills.

The test is stated to be valid to the extent that mastery of certain basic skills of learning is an objective of every school. It may be a useful instrument if a school has a minimum competency in mathematics requirement for graduation or for admission to a particular curriculum program. However, for the majority of students mastery of mathematics at the modern secondary school level involves more than mere mastery of the fundamental operations. Thus, the test would be a valid instrument for only a small portion of the secondary school population. It would appear to be of extremely limited value for the better students; it could only serve to confirm an already known fact about their mastery of the basic skills. The test may be useful for placement of lower ability students in courses designed to devote considerable attention to the strengthening of basic mathematical skills.

To a large extent the publishers have based their case for validity of the abbreviated test upon the fact that the parent instrument from which the items were drawn is valid. This is a dubious basis upon which to establish the validity of a test consisting of only a fraction of the number of items which comprise the longer test.

Despite the fact that the items deal with simple arithmetic problems, it is questionable whether or not the time limit of 35 to 38 minutes (depending upon the manner in which answers are recorded) to solve 70 exercises is adequate for the general population of high school students. If speed is a factor, the scores will be partially attributable to it and not all to power as suggested in the manual. Likewise, the Kuder-Richardson formula 21 reliability estimate of .90 provided for grade 11 will be inappropriate. The effect of speed upon the reliability coefficients estimated in this manner may be greater for grades 9 and 10 if the scores reflect general educational maturation more than achievement in specific courses. A coefficient of equivalence of .82 is reported, based upon students from grades 9–12. This offers a more desirable and meaningful estimate of reliability but is somewhat lower than would be expected in view of the range of ability represented by grades 9–12.

The norms are based upon standardization samples selected with respect to geographical location, size of community, grade placement, chronological age, and mental age. Grade equivalents, percentile ranks, and normalized standard scores are provided. From the information in the manual it is questionable whether or not the tenth and twelfth grade samples are comparable to the ninth and eleventh grade samples since the population was stratified into four groups prior to the selection of the former sample and into only two subgroups prior to the selection of the latter sample. More detailed information should be provided in the manual relative to this situation. Also, a more complete description of the dual stage sampling technique employed would be of value. Amplification along these lines would permit the user more assurance in making decisions concerning the adequacy of the national norms as well as enabling a more valid interpretation of a specific school's or class's performance on the test.

In summary, the two forms of the *Survey of Mathematics Achievement* are highly equivalent and each provide a readily obtained and reasonably reliable score representative of a student's proficiency in the basic skills. They are limited in their utility due to the nature of the behavior elicited.

[592]

★**T.C. Mathematics Test.** Teachers college entrants; 1955–58; most items selected or adapted from an out of print form of *Cooperative Mathematics Tests for Grades 7, 8, and 9;* "level of knowledge of simple mathematical procedures"; 12 scores: fractions, decimals, volume, percentage, geometry, graphs, area, algebra, number, perimeter, terms and definitions, total; 1 form ['56, 6 pages]; mimeographed manual ['58, 7 pages]; no data on reliability; no norms for subscores; distribution restricted to teacher training institutions; separate answer sheets must be used; 6*s.* per 10 tests; 2*s.* per 10 answer sheets; 4*s.* per key; 2*s.* 6*d.* per manual; 7*s.* 6*d.* per specimen set; postpaid within Australia; 35(40) minutes; Australian Council for Educational Research. *

[Other Tests]

For tests not listed above, see the following entries in *Tests in Print:* 946, 948, 951, 954–5, 957–8, 960–1, 968, 971, 975, and 977; out of print: 945, 947, 950, 962–3, and 973; status unknown: 969.

ALGEBRA

[593]

***Advanced Algebra: Minnesota High School Achievement Examinations.** High school; 1952–63; series formerly called *Midwest High School Achievement Examinations;* new form issued each May; norms available in June following release of new form; Form F ('63, 4 pages) used in 1963 testing; no specific manual; series manual ('63, 4 pages); series norms ['63, 4 pages]; series cumulative profile ('62, 2 pages); no data on reliability; no description of normative population; 12¢ per test; $2.50 per 100 profiles; postage extra; 20¢ per specimen set, postpaid; 60(65) minutes; American Guidance Service, Inc. *

LYNNETTE B. PLUMLEE, *Personnel Research and Testing Division, Sandia Corporation, Albuquerque, New Mexico.* [Review of Forms E and F.]

These tests cover the traditional content of a second year algebra textbook. The two forms differ somewhat in content; for example, Form F includes questions on logarithms and trigonometry, topics not covered in Form E.

The test questions as a whole appear to have been carefully prepared and edited, and the answer key appears to be correct. While the majority of the items test important concepts or processes, a few items in Form E are too trivial to warrant inclusion. Some questions in this form can be answered with a knowledge of arithmetic only. The majority of questions in both forms test learned processes and definitions with little test of ability to apply these concepts in novel situations. Two or three questions contain two equivalent wrong answers. If the examinee recognizes this equivalence he can immediately eliminate these two options. The reviewer prefers Form F over Form E as a measure of algebraic knowledge.

Although the manual implies that the tests may be used for group diagnostic purposes, some sections of the test contain as few as two or three items. The user would do well to review the test carefully to acquaint himself with the content of the test before attempting to use it for this purpose.

No information is provided in the manual on speededness, although the editor of the test series stated in a letter to the reviewer that all tests in the series were planned so that "all or nearly all could finish." Both Forms E and F appear to place some premium on speed, with 68 and 63 items, respectively, to be completed in one hour. The fact that the 99th percentile is equivalent to 53 and 48 items, respectively, suggests a speeded test, especially where items cover conventional subject matter.

The student who does not check his work or who can quickly identify time-consuming items and skip these initially stands a better chance of increasing his score. If the user wishes to evaluate student or class knowledge of specific concepts, it is recommended that the test be administered under essentially untimed conditions.

Form F contains two typographical errors which will probably not cause the student difficulty. Of more seriousness is the poor typesetting. The denominators of most algebraic equations have been dropped below the line of print. Some of the exponents seem unnecessarily small. Spacing within test questions also falls below the standards one would like to set for commercial tests.

The four-page manual is disappointing, both in scope and clarity. The one manual covers 27 tests (Form F) in a variety of subjects. A manual which makes only those statements which can apply to all such tests cannot do justice to any one test. The section entitled "Content Validity" provides little information on how or whether this validity goal was achieved. In a letter to the reviewer, the editor stated that many of the authors eliminated questions which were answered correctly by fewer in the top than in the bottom quarter of their students. (It was not stated whether this procedure was followed for the mathematics test.) This statistical procedure of course does not insure "content validity," which is ordinarily obtained by asking "experts" to compare test content against test objectives. The editor stated that he and three other professional persons checked the items "for validity," but he did not explain the criterion used for evaluating validity.

The emphasis of the manual is on the use and limitations of the tests in evaluating local course content. This discussion contains little helpful information. The manual is, however, to be commended on its advice against evaluating teachers on the basis of test results.

The norms are based on scores submitted to the publisher, but the populations are not described in the manual. According to the editor's letter to the reviewer, norms were established primarily on schools in Minnesota. The number of students "used for the norms of Forms E and F varied between 500 and 4000."

More specifically, the reviewer would like to see the manual provide information on individual tests in the series, including information on: qualifications of the authors and reviewers; the statistical procedures used in test development; procedures used to determine content validity; geographical, ability, and educational nature of the norms populations; controls on norms administration; detailed description of the content (especially important for diagnostic tests); statistical information on speededness; and information on the standard error of measurement of the tests. Cautions should also be included regarding limitations in diagnostic use of the test, especially on an individual basis.

In summary, Form F tests a reasonable sampling of concepts covered in the traditional second year algebra course, though sampling of more advanced topics is sketchy and few problems measure ability to use the concepts. The manual is of little value and the norms tables should be used with caution.

James P. Rizzo, *Mathematics Instructor, The Lawrenceville School, Lawrenceville, New Jersey.* [Review of Forms E and F.]

If one looks to the manual for this series for information addressed to specific characteristics of this test, or others in the series, he is doomed to disappointment. The following paragraph, quoted from the manual, is in the section subtitled "Uses of the Tests" and is not atypical:

> High achievement in one or more units taught with relatively low achievement in other units taught might mean an undue balance of emphasis at the local level or an absence of appropriate materials to teach units in which achievement was low. A local school system could then decide whether this somewhat unusual emphasis is desirable at the local level or whether some changes should be made in the future offerings of this course.

Of the four paragraphs in the section subtitled "Content Validity," the one cited below constitutes the principal supporting evidence given by the publisher in this area:

> The authors of many of the tests gave the entire test of selected items experimentally to students locally in order to include only those items in the final edition which seemed to carry a high degree of validity. The editors further eliminated no fewer than 10 per cent of the questions on the basis that these did not carry as high validity as desirable. In some tests the number of questions eliminated came to nearly 25 per cent.

The percentile norms were computed from scores submitted by representative schools. The number of cases is not specified, and data are not provided with regard to other statistical properties of the distribution.

The printing of the tests leaves something to be desired. In Form F the items appear crowded, the practice of boxing them used in Form E having been discarded. In both forms the separation between each response and its designating letter is minimal, and representation of exponents is not uniformly clear. It is unfortunate that the slash is used in some fractions without grouping symbols to indicate the desired product or quotient: in using 2/3x the tester intends (2/3)x but a good case can be made for 2/(3x). All these characteristics contribute to unnecessary ambiguity or difficulty of reading and militate against the testee.

The score is the number right, and the answers are entered in a single column to the right on each page. The arrangement of the answer column makes the task of scoring with the folded key an easy one but may be a disadvantage to the testee since the items are arranged in double columns.

Both forms are divided into units of from 2 to 17 items. The units have titles which read very much like the chapter headings, or combinations thereof, in most traditional textbooks on a second course in algebra. Form F contains a 5-item unit on logarithms and trigonometry which is not a part of the earlier Form E. The practice of dividing the test into subtitled units, while providing a quick identification of areas of unusually low, or high, achievement—the publisher's intent according to the manual—carries with it the concomitant disadvantage of reinforcing the tendencies to teach and learn by compartmentalized techniques rather than seeking the principles which relate such units, and reduces the effectiveness of the test as a comprehensive survey and measure of the student's achievement in the year's work.

The items of both forms lean heavily upon manipulative skills. The coverage in this vein—fractions, factoring, radicals, etc.—is more than adequate. A laudable effort has been made to incorporate items which test recognition of definitions and understanding of concepts, but with somewhat mixed results. The items on identification of types of variation seem to rely more on a conditioned response to a familiar formula or relation than on real understanding of the language of variation since in no instance are the constants or variables defined. Also, this reviewer found it difficult to accept the expression "is increased 8 times" in lieu of the unambiguous multiplied by 8, which was the intent of the response. With few exceptions those questions about graphs of equations or their interpretation for use in solutions of particular values of polynomials of one variable tend to the stereotyped or lack precision of statement, neglecting the fact that a family of curves may be associated with a particular value of a polynomial or that a single curve may be used to relate polynomials differing only by a constant.

In view of the trend in secondary school mathematics over the past 10 years, particularly in algebra, inclusion of algebraic and graphic items on systems of inequalities, greater use of the more effective modern terminology, and inclusion of more items which emphasize the structural properties of algebra would be desirable in replacing some of the manipulative items.

The heavy emphasis on almost purely manipulative skills, the relative lack of success in framing items testing concepts and their interrelations, the format of the test, and the paucity of data on its characteristics mark this as a standardized test of limited usefulness.

For a review by Emma Spaney of earlier forms, see 5:442.

[594]

★Algebra: Cooperative Mathematics Tests. Grades 8–9, high school, high school and college; 1962–64; IBM; Forms A (7 pages), B (6 pages); 3 levels; no specific manual; series directions for administration ('62, 9 pages); series handbook ('64, 78 pages); separate answer sheets must be used; $4 per 20 tests; $1 per 20 IBM scorable answer sheets; $1 per 10 scoring stencils (answer pattern must be punched out locally); $1 per handbook; postage extra; $2 per specimen set of this and 6 other mathematics tests, cash orders postpaid; 40(45) minutes; Cooperative Test Division. *
a) ALGEBRA I. Grades 8–9; Forms A, B, ('62).
b) ALGEBRA II. High school; Forms A, B, ('62).
c) ALGEBRA III. High school and college; Forms A, B, ('63).

PAUL BLOMMERS, *Professor of Education, State University of Iowa, Iowa City, Iowa.* [Review of tests I and II.]

These tests deal respectively with the content of first and second courses in high school algebra. They are members of a new set of mathematics tests under development by the Cooperative Test Division of Educational Testing Service. CTD followed its usual practice of calling on selected classroom teachers of mathematics to assist in the preparation of the items. The content specifications were reviewed by a committee of noted mathematics educators.

This approach has unquestionably been helpful to CTD in coping with a test development problem which, while not unique to the field of mathematics certainly, currently presents special difficulties in that field, namely, the problem of testing over both modern and traditional content with the same instrument. The resulting product in this instance consisted of tests which should be reasonably fair for students whose first or second courses in algebra were either of the traditional or modern kind. While the content of both tests is largely traditional in character, yet it is content which the student of modern courses can scarcely be excused from knowing. Where the items deal with matters that are given greater emphasis in the newer programs—as, for example, inequalities—they are put in such a way as to be solvable by any student of a traditional program who has acquired a reasonable degree of insight into the number system. No items have been included which treat those aspects of the newer mathematics that are more or less unique to it, such as concepts of set algebra. On the whole the items appear to be of excellent quality, the emphasis throughout being on understanding of algebraic concepts as contrasted with manipulative skill. Speed as a possible factor is minimized by a time limit (40 minutes for 40 five-response multiple choice problems for both tests I and II) which should prove more than ample for any student who has truly attained such understanding.

While CTD literature pertaining to these tests [1] makes no specific suggestion regarding their use, it must be presumed that they are intended as standardized external end-of-course examinations which could be helpful to a teacher in evaluating the relative achievement of his pupils not only as compared with one another but also as compared with pupils from the classrooms of other similar school systems. Insofar as within-class comparisons are concerned the tests appear to have excellent content validity. No information is given on the degree to which the test performance rankings of the pupils of a given class would tend to conform to the judgments of their teachers or to correlate with subsequent success in the study of mathematics. Granting content validity and a reasonable degree of reliability, the usefulness of these tests as a basis for comparisons between pupils from a classroom in one school system and those of another classroom in a similar school system depends, of course, primarily on the adequacy of the normative data. The normative data currently available for these tests are definitely on the skimpy side. Tables giving raw score percentile ranks are provided for each form of both tests for each of three types of systems—suburban, urban, and rural. In the case of Algebra I, only 13 suburban, 11 urban, and 10 rural systems, fairly well scattered throughout the United States, are represented. The total numbers of pupils involved are less than 1,000 in the case of each of the suburban and urban samples and less than 500 in the case of the rural sample. The situation is even worse in the case of Algebra II, the norms currently available being based on only 6 suburban, 6 urban, and 8 rural systems. The numbers of pupils involved are roughly 700 suburban, 400 urban, and only 200 rural. However, in all fairness it is important to note that CTD clearly labels these data as *preliminary* and promises an early forthcoming comprehensive interpretive manual and detailed technical report to be based on the results of an extensive nationwide testing program.

Kuder-Richardson formula 20 reliability coefficients based on the preliminary normative data described above are given separately for each form of each test and each type of school system. The values of these coefficients range from .80 to .85, which is probably just about par for algebra tests of this length (40 items).

The two forms of both these tests are far more closely parallel than would be expected were they derived by the independent selection of items fitting the categories of a given set of content specifications. Granting that there should be nothing unique about the true variances of equivalent forms, the practice of constructing such forms by using highly similar items remains of questionable value. Considering strictly from a practical point of view, the possible uses to which second forms of end-of-course algebra tests might be put, it seems clear that the greater the degree of similarity between corresponding pairs of items in the two forms, the less point there is in having two forms at all. Forms A and B of both these algebra tests may not be as vulnerable to criticism of this kind as are some published tests,

[1] This review was prepared on the basis of materials being sold in 1963 and does not cover the 1964 handbook referred to in the entry preceding this review.—Editor.

but they certainly are approaching an undesirable degree of similarity of this type.

In summary, these end-of-course algebra tests may be said to be of excellent quality. They appear to be reasonably valid for students whose training in algebra was either of the traditional or modern type. The major weakness consists of the limited character of normative data currently available.

[595]

★Algebra Test for Engineering and Science: National Achievement Tests. College entrants; 1958–61; 2 scores: part 1, total; 1 form ('61, 16 pages, identical with test copyrighted in 1958 except for option order for some items and use of letters to designate options); manual ('58, 4 pages); $5 per 25 tests; 25¢ per manual; 50¢ per specimen set; postage extra; 50(55) minutes for part 1, 80(85) minutes for total test; A. B. Lonski; [Psychometric Affiliates]. *

PETER A. LAPPAN, JR., *Assistant Professor of Mathematics, Lehigh University, Bethlehem, Pennsylvania.*

This is a 5-choice multiple choice test consisting of two parts, the first with 50 questions to be answered in 50 minutes, and the second with 15 questions to be answered in 30 minutes.

The test seems to measure manipulative ability in elementary algebra and understanding of the notation of algebra. Part 1 is basically a test of manipulation of algebraic symbols and contains no more material than might be found in a good first course in algebra. Part 2 is more of an attempt to measure understanding of algebraic notation using more advanced concepts than those of Part 1.

The test deals with a wide variety of topics, attempting to touch most types of manipulative problems which might occur in the usual mathematics courses. As a result, no single topic is covered in depth.

The questions consist mainly of symbols to be manipulated, and little attempt is made to tap understanding of what the symbols mean, or even the meaning of the manipulation procedure. There seems to be no attempt to measure reasoning ability, except for an occasional question in Part 2. However, the coverage seems as adequate as possible for a test of this relatively short length. There is a noticeable lack of emphasis on such important topics as graphing (one question) and simultaneous linear equations (one question), but no other serious omissions are apparent to the reviewer.

As questions are generally short and very simply phrased, there seems to be little chance that such factors as verbal deficiency (other than total illiteracy) or misinterpretation of the question would enter significantly into a student's score. There is one serious ambiguity on a question in Part 2, but this is the only case where there is an urgent need for rephrasing among the 65 questions. However, the printing of the test leaves much to be desired, as fractions and exponents appear disproportionately small and faint.

The norms given in the instruction manual should be used with extreme care. The statistical information says little about the population on which the test was normed, and the information given in tables 1 through 4 in the manual is virtually useless to one unfamiliar with the courses to which the statistical data apply. The user might be well advised to interpret scores on the basis of his own individual needs rather than to rely on norms tailor-made for courses for which he may have little use.

On the whole, the test appears to be adequate as a measure of minimum level of achievement in algebra. As such, it may be used as a placement test, particularly for courses where the emphasis is to be placed on algebraic manipulation. However, the test does not seem to attempt to measure reasoning ability, so that it is totally unsuitable as a predictor of success in a course where the emphasis will be on reasoning in an algebraic setting.

[596]

***Elementary Algebra: Every Pupil Test.** High school; 1929–64; new form (2–4 pages) usually issued each December and April; forms from previous testing programs also available; general directions sheet ('63, 2 pages); no data on reliability; Ohio norms for new forms available following testing program; 5¢ per test; 3¢ per key; postpaid; 40(45) minutes; Ohio Scholarship Tests. *

[597]

***Elementary Algebra: Minnesota High School Achievement Examinations.** High school; 1955–63; series formerly called *Midwest High School Achievement Examinations;* new form issued each May; norms available in June following release of new form; Form F ('63, 4 pages) used in 1963 testing; no specific manual; series manual ('63, 4 pages); series norms ['63, 4 pages]; series cumulative profile ('62, 2 pages); no data on reliability; no description of normative population; 12¢ per test; $2.50 per 100 profiles; postage extra; 20¢ per specimen set, postpaid; 60(65) minutes; American Guidance Service, Inc. *

For a review by Lynnette B. Plumlee of earlier forms, see 5:448.

[598]

★Elementary Algebra Test: Affiliation Testing Program for Catholic Secondary Schools. Grades 9–12 and students who are candidates for the high school diploma issued by the Catholic University of America; 1949–63; administered annually in May at individual schools; IBM; new form issued annually; Form Z ('63, 11 pages) used in 1963 program; separate answer sheets must be used; 50¢ per test and IBM answer sheet; postpaid; fee includes purchase of test booklets, scoring, and other services; for more complete information, see 758; specimen set of the complete battery free; 90(100) minutes; Program of Affiliation, Catholic University of America. *

REFERENCES

1. BUDDEKE, RITA. *Differential Factorial Patterns of Boys and Girls in Algebraic Computation.* Catholic University of America, Educational Research Monograph, Vol. 23, No. 1. Washington, D.C.: Catholic University of America Press, 1960. Pp. vii, 53. *

2. NOVELLO, RUSSELL R. *Differential Factors in Algebraic Computation for High-Achieving Boys and Girls.* Catholic University of America, Educational Research Monograph, Vol. 23, No. 2. Washington, D.C.: Catholic University of America Press, Inc., 1960. Pp. viii, 69. *

HENRY CHAUNCEY, *President, Educational Testing Service, Princeton, New Jersey.* [Review of Forms Y and Z.]

In these days of mathematical curricular change, a critique of a mathematics test should include an external assessment of the course upon which the test is based. This is especially true in view of the important uses for the tests in the Affiliation Testing Program, which make their influence quite strong. The suggested course outline provided for elementary algebra is quite conservative, and it reflects none of the more modern improvements which characterize the best of the contemporary programs. The absence of any work on inequalities, except as an optional topic in geometry, is the most obvious deficiency. By 1958 (publication date of the booklet in which the outline appears) some attention should also have been given to graphs on the number line. Neither of these improvements needed to await the further development of current, contemporary programs. In the long run, it would probably be easier for mathematics staffs to gradually evolve and modernize their programs than to suddenly shift, by adoption of a new program in its entirety.

The absence of the above topics in Forms Y and Z should, therefore, be construed as an external criticism of the test. Internally, both forms emphasize heavily the manipulative and routine aspects of algebra. This emphasis is enhanced by the use of "none of these answers" as a fifth choice in most questions. Good students making trivial clerical errors are attracted to this choice, when otherwise they would be led to recheck their work. This bad effect defeats the purpose of this choice, namely, to draw all those students making significant errors which are not anticipated by the testmaker.

The later form, Form Z (1963), shows a marked improvement over Form Y in the conceptual nature of many of the items. Some of the best of these items deal with positive and negative numbers, odds and evens, absolute value, and the function concept. With the changes in the suggested course currently being planned in the Affiliation Program, and with the continued improvement in the quality of this test as indicated by Form Z, it is likely that the test will become a better and better instrument of evaluation.

For a review of the complete program, see 758.

[599]

***First Year Algebra: Every Pupil Scholarship Test.** 1 year high school; 1926–64; new form (2–4 pages) usually issued each January and April; forms from previous testing programs also available; general directions sheet ['63, 2 pages]; no data on reliability; norms for new forms available following testing program; 4¢ per test; 4¢ per key; postage extra; 40(45) minutes; Bureau of Educational Measurements. *

[600]

★First Year Algebra Test: National Achievement Tests. 1 year high school; 1958–62; Forms A ('62, c1958–62, identical with test copyrighted in 1958), B ('59), (8 pages); class record-keys: Forms A ('60, identical with sheet copyrighted in 1958), B ['59]; no specific manual; combined manual ['58, 12 pages] for this test and tests 650, 653, and 656; $3.50 per 25 tests; 85¢ per manual; 50¢ per specimen set (without manual); postage extra; 40(45) minutes; Ray Webb and Julius H. Hlavaty; [Psychometric Affiliates]. *

DONALD L. MEYER, *Assistant Professor of Education, Syracuse University, Syracuse, New York.*

This test consists of 48 items dealing with basic algebra skills. These skills seem to be adequately represented except for graphing. Only one item depends on the pupil's "understanding" of graphs. The few items which test application generally involve simultaneous equations and are near or at the end of the test. Since the time limit is short (40 minutes) it is doubtful that the majority of students will attempt these items.

The two forms of the test parallel each other quite closely in content, although Form B is somewhat easier. Both forms are difficult

—the reported medians being 21.7 and 23.5 for Forms A and B, respectively. The tables of percentile ranks are given in groups of 10 percentage points. For Form B the percentile ranks 31–40 correspond with the raw scores 21–23 and the percentile ranks 41–50 correspond with the raw score 24, which is curious in light of the reported median.

There are yet other curiosities. The manual gives the teacher the option of scoring the test using a correction for guessing formula. Additional tables of percentile ranks are furnished together with instructions on scoring procedures. The two examples shown are based upon tests having 50 and 51 items. (Recall that the test contains 48 items.) In addition, the supplementary table of percentile ranks for Form A lists the raw scores 2–6 corresponding to percentile ranks 0–10, while the table for simply number correct gives the raw scores 1–11 for the range 0–10. This must, of course, be incorrect. It is not surprising that neither the test booklet nor the manual contains any directions or instructions to the students regarding guessing. No information is given on why one might prefer one scoring procedure to the other.

The answer sheet for Form B says that a perfect score for the test is 120 points and that each correct answer counts one point. Perhaps this is the result from another scoring formula not reported!

Under the heading "Validity" the manual reports that the test was originally administered as a completion type test and the pupils' answers were the basis for the multiple choice distractors. It goes on to say that difficulty, discrimination, and validity indices were computed for each item. This is essentially all the manual says about validity. This is unfortunate since it would be most interesting to know how the validity indices were computed and what the results were. The reliability, using stepped-up split-half coefficients, is reported as .91 for both forms.

There is no discussion of the norm group used except for a general statement in the publisher's catalogue to the effect that, for all of the publisher's achievement tests, selected schools were chosen to represent "an average cross section of pupils" of high, average, and low ability. The catalogue goes on to say, "We have found that this method gives more reliable norms than a larger number of schools chosen at random."

In summary, there is no reason why anyone should use this test and several reasons why one should not. The advantages of using a standardized test rather than one constructed by the teacher are not apparent in this test. Indeed, many teachers probably have objectives other than those included in this test in which case its use would be disadvantageous.

[601]

Seattle Algebra Test: Evaluation and Adjustment Series. 1 semester high school; 1951–54; IBM; Forms AM ('51), BM ('52), (4 pages); manual ('51, 7 pages); expectancy chart ['54, 2 pages]; separate answer sheets must be used; $3.40 per 35 tests; $1.55 per 35 IBM answer sheets; 40¢ per specimen set; postage extra; 40(50) minutes; Harold B. Jeffery, Earl E. Kirschner, Phillip Stucky, John R. Rushing, David B. Scott, and Otie P. Van Orsdall; [Harcourt, Brace & World, Inc.] *

REFERENCES

1. McNamara, Walter J. "Retraining of Industrial Personnel." *Personnel Psychol* 16:233–47 au '63. * (*PA* 38:6728)

Sheldon S. Myers, *Head, Mathematics Section, Test Development Division, Educational Testing Service, Princeton, New Jersey.*

The two forms of this test cover the first half year of a beginning algebra course as conceived 20 years ago. The tests are well printed and well edited. They are pitched to the ability of average and below average classes. They are decidedly too easy for college preparatory students taking the contemporary *College Entrance Examination Board Scholastic Aptitude Test*.

The final product, as well as the descriptive evidence in the manual, indicates that the two forms were developed with considerable care in terms of content sources, balance, coverage, pretesting, item analysis, editing, and norming. Considering the nature of the algebra course being tested and the population for which the test was designed, the tests are of high quality and should provide useful surveys of midyear student progress in basic fundamentals.

However, in terms of usefulness in today's modern algebra programs, they are very much out of date. They do not contain any questions on such important contemporary emphases as the number line, inequalities, coordinates, graphs, the properties of a field, and simple deductive reasoning. An up-to-date algebra test should include these topics, even at midyear. Another weakness is that few, if any questions require original thinking or sophistication. Most of the questions require straightforward recall of facts and use of formal procedures.

The tests have a few technical weaknesses. In an attempt to achieve close parallelism of forms and consequent equivalence of scores, most of the items are paralleled too closely and many are almost identical. This would probably lead to a considerable practice effect from one form to the other. It is possible by careful pretesting and detailed item analysis to achieve parallelism by controlling and balancing discrimination, mean difficulty, standard deviation, and distribution of difficulty without requiring such close paralleling of item structure and content. Another weakness is in the extensive use of "none of the above" as a choice (33 out of 47 questions on Form AM and 42 of 47 on Form BM). It is true that when the testmaker cannot think of, or does not have room for, all the plausible wrong answers students might get, "none of the above" will draw these responses. But the difficulty is that this choice will also draw good students making trivial errors. Long experience with the item analyses of this type of question, in which the ability levels of students taking each choice are computed, shows that the discrimination power of a question is often lowered for this reason.

The manual is thorough and well done. It is particularly good in the section "Using the Test Results."

In summary, these tests are easy midyear surveys of the elementary processes and facts of a very traditional algebra course. They should provide useful surveys of the weaknesses of an average class in the basic fundamentals of elementary algebra at the half-year point.

WILLARD G. WARRINGTON, *Director, Office of Evaluation Services, Michigan State University, East Lansing, Michigan.*

The *Seattle Algebra Test* is "designed to measure the achievement of students in the important objectives of the first half year of a high school course in beginning algebra." According to the manual, the items to measure these important objectives "were constructed only after a thorough analysis of varied instructional materials and authoritative pronouncements in the mathematics field." The sources used in almost all cases were written in the early 1940's. Consequently, the appropriateness of this test depends primarily upon the extent to which the important objectives of that era are still the important objectives of today's first year algebra course.

The test purports to measure student mastery in four areas: Part A, Vocabulary; Part B, Fundamental Processes; Part C, Equations; and Part D, Algebraic Representation and Problems. While it would be possible to obtain part scores for each area, the manual is commendable in that it specifically cautions against using such results as a diagnostic procedure for individual guidance. The manual does, however, provide constructive suggestions as to how the results from this test can be used to evaluate and improve the total instructional program.

The test items, in general, are well constructed and, with the possible exception of a few of the vocabulary items, present meaningful tasks to the student. The clarity of directions for administration and scoring of the test, along with the 50-minute administration time, should make this a convenient test to use. This overall usefulness is further enhanced by the two forms of the test which appear to be quite similar in content and, according to the manual, which are sufficiently equivalent to be used interchangeably.

The material in the manual on reliability is adequate and, in particular, the discussion of the standard error of measurement concept is a welcome addition. Unfortunately, the sections on standard scores and percentile norms are considerably less precise and will very likely confuse the average user. Furthermore, the Expectancy Chart which accompanies the test and shows the relationship between learning ability and achievement in algebra is even more confusing and unnecessarily complicated. Undoubtedly the greatest weakness of this test is the complete lack of data relevant to predictive validity. This reviewer would argue that publishers of achievement tests have an obligation to provide such data and that these data should be presented in a format so that even the relatively unsophisticated user can find them useful.

To summarize, this reviewer feels that the *Seattle Algebra Test* is a well constructed, although somewhat mechanical, test that should be very useful both as a pretest and as an end-of-semester test for the beginning algebra course. However, the test seems somewhat limited as to its objectives, and, as stated in the manual, many teachers will want "to supplement the standardized test with measures designed to cover the specific local standards which are not properly represented in the standardized test."

For a review by Albert E. Meder, Jr., see 5:452.

[602]

★Survey Test of Algebraic Aptitude: California Survey Series. Grade 8; 1959; IBM and Grade-O-Mat; 1 form (8 pages); manual (18 pages); $2.80 per 35 tests; separate answer sheets or cards may be used; 5¢ per IBM answer sheet; 2¢ per Cal-Card; 20¢ per scoring stencil for answer sheets; 20¢ per hand scoring stencil for Cal-Cards; 2¢ per Grade-O-Mat scorable punch-out card; 6¢ per stylus; 6¢ per backing pad; 10¢ per series class record sheet; 2¢ per series individual record sheet; postage extra; 50¢ per specimen set, postpaid; 40(45) minutes; Robert E. Dinkel; California Test Bureau. *

Cyril J. Hoyt, *Professor of Educational Psychology, University of Minnesota, Minneapolis, Minnesota.*

The *Survey Test of Algebraic Aptitude* is published in a single form for use in the latter part of the eighth grade or beginning ninth grade. The test "is designed to determine the degree of success to be anticipated in the initial course in algebra." The manual reports a correlation of .69 between first semester algebra grades and test scores for a group of 129 ninth graders in college preparatory algebra. When most of the 27 pupils taking noncollege preparatory algebra were combined with these (thus enhancing the standard deviation from 6.5 to 8.3) the correlation with second semester grades was .64 for the 146 pupils in the combined group. The reviewer obtained a correlation of .58 between STAA and first quarter algebra grades for 150 pupils out of a class of 325 in one junior high school in an upper middle class suburb in Ramsey County, Minnesota. The mean and standard deviation for this group were 49.8 and 6.0 as compared to 49.0 and 6.5 for the college preparatory group of 129 cited above. Adjustment for the difference in variability of the two groups makes the reviewer's coefficient .65. A recent study [1] indicates that pre-algebra teachers' grades and recommendations have a predictive power of .63 for ninth grade algebra achievement.

1 Barnes, Ward Ewing, and Asher, John William. "Predicting Students' Success in First-Year Algebra." *Math Teach* 55:651–4 D '62. *

The manual indicates that the 60 items in the test were selected from among 70 tried, so that only 14 per cent were discarded. The reported phi coefficients are not indicative of high quality items. In fact, the item analysis data given are in no way indicative of the test's construct validity as claimed by the author.

The section reporting concurrent validity uses the pupil responses employed in the item selection for determining predictive validity. Such multiple use of data takes unwarranted advantages of the effects of sampling errors to enhance correlations.

Table 4 of the manual reports means for the six different groups into which the 332 ninth graders providing the item analysis data had been placed for mathematics instruction. The arrangement of the lines in this table is misleading because the section composed entirely of pupils whom the counselors judged as 3 on a 5-point scale (from 1, highest mathematics potential, to 4 and R, needing remedial instruction) actually earned a higher mean score than two sections (placed higher in the table) which included some pupils rated as 1 and 2 by the counselors, as well as some judged as 3. The text states that "the group mean scores *produce the expected progression* from the lowest to the highest levels" (reviewer's italics). This statement correctly expresses the relation of mean STAA scores to the table arrangement but does not express the relation of STAA means to the reviewer's interpretation of the counselors' judgment of the probable mathematics potential of the pupils.

The subsequent agreement of actual enrollment (based on eighth grade teachers' recommendations, grades, and general mental ability) with sectioning based on STAA scores or their use in conjunction with other information is not reported clearly though such data were available to the publisher. When the reviewer used the information from Table 5 (which presents the means of 259 of the above pupils grouped into three instructional categories), along with the assumption of a normal distribution of scores, he estimated that approximately 20 per cent of the pupils would have been placed in unsuitable sections if the STAA scores were used alone. The manual describes such results by saying, "the distributions overlapped very little."

The manual makes unwarranted claims for the effectiveness of the test scores. For example, the statement is made that the test "is an ideal instrument for advisement purposes with individual students." This statement seems more appropriate for a sales promotion brochure than for a test manual. The succeeding paragraphs contain advice to counselors on just what the author of the manual considers an appropriate role for the counselor. Further, the manual states that this test "can serve as one reliable source of information" for grouping "students according to ability," though only very unconvincing empirical evidence is cited in Table 5 to show how effectively the test functions in this capacity. If, however, for the pupils of Table 5 the concurrent frequencies of actual enrollment had been reported along with figures for enrollment previously suggested on the basis of STAA scores, the reviewer would have said that some useful empirical evidence was presented relevant to this test's effectiveness for grouping "students according to ability."

If the user recognizes that numerous statements in the manual are not accompanied by supporting evidence, he will find that the STAA is a reasonably satisfactory test which can be useful in situations where teacher recommendations and a uniform grading system for the pre-algebra instruction are not available. The publishers have not presented evidence that this test can provide any additional information on expected success in algebra that is not available from teachers' grades and recommendations in a good junior high school mathematics department, though the original data summarized in the manual as the basis for concurrent validity could have yielded such information. Though the predictive validity coefficient reported for STAA (on the item analysis sample) is negligibly lower than that for the *Portland Prognostic Test for Mathematics,* the publisher of the latter has shown that teachers' judgments combined with the test results enhance the predictive power to .76. Hence, the Portland test would be preferred in the absence of information on the STAA.

DONALD L. MEYER, *Assistant Professor of Education, Syracuse University, Syracuse, New York.*

This test is composed of 60 items which can be classified into two main groups: those dealing with the usual seventh and eighth grade subject matter (arithmetic, simple formulae) and those dealing with "symbol reasoning or manipulation" (binary arithmetic, code substitution). Since past achievement usually predicts future achievement fairly well and the usual algebra course involves a goodly amount of "symbol reasoning or manipulation," this test certainly has face validity for predicting algebra achievement. The manual accompanying the test gives a discussion of the other types of validity.

For construct validity a résumé of the development of the test is presented together with correlations between a preliminary 24-item form of the aptitude test and two algebra achievement tests. It is unfortunate that these correlations are not reported for the final 60-item test. Correlations of the final form with three other algebra aptitude tests are given, however. These correlations range from .73 to .81.

The concurrent validity of the test is demonstrated by the presentation of summary statistics resulting from the administration of the test to six groups of ninth grade mathematics students at a particular high school. These students had previously been placed by school personnel into classes ranging from "remedial mathematics" through "general mathematics" to algebra. The means for these groups on the test consistently increase from 20.2 for the remedial group to 49.0 for the top algebra class.

The most important type of validity for an aptitude test is, of course, its predictive validity. The discussion of the test's predictive power is fairly short. Three correlations between end-of-term school marks and scores on the test are reported. These correlations, which range from .68 to .74, were calculated using the data from the school mentioned previously. Considering all the difficulties associated with teachers' marks, the evidence presented is certainly indicative of high predictive validity.

The evidence that is lacking, however, is that which would convince one that a test of algebra aptitude is worthwhile administering at all. A group test of mental ability is usually a part of every school testing program and if it correlates as highly with achievement as the aptitude test, then it could be argued that a school testing program needn't include a test such as the *Survey Test of Algebraic Aptitude.* It would seem that any publisher of an aptitude test should report the additional variance in achievement measures accounted for by their aptitude test after a group intelligence test and, possibly, past achievement measures have been considered. The time required for the administration of any additional test must be well justified. In the present instance, no correlations of the total test with either achievement test scores or with an intelligence test have been reported. In the section on concurrent validity discussed above, the classes were formed on the basis of *California Short-Form Test of Mental Maturity* scores, teachers' recommendations, and arithmetic marks earned in previous years. The conclusion was that the survey test had concurrent validity with the grouping process used. Another tentative conclusion is that we can get along without the survey test.

The 60 items have been constructed so that the last 30 parallel the first 30 in content. The manual suggests that a comparison of the resulting part scores would identify, e.g., the "fast and inaccurate" and the "slow and accurate" pupils. Since the test is timed and norms are not available on the part scores, this comparison would be difficult.

The physical layout of the test is good, but some of the items suffer from technical imperfections. "None of these" or "impossible" as an alternative is used once in the first 30 items and three times in the last 30 items. It is keyed as the answer when it is last used. One gets the impression that this alternative has been used as a "space-filler." An implausible distractor occurs in two parallel items requiring the pupil to change from one unit of measure to another. The distractor, 1 rod, is not a likely response.

An item in the first 30 items requires the pupil to choose the largest of five given numbers, and an item in the second 30 requires the pupil to choose the smallest of the same five numbers. The intercorrelation of these items is likely to be spuriously high. The stems in five of the items are such that the pupil does not know the point of the question until he has read the accompanying alternatives.

In summary, the *Survey Test of Algebraic Aptitude* has high validity for assessing current and future status of pupils in ninth grade algebra, granting the generalizability of the norm group data. If one desires to include an algebra aptitude test in the school testing program, this test should be seriously considered. What unique contribution the test can make to the program, however, is unknown.

[603]

***The Votaw Algebra Test: Elementary Algebra.** High school; 1939–59; IBM; Forms D, E, F, ('59, 6 pages); manual ('59, 2 pages); $2.50 per 25 tests; separate answer sheets may be used; 2¢ per IBM answer sheet; 15¢ per scoring stencil; 25¢ per specimen set; cash orders postpaid; 45(50) minutes; David F. Votaw, Sr. and David F. Votaw, Jr.; Steck Co. *

KENNETH F. MCLAUGHLIN, *Specialist, Appraisal of the Individual, United States Office of Education, Washington, D.C.*[1]

This 45-minute test (with three forms) is a 1959 revision of a test issued in 1939. It covers the topics customarily included in a traditional first year algebra course. There is no attempt to include the new symbols or concepts of the "new-type" mathematics courses.

A number of the problems which were included in the old Form A (which was the only early form available to the reviewer) are included in Form D.

Each of the new forms has 60 five-choice items. The fifth choice for each problem is "Different answer." This fifth choice is the correct one for approximately one fifth of the questions in each form. This large number of fifth choice correct answers may be upsetting for those students who also have been unable to find their choices listed on many other items of the test.

The manual of directions and norms consists of two pages. The directions for administration are very general in nature so that no two teachers would probably administer the test in the same manner. The procedure would be improved if the authors would give precise instructions to be read to the students.

The norms for the 1939 edition indicated different means and standard deviations for students answering on the test booklet or on cards for machine scoring. No such differences are suggested for the 1959 tests.

Few details are given to support the various validity statements which are made. Under "content validity" there is an indication of the kinds of materials examined before writing the items. After the item pool was administered to 600 pupils, the test results were used to determine the internal consistency of each item and to eliminate nondiscriminating items. How-

1 Opinions stated in this review do not represent United States Office of Education position or policy.

ever, there is no indication as to the population of schools from which these pupils were selected.

Under "concurrent validity" the authors do not specify the definition of "gifted" which was used by mathematics teachers or principals in selecting certain of their best students. However, three fourths of such "gifted" students were found to exceed a raw score of 54. There is no indication of the level of ability needed to be on the general scholastic honor rolls of various high schools—which is another basis for showing the concurrent validity of the test.

In discussing "statistical validity" the authors indicate that for 402 pupils (the number, type, or location of schools which these pupils attended is not given) there was a correlation of .80 between the pupils' algebra test scores (probably at the end of the course) and course grades.

The reliability coefficient of .88 was computed by averaging the intercorrelations of the three forms by pairs, which were .897, .870, and .883. This lends support to the claim that the forms are equivalent.

The test title suggests that the test is suitable as a first semester and second semester test. However, percentile rank norms, for boys, girls, and total, are given only for the end of the second semester. There is a table of "Central Tendencies and Variabilities" for each semester which indicates that the difference in means for the two groups is 7.2 raw score units—which would appear to be a rather small change as the result of an extra semester's work.

In order for the test to be useful for diagnostic purposes, as is suggested by the authors, it would be helpful to have available in the manual a table of specifications which would indicate the skills or concepts which each test item covers.

This reviewer would recommend this test for use at the end of the second semester of a traditional first year algebra course. Local norms should be developed to supplement those given. This test would be useful at other times in the course as a diagnostic instrument to determine areas of error for the individual student in the mechanical application of the rules of algebra. It should not be considered as an adequate measure of the ability of a student to use algebraic techniques in the solution of written problems.

For reviews by Richard M. Drake and Nathan Morrison of earlier forms, see 3:329.

[Other Tests]

For tests not listed above, see the following entries in *Tests in Print:* 979, 981–4, 986–8, 992, 994, 997–9, 1001–8, 1010, and 1012; out of print: 978 and 989–91.

ARITHMETIC

[604]

★**American Numerical Test.** Adults in "that great middle and upper middle block of vocations which emphasize shop and white collar skills involving number competence"; 1962; 1 form (3 pages); manual (2 pages); no data on reliability; $3 per 25 tests; $1 per specimen set of 5 tests (must be purchased to obtain manual); cash orders postpaid; 4(10) minutes; John J. McCarty; Psychometric Affiliates. *

MARVIN D. GLOCK, *Professor of Educational Psychology, Cornell University, Ithaca, New York.*

PURPOSE. The test is purported to measure fluency in dealing with numbers; that is, the ability to shift from one type of arithmetic operation to another, such as from addition to multiplication. The uses for such a test are not mentioned specifically, but the norms and validity sample imply vocational usage. The norms "probably are rather representative of that great middle and upper middle block of vocations which emphasize shop and white collar skills involving number competence."

VALIDITY. The test was validated using instructor rankings of classroom performance at the Vocational Technical Institute of Southern Illinois University. The rankings were transmuted to derive a mean and standard deviation, and Pearson product-moment coefficients of correlation ranging from .26 to .90 were obtained.

RELIABILITY. There is no mention of reliability.

NORMS. The norms "are computed on 672 vocational specialists (secretarial, automotive, construction, accounting, machine tool design, etc.)." The manual does not indicate where this sample was obtained or what the distribution is among the mentioned vocations.

ADMINISTRATION AND SCORING. The test is easy to administer. There are 60 fill-in items and they are hand scored. Unfortunately there is an error in the key for item 59.

TEST CONTENT. The items are very simple multiplication, addition, division, and subtraction problems which alternate in that order throughout the test. The main purpose of the test is to measure ability to shift arithmetic operations fluently, but the test is not designed in such a way as to prevent the examinee from working, in order, all of those items of a given type, e.g., addition. There is, indeed, a definite advantage to working easier types first. This criticism could have been overcome by clearly instructing examinees to work the problems in the order of appearance and by scoring any skipped items as wrong with a consequent penalty. Items after the last attempted item would not be scored.

EVALUATION. The test seems to have little usefulness. The sample from which the norms were derived is too vaguely defined to allow interpretation of the percentile scores. The validity studies were performed on a small sample and the criterion used was ratings of classroom success in specific fields. The test is not purported to be designed to measure vocational success in specific fields, but fluency in dealing with numbers. The particular feature of mixed arithmetic operations is ineffective if the examinee works the problems by arithmetic type instead of in order of presentation.

RICHARD T. JOHNSON, *Assistant Professor of Education, Rutgers, The State University, New Brunswick, New Jersey.*

The singular brevity of the *American Numerical Test* manual, the lack of a concrete statement of purpose other than that implied in the title, and the content of the test, make it difficult to assess just what the author had in mind in constructing it. Somewhat oblique references are made to measuring "numerical competence" and "numerical adaptability," but inspection of the items still leaves the purpose of the test in doubt.

Sixty simple problems comprise the test; no information is given on how these were selected. Problems are "arranged in sequences of the four basic arithmetical processes" (addition, subtraction, multiplication, and division), supposedly to insure a rapid change in orientation. However, because the difficulty is the same throughout, the examinee could answer every fourth item (which is multiplication of a two-digit number by a single digit one) throughout the test, then go back and do every fourth item beginning with the second one (which is addition of two two-digit numbers), etc.

The division problems are all of a three-digit dividend and a single digit divisor, the subtraction ones mainly of a two-digit subtrahend and a three-digit minuend (except for five two-digit minuend problems). The apparent homogeneity of items in format, sequence, and simplicity, combined with a four-minute time limit seem to suggest that a title of "Basic Arithmetic Speed Test" would be more appropriate.

The author states that the 60 problems "were found to provide excellent challenge even for accounting students and to distribute individuals of various backgrounds well over the numerical competence continuum," but inspection of the mean and standard deviation for his accounting group indicates that about 16 per cent of the group received scores of either 59 or 60 correct.

Validity coefficients (Pearson product-moment) between test scores and transmuted instructor ratings of students at the Vocational Technical Institute of Southern Illinois University for six vocational groups range from .26 to .90, with a reported median value of .33. No information is given on how the instructor rankings were made, the transmutation, criteria, or anything beyond the fact that something was done. No mention whatever of any reliability values occurs under the manual heading of "Reliability and Validity."

Administration is fairly simple, and answers are worked out and written directly on the test booklet. The answers are printed around the margin of the scoring sheet, and scoring is done by hand. Answer number 59 is incorrect, and seems to exemplify the lack of care which has gone into the production of the test and manual.

Although norms are given for 672 vocational students, no information is given on sex differences, proportion of each vocation sampled, background, or anything else which one would need to know in order to make even the most shallow interpretation. Apparently all of the students were enrolled at Southern Illinois University. The interpretation that these students "are rather representative of that great middle and upper middle block of vocations which emphasize shop and white collar skills involving number competence" seems entirely unjustified. The implication is that the test is useful for classifying people on the job, in spite of the fact that all the norms are based on student scores. These would be appropriate for predicting instructor rankings at Southern Illinois University and for little else.

As the test now stands, it is lacking in the characteristics most essential for use by consumers: evidence of appropriate and sufficiently high validity and reliability estimates, clearly defined situations for which the test is appropriate, and items which represent a value greater than the cost of $3 per 25 tests. A potential user would undoubtedly do better by using his own sets of random numbers with arithmetical operation signs attached, and doing his own validity and reliability studies for his particular application, than to purchase the *American Numerical Test* in its present form.

[605]

***American School Achievement Tests: Part 2, Arithmetic.** Grades 2–3, 4–6, 7–9; 1941–63; 3 scores: computation, problems, total; 4 forms (2 sheets); Forms D, E, and F are identical with Forms A, B, and C copyrighted 14 years earlier except for format; 3 levels; 50¢ per specimen set of any one level; postage extra; Willis E. Pratt, Robert V. Young, and Clara E. Cockerille (manuals for *b* and *c*); Bobbs-Merrill Co., Inc. *

a) PRIMARY BATTERY 2. Grades 2–3; Forms D ('55), E ('56), F ('57), G ('58); battery manual ('58, c1955–58, 13 pages); $2.75 per 35 tests; 24(35) minutes.

b) INTERMEDIATE BATTERY. Grades 4–6; Forms D ('55), E ('56), F ('55), G ('58); battery manual ('61, 17 pages); $3 per 35 tests; 50(60) minutes.

c) ADVANCED BATTERY. Grades 7–9; Forms D ('55), E ('56), F ('55), G ('58); battery manual ('63, 17 pages); $3 per 35 tests; 60(70) minutes.

REFERENCES

1. CLELAND, DONALD L., AND TOUSSAINT, ISABELLA H. "The Interrelationships of Reading, Listening, Arithmetic Computation and Intelligence." *Reading Teach* 15:228–31 Ja '62. *

For reviews by Joseph Justman and J. Fred Weaver, see 5:456. For reviews of the complete battery, see 2, 5:1, 4:1, and 3:1.

[606]

***Arithmetic Computation: Public School Achievement Tests.** Grades 3–8; 1928–59; subtest of *Public School Achievement Tests;* Forms 1 ['28], 2 ('28), (4 pages); battery manual ('59, 20 pages, essentially the same—including norms—as 1928 manual); no data on reliability; $2.45 per 35 tests; 25¢ per battery manual; 50¢ per specimen set; postage extra; 40(45) minutes; Jacob S. Orleans; Bobbs-Merrill Co., Inc. *

For reviews of the complete battery, see 40:1194.

[607]

★Arithmetic: Cooperative Mathematics Tests. Grades 7–9; 1962–64; IBM; Forms A, B, C, ('62, 8 pages); no specific manual; series directions for administration ('62, 9 pages); series handbook ('64, 78 pages); separate answer sheets must be used; $4 per 20 tests; $1 per 20 IBM scorable answer sheets; $1 per 10 scoring stencils (answer pattern must be punched out locally); $1 per handbook; postage extra; $2 per specimen set of this and 6 other mathematics tests, cash orders postpaid; 40(45) minutes; Cooperative Test Division. *

O. F. ANDERHALTER, *Professor of Education, and Director, Bureau of Institutional Research, St. Louis University, St. Louis, Missouri.*

These 50-item tests cover a wide range of arithmetic skills. The publishers state that "unlike tests which measure routine manipulation of symbols or the recall of specific information, these tests emphasize the student's understanding of mathematics ideas and his ability to reason with insight." While the tests include numerous items not unlike the traditional type used in measuring computational and word problems skills, there are also a sizable number of items which do represent a unique approach. In some, the effort appears to fall short of the purpose. Thus, for example, item 2 on Form A merely calls for a verbalization of a procedure. In numerous others, however, the authors do appear to be approaching their objective. Item 34 on Form A, for example, is an item measuring the understanding of the distributive property of multiplication and addition. Many similar types of items can be found. The authors are to be commended for their efforts in this direction. To the reviewer, the test is directed toward the measurement of basic understandings and insights.

Little information is available concerning the construction and standardization of the test. Preliminary interpretative data are published in an 8-page manual, dated 1962, and based upon data collected in May 1961.[1]

In the preliminary manual, percentile norms are provided for each of grades 7, 8, and 9, separately for rural, urban, and suburban schools. The number of schools in the norm groups ranges from a low of 4 to a high of 9, with the number of students ranging from a low of 77 to a high of 569. The norms, along with reported mean scores, tend to make the use of the test at grade 9 questionable. For Form A, as an example, the average scores for urban students in grades 7 through 9 are 22.8, 25.3, and 23.5, respectively. For all three forms, and for all three groups, the grade 9 averages are lower than the corresponding grade 8 aver-

1 This review was completed before the 1964 series handbook referred to in the entry was published.—Editor.

ages. In three of the nine comparisons, the grade 9 average is actually lower than the corresponding grade 7 average. While the number of cases in all groups is relatively small, there is a consistent pattern in this direction.

The preliminary manual provides Kuder-Richardson 20 reliability coefficients for all norm groups. Coefficients range from a low of .80 to a high of .91, with most centering in the .86 to .89 range. The tests appear to be adequate in this respect.

Little other information is given in the preliminary manual. While technical and interpretive data were to be gathered in May 1962, no technical report was available as of December 1963.

In summary, the reviewer feels that in terms of the expressed purpose—to emphasize the student's understanding of mathematics ideas and his ability to reason with insight—the test content is superior to that of other survey tests in arithmetic with which he is familiar. This is particularly true with respect to some of the insights underlying our number system and numerical manipulations. If, as in many cases, however, the user is interested in skill in carrying out the manipulations—either separately or in contrived and verbalized situations (the latter, of course, also requiring some degree of insight)—he would find the sampling of such skills inadequate.

The reviewer consequently would find it difficult to recommend the tests as a replacement for the conventional skills tests for many school uses, but he can see considerable merit to their use as a supplemental measure adding at least a partially new dimension to the measurement program. Any general recommendation for such a use would have to be made with some reservations pending publication of more adequate technical information and interpretative materials.

[608]

***Arithmetic: Every Pupil Scholarship Test.** Grades 4–6, 7–8; 1928–64; new form (4 pages) usually issued each January and April; forms from previous testing programs also available; 2 levels; general directions sheet ['63, 2 pages]; no data on reliability; norms for new forms available following testing program; 4¢ per test; 4¢ per key; postage extra; 40(45) or 50(55) minutes; Bureau of Educational Measurements. *

[609]

***Arithmetic: Every Pupil Test.** Grades 3, 4, 5, 6; 1930–64; new form (4 pages) usually issued each December and April; forms from previous testing programs also available; 4 levels; general directions sheet ('63, 2 pages); no data on reliability; Ohio norms for new forms available following testing program; 5¢ per test; 3¢ per key; postpaid; 40(45) minutes; Ohio Scholarship Tests. *

[610]

***Arithmetic Progress Test.** Ages 8-6 to 10-0, 9-0 to 10-8, 10-0 to 11-6; 1952–62; 3 levels; 5*s.* per 12 tests; 6*d.* per single copy; 1*s.* per manual for any one test; prices include purchase tax; postage extra; Valerie Land (*a*) and G. A. V. Morgan (*c*); published for the National Foundation for Educational Research in England and Wales; Newnes Educational Publishing Co. Ltd. *

a) ARITHMETIC PROGRESS TEST A1. Ages 8-6 to 10-0; 1962; 1 form ['62, 4 pages]; manual ('62, 7 pages); 40(50) minutes.

b) ARITHMETIC PROGRESS TESTS B1 AND B2. Ages 9-0 to 10-8; 1958–62; forms B1, B2, ['58, 4 pages]; revised manual ('62, 7 pages); 40(45) minutes.

c) ARITHMETIC PROGRESS TESTS C1 AND C2. Ages 10-0 to 11-6; 1952–58; C1 formerly called *Arithmetic Grading Test 1;* forms C1 ['52], C2 ['53], (4 pages); revised manual ('58, 7 pages) for C1; manual ['54, 5 pages] for C2; no data on reliability of C2; 30(40) minutes.

For reviews by William Curr and John Sutherland of Tests C1 and C2, see 5:461.

[611]

★Arithmetic Reasoning. Business and industry; 1948–63; 1 form ('61, 5 pages); manual ['63, 13 unnumbered pages]; $3.50 per 25 tests; 10¢ per key; $1 per manual; postage extra; $1 per specimen set, postpaid; 15(20) minutes; Richardson, Bellows, Henry & Co., Inc. *

[612]

***Arithmetic Reasoning: Public School Achievement Tests.** Grades 3–8; 1928–59; subtest of *Public School Achievement Tests;* Forms 1 ('28), 2 ['29], (4 pages); battery manual ('59, 20 pages, essentially the same—including norms—as 1928 manual); no data on reliability; $2.45 per 35 tests; 25¢ per battery manual; 50¢ per specimen set; postage extra; 40(45) minutes; Jacob S. Orleans; Bobbs-Merrill Co., Inc. *

For reviews of the complete battery, see 40:1194.

[613]

***Arithmetic Test: National Achievement Tests.** Grades 3–8; 1936–61; 2 forms; 2 tests; no manual; no data on reliability; no norms for part scores; $3.50 per 25 tests; 50¢ per specimen set; postage extra; Robert K. Speer and Samuel Smith; [Psychometric Affiliates]. *

a) FUNDAMENTALS. 1938–61; 4 scores: fundamentals-speed, number comparisons, fundamentals-skills, total; Forms A ('60, c1938–60, 6 pages, identical with test copyrighted in 1938), B ('58, c1938–58, 6 pages, identical with test copyrighted in 1938); directions-norms sheets (2 pages): Form A ('61, c1938–61, identical with sheet copyrighted in 1938), Form B ('38); (55–85) minutes.

b) REASONING. 1936–60; 5 scores: comparisons, problem analysis, finding problem key, problems, total; Forms A ('50, c1938–50, 8 pages, identical with test copyrighted in 1938), B ('54, c1938–54, 8 pages, identical with test copyrighted in 1938 except for item 6, Part 4); directions-norms sheets (2 pages): Form A ('60, c1938–60, identical with sheet copyrighted in 1938), Form B ('38); (40) minutes.

For reviews by R. L. Morton and Leroy H. Schnell, see 40:1449; for reviews by William A. Brownell and W. J. Osburn, see 38:889.

[614]

***Arithmetic Tests 1–2, 4–13.** Ages 10 to 11-11; 1951–63; 12 series; new series published annually; distribution restricted to directors of education; 8*s.* per 12 copies any one test except 7E; 9*d.* per single copy; 1*s.* 3*d.* per manual for any one test except 1 and 2; prices include purchase tax; postage extra; G. A. V. Morgan (*a–d*), M. A. Brimer (*e*), and others; published for the National Foundation for Educational Research in England and Wales; Newnes Educational Publishing Co. Ltd. *

a) ARITHMETIC TEST 1. 1951–54; 1 form ['51, 11 pages]; revised manual ('54, 8 pages); 1*s.* per manual; 40(45) minutes.

b) ARITHMETIC TEST 2. 1952–55; 1 form ['52, 8 pages]; manual ['55, 7 pages]; 1*s.* per manual; 50(55) minutes.

c) ARITHMETIC TEST 4. 1954–57; 1 form ['53, 8 pages]; manual ('57, 9 pages); 50(55) minutes.

d) ARITHMETIC TEST 5. 1954–55; 1 form ['54, 8 pages]; manual ('55, 11 pages); no norms for ages 11-10 to 11-11; 50(55) minutes.

e) ARITHMETIC TEST 6. 1955–56; 1 form ['55, 8 pages]; manual ('56, 11 pages); no norms for ages 11-10 to 11-11; 50(55) minutes.

f) [SERIES 7.] 1957–61; 2 tests.

1) *Arithmetic Test 7.* 1957–59; 1 form ['57, 8 pages]; manual ('59, 11 pages, identical with 1957 manual); 50(55) minutes.

2) *Arithmetic Test 7E.* 1957–61; 27 scores: 2 subscores (mechanical, problem) and total in each of 6 areas (number, linear, money, weight, time, liquid), mechanical total, problem total, 6 process scores, total; 1 form ['57, 8 pages]; manual ('61, 9 pages, identical with 1957 manual except for omission of practice exercise); no data on reliability of subscores; 10*s.* per 12 tests; 1*s.* per single copy; 48(55) minutes.

g) ARITHMETIC TEST 8. 1957–59; 1 form ['57, 8 pages]; manual ('59, 11 pages, identical with 1958 manual); 50(55) minutes.

h) ARITHMETIC TEST 9. 1958–59; 1 form ['58, 8 pages]; manual ('59, 11 pages); 50(55) minutes.

i) [SERIES 10.] 1959–60; 2 tests.

1) *Arithmetic Test 10.* 1959–60; 1 form ['59, 8 pages]; manual ('60, 11 pages); 50(55) minutes.

2) *Arithmetic Test 10E.* 1959–60; 27 scores: same as for 7E; 1 form ['59, 8 pages]; manual ('60, 9 pages); no data on reliability of subscores; 48(55) minutes.

j) [SERIES 11.] 1960–61; 2 tests.

1) *Arithmetic Test 11.* 1960–61; 1 form ['60, 8 pages]; manual ('61, 11 pages); 50(55) minutes.

2) *Arithmetic Test 11E.* 1960–61; 25 scores: 3 scores (mechanical, problem, total) in each of 5 areas (number, money, weight, time and capacity, linear), problem understanding, problem total, mechanical total, 6 process scores, total; 1 form ['60, 8 pages]; manual ('61, 10 pages); no data on reliability of subscores; 48(55) minutes.

k) [SERIES 12.] 1961–62; 2 tests.

1) *Arithmetic Test 12.* 1961–62; 1 form ['61, 8 pages]; manual ('62, 11 pages); 50(55) minutes.

2) *Arithmetic Test 12E.* 1961–62; 25 scores: same as for 11E; 1 form ['61, 8 pages]; manual ('62, 10 pages); no data on reliability of subscores; 48(55) minutes.

l) [SERIES 13.] 1962–63; 2 tests.

1) *Arithmetic Test 13.* 1962–63; 1 form ('62, 8 pages); manual ('63, 12 pages); 50(55) minutes.

2) *Arithmetic Test 13E.* 1962–63; 23 scores: 3 scores (mechanical, problem, total) in each of 4 areas (number, money, weight and linear, time and capacity), mechanical total, problem understanding, problem mathematics, problem total, 6 process scores, total; no data on reliability of subscores; 1 form ('62, 8 pages); manual ('63, 10 pages); 48(55) minutes.

REFERENCES

1. MORETON, C. ANNE, AND BUTCHER, H. J. "Are Rural Children Handicapped by the Use of Speeded Tests in Selection Procedures?" *Brit J Ed Psychol* 33:22–30 F '63. * (*PA* 38:684)

[615]

★Bobbs-Merrill Arithmetic Achievement Tests. Grades 1, 2, 3, 4, 5, 6, 7, 8–9; 1963; 3 scores: concepts and problems, computation, total; IBM for grades 4–9; Forms A, B; 8 levels; no data on reliability of subscores; separate answer sheets must be used in grades 4–9; $3.20 per 35 tests of levels 1, 2, or 3; $3.40 per 35 tests of levels 4, 5, or 6; $3.60 per 35 tests of levels 7 or 8; $1 per set of scoring templates for levels 1 or 2; $1.50 per set of scoring templates for level 3; $1.75 per 35 IBM answer sheets for levels 4–8; 25¢ per scoring stencil; 50¢ per specimen set of any one level; $3.50 per specimen set of all levels; postage extra; William E. Kline and Harry J. Baker; Bobbs-Merrill Co., Inc. *

a) LEVEL 1. Grade 1; Forms A, B, (4 pages); manual (11 pages) for each form; (50–65) minutes in 2 sessions.

b) LEVEL 2. Grade 2; Forms A, B, (4 pages); manual (11 pages) for each form; (50–65) minutes in 2 sessions.

c) LEVEL 3. Grade 3; Forms A, B, (7 pages); manual (12 pages); 40(45) minutes in 2 sessions.

d) LEVEL 4. Grade 4; IBM; Forms A, B, (8 pages); combined manual (17 pages) for levels 4–6; 50(55) minutes.

e) LEVEL 5. Grade 5; IBM; Forms A, B, (11 pages); combined manual (17 pages) for levels 4–6; 50(55) minutes.

f) LEVEL 6. Grade 6; details same as for level 5.

g) LEVEL 7. Grade 7; IBM; Forms A, B, (11 pages); combined manual (17 pages) for levels 7–8; 60(65) minutes.

h) LEVEL 8. Grades 8–9; IBM; Forms A, B, (12 pages); combined manual (17 pages) for levels 7–8; 60(65) minutes.

[616]

***California Arithmetic Test: 1957 Edition With 1963 Norms.** Grades 1–2, 2.5–4.5, 4–6, 7–9; 1933–63; subtest of *California Achievement Tests;* 3 scores: reasoning, fundamentals, total; IBM and Grade-O-Mat for grades 4–9; 2–4 forms ('63 printings, c1957–63, are identical with tests copyrighted in 1957 except for profile); 4 levels; battery manual ('63, c1957–63, 53–64 pages) for each level; battery technical report ('57, 48 pages) on 1957 edition with 1957 norms; battery individual profile ('63, 2 pages) for each level; separate answer sheets or cards may be used in grades 4–9; 5¢ per IBM answer sheet; 9¢ per Scoreze answer sheet; 3¢ per set of Cal-Cards; 4¢ per set of Grade-O-Mat scorable punch-out cards; 20¢ per either IBM answer sheet or Cal-Card hand scoring stencil; 60¢ per either IBM answer sheet or Grade-O-Mat machine scoring stencil; 2¢ per profile; postage extra; technical report free; 75¢ per specimen set of *a* or *b*, $1 per specimen set of *c* or *d;* postpaid; Ernest W. Tiegs and Willis W. Clark; California Test Bureau. *

a) LOWER PRIMARY. Grades 1–2; Forms W, X, ('63, 9 pages); $2.80 per 35 tests; 39(50) minutes.

b) UPPER PRIMARY. Grades 2.5–4.5; Forms W ('63), X ('57), (11 pages); $2.80 per 35 tests; 54(65) minutes.

c) ELEMENTARY. Grades 4–6; IBM and Grade-O-Mat; Forms W, X, Y, Z, ('63, 10 pages); $3.15 per 35 tests; 70(80) minutes.

d) JUNIOR HIGH LEVEL. Grades 7–9; IBM and Grade-O-Mat; Forms W ('63), X ('57), Y ('57), Z ('57), (11 pages); $3.15 per 35 tests; 78(88) minutes.

REFERENCES

1. PETA, STEPHEN BENJAMIN. "An Evaluation of Arithmetical Competence in the Junior High Schools of Lethbridge." *Alberta J Ed Res* 2:114–28 Je '56. *

2. ANDERSON, HARRY E., JR. "The Prediction of Reading and Language From the California Tests." *Ed & Psychol Meas* 21:1035–6 w '61. *

3. ANDERSON, HARRY E., JR. "A Study of Language and Nonlanguage Achievement." *Ed & Psychol Meas* 21:1037–8 w '61. *

4. BALDAUF, ROBERT J. "Predicting Success in Eighth Grade Algebra." *Psychol Rep* 12:810 Je '63. * (*PA* 38:6580)

For a review by Robert D. North, see 5:468; for a review by Robert L. Burch of the 1950 edition, see 4:411; for reviews by C. L. Thiele and Harry Grove Wheat of an earlier edition, see 40:1459; for a review by William A. Brownell, see 38:893. For reviews of the complete battery, see 3, 5:2, 4:2, 3:15, 40:1193, and 38:876.

[617]

*__Cardall Arithmetic Reasoning Test.__ College and adults; 1941–60; formerly published by Science Research Associates, Inc. (see 4:407); Forms A ('41), B ('60, same as test copyrighted in 1941), (1 page); manual ('60, 2 pages, same as preliminary manual copyrighted in 1942); college freshman norms only; $6 per 100 tests; $1 per specimen set; postage extra; 40(45) minutes; Alfred J. Cardall; Cardall Associates. *

For a review by William L. Schaaf, see 4:407.

[618]

★**Computation Test A/67.** Job applicants with at least 6 years of education; 1956–63; multiplication; 1 form ['56, 2 pages, combined English-Afrikaans edition]; no manual; mimeographed norms ('63); R5 per 100 tests; 30c per specimen set; postpaid; 7(10) minutes; National Institute for Personnel Research. *

[619]

★**Diagnostic Arithmetic Tests.** Standards 2–5; 1951–63; 8 tests (Afrikaans edition, '51; English edition, '58) in separate booklets (3–6 pages): addition, subtraction, multiplication, division, weights and measures, fractions, decimals, percentages; mimeographed instructions ['63, 7 pages]; no keys; no data on reliability; no norms; prices vary from 61c to R1.28 per 100 copies of any one test, postpaid; manual free; specimen set not available; administration time not reported; National Bureau of Educational and Social Research. *

[620]

★**Diagnostic Tests in Money.** Ages 10–12; 1960; 7 scores: addition, subtraction, multiplication (2 scores), division (2 scores), changing money; 1 form (10 pages); manual (35 pages); *7d.* per test; *2s. 6d.* per manual; postage and purchase tax extra; administration time (in 3–5 sessions): 36(50) minutes for age 10, 28(45) minutes for age 11, 25(40) minutes for age 12; F. J. Schonell, J. A. Richardson, and K. P. O'Connor; Oliver & Boyd Ltd. *

KENNETH LOVELL, *Lecturer in Educational Psychology, University of Leeds, Leeds, England.*

According to the authors the chief purpose of the tests is to enable the psychologist or teacher to discover, quickly, "the various types of errors made by pupils in applying their basic number knowledge to operations involving money." The tests were designed for the middle and upper classes of the primary school and the lower forms of secondary school.

The manual does not give adequate data regarding the construction of these tests. No information is given concerning either the criteria by which items were accepted in the first draft as representing distinct steps, or the criteria by which items were regarded as redundant and eliminated. Likewise, nothing is said about the socioeconomic background, intelligence, sex, or even nationality of the 100 children in each of 4 classes—ranging in age from 9 to 13½ years—to whom the first draft was applied. No details are available regarding the bases on which "items of low diagnostic utility were omitted" in the preparation of the second draft, nor is the reader told anything about the population (involving some 600 children) to which this and two subsequent drafts were given.

Reliability coefficients (together with standard errors) are given for the tests. These range from .81 to .96 and were obtained from the results of 100 children aged 12+ years retested after an interval of two months but we do not know if these figures were obtained under timed or untimed conditions. No information is given about these children, nor is there any indication that the reliability is the same at 10 as at 13 years of age. Mean scores and standard deviations of raw scores are not available. The manual does give a general analysis of the main errors made by 600 children (those on whom the second and subsequent drafts were tried out), but since we know nothing of this population these data are of limited value. When the tests are given to determine the pupils' mastery of processes they are given with unlimited time, but if it is required to assess speed and accuracy time limits are imposed. Such limits are stated for each test at ages 10, 11, and 12, while with testees of 13 years of age and over the times for the 12-year-olds are to be used. These times are based on the performance of the best 25 per cent of the 10-, 11-, and 12-year-old children in the final standardization. Unfortunately nothing is known of the nature of the group used for this purpose.

On the credit side it can be said that the tests are well printed, the instructions to the pupils are clear, and the tests certainly cover many of the steps and processes that pupils find difficult in the four rules applied to money and also in changing money. There are no other diagnostic tests available in Great Britain that keep to only money as these tests do, although there are well graded textbooks that carefully cover the steps and processes concerned.

In conclusion it may be said that the construction and standardization of these tests are quite inadequate judged by the information available in the manual. The presentation of the items and the instructions to the pupils, however, are satisfactory. Perhaps these tests are best regarded as a very useful set of graded exercises with which to probe children's ability to work specific steps and processes, rather than as psychological tests in the psychometric sense. It must also be stressed that high scores on these tests do not ensure understanding of the concepts involved; high scores may be obtained by pupils who have been well drilled and who perform the operations involved by rote. Even when particular types of examples are practised after errors have been diagnosed, it does not necessarily follow that a better grasp of basic notions will result, although pupils may well work these examples with greater facility.

G. A. V. Morgan, *Former Principal Psychologist, North Wales Child Guidance Service, Denbighshire, Wales.*

Not unexpectedly, in view of the valuable pioneering contribution of the senior author, Professor Schonell, to diagnostic and remedial work in language and number, this test rests on a background of thorough preparation. Arithmetic textbooks, curricula, and tests were analysed in detail to establish items of high diagnostic utility representing progressive steps in attainment. In a series of four thorough tryouts, half the original material was eliminated, modified, or refined. The test is based on careful analysis of the steps in learning and difficulties likely to occur; it is intended that remedial work should be planned by reference to these steps and the detailed analysis of errors made on the test.

The retest reliability coefficients of the subtests, on a group of 100 twelve-year-old children, are satisfactory (median .88) in view of the small number of items (22 to 25) in each test and indicate a very satisfactory reliability for the test as a whole. It is not shown, however, whether reliability estimates are based on timed or untimed versions of the test.

Given untimed, the subtests provide diagnostic information; timed, they are intended to provide estimates of speed and facility in computation. No standardization data are quoted. This would be reasonable if the test were for diagnostic purposes only, that is, for locating the specific errors and misconceptions of individual children and indicating the steps that require special attention in teaching. It is suggested, however, that the tests can be used "to assess attainment level in the four basic processes applied to money." This is ambiguous without reference to limits of score and the proportions likely to reach these. It is probable that the tests will need to be restandardized in Britain.

Insufficient detail is given in the manual of the experimental groups used in developing the test. At the present stage in test development, it should be essential to provide data on the experimental groups used. Furthermore, in standardization it would appear as relevant to establish the representative nature of the sample used and the way the sample was drawn as to quote the number of children. Modern practice, following statistical theory, suggests that the number of schools represented in a sample is more important than the total number of children tested. The first item analysis of this test was based on four classes only.

Analyses of the social utility of arithmetic consistently show that competence in simple money situations is the most frequently used and important of elementary number skills, especially among the less able and less educated part of the population. This test therefore reflects an important aspect of the school curriculum. It represents, however, only one aspect of "money" skill and that is computation in mechanical aspects. Mechanical facility based on paper and pencil work is only indirectly linked with ability to handle simple "problems" or even practical social situations involving money. The test is based on the "logical" steps of a standard curriculum, which would be quite rigid in the succession and timing of topics, and measures facility in mechanical processes based on the assumption of standard "processes." It is even implied, in reference to "borrowing" in describing errors in working, that the items may be worked by one standard method. There is relatively little scope in the test to accommodate money situations in "social arithmetic" which may be computationally simple but requires flexibility of thought and grasp of recurrent "patterns." In particular, the section on "changing money" provides opportunity for computation with fairly difficult number relationships involved in money, sufficient to stretch the brighter pupils, but represents few of the actual situations likely to be met with in everyday changing of money; several items on the conversion of large quantities of small denominations are unrealistic or "textbook" examples, representing neither the demands of social utility on the one hand nor the mathematical development of the child on the other. Even long division of money, it might be noted, rarely occurs in situations outside a book.

In the remedial treatment, an arithmetic text is linked with the test, with carefully planned practice material for each step in an item likely to present difficulty. The analysis of errors, done with great thoroughness, will be of considerable interest to psychologist and teacher in remedial work. (The various opportunities for error in the British money system must be a source of wonder to observers fortunate enough to possess a decimal coinage. It seems significant that American tests of attainment appear to devote relatively less space to money and emphasise problems rather than computation.) Most of the errors, never less than 40 per cent, appear to be related to notation, place value, and number base in various forms; confusion of 10 and other bases, about 20 per cent in most subtests, rises to 39 per cent in easier division.

Tests of mechanical facility in arithmetic have been widely used in Britain, particularly for assessing and diagnosing the attainment of the educationally retarded since such tests are relatively free from reading difficulties and since teachers assume that number facility based solely on computation is an adequate measure of number skill. This quite frequently leads to the paradox of educationally subnormal children who are profiting from excellent schemes of practical number work, based on social utility and relevant to their level of understanding, being assessed on tests of arithmetical computation which are only partly relevant, if at all. It is this danger, of which the authors are doubtless aware, that needs to be guarded against in a routine use of tests measuring only computation.

The principle of diagnostic testing of attainment is now accepted. Earlier tests have stimulated British test sources such as the National Foundation for Educational Research to incorporate the diagnostic principle in test batteries. The present test appears to be the only available up to date one dealing solely with money. It should have a most valuable contribution to make to diagnostic and remedial work, particularly in the normal classroom, as far as mechanical computation, and what this implies, is in question. For the remedial teacher and teacher of the educationally retarded, however, it represents only part of the diagnostic evidence needed; similarly, those undertaking "remedial" teaching or devising appropriate sequences for the slower learning child may need to consider not simply graded practices on specific items or errors, but also wider aspects of understanding and use. In this field, possibly, the future will be with diagnostic and attainment tests depending on oral tests and "practical" assessments. (Neglected since the first attempts by Burt half a century ago.)

[621]

★**Intermediate Diagnostic Arithmetic Test.** Ages 10–12.5; 1959; 18 scores: mechanical (10 subscores plus total), processes (5 subscores), problems, total; 1 form ['59, 11 pages]; manual ('59, 10 pages); 8*s.* 6*d.* per 12 tests; 10*d.* per single copy; 1*s.* 3*d.* per manual; prices include purchase tax; postage extra; 85(95) minutes; Roy Harris (test); published for the National Foundation for Educational Research in England and Wales; Newnes Educational Publishing Co. Ltd. *

STANLEY NISBET, *Professor of Education, University of Glasgow, Glasgow, Scotland.*

This test, which may be used as an achievement test or as a diagnostic test, is designed for English children at the end of primary school or at the beginning of secondary school. The test is in five parts (10, 15, 20, 20, and 20 minutes, respectively) and gives each pupil not only a total score but subscores (*a*) in 10 different fields (number, fractions, decimals, weight, money, capacity, length, averages, percentages, area), (*b*) in 5 processes (addition, subtraction, multiplication, division, place value), (*c*) in mechanical arithmetic as a whole, and (*d*) in problem arithmetic as a whole. A well designed scoring chart, printed on the inner side of the front page of the test booklet, on which the pupil's name and other particulars are entered in the normal way, provides the essential information at a glance. A table of norms translates total scores into standardized scores and a "Table of Grade Equivalents" provides a rough-and-ready ABC grading for each subscore.

This test will probably be most valuable as a diagnostic test, with the norms used only as an approximate indication of absolute attainment. The standardization was made on 1,677 children "in a selected area." However, attainment levels in arithmetic as a whole and in its various aspects tend to vary from area to area, and norms based on a single area, however well chosen, would have to be used with great caution.

A few minor criticisms may be listed: (*a*) the scoring chart would be clearer if its divisions and subdivisions were indicated by differentiated lettering and thicknesses of line; (*b*) pupils who understand the place value of figures well enough in practice may yet be puzzled by such a question as "In this number, 3060, how many times greater than the 6 is the 3?"; (*c*) in items 20 and 31 more space should be left for working the problem; (*d*) the wording of items 22 and 23 might not be acceptable to all teachers, though it has presumably been found to work satisfactorily; (*e*) items of the form "Subtract 1⅛ − ¾ =   " will seem strange to some pupils and might even lead a few to think that in this case the minus means "from"; (*f*) division sums set out with the division sign in front of the divisor (for example, item 21) look odd; (*g*) item 32, set out in the form "÷ 1.3) 19.5" (with space underneath), suggests that the pupil should go ahead with the sum as it is, whereas most schools will have taught him to make the divisor a whole number first; (*h*) some teachers will object to sums dealing with yards *and* feet *and* inches, or gallons *and* quarts *and* pints, on the ground that such combinations of measures are not found in real life, and they will object to "a flight of stairs 5 yd. high" as equally artificial; (*i*) the last part of the "Directions for Use of Marking Key" is not clear.

All in all, this test can be recommended for those who have to obtain a quick picture of the pattern of strengths and weaknesses in arithmetic of a group of pupils at the transition stage from primary to secondary school. At this stage there is the greatest need for educational guidance and a group test like this, which is easy to administer, which takes little time, and which yields the maximum of helpful information, should be valuable to teachers and others responsible for such guidance.

[622]

Los Angeles Diagnostic Tests: Fundamentals of Arithmetic. Grades 2–8; 1925–47; 5 scores: addition, subtraction, multiplication, division, total; Forms 1, 2, ('25, 8 pages); manual ('47, 8 pages); record blank ('25, 2 pages); $2.80 per 35 tests, postage extra; 25¢ per specimen set, postpaid; 40(45) or (40–60) minutes; Caroline Armstrong and Willis W. Clark; California Test Bureau. *

[623]

Los Angeles Diagnostic Tests: Reasoning in Arithmetic. Grades 3–9; 1926; Forms 1, 2, (8 pages); directions sheet for each form ['26, 1 page]; record blank (2 pages); no data on reliability; $2.80 per 35 tests, postage extra; 25¢ per specimen set, postpaid; 30(40) minutes for grades 3–5; 40(50) minutes for grades 6–9; Caroline Armstrong; California Test Bureau. *

[624]

Madden-Peak Arithmetic Computation Test: Evaluation and Adjustment Series. Grades 7.5 and over; 1954–57; 6 scores: addition and subtraction, multiplication and division, common fractions, decimal fractions-mixed decimals-percentages, mental computation and estimation, total; IBM; Forms AM, BM, ('54, 6 pages); manual ('56, 20 pages); 2 sheets of supplementary norms ['57, 1 page each]; no norms for grades 13 and over; tentative norms for grades 7–8; $3.80 per 35 tests; separate answer sheets may be used; $1.55 per 35 IBM answer sheets; 20¢ per machine scoring stencil; 40¢ per specimen set; postage extra; 49(60) minutes; Richard Madden and Philip Peak; [Harcourt, Brace & World, Inc.]. *

For reviews by Theodore E. Kellogg and Albert E. Meder, Jr., see 5:478.

[625]

★Manchester Mechanical Arithmetic Test (Sen.) 1. Ages 13.5–15; 1959; 1 form (10 pages); manual (8 pages); 15*s.* per 25 tests; 10*d.* per single copy; 1*s.* 6*d.* per manual; postage extra; 60(65) minutes; Jack Wrigley (test) and Stephen Wiseman; University of London Press Ltd. *

[626]

***[Mechanical Arithmetic Tests.]** Ages 7 to 8-8, 8 to 9-2, 8 to 10-0; 1949–61; title on manuals for *b* and *c* is *Tests of Mechanical Arithmetic;* 3 levels; prices include purchase tax; postage extra; G. A. V. Morgan (*b*) and Miriam E. Highfield (*c*); published for the National Foundation for Educational Research in England and Wales; Newnes Educational Publishing Co. Ltd. *

a) MECHANICAL ARITHMETIC TESTS 2A AND 2B. Ages 7 to 8-8; 1958; forms 2A, 2B, ['58, 4 pages]; manual ('58, 7 pages); 5*s*. per 12 tests; 6*d*. per single copy; 1*s*. per manual; 30(35) minutes.

b) MECHANICAL ARITHMETIC TESTS 1C AND 1D. Ages 8 to 9-2; 1952–57; forms 1C, 1D, ['52, 2 pages]; manual ['57, 4 pages]; 2*s*. 6*d*. per 12 tests; 4*d*. per single copy; 8*d*. per manual; 25(30) minutes.

c) MECHANICAL ARITHMETIC TESTS 1A AND 1B. Ages 8 to 10-0; 1949–61; forms 1A, 1B, ['49, 2 pages]; manual ['61, 4 pages, same as 1950 manual except for organization]; 2*s*. 6*d*. per 12 tests; 4*d*. per single copy; 8*d*. per manual; 30(35) minutes.

For reviews by George W. Sturrock and Jack Wrigley, see 5:489.

[627]

***Metropolitan Achievement Tests: [Arithmetic].** Grades 3–4, 5–6, 7–9; 1932–62; subtest of *Metropolitan Achievement Tests;* 2 scores: computation, problem solving and concepts; IBM and MRC for grades 5–9; 2 editions; directions for administering ('59, 8 pages) for elementary level; combined directions for administering ('59, 12 pages) for both levels and both editions of intermediate and advanced levels; battery manual for interpreting ('62, 121 pages); 40¢ per specimen set of any one level of either edition; $1.20 per manual for interpreting; postage extra; Walter N. Durost, Harold H. Bixler, Gertrude H. Hildreth, Kenneth W. Lund, and J. Wayne Wrightstone; Harcourt, Brace & World, Inc. *

a) REGULAR EDITION. Grades 3–4, 5–6, 7–9; 1932–62; Forms A ('60), B ('60), C ('61), (7 pages); 3 levels; $4.30 per 35 tests.

1) *Elementary Arithmetic Test.* Grades 3–4; 1937–62; 56(65) minutes in 2 sessions.
2) *Intermediate Arithmetic Test.* Grades 5–6; 1932–62; 108(125) minutes in 2 sessions.
3) *Advanced Arithmetic Test.* Grades 7–9; 1932–62; 108(125) minutes in 2 sessions.

b) SEPARATE ANSWER SHEET EDITION. Grades 5–6, 7–9; 1932–62; IBM and MRC; Forms AM ('60, c1958), BM ('59), CM ('61), (7 pages); 2 levels; separate answer sheets or cards must be used; $4.50 per 35 tests; $1.50 per 35 IBM answer sheets; 20¢ per scoring stencil; $2 per 100 Harbor answer cards (machine scoring service, by Measurement Research Center, Inc., may be arranged through the publisher); $1.60 per 35 optional computation worksheets; 108(125) minutes in 2 sessions.

1) *Intermediate Arithmetic Test.* Grades 5–6.
2) *Advanced Arithmetic Test.* Grades 7–9.

REFERENCES

1. JACOBS, JAMES N. "Aptitude and Achievement Measures in Predicting High School Academic Success." *Personnel & Guid J* 37:334–41 Ja '59. * (*PA* 35:1263)

O. F. ANDERHALTER, *Professor of Education, and Director, Bureau of Institutional Research, St. Louis University, St. Louis, Missouri.*

The test booklets are attractive and create a favorable impression. Item positioning, type size, and coloring add to the readability. The manual providing directions for administering the tests follows good testing practices. Directions are clear and precise. The section dealing with use and interpretation of results is adequate, particularly when used in conjunction with the larger manual for interpreting, which deals with the entire battery.

The tests provide two scores: computation, and problem solving and concepts. The format follows traditional techniques used to measure such skills. Computational problems stay well within the scope of the grade for which each level is intended. Thus, the elementary level (grades 3 and 4) deals almost exclusively with fundamental operations involving whole numbers; the intermediate level (grades 5 and 6) adds an appropriate emphasis upon fractions, mixed numbers, and decimals; and the advanced level (grades 7 to 9) gives increasing weight to such matters as decimals and percentages. About a third of the items in the problems and concepts sections deal with concepts. These range from elementary number concepts to decimal-fraction-percentage relationships, with other terms and concepts appearing appropriately. Word problems are closely associated with computational skills at each level. In general, the content of the tests adheres well to the content of the traditional arithmetic program in the elementary school.

Standardization procedures involving test construction, analyses of items, equating of forms, and derivation of norms, appear to have been well planned and carried out. Size and representativeness of the norm sample are adequate. Provision for percentile and especially stanine norms, in addition to grade equivalents, is to be commended and should promote a sound use of results.

All reliability coefficients are "corrected split-half" coefficients. Median single grade coefficients range from .80 to .92, with individual single grade coefficients ranging from .82 to .95. While the manual states that "this test battery is not intended to measure the speed with which children can answer test questions," and again, "there is no speed factor involved in most of the tests in this battery," some evidence relating to the extent of speededness is desirable when split-half coefficients are used as the sole evidence of reliability. With multiple forms at each level, interform coefficients would appear to be worthwhile additions.

Validity is supported in terms of curricula by data relating to the selection of content at each level, and statistically by correlations between test scores and various mental ability tests. Curricular validity evidence, discussed earlier, is adequate. Correlations with other appropriate arithmetic criteria would be helpful.

The manual dealing with the full battery is a very worthwhile attempt to insure sound use of results. The authors are to be commended for this type of supplementary material.

These tests represent a sound measure of traditional arithmetic skills. Content is well suited to grade level, and the care taken in the development and norming program is evident. Supplementary materials follow good testing practices. The many strong points override the minor reservations expressed in this review.

E. W. HAMILTON, *Head, Department of Mathematics, State College of Iowa, Cedar Falls, Iowa.*

Materials making up this edition of the *Metropolitan Achievement Tests: Arithmetic* were copyrighted in 1958–62. As in former editions, the format is attractive and the accompanying manual for interpreting the results is excellent and comprehensive. A person interested in tests, be he teacher, administrator, or college student, could hunt at length for a better summary of the intricacies of testmaking. A new feature of the interpreter's manual is the inclusion of stanines in addition to the more traditional percentiles and correlation coefficients.

Reliabilities are high (approximately .90) and interesting evidence is presented to support the argument that students really do work honestly even though they use answer sheets and don't have to show their work.

One might wish that the resources and obvious skill of the authors were directed more toward some of the mathematical topics and pedagogical niceties of the last 20 years. It is easy to see why very recent material may be ignored. Much of it hasn't gained wide acceptance or is so new as to be newer than the tests. It takes time to build and standardize instruments of this calibre and they must last several years. However, attention to concepts, generalizations, and understanding has been a part of the curriculum makers' objectives long enough to deserve considerable recognition. A few items in section 2 of the various tests touch on simple concepts like place value, but most of the questions are very routine verbal problems.

There do not seem to be any great demands made upon the reading skill of the student, even in the advanced tests. However, the very simplicity of the problems makes it difficult to be sure that students will not solve them by random or fortuitous choice of operations.

This test will identify the popular arithmetic virtues of the parents' generation. Whether it will serve to guide and direct the present generation of children remains to be seen.

For a review by Robert L. Burch of the 1947 edition, see 4:416; for reviews by Peter L. Spencer and Harry Grove Wheat of an earlier edition, see 40:1458.1; for reviews by Foster E. Grossnickle and Guy M. Wilson, see 38:892. For reviews of the complete battery, see 15; for reviews of earlier editions of the complete battery, see 4:18, 40:1189, and 38:874.

[628]

*[**Moray House Arithmetic Tests.**] Ages 8.5–10.5, 10–12, 12–14; 1935–63; 3 levels; distribution restricted to education authorities; 37*s.* 6*d.* per 100 tests; 8*d.* per single copy; 1*s.* 9*d.* per manual for any one form of any one test; postpaid; purchase tax extra; Department of Education, University of Edinburgh; University of London Press Ltd. *

a) MORAY HOUSE JUNIOR ARITHMETIC TEST. Ages 8.5–10.5; 1949–58; title on test is *Junior Arithmetic Test;* forms 1 ['52], 2 ['58], (8 pages); manual (dates same as for tests, 12 pages) for each form; 40(50) minutes.

b) MORAY HOUSE ARITHMETIC TEST. Ages 10–12; 1935–63; 1–2 new forms issued annually; 15 forms (8 pages) currently available: forms 19 ['49], 20 ['50], 21 ['51], 24 ['54], 25 ['55], 26 ['56], 27 ['57], 28 ['58], 29 ['58], 30 ['59], 31 ['60], 32 ['60], 33 ['61], 34 ['62], 35 ['63]; manual (dates same as for tests, 12 pages) for each form; 40(50) minutes.

c) MORAY HOUSE ARITHMETIC TEST (ADV.). Ages 12–14; 1947–58; forms 1 ['50], 2 ['58], (8 pages); manual (dates same as for tests, 12 pages) for each form; 60(70) minutes.

REFERENCES

1. THOMSON, GODFREY H. *What Are Moray House Tests?* London: University of London Press, [no date]. Pp. 8. *

2. THOMSON, GODFREY H. "The Standardization of Group Tests and the Scatter of Intelligence Quotients." *Brit J Ed Psychol* 2:92–112, 125–38 F, Je '32. * (*PA* 6:3031)

3. LAMBERT, CONSTANCE M. "Symposium on Selection of Pupils for Different Types of Secondary Schools: 7, A Survey of Ability and Interest at the Stage of Transfer." *Brit J Ed Psychol* 19:67–81 Je '49. *

4. PILLINER, A. E. G. "The Position and Size of the Border-Line Group in an Examination." *Brit J Ed Psychol* 20:133–6 Je '50. * (*PA* 25:1281)

5. SUTHERLAND, JOHN. "A Comparison of Pupils' Arithmetical Ability in the Secondary School With Their Ability at the Time of Their Transfer From Primary Schools." *Brit J Ed Psychol* 21:3–8 F '51. * (*PA* 25:7659)

6. EMMETT, W. G., AND WILMUT, F. S. "The Prediction of School Certificate Performance in Specific Subjects." *Brit J Ed Psychol* 22:52–62 F '52. * (*PA* 27:667)

7. SUTHERLAND, JOHN. "An Investigation Into the Prognostic Value of Certain Arithmetic Tests at the Age of Eleven

Plus." *Brit J Psychol, Stat Sect* 5:189–96 N '52. * (*PA* 27:6782)
8. EMMETT, W. G. "Secondary Modern and Grammar School Performance Predicted by Tests Given in Primary Schools." *Brit J Ed Psychol* 24:91–8 Je '54. * (*PA* 29:3036)
9. NISBET, JOHN, AND BUCHAN, JIM. "The Long-Term Follow-Up of Assessments at Age Eleven." *Brit J Ed Psychol* 29:1–8 F '59. * (*PA* 34:3444)

For a review by John Cohen of earlier forms of b, *see 3:346.*

[629]

★**N.B. Arithmetic Tests.** Standards 2–3 (ages 9–11), 4–5 (ages 11–13), 6–8 (ages 13–15); 1961–63; 4 scores: ready knowledge, fundamentals, mechanical computations and problems, total; Forms A, B, ['62, 8 pages]; 3 levels: series 2, 3, 4; preliminary manual ['63, 20 pages]; prices range from R1.35 to R1.80 per 100 tests and from R5.54 to R6.67 per 100 answer booklets; postpaid; specimen set not available; Afrikaans edition available; 35(40) minutes for series 2 and 3, 45(50) minutes for series 4; National Bureau of Educational and Social Research. *

[630]

***Primary Arithmetic: Every Pupil Scholarship Test.** Grades 1, 2–3; 1935–64; new form (4 pages) usually issued each January and April; forms from previous testing programs also available; 2 levels; mimeographed directions for each level ['63, 1–2 pages]; general directions sheet ['63, 2 pages]; no data on reliability; norms for new forms available following testing program; 4¢ per test; 4¢ per key; postage extra; (60) minutes; Bureau of Educational Measurements. *

[631]

***Revised Southend Attainment Test in Mechanical Arithmetic.** Ages 7–15; 1939–50; 1 form ['50]; 2 parts: Sheets 1 (same as Sheet 1 of *The Staffordshire Arithmetic Test*), 2, (2 pages); manual discontinued; no data on reliability and validity; no norms; 5*s*. per 50 copies of either part, postage extra; specimen set not available; administration time not reported; [M. E. Hebron]; George G. Harrap & Co. Ltd. *

For a review by Stephen Wiseman of the original edition, see 3:352.

[632]

***SRA Achievement Series: Arithmetic.** Grades 1–2, 2–4, 4–6, 6–9; 1954–64; subtest of *SRA Achievement Series;* title on tests for grades 2–6 is *Let's Figure This Out;* 3 or 4 scores: concepts, reasoning, computation, total (Forms C and D only); 2 editions; battery teacher's handbook ['64, c1955, 47 pages] for both editions; 50¢ per teacher's handbook; postage extra; Louis P. Thorpe, D. Welty Lefever, and Robert A. Naslund; Science Research Associates, Inc. *

a) FORMS A AND B. Grades 1–2, 2–4, 4–6, 6–9; 1954–64; IBM for grades 4–9; 4 levels; battery school administrator's manual ('58, c1955–56, 32 pages); battery technical supplement, second edition ('57, 45 pages); battery pupil progress and profile charts ('59, c1955–59, 4 pages); separate answer sheets must be used in grades 4–9; 90¢ per 20 pupil progress and profile charts; 50¢ per school administrator's manual; $1 per technical supplement; $1.50 per specimen set of any one level of the complete battery.

1) *Grades 1–2.* 1958–61; Form A ('58, 17 pages); battery examiner's manual ('58, revised '61, 21 pages); mimeographed technical data supplement ('59, 3 pages) for the battery; $2.50 per 20 tests; 105(155) minutes in 3 sessions.

2) *Grades 2–4.* 1955–60; Forms A ('55), B ('57), (15 pages); battery examiner's manual, third edition ('60, c1955–60, 27 pages); $2 per 20 tests; 50¢ per hand scoring stencil; 115(165) minutes in 3 sessions.

3) *Grades 4–6.* 1954–60; IBM; Forms A ('54), B ('56), (16 pages); battery examiner's manual, second edition ('56, c1954–56, revised '60, 39 pages); $2.15 per 20 tests; $5 per 100 IBM scorable answer sheets; $1 per set of machine scoring stencils; 50¢ per hand scoring stencil; 120(150) minutes in 2 sessions.

4) *Grades 6–9.* 1954–60; IBM; Forms A ['55], B ('56), (21 pages); battery examiner's manual, second edition ('56, c1955–56, revised '60, 39 pages); $2 per 20 tests; $5 per 100 IBM scorable answer sheets; $1 per set of machine scoring stencils; 50¢ per hand scoring stencil; 105(125) minutes in 2 sessions.

b) FORMS C AND D. Grades 1–2, 2–4; 1955–64; 2 levels; battery test coordinator's manual ('64, c1961–64, 64 pages); battery pupil progress and profile charts ('64, c1955–64, 4 pages); 90¢ per 20 pupil progress and profile charts; 50¢ per test coordinator's manual; $2 per specimen set of both levels of the complete battery.

1) *Grades 1–2.* 1958–64; Forms C ('58, revised '63), D ('63), (21 pages); Form C is essentially the same as the 1958 Form A except for typography, art work, vocabulary changes in most orally presented items, and option order changes in one-third of the items; battery examiner's manuals (45 pages): Form C ('58, revised '64), Form D ('63, c1958–63, revised '64); $2.50 per 20 tests; 105(155) minutes in 3 sessions.

2) *Grades 2–4.* 1955–64; Forms C ('55, revised '63), D ('57, revised '63), (21 pages); tests are revisions, with approximately 24 per cent new items, of Forms A and B published in 1955 and 1957, respectively; battery examiner's manual ('64, c1955–64, 43 pages) for each form; $2 per 20 tests; 110(160) minutes in 3 sessions.

REFERENCES

1. HOPEN, HAROLD M. *The SRA Achievement Tests for Appraising Arithmetic Computation: As Applied to Grades Six, Seven, and Eight in Russellville Public Schools (Oregon).* Master's thesis, Lewis and Clark College (Portland, Ore.), 1957.

E. W. HAMILTON, *Head, Department of Mathematics, State College of Iowa, Cedar Falls, Iowa.* [*Review of Forms A and B.*]

The current edition of the *SRA Achievement Series: Arithmetic* was produced between 1954 and 1958 according to the copyright dates on the test booklets.

A manual for school administrators, consisting largely of tables of specifications regarding grade placement of test items, is provided. The examiner's manuals are very adequate; the teacher's handbook for diagnostic work after testing should be helpful; and the technical supplement provides information on standardization and the usual information on reliability, as well as correlation matrices for all parts of the test battery. Profile charts are provided and schools are encouraged to study year-by-year growth.

In general, the format is engaging and Part 1 of the various tests is somewhat different. Information is listed; then follows a series of seven questions requiring organization, comparison, and computation. This process is repeated in several situations, thus making a very adequate test of ability to formulate and solve problems. There is some premium on reading in such tests above grade 4.

Whether or not one cares to test formally as low as grades 1–2, or whether or not one should, at least these authors have provided a rather ingenious test and manual to try to avoid the reading problem and to canvass the child's ability to recognize number symbols, understand cardinal and ordinal use of number, and handle time, money, easy combinations, and a few comparisons of quantity.

On the whole, there is good coverage of traditional arithmetic. However, with the possible exception of 2 out of 50 items in Part 3 of the 6–9 test, there is nothing that could be identified as having entered the arithmetic curriculum since 1930. Anyone who has endeavored to follow new trends in the last few years will have to look elsewhere to find measures of these outcomes. If, however, the purpose is to discover whether the pupils are learning the same things as formerly in spite of changes in curriculum, these tests should be a valuable aid, at least in those cases where previous records are available for comparison.

For reviews by Robert D. North and J. Fred Weaver of Forms A and B, see 5:483. For reviews of Forms A and B of the complete battery, see 21 and 5:21.

[633]

*__Scholastic Achievement Series: Arithmetic.__ Grades 2.5–3, 4–6, 7–9; 1954–59; various titles used by publisher; for Catholic schools; subtest of *Scholastic Achievement Series;* 3 scores: computation, reasoning, total; IBM for grades 4–9; 3 levels; $2 per 20 tests; separate answer sheets may be used in grades 4–9; $1 per 20 IBM scorable answer sheets; 50¢ per specimen set of any one level; postage extra; Oliver F. Anderhalter, R. Stephen Gawkoski, and John O'Brien; Scholastic Testing Service, Inc. *

a) PRIMARY TEST. Grades 2.5–3; Forms A ('54), B ('55), (8 pages); battery manual ('59, 12 pages); 43(55) minutes.

b) ELEMENTARY TEST. Grades 4–6; IBM; Forms A ('54, 11 pages), B ('55, 12 pages); battery manual ('58, 21 pages, technical data and norms same as in 1955 manual); 24¢ per scoring stencil; 53(65) minutes.

c) ADVANCED TEST. Grades 7–9; IBM; Forms A ('54, 8 pages), B ('55, 9 pages); battery manual ('59, 22 pages, technical data and norms same as in 1955 manual); 12¢ per scoring stencil; 53(65) minutes.

For reviews by Joseph Justman and Charles S. Ross, see 5:484. For reviews of the complete battery, see 23 and 5:23.

[634]

*__Schrammel-Otterstrom Arithmetic Test.__ Grades 4–6, 7–8; 1945–52; 4 scores: computation, comprehension, problems, total; IBM; hand scored Forms A, B, ('45, 4 pages); machine scorable Forms C, D, ('52, 6 pages); 2 levels labeled Tests 2, 3; manual ('45, 10 pages); mimeographed supplement ('52, 8 pages) for Forms C and D; $1.20 per 25 tests; separate answer sheets may be used with Forms C and D; 85¢ per 25 IBM answer sheets; 30¢ per scoring stencil; postage extra; 35¢ per specimen set, postpaid; 50(55) minutes; H. E. Schrammel, Ruth E. Otterstrom, and Virginia Reed (Test 3, Forms C, D); Bureau of Educational Measurements. *

For a review by William A. Brownell, see 3:351.

[635]

★**Seeing Through Arithmetic Tests.** Grades 3, 4, 5, 6; 1960–62; 7 scores: problem solving, computation, selecting equations, solving equations, information, concepts, total; 1 form ('60, 8 pages); 4 levels; teacher's guide ('60, 8 pages); norms ('62, 1 page); cumulative individual record ('60, 1 page); no data on reliability; revised norms issued annually and available free to users who send in report forms; $2 per 25 tests; $2 per 40 cumulative records; $1 per specimen set; postage extra; 80(90) minutes in 2 sessions; Maurice L. Hartung, Henry Van Engen, E. Glenadine Gibb, and Lois Knowles; Scott, Foresman & Co. *

WILLIAM H. LUCIO, *Professor of Education, University of California, Los Angeles, California.*

The *Seeing Through Arithmetic Tests* are designed to meet the needs of a modern arithmetic program and, more specifically, to be used in connection with Books 3 through 6 of the *Seeing Through Arithmetic* textbook series. The test manual states that "An arithmetic test has long been needed that would do more than test pupils' ability to compute." The STAT "are designed to test all aspects of pupils' competence in arithmetic." The STAT appear to achieve their general purposes of testing mathematical concepts and problem solving to a commendable degree.

The general physical format of the tests is excellent. Each test booklet consists of eight pages, printed on good quality paper. The same uniform sharp black type is used for all four tests. A light grey border, approximately one half inch in width, outlines each page and serves to focus visual attention on the darker type used for the test items. All items are of the multiple choice type and answered by checking appropriate boxes in the test booklet. Adequate space is provided for computation. Scores are determined by the number of correct responses. A single sheet scoring template is provided for each of the four tests and Cumulative Individual Records are available on which to maintain a four-year record of individual achievement. The scoring template and record card are well designed, easy to use, and printed on a heavy quality tagboard. All materials in the test packets are printed on 8½ by 11 inch stock, a feature making for ease of handling and filing.

The manual provides a concise description of the purposes of each of the six test sections and precise directions for administration and scoring. Test interpretation is based on comparisons with national norms; more extensive information for test interpretation should be incorporated in future manuals.

Data indicate that the tests are valid instruments to assess achievement of pupils using the Scott, Foresman arithmetic textbooks. Test construction procedures appear to have insured content validity and item discriminatory power. The items were initially tried out in pilot classrooms to determine "order of difficulty" and "working time required." Experimental test booklets were then prepared for tryout on a national scale in the spring of 1959. Approximately 50,000 pupils and over 1,000 schools were involved in the national norming, including both users and non-users of the publisher's arithmetic texts. Before the final forms of the STAT were prepared, the results from the national norming procedure were "tabulated on the basis of established controls, the suggestions of participating teachers were analyzed and acted upon," the relative order of difficulty for test items in each part of each test was established, required working time was determined, and preliminary norms plotted. The manual states that "A fixed, established norm is not provided for these tests. Instead, test users, each year, will be provided with a report on achievement for the current year. Thus, each year, users can compare the achievement level of their pupils with the national achievement level." The national means have been provided for each year since 1959. Detailed information on the size of sample or the types and numbers of schools involved in these yearly summaries is not provided in current test manuals; it can only be assumed that adequate sampling procedures were followed and that the samples are of the same order as those of the original norming population. No reliability data are currently provided in the manual.

Both selection and arrangement of test content are excellent. All four tests contain the same six parts with an identical number of items in each part. Each part is designed to test a particular mathematical competency in the following order: Part 1, ability to find the answer to a problem (computation is necessary); Part 2, computational ability; Part 3, ability to select the equation that shows the structure of a problem (no computation required); Part 4, ability to find the numerical replacement for the placeholder in an equation (computation is necessary); Part 5, mastery of certain arithmetical information necessary for efficient work in arithmetic; and Part 6, ability to deal with basic concepts and generalizations in arithmetic.

A number of features of the STAT deserve favorable mention. The publisher's procedure of providing yearly norms based on collation of nationwide test results helps to maintain the currency of the tests and to provide data for needed revisions. The tests have been designed so that (*a*) each of the six sections in each test is discrete, concentrating on a particular function, (*b*) the child does not have to transfer his answers to an answer sheet, (*c*) space is provided in the tests for necessary computation, (*d*) devices labeled "stop signs" appear at the end of each part, and (*e*) tests are administered in two different class periods on two successive days with generous time allotments.

The items, with minor exceptions, are expertly written and realistic for the intended age level. For example: "When ⅔ is multiplied by another number greater than zero, which of these statements is always true of the answer?" The pupil then has the choice of the following five answers: "The answer is always greater than 1." "The answer is always less than 1." "The answer is always less than ⅔." "The answer is always greater than ⅔." "None of these." The authors have used variations in language to provide clues for solving items and to express various processes. The questions "How many more?" "How many less?" "How many fewer?" illustrate how language may be used to express the subtraction process, avoiding cliches such as "How many are left?"

Other pertinent items require the child to solve problems when the unknown quantity is placed in various positions in an equation and test the commutative property of addition. Contemporary mathematical thought is applied in a number of items. For example, the grade 5 test uses *n* as a symbol for the replacement numeral and includes ratio items, all appropriately introduced. The grade 6 test uses parentheses in various formulas, the *n* symbol, geometrical figures, and symbols for "greater than" and "number of pairs." It should be noted that because some of these concepts may be relatively advanced, pupils instructed in traditional programs may be at a disadvantage when taking the STAT; therefore, users of these tests should be aware of the precise outcomes assessed by the tests in order to teach for appropriate transfer.

Shortcomings of the STAT are few (detracting little from their overall quality); for instance, (*a*) decimal points in certain equations could be larger in order to distinguish them from ordinary printed periods; (*b*) the grade 3 test might be improved by including items focusing more sharply on interpretation and positional value; (*c*) the grade 4 test could include items dealing with temperature, inches, feet, yards, and miles; and (*d*) there should be more precision in the use of terms, such as using "greatest value" instead of "most things."

Though the STAT are designed to assess the explicit outcomes of instruction based on the use of the Scott, Foresman *Seeing Through Arithmetic* textbook series, nevertheless they should be of value for assessing pupil achievement in any modern arithmetic program because of their comprehensive coverage of concepts and processes. The reviewer considers that these tests reflect expert skill in test construction, and that they should facilitate more effective measurement of mathematical behavior of elementary school pupils.

[636]

★Shop Arithmetic Test. Industry; 1948–63; Forms 1 ('48), 2 ('51), (5 pages); Form 2 is a slightly easier form rather than a parallel form; manual ['63, 11 unnumbered pages]; norms for males only; $3.50 per 25 tests; 10¢ per key; $1 per manual; postage extra; $1 per specimen set, postpaid; 15(20) minutes; Richardson, Bellows, Henry & Co., Inc. *

REFERENCES

1. Cuomo, Sylvia. "Validity Information Exchange, No. 8–17: D.O.T. Code 5-92.601, Foreman II." *Personnel Psychol* 8:268 su '55. *

2. Cuomo, Sylvia, and Meyer, Herbert H. "Validity Information Exchange, No. 8-16: D.O.T. Code 5-92.601, Foreman II." *Personnel Psychol* 8:267 su '55. *

[637]

***Stanford Achievement Test: Arithmetic Tests.** Grades 4–5.5, 5.5–6.9, 7–9; 1923–64; same as arithmetic subtests of *Stanford Achievement Test, [1964 Revision]*; 1953 revision (see 5:487) still available; 3 scores: computation, concepts, applications; IBM and MRC; Form W ('64, 8 pages); 3 levels; manual ['64, 8 pages] for each level; supplementary directions ['64, 1 page each] for use with IBM answer sheets, Harbor answer cards; $4.30 per 35 tests; separate answer sheets or cards may be used; $1.50 per 35 IBM answer sheets; 20¢ per scoring stencil; $2 per 100 Harbor answer cards (machine scoring service, by Measurement Research Center, Inc., may be arranged through the publisher); 40¢ per specimen set of any one level; postage extra; Truman L. Kelley, Richard Madden, Eric F. Gardner, and Herbert C. Rudman; Harcourt, Brace & World, Inc. *

a) INTERMEDIATE 1. Grades 4–5.5; 85(95) minutes in 2 sessions.

b) INTERMEDIATE 2. Grades 5.5–6.9; 87(95) minutes in 2 sessions.

c) ADVANCED. Grades 7–9; 87(95) minutes in 2 sessions.

REFERENCES

1. Laney, Arthur R., Jr. "Validity of Employment Tests for Gas-Appliance Service Personnel." *Personnel Psychol* 4:199–208 su '51. * (*PA* 26:1735)

2. Gowan, J. C. "Intercorrelations and Factor Analysis of Tests Given to Teaching Candidates." *J Exp Ed* 27:1–22 S '58. * (*PA* 33:9299)

3. Emm, M. Eloise. *A Factorial Study of the Problem-Solving Ability of Fifth Grade Boys.* Catholic University of America, Educational Research Monograph, Vol. 22, No. 1. Washington, D.C.: Catholic University of America Press, April 1959. Pp. vi, 57. * (*PA* 35:672)

4. McTaggart, Helen Patricia. *A Factorial Study of the Problem-Solving Ability of Fifth-Grade Girls.* Washington, D.C.: Catholic University of America Press, 1959. Pp. viii, 27. *

5. Nolan, Carson Y. "Achievement in Arithmetic Computation: Analysis of School Differences and Identification of Areas of Low Achievement." *Int J Ed Blind* 8:125–8 My '59. *

6. Nolan, Carson Y., and Ashcroft, Samuel C. "The Stanford Achievement Arithmetic Computation Tests: A Study of an Experimental Adaption for Braille Administration." *Int J Ed Blind* 8:89–92 Mr '59. *

7. Rudd, John Paul. *A Study of the Validity of Selected Predictors for Placement in Three-Rail Curricula.* Doctor's research study No. 1, Colorado State College (Greeley, Colo.), 1962. (*DA* 24:184)

C. Alan Riedesel, *Assistant Professor of Education, Pennsylvania State University, University Park, Pennsylvania.* [Review of 1953 edition.]

The arithmetic subtests of the *Stanford Achievement Test* are developed at four levels and designated to be appropriate for grades 3.0 to 9.9. Each arithmetic achievement test consists of two subtests. The first subtest, labeled "Reasoning," consists of items designed to measure understanding of the number system, arithmetic background, and verbal problems. The second, titled "Arithmetic Computation," consists of computational exercises.

REASONING. In general the verbal problem items are well constructed. In each form and level there are several problems demanding more than just the ability to juggle the numbers contained in the problem.

The portion devoted to the informational background and understanding of the number system falls well below the caliber of the problem solving section. The reviewer feels that a better estimate of a pupil's ability could be gained if there were a score for "problem solving" and a separate score on the informational section. It is difficult to see why items such as "How many cookies in a dozen?" and "A yard is how many inches?" are appropriate items for a "reasoning" subtest. Such items might better be labeled "arithmetic information."

Missing from the entire test are items which adequately measure understanding of place value, including "borrowing" and "carrying," and understanding of the rationale of the fundamental operations. At no time are the examinees asked to display resourcefulness and knowledge of number relationships in answering the "reasoning" exercises.

Since the items were written in the early 1950's, topics such as nonmetric geometry are not surveyed. Teachers and pupils who emphasize a distinction between number and numeral will find the wording of the tests to be imprecise.

COMPUTATION. The computation section consists of an average of 45 items in which the pupil is required to find the answer to a computation situation. Approximately one half of the entire arithmetic test at each level is devoted to the measurement of computational skill. With the present inconsistencies of grade placement in arithmetic curriculums the great emphasis upon this phase of the arithmetic program is questionable. This computational subtest is appropriate for those schools that follow the typical grade placement of 1950–1951. Since considerable space is devoted to an aspect of arithmetic that the teacher can easily survey, the reviewer feels that an analysis of the skills measured by each item, such as that contained in the manual for the *Iowa Tests of Basic Skills,* would help in applying findings of the test.

RELIABILITY. Each manual presents split-half reliability coefficients for each subtest and grade level. The coefficients are based on a random sampling of about 250 pupils selected from as many as 34 school systems. Reliability coefficients range from .86 to .93. In grades 1 and 2 the reliability coefficients for the reasoning subtest are .66 and .79, respectively. A reliability coefficient based on a comparison of the alternate form is not given.

EQUIVALENCE OF FORMS. The manual states that "Comparability of scores from battery to battery was determined in a separate study of the overlapping between adjacent batteries, results of which were incorporated in the K-scores to insure proper articulation of results from the several batteries." The correlation coefficients are not reported.

INTERPRETATION OF RESULTS. The standardization sample school systems were selected from four geographic regions and five system types. The sample per grade ranged from a low of 3,352 in grade 9 to a high of 16,175 in grade 4. Grade 9 was the only sample of less than 9,000 pupils. The test was administered to the group in April and May of 1952. The tests may be interpreted in terms of: Modal-age grade norms, total-age grade norms, percentile ranks, and K-scores.

SUMMARY. This arithmetic test is a dependable test for a school system using traditional methods and content. The interpretation of the tests could be improved by providing a separate problem solving score. Too great a proportion of the test is devoted to the measurement of computational skills.

The norms were established over 10 years ago and the elementary school arithmetic curriculum has undergone many changes in both content and method during this time. Thus, the test user should carefully check the test against the objectives of his present arithmetic program.

For a review by Robert L. Burch of the 1946 edition, see 4:419. For a review of the complete battery, see 26; for a review of the 1953 revision, see 5:25; for reviews of earlier editions, see 4:25 and 3:18.

[638]

★Survey of Arithmetic Achievement: California Survey Series. Grades 7–9; 1959; all items from *California Arithmetic Test, 1957 Edition;* IBM; Forms 1, 2, (8 pages); no specific manual; combined manual (20 pages) for this test and the junior high level of tests 280 and 815; $2.45 per 35 tests; separate answer sheets may be used; 5¢ per IBM answer sheet;

20¢ per scoring stencil; 10¢ per series class record sheet; 2¢ per series individual record sheet; postage extra; 50¢ per specimen set, postpaid; 38(43) minutes with answer sheets, 35(40) minutes without answer sheets; Ernest W. Tiegs and Willis W. Clark; California Test Bureau. *

C. ALAN RIEDESEL, *Assistant Professor of Education, Pennsylvania State University, University Park, Pennsylvania.*

This test is a 70-item survey of arithmetic achievement. The manual states, "The purpose ....is to obtain a general, but accurate, estimate of the extent to which an individual or a group has acquired knowledge and understandings with regard to a specific subject or area of learning." Thus, this test is not designed for diagnostic analysis of individual difficulties. The teacher who wishes to make an evaluation of individual difficulties in arithmetic will receive little aid from this instrument.

The items, largely computational in nature, were selected from the *California Achievement Test, 1957 Edition.* Included are items which survey computation involving addition, subtraction, multiplication, and division of the positive integers, fractions, and decimals; addition and division of negative integers; addition, subtraction, and multiplication of denominate numbers; all three types of computation with cents; and finding the square root of positive integers. The reading and writing of Hindu-Arabic and Roman numerals as well as vocabulary items are included. Ten verbal problems survey area, finding averages, volume, each type of per cent situation, and the solution of single and multi-step problems.

The manual does not include an analysis of skills measured by specific items other than to state that reasoning and skill in the fundamental processes are included. An analysis of the skills measured by specific items would speed the examination of the test and help teachers in surveying pupil achievement.

Since the test items were written during or before 1957 the test is not adequate in scope to measure the arithmetic achievement of children in an up-to-date program. One would hope that a measure of junior high arithmetic achievement would include a greater number of items measuring understanding. Other content which the reviewer would expect to see surveyed more adequately includes place value concepts, ratio and proportion, and the relationships of the fundamental operations. Also, it would be hoped that more of the verbal problems would be thought provoking.

It should be noted that essentially this is a test of *arithmetic*. The better "traditional" and "modern" programs for the junior high level spend an extensive amount of time on geometrical concepts. This test surveys few of these concepts.

The majority of the items are well written and should be understandable to the students. Pupils and teachers who emphasize the distinction between number and numeral will find items 6 and 43 in both forms to be imprecise. However, the wording of these items should not cause incorrect responses by students.

The reliability coefficient of .92 is based on data from 183 students at the eighth grade-seventh month level. The Kuder-Richardson formula 21 was used in computation. A reliability coefficient based on a comparison of the alternate forms is not given.

Equivalence of forms was checked by an administration to two classes each of seventh, eighth, and ninth grade students. A comparison at five key percentile points revealed "sufficient" comparability. The correlation coefficients are not reported. The "equivalent" forms might better be called paraphrased forms in that they appear to have been constructed by matching item by item, rather than by random assignment of items to forms by category in the table of specifications.

The standardization was conducted in 1959 as a part of a dual testing project with the *California Short-Form Test of Mental Maturity.* This adds a control to the use of mental maturity. The sample was obtained with respect to geographical location, size of community, grade assignment, chronological age, and mental age. A total of 100 classrooms and 3,420 individuals were sampled. The manual states that "Special efforts were made to include only the designated normal or typical classes for the community. Neither accelerated nor retarded classes were included * The purpose of this restriction was to maintain the normal homogeneity of classroom units in the standardization program." Since these limitations were placed on the standardization group the test norms are only appropriate for "average" junior high school classes. Advanced classes using the test will probably receive spuriously high grade equivalents and percentile ranks. Below average classes may rank spuriously low.

As a survey of the arithmetic achievement of average junior high school classes when arithmetic is viewed as a tool, this test is satisfactory. As a measure of a comprehensive junior high school mathematics program in which understandings are emphasized, the *Survey of Arithmetic Achievement* is inadequate. The California test, like many other tests of the same nature, measures performance and recognition of symbols and assumes understanding.

HAROLD C. TRIMBLE, *Professor of Mathematics Education, Ohio State University, Columbus, Ohio.*

This test is one of four tests in the California Survey Series developed from items taken from the junior high level of the *California Achievement Tests, 1957 Edition.* The 70 items for this test were selected from the much longer *California Arithmetic Test,* a subtest of the CAT battery, "using the criteria of item difficulty and item discrimination." Although the shorter test loses whatever diagnostic value the longer test had, it retains many of its most effective items and gains in efficiency. There is a saving of time without a proportional loss of information.

The norms for this and the other tests based on the CAT battery were derived with exceptional care. The research design involved the selection of a representative sample of students from grades 7–9. Attention was paid to geographic location, size of community, grade assignment, and chronological and mental age. Each student took the four achievement tests and the *California Short-Form Test of Mental Maturity.* Care was taken with test administration in each locality. Undue influence upon the norms by any one school system was avoided.

The manual deals with the three tests as a battery rather than the single test of arithmetic achievement. It provides complete information with respect to norms. Using the statistical tables for the arithmetic test, it is easy to compare students in any particular school with students in the norm sample, and hence to make allowances for possible differences in chronological age, mental age, special type of school, or the like. Raw scores are easily converted to grade placements, chronological ages, percentile scores, or standard scores. Hence the norms are outstanding both in quality and convenience of presentation.

All that has been said up to this point deals with the statistical quality of the test. It is well to keep in mind that the things people can measure most accurately are not necessarily the things they will believe to be worth measuring. Hence it is important to ask, "Does this test measure significant outcomes of instruction in arithmetic?"

In this connection the prospective user should bear in mind that all items on this test were taken from the 1957 edition of the *California Arithmetic Test.* This 1957 version was criticized by Robert D. North (5:468) as less suitable for the brighter pupils than other tests such as the Stanford and Cooperative series. Moreover, the 1957 version was based almost entirely upon an edition of 1950 which was considered by Robert L. Burch (4:411) to be outdated by "newer" developments in the arithmetic curriculum.

There have been two major changes in thinking about the teaching of arithmetic since the pattern of item selection for this test was set about 1940. Revisions of the test do not adequately reflect either of these changes.

An emphasis upon "meanings" in arithmetic was increasingly evident beginning about 1938. For the most part, this took the form of asking pupils to explain the "whys" of the algorithms. Burch seems to have felt that the 1950 edition of the *California Arithmetic Test* failed to reflect this emphasis. This 1959 test also fails to require pupils to explain, or even to understand, the effects of the place value system of numeration upon the algorithms for the "fundamental" operations.

More recently there has been a growing concern in the profession that pupils understand properties of numbers as well as properties of numerals. Especially in grades 7–9 a number system is increasingly viewed as a mathematical structure with special properties. Meanwhile the emphasis upon systems of numeration has continued and been extended.

This test reflects neither of these two developments. In fact, pupils studying from texts in arithmetic published as much as 15 years ago may be confused by some of the questions on the test. Questions given in the test in the form $\begin{array}{r}321\\ \underline{+69}\end{array}$ are now more commonly stated in the form 321 + 69. Questions with "ragged" decimals, like "78.06 – 8.0425," are rarely used nowadays. Considerations of precision of measurement make such questions practical absurdities. The items which require pupils to work with positive and negative numbers are asked in mathematically awkward ways. The pupil is also asked to solve an equation like $x^2 = 81$ for x, but not told what sorts of replacements of x are permissible. This reviewer would be inclined, in this context, to give as the answer: $x = 9$ or $x = -9$. The test key gives only the answer $x = 9$. Further examples of the conflict of this test with the newer programs in elementary mathematics could be given. A question like "10% of 40 + 10% of 90" will be genuinely puzzling to many pupils who have a thorough understanding of per cent. The difficulty is not with the ideas but with the form of the question.

This test measures efficiently and precisely the outcomes of an arithmetic program that is, by some standards, at least 20 years out of date. Scores obtained will still be somewhat valid because well-educated pupils will be able to adapt to most of the test items and to guess what it is they are being asked to do. The trouble is that many badly-educated pupils will also achieve distinction in arithmetic if this test is the only criterion for excellence.

[639]

★Test A/8: Arithmetic. Technical college students and applicants for clerical and trade positions with 8–12 years of education; 1943–57; forms 1 ['43], 2 ['44], (5 pages); mimeographed manual ['50, 5 pages]; mimeographed norms ('57); R10.00 per 100 tests; R.50 per specimen set; postage extra; Afrikaans edition available; 30(35) minutes for technical college students, 40(45) minutes for others; National Institute for Personnel Research. *

[640]

★Test of Arithmetic Fundamentals. Business and industry; 1951–63; Forms 1 ('51), 2 ('59), (5 pages); manual ['63, 8 unnumbered pages]; no data on reliability of Form 2; $3.50 per 25 tests; 10¢ per key; $1 per manual; postage extra; $1 per specimen set, postpaid; Spanish edition available; 20(25) minutes; Richardson, Bellows, Henry & Co., Inc. *

[641]

★Understanding the Meanings in Arithmetic: A Diagnostic Test. Grades 7–12; 1959; 1 form (10 pages); manual (19 pages); reliability data reported for this test are actually for a longer preliminary form; no norms (use of norms not recommended); $3.50 per 20 tests; 50¢ per specimen set; postage extra; (75) minutes in 2 sessions 1 day apart; David Rappaport; Science Research Associates, Inc. *

REFERENCES

1. RAPPAPORT, DAVID. *An Investigation of the Degree of Understanding of Meanings in Arithmetic of Pupils in Selected Elementary Schools.* Doctor's thesis, Northwestern University (Evanston, Ill.), 1957. (*DA* 18:1322)
2. RAPPAPORT, DAVID. "Testing for Meanings in Arithmetic." *Arith Teach* 6:140–3 Ap '59. *

RICHARD T. JOHNSON, *Assistant Professor of Education, Rutgers, The State University, New Brunswick, New Jersey.*

The 65 diagnostic items in *Understanding the Meanings in Arithmetic* were selected from the 72 used by David Rappaport for his dissertation at Northwestern University. In general they represent an excellent approach to measuring the ability of junior and senior high school students to understand basic concepts and processes of arithmetic.

The probem of showing validity by the selection of items is a formidable one. The test author used questions which "fifteen specialists in arithmetic" rated high in validity as his approach to it. However, some of his questions were considered by his judges to be too involved, and some were so ambiguous as to allow for several quite different interpretations (*2*). No mention could be found of whether the poorer questions were included in the seven items which were dropped from his first test form.

The value of the test to a user seems to hinge on his estimation of the similarity of the concept tested to his own methods of teaching and interpretation of theory. For instance, most teachers prefer teaching division by fractions using the method of multiplying by the inverse of the divisor, but the test assumes the teaching by the common denominator method. Similarly, in dividing by a decimal divisor, most teachers would use the multiplication by a power of 10 to clear the divisor of decimals, but the test assumes otherwise. However, the questionable items are in a distinct minority.

In some of the items, the author approaches the problem of testing concepts by giving the answer to an arithmetic problem and then asking the student to describe the process of obtaining that answer. For example, 16 and 18 may be added with the answer 34 given. The student is then asked to describe how the 6 and 8 are added to get 14 ones, and 10 of the ones exchanged for 1 ten.

The data given in the abstract of the author's dissertation (*1*) suggest that the test is better for diagnosis of individuals low in computational skills than for those who are high, which would be a valuable attribute. A study of possible increase in computational skills for individuals subjected to a remedial program based on diagnosis from this test would add much to validity information.

Although the manual does not so state, the reliability is based on corrected split-half estimates using the original 72 items. A seventh grade estimate of .89 and an eighth grade estimate of .90 are reported, but comparable values computed on the actual test of 65 items are needed for each of the grades from 7 to 12.

In other realms of providing information, the manual does fairly well. Examples of a class record, and a paragraph definition of each concept are given. Scoring guides are on tear-out sheets which cannot be torn out easily, and students' answers are written directly in the test booklet. The manual must therefore be lined up with each page of the student booklet in order to correct the answers. A fold-out sheet which facilitates marking concepts which are inadequately mastered is attached to the test booklet.

The directions (to be read aloud) state that the students have 40 minutes for the first section of the test, but the examiner then is instructed to allow them extra time as needed. The rationale apparently is that such directions will prevent the examinee from spending undue time on questions for which he does not know the answer.

In spite of these limitations, the test seems a convenient way of assessing a number of arithmetical skills at one time, pinpointing basic concepts which have not been mastered, and providing a guide for the teacher's use for remedial instruction. Provided the teacher is committed to the methods underlying the choice of test items, he should find the test a useful adjunct to his own methods of finding out just what his students don't know.

HAROLD C. TRIMBLE, *Professor of Mathematics Education, Ohio State University, Columbus, Ohio.*

According to the author, this test "is designed to measure the pupil's (1) understanding of the essential meanings (concepts) in arithmetic, and (2) thought processes involved in performing calculations."

It is not a standardized test in the usual sense of the term; that is, it "does not present norms describing the *average* performance of particular groups of pupils at different grade levels." Rather, "the *standard of performance* on this test is a correct answer for every question." Incorrect answers are identified by reference to a convenient key. These answers are then recorded on a class record sheet and classified as relating to one or more of the following 16 concepts: cardinal number, ordinal number, place value, decimal system place value, different concepts of a number, process of exchange, addition, subtraction, multiplication, division, fractions, addition of fractions, subtraction of fractions, multiplication of fractions, division of fractions, and decimals. The pattern of marks on the class record sheet is interpreted to locate lack of understanding of particular concepts by individual pupils or classes.

The aims of this test are excellent. The author does not propose to supplant, but rather to supplement, the familiar tests of basic skills. He works out a feasible system of scoring and recording of the data aimed to locate and categorize deficiencies in understanding.

It is a good thing to try to test some of the less tangible objectives of instruction in arithmetic. But if the test is taken too seriously, it may do more harm than good. Some of the questions a prospective user of the test might well ask are: Are the 16 concepts named by the author really basic? (For that matter, are they really concepts?) Should the analysis be limited to "basic concepts and operations derived from our Hindu-Arabic number system?" Or, should properties of numbers, apart from the system of numeration used, be considered as even more basic? Is the approach to an algorithm taken in this test unique? If not, is it the most basic approach possible? For example, should addition and subtraction be related to working with "like size units," or should they be related to the distributive law as is becoming more common? Should comparison by subtraction involve a one-to-one correspondence step followed by take-away, as in several published texts, rather than forcing the solution by addition? Should division of fractions be based upon working with like units, or should it be based upon working with the inverse for multiplication, or upon another of the several available principles?

This test would seem most useful in classes taught by its author or his students. As an outsider, this reviewer would take exception to a great many of the definitions and choices of procedure presented in the manual as *the* correct ones. Hence he would not accept excellent performance on this test as a valid measure of an understanding of the essential meanings of arithmetic.

It is recommended, then, that a prospective user of this test first take the test himself, and then read the manual. Only if he feels that his ideas about what comprise basic concepts in arithmetic agree with those measured by the test should he take results on this test at face value.

It is hoped that tests of this sort become more common. It is important that workers in the profession *experiment* with a more careful formulation of basic concepts and endeavor to measure behaviors relevant to their acquisition. It is equally important to avoid a premature dogma in these matters. In particular, this reviewer differs sharply with some of *the* ways to view the calculations of arithmetic that are encouraged in this test. He is further dismayed by the failure to separate properties of numbers from properties of numeration.

[642]

★**The Wirral Mechanical Arithmetic Tests.** Ages 7, 8, 9, 10; 1962; forms A, B, (4 pages); 4 levels, labeled Tests 1–4; manual (60 pages); norms for combined forms also presented; 3*d.* per test; 2*s.* 3*d.* per manual; postage and purchase tax extra; 20(25) minutes; Fred J. Schonell and John McLeod; Oliver & Boyd Ltd. *

JOHN SUTHERLAND, *Principal Lecturer in Education, Moray House College of Education, Edinburgh, Scotland.*

The authors claim that the two forms at each age level are complementary rather than parallel and that the use of both will give a rather more reliable estimate of the pupils' arithmetical ability than the use of either one alone. The items cover the same general field but a different selection is made in each of the forms. At the same time the intercorrelations between the two forms are high, ranging from .89 to .94, indicating a large common factor in the performance of each. Having claimed that the two forms are complementary, however, the authors are hardly justified in using the intercorrelations between them as a measure of the reliability of the tests. They are, on the other hand, quite entitled to use the Kuder-Richardson formula, for the two forms can quite legitimately be treated as one test.

Norms for each test and for each pair of tests used together are provided either in the form of arithmetic quotients or percentile ranks for different age groups.

Whether or not the test is valid depends, of course, upon whether the test fits the syllabus of instruction used in the area in which the test is being used. The teaching of arithmetic is in a state of flux at the moment. There are many new ideas being tried out, much lumber being eliminated, and new material being introduced. It is becoming increasingly difficult, therefore, to get a test which can be applied over a wide area and at the same time cover the entire curriculum adequately. These tests contain many items which are not taught in all parts of Britain to children under the age of 12, which would invalidate the tests in these areas. Such items include, for example, the items on square measure, percentages, averages, and some of the items on decimals. There are also items which make use of terms which many people are today rejecting, such as chains in the table of length and quarters in the table of weight. Anyone wishing to use the tests, therefore, should examine them carefully to check whether they fit the curriculum being taught.

While the distribution of items in the earlier tests is reasonable, in the more advanced tests (4A and 4B) there is a very steep gradient from the very easy items to the very difficult. In the course of 30 items the test ranges from simple one-figure multiplication by three to complex vulgar and decimal fractions and percentages. This means that there are very few items of each type. Anyone testing 11-year-olds would be well advised to use both tests 4A and 4B.

The authors' claim for the validity of the tests by describing validity as a concept that is "conducive to estimation more by induction and observation than by mechanical statistical calculation" seems to be somewhat doubtful. In some cases this may be the only course open, but in the case of arithmetic tests administered at the ages of 7–10, one would have thought that there must be an element of prediction involved and that the validity of the tests would therefore be determined quite precisely by means of a follow-up study.

The tests in their final form were administered to children in one area of the country only and, in order to produce conversion tables which could be used in any part of the country, the results were compared with the results of the 11+ test applied on each of the previous four years to pupils in this area. The results over the four years had been very steady (a range of mean AQ of only .84 points and a range of standard deviation of only 1.67 points). The authors therefore made the assumption that the distribution of ability in terms of national AQ's would be the same on this occasion. Not only this, but they assumed that the distribution of ability among 7-, 8-, 9-, and 10-year-olds would be the same as that for the 11-year-olds. On this assumption they were able to convert local norms into national norms. The assumptions made appear to be pretty radical, and the norms provided must therefore be used with great discretion. The younger the children the less faith can we place in the quotients obtained.

A lot of care and thought has gone into the construction of the tests. Provided that they are suitable for the curriculum being taught, they should provide the teacher with a measuring instrument which will at least give him an accurate order of merit within his class. The accuracy of any measure of achievement relative to the national average, however, must remain in doubt.

[Other Tests]

For tests not listed above, see the following entries in *Tests in Print:* 1014–7, 1020, 1022, 1025–6, 1028, 1030–3, 1036, 1038, 1040–2, 1045–7, 1050–1, 1053–5, 1057–62, 1066–7, 1075, 1077–8, 1084, 1087–9, 1092, 1094, 1096, and 1098–9; out of print: 1019, 1049, 1064–5, 1073, and 1076; status unknown: 1039 and 1080.

GEOMETRY

[643]

★Analytic Geometry: Cooperative Mathematics Tests. High school and college; 1962–64; IBM; Forms A, B, ('63, 6 pages); no specific manual; series directions for administration ('62, 9 pages); series handbook ('64, 78 pages); separate answer sheets must be used; $4 per 20 tests; $1 per 20 IBM scorable answer sheets; $1 per 10 scoring stencils (answer pattern must be punched out locally); $1 per handbook; postage extra; $2 per specimen set of this and 6 other mathematics tests, cash orders postpaid; 40(45) minutes; Cooperative Test Division. *

[644]

★Diagnostic Test in Basic Geometry. 1, 2 years high school; 1962; 1 form; 2 levels: parts 1, 2, (2 pages) for first year students, parts 3, 4, (2 pages) for second year students; manual (24 pages); no data on reliability; no norms; 2*s.* 6*d.* per 10 copies of any one part; 1*s.* 6*d.* per key for any one part; 4*s.* 6*d.* per manual; 11*s.* 6*d.* per specimen set; postpaid within Australia; (10–30) minutes per part; John H. Henshaw; Australian Council for Educational Research. *

[645]

★Geometry: Cooperative Mathematics Tests. High school; 1962–64; 2 scores: Part 1, total; IBM; Forms A, B, ('62, 16 pages); no specific manual; series directions for administration ('62, 9 pages); series handbook ('64, 78 pages); separate answer sheets must be used; $4 per 20 tests; $1 per 20 IBM scorable answer sheets; $1 per 10 scoring stencils (answer pattern must be punched out locally); $1 per handbook; postage extra; $2 per specimen set of this and 6 other mathematics tests, cash orders postpaid; 40(45) minutes; Cooperative Test Division. *

REFERENCES

1. Traxler, Arthur E. "Difficulty, Reliability, and Validity of the Cooperative Mathematics Tests: Geometry, Form A, Among Independent School Pupils." *Ed Rec B* 84:63–6 Jl '63. *

[646]

***Geometry: Every Pupil Test.** High school; 1929–64; new form (4 pages) usually issued each December and April; forms from previous testing programs also available; general directions sheet ('63, 2 pages); no data on reliability; Ohio norms for new forms available following testing program; 5¢ per test; 3¢ per key; postpaid; 40(45) minutes; Ohio Scholarship Tests. *

[647]

***Lee Test of Geometric Aptitude, 1963 Revision.** High school; 1930–63; IBM; 1 form ('63, 12 pages); manual ('63, 19 pages); norms for grade 9 only (publisher recommends use of local norms); $3.50 per 35 tests; separate answer sheets or cards may be used; 5¢ per IBM answer sheet; 2¢ per Cal-Card; 20¢ per set of answer sheet scoring stencils; 20¢ per Cal-Card hand scoring stencil; postage extra; 50¢ per specimen set, postpaid; 26(40) minutes; J. Murray Lee and Dorris M. Lee; California Test Bureau. *

REFERENCES

1. Lee, J. Murray, and Lee, Dorris May. "The Construction and Validation of a Test of Geometric Aptitude." *Math Teach* 25:193–203 Ap '32. *
2. Goddeyne, Loretta Marie, and Nemzek, Claude L. "The Comparative Value of Two Geometry Prognosis Tests in Predicting Success in Plane Geometry." *J Social Psychol* 20:283-7 N '44. * (*PA* 19:798)
3. Gibney, Esther F. "Aptitude Tests in Relation to the Teaching of Plane Geometry." *Math Teach* 42:181–6 Ap '49. *
4. Gorecki, Audrey G. *The Lee Test of Geometric Aptitude: A Study of Its Use in Predicting Class Success and Its Use in Guidance in the Winona Public School.* Master's thesis, Winona State College (Winona, Minn.), 1959.
5. Hohman, Marie. *The Comparative Value of Three Geometry Prognosis Tests and an Arithmetic Achievement Test in Predicting Success in Plane Geometry.* Master's thesis, Catholic University of America (Washington, D.C.), 1959. (Abstract: *Cath Ed R* 59:621)

Kenneth F. McLaughlin, *Specialist, Appraisal of the Individual, United States Office of Education, Washington, D.C.*[1]

This test is a revision of a test which was first available in 1931. There have been a number of changes and improvements. Completion type questions have been replaced with four- and five-option multiple choice items which can be answered in the test booklet, or on a machine scorable IBM 805 answer sheet or mark-sense Cal-Cards. Both the old and new forms have 50 questions. Based upon research, seven of

1 Points of view or opinions stated in this review do not represent United States Office of Education position or policy.

the original questions have been replaced in the new edition and the item order changed. Items are no longer weighted in the new revision.

The same four types of questions in the early test (selected by a multiple regression technique) are retained in the 1963 revision. In Part 1, items in spatial relationships are concerned with the equivalency of angles or angle sizes in three simple geometric figures. In Part 2, items are referred to a price list (updated to 1963) of various fruits and vegetables. This part "measures the ability to manipulate numerical quantities and to solve problems with fractions." In Part 3, items are referred to a figure composed of triangles and parallelograms from which the student is to determine lengths and perimeters by means of "intuitive geometry." Items in Part 4 are a series of written problems involving simple lengths, areas, and volumes for which definitions and written formulas are given which test "the student's general capacity to think in terms of geometric abstractions."

Part 2 lacks face validity for this reviewer and appears to test a particular arithmetic skill in fractions. However, as often happens, some of the least obvious types of questions may serve as good predictors of specific abilities.

The format and drawings of the 1963 revision are much improved over the older form. However, in Part 1, item 7 could be made clearer to the student who is under the pressure of time by saying: "You may use the information available in problems 5 and 6," rather than using the vague statement "(The necessary information has been given in previous problems)." A similar statement can be made concerning item 11 for which the information in items 1, 3, and 4 may be helpful, but the items occur on a preceding page to which the student must return. There is no apparent reason that related problems could not be grouped together on the same page.

Sample C of Part 3 might confuse some students since all of the information needed is not included with the problem but is imbedded in some explanatory information which may or may not apply to the sample problem. In several problems in Part 3, the solution to a problem has already been found by the student in solving the problem directly preceding, as occurs, for example, in problems 26 and 27, 29 and 30. As a result, these pairs of items are not entirely independent and the student marking one correctly would probably answer the other properly also.

In Part 4, the wording of questions 45 and 47 might be improved so that the problems would be clearer to the student.

The manual describes the procedures followed in determining the types of items to be included in this test and indicates for one study the number of students (291) who took both the old and new forms. The manual discussion includes cautions to be considered in interpreting these experimental data. The students from ninth grade classes in two high schools took the test under standardized conditions in May 1961. (In one school, some of the students were participating in an accelerated mathematics program.) Predictive validity coefficients with second semester plane geometry marks were obtained with values of .51 and .55. In Part 2 of the manual, "Uses of Test Results," the data from each of these classes are used to illustrate the procedures for making local scattergrams, tables, and expectancy charts which may be used to predict the percentage of students in each of four score groups who will make each of five letter grades. Suggested cautions presented include the fact that a score may be misplaced one step interval because of the standard error of measurement and that a prediction based upon a test score may prove incorrect because of the unusual effort, or lack of effort, of the student when taking geometry. The manual also recommends that each school produce its own tables.

The directions for administration of the test are carefully written and should be closely followed by the test administrator.

The norms presented are based upon a ninth grade population from 10 different secondary schools in three states: Pennsylvania, Wisconsin, and California. There is no description of these schools or their curricula. The norms are presented in terms of percentiles, standard scores, and stanines. It is pointed out again that since mathematics programs differ in many schools the test will prove most effective if local norms are developed. This is especially true since recently new mathematics programs have been developed in which geometric concepts are often introduced in elementary grades.

It would seem to this reviewer that a school wishing to use this predictor of geometric aptitude *must* construct its own local norms to fit the local curriculum, develop its own expectancy charts, and exercise all the cautions of interpretations which are so carefully suggested in the manual.

LYNNETTE B. PLUMLEE, *Personnel Research and Testing Division, Sandia Corporation, Albuquerque, New Mexico.*

This test is a revision of a test originally constructed in 1930 to predict the success of students in plane geometry. The revision converts the test from completion type items to multiple choice type items and makes other "technical improvements," but apparently does not question the basic content established over 30 years ago. Validity coefficients for the revised test for two schools were .51 and .55 for 94 and 72 cases, respectively, using second semester marks in geometry as a criterion. The publisher wisely recommends that users develop local expectancy charts for interpreting the predictive value of the test for local use, and helpful instructions are provided for developing such charts.

The 19-page manual includes information on the construction and validation of the test. The description is extensive though not always explicit or clear. It is noted that eight experimental tests were tried for the original 1930 edition, but the manual does not describe the types of material in the four tests which were eliminated.

In view of recent changes in the mathematics curriculum through the first eight grades, one wonders whether the original content would still be selected on the basis of a current survey. Also, would a greater variety of content have resulted in greater predictive validity? Restriction to four types of test content, each of which is highly homogeneous, places a heavy emphasis on the examinee's grasping the idea of each type. If other standard mathematical aptitude or perceptual ability tests were included in any of the experimental validity studies, we are not told about it. One can only conjecture whether some of these might have had equal predictive value.

The manual states that "Some individuals of high intelligence may not do well on this test if they do not have the requisite background," but no information is given regarding what is considered requisite background, except that the test "presumes no previous introduction to geometric symbols or concepts." Timing is such that there appears to be an advantage to the person with a background in geometry. No evidence is presented regarding the possible influence of previous training in geometry on the validity of the test. Since so many junior high school mathematics curricula include some introduction to geometry, any assumption of unfamiliarity with geometry would seem unwarranted. The editors wisely emphasize the need to take other information into consideration in advising students regarding enrollment in geometry. Evidence provided in the manual seems hardly sufficient to warrant using this test to screen students for a high school course in geometry.

The directions for Part 3 are imprecise. A few values are provided on a complex figure from which the student is to deduce other dimensions. To solve the questions, the student must assume (without instruction to do so) that what looks like a parallelogram or square is, in fact, such. Otherwise the questions are not soluble. Without instructions to assume parallelism, an alert student may also be confused by noting that an apparent square, with sides labeled 17, has its diagonal labeled 24.

Methods used in deriving some of the normative data presented in the manual are not clear. For example, the reason is not given for the lack of correspondence between the percentile rank and the percentile range in some instances. By way of illustration, a range of 93.9 to 94.9 is shown as equivalent to a rank of 95.

In summary, this test revision makes "technical improvements" on a 30-year-old test, apparently without reexamining the current appropriateness of the original experimental data. Any potential user is advised to conduct his own validity study, comparing the usefulness of this test with that of other mathematical aptitude material.

For reviews by Edward E. Cureton and Charles C. Weidemann of the original edition, see 40:1470.

[648]

***Plane Geometry: Every Pupil Scholarship Test.** High school; 1926–64; new form (4 pages) usually issued each January and April; forms from previous testing programs also available; general directions sheet ['63, 2 pages]; no data on reliability; norms for new forms available following testing program; 4¢ per test; 4¢ per key; postage extra; 40(45) minutes; Bureau of Educational Measurements. *

[649]

***Plane Geometry: Minnesota High School Achievement Examinations.** High school; 1955–63; series formerly called *Midwest High School*

Achievement Examinations; new form issued each May; norms available in June following release of new form; Form F ('63, 4 pages) used in 1963 testing; no specific manual; series manual ('63, 4 pages); series norms ['63, 4 pages]; series cumulative profile ('62, 2 pages); no data on reliability; no description of normative population; 12¢ per test; $2.50 per 100 profiles; postage extra; 20¢ per specimen set, postpaid; 60(65) minutes; American Guidance Service, Inc. *

For a review by Harold P. Fawcett of earlier forms, see 5:495.

[650]

★Plane Geometry: National Achievement Tests. High school; 1958–60; Forms A ('60, c1958–60, identical with test copyrighted in 1958), B ('59), (8 pages); no specific manual; combined manual ['58, 12 pages] for this test and tests 600, 653, and 656; class record-keys (2 pages): Form A ('60, identical with sheet copyrighted in 1959), Form B ['59]; $3.50 per 25 tests; 85¢ per manual; 50¢ per specimen set (without manual); postage extra; 40(45) minutes; Ray Webb and Julius H. Hlavaty; [Psychometric Affiliates]. *

[651]

★Plane Geometry Test: Affiliation Testing Program for Catholic Secondary Schools. Grades 9–12 and students who are candidates for the high school diploma issued by the Catholic University of America; 1949–63; administered annually in May at individual schools; IBM; new form issued annually; Form Z ('63, 11 pages) used in 1963 program; separate answer sheets must be used; 50¢ per test and IBM answer sheet; postpaid; fee includes purchase of test booklets, scoring, and other services; for more complete information, see 758; specimen set of the complete battery free; 90(100) minutes; Program of Affiliation, Catholic University of America. *

HENRY CHAUNCEY, *President, Educational Testing Service, Princeton, New Jersey.* [Review of Forms Y and Z.]

Forms Y and Z of the Plane Geometry Test are better than most currently available tests in this area; this is because of the number of items emphasizing reasoning and conceptual ideas. In Form Y, six items get at important aspects of proof. Form Z contains items that are ingenious, involving proof and propositional logic.

There are, however, some technical flaws which should be pointed out. In the six occasions in Form Z when the choice indicating insufficiency of data is used, this choice never occurs as the key. This is not the case in Form Y, where the first item has such a key. Another defect arises in connection with the format of the items, which is sentence completion. Normally one selects as a key the choice which makes the sentence true. This is not followed in many of the items. For example, one item reads: "In a rhombus the diagonals (1) are equal, (2) are perpendicular, (3) bisect each other, (4) have two of these properties, (5) have all three of these properties." Choice 1 is true; choice 2 is also true; choice 3 is false; and 4 is the key. It is doubtful that the stipulation in the directions, "choose the answer *which most satisfactorily completes the statement,*" adequately covers this situation. It would probably be better to use the word "only" in some way, to make the "true" options false by insufficiency.

These days candidates are getting much sharper at detecting mathematical flaws and loopholes in test questions. It is becoming increasingly necessary to word questions in tighter language. In algebra this takes the form of $x \neq y$ in questions involving algebraic fractions such as $1/(x - y)$. In geometry this takes the form of specifying which are the equal sides or equal angles in an isosceles triangle. Thus in Form Y, item 59, "In isosceles triangle ABC, the exterior angle at vertex B is acute" is not adequate to specify which are the equal angles and, therefore, choice 5, "not enough is given to tell," is justified, as well as the intended key. "Vertex B" is not enough since A and C are also vertexes. The failure to distinguish between the name of a thing and its measure, as is done in most contemporary programs, is not so much an internal fault of the test as a characteristic of the course being evaluated.

At a time when textbooks and curricula in geometry are undergoing extensive changes, it is even more necessary for a teacher to examine closely prospective tests before selection. If these tests, after such an inspection, seem to be fair measures of the content and emphases of a particular course, then they should provide useful achievement scores in that course.

For reviews of the complete program, see 758.

[652]

***Solid Geometry: Minnesota High School Achievement Examinations.** High school; 1952–63; series formerly called *Midwest High School Achievement Examinations;* new form issued each May; norms available in June following release of new form; Form F ('63, 4 pages) used in 1963 testing; no specific manual; series manual ('63, 4 pages); series norms ['63, 4 pages]; series cumulative profile ('62, 2 pages); no data on reliability; no description of normative population; 12¢ per test; $2.50 per 100 profiles; postage extra; 20¢ per specimen set, postpaid; 60(65) minutes; American Guidance Service, Inc. *

[653]

★Solid Geometry: National Achievement Tests. High school; 1958–60; Forms A ('60, c1958–60, identical with test copyrighted in 1958), B ('59), (8 pages); class record-keys: Forms A ('58), B ['59]; no specific manual; combined manual ['58, 12 pages] for this test and tests 600, 650 and 656; $3.50 per 25 tests; 85¢ per manual; 50¢ per specimen set (without manual); postage extra; 40(45) minutes; Ray Webb and Julius H. Hlavaty (manual); [Psychometric Affiliates]. *

SHELDON S. MYERS, *Head, Mathematics Section, Test Development Division, Educational Testing Service, Princeton, New Jersey.*

In both forms of this test, 48 questions are to be worked in 40 minutes, an allowance of about 50 seconds per question. In view of the average difficulty of the questions in each form (mean raw scores are 27.6 and 25.6), the tests appear to be somewhat speeded. The reliabilities (.84 and .85) therefore appear to contain a speed factor.

Although solid geometry has been declining as a separate subject, with important aspects of it incorporated at other points in the curriculum, this test should not be criticized on this ground. However, the actual content of the two forms raises a serious question about the mathematical objectives of the course being tested. There is nothing in either form on proof, mathematical structure, or those aspects—such as coordinates in 3-space—which would link it with the main stream of mathematics. Instead, the emphasis is mainly on a collection of mensurational procedures, with 36 questions in one form and 33 in the other requiring computations with numerical measures.

The forms are fairly strong on locus (8 and 5 questions) and imbalanced with respect to spherical geometry (6 and 2 questions). It is encouraging to note that a dozen questions in both forms require skill in one important aspect of solid geometry—space perception. The forms are weak with respect to the use of algebra and neglect entirely such important contemporary topics as inequalities, coordinates in 3-space, and proof.

Perhaps the best feature of the two forms is that practically all the questions require reasoning and the application of concepts rather than the mere recall of facts. For this reason, the tests would be useful for practice and the strengthening of certain skills. For evaluation, considerable caution should be exercised with regard to the meaning of the total scores. Much more fruitful would be an analysis of the errors made by students.

Question 3 in Form A has no solution, since it neglects to specify that the plane which bisects the altitude of the pyramid is parallel to the base. In the choices of question 43, Form A, the inch symbols should not be inside the radicals. These errors, along with several misprints in each form, can easily be corrected at the time of administration.

The Manual of Directions is a 12-page pamphlet covering four achievement tests. Aside from percentile tables and statistical tables giving means, medians, standard deviation of raw scores, reliability, range, and size of norms samples for each test, there is very little descriptive information about each test. One looks in vain for descriptions of test content and rationales. There is little on test development; however, one good procedure described was that the four choices in each question were derived from a frequency count of student choices on completion type pretests.

In summary, these are difficult tests of a rather conservative solid geometry course, but they should provide useful practice in the application of concepts and processes.

[Other Tests]

For tests not listed above, see the following entries in *Tests in Print:* 1105, 1107–10, 1112, 1114–6, 1119–26, and 1129–30; out of print: 1100–4.

MISCELLANEOUS

[654]

★Calculus: Cooperative Mathematics Tests. High school and college; 1962–64; IBM; Forms A, B, ('63, 10 pages); no specific manual; series directions for administration ('62, 9 pages); series handbook ('64, 78 pages); separate answer sheets must be used; $4 per 20 tests; $1 per 20 IBM scorable answer sheets; $1 per 10 scoring stencils (answer pattern must be punched out locally); $1 per handbook; postage extra; $2 per specimen set of this and 6 other mathematics tests, cash orders postpaid; 40(45) minutes; Cooperative Test Division. *

[655]

★Structure of the Number System: Cooperative Mathematics Tests. Grades 7–8; 1962–64; IBM; Forms A, B, ('63, 6 pages); no specific manual; series directions for administration ('62, 9 pages); series handbook ('64, 78 pages); separate answer sheets must be used; $4 per 20 tests; $1 per 20 IBM scorable answer sheets; $1 per 10 scoring stencils (answer pattern must be punched out locally); $1 per handbook; postage extra; $2 per specimen set of this and 6 other mathematics tests, cash orders postpaid; 40(45) minutes; Cooperative Test Division. *

TRIGONOMETRY

[656]

★**Plane Trigonometry: National Achievement Tests.** Grades 10–16; 1958–60; Forms A ('60, c1959–60, identical with test copyrighted in 1959), B ('59), (8 pages); no specific manual; class record-key ['59] for each form; combined manual ['58, 12 pages] for this test and tests 600, 650, and 653; $4.50 per 25 tests; 85¢ per manual; 50¢ per specimen set (without manual); postage extra; 40(45) minutes; Ray Webb and Julius H. Hlavaty; [Psychometric Affiliates]. *

[657]

★**Trigonometry: Cooperative Mathematics Tests.** High school and college; 1962–64; IBM; Forms A, B, ('62, 7 pages); no specific manual; series directions for administration ('62, 9 pages); series handbook ('64, 78 pages); separate answer sheets must be used; $4 per 20 tests; $1 per 20 IBM scorable answer sheets; $1 per 10 scoring stencils (answer pattern must be punched out locally); $1 per handbook; postage extra; $2 per specimen set of this and 6 other mathematics tests, cash orders postpaid; 40(45) minutes; Cooperative Test Division. *

[658]

★**Trigonometry: Minnesota High School Achievement Examinations.** High school; 1961–63; series formerly called *Midwest High School Achievement Examinations;* new form issued each May; norms available in June following release of new form; Form F ('63, 4 pages) used in 1963 testing; no specific manual; series manual ('63, 4 pages); series norms ['63, 4 pages]; series cumulative profile ('62, 2 pages); no data on reliability; no description of normative population; 12¢ per test; $2.50 per 100 profiles; postage extra; 20¢ per specimen set, postpaid; 60(65) minutes; American Guidance Service, Inc. *

[Other Tests]

For tests not listed above, see the following entries in *Tests in Print:* 1134–5 and 1137; out of print: 1131–2.

MISCELLANEOUS

Reviews by *Clifford R. Adams, James E. Bryan, Robert C. Challman, Henry Chauncey, Stanley E. Davis, Lester W. Dearborn, Dorothy Eichorn, Albert Ellis, Benno G. Fricke, Elizabeth Hagen, Robert A. Harper, Theodore L. Harris, James R. Hayden, David O. Herman, John D. Krumboltz, D. Welty Lefever, Peter G. Loret, C. Robert Pace, William R. Reevy, Harold Seashore, and Dean K. Whitla.*

[Other Tests]

For tests not listed above, see the following entries in *Tests in Print:* 1138–42.

AGRICULTURE

[659]

***Agriculture: Every Pupil Scholarship Test.** High school; 1927–57; 1 form ('57, 2 pages); general directions sheet ['63, 2 pages]; no data on reliability; 4¢ per test; 4¢ per key; postage extra; 40(45) minutes; Bureau of Educational Measurements. *

[Other Tests]

For tests not listed above, see the following entries in *Tests in Print:* 1144–5 (out of print).

COMPUTATIONAL AND SCORING DEVICES

[660]

★**Chronological Age Computer.** Grades kgn–3, 4–6, 7–9, 9–12; 1961; for determining CA's at month of testing from birthdates; new set of computing slides issued each September; $1.40 per set of computing slides for current year; $2 per complete set; postage extra; B. A. Linsday; American Guidance Service, Inc. *

[661]

★**Digitek Optical Test Scoring and Document Scanning System.** 1963–64; for scoring special Digitek answer sheets marked with ordinary lead pencils; reads alphabetic as well as numeric grids on answer sheets and other kinds of data sheets and will also score IBM-type 805 answer sheets; model 100 (basic machine); model 100A optical scanning unit (basic machine with card punch, item analysis mode, and other features); operation manual ['63, 15 pages]; reference manual ('64, 15 pages); purchase (monthly rental) prices: $17,985 ($297) for basic machine, $39,780 ($657) for model 100A optical scanning unit, $41,630 ($687) for system with computer magnetic tape output; standard answer sheets printed on one side vary in price from $30.60 per 1,000 when minimum of 1,000 are purchased to $7.40 per 1,000 when 100,000 are purchased; corresponding prices for standard answer sheets printed on two sides vary from $39.60 to $9.45; postage and freight charges extra; Digitek Corporation. *

[662]

★**Dominion Table for Converting Mental Age to I.Q.** 1948; for determining IQ's from MA's and CA's between 5 and 17; 1 form (7 pages); 15¢ per copy, postage extra; Department of Educational Research, Ontario College of Education, University of Toronto; distributed by Guidance Centre. *

[663]

★**The EB Punch-Key Scoring and Answer Sheet System.** 1958; special answer sheets for 5-option multiple choice items and equipment for perforating them for hand scoring; 4 perforating methods; mimeographed manual (12 pages); 2 types of answer sheets: No. 1 (90 items), No. 2 (150 items); other answer sheets may be adapted for use with *b–d;* $2.50 per 500 answer sheets of either kind; manual free; Edvin Brye; the Author. *

a) EB TWO-IN-ONE SCORING BOARD. Punchboard for use in perforating answer sheets; may be used only with the special answer sheets; $14.

b) EB DEEP THROAT HEAVY-DUTY PUNCH. Special punch for perforating up to 150 answer sheets at one time; $75.

c) EB HOLLOW PAPER DRILL ADAPTER. Paper drilling attachment for use with drill press; $15.

d) EB SPECIAL ANSWER SHEET DRILLING MACHINE. Portable machine available only on special order; $150.

[664]

★**[Grade Averaging Charts.]** 1956–61; 3 charts; 10 or more copies, 90¢ each; $1 per single copy; postage extra; E. P. Harvey; Teaching Aids Co. *

a) SCORE-QUICK GRADER. 1961; for determining per cent correct from number wrong.

b) QUICK PER CENT GRADE AVERAGING CHART. 1960; for averaging per cent grades.

c) TIME-SAVER GRADE AVERAGING CHART. 1956; for averaging letter grades.

[665]

★**Grade Master.** 1962; for scoring special 50-item answer sheets; may be used with teacher-made and standardized tests composed of 2- to 5-choice items; provides dry-process marking of wrong answers and printing of total wrong; instruction manual (8 pages); electrographic lead pencils recommended for preparation of answer master (answer sheets are marked with No. 1 or 2 pencils); $1,495 per machine; $7.50 per 500 answer sheets; 1½¢ per single copy; $15 per 500 answer masters; 3¢ per single copy; $1 per 12 electrographic lead pencils; postage extra; Electronics for Education, Inc. *

[666]

★**Grade-O-Mat.** 1960; portable machine for scoring IBM punch answer cards; students encircle responses during test administration and then, after test time has elapsed, punch out encircled options; Model 250 ['60]; instruction manual ['60, 7 pages]; directions for administering tests using punch cards ['60, 1 page]; 5 types of standard answer cards: 224-item true-false, 150-item 3-choice multiple choice, 112-item 4-choice multiple choice, 90-item 5-choice multiple choice (A–E), 90-item 5-choice multiple choice (1–5); $595 per machine; 1¢ per answer card; 6¢ per stylus; 6¢ per backing pad; specially printed cards for *Sequential Tests of Educational Progress* and *Cooperative School and College Ability Tests:* 2¢ per card for any one STEP test, 4¢ per set of cards for SCAT; postage extra; Grade-O-Mat Division, Burgess Cellulose Co. *

[667]

***Hankes Answer Sheets.** 1946–62; special answer sheets, scoring services, and profiles for 3 tests (listed below); $1 for scoring and profiling 1 Hankes answer sheet; $1.20 for scoring and profiling 1 IBM answer sheet; $1.20 for scoring and profiling directly from test booklet; economy coupon payment plan (35¢ to 60¢ per answer sheet) also available; coupon and cash orders postpaid one way; scoring service for other types of answer sheets available; E. J. Hankes; Testscor. *

a) STRONG VOCATIONAL INTEREST BLANK. $2.25 per 50 Hankes answer sheets; 2 copies of profile per answer sheet included as part of scoring service.

b) THE PERSONALITY INVENTORY. $1.50 per 50 Hankes answer sheets; only raw scores reported.

c) MINNESOTA MULTIPHASIC PERSONALITY INVENTORY. $1.90 per 50 Hankes answer sheets; 1 copy of profile per answer sheet included as part of scoring service.

REFERENCES

1–5. See 4:466.
6. See 5:529.

[668]

★**IBM Optical Mark Scoring Reader.** 1962–63; for scoring special IBM answer sheets marked with ordinary lead pencils; also adaptable to use with IBM card punch; model 1230 ['62]; manual ('63, 33 pages); purchase (monthly rental) prices: $15,400 ($220) for model 1230, $3,650 ($70) for model 534 card punch, $6,950 ($120) for optional card punch attachment, $2,800 ($40) for optional formula counter, $1,400 ($20) for optional second rights-wrongs-omits counter (single counter is standard equipment), $1,400 ($20) for optional storage feature for part scoring; standard answer sheets printed on one side vary in price from $21.27 per 1,000 when minimum of 500 are purchased to $6.91 per 1,000 when 50,000 or more are purchased; corresponding prices for standard answer sheets printed on two sides vary from $31 to $7.56; postage and freight charges extra; International Business Machines Corporation. * [The expression "IBM" in the test entries in this volume may mean either that the test is scorable by IBM 1230 Optical Mark Scoring Reader or that it is scorable by IBM 805 Test Scoring Machine (see 669). Except for the prices of standard 1230 answer sheets given in this entry, all prices given for IBM answer sheets refer to 805 answer sheets. Price information for most 1230 answer sheets designed to be used with specific tests was not available when these entries were prepared. Users of tests marked "IBM" should check with the publishers of these tests to determine which type IBM answer sheet is available.]

[669]

***IBM Test Scoring Machine.** 1937–61; for scoring IBM answer sheets marked with special electrographic lead pencils; formerly called *International Test Scoring Machine;* may also be equipped with Type 807 Graphic Item Counter to provide item analysis data; model 805 ['37]; manual ('61, c1954–61, 35 pages); purchase (monthly rental) prices: $3,000 ($50) for model 805, $4,500 ($75) when equipped with Graphic Item Counter; fees to colleges and universities are 20 per cent lower; standard answer sheets printed on one side vary in price from $11.22 per 1,000 when minimum of 500 are purchased to $5.92 per 1,000 when 50,000 or more are purchased; corresponding prices for standard answer sheets printed on two sides vary from $11.43 to $6.34; wooden pencils (filled with electrographic lead) vary from $4.25 per half gross to $7.75 per gross for 25 or more gross; mechanical pencils vary from $4 per dozen to $39 per gross in lots of over 12 gross; $6 per carton of 432 electrographic leads; $6.50 per 1,000 graphic item count records; $2.25 per 100 special carbons for use with graphic item count records; postage and freight charges extra; International Business Machines Corporation. * [The expression "IBM" in the test entries in this volume may mean either that the test is scorable by IBM 805 Test Scoring Machine or that it is scorable by IBM

1230 Optical Mark Scoring Reader (see 668). Except for the prices of standard 1230 answer sheets given in the entry for model 1230, all prices given for IBM answer sheets refer to 805 answer sheets. Price information for most 1230 answer sheets designed to be used with specific tests was not available when these entries were prepared. Users of tests marked "IBM" should check with the publishers of these tests to determine which type IBM answer sheet is available.]

REFERENCES

1–14. See 40:1492.
15–36. See 3:397.
37–51. See 5:530.
52. WHITCOMB, MILTON A. "The IBM Answer Sheet as a Major Source of Variance on Highly Speeded Tests." *Ed & Psychol Meas* 18:757–9 w '58. * (*PA* 34:181)
53. DINGMAN, HARVEY F.; HOYT, WILLIAM G.; AND THOMSON, KENNETH F. "A Control Chart for Errors in IBM Test Scoring Machines." *J Exp Ed* 27:241–3 Mr '59. * (*PA* 35:58)
54. MILLER, IRWIN, AND MINOR, FRANK J. "Influence of Multiple-Choice Answer Form Design on Answer-Marking Performance." *J Appl Psychol* 47:374–9 D '63. * (*PA* 38:6646)

For a review by Arthur E. Traxler, see 3:397; for reviews by John G. Darley and H. T. Manuel, see 40:1492.

[670]

★[**MRC Test Processing Service.**] 1956–63; scoring services for certain levels and forms of the following tests: *American College Testing Program Examination, Differential Aptitude Tests, Henmon-Nelson Tests of Mental Ability, Revised Edition, Iowa Silent Reading Tests: New Edition, Iowa Tests of Basic Skills, Iowa Tests of Educational Development, Lorge-Thorndike Intelligence Tests, Metropolitan Achievement Tests, National Merit Scholarship Qualifying Test, Nelson-Denny Reading Test, Otis Quick-Scoring Mental Ability Tests, New Edition, Purdue High School English Test, Stanford Achievement Test,* and *Strong Vocational Interest Blank;* service requires use of special MRC answer sheets in all cases except the Henmon-Nelson, Nelson-Denny, Otis, and Purdue tests and certain forms of the Metropolitan tests, which require special answer cards; sponsors of large-scale testing programs may arrange for MRC scoring of other tests; answer sheets, cards, and prices must be secured directly from the test publishers, except in the case of the SVIB; SVIB prices: $1.50 per set of 25 MRC answer sheets and preliminary manual ('63, 17 pages) for using MRC answer sheets with SVIB; SVIB scoring fee (per answer sheet and providing individual report of 31 scores for women and 55 scores for men): 30¢ for card report, 35¢ for profile report, 40¢ for card and profile report; postage and $1 processing fee extra; Measurement Research Center, Inc. *

[671]

★**NCS Digital Test Scoring and Data Processing.** 1962–64; special answer sheets, scoring and reporting services, and profiles for 16 tests: *Adjective Check List* (ACL), *California Achievement Tests* (CAT), *California Psychological Inventory* (CPI), *California Short-Form Test of Mental Maturity* (CTMM-SF), *Cooperative School and College Ability Tests* (SCAT), *Edwards Personal Preference Schedule* (EPPS), *General Aptitude Test Battery* (GATB), *LYR Youth Inventory* (LYR), *Minnesota Multiphasic Personality Inventory* (MMPI), *Omnibus Personality Inventory* (OPI), *Opinion, Attitude and Interest Survey* (OAIS), *Sequential Tests of Educational Progress* (STEP), *Sixteen Personality Factor Questionnaire* (16 PF), *Stern Activities Index* (SAI), *Stern Environment Indexes* (SEI), *Strong Vocational Interest Blank* (SVIB); $3.25 per 50 NCS answer sheets for any one test except OAIS ($2.50), GATB ($3), ACL ($4.75), SCAT and STEP ($2 per 20 combined answer sheets for SCAT and STEP battery), CAT and CTMM-SF (5¢ each for CTMM-SF, 10¢ each for CAT battery, and 10¢ each for combined answer sheet for CTMM-SF and CAT battery when ordered for handscoring, free when ordered for NCS scoring), and LYR ($1 to $1.50 per examinee depending on quantity—includes test, answer sheet, and scoring service); answer sheets for most tests may also be purchased from the test publishers; scoring and profiling fees per answer sheet, depending on quantity or services: 20¢ for CTMM-SF, 25¢ for GATB, 30¢ to 35¢ for CPI or MMPI, 30¢ to 40¢ for SCAT and STEP battery combined, 44¢ for CAT battery, 45¢ to 55¢ for OPI, 45¢ to 65¢ for EPPS or 16 PF, 60¢ for CAT battery and CTMM-SF combined, 60¢ to 65¢ for SVIB, 60¢ to 80¢ for ACL, 75¢ to 95¢ for SAI or SEI, 80¢ for OAIS, $1 to $1.50 for LYR (includes test and answer sheet); other services available (for CAT, CPI, CTMM-SF, EPPS, MMPI, SAI, SCAT, SEI, 16 PF, and STEP) when 25 or more examinees have been tested: report of means and standard deviations (14¢ to 20¢ per examinee, except for CAT, 5¢, CTMM-SF, 4¢, and SCAT and STEP, quotations on request), report of frequency distributions (12¢ to 18¢ per examinee, except for CAT, 3¢, CTMM-SF, 2¢, and SCAT and STEP, quotations on request); MMPI profile coding for 25 or more examinees: 10¢ to 15¢ per examinee; report of OAIS scores to the student's high school and up to 4 colleges: $1.50 per examinee; CAT right response record: 20¢ per examinee; 5¢ per extra report for any one test; hand scoring stencils: $1 for SCAT or STEP, 60¢ for CAT, 20¢ for CTMM-SF, 50¢ for GATB; postage extra; scoring service for other types of answer sheets available; National Computer Systems. *

[672]

★**Psychometric Research and Service Chart Showing the Davis Difficulty and Discrimination Indices for Item Analysis.** 1962; 1 chart ['62, 1 page]; instructions ('62, 8 pages); Rs. 3.95 per set of chart, plastic sliding scale ruler, and instructions; postage extra; A. Edwin Harper, Jr., S. P. Sangal, and B. Das Gupta; Manasayan. *

Manas 9:64 '62. Based on Davis's method of item analysis, this chart has been prepared by the authors from which it is possible to find out directly, in a very easy operation the difficulty and discriminative indices of each item in an objective test, thus saving a tremendous amount of monotonous work. In fact, the chart is [based] upon the well known works of Davis, Fan and Flanagan. It should prove to be a very good aid for persons engaged in psychometric research especially construction of objective type tests particularly in this country where non-availability of such tools and lack of facilities of statistical work handicaps the worker very much. The instructions pamphlet describes when to use, when not to use the chart and how this chart was constructed etc. The reading of the chart is much facilitated by a specially made plastic sliding scale. All the items are supplied in a protective folder. The publishers and the authors are to be complimented, as also the Indian Statistical Institute (who originally published the chart and who have now authorised Manasayan to publish this new and improved edition) all of whom have combined to bring this important tool to Indian psychologists, and *at such a low cost.* We understand that [the] chart is being sold on a non-profit basis.

[673]

★**The Rapid-Rater.** 1961; special answer sheets and hand punch device for use with classroom tests and for self-testing; may be used with any test composed of 80 or fewer 4-choice multiple choice questions keyed to 1 of 32 fixed answer patterns; group testing requires 1 device for each student; 1 model ['61]; instruction manual ['61, 12 pages]; 13 or more instruments, $3.50 each; 1–12 instruments, $4.50 each; prices include 25 answer sheets and 2 scoring keys (used in varying positions to produce 32 possible keys); 90¢ per 100 additional answer sheets (may also be produced locally); $1 per manual (free with 10 instruments); postage extra; Shaw Laboratories, Inc. *

[674]

★**STAR Score Teach Answer Record.** 1962; special answer sheets and battery-operated punch device which causes a light to flash when a correct response is selected; may be used with any test composed of 2- to 5-choice multiple choice items keyed to 1 of 12 fixed answer patterns; group testing requires 1 device for each student; Models 2761 (for scoring number wrong), 2762 (for scoring number right and number wrong), 2760 (no counters, teaching device only); manual ['62, 15 pages]; 3 types of answer sheets (each with a special answer board and key): No. 58534 (up to 60 items), No. 58533 (up to 102 items), No. 58532 (up to 210 items); $33.50 for Model 2760, $49.50 for Model 2761, $69.50 for Model 2762; prices include answer board and key for pattern of purchaser's choice and 50 answer sheets; $7.50 per additional answer board; $1.50 per additional key; $15 per 500 answer sheets; $10 per carrying case; postage extra; custom made answer boards available; [Arthur M. Wellington and James Bruce]; HRB-Singer, Inc. *

[Other Tests]

For tests not listed above, see the following entries in *Tests in Print:* 1148, 1151, 1154, and 1158–60; out of print: 1146–7, 1155–6, and 1161.

COURTSHIP AND MARRIAGE

[675]

★**A Courtship Analysis.** Adults; 1961; unscored counseling and teaching aid for analysis of the attitudes and behavior traits of each partner as seen by the other; experimental form; 1 form (8 pages); combined counselors' and teachers' guide (7 pages) for this test and test 676; no data on reliability; no norms; $1.25 per 10 forms; 35¢ per specimen set; postage extra; [25–30] minutes; Gelolo McHugh; Family Life Publications, Inc. *

WILLIAM R. REEVY, *Associate Professor of Psychology, State University of New York, Cortland, New York.*

The *Courtship Analysis* is a list of 127 items which present to courting persons the opportunity of analyzing premarital factors which might influence adjustment in marriage. Broadly speaking, the items can be classified as attitudes, traits, behaviors, and conditions which the author believes should be considered by individuals prior to engagement. A young person is to decide how each item applies to his (or her) partner by responding in one of four ways: (*a*) "This makes me happy," (*b*) "Sometimes I worry about this," (*c*) "This bothers me a lot," (*d*) "I don't know about this." Twelve categories of items are covered with a range of 5 to 18 items found in each class.

The present edition of the schedule is considered experimental for use as: (*a*) a communication device, (*b*) a teaching aid, (*c*) a counseling tool, and (*d*) a research device. Not enough emphasis, however, is given to the fact that the schedule is very much an experimental form. It is easy for one to get the impression, particularly from the schedule itself, that the list identifies problem areas causal to adjustment or maladjustment in future marriage. A schedule which would do this would be an extremely valuable tool, but, as yet, none has been constructed which does this to any significant degree.

Had the author given specific information as to the actual sources of the topics and items, one might be better able to check on their possible worth and validity. If the schedule were to be used for research purposes only, one would not be so concerned about its content. No evidence of the validity of the items is given in the manual, but the schedule does appear to have some content validity. To some extent the author has drawn on the research in marital success for his topic areas. This is shown by the fact that religion, common interests, and background are factors which get the more extended treatment in the list. However, some idiosyncrasy in choice of problem areas and items is shown by the inclusion of topics such as "sense of humor" and "ambition." Inclusion of such matters suggests that another major source of items and areas is the collated opinions of youth themselves as modified by the author's personal and clinical judgment and reflection upon these opinions.

Even if the author dealt with just those factors shown by research to be associated with marital success, "75% of the factors that count for marital success would yet be left unaccounted for." [1] But since he included many factors which don't derive from empirical research, the probability is that no more than one quarter of the factors being discussed are important for adjustment in marriage. It is possible, however, that by rational methods he may have chanced upon factors that are more important influences than have been revealed by research thus far. But this is unlikely. And if he has, he gives no proof of such discovery. So, it seems that the most these items do is make the courting persons do some thinking about marriage, but not much. However, this schedule is neither better nor worse than any other such device in focusing the couple on a sufficient majority of the known variables that make for marital success and happiness.

One must also take into account, as the author himself points out, that the list will not: (*a*) reveal problems that the counselee will not admit, (*b*) tell one whether the problems marked are real problems or symptoms of unknown problems, or (*c*) give the relative strengths of the seriousness of problems. What then is it that the specific items are telling the counselee and the counselor which is of value? Not a great deal. The counselee cannot tell how adjusted or maladjusted he is in courtship, he cannot tell how, in relation to others, he stands in readiness for marriage, he cannot even guess, nor can the counselor help him learn through depending on the list, what the chances for him and his partner are to achieve happiness in marriage. Again, as in the instance of the *Otto Pre-Marital Counseling Schedules,* the *Courtship Analysis* is, in general, no better an aid to counseling than the counselor alone. It means little for the author to say that it is not a substitute for counseling since no experienced counselor will so construe it. But the inexperienced counselor, the one who most needs this cautionary advice, is the one who most likely will lean on it as a prognostic and diagnostic instrument which it definitely is not.

SUMMARY. The *Courtship Analysis,* which has approximately half of its areas in common with the *Otto Pre-Marital Counseling Schedules,* gives considerably more weight to personality, background, and attitudinal factors. It has more inherent and psychological interest than the Otto Schedules. For no other reason, however, is it to be generally recommended over its competitor.

In some cases the Analysis will be of some value in helping skilled counselors identify premarital factors which forbode maladjustment in future marriage. Again, as in the case of the Otto Schedules, the use of the *Courtship Analysis* by the unskilled is not recommended. The Analysis has limited use in research.

1 WALLER, WILLARD; revised by Reuben Hill. *The Family: A Dynamic Interpretation,* p. 359. New York: Dryden Press, Inc., 1951. Pp. xviii, 637. *

[676]

★A Dating Problems Checklist. High school and college; 1961; unscored counseling and teaching aid; experimental form; 1 form (8 pages); combined counselors' and teachers' guide (7 pages) for this test and test 675; no data on reliability; no norms; $1.25 per 10 forms; 35¢ per specimen set; postage extra; [25–30] minutes; Gelolo McHugh; Family Life Publications, Inc. *

CLIFFORD R. ADAMS, *Professor of Psychology, The Pennsylvania State University, University Park, Pennsylvania.*

The 128 items that comprise *A Dating Problems Checklist* (DPC) were "collected from groups of young people throughout the United States who were working with the author in the area of boy-girl relations." Presumably, each item represents or relates to some problem that has been or may be encountered in dating. The items have been conveniently aggregated under seven types of problems: 21 items apply to "Dating Conditions"; 25 items relate to "Home, Parents, and Family"; 17 items reflect maladjustment of "Personality and Emotional Self"; 19 items deal with "Sexual Attitudes"; 12 items bear upon "Social Poise"; 8 items are devoted to "Physical Self"; and the remaining 26 items explore "Dating and Definite Commitments." The inventory was designed for use with high school and college students.

In the administration of the DPC, the subject is asked to check each problem that he or she presently has "in dating or in connection with dating." Space is provided below the last item for the respondent to list any dating problems that are being experienced which have not been covered by the questionnaire. The individual is then told to reread all marked statements and to add a second check by those dating problems which are most bothersome. Below this direction, the student reads that if help is wanted "in deciding whether to become engaged," it may be available through completing another form, *A Courtship Analysis,* with the dating partner.

There is a seven-page guide for counselors and teachers who employ *A Courtship Analysis* or the DPC in their work. About one and one half pages are given to the use of the DPC, or about 40 per cent less space than is devoted to advertising other publications also available from the distributor.

The author states that the DPC can be used to encourage interest and discussion in areas that might not be considered in unstructured counseling or teaching situations. He feels that its use will also enable a group leader to identify in a minimum of time "the interests and needs of the group to be led in a study of dating and courtship." There is little doubt that these objectives have basic merit and that they can probably be achieved through the use of the DPC. The author creditably warns against any attempt to score the form and emphasizes that the number of problems checked is only an indication of the ones that "the individual can recognize and is willing to discuss." He points out that any insights to be gained from the DPC will be most useful only when combined with other data in formulating some remedial plan directed toward improving the "whole social relationship rather than in the area of dating alone."

No data are given regarding either validity or reliability. While it can be argued that the nature of the items themselves suggests inherent validity, it is regrettable that some measure of reliability was not sought. The author may have thought this was unnecessary (or that reliability would be too transient in the case of a given individual) since he feels the form has only "limited use in research."

In respect to the purposes for which the DPC is intended, there appears to be justification for its use as a teaching device or counseling aid, although some items are not well differentiated; for example, "I want to break up with someone but don't know how" and "I want to stop going steady." For individual diagnosis in counseling, the questionnaire will have limited value since no norms are provided. If a client were to present a counselor with a written list of specific worrisome problems, the information might be fully as valuable as a checklist and might have the further value of not suggesting problems of little or no consequence.

Robert A. Harper, *Consulting Psychologist, 3000 Connecticut Avenue, N.W., Washington, D.C.*

The author of this list of 128 statements about dating contends that it could serve as a valuable starting point for counseling with teenagers. The reviewer believes that an experienced and well-trained counselor could spontaneously devise questions effectively geared to the situations of his teenage clients. While the checklist might be helpful to an untrained, inexperienced, and unimaginative counselor, it is appropriate to question whether or not such a person should be counseling teenagers with or without this checklist.

The author is to be commended for pointing out explicitly in the Counselors' and Teachers' Guide which accompanies the checklist that "the temptation to treat the number of problems checked as a score must be avoided." This checklist, then, is to be viewed as a stimulus to teenage interest and discussion. However, in the reviewer's steady counseling and teaching experiences over a quarter of a century in the areas of courtship and marriage, he has yet to encounter young people as individuals or groups who need their interest specifically stimulated along the lines of sex, dating, and related problems.

The 128 items of the checklist have been divided into seven problem areas: dating conditions; home, parents, family; personality and emotional self; sex attitudes; social poise; physical self; and dating and definite commitments. These categories not only seem to be overlapping, but go completely undefined.

Some psychologists and other professional persons at times defend such "tests" as this as an aid to those persons who will proceed, without training or supervision, to teach or counsel. Such people, it is argued, will function professionally whether professional people like it or not, and the latter should, therefore, welcome a test or two that will reduce the resulting pedagogical or therapeutic atrocities. This is somewhat comparable to resigning oneself to thievery and assuaging one's conscience by approving a guide on "Honor Among Thieves."

In summary, such an unscored test, without norms or data on either reliability or validity, cannot be considered of any value whatever to competent counselors and teachers. Should it be used "to stimulate interest and to provide discussional openings to many areas that might be overlooked," as the author proposes? No! It would give unqualified practitioners a false sense of emotional security and competency with which to misteach and miscounsel teenagers.

[677]

★The El Senoussi Multiphasic Marital Inventory. Premarital and marital counselees; 1963; 10 scores: frustration and chronic projection, cumulative ego strain, adolescent hangover or immaturity, revolt against femininity, flight into rejection, early conditioning against marriage, will-o'-the-wisp, sex dissatisfaction, sex dissatisfaction and projection, total; 1 form (12 pages); manual (33 pages plus copy of test and protocol booklet); protocol booklet (4 pages); no data on reliability; $18.50 per examiner's kit of 25 tests, 25 protocol booklets, and manual; $10 per 25 tests; $6.50 per 25 protocol booklets; $4 per manual; postpaid; [30] minutes; Ahmed El Senoussi; Western Psychological Services. *

[678]

★Individual and Marriage Counseling Inventory. Adult counselees; 1956; a biographical data blank and record form; 1 form (4 pages); no manual; $1.25 per 20 inventories; 10¢ per single copy; postpaid; [15] minutes; Aaron L. Rutledge; Merrill-Palmer Institute. *

[679]

★The Male Impotence Test. Adult males; 1964; title on test is *MIT;* 5 scores: reaction to female rejection, flight from male role, reaction to male inadequacy, organic factor, total; 1 form (4 pages); manual (39 pages); no data on reliability; $10 per 25 tests and manual; $4 per manual; [15] minutes; Ahmed El Senoussi; Western Psychological Services. *

[680]

★Marital Roles Inventory. Marriage counselees; 1961; 4 derived scores: index of marital strain, index of deviation of role performances, index of deviation of role expectations, corrected index of marital strain; separate forms (Forms H, W, 2 pages) for men and women; husband and wife must both take inventory to obtain marital strain score; scoring-history form (4 pages); mimeographed manual (21 pages); no data on reliability; validity data based on an earlier form and scoring method; $3.50 per 25 tests; $6.50 per 25 scoring forms; $3 per manual; postpaid; specimen set not available; (20) minutes; Nathan Hurvitz; Western Psychological Services. *

REFERENCES

1. Hurvitz, Nathan. "The Index of Strain as a Measure of Marital Satisfaction." *Sociol & Social Res* 44:106–11 N–D '59. * (*PA* 35:6683)
2. Hurvitz, Nathan. "The Marital Roles Inventory and the Measurement of Marital Adjustment." *J Clin Psychol* 16:377–80 O '60. * (*PA* 37:3454)
3. Hurvitz, Nathan. "The Measurement of Marital Strain." *Am J Sociol* 65:610–5 My '60. * (*PA* 35:6684)

Robert A. Harper, *Consulting Psychologist, 3000 Connecticut Avenue, N.W., Washington, D.C.*

The author of this test asserts that what is measured is important for marital counseling, but he offers no scientific evidence for his assertion. What the author refers to as "validation" of the test is stated to be based upon the original *Marital Roles Inventory* (MRI), but no description is given in the manual of how this original MRI differs from the current one. The only external criteria used were from another test of quite doubtful validity.[1] The author obtained quite unimpressive negative correlations between what Wallace and Locke call marital happiness and what Hurvitz designates as indices of marital strain.

The MRI consists of 11 statements about the husband and 11 about the wife. Each spouse rates the statements about himself (herself) in the order of importance in which each thinks he (she) actually carries out his (her) own "roles" in marriage. Each then ranks the 11 statements about his or her spouse in the order of importance in which he or she wants or prefers the spouse to carry out the spouse's roles.

Four scores are obtained with MRI, each applicable to both the husband and the wife. These score descriptions follow: (*a*) Index of Marital Strain (IMS). "This score is obtained by comparing one spouse's ranking of his own roles with the other spouse's ranking of these roles. The husband's IMS is the difference between his ranking of his own roles and his wife's ranking of his roles; the wife's IMS is the difference between her ranking of her own roles and her husband's ranking of her roles." (*b*) Index of Deviation of Role Performances (IDRP). "This score is obtained by comparing a spouse's ranking of his (her) role-set with the modal ranking of these roles by the normative group" (which consisted of a group of 104 couples selected by an undescribed sampling method and given the undescribed "original" MRI). (*c*) Index of Deviation of Role Expectations (IDRE). "This score is obtained by comparing a spouse's ranking of the roles in his (her) mate's role-set with the modal ranking of these roles by the normative group." (*d*) Corrected Index of Marital Strain (C-IMS). This score is obtained by adding the IMS, IDRP, and IDRE. The sum is the C-IMS. The rationale for this procedure is that where husband and wife have

1 Locke, Harvey J., and Wallace, Karl M. "Short Marital-Adjustment and Prediction Tests: Their Reliability and Validity." *Marriage & Family Living* 21:251–5 Ag '59.

atypical, but closely coinciding, rankings of their roles and role expectations, the IMS will not catch marital strain, but the C-IMS will. According to the manual, "Although there is no difference between their performance and expectation, experience and research underlying the MRI indicates that marital strain exists." The nature of this experience and research goes undescribed.

Three score ranges are given for each of the foregoing four scores: limited strain, general incompatibility, and serious problems. A footnote to these categories of ranges states that they are "based upon clinical experience and not upon experimental findings."

The author also offers sociologically ideal or "constructed-type" interpretations of the 11 roles for each spouse. It is quite doubtful that such interpretations of the simple "role statements" would be even vaguely present in the minds of an actual couple unless both husband and wife were trained as sociologists.

In summary, MRI with its statistical tables and computations and its various categories of "objective" scores of marital strain could readily lead the untrained and inexperienced counselor to believe he had found a "scientific" counseling aid. With no discernible evidence of true validity or reliability, however, MRI can bring to the trained and experienced counselor only a sense of frustration and disappointment.

[681]

★A Marriage Adjustment Form. Adults; 1939–61; problems checklist; 1 form ['61, 8 pages, reprinted from the author's *Predicting Success or Failure in Marriage* ('39), see *1* below]; combined manual ['61, 4 pages] for this test and test 684; no data on reliability; $1.25 per 10 tests; 35¢ per specimen set; postage extra; (30–50) minutes; Ernest W. Burgess; distributed by Family Life Publications, Inc. *

REFERENCES

1. Burgess, Ernest W., and Cottrell, Leonard S., Jr. *Predicting Success or Failure in Marriage.* New York: Prentice-Hall, Inc., 1939. Pp. xxiii, 472. * (*PA* 14:404)

Lester W. Dearborn, *Director, Counseling Service, 316 Huntington Avenue, Boston, Massachusetts.*

The items in the *Marriage Adjustment Form* are unrealistic in the sense of expecting a person to be able to answer them with any degree of accuracy, and even more than this, because the answers are to be broken down into degrees of evaluation which would require the testee to make an impossible subjective assessment of his feelings. Take the case of question 21: "Everything considered, how happy has your marriage been *for you?*" (Check): (i) extraordinarily happy; (k) decidedly happy; (m) happy; (n) somewhat happy; (o) average; (p) somewhat unhappy; (q) unhappy; (r) decidedly unhappy; (s) extremely unhappy." Now anyone might ask what is the difference between *decidedly unhappy* and *extremely unhappy*. How can anyone decide between whether he is *extraordinarily happy* or *decidedly happy?* Or *somewhat unhappy* or *extremely unhappy?* Furthermore, the testee is expected to make not only such an evaluation of his own feelings but he is expected in addition to be able to project his feelings so that he can make the same critical comment concerning the feelings of his spouse.

Happiness is a matter of feeling for which there never has been nor could there ever be any established norms. It is a completely individual matter. Most of the questions are very similar and are based on the same error of reasoning, and therefore I do not believe this kind of a form has any real value. It is to be noted that this form was first published in 1939 and, as in the case of the *Marriage Prediction Schedule,* has never been validated nor has the matter of reliability ever been established.

In the second part of the form the arrangement is a bit different, and here there are a number of questions which the client might answer on the basis of whether or not he believes that the suggested conditions have or have not interfered with his happiness in marriage. The answers in Part 2 could furnish some information which would be helpful to any counselor, and he might well use the second part for a quick rundown by the client preliminary to going into a counseling session.

[682]

★The Marriage Adjustment Inventory. Marriage counselees; 1962; problems checklist; 52 scores: 4 scores (self-evaluation, spouse-evaluation, husband-wife evaluation, total) in each of 12 areas (family relationships, dominance, immaturity, neurotic traits, sociopathic traits, money-management, children, interests, physical, abilities, sexual, incompatibility) and total scores for self-evaluation, spouse-evaluation, husband-wife evaluation, total; separate forms (Forms H, W, 4 pages, identical except for booklet color) for husbands and wives; mimeographed manual (12 pages); no data on reliability; $6.50 per 25 tests; $2 per manual; postpaid; specimen set not available; (10–30) minutes; Morse P. Manson and Arthur Lerner; Western Psychological Services. *

Clifford R. Adams, *Professor of Psychology, The Pennsylvania State University, University Park, Pennsylvania.*

The construction of the *Marriage Adjustment Inventory* (MAI) began with the selection of some 600 items from varied sources, including tests, questionnaires, publications relating to marriage and its problems, clinical experiences, and interviews with professional workers from several different disciplines. Although the manual states that "these items were screened and the most significant adapted for use in preliminary questionnaire surveys," no information is given regarding the 255 items that "survived" the original screening nor how this number was subsequently reduced to the 157 items that comprise the present MAI.

Each item or "question-problem" is phrased negatively to point up some attitude, feeling, or behavioral attribute that would presumably make for marital unhappiness or maladjustment. Following each item are the letters H-W. By circling H or W, or H-W, the individual indicates if the husband or wife, or both, possess this negative characteristic. The sum of the circles applying to self is the SE (self-evaluation) score, and the sum of the circles applying to the mate is the SPE (spouse-evaluation) score. The sum of the H-W circles (supposedly characteristic of both spouses) is the H-WE (husband-wife evaluation) score. The TE (total evaluation) score is the sum of all circled responses. In addition to these four major scores, 48 "cluster" scores may also be determined for each person completing the form.

Twelve areas or "clusters" of marital problems are said to be measured, the first six by items 1–89 and the second six by items 90–157. One cluster, identified as "dominance," contains only 6 items but the largest cluster, termed "immaturity," consists of 28 items. The median number of items per cluster is 13. Though no item in any cluster is repeated in another, several items appear to be closely related. No explanation of how the separate clusters were segregated nor the criteria for inclusion of specific items within a cluster is presented in the manual. The sum of circled answers under each cluster heading is a rough index of the contribution of the cluster to each of the four "evaluation" scores.

Other than any inherent validity of the separate items, the validity of major and cluster scores seems to depend solely upon self-ratings of happiness on a 5-point scale ranging from "very happy" to "very unhappy." By such ratings, the 120 males (101 married, 14 divorced, 5 separated) and 117 females (95 married, 20 divorced, 2 separated) were classified, by sex, into "happily adjusted," "average adjusted," and "unhappily adjusted" groups. On this basis, 67 per cent of the men and 59 per cent of the women were considered happily adjusted with respective proportions of 20 and 21 per cent judged to be unhappily adjusted. Only 13 per cent of the men and 20 per cent of the women were found to be average in adjustment.

By cluster and group, the two sexes were contrasted in respect to their mean scores on SE, SPE, H-WE, and TE. Generally, the separate cluster means showed less maladjustment among the happy than the unhappy but several discrepancies or reversals were noted between the extreme groups and the average adjusted group. When the separate cluster means were summed under each of the four major scores, the differences between groups appeared to be satisfactory except in respect to the H-WE score for each sex. But the manual reports too little data to appraise the significance of these differences.

Percentile equivalents of the four evaluative scores by sex and each of the three adjustment levels are given in the manual. On the last page of the MAI test form, space is provided to summarize these scores and their percentile equivalents at each of the three adjustment levels. Critical scores by sex are suggested on a comparative basis; for example, the critical score on self-evaluation is set at 20 since 90 per cent of the happily adjusted in both sexes made raw scores of 20 or less in contrast to 30 per cent of the unhappily adjusted men and women.

In view of the lack of any data on reliability and the fact that validity is limited to inherent content of items, marital status, and self-ratings, there is some question about the use of the MAI in individual diagnosis for therapeutic purposes. There is no evidence of cross validation and this must be regarded as a serious shortcoming. The authors of the questionnaire state that it was designed with 12 purposes in mind, none of which seems to be completely fulfilled. But the paucity of test materials in the field of marriage counseling justifies the experimental use of the MAI. The experienced therapist will find this form useful as a point of departure even though he may deplore its failure to emphasize any of the positive qualities that go into successful marriage. It is doubtful that the MAI, although of recent vintage, represents a decided improvement over the pioneer efforts a quarter of a century ago of Lewis M. Terman and of Burgess and Cottrell. In spite of these reservations, the MAI is a welcome addition to the armentarium of the counselor and therapist.

ALBERT ELLIS, *Consulting Psychologist, 333 West 56th Street, New York, New York.*

This inventory consists of 157 questions of the type: "Is chiefly interested in money"; "Is unfair in many ways"; and "Feels lonely most of the time." Each question proposes a problem that may exist in a marital relationship; and the counselee who uses the test is supposed to state whether the problem is that of the husband, the wife, or both the husband and wife. The inventory is designed to be used with clients of a marriage counselor, and to indicate to the counselor the main problems existing, as self-appraised and as spouse-appraised, in a given marriage. Four scores in each of 12 areas (as listed in the heading above) are obtained by simple scoring procedures.

The inventory was standardized on 120 men and 117 women, the great majority of whom were married and living together at the time of their being tested. These individuals rated themselves on their own marriage adjustment; their ratings were then used as criteria for the validity of the evaluative scores. The authors note that

> from the samples used in this standardization, it appears that better adjusted marriages, happier marriages, not only are characterized by *low scores* but also show a tendency by each spouse to minimize the problems of the mate. This is seen in the higher mean Self-Evaluation Scores. This may indicate a halo effect is in operation, and that in happy marriages each spouse, more or less, idealizes the mate. Ninety per cent of Happily Adjusted men made SE scores of 20 or less. Scores of 20 and higher, in a very large percentage of cases, indicate severe marital maladjustment in men. Ninety per cent of the Happily Adjusted women made scores of 20 or less, while only 30 per cent of the Unhappily Adjusted women made scores of 20 or less. As in the case of the men, scores of 20 and higher for women, in a very large percentage indicated severe marital maladjustment.

From these figures, it is apparent that the test has a high degree of validity—as measured by the criterion of the subjects' ratings of the happiness of their own marriage. It is questionable, however, whether this criterion has much meaning, so that all the test basically seems to show is that individuals who rate themselves as being happily married also rate themselves as having relatively few marital problems. This is hardly a surprising finding!

The main purposes of the inventory seem to be "to enable the Counselor to identify and define causes of tension and stress in marriage" and "to provide an economical approach to obtain useful marriage adjustment information and reduce costs and time of counseling." Although the first of these purposes may well be served by the inventory, it is highly questionable how well the second is served. Most competent marriage counselors will be able to obtain the information gathered through the use of this inventory more quickly and economically by their own incisive questioning in the course of counseling sessions and by observing the tones and overtones of the answers they thereby receive. They will almost certainly obtain more valid marital information than the test makes available. For research in the field of marriage counseling, however, the inventory may prove to be of distinct use.

[683]

★The Marriage Adjustment Sentence Completion Survey. Marriage counselees; 1962; separate forms (Forms H, W, 4 pages, identical except for sex references) for husbands and wives; profile-summary (4 pages); mimeographed manual (14 pages); no data on reliability and validity; no norms; $14 per set of 26 tests (13 of each form), 26 profiles, and manual; $2 per manual; postpaid; specimen set not available; (20–40) minutes; Morse P. Manson and Arthur Lerner; Western Psychological Services. *

ALBERT ELLIS, *Consulting Psychologist, 333 West 56th Street, New York, New York.*

The *Marriage Adjustment Sentence Completion Survey* consists of 100 incomplete sentences of the type: "To me the important things in marriage are"; "I am very unhappy because"; "Why don't I"; and "I need most." The survey is designed to be used by a professional marriage counselor with his clients. A system of rating is presented through which both husband and wife may be evaluated on five different continua: Needs, Problems, Maturity Level, Goals, and Values. Since the survey is a projective technique rather than a more objective paper and pencil personality test, the rating system is suggestive and subjective rather than more precise and uses the categories Low, Weak, Fair, Good, and Excellent rather than quantitative scores.

The survey was standardized on 120 males and 117 females, all of whom had at one time been married, and the great majority of whom were still married and living together at the time of their being tested. This is apparently the same group of subjects as that used in the standardization of the same authors' *Marriage Adjustment Inventory*. All the subjects rated themselves on their own marriage adjustment; but no attempt was made to use their self-ratings, or any other criterion, as the basis for a validity study. No reliability data are presented either.

The main purposes of the survey are to provide the counselor "with a considerable amount of data pertaining to the specific marriage and the people in it. These data are so organized that major areas of involvement are identified by the Counselor. * It enables the Counselor to identify underlying causes of tension and stress in marriage, thus facilitating the more penetrating processes of counseling and psychotherapy. It provides insights to husband and wife evoked by the process of completing the MASCS." Although it may well be that these purposes are adequately realized in the course of the test's being used by a competent marriage counselor, the manual presents no evidence that this is true. Even if the MASCS does serve the purposes for which it was designed, there is also no evidence that it does so more economically or successfully than if it were dispensed with entirely and the time taken to score and interpret it were used by the counselor in a simple interviewing procedure. As a research tool, the MASCS may possibly be quite valuable, but its clinical usefulness is as yet entirely unproven.

[684]

A Marriage Prediction Schedule. Adults; 1939–61; reprinted from *Predicting Success or Failure in Marriage* (see *1*); 1 form ['39, 8 pages]; combined manual ['61, 4 pages] for this test and test 681; no data on reliability and validity; $2.50 per 25 tests; 35¢ per specimen set; postage extra; (30–50) minutes; Ernest W. Burgess; Family Life Publications, Inc. *

REFERENCES

1–8. See 5:84.

LESTER W. DEARBORN, *Director, Counseling Service, 316 Huntington Avenue, Boston, Massachusetts.*

In reviewing *A Marriage Prediction Schedule*, I must say that I start the review with a prejudice. I do not believe that there is any value in attempting to make prediction of success or failure in marriage by a written test, no matter how well prepared it is. In stating my prejudice I would not be dealing fairly if I did not admit to the caution by the author who says, "The prediction schedule is far from a perfect guide for deciding whether a certain couple should or should not marry." With this the reviewer has no disagreement. In addition, I find that there are no data on its reliability or validity. It would appear that all that can honestly be said is that while this is called a prediction schedule I don't think it has much predictive value.

In an attempt to establish a method of scoring, the subject is asked to evaluate a rather incomprehensible series of choices to be marked by degrees; certainly here we have a question of semantics. For instance, to ask a person to evaluate his feeling toward his father when the subject was a child and break it down into mild attachment and mild hostility, etc. is anticipating an incredible ability to associate and identify feelings of a period long past. I would contend that answers to such a question have little or no meaning.

Under item 15 I find myself quite disturbed at a person's having to determine whether or not the sex information he received was *wholesome* or *unwholesome* or whether he received the information from *pernicious* reading. The words wholesome, unwholesome, pernicious, etc. are descriptive adjectives that would defy any objective appraisal, and certainly they are judgmental in character and have no place in a schedule of this kind.

The manual states that scores above 630 are favorable to marriage adjustment and that 75 per cent of engaged persons with scores of 630 or higher were later found well adjusted in marriage. No evidence in support of this claim has been presented. If such evidence exists it should be made available.

I would say that this schedule, which is over 25 years old, is outmoded and should not be used as a marriage prediction device but might, however, be used as a tool for obtaining a personal history that could be used by the counselor in the process of counseling.

[685]

★Marriage Role Expectation Inventory. Adolescents and adults; 1960–63; role expectations in 7 areas (authority, homemaking, care of children, personal characteristics, social participation, education, employment and support) yielding an equalitarian-traditional rating; Forms M (for males), W (for females), ('63, 4 pages, identical except for wording changes); originally published in *2* below; teacher's and counselor's guide ('63, 7 pages); no data on reliability of subscores; no norms (author recommends the use of local norms); $2.50 per 26 tests; 35¢ per specimen set of both forms; cash orders postpaid; (25-50) minutes; Marie S. Dunn; Family Life Publications, Inc. *

REFERENCES

1. DUNN, MARIE S. *Marriage Role Expectations of Adolescents.* Doctor's thesis, Florida State University (Tallahassee, Fla.), 1959. (*DA* 20:3277)
2. DUNN, MARIE S. "Marriage Role Expectations of Adolescents." *Marriage & Family Living* 22:99-111 My '60. *
3. MOSER, ALVIN J. *Marriage Role Expectations of High School Students.* Master's thesis, Florida State University (Tallahassee, Fla.), 1960.
4. GOULD, NORMAN S. *Marriage Role Expectations of Single College Students as Related to Selected Social Factors.* Doctor's thesis, Florida State University (Tallahassee, Fla.), 1961. (*DA* 22:2906)
5. MOSER, ALVIN J. "Marriage Role Expectations of High School Students." *Marriage & Family Living* 23:42-3 F '61. * (*PA* 36:3FH42M)
6. BUSBICE, JUANITA J. *Marriage Role Expectations and Personality Adjustments.* Master's thesis, Northwestern State College (Natchitoches, La.), 1962.

ROBERT C. CHALLMAN, *Clinical Psychologist, 301 Kenwood Parkway, Minneapolis, Minnesota.*

According to the author, this inventory "does not determine readiness for marriage" nor predict marriage success. She intends it to be used in marriage and family classes so students may learn about the differing conceptions of masculine and feminine roles and realize that their own ideas are not necessarily "right" or "wrong." She also offers it for use in premarital counseling and for use with "couples who are in trouble with their marriage."

The (corrected) odd-even reliability of the total score—the basic measure of equalitarian-traditional role expectations—is stated to be .975. Intrinsic validity is claimed on the basis of the way in which the items were selected (which included a consensus of qualified judges) and on the fact that all the final 71 items met the criterion of differentiating between "high" and "low" groups of adolescent testees at the 5 per cent level of significance.

It is relatively easy to apply the scoring key in order to get the total score. It is time consuming and awkward to obtain the subscores for the seven areas mentioned above. Still more time is required because the scoring directions in the manual are not in accord with the scoring key.

Although no norms are offered and no data given as to the distribution of total scores of any subjects, the author provides a scheme for interpreting scores based on a simple division of the total possible range of scores into four approximately equal parts and labeling each part. Since no rationale is given for this method of interpretation, it is difficult to evaluate its significance.

There is no evidence that the inventory has been used with adult subjects beyond the college years, nor is there any indication that it has been used as an aid in premarital or marital counseling. At least six of the eight studies cited in the manual involving the use of the inventory deal with surveys of adolescents.

In marriage and family classes, the inventory may well serve a useful purpose. Since each student would presumably have an opportunity to compare his responses with those of the class and to discuss the items, he might thereby increase his self-knowledge.

As an instrument for premarital counseling with "normal" engaged couples, the differences in answers to the same item might be used as a basis for discussion leading to compromise or acceptance. Presumably such couples would be found primarily in church groups. Premarital counseling in clinical settings usually involves problems of a more severe kind, making the use of this inventory of doubtful value.

For marital counseling, the serviceability of the inventory is markedly impaired by the presence of a number of questions referring to "after marriage" and a number which assume that the testee is in high school, such as "being married will not keep my husband from going to college." If it were modified in such a way as to eliminate or rephrase inappropriate questions, it might become a part of the counseling process, at least with an occasional couple seen in a clinical setting.

On the whole, the *Marriage Role Expectation Inventory* may serve as a helpful technique in marriage and family classes and with "normal" engaged couples. In its present form, it is less suitable for marital counseling. The total score (without norms) has an uncertain meaning and the subscores are probably not worth the effort of determining. The author states, "it seems particularly important [for the counselor] to note and discuss the responses to specific items." With that statement the reviewer agrees.

[686]

★Otto Pre-Marital Counseling Schedules. Adult couples; 1961, c1951-61; checklist for use as a discussion stimulator; 1 form ('61, c1951); 3 parts; manual ('59, 31 pages); no data on reliability; no norms; $8.75 per 25 sets of all 3 parts; $4.75 per 25 copies of *a*; $2.25 per 25 copies of *b* or *c*; $2 per manual; 75¢ per specimen set (includes descriptive summary but not manual); postage extra; (60) minutes; Herbert A. Otto; Consulting Psychologists Press, Inc. *

a) PRE-MARITAL SURVEY SECTION. 4 pages.
b) FAMILY FINANCE SECTION. 1 page.
c) SEXUAL ADJUSTMENT SECTION. 2 pages.

REFERENCES

1. OTTO, HERBERT A. *The Development, Application and Appraisal of Pre-Marital Counseling Schedules.* Doctor's thesis, Florida State University (Tallahassee, Fla.), 1956. (*DA* 16:795)
2. OTTO, HERBERT A. "The Use of Inter-Action Centered Schedules in Group Work With Pre-Marital Couples." *Group Psychother* 12:223-9 S '59. *

ROBERT C. CHALLMAN, *Clinical Psychologist, 301 Kenwood Parkway, Minneapolis, Minnesota.*

The Pre-Marital Survey Section provides a checklist of three to six items grouped under the following headings: housing, money matters, our relationships, education, employment, health, religious matters, in-laws, children, sexual adjustment, leisure time, and wedding preparations. The Family Finance Section is a separate schedule which supplements the less detailed money matters material. The supplementary Sexual Adjustment Section consists of 14 statements of implicitly recommended sexual techniques and attitudes, apparently intended to educate the engaged couple while providing a basis for counseling if needed and desired. Because of the nature of the schedules, normative and reliability data are irrelevant. The author claims that the schedules provide a means for engaged couples to "undertake a systematic exploration of their goals, needs, and expectancies in relation to marriage," which he believes most couples do not do. He stresses the value of the couple working on the schedules together in making this "exploration."

The survey section covers such obvious topics that only the most naïve couples would not have already discussed them fully enough for their purposes. Some of the items need not be discussed before the wedding, e.g., "Agreeing on how to spend most of our leisure time." The two supplementary schedules might uncover a few topics that needed further exploration with a counselor or be suggestive of some aspect previously overlooked.

It is probable that these schedules would have limited usefulness in a clinical setting, intended as they were for "normal" engaged couples. In all likelihood they would be more frequently used as counseling aids by ministers rather than by psychologists, social workers, or marriage counselors. Thus one is not surprised to find that five of the seven books on premarital counseling recommended in the manual are written for ministers.

WILLIAM R. REEVY, *Associate Professor of Psychology, State University of New York, Cortland, New York.*

The premarital schedules are related interview guides designed for use in educational programs of marriage preparation and as tools in premarital counseling. Comprised of three sections, they are to be used separately or in any combination, depending on client needs. The major one, the Pre-Marital Survey Section, is a catalog of items classified around 12 problem areas with which counselees are to be acquainted. Focus on these areas is meant to help the counselor assess the client's primary problems. The two supplemental schedules give more extended coverage to two areas in the main section.

The schedules are built on the belief that communication during courtship for assessment of compatibility will lead to emotional growth. And so the author concentrated on the matter of enhancing communication through the arrangement of the format and items. For example, after interchange about the items of the Pre-Marital Survey Section, the couple are to check under one of two headings: "We have worked this out pretty well" or "We need to talk about this more." The progression within the schedule is from the less to the more personal, the questions are open ended, and space is provided for the writing of further questions and comments.

Though the counselor gets an assist from the format it is still mainly his and the counselees' job to bring about communication regarding primary problems. The schedules have no predictive value and practically no diagnostic value and are only as useful as the counselor is skilled. Skilled counselors would not need these guides for discussion. A proficient counselor would use his time to greater advantage for the couple otherwise than in spending an hour or two in discussing the schedules.

The author, not content with the more modest notion of the use of the schedules with couples only, gives numerous suggestions in the manual for their use in miscellaneous programs and with groups for education, discussions, and counseling. However, the schedules were developed principally within a framework of premarital counseling.

The schedules are not personality inventories or tests; they provide no scores and hence no normative or correlative data. As the usual concepts of validity are not applicable in judging the degree to which the author achieved his aims and purposes, the schedules must be judged otherwise. The ultimate worth of the areas and the items in bringing to light the factors most highly associated with adjustment in marriage depends finally upon the validity of the research conclusions and the expert opinions upon which the author drew.

In attempting to find significant areas and items the author proceeded empirically enough —especially so, as the first unpublished version of these schedules appeared when there were no published studies pertaining to the construction of premarital counseling schedules. The areas for the Pre-Marital Survey Section were selected mainly on the basis of research studies done before 1950, drawing largely upon two of the best, those of Burgess and Cottrell [1] and Locke.[2] The actual items both in the main and supplemental sections are derived from approximately a dozen standard texts in family life education and some good sex manuals. Good judgment was exercised in leaning heavily on very frequently used and respected texts. But in his culling for items the author did not sample enough texts, nor did he tally the frequency with which like opinions were repeated so as to rank their relative importance.

The areas which the author chose represent areas of family life on which the degree of spousal agreement might be estimated. They correlate on the average with limited, selected criteria of marital happiness to a degree of about .50. This low correlation shows that much of what makes for adjustment in marriage, especially for an individual couple, is not specifically known. Much remains to be learned about what is causal to adjustment in marriage, and therefore such schedules, except for research purposes, are premature.

All sections of the schedule, and particularly the supplemental sections, were constructed, the author says, with a view to providing information. And he gives extended and numerous suggestions in the manual for use of the schedules with educational groups and thus unduly emphasizes their use in instruction.

The reviewer doubts their value as tools in education and counseling in preparation for marriage, even considering the author's statements in his dissertation (*1*) that: (*a*) the *Otto Pre-Marital Counseling Schedules* increased communication, (*b*) they were especially effective in facilitating rapport, and (*c*) client reactions, as tabulated, to the separate schedules were overwhelmingly positive. The instructional aspect in the schedules seems principally to take into account the practical necessities in beginning a marriage; such schedules might better probe more dynamic factors.

The reviewer does not share the author's belief that instruction is the corrective it is touted to be. Take as one example sexual instruction and the area of sexual adjustment which gets weight in the schedule. Improved sexual adjustment and happiness in marriage have not been achieved by four decades of sex instruction in high school and in college family education courses. Yet the author has ignored such knowledge and has centered much schedule material and suggestions in the manual around the idea of instruction.

The use of the schedules seems mainly for persons relatively unskilled in counseling, as suggested by the author in the manual. However, this reviewer raises the serious question about their use by such persons. These schedules lend themselves to "trapping" the unskilled counselor into deceiving himself into thinking he has surely probed the problem and, therefore, done a good job. Marital and premarital counseling are professional specialities in their own right and require a high degree of skill. Certainly competency therein calls for training and experience at least equal to that in psychiatry, social work, or clinical psychology. And so, any "tools" which give anyone the idea that such counseling can be done by those relatively untrained in psychotherapy are not, generally, to be lauded.

SUMMARY. The author is to be given credit for his empirical approach in constructing a premarital counseling schedule during a time period when he did not have many guides. At times and with some cases the schedules might be useful in helping a skilled counselor quickly

1 BURGESS, ERNEST W., AND COTTRELL, LEONARD S., JR. *Predicting Success or Failure in Marriage.* New York: Prentice-Hall, Inc., 1939. Pp. xxiii, 472. *

2 LOCKE, HARVEY J. *Predicting Adjustment in Marriage: A Comparison of a Divorced and a Happily Married Group.* New York: Henry Holt & Co., Inc., 1951. Pp. xx, 407. *

to identify possible areas of future maladjustment. Their use is not recommended for the unskilled. At this stage of our knowledge about marital adjustment they are best used in research.

[687]

***Sex Knowledge Inventory, Experimental Edition.** Sex education classes in high school and college and adults; 1950–60; 1 form; 2 tests (labeled Forms X and Y); $2.75 per specimen set of both tests; cash orders postpaid; Gelolo McHugh; Family Life Publications, Inc. *

a) SEX KNOWLEDGE INVENTORY: FOR MARRIAGE COUNSELING. 1950–60; Form X ('50, 10 pages); counselor's manual ('60, 68 pages, identical with manual published in 1950 except for bibliography); tentative norms ('52, 1 page); separate answer sheets must be used; 1–10 tests, 85¢ each; $1 per 10 answer sheets; $3.80 per specimen set including 2 tests and 12 answer sheets (this or combined specimen set must be purchased to obtain manual); [45] minutes.

b) SEX KNOWLEDGE INVENTORY: VOCABULARY AND ANATOMY, SECOND REVISION. 1950–56; Form Y ('55, 4 pages, identical with first revision except for format); directions sheet ['55, 1 page]; tentative norms (no date) based on first revision; no norms for college men and adults; $2.25 per 25 tests; $1.20 per specimen set including 10 tests.

REFERENCES

1. PARMER, CHARLES H. *The Relation Between Scores on the McHugh Inventory and Self-Ratings of Marital Satisfaction.* Doctor's thesis, Pennsylvania State College (State College, Pa.), 1953.
2. CUTHBERT, BETTY L. "Sex Knowledge of a Class of Student Nurses." *Nursing Res* 10:145–50 su '61. *
3. SHATIN, LEO, AND SOUTHWORTH, J. A. "Sex Knowledge, Intelligence, and Sexual Adjustment." *J Social Psychol* 54:219–33 Ag '61. * (*PA* 36:3JP19S)

CLIFFORD R. ADAMS, *Professor of Psychology, The Pennsylvania State University, University Park, Pennsylvania.*

Although Form X of the *Sex Knowledge Inventory* is labeled as an "experimental edition" designed as a tool for marriage counseling, it can be used to explore the sex knowledge, and to some extent the sexual attitudes, of literate adults and college and senior high school students. There are 80 questions, each followed by five answer choices of which only one is adjudged to be correct. According to the comprehensive 68-page manual, the first five questions are general and deal with matters "often....uppermost in the minds of prospective marriage partners." Thereafter, in order, 5 questions relate to "sex-act techniques"; 4 items concern the hymen; 13 questions are devoted to "possible causes of poor sexual adjustment" followed by 3 items concerning sex dreams; questions 31–36 deal with birth control; questions 37–39 deal with sterilization and circumcision; 12 items ask about menstruation in contrast to 13 questions about conception, pregnancy, and childbirth; some 7 items relate to superstitions, misconceptions, and misinformation in contrast to only 3 questions about masturbation; and finally, there are 4 questions about venereal diseases followed by 2 items dealing with the "effects of menopause on sex life."

The separate answer sheet that must be used in conjunction with Form X is well designed and easily scored. Directions for answering the inventory are clear, and a 30-word glossary is provided to explain certain technical terms that might be unfamiliar to individuals taking the test. (This word list might be more convenient to use if it were printed inside the front cover rather than the back cover of the test booklet.)

A percentile table based on raw scores of 1,002 men (median chronological age 21 years, median educational age 14 years) and of 1,061 women (median CA 20 years, median EA 13 years) is printed on the back of each answer sheet. Reliability of the test, computed on a mixed group of 441 subjects, is quite satisfactory, with the coefficients of reliability averaging .88.

The author believes that the inventory will identify areas in which a subject's knowledge is deficient or in which his attitudes need reorientation. It is emphasized that this instrument "is not intended as a measure of individual ability to establish a satisfactory sexual relationship, nor is it designed for making predictions about a couple's chance of success in their sex lives together." But the author does say that the inventory should be useful in helping to free a couple (or individual) "from handicapping ignorance and attitudes about sex." Granting that this type of a priori validity is more suggestive than conclusive, it is reasonable to assume that discussion between a counselor and a counselee of the latter's wrong answers to questions would not only enhance the knowledge of the subject but also provide a start toward the development of more constructive attitudes.

A few items in the inventory might well be revised to take advantage of recent sexual research findings, particularly those of William H. Masters and others of the Washington University Medical School in respect to the anatomy and physiology of sexual response and of other investigators relating to contraception (e.g., the birth control "pill" and aerosol vaginal foam). With the lapse of time since the form began to be used, it would be expected that some objective measures of validity would soon be available. But there can be little doubt that the inventory is the best instrument of its kind available to marriage counselors and teachers of sex education.

Especially to be commended is the extensive manual for the guidance of users of the inventory. Each of the 80 items in the form and the 13 categories that they comprise is discussed in detail. This comprehensive treatment contains many hints and suggestions of great value to the beginning counselor and of considerable value even to experienced therapists. In nearly all cases, suggestions and comments are keyed to five books that should already be in the library of most teachers and counselors interested in sex and marriage.

Form Y of the *Sex Knowledge Inventory* is strictly a limited measure of the more basic facts of sex and reproduction as they pertain to anatomy and vocabulary. It is not a substitute for Form X but may be used in conjunction with it. Part 1 of the test asks the subject to identify by name 11 male and 9 female sexual parts as depicted by numbers on two graphic illustrations (cross sections) of the sex organs and structures of the male and female.

Part 2 of Form Y consists of 12 questions about the male sexual parts and 20 questions about the female sexual parts, which are answered by reference to the numbers on the two drawings contained in Part 1. These questions deal, for the most part, with physiology and function of the various sex organs and structures.

In Part 3, the subject matches some 40 of 48 numbered words (including several distractors) to definitions presented by 37 items. The words are varied, ranging from adultery and douche to impotence and incest. A few of the definitions (e.g., for miscarriage and syphilis) lack precision.

According to the author, "this test measures individual understanding of the human reproductive system, knowledge of how sex parts function, and vocabulary pertaining to sexual activity." While there is undoubtedly some correlation between it and Form X, either form may be used independently or as a supplement to the other. One unique feature of Form Y is that its format provides some measure of information and understanding of sex structure and function "even where vocabulary is lacking." No items in this particular form deal with sex techniques or birth control. In the instructions to users of the inventory, as was the case with Form X, it is stressed that the "absence of understanding of important facts of sex" is not evidence that lack of knowledge "always indicates poor adjustment."

The instructions state that Form Y may be applicable to many research projects and that it is useful as "a teaching aid in mental hygiene, human biology, family life, or sex education classes at the high school and college levels."

Although current norms for this second revision are in preparation, available norms are based on the first revision of the test. It is said that the reliability coefficient of the present revision "is about .92," a slightly higher figure than that claimed for Form X.

The possible value of the two forms of the *Sex Knowledge Inventory,* according to one commentator, is that "these tests make a major therapeutic contribution" through modifying individual concern about sex and through de-emotionalizing "sex from fear provoking attitudes and beliefs to a matter of fact consideration." This optimistic summary, it is hoped, will soon be substantiated by more objective studies of validity.

For a review by Albert Ellis, see 4:488 (1 excerpt).

[688]

★**Sex Knowledge Test.** Adults, particularly marriage counselees; 1958; self-scored discussion aid; 1 form (4 pages); no manual; no data on reliability; no norms; 1–12 copies free (except for postage) to persons engaged in marriage counseling; [20] minutes; medical advisors of *Sexology Magazine;* Sexology Corporation. *

[Other Tests]

For tests not listed above, see the following entry in *Tests in Print:* 1288.

DRIVING AND SAFETY EDUCATION

[689]

★**Driver Attitude Survey.** Drivers; 1962; 6 scores: violations, accidents, alcohol, faking, deviance, misses; IBM; 1 form (4 pages); manual (7 pages); no data on reliability; tentative norms; separate answer sheets must be used; $3.50 per 25 tests; 5¢ per IBM answer sheet; $2.50 per set of scoring stencils; 35¢ per manual; 60¢ per specimen set; postage extra; (30–60) minutes; Donald H. Schuster and J. P. Guilford; Sheridan Supply Co. *

[690]

★**Hannaford Industrial Safety Attitude Scales.** Industry; 1959; attitude toward safety; 2 editions; manual (4 pages) for each edition; $2.25 per 25 tests; specimen set not available; prepaid orders only; (15) minutes; Earle S. Hannaford; Center for Safety Education. *

a) INDUSTRIAL SAFETY ATTITUDE SCALE FOR MALE EMPLOYEES. Forms EA, EB, (2 pages).

b) INDUSTRIAL SAFETY ATTITUDE SCALE FOR MALE SUPERVISORS. Forms SA, SB, (2 pages).

DAVID O. HERMAN, *Staff Psychologist, The Psychological Corporation, New York, New York.*

According to their manuals, the Hannaford scales may be used to locate workers who are accident risks (or supervisors who may not motivate their men to work safely), to measure the effectiveness of safety training programs, and to provide discussion points for safety meetings. They were developed by a Thurstone scaling procedure: a large number of statements about safety were collected, and were rated by judges according to their favorableness or unfavorableness toward safety. The 20 statements chosen for each one of the final forms were selected so as to reflect a wide range of positive and negative attitudes. Inspection of the published scale values of the 20 items in each form shows that a wide attitude range is indeed represented. It can also be verified that the two parallel forms of both the supervisor's and the employee's editions are quite closely matched in their distributions of scale values.

Administration is simple—the examinee merely indicates agreement or disagreement with each statement. For all statements with which the subject has agreed the scorer lists the scale values, which are published in the manuals. The median of these values is the final score. There are no norms as such, but rather, a brief table indicates the approximate meaning of certain ranges of scores: scores of 0 through 2.9 indicate enthusiasm toward safety, scores of 5.0 through 5.9 indicate indifference, and so on. Presumably this table defines the categories used by the judges during the scale construction.

Such a table does not constitute satisfactory norms. For one thing, examinees may not approach the items in the same way as did the impartial judges. Furthermore, a general acquiescence set, or tendency to agree with presented items, will affect scores; other things being equal, subjects who agree with more statements will tend to score closer to the middle or neutral point on the scale. Thus, extreme scores will be rare and scores of 0 to 2.9 (enthusiasm) or 8.0 to 11.0 (antagonism) may hardly ever occur, which means that the end categories in the norms may be misleading. In any case, the norms (really "standards") given in the manuals are likely only to be first approximations of norms based on actual distributions of obtained scores.

Retest and parallel-form reliability coefficients range between .83 and .88. These coefficients indicate a high degree of consistency for such short scales.

Pooled data from about 50 companies show that mean scores of contrasted groups differ significantly in the expected direction. Supervisors of injury-free employees had a lower average score on the supervisor's edition than did supervisors of workers who had incurred injuries; injury-free employees averaged a lower score on the employee's edition than did employees who had incurred injuries. Although encouraging, these studies are not truly predictive in nature, but were conducted on samples for which the criterion measures were already available at the time of testing. This point is important because most of the items are rather transparent, especially the ones with extreme scale values, such as "Safety does not benefit the worker" and "A supervisor who does not enforce safety should be demoted." There is no attempt to control for response bias, such as deliberate falsification, and it is most likely that while scores indicating poor safety attitudes will be valid, one cannot have equal confidence in scores at the opposite end of the scale. Therefore, the scales should be used either in situations in which examinees are motivated to answer honestly, or else with groups of sufficient size that one may assume that response bias affects all group means equally. Thus, if employees in one department of a plant are compared with those in other departments, an examination of group means should help identify groups which could benefit from safety training.

Actually, in listing possible uses of the attitude scales, the manuals quite properly do not suggest that they may be employed in personnel selection. The uses suggested are all in connection with current employees, for evaluating the effectiveness of training programs and providing discussion points for safety meetings, in which falsification may be kept to a minimum.

SUMMARY. These short 20-item attitude scales appear to be carefully constructed by conventional Thurstone methods. However, although normative standards are in a sense implied by the manner of construction, the tables of norms given in the manuals are not really norms as they are ordinarily conceived. The validity and reliability figures are encouraging, but the validity studies are rather limited in scope, and the satisfactory retest coefficients may have been affected by response bias.

If an industrial manager wishes to measure safety attitudes and can persuade examinees to answer honestly (or, as mentioned above, wishes to contrast groups or use the scales as an aid in safety discussions) these scales should be useful for his purposes.

[691]

★The McGlade Road Test for Use in Driver Licensing, Education and Employment. Prospective drivers; 1961–62; manual title is *A New Road Test for Use in Driver Licensing, Education & Employment;* 1 form; score sheet ('62, 2 pages); manual ('61, 28 pages); no data on reliability of scores; $2 per 25 tests (must be purchased to obtain manual); 8¢ per single copy; prepaid orders only; (16) minutes; Francis S. McGlade; published in cooperation with Shell Traffic Safety Center; Center for Safety Education. *

REFERENCES

1. McGlade, Francis Stanley. *An Evaluation of the Road Test Phase of the Driver Licensing Examinations of the Various States: An Investigation of Current Road Tests and Testing Procedures, and the Development of a Valid and Reliable Road Test Based on Derived Implications.* Doctor's thesis, New York University (New York, N.Y.), 1960. (*DA* 21:1101)

[692]

★National Test in Driver Education (Preliminary Form). Student and adult drivers; 1940–63; revision of *Knowledge Test for Automobile Drivers;* Short Form ('61, 4 pages); mimeographed manual ('63, 1 page); no data on reliability; $2 per 25 tests (must be purchased to obtain manual); 8¢ per single copy; prepaid orders only; (20) minutes; Center for Safety Education. *

[693]

***Siebrecht Attitude Scale.** Grades 9–16 and adults; 1941–58; attitude toward safe driving practices; 1 form ('41, 4 pages); manual ('41, 4 pages); revised scoring method ('58, 1 mimeographed page); tentative norms; $2 per 25 tests, prepaid orders only; specimen set not available; (10) minutes; Elmer B. Siebrecht; Center for Safety Education. *

REFERENCES

1. Siebrecht, Elmer B. *The Construction and Validation of a Scale for the Measurement of Attitudes Toward Safety in Automobile Driving.* Doctor's thesis, New York University (New York, N.Y.), 1941.

2. Siebrecht, Elmer B. *Measuring Driver Attitudes.* New York University, Division of General Education, Center for Safety Education, Research Contributions to Safety Education, Vol. 2, No. 3. New York: the Center, 1941. Pp. 29. * (*PA* 16:738)

3. Forlano, George, and Wrightstone, J. Wayne. "Relationship of Driver Attitude to Aspects of Personality, Driver Knowledge, and Intelligence." *J Ed Res* 50:183–9 N '56. * (*PA* 32:205)

[694]

★Student Record in Driver Education. Student drivers; 1956; record form for use by driving teachers; 1 form ['56, 2 pages]; instructions (4 pages); $2 per 25 records (must be purchased to obtain instructions); 8¢ per single copy; prepaid orders only; Earl D. Heath; Center for Safety Education. *

[Other Tests]

For tests not listed above, see the following entries in *Tests in Print:* 1162, 1162a, 1164–5, 1169, 1171, 1173, and 1176; out of print: 1163, 1168, 1170, and 1172.

EDUCATION

[695]

★College and University Environment Scales (CUES). College; 1962–63; an adaptation of the *College Characteristics Index,* from which all items are selected; students' conceptions of "the prevailing atmosphere or climate of the campus"; 5 scores: practicality, community, awareness, propriety, scholarship; IBM; Form X-1 ('62, 7 pages); preliminary technical manual ('63, 83 pages); separate answer sheets must be used; 20¢ per test; 4¢ per IBM scorable answer sheet; $2.50 per set of scoring stencils; $2.50 per manual; postage extra; $3 per specimen set, postpaid; Scribe answer sheets (scored by the publisher only) free; fee for Scribe scoring service: 60¢ per answer sheet; (20–25) minutes; C. Robert Pace; Educational Testing Service. *

REFERENCES

1. Fisher, M. Scott. *The Relationship of Satisfaction, Achievement, and Attrition to Anticipated Environmental Press.* Master's thesis, Brigham Young University (Provo, Utah), 1961.

2. Standing, G. Robert. *A Study of the Environment at Brigham Young University as Perceived by Its Students and as Anticipated by Entering Students.* Master's thesis, Brigham Young University (Provo, Utah), 1962.

[696]

Diagnostic Teacher-Rating Scale. Grades 4–12; 1938–52; ratings by pupils; originally published in 1938 for use in grades 4–8; 8 ratings: liking for teacher, ability to explain, kindness-friendliness-understanding, fairness in grading, discipline, work required, liking for lessons, total; Forms A, B, ['52, 2 pages, identical with forms published in 1938 except for format and revision in directions]; 2 parts on one sheet: Area Scale, Diagnostic Check List (Area Scale is the same for both forms); manual ['52, 4 pages]; no data on reliability and validity; tentative norms ['38] based on use in grades 4–8; $3.15 per 35 scales; 35¢ per specimen set; postpaid; administration time not reported; Mary Amatora; Educators'-Employers' Tests & Services Associates. *

REFERENCES

1–2. See 4:795.
3–7. See 5:534.

For a review by Dorothy M. Clendenen, see 5:534.

[697]

***Faculty Morale Scale for Institutional Improvement.** College faculty; 1954–63; 1 form ('54, 1 page); manual ('63, 4 pages); $3 per 30 tests; $1 per specimen set (must be purchased to obtain manual); cash orders postpaid; [12] minutes; A Local Chapter Committee, American Association of University Professors; Psychometric Affiliates. *

[698]

***The Graduate Record Examinations Advanced Tests: Education.** Grades 16–17; 1946–63; for more complete information, see 762; 180(200) minutes; Educational Testing Service. *

REFERENCES

1. SAUM, JAMES A. "The Graduate Record Examination and Its Application in the Stanford School of Education." Abstract. *Calif J Ed Res* 2:183 S '51. *
2. SAUM, JAMES ARTHUR. *Selection Techniques and Their Application in the Stanford School of Education.* Doctor's thesis, Stanford University (Stanford, Calif.), 1951.
3. TREACY, JOHN P. "Interpretation of Scores on Advanced Test in Education." *Cath Ed R* 49:171–4 Mr '51. *
4. MANUEL, HERSCHEL T. "A Study of an Examination for Admission to Candidacy for the Doctorate in Education." *Yearb Nat Council Meas Used Ed* 11:15–8 '54. *
5. LANNHOLM, GERALD V. "The Development of an Advanced Level Test in Education." *J Ed Res* 49:311–3 D '55. * (*PA* 30:7767)
6. SCHULTZ, MARGARET K., AND ANGOFF, WILLIAM H. "The Development of New Scales for the Aptitude and Advanced Tests of the Graduate Record Examinations." *J Ed Psychol* 47:285–94 My '56. * (*PA* 32:2127)
7. CAPPS, MARIAN P., AND DECOSTA, FRANK A. "Contributions of the Graduate Record Examinations and the National Teacher Examinations to the Prediction of Graduate School Success." *J Ed Res* 50:383–9 Ja '57. * (*PA* 32:937)

D. WELTY LEFEVER, *Professor of Education, University of Southern California, Los Angeles, California.* [Review of Forms GGR and LGR1.]

The GRE test in education consists of 200 five-choice items administered under a single three-hour time limit. Raw scores are converted to scaled scores with a mean 500 and a standard deviation 100. The reference group on which the scaled scores are based consisted of 2,095 seniors from 11 colleges tested in 1952. This procedure provides a certain degree of stability as well as comparability among the several forms of the advanced education test. Care must be exercised, however, in interpreting the scores, particularly for graduate students from institutions differing from those in the reference group. These summaries describe admittedly heterogeneous groups characterized by different kinds of undergraduate preparation, standards of selection, and amounts of specialized study. Curricula in education vary considerably in both scope and sequence.

The data on reliability of the several forms of the advanced education test indicate a highly reliable examination. The K-R 20 coefficients range from .90 to .95.

As is generally true, questions relating to validity are the most important and intriguing as well as the most difficult to answer. Little evidence has been reported concerning the predictive validity of the advanced education test.

It is interesting to compare the scaled scores on the advanced education test for a sample of 1,206 applicants for admission to graduate school with those of a sample of 323 second year graduate students. The second year group obtained scaled score quartiles approximately 70 points higher than candidates for admission to graduate work. Both groups took the Aptitude Test and the Advanced Test in education (the second year students sometime in the period 1953–55 and the applicants during the 1960–61 national program), thus providing a basis for speculating about the relative selectivity of each sample. The two groups differed by about the same number of scaled score points on the verbal score of the Aptitude Test. Thus, unless the difficulty of the forms used over the period 1953–61 has changed considerably, one might infer that the superiority in achievement shown by the second year graduates is more likely to represent a difference in the selectivity of the samples than a substantial gain in professional knowledge. If this line of reasoning is sound, a question could be raised regarding the validity of the education test as a measure of growth in professional information and understanding beyond the first graduate year.

The *Handbook for Deans and Examiners* states that the Advanced Tests are designed to cover "the basic concepts and fundamental principles of the subject [tested] and to include many questions requiring reasoning with, and application of, these facts and principles."

At least two thirds of the test questions appear to require considerable breadth of background information and some understanding of concepts or generalizations. The GRE education test is exceptionally comprehensive in its treatment of educational problems, including key ideas from the history of education, acquaintance with different points of view and philosophic positions, knowledge of important findings of psychology and measurement, and understanding of the significance of representative policies and practices concerning curriculum content and instructional methodology. Technical subject matter and detailed research outcomes have been avoided. Also, little emphasis has been given critical thinking and problem analysis on an advanced level. It would, undoubtedly, be very difficult to develop a sampling of content from second or third year graduate courses which would be sufficiently representative of major programs.

Although quality of item writing is decidedly superior, a few criticisms seem appropriate. Several items contain time references such as "new," "today," and "traditional." Other items deal with trends which may actually be moving in contrary directions in different regions and communities. In some instances it may be difficult for the student to deal intelligently with subject matter regarded as controversial in many localities, unless he is given a suitable frame of reference which frees him from the necessity of deciding which side of an issue the item writer is taking. A few items depend for their answer on a relatively small number of studies whose findings at best might be called inconclusive.

Perhaps the most serious criticism relates to the use of pedagogical phrases which may well have the effect of specific determiners which help the student select the correct response. A list of such phrases may include: "provide effectively for individual needs," "practice in democratic procedures," "meaningful experiences," "effective living," "meet needs of the community," "adequate integration of learning experiences," "persistent problems of living," "accept all pupils," "adjust to problem situations," "the insecure person," "more secure," "common values." These phrases may tend to represent a fairly systematic point of view about the goals and program of education. It happens that this reviewer finds himself in basic accord with such a philosophy and finds the type of question reflecting this viewpoint more stimulating and valuable professionally than the factual recall item. Perhaps the hypothesis concerning specific determiners should be checked. It may be possible to balance out any such influence by using similar phrasing in the distractors.

The advanced education test represents the product of a high level of professional craftsmanship. The test as a whole represents a definite departure from the typical stress on factual recall items. The coverage of education course content is reasonably well achieved, at least so far as the first year of graduate work is concerned. This reviewer, however, seriously questions its suitability as a screening test for doctoral candidates. The emphasis of the test seems to be that of a general orientation to the introductory aspects of education as a professional field.

For a review by Harry N. Rivlin of an earlier form, see 5:537. For a review of the testing program, see 5:601.

[699]

Minnesota Teacher Attitude Inventory. Elementary and secondary school teachers and students in grades 12–17; 1951; IBM; Form A (6 pages); manual (15 pages); separate answer sheets must be used; $3 per 25 tests; $2 per 50 IBM answer sheets; 60¢ per set of stencils and manual; 75¢ per specimen set; postpaid; (20–30) minutes; Walter W. Cook, Carroll H. Leeds, and Robert Callis; Psychological Corporation. *

REFERENCES

1–9. See 4:801.

10. Cook, Walter W.; Leeds, Carroll H.; and Callis, Robert. Chap. 4, "Predicting Teacher-Pupil Relations," pp. 66–80. In *The Evaluation of Student Teaching: Twenty-Eighth Annual Yearbook of the Association for Student Teaching.* Lock Haven, Pa.: the Association (State Teachers College), 1949. Pp. ii, 190. *

11. Cook, Walter W., and Hoyt, Cyril J. "Procedure for Determining Number and Nature of Norm Groups for the Minnesota Teacher Attitude Inventory." *Ed & Psychol Meas* 12:562–73 w '52. *

12. Gibby, Mabel Kunce. *The Use of the Minnesota Teacher Attitude Inventory in Appraising Counselor Attitudes.* Doctor's thesis, University of Missouri (Columbia, Mo.), 1952. (*DA* 12:534)

13. Leeds, Carroll H. "A Second Validity Study of the Minnesota Teacher Attitude Inventory." *El Sch J* 52:398–405 Mr '52. * (*PA* 27:5428)

14. Mitzel, Harold Eugene. *Interest Factors Predictive of Teachers' Rapport With Pupils.* Doctor's thesis, University of Minnesota (Minneapolis, Minn.), 1952. (*DA* 12:712)

15. Shaw, Jack; Klausmeier, Herbert J.; Luker, Arno H.; and Reid, Howard T. "Changes Occurring in Teacher-Pupil Attitudes During a Two-Weeks Guidance Workshop." *J Appl Psychol* 36:304–6 O '52. * (*PA* 27:5433)

16. Callis, Robert. "The Efficiency of the Minnesota Teacher Attitude Inventory for Predicting Interpersonal Relations in the Classroom." *J Appl Psychol* 37:82–5 Ap '53. * (*PA* 28:1584)

17. Downie, N. M., and Bell, C. R. "The Minnesota Teacher Attitude Inventory as an Aid in the Selection of Teachers." *J Ed Res* 46:699–704 My '53. * (*PA* 28:3305)

18. Ferguson, John L., Jr. *A Factorial Study of the Minnesota Teacher Attitude Inventory.* Doctor's thesis, University of Missouri (Columbia, Mo.), 1953. (*DA* 13:1087)

19. Sandgren, Duane. *Student Teachers' Attitude Inventory Scores: Their Changes as a Result of Practice Teaching and Their Relation to Critic Teachers' Ratings of Teaching Ability.* Doctor's thesis, Indiana University (Bloomington, Ind.), 1953.

20. Smith, Floyd Ray. *Changes in Some Personal Qualities of Student Teachers at the University of Missouri.* Doctor's thesis, University of Missouri (Columbia, Mo.), 1953. (*DA* 13:1107)

21. Tollett, Jane. *Relation of Minnesota Teacher Attitude Inventory Scores to the Boy-Girl Failure Ratio in Elementary Schools of Cumberland County, Tennessee.* Master's thesis, University of Tennessee (Knoxville, Tenn.), 1953.

22. Brammer, Lawrence M., and Klingelhofer, E. L. "Some Aspects of the Reliability and Validity of the Minnesota Teacher Attitude Inventory." Abstract. *Calif J Ed Res* 5:184–5 S '54. *

23. Coleman, William. "Susceptibility of the Minnesota Teacher Attitude Inventory to 'Faking' With Experienced Teachers." *Ed Adm & Sup* 40:234–7 Ap '54. * (*PA* 29:3066)

24. Garrett, Mary E. *A Study of the Responses of Counselors to the Minnesota Teacher Attitude Inventory.* Master's thesis, University of Texas (Austin, Tex.), 1953.

25. Moffett, Charles R. *Operational Characteristics of Beginning Master's Students in Educational Administration and Supervision.* Doctor's thesis, University of Tennessee (Knoxville, Tenn.), 1954.

26. Rabinowitz, William. "The Fakability of the Minnesota Teacher Attitude Inventory." *Ed & Psychol Meas* 14:657–64 w '54. * (*PA* 29:8000)

27. ROCCHIO, PATRICK DOMINIC. *Teacher-Pupil Attitudes as Related to Teachers' Personal Characteristics and Pupil Adjustment.* Doctor's thesis, University of Minnesota (Minneapolis, Minn.), 1954. (*DA* 16:711)
28. COOK, WALTER W., AND MEDLEY, DONALD M. "The Relationship Between Minnesota Teacher Attitude Inventory Scores and Scores on Certain Scales of the Minnesota Multiphasic Personality Inventory." *J Appl Psychol* 39:123-9 Ap '55. * (*PA* 30:1642)
29. DELLA PIANA, G. M., AND GAGE, N. L. "Pupils' Values and the Validity of the Minnesota Teacher Attitude Inventory." *J Ed Psychol* 46:167-78 Mr '55. * (*PA* 30:1644)
30. HARDY, JAMES. *A Validation Study of the Minnesota Teacher Attitude Inventory in Manitoba.* Master's thesis, University of Manitoba (Winnipeg, Man., Canada), 1955.
31. KEARNEY, NOLAN C., AND ROCCHIO, PATRICK D. "Relation Between a Teacher-Attitude Inventory and Pupil's Ratings of Teachers." *Sch R* 63:443-5 N '55. *
32. KEARNEY, NOLAN C., AND ROCCHIO, PATRICK D. "The Relation Between the Minnesota Teacher Attitude Inventory and Subject Matter Taught by Elementary Teachers." *Ed Adm & Sup* 41:358-60 O '55. * (*PA* 31:1786)
33. KEARNEY, NOLAN C., AND ROCCHIO, PATRICK D. "Using the Minnesota Teacher Attitude Inventory in Counseling Prospective Teachers." *Personnel & Guid J* 34:159-60 N '55. * (*PA* 30:6353)
34. LUTON, JAMES N. *A Study of the Use of Standardized Tests in the Selection of Potential Educational Administrators.* Doctor's thesis, University of Tennessee (Knoxville, Tenn.), 1955.
35. MITZEL, HAROLD E.; RABINOWITZ, WILLIAM; AND OSTREICHER, LEONARD M. *Effect of Certain Response Sets on Valid Test Variance.* College of the City of New York, Division of Teacher Education, Office of Research and Evaluation, Publication No. 26. New York: Office of Research and Evaluation, the Division, February 1955. Pp. ii, 23. * (*PA* 30:118)
36. PICERNO, VINCENT JOSEPH. *Personal Characteristics of Some Successful Music Teachers in Erie County, New York.* Doctor's thesis, Northwestern University (Evanston, Ill.), 1955. (*DA* 16:74)
37. ROCCHIO, PATRICK D., AND KEARNEY, NOLAN C. "Using an Attitude Inventory in Selecting Teachers." *El Sch J* 56:76-8 O '55. * (*PA* 30:6359)
38. CANDLAND, DOROTHY NELSON. *The Relationship Between the Dominative-Supportive Dimension of Personality and Student-Teachers' Classroom Behavior.* Doctor's thesis, Stanford University (Stanford, Calif.), 1956. (*DA* 16:914)
39. CLARKE, ALBERT THOMPSON. *A Study of the Validity of the Minnesota Teacher Attitude Inventory as an Instrument to Aid in the Selection of Directing Teachers.* Doctor's thesis, Florida State University (Tallahassee, Fla.), 1956. (*DA* 16:1404)
40. COOK, WALTER W.; HOYT, CYRIL J.; AND EIKAAS, ALF. "Studies of Predictive Validity of the Minnesota Teacher Attitude Inventory." *J Teach Ed* 7:167-72 Je '56. * (*PA* 32:5993)
41. COOK, WALTER W.; KEARNEY, NOLAN C.; ROCCHIO, PATRICK D.; AND THOMPSON, ANTON. "Significant Factors in Teachers' Classroom Attitudes." *J Teach Ed* 7:274-9 S '56. *
42. DAY, HARRY P. *A Study of the Validity of the Minnesota Teacher Attitude Inventory as a Predictive Instrument in the Selection of Good Teaching Prospects From Among College Undergraduates.* Doctor's thesis, Florida State University (Tallahassee, Fla.), 1956. (*DA* 16:500)
43. ESON, MORRIS E. "The Minnesota Teacher Attitude Inventory in Evaluating the Teaching of Educational Psychology." *J Ed Psychol* 47:271-5 My '56. * (*PA* 32:2144)
44. FURST, EDWARD J., AND FRICKE, BENNO G. "Development and Applications of Structured Tests of Personality." *R Ed Res* 26:26-55 F '56. * (*PA* 31:6081)
45. GERDES, BERNHARD WILLIAM. *The Parent-Teacher Conference: Attitudes of Parents and Teachers as Associated With Success in the Conference.* Doctor's thesis, Stanford University (Stanford, Calif.), 1956. (*DA* 17:92)
46. GRAY, W. MAXINE. *The Use of the Minnesota Teacher Attitude Inventory in the Selection, Counseling, and Placement of Student Teachers.* Doctor's thesis, Wayne University (Detroit, Mich.), 1956. (*DA* 17:102)
47. KEARNEY, NOLAN C., AND ROCCHIO, PATRICK D. "The Effect of Teacher Education on the Teacher's Attitude." *J Ed Res* 49:703-8 My '56. * (*PA* 31:3839)
48. LAMBERT, HAZEL M. "An Item Analysis of the Minnesota Teacher Attitude Inventory." Abstract. *Calif J Ed Res* 7:132-3 My '56. *
49. LEEDS, CARROLL H. "Teacher Attitudes and Temperament as a Measure of Teacher-Pupil Rapport." *J Appl Psychol* 40:333-7 O '56. * (*PA* 31:8873)
50. MITZEL, HAROLD E.; RABINOWITZ, WILLIAM; AND OSTREICHER, LEONARD M. "The Effects of Response Sets on the Validity of the Minnesota Teacher Attitude Inventory." *Ed & Psychol Meas* 16:501-15 w '56. * (*PA* 32:968)
51. OELKE, MERRITT C. "A Study of Student Teachers' Attitudes Toward Children." *J Ed Psychol* 47:193-8 Ap '56. * (*PA* 32:2154)
52. PHILLIPS, RAYMOND V. *A Study of Attitude and Personality Variables Among In-Service Teachers.* Doctor's thesis, Temple University (Philadelphia, Pa.), 1956. (*DA* 16:2528)
53. POTTER, DONALD R. *Evaluation of the Minnesota Teacher Attitude Inventory as a Predictor of Achievement in a First Course in Education.* Master's thesis, Iowa State College (Ames, Iowa), 1956.
54. PRICE, MONROE SAMUEL. *The Susceptibility to Distortion of the Minnesota Teacher Attitude Inventory.* Doctor's thesis, University of Michigan (Ann Arbor, Mich.), 1956. (*DA* 17:1267)
55. ROCCHIO, PATRICK D., AND KEARNEY, NOLAN C. "Does a Course in Mental Hygiene Help Teachers?" *Understanding the Child* 25:91-4 Je '56. *
56. ROCCHIO, PATRICK D., AND KEARNEY, NOLAN C. "Teacher-Pupil Attitudes as Related to Nonpromotion of Secondary School Pupils." *Ed & Psychol Meas* 16:244-52 su '56. * (*PA* 31:5164)
57. ROGERS, VINCENT R., AND SMITH, JAMES A. "Professional Attitudes of Students in an Intensive Teacher-Training Program." *El Sch J* 57:100-1 N '56. *
58. SANDGREN, DUANE L., AND SCHMIDT, LOUIS G. "Does Practice Teaching Change Attitudes Toward Teaching?" *J Ed Res* 49:673-80 My '56. * (*PA* 31:3846)
59. SORENSON, A. GARTH. "A Note on the 'Fakability' of the Minnesota Teacher Attitude Inventory." *J Appl Psychol* 40:192-4 Je '56. * (*PA* 31:6696)
60. ANDREWS, JOHN H. M. "Administrative Significance of Psychological Differences Between Secondary Teachers of Different Subject Matter Fields." *Alberta J Ed Res* 3:199-208 D '57. *
61. BEAMER, GEORGE C., AND LEDBETTER, ELAINE W. "The Relation Between Teacher Attitudes and the Social Service Interest." *J Ed Res* 50:655-66 My '57. *
62. CONDELL, JAMES F. "Use of the Minnesota Teacher Attitude Inventory (MTAI)." *Psychol Rep* 3:411-2 S '57. * (*PA* 32:4636)
63. CRIST, ROBERT L. *A Study of Mean Differences in the R, S, and T Traits of the Guilford-Zimmerman Temperament Survey for Upper and Lower Quarter Students on the Minnesota Teacher Attitude Inventory.* Master's thesis, Purdue University (Lafayette, Ind.), 1957.
64. EIKAAS, ALF INGVALD. *A Study of Personality Dimensions Related to Teacher-Pupil Rapport.* Doctor's thesis, University of Minnesota (Minneapolis, Minn.), 1957. (*DA* 17:2495)
65. FISHMAN, JOSHUA A. "The MTAI in an American Minority-Group School Setting: 1, Differences Between Test Characteristics for Norm and Non-Norm Populations." *J Ed Psychol* 48:41-51 Ja '57. * (*PA* 32:4639)
66. GAGE, N. L. "Logical Versus Empirical Scoring Keys: The Case of the MTAI." *J Ed Psychol* 48:213-6 Ap '57. * (*PA* 33:4692)
67. GAGE, N. L.; LEAVITT, GEORGE S.; AND STONE, GEORGE C. "The Psychological Meaning of Acquiescence Set for Authoritarianism." *J Abn & Social Psychol* 55:98-103 Jl '57. * (*PA* 32:466)
68. MAZZITELLI, DOMINICK, JR. *A Forced-Choice Approach to the Measurement of Teacher Attitudes.* Doctor's thesis, University of Illinois (Urbana, Ill.), 1957. (*DA* 18:498)
69. MURRAY, ALFRED J. *An Analysis of Attitude for Success in Teaching as Measured by the Minnesota Teacher Attitude Inventory.* Master's thesis, Montana State University (Missoula, Mont.), 1957.
70. SHELDON, M. STEPHEN, AND SORENSON, A. GARTH. "Conditions Affecting the Fakability of the Minnesota Teacher Attitude Inventory." *Calif J Ed Res* 8:130 My '57. *
71. STEIN, HARRY L., AND HARDY, JAMES. "A Validation Study of the Minnesota Teacher Attitude Inventory in Manitoba." *J Ed Res* 50:321-38 Ja '57. * (*PA* 32:901)
72. BUDD, WILLIAM C., AND BLAKELY, LYNDA S. "The Relationship Between Ascendancy and Response Choice on the Minnesota Teacher Attitude Inventory." *J Ed Res* 52:73-4 O '58. * (*PA* 34:2027)
73. BUDD, WILLIAM C., AND BLAKELY, LYNDA S. "Response Bias in the Minnesota Teacher Attitude Inventory." *J Ed Res* 51:707-9 My '58. * (*PA* 33:11043)
74. CHANSKY, NORMAN M. "The Attitudes Students Assign to Their Teacher." *J Ed Psychol* 49:13-6 F '58. * (*PA* 36:2KD13C)
75. DEL POPOLO, JOSEPH ANTHONY. *Authoritarian Trends in Personality as Related to Attitudinal and Behavioral Traits of Student Teachers.* Doctor's thesis, Pennsylvania State University (University Park, Pa.), 1958. (*DA* 19:86)
76. DONAT, GERTRUDE MCADAM. *Factors Related to Measured Masculinity Among Students Majoring in Secondary Education.* Doctor's thesis, University of Minnesota (Minneapolis, Minn.), 1958. (*DA* 19:1834)
77. EVANS, K. M. "An Examination of the Minnesota Teacher Attitude Inventory." *Brit J Ed Psychol* 28:253-7 N '58. * (*PA* 34:3457)
78. FISHMAN, JOSHUA A. "The Minnesota Teacher Attitude Inventory in an American Minority-Group School Setting: 2, Indirect Validation as a Test of Pupil-Directedness." *J General Psychol* 59:219-27 O '58. * (*PA* 36:2KM19F)
79. LETON, DONALD A. "A Study of the Validity of Parent

Attitude Measurement." *Child Develop* 29:515–20 D '58. * (*PA* 34:4131)
80. NUNNERY, MICHAEL Y. *A Study in the Use of Psychological Tests in Determining Effectiveness and Ineffectiveness Among Practicing School Administrators.* Doctor's thesis, University of Tennessee (Knoxville, Tenn.), 1958. (*DA* 19:1276)
81. PETERSON, TED TANGWALL. *Selecting School Administrators: An Evaluation of Six Tests.* Doctor's thesis, Stanford University (Stanford, Calif.), 1958. (*DA* 19:262)
82. RABINOWITZ, WILLIAM, AND ROSENBAUM, IRA. "A Failure in the Prediction of Pupil-Teacher Rapport." *J Ed Psychol* 49:93–8 Ap '58. * (*PA* 36:2KM93R)
83. SORENSON, A. G., AND SHELDON, M. S. "A Further Note on the Fakability of the MTAI." *J Appl Psychol* 42:74–8 Ap '58. * (*PA* 33:7021)
84. STAFFORD, KENNETH R. "The Minnesota Teacher Attitude Inventory Scores of Negro and White Fifth Year Students in the Arkansas Experiment in Teacher Education." *J Ed Res* 51:633–4 Ap '58. * (*PA* 33:9002)
85. WALTHEW, JOHN K., JR. *An Analysis of Changes Between Initial and Final Minnesota Teacher Attitude Inventory Scores of Tests Administered to Undergraduate Teacher Trainees in a Course in Educational Psychology at Cornell University, and the Relationship of These Changes to the Subject Matter and Objectives of Educational Psychology.* Master's thesis, Cornell University (Ithaca, N.Y.), 1958.
86. WILLIAMS, RAYMOND EDMUND. *The Measurement and Prediction of Cooperating Teacher Effectiveness in Music Teacher Education.* Doctor's thesis, University of Illinois Urbana, Ill.), 1958. (*DA* 19:1023)
87. ANDREWS, JOHN H. M., AND BROWN, ALAN F. "Can Principals Exclude Their Own Personality Characteristics When They Rate Their Teachers?" *Ed Adm & Sup* 45:234–42 Jl '59. * (*PA* 34:6579)
88. BADAL, ALDEN WESLEY. *The Relationship of Selected Test Measures to Administrator Success in the Elementary School.* Doctor's thesis, Stanford University (Stanford, Calif.), 1959. (*DA* 20:1263)
89. COLEMAN, WILLIAM, AND COLLETT, DOROTHY MANLEY. "Development and Applications of Structured Tests of Personality." *R Ed Res* 29:57–72 F '59. * (*PA* 34:5604)
90. COSS, ARTHUR FULTON. *A Comparative Analysis of the Expressed Attitudes of Elementary Education Students, Their University Instructors, and Their Supervising Teachers Toward Pupil-Teacher Relations as Measured by the Minnesota Teacher Attitude Inventory.* Doctor's thesis, Indiana University (Bloomington, Ind.), 1959. (*DA* 20:1278)
91. DAY, HARRY P. "Attitude Changes of Beginning Teachers After Initial Teaching Experience." *J Teach Ed* 10:326–8 S '59. * (*PA* 34:8414)
92. DAY, HARRY P. "A Study of Predictive Validity of the Minnesota Teacher Attitude Inventory." *J Ed Res* 53:37–8 S '59. *
93. GRUBER, JOSEPH JOHN, JR. *A Comparative Study of Employed Male Physical Education Graduates and Physical Education Undergraduate Students on Selected Instruments.* Doctor's thesis, Purdue University (Lafayette, Ind.), 1959. (*DA* 20:2676)
94. HOOKER, WILLIAM DOUGLAS. *A Study of Certain Personal Characteristics and Attitudes of Full-Time and Part-Time Student Teachers and Certified Beginning Teachers.* Doctor's thesis, University of Texas (Austin, Tex.), 1959. (*DA* 20:2677)
95. HOYT, CYRIL J., AND COOK, WALTER W. "The Predictive Validity of the Minnesota Teacher Attitude Inventory Based on Pupil Attitude Toward School." *J Teach Ed* 10:42–4 Mr '59. * (*PA* 34:2038)
96. ISENBERGER, WILMA. "Self-Attitudes of Women Physical Education Major Students as Related to Measures of Interest and Success." *Res Q* 30:167–78 My '59. *
97. JOHNSON, DONALD V. *The Relationship of the Minnesota Teacher Attitude Inventory Scores to the Marks of Student Teachers.* Master's thesis, Ohio University (Athens, Ohio), 1959.
98. MUNSON, HOWARD ROGER. *Comparison of Interest and Attitude Patterns of Three Selected Groups of Teacher Candidates.* Doctor's thesis, State College of Washington (Pullman, Wash.), 1959. (*DA* 19:3237)
99. NUNNERY, MICHAEL Y. "How Useful Are Standardized Psychological Tests in the Selection of School Administrators." *Ed Adm & Sup* 45:349–56 N '59. * (*PA* 35:7092)
100. OSMON, ROBERT VANCE. *Associative Factors in Changes of Student Teachers' Attitudes During Student Teaching.* Doctor's thesis, Indiana University (Bloomington, Ind.), 1959. (*DA* 20:1281)
101. PALACIOS, JOHN RAYMOND. *A Validation Study of Selected Tests for Possible Use in Admission to Professional Education Sequences at Purdue University.* Doctor's thesis, Purdue University (Lafayette, Ind.), 1959. (*DA* 20:2679)
102. RICCIO, ANTHONY C., AND PETERS, HERMAN J. "Freshman Teacher Education Norms for the Minnesota Teacher Attitude Inventory." *J Ed Res* 52:361 My '59. *
103. RICCIO, ANTHONY C., AND PETERS, HERMAN J. "Vocational Guidance and Familial Influences." *Voc Guid Q* 8:70–1 w '59–60. *
104. RICCIO, ANTHONY CARMINE. *The Relationship of Selected Variables to Attitudes Toward Teaching.* Doctor's thesis, Ohio State University (Columbus, Ohio), 1959. (*DA* 20:2159)
105. SHELDON, M. STEPHEN. "Conditions Affecting the Fakability of Teacher-Selection Inventories." *Ed & Psychol Meas* 19:207–19 su '59. * (*PA* 34:4093)
106. SHELDON, M. STEPHEN; COALE, JACK M.; AND COPPLE, ROCKNE. "Concurrent Validity of the 'Warm Teacher Scale.'" *J Ed Psychol* 50:37–40 F '59. * (*PA* 35:2810)
107. STANDLEE, LLOYD S., AND POPHAM, W. JAMES. "The MTAI as a Predictor of Over-All Teacher Effectiveness." *J Ed Res* 52:319–20 Ap '59. *
108. WAGGONER, GLEN HASTINGS. *Administrator's Scores on Selected Standardized Tests and His Administrative Performance as Reported by Classroom Teachers.* Doctor's thesis, Stanford University (Stanford, Calif.), 1959. (*DA* 20:3169)
109. BARTLETT, CLAUDE J.; RONNING, ROYCE R.; AND HURST, JOHN G. "A Study of Classroom Evaluation Techniques With Special Reference to Application of Knowledge." *J Ed Psychol* 51:152–8 Je '60. * (*PA* 35:3871)
110. BOYCE, RICHARD DUDLEY. *An Empirical Evaluation of Five Tests for Administrator Selection: The Composite Study.* Doctor's thesis, Stanford University (Stanford, Calif.), 1960. (*DA* 21:2546)
111. EBERT, FRANCIS JOHN. *An Empirical Evaluation of Five Tests for the Selection of Elementary School Principals.* Doctor's thesis, Stanford University (Stanford, Calif.), 1960. (*DA* 21:2548)
112. GARDNER, MARGARET SEYMOUR. *Factors Associated With Success in First Grade Teaching.* Doctor's thesis, Northwestern University (Evanston, Ill.), 1960. (*DA* 21:2609)
113. GRUBER, JOSEPH JOHN. "Personality Traits and Teaching Attitudes." *Res Q* 31:434–9 O '60. *
114. HARDER, NANCY ALLIENE. *A Comparison of Learner-Centeredness in Teacher Attitudes and Verbal Behavior.* Doctor's thesis, North Texas State College (Denton, Tex.), 1960. (*DA* 21:2589)
115. HEATH, EARL JOSEPH. *A Study of Attitudes Toward Teacher-Pupil Relationships Utilizing Q-Technique With the Items of the MTAI.* Doctor's thesis, Indiana University (Bloomington, Ind.), 1960. (*DA* 21:2591)
116. HOYT, CYRIL J., AND COOK, WALTER W. "The Stability of MTAI Scores During Two to Seven Years of Teaching." *J Teach Ed* 11:487–91 D '60. * (*PA* 35:7133)
117. JAMES, KENNETH RAYMOND. *An Empirical Evaluation of Five Tests for Administrator Selection in a Metropolitan School District.* Doctor's thesis, Stanford University (Stanford, Calif.), 1960. (*DA* 21:2556)
118. KAPLAN, DONALD MARTIN. *Differences in Attitudes and Personality of "Subject-Oriented" and "Pupil-Oriented" Secondary School Teachers: A Comparative Analysis of Two Groups of Secondary School Teachers With the Minnesota Teacher Attitude Inventory and the Rorschach.* Doctor's thesis, New York University (New York, N.Y.), 1960. (*DA* 21:2988)
119. KINGSTON, ALBERT J., AND NEWSOME, GEORGE L. "The Relationship of Two Measures of Authoritarianism to the Minnesota Teacher Attitude Inventory." *J Psychol* 49:333–8 Ap '60. * (*PA* 34:7640)
120. MARKWARDT, FREDERICK CHARLES, JR. *Pattern Analysis Techniques in the Prediction of College Success.* Doctor's thesis, University of Minnesota (Minneapolis, Minn.), 1960. (*DA* 21:2990)
121. POLMANTIER, PAUL C., AND FERGUSON, JOHN L. "Faking the Minnesota Teacher Attitude Inventory." *Ed & Psychol Meas* 20:79–82 sp '60. * (*PA* 34:8425)
122. POPHAM, W. JAMES, AND TRIMBLE, ROBERT R. "The Minnesota Teacher Attitude Inventory as an Index of General Teaching Competence." *Ed & Psychol Meas* 20:509–12 au '60. * (*PA* 35:4001)
123. PRICE, ROBERT DAVID. *Relations Between Cooperating Teachers' and Student Teachers' Attitudes and Performances.* Doctor's thesis, University of Texas (Austin, Tex.), 1960. (*DA* 21:2615)
124. RABINOWITZ, WILLIAM, AND ROSENBAUM, IRA. "Teaching Experience and Teachers' Attitudes." *El Sch J* 60:313–9 Mr '60. *
125. RICCIO, ANTHONY C., AND PETERS, HERMAN J. "The Study of Values and the Minnesota Teacher Attitude Inventory." *Ed Res B* 39:101–3 Ap '60. *
126. RIPPY, MARK LEO, JR. *Certain Relationships Between Classroom Behavior and Attitude and Personality Characteristics of Selected Elementary Teachers.* Doctor's thesis, George Peabody College for Teachers (Nashville, Tenn.), 1960. (*DA* 21:814)
127. SCOTT, OWEN, AND BRINKLEY, STERLING G. "Attitude Changes of Student Teachers and the Validity of the Minnesota Teacher Attitude Inventory." *J Ed Psychol* 51:76–81 Ap '60. * (*PA* 35:2809)
128. SEWARD, THOMAS CLINTON. *The Effect of Instructor-Student Value Discrepancy on the Attitude Change of Prospective Teachers.* Doctor's thesis, Michigan State University (East Lansing, Mich.), 1960. (*DA* 21:1127)
129. BESSENT, EDGAR WAILAND. *The Predictability of Selected Elementary School Principals' Administrative Behavior.*

Doctor's thesis, University of Texas (Austin, Tex.), 1961. (*DA* 22:3479)
130. BILLINGSLY, LEON COMMODORE. *Characteristics of Teacher Effectiveness.* Doctor's thesis, University of Arkansas (Fayetteville, Ark.), 1961. (*DA* 22:1082)
131. CAMPBELL, ROBERT E., AND HORROCKS, JOHN E. "A Note on Relationships Between Student and Parent Minnesota Teacher Attitude Inventory Scores." *J Ed Psychol* 52:199–200 Ag '61. * (*PA* 38:2461)
132. DARROW, HARRIET DRISKELL. *The Relationship of Certain Factors to Performance of Elementary Student Teachers With Contrasting Success Records in Student Teaching.* Doctor's thesis, Indiana University (Bloomington, Ind.), 1961. (*DA* 22:3934)
133. DAVIES, LILLIAN SCHOLLJEGERDES. *Some Relationships Between Attitudes, Personality Characteristics, and Verbal Behavior of Selected Teachers.* Doctor's thesis, University of Minnesota (Minneapolis, Minn.), 1961. (*DA* 22:3943)
134. DUDA, WALTER BOLESLAV. *The Prediction of Three Major Dimensions of Teacher Behavior for Student Teachers in Music Education.* Doctor's thesis, University of Illinois (Urbana, Ill.), 1961. (*DA* 22:1518)
135. FOX, AUGUSTA MEREDITH. *Relationships Between Personality and Leader Behavior of Elementary School Principals.* Doctor's thesis, North Texas State College (Denton, Tex.), 1961. (*DA* 22:2263)
136. HILL, THOMAS BARLOW, JR. *The Relationships Between Teacher Morale and the Ability to Establish Rapport With Pupils and Other Selected Variables.* Doctor's thesis, North Texas State College (Denton, Tex.), 1961. (*DA* 22:789)
137. VERTEIN, LESTER DALE. "A Study of the Personal-Social and Intellectual Characteristics of a Group of State College Students Preparing to Teach." *J Exp Ed* 30:159–92 D '61. *
138. BIXBY, ARTHUR PORTER. *Effect of Supervision Upon Attitudes of Teachers Toward Children.* Doctor's thesis, University of Connecticut (Storrs, Conn.), 1962. (*DA* 23:1567)
139. BOWMAN, VINCENT JOSEPH. *A Study of Preservice Secondary Education Majors Relative to Their Scores on the Minnesota Teacher Attitude Inventory.* Doctor's thesis, University of Kansas (Lawrence, Kan.), 1962. (*DA* 23:3231)
140. COOK, DESMOND L. "A Note on the Relationships Between MTAI and GZTS Scores for Three Levels of Teacher Experience." *J Ed Res* 55:363–7 My '62. * (*PA* 37:5678)
141. CRANE, WILLIAM J. "Screening Devices for Occupational Therapy Majors." *Am J Occup Ther* 16:131–2 My–Je '62. * (*PA* 37:4078)
142. FORD, ROXANA R. "Attitudes of Home Economics Teachers Towards Children." *J Home Econ* 54:466–9 Je '62. *
143. RICCIO, ANTHONY C., AND LARSON, RICHARD F. "Peer Evaluation and Performance on the MTAI." *J Ed Sociol* 35:377–80 Ap '62. *
144. ROBINSON, WILLIS. *A Validity Study of the Testing Program for the Selection of Students for Teacher Education.* Doctor's thesis, Purdue University (Lafayette, Ind.), 1962. (*DA* 23:2812)
145. WEBB, JOHN RANKIN. *A Study of the Relationship of Teaching Difficulties Reported by Beginning Secondary Teachers to Teacher-Pupil Attitudes and Other Variables.* Doctor's thesis, University of Arkansas (Fayetteville, Ark.), 1962. (*DA* 23:3254)
146. WILLIAMS, DONALD EARL. *The Interrelatedness of Student Teachers' Temperament Traits, Their Attitudes Toward Youth, and Their Teacher-Pupil Interpersonal Problems.* Doctor's thesis, North Texas State University (Denton, Tex.), 1962. (*DA* 23:3255)
147. DURFLINGER, GLENN W. "Academic and Personality Differences Between Women Students Who Do Complete the Elementary Teaching Credential Program and Those Who Do Not." *Ed & Psychol Meas* 23:775–83 w '63. *
148. DURFLINGER, GLENN W. "Personality Correlates of Success in Student-Teaching." *Ed & Psychol Meas* 23:383–90 su '63. * (*PA* 38:1427)
149. GETZELS, J. W., AND JACKSON, P. W. "The Minnesota Teacher Attitude Inventory," pp. 508–22. In *Handbook of Research on Teaching.* Edited by N. L. Gage. Chicago, Ill.: Rand McNally Co., 1963. Pp. xiii, 1218. * (*PA* 38:9132)
150. HERBERT, N., AND TURNBULL, G. H. "Personality Factors and Effective Progress in Teaching." *Ed R* 16:24–31 N '63. *
151. HUGHES, BILLIE EDWARD. *Predicting Achievement in a Graduate School of Education.* Doctor's thesis, North Texas State University (Denton, Tex.), 1963. (*DA* 24:1448)
152. NOLL, VICTOR H., AND NOLL, RACHEL P. "The Social Background and Values of Prospective Teachers." *Yearb Nat Council Meas Ed* 20:108–14 '63. * (*PA* 38:9297)
153. OFCHUS, LEON T., AND GNAGEY, WILLIAM J. "Factors Related to the Shift of Professional Attitudes of Students in Teacher Education." *J Ed Psychol* 54:149–53 Je '63. * (*PA* 38:1429)
154. PIVETZ, MILDRED E. *The Relationship Between Teachers' Attitudes and Effectiveness in the Classroom.* Doctor's thesis, State University of New York at Buffalo (Buffalo, N.Y.), 1963. (*DA* 24:2340)
155. ZACHAREWICZ, MARY MISAELA. *Relations Between Teaching Attitudes of Prospective Teachers and Their Self Descriptions.* Doctor's thesis, Fordham University (New York, N.Y.), 1963. (*DA* 24:876)

For reviews by Dwight L. Arnold and Lee J. Cronbach, see 4:801.

[700]

***National Teacher Examinations.** College seniors and teachers; 1940–64; tests administered 4 times a year (March, July, October, December) at centers established by the publisher; tests may also be locally administered by arrangement; supervisor's manual ['63, 27 pages]; handbook for school and college officials ('61, 42 pages); bulletin of information for candidates ('64, 34 pages); score interpretation leaflet ['63, 6 pages]; separate Scribe answer sheets must be used; examination fees: $5 plus $4 for the Common Examinations and $2 for each Area Examination; fee includes report of scores to the examinee and 1–3 school systems or colleges designated at time of application; $1 per additional report; Educational Testing Service. *

a) COMMON EXAMINATIONS. 6 scores: professional information, English expression, social studies-literature-fine arts, science and mathematics, nonverbal reasoning, weighted total; 190(215) minutes.

b) TEACHING AREA EXAMINATIONS. Formerly called Optional Examinations; 13 tests (candidates elect 1 or 2): Education in the Elementary School, Early Childhood Education, Biology and General Science (see 868), English Language and Literature (see 259), Industrial Arts Education (see 736), Mathematics (see 583), Chemistry-Physics-and General Science (see 869), Social Studies (see 974), Physical Education (see 727), Business Education (see 28), Music Education (see 350), Home Economics Education (see 734), Art Education (see 345); 80(90) minutes.

REFERENCES

1–43. See 4:802.
44–49. See 5:538.
50. FENSTERMACHER, GUY M., AND SWINEFORD, FRANCES. "The National Teacher Examinations and the Appraisal of Teacher Preparation." *J Teach Ed* 9:429–34 D '58. *
51. MCCAMEY, JAMES E. *The Correlation Between Certain Academic Factors and Scores on the 1957 National Teacher Examinations of the 1957 Graduates of the University of Hawaii Teachers College.* Master's thesis, University of Hawaii (Honolulu, Hawaii), 1958.
52. STARCHER, GENEVIEVE. "National Teacher Examinations: A Certification Instrument in West Virginia." *J Teach Ed* 10:102–6 Mr '59. *
53. GRUBER, EDWARD C. *How to Score High on the National Teacher Examination.* New York: Arco Publishing Co., Inc., 1962. Pp. vi, 167, plus supplements. *
54. SIMPSON, HAZEL DEAL. *An Analysis of the Relationship Between Scores Attained on the National Teacher Examinations and Certain Other Factors.* Doctor's thesis, University of Georgia (Athens, Ga.), 1963. (*DA* 24:2369)

HAROLD SEASHORE, *Director, Test Division, The Psychological Corporation, New York, New York.* [Review of two of the following forms of each test: Forms HNT, INT, JNT, KNT, and LNT.]

The National Teacher Examinations aim "to provide objective examinations of measureable intellectual competencies which are commonly considered basic to effective classroom teaching." The component tests assess preparation in the usual academic and vocational subjects and in professional education; they also include measures for separate appraisal of mental ability.

The NTE is a "secure" program, with the tests given on scheduled days by qualified examiners in a large number of centers across the country. Under some circumstances, colleges and universities can schedule special testings to embrace whole groups, such as seniors majoring in education or new graduate students in education. This review will not include any further comment on the program aspects of the NTE except to note that the procedures, information bulletins, manuals for administration, and rules for storage and retrieval of test scores are similar to those for other secure programs operated by the Educational Testing Service, a statement which is intended as a compliment.

The examinee who completes the usual program will first spend about three hours in the morning on the Common Examinations, which include five parts in a single booklet: Professional Information (90 items), English Expression (45 items), Social Studies, Literature, and Fine Arts (60 items), Science and Mathematics (50 items), and Nonverbal Reasoning (29 items). Each of these yields a reasonably reliable score; K-R 20 values are in the upper .80's. A weighted total score is computed with the five tests, in the order above, weighted 4, 1, 2, 2, and 1. Multipliers are applied to the scaled scores based on the standardizing population. The Handbook for School and College Officials wisely notes that any school system or university using the common tests can develop local weighting to serve its own needs. Indeed, the rationale of the above formula is not stated.

In the afternoon, the examinee will take either one or two 80-minute Optional Examinations. He elects to be examined in the fields in which he claims the greatest competence for teaching. These tests are available in 13 teaching fields. The first two are age oriented: Education in the Elementary School and Early Childhood Education. These two tests cover professional knowledge and methodology of teaching primarily, but also survey content in science, mathematics, literature, etc., appropriate for the grades.

The other optional tests are in academic or vocational fields as listed in the above entry. These subject-oriented tests are meant to measure mastery of the subject matter itself and of the principles, objectives, and methods of teaching these subjects at the secondary level. Reliability coefficients for these 13 tests (which have from 85 to 120 items each) are reported for samples of about 300 cases; the K-R 20 values in various reports range from .80 to .94 with the median value about .88.

The scaled score systems for the NTE need description because they are not as simple as they may first seem. Raw scores on each of the 5 common and 13 optional tests are converted to scaled scores with a mean of 60 and a standard deviation of 10 for the standardizing population. The "standardizing population" is not the same for the common tests and the optionals. For the Common Examinations, 60 is equated to the mean score of the group tested when the program was inaugurated. The date is not given but, from other sources, it is in the early 1940's. The schools included are not listed in current manuals. The 1960 and 1959 test analysis reports show that the current form is tied to the original scaling through 50 items which are common to the once-before form, which, in turn, is tied through 62 overlapping items to its predecessor.

The main problem with this plan is not the technical one of deriving statistically useful scaled scores, but of interpretation of scores on the Common Examinations. The less sophisticated user may assume that 60 is the average score of current samples of education students and teachers. A dean notes that his seniors only score between 54 and 56 on the five parts. Is his group low? Assuming no loss in accuracy of scaling over many generations of test forms, his group is low in comparison with an undefined, prewar population. But if he turns to page 17 of the 1961 handbook, he finds that the rounded mean scores on the five tests for 300 random cases in 1960 were 56, 57, 55, 58, and 57. Now he might conclude that on the average his seniors "look like" current nationwide candidates—but since the idea of "mean is 60" is so persistent, he, his colleagues, and especially his critics may still make erroneous inferences about standards of teacher training in this decade. Since scaled scores for anchoring tests to each other have merits and several uses, about all one can ask for is effective and clear explanations for the general readers of the manuals and the consumers of test scores. This reviewer finds no technical fault with the exposition in the handbook, but would hope that the editors will strive for greater clarity. That clarity, in fact accuracy, is called for is seen in this quotation from the 1963 Bulletin of Information for Candidates [1]: "The scale of scores for each test ranges approximately from 30 to 90, with an average of about 60." The error is that 60 on the Common Examinations refers to an unidentified group tested on different forms more than a couple of decades ago. According to the handbook, many more than half the examinees will rate under 60 in the common tests. Perhaps no harm is done, but why cannot ETS report in terms of adequately determined percentile ranks based on the edition of the test the candidate writes? This reviewer has not seen the actual reports sent to the examinees; they may be more accurate and less discouraging to a fair percentage. As shown below, 60 is clearly a proper statement of the mean of relevant groups on the Optional Examinations.

Two paragraphs back, the quasi-norms on page 17 of the handbook were referred to. However, on page 20, a table of percentile equivalents for various scaled scores on each of the five common tests and the weighted score is provided, based on testing during 1956–60. Knowing that during this period ETS tested tens of thousands of cases with the NTE, it is surprising that the table is based on a stratified sample of institutions which tested nearly all their full-time seniors preparing to teach rather than on a good nationwide sample. The casual reader might accept this as a table of national norms. The sample includes 3,505 cases distributed regionally as follows: New England, 8 per cent; Middle Atlantic, 51 per cent; North Central, 8 per cent; Southern, 34 per cent; Western, *none*. While this sample has been completely described, the resulting data could be misleading to those seeking useful national norms, and, above all, the limited nature of the sample reflects a seeming unwillingness on the part of ETS to spend much of its $9 to $13 fee on computing useful data from the huge number of cases secured each year.

Turning to the matter of scaled scores for the optional tests, another frame of reference is apparent. The scaled scores for the optional tests are derived from scores of all candidates in the most recent nationwide administration who indicated for a particular test that it was in the field which they were best prepared to teach. This is a rational basis. The mean scaled score of 60 is the average of an identified group of current "majors." The handbook does not say whether the norming process occurs each year, or just in the year when a new form is first used. The percentile rank equivalents for these scaled scores are straightforward transformations. In view of the fact that scaled scores for optional tests cannot be compared *across* tests, one wonders why tables for converting raw scores directly to percentiles are not given. One cannot compare these scaled scores across tests because each test is necessarily normed on a different population—those who took the test. The handbook explains this in several places. Quite properly, no attempt is made to equate physics majors on the physics test with art majors on the art test. The average physics major is in the middle of his group; the average art major is in the middle of his group.

There is in the handbook a table which reports the mean scaled scores on the parts and total of the Common Examinations for candidates who elected each of the 13 specialties. Not unexpectedly, the results show teacher candidates in sciences, mathematics, English, and foreign languages scoring highest on the general tests, and those in business education, home economics, industrial arts, and physical education ranking lowest.

The validation data are sparse for reasons well understood by those who have tried to evaluate success in teaching. In fact, no claim is made that the NTE tests measure teaching ability; rather they assess knowledge of subjects, professional understandings, and mental abilities which experts and common sense would agree are requisite for good teaching. That is, the tests are justified first on the basis of content validity, derived from expert consultation. One table shows that mean weighted total scores on the common tests are higher for those with more professional education. However, the data pose a problem. This was not a longitudinal study. The master's and doctoral student sample includes only 412 cases whereas the senior group has 8,459 cases. This reviewer hopes it is a matter of poor sampling rather than a fact that the graduate students in education score lower than the senior teacher candidates on two of these five tests! ETS can be expected to draw some samples on some other than a fortuitous basis. This will never be a simple task, but attempts along several dimen-

1 This statement appeared in the 1963 bulletin of information (which was used with the latest of the test forms reviewed) and in earlier bulletins. The statement has been omitted from the 1964 bulletin referred to in the entry preceding this review. The 1964 bulletin was published since this review was written. —Editor.

sions of level and locus of training are needed. Apart from information in the public manuals, there probably are files of validation data which have been developed for individual institutions. On the consumer side, school systems which have used the tests as part of selection programs should by this time have generated some validity studies. ETS probably finds the collection and evaluation of such data as difficult a task as do others who seek validation data for personnel tests used in companies.

It is not the purpose of this review to analyze each test of the NTE. However, a few comments are in order. The Common Examinations have one professionally loaded test and four other parts which tap substantive content of the fields. They constitute a sort of general culture battery. The items in the optional series fall into three gross classes. Each test has *substantive* items based on knowledge unique to the field, such as chemical processes, biological concepts, terminology in dressmaking. Each test has *mixed* items in which methods of classroom management are directly related to substantive content, such as an item on choice of laboratory or literary topics to accomplish a specific goal. Each test has some *pure methodology* items based not on course content but on how to structure or handle stated teaching situations. A happy generalization is that the substantive items are clearly dominant, the mixed items next, and the pure methodology items not only fewest, but few.

The foregoing generalization is truest of the tests for the old-line academic fields, less so for the applied fields (such as Home Economics Education, Industrial Arts Education, and Business Education), and least so, quite expectedly, for the two professional fields (Early Childhood Education and Education in the Elementary School).

Anyone who has attempted to write items to measure professional practice knows that, in comparison with items for classroom subject matter fields, such items are more likely to evoke dispute as to keying and criticisms as to clarity of statement. This is reflected, of course, in item analysis. In the technical reports for the latest forms of the 13 optional tests, it is evident that there are more discriminating items for the tests in the so-called "solid" fields than for the tests in the applied and professional fields.

In attempting to evaluate the items of the tests, the reviewer, however, came upon a matter that is of concern. He had assumed that each new form of a component test would have had its item content "cleaned up" by extensive pretrials of the items. The technical reports indicate that this has been done rather thoroughly for the substantive parts of the Common Examinations since the distributions of biserial *r*'s for these items show relatively few items with values under .30. In Form INT of the Common Examinations, for example, 50 of the 274 items have discrimination indices of .29 and below, of which 36 are in the 90-item Professional Information section.

In the newest forms of the Optional Examinations (Forms KNT and LNT) a large number of discrimination indices are .29 and lower. For example, for Form LNT 47 of the 110 Business Education *r*'s are .29 and below; 40 of the 95 Home Economics *r*'s are that low, with 16 of them below .20. Of the 13 tests, only Mathematics seems to have a reasonably small number of less discriminating items, 10 out of 85 for Form KNT. These data suggest that the definitive item analyses are performed after the tests have been used operationally for the first time. Recognizing the problems of adequately pretesting items when new forms are needed annually, one can still wonder as to the quality and efficiency of these tests. Considering that the items are in general well edited, is it a matter of appropriateness of level and choice of content? Thousands of examinees a year complete these examinations. Could not the batches of new items be tried out a year in advance by embedding them in the operational copies? Given the power of ETS to persuade colleges to participate in experimental runs, one wonders why a sufficient number of new items could not be tried out well in advance and only those which meet an acceptable criterion of discrimination retained. There are problems, and costly ones, but ETS can be expected to perform at this level in preparing tests which are important in decision making.

In summary, the National Teacher Examinations are a battery of secure tests which are well conceived for their purposes—that is, to measure the substrata of professional and academic learning a prospective teacher brings to his or her employment. More specific validity studies are needed. More pretesting of items is called for. The scoring and normative system is not simple, but workable. The NTE deserves use in evaluations of institutions and of individual seniors and graduate students. It should be helpful to school systems as a supplement to the other information used in selecting teachers. The reviewer's prejudice is that if he were a dean or superintendent, he would take scores on the NTE seriously and weight them heavily.

For reviews by William A. Brownell, Walter W. Cook, and Lawrence G. Derthick of earlier forms, see 5:538; for a review by Harry N. Rivlin, see 4:802. For reviews of individual tests, see 259, 345, 350, 583, and 974.

[701]

Pictographic Self Rating Scale. High school and college; 1955–57; attitude toward classroom and study activities; Experimental Form A ('55, 4 pages); manual ('57, 2 pages); no college norms; separate answer sheets must be used; $3.50 per 25 tests; $1.50 per 25 answer sheets; 25¢ per manual; 50¢ per specimen set; postage extra; (35) minutes; Einar R. Ryden; [Psychometric Affiliates]. *

REFERENCES

1. Romanowski, Walter V. *The Revision and Factor Analysis of a Pictographic Self Rating Scale.* Doctor's thesis, Purdue University (Lafayette, Ind.), 1955. (*DA* 16:1278)
2. Sales, Robert C. *A Validity Study of a Pictographic Self Rating Scale.* Master's thesis, Purdue University (Lafayette, Ind.), 1955.

Stanley E. Davis, *Reading and Study Skills Counseling Director, University Counseling Center, The Ohio State University, Columbus, Ohio.*

The *Pictographic Self Rating Scale* is intended to make it "possible for the pupil to take an active part in the analysis of his progress in any school subject" and to aid "the teacher quickly and easily to obtain an estimate of how each pupil in his class feels about the subject being taught."

The pupil rates himself on each of 15 items pertaining to learning procedures and attitudes toward the subject, by selecting one of five illustrated statements that most accurately describes him. While it appears that the 15 items are concerned with characteristics that have relevance to learning in any course, no explanation is given of the rationale underlying the selection of the items.

According to the abstract of Romanowski's thesis (*1*) in *Dissertation Abstracts* (*DA* 16:1278), a correlation of .60 between student self-evaluations and ratings of the students by teachers, both groups using the PSRS for making the ratings, was obtained in a study involving 302 high school students. This finding may be interpreted to mean that a teacher should not have too much confidence in his own impressions of how students feel about his subject and about themselves in his class.

The two-page manual reports a test-retest reliability coefficient of .87. According, again, to *DA* 16:1278, this study involved 194 high school students and a four-week interval between testings. This finding suggests that this instrument is sufficiently reliable for its purposes.

The format of the test booklet and of the answer sheet are satisfactory. The verbal statements used as response alternatives are cogently phrased, and the illustrations are cleverly executed in comic strip form. Reactions of high school students regarding the wording and illustrations were elicited and used during the construction of the items.

The feature of pictorial as well as verbal printed presentation of response alternatives is probably attractive to students in early high school. It is possible that students in the last year of high school and in college may find the drawings, whose central character appears to be an early teen-ager, a bit too juvenile for their tastes.

The problem of "faking" is met reasonably well by the following statement in the instructions to the student: "This is not a test and the results will not affect your grade." However, the fact that the point values of response alternatives are printed on the answer sheet (for the convenience of the scorer) may tend to aggravate rather than alleviate the faking problem.

In short, the PSRS is a convenient device for anyone who wants to assess how high school students feel about a particular course and about their study procedures in that course, or who wants to encourage students to think along these lines. Most high school students will probably enjoy filling it out. Its usefulness at the college level is somewhat in doubt, and remains to be demonstrated. Until such time as considerably more data bearing upon the characteristics of the instrument become available, the appearance of "Experimental" on the test booklet sets the proper tone for the use of the PSRS.

John D. Krumboltz, *Associate Professor of Education and Psychology, Stanford University, Stanford, California.*

This scale is a simple 15-item questionnaire which a teacher might use to obtain student reactions about a course. It asks students to rate themselves on how well they are comprehending the subject, how interested they are in the subject matter, and how willing they are to participate in class activities. Students are asked to respond to each question on a 5-point scale.

The only thing that makes this scale different from something a teacher might construct himself in 10 minutes is that each point on the 5-point scale for each item is accompanied by a cartoon designed to illustrate in a semihumorous manner the degree of the student's reaction. It is doubtful that the cartoons add anything to the usefulness of the test except perhaps to make responding to the scale more entertaining to the students. The cartoons do not reduce the reading difficulty of the questions since it is still necessary to read each item and its five alternatives in order to understand what the item is asking. While most of the cartoons accompanying the scale points are reasonably pertinent, there are a few which may actually mislead students who would prefer to look at cartoons rather than read carefully the verbal descriptions beneath them. For example, the five cartoons for item 12, "willingness to learn," show a boy in five degrees of activity while fishing. Since fishing is often considered a way of escaping from learning, some students could be confused as to the intent of the item.

The manual presents data showing that scores on the scale correlate with IQ scores, with academic attainment, and with teachers' ratings of students' need for assistance. The evidence seems pretty clear that bright, academically attaining students who have little need for special teacher assistance rate themselves higher on this scale than their opposite numbers. Unfortunately, this information is not particularly pertinent in judging whether the scale would be useful to a given teacher. These "validity" data mean merely that students who are doing well in a course rate themselves as comprehending it better than students who are not doing well in the course; students who are having difficulty know they are having difficulty.

One of the suggested uses of this scale is that the teacher can locate areas of difficulty as the pupil sees them. Even here it is doubtful that the scale would be as useful as one the teacher himself might construct in just a few minutes. The items solicit rather broad diffuse reactions to the subject matter rather than pinpointing specific remediable teacher activities. For example, items concerned with the "willingness to learn," "difficulty in learning," and "value of the subject to you" ask the student to give his overall reaction to the class. There are no specific items which suggest remedial action; for example, there are no questions about the quantity of homework assigned, whether test questions are too trivial, or whether the teacher discourages students from asking questions. After administering the *Pictographic Self Rating Scale* to his class, a teacher might have some general idea as to how well the students liked the class, but he would have no idea as to what specifically he might be able to do to remedy the situation.

The manual is inadequate in several respects: (*a*) The administrative directions and the description of possible uses of the scale state that the scale contains 14 items, whereas in fact it contains 15 items. (*b*) The reliability of the scale is reported as a test-retest reliability coefficient of .87 obtained from high school students. No description is given of the kind of classes involved, the number of students, the number of classes, or the time interval between test and retest. The information does happen to be in Romanowski's unpublished thesis (*1*), referred to in a footnote, but the ordinary user of the test would have no access to this information. (*c*) No tables of norms are provided so that a teacher might compare his classes' reactions to the reactions of some other defined group of classes. (*d*) The tables which report the mean scores of pupils of various IQ levels and attainment levels contain no information about the range of scores within each level. Standard deviations at each level would have been helpful. (*e*) The manual reports that "the grade level seems to make no difference in the way pupils rate themselves." The statement is ambiguous and might lead some teachers to believe that pupils do not change their self-rating as they move from one grade to the other. Actually, the statement means that the average self-ratings of pupils concurrently enrolled in grades 9, 10, 11, and 12 were not significantly different from each other. (*f*) The manual states that "it has also been demonstrated that the nature and content of a given school subject does not affect pupils' evaluations of themselves." It might be assumed that pupils rate themselves the same regardless of the school subject in which they find themselves. In actual fact, ratings were not obtained from any pupil in more than one subject. The quoted statement merely means that the average ratings in the history, English, mathematics and laboratory science courses chosen by Romanowski were not significantly different from each other. Only by obtaining Romanowski's thesis, however, could one determine exactly what was meant by the quoted statements.

In summary, a teacher who wanted to obtain student reactions to his course could certainly design a more useful and less expensive device himself by preparing a few questions about policies or practices that the teacher could change.

[702]

***A Pupil's Rating Scale of an Instructor.** High school and college; 1952–61; 1 form ('61, 1 page); no manual; no data on reliability and validity; $3.50 per 100 scales, postage extra; specimen set not available; [5–10] minutes; Russell M. Eidsmoe; the Author. *

JAMES R. HAYDEN, *Superintendent of Schools, New Bedford Public Schools, New Bedford, Massachusetts.*

A Pupil's Rating Scale of an Instructor is a single sheet listing 17 qualities of instruction, each of which may be scored on a scale from 1 to 9. This scaling is divided into three sections by means of which the numbers have value definitions, e.g., for Organization of Course, "carefully planned; well organized" may be rated 1, 2, or 3, while "some organization but not always clear" may be rated 4, 5, or 6, and "lack organization and planning" may be rated 7, 8, or 9.

Since the scale is intended for high school and college, substitution of the word "student" for "pupil" is recommended in the title. No accompanying information was furnished to indicate if and when or where the instrument was used or with what results. The format is good, the qualities of instruction are well chosen, and the results could be very interesting if compared with supervisor's ratings, jury ratings, or some group of trained observers all using the same scales.

While the intent is laudable, one cannot but wonder under the circumstances, how much superior this scale is to a single piece of blank paper given to the pupil at the end of the course with the instruction to answer these three questions: (*a*) What did you like most? (*b*) What did you like least? (*c*) How do you rate your instructor on a scale of 1–5? The reviewer has used this method and found it not only cheaper but has been surprised at the depth of the answers penetrating areas which no scale could ever portray.

Undoubtedly, this scale will direct the student's evaluation along very specific lines, such as "speech, tolerance, poise, etc." However, since the scale is offered to the instructor for the evident purpose of introspection only, its contribution to the field of measurement must still remain speculative.

[703]

★Purdue Instructional Television Attitude Scale. Adults; 1957–58; Forms C, D, ('58, 1 page); mimeographed instructions and scoring procedures ('57, 4 pages); experimental scoring keys; 2¢ per scale, postpaid; [5–10] minutes; Purdue Research Foundation; distributed by Instructional Media Research Unit. *

[704]

★The Purdue Instructor Performance Indicator. College teachers; 1960; ratings by students; Forms A, B, (2 pages); mimeographed manual (13 pages); $2.50 per 25 tests, postage extra; 75¢ per specimen set, postpaid; (20) minutes; John H. Snedeker and H. H. Remmers; University Book Store. *

REFERENCES

1. SNEDEKER, JOHN H. *The Construction of a Forced-Choice Rating Scale for College Instruction.* Doctor's thesis, Indiana University (Bloomington, Ind.), 1959. (*DA* 20:1273)

2. LEFTWICH, WILLIAM H., AND REMMERS, HERMANN H. *A Comparison of Graphic and Forced-Choice Ratings of Teaching Performance at the College and University Level.* Purdue University, Division of Educational Reference, Studies in Higher Education 92. Lafayette, Ind.: the Division, June 1962. Pp. 35. * (*PA* 37:5683)

3. LEFTWICH, WILLIAM HENSLEY. *A Comparison of Graphic and Forced-Choice Ratings of Teaching Performance at the College and University Level.* Doctor's thesis, Purdue University (Lafayette, Ind.), 1962. (*DA* 23:692)

C. ROBERT PACE, *Professor of Higher Education, University of California, Los Angeles, California.*

This is a forced-choice rating scale. It consists of twelve groups of four statements each. From each group of four statements, students choose two which best describe or apply to their instructor.

The content and arrangement of test items were determined in the following manner. Senior students in one large university were asked to write descriptive statements of the behavior of college teachers, some of these being favorable and others unfavorable. When this collection of statements was consolidated, 552 potentially usable items were obtained. These items were then judged by 50 faculty members as to whether they were relevant to one or more of the 10 categories described in the *Purdue Rating Scale for Instruction* which is said to consist of the principal factors comprising the teaching process. The 164 items which survived this screening process were then submitted to 100 students and 25 faculty members at one university who rated each item on a 5-point scale for "favorability" or social acceptability. Another group of 100 students and 25 faculty members from the same university then rated on a 5-point scale the applicability of each item to the best college instructor they knew. Still another group of judges rated the applicability of each item to the worst college instructor they knew. The final selection of items for the scale consisted of 24 statements which discriminated significantly between best and worst teachers, plus 24 statements which did not discriminate significantly between best and worst teachers, these 48 statements then being arranged in groups of four (two discriminating statements with two nondiscriminating statements) chosen so that all four in a group were similar in social acceptability.

The final test was then given in 112 classes at a large midwestern college. The mean scores for the instructors of these classes yielded a normal distribution ranging from approximately 8 to 18 out of a possible range of 0 to 24. Percentile ranks assigned to these scores are shown in the test manual as norms.

The test is printed in two forms, A and B, but since each form consists of the same 48 items, arranged in the same 12 blocks of 4 items each, there appears to be no reason for having two forms.

The virtue of this instrument lies almost entirely in the careful forced-choice arrangement of items, a feature which does in fact result in a normal distribution of scores, and in a high reliability for the mean ratings of a class.

In the manual, the authors conclude a discussion of validity by saying that for the purposes of this scale reliability and validity are synonymous. This is true, however, only if one is willing to accept the method of item selection and scoring as a sufficient definition of validity. The item content came first of all from statements by college seniors in one school. Then much of this item content was eliminated because it was not classifiable under the 10 headings which a group of judges in 1926 had said were the principal factors in the teaching process. Then, the decision as to whether or not an item would count in the score was based on the ideas about best and worst teachers obtained from some students and faculty members at one school. And finally, many items were eliminated because of differences in their social acceptability. The end product is a definition of effective teaching which some, and perhaps many, college professors may be unwilling to accept.

Four examples which illustrate how effective teaching is defined will enable potential test users to judge for themselves the validity of what is being measured. If your students say that you are interested in your subject matter instead of saying that you are willing to help those who are slow to learn, you are not an effective teacher. If your students say that you have confidence in yourself instead of saying that there is good fellowship between you and your students, you are not an effective teacher. If your students say that you know your subject instead of saying that you have a clear and pleasant voice, you are not an effective teacher. If your students say that you base your grades on work done, not personal feelings, instead of saying that you have a sense of humor, you are not an effective teacher. This is not to say that knowledge and interest in one's subject, self-confidence, and fair grading are unimportant or unrelated to good teaching. It is to say, however, that the possession of these attributes contributes nothing toward obtaining a good score for teaching effectiveness as defined by the Purdue test.

[705]

***The Purdue Rating Scale for Instruction.** College teachers; 1927–60; student ratings on 26 characteristics of the instructor and teaching situation; IBM; 1 form ('50, 2 pages); revised manual ('60, 17 pages, tentative norms gathered in 1947); report form ['50, 4 pages]; $2 per 25 IBM scorable test-answer sheets, postage extra; 75¢ per specimen set, postpaid; (20) minutes; H. H. Remmers and D. N. Elliott (scale); University Book Store. *

REFERENCES

1–26. See 4:803.
27. Bendig, A. W. "Comparison of Psychology Instructors and National Norms on the Purdue Rating Scale." *J Ed Psychol* 44:435–9 N '53. * (*PA* 28:6601)
28. Bendig, A. W. "A Factor Analysis of Student Ratings of Psychology Instructors on the Purdue Scale." *J Ed Psychol* 45:385–93 N '54. * (*PA* 29:6558)
29. Elkin, Albert. "A Longitudinal Study of the Purdue Rating Scale for Instructors." Abstract. *Am Psychologist* 11:412 Ag '56. *
30. Leftwich, William H., and Remmers, Hermann H. *A Comparison of Graphic and Forced-Choice Ratings of Teaching Performance at the College and University Level.* Purdue University, Division of Educational Reference, Studies in Higher Education 92. Lafayette, Ind.: the Division, June 1962. Pp. 35. * (*PA* 37:5683)
31. Leftwich, William Hensley. *A Comparison of Graphic and Forced-Choice Ratings of Teaching Performance at the College and University Level.* Doctor's thesis, Purdue University (Lafayette, Ind.), 1962. (*DA* 23:692)

C. ROBERT PACE, *Professor of Higher Education, University of California, Los Angeles, California.*

The first 10 items in the scale have been in use since 1927. They deal with such qualities of the teacher as "interest in subject," "fairness in grading," "self-reliance and confidence," "stimulating intellectual curiosity." The next 16 items were incorporated in the 1950 printing. They deal with somewhat more specific aspects of a course, such as "suitability of the reference materials," "the weights given to tests in determining the final grade," "the degree to which the objectives of the course were clarified and discussed." The items are intended to reflect aspects, traits, skills, and conditions that students, instructors, and administrators agree should be included in the evaluation of an instructor and a course by students.

The test manual, published in 1960, cites 22 studies in which the scale has been used. All but one of the references are to studies reported prior to 1951. A table of percentile norms is presumably based on the ratings of 460 instructors in 10 different Indiana institutions in 1948.

Although the ratings on the first 10 items are theoretically distributed along a 10-point scale, little actual use is apparently made of the lower half of the scale because the zero percentiles in the norm group correspond, in almost all cases, to values of 5, 6, and 7 on the actual rating scale. Thus, only the top 4 to 6 points on the 10-point scale appear to be functional. On the last 16 items the ratings are expressed along a 5-point scale. Here again, the lowest categories are nonfunctional. On one item the difference between the zero and 100th percentiles is represented by a difference of less than one point on the 5-point scale, and on 6 of the 16 items the difference is less than 2 points.

For a test which has been in existence for so many years, and has been widely used, it is both surprising and unfortunate that a more discriminating set of ratings has not been developed and that the norms provide such a limited reference group.

On the other hand, the items in the scale have a certain intrinsic interest for the college teacher; and the individual instructor can profitably study the responses of his own students without regard to normative information. Also, the fact that there have been a good many studies using the Purdue scales enables the author to suggest answers in the manual to a number of questions which professors nearly always ask about student ratings; for example, that there is little relationship between the ratings and the difficulty of the course or the grades that students receive, and that alumni rate their former instructors in the same way as do the present students.

Useful as the scales are, even in their present form, it is obvious that little or nothing has been done over the past 12 to 15 years to improve their content, increase their discriminating power, or provide up-to-date norms. Moreover, the varied and changing patterns of college instruction—lectures, discussions, laboratories, TV, programmed learning, independent study, and other practices—may rapidly make the Purdue scales obsolete for many instructors and courses.

For a review by Kenneth L. Heaton, see 4:803.

[706]

★The Purdue Teacher Morale Inventory. High school teachers; 1961; title on test is *Purdue Teacher Opinionaire;* 9 scores: teaching as an occupation, relationships with students, relationships with other teachers, administration policies and practices, curriculum factors, relationships with community, working conditions, economic factors, total; Form A (8 pages); manual (13 pages); no norms for subscores; $4.50 per 25 tests, postage extra; $1 per specimen set, postpaid; (20–30) minutes; Ralph R. Bentley, Averno M. Rempel, and Ned A. Rosen; University Book Store. *

[707]

★Remmlein's School Law Test. Teacher education classes in school law; 1957; 3 or 4 scores: acquaintance with legal terms, knowledge of principles and cases, use of law books (optional), total; 1 form (30 pages); manual (22 pages); no data on reliability; validity data and norms based upon a 1956 experimental form, of which the current form is said to be a minor revision; 20¢ per test; 15¢ per key; 50¢ per manual; cash orders postpaid; 60(65) minutes; [Madaline Kinter Remmlein]; Interstate Printers & Publishers, Inc. *

[708]

★Sizing Up Your School Subjects. Grades 7–14; 1958; disguised test of reactions to instruction by television; 1 form (17 pages); manual (15 pages); no norms; 20¢ per test; $1 per manual; postage extra; $1 per specimen set, postpaid; 30(40) minutes; Henry S. Dyer and Anne H. Ferris; Educational Testing Service. *

[709]

***Teacher Education Examination Program.** College seniors preparing to teach; 1957–63; IBM; tests administered at any time by participating institutions; program utilizes reprints or slight modifications of inactive forms of the *National Teacher Examinations;* 14 tests; handbook for presidents, deans, and department heads ('62, 15 pages); score interpretation booklet for college officials, revised edition ('62, 14 pages);

supplement ('63, 1 page); score interpretation leaflet for students ['57, 6 pages]; supervisor's manual (no date, 21 pages); instructions to students (no date, 8 pages); no data on reliability of tests in physical science, French, and Spanish; examination fees (charged to the participating institutions): $5 per student for general examination with or without 1 field test, $6 per student for general examination and any 2 field tests, $5 per student for any 1 or 2 field tests; postpaid; fee includes reporting of scores to the participating institution; special normative services available at fees ranging from $25 to $40; Educational Testing Service. *

a) GENERAL PROFESSIONAL EXAMINATIONS. 7 scores: foundations of education, child development and educational psychology, guidance and measurement, instructional methods, English, history-literature-fine arts, science and mathematics; 185(245) minutes.

b) TEACHING FIELD TESTS. 13 tests: Early Childhood Education, Elementary School Education, English Language and Literature (see 260), Social Studies (see 975), Biological Science (see 887), Physical Science (see 878), Mathematics (see 584), French (see 374), Spanish (see 430), Industrial Arts (see 738), Physical Education (see 728), Business Education (see 29), Music Education (see 351); 80(95) minutes.

For a review by Walter W. Cook, see 5:543. For reviews of the National Teacher Examinations, *see 700, 5:538, and 4:802.*

[710]

A Test on Adult Attitudes Toward Children. Teachers and parents and classes in child development. 1957; 1 form (4 pages); directions sheet ['57, 2 pages]; $2 per 25 tests; 25¢ per specimen set; cash orders postpaid; David F. Votaw, Sr.; (15) minutes; Steck Co. *

ELIZABETH HAGEN, *Professor of Psychology and Education, Teachers College, Columbia University, New York, New York.*

The title of this instrument is misleading because the test consists of 54 true-false statements that primarily test knowledge of what experts in child development think are desirable actions to take in relation to some behavior on the part of the child or knowledge of very general developmental trends of children. Neither the content of the instrument nor the manual (consisting of a single sheet) justifies calling it *A Test on Adult Attitudes Toward Children.*

Data provided in the manual show that the mean scores of women exceed those of men and that the mean scores of persons who have completed a course in child development exceed those of persons who have not had such a course. The manual also states that the mean score of 78 parents was significantly higher than the mean score of 201 childless persons. The purpose of the test's author in presenting these data is not clear, because in spite of these reported differences only one set of norms is provided and the sample on which the norms are based is not specified by sex, parenthood, or previous formal instruction in child development. Data such as these also do not help to establish the validity of the instrument as a measure of attitude.

Although the author reports a split-half reliability of .78, he does not provide any information as to the number or nature of the sample on which it is based.

In summary, one can state that *A Test on Adult Attitudes Toward Children* is not recommended for use since the data provided by the author fail to show that it is a valid measure of adult attitudes toward children.

[711]

***The Wilson Teacher-Appraisal Scale.** Rating of instructors by themselves and by students in grades 7–11, 12–16; 1948–57; rating forms for teachers taken from *A Self Appraisal Scale for Teachers;* 1 form; 2 levels; no manual; no data on reliability; no norms; $1.50 per 50 scales for students; 10¢ per scale for teachers; sample scale free; postpaid; [10–15] minutes; Howard Wilson; Administrative Research Associates. *

a) JUNIOR EDITION. Grades 7–11; 1948–57; 1 form ('57, 1 page) for students; 1 form ('57, 2 pages) for teachers.

b) [COLLEGE EDITION.] Grades 12–16; 1957; 1 form ('57, 1 page, essentially the same as form copyrighted 1948) for students; 1 form ('57, 2 pages) for teachers.

JAMES R. HAYDEN, *Superintendent of Schools, New Bedford Public Schools, New Bedford, Massachusetts.*

The *Wilson Teacher-Appraisal Scale,* junior edition, is divided into three sections labeled Personal Appraisal, Course Appraisal, and Teacher Rank. The senior edition has the same section headings plus Assignments and Examinations. Assignments and examinations are also a part of the junior form but placed in the section labeled Course Appraisal. The senior form lists 18 qualities while the junior form lists 14 qualities. These quality appraisals require a selection on a descriptive word scale which varies from two to five choices.

While the author indicates that since 1948 some 200,000 students have evaluated their instructors, no information is furnished as to teacher reaction, nor in what manner these particular qualities of teacher performance were selected. Did he research the literature? Was a free writing situation the first source? Were juries set up and some selection technique used? Would this scale be of value to a teacher planning to apply for a super-maximum in a system employing some form of merit rating? Granted the research on the recognizable qualities of a good teacher is far from unanimity, there is considerable work in progress. How much research was used in constructing this instrument and what good uses have resulted since it has been on the market, the current user is not informed by the publisher.

Students using this scale must be in a well lighted room and have good eyesight. While the qualities to be appraised are readable, the value definitions are in extremely small type.

Before a teacher invests his own money to purchase this scale or an administrator invests public funds to furnish his faculty with the scale, some of the possibilities, even exciting implications, should be spelled out by the author. Otherwise, my reaction is the same as when I receive a long, detailed form upon which I am asked to rate a former teacher. My usual reply is to turn over the page, write a paragraph giving two or three specifics and a recommendation to hire without reservation, with reservation, or to avoid him like the plague. I do not mean to disdain all the scales which have been constructed and profitably used by trained observers. However, when it comes to asking students for an evaluation, I believe a blank piece of paper in a free writing situation will reveal in depth as much as, if not more than, a scale offering no evidence of research and requiring the expenditure of private or public funds.

[Other Tests]

For tests not listed above, see the following entries in *Tests in Print:* 1177, 1180–1, 1183, 1187–8, 1193–4, 1201, 1203–4, 1206–9, and 1211; out of print: 1179, 1184, 1189–90, and 1200; status unknown: 1178.

ETIQUETTE

[Other Tests]

For tests not listed above, see the following entries in *Tests in Print:* 1213–6.

HANDWRITING

[712]

★The American Handwriting Scale. Grades 2–8; 1929–57; 2 scores: rate, quality; 1 form; manual ('57, 20 pages, same as manual with earlier copyright); combined rating scale for grades 2–8 ('57, 1 chart, same as chart copyrighted in 1929); separate rating scales for grades 2–4, 3–5, 4–6, 5–7, 6–8 (same as combined rating scale); record booklet ('49, 5 pages); no data on reliability; tentative rate norms; 55¢ per set of combined rating scale, record booklet, and manual; 20¢ per separate rating scale; postage extra; (15–20) minutes plus time to memorize passage; Paul V. West; A. N. Palmer Co. *

Theodore L. Harris, *Professor of Educational Psychology and Education, The University of Wisconsin, Madison, Wisconsin.*

The full *American Handwriting Scale* includes seven scales consisting of seven samples of cursive handwriting for each of grades 2 through 8. Abbreviated scales made up of three adjoining grade scales are also available for use at each of several grade levels. The original sample on which the scale was based included specimens written by right-handed and left-handed boys and girls at the grade levels indicated on the scale. The writing sample, obtained in a two-minute writing interval, represents different content judged to be of interest to each grade level and includes most letters of the alphabet. Two criteria, quality and speed, are incorporated in each scale at each grade level, the scale samples ranging within grade from the poorest sample with the slowest speed to the best sample with the fastest speed. The tentative rate norms are a cardinal ordering of 644 or more samples per grade level into seven scale values representing rate intervals of .714 SD.

The use of quality and speed in determining placement of a handwriting sample is a distinctive feature of this scale. While there is a certain practical value in knowing the speed at which handwriting is produced, the assumption of a linear relationship between handwriting speed and quality does not conform to present evidence that handwriting quality deteriorates as a pupil writes either too slowly or too fast. Misinterpretation of this relationship by users of this scale might lead to unfortunate implications of the role of speed in the improvement of handwriting quality.

The quality scale itself is an ordinal scale derived from 50 specimens per grade level selected as representative of the normal distribution of the rate scale. While some 42,000 quality judgments were made by teachers, supervisors, and handwriting experts of the selected specimens, it is evident that the range of quality represented on the scale was necessarily limited by the prior screening for rate, and that the ordinal method of ranking sample against sample yielded no guarantee of equal intervals between the quality scale items. Inspection of the scale items, furthermore, reveals that they are not representative of the range of handwriting slant and size actually found in schools today. For this reason, a quality judgment of "that sample which most nearly agrees with the specimen in general appearance" is difficult if not impossible for specimens which do not conform to the medium to large size and the moderate forward slant of most of the scale samples.

It would appear, therefore, that this scale possesses several deficiencies not the least of which is the attempt to include the factor of speed in the selection of scale items. Realistic and accurate quality judgments are difficult not because of sample size but because of the limited power of the sample to adequately represent the various dimensions of handwriting quality. Furthermore, the assumption that handwriting quality is normally distributed and is amenable to the application of the "same scale distances and values....used as in constructing the rate scale" appears untenable since it imposes a cardinal scale value upon an ordinal ranking not demonstrated to represent cardinal, or equal, quality intervals. It is hoped that these deficiencies and others, such as the lack of data on scaling reliability, the questionable policy of including both right-handed and left-handed writers in the original sample, the desirability of more attractive copy content, and the obvious need for a manuscript scale in grades 1 and 2, will be remedied insofar as possible in the contemplated revision of this scale.

[713]

Evaluation Scales for Guiding Growth in Handwriting. Grades 1, 2, 3, 4, 5, 6, 7, 8–9; 1958; 1 form (1 page); 8 levels; no manual; no data on reliability; 45¢ per scale; $3.25 per specimen set; postpaid; 2(10) minutes; Frank N. Freeman; Zaner-Bloser Co. *

REFERENCES

1. Freeman, Frank N. "A New Handwriting Scale." *El Sch J* 59:218–21 Ja '59. *
2. Feldt, Leonard S. "The Reliability of Measures of Handwriting Quality." *J Ed Psychol* 53:288–92 D '62. * (*PA* 37:5649)

Theodore L. Harris, *Professor of Educational Psychology and Education, The University of Wisconsin, Madison, Wisconsin.*

The Evaluation Scales are a series of seven separate scales for each of grades 1–7 and one scale for use in grades 8–9. The scales for grades 1 and 2 are for manuscript writing while those of higher grade levels are for cursive writing. The range of grade levels to which the scales may be applied, and the inclusion of the two major writing styles, manuscript and cursive, are notable features of these scales.

The combined scales were drawn from an original sample of 135,491 specimens of representative schools from 162 cities in 43 states. Copy judged appropriate for each grade level was memorized, and the more representative of two specimens of each pupil's handwriting secured in a two minute write-out was used in the development of the scale. The 10,000 or more specimens obtained at each grade level were successively sorted into five quality groups, each of which was then re-sorted to obtain median quality scale samples for each fifth of the distribution. The final scale for each grade is an example of the "middle quality of each of the five quality grades of the original sorting."

The basic criterion for the selection of scale samples was "general merit" with primary consideration given to legibility and form, and secondary consideration given to ease and fluency. A further specification in scale sample selection was that they "should show a balance among all the elements of form: spacing, alignment, letter formation, and uniformity in size and slant."

The scales possess several merits. They have the virtue of simplicity through the use of only five reference points, thus tending to make the teacher's and pupil's discriminating task easier than that for scales employing a greater number of quality levels. For greater ease in determining comparable legibility, each scale item is a grammatically complete writing sample rather than a partial one. A single criterion of general quality or effectiveness is employed in scaling judgments, and an attempt is also made to define the components of this nebulous concept, handwriting quality, and to indicate the priorities among these in using the scale. In addition, the simplicity and attractive format of the individual scales, together with the broad grade range to which they are applicable, enhance their use in the classroom.

The scales likewise have two major shortcomings. While the size of the original sample was large, it is representative of only a narrow range of handwriting size and slant. Thus while the scale is helpful in making judgments of cursive handwriting specimens of moderate to large size and moderate forward slant, it is not appropriate, for example, for judging the quality of small handwriting with a backward slant.

In this sense, it is not as useful for making quality judgments about the wide range size and slant found in the classroom as would be a scale specifically designed to account for these variations.

The discriminative power of the scale is limited in another way because the ordinal sample-against-sample ranking procedure does not define how much different a given scale sample is from another, nor how comparable are samples of a given rank across grade levels. While Freeman appears to argue that a cardinal ordering of handwriting samples has no practical value, failure to account for this factor weakens the discriminative value of the instrument and complicates the teacher's task in making accurate and reliable judgments. A similar question may be raised about the reliability of judgments in the original scaling, a matter on which no data are given.

These scales, then, have value in assisting the teacher to make gross judgments of the handwriting quality of writing specimens which conform most closely to the relatively uniform size and slant of the scale models. The manuscript scales, furthermore, provide useful reference for judging early writing activity. The adherence to a single criterion of quality and to as few as five quality levels in making handwriting quality judgments appears sound. More widespread, discriminative, and reliable scaling of handwriting samples would be encouraged, however, through the use of a cardinal rather than an ordinal scaling technique and its application to samples differentiated according to the size and slant of the handwriting.

[714]

Normal Handwriting Scale. Grades 4–8; 1947; Form A (2 pages); mimeographed directions sheet ['47, 1 page]; no data on reliability; tentative norms; 20¢ per scale, postpaid; Albert Grant; Zaner-Bloser Co. *

Theodore L. Harris, *Professor of Educational Psychology and Education, The University of Wisconsin, Madison, Wisconsin.*

The chief purpose of the *Normal Handwriting Scale* is to "make pupils able to judge their own writing." It provides pupils with a quick and accessible means of rating the quality of words they frequently write. The scale comprises eight simple words, cursive handwriting samples at each of five quality levels, and is printed upon a stiff cardboard filler designed to be kept in the pupil's notebook. The scale card is perforated at intervals to allow the pupil's sample to be placed close to the scale item for comparison.

The scales are for the following words: *the, and, have, will, are, you, is,* and *of*. Ratings are made for several samples of each word and the ratings averaged for each word. A total average score may then be computed for comparison with tentative midyear norms for grades 4–8. It is suggested that the pupil make these ratings several times a year and note his progress.

No evidence is presented of the scale's derivation, development, or standardization. It is to be presumed that the scale is an ordinal one. It includes, however, samples of a wider range of handwriting size, slant, and quality than does the typical handwriting scale available for school use.

The scale is most useful as a self-diagnostic device for focusing the pupil's attention particularly upon the characteristic of handwriting form and for judging the relative quality of frequently written and presumably habituated words. The emphasis of the scale upon the word as the unit of quality is not, however, consistent with the usually held position that handwriting quality represents something more than the sum of the quality ratings of its individual word parts.

[Other Tests]

For tests not listed above, see the following entries in *Tests in Print:* 1218 and 1220.

HEALTH AND PHYSICAL EDUCATION

[715]

★AAHPER Youth Fitness Test. Ages 10–30; 1958–62; 7–8 scores: pull-up, sit-up, shuttle run, standing broad jump, 50-yard dash, softball throw, 600-yard run-walk, swimming (optional); largely individual; 1 form ('58); revised manual ('61, 64 pages); record form ('58, 4 pages); college norms supplement to 1958 manual ('61, 4 pages); personal fitness record ('58, 4 pages); cumulative fitness record ['60, 4 pages]; fitness test dials ('62, separate dials for boys and girls) for determining percentile rank from age and test time, ages 10–17; no data on reliability; no norms for swimming; $1 per 25 college norm supplements; 5¢ per personal fitness record; 75¢ per 25 class records; $2 per 25 cumulative fitness records for grades 5–12; $1 per fitness test dial; 75¢ per manual; cash orders postpaid; specimen set not available (manual contains samples of record forms); (5–15) minutes per student, (100) minutes in 2 sessions per class of 35 (excluding swimming); dials by Paul Smith;

AAHPER Youth Fitness Project; American Association for Health, Physical Education, and Recreation. *

REFERENCES

1. AMERICAN ASSOCIATION FOR HEALTH, PHYSICAL EDUCATION, AND RECREATION, YOUTH FITNESS PROJECT, PAUL A. HUNSICKER, DIRECTOR. *AAHPER Youth Fitness Test Manual.* Washington, D.C.: the Association, 1958. Pp. v, 55. * For latest edition, see 10.
2. HUNSICKER, PAUL. "First Nationwide Tabulations From the AAHPER Physical Fitness Test Battery." *J Health Phys Ed & Rec* 29:24–5 S '58. *
3. BAKER, JOE G. *The Relationship Between the New York State Physical Fitness Test and the AAHPER Physical Fitness Test.* Master's thesis, University of Kansas (Lawrence, Kan.), 1959.
4. STARR, HELEN M. "How to Fit in Fitness Testing." *J Health Phys Ed & Rec* 30:18–20 Mr '59. *
5. ESSLINGER, ARTHUR A. "Perspective on Testing." *J Health Phys Ed & Rec* 31:36–7 S '60. *
6. HUNSICKER, PAUL A. "Fitness Norms for College Men." *J Health Phys Ed & Rec* 31:38 S '60. *
7. MESSINA, VINCENT J. *The Establishment of Norms for Bowling Green State University Freshmen Men and Women in the Youth Fitness Test of the American Association for Health, Physical Education and Recreation.* Master's thesis, Bowling Green State University (Bowling Green, Ohio), 1960.
8. NEHOWIG, DONALD. *A Comparative Analysis of Performance by the Madelia Public School Students on the Kraus-Weber Test and the AAHPER Fitness Test.* Master's thesis, South Dakota State College (Brookings, S.D.), 1960.
9. SPILKER, OTTO HUGH. *Elementary School Health and Physical Education Program Standards and Related Variables Compared With Pupil Achievement on Five Items of the AAHPER Youth Fitness Test.* Doctor's thesis, Indiana University (Bloomington, Ind.), 1960. (*DA* 21:1835)
10. AMERICAN ASSOCIATION FOR HEALTH, PHYSICAL EDUCATION, AND RECREATION, YOUTH FITNESS PROJECT, PAUL A. HUNSIKER, DIRECTOR. *AAHPER Youth Fitness Manual, Revised Edition.* Washington, D.C.: the Association, 1961. Pp. iv, 60. *
11. KNUTTGEN, HOWARD G. "Comparison of Fitness of Danish and American School Children." *Res Q* 32:190–6 My '61. *
12. MOHR, DOROTHY R. "Fitness Test Norms for College Women." *J Health Phys Ed & Rec* 32:28–9 S '61. *
13. MUNDT, SHARON A. *A Comparative Analysis of Performance of College Women on the Kraus-Weber Test and the AAHPER Test.* Master's thesis, South Dakota State College (Brookings, S.D.), 1961.
14. ROUTLEDGE, ROBERT H. *A Study to Establish Norms, for Edmonton Public Secondary School Boys, of the Youth Fitness Tests of the American Association for Health, Physical Education, and Recreation.* Master's thesis, University of Alberta (Edmonton, Alta., Canada), 1961.
15. SPERLICH, WILLIAM C. *A Study of the Performance of Fairmont, Minnesota, Sixth Grade Boys and Girls on the AAHPER Test and the Relationship of These Results to Social Standing in Class and to Intelligence.* Master's thesis, Mankato State College (Mankato, Minn.), 1961.
16. COWAN, MARY. *A Study of the AAHPER Youth Fitness Test Ratings of Three Groups of College Men Before and After a Semester of Flickerball, Weight Training, and Physical Fitness Training, Respectively.* Master's thesis, University of New Mexico (Albuquerque, N.M.), 1962.
17. GROSS, ELMER A., AND CASCIANI, JEROME A. "The Value of Age, Height, and Weight as a Classification Device for Secondary School Students in the Seven AAHPER Youth Fitness Tests." *Res Q* 33:51–8 Mr '62. *
18. O'DONNELL, CORNELIUS R. *An Analysis of the Change in Percentile Ranking in Three Test Items of the American Association for Health, Physical Education and Recreation National Fitness Test in One Year Based on Increased Physical Education Classes.* Master's thesis, Newark State College (Union, N.J.), 1962.
19. COLEMAN, JAMES C.; KEOGH, JACK F.; AND MANSFIELD, JOHN. "Motor Performance and Social Adjustment Among Boys Experiencing Serious Learning Difficulties." *Res Q* 34:516–7 D '63. *
20. PONTHIEUX, N. A., AND BARKER, D. G. "An Analysis of the AAHPER Youth Fitness Test." *Res Q* 34:525–6 D '63. *
21. STRONG, CLINTON H. "Motivation Related to Performance of Physical Fitness Tests." *Res Q* 34:497–507 D '63. * (*PA* 38:9160)

[716]

★**Action-Choice Tests for Competitive Sports Situations.** High school and college; 1960; sportsmanship; Forms A, B, (8 pages); mimeographed norms-score report sheet (1 page); no data on reliability and validity; no norms for high school students; separate answer sheets must be used; 30¢ per set of 25 tests of each form; 1¢ per answer sheet; $1 per specimen set of both forms; postpaid; (20–30) minutes; Mary Jane Haskins and Betty Grant Hartman; Mary Jane Haskins. *

REFERENCES

1. HASKINS, MARY JANE. *A Problem-Solving Test of Sportsmanship.* Doctor's thesis, Ohio State University (Columbus, Ohio), 1959.
2. HASKINS, MARY JANE. "Problem-Solving Test of Sportsmanship." *Res Q* 31:601–6 D '60. *

[716a]

★**Basic Fitness Tests.** Ages 12–18; 1964; 11 scores: extent flexibility, dynamic flexibility, shuttle run (explosive strength), softball throw (explosive strength), hand grip (static strength), pull-ups (dynamic strength), leg lifts (trunk strength), cable jump (coordination), balance A (equilibrium), 600-yard run-walk (stamina), fitness index; largely individual; 1 form; manual (55 pages); performance record (4 pages); norms for 6 of the tests begin at age 13 or 14; 10¢ per performance record; $1.95 per manual; postage extra; "it is possible to process through complete classes of fifty students in less than two classroom hours"; Edwin A. Fleishman; Prentice-Hall, Inc. *

REFERENCES

1. FLEISHMAN, EDWIN A. *The Structure and Measurement of Physical Fitness.* Englewood Cliffs, N.J.: Prentice-Hall, Inc., 1964. Pp. xv, 207. *

[717]

★**Belmont Measures of Athletic Performance: Field Hockey Scale.** High school and college women; 1963; ratings by 6 classmates; 1 form (1 page); manual (2 pages); $3 per 50 scales; $1 per specimen set (must be purchased to obtain manual); cash orders postpaid; (3–5) minutes for rating 1 classmate; Logan Wright and Patsy K. Wright; Psychometric Affiliates. *

[718]

***College Health Knowledge Test, Personal Health.** College; 1950–59; 12 scores: social and biological background, nutrition and diet, excretion and cleanliness, exercise and body mechanics, fatigue and rest, mental hygiene, reproduction and heredity, prevention and control of disease, eye-ear-teeth hygiene, hygiene of environment, use of medical care, total; 1 form ('59, 8 pages); revised manual ('59, 3 pages); no reliability data or norms for part scores; 1–99 tests, 15¢ each; 10¢ per key; 10¢ per manual; cash orders postpaid; (28–50) minutes; Terry H. Dearborn; Stanford University Press. *

REFERENCES

1. DEARBORN, TERRY HAMILTON. *The Measurement of Health Knowledge.* Doctor's thesis, Stanford University (Stanford, Calif.), 1950.
2. DEARBORN, TERRY H. "Personal Health Knowledge of College Students Before Instruction." *Res Q* 29:154–9 My '58. *
3. DEARBORN, TERRY H. "Comparative Class Performances and Gains in Junior College Health Education." *Res Q* 34:299–304 O '63. *
4. DEARBORN, TERRY H. "Junior College Health Knowledge Study in California." *J Sch Health* 33:90–2 F '63. *

JAMES E. BRYAN, *Training Administrator, United States Public Health Service, Division of Foreign Quarantine, United States Quarantine Station, Staten Island, New York.*

This test is aptly described by its title. It is a health knowledge test and it goes no further. The items are of the multiple choice completion type, with the emphasis on completion in too many instances; e.g., 22 items, almost a quarter of the whole test, have stems consisting of from one to three words, such as "Health," "Digestion is," or "The thyroid gland," each followed by five choices to complete sentences that may wander off in any direction. The test would be greatly improved if the items were revised so that the stems called for specific answers, or at least revised so that the stems supplied sufficient information to indicate to the informed student what answers were expected.

Five-choice items are generally considered better than items with fewer choices, but this ceases to be the case when it becomes necessary to use "forced foils" in order to get the fifth choice. Although in most cases the author has given parallel choices that are well selected, there are exceptions which appear to have been made in order to supply a fifth one. For example, the stem of item 36, "The principal harm which may result from chronic poor posture in adults is," is followed by four plausible, parallel choices concerned with body structure or function, but the fifth one, "poor fit and appearance of clothes," seems completely out of place. Item 56 is another example of unfortunate construction. The stem reads: "A junior college freshman with an I.Q. of 100 studies hard and receives average grades. He makes a 'B' in biology and believes he would like to become a doctor. His parents cannot afford to pay his expenses beyond junior college. He should be helped by his school counselor to." Even after introducing interest, aptitude, and financial responsibility, in order to have five choices, it seems to have been necessary to relate the fifth choice, "take the clerking job for a year, saving his money to enter a university at that time," to the fourth, "realize the impracticability of this goal, and to be satisfied with a clerking job offered him," rather than to the stem.

In a few cases there is more than one correct answer, or at least room to question the correctness of other choices. For example (item 71), "rheumatic fever" is a frequent cause of heart disease; but "syphilis," one of the foils, was a frequent cause of heart disease before the advent of the "wonder drugs," and still is in cases of inadequate treatment. Also (item 78), iodine *is* added to drinking water in some areas to "prevent goiter," but it is also used in some areas to "kill bacteria" when better methods of providing safe drinking water are not available. For item 97, which calls for the least important criterion for judging the soundness of a piece of health advice, the foil "its acceptance by one's friends" would seem to have as little scientific basis as "the extent of its advertisement," keyed as the answer. According to item 76, tuberculosis is "the disease which is the most frequent cause of death in the high-school and college age group." According to the Communicable Disease Center of the United States Public Health Service, this is no longer correct.

According to the manual, the test is "a valid, reliable, and comprehensive measure of achievement and diagnosis in the field of personal health knowledge." Mean coefficients of .89 for reliability and .75 for validity are given. On the basis of total score these are acceptable coefficients for a measure of achievement. There are no similar data for section scores. With 6 of the 11 sections made up of seven or fewer items, the description of this test as a diagnostic measure does not seem justified. The manual also suggests using the test for pretesting to determine the student's beginning level of health knowledge and the same test or an equivalent form for posttesting to determine whether achievement has been satisfactory. The use of the same test for both pretesting and posttesting is questionable, and there is no indication that an equivalent form is available.

Standardization was carried out mostly in California institutions. Wider geographical distribution of institutions would have been desirable.

In the opinion of this reviewer, the test is a rather comprehensive measure of achievement, and the distribution of items among the various areas is good when the overall length of the test is considered. Most, if not all, of the adverse criticisms of individual items could be corrected relatively easily. To qualify as a diagnostic tool, the test would need to be made long enough to insure adequate reliability of section scores.

PETER G. LORET, *Program Director, Educational Testing Service, Princeton, New Jersey.*

This test is described in its manual as having been constructed specifically for the college level to provide "a valid, reliable, and comprehensive measure of achievement and diagnosis in the field of personal health knowledge." It consists of 100 items (5-choice) sampling 11 areas of health knowledge; these items were selected from some 1,200 questions administered to college, university, and junior college students during the period 1936–50. Standardization of the original edition of the test was carried out from 1948 to 1950. Revision of seven items and substitution of two other items constitutes the 1959 revision of this instrument.

The content of the test appears adequate in terms of subject matter covered; its applicability as a reliable diagnostic instrument designed to evaluate knowledge in specific areas is, however, quite doubtful as has already been noted by Clarke in his review of the original edition (see 4:478), particularly when such area subscores as may be obtained are based on as few as five items.

One wishes that the author had applied a strong hand in editing test questions from various sources. There appears to be little consistency in the style of item presentation, with a number of the items violating the ground rule of including in the item "stem" the specific problem posed or the question intended. On this basis, one may question items with stems such as "Health" (item 6), "Emotions" (item 53), and "Colds" (item 72), and a number of others which are poorly presented.

Several other comments regarding content appear to be in order. With the rapid advances of medicine and the health sciences in general, any test in this area is likely to run the risk of being somewhat outdated at the time of publication; this test is no exception. For example, the stem and keyed response to item 73 indicate that tuberculosis is best treated by rest and proper food, whereas the current treatment of choice is one best described on a simple level as "medication and rest." One cannot help but question the promulgation of puritanical attitudes relative to sex as reflected by items and keyed correct responses which lead to such blanket statements as (item 58) "The delay of sexual relations after biological maturity causes no mental or physical ill effects" or (item 60) "Sexual promiscuity is properly considered as being a physical and psychological hazard."

Items do not appear to be arranged in order of difficulty; if they are, no statement to this effect appears in the manual.

If the test requires minor revisions in content, then the manual which accompanies it requires revisions of a major magnitude. It suggests, for example, that the test be used as a "pretest" to "reveal the initial achievement of the class and of each student," that at the conclusion of the course in personal hygiene "sections of the test, or equivalent form" may be given, and that "such individual progress is one basis for grading students in the course." In the absence of *any* equivalent form such a recommendation is meaningless, while the reuse of the same form of the test for grading students at the conclusion of the course is completely naïve, ignoring the effects of both practice and growth.

The statement, "A correction formula is not usually applied to items having as many as five choices, but may be used to retard guessing, if desired" is presented in the absence of any evidence to warrant such an assumption, either for this test or, for that matter, any test.

Although the construction of the test is discussed in some detail, the manual fails to provide adequate descriptions of the sample ("Standardization was carried out from 1948 to 1950 using some two thousand students in 55 hygiene classes in eight institutions, mostly in California"). The final form of the test is described as having been administered to "more than two thousand students at the close of their courses in personal hygiene in eight junior colleges, colleges, and universities, to establish norms and correlations for validity and reliability." Such a limited description of the normative sample is, quite obviously, inadequate, particularly in view of the fact that neither the specific number of colleges nor number of students from each is provided either in the text or tables; for that matter, neither are the standard deviations given for the norms groups.

The failure of the manual to include the appropriate standard deviations and other data for the groups upon which reliability coefficients are based makes any attempt to evaluate the data a hopeless task. Corrected split-half reliabilities are reported "for a four-group sample of 28 percent....with a mean coefficient of .89, very satisfactory." The "28 percent" is not identified further; thus, there is some doubt as to whether this was a sample of 28 per cent of the total standardization group, whether there were four standardization groups from each of which 28 per cent were selected, or whether some other method was utilized. The statement that the reliability of the test is "very satisfactory" does not compensate for the lack of data.

Validity coefficients for the normative sample are reported as ranging from .64 to .87, with mean .75, against the criterion of final grades in hygiene courses. The reader is left in doubt as to what part, if any, the test results may have played in the assignment of final grades in the courses, thus contaminating the criterion, and furthermore, as to whether some of the instructors in the normative group may not indeed have used the instrument as a pretest at the beginning of the course as suggested in the manual.

SUMMARY. This test may well prove to be helpful if used at the beginning of a personal hygiene course to assist the instructor in determining the general level of the students' knowledge of the subject; analysis of individual item responses may reveal fallacious beliefs existing among the students and specific concepts to be emphasized in the course. Use of the test for other purposes, and use of the normative data presented in the manual, however, is not recommended.

For a review by H. Harrison Clarke, see 4:478.

[719]

Cornell Medical Index—Health Questionnaire. Ages 14 and over; 1949–56; medical questionnaire to be used by examining physician; separate forms ('49, 4 pages) for men and women; revised manual ('56, 15 pages including sample questionnaire and diagnostic sheet); no data on reliability; diagnostic sheet ['53, 1 page]; $2.50 per 50 questionnaires; $1 per 50 diagnostic sheets; postpaid; specimen set free; Spanish edition available; (10–30) minutes; Keeve Brodman, Albert J. Erdmann, Jr., and Harold G. Wolff; Cornell University Medical College.

REFERENCES

1. BRODMAN, KEEVE; ERDMANN, ALBERT J., JR.; LORGE, IRVING; GERSHENSON, CHARLES P.; AND WOLFF, HAROLD G.; WITH THE TECHNICAL ASSISTANCE OF BARBARA CAPLES. "The Cornell Medical Index—Health Questionnaire: 3, The Evaluation of Emotional Disturbances." *J Clin Psychol* 8:119–24 Ap '52. * (*PA* 27:1951)

2. BRODMAN, KEEVE; ERDMANN, ALBERT J., JR.; LORGE, IRVING; GERSHENSON, CHARLES P.; AND WOLFF, HAROLD G.; WITH THE TECHNICAL ASSISTANCE OF TODD H. BROADBENT. "The Cornell Medical Index—Health Questionnaire: 4, The Recognition of Emotional Disturbances in a General Hospital." *J Clin Psychol* 8:289–93 Jl '52. * (*PA* 27:5858)

3. ERDMANN, A. J., JR.; BRODMAN, K.; LORGE, I.; AND WOLFF, H. G. "Cornell Medical Index—Health Questionnaire: 5, Outpatient Admitting Department of a General Hospital." *J Am Med Assn* 149:550–1 Je 7 '52. *

4. BRODMAN, KEEVE. "Cornell Medical Index—Health Questionnaire," pp. 568–76. (*PA* 27:7756) In *Contributions Toward Medical Psychology: Theory and Psychodiagnostic Methods, Vol. II.* Edited by Arthur Weider. New York: Ronald Press Co., 1953. Pp. xi, 459–885. *

5. BRODMAN, KEEVE; ERDMANN, ALBERT J., JR.; LORGE, IRVING; AND WOLFF, HAROLD G. "The Cornell Medical Index—Health Questionnaire: 6, The Relation of Patients' Complaints to Age, Sex, Race, and Education." *J Gerontol* 8:339–42 Jl '53. * (*PA* 28:7916)

6. BRODMAN, KEEVE; DEUTSCHBERGER, JEROME; ERDMANN, ALBERT J.; LORGE, IRVING; AND WOLFF, HAROLD G. "Prediction of Adequacy for Military Service: Use of the Cornell Medical Index—Health Questionnaire." *U S Armed Forces Med J* 5:1802–8 D '54. * (*PA* 29:8052)

7. BRODMAN, KEEVE; ERDMANN, ALBERT J., JR.; LORGE, IRVING; DEUTSCHBERGER, JEROME; AND WOLFF, HAROLD G. "The Cornell Medical Index—Health Questionnaire: 7, The Prediction of Psychosomatic and Psychiatric Disabilities in Army Training." Discussion by Ruth Tolman. *Am J Psychiatry* 111:37–40 Jl '54. * (*PA* 29:2437)

8. ARNHOFF, FRANKLYN N.; STROUGH, LA VERN C.; AND SEYMOUR, RICHARD B. "The Cornell Medical Index in a Psychiatric Outpatient Clinic." *J Clin Psychol* 12:263–8 Jl '56. * (*PA* 31:6055)

9. HOLMES, THOMAS H. Chap. 6, "Multidiscipline Studies of Tuberculosis," pp. 65–152. In *Personality, Stress, and Tuberculosis.* Edited by Phineas J. Sparer. New York: International Universities Press, Inc., 1956. Pp. xviii, 629. *

10. LEIGH, DENIS, AND MARLEY, EDWARD. "A Psychiatric Assessment of Adult Asthmatics: A Statistical Study." *J Psychosom Res* 1:128–36 Je '56. * (*PA* 31:6482)

11. BARD, MORTON, AND WAXENBERG, SHELDON E. "Relationship of Cornell Medical Index Responses to Postsurgical Invalidism." *J Clin Psychol* 13:151–3 Ap '57. * (*PA* 32:2884)

12. SUCHMAN, EDWARD A.; PHILLIPS, BERNARD S.; AND STREIB, GORDON F. "An Analysis of the Validity of Health Questionnaires." *Social Forces* 36:223–32 Mr '58. *

13. WHITE, COLIN; REZNIKOFF, MARVIN; AND EWELL, JOHN W. "Usefulness of the Cornell Medical Index—Health Questionnaire in a College Health Department." *Mental Hyg* 42:94–105 Ja '58. * (*PA* 33:8425)

14. LAWTON, M. POWELL. "The Screening Value of the Cornell Medical Index." *J Consult Psychol* 23:352–6 Ag '59. * (*PA* 34:4344)

15. CROOG, SYDNEY H. "Ethnic Origins, Educational Level, and Responses to a Health Questionnaire." *Hum Org* 20:65–9 su '61. *

16. MATARAZZO, RUTH G. "The Relationship Between Medical and Psychiatric Symptomatology in Medical and Psychiatric Patients." Abstract. *Acta Psychologica* 19:863–4 '61. *

17. MATARAZZO, RUTH G.; MATARAZZO, JOSEPH D.; AND SASLOW, GEORGE. "The Relationship Between Medical and Psychiatric Symptoms." *J Abn & Social Psychol* 62:55–61 Ja '61. * (*PA* 36:3HI55M)

18. RHUDICK, PAUL J., AND DIBNER, ANDREW S. "Age, Personality, and Health Correlates of Death Concerns in Normal Aged Individuals." *J Gerontol* 16:44–9 Ja '61. * (*PA* 35:6241)

19. BROWN, A. C., AND FRY, JOHN. "The Cornell Medical Index—Health Questionnaire in the Identification of Neurotic Patients in General Practice." *J Psychosom Res* 6:185–90 Jl–S '62. * (*PA* 37:8200)

20. CHANCE, NORMAN A. "Conceptual and Methodological Problems in Cross-Cultural Health Research." *Am J Pub Health* 52:410–7 Mr '62. *

21. HAMILTON, M.; POND, D. A.; AND RYLE, A. "Relation of C.M.I. Responses to Some Social and Psychological Factors." *J Psychosom Res* 6:157–65 Jl–S '62. * (*PA* 37:8030)

22. RYLE, ANTHONY, AND HAMILTON, MADGE. "Neurosis in Fifty Married Couples: Assessed From General Practice Records, Interviews by a Psychiatric Social Worker and the Use of the Cornell Medical Index." *J Mental Sci* 108:265–73 My '62. * (*PA* 37:3725)

23. SKLAR, MAURICE, AND EDWARDS, ALLAN E. "Presbycusis: A Factor Analysis of Hearing and Psychological Characteristics of Men Over 65 Years Old." *J Auditory Res* 2:194–207 Jl '62. *

24. DESROCHES, HARRY F., AND LARSEN, ERNEST R. "The Cornell Medical Index as a Screening Device in a VA Population." *J Clin Psychol* 19:416–20 O '63. *

25. KASSARJIAN, HAROLD H. "Success, Failure, and Personality." *Psychol Rep* 13:567–74 O '63. * (*PA* 38:8591)

26. KNOX, STAFFORD J. "Psychiatric Aspects of Mitral Valvotomy." *Brit J Psychiatry* 109:656–68 S '63. * (*PA* 38:6366)

27. KOLE, DELBERT M., AND MATARAZZO, J. D. "Intellectual and Personality Characteristics of Medical Students." Abstract. *J Med Ed* 38:138–9 F '63. *

28. MATARAZZO, RUTH G.; BRISTOW, DAVID; AND REAUME, RALPH. "Medical Factors Relevant to Psychological Reactions in Mitral Valve Disease." *J Nerv & Mental Dis* 137:380–8 O '63. *

29. POND, D. A.; RYLE, A.; AND HAMILTON, MADGE. "Marriage and Neurosis in a Working-Class Population." *Brit J Psychiatry* 109:592–8 S '63. * (*PA* 38:6540)

30. POND, D. A.; RYLE, A.; AND HAMILTON, MADGE. "Social Factors and Neurosis in a Working-Class Population." *Brit J Psychiatry* 109:587–91 S '63. * (*PA* 38:6539)

31. SCOTCH, NORMAN A., AND GEIGER, H. JACK. "An Index of Symptom and Disease in Zulu Culture." *Hum Org* 22:304–11 w '63–64. *

[720]

★Cowell Test of Ability to Recognize the Operation of Certain Principles Important to Physical Education. Physical education majors; 1961–62; 1 form ('61, 20 pages); instructor's copy ('61, 22 pages consisting of 2 pages of description and technical data bound around the test booklet); supplementary data and norms ['62, 5 pages]; separate answer sheets must be used; $3.65 per set of 10 tests and instructor's copy; $1.60 per 100 answer sheets; 50¢ per sample instructor's copy; postpaid; (50-60) minutes; Charles C. Cowell; distributed by Tri-State Offset Co. *

REFERENCES

1. Cowell, Charles C. "Test of Ability to Recognize the Operation of Certain Principles Important to Physical Education." *Res Q* 33:376-80 O '62. * (*PA* 37:5647)

[721]

***Elementary Health: Every Pupil Scholarship Test.** Grades 6-8; 1933-64; new form (2 pages) usually issued each January and April; forms from previous testing programs also available; general directions sheet ['63, 2 pages]; no data on reliability; norms for new forms available following testing program; 4¢ per test; 4¢ per key; postage extra; 30(35) minutes; Bureau of Educational Measurements. *

[722]

★The Graduate Record Examinations Advanced Tests: Physical Education. Grades 16-17; 1962; for more complete information, see 762; 180(200) minutes; Educational Testing Service. *

For a review of the testing program, see 5:601.

[723]

★Health Behavior Inventory. Grades 3-6, 7-9, 10-12; 1962-64; IBM; 1 form ('62, 14-17 pages); 3 levels; manual ('64, 15-19 pages) for each level; no data on reliability of elementary and senior high level subscores; reliability data for junior high level total and subtotal scores only; norms based on grades 6 (elementary level), 9 (junior high level), and 12 (senior high level) only; $5.25 per 35 tests; separate answer sheets may be used; 5¢ per IBM answer sheet; 20¢ per scoring stencil; postage extra; 75¢ per specimen set of any one level, postpaid; Sylvia Yellen (*a*), Albert D. Colebank (*b*), E. Harold LeMaistre (*c*), and Marion B. Pollock (*c*); California Test Bureau. *

a) ELEMENTARY LEVEL. Grades 3-6; 9 scores: personal health, personal cleanliness, nutrition, safety, community health, infection and disease, mental health, dental health, total; (20-30) minutes.

b) JUNIOR HIGH LEVEL. Grades 7-9; 15 scores: nutrition, personal cleanliness and skin care, mental health, personal health, community health, smoking and drinking, infection and disease, safety, care of eyes, dental health, rest and recreation, practices total, attitudes total, knowledge total, total; (30-50) minutes.

c) SENIOR HIGH LEVEL. Grades 10-12; 11 scores: personal health, safety and first aid, family health, infection and disease, mental health, nutrition, community health, exercise-rest-recreation, drinking-smoking-narcotics, dental health, total; (35-45) minutes.

JAMES E. BRYAN, *Training Administrator, United States Public Health Service, Division of Foreign Quarantine, United States Quarantine Station, Staten Island, New York.*

The manual for each level of the *Health Behavior Inventory* gives detailed directions for the preparation and use of both individual and group profiles, including a sample work sheet and profile designed to permit comparison by content area with female, male, and composite group norms. A similar sheet appears on the back of each test booklet. Although each manual carries a footnote to the effect that many items in an inventory of this type cannot be considered as absolutely right or wrong, scores are based on per cent of preferred responses specified by the author. All manuals report that samples for normative testing were taken from "38 states across the nation," with over 7,000 cases at the elementary level, over 6,000 cases at the junior high school level, and almost 4,500 cases at the senior high school level. The norms shown are those for the top grade for each level. The manuals report that since additional samples taken from other grades indicate little or no difference in scores of pupils in the various grades for which each level is designed, the norms for the top grade apply equally well to all grades for the level. Each manual reports reliability coefficients based on subsamples of 1,000 males and 1,000 females drawn from the "nationwide" samples. All manuals indicate that appropriate steps were taken to establish content validity and that statistical validation of the items was determined through discrimination indices, but they give no statistical data regarding the latter. The authors make no attempt in the tests themselves to segregate and categorize items according to content areas. Instead they show the item numbers under appropriate headings on the work sheet. In this way they show that an item may properly fit into more than one area. By this technique they avoid the problems so often encountered in the placement of overlapping items in tests that are divided into content areas.

Specific information and comments on the individual inventories are given below.

ELEMENTARY LEVEL. The manual for this level reports reliability coefficients for total scores as follows: males, .78, females, .79, and composite, .78. The inventory for this level consists of 40 questions, each illustrated by a picture of a child or of children carrying out the health practice with which the question is concerned. For each question the examinee selects one of three choices to show whether a particular practice is habitual, occasional, or nonexistent so far as he is concerned. The inventory has been carefully prepared and is fairly comprehensive. There are, however, certain items for which changes might be indicated or areas in which the teacher, in considering individual profiles, should take into consideration facts not elicited by the inventory.

In items 2, 5, and 8, which ask if the examinee eats all of the food served at each of his meals, the author apparently assumes that the meals have been properly prepared for the individual in question with regard to both content and quantity. Although later questions do inquire about items of diet in general, they are not designed to show whether the examinee eats balanced meals, whether the food items suggested are available to him, or whether the quantity served is correct for him. Statements that he does not eat foods he has not tried before, that he does not drink three or four glasses of milk every day, or that he does not eat fruit or vegetables between meals may mean either that he has been permitted to develop poor eating habits or that he has no opportunity to eat such a variety of foods. With regard to quantity, the meals served may have been grossly inadequate or excessive for the individual's needs.

Although there is a question about handwashing after going to the toilet, there is nothing about elimination habits. (This may have been omitted because of illustration problems.) Question 25 asks, "Do you put a handkerchief or tissue over your mouth when you sneeze or cough?" The nose should be covered when sneezing. Question 26 asks, "Do you stay at home when you are sick even when you have a cold?" Parental attitude rather than the child's feelings might result in a negative answer.

JUNIOR HIGH LEVEL. This inventory is divided into three parts: Practices, Attitudes, and Knowledge. The manual reports reliability coefficients for males, females, and composite for each part and for the total test. Coefficients for the total test are given as: males, .88, females, .82, and composite, .87. The manual also reports per cents of preferred responses for each of these groups by content area.

The first part is composed of 25 questions intended to show health practices. Each question is to be answered by selecting one of three choices, "usually," "sometimes," and "never," with the answers to be based on actual practice. The second part is made up of 25 statements toward which the examinee is expected to show his attitude by indicating one of three choices, expressing agreement, uncertainty, or disagreement. Most of the statements in the second part are designed so that replies indicate an attitude toward a specific practice about which the first part contained a question. Several questions in the first part, however, have no corresponding attitude statement in the second part. This reviewer would favor the paralleling of every question in Part 1 with a statement in Part 2 in order to permit the comparing of habits and attitudes. For example, would a pupil's reply that he never eats "at least two servings of vegetables, including one green leafy vegetable," indicate that he does not eat them because of his attitude toward them, or because they are not available to him?

The third part includes 50 four-choice multiple choice items designed to measure general knowledge about health. This part is much more comprehensive than the first two parts—but it contains as many items as the first two parts combined. Most of these items relate to items in either Part 1 or Part 2, and some relate to items in both parts. What a test this would be if each item in each part related to an item in each of the other parts!

A few critical comments concerning item construction are offered. Several of the stems do not provide enough direction for the examinee. These are of the "Traffic signals" (item 78) or "Coffee" (item 92) type and of the "Playing in the street is" (item 79) or "Rubbing the eyes with the hands is" (item 84) type. One of the items (93) has at least two correct answers: "The drinking of alcoholic beverages can result in 1. rotting the lining of the stomach. 2. destruction of brain cells. 3. a habit that is very difficult to overcome. 4. an unhealthful effect upon the brain, nervous system, heart and circulatory system." While choice 4 is keyed as the correct answer, certainly 3 is also correct. For item 61, the stem of which reads, "In cleaning the inner and outer surfaces of the teeth, the toothbrush should be," choice 1, "rolled or drawn from the gum line to the biting edges," is given as the correct answer. In view of the different actions of electric tooth brushes now on the market and recommended by various dentists, this item appears to be controversial and should probably be omitted from the inventory until the dental profession has reached substantial agreement on the preferred method of cleaning teeth. According to item 97, "Removing wax from the ear by using a damp washcloth held over the index finger is a.... 2. poor practice, because the roughness of the cloth may irritate the lining of the ear." This choice is the only one that can possibly be correct, but how many people can insert an index finger wrapped in a washcloth into the ear far enough to cause injury?

SENIOR HIGH LEVEL. The manual for this level gives the same type of information reported for the Junior High Level. It reports reliability coefficients as follows: males, .89, females, .80, and composite, .89. In this inventory there are 75 five-choice multiple choice items. The subject matter coverage is rather comprehensive, and in most cases the foils are good. The quality of the test is not enhanced by building it around John and Sue, a high school boy and girl looking forward to marriage, reference to one or both of whom in every item may very well result in making the test somewhat more interesting to read and more palatable to take but which most certainly results in a good deal of window dressing and considerable switching from the third to the second person in item stems. There are serious flaws in several items. Specific examples are cited: (*a*) In item 9, just seeing how milk is pasteurized and bottled is not going to make John and Sue understand whether pasteurization is done primarily to kill pathogenic organisms or to kill all organisms present. (*b*) The stem of item 11 reads, "Sue's weight is now normal, thanks to treatment she followed when underweight. You feel that Sue should now.... 3. avoid skipping meals as a means of controlling her weight. 4. take calorie-controlled diet preparations if she begins to gain weight." This seems like a rather sudden shift from concern about being underweight to concern about being overweight. And even if there should be good reason for such a shift of concern, Sue's physician would most likely give her the advice included in choice 4 as well as that given in choice 3, which is keyed as correct. (*c*) For item 26, the stem of which reads, "Sue and John were surprised to learn that one out of two hospital beds in this country is occupied by a mental patient. You understand that," choice 4, "mental illness is as curable as any other kind of illness," is keyed as correct. This is such a broad statement that it is doubtful if many doctors would support it. In addition, the first three choices are open to question—many patients are in mental hospitals because they are dangerous to themselves or to others; in many states people can be legally classified as "sane" or "insane"; and there is still uncertainty in medical circles as to whether or not certain mental illnesses are hereditary. (*d*) The stem of item 40, "John learned in health class that the venereal disease rate has increased alarmingly in the past few years, particularly among high school students. If you were John you would believe," contains nothing to indicate that John has any reason to select choice 2, "prompt diagnosis and treatment with penicillin can completely cure venereal disease." In addition, penicillin is not the drug of choice for the treatment of *all* venereal diseases, and some people cannot tolerate penicillin. Also, choice 4, "venereal disease symptoms will eventually disappear if not treated," is partially correct since the symptoms of the first and second stages of syphilis and sometimes the symptoms of chancroid will disappear without treatment. (*e*) In item 60, Sue is going to visit the local health department where "she will learn that the responsibility for community health is shared by 1. the local public health department and the schools. 2. the doctors in the community. 3. local and state governments. 4. all community health agencies. 5. every person living in the community." The last choice, which is keyed as correct, encompasses all of the others, with the result that there are five correct responses. (*f*) In item 64, "John and Sue have been working on a school project concerned with commercial medicines. You believe that such medicines should be purchased only when 1. prescribed by a physician.... 4. made by a reputable company....," the former response is keyed as correct but there is room for argument that the latter response is also correct.

CONCLUSION. Although this reviewer's comments may appear rather harsh, especially for the Senior High Level inventory, he considers the inventories to be quite comprehensive and basically sound. Even though certain of the criticisms are serious, the flaws are correctible, and most of the comments are offered more as suggestions for possible improvement in later editions than as serious criticisms of the inventories as they stand. The reviewer is of the opinion that the inventories will yield interesting and valuable information regarding the health habits, attitudes, and knowledge of pupils to teachers who make themselves well acquainted with the inventories and study individual and group responses to them.

PETER G. LORET, *Program Director, Educational Testing Service, Princeton, New Jersey.*

The three distinct forms in this series, which constitute the work of several authors on tests for junior and senior high school students, aim to evaluate knowledge and attitudes related to health matters and, in the case of the Elementary Level (grades 1–6), to yield a measure of what the pupil actually does rather than what he has learned or heard. The three tests differ both in style and in content (and are therefore separately reviewed below), but they have a number of aspects in common which may be summarized.

Following initial development of the tests by their respective authors, all were first utilized in their original form in the School Health Education Evaluative Study conducted in the Los Angeles area. Later, revisions of the tests were used in the nationwide School Health Education Study, in which both urban and rural students from all sections of the country took part. Normative data for the tests are based primarily on randomly selected classes of students from the latter study; separate percentile rank and standard score norms for males and females were obtained for grade 6 (38 states, 115 school systems, $n = 7{,}145$), grade 9 (38 states, 97 school systems, $n = 6{,}013$), and grade 12 (38 states, 97 school systems, $n = 4{,}476$). The publisher reports that little or no difference in performance was found among various sizes of school systems sampled. Additional sampling at other grade levels and analysis of distributions of scores is reported to indicate little or no difference in scores obtained by students in grades other than those for which normative data are presented at each level; thus, it is indicated that twelfth grade norms are equally applicable to grades 10 and 11, that ninth grade norms may be used for grades 7 and 8, and that sixth grade norms may be used for grades 1 through 6. These data, however, are not presented in the manual.

Reliability of total test score (based on number right) for the three levels is more than adequate for most purposes, ranging from .78 for the 40-item Elementary Level to .89 for the 75-item Senior High Level. In all cases, coefficients have been obtained through use of the Kuder-Richardson formula 20. It is interesting to note that for both junior and senior high school girls the tests appear to be somewhat less reliable than for boys; the differences in r are .06 at the junior high and .09 at the senior high level.

Validity data for the test series are derived primarily from the two uses of the inventory cited above. Techniques utilized include the selection of items from authoritative sources, screening of items by subject matter specialists, statistical validation through item analysis, and refinement of items subsequent to the administration of the tests to a nationwide sample of students. The user of the tests will wish to note that test results obtained in the Los Angeles study indicated that health knowledge scores in most instances were higher than health practice scores, that health practices appeared to lag behind both knowledge and attitudes, and that more improvement was noted in knowledge and attitudes than in practices following a period of instruction.

The manuals for this series are excellent, incorporating in each case a description of the test, suggestions for use and interpretation, directions for the examiner, normative data, and scoring keys. Test questions for each form are classified into content areas and it is suggested that the test user compute for each area the average per cent "preferred" response (i.e., the author's keyed response). For this purpose, the publisher has provided a table for converting number of students responding with the keyed response to per cent for classes of up to 50 students. Step-by-step procedures for carrying out such analyses both for individuals and groups are provided to assist the examiner in estimating health education strengths and deficiencies. For this purpose, normative data for each content area for males, females, and the composite group are provided in each manual.

ELEMENTARY LEVEL. This test, designed for grades 1–6, presents 40 questions (such as "Do you play in the street?"), each of which is presented both verbally and pictorially to the student. For each question, the testee is asked to indicate what he does, rather than what he thinks ought to be done; he indicates his answer by underlining the most appropriate of three responses: "Most of the time I do," "Sometimes I do," and "No, I never do." The questions are clearly presented and the illustrations for each question are both appropriate and of high quality. The pictorial approach will prove particularly helpful to the younger student who might have difficulty reading the questions. The vocabulary used, however, should prove fairly easy for the great majority of the test takers.

Two other comments appear to be in order for potential users of this form. The original inventory used the phrase "Yes, I always do" as the positive end of the scale of responses. Although the manual indicates that the change to "Most of the time I do" was made prior to standardization of the test, it does not indicate the reason for such action. This substitution in wording may, at least for the child in the lower grades, introduce a minor element of confusion by requiring that he indicate that he behaves in a specified manner most of the time, when in fact he does so *all* the time; granted, however, that such consistent behavior in children of this age group is very unlikely.

The format and simplicity of the test appears to be a particularly desirable feature for use of the test in the lower grades, though for the average fifth or sixth grader the presentation may be somewhat oversimplified. This approach, however, is a necessary compromise when one attempts to cover a span of six grades with a single test, and it should not be considered as an extremely critical factor in the use of this instrument.

JUNIOR HIGH LEVEL. The test consists of three parts, dealing respectively with health practices (25 questions requiring responses of "Usually," "Sometimes," or "Never"), health attitudes (25 statements requiring responses of "Agree," "?," or "Disagree"), and health knowledge (50 questions, four-choice multiple choice).

Parts 1 and 2 are well executed and require no critical comment. Part 3, however, provides an unfortunate exception; one cannot quarrel with the validity of the content of the questions, but the violation of basic item writing rules through use of such "stems" as "Coffee," "It is not natural to want to," or "A bath or shower each day" leaves a great deal to be desired. One can only hope that the publisher will consider an editorial revision of this part of an otherwise excellent test at the earliest opportunity.

SENIOR HIGH LEVEL. Whatever the Junior High Level of the series may lack in reflecting good item writing practices is more than adequately compensated for by the general excellence of this test. With but a few exceptions, the questions are clearly written, pertinent, and challenging to the student. It seems particularly noteworthy and commendable that well written items on such "sensitive" topics as fluoridation of drinking water, effects of smoking, use of stimulants and depressants, and venereal disease are included.

Several points in the content of the test do deserve critical appraisal, however. In one case, the correct answer for an item (14), which asks the subject to indicate what he should do to keep in top physical condition, is given by the stem of the item immediately following (15), which states that "physical fitness can be promoted by regular, daily exercise."

The "preferred" response for item 21, which states that "During their first year of high school, there has been a change in the social behavior of both John and Sue. The best indication of this is that they," is given as "are cheerful and cooperative in their relationships with family and friends." In the absence of item analysis data, but in the light of the typical behavior of the high school freshman, it would seem more likely that the second option, "are at ease in social situations which they find interesting" is more applicable. Up to the point in time indicated, the typical pattern of behavior does seem to be one in which there is relatively little social interchange between the sexes; generally, prior to this time such interchange, if any, tends to be characterized by its awkwardness.

Among the otherwise excellent multiple choice questions, a series of matching items (67–71) fails on several counts: it presents five complaints (e.g., "persistent indigestion") which the student is asked to match with a series of five courses of action (e.g., "treat yourself"); even if more than a single course of action were the correct answer for all five items, and unfortunately in this case all are keyed with the same response of "Go to a medical doctor," the general rule for matching questions of this type requires that the number of concepts to be matched not be equal in number, since answering a single item correctly usually increases the probability of a correct guess on the remaining questions. The introduction of a single, poorly written set of this type in the midst of a test otherwise consisting entirely of five-choice questions appears neither particularly logical nor necessary.

SUMMARY. With the exception of specifics noted above, the majority of which can readily be corrected by judicious use of an editorial pen, this series consists of three carefully planned and well executed tests. Of the three levels in the series, the elementary and senior high tests should prove particularly helpful in their *present* form to those wishing to gain insight into the health knowledge, practices, and attitudes of their students. With a more thorough editorial revision, the junior high test, too, can be brought up to the standard of excellence represented by the other tests.

[724]

***Health and Safety Education Test: National Achievement Tests.** Grades 3–6; 1947–60; 5 scores: good habits, cause and effect, facts, application of rules, total; Form A ('60, c1947–60, identical with test copyrighted in 1947); no manual; directions-norms sheet ('59, c1947–59, 2 pages, identical with sheet copyrighted in 1947); no data on reliability; $3.50 per 25 tests; 50¢ per specimen set; postage extra; 40(45) minutes; Lester D. Crow and Loretta C. Ryan; [Psychometric Affiliates]. *

For a review by Clarence H. Nelson, see 5:555.

[725]

***Health Education and Hygiene: Every Pupil Test.** Grades 7–9; 1935–64; new form (4 pages) usually issued each December and April; forms from previous testing programs also available; general directions sheet ('63, 2 pages); no data on reliability; Ohio norms for new forms available following testing program; 5¢ per test; 3¢ per key; postpaid; 40(45) minutes; Ohio Scholarship Tests. *

[726]

***High School Health: Every Pupil Scholarship Test.** High school; 1938(?)–63; new form (2 pages) usually issued each April; forms from previous testing programs also available; general directions sheet ['63, 2 pages]; no data on reliability; norms for new forms available following testing program; 4¢ per test; 4¢ per key; postage extra; 40(45) minutes; Bureau of Educational Measurements.

[727]

***Physical Education: National Teacher Examinations.** College seniors and teachers; 1954–62; for more complete information, see 700; 80(90) minutes; Educational Testing Service. *

For reviews of the testing program, see 700, 5:538, and 4:802.

[728]

Physical Education: Teacher Education Examination Program. College seniors preparing to teach secondary school; 1957; an inactive form of *Physical Education: National Teacher Examinations;* for more complete information, see 709; IBM; 80(95) minutes; Educational Testing Service. *

For a review of the testing program, see 5:543. For reviews of the National Teacher Examinations, *see 700, 5:538, and 4:802.*

[729]

★Smoking Habits Questionnaire. Grades 7–12; 1959; 1 form ['59, 4 pages]; directions for administration ['59, 1 page]; no data on reliability; no norms; 1–199 copies, 15¢ each; 200–999 copies, 10¢ each; postpaid; [12–14] minutes; V. J. Sallak; the Author. *

[730]

★Veenker Health Knowledge Test for the Seventh Grade. Grade 7; 1960; IBM; Forms FA, FB, (9 pages); manual (4 pages); separate answer sheets must be used; $5.75 per 35 tests; IBM answer sheets must be purchased elsewhere; scoring stencils must be constructed locally; 50¢ per specimen set; postpaid; (45–50) minutes; C. H. Veenker; the Author. *

REFERENCES

1. VEENKER, C. HAROLD. "A Health Knowledge Test for the Seventh Grade." *Res Q* 30:338–48 O '59. *

[731]

[Wetzel Grid Charts.] Ages birth–3, 2–18; 1940–48; chart for evaluating physical growth and development; 2 levels; manual ('48, 113 pages, see *4* below); 1–99 copies, 30¢ each; $4.75 per manual; specimen set of grids free; postpaid; Norman C. Wetzel; NEA Service, Inc. *

a) THE BABY GRID: A GUIDE TO INDIVIDUAL PROGRESS DURING INFANCY. Ages birth–3; 1946–48; 1 form ('46, 2 pages).

b) GRID FOR EVALUATING PHYSICAL FITNESS IN TERMS OF PHYSIQUE (BODY BUILD), DEVELOPMENT LEVEL AND BASAL METABOLISM—A GUIDE TO INDIVIDUAL PROGRESS FROM INFANCY TO MATURITY. Ages 2–18; 1940–48; referred to by publisher as the "Big Grid"; 1 form ['49, c1940–48, 2 pages].

REFERENCES

1–9. See 4:489.

10. BRUCH, HILDE. "The Grid for Evaluating Physical Fitness (Wetzel): Application to Children With Abnormal Bodily Dimensions." *J Am Med Assn* 118:1289–93 Ap 11 '42. *

11. WETZEL, NORMAN C. "Appraisal of Growth and Development." *J Pediatrics* 22:741–8 Je '43. *

12. WETZEL, NORMAN C. "Assessing the Physical Condition of Children: 1, Case Demonstration of Failing Growth and the Determination of 'Par' by the Grid Method." *J Pediatrics* 22:82–110 Ja '43. *

13. WETZEL, NORMAN C. "Assessing the Physical Condition of Children: 2, Simple Malnutrition: A Problem of Failing Growth and Development." *J Pediatrics* 22:208–25 F '43. *

14. WETZEL, NORMAN C. "Assessing the Physical Condition of Children: 3, The Components of Physical Status and Physical Progress and Their Evaluation." *J Pediatrics* 22:329–61 Mr '43. *

15. STUART, HAROLD C., AND MEREDITH, HOWARD V. "Use of Body Measurements in the School Health Program." *Am J Pub Health* 36:1365–86 D '46. *

16. WETZEL, NORMAN C. "The Baby Grid: An Application of the Grid Technique to Growth and Development in Infants." *J Pediatrics* 29:439–54 O '46. *

17. LEESON, H. JEAN; MCHENRY, E. W.; AND MOSLEY, W. "The Value of the Wetzel Grid in the Examination of School Children." *Can J Pub Health* 38:491–5 O '47. *

18. FRIED, RALPH, AND MAYER, MORRIS F. "Socio-Emotional Factors Accounting for Growth Failure in Children Living in an Institution." *J Pediatrics* 33:444–56 O '48. * (*PA* 23:4694)

19. MANN, ARVIN W.; DREIZEN, SAMUEL; PYLE, S. IDELL; AND SPIES, TOM D. "The Red Graph and the Wetzel Grid as Methods of Determining the Symmetry of Status and Progress During Growth." *J Pediatrics* 32:137–50 F '48. * (*PA* 22:3855)

20. CASE, L. D. "The Wetzel Grid Chart: Something New in the Field of Guidance." *Assn Boys' Work J* 23:8–9 Ja '49. *

21. COLEMAN, ALLAN B. "Grid Prodrome Phenomenon in Celiac Disease: Report of Four Cases." *J Pediatrics* 35:165–8 Ag '49. *

22. SNODGRASSE, R. M. *Growth in Chicago Private School Boys With Special Reference to the Wetzel Grid.* Doctor's thesis, University of Chicago (Chicago, Ill.), 1950.

23. DAU, ANGIE WALDROM. *The Use of Wetzel Grids by a Classroom Teacher.* Master's thesis, Southern Methodist University (Dallas, Tex.), 1951.
24. GOFF, MILDRED E. *A Comparison of Status on the Wetzel Grid With Measures of Mental Ability, Motor Ability, and Personality Among High School Girls.* Master's thesis, University of Texas (Austin, Tex.), 1951.
25. DEISHER, ROBERT W., AND BRYAN, ELIZABETH. "The Value of the Wetzel Grid in a School Health Program and Problems Related to Its Use." *J Sch Health* 22:44–59 F '52. *
26. GARN, STANLEY MARION. "Individual and Group Deviations from 'Channelwise' Grid Progression in Girls." *Child Develop* 23:193–206 S '52. * (*PA* 27:7076)
27. HILL, D. A. "A Wetzel Grid Survey in Toronto." *Can J Pub Health* 44:285–94 Ag '53. *
28. ADAMS, FORREST H.; LUND, GEORGE W.; AND DISENHOUSE, ROBERT B. "Observations on the Physique and Growth of Children With Congenital Heart Disease." *J Pediatrics* 44:674–80 Je '54. *
29. PUGH, MOLLY C. "Charting Growth With the Wetzel Grid." *J Health Phys Ed & Rec* 25:47–8 Mr '54. *
30. EICHORN, DOROTHY H. "A Comparison of Laboratory Determinations and Wetzel Grid Estimates of Basal Metabolism Among Adolescents." *J Pediatrics* 46:146–54 F '55. * (*PA* 30:2533)
31. SMILLIE, DAVID. "An Evaluation of the Channel System on the Baby Grid." *Child Develop* 30:279–88 Je '59. *
32. SOLLEY, WILLIAM H. "Status of Physique, Change in Physique, and Speed in the Growth Patterns of School Children, Grades 1–8." *Res Q* 30:465–78 D '59. *
33. SOLLEY, WILLIAM H. "Relationship of Selected Factors in Growth Derivable From Age-Height-Weight Measurements." *Res Q* 31:92–100 Mr '60. *
34. BAER, MELVYN J.; TORGOFF, IRVING H.; AND HARRIS, DONNA J. "Differential Impact of Weight and Height on Wetzel Developmental Age." *Child Develop* 33:37–50 D '62. * (*PA* 37:6421)
35. WEAR, C. L., AND MILLER, KENNETH. "Relationship of Physique and Developmental Level to Physical Performance." *Res Q* 33:615–31 D '62. * (*PA* 38:1896)

DOROTHY EICHORN, *Associate Research Psychologist, and Administrator, Harold E. Jones Child Study Center, Institute of Human Development, University of California, Berkeley, California.*

These two growth charts are very similar in format and interpretation. The essential elements are the "grid" and "auxodrome" panels, but each chart has a table for recording height, weight, and age, an "energy" panel giving estimates of basal metabolism, and space for summarizing a considerable amount of developmental and clinical data. Two small graphs for plotting head and chest circumference are included on the Baby Grid.

The grid panel is a logarithmic plot of weight against height, subdivided into parallel "channels" across which run lines of "isodevelopmental level." Thus, any single weight-height point falls in some channel and at a certain developmental level. Channels represent physiques ranging from extremely thin to obese, and these in turn correspond to clinical ratings of physical status and nutrition. A developmental level is a number assigned to a body size, and the size represented is said to be surface area. On the auxodrome panel developmental level is plotted against age. A group of percentile size-age curves, called auxodromes, are provided as standards of reference. The 67 per cent auxodrome is taken as the average, and the developmental age corresponding to any developmental level can be derived by determining the age at which the 67 per cent curve crosses that level.

Empirical tests reveal that developmental level is primarily a function of weight.[1] Thus auxodromes are essentially weight-age curves and developmental age practically equivalent to a weight-age. Wetzel originally asserted (*1*) that developmental age "serves the purpose of, determinations of skeletal age." Later, presumably because research comparing skeletal age assessments with developmental age controverted this claim[2] (*10, 19*), he stated that equal developmental ages did not imply equal maturity (*12–4*). Grid estimates of basal metabolism from developmental level also deviate in certain systematic ways from actual determinations of metabolic rate (*10, 30*). These qualifications do not bear directly, however, on Wetzel's basic method of evaluating growth in terms of direction (channel course) and speed (gain in developmental level). He claims that in optimal growth a child gains at the rate of 12 levels per year while remaining "in channel." Tolerance limits are 2 to 3 levels per year and a shift of one half channel per 10 levels. Data from several sources seriously challenge the dictum of constancy of channel progression[3] (*6, 26*). For example, Garn (*26*) reports that among two groups of girls followed longitudinally, not more than 50 per cent remained in channel for even one year, and after longer intervals the proportions dropped to 10–30 per cent. Further, these were not random shifts, attributable to widespread "growth failure" or local conditions, because the longitudinal data and mean data from six different ethnic or regional groups showed a systematic pattern of change with age—down-channel from 6 to 12 years and up-channel thereafter. The reviewer has unpublished data from three longitudinal studies which confirm Garn's results for girls and show a similar, although less marked, arcuate curve of channel position with age for boys. The proportions of boys remaining in channel at successive years are, however,

1 SIMMONS, KATHERINE, AND GREULICH, WILLIAM WALTER. "Menarcheal Age and the Height, Weight, and Skeletal Age of Girls Age 7 to 17 Years." *J Pediatrics* 22:518–48 My '43. * TANNER, J. M. "The Assessment of Growth and Development in Children." *Arch Dis Childh* 27:10–33 F '52. *
2 SIMMONS AND GREULICH, op. cit.
3 ANDERSON, B. "Wetzels technic til bedömmelse at börns legemlige udvikling provet paa et dansk materiale." *Ugeskrift för Laeger* 104:981–4 '42.
DÖSSING, J. "Vurdering af Wetzels graefiske methode paa grundlag at 5082 danske börns horde og waegt." *Ugeskrift för Laeger* 110:695–9 '48.

equally as small as those for girls. Such shifts in channel imply that gain in level and constancy of auxodrome also are not maintained within the prescribed limits. Large scale surveys demonstrate that the Grid fails to identify some children with significant pathology and labels as "growth failures" children found on examination to be clinically fit (*27, 29*). Wetzel points out the former possibility, but makes no allowance for the latter. The research with longitudinal groups suggests that many "false positives," as well as some cases of diagnosed "growth failure" who apparently respond to treatment, are actually instances of normal maturational changes in weight-height ratio for which the Grid does not compensate.

Persons engaged in basic research on physical growth have criticized the statistical and mathematical foundations of the Grid, the use of cross-sectional data as longitudinal standards, and the evaluation of development solely by height and weight [4] (*6*) but all admit that a generally satisfactory growth chart has yet to be devised. Standard score forms are better research tools, but for many practical purposes, the Grid system is one of the best available. Separate scores do not have to be combined conceptually, and data cast in terms of body build and percentiles are more readily understood by children and adults untrained in statistical inference. Because of the emphasis on evaluation in terms of the individual's own curve, the Grid is less easily misused by the overzealous and underinformed than are conventional weight-age and height-age standards. As a clinical record, one sturdy chart on which progress can be visualized and a large body of relevant data summarized is a welcome substitute for a sheaf of papers in a folder.

[Other Tests]

For tests not listed above, see the following entries in *Tests in Print:* 1223, 1225, 1229, 1231, 1233, 1235–8, 1241–3, 1248, and 1252; out of print: 1224, 1234, 1240, 1246, and 1249; status unknown: 1253.

4 FALKNER, FRANK. "Measurement of Somatic Growth and Development in Children." *Courrier* 4:169–81 Ap '54. * TANNER, op. cit.

HOME ECONOMICS

[732]

***Clothing: Every Pupil Scholarship Test.** High school; 1927–63; new form (2–4 pages) usually issued each April; forms from previous testing programs also available; general directions sheet ['63, 2 pages]; no data on reliability; norms for new forms available following testing program; 4¢ per test; 4¢ per key; postage extra; 40(45) minutes; Bureau of Educational Measurements. *

[733]

***Foods: Every Pupil Scholarship Test.** High school; 1927–63; new form (2–4 pages) usually issued each April; forms from previous testing programs also available; general directions sheet ['63, 2 pages]; no data on reliability; norms for new forms available following testing program; 4¢ per test; 4¢ per key; postage extra; 40(45) minutes; Bureau of Educational Measurements. *

[734]

★Home Economics Education: National Teacher Examinations. College seniors and teachers; 1960–63; for more complete information, see 700; 80(90) minutes; Educational Testing Service. *

For reviews of the testing program, see 700, 5:538, and 4:802.

[735]

★Homemaking I and II: Every Pupil Scholarship Test. 1, 2 years high school; 1947–57; 1 form ('57, 2 pages); 2 levels; general directions sheet ['63, 2 pages]; no data on reliability; 4¢ per test; 4¢ per key; postage extra; 40(45) minutes; Bureau of Educational Measurements. *

[Other Tests]

For tests not listed above, see the following entries in *Tests in Print:* 1254–7, 1259–60, 1262–5, 1267, and 1270–4; out of print: 1266 and 1275.

INDUSTRIAL ARTS

[736]

***Industrial Arts Education: National Teacher Examinations.** College seniors and teachers; 1947–62; for more complete information, see 700; 80(90) minutes; Educational Testing Service. *

For reviews of the testing program, see 700, 5:538, and 4:802.

[737]

***Industrial Arts: Every Pupil Scholarship Test.** High school; 1926–63; new form (2–4 pages) usually issued each April; forms from previous testing programs also available; general directions sheet ['63, 2 pages]; no data on reliability; norms for new forms available following testing program; 4¢ per test; 4¢ per key; postage extra; 40(45) or 50(55) minutes; Bureau of Educational Measurements. *

[738]

Industrial Arts: Teacher Education Examination Program. College seniors preparing to teach secondary school; 1957; an inactive form of *Industrial Arts Education: National Teacher Examinations;* IBM; for more complete information, see 709; 80(95) minutes; Educational Testing Service. *

For a review of the testing program, see 5:543. For reviews of the National Teacher Examinations, *see 700, 5:538, and 4:802.*

[Other Tests]

For tests not listed above, see the following entries in *Tests in Print:* 1276 and 1280–2.

LISTENING COMPREHENSION

[739]

Brown-Carlsen Listening Comprehension Test: Evaluation and Adjustment Series. Grades 9–13; 1953–55; IBM; Forms AM ['53], BM ('55), (2 pages); manual ('55, 20 pages); expectancy chart ['54, 2 pages]; $1.90 per 35 IBM test-answer sheets; 20¢ per set of scoring stencils; 30¢ per manual; 60¢ per specimen set; postage extra; (45–50) minutes; James I. Brown and G. Robert Carlsen; [Harcourt, Brace & World, Inc.]. *

REFERENCES

1–13. See 5:577.

14. ROSE, ERVIN. *A Comparative Study of the Brown-Carlsen Listening Comprehension Test and Three Tests of Reading Comprehension.* Doctor's thesis, New York University (New York, N.Y.), 1958. (*DA* 19:2007)

15. DUNCAN, CHARLES HOWARD. *The Relationship Between Listening Ability and Shorthand Achievement.* Doctor's thesis, University of Pittsburgh (Pittsburgh, Pa.), 1959. (*DA* 20:1640)

16. HABERLAND, JOHN A. "A Comparison of Listening Tests With Standardized Tests." *J Ed Res* 52:299–302 Ap '59. * (*PA* 34:4812)

17. JONES, ROBERT A., AND MICHAEL, WILLIAM B. "The Validity of a Battery of Tests in Communication Skills for Foreign Students Attending an American University." *Ed & Psychol Meas* 21:493–6 su '61. * (*PA* 36:2KK93J)

18. MICHAEL, WILLIAM B., AND JONES, ROBERT A. "Linguistic Factors in Several Tests and Criterion Measures Pertaining to Communication Skills." *Ed & Psychol Meas* 21:1011–4 w '61. *

19. MURPHY, WILLIAM CARL. *A Study of the Relationships Between Listening Ability and High School Grades in Four Major Academic Areas.* Doctor's thesis, University of Alabama (University, Ala.), 1962. (*DA* 23:3693)

20. *Normative Information: Manager and Executive Testing.* New York: Richardson, Bellows, Henry & Co., Inc., May 1963. Pp. 45. *

21. JOHNSON, F. CRAIG, AND FRANDSEN, KENNETH. "Administering the Brown-Carlsen Listening Comprehension Test." *J Commun* 13:38–45 Mr '63. *

22. KELLY, CHARLES M. "Mental Ability and Personality Factors in Listening." *Q J Speech* 49:152–6 Ap '63. *

For reviews by E. F. Lindquist and Irving Lorge, see 5:577.

[740]

***Sequential Tests of Educational Progress: Listening.** Grades 4–6, 7–9, 10–12, 13–14; 1956–63; IBM, NCS, and Grade-O-Mat; Forms A, B, ('57, c1956–57, 7–11 pages); 4 levels; separate directions ('57, 22–24 pages) for each form at each level; interpretive manual ('57, 29 pages); battery technical report ('57, 58 pages); 1958 SCAT-STEP supplement ('58, 32 pages); 1962 SCAT-STEP supplement ('62, 49 pages); 1963 SCAT-STEP supplement of urban norms ('63, 16 pages); battery teacher's guide ('59, 85 pages); battery profile ('57, 1 page); battery student report ('58, 4 pages); no data on reliability of Form B; separate answer sheets must be used; $4 per 20 tests; $1 per 20 IBM scorable answer sheets; 25¢ per scoring stencil; see 671 for prices of NCS answer sheets and scoring services; see 666 for prices of Grade-O-Mat cards; $1 per 20 profiles; $1 per 20 student reports; $1 per interpretive manual; $1 per technical report; $1 per supplement; $1 per teacher's guide; postage extra; $2 per specimen set, cash orders postpaid; (90–100) minutes; Cooperative Test Division. *

a) LEVEL 4. Grades 4–6; Forms 4A, 4B.
b) LEVEL 3. Grades 7–9; Forms 3A, 3B.
c) LEVEL 2. Grades 10–12; Forms 2A, 2B.
d) LEVEL 1. Grades 13–14; Forms 1A, 1B.

REFERENCES

1. North, Robert D. "An Evaluation of the STEP Listening Test for the Independent School Testing Program." *Ed Rec B* 72:61–7 Jl '58. *

2. BALDAUF, ROBERT JOHN. *A Study of a Measure of Listening Comprehension and Its Relation to the School Achievement of Fifth Grade Pupils.* Doctor's thesis, University of Colorado (Boulder, Colo.), 1960. (*DA* 21:2979)

3. BONNER, MYRTLE CLARA STUDDARD. *A Critical Analysis of the Relationship of Reading Ability to Listening Ability.* Doctor's thesis, Auburn University (Auburn, Ala.), 1960. (*DA* 21:2167)

4. VINEYARD, EDWIN E., AND BAILEY, ROBERT B. "Interrelationships of Reading Ability, Listening Skill, Intelligence, and Scholastic Achievement." *J Develop Read* 3:174–8 sp '60. * (*PA* 35:1274)

5. MCGUIRE, CARSON. "The Prediction of Talented Behavior in the Junior High School." *Proc Inv Conf Testing Probl* 1960:46–67 '61. *

6. CLELAND, DONALD L., AND TOUSSAINT, ISABELLA H. "The Interrelationships of Reading, Listening, Arithmetic Computation and Intelligence." *Reading Teach* 15:228–31 Ja '62. *

7. SPEARRITT, DONALD. *Listening Comprehension—A Factorial Analysis.* A.C.E.R. Research Series No. 76. Melbourne, Australia: Australian Council for Educational Research, 1962. Pp. x, 149. *

8. ANDERSON, HAROLD M., AND BALDAUF, ROBERT J. "A Study of a Measure of Listening." *J Ed Res* 57:197–200 D '63. *

9. KELLY, CHARLES M. "Mental Ability and Personality Factors in Listening." *Q J Speech* 49:152–6 Ap '63. *

10. MICHAEL, WILLIAM B.; CATHCART, ROBERT; ZIMMERMAN, WAYNE S.; AND MILFS, MILO. "Gains in Various Measures of Communication Skills Relative to Three Curricular Patterns in College." *Ed & Psychol Meas* 23:365–74 su '63. * (*PA* 38:1384)

11. WEAVER, WENDELL W., AND KINGSTON, ALBERT J. "A Factor Analysis of the Cloze Procedure and Other Measures of Reading and Language Ability." *J Commun* 13:252–61 D '63. * (*PA* 39:188)

For reviews by E. F. Lindquist and Irving Lorge, see 5:578. For reviews of the complete battery, see 25 and 5:24.

PHILOSOPHY

[741]

***The Graduate Record Examinations Advanced Tests: Philosophy.** Grades 16–17; 1939–61; for more complete information, see 762; 180(200) minutes; Educational Testing Service. *

For a review of the testing program, see 5:601.

[742]

***The Graduate Record Examinations Advanced Tests: Scholastic Philosophy.** Grades 16–17; 1951–62; available only in the Institutional Testing Program; for more complete information, see 762; 180(200) minutes; Educational Testing Service. *

REFERENCES

1. MCGANNON, J. BARRY. *Graduate Record Scholastic Philosophy Test.* Master's thesis, Saint Louis University (Saint Louis, Mo.), 1952.

2. MCGANNON, J. BARRY. "Construction of an Objective Test in Scholastic Philosophy." *Cath Ed R* 52:456–79 O '54. *

For a review of the testing program, see 5:601.

PSYCHOLOGY

[743]

***The Graduate Record Examinations Advanced Tests: Psychology.** Grades 16–17; 1939–63; for more complete information, see 762; 180(200) minutes; Educational Testing Service. *

For a review by Harold Seashore, see 5:583.
For a review of the testing program, see 5:601.

[744]

★Psychology Test: Every Pupil Scholarship Test. High School; 1932–59; 1 form ('59, 2 pages); general directions sheet ['63, 2 pages]; no data on reliability; 4¢ per test; 4¢ per key; postage extra; 40(45) minutes; Bureau of Educational Measurements. *

[Other Tests]

For tests not listed above, see the following entries in *Tests in Print:* 1295; out of print: 1297–8.

RECORD AND REPORT FORMS

[745]

★A/9 Cumulative Record Folder. Grades kgn–12; 1951; 1 form ['51, 3 pages]; $9.50 per 100 folders, postage extra; sample copy free; American Guidance Service, Inc. *

[746]

★[Guidance Cumulative Folder and Record Forms.] Grades kgn–12; 1941–61; 1 folder (Form 100-R, '41, 4 pages) and 4 parts; 4 insert sheets; revised directions for using folder ('42, 2 pages); directions for using insert sheets ['50, 2 pages]; 1–99 folders, 10¢ each; $1 per 100 insert sheets; postage extra; specimen set free; Chronicle Guidance Publications, Inc. *
a) INTERVIEW RECORD SHEET. Form 101 ['58, 1 page].
b) OBSERVATION RECORD SHEET. Reports by teachers; Form 102 ['58, 1 page].
c) PERSONALITY REPORT SHEET. Ratings by teachers; Form 103 ['58, 1 page].
d) FOUR YEAR EDUCATIONAL PLAN. Form 104 ['61, 1 page].

[747]

★Ontario School Record System, 1960 Revision. Grades kgn–8, 9–13; 1950–60; 2 levels; manual ('60) consisting of a folder containing general information sheet (2 pages) and separate suggestions (4 pages) for completing records at each level; 5¢ per suggestions for either level; 15¢ per complete manual; 30¢ per complete specimen set; postage extra; Guidance Centre. *
a) OSRI, PART I. Grades kgn–8; 2 parts: *Ontario School Record Folder 1* ('60, c1950–60, 4 pages), *Ontario School Office Record, Part 1* ('60, c1955–60, 2 pages); $1.10 per 25 record folders; 22¢ per 25 office records.
b) OSR2, PART 2. Grades 9–13; 3 parts: *Ontario School Record Folder 2* ('60, c1950–60, 4 pages), *Ontario School Office Record 2* ('60, c1950–60, 2 pages), *Ontario School Record Student Information Form* ('60, c1950–60, 2 pages); $1.40 per 25 record folders; 22¢ per 25 office records; 36¢ per pad of 50 information forms.

[748]

★[Physical Growth Record.] Ages 4–17; 1947; 1 form ['47, 4 pages, directions included in record booklet]; 2 editions; 10¢ per record booklet; [5–10] minutes; Howard V. Meredith and the Joint Committee on Health Problems in Education of the National Education Association and the American Medical Association; published jointly by the National Education Association and the American Medical Association. *
a) PHYSICAL GROWTH RECORD FOR GIRLS.
b) PHYSICAL GROWTH RECORD FOR BOYS.

REFERENCES

1. MEREDITH, HOWARD V. "A 'Physical Growth Record' for Use in Elementary and High Schools." *Am J Pub Health* 39: 878–85 Jl '49. *

[Other Tests]

For tests not listed above, see the following entries in *Tests in Print:* 1301–2, 1303a, 1304–9, 1311–2, 1314–5, 1318, and 1320–1; out of print: 1316 and 1319; status unknown: 1303 and 1317.

RELIGIOUS EDUCATION

[749]

★Achievement Test in Jewish History. Junior high school; 1962; 4 scores: informational background, terms and concepts, personalities, total; IBM; Forms A, B, ('62, 11 pages); mimeographed manual ('62, 10 pages); mimeographed technical report ['62, 30 pages]; mimeographed norms supplement ('62, 1 page); reliability data for earlier experimental forms only; no norms for subscores; separate answer sheets must be used; 15¢ per test; 2¢ per IBM answer sheet; 25¢ per hand scoring stencil; 25¢ per manual; 50¢ per technical report; cash orders (plus 10% for postage) only; 35(45) minutes; original forms by Leon H. Spotts; revision, manual, and technical report by Gerhard Lang; National Curriculum Research Institute, American Association for Jewish Education. *

[750]

★Achievement Test for Weekday Afternoon Congregational Schools. End of grade 3; 1959–63; various titles used by publisher; IBM; Forms A ['62], B ['63], (11–12 pages); 3 tests; manuals: for Form A ['62], for Form B ['63], (16 pages); supplements: for Form A ('62), for Form B ['63], (4 pages); directions for administering ['61, 4 pages]; norms ('62, 5 pages) for Form A; no data on reliability; no norms for Form B; separate answer sheets must be used; 1 or more copies of all tests, 20¢ for New York City schools, 36¢ for out of town schools; $1 per specimen set; postage extra; [45–60] minutes; Jewish Education Committee of New York, Inc.; Jewish Education Committee Press. *
a) THE JEWISH PEOPLE.
b) JEWISH LIFE AND OBSERVANCES.
c) HEBREW LANGUAGE.

[751]

★Religion Test (Four-Year Course): Affiliation Testing Program for Catholic Secondary Schools. Grade 12 and students who are candidates for the high school diploma issued by the Catholic

University of America; 1949–63; administered annually in May at individual schools; IBM; new form issued annually; Form Z ('63, 14 pages) used in 1963 program; separate answer sheets must be used; 50¢ per test and IBM answer sheet; postpaid; fee includes purchase of test booklets, scoring, and other services; for more complete information, see 758; specimen set of the complete battery free; 90(100) minutes; Program of Affiliation, Catholic University of America. *

HENRY CHAUNCEY, *President, Educational Testing Service, Princeton, New Jersey.* [Review of Forms Y and Z.]

Form Y is reported to have a reliability of .90 (K-R 21) and a validity of .79 (based on pretests and measured against a criterion of teachers' grades). For Form Z the corresponding figures are .88 and .87. Nine major areas are covered in the test: morals, dogma, apologetics, the Bible, Church history, grace, the sacraments, liturgy, and the Mass. In Form Y, morals and dogma receive the greatest emphasis (about 16 per cent each); apologetics, the Bible, and the sacraments receive the next greatest emphasis (about 13 per cent each); and Church history, grace, liturgy, and the Mass receive the least emphasis (about 7 per cent each). In Form Z, morals receives 23 per cent emphasis; dogma, the Bible, grace, the sacraments, and liturgy, about 10–15 per cent each; and apologetics, Church history, and the Mass, about 5 per cent each.

The course of study outlined by the Program of Affiliation lists as the main objectives of the course in religion the development of Catholics who have an intelligent understanding of their faith, and the development of Catholics who practice their faith and feel its import in every aspect of daily life. One wonders whether a test designed to measure these objectives can do so effectively by testing primarily the student's ability to recall factual information. Very few items attempt to go beyond this very lowest level of comprehension. (This emphasis on purely factual, rote recall information may account for the extraordinarily high validity coefficients reported.) The good Catholic should, of course, have at his fingertips basic knowledge of his religion, but a test in religion that is measuring the stated objectives should probably not be so concerned to discover whether the student knows the meaning of the word *usury* (Form Z, item 72) as it should be to discover whether the student knows the implications of that particular sin in modern American life. Perhaps, however, the test merely reflects current methods of teaching religion.

Form Z also raises the question of whether adequate consideration has been given to sampling procedure. In this form, the student is asked, for instance, to identify differences in sins related to the eighth commandment (perjury, rash judgment, calumny, and detraction), but some other commandments are not considered even in a general fashion. Similarly, in that form, questions dealing with exactly the same aspects of birth control and abortion are repeated (compare items 31 and 98, and 29 and 97).

However, considered as a whole, the test deals with material that should be familiar to high school students who have completed a four-year course in religion similar to that outlined in the suggested course of study. In the light of the statistical information provided and in terms of a general review of the items, the test seems to be suitable for the population in regard to level of difficulty, and students should be able to complete it within the allotted time. However, no information has been provided concerning the discriminating power of individual items, although such information would be invaluable in judging the validity of the test. Many items in both forms appear to be specifically determined because of the distinctive length of the key (for example, Form Z, items 3, 11, 25, 34; Form Y, items 14, 17, 46). Others seem more likely to be difficult for the better student (for example, Form Y, item 9; Form Z, item 59). Some items (for example, Form Z, items 90 and 92) have options that are not restrictive and are actually a part of the key, even though an incomplete part.

In addition, the stems of many items are undirected: "The psalms . . . . ," "A priest may . . . . ," "Sanctifying grace . . . ." Furthermore, even considering the population for which the test is intended, many stems, particularly in Form Z, lack necessary qualification (for example, "Communism is wrong because it . . . ." could probably be more properly worded as "The basic reason the Church considers Communism wrong is that it . . . .").

The general instructions are, in some ways, unfair to the student. He is told to omit those topics he has not studied, rather than those with which he is unfamiliar. The student may not have studied, for instance, the parts of the Mass, but he may be quite capable of answering questions concerning the Mass on the basis of information provided in his missal. In Form Y, these directions may have resulted in students omitting whole blocks of items concerning the same subject matter. These omissions would make the test a different one for each student. It seems unjustifiable to compare scores when all students are not taking the same test. In Form Z, however, the presentation of blocks of items according to subject matter seems to have been eliminated.

In summary, the tests do fill a need in Catholic education by measuring an aspect of Catholic curriculum that is not measured by secular testing agencies. However, the test would probably be more useful in fulfilling its objectives if, in addition to following more carefully the standard rules for preparing items, the item writers made greater use of items that require the student to demonstrate his knowledge in contexts that utilize, insofar as possible, the relationship between factual information about Catholicism and the Christian life.

For a review of the complete program, see 758.

[752]

*Scholastic Achievement Series: Religion.** Grades 2.5–3, 4–6, 7–9; 1953–59; various titles used by publisher; for Catholic schools; subtest of *Scholastic Achievement Series;* IBM for grades 4–9; 3 levels; $2 per 20 tests; separate answer sheets may be used in grades 4–9; $1 per 20 IBM scorable answer sheets; 12¢ per scoring stencil; 50¢ per specimen set of any one level; postage extra; Oliver F. Anderhalter, R. Stephen Gawkoski, and John O'Brien; Scholastic Testing Service, Inc. *

a) PRIMARY TEST. Grades 2.5–3; 1953–59; 4 scores: concerning God, concerning incarnation and redemption, concerning sin and grace, total; Forms A ('53, 5 pages), B ('55, 4 pages); battery manual ('59, 12 pages); 27(35) minutes.

b) ELEMENTARY TEST. Grades 4–6; 1954–58; 4 scores: the Creed, the Sacraments, the Commandments, total; IBM; Forms A ('54, 8 pages), B ('55, 10 pages); battery manual ('58, 21 pages, technical data and norms same as in 1955 manual); 36(45) minutes.

c) ADVANCED TEST. Grades 7–9; 1954–59; 4 scores: same as for elementary test; IBM; Forms A, B, ('54, 8–9 pages); battery manual ('59, 22 pages, technical data and norms the same as in 1955 manual); 37(45) minutes.

For reviews of the complete battery, see 23 and 5:23.

[753]

★Standardized Bible Content Test. Bible college; 1956–61; Forms A ('56), B ('57), C ('58), D ('59), (10 pages); manual ('61, 47 pages); reliability data for Form A only; $12 per 100 tests; 15¢ per single copy; separate answer sheets may be used; $1.50 per 100 answer sheets; 2¢ per single copy; 50¢ per manual (free with 15 or more tests); postpaid; 45(50) minutes; Standardized Bible Content Test Committee of the Accrediting Association of Bible Colleges; distributed by Clarence E. Mason, Jr. *

[754]

★Test on Biblical Information. Grades 6–8; 1954–55; Forms A, B, ('54, 6 pages); 2 tests: New Testament, Old Testament; manual ('55, 6 pages); tentative norms; $3 per 35 tests; 60¢ per specimen set of both tests; postage extra; (20–30) minutes; Martin J. Maehr in collaboration with Theo. G. Stelzer and Herbert E. Kaiser; Concordia Publishing House. *

[755]

★Theological School Inventory. Incoming seminary students; 1962–64; motivation for entering the ministry; 12 scores (definiteness, natural leading, special leading, concept of the call, flexibility, acceptance by others, intellectual concern, self-fulfillment, leadership success, evangelistic witness, social reform, service to persons) plus unscored sections on biographical information and reactions to demands of the ministry; Form C ('62, 14 pages); manual ('64, 110 pages); 4 research supplements ('64, 6–20 pages each); separate answer sheets must be used; $1.50 per set of test and answer sheet; $5.50 per 25 additional answer sheets; $4 per set of scoring stencils; $4.85 per set of manual and supplements in a looseleaf binder; postage extra; (90–100) minutes; Educational Testing Service (test), James E. Dittes (manual and supplements), Frederick Kling (test and 1 supplement), Ellery Pierson (1 supplement), and Harry DeWire (1 supplement); Ministry Studies Board. *

[756]

★Unit Tests on Luther's Catechism. Grades 6–9; 1952–54; 7 tests, 11 scores for each: knowledge and skill (locating Bible references, spelling related words, quotations, applying quotations, Bible stories, vocabulary, understanding, ethical insight, total), attitudes, performance; Forms A, B, (8 pages); manual ('52, 8 pages); reliability data for *b* only; norms for *a* and *b* only; $1.75 per 25 tests; separate answer sheets may be used; $1 per 50 answer sheets; $1 per specimen set; postage extra; (50–55) minutes per test for grades 6–7, (40–45) minutes per test for grades 8–9; Committee on Tests and Measurements of the Board for Parish Education, Lutheran Church—Missouri Synod; Concordia Publishing House. *

a) CURRICULUM UNIT 1: OUR RELATION TO GOD (FIRST TABLE OF THE LAW). 1952; Henry J. Boettcher.

b) CURRICULUM UNIT 2: ACTIVE NEIGHBORLY LOVE (SECOND TABLE OF THE LAW). 1952; Henry J. Boettcher.

c) CURRICULUM UNIT 3: THE PERSON AND WORK OF GOD THE FATHER (FIRST ARTICLE OF THE CREED). 1954; Paul Groenke.

d) CURRICULUM UNIT 4: THE PERSON AND WORK OF JESUS CHRIST (SECOND ARTICLE OF THE CREED). 1954; F. W. Ibeling.

e) CURRICULUM UNIT 5: THE WORK OF THE HOLY GHOST (THIRD ARTICLE OF THE CREED). 1953; Roy C. Krause.

f) CURRICULUM UNIT 6: PRAYER. 1953; C. R. Marquardt.

g) CURRICULUM UNIT 7: THE SACRAMENTS. 1953; Paul Groenke.

REFERENCES

1. BOETTCHER, HENRY J. "Unit Tests on Luther's Catechism," pp. 61–7. In *Tests and Measurements in Lutheran Education.* Edited by Arthur L. Miller. Lutheran Education Association, Fourteenth Yearbook, 1957. River Forest, Ill.: the Association, 1959. Pp. xi, 115. *

[Other Tests]

For tests not listed above, see the following entries in *Tests in Print:* 1323–30; out of print: 1332 and 1335.

SOCIOECONOMIC STATUS

[757]

★Socio-Economic Status Scale. Urban students, adults, rural families; 1962–64; 2 editions; postage extra; specimen set not available; Manasayan. *

a) SOCIO-ECONOMIC STATUS SCALE (URBAN). Urban students, adults; 1962; 3 ratings (education, occupation, income) yielding a total status score; 2 levels ('62, 2 pages): Form A (for adults), Form B (for students); manual ('62, 18 pages); score card ('62, 1 page) for both editions; no data on reliability; Rs. 12.50 per set of 50 information blanks of each level, 50 score cards, and manual; administration time not reported; B. Kuppuswamy.

b) SOCIO-ECONOMIC STATUS SCALE (RURAL). Rural families; 1964; 9 ratings (caste, occupation, education, social participation, land, house, farm powers, material possessions, family type and size) yielding a total status score; 1 form ('64, 2 pages); manual ['64, 26 pages]; Rs. 10.50 per set of 50 information blanks and manual; (5–15) minutes; Udai Pareek and G. Trivedi.

Manas 9:64–6 '62. D. Gopal Rao. [Review of the urban edition.] Most of the investigations in the field of Social Sciences require the knowledge of the socio-economic background of an individual or a group. Without any such proper tool in India, the research workers had to have their conclusion solely on the basis of the income of the parents. Dr. Kuppuswamy's S.E.S. Scale has filled the lacuna that was prevalent in this field. * In a pragmatic society like America, where the status of an individual is measured in terms of his material possessions, it may be easy to develop a scale based upon the quality and quantity of such materials, viz, the possession of a car, telephone, radio or television. But in a country like India where the people tend to have a nonmaterialistic view of life and consequently different pattern of values as compared with other cultures, it becomes very difficult to assess the status of an individual. * Kuppuswamy deserves to be congratulated for developing a very much needed tool in the field of Social Sciences. The scale would be useful in ascertaining the status of the urban population. It has 3 variables namely, education, occupation and income. Each variable has been scaled on a seven point scale and weightage has been worked out for various points. * The scope of the scale needs to be extended to include the difference between the several graded cities (class A, B and C). In India, in terms of income significance, the value of income varies inversely with the increasing cost of living. * Income is not [an] absolute entity. It is a relative concept influenced by certain factors like the size of the family, and the number of dependents etc. In this scale no effort has been made to relate the income to these factors. The chief merit of Dr. Kuppuswamy's scale is its simplicity and objectivity. The scoring is rendered very comprehensive and easy by the use of a score card, on which the status score of an individual can be worked out. * The inventory is self-explanatory and has two forms, form A is meant for earners and form B is for non earners (mainly students). The manual in the form of a small booklet of 18 pages is attractive and it gives the details of the construction and use of the scale. Though the scale has certain shortcomings the efforts of the learned professor in constructing the tool, the only of its kind in India, is laudable. *

[Other Tests]

For tests not listed above, see the following entries in *Tests in Print:* 1336–7 and 1340; out of print: 1338–9.

TEST PROGRAMS

[758]

★The Affiliation Testing Program for Catholic Secondary Schools. Grades 9–12 and students who are candidates for the high school diploma issued by the Catholic University of America; 1949–63; administered annually in May at individual schools; except for those with diploma candidates, schools need not be affiliates; IBM; 13 tests (diploma candidates must take at least 7 over the 4 year high school period); new form issued annually; norms and item analysis data available in November following the testing program; Form Z ('63) used in 1963 program; manual ('63, 25 pages); directions for administering ['63, 2–5 pages] for each test; norms-item analysis report ['63, 26 pages] for Form Z tests; interpretive booklet for norms-item analysis report ('63, 20 pages); student profile [no date, 2 pages]; school profile ['63, 2 pages]; separate answer sheets must be used; 50¢ per test and IBM answer sheet; 10¢ per IBM electrographic pencil; postpaid; specimen set free; fees include purchase of test booklets (except in the case of *d* and *m*), scoring service, national item difficulty data for each test, and (for schools testing at least 90 per cent of students who are enrolled in a course corresponding to the test area) local item analysis data for

2–3 tests per year; stencils for local hand scoring also provided; $1 per diploma (optional); 90(100) minutes per test, (540) minutes in 3 sessions for the program; Program of Affiliation, Catholic University of America. *
a) RELIGION TEST (FOUR-YEAR COURSE). Grade 12; Form Z (14 pages).
b) ENGLISH TEST (FOUR-YEAR COURSE). Grade 12; Form Z (15 pages).
c) LATIN TEST (TWO-YEAR COURSE). Grades 10–12; Form Z (11 pages).
d) SPANISH TEST (TWO-YEAR COURSE). Grades 10–12; test booklets must be returned after use; Form Y ['62, 12 pages].
e) FRENCH TEST (TWO-YEAR COURSE). Grades 10–12; Form Z (13 pages).
f) ELEMENTARY ALGEBRA TEST. Grades 9–12; Form Z (11 pages).
g) PLANE GEOMETRY TEST. Grades 9–12; Form Z (11 pages).
h) BIOLOGY TEST. Grades 9–12; Form Z (15 pages).
i) CHEMISTRY TEST. Grades 9–12; Form Z (13 pages).
j) PHYSICS TEST (TRADITIONAL AND PSSC). Grades 9–12; Form Z (19 pages).
k) AMERICAN HISTORY TEST. Grades 9–12; Form Z (16 pages).
l) WORLD HISTORY TEST. Grades 9–12; Form Z (12 pages).
m) CHRISTIAN DEMOCRACY TEST (CIVICS, SOCIOLOGY, ECONOMICS). Grades 9–12; test booklets must be returned after use; Form Z (16 pages).

HENRY CHAUNCEY, *President, Educational Testing Service, Princeton, New Jersey.* [Review of Forms Y and Z.]

The Affiliation Testing Program is an optional service to Catholic secondary schools. Its purpose is "to fill the need for standard achievement tests based on a Catholic philosophy of education, Catholic secondary school objectives, and Catholic secondary school content." [1] The three objectives of this program are to make possible the comparison of the achievement of individual students with that of other students with similar educational backgrounds, to provide the basis for comparative studies of class achievement, and to furnish data for comparative study of teachers' grades and test scores.

The battery of tests quite comprehensively covers subjects studied in high school, except for advanced work in mathematics and foreign languages. Mathematics tests are available only in algebra and plane geometry. The tests in Latin, French, and Spanish are all intended for students who have had only two years of study. With the clear need at the present time for more advanced work in mathematics and foreign languages, it seems unfortunate that advanced work in these fields is, in effect, discouraged for lack of appropriate tests.

Each test is based on a course outline that has been prepared as a result of a study of courses given in Catholic secondary schools. The outlines are concise and cover only the topics recognized as being essential. It is made clear that the outlines should be "liberally interpreted as indicating in a general way the nature and extent of preparation considered necessary." The tests are not intended to encourage conformity to a prescribed curriculum, but rather to provide considerable latitude in both the selection of the textbook and the handling of the course.

It is stated that the objectives of the tests include "the measuring of knowledge acquired on basic content material, the understanding of basic principles within the field, the application of both knowledge and principles to related problems, and the skills involved in such application."

Pretests are constructed a year in advance and are administered at a representative sample of 30 Catholic high schools. As a result of detailed item analysis and teacher opinionaires, each test is revised prior to issuance for general use the following year.

Each test requires 90 minutes for administration. The number of items varies from 60 to 150. Reports to schools are in terms of standard scores with mean 50 and standard deviation 10. Percentile equivalents are also reported. The norms that are implicit in the standard scores and percentiles are believed to be representative of achievement of Catholic secondary school students, although only somewhat over 25,000 students participated in the 1962 program, and although only a somewhat smaller number of students are included in standardization procedures (students in classes where 90 per cent or more of the students took the tests). Since the norms are based, in any case, on students from Catholic schools which participated in the program on a voluntary basis, there is no assurance that the norms are truly national or that they represent all Catholic secondary education. This may not, however, be a very important matter to the users of the program, and it is likely that there is relatively good comparability from year to year, as the participating schools probably remain quite constant.

1 This quotation and the quotations elsewhere in this review and in the reviewer's separate evaluations of the tests comprising the ATP are from the 1958 edition of the booklet *Program of Affiliation*. The 1964 edition which has now been published was still in preparation when these reviews were written.—**Editor.**

The report to the school includes the mean standard score of the school for each test in which its students participated, and a table giving percentile rank for school means in each test field is also made available. Data on item difficulty for the norms sample are reported for each test each year and local item analysis data are provided for each test once every five years to determine student achievement within various content areas of each test.

Kuder-Richardson formula 21 reliabilities are calculated each year for each pretest and for a stratified sample of students taking the final form of each test. For Form Y the reliabilities range from .82 to .93, with only five under .90. Form Z reliabilities range from .78 to .95, with seven under .90. In the manuals for Forms Y and Z, split-half reliabilities for Form S of the tests are also reported. They range from .83 in world history to .96 in French. All but four of the Form S tests had reliabilities of .90 or higher. In view of the length of the tests and the range of abilities of the students, these would seem to be about what one would expect.

Validities of the tests have been obtained by correlating test scores with teachers' grades in the corresponding courses and with average grades. A study was made of Form T of the test administered in 1957. Average grades for each student (300–500 students from over 100 schools "distributed throughout wide geographical areas") were transmuted into normalized scores for each school in order to eliminate variability of marking systems. The resulting coefficients are: .51 in Spanish, .56 in algebra, .58 in American history, .61 in religion and English, .68 in geometry, .70 in world history, .75 in French, .83 in chemistry, .89 in Latin and biology, .90 in Christian democracy, and .93 in physics. These are remarkably high validities, which the author of the manual attempts to make look even better by correcting for attenuation of the criterion, using .60 as an estimate of the reliability of the teachers' grades. This has the awkward effect of making five of the correlations higher than 1.00, so that in the column of figures given the corrected coefficients the original uncorrected coefficients are used in these instances. Corrections for the vaguely estimated reliability of the criterion probably give an overly favorable picture of the validity of a test.

Such high validity coefficients suggest that the range of ability and accomplishment of the students is very great, and also that the courses are much more standard from school to school than the sponsors of the Affiliation Testing Program consider desirable, according to statements in the manual. It would also suggest that the tests are heavily factual in content, and this is borne out in the review of the tests themselves.

The manual contains five main sections that are pretty much the same from year to year: (*a*) the purposes, nature, and development of the tests; (*b*) materials, costs, and procedures; (*c*) directions for administering the tests and advice to students; (*d*) explanation of the data that are reported, interpretation, and special studies; (*e*) a summary of the steps that must be taken by participating schools from the first ordering of the tests to the final return of unused test booklets. There is also a two-page supplement that provides the latest validity, reliability, and norms data. In general, the manual is adequate, although not as clear and thorough in its explanation of the studies that have been made as would be desirable.

So far as is known, there are no sample questions given out in advance to enable students to understand the directions for each type of question used. Since some of the item forms are quite complicated, a practice booklet made available to the students before they take the tests would be desirable.

The separate tests in this extensive battery are generally good, although somewhat uneven in their quality. By and large, they are appropriate for students who have taken traditional courses. Some of the questions, however, are quite imaginative. Specific comments are presented in the reviewer's separate evaluations of each of the tests.

For reviews of the separate tests, see 263, 375, 410, 431, 598, 651, 751, 891, 913, 935, 964, 998, and 1013.

[759]

★College Board Placement Tests. Entering college freshmen; 1962–63; all tests (except 2 forms of the tests in French, Spanish, and German listening comprehension) are reprints of inactive forms of tests from the *College Entrance Examination Board Admissions Testing Program;* tests rented to colleges for local administration and scoring at any time; IBM; 18 tests: Biology (see 894), Chemistry (see 916), English Composition (see 288), French Listening Comprehension (see 369), French Reading (see 370), German Listening Comprehension (see 386),

German Reading (see 387), Greek (see 395), Italian (see 401), Italian Listening Comprehension (see 400), Latin Reading (see 406), Advanced Mathematics (see 571), Intermediate Mathematics (see 572), Physics (see 928), Russian Listening Comprehension (see 414), Spanish Listening Comprehension (see 422), Spanish Reading (see 423), Spatial Relations (see 1084); administration and scoring manual ('63, 34 pages); interpretation manual ('63, 18 pages); bulletin of information ('63, 13 pages); Admissions Testing Program score report booklet for counselors ('63, 40 pages) is also distributed with test materials; no norms based on program participants (publisher recommends use of local norms and conditional use of normative data from the Admissions Testing Program); separate answer sheets must be used; rental fee: 25¢ per test, postpaid; scoring service available; 30(40) minutes for listening comprehension tests, 60(70) minutes for other tests; program administered for the College Entrance Examination Board by Educational Testing Service. *

[760]

***College Entrance Examination Board Admissions Testing Program.** Candidates for college entrance; 1901–64; tests (except those under *c* below) administered from 1 to 5 times annually (January, March, May, July, December) at centers established by the publisher; supervisor's manual ('63, 47 pages) for *a* and *b;* examiner's manual ('62, 18 pages) for *c;* score report booklet for students ('63, 20 pages); score report booklet for counselors ('63, 40 pages, also covers the *Preliminary Scholastic Aptitude Test*); score report booklet for admissions officers ('62, 20 pages); bulletin of information ('63, 86 pages); separate descriptive booklets ('63, 52–122 pages) for *a, b,* and *c;* separate Scribe answer sheets must be used; examination fees for *a* and *b:* $5 for morning session (SAT), $7.50 for afternoon session (any 1 to 3 achievement tests or Writing Sample and any 1 or 2 achievement tests), $2 for Writing Sample if taken alone; fees include reporting of scores (except for the Writing Sample, a copy of which is sent ungraded to each score recipient) to the student's secondary school and 1–3 colleges or scholarship programs designated at time of application; $1 per additional report; scores not reported to the candidate but may be released by the secondary school at its discretion; program administered for the College Entrance Examination Board by Educational Testing Service. * See separate test entries referred to below for references on specific tests.

a) SCHOLASTIC APTITUDE TEST. See 449; 1926–63; 2 scores: verbal, mathematical; special editions for the blind and special administration arrangements for the physically handicapped available; 180(240) minutes.

b) ACHIEVEMENT TESTS. 1901–64; 15 tests (candidates elect 1–3 tests as specified by individual college or scholarship program requirements): American History and Social Studies (see 966), Biology (see 892), Chemistry (see 914), English Composition (see 287), European History and World Cultures (see 967, available only in January and May testing programs), French (see 366), German (see 383), Hebrew (see 396, available only in January testing program), Latin (see 404), Advanced Mathematics (see 568), Intermediate Mathematics (see 569), Physics (see 926), Russian (see 412, available only in January testing program), Spanish (see 419), Writing Sample (see 289); 60(80) minutes.

c) SUPPLEMENTARY ACHIEVEMENT TESTS. 1960–63; tests administered at the local secondary school on a specified date in February; candidates must also be registered to take one or more achievement tests in one of the regular program administrations; 7 tests: French Listening Comprehension (see 367), German Listening Comprehension (see 384), Greek (see 394), Italian Listening Comprehension (see 398), Italian Reading and Essay (see 399), Russian Listening Comprehension (see 413), Spanish Listening Comprehension (see 420); no data on reliability of tests in Greek, Italian Listening Comprehension, Italian Reading and Essay, and Russian Listening Comprehension; listening comprehension tests administered by 7½ ips tape; demonstration tape (3¾ ips) available to schools on request; no additional fees for supplementary tests; (30–40) minutes for listening comprehension tests, 90(100) minutes for Greek and Italian achievement tests.

REFERENCES

1–9. See 4:526.
10–12. See 5:599.
13. *Reviews of College Board Tests From The Fifth Mental Measurements Yearbook.* Introduction by John A. Valentine. Comments on the reviews by William E. Coffman. New York: College Entrance Examination Board, 1959. Pp. 40. *
14. BLACK, D. B. "A Comparison of the Performance on Selected Standardized Tests to That on the Alberta Grade XII Departmental Examination of a Select Group of University of Alberta Freshmen." *Alberta J Ed Res* 5:180–90 S '59. * (*PA* 34:6559)
15. KENDRICK, S. A. "College Board Tests Today." *Col Board R* 39:17–21 f '59. *
16. COLLEGE ENTRANCE EXAMINATION BOARD. Review of College Board Research, 1952–60. New York: the Board, 1961. Pp. iv, 67. Paper. Gratis. * (A revision of *Review of the Research Activities of the College Entrance Examination Board, 1952–57* by Joshua A. Fishman.)
17. BROWNSTEIN, SAMUEL C., AND WEINER, MITCHELL. *Barron's How to Prepare for College Entrance Examinations, Third Edition.* Great Neck, N.Y.: Barron's Educational Series, Inc., 1962. Pp. 443. *
18. COLLEGE ENTRANCE EXAMINATION BOARD. *College Board Score Reports: A Guide for Admission Officers.* Princeton, N.J.: the Board, 1962. Pp. 20. *
19. DYER, HENRY S. "How Adequate Are the Admissions Tests?" *Col Board R* 47:3–7 sp '62. *
20. *Manual of Freshman Class Profiles, 1963 Edition.* Princeton, N.J.: College Entrance Examination Board, 1963. Pp. 642. *
21. COLLEGE ENTRANCE EXAMINATION BOARD. *College Board Score Reports: A Guide for Counselors: Preliminary Scholastic Aptitude Tests, Scholastic Aptitude Test, and Achievement Tests.* Princeton, N.J.: the Board, 1963. Pp. 44. *
22. COLLEGE ENTRANCE EXAMINATION BOARD. *A Description of the College Board Achievement Tests.* Princeton, N.J.: the Board, 1963. Pp. 120. *
23. COLLEGE ENTRANCE EXAMINATION BOARD. *A Description of the College Board Scholastic Aptitude Test.* Princeton, N.J.: the Board, 1963. Pp. 53. *
24. COLLEGE ENTRANCE EXAMINATION BOARD. *A Description of the College Board Supplementary Achievement Tests.* Princeton, N.J.: the Board, 1963. Pp. 62. *

BENNO G. FRICKE, *Associate Professor of Psychology, and Chief, Evaluation and Examinations Division, The University of Michigan, Ann Arbor, Michigan.*

This review of the CEEB Admissions Testing Program provides primarily an *overall* evaluation of the validity and utility of the Board's Scholastic Aptitude Test (SAT) and the achievement tests. Separate reviews of the individual tests of the College Board program are given elsewhere in this volume and in the Fourth and Fifth MMY's. Although the CEEB Admissions Testing Program has appeared as an entry in the two previous MMY's, this is the first MMY to give readers an estimate of the quality of the Board's *total* admissions test package. It is essential, in my opinion, to take into account results from several presumably different tests (and academic criteria) before defensible conclusions may be drawn about the special worth of any one of them.

PUBLICATIONS OF THE CEEB AND ETS. A rapid examination of the extensive literature distributed by the College Board and Educational Testing Service concerning the CEEB admissions tests cannot help but make a favorable impression. In particular, the material prepared for college-bound students is extremely well done (e.g., the 1963–64 Bulletin of Information: Admissions Testing Program). The writing in practically all CEEB publications is clear and the quality of printing and paper is very good. Because the literature on the CEEB tests and testing program is widely distributed and easily available (much of it is free) and since other pertinent reviews appear in this volume there is little need to provide detailed descriptive data in this review. The limited space will be used primarily to focus attention on more important matters, namely research evidence disclosing the quality of the tests.

NEW LANGUAGE LISTENING TESTS. First, however, a few comments should be made about some of the newer tests now included in the program—the Supplementary Achievement Tests. There are as yet no validity data for these tests, at least I have found none and none were supplied to me by the producers of the tests. All but two (Greek and Italian Reading and Essay) of these relatively unknown and little used tests are listening comprehension tests in the foreign languages. They seem to differ sufficiently from other CEEB tests to merit separate existence and, possibly, wide usage. The major difference between these tests and the others is that the stimulus material is heard, not read. Proper administration of these tests is, necessarily, more complicated than the others, and is accomplished through tape recordings. Unlike the others, the language listening tests are administered by the secondary schools. Completed answer sheets are sent to Princeton where they are scored; a student's scores are then sent to his high school and up to three colleges.

Although the possibility exists for improper use of test materials in such nonsecure situations, it is refreshing to see not only new evidence of faith in school authorities but also a willingness by schools to cooperate with a national testing program. Procedures and devices which yield information benefiting students, schools, and colleges deserve widespread support, and it is to be hoped that the present handling of the listening tests represents a step in the direction of returning to the schools the responsibility for supervising all testing. Considerable confidence in the schools already exists, for if it did not, the successful administration of the *Preliminary Scholastic Aptitude Test* and the *National Merit Scholarship Qualifying Test* would not be possible. (It may be worth noting here that the validity coefficients which I have seen for these two tests do not differ significantly from the validity coefficients of their secure counterparts, the SAT and ACT, respectively.) It seems unfortunate, however, that the admissions tests which the CEEB has agreed to turn over to the schools for administration are the most difficult ones to manage.

RESEARCH RESULTS. While the CEEB and ETS may not yet have had enough time to collect and report adequate data bearing on the validity of the language listening tests, more than ample time has elapsed since the SAT and achievement tests were first issued to permit a final judgment of their nature and merit. Unfortunately, and surprisingly, while most of these tests have been in existence for over 20 years, there is relatively little research evidence on which to base a judgment. Although pertinent research on the development and effectiveness of the CEEB tests has not been assembled into the familiar test manual or handbook, a number of CEEB and ETS publications provide some of the needed data.

Perhaps most useful for most purposes are the 70-page volume entitled *College Board Scores: Their Use and Interpretation*, authored by Henry S. Dyer and published in 1953 (*10*), the 192-page revision of it by Dyer and Richard King in 1955 (*11*), and the 206-page supplement to it by Joshua Fishman in 1957 (*12*). Each of these publications shows that (*a*) the SAT has acceptable validity for predicting freshman grade-point averages (validity coefficients usually range between .30 and .55), and (*b*) the achievement tests have acceptable validity for predicting grades in appropriate subjects (coefficients also usually range between .30 and .55). A number of other publications in the 1950's by the CEEB, ETS, and independent researchers report similar findings.

This may be the place to emphasize that most of the recent studies which show the SAT to have *lower* coefficients than indicated above *cannot* be used as evidence that the SAT is now a poorer test than formerly. Lower predictive coefficients probably stem from increased use in recent years of SAT scores in arriving at admissions decisions. The substantial growth in the number of applicants to selective colleges has permitted them to admit more *uniformly* able students; consequently, there is relatively little valid variance left in the SAT scores of enrolled students. Also, because most colleges which require the CEEB tests have made greater use of the SAT than the achievement tests in selecting students, meaningful research on the relative validity or contribution of these tests can no longer be done in these institutions. Uncontaminated research results are needed, preferably from institutions which do not rely on test data in arriving at admissions decisions, in order to make a precise comparison of the utility of the SAT and the achievement tests.

Although my concern in this review is mainly with the special significance of the various subtests and parts of the SAT and the achievement tests, it is pertinent to note here that Indiana University, an institution which has not used Board test scores for admissions purposes, recently completed a significant validity study [1] of the SAT and obtained validity coefficients of .54 and .41 for SAT-Verbal and SAT-Mathematical, respectively. The validity of the *total score* on SAT was .54. These Indiana figures are similar to those obtained at most of the major private colleges in the late 1940's and early 1950's, before the present favorable selection ratio existed.

For the benefit of those who may be interested in comparing the SAT with other academic ability tests, it should be mentioned that the validity of the *total score* on the *American College Testing Program Examination* was .61 at Indiana. The superiority of ACT, however, is almost certainly less than the difference of .07 might suggest, for while random samples of almost 1,500 freshmen took each test, evidence from other sources indicates that the success of students who took the SAT was somewhat *less* predictable than the success of students who took the ACT test. For example, the validity coefficient for high school record was .55 for the group that took the SAT, and .58 for the group that took the ACT test; the corresponding coefficients for an English usage test were .50 and .53.

DIFFERENTIAL VALIDITY OF SAT-V AND SAT-M. Research with many tests and varieties of test content over the years shows that it is possible to construct subtests which measure at least two academically important aptitudes, usually referred to as verbal (or linguistic), and mathematical (or quantitative) aptitude. How well does the SAT measure these aptitudes? At least two types of evidence are relevant. One has to do with the extent to which scores from the SAT-V and M correlate with each other *and* with themselves (i.e., their reliability), and the other has to do with the extent to which SAT-V and M scores correlate with performance in appropriate and inappropriate courses.

Clearly, if the correlation between V and M is very high, say approaching the average reliability of V and M, then there would be little need to seek further evidence, for it would be reasonably clear that both parts measure essentially the same attributes even though the item content appears to sample different dimensions. If the correlation between V and M is very low or zero, then it would be clear that different attributes are being measured (on the assumption that V and M have adequate reliability), although further evidence would still be needed to determine what, specifically, is being measured by each part. According to the statistical data in a February 1963 report,[2] the median correlation between V and M for the 14 forms of the SAT administered in the period 1959–62 is .64; about ten years ago the average correlation for a comparable three-year period was .54. Noteworthy changes in the internal consistency reliability coefficients have not taken place; the median coefficients for the 14 forms used in 1959–62 are .90 for SAT-V, and .89 for SAT-M. Although I have been unable to find test-retest reliability coefficients for SAT-V and M, there is a brief report [3] of a study by Richard S. Levine in which the verbal and mathematical aptitude scores of the *Scholarship Qualifying Test* (SQT) were correlated with

1 CHASE, CLINTON I.; LUDLOW, H. GLENN; POMEROY, MARTHA C.; AND BARRITT, L. SPENCER. *Predicting Success for University Freshmen.* Indiana Studies in Prediction No. 1. Bloomington, Ind.: Bureau of Educational Studies and Testing, 1963. Pp. vi, 47. *

2 SWINEFORD, FRANCES. *College Entrance Examination Board Scholastic Aptitude Test, August 1959 to May 1962.* Unpublished report, Educational Testing Service, Princeton, N.J., February 1963. Pp. 9. *

3 "SQT, SAT Scores Compared." Abstract of an unpublished study by Richard S. Levine. *Col Board R* 34:2 w '58. *

the two SAT scores. According to this report, "The correlations between the two parts of the SQT and similar sections of the SAT proved to be very high, the SAT-V and the SQT-V showing a correlation of .85 and the SAT-M and the SQT-M a correlation of .81."

Although it is clear from the correlations for V and M that the two parts are not measuring the same thing, it is also clear that whatever is being measured by one is also being measured by the other to a considerable extent. Correlations of .54 to .64 between measures of presumably different aptitudes are not a good sign. The overlap in variables is undesirably high.

More important than the correlation between V and M is the correlation V and M have with grades in appropriate and inappropriate subjects. As indicated earlier there is relatively little evidence of this type available, and none in *College Board Scores* and its supplements referred to above. Two 1957 research reports[4] by John W. French of ETS show the validity of V and M for: (*a*) high school grades of college-bound applicants for admission to college, (*b*) first-year college grades of college freshmen, and (*c*) third- and fourth-year major field grades of college graduates. For these three groups the validity coefficients of SAT-V and M for science-mathematics grades, social science grades, and humanities-English grades suggest some, but slight, differential validity. The approximate median validity coefficients of SAT-V for high school grades in the three course areas are .37, .49, and .56; corresponding coefficients for SAT-M are .45, .39, and .40. According to French the average SAT-V coefficients for first-year college grades in the three areas are .36, .43, and .39; corresponding SAT-M coefficients are .37, .20, and .18. The average SAT-V coefficients for third- and fourth-year major field grades in the three areas are .35, .43, and .34; corresponding SAT-M coefficients are .34, .26, and .23. The evidence shows that the verbal aptitude subtest predicts grades in the two linguistic course areas somewhat better than it predicts grades in the quantitative course area, and that M predicts grades in the quantitative course area somewhat better than it predicts grades in the two linguistic course areas. However, it is to be noted that grades in science-mathematics are *not* predicted significantly better by SAT-M than by SAT-V. There is much room for improvement here. More will be said on this later. For the present it will suffice to say that both parts of the SAT seem to be mainly measures of *general* academic ability.

DIFFERENTIAL VALIDITY OF THE ACHIEVEMENT TESTS. While there is relatively little data on the construct validity of the two aptitude tests, there is even less information on the specific or distinctive validity of each of the achievement tests. What is needed are studies which show the correlation between scores from the achievement tests and grades in appropriate and inappropriate courses. According to Dyer (*10*): "Data on the validity of the afternoon tests [the achievement tests] are not very complete. Most of the studies show the power of a given test to predict the grades in some appropriate college course." A table giving 21 validity coefficients for five achievement tests supports Dyer's statement that the tests predict grades in appropriate courses. Two years later (*11*) two new sentences were sandwiched between slightly modified versions of the two sentences in Dyer's report. The same table of 21 coefficients is reproduced. The new material is as follows: "Additional data will become available for publication after more empirical validity studies made at the colleges are reported to the College Board. There is always assurance, of course, that the tests possess the inherent validity which results from the judgment and scholarship of the school and college teachers who construct them." Evidence is needed, not reassurance.

In the 1957 supplement (*12*) a new table containing 63 correlation coefficients shows the relation between achievement test scores and course grades at 13 colleges. While this table permits some tentative (negative) judgments to be made concerning the purity of the College Board tests, results from only one institution (scattered over two pages in the supplement) seem satisfactory with respect to sample size and variety of courses and tests involved. Table 1, which presents results for this institution, suggests that if the Board's achievement tests measure different things, what they measure is not readily apparent. The correla-

4 FRENCH, JOHN W. *The Relation of Ratings and Experience Variables to* Tests of Developed Ability *Profiles.* Unpublished research bulletin, Educational Testing Service, Princeton, N.J., November 1957. Pp. iii, 57, viii. *
FRENCH, JOHN W. *Validation of the SAT and New Item Types Against Four-Year Academic Criteria.* Unpublished research bulletin, Educational Testing Service, Princeton, N.J., May 1957. Pp. 46, xvii. *

tions between course grades and appropriate tests are essentially the same as the correlations between grades and *inappropriate* tests.

Table 1
Validity of Four CEEB Achievement Tests

Students	Test	Course	Correlation
147	Chemistry	General Chemistry	.32
147	Advanced Mathematics	General Chemistry	.33
331	Physics	Physics: Mechanics	.34
331	Advanced Mathematics	Physics: Mechanics	.41
472	Advanced Mathematics	Physics: Mechanics	.41
472	Advanced Mathematics	Analytic Geometry and Calculus	.54
472	Advanced Mathematics	General Chemistry	.38
472	English Composition	Humanities	.33

The May 1957 research report by French referred to earlier gives the correlations between scores from the English Composition Test (ECT) and junior and senior major field grades in science and mathematics, social science, and humanities and languages; the validity coefficients are .35, .36, and .35, respectively. It appears that the ECT does not have specific validity; it seems to be a measure of *general* academic ability.

The scarcity of data on the achievement tests led the reviewer to carry out a series of studies on freshmen enrolled at the University of Michigan in 1961–62. Scores of the 1961 entrants were acceptable for a study of the CEEB tests because they were used relatively little for admissions purposes. The correlations between various achievement tests and grades in the two courses elected by the *largest* number of freshmen will illustrate the nature of the Michigan findings. Here are the achievement test validity coefficients for inorganic chemistry grades: Biology, .58; Chemistry, .55; Social Studies, .50; Physics, .49; Advanced Mathematics, .48; and ECT, .38. These coefficients show that scores from Chemistry do not correlate appreciably higher with grades in chemistry than do scores from tests purporting to measure other things. As a matter of fact the test which proved to be the best indicator of success in chemistry was Biology. There are few significant differences between the one appropriate and five inappropriate validity coefficients. Thus the Michigan results in the science area are similar to those reported earlier by Fishman (*12*). It is of more than incidental interest to note that scores from Social Studies, which correlate .50 with grades in chemistry, correlate .53 with grades in history and .53 with grades in political science.

The Michigan validity coefficients for freshman English grades are as follows: ECT, .45; Social Studies, .38; French, .33; Biology, .31; Chemistry, .28; Physics, .26; and Advanced Mathematics, .24. These coefficients clearly show that while the ECT does not have marked superiority over Social Studies and French, it does provide a better indication of success in English than do the advanced mathematics and physics tests. It should be observed, however, that the ECT does not provide appreciably better predictions for success in English (the coefficient is .45) than it does for success in chemistry (the coefficient is .38). In this respect the Michigan results for ECT are similar to those reported in the May 1957 study by French. Also noteworthy is the finding that the validity of the French test for grades in French courses at Michigan averages about .34, and the validity of the biology test for grades in zoology is .25; these appropriate validities are essentially the same as the inappropriate ones for grades in English (.33 and .31, respectively).

Despite widespread use, there seems to be little evidence for believing that a particular achievement test of the CEEB measures specifically what it purports to measure. The available evidence indicates that the achievement tests are *not* good measures of proficiency in specific subjects. Each test seems to be mainly a measure of *general* ability.

SIMILARITY OF SAT AND THE ACHIEVEMENT TESTS. Unlike the previous two sections, this one is concerned with the relationship between the CEEB tests labeled aptitude and the CEEB tests labeled achievement. The important question to be answered is, "Do these tests measure essentially the same or different characteristics of students?" The most direct and perhaps best answer to the question is provided by an examination of the correlations between scores from the parts of the SAT and scores from the individual achievement tests. The most recent correlations I have seen for the CEEB *candidate* population were assembled by Watkins and Waite in 1959 and are included in the 1961 report entitled *Scaling and Equating College Board Tests.*[5] It is important to consider scores

5 WATKINS, R. W., AND WAITE, ANNETTE. Appendix 12, "Comparison of Scaling and Equating of the College Board Achievement Tests," pp. 162–76. In *Scaling and Equating of College Board Tests* by S. S. Wilks and others. Unpublished report, Educational Testing Service, Princeton, N.J., 1961. Pp. vi, 195. *

of the applicant group so that factors connected with self- and other-selection may be ruled out. Lower correlations for students enrolled at particular institutions will be the rule; since there are no reliability statistics for CEEB test scores at particular institutions, it is not possible to make a fully meaningful local evaluation of correlations between SAT and the achievement tests.

Before the Watkins and Waite correlations are given, however, this reminder: a precise interpretation of them cannot be made unless the reliability of the variables being correlated is known; the preferred reliability estimate would be alternate form with time lapse. Although it does not seem that such coefficients have been computed, other evidence suggests that the average coefficients for SAT and achievement test pairings would *not* be greater than about .80 to .83, since alternate form reliability coefficients with time lapse are almost always lower than internal consistency or test-retest reliability coefficients. (Recall in this connection the internal consistency and test-retest reliability figures for the SAT: internal consistency—.90 for V, .89 for M, and test-retest—.85 for V, .81 for M. Also relevant is the only test-retest coefficient I have been able to find for the achievement tests; it is .82 and it is for Chemistry, reported by Fishman.[9] The spirit of the main point here can be summarized very briefly. A test (in its various forms and administerings) must correlate more highly with itself than it does with presumably different tests. If it does not, the tests presumed to measure different things do not do so.

Here are the Watkins and Waite correlations between scores from the main achievement tests and the SAT-V: ECT, .76; Social Studies, .78; French, .60; Chemistry, .65; Physics, .67; Intermediate Mathematics, .53; and Advanced Mathematics, .54. The corresponding correlations for SAT-M are: .55, .64, .46, .72, .69, .80, and .75. (Correlations similar to these are also found in references *10–2*.) These almost unbelievably high correlations suggest that whatever is measured by the ECT and the social studies test is also measured by the SAT-V, and that whatever is measured by the intermediate and advanced mathematics tests is also measured by the SAT-M. It also appears from the high correlations between the two science tests and *both* SAT-V and M that a combination of the latter two scores (perhaps even a simple average of them) would account for almost all of the valid variance in the chemistry and physics test scores. Of the tests included in this study, the French test is the only CEEB achievement test taken by a significant percentage of the candiate population which appears to measure something not already adequately reflected in the SAT. Since a relatively small proportion (26.7 per cent in 1962-63) of all the achievement tests taken by CEEB candidates are selected from tests other than ECT, Social Studies, and Intermediate and Advanced Mathematics, the absolute loss in dropping all the achievement tests from the Board's test offering would not seem to be great, especially when factors other than correlations between SAT and achievement tests are taken into account, and if needed changes in the SAT are made.

Before attention is turned to some of these other factors, it should be observed that the SAT-achievement test correlations suggest that if one wishes to know what a student's score would be on the ECT or the social studies test, the SAT-Verbal score will provide it with relatively little error. At least the error would not be much greater than the difference between the scores obtained on alternate forms of the ECT or social studies test, if a student were to take the achievement test twice, at different times.

One of the important factors beyond the SAT-achievement test correlations which should be taken into account in deciding whether these tests provide mainly multiple measurements of the same thing is their validity for predicting individual course grades, and overall grade-point average. Unfortunately, as indicated earlier, there are few studies which permit a fair comparison of the relative validity of the SAT and the achievement tests. According to the admissions literature and research evidence, colleges which have required applicants to submit scores for both SAT and the achievement tests have relied mainly on SAT scores in arriving at admissions decisions. The usual statistical corrections for "restriction of range" are simply not satisfactory. It is possible for heavy use to be made of a variable in selection work, yet the variability of scores for it may actually increase. Additional comment on this subject has been given elsewhere.[6]

6 FRICKE, BENNO G. "Qualification for Law School and the Bar: How Should It Be Determined," pp. 175–99. In *The*

It is appropriate here to again emphasize the long standing need for CEEB sponsored studies at varied institutions which do *not* require applicants for admission to submit Board test scores. Ideally, all incoming freshmen at these institutions should be given the SAT and as many achievement tests as appropriate, perhaps five or six per student. This would make it possible to see a study (correlation matrix) in which one might find, for example, the correlation between *scores* from SAT-V, SAT-M, ECT, Chemistry, and Advanced Mathematics, and *grades* in freshman English, chemistry, and mathematics.

There are probably more acceptable and directly comparable findings for the ECT and SAT-V as indicators of proficiency in English than any other achievement test-SAT pair. Many relevant studies have been completed, especially in the 1940's. Although Dyer (*10*) does not give pertinent correlations, his comment concerning the ECT and other assessment variables is somewhat similar to one I would make on the basis of studies I have seen. He says: "We know from a number of carefully controlled studies conducted by the College Board and others that the best single predictor of Freshman English marks is the SAT-Verbal score."

The Michigan study referred to earlier produced identical coefficients for ECT and SAT-V; the correlation with English grades was .45 for both tests. This finding suggests that when there is a difference between ECT and SAT-V scores, each one is more accurate about half the time. Since the tests function in the same way, it matters little which one is used—there seems to be nothing to be said for obtaining scores from both SAT-V and ECT.

Further evidence that the SAT-V and ECT measure highly similar (if not identical) qualities for all practical purposes is contained in some unpublished research by Swineford.[7] A relatively minor point about the Swineford research is that scores from the PSAT-Verbal rather than the SAT-Verbal were compared with scores from eight ECT item-type sections (including two interlinears). For a sample of 211 high school seniors, PSAT-V correlated more highly with an essay criterion of writing ability than *any one* of the eight ECT 20-minute subtests; for 262 juniors PSAT-V provided a better assessment than six of the eight sections, including both interlinears. According to Swineford, the ECT "normally consists of three different sections" and for the reported research "three combinations, each including an interlinear section" were selected because an earlier analysis of the data by Godshalk showed that "combinations that include one of the interlinear sections are generally more valid than those that do not." The median validity coefficient of the three selected combinations for both groups was .71. The PSAT-V coefficients were .70 for the seniors and .64 for the juniors. It is to be noted that for the seniors, who are the ones normally tested with the ECT, the validities are almost identical; for the juniors, who have yet to take another year of English, the ECT combinations provide superior assessments of writing ability.

It cannot be emphasized too strongly, however, that the combinations reported on by Swineford are from among the *better* combinations disclosed by the earlier analysis in which seniors and juniors were lumped together. For the entire group, 2 of the 3 combinations had actually ranked among the *top 7* of the 50 acceptable combinations for an ECT, and the third had had average validity. The important point is that the validity coefficients cited above do not show how the PSAT-V compares with acceptable combinations of ECT subtests (or even acceptable combinations including an interlinear), but rather how the PSAT-V compares with combinations drawn from among the better ones. In a single data set and analysis, chance and selective factors alone may produce combinations which *appear* to have substantially more validity than they actually do. Before one could conclude that these particular ECT subtest combinations provide results superior to, or even equal to, the PSAT-V results, it would be necessary to collect data for a new sample, preferably a large sample of *seniors* only. Nevertheless, one cannot help but be extremely impressed by the slight, possibly biased, differences now before us.

Very little acceptable data for comparing the SAT with achievement tests other than the ECT are available. The Michigan results are

Law Schools Look Ahead: 1959 Conference on Legal Education. Ann Arbor, Mich.: University of Michigan Law School, 1959. Pp. xii, 328. *

MILHOLLAND, JOHN E., AND FRICKE, BENNO G. "Development and Application of Tests of Special Aptitude." *R Ed Res* 32:25–39 F '62. *

7 SWINEFORD, FRANCES. *Validity of the Interlinear, Supplementary Report.* Draft of an unpublished report, Educational Testing Service, Princeton, N.J., April 1962. Pp. 6.

probably the least distorted by test score use in selection. A complete listing of the validity coefficients is unnecessary for the differences are small, some favoring one of the parts of the SAT, some favoring the achievement tests, with a slight tendency for the achievement tests to have the higher validity coefficients. The coefficients for the two largest course groups are illustrative: for chemistry grades the chemistry test's coefficient was .55, and the SAT-M's coefficient was .54; for grades in history the social studies test's coefficient was .53, and the SAT-V's coefficient was .46.

Also relevant for judging the overlap in the SAT and achievement tests are the results from multiple regression equations derived to predict overall grade-point average. For two samples at Michigan, totaling 1,575 freshmen (for whom the validity coefficient of high school record was about .385), the multiple validity coefficient for HSR and SAT was about .505; for HSR and the achievement tests it was about .515. The similar gains in multiple correlations do not by themselves necessarily indicate similarity of SAT and the achievement tests, for the tests could be measuring quite different things and still produce *identical* gains over HSR alone. Similarity is shown, however, when all three predictors are combined to predict grades. For HSR, SAT, and the achievement tests the multiple correlation with GPA was about .535, a relatively slight gain, which suggests that the tests are measuring largely similar matters. Nevertheless, the increase of .03 (from .505 to .535) indicates that scores from the achievement tests reflect something not already reflected in the present SAT. Whether the amount of gain in prediction is sufficient to justify the substantial cost and inconvenience of obtaining the achievement test scores is, I submit, debatable.

It should perhaps be mentioned that the gains in multiple correlation in no way prove that the achievement tests measure specific achievement, or something basically different from what is measured by the SAT. It is pertinent to note that similar gains have come from the use of additional aptitude and general ability tests (see, for example, the May 1957 report by French referred to above, and Olsen's 1957 report [8]). Also relevant to the general problem of effective assessment and prediction are the Michigan results for a fourth predictor, the Achiever Personality scale of the *Opinion, Attitude and Interest Survey* (OAIS). When scores from this scale are added to those from HSR and SAT the multiple correlation with GPA is about .565; the gain of .06 over the multiple correlation for HSR and SAT seems large enough to be of practical importance.

Although the SAT (and to some extent the achievement tests) were used for evaluating applicants in the 11 institutions reported on in Olsen's report, a few comments on her findings might be justified. In predicting first term average grades, the median gain over HSR alone produced by combining HSR and SAT was .105 at the four colleges having the largest number of freshmen (at least 308) and .08 for all 16 groups studied. The median gain over HSR and SAT produced by the achievement tests (the ECT and the average of scores on whatever other two achievement tests were taken) was .050 at these four colleges (.06 for the 13 groups for which comparisons were made). At Michigan, where SAT scores received less weight in admissions decisions, the corresponding gains were .12 and .03. The median gains in the Olsen study are about the same before and after correction of the coefficients for shrinkage. For three of the groups studied the coefficients were also "corrected" for restriction of range due to selection on the SAT; the median gain was reduced to .03, the same gain obtained at Michigan.

A very interesting and puzzling aspect of the regression equations Olsen reports for each of the institutions is that when the achievement tests are not included SAT-M has a positive beta weight, as do SAT-V and HSR; when the achievement tests are included and HSR omitted, SAT-M generally still has a positive weight; but when the achievement tests and HSR are both in the combination, SAT-M generally has a *negative* beta weight! This means, among other things, that if two students have identical scores on SAT-V, the achievement tests, and HSR but different scores on SAT-M, the forecast or predicted grade-point average is *best* or *highest* for the student who has the *lower* SAT-M score. Most admissions officers normally pick students who score high. A major point here is that the gain in multiple correlation accruing from use of scores from highly

8 OLSEN, MARJORIE. *Summary of Main Findings on the Validity of the CEEB Tests of Developed Ability as Predictors of College Grades.* Unpublished report, Educational Testing Service, Princeton, N.J., October 1957. Pp. 59. *

similar variables is the end result of a very complex network of statistical interactions; if test users depart from the beta weights, even the small potential gain in selection efficiency is lost.

It seems clear from the results of the multiple regression studies cited here that there is relatively little new information provided by the achievement tests over and above that obtained from the SAT and high school record.

GENERAL COMMENT UPON STATISTICAL FINDINGS. The available research evidence suggests that the SAT and the achievement tests are *not* good tests for making differential predictions of college achievement. Each one seems to be primarily a measure of *general academic ability* rather than specific aptitude or achievement. Scores from most tests correlate very highly with scores from the other tests or subtests which purport to measure different things. Furthermore, scores from the various tests and subtests correlate about the same with grades in inappropriate courses as they do with grades in appropriate courses. There is, however, a slight tendency for both the SAT and achievement tests to reflect two aspects of ability: linguistic (or verbal) ability, and quantitative (or mathematical) ability. The unique variance contributed by the SAT and the achievement tests seems inadequate. Data assembled over the last 20 years suggest that there is little or no need for both SAT and achievement test scores, especially if a new one- or two-score scholastic ability test is prepared along the lines suggested below.

ITEM ANALYSIS PROCEDURES: PROBLEMS AND PROPOSALS. Probably the major explanation for the high correlations between the various CEEB tests and for their lack of differential validity is to be found in the item analysis procedures ETS uses to construct new forms. These procedures, instituted in the 1920's and apparently followed more or less faithfully ever since, involve contrasting the responses of students who do well with those who do poorly on the total test or on an earlier form. Perhaps the most succinct statement concerning the statistical analysis made to pretest items for the CEEB tests is given in the 1962 edition of *A Description of the College Board Achievement Tests.* This 160-page booklet is designed primarily for students but it is available to others as well, free of charge. The most pertinent part, on page 12 in a section headed "To the student," is as follows:

> A question is considered effective to the extent that good students, as judged by their total score on the test, answer the question correctly and poor students do not. If as many poor students as good students answer a question correctlv, obviously such a question will add nothing to the effectiveness of a test, and it is discarded.

Similar statements appear in earlier editions of the booklet; however, interestingly, only a brief and confused statement concerning item analysis appears in the 1963–64 edition. The statement is given on the last page of the booklet and is included in a new section headed "To the Teacher."

Allowing an *internal* rather than an *external* criterion to influence which items are to be selected for new forms makes it likely that each new test will reflect primarily a general academic ability, and perhaps even a general test taking ability. Use of a test-score criterion encourages considerable "inbreeding" of test items. The new items that are selected measure largely whatever is measured by most of the old items. A potentially excellent item, which measures an important aspect *not* reflected in the old items, is eliminated by the internal consistency criterion method of test construction, for such an item does not correlate appreciably with the total test score. Consequently, tests constructed by means of a test-score criterion become anchored to general test ability rather than to academic behavior as evaluated by professors and teachers in the classroom. Scores from such tests are homogeneous and highly reliable, but not highly valid for external criteria such as college grades. Over the years ETS researchers and CEEB officers have been overly preoccupied with the importance of high reliability, in my opinion; they have given relatively little attention to procedures which produce tests and subtests having high validity—the only aspect of a test that really matters. If a test has adequate validity it necessarily must have adequate reliability.

It should be noted here that the discriminating power of items to be incorporated into future test forms is largely determined from relatively small samples of student answer sheets. For most item analyses 370 cases are selected. The item responses of the 100 students from this sample who obtain the highest total scores are contrasted with the item responses of the 100 who obtain the lowest total scores.

Items which discriminate well between these groups are best, I am sure, for doing what most of the items in the test do, but I am equally sure that they are *not* best for doing what most test users want them to do, namely to discriminate the good students from the poor students *in college*. Such items measure few dimensions of consequence in college success and duplicate each other to such an extent that probably very few of them are actually functioning.

A few suggestions for improvement may be appropriate. A better item analysis procedure, I think, would be to assemble the answer sheets of 370 students as before (I would prefer *many* more than 370), and then identify not the top and bottom 100 students according to their score on the total test, but the top and bottom 100 students according to their *grades in college*. Items which best separate successful from unsuccessful students would then be selected for subsequent test forms. Actually, several additional item analyses should be carried out to be certain that the tests have *differential* or specific validity. For example, in selecting items for the SAT-Verbal test one should select items which do a much better job in predicting success in verbally oriented courses such as history, English, and the foreign languages, than they do in predicting success in mathematically oriented courses such as chemistry, physics, and trigonometry. One should also want to select items which have a relatively *low* correlation with the total score on the SAT-V—that is, one should *seek* items now judged unsuitable by the ETS test constructors (providing the items have already met a satisfactory standard of external validity, a standard not now set by ETS). Items should be selected for SAT-V which have not only a relatively *low* correlation with the total score on SAT-V, but also *very little* correlation with tests designed to measure different criteria. (The scales of the OAIS, referred to earlier, were constructed in a manner similar to that suggested here.)

NONSTATISTICAL EVALUATION OF CEEB TESTS. A judgment of the merit of the SAT and achievement tests from an inspection of the content of the test items is difficult. While specific items may be found in the tests which seem inadequate in some respects (there has been much criticism of the tests on these grounds), my opinion is that, in general, the face validity of the questions is very good. However, I would prefer to see, for example, the use of many more short questions and a much greater variety of item types in the SAT-Verbal. The general content of each of the achievement tests seems quite appropriate—the biology test contains questions about botany and zoology, not chemistry and physics; the chemistry test contains questions about chemistry, not English usage and mathematics; etc. I would expect that students who *have not had* a course (or a substantial part of one) in biology or chemistry would do poorly on the appropriate achievement test.

However, while each of the tests at first glance seems to assess what it purports to, on further study a serious question arises as to just what determines who gets a high score and who gets a low score. For example, what basic factors account for the variance of scores on the biology, chemistry, and mathematics tests for students who have had courses in these subjects? While each achievement test may be useful for determining whether a student has had a relevant course, there are other much more economical ways of doing this: one is to look at the student's transcript. It is my opinion that *for students who have had a relevant course,* each achievement test functions mainly as a *general* academic ability test.

Similar opinions about the various achievement tests have been expressed elsewhere. For example, in the only previous MMY review of the ECT (see 4:178), Frederick B. Davis and Charlotte Croon Davis had this to say: "Some types of items do not seem to measure primarily aspects of English composition. * These items [previously described], though interesting and well-constructed, appear to measure aspects of literary appreciation and comprehension rather than composition." In the same volume, Robert L. Thorndike (see 4:662) had this to say about the social studies test: "These skills [reading and interpretation skills] are certainly important for college work. Whether the social studies test is the point at which they should be evaluated, rather than the verbal section of the *Scholastic Aptitude Test,* may, perhaps, be debated." The only other previous MMY review of the social studies test (see 5:786) contains additional comment of a related nature by Ralph W. Tyler. Among other things, Tyler felt there was too much emphasis on American history in the test. The social studies test has now been replaced by two tests: American History and Social Studies, and European History and World Cultures. The former title fits better, phenotypically; genotypically, however, American History and Social Studies seems to remain primarily a measure of general verbal ability. Incidentally, pertinent research evidence is not yet available for the new social studies tests, but there seems to be no reason to believe that the results will be either more or less favorable than indicated for the single social studies test in this review.

Readers may find especially interesting the judgmental data I collected for this review. It has to do with what is being measured by the fourth major achievement test of the CEEB, Advanced Mathematics, and by SAT-M. After puzzling over what was really being measured by the items in these tests, I selected 34 of the 50 items in the advanced mathematics test and an equal number from SAT-M and mixed them up for presentation to others. Each of the 68 items was placed on a separate sheet and the problem was to identify which questions were aptitude and which were achievement. It was not surprising for me to see how well the so-called aptitude and so-called achievement test items could be separated. There is no need to give detailed data on the sortings of non-mathematicians beyond saying that some scored near the chance level and that some did about as well as one of the members of the University's mathematics department.

Two members of Michigan's Department of Mathematics were asked to participate. One is an associate professor who has been the University's mathematics placement expert for a number of years and who recently completed a major text for college freshmen; the other is a full professor and chairman of the department. Both men are familiar with the subject matter incoming freshmen must know; about eight years ago they prepared the first edition of the University's mathematics placement examination.

Before the items were classified as either aptitude or achievement the mathematicians were told that the questions appear in the CEEB tests and that between 25 and 75 per cent are classified there as either aptitude or achievement. *By chance sorting alone,* on the average, 34 of the 68 items would be classified *incorrectly,* for one can only be right or wrong about each item (i.e., the classification of 34 items would disagree with the way they are categorized in the tests). After all items were classified the number of disagreements was determined: one mathematician had 18 disagreements, and the other had 24. A total of 33 different questions produced disagreement with the aptitude-achievement classification by the test constructors; both Michigan mathematicians agreed in their disagreement on 9 items. Certainly it is obvious that it is *not obvious* what is measured by many of the questions in the advanced mathematics test and SAT-M.

No one should get the impression from the preceding paragraphs that it would be similarly difficult to distinguish SAT-M items from chemistry test items—it would not. But simply looking at the questions is not good enough for determining what is really being measured. In my opinion the *best evidence* on the nature and quality of the CEEB tests is provided by the statistical data already analyzed.

Perhaps the most dramatic item bearing on the merit of a CEEB achievement test is found in Joshua Fishman's *Research Activities of the College Entrance Examination Board: 1952–57.*[9] It is as follows:

> Candidates taking the physics achievement test in the spring differ in their preparation. This is due to two factors. In some schools with large college-aspiring groups the entire semester's work is crammed into the pretest period. In other schools, pupils still have several months of physics study to complete after their CEEB examination. Furthermore, schools differ somewhat in the exact sequencing of topics in their physics courses, so that, again, certain candidates will have studied given topics by test time, whereas others will not have. What are the score consequences of these differences in pupil preparation? Neither the differences in sequencing of topics, nor the cramming of the entire course into the pretest period produces significantly different test scores.

If the physics test is a good measure of what it purports to measure, differences would have been found. If scores on the test are due mainly to *general academic ability,* differences would not be found. Imagine, for contrast, what would happen if a sample of students in a college physics course were given the instructor's final examination for the course after only two months, and some others were given the examination after four months. The scores on such an achievement examination would almost certainly show rather striking differences.

9 FISHMAN, JOSHUA A. *Research Activities of the College Entrance Examination Board, 1952–57.* Unpublished report, College Entrance Examination Board, New York, N.Y., 1958. Pp. 117. *

MULTIPLE TEST SCORES: UNFORTUNATE CONSEQUENCES. The use of scores from the SAT-V, SAT-M, and, typically, three achievement tests by admissions officers, guidance counselors, and others may be a *major* factor in putting students in inappropriate colleges. If these five tests are mainly measures of general academic ability, but test users believe them to be measures of verbal and mathematical *aptitude* and measures of *proficiency* in, for example, English, history, and chemistry, many incorrect inferences may be drawn. Tests are increasingly being criticized by laymen for isolated but dramatic instances of improper use of test scores. Test producers can be held responsible for only a very few of these relatively rare cases, but they do carry heavy responsibility for the quality of nearly all the decisions made by and about students who take their tests. In my opinion, the amount of damage arising from the *occasional misuse* of CEEB test scores is negligible by comparison with the damage arising from the *routine and intended use* of the SAT and the achievement tests.

Picture a student whose scores on SAT-V and M are high and whose high school grade record is only average. Often the student's high scores on the achievement tests—and they are almost certain to be high if the SAT scores are high—will lead an admissions officer to conclude, "This fellow seems to have learned a lot but the school probably has many able students so his rank underestimates his performance," or, "This fellow seems to have learned a lot but the teachers for some reason did not grade him properly—perhaps he's creative and disruptive." Similarly, there are other students who are not admitted to the college of their choice and the college which is in line with their "total academic promise" because, despite their very superior school record, fine recommendations, etc., they have low scores on not one, not two, but *five* tests! It is quite a different matter, however, to have five low scores (or five high scores) on relatively independent tests, each having specific validity.

Much harm also comes from the judgments that students make about themselves. I shudder to think of the large number of students whose self-conceptions are incorrectly influenced by the CEEB test scores. Picture, for example, the conscientious student who normally scores satisfactorily but not high on tests of intelligence or academic aptitude and whose performance in school is usually superior. He does not expect to do particularly well on the SAT (because he normally does not do particularly well on indicators of aptitude) but he expects to do well on the achievement tests (because he normally does well on indicators of achievement). The relatively low scores he obtains on the achievement tests—and they are almost certain to be low if the SAT scores are low—will shock him as well as his teachers, parents, and others who have seen many evidences of his academic behavior. But here are the highly regarded College Board scores. They indicate a fairly general weakness. The student does not know what the statistical evidence shows about the lack of differential validity in the SAT and the achievement tests and is left to draw his own conclusions from the test titles.

Similarly, there are many poor but bright students who are needlessly encouraged to think of themselves as superior students. After such students get their CEEB scores they often find it possible to rationalize their poor school grades and to criticize their school teachers for not evaluating them properly in the past.

I contend that having multiple measurements of essentially the *same* general ability is a most serious matter. It has led to excessive weight being given to test ability and, probably, test-wiseness. Tested ability is an important factor, but it is not something which should be weighted many more times than is justified. It would be much better to have *one* valid ability test score (such as one might get by obtaining a *total score* from all the items in the SAT-V, SAT-M, and the three achievement tests).

I think it is very important not to report to test users scores which have little or no distinctive meaning. Unless tests have differential validity they should not have different names. That is, I do not believe it wise to report the five CEEB test scores (two "aptitude," three "achievement") *along with* a total score, or an average score. *Only* a total or average score should be reported for the CEEB tests currently available. The use of too many tests to measure general academic ability for admissions purposes is as bad as not using any.

PROPOSED SCHOLASTIC ABILITY TEST. I have already indicated that the research evidence suggests that it is possible to construct satisfactory linguistic and quantitative ability subtests. I would favor the CEEB reporting *two scores* for admissions and guidance purposes. There may be merit in keeping the old subtest labels, Verbal and Mathematical, but in order to convey more accurately its nature, the title of the SAT should probably be changed to Scholastic Ability Test. If major reliance is placed upon *external* rather than *internal* item analysis procedures, as outlined earlier, I am optimistic that two subtests could be developed which would be reasonably independent (i.e., scores would correlate less than .30 with each other, rather than about .65 as is the case with current forms of SAT-V and M) and which would have considerable *differential* validity. A properly revised SAT, containing much more varied content than the present SAT, would probably produce scores sufficiently valid that there would be no statistical advantage in having achievement test scores for the prediction of overall grade-point average.

The new verbal (or linguistic) test might well contain material of the type now in the SAT-V, the English Composition Test, and the two history-social studies tests, as well as new material such as ETS has experimented with (e.g., "literature information," "government information," and "best arguments"). The new mathematical (or quantitative) test probably should contain mostly material of the type now in the SAT-M and the intermediate and advanced mathematics tests.

There is much to be said for having such a revised SAT scheduled three or four times in November and December and restricted to only college-bound students in their *senior* year. It is also suggested that a student *not* be allowed to take this major admissions examination more than once. All students, however, should be encouraged or required to take the PSAT (revised in a manner similar to that suggested for the SAT) in their *junior* year. Since the proposed SAT and PSAT would give similar results (as do the present ones), institutions which desire to inform students early of their chances of admission could do so; final decisions could be made on the basis of the final SAT, high school record, and other information. It is also suggested that the administration of the SAT be handled by high school officials in essentially the same way as the PSAT and language listening tests.

PROPOSED ACHIEVEMENT TESTS. It is my overall feeling that *achievement* tests cannot be constructed which will be satisfactory for college *admissions* purposes, especially if students take such tests at different times during the junior and senior year, even before some have completed the pertinent courses in school, as is now fairly common. The material in the CEEB tests must, almost of necessity, be very "broad-based" (i.e., must contain general ability test material with a little content flavoring) in order to be fair to all applicants. Schools differ markedly in what they teach in courses labeled social studies, English, mathematics, chemistry, biology, French, etc., and tests which are to appear appropriate to them all are not likely to provide good measures of subject matter proficiency in any one of them. The present achievement tests of the CEEB, built so as not to be perceived as too provincial by any group of secondary schools and colleges, are not the kind of achievement tests which will help improve the transition of students to the instructional programs of the colleges.

I would like to see the College Board arrange for the development of about 50 different objective proficiency tests of the type which a college or high school teacher might prepare as a final examination. The tests, each about 45 minutes long, should cover 15 to 20 subjects (e.g., American history, English composition, chemistry, algebra, trigonometry, calculus, and German); there could be two to four examinations for each subject, from which a college would choose the one its students would take. These tests should be administered *no earlier* than May of the senior year to all students *already admitted* to a college; administration should be by officials in each school. The scores would be used for placement and guidance only, not admission.

Each college would examine the tests and specify certain of them (perhaps five to seven) to be taken by *all students* it has admitted and will enroll in the fall. Since there would be only one administration of the tests, and since score reports would be sent only to one college (about July 1, perhaps), the cost of the program would not be great, at least by comparison with the present program. It is suggested that the tests be constructed by subject matter experts *and* test experts who would give adequate attention to the problem of undesirably high correlations among the tests of proficiency, and between the proficiency tests and the Board's main admissions test, the proposed

Scholastic Ability Test. Because each of the present Board achievement tests is constructed more or less independently, it is not surprising that they all tend to measure a more or less *common* academic ability factor. While it is not easy to prepare subject matter tests with specific and appropriate validity, I am confident that it can be done. No agency is better equipped to do it than ETS.

SUMMARY AND CONCLUSION. Surprising as it may seem, there is relatively little research evidence on the merit of the most influential tests used in the United States today. The academic destiny of literally millions of students has been affected by tests which appear to have been inadequately investigated and evaluated. Available research results strongly suggest that the College Board examinations do *not* meet the minimum test standards commonly accepted by members of the testing fraternity. Such a state of affairs is not a happy one to report upon, for the major architect and producer of the tests and research is the Educational Testing Service, a leading force in the struggle for better tests. Over the years many members of ETS have made important contributions to testing; it is disappointing indeed to find that the combined effort of some of them must be judged unsatisfactory.

It would be kind to say that the tests have not been in existence long enough to permit their utility to be demonstrated, but it would be incorrect. An objective appraisal by the officers of the CEEB and ETS of the Board's testing program is urgently needed, and long overdue. It is to be hoped that such a self-study would culminate not only in fewer tests measuring general academic ability, but also in a more varied test offering, including measures of personality and interest factors which are important in the academic setting. The competitive situation created a few years ago by the introduction of the American College Testing Program will, hopefully, stimulate a number of improvements. Many opportunities exist. The needs of higher education in this country require a more creative approach than is apparent in the tradition-laden test offering which the CEEB pioneered many years ago.

I should hasten to add, before I am misinterpreted, that I do not regard the present CEEB-ETS tests as inferior to the ACT tests. Figures are not yet available to make a proper comparison. Several bits of evidence I have seen suggest that the tests will not differ significantly with respect to either predictive or differential validity (i.e., both appear to have adequate predictive validity and inadequate differential validity).

With respect to the CEEB tests, my advice to colleges is to require the SAT (even if it is not revised as suggested herein), and not to require the achievement tests (even though minor changes in the tests continue to be made). The SAT and the achievement tests duplicate each other to an extreme degree. Because the achievement tests are not good measures of what they purport to measure, they should not be used for admission, placement, or guidance purposes. In this reviewer's opinion, more harm than good results from their use. Certainly the substantial fees charged students should have enabled the Board to produce superior assessment devices. If a better testing program cannot be imagined and developed by the officers of the CEEB and ETS, then many needlessly erroneous decisions with far-reaching effects will continue to be made.

DEAN K. WHITLA, *Director, Office of Tests, Harvard University, Cambridge, Massachusetts.*

The current aptitude and achievement test battery of the College Entrance Examination Board represents several decades of effort on the part of member colleges and testing specialists to devise instruments for assessing the academic preparation and promise of college applicants. The importance of this testing program in current college admission work is highlighted when we consider that in 1946 Board membership was comprised of 53 colleges, while as of 1963, 543 institutions of higher education (as well as 204 secondary schools and 43 educational associations) belonged to this organization.

As the program has expanded, the impact of the College Board tests has become multifaceted. While they had their genesis as selection devices for college admissions, they have now assumed concomitant or, as critics have suggested, displaced roles in education: they serve also as bench marks for evaluating the quality of secondary school instruction, as determinants of curriculum, as the focus for special tutoring instruction, and as instruments for placement within the college curriculum. Some critics see the tests' effects as even more profound and criticize them for the sterility they produce in thinking as a result of their multiple choice format and their demands for convergent, rather than divergent, thinking.

The degree of interest evidenced today is a function of the increased importance these tests play or seem to play in admissions decisions. When the number of candidates was few and the number of colleges requiring these tests was also few, the impact of the tests at the national level was negligible. Now, however, with the growing number of colleges and candidates involved and with the national cognizance of the College Board program, the Board serves as both a filter for ideas in higher education as they reach out to the secondary school systems and as a feedback system from these schools to the colleges. An important aspect of this organization, then, is that in a real sense it is a resonating board, presenting in its work and testing program a blending of demands made or expectations expressed by a variety of colleges serving various regions of the country, and influencing school programs by way of its expressions of college concerns.

While the College Board is a membership organization, its operations are run by professional and technical personnel staffing the parent office and the operating organization, Educational Testing Service. The membership guides policy, and representatives of the member colleges actively contribute by serving on test committees that oversee new developments in the tests and participate in test construction. While the professional staff has attempted, through seminars, to create among member colleges a dialogue whereby prediction techniques and such problems as interpretation and uses of scores can be considered, such programs and associated research could well be extended and made even more comprehensive.

The College Board tests are administered in two sections—the morning session or Scholastic Aptitude Test and the afternoon or achievement testing program. There are five major administrations during the year at testing centers throughout the country and the world.

Test scheduling presents problems of two types. To take the tests, a candidate must register well in advance of the testing date. Clerical tasks—the shipping of tests, the mailing of tickets for admission to the center—take time, time which is normally available; however, final registration dates closer to the actual administration would be advantageous. Second, there is a considerable delay between the date of test administration and the date scores are reported to schools and colleges. The facility with which ETS handles the volume of testing is certainly creditable, but, hopefully, new techniques can be employed which will expedite the score reporting process even more.

In 1962–63, 933,839 SAT's were administered, of which 56.9 per cent were taken by boys and 43.1 per cent by girls. In addition, 364,279 candidates sat for an achievement test series. The growth of the achievement testing program has been greater over a four-year period (1959–63) than that of the SAT. The difference in rates of growth was most marked between 1960–61 and 1961–62 when aptitude testing increased 11.2 per cent while achievement testing increased 29.6 per cent. Growth from 1961–62 to 1962–63 was at the rate of 16.3 per cent and 18.5 per cent for the SAT and the achievement tests, respectively. The ECT is the most popular of the achievement series; it was taken by 75.8 per cent of those who took Board achievement tests in 1962–63. Intermediate Mathematics was the second most popular test, taken by 46.5 per cent of the group taking achievement tests in 1962–63. The language listening tests, administered only once a year and given at the student's high school, show large percentage increases since their introduction in 1960, though they obviously account for a very small portion of the CEEB testing program (about 24,000 students took a listening test in 1962–63 as compared with about 18,000 in 1961–62). The listening tests seem to have met with the approval of language teachers; more frequent administrations of these tests should be encouraged.

THE SAT AND PSAT. In June of 1926, 8,000 candidates sat for the first administration of the SAT. As previously mentioned, over 900,000 candidates took this test in 1962–63, with over 850,000 students sitting for the *Preliminary Scholastic Aptitude Test* (a shorter and somewhat less difficult instrument taken by secondary school students, primarily juniors). The availability of the PSAT gives the candidate an opportunity to "practice" in his junior year or very early in his senior year at one fifth the cost of the SAT, as well as giving him information for guidance purposes. One limitation to this pattern of testing is that the PSAT does not constitute an acceptable substitute for the SAT; the latter must be taken in the senior year. Most colleges will, however, accept scores from the SAT taken in the junior year if a candidate wishes to submit them for admissions purposes.

The SAT is designed to measure "the general ability to use language and mathematical concepts in the solution of the kinds of intellectual problems the candidate would encounter in college." From its inception, it has been an evolving test with provisions for maintaining stability of scores. An interesting illustration of the way in which the SAT evolves in response to educational need is reported by Coffman.[1] In the early 1940's educators at large were acknowledging that coaching by teachers in vocabulary and techniques was possible (though there was little evidence of its success) because of known characteristics of the test, such as "double definition" items. The test of 1947, therefore, differed considerably from previous forms; candidates were required to read prose passages of graded difficulty and answer content-based questions (types of exercises not previously used). Such passages have since become standard SAT fare. Recent studies of the effects of tutoring[2] have indicated that the improvement in scores of tutored students is less than the standard error of measurement of the test.

SAT CONTENT.[3] Of all the types of verbal items which have appeared in the SAT, the antonym has the longest history of continuous usage. Except for a brief period in the early 1930's, all the operational sections of the SAT have also included some form of analogy items. As noted above, reading comprehension items began to be used in 1947 and have been part of the test since that year.

On the mathematical portions of the test, five-choice items covering arithmetic, algebra, and geometry have been used since 1943. Early forms of the test utilized fairly simple word problems and number series completion items, and, for a period, candidates were asked to provide free responses to word and computation problems. It is interesting that in 1928 and 1929 and from 1936 to 1941, the SAT content was limited to verbal items; during the latter period, a separate mathematics attainment test was used. From 1926 to 1960, 65 editions of the test containing 38 different major item types had been prepared.

In creating present-day forms of the SAT, the test constructors attempt a stratified sampling of content. In describing current test content and its evolution Loret states:

> current editions of the SAT contain approximately equal numbers of items from the aesthetic-philosophical, human relationships area, scientific world, and world of practical affairs....passages for the reading comprehension items are drawn systematically from material in four areas: biological science, physical science, social studies, and the humanities. Within each area, insofar as possible, three types of writing are sampled: narration, exposition, and argumentation. * the mathematical sections have tended to move away from common use of computational problems.... toward considerably greater emphasis on other aspects of mathematical aptitude *

Separate verbal and mathematical scores have been reported since 1942.

CULTURAL BIAS. Coffman's recent review of the SAT suggests that the test is generally uncontaminated by cultural bias and contends that any cultural bias that might exist does not invalidate the test as a college admission device, for it is equally predictive of grades for any type of candidate. Two of the studies he reports, however, seem to suggest contradictory findings in this area. One study concluded that candidates with foreign born parents do better in college than would have been predicted from their SAT scores and high school record. The second study concluded that working class and rural men did not do as well in college as would be expected on the basis of SAT scores and high school rank. I can only suggest that we are presented here with a moot question.

At present what we know about the SAT and its functioning is essentially pragmatic: scores can generally be accepted as indicative of level of academic potential for college work and they do indicate verbal and mathematical aptitudes. To date we do not have a firm idea of the differentiated and fundamental mental processes the test is assessing. Its content is structured along lines that reflect the education

1 COFFMAN, WILLIAM E. *The Scholastic Aptitude Test—1926–62.* Unpublished report, Educational Testing Service, Princeton, N.J., June 1963. Pp. 26. *

2 See, for example, the reviewer's article, "Effect of Tutoring on Scholastic Aptitude Test Scores." *Personnel & Guid J* 41:32–7 S '62. *

3 The information in this section is drawn from *A History of the Content of the Scholastic Aptitude Test*, by Peter G. Loret. Unpublished report, Educational Testing Service, Princeton, N.J., October 1960. Pp. ii, 132. *

given throughout our public and independent schools.

Another point of view on the problem of cultural bias has implications for admissions as a whole. While the test is not designed to identify undeveloped talent, it has still made a significant social contribution. The most vehement of the critics of the multiple choice aptitude and achievement tests, and of the College Board tests in particular, have, it seems to this reviewer, ignored an important service rendered by these tests: youth from all the social strata of this country know the opportunity for higher education has been transformed—from a dream in the early years of this century to a growing reality in this decade—in goodly measure through the use of these instruments. Such testing has had, in short, a tremendous favorable influence on the great sorting process that is college admissions, for it encourages an ability sort rather than a social strata sort.

ACHIEVEMENT TESTS. ETS, serving as the operating arm of the CEEB, places the responsibility for achievement test items on committees composed of selected members from secondary school and college faculties. Such committees, with supporting psychometric personnel from the ETS staff, make an interesting amalgamation of effort.

Three of the examiners on each committee are college teachers, one is a public school teacher, and one is a teacher in an independent secondary school. Committee members are selected not only for excellence in their subject areas, but also for their knowledge of the subject curriculum in secondary schools and colleges. Their domain covers the questions that will compose each test, and their decisions are thus concerned with the topics to be covered in the test in their field and the emphasis to be given each topic. Some of the new questions for test forms are written by these examiners; others are written by the staff at ETS. A tryout test is administered to several hundred students. Then this set of questions is subjected to item analysis to determine the difficulty of each item and its effectiveness in discriminating between good and poor students judged on the basis of total score on the test.

In response to the rapidly changing curriculum in secondary schools, the last several years have brought marked changes in the achievement tests. There are, however, difficulties inherent in responding to changes in secondary instruction that arise in locally autonomous school systems, for it is impossible to have a limited series of achievement tests that will correspond to the objectives of such a variety of curricula.

Another dilemma concerning the achievement tests is that of scheduling. Cause for concern is the discrepancy between the ideal time for administering the tests, which would be late spring (especially for subjects studied only one year in secondary school, such as chemistry and physics), and the date earlier in the academic year by which colleges must have the scores if they are to be part of the admission process. The achievement test scores have become widely used not only for selecting among applicants but also for college placement.

THE ENGLISH COMPOSITION TEST AND THE WRITING SAMPLE. Two associated tests, the ECT and the Writing Sample, undoubtedly constitute the Board's most controversial offerings. Critics have often assailed the validity of multiple choice tests as measures of candidates' ability to write. Furthermore, it is argued that the multiple choice approach might encourage schools to avoid their instructional responsibilities in composition.

The forms of the ECT for the past several years have been mainly of multiple choice type, sometimes including a prose passage containing mistakes and garbled material, which the student must change and correct on the test booklet and which is hand graded. The ECT form I inspected included this 30-minute "interlinear" exercise and two other sections covering correct usage of words, grammar or idiom, and recognition of errors in diction, grammar, sentence structure, and style (as the test directions indicate, verbosity, redundancy, clichés, and abused metaphors). Paragraph organization, construction shift, and prose groups (where the student selects from four possible answers the most appropriate one to take the place of a missing sentence in a paragraph) are other types of items frequently used.

Because the ECT has been especially open to criticism, a Committee of Examiners has recently completed a study to determine its effectiveness as a measure of writing ability. For a lucid and complete review by a College Board staff member of current developments in the test and of the research that has been carried out during this study, I refer the reader to an article by Edward S. Noyes in the *College Board Review*.[4] The study was especially relevant because it attacked the problem of test validity by attempting to solve first, the criterion problem: an appropriate alternate measure of writing ability. Five different readers scored five essays for each of a sample of 646 students from eleventh and twelfth grades in 24 schools. The readers used holistic (scores of 3, 2, 1) scoring and the 25 ratings (5 ratings on each of 5 essays) were added to obtain a student's total essay score. The total score became the "pure" criterion of writing ability against which scores on eight types of ECT subtests (all but one, the interlinear exercise, of objective type) and, later, a single essay or combination of the essays, were compared. Correlations between the eight subtests and the criterion of writing ability ranged from .71 to .46. The best prediction of writing ability was obtained when a 20-minute essay plus objective subsections were combined with the PSAT or SAT Verbal score; such a combination produced multiple correlations ranging from .73 to .79. In the light of these results, the Board's Committee on Examinations has authorized the examiners in English to use a theme as one of the subtests of the ECT.

If an essay is included as part of the ECT, it is hard to justify the use of the Writing Sample, especially in the light of a recent study at Amherst which explored this test and its relevancy to admissions. The Writing Sample requires the student to write a composition on one of several alternate topics. A copy of the essay is sent, ungraded, to the admissions offices of colleges to which the candidate is applying. Dean Wilson of Amherst read and graded Writing Sample essays of candidates for admissions in 1961. His ratings of these essays were subjected to a validity study conducted by Dyer at Educational Testing Service.[5] Dyer found that adding grades given on the Writing Sample to the usual objective measures used in predicting college grades produced practically no increase in the prediction of grade averages. When the Writing Sample was substituted for the ECT it did not increase the prediction at all. A small increase was found in the prediction of English grades, but even this was not significant. Stressing that I am dealing here only with problems of academic grade prediction, I must conclude that, in this one documented case at least, an essay examination graded at the admitting college did not reveal or contribute new insights into a candidate's potential for college level work.

These findings provoke questions that the ECT study cannot answer, for college grades were not the criterion in that study. Since the Dyer study demonstrated that at Amherst the Writing Sample did not add to grade prediction beyond that possible using the ECT without the essay, the need for additional research in naturalistic settings seems apparent.

VALIDITY. Over the long history of the SAT, there has been a policy of encouraging continuous study by colleges of the validity of the test for their own students. The rationale for such a policy is simply that the criterion of "college success" is varying and complex. Colleges have accepted this suggestion and, from a variety of CEEB and ETS sources, there is evidence that thousands of such studies have been conducted. Unfortunately, the results of these studies have not been summarized and made accessible. It is impossible to determine whether the fluctuation in the ability of any test or performance variable to predict college grades is due to differences in admission procedures, student populations, or college environments.

Because it is difficult to obtain good criterion measures, there has been a tendency to use the test specifications as their own justification, as indicated in such statements as the following which appears in *College Board Score Reports: A Guide for Admissions Officers:* "A test prepared by teachers competent in the subject matter area covered normally has a high degree of apparent validity independent of any statistical verification." There have been encouraging signs that external criteria are being used more frequently, as in the study of the ECT.

As a brief overview of the magnitude of correlations that have been found in recent research by Olsen,[6] French,[7] and others, summaries are provided in Table 1.

Table 1 indicates that SAT-Verbal is in

4 NOYES, EDWARD S. "Essay and Objective Tests in English." *Col Board R* 49:7–11 w '63. *
5 "Advocate of Writing Sample Puts Judgment to the Test." *ETS Develop* 11:2 Ja '63. *

6 OLSEN, MARJORIE. *Summary of Main Findings on the Validity of the CEEB Tests of Developed Ability as Predictors of College Grades.* Unpublished report, Educational Testing Service, Princeton, N.J., October 1957. Pp. 59. *
7 FRENCH, JOHN W. *The Validity of New Tests for the Performance of College Students With High-Level Aptitude.* Unpublished report, Educational Testing Service, Princeton, N.J., March 1963. Pp. iii, 32, plus appendix. *

Table 1
Median Correlations Between College Grades and SAT-V, SAT-M, High School Grades, and Linear Combinations of These Predictors With and Without Achievement Tests

Predictors	Engineering Men	Liberal Arts Men	Liberal Arts Women
SAT-V	.22 (n = 17)	.38 (25)	.36 (14)
SAT-M	.28 (16)	.31 (25)	.27 (14)
SAT-V, M	.40 (5)	.50 (7)	.39 (6)
HS Grades	.39 (18)	.48 (43)	.48 (34)
SAT-V, M, HS Grades	.58 (9)	.59 (25)	.67 (29)
SAT-V, M, HS Grades, Achievement Tests	.58 (14)	.64 (8)	.67 (6)

Note: n = number of colleges.

general a better predictor of liberal arts college grades than is SAT-Mathematical, while the reverse is true for engineering colleges. The best linear combination of V and M scores is of comparable predictive power to high school grades for the men's colleges (liberal arts and engineering) but is of less value for women's colleges. When these three variables are combined, they improve the prediction of grades over that of the SAT-V and M or high school grades alone. There also tends to be a slight improvement when achievement test scores are added as a fourth predictor variable.

The fact that three hours of paper and pencil aptitude testing produces as powerful a predictor of college achievement as does the high school record testifies to the validity of the SAT. That such a phenomenon continues to hold over long experience with the CEEB tests supports claims of their relevance as assessors of the educational process.

This table, however, had to be assembled by the writer from data scattered through various ETS-CEEB reports which are not generally available, and it constitutes only a rough approximation of the table that should have been available to test users, had the problem of validity been given the concerted attention it deserves.

There are some inherent limitations in the above data. The sample of colleges was arbitrary, including schools where ETS was conducting some research project or schools which, having completed their own studies, made the results available in response to interest expressed by the CEEB. While colleges located in all areas of the country are included, the New England and Atlantic states are overrepresented. Colleges with a variety of mean scores are included but the means tend to be somewhat higher than those of CEEB colleges in general. A further limitation is that the studies summarized in the table cover a span of years—a period of great change for many schools—and include schools with different selection criteria, a factor which tends to influence the standard deviation of the scores and consequently the magnitude of the correlations. Clearly the effects of candidates' choice of college and college admissions procedures (both generally tending to increase homogeneity of the student group) increase the problem of validity for a particular college population.

One of the questions always asked of a multitest battery concerns the size of the correlations among the subtests. The correlations between SAT-V and M have ranged from a low of .38 in December 1946 to a high of .77 in June 1949. During the most recent five-year period for which data were available (1958–62), a period during which the SAT specifications have been similar to the current forms, the V and M scores have had a median intercorrelation of .64. Analyses of subscores by item types have indicated that changing item style has not increased the correlations between the two parts of the test.

Data from a number of studies at various colleges show that while the V-M correlation is less than that reported from the College Board sample (as would be expected because of range restriction in individual college populations), interestingly the magnitude of these correlations is not a simple function of the heterogeneity of those enrolled in the colleges. However, this finding may be an artifact of the action of college admissions committees since this material was compiled on enrolled students. Research, therefore, should be directed not only toward understanding the changes in the V-M relationships; it should also encompass examination of the interrelationships among the total battery. At those colleges requiring the achievement tests as well as the SAT, the test user makes an overall evaluation of the candidates' scores, seldom basing his assessment on the presence of a single strong or weak score. Since the aptitude and achievement series can effectively be considered a battery, the absence of an intercorrelation matrix constitutes a serious limitation in the currently available information. With the exception of the V and M relationship and the PSAT-SAT relationship, only incidental evidence has been accumulated for the series.

SCALING. From the first offering of the SAT in 1926, scores have been reported on a scale with a mean of 500 and a standard deviation of 100. Until 1941 this scale was reestablished on the basis of each group tested; in 1941 the scale was fixed in terms of the group of students examined in April of that year. To retain the 1941 frame of reference there has been a linkage of items between successive forms of the test. Since 1955 a more elegant system of equating has been employed, called "double part-score equating." [8] Essentially, this method calls for two independent equating procedures to be conducted for each form of the test. Data are collected from four samples of students, two of which take the new form of the test, plus a set of equating items (a different set for each group), while the two other groups take an old form (a different form for each group) plus the equating items. From these data, two equations are obtained; the conversion equation is derived from the line which bisects these two derivations. This process uses one "old" form a year old and a second "old" form three or four years old, thus minimizing any chance of drift in scores. In addition, for this interlocking procedure old forms are alternated. This procedure has inherent self-correcting properties, the effect of which is demonstrated by the great proximity of conversion lines derived.

In simpler terms, the equating procedure means that, regardless of test difficulty or ability level of the particular group taking the test at any administration, a student's score on a particular SAT form "represents the same level of performance as that same score on any other form of the test." The research efforts in this area have had to deal with the special problems of changing student populations and forms of the test.

The achievement tests consisted of essay tests until lack of readers during the war forced the replacement of essays by multiple choice tests. At that time the new achievement tests were scaled to the SAT. When the SAT scores of groups of students taking the various achievement tests were examined, it became evident that these groups did not possess equal aptitude; students who took the Latin test had higher abilities (SAT scores) than did those taking the Spanish test; similarly those taking Advanced Mathematics had higher abilities than those who took Intermediate Mathematics. To eliminate the effect of the differences in SAT scores of groups taking the various tests, the achievement tests were scaled by regression equations to the SAT. The use of a regression equation insures that achievement tests which correlate highly with the SAT-V or M will have mean scaled scores similar to the SAT-V or M score of the tested groups of students; if the SAT-V and M scores have no correlation with an achievement test, the mean of that test will be 500 and the sigma 100.

Since that initial scaling procedure, the achievement tests have been scaled using the scores on items common to both the old and new forms of the tests. There is no evidence that the complicated "double part-score" scaling system has been used with the achievement tests. Some long overdue experimental procedures are now underway to determine whether, over a period of years, the scales of the achievement tests have drifted from their original scaling ties to the SAT scale.

While the equivalency of scores among all of these tests has been widely accepted, there remains an underlying illogicalness to the idea that a physics test score is comparable to a Latin test score. In fairness to the CEEB, it should be noted that the Board has recognized this limitation and recommends that scrupulous attention be given the normative data which are available.

NORMS. The long and widespread use of the CEEB series has provided an opportunity for the compilation of an extensive set of supporting statistics. The most recent published norming data are based on the results of the December 1960 and March 1961 tests. Another source of norms as well as other information supplied by the colleges themselves is the *Manual of Freshman Class Profiles* (*20*), an excellent addition to the CEEB series of publications. In *College Board Scores* (*11–2*), norms (based on 1952–56 testing) are available for many of the tests for groups separated by amount of educational preparation, sex, and public-independent school background. For some of the achievement tests, the number of categories for

[8] ANGOFF, WILLIAM H., AND WAITE, ANNETTE C. *A Study of Double Part-Score Equating for the Scholastic Aptitude Test.* Unpublished report, Educational Testing Service, Princeton, N.J., August 1959. Pp. 12. *

which norms are available is impressive. This is exemplified by those given for the ECT (*11*); there are means for candidates grouped by the extent to which their schools use essay examinations, by the number of American and British prose writers read, by number of poets read, by extent of Bible reading, by number of Shakespearian plays read, by amount of long and short theme writing, by time and courses devoted to creative writing, and by amount of speech making and dramatics, and percentile norms for candidates grouped by interest in English, by amount of writing and reading, and by amount of foreign language studied, as well as by the usual categories. Helpful summations and evaluations of this material are also available, showing that girls perform better than boys on the ECT; that independent school students perform better than those from public schools; that those who did more writing and had more interest in English did better on the ECT than their comparable counterparts; that the group interested in writing had higher scores than the actual writers; and that the group that did the most reading also scored higher than did those who wrote more. These findings are interesting since they represent differences found for groups with comparable SAT-V scores.

While norms are available for many different student groupings, most noticeably ~~absent~~ are categorizations by social data. Some measure of socioeconomic status should have been used in addition to public-private secondary school attendance, for this latter breakdown does not successfully differentiate between students of middle class background and those of disadvantaged background. Categorizations by amount of parental education and income and by regional grouping would also be informative. Such data could have favorable effects on educational offerings as well as provide an index for evaluating the strength of a candidate's performance within his own cultural setting (the same dimension involved in the use of rank in class). These data would also make available for the serious student of norms a method of evaluating the degree of cultural bias in the tests.

According to a national norming study conducted in 1959 and based on a random sample of secondary school seniors, the SAT-V score of 500 was at the 85th percentile. To give another perspective, the average secondary school senior received a score of 360, with the standard deviation for the group approximating 120 points. Thus a score of 800 would be 3.7 standard deviations above the mean, while one of 200 would be 1.3 standard deviations below the mean. Less than 15 per cent of these unselected seniors would be expected to score below 200.

RELIABILITY. The Kuder-Richardson formula 20 coefficients of reliability for the 14 forms of the SAT administered between 1959 and 1962 varied from a low of .88 to a high of .91 for Verbal and from a low of .87 to a high of .91 for Mathematical. The corresponding standard errors of measurement ranged from 30 to 34 scaled score points for SAT-V and from 31 to 37 points for SAT-M. These measures seem relatively stable; test-retest correlations for two forms administered with an intervening interval of up to 10 months are reported by Coffman to have run about .89 for SAT-V and .85 for the SAT-M.

Average reliabilities of the achievement tests administered in 1960 and 1961 range from .85 to .96 with a median of .90. The ECT is one of the two tests with the lowest average reliability (.85), a factor seriously limiting the upper bound of validity that can be obtained with this test and, consequently, making the findings of the ECT study very remarkable. (The 1962 form of the ECT, however, had a reliability of .90.) The shorter timing of the PSAT-Verbal test undoubtedly is the cause for its average reliability (.86) being less than that of the SAT-V (.90). The other tests showing average reliabilities below .90 are those gauging mathematical skills (SAT-M, Advanced Mathematics, and Intermediate Mathematics) and two of the language listening tests (French and Spanish). The reason cited for the lower reliabilities of the mathematics tests is that it takes longer for students to respond to items of a mathematical type; consequently, there is less opportunity for the test to sample as widely the extent of their knowledge in a test period as can other achievement tests. Conversely, however, it would seem that the domain of mathematical knowledge would be more easily encompassed than that of the verbal areas of knowledge.

Considering the score range of 600 points (200–800) and the general positioning of the scale (a mean of 500 in the original standardizing population or a 360 mean for an unselected secondary school senior population), we would expect that standard errors ranging from 30 to 35 points would adequately meet college needs for differentiating among students. Due to the homogeneity of scores among college applicant groups, however, the ratio of the error to the score sigma for many colleges falls in the range of 1:2 (35:70) rather than 1:3 (35:100) as in the candidate population. If the trend toward score homogeneity continues, reliability as well as validity can become a problem of significant proportions.

SUMMARY. The public criticisms of testing programs, of which the CEEB tests have been a major target, are by and large unfounded. The criticism should rather be directed to the source of the antagonism, those admission officers who avoid their responsibilities in the assessment process by overemphasizing the importance of scores and accepting test results as infallible judgments of aptitude and achievement. The CEEB admissions series merits the respect it has received from the educational community. There is extensive evidence that the great care and expertise exercised in the preparation of these tests have produced an outstanding battery. While the series of achievement tests has a history of innovative change that is not equaled by the Scholastic Aptitude Test, the arguments for stressing stability and evolutionary change in the latter instrument are persuasive, especially since it is a good test in its current form.

For reviews of individual tests, see 287, 289, 383–4, 449, 568–9, 914, and 966–7; for reviews of earlier forms, see 5:272, 5:277, 5:280, 5:318, 5:723, 5:742, 5:749, 5:786, 4:178, 4:237, and 4:367.

[761]

***College Entrance Examination Board Advanced Placement Examinations.** High school students desiring credit for college level courses or admission to advanced courses; 1954–63; tests administered annually in May at participating secondary schools and other centers established by the publisher; 11 tests: American History (see 1000), Biology (see 893), Chemistry (see 915), English (see 254), European History (see 1001), French (see 368), German (see 385), Latin (see 405), Mathematics (see 570), Physics (see 927), Spanish (see 421); coordinator's manual ('62, 47 pages); bulletin of information for coordinators ('63, 12 pages); bulletin of information for students ('63, 11 pages); course and examination description booklet ('62, 151 pages); no technical data distributed with test materials; separate Scribe answer sheets must be used for objective sections of tests; examination fee: $5 plus $10 for each test taken; fee includes reporting of scores to the college the candidate plans to attend (the candidate's graded test booklets and his secondary school's recommendations and description of courses taken are also supplied); scores also reported, at a later date, to the secondary school; specimen sets of the essay sections of previous tests available at $2 per complete set of essay sections from all tests or $1 per 5 copies of the essay section of any one test; specimen sets of objective sections not available; $6 per tape for listening comprehension section of previous test in Spanish (tapes for other language tests not available); $1.50 per course and examination description booklet; postpaid; 180(200) minutes; program administered for the College Entrance Examination Board by Educational Testing Service. *

REFERENCES

1. COLLEGE ENTRANCE EXAMINATION BOARD, COMMISSION ON ADVANCED PLACEMENT, BAYES M. NORTON, CHAIRMAN. *Advanced Placement Program.* New York: the Board, 1956. Pp. 136. * (*PA* 30:7756)
2. PEARSON, RICHARD. "Advanced Placement Program: Opportunities Ahead." *Col Board R* 39:24–6 f '59. *
3. WILCOX, EDWARD T. "Advanced Placement at Harvard." *Col Board R* 41:17–20 sp '60. *
4. CAMERON, BEN F., JR. "Advanced Placement Examinations." *Ed Leadership* 20:30–3+ O '62. *
5. COLLEGE ENTRANCE EXAMINATION BOARD, COMMITTEE ON ADVANCED PLACEMENT, 1962, THOMAS C. MENDENHALL, CHAIRMAN. *Advanced Placement Program: Course Descriptions.* New York: the Board, 1963. Pp. 152. *

For reviews of individual tests, see 893 and 1000; for reviews of earlier forms, see 5:205, 5:211, 5:273, 5:419, 5:724, 5:743, 5:750, and 5:812.

[762]

***The Graduate Record Examinations.** College through graduate school; 1937–64; 2 programs; score interpretation booklet ('58, 25 pages); supplement ('59, 18 pages); revised supervisor's manual ('63, 24 pages); separate Scribe answer sheets must be used; Educational Testing Service. * See separate test entries referred to below for references on specific tests.

a) NATIONAL PROGRAM FOR GRADUATE SCHOOL SELECTION. Graduate school entrants; 1942–64; tests administered 5 times annually (November, January, March, April, July) at centers established by the publisher; prospectus for deans and advisers ('63, 13 pages); bulletin of information for candidates ('63, 34 pages); score interpretation leaflet for candidates (no date, 6 pages); examination fees: $7 for morning session (Aptitude Test), $8 for afternoon session (1 Advanced Test), $12 for both morning and afternoon sessions; fees include reporting of scores to the candidate and 1–3 schools designated at time of application; $1 per additional report; postpaid.

1) *Aptitude Test.* See 461; 1949–63; 2 scores: verbal, quantitative; 150(170) minutes.

2) *Advanced Tests.* 1939–64; candidates elect 1 test as specified by individual college requirements; 17 tests: Biology (see 896), Chemistry (see 919), Economics (see 987), Education (see 698), Engineering (see 1132), French (see 376), Geology (see 922), Government (see 1018), History (see 1003), Literature (see 299), Mathematics (see 578), Philosophy (see 741), Physical Education (see 722), Physics (see 931), Psychology (see 743), Sociology (see 1021), Spanish (see 425); 180(200) minutes.

b) INSTITUTIONAL TESTING PROGRAM. College and graduate school; 1937–64; tests available for institutional testing at any time except dates on which National Program for Graduate School Selection is scheduled;

institution must agree to test all students in at least one administrative group; 3 parts; examiner's manual ('63, 42 pages); handbook for deans and examiners ('63, 11 pages); prospectus for students (no date, 8 pages); score interpretation leaflet for students ('62, 6 pages); $2.50 per any 1 test (Area Tests, Aptitude Test, an Advanced Test); $4.50 per any 2 tests; $6 per any 3 tests; fees include scoring service and report of scores to the institution; individual students may have transcripts (Aptitude Test and Advanced Test scores only) sent to other institutions for a fee of $1 per transcript; postage extra; administration must be completed within 1 week.

1) *The Area Tests.* See 9; 1954–63; 3 scores: social science, humanities, natural science; 210(240) minutes.

2) *Aptitude Test.* See *a1* above.

3) *Advanced Tests.* 20 tests: same as *a2* above plus Music (see 348), Scholastic Philosophy (see 742), Speech (see 309); 180(200) minutes except for Music, 105(125) minutes.

REFERENCES

1–24. See 4:527.
25–36. See 5:601.
37. GRUBER, EDWARD C. *How to Pass High on the Graduate Record Examination.* New York: Arco Publishing Co., Inc., 1962. Pp. iv, 164, plus supplements. *

For a review by Harold Seashore, see 5:601. For reviews of individual tests, see 9, 376, 461, 578, 698, 919, 931, and 1021; for reviews of earlier forms, see 5:10, 5:215, 5:220, 5:247, 5:270, 5:336, 5:427, 5:537, 5:583, 5:727, 5:754, 5:818, and 5:835.

[763]

★National Guidance Testing Program. Grades 4–14; 1958–64; a scoring service for the *Cooperative School and College Ability Tests* and the *Sequential Tests of Educational Progress;* tests administered during 2 periods (September–November or February–May) by individual schools (may be administered at other times with delayed scoring service); score reports based on the regular norms available for the tests administered; local means and standard deviations reported to schools (no data summarizing the program test results are gathered or reported); bulletin of information ['64, 11 pages] for schools; separate Scribe answer sheets must be used (a single answer sheet is used regardless of number of tests administered); $2 per 20 Scribe answer sheets; scoring fee: 30¢ per student; postage extra; fee includes scoring service, 4 list reports of scores, permanent record slip for each student, and report of means and standard deviations for groups of 25 or more; 5¢ per student for duplicate permanent record slip; 2¢ per student for optional IBM work card; 20¢ per student for report of local norms (service available only when 100 or more students per grade have been tested); tests, manuals, and other accessories extra (see STEP and SCAT entries for prices); 70–490(80–560) minutes depending on number of tests administered; Cooperative Test Division. *

[764]

★Project Talent Test Battery: A National Inventory of Aptitudes and Abilities. Grades 9–12; 1960–61; for research use and normative studies only; MRC; 5 booklets containing 21 tests and 3 questionnaires; teachers' guide ('60, 41 pages); appendix ('60, 8 pages); counselor's technical manual ('61, 50 pages) for interpreting scores from the national testing program; tentative norms; separate answer sheets must be used; tests loaned and scored by publisher only; details available from publisher; $3 per specimen set, postpaid; 4 half-day sessions for the complete battery; University of Pittsburgh Project Talent Office. *

a) TEST BOOKLET A. 1 form ('60, 16 pages); 3 tests, 26 scores; 113(125) minutes.

1) *Information Test—Part 1.* 16 scores: screening, vocabulary, literature, music, social studies, mathematics, physical science, biological science, scientific attitude, aeronautics and space, electricity and electronics, mechanics, farming, home economics, sports, total; 90(95) minutes.

2) *Student Activities Inventory.* 10 scores: sociability, social sensitivity, impulsiveness, vigor, calmness, tidiness, culture, leadership, self-confidence, mature personality; 20(25) minutes.

3) [*Preferences Test.*] Characteristics preferred in friends and associates; 3(5) minutes.

b) TEST BOOKLET B. 1 form ('60, 32 pages); 3 tests, 30 scores; 135(150) minutes.

1) *Interest Inventory.* 17 scores: physical science-engineering, biological science-medicine, computation, mechanical-technical, skilled trades, literary-linguistic, social service, public service, musical, artistic, business management, sales, office work, labor, farming, outdoor recreation, sports; 20(25) minutes.

2) *Information Test—Part 2.* 13 scores: art, law, medicine, engineering, architecture, military, accounting-business-sales, Bible, hunting and fishing, other outdoor activities, theater and ballet, miscellaneous, total; 35(40) minutes.

3) *Student Information Blank.* Personal and family background data, activities, experiences, and plans; supplement ['60, 7 pages]; directions for using supplement ['60, 2 pages]; 80(85) minutes.

c) TEST BOOKLET C1-X. 1 test (arithmetic computation) plus study materials for memory for words and memory for sentences below; 1 form ('60, 4 pages); 19(25) minutes.

d) TEST BOOKLET C1. 4 tests, 12 scores: memory for words, memory for sentences, mathematics (arithmetic reasoning, introductory, advanced, total), English (usage, effective expression, punctuation, spelling, capitalization, total); 1 form ('60, 16 pages); 112(130) minutes.

e) TEST BOOKLET C2. 11 tests, 11 scores: abstract reasoning, mechanical reasoning, disguised words, creativity, clerical checking, visualization in 2 dimensions, reading comprehension, visualization in 3 dimensions, word functions in sentences, table reading, object inspection; 1 form ('60, 41 pages); 112(145) minutes.

f) SCHOOL QUESTIONNAIRE: GENERAL SCHOOL CHARACTERISTICS. Principals; 1 form ('60, 32 pages).

g) SCHOOL QUESTIONNAIRE: GUIDANCE PROGRAM. Guidance counselors; 1 form ('60, 15 pages).

h) SCHOOL QUESTIONNAIRE: COUNSELOR'S QUESTIONNAIRE. Guidance counselors; 1 form ('60, 6 pages).

REFERENCES

1. FLANAGAN, JOHN C. "Project Talent: The First National Census of Aptitudes and Abilities." *Yearb Nat Council Meas Used Ed* 17:37–44 '60. *
2. FLANAGAN, JOHN C. "Maximizing Human Talents." *J Teach Ed* 13:209–15 Je '62. *
3. FLANAGAN, JOHN C.; DAILEY, JOHN T.; SHAYCOFT, MARION F.; GORHAM, WILLIAM A.; ORR, DAVID B.; AND GOLDBERG, ISADORE. *Design for a Study of American Youth: 1, The Talents of American Youth.* Boston, Mass.: Houghton Mifflin Co., 1962. Pp. 240. * (*PA* 37:2001)
4. FLANAGAN, JOHN C.; DAILEY, JOHN T.; SHAYCOFT, MARION F.; ORR, DAVID B.; AND GOLDBERG, ISADORE. *Studies of the American High School: A Survey and Follow-Up of Educational Plans and Decisions in Relation to Aptitude Pat-*

terns. Cooperative Research Project No. 226. Pittsburgh, Pa.: Project Talent Office, University of Pittsburgh, 1962. Variously paged. *

5. SHAYCOFT, MARION F.; DAILEY, JOHN T.; ORR, DAVID B.; NEYMAN, CLINTON A., JR.; AND SHERMAN, STUART E. *Studies of a Complete Age Group—Age 15: The Identification, Development, and Utilization of Human Talents.* Cooperative Research Project No. 566. Pittsburgh, Pa.: Project Talent Office, University of Pittsburgh, 1963. Variously paged. *

For excerpts from related book reviews, see B178.

[765]

★[Science Talent Search Program.] High school seniors who are candidates for Westinghouse Electric Corporation science scholarships and awards; 1942–60; program administered annually in December at individual schools; candidates must take the *Science Aptitude Examination* (new form issued annually; 22nd form, '62, 11 pages, used in 1963 program) and submit a personal data report and a report on a scientific project; instructional leaflet ('62, 5 pages) and *Personal Data Blank* ('59, 8 pages, data supplied by the student and his teachers and principal) available only to program participants; previous examinations may be purchased following program use; no data on reliability; norms available following the program; separate answer sheets must be used for program (may be used thereafter); materials and scoring service free to program participants; examinations from the following programs are available for purchase: 14th ('54, 16 pages), 16th ('56, 16 pages), 18th ('58, 12 pages), 19th ('59, 12 pages), 20th ('60, 12 pages), 21st ('61, 12 pages), 22nd ('62, 11 pages); no manual for purchasable forms; mimeographed key-norms sheets from each program: 14th ('55), 16th ('57), 18th ('59), 19th ('60), 20th ('60), 21st ('62), 22nd ('63); 15¢ per test with answer sheet and key-norms sheet, cash orders only; 150(160) minutes; Harold A. Edgerton; Science Service, Inc. *

[Other Tests]

For tests not listed above, see the following entries in *Tests in Print:* 1341–2, 1344, 1347, 1349–52, 1354–7, 1360–2, and 1365–6; out of print: 1348 and 1363.

MULTI-APTITUDE BATTERIES

REVIEWS BY *Dorothy C. Adkins, Anne Anastasi, Harold P. Bechtoldt, John B. Carroll, S. S. Dunn, Norman Frederiksen, Leo Goldman, William H. Helme, Lloyd G. Humphreys, J. A. Keats, Benjamin Kleinmuntz, William B. Michael, John E. Milholland, Joseph E. Moore, Paul F. Ross, Stanley I. Rubin, Richard E. Schutz, Julian C. Stanley, Erwin K. Taylor, William W. Turnbull, and Leroy Wolins.*

[766]

★Academic Promise Tests. Grades 6–9; 1961–62, c1959–62; 7 scores: abstract reasoning, numerical, nonverbal total, language usage, verbal, verbal total, total; IBM; Forms A, B, ('61, 20 pages); manual ('62, 54 pages); separate answer sheets must be used; $4.50 per 25 tests; $3.75 per 50 IBM answer sheets; $1.10 per 50 student report forms; 50¢ per set of manual and scoring stencil; 90¢ per specimen set; postpaid; 90(120) minutes; George K. Bennett, Marjorie G. Bennett, Dorothy M. Clendenen, Jerome E. Doppelt, James H. Ricks, Jr., Harold G. Seashore, and Alexander G. Wesman; Psychological Corporation. *

JULIAN C. STANLEY, *Professor of Educational Psychology, and Director, Laboratory of Experimental Design, University of Wisconsin, Madison, Wisconsin.*

Three subtests, Abstract Reasoning (AR), Numerical (N), and Verbal (V), of the *Academic Promise Tests* (APT) represent a welcome downward extension of the *Differential Aptitude Tests.* This reviewer wonders whether the 60-item fourth subtest, Language Usage (LU), containing 24 grammar items, 23 spelling items, 8 capitalization and punctuation items, and 5 correct sentences items in Form A, is as good from the standpoint of content, even though its correlation with school marks is relatively high. In particular, the misspelled words seem to test clerical ability for minor details of a sentence. Ten of the 23 are as follows, in order of their appearance in Form A: shoping, efect, strugle, comunicate, apeal, compeled, acompany, arive, generaly, and posibility. The authors do not tell why they chose these words and the other 13 [allways, clamed, telagram, reseption, regester, hight, greif, compaired, insurence, anyway (for "any way"), when ever, celler, and talant], except to mention "careful editorial scrutiny," difficulty, and discrimination of more able from less able students. Some explicit content validity rationale for choosing the items themselves seems needed.

One also would like to know the basis for including at least 15 verb items among the 24 grammatically faulty sentences. Were content specifications drawn up initially and adhered to throughout the tryout phase? Without such information, and on the basis of my content analysis of the Form A language usage items, I would prefer to substitute a reading comprehension test for LU.

The content of the other three subtests (AR, N, and V) seems considerably better. Abstract Reasoning consists of 60 ingenious plane geometry items, for each of which the examinee must decide which one of four "answer figures" goes with the three "problem figures." Inductive reasoning and spatial relations ability both seem to play a considerable part in these.

One fourth of the N items in Form A are number series. The remaining 45 are straightforward arithmetical computation or arithmetical reasoning items of the same sort as that pioneered by A. S. Otis and E. L. Thorndike, as contrasted with the various new-type quantitative reasoning items in the mathematical subtest of the *College Entrance Examination Board Scholastic Aptitude Test.* Only five items are accompanied by figures, perhaps in an attempt to keep overlap with AR minimal.

For each of the 60 N items, the last option is "D. None of these." On Form A, D is the keyed option for items 2, 7, 10, 14, and 19 of the N subtest—only 5 times instead of 60/4 = 15. LU has exactly the same arrangement: 21 keyed A's, 19 B's, 15 C's, and 5 D's. Thus, response biases of examinees may affect their N and LU scores considerably. The keyed A, B, C, D option positions for AR and V are much better balanced: 13, 17, 15, and 15.

While generally good, the 60 V items in Form A, all analogies, could have benefited from more careful editing. Items 11 and 37 have as the first part of their stems "HAMMER is to NAIL" and "HOUSE is to NAILS," respectively. "Mississippi" appears in the stem of item 9 and as an option in item 26. "Wilson" (the president) appears in the stem of item 23 and as an option in item 52.

Item 23, "WORLD WAR I is to WORLD WAR II as WILSON is to (A) Lincoln, (B) Roosevelt, (C) Grant, (D) Eisenhower," may become more difficult as time goes by. Item 52, "JOHNSON is to LINCOLN as ARTHUR is to (A) Adams, (B) Tyler, (C) Wilson, (D) Garfield," may now be confusing.

Item 54 can be answered correctly without knowing who Allen is if the examinee remembers that Marion was called the "Swamp Fox": "MOUNTAIN is to SWAMP as ALLEN is to (A) Wolfe, (B) Marion, (C) Burgoyne, (D) Sheridan."

Because no correction for chance is employed ("If you are not sure of an answer, select the choice which is your best guess"), a sixth grade student who guesses at all 240 items with the expected degree of success (15 marked according to the key for each subtest) would obtain higher percentile ranks on AR, N, V, and LU than if he marked nothing: 20, 30, 15, and 20 versus 1, 1, 1, and 1.

The comprehensive APT manual provides excellent information on predictive validity for school marks, comparable forms reliability for single grade groups, standard errors of measurement, practice effects, and APT-WISC equivalence. The detailed validity data for schools of various types all over the country occupy 18 large pages of the manual. Percentile norms for each of the four grades are given for AR, N, AR + N, V, LU, V + LU, and AR + N + V + LU.

The *Academic Promise Tests* resemble the analogous grade levels of the *Cooperative School and College Ability Tests,* but offer in addition the nonverbal AR subtest, which to this reviewer appears greatly superior to the nonverbal material of the *California Test of Mental Maturity.* APT's LU portion seems rather out of date and out of place among AR, N, and V, but it certainly does correlate well with school grades—particularly in English, where the median *r*'s are .60 for LU, .50 for N, .45 for V, and .31 for AR. Even for mathematics it is excelled only by N (.41 versus .58).

Everything considered, this excellent new battery offers schools convenient, attractive, predictively valid, reliable measurement in four areas.

William W. Turnbull, *Executive Vice President, Educational Testing Service, Princeton, New Jersey.*

The new *Academic Promise Tests* should prove to be a quick and economical way to identify talented students and those who need remedial help. They are well designed and produced. Instructions are clear, the format is attractive, and several features have been introduced to simplify giving, scoring, and interpreting the tests.

Four separate scores are derived: Abstract Reasoning (AR), Numerical (N), Verbal (V), and Language Usage (LU). In addition, the first two scores (AR + N) are summed to provide a measure of nonverbal reasoning ability and the last two (V + LU) to afford a measure of competence with verbal materials. Finally, a total score is derived from all four parts. Although the time limits are short, the reliabilities are acceptably high, even on the individual sections where a rigorous test of reliability (parallel forms correlated within a single school grade) is employed. The validity data given are extensive and the correlations with school grades are very satisfactory. It should be noted that predictions over more than a few months have not yet been undertaken but presumably will be consistent with the short-run predictions now available.

While the tests are generally well made, the logic underlying the composition of the battery and the derivation of its two subtotal scores seems open to some question. To begin with, the purposes for which the tests are recommended include sectioning and grouping for instructional purposes. For this use, it would seem important to tap at least the student's mathematical achievement (whether "new" or "traditional") and his attainments in science and social studies. These are not separately represented in this battery. Thus for sectioning and placement, the user will need to supplement the *Academic Promise Tests* with more specific measures of academic achievement.

A real problem concerns the inclusion of Abstract Reasoning in the battery. This is a well constructed and edited test of figure classification. The manual states: "Then, there are students whose educational background has been such as to arouse doubt that verbal or numerical tests are adequate measures of their potential learning ability, or whose strengths are better represented by nonverbal performance tasks. To provide description of nonverbal, non-numerical competence, the Abstract Reasoning test has been designed." In principle, this seems reasonable. The manual provides no evidence about the usefulness of the test for students with unusual educational backgrounds, however. Instead, it includes coefficients of correlation between each score (including Abstract Reasoning) and school grades achieved by regular students in regular classes, grades 6 through 9. Here the evidence is that the AR score is not particularly useful: it yields correlations whose median is about .30 in contrast to about .45 for the other three scores taken singly. Moreover, this pattern seems to hold quite consistently over the major subject areas where the data are extensive enough to permit conclusions. It is possible that later research will justify retention of this section, but unfortunately the disappointing results reported in the manual are fairly typical of what has usually been found in attempts to measure academic potential by abstract reasoning tests of the nonverbal and non-numerical variety. On the evidence at hand, it is hard to escape the conclusion that inclusion of Abstract Reasoning represents a triumph of hope over experience and that the testing time could have been better utilized for other purposes.

The second section, Numerical, is a well made test with good variety in its items. From the validity data, moreover, it appears to be performing just as one would hope a good quantitative test would perform. When the scores are lumped together with those from the AR section to provide a nonverbal subtotal, however, both their meaning and a degree of their utility is lost. The data in the manual show that invariably the combined score is less valid than the score of the numerical section taken alone. As suggested in the previous paragraph, one way to prevent this erosion of validity would be to drop the AR section entirely.

The verbal test is composed of well written analogies. As the manual states, "The analogy process *per se* is a kind of reasoning; the content to which the reasoning is applied may be as varied as desired." Capitalizing on this feature, the authors have drawn upon the materials of science, mathematics, history, and geography as well as upon everyday word relationships for their verbal test items. One consequence is that the test appears to stress general verbal reasoning and general information rather than word relationships more narrowly defined. The validity coefficients show that the resulting composite is indeed predictive of school grades. Whether or not the scores from this wide-coverage test should be combined with LU to yield an overall "verbal" score is, however, debatable. It should be noted that the single V score correlates more highly with N ($r = .69$) than with LU ($r = .63$). This fact points up the question of whether or not a combination of V and LU is especially appropriate and reinforces the observation that V is more a test of reasoning than of word understanding per se.

The test of "Language Usage" combines items on spelling, grammar, and punctuation. Generally, it is a competently written test, although more careful editing might have improved an ambiguous item here and there. Both reliability and validity coefficients are satisfactory, however, and the test scores should be helpful for the purposes stated for the battery —including, in this instance, pupil sectioning.

The manual accompanying the battery is unusually good in several respects; notably, in the completeness of the data given (e.g., on practice effect, reliability of differences between pairs of scores, and relations with scores on other tests) and in its clear discussion of such points as the contruction of expectancy tables. The techniques of reporting and profiling scores are efficient and clearly described. Inclusion of instructions for the use of score bands (within which the true score is likely to lie) rather than exact score points is a welcome feature.

In summary, the *Academic Promise Tests* are well prepared and produced with a professional touch. Validity data involving predictions over three to four months are encouraging. Generally, the individual scores may be found more revealing than their sums. The usefulness of Abstract Reasoning is questioned and the view is presented that the APT would be improved by its omission. Overall, however, the tests should have real utility as relatively brief measures of general academic development and promise and should be of supplementary help in sectioning and placement.

[767]

***Differential Aptitude Tests.** Grades 8–13 and adults; 1947–63; 9 scores: verbal reasoning, numerical ability, total (scholastic aptitude), abstract reasoning, space relations, mechanical reasoning, clerical speed and accuracy, language usage (spelling, sentences); IBM and (Form L only) MRC; Forms A ('47), B ('47), L ('62, c1947–62), M ('62, c1947–62); Forms L and M are revisions of Forms A and B, respectively; manual, third edition ('59, c1947–59, 98 pages, based on Forms A and B but also used with Forms L and M); individual report forms (2 pages): for Forms A and B ('61), for Forms L and M ('63, c1961–63); individual report folder ('61, 6 pages) for Forms A and B; casebook ('51, 93 pages, see *29* below); separate answer sheets must be used; $1.25 per 50 individual report forms; $3 per 50 individual report folders; $1.75 per casebook; $2 per manual; postpaid; George K. Bennett, Harold G. Seashore, and Alexander G. Wesman; Psychological Corporation. *

a) FORMS A AND B. 1947–61; IBM; 2 editions; directions for administration and scoring, third edition ('59, 23 pages, reprinted from manual); $3 per specimen set; Spanish edition available; 186(240–270) minutes in 2–6 sessions.

1) *Combined Booklet Edition.* 3 booklets; 50¢ per set of either hand or machine scoring stencils for any one booklet; $1 per set of hand scoring stencils for all 3 booklets; $1.10 per set of machine scoring stencils for all 3 booklets.

(*a*) Combination 1—VN. 3 scores: verbal reasoning, numerical ability, total (scholastic aptitude); 9 pages; $4 per 25 tests; $2.85 per 50 IBM answer sheets; 60(85) minutes.

(*b*) Combination 2—MR-LU-SR. 4 scores: mechanical reasoning, space relations, language usage (spelling, sentences); 34 pages; $7.50 per 25 tests; $4.45 per 50 IBM answer sheets; 95(135) minutes.

(*c*) Combination 3—CSA-AR. 2 scores: clerical speed and accuracy, abstract reasoning; 12 pages; $4.50 per 25 tests; $4 per 50 sets of IBM answer sheets; 31(50) minutes.

2) *Separate Booklet Edition.* 7 booklets; $2 per 50 IBM answer sheets for any one booklet; 50¢ per hand or machine scoring stencil for any one booklet; $1.25 per complete set of hand scoring stencils; $1.40 per complete set of machine scoring stencils; 50¢ per specimen set of any one booklet (includes directions but not manual).

(*a*) Verbal Reasoning. 6 pages; $3 per 25 tests; 30(40) minutes.

(*b*) Numerical Ability. 3 pages; $2.25 per 25 tests; 30(35) minutes.

(*c*) Abstract Reasoning. 7 pages; $3 per 25 tests; 25(30) minutes.

(*d*) Space Relations. 11 pages; $3.50 per 25 tests; 30(40) minutes.

(*e*) Mechanical Reasoning. 19 pages; $3.75 per 25 tests; 30(35) minutes.

(*f*) Clerical Speed and Accuracy. 6 pages; $3 per 25 tests; 6(15) minutes.

(*g*) Language Usage. 2 scores: spelling, sentences; 7 pages; $3 per 25 tests; 35(45) minutes.

b) FORMS L AND M. 1947–63; also called *Two-Booklet Edition* and *Differential Aptitude Tests, 1963 Edition;* IBM and (Form L only) MRC; 2 booklets (a separate booklet combination of verbal reasoning and numerical ability subtests is also available); directions and norms ('63, c1947–63, 34 pages); directions ('63, 4 pages) for use of MRC answer sheets with Form L; no data on reliability; norms for grades 8–12 only; $7.75 per 25 tests of either booklet; 60¢ per set of scoring stencils for IBM answer sheets; $8 per 50 MRC answer sheets; $1 per set of stencils for hand scoring MRC answer sheets (machine scoring service, by Measurement Research Center, Inc., may be arranged through the publisher); $3 per specimen set with manual for *a;* $1.50 per specimen set without manual; 181(235–245) minutes in 2–6 sessions.

1) *Booklet 1.* 1961, c1947–61, 21 pages; 4 scores: verbal reasoning, numerical ability, abstract reasoning, clerical speed and accuracy; $5.50 per 50 IBM answer sheets; 91(120) minutes.

2) *Booklet 2.* 1962, c1947–62, 38 pages; 4 scores: mechanical reasoning, space relations, language usage (spelling, grammar); $4.50 per 50 IBM answer sheets; 90(115) minutes.

REFERENCES

1–28. See 4:711.

29–77. See 5:605.

78. CHOTHIA, F. S. "Predicting Success in Multi-Purpose Schools." *Indian J Psychol* 31:139–40 Jl–D '56. *

79. CURETON, EDWARD E. "Service Tests of Multiple Aptitudes." *Proc Inv Conf Testing Probl* 1955:22–39 '56. * (*PA* 31:3017)

80. JACOBS, JAMES NAJEEB. *An Evaluation of Certain Measures of Aptitude and Achievement in the Prediction of Scholastic Success.* Doctor's thesis, Michigan State University (East Lansing, Mich.), 1957. (*DA* 22:4268)

81. SININGER, ROLLIN ALBERT. *Development and Evaluation of Visual Aids for Interpreting the Differential Aptitude Test and Kuder Preference Record.* Master's thesis, University of Texas (Austin, Tex.), 1957.
82. VINEYARD, EDWIN E., AND MASSEY, HAROLD W. "The Interrelationship of Certain Linguistic Skills and Their Relationship With Scholastic Achievement When Intelligence Is Ruled Constant." *J Ed Psychol* 48:279–86 My '57. * (*PA* 33:2200)
83. WEEKS, WILLIAM R. *A Study of the Predictability of High School Grades and the Differential Aptitude Tests for Predicting Success in a Two-Year Terminal Program at Western Michigan University.* Master's thesis, Western Michigan University (Kalamazoo, Mich.), 1957.
84. CATTELL, RAYMOND B., AND SCHEIER, IVAN H. "The Objective Test Measurement of Neuroticism, U.I. 23 (—)." *Indian J Psychol* 33:217–36 pt 4 '58. *
85. MYERS, MAURICE. *A Comparison of Differential Aptitude Test Patterns of Junior College Students in Five Semi-Professional Fields.* Doctor's thesis, New York University (New York, N.Y.), 1958. (*DA* 19:3218)
86. SMITH, D. D. "Abilities and Interests: 2, Validation of Factors." *Can J Psychol* 12:253–8 D '58. * (*PA* 33:9347)
87. CALIA, VINCENT FRANK. *The Use of Discriminant Analysis in the Prediction of Performance of Junior College Students in a Program of General Education at Boston University Junior College.* Doctor's thesis, Boston University (Boston, Mass.), 1959. (*DA* 20:3190)
88. DOPPELT, JEROME E., AND SEASHORE, HAROLD G. "Psychological Testing in Correctional Institutions." *J Counsel Psychol* 6:81–92 sp '59. * (*PA* 34:6012)
89. DOPPELT, JEROME E.; SEASHORE, HAROLD G.; AND ODGERS, JOHN G. "Validation of the Differential Aptitude Tests for Auto Mechanics and Machine Shop Students." *Personnel & Guid J* 37:648–55 My '59. * (*PA* 35:2775)
90. FRIESEN, DAVID. *The Differential Aptitude Tests as Predictors in Education I at the University of Manitoba.* Master's thesis, University of Manitoba (Winnipeg, Man., Canada), 1959.
91. HASCALL, EDWARD ORSON, JR. *Predicting Success in High School Foreign Language Study.* Doctor's thesis, University of Michigan (Ann Arbor, Mich.), 1959. (*DA* 19:3245)
92. JACOBS, JAMES N. "Aptitude and Achievement Measures in Predicting High School Academic Success." *Personnel & Guid J* 37:334–41 Ja '59. * (*PA* 35:1263)
93. JAYALAKSHMI, G. "Correlation of Tests of Psychomotor Ability With Intelligence and Non-motor Tests." *J Psychol Res* 3:78–84 S '59. *
94. MOSHIN, S. M. "Plea for a Scientific Aptitude Test and a Preliminary Report of the Development of Such Test." *Indian J Psychol* 34:36–42 pt 1 '59. *
95. NORTON, DANIEL P. "The Relationship of Study Habits and Other Measures to Achievement in Ninth-Grade General Science." *J Exp Ed* 27:211–7 Mr '59. * (*PA* 35:1283)
96. OAKES, FREDERICK, JR. *The Contribution of Certain Variables to the Academic Achievement of Gifted Seventh Grade Students in an Accelerated General Science Curriculum.* Doctor's thesis, New York University (New York, N.Y.), 1959. (*DA* 20:4002)
97. SMITH, D. D. "Traits and College Achievement." *Can J Psychol* 13:93–101 Je '59. * (*PA* 34:4780)
98. STINSON, PAIRLEE J., AND MORRISON, MILDRED M. "Sex Differences Among High School Seniors." *J Ed Res* 53:103–8 N '59. *
99. STOCKSTILL, KIAH, JR.; FRYE, ROLAND L.; AND STRITCH, THOMAS M. "Comparison of Differential Aptitude Test Scores for Junior High School Students." *Psychol Rep* 5:765–8 D '59. * (*PA* 34:6174)
100. BOURNE, ROBERT K., AND ROTHNEY, JOHN W. M. "Assessments of Counselees Writing Skills by Tests and Essays." *Voc Guid Q* 9:21–4 au '60. *
101. CALIA, VINCENT F. "The Use of Discriminant Analysis in the Prediction of Scholastic Performance." Comments by David V. Tiedeman. *Personnel & Guid J* 39:184–92 N '60. * (*PA* 35:3949)
102. CASSEL, RUSSELL N., AND STANCIK, EDWARD J. "Factorial Content of the Iowa Tests of Educational Development and Other Tests." *J Exp Ed* 29:193–6 D '60. *
103. FILELLA, JAMES F. "Educational and Sex Differences in the Organization of Abilities in Technical and Academic Students in Colombia, South America." *Genetic Psychol Monogr* 61:115–63 F '60. * (*PA* 34:7630)
104. FOOTE, RICHARD PAUL. *The Prediction of Success in Automotive Mechanics in a Vocational-Industrial Curriculum on the Secondary School Level.* Doctor's thesis, New York University (New York, N.Y.), 1960. (*DA* 21:3014)
105. HARRIS, YEUELL Y., AND DOLE, ARTHUR A. "A Pilot Study in Local Research With the Differential Aptitude Test Battery." *Personnel & Guid J* 39:128–32 O '60. * (*PA* 35:5366)
106. HUGHES, HERBERT HOWARD. *Expectancy, Reward, and Differential Aptitude Tests Performance of Low and High Achievers With High Ability.* Doctor's thesis, Florida State University (Tallahassee, Fla.), 1960. (*DA* 21:2358)
107. MILTON, OHMER. "Primitive Thinking and Reasoning Among College Students." *J Higher Ed* 31:218–20 Ap '60. *
108. ROSINSKI, EDWIN F. "Must All Tests Be Multi-Factor Batteries?" *J Exp Ed* 28:235–40 Mr '60. *
109. BRIM, CHARLES WILLIAM. *Inter-High School Variability and Its Effect on the Prediction of College Achievement.* Doctor's thesis, University of Illinois (Urbana, Ill.), 1961. (*DA* 22:3466)
110. EELLS, KENNETH. "How Effective Is Differential Prediction in Three Types of College Curricula?" *Ed & Psychol Meas* 21:459–71 su '61. * (*PA* 36:2KJ59E)
111. EWALD, HATTIE HOFF. *The Relationship of Scores on the Differential Aptitude Tests to Scholarship in High School and Freshman College.* Doctor's thesis, University of South Dakota (Vermillion, S.D.), 1961. (*DA* 22:800)
112. HAGER, CHARLES WILLIAM. *Correlation of Personality and Character Traits With Differential Achievement in High School.* Doctor's thesis, University of Texas (Austin, Tex.), 1961. (*DA* 22:3520)
113. HASCALL, EDWARD O. "Predicting Success in High School Foreign Language Study." *Personnel & Guid J* 40:361–7 D '61. * (*PA* 36:4KL61H)
114. MCGUIRE, CARSON. "The Prediction of Talented Behavior in the Junior High School." *Proc Inv Conf Testing Probl* 1960:46–67 '61. *
115. NUGENT, FRANK A. "The Relationship of Discrepancies Between Interest and Aptitude Scores to Other Selected Personality Variables." *Personnel & Guid J* 39:388–95 Ja '61. * (*PA* 35:6212)
116. BROMER, JOHN A.; JOHNSON, J. MYRON; AND SEVRANSKY, PAUL. "Validity Information Exchange, No. 15-02: D.O.T. Code 4-97.010, 4-75.120, 4-85.040, Craft Foremen Correspond to Foremen I; 5-91.875, 5-91.088, 5-91.091, 5-91.831, 5-91.812, Process, Production, and Warehouse Foremen Correspond to Foremen II." *Personnel Psychol* 15:107–9 sp '62. *
117. COBB, BART B. "Problems in Air Traffic Management: 2, Prediction of Success in Air Traffic Controller School." *Aerospace Med* 33:702–13 Je '62. *
118. MERENDA, PETER F.; HALL, CHARLES E.; CLARKE, WALTER V.; AND PASCALE, ALFRED C. "Relative Predictive Efficiency of the DAT and a Short Multifactor Battery of Tests." *Psychol Rep* 11:71–81 Ag '62. * (*PA* 37:5665)
119. MUKHERJEE, B. N. "The Factorial Structure of Aptitude Tests at Successive Grade Levels." *Brit J Stat Psychol* 15:59–65 My '62. * (*PA* 37:7182)
120. RUDD, JOHN PAUL. *A Study of the Validity of Selected Predictors for Placement in Three-Rail Curricula.* Doctor's research study No. 1, Colorado State College (Greeley, Colo.), 1962. (*DA* 24:184)
121. SPRINGOB, H. KARL, AND JACKSON, CLIFTON W. "Measured Abilities and Inventoried Interests of Ninth Grade Boys." *Voc Guid Q* 11:37–40 au '62. * (*PA* 37:8279)
122. SUPER, DONALD E., AND CRITES, JOHN O. *Appraising Vocational Fitness by Means of Psychological Tests, Revised Edition,* pp. 339–49. New York: Harper & Brothers, 1962. Pp. xv, 688. * (*PA* 37:2038)
123. YOUNG, CHARLES RAY. *Factors Associated With Achievement and Underachievement Among Intellectually Superior Boys.* Doctor's thesis, University of Missouri (Columbia, Mo.), 1962. (*DA* 23:2406)
124. AIJAZ, SAIYID MOHAMMAD. *Predictive Validity of the Three Versions of the "Verbal Reasoning" and the "Numerical Ability" Subtests of the* Differential Aptitude Tests *for East Pakistan.* Doctor's research study No. 1, Colorado State College (Greeley, Colo.), 1963. (*DA* 24:1068)
125. ALVI, SABIR ALI. *Traditional and "Culture Fair" Aptitude Test Performance of College Students From Different Academic and Cultural Backgrounds.* Doctor's thesis, Indiana University (Bloomington, Ind.), 1963. (*DA* 24:2775)
126. BLOSSER, GEORGE H. "Group Intelligence Tests as Screening Devices in Locating Gifted and Superior Students in the Ninth Grade." *Excep Child* 29:282–6 F '63. * (*PA* 38:2434)
127. CHENEY, TRUMAN M., AND GOODISH, NAOMI. "Analysis—Between Certain Variables and Achievement in Beginning Shorthand." *J Bus Ed* 38:317–9 My '63. *
128. LUNDY, CHARLES T., AND SHERTZER, BRUCE. "Making Test Data Useful." *Personnel & Guid J* 42:62–3 S '63. *
129. OSBURN, H. G., AND MELTON, R. S. "Prediction of Proficiency in a Modern and Traditional Course in Beginning Algebra." *Ed & Psychol Meas* 23:277–87 su '63. * (*PA* 38:1386)

J. A. KEATS, *Reader in Psychology, University of Queensland, Brisbane, Queensland, Australia.*

The revised forms of the *Differential Aptitude Tests* contain only minor changes in the tests themselves. Possibly the major change which necessitated the production of the revised forms was the decision to change from a score "corrected" for guessing to a score equal to the number of correct responses for all tests. Such a change necessitated extensive changes in norms and these alone would have required a revised edition. The content of four of the eight tests is unchanged—these are Numerical Ability, Abstract Reasoning, Mechanical Reasoning, and Language Usage 1: Spelling. Verbal Reasoning still consists of double ended analogies of the form "? : word 1 :: word 2 : ?" but the alternatives are now listed as five pairs of words, the first of each pair corresponding to a possible first word of the analogy and the second word of the pair corresponding to a possible last word in the analogy. In the previous edition the subject had to seek two words from 16 options. Language Usage 2: Grammar (formerly entitled Sentences) and Space Relations have more items with only one correct response per item (instead of a varying number). Clerical Speed and Accuracy has been reset in clearer type. Norms for the new edition, based on over 50,000 cases from 195 schools in 43 states are presented with the new forms but the necessary revisions to the manual were not available at the time this review was written.

In this review it is not proposed to restate the many advantages of a battery of tests based on research results and on which research is continuing. The *Differential Aptitude Tests* have been in use for more than 16 years and many reviewers in these yearbooks and elsewhere have stressed the value of the contribution made by this battery. This reviewer agrees with most of the advantages claimed, but rather than restate these, he wishes to make suggestions for further research and development.

The practice of using "corrected" scores rather than simply the number of correct responses has been commented on by other reviewers in this series and elsewhere. It is gratifying to see a change to the latter procedure in the revised edition. The change in the analogies items of Verbal Reasoning also follows a questioning of the possible factorial complexity of the earlier items by a previous reviewer in this series. However, no evidence has been given to show that this present change goes far enough in the direction of reducing possible factorial complexity. Perhaps this evidence is given in the new manual but, unless results of research are available on this point, there is always the question as to whether the change is simply one towards the conventional rather than one resulting from scientific findings. The changes in Spatial Relationships and Language Usage 2: Grammar do follow the important point made by a previous reviewer that in the original form each *option* became a true-false item and could be scored as such. The value of continuous research and review of a soundly based test battery is well illustrated by these changes. A further example was noted in the provision of correlations with *SRA Primary Mental Abilities* following the suggestion of an MMY reviewer.

There are, however, a number of points made by previous reviewers which have not been met by this revision. The criticism that Language Usage 2: Grammar tends to accept out-of-date standards of usage does not seem to have been met. Indeed, the item used by an earlier reviewer as an example of this tendency still appears in the revised form. There are, of course, difficulties of changes in usage inherent in testing grammar, but surely these can be avoided by experienced item writers. A second point concerns the possibility of an acquiescence response set in both parts of Language Usage. It would be of considerable interest to know the correlation between the two parts of the spelling test obtained by separating items for which R (right) is the correct response from those for which W (wrong) is the correct response. Do these two sets of items combine to produce a homogeneous test? A similar question arises for the grammar items, since the "no error" option is sometimes correct.

Earlier comments have raised the question of the homogeneity of the items in the tests. Superficial homogeneity obtained by having all items of the same type in each of the eight tests does not necessarily guarantee homogeneity (or unidimensionality) in the sense of Lazarsfeld's definition,[1] which requires that pairs of items should be essentially zero correlated for persons at the same ability level. This property may be checked experimentally by methods used by Lord,[2] which are essentially factor analytic in form. If this check has not been made for the revised form—and there is no evidence that it has—then this is a further task in the improvement of this already important battery. It is

1 Lazarsfeld, Paul F. Chap. 10, "The Logical and Mathematical Foundation of Latent Structure Analysis," pp. 362–412. In *Measurement and Prediction*. By Samuel A. Stouffer and others. Princeton, N.J.: Princeton University Press, 1950. Pp. x, 756. *

2 Lord, Frederic. "A Theory of Test Scores." *Psychometric Monographs,* No. 7. Princeton, N.J.: Psychometric Society, 1953. Pp. x, 84. *

not intended to imply that all, or even any, of the tests are not homogeneous but merely to stress the point that it is the responsibility of the test constructor to investigate the question and so be able to assure users that the test scores have an unambiguous meaning—at least in this sense. The research required is certainly not beyond present methods of analysis, either theoretically or computationally.

A feature of the present manual is the presentation of standard errors of measurement as well as reliability coefficients for each test (Forms A and B) at each of the grade levels tested. This feature has drawn favourable comment from previous reviewers which this reviewer echoes as far as the presentation of standard errors of measurement is concerned. There is, however, evidence that the standard error of measurement depends on the particular score obtained and that these variations would be greater than the variation in standard error between grade groups. If there is variation in standard error with score value of the kind found in experimental studies, this would account—in part at least—for variations in standard error between grades and so would be a more basic measure to report for at least some different score levels. This practice has already been adopted by at least one test publisher and is recommended for this battery, particularly in view of the stress placed on profile interpretation.

A further feature of the present manual that has attracted favourable comment is that continuous up-to-date information is provided from validity studies. This acknowledgment of responsibility to keep users informed of current results is commendable and the criticism that virtually all of the studies are carried out by the publisher's staff is not entirely valid. There is always the rebuttal that only in this way can the publisher be sure of the soundness of the research he is reporting. However, there is an obligation in this situation for the publisher to ensure that all relevant research methods are tried and at least a representative sample of the results reported. Previous reviewers in this series have commented on the absence of multiple correlations in the validity data presented. The use of discriminant function analysis seems also to be pertinent, but published results of such analyses are absent from the manual. The availability of these data would greatly assist the sophisticated user in establishing the guidance programme most efficient for his particular situation. Considerations such as testing time available might cause him to reject the full battery for a particular purpose, whereas a selection of the tests, based on multiple correlation data, might indicate that a sub-battery would prove to be just as efficient. Perhaps the new manual will remedy this deficiency. A further advantage of using these more advanced techniques is that they may help to condense the enormous amount of validity data presently published for this battery and so assist the user in gaining a clearer impression of the established usefulness of the programme. Of course, no user can complain at having too much validity data, but the more sophisticated user is well aware that first order correlations are not necessarily a true indication of the relative contributions of the tests to the information provided by the battery as a whole.

The need to explore and report applications of modern research methods arises also in connection with establishing the percentiles which form the basis of the norms presented. Presumably, these have been estimated from the cumulative frequency distribution of the observed data. An overall standardisation sample of more than 50,000 cases seems very substantial indeed but when it is subdivided by grade, sex, and time of testing it is found that each set of norms is based on little more than 2,000 cases. Even these samples are quite adequate and probably larger than those used by most other agencies. However, in the reviewer's experience even distributions of this size show many irregularities and the raw percentiles, particularly those at the extremes, are likely to be somewhat unstable and possibly biased. This problem has received too little attention from theorists. Some theoretical distributions have been proposed [3] but until more work is done in theory and application, the problem of the stability of norms will remain. It is by large organisations using well established tests that the necessary applied work must be carried out.

In summary, the *Differential Aptitude Tests* were founded on the findings of research up to 1947 and most of the minor changes in the revised battery are based on research. The re-

3 KEATS, J. A. *A Statistical Theory of Objective Test Scores*. Melbourne, Australia: Australian Council for Educational Research, 1951. Pp. viii, 48. *
KEATS, J. A., AND LORD, FREDERIC M. "A Theoretical Distribution for Mental Test Scores." *Psychometrika* 27:59–72 Mr '62. *

viewer is of the opinion that more changes and more evidence for the changes made, as well as for retaining old forms, are called for to enable the battery to represent the standard to which others should aspire. Much of the material required could well appear in the revised manual which was, of course, not available to the reviewer. In any case, the battery will be widely used and the extensive preparation and renorming of the revised forms justify this choice.

RICHARD E. SCHUTZ, *Professor of Education, and Director, Testing Service, Arizona State University, Tempe, Arizona.*

The additions to the DAT which have appeared since the battery was reviewed in *The Fifth Mental Measurements Yearbook* simply add to the thickness of the frosting on an already well frosted cake. Revised Forms L and M have been produced, a revised manual was published in 1959 with another promised in 1964, and a new pamphlet for use in reporting and interpreting scores to students, parents, and teachers has appeared.

The revisions incorporated into the revised Forms L and M serve to increase the practical usability of the tests. The single booklet edition has given way completely to a two-booklet edition, although a VR-NA combination is still available as a separate. The responses to the entire battery are recorded on both sides of two answer sheets.

The new Form L is based on the content of the original Form A, while Form M is based on Form B. Content modification varies from test to test. In Verbal Reasoning, the stems of the double-ended analogies have been retained intact, but the 16 options previously available in the combinations of the 4 choices for opening and 4 for closing the analogy have been reduced to 5 fixed pairs.

The content of Numerical Ability and Abstract Reasoning is unchanged, but the layout of NA has been improved to increase the amount of white space on each page.

The items in Space Relations have been completely reworked to convert them to single-keyed responses, and the number of items has been increased from 40 to 60. Mechanical Reasoning is reproduced intact. The content of Clerical Speed and Accuracy remains unchanged but the items have been reset in a smaller non-serifed type face and printed on one page rather than two. No change has been made in the spelling subtest of Language Usage. The sentences subtest has been retitled "Grammar." In addition, the multiple-keyed items have been converted to single-keyed responses and the number of items increased from 50 to 60.

The new forms have been standardized with even greater care than was exercised in the 1952 standardization. More than 50,000 students from 195 schools in 95 communities representing 43 states were tested. Tables are presented demonstrating that the standardization sample is representative of the U.S. population with respect to geographic distribution and community size. Almost all of the tests were administered in October, November, and December rather than throughout the year as in 1952. Thus the norms are most relevant for fall testing programs. Tables of spring norms, also provided, were obtained by interpolating between successive grades tested in the fall. Although only interpolations, the spring norms are probably more accurate than were previous "windage" allowances. As in the original edition, percentile norms are presented for boys and girls separately.

Previous reviewers have been hard pressed to find valid criticisms of the DAT. The new DAT materials appear to eliminate some of these criticisms including the following:

a) *No evidence is presented to demonstrate that subtracting wrong responses is of any value in scoring the power tests.* Apparently, there was no such evidence to be presented. All eight tests of Forms L and M are scored rights only.

b) *Few correlations with other tests are presented.* The 1959 manual presents four full-page tables reporting the correlations of Forms A and B with a wide variety of intelligence, aptitude, achievement, and interest tests.

c) *The authors fail to come to grips with operational problems in interpreting the test results.* The new six-page student report folder represents an important step towards overcoming this criticism. The folder is evaluated more fully later in the review.

The following criticisms made by previous reviewers are still judged to be relevant:

d) *No information is given concerning item analysis techniques used in constructing the tests.* Although the 1959 manual includes a brief section on "Principles Governing the Test

Construction," it remains silent concerning the details of item analysis procedures and criteria. Possibly the 1964 manual will include additional information in this area.

e) There is an undue amount of overlap and high correlation between tests. This is a criticism which is not likely to be overcome, since it is inherent in the overall structure of the battery. The criticism is, of course, a relative one. Since one has no control over the obtained correlations after the test content has been definitely established, the criticism can best be avoided by demonstrating that the tests have adequate validity despite the overlap and correlation. This in turn involves attending to the next listed criticism.

f) No use has been made of multiple regression and discriminant analysis procedures in establishing the validity of the various tests. Although the 1959 manual presents numerous impressive arrays of predictive validity coefficients, only a single set of multiple regression equations is included. The equations involve the use of the DAT given in grade 10 as predictors of scores on the *College Entrance Examination Board Scholastic Aptitude Test* taken in grade 12. Two equations based on the performance of 85 boys are given and another two based on the performance of 60 girls from a single school. Optimal weighting of Verbal Reasoning, Spelling, and Sentences produced a multiple correlation coefficient of .79 between predicted and actual SAT Verbal scores. Weighting Numerical Ability, Verbal Reasoning, and Space Relations produced a multiple correlation of .85 with SAT Mathematics scores. These are quite respectable correlations. Unfortunately, no information is given concerning the first-order correlations between the DAT and SAT for the two groups so that it is impossible to evaluate the increased efficiency provided by using the multiple tests. Nor is it possible to even guess what the multiple correlations might look like for criteria other than a scholastic aptitude test.

Thus, despite the extensive predictive validity coefficients for separate DAT subtests, the *differential* validity of the tests in predicting various criteria is still without substantiation. Moreover, visual inspection of the patterns of correlations that are presented in the 1959 manual casts doubt that the battery does provide the differential utility implied in its title.

The 1959 manual steers the user in the direction of expectancy charts rather than regression equations. Although only illustrative samples of such charts are included in the manual, users are encouraged to prepare charts based on local data and references for the construction of such charts are given. While expectancy charts are unquestionably more feasible than regression equations for school people working by hand, the increasingly widespread availability of electronic data processing equipment in even the smaller school districts makes more sophisticated statistical procedures a thoroughly reasonable possibility. It is hoped that the DAT authors and publisher will help reduce the technological lag by continuing to exercise professional leadership in encouraging DAT users to utilize the best available resources for analyzing test results. The kind of operationally useful suggestions included in previous supplements and other auxiliary materials are most commendable.

g) Adequate occupational validity and normative data are lacking. The DAT was born and has been reared in an educational context. No occupational validity data are reported in the 1959 manual. The only occupational normative data presented are of a follow-back variety. These were obtained from a 5-year questionnaire follow-up of 2,900 juniors and seniors in 6 cities, and a 7-year follow-up on 2,386 of the same students in 5 of the cities. A return of about 60 per cent was obtained in each study. Since no criterion measures were available, the study yielded only descriptive characteristics of various subsamples in terms of their high school DAT scores. With the huge number of DAT's that have been administered by school districts in continuous testing programs for more than 15 years, data are certainly available for more definitive occupational validity studies.

So much for the current status of the DAT. Probably the most important innovation in DAT usage as far as the individual examinee is concerned will be found in the simple little six-page student report folder. Teachers, parents, and students are usually left cold by impressive psychometric characteristics of a test. They want to know what the results mean for them personally. All other data are of secondary importance. Although one can only speculate about the nature of the conclusions that users draw from the DAT, the new individual report folder provides some clear clues concerning the authors' philosophy and practice in interpreting DAT results.

I am frankly ambivalent concerning the contents of the folder. When one explicitly outlines the specific inferences he derives from test results, he reveals the nude consequences of the test. I feel the authors are to be commended for being forthright and specific in their generalizations, but nudity is a vulnerable form. The following statements are illustrative: "A student who wants to major in such fields as mathematics, physics, chemistry, or any branch of engineering, may expect to encounter some difficulty if his NA score is not in the top third or top quarter." "Students who do well on SR should have an advantage in work such as drafting, dress designing, architecture, mechanical engineering, die-making, building construction, and some branches of art and decoration." "If you do well on both these tests [Language Usage] and on VR, you should be able to do almost any kind of practical writing provided you have a knowledge of your topic and a desire to write about it."

Although the folder is sprinkled with almost as many disclaimers and cautions as a typical stock market advice sheet, I have an uneasy feeling that students and parents, who are certain to be highly involved emotionally and completely naïve statistically, run a high probability of making unjustified decisions on the basis of the material included in the folder. Optimally, of course, an expert counselor should be available to assist in the interpretation. But will he be available, and can he be expected to be as accurate in his inferences or as effective in communicating them as the report folder? Although I would not argue the soundness of any of the inferences included in the folder, I cannot find data in the 1959 manual to support many of them directly. This adds to my ambivalence, since undeniably I, along with every other DAT user, have drawn much wilder inferences on the basis of less substantial evidence.

I am able to resolve this ambiguity only by exercising both an absolute and a relative evaluation criterion, a discrimination which extends to my evaluation of the DAT in general. From a relative point of view, this is the best we can currently offer; no alternative procedures of any sort which possess greater utility can be suggested at the present time. From an absolute point of view, we have a long way to go to achieve optimal effectiveness. Fortunately, the road toward improvement appears to be sufficiently well defined to permit a few additional steps.

For reviews by John B. Carroll and Norman Frederiksen, see 5:605; for reviews by Harold Bechtoldt, Ralph F. Berdie, and Lloyd G. Humphreys, see 4:711; see also 3:620 (1 excerpt).

[768]

***Differential Test Battery.** Ages 11 to "top university level" (range for Test 1 extends downward to age 7); 1955–59; 12 tests in 7 booklets; battery manual ('55, 53 pages, including 12 pages of provisional norms for the Speed Tests which are now superseded by the norms in the separate manual); no data on validity; 8*s*. per battery manual; 86*s*. per specimen set; prices include purchase tax; postpaid within U.K.; 136.5(200) minutes; J. R. Morrisby; distributed by the National Foundation for Educational Research in England and Wales. *

a) TEST 1, COMPOUND SERIES TEST. Ages 7 and over; "mental work power"; 1955; 1 form ('55, 68 pages); manual ('55, 22 pages); separate answer sheets must be used; 39*s*. per test; 7*s*. per 25 answer sheets; 4*s*. per set of key and manual; 30(40) minutes.

b) GENERAL ABILITY TESTS. Ages 11 and over; 1955; 3 tests; manual ('55, 32 pages); 39*s*. per 25 tests; 15*s*. per set of scoring stencils and manual for all 3 tests.

1) *Test 2, General Ability Tests: Verbal.* 1 form ('55, 9 pages); 12(20) minutes.

2) *Test 3, General Ability Tests: Numerical.* 1 form ('55, 8 pages); 29(40) minutes.

3) *Test 4, General Ability Tests: Perceptual.* 1 form ('55, 9 pages); 23(35) minutes.

c) TEST 5, SHAPES TEST. Ages 11 and over; 1955; spatial ability; 1 form ('55, 13 pages); manual ('55, 13 pages); separate answer sheets must be used; 9*s*. per test; 8*s*. per 25 answer sheets; 10*s*. per set of scoring stencil and manual; 10(15) minutes.

d) TEST 6, MECHANICAL ABILITY TEST. Ages 11 and over; 1955; 1 form ('55, 10 pages); manual ('55, 11 pages); separate answer sheets must be used; 7*s*. per test; 8*s*. per 25 answer sheets; 6*s*. per set of key and manual; 15(20) minutes.

e) SPEED TESTS. Ages 11 and over; 1955–59; 6 tests in a single booklet ('55, 16 pages); manual ('59, 32 pages); no data on reliability; 59*s*. per 25 tests; 8*s*. per set of manual and key for Test 7 (no keys necessary for other tests); 17.5(30) minutes.

1) *Test 7 (Speed Test 1), Routine Number and Name Checking.*
2) *Test 8 (Speed Test 2), Perseveration.*
3) *Test 9 (Speed Test 3), Word Fluency.*
4) *Test 10 (Speed Test 4), Ideational Fluency.*
5) *Test 11 (Speed Test 5), Motor Speed.*
6) *Test 12 (Speed Test 6), Motor Skill.*

For reviews by E. A. Peel, Donald E. Super, and Philip E. Vernon, see 5:606.

[769]

***Employee Aptitude Survey.** Ages 16 and over; 1952–63; IBM; 10 tests (2 pages); battery manual ['63, 25 pages]; technical report ('63, 81 pages);

$2.50 per 25 test-answer sheets; 40¢ per set of scoring stencils for any one test; 50¢ per manual; $2 per technical report; $3 per specimen set of all tests (without technical report); postage extra; G. Grimsley (*a–h*), F. L. Ruch (*a–g, i, j*), N. D. Warren (*a–g*), and J. S. Ford (*a, c, e–g, j*); Psychological Services, Inc. *

a) TEST 1, VERBAL COMPREHENSION. 1952–63; IBM; Forms A Revised, B Revised, ('56); 5(10) minutes.
b) TEST 2, NUMERICAL ABILITY. 1952–63; IBM; Forms A ('52), B ('56); 10(15) minutes.
c) TEST 3, VISUAL PURSUIT. 1956–63; IBM; Forms A ('56), B ('57); 5(10) minutes.
d) TEST 4, VISUAL SPEED AND ACCURACY. 1952–63; IBM; Forms A ('52), B ('56); 5(10) minutes.
e) TEST 5, SPACE VISUALIZATION. 1952–63; IBM; Forms A Revised, B Revised, ('57); 5(10) minutes.
f) TEST 6, NUMERICAL REASONING. 1952–63; IBM; Forms A Revised, B Revised, ('57); 5(10) minutes.
g) TEST 7, VERBAL REASONING. 1952–63; IBM; Forms A Revised, B Revised, ('57); 5(10) minutes.
h) TEST 8, WORD FLUENCY. 1953–63; 3 forms; the same test blank ('53) is used with all 3 forms; 5(10) minutes.
i) TEST 9, MANUAL SPEED AND ACCURACY. 1953–63; 1 form ('56); 5(10) minutes.
j) TEST 10, SYMBOLIC REASONING. 1956–63; IBM; Forms A, B, ('57); 5(10) minutes.

REFERENCES

1. RUCH, FLOYD L. "Validity Information Exchange, No. 13-02: D.O.T. Code 0-48.18, Engineering Draftsman (Trainee)." *Personnel Psychol* 13:448 w '60. *
2. RUCH, FLOYD L., AND RUCH, WILLIAM W. "Predicting Success in Draftsman Training With Short Time Limit Aptitude Tests." *Ed & Psychol Meas* 20:827–33 w '60. * (*PA* 35:4068)
3. HANEY, RUSSELL; MICHAEL, WILLIAM B.; AND GERSHON, ARTHUR. "Achievement, Aptitude, and Personality Measures as Predictors of Success in Nursing Training." *Ed & Psychol Meas* 22:389–92 su '62. * (*PA* 37:3869)
4. MICHAEL, WILLIAM B.; HANEY, RUSSELL; AND GERSHON, ARTHUR. "Intellective and Non-Intellective Predictors of Success in Nursing Training." *Ed & Psychol Meas* 23:817–21 w '63. *

PAUL F. ROSS, *Industrial Psychologist, Imperial Oil Limited, Toronto, Ontario, Canada.*

The *Employee Aptitude Survey* (EAS) multitest battery was reviewed in *The Fifth Mental Measurements Yearbook* by Dorothy C. Adkins and by S. Rains Wallace. Since those reviews, the original 10 examiner's manuals, one for each test, have been combined into one Examiner's Manual describing test administration and scoring, and the technical information about the tests has been published in a Technical Report. The test battery itself remains unchanged except for one test, Word Fluency (Test 8), which has been standardized using a third letter of the alphabet as the starting, or stimulus, letter. Thus the battery contains eight tests with two forms each, one test with three forms (Word Fluency, Test 8), and one test (Manual Speed and Accuracy, or dotting, Test 9) with one form. This review was prepared after examining the 10 tests in their several forms, the Examiner's Manual (no date of publication), the Technical Report (1963), the Manual for Interpreting the Employee Aptitude Survey (Lockheed Aircraft Corporation, 1957), and the 1963–64 test catalog describing the EAS battery.

The Examiner's Manual is easy to read, presenting instructions for the administration of a test on one side of a page and scoring instructions on the back side of the same page. General instructions describe such practical matters as writing down start and stop times when a watch with a sweep second hand is used for timing and having two pencils for each examinee. Calculating raw scores from rights and wrongs using scoring formulae with fractions is made easy by a fold-out table on the inside back cover; raw scores for all but three tests can be read directly from the table. The 78-page Technical Report contains five chapters and a list of 13 references. Chapters present the rationale for the test battery, its reliability and factorial content, norms by occupation and educational level, validity data, and correlations with other tests. Alternate form correlations (reliability estimates) vary from .75 to .91 for the 10 tests, these correlations coming from samples of 853 to 1,885 examinees. The alternate form correlations are higher than those previously reported, with two relatively unimportant exceptions. The "50-odd correlations with measures other than standardized tests," which Adkins called "a rather impressive array" of validity data, have increased at least five-fold (see comments about validity data below). Most impressive of all, norms covering 45 jobs and 7 educational and industrial groups and "based on over 100,000 test scores" are presented. The jobs are described with a job code from the *Dictionary of Occupational Titles* and a short, one or two sentence job description. The sexes are kept separate in reporting norm data.

Adkins remarked about the many convenient features for using the EAS battery, and Wallace summarized his comments by saying: "This is an outstandingly well thought out and well constructed battery of tests based upon unusually competent analysis. The format, instructions, and scoring keys are uniformly excellent. It deserves the attention of anyone who has a selection problem, particularly for a wide variety of occupations." This reviewer agrees.

But no review is complete without criticisms, and important criticisms can be made of the technical data about this test battery. A summary of the criticisms by Adkins and Wallace can serve as a starting place. They found the battery could be criticized because (*a*) criteria for judging validity of the tests were frequently training criteria rather than on-the-job measures of performance, (*b*) minimum hiring scores, or cutting scores, were recommended for occupations for which no validity data were reported, (*c*) one test (Word Fluency, Test 8) had no validity data reported for it, (*d*) the factor analysis reported was something less than satisfying to the reviewers, and (*e*) general college students do as well as engineers in Space Visualization (Test 5) when Adkins' guesses seem to be that the engineers should do better than general college students. Adkins goes on to say that (*f*) Verbal Comprehension (Test 1) is too easy, (*g*) Symbolic Reasoning (Test 10) "could be improved by adjustment of the item difficulties," which must mean that the test is too difficult, (*h*) the three separately timed parts of the numerical ability test (Test 2) probably should not be printed side by side on an answer sheet, but rather should be in cyclic omnibus order under one time limit, and (*i*) some correct answers for the number series items (Numerical Reasoning, Test 6) are not shown among the answer alternatives.

The test authors appear to have responded to these criticisms. They have increased the amount of validity data reported, and on-the-job ratings of performance are included as criteria. A few validity coefficients are reported for Word Fluency (Test 8). *Suggested cutting scores have been dropped altogether.* The authors discuss why some of the right answers to the number series items are not among the alternatives; the discussion is presented in the Technical Report. But, in this reviewer's opinion, a number of the Adkins-Wallace observations and criticisms can still be made. Validity data based on on-the-job performance measures are still quite thin; the factor analysis may be misleading; Verbal Comprehension is quite easy and Symbolic Reasoning quite difficult (for example, office managers get a mean Verbal Comprehension score of 24 out of a maximum of 30 points, and a mean Symbolic Reasoning score of 9 out of 30 points); Numerical Ability would be easier to administer and perhaps could be shortened to five minutes if it were administered under one time limit with the item types (integers, decimals, fractions) in cyclic omnibus form; engineers, design engineers, and draftsmen now have Space Visualization (Test 5) mean scores which are approximately half a standard deviation higher than the mean scores for male college students and top and middle management.

The factor analysis reported in the Technical Report is the same factor analysis reported in earlier manuals for the EAS battery. The new report seems to be somewhat more complete. But the factor matrix, as reported, could be misleading. The authors omit reporting whether the "factors" are independent (orthogonal) or correlated (oblique) after rotation. The reported factor loadings convey the impression that the tests are virtually factor pure; only three out of nine tests have loadings on more than one factor. If the factors are assumed to be orthogonal, the reader could conclude from the factor matrix that the test intercorrelations are virtually zero. Yet in examining the intercorrelations among the 10 tests, particularly when based on samples of industrial leadmen or utility clerks, it is quite clear that there is a "general factor" present in most of the tests as attested by the moderate, all positive, intercorrelations among most tests in the battery. The modestly high test intercorrelations observed with industrial leadmen are reduced appreciably when the test intercorrelations are based upon persons like General Motors Institute engineering students; that is, the effects of the "general factor" are substantially reduced. Do these tests have enough "ceiling" for the GMI students and other persons with high general ability? Further examination of several sets of intercorrelations among the EAS battery suggests that Test 3 has loadings on two or more common factors just as Tests 2, 4, and 7 have already been found to be factorially complex. The authors need to consider doing additional factor analytic studies of their test battery.

The validity data are contained in 270 correlation coefficients. On-the-job criteria of job performance have been used to estimate 83 of the 270 validity coefficients; 187 coefficients are based on training criteria such as course grades and instructor's ratings. Of the 83 validity coefficients based upon on-the-job criteria, 10 are based on "large" samples of 80 or more people, 18 come from samples of 40 to 79 people, 27 come from samples of 21 to 39 people, and 28 "validity coefficients" come from samples of 20 or fewer people! It seems fair to conclude that there is rather little validity data based upon on-the-job measures of job performance with samples of reasonable size.

Criticism of validity data is not ended with a criticism of the overuse of training criteria or the small samples. The statistical significance of validity coefficients is not called to the reader's attention, thus making it quite possible to examine a "validity" coefficient of .68 based upon a sample of nine people without realizing that the coefficient is not significantly different from zero. Often ratings of job performance were obtained by asking the supervisor to place subordinates in upper and lower groups based on overall job performance, or classroom performance. Using this dichotomized criterion, biserial and tetrachoric correlation coefficients are calculated to report 109 of the 270 validity coefficients. It would seem that there would be little extra work in obtaining ratings on a graphic scale, or ranks, thus improving somewhat on the criterion measurement and making possible the use of the Pearson product-moment or the Spearman rank-order correlation coefficients. One of the reasons why test batteries of this kind are attractive is that the multiple, independent dimensions of human abilities measured by the battery hold the promise of increased validities through the combination of scores from several tests. It is of interest to the reviewer that no validity data are reported for cross-validated combinations of test scores. Not even multiple correlation coefficients are reported among the validity data. The authors present the validity data in such a way that it is impossible to tell which work was done under their own supervision and which was done under the supervision of other researchers. It is very difficult to tell which is new validity information and which has appeared in previous editions of the test manuals. It would seem that the methods of research report writing and citation of bibliographic references common to publication in scientific journals could be used to better advantage in the Technical Report. Validation studies are reported in outlines describing the job, sample, criterion, and validity. The resulting reports can be scanned quickly, and are convenient in that sense. But criteria described as "supervisor's ratings based on over-all job proficiency" or "instructor's ratings" are vaguely described at best and are impossible to reproduce in another study. Extensive use of references to a much enlarged list of sources is desirable.

The normative information supplied in the Technical Report is the most valuable part of the new information contained in the report. Few test publishers have assembled so much norm data for a test or test battery. The norms by occupation and sex make the data particularly valuable. To continue in the role of the critic, however, this reviewer thinks that norm data showing the relationship of test scores to age should be provided; no data of this kind are presented. The addition of a report of the mean and standard deviation of age, educational level, and job service for persons included in a norm group, reporting sex and occupation as already provided, would make an individual's scores even more interpretable. (The norms by educational level have not been overlooked; information obtained by examining them supports the notion of reporting the mean and standard deviation of educational level for all occupational norm groups.) For example, if test data are included in specific occupational norms only after individuals have survived several years in the occupation, it may be possible for vocational counselors and employers to use the norm data as guidelines and thereby add operational definition to the idea of being "over qualified" or "under qualified" for a job. Test users would be fortunate if the test authors have some of the age, educational level, and occupational service information available for the large amount of occupational norm data already published.

Several miscellaneous criticisms can be made. The catalog suggests that certain tests should be used as a battery for certain occupations, 21 occupations altogether being named in this way, but too many of the suggestions are not supported with *validity* data based on either training or on-the-job performance criteria. The third form of Word Fluency (Test 8), which has been added since the last review of this test in the MMY, is not described in terms of either reliability or validity in the Technical Report. The qualifications of the test administrator are not described, nor are the qualifications of the tests' interpreter described. The catalog states: "All orders from recognized business firms (other than employment agencies) and from members of the American Psychological Association will be filled immediately." Is this adequate control over the qualifications of the test purchaser, particularly when any "recognized business firm" can order tests? Is the investment that private (industrial) users make in norming and validating the tests for their own use adequately protected by this sales policy? It may be that the sales policy is appropriate; the reviewer would like to point out that the sales policy cannot be adequately assessed by an examination of the test catalog.

Potential purchasers of the EAS battery will want to compare it with competing test batteries in terms of administration time, administration convenience, apparent factorial content, normative data, validity data, cost, and publisher's sales policy. The long and venerable genealogy of useful tests from which this test battery has descended cannot be overlooked when considering the validity data (which are given a bit of knocking about in this review). The technical data are an improved product over what they were when last reviewed in the MMY, and the test battery itself was appropriately described at that time as "an outstandingly well thought out and well constructed battery of tests based upon unusually competent analysis." The authors and publisher appear to have responded constructively to a few of the criticisms previously offered, thereby improving the technical data and promising, by their behavior, more improvement for the future. The criticisms contained in this review are offered for the attention of the potential purchaser of the tests, who is assumed to be technically qualified to evaluate tests and criticism of tests. The criticisms should not be taken by the casual reader as indicating an overall negative opinion of this battery nor as reflecting doubt about the practical usefulness of the tests.

ERWIN K. TAYLOR, *President, Personnel Research and Development Corporation, Cleveland, Ohio.*

This battery of 10 short tests (nine have a 5-minute time limit and one a 10-minute limit) was comprehensively and quite analytically reviewed in *The Fifth Mental Measurements Yearbook.* It is being reconsidered at this time because of the publication of a 78-page technical manual for which a nominal charge of two dollars per copy is made. Since the reviewer would have nothing of significance to add to what the previous MMY reviewers of this battery said, he will confine his remarks to the technical manual.

The manual consists of five chapters covering the following areas: Rationale of the *Employee Aptitude Survey,* Test Battery Statistics, Occupational and Educational Norms, Validity, and Correlations with Other Tests.

The first chapter, after devoting a page to ease of administration and scoring, availability of alternate forms, face validity, and the existence of short time limits, goes into a rather elaborate rationale for the use of short tests of low intertest correlation. It demonstrates the well documented, but infrequently considered, fact that increases in reliability beyond the value of .70 add very little to a test's potential validity. The manual goes on to demonstrate that by the use of short tests with low intertest correlations, higher validity can be obtained through multiple correlation than through the use of more reliable tests of greater length. This point is—in part, at least—denied by the manual's authors in that they say in the same section that in vocational guidance, which they refer to as "usually a leisurely process," "it is often advisable to use two forms of each EAS test to gain the advantage of greater reliability." It is also noted that in the fourth chapter, which reports a variety of validation studies, only zero order validities, rather than multiple correlations, are reported. The remainder of the first chapter is devoted to a description of the rationale and content of each of the 10 tests in the battery.

The second chapter is devoted to reliability, intercorrelations, and factorial content. Alternate form reliability information is provided for 9 of the 10 tests and test-retest data for the tenth. Based on samples ranging from 853 to 1,885, reliabilities range from .75 to .91. The means and standard deviations of the reliability sample, as well as the standard error of measurement, are given for each. Considering that the tests were apparently administered on a time rather than a power basis these reliabilities may be somewhat inflated by the speed factor. In any event, it would appear that the tests are sufficiently reliable to support substantial validity.

To provide information on the intercorrelations among the tests, the manual contains the equivalent of seven intercorrelation matrices. These are conveniently arranged to give the seven sets of correlations of each test with all the others. Samples range in size from a group of 138 security sales applicants to 335 engineering students. It is interesting to note the wide variability of the intercorrelations in these seven populations. For example, the correlation of Test 1 with Test 2 ranges from .12 to .49, the correlation of Test 3 with Test 10 ranges from .04 to .45, and the correlation of Test 1 with Test 5 ranges from −.01 to .41. Unfortunately, since the manual does not provide the means and standard deviations for these seven groups, there is no opportunity to determine the extent to which the instability of the intertest correlations is a function of the level and homogeneity of the group tested. Nevertheless, it is noteworthy that the manual does provide the reader with a basis for reaching the valid conclusion that the intercorrelations of the tests are not as fixed and final as most test manuals would lead us to believe.

The intercorrelations among the tests are summarized in a single matrix in which the entries are z transformed averages of the equivalent entries from the seven individual matrices.

In the light of the instability of the test intercorrelations demonstrated in the preceding section, one might question the stability of a single factor analysis based on only 90 cases in what is apparently a homogeneous population. It does not appear unlikely that additional factor analysis with larger, different populations might yield considerably different results from the evidence given in the manual.

Both forms of the nine tests for which alternate forms are available were administered to 330 junior college students, half taking each form first. For Test 1 there was no significant difference between the means. For each of the other tests, however, highly significant differences were found. This finding was attributed to a practice or warm-up effect which apparently operated differently at various score levels. It might be noted parenthetically at this point that to the extent that a practice effect existed, the manual's claims with respect to the relationship of reliability and validity to the length of testing time may not be wholly true. A rather extensive table is given for each test, enabling the user to equate the two forms where both are given. Apparently, this difference is purely a function of order of administration, rather than of any lack of equivalence of the two forms.

Chapter 3, "Occupational and Educational Norms," presents 47 sets of norms on employed personnel and 5 on various categories of students. Norms are conveniently arranged by major groupings and are listed in a table of contents at the beginning of the chapter. Accompanying each set of norms is the job title, its DOT code, the sex of the population, and a brief job description. The variability in the n for the several tests for each group suggests that some of the norms groups are apparently composites of smaller populations. The n's vary from a low of 40 "test pilots—jet aircraft" to a high of 2,739 employees of the Denver Division of the Martin-Marietta Corporation. Not all tests were administered to all populations and the number of tests on which norms are available vary from only 3 for telephone operators and electric truck operators up to 9 or 10 for many occupations. It is apparent that a number of the tests, even with their fairly rigid time limits, are somewhat on the easy side and do not provide adequate ceiling for higher level jobs. Thus, the tests appear more appropriate for clerical, semiskilled, skilled, technical, and some sales jobs than for positions at higher levels of technical, managerial, and executive responsibility.

Chapter 4 presents the validity of various tests within the battery for 31 samples from a wide variety of occupational situations. Samples vary from as few as 9 programmers to as many as 474 students at a Texas state college. Most of the validities are against supervisors' ratings or actions of some sort. Many of the correlations reported are biserials. A few are tetrachorics and some are product-moments. Each study names the job, describes the size and nature of the population, and indicates whether the validity is of a concurrent or follow-up nature. Unfortunately, either no other predictors than the EAS tests were incorporated in any of the studies or, if they were, the authors neglected to report them, so that the validity of the EAS tests cannot be compared with that of other instruments which might have been used along with it. In each case only zero order validities are reported and, as previously noted, in spite of the author's earlier plug for multiple correlations, none is presented in the validity chapter.

Validities are quite variable, ranging in one study of 44 male computer programmers from

−.24 for Test 5, Space Visualization, to .41 for Test 6, Numerical Reasoning. Since no credits are given anywhere in this chapter to other researchers, all of the validity data presented were apparently collected by the authors; the claim is made that "more than 2,000,000 EAS tests have been administered since the publication of the 1958 Manuals," and that "many of the results have been made available to the publishers." It would seem logical to assume that additional validity research has been accomplished; it is surprising that so little independent research has been reported in the literature. It seems rather unfortunate that in preparing the manual, and particularly the chapter on validity, the authors did not track down the results obtained by others who may have performed validity studies of these tests.

The final section of the manual deals with the correlational relation of the EAS with such other tests as the *SRA Primary Mental Abilities* and the *California Tests of Mental Maturity* as used on the factor analysis population, as well as scattered reports on Bennett's *Tests of Mechanical Comprehension,* the *Otis Employment Tests,* the *Minnesota Clerical Test,* and the DAT Clerical Speed and Accuracy. The relationships are about what would be expected.

While in reviewing this manual I have found occasion here and there to criticize negatively, my overall impression is highly favorable. The manual certainly does not achieve perfection; however, it presents more industrial data in a more honest and straightforward fashion than does the manual for any other general aptitude battery prepared for industrial use. The authors are to be congratulated for not endeavoring to group similar sounding job titles into so-called "job families" on an armchair basis and then arbitrarily assuming specified tests in their battery to have ubiquitous validity for any position, regardless of level or complexity, that happens to carry the title of one of the jobs in one of the families.

This manual could well serve as a model that publishers of other tests intended for industrial selection use would do well to copy.

J Counsel Psychol 10:407–8 w '63. John O. Crites. [Review of 1963 Technical Report.] * The Technical Report....is a well-organized and well-written manual which presents data on the EAS in a straightforward and professional manner. Unlike some test manuals, its shortcomings are more the result of omission than commission * The reliability estimates are.... quite acceptable, being in the .80's and .90's for all but two of the tests. Data on the interrelationships of the tests are equally favorable, in that they support their independence. Only three tests correlate with each other as high as .40, in contrast to a median *r* of .50 for the entire DAT battery, and these are ones which might be expected to be interrelated (e.g., Verbal Comprehension and Verbal Reasoning). The factor loadings of the EAS battery on appropriate reference variables are generally impressive and further substantiate the essential statistical purity of the tests. * contains norm tables for various occupational groups * Each table includes a job description and DOT code for the occupation, along with centile norms, *N*'s, means, and standard deviations for the EAS tests which are most relevant to the occupation. How the tests were selected, however, and how the norms should be used are not clear, since there is no discussion of them in the report. The implication is that a comparison of an examinee's score with an occupational norm group is in some way meaningful. Actually, about the only information this procedure gives is the relative standing of the examinee in the group: he may rank at the top, in the middle, or at the bottom. How successful he might be in the occupation is not indicated by the normative data, since the groups were not selected on some criterion of success. Even if they had been, there would be the problem of deciding what cut-off scores to use and whether to weight scores on some tests more than others. In short, occupational norms for a multifactor aptitude battery such as the EAS not only have little or no practical utility but they mislead some test users into interpreting them as validity data. * chapter [4] summarizes the relationships of the EAS tests to job performance criteria in clerical, sales, management and supervisory, skilled and semiskilled, and technical occupations. The intent of the chapter is to establish the validity of the battery as a predictor of success in a variety of jobs, but unfortunately the evidence which is presented is not very convincing, for three reasons. First, the *N*'s for the validation samples are, in most cases, very small. Throughout the chapter, the test authors report r's based upon samples with as few subjects as 9, 10, 18, 19, 20, 29, 30, 31, 35, and 36. Not only are r's computed on such N's very unstable, but they often tend to be spuriously high. Second, no significance levels for the r's are reported, and no indication is given that the biserial r's derived from a comparison of more and less successful workers are for extreme groups. If they are not, then they are inflated. Third, and most important, no multiple correlations are reported for the EAS tests, despite the rationale for the battery that less reliable measures should be combined for optimal predictive efficiency. * The EAS is based upon a sound rationale and consists of tests which have proven validity when used separately. As a battery, however, much remains to be demonstrated as far as its usefulness is concerned. In particular, multiple correlations of the tests with job success criteria in large samples need to be conducted and then replicated to establish the magnitude of the R's and the stability of the Beta's for predictive purposes. Until such data are available, personnel workers and counselors should use the EAS as a battery with caution.

For reviews by Dorothy C. Adkins and S. Rains Wallace, see 5:607.

[770]

***Flanagan Aptitude Classification Tests.** Grades 9–12, 10–12 and adults; 1951–60; also called FACT; 2 editions; postage extra; John C. Flanagan; Science Research Associates, Inc. *

a) [SEPARATE BOOKLET 16-TEST EDITION.] Grades 10–12 and adults; 1951–60; 16 tests; examiner's manual ('53, 27 pages); technical supplement ('54, 16 pages); supplementary manuals, preliminary editions ('60, 6 pages) for Tests 15 and 16; counselor's booklet ('53, 35 pages); personnel director's booklet ('53, 27 pages); manual for interpreting scores ('56, 12 pages); aptitude classification sheet ('53, 1 page); student's booklet for interpreting scores ('53, 20 pages); $2.55 per 20 self-marking tests; 60¢ per 20 classification sheets; 30¢ per technical supplement; 25¢ per supplementary manual for either 15 or 16; 40¢ per counselor's booklet; 25¢ per manual for interpreting scores; 25¢ per student's booklet; 50¢ per personnel director's booklet; $3 per educational specimen set; $5.75 per industrial specimen set; 258(388) minutes in 2 sessions.

1) *FACT 1A, Inspection.* 1953–56; form A ('53, 6 pages); 6(12) minutes.
2) *FACT 2A and 2B, Coding.* 1953–56; forms A ('53), B ('54), (6 pages); 10(30) minutes.
3) *FACT 3A and 3B, Memory.* 1953–56; forms A ('53), B ('54), (3 pages); 4(5) minutes.
4) *FACT 4A, Precision.* 1953–56; form A ('53, 4 pages); 8(15) minutes.
5) *FACT 5A, Assembly.* 1953–56; form A ('53, 6 pages); 12(18) minutes.
6) *FACT 6A, Scales.* 1953–56; form A ('53, 6 pages); 16(28) minutes.
7) *FACT 7A, Coordination.* 1953–56; form A ('53, 8 pages); 2⅔(8) minutes.
8) *FACT 8A, Judgment and Comprehension.* 1953–56; form A ('53, 7 pages); (35–40) minutes.
9) *FACT 9A, Arithmetic.* 1953–56; form A ('53, 6 pages); 10(20) minutes.
10) *FACT 10A, Patterns.* 1953–56; form A ('53, 6 pages); 20(28) minutes.
11) *FACT 11A, Components.* 1953–56; form A ('53, 6 pages); 20(24) minutes.
12) *FACT 12A, Tables.* 1953–56; form A ('53, 6 pages); 10(15) minutes.
13) *FACT 13A and 13B, Mechanics.* 1953–56; forms A ('53), B ('54), (6 pages); 20(25) minutes.
14) *FACT 14A, Expression.* 1953–56; form A ('53, 6 pages); (35–45) minutes.
15) *FACT 15A, Reasoning.* 1957–60; form A ('57, 6 pages); 24(30) minutes.
16) *FACT 16A, Ingenuity.* 1957–60; form A ('57, 7 pages); 24(30) minutes.

b) [19-TEST EDITION.] Grades 9–12; 1957–60; MRC; 19 tests (same as for *a* plus vocabulary, planning, alertness) in 2 booklets: gray book ('57, 64 pages), blue book ('57, 24 pages); examiner's manual ('58, 70 pages); mimeographed norms ['58, 23 pages]; administrator's manual ('58, 17 pages); technical report, first edition ('59, 65 pages); mimeographed manual for planning short batteries ('60, 10 pages); student's booklet for interpreting scores ('58, 25 pages); separate answer sheets must be used with gray book (blue book, containing Tests 14–19, is scored by students); 60¢ per gray book; 20¢ per blue book; 8¢ per MRC answer sheet; $1.03 per set of stencils for hand scoring MRC answer sheets (machine scoring through the publisher only; fees: $1 per student including copy of student's booklet for each student, 70¢ per student without student's booklet); 35¢ per student's booklet; 50¢ per examiner's manual; 35¢ per administrator's manual; $2 per technical report; $3 per specimen set; manual for planning short batteries free; (630) minutes in 3 sessions.

REFERENCES

1. LATHAM, ALBERT J. *Job Appropriateness: A One-Year Follow-Up of High School Graduates.* Doctor's thesis, University of Pittsburgh (Pittsburgh, Pa.), 1948.
2. VOLKIN, LEONARD. *A Validation Study of Selected Test Batteries Applied to Fields of Work.* Doctor's thesis, University of Pittsburgh (Pittsburgh, Pa.), 1951.
3. FLANAGAN, JOHN C. "Job Element Aptitude Classification Tests." *Personnel Psychol* 7:1–14 sp '54. * (PA 29:3127)
4. CURETON, EDWARD E. "Service Tests of Multiple Aptitudes." *Proc Inv Conf Testing Probl* 1955:22–39 '56. * (PA 31:3017)
5. FLANAGAN, JOHN C. "The Flanagan Aptitude Classification Tests." Comments by Donald E. Super. *Personnel & Guid J* 35:495–507 Ap '57. *
6. WHITE, ARDEN JUNIOR. *A Comparison of the Flanagan Aptitude Classification Tests With the Wechsler Adult Intelligence Scale, the School and College Ability Test, and Three Other Measures of Mental Variables at the High School Level.* Doctor's research study No. 1, Colorado State College (Greeley, Colo.), 1959.
7. BOLTON, FLOYD B. "Value of a Vocational Aptitude Test Battery for Predicting High School Achievement." *Personnel & Guid J* 42:280–4 N '63. *

NORMAN FREDERIKSEN, *Director of Research, Educational Testing Service, Princeton, New Jersey.* [Review of the 19-Test Edition.]

FACT (the *Flanagan Aptitude Classification Tests*) is a battery of tests intended for use in counseling high school students with respect to educational and vocational plans. Guidance materials have been prepared that lead to specific predictions of success in 37 occupational areas, 20 of which require college preparation and 17 of which do not. The earlier (1953) edition of FACT contained 14 tests [1] and was somewhat lacking in predictors of academic achievement. The 1958 version contains 19 tests. The added tests, which bear the titles Reasoning, Vocabulary, Planning, Ingenuity, and Alertness, appear to make up this deficiency. Most, but not all, FACT tests are multiple choice tests with five options. The time required for administration is about 10½ hours. The suggested procedure is to give the tests in three 3½-hour sessions.

Each FACT test corresponds to an aptitude, or job element. According to the Technical Report, job elements are identified by a method that includes (*a*) listing the critical behaviors in a job, (*b*) translating the critical behaviors into hypotheses about the nature of the aptitudes involved, and (*c*) testing the hypothesis that variations in job performance are correlated with measures of the related aptitude. Since it is not usually possible to test hypotheses about the relationships between aptitude and job performance with a high degree of rigor (because satisfactory criteria of job performance are lacking), and since the identification of "critical" behaviors and the generation of hypotheses about the relevant aptitudes are both rather subjective procedures, the test selection does not have a strong empirical foundation. The author regards this as an advantage and is inclined to disparage heavy dependence on empirical studies. Whether or not one agrees with the rationale of the procedure described, the test selection in general seems sensible. Indirectly it does have considerable empirical foundation through the author's extensive experience in Air Force selection during World War II.

Test 1, Inspection, is supposed to measure ability to spot flaws in articles quickly and accurately. The 80 items consist of small pictures —120 to a page—of objects such as safety pins, screws, and buckles. The task is to identify the one in each set of five that is not like the model. Test 2, Mechanics, consists of four-choice items about diagrams depicting devices such as an electric motor and a pressure gauge. The test is rather difficult; according to the norms, ninth graders get 9 of the 30 items right, on the average, while twelfth graders get 11 right. Test 3, Tables, requires the student to look up cell entries in tables. Test 4, Reasoning, requires the student to translate problems stated in words into mathematical notation. It contains 24 five-choice items. Ninth graders on the average get 6 items right and twelfth graders get 9 right. Test 5, Vocabulary, is a conventional synonyms test of 60 five-choice items. This test is also rather difficult for high school students, the median raw score for ninth graders being 13 and for twelfth graders 20. Each item of Test 6, Assembly, requires the student to choose the one of five pictures that represents how several solid parts would look when properly assembled. Drawings are reasonably clear and accurate, but with 10 items per page they are quite small. Test 7, Judgment and Comprehension, is a reading comprehension test, with 4 items based on each of 6 paragraphs. Test 8, Components, is a variation of a hidden figures test. It contains 40 five-choice items and is rather difficult, the figures being hidden in rather complex drawings. The mean is 17 for ninth graders and 22 for twelfth graders. Test 9, Planning, requires the student to rearrange steps in the execution of a task, such as making a cake or building a patio, into a good order. Test 10, Arithmetic, measures speed and accuracy in adding, subtracting, multiplying, and dividing. Test 11, Ingenuity, is supposed to measure ability to devise ingenious solutions to problems presented in short paragraphs. The solution to each problem must be expressed in a word or so, and the multiple choice answer is selected on the basis of first and last letters of the words. Test 12, Scales, requires the student to read values from graphs. The median raw scores for ninth and twelfth graders on the 72 items are 19 and 25, respectively. Test 13, Expression, measures knowledge of English grammar, usage, and sentence structure. Items consist of sentences; some are to be evaluated as right or wrong from the standpoint of grammar, and some are to be ranked in sets of three in terms of clarity and smoothness. All the above 13 tests are printed in one test booklet for use with a separate answer sheet.

1 The 16-Test Edition referred to in the entry preceding the review contains two additional tests which were added in 1957.—Editor.

A second booklet contains tests that do not require a separate answer sheet. Test 14, Precision, is supposed to measure ability to do precision work with small objects. The task is to draw lines rapidly between guide lines in small circular and square patterns. Test 15, Alertness, consists of 36 pictures, each of which depicts a potentially dangerous situation, such as a frayed electric cord, in a complex setting. The task is to identify the dangerous object in each picture. Test 16, Coordination, is another tracing task, this one requiring hand and arm movements. Test 17, Patterns, is a test in which the student reproduces geometrical designs, some of them upside down, on a grid. The instructions for Test 18, Coding, tell the student to mark the correct code numbers for sales districts, paint colors, etc., memorizing them as he goes along. It is possible, and perhaps more efficient, to perform the task without memorizing. The last test, Memory, demands that the student use the correct code numbers from the previous test without the possibility of looking them up. Performance on Memory thus depends in part upon how the student chose to do the coding in the previous test.

No information is given about item difficulties or item validities; in fact, there is nothing in the Technical Report to suggest that item analyses were made. Information from the norms tables suggests that a number of the tests are rather difficult even for high school seniors and that a selection of items that are less difficult might have improved the reliability of some of the tests. Nevertheless the test construction job in general appears to have been well done. The directions to supervisors seem clear and complete, and instructions to students seem satisfactory.

National norms tables are presented for ninth, tenth, eleventh, and twelfth grades, from which raw scores on each test may be converted to percentiles and stanines. These "general national norms" were based on a standardization group said to be "as typical as possible of ninth-, tenth-, eleventh-, and twelfth-grade students throughout the country." The group is described as including almost 11,000 students from 11 states—1 in the East, 5 in the South, 3 in the Middle West, and 2 in the West. From a statement in the Acknowledgments it is possible to deduce that the East is represented by West Virginia; the South by Mississippi, Kentucky, Oklahoma, Georgia, and South Carolina; the Middle West by Illinois, Michigan, and Wisconsin; and the West by Utah and California. Some of these states contributed very few cases, the smallest number being 59. Two school systems in two states contributed almost 7,000 of the 11,000 cases. Labeling these data as "national" norms is questionable.

Most of the reliabilities that are reported are based on correlations between separately timed parts, which is appropriate in view of the fact that most of the tests are speeded. Odd-even correlations are used in the case of two unspeeded tests—Judgment and Comprehension, and Expression. Alternate form reliabilities from an earlier study of twelfth graders are reported for Coding and Memory. The median of the 17 reliability coefficients reported for ninth graders is .75, with a range from .52 (for Mechanics) to .86 (for Coordination). The comparable values for the 19 tests for the twelfth grade (including the earlier data for Coding and Memory) are .75, .55 (for Memory), and .91 (for Vocabulary). The reliabilities tend to be rather low for tests intended for use in counseling. The author states, however, that the tests are not intended for use separately but rather in combinations selected for various occupational fields. Reliabilities for several combinations are presented. The reliability (for twelfth grade students) of the combination of seven tests for chemist is reported to be .93, of the four tests for office clerk .87, and of the six tests for mechanic .91, to cite a few.

Intercorrelations of the 19 tests are reported separately for ninth and twelfth grades, based on about 1,000 students in each grade from the two school systems that contributed most of the norms data. Intercorrelations are in general fairly low; the median correlations are .20 and .31 for ninth and twelfth grades, respectively. Pairs of tests such as Arithmetic and Tables ($r = .60$), Ingenuity and Vocabulary ($r = .62$), and Reasoning and Judgment and Comprehension ($r = .58$) have correlations that are relatively high. Among the less academic tests, correlations of Patterns with Scales ($r = .49$) and Coding with Memory ($r = .51$) are fairly high, the latter partly because of experimental dependence. (The r's reported above are for twelfth grade students.)

The information on reliability and intercorrelations is summarized in a meaningful way by dividing the variance of each test into three parts: error variance, overlapping variance, and unique variance. Inspection of the table for ninth graders reveals, for example, that 48 per cent of the variance of Mechanics is attributable to error, 27 per cent is overlapping variance (i.e., can be predicted by other tests in the battery), and 25 per cent is unique variance (variance potentially useful for prediction and not found in other parts of the battery). We find in the twelfth grade table that 10 per cent of the variance for Expression is error variance, 39 per cent is overlapping variance, and 51 per cent is unique; while for Reasoning 26 per cent is error variance, 65 per cent is overlapping, and 9 per cent is unique. The usefulness of such information in test battery construction is apparent. The information about FACT tests might logically have led to a battery with fewer than 19 tests.

FACT tests are intended to be used in combination, and recommendations are made as to how the tests are to be combined into occupational aptitude scores. The recommendations are based on a survey of follow-up studies, concurrent validity studies, and job analysis findings. According to the Technical Report, the recommendations are to be viewed as working hypotheses that are subject to revision as the results of validity studies accumulate. The recommendations seem sensible. For the occupational area engineer, for example, the recommended tests are Mechanics, Reasoning, Assembly, Judgment and Comprehension, Components, Scales, and Patterns. For clergyman, the tests are Vocabulary, Judgment and Comprehension, Expression, and Memory; and for printer they are Inspection, Mechanics, Scales, and Precision. Although the recommendations viewed one at a time seem eminently reasonable, comparisons of recommendations for similar occupations yield a few surprises. For example, it seems strange that Planning is judged to be important for physicist but not for engineer, that Ingenuity is required for psychologist but not for lawyer, and that Precision is important for electrician but not for draftsman. It appears that some effort was made to reduce overlap in the recommendations; the more overlap, the less differential prediction is possible.

The intercorrelations of the composite occupational aptitude scores are very high for occupations requiring college training, largely because of similarities in the test recommendations. In one case (for humanities teacher and clergyman) the tests recommended are exactly the same and the correlation is of course 1.00. Of the 210 correlations in the twelfth graders' table for college occupations, 74 are .90 or greater and 149 are .80 or greater. The correlation between composites for teacher and business administrator is .97; between physician and artist, .96; and between physicist and lawyer, .95. The student seeking some basis for a choice between such pairs of occupations will get little help from FACT. Intercorrelations of composites for non-college jobs are much lower; they range from .34 to .98, with a median of .70, for twelfth grade data.

Predictive validity studies have been conducted, using data from students tested in 1952 with the earlier version of FACT. For college-level occupations, the criteria used combined measures of progress in the field and performance as measured by college grades. College achievement must have accounted for most of the variation in the criteria, since, for the period of time covered, progress in the field is largely progress in academic training. The number of cases is usually small because the 1,200 students studied entered a large number of different occupations. With n's ranging from 24 to 133, the nine correlations between the criterion and occupational stanine scores ranged from .04 to .65. An attempt was also made to build criteria based on salary and promotion for non-college occupations. Correlations with occupational stanines for five business and clerical fields approximated zero, but somewhat better luck was obtained with three technical fields. A large number of concurrent validity studies, mostly with grade criteria, are also described, as well as correlations with other tests. The report of all these studies leaves one with two impressions: (*a*) that academic criteria can be predicted with certain FACT tests about as well as with conventional scholastic aptitude tests; and (*b*) that better solutions to criterion problems in occupational areas will have to be found before the results of validity studies will be very useful in guiding aptitude test development.

The Student's Booklet provides the student with a simple procedure for interpreting his test scores in terms of predicted success and satisfaction in the 37 occupational areas. The cover of the booklet extends an inch above the inside pages, and in this space the student places a gummed strip containing a report of his percentile scores. The scores are thus visible no matter where the booklet is opened. The pages contain sections corresponding to the occupational areas. The section for each area includes a short job description, a list of related job titles, and a list of the FACT tests that have been chosen to form the occupational test composite. The student copies his scores in spaces opposite the names of the tests. Then he rearranges the percentiles in rank order and finds the median, which is his occupational score. Finally, he compares the median percentile with the cutting score given for that occupation.

The method of combining test scores to form occupational composites that was used in obtaining reliabilities, intercorrelations, and validities is not specified in the Technical Report, but it seems unlikely that medians were used. Judging from the method used for the earlier version of FACT, it is more likely that occupational scores were formed by combining stanine scores with equal weights. If this assumption is true, the reliabilities, intercorrelations, and validities would all be slightly lower for scores produced by the method described in the Student's Booklet, since the median has a larger error than a mean.

The Administrator's Manual describes the cutting scores by saying that "of those students who entered and succeeded in the occupation, 80 percent exceeded the cut-off score; 20 percent did not." This statement implies the existence of data supporting the choice of each cutting score; but one looks in vain to find it. Score distributions are shown for "students subsequently identified as satisfied and successful members of certain occupational groups," but the data obviously do not justify the "80 percent" interpretation of the cutting scores for most areas. For example, one table presents score distributions for students subsequently identified as satisfied and successful engineers and scientists. The table is based on only 22 cases—17 engineers, 4 chemists, and 1 biologist. But separate cutting scores are given in the Student's Booklet for engineers, chemists, and biologists (to say nothing of physicists, for whom no data are reported). Predictive validity data for single specific occupations, with *n*'s varying from 1 to 312, are presented for fewer than half of the 37 occupations for which cutting scores are recommended. Even when concurrent validity studies and studies reported in a section called "Validity Exchange" are considered, there are still a substantial number of occupations for which recommended cutting scores are included in the Student's Booklet but no validity data are reported. A statement in the Technical Report that many of the recommendations are based only on job analyses, and not on validity studies, seems to be more accurate than the statement in the Administrator's Manual.

From many points of view, the FACT battery is of high quality. There is a defensible rationale for the tests, they are for the most part good tests, the accessory materials are well planned, and the statistical analyses are competent. But there is less empirical justification for using FACT as the basis for a counseling program than seems at first glance to be supplied by the Technical Report. The informed judgment of an experienced psychologist is the real basis for the FACT tests and the recommendations for their use.

WILLIAM B. MICHAEL, *Professor of Education and Psychology, University of California, Santa Barbara, California.* [Review of the 19-Test Edition.]

In comparison with the 1953 edition of the *Flanagan Aptitude Classification Tests* (FACT), which consisted of 14 tests printed in separate booklets, the 1958 edition is composed of 19 tests which have been issued in two booklets. The "gray book" includes the first 13 tests, which may be completed on separate answer sheets designed for machine scoring. These tests may be reused many times. The "blue book" includes the remaining six tests, which are not reusable and which are to be hand scored by the examinees themselves.

The five new tests include Reasoning (Test 4), Vocabulary (Test 5), Planning (Test 9), Ingenuity (Test 11), and Alertness (Test 15). That Tests 4 and 5, and possibly Tests 9 and 11, reflect academic aptitudes should serve substantially to correct a major weakness of the first edition as a predictor of success in college work—a shortcoming that Carroll pointed out in his review of the 1953 edition of the FACT battery in *The Fifth Mental Measurements Yearbook*. Although Flanagan's total testing program called for the coverage of 21 job elements, two measures, Carving and Tapping, have not been included in the present battery, since they are not pencil and paper tests.

There are many commendable features in the 1958 edition—especially the elegant format of both the test materials and manuals and the mechanics of administration, scoring, reporting, and interpretation. Both the Administrator's Manual and the Examiner's Manual are comprehensive and clear. Whether or not one agrees with Flanagan's rationale concerning the construction of tests and the interpretation of their scores around critical job requirements, the Student's Booklet offers a straightforward and stimulating appraisal of the meaning of scores on sub-batteries—typically three to seven tests—considered to be pertinent to 37 different job families (the activities of which are lucidly described in operational terms in the Student's Booklet). The examinee simply places in rank order the centiles he has earned on each test of the sub-battery and determines whether his median centile is above or below a value that is recommended for success in the occupation cited. Although serious questions may be raised concerning the accuracy of the recommended cutting score, examinees are taking an active part in determining their own potentialities and in discovering their own relative strengths or weaknesses on each of the tests of the battery, in the general college aptitude composite, and in each of 37 occupational composites. Despite the fact that students are warned in their own manual that the scores are not absolute, it appears that the emphasis has not been strong enough. Of course, if the teachers and counselors utilize the group counseling sessions in terms of the specific directions and cautions cited and follow other suggestions in the Administrator's Manual, the risk of misinterpretation should be minimized.

The major weaknesses in the program of FACT lie in the inadequacy of the norms, in the degree of reliability of several of the subtests, and particularly in the *evidence* presented concerning the validity both of the job element approach and of the tests themselves. In fairness it should be emphasized that there have been substantial improvements—especially in the new normative data.

In the Technical Report the data for a national standardization of the test on a group of 10,972 students from 17 schools representing 11 school systems and 11 states are reported for ninth, tenth, eleventh, and twelfth grades. The attempt was made to select this norm group in order that at the eleventh grade level it would be nearly equivalent to a much larger national sample on which the *Iowa Tests of Educational Development* had been standardized. Normative data are presented in terms of both centile and stanine values. (Most of the individuals in the original normative samples, which included a group of approximately 1,400 Pittsburgh students tested in December 1952, participated in one-year and five-year follow-up studies of occupational success. The resulting data are reported in the validity section of the Technical Report.)

From an inspection of the normative data for each test it appears that most of the tests yield for each grade level in high school a substantial range of scores, an adequate basis for differentiation among individuals, and relatively symmetrical distributions of scores. There are exceptions. Tests 5 and 18, Vocabulary and Coding, furnish, respectively, positively and negatively skewed distribution of scores. With only 30 four-response items, the normative data for Mechanics reveal the 50th and 99th percentiles of raw scores to be 9 and 20, respectively, for ninth graders, and 11 and 25, respectively, for twelfth graders. Reliability estimates of only .52 and .67 for ninth and twelfth graders, respectively, are reported. (The reviewer was unable to find any information concerning the nature of the scoring formula used.) Similar comments might also be made concerning the 24-item Test 4, Reasoning. Serious doubt is cast on the usefulness of either one of these tests as a separate unit for assessment purposes.

A comparison of the estimates of reliability furnished for the 1953 and 1958 editions reveals similar values. For ninth graders and twelfth graders, respectively, the range of the 17 estimated reliabilities in the 1958 normative group (no 1958 figures are reported for Coding and Memory) was from .52 to .86 and from .61 to .91, median values being .75 and .77, respectively. Flanagan has proposed using composites of three or more tests for the purpose of occupational classification; the reliabilities of the composites are probably adequate. Lacking information concerning either item analysis statistics or any revisions of items in light of preliminary tryouts of test material, one wonders how much the estimates of reliability of individual tests might have been improved through additional efforts in test construction.

The greatest potential weakness of the FACT program may well rest on its validity, although admittedly differences in theoretical position or philosophical orientation concerning what is meant by the term validity will not permit a definitive conclusion. The reliance in both the 1953 and 1958 editions on development of test items that can be matched against descriptions of hypothesized psychological activities in a given occupation will be challenged by many who prefer either empirical studies or the utilization of the factor analytic model. Since in *The Fifth Mental Measurements Yearbook* both Bechtoldt and Carroll presented detailed critiques of Flanagan's job element position, further comment seems superfluous.

Those who favor empirical procedures will take some measure of satisfaction from a limited amount of empirical data in the Technical Report, which, as mentioned previously, consisted of one-year and five-year follow-up studies. A numerical code for progress was developed and applied to several different occupational areas, and predictive validities of occupational stanines relative to the constructed criterion measures were obtained for many relatively small groups of individuals taken from the 1952 Pittsburgh standardization sample. These predictive validities showed about as much promise as those indices one may find for competing test batteries. Reported in a separate section of the Technical Report are validity studies in which concurrent criteria such as grades in various high school courses were correlated with scores on individual test units. An extensive collection of concurrent validity coefficients of the FACT scales with test measures from other batteries is also presented. Again the results seem to compare favorably with those revealed by competing publishers for their tests.

Somewhat less satisfactory to many measurement specialists as evidence of validity are the data in the Technical Report concerning the proportion of *unique variance* and *error variance* in each test. The application of a correction for attenuation of the multiple correlation coefficient of each composite of 18 tests with the single test not in the composite was made to allow for errors of measurement in the composite. The unique variance is equal to the difference between the reliability estimate for a single test and the ratio of the coefficient of multiple determination to the reliability of the composite. Since corrections for attenuation can be deceptive, there is considerable doubt in the reviewer's mind concerning the helpfulness to the test consumer of this approach. Additional evidence for the uniqueness of each of the 19 tests is furnished by the relatively low intercorrelations which, to a considerable extent, were probably facilitated by the relatively low reliabilities of certain test units.

Finally, the validity of these tests may be viewed in terms of whether other test specialists agree with Flanagan and his associates concerning the job elements these tests measure. No such evidence has been presented. Careful reading of Carroll's detailed analysis in *The Fifth Mental Measurements Yearbook* of the content in each of the 14 tests in the 1953 edition of FACT would indicate that there may be room for considerable disagreement. As nearly as the reviewer can determine, relatively few changes have been made in the content of the items in the tests common to the 1953 and 1958 editions. Apparently Carroll's criticisms of Coding have not been given serious study, and certainly the carry-over of Coding's defects to the Memory test, in which the examinee must respond in terms of the codes, has not been remedied.

What may be said of the content of the five new tests in the 1958 edition? Reasoning and Vocabulary appear to be similar to those that bear the same names in competing batteries, although the reliability of the former test is relatively low, probably because of its containing only 30 items. Planning, which requires the examinee's placing in an appropriate order the steps involved in designing or carrying out a certain project, suggests alternatives that may not necessarily have a single best sequence. In this test the four problem situations associated with only 32 items have yielded scores with reliability estimates of only .73 and .66 for ninth and twelfth graders, respectively. To the reviewer the test titled Ingenuity, which appears to be highly complex factorially, demands of the examinee a high level of reading comprehension, a substantial vocabulary, possession of considerable general information, and a fluency with words. The reviewer would be at a loss to match the items of this test with the hypothesized psychological processes underlying elements of particular job families, although the instrument might be expected to display substantial predictive validity in certain college curricula. In the fifth new test, Alertness, 36 pictures are presented; in each, the task is to pick the one of five lettered objects which presents a potential danger or detrimental influence. The low estimates of reliability of .63 and .61 for ninth and twelfth graders, respectively, may be a function of the exceedingly short time limit of three minutes, although the range of scores is substantial.

In summary, the 19 FACT tests cover a variety of different aptitudes, the measurement of which has been anchored to a rationale for the construction of items around critical job activities. The detailed and explicit manuals for the examiner, administrator, and student, as well as careful application of information in the Technical Report, may be expected to result in a program which is highly efficient in the mechanics not only of administering and scoring tests, but also of reporting and interpreting their results. Although under adequate supervision the instructional and guidance value of the FACT program for the high school student should be substantial, several of the individual tests could be improved from the standpoint of revamping certain blocks of items, furnishing up-to-date normative information, increasing the level of reliability of the scales, and obtaining additional estimates of their predictive validities. Despite the limitations cited, the FACT battery compares favorably with other batteries that are being marketed by competing test publishers.

For reviews by Harold P. Bechtoldt, Ralph F. Berdie, and John B. Carroll of a, *see 5:608.*

[771]

***General Aptitude Test Battery.** Ages 16 and over, grades 9–12 and adults; 1946–63; developed for use in the occupational counseling program of the United States Employment Service and released in 1947 (*a*) and 1952 (*b*) for use by State Employment Services; IBM, NCS, and DocuTran for *b;* 2 editions; manual in 3 sections: section 1, administration and scoring ('63, 63 pages for *a;* '62, 68 pages for *b*) and sections 2, norms-occupational aptitude pattern structure ('62, 113 pages) and 3, development ('62, 237 pages) for *b* but also used with *a;* record blank ['61, 2 pages] for apparatus tests of both editions; tests (except for separate booklet edition of *b*) available to nonprofit institutions for counseling purposes; no testing fee for applicants tested through the facilities of State Employment Service offices; institutions using their own facilities must purchase tests and employ trained testing supervisors; manual available for unrestricted sale at 45¢ for either edition of section 1, 70¢ for section 2, and $2 for section 3; orders for tests and all other accessories must be cleared through State Employment Service offices, from which details may be secured; postpaid; specimen set not available; 51(135) minutes; United States Employment Service; test materials except for performance tests distributed for the Service by United States Government Printing Office. *

a) GATB, B-1001, [EXPENDABLE BOOKLET EDITION]. Ages 16 and over; 1947–63; 10 scores: intelligence, verbal, numerical, spatial, form perception, clerical perception, aiming, motor speed, finger dexterity, manual dexterity; 1 form ('46); 15 tests: 11 tests in 2 booklets plus 4 performance tests; revised profile card ('61, 2 pages); revised adult aptitude pattern card ('61, 2 pages).

1) *Book 1.* 1 form (34 pages); 5 tests: tool matching, name comparison, H markings, computation, two-dimensional space; $18.75 per 100 tests.

2) *Book 2.* 1 form (27 pages); 6 tests: speed, three-dimensional space, arithmetic reasoning, vocabulary, mark making, form matching; $15 per 100 tests.

3) *Pegboard.* 2 tests: place, turn; $18.50 per set of testing materials; distributed by Specialty Case Manufacturing Co. Test Equipment and Warwick Products Co.

4) *Finger Dexterity Board.* 2 tests: assemble, disassemble; $8.65 per set of testing materials; distributed by Specialty Case Manufacturing Co. Test Equipment and Warwick Products Co.

b) GATB, B-1002, [SEPARATE ANSWER SHEET EDITION]. Grades 9–12 and adults; 1952–63; 9 scores: same as for *a* above except for omission of aiming and motor speed; IBM, NCS, and DocuTran except for part 8 and performance tests; Forms A ('52), B ('53) of paper and pencil tests; 12 tests: 8 tests in 3 booklets plus 4 performance tests; paper and pencil tests also available in 8 separate booklets for restricted use by State Employment Services in testing adults; supplement to section 1 ['62, 30 pages] of the manual, for use when DocuTran scoring service is employed; supplement to section 1 ['63, 38 pages] of the manual, for use with NCS answer sheets; revised profile card ('61, 2 pages); revised aptitude pattern cards ('61, 2 pages) for grades 9, 10, adults (only the card for adults is used with the separate booklet edition); separate IBM, NCS, or (combined booklet edition only) DocuTran answer sheets must be used; $9.50 per 500 IBM answer sheets; (NCS accessories and scoring service available through National Computer Systems: fee, 25¢ per examinee, plus $3 per 100 NCS answer sheets, $2 per 100 test center identification sheets, 50¢ per optional hand scoring stencil, 25¢ per NCS supplement to section 1 of the manual, postage extra; DocuTran accessories and scoring service available through Science Research Associates, Inc.: fee, 25¢ per examinee, plus $2 per 100 DocuTran answer sheets, 60¢ per 20 test center identification sheets, 50¢ per set of optional hand scoring keys, 25¢ per DocuTran supplement to section 1 of the manual, postage extra); *separate booklet edition prices:* $4.25 ($5.50) per 100 tests of Form A (Form B) name perception, computation, or arithmetic reasoning, $2.50 ($2.75) per 100 tests of Form A (Form B) vocabulary or form matching, $7.50 ($8.75) per 100 tests of Form A (Form B) three-dimensional space or tool matching, $2.75 per 100 tests of part 8.

1) *Book 1.* 2 forms (24 pages); 4 tests: name perception, computation, three-dimensional space, vocabulary; $14 per 100 tests of Form A; $15 per 100 tests of Form B.

2) *Book 2.* 2 forms (17 pages); 3 tests: tool matching, arithmetic reasoning, form matching; $10 per 100 tests of Form A; $12 per 100 tests of Form B.

3) *Part 8* [*Mark Making*]. 1 form (4 pages); $2.75 per 100 tests.

4) *Pegboard.* Same as a3 above.

5) *Finger Dexterity Board.* Same as a4 above.

REFERENCES

1–33. See 4:714.

34–209. See 5:609.

210. SENIOR, NOËL. *An Analysis of the Effect of Four Years of College Training on General Aptitude Test Battery Scores.* Master's thesis, University of Utah (Salt Lake City, Utah), 1952.

211. BEAMER, GEORGE C., AND ROSE, TOM. "The Use of the GATB and the AIA Tests in Predicting Success in Accounting." *Acctg R* 30:533–5 Jl '55. *

212. ANDERSON, PAULINE K. "The Use of the General Aptitude Test Battery in the Employment Service." *Proc Inv Conf Testing Probl* 1955:16–21 '56. * (*PA* 31:3202)

213. CURETON, EDWARD E. "Service Tests of Multiple Aptitudes." *Proc Inv Conf Testing Probl* 1955:22–39 '56. * (*PA* 31:3017)

214. JEX, FRANK B. *University of Utah Studies in the Prediction of Academic Success.* University of Utah Research Monographs in Education, Vol. 1, No. 1. Salt Lake City, Utah: the University, July 1957. Pp. ix, 51. *

215. HIRT, MICHAEL LEONARD. *Use of the General Aptitude Test Battery to Determine Aptitude Changes With Age and to Predict Job Performance.* Doctor's thesis, University of Nebraska (Lincoln, Neb.), 1958. (*DA* 19:1436)

216. PICKETT, LOUIS M. *The General Aptitude Test Battery as a Predictor of College Success.* Master's thesis, Utah State University (Logan, Utah), 1958.

217. UNITED STATES EMPLOYMENT SERVICE. "Validity Information Exchange, No. 11-25: D.O.T. Code 4-15.020, Weaver; 6-19.635, Weaver." *Personnel Psychol* 11:440–1 au '58. *

218. UNITED STATES EMPLOYMENT SERVICE. "Validity Information Exchange, No. 11-26: D.O.T. Code 6-14.420, Looper." *Personnel Psychol* 11:581–2 w '58. *

219. UNITED STATES EMPLOYMENT SERVICE. "Validity Information Exchange, No. 11-27: D.O.T. Code 6-98.251, Grid Operator." *Personnel Psychol* 11:583–4 w '58. *

220. UNITED STATES EMPLOYMENT SERVICE. "Validity Information Exchange, No. 11-28: D.O.T. Code 7-76.110, Egg Candler." *Personnel Psychol* 11:585 w '58. *

221. UNITED STATES EMPLOYMENT SERVICE. "Validity Information Exchange, No. 11-30: D.O.T. Code 9-68.60, Fruit Sorter; 9-68.60, Olive Sorter; 9-68.35, Packer (Agric.)." *Personnel Psychol* 11:587–90 w '58. *

222. HIRT, MICHAEL. "Another Look at the Relationship Between Interests and Aptitudes." *Voc Guid Q* 7:171–3 sp '59. *

223. HIRT, MICHAEL. "Use of the General Aptitude Test Battery to Determine Aptitude Changes With Age and to Predict Job Performance." *J Appl Psychol* 43:36–9 F '59. * (*PA* 34:4828)

224. NICKSICK, THEODORE, JR., AND BEAMER, GEORGE C. "Aptitude Patterns for Selected Major Fields of Study." *Personnel & Guid J* 38:43–5 S '59. *

225. SHARP, H. C., AND PICKETT, L. M. "The General Aptitude Test Battery as a Predictor of College Success." *Ed & Psychol Meas* 19:617–23 w '59. * (*PA* 34:6573)

226. UNITED STATES EMPLOYMENT SERVICE. "Validity Information Exchange, No. 12-8: D.O.T. Code 2-63.10, Fireman II." *Personnel Psychol* 12:313–4 su '59. *

227. UNITED STATES EMPLOYMENT SERVICE. "Validity Information Exchange, No. 12-9: D.O.T. Code 4-44.110, Linotype Operator." *Personnel Psychol* 12:315 su '59. *

228. UNITED STATES EMPLOYMENT SERVICE. "Validity Information Exchange, No. 12-10: D.O.T. Code 5-83.641, Packaging-Machine Mechanic." *Personnel Psychol* 12:316 su '59. *

229. UNITED STATES EMPLOYMENT SERVICE. "Validity Information Exchange, No. 12-11: D.O.T. Code 6-14.063, Transfer Knitter." *Personnel Psychol* 12:317 su '59. *

230. UNITED STATES EMPLOYMENT SERVICE. "Validity Information Exchange, No. 12-12: D.O.T. Code 6-14.064, Seamless-Hosiery Knitter." *Personnel Psychol* 12:318–9 su '59. *

231. UNITED STATES EMPLOYMENT SERVICE. "Validity Information Exchange, No. 12-13: D.O.T. Code 6-62.055, Clicking-Machine Operator." *Personnel Psychol* 12:320–1 su '59. *

232. UNITED STATES EMPLOYMENT SERVICE. "Validity Information Exchange, No. 12-14: D.O.T. Code 6-94.682, Production Assembler." *Personnel Psychol* 12:322 su '59. *

233. UNITED STATES EMPLOYMENT SERVICE. "Validity Information Exchange, No. 12-15: D.O.T. Code 7-36.240, Petroleum Transport Driver." *Personnel Psychol* 12:323 su '59. *

234. UNITED STATES EMPLOYMENT SERVICE. "Validity Information Exchange, No. 12-16: D.O.T. Code 7-88.414, Fork-Lift Truck Operator." *Personnel Psychol* 12:324 su '59. *

235. UNITED STATES EMPLOYMENT SERVICE. "Validity Information Exchange, No. 12-17: D.O.T. Code 9-68.30, Cereal Packer." *Personnel Psychol* 12:325 su '59. *

236. UNITED STATES EMPLOYMENT SERVICE. "Validity Information Exchange, No. 12-20: D.O.T. Code 4-85.040, Welder, Combination." *Personnel Psychol* 12:484–5 au '59. *

237. UNITED STATES EMPLOYMENT SERVICE. "Validity Information Exchange, No. 12-21: D.O.T. Code 5-00.020, Units Mechanic." *Personnel Psychol* 12:486 au '59. *

238. UNITED STATES EMPLOYMENT SERVICE. "Validity Information Exchange, No. 12-22: D.O.T. Code 5-17.010, Patternmaker, Metal; 5-17.020, Patternmaker, Wood." *Personnel Psychol* 12:487–8 au '59. *

239. UNITED STATES EMPLOYMENT SERVICE. "Validity Information Exchange, No. 12-23: D.O.T. Code 6-78.905, Machine Operator, General." *Personnel Psychol* 12:489 au '59. *

240. UNITED STATES EMPLOYMENT SERVICE. "Validity Information Exchange, No. 12-24: D.O.T. Code 8-04.10, Corn-Cutting-Machine Operator; 8-04.10, Corn-Husking-Machine Operator; 8-04.10, Cutter, Machine." *Personnel Psychol* 12:490–1 au '59. *

241. UNITED STATES EMPLOYMENT SERVICE. "Validity Information Exchange, No. 12-25: D.O.T. Code 8-04.10, Cutter, Hand; 9-68.60, Inspector, Belt; 9-68.60, Sorter, Food Products; 8-04.10, Trimmer; 8-04.10, Vegetable Packer; 9-68.01, Weight Checker." *Personnel Psychol* 12:492–4 au '59. *

242. UNITED STATES EMPLOYMENT SERVICE. "Validity Information Exchange, No. 12-26: D.O.T. Code 9-13.01, Assembler (Toys and Games); 9-13.01, Model Airplane Assembler; 7-00.971, Toy Train Assembler." *Personnel Psychol* 12:495–6 au '59. *

243. UNITED STATES EMPLOYMENT SERVICE. "Validity Information Exchange, No. 12-27: D.O.T. Code 1-05.01, Clerk, General Office." *Personnel Psychol* 12:629 w '59. *

244. UNITED STATES EMPLOYMENT SERVICE. "Validity Information Exchange, No. 12-28: D.O.T. Code 4-46.205, Stripper (Print. & Pub.) II." *Personnel Psychol* 12:630 w '59. *

245. UNITED STATES EMPLOYMENT SERVICE. "Validity Information Exchange, No. 12-29: D.O.T. Codes 5-27.010 and 5-28.100, Painter-Decorator." *Personnel Psychol* 12:631 w '59. *

246. UNITED STATES EMPLOYMENT SERVICE. "Validity Information Exchange, No. 12-30: D.O.T. Code 6-42.420, Bag-Making-Machine Operator; 4-42.400, Cellophane-Bag-Machine Operator; 4-42.400, Waxed-Bag-Machine Operator." *Personnel Psychol* 12:632–3 w '59. *

247. UNITED STATES EMPLOYMENT SERVICE. "Validity Information Exchange, No. 12-31: D.O.T. Code 6-72.333, Jewelry Assembler." *Personnel Psychol* 12:634 w '59. *

248. UNITED STATES EMPLOYMENT SERVICE. "Validity Information Exchange, No. 12-32: D.O.T. Code 6-93.404, Luggage-Hardware Assembler." *Personnel Psychol* 12:635 w '59. *

249. UNITED STATES EMPLOYMENT SERVICE. "Validity Information Exchange, No. 12-33: D.O.T. Code 6-94.352, Power Lawn Mower Assembler." *Personnel Psychol* 12:636–7 w '59. *

250. UNITED STATES EMPLOYMENT SERVICE. "Validity Information Exchange, No. 12-34: D.O.T. Code 6-95.001, Solderer I." *Personnel Psychol* 12:638 w '59. *

251. UNITED STATES EMPLOYMENT SERVICE. "Validity Information Exchange, No. 12-35: D.O.T. Code 7-54.621, Water Filterer." *Personnel Psychol* 12:639 w '59. *

252. UNITED STATES EMPLOYMENT SERVICE. "Validity Information Exchange, No. 12-36: D.O.T. Code 7-57.501, Presser, Hand; 7-57.501, Silk Finisher, Hand." *Personnel Psychol* 12:640–1 w '59. *

253. DROEGE, ROBERT C. "G.A.T.B. Norms for Lower High School Grades." Comments by Albert S. Thompson. *Personnel & Guid J* 39:30–6 S '60. * (*PA* 35:3969)

254. MCDANIEL, ERNEST D., AND STEPHENSON, HOWARD W. "Prediction of Scholastic Achievement in Pharmacy at the University of Kentucky." *Am J Pharm Ed* 24:162–9 sp '60. *

255. SOUEIF, M. I., AND METWALLY, A. "Testing for Organicity in Egyptian Psychiatric Patients." *Acta Psychologica* 18(4):285–96 '61. * (*PA* 36:5JG85S)

256. MCNAMARA, THOMAS A. "Identification of Vocational Aptitudes," pp. 330–7. In *Education and National Purpose: Forty-Ninth Annual Schoolmen's Week Proceedings.* Edited

by Helen Hus. Philadelphia, Pa.: University of Pennsylvania Press, 1962. Pp. 358. *

257. RUSSO, J. ROBERT. "Two Governmental Sources for Aptitude Testing." *Sch Counselor* 9:140–1 My '62. *

258. STEIN, CARROLL I. "The GATB: The Effect of Age on Intersample Variations." Comments by Robert C. Droege. *Personnel & Guid J* 40:779–85 My '62. * (*PA* 37:2964)

259. SUPER, DONALD E., AND CRITES, JOHN O. *Appraising Vocational Fitness by Means of Psychological Tests, Revised Edition,* pp. 330–9. New York: Harper & Brothers, 1962. Pp. xv, 688. * (*PA* 37:2038)

260. BELL, FOREST O.; HOFF, ALVIN L.; AND HOYT, KENNETH B. "A Comparison of Three Approaches to Criterion Measurement." *J Appl Psychol* 47:416–8 D '63. * (*PA* 38:6737)

261. BURT, SAMUEL M. "Aptitude Test for Selection of Vocational-Technical School Printing Students." *Am Voc J* 38:23 N '63. *

262. DROEGE, ROBERT C.; CRAMBERT, ALBERT C.; AND HENKIN, JAMES B. "Relationship Between G.A.T.B. Aptitude Scores and Age for Adults." *Personnel & Guid J* 41:502–8 F '63. * (*PA* 39:1384)

263. GAVURIN, EDWARD, AND POCKELL, NORMAN E. "Comparison of Bare-Handed and Glove-Handed Finger Dexterity." Abstract. *Percept & Motor Skills* 16:246 F '63. *

264. TAYLOR, FRED R. "The General Aptitude Test Battery as Predictor of Vocational Readjustment by Psychiatric Patients." *J Clin Psychol* 19:130 Ja '63. * (*PA* 39:2368)

HAROLD P. BECHTOLDT, *Professor of Psychology, University of Iowa, Iowa City, Iowa.* [Review of Edition B-1002.]

The *General Aptitude Test Battery* (GATB) of the United States Employment Service (USES) represents the outcome of one of the longest programs of test battery development in existence. The change from battery B-1001 to the revised one, B-1002, was reviewed in *The Fifth Mental Measurements Yearbook* by Humphreys, Comrey, and Froehlich. Since available information listed in the three sections of the Guide to the Use of the General Aptitude Test Battery, dated January and October 1962, indicate little, if any, further change from the material of the earlier reviews, the present set of comments will cover the few additional data and amplify the more crucial points of the previous reviews. This restatement seems desirable since the current manuals and recent studies are still open to serious criticism.

The relationships of the GATB test scores to scores of a variety of other tests, to educational level, to sex, and to age are treated briefly in the Guide, but with incomplete data reporting. The discussions generally are considered and cautious. The serious problems associated with attempting to conduct acceptable research studies in a variety of field units with field personnel are recognized. Studies of test stability and of equivalence of forms indicate values comparable to those found in other test batteries. The successive-step procedure, however, introduces untested assumptions. Changes in means and variances are noted with respect to practice effects but the discussion of the effect of heterogeneity on "reliability" coefficients is inadequate. Reports of the standard errors of measurement are needed. A brief, but inadequate, discussion deals with the possible influence both of experience on the job and of specific academic courses on GATB scores. The positive relationship of educational level to GATB scores is noted at several points, but this point is not pursued. A longitudinal follow-up study of job placement of high school students was started in 1958, but the results are not yet available. The use of minimum qualifying scores for each occupational group simplifies the clerical use of the test results to the greatest possible extent; these qualifying norms are said to include only "the most significant aptitudes" that are required by the occupation. The Guide points out that "a deficiency in one significant aptitude cannot be compensated for by a superabundance of another." All available data other than GATB scores are to be integrated or interpreted by the counselor; large scale studies have regularly shown such judgments to be a serious source of error in a prediction situation.

The more important comments deal primarily with certain procedures and points of view in the three parts of the Guide available to the user. These comments are made possible by the extensive report of the work which has been done by the USES organization on the development of the GATB.

PURPOSE. The present manual indicates that a change in objective has developed since 1940. Whereas the task of the Employment Service was previously stated "to promote the satisfactory placement of work seekers in jobs," [1] the Guide indicates the USES is now interested "not only in establishing test norms for a single occupation, but also in relating a given set of occupational norms to the norm structure for groups of occupations." The test norms purport to involve job performance by expressing minimum levels on essential aptitudes for each of a large number of occupations. However, no acceptable evidence is presented to indicate that these values define *minimum* levels of *essential* aptitudes. The USES aptitude tests "are designed to measure capacities to learn various jobs," yet only a few of the many studies attempt to predict performance on the

1 STEAD, WILLIAM H., AND ASSOCIATES. *Occupational Counseling Techniques.* New York: American Book Co., Inc., 1940. Pp. ix, 273. *

job after training. The presentation of validity data indicates a primary objective of the USES is the empirical prediction of a criterion defined mainly by ratings of supervisors. The use of such inadequate criteria of worker "job performance" probably is responsible in part for the failure to use predictors other than GATB scores. The evidence offered of the success with which the predictions are achieved consists of sets of tetrachoric correlations summarized in Tables 34 to 37, Section 3 of the Guide. Other data appear in a technical report *Selecting Employees for Developmental Opportunities.*[2] The previous cogent criticism of the use of tetrachoric correlations in this connection has led to statements that the more appropriate phi coefficients are currently being used. The use of point-biserial or other product-moment correlations with multiple-level criteria would be even more informative.

CONCEPTUAL FRAMEWORK. A preliminary comment is needed regarding the term aptitude. A discussion in the manuals and in the most recent study of the battery is characteristic of the "hypothetical underlying trait" approach found in the writings of some factor analysts. The empirically untenable positions of postulated innate abilities and of a distinction between ability and performance are presented. One current dictionary of psychological terms[3] points out that the words aptitude, capacity, and ability have many referents; the preferred position, consistent with an APA definition of a test,[4] is that these terms are referring either to observed or to predicted (and observable) performance. This view is represented by the USES selection of one, two, or three test scores to define the aptitudes. The aptitudes so defined may be named as response-defined or behavioral variables. In the GATB B-1002, nine aptitudes are defined by linear functions of a set of 12 test scores. The overriding commitment to the older notion of aptitudes is evident, however, in the restrictions as to predictor variables to be used. No historical, biographical, or situational variables are used in any of the prediction functions.

2 UNITED STATES ARMY ORDNANCE CORPS. *Selecting Employees for Developmental Opportunities.* Technical Report. Rock Island, Ill.: Rock Island Arsenal, July 1962.

3 ENGLISH, HORACE B., AND ENGLISH, AVA CHAMPNEY. *A Comprehensive Dictionary of Psychological and Psychoanalytic Terms.* New York: Longmans, Green & Co., Inc., 1958. Pp. xiv, 594. *

4 AMERICAN PSYCHOLOGICAL ASSOCIATION. "Report of Testimony at a Congressional Hearing." *Am Psychologist* 13:217–23 My '58. *

The hunches or guesses of an investigator about relationships of defined behavioral variables to environmental or training concepts and to other behavioral concepts (called criteria) defined by performance on the job are examples of hypotheses about relationships involving two or more empirical and observed variables. As noted by Humphreys, once the definitions of any set of predictors are provided, the hunches or procedures leading to the definitions are of little, if any, concern. What is of concern then is the usefulness of these definitions; for the USES problems, usefulness is primarily accuracy of prediction of the criterion variable. However, too little consideration is given to the acceptability of ratings as criterion variables.

The reduction of nearly 100 tests (of the pre-1940 era) to a set of 15 (B-1001) and then to 12 (B-1002) represents a simplification which potentially is of value for theoretical purposes as well as for the pragmatic objectives of absolute and differential prediction. The adequacy of this formulation is not, however, indicated by an internal analysis using some factor analysis technique. The factor analysis results may provide hypotheses (as to possibly useful sets of variables) that are subsequently confirmed, but these factor analysis results are *not* substitutes for appropriate empirical evidence of criterion prediction.

It seems clear that if linear or nonlinear regression procedures were to be used, the cogency of the previous criticisms of the USES formulations would be evident. For example, Humphreys points out that no definition of mechanical information or comprehension is included; such test defined concepts have been found useful for the USES type of problem by other investigators. This and other possibly serious omissions are clearly indicated in the study reported in Section 3 (Wherry and Black) and by the work of other investigators. A second problem, also noted by Humphreys, is the "experimental dependence" resulting from the definition of G (intelligence) as a linear combination of scores also used to define F (finger dexterity), N (numerical aptitude), and S (spatial aptitude). This dependence precludes the use of efficient regression procedures and introduces into the system the problem of correlated errors and of linear constraints. One solution is to develop a new test to define "G." A third problem is the use of "multiple cut-off" scores instead of linear or nonlinear continuous functions of the predictors to develop the estimated (or predicted) criterion variable. The criterion variable is also dichotomized. As a result, only predictions of high or of low standing are provided. The available data indicate that more than two levels of job performance may be consistently and usefully observed. In addition, the usefulness of defining an ability by performance on a single task or test situation could also be evaluated by empirical data in the suggested regression framework.

RESTRICTION OF VARIABLES TO APTITUDES. Prior to 1940, the USES used a combination of aptitude tests and trade tests in their counseling activities. Aptitude tests were used to define properties of performance of individuals who had not had relevant job experiences. Trade tests defined behavioral variables which were involved in specific job experiences. The orientation since 1945, as indicated by the statements in Section 3, is on aptitudes whose high relationship to job success is to be independent of variations in amount or kind of job training. It is assumed that the GATB scores are such aptitudes. If so, then the usefulness or "validity" of the aptitude test scores can be evaluated by testing workers already on the job in the "concurrent validity" type of design. The substitution of concurrent validation studies (using relatively homogeneous groups of workers on the job) for longitudinal or actual prediction studies is justified in the Guide by reference to a similar statement by Ghiselli and Brown. If the assumed invariance of linear relationships tends to hold, then the correlation coefficients will increase when more heterogeneous groups of applicants are used.

Three comments are indicated with respect to this assumption: First, this reviewer knows of no acceptable evidence tending to support this assumption of relationships being independent of experience *in general.* Skills required for learning a job are not necessarily those skills which differentiate between job performances after a period of time on the job. Such differences are often indicated when performance, rather than rating criteria, are used. Second, skills required to learn a job would be observed prior to being on the job. The evaluation would be in terms of performance change during a period of training on the job. Third, both laboratory and industrial studies indicate that experience or practice on one task will influence performance on some other tasks. The criterion used is important in such studies. That this assumption is also considered questionable by the USES is indicated in several statements in which the greater cogency of "longitudinal validity" paradigms, as opposed to the concurrent validation designs, is recognized.

In specific cases, there may be some test performances relevant to either rate of acquisition or rate of skilled performance, which are not strongly influenced by specific or general skills acquired on the job. The data of Table 34, however, suggest that both educational level and experience on the job will change the mean values, as well as the standard deviations and possibly the relationships involving performances on some of these GATB scores. Furthermore, the relationships of age and education to test performance shown in the Ordnance Corps technical report suggest that some of these aptitude performances can be replaced by the simple and gross variable "number of years of education." Partial correlations with education held constant then would indicate any additional relationships attributable to these tests as such.

If the desired levels of absolute and differential prediction of adjustment to the job, of tenure in the job, or of actual performance on the job are to be achieved, it is likely that variables in addition to the nine currently used will be required. The simplest of these additional variables will be the educational level and present technical skill and previous experience (on the job). It may be necessary to define these technical and job-acquired skills by several trade or information tests and by biographical (historical) data.

USE OF MULTIPLE CUTOFF SCORES. A serious question can be raised regarding the appropriateness of the wholesale application of the technique of multiple cutoff scores for the problem of predicting "job success" by specifying a set of occupational norms. One reason offered for this technique is the simplification of the advising procedure in the several field offices of the USES. The clerks have only to compare the several aptitude scores, which require at most the addition of two or three values, with the GATB B-1002 cutoff values. A more important reason is the notion that noncompensatory sets of skills are characteristic of *all* occupations; minimum levels on a set of essential skills are implied for all jobs. This reviewer knows of no evidence involving test scores such as those of the GATB, which supports this assumption even for *one* occupation. The published evidence indicates that linear and nonlinear functions of test scores in a compensatory combination are as useful as or more useful than the multiple cutoff procedures. For some prediction problems, nonlinear functions are more useful than linear ones.

References are made in the Guide to articles from 1950 to 1953 in support of the use of multiple cutoff procedures. Since 1953, psychologists generally have become aware of several useful alternative procedures, such as nonlinear transformation of scores and nonlinear functions involving the use of powers and products of variables in a regression equation. The details of these procedures are given by statisticians such as Rao [5] and Williams.[6] Computer programs are available. Examples also have been provided by Horst [7] and by other psychologists. Horst [8] and his associates have also considered the linear prediction problem at some length. More recently, Lord [9] has pointed out the theoretical inadequacy of the cutting score techniques for the case of such "fallible" variables as test scores and job performances. Since the entire GATB was administered to all subjects used in the several validity studies, a systematic reanalysis of the better of these studies by more adequate techniques would appear to be indicated. Simplification of the regression equation for office use by clerks might then be developed so that the effected loss in accuracy would be tolerable and known.

The combination of a large number of variables in a multiple linear or nonlinear regression function developed on small samples will often lead to marked shrinkage of the correlation coefficient in subsequent cross validation trials in part from the effects of correlated errors. Humphrey's point that shrinkage can also be expected in the multiple cutoff values in the small USES samples seems sound; selection of a subset of variables from a larger set is involved. However, at least three cross validation studies are reported in Section 3 of the manual. These studies, as presented, indicate either no shrinkage or a significant increase in accuracy of prediction on the subsequent studies. The use of judgmental (logical) criteria in the battery selection may have reduced the effects of correlated errors in the data. Section 3, however, discusses what has been called "double cross-validation." It is, therefore, not clear whether the cutoff values determined in the first study were actually retained for use in the subsequent studies. One possibility is that adjustments were made on the two or more successive studies, to obtain the best separation of the "high" and "low" workers. The point is that the cross validation data and the validity values reported in Table 34 are simply not consistent with those of other comparable investigations. The use of small samples and of the multiple cutoff procedures by other organizations does not lead to such favorable results even when the inappropriate tetrachoric correlation coefficient is used.

SELECTION OF SUBSETS OF APTITUDES. For the purpose of simplifying the advising procedures, cutoff scores are proposed only for subsets of two to four of the nine aptitudes. The procedures used in this selection of a subset, as detailed both in the Guide (Section 3) and in the Ordnance Corps technical report, involve the application of four criteria. These include a relatively high mean test score, a relatively low test score standard deviation, a significant correlation of the test score with the criteria, and a logical judgment of importance of an aptitude (test score) on the basis of job analysis description. The first three of these criteria might be justified. Relatively high scores for workers on the job may arise either from the effect of job experience on the test or from a level of pre-job performance that is indicative of success on the job. However, low scores may also provide useful predictions. A relatively low standard deviation implies reduced variability which might be expected in certain job skills; such reduced variability could then also appear in the test data. Such reduced variability may be achieved

5 RAO, C. RADHAKRISHNA. *Advanced Statistical Methods in Biometric Research.* New York: John Wiley & Sons, Inc., 1952. Pp. xvii, 390. *

6 WILLIAMS, E. J. *Regression Analysis.* New York: John Wiley & Sons, Inc., 1959. Pp. ix, 214. *

7 HORST, PAUL. "Pattern Analysis and Configural Scoring." *J Clin Psychol* 10:1–11 Ja '54. *

8 HORST, PAUL. "A Technique for the Development of a Differential Prediction Battery." *Psychol Monogr* 68(9):1–31 '54. *

HORST, PAUL, AND MACEWAN, CHARLOTTE. "Predictor Elimination Techniques for Determining Multiple Prediction Batteries." *Psychol Rep* 7:19–50 Ag '60. *

9 LORD, FREDERIC M. "Cutting Scores and Errors of Measurement." *Psychometrika* 27:19–30 Mr '62. *

LORD, FREDERIC M. "Cutting Scores and Errors of Measurement—A Second Case." *Ed & Psychol Meas* 23:63–8 sp '63. *

by eliminating cases from either end (or both ends) of a test distribution directly or indirectly through some selective process involving attributes characteristic of the job. In terms of the variation in job and test performances actually observed, significant linear (correlation) or nonlinear (correlation ratio) coefficients are useful indices of the desired empirical relationships.

Variation in job skills, however, does not mean that any of the workers on the job are "unsatisfactory." Changes in the classification of given workers (as high or satisfactory and low or unsatisfactory) may develop from changes in the job market, in the job (by simplification and by automation), and in the interpersonal aspects (by labor relations). There is no indication in these manuals that the influence of such changes is considered relevant to evaluating the prediction of success on the job.

The questionable criterion for selecting subsets of variables is the introduction of a rating of logical appropriateness by a job analyst. Such judgments restrict the set of possible empirical relationships to those in line with preconceptions of fallible individuals having vested interests in certain job analysis and ability-performance formulations. It is generally accepted that it is human to err; job analysts are human. The effects of these restrictive (armchair) analyses are clearly shown both in the Guide and in the Ordnance Corps technical report. Additional inadequate criteria used in the Ordnance study also involve the wrong regression line; pass and fail test score categories are "predicted" (fitted to the sample data) *from* concurrent high and low supervisory ratings.

SUMMARY. The present reviewer concurs in general with the earlier reviews by Humphreys and Comrey (5:609) with respect both to the strengths and weaknesses of the test battery. The tests provided are fairly well constructed; the empirical data are as complete as, or more complete than, those for any other available test battery. The results to be expected from using the tests, either as recommended or as they might be used, are probably as good as those from the use of any other existing test battery.

JOHN B. CARROLL, *Professor of Educational Psychology, Harvard University, Cambridge, Massachusetts.* [Review of Edition B-1002.]

The *General Aptitude Test Battery* was rather completely described, and reviewed in generally favorable terms, in both *The Fourth* and *The Fifth Mental Measurements Yearbooks.* The chief complaint of the reviewers was that the research data on reliability, validity, occupational aptitude patterns, and so forth were either too scanty or too widely scattered. The publication, in October 1962, of Section 3 of the Guide to the Use of the General Aptitude Test Battery, with the title Development, certainly goes far in satisfying these complaints. This publication of 217 pages plus numerous fold-out tables is a rich source of information about all aspects of the GATB, including history, methods of construction, item analysis and factor analysis studies, development of norms, intercorrelations of tests, validity studies for numerous occupations, reliability and effects of practice, effect of training, effect of aging, and use of the test. It is, in fact, to be highly recommended as outside reading in courses in tests and measurement and in individual differences. One of the major faults of Section 3 of the Guide is that it lacks an index.

From this manual it will be abundantly evident that even though the GATB is widely operational in United States Employment Service offices and cooperating institutions, it is also regarded as a research test by its makers. New validity data are being collected continually, in both concurrent and longitudinal designs. In the light of these studies, the Occupational Aptitude Pattern structure is revised periodically; the most recent revision, according to this manual, was made in 1961. A major longitudinal study involving 36,000 high school students is now under way in order to secure data on the long-term validity of the GATB given in high school as a predictor of occupational success. Various interesting questions about the battery are being pursued by the research staff in the USES and also by numerous independent investigators throughout the country. In fact, the GATB seems to be a very popular object of study in master's and doctor's theses. Of particular interest are the data presented in the Guide on the effects of aging: it is shown that even when educational level is controlled, there are significant decrements in nearly all the factors measured by the GATB. Only Verbal Aptitude (V) seems to be impervious to the effects of aging, a finding which squares with those obtained elsewhere.

Likewise, interesting data on reliability and the effects of practice are presented. The authors continue to offer reliability data only on aptitude scores and not on individual tests from which the aptitude scores are derived; I would defend their position on this point on the ground that publication of reliability data on individual tests might tend to encourage the possibly ill-advised use of such tests singly. Actually, four factors (V, S, Q, and K) are defined by single tests, and their reliabilities are satisfactory. The authors are to be applauded for presenting most of their reliability data in the form of coefficients of stability, i.e., test-retest coefficients for periods from a week to a year. The fact that nearly all these coefficients are in the range of .80 to .90 speaks well for the measurement characteristics of the tests. On the other hand, these coefficients are generally derived from very heterogeneous samples, and I cannot find a single mention of a standard error of measurement; there is some question in my mind about the possible imprecision of the scores and its consequences for the assignment of people to Occupational Aptitude Patterns.

It is reported that a practice effect was consistently observed for all aptitudes. Such practice effects can hardly be avoided and it is a good thing that the magnitudes of the practice effects are reported here so that they can be taken into account by counselors in interpreting retest scores.

It is unfortunate that so little could be reported concerning the effects of training on GATB scores. The authors apparently had to rely on the meager research on the problem conducted outside the government.

With a degree of immodesty that is only partly excused by the inclusion of supporting references to the comments of favorable independent reviewers, the Guide (Section 3, p. 176) makes the following statement: "The GATB probably comes closer than any other multi-factor test battery to meeting the requirement of validity for success in a variety of occupations." The information contained in the Guide now makes it possible to assess the claims of the GATB itself; the Guide does not pretend to present comparative validity data for other multifactor test batteries, although it devotes a chapter to the presentation and discussion of correlations between the GATB and other tests.

Extensive validity data are reported for 198 specific occupations or clusters of highly similar occupations. These data are reported in two forms: (*a*) tetrachoric *r*'s resulting from the cross classification of a dichotomous criterion with qualification versus nonqualification in terms of an individual's meeting a series of cutoff scores; and (*b*) Pearsonian *r*'s for aptitude scores against a continuum-measured criterion (ratings, work sample, production record, etc.). Reviewers of the GATB in previous yearbooks have already complained about the inexactitude of the multiple cutoff procedure, but the authors of the Guide defend it in terms of practicality, and they have a point. Counselors probably have enough trouble with the relatively simple procedures whereby a profile of scores is matched against Occupational Aptitude Patterns, without getting into the computation of multiple regression equations even in a simplified form. Nevertheless, with the era of the computer already well under way one would think that the facilities of the USES could include means of feeding GATB data into an electronic processing system to yield something more informative and precise than the occupational classifications yielded by the present system. In fact, it is now possible to have GATB tests scored by Science Research Associates' DocuTran or by National Computer Systems' machines, either of which surely could be geared to produce classifications based upon multiple regressions.

For the moment, however, we must be satisfied with the tetrachoric correlations listed in the voluminous tables of the Guide. In all, Table 34 presents 317 tetrachoric correlations with values ranging from .24 to .96 and with a median of about .65. Taken at face value, these results are truly impressive. One could have thought that a great many more low validity coefficients would have been obtained; actually only 11 out of the 317 coefficients are less than .40. Nearly all the correlations are based on concurrent validity designs; the median of the 39 coefficients listed as "predictive" validities based on longitudinal designs is .71, somewhat higher than the median of the concurrent validities. But one is justified in harboring certain misgivings about all these results. Each tetrachoric *r* listed in Table 34 is matched by a series of Pearsonian correlations in Table 36. Examination of these data reveals that the tetrachoric *r* may often be spuriously high, due to capitalization on error. Consider, for example, the tetrachoric *r* of .96 given as the predictive validity of the GATB "norms" (cutting scores) for laborer (fireworks) against supervisory ratings. In Table 36, however, the criterion correlations for the two aptitude scores involved in the norms for this occupation are .69 and .57, respectively; even if these two scores (F and M) were correlated zero, which is unlikely, the multiple correlation could not be higher than about .89. An even stranger contrast is afforded by the data for stenographer, where for a sample labeled Cross-Validation II the tetrachoric *r* is given as .62, but the Pearsonian *r*'s for the aptitude scores are for the most part significantly *negative!* (These are only examples of a number of cases that could be cited.)

Previous reviewers have pointed out that the tetrachoric *r* is not the best statistic to characterize prediction in a 2 by 2 table; although the authors of the Guide state that in recent studies they have been using the phi coefficient, they do not present any such coefficients in their statistical tables.

All in all, the data now available on the GATB support the claim that it is indeed comprehensive in the sense that it measures most of the ability traits that are important in predicting success in a substantial sample of occupations that can be identified. Further, the subtests have been demonstrated to be reliable and valid enough to yield highly significant and useful results in the hands of the employment or guidance counselor who knows how to use and interpret them. Whether the battery could be improved by the inclusion of measurements of further factors (e.g., rote memory, mechanical knowledge) is uncertain. One hopes that the USES test construction staff will continue to maintain this test by providing additional alternate forms and further validity results. In particular, they need to give attention to the problem of identifying the skills of workers technologically unemployed by automation. Although validity coefficients are given for certain occupations catering to the new leisure (e.g., fishing rod assembler) there are no data on how to select computing machine operators or programmers.

One hopes also that the USES will make provision for the test results to be used with more discrimination; if, as the authors claim, the test results predict a dichotomous criterion so well, they could surely be even better used in predicting a continuous criterion. In this way a counselor could make better estimates of the probabilities of success in an occupation or occupational group than he can with the present system.

For reviews by Andrew L. Comrey, Clifford P. Froehlich, and Lloyd G. Humphreys of b, *see 5:609; for reviews by Milton L. Blum, Edward B. Greene, and Howard R. Taylor of* a, *see 4:714.*

[772]

***The Guilford-Zimmerman Aptitude Survey.** Grades 9–16 and adults; 1947–56; IBM except for parts 3 and 4; 7 parts; manual, second edition ('56, 7 pages); separate answer sheets may be used except for parts 3 and 4; 4¢ per IBM answer sheet for any one part; 75¢ per scoring stencil for any one part except parts 3 and 4 ($1); 40¢ per manual; $2.35 per complete specimen set; postage extra; J. P. Guilford and Wayne S. Zimmerman; Sheridan Supply Co. *
a) PART 1, VERBAL COMPREHENSION. IBM; Form A ('47, 4 pages); $2.50 per 25 tests; 75¢ per specimen set; 25(30) minutes.
b) PART 2, GENERAL REASONING. IBM; Form A ('47, 4 pages); $2.50 per 25 tests; 65¢ per specimen set; 35(40) minutes.
c) PART 3, NUMERICAL OPERATIONS. Form A ('47, 4 pages); $2.50 per 25 tests; 60¢ per specimen set; 8(13) minutes.
d) PART 4, PERCEPTUAL SPEED. Form A ('47, 4 pages); $2.50 per 25 tests; 60¢ per specimen set; 5(10) minutes.
e) PART 5, SPATIAL ORIENTATION. IBM; Form A ('47, 8 pages); $4 per 25 tests; 75¢ per specimen set; 10(20) minutes.
f) PART 6, SPATIAL VISUALIZATION. IBM; Form B ('53, 7 pages); $4 per 25 tests; 75¢ per specimen set; 10(15) minutes.
g) PART 7, MECHANICAL KNOWLEDGE. IBM; Form A ('47, 8 pages); $4 per 25 tests; 75¢ per specimen set; 30(35) minutes.

REFERENCES

1–15. See 4:715.
16. BALL, JOE M. *An Experimental Study of the Relationship Between the Ability to Impart Information Orally and the Primary Mental Abilities, Verbal Comprehension and General Reasoning.* Doctor's thesis, University of Southern California (Los Angeles, Calif.), 1951.
17. MARTIN, GLENN C. "Test Batteries for Trainees in Auto Mechanics and Apparel Design." *J Appl Psychol* 35:20–2 F '51. * (*PA* 25:7123)
18. TOMKINS, SILVAN S. Chap. 6, "Personality and Intelligence: Integration and Psychometric Technics," pp. 87–95. (*PA* 27:445) Discussion by Joseph Zubin (pp. 103–4). In *Relation of Psychological Tests to Psychiatry.* Edited by Paul H. Hoch and Joseph Zubin. New York: Grune & Stratton, Inc., 1952. Pp. viii, 301. *
19. CURETON, EDWARD E. "Service Tests of Multiple Aptitudes." *Proc Inv Conf Testing Probl* 1955:22–39 '56. * (*PA* 31:3017)
20. GUILFORD, J. P. "The Guilford-Zimmerman Aptitude Survey." Comments by Donald E. Super. *Personnel & Guid J* 35:219–24 D '56. * (*PA* 31:7919)
21. BERGER, R. M.; GUILFORD, J. P.; AND CHRISTENSEN, P. R. "A Factor-Analytic Study of Planning Abilities." *Psychol Monogr* 71(6):1–31 '57. * (*PA* 33:6967)
22. HILLS, JOHN R. "Factor-Analyzed Abilities and Success in College Mathematics." *Ed & Psychol Meas* 17:615–22 w '57. * (*PA* 33:4696)
23. MILLER, ROBERT S., AND COTTLE, WILLIAM C. "Relationships Between MMPI Scales and GZTS Scales: An Adult Female Sample." *Univ Kans B Ed* 11:54–9 F '57. *
24. BALL, JOE M. "The Relationship Between the Ability

to Speak Effectively and the Primary Mental Abilities, Verbal Comprehension and General Reasoning." *Speech Monogr* 25:285–90 N '58. * (*PA* 33:9492)
25. STINSON, PAIRLEE J. "A Method for Counseling Engineering Students." *Personnel & Guid J* 37:294–5 D '58. * (*PA* 36:2KI94S)
26. GUILFORD, J. P. *Personality.* New York: McGraw-Hill Book Co., Inc., 1959. Pp. xiii, 562. *
27. HANEY, RUSSELL; MICHAEL, WILLIAM B.; AND JONES, ROBERT A. "Identification of Aptitude and Achievement Factors in the Prediction of the Success of Nursing Trainees." *Ed & Psychol Meas* 19:645–7 w '59. * (*PA* 34:6164)
28. MICHAEL, WILLIAM B.; JONES, ROBERT A.; AND HANEY, RUSSELL. "The Development and Validation of a Test Battery for Selection of Student Nurses." *Ed & Psychol Meas* 19:641–3 w '59. * (*PA* 34:6171)
29. WILSON, JOHN E. "Evaluating a Four Year Sales Selection Program." *Personnel Psychol* 12:97–104 sp '59. * (*PA* 34:3533)
30. LONG, JOHN MARSHALL. *The Prediction of College Success From a Battery of Tests and From High School Achievement.* Doctor's thesis, University of Virginia (Charlottesville, Va.), 1960. (*DA* 21:1100)
31. MERRIFIELD, P. R.; GUILFORD, J. P.; CHRISTENSEN, P. R.; AND FRICK, J. W. "The Role of Intellectual Factors in Problem Solving." *Psychol Monogr* 76(10):1–21 '62. *
32. *Normative Information: Manager and Executive Testing.* New York: Richardson, Bellows, Henry & Co., Inc., May 1963. Pp. 45. *

For reviews by Anne Anastasi, Harold Bechtoldt, John B. Carroll, and P. E. Vernon, see 4:715.

[773]

***The Jastak Test of Potential Ability and Behavior Stability.** Ages 11.5–14.5; 1958–59; test booklet title is *The Jastak Test;* 16 scores: 10 direct scores (vocabulary, number series, coding, picture reasoning, space series, verbal reasoning, social concept, arithmetic, space completion, spelling) and 6 derived scores (language, reality, motivation, psychomotor, intelligence, capacity); 1 form ('59, 14 pages, called short form, all items selected from the original 1958 long form); manual ('59, 59 pages); three fourths of the technical data reported (excluding norms) relate to the long form; $4 per 25 tests; $1 per set of keys; $1.50 per manual; postage extra; $1.50 per specimen set, postpaid; 35(50) minutes; J. F. Jastak; Educational Test Bureau. *

REFERENCES

1. STRETCH, LORENA B. "The Jastak Test." *Peabody J Ed* 36:268–71 Mr '59. *
2. CONDELL, JAMES F. "Comparison of Henmon-Nelson and Jastak Scores of Seventh Graders." *Psychol Rep* 9:622 D '61. *
3. O'BLOCK, FRANCIS R. *Reality Scores on the Jastak Test of Potential Ability and Behavior Stability as Associated With Teachers' Judgment of Social and Personal Adjustment.* Master's thesis, Bowling Green State University (Bowling Green, Ohio), 1962.

ANNE ANASTASI, *Professor of Psychology, Fordham University, New York, New York.*

The item types employed in the Jastak test are quite similar to those encountered in intelligence tests, although the scores are treated and interpreted in some unusual ways. The scores from the 10 subtests are first reduced to standard scores with mean 10 and standard deviation 2.5 and then further manipulated to yield three types of measures designated as intelligence, capacity, and stability scores. Intelligence is measured by a deviation IQ based on the sum of the 10 subtest standard scores. Although these IQ's are not simply the sum of the 10 scores, but are found from a conversion table, it is not clear what their SD is. The manual reports 16.61 (a strange value to choose if it refers to the converted scale) and elsewhere gives SD's ranging from 16.25 to 17.97 for different age and sex groups. Which, if any, of these values refer to deviation IQ's and which to sums of scores cannot be determined from the manual.

Even more puzzling are the procedures employed in computing capacity and stability scores. "Capacity" is estimated through a comparative analysis of the subject's performance on the 10 subtests, which differ widely in the intellectual functions covered. Quite apart from the dubious rationale of such intertest comparisons and the theoretically questionable concept of potentiality itself, the specific procedure followed in computing the capacity score makes its meaning highly suspect. The individual's standard scores on the 10 subtests are first ranked from highest to lowest and each score is then converted to an equivalent score in terms of normative values for the 10 ranks. The individual's highest equivalent score is taken as his capacity score (regardless of which subtest he obtained it on). If this score is appreciably higher than his other equivalent scores, the conclusion is that he is performing below capacity. According to this procedure, an individual will appear to be functioning below capacity if his 10 scores cover a wide range (when his top score will therefore be relatively high), or if they cover a narrow range (when his bottom score will be relatively high), or if he has a run of equal scores in any rank position (when the lowest of the scores in this run will be relatively high). It is difficult to see what a "capacity score" so derived could possibly mean. Yet the manual asserts categorically: "A large discrepancy between the intelligence score and the capacity score is always indicative of adjustment problems."

The procedures followed in computing stability scores are more complex and still more obscure. Their underlying rationale seems to be that profile irregularities indicate emotional instability. It is well known that scatter analysis as an approach to personality diagnosis has not proved fruitful when applied to other instruments, such as the Wechsler scales. As applied to the Jastak test, it seems totally without foundation. Elaborate interpretations of low or high performance in different groups of subtests are offered, with no supporting evidence. Although the manual includes one table giving the results of a factor analysis, the group-factor loadings required to justify the combination of subtests into groups to obtain stability scores are missing. Yet by different groupings of the 10 subtests, the author derives what he terms "language," "reality," "motivation," and "psychomotor" scores. And the individual's relative standing in these four stability scores provides the basis for detailed personality descriptions.

All norms are based on a national sample of 3,000 school children, chosen so as to approximate the 1955 census distribution with regard to geographical areas. The sample consists of 500 boys and 500 girls at each year of age from 12 to 14. Although schools were selected so as to represent high, average, and low socioeconomic levels, no data on parental occupation or other socioeconomic indices are provided.

Split-half subtest reliabilities within single age groups are all in the .80's, but these coefficients are difficult to interpret because of a number of questionable procedures. In fact, if reliability was actually computed by the procedures described in the manual (p. 54), then the coefficients must be incorrect for all but 3 of the 10 subtests. It might also be added that all reliabilities were computed with a longer form of the test, about which nothing is reported other than that it correlated .97 with the present form. No information is given about the relative length of the two forms, how the short form was developed, or the conditions under which the correlation of .97 was obtained. The manual contains no mention of validity, nor any data permitting an evaluation of the test's validity. It ends with a chronological list of the author's publications, but there is no indication of which of these publications (if any) provide material relevant to the test.

While this test offers some ingenious adaptations of intelligence test items that may be of interest to research workers and test constructors, it does not appear to be ready for general use. The manual is quite unclear regarding technical aspects of test construction and evaluating; and it abounds in loose statements and unsupported interpretations. Some of the numerical juggling of subtest scores appears to yield meaningless results. Several statistical procedures are either incorrectly reported or simply incorrect. There is a conspicuous lack of validity data. Yet the tone of the manual makes it evident that the test is being offered, not as a research instrument, but for immediate operational use in the schools. Much of the discussion is addressed to teachers and guidance counselors, who are presumably regarded as the test's chief users. In a personal communication, the test author states that he plans to publish a major study in the future, explaining the complete test construction procedures he followed. It is unfortunate that publication of the test for general use was not delayed until this technical report became available.

BENJAMIN KLEINMUNTZ, *Associate Professor of Psychology, Carnegie Institute of Technology, Pittsburgh, Pennsylvania.*

The Jastak test is in the tradition of multiple aptitude batteries and consists of 10 tests which provide 10 separate scores which in turn yield 6 derived scores. The tests are intended for youngsters between the ages of 11.5 and 14.5. A longer version of essentially the same test was published in 1958; the present form can be administered in about one half the time of the earlier test (35 versus 65 minutes). Most of the statistical data reported in the 1959 manual are relevant to the earlier version, and this reviewer could find no explanation in the manual for the abridgment of the long form. It seems that the time spent in abridging the 1958 form might have been more profitably put to use had the test author worked in the direction of furnishing the potential test user with data on the validation of the earlier batteries and perhaps in providing an alternate form of the earlier version of the test.

The 10 direct scores are gotten from tests of vocabulary, number series, coding, picture reasoning, space series, verbal reasoning, social concept, arithmetic, space completion, and spelling; and the derived scores consist of intelligence, capacity, language, reality, motivation, and psychomotor factors. The standard score equivalents for each of the subtest raw scores can be obtained by consulting the appropriate tables, and the intelligence score is obtained by totaling these standard scores and consulting another table. The capacity score is derived by rank ordering the standard scores and finding the capacity score equivalents in a table prepared for that purpose. The correlation between intelligence and capacity scores is reported as .93, and presumably the capacity score, which on the average is 9.68 higher than the intelligence score, is "a measure of optimum potential." A large discrepancy between the intelligence and the capacity scores, according to the manual, is "always indicative of adjustment problems." No empirical evidence is offered to substantiate this interpretation.

Four other derived scores—language, reality, motivation, and psychomotor—are referred to as stability factors. The manual is not at all clear as to the origin of these "factors," but the one thing that seems certain about these scores is that they were not obtained from any of the conventional forms of factor analysis. Here the manual would have one believe that linear transformations of standard scores to regressed scores, which in turn yield "range" scores, are equivalent to extracting factors. To make the illusion of factor analysis complete, there is a statement that the "quartimax method" of factor analysis was made and that factor variances "were obtained from the 'psycho-logical' method of successive score transformations." If a factor analysis was performed by the quartimax method, which is really nothing more than a variation on Thurstone's simple structure in which the sum of *fourth* powers of elements in the rotated matrix is maximized, the test author has certainly done a good job of obscuring this fact in the test manual.

Each of the 10 subtests, except the spelling test, is timed for either 2, 3, or 4 minutes. The directions for administering the test are carefully prepared and clearly presented in the manual. The test booklet is a 15-page expendable form which the examinee will find quite readable and on which his summary statistics can be conveniently entered. Of questionable usefulness is the visual aid provided in the form of a circular graph which allows for the plotting of test scores. This circular graph has 10 radii, one for each of the subtests, which fan out from the middle and which are marked off numerically in accordance with the standard scores 6, 10, and 14. The number 10 circle represents average ability, and the number 6 and 14 circles represent mental retardation and superiority, respectively. These test profiles are inappropriately referred to as "personality profiles" by the test author. Most of the subtests have appeared elsewhere before, and no rationale for their present appearance in the form of the Jastak test is presented in the manual.

The vocabulary test consists of six pictures and a list of 21 words underneath. The student is required to identify the meaning of each word by correctly specifying the picture in which it occurs. For example, the word "instruction" is correctly identified in the picture in which an instructor is lecturing about geography. Unfortunately, due to a combination of poor artistic workmanship, unclear reproduction, and oversight, matters are not always that unambiguous. For instance there are four pictures in which the word "peruse" could plausibly be identified, but only one of these pictures is considered the correct answer. In one of these pictures a man is standing near a newstand with a newspaper, and his eyes seem to be on the reading matter; however, one learns from a subsequent answer that he is apparently reaching in his pocket for money, and the newspaper is under his arm. "Remuneration" seems to be the correct identification here. In two other pictures possibly relevant to the word "peruse," a nurse is reading a patient's chart, and a group of men is looking at a map of the United States. None of these identifications is correct, and the appropriate picture is one in which a man is reading a newspaper while sitting on the train. The reproduction of the picture has blotted out his eyes, however, and it is not obvious that he is not sleeping behind that paper and therefore a candidate for a subsequent word, "indolent."

The number series test consists of 15 rows of four numbers arranged according to some order. In order for the student to furnish numbers for two blank lines following the four number series, he must discover the principle that accounts for the ordering of the series. The coding test consists of a key with nine pairs of nonsense marks, and the task requires the student to consult this key in order to respond with the correct symbol when given one of the symbols in a pair. This is an interesting and more difficult version of the digit-symbol coding task.

The picture reasoning subtest consists of 10 series of five pictures each. The pictures within each of the 10 items can be arranged in some logical order, and ranked from 1 to 5. In this test as well as in the social concept test, none of the objections which were raised earlier concerning the quality of the artistic workmanship and reproduction are valid. The drawings and the format are quite clear and errors are strictly a function of the individual's abilities. A series of 13 rows of 10 geometric figures make up the space series test. The first five figures in each row change in some consistent order, and the examinee has to identify two of the remaining five figures that fit in with the changing pattern. The verbal reasoning test has 14 items and for each of these words the student has to select from among five words one that is the same and one that is opposite to the meaning of the first word on each line.

The social concept test is comprised of 11 rows of four pictures. Each row of pictures deals with some form of human action, attitude, or convention and the examinee has to identify the one picture out of four which does not fit the social concept pictured in the other three. The arithmetic test is a straight computation exercise in which 22 problems are arranged in order of complexity. Two other tests complete the batteries and these are the space completion and spelling tests. The former test consists of 11 problems in which the student has to find the two or more parts which go together to make up the stimulus figure. In the spelling test 22 words are dictated to the students to be written in their correct spelling on the lines provided for them.

In view of the fact that all except one (spelling) of the above are speeded tests, the test author's use of odd-even reliability coefficients is a questionable procedure. To the extent that individual differences in the obtained test scores depend upon speed of performance, the reliability coefficients found by this method will be spuriously high. The use of an equivalent forms reliability estimate would, of course, have been the method of choice; however, since no alternate form has been devised, the author could have split the test into times rather than into odd and even items. There are two ways to accomplish this. One way is to split each of the subtests into two half tests and to observe separate time limits. Each form would then be half the length of the complete test and therefore a Spearman-Brown or some such other correction formula could be used to estimate the reliability of the complete test. An alternative to this procedure would be to divide the total time into quarters, and to find the score for each of the four quarters. Both methods require some planning, and it would seem almost as easy to develop an equivalent form. The absence of the latter, however, does not serve as a license to use an inappropriate procedure. Having said this, it is important to point out that the odd-even reliability coefficients reported in this manual are not relevant to the present test, and therefore no stability data for any of the scores are available.

The principal weakness of the Jastak test is the lack of convincing evidence for the validity of either the individual subtest scores or any of the composite or derived scores. Unless this reviewer has missed something in the manual, the only evidence presented for the validity of the present battery is its correlation with two other tests and with the long form of this test. Correlations are reported of .87 between the short form of the Jastak test and the *California Test of Mental Maturity*, and .89 between the Jastak test (short form?) and the *Kuhlmann-Finch Tests*. The long form and the short form intelligence scores of the Jastak test yielded a coefficient of .97. In the Statistical Appendix of the manual, the latter correlation gave rise to this statement: "Except where indicated the statistical data here presented apply to the long form of the Jastak Test. Since the two forms are highly correlated ($r = .97$), the results are similar for both tests." There is no trace of either concurrent or predictive validity evidence; to the extent that factor analysis could be considered construct validity evidence, a gesture in the direction of providing construct validity is made in the form of correlation matrices which report the intercorrelation coefficients of the various subtests. No factor loadings are reported and there were probably no matrix rotations. Neither these incomplete factorial data nor the correlations between the Jastak and other tests are offered as validity evidence. As a matter of fact, except in the very loosest sense, the word validity is not mentioned in the manual.

In this light it is difficult to understand the test author's rather extensive 15-page section on the interpretation of test results. In the introductory remarks to that section, Jastak promises the reader that "if these pages are diligently studied and properly understood, considerable benefits will accrue to the examiner and the examined child." And for his efforts, the reader is rewarded with such incredibly muddled information as the following:

> The primary purpose of psychological testing is to know the child as well as possible and to help him improve his learning behavior.
>
> A disturbed individual will be more intelligently disturbed if he is bright than if he is dull. Intelligence enhances the symptoms of mental illness. It is of little value in overcoming them.
>
> We favor a definition of intelligence in ethically neutral terms. Biologically, intelligence represents the quantity, variety, and speed of responses and their manifold relationships available to the individual.
>
> Ability and personality adjustments are nearly identical. Personality differences are known to us only through the study of behavior reactions in response to many different tasks and situations.

On the other hand, the section which describes the collection of normative data and the standardization procedure itself are in the best tradition of psychological test development. The student population upon which this test was standardized consisted of boys and girls between the ages of 11.5 and 14.5. In order "to obtain the desired sampling, the United States was divided into nine population regions * A representative cross section within each region was selected," and care was exercised to consult the appropriate sources (e.g., U.S. Census Bureau and state census agencies) in order to divide the sample into high, middle, and low socioeconomic standing. A total of 8,500 tests were completed and from this sample, 3,000 records were randomly chosen for the derivation of the norms. The selection was designed to furnish 1,000 students (500 boys and 500 girls) for each of three age levels. An additional 600 children (200 for each age) "were selected to represent all levels of intelligence," and the statistical tables presenting the total normative sample of 3,600 cases are conveniently arranged so that the test user can easily obtain standard score equivalents for raw scores.

In summary then, it may be said that the Jastak test has technical faults which it shares with many of the multiple aptitude batteries that have evolved from the pioneer studies of L. L. Thurstone. True to the direction of the evolution of the subsequent versions of the primary mental abilities tests, the present edition of the Jastak test offers an abridgment and simplification of its own earlier form rather than providing the much needed empirical validation and technical refinements. Some of the shortcomings of the Jastak test are improper procedures for computing reliability of speeded tests (actually no reliability data are reported for the short form), meager validity data, and unsupported interpretations. The format of the test booklet and manual and the collection and presentation of the normative data are the battery's chief assets.

Am J Mental Def 65:300 S '60. Earl C. Butterfield. In issuing this shorter, group form of his intelligence test, Jastak reaffirms his faith that people, including the retarded, possess an intellectual potential which is greater than that which they reveal on the standard intelligence measure. Unfortunately, Jastak's test manual does little to convince us that his faith is founded in fact. He offers no evidence of the empirical validity of the capacity scores which his test yields. His test must therefore be considered an *experimental instrument* which has yet to be put to a telling test. Although the test's ten subscales are all composed of academic or intelligence test type items, Jastak purports to derive personality measures from them. He does demonstrate that these personality scores (Reality, Motivation, and Psychomotor) are relatively independent of or uncorrelated with the intellectual indices. Again, however, he does not offer any empirical evidence for the validity of these scores. In considering the probability of such validity demonstrations, it should be pointed out that Jastak, in proposing to measure personality from intelligence test subscale scatter (or stability as he calls it), is launching himself upon the same flight from which Wechsler and Rappaport have so recently and frequently been shot down. Is Jastak's flight also one of fantasy? Only *future* research will tell. The test's manual is written to educators. Whether by intent or not, it seems ideally suited to the seduction of the psychometrically unsophisticated teacher. It is a frightening, if ingenious, piece of propaganda for the "mental measurement movement" in general, and this test in particular. It timidly tackles the educator's coveted concept of the "whole child" in an effort to convince the conservative that the whole is not greater than the sum of its parts, but rather that the whole (child) can best be understood as parts and their inter-relationships. It reaches unparalleled heights in making complex statistical procedures such as factor analysis *seem* comprehensible to the unbaptised. It speaks to the teacher in her own idiom, that of the individual child, by presenting both pathetic and inspiring case studies in which the Jastak test is always "right." By virtue of its very effectiveness in tapping teachers' beliefs in "diagnosis," "individual pupil planning," and the "whole child," the manual becomes unfit for distribution to *unsuspecting* teachers. This is because it is highly likely that the manual will leave such teachers with the impression that this test has some demonstrated practical utility, while, in fact, it has no such thing. Being an experimental instrument, the most that can be said for it is that it has "potential" utility. Among the test's ten subscales are some ingenious modifications of item types which have heretofore been used almost exclusively in individual rather than group tests. The group test constructor would do well to examine Jastak's Vocabulary, Picture Reasoning and Social Concept subscales. They reflect a real originality. It should be noted that this test is of limited utility to those people interested primarily in mental retardation. It is built for just the age range of 11½ to 14½ and is a group test intended primarily for use in normal populations. Those investigators interested in the relationships of functional and potential intellectual levels and personality variables might well view this test as a welcome aid, however.

J Consult Psychol 24:466 O '60. Edward S. Bordin. This briefer form of the 1958 edition ....is reported to correlate .97 with its parent. This correlation and the extremely high reliability coefficients reported are fallaciously high estimates because they were computed on the same sample that provided the data for item analysis on the basis of which the items to be included in this form were selected. The manual is essentially unchanged. I must repeat my conclusion regarding the long form: without further validation data, the *Jastak Test* cannot be accepted as a way of obtaining inferences other than general level of ability.

[774]

***Job-Tests Program.** Adults; 1947–60; battery of aptitude tests, personality tests, and biographical forms used in various combinations in different jobs in business and industry; 1 form; 3 series; manual ('56, 8 looseleaf pages); directions for administering ('60, 4 looseleaf pages); hiring summary worksheets ('60, 1 page) for 24 job fields: numbers clerk, junior clerk, office machine operator, contact clerk, senior clerk, secretary, unskilled worker, semiskilled worker, factory machine operator, vehicle operator, inspector, skilled worker, sales clerk, salesman, sales engineer, scientist, engineer, office technical, writer, designer, instructor, office supervisor, sales supervisor, factory supervisor; no data on reliability presented in manual; $15 per complete set of aptitude tests, personality tests, biographical forms, hiring summary worksheets, scoring stencils, manual, and rating forms from the *Merit Rating Series;* $5 per set of aptitude tests, personality tests, biographical form, hiring summary worksheet, scoring stencil, and manual for a particular job field; $3 per set of aptitude tests, hiring summary worksheet, scoring stencil, and manual for a particular job field; postage extra; Industrial Psychology, Inc. *

a) FACTORED APTITUDE SERIES. Formerly listed as [*Aptitude Intelligence Tests*]; 15 tests; $5 per 20 tests; French and Spanish editions available; Joseph E. King (1–2, 4–15) and H. B. Osborn, Jr. (3).

1) *Office Terms.* 1947–56; 1 form ('56, 3 pages); 5(10) minutes.

2) *Sales Terms.* 1948–56; 1 form ('56, 3 pages); 5(10) minutes.

3) *Factory Terms.* 1957; 1 form (3 pages); 10(15) minutes.

4) *Tools.* 1948–56; 1 form ('56, 3 pages); 5(10) minutes.

5) *Numbers.* 1947–56; 1 form ('56, 3 pages); 5(10) minutes.

6) *Perception.* 1948–56; 1 form ('56, 3 pages); 5(10) minutes.

7) *Judgment.* 1947–56; 1 form ('56, 3 pages); 5(10) minutes.

8) *Precision.* 1947–56; 1 form ('56, 3 pages); 5(10) minutes.

9) *Fluency.* 1947–56; 2 scores: words ending in tion and jobs, or words beginning with pre and equipment; 1 form ('56, 3 pages, contains 4 parts of which examinee takes only 2); 6(10) minutes.

10) *Memory.* 1948–56; 1 form ('56, 4 pages); 5(10) minutes.

11) *Parts.* 1949–56; 1 form ('56, 3 pages); 5(10) minutes.

12) *Blocks.* 1948–56; 1 form ('56, 3 pages, adapted from *Army General Classification Test*); 5(10) minutes.

13) *Dimension.* 1947–56; 1 form ('56, 3 pages); 5(10) minutes.

14) *Dexterity.* 1949–56; 3 scores: maze, checks, dots; 1 form ('56, 4 pages); 3(10) minutes.

15) *Motor.* 1948–56; 1 form ('56, 4 pages, plus motor apparatus); $20 per set of motor apparatus; 6(10) minutes.

b) EMPLOYEE ATTITUDE SERIES. 3 tests; $5 per 20 tests of CPF or NPF; $10 per 20 tests of 16 PF; French and Spanish editions available; R. B. Cattell, J. E. King (1–2), and A. K. Schuettler (1–2).

1) *CPF.* 1954; 1 form ('54, 3 pages, published also by Institute for Personality and Ability Testing as Form A of *IPAT Contact Personality Factor Test*); combined interpretation sheet for CPF and NPF [no date, 2 pages]; (4–10) minutes.

2) *NPF.* 1954; 1 form ('54, 3 pages, published also by Institute for Personality and Ability Testing as *IPAT Neurotic Personality Factor Test* bearing 1955 copyright); combined interpretation sheet for CPF and NPF [no date, 2 pages]; (4–15) minutes.

3) *16 PF.* 1956–60; special printing with new item format, labeled Industrial Edition A, of *Sixteen Personality Factor Questionnaire,* Form C; revised interpretation sheets ('60, 4 pages); (20–30) minutes.

c) APPLICATION-INTERVIEW SERIES. 1948–56; questions in 8 areas: job stability, job experience, education, financial maturity, health-physical condition, family, domestic, activities; 1 form ('56, 4 pages); 5 biogra-

phy booklets; descriptive sheets ('56, 3 pages); no norms for part scores; $5 per 20 biography booklets; (15–20) minutes; Joseph E. King.
1) *Biography-Clerical.*
2) *Biography-Mechanical.*
3) *Biography-Sales.*
4) *Biography-Technical.*
5) *Biography-Supervisor.*

WILLIAM H. HELME, *Supervisory Research Psychologist, United States Army Personnel Research Office, Washington, D.C.*

In the *Job-Tests Program* the authors have assembled a comprehensive set of ability measures, personality-attitude questionnaires, and background-experience questionnaires for use in selection for a wide variety of business and industrial jobs. Many of the instruments have been adapted from earlier tests on which originators conducted extensive reliability and factor analysis studies. Some, such as Cattell's personality measures, have been incorporated without further change. All are carefully constructed and presented with clear and concise instructions for administration and scoring. Moreover, these sets of measures are reported by the present authors to have been used in some 5,000 industrial concerns. In short, the stage appears all set for presentation of an impressive, well documented battery with clear guidelines for wide industrial application.

But the presentation never comes off. The reason is the absence of adequate validation. Seventeen research bulletins on validation for particular jobs are presented. Sample sizes in the studies range from 16 to 106. Validity coefficients are reported for only a small number of measures for each sample. Several of the samples are of relatively routine clerical jobs; other studies are concerned with electrical assemblers, salesmen, sales managers, printing estimators, policemen, and engineering supervisors. In each sample a few unbiased zero-order coefficients of correlation with performance ratings are reported. These findings can perhaps be characterized as "promising" individual instances of validity, but scarcely as a basis for supporting or recommending wide use.

The research bulletins also present both nonlinear correlations and validity coefficients of weighted test composites. Since there is likelihood of substantial shrinkage in the correlation ratio for a single test validity or in the validity of a weighted composite on samples of this size, these validity estimates should be discounted. This error is perpetuated in the manual, in a section entitled "How to Tailor Personnel Tests to Your Company Operation." This section recommends the practice of obtaining "tailored" weights on samples of 40 or more cases, and also illustrates the use of nonlinear correlations, without mention of the shrinkage in validity to be expected when the weights are applied to new samples. There is a statement that the statistical correlations and derivation of weights is "best carried out by a trained industrial psychologist or psychometrician"—but the best trained psychologist can scarcely make up for the inadequate data or design.

The reviewer feels that little purpose would be served by more detailed discussion of the *Job-Tests Program* at this time. As pointed out in earlier reviews in the *Mental Measurements Yearbook,* what is needed is thorough and conscientious validation if this set of measures is to be put on a sound scientific basis for industrial use. With all the participating companies, and with use of other research resources, it is hard to see why a really comprehensive validation program has not already been carried out in the more than 15 years since these tests were released "for general use in business and industry." Until this is done, industrial users would be well advised to be wary of applying these measures without application of standard statistical methods for their evaluation, or, as an alternative, utilizing one of the other industrial batteries such as the *Flanagan Aptitude Classification Tests* or other selection battery for which more adequate information is available.

STANLEY I. RUBIN, *Coordinator, Assessment Services, Personnel Research and Development Corporation, Cleveland, Ohio.*

The "Complete" *Job-Tests Program* offers a series of tests for each of 24 job fields which are broadly categorized as Clerical, Mechanical, Sales, Technical, and Supervisory. In all, there are 23 tests and forms which are used in different combinations and which include aptitude, intelligence, and personality tests, and biographical forms.

The fundamental rationale for the various tests is based upon the theory of factor analysis. Thus, for the aptitude-intelligence portion of the series, the tests attempt to measure eight essentials which "are very important tests for every job field, since they indicate if the applicant has the basic brainpower to learn and perform the assignments in that job field."

The personality measures are predicated on the factorial studies conducted by R. B. Cattell, and are designed to "find out if the applicant is personally adjusted and how he gets along and deals with poeple." Three different personality "tests" are offered: the CPF test measuring extroversion-introversion, the NPF test measuring stability-neuroticism, and the 16 PF test measuring 16 different personality factors. The latter test also offers a distortion or "lie" factor as well as six "complex" personality scores which "tap broader areas of personality significant at certain job assignments."

Finally, there are five biographical forms, one for each of the job categories mentioned above. The data obtained from these forms (each item is weighted) are designed to reveal information relative to a person's job stability, job experience, educational background, financial maturity, health and physical condition, family background, domestic situation, and outside activities. This in turn is used to determine the adequacy of an applicant's background for a particular job field.

The tests in the "Program" are geared primarily for use in business and industry. The publisher appeals to the cost conscious personnel manager and advises that the various combinations of tests will assist management in making better initial selections by utilizing "scientific methods for psychological testing and interviewing." In addition to suggesting tests to be used in determining an applicant's suitability for a particular job field, the publisher presents some interesting notions and tips for personnel clerks on such topics as recruiting, hiring, test administration, and follow-up procedures.

With few exceptions, the tests offer the advantage of little administration time since only five minutes is required for each measure. In addition, for each job area there is a "Hiring Summary Worksheet" complete with a qualification grid on which an applicant's raw scores are quickly weighted and converted to stanine scores. Once they have been obtained, a simple technique is followed for determining whether the applicant is under-qualified, minimum-qualified, well-qualified, best-qualified, or over-qualified for the field in which he is being tested. According to the manual, the "qualification level" provides an easy method for determining the extent to which an applicant measures up to successful workers in a particular field, as well as comparing him with other applicants.

STRONG POINTS. The major advantage that the "Complete" *Job-Tests Program* has to offer is its typography. All of the materials are attractive, easy to read, and presented in a well written style. The publisher has apparently taken great pains to develop clear "how to do it" procedures designed to appeal to personnel clerks in industry. The tests are simple to administer and score, and any individual taking them will find the instructions easy to understand. Similarly, the inclusion of a Hiring Summary Worksheet enables the personnel clerk to obtain a "quick fix" on an applicant's suitability for a particular position, and to determine whether further testing is justified. Furthermore, companies utilizing the program are encouraged to establish individual standards specifically tailored for their own organizations. In fact, the various steps necessary to carry out such a project are presented in concise form.

The tests in the program offer the advantage of providing a certain amount of face validity. That is, most of the items in the aptitude-intelligence portion of the series give the appearance of appropriateness.

It is the opinion of this reviewer that the major strong point about the program is that it is a clearly written, easily administered "do it yourself" testing program that requires a minimum of sophistication on the part of its users.

WEAK POINTS. Two previous reviews of the aptitude series portion of the program, one in 1953 by D. Welty Lefever and another in 1959 by Harold P. Bechtoldt, criticized the authors for making too many claims about the predictive value of the instruments in the absence of supportive evidence. Once again this criticism is justified in view of the sparsity of data and published studies about the series in recognized professional journals. In the manual, the phrase "validation studies" appears time and time again, but no statement is made as to where these are published in the professional literature.

Second, there is the question of the job test fields themselves. The manual lists a number of job titles, 800 to be exact, that exist in industry. Then, on an a priori basis, these 800 titles are assigned to the 24 job test fields. The assumption made is that the job test fields are sufficiently basic to be used in such a manner. Furthermore, it is assumed that the various tests suggested for each of these fields is appropriate. For example, users are advised that they can use the tests in the job area labeled Sales Engineer to test a man being considered for a job as an underwriter, as well as for such divergent positions as lawyer, jobber, industrial engineer, manuscript reader, optometrist, purchasing agent, securities broker, and others. Such a broad claim requires much more substantiating evidence than is provided in the manual.

The manual also fails to take into consideration the fact that within each field of work there exist various levels of complexity. For example, in suggesting tests to be used for selecting secretaries, no attempt is made to account for the differences in complexity of duties to be performed or in the caliber of person required under differing employment conditions or work environments. Surely one would expect more from a secretary to the president of a large corporation than a secretary who works for one of the salesmen.

Third, there is the matter of claiming purity of items by the technique of name similarity. While the manual does admit that this series "was not developed from a full scale factor analysis," the publisher implies that it was by calling it a "Factored Aptitude Series." It would appear that an effort was made to approximate "purity" by developing "item-types." What this apparently means is that in lieu of a factor analysis on this series, the publisher has settled for second best in the hope that the items created for a particular aptitude would closely approximate those emerging from other factorial studies. The authors fail to realize, however, that items and not types are factorially pure. In the opinion of this reviewer, it is misleading to label the series "Factored Aptitude Series" when the items in the tests have not been subjected to a factor analysis.

In the discussion of the intercorrelations between the various tests in the aptitude series the manual reports that the "average intercorrelation between the factors is in the neighborhood of .35." Reporting this statistic is of little value unless one has an opportunity to examine the intercorrelation matrix for the eight so-called "factors" involved. Once again no mention is made of any publication, in professional literature, where this matrix can be examined.

In an effort to make the personnel man's job easier, the publisher offers "pre-set" weights and standards established on the series of tests for each of 24 job fields. Again in the absence of published studies, the authors claim to have differentiated successful from unsuccessful employees in each of these job fields. What they suggest is that in the absence of a validation study within a company, the personnel man should utilize the pre-set standards which they have "researched out." This "Procrustean Bed" is nothing more than an inappropriate generalization when one considers that the standards used in selecting industrial salesmen operating out of a large metropolitan office in New York City can be expected to differ significantly from those utilized in selecting industrial salesmen working out of a small city in Mississippi.

Finally, there is the matter of the 16 PF test or, as the manual states, "sixteen unitary, independent, and source traits of personality." Not only are many of the items in this test of Lilliputian stature when considering the complex nature of an individual's personality, but they are downright insulting to the intelligence of most individuals capable of coping with even the simplest of problems in logic. One of the items in this test is as follows: "Are you always a sound sleeper, who does not walk or talk in his sleep?" The respondent is then asked to answer (A) Yes; (B) In between; (C) No.

This reviewer believes that the authors are guilty of gross over simplification in the technique they suggest for measuring the complex dimensions of an individual's personality. They would have us believe that all an untrained person has to do to determine the complexities of a personality is to add up the rank scores on four variables, compute the total, obtain the combined rank, then make an interpretation. For example, to determine a person's stability, add Factors C (mature), L (trustful), E (dominant), and O (self-confident). If a high rank is obtained, by means of simple addition, then the individual has a "non-neurotic personality." This same method is suggested for measuring extroversion, anxiety level, leadership, research creativity, and initiative-drive.

The authors make the error of assuming that a person's personality is a static entity unaffected by a multitude of needs and environmental conditions. Furthermore, little appreciation is offered for the commonly accepted notion among professionals that "the whole is greater than the sum of its parts." Kenneth S. Nickerson [1] commenting on the 16 PF has aptly stated, "a significant aspect of complex human behavior cannot be measured by six abstruse items, and sixteen such measures do not make a personality." This reviewer is in full agreement.

SUMMARY. The "Complete" *Job-Tests Program* offers a well written, easy to administer, and simple to score group of tests that are presented in stylish fashion. It has been developed with great concern for the problems of the personnel man in industry. In fact, the series is probably the most attractive one on the market today. It has a great deal of face validity, but the authors have failed to make available, in sufficient quantity and in recognized professional journals, the kind of data that one must submit for professional scrutiny before claims of validity can be voiced. Indeed, it is unfortunate that the authors, talented writers who have taken the time, effort, and pains to communicate so much to personnel clerks on how to administer and score the *Job-Tests Program*, have failed to make available evidence of validity.

In the opinion of this reviewer, the program does have something to offer for a personnel man interested in conducting a validity study within his plant on current employees. However, until further evidence is submitted to substantiate the numerous claims about the predictive value of the series, it cannot be recommended as a selection device for general use in industry.

For a review by Harold P. Bechtoldt of the Factored Aptitude Series, *see 5:602; for a review by D. Welty Lefever of an earlier edition of this series, see 4:712 (1 excerpt); for reviews of the personality tests, see 174, 5:71, 5:74, 5:112, and 4:87.*

[775]

★Measurement of Skill: A Battery of Placement Tests for Business, Industrial and Educational Use. Adults; 1958–62, c1956–62; 8 tests (3 pages except for *g*); manual ('62, c1960–62, 42 looseleaf pages); revised profile card ('62, c1960, 1 page); Skillsort cards ('62, 54 cards) and manual ('62, 9 pages) for job profile determination; $3.75 per 25 tests; $20 per set of scoring stencils for all tests; $8 per 100 profiles; $7.50 per set of Skillsort cards; $5 per manual (including any supplements issued during year following purchase); $1 per specimen set of tests only; $25 per specimen set of tests, manual, and stencils; postpaid; 5(10) minutes per test (except for *g*); Walter V. Clarke Associates, Inc.; AVA Publications, Inc. *

a) SKILL WITH VOCABULARY. Form MOS-1 ('59, c1956–59).
b) SKILL WITH NUMBERS. Form MOS-2 ('59, c1956–59).
c) SKILL WITH SHAPE. Form MOS-3 ('59, c1956–59).
d) SPEED AND ACCURACY. Form MOS-4 ('59, c1956–59).
e) SKILL IN ORIENTATION. Form MOS-5 ('59, c1958–59).
f) SKILL IN THINKING. Form MOS-6 ('58, c1957–58).
g) SKILL WITH MEMORY. Form MOS-7 revised ('61, c1960, 5 pages); 7(12) minutes.
h) SKILL WITH FINGERS. Form MOS-8 ('59, c1956–59).

REFERENCES

1. MERENDA, PETER F. "Relative Predictive Efficiency of a Short Versus a Long Test Battery for High School Students." *Psychol Rep* 8:62 F '61. * (*PA* 36:1KJ62M)
2. MERENDA, PETER F.; HALL, CHARLES E.; CLARKE, WALTER V.; AND PASCALE, ALFRED C. "Relative Predictive Efficiency of the DAT and a Short Multifactor Battery of Tests." *Psychol Rep* 11:71–81 Ag '62. * (*PA* 37:5665)

DOROTHY C. ADKINS, *Professor of Psychology, The University of North Carolina, Chapel Hill, North Carolina.*

That the *Measurement of Skill* battery has been prematurely made available to prospective purchasers and submitted for review in this compendium is unfortunate. It consists of eight short subtests, for five of which the only estimate of reliability is based upon test-retest correlation, with a four-week interval, for 36 summer-school college students! For one test an additional test-retest estimate is given for 30 college students and a five-week interval. For the memory test, three test-retest estimates (for 56 undescribed cases after four weeks, 26 undescribed cases after five weeks, and 71 salesmen after a two-day memory course) are offered. For the eighth test, a six-month interval and 102 high school students were used. Whether or not the college students are representative of the job applicants for which the test is presumably designed may also be questioned.

In the reviewer's opinion, the test-retest method is useful principally as a device for introducing the meaning of the concept of reliability to undergraduate students. With brief tests as simple and economical to develop and reproduce as the ones under consideration, no

1 NICKERSON, KENNETH S. "Comments on the Brain Watchers." Letter. *Am Psychologist* 18:529–31 Ag '63. *

reasonable excuse occurs to one for failure to determine estimates of reliability from correlations between different forms of the tests.

The manual states that the tests were designed "primarily as aids in the proper selection, classification, and assignment of business and industrial employees at *all levels* of the occupational hierarchy" (reviewer's italics) and that "in addition they show promise for use in predicting high school achievement." Centile norms are provided for each test for from five to nine groups, in each case including a group designated "General Industrial and Business Employees," which evidently contains the individuals in other employee groups classified as professional, executives and managerial, general office, and skilled and semiskilled. For six tests, the total group n is at least 759, while the other two n's are 176 and 589. Means and standard deviations of each test for each group are also given.

The individual using a table of norms for a test is instructed to read off the "percentile" score in the column for the group with which the subject is being compared. Following the description of the norms appear four pages that are marked "Restricted to AVA Analysts Only." These discuss ipsative profile interpretation and observe that the mean score "has been found to be related to intelligence as a general concept ($r = .55$)"—whatever that means! Before the scores are averaged, they are converted to a scale of numbers ranging from 0 to 100 by means of the MOS Record Summary Card. The reviewer was unable to determine exactly what kind of "standard score equivalents" these converted scores represent. The converted score of 50, for example, uniformly corresponds to neither the mean score nor the 50th centile point.

These same pages present a table from which an approximation of IQ score as measured by the Otis can be found at the intersection of the column containing an individual's mean MOS score and the row containing his AVA Resultant Activity Score. Elsewhere it is mentioned that the multiple correlation of these two scores with the *Wonderlic Personnel Test* was .59 for 244 cases. In any case, the suggestion that what is ordinarily meant by the symbol IQ can be inferred from the mean MOS score and the AVA Resultant Activity Score is unfounded.

Arguing that the usefulness of a battery of tests is a function of the differences among them, the authors present a table of "coefficients of independence," based upon the average intercorrelations from four samples. The coefficients given range from 0 to 100 for perfect independence or maximum possible difference. The coefficient may be simply $100(1 - r)$ but it is more likely to equal $100(1 - r^2)$, what is sometimes called the coefficient of nondetermination. This would mean that the intercorrelation coefficients corresponding to the tabled values 78 to 99 range from about .10 to about .47. The original correlation coefficients and the method used for averaging them might well have been presented.

As to validity, the manual first states that the tests have been carefully designed to insure face validity, claiming that the nature of the tasks is consistent with the test titles and is homogeneous within each test. In the case of certain tests, however, the tasks do not represent what psychologists would expect from the title or even from the manual's descriptions of the tests. The "Skill With Vocabulary" test is referred to as a test of verbal fluency. Each item consists of definitions of a word, with the first letter and the number of letters given. Unlike the usual vocabulary test, this test does indeed seem to draw upon fluency, not to mention spelling ability. The "Speed and Accuracy" test calls for identifying the number of X's embedded in rows of letters of the alphabet. A better name for this test might connote its perceptual or visual character—Perceptual Speed, for example. The "Skill With Fingers" test, intended to test finger dexterity, requires the subject to write in blank squares as many figure 4's as he can in the allotted time.

But, as the authors recognize, mere face validity (however defined) is not sufficient. Hence they report that "empirical statistical validity studies against well defined criteria are being made." Except in the case of predicting high school scholarship (see below), these important studies were not yet available when the manual was released. In the meantime, it is argued that the validity of the series and of parts of it is attested to by combinations of MOS tests correlated with other single tests. For various subtests, correlations are reported with such tests as the *Wonderlic Personnel Test*, Bennett's *Tests of Mechanical Comprehension*, *Revised Minnesota Paper Form Board*

Test, and *Minnesota Clerical Test,* with *n*'s ranging from 25 to 175. Multiple correlations for composites of various tests of the MOS series with other tests are presented. The value of such coefficients (based upon as few as 25 cases, with the zero-order coefficients corrected for restriction in range) is highly questionable. Estimating the standard deviations on MOS tests for an *n* of 8,597 cases (a composite of normative samples for the *Revised Minnesota Paper Form Board Test*) from data for 25 cases and then using these estimates in reaching a multiple correlation is attempting to squeeze too much out of a limited amount of raw information.

Also reported in the manual is what purports to be a comparative study of the validity of the MOS battery and the substantially longer *Differential Aptitude Tests.* The MOS battery was administered in the spring of 1960 to the eleventh graders of a large city high school. The tests were correlated with marks in different courses achieved by these students in the tenth, eleventh, and twelfth grades. The manual states that the class had previously taken the DAT battery of eight tests, which also could be correlated with course marks. The two sets of zero-order and multiple correlations are of about the same order. Only upon reference to two articles in *Psychological Reports* (*1–2*) does one learn that the DAT was administered when the subjects were in the eighth grade!

In the 1962 article (*2*) the authors make much of their finding that the coefficients of independence (see above) for the MOS tests are greater than for the DAT tests. Perhaps it will be sufficient to observe that the anticipated coefficients of independence for a battery of tests all of zero reliability would be 100. The 1962 article also observes from factor analyses that the uniqueness values for the tests in the DAT battery are substantially lower than the communalities, whereas the converse is generally true for the tests in the MOS series. Since the uniqueness of a test consists not only of any factors specific to it but also of a variable error factor, a finding that less reliable tests have greater U^2 values is exactly what should be expected, other things being equal.

We turn to a few features of the tests as gleaned from inspection. Skill With Vocabulary, first copyrighted in 1956, still contains what appear to be serious errors. In one item, for example, the answer "renegade" is to be given for a definition that includes "turncoat." In the very next item, "turncoat" is to be given for a definition that includes "renegade." In general, the items contain many specific determiners. Some of these are so obvious that one wonders whether for some subtle reason they were intentional.

In the case of Skill With Numbers, an improved test design could produce many more than a maximum of 48 responses in the five-minute time limit. Moreover, the suggestion that part scores be obtained for sets of 12 simple items on the four basic arithmetic operations is unwise.

The figures in Skill With Shape are unduly small; and the drafting is far from perfect, so that the sizes of areas that are supposed to be the same are not. One also wonders about the variance introduced by having the subject indicate the answer by shading the areas within the complex figures that correspond to black areas shown at their right. Some will make a few rough lines, others do meticulous shading.

The perceptual ability required for MOS-4, Speed and Accuracy, may be confounded with a numerical factor, since the subject must count the number of *X*'s in each row. The number of separate items in the "Orientation" test (10) is too small. The test should be redesigned or another format substituted to yield more responses per unit of time. Skill in Thinking probably involves a specific algebraic skill. The scoring of Skill With Memory could be simplified by casting it in multiple choice form. The number "4" seems a poor choice for Skill With Fingers since it can be written in two ways.

Accompanying the MOS test battery is a set of 54 Skillsort cards and a sorting tray. The cards contain statements like "Operates a variety of machines," "Compiles statistical data," and so on. On the back of each card are three numbers that apparently represent the tests in the MOS battery that have been judged to test the ability to perform the duty described on the face of the card. According to the "Instructions for Skillsort Profile Determination," one decides for each card whether it does or does not describe some aspect of a job under consideration and then tallies the test numbers on the backs of the selected cards. Each of the frequencies is multiplied by one of a set of weights that range from .03 to .13 and that appear to be inversely but not linearly related to the frequency of occurrence of the test numbers on the backs of the cards. The weighted frequencies are converted by means of a table to "C scores" that range from 31 through 78. These possibly represent some form of normalized scores with a mean of 50 and a standard deviation of 10. The sum of the C scores is multiplied by .125 (although the directions say .0125), and the resulting average C score is indicated by a line on a profile form that contains a scale ranging from 20 to 80. The C scores for the eight separate tests are plotted and the points connected by lines. Presumably this profile is supposed to suggest which MOS tests should be used or weighted most heavily for the job under consideration.

The design and physical quality of all these materials are exceptionally good.

LLOYD G. HUMPHREYS, *Professor of Psychology and Head of the Department, University of Illinois, Urbana, Illinois.*

The *Measurement of Skill* test battery has as a subtitle "A Battery of Placement Tests for Business, Industrial and Educational Use." There are eight subtests of varying numbers of items, each of which requires five minutes for administration. The manual recommends these tests as substitutes for longer test batteries, such as the DAT. The adjectives "short" and "practical" are used liberally in the manual. Data of a sort are presented under headings drawn from the APA's test standards, and the claim is made that these tests perform at least as well if not better than longer and more complex instruments. There is ample sales appeal for the unwary personnel manager or school administrator. Unfortunately, however, the MOS battery represents a poor professional job of test construction, validation, standardization, and manual writing.

Reliabilities are test-retest, interval is typically about four weeks, n is typically 36. Most item types are easily remembered, and the number of items to remember is frequently small. Reliabilities reported vary from .44 to .82, but this reviewer strongly suspects that larger n's and parallel forms coefficients would result in values *much* lower than these in any reasonable sort of population.

The validation section is in each case woefully weak. Apparently, the *Measurement of Skill* tests were correlated with whatever ability tests happened to be available. The Wonderlic is used frequently and appears to be as satisfactory a reference test for Skill With Shape or Skill in Orientation as it is for Skill With Vocabulary.

Intercorrelations of the tests in the battery are low because the reliabilities of the tests are low, though the authors report coefficients of independence in place of the usual correlation coefficients. The root of the quantity $(1 - r^2)$ has the very satisfying property, from the point of view of the salesman, of approaching unity quite closely even for moderate values of r.

The authors discuss the values in the use of a battery of tests. One of these is the possibility of using differential weights for the prediction of different criteria. Unfortunately, the tests are so short and reliabilities are presumably so low that stable differential weighting cannot be accomplished on samples of the size typically found in business and in education. The authors also state, in one place, that short tests with low reliabilities should not be used in isolation. However, norms are presented for each of the tests individually; a section is devoted to the ipsative interpretation of test profiles; and the user is even encouraged to obtain part scores on Skill With Numbers.

One study of the comparative validity of the DAT and the MOS batteries has been accomplished. School grades were used as criteria. The study is discussed in the manual and is also to be found in *Psychological Reports* (*1–2*). Unfortunately, there is a major flaw in the design. The DAT was administered during the eighth grade; the *Measurement of Skill* was administered during the spring semester of the eleventh grade; criteria used were grades at the end of the tenth, eleventh, and twelfth grades. The difference in time interval between the two test administrations and the criterion performances makes the data basically worthless. Furthermore, in the tenth grade, where the time interval difference is smallest, comparisons are between correlations computed on overlapping but nonidentical samples.

In summary, the *Measurement of Skill* should not be used; it should not have been published; it should not be sold.

JOSEPH E. MOORE, *Regents Professor of Psychology, Georgia Institute of Technology, Atlanta, Georgia.*

According to the manual, these tests were developed "primarily as aids in the proper selection, classification and assignment of business and industrial employees at all levels of the occupational hierarchy. In addition they show promise for use in predicting high school achievement." The claim of face validity is made for all of the tests and concurrent validity data are presented for several of them. However, predictive validity data based on business or industrial use do not appear for any of the tests. The authors state that "since face validity alone is not sufficient evidence that the series will perform as expected, empirical statistical validity studies against well defined criteria are being made." It is most unfortunate that the manual does not contain at least one such study. A rather loosely designed study of predictive validity is presented for one high school in Rhode Island. In this, scores from the MOS and the *Differential Aptitude Tests* were compared with later success in certain subject matter areas. No cross validation is reported on any of these tests.

For the authors to administer a series of tests to so many hundreds of workers and publish business and industrial norms without reporting a single study against job performance criteria is unfortunate, if not inexcusable. To say that such studies are being made and will be published later does not excuse these authors. The claim that the eight separate tests measure separate skills of some kind should have been verified on different jobs against meaningful performance criteria. Evidence of predictive validity in the business and industrial area is, at this time, entirely lacking.

A rather ingenious procedure for rating job characteristics is also available for use in conjunction with the MOS. The material consists of 54 cards containing descriptive phrases. The rater sorts these cards into seven boxes representing his judgment of the significance or importance to the job of each descriptive phrase. Each card also has on its back side a code for the particular MOS test which seems to be required by the particular characteristic. These codes are tallied and the resultant frequencies are given C score ratings from which a "Skillsort profile" is drawn for all eight tests. It is unfortunate that no rationale is given for the Skillsort technique. No data are given showing the reliability of the ratings by such a method. Furthermore, no data are presented to show that the MOS coded characteristics differentiate between jobs in the expected direction. The general description of the Skillsort method and the use of terms are remarkably close to the old United States Employment Service job analysis procedure. This similarity should make the Skillsort somewhat more understandable and meaningful to many users.

The general instructions for each of the MOS tests are clear and concise. The exact statements the tester is to say are presented in boldface type that is easy to read. The instructions for scoring are clearly given and the use of plastic stencils that fit over the test sheets makes scoring very rapid.

It very well could be that the authors might have made a strong case for the MOS and the Skillsort procedures if they had shown that such instruments and C score ratings clearly differentiate performance ratings of superior and inferior personnel on specific jobs. Since they have not done so, however, use of the MOS and the Skillsort procedure by business or industry *cannot* be recommended. There are no data to show that these instruments differentiate at all between jobs. Certainly one should not use these instruments until the authors have made good their promise to furnish "empirical statistical validity studies against well defined criteria."

[776]

***Multiple Aptitude Tests, 1959 Edition.** Grades 7–13; 1955–60; tests identical with those of 1955 edition except for booklet organization; 14 scores: scholastic potential plus 13 scores listed below; IBM and Grade-O-Mat; 1 form ('59); 9 tests in 4 booklets; administration and scoring manual ('59, 24 pages); interpretation manual ('60, 55 pages); technical report ['60, 79 pages]; extended profile ('59, 1 page); student report ('60, 4 pages); separate answer sheets or cards may be used; 10¢ per set of IBM answer sheets; 10¢ per set of Cal-Cards; 75¢ per set of either hand or machine scoring stencils for answer sheets; 75¢ per set of hand scoring stencils for Cal-Cards; 14¢ per set of Grade-O-Mat scorable punch-out cards; 6¢ per stylus; 6¢ per backing pad; 2¢ per extended profile (free on request with all 4 booklets); 2¢ per transparent profile (no date); 3¢ per student's report; 50¢ per interpretation manual; postage extra; $1.25 per complete specimen set, postpaid; technical report free; 175.5–177(220–222) minutes in 2–3 sessions; David Segel and Evelyn Raskin; California Test Bureau. *

a) FACTOR 1, VERBAL COMPREHENSION. 3 scores: word meaning, paragraph meaning, total; 1 form (12 pages); $4.20 per 35 tests; 42(52) minutes.

b) FACTOR 2, PERCEPTUAL SPEED. 3 scores: language usage, routine clerical facility, total; 1 form (12 pages); $4.20 per 35 tests; 33(43) minutes.
c) FACTOR 3, NUMERICAL REASONING. 3 scores: arithmetic reasoning, arithmetic computation, total; 1 form (12 pages); $4.20 per 35 tests; 52(62) minutes.
d) FACTOR 4, SPATIAL VISUALIZATION. 4 scores: applied science and mechanics, 2-dimensional spatial relations, 3-dimensional spatial relations, total; 1 form (32 pages); $8.40 per 35 tests; 50(65) minutes.

REFERENCES

1. MENDENHALL, GEORGE V. *A Statistical Investigation of Interrelationships in the Multiple Aptitude Tests.* Master's thesis, University of Southern California (Los Angeles, Calif.), 1952.
2. CURETON, EDWARD E. "Service Tests of Multiple Aptitudes." *Proc Inv Conf Testing Probl* 1955:22-39 '56. * (*PA* 31:3017)
3. SEGEL, DAVID. "The Multiple Aptitude Tests." Comments by Donald E. Super. *Personnel & Guid J* 35:424-34 Mr '57. * (*PA* 32:1645)
4. D'AMICO, LOUIS A.; BRYANT, J. HOWARD; AND PRAHL, MARIE R. "The Relationship Between MAT Scores and Achievement in Junior College Subjects." *Ed & Psychol Meas* 19:611-6 w '59. * (*PA* 34:6564)
5. KHAN, LILIAN. *Factor Analysis of Certain Aptitude and Personality Variables.* Doctor's thesis, University of Southern California (Los Angeles, Calif.), 1959. (*DA* 20:2889)
6. MINER, JOHN B. "The Concurrent Validity of the PAT in the Selection of Tabulating Machine Operators." *J Proj Tech* 24:409-18 D '60. * (*PA* 35:5391)
7. KHAN, LILIAN. "Factor Analysis of Certain Aptitude and Personality Variables." *Indian J Psychol* 37:27-38 Mr '62. * (*PA* 37:6716)
8. CAPLAN, STANLEY W.; RUBLE, RONALD A.; AND SEGEL, DAVID. "A Theory of Educational and Vocational Choice in Junior High School." *Personnel & Guid J* 42:129-35 O '63. *

S. S. DUNN, *Assistant Director, Australian Council for Educational Research, Hawthorn, Victoria, Australia.*

The tests in the 1959 edition are identical with those used in 1955 but are now published in four booklets each containing the tests for one factor. Test 3, Language Usage, is dropped from Factor 1 and with Test 4, Routine Clerical Facility, provides the basis for Factor 2, Perceptual Speed.

The material about the tests now appears in three parts—a manual, a guide to interpretation, and a technical report. The manual, which sets out very carefully the directions for administration and scoring, lists 10 changes in the 1959 edition, and it can be assumed that these represent an improvement or additional data since the 1955 printing.

The appearance of the material is pleasant. A glance at the technical report reveals no less than three chapters on validity—construct, concurrent, predictive—and 63 tables. One might be pardoned for thinking that the report has been prepared with an eye on *The Mental Measurements Yearbook*. Undoubtedly the reviewers of the 1955 edition will find that attempts have been made to remedy most of their criticisms, except the need for two forms of the tests.

Nevertheless, the reviewer was frankly worried by the vast superstructure of statistics and the small amount of space devoted to discussing the nature of the "aptitudes" measured and the extent to which they are affected by good teaching or superior environment.

The word aptitude is subject to a good deal of misunderstanding by lay people, and probably by many professionals. From certain incidental references one can guess that the authors probably intend to use it in the sense that any test used to predict is an "aptitude" test. However, although they do not clearly say this and follow up the implications, other references give the impression that they believe the factors have been responsible for *determining* school performance.

The verbal comprehension factor has two tests, Word Meaning and Paragraph Meaning. The same two item types are the basis of most reading achievement tests. Because success in most school subjects will depend in part on reading skills, such tests are useful predictors of later success. However, differences in reading scores are due to multiple influences and for many pupils scores can be changed significantly under appropriate conditions. Thus children from culturally impoverished homes or from a school where the teaching has been poor can be helped. The MAT report does not give attention to this problem.

Likewise, the Factor 3 tests—Arithmetic Reasoning and Arithmetic Computation—are typical of tests a teacher would use in assessing arithmetic achievement. In discussing a case a reference is made to the possibility of improvement in computation. Now, there is no reason why tests of achievement in reading and arithmetic should not be given and used to predict future success. The English have been doing it for years with children at 11+ and obtaining validity coefficients higher than the typical figures quoted for these tests. But if the tests are referred to as aptitude tests rather than achievement tests, it would not be surprising if teachers and pupils *act in different ways* about what is in fact an identical score.

There are certain advantages to be gained by separating the technical report from the rest of the material on the test, but one doubts the value of separating the manual and the guide to interpretation. Users of the test surely need both of these.

A mass of correlation data is given in the

technical report. In fact, with 63 tables and 42 graphs for occupational groups, it is doubtful if anybody other than a reviewer would be willing to tackle it at a sitting. Evaluation of these data by the authors, however, is not adequate. There is no satisfactory discussion of the relationship of scores to performance in school subjects and the probable reasons for the figures discovered. Thus, Test 3, Language Usage, is likely to predict English grades to the extent that the criterion test emphasizes usage.

The dangers in using the occupational data are not sufficiently stressed. A paragraph in the technical report states that since the samples used come from the same geographical locale they are not representative samples. This information is not repeated in the interpretive guide. The occupational information is valuable but more discussion and evaluation of it is warranted. The authors should be able to do this more competently than the vast majority of users.

The quality of the tests is undoubtedly as good as most of their kind; the correlation data are exceeded by those of few tests. The psychometrics are impressive. In fact, the burden of the reviewer's complaint is that the psychometric erudition is not matched by an equivalent understanding of the educational process.

LEROY WOLINS, *Associate Professor of Psychology and Statistics, Iowa State University, Ames, Iowa.*

The improvements brought about by the revision are apparently relevant to criticisms made by the users of this battery as well as reviewers. The user will find the test easier to administer since directions for each subtest are printed on the test booklet. The user also will find scoring facilitated by allowing the subjects to respond on either IBM cards or the conventional answer sheets. Responding on cards may also facilitate research, since it potentially makes the expensive process of key punching of test scores and item responses unnecessary.

In the technical report is included substantial evidence for the various kinds of validity and reliability required of a good test battery. Of special interest is the new information on predictive validity using grades in individual courses and the grade-point average as criteria. The data presented for predictive validity are based on many samples, each of which came from a single school and some of which apparently came from a single classroom. Only the zero-order correlations with the criterion are presented for each part of the battery. It is highly appropriate that such samples as these be used in validating a test since the user of this test is interested in distinguishing among individuals within such samples. However, since such samples of necessity are often small, the wide fluctuations that might be anticipated are observed in the reported validities.

Although no new normative data were ostensibly collected, the original samples of males and females were combined and norms based on both sexes are reported. Also, for each sample used in the validity study, means and standard deviations are reported; the user of this test may find useful normative information by examining these statistics from homogeneous samples.

Multiple correlations are not reported but they should be. A major justification for deriving several scores rather than one is that the proper weighting of several scores will result in better prediction than a single score. It is true that multiple correlations would be subject to even greater fluctuations than the zero-order correlations. However, not all the samples were small; several involved over 100 individuals and two involved over 300 individuals. Despite this, evidence for incremental validity of the separate parts of the test comes from two sources: a study (*4*) involving this battery at a junior college where individual course grades were predicted and multiple correlations were computed, and inspection of the relative values of the zero-order coefficients reported using various criteria and noting that they generally make sense.

Also included in the technical report are many figures depicting the relative performance of various occupational groups on the parts of the battery. It is stated that this presentation shows that occupational differences and differences in performance on the several parts of the battery within any one occupation make sense relative to the traits being measured. Since these data are not derived from random samples, the authors and publisher deserve commendation for not presenting them in tabular form and for presenting a minimum amount of scale information. Thereby they avoid inviting the user of the battery to use this information normatively.

The guide to interpretation is excellent. It contains several case studies in which scores are interpreted in the context of other information. It contains abacs for testing significance of differences between points on a profile and discussion of procedures for using ancillary materials. Throughout this guide the reader is explicitly reminded of the fallibility of test scores and warned against common errors of interpretation.

Thus, in terms of content, analyses, and supplementary materials, this reviewer judges this battery to be excellent. Its utility is limited, however, in that only one form of the test is available. It would seem that scores in the numerical reasoning factor, in particular, would increase as a function of practice.

J Counsel Psychol 8:92 sp '61. Laurence Siegel. * The battery in its present form is the culmination of research by the senior author spanning a twenty-five year period. The fact that MAT was developed with extreme care rather than in haste is apparent throughout, and particularly in the excellent Technical Report. * Demonstrations of the validity of this battery are impressive. * may be used for studies of inter-individual or intra-individual differences. Analyses of the latter type should prove to be particularly valuable for counseling at the high school and early college levels. Users of the battery are provided with a separate publication concerning the interpretation of MAT scores. This helpful supplement to the Technical Report and Manual contains discussions and illustrations of the ways in which factor and test scores may be interpreted. There is always the danger that such a supplement may be used by unqualified persons who come to regard themselves as expert counselors by virtue of this short course in test interpretation. A kind of internal safeguard against this is provided by the level at which this supplement is written. It will seem like gibberish to persons who are only slightly familiar with test theory. Furthermore, it contains a discussion of the necessity for supplementing aptitude data with other kinds of evidence before attempting to counsel individual students.

For reviews by Ralph F. Berdie and Benjamin Fruchter of the original edition, see 5:613.

[777]

★N.B. Aptitude Tests (Junior). Standards 4–8; 1961–62; 12 scores: reasoning, classification, computations, spare parts, synonyms, squares, name comparison, figure perception, memory for names and faces, word fluency, coordination, writing speed; 1 form ['62, 32 pages, Afrikaans and English in 1 booklet]; manual ['62, 53 pages, 26 pages in Afrikaans and 26 in English]; separate answer sheets must be used; R8.21 per 100 tests; 14c per manual; postpaid; specimen set not available; 104(135) minutes in 3 sessions; National Bureau of Educational and Social Research. *

[778]

★National Institute for Personnel Research High Level Battery. Adults with at least 12 years of education; 1960–62; 4 tests in a single booklet: mental alertness, arithmetical problems, reading comprehension, vocabulary; 1 form ('60, 28 pages); no manual; mimeographed norms ('61–62, 7 pages); separate answer sheets must be used; R200 per 100 tests; R5 per 100 answer sheets; R2.25 per specimen set; postpaid; 117(130) minutes; National Institute for Personnel Research. *

REFERENCES

1. SCHEPERS, J. M. "A Components Analysis of a Complex Psychomotor Learning Task." *Psychologia Africana* 9:294–329 '62. * (*PA* 37:4314)

[779]

★National Institute for Personnel Research Normal Battery. Standards 6–10 and job applicants with 8–11 years of education; 1960–62; 5 tests in a single booklet: mental alertness, comprehension, vocabulary, spelling, computation; 1 form ['60, 30 pages]; no manual; mimeographed norms ('62, 5 pages); separate answer sheets must be used; R130 per 100 tests; R5 per 100 answer sheets; R1.50 per specimen set; postpaid; Afrikaans edition available; 115(140) minutes; National Institute for Personnel Research. *

[780]

***SRA Primary Mental Abilities, Revised.** Grades kgn–1, 2–4, 4–6, 6–9, 9–12; 1946–63; previous edition (see 5:614) still available; earlier editions titled *Tests for Primary Mental Abilities* and *Chicago Tests of Primary Mental Abilities;* IBM for grades 4–12; 5 levels; no data on reliability and validity of present edition; postage extra; L. L. Thurstone (earlier editions) and Thelma Gwinn Thurstone; Science Research Associates, Inc. *

a) GRADES K–1. 5 scores: verbal meaning, perceptual speed, number facility, spatial relations, total; 1 form ('62, c1946–62, 24 pages); manual ('63, 31 pages); $3 per 20 tests; 50¢ per specimen set; (65–75) minutes in 2 sessions.

b) GRADES 2–4. 5 scores: same as for grades kgn–1; 1 form ('62, c1946–62, 32 pages); manual ('63, 39 pages); prices and time same as for grades kgn–1.

c) GRADES 4–6. 1946–63; 6 scores: same as for grades kgn–1 plus reasoning; IBM; 1 form ['62, 41 pages]; manual ('63, 46 pages); profile ('63, 2 pages); separate answer sheets must be used; $11 per 20 tests; $5 per 100 IBM scorable answer sheets; $1 per set of scoring stencils; 70¢ per 20 profiles; $1 per specimen set; 52(107) minutes.

d) GRADES 6–9. 5 scores: verbal meaning, number facility, reasoning, spatial relations, total; IBM; 1 form ('62, c1946–62, 24 pages); manual ('63, 40 pages); profile ('63, 2 pages); prices same as for grades 4–6; 35(75) minutes.

e) GRADES 9–12. 5 scores: same as for grades 6–9; IBM; 1 form ('62, c1946–62, 24 pages); manual ('63, 40 pages); profile ('63, 2 pages); prices same as for grades 4–6; 34(74) minutes.

REFERENCES

1–10. See 40:1427.
11–60. See 3:225.
61–102. See 4:716.
103–161. See 5:614.
162. CURETON, EDWARD E. "Service Tests of Multiple Aptitudes." *Proc Inv Conf Testing Probl* 1955:22–39 '56. * (*PA* 31:3017)
163. TAYLOR, PRESTON L. *A Study of the Relationship Between Intelligence as Measured by SRA Primary Mental Abilities Tests and Validity Scores on the Kuder Vocational Preference Record.* Master's thesis, Texas Southern University (Houston, Tex.), 1956.
164. ROWAN, T. C. "Psychological Tests and Selection of Computer Programmers." *J Assn Comput Mach* 4:348–53 Jl '57. *
165. STROTHER, CHARLES R.; SCHAIE, K. WARNER; AND HORST, PAUL. "The Relationship Between Advanced Age and Mental Abilities." *J Abn & Social Psychol* 55:166–70 S '57. * (*PA* 33:3294)
166. HUTTNER, LUDWIG, AND STENE, D. MIRIAM. "Foremen Selection in Light of a Theory of Supervision." *Personnel Psychol* 11:403–9 au '58. * (*PA* 33:11090)
167. KACZKOWSKI, HENRY R., AND CONNERY, THOMAS F. "PMA Factors as Predictors of High School Workshop Performance." *Psychol Newsl* 9:232–3 Jl–Ag '58. * (*PA* 33:4811)
168. LLOYD, CLAUDE J. *The Relationship Between the Scores Made by Pupils on the Primary Mental Abilities Test, the Metropolitan Achievement Reading Test, and the Kuhlmann-Anderson Intelligence Test.* Master's thesis, University of Southern California (Los Angeles, Calif.), 1958.
169. SCHAIE, K. WARNER. "Occupational Level and the Primary Mental Abilities." *J Ed Psychol* 49:299–303 D '58. * (*PA* 36:2LB99S)
170. SCHAIE, K. WARNER. "Rigidity-Flexibility and Intelligence: A Cross-Sectional Study of the Adult Life Span From 20 to 70 Years." *Psychol Monogr* 72(9):1–26 '58. * (*PA* 33:9923)
171. SMITH, D. D. "Abilities and Interests: 2, Validation of Factors." *Can J Psychol* 12:253–8 D '58. * (*PA* 33:9347)
172. TYLER, LEONA E. "The Stability of Patterns of Primary Mental Abilities Among Grade School Children." *Ed & Psychol Meas* 18:769–74 w '58. * (*PA* 34:2122)
173. WILSON, JOHN A. R. "Differences in Achievement Attributable to Different Educational Environments." *J Ed Res* 52:83–93 N '58. * (*PA* 33:10949)
174. CHAMBERS, JACK A. "Preliminary Screening Methods in the Identification of Intellectually Superior Children." *Excep Child* 26:145–50 N '59. * (*PA* 35:3249)
175. COLEMAN, JAMES C. "Perceptual Retardation in Reading Disability." *Percept & Motor Skills* 9:117 Je '59. *
176. EMM, M. ELOISE. *A Factorial Study of the Problem-Solving Ability of Fifth Grade Boys.* Catholic University of America, Educational Research Monograph, Vol. 22, No. 1. Washington, D.C.: Catholic University of America Press, April 1959. Pp. vi, 57. * (*PA* 35:672)
177. HARRIS, DALE B. "A Note on Some Ability Correlates of the Raven Progressive Matrices (1947) in the Kindergarten." *J Ed Psychol* 50:228–9 O '59. * (*PA* 36:1FE28H)
178. KELLY, E. LOWELL, AND GOLDBERG, LEWIS R. "Correlates of Later Performance and Specialization in Psychology: A Follow-Up Study of the Trainees Assessed in the VA Selection Research Project." *Psychol Monogr* 73(12):1–32 '59. * (*PA* 34:7952)
179. LORANGER, ARMAND W., AND MISIAK, HENRYK. "Critical Flicker Frequency and Some Intellectual Functions in Old Age." *J Gerontol* 14:323–7 Jl '59. * (*PA* 34:4153)
180. MCTAGGART, HELEN PATRICIA. *A Factorial Study of the Problem-Solving Ability of Fifth-Grade Girls.* Washington, D.C.: Catholic University of America Press, 1959. Pp. viii, 27. *
181. RACKY, DONALD J. "Predictions of Ninth Grade Woodshop Performance From Aptitude and Interest Measures." *Ed & Psychol Meas* 19:629–36 w '59. * (*PA* 34:6572)
182. SCHAIE, K. WARNER. "Cross-Sectional Methods in the Study of Psychological Aspects of Aging." *J Gerontol* 14:208–15 Ap '59. * (*PA* 34:1144)
183. VANDENBERG, STEVEN G. "The Primary Mental Abilities of Chinese Students: A Comparative Study of the Stability of a Factor Structure." *Ann N Y Acad Sci* 79:257–304 O 31 '59. * (*PA* 35:3420; 36:3HD57V)
184. WILKINS, MURIEL F. *Is There a Schizophrenic Pattern on the PMA?* Master's thesis, University of Ottawa (Ottawa, Ont., Canada), 1959.
185. CHASE, CLINTON I. "The Position of Certain Variables in the Prediction of Problem-Solving in Arithmetic." *J Ed Res* 54:9–14 S '60. *
186. DURKIN, DOLORES. "A Case-Study Approach Toward an Identification of Factors Associated With Success and Failure in Learning to Read." *Calif J Ed Res* 11:26–33 Ja '60. * (*PA* 34:8336)
187. HARBILAS, JOHN N. *The Iowa Tests of Basic Skills and the SRA Primary Mental Abilities as Predictors of Success in Seventh Grade Science.* Master's thesis, Stetson University (DeLand, Fla.), 1960.
188. JACOBS, RONALD E. "A Comparison of Tests: The Primary Mental Abilities: The Pintner Mental Abilities: The California Test of Mental Abilities." *Sch Counselor* 8:12–8 O '60. *
189. LORANGER, ARMAND W., AND MISIAK, HENRYK. "The Performance of Aged Females on Five Non-Language Tests of Intellectual Functions." *J Clin Psychol* 16:189–91 Ap '60. * (*PA* 36:2FI89L)
190. MEYER, WILLIAM J. "The Stability of Patterns of Primary Mental Abilities Among Junior High and Senior High School Students." *Ed & Psychol Meas* 20:795–800 w '60. * (*PA* 35:3278)
191. SARASON, SEYMOUR B.; DAVIDSON, KENNETH S.; LIGHTHALL, FREDERICK K.; WAITE, RICHARD R.; AND RUEBUSH, BRITTON K. *Anxiety in Elementary School Children: A Report of Research,* pp. 136–47, 313–9. New York: John Wiley & Sons, Inc., 1960. Pp. viii, 351. * (*PA* 34:7494)
192. AVAKIAN, SONIA ASTRID. "An Investigation of Trait Relationships Among Six-Year-Old Children." *Genetic Psychol Monogr* 63:339–94 My '61. * (*PA* 36:1FF39A)
193. BURGESS, THOMAS C. "Retest Reliability of the Primary Mental Abilities Tests." *Psychol Rep* 9:678 D '61. *
194. CLARK, PHILIP J.; VANDENBERG, STEVEN G.; AND PROCTOR, CHARLES H. "On the Relationship of Scores on Certain Psychological Tests With a Number of Anthropometric Characters and Birth Order in Twins." *Hum Biol* 33:163–80 My '61. * (*PA* 36:3DP63C)
195. MEYER, WILLIAM J., AND BENDIG, A. W. "A Longitudinal Study of the Primary Mental Abilities Test." *J Ed Psychol* 52:50–60 F '61. * (*PA* 36:2HD50M)
196. SILVERSTEIN, A. B. "Test Anxiety and the Primary Mental Abilities." *Psychol Rep* 8:415–7 Je '61. * (*PA* 36:2HK15S)
197. CANISIA, M. "Mathematical Ability as Related to Reasoning and Use of Symbols." *Ed & Psychol Meas* 22:105–27 sp '62. * (*PA* 37:1212)
198. CLELAND, DONALD L., AND TOUSSAINT, ISABELLA H. "The Interrelationships of Reading, Listening, Arithmetic Computation and Intelligence." *Reading Teach* 15:228–31 Ja '62. *
199. DERRICK, MURIEL W., AND GODIN, MALCOLM A. "A Cross-Validation Study of a Diagnostic Pattern on the P.M.A." *Ont Hosp Psychol B* 8:13–5 D '62. *
200. DONALD, MERLIN W., AND LAGAN, ANTHONY E. "A Study of the Diagnostic Efficiency of a Schizophrenic Pattern on the PMA." *Ont Hosp Psychol B* 7:5–7 Ap '62. *
201. MCFARLAND, ROBERT L.; NELSON, CHARLES L.; AND ROSSI, ASCANIO M. "Prediction of Participation in Group Psychotherapy From Measures of Intelligence and Verbal Behavior." *Psychol Rep* 11:291–8 Ag '62. * (*PA* 37:5190)
202. MEYERS, E.; ORPET, R. E.; ATTWELL, A. A.; AND DINGMAN, H. F. *Primary Abilities at Mental Age Six.* Monographs of the Society for Research in Child Development, Vol. 27, No. 1, Serial No. 82. Lafayette, Ind.: Child Development Publications, 1962. Pp. 40. * (*PA* 38:8462)
203. SUPER, DONALD E., AND CRITES, JOHN O. *Appraising Vocational Fitness by Means of Psychological Tests, Revised Edition,* pp. 129–38. New York: Harper & Brothers, 1962. Pp. xv, 688. * (*PA* 37:2038)
204. WAGNER, ROSE M. *A Study of the Long Range Predictive Value of Various Factors of the Primary Mental Abilities Test Given in Grade Five.* Master's thesis, University of Washington (Seattle, Wash.), 1962.
205. WILSON, JOHN A. R., AND STIER, LEALAND D. "Instability of Sub-Scores on Forms of SRA Primary Mental Ability Tests: Significance for Guidance." *Personnel & Guid J* 40:708–11 Ap '62. * (*PA* 37:1984)
206. BENDIG, A. W., AND MEYER, WILLIAM J. "The Factorial Structure of the Scales of the Primary Mental Abilities, Guilford Zimmerman Temperament Survey, and Kuder Preference Record." *J General Psychol* 68:195–201 Ap '63. * (*PA* 38:53)
207. CATTELL, RAYMOND B. "Theory of Fluid and Crystallized Intelligence: A Critical Experiment." *J Ed Psychol* 54:1–22 F '63. * (*PA* 37:7991)
208. CENTER, WILLIAM RUSSELL. *A Factor Analysis of Three Language and Communication Batteries.* Doctor's thesis, University of Georgia (Athens, Ga.), 1963. (*DA* 24:1918)
209. OSBURN, H. G., AND MELTON, R. S. "Prediction of Proficiency in a Modern and Traditional Course in Beginning Algebra." *Ed & Psychol Meas* 23:277–87 su '63. * (*PA* 38:1386)
210. SANDERS, RICHARD M. "The Use of Intelligence Tests." *J Ed Res* 56:500 My–Je '63. *
211. WHITE, HORTENSE G. "Typing Performance as Related to Mental Abilities and Interests: A Preliminary Study." *J Ed Res* 56:535–9 Jl–Ag '63. *

John E. Milholland, *Professor of Psychology, The University of Michigan, Ann Arbor, Michigan.*

The 1953–54 edition of these tests had three levels: ages 5–7, 7–11, and 11–17. The 1962–63 edition has five levels identified by school grades rather than by age: K–1, 2–4, 4–6, 6–9, and 9–12. "The motor test has been dropped from the lowest level and the verbal fluency test from the highest. Verbal, number, and spatial scores are now provided for every level." There is a perceptual speed test in each of the K–1, 2–4, and 4–6 levels, and a reasoning test in the 4–6, 6–9, and 9–12 levels. Tests for the upper three levels are printed in reusable booklets suitable for use with separate answer sheets; the tests for the K–1 and 2–4 levels are printed in consumable booklets.

Five "primary mental abilities" labels are used to designate the subtests. The presence of and emphasis given to each of the abilities in the various levels reflect the judgment of the authors with respect to the relative importance of these abilities at the indicated grade levels.

Claims are still made for the differential utilities of the subtest scores. All of the examiners' manuals contain the statement "The profile of five primary mental abilities helps counselors and teachers to evaluate, understand, and interpret the often puzzling individual differences in behavior and performance among children who appear to be of comparable intelligence." The manual for the lowest level also contains the statement that "individual subtest scores provide a helpful index of [a child's] readiness for certain kinds of school tasks such as reading, writing, and arithmetic; they indicate the areas where he has the ability to learn most easily and those where he may need help." A similar statement is included in the manual for grades 2–4. In the case of the three upper level tests, the claims are made in a profile interpretation sheet that is intended to be given to pupils who take the test: "Looking at your high scores can give you an idea of the kind of school subjects you'll probably do best in. Verbal Meaning (V), for example, is particularly important in English, foreign languages, and social studies. Number Facility (N) is important in math." The advice is also given that a pupil making a total stanine score of 7 or above has an indication that he has "the mental ability to do well on college entrance examinations and to do good college work." Those with stanine scores of 5 or 6 may find it "difficult to gain admission to a highly selective college." Those with stanine scores below 4, however, and with school grades and other test scores generally low are advised that "it is somewhat doubtful that other factors could compensate sufficiently to enable you to do college-level work successfully."

There are two bases on which claims such as these may be substantiated. One is logical, that the verbal meaning factor *ought* to be important in English, foreign language, and social studies, the numerical factor important in math, etc. In this case the focus would be on how well the subtests were measuring the factors whose labels they carried. The only assurance we have that they are doing this is the similarity of the items to those originally used by Thurstone and the fact that an item was included in the tests only when three judges agreed on its appropriateness. A more convincing procedure would be a factor analysis of current PMA subtests along with the original ones.

The second basis for justification of the claims is empirical—the demonstration that persons with particular kinds of profiles do in fact perform better in the areas characterized by their high scores. Practically all the data here merely show that persons high in V, for example, do better in English than persons low in it, or that those high in N do better than those low in it in math. Such studies as these, even, are relatively rare, and their results are often inconclusive. None of them is described in the manuals.

In all the manuals the promise is made that a technical supplement will be available shortly, but as of this writing (January 1964) it has not been issued. Through the courtesy of the publishers I have, however, seen a preliminary draft of portions of it. In a section on how to use the test results, the following statement appears: "The validity studies make it possible to form some judgments about the newly revised PMA scores in factors that most affect achievement in various courses." The discussion goes on to point out that verbal meaning is necessary to almost all school subjects and has generally been found most highly related to achievement in almost all academic courses. Reasoning is also highly related to achievement. The relationship of spatial relations to drafting, geometry, and trigonometry is probably significant and number facility appears to be most useful in predicting arithmetic grades. Perceptual speed is considered to be important in the early grades in areas where a child is beginning to learn symbols such as letters, words, and numbers. The support for this conclusion is found in the validity studies in the lower grades, where perceptual speed correlates about as well with reading grades as verbal meaning does. Some appropriate cautions are given about the likelihood of different results under different situations and the danger of relying too much on a single test score. The only data presented in this section are from a study of reading readiness carried out on a sample of 377 pupils who took the PMA K–1 and who 13 months later were given the *SRA Achievement Series: Reading*. The results show a satisfactory but, of course, not unexpected relationship between total PMA scores and the reading test scores. There is no treatment whatever of subtest validities.

There is, however, a separate section of the technical supplement devoted to validity. Here the same reading readiness study is referred to and subtest correlations are given. The conclusion is "the single PMA total score was an effective predictor of reading scores." An inspection of the correlations themselves confirms the lack of differential validity for the separate PMA scores.

Data are also presented showing the correlation between PMA subtest and total scores and elementary and high school grades in various subjects. Three elementary schools and one high school were used. In the elementary schools there were only two exceptions (Reasoning versus reading and Reasoning versus language arts —both in the same school) to the superiority of total score over any subtest for predicting grades in the separate subjects. The median subtest–subject grade correlation was .45; the median total score-grade correlation was .59. In the high school, the subtests showed up a little better, although the validities were generally too low (–.18 to .39, median .22) to be of much use in prediction. It makes some sense, however, that the numerical and reasoning subtests should correlate highest of the five subtests with grades in college preparatory mathematics (.30 and .29) and in science (.23 and .24) and that the reasoning and verbal subtests should be the best predictors of English (.37 and .39) and of social studies (.35 and .27). The median correlation of total scores with high school subject grades was .22.

It does not seem to me that the correlations of subtests with grades in various subjects shed much light on the soundness of the rationale for saying that different primary mental abilities are required for different subjects. The research that would demonstrate the utility of PMA profiles for counseling has not been done yet. In the meantime, counselors would be well advised to follow leads furnished by such things as interest and background in advising students to enter certain lines of work. Scores on the PMA subtests might provide only some inkling of areas that might be worthwhile to explore. The evidence in the preliminary draft of the technical supplement (and other studies done in the past) provides no justification for reporting separate PMA scores in elementary school. If the correlation is taken as a measure, the total score gives more information about any subject than the primary mental ability score supposedly most relevant for it. Probably the most useful kind of multiscore test for elementary school is one that provides just a verbal and a nonverbal measure.

The draft of the technical supplement also contains a section on reliability. Data presented there meet the criticism of earlier reviewers of the tests, that because of speededness internal consistency estimates of reliability were too high and should be replaced by test-retest estimates. A test-retest study was done in the public schools of Goldsboro, North Carolina. The verbal subtest showed up best, with reliabilities varying from .73 to .93 in the different grades and IQ standard errors of measurement for the different test *levels* going from 4.14 to 6.01. The perceptual speed subtest was poorest, with reliabilities from .51 to .81 and standard errors from 5.29 to 9.42, the latter in the K–1 level, where perceptual speed is thought to be particularly important. Total score single grade reliabilities go from .84 to .94; level standard errors from 3.65 to 4.56. Total score reliability, at least, is satisfactory.

Although the supplement is sprinkled with admonitions urging caution, the following statement also appears: "The subtests are often used for differential diagnostic and predictive purposes." In furtherance of this practice, tables of reliabilities and standard errors of difference scores are given. An interesting feature is a set of tables which are supposed to give the probabilities that differences of 10 or 20 IQ points are due to true score differences rather than to error. The technique for determining the probabilities is not explained, and I suspect a faulty rationale. It is true that the probabilities of differences of 10 or 20 points due to error can be calculated, but the complements of these are the probabilities that errors will be less than 10 or 20 points, not that the 10 or 20 point differences are due to true score differences.

If even as rudimentary a technical supplement as I examined is published, it will represent at least a small step toward psychometric respectability on the part of those responsible for PMA. They still have a long way to go before they come up to levels already reached by a number of the better test producers on the scene today. Carrying out the research and development necessary to meet technical standards is a costly process, and the producers of PMA may regard it as prohibitively expensive.

For reviews by Norman Frederiksen and Albert K. Kurtz of the previous edition, see 5:614; for reviews by Anne Anastasi, Ralph F. Berdie, John B. Carroll, Stuart A. Courtis, and P. E. Vernon, see 4:716; for reviews by Cyril Burt, Florence L. Goodenough, James R. Hobson, and F. L. Wells of an earlier edition, see 3:225 and 3:264; for reviews by Henry E. Garrett, Truman L. Kelley, C. Spearman, Godfrey H. Thomson, and Robert C. Tryon, see 40:1427 (3 excerpts); for excerpts from related book reviews, see 40:B1099 and 38:B503.

[781]

★**Vocational Guidance Program.** Grades 10–16; 1947–62; a battery of aptitude and personality tests; except for modification noted in *a* below, two title changes, and directions for all tests, tests *a–h* are identical with corresponding tests of the *Factored Aptitude Series* (1947–57) which are also used in the *Job-Tests Program;* tests *i* and *j* are identical, except for directions, with two other tests of the *Job-Tests Program;* 1 form; 10 tests ('62, 3 pages except *h,* 4 pages) used in various combinations for different job areas; 4 bulletins serve as manual and interpretive materials: bulletin 1 ['62, 4 pages], how program operates, bulletin 2 ['62, 4 pages], job fields checklist for students, bulletin 3 ['62, 2 pages], directions for administering and scoring, bulletin 4 ('62, 4 pages), job qualification profiles; no data on reliability and validity presented with tests (data based on use of the corresponding tests in the *Job-Tests Program* available on request); norms, based on employees, the same as those reported with the *Job-Tests Program;* separate answer sheets must be used (except with *h*); $2 per 20 copies of any one test except *h;* $1 per 20 copies of *h;* $2 per 20 self-marking answer sheets; 75¢ per 20 copies of either bulletin 2 or bulletin 4; $2 per "manual" consisting of all 4 bulletins, single copies of each test, and 4 answer sheets; postage extra; 7(10) minutes per test except for *h–j;* Joseph E. King; Industrial Psychology, Inc. *

a) BUSINESS TERMS. A combination of items (two-thirds of them with revised option order) from *Sales Terms* and *Office Terms* of the *Factored Aptitude Series.*
b) SYSTEMS. Identical with *Numbers* test of the *Factored Aptitude Series.*
c) PERCEPTION.
d) JUDGMENT.
e) TOOLS.
f) PRECISION.
g) PARTS.
h) DEXTERITY. 3(10) minutes.
i) CPF. A special printing of *IPAT Contact Personality Factor Test* (see 123); (5–10) minutes.
j) NPF. A special printing of *IPAT Neurotic Personality Factor Test* (see 5:74); (5–10) minutes.

LEO GOLDMAN, *Associate Professor of Education, Brooklyn College, Brooklyn, New York.*

Except for directions, title changes, and a modification of one test, this battery of tests is identical to those in the *Job-Tests Program,* a battery developed for industrial selection. The tests themselves seem, like their predecessors, to be for the most part well constructed, both in their items and in the mechanics of administration and scoring. Since the parent tests have been used in industry for some 16 years, they could provide a good foundation for vocational guidance testing in high schools.

There is, however, almost none of the evidence that one would require before using these adult selection tests in counseling with high school students. There are, for example, no high school norms; there is only the statement in Bulletin 1 that "The psychological factors measured by the tests mature by age 16 or 17, and rarely change after that. Thus, what the student ranks when you test him at 16, is what he will be for the rest of his life." Anyone who has taken even a first measurement course should be able to recognize the illogic of that statement and the absurdity of its conclusion.

Furthermore, one might ask for validity studies based on a follow-up of high school students into jobs. These would be especially necessary with those tests, such as Business Terms and Perception, which are most sensitive to experience on related jobs. All that is offered is a group of reprints and summaries of validity studies done in industry. These do not suffice. These earlier studies bear little enough evidence of the usefulness for industrial selection of the parent series. There is even less evidence to support the vocational guidance interpretations which are now suggested. The Job Qualification tables, for example, show desirable profiles for each of 24 job fields but nowhere does one find either a rationale or documentary evidence to support these tables.

One would expect information about the reliability of these tests with high school students. Nothing is presented except a summary of the earlier reliability studies, presumably done with adults during the initial standardization of these tests. Even those data are inadequately reported (lacking description of the samples used). For what they are worth, the retest correlations range from .79 to .91, with the median being .83. Although these are impressive reliability correlations for seven-minute tests, they are below the level expected for counseling use.

We can guess that one of the adaptations which the author made for the application of these tests to vocational guidance students is a table (Bulletin 3) which tells how to obtain an IQ for Business Terms and Judgment (one IQ for each), and a nonlanguage IQ for Parts. This is quite a tour de force when one realizes that Business Terms is merely a business vocabulary test, Judgment a letter and number series reasoning test, and Parts a spatial visualization test. There is no explanation of the derivation of these IQ's, nor any rationale for their use. And, oh yes, the IQ table classifies IQ's of 130 and up as genius!

The sparsity of research on norms, reliability, validity, and all the other standardization topics has not prevented the author and publisher from making some of the most naïve and unfounded claims this reviewer has seen in a long time. They report, for example, that "Averaging the Judgment and Parts test ranks gives an index of the student's creative thinking or research ability." These, remember, are a test of letter and number series reasoning, and a test of spatial visualization, respectively!

Elsewhere one is told that validity correlations of .26 to .39 permit a "definite prediction of job performance, and thus [the] test can differentiate applicants who will become good vs. poor performers." Furthermore, validity coefficients from .40 to .55 permit "excellent prediction of job performance." Although recognizing with the author that validity correlations higher than .55 are rare, one doesn't conclude that therefore the best coefficients available provide "excellent predictions."

One could cite many more such unwarranted claims, oversimplifications, and violations of basic principles of measurement. The flaws of the original tests have been multiplied in this so-called adaptation for guidance use. The "manual" for the *Vocational Guidance Program* is not a manual at all, but a grab-bag: except for the instructions for test selection, administration, scoring, and interpretation, there is only a collection of unbound summaries and reprints of studies done with the parent series.

These tests were judged by earlier reviewers to be inadequate for industrial selection applications. They are even less adequate for guidance use. Practically all of the modern multifactor batteries are far superior to this one. This battery is not ready for guidance use in schools, or anyplace else, for that matter.

For reviews by William H. Helme and Stanley I. Rubin of the Job-Tests Program, *see 774; for a review by Harold P. Bechtoldt of the* Factored Aptitude Series, *see 5:602; for a review by D. Welty Lefever of an earlier edition of the* Factored Aptitude Series, *see 4:712 (one excerpt); for reviews of the personality tests, see 174, 5:71, 5:74, 5:112, and 4:87.*

[Other Tests]

For tests not listed above, see the following entries in *Tests in Print:* 1368–9, 1378, and 1380; out of print: 1370, 1374, and 1385–6.

READING

REVIEWS BY *Ira E. Aaron, Mary C. Austin, Thomas C. Barrett, Emmett Albert Betts, L. B. Birch, Emery P. Bliesmer, M. Alan Brimer, Charles M. Brown, N. Dale Bryant, W. V. Clemans, William E. Coffman, Thomas E. Culliton, Jr., Stanley E. Davis, Gabriel M. Della-Piana, Clarence Derrick, William Eller, W. G. Fleming, Edward B. Fry, J. Raymond Gerberich, Albert J. Harris, A. N. Hieronymus, Kenneth D. Hopkins, Worth R. Jones, C. E. Jurgensen, Albert J. Kingston, John D. Krumboltz, Charles R. Langmuir, Paul R. Lohnes, Arthur S. McDonald, Jason Millman, Coleman Morrison, David B. Orr, David A. Payne, M. L. Kellmer Pringle, Alton L. Raygor, H. Alan Robinson, Donald E. P. Smith, George D. Spache, Russell G. Stauffer, Agatha Townsend, Arthur E. Traxler, B. H. Van Roekel, Magdalen D. Vernon, and Morey J. Wantman.*

[782]

***A.C.E.R. Silent Reading Tests, Forms C and D.** Ages 10–13; 1946–63; Forms C ['46], D ['63]; 3 parts; manual ['63, 38 pages]; 13*s.* per 10 sets of all 3 parts; 2*s.* 6*d.* per key; 5*s.* per manual; 8*s.* 9*d.* per specimen set; postpaid within Australia; Australian Council for Educational Research. *

a) PART 1, WORD KNOWLEDGE. 4 pages; 3*s.* 6*d.* per 10 tests; 10(20) minutes.

b) PART 2, SPEED OF READING. 8 pages; 4*s.* 6*d.* per 10 tests; 6(15) minutes.

c) PART 3, READING FOR MEANING. 8 pages; 6*s.* per 10 tests; 20(30) minutes.

REFERENCES

1. WHEELER, D. K. "Reading Speed of W. A. Children." *Educand* 2:4–9 N '54.

For reviews by Fred J. Schonell and D. K. Wheeler, see 5:617.

[783]

***American School Achievement Tests: Part 1, Reading.** Grades 2–3, 4–6, 7–9; 1941–63; subtest of *American School Achievement Tests;* 3 scores: sentence and word meaning, paragraph meaning, total; Forms D ('55), E ('56), F ('57), G ('58, except for Primary Battery 2, '55), (2 sheets); Forms D, E, and F are essentially the same as Forms A, B, and C copyrighted in 1941–43; 3 levels; 50¢ per specimen set of any one level; postage extra; Willis E. Pratt, Robert V. Young, and Clara E. Cockerille (manuals for *b* and *c*); Bobbs-Merrill Co., Inc. *

a) PRIMARY BATTERY 2. Grades 2–3; battery manual ('58, c1955–58, 13 pages); $2.75 per 35 tests; 25(35) minutes.

b) INTERMEDIATE BATTERY. Grades 4–6; battery manual ('61, 17 pages); $3 per 35 tests; 25(35) minutes.

c) ADVANCED BATTERY. Grades 7–9; battery manual ('63, 17 pages); $3 per 35 tests; 30(40) minutes.

For reviews by Russell G. Stauffer and Agatha Townsend, see 5:620. For reviews of the complete battery, see 2, 5:1, 4:1, and 3:1.

[784]

***California Reading Test, 1957 Edition With 1963 Norms.** Grades 1–2, 2.5–4.5, 4–6, 7–9, 9–14; 1933–63; subtest of *California Achievement Tests;* 3 scores: vocabulary, comprehension, total; IBM and Grade-O-Mat for grades 4–14; 2–4 forms ('63, c1957–63, identical with tests copyrighted in 1957 except for profile on all test booklets and revision of junior high level Form X); 5 levels; battery manual ('63, c1957–63, 53–70 pages) for each level; battery technical report ('57, 48 pages) on 1957 edition with 1957 norms; battery individual profile ('63, 2 pages) for each level; no norms for grades 13–14; separate answer sheets or cards may be used in grades 4–14; 5¢ per IBM answer sheet; 9¢ per Scoreze answer sheet; 3¢ per set of Cal-Cards; 4¢ per set of Grade-O-Mat scorable punch-out cards; 20¢ per set of either IBM answer sheet or Cal-Card hand scoring stencils; 40¢ per set of either IBM answer sheet or Grade-O-Mat machine scoring stencils; 2¢ per profile; postage extra; technical report free; 75¢ per specimen set of *a* or *b;* $1 per specimen set of *c, d,* or *e;* postpaid; Ernest W. Tiegs and Willis W. Clark; California Test Bureau. *

a) LOWER PRIMARY. Grades 1–2; Forms W, X, ('63, c1957–63, 9 pages); $2.80 per 35 tests; 23(35) minutes.

b) UPPER PRIMARY. Grades 2.5–4.5; Forms W, X, ('63, c1957–63, 13 pages); $3.15 per 35 tests; 40(50) minutes.

c) ELEMENTARY. Grades 4–6; IBM and Grade-O-Mat; Forms W, X, Y, Z, ('63, c1957–63, 14 pages); $3.50 per 35 tests; 50(60) minutes.

d) JUNIOR HIGH LEVEL. Grades 7–9; IBM and Grade-O-Mat; Forms W, X, Y, Z, ('63, c1957–63, 18 pages); $3.50 per 35 tests; 68(80) minutes.

e) ADVANCED. Grades 9–14; IBM and Grade-O-Mat; Forms W, X, Y, ('63, c1957–63, 19 pages); $3.50 per 35 tests; 68(80) minutes.

REFERENCES

1–5. See 5:622.

6. BLACK, D. B. "A Study of the Relationship of the Grade IX Principal's Rating to Performance on the Alberta Grade IX Departmental Examinations." *Alberta J Ed Res* 4:227–36 D '58. * (*PA* 34:2089)

7. HANEY, RUSSELL; MICHAEL, WILLIAM B.; AND JONES, ROBERT A. "Identification of Aptitude and Achievement Factors in the Prediction of the Success of Nursing Trainees." *Ed & Psychol Meas* 19:645–7 w '59. * (*PA* 34:6164)

8. MAKLEY, MARGARET. *A Comparison of California Reading Achievement Scores With Reading Performance in Grades Three and Four.* Master's thesis, Fresno State College (Fresno, Calif.), 1959.

9. MICHAEL, WILLIAM B.; JONES, ROBERT A.; AND HANEY, RUSSELL. "The Development and Validation of a Test Battery for Selection of Student Nurses." *Ed & Psychol Meas* 19:641–3 w '59. * (*PA* 34:6171)

10. HANEY, RUSSELL; MICHAEL, WILLIAM B.; JONES, ROBERT A.; AND GADDIS, L. WESLEY. "Cognitive and Non-Cognitive Predictors of Achievement in Student Nursing." *Ed & Psychol Meas* 20:387–9 su '60. * (*PA* 35:7120)

11. ANDERSON, HARRY E., JR. "The Prediction of Reading

and Language From the California Tests." *Ed & Psychol Meas* 21:1035–6 w '61. *
12. ANDERSON, HARRY E., JR. "A Study of Language and Nonlanguage Achievement." *Ed & Psychol Meas* 21:1037–8 w '61. *
13. JONES, ROBERT A., AND MICHAEL, WILLIAM B. "The Validity of a Battery of Tests in Communication Skills for Foreign Students Attending an American University." *Ed & Psychol Meas* 21:493–6 su '61. * (*PA* 36:2KK93J)
14. MICHAEL, WILLIAM B., AND JONES, ROBERT A. "Linguistic Factors in Several Tests and Criterion Measures Pertaining to Communication Skills." *Ed & Psychol Meas* 21:1011–4 w '61. *
15. MICHAEL, WILLIAM B.; JONES, ROBERT A.; GETTINGER, TED, JR.; HODGES, JOHN D., JR.; KOLESNIK, PETER E.; AND SEPPALA, JAMES. "The Prediction of Success in Selected Courses in a Teacher Training Program From Scores in Achievement Tests and From Ratings on a Scale of Directed Teaching Performance." *Ed & Psychol Meas* 21:995–9 w '61. *
16. HANEY, RUSSELL; MICHAEL, WILLIAM B.; AND GERSHON, ARTHUR. "Achievement, Aptitude, and Personality Measures as Predictors of Success in Nursing Training." *Ed & Psychol Meas* 22:389–92 su '62. * (*PA* 37:3869)
17. MICHAEL, WILLIAM B.; HANEY, RUSSELL; AND GERSHON, ARTHUR. "Intellective and Non-Intellective Predictors of Success in Nursing Training." *Ed & Psychol Meas* 23:817–21 w '63. *
18. SHEPPARD, CHARLES, AND CAMPBELL, WILLIAM J. "An Evaluation of the California Achievement Test, Elementary, Form W, Reading Vocabulary." *J Ed Res* 56:481–3 My–Je '63. *

For reviews by John C. Flanagan and James R. Hobson of the 1950 edition, see 4:530 (1 excerpt); for a review by Frederick B. Davis of an earlier edition, see 40:1563; for reviews by Ivan A. Booker and Joseph C. Dewey, see 38:1110. For reviews of the complete battery, see 3, 5:2, 4:2, 3:15, 40:1193, and 38:876.

[785]

★**Comprehension Test for Training College Students.** Training college students and applicants for admission; 1962; 1 form (8 pages); manual (12 pages); 17*s*. per 25 tests; 7*s*. per manual; 7*s*. per specimen set; prices include purchase tax; postpaid within U.K.; 45(50) minutes; E. L. Black; distributed by National Foundation for Educational Research in England and Wales. *

[786]

***Davis Reading Test.** Grades 8–11, 11–13; 1956–62; 2 scores: level of comprehension, speed of comprehension; IBM; 2 levels; manual ('62, c1958–62, 31 pages); separate answer sheets must be used; $3.50 per 25 tests; $2 per 50 IBM answer sheets; 50¢ per set of scoring stencils and manual; 75¢ per specimen set; postpaid; 40(55) minutes; Frederick B. Davis and Charlotte Croon Davis; Psychological Corporation. *

a) SERIES 1. Grades 11–13; 1956–62; Forms 1A, 1B, 1C, 1D, ('57, c1956–57, 10 pages).
b) SERIES 2. Grades 8–11; 1961–62; Forms 2A, 2B, 2C, 2D, ('61, c1960–61, 11 pages).

REFERENCES

1. KETCHAM, HERBERT E., (MRS.) "Reading Tests and College Performance," pp. 63–6. In *Research and Evaluation in College Reading*. Ninth Yearbook of the National Reading Conference for College and Adults. Fort Worth, Tex.: Texas Christian University Press, 1960. Pp. 137. *
2. WEAVER, WENDELL W., AND KINGSTON, ALBERT J. "A Factor Analysis of the Cloze Procedure and Other Measures of Reading and Language Ability." *J Commun* 13:252–61 D '63. * (*PA* 39:188)

WILLIAM E. COFFMAN, *Director of Research and Development, College Board Programs Division, Educational Testing Service, Princeton, New Jersey.*

The modern standardized test is so much the product of a highly developed technology that one is likely to overlook the fact that the central core of every good test is the collection of test questions—products of creative effort by artist-writers. The *Davis Reading Test* is supported by an unusually comprehensive array of technical data. The manual for the test is a 31-page booklet of which more than 19 pages are devoted to technical information. Six pages are needed for such formal aspects as covers and table of contents, three for directions for administration and scoring, and almost two for acknowledgments. There remains only about two pages for the authors to discuss what they are about.

It is only when one actually takes several forms of the test that he becomes conscious of how much these tests carry the mark of the artist-writer. There is a freshness about the stimulus passages and a challenge to the questions which makes the task of marking answers an encounter with an interesting adversary. On a subjective basis alone one concludes that these are unusually effective collections of passages and questions for assessing the ability of adolescents to garner meaning from the printed page.

But one does not need to depend on subjective impressions only. According to the evidence presented in the manual, the test will do what the authors claim and probably more. Data are presented with respect to scaling, reliability, and validity. The user is provided with detailed guidance as to how to use the test to best advantage. The normative data are appropriate. Let me illustrate.

Most published tests which are offered for use over a span of grades are pitched in difficulty at the middle of the range; thus one has to be careful not to exceed the effective range, especially when using the test with atypical groups. The *Davis Reading Test,* in contrast, has its two levels anchored at the ends of the range. Series 1 is of middle difficulty for the grade 13 norms group; Series 2 is ideal for the grade 8 group. And there is a comfortable overlap for the grade 11 sample in the middle. It is likely that the Series 1 forms will be suitable for many upper class college groups and the

Series 2 forms for many groups below eighth grade.

Some users may object to the fact that the norms samples are defined only by the names of the institutions participating in the norms administrations. One may doubt, however, whether a rigorously drawn national sample would have any clear advantage over a sample which is well distributed geographically and which consists of students in schools which are willing to cooperate. The major values of a test of this type depend on the existence of a sound score scale which will permit comparisons within a school system and over a period of time. The scale for the *Davis Reading Test* meets this requirement; a table relating the scaled scores to those for the *College Qualification Tests* provides additional flexibility.

In response to recommendations of professional groups, most test publishers now provide data on the reliability of a test for within-grade samples. The publishers of the *Davis Reading Test* have based their coefficients on 28 carefully designed experiments involving all eight forms. Furthermore, standard errors of measurement are provided, not only for single forms but also for combinations of two, three, and four forms. The experimenter who wishes to achieve high reliability by administering more than one form has the necessary information at his finger tips.

Evidence is provided regarding both predictive and construct validity. Correlations with English grades are presented for 70 different groups. Correlations with six other tests based on Series 1 scores and with eight other tests based on Series 2 scores appear reasonable. As to content validity, the tests seem to speak for themselves. If there is any question regarding validity, it is that there is no objective evidence to support the differentiation of a level and a speed score.

Each form of the test consists of two parallel halves of 40 questions each. Almost all students complete the first half and almost nobody completes the second half. Therefore, score on the first half is taken as a measure of accuracy or depth of comprehension while score on the total test measures both speed and accuracy. It is argued that "Level score indicates the degree of comprehension attained while progressing at a self-determined rate of working as rapidly as possible without making careless mistakes." It would be enlightening to study the perceptions of test takers regarding the meaning of the instructions to "work as rapidly as you can without making careless mistakes." It would also be worthwhile to search for criteria against which the level score proves more valid than the speed score.

This test is an outstanding example of the test writer's art. Evidence presented in the manual indicates that the several forms meet high standards of reliability and validity and are of appropriate difficulty for the recommended uses. One may wish to look behind differences between speed and level scores to the perceptions which guided the student at the time he took the test, but it is doubtful that one can find a better reading test for use in grades 8–13.

ALTON L. RAYGOR, *Associate Professor of Educational Psychology, and Coordinator, Reading and Study Skills Center, University of Minnesota, Minneapolis, Minnesota.*

One expects good tests from Fred Davis. Editorship of earlier Cooperative reading tests qualifies him as an expert in the field, as do other pieces of evidence concerning his professional life. He has been very much interested in the problem of measuring gain in reading improvement programs; in fact, he includes in the manual for this test a brief discussion of the problem and refers the reader to a more lengthy treatment of it in another source.

These tests and the manual which goes with them testify to the care with which Davis and his wife go about constructing achievement tests. It is gratifying to see that some of the most typical pitfalls of test constructors are avoided, particularly those in which quality is sacrificed to produce ease of administration and scoring. The use of scaled scores to achieve equivalence of forms is a great deal preferable to the technique of some other reading test authors, who use some system for determining the difficulty level of items and then build equivalent forms on the assumption that one can do this as a random process.

The Davis test is also very simple to administer and to score. Hand scoring with the correction formula is made easy by the provision of a table in the manual which even tells the scorer how many to subtract from the right answers in the case of a given number of wrong answers.

The test seems well standardized on an adequate number of students representing what seems to be a good selection of schools and colleges. One could always hope that such a standardization sample could be demonstrated to be a stratified random sample of a nationwide population, but the difficulty of achieving such sampling is certainly a major factor to be considered.

The section in the manual on interpretation of scores is clearly written and does a good job of indicating the limits on the accuracy of measurement of an individual score. The discussion on the standard error of measurement is particularly clear. The section in which the reliability of the test is discussed in terms of increases in reliability to be gained by use of more than one form is very useful in that it is likely not only to encourage the realization of the limits of reliability, but might also result in longer and more reliable testing on the part of the typical user.

Concerning validity the manual states, "The content validity of a reading test depends on whether mental activities required to answer the questions constitute a representative sample of those called into play during the process of understanding material of a defined type. * the content of the *Davis Reading Test* has been carefully designed to bring this about. Factoral studies have provided evidence that tests of this kind are excellent measures of verbal aptitude."

The question which bothers this reviewer about the Davis test is why it was built at all. Davis worked very hard on the development of the Cooperative reading tests which measure the same variables except for the exclusion of the vocabulary in the Davis. A strong criticism of the Cooperative test was that the subscores were based on the same items and that they were extremely difficult to interpret. The speed of comprehension score was commonly mistaken for a speed of reading score and it seems to this reviewer that this confusion is fostered by the word "speed" in the name of the score. In the present test, the level of comprehension score uses a varying proportion of items that overlap with the speed of comprehension score. For the subject who does exactly 40 of the items, both scores are computed on precisely the same items. On the other hand, if the subject completes the whole test, only half of the items are used on the level of comprehension score. The statement that the level of comprehension score "indicates the depths of understanding displayed by a student in reading the kinds of material he is ordinarily required to read in high school and college" seems to this reviewer to leave a great deal to be desired in the explanation about the scores in a fashion which will enable the user to successfully discriminate between them and understand the factors which produce differences between the speed score and the level score. This is particularly troublesome when one finds that the two scores are correlated with each other at between .74 and .80, close to the limits of reliability for each score.

To summarize, this seems like a very well built test by competent authors, with adequate reliability and validity, and standardized on an adequate sample of what appear to be representative students, but it suffers the same difficulty in interpretation and overlap in measured skills as the earlier reading test constructed by Davis.

For a review by Benjamin Rosner of a, *see* *5:625.*

[787]

***Developmental Reading Tests.** Grades 1.5, 1.5–2.5, 2.5–3, 4–6; 1955–61; 4 levels; the 1961 forms of *a–c* are single-booklet printings of the 1955 three-part forms; no specific manual (directions and norms printed on test booklets); no data on reliability; preliminary norms; $5 per 35 tests (except for *d,* $4 per 35 tests); $1 per set of scoring cards; $1 per 50 class records; 40¢ per specimen set of any one level; postage extra; 40(55) minutes in 3 sessions 1–2 days apart for *a–c,* 32(50) minutes for *d;* [Guy L. Bond, Theodore Clymer, and Cyril Hoyt]; Lyons & Carnahan. *

a) PRIMER READING. Grade 1.5; 1955–61; 3 scores: basic vocabulary, general comprehension, specific comprehension; Form P-A ('61, 14 pages).

b) LOWER PRIMARY READING. Grades 1.5–2.5; 1955–61; 3 scores: same as for *a;* Form L-A ('61, 14 pages).

c) UPPER PRIMARY READING. Grades 2.5–3; 1955–61; 3 scores: same as for *a;* Form U-A ('61, 14 pages).

d) [INTERMEDIATE READING.] Grades 4–6; 1959; 6 scores: basic vocabulary, reading to retain information, reading to organize, reading to evaluate-interpret, reading to appreciate, average comprehension; Forms IR-A, IR-B, ('59, 16 pages).

EDWARD B. FRY, *Professor of Education, Rutgers, The State University, New Brunswick, New Jersey.*

The *Developmental Reading Tests* are good examples of tests that do not have a specific purpose.

There are several reasons why a teacher or a school system might want to use a reading achievement test. One is to compare their students' present achievement, either individually or in groups, with other students who have taken the same test (the standardization group). A second reason might be to see how students are progressing through the curriculum. Teachers might want an answer to such a legitimate question as "Is Johnny ready to start using the second grade book?" A third use of such tests might be to better enable teachers to discern relative differences between students. This would answer the questions "Can Johnny read better than Mary?" and "Which students are my best readers?" Finally, the reading achievement test might be diagnostic in certain specified skills, providing such useful information as "Johnny's sight recognition vocabulary is good but his understanding of a paragraph is poor."

Now if these are some of the ultimate purposes of a reading achievement test, how do the *Developmental Reading Tests* fulfill them?

First, the publisher provides no information about the standardization group. Were the norms obtained on children from one rich district where 90 per cent of the fathers are in the professional class? Or were they obtained in two poor rural communities where the teachers, the school buildings, and the parents' incomes are all well below national norms? It is impossible to tell from the teacher's manual (or rather lack of manual). Hence, it is suggested that the norms provided are valueless and do not represent anything but the authors' or publisher's opinion. Nor do the authors state how this test compares with other tests—it might be much easier, it might be much harder.

From a technical standpoint, there is also a serious flaw in that no reliability data are provided. A student might take the test on one day and do very well, only to be an abject failure another time. Hence, the teacher cannot be sure that Johnny can read better than Mary. There is no information about comparability of the alternate forms provided at the intermediate level. Is one form easier than the other?

In short, as standardized tests, these tests fall far short of the mark.

But there is another valid function of tests and that is to show progress through the curriculum. Presumably, this is one function that the *Developmental Reading Tests* could perform admirably, as there is interlocking authorship with the Developmental Reading Series (textbooks) published by the same publisher. But one looks in vain for such help or statement that this could or should be done. There is one strong hint in some of the publisher's descriptive material to the effect that "The vocabulary of the tests was selected....[from] the same word lists that were used in writing the Developmental Reading Series." But this is not the same as saying that if a student scores 2.5 on the primer level test, he is ready for the upper second grade book. Hence, as purely curriculum development tests, these tests do not give the type of information that is useful.

These tests also suffer from faults common among all too many reading achievement tests: (*a*) The subtests have meaningless names. What is the difference between "General Comprehension" and "Specific Comprehension"? (*b*) The subtests are too short. In the intermediate test, for example, Reading to Evaluate—Interpret has 18 items, and Reading to Appreciate has 18 items. Teachers are given grade scores for each of these, and are instructed to plot them on a profile. Statistically, an 18-item subtest is questionable, and logically, the diagnostic value of the stated names is questionable. Wouldn't it be better to use only average comprehension (which is composed of four such subtests)? It would give much more accurate information to teachers and administrators. (*c*) There is no bottom cutoff score. Anyone who has administered a number of multiple choice tests in a school has seen the dullest child simply go through and mark items at random, often without even bothering to read them. If he did this on the primary form, on the average he would get a 1.45 reading grade score in General Comprehension. But if he managed to sit in the class until the fourth grade where he might be administered the intermediate form, by using the same process he would average 4.7 in Reading to Organize. Now, there is a real measure of reading progress! He grew three years in achievement in three school years—a fact in which the teacher and the superintendent can really take pride. How long are teachers, administrators, and test publishers going to permit this ridiculous situation to exist? (What should be done? For any raw score below 8, the scoring directions should simply state: "This test not valid below grade 5.0; use a lower form.")

The directions for administering and scoring are clear. The printing is good. Graphic profiles of subtest scores are printed on the front of each booklet. In fact, in most respects, the *Developmental Reading Tests* "look" like well-made standardized tests and this is perhaps what is so insidious. The teacher follows the directions, the students mark the booklet, the tests are scored, and Johnny gets a reading grade of 1.9. What on earth does this mean?

If the test authors and publisher would only decide whether they want to have a standardized test or a test that measures curriculum development against some criterion (such as their reading textbooks), the school administrators, teachers, and children would certainly profit by such a decision.

Agatha Townsend, *Consultant, Educational Records Bureau, New York, New York.*

The *Developmental Reading Tests* as now in print could be used as the raw material from which to manufacture a set of acceptable reading tests for the primary and intermediate grades. Basically, the test content is good; the format, although in need of a few modifications, is clear and quite suitable; and the concept of reading which is implicit in the battery is worth more attention than it can receive in its present form. The authors are, of course, highly qualified.

This review will consider briefly the changes which might be made, beginning with the major gaps in the present materials. The lacks, then, seem to lie primarily in the low esteem in which the authors, or perhaps the publishers, hold the classroom teacher. Evidently the elementary school teacher is not willing to bother himself with details such as the basis for grade equivalence tables, the possible reliability of scores, or any information about test construction. There is no test manual. The sole explanatory item furnished appears on the envelope containing the specimen set. After assuring the teacher that the test construction conforms to modern principles, the two pertinent sentences read: "The vocabulary of the tests was selected by use of the Thorndike, Dale-Chall, and other scientific word lists. These are the same word lists that were used in writing the Developmental Reading Series by Bond et al., which is published by Lyons and Carnahan."

The teacher is evidently expected to refer to manuals for the reading series and his own experience in order to improve scores which are not within the "allowable variation." That term is a new one to this reviewer who is accustomed to classes which are allowed to include pupils of a wide range of reading skills (not that this is necessarily an ideal situation). The description of what is allowable variation (four to six months either side of grade placement for the primary grades, six to eight months for higher grades) appears on the cover page of the booklets. Though it does not appear on the booklet for the intermediate grades, one of the statements refers to this grade range: "If the pupil's placement in grade is between 3.5 and 5.4, variation may be 8 months either way." Since, as mentioned earlier, there is no description of the basis for the grade equivalents, it is not clear if this allowable variation is a way of expressing the standard error of scores, or based on the distributions and related to a percentile band interpretation. Probably many teachers using the test interpret it conservatively enough, to mean that if the score falls within these limits it probably reflects about average performance for classes using Lyons and Carnahan readers.

When one turns to the booklet content, the picture of the tests is a far happier one. The primary tests are similar in appearance and in approach to the *Gates Primary Reading Tests*. The three scores, Basic Vocabulary, General Comprehension, and Specific Comprehension, are based on parts which seem long enough and internally consistent enough so that the scores are probably useful. There are no word attack materials, a serious omission. The intermediate test retains the vocabulary part, and has four brief comprehension parts, which are designed to test, and probably do measure, reading to retain information, to organize, to evaluate and interpret, and to appreciate. There is an average comprehension score obtained by averaging these four parts. Part 3, Reading to Organize, is based on 30 items, but the other sections may be too short for adequate reliability.

Throughout, the battery would be improved by some simple steps to make the teacher's task easier. No score boxes are provided. In most of the parts, the items are not numbered in sequence, making checking for accuracy of scoring difficult. It seems cumbersome, especially since there is no place to record the raw scores, to have to refer to the back cover for the grade rating and then to the front in order to enter it on the profile chart. Grade scales could easily be added to the stencil keys. The boxes on the keys through which the answers appear should also be numbered. The intermediate test could easily be adapted to use of a separate answer sheet.

There is only one form for the three tests below the intermediate level. Hence, reteaching on the basis of the scores would have to be evaluated by repeating the same form, or using another measure altogether. The two forms of the intermediate test are not identical in the range of the grade equivalents. Form A is apparently easier. This circumstance should be pointed out to the user, who might wish to start with Form A for grade 4 to take advantage of it.

Lyons and Carnahan is not the only publisher of textbooks to enter the testing field. It would probably be worthwhile for the firm to review similar publications for competing series. Ginn and Company supplement their basic reading series by tests written by McCullough and Russell, who have written adequate manuals for interpretation and have provided at least minimal information on standardization and test construction.

In summary, since the *Developmental Reading Tests* are not inextricably woven into a single reading series, it might be worthwhile to urge their further improvement into a full-fledged reading achievement test. At the present stage, however, this reviewer is convinced that teachers using the Lyons and Carnahan texts would secure better measurement of reading skills by using a more fully standardized battery issued by publishers who are test specialists.

[788]

***Elementary Reading: Every Pupil Scholarship Test.** Grades 4–6, 7–8; 1928–64; new form (4 pages) usually issued each January and April; forms from previous testing programs also available; 2 levels; general directions sheet ['63, 2 pages]; no data on reliability; norms for new forms available following testing program; 4¢ per test; 4¢ per key; postage extra; 15(20) or 25(30) minutes; Bureau of Educational Measurements. *

[789]

***Elementary Reading: Every Pupil Test.** Grades 4–6; 1936–64; new form (4–8 pages) usually issued each December and April; forms from previous testing programs also available; 2 tests; general directions sheet ('63, 2 pages); no data on reliability; Ohio norms for new forms available following testing program; 5¢ per test; 3¢ per key; postpaid; Ohio Scholarship Tests. *

a) GENERAL ABILITY. 22(40) minutes.

b) SPEED AND COMPREHENSION. 2 scores: speed, comprehension; 6(15) minutes.

[790]

Gates Advanced Primary Reading Tests. Grades 2.5–3; 1926–58; Forms 1, 2, 3, ('58, 4 pages); 2 tests; manual ('58, 12 pages); series supplement ('58, 5 pages); $1.50 per 35 tests; 50¢ per specimen set of both tests; cash orders postpaid; 40(60) minutes; Arthur I. Gates; Bureau of Publications. *

a) TYPE AWR, WORD RECOGNITION. 15(25) minutes.

b) TYPE APR, PARAGRAPH READING. 25(35) minutes.

REFERENCES

1–3. See 5:630.
4. NORTH, ROBERT D. "Difficulty and Reliability of the Gates Primary and Advanced Primary Reading Tests, 1958 Edition, for Independent School Pupils." *Ed Rec B* 76:45–51 F '60. *

KENNETH D. HOPKINS, *Associate Professor of Educational Psychology, University of Southern California, Los Angeles, California.*

The 1958 edition of the *Gates Advanced Primary Reading Tests* is patterned closely after earlier editions. The content has been updated and percentile norms are available for the first time.

ADMINISTRATION AND SCORING. The procedures for administration are clear and explicit. Several practice exercises are included for the examinee, to insure understanding of the directions. The manual recommends that colored pencils be used to facilitate scoring, which seems somewhat impracticable; having the print of the tests a nonblack color would have better served the purpose.

Since the two subtests (Word Recognition and Paragraph Reading) are usually given together, a combined booklet would have been easier to use. The manual indicates that the usual order of the tests can be changed if desired, yet no empirical findings are presented to support the assumed lack of ordering and practice effects.

The suggestions in the manual for practical use of the test results are excellent, e.g., improving word recognition. A supplementary manual gives more detailed and technical information. Unfortunately this is a single composite supplement serving the purposes of all the several Gates tests; consequently the interspersed data are not always clearly and well defined. The reader is not always certain whether a statement applies to a specific test or to all Gates' tests. The tables are especially inadequately labeled and interpreted.

STANDARDIZATION AND NORMS. Twenty carefully selected schools served as the reference group on whom the normative data were obtained. Consideration was given to representative IQ scores and socioeconomic status. The manual appears to claim too much in indicating that the results from this relatively small sample of stratified schools were "for all practical purposes" as good as those which would have been obtained if all of the approximately 100 stratified schools had been used. Although the normative sample is purported to be "fairly representative of the nation's total school population," substantiating descriptive data are omitted. The norms are based, in part, on an actual group who took the tests (n = 3,300), and partially inferred from other "key" tests on which interrelationships had been previously established (n = 2,500). Greater explanation regarding this process would have been desirable. The assumption of equal correlation with the "key" tests on other groups may not be completely justifiable due to the curricular specificity of school districts.

Reading grade equivalents, reading ages, and percentile norms are provided. Percentile norms are given at grades 2.5, 2.8, 3.2, 3.5, and 3.8, although it is not made clear whether any of the values are interpolated or extrapolated.

The manual indicates that scores on the present edition "differ materially from those used in earlier editions, reflecting the changes in promotion policy." Additional information regarding the extent of the differences should have been provided so that users accustomed to the earlier editions could more appropriately interpret scores on the current forms.

In some cases, grade equivalents are given to the second decimal place. The validity of this procedure is seriously questioned. A false sense of precision is apt to be inferred from such scores.

RELIABILITY. The tests are to be commended on their use of the most rigorous and appropriate method of reliability determination, the alternate form approach. The manual, however, gives no indication as to which of the three forms were used for the reliability coefficients presented. Unfortunately, reliability data are not given for grade 2, although the tests are designed for grades 2.5–3.9. Difficulty factors would almost certainly make coefficients lower than for grade 3. The samples on which the reliabilities were determined were small and they are inadequately described, but the resulting coefficients, although high, would appear to be conservative since the corresponding standard deviations are usually only about one half the values for the normative sample as estimated from the percentile norms. Data are missing to support the equality of means and standard deviations for the various forms. This is very important since the same conversion table is used for all forms of the tests.

Although the manual states that the tests are diagnostic, its treatment of difference scores is not precise. The values for the difference scores that "may be regarded as both statistically reliable and practically significant" are probably too small; the .15 level of significance is used for these scores. No basis is given for the claim of practical significance.

VALIDITY. The content universe which the items sample is not defined. In fact, no mention of content validity is made, although the items appear to possess face validity. The basis of item selection is given only in general terms; item statistics are not reported.

Although the manual states that the tests are not primarily tests of speed, no empirical data are reported to indicate the influence of speed. The measures are to be commended for not attempting to span several grades with a single test.

No evidence for concurrent or predictive validity appears. No mention is made of the technical recommendations of the AERA or APA. The present tests do not appear to adequately meet the following specifications for achievement tests: A1, B1.2, B1.3, B5, C2.1, C2.3, C3, C4, C4.1, C4.2, C4.6, C5.1, C11, C16.1, D1.2, D1.3, D3, D7, E1, E2, F1, F3, F4, F5, F8, F8.3, F8.6, F8.7, F8.8.

The 15-minute word recognition subtest is composed of attractive drawings from each of which a line is to be drawn to its name. The distributions are skewed positively at grade 2. The 25-minute paragraph reading subtest is composed of 24 items of increasing length in which the examinee performs a straightforward task requiring no inference or abstraction, e.g., "Draw a line under the little book."

SUMMARY. The *Gates Advanced Primary Reading Tests* are attractive, easily administered, and easily scored. Reliability is excellent, although the standardization and norming leave some unanswered questions which limit generalizability and interpretation. More information regarding content validity would have been desirable, yet the tests appear to be useful survey measures.

For reviews by Virginia Seavey and George Spache of the previous edition, see 3:484.

[791]

Gates Basic Reading Tests. Grades 3.5–8; 1926–58; revision of *Gates Silent Reading Tests;* Forms 1, 2, 3, ('58, 4 pages); 5 tests; Types GS, UD, and ND are scored for percentage of attempts correct; manual ('58, 21 pages); series supplement ('58, 5 pages); $1.50 per 35 copies of any one test; 50¢ per specimen set of all 5 tests; cash orders postpaid; Arthur I. Gates; Bureau of Publications. *

a) TYPE GS, READING TO APPRECIATE GENERAL SIGNIFICANCE. 10(15) minutes for grades 3–4, 8(15) minutes for grades 5–8.
b) TYPE UD, READING TO UNDERSTAND PRECISE DIRECTIONS. 10(15) minutes for grades 3–4, 8(15) minutes for grades 5–8.
c) TYPE ND, READING TO NOTE DETAILS. 10(15) minutes for grades 3–4, 8(15) minutes for grades 5–8.
d) TYPE RV, READING VOCABULARY. (20) minutes.
e) TYPE LC, LEVEL OF COMPREHENSION. (20) minutes.

REFERENCES

1–5. See 40:1539.
6–7. See 3:485.
8. See 5:631.
9. CHASE, CLINTON I. "The Position of Certain Variables in the Prediction of Problem-Solving in Arithmetic." *J Ed Res* 54:9–14 S '60. *

ALBERT N. HIERONYMUS, *Professor of Education and Psychology, State University of Iowa, Iowa City, Iowa.*

These tests were very competently reviewed in their present form in *The Fifth Mental Measurements Yearbook.* Some of the minor faults of the manuals which were criticized have apparently been corrected. The major faults of the tests themselves persist.

The most severe limitation of these tests is that they attempt to serve too wide a grade range. Generally speaking, the tests are far too difficult for the lower grades in the intended range (grades 3–8), and not particularly interesting or challenging for the upper grades. In two of the tests only 24 items are used to separate a population which is extremely heterogeneous (grade equivalent range of 2.0 to 12.4 or 12.5) in reading proficiency.

Type GS, Reading to Appreciate General Significance, is presented as requiring "thorough understanding of and real thinking about the content." Yet most of the passages consist of from three to five short sentences which hardly set the stage for very complex understanding. Furthermore, many of the items can be marked without even reading the passage, as for example: "Draw a line under another invention of the kind that usually does not impress people—paper clip, car, airplane, dynamo, camera." For measuring such a complex skill, the form of items is quite inadequate. It is virtually impossible to ask a genuinely searching question about a passage when the question can be answered in one word. The short passages and the one word responses do not do justice to the standards usually set for appreciating general significance of materials which upper grade children are expected to handle.

On Type GS, the median grade 3.4 score is only 5/24, which is chance. With 10-minute time limits, the median grade 8.7 score is 22/24, but the scores at the top are spread considerably with an 8-minute time limit. With an 8-minute time limit, however, children have to average approximately 250 words per minute to complete the test if they read without looking back. This would seem to put quite heavy emphasis upon speed in a test purported to measure thinking and understanding.

Type UD, Reading to Understand Precise Directions, is presented as a test of the "kind of reading the child should be able to do when he reads the instructions for assembling a toy or gadget, operating a television set, [etc.]." This test appears to be misnamed; the only directions used are "put an x on," "draw a line under," "draw a line from [one object] to [another]," and "draw a line around." It is usually, although not always, necessary to read the short selection, but the selections themselves do not constitute directions as such, nor do the items require "exact memory of details in sequential order," as stated in the manual.

In Type ND, Reading to Note Details, most of the 54 items can be marked without reading the passages. This is caused to a large extent by the use of weak distractors. For example, the four responses to the question, "What may air conditioning add to air?" are "radio," "moisture," "mustache," and "pencil"!

If the first three tests are considered primarily as speed tests, these criticisms are less important than if they are regarded as measuring comprehension skills of the types named in the titles. And if they are considered to be speed tests, it is notable that they sample speed under three different explicitly stated purposes.

Type LC, Level of Comprehension, appears to be much better adapted to the grade range than the first three. The test is strictly a power test, untimed, with increasingly difficult passages. The content is interesting and challenging. The items require close reading and a genuine understanding of the content of the passages. As in Type GS, however, the short passages and the one word responses limit the *range* of comprehension skills which can be assessed and do not do justice to a complex definition of comprehension.

Type RV, Reading Vocabulary, is the traditional type of vocabulary test, competently constructed.

The manual and the supplement to the manual are quite complete, well organized, and written in a style understandable to the typical user. As might be expected, the tests are highly intercorrelated, and in some instances the intertest correlations approach very closely the reliabilities of the tests. (In one of the more extreme situations, the correlation between Type RV and Type LC is reported as .89, which value is also reported for the equivalent forms reliability of each of the tests.) It is to the credit of the author that equivalent forms reliabilities, intercorrelations, and critical differences are reported, although the value of the data is somewhat restricted by small *n*'s and lack of comparability of the many samples employed.

In the section on the interpretation of percentile ranks, the recommendation of a percentile band of ±5 percentile ranks seems extremely conservative. On Type GS, at grade 6.2, for example, this would average approximately ±.9 of a raw score unit, which is about one half the standard error of measurement (1.7).

SUMMARY. Three of the five tests put considerable emphasis on speed of comprehension, although they purport to measure thinking and understanding. In addition, the tests appear to be much better suited for use in grades 5 and 6 than in the other grades for which they are intended. Teachers and reading specialists, however, will find the tests useful as a diagnostic supplement to reading tests published as a part of achievement test batteries. The latter generally provide a more satisfactory measure of a greater variety of comprehension skills on longer passages.

ARTHUR E. TRAXLER, *Executive Director, Educational Records Bureau, New York, New York.*

The *Gates Basic Reading Tests,* designed for grades 3.5 to 8, are a second revision of the *Gates Silent Reading Tests,* first published in 1926 and revised in 1943. The present revision, issued in 1958, has evidently taken into account various suggestions made by reviewers in earlier yearbooks, and the resulting tests represent a considerable improvement over the original ones, although certain limitations that still exist will be mentioned in this review.

DESCRIPTION OF THE TESTS. The current edition is published in five separate booklets, each designed to measure a separate type of reading ability. The author recommends that all five be used as a team, although they are available individually or in any combination. The first three —GS, Reading to Appreciate General Significance; UD, Reading to Understand Precise Directions; and ND, Reading to Note Details— are intended to measure speed and accuracy of reading material of approximately uniform difficulty. The last two—RV, Reading Vocabulary, and LC, Level of Comprehension—consist of items of increasing difficulty and are designed as power tests.

All responses are recorded in the test booklets. No provision is made for separate answer sheets or machine scoring, although all except Type UD could readily be adapted to answer sheets. Scoring is done with strip keys except in the case of Type UD, where a transparent overlay key is used.

Each type exists in three forms, known as Forms 1, 2, and 3. The raw scores on these forms are reputed to be comparable, and the same norms are used with all three forms. The test construction procedures, as reported in the manual, should make for close comparability of the forms, but more evidence is needed concerning the relative difficulty of the three forms.

The tests are accompanied by a comprehensive 21-page manual and a 5-page supplement. The manual includes a brief description of the abilities tested, careful and detailed directions for giving and scoring the tests, grade and age norms, accuracy scores (percentages of exercises correct) and norms, percentile norms, instructions for interpreting the scores and ratings, suggestions for improving the abilities tested, a brief statement about the procedure used in the development of the norms, and other information.

The supplement is a more technical document. It gives a longer explanation of the preparation of the tests and the development of norms and discusses reliability coefficients, intercorrelations, standard errors of measurement, and the reliability and significance of differences between test scores. The supplement is a welcome addition to the Gates tests, which in earlier editions were notably lacking in statistical data on reliability and validity.

STRENGTHS OF THIS SERIES. The reading materials in the Gates tests reflect the competence of their author. The passages are well chosen and prepared, as would be expected from a person of Gates' stature in the reading field. Three of the five booklets, RS, UD, and ND, reflect some 35 years of experience in testing reading abilities of these particular types. Although data are not available concerning the importance of the five types of reading which these tests purport to measure, Gates, as a leading authority on reading, is in a favorable position to say what reading abilities are important, and this reviewer believes that the ones he has chosen would find wide acceptance among reading specialists.

Perhaps the greatest single strength of these tests lies in the sections of the manual in which suggestions for diagnosing abilities and deficiencies are made and guidance in improving the tested abilities is given. These sections should be of much help to teachers in interpreting the scores and making effective use of the results.

The normative population was apparently chosen with care, and it is believed that the norms should be representative of reading achievement in a nationwide sampling of public school pupils at these grade levels.

The format of the tests is good. They are clearly printed on paper stock of good quality. Through judicious use of some blue lines on the cover page, the tests are given a bright, attractive appearance, while, at the same time, their appearance is more reserved and professional than that of some of the modern tests prepared for use by elementary and junior high school pupils.

LIMITATIONS. Some essential statistical data for the basic tests either are lacking or are not especially impressive. All reliability coefficients reported in the supplement are above .80, but none reach .90, the point usually regarded as the reliability desirable for tests used in the study of individual pupils. However, since reliability was computed by the alternate form method, which tends to yield lower reliability coefficients than the split-half method, these coefficients may be regarded as fairly satisfactory.

As already mentioned, statistical evidence concerning the relative difficulty of the three forms of each type seems to be lacking. Since the scores are reported as raw scores and since the same norms are used for all three forms, this is an omission of some importance. Remedial teachers in particular might draw erroneous conclusions concerning progress if they simply assumed all forms to be equivalent without definite evidence concerning this point.

The intercorrelations among the types raise a question as to whether these types of reading ability differ enough to make separate measurement worthwhile. The correlations between Reading Vocabulary and Level of Comprehension, for example, are almost as high as the reliability coefficients. It should be said, parenthetically, that this sort of outcome is by no means unique to the Gates tests; this oneness—this unity of the reading process—is at once the comfort and the despair of every person who has ever constructed a reading test.

Finally, among the limitations must be listed the structure of some of the tests themselves. In all educational measurement, when we have determined the objectives, scope, and relative emphases of the field to be measured, the goodness of a test comes down pretty much to how well prepared and useful the individual items are. In this respect, Type GS and Type LC are superior. The tests of the other three types seem to fare less well. In Type UD, a high score can be obtained simply by responding to the last sentence of each paragraph without reading the rest of the paragraph at all. Likewise, a good many of the questions in Type ND can be answered by a comparatively mature reader from general knowledge, without reading, or by very hastily skimming, the paragraphs. In these times when test taking begins in the cradle and stops only short of the grave, youngsters in the intermediate and upper grades are, one suspects, testwise enough to take full advantage of this situation.

The structure of Type RV, Reading Vocabulary, leaves most to be desired. Space limitations prevent expansion on this point. Suffice it to say that many of the items seem more nearly classification items than items testing incisive knowledge of word meaning and that one can be almost sure without an item analysis that many of the decoys are nonfunctioning. To take just one example from Form 2, item 11: "GIANT (1) big man, (2) fireman, (3) music, (4) bad man, (5) slowly." What eight- or nine-year-old, if he can recognize words at all, is going to choose "music" or "slowly" as a synonym for "giant"? Decoys usually serve the purpose better when they are more attractive than some of these seem to be. Notwithstanding these limitations, the available data indicate that the vocabulary scores are among the more reliable and valid scores yielded by this battery.

OVERALL APPRAISAL. On balance, the strengths of the *Gates Basic Reading Tests* outweigh their limitations. Such limitations as have been mentioned in this review arise partly from the unitary nature of the reading process itself, which tends to defy attempts to analyze it into types, partly from the testing technique used in certain booklets, and partly from one or two noteworthy statistical omissions or seeming inadequacies. The strengths come from the expert knowledge of the test author concerning what the important areas of reading development are and from his insight into the diagnosis and correction of the reading weaknesses indicated by the tests and his ability to convey this understanding to others through discussion in the manual.

For a review by S. S. Dunn, see 5:631; for reviews by George Spache, Herbert F. Spitzer, and T. L. Torgerson of an earlier edition, see 3:485; for reviews by Joseph C. Dewey and James R. Hobson of the original edition, see 40:1539 (1 excerpt).

[792]

Gates Primary Reading Tests. Grades 1–2.5; 1926–58; 3 scores: word recognition, sentence reading, paragraph reading; Forms 1, 2, 3, ('58, 4 pages); 3 tests; manual ('58, 14 pages); series supplement ('58, 5 pages); $1.50 per 35 tests; 50¢ per specimen set of all 3 tests; cash orders postpaid; 50(80) minutes; Arthur I. Gates; Bureau of Publications. *

a) TYPE PWR, WORD RECOGNITION. 15(25) minutes.
b) TYPE PSR, SENTENCE READING. 15(25) minutes.
c) TYPE PPR, PARAGRAPH READING. 20(30) minutes.

REFERENCES

1–7. See 3:486.
8–9. See 5:632.
10. NORTH, ROBERT D. "Difficulty and Reliability of the Gates Primary and Advanced Primary Reading Tests, 1958 Edition, for Independent School Pupils." *Ed Rec B* 76:45–51 F '60. *

WILLIAM ELLER, *Professor of Education, State University of New York at Buffalo, Buffalo, New York.*

In the extensive sequence of reading tests developed by Gates and his associates for use from kindergarten through grade 10, the *Gates Primary Reading Tests* were planned for grade 1 and the first half of grade 2. However, examination of the items and the norms indicates that in many American schools the tests could not profitably be administered earlier than about December of the first grade year.

Three 4-page booklets, each devoted to a certain reading subskill and each available in three equivalent forms, constitute the *Gates Primary Reading Tests*. The first, Type PWR was "designed to sample the ability to read words representative of the primary vocabulary." Each item consists of a picture accompanied by four words, and the pupil's task is to select the one word which "tells the most about the picture." The sight vocabulary tested is restricted to words which can be defined easily with pictures, with the result that about 75 per cent of the correct answers are nouns, and almost another fourth are verbs in each form. While a balanced representation of the different parts of speech may not be important, it is unfortunate that Type PWR cannot include any of the short, abstract words (these, from, was, etc.) which account for a large proportion of word recognition errors in grades 1 and 2.

Type PSR, Sentence Reading, consists of 45 sentences, each of which describes a picture which the child selects from a set of six pictures in a multiple choice arrangement. Typical picture-matched sentences are "Father is mending the gate" and "This is a dog." About a fifth of the sentences begin with "This is a," which means that only the ending poses a unique reading task in such sentences. If the common 3-word beginning had been used fewer times, Type PSR would test a greater variety of sentences, and the examinee would be forced to read all of each sentence.

Although Type PPR is described as a measure of paragraph reading, it could just as reasonably be titled a test of ability to follow printed directions, since each item instructs the reader to carry out some act with his pencil (draw a line, make an X). As in the two preceding tests, the items seem well graduated in difficulty. The manual includes two paragraphs which explain why the reading of paragraphs requires more advanced reading ability than the reading of single sentences as in Type PSR. Yet about 40 per cent of the items in each form of PPR are one-sentence items, although they appear to be more complex and time consuming than the single sentences of Type PSR.

The manual includes rather generous claims for the diagnostic potential of the tests. The author suggests that comparisons of results from Types PWR, PSR, and PPR will reveal the instructional needs of individuals and groups, because "the three tests measure different phases of reading ability." However, the supplement to the manual lists the following intercorrelations: between PWR and PSR, .80; between PWR and PPR, .82; between PSR and PPR, .84. Intercorrelations of these magnitudes indicate that the three tests do not measure three discrete abilities but are very nearly testing the same skill. Further, the reported intercorrelations so nearly approach the alternate forms reliabilities of the three types (.86, .87, and .89) that sizeable grade-level differences between the three types for any given pupil should be interpreted as errors of measurement and not as diagnostic revelations. Because the three types are evidently measuring the same basic ability, they should be perceived as three parts of a single test, and the publisher should provide a scheme for weighting them into one composite score.

Teachers and supervisors who have used the *Gates Primary Reading Tests* for several years report that they are easy to administer because the directions in the manual are clear and complete and because the examiner does not have to possess much sophistication about measurement. Test users in the field also comment that the tests correlate well with other measures of reading ability, including overall appraisals by classroom teachers.

The *Gates Primary Reading Tests* have enjoyed considerable popularity for many years, and it is likely that they will continue to be regarded favorably by teachers and administrators for certain practical reasons: (*a*) All three tests can be administered in a total of 50 minutes (plus explanation time). (*b*) The items require examinee activities that teachers consider to be valid measures of primary reading skill. (*c*) Information concerning norms is plentiful and easy to interpret. (*d*) The manual includes pedagogic suggestions for improving the specific abilities identified by the tests.

COLEMAN MORRISON, *Assistant Professor of Education, Rhode Island College, Providence, Rhode Island.*

Although the general purpose of these tests is described as diagnostic, the end result falls far short of this objective. One of the chief characteristics of a diagnostic test is to provide the tester with some of the causal factors relating to failure. Yet this element is missing as the present tests are designed. Essentially the tests consist of three parts, Word Recognition, Sentence Reading, and Paragraph Reading. The tester can determine the extent to which the student does well or poorly on each of these areas, but in those instances where he does poorly no rationale is available to ascertain why. In this respect the tests might best be labeled as "survey" rather than diagnostic. It is altogether possible, however, that the author had some different concept of diagnosis than the reviewer since the examples of "diagnosis" that are included in the manual merely point up the obvious (e.g., "Pupil B is retarded in reading....and about equally weak in all three abilities").

There is also some question relating to the accuracy of other statements found in the manual—particularly those relating to the paragraph reading and sentence reading subtests. In this respect the contention in the manual that "the third test [paragraph reading] requires the reading of paragraphs" is very misleading. Actually, of the 26 paragraph items, 11 are of the one-sentence variety and of the remaining 15, 8 can be answered by identifying only one sentence (e.g., "A teacher told the boy to jump into the water for the ball. Draw a line from the boy to the ball").

Similarly, in the sentence reading subtest students can, by identifying one word as opposed to the entire sentence, score correct responses. Admittedly this may involve superior intelligence on the part of the testee, but invariably illustrations that accompany such items are so unequivocal as to almost preclude the possibility of the student making any other selection if he can identify one key word.

Although the manual consistently refers to "representative vocabulary," "representative pupils," "representative passages," "representative sentences," without further elaboration, more detailed information is given in a supplementary manual ("for readers who desire a more extended description of norms, the test reliability data, and the standardization procedures"), which helps clarify some of these obscure phrases. Yet one is never really clear as to what the test vocabulary is actually representative of!

On the other hand, the manual does provide some helpful suggestions for teachers to assist children to overcome word recognition and comprehension difficulties. Similarly helpful is the discussion of the conversion of raw scores into age, grade, and percentile scores.

If teachers follow scoring directions as indicated, the process in correcting 30 or more tests could be extremely time consuming since marks must be made for both right and wrong answers for Word Recognition. In addition, for Paragraph Reading, the scorer is asked to indicate the number of test items that the testee attempted although no subsequent use is made of this information in the scoring. Although overlays are provided which facilitate the scoring process, guides to assist in the interpretation of children's marks are complicated and unnecessary.

One minor point—the words "pencil" and "crayon" are used interchangeably, a practice that could conceivably confuse some young children taking the tests. One might also question the standardization of the tests, especially since the tester is given the liberty to "supplement or to alter the directions or illustrative procedures" and to provide "extra time" for some children.

In summary, these tests have certain advantages as survey tests but leave much to be desired as diagnostic instruments.

For reviews by William S. Gray and George Spache of an earlier edition, see 3:486.

[793]

***Gates Reading Survey.** Grades 3.5–10; 1939–60; 5 scores: speed and accuracy, accuracy, vocabulary, level of comprehension, total; IBM for grades 4–10; 2 editions; series manual supplement ('58, 5 pages); $2.75 per 35 tests; postpaid; Arthur I. Gates; Bureau of Publications. *

a) HAND SCORED EDITION. Grades 3.5–10; Forms 1, 2, 3, ('58, 8 pages); revised manual ('60, c1958, 15 pages); 50¢ per specimen set; (50–60) minutes.

b) MACHINE SCORED EDITION. Grades 4–10; Forms M1, M2, M3, ('58, 8 pages); revised manual ('60, c1958, 16 pages); separate answer sheets must be used; $1.25 per 35 IBM answer sheets; $1 per set of scoring stencils; $1 per specimen set; (60–70) minutes.

REFERENCES

1. GATES, ARTHUR I. *The Improvement of Reading: A Program of Diagnostic and Remedial Methods, Third Edition.* New York: Macmillan Co., 1947. Pp. xxi, 657. * (*PA* 22:3195)
2. MCQUEEN, ROBERT, AND WILLIAMS, KENNETH C. "Predicting Success in Beginning High School Algebra." *Psychol Rep* 4:603–6 D '58. * (*PA* 34:2009)
3. WEST, DORAL N. "Reducing Chance in Test Selection." *Personnel & Guid J* 36:420–1 F '58. *
4. BARRETT, HARRY O. "The Predictive Efficiency of Grade 8 Objective Tests in Terms of Grade 9 Achievement." *Ont J Ed Res* 2:101–7 Ap '60. *
5. CLELAND, DONALD L., AND TOUSSAINT, ISABELLA H. "The Interrelationships of Reading, Listening, Arithmetic Computation and Intelligence." *Reading Teach* 15:228–31 Ja '62. *
6. TRELA, THADDEUS MICHAEL. *A Comparison of Ninth Grade Achievement on Selected Measures of General Reading Comprehension, Critical Thinking, and General Educational Development.* Doctor's thesis, University of Missouri (Columbia, Mo.), 1962. (*DA* 23:2382)
7. FORTENBERRY, WARREN D., AND BROOME, BILLY J. "Comparison of the Gates Reading Survey and the Reading Section of the Wide Range Achievement Test." *J Develop Read* 7:66–8 au '63. *

GEORGE D. SPACHE, *Professor of Education, and Head, Reading Laboratory and Clinic, University of Florida, Gainesville, Florida.*

This version of the *Gates Reading Survey* represents a 1960 revision or, more properly, a 1960 reprinting of the 1958 edition. The most extensive change in the latest edition is a simplification of a table on page 10 of the manual to clarify the significance of differences among subtest scores.

The 1958 test does not differ materially from the edition of 20 years ago in type of content, rationale, and structure. There are still three subtests: a 36-item speed and accuracy test, a 60-item vocabulary test (65 in the hand scoring edition), and a 43-item level of comprehension test. The speed and accuracy test requires the reading of two- to three-sentence paragraphs, all of similar difficulty, each followed by a simple multiple choice question measuring comprehension of the inferential type. The level of comprehension subtest involves very short paragraphs of increasing difficulty in which comprehension is measured by choosing appropriate words to fit two or three blanks in the paragraphs. The vocabulary subtest requires the simple matching of a word with a synonymous word among the five given choices.

Some of the criticisms of the early edition have been recognized in this revision by supplying a printed scoring key and by clarifying directions slightly. Other objections have not been met, such as the need for instructing the student that the vocabulary and level of comprehension tests are not speed tests, or that he is not to proceed to the next subtest if he finishes quickly, or that the range of items extends up to the tenth grade and therefore he may not be expected to do all items. The use of rather vague directions regarding the time limit for the two power type tests has also persisted. Recent research has shown that the use of the cloze procedure (supplying words for blanks in reading material) as used in the level of comprehension test is a valid reading measure, despite earlier objections.

The author has persisted in the use of some reading tasks of a highly artificial nature with the result that estimates of reading ability are yielded which, in the opinion of many users of the earlier edition, exceed or are unrelated to the pupil's classroom functioning. The speed of comprehension test is particularly susceptible to this criticism. The simplicity of the test may permit good, rapid readers of, say, the third and fourth grades to achieve rather exalted scores in this task, in this reviewer's experience. The correction of the accuracy score on this test for possible guessing is only partially successful in combating this tendency.

Both measures of speed and level of comprehension require largely inferential thinking, a legitimate type of comprehension question but one seldom stressed in the average classroom. The relationship between this mode of testing and the skills of immediate recall of details and main ideas is unknown. Thus the value of these tests in predicting classroom performances, as these are commonly judged by the teacher, is questionable.

The assigning of a grade score to a raw score of zero on each test is hardly defensible, even though the manual does suggest caution in interpreting scores at either extreme. Most teachers do not read manuals very carefully, except perhaps for the directions for administering the tests. Furthermore, many teachers are very naïve in their wholehearted acceptance of test scores as accurate reflections of pupil performances.

The reliability coefficients for each of the subtests for each grade from third to eighth are in the .80's and certainly adequate for most testing purposes. In addition, unlike many test authors, Gates supplies a table indicating the minimum differences necessary for significant variations among subtest scores.

The data on the intercorrelations of the three subtests indicate moderate relationships between speed and level of comprehension (.63–.71) and marked relationship between vocabulary and level of comprehension (in the .80's). These facts seem to imply that there is a justification for reporting the two comprehension scores separately. There is no apparent explanation for the high correlations between the vocabulary and level of comprehension tests.

The inherent difficulty of the scaling of the test items, particularly in the level of comprehension and vocabulary subtests, raises some questions regarding the effective range of use of the test. Upper third grade pupils, the youngest for whom the test is offered, will succeed with approximately 25 per cent of the items in each subtest. At this level, the test would appear to be very difficult and discouraging for such pupils. There is also the question of the validity of the scores for these children, or for those third graders of lesser achievement, as the author himself suggests. Since mid-fourth graders will achieve 33–39 per cent of the items of the tests, it would appear that this level is preferable as the lower limit of the range of applicability.

Despite the many minor limitations, this test will probably continue to find wide and profitable use in survey testing and in evaluations of reading programs and of school systems, even though it lacks diagnostic features and may lack close relationships to teacher estimates.

Morey J. Wantman, *Director of Advisory and Instructional Programs, Educational Testing Service, Princeton, New Jersey.*

The stated purpose of the *Gates Reading Survey* is "to reveal specific strengths and weaknesses in reading abilities, and thereby to indicate the type of training most needed by a class or individual pupil. The tests....are, in other words, diagnostic."

The speed and accuracy score is equal to the number of correct answers on 36 reading comprehension type items. The "accuracy" score is equal to the speed and accuracy score divided by the total number of the correct and incorrect responses. The time limit for this test is from four minutes to eight minutes, depending on the grade level and whether the hand scored or machine scored edition is used. The vocabulary score is based on 60 or 65 words, for which "another word....that means the same or nearly the same" is to be determined. The level of comprehension score is based on 21 passages in which two or three blanks are to be filled in with words that make "the best sense" for the passage. The maximum possible score for level of comprehension is 43. Both the vocabulary and level of comprehension tests are untimed, but about 20 to 25 minutes is suggested. The "total" score is an average score and is based on the reading grade scores for speed and accuracy, vocabulary, and comprehension.

CONTENT. The materials for the tests were carefully selected and subjected to tryout, analysis, and revision. Nevertheless, in view of the directions for the vocabulary test, some of the items are questionable and might cause difficulties for good readers at the higher grade levels. The directions for this test (see above) are likely to be interpreted by pupils to mean that they are to supply synonyms for the words in the stem of the questions. In all three forms of the vocabulary test the correct response is not always a synonym of the stem word but sometimes is either a general term for the stem word or a specific example of the stem word. For example, both the words "three" and "sixteen" appear as stem words in Form M2 and the correct answer for each of these is "number"; and for the stem word "animal," the correct answer is "horse." The directions for the vocabulary test should be revised so pupils will not expect the correct response always to be a synonym.

The tests are intended for grades 3.5 to 10; a wide range of difficulty of content material has therefore been included. The questions appearing early in the tests are far too easy for pupils in grades 9 and 10, and the questions at the end of the test are much too difficult for the youngest pupils. This situation, together with evidence cited below regarding the tables of norms, forces one to question the appropriateness of the tests for grades 3, 4, 9, and 10.

FORMAT. The format of the tests is good. The machine scored edition has one continuous numbering system for the questions of the three tests and has different designations for the options in adjacent questions, thus minimizing the chances of a pupil's marking his response in the wrong position on the answer sheet.

Directions to the teacher for administration of the tests also appear on the front cover of the test booklet for all forms. It seems unwise to have material on the test booklet which is not intended for the pupil.

SCORING. The scoring of the tests for the hand scored edition is cumbersome. The method for handling fractional scores for the vocabulary test and the level of comprehension test is not consistent for the hand scored and machine scored editions; it is not clear why the same rounding rules were not used for the two editions.

NORMS. An attempt was made to base the norms for the tests on a nationwide sampling of schools so that representative types of instruction, socioeconomic status, and levels of intelligence are appropriately sampled. The normative figures are based on 23,100 cases. However, the tables of norms contain flaws and inconsistencies which trouble this reviewer.

The maximum possible score on the speed and accuracy test is 36 and there are four options in each question; thus, the "chance score" is 9. Since there is no correction for wrong responses, a score below 10 is not meaningful. Nevertheless, in one of the tables for this test a reading grade score as high as 4.8 is presented as equivalent to a raw score of 9.

For grades 4 and 5 the table of norms for the speed and accuracy test for the machine scored edition is identical to the corresponding table of the hand scored edition even though there are different time allowances for the two editions. On the other hand, for grades 6–10 the machine scored edition norms and the hand scored edition norms are different for this test.

Discrepancies between the machine and hand scored editions also appear in the norms tables of the vocabulary test. The machine scored and hand scored editions are reported to be identical item for item. Actually, there are 65 items in the vocabulary test of the hand scored edition, of which only 60 appear in the machine scored edition. In spite of this difference, it is difficult to understand, in view of the fact that the "items are arranged in order of increasing difficulty," why a raw score of 10 yields a reading grade of 2.8 on the hand scored edition and a reading grade of 3.1 for the machine scored edition. A similar situation occurs for the comprehension test: a raw score of 10 on the hand scored edition yields a reading grade of 3.3, and the same raw score on the machine scored edition yields a reading grade of 3.7. In the case of the comprehension test the items in the hand scored and machine scored editions are identical, and there is no time limit for either edition.

The percentile norms provided are presented in a form which makes their use unnecessarily involved. (*a*) A conversion of the raw score to a reading grade must be made in one table and then the reading grade converted to a percentile rank by use of a different table. In this connection a description of the use of percentile ranks in the manual implies that the percentile rank is known and that one can interpret something from it about the reading grade level. The situation is just the reverse: the reading grade is known before the percentile rank is obtained. (*b*) The percentile tables provide only data for percentile ranks which are multiples of five. A teacher would therefore sometimes be unable to find the entry he was looking for in the body of the table.

It is not clear from the descriptions in the manuals and supplement exactly how the percentiles were determined. In the percentile tables for the hand scored edition, entries are provided for grade positions from 3.5 through 10.8. There are 23 different grade position sets of percentiles. The data for each grade position is labeled at the top of the column. The entry for the 50th percentile for a given column usually agrees exactly with the column designation, but this is not always the case. The largest discrepancy occurs in Table 6 in the manual for the hand scored edition: for grade position 10.8 of the speed and accuracy test, the 50th percentile is reported as 10.4. Whether or not any such discrepancies could or should occur depends on the method of deriving the percentile ranks and the median reading grades.

The manuals illustrate the averaging of percentile ranks to obtain an overall score for speed, vocabulary, and comprehension. This procedure is highly questionable.

No data are provided for school or group norms, and the manuals' instructions for interpretation of group results imply that the tables for individual norms should be used. Such use could lead to erroneous interpretations.

The description of procedures for the development of norms for the machine scored edition implies that the machine scored edition was not used in the norming process. The norms for the machine scored tests are "adjusted to take account of the differences in the two editions." The discussion of norms for the machine scored edition is again not specific enough to make clear the method by which they were obtained.

RELIABILITY. The reliability figures presented in the supplement are equivalent forms reliabilities. They are presented for five different grade positions for each test and they range from a low of .82 to a high of .89. These reliability coefficients are certainly acceptable. The author rightly points out that competing tests may be reporting split-half reliability figures, which of course would be much higher for his tests if he had reported them. Furthermore, in a conservative discussion of reliability, the author warns that a wider range of reading ability in given school systems "would probably yield larger standard deviations and standard errors of measurement." Such systems may not in fact "yield larger standard errors of measurement" because the coefficient of reliability may be higher.

In discussing reliability and sources of unreliability, the author consistently omits the factor which is, to this reviewer, the most important—viz., the sampling of questions. In short, the use of different forms of the tests could result in different scores because of this factor alone. In this connection, it should be pointed out that no evidence for the equivalence of forms is presented. The forms are merely stated to be equivalent.

The discussion in the manuals on the reliability of differences with respect to pupil averages at times is excellent and extremely conservative, and the emphasis on practical significance as opposed to statistical significance is commendable. On the other hand, the discussion on reliability of differences is sometimes vague and not always consistent with the figures presented for standard errors of measurement.

Reliability figures are presented in the supplement to the manuals as if the figures applied equally well to the machine and hand scored editions. A question therefore arises as to why the two editions differ in the figures presented for "Smallest Difference Between Reading Grade Scores That May Be Regarded as Both Statistically and Practically Significant."

VALIDITY. Neither the manuals nor the supplement presents any data on the validity of the tests. The supplement makes the claim that studies of the tests have been carried on since 1928 and that the number is so large that listing them all would be prohibitive. A partial list is presented, but the most recent entry is more than 15 years old.

SUMMARY. The *Gates Reading Survey* is a useful instrument for determining the level of competence in reading of a group of pupils. The reliability coefficients are satisfactory, and the material in the tests has face validity. On the other hand, the tests are probably not appropriate for grades 3, 4, 9, and 10, and the scores are not likely to prove very helpful for individual diagnosis. This reviewer would like to see more information presented on the methods for establishing the tables of norms, particularly the percentile tables, and evidence on the equivalence of the different forms of the tests.

For reviews by Dorothy E. Holberg and Herbert F. Spitzer of an earlier edition, see 3:487.

[794]

***Iowa Silent Reading Tests: New Edition.** Grades 4–8, 9–14; 1927–56; IBM and (grades 4–8) MRC; Forms AM Revised, BM Revised, ('43, c1927–39), CM, DM, ('43, c1942); 2 levels; manual ('43, 16 pages) for each level; separate answer sheets may be used; $2.45 per 35 IBM answer sheets; 60¢ per set of scoring stencils; 40¢ per specimen set of either level; postage extra; H. A. Greene, A. N. Jorgensen (*b*), and V. H. Kelley; [Harcourt, Brace & World, Inc.]. *

a) ELEMENTARY TEST. Grades 4–8; 1933–56; IBM and MRC; 4 forms (12 pages); 9 scores: rate, comprehension, directed reading, word meaning, paragraph comprehension, sentence meaning, alphabetizing, use of index, total; supplementary directions ('56, 4 pages) for use with separate answer sheets; $4.10 per 35 tests; $8 per 100 MRC answer sheets; $1.60 per set of MRC stencils for hand scoring (machine scoring service, by Measurement Research Center, Inc., may be arranged through the publisher); 49(60) minutes.

b) ADVANCED TEST. Grades 9–14; 1927–43; IBM; 4 forms (16 pages); 10 scores: rate, comprehension, directed reading, poetry comprehension, word meaning, sentence meaning, paragraph comprehension, use of index, selection of key words, total; $5.40 per 35 tests; 45(60) minutes.

REFERENCES

1–6. See 40:1547.
7–27. See 3:489.
28. TERRY, PAUL W. "The Prognostic Value of Different Types of Tests in Courses in Educational Psychology." *J Appl Psychol* 18:231–40 Ap '34. * (*PA* 8:5251)
29. TRAXLER, ARTHUR E. "Sex Differences in Rate of Reading in the High School." *J Appl Psychol* 19:351–2 Je '35. * (*PA* 10:625)
30. GARRISON, K. C. "The Use of Psychological Tests in the Selection of Student-Nurses." *J Appl Psychol* 23:461–72 Ag '39. * (*PA* 13:6426)
31. SHERMAN, ORPHA. "A Comparative Study of the A.C.E. Test and the Iowa Silent Reading Test." *Proc Iowa Acad Sci* 46:291–3 '39. *
32. MOORE, JOSEPH E. "A Study of Sex Differences in Speed of Reading." *Peabody J Ed* 17:359–63 My '40. * (*PA* 14:6218)
33. SLOCUM, ROGER LEON. *Reading Status of University of Wisconsin Freshmen.* Doctor's thesis, University of Wisconsin (Madison, Wis.), 1940.
34. LANGSAM, ROSALIND STREEP. *A Factorial Analysis of Reading Ability.* Doctor's thesis, New York University (New York, N.Y.), 1941.
35. ADAMS, MICHAEL. "The Prediction of Scholastic Success in a College of Law." *Proc Iowa Acad Sci* 49:385–9 '42. * (*PA* 17:2871)
36. GIESECKE, G. E.; LARSEN, R. P.; AND WITTENBORN, J. R. "Factors Contributing to Achievement in the Study of Elementary German." *Mod Lang J* 27:254–62 Ap '43. *
37. HAVIGHURST, ROBERT J., AND JANKE, LEOTA LONG. "Relations Between Ability and Social Status in a Midwestern Community: 1, Ten-Year-Old Children." *J Ed Psychol* 35:357–68 S '44. * (*PA* 19:476)
38. HUMBER, WILBUR J. "The Relationship Between Reading Efficiency and Academic Success in Selected University Curricula." *J Ed Psychol* 35:17–26 Ja '44. * (*PA* 18:2581)
39. SOLOMON, LEWIS E. *Some Relationships Between Reading Ability and Degree of Academic Success in College.* Doctor's thesis, University of Colorado (Boulder, Colo.), 1944.
40. GLADFELTER, MILLARD E. "An Analysis of Reading and English Changes That Occur During the Freshman Year in College." *J Am Assn Col Reg* 20:527–43 Jl '45. * (*PA* 20:2073)
41. JANKE, LEOTA LONG, AND HAVIGHURST, ROBERT J. "Relations Between Ability and Social Status in a Mid-Western Community: 2, Sixteen-Year-Old Boys and Girls." *J Ed Psychol* 36:499–509 N '45. * (*PA* 20:1999)
42. SMITH, FRANCIS F. "The Use of Previous Record in Estimating College Success." *J Ed Psychol* 36:167–76 Mr '45. * (*PA* 19:2377)
43. PRESTON, RALPH C., AND TUFT, EDWIN N. "The Reading Habits of Superior College Students." *J Exp Ed* 16:196–202 Mr '48. * (*PA* 20:5126)
44. *Selection and Training of Shorthand Students in Ontario Secondary Schools.* A study conducted by the Shorthand Survey Committee of the Ontario Commercial Teachers' Association and the Department of Educational Research, Ontario College of Education, University of Toronto. Toronto, Canada: Sir Isaac Pitman & Sons (Canada) Ltd., 1949. Pp. vii, 68. *
45. BUTLER, ALFRED JAMES. *An Analysis of the Iowa Silent Reading Advanced Tests, Form Cm.* Master's thesis, University of British Columbia (Vancouver, B.C., Canada), 1949.
46. PFLIEGER, ELMER F. "A Study of Reading Grade Levels." *J Ed Res* 42:541–6 Mr '49. * (*PA* 23:5752)
47. TRAXLER, ARTHUR E. "Correlations Between Scores on Various Reading Tests Administered Several Months Apart." *Ed Rec B* 52:78–82 Jl '49. * (*PA* 24:748)
48. TREUMANN, MILDRED JENKINS, AND SULLIVAN, BEN A. "Use of the Engineering and Physical Science Aptitude Test as a Predictor of Academic Achievement of Freshman Engineering Students." *J Ed Res* 43:129–33 O '49. * (*PA* 24:2804)
49. TRAXLER, ARTHUR E. "Intercorrelations and Validity of Scores on Three Reading Tests." *Ed Rec B* 56:79–89 Ja '51. * (*PA* 25:6416)
50. MANSON, WILLIAM Y. *A Survey of the Use of the Iowa Silent Reading Test in Virginia Group III High Schools.* Master's thesis, University of Richmond (Richmond, Va.), 1951.
51. BARBE, WALTER, AND GRILK, WERNER. "Correlations Between Reading Factors and IQ." *Sch & Soc* 75:134–6 Mr 1 '52. *
52. PRESTON, RALPH C., AND BOTEL, MORTON. "The Relation of Reading Skill and Other Factors to the Academic Achievement of 2048 College Students." *J Exp Ed* 20:363–71 Je '52. * (*PA* 27:2967)
53. RIDLEY, WALTER NATHANIEL. *Prognostic Values of Freshman Tests Used at Virginia State College.* Doctor's thesis, University of Virginia (Charlottesville, Va.), 1953. (*DA* 14:1042)
54. CHAPMAN, HAROLD M. "The Prediction of Freshman Achievement From a Combination of Test Scores and High School Grades." Abstract. *Am Psychologist* 10:373 Ag '55. *
55. CHAPMAN, HAROLD MARTIN. *The Prediction of Freshman Scholarship From a Combination of Standardized Test Scores and High School Grades.* Doctor's thesis, University of Houston (Houston, Tex.), 1955. (*DA* 15:1201)
56. DUNGAN, EARL WILLIAM. *An Evaluation of the Orientation Test Battery at Dickinson State Teachers College for Purposes of Prediction and Counseling.* Doctor's field study, Colorado State College of Education (Greeley, Colo.), 1955.
57. ANDERSON, RODNEY EBON. *The Use of Entrance Tests in the Differential Prediction of Freshman College Achievement, and the Effect of an Item Analysis on the Efficiency of the Predictive Batteries.* Doctor's thesis, Indiana University (Bloomington, Ind.), 1956. (*DA* 16:2344)
58. BONNER, LEON WILLIAM. *Factors Associated With the Academic Achievement of Freshmen Students at a Southern Agricultural College.* Doctor's thesis, Pennsylvania State University (State College, Pa.), 1956. (*DA* 17:266)
59. SHAW, GERALDINE SAX. "Prediction of Success in Elementary Algebra." *Math Teach* 49:173–8 Mr '56. *
60. GOWAN, J. C. "Intelligence, Interests, and Reading Ability in Relation to Scholastic Achievement." *Psychol Newsl* 8:85–7 Mr–Ap '57. * (*PA* 32:3346)
61. CAMPBELL, ROBERT J. *An Analysis to Determine the Value of Otis I.Q. Test and the Iowa Silent Reading Test in Predicting Final Academic Success of Adams State College Students.* Master's thesis, Adams State College (Alamosa, Colo.), 1958.
62. CHAMPION, JOHN MILLS. *A Method for Predicting Success of Commerce Students.* Doctor's thesis, Purdue University (Lafayette, Ind.), 1958. (*DA* 19:2134)
63. NORTON, DANIEL P. "The Relationship of Study Habits and Other Measures to Achievement in Ninth-Grade General Science." *J Exp Ed* 27:211–7 Mr '59. * (*PA* 35:1283)
64. GARRETT, WILEY S. "Prediction of Academic Success in a School of Nursing." *Personnel & Guid J* 38:500–3 F '60. * (*PA* 35:3954)
65. SCARBOROUGH, ROSA L. *A Comparative Study of the Results of the Iowa Silent Reading Tests, Forms AM and BM Administered to the 9th and 12th Grades of the Booker T. Washington High School, Reidsville, North Carolina, 1960.* Master's thesis, Agricultural and Technical College (Greensboro, N.C.), 1961.

66. CRANE, WILLIAM J. "Screening Devices for Occupational Therapy Majors." *Am J Occup Ther* 16:131–2 My–Je '62. * (*PA* 37:4078)
67. JONES, KENNETH J. "Predicting Achievement in Chemistry: A Model." *J Res Sci Teach* 1:226–31 S '63. *

WORTH R. JONES, *Professor of Education, University of Cincinnati, Cincinnati, Ohio.*

Except for the supplementary directions for use with machine scored answer sheets, the *Iowa Silent Reading Tests* and manuals have been unchanged since last reviewed by Davis and Turnbull in *The Third Mental Measurements Yearbook* (3:489). The reader should note also the reviews by Booker and Roberts (40:1547). Pertinent comments regarding the content, the validity, and the reliability of these tests have been expressed adequately by these men. The major purpose of this review will be that of attempting to evaluate the role that these tests have today.

Upon examination it soon becomes evident that some of the paragraphs and statements used in the tests contain informational material which is considerably outdated. For example, in the Elementary Test both Forms CM and DM have sections describing dictating machines using revolving wax cylinders. Machines in use today have magnetic tapes, wires, and plastic belts. Several other instances of antiquated material and ambiguous references could be cited in the tests where items pertain to such things as "the League of Nations," "the production of corn," and "The World War." Also, it is felt that the paragraph comprehension subtests are somewhat jumbled, and the sentence meaning subtests contain too many specific determiners which tend to give away the correct answers.

The availability of four alternative forms at each level is a desirable feature of these tests, but it is important to note that the forms were equated, scaled, and standardized in 1942. According to the manuals, the standardization groups were located in communities and states "widely distributed geographically." The manuals fail to give adequate information concerning the identity of these communities and states. The claim is made, however, that "These data represent a wide sampling of the elementary school population [and the high school population] of the United States." The only two communities identified are Salem, Massachusetts, and Rochester, New Hampshire. Furthermore, the lack of representative norms for grade 13 is a decided weakness.

Because of the limitations and weaknesses mentioned, it is the opinion of this reviewer that the *Iowa Silent Reading Tests* should not be used unless they are thoroughly revised. Readers who are primarily interested in selecting a test for high school and college students which measures reading comprehension and speed of comprehension might consider the *Davis Reading Test* or the *Nelson-Denny Reading Test.* Both of these tests can be administered during a regular class period, and adequate standardization data are included in the manuals.

Several of the available achievement test batteries include reading tests which may be used effectively to measure important skills in reading at elementary school grade levels. Some of those containing subtests similar to the ones found in the *Iowa Silent Reading Tests* are the *Iowa Tests of Basic Skills,* the *Stanford Achievement Test,* and the *Metropolitan Achievement Tests.* The *Stanford Achievement Test* (1964 edition) has an attractive, new format and new norms. It seems to offer excellent possibilities for future use.

The *SRA Achievement Series* and the *Sequential Tests of Educational Progress* also include rather good tests of reading comprehension. One limitation of these tests, however, is the fact that they require more than one class period to administer.

In summary, this reviewer is of the opinion that the *Iowa Silent Reading Tests,* in their present form, no longer serve the purpose for which they were intended.

For reviews by Frederick B. Davis and William W. Turnbull, see 3:489 (2 excerpts); for reviews by Ivan A. Booker and Holland D. Roberts of an earlier edition, see 40:1547.

[795]

Lee-Clark Reading Test, 1958 Revision. Grades 1, 1–2; 1931–58; Forms A, B, ('58, 6–8 pages); 2 levels; manual ('58, 12 pages) for each level; $2.80 per 35 tests, postage extra; 25¢ per specimen set, postpaid; (20–30) minutes; J. Murray Lee and Willis W. Clark; California Test Bureau. *
a) PRIMER. Grade 1; 4 scores: auditory stimuli, visual stimuli, following directions, total.
b) FIRST READER. Grades 1–2; 6 scores: same as for primer level plus completion, inference.

THOMAS C. BARRETT, *Assistant Professor of Education, The University of Wisconsin, Madison, Wisconsin.*

The *Lee-Clark Reading Test,* Primer and First Reader, is designed to determine in an objective manner the reading ability of first and second grade students. The Primer has three parts: (*a*) Auditory Stimuli tests the subject's ability to hear, remember, and select from four alternatives a word pronounced by the teacher; (*b*) Visual Stimuli measures word recognition by requiring subjects to relate a number of words to a number of pictures; and (*c*) Following Directions involves the marking of pictures in prescribed ways on the basis of directions given in sentence form. In addition to the three parts just described, the First Reader provides two additional parts: (*a*) Completion requires the subject to choose from three alternatives a word that best completes a sentence; and (*b*) Inferences measures the ability to select a word from three choices that best completes the second sentence in a two sentence story.

Reliability coefficients of .83 and .90 were obtained for the Primer and First Reader, respectively, using the K-R 21. The number of subjects, grade placements, means, standard deviations, and standard errors of measurement are reported for both of these studies. Although the magnitudes of the reliability coefficients appear to be adequate, the test user should interpret them with several facts in mind. First, the samples used in the two investigations were relatively small and the process used in selecting the samples is not described. Second, the possibility that the time limits placed on the parts of the tests might produce spuriously high reliability coefficients is open to question. Finally, the forms of the tests used in these reliability studies are not given.

Content validity of the tests was determined through a comparison of the vocabulary used in the tests with the vocabularies found in first and second grade books of three widely used basic reading series and with Gates' *Reading Vocabulary for the Primary Grades.* The results of the analyses indicated that the vast majority of words used in the *Lee-Clark Reading Test* were common to both the criteria used. It should be noted, however, that the Gates Reading Vocabulary was published in 1926 and that no dates are given for the readers used.

Another facet of validity of both the Primer and First Reader tests is demonstrated by comparing results on the tests with the results on a number of other standardized reading achievement tests. Twenty studies involved the Primer, Form A, while 18 studies utilized an unidentified form of the First Reader. The correlation coefficients range from .35 to .91 for the former and from .64 to .88 for the latter. Adequate information regarding the grade placements, numbers, means, and standard deviations for the subjects involved in each study is reported in the manual. Test users will have to make their own judgments with respect to adequacy of the results of these studies on the basis of their knowledge of the reliability and validity of the criterion measures, since this information is not provided. Furthermore, any judgments should take into consideration the relatively small number of subjects used in the majority of these studies and the lack of information about their selection.

Percentile and grade placement norms are provided for both the Primer and the First Reader. Grade placement norms are based on two groups of students for each test. The first group is described as normal in intelligence and as a representative national sample with respect to the various types of reading instruction encountered throughout the country. Subjects in the second group are pictured as being representative of above average students enrolled in schools where reading instruction is introduced early in first grade. Although the availability of norms for two different groups of first and second grade readers is most worthwhile, there is, unfortunately, no detailed description of the characteristics of the subjects or the means of selecting them. Therefore, the test user must rely on the judgment of the authors with regard to the adequacy of the standardization sample and the resulting norms.

The manuals provide helpful discussions with respect to test interpretation and the use of test results, e.g., the intelligence of subjects as a factor in interpreting test results and the diagnostic value of part scores. The former discussion should be particularly helpful to the test user since it points out the different meanings of norms for different groups of children depending on their intellectual abilities. Regarding an analysis of part scores on either test, teachers may be able to detect gross intra-individual differences for a student, as the authors suggest, but they should be careful about accepting minute differences on the part scores as indicative of definite differences in the reading abilities measured, since the reliability of part scores and the intercorrelations among the parts are not provided.

In general, the Primer and First Reader tests sample the types of reading behavior that are customarily accepted as being representative of first and second grade reading development and appear to provide an adequate survey of these reading skills. Teachers should have no difficulty with the mechanics of administering and scoring the tests. Furthermore, the technical aspects of the tests appear to be relatively adequate when compared to other tests of this nature; however, test users should keep in mind the shortcomings mentioned above, particularly the lack of information about the subjects upon which the norms were based, when test results are interpreted.

Coleman Morrison, *Assistant Professor of Education, Rhode Island College, Providence, Rhode Island.*

Of the several weaknesses inherent in these tests the most outstanding appears to be the difficulty in interpreting test norms. To determine grade placement of children taking either the Primer or the First Reader tests, the testees can be assigned to either of two groups. To be assigned to "group 2" are those "above average" pupils who are introduced to "formal reading" during the first grade (by example this is indicated to be "late in the first semester" in the Primer manual, and "late in the second semester" in the First Reader manual). To be assigned to group 1 are children of "normal intelligence" who as a group begin "formal reading" after children in group 2, by implication, at some undisclosed time *after* the first grade.

Perhaps much of the confusion that ensues in attempting to assign a pupil to a particular group stems from the absence of any clearly defined explanation of what constitutes "formal reading," what is meant by "above average groups of children," and the altogether amorphous starting time when the two "fairly representative groups" of children begin reading. Additionally there would appear to be no norms to determine the grade placement of children who had been taught to read in the kindergarten or very early in the first grade, or for groups of children introduced to reading at various times during grade 1.

Apart from grade placement norms, "age in months" figures are provided, but without any corresponding information as to how such figures should be utilized. Still another table is provided to adjust the grade norms in relation to intelligence quotient medians. This might have been helpful if figures which represent "fractions of a year above (+) and below (−) the test norms for pupils of average ability" were spelled out more explicitly.

Aside from the need for more adequate information in the areas noted above, it would be desirable to know something of the selective process and representativeness of the original population sample since samples of only 118 and 120 were used in determining the reliability of the Primer and First Reader tests, respectively.

An analysis presented in the manuals of the vocabulary selection used in both tests indicates that all but 8 of the 86 words found in the Primer and all but 16 of the 194 words in the First Reader were also introduced in 21 books (comprised of preprimers, primers, and first and second readers from three basal reading series) used for comparative purposes. No copyright date is given, however, for any of the 21 books used. In any event it is unlikely that many children would be exposed to all such books. Aside from this at least one of the three series (Scott, Foresman) has been revised since the publication of these tests and another (Macmillan) cannot currently be considered to be "widely used" as the manuals report. A further analysis of words was carried out by comparing test vocabulary with the position of the words on the Gates Reading Vocabulary. Since the latter list was compiled in 1926 it is doubtful that such a comparison would provide any valid rationale for determining vocabulary items in 1958.

Of the 38 items tested in the Primer and 59 in the First Reader, 68 and 51 per cent, respectively, involve the identification of words in isolation, a practice of very questionable merit. Furthermore, 15 of the 38 items in the Primer and 15 of the 59 items in the First Reader are pronounced by the test administrator, thereby tending to place excessive emphasis on this particular type of auditory stimuli.

Despite the ease in administering and scoring these tests, the weaknesses noted above far outweigh these advantages and the tests cannot be recommended.

For a review by Ruth Lowes of the 1943 edition of the primer level, see 3:490.

[796]

★Manchester Reading Comprehension Test (Sen.) 1. Ages 13.5–15; 1959; 1 form (8 pages); manual (8 pages); 10*s*. 6*d*. per 25 tests; 7*d*. per single copy; 1*s*. 6*d*. per manual; postage and purchase tax extra; 45(50) minutes; Stephen Wiseman and Jack Wrigley (test); University of London Press Ltd. *

REFERENCES

1. WRIGLEY, JACK. "The Factorial Nature of Ability in Elementary Mathematics." *Brit J Ed Psychol* 28:61–78 F '58. * (*PA* 33:6845)

[797]

***Metropolitan Achievement Tests: [Reading].** Grades 2, 3–4, 5–6, 7–9; 1932–62; subtest of *Metropolitan Achievement Tests;* 2–3 scores: word knowledge, word discrimination (grade 2 only), reading; IBM and MRC for grades 5–9; 4 levels; battery manual for interpreting ('62, 121 pages); 40¢ per specimen set of any one level; $1.20 per manual for interpreting; postage extra; Walter N. Durost, Harold H. Bixler, Gertrude H. Hildreth, Kenneth W. Lund, and J. Wayne Wrightstone; [Harcourt, Brace & World, Inc.]. *

a) UPPER PRIMARY READING TEST. Grade 2; 1932–62; Form C ('61, 12 pages); directions for administering ('59, 12 pages); $5.40 per 35 tests; (79–84) minutes in 3 sessions.

b) ELEMENTARY READING TEST. Grades 3–4; 1932–62; Forms A ('60, c1958), B ('59), C ('61), (8 pages); directions for administering ('59, 8 pages); supplementary directions for use with deaf children available on request; $4.60 per 35 tests; 37(43) minutes.

c) INTERMEDIATE READING TEST. Grades 5–6; 1933–62; IBM and MRC; Forms AM ('60, c1958), BM ('59), CM ('61), (8 pages); combined directions for administering ('59, 11 pages) for this level and the advanced level; $4.60 per 35 tests; separate answer sheets or cards may be used; $1.75 per 35 IBM answer sheets; 20¢ per scoring stencil; $2 per 100 Harbor answer cards (machine scoring service, by Measurement Research Center, Inc., may be arranged through the publisher); 39(46) minutes.

d) ADVANCED READING TEST. Grades 7–9; 1933–62; forms, prices, and administration time same as for intermediate level.

REFERENCES

1. SPACHE, GEORGE. "Deriving Comprehension, Rate and Accuracy of Reading Norms for a Short Form of the Metropolitan Achievement Reading Test." *J Ed Psychol* 32:359–64 My '41. * (*PA* 16:1207)
2. STONE, CLARENCE R. "Validity of Tests in Beginning Reading." *El Sch J* 43:361–5 F '43. * (*PA* 18:2605)
3. LLOYD, CLAUDE J. *The Relationship Between the Scores Made by Pupils on the Primary Mental Abilities Test, the Metropolitan Achievement Reading Test, and the Kuhlmann-Anderson Intelligence Test.* Master's thesis, University of Southern California (Los Angeles, Calif.), 1958.
4. WRIGHTSTONE, J. WAYNE; ARONOW, MIRIAM S.; AND MOSKOWITZ, SUE. "Developing Reading Test Norms for Deaf Children." *Am Ann Deaf* 108:311–6 My '63. * (*PA* 38:1410)

H. ALAN ROBINSON, *Assistant Professor of Education, The University of Chicago, Chicago, Illinois.*

This test, part of a larger battery, is a good survey instrument yielding three scores (Word Knowledge, Word Discrimination, Reading) at the primary level and two scores (Word Knowledge and Reading) at upper levels. Each score is treated separately although this group of subtests is printed in one booklet. The subtest Reading, which should not be confused with the total reading test, is a measure of sentence and paragraph meaning at the primary level, paragraph meaning at the elementary level, and paragraph plus larger selection comprehension at intermediate and advanced levels. Word Knowledge measures vocabulary and word recognition. Word Discrimination is actually a measure of phonic ability.

No clear reason is advanced by the authors for the exclusion of Word Discrimination from the elementary form; according to the manual's description of the total achievement battery, a word discrimination test is part of the elementary level. Nor do the authors indicate why the reading test at intermediate and advanced levels might not also include Language Study Skills and possibly Social Studies Study Skills, both of which subtests are part of the total achievement battery and measure reading skills. Teachers, supervisors, consultants, and administrators particularly interested in evaluating results in reading might want to add such subtests for fuller coverage.

The test is not a diagnostic instrument, nor does it purport to be one. On the other hand, it offers possibilities for analysis of weaknesses and strengths for given individuals and classes. It might have been helpful for the teacher if some device for analysis had been worked into the scoring of the test, a device such as the one used in the *California Reading Test.*

The test has further diagnostic features: (*a*) Reliability for each subtest is good (.79 to .96) and a measure of validity has been obtained through careful study of curricula, judgment of experts, and repeated experimentation (although the measure of validity of the word discrimination subtest is a little vague). Hence, the examiner has some indication of strengths and weaknesses through examination of the subtests included in the reading test. (*b*) The primary subtest Reading includes a section on sentence reading (14 items), and a section on paragraph reading (51 items). Although the 14 items on sentence reading represent a very small sample, a teacher can get some subjective evidence of performance from the two parts. (*c*) At all upper levels the subtest Reading contains questions aimed at the measurement of just four comprehension skills: main thought, details, inferences, and meaning of words from context. Even though the authors of the test do not provide methods of analyzing strengths and weaknesses in the four skills, the teacher can work out a method for doing this on his own.

The diagnostic features of a survey test such as this are, however, a bonus. The test has much to offer in its own right as a rough measurement of reading achievement. Some important considerations are that: (*a*) The Manual for Interpreting is exceptionally well done; it serves to explain these tests and also provides excellent material about the use of tests in general. (*b*) Directions for administration and scoring are clear and not complicated. (*c*) Results are reported in the three most common ways (grade equivalents, percentiles, stanines), and therefore are most flexible and useful for a variety of interpretive purposes. (*d*) Standardization has been scientifically executed: experimental forms tried with about 27,000 students; item analyses carried out to select items for final forms; tests then administered to about 500,000 students in 225 school systems throughout 49 states; norm sample based on about 25 per cent of the students tested in each class. (*e*) The test booklets are modern in appearance, well arranged, and simple to follow.

Although the advanced forms of the test do not appear to discriminate well among those students reading at ninth grade level or above, the *Metropolitan Reading Test* is one of the best survey tests of reading achievement on the market today for the elementary grades. It has been carefully planned, carefully tested, and well produced. It serves its purpose as a rough measure of reading achievement for comparative purposes and as a tool of identification upon which further evaluation may be based.

For reviews by James R. Hobson and Margaret G. McKim of the 1947 edition, see 4:543; for a review by D. A. Worcester of an earlier edition, see 40:1551; for reviews by Ivan A. Booker and Joseph C. Dewey, see 38:1105. For reviews of the complete battery, see 15; for reviews of earlier editions, see 4:18, 40:1189, and 38:874.

[798]

***Monroe's Standardized Silent Reading Test.** Grades 3-5, 6-8, 9-12; 1919-59; 2 scores: rate, comprehension; 3 levels; no data on reliability; $3.50 per 35 tests of Tests 1 or 2; $2.80 per 35 tests of Test 3; 50¢ per specimen set of any one level; postage extra; Walter S. Monroe; Bobbs-Merrill Co., Inc. *

a) TEST 1. Grades 3-5; 1919-59; self-marking Forms 4, 5, 6, ('58, 4 pages); combined manual ('59, 4 pages) for this test and Test 2 below; no description of normative population; 4(10) minutes.

b) TEST 2. Grades 6-8; 1919-59; details same as for Test 1.

c) TEST 3. Grades 9-12; 1919-21; Forms 1, 2, (no date, 4 pages, same as 1919-20 tests except for directions); instructions-norms sheet ['21, 2 pages]; 5(10) minutes.

REFERENCES

1. MONROE, WALTER S. "Monroe's Standardized Silent Reading Tests." *J Ed Psychol* 9:303-12 Je '18. *
2. WITHAM, ERNEST C. "Scoring the Monroe Silent Reading Test." *J Ed Psychol* 9:516-8 D '18. *
3. PRESSEY, S. L., AND PRESSEY, L. W. "The Relative Value of Rate and Comprehension Scores in Monroe's Silent Reading Test as Measures of Reading Ability." *Sch & Soc* 11:747-9 Je 19 '20. *
4. WEST, PAUL V. "The Monroe Silent Reading Test." *Sch & Soc* 13:510 Ap 23 '21. *
5. BALLENGER, H. L. "A Comparative Study of the Vocabulary Content of Certain Standard Reading Tests." *El Sch J* 23:522-34 Mr '23. *

CHARLES R. LANGMUIR, *Director of Special Projects, The Psychological Corporation, New York, New York.*

There are two points of interest about this set of tests. First, it is an antiquity which reveals the meaning of "standardized" as applied to tests 45 years ago. Second, comparison of the original and the current issue, advertised as "revised" by its new publisher, reveals a classic example of editorial stability which might better be termed total resistance to a half century's development of psychometric concepts, techniques, and standards of professional reporting.

Test 1 for grades 3-5 and Test 2 for grades 6-8 consist of short passages, each followed by a five-choice item. The several forms vary in length from 16 items totaling 825 words to 21 items totaling 1,003 words. The item content is almost identical with the original tests. In the 1920 edition the pupil underlined the word which answered the question. In the new edition the options have been numbered and the pupil marks an "X" in a numbered box. The practice exercises have been changed. That is the extent of the revision.

The original manual supplied some kind of central tendency scores called "standards" for middle of the year and end of the year in each grade, 3 through 12, and it described the table with the heading: "Standards based on 130,000 scores, October, 1920." The new manual for Tests 1 and 2 contains tables of grade equivalent scores for rate and comprehension without any information whatever to support the entries. In short, no data.

Except for the practice exercise, the two forms of Test 3 for grades 9–12 are identical with the original. Each form contains 12 paragraphs averaging about 60 words and one question, generally two-choice, on each passage. The "standards" for middle of the year and end of the year in grades 9–12 are copied from the original manual, along with the assertion that they are "based on 130,000 scores, October, 1920." It is evident from the original manual that the 65,000 pupils were distributed over all grades, 3–12, so that an unknown but certainly large fraction of the 130,000 scores have no relevance whatever to Test 3.

It is not precisely true that the content of Test 3 is exactly the same as the original. In one form the word "parenthesis" is changed to the plural spelling, doubtless to gain grammatical accuracy. The reviewer contrasts this editorial feat with the folly of perpetuating a science paragraph containing the statement: the barometer registered ten degrees lower. It is a curious fact that the author's blue pencil missed this absurdity in 1919; it is fantastic that a test publisher retained the item intact for 45 years.

AGATHA TOWNSEND, *Consultant, Educational Records Bureau, New York, New York.*

Since it seems quite unlikely that any teacher or reading supervisor examining these tests will today select them for use, it seems appropriate to review them as what they are, a landmark in educational history, or—better still—one living specimen representative of an extinct species. Since the tests are still in print, and distributed by the test division of a well-known publisher, it seems impossible to avoid questioning the purpose, even the plausibility, of keeping them on the market, but this will be a secondary aim of the review.

What was reading like in 1920, and how was it tested? What relation exists between norms for those days and for these? A trial administration of the two elementary school levels to a group of sixth graders provides some evidence that the 1920 norms were probably once fairly representative. This statement is based, it is true, on reasoning by analogy from other comments and studies. There seems to be general agreement that the school grades of the early 1920's were reading, on the average, about one year above the level of grades similarly designated today. The finding is in line with Gates' summary, which indicated that pupils in the early 1960's are just about one year younger at a given grade placement than were their grandparents. At any rate, trial by this reviewer tended to place sixth graders of about average reading skills for modern test norms at about the fifth grade level on Test 1, which is designed for grades 3 to 5, according to the publisher, and at about the median for grade 6 according to the 1920 standards on the higher level, Test 2, for grades 6 to 8.

Placement in the norms, of course, is not the only dislocation for today's pupils trying out the tests. The material, its style and content, seems to reflect a seriousness of purpose, and preference for the literary and moral paragraph, which is unfamiliar today. Whatever one may conclude about the relative values involved, it is undoubtedly true that our sixth graders were faced with problems different from what was difficult for the earlier testees. The first paragraph in one of the upper level tests, for instance, found several pupils grinding to a halt before they were well begun: "It was the garden-land of Antioch. Even the hedges, besides the lure of shade...." To the historian, some of the paragraphs are attractive, though nostalgic, but they must have been almost as distant from the everyday life of yesterday's youngsters as they are from ours. Moreover, the difficulty of the paragraphs does not lie exclusively in wording or setting. Not all the test questions ask for understanding of the details or main ideas presented. Some are aimed at inference, and even though Monroe's insight was generally good, there are misleading paragraphs and responses. An obscure little passage is supposed to be identified as coming from Russia, but the only clue is a reference to reindeer skins; coupled with a proper name, Lars, this tends to lead the child up a blind alley. Several of our sixth graders also boggled when the term "equinox" was used among the choices for items asking them to identify the "season of the year" pictured in a poem.

It is more interesting for the test specialist, however, to compare the characteristics of the two scores on the tests with those of tests made more recently. The test purports to give the teacher information on both rate and comprehension. The rate score for the lower levels of the test is expressed as words read per minute—a figure derived by dividing the total number of words read throughout the working period by four, the total elapsed minutes for the test. It will be seen that this is a far cry from the usual words per minute score based on a connected passage. No account is taken of the varying character (expository prose, narrative, or poetry) of the portions of the test read, the variations in difficulty (for the passages do not very dependably rise in difficulty as one proceeds), or the fact that a pupil may stop longer to ponder one response or another. It is true, of course, that this method of deriving a rate score has its descendants in modern tests. The speed of comprehension score of the *Cooperative English Tests* and that of the *Davis Reading Test* come immediately to mind. In such tests, the speed score is made less misleading by reporting it as a score which must be related to the norms for its interpretation. The Monroe elementary test did not come to grips with the problem of understanding a reading rate which is called by the same name as other words-read-per-minute scores. The rate score can be translated into a grade equivalent but it still was undoubtedly used as rate per minute.

It is apparent that Monroe himself realized some of the difficulties created by the speed score on the elementary school test. The secondary school test still depends for its rate score on the amount of the test completed, but the score itself is expressed by an arbitrary number which must be translated into a grade rating for use.

Comments have been made above about the types of passages used in the elementary school tests. Test 3, designed for grades 9 to 12, departs even farther from the familiar methods used to test understanding of passages. Several of the paragraphs take on the guise of verbal puzzles like: "If he should stand, underline smoke. If he should lie on the floor, underline air." In such cases, the additional answer choices perform no visible function. Other items require the identification of the main idea. Several are really disguised vocabulary items. Each of the two forms of Test 3 includes only 12 items; choice ranges from two to five; there are several write-in items interspersed, and other devices are used. The forms of Tests 1 and 2, which were adapted at some unspecified date for a self-scoring device using carbon-backed paper, are all made up of standard five-choice items.

It is not surprising, probably, that this early test carries no indication of reliability or validity. An effort was made to equate the two forms of Test 3. The materials for interpretation include directions (misprinted, by the way) for converting the score on one form to that on the other. The only norms are "Standards based on 130,000 scores, October, 1920" and consist of middle-of-the-year scores, which are not identified as means or medians, for each form for grades 9 through 12. There is a similar set of eight scores for "end of the year," though no explanation is given how either mid-year or end-of-year scores were secured in October. The teacher is urged to distribute the rate and comprehension scores for each class, and compute the medians. No directions are given for interpreting the range of results except for the reporting of the "standards" already described.

The interpretation of Tests 1 and 2 is presumably facilitated by tables assigning grade equivalents to the two scores on each form. Absolutely no data are given for the origin of these norms. It seems probable, however, that they bear no relation whatever to the 1959 copyright date carried by the manual.

Reviewing *Monroe's Standardized Silent Reading Test* has proven a fascinating exercise in the history of testing. Teachers of measurement should take advantage of the test's availability to secure copies for use with their classes. This is where educational testing began. Here is a test which in its time was undoubtedly administered to millions of pupils. It bears no data on reliability and validity. Items are not arranged in order of difficulty, in spite of a strikingly brief time limit. There is no consistent pattern of response or method of rationalizing results on completion items, items with different numbers of choices, or other variants. There are no percentile norms, and the character of the groups on which the scanty medians and the grade equivalents are based is nowhere discussed. All these items and others which might be introduced (such as the implications of the rate score) would certainly provide an interesting session.

On the other hand, the availability of the test may actually be dangerous for the unwary school system. It was devised by a distinguished educator (though one teacher ascribed it to Marion Monroe, since Tests 1 and 2 have mercifully dropped the author's full name). Its simplicity of scoring and its unassuming appearance may recommend it to the timid teacher or to the unsympathetic administrator who may feel that tests are getting altogether too elaborate. And, to tell the truth, anyone must be entitled to wonder why a supposedly responsible publisher still keeps it in stock. It belongs in the archives of testing, where it should rest in peace.

[799]

★N.B. Silent Reading Tests (Beginners): Reading Comprehension Test. Standard 1 (grades 1–2); 1961–62; Forms A, B, ['62, 7 pages]; mimeographed manual ['62, 13 pages]; R2.45 per 100 tests of Form A; R2.15 per 100 tests of Form B; postpaid; specimen set not available; Afrikaans edition available; administration time not reported; National Bureau of Educational and Social Research. *

[800]

***The Nelson-Denny Reading Test: Vocabulary-Comprehension-Rate.** Grades 9–16 and adults; 1929–60; previous edition (see 4:544) still available; 4 scores: vocabulary, comprehension, total, rate; IBM and MRC; Forms A, B, ('60, 12 pages); manual ('60, 30 pages); supplementary profile-norms sheet ('60) for adults; adult norms based on cut-time administration only; separate answer sheets or cards must be used; $4.20 per 35 tests; $2.49 per 35 self-marking answer sheets; $3.15 per 100 IBM answer sheets; 45¢ per scoring stencil; $2.55 per 100 MRC answer cards (machine scoring service, by Measurement Research Center, Inc., may be arranged through the publisher); $1.20 per 35 adult profile-norms sheets; 75¢ per specimen set; postage extra; 30(35) minutes for regular administration, 22½(27½) minutes for reading efficiency classes; original edition by M. J. Nelson and E. C. Denny; revision by James I. Brown; Houghton Mifflin Co. *

REFERENCES

1–6. See 40:1557.
7–23. See 4:544.
24. FREEHILL, MAURICE F. "Student Self-Estimates as Guidance in Selecting Courses." *Col & Univ* 27:233–42 Ja '52. *
25. DURNALL, EDWARD J., JR. "A Testing Program for Junior College for Women." *Jun Col J* 23:261–7 Ja '53. *
26. MUNGER, PAUL F. "Factors Related to Persistence in College of Students Who Ranked in the Lower Third of Their High School Class." *J Counsel Psychol* 1:132–6 f '54. * (*PA* 29:6258)
27. VINEYARD, EDWIN E., AND MASSEY, HAROLD W. "The Interrelationship of Certain Linguistic Skills and Their Relationship With Scholastic Achievement When Intelligence Is Ruled Constant." *J Ed Psychol* 48:279–86 My '57. * (*PA* 33:2200)
28. FLEMING, W. G. *Aptitude and Achievement Scores Related to Immediate Educational and Occupational Choices of Ontario Grade 13 Students.* Atkinson Study of Utilization of Student Resources, Report No. 3. Toronto, Canada: Department of Educational Research, Ontario College of Education, University of Toronto, 1958. Pp. xix, 380. *
29. FLEMING, W. G. *Ontario Grade 13 Students: Their Aptitude, Achievement, and Immediate Destination.* Atkinson Study of Utilization of Student Resources, Report No. 4. Toronto, Canada: Department of Educational Research, Ontario College of Education, University of Toronto, 1958. Pp. ix, 55. *
30. FLEMING, W. G. *Personal and Academic Factors as Predictors of First Year Success in Ontario Universities.* Atkinson Study of Utilization of Student Resources, Report No. 5. Toronto, Canada: Department of Educational Research, Ontario College of Education, University of Toronto, 1959. Pp. xi, 137. *
31. PALACIOS, JOHN RAYMOND. *A Validation Study of Selected Tests for Possible Use in Admission to Professional Education Sequences at Purdue University.* Doctor's thesis, Purdue University (Lafayette, Ind.), 1959. (*DA* 20:2679)
32. SMITH, D. D. "Traits and College Achievement." *Can J Psychol* 13:93–101 Je '59. * (*PA* 34:4780)
33. PIPHER, J. A. "An Appraisal of the Use of the Dominion Group Test of Learning Capacity (Advanced) in the Atkinson Study of Utilization of Student Resources." *Ont J Ed Res* 3:17–23 O '60. *
34. BEAMER, BEN A. *The Relative Value of the Nelson-Denny Test and the Cooperative Reading Test in the Freshman Test Battery at Virginia State College.* Master's thesis, Virginia State College (Petersburg, Va.), 1961.
35. FLEMING, W. G. *The Use of Predictive Factors for the Improvement of University Admission Requirements.* Atkinson Study of Utilization of Student Resources, Report No. 9. Toronto, Canada: Department of Educational Research, Ontario College of Education, University of Toronto, 1962. Pp. xi, 76. *
36. ROBINSON, WILLIS. *A Validity Study of the Testing Program for the Selection of Students for Teacher Education.* Doctor's thesis, Purdue University (Lafayette, Ind.), 1962. (*DA* 23:2812)

DAVID B. ORR, *Senior Research Scientist, American Institute for Research; and Director of School and Survey Research, University of Pittsburgh Project Talent Office; Washington, D.C.*

This test represents a revision and improvement of one already well known and widely used. It is composed of a 100-item vocabulary section and a 36-item reading comprehension section, both of traditional multiple choice types. New features of this revision are the addition of a reading rate score, more complete norms, and some attention to the special case of adults studying "efficient" or "rapid" reading.

The test shows evidence of careful construction. Data on the development and standardization of the revised forms are presented along with reliabilities, difficulties, and standard errors of measurement. In general the format is clear and workable, and, with a few exceptions, the items seem well constructed and unambiguous. Earlier criticisms of the form of the norms and of the lack of discussion of diagnostic uses of the test have been taken care of in the new manual.

Both self-scoring and machine scorable answer sheets are available, making the test economical and convenient to use.

One criticism of the content of the reading comprehension portion of the test is that some of the passages draw their difficulty from what is essentially poor writing, i.e., long, involved, and somewhat awkward sentences and constructions. This reviewer feels that the essence of reading comprehension lies more in the reader's ability to grasp ideas and their implications than in his ability to thread his way through grammatical complexities.

There is little to criticize in the standardization of the test, though the total groups employed were relatively small. A stratified random sampling procedure was used for grades 9–12 based on school enrollment by region and community size. Data are presented. For college levels, enrollment by five types of colleges was used as the basis of stratification. Special adult norms are given for administration of the test to adults in "efficient reading" classes in less than the usual time. These are based on 961 adult students in the University of Minnesota Extension Division Efficient Reading Classes (about half for each of the two available forms).

A considerable amount of technical data about the revision is presented in the manual. Since both the vocabulary and comprehension parts of the test tend to be somewhat speeded, the authors have commendably chosen alternate form reliability rather than split-half. Reliabilities for reading rate, vocabulary, and total score are acceptably high (.92 to .93), but comprehension leaves something to be desired (.81), particularly for individual work. However, standard errors of measurement are presented by form by grade and their use explained. Correlations with English and IQ tests are also given, but these, like the reliabilities, are based on unnecessarily small samples and may not be very dependable.

Comparative data are presented with respect to the mean item difficulty and "validity" of Forms A and B original and Forms A and B revised. This reviewer would like to emphasize his dislike for the use of the terms validity, validity index, or validity coefficient to represent the correlation between an item score and a total score. Such a correlation is more properly referred to as an internal consistency coefficient and does not measure validity in the same sense as either item-criterion correlations or test-criterion correlations. However, the data presented do show considerable improvement in the range for these coefficients for both vocabulary and comprehension sections over the original forms. The mean value for the vocabulary section has been raised from about .38 to .47 which is now more comparable to the comprehension sections (.45). Mean difficulties in terms of per cent passing the item have been made somewhat easier for the revised vocabulary sections (62) and have remained about the same for the comprehension sections (about 71). All of these values seem satisfactory, though the present difficulty indices show that the comprehension sections are a little on the easy side.

Perhaps the most disappointing aspect of the present manual is its failure to include more data on the predictive and concurrent validity of the test. Only one predictive study is cited and the small group correlations with the ACE, "Otis IQ," and "Coop English" (not further identified) do not really fill the latter need. The authors do not even address themselves, except incidentally, to topics of content or construct validity in describing the development of the test. This reviewer considers these to be regrettable lacks in the manual.

A further deficiency in the manual is the fact that, try as he might, this reviewer could find no information on the intercorrelations of the three Nelson-Denny scores. This is an unfortunate omission as the user may well ask to what extent the information provided by these individual scores is being duplicated from one to another.

In summary, in spite of certain defects, this test is one of the better of its kind and represents a useful improvement of an already useful test. Some care should be exercised in the comprehension score for individual diagnosis, and appropriate standard errors should be kept in mind. In general the test may be expected to provide useful information at a reasonable cost and will doubtlessly continue to find a place in the test user's repertoire.

Agatha Townsend, *Consultant, Educational Records Bureau, New York, New York.*

The current revision of the old standby for college testing, the *Nelson-Denny Reading Test,* will probably be welcomed by the chief clientele for its predecessor, teachers of college-bound pupils in grades 11 and 12, and those of college English classes; it may also be useful for college placement. It is a good test for a limited audience, and it should be stated at the outset that most of the criticisms which it has incurred, some of which are noted below, have arisen because of an attempt made to increase the sale of the test by appeals to other groups.

The simple structure is well adapted to the survey purposes to which the test has always held. It consists of a long (100-item) vocabulary test and a series of reading passages on which comprehension questions are asked. In both the old and revised editions, the raw score on comprehension is multiplied by two and added to the vocabulary score for a total. This weighting of the comprehension factor is probably justifiable since it brings the two scores fairly closely in line, though the total score for a good reader, or at least one answering most of the questions correctly, will be weighted more heavily with vocabulary.

The new test also includes a rate score. This is an approximation of words read per minute, though for some undisclosed reason, it is not based on an accurate count of the words in the rate passage, which also serves as the first comprehension passage. The manual points out quite correctly that the rate score should be regarded like any other piece of raw data, and interpreted through reference to the percentile tables. The teacher using the rate score, however, should also be warned that the rate passages have a Dale-Chall readability index which places them at the college level; hence comparisons with other rate scores should be made very cautiously. One should not be misled by the statement that the grade norms "represent a convenient way of rendering scores on several tests 'comparable.'" It should also be noted that the rate score is based on a testing time of only one minute, although there is considerable evidence to suggest that such a brief sample is not so reliable as rate measurement over a longer interval. Moreover, interestingly enough, the source which the author quotes in justification for a one-minute limit does not report favorable reliability data on limits less than four minutes.

Except for the limitations noted about the rate score, the data on reliability for the test indicate that the part scores may be used with considerable confidence. The confidence is increased by observing that the percentile norms seem to have been carefully constructed and the populations on which they are based carefully described. Standard error of measurement figures are reported in addition to reliability data; this is a valuable and praiseworthy addition to the manual.

Decisions about the usefulness of this test should be made, in the opinion of this reviewer, only after careful study of both the test and the students with whom it might be employed. Reference has already been made to the measured difficulty of the passage on which the rate score is based. The manual points out that this passage is about median in difficulty for the series of passages—as judged, however, by the difficulty of the comprehension items. This method of estimating difficulty has its obvious shortcomings, and in fact, the fifth of the eight passages in each form (the only one based on general material typical of newspaper or magazine reporting) seems to be markedly easier than the others. The manual makes no mention of controlling difficulty through reference to any readability formula. Both the comprehension passages and the vocabulary part appear to be suitable for colleges but are almost certainly too difficult for average ninth and tenth grades. This statement is borne out indirectly by the norms. The average score for ninth grade pupils is from 15 to 18 (out of 100) in vocabulary, and represents about 12 of the 36 comprehension items answered correctly. Certainly most teachers will seek a test which samples these abilities more adequately for younger students.

Although the manual points out that "reading range at any one grade level is likely to extend over six to eight grades," all grade equivalents below 9.0 are marked "extrapolated" in the norms table, and there is no indication of any tryout below grade 9. This reviewer considers the use of grade equivalents as misleading and unnecessary, at least above grade 6, and is favorably impressed that these tables are not stressed in the interpretation. The grade norms for comprehension and rate, in any event, are so coarse as to have little attractiveness for most users.

Even though the percentile norms appear to indicate an adequate spread of scores and although suitable reliability figures are reported for grade 11 and above, the restricted content may still make the test unsatisfactory for use with any high school groups except those which are clearly college preparatory, and barely suitable for modern programs with those groups. There is a very sparse scattering of terms from science in the vocabulary test, which is chiefly general and somewhat literary in character. The comprehension passages are limited to history, formal economics, semihistorical passages on literature, two extracts in each form which might be called sociology and anthropology, and the one general passage mentioned above. They seem to give adequate representation for standard college textbook materials in a limited number of fields.

The high school or college teacher who turns to the manual for suggestions on the use of scores in instruction will be disappointed. In an essay on reading improvement, "Some Uses of the Test," the author makes some curious statements about the rise in rate and comprehension which can be expected in reading improvement courses (undescribed), offers an obscure comment about the use of high school rank in place of a measure of intelligence, and refers to an unidentified listening test (from internal evidence this is probably the Brown-Carlsen, since the author participated in the construction of this measure) and its relation to Nelson-Denny scores. Although the essay is interesting, it scarcely lives up to its title.

This review should not close without mentioning the striking new material which has been prepared for use of the Nelson-Denny with adult reading improvement classes. The profile and interpretation sheets as they now stand need improvement. It will be seen that Brown's adult classes are unusual, as it is clearly stated that the adult norms are based on highly selected groups of professional people, chiefly students who read better than the average college senior, and "more than half have one or more college degrees." Bearing this limitation clearly in mind, it seems as if the Nelson-Denny might be appropriate for use in some adult courses; additional norms would be needed for many groups, or reference should be made to the existing grade or college norms.

Unfortunately, the recommendation of the author is that when the test is employed for adults, administration time should be shortened to 7½ minutes for vocabulary, and 15 minutes for rate plus comprehension. The surprising statement is added that this cut-time administration adds "sensitivity" to the test. Considering the small number of comprehension items to begin with and the steep difficulty of the vocabulary part, this conclusion seems questionable. Cutting the time will artificially increase the ceiling of the test but will do so by making it farther than ever from a power test. The suggestions for use in teaching adults are as vague as those for the school and college situation.

In summary, with the new revision, the Nelson-Denny seems to be very much what it was before. It was and is a challenging test with a highly academic flavor, useful for good readers who expect to use their reading in liberal arts fields, though not in the sciences. The rate score may prove useful for college textbook reading. The percentile norms seem adequate for grade 11 and above, and the test may facilitate a survey of a field where we admittedly lack good information—the growth of reading power in the college years. It is not a test which will adequately differentiate among the reading skills of college students, but it has its place for screening. Without further evidence, it can be recommended to only a limited number of teachers working with adult classes, and then only when the character of the adult enrollment is similar to that of the sample on which the norms are based. The question of carryover from this textbook type of reading to business and professional reading remains unanswered. The explanatory materials which accompany the test are not as good as the norms. The suggestions for teaching are not adequate for the instructor with a limited background in reading improvement, and a teacher with adequate preparation will find them unnecessary.

J Counsel Psychol 10:203–4 su '63. John O. Crites. * extensively up-dated and improved * Unusually complete normative data are given for the test, which was standardized upon large numbers of Ss. * Reliabilities for the test ....based upon a carefully conducted study of 110 college students....seem to be adequate for both general screening purposes with the total scale and diagnostic work with the subscales. With respect to the latter, the validity data on the test, which consists primarily of item analyses indicates that it can be used to identify differential difficulties in vocabulary and comprehension. The value of the rate score is less certain, since no data on its correlation with comprehension are reported, but its expected relationship would be high. Although the Manual (p. 22) attempts to convey the impression that the Nelson-Denny usually correlates with scholastic achievement in the .60's, the data which are cited are far from conclusive. The correlation is more likely in the .40's. * a well constructed and excellently standardized measure which can be confidently recommended to counselors. Its scores appear to be quite reliable, and there is some evidence of its validity for a variety of purposes. If there is a shortcoming in the work which has been done on the test, it is in certain unverified statements which are made in the Manual. For example, on page 22, studies on the relationship of the Nelson-Denny and other tests to academic achievement are summarized and then the following conclusion is drawn: "These findings suggest that the inclusion of this test [the Nelson-Denny] in any college entrance battery should noticeably improve its predictive accuracy." There is no basis for this inference, which would require data on the differential contributions of tests to a battery, such as are determined by a procedure like the Wherry-Doolittle. Consequently, the Manual should be read critically and discriminatingly, since parts of it are misleading, but this should not unduly detract from the over-all high quality of the test.

For a review by Ivan A. Booker of the earlier edition, see 4:544; for a review by Hans C. Gordon, see 40:1557.

[801]

Nelson-Lohmann Reading Test: Coordinated Scales of Attainment. Grades 4, 5, 6, 7, 8; 1946–54; identical with reading sections of *Coordinated Scales of Attainment;* IBM; Form A ('53, 4 pages, identical with test copyrighted in 1946 except for title); 5 levels; directions for administering ('53, 4 pages); battery manual ('54, 24 pages); separate answer sheets must be used; $2.35 per 25 tests; $1.45 per 25 IBM scorable answer sheets; 25¢ per scoring stencil; $1.50 per battery manual; postage extra; 75¢ per specimen set, postpaid; (45) minutes; Ethel V. Nelson and Victor L. Lohmann; Educational Test Bureau. *

JASON MILLMAN, *Assistant Professor of Educational Psychology and Measurement, Cornell University, Ithaca, New York.*

The *Nelson-Lohmann Reading Test* is identical to the reading test in the *Coordinated Scales of Attainment.* A separate test of 60 multiple choice items, based upon 10 to 13 one-paragraph episodes, is provided for each of grades 4 through 8. Directions for each test are identical. While the tests are essentially untimed, 45 minutes are suggested as being "sufficient for all but the slower classes."

Inspection of the items suggests that while the majority measure the ability to note details, a number of them require the ability to grasp the main idea, determine word meanings from context, and interpret beyond the printed word.

To help in the interpretation of the scores, age equivalent, grade equivalent and percentile rank norms are provided, together with profile charts. The charts will be of most value when the reading test is used in conjunction with the other tests in the *Coordinated Scales of Attainment.*

It is difficult to evaluate the test on more technical grounds since the only information provided is that compared to the earlier editions, "The current, revised edition....matches the original one in difficulty, item by item, and is much improved in other respects." We are further assured that "the same norms apply to both the new test as well as the old test."

Because individual items have been matched on difficulty with corresponding items in the older test is no guarantee that the distribution of total scores on which norms are based will be the same. Further, we have no assurance that the high empirical standards of item selection and the satisfactory levels of reliability associated with the first test are to be found with the present edition.

Only items of average or near average difficulty for the grade under consideration were retained for use in the older edition. Because the current edition matches these item difficulty levels, we can be sure each current test also measures a limited range of ability. Thus, the authors should be commended for warning against distorted interpretations of grade equivalents more than one grade above or below the grade for which the test was designed. This reviewer, however, is less pleased with the claim that the test is appropriate to measure a "wide range of individual differences" and that "the variations in attainment found in a typical class are fully taken into account."

In summary, the *Nelson-Lohmann Reading Test* appears to be a good measure of ability to comprehend nontechnical reading material in a situation where reading speed is minimized. This reviewer agrees that "*school norms* and *city or county norms* [should] be developed." The narrow range of difficulty of the items in each test suggests that accurate measurement of the reading ability of individual students who are much above or below the grade norm of the test will not be possible. A technical manual for the test is needed.

For a review by Alvin W. Schindler of the complete battery, see 4:8; for reviews by Roland L. Beck, Lavone A. Hanna, Gordon N. Mackenzie (with Glen Hass), and C. C. Ross of the batteries for grades 4–8, see 3:6.

[802]

***The Nelson Reading Test, Revised Edition: Vocabulary-Paragraph Comprehension.** Grades 3–9; 1931–62; revision of *The Nelson Silent Reading Test: Vocabulary and Paragraph: The Clapp-Young Self-Marking Tests,* which is still available; 3 scores: vocabulary, paragraph comprehension, total; IBM; Forms A, B, ('62, 19 pages); manual ('62, 23 pages); separate answer sheets must be used; $4.95 per 35 tests; $2.55 per set of 35 self-marking answer sheets and manual; $3.30 per 100 IBM answer sheets; 42¢ per set of scoring stencils; 42¢ per manual; 84¢ per specimen set; postage extra; 30(35) minutes; M. J. Nelson; Houghton Mifflin Co. *

H. ALAN ROBINSON, *Assistant Professor of Education, The University of Chicago, Chicago, Illinois.*

Although the test is said to be designed for grades 3–9, the requirement that separate answer sheets (either self-marking or IBM) be used places third and fourth graders at a disadvantage and makes the test more suitable for grades 5–9. No evidence of experimentation with and without separate answer sheets is reflected in the examiner's manual. In addition, the test is probably not suitable for junior high school students reading at levels beyond grade 9. Grade equivalents are not given above 10.5 and the most difficult passages in the paragraph comprehension section of the test appear to be rather easy for mature readers.

The revision of the test, however, has produced a paragraph comprehension section which contains a little more challenging and varied material than it did in the old test, and a vocabulary section composed of the best items, selected on the basis of item analyses, from the original forms. The fact that the revision resulted in two forms rather than three as in the earlier edition will make more limited the test-retest use of an instrument which spans seven grades.

The test, however, appears to be effective as a rough measure of reading achievement. The standardization procedure was meticulous and comprehensive. The manual contains percentiles and grade equivalents for vocabulary, paragraph comprehension, and total score. The test appears to be reliable and, when compared with other reading tests, gives some evidence of validity.

A better and more comprehensive measure of validity, however, might have included the study of curriculums in grades 3–9. Obviously there are many more important comprehension skills at these levels than the three measured: main thought, details, and prediction of outcome. In fact, the inclusion of "prediction of outcome" for each paragraph means that material needed to be structured for that purpose.

In a number of instances on this test, possible answers can easily be eliminated because they are nonsensical. One such answer is "went home," which occurs repeatedly in the "what do you think happened next?" type of question: "Durovitch went home"; "the man went home"; "Wilbur went home"; "the professor went home." Inspection of test items by a panel of expert judges might have strengthened the total test.

Although a third of the manual consists of norm tables, it also includes information about the test and its uses. A helpful table is provided which permits the teacher to ascertain students' weaknesses and strengths in the three particular comprehension skills. The author does not make claims, however, for diagnostic values over and above an analysis of scores from both parts of the test (vocabulary and paragraph comprehension). On the other hand, too many conclusions about deficiencies and possible remedies for them are drawn on the basis of this one survey test. A teacher would be ill-advised to plan an instructional program on the evidence presented by one test without further testing in specific skill areas.

This is not a diagnostic instrument. It is a test with some flaws, but it does seem to be an adequate gross measure of reading achievement. It is a decided improvement over the earlier edition especially in format and attractiveness.

For a review by William D. Sheldon of the earlier edition, see 4:545; for a review by Constance M. McCullough, see 3:492; see also 40:1558 (1 excerpt).

[803]

***Primary Reading: Every Pupil Scholarship Test.** Grades 1, 2–3; 1935–64; new form (4 pages) usually issued each January and April; forms from previous testing programs also available; 2 levels; special directions for grade 1 administration ['63, 3 pages]; general directions sheet ['63, 2 pages]; no data on reliability; norms for new forms available following testing program; 4¢ per test; 4¢ per key; postage extra; (40–60) minutes for grade 1, 15(20) minutes for grades 2–3; Bureau of Educational Measurements. *

[804]

*Primary Reading: Every Pupil Test.** Grades 2–3; 1936–64; new form (8 pages) usually issued each December and April; forms from previous testing programs also available; general directions sheet ('63, 2 pages); no data on reliability; Ohio norms for new forms available following testing program; 5¢ per test; 3¢ per key; postpaid; 16(30) minutes; Ohio Scholarship Tests. *

For reviews by William S. Gray and Virginia Seavey of the 1946 forms, see 3:493.

[805]

★Reading Adequacy "READ" Test: Individual Placement Series. Adults; 1961; 3 scores: reading rate, per cent of comprehension, corrected rate; Form C (4 pages); no manual; no data on reliability; no description of normative population; $4 per 25 tests; $1 per key; $2.25 per specimen set; postpaid; [10–15] minutes; J. H. Norman; the Author. *

[806]

***Reading Comprehension: Cooperative English Tests, [1960 Revision].** Grades 9–12, 13–14; 1940–60; separate booklet edition of reading subtest of *Cooperative English Tests, [1960 Revision]*; revision of *Reading Comprehension: Cooperative English Test: Lower and Higher Levels, C1 and C2*; 4 scores: vocabulary, level of comprehension, speed of comprehension, total; IBM; Forms A, B, C, ('60, 10–11 pages); 2 levels (tests labeled, say, for grades 13–14, Form 1A, for grades 9–12, Form 2A); battery directions for administering ('60, 16 pages); battery manual for interpreting ('60, 42 pages); battery technical report ('60, 35 pages); distribution of Form 1C restricted to colleges; separate answer sheets must be used; $4 per 20 tests; $1 per 20 IBM scorable answer sheets for the battery; 25¢ per scoring stencil; $1 per 20 Scribe answer sheets for the battery (scored by the publisher only); $1 per manual for interpreting; $1 per technical report; postage extra; $2 per specimen set of the battery, cash orders postpaid; 40(45) minutes; revision by Clarence Derrick, David P. Harris, and Biron Walker; Cooperative Test Division. * (Australian edition of the Higher Level of the earlier edition: Australian Council for Educational Research.)

REFERENCES

1–2. See 40:1564.
3–17. See 3:497.
18–37. See 4:547.
38–58. See 5:645.
59. STUCKY, MILO O., AND ANDERSON, KENNETH E. *A Study of Persistence in College Attendance in Relation to Placement-Test Scores and Grade-Point Averages.* University of Kansas, School of Education, Kansas Studies in Education, Vol. 9, No. 2. Lawrence, Kan.: the School, April 1959. Pp. 58. *
60. STUCKY, MILO O., AND ANDERSON, KENNETH E. "A Study of the Relationship Between Entrance-Test Scores and Grade-Point Averages and Length of Stay in College." *Yearb Nat Council Meas Used Ed* 16:164–70 '59. *
61. ANDERSON, A. W. "The Relationship of Age to Adult Reading Scores." *J Ed Psychol* 51:334–6 D '60. * (*PA* 36:1FA34A)
62. CASSEL, RUSSELL N., AND STANCIK, EDWARD J. "Factorial Content of the Iowa Tests of Educational Development and Other Tests." *J Exp Ed* 29:193–6 D '60. *
63. MARKWARDT, FREDERICK CHARLES, JR. *Pattern Analysis Techniques in the Prediction of College Success.* Doctor's thesis, University of Minnesota (Minneapolis, Minn.), 1960. (*DA* 21:2990)
64. BARNHART, E. L., AND ANDERSON, KENNETH E. *A Study of the Relationships Between Grade-Point Averages, Placement-Test Scores, Semester Hours Earned, and Area of Major Interest for the Group Who Entered the University of Kansas in the Fall of 1954.* University of Kansas, School of Education, Kansas Studies in Education, Vol. 11, No. 1. Lawrence, Kan.: the School, January 1961. Pp. 36. *
65. BEAMER, BEN A. *The Relative Value of the Nelson-Denny Test and the Cooperative Reading Test in the Freshman Test Battery at Virginia State College.* Master's thesis, Virginia State College (Petersburg, Va.), 1961.
66. COOLEY, JOHN C. "A Study of the Relation Between Certain Mental and Personality Traits and Ratings of Musical Abilities." *J Res Music Ed* 9:108–17 f '61. *
67. CAMPBELL, JOEL T.; OTIS, JAY L.; LISKE, RALPH E.; AND PRIEN, ERICH P. "Assessments of Higher-Level Personnel: 2, Validity of the Over-All Assessment Process." *Personnel Psychol* 15:63–74 sp '62. * (*PA* 37:3908)
68. PRESTON, RALPH C. "A New Approach to Judging the Validity of Reading Comprehension Tests: Summary of an Investigation." *Int Rdg Assn Conf Proc* 7:166–7 '62. *
69. OSBORN, LYNN R. "An Analysis of the Relationship Between Speech Performance and Performance on Written Examinations of Course Content in a Beginning College Speech Course as Reflected in Assigned Grades." *Univ Kans B Ed* 17:68–71 F '63. *
70. RANKIN, EARL F., JR. "Reading Test Reliability and Validity as Function of Introversion-Extroversion." *J Develop Read* 6:106–17 w '63. *

W. V. CLEMANS, *Director, Test Department, Science Research Associates, Inc., Chicago, Illinois.*

The 1960 series of *Cooperative English Tests* continues the format of similar Cooperative tests first developed in the 1930's. The Manual for Interpreting Scores states that "most of the items in the Reading Comprehension tests are simply revisions of items in previous forms, and the 1960 reading passages include a selection of the best passages from previous forms." But it also states that no item in the 1960 series is identical to an item in an earlier form.

The series contains three forms at each of two levels. Forms 2A, 2B, and 2C were designed for grades 9 through 12, and Forms 1A, 1B, and 1C for college freshmen and sophomores. It is suggested in the Directions for Administering and Scoring that for above average twelfth graders the examiner might prefer the upper series. This reviewer takes a much stronger position: the upper series *should* be used in such instances; in fact, a strong argument can be made that it should be used with average twelfth grade students as well, for the lower level forms contain some passages that border on the childish, and lack ceiling for twelfth graders. For example, the range of raw scores for twelfth grade students scoring in the highest quarter on the level of comprehension section of Form 2A is from 27 to the maximum of 30—hardly enough for valid discrimination. Of course, the tests in the lower series can and probably should be used with below average twelfth graders.

Aside from the problem of form selection, the instructions for administration and scoring are explicit and complete.

Raw scores on all forms are converted to a common scale. The statement in the manual that the scores are directly comparable from form to form can be misleading, because the forms do not have the same range of converted scores. But even for that section of the range where pairs of scores exist the claim can be questioned. For example, a student taking 2A must get 30 per cent of the level of comprehension questions correct to earn a converted score equivalent to zero correct on Form 1B. In fact, more than half of the converted score scale for the Form 2A level of comprehension test is related to a raw score performance on Form 1B that is at chance or below. The term "directly comparable" applies better to other sections of the range.

The samples used for norming the tests were well selected and adequately described. Tables are presented by grade giving percentile bands for converted score equivalents. The upper limit of each band corresponds to a score approximately one standard error of measurement above the midpoint of the converted score interval and the lower limit is a like distance below the midpoint. Referring to these bands the Technical Report states, "It is hoped that this form of presentation will encourage more realistic interpretation of scores." This is a worthy goal, but its achievement is impeded by the directions given for interpreting the bands. To illustrate, in the Manual for Interpreting Scores it is stated, "Stanley's score falls between the 75th and 90th percentiles for this group. This means that only about 10 per cent of freshmen in the norms group score higher and about 75 per cent score lower."

This statement is misleading. It confuses two concepts, namely, percentile rank and the probable location of a "true" percentile rank. Percentile rank for an individual will vary between administrations of the same test as well as between parallel forms, and it is important to make this clear. But the percentile rank for *any* individual on *one administration* is a point on the percentile scale. The percentile band could have been made wider—for example, plus and minus two standard errors of measurement. If the wider band were used, this would not mean that a smaller percentage of the norm group scored above and below Stanley. It would merely mean that the band is more likely to include the percentile corresponding to Stanley's "true" score. If Stanley's performance on a single administration of a test is equivalent to a percentile rank of 84, it can be said that on that particular test at a particular point in time he marked more questions correctly than 84 per cent of the norm population. If his percentile band is 75–90 it can also be said that it is likely that the percentile corresponding to the mean score he would obtain based on repeated administrations of similar forms would fall in this range. But it should not be stated nor implied that "only about 10 per cent of freshmen in the norms group score higher and about 75 per cent lower." This statement misinterprets the significance of the band. Earlier in the manual, in a section explaining why the publisher lists percentile bands, a more accurate description of their meaning is presented.

The reliability coefficients (test-retest) reported are very much the same from form to form. Typical are the values reported for Form 1C based on twelfth graders: vocabulary, .88; level, .77; speed, .83; and total, .92. No reliability coefficients are reported for college students.

Because of the nature of the tests, validity is defended largely on the basis of "relying on well-qualified people to construct the tests." A summary of several validity studies relating to earlier forms is given.

In summary, with some exceptions, the manuals are quite good. The tests, on the other hand, leave something to be desired. By the nature of the scores reported, a major purpose seems to be the differentiation of speed and level of comprehension, and yet the data supplied suggest that except for unreliability these two variables are perfectly correlated. Good manuals can help assure that the basic qualities of a test will be realized, but the best of manuals can do nothing to improve those qualities.

W. G. Fleming, *Assistant Director, Department of Educational Research, Ontario College of Education, University of Toronto, Toronto, Ontario, Canada.*

The *Cooperative English Tests* have been in use for many years. During this time they have undergone substantial revisions, and a great deal of background and interpretative information has been accumulated. A number of critics have commented on successive editions in *The Mental Measurements Yearbook*. It seems reasonable to examine the 1960 edition with particular reference to the points raised by these critics.

There has been frequent comment on the care taken to obtain the services of highly competent people to construct and edit the items. The most up-to-date and appropriate statistical techniques have been applied in the tryout and analysis of the items. As a result, the finished product has been unusually free from the kind of flaw that proves irritating in so many standardized tests.

The new edition gives even more grounds for satisfaction with the competence shown in construction and editing of the items, the format, and the adequacy of instructions for administration and interpretation of results. The Manual for Interpreting Scores should make a real contribution to the education of teacher-users with little training in statistics and measurement. In particular, the explanation of the use of the percentile band should help to improve understanding of the meaning and importance of errors of measurement.

Some of the earlier critics were concerned about the validity of the tests. Perhaps their main apprehensions had to do with the test of English expression, which the present reviewer does not propose to deal with, as a measure of the student's ability in written expression. The question of validity is also very important for the reading comprehension test. Validity coefficients obtained from a number of studies are presented in the Technical Report, not only for total reading, but also for vocabulary, level of comprehension, and speed of comprehension. These studies are based on earlier editions of the tests, but it is claimed, not unreasonably, that the latest edition is enough like these that the findings may be considered relevant. While some of the reported validity coefficients are reasonably high, both in absolute terms and in comparison with those based on other similar test scores, others are not particularly impressive. They tend to reinforce existing evidence that the user of the tests should not rely on them to the exclusion of other forms of examinations, whatever the defects of the latter may be, if he wants to obtain a satisfactory evaluation of the many facets of a student's development in English. Of course it has never been reasonable to complain, and certainly cannot now be suggested, that the publishers have made exaggerated claims about the meaning or value of the scores.

An area of potentially fruitful study in the continuing process of improving and perfecting the tests has to do with the degree of emphasis on different types of items. One aspect of this problem concerns the optimum balance between vocabulary and reading comprehension items, assuming that there are no other categories that deserve inclusion along with these two. There must necessarily be a degree of arbitrariness in the decision to have 60 items in each of the two subsections. A continuing examination of statistical evidence and of informed opinion on the advisability of maintaining the present arrangement is indicated.

Another aspect of the same problem has to do with the degree of emphasis on different types of reading passages, such as exposition, narration, and argumentation, and, as a parallel in the vocabulary section, on words commonly used as conveyors of objective information as opposed to those generally used to communicate feeling or emotion. It seems to the reviewer that the utilitarian aspects of the language have predominated in the construction of the tests to the extent that teachers who place a high value on reading for inspirational or aesthetic purposes may be somewhat unhappy with the result. Even though it may be validly pointed out that a very large proportion of reading is done for the "practical" purposes of obtaining information or ideas, there are good arguments for a higher proportion of passages intended to produce emotional effects. More feeling-toned words in the vocabulary section might also tend to meet criticism of this type.

Assuming the appropriateness of the chosen frame of reference, the reading passages are quite satisfactory. On the whole, they are good examples of clear, straightforward language. The item writers have avoided resorting to obscurity or muddiness in their search for difficulty.

Past criticisms of inadequacies in information on reliability have been met. Reliability coefficients between alternative forms are presented for different parts of the tests and for different grade groups. These are satisfactorily high.

Norms information was also criticized at one time for lack of sufficient detail on the types of schools selected. Such information cannot now be considered unsatisfactory. The approach has been to use rather small numbers of students from a relatively large number of institutions. Also, the limitations of "national" norms and the advisability of obtaining and using local norms are pointed out.

In general, it is evident that the test producers have been keenly alert for weaknesses suggested by critics and by users of the tests in practical situations, and have gone to considerable lengths to correct these. The latest edition of *Reading Comprehension: Cooperative English Tests* will be welcomed as a definite contribution to the science of measurement.

For reviews by Robert Murray Bear and J. B. Stroud of the earlier edition, see 3:497. For reviews of the complete battery, see 256; for reviews of earlier editions, see 3:120.

[807]

***Reading: Public School Achievement Tests.** Grades 3–8; 1928–59; subtest of *Public School Achievement Tests;* Forms 1, 2, ['28, 8 pages]; battery manual ('59, 20 pages, essentially the same—including norms—as 1928 manual); no data on reliability; $3.50 per 35 tests; 25¢ per battery manual; 50¢ per specimen set; postage extra; 40(45) minutes; Jacob S. Orleans; Bobbs-Merrill Co., Inc. *

For reviews of the complete battery, see 40:1194.

[808]

***SRA Achievement Series: Reading.** Grades 1–2, 2–4, 4–6, 6–9; 1954–64; subtest of *SRA Achievement Series;* title on tests for grades 2–6 is *What Is This About?;* 2–5 scores: comprehension, vocabulary, verbal-pictorial association (grades 1–2 only), language perception (grades 1–2 only), total (Forms C and D only); 2 editions; battery teacher's handbook ['64, c1955, 47 pages] for both editions; 50¢ per teacher's handbook; postage extra; Louis P. Thorpe, D. Welty Lefever, and Robert A. Naslund; Science Research Associates, Inc. *

a) FORMS A AND B. Grades 1–2, 2–4, 4–6, 6–9; 1954–64; IBM for grades 4–9; 4 levels; battery school administrator's manual ('58, c1955–56, 32 pages); battery technical supplement, second edition ('57, 45 pages); battery pupil progress and profile charts ('59, c1955–59, 4 pages); separate answer sheets must be used in grades 4–9; 90¢ per 20 pupil progress and profile charts; 50¢ per school administrator's manual; $1 per technical supplement; $1.50 per specimen set of any one level of the complete battery.

1) *Grades 1–2.* 1958–61; Form A ('58, 29 pages); battery examiner's manual ('58, revised '61, 21 pages); mimeographed technical data supplement ('59, 3 pages) for the battery; $3.50 per 20 tests; 120(185) minutes in 4 sessions.

2) *Grades 2–4.* 1955–60; Forms A ('55), B ('57), (15 pages); battery examiner's manual, third edition ('60, c1955–60, 27 pages); $2 per 20 tests; 50¢ per hand scoring stencil; 90(130) minutes in 2 sessions.

3) *Grades 4–6.* 1954–60; IBM; Forms A ('54), B ('56), (16 pages); battery examiner's manual, second edition ('56, c1954–56, revised '60, 39 pages); $2.15 per 20 tests; $5 per 100 IBM scorable answer sheets; $1 per set of machine scoring stencils; 50¢ per hand scoring stencil; 65(80) minutes.

4) *Grades 6–9.* 1954–60; IBM; Forms A ['55], B ('56), (18 pages); battery examiner's manual, second edition ('56, c1955–56, revised '60, 39 pages); $2 per 20 tests; $5 per 100 IBM scorable answer sheets; 50¢ per either hand or machine scoring stencil; 70(80) minutes.

b) FORMS C AND D. Grades 1–2, 2–4; 1955–64; 2 levels; battery test coordinator's manual ('64, c1961–64, 64 pages); battery pupil progress and profile charts ('64, c1955–64, 4 pages); 90¢ per 20 pupil progress and profile charts; 50¢ per test coordinator's manual; $2 per specimen set of both levels of the complete battery.

1) *Grades 1–2.* 1958–64; Forms C ('58, revised '63), D ('63), (36 pages); Form C is essentially the same as the 1958 Form A except for typography, art work, 1 new item, revision in 13 items, and option order changes in 3 sets of items; battery examiner's manuals (45 pages): Form C ('58, revised '64), Form D ('63, c1958–63, revised '64); $3.50 per 20 tests; 120(185) minutes in 4 sessions.

2) *Grades 2–4.* 1955–64; Forms C ('55, revised '63), D ('57, revised '63), (25 pages); tests are revisions, with approximately 24 per cent new items, of Forms A and B published in 1955 and 1957, respectively; battery examiner's manual ('64, c1955–64, 43 pages) for each form; $2 per 20 tests; 90(120) minutes in 2 sessions.

EDWARD B. FRY, *Professor of Education, Rutgers, The State University, New Brunswick, New Jersey.* [Review of Forms A and B.]

The reading tests of the *SRA Achievement Series* are carefully thought out, nicely prepared, and widely standardized. They can be recommended for group testing of average and above average pupils subject to the limitations stated below.

The authors have done an excellent job of stating objectives and in attempting to keep them in harmony with well known curriculum committee recommendations. The reading items have been classified according to types of skills required to answer them, and thus the tests go a long way to refute the critics of multiple choice testing who can only see that type of item as valid for examination of simple facts. One might wonder why more use was not made of Bloom's *Taxonomy of Educational Objectives* when classifying items, but nonetheless, a creditable job was done.

However, the fact that the individual items cover a wide range of skills does not justify the statement found in the administrator's manual that "Test Scores provide a basis for discovering and correcting the causes of poor achievement." In fact, only in the broadest sense can this statement be made. A counselor might do a gross kind of diagnosis in certain cases; for example, if all reading scores were down and all or most arithmetic scores were up.

There is apparently much overlap between vocabulary and comprehension, the only two reading scores given above grade 2. Product-moment correlations between vocabulary and comprehension range from .75 to .81 for various grade levels between second and ninth grade. Probably much of this is due to the authors' "holistic approach" which means that comprehension is based on items immediately following the reading of a paragraph or two, and vocabulary is tested on words used (and underlined) in the same sample paragraph. In brief, the vocabulary subtest and the comprehension subtest seem to be measuring much the same thing; this is not necessarily bad, as they are both important reading comprehension skills and taken together they undoubtedly give important information about the student's reading ability. The teacher, however, should not assume that he is measuring two different skills.

These reading tests should not be used with below average pupils. There are several reasons for this. First, the authors state in the Technical Manual:

> Each battery has been so constructed that it does not contain easy items suitable for the seriously retarded pupil to answer correctly, and only a relatively few items simple enough for the low-average learner to handle successfully. However, the upper level of each test battery has been extended sufficiently so that it overlaps the next higher battery to a considerable extent.

The second reason for being wary and often, in fact, disregarding low scores, is that these tests, in common with most achievement tests, do not have a cutoff point at the chance guessing probability score. For example, if a student just guessed at each item on the reading vocabulary section for the grades 1–2 test, on the average he would get a raw score of 10 (there are 41 four-choice items) and this would yield a grade level score of 1.6. On the grades 2–4 form his guessing score for vocabulary would place him at grade level 2.1; on the 4–6 form it would be 3.9, and on the 6–9 form his guessing vocabulary score would be 5.7. Notice what nice progress the nonreading student can make by just guessing at higher forms. Is it any wonder that school superintendents refuse to have remedial reading programs based on such evidence?

It seems to this reviewer that publishers and authors should stop putting out this type of misinformation since, unfortunately, some teachers and school administrators will think that a reading vocabulary score of 5.7 is telling them something about the student when in fact it may only mean that the student was adroit enough to fill in one blank for each question. A cutoff point at least one standard error above the guessing probability score would remedy most of this, and the fact that the user was refused a grade level score would more often force him to give the next lower level test, as should be done anyway.

It is very difficult to assess reading ability with nationally standardized tests at the very beginning reading levels (under grade 3) because the child's knowledge of words is so constricted by the particular reading series of textbooks in which he has received instruction. This reviewer, having spent a good many hours with his knees forced under a little table and a primer in hand, was somewhat bothered by the vocabulary used in the grades 1–2 form of the test. The fourth item in the verbal-pictorial association subtest, for example, asks the child to connect one of eight pictures to each of the four following words: "bride, geyser, dairy, incline." This opinion about word difficulty was substantiated by *The Teacher's Word Book of 30,000 Words* by Thorndike and Lorge, who state that those words should be taught at grades 5, 8, 6, and 4, respectively. To a lesser extent this criticism is also true of the other subtests at the 1–2 level. The Spache readability formula for the two longer and more difficult (of five) sample paragraphs used in the comprehension subtest are at difficulty level 2.5 and 3.3.

The supplementary material such as scoring keys and manuals for the examiner, teacher, and administrator, and the Technical Supplement are all well done and helpful.

In summary, the SRA reading tests are good for measuring general reading ability of average and above average students. They are not recommended for below average pupils as the results are sometimes questionable and sometimes worthless unless extreme care is taken in selecting the proper form. A seventh grader with only a very mild reading problem should be given the 4–6 form and even lower if necessary. Similarly, a teacher with an average fourth grade should use the 2–4 form rather than the 4–6 form.

The difference between the reading vocabulary and reading comprehension sections is not very meaningful, but, separately or together, they give a useful measure of silent reading ability.

The use of the tests in first grade is very questionable and their use before the end of the second grade is somewhat questionable.

For reviews by N. Dale Bryant and Clarence Derrick of Forms A and B, see 5:649. For reviews of Forms A and B of the complete battery, see 21 and 5:21.

[809]

***Sentence Reading Test 1.** Ages 7-6 to 11-1; 1956–60; 1 form ['60, 4 pages, identical with test published in 1956 except for format]; manual ['56, 8 pages]; 5*s.* per 12 tests; 6*d.* per single copy; 1*s.* per manual; prices include purchase tax; postage extra; 15(25) minutes; A. F. Watts; published for the National Foundation for Educational Research in England and Wales; Newnes Educational Publishing Co. Ltd. *

For reviews by Reginald R. Dale and Stephen Wiseman, see 5:652.

[810]

***Sequential Tests of Educational Progress: Reading.** Grades 4–6, 7–9, 10–12, 13–14; 1956–63; IBM, NCS, and Grade-O-Mat; Forms A, B, ('57, c1956–57, 12–18 pages); 4 levels; battery directions ('57, 12 pages); interpretive manual ('57, 30 pages); battery technical report ('57, 58 pages); 1958 SCAT-STEP supplement ('58, 32 pages); 1962 SCAT-STEP supplement ('62, 49 pages); 1963 SCAT-STEP supplement of urban norms ('63, 16 pages); battery teacher's guide ('59, 85 pages); battery profile ('57, 1 page); battery student report ('58, 4 pages); no data on reliability of Form B; separate answer sheets or cards must be used; $4 per 20 tests; $1 per 20 IBM scorable answer sheets; 25¢ per scoring stencil; see 671 for prices of NCS answer sheets and scoring services; see 666 for prices of Grade-O-Mat cards; $1 per 20 profiles; $1 per 20 student reports; $1 per interpretive manual; $1 per technical report; $1 per supplement; $1 per teacher's guide; postage extra; $2 per specimen set, cash orders postpaid; 70(90–100) minutes; Cooperative Test Division. *

a) LEVEL 4. Grades 4–6; Forms 4A, 4B.
b) LEVEL 3. Grades 7–9; Forms 3A, 3B.
c) LEVEL 2. Grades 10–12; Forms 2A, 2B.
d) LEVEL 1. Grades 13–14; Forms 1A, 1B.

REFERENCES

1. MAYER, ROBERT W. "A Study of the STEP Reading, SCAT and WISC Tests, and School Grades." *Reading Teach* 12:117+ D '58. * (*PA* 34:3441)

2. O'SHAUGHNESSY, MARY MICHAEL. *Some Effects of Praise and Reproof on Test Performances on School Ability and Reading Achievement Tests.* Catholic University of America, Educational Research Monograph, Vol. 24, No. 2. Washington, D.C.: Catholic University of America Press, December 2, 1960. Pp. x, 114. *

3. RUDD, JOHN PAUL. *A Study of the Validity of Selected Predictors for Placement in Three-Rail Curricula.* Doctor's research study No. 1, Colorado State College (Greeley, Colo.), 1962. (*DA* 24:184)

4. TRELA, THADDEUS MICHAEL. *A Comparison of Ninth Grade Achievement on Selected Measures of General Reading Comprehension, Critical Thinking, and General Educational Development.* Doctor's thesis, University of Missouri (Columbia, Mo.), 1962. (*DA* 23:2382)

5. ENDLER, NORMAN S., AND STEINBERG, DANNY. "Prediction of Academic Achievement at the University Level." *Personnel & Guid J* 41:694–9 Ap '63. * (*PA* 39:2888)

6. MICHAEL, WILLIAM B.; CATHCART, ROBERT; ZIMMERMAN, WAYNE S.; AND MILFS, MILO. "Gains in Various Measures of Communication Skills Relative to Three Curricular Patterns in College." *Ed & Psychol Meas* 23:365–74 su '63. * (*PA* 38:1384)

EMMETT ALBERT BETTS, *Research Professor, University of Miami, Coral Gables, Florida.*

One of the special features of the STEP series of tests is the inclusion of both reading and listening tests. This attention to listening permits the teacher to note a discrepancy between reading and listening achievement and to take steps to correct the deficit in reading ability. Moreover, the listening test may reveal causes of low achievement in reading, even among so-called superior students.

STEP Reading provides a wide range of types of material: fiction, poetry, rhymes, plays, letters, directions for doing something, announcements, articles of opinion, explanations, and information. These presentations probably are of sufficient length to provide relatively high reliability and to measure the pupil's achievement in dealing with units of material longer than the paragraph.

The test materials appear to be well written by competent craftsmen and interesting to the pupils. At Level 4, for example, there are selections on history, games (horseshoes), a canary and a whale, a railroad yard, safety, how a camera operates, plants, and Edison's birthday, as well as verse, poetry, and a play.

These reading tests provide an adequate coverage of certain thinking abilities. Moreover, these specific learnings are identified by item numbers under appropriate categories in the Teacher's Guide, permitting the teacher to identify "need" areas for teaching purposes. However, the causes of these deficits are not necessarily identified; for example, low achievement on some time test items may indicate a need for word perception skills rather than for "analyzing motivation" or critical reading. These hazards are not identified in the well written materials for the use and interpretation of the tests. In short, these tests, like other achievement tests, have limited use for diagnostic purposes and, therefore, require considerable sophistication on the part of the teacher who interprets them.

STEP Reading is purported to measure five major categories of comprehension skills, abilities, and attitudes: (*a*) ability to recall ideas, (*b*) ability to translate ideas and make inferences, (*c*) ability to analyze motivation (of the author), (*d*) ability to analyze presentation, and (*e*) ability to criticize (constructively). Specific test items, not always sequentially grouped, deal with mood, intent, and tone (i.e., reader relationship to author), ability to visualize, relevance of ideas, sequence of ideas (e.g., in learning to play horseshoes), idiomatic and figurative expressions, and drawing conclusions (related facts and cause-effect).

The above achievements are quite thoroughly examined; however, many important reading-study learnings are untapped: organization (e.g., outlining, charts, etc.), rate and purpose (e.g., skimming, rapid reading, and study-type reading—except by inference on the part of the interpreter), word perception, vocabulary, etc. In short, very little is done on the concept that "reading is thinking in a language."

Users of these tests need to select them with caution. For example, Level 4 tests purportedly are designed for grades 4, 5, and 6, where the range of reading achievement may be from beginning reading to at least twelfth grade. However, the vocabulary of the first selection in Form 4B includes *holiday, swimming, experiments, discovery, invention,* and a number of other words which, in terms of word perception skills, will frustrate the lowest 15 to 20 per cent of a fourth grade class. On the other hand, the most difficult items may not challenge the upper 10 to 20 per cent. Hence, these tests are not wide range tests and are not designed for estimating either a pupil's independent reading level or his instructional reading level. However, they may be used to compare the performance of groups and to screen out those pupils at the "tails" of a distribution.

Hence, caution should be observed in selecting pupils for the administration of a given test. Users of these tests are given sound advice that "the tests at a given level are designed for *typical* students in the grade range indicated." Unfortunately, no provision is made for testing the lower achievers, especially in grade 4, but this point is not made in the guide materials.

PAUL R. LOHNES, *Associate Professor of Education, State University of New York at Buffalo, Buffalo, New York.*

Excellent previous MMY reviews of STEP Reading provide the background for these supplementary comments and must be consulted (see 5:24 and 5:653). The consensus of earlier opinions seemed to be that these were carefully and skillfully constructed reading tests of high quality and promise, but that ETS had not furnished sufficient research evidence of validities. The usefulness of the converted scores was questioned because all interpretations of scores depended on percentile bands. The failure to provide alternate forms reliabilities was scored. This reviewer concurs with the earlier reviews in general, and will attempt to critique the present adequacy of STEP Reading research, as reported in all manuals now available. Since scores from a particular test are only meaningful when we know how they relate to scores from other sources, the research in question must be concerned with the SCAT-STEP battery and other school achievement measures, and not solely with STEP Reading. Two major deficiencies of the original published SCAT-STEP research which have not been reduced by more recent publications continue to plague users of STEP Reading, and the delineation of these two problems constitutes the burden of this review.

The first deficiency is the total lack of evidence regarding the factorial compositions of the reading tests. It is admitted that the tests measure a complex set of reading skills, but no evidence is forthcoming to support the contention that the chosen "five major reading-for-comprehension skills" are major components of reading ability, or that the STEP reading tests do actually "weight these five kinds of skills approximately equally." All we know is that a committee of authorities agreed on this breakdown of reading into component skills. With due respect for the committee, it would be highly desirable to have their judgments tested and supported by empirical evidence. This reviewer is surprised that ETS researchers who are so productive of sophisticated factor-analytic studies, testifying to their confidence in the significance of such studies, have allowed a major new test program to be launched and continued for years with no indication that factor analysis is considered pertinent to the establishment of the dimensions of school-developed abilities. Specifically, the claim that five components of reading ability are equally weighted in STEP Reading deserves the empirical test of a factor analysis of the item intercorrelations at each level. The meaningfulness of the results would be greater if the SCAT Verbal were also included. This reviewer suspects that ETS has such research results but has not shared them with STEP Reading users. Possibly the results are embarrassing. If positive support for the design of the reading tests is available in factor-analytic studies, ETS may be hesitant to involve users in the complexities of reports of these results. If so, the agency does educators a disservice, for the ability of ETS staffers to write explanations of technical matters which make those matters comprehensible to lay readers is well proven, and here is an opportunity to educate users on a very important matter, the factorial validities of tests. Since an earlier reviewer charged that the SCAT-STEP battery perhaps provided "a set of measures of general intelligence" (R. W. B. Jackson, see 5:24), it would seem that ETS would have moved to close this gap in the research documentation of the series. This earlier critique was based on inspection of reported correlations between SCAT and STEP tests. To date, no STEP manual reports intercorrelations among the STEP tests. ETS should accept responsibility to contribute, through the SCAT-STEP publications, to users' understanding of the trait composition and organization of the domain of school-developed abilities.

Mention of SCAT-STEP intercorrelations supports the charge of a second major deficiency of the research basis for the test battery, which is the failure to demonstrate differential predictive validities for the tests, and especially for STEP Reading versus SCAT Verbal. The correlations between these tests average about .80 (among 26 coefficients reported on page 13 of the 1957 Technical Report the highest is .87 and the lowest is .72), suggesting the possibility of very similar predictive validities. The one study of comparative validities reported (by R. W. Mayer, 1958 SCAT-STEP Supplement, p. 26) showed both tests correlated .70 with average grades for 271 seventh graders. If this result proved generalizable, it would be possible for the STEP Reading manual to provide instructions for predicting future achievements, making SCAT Verbal scores redundant and unnecessary. This reviewer suspects that little emphasis has been given to predictive validities of STEP Reading in order to avoid raising this question for the user. ETS should accept responsibility to face the challenge of current discussions of school testing programs which imply that the older distinction between aptitude and achievement batteries and the requirement that schools employ both may now be practically unnecessary and theoretically confusing. By describing the SCAT tests as measures of school-developed abilities ETS has moved in this direction, but the question of whether all uses of SCAT could be developed from STEP remains unanswered. A byproduct of a complete merger of scholastic aptitude and achievement tests might be the abandonment of the over- and under-achievement mythology, now fostered by the proposal for comparing STEP Reading and SCAT Verbal scores for individuals (1957 Interpretive Manual, p. 9).

Some other points on STEP Reading: (*a*) Users should ponder the report of marked sex differences at all grades (1957 Technical Report, p. 23). Should separate sex norms be prepared? (*b*) Ponder also the excellent report on reliabilities of difference scores (1958 SCAT-STEP Supplement, pp. 27–9) before interpreting profiles, especially reading versus writing differences, where the reported reliability is .04. (*c*) The report of a study by J. R. Cleary showing high alternate forms reliabilities in a particular situation, although not definitive, is comforting (1962 SCAT-STEP Supplement, p. 30).

This review has not summarized the many positive features of the STEP reading tests and manuals because they have been reviewed before. It has been argued that ETS should document the factorial composition and predictive validities of the tests.

For reviews by Eric F. Gardner, James R. Hobson, and Stephen Wiseman, see 5:653. For reviews of the complete battery, see 25 and 5:24.

[811]

***Silent Reading Tests.** Standards 1–3 (ages 7–10), 3–8 (ages 10–15), 6–10 (ages 13–17); 1947–63; 3 levels; postpaid; specimen set not available; Afrikaans edition available; National Bureau of Educational and Social Research. *

a) SILENT READING TEST (ELEMENTARY). Standards 1–3; 1947–63; 4 tests; instructions and norms ['62, 13 pages]; no data on reliability; prices range from R1.38 to R2.73 per 100 tests.
1) *Paragraphs.* Forms A ['63], B ['51], (7 pages, essentially the same as 1947 tests); 20(30) minutes.
2) *Sentences.* Forms A, B, ['51, 5 pages, essentially the same as 1947 tests]; 15(20) minutes.
3) *Vocabulary.* Forms A, B, ['61, 4–5 pages, essentially the same as 1947–51 tests]; 10(15) minutes.
4) *Speed.* Forms A, B, ['51, 4 pages]; 4(7) minutes.
b) SILENT READING TESTS (REVISED EDITION). Standards 3–8, 6–10; 1947–63; 3–4 scores: vocabulary, paragraphs, sentences (junior level only), language usage; items of vocabulary, paragraphs, and sentences subtests taken from 1947 forms of the earlier edition; 2 levels; revised manual ('63, 42 pages); separate answer sheets must be used; R0.47 per 100 answer sheets; R0.06 per scoring stencil.
1) *Junior.* Standards 3–8; 1947–63; Forms A, B, ['58, 25 pages]; R5.00 per 100 tests of Form A; R8.98 per 100 tests of Form B; 90(95) minutes.
2) *Senior.* Standards 6–10; 1951–63; Forms A, B, ['58, 20 pages]; R5.00 per 100 tests; 72(77) minutes.

[812]

★**Southgate Group Reading Tests.** Ages 6-0 to 7-6, 7-0 to 8-11; 1959–62; 2 tests; postage and purchase tax extra; Vera Southgate; University of London Press Ltd. *
a) TEST 1—WORD SELECTION. Ages 6-0 to 7-6; 1959; Forms A, B, C, (4 pages); manual (23 pages); 6*s.* 3*d.* per 25 tests; 4*d.* per single copy; 2*s.* 6*d.* per manual; (15–20) minutes.
b) TEST 2—SENTENCE COMPLETION TEST. Ages 7-0 to 8-11; 1962; Forms A, B, (4 pages); manual (20 pages); 7*s.* 6*d.* per 25 tests; 6*d.* per single copy; 2*s.* 6*d.* per manual; 15(30) minutes.

M. L. KELLMER PRINGLE, *Director, National Bureau for Co-operation in Child Care, London, England.*

The aim of Test 1 of the *Southgate Group Reading Tests* is to provide teachers with a simple and speedy method of making a preliminary assessment of the reading ability of young children who are in the initial stages of mastering the subject. The author's purpose was to fill a need which existed in England since there was no group test available with norms extending much below the seven year level. In the manual it is suggested that the test is most useful for average children between the ages of 6 and 7½ years and for older children up to 14 years who are slow in learning to read. Norms are given for reading ages of 5 years 9 months to 7 years 9 months. To facilitate retesting, three parallel forms are provided. They each contain 30 items, which consist of five words, one of which is read aloud by the teacher and ringed by the pupil; 16 of the items are accompanied by a drawing illustrating the correct word. The design and layout are excellent, the printing and the drawings being bold, clear, and well spaced out. The manual states that the 450 words were selected from 676 items on the basis of item analyses. While the words appear to be well within the comprehension of 6- to 8-year-olds, no information is given as to how they were chosen in the first place. Otherwise the manual contains all the required basic information which is set out simply and lucidly. However, one point needs attention when the instructions for administering the test are reprinted: it is stated that the key word is to be repeated twice; in fact, in the first 10 items, for which the instructions are given in full, the key word is repeated three times for three items and four times for one item. Since this applies to all three forms, it appears to be deliberate. There may well be a good reason for this, but in that case it should be given and the wrong instruction deleted.

The standardisation sample consisted of all the children in Worcester's 32 infant and primary schools who were between the ages of 5 years 8 months and 8 years 1 month; the total number was 2,329. Each pupil completed two of the three parallel forms of the test. It is regrettable that the correlation coefficients are not given if they were worked out. Instead, in discussing the reliability of the test, it is stated that a group of 96 children in one school were given two of the parallel forms on different days and that the product-moment correlation coefficient between raw scores was .95.

Test 2 has been designed for use in conjunction with Test 1. Indeed, the author suggests that "when a teacher is in doubt about the ability of the pupils whom he wishes to test, it is kinder to commence by administering Test 1, and to follow it with Test 2 for those who achieve high scores on Test 1, rather than to reverse this procedure." Since each test takes only about a quarter of an hour, this procedure is quite practicable. Norms are given for reading ages of 7 years 0 months to 9 years 7 months. For Test 1 the author recommends that no more than 15 to 20 children should be tested at one sitting. On the other hand, Test 2 can be taken by an entire class of 40 to 50 pupils, but to prevent cheating a simple but ingenious device is used: the practice examples and instructions for administration are identical for the two parallel forms but Form A has been printed on white and Form B on blue paper; thus, when distributing the test booklets the teacher can readily check that children sitting next to each other do not have the same form of the test. The alternative form of the test can of course also be used for retesting but one would have to ensure that children sit in exactly the same position as on the first occasion if the anti-cheating device is to be employed again.

Each form of Test 2 consists of 42 sentences with a choice of five words at the end, from which the child has to choose one to complete the sentence. They are arranged in order of increasing difficulty. Again it is not made clear how the multiple choice items were selected but the author states that "10 separate tests, comprising 584 items, were devised and administered to children within the age range of 6-0 to 10-11 years." It is not clear whether "item" in this context refers to the sentence or to each of the five words accompanying each sentence.

The standardisation of all the tests was carried out in one small cathedral town in the Midlands (population 67,050). "There is no reason to believe," states the author, "that the reading ability of children in Worcester differs markedly from the reading ability of children elsewhere in the country." Since there were no pupils from rural or highly industrialised or metropolitan areas, one would feel more ready to accept this opinion if it were supported by some factual evidence. After all, it is known that there are differences in attainment in different parts of the country.

On all the tests girls tended to achieve higher scores than boys; on Test 2, this difference reached the 5 per cent level of significance on Form B for the age group 8–11. Though the question of establishing separate norms for boys and girls was considered, the author decided against this mainly on the grounds that teachers would find it of greater practical utility to have a level of attainment for their pupils irrespective of sex.

In summary, these reading tests are welcome additions in the armoury of teachers who wish to group large numbers of pupils and to screen for further individual attention those who are backward in the subject. The tests are well presented, statistically adequate, and both easy and quick to administer. Test 1 has the added merit of making possible the group testing of younger or more backward children than has hitherto been feasible in this country, while Test 2 is distinguished for its "anti-cheating" device.

MAGDALEN D. VERNON, *Professor of Psychology, University of Reading, Reading, England.*

These two group tests are intended for British teachers who wish to gain a general idea as to the achievement of children in the early stages of learning to read, and who have no opportunity for individual testing. The first test especially will be of considerable value since there are few if any group tests for beginners available with British norms.

In Test 1, a test for word recognition, the children, who can be tested in groups up to 20, have to select from five alternatives the word spoken to them in each item. In 16 out of 30 items the correct word is also illustrated by a picture. Preliminary examples are given for practice. There is no time limit for the test, but it normally takes 15–20 minutes. Norms are provided for converting scores into reading ages 5-9 to 7-9.

Test 2, a test of reading comprehension, can be used for larger groups by distributing the alternative forms, A and B, so that children sitting side by side have different forms. After preliminary instructions (the same for A and B) as to which word they should choose to complete short sentences, the children work the 42 test items silently within a time limit of 15 minutes. Norms are given for reading ages 7-0 to 9-7. In both tests the norms have been based on the median, not the mean, scores since a number of children on whom the tests were standardized achieved scores of zero or full scores.

The test manuals are extremely clear and readily comprehensible. The author is to be commended for employing no time limit in Test 1, since little children are confused by haste. Presumably she considered that the older children for whom Test 2 is intended are accustomed to speeded performance.

The process of construction appears to have been satisfactory for both tests. Item analysis was carried out with 500–600 trial items, and the items selected with high validity values to cover the required range of difficulty. Reliability for both tests, as calculated by product-moment correlations between alternative forms, is of the order of .95. Mean scores for alternative forms show no significant differences.

The validity of the first test was measured by correlation with performance on five individual word reading tests, the average correlation being .90, and with teachers' estimates of reading ability (rank correlations of .87 and .95 for an earlier duplicated form of the test). The second test was correlated with another sentence completion test and with an individual word reading test, giving correlations of .82 and .88. It is perhaps unfortunate that more tests were not used for validation.

It should be noted that standardization was carried out in one locality only, the city of Worcester. This procedure obviated sampling difficulties since every child in the city schools within the age ranges of 5-8 to 8-1 (2,329 children) for Test 1 and 7-0 to 10-11 (3,751 children) for Test 2 was tested. However, the procedure does raise the question of representativeness. Several investigations have shown that reading achievement varies considerably in different parts of Britain; it is not possible to determine where, other than in Worcester, the norms for these tests are applicable. Again, it is not stated whether the norms were obtained from children taught mainly by look-and-say methods or phonic methods, or both types of methods. It is the reviewer's impression that Test 1 particularly might be easier for children taught by look-and-say since it includes some words, such as "umbrella" and "cigarette," which might be discriminated by length alone, and other words, such as "thought" and "rough," which are so irregular as to be difficult for phonically taught children. Performance on the test might also be affected by differences in familiarity with the test words resulting from the reading books customarily given to the children. Again, we are not informed as to whether a wide or restricted range of these is used in the Worcester schools.

To summarize: The two tests provide a useful coverage for British children in the early stages of learning to read, and they should be valuable to teachers who wish to obtain a general assessment of reading achievement in their classes. Test 1 is probably the best of its kind available. There are other alternatives to Test 2, and its validity is not entirely satisfactory. However, it would certainly be advisable also to apply individual tests to children showing poor achievement, in order to ascertain if they are really backward or were nervous and confused by the group testing situation. Some check on the norms, involving children in other areas and children taught by different methods, would also seem desirable.

Brit J Ed Psychol 30:188 Je '60. P. E. Vernon. [Review of Test 1.] * a useful job * It is a pity, perhaps, that no information is given on the effects of children's familiarity with the tester's pronunciation and of the clarity of his enunciation. The high reliability quoted as between different testers is meaningless, since it is based on a wide age range. However, about half the items are accompanied by pictures; and the correlations of around 0.90 (in a 6-year age group) with individual oral tests, are reassuring. With reading comprehension, as might be expected, the correlation appears to be much lower though the quoted figure—is again—meaningless. The thirty items in each form provide fair discrimination, namely about one to two months per item. Standardisation was based on over two thousand children in the City of Worcester. One wonders whether the assumption that this sample is representative of the country is legitimate, but it had the advantage of being a complete population. The author might also have provided percentiles at successive age levels. She claims, reasonably enough, that teachers do not understand standard scores; but one fears that the absence of indications of spread mean that there is little discrimination among below-average younger, or above-average older, readers.

[813]

***Stanford Achievement Test: [Reading Tests].** Grades 4–5.5, 5.5–6.9, 7–9; 1922–64; same as paragraph meaning and (grades 4–6.9 only) word meaning subtests of *Stanford Achievement Test, [1964 Revision]*; 1953 revision (see 5:656) still available; IBM and MRC; 3 levels; manual ['64, 8 pages] for each level; supplementary directions ['64, 1 page each] for using IBM answer sheets, Harbor answer cards; separate answer sheets or cards may be used; $1.50 per 35 IBM answer sheets; 20¢ per scoring stencil; $2 per 100 Harbor answer cards (machine scoring service, by Measurement Research Center, Inc., may be arranged through the publisher); 40¢ per specimen set of any one level; postage extra; Truman L. Kelley, Richard Madden, Eric F. Gardner, and Herbert C. Rudman; Harcourt, Brace & World, Inc. *

a) INTERMEDIATE 1 READING TESTS. Grades 4–5.5; 2 scores: word meaning, paragraph meaning; Form W ('64, 8 pages); $4.30 per 35 tests; 40(48) minutes.

b) INTERMEDIATE 2 READING TESTS. Grades 5.5–6.9; 2 scores: word meaning, paragraph meaning; Form W ('64, 8 pages); $4.30 per 35 tests; 42(50) minutes.

c) ADVANCED PARAGRAPH MEANING TEST. Grades 7–9; Form W ('64, 5 pages); $4 per 35 tests; 30(35) minutes.

REFERENCES

1–4. See 4:555.
5. TRELA, THADDEUS MICHAEL. *A Comparison of Ninth Grade Achievement on Selected Measures of General Reading Comprehension, Critical Thinking, and General Educational Development.* Doctor's thesis, University of Missouri (Columbia, Mo.), 1962. (*DA* 23:2382)

For reviews by Helen M. Robinson and Agatha Townsend of the 1953 revision, see 5:656; for a review by James R. Hobson of the previous edition, see 4:555; for a review by Margaret G. McKim, see 3:503. For a review of the complete battery, see 26; for a review of the 1953 revision, see 5:25; for reviews of earlier editions, see 4:25 and 3:18.

[814]

★Survey of Primary Reading Development. Grades 1–3.5; 1957; Forms A-1, B-1, (15 pages); manual (48 pages); $2.75 per 20 tests; 50¢ per manual; $1 per specimen set; postage extra; (30–60) minutes in 1–2 sessions; J. Richard Harsh and Dorothy Soeberg; Educational Testing Service (Western Office). *

THOMAS C. BARRETT, *Assistant Professor of Education, The University of Wisconsin, Madison, Wisconsin.*

The *Survey of Primary Reading Development* (SPRD) employs six tests to determine the reading ability of primary grade children. Test 1, Form Comparison, and Test 2, Word Form Comparison, require the student to visually discriminate between pairs of geometric forms and words respectively. Tests 3 and 4, Word Recognition and Sentence Recognition, evaluate the child's ability to hear, remember, and select from among several alternatives a word or sentence pronounced by the tester. Test 5, Sentence Comprehension, measures the ability to select from among three alternatives for each item a word or, in one instance on each form, a group of words which best completes a statement. Test 6, Story Comprehension, includes five stories in each of the two forms. Four to nine statements follow each story and the student is asked to designate from these statements the ones that are true on the basis of what was read.

The manual presents the directions for the six tests in a straightforward, easy to follow manner. Scoring procedures are handled in a similar fashion, and the test user should have little difficulty with the correction process with one possible exception, Test 6, Story Comprehension. Regarding this test, the manual states that it is necessary to determine how many stories a subject actually reads. To achieve this objective, the manual indicates that the subject must circle at least one statement following a story before all the items relating to that story are to be scored. Since only the correct statements are marked by the student, it seems possible that he might read a story and not choose to mark any statements. Potential test users should be alert to this, and the authors might consider altering the directions on this test in future editions so that students will mark both right and wrong statements following the stories.

The SPRD manual presents a discussion of validity under three headings: (*a*) content validity, (*b*) instrumental validity, and (*c*) predictive validity. With respect to content validity, the authors concentrate on the selection of the vocabulary used in the SPRD. They indicate that a composite vocabulary for the SPRD was drawn from samples of dictated stories of primary children and from the most commonly used series of readers. Although this is helpful information, it would have been more useful had the authors stated the number and sources of the experience charts utilized and the number of basic reading series involved, and given a description of the final composite vocabulary. No other information is provided with respect to content validity; therefore, the potential test user is not provided with the authors' rationale for the selection and the weighting of the six tests.

Instrumental validity deals with the concern of the authors to provide the students with a simple and consistent means of indicating responses to the items so that the ability to follow directions does not confound the results. This is commendable; however, as indicated above the simplicity of this means of indicating responses may be detrimental to the scoring of Test 6.

Regarding predictive validity, the manual reports a correlation coefficient of .79 between the SPRD and the assigned levels of reading competency of each child in an unidentified sample of children determined by a reading specialist using a diagnostic battery of reading tests, which is not described in terms of validity and reliability. The lack of information about the sample, the criterion, and the procedures used to obtain the validity coefficient leaves much to be desired.

Three reliability coefficients for the SPRD

are reported in the manual. Two of these are coefficients of internal consistency based on *n*'s of 87 and 304 and obtained by split-half analyses. The coefficients in these two instances are both .91; however, no information about the subjects sampled or the form or forms of the SPRD used in the analyses are provided. A third reliability coefficient of .88 is reported for a test-retest analysis of Form A-1 involving a sample of 128 subjects. In general, the reliability information for the SPRD is inadequate. Moreover, no reliability coefficients regarding the equivalence of the two forms, A-1 and B-1, are made available; thus, comparability of the two forms is left in doubt.

Grade placement norms are provided for both forms. These norms are based on relatively large samples of first, second, and third grade children drawn from eight school systems in Los Angeles County. Although mention is made of the intent to obtain a representative sample in terms of socioeconomic status, community size, population mobility, and scholastic characteristics, the only specific information about the standardization sample offered is: a brief description of six communities used in the sample; a statement that the average age of the sample upon entering first grade was six years and two months; and a statement that the standardization sample had a normal distribution of intelligence with a mean of 101 and a standard deviation of 15 on an unidentified intelligence test. Fortunately, the manual does recommend that communities using the SPRD would benefit if local norms were developed because of the nature of standardization sample.

In addition to the grade placement norms, the manual presents a scale which places students in six descriptive levels of reading development on the basis of their total scores on the SPRD. These levels of reading development are then related to instructional activities presented in the last 13 pages of the manual. Although the levels of reading development and the correlated instructional activities would be helpful to the classroom teacher, the accuracy of the SPRD in indicating such levels is not verified by the technical information in the manual.

In conclusion, the SPRD has a number of apparent technical limitations, e.g., inadequate information concerning reliability and validity, and a standardization sample drawn from a provincial population. Nevertheless the SPRD does sample behaviors that are accepted characteristics of reading development in the primary grades, and it may be useful, at best, as a supplementary instrument for estimating reading development for primary grade students.

RUSSELL G. STAUFFER, *Professor of Education, and Director, The Reading Study Center, University of Delaware, Newark, Delaware.*

The principal use of this test is, as the test name implies, to survey reading development and, as the manual indicates, the survey is for all children in the first, second, and beginning third grade. It is also suggested that the test might be used with special training class pupils, middle and upper grade elementary pupils who are low achievers, and as part of a battery of tests for individual pupil study. To serve in these different ways the test is designed in six parts so as to "offer some success to a child regardless of his level of reading * the variety of exercises allows the child at the beginning level of reading development to complete some items successfully and also provides some challenge for the student at a more advanced level."

The word "survey" as used in this test seems to apply then to the range of skills exemplified by the six parts and not to the range of achievement that might be found in a typical population such as that used in the standardization. The test does not have enough top to allow a capable third grade level pupil to show his achievement. It is a well established fact that pupils at the first grade level typically display a range of reading achievement of five years. This being the case, this test may survey range of achievement only for first grade level pupils, since it does not have enough top to survey the range of pupils at a second or third grade level.

Examination of the six parts shows that the first four parts are not really tests of ability to read. Part one deals with geometric form discrimination and, as the accompanying manual states: "High scores may be made by children ....even though they may be unable to read." The second part requires pupils to recognize whether words, rather than geometrical forms, are alike or different in appearance. Again, good scores may be obtained by children "even though they may be unable to attach meanings to the words." Tests 3 and 4 require the pupil to listen to the examiner pronounce either a word or a short sentence and then mark in the test the word or sentence that says the same thing. This kind of aid to recognition whereby the teacher does the reading orally falls far short of a test in which a pupil must either use a picture as a stimulus or deal on his own with printed words. Parts five and six require pupil ability to read. However, the number of items is limited to nine and five, respectively, and their structure is quite simple.

Each part is scored separately. A total raw score can be converted into a grade placement equivalent. Test users are cautioned about the use of grade placements for individual children because, for example, "a grade placement of 2.3 does not have a statistically significant deviation from 2.4 or 2.2 for an individual child." The manual also says that a total score usually describes a "frustration level" rather than an "instructional level" for a pupil. No evidence is provided to support this claim. A scattergram analysis is provided to allow pupil placement at one of six levels. Each level is briefly described. Again, no evidence is cited to support either the levels or skills listed for instructional purposes at the different levels.

It is claimed that a feature of this test is the suggested instructional activities recommended for use with pupils placing at one or another of the six different levels. These activities are located in the manual of instructions. They are not to be thought of as remedial in nature. Predictive validity for such subclassifications of pupils and recommended instructional activities are based on one validity study conducted by a reading specialist in a summer workshop. This is hardly an adequate means of determining validity.

[815]

★Survey of Reading Achievement: California Survey Series. Grades 7–9, 9–12; 1959; all items from *California Reading Test, 1957 Edition;* IBM; 2 levels; $2.80 per 35 tests; separate answer sheets may be used; 5¢ per IBM answer sheet; 20¢ per scoring stencil; 10¢ per series class record sheet; 2¢ per series individual record sheet; postage extra; 50¢ per specimen set of either level, postpaid; 40(45) minutes with answer sheets, 37(42) minutes without answer sheets; Ernest W. Tiegs and Willis W. Clark; California Test Bureau. *

a) JUNIOR HIGH LEVEL. Grades 7–9; Forms 1, 2, (11 pages); no specific manual; combined manual (20 pages) for this test, test 638, and the junior high level of test 280.

b) ADVANCED. Grades 9–12; Forms 1, 2, (12 pages); no specific manual; combined manual (20 pages) for this test, test 591, and the advanced level of test 280.

CLARENCE DERRICK, *Professor of English, and Chairman, Humanities Department, University of Florida, Gainesville, Florida.*

The *Survey of Reading Achievement,* one of four separate tests adapted from the longer *California Achievement Tests,* is a 40-minute, 100-item test designed to measure achievement in vocabulary and reading comprehension. The items are "spiraled," i.e., arranged in blocks—vocabulary, comprehension, vocabulary, comprehension. A variety of skills are sampled—ability to recognize synonyms and antonyms; ability to follow directions and use the dictionary; ability to interpret graphs, charts, and maps; ability to draw inferences and deductions in reading. A 20-page manual for each level provides information on reliability, validity, and equivalence of forms, and directions for administering, scoring, and interpreting the test results. The normative population is described; and percentile, standard score, grade placement, and age norms tables are supplied.

Test items can always be criticized. The general rule is that no one ever likes an item written by someone else. The items in this series are distinctly above average, but there are flaws. A useful technique is to attempt to answer reading comprehension items *before* reading the selection (I wish the publishers would stop calling their selections "stories"). On Form 1, grades 7–8–9, items 59–67, this reviewer answered correctly 8 out of the 9 questions about Switzerland without looking at the passage. Fortunately, most of the items in the test stood up better when examined by this technique. The map in this same form is too small. Again fortunately, comparable items in the other forms did not have this defect. Some of the "following directions" items have the flavor of aptitude tests. The number of items testing a particular study skill is necessarily small, but this is a survey test reporting only a single score.

The statistical data are reasonably adequate. One might ask whether it is advisable to report scores in such a variety of ways. In the ancient days, grade placement and age norms were used. Standard scores and percentile ranks are improvements. One suspects that the publisher is listening to the voice of the uninformed consumer, but publishers have an obligation to lead, not follow.

These criticisms are minor. All in all, the

Survey of Reading Achievement is a good test which can serve an important and useful function.

J. RAYMOND GERBERICH, *Visiting Professor of Education, University of Maryland, College Park, Maryland.*

In an era of linear and branching programs, it seems appropriate to trace the genealogy of this test in similar terms. The stock goes back to the *Progressive Achievement Tests,* published in 1933 at four different levels. One of the three parts was also published separately as the *Progressive Reading Test.* Two revisions followed according to the same pattern, the second one in 1943. The Progressive series was followed by the *California Achievement Tests,* almost identical to their immediate predecessors, in 1950. A 1957 revision in which four levels of CAT were expanded to five brought the linear phase of the test series to a close up to the present.

Parallelism, a linear concept, is represented in the quarter century of test history recounted above, except for the minor digressions represented by splitting one level into two in the 1957 edition and by putting out an unrevised hand scoring edition for the elementary and intermediate grades, called the *California Basic Skills Tests.* True branching, however, did not occur until the *Surveys of Achievement* appeared in 1959, to place emphasis on a survey as contrasted with a diagnostic function. The *Survey of Reading Achievement* at two levels, covering grades 7 to 12, is paralleled by survey tests in language and mathematics.

An evaluation of the current reading test that does not take this background into account and that fails to recognize differences between the old and the new seems inadequate to this reviewer. Five reviews of the 1933, 1937, and 1950 editions of the reading tests have appeared in earlier yearbooks of the MMY series. Mention of separate tests in reviews of various editions of the batteries brings critical judgments about the reading tests in the MMY to more than a dozen. It seems appropriate here to examine the current reading test first and then to consider why and how the *Survey of Reading Achievement*—the first test under this title—evolved from the earlier tests of receptive language skills.

The current reading test, paralleled by tests in the areas of mathematics and language, appears at two overlapping levels—"Junior High Level" for grades 7 to 9 and "Advanced" for grades 9 to 12, and in Forms 1 and 2 at each level. Why names for the two levels are not more harmonious does not seem clear, in view of the various name patterns that easily come to mind for the lower and upper portions of the grade 7 to 12 span. Each of the forms at each of the levels includes 100 items in an omnibus format that shifts back and forth, in clusters of from 9 to 20 items, from reading vocabulary to reading comprehension. Vocabulary and comprehension items contribute to the total, and only, score in the ratio of 60 to 40, even though the time necessary to respond to items in these two areas of reading proficiency may well be in the reverse ratio of 40 to 60. The test is timed for 40 minutes with answer sheets and 37 minutes when answers are recorded in booklets.

These tests appear in the two-column format and type styles that have characterized tests of this publisher for many years. The print is clear and legible and the format is in general pleasing. Some undesirable by-products result, however. An occasional item, even a short one, is started in one column and finished in the next. The three lines of directions for one group of items dangles at the bottom of one column and the 20 items fill the next column. Some individual test items are nearly a half column in depth, and in one instance five long items occurring together fill an entire page.

In another place, eight of the nine items based on a story appear on page 8 whereas the two-column story on which the items are based appears entirely on page 7. A pupil taking the test will need to waste much time, and will doubtless suffer some annoyance, in turning back and forth from questions to story as he follows the instructions, "You may look back to find the answers." Since the entire unit occupies slightly less than three and a half columns, the entirety of this exercise could have been put in the four columns of a two-page spread. More than a page and a half at the end of the booklet are unused, so there was no need for economizing on space.

Kuder-Richardson 21 reliability coefficients of .94 and .91 are reported for grade 8 and grade 11, respectively, at the two levels. Means, standard deviations, and standard errors of measurement are also reported for these grades, both in terms of raw scores and of grade placement. No such information appears for grades 7, 9, 10, and 12, however.

Correlations between scores on Forms 1 and 2 are given as .86 and .87 at the lower and higher levels and the means of raw scores are shown to differ only in minor degree. Raw score values at the 90th, 75th, 50th, 25th, and 10th percentiles are also given for the two forms; six of the differences are 1 or 0, three are 2, and one is 3. These data are based on pupils in grades 7 to 9 and grades 9 to 12 at the two levels, but neither the sizes of the samples nor the proportions of pupils at the various grade levels are given. It seems likely that the reduction in range of talent if data were presented for single grades would be reflected at least in lower between-forms correlations.

Evidence concerning test validity depends heavily on subject matter objectives, buttressed by opinions of curriculum specialists and other supposedly qualified critics and by data concerning item difficulty and discriminative power. Average percentages of correct responses to test items are reported as 62 and 64 for the lower and upper levels respectively. Average differences of 35 are shown between the percentages of correct responses for the upper and lower 27 per cent groups at both levels of the test. These indices of difficulty and discriminative power are both reported as averages for the range of grades covered by each level of the test. The dependence on content validity and item characteristics represented here seems not to be inappropriate in a test that purports to measure mastery of basic skills, although more attention could well have been directed toward less traditional and more dynamic instructional outcomes, and data on item characteristics could easily have been presented for the more homogeneous grade groups.

Eighteen geographical areas and four sizes of school communities were systematically sampled in setting up the normative group and a neat, two-stage procedure was used in the process. The results are shown in the 100 classes and 3,420 pupils and the 136 classes and 3,770 pupils involved in the samples for grades 7–9 and grades 9–12, respectively. A number of desirable precautions were also taken in the attempt to have the testing done under optimum conditions. Norms are presented in the form of grade equivalents, age equivalents, percentiles by grade levels, and normalized standard scores. The "band" principle of taking unreliability of scores into consideration is represented by a table of percentile ranges in the manual, but the report forms make no direct provision for recording these ranges.

Such supplementary materials as scoring keys, class record sheets, answer sheets, and test manuals are well printed and commendably precise in organization and format. Instructions for administering and scoring the tests, as well as information about reliability, validity, the normative sample, and the norms, are systematically presented in the manuals. However, the manuals fail to fulfill an obligation to test users when they substitute the statement, "the statistics by grades are available upon request" for data about reliability and intercorrelations at each separate grade level. Reliability data for one grade at each level and data on comparability and equivalence of forms for several adjacent grades combined could easily have been replaced by the more definitive and meaningful results for each of the grades that are presumably in the publisher's files.

Individual test items and exercises, consisting of a story or map and many dependent items, are drawn directly, or with minor editorial changes, from various forms of an earlier test in the series. A comparison of Form 2 of the *Survey of Reading Achievement* and Form W of the *California Reading Test,* 1957 edition, both at the junior high level, disclosed that at least 19 individual items and three groups of items totaling 22, two based on stories and one on a map, are either substantially the same or identical. The manual for the survey series points out that Forms 1 and 2 are "produced," respectively, from items in Forms Y and Z and Forms W and X of the longer and more diagnostic 1957 series. It goes on to show how duplication of items can be avoided by selection of the proper forms if pupils take a test in each series.

Two broad trends are evident in the 30-year history of these achievement tests: recognition of new methods of test scoring in their format, accessory materials, and accompanying services; and recognition of the distinction between diagnostic and survey tests in their titles, formats, and score patterns.

The first trend is shown by a progression including hand scoring of booklets, hand scoring of IBM answer sheets, and scoring IBM answer sheets electrically by using the International Test Scoring Machine. Only the first two of these methods are ordinarily practicable in a small school system; the more technical types of scoring services are available from the large-scale scoring centers that are now found in metropolitan areas throughout the country and from the test publisher.

The second trend—away from a professed diagnostic function and toward a survey purpose—may be in some degree a reaction by the authors and publisher to previous MMY reviews. A number of reviewers, both of the Progressive and the California series of achievement tests, pointed out that the tests were analytic rather than diagnostic and that the subtest scores, in the third echelon from the total reading score at the top, were deficient in reliability. It should be noted, however, that the survey tests are an offshoot from the current achievement series at the two upper levels and seem not at all to be designed as replacements for the multiscore tests of achievement.

It is somewhat disturbing to find significant duplication of items, exercises, and even forms among the several recent series of these tests—the 1957 achievement tests, the basic skills tests, and the survey tests. Although the overlaps are admitted in the test manuals, more than ordinary care is required of test users to avoid the possibility of an undesired second use of testing materials. More important, however, is the problem of singling out, from the batteries and tests with overlapping functions as well as content, the test or tests best calculated to fulfill a certain need. It is possible that time and money spent in the development of new forms, tests, and batteries and in greater differentiation among the various components would materially increase the stature and the reputation of this venerable series of achievement tests.

[816]

*__Techniques in Reading Comprehension: Every Pupil Test.__ Grades 7–9, 10–12; 1937–64; test booklet titles vary; new form (8 pages) usually issued each December and April; forms from previous testing programs also available; 2 levels; general directions sheet ('63, 2 pages); no data on reliability; Ohio norms for new forms available following testing program; 5¢ per test; 3¢ per key; postpaid; 40(45) minutes; Ohio Scholarship Tests. *

For reviews by Ivan A. Booker and James M. McCallister of the 1946 forms, see 3:505.

[817]

★**Test of Reading Comprehension.** Business and industry; 1951–63; 1 form ('51, 8 pages); manual ['63, 10 unnumbered pages]; $5.25 per 25 tests; 10¢ per key; $1 per manual; postage extra; $1.25 per specimen set, postpaid; 20(25) minutes; Richardson, Bellows, Henry & Co., Inc. *

[818]

*__Tests of Reading: Cooperative Inter-American Tests.__ Grades 1–3, 2–3, 4–7, 8–13, 10–13; 1950–63; Levels 2 and 5 (*b* and *e* below) called *Test of Reading: Inter-American Series;* a series of parallel tests and manuals in English and Spanish; IBM for grades 4–13; 5 levels; tentative norms (publisher recommends use of local norms); separate answer sheets must be used for grades 4–13; postage extra; 30¢ per specimen set of any one level, postpaid; prepared under the direction of Herschel T. Manuel; Guidance Testing Associates. *

a) PRIMARY LEVEL. Grades 1–3; 1950; 3 scores: vocabulary, comprehension, total; English language Forms AE, BE, ('50, 8 pages); Spanish language Forms AS, BS, ('50, 8 pages); directions ('50, 4 pages); series manual ('50, 18 pages); no data on reliability; no norms for subscores; $2.50 per 25 tests; 30¢ per set of keys; 16(25) minutes.

b) LEVEL 2—PRIMARY. Grades 2.5–3; 1962–63; 4 scores: level of comprehension, speed of comprehension, vocabulary, total; English language Form CE ('62, 12 pages); Spanish language Form CEs ('62, 12 pages); directions ['62, 4 pages]; tentative norms and technical data ['63, 2 pages]; no norms for grade 3; $3.50 per 25 tests; 23(35) minutes.

c) INTERMEDIATE LEVEL. Grades 4–7; 1950; 3 scores: vocabulary, comprehension, total; IBM; English language Forms AE, BE, ('50, 10 pages); Spanish language Forms AS, BS, ('50, 10 pages); combined directions ('50, 5 pages) for this and the advanced level; series manual ('50, 18 pages); no data on reliability; no norms for subscores; $3 per 25 tests; 4¢ per IBM answer sheet; 20¢ per scoring stencil; 40(50) minutes.

d) ADVANCED LEVEL. Grades 8–13; 1950; 3 scores: vocabulary, comprehension, total; IBM; English language Forms AE, BE, ('50, 12 pages); Spanish language Forms AS, BS, ('50, 12 pages); combined directions ('50, 5 pages) for this and the intermediate level; series manual ('50, 18 pages); no data on reliability; no norms for subscores; $3 per 25 tests; 4¢ per IBM answer sheet; 20¢ per scoring stencil; 40(50) minutes.

e) LEVEL 5—ADVANCED. Grades 10–13; 1962–63; 4 scores: level of comprehension, speed of comprehension, vocabulary, total; IBM; English language Form CE ('62, 14 pages); Spanish language Form CEs ('62, 14 pages); directions ['62, 4 pages]; tentative norms and technical data ['63, 7 pages] for this and the Level 5 general ability test of the series; $4 per 25 tests; 4¢ per IBM answer sheet; 20¢ per scoring stencil; 41(50) minutes.

REFERENCES

1–4. See 4:557.
5. CHENAULT, VIVIAN M. *A Study of the Cooperative Inter-American Tests of General Ability and Reading at the Primary Level.* Master's thesis, University of Texas (Austin, Tex.), 1952.
6. MANUEL, HERSCHEL T. "The Use of Parallel Tests in the Study of Foreign Language Teaching." *Ed & Psychol Meas* 13:431–6 au '53. * (*PA* 28:4842)
7. EINSPAHR, MARTIN HARLEY. *The Construction and Validation of Scales for Predicting Academic Success in College.* Doctor's thesis, University of Houston (Houston, Tex.), 1959. (*DA* 20:3366)
8. ZIMMERER, ANN MORGAN. *A Study of Selected Variables for Predicting Success in a College of Engineering.* Doctor's

thesis, University of Houston (Houston, Tex.), 1963. (*DA* 24:842)

For reviews by Jacob S. Orleans and Frederick L. Westover of a *and* c–d, *see 4:557.*

[819]

★W.A.L. English Comprehension Test. High school; 1962–63; 4 scores: vocabulary (2 scores), reading comprehension, total; Form 1 ['62, 8 pages]; mimeographed temporary manual in 2 parts: part 1 ['62, 5 pages], part 2 ['63, 11 pages]; no data on reliability; temporary norms; separate answer sheets must be used; 15*s.* per 10 tests; 3*s.* 6*d.* per 10 answer sheets; 3*s.* per scoring stencil; 4*s.* per manual; 9*s.* per specimen set; postpaid within Australia; 70(75) minutes; Australian Council for Educational Research. *

[Other Tests]

For tests not listed above, see the following entries in *Tests in Print:* 1387, 1389–90, 1392–3, 1397, 1399–400, 1406, 1412, 1415–7, 1419, 1422, 1424, 1428, 1431–4, 1437–8, 1440–1, 1443, 1446–7, 1450, 1456, and 1459–62; out of print: 1396, 1411, 1414, 1444, and 1454.

DIAGNOSTIC

[820]

★California Phonics Survey. Grades 7–12 and college; 1956–63; shortened version of *Stanford Diagnostic Phonics Survey, Research Edition;* 9 error analysis scores for Form 1 (Form 2 yields total score only): long-short vowel confusion, other vowel confusion, consonants-confusion with blends and digraphs, consonant-vowel reversals, configuration, endings, negatives-opposites-sight words, rigidity, total; IBM; Forms 1, 2, ('62) in a single booklet (8 pages); manual ('63, 44 pages); may be administered by examiner but tape recording is recommended; no data on reliability of subscores; $3.50 per 35 tests; $5.95 per tape; separate answer sheets may be used (must be used if tape recording is used); 5¢ per IBM answer sheet; $1.80 per set of scoring stencils; 9¢ per Scoreze answer sheet for Form 1 (not available for Form 2); 50¢ per specimen set without tape ($6.45 with tape), postpaid; (40–45) minutes; Grace M. Brown and Alice B. Cottrell; California Test Bureau. *

REFERENCES

1. Cottrell, Alice B. *A Group Test for Ascertaining Ability in Phonetic Analysis Among College Freshmen.* Doctor's thesis, Stanford University (Stanford, Calif.), 1958. (*DA* 18:1794)

Thomas E. Culliton, Jr., *Assistant Professor of Education, University of Illinois, Urbana, Illinois.*

The *California Phonics Survey* is the result of one of the pioneer attempts to measure the phonic knowledge of groups of students at the junior high through college level. The development of a group test to measure this basic component of reading and writing skill is a very worthwhile project. The substitution of a system involving evaluation of reading and listening for one based on reading and speaking has provided for the first time the opportunity to measure large groups of children. The reported correlation of .89 between the two testing methods is high.

The 75-item test "is divided into five units largely to provide variety in the mode of presentation and to obviate any fatigue effect." The five units do not measure different kinds of phonic skill but rather include items of different structural types. Provision is made for analysis of an individual's performance according to eight diagnostic categories. The pattern of the errors of an individual, when plotted on the profile sheet and interpreted according to the key given in the manual, is a basis for diagnosis and a starting point for remedial work. A detailed analysis of the phonic skills of individual examinees is made possible by the diagnostic keys. An examination of the profile and of the errors made in each category reveals phonic deficiencies which could hinder academic achievement. It indicates the type and extent of remedial work which might prove helpful in individual cases.

Since each of the 75 items on the test presents the possibility for more than one error, it is the specific wrong choice that is diagnostically significant. The test items in this survey "include all of the common speech sounds of the English language in their more usual spellings." Test items were kept simple by omitting spellings affected by regional pronunciations and by limiting the frequency of spellings that may be pronounced in more than one way. The *California Phonics Survey* may be administered by use of a magnetic tape recording or it may be presented orally by a competent language arts teacher. The authors note that "in areas where regional pronunciations, dialect or other speech differences are strongly noticeable, it is preferable" that the teacher present the test rather than utilize the tape recording. The test can be completed within a 45 minute period of time, a very practical consideration in terms of ordinary high school class period duration.

The directions for administering and scoring the test are clear and complete. The examiner is advised to be familiar with the samples, pronunciation, and pace of presentation, as well as the general instructions, before administering the test. Specific directions are given for administering the test by using the tape recording and by oral presentation by the teacher. Complete, clear, and precise directions are provided for machine or hand scoring and for the interpretation of the test results.

The standard error of measurement is used to establish the cutoff points to separate the students with adequate phonic skills from those with some phonic difficulty and those with serious or gross phonic disability.

The initial work on the *California Phonics Survey* was begun in 1954. Since that time, seven versions of the test have been written, administered, and analyzed both experimentally and diagnostically. The final version, the present test, was used in a national standardization program at various grade levels in both public and private schools to obtain the adequate reliability and validity data which are given.

This test was prepared to furnish teachers of grades 7 through college with essential information about the phonic ability of students at these levels. An individual's results will indicate the adequacy of the phonic skills of the student and provide information regarding the type and degree of disability, if one exists. Much care and attention have gone into the construction of this test. The selection of the test items to include all of the common speech sounds in their usual spelling, the careful analysis of the experimental results, and the analysis of diagnostic implications, the preparation of analytical data, and the other details of test construction and standardization appear to be well done. This diagnostic test is a much needed device for measuring a very important aspect of reading.

[821]

★Diagnostic Reading Scales. Grades 1–8 and retarded readers in grades 9–12; 1963; 10 or 11 scores: word recognition, instructional level (oral reading), independent level (silent reading), rate of silent reading (optional), potential level (auditory comprehension), and 6 phonics scores (consonant sounds, vowel sounds, consonant blends, common syllables, blending, letter sounds); individual; 1 form (28 pages); record booklet (29 pages); manual (27 pages); no data on reliability of rate of silent reading and phonics scores; $1 per test; $8.75 per 35 record booklets and manual; 25¢ per single copy of record booklet; 25¢ per manual; postage extra; (45) minutes; George D. Spache; California Test Bureau. *

N. Dale Bryant, *Executive Director, Study Center for Learning Disabilities, State University of New York at Albany and Albany Medical College, Albany, New York.*

These scales provide a logical and well organized approach to diagnosis of reading skills and difficulties. Four major scores and some supplementary measures are provided. Administration and scoring of the major scales is simple and takes relatively little time. The word recognition score is based upon one of three word lists of 40–50 words each. The lists are adequately scaled, and of reasonable reliability (.96, .87, .91, Kuder-Richardson formula 21). Word recognition norms provide grade level scores of 1.3 to 6.5. Only *immediate* responses are considered correct. Words correctly pronounced after a few seconds are counted as errors both in scoring and in determining when to stop testing (this latter point is not clear from the manual but was confirmed by the test author in personal communication with the reviewer). The immediate recognition measure used in this test is particularly valuable, but separate norms should also be given for untimed recognition as well.

It is particularly valuable that the other three major scores—oral reading, silent reading, and auditory comprehension—are based upon the same series of reading selections. Two selections are available at each level 1.6, 1.8, 2.3, 2.8, 3.3, 3.8, 4.5, 5.5, 6.5, 7.5, and 8.5, as determined by readability formulas reflecting vocabulary and sentence length.

Oral reading level is determined by the highest level selection an examinee can read with no more than the average number of errors (for children at that reading level) and with 60 per cent comprehension. The number of errors allowed seems very liberal and, in personal communication, the test author supplemented the manual's description by indicating that the average value referred to the mean plus one standard deviation. This is a logical procedure but one that influences interpretation and comparison with other scores. The manual should clarify this point. Oral reading errors include the standard omissions, additions, substitutions, reversals, repetitions (of more than one word), and aided words (given after five seconds delay). The crucial analysis of types of errors is aided by a checklist of difficulties, but it still requires considerable clinical experience and judgment.

Silent reading level and auditory comprehension level are based entirely upon obtaining 60 per cent comprehension (4 out of 7 or 5 out of 8) on the short answer type questions that follow each selection. Performance on a single selection determines level and this may sometimes produce inaccuracies because of variation in interest, background knowledge, attention, and the approach an examinee brings to a particular selection. Children with reading difficulties are often more variable than normal, so the test-retest (4–10 weeks) reliability of .84 or .88 is not completely reassuring. Test-retest is not the most appropriate measure for evaluating the reliability of comprehension measures since memory is an important factor (indicated in part by an increase in mean silent reading score from 3.5 to 4.1 between test and retest).

The experienced examiner will sometimes note that a child's errors in oral reading of a failed selection, or even in the comprehension test, are not consistent with his performance in previous selections and will, therefore, administer a second selection at the failed level. Such bracketing of the failure level, while not spelled out in the manual, is essential in a few cases, but it may use up the selections so that they are not available for determining silent reading levels or auditory comprehension level. Even one additional selection at each level would almost completely prevent this using up of selections and would increase the usefulness of the test.

The assumptions involved in labeling auditory comprehension as "potential reading level" are not well substantiated. However, this is an important clinical measure since it can detect difficulties in retention and organization of information which are independent of reading. In obtaining the auditory comprehension measure, the user should *not* consider the level of a selection as a grade level norm. While the manual does not discuss this problem, data from Table 7 in the manual make it apparent that regular classroom cases can understand material read to them on an average of two grade levels above their grade placement. In testing over 50 cases with this instrument, the reviewer finds that reading disability cases usually have auditory comprehension scores well above their grade placement, and it is clinically useful to treat any auditory comprehension score below grade placement as indicating a real comprehension problem (probably a general one and one which is likely to interfere with reading comprehension).

While no descriptive data are given on the standardization for the rate of silent reading scores, the time for each selection is classified as slow, average, or fast, and this is probably as specific as one should be on this measure.

The supplementary phonics tests are, as their names suggest, merely supplementary. They are probably as useful as comparable measures in other diagnostic reading tests, but they do not provide an adequate or systematic analysis of usable phonic skills. The experienced clinician, however, will obtain a great deal of information from these supplementary tests, particularly Test 4, Common Syllables, and Test 5, Blending.

There is a potpourri of validity and other studies within the manual which suggest that on normal classroom cases the *Diagnostic Reading Scales* give similar results to the *California Reading Test* and to ratings by first grade teachers, but give rather different results from the reading section of the *Metropolitan Achievement Tests* and the paragraph meaning section of the *Stanford Achievement Test.* Data from one study suggest that the mean instructional level (oral reading) is slightly higher than the mean independent level (silent reading) which contradicts assumptions in the manual and administrative directions. Implication of the data in various tables is not fully explored, and a much more systematic study of the test and more comprehensive manual would be extremely valuable to users. The manual should include particularly a description of the sample on which oral errors were tabulated and the mean and standard deviation of such errors. Also useful would be difficulty indices of test items administered without reading the selections as well as difficulty indices when normal administration is used.

In spite of minor difficulties and the need for a more systematic and effective manual, the four major scores (when accompanied by a clinical analysis of errors) provide one of the most quickly obtainable and most meaningful approaches presently available for the diagnosis of reading skills and difficulties.

[822]

***Diagnostic Reading Test: Pupil Progress Series.** Grades 1.9–2.1, 2.2–3, 4–6, 7–8; 1956–60; various titles used by publisher; some subtests also appear in *Scholastic Diagnostic Reading Test* for Catholic schools; IBM for grades 4–8; 2 forms; 4 levels; $2.40 per 20 tests; separate answer sheets may be used in grades 4–8; $1 per 20 IBM answer sheets; 12¢ per set of scoring stencils; 50¢ per specimen set of any one level; postage extra; Oliver F. Anderhalter, R. Stephen Gawkoski, and Ruth Colestock; Scholastic Testing Service, Inc. *

a) PRIMARY TEST I. Grades 1.9–2.1; 1956–57; referred to as Pre-Primary Test in manual for Form A; 9

scores: vocabulary (word recognition, word to content relation, words in use, total), rate of reading for meaning, comprehension (recalling information, locating information, reading for descriptions, total); Forms A ('56, 11 pages), B ('57, 12 pages); separate manuals for Forms A ('56), B ('57), (9 pages); (40–60) minutes.
b) PRIMARY TEST 2. Grades 2.2–3; 1956–57; referred to as Primary Test in manual for Form A above; 10 scores: vocabulary (words in use, word meaning, total), rate of reading for meaning, comprehension (same as for *a* plus following directions, reading for meaning); Forms A ('56, 12 pages), B ('57, 15 pages); separate manuals for Forms A ('56), B ('57), (11 pages); (40–60) minutes.
c) ELEMENTARY TEST. Grades 4–6; 1956–57; 13 scores: knowledge and use of sources (functions, best sources, use of index, use of table of contents, total), rate of reading for meaning, comprehension (same as for *a* plus word meaning, reading for meaning, reading for directions or procedures); IBM; Forms A ['56, 15 pages], B ('57, 18 pages); separate manuals ('57, 16 pages) for each form; 44(65) minutes for Form A, 48(70) minutes for Form B.
d) ADVANCED TEST. Grades 7–8; 1956–60; 13 scores: same as for *c*; IBM; Forms A ['56, 15 pages], B ('57, 18 pages); manual ['60, 8 pages]; 44(65) minutes for Form A, 48(70) minutes for Form B.

AGATHA TOWNSEND, *Consultant, Educational Records Bureau, New York, New York.*

Tests designated for the diagnosis of individual performance as well as for the description of class status in a field must face the most rigorous scrutiny. Not only must the scores obtained be highly reliable measures, but they must be valid in either curricular terms or in terms of the mental factors involved in the field; frequently, both kinds of validity are desirable. Unfortunately, the title of the *Diagnostic Reading Test: Pupil Progress Series* tends to mislead the user who will assume that the parts meet either of these criteria.

Stauffer, in a review (5:650) of the *Scholastic Diagnostic Reading Test* for Catholic schools, which includes most of the subtests used in the test under review here, observed that the analysis of reading functions was not satisfactory for clinical use, though he praised the curricular validity of certain of the tests at the upper level. Traxler, in the same volume, was critical of the reliability of the part scores. Both these reviews should be consulted; it seems unnecessary to repeat the comments made. It is unfortunate that the publisher has not profited from these suggestions for the improvement of the public school edition.

To the criticism that the test does not give a clinically sound picture of reading problems, this reviewer would like to add that the curricular suitability of the series is also questionable. Two points seem particularly serious. No matter how one conceives the process of learning to read, a good reliable test of word meaning is required in a battery for either survey or diagnostic use. The vocabulary, or word meaning, sections of this series are too short (30–35 items) at the primary 1 and elementary levels, a fact which is noticeable from the reliabilities reported, which average about .88 for each level. At the primary 2 level, however, where there are 65 items in the vocabulary subtests, reliability averages about .95. The brevity of the primary 1 and elementary parts inordinately restricts the word list, particularly at the elementary level. To return to the curricular criterion, I also note that in the absence of any auditory or word attack tests, the teacher is left with no data on the causes for a low word meaning score.

Again, the content of the subtests contributing to the total score related to comprehension, another score which is certainly a minimum requirement, may be questioned. There is undue weight given to factual detail items in all the parts which contribute to this subtotal in all three of the elementary school batteries.

If these two areas of the curriculum are not measured adequately, one is left with the third subtotal, an index of reading rate, which many teachers and reading specialists do not consider of much importance until at least the end of the grade range for the Elementary Test. The reliability of the brief "Rate of Reading for Meaning" part (based on two minutes of testing in grades 1 and 2, and on a sample of 30 seconds length added to another of one minute in the Elementary Test), is about .89 for primary 1, .88 for primary 2, and .94 for elementary.

It will be noted that no statements have as yet been made about the sections of the Advanced Test. While these are designed to continue the outline of the testing done in the primary and elementary levels, no reliability or standard error of measurement data whatever are included in the 1960 manual for the tests for grades 7 to 8 (such data did appear in the earlier, 1957, manuals but they are not repeated). As does the Elementary Test, the Advanced Test has four subtests (60 items) on "Knowledge and Use of Sources." There is much merit in these sections of the tests. Here, the advanced level seems to have greater face validity than the parallel parts of the elementary level. The questions asked are certainly far more realistic. For instance, the elementary level test on the use of the index asks a series of "On which page would you look to find" questions, beginning with (Form A) "how to fill out a job application form" and ending with "something about preparing for a job interview." (The items cited are for grades 4 to 6.) Questions on the advanced level ask "To which page would you turn if" and include such items as "your father was looking for work as a carpenter" and "you wanted to buy a pet rabbit."

The two reviewers for the forms used in Catholic schools also urged extension of the norms to a broader base. It is unfortunate that once again this reviewer must report that the public school forms also have norms based on a very small sampling. They are drawn from 37 schools in 9 states, with total number of pupils going as low as 531 for grade 9, from a high of 1,751 for grade 2.

Much could be done to improve these batteries. The addition of word attack or word analysis materials to the tests below grade 6 seems obvious advice to give. The strengthening of the norms would make it possible to provide fully worked out percentile tables, requiring less interpolation. The two forms could be equated. Most important, interpretive and statistical data could be added to the manual for the advanced level.

Until steps such as these are taken, competing tests should be preferred. Fuller measurement of vocabulary and inclusion of word attack skills is featured by the lower levels of the *Diagnostic Reading Tests,* produced by the Committee on Diagnostic Reading Tests, Inc. Better measurement for interpretation and critical reading is included in the STEP reading test from the Educational Testing Service. More analytical study skills measurement is possible through the *Iowa Tests of Basic Skills.* Moreover, normative data for all these batteries are far more extensive.

[823]

***Diagnostic Reading Tests.** Various grades kgn–13; 1947–63; IBM (except for section 4, part 1) for grades 2–13; 3 levels; interpretation booklet ('52, 42 pages); revised norms booklet ('63, 40 pages); $1 per interpretation booklet; 50¢ per norms booklet; postage extra; Committee on Diagnostic Reading Tests, Inc. *

a) DIAGNOSTIC READING TESTS: KINDERGARTEN THROUGH FOURTH GRADES. Various grades kgn–4 (except for section 4, part 1); 1957–63; 2 sections, 5 booklets; 20¢ per copy of any one booklet; 25¢ per key for any one booklet; 25¢ per directions for any one booklet; $2.50 per specimen set of all forms of all 5 booklets and directions for each.

1) *Survey Section.* Grades kgn–1, 1, 2, 3–4; 1957–63; 4 levels.

(*a*) Reading Readiness Booklet. Grades kgn–1; 5 scores: relationships, eye-hand coordination, visual discrimination, auditory discrimination, vocabulary; Form B ('57, 16 pages); mimeographed directions for administering ['57, 8 pages]; administration time not reported.

(*b*) Booklet 1. Grade 1; 12 scores: visual discrimination, auditory discrimination (3 subscores plus total), vocabulary (3 subscores plus total), story reading (2 subscores plus total); Form A ('57, 23 pages); mimeographed directions ['57, 10 pages]; reliability data for total subscores only; administration time not reported.

(*c*) Booklet 2. Grade 2; 3 scores: word recognition, comprehension, total; IBM; Forms A, B, ('57, 15 pages); mimeographed combined directions ['57, 10 pages] for this test and (*d*) below; separate test-answer sheets may be used; 4¢ per IBM answer sheet; 25¢ per scoring stencil; [30] minutes.

(*d*) Booklet 3. Grades 3–4; details same as for (*c*) above.

2) *Section 4: Word Attack, Part 1: Oral.* Grades 1–8; 1958; individual; Forms A, B, (8 pages); revised directions for administering (8 pages) for grades 1–13; no data on reliability; [20] minutes.

b) DIAGNOSTIC READING TESTS: LOWER LEVEL. Grades 4–8; 1947–63; 2 sections, 4 booklets; 25¢ per key for any one booklet; 25¢ per directions for any one booklet; $1.75 per specimen set of all 4 booklets and directions for each.

1) *Survey Section.* Grades 4–8; 1952–63; IBM; 2 booklets; directions for administering ('61, 14 pages, same as directions published in 1958 except for some wording and typographical changes); 20¢ per copy of either booklet; separate answer sheets may be used; 4¢ per IBM answer sheet; 25¢ per scoring stencil; (30) minutes per booklet.

(*a*) Booklet 1: Part 1, Word Recognition and Comprehension. 2 scores: word recognition, comprehension; Forms A, B, C, D, ('57, 12 pages, Form B identical with test copyrighted in 1952 except for format and cover page).

(*b*) Booklet 2: Parts 2 and 3, Vocabulary-Story Reading. 3 scores: vocabulary, rate of reading, story comprehension; Forms A ('52), B ('57, identical with test copyrighted in 1952 except for cover page and, in vocabulary section, revised option order in most items and minor revision in 1 item), C ('57), D ('57), (12 pages).

2) *Section 4: Word Attack.* Various grades 1–13; 1947–63; 2 parts.

(*a*) Part 1, Oral. Grades 1–8; see *a*2 above.

(*b*) Part 2, Silent. Grades 4–13; 1947–63; 3 scores: identification of sounds, syllabication, total; IBM; Forms A, B, ('47, 6 pages); revised directions for administering ('58, 4 pages); 15¢ per test; separate answer sheets may be used; 4¢ per IBM answer sheet; 25¢ per scoring stencil; (30) minutes.

c) DIAGNOSTIC READING TESTS: [UPPER LEVEL]. Grades 7–13; 1947–63; IBM except for section 4, part 1; 5 sections, 6 booklets; separate answer sheets may be used with all except section 4, part 1; 4¢ per IBM answer sheet; 25¢ per scoring stencil; 25¢ per directions for any one booklet; $4.50 per specimen set of all 6 booklets and directions for each.

1) *Survey Section.* 1947–63; 5 scores: rate of reading, comprehension check, vocabulary, total comprehension, total; IBM; Forms A ('52, same as test copyrighted in 1950 except for cover page, revision

in 2 items, and minor change in directions), B ('47), C ('50), D ('50, some printings c1949), E ('52), F ('50), G ('50), H ('50), (22–23 pages); revised directions for administering ('56, c1947, 10 pages); 25¢ per test; 40(50) minutes. (Forms A and B were published in the high school and college educational edition of *Reader's Digest* in November 1949 and May 1950, respectively.)

2) *Section 1: Vocabulary (Revised).* 1947–63; 5 scores: English, mathematics, science, social studies, total; IBM; Forms A, B, ('52, 9 pages); mimeographed directions for administering ('56, 4 pages); no data on reliability of total score; 15¢ per test; 35(40) minutes.

3) *Section 2: Comprehension: Silent and Auditory.* 1947–63; IBM; revised Forms A, B, C, D, ('57, c1948, 28–34 pages); mimeographed directions for administering ['58, 8 pages]; may be administered as a listening comprehension test; no norms for grade 13; 25¢ per test; [30] minutes as a silent reading test.

4) *Section 3: Rates of Reading: Part 1, General.* 1947–63; IBM; 4 scores: normal rate of reading, comprehension at normal rate, maximum rate of reading, comprehension at maximum rate; Forms A, B, ('47, 14 pages); directions for administering ('48, 12 pages); 15¢ per test; 30(35) minutes.

5) *Section 4: Word Attack.* 1947–63; 2 parts.

(*a*) Part 1, Oral. 1948–58; individual; Forms A, B, ('48, 15 pages); revised directions for administering ('58, 6 pages) for grades 1–13; no data on reliability; no norms for grades 9–13; 20¢ per test; (20) minutes.

(*b*) Part 2, Silent. Grades 4–13; see *b*2(*b*) above.

REFERENCES

1–19. See 4:531.

20. COMMITTEE ON DIAGNOSTIC READING TESTS, INC. *Diagnostic Reading Tests: Their Interpretation and Use in the Teaching of Reading.* New York: the Committee, Inc., 1952. Pp. 44. * (*PA* 27:6739)

21. TRIGGS, FRANCES ORALIND. "The Development of Measured Word Recognition Skills, Grade Four Through the College Freshman Year." *Ed & Psychol Meas* 12:345–9 au '52. * (*PA* 27:6120)

22. BARRETT, DOROTHY M. "Correlation of Survey Section of Diagnostic Reading Tests and of Test C2: Reading Comprehension With College History Grades." *J Ed Res* 46:465–9 F '53. * (*PA* 28:1461)

23. TRAXLER, ARTHUR E. "Results of the Diagnostic Reading Tests for Grades 4, 5, and 6, Survey Section, Among Independent School Pupils." *Ed Rec B* 60:69–76 F '53. * (*PA* 28:1579)

24. ROGO, ROBERT A. *The Relationship of Scores of the Diagnostic Reading Tests: Survey Section and the American Council on Education Psychological Examination, to First Semester Freshman Honor Point Averages for Students in the College of Arts and Sciences at the University of Detroit.* Master's thesis, University of Detroit (Detroit, Mich.), 1954.

25. TRIGGS, FRANCES ORALIND; CARTEE, J. KEITH; BINKS, VIRGINIA; FOSTER, DESMOND; AND ADAMS, NICHOLAS A. "The Relationship Between Specific Reading Skills and General Ability at the Elementary and Junior-Senior High School Levels." *Ed & Psychol Meas* 14:176–85 sp '54. * (*PA* 28:8005)

26. WARD, LOUIS R. "Diagnostic Reading Tests." Letter. *Col Engl* 15:475–6 My '54. *

27. SAWIN, E. I. "Problems and Projected Plans in Air Force ROTC Evaluation." *Yearb Nat Council Meas Used Ed* 12:1–5 pt 1 '55. *

28. WALL, CLAIRE FRENCH. *The Relationship Between Certain Variables in Reading Improvement and Academic Grades at the College Level.* Master's thesis, Alabama Polytechnic Institute (Auburn, Ala.), 1955.

29. MCQUEEN, ROBERT. "Diagnostic Reading Scores and College Achievement." *Psychol Rep* 3:627–9 D '57. * (*PA* 33:4705)

30. TRIGGS, FRANCES ORALIND. "A Comparison of Auditory and Silent Presentations of Reading Comprehension Tests." *Yearb Nat Council Meas Used Ed* 14:1–7 '57. *

31. WALDMAN, JOHN, AND TRIGGS, FRANCES ORALIND. "Measurement of Word Attack Skills." *El Engl* 35:459–63 N '58. *

32. HINTON, EVELYN A. "Doubts About Equivalent Forms." *J Develop Read* 2:59–62 su '59. *

33. TRIGGS, FRANCES ORALIND. "The Relationship of Word Attack Skills as Measured by Silent and Oral Tests." *Yearb Nat Council Meas Used Ed* 16:134–9 '59. *

34. MILLER, ROBERT E. "Selection of Engineering Students for an Abbreviated Mathematics Sequence." *Personnel & Guid J* 39:224–5 N '60. *

35. ROBERTSON, MALCOLM H., AND HARRISON, MILDRED M. "Reading Skill as a Predictor of College Achievement." *J Ed Res* 53:258–62 Mr '60. *

36. BOAG, AUDREY K., AND NEILD, MARGARET. "The Influence of the Time Factor on the Scores of the Triggs Diagnostic Reading Test as Reflected in the Performance of Secondary School Pupils Grouped According to Ability." *J Ed Res* 55:181–3 D–Ja '62. * (*PA* 37:1986)

37. CASH, W. L., JR. "Predictive Efficiency of Freshman Entrance Tests." *J Psychol Studies* 13:111–6 Je '62 [issued F '64]. *

38. DREW, ALFRED STANISLAUS. *The Relationship of General Reading Ability and Other Factors to School and Job Performance of Machinist Apprentices.* Doctor's thesis, University of Wisconsin (Madison, Wis.), 1962. (*DA* 23:1261)

39. RANKIN, EARL F., JR. "Reading Test Reliability and Validity as Function of Introversion-Extroversion." *J Develop Read* 6:106–17 w '63. *

40. SEEGARS, JAMES E., JR., AND ROSE, HARRIETT A. "Verbal Comprehension and Academic Success in College." *Personnel & Guid J* 42:295–6 N '63. *

ALBERT J. KINGSTON, *Professor of Education, University of Georgia, Athens, Georgia.*

The *Diagnostic Reading Tests* consist of three separate test batteries designed to appraise reading abilities at all grade levels from kindergarten through the college freshman year. The basic plan for each battery includes a separate survey test designed to appraise a pupil's general reading proficiency and a number of supplemental tests for appraising specific reading skills. Teachers may employ all of the tests included in a given battery or merely select those they feel to be desirable. Obviously the development of these instruments required considerable ambition, knowledge, and perseverance. A characteristic of the Committee on Diagnostic Reading Tests has been its long term planning and continuous study of the reading process. As a result of the Committee's work, teachers have available for use a series of tests which possess a common design and theoretical basis for measuring longitudinal growth in reading.

The upper level battery was the first published and is widely employed in college and secondary school reading programs. The Survey Section often is employed for identifying pupils who need special assistance and for evaluating the effectiveness of various types of instruction. Eight different forms of the survey section are available. A number of writers, however, have criticized the claim of equivalency of the forms of the Survey Section. The upper level battery also includes tests (with alternate forms) of vocabulary, comprehension, rates of reading, and word attack skills. Generally the selections employed in appraising reading skills are varied and have been carefully selected. A few, however, need revision and should be brought up to date.

The lower level Survey Section, which is in two booklets with four comparable forms of each, yields measures of word recognition, comprehension, vocabulary, and rate of reading. As the Committee believed it was helpful to print both the reading selections and the comprehension questions pertaining to the passages on the same page, the selected passages tend to be crowded at the top of each page. The result is an unattractive and crowded format. The various sections of the lower level tests appear to have sufficient reliability for appraising general reading ability and for individual diagnosis.

At both the intermediate and primary grade levels, the identical test (Section 4: Word Attack, Part 1, which is available in two forms) is used for appraising oral word attack skills. An unusual feature of the oral word attack test is the availability of norms which are reported in terms of the mean number of errors made by pupils in various grades on each of the seven types of errors the test is scored for. How this information is used is uncertain. Presumably a teacher who diagnoses the reading skills of one of her pupils can use this information in determining the progress of a given student.

In the opinion of the reviewer, the battery designed for use in kindergarten through the fourth grade is less satisfactory than either the upper level or lower level batteries. Although two forms of the tests for use in grades 2–4 exist, there is only one form of the readiness test (for kindergarten and grade 1) and Booklet 1 (for grade 1) of this level of the Survey Section. The test booklets are printed on poor quality paper and the format is unattractive. Directions for administering the readiness and other survey tests are offset reproductions of typed copy, printed on a poor grade of paper and stapled in the upper left hand corner. Even if great care is used in handling the direction sheets it is likely that they will have to be restapled after being used once or twice. In addition, the direction sheets received by the reviewer were faintly printed and blurred, and a number of the words along the left margin were illegible. A further shortcoming is the lack of readily available information regarding the reliability and validity of this battery and its subtests. However, the latest norms booklet published in 1963 contains an insert sheet which presents median reliability coefficients for the various tests in the battery. The insert also suggests that "Test users who care to do so may find research studies in the literature reported both by the Committee and by independent users of the test." While it undoubtedly is difficult for test publishers to provide current information about their instruments, more adequate manuals would save test consumers considerable time and effort.

The norms distributed with the tests are continuously revised, and a revised norms booklet based on the scores of thousands of children was printed in 1963. Unlike many primary and intermediate grade level reading tests, these tests do not present norms in terms of grade-level equivalents. Quartiles and medians are employed for the readiness test and percentiles are reported for the other subtests. Certain primary grade teachers may be somewhat unhappy about this procedure.

The Committee is to be congratulated for its ambitious attempt to measure reading abilities at various grade levels. The *Diagnostic Reading Tests* represent a step in the right direction. One cannot help but feel that the overall planning which has gone into this vast project has been excellent. Unfortunately, a number of important details which would assist the average teacher in using these tests seem to have been overlooked. It is hoped that in the near future the Committee will concern itself with a number of details which would make these tests more usable to the average classroom teacher. Certain test selections and items need revision, and the format of certain tests should be improved. Above all, efforts should be made to develop manuals of instruction which are both complete and inexpensive. These generally useful tests deserve no less than the best manuals.

B. H. Van Roekel, *Professor of Education, Michigan State University, East Lansing, Michigan.*

Readers usually abhor prefatory comment but in this instance such comment seems appropriate.

The literature dealing directly with the administration, interpretation, and application of the *Diagnostic Reading Tests* is exceedingly voluminous and there is more to come, for apparently there are yet two tests to be printed. In sheer bulk, this reviewer examined 56 separate publications, including 11 manuals of directions, 38 test booklets, and 7 assorted pamphlets and bulletins dealing with test norms and the use and interpretation of test results in the teaching of reading.

The previous paragraph is not intended to exalt the dedication and diligence of the reviewer. It should alert the reader to the problems a reviewer faces in organizing and focusing comment in a manner useful to the prospective users of these tests. Especially, the reader should recognize the likelihood of oversight when a reviewer is confronted with so many pages.

The development of the *Diagnostic Reading Tests* represents one of the most ambitious attempts to help schools individualize reading instruction. It is truly a global effort in the sense that it not only purports to measure reading efficiency from kindergarten through college but it also attempts to provide specific suggestions for using the test scores to adapt instruction in reading to the abilities and needs of students. Unfortunately, the hundreds of pages which make up these tests and related literature tend to defeat the purposes for which the tests were built. The following itemizes the reactions of the reviewer to specific elements within the total framework represented by these tests.

a) One gets the impression that these tests are a bit like Topsy—they just grew. Nowhere did this reviewer find any evidence to suggest that the committee started with a clear cut plan which definitively structured the elements which were to make up this testing program. The best that one can do is to say that the Committee on Diagnostic Tests, Inc., began its work in 1943. Among its first efforts it canvassed the opinions of teachers and others actively involved in matters relating to the teaching of reading. From this survey the Committee concluded "that one of the greatest stumbling blocks to efficient teaching of reading was the inability of teachers to recognize the reading level of students and thus to apply the cardinal principle of all teaching, namely, to start where students are and proceed to a well-defined objective. The Committee therefore decided to construct measuring instruments for the skills already defined as the major areas of reading instruction." The Committee specifies that the tests are scored in areas of instruction in reading rather than in terms of "pure factors." The prospective test user is left to his own in concluding the distinction between instructional areas and "pure factors." The Committee also suggests that new tests will be built as the need arises but there is no specification as to what constitutes a need or how one determines when a need has arisen.

b) The manuals of directions, tables of norms, and other literature accompanying the tests hardly reflect professional standards. The manuals of directions and tables of norms are so poorly duplicated and the format is so cluttered one has difficulty reading them. Much of the literature dealing with the interpretation and application of test scores is clumsily written and, as Davis put it in a previous review (see 4:531), the materials "contain an admixture of information helpful to teachers and test users and misinformation about reading. The answer to Question 11 in 'Questions on Reading' will cause statisticians to shudder and will help make percentile norms seem incomprehensible to most teachers."

c) Many of the test items lack polish and some are faulty. An example is item 11 of Form C, Booklet 1, Survey Section: Lower Level, the stem of which asks "which word or words would help you to say the word *sprinkle?*" Apparently response 2 ("rink") is intended to be the correct response. If "rink" is the appropriate response, children must split a blend (spr) and a unique syllabic unit (kle), and thus violate basic elements of English structure.

d) The norms are inadequate. The variation and size of samples from which normative data for the various parts of the tests have been gathered provide almost no basis for comparability.

SUMMARY. The basic notion underlying the development of these tests is good. But some parts of these tests have now been on the market for at least a decade. One can hardly excuse the lack of refinement by saying that the tests are in the developmental stage. Ten years is long enough to develop them. These tests need a good overhaul.

For reviews by Frederick B. Davis, William W. Turnbull, and Henry Weitz of the tests for grades 7–13, see 4:531.

[824]

***Gates-McKillop Reading Diagnostic Tests.** Grades 2-0 to 6-0; 1926–62; revision of *Gates Reading*

Diagnostic Tests; 28 scores: omissions, additions, repetitions, 8 mispronunciation scores (reversals, partial reversals, total reversals, wrong beginnings, wrong middle, wrong ending, wrong in several parts, total mispronunciations), oral reading total, words—flash presentation, words—untimed presentation, phrases—flash presentation, recognizing and blending common word parts, giving letter sounds, naming capital letters, naming lower-case letters, 4 scores for recognizing the visual form of sounds (nonsense words, initial letters, final letters, vowels), auditory blending, spelling, oral vocabulary, syllabication, auditory discrimination; individual; Forms 1, 2, ('62, 9 pages); pupil record-response booklet ('62, 16 pages) for each form; manual ('62, 20 pages); no data on reliability; no norms for auditory discrimination score; separate record-response booklets must be used; $1.25 per test; 20¢ per record-response booklet; 10¢ per tachistoscope card for flash presentation subtests; 25¢ per manual; $2.50 per specimen set; postpaid; [30-60] minutes; Arthur I. Gates and Anne S. McKillop; Bureau of Publications. *

REFERENCES

1-3. See 3:510.
4-5. See 4:563.
6. Russell, David H. "Auditory Abilities and Achievement in Spelling in the Primary Grades." *J Ed Psychol* 49:315-9 D '58. * (*PA* 36:2KL15R)
7. Murray, Carol-Faith, and Karlsen, Bjorn. "A Concurrent Validity Study of the Silent Reading Tests and the Gates Reading Diagnostic Tests." *Reading Teach* 13:293-4+ Ap '60. * (*PA* 35:2751)

N. Dale Bryant, *Executive Director, Study Center for Learning Disabilities, State University of New York at Albany and Albany Medical College, Albany, New York.*

This collection of subtests is a minor revision of the *Gates Reading Diagnostic Tests* and, as such, keeps the advantages of being a familiar and widely used instrument. The manual is well organized but lacks needed descriptions of normative samples and studies as well as crucial reliability data.

The oral reading test uses stilted and unrepresentative reading selections at the higher levels and this may handicap some individuals far more than others. The reading selections have no comprehension tests; this not only influences examinee "set" but may also prevent identification of gross comprehension difficulties. One characteristic that is of particular value in the oral reading test is the analysis of types of errors made in the first four paragraphs read. Errors of omission, addition, repetition, and mispronunciations are compared as percentages of the total errors on the four paragraphs. In addition, seven types of mispronunciation (e.g., reversals, wrong beginnings, wrong in several parts, etc.) are analyzed in relation to the total number of mispronunciations in the four paragraphs. These normative values are particularly valuable if a diagnostician is sophisticated enough to associate the majority of errors of each type with probable causes, e.g., perceptual errors, difficulties with vowel sounds, careless mistakes from tension, and reading too rapidly. The norms provide guide lines of expected errors, and if cautiously used, can aid specific diagnosis of particular defects contributing to the reading difficulties.

Many of the subsequent subtest scores are interpreted with respect to the oral reading level and not to the child's age or grade level. This can be valuable but it can also be misleading (i.e., when no item is answered correctly on the subtest Recognizing and Blending Common Word Parts, a seventh grader, reading at beginning third grade level, may be rated as showing normal progress. This may be correct, but it can lead an unsophisticated teacher to ignore a possible basic difficulty.) An error in the oral test score gives a continual bias in interpreting later scores. Age differences are sometimes important in that an older child who is a poor reader may perform differently on certain subtests than would be expected of a younger child reading at the same oral reading level.

The word recognition subtest appears adequate and there is a checklist of difficulties which is useful. Word Recognition is both timed and untimed, the timed presentation using about a half second exposure through a slotted card. The difference between untimed word recognition and both timed word recognition and timed phrase recognition can help identify defects in rapid perception. The word recognition measures are not a measure of immediate recognition since children may sound out words (even after a flash) rather than recognizing them automatically.

The remaining subtests are useful but provide an incomplete analysis of component reading skills. The subtest Recognizing and Blending Common Word Parts can be particularly valuable. Auditory Blending can be useful for detecting gross blending defects, but the difficulty of administration makes for extreme variability between examiners. Giving letter sounds which are presented singly, as is done in some subtests, is not a good measure of usable phonic skills, especially when testing reading disability cases. Most of the remaining subtests depend upon the examiner pronouncing a word or sound and the examinee picking a response that corresponds to the presentation. Since production of sound from visual symbols (as in reading) is sometimes very different from identifying symbols to fit sounds, these scores may miss the identification of specific difficulties.

The supplementary tests, Spelling and Oral Vocabulary (actually auditory vocabulary), Syllabication, and Auditory Discrimination, are brief but useful in identifying gross defects but not necessarily in providing exact scores.

In summary, this is a well established test with alternate forms and a well organized manual which has a number of deficiencies. The many scores are useful but they can sometimes lead to misinterpretations, and several important aspects, such as comprehension difficulties, could be missed. As in any diagnostic reading test, clinical judgment is needed to get the most from the scores and the test performance, and this diagnostic test appears to require more sophistication than most.

GABRIEL M. DELLA-PIANA, *Associate Professor of Educational Psychology, University of Utah, Salt Lake City, Utah.*

This reading battery for individual diagnosis is a revision of the earlier *Gates Reading Diagnostic Tests* reviewed by Spache in *The Fifth Yearbook.* There are some major changes in the revision, although most of the test is much like the earlier version and Spache's criticisms remain relevant for the present edition, excepting for the reversal test which has been eliminated.

Subtests 1 (Oral Reading), 2 (Words: Flash Presentation), and 3 (Words: Untimed Presentation) are essentially identical to the earlier test except for order of appearance in the battery and an improvement in format of the pupil record booklet, including larger type and greater space between lines allowing greater ease in legibility and recording of pupil responses by the examiner.

The oral reading test is scored for errors but not time or comprehension in arriving at an oral reading grade equivalent. Norms are given for omissions, additions, repetitions, and seven mispronunciation scores for errors on the first four paragraphs. The norms are rough comparisons of the errors of a given child with those made by the average child making the same number of total errors. The norm group, however, is not defined beyond this.

Subtest 4 (Phrases: Flash Presentation), is also essentially the same as in the earlier edition of the test. The procedure for administration is similar to the flash presentation of words in which the examiner covers the word with a card and moves the card past the word for a half second exposure through an opening on the card. It is a little awkward to cover all other words on the page while exposing one, but the procedure can be mastered with a little practice. With the unreliability of exposure time and the doubtful diagnostic value of flash presentation, the reviewer prefers the approach of Spache's *Diagnostic Reading Scales* which omits flash presentation of words or phrases.

Subtest 5 (Knowledge of Word Parts: Word Attack) has four sections. The first section (Recognizing and Blending Common Word Parts) requires the child to read orally a column of nonsense words and if he misses any he tries sounding out and blending the parts presented to him separately. Thus, if "spack" is missed, the child is given *sp* and *ack* and asked to sound them separately and blend them. If performance on this test is good, the next three sections are omitted: 2, Giving Letter Sounds; 3, Naming Capital Letters; and 4, Naming Lower Case Letters. The first section of this subtest is new in this revision but the other three sections are the same as in the earlier edition except for changes in order of presentation of the letters. The rationale for changing order is not given, but it appears that beginning with *s, t,* and *n,* instead of the earlier *u, o,* and *y,* makes the task easier to begin with in the "letter sounds" test. Also, the change to *X, G, O,* and *K,* from the earlier *A, E, I, O, U,* seems to avoid the familiar sequence prompt in the "naming capital letters" test. Norms for these tests compare errors with those of students with like oral reading grade or actual grade level. However, nowhere in the manual is the norm group clearly identified for this subtest or others.

Subtest 6 (Recognizing the Visual Form or Word Equivalents of Sounds) differs from subtest 5 in that the former requires supplying sounds and this test requires recognition of sounds heard and association with their visual forms. Interpretations are wisely treated as hypotheses to be tested in other ways.

Subtest 7 (Auditory Blending) shows some improvement over the earlier version. Thus, "fry" is presented as *fr-i* instead of *f-r-y* and "dance" is *d-an-s* instead of *d-a-n-c-e.*

Subtest 8 includes supplementary tests on spelling (oral spelling of words read to the child from the earlier Words: Untimed Presentation), oral vocabulary (the examiner reads twice a sentence with four alternative completions, such as "A *head* is part of a: coat, saw, man, box"), syllabication (a condensed version of a test from the earlier edition in which the child reads orally nonsense words like "adon," and "ligarind," and auditory discrimination (in which the child is to say "same" or "different" to pairs of words some of which differ in beginning, ending, or middle sounds).

One of the great strengths of this battery is the studding of suggestions for profile analysis throughout the manual. Even the user of other batteries would gain much from these sections. For example, it is suggested that performance on column 3 of subtest 5-1 (reading the middle and final elements of words, such as the *ack* in "spack") be compared with subtest 8-3, syllabication, to see whether "the pupil has more difficulty in finding and combining syllables in words (as in the syllabication test) than in recognizing the syllables when they are presented alone" (as in column 3 of subtest 5-1). Such suggestions improve one's ability in clinical diagnosis.

If this battery is used as intended, the user must interpret norms where the reference group is not entirely clear, needs to make decisions as to whether a test should be given and in what order, and needs to consider alternative interpretations of test scores. Thus, administering and interpreting this battery requires a sophisticated examiner willing to pay the price of considerable training, formal or informal. This judgment also holds for the *Durrell Analysis of Reading Difficulty* and Spache's *Diagnostic Reading Scales.*

Nevertheless, the sophisticated user must make a choice among these three batteries (or possibly others). The reviewer suggests getting experience with all three because of the training value in studying the different approaches of Gates, Durrell, and Spache. And the final choice at the present will depend in part on what other tests are routinely administered. Thus, the Gates-McKillop's lack of a reading comprehension measure is no serious problem if such measures are routinely available on your cases. If complete or self-contained batteries are desired, the Spache and Durrell tests are preferable.

The casual user (whether classroom teacher or psychologist) could, of course, use these tests very informally. In such a case, I would recommend the Durrell because it is easier to get acquainted with and presents a variety of standard reading tasks which cover many facets of the reading process.

For a review by George D. Spache of the earlier edition, see 5:662; for a review by Worth J. Osburn, see 4:563; for related reviews, see 4:564 (2 excerpts); for a review by T. L. Torgerson, see 3:510.

[825]

Group Diagnostic Reading Aptitude and Achievement Tests. Grades 3–9; 1939; 15 scores: reading (paragraph understanding, speed), word discrimination (vowels, consonants, reversals, additions and omissions), arithmetic, spelling, visual ability (letter memory, form memory), auditory ability (letter memory, discrimination and orientation), motor ability (copying text, crossing out letters), vocabulary; 1 form (16 pages); directions (2 pages); key-norms (12 pages); no data on reliability; tentative norms; no description of normative population; 15¢ per test; $1.50 per set of 22 cards for visual tests; 50¢ per key-norms; postage extra; (60–70) minutes; Marion Monroe and Eva Edith Sherman; C. H. Nevins Printing Co. *

[826]

★McCullough Word-Analysis Tests, Experimental Edition. Grades 4–6; 1962–63; c1960–63; 10 scores: initial blends and digraphs, phonetic discrimination, matching letters to vowel sounds, sounding whole words, interpreting phonetic symbols, phonetic analysis total, dividing words into syllables, root words in affixed forms, structural-analysis total, total; 1 form ('62, c1960–62, 8 pages); manual ('62, c1960–62, 10 pages); norms manual ('63, 11 pages); individual record ('62, c1960–62, 4 pages); $5.92 per 35 tests; 76¢ per specimen set; postage extra; [70] minutes in 7 sessions; Constance M. McCullough; Ginn & Co. *

EMERY P. BLIESMER, *Director, McGuffey Reading Clinic, University of Virginia, Charlottesville, Virginia.*

This battery consists of seven 30-item tests, five for diagnosing phonetic analysis skills and two for diagnosing structural analysis skills. The first four tests are intended for pupils who have at least fourth grade, and the last three for pupils with at least fifth grade, level reading skill or above. The tests may be given to groups or to individuals, with examinees recording their answers in an 8-page test booklet. The fourth test (Sounding Whole Words) involves ability to blend or apply the separate skills measured in the first three tests (hearing consonant blends or digraphs and vowels and identifying letters which make their sounds).

A pupil's individual record sheet is provided for compiling a record of performance on each specific item on each test. Two "cross-reference interpretation" pages are also included on the individual record sheet. The first cross reference sheet lists each item in Test 4 (Sounding Whole Words) and the specific item in each of the first three tests which relates to the given Test 4 item. In the second cross reference interpretation page each of the items in Test 5 (Interpreting Phonetic Symbols) is listed; and the specific items in Test 2 (Hearing Vowel Sounds) and Test 3 (Matching Letters to Vowel Sounds) is indicated. Illustrations for interpretation for each of the cross reference pages are also provided. Diagnoses for each of the tests are provided with the answer keys in the manual. For most tests, reference is made to "teachers' manuals or reader series" as a source of exercises or possibilities for adaptation for remedial work.

While the test was originally intended for use as an instructional or diagnostic aid in the classroom, requests for normative data apparently led to a "relatively modest, though technically precise" program for establishing norms; and the test is presented, with its norms, as "classroom-tests-plus-norms." Recommendation is made in the norms manual, however, that the test be used primarily as a classroom related device.

Preliminary tryout and analysis of the tests were accomplished by administering them to approximately 400 children in grades 4–6. For establishing norms, approximately 600 children in each of grades 4–6 were tested. One class for each grade was tested in 23 school systems in 21 states, with all classes tested being in schools in which the Ginn Basic Readers were used. Efforts were made to establish a norming sample representative of socioeconomic districts and distribution of mental ability found in the general population.

Norms are presented in terms of percentile ranks for each grade. The finding of a fairly consistent, although slight, difference in mean scores favoring girls led to provision of separate normative data for boys, girls, and total groups. Standard deviations of boys' scores were found to be greater than those of girls' scores on every test in grades 4 and 5, but not in grade 6; a similar dispersion pattern was found with respect to intelligence test scores.

Examination of the various tables of normative data indicates that scores on the various tests tend to cluster near the tops of distributions. For Test 1, for example, a perfect raw score of 30 corresponds to a percentile rank in the 60's. However, pupils in the norm group did not receive such a high proportion of top scores on the other six tests. It is suggested by the publisher that use of separate subtest scores rather than total scores ("total phonetic," "total structural," or "all tests") should lead to better diagnostic use of the tests, with individual scores deviating at least one standard deviation below the mean score for a subtest before being considered significantly low scores.

On Test 2, which requires that the pupil hear the sound of a given letter or pair of letters in a key word, there might be uncertainty in the case of some children as to whether one or two letters are underlined in some of the key words. Circling the key letter or letter pair, or use of some procedure other than underlining, might reduce the possibilities for confusion. On Test 3, more than one answer should be considered correct on several items unless knowing proper spelling of words spoken by the examiner is also required. For example, any one of the letters of item 11, "a," "o," "e," "ou," could precede *r* in words and have the same sound as *er* in "her," "were," "term." Several other similar instances could also be pointed out. However, this test seems unusually free of these types of errors or confusion possibilities, particularly when compared with the exercises or practice activities of word attack skills in many workbooks accompanying reading series or in supplementary practice materials used in many reading programs. Each page of the various test materials is an inch longer than the standard size, 8½ by 11 inches. Shortening of pages to a standard length in future editions would facilitate filing of test materials in case folders.

The test appears to be a carefully planned and well constructed one. Administration of the test will permit a more detailed analysis of word attack skill deficiencies than is possible with most other existing diagnostic tests. The relatively unique cross reference feature of the tests should be valuable not only for determining more specific elements or phases of weaknesses in poor readers but also for helping teachers become more aware of the diagnostic possibilities of word errors made in regular classroom situations.

ALBERT J. HARRIS, *Professor of Education, and Director, Office of Research and Evaluation, Division of Teacher Education, The City University of New York, New York, New York.*

This battery of seven subtests is intended to provide a basis for the group or individual measurement of pupil status and needs in word attack skills in the intermediate grades. The tests, designed for group administration without time limits, get at the following abilities: identifying the consonant combinations heard at the beginnings of words; identifying words with similar vowel sounds; deciding which vowel or vowel digraph represents the common vowel sound in three words; recognizing an artificial word that is a phonetic respelling of a meaningful word; using a dictionary-type pronunciation key; dividing words into syllables; and finding the root word in a word consisting of a root with a prefix or suffix. The tests seem well designed for their specific purposes. Four of them (1, 2, 3, and 6) may be given to grade 4 and up, while the other three are for grade 5 and up.

The test form is an 8-page booklet. The manual, scoring keys, and class record sheet are contained in a 12-page booklet, and there is a 4-page folder for use in analyzing an individual pupil's errors. The tentative norms manual was available to this reviewer in manuscript form.

These tests are ingenious in design and provide for group measurement of skills which previously have had to be measured individually, or by group tests so long and cumbersome as to discourage teachers from using them. They seem capable of providing diagnostically useful information about the instructional needs of a class, group, or individual pupil in word recognition skills. Although scoring is likely to be time consuming, it is probable that many teachers will be willing to exert the effort required. The total score and the subscores for phonics and structural analysis are likely to be less useful than the separate subtest scores, and these, in turn, less useful than individual pupil listings of specific items on which further learning is needed.

The norms manual reports a preliminary standardization which is quite respectable. The tests were administered to one class at each grade in 23 school systems, located in 21 states. Approximately 600 children were tested in each of grades 4–6. Within-grade reliabilities were found to be .94 or higher for total score; .68 to .97 for subtests. Means and standard deviations show slightly higher means and lower variability for girls than for boys; variability at each grade is considerably larger than change from one grade to the next. Percentile norms are given separately for boys and girls for each subtest at each grade; also for total score, and for phonics and structural analysis subscores. The percentile tables show generally skewed distributions; on Tests 1 and 3 the median is a perfect score of 30, indicating that most of the children had learned the skills measured by these tests before entering fourth grade.

The norms are based on classes of children all of whom had used the Ginn Basic Readers. The *Kuhlmann-Anderson Intelligence Tests* were given at about the same time and showed an average IQ of 108.5. The normative population is, therefore, somewhat untypical and the scores on which the norms are based are probably slightly higher than what might be found in a sample truly representative of the total intermediate grade population.

These tests should be welcomed by schools. They can provide diagnostically useful information on a group test basis, both in intermediate grades and in corrective and remedial reading classes in secondary schools. They seem to be well constructed and quite suitable for the uses for which they are intended. The tentative standardization indicates that many pupils need additional instruction in the skills tested, and these tests can be used to sharpen the focus of instructional efforts.

[827]

★**OC Diagnostic Syllable Test.** Grades 4–6; 1960; 1 form (1 page); directions-key (2 pages); no data on reliability; no norms; 2–100 tests, 6¢ each; 10¢ per directions-key; 25¢ per single copy and directions-key; cash orders (plus postage) only; (15–20) minutes; Katherine O'Connor; [O'Connor Reading Clinic Publishing Co.]. *

[828]

★**Phonics Knowledge Survey.** Grades 1–6; 1964; individual; content card (2 pages); response record (8 pages); manual (4 pages); no data on reliability; no norms; $3.75 per set of content card, 25 response records, and manual; 50¢ per specimen set; postpaid; (10–30) minutes; Dolores Durkin and Leonard Meshover; Bureau of Publications. *

[829]

***Phonovisual Diagnostic Test.** Grades 3–12; 1949–58; formerly called *Phonovisual Diagnostic Spelling Test;* phonetic weaknesses; no data on reliability; no norms; postage extra; [15] minutes; Lucille D.

Schoolfield and Josephine B. Timberlake; Phonovisual Products, Inc. *
a) [1949 EDITION.] 1 form ('49); error analysis sheet ('49, 1 page); instructions ('49, 4 pages); 75¢ per 50 error analysis sheets; 10¢ per single copy.
b) [1958 EDITION.] 1 form ('58); instructions-class error analysis chart ('58, 5 pages); 50¢ per chart.

CHARLES M. BROWN, *Associate Professor of Education, and Director, The Reading Center, University of Southern California, Los Angeles, California.*

That the *Phonovisual Diagnostic Test* should be included in the reading section is perhaps anomalous. Originally published as a spelling test, it is now called a diagnostic test. But diagnostic of what? The brief instructions to the teacher state that this test is "designed to discover [the pupil's] phonetic weaknesses." It appears to test a combination of skills in auditory discrimination and a knowledge of spelling conventions. At the conclusion of the test, however, the user cannot be certain which of these two factors he has measured.

The test is administered in groups to children from the high second grade up by dictating 17–20 words which purport to "test for all consonant sounds, the digraphs wh, th, sh, ch, ng, 9 initial blends, and 17 fundamental vowel sounds." Analysis of all the mistakes is made for each pupil and errors are summarized for the entire class.

No reliability, validity, or normative data are presented.

GEORGE D. SPACHE, *Professor of Education, and Head, Reading Laboratory and Clinic, University of Florida, Gainesville, Florida.*

The 1949 and 1958 editions of this spelling test are offered as a means of determining a pupil's phonic skills. Both editions are currently available and considered equivalent by the authors. Basically, the task is one of writing 17 words (1958) or 20 words (1949) at dictation. The items are very simple, monosyllabic words which can be spelled successfully, according to the authors, by any pupil above the second grade if he is familiar with the most frequently occurring sounds in the English language. The authors further claim that the tests measure all consonant sounds, 5 consonant digraphs, 9 initial blends, and the 17 fundamental vowel sounds.

Inspection of the test items reveals that the average grade placement of the items in the 1949 test is 4.9, and in the 1958 test, 4.0 according to Gates' *List of Spelling Difficulties in 3876 Words.* While Gates' study is admittedly old (1937), any error in the estimate of current grade placement of the test words is probably in the direction of underestimation because of the trend toward simplification of spelling vocabularies in the intervening years. Thus it appears that the score for an average pupil at the lower levels of use proposed for this test, who might not have been taught to spell these words, might not reflect a lack of phonic spelling knowledge.

Corollary questions regarding the validity of the tests are their lack of equivalence and their suitability for secondary or upper elementary pupils. It is quite possible that many such pupils may have learned to spell these very simple words, and yet lack adequate phonic skills.

The validity of the tests as complete diagnostic measures is also questionable since the items *do not* include all consonant sounds, and make no attempt to evaluate the pupil's knowledge of such phonic elements as vowel digraphs or silent consonants. Furthermore, the lists include only 2 or 3 examples of vowels with *r* and about 5 vowel diphthongs of the 25 to 30 such combinations commonly taught in primary reading programs. The consonant sounds tested include only the simplest 18 and omit the very common alternative sounds of *c, s, g,* and *z.* Thus, in all areas of phonic skills covered the tests are incomplete, and their content validity is questionable.

There is, however, a degree of face validity in the purpose of these tests in view of the research evidence of the frequency of weaker phonic skills among poor spellers. In such cases, when the test is not too simple, it may serve to reveal this weakness as it may manifest itself in spelling, at least in those items covered by the test. But the authors assume, as many of the test users would, that the test is diagnostic of phonic skills in both reading and spelling. This assumption will be incorrect in many individual cases, for the two processes are not identical and all pupils are not necessarily handicapped to the same degree in phonic skills in both reading and spelling. Some poor spellers are good readers, and occasionally a pupil who is poor in reading appears to show normal spelling ability. Some are ineffectual in applying phonic skills in the one area, yet seem to be able to do so in the other.

Thorough testing of phonic skills in reading

should involve evaluating the child's ability to hear, discriminate among, and identify all phonic elements, as well as the ability to translate mentally or orally a printed symbol into its equivalent sounds. The pupil must also be skilled in blending the separate sounds he may identify into a complete recognizable word. In contrast, the spelling process involves recognizing and discriminating among the auditory sounds which constitute words, knowing the common symbols used to represent these sounds and their frequent variants, and, finally, writing the proper letters to represent these sounds. It is widely recognized that this process may be disrupted by any of a half dozen factors such as poor auditory discrimination, handwriting errors, lapses of attention, poor auditory memory, certain visual defects, and the influence of defective articulation or pronunciation. The *Phonovisual Diagnostic Test* ignores all these contributing factors and assumes that any and all misspellings of the test words are due purely to weak phonic skills.

In summary, the tests appear to be inappropriate in difficulty for the range of grades for which they are offered, unequivalent in difficulty, incomplete in their sampling of phonic skills and facts, and lacking in coverage of the possible causal factors. Furthermore, the mode of testing is questionable for measuring phonic ability in both reading and spelling.

[830]

★Roswell-Chall Auditory Blending Test. Grades 1–4; 1963; individual; orally administered; 1 form (2 pages); manual (4 pages); $2.50 per 35 tests, postpaid; 50¢ per specimen set, prepaid orders only; administration time not reported; Florence G. Roswell and Jeanne S. Chall; Essay Press. *

REFERENCES

1. Huset, Martha K. *Relationship Between Difficulty in Auditory Blending and Some Diagnostic Indicators of Organicity in Children of Average or Superior Intelligence With Reading Disability.* Master's thesis, City College of New York (New York, N.Y.), 1961.

2. Chall, Jeanne; Roswell, Florence G.; and Blumenthal, Susan Hahn. "Auditory Blending Ability: A Factor in Success in Beginning Reading." *Reading Teach* 17:113–8 N '63. *

Ira E. Aaron, *Professor of Education, University of Georgia, Athens, Georgia.*

The purpose of this test is to assess a child's ability to blend sounds into whole words. It is suitable for use in grades 1 through 4 and with older children who have difficulty in recognizing words. The test is individual in nature and is presented orally. Though no estimate of administration time is given in the manual, it is likely that most children will complete the test in less than five minutes.

The test consists of three parts, each of which contains 10 words. The examiner presents the sounds in a word slowly and the child tells him what the word is. The words in Part 1 are divided into two sounds, one of these being the sound of a consonant letter and the other a vowel, vowel digraph, or diphthong sound (as *a-t*). Each word in Part 2 is subdivided into two parts, the sound of the initial consonant letter or consonant combination and the remainder of the word (as *f-at*). Part 3 words are subdivided into three elements with the initial sound being that of a single consonant, the second sound that of the middle vowel or vowel digraph, and the final sound that of a consonant or consonant combination (as *c-a-t*). The child's score is the number of correct words he gives. Instructions for giving the test are easy to follow.

A brief section on interpretation is included in the manual. By use of a table, raw scores may be interpreted as either "inferior" or "adequate." The table is based upon administration of the test to 62 children in the first grade, to 40 of these same children who were retested in grade 2 or 3 and in grade 4, and to a group of reading disability cases in grades 3–5. Auditory blending scores, on the average, increased with the grade, and correlations were found between auditory blending scores and oral reading, silent reading, and word analysis skills.

The dichotomy of "inferior blending" and "adequate blending" is not in keeping with reality. Six correct answers, for instance, is considered inferior for a first grader while seven correct is adequate. A division similar to those offered by some readiness test manuals in which up to five different categories are presented would be an improvement. Interpretation should be in terms of prediction of success in phonics instruction since the authors emphasize the test's suitability for this.

The usefulness of the table of interpretation is restricted further by the nonrepresentativeness of the samples. The longitudinal study involved 62 New York City Negro children thought to be from the lower to lower middle class, and the second sample consisted of 25 severely disabled readers. Though the helpfulness of the table for interpretation is limited, the explanations for poor blending ability and suggestions for fostering this ability are good.

Reliability coefficients, computed by the split-halves method, ranged from .86 to .93 for the children tested in grades 1–4. A coefficient of .94 was found for 25 severely retarded readers, using the same correlation technique. These appear to be the same children used in the development of the interpretation table. Data presented indicate that the test is reliable.

In an attempt to support the validity of the test, the authors computed correlations between the test and an oral reading test (Gray), a silent reading test (Metropolitan), and the *Roswell-Chall Diagnostic Reading Test of Word Analysis Skills.* These data were based upon the 40 children who were tested in grades 1–4. The sizes of the correlation coefficients were unimpressive, ranging from .26 to .66. Validity is specific, and any data on validity should involve the question, "Valid for what?" The only test of the three cited that deals with phonics, to which this test is supposed to be related, is the *Roswell-Chall Diagnostic Reading Test of Word Analysis Skills.* These correlations range from .46 to .66. A child who knows very few phonics skills may still do well on the other tests if he has a large sight vocabulary and uses other word attack skills well. A correlation coefficient of .70 was found between the auditory blending test and the Gray test for the 25 severely disabled readers in grades 3–5. The extent to which knowledge of phonics is related to the Gray test is not discussed in the manual. The authors refer to two additional sources for information about the reliability and validity of the test. One is a paper, available on request, delivered at a meeting of the American Educational Research Association, and the other is an unpublished master's thesis. Any additional data on reliability and validity contained in these two sources should have been included in the manual.

This test, more an informal inventory than a standardized test, is useful for evaluating a pupil's ability to blend sounds he hears into words. Though the authors do not present convincing data to support the validity of the test, the test is probably valid for this one purpose. No norms are offered, but a section on interpretation in the manual gives the examiner some help in interpreting raw scores.

B. H. VAN ROEKEL, *Professor of Education, Michigan State University, East Lansing, Michigan.*

Anyone contemplating using this test must resolve two issues. The first is the usual one of judging the degree to which the technical aspects of the test meet the standards of good test construction. The second is strictly a theoretical consideration where the prospective user must weigh the significance of that which the test purports to measure in relation to the reading act itself.

The term "auditory blending" occurs here and there in the literature and apparently is synonymous with the more commonly used expression "auditory perception." One can perhaps best define auditory blending by describing a child's behavior when he responds correctly to the items on this test.

The test is administered to children individually and all responses are oral. The test consists of 30 items divided equally among three parts. The items are single words which the teacher pronounces slowly so that the phonemes or, in some instances, combinations of phonemes are heard as more or less discrete sounds. To illustrate, the teacher pronounces the word "at" as *a-t,* "cow" as *c-ow,* "time" as *t-ime,* and "toast" as *t-oa-st.* The child's response is scored as correct if, in the first instance he responds with the usual sound people make when they respond orally to the visual stimulus *at,* in the second instance with the usual oral response to *cow,* and so on. The manual of instructions states that "the test is particularly useful for judging the ease or difficulty that pupils will experience in phonics instruction."

Auditory blending, as interpreted by this reviewer, is the mental act which the child performs when he synthesizes the phonemes prior to uttering the whole word vocally. Correct responses to the items in this test are merely manifestations that auditory blending has been accomplished.

The authors must feel that auditory blending is a significant factor in learning to read or they would not have built this test. The *Handbook of Research on Teaching*[1] cites some research which supports the authors of this test but the evidence is contradictory and far from conclusive.

The technical characteristics of the test are even less defensible than the rationale for re-

1 RUSSELL, DAVID H., AND FEA, HENRY R. "Auditory Perception," pp. 873–8. In *Handbook of Research on Teaching.* Edited by N. L. Gage. Chicago, Ill.: Rand McNally & Co., 1963. Pp. xiii, 1218. *

lating its content to the ease or difficulty pupils will experience in phonics instruction. The manual is almost devoid of information a prospective test user needs to make judgments about the usefulness of this test. The manual carries not even a hint regarding the selection of content, and data on the construction of the test are conspicuous by their complete absence. The norming group is described as "children in Grade 1 who were later retested in Grades 2 through 4 and....a group of children with reading disability in Grades 3, 4, and 5." The manual carries two references which provide additional information regarding the reliability and validity of this test.

In summary, the test reflects almost none of the characteristics of good test construction, the norming group is totally inadequate, and the manual of instructions falls far below reasonable technical standards.

[831]

***Roswell-Chall Diagnostic Reading Test of Word Analysis Skills.** Grades 2–6; 1956–59; individual; Forms 1, 2, ('59, c1956–59, 4 pages, identical with tests copyrighted in 1956); manual ('59, c1956–59, 4 pages, essentially the same as 1956 manual); supplement ('58, reprint of *1* below); $2.60 per 35 tests; 50¢ per specimen set; postpaid; supplement free on request; [5–10] minutes; Florence G. Roswell and Jeanne S. Chall; Essay Press. *

REFERENCES

1. CHALL, JEANNE S. "The Roswell-Chall Diagnostic Reading Test of Word Analysis Skills." *Reading Teach* 11:179–83 F '58. *

IRA E. AARON, *Professor of Education, University of Georgia, Athens, Georgia.*

This test is designed to assess strengths and weaknesses of selected word recognition skills. It is suited for children reading on approximately the second to sixth grade levels. The five subtests deal mainly with phonics skills.

Subtest 1 measures ability to give sounds of (*a*) consonant letters and (*b*) consonant combinations. All consonant letters except *q* and *x* are included in the first part, but only 10 consonant combinations (blends and digraphs) are used in the second part of the subtest. Equally important consonant combinations are omitted. The second part of subtest 1 is too brief to be of much value in diagnosis though it may serve as a screening device.

Subtest 2, assessing knowledge of vowel sounds, consists of three parts: (*a*) pronouncing one-syllable words having short vowel sounds, (*b*) reading sentences containing words with short vowel sounds, and (*c*) giving the sounds of vowel letters. A child having a large sight vocabulary may perform well on the first two parts of this subtest without knowing the short sounds. The third part indicates the child's knowledge of short sounds but not the extent to which he will use this knowledge in attacking words. Presenting short vowel sounds in nonsense "words" appears a more natural way of assessing the development of this skill.

In Subtest 3, concerned with the silent *e* rule, five pairs of one-syllable words are presented for pronunciation. The first of each pair contains the short vowel sound (as *fin*); the second of each pair is the same as the first except for final *e* and the long vowel sound (as *fine*). A child with a large sight vocabulary may pronounce all the words without knowing the influence of final *e* on the sound of the preceding vowel. Again, use of nonsense "words" would be more appropriate. No explanation is offered for including the silent *e* rule while omitting other rules often taught in the primary grades.

Subtest 4 consists of 12 one-syllable words containing vowel combinations. Eight words have vowel digraphs (as *feel* and *paid*) in which the long sound of the first vowel is heard; two words contain the *oi* diphthong; and two words, incongruous with what this subtest is purported to evaluate, have *ar* combinations. This section of the test, like the previous two subtests, would be ineffective with children who have large sight vocabularies.

Subtest 5, labeled "Syllabication," actually combines syllabication with several other skills. Eight multisyllabic words, difficult enough to challenge most children reading on primary grade level, are presented for the child to pronounce. The examiner observes the child as he puts into practice a combination of word recognition skills. If the purpose of this section is to determine how the child attacks unknown words, then it is effective only with children who do not know the words presented.

The manual does not present information on reliability and validity but does cite an article, available upon request from the publisher, that contains such data (*1*).

Correlation between the total scores of Forms 1 and 2 was found to be .98 for a small sample of 52 children receiving remedial reading instruction. These children ranged from third through eleventh grades in school and from first through eighth grade reading levels with an average reading level of 4.3. For these same subjects, subtest reliabilities were reported to range from .78 to .99. The reliability of the test appears adequate.

Validity data cited are based upon two second grade classes, two fifth grade classes, and the 52 remedial readers used in the reliability study. Correlations between the total scores on the Roswell-Chall test and other tests are presented. The validity coefficients for the clinic sample were lower than those for the second and fifth grades, though the test was designed for use with poor readers. Validity data are weak in that the same silent reading tests were not used at all levels and the number of cases was small. Despite these limitations, the authors have attempted to a greater extent than most authors of informal tests of word recognition to establish validity. However, the only way to check functional use of word attack skills is to confront children with unknown words. Many of the words used in this test would not be unknown to some of the children taking the test.

The manual is easy to follow though information offered on scoring and interpretation is limited. Normative data are not given, but the manual does include a sequence for teaching the skills tested. Both manual and tests appear to have been prepared without careful thought being given to the skills involved in word recognition.

In summary, this test assesses a limited number of word recognition skills and may be administered easily in a short period of time by an experienced teacher who knows the skills being measured. The test is similar to informal inventories of word recognition skills that many clinics and classroom teachers use. This test alone gives insufficient information to evaluate effectively the word recognition skills of a child.

EMMETT ALBERT BETTS, *Research Professor, University of Miami, Coral Gables, Florida.*

These individually administered tests are designed to assess phonic skills: consonants, vowels, syllables. The first subtest, requiring the pupil to produce in isolation the sounds usually represented by consonant letters, indicates a gross lack of linguistic sophistication on the part of the authors. The second subtest requires the pupil to say words illustrating the "short" vowel principle and to read two sentences containing words of this type. However, the pupil is requested to give the sound of *a*, with provision for only two possible responses. The third subtest requires the pupil to say "pin-pine" and other words contrasting short vowel and final *e* words. The fourth subtest presents mixed items including vowel digraphs, diphthongs, and vowel plus *r*—without help on interpretation. The last part covers syllabication with most of the emphasis on suffixes and inflectional endings.

This so-called standardized test suffers in comparison with both extant inventories and tests of word perception skills offered by publishers of basic textbooks in reading, and teacher-made informal inventories of phonic skills recommended by authors of textbooks on method. In these materials, systematic attention is given to (*a*) generalizations (e.g., the "at-cat-sat," "ate-mate-late," "eat-meat-heat" word patterns), (*b*) usual sounds represented by letters and syllables (e.g., the usual sound represented by *ir* in "bird"), and (*c*) syllable phonics. These types of skills put the "feed" into *feedback* as a factor in learning the relationships between sounds and letters—an everyday need in the classroom.

For a review by Byron H. Van Roekel, see 5:667.

[832]

Silent Reading Diagnostic Tests: The Developmental Reading Tests. Grades 3–8; 1955; 20 scores: recognition pattern (6 scores), error analysis (4 scores), recognition techniques (9 scores), word synthesis; 1 form (23 pages); manual (14 pages); tentative norms; $4 per 20 tests; $2 per set of scoring cards (optional); $1 per 100 tabulation sheets; postage extra; 40¢ per specimen set, postpaid; (90) minutes in 2 sessions; Guy L. Bond, Theodore Clymer, and Cyril J. Hoyt; Lyons & Carnahan. *

REFERENCES

1. MURRAY, CAROL-FAITH, AND KARLSEN, BJORN. "A Concurrent Validity Study of the Silent Reading Tests and the Gates Reading Diagnostic Tests." *Reading Teach* 13:293–4+ Ap '60. * (*PA* 35:2751)

EMERY P. BLIESMER, *Director, McGuffey Reading Clinic, University of Virginia, Charlottesville, Virginia.*

This test, intended for classroom diagnostic use and designed for children of beginning third grade "age" and above, is made up of 11 separate tests: 1, Recognition of Words In Isolation; 2, Recognition of Words In Context; 3, Recognition of Reversible Words In Context; 4, Locating Elements; 5, Syllabication; 6, Locating the Root Word; 7, Word Elements; 8, Beginning Sounds; 9, Rhyming

Sounds; 10, Letter Sounds, and 11, Word Synthesis. The test yields measures of various abilities concerning word recognition techniques and indications of parts of words where errors tend to be made.

Detailed directions for administering the tests are provided in the manual. It is advised that tests be administered in two sessions of approximately 45 minutes each. Administrators are instructed to "allow sufficient time for the children to attempt all items but not more than" a given number of minutes (7 or 5) on Tests 1–6 and 11. No time limits are suggested for Tests 7 through 10, on which tests the administrator has to read words or sound elements.

A great majority of items in Test 4, Locating Elements, which involves finding a little word in a big word below a picture, are ones in which several little words might be found in a big word; however, only one given response is indicated on the key as a correct one for each item. The advisability of permitting several responses to be scored as correct ones is especially highlighted with such words as "fellowship," "forebearance," "crowbar," "notebook," and "hairdressing." "City" as a little word in "scarcity" is also to be questioned. On Test 6, Locating the Root Word, children are instructed only to locate a "little word within the larger word from which the larger one was made"; and "root word" is not mentioned in the instructions. As in the case of Test 4, the key permits only one of several possible responses for a number of items to be considered as the correct one for each of those items, although several little words are to be found in each of a number of items.

Test 11, Word Synthesis, is somewhat unique. The test consists of 12 paragraphs, each followed by several comprehension questions. A number of lines in each paragraph end with a hyphenated word (frequently not divided between syllables). This then requires that the examinee be able to blend the hyphenated words, which words play an important part in answering the comprehension questions.

Scoring keys or stencils are provided for each of the 18 pages of the test booklet on which test questions appear. Only the test page for which the key is intended is designated on each key. Clear and definite designation of the test to which each key applies is desirable and would facilitate scoring and recording. Keys for a number of tests are somewhat cumbersome and awkward to handle. Some of the slots cut out to show a correct answer are large enough to include part of another word or element; this might lead to confusion as to which of two items is the correct one. Aids or cues for aligning answer keys on a page are missing and would be especially helpful in view of the scoring keys being slightly larger than the test pages.

Keys for Tests 1 and 2 indicate not only the correct response for each item but also give indications for the type of error (initial, ending, middle, or orientation) reflected by each of the wrong responses. This is the "error key." Having a larger symbol for the correct response, or using another method to have this symbol stand out more from the incorrect responses, would facilitate scoring on Tests 1 and 2. A considerable amount of time and effort is involved in scoring and analyzing performance on these two tests. Each of the items must be "key marked" in terms of whether it is correct or the type of error made; and a count of the rights, wrongs, omits, and the various key marks must be made.

A detailed graphic profile is to be found at the beginning of the pupil test booklet. This is broken into the following areas: (*a*) "recognition pattern," based on performance on Tests 1–3; (*b*) "error analysis," based on performance on Tests 1 and 2; (*c*) "recognition techniques," based on performance on three visual analysis tests, Tests 4–6, and on four phonetic knowledge tests, Tests 7–10; and (*d*) "word synthesis," based on performance on Test 11, which calls for finding word elements phonetically. Plotting the graphic profile for a given pupil involves obtaining or computing his grade placement level, chronological "grade," mental "grade," and various reading ability scores and "average reading score" obtained with other standardized reading tests. Grade equivalent reading scores are determined automatically for each of the scores from the *Silent Reading Diagnostic Tests* (individual test scores and scores based on a combination of tests) when the score on a given test or combination is checked on a horizontal scale.

The variations from "average reading" (for an individual) which are considered important range from one half grade when the average reading level is between 1.5 and 2.4, to one and one half grades when the average reading is 5.5 and above. These distances are also to be applied when considering how much below mental "grade" a child's reading grade needs to be before he is considered a remedial case.

Only brief treatment is given in the manual to interpretation of test performance and results (just slightly over a page) and to presentation and discussion of technical data (less than a page). Very meager information is given with regard to establishment of "tentative norms." Reportedly, tests were based upon research and experimental use, with five editions in experimental form having been used in the development of the tests. The only information presented concerning the norming population is that the group included "all children in a typical Midwestern community with a population of approximately 20,000, and two other groups from other representative communities." Reliability coefficients presented for a group of 49 third grade children range from .78 to .97, except for .67 on orientation errors (reversals) and .46 on syllabication. (For the latter test, a reliability coefficient of .84, based on 104 fifth grade children, is also presented.) The method of internal consistency (each item related both logically and statistically to the designated error pattern) was used for developing error keys for Tests 1 and 2.

The *Silent Reading Diagnostic Tests* afford good opportunities for detailed diagnoses of children with elementary grade level reading skills. Diagnosis in the detail or to the extent made possible with these tests will not be needed for all children in many classes; and the time and effort involved in scoring and analyzing some of the tests would preclude wholesale use in all classes in many school systems. As do some other diagnostic tests, these tests have considerable possibility for use as training instruments in graduate training programs in reading and in inservice training programs (partly by making teachers and others using the instruments more definitely aware of various skills, patterns, and relationships involved in some aspects of reading).

ALBERT J. KINGSTON, *Professor of Education, University of Georgia, Athens, Georgia.*

The *Silent Reading Diagnostic Tests* consist of 11 subtests designed for diagnosing the reading skills of pupils in grades 3 and above. One definite advantage of these tests is that, unlike most diagnostic measures, they are group measures. The tests are excellent for appraising word recognition and word attack skills but do not provide a measure of the reader's comprehension or his interpretation of materials in context settings. In order to obtain maximum value from these tests, a teacher must use them in conjunction with another test of reading ability, such as the *Developmental Reading Tests* by the same authors. In interpreting the results of these tests some measure of the pupil's mental ability also is recommended.

The format of the tests is attractive and the instructions for administering and scoring the tests are clearcut and well written. It is recommended that the tests be administered in two separate periods of 45 minutes each, a procedure which limits fatigue and makes their use more feasible in a typical elementary classroom. The first five tests are administered during the first period of testing, and the remainder of the tests are completed during the second testing session. A possible weakness lies in the format of the test. Tests 5 and 6 are printed on the same page. Faster pupils probably work Test 6 mentally while waiting for their classmates to finish the previous subtest. It is impossible to predict the degree to which they may be helped by such practice prior to being tested on Test 6 during the second testing session. However, since time limits for each subtest are generous, this criticism may not be too important.

Test 11, Word Synthesis, might be improved. This section seeks to evaluate the pupil's ability to blend words together both visually and phonetically. In order to achieve this goal words are presented in context, but a number are hyphenated in an artificial fashion. In the first selection, for example, the five test words employed are wagon, play, stick, pull, and with. Each of these words is the last word on a line. They are hyphenated as follows: wag-on, pl-ay, st-ick, p-ull, and w-ith. This format represents a highly artificial reading situation.

The manual which accompanies the tests is clearly written and more than adequate. The reliabilities of the tests are sufficient for individual diagnosis. Scoring is easy and can be accomplished in approximately 15 minutes per booklet. A set of window cards is furnished for scoring purposes. Norms are presented by half-grade intervals and a profile inside the test booklet lends itself to easy interpretation. It is essential, however, that the teacher also appraise the student's comprehension abilities not included in these measures if she is to obtain maximum value from the use of these tests.

In the opinion of the reviewer, these tests can be of great assistance to the elementary teacher. The results are readily obtained and constitute reliable and valid measures on the basis of which individualized reading instruction can be planned.

[833]

The Standard Reading Tests. Reading ages up to 9-0; 1958; individual; 1 form; 12 tests; manual (128 pages, see *1* below) includes all test materials; no data on reliability; norms for Tests 1, 11, and 12 only; 21*s.* per manual, postage extra; administration time not reported; J. C. Daniels and Hunter Diack; Chatto & Windus Ltd. *

a) TEST 1, THE STANDARD TEST OF READING SKILL.
b) TEST 2, COPYING ABSTRACT FIGURES.
c) TEST 3, COPYING A SENTENCE.
d) TEST 4, VISUAL DISCRIMINATION AND ORIENTATION TEST.
e) TEST 5, LETTER-RECOGNITION TEST.
f) TEST 6, AURAL DISCRIMINATION TEST.
g) TEST 7, DIAGNOSTIC WORD-RECOGNITION TESTS.
h) TEST 8, ORAL WORD-RECOGNITION TEST.
i) TEST 9, PICTURE WORD-RECOGNITION TEST.
j) TEST 10, SILENT PROSE-READING AND COMPREHENSION TEST.
k) TEST 11, GRADED SPELLING TEST.
l) TEST 12, GRADED TEST OF READING EXPERIENCE. (20) minutes.

REFERENCES

1. DANIELS, J. C., AND DIACK, HUNTER. *The Standard Reading Tests.* London: Chatto & Windus Ltd., 1958. Pp. 215. *

L. B. BIRCH, *Senior Lecturer in Educational Psychology, Institute of Education, University of Sheffield, Sheffield, England.*

There are 12 tests in this battery, 11 of reading and 1 of spelling. Only 3—the spelling test, a test of reading accuracy, and a comprehension test of the sentence completion type—have norms; the rest are diagnostic tests of visual and auditory discrimination, shape, letter, and word recognition.

Test 1, called the Standard Test of Reading Skill, consists of 36 items in the form of interrogative sentences. The answers to the questions are not important; if the sentence has been correctly read the answer is obvious. The purpose is to ensure that the children concentrate upon extracting the meaning from the words they read and to discourage concentration upon mere word recognition. The authors claim that the items are placed not only in a statistically derived order of difficulty but also in a logical one. Thus, polysyllabic words with digraphs and irregular phonic structure are placed later than monosyllables with single consonants and regular phonic structure. It is claimed that this arrangement makes it possible to evaluate a child's response in developmental terms as well as in the more familiar reading ages. There are tables of norms by which raw scores can be converted into reading ages from 5.0 to 9.0 years and into seven broad categories or "reading standards." These range from 0 for children having little functional reading skill to VI for those who have mastered the mechanics of reading and now require only practice to develop adult competence. The characteristics of each stage are described in the manual.

The second normed reading test, the Test of Reading Experience (Test 12) is a group test of 50 sentence completion items. The norms cover reading ages 6.0 to 14+, though it is stated that norms above reading age 10 are unreliable. Unfortunately, no standardisation details for any of the normed tests, and no estimates of reliability or validity, are given in the manual. There is no indication in the text where these data are published.

Of the more specifically diagnostic tests, Test 2 consists of four meaningless line diagrams, something like those in Bender's *Visual Motor Gestalt Test,* which have to be copied. In Test 3 the child has to copy a six-word sentence. Test 4 is a test of visual discrimination and orientation, in which the subject has to reorganise a stimulus shape which may be a drawing of a concrete object, an abstract, or group of letters from among four others which include the stimulus shape. Test 5 is a test of letter recognition which can be used in several ways. The children can be asked simply to name the letters, or to give their phonic values, or to indicate the initial and end letters of a list of stimulus words which are orally presented. Test 6 is of aural discrimination; the subject has to recognise which of three objects begins with a particular sound. There are eight subtests to Test 7, the word recognition test. The first part tests recognition of two- and three-letter words of phonically simple structure; subsequent subtests test recognition of more difficult words with various blends of consonants and with complex and irregular structure. Test 8 is a test of oral recognition in which subjects have to pick one orally presented stimulus word from a line of four. Test 9 is similar but the stimulus this time is a picture of a well known object. Test 10 consists of a short passage to be read silently and a set of comprehension questions. The normed spelling test is of 40 words ranging from *on* to *beautiful* and covering spelling ages of 5.0 to 12.3.

Each of the tests has clear instructions for administration and no special training is required. There is no doubt that a considerable clinical picture of a child's strengths and weaknesses may be built up from responses to these tests. Sometimes these findings can be clearly interpreted in the light of experience, at others the classroom teacher for whom the tests are designed will have to seek advice from the interpretations in the manual. These are usually cautiously stated, but often they are based upon the authors' own theories of the nature of the reading process which are not universally held.

[Other Tests]

For tests not listed above, see the following entries in *Tests in Print:* 1445, 1465–7, 1474, and 1476; out of print: 1473.

MISCELLANEOUS

[834]

★Botel Reading Inventory. Grades 1–12; 1961; reading instructional level and placement of reading materials; 3 tests; *b* and *c* yield 4 ratings: free reading level, highest instructional level, highest potential level, frustration level; manual (31 pages including class summary sheets); no data on reliability; $15 per set of manual and 100 copies of each test, postage extra; specimen set free; Morton Botel in cooperation with Cora L. Holsclaw and Gloria C. Cammarota; Follett Publishing Co. *

a) PHONICS MASTERY TEST. Individually administered in part; 1 form; 4 parts in one response booklet (4 pages): consonants, vowels, syllabication, nonsense words; nonsense words may be given alone in grades 3 and over as a screening test; [15–25] minutes; $4.20 per 100 tests.

b) WORD RECOGNITION TEST. Individual; 1 form (2 cards); scoring sheet (3 pages); [4–12] minutes; $4.20 per 100 tests.

c) WORD OPPOSITES TEST. May be administered as a reading or listening test; 2 forms: reading (4 pages), listening (2 pages); [20–30] minutes as a listening test; $7.20 per 100 sets of both forms.

IRA E. AARON, *Professor of Education, University of Georgia, Athens, Georgia.*

This three-part informal inventory is designed to aid the teacher in estimating the instructional, independent, and frustration reading levels of children and to evaluate knowledge of selected phonics and related skills. Though it may be used with pupils in grades 1–12, it is appropriate for use only with those whose reading levels are at the fourth or lower grade levels.

The Phonics Mastery Test assesses knowledge of sounds of single consonants, consonant blends, and consonant digraphs; rhyming elements; vowel sounds; and syllabication (number of syllables in words and accent). For parts of this test, the children write the letter or letters representing the beginning or vowel sounds in the words the examiner reads. Pupils also write words rhyming with each of several words presented in the test booklet. They also identify long and short vowel sounds. The fourth subtest, which must be administered individually, consists of nonsense words the child pronounces. If children are thought to be reading beyond third grade level, the examiner may administer this test first and omit the earlier subtests for children who perform well. This section appears to sample adequately the phonics skills.

The Word Recognition Test contains 20 words at each reading level from preprimer through fourth grade. The examiner asks the child to pronounce the words at appropriate levels, starting where he thinks the child can pronounce all words and ending when accuracy drops below 70 per cent at two successive levels. The lists of words appear to have been selected carefully. This test and the Word Opposites Test serve as a basis for estimating reading levels.

The Word Opposites Test is designed to give an estimate of word comprehension. At levels from first reader through senior high school, 10 multiple choice items at each level are presented. Each item consists of four or five words, and the child is asked to find a word in each line that is the opposite of the first word. No evidence is cited to show the degree of relationship between selecting opposite words in multiple choice items and comprehending sentences and paragraphs. The test may also be given as a listening test in order to estimate a potential level for reading.

The manual presents a table of standards for interpreting scores on the reading placement tests. A child who has from 95 to 100 per cent accuracy on the Word Recognition Test and from 90 to 100 per cent accuracy on the Word Opposites Test is at the independent or free reading level, that is, at a level where he can read without teacher assistance. The levels at which the child has from 70 to 90 per cent accuracy on the Word Recognition Test and from 70 to 80 per cent accuracy on the Word Opposites Test are the instructional levels, where the child can be instructed in reading under teacher supervision. Any level at which accuracy falls below 70 per cent on either of the two tests is a frustration level. Children should not be instructed or allowed to read at frustration level. These standards are modifications of those often used in informal inventories in which paragraphs instead of isolated words are read. The manual indicates that research supports the two criteria that have been modified by Botel in setting up the various reading levels. A thorough review of the literature in this area will reveal very little research evidence to support these criteria. However, actual experience on the part of teachers and reading specialists does indicate the appropriateness of these "standards."

The manual includes an interesting and appropriate discussion of the importance of giving each pupil the right book and of how informal tests help the teacher in selecting appropriate books for children. Its recommendation for individualized reading and concentrated word attack instruction during the first four to six weeks of the school year, because of loss during the vacation period, would not be appropriate in those communities in which children engage actively in reading during the summer months. The manual also includes a useful summary chart of the Phonics Mastery Test for class use.

In summary, the *Botel Reading Inventory* is a useful informal test that will give the classroom teacher an economical way to gather information for selecting reading materials for children and for assessing knowledge and use of word recognition skills. Information, however, is needed on reliability and validity.

Charles M. Brown, *Associate Professor of Education, and Director, The Reading Center, University of Southern California, Los Angeles, California.*

Each of the parts of the *Botel Reading Inventory* must be considered separately. The Phonics Mastery Test calls for the pupils to respond in a group situation to a series of spoken words by writing the first letter, the first two letters, or the vowel letters contained in the words; it further calls for the pupil to identify the number of syllables and the accented syllable in a series of spoken words. Beyond this, pupils may be asked in an individual oral situation to pronounce a series of nonsense words. These tests are "scored" by summarizing the particular sound-symbol elements which give trouble to the individual pupils. No norms are presented; 100 per cent mastery is said to be the goal.

The Word Recognition Test is a somewhat formalized individual informal reading inventory using several groups of graded words. The Word Opposites Test, which may be used as a silent reading comprehension estimate or as a listening potential test, consists of a series of graded words with multiple choice alternatives from which the pupil must select a word with the opposite meaning. The score on each grade level of these tests which the pupil completes is to be compared with a table of standards to determine, for each level of material administered, whether the pupil is at the free reading level ("can read with profit without any teacher help"), the instructional level ("usually needs teacher guidance for comprehension and interpretation"), or the frustration level ("cannot read with profit even with teacher help"). From this procedure the teacher is to determine each pupil's highest instructional level (highest grade level of words read at the instructional level) and highest potential level (highest instructional level on word opposites administered as a listening test).

Because there are no normative data, no information on how the standards for the reading level classifications were determined, no data on reliability or validity, and not even any anecdotal data indicative of tryouts, one wonders how this "instrument" would be any better than a simple application of informal reading inventory criteria to the oral and silent reading of graded material. The selection of appropriate instructional and free reading material on the basis of the scores on this inventory would be rather gross at best and, further, would be very dependent upon some evaluation of the readability level of those instructional materials.

[835]

★**Functional Readiness Questionnaire for School and College Students.** Grades 1-16; 1957; reports by pupil and teacher on physical and emotional problems related to reading difficulties and school problems; individual; 1 form (1 page, must be reproduced locally); manual (23 pages); no data on reliability and validity; $1 per manual (includes copy of questionnaire), postpaid; [5] minutes; Earl A. Taylor and Harold A. Solan; Reading and Study Skills Center, Inc. *

[836]

★**Learning Methods Test.** Grades kgn, 1, 2, 3; 1954-55; comparative effectiveness of four methods of teaching new words: visual, phonic, kinesthetic, combination; individual; 1 form ('55); 4 levels: primer (46 cards), grades 1 (120 cards), 2 (114 cards), 3 (130 cards); procedure consists of a pretest to select 40 unknown words, a 15-minute training session on each method, and post-tests of immediate and delayed recall for each method; mimeographed revised manual ('55, 13 pages); record form ('54, 1 page); $6 per set of cards for all 4 levels, 25 record forms, and manual; 25¢ per manual; postage extra; (85-100) minutes in 5 sessions for pretest, training, and post-tests; Robert E. Mills; Mills Center, Inc. *

REFERENCES

1. COLEMAN, JAMES C. "Learning Method as a Relevant Subject Variable in Learning Disorders." *Percept & Motor Skills* 14:263-9 Ap '62. * (*PA* 37:1870)

THOMAS E. CULLITON, JR., *Assistant Professor of Education, University of Illinois, Urbana, Illinois.*

This test was designed "to aid the remedial reading teacher in determining the student's ability to learn new words under different teaching procedures." The four teaching procedures used in this test are: the visual method, the phonic or auditory method, the kinesthetic or tracing method, and the combination method. Actually, the test is a series of teaching lessons with testing to determine immediate and delayed learning and the appropriateness of the various methods for different individuals.

The *Learning Methods Test* consists of four sets of picture word cards including primer, first, second, and third grade words. A test record form, for each child, is used to record the words selected and the results of the immediate and delayed recall tests.

The author's purpose as stated in the manual is to determine the method by which the individual child learns most easily. A pretest for the selection of test items is necessary. An examination of the four sets of words indicates that they would be in the speaking vocabulary (therefore, in the meaning vocabulary) of even kindergarten children. For this reason it seems unnecessary to use graded lists. The grade 3 set could be used with a child reading at a primer level because the words are going to be taught, and the method then tested.

The author suggests that the order of methods used be varied from child to child. There appears to be no valid reason for this since the test is an individual test and it is assumed that other children will not be present during the administration.

The Phonic Method Test as presented in the manual will probably present difficulty to an examiner. The directions to the examiner state, "Say, 'This is the letter ______. It makes a sound such as ______. The next letter is ______; it makes the sound of ______, etc.' Have the child repeat the separate sounds after you as you do them with each word. Then have the child try the entire word sound by sound, then blending the different sounds into one whole until it is a unified, complete word." One is left with the problem of what to do with silent letters (nos*e*), consonant digraphs (ben*ch*), vowel digraphs (gr*ai*n), vowel-consonant combinations (n*ur*se), and diphthongs (t*ow*el, rainb*ow*). In many of the words the individual letters have no separate sound of their own, but receive their value because of another letter in the word. Another difficulty might be the consonants that have multiple sounds (*c*ircus, *c*andy). If a child had no prior phonetic training, it seems that this might be too complex a task to cover in a 15-minute period. With all of the phonetic inconsistencies in the English language, perhaps a list of more phonetically regular words would be best for use with this test.

The Combination Method Test suggests, "Ask the child to find any common phonograms or little-words-in-big-words." Care must be taken in this exercise to see that children do not pick out little words that have a different pronunciation than that found in the larger word ("am" in game; "on" in pony; "on" in tongue; "on" in onion).

Reliability coefficients were obtained for all four methods by correlating the number of right responses for a particular method with the number of right responses for delayed recall for the same method. One might question the value of studies based on the responses of only 30 subjects. The author states that he administered all the tests, teaching procedures, and retests. The size of the sample and the single examiner may be limitations of the reliability data. A larger sample with other examiners would be advantageous since it would provide the opportunity for an inter-examiner reliability study to be made.

Research findings on the *Learning Methods Test* based on 58 subjects are included in the manual. Specific conclusions are drawn based on sex differences, differences in intelligence (low, average, and high), and differences in age (ages 7, 8, and 9). With the exception of the sex differences study, we have no idea of the number of children in each of these groups.

At one point, the author refers to one method as being the best "in a great number of cases." While the sampling may indicate tendencies, it must be noted that these should not be considered as specific conclusions as the manual implies.

An editorial correction in the manual should be made. The picture word cards are 2 by 4¼ inches rather than 4 by 6 inches.

In summary, the *Learning Methods Test* is a comparatively short, easily administered test to be used by the remedial reading teacher as an aid in determining the most effective method for teaching specific children new words. The criticisms raised here are not fundamental criticisms of the test but rather are directed to further study and analysis of more complete data and possible revision of parts of the current test.

William Eller, *Professor of Education, State University of New York at Buffalo, Buffalo, New York.*

Elementary teachers and reading specialists frequently observe a pupil's tendency to learn more readily from one method of teaching word recognition than from another. However, weeks or months may elapse before a teacher can detect the most efficient method for teaching a given pupil: therefore, Mills devised his *Learning Methods Test* to aid in the identification of the effective procedures for presenting new words to a given child. The four instructional methods compared are the visual, the phonetic (or auditory), the kinesthetic (or tracing), and a combination of all three.

With a large pack of graded word cards the examiner administers a pretest to identify a pool of words not known to the pupil. Forty words are selected at random from this pool and arranged into four sets of 10. Following any one of the four detailed methodologies set forth in the manual, the examiner next spends exactly 15 minutes teaching the first set of 10 unknown words. At the termination of the teaching interval an immediate recall test reveals the number of words learned, and a day or so later a delayed recall test provides a retention score. On subsequent days the other three methods are taught and tested in like manner except for the differences in teaching methodology. After the four delayed recall scores have been averaged, any single score can be compared with this mean to determine the relative efficiency of a certain instructional method for the particular pupil tested.

The distinctive *Learning Methods Test* can be quite useful to teachers of developmental or remedial reading since it provides evidence of a pupil's word learning rate and his retention of new words, in addition to giving an indication of his relative ability to learn from different teaching methods. The test is particularly appropriate for use with remedial cases or with pupils who seem for a time to be learning at a suspiciously low rate. However, the test is not a highly standardized, precision measure in the manner of the majority of instruments described in this yearbook, and it could perhaps more appropriately be titled "Learning Methods Inventory." Much of the lack of precision is attributable to the flexibility of the 15-minute interaction between examiner and examinee while the 10 new words are being taught. Although each teaching method is carefully defined in the test manual, variations in pupil responses interfere with the examiner's effort to develop a uniform procedure. If the test administrator is an experienced teacher, he will detect in himself a tendency to modify the procedure so that an unusually deficient reader will learn at least a few of the 10 words. Pupil deviation from the prescribed technique occurs chiefly when the child has developed one learning method extensively and thus favors that method. For example, if the pupil has considerable phonic ability and tends to attack strange words phonetically, the examiner will observe the learner "sounding" words to himself, no matter which of the four methods he is supposed to be using.

The limited number of items in each of the four subtests further restricts the precision of this instrument. Equivalent forms reliabilities ranging from .91 to .97 are reported for the four methods. Because it seems inconceivable that a test with so few items and so little rigidity of procedure could enjoy a reliability in excess of .95, this reviewer and a doctoral candidate calculated some reliability coefficients based on procedures very much like those described in the manual. Whereas the manual includes a reliability of .97 for the visual method subtest, the Buffalo data yielded .70, which is a more likely figure. Evidently the reliability values in the manual were influenced by factors not ordinarily included in reliability calculations.

[837]

★**The Reader Rater.** Ages 15 and over; 1959; self-administered survey of reading skills; 12 scores: speed, comprehension, reading habits, reading for details, reading for inferences, reading for main ideas and adjusting speed, summarizing, skimming, recall of information read, unspeeded vocabulary, speeded vocabulary, total; Form A (27 pages); no data on reliability; no norms; $3 per booklet containing test, self-marking answer sheet, and profile; postage extra; accessories not necessary; (60–120) minutes; Better Reading Program, Inc. *

[838]

★**The Reading Eye.** Grades 1, 2, 3, 4, 5, 6, 7–8, 9–16 and adults; 1959–60; an eye-movement camera with test materials; 5 reading component scores (fixations, regressions, average span of recognition, average duration of fixation, rate with comprehension), 3 ratings (grade level of fundamental reading skill, relative efficiency, directional attack), and 2 diagnostic categories (visual adjustment, general adjustment to reading); individual; 1 model ['59]; 8 test forms ('59, 1 card each) for each of 8 levels; manual ('60, 107 pages, see *3* below); graph analyzer ('59, 1 card); reliability data and norms for reading component scores only; $460 per camera; $64 per set of 64 cards (all test forms for all levels); $2.10 per graph analyzer; $27 per light box for use in analyzing graphs; $3.75 per manual; $700 per complete set of the preceding materials plus film, developing unit, carrying case, and other accessories; postage extra; [4] minutes; Stanford E. Taylor and [Helen Frackenpohl]; Educational Developmental Laboratories, Inc. * For a related test, see 839.

REFERENCES

1. TAYLOR, STANFORD E. "A Report on Two Studies of the Validity of Eye-Movement Photography as a Measurement of Reading Performance," pp. 240–5. In *Reading in a Changing Society*. Edited by J. Allen Figurel. International Reading Association Conference Proceedings, Vol. 4. New York: Scholastic Magazines, Inc., 1959. Pp. 264. *

2. SPACHE, GEORGE D. "Evaluation of Eye-Movement Photography in Reading Diagnosis and Reading Training," pp. 98–106. In *Research and Evaluation in College Reading*. Ninth Yearbook of the National Reading Conference for College and Adults. Fort Worth, Tex.: Texas Christian University Press, 1960. Pp. 137. *

3. TAYLOR, STANFORD E. *Eye-Movement Photography With the Reading Eye, Second Edition.* Appendices (EDL Research and Information Bulletins Nos. 2 and 3) by Stanford E. Taylor, Helen Frackenpohl, and James L. Pettee. Huntington, N.Y.: Educational Developmental Laboratories, Inc., 1960. Pp. 69, 12, iv, 22. *

ARTHUR S. MCDONALD, *Professor of Education, and Director of Reading Services, Marquette University, Milwaukee, Wisconsin.*

The *Reading Eye* camera serves four main purposes in the diagnostic and assessment procedures of reading. It (*a*) provides a survey of the individual's oculomotor efficiency in the reading act; (*b*) indicates the need for specific types of corrective or remedial treatment; (*c*) indicates the adequacy of visual functioning while reading; and (*d*) permits more finely discriminated research into aspects of the nature of reading performance. The *Reading Eye* photographic record reveals the efficiency of reading performance in terms of average number of fixations per line, frequency of regressions, duration of fixations, span of recognition, and adequacy of directional attack (consisting of left-to-right eye movements while reading).

Numerous research studies have demonstrated that eye-movement photographic records reflect accurately the individual's customary reading performance and that these oculomotor characteristics do not naturally improve with the reading instruction provided in the typical classroom.

The availability of several test forms and corresponding normative data enables the *Reading Eye* to be used at every level of instruction from first grade through graduate school. Alternate equated forms make retesting and study of progress practicable. The equated forms for measuring reading flexibility enable teachers to plan instruction to provide the specific kinds of developmental or corrective activities required to produce versatile readers and assess progress.

The test selections and comprehension questions were designed to insure equivalence of alternate selections at each level and a consistent increase of difficulty from level to level by use of readability formulae, vocabulary control, review by a number of test specialists, and item analysis based on two validation testings. In addition, general plot complexity and nature of content were matched at each level. The comprehension questions were designed to test all pertinent information presented in each selection. A research validation study showed that more than 30 percentage points separated the scores of those who read the selections and those guessing answers without reading the selections. On the basis of this study, scores below 70 per cent are recommended to be used with caution.

Norms for reading component scores are based on nationwide testing following a plan which seems to insure the representative nature of the samples with special attention to adequacy of geographical distribution, public-private school representation, and (in the case of the flexibility tests) appropriate proportions of students who had completed special developmental or corrective reading programs and those who had not. A commendable feature of the norms is the preparation of separate norms for males and females for each level based on actual testing at that level. This procedure avoids the hazards of statistical extrapolation over a range of grades and allows differential interpretation of reading performance without the obscuring factor of sex.

The test manual reports validity studies involving comparison of photographic measurements with scores on the Survey Section of the *Diagnostic Reading Tests* at the fourth, seventh, and tenth grade levels. Correlations ranging from .83 to .91 (uncorrected for attenuation) were obtained. Validity studies conducted by the reviewer and his associates on groups of high school, college, and adult students comparing photographic record data and performance on a number of standardized tests, including the reading comprehension test of the *Cooperative English Tests* and the Survey Section of the *Diagnostic Reading Tests,* as well as performance in lengthy selections from books on an immediate test-retest basis and on a time lag basis (after 3 months and after 1 year), resulted in correlations ranging from .85 to .93. A number of other research studies reported in the literature agree in indicating that students read similarly before and away from the eye-movement camera. They also agree in concluding that certain aspects of reading performance are difficult to assess without the use of photographic records or other more expensive measures.

Taylor has reported test-retest reliabilities ranging from .83 to .93 for the various component scores of his reading performance efficiency rating. Other researchers, including the reviewer, have found test-retest correlations of .80 to .91 for these components. Inasmuch as span of recognition is a mathematical computation from the fixation score, reliabilities have not been run on it since this score manifestly depends on the reliability of the fixation component.

The directions for using the camera, obtaining data, and interpreting scores are exceptionally clearly written and should enable teachers to correctly and efficiently use the instrument. In addition, for the researcher, a comprehensive bibliography of studies dealing with eye-movement photographic research is provided.

SUMMARY. The *Reading Eye* is a useful diagnostic and evaluative instrument for teachers and researchers at all levels. Characteristics of reading performance revealed by eye-movement photography correlate highly with reading competence and grade placement as judged by other criteria. Further, certain aspects of the functional and perceptual efficiency of a reader can be detected most effectively in the school situation by eye-movement photography. The reliability coefficients of the various component scores are high enough to permit individual diagnosis with confidence. Thus, the eye-movement camera has a number of unique contributions to make to the process of reading diagnosis, assessment, and research.

GEORGE D. SPACHE, *Professor of Education, and Head, Reading Laboratory and Clinic, University of Florida, Gainesville, Florida.*

The *Reading Eye* is a portable 35 mm. camera devised for the purpose of photographing a reader's eye movements. The permanent record obtained by the camera, the reading graph as it is called, serves four basic purposes: (*a*) to analyze in detail the individual's mechanical functioning in the reading act; (*b*) to obtain indications of the need for specific types of corrective instruction; (*c*) to give indications of difficulties in visual functioning in the reading act; and (*d*) to observe the reader's general adjustment to the reading situation.

In actual use, the subject is administered several trial reading selections chosen from among the 64 test selections ranging from first grade to college level. When an appropriate level is found, as measured by comprehension, a test selection is placed in the camera and read by the subject. The camera employs the principle of corneal reflection by which beads of light are reflected into the camera and onto the moving film, thus providing a permanent, objective record of visual behavior during the reading act. The portion of film may be removed from the camera immediately and developed in the processor supplied with the ensemble.

The reading graph is then analyzed in terms of number of fixations and regressions per 100 running words, the average span of recognition, the average duration of fixations, and the rate of reading. Comprehension is measured by 10 post-reading questions. Subsequent analysis of the graph may be made to judge relative efficiency of eye movements (rate divided by fixations plus regressions); and for directional attack (regressions divided by fixations). The individual's performances are then compared with the norms established by the testing of 12,000 cases ranging from first grade to college level.

Studies by Taylor (*1, 3*) support the validity of the technique by indicating high correlations between rate of reading in the camera and in ordinary reading tests. His studies also indicate consistency of performance of individuals reading materials at or below their grade levels, or in reading materials varying significantly in interest values. Consistency of performances was demonstrated in another sample when individuals read at their "usual" rate or when instructed to read carefully for comprehension. The pretesting to determine an appropriate test card further contributes to the reliability of the camera record. Formal data on reliability by test-retest or other means have not yet been established.

For training in the operation of the camera, purchasers are given a prepared list of training materials and instruction by the local EDL representatives. Actually, the technique is so simple that extended training is unnecessary.

In this reviewer's opinion, the *Reading Eye* adds certain dimensions to reading diagnosis and remediation not found in any other approach. It alone will serve to reveal the efficiency of the reader's functioning in the reading act in such details as excessive regressions, abnormal duration of fixation pauses, habitual regressions at recurring points, inaccuracy of return sweep, coordination and vergence problems, the effects of lateral or vertical imbalance and of variations in acuity, tendencies to suppression or monocular reading, and evidences of severe tension. The analysis of the reading graph also yields information regarding the need for training in directional attack, the effectiveness of mechanical training devices, and the outcomes of remedial training in reading.

For an excerpt from a related book review, see B478.

[839]

★Reading Versatility Test. Grades 6–10, 11–16 and adults; 1961–62; reading flexibility; 2 levels; manual ('62, 10 pages); no data on reliability; stopwatch or test timer (card booklet for indicating elapsed time) necessary for administration of *a*1 and *b;* 80¢ per test timer; postage extra; Arthur S. McDonald, Mary Alodia, George Zimny, Stanford E. Taylor, and James Byrne; Educational Developmental Laboratories, Inc. *

a) BASIC. Grades 6–10; 1961–62; 2 editions.

1) [*Paper and Pencil Edition.*] 7 scores: rate of reading (2 scores), comprehension (2 scores), scanning rate, skimming rate (2 scores); Forms A ('61), B ('61), AA ('62), BB ('62), (16 pages); test booklet title of Forms AA and BB is *Appraisal of Reading Versatility (Basic)*; distribution of Forms A and B restricted to schools; 16¢ per test; 50¢ per specimen set of 2 forms; [30] minutes.

2) [*Reading Eye Edition.*] Administered using the publisher's eye-movement camera (see 838); 29 scores: 5 scores (comprehension, rate, fixations per 100 words, duration of fixation, apparent number of lines) for each of 5 exercises, and 2 scores (regressions per 100 words, span of recognition) for each of 2 exercises; individual; Forms A, B, ('61, 15 pages); record sheet ['62, 2 pages]; separate answer folders must be used; $1 per test; 5¢ per answer folder; $460 per camera; $24 per special platen for this test; specimen set not available; [35] minutes.

b) ADVANCED. Grades 11–16 and adults; 1962; 6 scores: same as for *a*1 except only 1 skimming rate score; Forms C, D, CC, DD, (16 pages); test booklet title of Forms CC and DD is *Appraisal of Reading Versatility (Advanced)*; distribution of Forms C and D restricted to schools and colleges; 20¢ per test; 60¢ per specimen set of 2 forms; [30] minutes.

REFERENCES

1. THEOPHEMIA, MARY. "Testing Flexibility in Reading." *Int Rdg Assn Conf Proc* 7:138–9 '62. *

[840]

★Understanding Communication (Verbal Comprehension). Industrial employees at the skilled level or below; 1959, c1956–59; 1 form ('56, 4 pages); manual ('59, 13 pages); reliability data based on student group only; $3 per 20 tests, postage extra; $1 per specimen set, postpaid; 15(20) minutes; Thelma G. Thurstone (test) and Measurement Research Division, Industrial Relations Center, University of Chicago (manual); Education-Industry Service. *

C. E. JURGENSEN, *Assistant Vice President, Personnel, Minneapolis Gas Company, Minneapolis, Minnesota.*

This test purports to measure comprehension of verbal material in the form of short sentences and phrases. The items were selected on the basis of an item analysis of a 200-item test administered to over 500 children in grades 7–12. The test has been used in junior and senior high schools and in at least three industrial groups. Although developed on school children, the test is apparently intended for industrial use. Norms indicate that the range of scores allows the test to discriminate adequately between hourly industrial personnel (better between semiskilled than between persons on skilled levels) but not between executives or between professionals.

Validity data are weak, consisting of a correlation of .75 between scores on this test and an unnamed general scholastic achievement test for a group of 200 eighth grade children and correlations of .52 and .48 with a test of verbal reasoning for two groups of industrial employees (*n*'s of 193 and 45). No predictive or concurrent validity coefficients are given in the manual. Though this test is presumably intended for use in business and industry, there is little evidence on what the test measures or how well it measures whatever it does measure. Similarly there is a lack of evidence on relevance of scores to any criteria of job success. The fact that test scores differentiate within or between occupational groups is insufficient; conceivably, age or educational level might differentiate even better than scores on the test.

The manual, in reference to scores on this test, asserts that "speed of reading, vocabulary, and word fluency are of minor importance if the subject has good verbal comprehension," but no supporting evidence is given. Although the test is intended to measure understanding communication, and although the verbal comprehension factor has been identified in various factorial studies, no evidence is presented to the effect that this test will give more or additional or better information than any test of general mental ability, or even a test of reading ability.

In general, the manual is well written and is particularly commendable for its two-page discussion of standard score interpretation. It is unfortunate that the manual does not also present data on the meaning and use of the specific score obtained from this test.

In summary, though the test may be a useful addition to a battery intended for factor analyses in theoretical studies of the nature of cognitive processes, there is no evidence that it should be used in addition to or in place of other tests in a battery for employee selection or placement or for student counseling or guidance.

DONALD E. P. SMITH, *Associate Professor of Education, and Chief, Reading Improvement Service, The University of Michigan, Ann Arbor, Michigan.*

This test of silent reading comprehension runs the risk of being judged by its typography. That would be a mistake. The measuring technique, the content, and the evaluative evidence commend it as a standard for comparison by those who would measure reading skill. It was developed "to measure comprehension of verbal material in the form of short sentences and phrases * Marking the right answer does not depend on [delayed] memory or on recognizing the answer in the paragraph; rather, it depends on solving a problem presented in verbal form."

To appreciate the author's implied distinction between her strategy and that of other current measures, consider the following item: "The skill attained by the early smith in England is strikingly illustrated in the discovery of ornate hinges, an andiron with an oxhead design, and fragments of: (*a*) crude weapons, (*b*) beautiful tapestry, (*c*) engraved shields, (*d*) horseshoes." An analysis of the semantic and syntactic elements which must be discriminated in this item is inappropriate here, but the item deserves attention as a model for the reading comprehension task.

The test consists of 40 such items selected from 200 sample items tried out on children in grades 7–12. Four choices, consisting of a terminal word or phrase, follow each item. Distractors are excellent. Items appear to be arranged in order of complexity.

Split-half reliability on 300 students is reported as .91, unusually good for a measure of reading skill. Of interest are data gleaned from the norm table. Standard scores (normalized) are provided for a sample of nearly a thousand hourly industrial personnel. Four standard deviations embrace raw scores from 11 to 38 (of 40 possible). Since the score consists of rights only, a chance score (10) would place the subject at or below the 2nd percentile, where he belongs, a desirable though not necessarily common state of affairs.

Coefficients are provided indicating a substantial relationship with "general scholastic achievement scores" (.75), and with a test of verbal reasoning (.63, no reference given). Failure to compare this scale with others is understandable in light of the author's definition of reading comprehension.

The manual is clearly written and includes a simple explanation of standard scores and their interpretation, as well as a number of careful admonitions concerning interpretation. Print and leading are inappropriate. Minor visual problems, particularly tremor, are likely to penalize some subjects.

With improved typography, this scale deserves the widest possible use in high school, college, and industry.

[Other Tests]

For tests not listed above, see the following entries in *Tests in Print:* 1463–4, 1468, and 1471.

ORAL

[841]

★**Flash-X Sight Vocabulary Test.** Grades 1–2; 1961; 2 scores: sight vocabulary, experience vocabulary; individual; 1 form (3 discs); instruction booklet (9 pages); record sheet (2 pages); manual (12 pages); no data on reliability; $1.60 per test; $2 per 100 record sheets; $7.20 per tachistoscope with manual and demonstration disc; postage extra; [10] minutes; George D. Spache and Stanford E. Taylor; Educational Developmental Laboratories, Inc. *

[842]

★**Gray Oral Reading Test.** Grades 1–16 and adults; 1963; individual; Forms A, B, C, D; reading passage booklet (15 pages) for each form; record booklet (8 pages) for each form; manual (29 pages); tentative norms; $1.60 per reading passage booklet; $3.20 per set of 35 record booklets and manual; 50¢ per specimen set of record booklet and manual; postage extra; administration time not reported; edited by Helen M. Robinson; William S. Gray; Bobbs-Merrill Co., Inc. *

EMERY P. BLIESMER, *Director, McGuffey Reading Clinic, University of Virginia, Charlottesville, Virginia.*

While a promised "revision" or extension of the pioneer and widely used Gray *Standardized Oral Reading Paragraphs* has long been anticipated and awaited, this test, according to the publisher, represents a new test rather than a revision of the 1915 Gray test. Four forms are provided for this new test instead of only one, with each form containing 13 reading selections or passages. Four comprehension questions, intended to be checks on comprehension of literal meaning rather than accurate or precise measures of high level understanding, and a checklist or tallying column for various types of pronunciation errors accompany each passage. A separate booklet of reading passages for use by the examinee is provided with each form, as is also an 8-page examiner's record booklet. The latter contains the 13 reading passages for a given form, with the front page of the record booklet being a summary page for separate and total passage scores, types of errors, and observations.

The purported functions of the test are, first, to assess oral reading skill and, second, to aid in diagnosing reading difficulties. Detailed directions for administering and scoring the test and for interpreting and recording errors are given in the manual. Time needed for reading each passage, types of errors made, responses to comprehension questions, and other observations and comments are recorded by the examiner during administration of the test. Eight types of errors are noted: aid on words, gross and partial mispronunciations, omissions, insertions, substitutions, repetitions, and inversions. Each passage is scored on the basis of time required for reading it and the number of errors made. A total passage score is then used for converting to a grade equivalent score.

The reading passages were so constructed as to be of progressive levels of difficulty, ranging from a preprimer level to college or adult levels. Purportedly, the average case tested will read at least five passages before a terminal point is reached. One of the unique features of the test is the use of a picture to introduce the first selection, in line with regular classroom practice at beginning reading levels.

The "tentative norms" presented in the manual are based on results obtained by administering all four forms of the test to each of approximately 20 boys and 20 girls in each of grades 1–12. Grade equivalents of total passage scores on each form for each sex reflect slight differences in difficulty among forms. Subjects in the norming population were from two school districts in Florida and several schools in a Chicago suburb and metropolitan Chicago (all public schools). Attempts were made to have "average readers" for each given grade in the norming population; but the average mental level of subjects in each grade tended to be near the upper limit of the normal or average range.

A detailed and careful presentation of "interpretation of the scores" is provided in the manual. Some attention is given to causes for specific types of errors. Detailed interpretation of three illustrative examples or sample records of data is also included.

The size of the record booklet and manual pages is slightly larger than that of the standard 8½ by 11 inch sheet. Since more than ample room for recording errors, responses, and various scores is provided in the record booklet, cutting the booklet down to standard size could be done without detracting from recording and scoring procedures and would greatly facilitate keeping of the booklets in case folders and files.

The *Gray Oral Reading Test* should be viewed as a very welcome and useful addition to the stock of measuring tools in the field of reading. Development and construction of the test appears to have been done rather carefully and soundly. The suggestions in the manual that the test can be quite useful in giving estimates of oral reading ability, in suggesting difficulties requiring further analysis, and in giving insight in word perception skills, but that additional tests may be needed before recommendation for correction procedures can be made, seem rather modest ones. It is likely that this test will have an even greater use than did the *Standardized Oral Reading Paragraphs,* with its greatest use being found in remedial programs or in other work with youngsters with reading difficulties. Provision of more than one form is particularly welcome (especially in view of the apparently widespread practice of using the earlier Gray test as a pretest and post-test in remedial programs and in reported research studies), as is also the simpler and better explained scoring procedure.

ALBERT J. HARRIS, *Professor of Education, and Director, Office of Research and Evaluation, Division of Teacher Education, The City University of New York, New York, New York.*

The publisher states that the new *Gray Oral Reading Test* is not a revision of the *Standardized Oral Reading Paragraphs* (first published in 1915), which will remain available. The 1963 test is new in content and method of standardization. Nevertheless, a comparison shows many similarities with the older test. The similar features include the basic structure of a series of short selections for oral reading, ascending in difficulty from first grade through secondary school, and a scoring procedure in which raw scores are based on a combination of errors and rate.

There are, however, several important differences. These include: (*a*) the new test has four equivalent forms; (*b*) each form has a picture to introduce the easiest selection; (*c*) the 13 passages in each form include 3 of first grade level; (*d*) the material for the subject to read is printed on stiff, durable paper in a booklet, each passage on a separate page; (*e*) a record booklet is provided in which the subject's responses are recorded and scored; (*f*) four comprehension questions are asked on each passage, although comprehension is not included in the score; and (*g*) the new 29-page manual provides most of the information one likes to find in a manual.

The major purposes of the test are: "first, to provide an objective measure of growth in oral reading from early first grade to college; and second, to aid in the diagnosis of oral reading difficulties." For the latter purpose, errors are categorized under eight headings: aid, gross mispronunciation, partial mispronunciation, omission, insertion, substitution, repetition, and inverting word order. Hesitations, self-corrections, and repetitions of less than a word are not counted as errors, but affect the score by increasing the time taken.

Directions for administration and scoring are clear and explicit. One starts with an easy passage and gives enough passages to cover the range from reading without error to two passages read with seven or more errors each. The score for each passage is based on a combination of errors and time, with errors the major factor. The total raw score is the sum of the passage scores, with full credit given for passages below the one read perfectly.

The four comprehension questions to be asked after each passage have been intentionally limited to the literal meaning and are therefore not comparable to questions usually asked in silent reading tests of comprehension. For this reason, it is probably wise that no norms have been provided for the comprehension questions.

The content of the passages is varied, and in general the style of writing is appropriate. Difficulty ascends regularly and in fairly even steps. The length of the passages is quite similar, except at first grade level. The four forms seem quite equivalent in content as well as in form, although small differences in difficulty are reported.

The test's claim for validity rests on the steps taken in its construction, and its content. The steps taken to use appropriate vocabulary and content, provide steady and sequential progression in difficulty, and construct forms that are reasonably equivalent in content as well as statistically, represent test construction at a high level. The scoring procedure and methods of analysis provided are appropriate for the purposes of the test. Perhaps too much weight is given to time as compared to errors. Face and construct validity can be accepted as being high. At the same time, one can hope that data about this new test's relationship to other established measures of reading skills will be forthcoming.

Information about reliability is given mainly in terms of standard errors of measurement, which range from 1.98 raw score points for girls on Form A to 4.59 points for girls on Form B; 4.0 points is conservatively taken as the average value. In grade scores this is about .4 to .5 at first grade, increasing gradually to .6 or .7 at fourth grade, .8 at eighth grade, and more than a year at secondary levels. Although this may seem like a large margin of error, it compares favorably with the available data on other oral reading tests. For the entire range of scores, intercorrelations among forms average .97; reliability coefficients are not given for single grades.

The weakest feature of this test is the norms, which are presented as tentative. They are based on the testing of 502 children, 256 boys and 246 girls, averaging about 40 children per grade, chosen by means of random numbers from representative classes in schools in Florida, Chicago, and a Chicago suburb. Children with speech defects, serious health or emotional problems, or who had been double promoted or retarded were eliminated. Whether any Negro children were included is not stated. The population seems to have been above average intellectually, with average IQ's of 109.1 for boys and 111.6 for girls. Since the girls in general did better than the boys, separate norms are given for boys and girls. The differences are fairly substantial; a raw score of 40 points on Form B provides a grade equivalent of 5.1 for a boy but only 4.3 for a girl.

This reviewer questions the desirability of sex norms on an achievement test, for which one of the purposes is the proper placement of children in instructional groups. It does not seem likely that a boy scoring 5.1 on this test is any more capable of reading a fifth grade reader than a girl scoring 4.3. The use of separate norms by sex seems to reduce the test's possible usefulness in the selection of appropriate learning materials or in assigning children to instructional groups. This reviewer hopes that a set of combined norms will be added to the present separate norms for boys and girls.

Another difficulty in the norms is the severity of the standards for beginning readers. A boy needs a raw score of at least 11 to achieve a grade score above 1.0; on three of the four forms, a girl needs a raw score above 13 to do the same. This means that a child could read the preprimer passage perfectly and get partial credit on the primer passage, and still score 1.0, the same as a child unable to recognize a single word. It is to be hoped that when further normative studies are carried out, these difficulties with the present tentative norms will be eliminated.

Considering the test as a whole, this reviewer considers it a long-needed and very welcome addition to the very limited number of reasonably satisfactory oral reading tests.

PAUL R. LOHNES, *Associate Professor of Education, State University of New York at Buffalo, Buffalo, New York.*

The appearance of a new set of oral reading tests from a source as eminently qualified as the late William S. Gray and his colleagues at the University of Chicago is a significant event.

The technical preparation of these tests as described in the manual is excellent, as far as it goes. Four forms are provided, with grade norms for grades 1 through 12 for each sex. Although the forms are not equivalent in difficulty, the grade scores based on the various forms are comparable, and a standard error of measurement estimate is given for each grade score for each form and each sex. The norms are described as "tentative" because they are based on a total *n* of only 502, which breaks down to about 22 boys and 22 girls at each grade level, but considerable thought went into the design of the sample and the construction of the norms, which are judged adequate and useful, particularly as they adjust for sex and form differences in raw scores.

The complex analysis of variance by which the significances of these differences are established, the use of moving averages to smooth the curvilinear relationship of raw scores to grade levels, and the regression analysis employing score first-differences as a source of standard error of measurement estimates, all reported in commendable detail in the manual, will repay the closest study. Incidentally, besides locating sex and form problems, the analysis of variance overwhelmingly confirms the ability of the tests to discriminate among grade levels. Finally, intercorrelations among grade scores on the four forms are all in the neighborhood of .98, which leaves no doubt that the tests are measuring something systematically and similarly.

The problems of the Gray tests relate to questions about the nature of oral reading ability, questions which the manual raises but does not resolve. Internally, the tests produce scores which represent a nice blend of speed and accuracy aspects of performance, but the assumed relationship of fluency to accuracy is not explored. Eight types of errors are counted as sources of inaccuracy. A comprehension score is derived but not included as part of the total score. As the writings of Gray [1] testify, oral reading is a complex ability. Since diagnostic use of the tests is to be based on analysis of these details of performance there is a practical as well as a theoretical need for exposition of the precise interrelations among the components of oral reading ability. Externally, the biggest unanswered question concerns the relation of oral to silent reading, since a major justification for concern about oral reading is the claim that it is an important contributor to silent reading ability,[2] but other correlates of oral reading have been suggested and should be explored. For example, Winston [3] has suggested that "there is a direct relation between oral reading and personality development." Not only the manual is silent on the predictive validities and psychological meaning of oral reading ability; the two most recent reviews of reading research in *Review of Educational Research* [4] are also silent on these issues.

These are excellently prepared tests which will be particularly useful in the instrumentation of educational research into reading and its correlates, and in adding the dimension of oral reading scores to the cumulative school record on which research is frequently based. Perhaps a revision of the manual should review the existing research literature.

[843]

★**Neale Analysis of Reading Ability.** Ages 6–12; 1957–58; 3 scores (accuracy, comprehension, rate of reading) plus 3 optional supplementary tests (names and sounds of letters, auditory discrimination through simple spelling, blending and recognition of syllables); individual; Forms A, B, C, ('58, 46 pages in 1 booklet); individual record sheet ('57, 4 pages) for each form; manual ('58, 36 pages); no data on reliability of rate score and supplementary tests; no norms for supplementary tests; 5*s.* ($1) per test booklet; 5*d.* (25¢) per record sheet; 3*s.* 6*d.* (35¢) per manual; postage extra; (10–15) minutes; Marie D. Neale; Macmillan & Co. Ltd. * (United States publisher: St Martin's Press, Inc.)

1 Gray, William S. *The Teaching of Reading and Writing: An International Survey.* UNESCO Monographs on Fundamental Education, No. 10. Chicago, Ill.: Scott, Foresman & Co., 1956. Pp. 281. *
Gray, William S. "Reading," pp. 1086–1135. In *Encyclopedia of Educational Research, Third Edition.* Edited by Chester W. Harris. New York: Macmillan Co., 1960. Pp. xxxi, 1564. *
2 Heilman, Arthur W. *Principles and Practices of Teaching Reading,* pp. 146–9. Columbus, Ohio: Charles E. Merrill Books, Inc., 1961. Pp. xiii, 465. *
3 Winston, Gertrude C. "Oral Reading and Group Reading." *El Engl* 40:392–3+ Ap '63. *
4 Clymer, Theodore, and Robinson, Helen M. "Reading." *R Ed Res* 31:130–44 Ap '61. *
McCullough, Constance M. "Reading." *R Ed Res* 28:96–106 Ap '58.

M. Alan Brimer, *Senior Research Fellow in Education, University of Bristol, Bristol, England.*

The absence in Britain of an oral, diagnostic, reading test which would yield measures of reading attainment has handicapped teachers of reading for a number of years. It is this deficiency that the Neale test attempts to remedy, and which suggests the particular criteria for evaluating it.

The test booklet is well produced in spirally-bound, firm board. Black and white illustrations introduce the passages without revealing clues to comprehension. The type face is clear and the size and spacing of type is appropriately adjusted to the visual-perceptual skill requisite at the various reading levels. Each form contains six passages of graded difficulty and increasing length, which have been written to produce controlled variation of vocabulary and sentence structure. Each passage is a self-contained anecdote in which interest is coordinated with reading level.

In reference to the methods used to construct the test, the manual states that analysis of word difficulty, sentence structure, and optimum length of the test for each age level took place after preliminary trials and that statistical analysis followed further trials, but no account of the criteria or methods adopted is given. Some discussion of the rationale of securing three different measures from a single reading performance ought to have been included. Rate, accuracy, and comprehension are interdependent in oral reading, but this test allows them to vary together in an uncontrolled way. The child is allowed and encouraged to try words over when he hesitates, but only a limited time is allowed for word attack before the examiner supplies the word and records a refusal. Thus, inaccuracy reduces reading rate and possibly successful attempts at words are limited in the interests of rate. Comprehension is measured entirely through recall. The examiner is told to prevent the child from rereading the passage for clues to the answer. Consequently, the level of comprehension attained depends on the rate that the child adopts. It may be maintained that it is a representative sample of the child's oral reading that is being examined, and that it is more closely relevant to the child's reading in school to secure the three measures in this same context. Nevertheless, such a desirable intention has merit only insofar as the measures retain their distinct characteristics, and insofar as they are obtained in circumstances unequivocal for the child. It would probably have been better to have measured rate separately from accuracy and comprehension.

There are no difficulties in administration, though the classification of errors requires considerable experience if it is to keep pace with the rate of more rapid readers. A practice test would have improved task orientation. The instruction to "remember the story as you read it" is inadequate to induce the appropriate "set." Until the child has experienced the questions following the first passage and has realised that he may not look back (he is not told this), he does not appreciate the nature of the reading task that is being required of him. Scoring takes place as the test proceeds. For each passage, a ceiling level fixed by the accuracy score determines whether or not the child should proceed to the next passage. Such ceiling level decisions are rapidly made, and, apart from the rate score which rather unnecessarily requires the examiner to divide the number of words read by time, the summary scores are quickly obtained. A table relating time to rate for the six possible total numbers of words read would have facilitated rate scoring.

The reliability of the accuracy scores is good, none of the parallel forms reliabilities for year groups falling below .96. The reliabilities for the comprehension scores, while they are lower, are nevertheless adequate. The difference in the reliability levels may be attributable to the relative number of items. There are 100 scorable accuracy items, but only 42 comprehension items. The failure to quote the reliability of the rate scores or to make any reference to it can only be interpreted to the disadvantage of the test.

Validity was established by factor analysis studies of the performances of 9- and 11-year-old children, but details of the methods and results are not given. When criterion variables were selected and combined to form a complex criterion, the concomitant validity found for the test was high.

The standardisation sample consisted of over 2,000 children. While it is stated that size of school, area, social background, age, and sex were controlled, no account is given of the distribution of these characteristics in the sample. The standardisation sample must be judged small, particularly when it is realised that the numbers are distributed over three forms of the test (Form A, 1,221; Form B, 552; Form C, 489) and that the distribution of these over seven year groups results in an average of just under 200 per year group for Form A, and of less than 100 for Forms B and C.

Norms are given in the form of reading ages only, and it is to be regretted that no alternative form of expression is offered to test users. It may be that the numbers involved in standardisation would not have permitted more exact statistical forms. No account is given of the methods used to derive the norms. Such information would be desirable since, although reading ages are shown to ascend reasonably smoothly with score, some difficulty in smoothing the relationship might be expected from the use of discrete ceiling levels, which would tend to produce uneven trends in the increase of score with age.

Neale emphasizes that the objective score must be interpreted in relation to the child's personal history and that practical help is likely to arise from a study of the errors made rather than of the score. It is suggested that standard testing procedure might be abandoned in favour of more insightful pursuit of the child's difficulty. However, no guidance is offered as to the extremity or character of the errors that would warrant this. Similarly, the three supplementary tests are provided without explicit instructions for administration, scoring, or interpretation, and it is likely that an examiner sufficiently trained and experienced to make use of them would have more adequate tests at his disposal.

In summary, there are failings in construction, standardisation, and test reporting which prevent the test from satisfying the need in Britain that the author recognizes. Its best feature is the provision of standard reading passages within which the categories of reading errors can be recorded.

MAGDALEN D. VERNON, *Professor of Psychology, University of Reading, Reading, England.*

This is a test of individual oral reading rate, accuracy, and comprehension, standardized for British children. Each alternative form of the test consists of six passages of prose, graded in length and in difficulty of vocabulary and sentence structure. Each passage is illustrated by a picture to "set the scene" and arouse interest; the contents themselves also seem adequately interesting.

The child is required to read each passage aloud, and is scored for rate and accuracy. After each passage he answers eight questions (but only four on the first passage), the correctness of his answers indicating his degree of comprehension. There is no time limit, but each test should take about 15 to 20 minutes. The child is stopped after any passage in which he has made 16 errors of accuracy.

Though the instructions for this test are clear and comprehensible, the record sheets are not satisfactory. They give no space for recording the answers to the comprehension questions, though these may often be difficult to score while testing. The space for recording errors in reading is inadequate. Yet the tester may need to do this, since he is advised to classify the errors into six subgroups. The author is of the opinion that the type of error has some significance as to the nature of the child's reading processes. To investigate these further, she provides supplementary diagnostic tests of reading isolated letters, spelling, and blending. But no norms or standardized interpretations are given for these, nor any validation as to the particular type of defect they are supposed to indicate. Thus only a tester with extensive knowledge of reading defects can learn much from the child's performance on these supplementary tests. However, he may be able to obtain some useful information by studying discrepancies between accuracy and comprehension scores on the main test.

The main test seems on the whole to have been satisfactorily constructed, except that the sixth passage in each form appears to be far too difficult for even the older children to understand, and it is doubtful if they could score anything on it for comprehension. The forms were standardized on over 2,000 children, the sample being suitably controlled for region and social background. However, no children over 11 years appear to have been tested. The reading ages, given separately for the three scores, are based on extrapolation above age 11-10 for rate and comprehension, and above 11-11 for accuracy. In view of the aforesaid difficulty of the sixth passage, this seems a somewhat doubtful procedure.

Reliability for accuracy scores, which was calculated by correlating these scores on alternative forms of the test, is good (.98), and there is also a close correspondence between the mean scores on alternate forms for accuracy and comprehension at ages 7 to 11. Nothing is stated as to the correspondence of scores for rate, though it is shown that norms for rate are similar to those obtained on Ballard's *One-Minute Reading Test.* Validity was assessed by correlating a pooled score for rate, accuracy, and comprehension with pooled scores on the Ballard test, another word recognition test, and tests for comprehension, for 200 9-year-olds and 200 11-year-olds. The correlations are high (.95), but no explanation is given as to why scores for rate, accuracy, and comprehension were not separately validated. However, in the pilot study, accuracy scores for 9- to 11-year-olds showed correlations of .94 to .95 with scores on Schonell's *Graded Reading Vocabulary Test.*

It is doubtful whether measures of reading rate are of any particular significance for children of this age, and indeed it might be preferable to encourage them to read slowly and carefully. But the test may be found useful by busy clinicians in that it assesses accuracy and comprehension together in a short space of time and affords a direct comparison between these. The use of pictures also is probably valuable for the younger children. But the validation for comprehension is unsatisfactory, and the test is not clearly superior to any of the existing tests. It is not adequate for diagnostic purposes.

Brit J Ed Psychol 28:298 N '58. * a valuable addition to the educational psychologist's diagnostic battery. Indeed, it provides a better *individual* assessment of reading comprehension from R.A. 6½ to 13.0 than any other at present available (an average of six questions per year as contrasted with two questions in "My Dog"). It covers word pronunciation from 6 to 12½, as reliably as the conventional Graded Vocabulary tests. Norms are also provided for reading speed, but this measure is troublesome to record and calculate and is, in any case, discriminative only from R.A. 6½ to 9½. The material consists of three parallel series of six graded passages which, both by their content and their illustrations, should attract the child's interest. The printed record and score sheet seems unwieldy and expensive; and the clinic psychologist, or trained remedial teacher, will probably prefer to make her own analysis of types of reading error. The author claims that testing occupies ten to fifteen minutes per child. The tests have been carefully standardised and shown to have good reliability. It is a pity, however, that the opportunity was not taken to construct percentile or deviation norms for each age group instead of scoring purely in reading ages. The material is well printed, and the manual is clear, though one fears that unsophisticated teachers may sometimes fail to follow it correctly.

[844]

★Slosson Oral Reading Test (SORT). Grades 1-8 and high school; 1963; individual; 1 form (2 pages, test and examiner's directions and norms on a single sheet); no manual; 75¢ per pad of 20 tests, postpaid; (3) minutes; Richard L. Slosson; Slosson Educational Publications. *

[Other Tests]

For tests not listed above, see the following entries in *Tests in Print:* 1483-5 and 1488-91; out of print: 1486.

READINESS

[844a]

★The Anton Brenner Developmental Gestalt Test of School Readiness. Ages 5-6; 1964; individual; 1 form; manual (32 pages plus sample copies of record booklet and number recognition form); record booklet (3 pages); number recognition form (3 pages); $10 per set of 25 record booklets, 1 number recognition form, and manual; $3 per set of wooden cubes, pencil, and crayon (may also be assembled locally); $6.50 per 25 record booklets; $4 per manual; postpaid; (3-10) minutes; Anton Brenner; Western Psychological Services. *

REFERENCES

1. BRENNER, ANTON. "Reality Perception, Perceptual Differentiation and Readiness for School." *Merrill-Palmer Q* 4:196-209 su '58. *
2. HOFMANN, HELMUT. "Children's Drawings as an Indication of Readiness for First Grade." *Merrill-Palmer Q* 4:165-79 sp '58. *
3. VIEWAG, WILLIAM E., JR. "The Albion Study: A Longitudinal Study of Readiness for School Tasks as Measured by the Brenner-Gestalt Test; A Preliminary Report," pp. 75-88. In *Inter-Institutional Seminar in Child Development: Collected Papers, 1958.* Dearborn, Mich.: Educational Department, Henry Ford Museum and Greenfield Village, 1958. Pp. v, 122. *
4. BRENNER, ANTON. "A New Gestalt Test for Measuring Readiness for School." *Merrill-Palmer Q* 6:27-51 f '59. *
5. RALPH, JEAN SMITH. *The Brenner Gestalt Test as a Measure of Readiness for School.* Master's thesis, Wayne State University (Detroit, Mich.), 1960.
6. LUTTGEN, GERTRUDE. "Use of the Brenner Gestalt Test by a Classroom Teacher," pp. 102-14. In *The Inter-Institutional Seminar in Child Development: Collected Papers, 1960.* Greenfield Village, Mich.: Education Department, Henry Ford Museum, [1961]. Pp. vi, 272. *
7. RALPH, JEAN. "The Brenner-Gestalt Test as a Measure of Readiness for School," pp. 87-101. In *The Inter-Institutional Seminar in Child Development: Collected Papers, 1960.* Greenfield Village, Mich.: Education Department, Henry Ford Museum, [1961]. Pp. vi, 272. *
8. SANDHU, SWARAN SINGH. *Factors of Personality, Home and Culture as Related to the Early Identification of Under-Achievement.* Master's thesis, Wayne State University (Detroit, Mich.), 1963.

[845]

***Gates Reading Readiness Tests.** Grade 1; 1939-42; 5 scores: picture directions, word matching, word-card matching, rhyming, letters and numbers; 1 form ('39, 8 pages); revised manual ('42, 31 pages, essentially the same as 1939 manual except for norms); $2.25 per 35 tests; 50¢ per specimen set; postpaid; (50) minutes; Arthur I. Gates; Bureau of Publications. * (Australian edition: Australian Council for Educational Research.)

REFERENCES

1-5. See 40:1537.
6-8. See 3:516.
9. BALOW, IRVING H. "Sex Differences in First Grade Reading." *El Engl* 40:303-6+ Mr '63. *

For a review by F. J. Schonell (Australian edition, identical except for norms), see 4:566; for reviews by Marion Monroe Cox and Paul A. Witty, see 3:516; see also 40:1537 (2 excerpts).

[846]

***Lee-Clark Reading Readiness Test, 1962 Revision.** Grades kgn-1; 1931-63; 4 scores: letter symbols, concepts, word symbols, total; 1 form ('62, c1960, 11 pages, identical with tests copyrighted in 1943 and 1951 except for format changes and, in concepts subtest, revision of all art work and half of items); manual ('62, 16 pages); optional tape recorded directions for administration ('63, 3¾ ips); mimeographed manual ['63, 16 pages] for use with tape; $3.50 per 35 tests; $5.95 per tape; postage extra; 25¢ per specimen set without tape, $6.20 per specimen set with tape, postpaid; (20) minutes; J. Murray Lee and Willis W. Clark; California Test Bureau. *

REFERENCES

1. LEE, J. MURRAY; CLARK, WILLIS W.; AND LEE, DORRIS MAY. "Measuring Reading Readiness." *El Sch J* 34:656-66 My '34. * (*PA* 8:4741)
2. WILMORE, WALDO W. *Relative Validity of Three Group Readiness Tests in Predicting Reading Achievement.* Master's thesis, University of Kansas (Lawrence, Kan.), 1939.
3. HENIG, MAX S. "Predictive Value of a Reading-Readiness Test and of Teachers' Forecasts." *El Sch J* 50:41-6 S '49. * (*PA* 24:2060)
4. MOREAU, MARGARET. "Long Term Prediction of Reading Success." *Calif J Ed Res* 1:173-6 S '50. *
5. KOPPITZ, ELIZABETH M.; MARDIS, VERDENA; AND STEPHENS, THOMAS. "A Note on Screening School Beginners With the Bender Gestalt Test." *J Ed Psychol* 52:80-1 Ap '61. * (*PA* 38:3205)
6. PARSLEY, K. M., JR., AND POWELL, MARVIN. "Relationships Between the Lee-Clark Reading Readiness Test and the 1937 Revision of the Stanford-Binet Intelligence Test, Form L." *J Ed Res* 54:304-7 Ap '61. *
7. POWELL, MARVIN, AND PARSLEY, KENNETH M., JR. "The Relationships Between First Grade Reading Readiness and Second Grade Reading Achievement." *J Ed Res* 54:229-33 F '61. *
8. DOBSON, JAMES C., JR. *A Critical Evaluation of the Lee-Clark Reading Readiness Test.* Master's thesis, University of Southern California (Los Angeles, Calif.), 1962.

9. DOBSON, JAMES C., AND HOPKINS, KENNETH D. "The Reliability and Predictive Validity of the Lee-Clark Reading Readiness Test." *J Develop Read* 6:278–81 su '63. * (*PA* 39:1724)

For a review by James R. Hobson of the 1951 edition, see 5:678; for reviews by Marion Monroe Cox and David H. Russell of the 1943 edition, see 3:517.

[847]

***Maturity Level for School Entrance and Reading Readiness.** Grades kgn–1; 1950–59; revision of *School Readiness Inventory;* behavior checklist completed by teachers; 2 scores: maturity level, reading readiness; individual; 1 form ('59, 2 pages, essentially a combination of items from the two forms of the original edition); manual ('59, 7 pages); $3 per 50 records; 50¢ per manual; postage extra; 55¢ per specimen set, postpaid; (20) minutes; Katharine M. Banham; [American Guidance Service, Inc.]. *

For a review by David H. Russell of the original edition, see 4:572.

[848]

***Perceptual Forms Test.** Ages 6–8.5; 1955–63; revision of *Children's Perceptual Achievement Forms;* visual development; 1 form ['58, 8 cards]; teacher's manuals (both including test cards): 1963 edition ('63, 10 pages) for group testing, clinical guide, 1962 edition ('62, 23 pages) for individual testing; procedure manual, educational edition ('63, 52 pages); mimeographed procedure guide, clinical edition ['62, 75 pages]; mimeographed training manual, parents edition ['61, 22 pages]; incomplete forms sheet ['55, 2 pages]; $2 per teacher's manual of either edition; $2 per pad of 100 incomplete forms sheets; $3.50 per procedure manual; $5 per procedure guide; $3 per set of training manual and templates; cash orders postpaid; [10] minutes; Publication Committee, Winter Haven Lions Club; Winter Haven Lions Research Foundation, Inc. *

REFERENCES

1. LOWDER, ROBERT GLENN. *Perceptual Ability and School Achievement: An Exploratory Study.* Doctor's thesis, Purdue University (Lafayette, Ind.), 1956. (*DA* 16:2205)
2. ROBINSON, HELEN M.; LETTON, MILDRED C.; MOZZI, LUCILLE; AND ROSENBLOOM, ALFRED A. "An Evaluation of the Children's Visual Achievement Forms at Grade I." *Am J Optom* 35:515–25 O '58. *
3. KAGERER, RUDOLPH L. *The Relationship of Visual Perception Performance in Early Grades to Reading Level in Grade Four.* Winter Haven, Fla.: Winter Haven Lion's Publication Committee, [1960]. Pp. vii, 31. *
4. ROBINSON, HELEN M.; MOZZI, LUCILLE; WITTICK, MILDRED LETTON; AND ROSENBLOOM, ALFRED A. "Children's Perceptual Achievement Forms: A Three Year Study." *Am J Optom* 37:223–37 My '60. *
5. MANAS, LEO. "A New Method of Scoring Children's Visual Achievement Forms." *J Am Optom Assn* 32:713–8 Ap '61. *
6. HARVEY, JASPER. "Evaluation and Development of Techniques for Testing Visual Acuity of Trainable Mentally Retarded Children." *Am J Optom* 40:745–54 D '63. *

MARY C. AUSTIN, *Professor of Education, Western Reserve University, Cleveland, Ohio.*

This test, primarily intended to discover the child who lacks that degree of hand-eye coordination considered requisite for beginning school tasks, may be given as a group test or as an individual one. Each child is asked to reproduce seven geometric forms, one at a time, on a blank sheet of paper 8½ by 11 inches. Presented in a specific sequence, the figures include circle, cross, square, triangle, divided rectangle, horizontal diamond, and vertical diamond. Following the drawing of these forms, the child turns his paper over for the "Incomplete Forms" test, for which the teacher shows the same test cards to the pupil so he can finish each incomplete picture on the page provided.

The revised 1962 manual provides clearly outlined directions for testing, scoring, and interpreting the results. Nine sample sets of drawings are illustrated and discussed. The scoring scale, developed from an analysis of more than 7,000 sets of children's drawings, indicates that a child whose drawings rate a score of more than 60 can be expected to possess "a sensory-motor-perceptual pattern adequate for the tasks" related to beginning school activities. A total score of "significantly less than 60" indicates that a child "can be expected to achieve in the lowest third of his class." Age characteristics, organization, neatness, and size relationship of drawings are taken into account, along with the total score obtained on the forms. Having identified the child who is likely to experience problems in general school achievement—problems which may be related to perceptual difficulties—the teacher might delay the introduction of formal reading instruction until hand-eye coordination has been improved through template training. The latter is discussed in some detail in the manual.

The development of the *Perceptual Forms Test* began in 1953 when members of the Winter Haven Lions Club expressed concern about reports of reading failures among children. At that time a committee was established to undertake a four year project to gather data on the probable causes of failures in the primary grades. Preliminary editions of the test were tried in the first three grades during the next few years, and a Lions Club employee collected information about a large number of children, their performance on the forms, and their subsequent success in school.

The history of research and experimentation over a period of several years includes studies made at Purdue University under the direction of Newell C. Kephart, a number of classroom experiments, and a group of independent studies. Lowder (*1*) validated the use of the geometric forms as a predictor of school achievement. He found a significant relationship between copying performance and school achievement, with the divided rectangle and horizontal diamond being the best discriminators and the most difficult items. His observations resulted in some revisions of the test itself. He also raised a number of questions about the testing of perceptual ability. Two of these were "Since outline form perception seems to be a learned, developmental phenomenon, will formal, systematic perceptual training result in improved school achievement in the lower grades?" and "What is the relationship of outline form perception to school achievement in grades beyond one, two, and three?" These questions led Kagerer (*3*) to explore the relationships between visual performance in the early grades and reading level in grade 4. His findings indicated that copying ability in the first grade does not predict reading ability in the fourth grade. There is, however, a relationship between copying performance in the second and third grade and reading achievement in the fourth grade. Kagerer pointed out that the copying tests should not be used to classify children, but rather to identify those who may be exhibiting difficulty with visual perceptual development. He also suggested that the possibility of helping children who demonstrate perceptual difficulty should be investigated.

The results of independent studies (*4*, *5*) seem to indicate that scores below 58 or 60 on the test should be interpreted to mean poor general achievement in the future, rather than specific difficulties in reading or handwriting.

There can be no question regarding the values of measures of copying or reproduction ability as a predictor of school success. Tests of visual discrimination which do not determine simply the child's knowledge of letters and words are offered in several reading aptitude tests. The *Perceptual Forms Test* represents the first generally available test of visual perception or discrimination not found in the readiness tests. In its present form the test can be helpful in evaluating the perceptual ability of school beginners. That revision of the test may be desirable is indicated in some of the studies mentioned previously. It may be advisable, for example, to eliminate the cross and the square and to add more difficult items to improve the predictive ability of the test. The present test appears less effective above the ages of 8 and 9. Perhaps an extension of its effective age range, coupled with an increased accuracy of discrimination, will result in the kind of test instrument which has a broader range of applicability. The Winter Haven Lions Research Foundation intends to continue its work in this direction.

[849]

Reading Readiness Test. Grades kgn–1; 1957; 1 form (12 pages); manual (8 pages); $3 per 25 tests; 25¢ per specimen set; cash orders postpaid; (20) minutes; David F. Votaw, Sr. and Peggy Lou Moses; Steck Co. *

REFERENCES

1. BANHAM, KATHARINE M. "Maturity Level for Reading Readiness: A Check List for the Use of Teachers and Parents as a Supplement to Reading Readiness Tests." *Ed & Psychol Meas* 18:371–5 su '58. *

DAVID A. PAYNE, *Assistant Professor of Education, Syracuse University, Syracuse, New York.*

This test contains 92 items distributed among 10 logically sequenced subtests. The authors emphasize the necessity of treating the test as a "game." This is highly desirable in light of the lack of test sophistication of elementary students and the need to establish rapport. An evaluation of the directions and test tasks indicates that this purpose has been reasonably approached.

The test items, subtests, and directions are of variable quality and difficulty. Assessment of students' familiarity with names of objects (10 items) is extremely easy, but "contributes but little to the placement of a child on the score scale." Above functioning as an introductory "game" exercise, this subtest serves no purpose. The semantics of test directions are of critical importance in tests intended for use with the very young. The reviewer encountered several items measuring interpretation of spoken sentences (10 items) which are open to question. In one item directions call for the student to make a cross on the picture which shows a girl carrying her doll, when the picture has the girl standing and holding the doll. Superfluous words in the directions may confuse some students. In one item, directions require the selection of a picture where "Joe likes to ride his bicycle." This direction might justifiably apply to any of the four stimulus pictures. Perhaps the statement "Joe is riding his bike" would be sufficient. These kinds of word selection problems, together with sometimes confusing uses of plurals, are not uncommon. The four subtests evaluating visual discrimination (letters, pairs of letters, words, and phrases) are well constructed. Most of the items in the test, however, appear very easy.

The manual lacks adequate statistical data. Some of the data reported lack complete description, others are open to question regarding validity. A more comprehensive manual would seem to be in order.

A split-half reliability coefficient of .92 is reported. Evidence of stability reliability is not presented but would be highly desirable inasmuch as this instrument is offered for predictive purposes.

Discussion of content validity takes the inadequate form of describing the types of items included in the test. The authors define concurrent validity as a correlation of their test with an unnamed intelligence test ($r = .74$, $n = 66$). It would be interestng to know the correlation of the intelligence measure with later reading performance. Perhaps it could function as well or better than this test in evaluating reading readiness. Correlation with accepted reading readiness and performance tests would also yield very useful information.

The norms (reported in centile form) were based on a "rigidly controlled" sample of 703 children, "about evenly divided between boys and girls, of Southwest Texas." This reviewer wonders what variables were rigidly controlled, and whether this norm group could be considered as a representative national sample.

Interpretation of test results is facilitated by the use of a quasi-expectancy table. The table is constructed with six unequal centile limits being coupled with qualitative descriptions (superior readiness, lower average, definitely not ready, etc.). The first author stated in personal correspondence that this table was "empirically determined," but without elaboration on methodology.

Under the heading, Purpose of the Test, a list is provided describing factors which are very important in reading readiness. Few of these appear to be measured by the test. The untested factors are probably more important than the measured ones. If the test is used, a teacher may wish to augment the results with measures of letter knowledge, copying ability, and auditory perception, especially the latter if instruction is primarily phonics oriented.

Due to the uneven quality of test items, probable lack of an appropriate test ceiling, and insufficient normative and validity data, particularly with regard to interpretation, it is felt that the *Reading Readiness Test* may yield scores which might be considered equivocal, and in its present form it is not recommended for use with individual students.

[850]

***Scholastic Reading Readiness Test.** First grade entrants; 1953-60; various titles used by the publisher; for Catholic schools; Form A Revised ('60, 11 pages); revised directions for administering ('60, 6 pages); no data on reliability; $2.40 per 20 tests; 50¢ per specimen set; postage extra; [30-45] minutes; Oliver F. Anderhalter and Ruth Colestock; Scholastic Testing Service, Inc. *

DAVID A. PAYNE, *Assistant Professor of Education, Syracuse University, Syracuse, New York.*

Inasmuch as the first edition (1953) of this test has not been reviewed previously, an attempt will here be made to compare the original and the revised edition (1960). Most of the statistical data reported in this review were obtained in personal correspondence from the first author.

In comparing the manuals of the two editions an alarming fact is noted. Although the revised edition was published after the APA Technical Recommendations, it contains less basic information than the 1953, or pre-APA Recommendations, edition. The manual of the revised edition contains only directions for administering, scoring, and using an expectancy table. Basic information on reliability, validity, and item analysis techniques employed is lacking. Even the sample sizes and demographic data on students used in composing the norms (reported as percentiles) and in constructing the expectancy table of chances for success in formal reading are not presented. Such a failure to provide even the most elementary data must be considered serious.

Both 1953 and 1960 editions of this test contain 80 "items" distributed among six subtests. Thirty three identical items are found in the two editions. The procedure of Tests 4 and 5 has been modified, though the basic content remains the same. Elsewhere, in 13 items one of the stimulus elements has been changed, and 6 items retain the same content but with one or more of the elements changed in form (e.g., redrawing of pictorial stimuli). No data are reported on the comparability of editions. The first author, in personal correspondence, however, stated that one unpublished study yielded a correlation of .94 (n = 138). The directions for administering are very well presented in both editions, but no estimate of administration time is given.

Three general areas are tested, with two subtests for each. Items purporting to measure knowledge and understanding of facts and events appear to be very easy. With a great number of easy items, perhaps the only discriminations possible are between the totally inept and all others. The visual discrimination items appear adequate, but one wonders about the effect of changing the stimuli, as is done within subtests, e.g., changing from geometric designs to letters and numbers as the student progresses through the subtest. The last area tested is sound-symbol association ability. Successful performance on these items appears to be very much dependent upon auditory training, which will differentially influence item difficulty. Such an uncontrolled variable might contribute significantly to the errors of measurement. In addition, the use of blends of "*cl*ock" (subtest 5) and "*dr*ess" (subtest 6) might be objected to by many contemporary linguists or phonics specialists. The directions call for the examiner to make a "hard C" (subtest 5) sound and a "hard D" (subtest 6). It is unlikely that either consonant sound can be made in isolation; moreover, one wonders how a "hard D" sounds.

Several comments on the nature of the 1960 revision seem appropriate. An attempt was made to provide a higher ceiling to the test by eliminating items with difficulty indices above 93 per cent. No rationale for selecting the 93 per cent cutoff point is presented. There is no evidence that item discrimination was investigated. The effect of this procedure was to lower the mean by 10 raw score points. The restandardization involved data on 17,144 students in 514 elementary schools representing systems in Michigan, California, Maryland, Virginia, Kentucky, Missouri, and New Jersey. It is not known if the 1960 norm group was composed of kindergarten or first grade students, or, if both grades were used, in what proportion. The norm groups for the 1953 and 1960 editions are markedly different, except at the upper end of the distribution. Despite this difference, the expectancy tables are virtually identical. It is possible that the expectancy table reported in the revised edition was arrived at by interpolation of figures for the first edition.

Corrected estimates of internal consistency (split-half) ranging from .977 to a remarkable .996 are reported for the 1953 edition. A Kuder-Richardson coefficient (no formula number designation) of .91 for the 1960 edition was reported to the reviewer in personal correspondence. Evidence of stability reliability of the total score and of the individual subtests would be highly desirable.

As stated earlier, no validity data are reported in the 1960 manual. Data made available to the reviewer, however, included reports of correlations ranging from .49 to .61 (median = .54) between the *Scholastic Reading Readiness Test* and the *Scholastic Diagnostic Reading Test.* Coefficients of .64 (n = 89) with the *Metropolitan Readiness Test,* and .53 (n = 135) with end of year reading performance for the 1953 edition were also given. A general intelligence measure would probably yield correlations similar to the above criteria.

Since this test, despite the revision, does not appear to have a high enough ceiling, the user might desire near perfect test performance before initiating formal reading at the preprimer level. The three readiness areas assessed are those generally accepted as having the greatest prognostic value. It is suggested that future manuals include a somewhat extended discussion of the authors' rationale in developing their test so that the potential user can evaluate the test in terms of his own classroom philosophy. There is no evidence, for instance, that a table of specifications was developed prior to item construction. It might also be fruitful to include items or subtests measuring knowledge of letter names and of handwriting or copying ability. On the basis of available information, this test cannot be recommended for use and its publication must be considered premature. It is hoped that future publications relating to this test will meet the essential principle of the APA Technical Recommendations of reporting sufficient information necessary for sound evaluations of usefulness and interpretation.

[851]

★**Watson Reading-Readiness Test.** Grades kgn-1; 1960; 3 scores: subjective test (teacher's ratings of physical, social, emotional, and psychological readiness), objective test, total; 1 form (6 pages); manual

(12 pages); no data on reliability; $1.35 per 25 tests; 15¢ per manual; 25¢ per specimen set; postage extra; [50–60] minutes in 4 sessions 1 day apart for objective test; G. Milton Watson; Book Society of Canada Ltd. * (United States publisher: C. S. Hammond & Co.)

[Other Tests]

For tests not listed above, see the following entries in *Tests in Print:* 1492–3, 1496–7, 1500, 1502, and 1504; out of print: 1494, 1501, and 1507.

SPECIAL FIELDS

[852]

***The Iowa Tests of Educational Development: Test 5, Ability to Interpret Reading Materials in the Social Studies.** Grades 9–12; 1942–61; IBM; Forms X-3S, Y-3S, ('52, 9 pages); battery examiner's manual ('58, c1949–57, 23 pages); battery general manual ('59, 37 pages); student profile leaflet, sixth edition ('61, c1958, 2 pages); see the complete battery entry (14*b*) for other accessories; no data on reliability; separate answer sheets must be used; $2.40 per 20 tests; $5 per 100 IBM answer sheets; 50¢ per scoring stencil; $3 per specimen set of the complete battery; postage extra; 60(70) minutes for full length version, 40(50) minutes for class period version; prepared under the direction of E. F. Lindquist; Science Research Associates, Inc. *

For reviews of the complete battery, see 14 and 5:17; for reviews of earlier forms, see 4:17 and 3:12.

[853]

***The Iowa Tests of Educational Development: Test 6, Ability to Interpret Reading Materials in the Natural Sciences.** Grades 9–12; 1942–61; IBM; Forms X-3S, Y-3S, ('52, 9 pages); battery examiner's manual ('58, c1949–57, 23 pages); battery general manual ('59, 37 pages); student profile leaflet, sixth edition ('61, c1958, 2 pages); see the complete battery entry (14*b*) for other accessories; no data on reliability; separate answer sheets must be used; $2.40 per 20 tests; $5 per 100 IBM answer sheets; 50¢ per scoring stencil; $3 per specimen set of the complete battery; postage extra; 60(70) minutes for full length version, 40(50) minutes for class period version; prepared under the direction of E. F. Lindquist; Science Research Associates, Inc. *

For reviews of the complete battery, see 14 and 5:17; for reviews of earlier forms, see 4:17 and 3:12.

[854]

★Lorimer Braille Recognition Test: A Test of Ability in Reading Braille Contractions. Students (ages 7–13) in grade 2 Braille; 1962; individual; 1 form (2 pages); manual (27 pages, available in printed form or Braille); 3*d.* per test; 3*s.* per manual; postpaid; John Lorimer; College of Teachers of the Blind. *

REFERENCES

1. "Lorimer Braille Recognition Test." *Teach Blind* 51:36–7 O '62. *

[855]

★Tooze Braille Speed Test: A Test of Basic Ability in Reading Braille. Students (ages 7–13) in grades 1 or 2 Braille; 1962; individual; 1 form (2 pages); manual (24 pages, available in printed form or Braille); record sheet (1 page); 3*d.* per test; 3*s.* per manual; postpaid; 1(5) minutes; F. H. G. Tooze; College of Teachers of the Blind. *

[Other Tests]

For tests not listed above, see the following entries in *Tests in Print:* 1508–9 and 1512–4.

SPEED

[Other Tests]

For tests not listed above, see the following entries in *Tests in Print:* 1516 and 1518; out of print: 1515 and 1517.

STUDY SKILLS

[856]

Brown-Holtzman Survey of Study Habits and Attitudes. High school and college; 1953–56; IBM; 1 form ('53, 3 pages); revised manual ('56, 11 pages); separate answer sheets must be used; $2.25 per 25 tests; $2 per 50 IBM answer sheets; 60¢ per set of scoring stencils and manual; 75¢ per specimen set; postpaid; (25–35) minutes; William F. Brown and Wayne H. Holtzman; Psychological Corporation. *

REFERENCES

1–14. See 5:688.

15. Anderson, Robert P., and Kuntz, James E. "The 'Survey of Study Habits and Attitudes' in a College Counseling Center." *Personnel & Guid J* 37:365–8 Ja '59. * (*PA* 35:1207)

16. Calia, Vincent Frank. *The Use of Discriminant Analysis in the Prediction of Performance of Junior College Students in a Program of General Education at Boston University Junior College.* Doctor's thesis, Boston University (Boston, Mass.), 1959. (*DA* 20:3190)

17. Reid, Jackson B.; King, F. J.; and Wickwire, Pat. "Cognitive and Other Personality Characteristics of Creative Children." *Psychol Rep* 5:729–37 D '59. * (*PA* 34:5632)

18. Smith, D. D. "Traits and College Achievement." *Can J Psychol* 13:93–101 Je '59. * (*PA* 34:4780)

19. Curran, Ann Marie. *Non-Intellective Characteristics of Freshman Underachievers, Normal Achievers, and Overachievers at the College Level.* Doctor's thesis, University of Connecticut (Storrs, Conn.), 1960. (*DA* 21:2584)

20. Lum, Mabel K. M. "A Comparison of Under- and Overachieving Female College Students." *J Ed Psychol* 51:109–14 Je '60. * (*PA* 35:3985)

21. Popham, W. James. "The Validity of the SSHA With Scholastic Overachievers and Underachievers." *Ed Res B* 39:214–5 N '60. *

22. Popham, W. James, and Moore, Mary R. "A Validity Check on the Brown-Holtzman Survey of Study Habits and Attitudes and the Borow College Inventory of Academic Adjustment." *Personnel & Guid J* 38:552–4 Mr '60. * (*PA* 35:7094)

23. Anderson, Thelma Hill. *Dimensions of the Characteristics Related to the High- and Low-Achievement of a Selected Group of Negro College Students.* Doctor's thesis, University of Oklahoma (Norman, Okla.), 1961. (*DA* 22:1082)

24. Savage, H. W. *An Evaluation of the Brown-Holtzman Survey of Study Habits and Attitudes for Use in Ontario.* Atkinson Study of Utilization of Student Resources, Supplementary Report No. 3. Toronto, Canada: Department of Educational Research, Ontario College of Education, University of Toronto, 1961. Pp. viii, 34. *

25. De Sena, Paul Ambrose. *Identification of Non-Intellectual Characteristics of Consistent Over-, Under-, and Normal-Achievers Enrolled in Science Curriculums at the Pennsylvania State University.* Doctor's thesis, Pennsylvania State University (University Park, Pa.), 1963. (*DA* 24:3144)

26. Pemberton, W. A. *Ability, Values, and College Achieve-*

ment. University of Delaware Studies in Higher Education, No. 1. Newark, Del.: the University, 1963. Pp. xii, 77. * (*PA* 38:6573)

For reviews by James Deese and C. Gilbert Wrenn (with Roy D. Lewis), see 5:688.

[857]

California Study Methods Survey. Grades 7–13; 1958; 5 scores: attitudes toward school, mechanics of study, planning and system, total, verification; IBM and Grade-O-Mat; 1 form (8 pages); manual (16 pages); $3.50 per 35 tests; separate answer sheets or cards may be used; 5¢ per IBM answer sheet; 40¢ per set of scoring stencils; 2¢ per Cal-Card; 40¢ per set of hand scoring stencils for Cal-Cards; 2¢ per Grade-O-Mat scorable punch-out card; 6¢ per stylus; 6¢ per backing pad; postage extra; 50¢ per specimen set, postpaid; (35–50) minutes; Harold D. Carter; California Test Bureau. *

REFERENCES

1–7. See 5:689.
8. CARTER, HAROLD D. "Improving the Prediction of School Achievement by Use of the California Study Methods Survey." *Ed Adm & Sup* 45:255–60 S '59. * (*PA* 34:8397)
9. CARTER, HAROLD D. "Over-Achievers and Under-Achievers in the Junior High School." *Calif J Ed Res* 12:51–6 Mr '61. * (*PA* 36:1KL51C)

JOHN D. KRUMBOLTZ, *Associate Professor of Education and Psychology, Stanford University, Stanford, California.*

The CSMS contains 150 "Yes" or "No" questions about study methods and attitudes which discriminate between high achieving and low achieving students. It yields a verification score plus three other subscores: (*a*) attitudes toward school, (*b*) mechanics of study, and (*c*) planning and system.

The CSMS was validated essentially by correlating its items and subscales with academic success. In general, it shows consistently positive correlations, ranging from .32 to .58 against grade-point averages and from .11 to .48 against achievement test scores. To some extent the use of grade-point averages to validate a study methods survey involves some circularity. The very first question on the CSMS is "Are you well satisfied with the grades you get?" The keyed answer is "Yes," indicating that students who get good grades answer "Yes" to that question more often than students who get poor grades. Obviously the students who are doing well in school know that they are doing well and will say so when asked on an inventory. The fact that their answers to these questions correlate with their grades should be no surprise. Using grade-point averages to validate study methods surveys can therefore be questioned. The absurdity can be shown by imagining what would happen if we were to construct a survey that consisted of only one question: "What is your grade-point average?" It could easily be shown that answers to this question correlated very highly with actual grade-point averages, thereby validating the one-item questionnaire. Many of the questions in the CSMS are more indirect ways of asking this one basic question.

We have no way of knowing whether the use of study methods that are keyed actually help students to get better grades. For example, one of the items that makes up the "mechanics of study" subscale (although it sounds more like an attitude item) is as follows: "Do you like to be alone in a room when you study?" Although the question is keyed "Yes," we have no evidence that students do better when they study in a room alone. It is possible, for example, that good students get better grades when they study in a room alone but that poor students get better grades with the added reinforcement of more studious persons present. The study methods that are best for the good students may not necessarily be best for the poor students. The CSMS makes no claim of taking such factors as this into account, but the careful user must understand that the answers characteristic of good students may or may not provide helpful suggestions about study methods for poor students.

The use of the CSMS as a predictive instrument is also advocated in the manual: "The *Survey,* when combined with tests of ability and intelligence, yields better prediction than that obtained from any instrument alone." Of course, the same statement could be made for almost any instrument, especially when the equations have not been subjected to cross validation. However, it has been well established in hundreds of studies that the best predictor of future grade-point average is previous grade-point average. The critical question is this: Does the addition of the CSMS to previous grade-point averages yield a higher cross validated multiple correlation in predicting future grade-point averages than previous grade-point averages alone? The manual presents no information on this point, but Carter (*4*) reports evidence on 129 high school seniors showing that their fall 1949 GPA correlated .88 with their spring 1950 GPA, while a prior edition of the CSMS predicted the same criterion with an r of .54. A multiple correlation was not reported. The usefulness of the CSMS as a predictive instrument is established only when it adds significantly to already available predictors known to be highly valid, not when it adds to those predictors which are not as highly valid.

The reliability data include both test-retest and internal consistency information. Exact descriptions of the samples used in these reliability studies are not given nor do we know the interval between test and retest. The reported reliabilities are in the neighborhood of .87 for the total score. Reliabilities of the subscales range from .58 to .76. Since the intercorrelations of the subscales with each other are in the neighborhood of .50, the reliability of differences between subscales is very low. The manual does not point this out, however. In fact, the manual says that "The coefficients reveal some communality among the three scores but not enough to reduce the usefulness of the scales to any appreciable extent." Actually, the intercorrelations between scales approach the reliability of each scale, so that it would be unwise to interpret differences between a person's subscale scores.

Thirty of the 150 items are also keyed for a verification scale. If a student scores less than 17 on this scale, he is to be "questioned individually about his responses to the *Survey*." The manual states that students scoring below this critical score may indicate "the desire to fake an unduly favorable score." Such an interpretation is highly unlikely in view of the nature of the verification scale. If a student were trying to fake an unduly favorable score, he would attempt to give the same kind of answers that would be given by high achieving students. Yet 19 of the 30 verification scale items are keyed in the same way for the verification scale as they are for the high-achieving students. Thus, a student who was trying to fake a highly favorable score would certainly answer at least 19 of the verification scale items in the "right" direction and thus be above the critical cutting score of 17. His faking of a favorable score would go undetected.

A second use for the verification score is to identify indiscriminate or chance marking due to carelessness or a negative attitude. Even here it is doubtful that a high proportion of careless responders would be caught. Completely random responding to the inventory would yield an average score on the verification scale of 15. Since a score of only 17 is sufficiently high to put one above suspicion, there would be a substantial percentage of random responders who would escape detection. Furthermore, if a careless student had a response set to answer "Yes" to every question, he would obtain a score of 23 on the verification scale and thus be far above suspicion. Thus the user of this inventory cannot use the verification scale to find those students who are trying to fake a favorable score nor to identify a very large percentage of those who are engaging in indiscriminate responding. Perhaps the best way of preventing these occurrences is to administer the inventory under circumstances where students have nothing to gain and something to lose by carelessness or falsification.

Some users may question the appropriateness of having only "Yes" or "No" answers to questions. The manual justifies this procedure on the questionable grounds that "so many of the attitudes and habits operate on an all-or-none basis." Actually, prior editions of the CSMS required responses on a 5-point scale ranging from "Always" to "Never." The manual states that "careful comparative studies reveal that this relatively cumbersome method of responding to questions was not appreciably more effective than a straightforward 'Yes' or 'No' response method."

One use of this inventory that has not been specifically suggested in the manual is as a source of concrete suggestions of study methods to be tried out by an under-achieving student. While no one knows if a specific study method will be best for any given student, many students need some hints and suggestions of methods that are at least worthy of a tryout. Perhaps one of the most constructive uses of the inventory would be to have a student compare his answers with the keyed answers and make a list of the specific study habits that he would like to try out in the future.

In spite of some of the negative factors pointed out above, the CSMS is actually a well constructed instrument for its type. Many of the criticisms mentioned would apply equally well to other study attitudes and methods inventories.

The author has taken the precaution to avoid a bias due to "response set" by keying about an equal number of "Yes" and "No" items in the three subscales. Only the verification scale has a disproportionate balance.

The norms were carefully constructed from a large number of students taking the test in grades 8 through 13. However, recommended use has been extrapolated to grade 7 also. In the grades studied no significant differences were found between different grade levels or between boys and girls, and hence there was no reason to prepare separate sets of norms.

The administrative instructions and the directions for scoring and recording scores appear to be simple, clear, and complete.

In summary, the CSMS appears to be a simple and useful device for calling attention to study methods which pupils might profitably try. The reliability of the total score appears to be satisfactory, but interpretations of differences between subscales should be avoided. Its use as a predictor of grade-point average is questionable, and its verification scale needs to be taken with a grain of salt. Users must remember that the study methods practiced by good students are not necessarily the study methods best for the poor students.

Donald E. P. Smith, *Associate Professor of Education, and Chief, Reading Improvement Service, The University of Michigan, Ann Arbor, Michigan.*

This is "a self-report inventory designed to reveal the....study methods and attitudes" of students in high school and college. It consists of 150 items yielding scores: attitudes toward school, mechanics of study, and planning and system. A "verification" or negative lie scale consists of the number of "correct" answers to 30 popular responses.

The scales have been developed over a 10 year period, during which time the several parts have been administered to several thousand students. That extreme care was used in its construction may be inferred from the clarity, precision, and inclusiveness of the manual. With one exception, the manual abounds with evidence concerning construct, content, and concurrent validity. The exception is the verification scale which has not been validated.

In brief, test-retest and K-R 21 reliabilities have a central tendency of .70 for the subscales and .85 for the total. Factoring at one stage of development yielded a "Mechanics of Study" factor which correlated only .09 with grade-point average, while the other "attitudinal" factors predicted GPA quite well. The author remedied that. He built in a relationship between mechanics of study and GPA by developing a new scale. Study habits items discriminating high from low achievers were identified so that, this time, the items correlated with GPA (about .50). The total score raises the multiple correlation between GPA and intelligence (Henmon-Nelson) from .66 to .75 among high school students.

Use of the results in counseling is discussed. If a school or college counselor has use for a study habits inventory, this is a good one to use. The manual might also be useful in a graduate course on test construction, since it follows APA recommendations remarkably well.

J Consult Psychol 23:471 O '59. Edward S. Bordin. * A good deal of work seems to have gone into the development of this instrument; its reliability seems adequate, and there is encouraging evidence of its validity for use in educational diagnosis with high school students. Little evidence is offered to support the supposed function of the Verification score.

J Counsel Psychol 7:77 sp '60. Laurence Siegel. * The *CSMS* is simple to administer and to score. It may prove to be a useful adjunct to scholastic counseling when improper study habits or scholastic attitudes are suspected. Two unfortunate omissions from the Manual might well be corrected in the future. First, the results of several validity studies at the college level ought to be summarized. Secondly, the Manual makes no mention of studies wherein *CSMS* scores were correlated with scores obtained from other instruments designed to measure similar functions.

[858]

***The Iowa Tests of Educational Development: Test 9, Use of Sources of Information.** Grades 9–12; 1942–61; IBM; Forms X-3S, Y-3S, ('52, 4 pages); battery examiner's manual ('58, c1949–57, 23 pages); battery general manual ('59, 37 pages); student profile leaflet, sixth edition ('61, c1958, 2 pages); see the complete battery entry (14b) for other accessories; no data on reliability; separate answer sheets must be used; $2.40 per 20 tests; $5 per 100 IBM answer sheets; 50¢ per scoring stencil; $3 per specimen set of the complete battery; postage extra; 27(35) minutes; prepared under the direction of E. F. Lindquist; Science Research Associates, Inc. *

For reviews of the complete battery, see 14 and 5:17; for reviews of earlier forms, see 4:17 and 3:12.

[859]

***A Library Orientation Test for College Freshmen, 1955 Edition.** Grade 13; 1950–61; 1 form ('55, 12 pages); manual ('61, 7 pages); separate answer sheets must be used; $4.50 per 35 tests; 50¢ per specimen set; postpaid; (50–60) minutes; Ethel M. Feagley, Dorothy W. Curtiss, Mary V. Gaver, and Esther Greene; Bureau of Publications. *

REFERENCES

1. JOYCE, WILLIAM D. "A Study of Academic Achievement and Performance on a Test of Library Understandings." *J Ed Res* 54:198–9 Ja '61. *

MOREY J. WANTMAN, *Director of Advisory and Instructional Programs, Educational Testing Service, Princeton, New Jersey.*

The previous reviews of this test in *The Fifth Mental Measurements Yearbook* present a complete description of the content of this instrument. The criticisms of the test in those reviews regarding both content and format still apply because there has been no revision of the instrument itself. This reviewer would add the comment that the number of options in some parts of the test is far too great. In Part 3, for example, there are as many as 19 options for 9 questions. The reading time for these questions could be reduced by splitting the 9 questions into 3 sets of 3 and reducing the number of options per set to 6. The 19 options are obviously not equally attractive for each question. It can be assumed that item discrimination is not improved by the presence of the large number of options. In addition, the key provided for the test is awkward in its present form. Stencil keys for each side of the answer sheet would be more serviceable.

Even though the instrument itself has undergone no revision, some of the gaps in the manual noted by a previous reviewer have been filled. The manual has been expanded to include both norms and reliability data. The table of norms is based on data from 14 colleges in the United States, distributed geographically as follows: "Eastern 6, North Central 4, Far West 3, and South 1." Neither the names nor characteristics of the institutions are provided, so the representativeness of the norms group of college freshmen in the United States is uncertain.

The instructions in the manual for interpreting group means by use of the table of norms supplied may lead to errors of interpretation of group results. Percentiles based on a distribution of means of colleges are necessary for appropriate interpretation of group means. The variability of a distribution of group means will be far less than the variability shown in the table of norms for individuals. The deviation of a group mean from the mean of all scores would therefore be of much greater significance than the table of norms for individual scores would suggest.

In addition to supplying a table of norms, the authors have also added data on reliability. The reliability coefficient reported for the more than 4,000 cases used is .86, estimated by Kuder-Richardson formula 21, and the standard error of an individual score is 4.2 raw score points. The authors wisely recommend to users of the instrument that they compute reliability coefficients and standard errors for their own groups. The reliability coefficient for an individual college might well be lower than the .86 based on data for 14 colleges.

There is still no evidence of statistical validity presented in the manual. The only validity study located (*1*) is based on 64 seniors in a teachers college, for whom the correlation is .41 between "academic rank and performance on the library test."

This reviewer agrees with the previous reviewers that this test is probably superior to an informal test constructed by a local librarian and that it would provide the librarian with some information regarding the areas in and the extent to which college freshmen need instruction in the use of library resources. The authors have increased the instrument's usefulness by supplying a table of norms and reliability data in the present edition of the manual; they are now urged to furnish validity data in the next edition.

For reviews by Janet G. Afflerbach (with Lois Grimes Afflerbach) and J. Wayne Wrightstone, see 5:693.

[860]

★Nationwide Library Skills Examination. Grades 4–12; 1959–63; new form issued each April; norms available following the testing program; 1 form ('63, 2 pages); no manual; mimeographed norms ('63, 1 page); no data on reliability; 10¢ per test, postage extra; (40–45) minutes; [Donald R. Honz]; Educational Stimuli. *

[861]

★OC Diagnostic Dictionary Test. Grades 5–8; 1960; 1 form (1 page, reprinted from *Thorndike-*

Barnhart Junior Dictionary); manual (3 pages); no key; no data on reliability; no norms; 2–100 tests, 6¢ each; 15¢ per manual; 25¢ per single copy and manual; cash orders (plus postage) only; (20) minutes; Katherine O'Connor; [O'Connor Reading Clinic Publishing Co.]. *

[862]

***SRA Achievement Series: Work-Study Skills.** Grades 4–6, 6–9 (grades 4.7–6.6, 6.7–8.3, 8.4–9.9 for Forms C and D); 1954–64; subtest of *SRA Achievement Series;* 2–3 scores: references, charts, total (Forms C and D only); IBM; 2 editions; battery teacher's handbook ['64, c1955, 47 pages] for both editions; separate answer sheets must be used; 50¢ per teacher's handbook; postage extra; Louis P. Thorpe, D. Welty Lefever, and Robert A. Naslund; Science Research Associates, Inc. *

a) FORMS A AND B. Grades 4–6, 6–9; 1954–64; 2 levels; battery school administrator's manual ('58, c1955–56, 32 pages); battery technical supplement, second edition ('57, 45 pages); battery pupil progress and profile charts ('59, c1955–59, 4 pages); 90¢ per 20 pupil progress and profile charts; 50¢ per school administrator's manual; $1 per technical supplement; $1.50 per specimen set of any one level of the complete battery.

1) *Grades 4–6.* Forms A ['54], B ('56), (15 pages); battery examiner's manual, second edition ('56, c1954–56, revised '60, 39 pages); $2.15 per 20 tests; $5 per 100 IBM scorable answer sheets; $1 per set of machine scoring stencils; 50¢ per hand scoring stencil; 92(125) minutes in 2 sessions.

2) *Grades 6–9.* Form A ('55), B ('56), (19 pages); battery examiner's manual, second edition ('56, c1955–56, revised '60, 39 pages); $2 per 20 tests; $5 per 100 IBM scorable answer sheets; 50¢ per either hand or machine scoring stencil; 70(90) minutes.

b) FORMS C AND D. Grades 4.7–6.6, 6.7–8.3, 8.4–9.9; 1955–64; an optional supplement to the Multilevel Edition of the complete battery; Forms C, D, ('63, 32 pages); 3 levels (called blue, green, and red levels, after color of answer sheet used) in a single booklet; separate battery examiner's manuals for use with DocuTran answer sheets ('63, 43 pages), IBM 805 answer sheets ('64, c1963–64, 40 pages), IBM 1230 answer sheets ('64, c1963–64, 42 pages); battery test coordinator's manual ('64, c1961–64, 64 pages); battery manual on how to use the test results ('64, c1961–64, 34 pages); battery conversion tables booklet ('64, 38 pages) for each level; battery pupil progress and profile charts ('64, c1955–64, 4 pages); separate IBM or DocuTran answer sheets must be used; $6 per 20 tests; $18 per 100 sets of IBM 805 answer sheets for the complete battery; $3.50 per set of battery scoring stencils and conversion tables booklet for any one level; $14 per 100 sets of IBM 1230 answer sheets for the complete battery, set of battery master answer sheets for machine scoring, and conversion tables booklet for any one level; $2 per set of battery hand scoring stencils and conversion tables booklet for any one level; $8 per 100 DocuTran answer sheets for the complete battery; $2 per set of battery hand scoring templates and conversion tables booklet for any one level; 90¢ per 20 pupil progress and profile charts; 50¢ per examiner's manual; 50¢ per how-to-use manual; $3 per specimen set of the complete battery; scoring service available; 70(80) minutes.

For reviews by Robert L. Ebel and Ruth M. Strang of Forms A and B, see 5:696. For reviews of Forms A and B of the complete battery, see 21 and 5:21.

[863]

★Senior High School Library and Reference Skills Test. Grades 9–12; 1960; 8 scores: alphabetization, uses of the dictionary, the card catalogue, research vocabulary, reference books, Dewey Decimal System, periodicals, total; 1 form (4 pages); no manual; no data on reliability; no norms; separate answer sheets must be used; 5–99 tests with answer sheets, 15¢ each; 75¢ per 25 answer sheets; 15¢ per key; 30¢ per specimen set; cash orders postpaid; [40–50] minutes; Claude E. Stephenson; Perfection Form Co. *

[864]

Spitzer Study Skills Test: Evaluation and Adjustment Series. Grades 9–13; 1954–55; 6 scores: dictionary, index, graphs-tables-maps, sources of information, total, note taking; IBM; Forms AM ('54), BM ('55), (12 pages); manual ('54, 11 pages); no college norms; separate answer sheets must be used; $6 per 35 tests; $1.75 per 35 IBM answer sheets; 40¢ per specimen set; postage extra; 105(135) minutes in 3 sessions, 75(90) minutes in 2 sessions for subtests 1–4 only; Herbert F. Spitzer; [Harcourt, Brace & World, Inc.]. *

REFERENCES

1. CROOK, FRANCES E. "Interrelationships Among a Group of Language Arts Tests." *J Ed Res* 51:305–11 D '57. *

ALTON L. RAYGOR, *Associate Professor of Educational Psychology, and Coordinator, Reading and Study Skills Center, University of Minnesota, Minneapolis, Minnesota.*

This test consists of five sections claimed to represent achievement in important study skills: (*a*) Using the Dictionary, (*b*) Using the Index, (*c*) Understanding Graphs, Tables, and Maps, (*d*) Knowledge of Sources of Information, and (*e*) Organization of Facts in Note Taking. The fifth test (note taking) is optional.

Relatively little information is given in the manual about the construction of the tests and their standardization. Item analysis was apparently carried out on some 2,400 students in four high schools, but little more than that is said. The note taking test (optional) is particularly slighted, and one has the feeling it was somewhat of an afterthought. It is left out of the table of intercorrelations, the table showing mean item difficulties and "validity" indices, the table of split-half reliabilities, and the table of correlations with other tests. In view of the lack of information concerning this optional test, it would seem that its inclusion should be questioned seriously.

The manual indicates that the test was standardized on more than 5,000 students in 17 high schools in 14 states, but there is no further information about the nature or location of the schools. The authors do give age and IQ means for the various grade levels.

A rather unusual standard score distribution with a mean of 106 and a standard deviation of 13 is used in converting raw scores to standard scores. The standard score distribution was made to correspond to the Terman-McNemar IQ score distribution on the population on which the test was standardized—a very dubious procedure.

The manual states that the difficulty level of items was computed along with estimates of correlations between item and total scores, but only mean values for subtests are given. These internal consistency estimates are unfortunately listed as "validity indices." When one looks for validity information, he finds some correlations with other tests, but nothing else. The obvious criterion—school grades—does not appear anywhere, even though the test is described on the jacket of the specimen set as "a measure of ability to use skills that are fundamental to success in many areas of the high school and college curriculum."

To the potential user this test will probably seem to be better than nothing, but no substitute for an adequately constructed and well standardized instrument. It may be a good test, but one cannot support that conclusion using the information provided in the manual.

For a review by James Deese, see 5:697.

[865]

★The Study Skills Counseling Evaluation. High school and college; 1962; 1 form (4 pages); mimeographed manual (6 pages); $7 per 25 tests and manual; $1.50 per manual; postpaid; specimen set not available; (10–20) minutes; George Demos; Western Psychological Services. *

STANLEY E. DAVIS, *Reading and Study Skills Counseling Director, University Counseling Center, The Ohio State University, Columbus, Ohio.*

The SSCE is intended to "enable students.... to identify rapidly and objectively their study weaknesses," in study time distribution, study conditions, taking notes, handling examinations, and "other habits and attitudes."

There are 50 five-alternative, multiple choice items of the self-report variety. The student is to respond in terms of the frequency (from "very often" to "very seldom") with which he or she follows the study procedure, or holds the attitude, indicated in the item stem.

Most of the items pertain to study procedures, with a few being primarily concerned with attitudes toward study and school. In light of research by Brown, Holtzman, and others which suggests that attitude items tend to be more effective in differentiating between high and low students, one might wish that more of the items in this inventory dealt with attitudes and fewer with procedures.

Many potential users would probably like to know more than the manual tells about the rationale and procedures used in the selection of items for inclusion in the SSCE. Seventeen of the items were found to discriminate at a statistically significant level between a group of college students with "B" grade averages ($n = 65$) and a group with less than "C" averages ($n = 46$). This is encouraging, but some explanation of the reasons for the inclusion of the other items is needed.

Data on the reliability of the SSCE are promising, though somewhat scanty. Test-retest scores of 74 students in one college, with an interval of one week between testings, yielded a reliability coefficient of .94.

The reported validity data, while very limited, are at least moderately encouraging. A coefficient of .38 was obtained between SSCE total scores and midsemester grades of 172 students in one college. Another study revealed that a group of 65 students with "B" averages made a significantly higher mean total score than did another group of 46 students with grade averages below "C." No information is given about the sex, class level, major field, or other characteristics of the students in these two studies.

No reliability or validity studies with high school students are cited.

Very little information is given about the students comprising the high school and college norm groups.

A few improvements in the format and organization of the SSCE would probably enhance its usefulness. Randomizing the order of response alternatives, instead of having a progression from the most desirable (best score) response on the left to the least desirable on the right in every item, would help to encourage more careful reading and consideration of the items by some students. In addition, the elimination of the headings that are used to group the items and a random order of presentation of the items would probably help toward the same end.

Users of the SSCE could effect a considerable saving by consuming answer sheets rather than the test booklets.

All in all, the SSCE is a promising instrument for use as an aid in study skills counseling and instruction, but it is in need of a great deal of further refinement and validation. At the present time, the *Brown-Holtzman Survey of Study Habits and Attitudes* is a better developed instrument for essentially the same purposes.

W. G. Fleming, *Assistant Director, Department of Educational Research, Ontario College of Education, University of Toronto, Toronto, Ontario, Canada.*

The contribution to academic success of adequate study habits and of constructive attitudes is pointed out in the manual as a reason for further efforts to improve measurement in this area. The uses of the SSCE, listed rather repetitively, may be summarized as follows: to increase the student's knowledge and understanding of his own weaknesses and problems as a basis for self-improvement; to provide teachers, counselors, and psychotherapists with information which may be used to assist the student; to screen students for certain courses; and to facilitate research. The third point is fortunately not emphasized. A device which cannot be constructed in such a way as to ensure against falsification of responses is of course all too likely to produce unfortunate results if employed for screening.

The SSCE is printed on a four-page folder with instructions on the front page. The five possible responses (VERY OFTEN, OFTEN, SOMETIMES, SELDOM, VERY SELDOM) are shown, and the student is asked to indicate the one most appropriate for each item. He is told that he will have time to finish. It is apparently assumed that he will feel no serious sense of frustration in marking VERY OFTEN when "always" would seem to be the appropriate answer, and VERY SELDOM when he never engages in the practice referred to.

The 50 items are divided into 5 groups: Study-Time Distribution, Study Conditions, Taking Notes, Preparing and Taking Examinations, and Other Habits and Attitudes. The second of these groups contains only three items.

A total score is obtained by assigning to each response a weight of 1 to 5, depending on the degree to which it is supposed to identify good habits and attitudes. Possible scores range from 50, the best possible, to 250. There seems to be no good reason why the weighting system could not have been devised so that a high score represented the positive end of the scale instead of the reverse. An unnecessary source of confusion might have been avoided by adherence to the more common practice.

Some of the items appear to be less than perfectly designed. The very first one is worded as follows: "I distribute my time on my study courses so I do not study more than two hours at a time on a single course." Apart from objections to the use of "so" in this construction, one might wonder what answer to expect from a student who, for reasons other than an unsatisfactory distribution of his time, spends less than two hours at a time on a single course. Item 4 reads as follows: "I study about two hours a week for each unit of class work I take." Students who habitually spend more than this amount of time on each unit would presumably have to give the same response as those who habitually spend less. There appears to be a danger that both these items might group together students with quite dissimilar characteristics.

With reference to items 21 and 22, it is not clear to the casual observer whether taking notes on one side of the paper only or taking notes in ink should be considered under every possible circumstance as either a good or a bad practice. The use of "so" for "so that" recurs in item 23. The meaning of item 28 is ambiguous: "I change my answers when I take a test." Instructors might feel themselves accused of unsystematic work in item 47: "I study in a 'hit or miss' manner, doing what is demanded of me by the instructor."

The impression that some items lack face validity might of course be overruled by evidence of effective discrimination obtained by analyzing the responses of an adequate tryout group. To judge from information in the manual, however, this kind of work was inadequately done. Only two groups, one consisting of 65 college students, each with a "B" average, and the other of 46 college students, each with less than a "C" average, are mentioned in connection with an attempt to measure item discrimination.

A low positive correlation with academic achievement is accepted as evidence of validity. A coefficient of .38 was found between SSCE scores and grade-point averages of 172 college students. There is no indication of the relationship between these two variables with academic aptitude or general intelligence held constant. The reported correlation of .31 with scores on Wrenn's *Study Habits Inventory* is a finding that ought to be considered highly disturbing instead of being dismissed with the view that "since many items in the two scales differ markedly, a high correlation was not expected; nevertheless, a coefficient of correlation of .31 shows some degree of relationship." Even though some of the items are considerably different, two instruments so similar in stated purpose should show a much closer relationship.

The test-retest reliability coefficient on 74 students from one college is reported as .94, a satisfactory figure. A table of norms is provided, but information about how the norms group was selected is lacking.

The manual is poorly written. The following sentences appear under the heading Uses of the SSCE: "A major use of the SSCE is to identify in High School and College students study weaknesses and problems of studying and then assist such students in their study problem areas" and "The SSCE is used in classes designed to improve study habits; in study skills laboratories." In more than one place there appears to be confusion about the use of the colon and semicolon. Short, choppy paragraphs consisting of one or two sentences follow one another in quick succession.

With a number of modifications and additional information, the SSCE could undoubtedly perform a useful service in schools and colleges. Judged on the basis of whether or not it represents an advance over existing instruments of its kind, it should, however, be identified as an ill-considered and unnecessary addition to the clutter of mediocre instruments of measurement already in existence which merely serve to bewilder the teachers and counselors whose interests they are supposed to serve.

[866]

★A Test on Use of the Dictionary. High school and college; 1955–63; 6 scores: pronunciation, meaning, spelling, derivation, usage, total; Form A ['55, 4 pages, plus 8-page reprint of material from *Webster's New International Dictionary, Second Edition*]; hectographed manual ['63, 4 pages]; no data on reliability; tentative norms; separate answer sheets must be used; 5¢ per test; 1¢ per mimeographed answer sheet; 25¢ per manual; 35¢ per specimen set; postpaid; (30–40) minutes; George D. Spache; Reading Laboratory and Clinic. *

[867]

***Watson-Glaser Critical Thinking Appraisal.** Grades 9–16 and adults; 1942–64; 6 scores: inference, recognition of assumptions, deduction, interpretation, evaluation of arguments, total; IBM; 2 editions; separate answer sheets must be used; $1.80 per 35 IBM answer sheets; 40¢ per specimen set of either edition; postage extra; Goodwin Watson and Edward M. Glaser; Harcourt, Brace & World, Inc. *

a) [1952 EDITION.] Form AM ('52, c1949–52, 8 pages); manual ('52, 12 pages); no data on reliability of current form; $4.50 per 35 tests; (44–50) minutes.

b) [1963 REVISION.] Forms YM, ZM, ('64, c1951–61, 8 pages, revision of Form AM and out of print Form BM, respectively); manual ('64, 16 pages); $5 per 35 tests; 20¢ per scoring stencil; (50–60) minutes.

REFERENCES

1–3. See 3:544.
4–11. See 5:700.
12. MOFFETT, CHARLES R. *Operational Characteristics of Beginning Master's Students in Educational Administration and Supervision.* Doctor's thesis, University of Tennessee (Knoxville, Tenn.), 1954.
13. LUTON, JAMES N. *A Study of the Use of Standardized Tests in the Selection of Potential Educational Administrators.* Doctor's thesis, University of Tennessee (Knoxville, Tenn.), 1955.
14. CRAWFORD, C. DELISLE. *Critical Thinking and Personal Values in a Listening Situation: An Exploratory Investigation Into the Relationships of Three Theoretical Variables in Human Communication, as Indicated by the Relation Between Measurements on the Allport-Vernon-Lindzey Study of Values and the Watson-Glaser Critical Thinking Appraisal, and Similar Measurements of Responses to a Recorded Radio News Commentary.* Doctor's thesis, New York University (New York, N.Y.), 1956. (*DA* 19:1845)
15. FRIEND, CELIA M., AND ZUBEK, JOHN P. "The Effects of Age on Critical Thinking Ability." *J Gerontol* 13:407–13 O '58. * (*PA* 33:10067)
16. JUERGENSON, ELWOOD M. *The Relationship Between Success in Teaching Vocational Agriculture and Ability to Make Sound Judgments as Measured by Selected Instruments.* Doctor's thesis, Pennsylvania State University (University Park, Pa.), 1958. (*DA* 19:96)
17. NUNNERY, MICHAEL Y. *A Study in the Use of Psychological Tests in Determining Effectiveness and Ineffectiveness Among Practicing School Administrators.* Doctor's thesis, University of Tennessee (Knoxville, Tenn.), 1958. (*DA* 19:1276)
18. BASS, JUET CARL. *An Analysis of Critical Thinking in a College General Zoology Class.* Doctor's thesis, University of Oklahoma (Norman, Okla.), 1959. (*DA* 20:963)
19. HERBER, HAROLD L. *An Inquiry Into the Effect of Instruction in Critical Thinking Upon Students in Grades Ten, Eleven, and Twelve.* Doctor's thesis, Boston University (Boston, Mass.), 1959. (*DA* 20:2174)
20. NUNNERY, MICHAEL Y. "How Useful Are Standardized Psychological Tests in the Selection of School Administrators." *Ed Adm & Sup* 45:349–56 N '59. * (*PA* 35:7092)
21. RODD, WILLIAM G. "A Cross-Cultural Study of Taiwan's Schools." *J Social Psychol* 50:3–36 Ag '59. * (*PA* 35:3960)
22. RUST, VELMA IRENE. *Factor Analyses of Three Tests of Critical Thinking.* Doctor's thesis, University of Illinois (Urbana, Ill.), 1959. (*DA* 20:225)
23. BERGMAN, LUCY MAE ERICKSON. *A Study of the Relationship Between Selected Language Variables in Extemporaneous Speech and Critical Thinking Ability.* Doctor's thesis, University of Minnesota (Minneapolis, Minn.), 1960. (*DA* 21:3552)
24. MILTON, OHMER. "Primitive Thinking and Reasoning Among College Students." *J Higher Ed* 31:218–20 Ap '60. *
25. RUST, VELMA I. "Factor Analyses of Three Tests of

Critical Thinking." *J Exp Ed* 29:177–82 D '60. * (*PA* 35:4466)
26. BESSENT, EDGAR WAILAND. *The Predictability of Selected Elementary School Principals' Administrative Behavior.* Doctor's thesis, University of Texas (Austin, Tex.), 1961. (*DA* 22:3479)
27. JACKSON, TEDDY RANDOLPH. *The Effects of Intercollegiate Debating on Critical Thinking Ability.* Doctor's thesis, University of Wisconsin (Madison, Wis.), 1961. (*DA* 21:3556)
28. RUST, VELMA I. "A Study of Pathological Doubting as a Response Set." *J Exp Ed* 29:393–400 Je '61. *
29. CRANE, WILLIAM J. "Screening Devices for Occupational Therapy Majors." *Am J Occup Ther* 16:131–2 My–Je '62. * (*PA* 37:4078)
30. RUST, VELMA I.; JONES, R. STEWART; AND KAISER, HENRY F. "A Factor-Analytic Study of Critical Thinking." *J Ed Res* 55:253–9 Mr '62. *
31. SHOCKLEY, JAMES T. "Behavioral Rigidity in Relation to Student Success in College Physical Science." *Sci Ed* 46:67–70 F '62. *
32. TRELA, THADDEUS MICHAEL. *A Comparison of Ninth Grade Achievement on Selected Measures of General Reading Comprehension, Critical Thinking, and General Educational Development.* Doctor's thesis, University of Missouri (Columbia, Mo.), 1962. (*DA* 23:2382)
33. *Normative Information: Manager and Executive Testing.* New York: Richardson, Bellows, Henry & Co., Inc., May 1963. Pp. 45. *
34. QUINN, PATRICK VINCENT. *Critical Thinking and Openmindedness in Pupils From Public and Catholic Secondary Schools.* Doctor's thesis, Columbia University (New York, N.Y.), 1963. (*DA* 24:2789)
35. SMITH, PAUL M., JR. "Critical Thinking and the Science Intangibles." *Sci Ed* 47:405–8 O '63. *

For reviews by Walker H. Hill and Carl I. Hovland of the 1952 edition, see 5:700; for a review by Robert H. Thouless of the original edition, see 3:544 (1 excerpt).

[Other Tests]

For tests not listed above, see the following entries in *Tests in Print:* 1519–20, 1525, 1529–30, 1536–39, 1541–2, and 1544; out of print: 1523–4, 1528, 1534, and 1540.

SCIENCE

REVIEWS BY *Kenneth E. Anderson, J. A. Campbell, Henry Chauncey, William W. Cooley, William R. Crawford, Max D. Engelhart, Barbara F. Esser, John C. Flanagan, Frank J. Fornoff, Elizabeth Hagen, Lloyd H. Heidgerd, William Hered, Kenneth J. Jones, Irvin J. Lehmann, George G. Mallinson, Jacqueline V. Mallinson, Leo Nedelsky, Clarence H. Nelson, and Theodore G. Phillips.*

[867a]

★Advanced General Science: Cooperative Science Tests. Grades 8–9; 1962–64; IBM; Forms A, B, ('62, 20–23 pages); no specific manual; series handbook ('64, 76 pages); separate answer sheets must be used; $4 per 20 tests; $1 per 20 IBM scorable answer sheets; $1 per 10 scoring stencils (answer pattern must be punched out locally); $1 per handbook; postage extra; $2 per specimen set of this and 4 other science tests, cash orders postpaid; 80(92) minutes in 1 or 2 sessions; Cooperative Test Division. *

[868]

***Biology and General Science: National Teacher Examinations.** College seniors and teachers; 1940–63; for more complete information, see 700; 80(90) minutes; Educational Testing Service. *

For reviews of the testing program, see 700, 5:538, and 4:802.

[869]

***Chemistry, Physics and General Science: National Teacher Examinations.** College seniors and teachers; 1940–63; for more complete information, see 700; 80(90) minutes; Educational Testing Service. *

For reviews of the testing program, see 700, 5:538, and 4:802.

[870]

Cooperative General Achievement Tests: Test 2, Natural Science. Grades 9–12 and college entrants; 1937–56; formerly called *A Test of General Proficiency in the Field of Natural Science;* IBM; Forms XX ('53, c1947–53, 7 pages, revision of Form X), YZ ('55, c1948–51, 7 pages, revision of Forms Y and Z, identical with test copyrighted in 1951); battery manual ('56, 16 pages); high school norms same as those published in 1938; separate answer sheets must be used; $4 per 25 tests; $1 per 25 IBM answer sheets; 25¢ per scoring stencil; postage extra; $1 per specimen set, cash orders postpaid; 40(50) minutes; Paul J. Burke (XX), [Carl A. Pearson, and John Zimmerman]; Cooperative Test Division. *

REFERENCES

1. HERTEL, J. P., AND DIVESTA, FRANCIS J. "An Evaluation of Five Factors for Predicting the Success of Students Entering the New York State College of Agriculture." *Ed & Psychol Meas* 8:389–95 au '48. * (*PA* 23:4412)
2. LEPLEY, WILLIAM M. "Predicting Success in Nurses Training." *J Psychol* 48:121–4 Jl '59. * (*PA* 34:6169)
3. WOLINS, LEROY; MACKINNEY, A. C.; AND STEPHANS, PAUL. "Factor Analyses of High School Science Achievement Measures." *J Ed Res* 54:173–7 Ja '61. * (*PA* 35:7129)
4. TAULBEE, GEORGE C., SR. *Construction and Validation of a Scale for Predicting Graduation From a College of Optometry.* Doctor's thesis, University of Houston (Houston, Tex.), 1963. (*DA* 24:387)

For a review by Palmer O. Johnson of earlier forms, see 3:548. For reviews of the complete battery, see 7, 5:6, 4:5, and 3:3.

[871]

***Elementary Science: Every Pupil Scholarship Test.** Grades 4–6; 1935–64; new form (4 pages) usually issued each January and April; forms from previous testing programs also available; general directions sheet ['63, 2 pages]; no data on reliability; norms for new forms available following testing program; 4¢ per test; 4¢ per key; postage extra; 40(45) minutes; Bureau of Educational Measurements. *

[872]

***Elementary Science and Health: Every Pupil Test.** Grades 4–6; 1935–64; new form (4 pages) usually issued each December and April; forms from previous testing programs also available; general directions sheet ('63, 2 pages); no data on reliability; Ohio norms for new forms available following testing program; 5¢ per test; 3¢ per key; postpaid; 40(45) minutes; Ohio Scholarship Tests. *

[872a]

★General Science: Cooperative Science Tests. Grades 7–9; 1962–64; IBM; Forms A, B, ('62, 10–11 pages); no specific manual; series handbook ('64, 76 pages); separate answer sheets must be used; $4 per 20 tests; $1 per 20 IBM scorable answer sheets; $1 per 10 scoring stencils (answer pattern must be punched out locally); $1 per handbook; postage extra; $2 per specimen set of this and 4 other science tests, cash orders postpaid; 40(45) minutes; Cooperative Test Division. *

[873]

***General Science: Every Pupil Scholarship Test.** High school; 1926–64; new form (2 pages) usually issued each January and April; forms from previous testing programs also available; general directions sheet ['63, 2 pages]; no data on reliability; norms for new forms available following testing programs; 4¢ per test; 4¢ per key; postage extra; 40(45) minutes; Bureau of Educational Measurements. *

[874]

***General Science: Every Pupil Test.** High school; 1929-64; new form (4 pages) usually issued each December and April; forms from previous testing programs also available; general directions sheet ('63, 2 pages); no data on reliability; Ohio norms for new forms available following testing program; 5¢ per test; 3¢ per key; postpaid; 40(45) minutes; Ohio Scholarship Tests. *

[875]

***General Science: Minnesota High School Achievement Examinations.** Grade 9; 1955–63; series formerly called *Midwest High School Achievement Examinations;* new form issued each May; norms available in June following release of new form; Form F ('63, 6 pages) used in 1963 testing; no specific manual; series manual ('63, 4 pages); series norms ['63, 4 pages]; series cumulative profile ('62, 2 pages); no data on reliability; no description of normative population; 12¢ per test; $2.50 per 100 profiles; postage extra; 20¢ per specimen set, postpaid; 60(65) minutes; American Guidance Service, Inc. *

[876]

***The Iowa Tests of Educational Development: Test 2, General Background in the Natural Sciences.** Grades 9–12; 1942–61; IBM; Forms X-3S, Y-3S, ('52, 7 pages); battery examiner's manual ('58, c1949–57, 23 pages); battery general manual ('59, 37 pages); student profile leaflet, sixth edition ('61, c1958, 2 pages); see the complete battery entry (14*b*) for other accessories; no data on reliability; separate answer sheets must be used; $2.40 per 20 tests; $5 per 100 IBM answer sheets; 50¢ per scoring stencil; $3 per specimen set of the complete battery; postage extra; 60(70) minutes for full length version, 40(50) minutes for class period version; prepared under the direction of E. F. Lindquist; Science Research Associates, Inc. *

REFERENCES

1. French, Joseph L. "A Predictive Test Battery." *Nursing Res* 10:104–5 sp '61. *

Lloyd H. Heidgerd, *Assistant Professor of Natural Science, Michigan State University, East Lansing, Michigan.*

Reading the title of this test raises the question, "What is meant by General Background in the Natural Sciences?" The General Manual states, "Like the test of social concepts, its content is not restricted to the content of the present high school curriculum." How then was its content selected? The manual does not explain, nor does it give any references where an explanation can be found. For the intelligent and trained test user such an omission is serious.

An examination of the two forms produced a reasonably balanced outline of general science content, approximately 40 per cent of the questions being on biological topics, 28 per cent on physics, 12 per cent on chemistry, and the remaining 20 per cent on astronomy and earth science. Approximately 35 per cent of the questions emphasize medical and engineering applications. This percentage and the general science content percentages are essentially the same for both forms.

On the basis of the Bloom taxonomy,[1] the reviewer classified about 25 per cent of the questions in each form in categories higher than knowledge. Since classification on the basis of the Taxonomy is somewhat subjective, the reviewer classified the questions of another publisher's natural science test designed for use in secondary schools. In the latter, about 50 per cent of the items were classified in categories higher than knowledge. The smaller number of questions in the higher taxonomic categories in the test being reviewed may or may not constitute a weakness depending on the basis for the validity of the test.

Technically, the questions themselves are relatively good in that the reviewer was able to find only three or four in each form that he considered to be ambiguous, incorrect, or too controversial for use in a nationally standardized test.

Both forms contain 90 questions. Obviously

1 Bloom, Benjamin S.; Engelhart, Max D.; Furst, Edward J.; Hill, Walker H.; and Krathwohl, David R. *Taxonomy of Educational Objectives: The Classification of Educational Goals: Handbook I, Cognitive Domain.* New York: Longmans, Green & Co., Inc., 1956. Pp. xiii, 207. *

the test is too long for administration within a single class period. To permit use within a single class period, a shortened version is available in the first 60 questions of each form. The content distribution within these questions is approximately that of the total test. Special administration instructions and conversions to standard scores are furnished for the shortened versions, but no data are given for the relative reliabilities other than a statement to the effect that the longer test is more reliable.

The administrator's manual is a model of clarity. The previously mentioned General Manual is written in clear, explicit English, and is easy to read. The topics covered are topics that teachers and guidance people like to see covered. It contains norms which convert standard scores to percentiles and which include all the grade levels for which the test is suggested. The scoring procedure is such that the same norms can be used for both the long and short versions.

It is at this point that the reviewer began to ask questions that the manual did not answer. What was the norming population like? The manual is vague. What was the standard error of measurement? The manual did not say. Both these deficiencies are serious. The teacher or counselor needs to know with what sort of students he is comparing his own students. He also needs to know how large a difference in percentile rank is necessary for statistical significance.

As indicated above in the test entry, no reliability data are furnished. Again it is necessary to report a serious deficiency.

Searching the manual for validity information is futile; that is, if you prefer data to overstatement. The following are some examples of the latter (the italics are the reviewer's): "The test results point up *any* need for curriculum revision that may exist"; "Accordingly, it is extremely important that every teacher acquire a thorough acquaintance with each of his students. To this end, he needs a comprehensive description of each student's intellectual development. With respect to *all* broad aspects of educational development that are readily measurable, the *Iowa Tests of Educational Development* meet this need." In effect, the teacher or administrator using the test results according to the manual is forced to rely on such statements as these in lieu of other validity data.

The guidance counselor fares somewhat better than the teacher. The publisher offers a separate booklet entitled, *Using the Iowa Tests of Educational Development for College Planning.* In it a number of studies are reported which indicate the test may have some predictive validity when it is used as part of the complete ITED battery. It is interesting that reliabilities are reported in this booklet though they are not properly defined according to the standards of the American Psychological Association.

In the introduction, "Overview," to *Using the Iowa Tests of Educational Development for College Planning* the statement is made that,

> The Iowa Tests of Educational Development were originally developed to serve two major educational purposes: For teachers and counselors—to provide reliable information regarding each high school student's general educational progress. For school administrators—to provide a dependable and objective basis for evaluating the curriculum programs of individual high schools.

If these are indeed the purposes of the tests in this series, it would seem desirable to supply data in the test manual which show how well these rather ambitious purposes are met. Within the limitations of the questions themselves, the science test in the series may be a very good one. However, because of the weaknesses of the manual that is supplied with it, the prospective user is left with doubt regarding the quality and the usefulness of the test.

JACQUELINE V. MALLINSON, *Assistant Professor of Science, Western Michigan University, Kalamazoo, Michigan.*

This test is one of nine parts comprising the battery of the *Iowa Tests of Educational Development*. In the words of the General Manual, "The battery as a whole is concerned not so much with what the student *knows* as with what he can *do*." The tests are designed for use in grades 9–12.

The two separate booklet edition forms of the science test, Forms Y-3S and X-3S, are composed of four-option multiple choice items. Each form has a total of 90 items, designed to consume a 60-minute testing period. However, each form also has a "stopping point" at the end of 60 items, in the event that the test administrator desires to give the test in one 40-minute (typical class) period.

The manual states, "This test is designed to measure the student's general knowledge and understanding of scientific terms and principles, of common natural phenomena and industrial applications, and of the place of science in modern civilization." Further, the publishers purport that the student's performance on the test indicates his background for further science courses, his interest in the natural sciences, and his aptitude for scientific study. Truly an amazing feat for one evaluative device!

A review of the individual items indicates that both forms contain about equal numbers of biological science items and physical science items. However, there is a noticeable lack of items dealing with the earth sciences (astronomy, meteorology, oceanography, and geology). These fields of science have assumed increasing importance in the secondary school science curriculum since the International Geophysical Year (IGY). Hence, this omission detracts from the total value of the test. In fairness to the publisher, however, it should be noted that these tests are now over 10 years old. If the separate booklet edition forms are to be revised, one can only hope that these modern areas of science will be given greater emphasis.

The stems of almost all items are in the form of questions. In the opinion of the reviewer, the options are unwarrantedly long. It would appear that the amount of reading required of a student would detract from the value of the test.

The items appear to range in difficulty from extremely easy to quite difficult. For example, item 2 in Form Y-3S is probably easy enough even for an elementary school student to answer. It reads, "For what is a *thermostat* used?" In contrast, item 52 is a relatively difficult one: "What commercial process depends on polymerization?" Since the tests are designed for use in grades 9–12, a range of difficulty is, of course, necessary. However, in the opinion of the reviewer, the range in these two forms is extremely wide.

Some of the items may best be described as "trivial." An example is item 17, Form X-3S: "Which best describes the nationality of the men who worked to produce the atom bomb? (1) They were almost all Germans. (2) They were almost all Americans. (3) They were almost all British. (4) They were from various countries." While such information may be of some interest, it is difficult to understand how a correct response to this item could indicate a student's background, interest, or aptitude for scientific study.

The manual provides percentile norms for student scores and percentile norms for school average scores. Hence, the tests can be used to interpret results for individuals or for entire school groups.

For a number of years this reviewer has decried the fact that there is a distinct dearth of "good" evaluative devices designed to measure both factual knowledge and *performance skills* in the area of general science. There are several tests on the market that do an adequate job of testing for factual recall. This is one of them. However, few tests adequately measure thinking and reasoning ability. This test falls by the wayside with the others in this respect.

The reviewer cannot agree with the manual that the test measures interest and aptitude in science. But, for a general measure of factual knowledge in the broad areas of science, it is probably as adequate as any other test now on the market.

For reviews of the complete battery, see 14 and 5:17; for reviews of earlier forms, see 4:17 and 3:12.

[877]

***Metropolitan Achievement Tests: [Science].** Grades 5–6, 7–9, 9–12; 1932–64; subtest of *Metropolitan Achievement Tests;* IBM and MRC; 3 levels; $2 per 100 Harbor answer cards (machine scoring service, by Measurement Research Center, Inc., may be arranged through the publisher); 40¢ per specimen set of any one level; postage extra; Walter N. Durost, (for *a* and *b*) Harold H. Bixler, Gertrude H. Hildreth, Kenneth W. Lund, and J. Wayne Wrightstone, and (*c* only) William H. Evans, James D. Leake, Howard A. Bowman, Clarke Cosgrove, and John G. Read; Harcourt, Brace & World, Inc. *

a) INTERMEDIATE SCIENCE TEST. Grades 5–6; 1932–62; Forms AM ('60, c1958), BM ('59), CM ('61), (5 pages); combined directions for administering ('59, 10 pages) for this and the advanced level; battery manual for interpreting ('62, 121 pages); $4 per 35 tests; separate answer sheets or cards may be used; $1.75 per 35 IBM answer sheets; 20¢ per scoring stencil; $1.20 per manual for interpreting; 20(25) minutes.

b) ADVANCED SCIENCE TEST. Grades 7–9; 1932–62; details same as for intermediate level.

c) HIGH SCHOOL SCIENCE TESTS. Grades 9–12; 1962–64; 2 scores: concepts and understandings, information; Forms AM ('62), BM ('63), (7 pages); manual ('64, c1962–64, 22 pages); content outline ['64, 4 pages];

revised interpretive manual for the battery ('64, c1962–64, 16 pages); separate answer sheets or cards must be used; $4.50 per 35 tests; $1.80 per 35 IBM answer sheets; 20¢ per scoring stencil; 45(55) minutes.

WILLIAM W. COOLEY, *Program Director, University of Pittsburgh Project Talent Office, Pittsburgh, Pennsylvania.* [Review of the intermediate and advanced levels.]

The intermediate and advanced science tests of this series illustrate a major problem with many of today's achievement tests. Almost all of the extensive supplementary materials for the test, including a battery manual of over 100 pages, either are concerned with the statistical characteristics of the tests or describe things to do with the numbers once the tests are scored. This test series will probably satisfy anyone concerned with questions of reliability, item analysis, and norms.

The problem is that the heart of the test, the items and the behaviors they are sampling, are treated as "givens." That is, there are very few cues to the science education objectives being assessed. There is simply the assurance that "exhaustive analyses were made of courses of study in terms of content as well as of purposes or aims." There is then the reference to a "grid of aims and purposes on one axis and content on the other" axis, used to classify items as they were written. A footnote suggests that the details of the content analyses are available from the publisher upon request. This reviewer made such a request and promptly received a list of the science content involved in each item; item 1 is on earth science, item 2 is on life science, etc. This list, plus a tabulation of item numbers classified into one of five such content areas, constituted the content analyses available for these science tests. This reviewer is simply taking this opportunity to point out that authors of the *Metropolitan Achievement Tests* have been far too concerned with the standardization process, while item content and validity appear to have been almost completely ignored. The tests are, therefore, open to very serious criticism regarding the nature of the items and the knowledge and abilities assessed.

Tests such as these would be greatly improved if a larger fraction of the money put into experimental tryout and standardization were used in the development of behavioral objectives and *valid* items in the first place. The philosophy seems to be that if you start out with a sufficiently large pool of mediocre items a good test will result from the application of very sophisticated statistical techniques. This approach almost inevitably ends up with a collection of items such as (from Form A, advanced level): "26. Ethyl is a compound used in—[e] building houses [f] improving paint [g] making plastics [h] improving gasoline." Content analysis becomes a concern here not only because some items appear to have invalid content (e.g., *ethyl* is not a compound), but also because the items reflect a very narrow view of the nature of science achievement.

Unfortunately, in spite of these serious shortcomings, these tests are among the better ones available for upper elementary and junior high school science.

GEORGE G. MALLINSON, *Dean, School of Graduate Studies, Western Michigan University, Kalamazoo, Michigan.* [Review of the intermediate and advanced levels.]

The *Metropolitan Achievement Tests* in science consist of an Intermediate Science Test for grades 5 and 6, an Advanced Science Test for grades 7–9, and High School Science Tests for grades 9–12. Only the intermediate and advanced tests are covered in this review. Each test is available in three parallel forms, A, B, and C. The tests consist of 55 four-option multiple choice items which, according to the Directions for Administering, can be administered in a 20-minute period. It should be noted that many test experts suggest that the use of a *five*-option item will, to a marked degree, reduce the "chance guess" factor.

The tests are attractive in appearance, having a two-color format. Items are printed in large, legible type, with options clearly marked. The test is printed on one large sheet of paper, approximately 11 by 25 inches, rather than as a booklet. This sheet is folded into thirds, so that before opening, the test is the typical 8½ by 11 inch size. However, the student must do much "flipping and folding" of pages in order to complete the test. In the opinion of the reviewer, this may be time consuming and difficult for the children, and also may cause them to lose their places.

A major concern of the user of a science test is the distribution of items in the science areas with which the test is concerned. A small brochure, entitled Using Metropolitan Science

Tests in Elementary Schools, indicates the following percentage distribution in the intermediate and advanced tests, respectively: life science, 21 and 18; earth science, 19 and 19; physical science, 28 and 36; conservation, 6 and 6; and health, 26 and 21. The areas of health and conservation are commonly considered topics of biological science. Hence, if the "Life Science," "Conservation," and "Health" percentages are combined, it is evident that the test is heavily weighted in biological science.

As a cross-check of these distributions, the reviewer analyzed each of the six forms of the two tests and categorized the items into three broad areas, biological science, earth science (including astronomy and meteorology), and physical science. With all six forms, almost 50 per cent of the items were in biological science. There are few items that deal with up-to-date topics of astronomy and meteorology. Currently, most science educators believe that well-rounded programs of elementary and junior high school science should consist of about one third biological science; one third earth science; and one third physical science. Hence, it would appear that the items are not distributed appropriately.

About *one half* of the items in the advanced forms are duplicates of items in the intermediate forms. A testmaker might defend some overlap between the two levels, but it is difficult to justify an overlap of almost 50 per cent. The ninth grade general science student should be able to handle topics far more advanced than should the typical fifth grade student. It is doubtful whether tests with this extent of overlap will have the suitable discriminating power.

Many of the test items are ambiguous, misleading half-truths, and, in some cases, incorrect. For example, on intermediate Form B this item appears: "The watery liquid which travels upward through many trees is called—[e] juice [f] foam [g] sap [h] lymph." The scoring key lists "[g] sap" as the correct response. This is scientifically incorrect, since the term *sap* refers to the liquid that travels *down* the stem from the leaves. Hence, no correct answer is given.

The same test includes this item: "A person who has been trained to treat sick animals is called—[a] a zoologist [b] a veterinarian [c] a biologist [d] an astronomer." Obviously, the response desired is "[b] a veterinarian." However, technically, options [a] and [c] might also be correct. Even if the ambiguity were removed, it is doubtful whether the item could be classified as anything but trivial.

Similar examples could be cited, if space permitted, from all other forms of the two tests. Suffice to say, the quality of the items leaves much to be desired.

Users of science tests are interested also in the philosophic objectives of the test and the degree to which these objectives are measured. The brochure that describes these tests indicates, "Some items call for the recall of generalizations, concepts, understandings, etc. * Other items require the application of concepts, understandings, and generalizations to problem situations. Items of this latter kind might be called problem-solving items." An example of this latter type of item is given in the brochure: "The seesaw is a simple machine which is called a lever. Another example of a lever is the—[e] wood screw [f] pencil sharpener [g] automobile wheel [h] baseball bat." In the opinion of the reviewer, this is far from a "problem solving" item. Further, it does *not* contain a correct option. The scoring key lists baseball bat as the correct response. However, technically this is *not* true. The bat itself has no fulcrum (the essential part of any lever). The fulcrum is actually the wrist of the batter. One could also argue defensibly that a baseball bat is as much a wheel and axle as it is a lever.

The test battery includes a Manual for Interpreting Metropolitan Achievement Tests, which is more than 100 pages in length and filled with much technical information. As with analogous materials for other standardized tests, the discussions of reliability and validity are so long and involved, and couched in so much technical jargon that it is doubtful whether the typical user will bother to "wade through them."

In summary, the reviewer believes that these tests are at best mediocre. The items primarily measure factual retention, and they are characterized by many misconceptions and half-truths. The tests are weighted too heavily with topics of biological science and there is far too much overlap between the intermediate forms and the advanced forms. In brief, this reviewer could not recommend the tests' use in an elementary or junior high school desiring to obtain a valid assessment of students' achievement in science.

For reviews of the complete battery, see 15; for reviews of earlier editions, see 4:18, 40:1189, and 38:874.

[878]

Physical Science: Teacher Education Examination Program. College seniors preparing to teach secondary school; 1957; an inactive form of *Chemistry, Physics and General Science: National Teacher Examinations;* for more complete information, see 709; IBM; 80(95) minutes; Educational Testing Service. *

For a review of the testing program, see 5:543. For reviews of the National Teacher Examinations, *see 700, 5:538, and 4:802.*

[879]

★**Purdue Physical Science Aptitude Test.** Grades 9–13; 1943–60; formerly called *Purdue Science Aptitude Test for High School and College;* IBM; Forms 1, 2, ['60, 11 pages]; manual ('60, 15 pages); separate answer sheets must be used; $5 per 25 tests; $1.25 per 25 IBM answer sheets; postage extra; 75¢ per specimen set, postpaid; 60(65) minutes; H. H. Remmers and Ned A. Rosen; University Book Store. * (Test is now out of print.)

REFERENCES

1. Remmers, H. H., and Gage, N. L. "The Abilities and Interests of Pharmacy Freshmen." *Am J Pharm Ed* 12:1–65 Ja '48. * (*PA* 22:4107)
2. Davenport, K. S. "The Influence of Mathematics Training on Achievement in Chemistry of First-Year Students in Home Economics," pp. 7–16. (*PA* 25:2652) In *Student Achievement and Instructor Evaluation in Chemistry.* Edited by H. H. Remmers. Purdue University, Division of Educational Reference, Studies in Higher Education, No. 66. Lafayette, Ind.: the Division, July 1949. Pp. 26. *
3. Remmers, H. H., and Gage, N. L. "Student Personnel Studies of the Pharmaceutical Survey." *Am J Pharm Ed* 13:6–126 Ja '49. * (*PA* 23:1004)
4. Remmers, H. H.; Elliott, D. N.; and Gage, N. L. "Curricular Differences in Predicting Scholastic Achievement: Applications to Counseling." *J Ed Psychol* 40:385–94 N '49. * (*PA* 24:3407)
5. Belman, H. S., and Evans, R. N. "Selection of Students for a Trade and Industrial Education Curriculum," pp. 9–14. In *Motives and Aptitudes in Education: Four Studies.* Edited by H. H. Remmers. Purdue University, Division of Educational Reference, Studies in Higher Education, No. 74. Lafayette, Ind.: the Division, December 1950. Pp. iii, 63. * (*PA* 26:3010)
6. Belman, H. S., and Evans, R. N. "Selection of Students for a Trade and Industrial Educational Curriculum." *J Ed Psychol* 42:52–8 Ja '51. * (*PA* 25:6486)
7. Johnson, A. Pemberton. "Counseling Engineering Freshmen." *Ed & Psychol Meas* 13:133–44 sp '53. * (*PA* 28:1566)
8. Baker, Paul Cleo. *Experiments in Variable Selection for Prediction of Academic Achievement.* Doctor's thesis, Purdue University (Lafayette, Ind.), 1955. (*DA* 15:2565)

William W. Cooley, *Program Director, University of Pittsburgh Project Talent Office, Pittsburgh, Pennsylvania.*

The *Purdue Physical Science Aptitude Test* "was designed as a tool for the selection and guidance of those capable of being adequately educated for technological and professional scientific work." The test assesses student knowledge and ability in the following areas: basic mathematical operations, mathematical problem analysis, science vocabulary, and scientific facts and principles. However, only a total score is provided. Over one half of the test is devoted to the mathematical portions, which leaves about 20 minutes to sample directly the scientific knowledge of the student.

Arguments presented in the manual for the content validity of the test are primarily in terms of knowledge and ability needed for achievement in science courses at the introductory level, either senior high school or junior college. This emphasis on high school science achievement is also found in the section on predictive validity. The exception here is a surprising and extensive consideration of the relation of this test to success in pharmaceutical colleges. In fact, one full page of this brief manual is devoted to the correlations between this test and grades at 15 such institutions. The coefficients range from .70 (based on 8 students) to −.15 (for 12 students). The authors were cheered by the fact that "in 10 of the 15 institutions the validity coefficient was significantly different from zero beyond the .05 level." This reviewer has the impression that the authors are rather hard pressed for validity information. If they choose to call this an aptitude test, they will have to provide more convincing evidence than that now available in the manual.

Reliability information is satisfactory; a K-R 21 coefficient of .86 is reported for over 2,000 high school students. The reliability appears to increase from the ninth grade to the twelfth grade. Information on the equivalence of the two forms is also adequate.

High school norms, in the form of percentile bands, are available for grades 9, 10, 11, and 12, for both boys and girls. The size of the norm groups ranged from 216 to 411. Since these represent a nationwide stratified random sample, the high school norms may be considered adequate for some purposes. However, the college "norms" are completely inadequate, unless one is interested in making comparisons with approximately 1,000 entering freshmen at Purdue University.

In summary, this test cannot be recommended for purposes of individual guidance with respect to scientific careers. One place where it might have a legitimate function is for gross tasks such as sectioning students according to ability for a course like college freshman chemistry or physics.

[880]

★Science Background: A Science Service Test to Identify Potential Scientific and Technical Talent. Grades 4–9; 1957–58; experimental edition; 2 tests; manual ('58, 4 pages) for each test; no data on reliability; tentative norms for grades 6 and 7 only; $4.75 per 25 sets of both tests, postpaid; specimen set not available; administration time not reported; Science Service, Inc. *

a) SCIENCE BACKGROUND—1A: THINGS DONE. Activities checklist; 1 form ('57, 4 pages).

b) SCIENCE BACKGROUND—2A: VOCABULARY. 1 form ('57, 4 pages).

[881]

★Science: Minnesota High School Achievement Examinations. Grades 7, 8; 1962–63; series formerly called *Midwest High School Achievement Examinations;* new form issued each May; norms available in June following release of new form; Form F ('63, 6 pages) used in 1963 testing; 2 levels; no specific manual; series manual ('63, 4 pages); series norms ['63, 4 pages]; series cumulative profile ('62, 2 pages); no data on reliability; no description of normative population; 12¢ per test; $2.50 per 100 profiles; postage extra; 20¢ per specimen set, postpaid; 60(65) minutes; American Guidance Service, Inc. *

ELIZABETH HAGEN, *Professor of Psychology and Education, Teachers College, Columbia University, New York, New York.* [Review of Form F.]

The tests appear to be constructed for what is usually called a general science curriculum in grades 7 and 8. The grade 7 test contains 113 items under five unit headings: Matter (20 items); The Earth and the Universe (17 items); Energy (13 items); Health (30 items); and General Biology (33 items). The grade 8 test contains 118 items under seven unit headings: Methods and Meanings of Science (16 items); Astronomy and Space (22 items); Meteorology (24 items); Botany (15 items); The Nature and Prevention of Diseases (20 items); Heat Engines, Pumps, and Pressure (11 items); and Conservation (10 items). The basis on which inclusion of units was decided is not specified for either test. The manual appears to be a very general one that is the same for all other subject matter tests in the battery; therefore, relevant material on content validity is limited to a single sentence which states that items were chosen because they measured the subject matter objectives of the curriculum. From another section of the manual, headed "The Authors," one obtains the impression that most of the items for the test were constructed by one or more teachers of the subject. Since the title of the test has changed from "Midwest" to "Minnesota" one would assume that the statements in the manual apply only to the state of Minnesota, but this is never specifically stated.

The tests for both grades 7 and 8 appear to be constructed for a very traditional general science course. Except for one item on the grade 7 test and five items on the grade 8 test that relate to space and space travel, all the items could have been answered by a student taking general science 30 years ago. None of the new discoveries or advances in the physical or biological sciences is included in the tests. The test items themselves measure primarily the recall of specific factual information; the methods of science, the broader concepts and generalizations of science, and reasoning and application are not measured at all by the tests.

The construction of the items tends to be poor. Many of the stems do not pose specific problems to the examinee. In the grade 7 test the option, "None of these, A–D" appears in about 10 per cent of the items and is never keyed as the correct answer. In the same test, almost 10 per cent of the items use the option "All of these, A–D" which is keyed as the correct answer more than half of the time.

Although percentile norms are provided, they are not available until after the test has been given and schools send scores to the publisher. The sample on which the norms are based appears to be a volunteer one and no evidence is provided as to how representative it is of any population; nor is any information given as to how many schools or individuals are included.

The manual accompanying the test is completely unsatisfactory. It provides no adequate data on validity and absolutely no data on reliability or the normative sample. It includes, however, a number of questionable statements about the relationship of interests and aptitudes and achievement and the general nature of evaluation. Overall, the Minnesota High School Achievement Examinations in science for grades 7 and 8 have little or nothing to recommend them for use in schools.

JACQUELINE V. MALLINSON, *Assistant Professor of Science, Western Michigan University,*

Kalamazoo, Michigan. [Review of Forms E and F.]

These four tests, Forms E and F for each of grades 7 and 8, are five-option multiple choice tests. They are designed as end-of-year subject matter achievement examinations. According to the publisher, "The intent in the use of these tests is to serve as an aid to instruction. They may be used to compare a student's achievement with other students in a class or throughout the State."

The tests are printed on large sheets of triple-fold paper, rather than employing the more common booklet format. This arrangement might prove to be somewhat awkward for students to handle. In addition, the student is required to indicate his answers in the appropriate blanks to the far right of each page. Such an arrangement might be confusing to a junior high school student. Also, the fact that no answer sheets are provided means that all tests must be hand scored.

The items require far less reading than many other science tests prepared for this level. In the opinion of this reviewer, this factor is a definite advantage. The stems and options of the items are all relatively short. Hence, a student is not required to "wade through" a vast amount of verbal material before reaching the "meat" of the item.

The rationale behind the categories into which the items are classified evades this reviewer. No statement could be found in any of the publisher's printed material that explains the classifications. Further, some items seem to be misplaced. For example, Form E for grade 7 includes the following item under Unit 1, Matter: "The coriolis effect given to winds is caused by A the revolution of the earth, B the rotation of the earth, C night and day, D the seasons, E the equinox." The classification of this item under the heading Matter is certainly questionable. In addition, any experienced general science teacher could undoubtedly criticize the item for the wording of the stem.

The section Earth and the Universe in Form E for grade 7 is entirely devoted to geology items. Although the heading might suggest the inclusion of some astronomy questions, none appear. Similar examples could be cited from the eighth grade examinations.

A survey of the subject matter areas covered in each of the four examinations indicates that the tests are heavily weighted with biological science items. An analysis of the items revealed that there are almost twice as many biology items as physical science or earth science items. Present-day curriculum experts suggest that the typical general science program should include approximately equal amounts of biological science, physical science, and earth science. Hence, the content of these tests is not consistent with curriculum trends. Also, there is a noticeable lack of items reflecting recent advances in modern science.

The items in these tests place great emphasis on a student's knowledge of scientific terminology and vocabulary. While the increase in vocabulary is an admirable outcome of science instruction, mere knowledge of terms is no guarantee of *understanding*. A great many stems of items end in phrases such as "is known as" or "is called." One wonders how valid a measure of true *understanding* results from measuring only knowledge of terms.

Some of the items are ambiguous; others include poor options; and in still others the answers are "telegraphed." In the opinion of the reviewer, an example of a poor item is number 41 in Form E for grade 7: "The best agent of erosion is A freezing, B thawing, C water, D wind, E sun." Most science educators will probably agree that the use of the term "best" in this stem is highly questionable. Many similar examples could be cited.

Norms are not made available at the time a new form of these tests is issued. Rather, results from actual use of the test are used to prepare norms which become available at least a month after a new form is released. Hence, a teacher must use an old form of the test if he wishes to have normative data immediately available with which to compare the achievement of his students.

One rather strange feature of the four tests reviewed is the fact that they do not contain equal numbers of items. Form E for grade 7 includes 86 items; Form F, 113 items. Form E for grade 8 contains 132 items; Form F, 118. Under the circumstances one wonders how results from one test administration to another can possibly be compared.

In summary, these tests for science 7 and 8 are, at best, mediocre measures of factual retention. The format is somewhat awkward, and the tests require hand scoring. Since few good standardized general science tests are available, teachers might use these tests for lack of a better evaluation device. It should be recognized, however, that the tests measure only factual recall, are heavily weighted with vocabulary items, and include far more biological science items than physical science or earth science. In other words, they do no more than a good teacher-made examination—and perhaps less.

[882]

***Sequential Tests of Educational Progress: Science.** Grades 4-6, 7-9, 10-12, 13-14; 1956-63; IBM, NCS, and Grade-O-Mat; Forms A, B, ('57, c1956-57, 11-15 pages); 4 levels; battery directions ('57, 12 pages); interpretive manual ('57, 31 pages); battery technical report ('57, 58 pages); 1958 SCAT-STEP supplement ('58, 32 pages); 1962 SCAT-STEP supplement ('62, 49 pages); 1963 SCAT-STEP supplement of urban norms ('63, 16 pages); battery teacher's guide ('59, 85 pages); battery profile ('57, 1 page); battery student report ('58, 4 pages); no data on reliability of Form B; separate answer sheets or cards must be used; $4 per 20 tests; $1 per 20 IBM scorable answer sheets; 25¢ per scoring stencil; see 671 for prices of NCS answer sheets and scoring services; see 666 for prices of Grade-O-Mat cards; $1 per 20 profiles; $1 per 20 student reports; $1 per interpretive manual; $1 per technical report; $1 per supplement; $1 per teacher's guide; postage extra; $2 per specimen set, cash orders postpaid; 70(90-100) minutes; Cooperative Test Division. *

a) LEVEL 4. Grades 4-6; Forms 4A, 4B.
b) LEVEL 3. Grades 7-9; Forms 3A, 3B.
c) LEVEL 2. Grades 10-12; Forms 2A, 2B.
d) LEVEL 1. Grades 13-14; Forms 1A, 1B.

REFERENCES

1. GEGA, PETER C., AND KARLSEN, BJORN. "Situational vs. Non-Situational Casting of Items in the STEP: Elementary Science." *Calif J Ed Res* 13:99-104 My '62. * (*PA* 37:3884)
2. LIGGITT, WILLIAM A. "An Evaluation of General Education in Elementary Teacher Preparation." *J Ed Res* 57:156-9 N '63. *

JOHN C. FLANAGAN, *President, American Institute for Research; and Professor of Psychology, University of Pittsburgh; Pittsburgh, Pennsylvania.*

The plan for the STEP series was to develop tests that "would emphasize broad understandings and abilities to utilize learned skills in solving new problems." According to the manual, the science tests of this series were designed to measure six skill categories: (*a*) "Ability to identify and define scientific problems"; (*b*) "Ability to suggest or screen hypotheses"; (*c*) "Ability to select valid procedures"; (*d*) "Ability to interpret data and draw conclusions"; (*e*) "Ability to evaluate critically claims or statements made by others"; (*f*) "Ability to reason quantitatively and symbolically." The general plan for these tests was described in *The Fifth Mental Measurements Yearbook* and will not be repeated here.

The impression of this reviewer is that the summer workshop method used for the writing and editing of these items was not effective in fulfilling these aims. As indicated by Julian C. Stanley in his review of this test in *The Fifth Yearbook,* a majority of the items appear to measure knowledge of specific facts or the execution of specific procedures. Although a thorough editorial review of these items is beyond the scope of the present review, some of the deficiencies are illustrated by the three items discussed below.

In Form 4A (for grades 4, 5, and 6) there is, following a graph about natural resources, an item which reads, "From the picture can we tell about how much of our rich top soil has been used up?" Clearly, this question calls for a "yes" or "no" answer. However, instead we find the choices are "(E) All of it (F) One-third of it (G) One-half of it (H) None of it." To make things more difficult for the child who has developed with respect to skill category *e* as listed above, the graph merely shows that we have used 33 per cent of our "top soil." Thus, the student, since he is given no "can't tell from the information given" option, is forced to conclude that the item writers didn't really mean "rich top soil" but just "top soil" in the stem, and so forth. The item may measure understanding of symbolic information presented in graph form but in an unsatisfactory way for the alert student.

Turning to Form 3B (for grades 7, 8, and 9) we find following two items on fertilizers an item which is stated as follows: "Tom knew that green plants make their own food. He knew that when the plants make food they must use all of the following EXCEPT (A) sunlight (B) carbon dioxide and moisture (C) oxygen (D) chlorophyll." The manual states the item is intended to measure skill category *b*. The very small number of students at this level who get the item correct by selecting "oxygen" as the exception very likely do it without anything resembling "screening hypotheses," but entirely from remembering a textbook description of photosynthesis.

At the college level (grades 13 and 14) in Form 1A, the following item is found: "The water level in the plant's cylindrical water tower is 50 feet above the ground. If the density of water is 62.4 lbs. per cu. ft., the force of the water on the bottom of the tower at ground level is (A) 50 × 62.4 lbs. per sq. ft. (B) not calculable unless the diameter of the tank is also known." The two other options are definitely incorrect but it appears that the two quoted here are *both* correct, although only B is keyed as correct. The force on each square foot on the bottom is given in A but to find the total force on the bottom, the diameter would be necessary. The item merely asks for "the force of the water on the bottom." It is stated that this item is designed to measure skill category *f*. It certainly should confuse the student. Again, his main problem in answering the question would be to try to guess the intention of the item writer.

Turning from the editorial to the technical aspects of the development of these tests, the findings are even more disappointing. The item analysis results were based on "100 case random samples" for the pretest forms. In one grade for each form, counts were made of the number of examinees in the high and low scoring 50 choosing each alternative for each item. For the other one or two grades tested with each form, counts were not made separately for high and low scoring groups. Thus, the standard errors of the item difficulties obtained were around five percentage points in the middle range of difficulty and the item internal consistency coefficients had standard errors of measurement of about .15. Good practice in this field has long indicated that samples of 400–600 cases are desirable to get satisfactorily reliable estimates of item characteristics. The use of high and low 50 per cent—instead of something like high and low 27 per cent or the more accurate high and low 9–20 per cent—is difficult to understand, since, with less effort, more accurate coefficients could have been obtained.

The alternate forms constructed from these relatively unstable statistics cannot be expected to be closely parallel. Therefore, the final forms were equated. The Technical Report does not indicate the number of students used in the equating program. It does state that linear conversions based on the means and standard deviations for the two forms were used as the basis for obtaining "equivalent" scores on the two forms. This linear method gives very poor results when the distributions of scores for the two forms are different. Therefore, area transformations would seem much more appropriate, especially in view of the unreliability of the item statistics and other content considerations which prevented obtaining closely parallel forms. The review by Wilbur L. Layton in *The Fifth Yearbook* also pointed out these deficiencies in equating procedures.

Although "uniform scaling procedures" were used to develop a score scale to be used for all levels, this score scale has no particularly useful properties. As Layton pointed out, the increments of growth for the various scales are quite uneven and comparable score scales were not achieved.

Reliability coefficients were calculated for the Form A tests only. The statement is made that similar results could be expected from Form B. Since the Technical Report does not give means and standard deviations for Form B on any of the samples, it is difficult to evaluate this assertion. However, the disparity in the "equivalent" converted scores for Forms A and B of the selected raw scores given in Table 2 raises considerable doubt on this point for the forms at some of the levels. Reliability coefficients were reported for the middle grade for which the tests were developed. They could be expected to be somewhat lower for the other grades. The Technical Report states that the reliability estimates were based on *all* students in the norms group for the grade. The *n*'s given in Table 1 range from 99 to 474 for the science tests. The reliability coefficients reported are .80, .81, .89, and .91. It is also noted that the item statistics used in computing these reliabilities were based on a special 100-case sample, rather than the same sample from which the mean and standard deviation were obtained. Why such methods were used is a real mystery, especially when it was reported that Forms A and B were given to a number of students for the equating program. Although previous reviewers have raised questions regarding these methods, apparently no effort has been made in the more than five years since the initial publication to compute alternate forms reliability coefficients.

The discussion of "Norming the Final Forms" in the Technical Report is very technical and will certainly overawe the average user of these tests. In spite of all the "sampling" corrections and discussion of reliability of grade means, previous reviewers, such as Palmer O. Johnson and Wilbur L. Layton, have been very critical of the methods used and the reporting of this norming project. The method of norming five tests by administering them simultaneously to the same class at the same time and of giving half Form A and half Form B is certainly an efficient one.

Unfortunately, the number of schools used was not very large, about "50 schools in each grade from 4 through 12." Even more disappointing is the failure to stratify these schools except in the crudest fashion on a single variable, region. The Technical Report states, "schools in the norms sample were so chosen that the representation from each of the nine regions is similar to the proportions in the United States." However, Table 9 shows that the norms sample of students deviates by including, for example, 42 per cent from the central states in grade 11, while the population value in these states is only 30 per cent. The South and the Far West have 24 per cent and 8 per cent of the norms sample as compared with values in the population of 30 and 14 per cent, respectively. There appears to be no mention of any correction of these biases by using a weighting procedure.

It is difficult to conceive of a national norms project of this type being undertaken without any technical effort at securing a representative sample of the performance of the nation's school children. No mention is made of the proportion of refusals in the schools invited to participate in the study and there is also no discussion of the types of schools which did participate. Stratification of the total population of schools in the country on such factors as student holding power, socioeconomic status of the community, or similar variables would certainly have made it possible to obtain more representative norms at little increase in expense.

In the colleges an even more radical step was taken. Nearly all the colleges and universities in the country were asked if they would test 12 freshmen and 12 sophomores to be selected at random according to a procedure devised by the Educational Testing Service. Each student was asked to take either the A or B form of one of the six achievement tests in the norms project. In addition to stratifying on region of the country and on type of college (two-year or four-year course), colleges were stratified on number of students enrolled. In selecting the final sample from the colleges willing to participate, nearly all of the "large" colleges were included, but only a sample was selected from among the small colleges. The nature of the sample as reported in Appendix Table C3 will surprise most students of higher education. Without making a detailed analysis of the list of nearly 100 colleges, one is impressed that the University of Maryland, the University of Idaho, and the University of North Dakota, along with the Pennsylvania State University and the Oregon State University, are the only representatives of our large state supported universities. Weighting procedures were used with the stratification, but a glance at the list suggests the lack of representativeness of the resulting norms. Here again, stratification on other characteristics of these colleges, such as instructor-student ratio, per student expenditure, etc., would probably have given these norms a little more value.

The percentile norms and means as published indicate very similar or slightly better performance on the part of eleventh grade students than twelfth grade students. This is contrary to all available evidence regarding student achievement in science in high school. For a battery intended to measure growth and progress, this is a relatively serious inconsistency and makes further difficulty for the test user trying to interpret student performance.

In the 1963 supplement entitled Test Performance in Urban Schools, norms are reported for schools in cities having more than 100,000 population. In each of the city school systems that agreed to participate (59 out of 130), three classes were selected in each of the odd grades 5, 7, 9, and 11 in one school in the system. All selections were made in a random fashion. The results for each school system were weighted in accordance with the city's total population. This represents another interesting attempt to improve the efficiency of the norming process. Unfortunately, it suffers from many of the same defects as the earlier norms studies: (*a*) no stratification of the population sampled, (*b*) inadequate numbers (for example, only one of the five big cities which represent nearly 40 per cent of the "urban" population was included, and thus about 90 students per grade are the only representatives of this large section of the urban schools, and these were weighted in accordance with the size of this one city, not the combined five largest cities), (*c*) no discussion of the nature of the biases represented in the group willing to participate.

In conclusion, this reviewer feels that the purposes and some of the innovations involved in developing these tests should certainly be commended. It is hoped that some of the deficiencies pointed out by various reviewers can be overcome in later editions.

George G. Mallinson, *Dean, School of Graduate Studies, Western Michigan University, Kalamazoo, Michigan.*

The STEP tests include a sequential battery of measures of science achievement consisting of eight tests. These eight tests consist of two parallel forms at each of these levels: grades 4–6, grades 7–9, grades 10–12, and college freshman and sophomore. Theoretically the tests could be used to trace the growth in science achievement of a group of students from the fourth grade through the second year of college, with measures that are similar in general format, areas of subject matter covered, and philosophical objectives.

Each test consists of 60 items, divided into two sections. The division is to facilitate the administration of each test within two class periods of average length. If time permits, each test may be administered in one sitting.

All items are four-option multiple choice. It should be noted here that many test experts believe that a five-option multiple choice item reduces the "chance guess" factor to a marked degree. The items are arranged in sets, ranging from 3 to 10 per set. Each set is introduced by a brief anecdote of a practical situation, on which the items are based. In theory, this plan is designed to make the tests more interesting to the testee and "to make possible the development of questions which cut across the conventional dividing lines between the sciences." In the opinion of the reviewer, the attempt to base the items on a practical situation has proved to be more of a detriment than a positive attribute to the science battery. For example, in Forms 4A and 4B (for grades 4–6), students must do a vast amount of reading before they come to grips with the science concepts. This arrangement is objectionable not only because of the time consumed in reading, but also because the science is frequently buried so deeply in the "practical situation" that it is almost unrecognizable.

Often the options for the multiple choice items are naïve or ridiculous. For example, in one set dealing with two children, one of whom is sick, an item reads: "Jane called to Bill from the bedroom, 'Please come sit here on my bed and play with me.' Mother would not let Bill be close to Jane because Jane was (E) cross (F) coughing and sneezing (G) unhappy (H) younger than Bill." If one "follows through" with the practical setting, it is entirely possible that option (E) might be correct. Even in the eyes of an upper elementary school student, such items may appear trivial.

At the high school and college levels, the "practical situation" approach may also prove to be inappropriate. It is doubtful whether present-day sophisticated high school students will be stimulated by "practical situations" such as, "Sarah is taking a course in home economics and finds it helpful in understanding more about cooking at home" (Form 2A); or "Jack decided to build a jet-propelled model airplane to enter in a contest" (Form 2B).

Similarly, college students are not likely to be enthusiastic about practical situations like, "A girl scout committee was planning the development of a new camp site having a stream running through it" (Form 1A); or "George Jones has asked the county agricultural agent's advice on increasing the productivity of his farm" (Form 1A). Hence, in this attempt to make an "interesting" test, the testmakers may have reduced the validity of the tests for measuring science achievement. They might better have dealt with clear, concise statements of the concepts to be measured.

The Manual for Interpreting Scores indicates the percentages of items in the various areas of science covered by the STEP science tests. In the opinion of the reviewer, the distribution of items seems reasonable.

A slightly different type of analysis of coverage was made by the reviewer. It is generally agreed that elementary and junior high school science programs should consist of about one third biological science, one third earth science (including astronomy and meteorology), and one third physical science. An analysis of all items in forms 4A, 4B, 3A, and 3B indicates that this distribution is adequately maintained. Similiar analyses were made for the high school and college levels. Here again, the test items were distributed adequately over these three areas.

In the opinion of the reviewer, a major subject matter weakness of the tests is the lack of consideration of emerging curriculum patterns in science. Reference is made specifically to the results of curriculum studies supported by the National Science Foundation. Also, few items reflect the newer developments in science. In fairness to the publisher, however, it should be noted that these tests are now relatively old, having been first published in 1957.

Two basic criteria for judging a test concern the underlying philosophic objectives and the degree to which these objectives are measured. The Teacher's Guide outlines an elaborate classification system in which every test item is categorized according to skill objectives and subject matter objectives. At first glance, one is impressed with the care and detail with which the classification is made. However, careful scrutiny indicates that the categories of science skills are, to a marked degree, the classic steps in "*The* Scientific Method." In the opinion of the reviewer, the STEP science tests are subject to criticisms leveled in the past at most standardized science tests. The tests pay lip service to measuring performance skills, but primarily measure retention of facts and the ability to recognize an element of scientific inquiry in a verbal context.

The STEP tests include an extensive group of supplemental materials, including a Teacher's Guide; a Manual for Interpreting Scores; a Technical Report; and 1958, 1962, and 1963 Supplements to the Technical Report. All these materials include vast amounts of normative data and instructions and suggestions for use of the test results. However, specific information about the reliability and validity of the science tests is scanty and inconclusive. Further, it is buried in remote corners of the Technical Reports, making it difficult for the average teacher to locate the information and understand it.

In summary, the reviewer believes that more time, effort, and finances have been invested in the development of the STEP tests than in any other set of science achievement tests thus far published. The tests have a distinct advantage in providing a sequential measure of science achievement from grade 4 through the sophomore college level. They have distinct weaknesses in that the items (*a*) are based on somewhat naïve "practical situations"; (*b*) fail to reflect modern curriculum trends; and (*c*) fail to measure some of the important performance skills that are objectives of science teaching. However, since there is a dearth of suitable evaluative devices for science, and since these are the only sequential measures available, the STEP tests may probably be considered the best of a poor lot. Their use is recommended because of the lack of other suitable tests.

For reviews by Palmer O. Johnson, Julian C. Stanley (with M. Jacinta Mann), and Robert M. W. Travers, see 5:716. For reviews of the complete battery, see 25 and 5:24.

[883]

***Stanford Achievement Test: Science.** Grades 5.5–6.9, 7–9; 1941–64, c1940–64; subtest of *Stanford Achievement Test, [1964 Revision]*; 1953 revision (see 5:717) still available; IBM and MRC; Form W ('64, 5 pages); 2 levels: Intermediate 2, Advanced; manual ['64, 8 pages] for each level; supplementary directions ['64, 1 page each] for use with IBM answer sheets, Harbor answer cards; $4 per 35 tests; separate answer sheets or cards may be used; $1.50 per 35 IBM answer sheets; 20¢ per scoring stencil; $2 per 100 Harbor answer cards (machine scoring service, by Measurement Research Center, Inc., may be arranged through the publisher); 40¢ per specimen set of either level; postage extra; 25(30) minutes; Truman L. Kelley, Richard Madden, Eric F. Gardner, and Herbert C. Rudman; Harcourt, Brace & World, Inc. *

For reviews by Bertram Epstein and Paul E. Kambly of the 1940 edition, see 4:593. For a review of the 1964 revision of the complete battery, see 26; for a review of the 1953 revision, see 5:25; for reviews of earlier editions, see 4:25 and 3:18.

[884]

***Survey Test in Introductory Science: California Survey Series.** Grades 7–9; 1946–59; subtest 6 of the elementary level (for grades 4–8) of *California Tests in Social and Related Sciences,* Form AA; IBM; Form 1 ('59, 7 pages, identical with test copyrighted in 1953 and identical with test copyrighted in 1946 except for format and wording changes in one sixth of the items); no specific manual; combined manual ('59, 19 pages) for this test and tests 885 and 897; $2.45 per 35 tests; separate answer sheets may be used; 5¢ per IBM answer sheet; 20¢ per scoring stencil; 10¢ per series class record sheet; 2¢ per series individual record sheet; postage extra; 50¢ per specimen set, postpaid; 23(28) minutes; Georgia Sachs Adams and John A. Sexson; California Test Bureau. *

Kenneth E. Anderson, *Dean, School of Education, The University of Kansas, Lawrence, Kansas.*

The test contains 65 items of the multiple choice and true-false types requiring 23 minutes of administration time. The items are devoted largely to testing factual information in two areas: (*a*) biology, or "the effects of plants, animals, etc., on the world in which we live," and (*b*) physical science, or "man's efforts to conquer and profit from the forces of nature."

The test was originally published in 1946 as a part of the *Progressive Tests in Social and Related Sciences* for use in grades 4–8. A revision of the battery, published in 1953 under the title *California Tests in Social and Related Sciences,* was identical to the 1946 version except for some minor changes. The fact that the present test is identical with subtest 6 of the 1953 revision for use in grades 4–8 makes one seriously question the validity of the test for present use in grades 7, 8, and 9. The opinion that the validity of the 1946 version of the battery was justified in terms of the techniques used at that time (see the review by Gerberich, 4:23) does not establish the validity of the present test, for much change has taken place in science instruction since 1953. A test valid for use in grades 4–8 in the pre-Sputnik era can hardly be considered valid for the same grades in the post-Sputnik age. It follows, therefore, that the same test cannot be valid for use in grades 7, 8, and 9 in today's schools.

Coefficients of reliability via the Kuder-Richardson formula 21 are reported as .83, .83, and .84 for grades 7, 8, and 9. The *r*'s are based on slightly over 500 cases in each grade. Age-grade, percentile, and standard score norms are available. These become rather meaningless, however, if the purpose of the test is that of surveying knowledge for the junior high school level, for the knowledge tested cannot be judged as modern or up to date when the test is based on items largely constructed in 1946.

Lloyd H. Heidgerd, *Assistant Professor of Natural Science, Michigan State University, East Lansing, Michigan.*

The notation "Grades 7-8-9" on the cover page could easily be misinterpreted. In the opinion of the reviewer, the test is not appropriate for general use in all three junior high school years. Originally, the test was constructed as part of the elementary battery (grades 4–8) of the *Progressive Tests in Social and Related Sciences,* which later became known as the *California Tests in Social and Related Sciences.* It probably is most suited for evaluating the science background of students entering the seventh grade. At the higher grade levels, it might be useful in work with nonacademic classes.

In describing the potential applications of this test in the catalog and in the manual, the test publisher implies that less capable students identified by the test should be counseled into non-laboratory science courses. Many educators would say just the opposite: that such students should be counseled into laboratory courses designed for their capabilities. In any event, it is the opinion of this reviewer that such an implication is outside the province of a test publisher. This opinion, of course, reflects in no way upon the quality of the test.

For whatever use this test is applied, the content should be examined by the teachers who worked with the pupils before the test was taken and by the teachers responsible for further work with them. The content covered is of such a nature and so distributed that this test can easily serve to point up the need for such a preliminary examination before any standardized test is used. About half of the 65 questions are based on biology, and most of these concern natural history; e.g., there are 3 questions which involve bird migration. The 10 questions in the next largest block serve to examine the student's knowledge of the history of inventions. There are 9 questions on astronomy, mostly on the relationships of the sun, earth, and moon. The remaining questions are about evenly divided among physics, chemistry, and earth science. Unfortunately, at least 6 of the questions appeared to the reviewer to be ambiguous or even incorrect. It is perhaps important to note that since most of the questions originated prior to 1946 (publication date of the *Progressive Tests in Social and Related Sciences*), the test is probably out of date in respect to many modern elementary science curricula.

Forty of the 65 questions require selection of the one intended answer among four options. The remaining 25 questions are of the true-false type. Almost all of the questions demand no more than the selection of an answer that the student ostensibly has been taught.

The reliabilities of .83 and .84 given for each grade level at which the test is likely to be used are not the lowest exhibited by useful tests. It might be expected that they would be higher, since there are several groups of questions within which the content is rather closely related. The publisher is to be complimented for reporting separate reliabilities for each grade level at which the test is likely to be used.

When it comes to reporting validity, the publisher is seriously deficient. There is the explanation that the items for this test and the other two science tests which the manual covers were rated as to suitability by experts. Nothing is said about the distribution of content except that the authors selected the questions from those approved by the "expert judgment" of supervisors, teachers, and college professors. Moreover, the manual doesn't say when the items were selected. As has been implied, in this age of rapid change, datedness should be considered in evaluating science tests. While the manual includes the statement, "An achievement test should show high positive relationships with other standardized tests in the same achievement area," no such relationships are reported for the *Survey Test in Introductory Science.*

The norming sample used for establishing percentiles has a reasonable geographic distribution, but there is good reason for not accepting the norms at face value. This is particularly true if they are to be used to evaluate a science program. There is wide range in what is considered desirable in an elementary science program. From the manual one cannot tell what type of program was considered desirable in the schools which were included in the norming sample. Moreover, one cannot determine in what percentage of the schools an elementary science program was offered.

In using the norms teachers will do well to keep in mind the standard errors of measurement for the various grade levels. For the seventh grade the standard error reported in the manual is 3.6 raw score points. According to the grade placement norms given for the seventh grade level—the level at which the test is most likely to be used—the chances are two in three that the error of placement is not more than one grade. In the percentile norms, the same probability prevails for differences as much as or more than 10 percentile points. With this test, as with most other tests, the standard error of measurement should be food for thought among those who are inclined to look at test scores as precise measurements.

The manual supplied with this test is somewhat less than adequate. The reviewer feels that the data on standard error should have been placed closer to the norms and explained in connection with them. Also, raw score entries in the tables are not clearly indicated. It seems to this reviewer that, if only one reference is given for instructions on preparing local norms, it should be an edition which the publisher has made certain is in print. Better still, adequate instructions should be given in the manual. The publisher has failed to meet either of these criteria for this test.

The instructions given for administering the test are clear except that the need for the use of electrographic pencils when IBM answer sheets or mark-sense cards are to be machine scored should be more strongly emphasized.

In summary, this test is a convenient one to use. It can be easily administered within a class period. Easily-used scoring and record-keeping aids are available. By examining the science content of the test and by thoroughly studying the manual, teachers can decide whether the test covers what they consider important for their objectives. If it does, the test may be useful and valuable, particularly if local norms are established.

For a review by David R. Krathwohl of the California Tests in Social and Related Sciences, *see 5:4; for reviews by Harry D. Berg and J. Raymond Gerberich of an earlier edition of the elementary level, see 4:23.*

[885]

***Survey Test in Physical Science: California Survey Series.** Grades 7–10; 1946–59; subtest 5 of the advanced level (for grades 9–12) of *California Tests in Social and Related Sciences,* Form AA; IBM; Form 1 ('59, 11 pages, identical with test copyrighted in 1953); no specific manual; combined manual ('59, 19 pages) for this test and tests 884 and 897; $2.80 per 35 tests; separate answer sheets may be used; 5¢ per IBM answer sheet; 20¢ per scoring stencil; 10¢ per series class record sheet; 2¢ per series individual record sheet; postage extra; 50¢ per specimen set, postpaid; 40(45) minutes; Georgia Sachs Adams, William E. Keeley, and John A. Sexson; California Test Bureau. *

IRVIN J. LEHMANN, *Associate Professor in Evaluation Services, Michigan State University, East Lansing, Michigan.*

This test consists of 45 items (requiring 70 responses) to be done in 40 minutes. The test was designed to measure the "student's understanding of and his ability to apply his knowledge of basic facts about the physical environment." Although the name of the test suggests that knowledge in the physical sciences, such as physics, chemistry, earth sciences, and astronomy, will be measured, this title might be misleading since the major emphasis in this test centers about physics and the solar system—38 per cent and 27 per cent of the responses, respectively. Unless the curriculum has changed markedly in the past few years, it would appear that there is overemphasis in physics and underemphasis in the earth sciences.

Although the test is *supposed* to measure the student's ability to apply principles of science, only 2 of the 70 responses are specifically devoted to this operation. Some of the other items require a quasi-scientific application, but, even so, it would appear that this test measures knowledge of facts per se. There are three items (8 per cent of the responses) that have very little bearing upon physical science, viz., important considerations for supplying a city with water, and fire safety. Some of the items, for example, the items on safety factors and some of the items pertaining to the use of scientific instruments, require no general science knowledge but just general knowledge.

The test format leaves something to be desired. For example, some of the items require a single answer while others require two answers. Although the items of each type occur in groups, the groups are alternated throughout the test; it would appear that grouping all items of one type under Part 1 and all of the other type under Part 2 could help prevent misunderstanding on the part of the students. Even though items requiring a single response have a single line on which the response is to be written and those requiring two responses have a split line, and even though it could be argued that this should keep the student informed, due to typographical errors, questions 16 and 17 each have a single response line even though *two* answers are required. Throughout the test, it is readily evident that some of the item options do not display some of the elementary principles of test construction, such as, every answer should be plausible, to measure the higher levels of understanding the homogeneity of the options should be increased, and all items with the same number of choices should be grouped together.

Although the keying of most of the items is adequate, there are two items where the wording of the options may result in some difficulty. In item 27 the first option, "methods of purifying water so that it will be chemically pure," is partly correct as an important consideration in supplying a city with water, but the response is not totally correct because chemical purity is not economically possible or even feasible. Item 28, which deals with rules for the control and prevention of fire, has a distractor ("A rubbish pile near an incinerator is permissible if a garden hose is handy in case of fire") which, it can be argued, is also a correct response. This being the case, it would be advisable to rewrite these two options.

Several means of assuring validity are reported in the manual. Courses of study, current leading textbooks, and research studies on the content of required high school courses were consulted in the preparation of the preliminary form. Many more items than needed were constructed and tried out (apparently prior to 1953, publication date of the original test from which this test is taken). Item analysis was then used to select the best items. "Experts" (college professors, supervisors, curriculum workers, and classroom teachers) were also used to rate the items along a 5-point continuum ranging from essential concepts that should be learned by every high school student to inconsequential concepts that should be deleted. Finally, correlations with another standardized science achievement test and teachers' marks were computed. The validity coefficients reported range from .53 to .66. Although these coefficients are fairly substantial, they leave much to be desired since the highest correlation was that between the test and another standardized achievement test.

Kuder-Richardson formula 21 reliability coefficients are reported for grades 7, 8, and 9, but not for grade 10. The reliabilities, which range from .81 to .83, are somewhat lower than would be expected in this area. Although this form of reliability estimate takes into account both the equivalence and homogeneity of the test items, it does not give any information regarding temporal fluctuations. The authors also report the standard error of measurement, which permits the user to attach to an obtained score a probability statement regarding the degree of accuracy of the obtained score in relation to the true score. The reported errors of measurement suggest that the test is quite reliable for general purposes.

Obtained scores may be converted to percentile norms, standard score norms, grade norms, and age norms. Although one table of percentile and standard score norms is said to be appropriate for "ninth- and tenth-grade students who have completed courses in general science," no mention is made of tenth graders in describing the normative populations, and the tables providing separate norms by grade do not include grade 10. Nevertheless, the authors are to be commended for providing several types of normative data, although, in the final analysis, teachers might wish to construct local norms. It would appear that the norming population might be underrepresentative of schools in the Middle West and the South.

Directions for administration and scoring are lucid, as are the descriptions of the various norms. The instructions for interpretation are straightforward and should be understandable to the unsophisticated user. Only the total score is interpreted even though four subscores can be obtained. There is both a class and individual score sheet with this test. Although the test is timed, the authors contend that it is a power test. This is not necessarily the case since the items do not progressively increase in difficulty.

Teachers contemplating using this test should be cognizant of the fact that the test measures only a limited portion of the range of objectives for the teaching of science. In addition, lack of separate normative data for the tenth graders suggests that the test not be seriously considered for use at this level. However, in the final analysis, the decision is up to the individual user. If all that is wanted is a test of general knowledge and familiarity with science, this test suffices this minimal objective. However, if the objectives are broader, then this test must be considered weak in many areas. The test appears to be much more heavily oriented to recall of factual material than to the understanding of or application of basic fundamental scientific principles.

For a review by David R. Krathwohl of the California Tests in Social and Related Sciences, *see 5:4.*

[886]

★T.C. General Science Test. Teachers college entrants; 1955–58; many items selected or adapted from out of print forms of *Cooperative General Science Test* and *Cooperative Chemistry Test;* 6 scores: natural science, physics, chemistry, biology, scientific reasoning, total; 1 form ['56, 6 pages]; mimeographed manual ['58, 7 pages]; no data on reliability; no norms for subscores; distribution restricted to teacher training institutions; separate answer sheets must be used; 6*s.* per 10 tests; 2*s.* per 10 answer sheets; 4*s.* per key; 2*s.* 6*d.* per manual; 7*s.* 6*d.* per specimen set; postpaid within Australia; 40(45) minutes; Australian Council for Educational Research. *

[Other Tests]

For tests not listed above, see the following entries in *Tests in Print:* 1554, 1557–8, 1560–2, 1567, and 1570; out of print: 1545, 1549–51, 1559, and 1565.

BIOLOGY

[887]

Biological Science: Teacher Education Examination Program. College seniors preparing to teach secondary school; 1957; an inactive form of *Biology and General Science: National Teacher Examinations;* for more complete information, see 709; IBM; 80(95) minutes; Educational Testing Service. *

For a review of the testing program, see 5:543. For reviews of the National Teacher Examinations, *see 700, 5:538, and 4:802.*

[887a]

★Biology: Cooperative Science Tests. High school; 1963–64; 3 scores: general and human biology, the diversity of life, total; IBM; Forms A, B, ('63, 16 pages); no specific manual; series handbook ('64, 76 pages); separate answer sheets must be used; $4 per 20 tests; $1 per 20 IBM scorable answer sheets; $1 per 10 scoring stencils (answer pattern must be punched out locally); $1 per handbook; postage extra; $2 per specimen set of this and 4 other science tests, cash orders postpaid; 80(92) minutes in 1 or 2 sessions; Cooperative Test Division. *

[888]

***Biology: Every Pupil Scholarship Test.** High school; 1926–64; new form (2 pages) usually issued each January and April; forms from previous testing programs also available; general directions sheet ['63, 2 pages]; no data on reliability; norms for new forms available following testing program; 4¢ per test; 4¢ per key; postage extra; 40(45) minutes; Bureau of Educational Measurements. *

[889]

***Biology: Every Pupil Test.** High school; 1935–64; new form (4 pages) usually issued each December and April; forms from previous testing programs also available; general directions sheet ('63, 2 pages); no data on reliability; Ohio norms for new forms available following testing program; 5¢ per test; 3¢ per key; postpaid; 40(45) minutes; Ohio Scholarship Tests. *

[890]

***Biology: Minnesota High School Achievement Examinations.** High school; 1955-63; series formerly called *Midwest High School Achievement Examinations;* new form issued each May; norms available in June following release of new forms; Form F ('63, 6 pages) used in 1963 testing; no specific manual; series manual ('63, 4 pages); series norms ['63, 4 pages]; series cumulative profile ('62, 2 pages); no data on reliability; no description of normative population; 12¢ per test; $2.50 per 100 profiles; postage extra; 20¢ per specimen set, postpaid; 60(65) minutes; American Guidance Service, Inc. *

BARBARA F. ESSER, *Professional Associate, Educational Testing Service, Princeton, New Jersey.* [Review of Forms E and F.]

The test under review here would seem to satisfy few, if any, of the criteria for standardized tests. The authorship is cloaked in anonymity. The rationale for the test is limited essentially to the statement, "The items....were chosen because they measured the subject matter objectives of the curriculum." We are not told just *what* curriculum, but it is obvious that it is a rather conventional one and that it has a strong Midwestern flavor, which might limit the test's appeal for a large number of users even if the test did not suffer from a great many other defects.

No information is provided in the manual as to the reliability of the test, its validity, its correlation with other measures, its standard error of measurement, or any of the other information which the conscientious test user has a right to expect of a test publisher. Some percentile rank norms of dubious merit are provided to test users after "the receipt of scores from a sufficiently large number of schools using the test." No details are provided as to the sampling plan used in deriving these norms, except for the statement that the ratio of small to large schools used approximates that of the actual test users. It is apparent from examining these norms that the successive test forms are not parallel to one another. This is also apparent in the composition of the two forms. Each is divided into eight units, but these units differ both in subject matter and in the number of items assigned. Separate norms are not provided for the individual units, although the manual encourages the user to study the subscores to spot those units on which students did well or poorly. One subscore is based on five items.

The brief four-page manual seems amateurish in the extreme. Although the reader is assured that "All questions were edited very carefully," editorial perfection is apparent neither in the test items nor in the manual. The manual contains numerous serious grammatical flaws and typographical errors. These are carefully carried over from the Form E manual to that for Form F, where some further garbling occurs as a result of a change in layout. The test booklets themselves are printed with a type face that is much too small for easy reading. Provision is made for recording answers directly in the test booklet rather than on separate answer sheets.

The test items themselves are not without merit. The five-choice format is used throughout, and each form contains sufficient items (Form E has 107 and Form F, 106) to produce reliable scores if the tests were more carefully constructed and standardized. The testing time in each case is one hour, although standardized directions for administering the test under conditions that would ensure the provision of exactly an hour are not to be found in the materials supplied to this reviewer.

Apparently the authors gave special attention to the goal of producing "thought" questions in addition to purely factual items. In this attempt they have been moderately successful. The manual also states that a concerted attempt was made to render the items clear and unambiguous, but in this the editors were only very moderately successful. Some items definitely have multiple keys, depending on the way the wording is interpreted. On the whole, however, the defects to be found in the items tend to be more editorial than biological. The manual makes the interesting statement that the items were so selected as to include in the final edition only those which "seemed to carry a high degree of validity." The criterion of this "validity" is nowhere defined.

This test may find some application as a classroom test for the teacher who for one reason or another lacks the time necessary to construct his own. The uses for the test recommended by the manual fall primarily in the area of guidance, with the wholesome caution that the test not be used for the evaluation of teachers. Certainly the publishers have a lot of work to do if they intend to offer this test to the public as a standardized measure of achievement in high school biology.

[891]

★**Biology Test: Affiliation Testing Program for Catholic Secondary Schools.** Grades 9–12 and students who are candidates for the high school diploma issued by the Catholic University of America; 1949–63; administered annually in May at individual schools; IBM; new form issued annually; Form Z ('63, 15 pages) used in 1963 program; separate answer sheets must be used; 50¢ per test and IBM answer sheet; postpaid; fee includes purchase of test booklets, scoring, and other services; specimen set of the complete battery free; for more complete information, see 758; 90(100) minutes; Program of Affiliation, Catholic University of America. *

HENRY CHAUNCEY, *President, Educational Testing Service, Princeton, New Jersey.* [Review of Forms Y and Z.]

Judging from the course description given in the booklet describing the Program of Affiliation, Forms Y and Z of this test in general cover the subject matter they are intended to cover. However, the vast majority of questions fail to probe deeply enough to determine whether or not the student has obtained "an understanding....of major biological principles," although this aspect of the subject matter is by no means entirely neglected. Form Z seems to do better in this respect than Form Y.

Technically, a number of questions in both forms leave a lot to be desired. There are questions which have incorrect keys. For instance, item 1 in Form Y represents the relationship of clover and bees as being symbiotic. Most biologists would not agree. Sometimes the options associated with the questions are such that a single, isolated bit of knowledge can serve to eliminate several options. For instance, Form Y, item 41, reads as follows: "Examples of insects are 1. fly, spider, mosquito 2. mosquito, butterfly, tick 3. butterfly, tick, cochineal bug 4. tick, cochineal bug, mosquito 5. cochineal bug, mosquito, fly." When a student attempts this question, he can eliminate three options if he knows what a tick is. Sometimes options are used which obviously include one of the other options. In Form Y, the options of item 63, from which a match for the "study of birds" is to be selected, include both "ornithology" and "zoology." In Form Z, item 14, the student is supposed to select "metabolism," from a list which also contains "catabolism," for "The process that includes utilization of foods, release of energy, and the excretion of wastes." The aforementioned are only a few of the questions which display flaws in the two forms reviewed. While faulty items do not typify the entire test, there are enough of them to indicate that it could be vastly improved. In technical quality of items, as in content coverage, Form Z seems to be superior to Form Y.

Mean scores of 82.1 and 74 and standard deviations of 17.1 and 17, given in the reports on Forms Y and Z, respectively, reflect desirable statistical characteristics. The K-R 21 reliabilities of .88 for both forms and validities of .85 and .74 are relatively high for a test of this type. The validity figures (based on correlations between pretest scores and teachers' grades) are so high that one would expect more details to be given on the way they were derived. For one thing, corrections for attenuation are not clearly described.

In summary, Forms Y and Z of this test cover well the content their constructors ostensibly intended them to cover, with the possible exception of understandings at the level of generalizations and principles. Technically, the forms could stand improvement.

For a review of the complete program, see 758.

[892]

***College Entrance Examination Board Achievement Test: Biology.** Candidates for college entrance; 1915–64; for more complete information, see 760; 60(80) minutes; program administered for the College Entrance Examination Board by Educational Testing Service. *

REFERENCES

1. COLLEGE ENTRANCE EXAMINATION BOARD. *Science: A Description of the College Board Tests in Biology, Chemistry, and Physics.* Princeton, N.J.: the Board, September 1954. Pp. 39. * (*PA* 29:2958)
2. EVENSON, A. B., AND SMITH, D. E. "A Study of Matriculation in Alberta." *Alberta J Ed Res* 4:67–83 Je '58. *
3. BLEIFELD, MAURICE. *How to Prepare for College Board Achievement Tests: Biology.* Great Neck, N.Y.: Barron's Educational Series, Inc., 1963. Pp. vi, 250. *

For a review by Elizabeth Hagen of an earlier form, see 5:723; for a review by Clark W. Horton, see 4:600. For reviews of the testing program, see 760.

[893]

***College Entrance Examination Board Advanced Placement Examination: Biology.** High school students desiring credit for college level courses or admission to advanced courses; 1956–63; for more complete information, see 761; 180(200) minutes; program administered for the College Entrance Examination Board by Educational Testing Service. *

REFERENCES
1. VALLEY, JOHN R. "A Report on CEEB Advanced Placement Mathematics and Natural Sciences Examinations Candidates, May 1958." *Sci Teach* 26:399–402 O '59. *

CLARENCE H. NELSON, *Professor, Office of Evaluation Services, Michigan State University, East Lansing, Michigan.* [Review of Forms KBP and LBP.]

The 1962 Form KBP and the 1963 Form LBP of the *College Entrance Examination Board Advanced Placement Examination: Biology* were designed to be administered to high school seniors who had completed a college level biology course while still in high school, and who were applying either for college credit, for advanced standing in college biology, or for both. The specifications for this examination were presumably derived from the course description which appears in the CEEB handbook entitled *Advanced Placement Program: Course Descriptions.* Following are a few excerpts from the specifications included in this book:

[the course] should have three class meetings and three hours of laboratory a week for 30 weeks * The overall approach should be dynamic * Living materials, and field work if feasible, should be an integral part of the laboratory work. * Evolution should be a fundamental theme or framework * the interdependence of organisms and environment should receive constant attention * Evolutionary changes....are brought about by the interaction of random mutations occurring within and selection pressures operating upon a population. * Genetics....plant, animal and human examples should be considered.

While the list includes many more statements, all of the foregoing at least suggest a functional, dynamic emphasis. The examination, in the main, tends to reflect more of a descriptive, definitional, conservative emphasis.

The 1962 and 1963 forms are similar in that each has two sections—one objective and one essay. Section 1 consists of 100 items to be answered in one hour. Section 2 consists of seven essay questions, four of which are to be answered in the two-hour time allotment. All examinees are required to answer the first question, and three additional questions each selected from a different pair of alternative questions. According to the Test Analysis of the May 1962 administration of Form KBP, a composite score was derived from the two sections in such a way as to make the highest possible converted score on the objective section one third, and the highest possible raw score on the essay section two thirds, of the maximum possible composite score.

SECTION 1. The objective type items comprising this portion of the examination reflect, on the whole, careful workmanship and conformity to the rules of test construction. Only two slight flaws were detected in the 1962 edition, in which two items contain minor irrelevant clues to the answers. About 90 per cent of the items in each of the two editions are answerable on the basis of very precisely memorized fundamental factual knowledge. Less than 10 per cent of the items in Section 1 of either form involve reasoning, critical analysis, or problem solving ability. Statistical data, based upon a spaced sample of 370 students out of a population of 1,058 who took the 1962 examination (data were not yet available for the 1963 edition) showed a reliability estimate of .88, a standard deviation of 15.5, and a mean for the 100 objective items of 40.9. A skewness to the right of this magnitude indicates that Section 1 proved to be very difficult for the group, but this is explained as being desirable in a situation where it is essential to distinguish among the more able candidates. The 1963 edition contained a selection of anchor items, repeated from the 1962 form, which will evidently provide a basis for judging comparability of the test populations in the two successive years.

SECTION 2. The first essay question in both forms was answered by all examinees. In each instance this question pertains to a situation from the very forefront of present-day research activity, so recent, in fact, that it is just beginning to find its way into the newest editions of the textbooks. Unless the student had done supplementary reading in new reference books or very recent issues of professional journals, he would have had very little basis for answering the first question satisfactorily. Perhaps it was the intent of the examiners to thus separate the students who read current research journals from those who do not. It would seem more appropriate, however, to include a question on current research materials in which some of the experimental procedures are described in the examination booklet and the students are then asked to make an analysis of the rationale—the how, the why, the significance of the steps in the procedure, and an appraisal of the experimental results. If this were done, all the students would be on the same footing, whether the experiment described happened to involve recent research or a classical situation from the textbooks. Since the students who took Forms KBP and LBP had a choice of questions 2 or 3, 4 or 5, and 6 or 7, it is difficult to see how there would be sufficient comparability in the students' combinations of answers to yield very meaningful scores. The readers entrusted with the scoring of these essay answers, however, were exceedingly conscientious in their efforts to get as high reliability as possible. A different reader read each of the four essay answers on any one paper. This procedure tended to eliminate the "halo" effect which, as the Test Analysis of Form KBP points out, "is almost certain to be present when two or more questions on a paper are graded by the same reader."

EXAMINATION AS A WHOLE. The overwhelming emphasis in this examination appears to be on the descriptive aspects of biology—anatomy, morphology, and embryology, in particular. The student is asked to name, describe, discuss, define, and compare. He is seldom asked to solve a problem or sequence of related problems, to criticize experimental procedures, to judge outcomes of experiments, or to analyze the logicality of the reasoning employed. The entire examination, both Section 1 and Section 2, is generally concerned with assessment of the student's fund of precise memorized factual knowledge rather than with his ability to evaluate methodology used in the creation of new science knowledge or his ability to apply knowledge to the solution of problem situations.

From the standpoint of assessing students' knowledge and ability in the area of biology, it is doubtful whether the essay portion of this examination contributes enough to justify the tremendous expenditure in time, effort, and money involved in scoring it. Section 1, as now constituted, serves its purpose exceedingly well and should be retained. If Section 2 could be made to include 100 objective items that would involve the student in application of knowledge to the solution of problems (sequences of 8–10 related problems bearing on the same situation), interpretation of data, and critical analysis of experimental procedures, the two sections would complement each other and together might constitute an examination that could yield a more meaningful estimate of the student's knowledge and ability. If a sample of the student's writing is of crucial significance to the college, the student could be given a half hour in which to write the answer to one of seven questions such as now appear in Section 2, and this could be sent unscored to the college of the student's choice for separate consideration in judging the student's ability.

For a review by Clark W. Horton of an earlier form, see 5:724.

[894]

★College Entrance Examination Board Placement Tests: Biology. Entering college freshmen; 1962–63, c1961–63; IBM; Form JPL (c1961, 8 pages, a reprint of an inactive form of *College Entrance Examination Board Achievement Test: Biology*); for more complete information, see 759; 60(70) minutes; program administered for the College Entrance Examination Board by Educational Testing Service. *

For reviews of the College Entrance Examination Board Achievement Test: Biology, *see 5:723 and 4:600.*

[895]

***Cooperative Biology Test: Educational Records Bureau Edition.** High school; 1941–62; IBM; Forms ERB-RY ('57, c1941–57, 7 pages, revision of the 1948 Form ERB-RX), ERB-SY ('58, c1942–58, 8 pages, revision of the 1949 Form ERB-SX), ERB-TY ('59, c1943–59, 8 pages, revision of the 1950 Form ERB-TX); no specific manual; general Cooperative manual ('51, 8 pages); no data on reliability presented in manual; norms: Form ERB-RY ('60), Form ERB-SY ('61), Form ERB-TY ('62); 12¢ per test; separate answer sheets may be used; 4¢ per IBM answer sheet; 50¢ per specimen set; postage extra; 40(45) minutes; Committee on Biology Tests of the Educational Records Bureau; Educational Records Bureau. *

REFERENCES

1–2. See 4:602.
3. See 5:725.

[896]

***The Graduate Record Examinations Advanced Tests: Biology.** Grades 16–17; 1939–63; for more complete information, see 762; 180(200) minutes; Educational Testing Service. *

For a review by Clark W. Horton of an earlier form, see 5:727. For a review of the testing program, see 5:601.

[897]

***Survey Test in Biological Science: California Survey Series.** Grades 7–10; 1946–59; subtest 6 of the advanced level (for grades 9–12) of *California Tests in Social and Related Sciences,* Form AA; IBM; Form 1 ('59, 9 pages, identical with test copyrighted in 1953); no specific manual; combined manual ('59, 19 pages) for this test and tests 884–5; $2.80 per 35 tests; separate answer sheets may be used; 5¢ per IBM answer sheet; 20¢ per scoring stencil; 10¢ per series class record sheet; 2¢ per series individual record sheet; postage extra; 50¢ per specimen set, postpaid; 40(45) minutes; Georgia Sachs Adams, William E. Keeley, and John A. Sexson; California Test Bureau. *

BARBARA F. ESSER, *Professional Associate, Educational Testing Service, Princeton, New Jersey.*

Since a previous reviewer of the battery of which this test is part (Krathwohl, see 5:4) devoted his attention primarily to statistical considerations, with only a passing caution that "potential users should examine the content carefully to determine its validity for their purposes," it seems advisable at this time to look more carefully into the content validity of this test of "biological science."

Even a superficial examination of the individual items within the test reveals an alarming lack of attention to factual accuracy on the part of the authors. A few examples will illustrate the nature of the inaccuracies and ambiguities which pervade the test. We find, for example, in the very first item this possible answer: "Non-living [*sic!*] things do not grow." While this may be considered true in the light of a strictly biological definition of the word "growth," it is certainly common for a physical scientist to speak of the "growth" of a crystal. The examinee is called upon to determine whether or not this statement represents a difference between living and nonliving things. Alas, his decision will probably have to be based on his talents for reading the minds of the test authors, since the statement is inherently ambiguous. A similar dilemma is presented in attempting to evaluate the truth or falsity of the assertion: "All living things are made up of one or more cells." This item is keyed as true, yet viruses, which are almost universally conceded to be living things, are clearly acellular in nature. Again, the statement "A typical cell cannot live long without a nucleus" presents problems. How typical is "typical" and how long is "long"? Erythrocytes function most usefully without nuclei. The statement "Living cells have been known to develop from non-living substances" is keyed false, yet students who have speculated seriously about the ultimate origin of life must surely be baffled in attempting to key this item. Further on, the problem of the cell nucleus comes up again in a diagram set where the response "F" (obviously meant to be a nucleus) "must be present in a living cell since it governs the activity of the cell" is keyed as true. Not only is this an even stronger statement than the one previously cited, but also it would seem to be subjecting the examinee to double jeopardy to include two questions so similar in nature on an examination of this type, especially when both are ambiguous. Several other examples of glaring duplication in the testing of concepts occur in the test.

To move from the area of ambiguity to one of outright technical accuracy, one might cite the statement "During the spawning season each [*sic!*] salmon lays thousands of eggs." Surely it would be an extremely "new" biology in which even male salmon possessed such remarkable ovarian productivity. In the section on health, the statement "Tonsils do not need attention unless a person is subject to frequent attacks of acute tonsillitis" is keyed false. Since this position is at best medically debatable, it would seem that the keyed answer is hardly defensible. Later one learns that if we "Expose bacteria to a direct flame for thirty seconds," the result will be that "both bacteria and spores will be killed." Not only does this seem an esoteric bit of information for the average high school student to possess, but it would appear to have no assured basis in fact, since it is well known that certain portions of a flame may be characterized by remarkably low temperatures.

This recital of defects could be extended considerably to include such flaws as the use of specific determiners (item 4, option 4; item 9, option 2; and item 12, option 4 are examples); poor format, such as the inclusion of a question based on a diagram appearing on a page which has just been turned out of view (item 7); mutually exclusive options in an item type where two correct statements out of four are to be selected (item 8, options 2 and 4); poor punctuation (item 16, where a clause which is obviously restrictive has nonetheless been set off by commas); and poor selection of item format. (Of the 105 possible responses to be made to the 93 items, 28 are out-and-out true-false in format and another 31 are functionally indistinguishable from this type. This distribution of item types would yield an expected chance score of approximately 39, a figure which is listed without apology as falling at the 34th percentile for seventh graders!)

It seems regrettable that the authors of this test did not subject it to more rigorous review by competent biologists and test construction specialists. Many of the defects pointed out here could have been avoided by simple editorial changes, rephrasing of ambiguous wording, more careful attention to pagination, and substitution of other items for those which produce undesirable duplication. Another matter, of course, is the wisdom of including so many true-false items, since these are almost inevitably ambiguous and are in poor repute among those who construct achievement tests. No doubt the desire to produce a relatively large number of scorable units in a 40-minute period influenced this decision.

Although the manual gives seemingly adequate information as to the reliability and "validity" of the test and provides age-grade, percentile rank, and standard score norms "making possible an interpretation of the results on both a longitudinal and a cross-sectional basis," when one considers the fundamental inadequacies of the test items themselves, interpretations of the sort advocated by the authors seem far from warranted, and it seems doubtful if the test can be valid for *any* purpose. One cannot help wondering whether the interesting statement, on page 11 of the manual, that one should "avoid discussing the specific test items after the test has been given" was motivated more by a sincere desire to protect the security of the test or by the realization that many of the test items would not bear objective scrutiny.

Until a revision is made to correct the numerous inaccuracies and ambiguities in this test, its use is not to be recommended at any level. Since it must be conceded that tests inevitably serve a teaching as well as an assessment function, continued use of this test in its present form, attractive in format as it may be, is much to be lamented.

CLARENCE H. NELSON, *Professor, Office of Evaluation Services, Michigan State University, East Lansing, Michigan.*

This test consists of 93 items. Since the first 12 are four-response multiple choice items requiring the student to select two answers, the number of scorable units in the test totals 105, which is quite substantial for 40 minutes of testing time. Thirty-five items are two-response: 28 true-false and 7 sound-unsound. The remaining items consist of clusters of 4 to 7 items with 5 common responses within each cluster. Practically all students should finish the test within a 40-minute period.

Test data are reported for tryouts in grades 7, 8, 9, and 10, the tryout populations numbering, respectively, 539, 611, 643, and 679. The respective means of 43.5, 51.0, 58.0, and 67.0 indicate that the test is quite difficult, as might be expected, for seventh graders, who have usually had only incidental exposure to biology in their general science classes, and moderately easy for tenth graders, most of whom have probably had a year's course in biology. The standard deviation of 17.7 and the reliability of .92 for the tenth grade group are both very good indeed, reflecting careful workmanship and craftsmanship in test refinement.

This test is designed for flexibility of administration. Answers may be marked either in the booklet itself or on a specially prepared IBM answer sheet. The format and editing of the test booklet reflect a standard of excellence for which California Test Bureau has long been distinguished in the field of test publishing.

While this test is generally accurate and on the whole conforms quite well to the rules of test construction, a few items might bear scrutiny. Item 14 should be very easy to answer merely by spotting in one of the responses the same word as appears in the item itself. In response A the phrase "that manufactures the *food*" locks readily into place with the phrase "perish from lack of food" in the item. The student would not have to understand either the role of chlorophyll or the parasitic habits of the yellow dodder in order to select the keyed answer. Item 20 reads in part, "If a plant is pulled up and transplanted, it will die." A scientist is usually more cautious and restrained and tries to avoid dogmatism. He would be more apt to say "it *may* die." Item 56 on the effect of wearing high heeled shoes and item 57 on what to do about blisters would seem to more properly belong in a hygiene test than in a biology test. Items 1–12 which are of the four-response, two-answer type, and items 48–82 which are either true-false or sound-unsound, lead one to wonder if there shouldn't be a correction for guessing, at least for these blocks of items. Because of the high probability of guessing the correct answer in two-response items, some test writers and editors tend to avoid the use of true-false items in standardized tests.

On the positive side, items 27–40 on animal classification, items 41–47 on functions of body systems, items 83–88 on causes of diseases, and items 89–93 on bacterial growth are carefully constructed and embody standard biological science subject matter.

The points contributing to the total score are apportioned among the subject matter categories as follows: Nature of Living Things (24), Plant Life and Its Importance (10), Animals and Their Relations to Man (18), Bodily Functions and Health (20), Diet and Health (15), and Diseases and Human Welfare (18).

Biology as a formal course is most often taught in grade 9 or 10. When offered in these grades by a highly professional teacher who has a major in biology, the course usually includes additional subject matter which appears in most standard high school textbooks and in many courses of study, but which has *not* been touched upon in this test. These areas are: reproduction (mitosis, meiosis, fertilization, embryological development), heredity (monohybrid and dihybrid crosses, linkage, sex-linkage, and blood type inheritance), evolution (fossil record, speciation, gene mutation), ecological interrelationships, and conservation of natural resources. Individuals well qualified to teach health, physical education, and recreation courses are often assigned to teach biology even though they have not taken the standard college biology courses. Such teachers often omit these additional areas and substitute instead a disproportionately heavy emphasis on disease, health and diet, films, excursions, reports, and projects. Fifty per cent of the items in the *Survey Test in Biological Science* are devoted to the areas of man's bodily functions, health, diet, diseases, and human welfare. In a standard biology course these topics would receive about 25 per cent of the total emphasis. The authors and publisher of this test imply that a permissiveness which results in this kind of course, which omits reproduction, heredity, evolution, ecology, and conservation, is highly desirable—an improvement, in fact, over more rigidly structured courses. If this is true, then the test has substantial validity—but only for such a hygiene-centered course. If, however, the judgment of textbook authors, course of study writers, and teachers who have majored in biology as to what properly belongs in a biology course is to be relied upon, then the coverage represented by the test is inadequate.

Based upon its content coverage, the *Survey Test in Biological Science* appears to be most valid for a course taught by a teacher who places a heavy emphasis on health and hygiene. It would be somewhat less appropriate for a biology course taught in grade 9 or 10 by a teacher who presents the standard content found in most biology textbooks and courses of study. This test would not be suitable at all for use in schools that have adopted the new Biological Science Curriculum Study materials. These BSCS materials represent a very high level of sophistication in biology and chemistry, and are infused with the theme "Science as Inquiry" which this test does not embody. Although all items are taken from a test designed for grades 9–12, the present test is designated as being appropriate for grades 7–10. The norming data seem to suggest that the test is most suitable for use in connection with the biology course taught in grades 9 and 10. While it includes a few topics taken up in junior high school general science, this test would not appear to be suitable for use in a general science course. The decision as to whether the *Survey Test in Biological Science* will be appropriate for a given situation must be made on the basis of the teacher's background and the kind of course that is offered in the particular school.

For a review by David R. Krathwohl of the California Tests in Social and Related Sciences, *see 5:4.*

[Other Tests]

For tests not listed above, see the following entries in *Tests in Print:* 1580–2, 1584–5, 1590, and 1592–3; out of print: 1588 and 1595.

CHEMISTRY

[898]

***A.C.S. Cooperative Examination: Biochemistry.** 1–2 semesters college; 1947–61; 3 scores: elementary, advanced, total; IBM; Form 1959 ('59, 12 pages); no specific manual; general A.C.S. directions ('61, 4 pages); norms ('59); separate answer sheets must be used; $6 per 25 tests; $1 per 25 IBM scorable answer sheets; 25¢ per scoring stencil; 50¢ per specimen set; postage extra; 100(110) minutes; Examinations Committee, Division of Chemical Education, American Chemical Society. *

REFERENCES

1. "Condensed Norms for A.C.S. Cooperative Examinations." *J Chem Ed* 34:144–6 Mr '57. *
2. "Condensed Norms: ACS Cooperative Examinations." *J Chem Ed* 37:166–7 Ap '60. *

J Chem Ed 37:167 Ap '60. Wilhelm R. Frisell. [Review of Form 1959.] * consists of 135 multiple choice questions divided into two parts, the first with 75 items and the second having 60 items * Part I is "elementary in character and designed for one-quarter or one-semester survey courses in Biochemistry, and Part II being more advanced and suitable (together with Part I) for intensive one-semester, two-quarter or one-year courses." Qualitatively, the two parts are very similar in the material covered and whether Part II really deserves the title of "advanced" might be questioned. Obviously, the task of sampling a student's comprehension of modern biochemistry with 135 questions represents a formidable challenge, and the examination committee has done a commendable job in trying to achieve a proper balance in the material covered by the test. However, in the reviewer's opinion, too great a proportion of the questions involves memory, and not enough emphasis is placed on broader aspects of molecular biology. To cite a few examples, topics such as the following receive little or no attention: current concepts of macromolecular structure (protein and DNA); principles of oxidation-reduction and the general role of dehydrogenation in biological systems; the role of equilibria and free energy changes in biochemical reactions; mechanisms of enzyme action; the catalytic nature of the citric acid cycle in energy production and the integrative functions of these reactions in the metabolism of carbohydrate, fat, and amino acids; etc. With such omissions it would be of interest to know whether the pattern of questions in the examination reflects the content of our present courses in elementary biochemistry. If it does, there might be cause for asking whether these courses need revision and also whether they have assumed their rightful relation to other chemistry and biology courses in undergraduate curricula. Such an inventory is long overdue under any circumstances. Regardless of the omission of certain topics, the 1959 edition of the Biochemistry Examination is a worthy contribution to the testing program of the Division of Chemical Education and should prove very helpful in the task of student counseling.

[899]

★**A.C.S. Cooperative Examination for Graduate Placement in Analytical Chemistry.** Entering graduate students; 1961–64; IBM; Forms 1961-A ('61, 7 mimeographed pages), 1964-A ('64, 6 pages); no manual; mimeographed interpretive data-norms sheet (dates as for tests, 2 pages) for each form; distribution restricted to colleges with doctoral programs in chemistry or chemical engineering; separate answer sheets must be used; $6 per 25 tests; $1 per 25 IBM scorable answer sheets; 25¢ per scoring stencil; 50¢ per specimen set; postage extra; 90(95) minutes for Form 1961-A, (120) minutes for Form 1964-A; Examinations Committee, Division of Chemical Education, American Chemical Society. *

REFERENCES

1. "Condensed Norms: ACS Cooperative Examinations." *J Chem Ed* 40:115–6 Mr '63. *

[900]

★**A.C.S. Cooperative Examination for Graduate Placement in Organic Chemistry.** Entering graduate students; 1961; IBM; Form 1961-O (10 pages, mimeographed); no manual; mimeographed interpretive data-norms sheet (2 pages); distribution restricted to colleges with doctoral programs in chemistry or chemical engineering; separate answer sheets must be used; $6 per 25 tests; $1 per 25 IBM scorable answer sheets; 25¢ per scoring stencil; 50¢ per specimen set; postage extra; 90(95) minutes; Examinations Committee, Division of Chemical Education, American Chemical Society. *

REFERENCES

1. "Condensed Norms: ACS Cooperative Examinations." *J Chem Ed* 40:115–6 Mr '63. *

[901]

★**A.C.S. Cooperative Examination for Graduate Placement in Physical Chemistry.** Entering graduate students; 1961–64; IBM; Forms 1961-P ('61, 5 pages), 1964-P ('64, 6 pages); no manual; mimeographed interpretive data-norms sheet (dates as for tests, 2 pages) for each form; distribution restricted to colleges with doctoral programs in chemistry or chemical engineering; separate answer sheets must be used; $6 per 25 tests; $1 per 25 IBM scorable answer sheets; 25¢ per scoring stencil; 50¢ per specimen set; postage extra; 90(95) minutes for Form 1961-P, (120) minutes for Form 1964-P; Examinations Committee, Division of Chemical Education, American Chemical Society. *

REFERENCES

1. "Condensed Norms: ACS Cooperative Examinations." *J Chem Ed* 40:115–6 Mr '63. *

[902]

***A.C.S. Cooperative Examination in General Chemistry.** 1 year college; 1934–63; 4 scores: information, application of principles, quantitative application of principles, total; IBM; Forms 1958 ('58), 1958S ('58), 1960 ('60), 1960S ('62), 1963 ('63), (12 pages); Forms 1958S and 1960S are identical with the corresponding Forms 1958 and 1960 except for order of items and responses; no specific manual; general A.C.S. directions ('61, 4 pages); norms: Forms 1958 ('58), 1960 ('60) 1963 ('63); separate answer sheets must be used; $6 per 25 tests; $1 per 25 IBM scorable answer sheets; 25¢ per scoring stencil; 50¢ per specimen set; postage extra; 105(110) minutes; Examinations Committee, Division of Chemical Education, American Chemical Society. *

REFERENCES

1–5. See 40:1593.
6–8. See 3:557.
9. See 4:610.
10–11. See 5:732.
12. "Condensed Norms for A.C.S. Cooperative Examinations." *J Chem Ed* 34:144–6 Mr '57. *

13. "Condensed Norms: ACS Cooperative Examinations." *J Chem Ed* 36:148 Mr '59. *
14. "Condensed Norms: ACS Cooperative Examinations." *J Chem Ed* 38:211 Ap '61 *

J. A. CAMPBELL, *Professor of Chemistry and Chairman of the Department, Harvey Mudd College, Claremont, California.* [Review of Forms 1958, 1960, and 1963.]

Although three separate forms (1958, 1960, and 1963) of this test are available currently, it is the opinion of this reviewer that schools would be making a mistake to use anything but the most recent form. Not only is the 1963 form better than the preceding two, but there are items in the 1958 and 1960 forms which are now out of date. For example, they are based on 16 as the defined atomic weight of oxygen and, in the 1960 form, there is a question asking what the basis of the atomic weight scale is. Each of the forms includes 100 items divided into roughly three equal parts. Part 1 emphasizes relatively detailed knowledge, Part 2, application of principles, and Part 3, chemical calculations. The tests are probably one of the best available sets at the college level and should provide an adequate measure of student accomplishment in most chemistry courses given to first year college students. The clarity, lack of ambiguity, coverage, and acceptability of the items increases regularly from the 1958 to 1963 forms, further suggesting that the 1963 form is the one which should be used.

This reviewer would class 79 items of the 1963 form as completely acceptable, 6 as having some question, but not such as would seriously bother any students, and 15 as involving ambiguities or misstatements which might cause difficulty, particularly to the better students. For example, 2p electrons can be represented not only as being in dumbbell shaped orbitals, but also in elliptical orbitals, as in the Bohr model, and in pyramidal orbitals, as in p^3 hybridization. Similar ambiguities arise when the possibility of barium chloride and copper sulfate undergoing an exchange reaction is presented along with the answer choice "none of the above." The barium chloride–copper sulfate reaction is only an exchange if one considers copper chloride as a weak electrolyte, which it normally is. It is unfortunate also that the test gives H_2F_2 as the formula of hydrogen fluoride. One more example will serve further to underline the problem met in writing multiple choice questions. The student is asked "which is a valid interpretation" of a graph comparing the boiling points of water, H_2S, H_2Se, and H_2Te. Which is a more valid interpretation, choice 1, "The higher boiling point of water is due to hydrogen bonding," or choice 2, "The higher boiling point of water is due to the *fact* that it is a liquid at ordinary temperatures" [reviewer's italics]?

The time for the examination, 105 minutes for 100 items, is short but probably adequate. The time per item certainly does not encourage much thought on the part of the student, but it does emphasize the worth of quick recall, even in those cases where it would be possible for the student to figure out the answer if he did not recall it.

The 1963 test has been prepared and reviewed by a competent set of people. It has been widely used and norms have been prepared. It is probably one of the best, if not the best, tests available at the college level. It would certainly be wise, however, to make sure that even more recent forms are not available before using the 1963 test, because the A.C.S. Examinations Committee is constantly engaged in revising the tests and issuing new editions.

WILLIAM HERED, *Associate Professor of Chemistry, Indiana University, Gary, Indiana; and Examiner, University of Chicago, Chicago, Illinois.* [Review of Forms 1960 and 1963.]

Forms 1960 and 1963 continue the admirable tradition established by their predecessors. The principal difference between these forms is that the more recent one places more emphasis on structural concepts and reaction rates.

The roster of chemists comprising the Examinations Committee and the General Chemistry Subcommittee is both long and impressive. Much of the success of the cooperative examinations may be attributed to the interplay of viewpoints possible because of the wide circle of participants. That the subcommittee does not include adequate representation from large universities and from the fermenting West Coast is, perhaps, a minor point in view of the test planning and item writing procedures adopted.

Since Forms 1960 and 1963 differ only slightly, only the content of the most recent form will be described. Part 1 consists of 30 items at the information level, almost all of which deal with useful facts. Trivia and purely descriptive material are virtually absent. The intellectual level of Part 2 is clearly above that of the first part. The 45 items are devoted to understanding and use of concepts and encompass most of the central principles and theories commonly taught. Part 3 consists of 25 numerical problems in a representative cross section of quantitative ideas.

The technical form throughout is excellent. Nearly all items are five-response multiple choice, permitting simple directions to the student and flexibility in the design of questions. Four items, however, are of the "evidence-explanation" type. The examinee selects from a set of five alternatives both the best experimental evidence for a given statement and the best theoretical explanation for it. Having a response group do double duty results in neither purpose being well served; the student is apt to be cornered into the correct responses by the paucity of attractive decoys.

Responses in numerical problems present a knotty puzzle to examiners. With the answers arranged in order of magnitude, an aid to reading, one often finds that response C is most often correct and responses A and E least often correct. This results from the tendency of item writers to make at least one decoy smaller than the correct answer and one larger. The alert student soon discovers the clue. It is a pleasure to note that no such maldistribution has occurred in the tests under review, which is further evidence of care in workmanship.

Another technical difficulty is not resolved, however. Where answers consist of mixed exponentials, for example, 4×10^{-10}, five responses do not permit sufficient variation in both terms of the answer, with the result that the correct response can often be found through either the integer or the exponential term. One remedy would split the answer into two parts by having the student select the integer from one set of responses and the exponential term from another. This device would be particularly useful in ionic equilibrium tests.

Time allowances are adequate and should not disturb the average examinee. To complete all items examinees will need to average 40 (Form 1960) to 50 (Form 1963) seconds per information item, 1 minute per application item, and 1.3 minutes per numerical problem. There are no absurdly simple items and few that would tax the most brilliant students. Keying is accurate. The balance of content, behavior, and numerical exercises is excellent.

Kuder-Richardson formula 21 reliabilities for both forms are high enough for any conceivable purpose: .82 and .84 for Part 1, .88 for Part 2, .82 and .84 for Part 3, and .93 and .94 for the total score. Percentile norms are based on 3,506 students from 41 institutions for Form 1960 and 2,683 students from 37 institutions for Form 1963. Students at the 50th percentile on Form 1963 had scores (corrected for chance guessing) representing 37 per cent of the maximum possible score on Part 1, 30 per cent of the maximum on Part 2, 30 per cent of the maximum on Part 3, and 32 per cent of the maximum overall. In comparison with the results on Form 1960, this represents a decline in percentage correct after correction for guessing of 13 per cent on Part 1, 13 per cent on Part 2, 6 per cent on Part 3, and 11 per cent overall. The decline is quite remarkable, particularly so because there is very little difference in these editions. Whether the apparent increase in difficulty of Form 1963 represents lower student quality, significant variation in content and behavior objectives, or other factors, needs to be explored.

In spite of the disturbing normative information, the reviewer regards Forms 1963 and 1960 as valid and reliable instruments for the range of subject matter and behavior included, and does not regard their demands as unreasonable. Clearly they cannot be the sole measure of achievement; the user will wish to supplement them for a better fit with his own goals.

J Chem Ed 38:210 Ap '61. S. L. Burson, Jr. [Review of Form 1960.] * The periodic table and atomic structure receive the greatest emphasis, followed by chemical bonding, equation balancing, and kinetic molecular theory. The remainder of the test affords a well-balanced coverage of the most important topics in the first year course in which organic chemistry is deemphasized. The trend in teaching general chemistry is away from encyclopedic treatment of descriptive chemistry toward an emphasis on concepts for interpretation and predictions. In this respect, it is gratifying that in this examination the recall primarily concerns tools for reasoning in chemistry. Several of the questions in Part II more appropriately belong in Part I, because the correct answers given among the choices are too obvious to require application of principles. Students should be required to extract some information from a graph; unfortunately, the correct answer to the single problem of this type can be ascertained without use of the graphic data, a phase diagram. "None of these" is offered as a choice only twice; more frequent use would be desirable. It is commendable that reading skill, as well as proficiency in chemistry, is required to answer a few questions. Form 1960 is printed in attractive, easily read type, a tremendous improvement over older examinations. The norms accompanying the test permit versatile use of the results for comparative evaluations: the sample is large (3506); subgroups within the sample are well classified. The test would not be an adequate challenge to students in a rigorous honors course. It is, however, an improvement over older examinations and is satisfactory for use with other general chemistry classes.

For reviews by Frank P. Cassaretto and Palmer O. Johnson of Form 1958 and earlier forms, see 5:732; for a review by Kenneth E. Anderson of earlier forms, see 4:610; for reviews by Sidney J. French and Florence E. Hooper, see 3:557.

[903]

★A.C.S. Cooperative Examination: Inorganic Chemistry. College; 1961; 3 scores: theory and periodicity, nomenclature and properties, total; IBM; Form 1961 (11 pages); no specific manual; general A.C.S. directions (4 pages); norms ('61); separate answer sheets must be used; $6 per 25 tests; $1 per 25 IBM scorable answer sheets; 25¢ per scoring stencil; 50¢ per specimen set; postage extra; 100(110) minutes; Examinations Committee, Division of Chemical Education, American Chemical Society. *

REFERENCES

1. "Condensed Norms: ACS Cooperative Examinations." *J Chem Ed* 39:151–2 Mr '62. *

FRANK J. FORNOFF, *Head, Science Section, Test Development Division, Educational Testing Service, Princeton, New Jersey.*

This examination consists of two parts. The first has 60 items to be completed in 60 minutes. The second contains 40 questions to be done in 40 minutes. All questions are five-choice, objective. The test description indicates that Part 1 covers theory and periodicity and that Part 2 covers nomenclature and descriptive chemistry. As with all such classifications, some uncertainty as to the proper placing of some of the items exists. A question on the Rutherford scattering experiment, for example, is in the chemical bond and structure section rather than among the nine questions on nuclear chemistry. Furthermore, a number of the periodicity questions and the descriptive chemistry questions appear very similar.

This reviewer questions the wisdom of the examiners' decision to ask 16 questions on periodicity when a periodic table is not provided. Students who have memorized large portions of the table would seem to have a major advantage. The examiners also appear to expect candidates to know the atomic numbers of elements, at least through the first transition group. This, too, seems to be an unfortunate requirement.

Norms data for two groups of students are presented. The first group of 70 or fewer students who have taken a one- or two-semester course in inorganic chemistry had a raw score of 43.7 at the 50th percentile. For these students the test was of appropriate difficulty. The second group, 129 entering chemistry graduate students, did considerably less well: the raw score for the 50th percentile rank was only 29.6. The reported Kuder-Richardson formula 21 reliabilities are in the low .90's or high .80's for each group and for each part and for the total test, although the norms groups are rather small for providing reliable data. The only description of the second norms group is a list of the universities which the students were entering. As with other American Chemical Society tests, the descriptive material available is less than would be desirable.

This reviewer found several questions that he felt could have been more carefully worded. A few examples follow. The number of the last element in the actinide series is not obvious unless one makes several assumptions, none of which are stated in the question. A question on the acidity of oxides probably is intended to refer to the acidity of the acids formed when the oxides dissolve in water. A periodicity question on strength of oxidizers would probably be stronger if the oxidizers used as options were less dependent on pH than are the chromate and molybdate ions. One can readily think of several properties in which

HF is more similar to water than NH_3 is, even though the keyed answer is NH_3. This reviewer would have thought that Pyrex-type glasses lost both borates and silicates when the glasses are exposed to caustic. Question 89 makes obvious the answer to question 69.

In the opinion of this reviewer, the test would provide better measurement of achievement in inorganic chemistry for a larger group of candidates if dependence on the recall factors mentioned above were reduced. With this limitation, the test appears to be a valuable one for most situations where an inorganic chemistry test is desired.

J Chem Ed 39:153 Mr '62. George B. Kauffman. With the publication of this test, the first ACS cooperative examination in a long-neglected field, Dr. S. Y. Tyree, Jr., his 12-man subcommittee, and 14 collaborators have successfully concluded a difficult assignment—the compilation of a test for an as-yet-unstandardized course given at either sophomore, junior, senior, or graduate level. Because of its comprehensive nature, this examination will undoubtedly be viewed by many chemical educators as an authoritative statement by a group of prominent inorganic chemists of the basic minimum contents of a modern inorganic chemistry course. This examination emphasizes trends and interpretation of observations rather than strict recall of isolated facts. Consisting of 100 multiple-choice items (five choices, one correct response), it is divided into two parts: (1) Theory and Periodicity (60 items, 60 minutes) and (2) Nomenclature and Properties of the Elements and Their Compounds (40 items, 40 minutes). These are sub-divided into nuclear chemistry (9 items), periodicity (16 items), chemical bond and structure (25 items), acid-base theory (10 items), nomenclature (10 items), and descriptive chemistry (30 items). A rough idea of the coverage may be gained from a partial list of topics considered—atomic and ionic sizes, oxidation and ionization potentials, hydrogen bonding, electronegativity, ionic and covalent character, dipole and magnetic moments, complexes and stereochemistry, orbital hybridization, physical measurements and their use, and nonaqueous solvents. Fields of current concentrated research activity which are represented include interstitial compounds, interhalogens, carbonyls, and hydrides of boron and silicon. Future revisions of this new examination will undoubtedly result in improvement. The 10 questions devoted to nomenclature seem excessive to this reviewer, considering the omission of equations, "unusual" oxidation states, "sandwich" compounds, and quantitative problems. It is understandable that the sub-committee should wish to further the adoption of the IUPAC nomenclature, but question 68 seems rather pedantic since two of the choices other than the correct one are in wide usage; incidentally, the anion in the correct answer should be written as one word. Also, the designation "hydroxyl" for the OH^- ion (question 51) is incorrect according to the IUPAC. The answer to question 67 is incorrect on this reviewer's copy of the key.

[904]

***A.C.S. Cooperative Examination in Physical Chemistry.** College; 1946–64; 4 scores: states of matter and solutions, thermodynamics-equilibrium-electrochemistry, structure of matter and kinetics, total; IBM; Forms L ('55, 12 pages), 1964 ('64, 8 pages); no specific manual; general A.C.S. directions ('61, 4 pages); norms: Form L ('61), Form 1964 ('64); separate answer sheets must be used; $6 per 25 tests; $1 per 25 IBM scorable answer sheets; 25¢ per scoring stencil; 50¢ per specimen set; postage extra; 110(120) minutes; Examinations Committee, Division of Chemical Education, American Chemical Society. *

REFERENCES

1. "Condensed Norms for A.C.S. Cooperative Examinations." *J Chem Ed* 34:144–6 Mr '57. *

For a review by Alfred S. Brown of an earlier form, see 3:559.

[905]

*[**A.C.S. Cooperative Examinations in Organic Chemistry.**] 1, 2 semesters college; 1942–62; IBM; 2 levels; no specific manual; general A.C.S. directions ('61, 4 pages); separate answer sheets must be used; $6 per 25 tests; $1 per 100 IBM scorable answer sheets; 25¢ per scoring stencil; 50¢ per specimen set; postage extra; 100(110) minutes; Examinations Committee, Division of Chemical Education, American Chemical Society. *

a) A.C.S. COOPERATIVE EXAMINATION FOR THE BRIEF COURSE IN ORGANIC CHEMISTRY. 1 semester college; 1956–61; 3 scores: part 1, part 2, total; Form 1961B ('61, 12 pages); norms ('61).

b) A.C.S. COOPERATIVE EXAMINATION: ORGANIC CHEMISTRY. 2 semesters college; 1942–64; earlier tests called *A.C.S. Cooperative Organic Chemistry Test;* 3 scores: part 1, part 2, total; Forms 1958 ('58), 1962 ('62), 1964 ('64), (12–15 pages); norms: Forms 1958 ('58), 1962 ('62), 1964 ('64).

REFERENCES

1. "Condensed Norms for A.C.S. Cooperative Examinations." *J Chem Ed* 34:144–6 Mr '57. *
2. "Condensed Norms: ACS Cooperative Examinations." *J Chem Ed* 36:148 Mr '59. *
3. "Condensed Norms: ACS Cooperative Examinations." *J Chem Ed* 39:151–2 Mr '62. *

4. "Condensed Norms: ACS Cooperative Examinations." *J Chem Ed* 40:115–6 Mr '63. *

J Chem Ed 39:152 Mr '62. LeRoy D. Johnson. [Review of test for the brief course, Form 1961B.] * The test comprises 100 well-selected questions which may be used as a final examination in the field. For the convenience of administration, Part I consists of 50 questions to be answered in 50 minutes. An equal amount of time is allowed for the 50 questions in Part II. To thoroughly cover the field and to assure reliability of test results, both parts must be given, and all 100 questions should be answered. Adequate directions are provided for the student so that the test may be machine or hand scored. A balance in difficulty and time requirements in Part I and Part II is well kept. The questions are the usual multiple-choice type. There is no attempt to separate aliphatic and aromatic chemistry. Questions involving nomenclature, proof of structure, quantitative results, simple syntheses, functional group tests, and reaction principles are thought-provoking, well-chosen, and distributed well throughout the test. There are relatively few questions involving reaction mechanisms, laboratory methods, name reactions, organic industrial processes, and theoretical principles as might be expected in a brief course. For the teacher who integrates aliphatic and aromatic subject matter in a brief course, this test should be a welcome addition.

For a review by Shailer Peterson of an earlier form of b, *see 3:558.*

[906]

*[**A.C.S. Cooperative Examinations in Qualitative Analysis.]** 1–2 semesters college; 1943–64; IBM; 3 tests; no specific manual; general A.C.S. directions ('61, 4 pages); separate answer sheets must be used; $1 per 25 IBM scorable answer sheets; 25¢ per scoring stencil; 50¢ per specimen set; postage extra; Examinations Committee, Division of Chemical Education, American Chemical Society. *

a) A.C.S. COOPERATIVE EXAMINATION: QUALITATIVE ANALYSIS. 1943–60; formerly called *A.C.S. Cooperative Chemistry Test in Qualitative Analysis;* 2 tests (8 pages) labeled forms; $6 per 25 tests.

1) *Form H.* 1953; part 1 identical with *c* below; 3 scores: part 1 (second semester general chemistry), part 2, total; norms ('53); no data on reliability; 75(85) minutes.

2) *Form 1960.* 1960; 4 scores: information-balancing equations, qualitative application of principles, quantitative application of principles, total; norms ('60); 105(110) minutes.

b) A.C.S. COOPERATIVE EXAMINATION: BRIEF QUALITATIVE ANALYSIS. 1961–64; Forms 1961 ('61), 1964 ('64), (7 pages); norms: Form 1961 ('61), Form 1964 ('64); $4 per 25 tests; 50(55) minutes.

c) [QUALITATIVE ANALYSIS SUPPLEMENT FOR GENERAL CHEMISTRY.] 1953; Form J ['53, 4 pages, identical with part 1 of Form H of *a*]; norms ('53); no data on reliability; $4 per 25 tests; 45(50) minutes.

REFERENCES

1. "Condensed Norms for A.C.S. Cooperative Examinations." *J Chem Ed* 34:144–6 Mr '57. *
2. "Condensed Norms: A.C.S. Cooperative Examinations." *J Chem Ed* 35:244–5 My '58. *
3. "Condensed Norms: ACS Cooperative Examinations." *J Chem Ed* 38:211 Ap '61. *
4. "Condensed Norms: ACS Cooperative Examinations." *J Chem Ed* 39:151–2 Mr '62. *

J Chem Ed 38:210 Ap '61. Richard E. Frank. [Review of Qualitative Analysis Form 1960.] * This test excels in a number of ways, some of which indicate progress compared with previous forms; e.g., the student is told how much credit each part carries, so he can distribute his efforts wisely. Total credit adds up to 100 points, making the scores immediately comparable with those of other tests given on that same basis. The total number of items was reduced from 80 to 60, and the time allowed to answer them was increased from 100 to 105 minutes. Time, therefore, is not the limiting factor any more, and a good student may be expected to get the whole test done and to achieve a score of 90 to 100 points. The material covered in the test offers a rather complete cross section of the knowledge and the abilities expected at the end of a qualitative analysis course. The balance of subjects could perhaps be improved in future editions by reducing somewhat the number of questions dealing with amino complexes, amphoterism, and hydroxide precipitation (about 20% now). The phrasing of the questions is simple, clear, and unambiguous, and the answers to choose from are so carefully worded that they do not lead, and a multiple choice really exists. In this respect the test is so well done that it may help some of the instructors who do not really like multiple choice tests become reconciled to the ever-mounting necessity to save time by using them. The problems in part III, testing for comprehension of the laws and correct setting-up of equations, avoid lengthy arithmetic. The slide rule, the use of which is permitted, will not be very busy. Since the emphasis of the whole examination is strongly on the intelligent application of principles, the test may also be used to advantage in qualification exams of new graduate students, preferably in combination with a few essay type questions on more advanced concepts.

J Chem Ed 39:153 Mr '62. W. H. Waggoner. [Review of Brief Qualitative Analysis Form 1961.] * This test consists of 50 items with a 50 minute time limit. Although there is no formal division into parts, questions dealing with similar subject matter are grouped together. Thus the group of questions involving "paper unknowns" (10 items) is readily identified. The problems which require numerical answers (5 items) and the equations to be balanced (5 items) are other obvious groups. The balance of the test is evenly divided between descriptive information on ions and reagents and the application of equilibrium principles. The test achieves a good balance between laboratory and classroom materials, one-half the total credit being drawn from each. The 50 minute time limit should be adequate for the average student. The questions are clearly and concisely stated, the answers unambiguous and definite. Teachers who are using laboratory schemes which employ thioacetamide or some other group reagent rather than the traditional hydrogen sulfide will find this test satisfactory. As would be expected, sulfide precipitates are mentioned but the specific reagents required for their formation are not. In line with usual qualitative laboratory practice, cations receive more attention than do anions. The questions involving separations and confirmations use only the more common inorganic ions; organic reagents are not mentioned. The redox equations to be balanced are representative of actual laboratory reactions and are given in ionic form. The calculations required for the problems are of the fundamental types and are not lengthy or cumbersome. The use of a slide rule is permitted but hardly necessary. While many teachers will question the inclusion of only five problems, it is difficult to see how more calculations could be included within the time allowed. Form 1961 is aptly designated as brief. Its obvious appeal is the fact that it may be administered during a single class period. The total test credit of 50 rather than 100 is difficult to understand since all items are of equal weight but the scores are readily convertible for direct comparison with results of other tests. The test would not be adequate for a full course in qualitative analysis. *

For a review by William Rieman III of earlier forms of a, *see 4:608; for reviews by William B. Meldrum and William Rieman III, see 3:562. For reviews by Frank P. Cassaretto and Palmer O. Johnson of* A.C.S. Cooperative Examination in General Chemistry *and* c, *see 5:732.*

[907]

***A.C.S. Cooperative Examination in Quantitative Analysis.** College; 1944-61; 3 scores: theory, problems, total; IBM; Forms G ('52), N ('57), (12 pages); no specific manual; general A.C.S. directions ('61, 4 pages); no data on reliability of Form G; norms: Forms G ('52), N ('61); separate answer sheets must be used; $6 per 25 tests; $1 per 25 IBM scorable answer sheets; 25¢ per scoring stencil; 50¢ per specimen set; postage extra; 110(120) minutes; Examinations Committee, Division of Chemical Education, American Chemical Society. *

REFERENCES

1. "Condensed Norms for A.C.S. Cooperative Examinations." *J Chem Ed* 34:144-6 Mr '57. *

See 5:735 (1 excerpt); for reviews by William B. Meldrum and William Rieman III of an earlier form, see 3:563.

[908]

***A.C.S.–N.S.T.A. Cooperative Examination: High School Chemistry.** 1 year high school; 1957-63; IBM; for an upper level test in the same area, see 909; Forms N ('58, c1957, 10 pages, essentially the same as test published in 1957 except for printing and editorial changes), 1959 ('59), 1959S ('60), 1961 ('61), 1961S ('62), 1963 ('63), 1963S ('63), (12 pages); Forms 1959S, 1961S, and 1963S are identical with the corresponding Forms 1959, 1961, and 1963 except for item order; 2 parallel parts in 1 booklet, either or both of which may be administered; no specific manual; general A.C.S. directions ('61, 4 pages); norms: Forms N ('59), 1959 ('59), 1961 ('61), 1963 ('63); separate answer sheets must be used; $4 per 25 tests; $1 per 25 IBM scorable answer sheets; 25¢ per scoring stencil; 50¢ per specimen set; postage extra; 90(100) minutes for Form N, 80(90) minutes for other forms; sponsored jointly with the National Science Teachers Association; Examinations Committee, Division of Chemical Education, American Chemical Society. *

REFERENCES

1. "Condensed Norms: A.C.S. Cooperative Examinations." *J Chem Ed* 35:244-5 My '58. *
2. EDWIN, H.; MARTIN, ARNOLD M.; AND MARIE, JOANNA. "Norms of the High School Chemistry Test, Form N." *Sci Teach* 25:32-4 F '58. *
3. "Condensed Norms: ACS Cooperative Examinations." *J Chem Ed* 37:166-7 Ap '60. *
4. "Condensed Norms: ACS Cooperative Examinations." *J Chem Ed* 39:151-2 Mr '62. *
5. JONES, KENNETH J. "Predicting Achievement in Chemistry: A Model." *J Res Sci Teach* 1:226-31 S '63. *

FRANK J. FORNOFF, *Head, Science Section, Test Development Division, Educational Testing Service, Princeton, New Jersey.*

These forms of the *ACS-NSTA Cooperative Examination: High School Chemistry* have been prepared by large committees, most of the members of which are high school teachers. The only evidence of the validity of the tests stems from this fact. Major weaknesses of this series of tests are the lack of validity evidence and the absence of a description of the test content and of the basis for item selection.

The several forms are similar in organization and content. All the questions are multiple choice and have five options. Timing and numbers of questions vary as follows: Form N (90 items, 90 minutes), 1959 forms (100, 80), 1961 forms (100, 80), and Form 1963 (90, 80).

Each of the forms is divided into two parts of equal length to permit administration during two class periods, if necessary. The descriptions of the test suggest that only one of the parts may be used if desired. The norms indicate, however, that the two parts of any one form differ somewhat in difficulty, and inspection indicates that they also differ in content.

Norms for the two parts of each form are provided for several groups and for a total group. The groups differ in high school grade level and in mathematics and physics training. Each of the norms groups is described as to sex, weekly time in chemistry classes and laboratory, type of secondary school, and professional goals.

Kuder-Richardson formula 21 reliabilities for most of the norms groups are in the .90's, even for the 45- to 50-item parts. Although data are not presented, this reviewer would judge that the tests are not unduly speeded.

To determine what changes have taken place in the tests in this series since 1957, when Form N appeared, Form N and Form 1963 have been studied in some detail by the reviewer. The items were classified using the Bloom [1] cognitive categories. These two tests differ little in this dimension. Recall of knowledge, comprehension, and application each have about a third of the questions. Most of the questions have quite short stems. A test composed of such questions reduces the amount of reading required of the candidates; on the other hand, such questions can rarely probe the analysis or evaluation levels of the Bloom taxonomy. Only one or two questions in each of these two forms fall into these higher categories.

When the questions in these same forms are classified as to content, one learns that the number of questions in each of the two categories, atomic-molecular structure and kinetic-molecular theory, has doubled from Form N to Form 1963. The number of questions dealing with solutions has increased somewhat, and the emphasis has shifted toward solutions of ions. To make room for the increased emphasis on these categories, the number of questions on the chemistry of the nonmetals and of the metals has been reduced by more than 50 per cent. These changes are in line with recent curricular developments. In general, distribution of questions among the various content areas seems satisfactory.

If the "Entire Groups" used for the norms are comparable, the newer forms are more difficult than the first one. Median scores in the norms groups may be expressed in terms of percentage of possible score as follows: Form N, 42 per cent; 1959 forms, 38 per cent; 1961 forms, 39 per cent; and Form 1963, 29 per cent. Either the question writers or the curriculum revisers—or both—are getting ahead of the norms group candidates. One may hope that this trend toward increasing difficulty will not be allowed to continue.

The relative freedom from error of the tests reflects the careful review that they have undoubtedly received, though one can find a few points worthy of comment. For instance, in the 1963 form, one is surprised to find that question 1 asks for the molecular weight of magnesium acetate. Why not at least include "formula weight" in parentheses for those students who have been taught this term for ionic substances? The "correct" definition for a polar molecule in question 3 is hardly elegant. Question 16 might have been a bit better if the possibility of a tetroprotic acid had been eliminated. Question 39, which asks about the density of a particular gas at 27° C and standard pressure, really has only three options, since the density must surely be one of the exhaustive set: greater than, equal to, or less than the density of the gas at standard conditions. In question 48, since a formula may represent a "molecule," a mole, or several other sizes of samples, the request for the number of atoms represented by a formula may not be as clear as is desirable.

Atomic weights are given only in a periodic table reproduced in the middle of the test. Hunting the appropriate atomic weights may

1 Bloom, Benjamin S.; Engelhart, Max D.; Furst, Edward J.; Hill, Walker H.; and Krathwohl, David R. *Taxonomy of Educational Objectives: The Classification of Educational Goals: Handbook I, Cognitive Domain.* New York: Longmans, Green & Co., Inc., 1956. Pp. xiii, 207. *

slow candidates unnecessarily in a timed test. The test committee should also consider the problem of significant figures in a printed test. What do "one liter" and "400 liters" mean?

Although the newest test is rather difficult and several more imaginative questions in all the forms might be desirable, these tests should be considered good measures of achievement in high school chemistry.

WILLIAM HERED, *Associate Professor of Chemistry, Indiana University, Gary, Indiana; and Examiner, University of Chicago, Chicago, Illinois.*

Form 1963, as well as Forms N, 1959, and 1961, represents the cooperative effort of 45 to 60 teachers selected by the Examinations Committee of the American Chemical Society and the National Science Teachers Association. The strength of their efforts is reflected in the character of the examinations.

The current trend in chemical education toward concentration on relatively few but central concepts, principles, and theories, rather than on a wide range of descriptive matter, is well represented. The content is meaningful and is treated at a number of intellectual levels. Only 2 of the 90 items in Form 1963 are nonfunctional bits of information. Nine per cent of the items require knowledge of basic information; 47 per cent require a degree of understanding; 13 per cent involve application; 31 per cent are numerical exercises. By contrast, the figures for the 1961 version are information, 30 per cent; understanding, 36 per cent; application, 8 per cent; and numerical exercises, 20 per cent.

Form 1963 consists of two equivalent, 45-item parts. Content and behavior sampling are so closely equivalent in the two parts that the committee recommends administration of the entire test to increase reliability. The reviewer would prefer a single 90-item test dealing with a wider variety of situations than is possible with the split format. The need for equivalence in the present scheme restricts the opportunity for more extensive coverage and exploration of a greater range of intellectual abilities. One finds no questions in the present test, for instance, requiring "thinking through" an unfamiliar problem situation or applying analytical reasoning in new contexts.

The exclusive use of multiple choice items permits instructions to be simple, natural, and direct; the student is permitted thereby to concentrate on substance rather than to exercise testmanship. Time allowances are adequate.

The medians on Form 1963, corrected for chance, are approximately 34 per cent of maximum for students with a minimum of mathematics and no physics to 45 per cent for those having six to eight semesters of mathematics and two semesters of physics. Oddly enough, the students having four to six semesters of mathematics and no physics achieved the lowest median, 28 per cent—no doubt a reflection on the sampling procedure. The median for the entire group was 29 per cent. These medians are significantly lower than for Form 1961, the declines being 13 per cent for the best prepared group and nearly 10 per cent for the entire group.

Since the newer tests do not appear to be significantly different or unreasonable in their expectations, both the low level of performance on these tests and the decline in medians from previous tests have educational implications. One suspects that descriptive chemistry still plays a large part in high school curricula. This emphasis reduces time available for study of concepts and principles and goes largely unrewarded in Forms 1963 and 1961. Perhaps the committee should officially recognize the "cultural lag" and append a frankly descriptive section for those desiring it.

Form 1963 appears to be quite satisfactory as a measure of the more enduring objectives of the conventional high school chemistry course.

J Chem Ed 37:167 Ap '60. Christine Jansing. [Review of Form 1959.] * is well planned and includes all important concepts developed in the first year. Objective exercises include recall of information, application of principles, and quantitative application of principles. * The questions, all multiple choice, are free from the ambiguity which often plagues the student when this type of question is used. A well-prepared class will not find the test so difficult as to be frustrating and discouraging. It is deplorable that many high schools have eliminated mid-year and final examinations. Retention is short-lived without frequent review, and often the logical development which makes science courses stimulating and interesting is missed when the student is not required to organize and review large areas of material. This examination is a reliable objective measure of pupil mastery of concepts and skills and an effective summation of the year's work.

J Chem Ed 39:152 Mr '62. Joseph Schmuckler. [Review of Form 1961.] * divided into two parts of 50 items per part * Both parts of the examination start with recall type questions, easy at first and becoming more comprehensive as the exam progresses. Each part is well interspersed with questions which require applications of principles, and both parts of the examination end with problems dealing with quantitative applications. The reading of plotted data is required from a graph showing solubilities of various solutes in a solvent at varying temperatures. The subject material covered by the exam includes nearly every topic that would be covered in a good high school presenting the traditional approach toward the teaching of chemistry. The questions require the student to be familiar with atomic structure and to understand the value and use of the periodic chart. The periodic chart may be available to the student during the examination. This is a very desirable feature of the examination procedure. The student must also be well grounded in reaction types. The quantitative questions re-emphasize the understanding of the basic principles being tested in the other parts of the examination. The test can well serve as a final examination to be used in conjunction with the teacher's own. This will provide the teacher with a standard to compare his and his students' achievements.

For reviews by Edward G. Rietz and Willard G. Warrington, see 5:729.

[909]

★ACS-NSTA Cooperative Examination: High School Chemistry [Advanced Level]. High school advanced placement classes; 1963; for a lower level test in the same area, see 908; experimental form; IBM; Form 1963 Adv (12 pages); no specific manual; general A.C.S. directions ('61, 4 pages); mimeographed norms (4 pages); separate answer sheets must be used; $4 per 25 tests; $1 per 25 IBM scorable answer sheets; 25¢ per scoring stencil; 50¢ per specimen set; postage extra; 80(90) minutes; sponsored jointly with the National Science Teachers Association; Examinations Committee, Division of Chemical Education, American Chemical Society. *

FRANK J. FORNOFF, *Head, Science Section, Test Development Division, Educational Testing Service, Princeton, New Jersey.*

This test is described as "an experimental test constructed specifically for advanced placement high school chemistry courses and....the first test in this area * designed to meet the demand for a higher level, more difficult test. Since high school chemistry courses throughout the United States vary so much in precept and scope, the test may be suitable for regular classes in many schools."

The test consists of 70 five-choice objective questions, divided into two parts of 40 and 30 questions. Questions in the first part count 1 point each, those in the second part 2 points each, thus giving a maximum raw score of 100. Each part is to be administered in 40 minutes.

The test description makes clear that both parts must be used for complete coverage. The accuracy of this statement is easily confirmed. Ten questions (20 points) in the second part are based on a page of material on electrochemistry: a cell diagram, a paragraph, and a table of oxidation potentials. There is no such passage in the first part. This passage is prefaced by advice to candidates to ignore the material if they can answer the questions without it. One may question the wisdom of including so many questions which only some students can answer without reading the accompanying passage.

The content areas which are emphasized in the test are atomic and molecular structure, ionic solutions, and electrochemistry. Although recent curricular developments have brought increased emphasis on these topics, this reviewer believes that other topics merit more attention than they receive in this test.

Data on two norms subgroups and on the total group are presented. About three fourths of the candidates in subgroup A had had only two semesters of chemistry. The median raw score for this group is only 23 out of 100. Subgroup B, students who had had three or four semesters of chemistry, achieved a median raw score of 45.8. Although the norms subgroups are described with respect to high school class, sex, weekly times in laboratory and class, type of secondary school, and semesters of chemistry, physics, and mathematics, one can wish for information as to how many of the students in subgroup A had taken Chemical Bond Approach or Chemical Education Material Study courses. The test was too difficult for the first year students who took it, but one cannot tell whether it would be as difficult for groups containing only students who had studied the new curricula.

Kuder-Richardson 21 reliabilities reported for both subgroups and the total group and for both parts and the total test range from .86 to .96. No validity data or rationale of the test content are available.

Although the test is difficult for first year students, the reviewer believes that it is somewhat less demanding than the objective section of the *College Entrance Examination Board Advanced Placement Examination: Chemistry.* Certainly the distribution of questions among the various content areas is not the same for the two tests.

The test is unusually free of questions that this reviewer considered unclear, but there are a few. In question 42, I doubt that any of the choices can be selected, "from periodic table positions *alone.*" One wonders why the physical state of water in the fifth option of question 23 is not specified when such descriptions are given for all the other substances mentioned in the question. Perhaps a particle with zero nuclear charge and a negative mass number should not be listed as an option when the stem calls for an element.

Teachers of high school courses which emphasize the content topics mentioned above will find this test well worth serious consideration. Other teachers of high school chemistry will probably prefer the regular high school test or the college level general chemistry test in the American Chemical Society offerings.

WILLIAM HERED, *Associate Professor of Chemistry, Indiana University, Gary, Indiana; and Examiner, University of Chicago, Chicago, Illinois.*

This is the first test in a series designed for advanced placement courses and sections of superior students. Part 1 consists of 40 items and Part 2 of 30 items, both parts to be completed in a total of 80 minutes. No sharp division is discernible between the two parts, although the items in Part 2 are at a somewhat higher level and include two situations in which items are grouped.

There is greater emphasis on reasoning than in Form 1963 of the lower level test. One fourth of the exercises are numerical problems, one fourth deal with qualitative application of principles, and one half involve comprehension only. A single strictly factual question is included.

Advanced tests should provide abundant opportunity for students to reason analytically and to exercise judgment. This test falls short in this respect; few of the test situations are unfamiliar enough to demand these abilities. The contexts are textbookish in general. A set of 10 items based on an exposition of a basic principle fails to be challenging because the exposition is too brief to be comprehensible to those who have not encountered it before and too elementary for those who have studied this area. Readings are excellent as a springboard for high level questions, but they must be unfamiliar and reasonably complete.

Although individually the items on this test show evidence of careful selection, the general impression is of heterogeneity. Content changes sharply from item to item. For instance, a low level question on Avogadro's number is followed by an application item on radioactivity. Subject matter is too extensive for the time available and depth has suffered.

Form 1963 Adv was administered to 906 students in 33 institutions. The median raw score, corrected for guessing, was 23 per cent of the possible score for 675 students with two semesters of chemistry and 46 per cent for 231 students having three to four semesters. This is most encouraging and indicates that this instrument probes well the content and behavior objectives of advanced curricula. The reliability coefficients, .94 to .96 for the total score and .86 to .94 for the subscores, are also satisfactory.

Although the test would be improved by better organization, by less concern for content sampling, and by increased attention to the more sophisticated levels of reasoning, its present form is a most excellent beginning.

[909a]

★Chemistry: Cooperative Science Tests. High school; 1963–64; 3 scores: general concepts and principles, laboratory, total; IBM; Forms A, B, ('63, 20 pages); no specific manual; series handbook ('64, 76 pages); separate answer sheets must be used; $4 per 20 tests; $1 per 20 IBM scorable answer sheets; $1 per 10 scoring stencils (answer pattern must be punched out locally); $1 per handbook; postage extra; $2 per specimen set of this and 4 other science tests, cash orders postpaid; 80(92) minutes in 1 or 2 sessions; Cooperative Test Division. *

[910]

***Chemistry: Every Pupil Scholarship Test.** High school; 1928–64; new form (4 pages) usually issued each January and April; forms from previous testing programs also available; general directions sheet ['63, 2 pages]; no data on reliability; norms for new forms available following testing program; 4¢ per test; 4¢ per key; postage extra; 40(45) minutes; Bureau of Educational Measurements. *

[911]

***Chemistry: Every Pupil Test.** High school; 1929–64; new form (4 pages) usually issued each December and April; forms from previous testing programs also available; general directions sheet ('63, 2 pages); no data on reliability; Ohio norms for new forms available following testing program; 5¢ per test; 3¢ per key; postpaid; 40(45) minutes; Ohio Scholarship Tests. *

[912]

***Chemistry: Minnesota High School Achievement Examinations.** High school; 1955–63; series formerly called *Midwest High School Achievement Examinations;* new form issued each May; norms available in June following release of new form; Form F ('63, 6 pages) used in 1963 testing; no specific manual; series manual ('63, 4 pages); series norms ['63, 4 pages]; series cumulative profile ('62, 2 pages); no data on reliability; no description of normative population; 12¢ per test; $2.50 per 100 profiles; postage extra; 20¢ per specimen set, postpaid; 60(65) minutes; American Guidance Service, Inc. *

For a review by Edward G. Rietz of earlier forms, see 5:741.

[913]

★Chemistry Test: Affiliation Testing Program for Catholic Secondary Schools. Grades 9–12 and students who are candidates for the high school diploma issued by the Catholic University of America; 1949–63; administered annually in May at individual schools; IBM; new form issued annually; Form Z ('63, 13 pages) used in 1963 program; separate answer sheets must be used; 50¢ per test and IBM answer sheet; postpaid; fee includes purchase of test booklets, scoring, and other services; specimen set of the complete battery free; for more complete information, see 758; 90(100) minutes; Program of Affiliation, Catholic University of America. *

HENRY CHAUNCEY, *President, Educational Testing Service, Princeton, New Jersey.* [Review of Forms Y and Z.]

According to the published description of the course for which the ATP Chemistry Test is designed, the purpose of the course is to "acquaint the student with the authentic body of fact and theory which constitutes the science of chemistry." Practical applications of chemistry are to be emphasized, and the chemical properties to be studied are to be primarily those which "serve for recognition, illustrate a chemical principle, or relate to some important household or industrial use." In general, the test seems appropriate for such a course.

The test samples well across the topics listed in the syllabus; the level of difficulty seems appropriate (means of 44.3 on Form Y and 44 on Form Z out of 100 items). Although no data on speededness are provided, it seems likely that most students could answer the 100 questions in the 90 minutes allowed. The instructions given are clear, but there is no statement concerning guessing.

The data reported for Forms Y and Z are quite impressive. For Form Y, reliability (K-R 21) is given as .83 and validity (correlation between teacher ratings and pretest scores) as .87. The figures for Form Z are reported as .84 and .70. The validity figures are difficult to accept at face value. The literature does not make it clear that the teachers could not have used the test scores in making their ratings. Those who prepared the statistical report are obviously aware of the kinds of data which should be reported. In several instances, however, it is impossible to ascertain exactly what procedures were used. Consequently, it is difficult or impossible to be sure what some of the data mean.

If one taught the course outlined in the chemistry syllabus, one would be disappointed if none of his students scored above 79 (the highest score obtained). While most chemistry teachers today would not use this test for the chemistry course which they might teach, the test does seem rather well suited to the course outline.

For a review of the complete program, see 758.

[914]

***College Entrance Examination Board Achievement Test: Chemistry.** Candidates for college entrance; 1901–64; for more complete information, see 760; 60(80) minutes; program administered for the College Entrance Examination Board by Educational Testing Service. *

REFERENCES

1–4. See 4:617.
5–6. See 5:742.
7. BLACK, D. B. "A Comparison of the Performance on Selected Standardized Tests to That on the Alberta Grade XII Departmental Examination of a Select Group of University of Alberta Freshmen." *Alberta J Ed Res* 5:180–90 S '59. * (*PA* 34:6559)
8. GILBERT, ARTHUR C. F. "The Efficiency of Certain Variables in Predicting Survival in an Engineering School." *Psychol Newsl* 10:311–3 My–Je '59. * (*PA* 34:1992)
9. BLACK, DONALD B. "The Prediction of Freshman Success in the University of Alberta From Grade XII Departmental Results." *Alberta J Ed Res* 6:38–53 Mr '60. *
10. JONES, KENNETH J. "Predicting Achievement in Chemistry: A Model." *J Res Sci Teach* 1:226–31 S '63. *

WILLIAM HERED, *Associate Professor of Chemistry, Indiana University, Gary, Indiana;*

and Examiner, University of Chicago, Chicago, Illinois. [Review of Forms FAC, KAC2, and LAC.]

The review of CEEB tests involves a great responsibility. Not only do the scores derived play a central role in admission to college, but also the character of these tests cannot fail to influence curriculum and evaluation at the local level. Since CEEB tests are generally not open to scrutiny by the teaching profession, the reviewer must act as surrogate for his colleagues in his assessment.

Accordingly, a painstaking study of the achievement tests in chemistry has been undertaken, with primary concern to the question of the extent to which the individual items and the tests as a whole reflect present-day objectives. Form KAC2 has been selected for comment, although the conclusions reached apply with full force to the other equivalent forms.

Content coverage samples aspects of traditional chemistry fairly well. Purely descriptive matter is at a satisfactory minimum, with due attention being paid to questions dealing with basic concepts and generalizations. One finds few items on solutions of electrolytes, reaction rate principles, and equilibrium, and little indication of the growing importance of molecular structure theory as a correlating principle. On the whole, however, subject matter is widely sampled.

Consideration of the levels of intellectual ability examined discloses great emphasis on basic knowledge and understanding at the expense of the higher levels. This finding is at variance with the statements found on page 139 of the booklet entitled *A Description of the College Board Achievement Tests:* "Very few questions in the present science tests ask solely for factual information. * emphasis will be on questions that require you to demonstrate understanding of the facts and ability to reason with them, rather than on questions that require you simply to recognize facts." The booklet lists the behavioral objectives of the science tests as: (*a*) understanding of basic concepts and principles; (*b*) ability to apply them to familiar and unfamiliar situations; (*c*) ability to solve numerical problems; (*d*) ability to interpret cause and effect relationships; (*e*) ability to interpret experimental data; and (*f*) ability to apply laboratory procedures to problems arising in each field.

The reviewer attempted classification of the items in Form KAC2 in these categories but was forced to add a category, "recognition of facts," falling below category *a* above. Forty-eight per cent of the items were found to require no more than recognition of facts; 23 per cent require some degree of understanding; 11 per cent involve application, but none to unfamiliar situations; 18 per cent are numerical problems. No representation of categories *d*, *e*, and *f* occurs and the opportunities for analytical or creative reasoning are virtually nil. This distribution is to be contrasted with that in Form 1963 of the *A.C.S.-N.S.T.A. Cooperative Examination: High School Chemistry:* 4 per cent recognition of facts, 47 per cent understanding; 6 per cent application, and 31 per cent numerical problems—and this is *not* the advanced version.

From the heavy weighting at the lower end of the intellectual scale and the absence of truly challenging questions, one would anticipate lower scores from students having had progressive and experimental courses than those whose preparation emphasized facts. Comparative data for Form KAC2 are available on this point. Students having completed the Chemical Bond Approach and Chemical Education Materials Study courses showed mean scores of 544 and 533, respectively, while the "regulars" achieved 581. A further finding is that, although the time allotment appears insufficient for all groups, the experimental course groups were most at a disadvantage; 38.5 per cent of the CBA's, 44.0 per cent of the CHEMS's, and 54.1 per cent of the "regulars" finished all of the items.

In view of the serious deficiencies indicated above, it is perhaps superfluous to discuss the technical character of the test items of Form KAC2. Two defects are so serious, however, that their perpetuation in future tests will make improvement doubly difficult. One is found in the structure of the 12 items making up Part B and described also on page 142 of the descriptive booklet. Each item consists of a statement followed by four numbered completions. Option A is to be marked if completions 1, 2, and 3 are correct, B if 1 and 3 are correct, C if 2 and 4 are correct, D if only 4 is correct, and E for all other cases. One can readily calculate that E may be marked by a student for 11 different reasons; if E is keyed correct and so marked by the student, there is no way of knowing whether he reasoned correctly or not. This results in an excessive contribution to uncertainty in Form KAC2, since four questions are keyed E.

The other major structural weakness is present in the 12 items of Part D—a format illustrated on page 149 of the descriptive booklet. Each item consists of an assertion followed by a reason or explanation, presumably related as cause and effect. However, the first decision to be made is whether both parts of each item are true statements. If either or both are false, the student is spared the cause-effect decision. In no less than 10 of the 12 items of Part D, a false statement appears and reduces the level of the item to recognition of fact. The other forms are only slightly better, 7 items operating at the cause-effect level in LCB3 and 6 in FAC. One may doubt, moreover, that the ability to discern cause-effect relationships is distinguishable in any case from the category of understanding.

The reviewer concludes that the CEEB chemistry test is acceptable only for evaluation of factual knowledge, elementary understandings, and the solution of conventional numerical problems, within the content framework of traditional courses. It is inappropriate as a measure of achievement in the CBA, the CHEM Study, and other curricula stressing reasoning. It cannot be expected to predict success in college chemistry. Only a complete reconsideration of content, aims, and objectives can lead to the construction of an instrument which has the requisite accuracy and precision.

For a review by Max D. Engelhart of an earlier form, see 5:742; for a review by Evelyn Raskin, see 4:617. For reviews of the testing program, see 760.

[915]

***College Entrance Examination Board Advanced Placement Examination: Chemistry.** High school students desiring credit for college level courses or admission to advanced courses; 1954–63; for more complete information, see 761; 180(200) minutes; program administered for the College Entrance Examination Board by Educational Testing Service. *

REFERENCES

1. VALLEY, JOHN R. "A Report on CEEB Advanced Placement Mathematics and Natural Sciences Examinations Candidates, May 1958." *Sci Teach* 26:399–402 O '59. *

For a review by Theo. A. Ashford of an earlier form, see 5:743.

[916]

★College Entrance Examination Board Placement Tests: Chemistry Test. Entering college freshmen; 1962–63, c1956–63; tests are reprints of inactive forms of *College Entrance Examination Board Achievement Test: Chemistry;* IBM; Forms KPL1, KPL2 in a single booklet (c1956–57, 23 pages); for more complete information, see 759; 60(70) minutes; program administered for the College Entrance Examination Board by Educational Testing Service. *

For reviews of the College Entrance Examination Board Achievement Test: Chemistry, *see 914, 5:742, and 4:617.*

[917]

***Cooperative Chemistry Test: Educational Records Bureau Edition.** High school; 1941–62; IBM; Forms ERB-RY ('57, c1941–57, 8 pages, revision of the 1948 Form ERB-RX), ERB-SY ('58, c1942–58, 8 pages, revision of the 1949 Form ERB-SX), ERB-TY ('59, c1943–59, 8 pages, revision of the 1950 Form ERB-TX); no specific manual; general Cooperative manual ('51, 8 pages); no data on reliability presented in manual; norms: Form ERB-RY ('60), Form ERB-SY ('61), Form ERB-TY ('62); 12¢ per test; separate answer sheets may be used; 4¢ per IBM answer sheet; 50¢ per specimen set; postage extra; 80(85) minutes; Committee on Chemistry Tests of the Educational Records Bureau; Educational Records Bureau. *

REFERENCES

1–2. See 4:619.
3. See 5:745.

KENNETH J. JONES, *Research Associate, Graduate School of Education, Harvard University, Cambridge, Massachusetts.*

This test is composed of 74 items in two parts. The format is five-option multiple choice. The first 45 items are primarily of a factual recall nature, while the last 29 are numerical problems. A perusal of the individual items reveals that the test is intended for the "standard" type of chemistry course—that is, one which emphasizes the descriptive and numerical aspects of the subject, as opposed to the theoretical. There were only four items which the reviewer could classify as having to do with atomic structure. With the impact of the new curricula in chemistry (CHEM, CBA), the character of most courses is changing. This fact restricts the usefulness of this test to those courses which are using pre-Sputnik texts.

This reviewer found several minor, but irritating, ambiguities among the items. Since by design there may be more than one "correct" answer to some of the items, the student must not be satisfied by choosing the best answer among the several foils. He must consider all options carefully. This can be both an advantage and a disadvantage. On the one hand, it mitigates against "testwiseness," but it often leads to some highly debatable items. For example, item 2 of Form ERB-TY lists both potassium and calcium as "metals which react *vigorously* with water at *room temperature.*" Calcium will react with modest vigor, but only if its surface is free of oxide. This may be nitpicking, but it is just what is being done in the popular literature. In this test, the problem could be eliminated merely by avoiding such items.

The test manual provides little information other than directions for administration. However, Traxler (*3*) gives reliability and validity information derived from a study in a sample of independent schools. For the most part the reliabilities were high (on the order of .90). Likewise the correlation with chemistry grades was moderate (.60). Clearly the test is reflecting some part of what goes into—or did in 1957—an independent school chemistry grade.

This reviewer used this test as a final test in chemistry in 1957, but employed an American Chemical Society test in subsequent years because it was felt that the latter better represented the theoretical aspects of the course. However, for many chemistry courses this test may adequately reflect the goals of instruction.

[918]

★General Chemistry Test: National Achievement Tests. Grades 10–16; 1958–59; 4 scores: uses-processes-results, formulae and valence, miscellaneous facts, total; Form A ('58, 12 pages); no manual; combined directions ('59, 1 page) for this test and test 930; class record-key ['58, 2 pages]; no data on reliability; no norms; $7.50 per 25 tests; 50¢ per specimen set; postage extra; 40(45) minutes; Lester D. Crow and Roy S. Cook; [Psychometric Affiliates]. *

J. A. CAMPBELL, *Professor of Chemistry and Chairman of the Department, Harvey Mudd College, Claremont, California.*

This test would seem to be of little use in any course other than one emphasizing a great deal of descriptive chemistry and pure recall of information. It contains a total of 120 questions divided into three parts: (*a*) Uses, Processes, and Results (50 questions), (*b*) Formulae and Valence (20 questions), and (*c*) Miscellaneous Facts (50 questions).

Not only are the great majority of the questions matters of recall and detailed items of descriptive chemistry, but the test is replete with typographical and scientific errors. In every item in which the symbol for chlorine occurs except one, the symbol CL is used, although any chemist would use Cl. In the question asking what is formed when magnesium burns in air, not only is magnesium oxide an answer but so too are magnesium hydroxide and magnesium carbonate, two other choices. Again, three of the possible answers to a question concerning the uses of electrolysis are valid; not only may it be used to purify copper, but also to promote osmosis and to produce death. In still another question related to chemicals often used by dentists, laughing gas (the keyed answer) is certainly a possible answer, but so also is fluorine (another choice), which is used in the form of fluorides. Coke is certainly a possible answer to the question concerning the chief fuel used in blast furnaces in metallurgy, but in many countries charcoal (a suggested answer) is also used. Typographical errors such as spelling ethyl as "ethyle" in one question and using SlO_2 as the formula for silicon dioxide also occur.

It is not, however, the errors in the test, which could occur in almost any test and do in most, which detract most from its value. It is rather the emphasis on what many chemists think are trivial bits of information which will be increasingly less important in chemistry courses of the future. Every test author is, of course, trapped by the textbooks which students are using. There are certainly some texts that provide the background which would lead a student to expect this kind of test. However, even the most descriptive of current books surely has more chemical principles in it than the authors of this test felt desirable to include. Surely, too, there must be other tests which will provide a more valid measurement of student accomplishments in courses currently being given in high school and college chemistry. The tests put out by the Examinations Committee of the American Chemical Society are certainly more up to date and much more widely tested.

The working time for the test, 40 minutes for 120 questions, is a sad indication of the very high rate of recall necessary for adequate performance on this kind of test. It surely is expecting too much to anticipate that students will do any appreciable amount of thinking when they are restricted to 20 seconds per question, a significant fraction of which time is normally spent reading the question.

A further drawback is the absence of normative data which might allow a person, if he insisted on using the test, to compare the performance of his students with that of others.

In the light of its deficiencies and the existence of much more reliable testing devices, the reviewer could not recommend this test for use in any high school course with which he is familiar.

[919]

***The Graduate Record Examinations Advanced Tests: Chemistry.** Grades 16–17; 1939–63; for more complete information, see 762; 180(200) minutes; Educational Testing Service. *

MAX D. ENGELHART, *Director, Division of Institutional Research and Evaluation, Department of Higher Education, Chicago Public Schools, Chicago, Illinois.*[1] [Review of Forms HGR and LGR1.]

The Advanced Test in chemistry of the Graduate Record Examinations is among the 20 optional tests employed in the National Program for Graduate School Selection and the Institutional Testing Program. As part of the National Program, the tests are used to assist in appraising the qualifications of applicants for admission and to aid certain organizations, such as the National Science Foundation, in awarding graduate fellowships. They are also used in the Institutional Testing Program for examining entire groups of regularly enrolled students in a given field, for example, all second semester seniors or first year graduate students. The data obtained in the Institutional Testing Program serve in the evaluation of achievement, of growth in achievement, and in guidance. The data also aid in selecting candidates for advanced degrees. It is obvious that the Advanced Tests, such as the one in chemistry, have very important functions.

The successive forms of these tests in chemistry are prepared by committees of specialists selected with the cooperation of the American Chemical Society. The committees are given technical assistance by staff members of the Educational Testing Service. Decisions concerning distributions of items among the various fields of chemistry are made by the committee, and the appropriate members prepare detailed content outlines of the various areas. These outlines are reviewed as changes are made in committee membership.

The distribution of items in Form LGR1 approximates 27 per cent in inorganic chemistry, 13 per cent in analytical chemistry, 30 per cent in organic chemistry, and 30 per cent in physical chemistry. Form HGR has a slightly higher percentage in analytical chemistry and slightly lower percentages in the other fields.

Form HGR contains 160 five-response multiple choice items for a testing time of three hours. In general, the items are extremely well written. Almost always the problem of the item is in the item stem. For the most part the listed answers are brief, plausible, and of parallel construction. Only a few are built in negative form requiring the student to select an exceptional or incorrect answer. There are a number of quantitative problems requiring computation or identification of the correct method of computation. Item analysis data reveal that only 19 per cent of the items have biserial *r*'s below .30, and only 8 per cent have *r*'s below .20. The coefficient of reliability of the test as a whole, estimated by means of a modification of the Kuder-Richardson formula 20, is .94, and the standard error of measurement in scaled score units is 30. In the test analysis it is reported that Form HGR was "rather difficult for fellowship applicants, very difficult for National Program candidates, and extremely difficult for Institutional Program candidates." The distributions of scores, however, were not markedly skewed. While omissions were large, evidence supplied in the test analysis supports the claim that speed is not a significant factor.

Study of the item data of Form HGR seems to indicate that most of the items having item-test correlations below .30 lack discriminating power because of their excessive difficulty rather than because of inadequate form or phraseology. One of the items asks the student to distinguish in terms of a certain property between pairs of compounds whose formulas are given. It is possible that some superior students were confused as to whether a given pair was to be distinguished from all the other pairs; or, as was actually the case, the members of a given pair were to be distinguished from each other. The biserial *r* was .26. Another

1 The author expresses his appreciation to Dr. Frank W. Dobbs, Associate Professor of Chemistry, Chicago Teachers College North, for aid in evaluating the content of Forms HGR and LGR1.

item, relevant to an important principle, lists as the stated correct answer one that is not as explicit as this reviewer would prefer. This may account for its biserial *r* of .09. No other items seem characterized by such defects.

Form LGR1 is similar to Form HGR though the number of items is 150 rather than 160. Form LGR1 also differs in having several groups of two or three items each relevant to the same general problem. This reviewer was especially impressed with items concerning alternative processes leading to the production of a certain compound, items involving manipulation of apparatus, items requiring analysis of a diagram, and items requiring interpretation of data in a chart or listed below the chart.

While the kind of data available with reference to Form HGR is not as yet available for Form LGR1, in the judgment of this reviewer the latter is a somewhat better test. Although both tests cover "basic concepts and fundamental principles of the subject," Form LGR1 has moved farther in the direction of including items "which require reasoning with the application of these facts and principles." There should be much more effort in this direction. The detailed content outlines referred to in an earlier paragraph are excellent in defining the subject matter content to be covered in the various areas of chemistry, but they define instructional objectives only on the level of knowledge. There is no indication that objectives on the level of intellectual skills have been explicitly considered. There has been no previous review of the advanced chemistry test, but the excellent review of the advanced physics test by Leo Nedelsky in *The Fifth Yearbook* should have had impact on the chemistry committee!

In the judgment of this reviewer, there should be series of items requiring interpretation of data and application of principles to novel problems. There should be items more directly concerned with experimental techniques in chemistry and the major aspects of scientific method as applied in chemistry. It is possible that a more effective test could be so organized that its major part would contain items relevant to basic concepts and principles and their applications to novel problems including interpretation of data. Such a test would be fair to *all* students regardless of their specializations in the various fields of chemistry. Separate and equivalent parts, optional to each student, could go beyond the general into the special fields. Many of the current items in physical chemistry must baffle students with major interests in organic chemistry, and the converse is true. Similarly, as seniors, superior students have forgotten many of the factual details of inorganic and analytical chemistry. The type of test suggested might help solve this problem. Furthermore, one hopes that candidates for admission to graduate study in chemistry with high scores on the *Graduate Record Examinations Aptitude Test* gain admission in spite of relatively lower scores on the Advanced Test in chemistry. The student with a high score on this test, however, is likely to be a superior graduate student whether or not he has the other qualities necessary for original contributions to the field.

Data with reference to the prognostic value of the Advanced Test in chemistry are beginning to be available. Some of these data are reported in the Graduate Record Examinations Special Reports of November 1960, and October 1962.[2] The earlier report includes a chart showing the relationship between chemistry scores of 59 graduate students and the letter marks of A, B, and C as measures of graduate school performance. This reviewer obtained a contingency coefficient for the 3 by 3 table of .60. A study made of the relationships between undergraduate grade-point averages in chemistry, the quantitative scores of the GRE Aptitude Test, scores on the Advanced Test in chemistry, and the graduate grade-point averages in chemistry for 35 students earning the master's degree in chemistry resulted in a multiple correlation of .63. The correlation between chemistry test scores and graduate grade-point averages in chemistry was .40. The second of the reports referred to above gives information concerning admissions practices of a number of graduate schools and a series of interesting case reports on score use. It is admittedly troublesome to obtain data concerning the predictive validity of a test such as the one being discussed. A major difficulty is the

2 LANNHOLM, GERALD V. *Abstracts of Selected Studies on the Relationship Between Scores on the Graduate Record Examinations and Graduate School Performance.* Graduate Record Examinations Special Report 60-3, Educational Testing Service, Princeton, N.J., November 1960. * ["An unpublished report."]

LANNHOLM, GERALD V. *The Use of Graduate Record Examinations in Appraising Graduate Study Candidates.* Graduate Record Examinations Special Report 62–3, Educational Testing Service, Princeton, N.J., October 1962. * ["An unpublished report."]

narrow range and uncertain validity of graduate school marks. Possibly what is needed is some other criterion of graduate school performance—for example, scores on locally constructed comprehensive or qualifying examinations or detailed ratings of various aspects of graduate school performance.

Especially commendable is the honest handling of the problem of norms for the Advanced Tests and others of the Graduate Record Examinations. Percentile ranks of scaled scores are reported for basic and supplementary reference groups. The norms are not represented as "national norms." "No claim is made that the reference institutions are a representative cross-section of all colleges in the country." It is also possible for a college official whose school participated in the Institutional Testing Program to obtain, for a particular test and level, a combined distribution of scores for students in colleges similar to his own.

While certain limitations have been mentioned with reference to Forms HGR and LGR1 of the Advanced Test in chemistry and certain suggestions have been made, encomiums are well deserved for those participating in the attack on the extremely difficult and important problem of selection of graduate students of chemistry. This reviewer would not welcome the task of asking full professors of chemistry to define their instructional objectives and to improve their evaluations of the achievements of graduate students even though these things are as necessary as the improvement of tests to permit more efficient prediction of graduate school success.

For a review of the testing program, see 5:601.

[920]

★Toledo Chemistry Placement Examination. College entrants with 1 year high school chemistry and algebra; 1959–63; 7 scores: arithmetic and algebra, general knowledge, formulas and nomenclature, equations, algebraic formulations, chemical problems, total; IBM; 2 forms: 1959 (8 pages), 1963 (7 pages); Form 1963 is a revision of form 1959; directions ['63, 4 pages]; norms ['62] based on form 1959; no data on reliability of Form 1963; no norms for part scores; separate answer sheets must be used; $5 per 25 tests; $1 per 25 IBM answer sheets; 25¢ per hand scoring stencil; 50¢ per machine scoring stencil; 50¢ per specimen set; cash orders postpaid; 55(60) minutes; Nelson W. Hovey, Albertine Krohn, and Glenn E. Mowers (form 1959); distributed by Research Foundation, University of Toledo. *

REFERENCES

1. Hovey, Nelson W., and Krohn, Albertine. "An Evaluation of the Toledo Chemistry Placement Examination." *J Chem Ed* 40:370–2 Jl '63. *

Kenneth E. Anderson, *Dean, School of Education, The University of Kansas, Lawrence, Kansas.*

This is a placement test designed primarily to determine which students among those with entrance credit in high school chemistry have little chance of success in college general chemistry. The two forms of the test are "designed specifically to measure knowledge of and aptitude for chemistry." Since use of the test has reduced the number of failures in general chemistry at the University of Toledo from 30 to 10 per cent, the test possesses some validity as used there.

Norms are now available and a reliability coefficient of .92 is reported. The norms are based on the administration of the 1959 form and supposedly the norms and reliability coefficient will hold for Form 1963, since the questions in both forms are essentially the same. The authors consider the 1963 form as an alternate form rather than as a replacement for the 1959 form.

Each form of the test has six sections with the number of items and point values indicated as follows: 1, Arithmetic and Algebra (15, 15); 2, General Knowledge (25, 25); 3, Formulas and Nomenclature (10, 10); 4, Equations (6, 12); 5, Algebraic Formulations (6, 12); and 6, Chemical Problems (5, 20).

The items in Parts 4, 5, and 6 are weighted for scoring purposes on the supposition that this tends to prevent crowding of scores at the lower end of the performance scale where discrimination is most needed in terms of the expressed purpose of the test. Whether the weighting is an artifact or does do the intended job is not spelled out.

In terms of points earnable per item, the authors have, in effect, placed greater value on the student's ability to solve equations, deal with algebraic formulations, and solve chemical problems than on whatever abilities are reflected in the other sections of the test. It would seem that the purposes of providing better discrimination among low scorers and of making Parts 4–6 contribute to the total score in a manner similar to Parts 1–3 would be better accomplished by devoting more items to these phases of chemistry, and at the same time making the items more difficult, than by weighting the few items now included in Parts 4–6. This procedure, it would seem, would make the test more valid in terms of the expressed purpose of the test.

The reliability of the test should be greater. Too, the number of items in the general knowledge section might be increased so as to reflect the newer developments in chemistry. Such an addition could only enhance validity and reliability as well. As the test now stands, it probably reflects what the authors consider to be the status of instruction in high school chemistry. It seems likely, in view of the new curricular developments in chemistry (such as the CHEM Study and the Chemical Bond Approach) and in mathematics, with a reportedly higher level of achievement of students today in these areas, that in the near future the *Toledo Chemistry Placement Examination* may not perform as efficiently as it now does the service for which it was designed. This may mean that the cutoff score of 40 may need to be raised. At the University of Toledo, the use of a cutoff score of 40 is based on the supposition that it is unlikely that more than a small percentage of students scoring less than 40 would survive "a reasonably rigorous course in general chemistry."

An alternate approach to the problem would be to revise the test so that it reflects the modern curricular developments in science and mathematics. These considerations are only important if the general college chemistry course in an institution reflects the new developments in science and mathematics.

In summary, it must be said that the test does measure some of the fundamental knowledge of chemistry as presently offered in many high schools. If the general college chemistry course in an institution reflects the same status, the test possesses validity as an instrument for screening students for entrance into the first course. If, however, the general college chemistry course reflects a higher level of knowledge as now taught in the more up-to-date high schools, the test will not possess as high a validity for screening purposes.

William R. Crawford, *Office of Research in Medical Education, University of Illinois College of Medicine, Chicago, Illinois.*

The *Toledo Chemistry Placement Examination* is described by the authors as an instrument designed to aid college chemistry instructors in their precourse evaluation of freshman students who have taken one year of high school chemistry and one year of high school algebra. The authors propose that it be used as a screening device for selecting students who are "ready" to take a general course in freshman chemistry, especially in colleges which do not have selective admission policies. The test was designed to fit the specific needs of the University of Toledo and was subsequently published in response to requests for information which followed publication of the initial results from that institution.

Both so-called "alternate forms" of the instrument consist of 67 items divided into six sections as follows: 1, Arithmetic and Algebra, 15 items; 2, General Knowledge, 25 items; 3, Formulas and Nomenclature, 10 items; 4, Equations, 6 items; 5, Algebraic Formulations, 6 items; and 6, Chemical Problems, 5 items. The brochure accompanying the test (no manual is provided) states: "Although it includes some mathematics items which test aptitude for the kind of reasoning required in chemistry, it is not primarily designed for the evaluation of aptitude of students without some chemistry background." This is an understatement! It is inconceivable that a student without some chemistry background really could perform well on this test, since most of the items deal with simple recall of specific facts presented in general chemistry courses, and few, if any, require a substantial amount of reasoning for their solution.

In Part 1, Arithmetic and Algebra, the reviewer could not find a single item which, in his opinion, measured anything more intellectually complex than simple recall of the manner in which algebraic manipulations should be performed. Part 2, General Knowledge, could, perhaps, better be called "Specific Knowledge," since the items are based on specific bits of information which must be recalled. For example, one item reads: "The approximate equivalent of one inch" (followed by four choices); another is: "The formula for Epsom salts" (followed by four choices). Again in this section the items seem designed to measure only recall of information and not the reasoning ability of the student. Part 3, Formulas and Nomenclature, calls for little more than the recall of names and formulas for specific compounds which are generally encountered in high school chemistry courses. Only six equations to be balanced are presented in Part 4, Equations, but these are representative of the types of balancing required in high school courses in general chemistry. Some of the problems in Part 5, Algebraic Formulations, impressed this reviewer as being designed to determine the student's ability to sort verbal material rather than to formulate algebraic relationships. They were uncomfortably reminiscent of tricky word problems sometimes found in elementary arithmetic and algebra texts. For example, the student is asked to select from four given choices the answer to this problem: "The volume of the larger of two beakers is 10 units greater than three times that of the smaller. Express the volume of the larger beaker if the volume of the smaller is represented by x." The reviewer is at somewhat of a loss to determine just what this type of item might really be measuring. More importantly, he questions whether the ability to solve this type of verbally involved problem is really related to academic success in college chemistry. The problems found in Part 6, Chemical Problems, are all of the standard type encountered in most traditional high school chemistry courses.

The authors recommend using the total score for selecting those students who are likely to be "successful" in a freshman college chemistry course and suggest that scores on the subsections might be useful for diagnostic purposes. The total score is derived by multiplying each subscore by a weighting factor and summing the results. No information is provided describing the rationale underlying the weighting system, and the user is not told whether to use the weights if a diagnostic score from each subtest is desired. Since the subtests are based on very small numbers of items (5–10 in all sections except Part 1, 15, and Part 2, 25) and since no method is provided by which scores on the sections can be compared directly, the reviewer feels that the recommendation for using the subscores as diagnostic scores is completely unjustified. Neither norms nor information on reliability or validity are provided for the subscores. The only norms provided are for the total score, and these are based on "over 2000 students" at the University of Toledo. The authors suggest using a cutoff score of 40 raw score points for determining "which students should be denied direct admission to the general chemistry course." They state that: "If there is no selection of students entering, between 10 and 20 per cent [of students tested] will be below this score. Only a few of these (less than 10%) would survive the average course in general chemistry. The exclusion of these poorly-prepared students will raise the level of the general chemistry course and improve the morale of both students and instructors." This reviewer cannot agree with the recommendation since it is apparently based on conditions at Toledo and he sees no justification for extrapolating these data to other schools, regardless of their policy concerning selective admissions.

Statistical data provided with the test are sparse. Percentile ranks, a standard deviation, a reliability coefficient, and item data (for the 1959 form only) comprise the total information provided. (The item analysis data supplied for review are not generally distributed with the test materials.) No mention is made of the way in which the reliability was computed. Furthermore, the data presented for the two forms are *identical,* and one must assume that the data for the 1959 form were simply applied to the 1963 form without further testing. Of the 67 items in the 1959 form, 20 had difficulty values in excess of .70, 4 had values less than .30, and 4 had discrimination index values less than .30. No information is provided with respect to the method for computing the discrimination indexes, and four had values less than .30. In preparing the 1963 form the four items from the 1959 form with discrimination index values less than .30 were replaced with new items, and the remaining items were edited and reordered into ascending difficulty within each section. New item data were not provided for the 1963 form. This reviewer suspects that the introduction of new items, the reordering of previous items, and the rewording of some items from the previous form would substantially change the nature of the statistical data derived from the two forms. There seems to be no justification for calling the two tests alternate forms.

In summary, this test cannot be recommended for use in assessing the probable success of freshman students in general chemistry.

Most any good achievement test in high school chemistry (e.g., the *Anderson Chemistry Test*) would probably yield information more useful for this purpose. Certainly the norms provided should not be applied indiscriminately since they were obtained on a relatively restricted population.

[Other Tests]

For tests not listed above, see the following entries in *Tests in Print:* 1604, 1607–8, 1610–1, 1616–7, and 1620–2; out of print: 1614 and 1623.

MISCELLANEOUS

[921]

★The Facts About Science Test. Grades 7–10; 1958; for research use only; 3 scores: understanding of science as an institution, knowledge of scientists as an occupational group, total; IBM; 1 form (8 pages); mimeographed manual (7 pages); no data on reliability and validity; no norms; separate answer sheets must be used; $2.75 per 25 tests; $1 per 25 IBM scorable answer sheets; $2 per set of scoring stencils; 65¢ per manual; postage extra; $1.25 per specimen set, postpaid; (45–50) minutes; Glen Stice and others; Educational Testing Service. *

[922]

***The Graduate Record Examinations Advanced Tests: Geology.** Grades 16–17; 1939–62; for more complete information, see 762; 180(200) minutes; Educational Testing Service. *

For a review of the testing program, see 5:601.

[923]

★Test of Chemical Comprehension. Employee applicants and applicants for nurses training; 1951–62; "chemical facts" of an "everyday nature"; 1 form ('51, 5 pages); manual ['62, 7 unnumbered pages]; $3.50 per 25 tests; 10¢ per key; $1 per manual; postage extra; $1 per specimen set, postpaid; (20–30) minutes; Richardson, Bellows, Henry & Co., Inc. *

[924]

★Test of Reasoning in Conservation. Grades 9–12; 1961, c1960–61; IBM; Forms A, B, ('61, c1960, 8 pages); manual ('61, 23 pages); separate answer sheets must be used; $3.25 per set of 20 tests, 20 IBM scorable answer sheets, scoring stencil, and manual; postage extra; $1.75 per specimen set, postpaid; 40(45) minutes; Conservation Foundation and Educational Testing Service; Educational Testing Service. *

REFERENCES

1. BELT, SIDNEY L. "Teaching, Testing and Conservation." *Sci Teach* 27:29–35 Ap '60. *

[925]

★Test on Understanding Science (TOUS). Grades 9–12; 1961; for research use only; 4 understanding scores: the scientific enterprise, scientists, methods and aims of science, total; IBM; Form W (14 pages); manual (21 pages); reliability data and norms based on an earlier form, of which Form W is said to be a minor revision; tentative norms for total score only; separate answer sheets must be used; $4 per 25 tests and 25 IBM scorable answer sheets; $1.50 per set of scoring stencils; postage extra; $2 per specimen set, postpaid; 40(45–50) minutes; W. W. Cooley and L. E. Klopfer; Educational Testing Service. *

REFERENCES

1. COOLEY, WILLIAM W., AND KLOPFER, LEOPOLD E. "The Evaluation of Specific Educational Innovations." *J Res Sci Teach* 1:73–80 Mr '63. *
2. KLOPFER, LEOPOLD E., AND COOLEY, WILLIAM W. "The History of Science Cases for High Schools in the Development of Student Understanding of Science and Scientists: A Report on the HOSC Instruction Project." *J Res Sci Teach* 1:33–47 Mr '63. *
3. SMITH, PAUL M., JR. "Critical Thinking and the Science Intangibles." *Sci Ed* 47:405–8 O '63. *

[Other Tests]

For tests not listed above, see the following entry in *Tests in Print:* 1628 (out of print).

PHYSICS

[926]

***College Entrance Examination Board Achievement Test: Physics.** Candidates for college entrance; 1901–64; a separate edition for candidates who are taking the PSSC physics course is also offered on a special administration date in January and March; for more complete information, see 760; 60(80) minutes; program administered for the College Entrance Examination Board by Educational Testing Service. *

REFERENCES

1–3. See 4:633.
4–5. See 5:749.
6. BLACK, D. B. "A Comparison of the Performance on Selected Standardized Tests to That on the Alberta Grade XII Departmental Examination of a Select Group of University of Alberta Freshmen." *Alberta J Ed Res* 5:180–90 S '59. * (*PA* 34:6559)
7. GILBERT, ARTHUR C. F. "The Efficiency of Certain Variables in Predicting Survival in an Engineering School." *Psychol Newsl* 10:311–3 My–Je '59. * (*PA* 34:1992)
8. BLACK, DONALD B. "The Prediction of Freshman Success in the University of Alberta From Grade XII Departmental Results." *Alberta J Ed Res* 6:38–53 Mr '60. *
9. GEWIRTZ, HERMAN. *How to Prepare for College Board Achievement Tests: Physics.* Great Neck, N.Y.: Barron's Educational Series, Inc., 1963. Pp. iv, 147. *

For a review by Theodore G. Phillips of an earlier form, see 5:749; for a review by Palmer O. Johnson of earlier forms, see 4:633. For reviews of the testing program, see 760.

[927]

***College Entrance Examination Board Advanced Placement Examination: Physics.** High school students desiring credit for college level courses or admission to advanced courses; 1954–63; for more complete information, see 761; 180(200) minutes; program administered for the College Entrance Examination Board by Educational Testing Service. *

REFERENCES

1. VALLEY, JOHN R. "A Report on CEEB Advanced Placement Mathematics and Natural Sciences Examinations Candidates, May 1958." *Sci Teach* 26:399–402 O '59. *
2. GILBERT, ARTHUR C. F. "Predicting Graduation From an Engineering School." *J Psychol Studies* 11:229–31 Jl–Ag '60. * (*PA* 35:7045)

For a review by Leo Nedelsky of an earlier form, see 5:750.

[928]

★College Entrance Examination Board Placement Tests: Physics Test. Entering college freshmen; 1962–63, c1954–63; tests are reprints of inactive forms of *College Entrance Examination Board Achievement Test: Physics;* IBM; Forms KPL1, KPL2 in a single booklet (c1954–55, 19 pages); for more complete information, see 759; 60(70) minutes; program administered for the College Entrance Examination Board by Educational Testing Service. *

For reviews of the College Entrance Examination Board Achievement Test: Physics, *see 5:749 and 4:633.*

[929]

***Cooperative Physics Test: Educational Records Bureau Edition.** High school; 1941–62; IBM; Forms ERB-RY ('57, c1943–59, 12 pages, revision of the 1948 Form ERB-RX), ERB-SY ('58, c1942–58, 12 pages, revision of the 1949 Form ERB-SX), ERB-TY ('59, c1943–59, 14 pages, revision of the 1950 Form ERB-TX); no specific manual; general Cooperative manual ('51, 8 pages); no data on reliability presented in manual; norms: Form ERB-RY ('60), Form ERB-SY ('61), Form ERB-TY ('62); 12¢ per test; separate answer sheets may be used; 4¢ per IBM answer sheet; 50¢ per specimen set; postage extra; 80(85) minutes; Committee on Physics Tests of the Educational Records Bureau; Educational Records Bureau. *

REFERENCES

1–2. See 4:635.
3. See 5:752.

[930]

★General Physics Test: National Achievement Tests. Grades 10–16; 1958–62; 3 scores: uses and application of principles, miscellaneous facts and scientists, total; Form A ('58, 12 pages); no manual; combined directions ('59, 1 page) for this test and test 918; typewritten norms ['62, 1 page]; no data on reliability of subscores; no norms for subscores; no description of normative population; $7.50 per 25 tests; 50¢ per specimen set; postage extra; 40(45) minutes; Lester D. Crow and Roy S. Cook; [Psychometric Affiliates]. *

THEODORE G. PHILLIPS, *Assistant Dean, Amundsen Branch, Chicago City Junior College, Chicago, Illinois.*

No manual is provided with this test. A sheet of percentile norms, which includes a coefficient of reliability of .90, is provided but without any information regarding the size and character of the population from which they were computed. Since the test is intended for students in grades 10–12 and college, it is important to know the composition of the population; otherwise, these norms are meaningless.

The test teems with inaccuracies. A careful proofreader could have eliminated these and errors in sentence structure with a few strokes of the pen. In item 1 "electricity" is misspelled; in item 15 "block-in-tackle" should read "block and tackle"; de Forest spells his name with one r (items 71, 102), Hooke with an e (item 37). The correct choices to item 18 are "British Thermal Units," or "calories"—both are units of heat; the third choice should read just "ergs," or, preferably, be replaced. In item 24, "for" should be deleted. Item 32 lacks the degree symbol.

The serious shortcomings of the test are that many items are not written in the language of physics and that the many inaccuracies reflect a limited knowledge of physics. In item 22 "increases" should be replaced by "raises," and "decreases" by "lowers" or "depresses." Item 40 can be improved by reading "A whistle.... may emit the...." rather than "may have the following vibrations per second." In items such as 38 and 93 on the kinetic theory of gases, it is the average kinetic energy of translation of the molecules that is involved. With regard to item 37, Hooke's law does not explain the ratio between strain and stress of a spring but rather the manner in which strain and stress vary. In items whose answers are computed from rounded-off physical constants, "about" or "approximately" should be inserted in the stem, as in items 27 and 100. Item 45 is keyed incorrectly; the answer is choice 1. Item 43 is ambiguous; either 1 or 3 is correct. If the item is revised to state "a two element vacuum tube" the keyed choice is correct. A transformer may be used to step voltages up or down; hence item 51 needs revising. The use of "a" or "an" or "a(n)" in the stem of items 53 and 57 would avoid the give away of correct responses as the items now read. "Nonchromatic" in item 55 should read "monochromatic." Item 56 should read that a moving magnet *may* be used to induce current in a coil. Item 60 should be updated by removal of "small" in choices 3 and 4, for copper oxide rectifiers can be used today to produce *large* currents. Electrical energy is "utilized," not "found" in a telephone, as item 62 now reads. Item 64 should read "sound is produced by vibrating objects." Item 69 should be ungarbled. In item 71 one of the choices should be "Zworykin" and this should be keyed as the correct response. The coefficient of *kinetic* friction is involved in item 81. Item 83 disregards the fact that *one* use of measurement of air pressure is to determine altitude. Item 91 should read "an electrolyte is a solution [not necessarily water] that can conduct an electric current." The incredible "white liquid" of item 96 should be "white light." The keyed answer to item 98 is correct only if the ladder is vertical. "Article" in item 105 should be replaced by "object." Since the lowest note emitted by a vibrating string is called its "fundamental" or "first harmonic," there are two correct choices to item 107. For the keyed response to item 111, it is necessary for the forces to be equal. Item 113 should be revised; Dalton did not work with the atom as such. The illumination meter used in item 114 is more specifically a "foot-candle meter." Item 115 can be expressed more precisely by asking "for which state of matter is the coefficient of expansion practically constant?" The units of frequency should be specified in item 127 as "cycles per second." No response is correct for item 128 as it now reads; obviously the units should be in "miles per second," not "miles per hour."

Why is "croton" coined as a distractor when there is now a plethora of subatomic particles? Why are biological terms and names of biologists used for distractors? More appropriate distractors from physics can be used.

In general, the items require sheer memory and a nodding acquaintance with principles, physical constants, equations, and discoverers of physical laws and principles. There are 15 problems which can be solved simply by substituting numbers in basic formulas.

This instrument does not test a student's basic knowledge of physics and his ability to apply that knowledge at the level of high school physics, and certainly does not test his knowledge of college physics. This reviewer recommends that the test be scrapped and a new one written in the language of physics by someone trained in physics. The scope of the test should be determined by sampling recent physics texts at the level for which the test is intended rather than at the vaguely described level of description "grades 10–12 and college."

[931]

***The Graduate Record Examinations Advanced Tests: Physics.** Grades 16–17; 1939–62; for more complete information, see 762; 180(200) minutes; Educational Testing Service. *

THEODORE G. PHILLIPS, *Assistant Dean, Amundsen Branch, Chicago City Junior College, Chicago, Illinois.* [Review of Forms FGR and K-KGR.]

Two forms of the GRE test in physics are reviewed, Form FGR containing 117 items and Form K-KGR containing 100 items. Both forms are extremely difficult, but, for the most part, carefully prepared. They sample all fields of undergraduate physics; however, some items are on topics usually not covered in many undergraduate physics courses, such as relativity, quantum mechanics, electronics, and nuclear physics. The test is used in the National Program for Graduate School Selection, the Institutional Testing Program, and the fellowship testing program of the National Science Foundation.

The percentile norms and technical data presented in Graduate Record Examinations Scores for Basic Reference Groups are based on limited samples. Norms for physics were derived from the scores of 49 senior physics majors in 10 colleges. These norms, first printed in 1958, have gone through two printings (1960 and 1961) without any revision in the tables to reflect the results of larger sampling. A 1959 supplement provides additional norms, but, again, the number of students is small: for physics, 56 first year graduate students in 9 colleges. This is a serious shortcoming of the advanced tests not only in physics but also in other fields. Frequent complaints have been made by colleagues in fields other than physics that the norms and technical data are based on too small a sample. Reliability coefficients of .94 and .90 are reported for Form FGR and Form K-KGR, respectively.

Each of the two forms is of three hours duration. In order to complete Form FGR (117 items) the students must average about 92 seconds per item, whereas on Form K-KGR they are allowed 108 seconds per item for the 100 items. On Form K-KGR students are not only given more time because of the fewer number of items; they have another advantage in that most of the questions are arranged in groups with a diagram or a set of experimental data pertaining to several items. In one instance as many as seven items are based on a schematic figure and a paragraph of descriptive material. On the other hand, because in Form FGR all 117 items are distinct, the student must read a different stem before proceeding to the choices. Of course, for the student who has not mastered the physical principle that should guide him in answering the group of questions depending on it, there is no advantage in the grouping of items on Form K-KGR and it would be preferable for him to start each item with a different stem embodying a different physical concept.

A distinct disadvantage of Form FGR is that the examinee must go from one field of physics to another field item after item, whereas in Form K-KGR there are 20 groups containing from two to seven items under a single descriptive paragraph or schematic drawing. But in this form also, the student must jump from one field of physics to another as he proceeds from group to group. This difficulty could be obviated in both forms simply by rearranging the items and the groups systematically by field. There are only three items on Form K-KGR that test wave-motion and sound. There are about 21 items on electricity and magnetism, the largest number of items devoted to any of the major divisions of physics. Clearcut classification, of course, is not possible, and, aside from the cursory treatment of wave-motion and sound, the major fields of physics are adequately covered. In Form FGR, there are five items on wave-motion and sound, the smallest number devoted to a major field of physics. In mechanics there are 28 items, again with some question regarding classification. In this form, aside from the emphasis on mechanics, the major fields of physics are also adequately sampled.

While these tests adequately measure a student's knowledge of the contents of undergraduate physics lecture courses, they provide no measure of a student's skill in experimental procedures and techniques. Success in experimental or theoretical physics at the graduate level cannot be predicted by these instruments.

For a review by Leo Nedelsky of an earlier form, see 5:754. For a review of the testing program, see 5:601.

[931a]

★Physics: Cooperative Science Tests. High school; 1963–64; 3 scores: general concepts and principles, laboratory, total; IBM; Forms A, B, ('63, 20–22 pages); no specific manual; series handbook ('64, 76 pages); separate answer sheets must be used; $4 per 20 tests; $1 per 20 IBM scorable answer sheets; $1 per 10 scoring stencils (answer pattern must be punched out locally); $1 per handbook; postage extra; $2 per specimen set of this and 4 other science tests, cash orders postpaid; 80(92) minutes in 1 or 2 sessions; Cooperative Test Division. *

[932]

***Physics: Every Pupil Scholarship Test.** High school; 1926–64; new form (4 pages) usually issued each January and April; forms from previous testing programs also available; general directions sheet ['63, 2 pages]; no data on reliability; norms for new forms available following testing program; 4¢ per test; 4¢ per key; postage extra; 40(45) or 45(50) minutes; Bureau of Educational Measurements. *

[933]

***Physics: Every Pupil Test.** High school; 1929–64; new form (4 pages) usually issued each December and April; forms from previous testing programs also available; general directions sheet ('63, 2 pages); no data on reliability; Ohio norms for new forms available following testing program; 5¢ per test; 3¢ per key; postpaid; 40(45) minutes; Ohio Scholarship Tests. *

[934]

***Physics: Minnesota High School Achievement Examinations.** High school; 1955–63; series formerly called *Midwest High School Achievement Examinations;* new form issued each May; norms available in June following release of new form; Form F ('63, 5 pages) used in 1963 testing; no specific manual; series manual ('63, 4 pages); series norms ['63, 4 pages]; series cumulative profile ('62, 2 pages); no data on reliability; no description of normative population; 12¢ per test; $2.50 per 100 profiles; postage extra; 20¢ per specimen set, postpaid; 60(65) minutes; American Guidance Service, Inc. *

IRVIN J. LEHMANN, *Associate Professor in Evaluation Services, Michigan State University, East Lansing, Michigan.* [Review of Forms E and F.]

This test was formerly called *Physics: Midwest High School Achievement Examinations.* No doubt, the questionability of the norms to be discussed later might have been a mitigating factor in the series being completely renamed.

Form F consists of 80 items to be done in one hour while its predecessor (Form E) contained 122 items to be done in one hour. In both forms, the content is well specified and includes units on measurement, mechanics, structure of matter, heat, sound, light, wave motion, electricity, and magnetism. Although the content sampling was quite adequate, this reviewer feels that in Form F heat is underrepresented and structure of matter overrepresented (6 per cent and 20 per cent of the items, respectively). Unfortunately, no definitive statement can be made since the course objectives are not described in the 4-page manual. In fact, one of the most serious shortcomings of this series is the paucity of information contained in the manual.

The "manual" for each form states that

both "thought" and factual items were to be included in the forms. An analysis of the items suggests that, even though this might have been the general intent of the authors, the final product is a series of items that measure factual knowledge per se, or the ability to substitute numbers in a formula. Little attention is given to the measurement of the student's ability to apply the basic physical principles he has learned in terms of "thought" questions. Both forms are lacking in items that require the student to display his ability to deduce hypotheses, interpret data, find flaws in experiments, analyze and synthesize, read graphs—all of which should be objectives in any of the physical sciences.

There is no information concerning the validity and reliability of either form. In fact, other than a brief statement as to content validity, there is no information to enable the user to effectively evaluate these tests. Before one is able to ascertain how well the objectives are measured, it is necessary that he know what these objectives are. General statements as to how the validity of the items was established do not suffice. Nor does this material contained in the manual: "Authors of tests were urged to include not only factual items but also items that would evaluate concepts. * The editors.... eliminated no fewer than 10 per cent of the questions on the basis that these did not carry as high validity as desirable." Nowhere is the user given any indication of the criteria (item difficulty and/or item discrimination) employed. In addition, just because "x" per cent of the items are removed is no justification for making a case for validity.

In quality, Form F is much poorer than Form E. In fact, Form F is not up to the average commercial test in quality. It suffers primarily from lack of editing. Although some inadequacies will slip by even the best of editors, some of the items in this test lack precision in the usual scientific sense, some contain redundancies, some are just plain confusing to the reader, and some give the obvious answer by the wording of the item. An example follows:

36. Capillary action is the product of
A. surface tension
B. cohesion
C. adhesion
D. adhesion and surface tension
E. cohesion and surface tension

The word "product" automatically eliminates the first three responses. Another example:

34. A substance that is extremely malleable is
A. cast iron
B. gold
C. glass
D. polyethylene plastic
E. rubber

Although "B" is keyed as the correct response, it could also be "C" or "D," or "E" if the latter were in liquid form. The item should specify "at room temperature."

Due to the absence of empirical data, this reviewer is forced to conclude that the authors of both forms made no attempt to investigate the statistical properties of the test. Data on empirical validity, reliability, and the norming population are conspicuous by their absence. A percentile norm table covering all the tests in the series is furnished, but it is not broken down by age, sex, or grade.

The uses of the tests are briefly described in the manual. The major emphasis appears to be on the improvement of instruction. The authors are to be commended on this philosophy. At the same time, however, they appear to be naïve when they state that there should be a high correlation between this and teacher made tests. Surely, they recognize the limitations of teacher made tests and one wonders whether this is also indicative of the quality of these tests.

Although the manual implies a grades 7–12 range, it is obvious that this test should not be given before grade 11 unless it is given for pretest purposes. Since there are no grade norms accompanying the test, it is difficult to determine whether the authors felt the test was valid for use in the junior high school grades.

Although Form E is a better test than Form F (from the standpoint of content sampling, format, and construction), neither form is impressive in its present form. Possibly with further editing, inclusion of different activity-items, empirical evidence as to validity and reliability, and a thorough standardization on a representative sample of high school students, both forms could have some merit.

If one is only interested in surveying the extent to which students have absorbed and are able to regurgitate certain facts, this test suffices. However, if the course objectives in physics are broader than this, then physics teachers who are looking for a good standardized test would do well to continue their search.

[935]

★Physics Test (Traditional and PSSC): Affiliation Testing Program for Catholic Secondary Schools. Grades 9–12 and students who are candidates for the high school diploma issued by the Catholic University of America; 1949–63; administered annually in May at individual schools; IBM; new form issued annually; Form Z ('63, 19 pages) used in 1963 program; separate answer sheets must be used; 50¢ per test and IBM answer sheet; postpaid; fee includes purchase of test booklets, scoring, and other services; specimen set of the complete battery free; for more complete information, see 758; 90(100) minutes; Program of Affiliation, Catholic University of America. *

HENRY CHAUNCEY, *President, Educational Testing Service, Princeton, New Jersey.* [Review of Forms Y and Z.]

The distribution of items in the test in terms of the content areas commonly taught in secondary school physics is reasonable. In Form Y, 43 per cent of the questions pertain to mechanics, 19 per cent to electricity and magnetism, 13 per cent to light, 10 per cent to modern physics, 9 per cent to heat, and 6 per cent to sound. For Form Z, the percentages are: mechanics (37), electricity and magnetism (24), heat (17), light (9), sound (7), and modern physics (6). A substantial number of questions involve something more than the recall of a fact. Many questions call for interpretation; application of a principle, concept, model, or theory; or analysis of an experimental situation. In accordance with the stated objectives of the physics course this test is designed to cover, a fair number of test questions require numerical solutions or are concerned with practical applications of physics to student experiences in home, shop, sports, amusements, and vehicles. However, the number of practical applications is not excessive. Since the students can be reasonably expected to grasp what is asked for in most questions, and can recognize the material as similar or related to what they should have studied, the test should elicit a favorable reaction from the examinees. The test appears sufficiently challenging, but not inordinately difficult.

Both forms include five-choice completion items, matching items, and reading passages followed by sets of statements. The statements following the passages are to be classified as (*a*) true and following from the passage; (*b*) true, but based on information not in the passage; (*c*) contradicted by the passage; or (*d*) contradicted by information not in the passage. This last type of item is subject to ambiguities which are nearly impossible to avoid.

Form Z has three parts (not separately timed); Part 1, containing 75 items, is to be taken by all students, while Parts 2 and 3 (35 items each) are to be taken by non-PSSC and PSSC physics students, respectively. Part 1 of Form Z has 20 items which involve matching the names of 10 physicists with 20 descriptions; this is an excessive number of items measuring something not generally regarded as significant.

There are certain technical deficiencies in a few of the items, but in general they are satisfactory. Two questions give little indication of what is desired from the examinee. The stems of the items merely consist of statements about a situation, and the options are further statements about the situation. Presumably, one is to pick the option that states something true about the situation. Another question asks for a potential difference, but no units are included in the stem or options. A curve on a graph to which five items relate is described as indicating time values; it actually indicates acceleration values.

The difficulty of the test appears appropriate. The means on the 110-item test of 90 minutes are 51.4 for Form Y and 49 for Form Z, the standard deviations are 12.2 and 11, and the range is 15–88, all in raw score units. There is no specific information on speededness, but the other data seem to indicate that the timing is quite appropriate.

On the basis of a review of the test questions and the available statistical data, I would judge that the test confronts the intended examinees with significant tasks of appropriate difficulty. The test scores should be a fair indication of the degree to which the examinees have mastered the concepts and abilities which a good secondary school physics teacher would seek to impart and develop in his course.

For a review of the complete program, see 758.

[936]

★Tests of the Physical Science Study Committee. High school students taking the physics course developed by the Physical Science Study Committee; 1959; IBM; 1 form (8 pages); an alternate version, called Series S (identical except for item order), is also available; 10 tests: 8 tests listed below plus a comprehensive test on each half of the course (Test 5 for the first half, Test 10 for the second half); handbook (39 pages); no data on reliability; norms based on experimental forms; separate answer sheets must be used; $2 per set of tests; $1 per 20 IBM scorable answer sheets; 25¢ per scoring stencil for any one test; $1 per handbook; $2 per specimen set; postage extra; 45(55) minutes per test; Frederick L. Ferris, Jr., Sherman Frankel, Walter C. Michels, and Thomas H. Wood; Cooperative Test Division. *

a) TEST 1: SPACE, TIME, AND MOTION.
b) TEST 2: MASS AND MATTER.
c) TEST 3: THE BEHAVIOR OF LIGHT.
d) TEST 4: LIGHT AND WAVE MOTION.
e) TEST 6: FORCE AND MOMENTUM.
f) TEST 7: ENERGY.
g) TEST 8: ELECTRICITY AND MAGNETISM.
h) TEST 9: THE ATOM.

REFERENCES

1. FORNOFF, FRANK J. "Developing the New Physics Test." *Col Board R* 46:19–21 w '62. *

GEORGE G. MALLINSON, *Dean, School of Graduate Studies, Western Michigan University, Kalamazoo, Michigan.*

Tests 1–4 and 6–9 of the *Tests of the Physical Science Study Committee* cover Chapters 1–6, 7–10, 11–15, 16–19, 20–23, 24–26, 27–31, and 32–34, respectively, of the textbook developed by the Committee. Tests 5 and 10 are comprehensive tests covering Parts 1 and 2, "The Universe" and "Optics and Waves" (Chapters 1–19); and Parts 3 and 4, "Mechanics" and "Electricity and Atomic Structure" (Chapters 20–34) of the textbook. Each test consists of 35 multiple choice items and is designed to be administered in a 45-minute session, with an additional 5–10 minutes for distributing and collecting materials, and reading directions. The responses are made on separate IBM scorable answer sheets which may also be hand scored.

The test format involves a number of anecdotes or situations presented in verbal and/or graphic or diagrammatic form; each anecdote or situation serves as the basis for two or more specific items. The items are mathematically oriented to a high degree and are designed as specific measures of the knowledge and understanding of the materials in the textbook developed by the Committee. On some items the students are required to "wade through" much verbal and visual material in order to respond. Thus there is some question in the mind of the reviewer whether the 45-minute testing period is adequate.

In general, the items demand understanding and thought on the part of the testee, rather than factual retention. There are included a number of items that may seem more mathematically oriented than those typically found on a physics test. Yet, they are not unique in terms of the direction of modern physics.

The reviewer compared the tests with the materials in the chapters they were designed to measure and also with the objectives stated for the PSSC physics program. The items seemed to be consistent with the materials in the chapters and "face validity" could be attributed to them in terms of the stated objectives.

The handbook for test administrators is exceptionally well done and is unique in that solutions are given for each item, thus providing the rationale for each correct answer. The tests may, therefore, be used by the teacher as a true teaching device.

Norms are provided in a table of "Estimated Percentile Equivalents of Raw Scores" with a caution that the tests are revised editions of the original experimental editions and statistical data concerning their reliability and validity are not available. The estimates are based on statistical information from the original experimental tests.

It is doubtful that the tests are valid measures of the outcomes of traditional courses in high school physics. The coverage of such courses is dissimilar to that of the PSSC physics course. However, even with limited information about their reliabilities and validities, the tests seem to be more than adequate for measuring PSSC physics. As *science* tests they are among the very best that the reviewer has yet seen.

LEO NEDELSKY, *Professor of Physical Sciences, University of Chicago, Chicago, Illinois.*

These tests are over a high school physics course based on a particular text, the PSSC physics text, and can be used only by the students of the course. The principal abilities measured by the tests, if given to the students of the course, are probably the ability to work with mathematical representations—formulas and graphs—of physical generalizations and the *knowledge* of these generalizations. The acquisition of these abilities at the required level, however, is likely to be based for many, perhaps most, students on *understanding* of individual topics and principles taught in the course, especially if the students don't know what the tests are like. Thus, understanding is tested indirectly by most exercises; direct testing of it is much less prominent because the situations on which exercises are based often closely resemble those in the text. The range of understanding tested is narrow because the situations are very abstract. Weighting knowledge more than understanding is also furthered by the time element. The 80 seconds per item allowance is adequate if the student recognizes the problem as quite like those he has practiced on, but, for many items in the tests, it is too short if he finds the problem so novel that he must decide what principles are applicable and how to apply them. The *ability to learn* is measured only indirectly—insofar as the students have to learn from the text. Learning from the text is more likely to be important in those schools in which the text's treatment of physics is more sophisticated than the teacher's understanding of physics, probably not an unusual relation.

The text, whose content the tests have been designed to sample, has excellent discussions of the nature and structure of physics as a process of inquiry. The content of these discussions is sampled very inadequately indeed. Even the sampling of physics as a body of knowledge is strongly biased—in favor of formalisms. For example, only a small portion of a discussion of molecules and crystals is tested for; typically, that portion which has for its title the *geometry* of crystals.

The reviewer had no access to validity studies, if such have been conducted. The only data the handbook furnishes are five percentiles for each part score, excepting for Test 9. The reviewer ventures to predict, however, that the tests should be a valid measure, more valid than any other he knows, of the ability to major in physics as it is now taught in our colleges and a good predictor of academic success in other exact sciences. The competence measured by the tests would be of little value to a student outside the mathematical sciences and would be soon lost to him because it was not used. The reasoning is as follows. It is possible to classify types of understanding of physical generalizations and their relation to phenomena into intuitive or nonverbalizable, qualitative or verbalizable, and formal and mathematical. The PSSC tests deal almost entirely with the latter type; many situations are stripped of all physical content, except that expressible by a simple algebraic equation or graph, and it is often possible to substitute "apple" or even "glurg" for "electron" or "photon" without changing the problem or its solution. The abstractions of college physics are a major obstacle to many of its students; a student with high scores on the PSSC tests need not fear that obstacle. He may also be assured of good grades in college physics courses, for most of these, although not quite so extreme, are like the PSSC tests in that they also shy off the uncouth phenomena of physical reality and the problems of research, and preoccupy themselves with highly idealized, highly abstract representations. It may be added here that the PSSC tests are intellectually tough—considerably beyond, both in toughness and the quality of thinking required, most college physics course tests.

Technically, the tests are excellent, and the best answer is almost always unambiguously the right answer, a univocality that is usually restricted to highly formalized exercises. Teachers of college physics and the more advanced high school physics courses could supplement with profit their own tests with PSSC tests, if these were made more widely available. If the tests were given to the students of courses other than the PSSC course, the tests' center of gravity should markedly shift from knowledge to understanding, provided some quite parochial items were eliminated.

Although the reviewer has criticized the tests for their narrow range of objectives, the range is certainly wider than that of the usual tests over college or high school physics courses, whether homemade or bought. What I particularly object to is that the tests measure only a fraction of what students can learn from the excellent text and the supplementary materials that are used in the PSSC course. Nevertheless, I must admit that my criticism of the PSSC tests is probably too severe; I feel chagrined that so much talent, thought, and energy has gone into building that sharp and shiny but overspecialized tool—a Phillips screwdriver of a test.

[Other Tests]

For tests not listed above, see the following entries in *Tests in Print:* 1634, 1638–40, 1643–5, and 1647–8; out of print: 1632, 1635, and 1650.

SENSORY–MOTOR

REVIEWS BY *Louis M. DiCarlo and Helen M. Robinson.*

[937]

★Leavell Hand-Eye Coordinator Tests. Ages 8–14; 1958; for determining need for training on the *Leavell Hand-Eye Coordinator;* individual; 7 scores: hand-foot preference, eye-ear preference, hand dexterity preference, visual imagery (3 scores), total; 1 form (3 pages); manual for use of the coordinator (22 pages, 4 of which provide instructions for the tests); no data on reliability; no norms; $3 per manual; $15 per box of 500 record blanks; postage extra; (10) minutes; Ullin W. Leavell; Keystone View Co. *

[938]

Robbins Speech Sound Discrimination and Verbal Imagery Type Tests. Ages 4–8, 8 and over; 1948–58; individual; 1 form; 2 levels; revised manual ('58, 46 pages) contains all tests; no data on reliability; no norms; $1.50 per manual, postpaid; Samuel D. Robbins and Rosa Seymour Robbins; Expression Co. *

a) [SPEECH SOUND DISCRIMINATION TESTS FOR YOUNG CHILDREN.] Ages 4–8; 1948–58; 1 form (revised edition, '58); 2 tests; combined scoring sheet ['58, 2 pages]; 75¢ per 50 scoring sheets.

1) *Verbal Imagery Test for Young Children.* (30) minutes.

2) *Picture Speech Sound Discrimination Test for Young Children.* (60) minutes in 2 sessions.

b) SPEECH SOUND DISCRIMINATION TESTS FOR OLDER CHILDREN. Ages 8 and over; 1948; 1 form ('48); scoring booklet ('48, 8 pages); 25¢ per scoring booklet; (60) minutes.

LOUIS M. DICARLO, *Professor of Audiology and Speech Pathology, Syracuse University, Syracuse, New York.*

The purpose of the Robbins tests is twofold: (*a*) "to determine just which types of speech sounds a child who manifests a phonetic speech defect of sensory origin is unable to differentiate"; (*b*) "to help him see, hear, and feel the differences between the individual speech sounds which compose these groups." Inference: The tests have diagnostic and remedial properties.

The present combined test and manual is a 1958 revision of the edition first published in 1948. It contains a battery of nine subtests for children ages 4–8 and a battery of nine subtests for children ages 8 and over. The younger children indicate their responses to an item by pointing to pictures, while the older children indicate their responses by stating whether the three words (making up a given item) read aloud to them by the examiner sound alike and, if not, which differs from the other two.

The tests were constructed because "many of the older speech sound discrimination tests are inadequate for diagnostic purposes." The tests also are based on the concept of different but specific sound descriptions and different behavior modalities, "eye-minded," "ear-minded," "motor-minded."

Modern behavior theory is not explicit with respect to the dynamics governing the input and output processes. Tests constructed on the bases of "mixed mental imagery," "auditory verbal imagery," "visual verbal imagery," and "non-verbal mental imagery" have little meaning and lead one into philosophical considerations which can be neither verified nor refuted. Further description in such terms may be transcending an individual's language equipment.

Further, evaluating speech discriminations through identification of pictures is testing auditory recognition. A child may exhibit serious speech sound discrimination disability but yet identify the pictures correctly because of the many other cues inherent in such a task. A low level of discrimination may be involved in identifying pictures but pictures themselves provide clues which may tolerate distortion when spoken.

Also, the speech sound discrimination tests for the older children test more than discrimination. Since they test memory and association, the question of just what segments of behavior the tests are measuring immediately becomes pertinent. The presentation of the same kind of material for 60 minutes introduces variables involving motivation, fatigue, and error. Furthermore, conditions of maximum and minimum stimulation are not specified, as in the *Templin-Darley Screening and Diagnostic Tests of Articulation.* Wepman's *Auditory Discrimination Test,* the Bryngelson-Glaspey

Speech Improvement Cards, and other available material accomplish the same purposes much more easily and economically. Nevertheless, the Robbins material contains items that the skillful speech pathologist may adapt for individual usage.

After 10 years the test manual reports no data concerning reliability or validity. Such information would appear to be not only desirable but crucial.

[Other Tests]

For tests not listed above, see the following entries in *Tests in Print:* 1651 and 1653–4.

HEARING

[939]

★Ambco Audiometers. Ages 6 and over; 1954–62; individual except for Models 601-G, 1122, and 1150; reliability data for Model 700 only; postage extra; Ambco Electronics. *

a) OTOMETER. 1954–62; for screening and threshold testing in schools, industry, and physicians' offices; range: 0 to +80 decibels in 5-db steps at 6 frequencies from 500 to 6,000 cps; 4 models ['62, battery operated portable units]: Models 601-S (single earphone), 601-SD (1 live and 1 dummy earphone), 601-D (double earphones), 601-G (11 single earphones for group testing); operating instructions ['62, 1 card]; mimeographed directions for administering ['54, 2 pages]; audiogram ['54, 1 page]; $165 for Model 601-S, $175 for Model 601-SD, $185 for Model 601-D, $395 for Model 601-G; [5] minutes.

b) OTO-CHEK AUDITORY SCREENER. 1956; for two-frequency air conduction screening; range: 15 and 35 decibels at 2,000 and 4,000 cps; 2 models (transistorized, battery operated portable units): Models 700-S (single earphone), 700-D (double earphone); mimeographed directions for administering ['56, 2 pages]; $85 for Model 700-S, $120 for Model 700-D; [1] minute; Howard P. House and Aram Glorig.

c) DIAGNOSTIC AUDIOMETER. 1958–62; for pure tone air and bone conduction threshold and screening testing; range in 5-db steps (air conduction): −10 to +100 decibels at 11 frequencies from 125 to 8,000 cps; range in 5-db steps (bone conduction): −10 to +50 decibels at 8 frequencies from 250 to 4,000 cps; 5 models (transistorized, AC operated): Models 1150-S ['58, portable unit, air conduction only], 1150-D ['58, portable unit, air and bone conduction], 1150-D2 ['58, desk model, air and bone conduction], A-15S ['62, desk model, air conduction only]; A-15D ['62, desk model, air and bone conduction]; manual ['58, 18 pages] for 1150 models; manual ['62, 27 pages] for A-15 models; audiogram ['58, 1 page]; $485 for Model 1150-S, $535 for Model 1150-D, $560 for Model 1150-D2, $370 for Model A-15S, $395 for Model A-15D; standard equipment includes one set of double earphones, calibrated white noise masking, and (bone conduction models only) bone conduction receiver; $245 per set of 10 earphones for group testing; other accessories (including microphone, speech unit, and patient's signal cord) available; [2–15] minutes.

d) SPEECH AUDIOMETER. 1961; for air and bone conducting testing using live or recorded voice; adaptable to two-room testing installations; Model A-17 (transistorized, AC operated desk model); manual ['61, 39 pages]; $970 per instrument; standard equipment includes air and bone conduction receivers, calibrated white noise masking, speech monitor, microphone, record player, and patient's signal cord; administration time not reported.

e) "SCREEN-EAR" SCREENING AUDIOMETER. 1960–61; for air conduction screening and threshold testing in schools and industry; range: 0 to +80 decibels in 5-db steps at 8 frequencies from 250 to 8,000 cps; Model 1122 ['61, transistorized, AC operated portable unit]; manual ['61, 8 pages]; audiogram (1 page); $285 per instrument with one set of double earphones; group testing accessories available; [5] minutes.

[940]

★Auditory Discrimination Test. Ages 5–8; 1958; individual; orally administered; Forms 1, 2, (2 pages); preliminary manual (4 pages); $5 per 50 tests; 50¢ per specimen set; postage extra; (5–10) minutes; Joseph M. Wepman; [Language Research Associates]. *

REFERENCES

1. WEPMAN, JOSEPH M. "Auditory Discrimination, Speech, and Reading." *El Sch J* 60:325–33 Mr '60. *

2. MARTIN, FREDERICK N.; HAWKINS, RICHARD R.; AND BAILEY, H. A. TED, JR. "The Nonessentiality of the Carrier Phrase in Phonetically Balanced (PB) Word Testing." *J Auditory Res* 2:319–22 O '62. *

LOUIS M. DICARLO, *Professor of Audiology and Speech Pathology, Syracuse University, Syracuse, New York.*

The *Auditory Discrimination Test* purports to identify those children from 5 to 8 years of age with auditory discrimination deficits. Each form of the test contains 40 items comprising 40 three- to five-letter word pairs of the CVC variety. On each form the vowel or vowel sound is identical in 36 of the word pairs. Thirteen releasing consonants and 13 arresting consonants differ, while 10 word pairs are identical as false positive choices. The words comprising each pair were matched for: (*a*) familiarity, as determined by position in the Lorge-Thorndike list, (*b*) membership in the same phonetic category, and (*c*) length. Vowel comparisons were based on parts of the tongue raised, height of tongue, and position of lips.

The test is administered individually and requires only several minutes. A period of practice precedes the test. When the child understands the task, the test is given with the child's back to the examiner. The examiner reads the word pairs and the child indicates whether the words in each pair are the same or different.

Instructions for scoring are clear, precise, and unambiguous. The score achieved is determined by the number of errors the child makes in calling words which are different identical. (Errors in calling identical words different are counted only to determine whether the test results should be considered valid.) Inadequate auditory discrimination is indicated when 5-year-old children make more than 6 errors; 6-year-olds, more than 5 errors; 7-year-olds, more than 4 errors; and children 8 years old and older, more than 3 errors.

A test-retest coefficient of reliability on 109 subjects is reported as .91. Calculation of phoneme difficulty on the two forms resulted in a rank order correlation of .67 for 214 cases. Information on the relation between test results and intelligence ($r = .32$), articulatory disorders, and reading disability is reported as indicators of validity.

SUMMARY. The test provides a quick and accurate assessment of auditory discrimination among children from 5 to 8 years of age. It is easy to administer and score. The specificity of the task eliminates contamination of performance by auditory memory span. The information the author presents under validity suggests *relationships* between auditory discrimination and intelligence, hearing, speaking, and reading, but it does not necessarily support the validity of the test. Auditory discrimination may represent only one of the contributory variables for performance in these other areas. Some deaf individuals who exhibit severe deficit in auditory discrimination do well in these other areas. Moreover, some of the differences between test results and performance in the other areas are reported as statistically significant. While the differences may be statistically significant, in some instances they may not be practically significant.

Nevertheless, for a quick, inexpensive, easy to score, and accurate test of auditory discrimination, the *Auditory Discrimination Test* is highly recommended.

[941]

***Auditory Tests.** Grades 2 and over; 1951–56; also called *C.I.D. Auditory Tests;* individual; 3 tests on 2 sets of records; no data on reliability; $5.25 per single replacement record; postpaid; attenuator, amplifier, monitoring meter, and earphone or loudspeaker necessary for administration; Central Institute for the Deaf; Technisonic Studios, Inc. *

a) AUDITORY TESTS W-1 AND W-2: SPONDAIC WORD LISTS. Recorded adaptation of *Auditory Test No. 9* developed by Harvard University Psycho-Acoustic Laboratory; threshold for speech; 2 tests ['51, combined on three 12-inch, 33⅓ rpm records] each consisting of 6 arrangements of the same 36 words; manual ['56, 19 pages]; $12.75 per set of records and manual; (10) minutes for one 36-word list.

1) *Test W-1.* A "constant level" test in which sound intensity must be attenuated by examiner.

2) *Test W-2.* A "descending level" test in which sound intensity has been attenuated on the record in downward steps of 3 decibels.

b) AUDITORY TEST W-22: PHONETICALLY-BALANCED WORD LISTS. Words selected in part from lists developed by Harvard University Psycho-Acoustic Laboratory; discrimination for speech at levels above threshold; 1 test ['51, on six 12-inch, 33⅓ rpm records]; 24 forms (6 arrangements of each of 4 word lists) at least 2 of which should be used with each examinee; instructions ['56, 17 pages, same as 1951 instructions except for cover page]; $25 per set of records and manual; [30] minutes.

REFERENCES

1. FALCONER, GEORGE A. "The Reliability and Validity of Monitored Connected Discourse as a Test of the Threshold of Intelligibility." *J Speech & Hearing Disorders* 13:369–71 D '48. * (*PA* 23:3391)

2. ARTHUR, ROBERT HARWARD. *The Comparative Reliability of the C.I.D. Tape-Recorded and the Harvard #9 Live-Voice Speech Reception Tests.* Master's thesis, University of Maryland (College Park, Md.), 1951.

3. BENSON, R. W.; DAVIS, H.; HARRISON, C. E.; HIRSH, I. J.; REYNOLDS, E. G.; AND SILVERMAN, S. R. "C.I.D. Auditory Tests W-1 and W-2." *Laryngoscope* 61:838–41 Ag '51. *

4. BENSON, R. W.; DAVIS, H.; HARRISON, C. E.; HIRSH, I. J.; REYNOLDS, E. G.; AND SILVERMAN, S. R. "Letter to the Editor." *J Speech Disorders* 16:375–6 D '51. *

5. HIRSH, IRA J.; DAVIS, HALLOWELL; SILVERMAN, S. RICHARD; REYNOLDS, ELIZABETH G.; ELDERT, ELIZABETH; AND BENSON, ROBERT W. "Development of New Materials for Speech Audiometry." *J Speech & Hearing Disorders* 17:321–37 S '52. * (*PA* 27:4552)

6. BRANDT, ANN MARIE MURPHY. *The Comparative Reliability of the Central Institute for the Deaf Disc Recorded and Monitored Live Voice Auditory Test W-22 (Phonetically Balanced Word Lists).* Master's thesis, University of Maryland (College Park, Md.), 1953.

7. CORSO, JOHN F. "Confirmation of the Normal Threshold for Speech on C.I.D. Auditory Test W-2." *J Acoustical Soc Am* 29:368–70 Mr '57. * (*PA* 32:2842)

8. HUTTON, CHARLES; CURRY, E. THAYER; AND ARMSTRONG, MARY BETH. "Semi-Diagnostic Test Material for Aural Rehabilitation." *J Speech & Hearing Disorders* 24:319–29 N '59. * (*PA* 34:8288)

9. TILLMAN, TOM W., AND JERGER, JAMES F. "Some Factors Affecting the Spondee Threshold in Normal Hearing Subjects." *J Speech & Hearing Res* 2:141–6 Je '59. * (*PA* 34:5301)

10. ELPERN, BARRY S. "Differences in Difficulty Among the CID W-22 Auditory Tests." *Laryngoscope* 70:1560–5 N '60. *

11. BOWLING, LLOYD, AND ELPERN, BARRY S. "Relative Intelligibility of Items on CID Auditory Test W-1." *J Auditory Res* 1:152–7 Ja '61. *

12. MCNAMEE, JOANNE F. *An Investigation of the Use of the CID Auditory Test W-22 With Children.* Master's thesis, Ohio State University (Columbus, Ohio), 1961.

13. NOBER, E. HARRIS, AND NOBER, LINDA W. "Speech Reception Threshold and Discrimination Scores as a Function of Method of Presentation and Frequency Response." *J Auditory Res* 2:1–4 Ja '62. *

14. RESNICK, DAVID M. "Reliability of the Twenty-Five Word Phonetically Balanced Lists." *J Auditory Res* 2:5–12 Ja '62. *

15. ROSS, MARK, AND HUNTINGTON, DOROTHY A. "Concerning the Reliability and Equivalency of the CID W-22 Auditory Tests." *J Auditory Res* 2:220–8 Jl '62. *

16. ELLIOTT, LOIS L. "Prediction of Speech Discrimination Scores From Other Test Information." *J Auditory Res* 3:35–45 Ja '63. *

17. GIOLAS, THOMAS G., AND EPSTEIN, AUBREY. "Comparative Intelligibility of Word Lists and Continuous Discourse." *J Speech & Hearing Res* 6:349–58 D '63. *

18. GRUBB, PATTI. "A Phonemic Analysis of Half-List Speech Discrimination Tests." *J Speech & Hearing Res* 6:271–5 S '63. *

19. REDDELL, RAYFORD CLAYTON. *A Comparison of Three Auditory Tests of Speech Discrimination on Normal and Pathological Ears.* Doctor's thesis, Stanford University (Stanford, Calif.), 1963. (*DA* 24:436)

20. WEINHOUSE, IRIS, AND MILLER, MAURICE H. "Discrimination Scores for Two Lists of Phonetically Balanced Words." *J Auditory Res* 3:9–14 Ja '63. *

[942]

***Audivox Audiometers.** Grades 1 and over; 1924–61; successor to *Western Electric Audiometers* (see 3:475); for pure tone air and bone conduction testing;

range in 5-db steps (air conduction): −10 to +75 decibels at 125 and 8,000 cps, −10 to +95 decibels at 8 other frequencies; range in 5-db steps (bone conduction): −10 to +95 decibels at 7 frequencies from 250 to 4,000 cps; 2 models ['53, AC operated]: desk Model 7BD, portable Model 7BP; mimeographed manual ['61, 8 pages]; audiogram ['53, 2 pages]; no data on reliability; $490 for Model 7BD; $465 for Model 7BP; standard equipment includes one set of double earphones, complex noise generator, calibrated masking, and communication circuit; $205 per set of 10 earphones for group testing; $36.10 per receiver and accessories for bone conduction testing; $4 per 500 audiogram cards; accessory equipment (including microphone, patient's signal switch, speech monitor meter, and speech audiometer) available; postage extra; [15-30] minutes; Audivox, Inc. *

Louis M. DiCarlo, *Professor of Audiology and Speech Pathology, Syracuse University, Syracuse, New York.*[1]

Since hearing is related to processes such as reading and learning, counselors, psychologists, reading specialists, speech pathologists, nurses and personnel workers in industry, school nurses, school administrators, and other specialists—including medical personnel—participate in assessing hearing behavior. World War II provided great impetus for expansive research in all areas of auditory function and communication. For some time there has been extended discussion of reference levels for audiometers in the United States and Great Britain. The two standards differ by about 10 decibels because of the manner in which the criterion was obtained. The American standard was obtained empirically on a clinical population in field surveys, while the British standard was derived from testing populations in a laboratory situation. It is desirable to obtain some agreement which will be universally acceptable.

An audiometer is an instrument constructed to produce sounds of different frequency and intensity levels for the purpose of measuring auditory sensitivity. Minimum specifications for both diagnostic and screening audiometers are described in the *Journal of the American Medical Association*[2] and the American Standards Association report.[3]

[1] This review presents some preliminary comments on audiometers and hearing testing in general, followed by brief comments on portable screening audiometers manufactured by Audivox, Inc., Beltone Electronics Corporation, Maico Electronics, Inc., and Zenith Hearing Aid Sales Corporation. Prices and information on these and other audiometers designed by Beltone, Maico, and Zenith will be found in the entries referred to at the end of the description of each.—Editor.

[2] American Medical Association, Council on Physical Medicine and Rehabilitation. "Minimum Requirements for Acceptable Pure Tone Audiometers for Diagnostic Purposes: Report of the Council." *J Am Med Assn* 146:255-7 My 19 '51. *

[3] American Standards Association. *Audiometers for General Diagnostic Purposes.* American Standards Z24.5—1951. New York: the Association, Inc., 1951. Pp. v, 5.

Different varieties of audiometers have been devised. Diagnostic audiometers, which include single and multiple channels, perform a multiplicity of pure tone and speech tests. These audiometers contain many accessories, including bone conduction receivers, masking controls, and accessories for differential tests.

The purpose of a screening audiometer is to detect those individuals whose hearing deviates from the normal. Normal hearing is a statistical concept and is based on the measurement of a representative sample of individuals between 18 and 25 years of age who have no history of auditory impairment and who have no anomalies as revealed by comprehensive otological examination. In audiology, the decibel is generally employed when measuring auditory sensitivity. The decibel, unfortunately, has different connotations for different individuals. For the audiologist, a decibel represents a logarithmic ratio between two sounds, one of which acts as a reference sound and the other, the sound to be measured. When used as a term to indicate a level of electric power, some other references are indicated. When an engineer employs .0002 dynes/cm^2, he implies a reference which may be indirectly pertinent to the acoustic reference of audiometric zero. Fortunately, there is agreement today on matters of measurement among audiologists. This results from the close cooperation existing between engineers, electronic experts, and audiologists. The audiometer permits the audiologist to obtain an audiogram of an individual's hearing in terms of frequency and intensity characteristics. This represents qualitative and quantitative descriptions of the individual's hearing status.

The usual intensity level is 10 decibels for screening purposes, but this value will vary according to the testing environment. The screening audiometer functions to detect those individuals who require medical attention. The more stringent the criteria, the greater the number of false positive findings that will result. Research suggests that individual screening is the preferable method of screening for hearing loss. Speech may be used, but it offers certain limitations, especially difficulties with acoustic environment and sound value levels.

Audiometers for screening purposes should have provisions for producing identifiable frequencies of 125, 250, 500, 1,000, 2,000, 4,000, and 8,000 cycles per second to be delivered to earphones for air conduction measurements. Margin of error should not be greater than ±5 per cent at any frequency. The intensity is indicated by the decibel scale on the audiometer; no measurement should deviate by more than 2.5 decibels. The intensity scale on most audiometers is indicated in 5 decibel steps. Each audiometer possesses both frequency and intensity dials, a tone interrupter switch with satisfactory rise and decay time limits, and a power source. All audiometers are encased so as to prevent shock hazards.

The technical competence necessary for the administration of screening tests may be developed through an instructional period sufficient to acquaint the tester with the system and manipulation of the instrument. The administration of complete diagnostic tests and the interpretation of audiograms demands extensive and specialized training. Such tests will be required when screening has identified the individual suspected of hearing loss. The environment in which screening tests are administered becomes an important factor in assessing the efficacy of the screening program. Today, most tests are administered under fairly adequate conditions.

AUDIVOX MODEL 7BP. The Audivox 7BP is a well constructed portable instrument which will withstand much usage with careful handling. It is a well engineered instrument. Purity of tones and accuracy of output levels meet requirements for audiometers. The tone interrupter is in the middle of the instrument. When the audiometer is turned on, the dials light up. The intensity attenuator moves 360° without noise. The output limit is 95 db. The instrument may be used for either individual or group testing.

BELTONE MODEL 9-C. The Beltone 9-C is a basic audiometer for screening purposes. It is portable, durable, and easy to manipulate. The instrument has proved to be stable and drift free. Purity of tone and accuracy of output levels meet the criteria for screening audiometers. It has a slide wire attenuator and is easy to calibrate. The output limit is 100 db. (For further information, see 943.)

MAICO MODEL MA-2B. The Maico MA-2B is a sturdy, well constructed portable model. It has a 360° continuous dial rotation without stops. Purity of tones and accuracy of output levels meet requirements for audiometers. A very good feature is the construction of the interrupter switches at both ends of the instrument so that the tester may use either hand for interrupting the tone. Since this model has a peep window for the dial, one may have difficulty reading the figures if the light burns out. The step attenuator also generates slight clicks. The instrument may be employed either for screening single individuals or may be hooked up with other earphones for group testing. (For further information, see 947.)

ZENITH MODEL ZA-100-T. The Zenith ZA-100-T is an all-transistor portable audiometer. It is lightweight, easy to carry, and battery powered. It is easy to calibrate. The dials are well lighted; the tone interrupter action is clear and accurate. Both its construction and operation are consistent with accepted standards. Purity of tone and accuracy of output levels meet requirements for audiometers. Since it is battery operated, it is necessary to turn off the battery when not in use. (For further information, see 953.)

[943]

★**Beltone Audiometers.** Grades kgn and over; 1954–63; individual except for Model 11-C; 7 models (AC operated); range: −10 to +100 decibels in 1-db steps at 11 frequencies from 125 to 8,000 cps; audiogram card ['62, 2 pages] for use with all models; no data on reliability; narrow band masking generator available; $1.35 per pad of 100 audiograms; postage extra; administration time not reported; Beltone Electronics Corporation. *

a) BELTONE PORTABLE AUDIOMETERS. 4 models; instruction manual ('61, 19 pages).

1) *Screening Model 9-C.* 1961; for air conduction screening and threshold testing in schools and industry; $325 per instrument with one set of double earphones.

2) *Diagnostic Model 10-C.* 1961; for air and bone conduction testing by physicians; $395 per instrument; standard equipment includes one set of double earphones, complex noise generator, calibrated masking, and bone conduction vibrator.

3) *Group Screening Model 11-C.* 1961; for air conduction testing in schools and industry; may be used with up to 40 persons; separate answer sheets (must be reproduced locally) must be used; $355 per instrument with one set of double earphones; $250 per set of 10 additional earphones and accessories for group testing.

4) *Diagnostic Model 12-AC.* 1955–61; for air and bone conduction testing by physicians; 1 model ['61, similar to Model 10-C but with communication circuit]; $440 per instrument; standard equipment includes one set of double earphones, bone conduction vibrator, microphone, complex noise generator, and calibrated masking.

b) BELTONE CLINICAL AUDIOMETERS. For pure tone air conduction, bone conduction, and live and recorded speech testing; adaptable to two-room testing installations.

1) *Diagnostic Model 14.* 1958–63; Models 14-A ['62], 14-AW ['63]; instruction manual ('58, 21 pages); $595 for Model 14-A (with complex noise masking); $632.50 for Model 14-AW (with white noise masking); standard equipment includes masking, one set of double earphones, bone conduction receiver, patient's signal button, microphone, and monitor phone.
2) *Clinical Model 15-C.* 1960–63; 1 model ['60, a dual channel unit]; instruction manual ('63, 22 pages); $1,060 per instrument with complex noise masking; $1,095 per instrument with white noise masking; standard equipment includes masking, double air conduction receivers, bone conduction vibrator, microphone, patient's signal switch, and monitor phone.

For comments by Louis M. DiCarlo on screening audiometers in general and specific comments on Model 9-C and three other portable audiometers, see 942.

[944]

★The Children's Auditory Test. Ages 3–8; 1953; for speech-reception threshold measurement with a speech audiometer; 1 form (12-inch, 78 rpm record); mimeographed manual (4 pages); no data on reliability; no norms; $6.20 per set of record and manual, postpaid; [15] minutes; Edna K. Monsees; Volta Bureau. *

[945]

★Eckstein Audiometers. Grades kgn and over; 1959–62; individual except for Models 200 G, 250 G, and 350 G; 16 models; range (for all models except Models 45, 60, and 62): −10 to +100 decibels in 5-db steps at 11 frequencies from 125 to 8,000 cps; combined manual ['59, 8 pages] for 200, 300, and 310 Series models; audiogram ['59, 1 page] for all models except Model 45; no data on reliability; $225 per set of 10 single earphones in portable case for group audiometers; 25¢ per pad of audiograms; postage extra; [10–15] minutes; Eckstein Bros. *
a) TRITONE AUDIOMETER. 1962–63; for quick screening air conduction testing by physicians and in schools and industry; range: 15, 30, and 50 decibels at 500, 2,000, and 4,000 cps; Model 45 ('62, transistorized, battery operated portable unit); manual ['62, 4 pages]; audiogram ['63, 1 page]; $79.50 per instrument with single earphone.
b) 60 SERIES. 1961; for air and (Model 62 only) bone conduction testing; range: 0 to +80 decibels in 5-db steps at 7 frequencies from 250 to 6,000 cps; 2 models (transistorized, battery operated portable units); manual ['61, 13 pages].
1) *Single Headphone.* Model 62; $199.50 per instrument with single earphone, bone conductor, and batteries.
2) *Double Headphone.* Model 60; $185 per instrument with one set of double earphones and batteries.
c) 200 SERIES. 1959; for air and (Model 200 MB only) bone conduction testing in field or office; same as 250 Series models except in metal carrying case; 3 models (transistorized, battery operated portable units).
1) *Basic Model.* Model 200; $295 per instrument with one set of double earphones and batteries.
2) *Group Model.* Same as Model 200 with group output; Model 200 G; $315 per instrument.
3) *Diagnostic Model.* Same as Model 200 with white noise generator, masking, and bone conductor; Model 200 MB; $350 per instrument.
d) 250 SERIES. 1962; for air and (Model 250 MB only) bone conduction testing in field or office; 3 models (transistorized, battery operated portable units); no manual.
1) *Basic Model.* Model 250; $295 per instrument with one set of double earphones and batteries.
2) *Group Model.* Same as Model 250 with group output; Model 250 G; $315 per instrument.
3) *Diagnostic Model.* Same as Model 250 with white noise generator, masking, and bone conductor; Model 250 MB; $350 per instrument.
e) 300 SERIES. 1961; for air and (Model 300 MB only) bone conduction testing; 2 models (AC operated desk models).
1) *Basic Model.* Model 300; $295 per instrument with one set of double earphones.
2) *Diagnostic Model.* Same as Model 300 with white noise generator, masking, and bone conductor; Model 300 MB; $350 per instrument.
f) 310 SERIES. 1961; for air and (Model 310 MB only) bone conduction testing; 2 models (transistorized, battery operated desk models).
1) *Basic Model.* Model 310; $295 per instrument with one set of double earphones and batteries.
2) *Diagnostic Model.* Same as Model 310 with white noise generator, masking, and bone conductor; Model 310 MB; $350 per instrument.
g) 350 SERIES. 1962; same as 250 Series models except AC operated; 3 models; no manual.
1) *Basic Model.* Model 350; $295 per instrument with one set of double earphones.
2) *Group Model.* Same as Model 350 with group output; Model 350 G; $315 per instrument.
3) *Diagnostic Model.* Same as Model 350 with white noise generator, masking, and bone conductor; Model 350 MB; $350 per instrument.

[946]

★Grason-Stadler Audiometers. Ages infancy and over; 1950–63; for use by audiologists in speech and hearing clinics; 3 models (AC operated); no data on reliability; Grason-Stadler Co., Inc. *
a) SPEECH AUDIOMETER. Ages 6 and over; 1950–63; for use in a two-room testing installation for determining speech reception threshold and discrimination loss; range: −10 to +110 decibels in 2-db steps; Model 162 ('56, a dual channel model); manual ['63, 21 pages]; $1,200 per instrument; standard equipment includes earphone outlet box, microphone, phonograph, white and speech noise masking generator; *Auditory Tests W-1 and W-2: Spondaic Word Lists* and *Auditory Test W-22: Phonetically-Balanced Word Lists* included with instrument; [15–45] minutes.
b) BÉKÉSY AUDIOMETER. Ages 6 and over; 1955–63; for air conduction threshold testing with intensity controlled by subject and his adjustments automatically recorded; range: −25 to +95 decibels in .25-db steps at 100 to 10,000 cps; Model E800 ('55); manual ['63, 8 pages]; audiogram card ['57, 1 page]; $3,250 per instrument; standard equipment includes one set of double earphones, white noise masking generator, monitor meter, and extension box for two-room installation; $15 per 500 audiogram cards; [7–10] minutes on fast speed, [15–20] minutes on slow speed.
c) PSYCHOGALVANOMETRY. Ages infancy and over; 1954–62; portable unit employing classical conditioning techniques for testing and graphically recording reactions of subjects not responsive to ordinary hearing test methods; Model E664 ('54); manual ['62, 9 pages]; $1,000 per instrument including miscellaneous conditioning accessories; $8.50 per carton of recording paper; [15–45] minutes.

REFERENCES

1. JERGER, JAMES F. "Bekesy Audiometry in Analysis of Auditory Disorders." *J Speech & Hearing Res* 3:275–87 S '60. * (*PA* 35:2490)
2. JERGER, JAMES F., AND HERER, GILBERT. "Unexpected Dividend in Békésy Audiometry." *J Speech & Hearing Disorders* 26:390–1 N '61. *
3. JERGER, JAMES. "Hearing Tests in Otologic Diagnosis." *ASHA* 4:139–45 My '62. *
4. ROSE, DARRELL E. "Some Effects and Case Histories of Reversed Frequency Sweep in Békésy Audiometry." *J Auditory Res* 2:267–77 O '62. *
5. PRICE, LLOYD L. "Threshold Testing With Békésy Audiometer." *J Speech & Hearing Res* 6:64–9 Mr '63. * (*PA* 38:216)
6. PRICE, LLOYD L., AND FALCK, VILMA T. "Békésy Audiometry With Children." *J Speech & Hearing Res* 6:129–33 Je '63. * (*PA* 38:3592)

[947]

***Maico Audiometers.** Grades kgn and over; 1936–64; individual except for Models MA-2B and MA-12; 5 models (AC operated); audiogram card ('49, 2 pages); no data on reliability; $1.15 per 100 audiogram cards; postpaid; Maico Electronics, Inc. *

a) HEARING EVALUATOR. 1959–60; for air and bone conduction testing in clinical and research work; Model MA-8 ('59, a dual channel unit); range in 1-db steps (air conduction): −10 to +70 decibels at 125 cps, −10 to +80 decibels at 250, 6,000, and 8,000 cps, −10 to +100 decibels at 7 other frequencies; range in 1-db steps (bone conduction): −10 to +30 decibels at 250, 6,000, and 8,000 cps, −10 to +40 decibels at 500 and 4,000 cps, −10 to +60 decibels at 750 to 3,000 cps; manual ['60, 23 pages]; $1,820 per instrument; standard equipment includes one set of double earphones, bone conductor, white and complex noise generator, masking, two microphones, and patient's signal cord; narrow band noise accessory available.

b) PORTABLE AUDIOMETERS. 1956–64; for pure tone air and (Models MA-2B and MA-11 only) bone conduction threshold and sweep check testing in schools, public health services, and industry; 3 models; group testing accessories (for use in grades 3-12) available.

1) *Model MA-2B.* 1956–58; for air, bone, and speech testing; range in 5-db steps (air conduction): −10 to +70 decibels at 125 cps, −10 to +80 decibels at 250, 6,000, and 8,000 cps, −10 to +100 decibels at 7 other frequencies; range in 5-db steps (bone conduction): −10 to +80 decibels at 250 cps, −10 to +100 decibels at 7 other frequencies from 500 to 4,000 cps; manual ['56, 25 pages]; $358 per instrument with one set of double earphones and calibrated masking; $418 per deluxe instrument with one set of double earphones, calibrated masking, bone conduction receiver, speech circuit, and microphone.

2) *Model MA-11 Diagnostic Pure Tone and Speech Audiometer.* 1964; for air, bone, and speech testing; also available as a desk model; range in 2 ½-db steps (air conduction): −10 to +70 decibels at 125 cps, −10 to +80 decibels at 250 and 8,000 cps, −10 to +100 decibels at 8 other frequencies; range in 2 ½-db steps (bone conduction): −10 to +40 decibels at 250 cps, −10 to +65 decibels at 8 other frequencies from 500 to 6,000 cps; manual ['64, 38 pages]; $585 per instrument; standard equipment includes one set of double earphones, bone conduction receiver, white noise masking, connection for recorded speech, microphone, and speech monitor meter.

3) *Model MA-12.* 1964; transistorized unit for air conduction threshold testing; range in 5-db steps: −10 to +80 decibels at 250, 500, 6,000, and 8,000 cps, −10 to +100 decibels at 1,000 to 4,000 cps; manual ['64, 21 pages]; $298 per instrument with one set of double earphones.

c) PROFESSIONAL AUDIOMETER. 1962; for pure tone air and bone conduction testing and speech threshold testing by otologists and audiologists; adaptable to two-room testing installations; Model MA-10; range in 1-db steps (air conduction): −10 to +70 decibels at 125 cps, −10 to +80 decibels at 250, 6,000, and 8,000 cps, −10 to +100 decibels at 7 other frequencies; range in 1-db steps (bone conduction): −10 to +40 decibels at 250 cps, −10 to +65 decibels at 8 other frequencies from 500 to 6,000 cps; manual ['62, 45 pages]; $975 per instrument; standard equipment includes white or complex noise generator, calibrated masking, communication circuit, one set of double earphones, bone conductor, microphone, and patient's signal cord; narrow band noise accessory available.

REFERENCES

1–4. See 5:763.
5. WILLIAMS, HAROLD N. *Utilization of the Maico F-1 Deluxe Audiometer in Differentiating Between Functional and Organic Disorders of Hearing in Public Schools.* Doctor's thesis, Bradley University (Peoria, Ill.), 1957. (*DA* 17:2535)
6. HANLEY, CLAIR N., AND GADDIE, BARBARA G. "The Use of Single Frequency Audiometry in the Screening of School Children." *J Speech & Hearing Disorders* 27:258–64 Ag '62. * (*PA* 37:3487)

For comments by Louis M. DiCarlo on screening audiometers in general and specific comments on Model MA-2B and three other portable audiometers, see 942.

[948]

★Maico Hearing Impairment Calculator. 1959; for calculating per cent of single-ear or binaural impairment from hearing levels tested at frequencies of 500, 1,000, and 2,000 cps; $1 per calculator, postpaid; Maico Electronics, Inc. *

[949]

The Massachusetts Hearing Test. Grades 1–16 and adults; 1948; method of group screening (with 10, 20, 30, or 40 receivers) using prescribed forms of scoring, signal presentation, and calibration; any pure tone audiometer adapted to group testing may be used; method of testing and instructions for scoring and interpretation are presented in *1* below; (17) minutes; Philip W. Johnston; standardized instructions for administering (1 instructions sheet, 1 answer sheet, and 5 master sheets) available free of charge from Massachusetts Department of Public Health, Division of Maternal and Child Health. *

REFERENCES

1. JOHNSTON, P. W. "The Massachusetts Hearing Test." *J Acoust Soc Am* 20:697–703 S '48. *
2. BECKER, MARSHALL A. *An Investigation of the Efficiency of a Modified Form of the Massachusetts Group Pure Tone Screening Test, as Used in the Syracuse University Freshman Testing Program.* Master's thesis, Syracuse University (Syracuse, N.Y.), 1951.
3. JOHNSON, KENNETH OWEN. *The Relative Efficiency of the Western Electric 4CA Phonograph and Massachusetts Pure Tone Group Hearing Tests.* Doctor's thesis, Stanford University (Stanford, Calif.), 1952.
4. THOMAS, DONALD B. *A Study of the Use of the Massachusetts Group Hearing Test at Ohio University.* Master's thesis, Ohio University (Athens, Ohio), 1952.
5. DICARLO, LOUIS M., AND GARDNER, ERIC F. "The Efficiency of the Massachusetts Pure Tone Screening Test as Adapted for a University Testing Program." *J Speech & Hearing Disorders* 18:175–82 Je '53. * (*PA* 28:3151)
6. CAUSEY, GEORGE DONALD. *A Comparative Analysis of Group and Individual Hearing Test Results.* Doctor's thesis, Purdue University (Lafayette, Ind.), 1954. (*DA* 14:1843)
7. YANKAUER, ALFRED; GEYER, MARGARET L.; AND CHASE, HELEN C. "Comparative Evaluation of Three Screening Methods for Detection of Hearing Loss in School Children." *Am J Pub Health* 44:77–82 Ja '54. * (*PA* 29:1420)
8. DOWNS, MARION P. "The Familiar Sounds Test and

Other Techniques for Screening Hearing." *J Sch Health* 26: 77–87 Mr '56. * (*PA* 31:4207)
9. MEYERSON, LEE. "The Massachusetts Hearing Test," pp. 23–9. In his *Hearing for Speech in Children: A Verbal Audiometric Test.* Acta Oto-Laryngologica Supplementum 128. Copenhagen, Denmark: Ejnar Munksgaard Publishers, 1956. Pp. xv, 165. *
10. DICARLO, LOUIS M., AND GARDNER, ERIC F. "A Comparative Study of the Efficiency of Three Group Pure Tone Screening Tests for Public School Children." *Excep Child* 24:351–9 Ap '58. * (*PA* 33:5383)

[950]

★New Group Pure Tone Hearing Test. Grades 1 and over; 1952–58; procedure for testing 10 children using a group pure tone sweep check hearing test; any pure tone audiometer adapted to group testing may be used; directions for administering are presented in *1* below; [6–10] minutes; Philip W. Johnston; standardized instructions for administering ['58, 7 pages] available free of charge from Massachusetts Department of Public Health, Division of Maternal and Child Health. *

REFERENCES

1. JOHNSTON, PHILIP W. "An Efficient Group Screening Test." *J Speech & Hearing Disorders* 17:8–12 Mr '52. * (*PA* 26:7201)
2. DICARLO, LOUIS M., AND GARDNER, ERIC F. "A Comparative Study of the Efficiency of Three Group Pure Tone Screening Tests for Public School Children." *Excep Child* 24:351–9 Ap '58. * (*PA* 33:5383)
3. VENTRY, IRA M. *Evaluation of One- and Two-Frequency Audiometric Screening of School Children.* Doctor's thesis, Stanford University (Stanford, Calif.), 1958. (*DA* 19:2408)

[951]

★[Rush Hughes (PB 50): Phonetically Balanced Lists 5–12.] Grades 2 and over; 1951; auditory discrimination; 8 lists on two 12-inch (33⅓ rpm) records; no manual; no data on reliability; no norms; $6.75 per single record; $12.60 per set of records and mimeographed copy of word lists; postpaid; [4] minutes per list; [Central Institute for the Deaf]; [Technisonic Studios, Inc.]. *

REFERENCES

1. PALMER, JOHN M. "The Effect of Speaker Differences on the Intelligibility of Phonetically Balanced Word Lists." *J Speech & Hearing Disorders* 20:192–5 Je '55. * (*PA* 30:4494)
2. CAMPANELLI, PETER A. "A Measure of Intra-List Stability of Four PAL Word Lists." *J Auditory Res* 2:50–5 Ja '62. *
3. LYNN, GEORGE. "Paired PB-50 Discrimination Test: A Preliminary Report." *J Auditory Res* 2:34–6 Ja '62. *
4. ELLIOTT, LOIS L. "Prediction of Speech Discrimination Scores From Other Test Information." *J Auditory Res* 3:35–45 Ja '63. *
5. GIOLAS, THOMAS G., AND EPSTEIN, AUBREY. "Comparative Intelligibility of Word Lists and Continuous Discourse." *J Speech & Hearing Res* 6:349–58 D '63. *
6. WEINHOUSE, IRIS, AND MILLER, MAURICE H. "Discrimination Scores for Two Lists of Phonetically Balanced Words." *J Auditory Res* 3:9–14 Ja '63. *

[951a]

***Sonotone Pure-Tone Audiometers.** Ages 6 and over; 1941–63; individual; range in 5-db steps (air conduction): −20 to +100 decibels at 500 to 6,000 cps, −20 to +80 decibels at 250 and 8,000 cps, −20 to +70 decibels at 125 cps; range in 5-db steps (bone conduction, Model 91M only): −20 to +60 decibels at 500 to 6,000 cps, −20 to +40 decibels at 250 and 8,000 cps; 2 models (AC operated); mimeographed manual ['57, 12 pages]; audiogram ('41, 1 page); no data on reliability; $1 per set of 3 pads of 50 audiograms; postage extra; administration time not reported; Sonotone Corporation. *
a) DIAGNOSTIC AUDIOMETER. For pure tone air and bone conduction testing; Model 91M ['63, portable, modification of 1957 model]; $395 per instrument; standard equipment includes one set of air receivers, bone conduction receiver, complex noise generator, and calibrated masking.
b) SCREENING AUDIOMETER. For air conduction screening testing in schools and industry; Model 91D ['63, modification of 1957 model, same as Model 91M but without masking or receiver and accessories for bone conduction testing]; $350 per instrument.

[952]

★Stycar Hearing Tests. Normal and mentally retarded children of ages 6–14 months, 15–18 months, 19–24 months, 2, 3–4, 5–7; 1958–59; individual; 1 form (a series of toys, objects, pictures, and word-sentence lists divided into 6 levels); manual ('58, 15 pages); record blank ('59, 2 pages); no data on reliability; no norms; 50*s.* per set of testing materials, 25 record blanks, and manual; 9*s.* per 25 record blanks; 9*s.* per manual; prices include purchase tax; postpaid within U.K.; administration time not reported; Mary D. Sheridan; distributed by National Foundation for Educational Research in England and Wales. *

[953]

★Zenith Audiometers. Grades kgn and over; 1959–61; for use in schools, industry, clinics, and physicians' offices; 2 models; directions for basic hearing tests ['61, 7 pages]; audiogram ('59, 2 pages); no data on reliability; 75¢ per 25 audiograms; postage extra; administration time not reported; Zenith Hearing Aid Sales Corporation. *
a) ZENITH DIAGNOSTIC PORTABLE AUDIOMETER. 1961; for pure tone air and bone conduction testing; range in 5-db steps (air conduction): −10 to +65 decibels at 125 cps, −10 to +80 decibels at 250 and 8,000 cps, −10 to +100 decibels at all other frequencies; range in 5-db steps (bone conduction): −10 to +50 decibels at 250 through 4,000 cps; Model ZA-100-T (transistorized, battery operated portable unit); manual ['61, 12 pages]; $375 per instrument; standard equipment includes one set of double earphones, bone conduction receiver, complex noise generator, calibrated masking, and communication circuit; microphone and shoulder carrying strap available.
b) AUDIO ANALYZER. 1959; for pure tone air conduction, bone conduction, and live and recorded speech testing; range in 5-db steps (air conduction): −10 to +65 decibels at 125 cps, −10 to +80 decibels at 250 and 8,000 cps, −10 to +90 decibels at 6,000 cps, −10 to +100 decibels at all other frequencies; range in 5-db steps (bone conduction): −10 to +30 decibels at 125 cps, −10 to +40 decibels at 250 cps, −10 to +55 decibels at all other frequencies to 4,000 cps; Model ZA-200 (AC operated); manual ['59 36 pages]; $425 per instrument; standard equipment includes one set of double earphones, bone conduction receiver, noise generator, and calibrated masking; accessory equipment (including speech record playback unit, desk speaker, microphone, patient's signal cord, speech monitor, and equipment for two-room testing installation) also available.

For comments by Louis M. DiCarlo on screening audiometers in general and specific comments on Model ZA-100-T and three other portable audiometers, see 942.

[Other Tests]

For tests not listed above, see the following entries in *Tests in Print:* 1656 and 1662–3.

MOTOR

[Other Tests]

For tests not listed above, see the following entries in *Tests in Print:* 1669–76; out of print: 1668.

VISION

[954]

★The Atlantic City Eye Test. Grades 1 and over; 1953–61; individual; 1 form ('53); directions for administering ['61, 1 page]; no data on reliability; $95 per set of testing materials, postage extra; [1–5] minutes; Samuel M. Diskan; Freund Brothers. *

REFERENCES

1. DISKAN, SAMUEL M. "Eye Health Screening in Schools." *Med Times* 87:1311–6 O '59. *

[955]

***Dvorine Pseudo-Isochromatic Plates, Second Edition.** Ages 3 and over; 1944–58; revision of *Dvorine Color Perception Testing Charts;* also called *Dvorine Color Vision Test;* individual; 2 scores: nomenclature, color perception; 1 form ('53, 33 pages, manual and 24 color plates in 1 booklet); record form ('58, 1 page); no data on reliability presented in manual; $19.50 per set of testing materials; $1 per 35 record forms; postage extra; [3–5] minutes; Israel Dvorine; Harcourt, Brace & World, Inc. *

REFERENCES

1–4. See 3:462.
5–17. See 5:773.
18. PETERS, GEO. A., JR. "The New Dvorine Color Perception Test." *Optom Wkly* 45:1801–3 N 4 '54. * (*PA* 29:5123)
19. PETERS, GEORGE, JR. "Diagnostic Sensitivity of Color Perception Tests." *Optom Wkly* 46:136–7 Ja 27 '55. * (*PA* 29:5122)
20. SLOAN, LOUISE L., AND HABEL, ADELAIDE. "Tests for Color Deficiency Based on the Pseudoisochromatic Principle: A Comparative Study of Several New Tests." *A.M.A. Arch Ophthal* 55:229–39 F '56. * (*PA* 31:2292)
21. BELCHER, S. J.; GREENSHIELDS, K. W.; AND WRIGHT, W. D. "Colour Vision Survey Using the Ishihara, Dvorine, Boström and Kugelberg, Boström, and American-Optical Hardy-Rand-Rittler Tests." *Brit J Ophthal* 42:355–9 Je '58. *
22. LAKOWSKI, R. "Age and Colour Vision." *Advancement Sci* 15:231–6 D '58. *
23. HARVEY, JASPER ELLIOTT. *The Evaluation and Development of Techniques for Testing the Visual Acuity of Trainable Mentally Retarded Children.* Doctor's thesis, University of Texas (Austin, Tex.), 1960. (*DA* 20:4587)
24. WHITE, HELEN I., AND PRICE, A. COOPER. "Figure-Ground Confusion on a Test for Color Blindness as Related to Impairment on Perceptual Tests for Cortical Brain Damage." *Percept & Motor Skills* 11:131–6 O '60. * (*PA* 35:2528)
25. DVORINE, ISRAEL. "Color Naming and Color Matching in a Group of Color-Vision Defectives." *Optom Wkly* 52:1891–7, 1962–6 S 28, O 5 '61. *
26. DVORINE, ISRAEL. "What Is Color Blindness?" *Ed* 83:174–8 N '62. *
27. DVORINE, ISRAEL. "Quantitative Classification of the Color-Blind." *J General Psychol* 68:255–65 Ap '63. * (*PA* 38:180)
28. HARVEY, JASPER. "Evaluation and Development of Techniques for Testing Visual Acuity of Trainable Mentally Retarded Children." *Am J Optom* 40:745–54 D '63. *
29. WILSON, JOHN M., AND WOLFENSBERGER, WOLF. "Color-Blindness Testing as an Aid in the Etiological Diagnosis of Mental Retardation." *Am J Mental Def* 67:914–5 My '63. * (*PA* 38:1284)

See 5:773 (3 excerpts); for the original edition, see 3:462 (6 excerpts).

[956]

Eames Eye Test. Grades kgn-16 and adults; 1938–50; individual; 1 form (7 cards, '38, except near vision card, '50); revised manual ('50, 13 pages); no norms; $7 per set of testing materials; $1.50 per 35 record cards; postage extra; hand stereoscope necessary for administration; [10] minutes; Thomas H. Eames; [Harcourt, Brace & World, Inc.]. *

REFERENCES

1–5. See 3:463.
6–7. See 5:774.
8. EAMES, THOMAS H. "Eye Screening Test." *J Ed* 141:32–3 F '59. *

HELEN M. ROBINSON, *William S. Gray Research Professor of Reading, The University of Chicago, Chicago, Illinois.*

The *Eames Eye Test* is an inexpensive visual screening test, designed to be more effective than the Snellen Chart which has been used widely in schools to identify pupils who should be referred to an eye specialist for a complete examination.

The Eames test includes five subtests: Test 1, for visual acuity, intended to detect nearsightedness and related problems which interfere with clear distant seeing; Test 2, to detect farsightedness, using the same target as Test 1 with a plus 1.50 lens added; Test 3, for near visual acuity, to identify pupils with difficulties seeing at book and school desk distances; Test 4, for coordination, to determine whether the two eyes are likely to be directed toward the same target; and Test 5, for fusion, intended to determine whether each eye sees similar targets simultaneously. In the manual, the statement is made that all subtests are adaptations of standard ophthalmological tests. No information is available concerning differences which may be attributed to the adaptations.

Two optional or supplementary tests are provided: (*a*) an astigmatic chart on a card about 5½ by 8½ inches, including only the upper half of the conventional astigmatic chart; and (*b*) a test of eye preference, requiring the child, with arm fully extended, to look at the examiner from a distance of 10 feet through a ring formed by touching the index finger to the thumb. Studies of eye preference show that a single test is inadequate; furthermore, this test is contaminated by hand preference. Therefore, the supplementary preference test is not recommended, even as a screening device.

Finally, a list of 24 symptoms with which teachers should be familiar is given, with the recommendation that if any one is observed to continue for several days, the child should be referred to the school nurse.

In order to administer the battery of tests, a space of more than 20 feet is needed such that the targets may be hung at eye level in "good and even illumination," but not direct sunlight. In addition, a hand stereoscope must be borrowed or purchased and calibrated so that the targets for Tests 4 and 5 may be placed at a distance of 4½ inches from the front of the lenses.

In Tests 1–3, each eye is covered as the subject reads the six letters (or points in the direction of each *E*) exposed at 20 feet and also at reading distance. Both eyes are used for the coordination and fusion tests. Examination time is estimated at 10 minutes, but much less time is needed for some pupils, because whenever a pupil fails a subtest, no others are given. If there is one failure, the subject is referred for a professional eye examination, either through the school nurse or directly.

Under validity, the manual reports that in one study of 100 children the test gave 97 per cent agreement with the findings of an eye physician, based on a complete eye examination, of eye difficulties requiring corrective treatment. The reliability obtained by retesting the same 100 children is reported as 93 per cent agreement for the complete battery. However, the validity of four visual screening tests was studied by the reviewer, using 79 unselected school children about equally distributed in grades 1 through 8. Two professional eye examinations were made, and the chi-square statistic was used to determine the validity of the need for referral based on the total battery. The *Ortho-Rater,* the *Massachusetts Vision Test,* and the *Keystone Visual Survey Service* proved to be significantly valid while the *Eames Eye Test* did not. However, the 1940 edition of the latter was used, and it did not include a subtest for near acuity.

Instructions for administering and scoring the test are clearly written. However, considerable skill and care are required to calibrate the hand stereoscope and to be sure that distances and illumination are satisfactory. The 1950 edition includes a near acuity test. The directions for administering the supplementary test of astigmatism have changed in this edition so they are not suggestive of failing responses.

The Eames test is undoubtedly more effective than the Snellen Chart, which is often used in schools, because the Eames test identifies subjects who are farsighted and considers near acuity and the use of the two eyes together. Both farsightedness and binocular coordination have been shown repeatedly to differentiate good from poor readers, and, therefore, it is important to include them in a school visual screening battery. No comparisons of the validity of the revised Eames test with other screening batteries are available. The Eames test is not so widely used in schools as are the *Massachusetts Vision Test* and the *New York School Vision Tester.*

The space required for the Eames test is more than 20 feet, the same as the *Massachusetts Vision Test,* while the Keystone and the New York vision testers require approximately 4 square feet of space. Furthermore, variations in the amount of light on the targets of the Eames test may create some inconsistencies in results.

In spite of the possible inadequacies, the *Eames Eye Test* undoubtedly fulfills its stated purpose of being more discriminating than the Snellen Chart and of being particularly useful in identifying ocular difficulties of pupils having reading disability. However, its dependability has not been as fully studied or as clearly demonstrated as that of other tests mentioned earlier in this review.

For a review by Magdalen D. Vernon, see 5:774.

[957]

★Keystone Tests of Binocular Skill: An Adaptation of the Gray Oral Reading Check Tests for Use in the Keystone Telebinocular. Grades 1–2, 2–4, 4–6, 6 and over; 1938–49; based on *Standardized Oral Reading Check Tests;* 2 scores (time, errors) for monocular and binocular vision; individual; 1 form ['38, 4 stereograms for each grade level plus 4 preliminary stereograms for determining grade level]; 4 levels; manual ('49, 14 pages); record blank ('38, 1 page) for preliminary test and for each level; no data on reliability; tentative norms (same as those published in 1923 for the original Gray test); $60 per set of 20 stereograms, box of 500 record forms, and manual of all 4 levels; $15 per box of 500 record forms; specimen set not available; postage extra; [10–15] minutes; Keystone View Co. *

REFERENCES

1. ROBINSON, HELEN M. "Factors Related to Monocular and Binocular Reading Efficiency." *Am J Optom* 28:337–46 Jl '51. * (*PA* 26:2977)

[958]

New York School Vision Tester. Grades kgn and over; 1957; title on manual is *School Vision Tester;* individual; 1 form; manual ['57, 17 pages]; no data on reliability; $250 per set of testing materials; copy of manual supplied free; postage extra; (1–4) minutes; Bausch & Lomb Inc. *

REFERENCES

1. SULZMAN, JOHN H., AND DAVIS, C. JANE. "The New York School Vision Tester." *N Y State J Med* 58:833–7 Mr 15 '58. *
2. GENTILE, JAMES F., AND JOHNSTON, PHILIP W. "A Comparison of Two School Vision Screening Tests." *Am J Ophthal* 52:511–5 O '61. *

HELEN M. ROBINSON, *William S. Gray Research Professor of Reading, The University of Chicago, Chicago, Illinois.*

The *New York School Vision Tester* is an adaptation of the *Ortho-Rater,* differing only in the slides accompanying the instrument. It is also known as the *School Vision Tester,* as shown by the manual accompanying the slides. Both the instrument and slides were designed especially for children of school age. The instrument is based on the stereoscopic principle. Each eye may be tested individually while the other is covered. However, both may be used simultaneously with appropriate slides. Furthermore, there is an attachment into which lenses may be inserted for screening farsightedness. The slides automatically turn on the constant light when they are pushed into the proper apertures.

The three slides include: (*a*) an acuity or keenness of vision slide with targets for the right and left eyes, using the *E* pointing in different directions and measuring levels from 20/200 to 20/20; (*b*) a slide for phoria, or relative posture of the eyes, at distance, combining vertical and lateral tolerances, using a picture of a boy throwing a ball to his dog as a target; and (*c*) a similar phoria slide for near, or reading distance. Plus 1.75 diopter lenses may be slipped onto the instrument easily. A card to demonstrate the use of the *E* and an answer key accompany the test. All materials may be conveniently stored in the lower part of the instrument.

The three foregoing slides have been developed to reproduce the results obtained by the *Massachusetts Vision Test,* according to Sulzman and Davis (*1*). An additional acuity test uses the *Ortho-Rater* checkerboard acuity targets, shown by previous studies to be dependable both with children and adults.

The space required for testing is approximately 4 square feet, in contrast to more than 20 feet needed for the Snellen Chart and similar tests. The lighting is controlled and constant. Only strong glaring light which would reflect on the lens of the instrument or in the pupil's eyes must be avoided. Average testing time is estimated at less than 2 minutes per pupil.

The first test is for acuity of the right eye at the optical equivalent of 20 feet. It uses the first slide with the occluder, or mask, in front of the left eye. The second test is for acuity of the left eye and requires only the turning of the occluder because the targets are on the first slide. The third and fourth tests also use the same slide, but lenses are placed in the instrument to identify a substantial amount of farsightedness in either eye. The fifth test, also at far distance, is a gross estimate of phoria, or the ability of the eyes to be directed toward the same target. If the ball is inside the picture, the pupil shows less than 6 prism diopters of esophoria (eyes tending to turn inward), less than 4 prism diopters of exophoria (eyes tending to turn outward), and less than 1½ diopters of vertical phoria (one eye tending to turn above the other). The sixth test is similar to the fifth, except that it indicates the coordination of the two eyes at the optical distance of 13 inches.

The manual gives clear directions for the administration of the test and specifies the passing and failing norms. A section of the manual deals with problems in the use of the instrument and slides, offering suggestions to avoid technical errors. This section closes with the suggestion that children who fail any of the tests should be retested. The reviewer recommends this procedure, especially with children in third grade or below that level. There is no discussion of referral procedures. Neither validity nor reliability data are supplied in the manual.

Only one study (*1*) of the *New York Vision Tester* was located. In grades 1, 3, 5, and 7, 102 children were given this test and the *Massachusetts Vision Test.* The authors report that there was complete agreement of the two instruments on referral. Presumably, this study is expected to establish the validity of the *New York Vision Tester,* and does so to the extent that the *Massachusetts Vision Test* is valid. However, the study gives no evidence of the reliability of the test battery, except for comments on several individual pupils. The article closes with the statement that additional slides may be purchased for use in the instrument. Attention is called to the fact that these tests would be expected to locate a larger number of the children in need of eye care but would also increase over-referrals. For general visual screening, this may be a valid argument for using the limited number of slides, but for retarded readers, it is more important to identify as many as possible in need of visual examination than to be concerned about referring some who do not need such care.

No near acuity test is provided, as in the *Eames Eye Test* and the *Keystone Visual Survey Service*. For some children, especially retarded readers, a near acuity test should be included. In a study by the reviewer,[1] coefficients of correlation between far and near acuity for children at grades 4 and 7 ranged from .29 to .52, using the *Ortho-Rater* with the checkerboard targets. Thus, the omission of a near acuity test may increase the agreement with the Massachusetts test while, at the same time, it omits a target of considerable value to schools.

For wide use as a visual screening test for large numbers of school children, the *New York Vision Tester* is undoubtedly better than the Snellen Chart and as good as the *Massachusetts Vision Test*. Furthermore, it can be administered in a smaller space, with better control of light, and in a shorter time. However, no data are available concerning the reliability of the test or its validity compared to professional eye examinations. The test can be recommended only with these two limitations.

[959]

Spache Binocular Reading Test. Nonreaders and grade 1, grades 1.5–2, grades 3 and over; 1943–55; eye preference in reading; individual; 1 form; 3 levels; manual ('55, 13 pages); record blank ('55, 2 pages); $12 per set of 4 stereographs and manual; $15 per box of 500 record forms; postage extra; specimen set not available; stereoscope necessary for administration; [2–4] minutes; George D. Spache; Keystone View Co. *

a) TEST 1. Nonreaders and grade 1; 1 form ('55, 1 card).

b) TEST 2, MY BIG RED CAR. Grades 1.5–2; 1 form ('55, 1 card).

c) TEST 3, THE QUEEN. Grades 3 and over; 1 form ('43, 2 cards).

REFERENCES

1–4. See 3:461.
5–8. See 5:784.

HELEN M. ROBINSON, *William S. Gray Research Professor of Reading, The University of Chicago, Chicago, Illinois.*

This ingenious test consists of a story mounted on each of four stereoscopic cards. On Test 1, which the examiner reads to nonreaders, 10 pictures appear before the left eye, with blanks in corresponding positions before the right eye; a similar target is available for the right eye only. Test 2, for grades 1.5–2, has 10 words appearing before the left eye only and 10 others before the right eye only. The words are selected in such a way that the story makes good sense with or without the key words before either eye. Test 3, for grade 3 and above, is arranged like Test 2, but consists of two stereoscopic cards and has 20 words presented to each eye alone. All tests must be used in a stereoscope.

The purpose of the test is to detect the extent to which each eye functions when both eyes are being used in reading. In most instances, all pictures or words before each eye are reported. Occasionally, a few words are omitted by chance, but omission of a substantial number or all of the words is a symptom of a vision problem. Three major types of vision problems may be revealed: (*a*) difficulties in which the two eyes do not work together, such as vertical or lateral imbalance, squint, or fusional problems; (*b*) conditions in which there is complete or partial suppression, or lack of use of one eye; and (*c*) considerable differences in acuity in the two eyes. While this test is not diagnostic of these problems, the results provide a basis for the recommendation of a professional visual examination.

Validity is illustrated by case studies in which binocular incoordination or differences in acuity are demonstrated on other tests as well as on this one. No coefficients were calculated, nor is there a report of validation against professional findings for a group of unselected pupils. The reliability of the tests, based on correlation coefficients between scores on Tests 2 and 3, is .98 for the right eye and .77 for the left. Reliability and validity data are not reported for Test 1. Test-retest data, based on 10 pupils at each of the first eight grades tested by the reviewer, revealed a coefficient of .85, which is satisfactory.

The manual is clearly and simply written. The interpretation of the results is carefully done, with specific suggestions concerning referral to vision specialists. The responsibility of school personnel is clearly stated.

The manual shows the picture of the *Key-*

1 ROBINSON, HELEN M. "An Analysis of Four Visual Screening Tests at Grades Four and Seven." *Am J Optom* 30:177–87 Ap '53. *

stone Telebinocular as the proper instrument for use of the *Spache Binocular Reading Test.* However, information obtained from the publisher indicates that the standard ophthalmic stereoscope used with the Spache test is a hand stereoscope. The possibility of using the test with a relatively inexpensive instrument, rather than as an adjunct to the *Keystone Telebinocular,* enhances its value to schools.

The *Spache Binocular Reading Test* is unique; it has been shown to be useful to those who are concerned with school vision problems generally and especially with reading problems.

For a review by Albert J. Harris of Test 3, *see 3:461.*

[960]

★Stycar Vision Test. Normal and handicapped children of ages 3–5, 5–7; 1958–60; individual; 1 form ('58); 2 levels (10 miniature toys, near test, and single letter cards for ages 3–5, 9-letter chart and key card for ages 5–7); manual ('60, 10 pages); no data on reliability; 74*s.* per manual and set of testing materials for both levels; 7*s.* per manual; prices include purchase tax; postpaid within U.K.; administration time not reported; Mary D. Sheridan; distributed by National Foundation for Educational Research in England and Wales. *

[961]

★T/O Vision Testers. Ages 3–5 and retarded children, grades 1–6, grades 7–12 and adults, drivers; 1958–62; individual; 4 models (essentially the same except for slight modifications and test slides included in testing sets); test slides may be used on all models; no data on reliability; $25 to $27.50 per carrying case; postpaid; Titmus Optical Co. *

a) T/O PEDIATRIC MODEL VISION TESTER. Ages 3–5 and retarded children; 1960–62; Model OV7-P ['62]; 3 tests ['62, 3 slides]: acuity, vertical and lateral phoria (near, far), plus *Michigan Pre-School T/O Vision Tests* ['60, acuity, 2 editions of 4 slides each: 20/30 unit, 20/40 unit]; no specific manual (manual for *b* or *c* below is used); directions for preschool tests ['60, 2 pages]; record form ['62, 1 page]; preliminary training cards must be used with preschool tests; $312 per set of testing materials including 2 pads of 50 record forms and 10 sets of training cards; (5) minutes.

b) T/O SCHOOL VISION TESTER. Grades 1–6; 1958; Model OV7-S ['58]; 6 tests ['58, 3 slides, adaptation of *Massachusetts Vision Test*]: acuity (4 tests), vertical and lateral balance (far, near); manual ('58, 18 pages); $285 per set of tester and accessories; $245 per tester without accessories; (2) minutes.

c) [T/O PROFESSIONAL AND INDUSTRIAL VISION TESTER.] Grades 7–12 and adults; 1958–59; Models OV7-A, OV7-M ['58, identical except that test slides are rotated manually on OV7-M and either electrically or manually on OV7-A]; 11 tests ['58, 11 slides plus demonstration slide]: acuity (3 near tests, 3 far tests), stereopsis, color discrimination, vertical phoria, lateral phoria (near, far); manual ('59, 20 pages); job standards booklet ('59, 20 pages); record form ['58, 1 page]; tester with accessories: $492 for Model OV7-A, $395 for Model OV7-M; tester without accessories: $342 for Model OV7-A, $245 for Model OV7-M; (5) minutes.

d) T/O VISION TESTER: DRIVER ED MODEL. Driver education classes and applicants for licenses; 1 model ['62]; 7 tests ['62, 7 slides]: literacy, color discrimination, sign recognition and depth, Landolt ring acuity, Sloan letter acuity, color identification, combined acuity; instructions ['62, 5 pages]; $312 per set of tester and accessories; (2) minutes.

REFERENCES

1. SCHRIER, MELVIN. "Freshman Visual Screening Program at Columbia University." *Am J Optom* 37:245–53 My '60. *

[962]

★Test for Colour-Blindness. Ages 6 and over; 1917–64; congenital color vision deficiency; 4 editions (dates reported are probably printing dates): 38-plate complete edition ['64], 24-plate abbreviated edition ['64], 14-plate edition ['62], 12-plate edition for infants, ['63]; instructions (6–10 pages) for each edition; no data on reliability; $33 (105*s.*) per 38-plate edition, $22 (84*s.*) per 24-plate edition, $15.50 per 14-plate edition, $15 per 12-plate edition; postage extra; 3 seconds per plate used; Shinobu Ishihara; Kanehara Shuppan Co., Ltd.; United States distributor: Graham-Field Surgical Co., Inc. * (British distributor: H. K. Lewis & Co. Ltd.; Canadian distributor: Radionics Ltd.)

REFERENCES

1. CLARK, JANET H. "The Ishihara Test for Color Blindness." *Am J Physiol Optics* 5:269–76 Jl '24. *
2. HAUPT, ISTAR. "The Nela Test for Color Blindness Applied to School Children." *J Comp Psychol* 6:291–302 Ag '26. * (*PA* 1:536)
3. MILES, WALTER. "One Hundred Cases of Color-Blindness Detected With the Ishihara Test." *J General Psychol* 2:535–43 O '29. * (*PA* 4:986)
4. TERMAN, SIBYL WALCUTT. "A New Classification of the Red-Green Color-Blind." *Am J Psychol* 41:237–51 Ap '29. *
5. WOELFEL, FLORENCE. "An Adaptation of the Ishihara Color Test for Use With Children of Pre-School Age." *Child Develop* 1:144–51 Je '30. * (*PA* 4:4517)
6. JENNINGS, J. ELLIS. "Evaluation of Pseudo-Isochromatic Tests for the Detection of Color Blindness." *Am J Ophthal* 14:952–8 S '31. * (*PA* 6:4671)
7. MURRAY, ELSIE. "The Ishihara Test for Color-Blindness: A Point in Ethics." *Am J Psychol* 47:511–3 Jl '35. * (*PA* 10:24)
8. PHILIP, B. R. "A Comparison of Color-Blind Tests." *Am J Psychol* 51:482–8 Jl '38. * (*PA* 12:5785)
9. HARRIMAN, PHILIP LAWRENCE. "Hypnotic Induction of Color Vision Anomalies: 1, The Use of the Ishihara and the Jensen Tests to Verify the Acceptance of Suggested Color Blindness." *J General Psychol* 26:289–98 Ap '42. * (*PA* 16:4005)
10. LOKEN, ROBERT D. *The Nela Test of Color Vision.* Comparative Psychology Monographs, Vol. 17, No. 6, Serial No. 90. Berkeley, Calif.: University of California Press, September 1942. Pp. ii, 37. * (*PA* 17:50)
11. MURRAY, ELSIE. "Congenital and Acquired Deficiencies of Color Vision: A Protest." *Am J Psychol* 55:573–6 O '42. * (*PA* 17:1483)
12. MILES, W. R. "Color Blindness in Eleven Thousand Museum Visitors." *Yale J Biol Med* 16:59–76 O '43. * (*PA* 18:3400)
13. THOMAS, GARTH J. "Visual Sensitivity to Color: A Comparative Study of Four Tests." *Am J Psychol* 56:583–91 O '43. * (*PA* 18:422)
14. BACKENSTOE, G. S. "Preliminary Survey on the Color-Vision Plates of Shinobu Ishihara." *J Aviat Med* 15:272–8 Ag '44. * (*PA* 19:52)
15. HARRIS, ROBERT H. "Comparison of the Ishihara and the American Optical Company Series of Pseudoisochromatic Plates." *Arch Ophthal* 31:163–4 F '44. * (*PA* 18:2379)
16. PICKFORD, R. W. "The Ishihara Test for Colour Blindness." Letter. *Nature* 153:656–7 My 27 '44. * (*PA* 19:1635)
17. GRIEVE, JOHN. "Ishihara Test of Colour Vision." Letter. *Lancet* 248:480 Ap 14 '45. * (*PA* 19:2867)
18. HARDY, LEGRAND H.; RAND, GERTRUDE; AND RITTLER, M. CATHERINE. "Tests for the Detection and Analysis of Color-Blindness." *J Opt Soc Am* 35:268–75 Ap '45. * (*PA* 19:3281)
19. HARDY, LEGRAND H.; RAND, GERTRUDE; AND RITTLER, M. CATHERINE. "Tests for Detection and Analysis of Color

Blindness: 1, An Evaluation of the Ishihara Test." *Arch Ophthal* 34:295–302 O '45. * (*PA* 20:1399)
20. HARDY, LEGRAND H.; RAND, GERTRUDE; AND RITTLER, M. CATHERINE. "Tests for the Detection and Analysis of Color-Blindness: 2, The Ishihara Test: Comparison of Editions." *J Opt Soc Am* 35:351–6 My '45. * (*PA* 20:60)
21. FOSTER, HARRIET. "A Comparative Study of Three Tests for Color Vision." *J Appl Psychol* 30:135–43 Ap '46. * (*PA* 20:3028)
22. HARDY, LEGRAND H.; RAND, GERTRUDE; AND RITTLER, M. CATHERINE. "The Effect of Quality of Illumination on the Results of the Ishihara Test." *J Opt Soc Am* 36:86–94 F '46. * (*PA* 20:3037)
23. HARDY, LEGRAND H.; RAND, GERTRUDE; AND RITTLER, M. CATHERINE. "Tests for Detection and Analysis of Color Blindness: 2, Comparison of Editions of the Ishihara Test." *Arch Ophthal* 35:109–19 F '46. * (PA 20:2644)
24. OXLADE, M. "An Experiment in the Use of Psychological Tests in the Selection of Women Trainee Telephone Mechanics." *B Ind Psychol & Personnel Prac* 2:26–32 Mr '46. * (*PA* 20:4838)
25. BOICE, MARY LOU. *The Relationship of Color Vision to Age in Members of the Academic Faculty of the University of Minnesota.* Master's thesis, University of Minnesota (Minneapolis, Minn.), 1947.
26. HARDY, LEGRAND H.; RAND, GERTRUDE; AND RITTLER, M. CATHERINE. "The Ishihara Test as a Means of Detecting and Analyzing Defective Color Vision." *J General Psychol* 36:79–106 Ja '47. * (*PA* 21:4263)
27. JURGENSEN, CLIFFORD E. "Industrial Use of the Ishihara Tests for Color Blindness." *J Appl Psychol* 31:1–8 F '47. * (*PA* 21:2429)
28. NEUBERT, FRANK R. "Colour Vision in the Consulting Room." *Brit J Ophthal* 31:275–88 My '47. * (*PA* 21:2902)
29. VAN DEN AKKER, J. A.; TODD, J. EDWARD; NOLAN, PHILIP; AND WINK, WILLMER A. "Use of a Monochromatic Colorimeter for the Study of Color Blindness." *J Opt Soc Am* 37:363–87 My '47. * (*PA* 21:2909)
30. VOLK, DAVID, AND FRY, GLENN A. "Effect of Quality of Illumination and Distance of Observation Upon Performance in the Ishihara Test." *Am J Optom* 24:99–122 Mr '47. * (*PA* 21:3434)
31. BOICE, MARY L.; TINKER, MILES A.; AND PATERSON, DONALD G. "Color Vision and Age." *Am J Psychol* 61:520–6 O '48. * (*PA* 23:4053)
32. CHAPANIS, ALPHONSE. "A Comparative Study of Five Tests of Color Vision." *J Opt Soc Am* 38:626–49 Jl '48. * (*PA* 23:530)
33. HARDY, LEGRAND H.; RAND, GERTRUDE; AND RITTLER, M. CATHERINE. "Incidence of Color-Blindness Among Psychotic Subjects." *J General Psychol* 39:229–42 O '48. * (*PA* 23:2801)
34. MURRAY, ELSIE. "Mass-Testing of Color Vision: A Simplified and Accelerated Technique." *Am J Psychol* 61:370–85 Jl '48. * (*PA* 23:2104)
35. CHAPANIS, ALPHONSE. "Diagnosing Types of Color Deficiency by Means of Pseudo-Isochromatic Tests." *J Opt Soc Am* 39:242–9 Mr '49. * (*PA* 24:60)
36. PICKFORD, R. W. "A Study of the Ishihara Test for Colour Blindness." *Brit J Psychol* 40:71–80 D '49. * (*PA* 24:5686)
37. CHAPANIS, ALPHONSE. "Relationships Between Age, Visual Acuity and Color Vision." *Hum Biol* 22:1–33 F '50. * (*PA* 24:5045)
38. CRAWFORD, A. "The Ishihara Test and the Frequency of Colour Weakness." Abstract. *Adv Sci* 7:96 My '50. *
39. PICKFORD, R. W. "An Item-Analysis of the Ishihara Test." *Brit J Psychol* 41:52–62 S '50. * (*PA* 25:3634)
40. PICKFORD, R. W. "The Validity of the Ishihara Test for Colour Blindness." Abstract. *Adv Sci* 7:96 My '50. *
41. KEPHART, NEWELL C., AND TIESZEN, MELVIN J. "Ortho-Rater Color Vision Test Compared With the Ishihara and the Pseudo-Isochromatic Plates." *J Appl Psychol* 35:127–9 Ap '51. * (*PA* 25:7862)
42. MACLATCHY, R. S. "Colour Vision Testing." *Trans Ophthal Soc U K* 71:623–9 '51. * (*PA* 27:1717)
43. PICKFORD, R. W. *Individual Differences in Colour Vision,* pp. 103–8, 195–7, 300–3, 339–44, passim. New York: Macmillan Co., 1951. Pp. xviii, 386. * (*PA* 27:4016)
44. CAVANAGH, PETER. "The Ishihara Test and Defects of Colour Vision." *Occup Psychol* 29:43–57 Ja '55. * (*PA* 30:2122)
45. SLOAN, LOUISE L., and HABEL, ADELAIDE. "Tests for Color Deficiency Based on the Pseudoisochromatic Principle: A Comparative Study of Several New Tests." *A.M.A. Arch Ophthal* 55:229–39 F '56. * (*PA* 31:2292)
46. O'CONNOR, N. "Imbecility and Color Blindness." *Am J Mental Def* 62:83–7 Jl '57. *
47. BELCHER, S. J.; GREENSHIELDS, K. W.; AND WRIGHT, W. D. "Colour Vision Survey Using the Ishihara, Dvorine, Boström and Kugelberg, Boström, and American-Optical Hardy-Rand-Rittler Tests." *Brit J Ophthal* 42:355–9 Je '58. *
48. LAKOWSKI, R. "Age and Colour Vision." *Adv Sci* 15:231–6 D '58. *
49. BUSHNELL, R. J. "Ishihara Test." *Psychometric Res B* (6):[15–7] su '60. *
50. DAS, RHEA S. "Efficiency of the Ishihara Plates in Distinguishing Defects of Colour Vision." *J Psychol Res* 4:1–13 Ja '60. *
51. NAKAJIMA, AKIRA; ICHIKAWA, HIROSHI; NAKAGAWA, OSAMU; MAJIMA, AKIO; AND WATANABE, MASANOBU. "Ishihara Test in Color-Vision Defects: Studies on a Statistical Method for Evaluation of the Screening Efficiency of Several Plates." *Am J Ophthal* 49:921–9 My '60. *
52. CRONE, R. A. "Quantitative Diagnosis of Defective Color Vision: A Comparative Evaluation of the Ishihara Test, the Farnsworth Dichotomous Test and the Hardy-Rand-Rittler Polychromatic Plates." *Am J Ophthal* 51:298–305 F '61. *
53. DVORINE, ISRAEL. "Color Naming and Color Matching in a Group of Color-Vision Defectives." *Optom Wkly* 52:1891–7, 1962–6 S 28, O 5 '61. *
54. SLOAN, LOUISE L. "Efficiency of the Ishihara Test." Reply by Akira Nakajima. Letters. *Am J Ophthal* 51:340–2 F '61. *
55. ROSNER, ROBERT S. "Self-Testing Device for Screening Color Vision." *Am J Ophthal* 54:139–40 Jl '62. *
56. DRONAMRAJU, K. R. "Frequency of Colour Blindness in Orissa." *Ann Hum Genetics* 26:315–9 Je '63. * (*PA* 38:1782)
57. DRONAMRAJU, K. R. "Reading of Ishihara (1959) Plates 14 and 15: A New X-Linked Recessive Colour Vision Anomaly?" *Ann Hum Genetics* 27:113–7 N '63. * (*PA* 38:7156)
58. SLOAN, LOUISE L. "Testing for Deficient Color Perception in Children," pp. 697–705. In *Diagnostic Procedures in Pediatric Ophthalmology.* International Ophthalmology Clinics, Vol. 3, No. 4. Edited by Leonard Apt. Boston, Mass.: Little, Brown & Co. (Inc.), December 1963. Pp. xv, 697–1051. *

[Other Tests]

For tests not listed above, see the following entries in *Tests in Print:* 1677–8, 1680–1, 1683, 1686–92, 1694–5, 1698, and 1705; out of print: 1679, 1682, 1696, and 1704.

SOCIAL STUDIES

REVIEWS BY *Howard R. Anderson, Harry D. Berg, William C. Bingham, Henry Chauncey, Richard E. Gross, John H. Haefner, David K. Heenan, Christine McGuire, Jonathon C. McLendon, Donald W. Oliver, Robert J. Solomon, Morey J. Wantman, and J. Richard Wilmeth.*

[963]

***American School Achievement Tests: Part 4, Social Studies and Science.** Grades 4–6, 7–9; 1941–63; 2 scores: social studies, science; Forms D ('57), E ('57), F ('57), G ('58), (2 sheets); 2 levels; $3 per 35 self-marking tests; 50¢ per specimen set of either level; postage extra; 50(60) minutes; Willis E. Pratt, Robert V. Young (manuals), and Clara E. Cockerille; Bobbs-Merrill Co., Inc. *

a) INTERMEDIATE BATTERY. Grades 4–6; battery manual ('61, 17 pages).

b) ADVANCED BATTERY. Grades 7–9; battery manual ('63, 17 pages).

For reviews of the complete battery, see 2, 5:1, 4:1, and 3:1.

[964]

★Christian Democracy Test (Civics, Sociology, Economics): Affiliation Testing Program for Catholic Secondary Schools. Grades 9–12 and students who are candidates for the high school diploma issued by the Catholic University of America; 1949–63; administered annually in May at individual schools; IBM; Form Z ('63, 16 pages) used in 1963 program; tests loaned only; separate answer sheets must be used; 50¢ per test and IBM answer sheet; postpaid; fee includes scoring and other services; specimen set of the complete battery free; for more complete information, see 758; 90(100) minutes; Program of Affiliation, Catholic University of America. *

HENRY CHAUNCEY, *President, Educational Testing Service, Princeton, New Jersey.* [Review of Forms Y and Z.]

In the booklet describing the Program of Affiliation, it is stated that each ATP examination in social studies "seeks to measure the achievement of the student not only in the actual course content....but in the application of such content to special assignments in current events classes." If this purpose were achieved in the Christian Democracy Test, it might well represent a significant step forward in social studies tests. However, a review of these two test forms indicates that, although current situations provide the context or vehicle for the posing of many questions, the questions typically do not require the application of social science knowledge to understand, explain, or interpret current phenomena. Questions dealing with a current situation usually require the student to recall some fact about the situation. The following question is illustrative (Form Y, item 2): "If you are considering buying a home, you need to know about how the . . . operates. 1. PHA 2. FHA 3. HOLC 4. FDIC 5. FRS."

The major criticism that can be made of the Christian Democracy Test pertains to the superficiality of the knowledge required to deal with most of the questions; that is, it appears to the writer that most of the questions can be answered on the basis of a rote association between name and name, or name and object, or name and idea. However, it should be mentioned that some promising item types dealing with relationships among ideas, and between ideas and situations, are present in each of the two forms. These more significant item types comprise approximately one fourth of the test in each case.

A second criticism of the Christian Democracy Test refers to the mechanics of test construction; that is, it is generally considered desirable in writing the question to state the task required of the student in the item stem. If the student is required to formulate the item task on the basis of some relationship between the item stem and the options, then the probability of ambiguity or obscurity is increased. It is readily apparent that most of the item stems in this test are incomplete. Furthermore, it is also considered good practice in test construction to provide item options with parallel construction. In this fashion irrelevant syntactical and structural cues are more easily avoided. Forms X and Y of this test include far too many irrelevant cues of this kind.

In summary, due to the particular turn of many of its questions, the Christian Democracy Test is inappropriate for general school programs emphasizing democratic principles. This review raises the question whether, in the light of observed substantive and measurement gaps, the test adequately measures many objectives postulated for the Affiliation Testing Program.

For a review of the complete program, see 758.

[965]

★Citizenship: Every Pupil Scholarship Test. Grades 8–9; 1951–57; 2 forms: April '56, January '57, (2 pages); general directions sheet ['63, 2 pages]; no data on reliability; 4¢ per test; 4¢ per key; postage extra; 30(35) minutes; Bureau of Educational Measurements. *

[966]

***College Entrance Examination Board Achievement Test: American History and Social Studies.** Candidates for college entrance; 1901–64; this test and the test in European history and world cultures (see 967) replace the single test in social studies which was offered from 1937 to 1962; for more complete information, see 760; 60(80) minutes; program administered for the College Entrance Examination Board by Educational Testing Service. *

HOWARD R. ANDERSON, *Senior Consulting Editor, High School Department, Houghton Mifflin Company, Boston, Massachusetts.* [Review of Forms KAC and LAC1.]

The test is one of 15 in the regular series of subject matter achievement tests offered by the College Entrance Examination Board. Another test in this series concerns itself with European history and world cultures. From 1937 until these two tests were developed, the series included only a single test in the field of social studies—the test called Social Studies. For a review by Ralph W. Tyler of Form FAC of that examination, see 5:786. The major emphasis in the earlier test was on United States history.

The important change made in the CEEB program is of major interest to school administrators and social studies teachers. The new test on European history and world cultures gives recognition to the fact that a growing number of high school students are taking substantial courses in this broad field. Because many students tend to take CEEB tests earlier in their high school program than was the case formerly, many of them may prefer to take the new examination on non-American history. The fact that two examinations are being provided in the field of social studies has made it possible to test more adequately a broader sample of important concepts and skills in the current test on American history and social studies.

The scope of the new test is suggested by the relative emphasis given the six content areas identified by the CEEB American History and Social Studies Committee: (*a*) political institutions, principles, history (35 per cent), (*b*) economic principles and developments (20 per cent), (*c*) foreign affairs (20 per cent), (*d*) social movements (15 per cent), (*e*) cultural-intellectual developments (5 per cent), and (*f*) geography (5 per cent). About one fifth of the 100 items are based on knowledge derived from government, economics, sociology, and geography. However, a student who has had no formal courses in these subjects but has completed a good course in American history should be able to cope with these non-history items.

The current test places major emphasis on the ability to understand and use what has been learned, rather than on the recall of odds and ends of information.

The goal the Examination Committee set itself was to prepare an examination in which about one third of the items test perception of relationships (causal, chronological, means-ends, trends, historical continuity and change, attitudes-action situations); judgments of most or least appropriate options; and applications. About another third of the test items call for the interpretation of written materials.

The test is well edited. The Test Analysis for December 1962 Achievement Examinations reports for Form KAC a mean of 49.82 and a reliability of .91. This publication also makes the point that "The configuration of entries in the two-way table has the characteristics of a power test, as distinguished from a speeded one." In other words, this test is well suited to the group which takes it.

A reviewer who has taught history to both high school students and college freshmen may question that even the present CEEB test adequately samples important concepts and skills taught at the lower level and expected to be part of the preparation of college students. But it is hard to see how test builders can do more in a one-hour objective type examination. If the present test accurately identifies students who have received good high school preparation in American history and related social studies and who are likely to do well in college social science courses, the test is indeed performing a very useful service.

For a review by Ralph W. Tyler of an earlier form of the social studies test, see 5:786; for a review by Robert L. Thorndike, see 4:662. For reviews of the testing program, see 760.

[967]

***College Entrance Examination Board Achievement Test: European History and World Cultures.** Candidates for college entrance; 1901–64; available only in January and May testing programs; this test and the test in American history and social studies (see 966) replace the single test in social studies which was offered from 1937 to 1962; for more complete information, see 760; 60(80) minutes; program administered for the College Entrance Examination Board by Educational Testing Service. *

DAVID K. HEENAN, *Associate Professor, Office of Evaluation Services, Michigan State University, East Lansing, Michigan.* [Review of Forms LAC1 and LAC2.]

This test in European history and world cultures is a new addition to the College Board series of achievement tests. This is one of two new instruments—the other is American History and Social Studies—which were developed to replace the single test in social studies and which became available in January 1963.

The test consists of 100 items and has a time limitation of one hour. The test covers the material well; its items are searching and should discriminate well. Since there are no statistics available at the moment, one can only judge by appearances.

This examination is an improvement over its predecessor and most of the weaknesses of the old social studies test (see 5:786) have been eliminated. Although the student's knowledge is still tested by sampling from a large body of information, it appears that greater attention has been given to covering the most important objectives in the teaching of world history and related fields. While the content of the examination is history-oriented, it is not enough for a student merely to have a good background in historical details, for the test incorporates material outside the scope of traditional history courses, i.e., the content and objectives found in humanities or world culture courses now being offered in many secondary schools. The items which would be classified as belonging to "related fields"—e.g., religious beliefs, philosophical concepts, aesthetics, etc.—do not dominate the test but are sufficient in number to give a student who has read widely a better opportunity to score well on the examination. It is unlikely that most high school students would have read all the works which provide the substance of the "culture items," and one could reasonably expect a wide range of scores. This is not a criticism of the test—it is to be expected that few, if any, students will be able to answer all the questions correctly. The questions on art styles and techniques require only superficial knowledge, but the items dealing with religious beliefs and philosophical systems appear to be more penetrating.

Some attention is given to non-European history and non-European cultures. This is an important addition to the test and is in line with the recent change of opinion as to what constitutes world history. In the past the content of most world history courses centered on the development of the Western world; now textbooks and teachers attempt to cover, at least in general terms, Russia, Africa, India, China, Japan, and the Islamic civilization.

The primary emphasis is on the time period from 1500 to the present, but there are enough questions on ancient and medieval history to make it difficult for a student to score well unless he has some information about man and his world prior to the modern period.

The test is well edited and there is an unusually small number of items which need to be altered for clarity or accuracy. While most multiple choice items are founded on recall of knowledge, other skills are demanded of the student. There is a good balance of items which involve judgment, interpretation and identification of ideas, recognition of cause and effect relationships, analysis of trends, and the like.

In summary, this is a good test. The committee responsible for determining its content and form has done a fine job. This test provides an excellent guidepost for the kinds of objectives that should be stressed in the teaching of world history in the secondary schools.

For a review by Ralph W. Tyler of an earlier form of the social studies test, see 5:786; for a review by Robert L. Thorndike, see 4:662. For reviews of the testing program, see 760.

[968]

Cooperative General Achievement Tests: Test 1, Social Studies. Grades 9–12 and college entrants; 1937–56; formerly called *A Test of General Proficiency in the Field of Social Studies;* IBM; Forms XX ('53, c1947–53, 8 pages, revision of Form X), YZ ('55, c1948–51, 8 pages, revision of Forms Y and Z, identical with test copyrighted in 1951); battery manual ('56, 16 pages); high school norms same as those published in 1938; separate answer sheets must be used; $4 per 25 tests; $1 per 25 IBM answer sheets; 25¢ per scoring stencil; postage extra; $1 per specimen set, cash orders postpaid; 40(50) minutes; Jeanne M. Bradford (XX) and [Elaine Forsyth Cook]; Cooperative Test Division. *

For a review by Harry D. Berg of earlier forms, see 3:596. For reviews of the complete battery, see 7, 5:6, 4:5, and 3:3.

[969]

***The Iowa Tests of Educational Development: Test 1, Understanding of Basic Social Concepts.** Grades 9–12; 1942–61; IBM; Forms X-3S, Y-3S, ('52, 8 pages); battery examiner's manual ('58, c1949–57, 23 pages); battery general manual ('59, 37 pages); student profile leaflet, sixth edition ('61, c1958, 2 pages); see the complete battery entry (14*b*) for other accessories; no data on reliability; separate answer sheets must be used; $2.40 per 20 tests; $5 per 100 IBM answer sheets; 50¢ per scoring stencil; $3 per specimen set of the complete battery; postage extra; 55(65) minutes for full length version, 40(50) minutes for class period version; prepared under the direction of E. F. Lindquist; Science Research Associates, Inc. *

MOREY J. WANTMAN, *Director of Advisory and Instructional Programs, Educational Testing Service, Princeton, New Jersey.*

As noted in the test entry above, the copyright dates for this test, the Examiner's Manual, and the General Manual for this separate booklet edition are different from each other. The reader must note these differences lest he misjudge the currency of Test 1, Understanding of Basic Social Concepts. The General Manual for the separate booklet edition of the *Iowa Tests of Educational Development,* copyrighted in 1959, has the following paragraph on page 4: "To this end, Forms X-3S and Y-3S have been prepared to offer the user a *choice* of either a *Full Length Version* or a *Class Period Version.*" The reader might easily interpret this statement to mean that Forms X-3S and Y-3S were prepared just before this manual was issued. The fact is that these forms were seven years old when the above statement was made. Similiarly, in the Examiner's Manual for the separate booklet edition the following statement appears in the general introduction of the tests: "The tests are designed to be given to college freshmen as well as high school students." This may have once been the case, but there are no norms for grade 13 in the 1959 General Manual. Finally, the fact that the test was actually copyrighted in 1952 makes a number of questions out of date. For example, in Form X-3S: (*a*) Question 15, option 3 was written when there were only 48 states in the Union. (*b*) Question 48 relates to the control of countries in tropical areas of the world, most of which have earned their independence, thus making the key incorrect. (*c*) Options 2 and 3 of question 49 fail to take into account that the AFL and the CIO have merged into one organization. (*d*) With the recent strengthening of the Republican Party in the South, question 90 becomes dubious. In Form Y-3S: (*a*) Question 49 contains a reference to Albert Einstein as if he were still alive. (*b*) In question 85, Alaska and Hawaii are referred to as territories.

The above test entry indicates that the test can be administered either as a "full length version" requiring 55 minutes or as a "class period version" requiring 40 minutes. The claim is made on page 4 of the General Manual that "the two versions of each test are similar with respect to the average difficulty of test questions, the rate of work required to complete all questions in the version, and the standard and percentile scores obtained." The class period version uses the first 65 items of the 90 items in the full length version. These 65 items are actually 72.2 per cent of the 90 items. It is not clear from the conversion tables of raw scores to standard scores appearing on the scoring stencils how the raw score equivalents were obtained. For Form Y-3S a raw score for the class period version having a given standard score is 72.2 per cent of the raw score in the full length version having the same standard score. If the equivalents on the stencil for Form Y-3S were indeed obtained by use of the 72.2 per cent as a multiplying factor, the procedure is completely indefensible. In the case of Form X-3S, the 72.2 per cent multiplying factor seems to be operative from about the standard score of 11 and higher but it does not seem to be operative for lower standard scores. Incidentally, it should be pointed out in connection with the conversion of raw scores to standard scores that the directions for obtaining the standard score from the table given on the keys (pages 21 and 22 of the Examiner's Manual for the separate booklet edition) are confusing with respect to "columns."

The quality of the questions in the test is good. Aside from the out-dated options, the only error detected by this reviewer appears in the keyed option of question 69 of Form X-3S where "native-born" appears in place of "natural born," the term used in the United States Constitution.

On the last page of the Examiner's Manual a list of materials for "profiling and interpreting" is presented. Among these is the General Manual with Catalog Number 7-1024. The descriptive paragraph about the General Manual states that it contains, among other things, all of the statistics for the "reliabilities of the tests, the inter-correlations of the tests, the equivalence of versions." When one looks in the General Manual, Catalog Number 7-1024, he finds no data on reliabilities, intercorrelations, or equivalence of versions.

On page 15 the General Manual presents a profile of percentile ranks of grade averages of "Midtown High School, Grade 10." Average standard scores for this school are given. The reader learns from the next row of the profile and from the discussion on page 24 that an average standard score of 14.1 on Test 1 yields a 76th percentile on school averages. (The test, incidentally, changes its name here to "Social Studies Background.") The conversion table for this situation appearing on page 32 does not show any entry for 14.1 nor does it show a percentile rank of 76. A straight linear interpolation does yield the result. The reader should not have to infer the method for obtaining the result nor should he in fact be asked to do such computations if the authors intend him to use percentiles rather than the nearest decile. The 99 percentile values should be presented in the table.

In a leaflet which is made available to students, the last sentence is as follows: "Remember that a well-educated person is one who has equally high scores on all the *Iowa Tests.*" A student with "equally high scores" (for example, all at the 5th percentile) might be reassured by this statement but he hardly would be judged to be well educated.

CONCLUSION. This reviewer cannot recommend the use of this test. A test in this field which is more than 12 years old is of limited usefulness. Furthermore, the unavailability of statistical data in the auxiliary materials for this edition of the test limits the use of the test for most school purposes.

For reviews of the complete battery, see 14 and 5:17; for reviews of earlier forms, see 4:17 and 3:12.

[970]

***Metropolitan Achievement Tests: [Social Studies].** Grades 5–6, 7–9, 9–12; 1932–64; subtest of *Metropolitan Achievement Tests;* IBM and MRC; 3 levels; $2 per 100 Harbor answer cards (machine scoring service, by Measurement Research Center, Inc., may be arranged through the publisher); 40¢ per specimen set of any one level; postage extra; Walter N. Durost, (for *a* and *b*) Harold H. Bixler, Gertrude H. Hildreth, Kenneth W. Lund, and J. Wayne Wrightstone, and (*c* only) William H. Evans, James D. Leake, Howard A. Bowman, Clarke Cosgrove, and John G. Read; Harcourt, Brace & World, Inc. *

a) INTERMEDIATE SOCIAL STUDIES TEST. Grades 5–6; 1932–62; 2 scores: information, study skills; Forms AM ('60, c1958), BM ('59), CM ('61), (7–8 pages); combined directions for administering ('59, 11 pages) for this and the advanced level; battery manual for interpreting ('62, 121 pages); $4.60 per 35 tests; separate answer sheets or cards may be used; $1.75 per 35 IBM answer sheets; 20¢ per scoring stencil; $1.20 per manual for interpreting; 46(52) minutes.

b) ADVANCED SOCIAL STUDIES TEST. Grades 7–9; 1932–62; details same as for intermediate level except: 56(62) minutes.

c) HIGH SCHOOL SOCIAL STUDIES TESTS. Grades 9–12; 1962–64; 3 scores: study skills, vocabulary, information; Forms AM ('62), BM ('63), (9 pages); manual ('64, c1962–64, 22 pages); content outline ['64, 4 pages]; revised interpretive manual for the battery ('64, c1962–64, 16 pages); separate answer sheets or cards must be used; $6 per 35 tests; $1.80 per 35 IBM answer sheets; 40¢ per set of scoring stencils; 74(88) minutes.

RICHARD E. GROSS, *Associate Professor of Education, Stanford University, Stanford, California.* [Review of the intermediate and advanced levels.]

These tests are the separate social studies subtests of the *Metropolitan Achievement Tests* and appear for the first time as independent entities in these 1959–61 copyrighted forms. The tests are each separated into two parts: the first on factual knowledge of history, geography, and civics; the second on basic social studies skills. The information test at both the intermediate and advanced levels includes 60 items approximately evenly divided between the three above-mentioned subjects and requiring 20 minutes in either case. The skills tests at both levels are subdivided into two parts, the first being devoted to map reading and interpretation, the second to the reading and interpretation of tables, graphs, and charts.

The majority of items in the social studies information sections are four-foil completion type multiple choice questions. The duplication of items between intermediate and advanced levels varies but in some subsections goes well beyond the one third claimed to be common to both levels. For example, 11 of the 21 history items in Form AM of the advanced test are duplications of items found in Form AM of the intermediate test. While there is a clear progression of more difficult items in the advanced forms, one wonders if there is really sufficient differentiation between the capabilities at these age levels and particularly if the so-called advanced tests reveal what a true achievement test should. It is this reviewer's opinion that achievement tests must measure attainments and competencies far beyond subject matter recall and recollection and the limited skills called for in these tests. If teachers desire a broad assessment of pupil grasp of the many fundamental aims typically held for the social studies, they must go far beyond such tests in attempting to ascertain the attainment of purposes. The skill portions of these tests are quite good as far as they go; yet, coupled with the informational sections, in total these instruments are highly limited as comprehensive measures of achievement.

How well do our students read and comprehend in the social studies area? How well can they differentiate cause and effect? How well can they demonstrate the understanding of basic concepts and generalizations? Can they recognize propaganda? Can they decide if conclusions are warranted by the evidence? Can they state the relationships between former events and current issues? Do they hold the essential capabilities of analysis and attitudes of openmindedness fundamental for the resolution of social problems? These are the queries I would want to put when examining pupils for true achievement of my social studies goals and these are elements upon which these tests throw very little light. As long as standardized tests are so lacking in scope of measurement they promise not to provide the needed leadership towards improvement in curriculum and instruction, but rather to further inculcate the distressing fact-depository school of social studies "education."

As suggested above, the skills portions of these tests do a satisfactory job of screening abilities of map, chart, and tabular interpretation and in some ways go on towards the more adequate measurement this reviewer seeks. When the geography section of the informational part of the tests is coupled with the map queries in the skills portion, one does get a fairly good view of geographical attainment. In fact, geography is the only one of the social studies subjects that comes near adequate treatment in these tests. In view of the need to extend measurement to other areas and for questions of other types, it might well be wise to even cut some of the map reading in future editions unless the tests are materially extended. The road map reading exercises in the intermediate forms seem to be the most expendable to this reviewer. The last page of the advanced forms are now overly cluttered and may confuse testees; the content should be spread out over another page in revised editions. Even though the geography sections are the superior portions of the tests, individual items call for correction and up-dating. For example, item 4, intermediate Form BM, asks where a magnetic compass points: south, north, east, or west? It does not allow for the pupil who knows of the south polar attraction; item 17, intermediate Form CM, lists silk, seemingly in error, as Japan's biggest "money product." The "correct" answer for item 18, advanced Form CM, is in error, as the population of China now approaches one quarter of the total world population. There are some shades of out-of-style geographic determinism in certain queries. In general, as is typical of most objective type tests, the pupils who really know the most and who grasp the interrelationships and complexities overlooked by the test constructors may be frustrated by a number of the answers elicited in each of the subject matter portions of these tests.

If these tests are to be billed as a "social studies" test, this reviewer feels that further development of items in the areas of sociology, anthropology, and economics is called for and that these areas should be included in future editions. As it is, however, the history items are sadly short of what should be included for a comprehensive assessment of knowledge in just this discipline. Twenty items are included in each form to survey knowledge of world, as well as U.S., history from the Stone Age to the United Nations! Most of the items are on American history, but then one quarter of these precious few are used to identify battles and wars and the inventor of the telephone. In addition, in the "history" items there are questions about which South American country raises the most cattle (item 33, intermediate Form AM); on the other hand, in the civics sections there are items dealing with the New Deal (item 53, advanced Form AM, which, by the way, does not include as the correct answer the major reason behind the creation of the A.A.A.).

It is easy to carp about numerous items in these tests, but this should not be so if the items were really carefully scrutinized by experts, as is claimed. Pupils have to choose, for example, between the British Isles and the British Commonwealth in an answer to a query on the United Kingdom (item 39, intermediate Form CM) in which either answer is correct for the pupil who remembers that Ireland is a separate entity in the British Isles. What is the correct answer to item 60, intermediate Form BM, "Which of the following groups most recently obtained the right to vote in the United States?" The "correct" choice is "Women" from among the other foils of "Negroes," "Indians," and "aliens." The child who knows Indians only gained full voting rights as late as 1924 or who sees the daily papers or the TV screen full of civil rights and integration stories knows that it must be the Negroes or possibly the Indians, but how could it possibly be his Mommy? Certain questions are confusing because of factors stretching from vocabulary (item 10, advanced Form AM) to point of view (item 41, intermediate Form CM) and from bad concepts (item 40, intermediate Form BM) to oversights (item 25, advanced Form AM).

A number of roads towards the improvement of tests of this nature are open. The reviewer has indicated a number of these. They range from improved scope and more careful construction to better discrimination and a wider variety of items. It would also seem essential to review just what are the basic contributions and processes of each of the social sciences and then to be sure to include such in the items. When, for example, of all the history items in a form (20) only 3 or 4 seem to deal with cause and effect relationships, we have missed one of the major contributions that should come from exposure to history. Perhaps some form of subtotals in the scores on each of the extended sections would also be an aid. Very probably the best way to meet many of the criticisms of this reviewer would come through providing a large reservoir of tried items that could be selected and used in varying ways depending upon purposes of the teacher, emphases and type of course, kinds of pupils, and the use to which the test results are to be put. Equally important will be unending efforts to develop tests like STEP, which move toward the application of knowledge rather than its mere reproduction.

Robert J. Solomon, *Vice President, Educational Testing Service, Princeton, New Jersey.* [Review of the intermediate and advanced levels.]

The intermediate and advanced levels of the Metropolitan social studies tests are intended to measure the knowledge and skills that are the important outcomes of social studies instruction in grades 5 through 9. The Intermediate Social Studies Test is intended for grades 5 and 6; the Advanced Social Studies Test, for grades 7, 8, and 9.

The intermediate level test consists of the social studies information and study skills subtests from the Intermediate Battery of the *Metropolitan Achievement Tests.* The advanced level test is similarly taken from the Advanced Battery of the *Metropolitan Achievement Tests.* In actuality, each form of the intermediate and advanced tests consists of two tests, separately timed and separately scored tests of information and study skills, with separate norms for each. Each form of the information test contains 60 questions to be answered in 20 minutes. Each form of the study skills test for the intermediate level contains 29–30 questions to be answered in 26 minutes. Each form of the study skills test at the advanced level contains 39–40 questions to be answered in 36 minutes. (One wonders why Form AM for each level contains one more question than Forms BM or CM.)

Although no data on speededness are presented in the manual, the tests appear to satisfy the authors' objective that the tests are "not intended to measure the speed with which children can answer test questions." A rate of three questions per minute for the information tests may ordinarily seem high for the typical student in grades 5–9, but these questions are for the most part quite short and require relatively little reading time. In the skills tests, the pace of approximately one question per minute seems adequate. Also, in the skills tests provision is made for internal timing so that the student will not spend too much time on the first parts. Thirteen minutes before the end of each skills test, students are directed to turn to the last group of 14–15 questions.

No classroom teacher, guidance counselor, or school administrator should select an achievement test without a careful analysis of its content. In the opinion of this reviewer, the test authors are entirely accurate in their description of the test. Nevertheless, it remains for the test user to judge, by his examination of the test questions, the extent to which the content of the test is an appropriate and sufficient measure of social studies achievement. In the words of the authors, the test "seeks to measure attainment of certain important objectives of social studies instruction in the elementary and junior high school grades." These objectives "are largely in the realm of knowledge and study skills. The Social Studies Information Test is primarily a measure of the pupil's acquisition of certain factual information generally covered in social studies textbooks." The study skills test consists of two parts. "The first part....is a measure of the ability to read and interpret maps. * The second part provides a measure of ability to read and interpret information presented in the form of tables, charts, and graphs." The questions in the several forms of the skills test at each level are well constructed and appear to measure exactly what the authors intended them to measure. A major reservation one may have about this test concerns whether the two parts constitute a comprehensive measure of the important social studies study skills for the grades intended. To be fair, it must be noted that the authors do not claim that they do.

In deciding on the content of the information test, "the authors analyzed the content of all series of social studies textbooks in common use at the time the tests were developed." This analysis, "together with the opinions of social studies educators as to probable trends in social studies instruction and as to desirable distributions of emphasis among various content areas, made it possible to develop an outline of the content of both levels of the social studies test." Despite this effort, the result is disappointing. The authors' description of the test as a measure of the acquisition of certain factual information is all too accurate. Although it may appear unfair to expect that which was never promised, the information test at each level seems too little concerned with the measurement of understanding. Too many questions require the naming of a person, place, or event, and too few the knowledge, comprehension, or application of a principle, generalization, or concept.

Except for the study skills test at the intermediate level, the reliabilities reported for the tests are satisfactory. Although it is not so specified, these reliabilities are for Form AM of each test, but one would expect the reliabilities of the other forms to be very similar. The reliabilities reported for the intermediate study skills test range from .64 to .77. To quote the manual, "one must consider with skepticism the score on any test that has a reliability coefficient below .80." However, in comparing these reliabilities with those for other tests, one should keep in mind that the reliabilities reported for the Metropolitan series are, quite appropriately, based on single-school-system, single-grade groups. Such reliabilities tend to be lower than those based on more than one grade or more than one school system.

In the view of the authors, the validity of the Metropolitan social studies tests rests on their careful efforts to reflect in the content of the tests the important outcomes of social studies instruction. This emphasis on the content validity of tests is not unusual for achievement tests. Indeed, there is a school of thought that holds that the only criterion of validity for an achievement test is the test itself. For these tests, no evidence of other kinds of validity is offered, although it is likely that data could be obtained to show, for example, the extent to which performance on the tests will predict future social studies achievement. As for the content validity of these tests, as was indicated earlier, the user of the test will ultimately have to judge this for himself by his own careful analysis of test content.

An analysis of the content and statistics of the three forms for each level indicates that the forms may be considered parallel. In using the tests, one should be aware that there is significant item overlap between the forms of the intermediate and advanced tests having the same letter designation, but there is none between forms with different letter designations. The overlap between forms is mainly among the history questions and for one complete set of skills questions. However, should one have need to administer both an intermediate and advanced test to the same student within a span of time when the student may still remember the items on the first testing, the possibility of spuriously high scores on the second testing can be avoided by making certain that the second test administered does not have the same letter designation as the first.

In general, the format of the tests is good and the directions are simple and clear. Teachers should have no difficulty in administering the tests; students should have little difficulty in taking them. Perhaps it would have been better if the layout of the study skills tests had been less crowded, particularly in the intermediate tests where it would have been possible to use the back page of the test booklet, as was done in the advanced tests.

The manual for the tests deserves a special word of praise. Written by Walter H. Durost, it is not only a model of what a test manual should be, but it is an excellent short course in tests and measurements. It presents a wealth of sophisticated thinking concerning the meaning and use of test scores in a lucid, uncomplicated style that any intelligent reader should be able to comprehend. One hopes that teachers using the tests will take the time to study the manual.

Despite criticisms expressed or implied in this review, the Metropolitan social studies tests are the workmanlike products of professional testmakers. No *caveat emptor* applies here. The teacher who carefully examines the tests and the materials accompanying them will have no difficulty in making intelligent and effective use of them. And, if he will study the excellent manual, he will be able to use all tests more wisely.

For reviews of the complete battery, see 15; for reviews of earlier editions, see 4:18, 40:1189, and 38:874.

[971]

***Sequential Tests of Educational Progress: Social Studies.** Grades 4–6, 7–9, 10–12, 13–14; 1956–63; IBM, NCS, and Grade-O-Mat; Forms A, B, ('57, c1956–57, 15–19 pages); 4 levels; battery directions ('57, 12 pages); interpretive manual ('57, 31 pages); battery technical report ('57, 58 pages); 1958 SCAT-STEP supplement ('58, 32 pages); 1962 SCAT-STEP supplement ('62, 49 pages); 1963 SCAT-STEP supplement of urban norms ('63, 16 pages); battery teacher's guide ('59, 85 pages); battery profile ('57, 1 page); battery student report ('58, 4 pages); no data on reliability of Form B; separate answer sheets or cards must be used; $4 per 20 tests; $1 per 20 IBM scorable answer sheets; 25¢ per scoring stencil; see 671 for prices of NCS answer sheets and scoring services; see 666 for prices of Grade-O-Mat cards; $1 per 20 profiles; $1 per 20 student reports; $1 per interpretive manual; $1 per technical report; $1 per supplement; $1 per teacher's guide; postage extra; $2 per specimen set, cash orders postpaid; 70(90–100) minutes; Cooperative Test Division. *

a) LEVEL 4. Grades 4–6; Forms 4A, 4B.
b) LEVEL 3. Grades 7–9; Forms 3A, 3B.
c) LEVEL 2. Grades 10–12; Forms 2A, 2B.
d) LEVEL 1. Grades 13–14; Forms 1A, 1B.

REFERENCES

1. LIGGITT, WILLIAM A. "An Evaluation of General Education in Elementary Teacher Preparation." *J Ed Res* 57:156–9 N '63. *

JONATHON C. MCLENDON, *Professor of Social Science Education, Florida Atlantic University, Boca Raton, Florida.*

The STEP tests in social studies continue without peer, indeed almost without available counterparts, as the leading standardized series of skill tests in social studies. As previous reviewers have indicated, the STEP tests fulfill a distinctive need in social studies, a field in which tests have generally dealt mostly or only with knowledge and understanding of facts and concepts.

Content validity of the STEP tests is dependent on the soundness of judgment of those three dozen persons who participated in the test construction. While this group included several outstanding teachers and other leaders in social studies education, additional evidences of content validity would be welcome. In light of the heavy emphasis that teachers place on interpretation of reading materials in social studies, content validity is weakened by the extent (37 to 51 per cent) of items that involve interpretation of visual materials. Data on item validity are not reported. Construct, concurrent, and predictive validity are evident only by implication. Correlations with SCAT scores are interesting, and useful in some ways; but more closely related criteria would serve better to guide teachers and students in interpreting and applying test results. Ideally, the reporting of scores would facilitate recognition of levels of achievement by individuals and groups in the use of particular skills involving specified types of instructional materials or sources.

Although the STEP tests aim chiefly to measure indicated abilities, previous knowledge concerning the subject matter presented on the test doubtless aids many test takers. The seven types of skills and eight areas of understanding listed in the Manual for Interpreting Scores on the social studies tests provide no more than general and somewhat vague identifications of related behaviors; the statements of understandings appear to restate several proposed in 1957 by the Committee on Concepts and Values, National Council for the Social Studies. Hopefully the publishers of the STEP tests will be able to furnish in the foreseeable future, as promised seven years ago in their 1957 Technical Report, "empirical checks....relating test scores to suitable criterion measures," which data have not yet appeared in the SCAT-STEP Supplements.

Reliability correlations (Kuder-Richardson formula 20) of .84 to .93 on the A forms attest to high internal consistency. Equivalence of Forms A and B is presumed on the basis of a common score scale. Test users look forward to the appearance of correlational analyses indicating equivalence of the forms. While it involves more than one might reasonably expect a test publisher to produce, a longitudinal study would be highly beneficial, following students from the middle grades through college and reporting learning as indicated by the STEP tests in relation to the curricular content and instructional emphases of varying school programs.

This reviewer joins those who would like to see wider use and further refinement and expansion of the STEP tests. The apparent popularity of these tests suggests the practicability, as well as desirability, of applying the approach to other areas of skill development and to additional types of instructional material in social studies.

DONALD W. OLIVER, *Associate Professor of Education, Harvard University, Cambridge, Massachusetts.*

This social studies series is one of seven tests in the series *Sequential Tests of Educational Progress.* All were developed on the basis of certain common assumptions and presumably have similar properties. All assume that the focus of education is upon the development of critical skills and understandings rather than upon teaching only the facts of lesson material and that success in education is to be measured in terms of the student's ability to apply school-learned skills to the solution of "new problems." The tests are not to be tied to specific "courses," or to specific bodies of content.

This approach is, of course, not particularly radical. The explicitness of problem areas covered in the material, however, is novel and refreshing. The items for each level (there are four levels at median grade difficulties for grades 5, 8, 11, and 13) are categorized in terms of skills, understandings, type of material, and subject matter. The skills presumably measured are the ability to: identify generalizations, identify values, distinguish facts from opinions, assess data, compare data, and draw conclusions. The understandings are described as those involving social change, the geographic environment, forces of nature, democratic society, economic wants, interdependence, and those related to understanding one's environment. The items are further classified under the "type of material" on which items are based and "subject matter." Types of material include maps, graphs, cartoons, photographs and drawings, and text material. The subject matter is classified as American history, geography, social anthropology, government, economics, and world history. Items described by "understanding" and "subject matter" are often double classified; e.g., an item may be classified as both American history and government.

While the "skills" and "understandings" are those most commonly stated in lists of objectives compiled by "experts," one might question the actual utility of such a breakdown. For example, one skill is described as the ability to "identify, compare, and contrast underlying values, attitudes, assumptions, biases, and motives." Item 8 (Form 1A), which is classified as testing this objective, asks the question, "What is the likelihood that the problem depicted in the cartoon will exist and be significant ten years from now?" Item 2 (Form 2B), also classified under the same objective, asks "Which of the following is the main idea of Cartoon I?" More commonly, however, items classified under "identify values" require the student to infer the opinion or policy of the author of a statement. The point is that we have little assurance (and no information) regarding the validity of the process by which the questions were categorized. This situation is, of course, as much an indictment of the utility of objectives as stated by experts in the profession as it is a criticism of the tests; it raises the question of whether the testmaker is to lead or follow. In this case the testmakers probably chose to follow the leaders in the profession in the hope of encouraging teachers to state objectives in broader terms than subject matter content. Considering the present emphasis on analyzing the "structure" of the social science disciplines and on identifying the major procedures and concepts underlying these disciplines, one would expect that the use of the tests as a point of influence on the existing fact-oriented curriculum (which is implied on page 14 of the teacher's guide) is already an obsolete goal. Probably 70-item tests of all the social sciences, including both information and problem analysis, are much too gross to get at the structure of anything.

It should be pointed out that perhaps the strongest feature of the test series is the attempt to measure dimensions of social problem analysis, rather than recall or comprehension of facts or generalizations in standard social studies courses. (Obviously this is not true of all the items, or the tests would simply be general reasoning tests.) The fact that the series does emphasize general skills and understandings rather than specific fragments of knowledge, however, leads one to ask: Are these simply reading or intelligence tests rather than "social studies" tests? This question is answered in part in the Technical Report issued with the tests. Correlations ranging between .73 and .89 are reported for the relationship between STEP Social Studies and total SCAT, the latter of which is designed to measure general academic attitude. It is interesting to note that somewhat lower correlations are reported between STEP Reading and SCAT. In the 1958 SCAT-STEP Supplement a correlation of .77 is reported for one study between SCAT and WISC, WISC being a reputable standard measure of general intelligence. Moreover, in the same study, the correlation between a STEP social studies test and social studies grades is reported as .55, while the correlation between SCAT and average grades is reported as .70. Looking at these data, one gets the impression that the STEP social studies tests measure very little that is *unique* to the understanding of problem analysis in the social studies, and very much that is common to general measures of reading and academic aptitude. The irony is that what is unique to the social studies in this series is probably the technical knowledge and factual information which the tests are attempting to subordinate to the more general problem solving goals.

In summary, this is the most comprehensive and probably the most carefully constructed series of sequential social studies tests available in the field. It has the bonus of an excellent teacher's guide, including assistance on how to use the instrument for instructional diagnosis and as a teaching aid. Presently there is a Technical Report and three supplements, which include norms for urban schools. Within the field of existing commercial tests to measure general social studies skills and understandings, this series stands alone. It is important to note, however, that it is constructed on the same assumptions and format as many tests of general reasoning and critical thinking and probably reflects very little that is unique to social studies as a field of teaching or knowledge. The field of achievement testing in the social studies still awaits an analysis of objectives related to those concepts, intellectual processes, and skills that are uniquely the contribution made through the study of history and the social sciences. Until the time that such objectives can be defined and measured, we might ask whether or not it makes sense to call available instruments "social studies tests."

For reviews by Richard E. Gross, S. A. Rayner, and Ralph W. Tyler, see 5:792. For reviews of the complete battery, see 25 and 5:24.

[972]

***Social Studies: Every Pupil Scholarship Test.** Grades 7–8; 1935–64; new form (2 pages) usually issued each January and April; forms from previous testing programs also available; general directions sheet ['63, 2 pages]; no data on reliability; norms for new forms available following testing program; 4¢ per test; 4¢ per key; postage extra; 30(35) minutes; Bureau of Educational Measurements. *

[973]

★Social Studies: Minnesota High School Achievement Examinations. Grades 7, 8, 9; 1961–63; series formerly called *Midwest High School Achievement Examinations;* new form issued each May; norms available in June following release of new form; Form F ('63, 6–7 pages) used in 1963 testing; 3 levels; no specific manual; series manual ('63, 4 pages); series norms ['63, 4 pages]; series cumulative profile ('62, 2 pages); no data on reliability; no description of normative population; 12¢ per test; $2.50 per 100 profiles; postage extra; 20¢ per specimen set, postpaid; 60(65) minutes; American Guidance Service, Inc.

[974]

***Social Studies: National Teacher Examinations.** College seniors and teachers; 1940–63; for more complete information, see 700; 80(90) minutes; Educational Testing Service. *

HARRY D. BERG, *Professor, Office of Evaluation Services, Michigan State University, East Lansing, Michigan.* [Review of Form LNT.]

This is one of the optional tests of the National Teacher Examinations. It is intended to be given to college seniors who are applicants for teaching positions so that they may show their competency in a field of greatest strength. The test should be judged within the limited purposes set forth for it by the program directors. The Handbook for School and College Officials states that "the purpose of the NTE program is....to provide objective examinations of measurable intellectual competencies which are commonly considered basic to effective classroom teaching." The phrases "objective examinations" and "measurable intellectual competencies" should be noted. It is admitted without apology that the examinations in the series cannot measure all of the qualities which contribute to effective teaching. Many of these qualities are at present poorly defined and many will probably never become amenable to objective testing. One implication of the limited purpose of the test is that no attempt has been made to establish its validity on a basis of on-the-job success.

Whatever the nature of the other qualities of the good teacher, understanding of subject content and methodology is an essential quality and one that can be defined and measured. It is the opinion of this reviewer that the present test has great potentialities for providing needed data on teaching applicants within this area. The various fields of the social studies are covered in a well balanced fashion and the items are so constructed as to emphasize reasoned understanding rather than the mere recall of facts. Many of the items pose hypothetical classroom situations in which the applicant must choose from a number of courses of action. Other items require a knowledge of teaching materials and their most appropriate uses. The various ways in which social studies data may be presented to pupils have been explored; some items are based on reading passages and others on cartoons, maps, and graphs.

The available statistics are all good. The test requires 80 minutes and has 105 items. The mean raw score is 48.03 (correction is made for guessing). The K-R 20 reliability is .92 and the mean item discrimination index (biserial *r*) is .43. The format, directions, and provisions for scoring are of the usual high quality associated with the Educational Testing Service. National norms based on scaled scores are made available to the concerned colleges and secondary schools. Provision is made for making the scores comparable from form to form.

All things considered, this test should provide prospective employers with one piece of useful information on teacher candidates. It is instructive to note, in this connection, that mean scores show considerable variance from one teacher training institution to another.

For reviews of the testing program, see 700, 5:538, and 4:802.

[975]

Social Studies: Teacher Education Examination Program. College seniors preparing to teach secondary school; 1957; an inactive form of *Social Studies: National Teacher Examinations;* for more complete information, see 709; IBM; 80(95) minutes; Educational Testing Service. *

For a review of the testing program, see 5:543. For reviews of the National Teacher Examinations, *see 700, 5:538, and 4:802.*

[976]

***Social Studies 12 (American Problems): Minnesota High School Achievement Examinations.** Grade 12; 1955–63; series formerly called *Midwest High School Achievement Examinations;* new form issued each May; norms available in June following release of new form; Form F ('63, 7 pages) used in 1963 testing; no specific manual; series manual ('63, 4 pages); series norms ['63, 4 pages]; series cumulative profile ('62, 2 pages); no data on reliability; no description of normative population; 12¢ per test; $2.50 per 100 profiles; postage extra; 20¢ per specimen set, postpaid; 60(65) minutes; American Guidance Service, Inc. *

[977]

***Stanford Achievement Test: Social Studies Test.** Grades 5.5–6.9, 7–9; 1940–64; subtest of *Stanford Achievement Test [1964 Revision]*; previous edition (see 5:799) still available; IBM and MRC; 2 levels; manual ['64, 8 pages] for each level; supplementary directions ['64, 1 page each] for use with IBM answer sheets, Harbor answer cards; separate answer sheets or cards may be used; $1.50 per 35 IBM answer sheets; 20¢ per scoring stencil; $2 per 100 Harbor answer cards (machine scoring service, by Measurement Research Center, Inc., may be arranged through the publisher); 40¢ per specimen set of either level; postage extra; Truman L. Kelley, Richard Madden, Eric F. Gardner, and Herbert C. Rudman; Harcourt, Brace & World, Inc. *

a) INTERMEDIATE 2. Grades 5.5–6.9; Form W ('64, 6 pages); $4 per 35 tests; 50(56) minutes.

b) ADVANCED. Grades 7–9; Form W ('64, 9 pages); $6 per 35 tests; 52(58) minutes.

For a review by Harry D. Berg of the 1953 revision, see 5:799; for a review by Ray G. Wood of the previous edition, see 3:595. For a review of the complete battery, see 26; for a review of the 1953 revision, see 5:25; for reviews of earlier editions, see 4:25 and 3:18.

[978]

★T.C. Social Studies Test. Teachers college entrants; 1955–58; 5 scores: geography, civics, history, critical thinking, total; 1 form ['56, 6 pages]; mimeographed manual ['58, 7 pages]; no data on reliability; no norms for subscores; distribution restricted to teacher training institutions; separate answer sheets must be used; 6*s.* per 10 tests; 2*s.* per 10 answer sheets; 4*s.* per key; 2*s.* 6*d.* per manual; 7*s.* 6*d.* per specimen set; postpaid within Australia; 35(40) minutes; Australian Council for Educational Research. *

[Other Tests]

For tests not listed above, see the following entries in *Tests in Print:* 1706, 1711–3, 1717–8, and 1724–5; out of print: 1714 and 1720.

CONTEMPORARY AFFAIRS

[979]

***Contemporary Affairs: Every Pupil Test.** Grades 10-12; 1939-64; new test (4 pages) usually issued each December and April; general directions sheet ('63, 2 pages); no data on reliability; Ohio norms for new forms available following testing program; 5¢ per test; 3¢ per key; postpaid; 40(45) minutes; Ohio Scholarship Tests. *

[980]

★Cooperative Test on Foreign Affairs. Grade 16; 1962, c1960-62; IBM; Form IBI ('62, c1960, 14 pages); manual ('62, 23 pages); separate answer sheets must be used; $4 per 20 tests; $1 per 20 IBM scorable answer sheets; 25¢ per scoring stencil; $1 per manual; postage extra; $2 per specimen set, cash orders postpaid; (60-65) minutes; Cooperative Test Division. *

REFERENCES

1. Bidwell, Percy W. Appendix A, "A Test on Foreign Affairs," pp. 146-80. In his *Undergraduate Education in Foreign Affairs.* New York: King's Crown Press, 1962. Pp. viii, 215. *

Christine McGuire, *Assistant Director, Research in Medical Education, University of Illinois College of Medicine, Chicago, Illinois.*

According to the excellent accompanying manual, this test was developed "to determine to what extent seniors enrolled in the colleges [included in a recent study of undergraduate education in international relations] had acquired a background of information necessary for an understanding of international relations —and could apply it, even in an elementary way." The test was constructed by asking over a hundred "distinguished" scholars in the field to submit topics that warranted inclusion in an instrument designed to "cover a variety of information of *more than passing significance* for an understanding of American foreign policy [italics added]." The manual further advises that the materials included are "as varied as the sources of information about the international scene: cartoons, maps, charts, excerpts from important documents." The items "require students not only to recall facts but also to draw inferences and to apply their knowledge and understanding."

In several important respects the test achieves the promise implied in the statement of purpose and description of materials: many of the questions are challenging; many are based on data presented in a fresh and interesting form; many involve an unfamiliar juxtaposition of facts that requires the student to reorganize his information into a structure not frequently encountered in conventional instruction. Practically all of the items are technically satisfactory; the common pitfalls of test construction have generally been avoided in this highly professional product.

Unfortunately, the test also has certain deficiencies which appear to be a direct consequence of carrying to an extreme some of the same qualities that account for its excellence. In the attempt to provide an unusual context for essentially factual questions, some of the items have become unduly strained and contrived. In a number of cases, orientation to the graph or chart presented is often more complex than the question itself. For example, one rather simple question about the direction and volume of trade in specified resources is based on an intricate chart depicting flows of goods by means of arrows of varying widths superimposed on a map. Again, a quite complex graph showing variation over time with respect to political party affiliation is used as the basis of an elementary question about the political composition of four national legislatures. To this reviewer, only esthetic values would be compromised if such questions were asked more directly without the interposition of essentially irrelevant complications in the contextual materials. Secondly, an unduly large proportion of the questions based on cartoons or excerpts from documents are uncomfortably reminiscent of the game of "guess what I am thinking about." Third, the combination of facts required to answer some questions derives not from necessary relations in the content being sampled, but is imposed by artificialities in the item itself. For example, one question asks the student to select the pair of nations in which one is characterized by X and the other by Y; no comparison or relation is implied, merely simultaneous matching of discrete qualities with specified political units. Finally, there are some questions in which the complexity of the instructions presents the only real obstacle to a correct answer.

Quite aside from these somewhat carping criticisms of what is most certainly a stimulating and provocative test, this reviewer has certain reservations about the balance of items in a test purporting to measure *knowledge* and *understanding* of *international relations.* Approximately one quarter is devoted to "map questions": What countries have common borders? What is the likely date of a given map? Where are certain physical features located on a Mercator projection? The distribution of what resource is depicted by a given pattern of shading? Despite the ingenuity of some of these materials, they appear to be overemphasized, in view of the importance of political, cultural, ethnic, and other basic economic factors in the world situation. The relatively few questions on chronology suggest that the authors are striving to test the students' understanding of a sequence of events; one nevertheless suspects that students are often forced to answer in terms of isolated knowledge of specific dates, rather than in terms of the inexorable logic of events. Finally, despite this reviewer's special love for economics and economic geography, it must be said that the test seems to include an overly large proportion of questions that can be answered only in terms of some fairly detailed knowledge of resources, industrial production, and direction of trade.

The manual accompanying the test is superb. It contains very clear and detailed instructions for administration, scoring, and interpretation of results. The norms are based on a 1960 administration to 1,854 randomly selected seniors in 175 colleges. The data are appropriately organized to provide norms for various populations arranged according to curriculum (business, education, engineering, and liberal arts), major subject (social sciences, natural sciences, and humanities), type of institution (private universities, state universities, liberal arts colleges, etc.), and geographic location of institution. Both the item statistics and the total scores are separately reported for the several groups in each category. Differences among groups confirm our stereotypes: students in liberal arts colleges perform better than those in business or teachers colleges; students with a social science major achieve more than students in the natural sciences and humanities; students in the coastal regions score higher than students elsewhere; men are more fully informed in this area than women. That the differences among groups are in the expected direction and that the test yields a high reliability coefficient (.89, Kuder-Richardson formula 20) are both strong support for a favorable judgment about the technical and statistical adequacy of the test.

From the point of view of its technical excellence, the superior manual which accompanies it, and the aid the manual provides to useful interpretation of results, this test can be highly recommended to all who are interested in an assay of rather sophisticated information about international affairs. However, since most questions require new combinations of factual material rather than its interpretation and analysis, this reviewer cannot recommend the test as a valid measure of *understanding* of international relations and *ability to apply* that understanding to an interpretation of contemporary events. Finally, in the words of the manual, "this test was constructed for administration in 1960. The relevance and accuracy of some of the items will, of necessity, suffer with the passage of time." Consequently, specific items should be reviewed before use since, in the opinion of this reviewer, time is already beginning to impose its stamp.

J Counsel Psychol 9:283–4 f '62. Laurence Siegel. * The Handbook is an interesting document containing the kinds of information usually found in "administrators' manuals" and "technical manuals." In addition, five brief "Technical Notes" are boxed within its text. These notes, written for the relatively naive test user, concern (a) computation of *t*-ratio; (b) the meaning of standard deviation, median and quartile; (c) the concept of reliability; (d) the meaning of significance levels; (e) the use of item-test biserials for item analysis. The inclusion of these Technical Notes is an interesting device, and they are extremely well-written. Whether or not they will enhance the ability of relatively unsophisticated users to interpret data presented in the Handbook remains to be seen. * Researchers wishing to measure knowledge of foreign affairs will find the test well-suited to their needs. The fact that validity (other than content validity) is not established and that norms are not available for groups other than college seniors should not prove too disturbing to them. However, counselors wishing to assess achievement in this area may be exasperated by a test with tremendous potential but lacking certain fundamental corollary information prerequisite to its intelligent use by them. The normative data for college seniors are good, but the major thrust of counseling is experienced prior to the senior year. The counselor usually needs to know something about the test performance of standardization groups representative of high school seniors, college freshmen, and perhaps the general adult population. Many interesting validity studies are self-evident for the Test on Foreign Affairs. The Handbook stops short with evidence that, of liberal arts seniors, those majoring in the social sciences have a higher mean score than either natural science or humanities majors. However, this begs the question of the test's predictive usefulness for vocational attainment. Also concurrent validities, perhaps, involving well-known interest inventories as well as other cognitive measures, are not cited. It is at least conceivable that the Test on Foreign Affairs may share considerable variance with tests of general ability and verbal fluency. It is very difficult to judge the feasibility of including this test in either a counseling battery or a school-wide achievement battery without evidence on this point.

[981]

***Current Affairs: Every Pupil Scholarship Test.** High school; 1935–64; new form (2 pages) usually issued each January and April; general directions sheet ['63, 2 pages]; no data on reliability; norms available following testing program; 4¢ per test; 4¢ per key; postage extra 40(45) minutes; Bureau of Educational Measurements. *

[982]

★Nationwide Current Events Examination. Grades 4–12; 1960–63; new form issued each April; norms available following the testing program; 1 form ('63, 2 pages); no manual; mimeographed norms ('63, 1 page); no data on reliability; 10¢ per test, postage extra; (40–45) minutes; [Donald R. Honz]; Educational Stimuli. *

[983]

★New York Times Current Affairs Test. High school; 1947–64; new test (4 pages) issued monthly during school year; no data on reliability; no norms; distribution restricted to schools subscribing to the publisher's School Service Program; program includes daily copy of *The New York Times* for each student, monthly copy of the test for each student, and other teaching aids; subscription price: 25¢ per student per week, postpaid; (35–40) minutes; New York Times. *

[984]

★New York Times Current Affairs Test for Colleges. College; 1947–64; new test (4 pages) issued monthly during school year; no data on reliability; no norms; distribution restricted to schools subscribing to the publisher's School Service Program; program includes daily copy of *The New York Times* for each student, monthly copy of the test for each student, and other teaching aids; subscription price: 40¢ per student per week, postpaid; (35–55) minutes; New York Times. *

[985]

★Newsweek Current News Test. Grades 9–12; 1951–64; 2 new tests (8 pages) issued annually: spring term review (covering mid December–mid April) issued each May, fall term review (covering September–mid December) issued each January; no data on reliability; no norms; distribution restricted to schools subscribing to one of the publisher's quantity subscription plans; plans include subscriptions to *Newsweek* magazine for student use, semester copy of this test and monthly copy of test 986 for each subscription, and other teaching aids; subscriptions may be entered in bulk (mailed to the school) at 15¢ each per issue or by individual student (placed by the teacher but mailed to the student, cash orders only) at $1.75 for 17 weeks, $2.75 for 34 weeks, or $3.50 per year; 2-week trial subscription, 30¢ per student; postpaid; administration time not reported; Newsweek Educational Division. *

[986]

★Newsweek NewsQuiz. Grades 9–12; 1951–64; formerly called *Newsweek Monthly Objective Test;* new test (4 pages) issued monthly during school year; no data on reliability; no norms; distribution restricted to schools subscribing to one of the publisher's quantity subscription plans; plans include subscriptions to *Newsweek* magazine for student use, monthly copy of this test and semester copy of test 985 for each subscription, and other teaching aids; subscriptions may be entered in bulk (mailed to the school) at 15¢ each per issue or by individual student (placed by the teacher but mailed to the student, cash orders only) at $1.75 for 17 weeks, $2.75 for 34 weeks, or $3.50 per year; 2-week trial subscription, 30¢ per student; postpaid; administration time not reported; Newsweek Educational Division. *

[Other Tests]

For tests not listed above, see the following entry in *Tests in Print:* 1731.

ECONOMICS

[987]

***The Graduate Record Examinations Advanced Tests: Economics.** Grades 16–17; 1939–62; for more complete information, see 762; 180(200) minutes; Educational Testing Service. *

REFERENCES

1. RILEY, ROBERT C., AND LOVE, JEAN O. "The Predictive Value of College Test Scores." *J Higher Ed* 29:393–5+ O '58. *

For a review of the testing program, see 5:601.

[988]

★A Standard Achievement Test in Economic Understanding for Secondary Schools, Sixth Revision. High school; 1954–57; 1 form ('57, 9 pages, mimeographed); no manual; no data on reliability; no norms; separate answer sheets must be used; 25¢ per test, postpaid; [50] minutes; E. C. Alft and the Illinois Council on Economic Education; [Joint Council on Economic Education]. *

[989]

★Test of Economic Understanding, Preliminary Edition No. 2. High school and college and industry; 1963; IBM; Forms A, B, (13 pages); manual (7 pages); tentative norms based upon the first preliminary edition; no college or industrial norms; separate answer sheets must be used; $3 per 20 tests; $4 per 100 IBM scorable answer sheets; 25¢ per scoring stencil; 35¢ per manual; 75¢ per specimen set; postage extra; 60(70) minutes; Committee for Measurement of Economic Understanding, Joint Council on Economic Education (test); Science Research Associates, Inc. *

[Other Tests]

For tests not listed above, see the following entries in *Tests in Print:* 1736 and 1738–9.

GEOGRAPHY

[990]

★Brandywine Achievement Test in Geography for Secondary Schools. Grades 7–12; 1962; Forms A, B, (6 pages); no manual; no data on reliability; no norms; separate answer sheets must be used; $7 per 35 tests; 20¢ per specimen set; postpaid; [50–55] minutes; John A. Bonham and Harry R. Martini; [Brandywine Achievement Test]. *

[991]

***Geography: Every Pupil Scholarship Test.** Grades 5–7; 1933–64; new form (2 pages) usually issued each January and April; forms from previous testing programs also available; general directions sheet ['63, 2 pages]; no data on reliability; norms for new forms available following testing program; 4¢ per test; 4¢ per key; postage extra; 30(35) minutes; Bureau of Educational Measurements. *

[992]

***[Geography]: Every Pupil Test.** Grades 4–6, 7; 1935–64; new form (4 pages) usually issued each December and April; forms from previous testing programs (which included separate tests for grades 4, 5, 6, and 7) also available; 2 levels; general directions sheet ('63, 2 pages); no data on reliability; Ohio norms for new forms available following testing program; 5¢ per test; 3¢ per key; postpaid; 40(45) minutes; Ohio Scholarship Tests. *

a) GRADES 4–6. 2 tests.
  1) *Geography of the Americas.*
  2) *Geography of the Eastern Hemisphere.*

b) GEOGRAPHY OF THE WORLD. Grade 7.

[993]

★Physical Geography: Every Pupil Scholarship Test. High school; 1943; 1 form (2 pages); general directions sheet ['63, 2 pages]; no data on reliability; 4¢ per test; 4¢ per key; postage extra; 40(45) minutes; Bureau of Educational Measurements. *

[994]

***Survey Test in Geography: California Survey Series.** Grades 7–9; 1946–59; subtest 3 of the elementary level (for grades 4–8) of *California Tests in Social and Related Sciences,* Form AA; IBM; Form 1 ('59, 11 pages, identical with test copyrighted in 1953 and identical with test copyrighted in 1946 except for format, changes in option order, and revision of 13 items); combined manual ('59, 15 pages) for this test and test 1010; $2.80 per 35 tests; separate answer sheets may be used; 5¢ per IBM answer sheet; 20¢ per scoring stencil; 10¢ per series class record sheet; 2¢ per series individual record sheet; postage extra; 50¢ per specimen set, postpaid; 38(45) minutes; Georgia Sachs Adams and John A. Sexson; California Test Bureau. *

JONATHON C. MCLENDON, *Professor of Social Science Education, Florida Atlantic University, Boca Raton, Florida.*

Previously published tests in this series were reviewed in *The Fourth* and *The Fifth Mental Measurements Yearbooks,* with much of the comment there still applicable to the nature and construction of each test. Retention of content which is the same as that in the 1953 edition and essentially the same as that in the 1946 edition of the geography test is unfortunate in two respects particularly: (*a*) inaccuracy of such items as item 12 which is keyed to identify Chicago as important for its meat packing industry, and (*b*) general outdatedness of some of the content, with much attention to transportation by water and rail but little to air and motor vehicle transport, for example. Indeed, it is difficult to find, in this test, item content that was not equally usable a quarter of a century ago. While major natural features are relatively permanent, there have been significant shifts in man's relationships to them. The test content includes some relationships, but it consists preponderantly of factual items and geographical terms, largely achievable through memoriter learning.

The publishers report a commendable procedure for establishing validity, involving survey of courses of study and textbooks and reports of research, trials to determine item discrimination and difficulty, and the judgments of a sizable number of teachers and supervisors. Desirably, the test consultants would include geographers. The reviewer is tempted to speculate on the commonsensical character of several items; they appear as appropriate to a test of general intelligence as to an achievement test in geography. Current trends in teaching of geography, reported for example in the National Council for Geographic Education's *Curriculum Guide for Geographic Education,* indicate further the need for revising the contents of the test. Coverage of the test is full in relation to conventional emphases in geography. One may question the suitability of a test as long as 105 items, especially for the lower grades of the grades 7–9 range. The test format is generally satisfactory, though less so in readability of maps, especially that on page 5. While answer sheets are available, the provisions for recording of responses in the test booklet encourage a maximum but uneconomical rate of test booklet use and inefficient scoring.

The eight school systems listed as providing 1957 and 1958 data beyond the 1953 data obtained for the earlier test battery scarcely seem adequate to provide a desirably broad base for norms. No large city school systems are included in the later group. Ideally, there would be made available norms for different kinds of school systems in varying cultural environments.

Use of standard scores in reporting norms represents a step in the right direction. Many users, however, may find the tables giving raw and standard scores and percentile rank equivalents inconvenient, if not incomprehensible. More importantly, the sizable standard error of measurement makes difficult a meaningful interpretation of individual test scores. The grade placement and age norms reported are attributed vaguely to an "independent nationwide survey"; the arithmetical precision with which raw score advances almost exactly one point for each month of grade ranking from 4.7 to 10.2 suggests the possibility of as much speculation as careful establishment of norms. Statistically sophisticated users will not be satisfied with the normative data; other users may unhappily be misled.

In sum, the test appears appropriate for schools that have or desire in geographic instruction a considerable emphasis on memorization of facts and definitions. Those who wish a test with more up-to-date content and with greater stress on geographic understanding and a variety of skills will look elsewhere.

For a review by David R. Krathwohl of the California Tests in Social and Related Sciences, *see 5:4; for reviews by Harry D. Berg and J. Raymond Gerberich of an earlier edition of the elementary level, see 4:23.*

[995]

★**World Geography: Every Pupil Scholarship Test.** High school; 1952–59; 1 form ('59, 4 pages); general directions sheet ['63, 2 pages]; no data on reliability; 4¢ per test; 4¢ per key; postage extra; 50(55) minutes; Bureau of Educational Measurements. *

[Other Tests]

For tests not listed above, see the following entries in *Tests in Print:* 1742, 1747–8, and 1751; out of print: 1741 and 1743–4.

HISTORY

[996]

***American History: Every Pupil Scholarship Test.** High school; 1926–64; forms from previous testing programs also available; 2 tests; general directions sheet ['63, 2 pages]; no data on reliability; norms for new forms available following testing program; 4¢ per test; 4¢ per key; postage extra; 40(45) minutes; Bureau of Educational Measurements. *

a) AMERICAN HISTORY TO 1865. New form (4 pages) usually issued each January.

b) AMERICAN HISTORY SINCE 1865. New form (4 pages) usually issued each April.

[997]

***American History: Every Pupil Test.** Grades 7–9, 10–12; 1931–64; new form usually issued each December and April; 2 levels; general directions sheet ('63, 2 pages; no data on reliability; Ohio norms for new forms available following testing program; 5¢ per test; 3¢ per key; postpaid 40(45) minutes; Ohio Scholarship Tests. *

a) GRADES 7–9. 1935–64; test booklet titles vary.

b) GRADES 10–12. 1931–64.

[998]

★**American History Test: Affiliation Testing Program for Catholic Secondary Schools.** Grades 9–12 and students who are candidates for the high school diploma issued by the Catholic University of America; 1949–63; administered annually in May at individual schools; IBM; new form issued annually; Form Z ('63, 16 pages) used in 1963 program; separate answer sheets must be used; 50¢ per test and IBM answer sheet; postpaid; fee includes purchase of test booklets, scoring, and other services; specimen set of the complete battery free; for more complete information, see 758; 90(100) minutes; Program of Affiliation, Catholic University of America. *

HENRY CHAUNCEY, *President, Educational Testing Service, Princeton, New Jersey.* [Review of Forms Y and Z.]

In the introductory statement to the description of the American history course which this test is designed to cover, it is implied that the primary objectives of the course are to teach a student the facts of American history and an understanding of some of the causal connections between events in American history. The most serious criticism of these two forms of the test, which purport to measure a student's achievement in these areas, must be that none of the questions meet the laudable second objective. The tests are composed entirely of items requiring rote recall of factual-type information, such as "The Atlantic Charter dealt with" (Form Y, item 36) or "Washington's Cabinet included all of these men except" (Form Y, item 41). Completion questions which do ask about the effects of a particular policy or event merely require recall of memorized results, and not reasoned understanding of why one thing caused another; for example, "Jackson's policy toward the United States Bank resulted in 1. A shortage of farm credit 2. improved national banks 3. a sound monetary system 4. state control of banking activities" (Form Z, item 15).

Both forms also include sections made up of a less common item type which tries to deal with causal relations directly, but the novel format only overcomplicates the questioning and oversimplifies the events. For example, in Form Y, item 124 lists "one crop system" in one column and "industrial development of the South" in a second column; the connecting link (the key) is supposed to be "prevents.... [the second-column item] from occurring or coming into existence." The absence of any date makes the item ambiguous, since the situation differed in the nineteenth and twentieth centuries; moreover, the implication that a single factor caused a complicated, pervasive development is misleading, if not in error. (The instructions for this section are improved in Form Z, but the technique is still doubtful.)

Three further objectives described in the introductory statement to the course description suggest that students of American history should learn "the truth," as opposed to "opinion, or pious belief," should apply their learning to current events, and should become better informed citizens. These goals are nowhere more specifically defined, but neither form includes any questions which ask for application to novel situations of principles learned from history; such questions might reflect a student's achievement of these objectives.

With relation to the content which the test purports to cover, the balance seems faulty in terms of chronology and emphasis, both within and between the two forms. The introductory statement indicates that the courses taught in Catholic schools should divide American history at 1850 into two equal terms of work. Yet in Form Y, only a little more than one third of the items concern post-1850 history. More specifically, one seventh of the test covers the colonial period, which seems to be a larger proportion than is justified by the attention given to that period in typical high school courses. In comparison to this emphasis, the Revolution, the Constitution, and the 1920's are neglected. Form Z weights the distribution in the opposite direction, with nearly two thirds of the questions on post-1850 happenings. Thus, the forms are hardly parallel in content. Furthermore, neither form gives enough attention to two themes that are increasingly emphasized in newer textbooks, namely, the reasons for the ways in which the economy and the power of the Federal Government have developed.

The introduction to the American history course description also suggests that the course should encourage the student's appreciation of the contributions of Catholics to American life, and help "to correct the distortion and peculiar emphasis now found in so many high school textbooks." The test acknowledges this intention by including three items in Form Y and eight in Form Z on the history of the Church, but on the whole the items reflect no markedly different interpretation of United States history than that found in tests prepared for public as well as parochial schools.

Tables 1, 2, and 3 (giving data on the norms population and student and class norms) in the ATP American History Test and Item Analysis Report for Form Y are helpful for teachers who know how to use them, but Table 4 (providing item content classifications and difficulty indices) has a fundamental organizational problem which makes the findings therein often useless. The problem is that the content areas are vaguely defined and are used part of the time as straight chronological divisions and other times as strand divisions of American history. While there may be some logic to the system, the titles of the eight content categories (there are nine for Form Z) do not themselves provide a thorough enough explanation of what each category includes and why. For example, an item on the mugwumps (Form Y, item 29) and one on imperialism (Form Y, item 27) are both lumped together in a category labeled "Expansion"; a question on legislation of the Progressive period (Form Y, item 49) and one on the Korean War (Form Y, item 143) both fall into a group called "World Power." One fourth of the items are classified in categories which lead to this type of confusion. Consequently, the interpretation of subscores based on such categories is bound to be a misleading indication of the strengths and weaknesses of a class.

Overall, the test includes items which are weak in the following aspects of verbal construction: Some stems are not directive enough to tell the student clearly what he is to do (for example, Form Y, items 135 and 150); ambiguities in other stems make the keys debatable (for example, Form Y, items 3, 31, 32, and 94); answer options are not always written in parallel construction (for example, Form Y, items 10, 15, and 42); awkward construction unnecessarily complicates many issues (for example, Form Y, items 11, 17, 22, 27, 34, 44, 45, and 149).

Two difficulties occur in terms of factual content: (*a*) in a few instances, historical facts and interpretations appear to be faulty (for example, Form Y, items 16 and 139; the sample questions for 133–150), and (*b*) a few obscure titles make several items unjustifiably difficult (Form Y, items 109, Transcontinental Treaty, and 113, the abbreviation ODT; Form Z, item 65, Transcontinental Treaty, and 93, Glass-Owens Bill for the Federal Reserve Act).

The Affiliation Testing Program makes ambitious claims to measure students' historical and social attitudes, skills, and knowledge; but in fact, the tests demand only rote recall of tired maxims about the American past. The method of inquiry is equally conventional, and occasionally faulty, in terms of language, facts, interpretation, organization, and questioning technique.

For a review of the complete program, see 758.

[999]

★Ancient History: Every Pupil Scholarship Test. High school; 1933–58; 1 form ('58, 2 pages); general directions sheet ['63, 2 pages]; no data on reliability; 4¢ per test; 4¢ per key; postage extra; 40(45) minutes; Bureau of Educational Measurements. *

[1000]

***College Entrance Examination Board Advanced Placement Examination: American History.** High school students desiring credit for college level courses or admission to advanced courses; 1956–63; for more complete information, see 761; 180(200) minutes; program administered for the College Entrance Examination Board by Educational Testing Service. *

REFERENCES

1. "CEEB Advanced Placement Examination: American History." Reproduction of an earlier examination and commentary by Henry F. Graff. *Social Ed* 26:251–62 My '62. *

HARRY D. BERG, *Professor, Office of Evaluation Services, Michigan State University, East Lansing, Michigan.* [Review of Form KBP.]

The *College Entrance Examination Board Advanced Placement Examination: American History* is a three-hour test with objective and essay sections. The objective portion has 75 items with a 45-minute time allotment; during the remainder of the time the candidate is to write on three essay questions drawn from a limited number of options. After a rather complex scoring procedure, composite scores are reported to the colleges on a 5-point scale. The amount of time devoted to the test should be adequate for securing a reliable sample, and the items, both objective and essay, seem appropriate in difficulty and coverage for an introductory college course in American history.

The objective portion of the test is up to the high standards of the College Entrance Examination Board. It has a reliability of .85, a mean raw score of 33.7 (corrected for guessing), and an unusually high mean index of discrimination of .38 (biserial correlations of item scores with total raw scores). Except for a few key-list items, undoubtedly included to increase the number of scoring units, the items are of the multiple choice variety. The items do a good job of sampling the various forms in which American history data are presented. Some are grouped items based on cartoons, graphs, and reading selections, while others are discrete items which require the student to analyze quotations, make comparisons, draw inferences, and exhibit other like abilities. Nearly all measure for concepts of broad significance and emphasize reasoned understanding rather than memorized content detail. This reviewer's only criticism would be that the objective test should be given more of the time and have greater influence in arriving at the composite score.

The essay portion of the examination is more open to criticism, not on the grounds of question selection, which is excellent, but on the grounds of reader and reading reliability. Low reliability has always been the great shortcoming of essay tests, and particularly so when national programs are involved. Despite complex efforts to make scoring more objective and despite the accumulated experience of the Board and ETS, the problem seems not much closer to solution than ever. Two pieces of statistical evidence to support this conclusion are presented. First, the intercorrelations among the subscores of the three essay questions (each question answered by a student is graded by a different reader) is very low, ranging in the neighborhood of .30. Secondly, the means of the options which students may select differ widely. One would expect that each option would attract about the same range of ability. Unless some unexplained selective factor is at work, the conclusion can hardly be escaped that reader standards change from one option to another. In brief, students with the same writing ability and knowledge may be receiving different scores depending upon the options selected. The fact that students who did poorly on a particular option did well on the objective portion, and the reverse, helps to confirm the observation. Perhaps the use of options should be reexamined. What is gained in reliability in offering the student more opportunities for showing his writing ability may be more than lost in the increased difficulty of establishing reader standards.

The comments which have just been made are in no way intended to reflect on the value of the Advanced Placement Program. The program is needed in American education and it is well that it is growing. It should be added that the test scores are only one part of the information given to colleges. Secondary school grades and recommendations, as well as the test papers themselves, are provided. It is, therefore, on a wide array of evidence that decisions to give advanced placement or credit can be made. It speaks well for the program that the selected freshmen do as well or better in their advanced courses than do sophomores in the same courses.

For reviews by James A. Field, Jr. and Christine McGuire of an earlier form, see 5:812.

[1001]

***College Entrance Examination Board Advanced Placement Examination: European History.** High school students desiring credit for college level courses or admission to advanced courses; 1956-63; for more complete information, see 761; 180(200) minutes; program administered for the College Entrance Examination Board by Educational Testing Service. *

REFERENCES

1. "CEEB Advanced Placement Examination: European History." Reproduction of a 1958 Examination. *Social Ed* 25:335-43 N '61. *
2. WINKLER, HENRY R. "The Advanced Placement Program and Examination in European History." *Social Ed* 25:332-4 N '61. *

[1002]

★Cooperative Topical Tests in American History. High school; 1963; title on manual is *Topical Tests in American History;* 1 form; 8 tests (6-8 pages); manual (4 pages); no data on reliability; "the norm on any one of these tests is a perfect score for all items" the examiner considers relevant to his teaching objectives; 50¢ per set of all 8 tests; 50¢ per set of keys; $1 per specimen set of all 8 tests; postage extra; 40(45) minutes; Cooperative Test Division. *

a) TEST 1, EXPLORATION, COLONIZATION, AND INDEPENDENCE: 1450-1783.
b) TEST 2, FOUNDATIONS OF AMERICAN GOVERNMENT: 1781-1801.
c) TEST 3, GROWTH OF NATIONALISM AND DEMOCRACY: 1801-1840.
d) TEST 4, EXPANSION, CIVIL WAR, AND RECONSTRUCTION: 1840-1877.
e) TEST 5, DEVELOPMENT OF INDUSTRIAL AMERICA: 1865-1898.
f) TEST 6, IMPERIALISM, DOMESTIC REFORM, AND THE FIRST WORLD WAR: 1898-1920.
g) TEST 7, PROSPERITY, DEPRESSION, AND THE NEW DEAL: 1920-1940.
h) TEST 8, THE SECOND WORLD WAR AND AFTER.

[1003]

***The Graduate Record Examinations Advanced Tests: History.** Grades 16-17; 1939-60; for more complete information, see 762; 180(200) minutes; Educational Testing Service. *

For a review by Robert H. Ferrell of an earlier form, see 5:818. For a review of the testing program, see 5:601.

[1004]

***History: Every Pupil Scholarship Test.** Grades 5-6, 7-8; 1933-64; new form (2-4 pages) usually issued each January and April; forms from previous testing programs also available; 2 levels; general directions sheet ['63, 2 pages]; no data on reliability; norms for new forms available following testing program; 4¢ per test; 4¢ per key; postage extra; 30(35) or 40(45) minutes; Bureau of Educational Measurements. *

[1005]

***Kansas United States History Test.** 1, 2 semesters in grades 7-8; 1957-58; IBM; Forms A ('57), B ('58), (2 pages); 2 levels labeled Tests 1, 2; manual ('57, 5 pages); no data on reliability of Form B; no norms for Form B; $1.20 per 25 tests; separate answer sheets may be used; 85¢ per 25 IBM answer sheets; 30¢ per scoring stencil; postage extra; 25¢ per specimen set, postpaid; 30(35) minutes; Shirley Meares and M. W. Sanders; Bureau of Educational Measurements. *

For reviews by Wayne A. Frederick and John Manning, see 5:820.

[1006]

★Objective Tests in American History. 1, 2 semesters high school; 1960; 1 form; 13 tests: 10 unit tests (3-4 pages), 2 semester tests (4-6 pages), and a final examination (4 pages); no manual; no data on reliability; no norms; separate answer sheets must be used; 5 or more tests with answer sheet, 10¢ each; 75¢ per 25 answer sheets; 15¢ per key (free with 24 or more copies of any one test); $3.25 per specimen set; cash orders postpaid; [50] minutes per test for unit tests, [60] minutes per test for other tests; Earl Bridgewater; Perfection Form Co. *

[1007]

★Objective Tests in World History. 1, 2 semesters high school; 1961; 1 form; 16 tests: 13 unit tests (3–4 pages), 2 semester tests (4 pages), and a final examination (4 pages); no manual; no data on reliability; no norms; separate answer sheets must be used; 5 or more tests with answer sheet, 10¢ each; 75¢ per 25 answer sheets; 15¢ per key (free with 24 or more copies of any one test); $4.15 per specimen set; cash orders postpaid; [50] minutes per test for unit tests, [60] minutes per test for other tests; Earl Bridgewater; Perfection Form Co. *

[1008]

***Social Studies 10 (American History): Minnesota High School Achievement Examinations.** Grade 10; 1955–63; earlier forms called *American History: Midwest High School Achievement Examinations;* new form issued each May; norms available in June following release of new form; Form F ('63, 8 pages) used in 1963 testing; no specific manual; series manual ('63, 4 pages); series norms ['63, 4 pages]; series cumulative profile ('62, 2 pages); no data on reliability; no description of normative population; 12¢ per test; $2.50 per 100 profiles; postage extra; 20¢ per specimen set, postpaid; 60(65) minutes; American Guidance Service, Inc. *

For a review by Howard R. Anderson of earlier forms, see 5:810.

[1009]

***Social Studies 11 (World History): Minnesota High School Achievement Examinations.** Grade 11; 1955–63; earlier forms called *Modern World History: Midwest High School Achievement Examinations;* new form issued each May; norms available in June following release of new form; Form F ('63, 6 pages) used in 1963 testing; no specific manual; series manual ('63, 4 pages); series norms ['63, 4 pages]; series cumulative profile ('62, 2 pages); no data on reliability; no description of normative population; 12¢ per test; $2.50 per 100 profiles; postage extra; 20¢ per specimen set, postpaid; 60(65) minutes; American Guidance Service, Inc. *

[1010]

***Survey Test in Introductory American History: California Survey Series.** Grades 7–9; 1946–59; subtest 1 of the elementary level (for grades 4–8) of *California Tests in Social and Related Sciences,* Form AA; IBM; Form 1 ('59, 10 pages, identical with test copyrighted in 1953 and identical with test copyrighted in 1946 except for format, 2 new items, option order in 16 items, order of 2 items, wording changes in 15 items, and other revisions in 3 items); combined manual ('59, 15 pages) for this test and test 994; $2.80 per 35 tests; separate answer sheets may be used; 5¢ per IBM answer sheet; 20¢ per scoring stencil; 10¢ per series class record sheet; 2¢ per series individual record sheet; postage extra; 50¢ per specimen set, postpaid; 40(45) minutes; Georgia Sachs Adams and John A. Sexson; California Test Bureau. *

RICHARD E. GROSS, *Associate Professor of Education, Stanford University, Stanford, California.*

This test and the accompanying survey test in geography have been taken from the battery of the *California Tests in Social and Related Sciences* without any change of content from the material copyrighted in 1953 and with only modest changes from the original edition of that battery copyrighted in 1946. The tests are claimed to sample the pupil's ability to understand and apply principles as well as his knowledge of facts.

The 95 items would seem to parallel an outdated emphasis too typically found in elementary school United States history offerings and the test probably fails to satisfactorily differentiate between more recently recommended areas of concentration for the usual fifth grade and eighth grade American history offerings. Twenty-two items are devoted to the Colonial Period, 28 to the Westward Movement, and 20 to other aspects of our history stretching from before the Civil War to World War II. The test concludes with 25 items supposed to be related to the understanding of democracy and citizenship education, although several of these are historical also. It would seem that teachers who wish to include some history of the past quarter century, who do not want to just reemphasize much of the same content taught in the fifth grade course, and who want to teach in important areas going beyond a few key personalities and the problems of exploration, settlement, pioneers and Indians, and life on the plains would find this test quite unsatisfactory.

Most of the items are quite clear and vocabulary is certainly within the ken of junior high pupils. About two thirds of the items are multiple choice with four foils; the remaining are true-false. If one is satisfied with the content being tested, the majority of the items seem quite satisfactory. No dates are included as such, but pupils have to know sequence or the periods in which certain events happened. A number of questions require the testee to indicate if a development occurred before, after, or during the "War Between the States" or some other war; one would wish that other events besides wars, or perhaps even dates themselves, were used to so classify periods. It also seems imperative that teachers continue to use the outmoded term, the "War Between the States," placed in most such tests to get Southern sales, instead of the commonly accepted "Civil War." In items 32 and 84, "negroes" should be capitalized. Several other items call for alteration

—or should be rejected in future editions of the test. Items 64 and 65, for example, could confuse the bright pupil. In the former, among the results of the "War Between the States" the student is expected to pick the right answer from four choices, two of which are "The Union was preserved" and "Manufacturing was developed"; any good student knows that both were important results of the war. In the next item, pupils are expected to select the statement that is true "concerning the first World War"; the "correct" answer describes an event which occurred *after* the war.

On the other hand, some items are so clear as to the correct foil that one is led to question just what really important understandings they are expected to differentiate; examples are items 3, 34, and 86. Item 19 is one of the poorer examples of the objective item that penalizes the pupil who knows his history. It asks, "Which one of the following factors helped to bring about the discovery of America?" Among the choices are "the desire to obtain the wealth of the Orient" and "the adventurous spirit of the seamen of the day." Is the reference to the Vikings or to Columbus? In the latter case, were not both motivations? When will competent historians become more involved in such test construction?

Some will not like certain of the emphases and queries in the civics aspect of the test; but, in conclusion, the greatest fault of this test is its failure to include items and emphases that might help lead teachers to improved instruction that incorporates updated concepts and developments and social studies aims beyond primarily the reproduction of content.

For a review by David R. Krathwohl of the California Tests in Social and Related Sciences, *see 5:4; for reviews by Harry D. Berg and J. Raymond Gerberich of an earlier edition of the elementary level, see 4:23.*

[1011]

***World History: Every Pupil Scholarship Test.** High school; 1926–64; new form (4 pages) usually issued each January and April; forms from previous testing programs also available; general directions sheet ['63, 2 pages]; no data on reliability; norms for new forms available following testing program; 4¢ per test; 4¢ per key; postage extra; 40(45) minutes; Bureau of Educational Measurements. *

[1012]

***World History: Every Pupil Test.** High school; 1933–64; new form (4 pages) usually issued each December and April; forms from previous testing programs also available; general directions sheet ('63, 2 pages); no data on reliability; Ohio norms for new forms available following testing program; 5¢ per test; 3¢ per key; postpaid; 40(45) minutes; Ohio Scholarship Tests. *

[1013]

★World History Test: Affiliation Testing Program for Catholic Secondary Schools. Grades 9–12 and students who are candidates for the high school diploma issued by the Catholic University of America; 1949–63; administered annually in May at individual schools; IBM; new form issued annually; Form Z ('63, 12 pages) used in 1963 program; separate answer sheets must be used; 50¢ per test and IBM answer sheet; postpaid; fee includes purchase of test booklets, scoring, and other services; specimen set of the complete battery free; for more complete information, see 758; 90(100) minutes; Program of Affiliation, Catholic University of America. *

HENRY CHAUNCEY, *President, Educational Testing Service, Princeton, New Jersey.* [Review of Forms Y and Z.]

The test is probably not too difficult or too speeded for the educational level at which it is directed. If, however, a candidate's course has followed the general aims outlined in the publisher's statement about the world history course the test is designed to cover, he would presumably find much in the test which he has not covered in the required detail, and much which he has studied that is not covered by either form. Though called World History Test, both forms are really tests of western civilization, with very few questions on other areas, and a large number on ancient and medieval history. Similarly, according to the course description the second term covers history after the end of the French Revolution. Actually, only approximately one fifth of the questions in the test relate to the nineteenth and twentieth centuries. Also, the questions are of such a nature that they measure detail rather than broad historical developments—another contradiction of stated aims. Similarly, little attention is paid to economic and social history. Moreover, the two forms do not contain similar item types. The stated objectives of the course in world history could be more adequately tested by the broader subject matter coverage indicated above and by the use of item types which would require the candidate to use his historical knowledge in new situations. Form Y would be improved by questions, not purely factual in nature, based on maps, passages, and quotations. Form Z would be improved by questions such as those in Part 1 of Form Y, and by more searching questions on stimulus materials.

The instructions for taking the test are clear, with the following exceptions: The sample question given on the front cover of both forms, which purports to be a sample for all questions in the test, is actually a sample for Part 1, the other parts each having a different sample question. Also, samples indicate five answer positions, whereas some item types have but four options.

In Form Y the questions in Part 4 (which involve first picking out the option which does not belong with the others in the group and then ordering the remaining options chronologically) are time consuming and, within the sets, dependent on one another in such a way that one error can cause the loss of more than one point. Certain types of questions, notably those in Parts 2 and 4, which involve association or relation of individuals or ideas, require the candidate to think as the examiner has thought. In questions of this type the advantage is with the candidate whose information is more stereotyped, not with the candidate whose knowledge is more sophisticated. The questions in Part 5 frequently test only a knowledge of dates, not cause and effect, as is the stated purpose. Some options contain specific determiners (items 14, options 2 and 3, and 24, options 1 and 2), some answers seem very obvious (items 8 and 100), and some answers seem of questionable accuracy (item 50). A minor point: the name Bismarck is twice misspelled.

In Form Z, there are no questions like those in Part 1 of Form Y, which may be described as discrete informational questions. All questions are based on types of stimulus material or require the candidate to make an association of some sort. Also in Form Z, Part 4 purports to test chronological knowledge, but the periods are so large that for many questions there can be only one alternative. On the other hand, a few questions require an exact date close to the beginning or end of a period. The questions in Part 3, which are based on a world map, are poor. The five regions numbered as possible answers are so far apart that only occasionally would the candidate have to make any real choice among the options. Also, a single number may be used with more than one meaning (for example, 1 refers to the continent of Africa, which is also called a country, to Carthage, and to Morocco). Part 2 consists of spot quotations which must be identified. Quotations representing points of view or schools of thought, or describing places, people, or events would provide a better test of the candidate's historical understanding.

In view of the subject matter and the time span covered by this test and the types of questions employed, a potential user would be advised to review the test carefully to be sure it will meet his needs.

For a review of the complete program, see 758.

[Other Tests]

For tests not listed above, see the following entries in *Tests in Print:* 1755, 1757–9, 1763–6, 1768–9, 1775, 1777, 1779–81, 1787, and 1790–4; out of print: 1756, 1767, 1770, 1773–4, and 1785–6.

POLITICAL SCIENCE

[1013a]

American Civics and Government Tests for High Schools and Colleges, Revised Edition. High school and college; 1930–54; Forms A, B, ['54, 8 pages, same as forms copyrighted in 1949 except for minor changes]; directions sheet ['49, 2 pages]; reliability, validity, and normative data based on 1949 forms; $3.15 per 35 tests; 50¢ per specimen set; postage extra; high school: 40(50) minutes; college: 35(45) minutes; F. A. Magruder, R. J. Clinton, and M. M. Chambers; [Bobbs-Merrill Co., Inc.]. *

JOHN H. HAEFNER, *Professor of Social Studies Education, State University of Iowa, Iowa City, Iowa.*

Form A consists of 63 multiple response items, each with four responses, and 57 matching items grouped into five sections. The answer key, consisting of a single sheet with the correct responses printed in six columns, is exceedingly awkward to use and very inefficient in terms of teacher time. A single sheet of directions provides information concerning the purposes of the test, its construction, the norms employed; directions for administering and scoring the test; and a minimum of data on reliability and validity. A class record sheet also accompanies the test.

The 63 multiple response items test exclusively for memoriter recall of isolated, and for the most part relatively insignificant, factual material. None of the items in this part could properly be classified as testing any reflective abilities, or any understanding of the processes of government. Furthermore, the items do not adequately sample the subject matter of American government, leaving large areas such as federal-state relationships, the civil service, and government finances—to mention only a few—completely untested. The items throughout the test are completely unimaginative in format, and at least five (items 57, Part 1; 30, 32, 20, and 27, Part 2) are obsolescent and the keyed responses no longer correct. The format of the matching items in Part 2 does not conform with accepted practice today.

The information provided on the directions sheet is entirely inadequate. In two separate places the sheet claims diagnostic values for the test—an unsupported claim which is warranted only in the vaguest and most general sense. The reliability is reported as ".85 (240 cases)," without any additional information as to specific techniques used to arrive at this figure. Validity "was determined by correlating a known criterion (teachers' marks) with scores on the test." On this basis, validity is reported as .65, based on 109 cases.

Both high school and college and "normal school" norms are provided. High school norms were based on 2,016 high school students, but nothing further about the nature of this sample is reported. College and normal school norms are based on a sample of 616 students, and no other information about the sample is provided.

The directions sheet states, "Each item included is found in the majority of the commonly used textbooks now in use, and each was carefully analyzed before it was put in the preliminary form." This appears to be the only criterion employed in the construction and selection of the items included. By inference, therefore, the authors were concerned only with measuring students' ability to recall material appearing in textbooks. The claims that the test will measure "the effectiveness of classroom instruction," that it will "test a pupil's understanding in the field," that it "makes it easy for a teacher to diagnose the pupil's difficulties," and that it can be used to "measure pupil progress" are certainly inadequately supported, if not downright misleading.

Except as an indication of students' ability for memoriter recall, this test has little to recommend it for high school use, and even less for college use. In the judgment of this reviewer, the test should be removed from sale as a public service.

[1014]

***American Government and Citizenship: Every Pupil Test.** Grades 11–12; 1935–64; new form (4 pages) usually issued each April; forms from previous testing programs also available; general directions sheet ('63, 2 pages); no data on reliability; Ohio norms for new forms available following testing program; 5¢ per test; 3¢ per key; postpaid; 40(45) minutes; Ohio Scholarship Tests. *

For a review by Elizabeth C. Adams of the 1951 form, see 4:699.

[1015]

***American Government: Every Pupil Scholarship Test.** High school; 1930–63; new form (4 pages) usually issued each April; forms from previous testing programs also available; general directions sheet ['63, 2 pages]; no data on reliability; norms for new forms available following testing program; 4¢ per test; 4¢ per key; postage extra; 40(45) minutes; Bureau of Educational Measurements. *

[1016]

***Constitution: Every Pupil Scholarship Test.** High school; 1926–64; new form (4 pages) usually issued each January; forms from previous testing programs also available; general directions sheet ['63, 2 pages]; no data on reliability; norms for new forms available following testing program; 4¢ per test; 4¢ per key; postage extra; 40(45) minutes; Bureau of Educational Measurements. *

[1017]

★Duke University Political Science Information Test (American Government). Grade 13; 1958; 5 scores: federal government, constitutional system, politics, programs and policies, total; Forms A, B, (7 pages, must be reproduced locally from sample copy); mimeographed manual (8 pages); no data on reliability and no norms presented in manual; $1 per test and manual, postpaid; 40(50) minutes; Robert H. Connery, Richard H. Leach, and Henry Weitz; distributed by Richard H. Leach. *

[1018]

***The Graduate Record Examinations Advanced Tests: Government.** Grades 16–17; 1939–61; for more complete information, see 762; 180(200) minutes; Educational Testing Service. *

For a review by Christine McGuire of an earlier form, see 5:835. For a review of the testing program, see 5:601.

[1019]

Peltier-Durost Civics and Citizenship Test: Evaluation and Adjustment Series. High school; 1958; 2 scores: achievement, attitude; IBM; Forms AM, BM, (6 pages); manual (9 pages); expectancy chart (2 pages); separate answer sheets must be used; $4.10 per 35 tests; $1.45 per 35 IBM answer sheets; 40¢ per specimen set; postage extra; 55(65) minutes; Charles L. Peltier and Walter N. Durost; [Harcourt, Brace & World, Inc.]. *

Howard R. Anderson, *Senior Consulting Editor, High School Department, Houghton Mifflin Company, Boston, Massachusetts.*

The manual states that the *Peltier-Durost Civics and Citizenship Test* is designed to to measure three broad objectives: "the acquisition of information concerning the structure and functions of government at federal, state, and local levels; development of understanding of certain concepts and processes central to a democratic type of government; and development of certain attitudes considered to be characteristic of the good citizen in a democracy." This test is primarily intended for use in grade 9.

Each form of the test includes four parts. Part 1 is made up of 50 four-response multiple choice items. Part 2 contains 15 statements about the functions of officials. In each case the appropriate title is to be selected from an alphabetical list of 49 officials. Part 3 consists of 4 matching exercises, each made up of three statements and five responses. Part 4 includes 32 statements which briefly describe ways of behaving. The pupil is expected to mark each statement A (agree), D, ? (in some circumstances, agree; in others, disagree), DK (don't know), DU (don't understand).

The majority of the items in Part 1 test recall of information. For example, "Responsibility for protecting the President....rests with...." The answer is "Secret Service" (item 4, Form AM). The items have been carefully edited; e.g., the stems are well phrased and the wrong responses are plausible but not unfair.

To do well on Part 2 the pupil would need to be able to recall the titles of the officials identified, for it would be difficult and time consuming to "match" the right name in an alphabetized list of 49 items. The example provided for this exercise seems farfetched: "This official might help to determine the rate you would have to pay for shipping a crate of oranges from Florida to Illinois." The answer is "Interstate Commerce Commissioner." Somehow one does not associate one of the Commissioners with the setting in which a tourist normally sends a crate of oranges to a friend.

One of the matching exercises in Part 3 (Form AM) seems difficult, or dated, or both. The three questions asked concern (*a*) the number of countries in the UN in 1953, (*b*) the number of amendments to the U.S. Constitution in 1953, and (*c*) the number of states required to ratify a constitutional amendment. The answers are to be chosen from these numbers: 18, 22, 36, 48, 60. Perhaps a student should be able to figure out that 22 is the right answer for *b*. Ten years later few pupils would know, though some might guess, that 60 is the answer for *a*. But surely 36 is not the correct answer for *c*.

The statements of attitude in Part 4 include some directly related to the experiences of children but more that are related to the experiences of grownups. They are focused on significant issues. The directions state: "Be sure you answer just as you really feel. This section is not like the rest of the test, where there are definitely right or wrong answers. These statements are matters of opinion on which people may have different ideas." Although students are asked to indicate their attitudes by checking agree, disagree, don't know, or don't understand, all correct answers are either agree or disagree. Might it not be better to include statements that actually are so controversial that varying degrees of agreement could be indicated? It seems unfair, somehow, to suggest to the student that the "right answer" may be in doubt when actually it is not. Requiring a yes or no answer doubtless would affect the mind set of the pupils tested.

The manual describes how the test was validated. Content specifications were derived from an analysis of seven widely used civics textbooks. This analysis suggested the following distribution of content: 25 per cent economics, 40 per cent government, 20 per cent sociology, 10 per cent personal development, 5 per cent consumer education. One wonders if the percentage of content derived from government is not higher in present-day civics courses.

Preliminary forms of the test were administered to more than 2,500 New England pupils, and the items revised in the light of criticisms made by teachers as well as of statistical analysis. For standardization purposes the test was then administered to 2,500 students in 13 high schools in 10 states in May 1954. The manual includes a table for translating raw scores into standard scores and percentile ranks. It also provides difficulty values for all items in both tests. The medians of the several estimates of reliability are .88 for the achievement section and .76 for the attitude section.

Teachers who wish an estimate of how well their pupils have mastered traditional information can use the two forms of the Peltier-Durost test for beginning (or end) of the year testing. Because the junior high school civics course has long been fluid, it might be desirable to construct a test that places major emphasis on skills and includes selections providing the content on which test items are based.

CHRISTINE McGUIRE, *Assistant Director, Research in Medical Education, University of Illinois College of Medicine, Chicago, Illinois.*

In the opening paragraph of the manual, this test is described as one "designed to measure attainment of certain of the generally accepted outcomes of instruction in a civics and citizenship course such as is commonly offered in the 9th grade....[including] the acquisition of information concerning the structure and functions of government at federal, state, and local levels; development of understanding of certain concepts and processes central to a democratic type of government; and development of certain attitudes considered to be characteristic of the good citizen in a democracy." The test was developed through a review of seven textbooks in widest use at the time of its construction (now somewhat remote). Five major areas (economics, 25 per cent; government, 40 per cent; sociology, 20 per cent; personal development, 10 per cent; and consumer education, 5 per cent) were subdivided into several hundred specific subtopics. "Tabulation was then made of the frequency of occurrence of the subtopics in the seven selected textbooks."

The achievement section of the test gives evidence of a slavish conformity to this frequency count. The items are randomly arranged, uncoordinated, and extremely dull. For example, such questions as the following abound: "Responsibility for protecting the President of the United States and his family rests with the" (followed by the names of four agencies); "How many members were there in the United Nations in 1953?" (followed by five numbers); "The sheriff is the principal law enforcement agent for a" (followed by names of four territorial jurisdictions). Interspersed among the factual questions are a few questions which can only be regarded as articles of faith. For example, such a question as: "Which of the following is the best reason for staying in school until you graduate from high school?" must be viewed as a matter of opinion even though the "right" answer conforms to our most cherished stereotypes about the relationship between quantity of education and preparation for earning a living. Finally, in the achievement portion of the test there are a few questions requiring identification of an example or the definition of a basic concept; these are, by far, the least objectionable.

The last section of the test is designed to measure the "development of certain attitudes considered to be characteristic of the good citizen in a democracy." Throughout the manual there are many subtle and some explicit references to "right attitudes." In the opinion of this reviewer, uncritical acceptance of such a dangerous concept denies the philosophic position it purports to identify and vitiates valid efforts toward constructive citizenship education. The manual reports that:

> As a basis for defining the attitudinal outcomes to be measured by the test, the authors relied upon the report, "Characteristics of a Good Democratic Citizen," prepared by the Working Committee on Citizenship of the National Council for the Social Studies, National Education Association (February 1950). This statement lists understandings, beliefs, and actions of a good citizen in a democracy. On the basis of the committee report 78 declarative statements were composed to which the student [responds] by marking one of the five options * The answers considered "right" are those which agree with the point of view embodied in the National Council report.

In the words of the manual: "To the extent to which this report is an adequate description of the good citizen and to the extent to which the test items are representative of what is in the report, *the student's responses reflect the degree to which he espouses desirable citizenship attitudes.*" (Italics are those of the reviewer.) If so, either the authors of the report or the authors of the test, or both, have failed. These "declarative statements" have two serious deficiencies: most are such obvious platitudes (for example, "One who keeps well informed on current events is a better citizen than one who doesn't") as to lead this reviewer to have doubts about the brain rather than the heart of any ninth grade student who fails to respond in the "expected" manner. Other items (for example, those concerning the right to strike or the particular definition of property rights applicable to natural resources) deal superficially, in some cases almost flippantly, with serious issues. Such cavalier treatment of basic constitutional questions that still occupy the highest courts of the land can only be a disservice to legitimate goals of citizenship education. The implication that there is an easy "right answer" must be misleading to the thoughtful student.

In addition to these basic deficiencies, the test entails unnecessary complexities of administration including internal time limitations of undue precision (e.g., 23 minutes for Part 1, 7 minutes for Part 2). While the test is reported to have been standardized on the basis of an administration to several thousand students in a number of states, other than number of schools and states represented and grade level (ninth grade), mean IQ, and approximate size of the group, there is no specific description of the sample population.

The accompanying manual is formally complete in that it gives directions for administration, scoring, and interpretation of results, and reports data about reliability, standard scores, and correlation with other measures of aptitude and achievement, although on the whole, it is so poorly written as to be confusing to the uninitiated. More seriously, however, it recommends what this reviewer regards as a positive misuse of the test. It not only suggests, but encourages the use of this single examination in conjunction with an intelligence test to perpetuate the identification, at best dubious, of "under-achievers" and "over-achievers" in civics and citizenship classes.

In short, the test is not recommended for use with any group, since it offers neither intellectual challenge nor serious concern about the basic democratic values which it purports to sample. The parallel forms are strictly equivalent in this respect. The very misuses for which testing programs are responsibly criticized, are advocated. The concept of scoring attitudes as right or wrong rather than as multidirectional, patterned, and almost infinitely contingent, the implicit approval given to comparing individuals and groups to poorly identified norms, the advice given to use the test as an aid in the labeling of individuals as underachievers and overachievers, and, finally, the tacit encouragement to teachers to emphasize trivia and platitudes in their civics courses, can only be viewed as shocking.

[1020]

★**Principles of Democracy Test.** Grades 9–12; 1961, c1960–61; IBM; Form A ('61, c1960, 8 pages); manual ('61, 24 pages); separate answer sheets must be used; $3 per 20 tests; $4 per 100 IBM answer sheets; 25¢ per scoring stencil; 75¢ per specimen set; postage extra; 40(45) minutes; Nathaniel L. Gage, Neil F. Garvey, Charles B. Hagan, and Roland Payette; Science Research Associates, Inc. *

WILLIAM C. BINGHAM, *Lecturer in Education, Rutgers, The State University, New Brunswick, New Jersey.*

The *Principles of Democracy Test,* according to the authors, is "designed to measure student knowledge and understanding of democratic principles as they are interpreted in the United States." To a great extent, this purpose is achieved very adequately in that many of the items deal effectively with understandings and application of facts. This quality is highly desirable and should be incorporated in more achievement tests.

In general, the manual is very good. Directions for both administration and scoring are simple, clear, easy to follow, and adequate in all respects. Time limits are appropriate for high school classroom use and are liberal enough to permit most students an opportunity to attempt all items.

Standardization procedures are reported in more detail than is often found, but one or two improvements in this connection would be helpful to the test user. While the standardization group is appropriately representative as a national sample, more specific description of the groups composing that sample could assist the test user in determining how well his own group is represented. This is particularly so because the standardization group apparently includes some students who were, and others who were not, studying related subject matter when the data were collected. Thus, the teacher who uses this test in association with an appropriate instructional unit (probably the most frequent use that can be anticipated) is likely to overestimate the relative performance of his own students because of the extent to which "uninstructed" students are represented in the standardization population.

Percentile norms are reported for grades 9 through 12 with suggestions for interpretation. Although separate norms are not reported for boys and girls, it is demonstrated that differences in means and variances for the sexes are not significant. The authors offer helpful suggestions for the development of local norms, the need for which should be reaffirmed in view of the observation made in the preceding paragraph.

The manual includes a Discussion Guide which is designed to serve as a study aid to the teacher. The guide includes suggestions for reporting scores to students, rationale for discussion of correct answers, and an indication of the percentage of the national sample which responded correctly to each item. The basic idea of the Discussion Guide is a good one, but in the case of the reviewer's copy, the print-through on some pages made it difficult to read. If use of the Discussion Guide is to be maximized, it would be helpful to have local norms established for some point in time other than the end of the second semester, as is the case with the reported national norms. An appropriate time may be at the end of a related teaching unit in social studies classes.

While the data reported on reliability and validity are not based on the total standardization group, they are based on representative research samples selected from that group.

In terms of reliability, appropriate information is reported on both internal consistency and stability. In this connection, the test performs satisfactorily (e.g., *r*'s from .85 to .89).

Very appropriately, the authors caution the test user to make his own judgment about content validity, and that point bears repeating here. The test user, by examination of the test, should determine for himself whether the test samples the kind of content he is concerned with measuring. It would be helpful to the test user, however, if the title of the test more adequately represented the content. For example, this reviewer classified 49 of the 65 items as dealing with either content or interpretation of the United States Constitution. Most social studies teachers would probably regard a concept such as "principles of democracy" as having a somewhat broader base than the Constitution. A more specific title might reduce the danger of misleading relatively unsophisticated test users.

Part of the concurrent validity data includes correlation coefficients between this test and grades in a variety of social studies courses (*r*'s from .33 to .83). The usefulness of these data is limited to the extent that the proportion of each course devoted to relevant subject matter is unknown, and whether the people assigning the grades had access to the test scores is not reported. It is of interest that many of the courses bearing titles similar to that of the test appear to be highly related to it. However, it is of particular interest, in terms of face validity, that the lowest reported coefficient (.33) was observed between the test and a course bearing the identical title.

The authors should be commended for the inclusion of data relating the test to other standardized measures, but it should be noted that the relatively high correlation with ability tests (e.g., .71 with the *Terman-McNemar Test of Mental Ability*) may, to some extent, be related to the increase in scores through the school years.

In summary, the test has a number of important assets and also a number of notable limitations. The *Principles of Democracy Test,* in general, does what the authors claim for it. The manual is clear and can be used by the typical consumer of achievement tests. For the most part, the limitations are in the form of missing data, especially in the description of the standardization group. The test should be useful to classroom teachers, especially to those with the interest and sophistication to develop relevant local norms.

JOHN H. HAEFNER, *Professor of Social Studies Education, State University of Iowa, Iowa City, Iowa.*

Form A of this test consists of 65 multiple response items, divided into nine sections, as follows: Constitution and Fundamental Law of the United States (10), Elections, Voting, and Ballots (9), Congress (7), President and Executive Branch (5), Judiciary and Law-Enforcement (5), National Government Powers (7), State and Local Government (6), Declaration of Independence and Articles of Confederation (3), Civil Liberties and the Bill of Rights (13). Answer sheets, which can be used for either machine or hand scoring, are required. The punched stencil provided for hand scoring is conveniently arranged for easy use. A well prepared manual accompanies the test and gives information about the authors, the purposes and uses of the test, directions for administering, scoring, and interpreting the test, suggestions for using the test in the classroom, and excellent technical information.

The section Using the Test in the Classroom is particularly helpful. Each item in the test is reprinted with the correct response, often with the source indicated, and the authors' rationale for the item. In addition, the percentages of students in grades 9, 10, 11, and 12 responding correctly to the item are provided, alongside a space in which the teacher may record the performance of his own class on the item. The rationale for each item does provide, as the manual suggests, a useful takeoff for class discussion.

The section dealing with Technical Information is above average in the data it provides on the construction of the test and the provisions made for standardization and norming. The norms are based on the scores of 7,386 students in grades 9–12 from 20 schools in 13 states, "drawn from the population of all schools that had administered the *Iowa Tests of Educational Development* in the spring of 1960." Unfortunately, the 13 states are not identified and it is somewhat difficult to judge how well the various geographic regions of the United States were, in fact, represented in the sample. The research samples on which computations of reliability, validity, and other test characteristics are based consisted of four samples of 400 students, one sample for each grade 9 through 12.

The reliability coefficients were computed by using both the split-half technique and Kuder-Richardson formula 20. These reliability coefficients are satisfactorily high, ranging from .85 to .89 for both techniques.

Pearson product-moment correlations are provided to show the relationship of scores achieved by students on the *Principles of Democracy Test* and on other instruments. Tests used for comparative purposes include portions of the *Iowa Tests of Educational Development,* the *California Test of Mental Maturity,* the *Terman-McNemar Test of Mental Ability,* the *Differential Aptitude Tests,* and portions of the *SRA Tests of Educational Ability*. It is interesting to note, particularly in the light of subsequent comments, that the lowest correlations (.30 and .31 for grades 9 and 10, respectively) are to be found when comparison is made with results on the reasoning test of the *SRA Tests of Educational Ability*. The samples, however, are quite small (145 for grade 9 and 129 for grade 10).

The technical construction of the items is generally good. There appears to be no sound reason, however, why 9 of the 65 items should have five responses instead of four as the other items do. There are 7 "negative" items; the negative in the stem of each of the items is italicized, but no special directions or warnings to students are provided, and the items are not grouped together at the end of a section or of the test as a whole. Correction of these minor technicalities would prove helpful to students and could affect the test's validity.

Individual items do reveal weaknesses in construction. In taking the test, this reviewer found the stems of items 15, 23, 38, and 40 to be somewhat confusing and not as clearly formulated as they might be. On several items, notably 5, 22, 42, and 50, there is some reason to believe that experts would not all agree on the correct response, and these items would consequently penalize students with a more thorough knowledge of government and political science.

Perhaps the most disturbing items are those included under the heading "Civil Liberties and the Bill of Rights," particularly items 55–65. The purpose of these appears to be to test students on the meaning and significance of the provisions in the Bill of Rights. As written, however, the items do not clearly test knowledge of the constitutional amendments as they apply to hypothetical situations, but are cast in the form of items of opinion or judgment. This is particularly disturbing in an area as complex and controversial as that of civil rights, where even among knowledgeable adults there is considerable disagreement over what *is*, what *should be*, and what *can be*. These 10 items would be a good deal more effective in what purports to be an *achievement* examination if they tested for knowledge of the Bill of Rights rather than for the judgment of the student as to what ought to be done in a hypothetical situation.

In the manual accompanying the test, under the heading Validity, the authors state: "In the final analysis....each teacher who uses the instrument should attempt to judge its content validity for himself by evaluating how well each item individually, and all items collectively, relate to his own teaching objectives." This reviewer took this injunction seriously and classified the items into five broad categories, as follows: (*a*) Items which are almost wholly devoted to the recall of specific factual material; (*b*) items which require recognition of terms, or the definition of terms, but which go beyond mere recall of a textbook sentence or definition; (*c*) items which require some degree of thought or the application of simple reflective abilities beyond recall; (*d*) items which are sophisticated in that they demand considerable knowledge as well as the application of some of the more difficult reflective abilities; and (*e*) items which call for the expression of a judgment or opinion rather than a knowledge of the facts or issues involved. To be sure, these are somewhat fuzzy criteria and they must be subjectively applied. Using them as carefully as possible, however, this reviewer found that 23 of the items should be classified in category *a*, 8 in category *b*, and 21 in category *c*. At best, only 2 items should be classified in category *d*, and it would be doubtful if even these 2 would really qualify. The 10 items in category *e* do not properly belong in an achievement examination since they really test value judgments.

This analysis, inadequate as it is, suggests that the description of the test, a test of "*knowledge* and *understanding*" (italics supplied), is not entirely accurate. Overall, it is more nearly a test of information. With some exceptions, the facts tested are important to a knowledge of American governmental institutions. The arrangement of the test into sections keeps the items, in part, from testing unrelated or isolated facts. But the test could, and in this reviewer's opinion should, go further and test for students' ability to reason with the facts.

The authors do not seem to have formulated the educational objectives for teaching the principles of democracy before devising the items. If this were to be done in terms of understandings and skills or abilities, and if the objectives were to be phrased so concretely as to be amenable to measurement, then the number of items requiring more than mere recall would almost certainly be increased. In addition, if less emphasis in writing the items were placed on the way in which the information appears in typical textbooks, memoriter recall would be reduced.

In summary, this test is acceptable for purposes of meeting state legislative requirements that students must demonstrate familiarity with "the principles of representative government" before graduating. With adequate revision, it could become a very fine instrument for measuring the outcomes of topnotch instruction in American government and governmental institutions.

[Other Tests]

For tests not listed above, see the following entries in *Tests in Print:* 1801, 1805, 1808, 1810, and 1812-5; out of print: 1798-9, 1802, 1806-7, and 1809.

SOCIOLOGY

[1021]

***The Graduate Record Examinations Advanced Tests: Sociology.** Grades 16-17; 1939-61; for more complete information, see 762; 180(200) minutes; Educational Testing Service. *

J. RICHARD WILMETH, *Associate Professor of Sociology, State University of Iowa, Iowa City, Iowa.* [Review of Form JGR.]

This test provides a rigorous examination of the kinds of knowledge and skill which are typically developed during graduate study in sociology. Items cover a wide range of concepts, theory, and principles. The test faithfully reflects the importance of quantitative methods in contemporary sociological research. A few of the questions require a knowledge of elementary statistical techniques, but what is called for in a much broader sense is some evidence of the habit of quantitative thinking in the interpretation of data. The student who has never carefully examined a table or a graph will find himself seriously handicapped on many of the items.

The substantive areas covered are legitimately within the realm of sociology today, with a minimum of intrusion into the neighboring fields of economics, political science, and psychology. Some acquaintance with anthropological literature is expected, and this is thoroughly in accord with the merging interests of the two disciplines. While many sociologists might object to the particular "mix" represented by this test, few would argue that any particular item should be excluded.

Form JGR was first used in 1961 and a preliminary analysis indicates that it is much more difficult than earlier forms. This is not at all surprising and it is doubtful that the difficulty is the result of technical flaws in item building. On the contrary, the test shows every evidence of thorough competence in test construction. Very few items can be answered on the basis of a low level recognition of vocabulary, or names, or books. Basic concepts and principles are more often tested as they apply to illustrative examples and as they relate to other concepts and principles. If the difficulty of the test is a basis for criticism, it would be on the ground that the test is a measure of achievement in graduate study rather than of aptitude for graduate study. Thus it might be argued that a student who has an easy familiarity with the knowledge on which Form JGR is based is ready at least for his master's degree.

It should be noted that a considerable gap continues to exist between undergraduate and graduate work in sociology. A student may accumulate a respectable looking record in his undergraduate years and be exposed very little to quantitative methods or to the great theoretical issues. Such a background provides little basis on which to predict success in graduate school. On the other hand, an increasing number of students are being advised to begin serious preparation for graduate study before they complete the bachelor's degree, and for students in this category Form JGR is an appropriate test. Making the test less difficult would seriously interfere with the purpose for which it is designed. It should be added, however, that even the most intensive preparation at the undergraduate level is not likely to give a student both the breadth and depth which are are required for high performance in all parts of the test. Therefore, the reporting of subscores might be very useful both to the student and to a graduate faculty.

In the present state of the discipline, one cannot conclusively say that a low score on Form JGR indicates that a student will not do well in graduate school. It may only indicate the inappropriateness of his undergraduate experience. A high score, on the other hand, would be a very strong indicator of probable success. This positive value should not be jeopardized by making the test easier. Sociology is in a stage of very rapid development and it is entirely justifiable that the GRE test in sociology be designed with an eye on the future rather than on the past.

For a review of the testing program, see 5:601.

[1022]

Sare-Sanders Sociology Test. High school and college; 1958; IBM; Form A (4 pages); mimeographed manual (3 pages); $1.20 per 25 tests; separate answer sheets may be used; 85¢ per 25 IBM answer sheets; 30¢ per scoring stencil; postage extra; 25¢ per specimen set, postpaid; 40(45) minutes; Harold Sare and Merritt W. Sanders; Bureau of Educational Measurements. *

J. Richard Wilmeth, *Associate Professor of Sociology, State University of Iowa, Iowa City, Iowa.*

According to the manual, this is an achievement test for high school and college classes pursuing introductory courses in sociology. Preparing such a double-purpose test is a rather perplexing task in view of the sharp discontinuities which exist between high school and college sociology. For contrast, we may consider American history, a field in which it would certainly be less difficult to compare the achievement of high school and college students. Sociologists are generally agreed that students in high school have little exposure to their field of study, and at least a few of them argue that this is no great cause for professional concern. Nevertheless, there now exists a committee of the American Sociological Association which is attempting to develop improved resource materials for the high school social studies program. Much more intensive efforts have been made in the same direction by economists in recent years.

Constructing a test for both high school and college students of sociology calls into play a kind of pedagogical Gresham's Law. The process is quite apparent in the instrument under consideration here. It consists of 142 items which are to be completed in 40 minutes. The first 115 items are in multiple choice form with three or four responses (usually single words or brief phrases) and the remainder are true-false. Under this format, little can be accomplished beyond low-level testing for vocabulary and simple descriptive facts. But even if this limited purpose is accepted, the test still has a number of shortcomings.

The test as a whole seems to have a rather secondhand quality which may be explained by a statement in the manual that "the items were selected from the basic content of several leading textbooks." Reliance on textbooks rather than on a general familiarity with the field can lead to simple errors of fact (males do *not* outnumber females in the United States, as one item asserts) and to such embarrassing lapses as the use of "more" as the singular of "mores." Casual reference to both high school and college texts may account for the appearance of items on government, labor relations, and consumer economics. These might be included under the rubric of social studies, but the test is neither broad enough to justify this label nor is it restricted to the typical interests of practicing sociologists. Other items are based on implicit value judgments which most sociologists would prefer either to make explicit or to avoid altogether.

One may criticize the form as well as the content. It requires no special competence in test construction to point out that an instrument which is offered for sale should be free of grammatical errors or that items which require nothing more than the ability to read should be discarded. An item which is based on an association between two variables should specify the direction of association as well as asserting that the relationship exists. Using the completion form of multiple choice question offers a temptation toward greater and greater brevity of statement until in the extreme case a stem may consist of a single word. The extreme is reached in this examination.

Both sociology and objective testing have been the targets of severe criticism, the former on the ground that it merely elaborates what everybody knows already, and the latter because it does not discriminate between those who understand and those who do not. This test will not improve the reputation of either.

[Other Tests]

For tests not listed above, see the following entry in *Tests in Print:* 1818 (out of print).

VOCATIONS

REVIEWS BY *E. Anstey, Alexander W. Astin, Richard S. Barrett, Ralph F. Berdie, Arthur H. Brayfield, David P. Campbell, Joel T. Campbell, John O. Crites, Jerome E. Doppelt, Philip H. DuBois, Marvin D. Dunnette, Robert L. Ebel, Leonard W. Ferguson, John P. Foley, Jr., John W. French, Edward J. Furst, Leo Goldman, L. V. Gordon, Milton E. Hahn, John K. Hemphill, David O. Herman, John R. Hills, Kenneth B. Hoyt, Stephen Hunka, C. E. Jurgensen, Martin Katz, Raymond A. Katzell, William E. Kendall, Willard A. Kerr, Wayne K. Kirchner, Philip H. Kriedt, Albert K. Kurtz, Seymour Levy, Arthur C. MacKinney, Samuel T. Mayo, Richard S. Melton, Philip R. Merrifield, Joseph E. Moore, Warren T. Norman, William A. Owens, Jean Maier Palormo, Lyman W. Porter, Ray G. Price, Paul F. Ross, Douglas G. Schultz, D. H. Schuster, Benjamin Shimberg, I. Macfarlane Smith, Harry L. Stein, Donald E. Super, Paul W. Thayer, Albert S. Thompson, Leona E. Tyler, and Charles F. Warnath.*

[1023]

★**Airman Qualifying Examination.** Grade 12 (including girls); 1946–63; successor to *Airman Classification Battery;* test administered at high schools by United States Air Force personnel at any time (arrangements for test administration may be made through local United States Air Force Recruiting Office); 4 aptitude scores: electronic, mechanic, general, administrative; IBM; Form AF PRT 15 ('63, 36 pages); supervisor's manual ('62, 18 pages); descriptive booklet ['63, 13 pages]; comparison chart ['63, 1 sheet]; no charge for testing and reporting of scores to high school counselors; postpaid; 120(150) minutes; Air Force Personnel Research Laboratory; Headquarters, United States Air Force Recruiting Service (ATC). *

REFERENCES

1. RUSSO, J. ROBERT. "Two Governmental Sources for Aptitude Testing." *Sch Counselor* 9:140–1 My '62. *

[1024]

★**[Aptitude Inventory.]** Employee applicants; 1957–63; 1 test ('57, 4 pages) published in the same form under 3 titles; 4 scores for each test: intelligent job performance, leadership behavior, proper job attitudes, relations with others; manual ('61, 11 pages); no data on reliability based on present scoring keys; $35 per 100 tests; $1 per specimen set; postpaid; [15–20] minutes; John C. Denton; Psychological Business Research. *

a) MANAGEMENT APTITUDE INVENTORY. Applicants for management and supervisory positions; 1957–61.

b) EMPLOYMENT APTITUDE INVENTORY. Applicants for office and factory positions; 1957–61.

c) SALES APTITUDE INVENTORY. Applicants for sales positions; 1957–63; supplementary norms ['63, 1 page].

REFERENCES

1. DENTON, J. C. "Validity Information Exchange, No. 16-05: D.O.T. Code: Business Forms Salesman." *Personnel Psychol* 16:283–8 au '63. *

LEONARD W. FERGUSON, *Program Director, Research Division, Life Insurance Agency Management Association, Hartford, Connecticut.*

This test consists of 98 items. Fifty of them are in Section 1: "Which phrase [out of two] is more like you?" Twenty-five items are in Section 2: "Which phrase [out of two] would you like better?" Twenty-three items are in Section 3: "Mark 'Y' (Yes) if the phrase describes you; Mark 'N' (No) if it does *not.*"

According to the author, items in the test were derived from merit rating studies and, except for the fact that they are worded in the first person singular, are almost "verbatim" descriptions of good and poor performance as described by top management personnel in several companies. Under each of the three titles in which the test appears (*Employment Aptitude Inventory, Sales Aptitude Inventory,* and *Management Aptitude Inventory*), the purpose is to measure "four factors important to success on the job." According to the author, these four factors are: (*a*) Intelligent Job Performance, "the degree to which the individual's job behavior is alert, open-minded, mature in judgment, and analytical"; (*b*) Leadership Behavior, "the ability to gain respect, motivate associates and lead a group"; (*c*) Proper Job Attitudes, "willingness to work hard to get ahead; ambition and determination"; and (*d*) Relations with Others, "getting along well, tolerant, not critical." In the order just named, the number of items in each factor scale is 25, 28, 24, and 24. Only three items are utilized in more than one scale. Two of these items are common to the last two scales; the other item is common to the first two scales. On each scale, the score is the number of "right" answers. A table permits the conversion of each score into a percentile rank.

Validity data supplied in the manual are as follows: (*a*) Correlations with "a combined ranking from judgments made independently by the company president and executive vice president" for 31 managers and executives in a midwestern plastics manufacturing company. The coefficients reported are .03, .51, .28, and −.22 for each of the scales in the order named above. (*b*) Correlations with "an overall ranking obtained from the Sales Personnel Manager," for 27 men who had entered a training program two years before the ranking was obtained. The coefficients obtained were −.36, .43, .44, and −.06. (*c*) Correlations with an initial two-way classification of "potential for success" at the start of the training program mentioned above. Coefficients (biserial, apparently) were −.08, .20, .33, and .10. According to the author, "the 'true' validities" lie somewhere between the second and third sets of coefficients. Accepting the author at his word, and splitting the difference, this would make the "true" validities −.22, .32, .38, and .02.

At best, these validites have dubious meaning. The two highest coefficients, .32 and .38, *may* indicate that the scales concerned have a useful, practical, predictive validity in the sense that the scores yield results in the same direction as a supervisor's more general observation and rating. But, even if this be the case, in no sense do the coefficients validate the claim that the variables in question are, in fact, Leadership Behavior and Proper Job Attitudes. Conversely, the negative correlation of −.22 and the near-zero correlation of .02 do not indicate that the corresponding scales do *not* measure Intelligent Job Performance and Relations With Others. They merely indicate *lack* of relation between whatever variables are involved and overall ratings of job success as these overall ratings were secured in the author's studies.

On the basis of a factor analysis of the intercorrelations among merit rating items for 216 sales managers and salesmen, the author found the following intercorrelations among the four factors that his later scales were designed to measure: Between *a* and *b,* .69; *a* and *c,* .70; *a* and *d,* .55; *b* and *c,* .68; *b* and *d,* .64; *c* and *d,* .50. On a "pre-publication model" of the aptitude inventory, when "approximately" 400 individuals rated themselves, the corresponding correlations were as follows: .21, −.14, −.23, −.06, −.03, and −.40. In order "to change....the generally negative matrix of intercorrelations....to more positive values," the author conducted item analyses on two samples of 100 "typical professional and managerial people." He also increased the number of items in each scale and modified the scoring keys. He then obtained corresponding intercorrelations as follows: .13, −.14, −.26, .17, .02, and −.23. In view of these results, it is difficult to accept the author's implied claim that the factors measured by his inventory are the same as those isolated by his factor analysis of intercorrelations among merit items utilized by supervisory personnel.

For five groups of workers (one group of salesmen, three groups of factory workers, and one group of factory foremen), the author reports 20 validity coefficients. These range from −.44 to .38, and have a median value of .07. Cases in each group ranged from 22 to 38. For Intelligent Job Performance, these coefficients range from −.44 to .25 and have a median value of +.10. For Leadership Behavior, the coefficients range from −.24 to .37 and have a median value of +.20. For Proper Job Attitudes, the coefficients range from −.17 to .38 and have a median value of .03. For Relations With Others, the coefficients range from −.27 to .13 and have a median value of −.14. From the standpoint of correlations with overall job success, the most satisfactory scales are Leadership Behavior and Proper Job Attitudes. But, whether these scales measure that which their respective names imply, is an open question, as was indicated above. In a release dated April 5, 1963, the author states that "enough data are available for the *Sales Aptitude Inventory* that one would not begin with the hypothesis that the true population validities are zero." In view of the data presented by the author, one wonders: "Why not?"

C. E. Jurgensen, *Assistant Vice President, Personnel, Minneapolis Gas Company, Minneapolis, Minnesota.*

The test consists of 98 items: 50 pairs in forced-choice format in which the applicant is to indicate which item in each pair is more like him, 25 pairs to be responded to on the basis of which item in each pair is preferred, and 23 phrases to be checked as self-descriptive or nondescriptive. These self ratings are scored on four dimensions similar to those found by other investigators to emerge from factor analyses of supervisory descriptions of good and poor employees.

Most of the data in the manual on validity and reliability come from background research studies and a prepublication model of the inventory. Such data, of course, are of little value in evaluating the present test form which was changed from the prepublication model by increasing the number of items in each of the four keys, editing the questions, changing phrasing of phrases, and revising the scoring keys. These changes were based on item analyses conducted on two samples of 100 cases. This is an exceedingly small n for item analyses of this type, and it is possible that the revised test is actually inferior to the earlier form.

Although four years elapsed between publication of the test (1957) and the mimeographed manual (1961), evidence of the effectiveness of the published test is meager. Although the author states that citing specific information concerning the many studies on the inventory would be prohibitive, the selected evidence he gives is based on five situations wherein the n's ranged from 22 to 38 and validity coefficients ranged from −.44 to +.38. Validities of this magnitude and based on n's of this size cannot seriously be taken as evidence of test effectiveness. The manual also includes testimonial-type statements such as business managers expressing considerable confidence in the inventory, a sales manager refusing to hire a salesman unless he exceeds an established minimum score, and the management team of a manufacturing company being strengthened successfully and materially largely by the use of the inventories. As is well known, testimonials of this type frequently are not supported by objective evidence.

Test-retest reliabilities for 113 college students over a two-week period ranged from .61 to .66. Many test experts will not agree with the author that reliabilities of this magnitude are acceptable. The author points out that a composite score based on the sum of the scores on two of the scales has reliability of .80 for the students, and suggests use of a composite score in practical situations. However, this is inconsistent with norms, which are limited to the four single scales. It is also inconsistent with the author's emphasis on the *pattern* of abilities, and with his emphasis on the scale Proper Job Attitudes as the best single predictor of future sales volume.

One reason for low reliability is the narrow range of obtained scores. A difference of a single point can raise the score as much as 20 percentile points, and a change in 10 raw score points is enough or more than enough to raise the score from the 5th to the 95th percentile in each of the four dimensions.

In addition to data given in the manual, the test author supplied the reviewer with a mimeographed report of a study conducted by the test author in 1963. It is based on 68 salesmen and 35 sales trainees, and includes a total of 24 validity coefficients ranging from −.11 to .47, nine of the coefficients being negative. Instead of giving data on their significance, the author states: "A significance test for these validities is an irrelevant procedure. Enough data are available for the *Sales Aptitude Inventory* that one would not begin with the hypothesis that the true population validities are zero." Statisticians are likely to raise their eyebrows and smile, for such coefficients are typical of those obtained when the true validity is zero.

In summary, there appears to be little reason to recommend this test. Sales-like generalities regarding the value of the test are neither relevant nor backed up by data given in the manual or in a supplementary study. Sophisticated test users are not likely even to consider seriously use of a test for which so little and so unfavorable data are available so many years after publication.

J Counsel Psychol 6:319–20 w '59. Laurence Siegel. * This is, at its present stage of development, an inadequate instrument accompanied by a somewhat irksome manual [the 1958 preliminary manual]. The reviewer offers this opinion with full realization of the necessity for phrasing manuals for potential industrial clients in an abbreviated fashion and with a minimum of statistical jargon. There is, however, no excuse for misleading generalizations like the following: "Psychology has....run into some confusion factors in the study of leadership. * A systematic approach to most problems is conspicuously absent." * Specific validities for the published MAI are not given in the manual. Two multiple correlations supportive of predictive validity using the two most valid subscales as predictors of managerial ratings are cited, however, for the prepublication version of the test. It is a moot question whether these coefficients indicate anything about the validity of the MAI as a measure of managerial aptitude. This validation procedure seems merely to indicate that it is possible for persons to describe themselves in a way that corresponds with the descriptions of them made by managerial raters. There is an element of circularity in this type of validation. Perhaps the gravest deficiency of the MAI is inadequate norming. * The....Inventory is supposed to predict success of managerial and sales applicants. Perhaps it does. The presently available normative and validity data, however, prohibit its use without extensive research within each company wishing to try it out. It is, at its present stage of development, valueless as an instrument for use by high school and college counselors.

[1025]

★ETSA Tests. Job applicants; 1960, c1957–60; formerly called *Aptitests;* Form A ('60, c1957–59); 8 tests (4 pages except Test 1A, 3 pages); manual ['60, 23 pages]; norms booklet ('60, 19 pages); publisher recommends use of Tests 1A, 8A, and one other; $20 per 10 copies of Tests 1A, 8A, and any one other; $7 per 10 copies of any one tests; $2 per manual; $5 per specimen set; 50¢ per norms booklet; $1.50 per 12 application-record folders ('60); 15¢ per single copy; postpaid; S. Trevor Hadley, George A. W. Stouffer, Jr., and the Psychological Services Bureau of Indiana, Pa.; Educators'-Employers' Tests & Services Associates. *

a) ETSA TEST 1A, GENERAL MENTAL ABILITY TEST. (45) minutes.

b) ETSA TEST 2A, OFFICE ARITHMETIC TEST. 40(45) minutes.

c) ETSA TEST 3A, GENERAL CLERICAL ABILITY TEST. 20(25) minutes.

d) ETSA TEST 4A, STENOGRAPHIC SKILLS TEST. (45) minutes.

e) ETSA TEST 5A, MECHANICAL FAMILIARITY TEST. Validity data for males only; (60) minutes.

f) ETSA TEST 6A, MECHANICAL KNOWLEDGE TEST. Validity data and norms for males only; (90) minutes.

g) ETSA TEST 7A, SALES APTITUDE TEST. 8 scores: sales judgment, interest in selling, personality factors, occupational identification, level of aspiration, insight into human nature, awareness of sales approach, total; no data on reliability of part scores; (60) minutes.

h) ETSA TEST 8A, PERSONAL ADJUSTABILITY TEST. 8 scores: community spirit, attitude toward cooperation, attitude toward health, attitude toward authority, nervous tendencies, leadership, job stability, total; no data on reliability of part scores; (60) minutes.

Marvin D. Dunnette, *Professor of Psychology, University of Minnesota, Minneapolis, Minnesota.*

According to the manual, the *ETSA Tests* are classified as Level A instruments, available to any company official in charge of a personnel function. It seems unwise to include the Sales Aptitude Test and the Personal Adjustability Test in the A classification. They are obviously intended to assess interest and personality factors and their proper interpretation probably requires a greater amount of professional knowledge than would be possessed by the typical company personnel officer.

The tests are rather lengthy, requiring administration times ranging from 20 minutes for the General Clerical Ability Test to 90 minutes for the Mechanical Knowledge Test. According to the manual, however, "To measure all the important factors which indicate capable or incapable personnel, ETSA recommends that each testee be given test 1-A and the appropriate test or tests selected from 2-A through 7-A, depending on the requirements of the job under consideration. Test 8-A should also be given when the person's personality is important in your consideration."

The manual is primarily an administrator's manual as well as a sales package apparently designed to convince the typical businessman that the tests will solve many of his firm's personnel ills and that they are easily administered and readily interpreted by following the simple guidelines offered by the authors. Although no norms are offered in the manual, the score distributions for each of the tests are grouped into ranges and assigned the descriptive labels (from low to high) of poor, questionable, average, good, and excellent. For each of the categories, brief descriptive paragraphs are provided to facilitate easy interpretation of an examinee's scores. This grouping of scores for interpretation seems wise for it should help to overcome the common tendency among unsophisticated users to overinterpret the seemingly fine gradations among examinees shown by the raw score distributions. The manual offers *no* information concerning reliability or validity and gives *no* descriptions of the development of the tests nor of the groups on which they were normed. Thus, if one were to judge the relative merits of the *ETSA Tests* solely on the basis of evidence from the manual, one's conclusions would be unalterably negative.

Fortunately, however, the authors have published a comprehensive technical supplement to the manual entitled "The ETSA Tests Hand Book of Norms." In marked contrast to the test manual, the handbook does *not* give the reader the feeling that the authors are trying to pull the wool over his eyes. Quite to the contrary—one learns that the item content of the tests is based on careful content analyses of standard textbooks in a variety of fields and on interviewing experience with a large number of applicants. The tests have been extensively item analyzed, and reliabilities and validities have been estimated in a variety of situations and on many different groups of subjects. Although an impressive number of validity studies is reported for each of the tests, for the most part the studies have not been done in industrial settings; instead, the groups consist rather often of students enrolled in business courses and the criteria are instructor ratings. Even so, the validity coefficients are generally rather good (ranging in the .40's and .50's) and a sufficient number of industrial validations are reported to give the user confidence in the potential utility of the tests as aids in making industrial personnel decisions.

The Handbook of Norms serves most importantly, however, as a demonstration of the competence and research mindedness of the test authors. The tests appear to have been systematically and seriously constructed, and a continuing program of research appears to be underway. From this laudatory pattern of past behavior, a continuing accumulation of research studies and additional validity information can be expected in future editions of the technical supplement to the manual.

In summary, the *ETSA Tests* appear to have a good deal of merit for industrial use. Ideally, however, the buyer and user should be one who has the training to conduct individual validity studies in his own firm. I personally believe that the sales pitch of the test manual should be "toned down" and that the technical information from the supplement should be incorporated into it. On the other hand, the authors have developed what appear to be rather good tests and they have done more thorough research on them than is typical. Thus, their sins of omission in the test manual may be more excusable than would usually be the case.

RAYMOND A. KATZELL, *Professor of Psychology and Head of the Department, New York University, New York, New York.*

These eight tests are printed clearly on paper of good quality, and possess reasonably high reported reliability and face validity. This reviewer finds little else to commend them.

CONTENT. The manual advises that a battery be selected for each job, composed of the Personal Adjustability Test, the General Mental Ability Test, and one or more others corresponding to the type of job, i.e., clerical, mechanical, or sales. Why the first should be universally recommended is not clear, since it is a specimen of personality inventory which, as a class, has not been found predictive of job performance, save possibly in the sales category.

There is little evidence that psychometrically rigorous procedures were followed in the construction of the individual tests. In content, each is mostly a rehash of the kinds of items in one or more preexisting tests. For example, the General Mental Ability Test comprises vocabulary, number progressions, and general information; the General Clerical Ability Test contains short sections on alphabetizing, number matching, name matching, spelling, office vocabulary and mailing information; and so on for the other tests. Among the few out of the ordinary parts is one in the Personal Adjustability Test purporting to measure "attitude toward cooperation." Typical of the 15 items in this section is: "The government should promise everyone a decent job." A response of agreement to such an item counts toward being considered a "poor risk" for employment. Grave questions exist concerning the use to which such information might be put by a psychometrically and morally obtuse employment official.

VALIDITY. The foregoing observations might be considered as cavil were there substantial evidence of concurrent or predictive validity for the battery or its individual tests. However, only a few validity data are reported, and these are often on students rather than on employed samples such as those for which the tests are intended. In several instances, the major evidence for validity of the aptitude tests rests on the tenuous basis of a difference in the distributions of scores of an occupationally experienced and an inexperienced sample; this type of evidence is further weakened by the absence of indications that the contrasted samples were otherwise comparable. In other instances, the only evidence of validity lies in the correlation of ETSA tests with well known ones; examples include the correlations of the General Mental Abilities Test with the *American Council on Education Psychological Examination* ($r = .68$) and with the *Otis Employment Test* ($r = .78$), and the correlation of the Personal Adjustability Test with the *California Test of Personality* ($r = .72$). This type of validity evidence inevitably raises the question of why we are supposed to use the new test rather than the other, but no answer is suggested in the present case.

Only for the Sales Aptitude Test are data furnished comparing the test with an external criterion of success in employed samples. In two small samples, correlations between the test and employers' rankings turned out to be .71 and .82; in two other samples, the test correlated with salesmen's salaries to the extent of .72 and .61. These concurrent validity coefficients are surprisingly high, considering both the results of other test research on salesmen and the fact that these coefficients are in the neighborhood of the test's reliability (the corrected split-half correlation in a sample of salesmen is reported as .77). Indeed, so amazing are these results that it behooves us to suspend judgment on their generality until other investigations have been reported.

In view of the nature and extent of the evidence reported, this reviewer remains unconvinced of the validity of these tests in terms of their power to correlate appreciably with criteria of job performance.

MANUAL AND NORMS. What is usually contained in a single manual is here organized into two pamphlets. The test manual briefly introduces the nature of the battery, gives instructions on administration and scoring, and outlines a cookbook guide to interpreting the test results. The Handbook of Norms furnishes rather sketchy information on the construction and standardization of the tests. Reactions to its reports of construction, reliability, and validity have already been noted. There remains the need to comment on its normative and interpretative sections.

The only statistical norms provided for each test are the mean and standard deviation of a vaguely defined sample of between 200 and 400 adults ($n = 860$, and is better defined, in the case of Test 8A). The reason for this, we are told, is that "norms are unimportant" for the kinds of tests and uses offered. This curious position seems to be based on two arguments. One is that norms (e.g., percentile ranks) which permit an interpretation of the relative status of an individual score are statistically more fallible than those (e.g., fifths) which produce grosser categorizations. The other is that general norms are not useful when one is mainly interested in selecting the better candidates from a local pool of job applicants.

Each of these arguments is, of course, erroneous. Therefore so is the failure to develop and report adequate normative data. The manual proceeds to subdivide the range of raw scores on each test into five categories, ranging from "Poor" to "Excellent," apparently quite oblivious to its own argument that local experience should supersede general guidelines. To make matters worse, if any empirical foundations exist for this categorization, they are not made explicit. We are in effect expected to take on faith the assertion that a person, say, who scores below 66 on the Personal Adjustability Test is a "poor risk" for employment, whereas one who scores above 96 is an "excellent risk."

In addition to technical deficiencies, the manual and handbook are equivocal about the value and utility of these tests. On the one hand, we are reminded every so often that they have yet to be thoroughly investigated and tested. But at other points the prospective consumer is also assured that the "ETSA Tests are a proven series of aptitude tests" which "provide scientifically accurate facts on which to base your hiring, placing, and promoting decisions." The mailing piece and order form addressed to personnel managers further expostulates: "Reduce Hiring Costs—Stop Expensive Personnel Turnover—Wasted Training—Don't Guess—Test!!" This is surely a tone more in keeping with the huckstering of nostrums than with the dissemination of scientific devices.

SUMMARY. *Caveat emptor!*

[1026]

★**General Adaptability Battery.** Illiterate and semiliterate job applicants; 1949–58; tests administered at centers established by firms employing the publisher's consulting and training services; 2 batteries; manual ('58, 166 pages, largely mimeographed); no data on reliability and validity in manual; instructions provided in several languages; test materials may be constructed locally or purchased from the publisher at a cost of R40–R50 per set of materials for testing one candidate; R2 per manual; training courses, assistance in setting up testing centers, and local norms service available; details available from the publisher; National Institute for Personnel Research. *

a) GENERAL CLASSIFICATION BATTERY. Illiterate and semiliterate applicants for semiskilled and laboring jobs; 8 tests: *Nuts and Bolts, Sorting Test 1 (Mechanical Parts), Sorting Test 2 (Letters and Numbers),* [*N.I.P.R.*] *Cube Construction Test, Tripod Assembly Test, Formboards Test,* 2 modifications of Kohs' *Block-Design Test;* R40 per 16 mm. silent film; projector necessary for administration; [20] minutes.

b) [BOSSBOY SELECTION TESTS]. Illiterate and semiliterate applicants for bossboy and supervisory jobs who score in top category of *a* above; supervisory ability; 3 tests, called *Leaderless Group Test;* [30] minutes per test.

REFERENCES

1. GOTSMAN, E. "A Sequential Procedure for Selecting and Classifying African Industrial Workers and Labourers." *J Nat Inst Personnel Res* 8:117–21 D '60. * (*PA* 35:5388)

[1027]

★**Individual Placement Series.** Adults; 1957–61; 8 tests; profile ['61, 1 page]; record card ['61, 2 pages]; no description of normative population; separate answer sheets must be used (except with *c, e,* and *f*); $1 per 25 answer sheets; 75¢ per 25 profiles; $1.50 per 25 record cards; $1 per 25 tabulation sheets; $18 per complete specimen set (including 10 answer sheets for each test); postpaid; J. H. Norman; the Author. *

a) ACADEMIC ALERTNESS "AA." 1957–59; 7 scores: general knowledge, arithmetic, vocabulary, reasoning ability, logical sequence, accuracy, total; Forms A, B, ('57, 6 pages); preliminary manual ('59, 15 pages); no data on reliability; $20 per 25 tests; 50¢ per key; $2.50 per specimen set; 20(25) minutes.

b) PERFORMANCE ALERTNESS "PA" (WITH PICTURES). 1961; Form C ('61, 4 pages); no manual; no data on reliability and validity; $12.50 per 25 tests; $1 per key; $2.50 per specimen set; 12(17) minutes.

c) READING ADEQUACY "READ" TEST. 1961; 3 scores: reading rate, per cent of comprehension, corrected rate; Form C ('61, 4 pages); no manual; no data on reliability; $4 per 25 tests; $1 per key; $2.25 per specimen set; [10–15] minutes.

d) SURVEY OF CLERICAL SKILLS (SOCS). 1959; 5 scores: spelling, office math, office terms, filing, grammar; Form C ('59, 8 pages); no manual; no data on reliability; no norms; $20 per 25 tests; $1 per key; $3 per specimen set; 40(45) minutes.

e) TYPING TEST. 1959; Forms C, D, ('59, 2 pages); scoring instructions-norms ('59, 2 pages) for each form; no data on reliability; $10 per 25 tests; 50¢ per scoring instructions-norms; $2 per specimen set; 5(15) minutes;

f) SHORTHAND TEST. 1960; Forms A, B, ('60, 2 pages); also available on 33⅓ rpm records; no manual; no data on reliability; $10 per 25 tests; 50¢ per key; $10 per record containing both forms; $2 per specimen set without record; $12 per specimen set with record; (20–25) minutes.

g) SURVEY OF PERSONAL ATTITUDE "SPA" (WITH PICTURES). 1960; 3 scores: social attitude, personal frankness, aggressiveness; Form A ('60, 14 pages); no manual; no data on reliability and validity; $32.50 per 25 tests; $1 per key; $3.50 per specimen set; [20–25] minutes.

h) OCCUPATIONAL INTEREST SURVEY (WITH PICTURES). 1959; 9 scores: scientific, social service, literary, agricultural, business, mechanical, musical, clerical, artistic; Form A ('59, 14 pages); preliminary manual ['59, 8 pages]; $27.50 per 25 tests; $2.25 per specimen set; (15–20) minutes.

[1028]

★**Screening Tests for Apprentices.** Standards 5–10 (ages 14–20); 1957–60; 8 scores: arithmetic (computations, problems), form relations (form perception, two dimensions, three dimensions), synonyms (Afrikaans, English), mechanical aptitude; 1 form ['57, 34 pages, Afrikaans and English in 1 booklet]; mimeographed preliminary manual ['60, 28 pages, 14 pages each in Afrikaans and English]; no data on validity; separate answer sheets must be used; R10.52 per 100 tests and answer sheets, postage extra; manual free; specimen set not available; 81(120) minutes; National Bureau of Educational and Social Research. *

[1029]

★**Steward Personnel Tests (Short Form), 1958 Edition.** Applicants for sales and office positions;

1957–58; abbreviated version of *Steward Sales Aptitude Inventory* and *Steward Vocational Fitness Inventory;* 10 scores: business knowledge, arithmetic, occupational interests (clerical, artistic, supervisory, accounting, writing, selling, mechanical, selling activities); 1 form ('58, 4 pages); manual ('58, 4 pages); no data on reliability and validity; tentative norms for business knowledge part score; $3 per set of 5 tests and manual; $1.50 per manual; postage extra; (35–60) minutes; Verne Steward; Steward-Mortensen & Associates. *

LEONARD V. GORDON, *Chief, Behavioral Evaluation Research Laboratory, U.S. Army Personnel Research Office, Washington, D.C.*

The *Steward Personnel Tests (Short Form)* constitute essentially an abridged version of the *Steward Sales Aptitude Inventory* and the *Steward Basic Factors Inventory,* which was originally called the *Steward Vocational Fitness Inventory.* The battery measures (*a*) business knowledge, (*b*) arithmetic, and (*c*) occupational interests, and is intended for use in the selection of sales or office personnel.

The recommended procedures for using the battery are similar to those for the *Steward Basic Factors Inventory.* The caliber of the individual required for a given job is determined by the employer. Raw scores on the business knowledge and arithmetic tests are converted by means of a prepared chart into ratings of unqualified, borderline, acceptable, superior, or "more than needed." The occupational interest section is scored for seven interest areas, and standards are provided for rating the applicant's interest in selling, which is the total of his scores for "selling" and "supervisory." No standards are provided for evaluating interest in different types of office jobs. The scores for each of the seven fields of interest are to be examined, and ratings are to be assigned by the "direct judgment method." Several illustrations of the method are given.

The *Steward Personnel Tests (Short Form)* suffer from the same general deficiencies noted in the reviewer's evaluation of the *Steward Basic Factors Inventory* (see 1182). Directions for establishing the job level are inadequate; no validity or reliability data are presented in the manual for the short form; the validity section in the manual for the *Steward Sales Aptitude Inventory* (this manual was included in the materials supplied for review) does not include a single validity coefficient; descriptive statistics are lacking; and no information is provided regarding the development of the table for converting raw scores into ratings.

In view of the availability of a number of standardized and better documented short personnel tests, the reviewer cannot recommend use of the *Steward Personnel Tests (Short Form).*

LYMAN W. PORTER, *Associate Professor of Psychology, University of California, Berkeley, California.*

These tests consist of 35 items pertaining to "business knowledge"; 15 "practical business arithmetic computation" items; and 49 "job activity" interest items designed to measure vocational interests in seven areas. The business knowledge items are in multiple choice format, and the interest items require a "yes" or "no" response.

The four-page manual provides "values" for converting scores on each part of the test into one of five possible ratings: unqualified, borderline, acceptable, superior, and "more than needed" (a possible rating for the first two parts of the test only). Each of these values is adjusted for three different "caliber levels" of sales and office personnel. Thus, a score that might produce a rating of unqualified for a high level sales job such as "wholesale merchant" might produce a rating of acceptable for a "house-to-house route salesman." The interesting thing about these conversion tables is that nowhere in the manual do the authors provide information as to how the "conversion values" were developed. In fact, nothing is given in the manual itself pertaining to the development of the three subtests, let alone data on why a particular score should be given a rating of "acceptable" or any other specific rating. In short, there are no norms given in the manual.

In a 1958 manual for the *Steward Sales Aptitude Inventory* which was made available to this reviewer, some scanty norms are given for the business knowledge subtest. These norms provide median scores on five groups (total *n* for the five groups is 420), including eighth grade students, high school students, college students majoring in nonbusiness courses, college students majoring in business, and life insurance agents preparing for CLU examinations. Median scores increase from the first-mentioned group to the last-mentioned.

According to the authors, the scores made on this subtest are "estimated to have more than 50 per cent higher correlation with the degree of success achieved in sales work (determined by squares of correlation coefficients) than the scores made on a standard mental ability test." This might possibly be true, but there is certainly no way to determine the accuracy of such a statement from the data presented in this manual. This is because the manual gives no coefficients concerning the predictive ability of the business knowledge subtest, nor is it even clear from the quoted statement which specific mental ability test, if any, is being referred to. The 1958 manual fails to provide any norms on either of the other two subtests of the *Steward Personnel Tests (Short Form)*.

In summary, based on both the four-page manual accompanying the *Steward Personnel Tests (Short Form)* and the previous (but relevant) 1958 manual, there are simply insufficient reliability data, validity data, and norms to justify the use of these tests in selection.

[Other Tests]

For tests not listed above, see the following entries in *Tests in Print:* 1819, 1824, and 1826–7.

CLERICAL

[1030]

***A.C.E.R. Short Clerical Test.** Ages 13 and over; 1953–60; 2 scores: checking, arithmetic; Forms A ('53), B ('56), (4 pages); mimeographed manual ('60, 20 pages); no data on validity; distribution of Form A restricted; 8*s.* per 10 tests of Form A; 6*s.* per 10 tests of Form B; 1*s.* per key; 7*s.* 6*d.* per manual; 8*s.* 6*d.* per specimen set; postpaid within Australia; 10(15) minutes; Australian Council for Educational Research. *

[1031]

***A.C.E.R. Speed and Accuracy Tests.** Ages 13.5 and over; 1942–62; 2 scores: number checking, name checking; Forms A ['57], B ['61], (5 pages); revised mimeographed manual ('62, 25 pages); no norms for subscores; separate answer sheets must be used; 10*s.* per 10 tests; 2*s.* 3*d.* per 10 answer sheets; 2*s.* per scoring stencil; 5*s.* 6*d.* per specimen set; postpaid within Australia; 12(20) minutes; T. M. Whitford (revised manual) and the Australian Council for Educational Research; the Council. *

REFERENCES

1. HOHNE, H. H. *Success and Failure in Scientific Faculties of the University of Melbourne.* Melbourne, Australia: Australian Council for Educational Research, 1955. Pp. vii, 129. * (*PA* 31:3787)

2. BUCKLOW, MAXINE, AND DOUGHTY, PATRICIA. "The Use of Aptitude Tests in Clerical Employment: The Selection of Accounting Machinists." *Personnel Prac B* 13:35–44 S '57. *

For a review by D. W. McElwain of an earlier form, see 4:719.

[1032]

★Beginner's Clerical Test. Applicants for clerical positions; 1958; abbreviated adaptation of *Group Test 25 (Clerical)* (see 4:724); 1 form (4 pages); manual (3 pages); no data on reliability; $1 per 25 tests; 20¢ per specimen set; postage extra; 10(15) minutes; Herbert Moore; Guidance Centre. *

STEPHEN HUNKA, *Assistant Professor of Educational Psychology, University of Alberta, Edmonton, Alberta, Canada.*

The *Beginner's Clerical Test,* "an abbreviated version of the N.I.I.P. Clerical Test," is described by its author as an experimental test to be used as the first test in a two stage testing program for selecting clerical workers. The test contains eight subtests to which the reviewer has given the following names: number selection, number operations A, coding, proofreading, copying, number operations B, alphabetic arrangement, and message checking. The author claims that the test measures "general intelligence," "speed and accuracy with which elementary clerical operations are made," the ability to grasp the meaning of directions, and ability to "give simultaneous attention to a number of details." Since unit weighting is used in scoring the responses, the total test score tends to reflect to a great extent the candidate's ability to work with numbers. Because of the nature of certain subtests, scoring must be carried out manually.

The author has suggested that a raw score below 50 out of a maximum score of 71 is unsatisfactory and should indicate rejection of the candidate and therefore termination of any further data collection. If, however, the raw score is above this value, further data should be collected, using the N.I.I.P. clerical test, an interest inventory, an intelligence test, a personality questionnaire, and an interview by the office manager. Although this strategy may be a reasonable one, the decision rules are not specifically formulated beyond the first stage.

The efficacy of this instrument as a screening device is lacking. The user does not know what proportion of the candidates from a specific population can be expected to be missed and thus excluded from the second phase of testing. Similarly, there is no indication of the extent to which candidates who do well on this test do not do well on the N.I.I.P. or on other test variables at stage two and thus should have been excluded. Since the author suggests a pre-reject procedure, some evidence must be given concerning the two types of errors that might be incurred. These should be stated as probabilities of error for various groups that might be tested in order that the user may take these probabilities into account while attempting to maximize a specific utility function for his institution.

Information on technical characteristics is also lacking. Norms provided have been based on "the first thousand" cases. No information concerning the norming sample is given, even though it would be reasonable to expect norms for both sexes. Validity data, reliability data, the correlation between this test and the N.I.I.P., and directions to guide the final decision to accept or reject on the basis of the complete strategy are also lacking. In addition, means and standard deviations of the total test and its subtests are not reported. To state that this test has proven value because some companies have released low scoring candidates while other companies have reported early promotion for high scoring candidates is totally inadequate.

The reviewer suspects that unless this test and the strategy within which it is used are reconsidered in the light of institutional decision theory, in order to provide evidence which indicates that the test can be expected to cut selection and training costs and thus to show that it is possible to approach maximization of some institutional utility index, the test will continue to be of an "experimental nature." The test is worthy of further study since it does attempt to measure a variety of basic clerical skills. In light of the fact that this test is designed as a screening device in a specific pre-reject strategy, no other test can be suggested as preferable.

Harry L. Stein, *Professor of Education, and Director of Graduate Studies in Education, University of British Columbia, Vancouver, British Columbia, Canada.*

This clerical "quickie" is, according to the publisher's catalog, designed for applicants in the education range grade 8 and up. The norms in the manual, however, are based upon applicants and employees with secondary school graduation. In Canada, secondary school graduation can have almost a limitless variety of interpretations, not only from one province to another but within a single province. In British Columbia, for example, there are at least five different types of secondary schools or programs.

The very skimpy manual suggests that the test "has been used in an experimental form.... chiefly as an elimination tool rather than directly as a selection tool." The manual also reports that the "correlation between this Test and the Otis is 65 [no decimal point]," and that there is thus "some indication that the Test may measure level of intelligence." Little evidence is presented that it does, in fact, measure clerical ability or aptitude. The only evidence of validity is given in the statement that "as a measure of promise for elementary types of clerical work, it has *proven* [italics mine] value; companies have reported hiring students who did poorly on the Test and later being obliged to release them; and companies finding students with high scores report promoting them in less than average time."

The manual provides a table showing how to convert raw scores into percentages. This table is titled "Norms." The maximum possible raw score is 71. A raw score, for example, between 60 and 70 is equivalent to a percentage score of 91–100. However, these are not norms in the sense that they indicate typical performance at any given level. They are merely the result of "statistical checking of the first thousand cases," which were apparently secondary school graduates. Just what statistics were used in the checking is not indicated. Interpretation of scores of candidates in the early secondary grades would be quite difficult.

There are nine *apparent* subtests covering recognition of the size of numbers; simple arithmetic operations including two column additions, and one each of subtraction, multiplication, and division; an attempt at simple filing; checking of names; copying; alphabetizing; and checking errors in coded material. The time allotment is 10 minutes. Scoring is by no means simple and may be subject to many errors because of the format of the test and the scoring key.

As a quick, rough and ready screening test of clerical ability, the *Beginner's Clerical Test* does not compare favorably with a highly standardized instrument such as the *Minnesota Clerical Test.* The publisher is hardly justified in placing a test of this kind on the market until he can satisfy potential users more effectively than he does at present.

[1033]

★Cardall Test of Clerical Perception. Applicants for clerical positions; 1960; 2 scores: checking names and addresses, checking numbers; 1 form (4 pages); no manual; no data on reliability; norms-key ['60, 2 pages]; $8.50 per 100 tests; 25¢ per norms-key; 75¢ per specimen set; postage extra; 6(10) minutes; Alfred J. Cardall; Cardall Associates. *

[1034]

★Checking Test. Applicants for clerical and stenographic positions; 1948–63; 1 form ['48, 4 pages]; manual ['63, 7 unnumbered pages]; no data on reliability; $3 per 25 tests; 10¢ per key; 75¢ per manual; postage extra; $1 per specimen set, postpaid; 5(10) minutes; Richardson, Bellows, Henry & Co., Inc. *

[1035]

★Classifying Test. Business and industry; 1950–63; 3 scores; speed, accuracy, total; Forms 1 ('50), 2 ('57), (5 pages); manual ['63, 22 unnumbered pages]; no data on reliability of total score; $3.50 per 25 tests; 10¢ per key; $1.50 per manual; postage extra; $1 per specimen set, postpaid; 10(15) minutes; Richardson, Bellows, Henry & Co., Inc. *

[1036]

★Clerical Tests, Series N. Applicants for clerical positions not involving frequent use of typewriter or verbal skill; 1940–59; 5 tests and 1 application form; 5 scores: comparing names and numbers, copying names, copying numbers, addition and multiplication, mental ability; manual ['59, 8 pages, same as for *Clerical Tests, Series V*]; profile ('51, 1 page); norms ['51, 1 sheet]; no data on reliability; $8.50 per set of 10 copies of each test and application form; $1 per set of manual and keys; postage extra; specimen set not available; Stevens, Thurow & Associates Inc. *

a) INVENTORY E, COMPARING NAMES AND NUMBERS. 1951; 1 form (4 pages); 5(10) minutes.

b) INVENTORY F, COPYING NUMBERS. 1951; 1 form (3 pages); 3(5) minutes.

c) INVENTORY G, ADDITION AND MULTIPLICATION. 1951; 1 form (2 pages); 6(10) minutes.

d) INVENTORY H, COPYING NAMES. 1951; 1 form (3 pages); 4(10) minutes.

e) INVENTORY NO. 2. 1956; mental ability; 1 form ['56, 4 pages]; 15(20) minutes. See 463.

f) APPLICATION FOR POSITION. 1951; 1 form ['51, 2 pages]. See 1129.

[1037]

★Clerical Tests, Series V. Applicants for typing and stenographic positions; 1940–59; 5 tests and 1 application form; 5 scores: grammar, spelling, vocabulary, typing (words per minutes), mental ability; manual ['59, 8 pages, same as for *Clerical Tests, Series N*]; profile ('51, 1 page); norms ['51, 1 sheet]; no data on reliability; $8.50 per set of 10 copies of each test and application form; $1 per set of manual and keys; postage extra; specimen set not available; Stevens, Thurow & Associates Inc. *

a) INVENTORY A, GRAMMAR. 1951; 1 form (2 pages); 3(5) minutes.

b) INVENTORY B, SPELLING. 1951; 1 form (2 pages); 5(10) minutes.

c) INVENTORY C, VOCABULARY. 1951; 1 form (4 pages); [10–15] minutes.

d) TEST OF TYPEWRITING ABILITY. 1951; 1 form (2 pages); 10(20) minutes.

e) INVENTORY NO. 2. 1956; mental ability; 1 form ['56, 4 pages]; 15(20) minutes. See 463.

f) APPLICATION FOR POSITION. 1951; 1 form ['51, 2 pages]. See 1129.

[1038]

★Clerical Worker Examination. Clerical workers; 1962–63; test booklet title is *Clerical Worker;* 5 scores: clerical speed and accuracy, verbal ability, quantitative ability, total ability, total; IBM; 1 form; 2 parts (6 pages): booklet 1, clerical ('63), booklet 2, ability ('62); practice test for booklet 1 ['62, 1 page]; manual ['62, 23 pages]; candidate identification sheet ('62, 1 page); no data on reliability and validity; no norms for verbal and quantitative part scores; distribution restricted to municipalities, employers, and agencies for use in selection of personnel; separate IBM scorable answer sheets must be used; 10–49 tests, $1 each; specimen set loaned free; postpaid; 5(10) minutes for practice test for booklet 1, 10(15) minutes for booklet 1, 50(60) minutes for booklet 2; McCann Associates. *

[1039]

★Cross Reference Test. Clerical job applicants; 1959; 1 form (3 pages); manual (4 pages); $3 per 25 tests; $2 per specimen set of 10 tests and manual; cash orders postpaid; 5(10) minutes; James W. Curtis; Psychometric Affiliates. *

PHILIP H. KRIEDT, *Associate Director of Personnel Research, The Prudential Insurance Company, Newark, New Jersey.*

This test is intended for use with applicants for clerical and shop or warehouse positions. The author claims that the test has a Gestalt-like quality, that it measures the ability "to synthesize an emergent function—simultaneous combination of simple checking and arithmetical skill." As a consequence, according to the author, the test will supplement most existing clerical aptitude tests. This may or may not be so. No evidence of any kind is given in the test manual to support this claim. No correlations with other clerical tests are furnished.

The manual is brief and unimpressive in content. A test-retest reliability of .90 is reported. Norms are given for clerical applicants, unselected nonclerical applicants, and "employed and unemployed adults." The norms are presented as evidence of validity because the clerical applicants scored higher than the nonclerical applicants.

In a tryout of the test with a small group, the reviewer found that several subjects had difficulty in understanding the directions quickly. The task to be done is rather complicated and may cause problems even with fairly sophisticated subjects. Several of the subjects developed a set as they went along of obtaining only approximate answers in doing the simple mental arithmetic that is required. In most instances, this is all that is necessary to get the correct answer. The test appears to be most suitable as an indication of aptitude for work requiring fast but not necessarily precise mental arithmetic. As a selection device for jobs of this kind, the *Cross Reference Test* may prove useful. It will probably have little value for selecting employees to perform noncomputational clerical work.

[1040]

***Minnesota Clerical Test.** Grades 8–12 and adults; 1933–59; formerly called *Minnesota Vocational Test for Clerical Workers;* 2 scores: number comparison, name comparison; 1 form ('33, 5 pages); revised manual ('59, 11 pages); $2.15 per 25 tests; 50¢ per specimen set; postpaid; 15(20) minutes; Dorothy M. Andrew, Donald G. Paterson, and Howard P. Longstaff (test); Psychological Corporation. *

REFERENCES

1–18. See 40:1664.
19–40. See 3:627.
41–86. See 5:850.
87. Petro, Peter K. *Student Aptitudes and Abilities Correlated With Achievement in First Semester High School Bookkeeping.* Master's thesis, Iowa State Teachers College (Cedar Falls, Iowa), 1957.
88. Bender, W. R. G., and Loveless, H. E. "Validation Studies Involving Successive Classes of Trainee Stenographers." *Personnel Psychol* 11:491–508 w '58. * (*PA* 34:2143)
89. Champion, John Mills. *A Method For Predicting Success of Commerce Students.* Doctor's thesis, Purdue University (Lafayette, Ind.), 1958. (*DA* 19:2134)
90. Shore, Richard P. "Validity Information Exchange, No. 11-22: D.O.T. Code 1-02.01, Bookkeeping-Machine Operator (Banking)." *Personnel Psychol* 11:435–6 au '58. *
91. Shore, Richard P. "Validity Information Exchange, No. 11-23: D.O.T. Code 1-06.02, Teller." *Personnel Psychol* 11:437–9 au '58. *
92. Shore, Richard P. "Validity Information Exchange, No. 11-24: D.O.T. Code 1-25.68, Proof-Machine Operator." *Personnel Psychol* 11:438–9 au '58. *
93. Cass, John C., and Tiedeman, David V. "Vocational Development and the Election of a High School Curriculum." *Personnel & Guid J* 38:538–45 Mr '60. *
94. Garrett, Wiley S. "Prediction of Academic Success in a School of Nursing." *Personnel & Guid J* 38:500–3 F '60. * (*PA* 35:3954)
95. Crane, William J. "Screening Devices for Occupational Therapy Majors." *Am J Occup Ther* 16:131–2 My–Je '62. * (*PA* 37:4078)
96. Super, Donald E., and Crites, John O. *Appraising Vocational Fitness by Means of Psychological Tests, Revised Edition,* pp. 162–79. New York: Harper & Brothers, 1962. Pp. xv, 688. * (*PA* 37:2038)

For a review by Donald E. Super, see 5:850; for reviews by Thelma Hunt, R. B. Selover, Erwin K. Taylor, and E. F. Wonderlic, see 3:627; for a review by W. D. Commins, see 40:1664.

[1041]

***National Institute of Industrial Psychology Clerical Test (North American Revision).** Ages 16 and over; 1934–60; 8 scores: oral instructions, classification, arithmetic, copying, checking, filing, problems, total; 1 form ['60, identical—except for minor changes in item order—with *N.I.I.P. Clerical Test: American Revision* which was published in the United States in 1934 and which was a revision of an earlier form of *Group Test 25 (Clerical)*, see 4:724]; manual ['60, 11 pages]; no data on reliability; norms the same as those reported in the 1934 United States manual; $2.25 per 25 tests; 30¢ per specimen set; postage extra; (30) minutes; J. H. Moore; Guidance Centre. *

REFERENCES

1–2. See 40:1665.
3–6. See 3:628.

Harry L. Stein, *Professor of Education, and Director of Graduate Studies in Education, University of British Columbia, Vancouver, British Columbia, Canada.*

This test appears, on the surface, to have those qualities required of a good clerical test if a superficial comparison is made of its content with that of similar tests which have received considerable approbation either through wide acceptance and use or through satisfactory reviews in the literature of testing.

This is the North American revision of the long established British edition. There are, however, a few elements in the test where the revision appears to have fallen a little short for North American use. For example, in item 2 of Test 1, Oral Instructions, the use of the term "post" is not usual, even for Canada. In item 4, the use of the term "Messrs." may confuse the listener. Also, the uniformity of administration is questionable; different accents and different emphases might have an effect upon the norms for this subtest. In Test 2, a term like "Victrola Records" might date the item.

This revision of the N.I.I.P. clerical test has many of the earmarks of *Group Test 25 (Clerical)* first published in 1925. The order of presentation of the subtests has been changed. In reviewing this test in *The Fourth Yearbook,* E. G. Chambers says, "It seems very probable that Group Test 25 measures elements involved in certain types of clerical work. Whether or not short subtests (mostly 2½ minutes each) measure these adequately is another matter and one which cannot be decided on available evidence." Nothing has been seriously changed in the most recent revision to alter what Chambers has said. The manual is entirely inadequate from the standards set up by the APA. Users of tests are entitled to this much consideration. Validity, reliability, and norms reporting are practically nonexistent, or so limited as to be of little value to users.

The manual supplies a few norms in deciles for normal high school students. It does not say whether or not they are graduates. It is assumed that "normal" means that they are without business training. It would seem that high school students with business training would be the most likely applicants for clerical positions. The only information supplied for students of this kind is that their median score was 77. The highest and lowest scores attained are given, but the manual does not say from what group these scores were obtained. Frequencies upon which the meager norms are based are not given.

The last page of the manual makes the claim, on the basis of about 100 cases, that the test makes a "fairly definite distinction between.... satisfactory secretarial workers" and "fair" office workers, or those not regarded as secretarial material. This conclusion is based upon the results of two or three of the very short subtests whose reliability may be questioned seriously, because of their short time allotment. This is the extent of the validation information supplied in the manual.

The test may be useful on an experimental basis only if local norms are developed and if the user can satisfy himself as to the validity and reliability of the test.

For a review by R. B. Selover of the American revision, see 3:628; for a review by Donald G. Paterson, see 40:1665.

[1042]

★**Number Checking Test.** Business and industry; 1957–63; 2 scores: checking forward, checking backward; 1 form ('57, 5 pages); manual ['63, 13 unnumbered pages]; no data on reliability; $3.50 per 25 tests; 10¢ per key; $1 per manual; postage extra; $1 per specimen set, postpaid; 6(16) minutes; Richardson, Bellows, Henry & Co., Inc. *

[1043]

★**Office Skills Achievement Test.** Employees; 1962–63; 7 scores: business letter, grammar, checking, filing, arithmetic, written directions, total; Form A ('63, 8 pages); manual ('62, 4 pages); no data on reliability of part scores; $3 per 25 tests; $1 per specimen set; cash orders postpaid; 20(25) minutes; Paul L. Mellenbruch; Psychometric Affiliates. *

DOUGLAS G. SCHULTZ, *Associate Professor of Psychology, Western Reserve University, Cleveland, Ohio.*

This test is intended for use in the employment of general clerical workers, although the manual contains no explicit statement of the test's purpose or uses or of the basis for content selection. The parts cover subject matter that can reasonably be expected to be predictive of competence in general office work. Office machine skills (typewriter, adding machine, etc.) are not directly assessed.

The published test is the third revision of an original which contained more items and two additional sections that were later dropped. Some kind of item analysis was performed at each stage but the details are not clear from the manual. The two forms (only Form A was available at the time this review was prepared) "were matched with regard to form, content and difficulty" on the basis of the pretest data. The little evidence in the manual raises some doubt as to how well equivalence was achieved.[1]

The manual makes an attempt to present empirical data to support the test, but a careful reading raises many questions. Apparently most of the statistical data described in the manual are based on the pretest samples, even though a few items were substituted and the timing of two parts was changed in the published version. The various groups and test forms used are not clearly defined.

All the parts are highly speeded, which is appropriate for this kind of test. For the reliability of a speeded test it is proper to administer the test twice, using one form each time. But it is not clear what one can conclude about an office skills test from statistics based on nursing trainees and college students. As a result, only one of the four groups for whom reliability data are presented is appropriate. This group consisted of only 35 cases and they apparently took a pretest form. The resultant correlation of .76 between administrations of the two forms 10 weeks apart would seem to be marginally acceptable, at best, if the test is to be used for the evaluation of individuals. Three validity coefficients are reported against supervisors' ratings, but the groups are small and the data again are apparently derived from administration of a pretest form. Percentile norms, based on the same pretest group, are given for each part score and the total, although no reliability figures are given for the part scores; one would not expect the part reliabilities to meet acceptable levels in view of the small numbers of items and the very short time limits.

Many of the items are of poor quality. For example, the classification of errors required in answering the first part (Business Letter) in-

1 No second form is mentioned in the publisher's 1965 catalog received in October 1964.—Editor.

troduces an unnecessary element; the important office skill is the ability to detect (and correct), not to classify, errors. In Part 3 (Checking) the directions do not say how certain differences, like written versus printed copy and small versus capital letters, are to be handled. Other items involve ambiguous examples of the principle being tested and many are presented in a confusing manner. The items and answer spaces are poorly arranged on the page in several instances. The materials are frequently crowded or placed in such a way as to induce errors in marking answers. The directions are inadequate and the print is unclear.

The scoring formulas used are strange; the manual states that they were devised to produce equal weightings for the test parts. There are a few errors in the scoring key.

This is a good example of a test that should not have been published. If it is to be used at all, additional and better items need to be constructed, more and sounder analytical data developed, and a better designed test booklet and much more complete and explicit manual prepared. For the present, several other available tests, e.g., the *Short Employment Tests* or a combination of something like the *Minnesota Clerical Test* and the *Wonderlic Personnel Test,* do everything this test might do in approximately the same time and do it much better.

Paul W. Thayer, *Director of Human Resources Research, Life Insurance Agency Management Association, Hartford, Connecticut.*

According to the manual, "This 1962 instrument overcomes deficiencies of many previous clerical tests by broadening the base of task challenge to include business letter writing, English usage, checking, filing, simple arithmetic, and following written directions." By "broadening the base," Mellenbruch seems to have taken his own advice in *The Fifth Mental Measurements Yearbook,* that a broad slice of the verbal and clerical skills areas should be sampled.

The first impression upon examining the test is negative simply because of extremely inadequate reproduction. The test resembles a poor mimeographing job. It hardly sets a standard for an examinee taking an "Office Skills Achievement Test." The overlay scoring template should be made of more durable material. Correct responses are indicated by heavy black dots which apparently must be punched out by the test administrator before the template can be used. One gets the impression that every attempt was made to cut reproduction costs.

Although reference is made to Form B in the manual and alternate form reliabilities are reported involving Forms A and B, only Form A was available to the reviewer. Form B is "to be printed in 1963–64." Intercorrelations among the subtests for a sample of 132 office and industrial employees are reported, but it is not clear whether they apply to Form A or B. The intercorrelations are generally low, although some are in the low .40's. Part 2 (Grammar) correlations "may not now be altogether correct due to the fact that one half minute has been added to the administration time" so that almost 10 per cent could finish all items. Although the author feels that this change should not affect the intercorrelations to any great extent, it may increase the subtest-test correlation above its reported .49.

Alternate form reliabilities seem quite adequate. Correlations with Form A of the *Henmon-Nelson Tests of Mental Ability* are reported at .51 (Form A) and .54 (Form B), based on the scores of 42 psychology students. One wishes that data on the range of the mental ability test scores were given to permit assessment of their appropriateness for a population of clerical applicants. Assuming some range restriction and considering the subtest intercorrelations, it is possible that these two correlations are underestimates of the relation to mental ability and that the battery has a high verbal loading.

The only validity data presented are for 80 clerical employees broken into three groups according to job level and rated by their supervisors. The correlations are .46 (routine), .29 (semi-routine), and .37 (high level) and are "distressingly low." Evidence for restriction of the range of ratings is presented and the author also offers the "proper test score cut-off" argument to account for these correlations. The fact remains that the samples are too small (19, 45, and 16, respectively). In addition, they are concurrent validity data despite the recommendation that the test be used predictively.

Although subtest reliabilities are lacking, normative data are based on only 132 office employees, and validity data are deficient, the test author makes cautious recommendations as to approximate scoring patterns considered desirable for the three levels of clerical workers. The publisher's catalog is more extravagant: "Excellent for high school guidance, school and employment, vocational placement, upgrading clerical personnel, and as a check on clerical training." No evidence is offered to support the bulk of these claims.

The test author requests reports from test users, especially validity and reliability data so that they can be included in future manuals. In this reviewer's opinion, considerably more such data should have been gathered prior to publication. The author should also study the relationships of the subtests and battery with other tests to determine the unique contribution made, if any. This test seems somewhat broader than many clerical tests in use today and *may* be quite useful. Considerably greater use under research conditions is needed before any definite conclusions can be reached.

[1044]

***Office Worker Test.** Office workers; 1956–60; 11 scores: reading, vocabulary, reasoning, arithmetic, checking, filing, spelling, punctuation, usage, information, total; forms 30-A ('56), 30-B ('59), 30-C ('60), (19 pages plus foldout answer sheet); mimeographed manual ['56, 23 pages, formerly called preliminary manual]; mimeographed general PPA directions ['57, 7 pages]; norms ('58, 1 page, based on form 30-A); no data on reliability of current forms; 10–49 tests, 46¢ each; $2 per specimen set; postpaid; 90(100) minutes; Public Personnel Association. *

RAY G. PRICE, *Professor of Business Education, University of Minnesota, Minneapolis, Minnesota.*

The purpose of the *Office Worker Test* is to *assist* in the selection of office workers at the entrance level. As defined in the manual, office workers include "office clerks, typists, stenographers, and other miscellaneous office classes, e.g., receptionists, messengers, etc."

The test contains 100 multiple choice items divided into 10 subtests of 10 items each. In each subtest the items are arranged in ascending order of difficulty, from those answered correctly by 75 per cent of applicants tested to items answered correctly by only 50 per cent of applicants. The working time allowed for the actual test is 90 minutes. The emphasis is on level of performance rather than speed.

Construction of the test began with an analysis of tests for office workers developed by a selected group of 25 public personnel agencies. A tabulation was made of the amount and kinds of subject matter included in these tests. A tryout form of the test, containing 200 items covering the 10 topics measured by a majority of the agencies, was then reviewed by experts in each of the subject matter fields. Using item analysis, only the 100 most discriminating items were selected for the final test.

Content validity was established by submitting the tryout form to "authorities" for their judgment regarding whether or not the items did measure those knowledges and abilities important for successful office work. Unfortunately, no follow-up of individuals tested has been undertaken to determine their subsequent performance in the office. There is no evidence that those who make high scores will be better able to do office work than those who do less well on the test. Neither is evidence provided with respect to correlations between test scores and intelligence test scores. This reviewer is of the opinion that the correlation might be rather high. In addition, the *Office Worker Test* does not emphasize the speed factor.

The total information given on reliability follows: "Using the Kuder-Richardson formula, the median (eight samples) reliability coefficient for the total score on the try-out form of the test was .92, with a range from .87 ($N = 35$) to .96 ($N = 97$)." Although the test being reviewed is only half as long as the tryout form, the authors "estimate" the final form has higher reliability since only the "most discriminating items" were used. This should not have been left to conjecture. The evidence should have been provided.

Each of the three forms has the same number of items within each subgroup. But evidence of the extent to which the tests are "equivalent" forms is lacking. The limited evidence of validity and reliability that is provided applies only to one form of the test. Yet it is a well known fact that preparing equivalent test forms to measure equally the same thing is extremely difficult.

The manual contains detailed and complete directions for administering and scoring the test. Some information usually found in test manuals, however, is missing. For example, as indicated above, adequate statistical evidence of validity and reliability is not provided, nor is evidence of form equivalence and test norms cited.

The *Office Worker Test* has numerous limitations. This is not to say that the test has no merit. It is to say that its sphere of helpfulness is restricted, even as stated in its announced purpose, "to *assist* in the selection of office workers at the entrance level." For those wanting evidence of knowledge in areas covered by the test, it may be an adequate measuring instrument. For anyone wanting a more complete measure of the actual or potential competence of office workers, on the other hand, such information as the test provides will need to be supplemented with data from other sources—interviews, references, performance tests, etc.

DOUGLAS G. SCHULTZ, *Associate Professor of Psychology, Western Reserve University, Cleveland, Ohio.*

This test is one of a series offered for use by public personnel agencies and "qualified officials who are responsible for the selection of personnel." The purchaser signs a statement that he will use the test "exclusively for the official purposes of this agency" and that he will protect its security. The *Office Worker Test* is designed to assist in the selection of clerks, typists, stenographers, receptionists, etc. The selection of subject matter was based on a study of office worker tests developed by 25 public personnel agencies. The test's 10 parts measure such basic variables as general intelligence, clerical ability, knowledge of English, and simple office information. Specialized office skills, like typewriting and shorthand, are not included.

The test booklet is attractive but not fancy; the print is satisfactory. The answer sheet for form 30-A is a little crowded but the IBM format introduced in the other forms is a considerable improvement. The items are sound and appear to be well written, with generally good options. The time limits are ample, even for the parts like arithmetic reasoning, arithmetic computation, checking, and filing, which are usually speeded. The explanation for the de-emphasis of speed sounds sensible but would be more compelling if backed up with some empirical evidence.

Although the manual (undated) is designated as applying to all three forms, it seems apparent that the description of the test's development applies only to the first form (30-A). The original items were well prepared and pretested on a large sample of appropriate subjects. The publisher told this reviewer that no pretesting or item analysis was carried out on the items in forms 30-B and 30-C but that the items were written to parallel those of form 30-A. The purpose of the test is well presented in the manual and the features and parts well described. Elaborate, excellent directions are included for administering the test.

The great weakness of the test is the lack of adequate statistical analysis. The manual sections on using the test results, validity, and reliability do essentially nothing to help a potential user or a reviewer evaluate the test. No validity data are reported; only reasons why validity is difficult to establish are given, along with some poor statements about "content" validity. The only reliability figure given is a median Kuder-Richardson coefficient (formula number not specified) of .92 derived from eight agency samples for the total score on the *pretest* form, which was twice the length of the published test. This coefficient drops to .85 for a test half as long and it is likely the figure appropriate to the published test is nearer to that level than, as the manual "confidently" states, "even greater than that of the tryout form." No other reliability information is available, e.g., for forms 30-B and 30-C or for the part scores of any of the forms. This reviewer would consider it inadvisable to use part scores in any way whatsoever in spite of statements in the manual that they may be suggestive.

The only normative data that are available are contained in a "Test Service Memo" dated June 1958. This leaflet presents a distribution of 986 total scores on form 30-A, apparently reported by the users of the test. The sample is not specified beyond that. From this distribution it appears that the test discrimination is very good and the mean score about where it should be, with few scores in the chance range. Part score means and standard deviations were also computed and they look reasonable from the standpoint of the utilization of the score range; the sample size for the part score calculations is not given. The publisher told this reviewer that no further analyses of any of the tests are currently available, although data are still being received from the client agencies and plans are being made for additional analyses.

Public personnel agencies must operate within a legal, political, and ethical framework that militates against the collection of empirical data to support a test. The need for utmost security prior to test administration, the requirement that candidates be allowed to see the test after they have taken it, and other aspects of their field of operation make it difficult to accumulate the kinds of data which have come to be expected of good tests. Yet other groups who depend upon tests as much as merit system personnel (e.g., workers in college admission) face many of the same problems but have made valiant and successful efforts to overcome them. The public personnel field must provide the energy, time, and funds to produce empirical support for the tests they use. The publisher of this test is in an excellent position to demonstrate leadership in this respect.

In summary, this test appears to be sound to the editorial eye. But there are essentially no empirical data to support its acceptance or utility. For a test that has been on the market for seven years, statistical evidence to help users evaluate and interpret the scores is long overdue. This is clearly not a standardized or proven instrument.

[1045]

The Short Employment Tests. Applicants for clerical positions; 1951–56; Forms 1, 2, 3, 4, ('51); 3 tests: CA (clerical, 3 pages), N (numerical, 4 pages), V (verbal, 3 pages); revised manual ('56, 11 pages); distribution of Form 1 restricted to banks which are members of the American Bankers Association; $2.10 per 25 tests; 50¢ per specimen set; postpaid; 15(20) minutes; George K. Bennett and Marjorie Gelink; Psychological Corporation. *

REFERENCES

1–16. See 5:854.
17. Shore, Richard P. "Normative Data Information Exchange, Nos. 11-33, 11-34." *Personnel Psychol* 11:599–600 w '58. *
18. Shore, Richard P. "Validity Information Exchange, No. 11-22: D.O.T. Code 1-02.01, Bookkeeping-Machine Operator (Banking)." *Personnel Psychol* 11:435–6 au '58. *
19. Shore, Richard P. "Validity Information Exchange, No. 11-23: D.O.T. Code 1-06.02, Teller." *Personnel Psychol* 11:437–9 au '58. *
20. Shore, Richard P. "Validity Information Exchange, No. 11-24: D.O.T. Code 1-25.68, Proof-Machine Operator." *Personnel Psychol* 11:438–9 au '58. *
21. Buel, William D., and Stevens, Samuel N., Jr. "Normative Data Information Exchange, Nos. 12-28, 12-29, 12-30." *Personnel Psychol* 12:647–9 w '59. *
22. Shore, Richard P. "Normative Data Information Exchange, Nos. 12-5, 12-6, 12-7, 12-8." *Personnel Psychol* 12:148–51 sp '59. *
23. Ash, Philip. "Validity Information Exchange, No. 13-07, Stenographers, Typists, General Clerks, and Secretaries." *Personnel Psychol* 13:456 w '60. *
24. Harker, John B. "Cross-Validation of an IBM Proof Machine Test Battery." *J Appl Psychol* 44:237–40 Ag '60. * (*PA* 35:4055)
25. Kirchner, Wayne K., and Banas, Paul. "Prediction of Key-Punch Operator Performance." *Personnel Adm* 24:23–6 Ja–F '61. *

Leonard W. Ferguson, *Program Director, Research Division, Life Insurance Agency Management Association, Hartford, Connecticut.*

According to the manual, the purpose of the *Short Employment Tests* is to "provide the economy of short time limits without sacrificing accuracy of measurement." This purpose was accomplished, state the authors, "by selection of highly efficient item types, by very careful test construction, and by aiming the tests at a well-defined population—applicants for clerical jobs."

The authors had four objectives: (*a*) "that the entire battery should consume not over twenty minutes"; (*b*) "that the test-retest reliabilities should exceed .80"; (*c*) "that instructions and scoring should be simple"; and (*d*) "that content should encompass verbal, numerical and clerical skills."

To meet the fourth objective, the authors prepared test V (a verbal test) of 50 "items in which the applicant is asked to choose from among four words the one which means most nearly the same as the problem word"; test N (a numerical test) of 90 "simple computations involving the fundamental skills of addition, subtraction, multiplication, and short division"; and test CA (a clerical aptitude test) of 60 items, each of which "requires the subject to locate and verify a name in an alphabetic list, and to read and code the amount entered opposite that name." Four forms of each of these three tests were constructed, but the use of one of these forms is restricted to members of the American Bankers Association.

From the data presented in the manual, it would appear that the *Short Employment Tests* meet the objectives stated by the authors. Each test takes only 5 minutes to give, and each can be scored in about 30 seconds. The reliabilities (alternate forms) vary from .77 to .91, and average .88, .87, and .81 for the V, N, and CA tests, respectively. Test-retest reliabilities for a two year interval are reported as .84, .75, and .71 for the V, N, and CA tests, respectively.

The authors supply three types of data relative to the value of the tests in employment. These are (*a*) correlations with various criteria, (*b*) correlations with other well known tests, and (*c*) intercorrelations among the *Short Employment Tests.* Based on records secured in four groups, each with more than 200 cases, intercorrelations range from .08 to .51 and have a median value of .34. Least intercorrelated are the N and V tests (.08 to .34), next least intercorrelated are the V and CA tests (.13 to .36), and most highly intercorrelated are the N and CA tests (.37 to .51). "These coefficients," state the authors, "are sufficiently small to indicate that each test measures a relatively *independent aspect* [italics added] of clerical aptitude." If this really be the case, then one might wonder why correlations of apparently comparable magnitude are cited to show that the tests are *"effective* [italics mine] for the separation of good from poor individuals." But as soon as one recalls that the frame of reference for the interpretation of test intercorrelations is different from the frame of reference in terms of which validity coefficients must be interpreted, it can be seen that the validity coefficients are comparatively high, and that the test intercorrelations are comparatively low, even if not as independent as this word seems to suggest. In fact, the *Short Employment Tests* intercorrelate about as well as do typical groups of items in practically all short mental alertness (or intelligence) tests. Otherwise, they would not correlate as well as they do with scores on the *Wonderlic Personnel Test, Minnesota Clerical Test* (names and numbers), and the *Psychological Corporation General Clerical Test* (verbal, numerical, and total). These correlations, based on groups which vary in size from 100 to over 1,000, range from .53 to .91 and have a median value of .70.

The manual gives 72 validity coefficients, 24 for each of the three tests. Only one of these coefficients is negative (−.03), and only one is exactly .00. Thus, 70 of the coefficients are positive, with the highest value reported being .65. For the V test, the coefficients range from −.03 to .53; for the N test, they range from .08 to .65; and for the CA test, they range from .00 to .55. In this same order, the median coefficients are .27 (V), .36 (N), and .32 (CA).

Twelve of the 72 validity coefficients reported are based upon test scores secured before employment and upon criterion data secured after employment; 15 are based upon test scores secured subsequent to employment and upon criterion data secured at a later time; 24 are based on test scores of employees for whom criterion data were obtained concurrently; 18 are coefficients "appearing in the literature"; and 3 show the correlation between test scores and the certification of a group of secretarial students.

The most telling of these coefficients are, of course, the 12 first mentioned. Based upon four groups of applicants, with sample sizes varying from 40 to 131, these coefficients range from .08 to .45 and have median values of .24 (V), .28 (N), and .34 (CA). Roughly, these average coefficients can be said to be significant at about the .05 (two-tailed) level, based on an *n* of 50.

When employees were tested, but time was allowed to elapse before criterion data were secured, coefficients ranged from .00 to .55 and had median values of .33 (V), .35 (N), and .25 (CA). Concurrent validity coefficients range from .09 to .65 and have median values of .30 (V), .38 (N), and .42 (CA). Coefficients "appearing in the literature" range from −.03 to .49 and have median values of .12 (V), .35 (N), and .26 (CA).

In the table from which the above values were taken, the authors indicate that four types of criteria were employed. These were (*a*) certification at completion of training in a secretarial school, (*b*) job level and job grade, (*c*) a production index, and (*d*) supervisory ratings. Supervisory ratings were secured in the form of a checklist or overall appraisal or merit rating, as well from ratings of job performance, general aptitude, mental efficiency, quality and quantity of work, and "employability."

As generally has been found to be the case with mental alertness tests, correlations with job level or job grade tend to be among the highest: .33 and .53 for V, .49 and .60 for N, and .30 and .46 for CA. Thus, the *Short Employment Tests* would appear to be useful indicators of promotability. With a production index, correlations were .10, .26, and .34, and with a checklist score they were .24, .33, and .45 for the V, N, and CA tests, respectively. With certification status, the correlations were .15, .48, and .47. When the criterion consisted of some form of overall supervisory or merit rating, validity coefficients for V ranged from −.03 to .48 and had a median value of .27. For N, they ranged from .08 to .65 and had a median of .35. And for CA, they ranged from .00 to .55 and had a median of .29.

To many individuals (too many), these validity coefficients may not seem particularly high. Be that as it may, they are certainly large enough to command respect and in fact, on the average, are much larger than those of many tests now used in industry. As is well known, a correlation coefficient is a rather severe (too severe) index of test validity for most employment tests. It is to be regretted, therefore, that the authors did not provide an expectancy table, or a series of expectancy tables, to show what percentage of various test score groups could be expected to pass and fail critical levels in each of several criteria.

It is not surprising that the authors found, and reported, that a sum of the scores on all three tests yielded higher validity coefficients than did the separate tests. Thirteen such coefficients are reported. They range from .31 to .60 and have a median value of .46. Thus, the most accurate predictions come, not from the separate tests but from the composite score based on all three tests. In view of this fact, most employers (but not all employers) will be well advised to give all three tests and to utilize the score based on all three tests as a basis for employment.

For a review by P. L. Mellenbruch, see 5:854.

[1046]

★**Short Tests of Clerical Ability.** Applicants for office positions; 1959–60; Form A ('59); 7 tests; preliminary manual ('60, 12 pages); norms for female office workers only; $1.95 per 20 tests (except *d*, $2.50 per 20 tests); 25¢ per scoring template for any one test; 25¢ per manual; $1 per specimen set; postage extra; Jean Maier; Science Research Associates, Inc. *

a) CODING. 2 pages; 5(10) minutes.
b) CHECKING. 2 pages; 5(10) minutes.
c) FILING. 2 pages; 5(10) minutes.
d) DIRECTIONS—ORAL AND WRITTEN. 3 pages; 5(10) minutes.
e) ARITHMETIC. 3 scores: computation, business arithmetic, total; 2 pages; no data on reliability of total score; 9(14) minutes.
f) BUSINESS VOCABULARY. 2 pages; reliability data and norms based on experimental form; 5(10) minutes.
g) LANGUAGE. 2 pages; reliability data and norms based on experimental form; 5(10) minutes.

PHILIP H. KRIEDT, *Associate Director of Personnel Research, The Prudential Insurance Company, Newark, New Jersey.*

Tobacco companies have learned that it is profitable to offer a variety of cigarette brands to the public. Although the brands differ only slightly, they will attract different customers for one reason or another. Test publishers have apparently arrived at the same conclusion, and, as a result, they are turning out an ever-increasing number of tests which differ only slightly from those already on the market. The *Short Tests of Clerical Ability* are a good illustration. Five of the seven tests in this battery are much like other published tests, and they will provide a real contribution only if they prove to be superior to other tests measuring the same abilities.

The test manual is well prepared. It strikes a reasonable compromise between meeting the demands of commercial salesmanship and the standards suggested in the American Psychological Association publication, *Technical Recommendations for Psychological Tests and Diagnostic Techniques.* Considering the shortness of the tests, the reliability coefficients that are reported seem satisfactory. The reliability coefficients for Business Vocabulary and Language are based on preliminary forms, however. The results of an assortment of validity studies based on numbers varying from 17 to 54 are fairly typical for tests of this kind. No intercorrelations among these tests are given although such information is planned for the next manual. Norms are given for all tests based on groups of from 133 to 368 employed office personnel. Here also the Business Vocabulary and Language results are based on preliminary forms.

Transparent plastic keys are furnished for all tests. These keys are somewhat unsatisfactory as correct answers are circled but no holes are cut. Because of this, the test scorer cannot check correct items but must keep a count of them some other way. The plastic material also has an undesirable glare which interferes with scoring.

This reviewer first read through the tests and administrative material and was favorably impressed by them. The tests are attractive in appearance and format and on casual inspection seem to be well constructed and ready for use. After trying them out with a small group of subjects, however, a number of flaws came to light which had not been apparent previously. Several of the tests proved to be much more difficult to administer than was expected.

The most useful test in the battery in the opinion of this reviewer is Language. It fills the need for a short separately administered test measuring a combination of spelling, punctuation, and the grammar skills. It should be useful in screening candidates for stenographic jobs and other positions requiring language skills. The test cannot, of course, be used for diagnostic purposes to indicate specific language skill deficiencies. Two other tests, Business Vocabulary and Arithmetic, appear to be satisfactory tests. The arithmetic test, however, is somewhat awkward in that the computation and arithmetic reasoning sections, which have separate time limits, are presented on the same page.

Three tests in the battery can be classified as clerical speed and accuracy measures. These are Checking, Coding, and Filing. All three are more complicated and confusing than is desirable. The *Minnesota Clerical Test* and the clerical subtest of the *Short Employment Tests* are recommended as more easily administered measures of the clerical speed factor.

Directions—Oral and Written, the most original test in the group, is unfortunately the least ready for use. The administrator reads an orientation lecture on a company's office procedures and policies while the subject takes notes. Then the subject is given an objective test on the information. The instructions say that the lecture should be read in about seven minutes allowing about one second for each dash indicating a pause. In trying out this test the administrator found it impossible to follow the time standards suggested. A word count revealed that if a second were allowed for each dash indicating a pause one would have to read at a rate of 480 words per minute to finish this material in seven minutes! This is, of course, unreasonable, and one wonders how rapidly the material was dictated in obtaining the norm group results. One also wonders whether a person who can take shorthand will have an advantage over others. The test given on the lecture material is confusing and the time limit is restrictive. All in all, this is a frustrating test to administer and a frustrating test to take.

This battery of tests is promising in some ways, but it has been placed on the market before it is really ready. Bennett and Gelink's *Short Employment Tests* can be used with greater confidence in selecting employees for most clerical positions.

PAUL W. THAYER, *Director of Human Resources Research, Life Insurance Agency Management Association, Hartford, Connecticut.*

This battery is an attempt to broaden the sampling of abilities to be tested for clerical jobs and includes tests of business vocabulary, arithmetic, name and number checking, filing, oral and written directions, coding, and language usage. Norms are based only on samples of female employees ranging in number from 133 to 368, and those given for Business Vocabulary and Language are estimates based on the administration of experimental forms. Subtest reliabilities appear to be adequate with the exception of Part 2 of Arithmetic. The test-retest reliability of .68 is much too low for accurate interpretation of an individual score.

Concurrent validity data for supervisory ratings are reported for all subtests (except Business Vocabulary and Language) in the form of biserial correlations for office personnel in two manufacturing concerns. The samples consist of approximately 50 in each case. In addition, the manual clearly points out that the moderate validities reported would change under predictive conditions.

The manual, tests, and scoring stencils are reproduced well. Subtests are printed separately for flexibility of administration. The tone of the manual is conservative and deficiencies in the available data are clearly indicated, making the job of the reviewer and potential user considerably easier than with many other tests.

As noted above, the manual is a preliminary edition. Unfortunately, three to four years have passed and data promised in the manual are still not available on intercorrelations of subtest scores, normative data on applicants and additional employee groups of different job levels, validity data showing appropriate combinations of tests for various job classes, and correlations of the battery with other tests.

Such data would be extremely valuable in assessing the contribution of this battery to the solution of clerical selection problems. Predictive validities also are needed. This reviewer hopes that enough research will be done in the near future to determine whether this attempt to increase the variety of abilities sampled has been successful and whether such an increase does aid in the selection of clerical personnel of various types.

[1047]

★Survey of Clerical Skills (SOCS): Individual Placement Series (Area IV). Adults; 1959; 5 scores: spelling, office math, office terms, filing, grammar; Form C (8 pages); no manual; no data on reliability; no norms; separate answer sheets must be used; $20 per 25 tests; $1 per 25 answer sheets; $1 per key; $3 per specimen set; postpaid; 40(45) minutes; J. H. Norman; the Author. *

[Other Tests]

For tests not listed above, see the following entries in *Tests in Print:* 1831, 1834, 1836–9, 1844–9, and 1853–4; out of print: 1832; status unknown: 1833 and 1840.

INTERESTS

[1048]

★Burke Inventory of Vocational Development. Grades 9–16 and adults; 1958; unscored checklist of occupational titles for use prior to vocational counseling interview; 1 form (3 pages); directions (1 page); no data on reliability; 6¢ per copy with directions; 25¢ per specimen set; postpaid; (15–30) minutes; Charles Burke; the Author. *

[1049]

★Career Finder. Grades 9–16 and adults; 1960; a short adaptation of the *Qualifications Record;* self-administered checklist of interests, activities, and experiences; 45 scores classified under 7 headings: arts (music, art, dramatics, dancing, graphic arts, crafts), biology (physiology, zoology, botany, foods, sports), computation (accounting, mathematics, drafting, purchasing, records, dexterity), literary (journalism, language, transcription, advertising, research), physical (tools, machinery, transportation, strength, hazards), social (management, instruction, public contacts, sales, consulting, religion, services, investigation, discipline), technology (chemistry, astronomy, electricity, mechanics, construction, geology, physics, aeronautics, standards); 1 form (4 pages in a 2-page sleeve); instruction leaflet (2 pages); no data on reliability and validity; $14 per 12 copies; $2 per copy; cash orders (postpaid) only; (60) minutes; Keith Van Allyn; Personnel Research, Inc. *

Arthur C. MacKinney, *Associate Professor of Psychology, Iowa State University, Ames, Iowa.*

Since the *Career Finder* is a shortened version of the *Qualifications Record* (see 1068 for my review), and since there is even less information available on the *Career Finder* than on the parent test, an extensive review does not seem required or even possible. Since the *Qualifications Record* is inadequately researched and standardized, it is safest to assume that all its limitations are also present in the *Career Finder.* Some no doubt have been exaggerated by the shortening process. As a result, this reviewer recommends against using this test.

Charles F. Warnath, *Associate Professor of Psychology, and Director, Counseling Center, Oregon State University, Corvallis, Oregon.*

This is the self-administering, self-scoring form of the *Qualifications Record* reviewed under 1068. Except for the deletion of the achievement factor from the seven factors used to obtain scores on the so-called "45 basic vocational elements of the Qualifications Record," the content of this instrument is essentially the same as that of the Q/R.

The *Career Finder* is pretty much the "poor man's Q/R." A simple slide-through sleeve format turns up on one horizontal row the six factor questions related to 1 of the 45 basic vocational elements. The respondent places a check mark in the appropriate box if he can answer "yes" to the question. He then adds up the number of checked boxes for each of the six factors and indicates the score on a profile of the 45 elements printed on the sleeve.

On the inside of the two-page slide-through sheets on which the questions are asked is a listing of about 500 occupations, each followed by four numbers corresponding to 4 of the 45 basic vocational elements considered necessary for success in that occupation. The respondent circles any element number for which he has received a factor score of 4, 5, or 6 on the profile. He then lists those occupations on the interpretation leaflet for which he has checked all four of the elements and, in another column, those for which he has checked three. The scoring and interpretation leaflet states at this point: "The occupations you have listed above are suggested fields of endeavor which tend to meet with your basic patterns of knowledge and skills."

On the sleeve are presented questions related to education and employment records, military record, dependents, etc. What relevance this information has to the *Career Finder* results is not clear, as its use is not mentioned in any of the materials furnished the respondent. The instruction leaflet suggests that the respondent may wish to contact a vocational counselor or psychologist or to write to Personnel Research "for more specific information concerning your situation." It goes on to say: "This is necessary because of the influence [of] your personal finances, sex, age, education, experience and other factors which may affect your vocational objectives."

This last sentence is, perhaps, the most telling argument against the types of vocational guidance typified by this instrument. The job seeker is led to believe on the basis of the description furnished by the publisher that this instrument will give definite answers to questions related to finding an occupation. However, it is only in the last sentence of the information folder which comes with his purchase of the instrument that he discovers that finding a job in which he can be "successful" may involve more than this instrument can accomplish. Nothing is said in the informational materials about the cost of a more extensive analysis of the *Career Finder* results by the publisher.

As with its parent instrument, the *Qualifications Record,* there is no evidence offered that this instrument has any reliability. In fact, the statement at the top of the *Career Finder* sleeve can be quite misleading in its implications regarding the "analysis of over 281,000 case studies of traits in 3,000 key occupations," since no effort is made to relate this work to the occupations for which the *Career Finder* is keyed.

The conclusions reached in my review of the Q/R would also be relevant to the *Career Finder:* Until detailed, scientifically verifiable information related to reliability and validity is presented, it is impossible to support the publicity claims for this instrument.

[1050]

★**Chatterji's Non-Language Preference Record.** Ages 11–16; 1962; 10 scores: fine arts, literary, scientific, medical, agricultural, mechanical, crafts, outdoor, sports, household work; Form 962 ['62, 16 pages]; mimeographed tentative manual ['62, 24 pages]; profile ['62, 2 pages]; reliability and validity data and most norms based on an earlier form (author recommends use of local norms); separate answer sheets must be used; Rs. 25 per 25 tests; Rs. 5 per 100 answer sheets; Rs. 12.50 per set of scoring stencils; Rs. 4.50 per pad of 100 profiles; Rs. 6 per manual; Rs. 22.50 per specimen set with scoring stencils, Rs. 9.50 per specimen set without stencils; postage extra; (45–55) minutes; S. Chatterji; distributed by Manasayan. *

[1051]

★**College Planning Inventory, Senior College Edition.** High school seniors seeking counseling on choice of college; 1959; unscored checklist of college names and fields of study for use prior to educational counseling interview; 1 form (5 pages); directions (2 pages); no data on reliability; 10¢ per copy with directions; 25¢ per specimen set; postpaid; (15) minutes; Franklyn Graff and Charles Burke; Charles Burke. *

[1052]

★**Curtis Interest Scale.** Grades 9–16 and adults; 1959; 10 scores (business, mechanics, applied arts, direct sales, production, science, entertainment, interpersonal, computation, farming) and 1 rating (desire for responsibility); 1 form (4 pages); manual (4 pages); $3 per 25 tests; $1 per 25 profiles; $1 per specimen set of 7 tests, 7 profiles, and manual; cash orders postpaid; (10–15) minutes; James W. Curtis; Psychometric Affiliates. *

Warren T. Norman, *Associate Professor of Psychology, The University of Michigan, Ann Arbor, Michigan.*

Based on information presented in the very brief manual and profile sheet, the only published sources available at present, the most that can be said for this device is that it takes very little time to administer, is easy to score, and is probably capable of discriminating between *group averages* for samples drawn from dissimilar occupations. By way of contrast, the manual asserts that this instrument is "a means of providing insight into the vocational interest patterns of *individuals* [italics mine]." The published sources, however, provide no data whatever on interindividual variability for the scales and no measures of relationship reflecting covariation among individual scores either among the scales or between them and any external criteria. Indeed, the only direct support offered for the asserted interpretability of individual scores is the statement that test-retest reliabilities over a six-week interval range between .81 and .88 for the various occupational keys.

In support of validity, the manual reports only averages of raw scores for groups of persons in mixed occupations superficially related to the name of each key. For example, a mixed group of 275 "bookkeepers," "numbers clerks," and "bank tellers" has a reported average raw score of 37.40 on the computation scale and 32.33 on the business scale. But, in the absence of any general normative data, the only possible interpretational basis for these data derives from the item format and scoring procedures employed. The exhaustive scoring of rank-order responses to the 10 stems, one presumably reflective of each occupational field, in each of 5 blocks produces raw scores for which the *profile elevation* for each respondent is a constant—22.5. But the fact that the average *across the 10 keys* is a constant for any respondent in no way implies that *each (or any) scale* has an average value of 22.5 *over people* in any normative sample. However, the headnote to the table in the manual which presents these group averages asserts that a raw score of 22.5 indicates "average interest." The unwary reader is thus led to confuse these two senses of "average" and consequently is apt to misinterpret even that scanty bit of validity information which is presented.

On the profile sheet are presented mean profiles for 11 small occupational samples (numbers range from 17 to 56). But the absence of any data on the variability of scores on the several scales, the limited number of occupations included, the minimal sample sizes employed, and the complete absence of any information concerning the sources of these data, the demographic characteristics of the respondents or the method of their selection, together make these profiles very nearly worthless as an aid to score interpretation.

The manual alludes to additional validity studies in progress. In response to a request for data from these studies, the reviewer was sent four sets of validity coefficients against various criteria for samples of sales engineers in a large electronics firm and a table of correlations between the occupational keys and the scales of the ACE, the three Guilford-Martin inventories, the *Study of Values,* and Kuder-Vocational based on 31 personnel executives in a large mail order company. In the former studies the interpersonal scale appears to have a validity of about .20 against a criterion of "average annual increase in income since entering full-time employment" while no other scale appears to have any consistent validity against this or any other criterion employed. In the latter study, a fair degree of correspondence appears to exist between similarly labeled scales on the Curtis and Kuder inventories although absence of intra-inventory correlations and the small sample employed make judgments of convergent and discriminant relationships more than a bit hazardous.

The "Desire for Responsibility" scale is supported by no data presented in the manual save for a vague allusion to "a high coefficient of correlation between level so marked and actual willingness to assume responsibility, as determined by ratings of supervisors, foremen and other administrative superiors." Similarly, there are no data presented to support the statements that "experience has shown that scores above 30 may be considered as designating 'primary interests,' and those ranging from 24 through 29 as identifying 'secondary interests' " or that "scores below 15 frequently reflect an emotional rejection of the associated work area."

In short, there is very little firm evidence to support the routine use of this device in either guidance or personnel selection contexts at the present time. The *Kuder Preference Record—Vocational* and the *Strong Vocational Interest Blank* both provide far better sources of information on occupational interest patterns of individuals or groups than does the Curtis scale. Unfortunately, the brevity of the Curtis scale, the ease with which it can be scored, the superficial appearance of relevance of the item content to the names of the scales, and the oversimplified presentation of the "validity" data are apt to lead to its use in situations where its utility is as yet unknown but likely to be minute. As he reviews this instrument, one remembers with renewed anguish Stagner's classic paper [1] on "The Gullibility of Personnel Managers." The release of this device for other than research use appears to have been, at the very least, premature.

LEONA E. TYLER, *Professor of Psychology, University of Oregon, Eugene, Oregon.*

This very brief test consists of five sets of 10 items each plus a supplementary set of 5 items designed to indicate the level of responsibility at which the subject prefers to work. In the 10-item sets, each item refers to an activity required by one of the main occupational fields: applied arts, business, computation, direct sales, entertainment, farming, interpersonal, mechanics, production, and science. The subject is instructed to rank the 10 items in each of these sets. The sum of the ranks he gives each type of activity constitutes the score for the occupational field.

The brief manual gives very little technical information. The selection of these particular 10 fields is said to have "resulted from a careful study of job placements of several thousands of clients of a vocational rehabilitation agency in the state of Illinois during an eight year period. The fields selected accounted for over 95% of employer requests for trainees or employees."

1 STAGNER, ROSS. "The Gullibility of Personnel Managers." *Personnel Psychol* 11:347–52 au '58. *

Reliability and validity evidence is scanty and not very precise. Test-retest coefficients for "140 individuals who could be retested at a six week interval" (age, sex, educational level, and other characteristics not specified) are reported to be from .81 to .88 for the individual occupational fields. Preliminary data suggest that persons employed in occupations the author classifies as belonging to the 10 major fields show the kinds of average scores and profiles one would expect of them. But these data are deficient in many ways. Each average is based on a mixture of specific occupational groups apparently combined on the basis of the author's judgment alone. (For example, the interpersonal group includes ministers, psychologists, school teachers, physicians, and nurses. Strong's extensive studies would suggest that the interests of these groups are not much alike.) Furthermore, there is no way of judging the amount of overlapping between the various interest groups. Only mean scores are presented.

There are other deficiencies as well. The author gives no norms of any kind except for a set of comparison profiles. There is no indication that he has considered the possible influence of response sets, including outright faking, on a subject's performance. There is no attempt to link this instrument up with the extensive body of knowledge about interests that has accumulated around the Strong and Kuder blanks.

However, when a reviewer asks himself whether a test like this one, technically deficient in all respects, should be used for any purpose whatever, the answer is not quite an unqualified "No." Used strictly as an interview aid in a counseling situation, these questions might stimulate some constructive thinking about occupational goals. The trouble with the test, as things now stand, is that inadequately trained counselors and naïve clients may be tempted to attach more importance to these scores and profiles than they deserve.

[1053]

★**Fowler-Parmenter Self-Scoring Interest Record.** Grades 9 and over; 1958–61; formerly called *G.C. Self-Scoring Interest Record;* 12 scores: outdoor, managerial, social service, verbal, operative, skilled mechanical, scientific, persuasive, clerical, artistic, numerical, musical; Form 1 ('60, c1958, 20 pages including profile); manual ('60, 25 pages); supplementary interest-occupation chart ['61, 7 pages]; separate profile ('60, 2 pages); $3.10 per 25 tests; $1.25 per 25 punch pins; 95¢ per 25 backing boards; 47¢ per pad of 50 profiles; 30¢ per manual; 30¢ per specimen set; postage extra; (30–40) minutes; H. M. Fowler and M. D. Parmenter; distributed by Guidance Centre. *

REFERENCES

1. Fowler, H. M. "Interests of Grade 9 Boys as Measured by the G.C. Self-Scoring Interest Record in the University of Toronto Schools and the Central Technical School." *Sch Guid Worker* 14:32–40 Je '59. *
2. Fowler, H. M. "More About the G.C. Interest Record." *Sch Guid Worker* 15:27–32 My '60. *

David P. Campbell, *Associate Professor of Psychology, and Director, Center for Interest Measurement Research, University of Minnesota, Minneapolis, Minnesota.*

In past editions of *The Mental Measurements Yearbook,* reviewers have often fallen back on the label "promising" for those instruments that have little of proven value to recommend them. This reviewer would like to make it clear at the outset that he feels this is too complimentary a term to be applied to this inventory. This is not a case of an instrument being published prematurely before adequate psychometric data are available; rather the authors seem to believe that sort of information is not essential. Not only have they published a manual without it, but, from their statements, it seems unlikely that they will ever furnish it. Their viewpoint is expressed in the following quotes:

> Although the authors have no strong desire to provide comprehensive norms for the Record, they recognize that [they would be useful].
>
> The validity of any evaluative instrument may be determined either by procedures involving judgment or by estimates obtained from empirical evidence.
>
> It may be argued that, in the case of an interest test, a rational judgment of validity may be just as valuable as a coefficient obtained by using numerical evidence.
>
> In the final analysis, the validity of the Record may best be judged by those who use it.

This inventory consists of 238 statements of specific activities that the authors have assigned to the 12 scales listed above by arbitrarily deciding which interest they feel a given item is measuring. The student completes the record by using a pin punch to indicate whether he likes or dislikes each activity, punching twice to indicate a strong like or dislike. The same items and scales are used for both men and women. The booklet is cleverly arranged and the student can score his blank in a matter of minutes. Whether the scores are worth obtaining is another matter.

Two profiles are generated, one called the "Like Profile," the other the "Dislike Profile." Just why two profiles are used is not clear as they are virtual mirror images, varying from this only if the student punches twice for dislikes and once for likes, or vice versa. The profiles are based on norms, not of any specific criterion group, but simply on ninth grade students, a high score indicating that the student selected more of the items that the authors felt belonged in the scale than most other ninth grade students.

Norms for adults are available, based on 179 men and 134 women. Although the authors point out in a parenthetical comment in the text that these adults were "mostly teachers," the treatment of the results in the tables and profiles implies that these are men and women in general. To advise an adult man scoring high on the skilled mechanical scale that he has more mechanical interests than the average man when he, in fact, really only has more mechanical interests than the average teacher would be grossly misleading, but this is only one example of the errors that would be made routinely by anyone using this record.

Once the profile is constructed, the manual and other interpretive aids give the student or counselor some clues as to which occupations the student might enjoy. Again, it is an armchair approach with no research to buttress it. For example, if a student has high scores on the social service and scientific scales, some of the recommended occupations for him to consider are: chiropractor, clinical psychologist, detective, doctor, economist, pharmacist, secret service man, and social worker. This is a unique grouping of occupations by interests and, based on what is known about the organization of interests as shown by the Strong blank, it is very likely inaccurate.

The only validity data presented are tables showing that boys and girls differ in the expected way on the scales, e.g., boys score higher on the skilled mechanical scale and lower on the artistic scale than girls. Of these tables the authors say, "The results shown in Tables 3, 5 and 6 can hardly be considered completely legitimate norms," and go on to point out that they are based on small numbers that were not collected systematically. Yet a page or two later they say, "Tables 3, 5 and 6 provide presumptive evidence of validity."

No correlations between scales are given, although the authors' expressed intention was to build "reasonably independent" scales. Nor are there any correlations provided between the record and other interest inventories, or achievement and ability tests, or any other behavioral indices. The median K-R 21 reliability for the 12 scales is roughly .90. No indication of stability over time is provided.

The 1960 manual lists four "further improvements" that "have been made in recent months." One of those improvements was putting in a "kink" in the punch pin to prevent too enthusiastic punching; another was reducing the size of the backing board (placed under the record to protect desk tops) so that it could be stored in a file drawer. That the authors list these sorts of things as improvements is a far more eloquent evaluation of this inventory than anything the reviewer could say.

Clearly, either the *Strong Vocational Interest Blank* or the *Kuder Preference Record* would be a far wiser choice than this instrument for almost any situation. Even though this inventory was developed for Canadian use, this reviewer feels its weaknesses are so glaring that a user would be better off risking cultural differences in norms on the established inventories.

In summary, this instrument has been developed almost entirely by subjective methods and has all the flaws guaranteed by such an approach. Not only are the basic psychometric data missing, the authors—based on what they say in the manual—are not particularly concerned with providing them. In its present state, this instrument is of little value to any practitioner in any situation, particularly as far better blanks are available.

JOHN W. FRENCH, *Professor of Psychology, and College Examiner, New College, Sarasota, Florida.*

The authors of this inventory have written a manual that is exceptionally clear and honest. Because research on the inventory has not yet provided representative norms or predictive validity data, it is not possible to use the instrument for accurately comparing a student's interests with those of students in any standard groups, and it is not possible to advise students with regard to their expectancies for success or satisfaction in certain jobs. However, the manual does not claim these things for the instrument. It states a modest but very useful goal: to suggest occupations, courses, subjects, and leisure time pursuits worthy of special consideration in planning for the future and to provide useful pre-interview information for the counselor. While the interpretation of inventory scores should always be done with the aid of an experienced counselor, the manual for this instrument is written in such a way that even relatively naïve persons should be able to use it properly. The rules of testing ethics are well observed in the manual by repeatedly reminding the reader of the modest goals of the inventory and the need to consider aptitudes as well as interests in vocational planning.

Each of the 238 items briefly describes a vocational activity or a course leading up to a vocational activity. Since names of obscure vocations are avoided, students should have little trouble understanding what the activity is, even though most of the jobs described will be unfamiliar to them. The responses are made by pricking a hole through one or two circles marked "like" to indicate degree of liking, pricking through one or two circles marked "dislike" to indicate degree of disliking, or failing to prick through any circle to indicate a lack of decision. The inventory has 12 "like" scores and 12 "dislike" scores determined conveniently by counting pricks in chains of rectangles or ovals. Each of the 12 scores is derived from either 29 or 30 items. Thus, some items are used in two of the scores and a few are used in three. This multiple use of items, though perhaps not serious, seems contradictory to the goal of independent scores stated in the manual. No intercorrelations of scores are presented to show how independent the scores actually turned out to be.

The instructions for interpretation are well presented. Several examples of score profiles are given and sample case histories are discussed. The manual also makes clear the nature and limitations of the reliability and norming data that are provided. A warning is sounded in the manual that interest scores have relative, rather than absolute, meaning. Ipsatively scored instruments such as the *Kuder Preference Record* have scores that are entirely relative, for, in those instruments, the scores in one area of interest are depressed by high interest, or raised by meager interest, in other fields. In this instrument, on the other hand, the scores are relative only insofar as the subject himself compares his intensity of liking from field to field. It is at least possible for a subject to show a liking for all fields. To this extent the Fowler-Parmenter inventory provides a good compromise between the extremes of relative and absolute scores. The manual explains this situation carefully and provides sample case histories that show how to avoid misleading interpretations.

An unusual example of lucid instruction for interpretation of scores is presented with a table of means and standard deviations. The positively skewed nature of the score distributions, probably characteristic for this kind of inventory, is described, and the consequent greater significance of deviations above the mean as compared to deviations below the mean is pointed out.

While the content and presentation of the Fowler-Parmenter inventory look good to this reviewer, and the manual is thorough and honest, it is nevertheless true that the stated limitations do exist. It is to be hoped that validity data, in particular, will be supplied at some future time. It is true that some amount of content validity may be assured by examining the items. However, even when a counselor merely suggests that his client consider certain vocations, there is implied a prediction that the client is more likely to succeed at these vocations or to find them more satisfying than he would find other vocations. To fully justify such implications as this, a validity study, using success and satisfaction criteria, ought to be carried out in such a way that the part played by the interest scores and the part played by appropriate aptitude test scores can be determined empirically.

[1054]

★**The Geist Picture Interest Inventory, [1964 Revision].** Grades 8–16 and adults; 1959–64; 18 (males) or 19 (females) scores: 11 or 12 interest scores (persuasive, clerical, mechanical, musical, scientific, outdoor, literary, computational, artistic, social service, dramatic, personal service—females only) and 7 motivation scores (family, prestige, financial, intrinsic and personality, environmental, past experience, could not say); 1 form ('64); separate editions for males (11 pages) and females (9 pages); manual ('64, 56 pages); no data on reliability and validity of motivation scores; $12 per set of 10 tests of each edition and manual; $5 per 10 tests; $4 per manual; postpaid; specimen set not available; (40–65) minutes; Harold Geist; Western Psychological Services. * (Spanish edition published by Psychological Test Specialists.)

REFERENCES

1. ABDEL-MEGUID, SAAD GALAL MOHAMED. *The Reliability of an Experimental Picture Interest Inventory of Vocational Interests.* Master's thesis, Stanford University (Stanford, Calif.), 1951.
2. GEIST, HAROLD, AND MCDANIEL, H. B. "Construction and Validation of a Picture Vocational Interest Inventory." Abstract. *Am Psychologist* 7:383–4 Jl '52. *
3. CLARKE, CARL TELLES. *A Comparative Study of the Geist Pictorial Vocational Interest Test and the Kuder Preference Record.* Master's thesis, University of Hawaii (Honolulu, Hawaii), 1959.
4. GEIST, HAROLD. "The Geist Picture Interest Inventory: General Form: Male." *Psychol Rep* 5:413–38 S '59. * (*PA* 38:4265)
5. GEIST, HAROLD. "Research Implications of a Pictorial Interest Test." *Calif J Ed Res* 10:25–8 Ja '59. * (*PA* 34:2036)
6. GEIST, HAROLD. "A Comparison of Observations of Parents of Their Children's Interests and Scores on a Picture Interest Inventory." *Calif J Ed Res* 11:207–12 N '60. * (*PA* 35:4730)
7. MAGARY, JAMES FREDERICK. *An Analysis of the Vocational Interests of Educable Mentally Retarded Adolescent Boys From Three Occupational Classes.* Doctor's thesis, Indiana University (Bloomington, Ind.), 1960. (*DA* 21:3703)
8. GEIST, HAROLD. "An Exploratory Study of the Relationship Between Grades and a Pictorial Interest Test." *Calif J Ed Res* 12:91–6 Mr '61. * (*PA* 36:1KI91G)
9. GEIST, HAROLD. "A Five Year Follow-Up of the Geist Picture Interest Inventory." *Calif J Ed Res* 13:195–208 N '62. * (*PA* 37:7223)
10. GEIST, HAROLD. "An Occupational Validation of a Pictorial Interest Test." *Calif J Ed Res* 13:32–8 Ja '62. * (*PA* 36:5LB32G)
11. GEIST, HAROLD. "An 81-Variable Cluster Analysis of a Picture Interest Inventory." Abstract. *Psychol Rep* 12:40 F '63. * (*PA* 38:2474)
12. GEIST, HAROLD. "Work Satisfaction and Scores on a Picture Interest Inventory." *J Appl Psychol* 47:369–73 D '63. * (*PA* 38:6693)

MILTON E. HAHN, *Professor of Psychology, University of California, Los Angeles, California.* [Review of the 1959 edition published by Psychological Test Specialists and now withdrawn.]

The inventory is a test booklet containing 132 drawings organized into 44 triads. Although the inventory appears nonverbal, there are verbal directions which provide differing sets in which to make choices. Selection of one choice from a triad is to be indicated on an answer sheet which can be hand or machine scored. Areas in which the items are scored are the familiar ones employed by the *Kuder Preference Record:* Persuasive, Clerical, Mechanical, Musical, Scientific, Outdoor, Literary, Computational, Artistic, and Social Service. To these Geist adds Dramatic.

Items carry unit weights for the appropriate scales. The scores which one can obtain on the scales vary from 11 for Clerical and Social Service, to 20 for Computational.

A large 18 by 18 inch sheet is provided for the subject to indicate why he made a response. The motivational areas selected by Geist for reflecting these explanations are: Could Not Say, Family, Prestige, Financial, Intrinsic and Personality, Environment, and Past Experience. Although the manual makes suggestions that the qualitative checklist scores be interpreted by percentage of responses in the category, no norms are provided. Selection of the motivational areas reflects no theoretical position regarding the dimensions or structure of motivation, nor are there references in the manual to sources from which a structure for the selected areas can be inferred.

RELIABILITY. Reliability of the inventory is presented in terms of test-retest scores (six-month interval); the statements that "Consistency of response is likely to be much higher where the examinee is responding to stimuli which are closer to those he experiences in real life" and that "A good impression of a test's reliability in use can be obtained by computing the percentages of same responses given on retesting" need qualification. The first basis for reliability may lie in the distances between and among choices presented by some of the very ambiguous pictures. Although the manual states that "the author eliminated all photographs in which the occupation or hobby was not recognized correctly by at least 90% of those taking the inventory," he goes on to say: "Since many photographs were still ambiguous, it was decided to use drawings rather than photographs, retaining those which met the identification criterion, and substituting new drawings for those that did not." In taking the inventory, the reviewer was forced to resort to Table 1, Identifications of Drawings in the GPII, 29 times. This is far from a 90 per cent recognition rate, although the sample on which the recognition rate was determined might have reached the figure given. There are no data in the manual which deal with item analysis, either in terms of discriminating power or difficulty.

No proof is offered that the drawings represent "stimuli which are closer to those he experiences in real life." A simple test of this assumption would have been to offer a verbal form of the test with the items being the names of the occupations, or activities, represented by the drawings.

The third criterion of reliability, that the percentage of the respondents selecting the same items on retest is high, could suffer from the same difficulty which plagues the first—distances among and between choices are so great in some triads that it would be difficult *not* to reselect the original choice, e.g., potter, dentist, and musician.

VALIDITY. The case for validity is made by use of three criteria: (*a*) "Just as use of drawings should increase the reliability of the GPII by providing stimuli which are less ambiguous than those in typical all-verbal inventories, such use should contribute to the validity of the GPII"; (*b*) "since 10 of the 11 interest area scores provided by the GPII are similar to the scores for the 10 Kuder scales, it is possible roughly to evaluate the validity of the GPII by correlating the two sets of scores"; and (*c*) "examinees with reading problems will give more valid responses to the GPII than to highly verbal inventories."

The untested assumptions regarding the superiority of the particular drawings in the GPII, or drawings in general, are not confirmed by evidence presented in the manual. Moreover, that the scores correlate with scores with the same scale names on the *Kuder Preference Record* assumes that if A correlates highly with B, then C, which correlates with B, must also correlate highly with A. This does not hold in all cases. The validities of the Kuder and SVIB reside in establishing patterns based on scores from members of vocational, or avocational, groups. No evidence is presented that there are characteristic occupational patterns represented by patterns of scale scores on the GPII. Some evidence of this type might have been obtained by samples from those boys successful and satisfied in academic, general, clerical, and vocational curricula, as well as those from trade school and remedial reading groups.

Unless a clearer description is made available regarding the remedial reading sample, it is difficult to judge whether or not acceptable validity exists, even for a special group. The relationship between reading and general adjustment problems is such that this does not appear as a strong bit of evidence for general validity. The question here, too, is: "Validity for what?"

GENERAL EVALUATION. The *Geist Picture Interest Inventory* does not justify the statement in the manual, "The GPII has shown itself to be quite adequate in research as well as in counseling and guidance work, providing a quick and satisfactorily reliable and valid estimate of interest in 11 areas." (*a*) The hypothesis that drawings, or pictures, are closer to an undefined real life situation than are verbal cues is not tested. No supporting evidence is included in the manual, nor is any research from the literature cited to establish acceptance. (*b*) Reliabilities are not convincing. As high, or higher, correlations may be obtained by within-triad choices which are not scaled for distance in terms of general social desirability. Some scales are of too few items. Samples do not appear adequate in size or method of selection. (*c*) Validity is questionable if the inventory is intended for use in the vocational, avocational, or educational counseling or guidance of youth. It has been demonstrated that the scales will separate some secondary school males on the dimensions used, but the meaning of the differential scale patterns has not been established. Content validity is questionable; concurrent validity is not clearly demonstrated; construct validity is assumed; no predictive validity has been established in terms of environmental criteria. (*d*) No systematic approach is presented in the manual regarding the composition or size of standardization samples. The 615 mainland cases for grades 9–12 may be from a single school or school system. The mainland trade school sample has but 60 cases. Only 75 University of California freshmen and sophomores comprise the university sample. The remedial reading sample is from grades 8 and 10, with but 50 cases in each grade. Puerto Rican students number 340 cases, which provide norms for grades 8, 11, and 12, a trade school, and the University of Puerto Rico. The Hawaiian sample is from unnamed schools, grades 11 and 12, and has but 99 cases. (*e*) Statistical treatment reported in the manual is not impressive. There is no evidence as to the factor composition of the scales. No evidence is presented to demonstrate that a nonverbal, or essentially nonverbal, test measures the same dimensions or factors as does a verbal test. Rigorous research methodology is missing. (*f*) The references at the end of the manual do not include Bordin, Clark, Darley, Fryer, Holland, Strong, Super, Tyler, and other major contributors to the field of interest measurement. No mention is made of Weingarten's *Picture Interest Inventory,* a competitor in the field. No theoretical position is stated regarding the nature of interests. No important hypotheses are stated and accepted or rejected by the presentation of research.

SUMMARY OPINION. An experimental instrument in the first stages of development, this inventory is not ready for distribution for other than research uses.

BENJAMIN SHIMBERG, *Director of Educational Relations, Cooperative Test Division, Educational Testing Service, Princeton, New Jersey.* [Review of 1964 revision.]

DESCRIPTION. The *Geist Picture Interest Inventory* (GPII) is presented as an antidote to most of the existing inventories which require considerable verbal proficiency on the part of examinees. The author suggests that "disconcerting discrepancies often arise between real interests manifested by life behavior and 'interests' estimated from highly verbal interest inventories." Such inventories, he states, "are often used with children and adults who may have *limited verbal facility or who may be almost illiterate*" (italics mine).

Geist has approached interest measurement via occupationally oriented drawings. It is his belief that picture items are "less ambiguous with respect to life referents than most verbal items."

The 1964 edition of GPII comes in the form of two consumable booklets, one for men and another for women. Pictures are arranged in triads: 44 for men and 27 for women. The respondent is required to make a "forced choice" among the pictures in each triad by circling one of the pictures. Beneath each triad are captions such as: "If you had the ability, which would you rather do?" "Which man [or woman] would you rather be?" "Which picture is most interesting to you?" "About which would you rather study?" The author states that the questions have been varied to reduce task monotony and to avoid response repetition. There is no indication that the influence of question wording on response has been studied in a systematic fashion.

The scoring is in terms of broad fields of interest using Kuder's nomenclature. Geist has added two scales: Dramatic and Personal Service (for females only).

EVALUATION. Bauernfeind [1] has recently suggested some things to look for in reviewing an interest inventory. This reviewer has decided to follow Bauernfeind's suggestions with respect to the Geist inventory.

What are the intended purposes of the instrument as viewed by the author and publisher? The author stresses the advantages of the pictorial approach for young people and adults who have difficulty understanding highly verbal materials. One would, therefore, conclude that this is the special audience toward which the GPII is directed and that its purpose is to facilitate interest measurement where highly verbal instruments are inappropriate. However, the manual stakes out a larger domain. It states that GPII "is a highly reliable and valid instrument in the quantitative determination of occupational and avocational interests of male and female populations, ranging from the eighth grade, through high school and college, and with adult groups."

How well are the actual test questions aligned with the stated purpose? The drawings permit an individual to identify with people at work (man welding, sawing, fixing TV set, etc.). It is in this realm that the GPII shows considerable promise. However, in an effort to make the instrument applicable to a broad population group, the author has included many drawings (over 30 per cent in the form for males) depicting people engaged in activities which require a high degree of verbal facility or advanced professional training. These are not activities likely to appeal to those with verbal handicaps. Indeed, they would appear to narrow the range of meaningful choice for those in this group whose interests are being probed.

What are the score areas and what does each score really mean? The score areas are the same as those used by Kuder with two additions. Space does not permit a detailed analysis of what each scale score means, but a close look at one area may be indicative of the problems that are likely to arise in the interpretation of scores. The manual defines the outdoor scale as indicating a preference for "outdoor or open air activities." The pictures contributing to a high outdoor score include those of a tree surgeon, a door-to-door salesman, a recreation director, a commercial fisherman, a farmer, a surveyor, a telephone lineman, a baseball player, a track runner, a dog trainer, some botanical specimens, and a man receiving a set of Air Force wings. True, all of these have an out-of-doors referent, but one might well ask whether the outdoors interest depicted by a tree surgeon represents the same set of values as those of the athlete or the Air Force pilot. This

1 BAUERNFEIND, ROBERT H. "What to Look for in a Review of an Interest Inventory." *Personnel & Guid J* 42:925–7 My '64. *

reviewer's skepticism is compounded when he notes that the author selected physical education teachers to represent the "outdoor" category in his norming and validation studies.

Are the scores derived from forced choice items such that all students tend to attain a balance of "high" or "low" scores? The forced choice technique may have certain advantages when every item is paired with every other item or combination of items. However, it is difficult to follow the logic of forced choice when there does not appear to be any systematic pairing or rotation. The various areas are unevenly represented. In the form for men, the clerical area is represented by 12 pictures, the persuasive area by 22. In the form for women, the mechanical area is represented by 24 pictures, the literary area by 4.

Are general norms provided or is it expected that scores will be interpreted using local norms? The author provides T score norms for students in grades 8–12, for two remedial reading groups, for a trade school sample, and for a university group. These are referred to as "the U.S. Mainland sample," meaning students from schools and colleges located in California. There are also norms for similar groups of students in Puerto Rico and Hawaii. In addition, T score tables are provided to show how members of various occupational groups scored on the various scales.

In transforming raw scores into T scores, the author assumes that the interests he is measuring are normally distributed in the specific norms populations he has established. This is a highly questionable assumption, and it throws serious doubt on the usefulness of the norms that are provided.

Since the number of cases represented in the various norms groups is not stated explicitly, one is left with the impression that they were established on a representative sample of lawyers, librarians, engineers, scientists, etc. One discovers, after some digging, that these norms were probably based on responses from not more than 12 lawyers, 24 librarians, 31 engineers, and 57 scientists. The median *n* for these occupational groups is 38 cases—an extremely small sample when one considers the great amount of variability *within* the various groups.

Are various scale scores reliable? Test-retest reliabilities for each interest area after a six-month interval for males in the mainland sample fluctuate between .13 and .94. Agreement was highest for a sample of 75 university students and lowest for samples of trade school and remedial reading students. Median reliability was in the .60's. No reliability data are presented for female groups.

What types of follow-up validity studies have been reported? The author has attempted to demonstrate validity of GPII through the use of various criteria in five studies. (*a*) Manifest interest of children as reported by their parents. (*b*) GPII scores of individuals in occupations related to each interest area. (*c*) A five year follow-up of students tested in high school to determine (by questionnaire) the occupations in which they were currently engaged. (*d*) Correlation between GPII and Kuder scores. (*e*) Comparison of GPII scores and scores on a job satisfaction scale. The small number of cases used in each of these studies, problems of sampling, and other methodological questions make it difficult to interpret or place much credence in the results.

In the manifest interest study, for example, the author reports relatively high correlations on three scales: Persuasive (.71), Social Service (.62), and Musical (.42). He reports low correlations on Artistic (.17), Mechanical (.19), Clerical (.20), and Outdoor (.22). However, these results are based on only 101 cases which had to be further subdivided into 11 interest categories. The *n* for each category is not given.

The five year follow-up study was based on replies from 289 students out of a total group of 1,522 to whom questionnaires were sent. The author concludes that five of his scales are "highly valid," while two are "not at all valid." The reviewer does not feel that any meaningful conclusions can be reached on the basis of the very small, self-selected sample.

The occupational validation also suffers from inadequate sampling (see section on norms). Moreover, conclusions regarding validity seem to rest on relatively small differences in T scores. There is no indication that the standard error of measurement of the T scores has been taken into consideration in drawing conclusions regarding the significance of the differences under discussion.

Correlations between Kuder and GPII scores for men range from .24 to .38 for three groups of U.S. high school students, and between .49 and .65 for five groups of Hawaiian high school students. The author regards these positive correlations as evidence of validity. One might ask what merit there may be in attempting to predict Kuder scores when the meanings of such scores are themselves open to serious question.[2]

The author attaches special significance to the fact that his remedial reading groups in the U.S. ($n = 70$) and in Hawaii ($n = 76$) showed somewhat lower correlations with Kuder scores than did other groups. He concludes, "GPII scores are more valid than Kuder scores for individuals with reading handicaps." This statement may be true, but this reviewer fails to see how the author can make it on the basis of the evidence he has presented.

CONCLUSION. The author has devised two experimental instruments which may be useful in situations where individuals suffer from reading disabilities. However, he has not yet demonstrated their usefulness for this special purpose, nor has he demonstrated that they produce useful or meaningful results when used with a more general population.

This reviewer can see possibilities in using the GPII as a clinical tool with the poor readers. Any attempt to provide guidance on the basis of normative information currently available would be a serious mistake.

Personnel & Guid J 38:506-7 F '60. David V. Tiedeman. * Although I find that the *Inventory* has faults, both logical and technical, the set of picture stimuli intelligently used either clinically or more formally might: (1) assess interest in a fuller context than usual and hence predict choice better than we can now do; (2) help us separate interest and capacity; and (3) identify interests in occupations besides the professions if the picture repertoire were expanded. Because of this potential, I have directed your attention to this *Inventory*. Perhaps some of you may have opportunity to test some of this potential and to let others know about it. I think it may be profitable to orient investigations of occupational motivations to pictures of work situations. [See original review for critical comments not excerpted.]

2 BAUERNFEIND, ROBERT H. "The Matter of 'Ipsative Scores.'" *Personnel & Guid J* 41:210-7 N '62. * (*PA* 37:6919)
KATZ, MARTIN. "Interpreting Kuder Preference Record—Vocational Scores: Ipsative or Normative." *Voc Guid Q* 10:96-100 w '62. (*PA* 37:1972)

Personnel & Guid J 39:59 S '60. Harold Geist. [An unexcerpted criticism of the above review by David V. Tiedeman. Also an unexcerpted reply by David V. Tiedeman.]

[1055]

★Geist Picture Interest Inventory: Deaf Form: Male. Deaf and hard of hearing males (grades 7-16 and adults); 1962; adaptation of *Geist Picture Interest Inventory;* 10 scores: persuasive, clerical, mechanical, scientific, outdoor, literary, computational, artistic, social service, dramatic; 1 form (29 pages); optional card form (81 cards) for determining occupation most preferred; record booklet-answer sheet (4 pages); manual (41 pages); no data on reliability of card form; separate answer sheets must be used; $2 per test (booklet form); $6.50 per 25 record booklet-answer sheets; $2.50 per set of keys; $6.50 per set of cards; $3 per manual; postpaid; [30-50] minutes; Harold Geist; Western Psychological Services. *

REFERENCES

1. GEIST, HAROLD. "Occupational Interest Profiles of the Deaf." *Personnel & Guid J* 41:50-5 S '62. * (*PA* 37:5340)

[1056]

★Gordon Occupational Check List. High school students not planning to enter college; 1961-63; 5 or 11 scores: business, outdoor, arts, technology, service, and 6 optional response summarization scores (preceding 5 areas and total); 1 form ('63, 6 pages); manual ('63, 15 pages); no norms; $4 per 35 tests; 40¢ per specimen set; postage extra; (20-25) minutes; Leonard V. Gordon; Harcourt, Brace & World, Inc. *

JOHN O. CRITES, *Associate Professor of Psychology, University of Iowa, Iowa City, Iowa.*

Designed specifically for use with individuals who have a high school education or less, the *Gordon Occupational Check List* (OCL) is an interest inventory which contains 240 statements of job duties and tasks, such as "install or repair plumbing in houses" and "fire and tend a large commercial furnace," found in occupations at the middle and lower levels of skill and responsibility. The statements are classified into five broad occupational groupings (Business, Outdoor, Arts, Technology, and Service) which roughly correspond to the groups in Roe's occupational classification scheme. Rather than Roe's six levels of skill and responsibility being represented in OCL, however, it includes only the lower levels, 3 through 6, which means that the top level professional and managerial occupations are not included. Within each of the OCL groupings further clusterings of statements have been made on the basis of common factorial structure, level of performance required, and the worker characteristics required for performance of the tasks. The groupings of items are not made explicit to the examinee, who is instructed simply to underline the statements of activities he would like to do and then to go back and circle the numbers of statements he would like to do the most. These responses are summarized for interpretative purposes in boxes provided at the end of a row of statements. In this respect, as in several others, the OCL is patterned after the *Mooney Problem Check List.*

Several kinds of reliability data are reported in the manual, most of which indicate that responses are reasonably stable over time. The total test-retest reliabilities for 52 male and 45 female twelfth graders, for example, were .81 and .82, respectively, with a month's interval, the data being percentage of items underlined identically on the two occasions. As the manual points out, these reliability estimates are attenuated by two factors: they do not take into consideration either the items not marked by the examinee or changes in response between highly similar items. When the first factor is accounted for by including a count of identical responses which were both underlined and not underlined, the reliabilities increase appreciably to .97 for males and .97 for females. Again, however, these coefficients are somewhat spurious because only a relatively small proportion of items is usually underlined. Probably the best conclusion which can be drawn is that the reliability of the OCL is in the middle or high .80's and should be sufficient for most counseling and research purposes.

Evidence for the validity of the OCL is less extensive and convincing than that for its reliability, consisting primarily of logical arguments for the instrument's comprehensiveness, response selectivity, and acceptance by examinees. About the best that can be said is that the OCL samples a fairly wide range of occupations which are commonly entered, it elicits responses to about one third of the items, and it appears to be considered worthwhile by those who take it. The relationships of the OCL to other variables, such as intelligence, inventoried interests, curricular choice, and occupational entry, have not been studied, and consequently its validity and usefulness is largely unknown.

The concepts and purposes which guided the construction of the OCL are sound: there is definitely a need for an inventory of lower level interests which can be used with high school age students as well as with older individuals seen in rehabilitation centers and employment agencies. If the OCL is used as a checklist, which is its unique feature, it should have considerable value as an aid to interview discussions of specific job duties and tasks and their relative desirability to individuals who are headed for lower level occupations.

Kenneth B. Hoyt, *Professor of Education, University of Iowa, Iowa City, Iowa.*

This inventory represents an attempt to construct, through logical means, an instrument which can be used to assess occupational interests of high school students not planning to enter college. The logic consisted of selecting 240 occupations, using Roe's group and level schema of occupational classification, which: "(1) could be successfully pursued by an individual with no more than a high school or equivalent education; (2) were relatively widespread geographically; (3) existed in some reasonable number; and (4) would not be considered objectionable by young people." Activity items representing critical job duties for each occupation were then written for each of the 240 occupations using the 1949 *Dictionary of Occupational Titles* and the 1961 *Occupational Outlook Handbook* as guides. These items constitute the prime content of the inventory.

While not stated in the manual, it appears that one must also assume, as part of the logic underlying construction of this inventory, that: (*a*) the concept of occupational interest is appropriate as a reason for choosing one of these occupations; (*b*) high school students will be familiar with the occupational tasks comprising the items and will be able to read the items as they appear; and (*c*) the manner in which high school students respond to these items bears some relationship to their occupational future. The manual reports no tests of these additional assumptions.

The 240 items are unevenly distributed among five areas of occupational interest. Technology (with 96 items) is most heavily represented. Both Business and Service have half as many items as Technology, while Outdoor and Arts each have one fourth as many. Items are clustered both by area and by level in the inventory. Four questions requiring varying amounts of writing from the student are placed at the end. There are no time limits.

A preliminary form of the checklist was administered to more than 6,000 high school students. The final form was constructed on the basis of analyses of responses of these students. Seventeen item substitutions were made in the final form. All statistical data reported in the manual are based on results obtained using the preliminary form. Information gleaned from reliability data presented indicate that: (*a*) the total number of items underlined in a test-retest situation is about the same; (*b*) in a test-retest situation, about two thirds of the items underlined by the same individuals are identical; (*c*) there is a substantial relationship between the specific items to which samples of boys and girls respond in a test-retest situation; and (*d*) there is a high relationship between the individual items responded to by two samples of boys and a similarly high relationship for girls. The numbers of students represented here range from 45 to 100. All were twelfth graders.

There are no norms reported. Means and standard deviations of numbers of responses by area and for the entire checklist are presented for 161 boys and 133 girls in the twelfth grade. The standard deviations are almost as large, and in several cases considerably larger, than the means, indicating a markedly skewed distribution. Evidently, a few students must have underlined a great many items and many students must have underlined very few.

The manual states the criterion of response selectivity as one to be used in assessing validity of the checklist. These means and standards are presented as evidence that this criterion has been met. I would interpret them as meaning that this criterion was not met well.

A second claim for validity is made on the basis of comprehensiveness by showing that, when one sample of 172 high school students were given an opportunity to list other occupations in which they were interested, very few did so. In the third place, when students in another sample were asked to write at the end of the checklist the life work they would choose for themselves, their responses were "closely related" to the occupations students had just underlined in the checklist. Finally, a claim for validity is made on the basis of the fact that a majority of students reported they enjoyed answering the checklist. No evidence is presented with respect to such factors as relationships between responses on the checklist and entry or persistence in an occupation nor satisfaction with occupations. Those looking for these kinds of evidence of validity will conclude that, to date, there is no reason to believe the checklist to be a valid instrument.

The 240 occupations represented in the checklist are presented as ones which could be successfully pursued with no more than a high school or equivalent education. Many will question whether such occupations as occupational therapist, X-ray technician, literary writer, watchmaker, public relations man, clergyman, or hotel manager could really be so classified. It would seem that some distinctions might have been made between what is *possible* with no more than a high school education and what is likely to be attainable. Certainly, some distinction should be made between occupations requiring further specialty training (albeit, not at the college level) and those requiring only a high school education. Likewise, it would seem that consideration might be given to distinguishing between entry occupations and nonentry occupations in selection of items for the checklist. These are serious weakneses.

The manual states that "much of this same information could be elicited during the course of an interview." This would seem to be an honest representation of the value of the checklist at present.

[1057]

★**The Guilford-Zimmerman Interest Inventory.** Grades 10–16 and adults; 1962–63; 10 scores: mechanical, natural, aesthetic, service, clerical, mercantile, leadership, literary, scientific, creative; 1 form ('63, 4 pages); manual ('63, 5 pages, called preliminary in text); profile ('62, 1 page); reliability and validity data based on an earlier longer form; norms for college freshmen only; separate answer sheets must be used; $3.50 per 25 tests; 20¢ per single copy; 5¢ per IBM scorable answer sheet; $2.50 per set of scoring stencils; 5¢ per profile; 35¢ per manual; postage extra; (20–30) minutes; Joan S. Guilford and Wayne S. Zimmerman; Sheridan Supply Co. *

KENNETH B. HOYT, *Professor of Education, University of Iowa, Iowa City, Iowa.*

This is an interest inventory which, if used at present, must be largely accepted on faith. Such faith must encompass many dimensions. First, one must have faith that the 10 interest categories in which scores may be obtained are inclusive for the range of occupational interests. The authors present no evidence showing this to be the case.

Second, one must accept the authors' contention that the 150 items (15 for each of the 10 scales) are accurate representations of the interest each stands for. Certainly, there is no intuitive way of establishing this to be the case and, again, no evidence is presented by the authors. Items were selected for inclusion on the basis of those which discriminated best among a sample of approximately 800 college freshmen who were administered a "preliminary experimental form" consisting of 450 items.

Third, in seeking answers regarding reliability of the scales, one must accept the authors' contention that the intra-scale correlations will be high. The authors base this claim on their report of average intra-scale correlations in the preliminary experimental form ranging "from .68 to .88." No reliability data for the present published form are presented.

Fourth, one must accept the authors' statement that "useful external criteria have not been sufficiently developed for the establishment of validity data." Those conversant with the literature reported with reference to validity of the SVIB may have some difficulty here.

Fifth, one is asked to accept the authors' statement with respect to their norm group of about 800 college freshmen that "students in the two Southern California colleges....have, in previous testing, proved to be fairly representative of liberal arts college students throughout the United States." The authors do note that further standardization is in progress and its results will be reported later.

One major feature of this instrument is that it is a non-ipsative measure. Examinees are asked to mark one of four responses to each item. These responses are assigned constant weights. A "Definite Dislike" response is scored 0; a "No Interest or Mild Dislike" is scored 1; a "Some Interest or Slight Like" is scored 2; and a "Definite Like" is scored 3. With 15 items per scale, the possible range of scores for each scale runs from 0 to 45. No data are reported relative to the appropriateness of these assigned weights.

Another feature is the presence of a "Creative" scale. Some may find themselves wondering whether it is possible to build such items independent of other interests. For example, could not a highly creative person with no mechanical interests mark "Build a unique structure out of unconventional materials" as a "Definite Dislike," not because he is without creative interests, but simply because he has no interest in things mechanical? Other examples of items from this scale which could be similarly questioned include "Invent a new 'gadget'" and "Experiment with materials to produce a unique art object."

Other claims made in the manual include the fact that administration time is short, scoring is quick and easy, and the scales are built using factor analysis procedures. Each of these claims appears justified. Those who are satisfied with such claims may find this inventory acceptable.

The manual suggests that the inventory be used in grades 10 through college age groups. Why the authors feel this instrument to be appropriate at grade 10 in spite of the fact the norms are for college freshmen is not explained.

By and large, it would seem that this inventory may be intended to compete with the SVIB. However, before it can sensibly be expected to do so, it is in need of much further development.

[1058]

★Hackman-Gaither Vocational Interest Inventory, Revised Edition. Grades 9–12 and adults; 1962–64; 8 scores: business contact, artistic, scientific-technical, health and welfare, business clerical, mechanical, service, outdoor; IBM; 1 form ('64, 12 pages); manual ('63, c1962–63, 22 pages); scoring instructions ('64, 2 pages); technical report ('63, 40 pages); profile ('62, 2 pages); student summary—curricular group means chart ('64, 4 pages); job preference indicator ('62, 2 pages) for each score field; separate answer sheets must be used; $7 per 20 tests; $1.60 per 20 IBM scorable answer sheets; $1.20 per 20 profiles; 10¢ per student summary—curricular group means chart; $1 per 20 job preference indicators for any one score field; 30¢ per manual; 60¢ per technical report; postage extra; $1.75 per specimen set, postpaid; (25–30) minutes; Roy B. Hackman and James W. Gaither; Palmer Associates. *

REFERENCES

1. ARNS, JOSEPHINE. *A Factorial Analysis of the Vocational Interests of Two Hundred Adult Female Students.* Doctor's thesis, Temple University (Philadelphia, Pa.), 1958. (*DA* 19:562)

2. BERRIER, JOHN G. *A Factorial Analysis of the Occupational Interests of Two Hundred Vocationally Experienced Adult Male Students.* Doctor's thesis, Temple University (Philadelphia, Pa.), 1958. (*DA* 19:1645)

3. GAITHER, JAMES WALLACE. *A Factorial Analysis of the Occupational Interests of Two Hundred Vocationally Inexperienced Adult Male Students.* Doctor's thesis, Temple University (Philadelphia, Pa.), 1958. (*DA* 19:868)

4. COHEN, LEONARD MARLIN. *The Relationship Between Certain Personality Variables and Prior Occupational Stability of Prison Inmates.* Doctor's thesis, Temple University (Philadelphia, Pa.), 1959. (*DA* 20:3375)

[1059]

***How Well Do You Know Your Interests.** High school, college, adults; 1957–62; 54 scores: numerical, clerical, retail selling, outside selling, selling real estate, one-order selling, sales complaints, selling intangibles, buyer, labor management, production supervision, business management, machine operation, repair and construction, machine design, farm or ranch, gardening, hunting, adventure, social service, teaching service, medical service, nursing service, applied chemistry, basic chemical problems, basic biological problems, basic physical problems, basic psychological problems, philosophical, visual art appreciative, visual art productive, visual art decorative, amusement appreciative, amusement productive, amusement managerial, literary appreciative, literary productive, musical appreciative, musical performing, musical composing, sports appreciative, sports participative, domestic service, unskilled labor, disciplinary, power seeking, propaganda, self-aggrandizing, supervisory initiative, bargaining, arbitrative, persuasive, disputatious, masculinity (for males only) or femininity (for females only); Form B-22 (6 pages); 3 editions (identical except for profiles): secondary school ('58), college ('57), personnel ('57); manual ('57, 24 pages); educational guidance supplement ('58, 12 pages); technical summary ('62, 4 pages); no description of normative population for personnel edition; $7.50 per 30 tests; $2.50 per specimen set of any one edition; postage extra; (20–30) minutes; Thomas N. Jenkins; Executive Analysis Corporation. *

REFERENCES

1. MENDELSON, MARTIN A. *Personality and Interests of Air Force Personnel.* Doctor's thesis, New York University (New York, N.Y.), 1957. (*DA* 21:3844)

JOHN R. HILLS, *Director, Testing and Guidance, The University System of Georgia, Atlanta, Georgia.*

HWDYKYI purports to be an interest inventory based on the principles and application of factor analysis. The Manual of Instructions mentions "over 1,000 factor analyses," "about 3,000,000 correlations," and "a fifteen year investigation of personality and personality appraisal." However, in the manual, the Educational Guidance Supplement, and the Technical Summary, only one research report which appears to include this inventory is mentioned, that one being a 1957 doctoral thesis (*1*) with no indication that it was ever published. Query to the publisher resulted in reprints concerning factor analyses of personality, but not of interests.

The idea behind the instrument apparently was factor analyzing interest items into homogeneous groups and using two to four of the most highly loaded items on each factor to represent that factor in the inventory. This should be a route to efficient measurement of a wide variety of independent variables. The inventory provides 53 scores from 120 items, each used only once, except that an item may be reused to measure masculinity-femininity, the 54th score.

The basic idea is good. Why is the reviewer unenthusiastic? First, the manual, the Educational Guidance Supplement, and the Technical Summary don't agree in detail with each other, even though long sections duplicate each other. They are poorly edited, e.g., Table 5 is referred to in the Technical Summary but appears only in the manual; the Educational Guidance Supplement shows that 513 secondary school students were used to develop test-retest reliability coefficients, but the Technical Summary implies that 2,603 students participated in the reliability study. Other examples of this type could be cited.

Beside poor editing, other signs of carelessness appear in annoying numbers. The manual says, "A random sample of at least *200* employees is necessary for establishing an accurate set of local norms." Yet it states, "For those who prefer a more representative sample of young men throughout the United States, Table 3 has been included. These norms are based on a sample of *200* unmarried men from *29* states." Apparently, local norms require a random sample, but a representative sample of young men throughout the United States need not be random, nor even stratified by geographical region. The same casual approach appears in the case of secondary school norms. The Educational Guidance Supplement indicates that those norms are based on students from 8 western, 2 midwestern, 17 northeastern, and 1 southern secondary schools. Eight of the 28 schools were in New York City!

The Technical Summary and the Manual of Instructions both state, "The median value of the *53* mean validities is 79.5." This is mathematical nonsense in terms of factorial validities, the kind of validity coefficient stressed for this test. It apparently is an error in decimal placement, but occurs in two documents published over a five-year interval.

One could go on at length, but why must one bother with such tangential evidence of inadequacy? Why not discuss the factor analyses, the content of the items which were used in the "over 1,000 factor analyses," the interpretation of the factors, the appropriateness of the communality estimates, the method of extraction, the method of rotation, the criteria for stopping extraction, etc., as they apply to this inventory? These data would reveal what the test measures factorially. The reason is that one can't examine these basic issues. The data specific to this interest test are not presented nor given bibliographic citation in standard publications or otherwise, and cannot be obtained upon query of the organization responsible for the instrument. Since a reviewer or a potential user cannot examine the basic data, he must study what is available to him, and in this case it is grossly inadequate. Until this is remedied, it is of no consequence that the test may be clever, easy to use, comprehensive, economical, or otherwise superior.

A test is of no value unless one can ascertain reasonably clearly what its scores measure. For a factored test with little or no published empirical evidence of validity, the definition of score meaning comes from study of items and factor loadings. In this case, only two items and their loadings are given for most of the scores. The ordinary user cannot readily find out what sets of items these were chosen to represent, what sets were included in the factor analyses on which the inventory is based, or what the factor loadings were of the items on various factors. Correspondence with the publisher leaves one sympathetic with his problems, i.e., the cost of publishing all these data and the fact that others will "borrow" good items once they are published. While solutions to these problems would be welcomed, recognition of them is no help to the potential user. He must decide whether to use this unknown device with a client. The ethical decision can only be to use it only for experimental purposes until more information is released by the publisher or until the user's own research reveals the value of the instrument. The reviewer is left disappointed that such a good effort toward improved, modern measurement of interests was left incomplete by the death of the author!

J Counsel Psychol 7:154 su '60. Gordon V. Anderson. This interest inventory has been designed to give reliable information about vocational interests over the widest possible range of occupational possibilities with greatest convenience possible and maximum saving of time. It appears to have achieved this remarkably well. * perhaps we do here have a useful contribution to interest measurement * The vocabulary level does not appear to be above that of the secondary school level, and the activities described are easily understood and unambiguous. The directions for responding to the inventory are simple * when all factors are considered, the cost of an interest profile obtained from this inventory is probably as low as from any other comparable standard inventory. The manual is well written, and a high professional standard is set in the recommendations which are made in it. Information about the development of the inventory and the procedures used for its standardization is somewhat skimpy. * Regardless of the inventory used, counselors are not likely to accept the results obtained at face value. The very nature of attitudes makes us reluctant to generalize readily from a quantitative result. The score or the profile is useful primarily as a starting point for counseling. The Jenkins vocational interest inventory holds out attractive clinical promise, with studies of patterning, both within the principal interest domains and among them, offering interesting possibilities. It would seem likely that an insightful counselor would find the profile very helpful in working with students to help them understand themselves better. Its very complexity should serve to discourage overgeneralizations and unsound predictions.

For reviews by Jerome E. Doppelt and Henry S. Dyer, see 5:859.

[1060]

***Inventory of Vocational Interests: Acorn National Aptitude Tests.** Grades 7–16 and adults; 1943–60; 5 scores: mechanical, academic, artistic, business and economic, farm-agricultural; 1 form ('57, c1943–57, 4 pages, identical with test copyrighted 1943); manual ('60, c1943–60, 6 pages, identical with manual copyrighted in 1943); directions sheet ('60, c1943–60, 1 page, identical with sheet copyrighted in 1943); no data on reliability; $2.50 per 25 tests; 25¢ per manual; $1 per specimen set; postage extra; (35) minutes; Andrew Kobal, J. Wayne Wrightstone, and Karl R. Kunze; [Psychometric Affiliates]. *

JOHN W. FRENCH, *Professor of Psychology, and College Examiner, New College, Sarasota, Florida.*

Each of the 25 items of this inventory asks the subject to check the nature of his interest with respect to some very general piece of equipment, organization, or situation. In each item he is to check exactly 3 out of 10 activities, labeled *a* through *j*. These options are worded differently as appropriate for each item, but their nature and sequence are fixed: *a* and *b* are mechanical activities, *c* and *d* are academic, *e* and *f* are artistic, *g* and *h* are business and economic, and *i* and *j* are farm-agricultural. The scores are then simply the number of checks recorded in each of these five areas of interest. The highest possible score is 50, resulting, for example, from checking both *a* and *b* in every item. The manual considers a score of 35 in one field to indicate "an outstanding quantity of interest." When no score for a field reaches this amount, the two fields with the highest scores are to be considered. Vocational counseling is then done on the basis of a one-page "Index of Basic Occupations" that lists occupations for each of the five fields and for every combination of two fields. For example, "carpenter" is one of 17 occupations listed for mechanical; "psychologist" is one of 14 listed for academic; and chemist is one of 13 listed for the combination of these two fields.

Compared to other vocational interest inventories this one has some advantages and some important shortcomings. Its advantages are: (*a*) The time it takes to complete is relatively short. (*b*) The scoring is so simple that the students can be asked to score their own tests. (*c*) The items are written about activities that are familiar to students rather than written in terms of occupational titles. (*d*) The activities among which the subjects must choose are well balanced for their social or prestige appeal.

The disadvantages of this inventory include: (*a*) The scores are ipsative, that is, the scores in the five areas may be compared only within a subject; the scores are not such that the intensity of interest can be compared from subject to subject, because relative interest in one field causes a depressed score in another field. Conversely, very meager interest in four fields will make a very modest interest in the fifth field seem to be intense. (*b*) The fixed sequence for the 10 options in each item makes the subject very much aware at all times what interests he is revealing. At best this is distracting; at worst it leads the subject unconsciously to mold his interest scores to a preconceived pattern or allows him consciously to fake in order to attain some practical goal. (*c*) Reliability and validity data are inadequate. The manual claims that "validity" of the inventory is sufficiently high to warrant its application in individual diagnosis. This sounds more like a claim of reliability, and it is not supported by data. Validity is claimed on the basis of rather interesting data for 60 cases showing a flat interest pattern or lack of interest in educationally low graded individuals. Data on 120 subjects is used to show a correlation of .65 between test scores and previous job advancement and a correlation of .38 with wages. More cases, more different groups, predictive rather than concurrent validity, and more information about the subjects is required before validity of the test can be considered to be established. (*d*) In their present form and with their present description in the manual, the "norms" tables are misleading. They do not, as might be expected, indicate an individual's percentile with respect to the intensity of his interest in a given field as compared to the interest of other individuals in the same field. Because of the ipsative nature of the scoring, the norms tables indicate merely an individual's percentile with respect to the amount of imbalance among his own interests as compared to the amount of imbalance displayed by other individuals.

This is an interest inventory that is simple and pleasant to use. It should be an interesting candidate for trial in a vocational testing situation. However, a user should not put reliance on the scores until they have been shown to predict future job behavior in the situation for which the test is to be used.

For reviews by Marion A. Bills, Edward S. Bordin, Harold D. Carter, and Patrick Slater, see 3:638.

[1061]

★**Job Choice Inventory.** Male job applicants and employees in oil and chemical industries; 1951–63; 5 scores: general mechanical, electrical and precision, construction and handiwork, process and laboratory, vehicle operation; Form O-C ('51, 3 pages); manual ['63, 17 unnumbered pages]; $3 per 25 tests; $2.50 per set of keys; $1.25 per manual; postage extra; $3 per specimen set, postpaid; (25–30) minutes; Richardson, Bellows, Henry & Co., Inc. *

[1061a]

***Kuder General Interest Survey.** Grades 6–12; 1934–64; revision and downward extension of *Kuder Preference Record—Vocational,* Form C; 11 scores: outdoor, mechanical, computational, scientific, persuasive, artistic, literary, musical, social service, clerical, verification; form E ('63, 15 pages); manual ('64, 52 pages); separate profiles ('63, 4 pages) for grades 6–8, 9–12; separate answer pads must be used; $11 per 20 tests; $2.60 per 20 self-marking answer pads; 70¢ per 20 profiles; 75¢ per specimen set; postage extra; (45–60) minutes; G. Frederic Kuder; Science Research Associates, Inc. *

[1062]

***Kuder Preference Record — Occupational.** Grades 9–16 and adults; 1956–63; 51 scores: verification, county agricultural agent, farmer, forester, minister, newspaper editor, physician [revised], clinical psychologist, industrial psychologist, YMCA secretary, school superintendent, accountant, meteorologist, personnel manager, department store salesman, psychology professor, mechanical engineer, counseling psychologist, journalist, architect ['57], electrical engineer (revised), civil engineer, lawyer, retail clothier, insurance agent, dentist, veterinarian, industrial engineer, pediatrician, psychiatrist, radio station manager, interior decorator, high school counselor, high school science teacher, high school mathematics teacher, chemist, mining and metallurgical engineer, druggist, job printer ['58], bank cashier ('59), male librarian ('59), pharmaceutical salesman ('59), X-ray technician ('59), podiatrist ('61), florist ('61), heating and air conditioning engineer ('61), heating and air conditioning sales engineer ('61), auto mechanic ('61), long distance truck driver ('61), teaching sister ('63), teaching brother ('63); IBM; Form D ('56, 12 pages); manual, fourth edition ('61, c1956–59, 17 pages); special accessories for use in developing occupational keys: computation sheet booklet ('56, 26 pages), research handbook, second edition ('57, c1956, 47 pages); separate answer sheets must be used; $11 per 20 tests; $6.25 per 100 IBM answer sheets; $1 per scoring stencil for any one score; $2.50 per computation sheet booklet; $2.50 per research handbook; $2 per counseling specimen set; $6 per research specimen set; postage extra; (25–35) minutes; G. Frederic Kuder; Science Research Associates, Inc. *

REFERENCES

1. JONES, CHARLES W. *Kuder Preference Record Occupational Form D: Scoring for Secondary Teachers.* Master's thesis, Iowa State College of Agriculture and Mechanic Arts (Ames, Iowa), 1957.
2. BARTON, ERVIN M. *Development of a Kuder Preference Record Occupational Form D, Scoring Key for Secondary School Counselors.* Master's thesis, Iowa State University (Ames, Iowa), 1958.
3. BLANCHARD, ROBERT EUGENE. *The Development and Validation of Instruments for Selecting Farm Operators for Farm Management Services.* Doctor's thesis, Purdue University (Lafayette, Ind.), 1959. (*DA* 20:2884)
4. JAMES, FLEMING. *The Stability of the Civil, Electrical, and Mechanical Engineering Scales of the Kuder Preference Record Occupational, Form D, and Some Implications for Counseling.* Master's thesis, Duke University (Durham, N.C.), 1959.
5. JOSEPH, MICHAEL P. "The Strong Vocational Interest Blank and the Kuder Preference Record—Occupational (Form D): A Comparative Study of Eight Same-Named Scales." *Yearb Nat Council Meas Ed* 18:145–54 '61. *
6. WARD, GLEN R. *Interest Patterns of the Kuder Preference Record Occupational Form D.* Master's thesis, Utah State University (Logan, Utah), 1961.
7. BOYCE, RICHARD W. "The Construction and Validity of an Interest Key for Medical Technologists." *Am J Med Tech* 28:349–51 N–D '62.
8. CAMPBELL, JOEL T.; OTIS, JAY L.; LISKE, RALPH E.; AND PRIEN, ERICH P. "Assessments of Higher-Level Personnel: 2, Validity of the Over-All Assessment Process." *Personnel Psychol* 15:63–74 sp '62. * (*PA* 37:3908)
9. SCHUTZ, RICHARD E., AND BAKER, ROBERT L. "A Comparison of the Factor Structure of the Kuder Occupational, Form D for Males and Females." *Ed & Psychol Meas* 22:485–92 au '62. * (*PA* 37:5696)
10. SCHUTZ, RICHARD E., AND BAKER, ROBERT L. "A Factor Analysis of the Kuder Preference Record—Occupational, Form D." *Ed & Psychol Meas* 22:97–104 sp '62. * (*PA* 37:1265)
11. WALKER, ROBERT WILLIAM. *Development of a Vocational Agriculture Interest Inventory for Guidance of Eighth Grade Students.* Doctor's thesis, Pennsylvania State University (University Park, Pa.), 1962. (*DA* 23:3702)
12. KUDER, G. FREDERIC. "A Rationale for Evaluating Interests." *Ed & Psychol Meas* 23:3–12 sp '63. * (*PA* 38:3242)
13. TERWILLIGER, JAMES S. "Dimensions of Occupational Preference." *Ed & Psychol Meas* 23:525–42 au '63. * (*PA* 38:6698)

DAVID P. CAMPBELL, *Associate Professor of Psychology, and Director, Center for Interest Measurement Research, University of Minnesota, Minneapolis, Minnesota.*

The Kuder-Occupational is a 100 triad inventory requiring the respondent to choose one item in each triad as liked most and one as liked least. It is a derivative of earlier forms of the *Kuder Preference Record,* and, as in those earlier forms, the author has done a careful job of selecting items and developing scales.

Unlike earlier forms of the Kuder, and like the *Strong Vocational Interest Blank,* it is scored on occupational keys developed by comparing answers of men in specific occupations with a group of men in general. Thus it competes directly with the SVIB, and most of this review will be devoted to comparing these two instruments.

Only concurrent validity results are reported in the manual and these are quite satisfactory. The scales do separate occupational groups from men in general, and they hold up well on cross validation. No data are furnished on the predictive validity, an area well researched with positive results for the Strong. And, regrettably, there are no data useful in the construct validity sense; no scale intercorrelations are presented; there are no groupings of occupations into larger, more meaningful categories, a technique very useful in interpreting the Strong; there are no indications of sex or age differences.

There are bound to be differences in the validity of these two instruments since the correlations between scales with the same name are only moderately high; they are measuring different things. In one study (5) using 45 students, the median correlation between eight like-named Kuder and Strong scales was .50. Another study, reported in the same paper, using 164 students on 10 scales, reported a median correlation of .45. There is no way of knowing from these studies which scale is best. The Kuder has the advantage of being developed more recently and thus should capitalize on any changes in the makeup of the occupations, while the Strong has an overwhelming amount of research to show that its scales are valid.

Kuder argues clearly and cogently in his manual that reliability as measured by internal consistency measures is not important when the intent is to separate occupations, and neither he nor this reviewer is particularly uncomfortable that these reliabilities are somewhat low (median K-R 20 = .81). But reliability over time, test-retest stability, is another matter. In advising a student about his future plans, test users need to have some assurance that the qualities being measured are stable. The Strong blank has good data on this point for periods up to 18 years. The only data presented in the Kuder manual are for a one month interval, where the median test-retest correlation for college students is .85, slightly lower than comparable figures for the Strong. The Kuder has yet to be proven over a lengthy time span, and, from this one indication, its stability may be less than the Strong.

Kuder has done considerable thinking about how to assure that the individual's answers are honest and careful, and, to this end, he has developed a verification scale to identify careless or dishonest answers. From the data presented, this scale works well. This is a worthwhile feature, although its importance is exaggerated in the manual; more space is devoted to this topic than to either reliability or validity. No such detection key has been developed for the Strong.

In ease of administration and scoring the Kuder definitely has an edge over the Strong. It is shorter, and scoring is much simpler. Other features of the Kuder include a Research Handbook and computational sheets which should be quite helpful to anyone wishing to develop his own scales.

In summary, this inventory has been developed with careful attention to item selection and scale development and it has some useful features not found in other interest inventories. However, in the bread-and-butter areas of reliability, validity, and ease of interpretation, it is still not well established and falls far behind the *Strong Vocational Interest Blank*. Practitioners are advised to continue with the Strong until more developmental research eliminates some of the unanswered questions about this inventory.

For reviews by Edward S. Bordin and John W. Gustad, see 5:862.

[1063]

***Kuder Preference Record—Vocational.** Grades 9–16 and adults; 1934–62; IBM; 2 forms; 2 editions of each; separate answer sheets or pads must be used; $11 per 20 tests; 70¢ per 20 profiles; 75¢ per specimen set of any one edition; postage extra; (40–50) minutes; G. Frederic Kuder; Science Research Associates, Inc. *

a) FORM B [NINE SCALE EDITION]. 1934–60; 9 scores: mechanical, computational, scientific, persuasive, artistic, literary, musical, social service, clerical; masculinity-femininity score also obtainable; 1 form; 2 editions; revised manual ('60, 25 pages); profile for adults ('46, 2 pages); profile for children ('44, 2 pages).

1) [*Hand Scoring Edition.*] Form BB ('42, 15 pages, called Form BH in publisher's catalog); $2.60 per 20 self-marking answer pads; 75¢ per 20 punch pins; $1.65 per 20 backing cardboards.

2) [*Machine Scoring Edition.*] IBM; Form BM ('42, 19 pages); $5 per 100 IBM answer sheets; $7.50 per set of scoring stencils.

b) FORM C [ELEVEN SCALE EDITION]. 1934–62; revision and expansion of Form B; 11 scores: same as for Form B plus outdoor, verification; 1 form; 2 editions; revised manual ('60, 27 pages); profile for adults ('51, 2 pages); profile for children ('50, 2 pages); profile leaflets (4 pages) for adults ('54) and for children ('53) for comparing vocational and personal (see 132) scores.

1) [*Hand or DocuTran Scoring Edition.*] Form CH ('48, 15 pages); supplementary manual ('62, 15 pages) for use with DocuTran scoring service; $2.60 per 20 self-marking answer pads; fee for DocuTran scoring service: 25¢ per student; fee includes answer sheet, supplementary manual, and 3 copies of profile report of scores.

2) [*Machine Scoring Edition.*] IBM; Form CM ('48, 20 pages); $5 per 100 IBM answer sheets; $7.50 per set of scoring stencils; scoring service available.

REFERENCES

1–2. See 40:1671.
3–62. See 3:640.
63–208. See 4:742.
209–419. See 5:863.

420. McCarthy, Thomas N. *The Relationship of Vocational Interests to Personality Traits.* Master's thesis, Catholic University of America (Washington, D.C.), 1952.

421. D'Arcy, Paul F. *Constancy of Interest Factor Patterns Within the Specific Vocation of Foreign Missioner.* Catholic University of America, Studies in Psychology and Psychiatry, Vol. 9, No. 1. Washington, D.C.: Catholic University of America Press, 1954. Pp. ix, 54. * (*PA* 29:6444)

422. Jacobs, Robert, and Traxler, Arthur E. "What Manner of Man Is the Average Accountant." *J Accountancy* 97:465–9 Ap '54. *

423. Moffett, Charles R. *Operational Characteristics of Beginning Master's Students in Educational Administration and Supervision.* Doctor's thesis, University of Tennessee (Knoxville, Tenn.), 1954.

424. Luton, James N. *A Study of the Use of Standardized Tests in the Selection of Potential Educational Administrators.* Doctor's thesis, University of Tennessee (Knoxville, Tenn.), 1955.

425. Womer, Frank B., and Furst, Edward J. "Interest Profiles of Student Nurses." *Nursing Res* 3:125–6 F '55. *

426. Furst, Edward J., and Fricke, Benno G. "Development and Applications of Structured Tests of Personality." *R Ed Res* 26:26–55 F '56. * (*PA* 31:6081)

427. Garrett, Gene A. *A Study of the Causes of Unsatisfactory Verification Scores on the Kuder Preference Record Vocational.* Master's thesis, University of Missouri (Columbia, Mo.), 1956.

428. Taylor, Preston L. *A Study of the Relationship Between Intelligence as Measured by SRA Primary Mental Abilities Tests and Validity Scores on the Kuder Vocational Preference Record.* Master's thesis, Texas Southern University (Houston, Tex.), 1956.

429. Urschalitz, M. Odelia. *Measurement of General Interests and Interests Relevant to Vocation Aim Among Religious Women.* Master's thesis, Fordham University (New York, N.Y.), 1956.

430. Wauck, Le Roy. *An Investigation of the Usefulness of Psychological Tests in the Selection of Candidates for the Diocesan Priesthood.* Doctor's thesis, Loyola University (Chicago, Ill.), 1956.

431. Booth, Mary D. "A Study of the Relationship Between Certain Personality Factors and Success in Clinical Training of Occupational Therapy Students." *Am J Occup Ther* 11:93–6+ Mr–Ap '57. * (*PA* 32:4585)

432. Gowan, J. C. "A Summary of the Intensive Study of Twenty Highly Selected Elementary Women Teachers." *J Exp Ed* 26:115–24 D '57. * (*PA* 33:4731)

433. Lucio, William H., and Risch, Frank. "Relationships Among Tests of Intelligence, Vocational Interest and Aptitude." *Calif J Ed Res* 8:198–203 N '57. * (*PA* 33:7005)

434. Petro, Peter K. *Student Aptitudes and Abilities Correlated With Achievement in First Semester High School Bookkeeping.* Master's thesis, Iowa State Teachers College (Cedar Falls, Iowa), 1957.

435. Sininger, Rollin Albert. *Development and Evaluation of Visual Aids for Interpreting the Differential Aptitude Test and Kuder Preference Record.* Master's thesis, University of Texas (Austin, Tex.), 1957.

436. Anikeeff, Alexis M., and Bryan, John L. "Kuder Interest Pattern Analysis of Fire Protection Students and Graduates." *J Social Psychol* 48:195–8 N '58. * (*PA* 34:6157)

437. Champion, John Mills. *A Method For Predicting Success of Commerce Students.* Doctor's thesis, Purdue University (Lafayette, Ind.), 1958. (*DA* 19:2134)

438. Coulson, Roger Wayne. *Relationships Among Personality Traits, Ability and Academic Efficiency of College Seniors.* Doctor's thesis, State University of Iowa (Iowa City, Iowa), 1958. (*DA* 19:1647)

439. Gitlin, Sidney. *A Study of the Interrelationships of Parents' Measured Interest Patterns and Those of Their Children.* Doctor's thesis, Temple University (Philadelphia, Pa.), 1958. (*DA* 19:3352)

440. Hale, Peter P. "Profiling the Kuder." *Voc Guid Q* 7:76 w '58. *

441. Kennedy, Eugene C. *A Comparison of the Personality Traits of Successful and Unsuccessful Seminarians in a Foreign Mission Seminary.* Master's thesis, Catholic University of America (Washington, D.C.), 1958.

442. Namani, Abdel-Kader. *Factors Associated With High and Low Correlations Between Individuals' Scores on Two Interest Inventories.* Doctor's thesis, Cornell University (Ithaca, N.Y.), 1958. (*DA* 19:2538)

443. Ostlund, Leonard A. "Kuder Interest Patterns of Outstanding Science Teachers." *Peabody J Ed* 36:101–8 S '58. *

444. Risher, Charity Conrad. *Some Characteristics Which Differentiate Between Academically Successful and Unsuccessful College Business Students.* Doctor's thesis, University of Missouri (Columbia, Mo.), 1958. (*DA* 19:2006)

445. Smith, D. D. "Abilities and Interests: 2, Validation of Factors." *Can J Psychol* 12:253–8 D '58. * (*PA* 33:9347)

446. Stinson, Pairlee J. "A Method for Counseling Engineering Students." *Personnel & Guid J* 37:294–5 D '58. * (*PA* 36:2KI94S)

447. Thomas, Paul L. *The Development of a Covert Test for the Detection of Alcoholism by a Keying of the Kuder Preference Record.* Master's thesis, West Texas State College (Canyon, Tex.), 1958.

448. White, Robert Marshall. *The Predictive Relationship of Selected Variables to the Vocational Interest Stability of High School Students.* Doctor's thesis, University of Minnesota (Minneapolis, Minn.), 1958. (*DA* 19:2141)

449. Bendig, A. W. "Kuder Differences Between Honors and Pass Majors in Psychology." *J Ed Res* 52:199–202 Ja '59. * (*PA* 34:283)

450. Budd, William C. "Prediction of Interests Between Husband and Wife." *J Ed Sociol* 33:37–9 S '59. * (*PA* 36:1IQ37B)

451. Calia, Vincent Frank. *The Use of Discriminant Analysis in the Prediction of Performance of Junior College Students in a Program of General Education at Boston University Junior College.* Doctor's thesis, Boston University (Boston, Mass.), 1959. (*DA* 20:3190)

452. Cannon, William M. *A Study of the Responses of Blind and Sighted Individuals to the Kuder Preference Record.* Doctor's thesis, Duke University (Durham, N.C.), 1959. (*DA* 20:3815)

453. Cohen, Leonard Marlin. *The Relationship Between Certain Personality Variables and Prior Occupational Stability of Prison Inmates.* Doctor's thesis, Temple University (Philadelphia, Pa.), 1959. (*DA* 20:3375)

454. Fleming, W. G. *The Kuder Preference Record—Vocational as a Predictor of Post-High School Educational and Occupational Choices.* Atkinson Study of Utilization of Student Resources, Supplementary Report No. 2. Toronto, Canada: Department of Educational Research, Ontario College of Education, University of Toronto, 1959. Pp. vii, 49. *

455. Gehman, W. Scott. "Validity Generalization and Cross-Validation of the Kuder Electrical Engineering Scale for Counseling College Students." *Ed & Psychol Meas* 19:589–97 w '59. * (*PA* 34:6163)

456. Gehman, W. Scott; Kraybill, Edward K.; and Katzenmeyer, Wm. G. "Application of New Kuder Engineering Scales for Counseling University Students." *J Eng Ed* 50:166–9 N '59. *

457. Guilford, J. P. *Personality,* pp. 213–20. New York: McGraw-Hill Book Co., Inc., 1959. Pp. xiii, 562. *

458. Hascall, Edward Orson, Jr. *Predicting Success in High School Foreign Language Study.* Doctor's thesis, University of Michigan (Ann Arbor, Mich.), 1959. (*DA* 19:3245)

459. Hirt, Michael. "Another Look at the Relationship Between Interests and Aptitudes." *Voc Guid Q* 7:171–3 sp '59. *

460. Kenney, Charles E. *Differential Vocational Interest Patterns of Successful and Unsuccessful Foreign Mission Seminarians.* Doctor's thesis, Loyola University (Chicago, Ill.), 1959.

461. King, Paul; Norrell, Gwen; and Erlandson, F. L. "The Prediction of Academic Success in a Police Administration Curriculum." *Ed & Psychol Meas* 19:649–51 w '59. * (*PA* 34:6166)

462. Klugman, Samuel F. "A Profile Coding System for the Kuder Preference Record—Vocational." *Ed & Psychol Meas* 19:569–76 w '59. * (*PA* 34:6167)

463. Krause, Allen H., and Baxter, James L. "A Scale Ranking Method for Profiling the Kuder." *Voc Guid Q* 8:19 au '59. *

464. Lane, Paul Anthony. *The Relationship Among Some Measures of Preferred Interest, Vocational Objectives and Academic Performance.* Doctor's thesis, University of Connecticut (Storrs, Conn.), 1959. (*DA* 20:1431)

465. Lessing, Elise Elkins. "Mother-Daughter Similarity on the Kuder Vocational Interest Scales." *Ed & Psychol Meas* 19:395–400 au '59. * (*PA* 34:6170)

466. McRae, Glenn G. *The Relationship of Job Satisfaction and Earlier Measured Interests.* Doctor's thesis, University of Florida (Gainesville, Fla.), 1959. (*DA* 24:631)

467. Motto, Joseph J. "Interest Scores in Predicting Success in Vocational School Programs." *Personnel & Guid J* 37:674–6 My '59. * (*PA* 35:2766)

468. Munson, Howard Roger. *Comparison of Interest and Attitude Patterns of Three Selected Groups of Teacher Candidates.* Doctor's thesis, State College of Washington (Pullman, Wash.), 1959. (*DA* 19:3237)

469. Nunnery, Michael Y. "How Useful Are Standardized Psychological Tests in the Selection of School Administrators." *Ed Adm & Sup* 45:349–56 N '59. * (*PA* 35:7092)

470. Oakes, Frederick, Jr. *The Contribution of Certain Variables to the Academic Achievement of Gifted Seventh Grade Students in an Accelerated General Science Curriculum.* Doctor's thesis, New York University (New York, N.Y.), 1959. (*DA* 20:4002)

471. Patterson, C. H. "Kuder Patterns of Industrial Institute Students." *Personnel Psychol* 12:561–71 w '59. * (*PA* 34:6172)

472. Peterson, Martha Elizabeth. *An Evaluation of Relationships Between Test Data and Success as a Residence Hall Counselor.* Doctor's thesis, University of Kansas (Lawrence, Kan.), 1959. (*DA* 21:3364)

473. Pierce-Jones, John. "Socio-Economic Status and Adolescents' Interests." *Psychol Rep* 5:683 D '59. * (*PA* 34:5854)

474. Pierce-Jones, John. "Vocational Interest Correlates of Socio-Economic Status in Adolescence." *Ed & Psychol Meas* 19:65–71 sp '59. * (*PA* 34:2051)

475. Racky, Donald J. "Predictions of Ninth Grade Woodshop Performance From Aptitude and Interest Measures." *Ed & Psychol Meas* 19:629–36 w '59. * (*PA* 34:6572)

476. Shoemaker, Wilfred L. "Rejection of Vocational Interest Areas by High School Students." *Voc Guid Q* 8:72–4 w '59–60. *

477. Smith, D. D. "Traits and College Achievement." *Can J Psychol* 13:93–101 Je '59. * (*PA* 34:4780)

478. Stauffacher, James C., and Anderson, Clifford L. "The Performance of Schizophrenics on the Kuder Preference Record." *Ed & Psychol Meas* 19:253–7 su '59. * (*PA* 34:4701)

479. Tavris, Edward C. *D^2 as a Profile Similarity Measure of Kuder Scales.* Doctor's thesis, Illinois Institute of Technology (Chicago, Ill.), 1959.

480. Thrash, Patricia Ann. *Women Student Leaders at Northwestern University: Their Characteristics, Self-Concepts, and Attitudes Toward the University.* Doctor's thesis, Northwestern University (Evanston, Ill.), 1959. (*DA* 20:3638)

481. Vaughan, Lawrence E. *Relationship of Values to Leadership, Scholarship, and Vocational Choice.* Doctor's thesis, University of Nebraska (Lincoln, Neb.), 1959. (*DA* 20:209)

482. Voas, Robert B. "Vocational Interests of Naval Aviation Cadets: Final Results." *J Appl Psychol* 43:70–3 F '59. * (*PA* 34:4845)

483. Wagner, Edwin Eric. *Predicting Success for Young Executives From Objective Test Scores and Personal Data.* Doctor's thesis, Temple University (Philadelphia, Pa.), 1959. (*DA* 20:3371)

484. Calia, Vincent F. "The Use of Discriminant Analysis in the Prediction of Scholastic Performance." Comments by David V. Tiedeman. *Personnel & Guid J* 39:184–92 N '60. * (*PA* 35:3949)

485. Cass, John C., and Tiedeman, David V. "Vocational Development and the Election of a High School Curriculum." *Personnel & Guid J* 38:538–45 Mr '60. *

486. Clark, Kenneth E. "Problems of Method in Interest Measurement," pp. 146–62. In *The Strong Vocational Interest Blank: Research and Uses.* Edited by Wilbur L. Layton. Minnesota Studies in Student Personnel Work, No. 10. Minneapolis, Minn.: University of Minnesota Press, 1960. Pp. viii, 191. * (*PA* 36:1LC91L)

487. Costello, Charles G., and Anderson, Marian E. "The Vocational and Personal Preferences of Psychiatric and General Nurses." *Nursing Res* 9:155–6 su '60. *

488. Diener, Charles L. "Similiarities and Differences Between Over-Achieving and Under-Achieving Students." *Personnel & Guid J* 38:396–400 Ja '60. *

489. Foote, Richard Paul. *The Prediction of Success in Automotive Mechanics in a Vocational-Industrial Curriculum on the Secondary School Level.* Doctor's thesis, New York University (New York, N.Y.), 1960. (*DA* 21:3014)

490. Giblette, John Franklin. *Differences Among Above Average, Average, and Below Average Secondary School Counselors.* Doctor's thesis, University of Pennsylvania (Philadelphia, Pa.), 1960. (*DA* 21:812)

491. Golburgh, Stephen Jon. *A Study of the Vocational Interests of Four Types of Psychotic Subjects.* Doctor's thesis, Boston University (Boston, Mass.), 1960. (*DA* 21:3851)

492. Goldstein, Arnold P. "The Fakability of the Kuder Preference Record and the Vocational Apperception Test." *J Proj Tech* 24:133–6 Je '60. * (*PA* 35:1321)

493. Kimbell, Fontella Thompson. *The Use of Selected Standardized Tests as Predictors of Academic Success at Oklahoma College for Women.* Doctor's thesis, University of Oklahoma (Norman, Okla.), 1960. (*DA* 20:4335)

494. Klugman, Samuel F. "Comparison of Total Interest Profiles of a Psychotic and a Normal Group." *J Counsel Psychol* 7:283–8 w '60. * (*PA* 36:1JQ38K)

495. LeBlanc, Clifford R. "Vocational Interests of Ninth Grade and Twelfth Grade Students." *Sch Counselor* 7:60–4 Mr '60. *

496. Miner, John B. "The Kuder Preference Record in Management Appraisal." *Personnel Psychol* 13:187–96 su '60. * (*PA* 36:2LD87M)

497. Reed, Woodrow W.; Lewis, Edwin C.; and Wolins, Leroy. "Differential Interest Patterns of Engineering Graduates." *Personnel & Guid J* 38:571–3 Mr '60. * (*PA* 35:1221)

498. Sterne, David M. "Use of the Kuder Preference Record, Personal, With Police Officers." *J Appl Psychol* 44:323–4 O '60. * (*PA* 35:3444)

499. Wagner, Edwin E. "Differences Between Old and Young Executives on Objective Psychological Test Variables." *J Gerontol* 15:296–9 Jl '60. * (*PA* 35:1328)

500. Welna, Cecilia Theresa. *A Study of Reasons for Success or Failure in College Mathematics Courses.* Doctor's thesis, University of Connecticut (Storrs, Conn.), 1960. (*DA* 21:1811)

501. Allen, Roscoe Jackson. *An Analysis of the Relationship Between Selected Prognostic Measures and Achievement in the Freshman Program for Secretarial Majors at the Woman's College of the University of North Carolina.* Doctor's thesis, Pennsylvania State University (University Park, Pa.), 1961. (*DA* 23:122)

502. Anastasi, Anne. *Psychological Testing, Second Edition,* pp. 536–9. New York: Mamillan Co., 1961. Pp. xiii, 657. * (*PA* 36:1HA57A)

503. Barrilleaux, Louis E. "High School Science Achievement as Related to Interest and I.Q." *Ed & Psychol Meas* 21:929–36 w '61. * (*PA* 36:5KJ29B)

504. Bridgman, C. S., and Hollenbeck, G. P. "Effect of Simulated Applicant Status on Kuder Form D Occupational Interest Scores." *J Appl Psychol* 45:237–9 Ag '61. * (*PA* 36:4LB37B)

505. Brown, Thelma E. "Factors Relating to Turnover Among Veterans Administration Nursing Assistants." *J Clin & Exp Psychopathol* 22:226–34 D '61. *

506. Buel, William D., and Bachner, Virginia M. "The Assessment of Creativity in a Research Setting." *J Appl Psychol* 45:353–8 D '61. * (*PA* 37:1211)

507. Coats, J. E.; with the assistance of R. G. Garner. *A Study of the Nature of the Chemical Operator's Occupation and the Personal Qualities That Contribute to Successful Operator Performance.* Midland, Mich.: Dow Chemical Co., March 1961. Pp. iv, 112. *

508. Craven, Ethel Case. *The Use of Interest Inventories in Counseling.* Chicago, Ill.: Science Research Associates, Inc., 1961. Pp. iv, 44. *

509. Garrett, Gene Aubrey. *A Comparison of the Predictive Power of the Kuder Preference Record and the Strong Vocational Interest Blank in a Counseling Setting.* Doctor's thesis, University of Missouri (Columbia, Mo.), 1961. (*DA* 22:1506)

510. Gorman, John R. *A Study of Adjustment and Interests for Fourth Year Minor Seminarians Studying for the Diocesan Priesthood.* Master's thesis, Loyola University (Chicago, Ill.), 1961.

511. Hascall, Edward O. "Predicting Success in High School Foreign Language Study." *Personnel & Guid J* 40:361–7 D '61. * (*PA* 36:4KL61H)

512. Hornaday, John A., and Kuder, G. Frederic. "A Study of Male Occupational Interest Scales Applied to Women." *Ed & Psychol Meas* 21:859–64 w '61. * (*PA* 36:5LE59H)

513. Hosford, Prentiss McIntyre. *Characteristics of Science-Talented and Language-Talented Secondary School Students.* Doctor's thesis, University of Georgia (Athens, Ga.), 1961. (*DA* 22:2687)

514. Levinson, Boris M. "The Vocational Interests of Yeshiva College Freshmen." *J Genetic Psychol* 99:235–44 D '61. * (*PA* 36:3KD35L)

515. Lewis, Edwin C., and MacKinney, Arthur C. "Counselor vs. Statistical Predictions of Job Satisfaction in Engineering." *J Counsel Psychol* 8:224–30 f '61. * (*PA* 36:5KI24L)

516. McDonagh, Andrew J. *A Study of Adjustments and Interests of First-Year College Seminarians for the Diocesan Priesthood.* Master's thesis, Loyola University (Chicago, Ill.), 1961.

517. McMillen, Daniel Morris. *A Study of the Effectiveness of the Kuder Preference Record-Vocational in Discriminating Among Purdue Engineering Graduates.* Doctor's thesis, Purdue University (Lafayette, Ind.), 1961. (*DA* 22:162)

518. Mink, Oscar Gorton. *A Study of Certain Cognitive and Conative Factors Affecting Academic Progress in Chemical and Metallurgical Engineering at Cornell University.* Doctor's thesis, Cornell University (Ithaca, N.Y.), 1961. (*DA* 22:2695)

519. Novak, Daniel F. "A Comparison of Delinquent and Nondelinquent Vocational Interests." *Excep Child* 28:63–6 S '61. *

520. Nugent, Frank A. "The Relationship of Discrepancies Between Interest and Aptitude Scores to Other Selected Personality Variables." *Personnel & Guid J* 39:388–95 Ja '61. * (*PA* 35: 6212)

521. O'Loughlin, Daniel R. "Helping Students Understand the Kuder." *Sch Counselor* 9:60–1 D '61. *

522. Pierce-Jones, John. "Social Mobility Orientations and Interests of Adolescents." *J Counsel Psychol* 8:75–8 sp '61. * (*PA* 36:3FH75P)

523. Robbins, James E., and King, Donald C. "Validity Information Exchange, No. 14-02: D.O.T. Code 0-97.61, Manager, Sales." *Personnel Psychol* 14:217–9 su '61. *

524. Silver, Reuben J., and Casey, E. W. "Stability of the Kuder Vocational Preference Record in Psychiatric Patients." *Ed & Psychol Meas* 21:879–82 w '61. * (*PA* 36:5JP79S)

525. Sutter, Cyril Robert. *A Comparative Study of the Interest and Personality Patterns of Major Seminarians.* Doctor's thesis, Fordham University (New York, N.Y.), 1961. (*DA* 22:328)

526. Witherspoon, Robert Paul. *A Comparison of the Temperament Trait, Interest, Achievement, and Scholastic Aptitude Test Score Patterns of College Seniors Majoring in Different Fields at the Arkansas State Teachers College.* Doctor's thesis, University of Arkansas (Fayetteville, Ark.), 1961. (*DA* 22:1091)

527. Wolins, Leroy; MacKinney, A. C.; and Stephans, Paul. "Factor Analyses of High School Science Achievement Measures." *J Ed Res* 54:173–7 Ja '61. * (*PA* 35:7129)

528. Atkinson, John Allen. *Factors Related to the Prediction of Academic Success for Disabled Veterans in a Four Year College Engineering Program.* Doctor's thesis, University of Denver (Denver, Colo.), 1962. (*DA* 23:2786)

529. Bauernfeind, Robert H. "The Matter of 'Ipsative Scores.'" *Personnel & Guid J* 41:210–7 N '62. * (*PA* 37:6919)

530. Buckalew, Robert J. *An Investigation of the Interrelationships Among Measures of Interests, Intelligence, and Personality for a Sample of One Hundred Sixty-Two Eighth Grade Boys.* Doctor's thesis, Temple University (Philadelphia, Pa.), 1962. (*DA* 23:3232)

531. Campbell, Robert E. "Counselor Personality and Background and His Interview Subrole Behavior." *J Counsel Psychol* 9:329–34 w '62. * (*PA* 39:2294)

532. Chatterjee, S., and Mukerjee, Manjula. "Relation Between Kuder Preference Record and a Non-Verbal Interest Inventory Modelled After It to Suit Indian Condition." *J Psychol Res* 6:115–7 S '62. * (*PA* 38:8406)

533. Christensen, C. M. "Dimensions and Correlates of Texture Preferences." *J Consult Psychol* 26:498–504 D '62. * (*PA* 39:1723)

534. Coutts, Robert LaRoy. *Selected Characteristics of Counselor-Candidates in Relation to Levels and Types of Competency in the Counseling Practicum.* Doctor's thesis, Florida State University (Tallahassee, Fla.), 1962. (*DA* 23:1601)

535. Crane, William J. "Screening Devices for Occupational Therapy Majors." *Am J Occup Ther* 16:131–2 My–Je '62. * (*PA* 37:4078)

536. D'Arcy, Paul F. "Review of Research on the Vocational Interests of Priests, Brothers and Sisters," pp. 149–200. In *Screening Candidates for the Priesthood and Religious Life.* By Magda B. Arnold and others. Chicago, Ill.: Loyola University Press, 1962. Pp. x, 205. *

537. Drew, Alfred Stanislaus. *The Relationship of General Reading Ability and Other Factors to School and Job Performance of Machinist Apprentices.* Doctor's thesis, University of Wisconsin (Madison, Wis.), 1962. (*DA* 23:1261)

538. Freeman, Frank S. *Theory and Practice of Psychological Testing, Third Edition,* pp. 581–4, 588–96. New York: Holt, Rinehart & Winston, Inc., 1962. Pp. xix, 697. *

539. Katz, Martin. "Interpreting Kuder Preference Record Scores: Ipsative or Normative." *Voc Guid Q* 10:96–100 w '62. * (*PA* 37:1972)

540. Lanna, Matthew George. *Vocational Interests in Relation to Some Aspects of Personality and Adjustment.* Doctor's thesis, Columbia University (New York, N.Y.), 1962. (*DA* 23:4421)

541. O'Hara, Robert P. "Acceptance of Vocational Interest Areas by High School Students." *Voc Guid Q* 10:101–5 w '62. * (*PA* 37:1976)

542. Reid, John W.; Johnson, A. Pemberton; Entwisle, Frank N.; and Angers, William P. "A Four-Year Study of the Characteristics of Engineering Students." *Personnel & Guid J* 41:38–43 S '62. * (*PA* 37:5655)

543. Rohrs, Dennis Kerlin. *Predicting Academic Success in a Liberal Arts College Music Education Program.* Doctor's thesis, State University of Iowa (Iowa City, Iowa), 1962. (*DA* 23:2937)

544. Rupiper, Omer John. "A Psychometric Evaluation of Experienced Teachers." *J Ed Res* 55:368–71 My '62. *

545. Springob, H. Karl, and Jackson, Clifton W. "Meas-

ured Abilities and Inventoried Interests of Ninth Grade Boys." *Voc Guid Q* 11:37-40 au '62. * (*PA* 37:8279)
546. Super, Donald E., and Crites, John O. *Appraising Vocational Fitness by Means of Psychological Tests, Revised Edition,* pp. 461-92. New York: Harper & Brothers, 1962. Pp. xv, 688. * (*PA* 37:2038)
547. *Normative Information: Manager and Executive Testing.* New York: Richardson, Bellows, Henry & Co., Inc., May 1963. Pp. 45. *
548. Bauernfeind, Robert H. *Building a School Testing Program,* pp. 212-31. Boston, Mass.: Houghton Mifflin Co., 1963. Pp. xvii, 343. *
549. Becker, James A. "An Exploratory Factor Analytic Study of Interests, Intelligence, and Personality." *Psychol Rep* 13:847-51 D '63. * (*PA* 38:8399)
550. Bendig, A. W., and Meyer, William J. "The Factorial Structure of the Scales of the Primary Mental Abilities, Guilford Zimmerman Temperament Survey, and Kuder Preference Record." *J General Psychol* 68:195-201 Ap '63. * (*PA* 38:53)
551. Cassel, Russell N. "Comparing IBM Card and Hand Scoring Pad Administration of the Kuder Vocational Preference Record." *Calif J Ed Res* 14:31-5 Ja '63. * (*PA* 37:8259)
552. Ewens, William P. "Relationship of Interest to Aptitude by Profiles and by Interest Areas." *Personnel & Guid J* 42:359-63 D '63. * (*PA* 39:1660)
553. Gilbert, Joseph. "Vocational Archetypes: A Proposal for Clinical Integration of Interests and Values in Vocational Counseling and Selection." *Psychol Rep* 13:351-6 O '63. *
554. Hornaday, John A. "Interest Patterns of Dietitians." *J Am Dietetic Assn* 43:99-103 Ag '63. *
555. Ivey, Allen E. "Interests and Work Values." *Voc Guid Q* 11:121-4 w '63. * (*PA* 38:1441)
556. Jones, Kenneth J. "Predicting Achievement in Chemistry: A Model." *J Res Sci Teach* 1:226-31 S '63. *
557. King, Paul; Norrell, Gwendolyn; and Powers, G. Pat. "Relationships Between Twin Scales on the SVIB and the Kuder." *J Counsel Psychol* 10:395-401 w '63. * (*PA* 38:9342)
558. Miller, William G., and Hannum, Thomas E. "Characteristics of Homosexually Involved Incarcerated Females." Abstract. *J Consult Psychol* 27:277 Je '63. *
559. Moorman, Jane Douglas. *A Study of the Meaning of High and Low Social Service and Persuasive Scores on the Kuder Preference Record as Measured by the Semantic Differential.* Doctor's thesis, University of Kansas (Lawrence, Kan.), 1963.
560. Overall, John E. "A Masculinity-Femininity Scale for the Kuder Preference Record." *J General Psychol* 69:209-16 O '63. * (*PA* 39:1817)
561. Perry, Marian Louise. *The Relationship of Selected Variables to the Success of Camp Counselors.* Doctor's thesis, University of Southern California (Los Angeles, Calif.), 1963. (*DA* 24:613)
562. Radcliffe, J. A. "Some Properties of Ipsative Score Matrices and Their Relevance for Some Current Interest Tests." *Austral J Psychol* 15:1-11 Ap '63. *
563. Sassenrath, Julius M., and Fattu, Nicholas A. *Relationships Among Factors Obtained for Elementary and Secondary Student Teachers.* Bulletin of the School of Education, Indiana University, Vol. 39, No. 5. Bloomington, Ind.: Bureau of Educational Studies and Testing, the School, September 1963. Pp. vii, 34. * (*PA* 38:6666)
564. Springob, H. Karl. "Relationship of Interests as Measured by the Kuder Preference Record to Personality as Measured by the California Psychological Inventory Scales." *Personnel & Guid J* 41:624-8 Mr '63. * (*PA* 39:1760)
565. Warburton, F. W.; Butcher, H. J.; and Forrest, G. M. "Predicting Student Performance in a University Department of Education." *Brit J Ed Psychol* 33:68-79 F '63. * (*PA* 38:1416)
566. White, Hortense G. "Typing Performance as Related to Mental Abilities and Interests: A Preliminary Study." *J Ed Res* 56:535-9 Jl-Ag '63. *
567. Zimmerer, Ann Morgan. *A Study of Selected Variables for Predicting Success in a College of Engineering.* Doctor's thesis, University of Houston (Houston, Tex.), 1963. (*DA* 24:842)

Martin Katz, *Assistant Director, Evaluation and Advisory Service, Educational Testing Service, Princeton, New Jersey.*

Since a number of comprehensive reviews of the *Kuder Preference Record—Vocational* (KPR-V) are already available in previous editions of *The Mental Measurements Yearbooks* (as indicated below), this reviewer will focus on an important aspect of score interpretation that seems to have been overlooked.

Like most other inventories and tests, the KPR-V produces raw scores that are not regarded as meaningful in themselves. That is to say, the tally of preferences (in response to forced-choice triads) is not taken at simple face value as representing "how much" interest an individual has in each of the 9 or 10 "areas." Instead, the profile sheet provides for a conversion of the raw sums to percentile ranks in the norms sample. It then directs that scores above the 75th percentile be regarded as high, scores below the 25th percentile be regarded as low, and those in between be regarded as average. High, low, and average are, the reviewer recognizes, comparative rather than absolute terms. For interpretation, it is of course crucial to know the nature of the comparison being made.

The publisher tells us that "Scores may be profiled so that the student can see how his interests compare with each other as well as with the norm group." (1963-64 catalog; similar statements appear in promotional materials and on the profile sheet for Form C.) In other words, the user is invited to make two kinds of comparison.

One kind involves comparing an individual with other people. This is the familiar normative comparison that seems to be inherent in the very process of converting raw scores to percentiles. It would appear to answer such relevant questions as, "Does Joe have more or less scientific interest than Fred?" "How does he stand in relation to other high school boys generally?" "How does he stand in relation to a representative sample of physicists?" (In view of the age of this instrument and its extensive use—over 2,000,000 students tested in 10,000 schools each year, says the publisher—one might also be justified in asking, "How does Fred stand in relation to high school boys who later became physicists?")

The other kind of comparison is intraindividual—when we compare one person's interest in something with his interest in something else. For example, "Does Joe have more scientific than literary interest?" Cattell has dubbed this kind of comparison *ipsative.*

Normative interpretation. For interpretation of normative scores, knowledge of the nature of the reference group is crucial. Ideally, the information we would like to derive from an interest inventory used for guidance is whether the individual has "enough" potential interest in a given occupation, vocational area, school subject, major field, or whatever other variables the inventory scales presumably pertain to. For example, if he should enter such-and-such an occupation, will he derive "enough" satisfaction from the job activities themselves to stay in that occupation (unless another occupation offers superior extrinsic rewards)? Will he be attentive "enough" to his work (assuming sufficient ability) to satisfy his employer, customers, or clients? Or, conversely, will lack of interest tend to make him unhappy, ineffective, unstable in that occupation? These are "payoff" questions in educational and occupational choice. To answer such questions, validity studies of considerable scope and careful design are needed. Not to belabor the point here, this reviewer has previously commented on the inadequacy for this purpose of the catch-as-catch-can "occupational norms" provided in the manual (*539*).

In fact, empirical evidence often fails to substantiate the notion that a score above the 75th percentile promises satisfaction or success in a given occupation or school subject. Thus Diamond (*88*) points out that a score at the 75th percentile of the KPR-V Musical scale is more than two standard deviations below the mean of an occupational group of musicians. Conversely, in our culture a high school boy might have a low percentile rank on Mechanical and still have *enough* mechanical interest for success and satisfaction in occupations generally labeled mechanical. Bauernfeind (*529*), in a summary of studies relating KPR-V scores to subsequent academic performance or to job tenure and reports of job satisfaction, found that the scores "at best yield only anemic predictions." (For example, he cites Kuder's study —reported in the old Form B manual—showing virtually no significant differences in KPR-V scores between "satisfied" and "dissatisfied" workers in five occupational fields.)

To go an important step farther, even a more general normative interpretation is questionable. An individual's percentile rank on a KPR-V scale does not even indicate how strong an interest he has in comparison with the general population of his peers (high school students or adults of the same sex). For example, if Joe scores at the 85th percentile on Scientific, we cannot infer that his interest in whatever the Scientific items represent is necessarily higher than or as high as that of 85 per cent of the boys in the high school norms group. This rather elementary inference will often be incorrect simply because the KPR-V places certain artificial limits on the number of areas in which a student's interests may be high or low.

On the surface, the conversion of raw scores to percentile ranks and the subsequent interpretation of these derived percentile ranks as "high" or "low" seems quite analogous to the similar conversion and interpretation of achievement and aptitude test scores in respect to "national" norms. However, it is obvious that an individual's raw score on one test of an achievement battery is experimentally independent of his raw scores on the other tests of the battery. Thus, an individual might be high —say above the 95th percentile—in all the tests of an achievement battery.

KPR-V raw scores, on the other hand, are not independent. These scores, it will be remembered, are derived from a tally of preference responses when a statement representing one "area" is compared with a statement representing another "area," the statements being presented in triads. In the great majority of the triads a preference tallied for one "area" precludes a tally for another "area" represented by another statement. Thus, each raw score tally may be said to be made at the expense of another scale. Therefore, total raw score in each "area" is not experimentally independent of raw scores in other "areas."

For example, Joe's 85th percentile rank on the Scientific scale does not necessarily denote that he has "more" interest in the activities represented by that scale than Fred, who ranks at the 65th percentile. The more statements representing other areas Fred likes, the lower his Scientific raw score and percentile rank tend to be. In general, then, a person with many strong interests might be lower on a given scale than another person who has only mild interest in that "area" but even less in others. Thus, KPR-V scores would fail to reflect a generally high or low level of interest (in the sense of intensity or salience); for example, the evidence that high ability students tend to be characterized by many high interests[1] could not be properly reflected by KPR-V scores.

IPSATIVE INTERPRETATION. But, it may be claimed, the absolute height of the percentile ranks is not important, and interpersonal comparisons are not required: for individual guidance, only the relative heights among scores obtained by a single student should be used. In other words, this argument runs, interpretation should be ipsative, not normative; the individual need know only in what "areas" he is highest and lowest—not whether he is high "enough" or as high as some other person. This argument assumes a closed system in which all choices are encompassed and one of those choices must be made. It does not permit a remark like Samuel Johnson's when Boswell asked him whether he preferred Rousseau or Voltaire: "Sir," rumbled Johnson, "it is impossible to settle the proportion of iniquity between them!"

The forced choice response process is clearly ipsative. But the resulting raw scores for each "area" defy direct interpretation. Raw score comparisons are obscured by different numbers of statements representing the various "areas" and by considerable range in the frequency with which the various "areas" are pitted against each other in the triads. Nevertheless, it may be illuminating to consider two scales, the Outdoor and the Persuasive, for which identical maximum raw scores of 80 appear at the top of the "Male" columns on the profile sheet. Here we may see an interesting reversal between raw score and percentile rank. A raw score of 56 on Outdoor places a boy at the 70th percentile, while a raw score of 54 on Persuasive places him at the 90th percentile. Similar reversals can be found in other pairings. A striking example appears in a comparison between Literary and Mechanical. Converting raw scores to per cents of maximum possible raw scores in order to take into account differences in the number of statements representing each "area," we find that 40 per cent of the highest possible raw score for Literary would rank Joe at the 50th percentile on high school norms, while 50 per cent of the highest possible raw score for Mechanical would place him at only the 20th percentile. To say on the basis of the percentile ranks that Joe has "more" interest in Literary than in Mechanical activities flies in the face of the ipsative raw score comparison.

In the same way, if Mary obtains 50 per cent of the maximum possible raw score on both Mechanical and Social Service, she will be at the 89th percentile in Mechanical interest and at the 24th percentile in Social Service interest on the norms for high school girls. Does this mean that she is "high" in one and "low" in the other? The counselor who makes this interpretation will want to be sure-footed about what he means by "high" and "low."

Joe's and Mary's percentile ranks simply reflect a *general* tendency of American high school boys to prefer Mechanical over Literary activities and high school girls to prefer Social Service over Mechanical activities. The fact that Joe deviates more from the centroid of the norms group on Mechanical than on Literary does not mean that he has—in this case—less Mechanical than Literary interest. Joe might like ice cream less than most people do, but still clearly prefer it to spinach. So the normative conversion spoils ipsative interpretation.

At the same time, the fact that raw scores are derived from solipsistic forced choice preferences tends to block meaningful normative inferences. Fred, whose general appetite level is lustier than Joe's, might like both ice cream *and* spinach more than Joe does (according to such criteria as amount consumed, gusto with which eaten, etc.), and yet rank lower than Joe on an "ice cream" scale derived from forced choice preferences.

UTILITY OF THE INSTRUMENT. In brief, then, the KPR-V percentile scores are derived from an alternation of ipsative and normative procedures. Close scrutiny of attempts to interpret the scales in either ipsative or normative terms suggests that these procedures tend to nullify each other, making either type of comparison dubious.

One further point. Severe criticisms of the KPR-V sometimes seem to prompt the rather naïve defense that the scores are interpreted only tentatively, that the primary purpose in administering the inventory is exploratory—to stimulate students to think constructively about

1 FRYER, DOUGLAS. *The Measurement of Interests: In Relation to Human Adjustment.* New York: Henry Holt & Co., 1931. Pp. xxxvi, 488. *
STRONG, EDWARD K., JR. "Nineteen-Year Followup of Engineer Interests." *J Appl Psychol* 36:65–74 Ap '52. *
TERMAN, LEWIS M., EDITOR. *Genetic Studies of Genius: 1, Mental and Physical Traits of a Thousand Gifted Children.* Stanford, Calif.: Stanford University Press, 1925. Pp. xv, 648. *
WIEGERSMA, S., AND BARR, FRANK. "Interest Testing in Educational and Vocational Guidance." *Ed Res* 2:39–64 N '59. *

interests in relation to vocational development.

Let us grant immediately that the young student's experience is often too limited for informed and rational decision making. Many activities are outside his range and ken. Tryout—enlarged experience—is the logical remedy for this limitation. Thus, we might echo Emerson's urging to "eat of every apple."

However, interest inventories are rather ineffectual as tryouts. Some of the KPR-V statements, for example, may baffle the young student, especially when they do not describe specific activities which lend themselves to ready visualization but instead represent complex combinations that are virtually occupational titles. Consider as an illustration the following triad:

> Be the director of a group conducting research on propaganda methods
> Be a dean in a university
> Be an expert in color photography.

There are many similar "Be a...." items (e.g., "Be a chemist," "Be a salesman," "Be a bookkeeper"). Scores obtained from responses to such items seem redundant. The student can be forgiven if he says, "But that's why I'm taking the inventory—to predict whether I'd like this or that occupation." He is asked to invest the very coin he hopes to earn. Most of us want the payoff on our investments transmuted into something of greater utility than what we pay in.

If exploration is the primary objective, it seems possible to expose the student to more active and enlightening tryouts either of "the real thing" or of vivid simulations. Even straightforward verbal presentations, as in most occupational information materials, can offer the student better opportunities to visualize himself in specific educational or occupational activities and roles, to "taste" them, and judge whether he likes or dislikes what he has tasted. The point here is that inventories often provide a formal designation and classification of interests before the student has been exposed to a range and variety of experiences appropriate for making realistic, valid, and stable judgments of preference. Decisions based in large part on such premature judgments may serve to foreclose the opportunity for further experience in the very areas where it is most deficient.

If opportunities for a wide range of experiences were equally available to all, the very selectivity implicit in a person's narrow range would in itself be revealing of interests. This is the basis of "informational" interest tests: given fairly equal accessibility to different kinds of information, the individual will know more about topics which interest him. But despite the exploratory activities offered by schools, many students do not have much access to certain kinds of relevant experience, activity, or information. Evidence that inventoried interests have not stabilized in the early secondary school years is probably a consequence not so much of genetic immaturity as of insufficient exploration.

Use of an inventory like the KPR-V tends to assume that such exploration has already taken place—at least to a sufficient extent for meaningful comparisons between statements. The inventory items themselves do not contribute to discovery, do not tell the person "what his interests are." On the contrary, their hope of stability depends on his having already developed a firm consciousness of likes and dislikes among a wide range of activities. But there would be no need to give a student who had just completed courses in woodwork and French an interest inventory to find out which he liked better. Just ask him.

The rationale for use of the KPR-V assumes, however, that the student is unable on his own to classify his discrete likes and dislikes, to organize them, make sense out of them, and relate them to alternatives for choice (occupational or educational).

But, to recapitulate, how can the scores be interpreted when we see that (*a*) a student with a distinctly *higher* percentile rank than another student on a KPR-V scale may have distinctly *less* interest than the other student has in that area, and (*b*) a student may have *more* interest in an area represented by a scale on which his percentile rank is *low* than in another area represented by a scale on which his percentile rank is *high?* Bauernfeind (*548*) has tried manfully to indicate the kind of language a counselor must use in interpreting, say, a high school student's 90th percentile rank on Artistic: "Your interests in artistic activities are higher (we don't know how much higher) than your own average of interests (whatever that is) relative to the interests of other boys in the national norms group." This bit of gobbledygook represents, adds Bauernfeind, "a conscientious effort to interpret the

Kuder profile honestly; and it is guaranteed to chill the counseling session."

Finally, then, if scores are interpreted at all properly, the KPR-V does not stand up well for tentative exploration and stimulation. The problems involved in the derivation and interpretation of scores must rank it well below such other vocational interest inventories as the *Strong Vocational Interest Blank* and the *Kuder Preference Record—Occupational* in usefulness.

For reviews by Clifford P. Froehlich and John Pierce-Jones, see 5:863; for reviews by Edward S. Bordin, Harold D. Carter, and H. M. Fowler, see 4:742; for reviews by Ralph F. Berdie, E. G. Chambers, and Donald E. Super of a, *see 3:640 (1 excerpt); for reviews by A. B. Crawford and Arthur E. Traxler of an earlier edition, see 40:1671.*

[1064]

***Occupational Interest Inventory, 1956 Revision.** Grades 7–16 and adults, 9–16 and adults; 1943–58; 10 scores grouped in 3 categories: fields of interests (personal-social, natural, mechanical, business, the arts, the sciences), types of interests (verbal, manipulative, computational), level of interests; IBM; 1 form ('56, 14 pages); 2 levels: intermediate, advanced; manuals ('56): intermediate (28 pages), advanced (36 pages); interest analysis report ['58, 4 pages] for both levels; intermediate norms based upon norms for advanced form; $5.25 per 35 tests; separate answer sheets may be used; 5¢ per IBM answer sheet; 9¢ per Scoreze answer sheet; 75¢ per set of hand scoring stencils; 90¢ per set of machine scoring stencils; postage extra; 50¢ per specimen set of either level, postpaid; (30–40) minutes; Edwin A. Lee and Louis P. Thorpe; California Test Bureau. *

REFERENCES

1–20. See 4:743.
21–40. See 5:864.
41. Smith, John Allan, and Nash, Philip G. "Differences in Interest Patterns According to High School Major Sequences." *Calif J Ed Res* 9:179–85 S '58. * (*PA* 34:2053)
42. Boykin, Leander L., and Brazziel, William F., Jr. "Occupational Interests of 1741 Teacher Education Students as Revealed on the Lee-Thorpe Inventory." *J Negro Ed* 28:42–8 w '59. * (*PA* 36:3KD42B)
43. Weaver, Sampson Joseph. *Interests of Graduates of Eighteen Liberal Arts Concentration Fields as Indicated by the Lee-Thorpe Occupational Interest Inventory.* Master's thesis, Brown University (Providence, R.I.), 1959.
44. MacKinney, Arthur C., and Wolins, Leroy. "Validity Information Exchange, No. 13-01, Foreman II, Home Appliance Manufacturing." *Personnel Psychol* 13:443–7 w '60. *
45. Cassel, Russell N., and Hendsch, Gene. "A Comparative Analysis of Occupational Interest Scores Between Gifted and Typical 5th Grade Pupils." *J Psychol* 54:241–4 Jl '62. * (*PA* 37:3856)
46. Dunn, Frances E. "Interest Patterns of College Majors." *J Col Student Personnel* 4:79–85+ D '62. *

For reviews by Martin Katz and Wilbur L. Layton, see 5:864; for a review by Arthur H. Brayfield of the original edition, see 4:743; for reviews by Edward S. Bordin and Stanley G. Dulsky, see 3:643.

[1065]

★Occupational Interest Survey (With Pictures): Individual Placement Series (Area II). High school and adults; 1959; subtest of *Individual Placement Series;* 9 scores: scientific, social service, literary, agricultural, business, mechanical, musical, clerical, artistic; Form A ('59, 14 pages); preliminary manual ['59, 8 pages]; no description of normative population; separate answer sheets must be used; $27.50 per 25 tests; $1.10 per 25 answer sheets; $2.25 per specimen set; postpaid; (15–20) minutes; J. H. Norman; the Author. *

[1066]

Picture Interest Inventory. Grades 7 and over; 1958; 9 scores: interpersonal service, natural, mechanical, business, esthetic, scientific, verbal, computational, time perspective; IBM; 1 form (23 pages); manual (24 pages); separate answer sheets must be used; $5.25 per 35 tests; 5¢ per IBM answer sheet; $1 per set of either hand or machine scoring stencils; postage extra; 50¢ per specimen set, postpaid; (30–40) minutes; Kurt P. Weingarten; California Test Bureau. *

REFERENCES

1. Weingarten, Kurt P. *The Measurement of Interests in Non-Professional Vocations by Means of a Pictorial Inventory.* Doctor's thesis, University of Southern California (Los Angeles, Calif.), 1953.
2. Weingarten, Kurt P. "The Measurement of Interests in Nonprofessional Vocations by Means of a Pictorial Inventory." *Calif J Ed Res* 5:7–10 Ja '54. * (*PA* 28:7657)
3. Cassel, Russell N., and Hendsch, Gene. "A Comparative Analysis of Occupational Interest Scores Between Gifted and Typical 5th Grade Pupils." *J Psychol* 54:241–4 Jl '62. * (*PA* 37:3856)
4. Houston, Lawrence Nathaniel. *An Investigation of the Relationship Between the Vocational Interests and Homosexual Behavior of Institutionalized Youthful Offenders.* Doctor's thesis, Temple University (Philadelphia, Pa.), 1963. (*DA* 24:2984)

Ralph F. Berdie, *Professor of Psychology, and Director, Student Counseling Bureau, University of Minnesota, Minneapolis, Minnesota.*

The publication of Meehl's paper, "The Dynamics of 'Structured' Personality Tests," in the *Journal of Clinical Psychology* in 1945, gave explicit recognition to the principle that the apparent meaning or content of personality and interest inventory items are of minor importance compared to the empirical validity of the items and the derived scales. Only two interest inventories, the Strong and the Kuder, have several decades of research providing evidence of validity and the proved items in these blanks are verbal. In contrast, the inventory reviewed here, the *Picture Interest Inventory,* is almost completely nonverbal. The manual states, "One of the outstanding features of the *Picture Interest Inventory* is its completely non-verbal character. The examinee has no verbal symbols to interpret."

The use of any practical item type is justified if it serves the desired purpose. If items consisting of pictures do as well as or better than verbal items, their use is justified. A long history of research has demonstrated the validity of verbal items, however, and one wishing to introduce a different interest item has a responsibility to show that it is at least as effective as the proven verbal item.

Very little short term and no long term research has demonstrated that the pictorial items used in this inventory, or in the similar *Geist Picture Interest Inventory,* have validity comparable to that of verbal items. Authors of picture interest inventories should not be discouraged from exploring the potential of this approach, but they must be careful in statements concerning the validity of nonverbal items without such evidence.

Weingarten's inventory is based on his doctoral dissertation done at the University of Southern California in 1953 (*1*). Knowing this, one is not surprised that the *Picture Interest Inventory* is closely related to the *Occupational Interest Inventory,* a verbal inventory, or that the development and standardization of the *Picture Interest Inventory* were closely tied to the other publication from the California Test Bureau. The reviewer would feel more comfortable with the validity of the *Picture Interest Inventory* if he had greater confidence in the validity of the *Occupational Interest Inventory.*

The *Picture Interest Inventory* provides scores in six occupational interest fields. The manual does not specify how the decision was made to include activities in these fields. Questions can be raised concerning how unitary these fields are, particularly when one observes grouped in the business field activities related to "operating an adding machine, selling produce, typing, making a ledger entry, wrapping a shirt, selling an automobile, filing, sorting mail, showing real estate, and court reporting." Similarly, one can question how much reality the occupational interest field of interpersonal service has when this includes "teaching arithmetic, directing traffic, addressing a jury, cutting hair, giving room service, examining a patient, waiting on tables, umpiring a playground game, carrying luggage on a ship, and delivering a sermon." Groupings of occupational activities should have an empirical basis. Here they do not.

The tables presenting statistics concerning the reliability of the inventory are more impressive than some of the statements in the manual which more properly belong in a salespiece than in a test manual. For example, under reliability and validity appears the statement, "The data in these sections indicate the considerable confidence with which one may employ the scales of this instrument." The test author should present the supporting evidence and allow the reader to make his own inferences concerning its acceptability. The manual again reads more like a sales publication because of the generous use of the word "very" when statistics are described. For example, statements such as this appear frequently: "The time perspective scale has a very significant relationship with the Occupational Level key of the Strong Blank." (This correlation, based on 52 college freshmen, is .51.)

Test-retest correlations obtained after a one-week interval range from .69 to .92, somewhat lower than the correlations reported for the Kuder Vocational and about the same as those reported for the Strong blank over a two year period. The reliabilities of the *Picture Interest Inventory* are no higher and perhaps in some cases are lower than similar reliabilities of other interest inventories.

Available information concerning the validity of the inventory is limited to that contained in the manual as no publications reporting such information could be located in the literature and the publishers of the test, who reported some research in progress, could provide information on only one study using 41 subjects. Most of the discussion in the manual concerning validity refers to content validity, with some weight placed on concurrent validity as shown by correlations with other inventories.

One item analysis involved the comparison of responses of persons scoring high and low on relevant scales of the *Occupational Interest Inventory,* a heavy load to place on the questionable validity of this older test.

The manual presents selected correlation coefficients between scores on the *Picture Interest Inventory* and SVIB. Although most of these are in the expected direction and most of them of a size that could be anticipated, there are some exceptions. For example, the correlation between the score on the interpersonal service scale and the social worker scale is .61, though the correlation between the interpersonal service scale and the physician's scale is −.03. The correlation between the business scale and the accountant's scale is .49, but that between the business scale and the real estate salesman's scale is .26. The correlations between the esthetic scale and the artist's and architect's scale are, respectively, .28 and .13.

Reported correlations between the *Picture Interest Inventory* and the Kuder range between .13 and .68. The computational scale on the first inventory and the clerical scale on the second correlate .67, but the interpersonal service and social service scales correlate only .44. The business and computational scales correlate .28, whereas the business and persuasive scales correlate .51. These correlations all tend to be lower than the correlations between the *Picture Interest Inventory* and the *Occupational Interest Inventory,* where the correlations range from .56 to .77.

The method used in pretesting items, assigning items to scales, and standardizing the test appears satisfactory although the descriptions of these procedures in the manual are unnecessarily cumbersome.

Table 13 in the manual presents statistics which reveal a marked sex difference on eight of the nine scales. Norms are presented for girls but no profile or report form is available for this sex.

Information is not reported concerning the scores or profiles characteristic of students in different curricula or different schools, or men or women in different occupations. No validity data are reported concerning the predictive efficiency of the scores.

In summary, the *Picture Interest Inventory* is an intriguing experiment in interest measurement and provides a promising research instrument. The information in the manual on the validity of the inventory and the lack of systematic clinical experiences with the instrument do not justify the use of the scales for counseling purposes.

Donald E. Super, *Professor of Psychology and Education, Teachers College, Columbia University, New York, New York.*

This inventory relies on pictures of vocational activities to parallel the verbal *Occupational Interest Inventory* developed by Lee and Thorpe. The line drawings are large and clear. The answer sheet is easy to use and quickly scored by hand or machine.

The PII manual claims distinction on the ground that the inventory avoids problems of vocabulary (once directions are understood) by using pictures. This goal is generally but not quite achieved: for example, picture 13a requires that the subject understand what the terms "Set No. 1, Cafe" mean when seen on what could be a crate or a bit of stage scenery, and picture 24b demands that he know, or guess with the help of a picture of a gadget for which this reviewer does not know the name, the meaning of the term "Tensile Test." Furthermore, independence of vocabulary does not mean independence of the vocabulary-producing experience or of the knowledge normally expressed in words: for example, one must know that materials are tested for strength, and that stages have movable sets. But even relative independence of vocabulary should make the inventory more widely usable than existing verbal inventories.

The interests assessed by the PII are classified as in the Lee-Thorpe inventory. Lumped together in one category are business detail and business contact interests, in another are biological and physical sciences, and in another social and personal service are combined. No data are given to justify disregarding the evidence from occupational scales such as Strong's which show that differentiation rather than combination is desirable.

The interpersonal service field includes ministers, physicians, barbers, and janitors, all "concerned primarily" with "serving others" by preaching, examining eyes, cutting hair, and checking doors and windows. The grouping of these items is based on logic and on item analysis which showed that they differentiated between high and low scores on the appropriate a priori scales of the PII and of the OII. This empirical check is important, but item-scale correlation does not guarantee scale purity.

Time perspective is a new scale, using teacher ratings to supplement an a priori scale in the item analysis; it is described as preference for occupations involving extensive training and as related to level of vocational aspiration. Is it perhaps prestige need?

Reliability data (retest after one week) are quite satisfactory. But no data are given on stability over time, which has been shown to vary with age and with the method of measurement.

Validity receives a total of eight pages, a refreshing development in manuals. Content and concurrent types dominate, understandable in a recently published instrument. Construct validity arguments include a Chinese proverb and the claim that pictures avoid the halo effect associated with occupational titles, this without evidence despite the probability that a man in a white coat is a man in white.

Content validity data include the fact of item-scale correlation, the classification of pictures by occupational levels to avoid social desirability effects, and trial of both forced choice and like-dislike methods. Item-scale correlations are insufficient evidence of what a scale measures, but a good beginning has been made.

One predictive validity study is reported: the time perspective scale shows a promising correlation of .40 with teacher ratings 11 months after testing.

Concurrent validity data include correlations with SVIB, with the Kuder Vocational, and with the Lee-Thorpe. The sampling in the SVIB study is odd, for it consists of 52 male freshmen in two universities. Unfortunately, the only correlations which were computed were those which looked sizable or which corresponded logically. This last procedure appears to have been inadequate, for physicians were classified as interpersonal service despite the evidence of Strong's work, and the interpersonal service scale correlates only −.03 with the SVIB physician key, with which the scientific scale correlates .63.

However, the expected relationships tend to occur. The interpersonal service scale correlates .61 with the social worker and .59 with social science teacher scales; the scientific scale correlates .63 with physician and .63 with engineer; and time perspective correlates .51 with occupational level.

The Kuder Vocational has similar relationships. The Lee-Thorpe (intermediate level) correlations for similarly named scales range from .56 for the interpersonal service field to .77 for the natural field (median = .68), surprisingly low in view of the conceptual and empirical anchoring of the PII to the OII. For the advanced level of the OII the correlations are somewhat higher (median .71).

Intercorrelations of the various PII scales are also reported here, although this is content, not concurrent, validity. The mechanical and interpersonal service fields and the business and natural fields have substantial negative correlations, other field intercorrelations being negligible, but that of −.01 between mechanical and natural interests is surprising. Verbal and computational interests correlate .59, perhaps because of an intelligence factor.

Norms consist of data on 1,000 persons in secondary schools and colleges. The vague claim that there are no grade differences is surprising in view of Strong and Kuder data. A nationwide scattering of normative cases is noted, but that this is actually a sample rather than a scattering is not made evident.

Scores which exceed the 70th percentile are to be considered first "because of their direct significance," along with fields below the 30th. But their occupational significance is not demonstrated. No consideration is shown for the fact, frequently pointed out by critics of the Kuder, that elevation in relation to occupational groups is as important as ipsative or general normative elevation. The counselor is instructed to use his knowledge of occupations in using the verbal, computational, and time perspective scales to obtain "further information regarding occupational interest," but no help is given him in knowing what these scales can tell him.

Norms for 140 girls are available. The items depict only men, but administration to girls "has suggested" to the author that the inventory is usable with both sexes. Girls' means do differ in expected ways (interpersonal service is higher, mechanical lower, etc.), but whether the mechanical or scientific interests of girls are well tested by items selected for boys is a question.

No norms are given for persons from non-English-speaking cultures, nor for cultural groups which differ in other respects from the dominant American culture. Taken alone, this is an acceptable limitation. But the inventory is recommended in the manual as "ideally suitable" "wherever the examinee has little or no knowledge of English or wherever low reading ability may seriously interfere with assessment," disregarding the fact that these conditions may accompany lack of knowledge of other artifacts such as tensile strength tests or chemists' balances. The test is, as an occupational interest inventory must be, culture-laden.

In conclusion, the *Picture Interest Inventory* could be a promising beginning in the measurement of vocational interests by nonverbal methods. It would benefit from factor analysis and from the needed purification of the scales which this would make possible. It deserves to be used in research to throw further light on its concurrent validity. In addition, much research is needed on the stability of such interests at various age levels and on its predictive validity for various curricula and occupations. As a good deal is known about these aspects of interests as measured by Strong's blank and by the Kuder, it is incumbent upon the author and publishers of *this* instrument to conduct such research and to make the results available. The PII is not yet ready for use in counseling, despite the attractiveness of its content, its simple scoring, its retest reliability, and the persuasive (business contact but not social service!) approach of its manual.

J Counsel Psychol 6:166–7 su '59. Laurence Siegel. * an attempt to develop a nonverbal measure of occupational interest. As such, it is a good idea. Much remains to be done with it, however, before it can take a place along side such well-developed inventories as the Strong and the Kuder. The manual conveys the impression that the PII was published somewhat prematurely. The evidence now available does, to be sure, substantiate the potential utility of the instrument. The problem is that there is not yet enough evidence. Perhaps the most serious objections to this inventory stem from the fact that assertions are incautiously made in the manual and that deficiencies are not properly spotlighted. This is not yet the polished instrument that the author and publisher would have us believe it is.

[1067]

Primary Business Interests Test. Grades 9–16 and adults; 1941–42; 5 scores: accounting, collections and adjustments, sales-office, sales-store, stenographic-filing; 1 form ('41, 1 page); manual ['42, 4 pages]; norms for grades 12–13 only; $2.75 per 25 tests; $1 per specimen set; postage extra; (20–25) minutes; Alfred J. Cardall; Cardall Associates. *

REFERENCES

1. Cardall, Alfred J. *A Test for Primary Business Interests Based on a Functional Occupational Classification.* Doctor's thesis, Harvard University (Cambridge, Mass.), 1941.
2. Cardall, Alfred J. "A Test for Primary Business Interests Based on a Functional Occupational Classification." *Ed & Psychol Meas* 2:113–38 Ap '42. * (*PA* 16:3767)

For reviews by George K. Bennett, Glen U. Cleeton, and George A. Ferguson, see 3:645.

[1068]

***Qualifications Record, 1961 Revision.** Job applicants and employees; 1958–61; includes *Job Qualification Inventory* ('47); 45 scores classified under 7 headings: computation (accounting, mathematics, drafting, purchasing, records, dexterity), social (management, instruction, public contacts, sales, consulting, religion, services, investigation, discipline), literary (journalism, language, transcription, advertising, research), arts (music, art, dramatics, dancing, graphic arts, crafts), biology (physiology, zoology, botany, foods, sports), physical (tools, machinery, transportation, strength, hazards), technology (chemistry, astronomy, electricity, mechanics, construction, geology, physics, aeronautics, standards); Comprehensive Form XL8 ('61, c1957–61, 8 pages); scoring instructions ['61, 4 pages]; scoring form ('61, 1 page); no data on reliability; 3 procedures of use available: (*a*) completed records are sent to the publisher for scoring and interpretation, (*b*) publisher is commissioned to develop tailored job standards for particular jobs within an organization and records of future applicants are scored and interpreted locally using these standards, (*c*) records are scored and interpreted locally using published "industry-wide" job standards based on data accumulated by the publisher; 4 "industry-wide" job standard portfolios (45 pages, 28 of which are common to all portfolios) available: securities salesman ('61), department manager-industrial ('60), life insurance salesman ('61), electronic sales engineer ('61); $7.50 per 25 tests; 75¢ per 25 scoring forms; $1 per specimen set; $15–$100 per applicant for procedure *a*, depending on type of report requested; $250 per job standard portfolio; postpaid; fees for procedure *b* available from the publisher; (60) minutes; Keith Van Allyn; Personnel Research, Inc. * [As of July 1964, the "industry-wide" job standards which are referred to under procedure *c* and which are evaluated in the following reviews have been withdrawn from sale according to the publisher.]

Arthur C. MacKinney, *Associate Professor of Psychology, Iowa State University, Ames, Iowa.*

It must be that the publisher of the *Qualifications Record* has never heard of the APA *Technical Recommendations for Psychological Tests and Diagnostic Techniques.* Virtually none of the information labeled as "essential" in the Technical Recommendations is provided in the instruction leaflets or the "Job Standard portfolios."

The claims made for the Q/R, both in publicity pamphlets and in the Job Standards are outlandish. For example (from a publicity pamphlet): "It [the Q/R] exposes each person's interests, activities, ambitions, training, achievements and experience, and the four behaviour traits: social, emotional, mental and physical, in relation to the 45 vocational elements found in *all* occupations. By this means, it brings into focus all significant facts concerning a man's capabilities, limitations and potentialities." And elsewhere: "Why is the Q/R different from any and all other instruments of measurement? It is dramatically different because it exposes the individual to the full spectrum of traits, skills and knowledge found in *all* occupations in a single, all-inclusive examination." Many other similar examples could be cited.

The Q/R is extremely difficult to describe. It consists of 315 "items," roughly resembling life history and vocational interest items, providing scores on 45 "elements" classified under seven headings. The "elements" are profiled. But one interesting feature is the attempt to make the seven "items" scored under each "element" represent levels of response, from interest—representing wishful thinking—at the lowest level to relevant work experience at the highest. Unfortunately, however, the "items" do not appear to represent a hierarchy of levels, and no evidence is offered to support the contention. In some instances the keyed item content for a given element is *not* the same as what the manual says is keyed.

The word "items" is in quotes because they frequently are not items in the conventional sense. Some are standard interest-type items but the large majority have several, and occasionally many, components. For example, "Sports" (classified under "Biology") lists 57 sports activities and if the respondent has acquired "valid skills and knowledge through intensive effort" in any one he answers "yes" and receives a point on that "item" and "element."

This is unquestionably one of the slickest promotion and format jobs around. The promotional brochures have already been noted. Furthermore, these brochures are handsome and, because they contain unsupported generalities (e.g., the published material repeatedly insists that the Q/R is "readily verifiable"), they might sound very impressive to the lay user. The Job Standard books are beautifully bound in heavy, blue plastic with gold imprinting, and the norms are provided on acetate overlays.

In spite of the publisher's claim that the Q/R is "dramatically different," and "nothing comparable to it is available anywhere," I don't see anything new here. It is basically a series of complex stimuli, presumed to be arranged in spiral form, which are in turn somehow grouped into categories or "elements." The use of norms within occupational or job groups dates at least from the early 1930's. And the promotion is reminiscent of P. T. Barnum's approach.

VALIDITY. The claims for validity take generally three forms: (*a*) The norms are based on "superior" employees. Unfortunately, no mention is made of what use, if any, is made of the other-than-superior employees in the validation process. (*b*) The order of progression of the items up the hierarchy, mentioned earlier, is assumed to be a logical order (questionable) and, from this, validity is inferred (even more questionable). (*c*) The improvement that comes whenever the Q/R is used.

None of these presumed bases for validity are helpful. There is no evidence cited that this test is a valid predictor of any criterion, nor does this reviewer see any content or construct validity. Thus, neither empirical evidence nor theory provides bases for interpreting the meaning of scores from this test.

RELIABILITY. One of the advertising brochures claims "a reliability factor of better than 86%." There is no sure way of knowing what this statement means. Reliability is not appropriately reported this way. One clue from the manual says, "when Qualifications Record forms are submitted to a group of 'superior' employees in a given job classification, better than 86 per cent of these employees will consistently respond in the same manner to the same questions." Subsequent correspondence with the publisher verified that this statement *is* the basis for the reliability figure. Since items such as "How many heads do you have?" would evoke complete consistency of response from one administration to another, the proportion of consistent responses is irrelevant to reliability. On the other hand, the writer's correspondence with the publisher gives the reliability as .86 (test-retest), but fails to say of what this is the reliability. This gives no assurance that profiling 45 separate scores is justifiable.

LOGICAL DIFFICULTIES. (*a*) The clustering in the Q/R, both of elements and items, apparently has no firm basis. Certainly no data are presented for any empirical clustering attempts. (*b*) The degrees within each element, wherein the seven items represent levels of whatever is being measured, are not supported by evidence, and they do not appear to be levels of the same thing. (*c*) There are a very large number of stimuli included in most of the "items." The respondent does not have a reasonable task set for him by such complex items, and a score so derived is not interpretable. (*d*) The manual, publicity brochures, and other written materials tend to be loaded with word magic. The verbal footwork may sound impressive but it is short of meaning. (*e*) A one-hour sample from a lifetime of behavior is supposed to do almost everything: measure intelligence, interest, accident proneness, personality, and training needs.

SUMMARY. The basic questions concerning any measuring instrument are, of course, what is measured and how well. For the Q/R the flat statement can be made that there is no definitive information on what is being measured, nor on how well it is being measured. Furthermore, the test is loaded with logical inconsistencies. Since most other tests and inventories are virtually certain to be better than this one, the use of the Q/R is not indicated.

CHARLES F. WARNATH, *Associate Professor of Psychology, and Director, Counseling Center, Oregon State University, Corvallis, Oregon.*

The authors of the materials accompanying this instrument state: "The Qualifications Record is *not* a test but a complete inventory of the individual's qualifications." The Job Standard Profile, which is the profile developed from the answers given to the *Qualifications Record,* is described as: "a composite study of significant traits, knowledge and skills of personnel engaged in this occupation and rated 'superior' in performance by their employers."

The responses given to the 315 questions of the Q/R are designed to compare the answers of the person taking the inventory with the answers given by "superior" workers in various occupations. The method of determining "superior" workers is not described. Seven factors (interest, activity, ambition, training or education, experience, achievement, and work behavior) are related to "45 basic vocational elements." These 45 basic vocational elements fall into the seven major categories itemized in the above entry.

By summing the "yes" responses to the appropriate questions on the Q/R, the administrator gets an 0 to 7 score for each of the 45 elements. These are plotted on a Job Standard Profile and then a plastic sheet is dropped over the profile. Imprinted on the sheet are colored bars covering several contiguous numbers for each of the elements. If a score falls under the bar for an element, it is considered acceptable for that element on the basis of its similarity to the score for "superior" workers in the occupation for which the Job Standard was developed. Low scores outside the acceptable are reported to "indicate that the person lacks basic traits essential for the job and training may be the answer to build up the responses. Positive deviations indicate the person is overqualified in the element or trait designated."

As a replacement for the employment screening interview, the Q/R can probably do an adequate job, for its range of questions is broad and it is likely to be no less subject to error or distortion than an interview. However, the major problems connected to the Q/R other than the price (as indicated above) are those related to the lack of evaluation studies offered to the purchaser or reviewer. The approach is one of slickness and surface logic. The plastic covered "industry-wide" Job Standards give one the feel of solid accomplishment. But one will look in vain for reliability or validity figures except for a nonsupported "86% reliability" figure mentioned in some of the promotional material.

The materials have undoubtedly been developed with an eye toward the businessman who may not have a personnel director trained to develop his own testing program. At several points in the "Personnel Screening and Evaluation" section of the Job Standards, comments are made which indicate that nonacademic definitions are used (for intelligence and personality, for instance), because the more academic definitions are inappropriate in the area of vocations. Words seem to be defined to fit the inventory questions. However, as is usual with these materials, no evidence is presented to support such contentions as: Intelligence "is the sum total of the basic factors of Interest, Activity, Ambition, Training, Experience, Work Behavior and Achievement, reliably evidenced by performance."

It is commendable that the publisher encourages the purchaser to develop local job standards, but then the purchaser must pay Personnel Research, Inc. to analyze the Q/R's for superior employees of the company and to develop the local job standards for the company. If the company depends on the "industry-wide" Job Standards, it must take much on faith. The Job Standard for "Department Managers" indicates that it "represents a survey of 166 managers of departments in 11 industrial plants," but does not elaborate. The Job Standards for "Sales Engineer-Electronics" and "Salesman, Insurance" do not mention even the number or distribution of the norm groups.

This may be a good instrument, but in the absence of information related to its validity and reliability, it is impossible to support the publicity claims for the instrument. Tests and inventories purporting to do some job for the purchaser need to present more than simply layman logic and paraphrased summaries of "satisfied customer" statements as evidence for effectiveness.

[1069]

★Safran Vocational Interest Test. Grades 10–13; 1960–62; test booklet title is *"S" Interest Scale;* 11 scores: 7 interest scores (economic, technical, outdoor, service, humane, artistic, scientific) and 4 ability self-ratings (academic, mechanical, social, clerical); 1 form ('60, 8 mimeographed pages); mimeographed manual ['62, 6 pages, reprint of *1* below]; mimeographed occupations manual ('60, 4 pages); norms ('61, 8 pages) for college freshmen; norms ['62, 3 pages] for technology students; no norms for ability self-ratings; $10 per 100 tests with accessories; 10¢ per test without accessories; postage extra; (30) minutes; C. Safran; the Author. *

REFERENCES

1. STEWART, JAMES A., AND SAFRAN, CARL. "An Introduction to the Safran Vocational Interest Test and a Report of Its Administration to University of Alberta, Calgary, Freshmen (1961–62 Class)." *Alberta J Ed Res* 7:185–95 D '61. * (*PA* 36:5HB85S)

[1070]

***Strong Vocational Interest Blank for Men, Revised.** Ages 17 and over; 1927–63; 64 scoring scales (54 occupations, 6 occupational group scales, and 4 nonvocational scales): group 1: group scale ('38), artist ('38), psychologist ('28–'49) by P. H. Kriedt, architect ('38), physician ('38–'52), psychiatrist ('52), osteopath ('47), dentist ('38), veterinarian ('49) by T. E. Hannum, biologist ('62) by Carl A. Lindsay, Louis M. Herman, and Martin L. Zeigler; group 2: group scale ('39), physicist ('52), chemist ('38), mathematician ('38), engineer ('38); group 3: production manager ('38); group 4: farmer ('38), carpenter ('38), printer ('38), mathematics-science teacher ('38), policeman ('38), forest service man ('38), army officer ('52), aviator ('40); group 5: group scale ('38), Y.M.C.A. physical director ('38), personnel manager ('38), physical therapist ('58), public administrator ('44), vocational counselor ('52) by Clements D. Brown, Y.M.C.A. secretary ('38), social science high school teacher ('38), business education teacher ('59) by Robert V. Bacon, city school superintendent ('38), minister ('38), social worker ('54), rehabilitation counselor ('62) by Nathan E. Acree; group 6: music performer ('54), music teacher ('54); group 7: C.P.A. owner ('38); group 8: group scale ('38), senior C.P.A. ('49), junior accountant ('38), office worker ('38), purchasing agent ('38), banker ('38), mortician ('46), pharmacist ('49) by Milton Schwebel, credit manager ('59); group 9: group scale ('38), sales manager ('38), real estate salesman ('38), life insurance salesman ('38), association of chamber of commerce executive ('62) by the Clifton Corporation and the author; group 10: group scale ('38), advertising man ('38), lawyer ('38), author-journalist ('38), librarian ('63); group 11: president of manufacturing concern ('38); nonvocational scales: occupational level ('39), masculinity-femininity ('38), specialization level ('52) by Milton G. Holmen, interest maturity ('41); IBM, Hankes, MRC, NCS, and FAST; Form M; 2 editions: hand scored edition ('46, 8 pages), machine scored edition ('45, c1938–45, 7 pages); combined manual ('59, 40 pages) for this test and test 1071; profile ('45, c1938–45, 2 pages); interest global chart ('45, 2 pages); student's guide to profile interpretation ('62, 4 pages); separate answer sheets or cards must be used with machine scored edition; $4 per 25 expendable tests; $6 per 25 reusable tests; $2.50 per 50 IBM answer sheets; $3.25 per 50 NCS answer sheets (scored by National Computer Systems only, see 671); $4 per 50 sets of FAST answer cards; see 667 for prices of Hankes answer sheets and scoring services; see 670 for prices of MRC answer sheets and scoring services; hand scoring stencils: $1.25 per single scale, $10 per set of any 10 scales, $55 per complete set; IBM scoring stencils (IBM scoring of a large number of scales is not recommended): $3 per single scale, $28 per set of any 10 scales, $150 per complete set; $1.25 per 25 profiles; 85¢ per 25 interest global charts; $3.50 per 50 student's profile guides; $2.50 per manual; $1.50 per combined specimen set (includes description and student's profile guide but not manual or scoring stencils) of SVIB for men and for women; postage extra: special service available for end-of-year testing of high school juniors: fee, 75¢ per student (fee includes loan of tests, scoring service, profile report the following September, and copy of student's guide); (30–60) minutes; Edward K. Strong, Jr.; Consulting Psychologists Press, Inc. *

REFERENCES

1–71. See 40:1680.
72–175. See 3:647.
176–273. See 4:747.
274–426. See 5:868.

427. FARNSWORTH, PAUL R. "Rating Scales for Musical Interests." *J Psychol* 28:245–53 Jl '49. * (*PA* 24:528)

428. FISHER, SEYMOUR, AND HINDS, EDITH. "The Organization of Hostility Controls in Various Personality Structures." *Genetic Psychol Monogr* 44:3–68 Ag '51. * (*PA* 26:2889)

429. FRIEDL, FRANCIS P. *Vocational Interests of Successful and Unsuccessful Seminarians in a Foreign Mission Society.* Master's thesis, Catholic University of America (Washington, D.C.), 1952.

430. KOLB, ALFRED. *Vocational Interests of the Brothers of the Sacred Heart.* Master's thesis, Catholic University of America (Washington, D.C.), 1952.

431. MCCARTHY, THOMAS N. *The Relationship of Vocational Interests to Personality Traits.* Master's thesis, Catholic University of America (Washington, D.C.), 1952.

432. D'ARCY, PAUL F. *Constancy of Interest Factor Patterns Within the Specific Vocation of Foreign Missioner.* Catholic University of America, Studies in Psychology and Psychiatry, Vol. 9, No. 1. Washington, D.C.: Catholic University of America Press, 1954. Pp. ix, 54. * (*PA* 29:6444)

432a. HILTON, ANDREW C.; BOLIN, STANLEY F.; PARKER, JAMES W., JR.; TAYLOR, ERWIN K.; AND WALKER, WILLIAM B. "The Validity of Personnel Assessments by Professional Psychologists." *J Appl Psychol* 39:287–93 Ag '55. * (*PA* 30:5294)

433. CRITES, J. O. *Ability and Adjustment as Determinants of Vocational Interest Patterning in Late Adolescence.* Doctor's thesis, Columbia University (New York, N.Y.), 1957. (*DA* 17:1593)

434. MURRAY, JOHN B. *Training for the Priesthood and Personality Interest Test Manifestations.* Doctor's thesis, Fordham University (New York, N.Y.), 1957.

435. SCHOLL, CHARLES ELMER, JR. *The Development and Evaluation of Methods for Isolating Factors That Differentiate Between Successful and Unsuccessful Executive Trainees in a Large, Multibranch Bank.* Doctor's thesis, University of Michigan (Ann Arbor, Mich.), 1957. (*DA* 18:2034)

436. BACON, ROBERT V. *A Study of the Interest Patterns of Men Business Teachers in Public Secondary Schools.* Doctor's thesis, University of California (Los Angeles, Calif.), 1958.

437. CARNES, GILES DERWOOD. *The Relations of Chronicity, Morbidity, and Social Class to the Vocational Interests of Psychiatric Patients.* Doctor's thesis, University of Missouri (Columbia, Mo.), 1958. (*DA* 19:2142)

438. FERGUSON, LEONARD W. "Life Insurance Interest, Abil-

ity and Termination of Employment." *Personnel Psychol* 11:189–93 su '58. *

439. FORMICA, LOUIS ANTHONY. *A Comparative Study of Selected Factors in the Vocational Development of Intellectually Superior College Girls From the Working and Upper-Class Levels.* Doctor's thesis, University of Connecticut (Storrs, Conn.), 1958. (*DA* 19:1012)

440. HENDERSON, HAROLD L. *The Relationship Between Interests of Fathers and Sons and Sons' Identification With Fathers: The Relationship of the Adolescent Son's Identification With his Father to Father-Son Interest Similarity as Measured by the Strong Vocational Interest Blank.* Doctor's thesis, Columbia University (New York, N.Y.), 1958. (*DA* 19:361)

441. HOLT, ROBERT R., AND LUBORSKY, LESTER; WITH THE COLLABORATION OF WILLIAM R. MORROW, DAVID RAPAPORT, AND SIBYLLE K. ESCALONA. *Personality Patterns of Psychiatrists: A Study of Methods for Selecting Residents, Vol. 1.* New York: Basic Books, Inc., 1958. Pp. xiv, 386. * (*PA* 33:5751)

442. HUTTNER, LUDWIG, AND STENE, D. MIRIAM. "Foremen Selection in Light of a Theory of Supervision." *Personnel Psychol* 11:403–9 au '58. * (*PA* 33:11090)

443. KENNEDY, EUGENE C. *A Comparison of the Personality Traits of Successful and Unsuccessful Seminarians in a Foreign Mission Seminary.* Master's thesis, Catholic University of America (Washington, D.C.), 1958.

444. KNOWLES, REX HANNA. *Differential Characteristics of Successful and Unsuccessful Seminary Students.* Doctor's thesis, University of Nebraska (Lincoln, Neb.), 1958. (*DA* 19:1655)

445. MALONE, ROBERT LINCOLN. *A Configural Versus the Standard Method of Scoring the Strong Vocational Interest Blank.* Doctor's thesis, University of Illinois (Urbana, Ill.), 1958. (*DA* 19:1110)

446. METZGER, PAUL LYMAN. *An Investigation of Some Correlates of Vocational Interest Similarity Between Fathers and Sons.* Doctor's thesis, University of Oregon (Eugene, Ore.), 1958. (*DA* 19:1116)

447. NAMANI, ABDEL-KADER. *Factors Associated With High and Low Correlations Between Individuals' Scores on Two Interest Inventories.* Doctor's thesis, Cornell University (Ithaca, N.Y.), 1958. (*DA* 19:2538)

448. STEIMEL, RAYMOND J. *A Study of the Relationship of Recalled Childhood Identification and Association to Masculinity-Femininity of Interest Scores on the MMPI and SVIB Among Scholarship Finalists.* Doctor's thesis, University of Kansas (Lawrence, Kan.), 1958.

449. STEWART, LAWRENCE H. "Non-Occupation Scales of the Strong Vocational Interest Blank and Amount of College Education." *Calif J Ed Res* 9:137–40 My '58. * (*PA* 33:9028)

450. THOMAS, EDWIN RUSSELL. *The Relationship Between the Strong Vocational Interest Blank and the Guilford-Martin Personality Inventory Among Salesmen.* Doctor's thesis, Syracuse University (Syracuse, N.Y.), 1958. (*DA* 19:2139)

451. WEBB, SAM C., AND GOODLING, RICHARD A. "Test Validity in a Methodist Theology School." *Ed & Psychol Meas* 18:859–66 w '58. * (*PA* 34:2123)

452. WEISSMAN, MARTIN P. *An Approach to the Assessment of Intellectual Disposition Among Selected High Ability Students.* Doctor's thesis, University of California (Berkeley, Calif.), 1958.

453. WRIGHT, ROBERT MATTHEW. *The Development and Use of an Occupational Factors Rating Scale in College Counseling.* Doctor's thesis, University of Missouri (Columbia, Mo.), 1958. (*DA* 19:2141)

454. ARMATAS, JAMES PHILIP. *An Investigation of Personality Effects Related in L-I-D Response Patterns on the Strong Vocational Interest Blank.* Doctor's thesis, University of Kansas (Lawrence, Kan.), 1959.

455. CRITES, JOHN O. "A Coding System for Total Profile Analysis of the Strong Vocational Interest Blank." *J Appl Psychol* 43:176–9 Je '59. * (*PA* 34:5931)

456. CROFTCHIK, VICTOR PAUL. *A Study to Establish a Scoring Key for Male Elementary and Secondary Art Teachers to Be Used With the Strong Vocational Interest Blank.* Doctor's thesis, Michigan State University (East Lansing, Mich.), 1959. (*DA* 20:4593)

457. CROWDER, DOLORES GARCIA. "Prediction of First-Year Grades in a Medical College." *Ed & Psychol Meas* 19:637–9 w '59. * (*PA* 34:6563)

458. FILBECK, ROBERT WORTH. *The Differentiation of Freshman Curricular Groups by Means of Empirically Derived Academic Interest Scales.* Doctor's thesis, University of Missouri (Columbia, Mo.), 1959. (*DA* 20:2675)

459. GRAY, CLIFTON WELLINGTON. *Detection of Faking in Vocational Interest Measurement.* Doctor's thesis, University of Minnesota (Minneapolis, Minn.), 1959. (*DA* 20:1429)

460. GUILFORD, J. P. *Personality,* pp. 206–12. New York: McGraw-Hill Book Co., Inc., 1959. Pp. xiii, 562. *

461. GUTEKUNST, JOSEF GRANT. *The Prediction of Art Achievement of Art Education Students by Means of Standardized Tests.* Doctor's thesis, Temple University (Philadelphia, Pa.), 1959. (*DA* 20:3202)

462. KELLY, E. LOWELL, AND GOLDBERG, LEWIS R. "Correlates of Later Performance and Specialization in Psychology: A Follow-Up Study of the Trainees Assessed in the VA Selection Research Project." *Psychol Monogr* 73(12):1–32 '59. * (*PA* 34:7952)

463. KENNEY, CHARLES E. *Differential Vocational Interest Patterns of Successful and Unsuccessful Foreign Mission Seminarians.* Doctor's thesis, Loyola University (Chicago, Ill.), 1959.

464. KIRK, DANIEL. *A Study of the Interests of Brother Candidates and Professed Brothers, on the Strong Minister and Clerical Interest Scales.* Doctor's thesis, St. John's University (Brooklyn, N.Y.), 1959.

465. MCCORNACK, ROBERT L. "An Evaluation of Two Methods of Cross-Validation." *Psychol Rep* 5:127–30 Mr '59. * (*PA* 34:147)

466. NICKELS, JAMES BRADLEY. *Inventoried and Expressed Vocational Interests: Their Intra-Group Consistency and Inter-Predictability.* Doctor's thesis, University of Missouri (Columbia, Mo.), 1959. (*DA* 20:3820)

467. NOLAN, EDWARD GILLIGAN. *Uniqueness in Monozygotic Twins.* Doctor's thesis, Princeton University (Princeton, N.J.), 1959. (*DA* 21:247)

468. RODGERS, FRANK P. *A Psychometric Study of Certain Interest and Personality Variables Associated With Academic Achievement in a College Level Printing Curriculum.* Doctor's thesis, University of Buffalo (Buffalo, N.Y.), 1959. (*DA* 19:3219)

469. SCHUTZ, RICHARD ARLEN. *The Relationship of Self-Satisfaction to Stated Vocational Preferences.* Doctor's thesis, University of Minnesota (Minneapolis, Minn.), 1959. (*DA* 20:2148)

470. STEPHENSON, RICHARD RYLE. *A Comparison of the Strong VIB Profiles of High Ability Male S. L. A. Freshmen Who Change Expressed Vocational Choice With Those Who Do Not Change Such Expressions.* Doctor's thesis, University of Minnesota (Minneapolis, Minn.), 1959. (*DA* 20:4166)

471. STEWART, LAWRENCE H. "Interest Patterns of a Group of High-Ability, High-Achieving Students." *J Counsel Psychol* 6:132–9 su '59. * (*PA* 34:4799)

472. STEWART, LAWRENCE H. "Mother-Son Identification and Vocational Interest." *Genetic Psychol Monogr* 60:31–63 Ag '59. * (*PA* 34:4542)

473. STRUNK, ORLO, JR. "Interest and Personality Patterns of Preministerial Students." *Psychol Rep* 5:740 D '59. * (*PA* 34:5635)

474. TYLER, LEONA E. "Distinctive Patterns of Likes and Dislikes Over a Twenty-Two Year Period." *J Counsel Psychol* 6:234–7 f '59. * (*PA* 35:4037)

475. WHITLOCK, GLENN EVERETT. *The Relationship Between Passivity of Personality and Personal Factors Related to the Choice of the Ministry as a Vocation.* Doctor's thesis, University of Southern California (Los Angeles, Calif.), 1959. (*DA* 20:2392)

476. BARROWS, GORDON A., AND ZUCKERMAN, MARVIN. "Construct Validity of Three Masculinity-Femininity Tests." *J Consult Psychol* 24:441–5 O '60. * (*PA* 35:4891)

477. BERDIE, RALPH F. "Strong Vocational Interest Blank Scores of High School Seniors and Their Later Occupational Entry." *J Appl Psychol* 44:161–5 Je '60. * (*PA* 35:3920)

478. BERDIE, RALPH F. "Validities of the Strong Vocational Interest Blank," pp. 18–61. In *The Strong Vocational Interest Blank: Research and Uses.* Edited by Wilbur L. Layton. Minnesota Studies in Student Personnel Work, No. 10. Minneapolis, Minn.: University of Minnesota Press, 1960. Pp. viii, 191. * (*PA* 36:1LC91L)

479. BROWN, DONALD JAMES. *An Investigation of the Relationships Between Certain Personal Characteristics of Guidance Counselors and Performance in Supervised Counseling Interviews.* Doctor's thesis, Ohio State University (Columbus, Ohio), 1960. (*DA* 21:810)

480. BURDOCK, E. I.; CHEEK, FRANCES; AND ZUBIN, JOSEPH. "Predicting Success in Psychoanalytic Training," pp. 176–91. In *Current Approaches to Psychoanalysis.* Proceedings of the 48th Annual Meeting of the American Psychopathological Association Held in New York City, February 1958. Edited by Paul H. Hoch and Joseph Zubin. New York: Grune & Stratton, Inc., 1960. Pp. 207. * (*PA* 36:4IE07H)

481. CLARK, KENNETH E. "Problems of Method in Interest Measurement," pp. 146–62. In *The Strong Vocational Interest Blank: Research and Uses.* Edited by Wilbur L. Layton. Minnesota Studies in Student Personnel Work, No. 10. Minneapolis, Minn.: University of Minnesota Press, 1960. Pp. viii, 191. * (*PA* 36:1LC91L)

482. CRITES, JOHN O. "Ego-Strength in Relation to Vocational Interest Development." *J Counsel Psychol* 7:137–43 su '60. * (*PA* 35:4012)

483. DARLEY, JOHN G. "The Theoretical Basis of Interests," pp. 118–45. In *The Strong Vocational Interest Blank: Research and Uses.* Edited by Wilbur L. Layton. Minnesota Studies in Student Personnel Work, No. 10. Minneapolis, Minn.: University of Minnesota Press, 1960. Pp. viii, 191. * (*PA* 36:1LC91L)

484. DUNNETTE, MARVIN D., AND KIRCHNER, WAYNE K. "Psychological Test Differences Between Industrial Salesmen and Retail Salesmen." *J Appl Psychol* 44:121–5 Ap '60. * (*PA* 35:4029)

485. EDDY, RAYMOND T. "Interest Patterns of Rehabilitation

Counselors." *J Counsel Psychol* 7:202–8 f '60. * (*PA* 36: 1IP02E)

486. ENGLAND, GEORGE W. "The Interest Factor in Undergraduate Engineering Achievement." *Personnel & Guid J* 38: 401–5 Ja '60. *

487. FREDERIKSEN, NORMAN, AND GILBERT, ARTHUR C. F. "Replication of a Study of Differential Predictability." *Ed & Psychol Meas* 20:759–67 w '60. * (*PA* 35:7953)

488. HAGENAH, THEDA. "Normative Data, Patterning, and Use of the Strong Vocational Interest Blank," pp. 104–17. In *The Strong Vocational Interest Blank: Research and Uses.* Edited by Wilbur L. Layton. Minnesota Studies in Student Personnel Work, No. 10. Minneapolis, Minn.: University of Minnesota Press, 1960. Pp. viii, 191. * (*PA* 36:1LC91L)

489. HARRELL, THOMAS W. "The Relation of Test Scores to Sales Criteria." *Personnel Psychol* 13:65–9 sp '60. * (*PA* 35: 7192)

490. HEIST, PAUL. "Personality Characteristics of Dental Students." *Ed Rec* 41:240–52 Jl '60. * (*PA* 35:7081)

491. HOYT, DONALD P. "Measurement and Prediction of the Permanence of Interests," pp. 93–103. In *The Strong Vocational Interest Blank: Research and Uses.* Edited by Wilbur L. Layton. Minnesota Studies in Student Personnel Work, No. 10. Minneapolis, Minn.: University of Minnesota Press, 1960. Pp. viii, 191. * (*PA* 36:1LC91L)

492. KIRCHNER, WAYNE; HANSON, RICHARD; AND BENSON, DALE. "Selecting Foremen With Psychological Tests." *Personnel Adm* 23:27–30 N–D '60. *

493. KNAPP, ROBERT H., AND GREEN, SAMUEL. "Preferences for Styles of Abstract Art and Their Personality Correlates." *J Proj Tech* 24:396–402 D '60. * (*PA* 35:4841)

494. KULBERG, GORDON E., AND OWENS, WILLIAM A. "Some Life History Antecedents of Engineering Interests." *J Ed Psychol* 51:26–31 F '60. * (*PA* 34:7954; 35:2738)

495. LAYTON, WILBUR L., EDITOR. *The Strong Vocational Interest Blank: Research and Uses: Papers From the Institute on the Strong Vocational Interest Blank Held at the University of Minnesota in February 1955.* Minnesota Studies in Student Personnel Work, No. 10. Minneapolis, Minn.: University of Minnesota Press, 1960. Pp. viii, 191. * (*PA* 36: 1LC91L)

496. MACKINNEY, ARTHUR C., AND WOLINS, LEROY. "Validity Information Exchange, No. 13-01, Foreman II, Home Appliance Manufacturing." *Personnel Psychol* 13:443–7 w '60. *

497. MARKWARDT, FREDERICK CHARLES, JR. *Pattern Analysis Techniques in the Prediction of College Success.* Doctor's thesis, University of Minnesota (Minneapolis, Minn.), 1960. (*DA* 21:2990)

498. MAYFIELD, EUGENE CUNLIFFE. *Interests as a Predictor of Graduation in Engineering.* Doctor's thesis, Purdue University (Lafayette, Ind.), 1960. (*DA* 21:1248)

499. NORRELL, GWEN, AND GRATER, HARRY. "Interest Awareness as an Aspect of Self-Awareness." *J Counsel Psychol* 7: 289–92 w '60. * (*PA* 36:1HF89N)

500. PAPPAS, ANGELINE J., AND GYSBERS, NORMAN C. "A Worksheet for Interpreting the Strong Vocational Interest Blank." *Voc Guid Q* 8:129–31 sp '60. *

501. PERRY, DALLIS. "Problems of Item Form and Criterion Group Definition," pp. 163–77. In *The Strong Vocational Interest Blank: Research and Uses.* Edited by Wilbur L. Layton. Minnesota Studies in Student Personnel Work, No. 10. Minneapolis, Minn.: University of Minnesota Press, 1960. Pp. viii, 191. * (*PA* 36:1LC91L)

502. RALEY, COLEMAN LAVAN. *Personality Traits of High-Academic Achievers at Oklahoma Baptist University, 1958–1959.* Doctor's thesis, University of Oklahoma (Norman, Okla.), 1960. (*DA* 20:2680)

503. SHIRLEY, JACK HAROLD. *A Comparative Study of the Academic Achievements, Interests, and Personality Traits of Athletes and Non-Athletes.* Doctor's thesis, University of Oklahoma (Norman, Okla.), 1960. (*DA* 20:4005)

504. SMITH, STUART ELWOOD. *The Relationship Between Scores on the Strong Vocational Interest Blank and Academic Performance at the State University of New York College of Medicine at Syracuse.* Doctor's thesis, Syracuse University (Syracuse, N.Y.), 1960. (*DA* 22:166)

505. STEIMEL, RAYMOND J. "Childhood Experiences and Masculinity-Femininity Scores." *J Counsel Psychol* 7:212–7 f '60. * (*PA* 36:1HF12S)

506. STEWART, LAWRENCE H. "Modes of Response on the Strong Blank and Selected Personality Variables." *J Counsel Psychol* 7:127–31 su '60. * (*PA* 35:3461)

507. STONE, VERNON W. "Measured Vocational Interests in Relation to Intraoccupational Proficiency." *J Appl Psychol* 44:78–82 Ap '60. * (*PA* 35:4102)

508. STRONG, EDWARD K., JR. "An Eighteen-Year Longitudinal Report on Interests," pp. 3–17. In *The Strong Vocational Interest Blank: Research and Uses.* Edited by Wilbur L. Layton. Minnesota Studies in Student Personnel Work, No. 10. Minneapolis, Minn.: University of Minnesota Press, 1960. Pp. viii, 191. * (*PA* 36:1LC91L)

509. STRONG, EDWARD K., JR. "Use of the Strong Vocational Interest Blank in Counseling," pp. 178–91. In *The Strong Vocational Interest Blank: Research and Uses.* Edited by Wilbur L. Layton. Minnesota Studies in Student Personnel Work, No. 10. Minneapolis, Minn.: University of Minnesota Press, 1960. Pp. viii, 191. * (*PA* 36:1LC91L)

510. SUPER, DONALD E., AND MOSER, HELEN P. "Some Correlates of Interest Maturity in Early Adolescence," pp. 76–92. In *The Strong Vocational Interest Blank: Research and Uses.* Edited by Wilbur L. Layton. Minnesota Studies in Student Personnel Work, No. 10. Minneapolis, Minn.: University of Minnesota Press, 1960. Pp. viii, 191. * (*PA* 36:1LC91L)

511. WHITEHORN, JOHN C., AND BETZ, BARBARA J. "Further Studies of the Doctor as a Crucial Variable in the Outcome of Treatment With Schizophrenic Patients." *Am J Psychiatry* 117:215–23 S '60. *

512. ANASTASI, ANNE. *Psychological Testing, Second Edition,* pp. 529–36. New York: Macmillan Co., 1961. Pp. xiii, 657. * (*PA* 36:1HA57A)

513. BOYD, J. B. "Interests of Engineers Related to Turnover, Selection, and Management." *J Appl Psychol* 45:143–9 Je '61. * (*PA* 36: 4LI43B)

514. BROWN, FRED G. "A Note on Expectancy Ratios, Base Rates, and the SVIB." *J Counsel Psychol* 8:368–9 w '61. * (*PA* 37:3894)

515. BURACK, BENJAMIN. "Have You Checked Machine-Scoring Error Lately?" *Voc Guid Q* 9:191–3 sp '61. * (*PA* 36:1KI91B)

516. DUDA, WALTER BOLESLAV. *The Prediction of Three Major Dimensions of Teacher Behavior for Student Teachers in Music Education.* Doctor's thesis, University of Illinois (Urbana, Ill.), 1961. (*DA* 22:1518)

517. DUNKLEBERGER, CLARENCE J., AND TYLER, LEONA E. "Interest Stability and Personality Traits." *J Counsel Psychol* 8:70–4 sp '61. * (*PA* 36:3FF70D)

518. FILBECK, ROBERT W., AND CALLIS, ROBERT. "A Verification Scale for the Strong Vocational Interest Blank, Men's Form." *J Appl Psychol* 45:318–24 O '61. * (*PA* 36: 5LB18F)

519. FORER, BERTRAM R. "The Case of E1: Vocational Choice." *J Proj Tech* 25:371–4 D '61. *

520. GARRETT, GENE AUBREY. *A Comparison of the Predictive Power of the Kuder Preference Record and the Strong Vocational Interest Blank in a Counseling Setting.* Doctor's thesis, University of Missouri (Columbia, Mo.), 1961. (*DA* 22:1506)

521. GOODSTEIN, LEONARD D., AND KIRK, BARBARA A. "A Six-Year Follow-up Study of Graduate Students in Public Health Education." *J Appl Psychol* 45:240–3 Ag '61. * (*PA* 36:4LB40B)

522. HEIST, PAUL; MCCONNELL, T. R.; MATZLER, FRANK; AND WILLIAMS, PHOEBE. "Personality and Scholarship." *Sci* 133:362–7 F 10 '61. * (*PA* 36:2KD62H)

523. HEIST, PAUL A., AND WILLIAMS, PHOEBE A. "Variation in Achievement Within a Select and Homogeneous Student Body." *J Col Student Personnel* 3:50–9 D '61. *

524. JOHNSON, RICHARD WILBUR. *The Relationship Between Measured Interests and Differential Academic Achievement.* Doctor's thesis, University of Minnesota (Minneapolis, Minn.), 1961. (*DA* 22:3923)

525. JOSEPH, MICHAEL P. "The Strong Vocational Interest Blank and the Kuder Preference Record—Occupational (Form D): A Comparative Study of Eight Same-Named Scales." *Yearb Nat Council Meas Ed* 18:145–54 '61. *

526. KIRCHNER, WAYNE K. "'Real-Life' Faking on the Strong Vocational Interest Blank by Sales Applicants." *J Appl Psychol* 45:273–6 Ag '61. * (*PA* 36:4LB73K)

527. KIRK, BARBARA A.; GOODSTEIN, LEONARD D.; AND CUMMINGS, ROGER W. "The Strong Vocational Interest Blank and Collegiate Nursing Education." *Personnel & Guid J* 40:160–3 O '61. * (*PA* 36:4KJ60K)

528. LEWIS, EDWIN C., AND MACKINNEY, ARTHUR C. "Counselor vs. Statistical Predictions of Job Satisfaction in Engineering." *J Counsel Psychol* 8:224–30 f '61. * (*PA* 36: 5KI24L)

529. MACKINNON, DONALD W. "Fostering Creativity in Students of Engineering." *J Eng Ed* 52:129–42 D '61. * (*PA* 36:4HD29M)

530. MAHONEY, THOMAS A.; JERDEE, THOMAS H.; AND NASH, ALLAN N. *The Identification of Management Potential: A Research Approach to Management Development.* Dubuque, Iowa: Wm. C. Brown Co., 1961. Pp. xiii, 79. *

531. MUSSEN, PAUL. "Some Antecedents and Consequents of Masculine Sex-Typing in Adolescent Boys." *Psychol Monogr* 75(2):1–24 '61. * (*PA* 36:3FH24M)

532. PALUBINSKAS, ALICE L., AND EYDE, LORRAINE D. "SVIB Patterns of Medical School Applicants." *J Counsel Psychol* 8:159–63 su '61. * (*PA* 36:3KL59P)

533. PORTER, ALBERT. *Predictors of Organizational Leadership.* Doctor's thesis, Stanford University (Stanford, Calif.), 1961. (*DA* 22:457)

534. RAJU, NAMBURY SITARAMA. *Vocational Interests of Chamber of Commerce and Trade Association Executives as Measured by the Strong Vocational Interest Blank.* Master's thesis, Purdue University (Lafayette, Ind.), 1961.

535. SCHUTZ, RICHARD A., AND BLOCHER, DONALD H. "Self-Satisfaction and Level of Occupational Choice." *Personnel & Guid J* 39:595–8 Mr '61. * (*PA* 35:6308)

536. SPRINKLE, RONALD LEO. *Permanence of Measured Vocational Interests and Socio-Economic Background.* Doctor's

thesis, University of Missouri (Columbia, Mo.), 1961. (*DA* 22:3527)
537. STEPHENSON, RICHARD R. "Chance Versus Nonchance Scores on the SVIB." *J Appl Psychol* 45:415-9 D '61. * (*PA* 37:2037)
538. STEPHENSON, RICHARD R. "A New Pattern Analysis Technique for the SVIB." *J Counsel Psychol* 8:355-62 w '61. * (*PA* 37:3896)
539. STEPHENSON, RICHARD R. "Predicting S.V.I.B. Profiles of High Ability Male Arts College Freshmen." *Personnel & Guid J* 39:650-3 Ap '61. * (*PA* 36:1KD50S)
540. STONE, VERNON W. "The Strong Vocational Interest Blank and Occupational Proficiency." *J Ed Res* 55:138-40 N '61. * (*PA* 36:5LC38S)
541. WATLEY, DONIVAN JASON. *Prediction of Academic Success in a College of Business Administration.* Doctor's thesis, University of Denver (Denver, Colo.), 1961. (*DA* 22:3527)
542. WEGNER, KENNETH WALTER. *An Analysis of Interest Patterns and Psychological Need Structures Related to L-I-D Response Patterns on the Strong Vocational Interest Blank for Women.* Doctor's thesis, University of Kansas (Lawrence, Kan.), 1961. (*DA* 22:3931)
543. ARMATAS, JAMES P., AND COLLISTER, E. GORDON. "Personality Correlates of SVIB Patterns." *J Counsel Psychol* 9:149-54 su '62. * (*PA* 37:6710)
544. BEDROSIAN, HRACH. *An Analysis of Vocational Interests at Two Levels of Management.* Doctor's thesis, Columbia University (New York, N.Y.), 1962. (*DA* 23:1067)
545. BURK, KENNETH WINFIELD. *Biographic, Interest, and Personality Characteristics of Purdue Speech and Hearing Graduates.* Doctor's thesis, Purdue University (Lafayette, Ind.), 1962. (*DA* 23:3021)
546. CRITES, JOHN O. "Parental Identification in Relation to Vocational Interest Development." *J Ed Psychol* 53:262-70 D '62. * (*PA* 37:4744)
547. CUMMINGS, ROGER WESLEY. *The Relationship Between Authoritarianism and the Strong Vocational Interest Blanks.* Doctor's thesis, University of California (Berkeley, Calif.), 1962. (*DA* 24:1071)
548. D'ARCY, PAUL F. "Review of Research on the Vocational Interests of Priests, Brothers and Sisters," pp. 149-200. In *Screening Candidates for the Priesthood and Religious Life.* By Magda B. Arnold and others. Chicago, Ill.: Loyola University Press, 1962. Pp. x, 205. *
549. EADDY, MORRIS LEE. *An Investigation of the Cannot Say Scale of the Group Minnesota Multiphasic Personality Inventory.* Doctor's thesis, University of Florida (Gainesville, Fla.), 1962. (DA 23: 1070)
550. ENGEL, ILONA MARIA. *A Factor Analytic Study of Items From Five Masculinity-Femininity Tests.* Doctor's thesis, University of Michigan (Ann Arbor, Mich.), 1962. (*DA* 23:307)
551. FREEMAN, FRANK S. *Theory and Practice of Psychological Testing, Third Edition,* pp. 584-96. New York: Holt, Rinehart & Winston, Inc., 1962. Pp. xix, 697. *
552. HEMPHILL, JOHN K.; GRIFFITHS, DANIEL E.; AND FREDERIKSEN, NORMAN; WITH THE ASSISTANCE OF GLEN STICE, LAURENCE IANNACCONE, WILLIAM COFFIELD, AND SYDELL CARLTON. *Administrative Performance and Personality: A Study of the Principal in a Simulated Elementary School.* New York: Bureau of Publications, Teachers College, Columbia University, 1962. Pp. xix, 432. *
553. HERMAN, LOUIS M.; LINDSAY, CARL A.; AND ZEIGLER, MARTIN L. "A Vocational Interest Scale for Biologists." *J Appl Psychol* 46:170-4 Je '62. * (*PA* 37:2104)
554. HOLLAND, JOHN L., AND ASTIN, ALEXANDER W. "The Prediction of the Academic, Artistic, Scientific, and Social Achievement of Undergraduates of Superior Scholastic Aptitude." *J Ed Psychol* 53:132-43 Je '62. * (*PA* 37:2010)
555. KINNANE, JOHN F., AND SUZIEDELIS, ANTANAS. "Work Value Orientation and Inventoried Interests." *J Counsel Psychol* 9:144-8 su '62. * (*PA* 37:7226)
556. KLEIN, FREDERICK L.; MCNAIR, DOUGLAS M.; AND LORR, MAURICE. "SVIB Scores of Clinical Psychologists, Psychiatrists, and Social Workers." *J Counsel Psychol* 9:176-9 su '62. * (*PA* 37:5960)
557. KNAPP, ROBERT H.; GEWIRTZ, HERBERT; AND HOLZBERG, JULES D. "Some Personality Correlates of Styles of Interpersonal Thought." *J Proj Tech* 26:398-403 D '62. * (*PA* 37:6717)
558. KORN, HAROLD A. "Differences Between Majors in Engineering and Physical Sciences on CPI and SVIB Scores." *J Counsel Psychol* 9:306-12 w '62. * (*PA* 39:2870)
559. KORN, HAROLD A., AND PARKER, EDWIN B. "A Normative Study of the S.V.I.B. Using an Objective Method of Pattern Analysis." *Personnel & Guid J* 41:222-8 N '62. * (*PA* 37:7172)
560. LANNA, MATTHEW GEORGE. *Vocational Interests in Relation to Some Aspects of Personality and Adjustment.* Doctor's thesis, Columbia University (New York, N.Y.), 1962. (*DA* 23:4421)
561. MCNAIR, DOUGLAS M.; CALLAHAN, DANIEL M.; AND LORR, MAURICE. 'Therapist 'Type' and Patient Response to Psychotherapy." *J Consult Psychol* 26:425-9 O '62. * (*PA* 39:2070)
562. MARTIN, ANN MILDRED. *The Development and Cross-Validation of an Academic Interest Scale for the Strong Vocational Interest Blank.* Doctor's thesis, University of Pittsburgh (Pittsburgh, Pa.), 1962. (*DA* 24:384)
563. MORSE, PAUL KENNETH. *The Strong Vocational Interest Blank and Minnesota Multiphasic Personality Inventory as Measures of Persistence Toward the Ministry as a Vocational Goal.* Doctor's thesis, University of Michigan (Ann Arbor, Mich.), 1962. (*DA* 23:3239)
564. OLHEISER, MARY DAVID. *Development of a Sister Teacher Interest Scale for the Strong Vocational Interest Blank for Women.* Doctor's thesis, Boston College (Chestnut Hill, Mass.), 1962.
565. PATERSON, DONALD G. "Values and Interests in Vocational Guidance," pp. 118-25. (*PA* 37:5694) In *Industrial and Business Psychology.* Proceedings of the XIV International Congress of Applied Psychology, Vol. 5. Copenhagen, Denmark: Munksgaard, Ltd., 1962. Pp. 229. *
566. PATTERSON, C. H. "Test Characteristics of Rehabilitation Counselor Trainees." *J Rehabil* 28:15-6 S-O '62. * (*PA* 37:6953)
567. PORTER, ALBERT. "Effect of Organization Size on Validity of Masculinity-Femininity Score." *J Appl Psychol* 46:228-9 Je '62. * (*PA* 37:2135)
568. RUPIPER, OMER JOHN. "A Psychometric Evaluation of Experienced Teachers." *J Ed Res* 55:368-71 My '62. *
569. SCHUTZ, RICHARD E.; STAATS, ARTHUR W.; AND STAATS, CAROLYN K. "Conditionability of Responses to Occupational Scale Items of the Strong Vocational Interest Blank for Men." *Psychol Rep* 10:447-50 Ap '62. * (*PA* 37:3846)
570. SEEMAN, WILLIAM, AND MARKS, PHILIP A. "A Study of Some 'Test Dimensions' Conceptions." *J Proj Tech* 26:469-73 D '62. * (*PA* 37:6678)
571. SLIFE, WAYNE GORDON. *The Measurement of Identification and Its Relationship to Behavioral Indices of Personality Organization.* Doctor's thesis, University of Houston (Houston, Tex.), 1962. (*DA* 23:3505)
572. STEFFLRE, BUFORD; KING, PAUL; AND LEAFGREN, FRED. "Characteristics of Counselors Judged Effective by Their Peers." *J Counsel Psychol* 9:335-40 w '62. * (*PA* 39:2312)
573. STEPHENSON, RICHARD R. "Faking 'Chance' on the SVIB." *J Appl Psychol* 46:252-6 Ag '62. * (*PA* 37:3899)
574. STEWART, LAWRENCE H. "Relationship of Two Indices of Interest Stability to Self-Satisfaction and to Mother-Son Identification." *Calif J Ed Res* 13:51-6 Mr '62. * (*PA* 37:897)
575. STRONG, EDWARD K., JR. "Good and Poor Interest Items." *J Appl Psychol* 46:269-75 Ag '62. * (*PA* 37:3900)
576. SUPER, DONALD E., AND CRITES, JOHN O. *Appraising Vocational Fitness by Means of Psychological Tests, Revised Edition,* pp. 418-56. New York: Harper & Brothers, 1962. Pp. xv, 688. * (*PA* 37:2038)
577. TUCKER, ANTHONY C., AND STRONG, EDWARD K., JR. "Ten-Year Follow-Up of Vocational Interest Scores of 1950 Medical College Seniors." *J Appl Psychol* 46:81-6 Ap '62. *
578. WATLEY, DONIVAN J., AND MARTIN, H. T. "Prediction of Academic Success in a College of Business Administration." *Personnel & Guid J* 41:147-54 O '62. * (*PA* 37:5656)
579. WHITLOCK, GLENN E. "Passivity of Personality and Role Concepts in Vocational Choice." *J Counsel Psychol* 9:88-90 sp '62. * (*PA* 38:3249)
580. WINTERS, JOSEPH STEPHEN. *The Inventoried Interests of Male Librarians.* Doctor's thesis, New York University (New York, N.Y.), 1962. (*DA* 24:1484)
581. WOODS, JAMES EDWARD. *Strong Vocational Interest Blank Profiles of Vocational Rehabilitation Counselor Trainees.* Doctor's thesis, University of Illinois (Urbana, Ill.), 1962. (*DA* 23:4235)
582. ANKER, JAMES M.; TOWNSEND, JOHN C.; AND O'CONNOR, JAMES P. "A Multivariate Analysis of Decision Making and Related Measures." *J Psychol* 55:211-21 Ja '63. * (*PA* 37:6186)
583. BENDIG, A. W. "The Relation of Temperament Traits of Social Extraversion and Emotionality to Vocational Interests." *J General Psychol* 69:311-8 O '63. * (*PA* 39:1800)
584 BROWN, FREDERICK G. "Further Evidence on Strong V.I.B. Response Tendencies and Personality Characteristics." *J Counsel Psychol* 10:199-200 su '63. *
585. CAMPBELL, DAVID. "Chance on SVIB: Dice or Men?" *J Appl Psychol* 47:127-9 Ap '63. * (*PA* 37:8297)
586. CARKHUFF, ROBERT R., AND DRASGOW, JAMES. "The Confusing Literature on the OL Scale of the SVIB." *J Counsel Psychol* 10:283-8 f '63. * (*PA* 38:4742)
587. COOLEY, WILLIAM W. "Predicting Choice of a Career in Scientific Research." *Personnel & Guid J* 42:21-8 S '63. *
588. CRITES, JOHN O. "Vocational Interest in Relation to Vocational Motivation." *J Ed Psychol* 54:277-85 O '63. * (*PA* 38:4744)
589. DE SENA, PAUL AMBROSE. *Identification of Non-Intellectual Characteristics of Consistent Over-, Under-, and Normal-Achievers Enrolled in Science Curriculums at the Pennsylvania State University.* Doctor's thesis, Pennsylvania State University (University Park, Pa.), 1963. (*DA* 24:3144)
590. DUNNETTE, MARVIN D. "A Note on *The* Criterion." *J Appl Psychol* 47:251-4 Ag '63. * (*PA* 38:3219)
591. DURFLINGER, GLENN W. "Academic and Personality Differences Between Women Students Who Do Complete the

Elementary Teaching Credential Program and Those Who Do Not." *Ed & Psychol Meas* 23:775–83 w '63. *

592. Fein, Arthur; Lipton, Leonard; and Elton, Charles F. "Comparison of Strong Vocational Interest Patterns of Schizophrenics and Normals." *Psychol Rep* 13:887–94 D '63. * (*PA* 38:9044)

593. Funkenstein, Daniel H. "Mathematics, Quantitative Aptitudes and the Masculine Role." *Dis Nerv System* 24(Sect 2):140–6 Ap '63. *

594. Guthrie, George M., and McKendry, Margaret S. "Interest Patterns of Peace Corps Volunteers in a Teaching Project." *J Ed Psychol* 54:261–7 O '63. * (*PA* 38:4126)

595. Holland, John L. "Explorations of a Theory of Vocational Choice and Achievement: 2, A Four-Year Prediction Study." *Psychol Rep* 12:547–94 Ap '63. * (*PA* 38:4747)

596. King, Paul; Norrell, Gwendolyn; and Powers, G. Pat. "Relationships Between Twin Scales on the SVIB and the Kuder." *J Counsel Psychol* 10:395–401 w '63. * (*PA* 38:9342)

597. Kirk, Barbara A.; Cummings, Roger W.; and Hackett, Herbert R. "Personal and Vocational Characteristics of Dental Students." *Personnel & Guid J* 41:522–7 F '63. *

598. Kole, Delbert M., and Matarazzo, J. D. "Intellectual and Personality Characteristics of Medical Students." Abstract. *J Med Ed* 38:138–9 F '63. *

599. Laime, Barbara F., and Zytowski, Donald G. "Women's Scores on the M and F Forms of the SVIB." *Voc Guid Q* 12:116–8 w '63–64. * (*PA* 38:9344)

600. Launer, Philip T. *The Relationship of Given Interest-Patterns to Certain Aspects of Personality.* Doctor's thesis, New York University (New York, N.Y.), 1963. (*DA* 24:2564)

601. Lee, Eugene C. "Career Development of Science Teachers." *J Res Sci Teach* 1:54–63 Mr '63. *

602. Lester, Robert Andrew. *The Relationship of SVIB and ACT Scores to Differential Academic Achievement.* Doctor's thesis, University of Minnesota (Minneapolis, Minn.), 1963. (*DA* 24:1076)

603. Lind, Amy. "Measured Personality Characteristics of Occupational Therapy Graduates and Undergraduates at the University of North Dakota." *Univ N Dak Col Ed Rec* 48:69–73 F '63. *

604. Pollack, Irwin W., and Kiev, Ari. "Spatial Orientation and Psychotherapy: An Experimental Study of Perception." *J Nerv & Mental Dis* 137:93–7 Jl '63. *

605. Porter, Albert. "Effect of Organization Size on Validity of Occupational-Level Score." *Personnel & Guid J* 41:547–8 F '63. *

606. Schumacher, Charles F. "Interest and Personality Factors as Related to Choice of Medical Career." *J Med Ed* 38:932–42 N '63. *

607. Sherry, Nancy Marie. *Inconsistency Between Measured Interest and Choice of College Major.* Doctor's thesis, University of California (Berkeley, Calif.), 1963. (*DA* 24:2368)

608. Smith, Louis M., and Wientge, Kingsley M. "Some Observations on the Vocational Interests of Gifted Adolescents in an Intensive Summer Academic Experience." *Personnel & Guid J* 42:15–20 S '63. *

609. Steimel, Raymond J., and Suziedelis, Antanas. "Perceived Parental Influence and Inventoried Interests." *J Counsel Psychol* 10:289–95 f '63. * (*PA* 38:4751)

610. Strong, Edward K., Jr. "Reworded Versus New Interest Items." *J Appl Psychol* 47:111–6 Ap '63. * (*PA* 37:8300)

611. Suziedelis, Antanas, and Steimel, Raymond J. "The Relationship of Need Hierarchies to Inventoried Interests." *Personnel & Guid J* 42:393–6 D '63. * (*PA* 39:1761)

612. Taylor, Donald W. Chap. 19, "Variables Related to Creativity and Productivity Among Men in Two Research Laboratories," pp. 228–50. In *Scientific Creativity: Its Recognition and Development.* Edited by Calvin W. Taylor and Frank Barron. New York: John Wiley & Sons, Inc., 1963. Pp. xxiv, 419. * (*PA* 38:2689)

613. Whitlock, Glenn E. "Role and Self Concepts in the Choice of the Ministry as a Vocation." *J Pastoral Care* 17:208–12 w '63. * (*PA* 38:9350)

614. Callis, Robert; West, Doral N.; and Ricksecker, E. L. *The Counselor's Handbook: Profile Interpretation of the Strong Vocational Interest Blanks.* Urbana, Ill.: R. W. Parkinson & Associates, 1964. Pp. 100. Paper. *

Alexander W. Astin, *Director of Research, American Council on Education, Washington, D.C.*

The latest (1959) manual for the *Strong Vocational Interest Blank* is well organized and provides detailed information on the rationale, construction, reliability, and validity of the SVIB, as well as an informative section on use and interpretation of the test in counseling and personnel work. Recent major research studies (*365, 382, 495*), which are summarized only briefly in the manual, now make it clear that the SVIB is useful for predicting membership in given occupations over long periods of time, and of moderate value for predicting success within a few selected occupations.

The manual does contain a somewhat misleading interpretation of Strong's 18-year follow-up study (*382*): "the chances are 50-50 that a man will enter an occupation on which he has a B rating. The chances become greater as he obtains higher scores....and....less as he obtains lower scores." The reader should have been told that these conclusions assume a 50-50 base rate in the population (which is, of course, seldom the case for a single occupation in any population). In future editions of the manual, the publisher might also consider presenting these longitudinal data in expectancy tables showing the probabilities of entering and remaining in some of the more common occupations or occupational groups as a function of the relevant scale or group keys. In particular, knowledge of the extremely low probabilities associated with scale scores of "C" should be valuable to the user.

The SVIB has for many years been a popular instrument among personnel workers in colleges and universities; there now appear to be increased efforts by the publisher to promote the use of the blank in counseling at the secondary school level. Apparently, it is assumed that knowledge of the information contained in the SVIB blank and knowledge of the vast and impressive body of relevant research will somehow enable the student and his counselor to work out a better vocational plan for the student than would be possible without such knowledge. As far as this reviewer knows, however, there is no convincing evidence to support this assumption. While this lack of evidence applies to any other test which has been recommended for use in counseling, it is hoped that the advocates of the SVIB will continue their tradition of pioneering empirical research by initiating studies to evaluate the usefulness of the SVIB in counseling and guidance.

A criticism frequently made of the SVIB is that scoring is a tedious and costly procedure. However, there are now in existence several commercial firms which provide rapid and accurate scoring at a cost of approximately 65 cents per blank. Slightly lower rates are available if large numbers of blanks are scored at one time.

In comparison with competing tests, the major liability of the SVIB would seem to be the complex problem of interpreting a profile based on such a large number of scales, although the extensive work which has recently been done with group keys (*365*) has alleviated much of this difficulty. In any case, there is still little doubt that the SVIB remains as the best constructed and most thoroughly validated instrument of its kind.

EDWARD J. FURST, *Associate Professor of Psychology, The Ohio State University, Columbus, Ohio.*

During the 10-year period since the previous review, the vitality of this inventory has continued undiminished. Important publications include the author's *Vocational Interests 18 Years After College* (*382*), Darley and Hagenah's *Vocational Interest Measurement* (*365*), and a new manual. To these should be added such further interpretive aids as Layton's monograph (*495*), substantial treatments in testing books, such as that by Super and Crites (*576*), and upwards of a hundred research studies in periodicals and dissertations. Moreover, in 1958 a national committee was established to provide a clearing house and depository to facilitate research on the blank and to insure continuing evaluation of it; and, in 1962, Strong announced that a revised blank was to be published in the near future.

With a revision forthcoming, it may seem unnecessary to review the current form. There are, however, at least a few good reasons for doing so. One is that purposes, theory, and technique remain essentially the same. Strong still holds to his original position that the objective is not to measure interests as such, but to differentiate men engaged in different occupations and thus to aid young persons to find the occupation best suited to them. Another reason is that the current form may well be in use yet for some years. (Disregarding 43 items to be reworded only and scored as before, about 102 of the 400 items will be new. Existing scales, based upon the 298 carryover items, will continue in use until gradually replaced by new scales based upon the entire new form. Preliminary results on certain of the scales have shown that the elimination of the 102 items does not lower the validity.)

The current blank bears the copyright date 1946 but, except for minor changes on the score page, it is the same as the 1938 revision. The score page is even more up to date than the manual, as it now provides spaces for scores on 50 specific occupational scales. Prospective users of the inventory should appreciate that it is more than a survey of interests. An inspection of the 400 items, the vast majority of which are answered Like, Indifferent, or Dislike, reveals that most of them elicit attitudes about a great variety of stimuli not primarily vocational in content. The items are of a kind that could just as well appear on a "personality" inventory. It is not at all surprising, then, that the scores show high retest consistency in late adolescence and adulthood, nor that high and low scores on many scales correlate with outside ratings of personality.

The revised manual, running to 40 pages, impresses the reviewer as being comprehensive yet concise and functional. It combines the separate men's and women's manuals, and includes much more helpful material on interpretation than the earlier edition. The author was especially careful to indicate the limitations of the four nonoccupational scales—Interest Maturity, Occupational Level, Masculinity-Femininity, and Specialization Level, scales which, because of their ambiguity, could just as well have been dropped. Despite its thoroughness, the manual necessarily leaves out a great deal of background material which the professional user can best get from books and monographs on the inventory. On the interpretation of scores in the so-called chance range, the manual and the profile report form are not now up to date. Current research has shown that such scores are not random scores in the sense that tosses of dice are random (*537*, *585*).

The basic merit of the Strong is that it gives scores on specific occupational scales through a comprehensive inventory. At the same time, this feature invites an overemphasis upon occupational labels in counseling. Fortunately, modern counseling theory can forestall that tendency. There is also the problem of broadening the usefulness of the results beyond the specific occupational scales. To some extent, the use of "pattern analysis," the grouping of scales into clusters, and the provision of group keys will meet this need. But these refinements place a heavy demand upon the user, so that the Strong is not a suitable device for the untrained. Also, the present interest clusters are somewhat tentative and incomplete; they need to be clarified and their number increased. The proposed revision, through the substitution of 102 new items, should help realize these changes as well as provide for additional specific scales.

Scoring of the Strong is inherently laborious, even with the prospect of unit weights in lieu of the present −4 to +4 weights. However, the availability of fast and inexpensive electronic scoring services minimizes this handicap and, in fact, will permit a vastly greater exploitation of the instrument's possibilities. Users should be able to look forward to scoring keys that not only differentiate men in a given occupation from men in general, but also distinguish men in a given occupation from men in other specific occupations—a comparison which, as Kuder has recently argued, almost always reflects the kind of vocational decision the person must make. To be a truly multistage instrument, then, the Strong must provide these additional scales which permit finer differentiation of interests. With its 400 items, as against 100 in the Kuder Occupational (Form D), it would seem to have a splendid potential for this.

All in all, the Strong remains a solidly based but rather complex inventory suitable mainly for older adolescents and adults considering higher level occupations. It may be used with mature adolescents as young as 14 or 15 but is most widely used with college students. For such uses, the Strong is probably still preferable to its leading rival, the Kuder Vocational, but the latter has its own special advantages and uses. In any case, the two instruments differ enough as to justify using both in some cases. It is perhaps still too early to compare the Strong and the Kuder Occupational (Form D), as the latter is relatively new.

For reviews by Edward S. Bordin and Elmer D. Hinckley, see 4:747; for reviews by Harold D. Carter, John G. Darley, and N. W. Morton, see 40:1680; for a review by John G. Darley of an earlier edition, see 38:1178; for excerpts from related book reviews, see B304-5, 5:B115, 5:B414, 4:748, 3:648, 3:650, and 3:652.

[1071]

***Strong Vocational Interest Blank for Women, Revised.** Ages 17 and over; 1933–62; 31 scoring scales (30 occupational scales and 1 nonvocational scale): artist ('46), author ('46), librarian ('46), English teacher ('46), social worker ('46–'54), psychologist ('46), lawyer ('46), social science teacher ('46), Y.W.C.A. secretary ('46), life insurance saleswoman ('46), buyer ('46), housewife ('46), elementary teacher ('46) by Ralph Bedell, music performer ('54), music teacher ('54), office worker ('47), stenographer-secretary ('47), home economics teacher ('46), dietitian ('46), college physical education teacher ('55) by Rosena M. Wilson, high school physical education teacher ('46) by Patricia Collins, occupational therapist ('46), nurse ('46), mathematics-science teacher ('46), dentist ('46), laboratory technician ('46), physician ('46), business education teacher ('48) by H. F. Koepke, engineer ('54), physical therapist ('58), femininity-masculinity ('47); IBM, NCS, MRC, Hankes, and FAST; Form W ('46, c1933–46); 2 editions: hand scored edition (8 pages); machine scored edition (7 pages); combined manual ('59, 40 pages) for this test and 1070; profile ('46, 2 pages); student's guide to profile interpretation ('62, 4 pages); separate answer sheets or cards must be used with machine scored edition; $4 per 25 expendable tests; $6 per 25 reusable tests; $2.50 per 50 IBM answer sheets; $3.25 per 50 NCS answer sheets (scored by National Computer Systems only, see 671); $4 per 50 sets of FAST answer cards; see 667 for prices of Hankes answer sheets and scoring services; see 670 for prices of MRC answer sheets and scoring services; hand scoring stencils: $1.25 per single scale, $10 per set of any 10 scales, $25 per complete set; IBM scoring stencils (IBM scoring of a large number of scales is not recommended): $3 per single scale, $28 per set of any 10 scales, $75 per complete set; $1.25 per 25 profiles; $3.50 per 50 student's profile guides; $2.50 per manual; $1.50 per combined specimen set (includes description and student's profile guide but not manual or scoring stencils) of SVIB for men and for women: postage extra; special service available for end-of-year testing of high school juniors: fee, 75¢ per student (fee includes loan of tests, scoring service, profile report the following September, and copy of student's guide); (30–60) minutes; Edward K. Strong, Jr.; Consulting Psychologists Press, Inc. *

REFERENCES

1–9. See 40:1681.
10–45. See 3:649.
46–64. See 5:869.
65. BIRD, DOROTHY JEAN. *An Analysis of Psychological Needs of Groups of College Freshmen Women by SVIB-W Patterns.* Doctor's thesis, University of Kansas (Lawrence, Kan.), 1958.
66. HALL, OLIVE A. "Factors Related to Achievement of Home Economics Majors in Chemistry." *J Home Econ* 50:767–8 D '58. *
67. ISENBERGER, WILMA. "Self-Attitudes of Women Physical Education Major Students as Related to Measures of Interest and Success." *Res Q* 30:167–78 My '59. *
68. OBST, FRANCES. "A Study of Selected Psychometric Characteristics of Home Economics and Non-Home Economics Women at the University of California, Los Angeles." *Calif J Ed Res* 10:180–4+ S '59. * (*PA* 34:7957)
69. PETERSON, MARTHA ELIZABETH. *An Evaluation of Relationships Between Test Data and Success as a Residence Hall Counselor.* Doctor's thesis, University of Kansas (Lawrence, Kan.), 1959. (*DA* 21:3364)
70. WARREN, PHYLLIS ANN. "Vocational Interests and the Occupational Adjustment of College Women." *J Counsel Psychol* 6:140–7 su '59. * (*PA* 34:4543)
71. WHITE, BECKY J. "The Relationship of Self Concept and Parental Identification to Women's Vocational Interests." *J Counsel Psychol* 6:202–6 f '59. * (*PA* 35:3945)
72. PARKER, AILEEN WEBBER. *A Comparative Study of Selected Factors in the Vocational Development of College Women.* Doctor's thesis, Indiana University (Bloomington, Ind.), 1961. (*DA* 22:1087)
73. WEGNER, KENNETH WALTER. *An Analysis of Interest Patterns and Psychological Need Structures Related to L-I-D Response Patterns on the Strong Vocational Interest Blank for*

Women. Doctor's thesis, University of Kansas (Lawrence, Kan.), 1961. (*DA* 22:3931)
74. McCarthy, M. Kieran, and McCall, Raymond J. "Masculinity Faking on the FM Scale of an Interest Inventory." *Personnel & Guid J* 41:346–9 D '62. * (*PA* 37:7228)
75. Durflinger, Glenn W. "Personality Correlates of Success in Student-Teaching." *Ed & Psychol Meas* 23:383–90 su '63. * (*PA* 38:1427)
76. Laime, Barbara F., and Zytowski, Donald G. "Women's Scores on the M and F Forms of the SVIB." *Voc Guid Q* 12:116–8 w '63–64. * (*PA* 38:9344)

For a review by Gwendolen Schneidler Dickson, see 3:649; for a review by Ruth Strang of an earlier edition, see 40:1681; for a review by John G. Darley, see 38:1179; for excerpts from related book reviews, see B304-5, 3:650, and 3:652.

[1072]

★VALCAN Vocational Interest Profile (VIP). Ages 15 and over; 1960–61; title on manual and profile is *PSYCAN Vocational Interest Profile;* formerly called *WIPCO Vocational Interest Profile;* 9 scores: numerical, mechanical, scientific, clerical, persuasive, musical, literary, artistic, service; 1 form ('61, 4 pages, essentially the same as 1960 research edition); preliminary users' guide ('60, 8 pages); profile (2 pages); $3 per 35 tests; 3¢ per profile; 50¢ per specimen set; postage extra; (20–25) minutes; R. N. Smith and J. R. McIntosh; [Evaluation Institute of Canada (VALCAN)]. *

[1073]

★Vocational Sentence Completion Blank, Experimental Edition. High school and college; 1952–60; 28 scores: general self concern (problem, achievement, independence, satisfaction, material, obligation, effectiveness), general emphasis (intellectual, active, other people, recreational), specific preference area (outdoor, mechanical, computational, scientific, persuasive, artistic, literary, musical, social service, clerical, domestic, academic, negative academic), miscellaneous (other, negative, neutral, omit); Form D ('52, 4 pages); 6-part mimeographed manual ('59 except for 1 part copyrighted 1958, 139 pages); mimeographed norms supplement ('60, 2 pages); mimeographed profiles ['59, 1 page] for men, women; no data on reliability and validity in manual; no norms for high school; 5¢ per test; 1¢ per profile; postage extra; manual free; (40–55) minutes; Arthur A. Dole; test and profiles distributed by University of Hawaii Bookstore; manual distributed by the Author.

REFERENCES

1. Dole, Arthur A. *An Investigation of Sentence Completion as a Method of Measuring Certain Dimensions of the Normal Personality and as Applied to Prospective Teachers.* Doctor's thesis, Ohio State University (Columbus, Ohio), 1951.
2. Souza, S. P. *The Interests and Goals of Lower Division Women in Teachers College and the College of Business Administration at the University of Hawaii as Measured by the Vocational Sentence Completion Blank.* Master's thesis, University of Hawaii (Honolulu, Hawaii), 1953.
3. Dole, Arthur A., and Fletcher, Frank M., Jr. "Some Principles in the Construction of Incomplete Sentences." *Ed & Psychol Meas* 15:101–10 su '55. * (*PA* 30:2869)
4. Dole, Arthur A. "The Vocational Sentence Completion Blank in Counseling." *J Counsel Psychol* 5:200–5 f '58. * (*PA* 34:3147)

[1074]

★William, Lynde & Williams Analysis of Interest. Male adults; 1956–62; 8 scores: management, accounting, engineering, mechanical, sales, service, teaching, writing; 1 form ('60, 4 pages); mimeographed combined manual ('62, 8 pages) for this test and test 199; no data on reliability of present edition; $4 per 25 tests, postpaid; [15] minutes; R. W. Henderson; William, Lynde & Williams. *

[1075]

★Your Educational Plans. Grades 6–9, 9–12; 1958–61, c1956–61; for analysis of biographical data and environmental factors related to educational and vocational goals; 2 levels; no data on reliability; separate answer sheets must be used; examination fee: 65¢ per student; fee includes purchase of test materials and reporting of coded responses on counselor's worksheets; $1 per counselor's kit (kits for additional counselors in participating schools free); postage extra; Samuel A. Stouffer with the assistance of Paul D. Shea (counselor's manual for *b*); Science Research Associates, Inc. *
a) [junior high school edition.] Grades 6–9; 1959; also part of *Pupil Record of Educational Progress;* 1 form, second edition ('59, 8 pages); counselor's worksheet ('59, 4 carbon-interleafed pages); no data on validity; (30–35) minutes.
b) high school edition. Grades 9–12; 1958–61; 1 form ('58, 7 pages); counselor's version ('58, 8 pages); counselor's manual ('59, 43 pages); counselor's workbook ('59, 44 pages of sample worksheets and answer sheets); counselor's worksheet ('61, 4 carbon-interleafed pages); (40–45) minutes.

REFERENCES

1. Gikas, Athena M. *An Evaluative Study of the "Your Educational Plans Inventory."* Master's thesis, Chico State College (Chico, Calif.), 1959.

Leo Goldman, *Associate Professor of Education, Brooklyn College, Brooklyn, New York.* [Review of the High School Edition.]

This questionnaire attempts to reveal the degree of realism of a high school pupil's aspirations regarding college and to identify factors which may contribute toward unrealism. The authors and editors seem to have in mind those schools in which counselors do not have enough time to interview and be well acquainted with all their counselees. For such counselors, YEP is offered as an aid in organizing the counselor's limited time, locating students with problems regarding college orientation, and determining the counselor's strategy in counseling. In addition, the inventory can provide information about the college orientation of an entire class or school, for the guidance of curriculum specialists and administrators.

The pupil answers 31 multiple choice questions regarding his educational and occupational goals, his academic success in the past, and the attitudes of his parents regarding the student's educational future. Other questions seek information about the parents' education and occupations, siblings and their educational experiences, and the family's financial condition in relation to college attendance. The questions are well constructed and soundly reflect many of the insights which have come from psychological and sociological research. There is explicit attention given, for example, to the distinction between a family's ability to finance a college education and its attitudes regarding the importance of attending college. Other important variables which have been found to influence college going are also tapped, e.g., availability of a college within commuting distance, parental occupation, and the attitudes of close friends.

A carbon copy of the answer sheet is returned to the publisher, along with an IQ, or an achievement test percentile, for each pupil. The publisher prepares a Counselor's Worksheet via IBM equipment. The worksheet contains a tabulation of all pupils, first by grade, then within each grade by high school curriculum (college preparatory or not) and whether planning to attend college, and finally in decreasing order of IQ or achievement percentile. Each pupil's responses to 22 of the YEP items are given in tabular form, a single digit being used to represent each response. In general, the coding is such that the lowest numbers are those most favorable to college entrance.

The Counselor's Manual and Workbook contain a wealth of excellent illustrative material and suggestions for interpretation of individual and class data. Many counselors would find these materials instructive and sensitizing, even without using the inventory and the tabulating service.

In effect, then, YEP is a convenient service to overloaded counselors. It asks vital questions and tabulates the answers in functional form. The counselor can quickly spot those pupils who are most likely to be thinking and acting unrealistically regarding college. The preliminary edition of YEP for the junior high school aims at an even more vital target—the realism of choice of high school course of study.

But asking good questions and tabulating the responses are only parts of the project. The part that is not yet available will hopefully provide information regarding the reliability and validity of the responses. And here we have only the publisher's promise that "statistical norms" will be reported in revised editions of the manual when available. Illustrative data from a few high schools whet the appetite, but they also suggest that all we may ever get from the publisher are predictive validity data which show the relation between responses to specific items and actual college attendance, and tables which show the interrelationship between items of the questionnaire. There is no suggestion of plans to provide construct and concurrent validity data. There is an occasional indication in the manual that the authors collected much more data during the standardization period, but it is not clear why these have not been reported in the present manual.

For the rather high cost of the limited information provided in the YEP program, users are entitled to some assurance that the answers are dependable. Otherwise YEP has little more to offer at this time than convenience. Each school can easily enough make up its own questions about college orientation and tabulate the answers. In fact, there may, for some schools at least, be an advantage in using a local form: it can address itself more specifically to the facts and attitudes which are of particular importance and concern in that school and community.

YEP is, in summary, a well conceived and well designed questionnaire to get at the realism of a pupil's orientation toward college. The scoring and tabulating service appears to be well organized and to provide a great deal of important information in usable form. There is, however, almost no evidence regarding the reliability and validity of the instrument. Until such evidence is reported, this questionnaire must be considered tentative and should be interpreted with great caution.

Personnel & Guid J 38:754–8 My '60. Henry Borow and Donald E. Super. * The reviewers do not intend the foregoing catalogue of reservations [see original review for critical comments not excerpted] to convey general disapproval of Your Educational Plans or to imply that this instrument cannot be made useful to the working counselor. They believe it possesses considerable potential merit. The kinds of events and attitudes it draws upon to build its picture of the student are not new or of unknown validity. Experimental work with weighted application blanks, standardized interviews, and autobiographical records has been known to the literature for a quarter of a century or more. But while these approaches to the diagnosis and prediction of behavior have had some visible impact upon industrial and military personnel psychology, they have had peculiarly little influence upon the systematic practices of guidance counselors. And now comes this new tool which implicitly recognizes the restricted value of conventional psychometric devices as unilateral predictors of the major social choices and actions of youth and which attempts to do something about it. Your Educational Plans draws upon crucial social variables which bear upon college intentions and decisions and provides the counselor with one method of fusing the data they yield with findings derived from tests and grades. Judiciously used, such an ingathering and summarizing procedure permits the counselor to correct and enlarge his image of the student as an academic person and, consequently, to make sounder inferences about his educational prospects. Still, if it is to serve school counselors with maximum effectiveness, Your Educational Plans will have to undergo many of the modifications which the reviewers have proposed. The professional eminence of those associated with the development of this instrument, the impressive philanthropic foundation support from which it has benefited, the provisions which have been farsightedly evolved for insuring continuing work with it —all these produce bright expectations which the actual product, as it now stands, falls far short of fulfilling. Yet, these same conditions of strength make wholly possible and, indeed, even likely the refinement and expanding usefulness of Your Educational Plans which the reviewers are urging.

[Other Tests]

For tests not listed above, see the following entries in *Tests in Print:* 1856, 1859, 1862, 1864, 1867–9, 1871, 1877, 1881–3, 1886, and 1889–91; out of print: 1863, 1872, and 1876; status unknown: 1855 and 1880.

MANUAL DEXTERITY

[1076]

★APT Manual Dexterity Test. Automobile and truck mechanics and mechanics' helpers; 1960; 1 form; manual (4 pages); no data on reliability; distribution restricted to clients; $19.50 per set of testing materials, postage extra; (10–20) minutes; Associated Personnel Technicians, Inc. *

[1077]

***Minnesota Rate of Manipulation Test, [1946 Edition].** Adults; 1931–57; revision of the 1933 edition of the same title which is still available and which is a revision of *Minnesota Manual Dexterity Test* ('31); 5 scores: placing, turning, displacing, 1-hand turning and placing, 2-hand turning and placing; individual; 1 form ('33); manual ('57, 18 pages, identical with manual copyrighted in 1946 except for new norms for placing and turning); $34 per set of testing materials including manual; 75¢ per manual purchased separately; postage extra; (10–15) minutes; Gilbert L. Betts (manual) and W. A. Ziegler; Educational Test Bureau. *

REFERENCES

1–4. See 40:1662.
5–26. See 3:663.
27. MOORE, JOSEPH E. "A Test of Eye-Hand Coordination." *J Appl Psychol* 21:668–72 D '37. * (*PA* 12:2919)
28. HACKMAN, RAY CARTER. *The Differential Prediction of Success in Two Contrasting Vocational Areas.* Doctor's thesis, University of Minnesota (Minneapolis, Minn.), 1940.
29. TIFFIN, JOSEPH, AND ROGERS, H. B. "The Selection and Training of Inspectors." *Personnel* 18:14–31 Jl '41. *
30. WALKER, K. F., AND OXLADE, M. N. "A Tentative Battery of Tests for the Selection of Women for Cotton Textile Spinning." *B Ind Psychol & Personnel Prac* 2:6–27 Je '46. * (*PA* 20:4871)
31. STRANGE, J. R., AND SARTAIN, A. Q. "Veterans' Scores on the Purdue Pegboard Test." *J Appl Psychol* 32:35–40 F '48. * (*PA* 23:771)
32. GEIST, HAROLD. "The Performance of Amputees on Motor Dexterity Tests." *Ed & Psychol Meas* 9:765–72 w '49. * (*PA* 26:2950)
33. SUPER, DONALD E. *Appraising Vocational Fitness by Means of Psychological Tests,* pp. 187–203. New York: Harper & Brothers, 1949. Pp. xxiii, 727. * (*PA* 24:2130)
34. BAUMAN, MARY K. Chap. 8, "Mechanical and Manual Ability Tests for Use With the Blind," pp. 97–113. (*PA* 26: 487) In *Psychological Diagnosis and Counseling of the Adult Blind: Selected Papers From the Proceedings of the University of Michigan Conference for the Blind, 1947.* Edited by Wilma Donahue and Donald Dabelstein. New York: American Foundation for the Blind, Inc., 1950. Pp. vii, 173. *
35. WYNDHAM, A. J. "Selection Tests for Machine-Shop Operators." *B Ind Psychol & Personnel Prac* 8:12–21 S '52. * (*PA* 27:5454)
36. BODLEY, E. A. "Selection Tests for Women Packers." *B Ind Psychol & Personnel Prac* 9:24–32 Mr '53. *
37. FLEISHMAN, EDWIN A. "A Note on the Minnesota Rate of Manipulation Test as a Time Limit Test." *Ed & Psychol Meas* 14:156–60 sp '54. * (*PA* 28:7520)
38. FLEISHMAN, EDWIN A., AND HEMPEL, WALTER E. "A Factor Analysis of Dexterity Tests." *Personnel Psychol* 7: 15–32 sp '54. * (*PA* 29:2061)
39. TOPETZES, NICK JOHN. "A Program for the Selection of Trainees in Physical Medicine." *J Exp Ed* 25:263–311 Je '57. * (*PA* 33:7024)
40. BAUMAN, MARY K. *A Manual of Norms for Tests Used in Counseling Blind Persons.* AFB Publications, Research Series, No. 6. New York: American Foundation for the Blind, 1958. Pp. 40. * (*PA* 32:1949)
41. DISTEFANO, MICHAEL K., JR.; ELLIS, NORMAN R.; AND SLOAN, WILLIAM. "Motor Proficiency in Mental Defectives." *Percept & Motor Skills* 8:231–4 S '58. * (PA 33:5438)
42. SHORE, RICHARD P. "Validity Information Exchange, No. 11-24: D.O.T. Code 1-25.68, Proof-Machine Operator." *Personnel Psychol* 11:438–9 au '58. *
43. BOURASSA, G. LEE, AND GUION, ROBERT M. "A Factorial Study of Dexterity Tests." *J Appl Psychol* 43:199–204 Je '59. * (*PA* 34:6585)
44. DRUSSELL, RUTH D. "Relationship of Minnesota Rate of Manipulation Test With the Industrial Work Performance of the Adult Cerebral Palsied." *Am J Occup Ther* 13:93–6+ Mr–Ap '59. * (*PA* 34:1869)
45. JAYALAKSHMI, G. "Correlation of Tests of Psychomotor Ability With Intelligence and Non-motor Tests." *J Psychol Res* 3:78–84 S '59. *
46. JAYALAKSHMI, G. "Studies in Psychomotor Abilities." *J Psychol Res* 3:13–20 Ja '59. *
47. PARKER, JAMES F., JR., AND FLEISHMAN, EDWIN A. "Ability Factors and Component Performance Measures as Predictors of Complex Tracking Behavior." *Psychol Monogr* 74(16):1–36 '60. * (*PA* 36:2CD36P)
48. FLEISHMAN, EDWIN A., AND ELLISON, GAYLORD D. "A Factor Analysis of Fine Manipulative Tests." *J Appl Psychol* 46:96–105 Ap '62. *
49. SUPER, DONALD E., AND CRITES, JOHN O. *Appraising Vocational Fitness by Means of Psychological Tests, Revised Edition,* pp. 185–200. New York: Harper & Brothers, 1962. Pp. xv, 688. * (*PA* 37:2038)
50. WOLINS, LEROY, AND MACKINNEY, ARTHUR C. "Validity Information Exchange, No. 15-04: D.O.T. Code 9-68.30, Packer II." *Personnel Psychol* 15:227–9 su '62. *

For reviews by Edwin E. Ghiselli and John R. Kinzer, see 3:663 (1 excerpt); for reviews by Lorene Teegarden and Morris S. Viteles, see 40:1662.

[1078]

O'Connor Finger Dexterity Test. Ages 14 and over; 1920–26(?); individual; 1 form ['26?]; mimeographed manual ['26?, 4 pages, includes a 1940 reference]; no data on reliability; $20 per set of testing materials, postage extra; (8–16) minutes; Johnson O'Connor; C. H. Stoelting Co. *

REFERENCES

1–15. See 40:1659.
16. McCullough, Constance M. *Prediction of Success in the School of Dentistry at the University of Minnesota by Means of Tests and Certain Other Factors.* Doctor's thesis, University of Minnesota (Minneapolis, Minn.), 1938.
17. Thompson, Claude Edward. *A Study of Motor and Mechanical Abilities.* Doctor's thesis, Ohio State University (Columbus, Ohio), 1939.
18. Hackman, Ray Carter. *The Differential Prediction of Success in Two Contrasting Vocational Areas.* Doctor's thesis, University of Minnesota (Minneapolis, Minn.), 1940.
19. O'Connor, Johnson. *Unsolved Business Problems,* pp. 85–6. Boston, Mass.: Human Engineering Laboratory, Inc., 1940. Pp. x, 159. *
20. Stead, William H.; Shartle, Carroll L.; Otis, Jay L.; Ward, Raymond S.; Osborne, Herbert F.; Endler, O. L.; Dvorak, Beatrice J.; Cooper, John H.; Bellows, Roger M.; and Kolbe, Laverne E. *Occupational Counseling Techniques: Their Development and Application.* Published for the Technical Board of the Occupational Research Program, United States Employment Service. New York: American Book Co., 1940. Pp. ix, 273. *
21. Blum, Milton, and Candee, Beatrice. "The Selection of Department Store Packers and Wrappers With the Aid of Certain Psychological Tests." *J Appl Psychol* 25:76–85 F '41. * (*PA* 15:3104)
22. Blum, Milton L., and Candee, Beatrice. "The Selection of Department Store Packers and Wrappers With the Aid of Certain Psychological Tests: Study 2." *J Appl Psychol* 25:291–9 Je '41. * (*PA* 15:4336)
23. Morrow, Robert S. "An Experimental Analysis of the Theory of Independent Abilities." *J Ed Psychol* 32:495–512 O '41. * (*PA* 16:2209)
24. O'Connor, Johnson. *The Too Many Aptitude Woman,* pp. 47–53, passim. Boston, Mass.: Human Engineering Laboratory, Inc., 1941. Pp. xii, 185. *
25. Bennett, George K., and Cruikshank, Ruth M. *A Summary of Manual and Mechanical Ability Tests, Preliminary Form,* pp. 59–60. New York: Psychological Corporation, 1942. Pp. v, 74. *
26. Ghiselli, Edwin E. "Estimating the Minimal Reliability of a Total Test From the Intercorrelations Among, and the Standard Deviations of, the Component Parts." *J Appl Psychol* 26:332–7 Je '42. * (*PA* 16:3863)
27. Thompson, Claude Edward. "Motor and Mechanical Abilities in Professional Schools." *J Appl Psychol* 26:24–37 F '42. * (*PA* 16:2483)
28. Ghiselli, Edwin E. "The Use of the Minnesota Rate of Manipulation and the O'Connor Finger Dexterity Tests in the Selection of Package Wrappers." *J Appl Psychol* 27:33–4 F '43. * (*PA* 17:2851)
29. Jacobsen, Eldon E. "An Evaluation of Certain Tests in Predicting Mechanic Learner Achievement." *Ed & Psychol Meas* 3:259–67 au '43. * (*PA* 18:2537)
30. O'Connor, Johnson. *Structural Visualization,* pp. 51–5, passim. Boston, Mass.: Human Engineering Laboratory, Inc., 1943. Pp. xiv, 182. *
31. Ross, Lawrence W. "Results of Testing Machine-Tool Trainees." *Personnel J* 21:363–7 Ap '43. * (*PA* 17:2459)
32. Surgent, Louis Vincent. "The Use of Aptitude Tests in the Selection of Radio Tube Mounters." *Psychol Monogr* 61(2):1–40 '47. *
33. Tiffin, Joseph. *Industrial Psychology, Second Edition,* pp. 122–5, 131–44. New York: Prentice-Hall, Inc., 1947. Pp. xxi, 553. *
34. Rinsland, Henry D. "The Prediction of Veterans' Success From Test Scores at the University of Oklahoma." *Yearb Nat Council Meas Used Ed* 6:59–72 pt 1 '49. *
35. Super, Donald E. *Appraising Vocational Fitness by Means of Psychological Tests,* pp. 203–17. New York: Harper & Brothers, 1949. Pp. xxiii, 727. * (*PA* 24:2130)
36. Laney, Arthur R., Jr. "Validity of Employment Tests for Gas-Appliance Service Personnel." *Personnel Psychol* 4:199–208 su '51. * (*PA* 26:1735)
37. Bodley, E. A. "Selection Tests for Women Packers." *B Ind Psychol & Personnel Prac* 9:24–32 Mr '53. * (*PA* 29:1633)
38. Fleishman, Edwin A. "A Modified Administration Procedure for the O'Connor Finger Dexterity Test." *J Appl Psychol* 37:191–4 Je '53. * (*PA* 28:3349)
39. Fleishman, Edwin A., and Hempel, Walter E. "A Factor Analysis of Dexterity Tests." *Personnel Psychol* 7:15–32 sp '54. * (*PA* 29:2061)
40. Prakash, J. C. "Standardised Norms for Selected Psychological Tests." *Indian J Psychol* 31:147–8 Jl–D '56. * (*PA* 35:3975)
41. Bourassa, G. Lee, and Guion, Robert M. "A Factorial Study of Dexterity Tests." *J Appl Psychol* 43:199–204 Je '59. * (*PA* 34:6585)
42. Jayalakshmi, G. "Correlation of Tests of Psychomotor Ability With Intelligence and Non-motor Tests." *J Psychol Res* 3:78–84 S '59. *
43. Jayalakshmi, G. "Studies in Psychomotor Abilities." *J Psychol Res* 3:13–20 Ja '59. *
44. Parker, James F., Jr., and Fleishman, Edwin A. "Ability Factors and Component Performance Measures as Predictors of Complex Tracking Behavior." *Psychol Monogr* 74(16):1–36 '60. * (*PA* 36:2CD36P)
45. Fleishman, Edwin A., and Ellison, Gaylord D. "A Factor Analysis of Fine Manipulative Tests." *J Appl Psychol* 46:96–105 Ap '62. *
46. Rim, Y. "The Predictive Validity of Seven Manual Dexterity Tests." *Psychologia* 5:52–5 Mr '62. * (*PA* 38:1417)
47. Super, Donald E., and Crites, John O. *Appraising Vocational Fitness by Means of Psychological Tests, Revised Edition,* pp. 200–13. New York: Harper & Brothers, 1962. Pp. xv, 688. * (*PA* 37:2038)

For a review by Morris S. Viteles, see 40:1659.

[1079]

O'Connor Tweezer Dexterity Test. Ages 14 and over; 1920–28(?); individual; 1 form ['28?]; mimeographed manual ['28(?), 4 pages, includes a 1937 reference]; no data on reliability; $21 per set of testing materials, postage extra; (8–10) minutes; Johnson O'Connor; C. H. Stoelting Co. *

REFERENCES

1–13. See 40:1678.
14. McCullough, Constance M. *Prediction of Success in the School of Dentistry at the University of Minnesota by Means of Tests and Certain Other Factors.* Doctor's thesis, University of Minnesota (Minneapolis, Minn.), 1938.
15. Thompson, Claude Edward. *A Study of Motor and Mechanical Abilities.* Doctor's thesis, Ohio State University (Columbus, Ohio), 1939.
16. Hackman, Ray Carter. *The Differential Prediction of Success in Two Contrasting Vocational Areas.* Doctor's thesis, University of Minnesota (Minneapolis, Minn.), 1940.
17. O'Connor, Johnson. *Unsolved Business Problems,* pp. 87–9. Boston, Mass.: Human Engineering Laboratory, Inc., 1940. Pp. x, 159. *
18. Stead, William H.; Shartle, Carroll L.; Otis, Jay L.; Ward, Raymond S.; Osborne, Herbert F.; Endler, O. L.; Dvorak, Beatrice J.; Cooper, John H.; Bellows, Roger M.; and Kolbe, Laverne E. *Occupational Counseling Techniques: Their Development and Application.* Published for the Technical Board of the Occupational Research Program, United States Employment Service. New York: American Book Co., 1940. Pp. ix, 273. *
19. Morrow, Robert S. "An Experimental Analysis of the Theory of Independent Abilities." *J Ed Psychol* 32:495–512 O '41. * (*PA* 16:2209)
20. O'Connor, Johnson. *The Too Many Aptitude Woman,* pp. 53–4, passim. Boston, Mass.: Human Engineering Laboratory, Inc., 1941. Pp. xii, 185. *
21. Bennett, George K., and Cruikshank, Ruth M. *A Summary of Manual and Mechanical Ability Tests, Preliminary Form,* pp. 59–60. New York: Psychological Corporation, 1942. Pp. v, 74. *
22. Crissey, Orlo L. "Test Predictive of Success in Occupation of Job-Setter." Abstract. *Psychol B* 39:436 Jl '42. *
23. Thompson, Claude Edward. "Motor and Mechanical Abilities in Professional Schools." *J Appl Psychol* 26:24–37 F '42. * (*PA* 16:2483)
24. Jacobsen, Eldon E. "An Evaluation of Certain Tests in Predicting Mechanic Learner Achievement." *Ed & Psychol Meas* 3:259–67 au '43. * (*PA* 18:2537)
25. O'Connor, Johnson. *Structural Visualization,* pp. 51–5, passim. Boston, Mass.: Human Engineering Laboratory, Inc., 1943. Pp. xiv, 182. *
26. Surgent, Louis Vincent. "The Use of Aptitude Tests in the Selection of Radio Tube Mounters." *Psychol Monogr* 61(2):1–40 '47. *
27. Beamer, George C.; Edmonson, Lawrence D.; and Strother, George B. "Improving the Selection of Linotype Trainees." *J Appl Psychol* 32:130–4 Ap '48. * (*PA* 23:965)

28. SUPER, DONALD E. *Appraising Vocational Fitness by Means of Psychological Tests*, pp. 203–17. New York: Harper & Brothers, 1949. Pp. xxiii, 727. * (*PA* 24:2130)
29. PETRIE, ASENATH, AND POWELL, MURIEL B. "The Selection of Nurses in England." *J Appl Psychol* 35:281–6 Ag '51. * (*PA* 26:3090)
30. ALBRIGHT, LEWIS E. "Validity Information Exchange, No. 9-44: D.O.T. Code 0-66.93, Seed Analyst." *Personnel Psychol* 9:522–3 w '56. *
31. ALBRIGHT, LEWIS EDWIN. *The Development of a Selection Process for an Inspection Task.* Doctor's thesis, Purdue University (Lafayette, Ind.), 1956. (*DA* 16:2201)
32. PRAKASH, J. C. "Standardised Norms for Selected Psychological Tests." *Indian J Psychol* 31:147–8 Jl–D '56. * (*PA* 35:3975)
33. BOURASSA, G. LEE, AND GUION, ROBERT M. "A Factorial Study of Dexterity Tests." *J Appl Psychol* 43:199–204 Je '59. * (*PA* 34:6585)
34. LEE, TERENCE. "The Selection of Student Nurses: A Revised Procedure." *Occup Psychol* 33:209–16 O '59. *
35. RIM, Y. "The Predictive Validity of Seven Manual Dexterity Tests." *Psychologia* 5:52–5 Mr '62. * (*PA* 38:1417)
36. SUPER, DONALD E., AND CRITES, JOHN O. *Appraising Vocational Fitness by Means of Psychological Tests, Revised Edition*, pp. 200–13. New York: Harper & Brothers, 1962. Pp. xv, 688. * (*PA* 37:2038)

For a review by Morris S. Viteles, see 40:1678.

[1080]

★**Purdue Hand Precision Test.** Ages 17 and over; 1941; 3 scores: attempts, correct responses, error time; individual; apparatus ['41]; no manual; typewritten instructions (2 pages); no data on reliability; no norms; administration time not reported; $115 per instrument, postage extra; [Joseph Tiffin]; [Lafayette Instrument Co.]. *

REFERENCES

1. TIFFIN, JOSEPH, AND ROGERS, H. B. "The Selection and Training of Inspectors." *Personnel* 18:14–31 Jl '41. *
2. TIFFIN, JOSEPH. *Industrial Psychology, Second Edition*, pp. 76, 78, 128–9, 304–8. New York: Prentice-Hall, Inc., 1947. Pp. xxi, 553. * (*PA* 22:505)

[1081]

Purdue Pegboard. Grades 9–16 and adults; 1941–48; 5 scores: right hand, left hand, both hands, right plus left plus both hands, assembly; 1 form ('41); manual ('48, 8 pages); profile ('48, 2 pages); $18.95 per set of testing apparatus and manual; 95¢ per 20 profiles; postage extra; 2.5(10) or 7.5(20) minutes; Purdue Research Foundation under the direction of Joseph Tiffin; Science Research Associates, Inc. *

REFERENCES

1–3. See 3:666.
4–15. See 4:751.
16–26. See 5:873.
27. SHORE, RICHARD P. "Validity Information Exchange, No. 11-24: D.O.T. Code 1-25.68, Proof-Machine Operator." *Personnel Psychol* 11:438–9 au '58. *
28. BOURASSA, G. LEE, AND GUION, ROBERT M. "A Factorial Study of Dexterity Tests." *J Appl Psychol* 43:199–204 Je '59. * (*PA* 34:6585)
29. EYMAN, RICHARD K.; DINGMAN, HARVEY F.; AND WINDLE, CHARLES. "Manipulative Dexterity and Movement History of Mental Defectives." *Percept & Motor Skills* 9:291–4 S '59. * (*PA* 34:6216)
30. MAXFIELD, KATHRYN E., AND PERRY, JAMES D. "Performance of Blind Vocational Rehabilitation Clients on the Purdue Pegboard." *Percept & Motor Skills* 11:139–46 O '60. * (*PA* 35:2495)
31. PARKER, JAMES F., JR., AND FLEISHMAN, EDWIN A. "Ability Factors and Component Performance Measures as Predictors of Complex Tracking Behavior." *Psychol Monogr* 74(16):1–36 '60. * (*PA* 36:2CD36P)
32. TOBIAS, JACK, AND GORELICK, JACK. "The Effectiveness of the Purdue Pegboard in Evaluating Work Potential of Retarded Adults." *Training Sch B* 57:94–104 N '60. * (*PA* 35:3791)
33. HOAG, RALPH LYNN. *A Comparative Study of Certain Motor Skills of Deaf and Hearing Mentally Retarded Children.* Doctor's thesis, University of Arizona (Tucson, Ariz.), 1961. (*DA* 22:488)
34. MOFFIE, D. J. "The Selection of Employees in Industry." *Arch Environ Health* 3:94–9 Jl '61. *
35. ZUBIN, JOSEPH; SUTTON, SAMUEL; SALZINGER, KURT; SALZINGER, SUZANNE; BURDOCK, E. I.; AND PERETZ, DAVID. Chap. 10, "A Biometric Approach to Prognosis in Schizophrenia," pp. 143–203. In *Comparative Epidemiology of the Mental Disorders.* The Proceedings of the Forty-Ninth Annual Meeting of the American Psychopathological Association, Held in New York City, February 1959. Edited by Paul H. Hoch and Joseph Zubin. New York: Grune & Stratton, Inc., 1961. Pp. xvi, 290. * (*PA* 36:2JV90H)
36. FLEISHMAN, EDWIN A., AND ELLISON, GAYLORD D. "A Factor Analysis of Fine Manipulative Tests." *J Appl Psychol* 46:96–105 Ap '62. *
37. RIM, Y. "The Predictive Validity of Seven Manual Dexterity Tests." *Psychologia* 5:52–5 Mr '62. * (*PA* 38:1417)
38. SUPER, DONALD E., AND CRITES, JOHN O. *Appraising Vocational Fitness by Means of Psychological Tests, Revised Edition*, pp. 213–7. New York: Harper & Brothers, 1962. Pp. xv, 688. * (*PA* 37:2038)
39. VAUGHAN, HERBERT G., JR., AND COSTA, LOUIS D. "Performance of Patients With Lateralized Cerebral Lesions: 2, Sensory and Motor Tests." *J Nerv & Mental Dis* 134:237–43 Mr '62. * (*PA* 37:1664)
40. WOLINS, LEROY, AND MACKINNEY, ARTHUR C. "Validity Information Exchange, No. 15-04: D.O.T. Code 9-68.30, Packer II." *Personnel Psychol* 15:227–9 su '62. *
41. COSTA, LOUIS D.; VAUGHAN, HERBERT G., JR.; LEVITA, ERIC; AND FARBER, NORMAN. "Purdue Pegboard as a Predictor of the Presence and Laterality of Cerebral Lesions." *J Consult Psychol* 27:133–7 Ap '63. * (*PA* 37:8141)

For a review by Neil D. Warren, see 5:873; for reviews by Edwin E. Ghiselli, Thomas W. Harrell, and Albert Gibson Packard, see 3:666.

[Other Tests]

For tests not listed above, see the following entries in *Tests in Print:* 1898–9, 1902–3, 1905, 1908, and 1911; status unknown: 1897 and 1900–1.

MECHANICAL ABILITY

[1082]

*__A.C.E.R. Mechanical Reasoning Test.__ Ages 13-9 and over; 1951–62; abbreviated adaptation of *A.C.E.R. Mechanical Comprehension Test;* 1 form ['51, 4 pages]; revised manual ('62, 15 pages); separate answer sheets must be used; 6*s.* per 10 tests; 2*s.* per 10 answer sheets; 1*s.* per scoring stencil; 3*s.* per manual; 4*s.* 9*d.* per specimen set; postpaid within Australia; 20(30) minutes; T. M. Whitford (revised manual), Research and Guidance Branch, Queensland Department of Public Instruction (test), and the Australian Council for Educational Research; Australian Council for Educational Research. *

For reviews by John R. Jennings and Hayden S. Williams, see 5:875.

[1083]

*__Chriswell Structural Dexterity Test, 1963 Revision.__ Grades 7–9; 1953–63; identical with 1953 edition except for additional norms and technical data in manual; title on manual is *Structural Dexterity Test of Mechanical Ability;* individual; Form B ('53, revision of unpublished Form A); revised manual ('63, c1953–63, 12 pages); record card ['53, 1 page]; $30 per set of testing materials, 50 record cards, and manual; $2.50 per 50 record cards; $1 per manual; postage extra; 6.5(15) minutes; M. Irving Chriswell; Vocational Guidance Service. *

REFERENCES

1. CHRISWELL, M. IRVING. "Validity of a Structural Dexterity Test." *J Appl Psychol* 37:13–5 F '53. * (*PA* 28:1618)

For a review by A. Pemberton Johnson of the 1953 edition, see 5:876.

[1084]

★College Entrance Examination Board Placement Tests: Spatial Relations Test. Entering college freshmen; 1962–63, c1954–63; tests are reprints of 1954–55 forms of *College Entrance Examination Board Special Aptitude Test in Spatial Relations;* IBM; Forms KPL1, KPL2 in a single booklet (c1954–55, 27 pages); for more complete information, see 759; 60(70) minutes; program administered for the College Entrance Examination Board by Educational Testing Service. *

REFERENCES

1. NEWMAN, SIDNEY H.; FRENCH, JOHN W.; AND BOBBITT, JOSEPH M. "Analysis of Criteria for the Validation of Selection Measures at the United States Coast Guard Academy." *Ed & Psychol Meas* 12:394–407 au '52. * (*PA* 27:6159)
2. MYERS, CHARLES T. "A Note on a Spatial Relations Pretest and Posttest." *Ed & Psychol Meas* 13:596–600 w '53. * (*PA* 28:5656)
3. BLADE, MARY F., AND WATSON, WALTER S. "Increase in Spatial Relations Test Scores During Engineering Study." *Yearb Nat Council Meas Used Ed* 11:23–9 '54. *
4. BLADE, MARY F., AND WATSON, WALTER S. "Increase in Spatial Visualization Test Scores During Engineering Study." *Psychol Monogr* 69(12):1–13 '55. * (*PA* 30:5226)

For a review of the College Entrance Examination Board Special Aptitude Test in Spatial Relations, *see 4:808.*

[1085]

★[Curtis Object Completion and Space Form Tests.] Applicants for mechanical and technical jobs; 1960–61; 1 form ('60, 1 page); 2 tests; manual ('61, 4 pages); $3 per 50 tests; $1 per specimen set (must be purchased to obtain manual); cash orders postpaid; 1(5) minutes per test; James W. Curtis; Psychometric Affiliates. *

a) OBJECT-COMPLETION TEST.
b) SPACE FORM TEST.

RICHARD S. MELTON, *Assistant Director, Test Development Division, Educational Testing Service, Princeton, New Jersey.*

These two tests are intended to provide estimates of ability to visualize separated parts of two-dimensional figures as a whole figure and to relate three-dimensional figures to their two-dimensional patterns or "unfolded designs." Each test consists of a single page of drawings (items), 24 such items in the Object-Completion Test and 16 in the Space Form Test. Each test is administered with a one-minute time limit. No data on speededness are given in the manual, but it is evident that what is being tested is the speed with which an individual can perform these tasks. However, the subjects are not told that speed of performance is important, nor are they told that only one minute will be allowed.

The first item on each test is a trial item with the correct answer given. Provision is made for the examiner to assure himself at this point that all subjects understand why this is the correct answer and to explain the task further, if necessary. This provision is obviously intended to reduce errors of measurement due to failure to understand the task, but it can also lead to the opposite kind of error for an applicant who understands the task and uses the extra explanation time to study the remainder of the items for several minutes, possibly, before the examiner gives the signal to begin. (The wisdom of printing the answer keys to the two tests in large letters on the first and last pages of the manual may also be questioned, because if the examiner were ever to pick up the manual and refer to it while administering the test, an alert examinee sitting near him could easily read off the correct answers to the test.)

Test-retest reliability coefficients, based on one sample of 150 persons, are reported as .91 for the Object-Completion Test and .86 for the Space Form Test. However, the time intervals between testings are not reported; one week would seem to be a minimum interval for tests of this kind. The correlation between the two tests could also have been obtained from these data, as well as information on practice effects, which would be substantial on tests of this type. However, no such information is reported in the manual.

No validity data of the usual kind are reported, but the manual states that sizable percentages of those who scored above the 23rd percentile on both tests and were subsequently hired were considered by their superiors to be satisfactory (or better) employees, whereas the majority of the few who scored below the 23rd percentile and were subsequently hired were reported as having significant difficulties in adapting to the requirements of their jobs. Why the 23rd percentile was chosen for a cutoff, what number of workers was involved, what the nature of their jobs was, and how many companies were represented is not indicated; thus the significance of these statements, and hence the validity of the tests, cannot be evaluated.

The primary norm table for the Object-Completion Test is based on a general unselected group of 418 male and 82 female applicants for jobs or vocational training in mechanical fields. A second table of norms is described as based on 200 skilled applicants, although the manual text says that the group was of the general unselected type described above. Two norm tables are also given for the Space Form Test, one based on 450 unselected applicants and one based on 200 skilled applicants. The latter group is described in the manual as job applicants or potential trainees for skilled work; no description of the sample of 450 is given. The final paragraph in the interpretation section of the manual recommends the establishment of local norms by each organization using the test, a recommendation heartily to be endorsed. (Lacking local norms, most users would probably do best to use the norm tables based on the larger numbers of cases, as the minor differences between these and the tables based on 200 cases may represent little more than chance departures from the values in the primary norm tables.)

EVALUATION. On the basis of the data presented in the manual, there are no grounds for recommending these tests over other tests on which there are more data. The two reliability coefficients reported are of satisfactory magnitude, but the conditions under which they were obtained are not described. It would be desirable to have additional estimates based on other samples, particularly when the tests are as short as these. The primary norm tables are based on samples of reasonable size, but the description of the composition of the samples is quite meager. It might be surmised that the majority of the individuals were tested in connection with the test author's consulting practice, and that they therefore represent a limited geographical area. Most seriously, there is no quantified evidence of either the predictive or concurrent validity of the tests. Finally, there is good reason to believe that the mode of administration of the tests is such that sizable errors of measurement could easily occur as a result of a small lapse in alertness on the part of the examiner. For these reasons, these tests are not to be recommended for use in selection until they are more adequately standardized and validated.

I. MACFARLANE SMITH, *Principal Lecturer (Research), Garnett College for Training Technical Teachers, London, England.*

The test consists of two parts. The Space Form Test presents five drawings of "unfolded" boxes. Below these there are 16 representations of three-dimensional boxes, viewed from varying angles. The subject is given one minute to match as many boxes as he can with the "unfolded" patterns printed above. The Object-Completion Test presents eight simple closed figures differing from one another in shape. Below these are 24 drawings of incomplete circles or squares, each of which may be completed by fitting one of the eight figures given above. The subject is given one minute to identify the figure required to complete each of the 24 incomplete drawings.

Each subtest consists of one sheet, printed on one side, and the total time required to work both parts is only two minutes. The material is of a kind which has long been known to provide measures of a factor named Visualization (*Vz*) in America and Spatial (*k*) in Britain. The first subtest involves thinking about objects in three dimensions and the second involves two-dimensional thinking only. The long-standing argument as to whether these two types of test material should be regarded as providing measures of two distinct factors or simply of one factor does not appear to be settled as yet. The manual states that "these two tests have been devised to provide estimates of....competence in two basic areas of mechanical aptitude and pattern visualization, with a minimal demand upon the time of the examiner and examinee."

The aims of speed and simplicity of administration seem to have been achieved, however, by ignoring most of the precautions usually taken to ensure complete understanding of the instructions and adequate sampling of the abilities tested. In the reviewer's opinion, the tests are much too short to ensure adequate standards of reliability and validity. It is well known that particular care should be taken in constructing spatial tests of these types since they are very susceptible to disturbances caused by misunderstanding of instructions or by inadequate time allowances.

At the beginning of each test, there is one worked item and one practice item, the latter misleadingly referred to in the instructions as "the first item." The manual states that if the subject answers the practice item incorrectly, the examiner should assist him to decide the correct response and only then should give the starting signal. Obviously, when the test is being given to a group of subjects, it may be difficult to prevent work being done on the test proper before the starting signal is given. Thus the time actually taken to work the test may be somewhat imprecise, and a difference of a second or two may be important when the time allowance is only one minute.

The tests comprise 22 and 14 items, respectively. Since the number of items is so small one might expect that the figures would be carefully drawn; but in fact many have been drawn very badly indeed. Lines intended to be parallel are frequently not parallel and triangles intended to be isosceles are sometimes scalene. The sector of a circle shown in the top line of one test is obviously less than a quadrant, yet in line 3, the missing corresponding part is just as obviously greater than a quadrant. The isosceles triangle shown in the top line is only about half the area of the corresponding triangle which is missing from the square in line 4. A subject gifted with high spatial ability might well be handicapped in performing this test because there are no given figures which exactly fill the gaps in some of the drawings.

In view of the shortness of the tests and the limited provision for preliminary practice, it is astonishing that the reliability coefficients are as high as those reported (.86 and .91 by the test-retest method). No reference is made in the manual to standardized scores and it is presumed that the figures for reliability are based on raw scores only. Separate tables of percentile norms for two different groups are provided. One of these tables is based on the scores obtained by a "general unselected group" of 500 applicants for jobs in the fields of mechanics, assembly work, etc. The other table is based on the scores obtained by a group of 200 "skilled applicants." These groups were composed of both men and women. It is desirable that separate tables be provided for each sex, since tests of spatial ability almost invariably show highly significant differences in mean score as between men and women.

The evidence of validity given in the manual can scarcely be regarded as satisfactory. Making every allowance for the fact that sufficient time has not yet elapsed for the collection of data from follow-up studies, the information provided is distinctly meagre. Given cutoff scores are said to discriminate between workers considered "satisfactory" and those who had "difficulty in adapting to some performance phases of the job." We should like to know how these tests compare with other tests of this type or of other types. Data from studies involving correlational, factorial, or regression analysis would have been helpful in evaluating the tests.

Until such evidence is made available, the tests cannot be recommended in their present form. Their only advantages would appear to be ease of administration and scoring and the shortness of the time required to apply them. It is difficult to think of any situation in which these advantages would offset the tests' disadvantages.

[1086]

★**Flags: A Test of Space Thinking.** Industrial employees; 1959, c1956–59; Form A ('56, 6 pages); manual ('59, 9 pages); no data on reliability; no data on validity of current form; norms for males only; $4 per 20 tests, postage extra; $1 per specimen set, postpaid; 5(10) minutes; L. L. Thurstone (test), T. E. Jeffrey (test), and Measurement Research Division, Industrial Relations Center, University of Chicago (manual); Education-Industry Service. *

I. Macfarlane Smith, *Principal Lecturer (Research), Garnett College for Training Technical Teachers, London, England.*

This test is intended to measure one of the primary mental abilities concerned with visual orientation in space, viz., the first space factor identified by Thurstone in several factor analytic studies.

The test consists of 21 items, each calling for six responses, and yields a maximum raw score of 126. The time allowed for working the test is five minutes. Each of the 21 items presents a flag on the left. There are six other flags on the right and these represent either the same or the opposite side of the flag given on the left. All six flags are in different positions, and the subject has to decide which side, the same or opposite, is represented by each of these six flags and to record his answer by crossing out either "S" or "O" underneath each flag.

The instructions are clear and well set out. The difference between the two sides of a flag is illustrated by the device of printing two sides of a flag on the front and back of the first page. This device is certainly helpful for impressing on the examinees the difference in the appearance of the flag when it has been turned over. Practice exercises are provided with the stipulation that explanation be given if examinees make mistakes on these. Thus every opportunity is given to the subject to understand the task before he is expected to begin.

The manual has some other features for

which the authors must be commended. The provision of templates markedly facilitates scoring. Guessing is allowed for by basing the final raw score on the number of correct answers less the number of wrong answers. There is a table for converting raw scores to normalized standard scores with a mean of 50 and a standard deviation of 10. The norms are based on the scores made by 278 male industrial employees.

The manual contains no information regarding reliability and validity, though no doubt data could have been supplied for the older form of the test. The present form differs from the earlier in that a different flag design is used for each item. This innovation was intended to make the test more interesting and there is no reason to suppose that either the reliability or validity will have been affected by the change. Wisely, however, the authors have not quoted figures obtained from earlier studies, pending empirical confirmation that the present version does not differ essentially from the older one. At the date of publication of the manual (1959) there were no validation studies of the present version. It is unlikely that anyone who studies the form and content of the test will seriously question its reliability.

There might, however, be some difference of opinion regarding its validity. It is intended to measure Thurstone's first space factor, which was described by him as the ability to visualize a rigid configuration when it is moved into different positions. This factor was one of five which Thurstone claimed to have identified clearly in his research on mechanical aptitude. *Flags* was not included in this research, although several other tests of the first space factor were included. The authors of the new version of *Flags* state that though measurement of the first space factor "is not essential to the measurement of mechanical aptitude, tests of [this] factor did differentiate between the high and low mechanical interest and experience groups." This was shown in Thurstone's study, though tests of the second space factor S_2 (probably the same as *Vz* or *k*) provided the better differentiation. There have been subsequent studies, however, in which the spatial orientation factor, believed to be the same as the first space factor measured by *Flags,* has been shown to have substantial validity for various courses, e.g., in engineering and mathematics at college level. Thus, there is little reason to doubt that the test under review will be shown to have validity for certain types of courses and occupations.

The reviewer would support the authors' claim that this test is likely to be useful for selecting those with high mechanical interest and aptitude. He would add, however—and the authors would probably agree—that it should be used in conjunction with other tests, particularly of the second space factor, called by Thurstone S_2 and sometimes designated in America as *Vz* and in Britain as *k*.

[1087]

★Hazlehurst Primary Mechanical Ability Tests. Applicants for positions requiring mechanical ability; 1940–50; 5 scores: crosses, bolts, tools, missing lines, total; 1 form ('50, 4 pages); 4 tests; manual ('50, 20 pages); no data on reliability; $10 per set of 25 copies of each test; $1 per set of manual and keys; postage extra; specimen set not available; J. H. Hazlehurst; Stevens, Thurow & Associates Inc. *

a) TEST 1, CROSSES. 3(5) minutes.
b) TEST 2, BOLTS. 4.5(10) minutes.
c) TEST 3, TOOLS. 9(15) minutes.
d) TEST 4, MISSING LINES. 5(10) minutes.

[1088]

★Mechanical Information Questionnaire. Employee applicants; 1944–57; 11 scores: automotive information, bench work, building construction, electrical, foundry practice, industrial engineering, maintenance, metal working, pipe fitting, woodworking, total; Forms A ('44), B revised ('57), (4 pages); mimeographed instructions ['44, 2 pages]; no data on reliability and validity; no description of normative population; $4 per 10 tests, cash orders postpaid; specimen set not available; (30) minutes; Eugene J. Benge; [Management Service Co.]. *

[1089]

★Mechanical Movements: A Test of Mechanical Comprehension. Industrial employees; 1959–63, c1956–63; abbreviated version of a Thurstone test developed about 1918; Form A ('56, 4 pages); manual ('63, 14 pages); norms for males only; $3 per 20 tests, postage extra; $1 per specimen set, postpaid; 14(19) minutes; L. L. Thurstone (test), T. E. Jeffrey (test), and Measurement Research Division, Industrial Relations Center, University of Chicago (manual); Education-Industry Service. *

WILLIAM A. OWENS, *Professor of Psychology, Purdue University, Lafayette, Indiana.*

Mechanical Movements is a paper and pencil test designed specifically to measure mechanical comprehension. The test booklet contains one page of instructions and three pages of test items. Each of the 37 items has two, four, or six response options, and all are based upon a total of 11 drawings of mechanical types of apparatus. A subject responds by drawing a black line, on the test booklet, under a number representing the option of his choice. The test is timed and is alleged to be "a measure of both speed and ease of mechanical comprehension."

There are no obvious flaws in the test format. The directions for administration are clear and the two sample problems are appropriate. No special sophistication is required of the examiner. Testing time is 14 minutes and total time for administration is estimated at 17 minutes. The scoring key consists of three columns of answers each of which can be matched against a corresponding column on the test booklet.

Mechanical Movements was originally developed by Thurstone in 1918 as a test of visualization. It has been modified by subsequent research and the present form is about half as long as the original. This change may be unfortunate, since the authors report a split-half reliability of .85 in a study of engineering freshmen. Such an estimate is, of course, inflated to an unknown, but probably substantial, extent by speeding. In the absence of other evidence, it must be concluded that the intrinsic reliability of *Mechanical Movements* is unknown and is probably unsatisfactory. If this is indeed the case, several factors may be responsible. First, the test is relatively brief at 37 items and 14 minutes. Second, since as many as seven questions are sometimes based upon a single drawing, a failure to comprehend one of these could cause the subject to make not one, but seven, incorrect responses. The correlation of item errors thus introduced may be regarded either as decreasing the effective number of items or as increasing the error variance, per se. According to either conception it has the effect of reducing test reliability.

Relationships with representative measures of other psychological functions are not reported, although it is noted that *Mechanical Movements* has failed to load substantially on a verbal factor in five analyses and that scores may therefore be presumed to be relatively independent of verbal ability.

With respect to the all important requirement of validity, *Mechanical Movements* is difficult to evaluate because adequate evidence is not presented. The test undoubtedly has some construct validity since it is reported to have "high" loadings on Thurstone's second space factor, defined as the ability to visualize internal movement or displacement of parts within a flexible configuration. On the other hand, no correlations with external criteria of mechanical aptitude are provided. The closest approach is a statement indicating a probability less than .001 that groups with high versus low degrees of mechanical interest and experience would not be discriminated. Clearly, a statement of probability is not an estimate of magnitude, and a P-value of .001 really tells the reader nothing about differences between means, or the correlation of the test with the experience-interest criterion (which sounds truncated).

The only other evidence regarding validity comes from a norm table which indicates mean scores for professionals and managers, foremen, and hourly workers as being 20.32, 14.46, and 15.02, respectively. In evaluating these, it is somewhat disturbing to note that foremen do not outscore hourly employees, but that professionals and managers substantially outscore both groups. Since an unstated number of the professionals are engineers, some members of this top group may actually have a high degree of mechanical aptitude. Unhappily, it could equally well be that scores are fairly substantially related to some more general cognitive ability. It is hoped that further research with *Mechanical Movements* will clarify the extent of its relationship with both other representative tests and selected external criteria of mechanical ability.

The norms themselves are based upon the combined scores of the three occupational groups priorly identified. Since the groups are combined, the frame of reference for a particular score is rather fuzzy. As more data are gathered separate norms for various subgroups will hopefully be developed.

In summary, certain vital questions regarding the reliability and validity of *Mechanical Movements* remain to be answered. Until this is done the test must necessarily be granted a less enthusiastic endorsement than can be accorded such well documented devices as Bennett's *Tests of Mechanical Comprehension.*

[1090]

★**Moray House Space Test 2.** Ages 10.0–12.0; 1951–61; 1 form ['61, 11 pages]; manual ['61, 12 pages]; distribution restricted to education authorities; 56*s.* per 100 tests; 1*s.* 9*d.* per manual; purchase tax extra; postpaid; 49(55) minutes; Department of Education, University of Edinburgh; University of London Press Ltd. *

REFERENCES

1. EMMETT, W. C. "Evidence of a Space Factor at 11+ and Earlier." *Brit J Psychol, Stat Sect* 2:3–16 Mr '49. * (*PA* 23:4509)

2. SWANSON, Z. "Further Investigation of the Moray House Space Test." Abstract. *Adv Sci* 7:95 My '50. *

3. WRIGLEY, JACK. "The Factorial Nature of Ability in Elementary Mathematics." *Brit J Ed Psychol* 28:61–78 F '58. * (*PA* 33:6845)
4. SMITH, I. MACFARLANE. "The Validity of Tests of Spatial Ability as Predictors of Success on Technical Courses." *Brit J Ed Psychol* 30:138–45 Je '60. *

E. ANSTEY, *Chief Psychologist, Civil Service Commission, London, England.*

The test is intended to form one of a battery of selection tests in an 11+ examination for allocation to secondary schools. These tests often consist entirely of verbal reasoning, English, and arithmetic items, which are highly predictive of the degree of suitability for an academic type of education, but give no particular indication of suitability for a technical type of education. The *Moray House Space Test 2* was designed to meet this need, to identify among boys and girls aged between 10.0 and 12.0 those likely to be successful at scientific and technical subjects such as technical drawing, woodwork, and metal work.

Throughout the test the subject is required to appreciate shapes and the relationship between them. On 4 of the 10 pages the diagrams are in three dimensions, presented so that the subject has to visualise parts of a simple structure that are hidden from him or to imagine how pieces might fit together. Apart from the written instructions, there is little use of words, but on four pages counting is required. The test might therefore be expected to have a high spatial and some numerical content, but less verbal-educational content than most 11+ tests. Some evidence to this effect is quoted in the manual, in the form of rather lower correlations with other standard tests than these tests have with each other. As all the correlations exceed .75, however, it would be wrong to regard the test, on its own, as more than a pointer towards a child's particular bent. Combined with information about the child's performance in other tests, his interests, and his aspirations, it might well be a useful pointer.

One would like to see more research into the progress of children at different types of secondary schools, grammar, technical, and modern, or in the corresponding streams within comprehensive schools, and to assess the predictive value, for instance, of an index contrasting performance in a space test with that in a clerical test.

Technically, the test is excellent. The layout is attractive, the instructions and examples clear, and the answers totally free from ambiguity. One minor criticism relates to page 9 of the test. Although there are six shapes to choose from in answering any question, the effective choice, for any subject who has grasped what to do, is between the two shapes which are mirror images of each other, i.e., there might be nearly a 50 per cent chance of getting the answer right by guessing. This is not to say that in practice the children do guess, but the design of this page could easily be altered to eliminate this minor technical flaw.

The test has a split-half reliability coefficient of .97, and in the course of preparation it was found to correlate about .94 with a parallel form of test.[1] One would not want higher reliability coefficients than these. Indeed the test could probably be reduced in length and still remain a reliable indicator.

Trials with 5,719 boys and 5,528 girls established a highly significant difference in performance between the sexes of 5 raw score points in favour of boys, equivalent to about a sixth of the standard deviation of the standardised scores. In view of the superior performance of boys, it is unfortunate that separate norms are not provided for boys and girls.

The *Moray House Space Test 2* is of excellent design and carefully standardised. For the intended purpose of helping to identify among children aged between 10.0 and 12.0 those likely to be successful at scientific and technical subjects, it would make a reliable measuring instrument. But full account should be taken of all other information available about a child before making any decisions about his or her future education.

[1091]

O'Connor Wiggly Block. Ages 16 and over; 1928–51; individual; 1 form ['28]; mimeographed manual ['28(?), 3 pages]; record blank ('51, 1 page); no data on reliability; $25.25 per set of blocks, 50 record blanks, and manual; $1.50 per 50 record blanks; postage extra; [15–30] minutes; Johnson O'Connor; C. H. Stoelting Co. *

REFERENCES

1. KEANE, FRANCIS L., AND O'CONNOR, JOHNSON. "A Measure of Mechanical Aptitude." *Personnel J* 6:15–24 Je '27. * (*PA* 1:2090)
2. STOY, E. G. "Additional Tests for Mechanical Drawing Aptitude." *Personnel J* 6:361–6 F '28. * (*PA* 2:2660)
3. REMMERS, H. H., AND SCHELL, J. W. "Testing the O'Connor Wiggly Block Test." *Personnel J* 12:155–9 O '33. * (*PA* 8:1800)
4. VITELES, M. S. "The Measurement of Motor Ability." Abstract. *Psychol B* 30:569 O '33. *
5. O'CONNOR, JOHNSON. *Psychometrics: A Study of Psychological Measurements.* Cambridge, Mass.: Harvard University Press, 1934. Pp. xxxiv, 292. *
6. PHILIP, B. R. "A Comparison of an Electric Circuit Tracing Test With the O'Connor Wiggly Block Test." *J Appl Psychol* 19:148–65 Ap '35. * (*PA* 9:5365)

1 The reliability coefficient based upon alternate forms was reported to the writer by A. E. G. Pilliner.

7. Remmers, H. H., and Smith, J. M. "Reliability and Practice Effect in the O'Connor Wiggly Block Test." *J Appl Psychol* 20:591–8 O '36. * (*PA* 11:2981)
8. Frye, Ellis K. "The Mechanical Abilities of Siblings." *J Genetic Psychol* 50:293–306 Je '37. * (*PA* 11:6020)
9. Harrell, Willard. "The Validity of Certain Mechanical Ability Tests for Selecting Cotton Mill Machine Fixers." *J Social Psychol* 8:279–82 My '37. * (*PA* 11:5311)
10. Harris, Albert J. "The Relative Significance of Measures of Mechanical Aptitude, Intelligence, and Previous Scholarship for Predicting Achievement in Dental School." *J Appl Psychol* 21:513–21 O '37. * (*PA* 12:2113)
11. Harrell, Willard. "A Factor Analysis of Mechanical Ability Tests." *Psychometrika* 5:17–33 Mr '40. * (*PA* 14:4285) (Abstract: *Psychol B* 36:524)
12. Brush, Edward N. "Mechanical Ability as a Factor in Engineering Aptitude." *J Appl Psychol* 25:300–12 Je '41. * (*PA* 15:4377)
13. Giese, William James. "A New Method for Scoring the Wiggly Block." Abstract. *Psychol B* 38:721 O '41. *
14. Bennett, George K., and Cruikshank, Ruth M. *A Summary of Manual and Mechanical Ability Tests, Preliminary Form*, pp. 57–8. New York: Psychological Corporation, 1942. Pp. v, 74. *
15. Estes, Stanley G. "A Study of Five Tests of 'Spatial' Ability." *J Psychol* 13:265–71 Ap '42. * (*PA* 16:3771)
16. Bates, Justine; Wallace, Marjorie; and Henderson, Mack T. "A Statistical Study of Four Mechanical Ability Tests." *Proc Iowa Acad Sci* 50:299–301 '43. * (*PA* 18:3276)
17. O'Connor, Johnson. *Structural Visualization*, pp. 1–46. Boston, Mass.: Human Engineering Laboratory, Inc., 1943. Pp. xiv, 182. *
18. Licht, Marie. *The Relation of Wiggly Block to Black Cube.* Human Engineering Laboratory, Inc., Technical Report No. 194. Boston, Mass.: the Laboratory, December 1945. Pp. 4. *
19. Licht, Marie. *The Relationship of Vocabulary and Wiggly Block Scores of Seven Test Administrators.* Human Engineering Laboratory, Inc., Technical Report No. 177. Boston, Mass.: the Laboratory, October 1945. Pp. 7. *
20. Khan, Hakim I. A. "The Correlation Between Wiggley Block Test and School Achievement." Abstract. *Proc 34th Indian Sci Congr, Delhi, 1947* 34:3 '46. *
21. Miller, Charles, and Lauer, A. R. "The Mechanical Aptitude of Drivers in Relation to Performance at the Wheel." *Proc Iowa Acad Sci* 53:273–5 '46. * (*PA* 23:991)
22. Bittel, Jane. *Standard Error on Worksample No. Three.* Human Engineering Laboratory, Inc., Technical Report No. 367. Boston, Mass.: the Laboratory, February 1947. Pp. 27. *
23. Foley, Jeanne. *A Description of a New Technique in Obtaining Practice and Conversion Factors for All Trials of Wiggly Block Beginning With Worksample 3: The Preliminary Factors.* Human Engineering Laboratory, Inc., Technical Report No. 364. Boston, Mass.: the Laboratory, January 1947. Pp. i, 25. *
24. McIntosh, W. John. "Use of Manual Dexterity and Mechanical Aptitude Tests in Shop Counseling of Mentally Retarded Adolescent Boys." *J Excep Child* 14:81–4 D '47. * (*PA* 22:4481)
25. Bunch, Richard H.; Kjerland, R. N.; and Lauer, A. R. "Reliability of the O'Connor Block Test." *Proc Iowa Acad Sci* 57:353–6 '50. *
26. Kjerland, R. N. "Age and Sex Difference in Performance in the O'Connor Blocks." *Proc Iowa Acad Sci* 58:371–4 '51. *
27. Phillips, J. J.; Green, M. C.; and Kjerland, R. N. "The Validity of a Pencil and Paper Version of the O'Connor Block Test." Abstract. *Proc Iowa Acad Sci* 59:392 '52. *

[1092]

Revised Minnesota Paper Form Board Test. Grades 9–16 and adults; 1930–48; IBM; 2 forms; 2 editions; manual ('48, 16 pages); 75¢ per specimen set of both editions; postpaid; 20(25) minutes; original test by Donald G. Paterson, Richard M. Elliott, L. Dewey Anderson, Herbert A. Toops, and Edna Heidbreder; revision by Rensis Likert and William H. Quasha; Psychological Corporation. * (Australian edition: Australian Council for Educational Research.)
a) [HAND SCORING EDITION.] 1930–48; Forms AA ('41), BB ('41), (6 pages); French-Canadian edition (Forms AA-FE, BB-FE, '55) available; $2.50 per 25 tests.
b) [MACHINE SCORABLE EDITION.] 1941–48; IBM; Forms MA ('41), MB ('41), (6 pages); separate answer sheets must be used; $3.50 per 25 tests; $2 per 50 IBM answer sheets; 40¢ per set of manual and scoring stencils.

REFERENCES

1–9. See 40:1673.
10–57. See 3:677.
58–95. See 4:763.
96–124. See 5:884.
125. Chothia, F. S. "Predicting Success in Multi-Purpose Schools." *Indian J Psychol* 31:139–40 Jl–D '56. *
126. Newall, K. "Selection Testing of Sewing Machinists." *Personnel Prac B* 14:36–8 D '58. * (*PA* 34:2164)
127. Skolnicki, John. "Normative Data Information Exchange, Nos. 11-23, 11-24." *Personnel Psychol* 11:453–4 au '58. *
128. Albright, Lewis E.; Smith, Wallace J.; and Glennon, J. R. "A Follow-Up on Some 'Invalid' Tests for Selecting Salesmen." *Personnel Psychol* 12:105–12 sp '59. * (*PA* 34:3463)
129. Smith, Wallace J.; Glennon, J. R.; and Albright, Lewis E. "Normative Data Information Exchange, Nos. 12-9, 12-10." *Personnel Psychol* 12:152–3 sp '59. *
130. Ash, Philip. "Validity Information Exchange, No. 13-06: D.O.T. Code 5-83.127, Typewriter Serviceman." *Personnel Psychol* 13:455 w '60. *
131. Cass, John C., and Tiedeman, David V. "Vocational Development and the Election of a High School Curriculum." *Personnel & Guid J* 38:538–45 Mr '60. *
132. Hakkinen, Sauli, and Toivainen, Yrjo. "Psychological Factors Causing Labour Turnover Among Underground Workers." *Occup Psychol* 34:15–30 Ja '60. * (*PA* 35:7162)
133. MacKinney, Arthur C., and Wolins, Leroy. "Validity Information Exchange, No. 13-01, Foreman II, Home Appliance Manufacturing." *Personnel Psychol* 13:443–7 w '60. *
134. Mason, P. L., and Casey, D. L. "The Use of Psychological Tests for Selecting Tabulating Machine Operators." *Personnel Prac B* 16:39–41 S '60. * (*PA* 35:4063)
135. Tyler, Donald J. *An Experimental Investigation of the Effects of a Course in Mechanical Drawing on the Interform Reliability of the Revised Minnesota Paper Form Board Test.* Master's thesis, Western Illinois University (Macomb, Ill.), 1960.
136. Watley, Donivan Jason. *Prediction of Academic Success in a College of Business Administration.* Doctor's thesis, University of Denver (Denver, Colo.), 1961. (*DA* 22:3527)
137. Reid, John W.; Johnson, A. Pemberton; Entwisle, Frank N.; and Angers, William P. "A Four-Year Study of the Characteristics of Engineering Students." *Personnel & Guid J* 41:38–43 S '62. * (*PA* 37:5655)
138. Saxena, K. N. "Predictive Efficiency of Revised Minnesota Paper Form Board Test (AA Series) for Achievement in Science for Delta Class Students." *Manas* 9:55–6 '62. * (*PA* 38:4702)
139. Super, Donald E., and Crites, John O. *Appraising Vocational Fitness by Means of Psychological Tests, Revised Edition*, pp. 290–300. New York: Harper & Brothers, 1962. Pp. xv, 688. * (*PA* 37:2038)
140. Watley, Donivan J., and Martin, H. T. "Prediction of Academic Success in a College of Business Administration." *Personnel & Guid J* 41:147–54 O '62. * (*PA* 37:5656)

For a review by D. W. McElwain, see 5:884; for reviews by Clifford E. Jurgensen and Raymond A. Katzell, see 4:763; for a review by Dewey B. Stuit, see 3:677; for a review by Alec Rodger, see 40:1673.

[1093]

***Spatial Tests 1, 2, and 3.** Ages 11-0 to 13-11, 10-7 to 13-11, 10-0 to 11-11; 1950–59; 1 form; 3 tests; distribution restricted to directors of education; prices include purchase tax; postage extra; published for the National Foundation for Educational Research in England and Wales; Newnes Educational Publishing Co. Ltd. *
a) SPATIAL TEST 1. Ages 11-0 to 13-11; 1950–59; 1 form ['50, 23 pages]; revised manual ('59, 24 pages); 17*s.* 6*d.* per 12 tests; 1*s.* 9*d.* per single copy; 3*s.* per manual; 41(60) minutes; I. Macfarlane Smith.
b) SPATIAL TEST 2 (THREE-DIMENSIONAL). Ages 10-7 to 13-11; 1950–56; 1 form ['51, 20 pages]; manual ['51, 13 pages]; provisional norms ['56] for ages 10-7 to 11-6; norms ['55] for ages 13-0 to 13-11; no data on reliability and validity; no norms for ages 11-7 to 12-11; 15*s.* per 12 tests; 1*s.* 6*d.* per single copy; 1*s.* 6*d.* per manual; 26.5(45) minutes; A. F. Watts with

the assistance of D. A. Pidgeon and M. K. B. Richards.

c) SPATIAL TEST 3 (NEWCASTLE SPATIAL TEST). Ages 10-0 to 11-11; 1958-59; 1 form ['58, 23 pages]; manual ('59, 11 pages); no norms for ages 11-4 to 11-11; 17*s.* 6*d.* per 12 tests; 1*s.* 9*d.* per single copy; 1*s.* 3*d.* per manual; 39(60) minutes; I. Macfarlane Smith and J. S. Lawes.

REFERENCES

1. SMITH, I. MACFARLANE. "Measuring Spatial Ability in School Pupils." *Occup Psychol* 22:150-9 Jl '48. * (*PA* 23:1181)

2. SMITH, I. MACFARLANE. "The Validity of Tests of Spatial Ability as Predictors of Success on Technical Courses." *Brit J Ed Psychol* 30:138-45 Je '60. *

3. TAYLOR, C. COLIN. "A Study of the Nature of Spatial Ability and Its Relationship to Attainment in Geography." Abstract of master's thesis. *Brit J Ed Psychol* 30:266-70 N '60. *

4. LAWES, J. S. "The Construction and Validation of a Spatial Test." Abstract of master's thesis. *Brit J Ed Psychol* 31:297-9 N '61. *

For reviews by E. G. Chambers and Charles T. Myers of tests 1 and 2, see 5:885; for a review by E. A. Peel of test 1, see 4:753.

[1094]

Tests of Mechanical Comprehension. Grades 9 and over; 1940-54; IBM; 4 editions; separate answer sheets must be used; $4.75 per 25 tests; $2 per 50 IBM answer sheets; 40¢ per set of manual and scoring stencils; 50¢ per specimen set; postpaid; (25-45) minutes; George K. Bennett, Dinah E. Fry (*b*, test only; *d*), and William A. Owens (*c*); Psychological Corporation. *

a) FORM AA. Grades 9 and over; 1940-54; 1 form ('40, 16 pages); manual ['47, 8 pages]; supplement ('54, 1 page); Spanish edition and bilingual French-English edition available.

b) FORM BB. Men in grades 13 and over; 1941-51; 1 form ('41, 16 pages); revised manual ('51, 8 pages); Spanish edition available.

c) FORM CC. Men in engineering schools; 1949; 1 form (15 pages); manual ['49, 4 pages].

d) FORM W-1. Women in grades 9 and over; 1942-47; 1 form ('42, 16 pages); manual ['47, 4 pages].

REFERENCES

1-19. See 3:683.

20-47. See 4:766.

48-93. See 5:889.

94. GLENNON, J. R.; SMITH, WALLACE J.; AND ALBRIGHT, LEWIS E. "Normative Data Information Exchange, Nos. 11-35, 11-36." *Personnel Psychol* 11:601-2 w '58. *

95. JUERGENSON, ELWOOD M. *The Relationship Between Success in Teaching Vocational Agriculture and Ability to Make Sound Judgments as Measured by Selected Instruments.* Doctor's thesis, Pennsylvania State University (University Park, Pa.), 1958. (*DA* 19:96)

96. KAZMIER, LEONARD J. "Normative Data Information Exchange, No. 12-23." *Personnel Psychol* 12:505 au '59. *

97. OWENS, W. A. "A Comment on the Recent Study of the Mechanical Comprehension Test (CC) by R. L. Decker." *J Appl Psychol* 43:31 F '59. * (*PA* 34:4842)

98. ASH, PHILIP. "Validity Information Exchange, No. 13-06: D.O.T. Code 5-83.127, Typewriter Serviceman." *Personnel Psychol* 13:455 w '60. *

99. CASS, JOHN C., AND TIEDEMAN, DAVID V. "Vocational Development and the Election of a High School Curriculum." *Personnel & Guid J* 38:538-45 Mr '60. *

100. MACKINNEY, ARTHUR C., AND WOLINS, LEROY. "Validity Information Exchange, No. 13-01, Foreman II, Home Appliance Manufacturing." *Personnel Psychol* 13:443-7 w '60. *

101. DURRETT, HAROLD L. "Validity Information Exchange, No. 14-03: D.O.T. Code 5-21.010, Continuous Miner Operator (Bituminous Coal Industry)." *Personnel Psychol* 14:453-5 w '61. *

102. CLEGG, HERMAN D., AND DECKER, ROBERT L. "The Evaluation of a Psychological Test Battery as a Selective Device for Foremen in the Mining Industry." *Proc W Va Acad Sci* 34:178-82 N '62. *

103. CRANE, WILLIAM J. "Screening Devices for Occupational Therapy Majors." *Am J Occup Ther* 16:131-2 My-Je '62. * (*PA* 37:4078)

104. DREW, ALFRED STANISLAUS. *The Relationship of General Reading Ability and Other Factors to School and Job Performance of Machinist Apprentices.* Doctor's thesis, University of Wisconsin (Madison, Wis.), 1962. (*DA* 23:1261)

105. SUPER, DONALD E., AND CRITES, JOHN O. *Appraising Vocational Fitness by Means of Psychological Tests, Revised Edition,* pp. 242-56. New York: Harper & Brothers, 1962. Pp. xv, 688. * (*PA* 37:2038)

106. *Normative Information: Manager and Executive Testing.* New York: Richardson, Bellows, Henry & Co., Inc., May 1963. Pp. 45. *

107. CAMPBELL, JOEL T. "Validity Information Exchange, No. 16-04: D.O.T. Code 7-36.250, Gas Deliveryman." *Personnel Psychol* 16:181-3 su '63. *

108. TAYLOR, DONALD W. Chap. 19, "Variables Related to Creativity and Productivity Among Men in Two Research Laboratories," pp. 228-50. In *Scientific Creativity: Its Recognition and Development.* Edited by Calvin W. Taylor and Frank Barron. New York: John Wiley & Sons, Inc., 1963. Pp. xxiv, 419. * (*PA* 38:2689)

For a review by N. W. Morton, see 4:766; for reviews by Charles M. Harsh, Lloyd G. Humphreys, and George A. Satter, see 3:683.

[1095]

★Three-Dimensional Space Test. Industrial workers in mechanical fields; 1950-63; 1 form ('50, 6 pages); manual ['63, 4 unnumbered pages]; no data on reliability; $4.25 per 25 tests; 10¢ per key; 75¢ per manual; postage extra; $1 per specimen set, postpaid; 10(15) minutes; Richardson, Bellows, Henry & Co., Inc. *

[1096]

★Tool Knowledge Test. Industry; 1951-63; 1 form ('51, 12 pages); manual ['63, 4 unnumbered pages]; $7.25 per 25 tests; 10¢ per key; 75¢ per manual; postage extra; $1.25 per specimen set, postpaid; (20-25) minutes; Richardson, Bellows, Henry & Co., Inc. *

[1097]

★Two-Dimensional Space Test. Business and industry; 1948-63; 1 form ('48, 5 pages); manual ['63, 5 unnumbered pages]; norms for males only; $3.50 per 25 tests; 10¢ per key; 75¢ per manual; postage extra; $1 per specimen set, postpaid; Spanish edition available; 10(15) minutes; Richardson, Bellows, Henry & Co., Inc. *

[1098]

★Weights and Pulleys: A Test of Intuitive Mechanics. Engineering students and industrial employees; 1959, c1956-59; Form A ('56, 3 pages); manual ('59, 10 pages); no data on reliability of current form; norms for male industrial employees only; $3 per 20 tests, postage extra; $1 per specimen set, postpaid; 3(8) minutes; L. L. Thurstone (test), T. E. Jeffrey (test), and Measurement Research Division, Industrial Relations Center, University of Chicago (manual); Education-Industry Service. *

WILLIAM A. OWENS, *Professor of Psychology, Purdue University, Lafayette, Indiana.*

As the manual states, "The test consists of one page of instructions and practice exercises and two pages of test items. There are 32 items in the test proper. Each item shows a diagram of a system of weights and pulleys. The subject decides whether the system is 'stable' or 'unstable' * The test is timed, and thus is a measure of the speed and ease with which the subject can visualize stability or change in the diagrams."

In format the test is simple and well arranged, and the items are clear and intelligible line drawings. Instructions for administration and sample problems, of which there are three, are adequate, and should require a minimum of examiner sophistication. Testing time, per se, is three minutes, and estimated total time for administration is six minutes. Since no answer sheet is utilized, scoring involves the use of two simple lay-over stencils which are provided.

The background of basic research which sired *Weights and Pulleys* is impressive; it was specifically developed as a measure of the second space factor identified by Thurstone in his analysis of mechanical aptitude. However, the test itself seems to have been marketed prior to the provision of several very critical types of interpretative data. Norms are based upon the scores of 285 industrial employees from five categories: professional, executive, junior executive, foreman, and hourly. The smallest group is 28 and the largest 103. If the groups are combined, the standard of comparison is very vague; if they are not combined, the *n*'s are inadequate.

For reliabilities of two shorter forms of the test Thurstone earlier reported estimates of .60 and .85 among engineering freshmen. It is implied that the present form is more reliable because it is twice as long. Correcting the lower figure for length still yields only .75, which is relatively unsatisfactory and completely speculative in view of the fact that *no direct estimate is reported*. Similarly, no correlations with cognitive measures are reported, although reference is made to a correlation of .40 with *Mechanical Movements* in a sample of 112 "industrial men."

Evidence as to the validity of *Weights and Pulleys* is somewhat scattered. Inferentially, it has construct validity, since tests with comparable items load highly on Thurstone's second space factor, defined as the ability to visualize movement or displacement within a flexible configuration. On the other hand, the manual states that there has been no industrial validation; and no direct evidence to the effect that the test will discriminate groups known or presumed to differ in mechanical aptitude is provided. A relevant examination of the hierarchy of means of the norm subgroups is disturbing, since it shows foremen only slightly more than 1 point above hourly workers and nearly 3 points below junior executives. It may be, as suggested by the publisher, that this sample of executives which was drawn largely from among chemical engineers has a high level of mechanical aptitude. Or, alternatively, it is equally possible that the test is relatively heavily saturated with a more general, intellective ability. In any event, the mean differences are small and their implication is dubious.

As things stand, the greatest weakness of *Weights and Pulleys* is that experience with it has apparently not been adequate to permit the answering of vital questions regarding its reliability and validity. Hopefully, time and the collection of further data will provide answers to these questions, pro or con. In the meantime it is not possible to recommend the use of this test as alternative to the use of an instrument of such well documented merit as Bennett's *Tests of Mechanical Comprehension.*

[Other Tests]

For tests not listed above, see the following entries in *Tests in Print:* 1912, 1915, 1917, 1919–23, 1925, 1927, 1929–30, 1932, 1934, 1936–7, 1940, 1943–5, 1947, and 1950; out of print: 1928, 1935, 1938, 1942, and 1948–9.

MISCELLANEOUS

[1099]

★**The Biographical Index.** College and industry; 1961–62; 5 scores: drive to excel, financial status, human relations orientation, personal adjustment, stability; 1 form ('61, 8 pages); manual ('61, 8 pages, including 1962 norms); separate answer sheets must be used; $10 per 25 tests; $2 per 25 answer sheets; $2 per specimen set (must be purchased to obtain manual); cash orders postpaid; (10–20) minutes; Willard A. Kerr; William James Press. *

JOHN K. HEMPHILL, *Director, Developmental Research Division, Educational Testing Service, Princeton, New Jersey.*

The *Biographical Index* is a collection of 79 biographical items, the responses to which are keyed to yield scores on five index areas: Drive to Excel, Financial Status, Human Relations Orientation, Personal Adjustment, and Stability, but none of these scores is further described or adequately defined. A total or composite score, made up of the sum of the five index scores is also suggested.

The index was developed by "reworking" a pool of biographical items that had been assembled by a search of the research literature for items that had, at one time or another, been shown to be correlated with some criterion of job success. A preliminary edition was administered to 38 executives and 62 students. Responses to each item were correlated with six hypothesized basic scores (the above five plus Energy Level) and items were then reassigned if "misplaced."

It is extremely difficult to determine the meaning of any one of the five scores, either by resort to reasoning from the title given to the index area or by examination of the item area correlation data for the preliminary form given in an appendix to the manual. For example, we find that having held a full time job before is keyed toward a high score in Human Relations Orientation, as is living in the same general community as the present job location, or the ability to list all past immediate supervisors and how they might still be reached. These items would not define a high human relations score for most reasonable people and indeed appear to be extremely strange bedfellows. If, then, we abandon reason for dust bowl empiricism and look at the item versus area index score correlation statistics we find, for example, that getting a master's degree within one year after the bachelor's degree has a .05 correlation with Drive to Excel, for which it is keyed in the present form, but also a .10 correlation with Financial Status, for which it is not; or that having reached the age of 30 or over is keyed for Stability, with which it correlates .64, but not for Financial Status, with which it correlates .95. The author's statements, "On the basis of the size of these correlations of items with basic area, items were re-assigned objectively to their quantitatively appropriate area" and "A few items correlating equally well with two or more basic areas were assigned on the basis of face validity" seem difficult to interpret.

The manual contains a review of studies of the validity of biographical items against job success criteria, presumably for the purpose of establishing the reasonableness of the procedure used to develop the index. About two pages of the eight-page manual are devoted to this review, contrasting sharply with less than a third of a column on reliability, and about two thirds of a column giving the results of two validity studies (using one sample of 36 executives and another of 26 executives). The norms provided are also quite inadequate. One norm group is simply described as 85 sales and executive personnel, and another as 93 college upperclassmen. The 1962 supplementary norms are based on 501 cases described as "managerial personnel" ($n = 107$) and "candidates for important sales positions." These later norms are organized by 41 specific age groups, but without note of the number of cases contained within each group.

Split-half reliability coefficients ($n = 100$) reported for the five scores range from .42 for Personal Adjustment to .74 for Stability and Drive to Excel. (The reliability for the combined five scores is reported as .88.) Intercorrelations among the scores are not provided. Validity coefficients for a criterion described as "the average annual increment to monthly salary of executives during their entire full-time working careers" range from −.10 to .50 for 36 executives from the Chicago area, and from −.15 to .60 for 26 executives from "all over the country." The highest coefficients for both groups (.50 and .60) were obtained for Personal Adjustment, but this score also has the lowest estimated reliability. These data leave much to be desired when presented as evidence of the potential usefulness of the test.

There is little that this reviewer can find in the description of the way the index was developed, or in the other information provided in the manual, that would support a recommendation for its use as a means of indicating individuals who "tend to be good job risks with superior probability of winning unusual merit increases and accumulating steady years of faithful service."

RICHARD S. MELTON, *Assistant Director, Test Development Division, Educational Testing Service, Princeton, New Jersey.*[1]

This inventory provides, as the manual states, "an objective quantification of background data." It consists of five scales which were originally formed on an a priori basis but modified subsequently in the light of item-scale correlations. Split-half reliability coefficients for the five scales, based on 100 cases, range from .42 to .74. In view of the diversity of the items and of the weights assigned to different items, the use of the split-half technique is questionable, and the absence of any other re-

1 At the time this review was requested the reviewer was Assistant Director, Professional Examinations Division, The Psychological Corporation, New York, New York.

liability data raises a serious question about the use of the index in making personnel decisions. The reliability of a composite score, which is presumably based on a sum of the five scale scores, is reported as .88, but no validity data or norms are given for this composite.

The validity data for the five scales consist of two sets of correlations with a criterion measure obtained on the answer sheet, the individual's annual increment to monthly salary. One set of correlations was based on 36 Chicago executives, and the other set was based on a "national" sample of 26 executives; both groups were participants in a management development seminar. The 10 correlations ranged from −.15 to .60, four being statistically significant. However, only one scale, Personal Adjustment, showed consistent significant results in both samples.

Three sets of norms are provided, one based on 85 sales and executive personnel, one on 93 college upperclassmen, and the third, a set of age norms, based on 501 "upper level sales applicants," including 107 managerial personnel. The third table, which shows that scores on all five scales increase with age, is clearly the best of the three. However, inasmuch as it includes ages 18 to 58, the average number of cases at each age is less than 13. (A personal communication from the test author indicates that the entries in the table were obtained by a moving average curve fitting technique.) The table also indicates that in many age brackets the score variability is frequently less than would be desired; in one extreme case a 1-point increment in raw score increases the percentile rank by 50 points. Clearly an age norm table based on more substantial numbers of cases is a necessity for the proper interpretation of scores on these scales.

No intercorrelations among the five scales are reported; means, standard deviations, and standard errors of measurement must be estimated by the user from the norm tables and the reliability coefficients reported. The "background research" summarized in the manual consists of brief reviews of research done on biographical inventories as far back as 1925; the purpose of including this extended review appears to be that of convincing potential users of the index that there is a long history of positive results with biographical data. More convincing evidence of the value of the present instrument would be much more welcome.

While the authors are to be commended for including a complete table of item-scale correlations ($n = 100$) and item-criterion correlations ($n = 38$), it would also have been desirable to include the percentages of responses to each of the keyed options. Such data would, among other things, help describe the nature of the sample. For example, it can be inferred from the correlations reported that at least one of the 38 executives earned a Ph.D. in three years. It would be of interest to know how many reported this (and other) achievements.

A review of the items in the index indicates a number of problems, including ambiguities which should not be left to the discretion of the individual or the examiner. One of these arises in connection with those items to which multiple responses are permissible and the score consists of the number of response categories checked. Not all such items make it clear that multiple responses are permissible. Some items call for comparisons with brothers or sisters. The individual having no siblings is presumably not to respond to such items, but the inclusion of items which are obviously not applicable to certain individuals raises obvious questions about the meaning of the scores.

The use of multiple response items also creates other problems. In one scale having a mean of approximately 11, 9 points can be obtained from a single item by checking every response category.

The naming of the scales was apparently done by inspection of the item content. This procedure is not without its defense, but when it leads to a 16-item scale measuring Personal Adjustment, the procedure must be questioned.

In summary, there is good reason to believe that an objective quantification of background data can be useful in the selection of certain classes of employees, but the suggestion on page 1 of the *Biographical Index* manual that "individuals who score high" on this instrument "tend to be good job risks with superior probability of winning unusual merit increases and accumulating steady years of faithful service" is not substantiated by the data reported on the following pages. The reliability data reported are such as to raise a serious question about the use of the instrument with individuals, the validation evidence is extremely meager, the norms are inadequate, and the nature of some of the items and of the scoring weights is such as to lead to some uncertainty about the meaning of the scores obtained. The index should be considered as a research instrument only, and this should be clearly designated in the manual and in any auxiliary publications.

[1100]

★Breadth of Information. Business and industry; 1957–63; "practical intelligence and attention to the ordinary happenings of the world"; 1 form ('57, 5 pages); manual ['63, 12 unnumbered pages]; $3.50 per 25 tests; 10¢ per key; $1 per manual; postage extra; $1 per specimen set, postpaid; (20–25) minutes; Richardson, Bellows, Henry & Co., Inc. *

[1101]

***Business Judgment Test.** Adults; 1953–65; 1 form ('53, 4 pages); revised manual ('65, 12 pages); $5 per 25 tests; 25¢ per revised scoring key ['56]; $1.75 per manual; $2.50 per specimen set; cash orders postpaid; Portuguese edition available; (10–20) minutes; Martin M. Bruce; the Author. *

REFERENCES

1. BRUCE, MARTIN M. "Normative Data Information Exchange, No. 25." *Personnel Psychol* 9:404–5 au '56. *
2. BRUCE, MARTIN M., AND FRIESEN, EDWARD P. "Validity Information Exchange, No. 9-35: D.O.T. Code 1-55.10, Salesman, House-to-House." *Personnel Psychol* 9:380 au '56. *
3. WATLEY, DONIVAN JASON. *Prediction of Academic Success in a College of Business Administration.* Doctor's thesis, University of Denver (Denver, Colo.), 1961. (*DA* 22:3527)
4. WATLEY, DONIVAN J., AND MARTIN, H. T. "Prediction of Academic Success in a College of Business Administration." *Personnel & Guid J* 41:147–54 O '62. * (*PA* 37:5656)

For a review by Edward B. Greene, see 5:893.

[1102]

***Cardall Test of Practical Judgment.** Adults in business and industry; 1942–62; 3 scores: factual, empathic, total; Form 62 ('62, 4 pages); manual ('61, 4 pages); $12 per 100 tests; $1.50 per specimen set; postage extra; (30–40) minutes; Alfred J. Cardall; Cardall Associates. *

REFERENCES

1–6. See 4:784.
7. GLADSTONE, ROY. "A Note on Certain Test Score Relationships and Their Implications for Research in Teacher Selection." *J Ed Psychol* 43:116–8 F '52. * (*PA* 26:7242)
8. RUSMORE, JAY T. "Validity Information Exchange, No. 8-04: D.O.T. Code 1-18.68, Service-Order Dispatcher." *Personnel Psychol* 8:112 sp '55. *
9. TOPETZES, NICK JOHN. "A Program for the Selection of Trainees in Physical Medicine." *J Exp Ed* 25:263–311 Je '57. * (*PA* 33:7024)
10. RUSMORE, JAY T. "A Note on the 'Test of Practical Judgment.'" *Personnel Psychol* 11:37 sp '58. * (*PA* 33:9101)

For reviews by Glen U. Cleeton and Howard R. Taylor of an earlier edition, see 3:694.

[1103]

★Conference Meeting Rating Scale. Conference leaders and participants; 1959; 1 form (2 pages); manual (2 pages); no data on reliability; $3 per 50 scales; $1 per specimen set of 10 scales and manual; cash orders postpaid; (10) minutes; B. J. Speroff; Psychometric Affiliates. *

[1104]

★Dartnell Self-Administered Employee Opinion Unit. Industry; 1955–58; attitudes toward job; 2 editions; administration manual ('58, 8 pages); handbook, *Planning and Conducting Employee Opinion Surveys* ('57, 218 pages); no data on reliability; 50¢ per set of scoring stencils; 50¢ per administration manual; $24 per handbook; postage extra; (35–60) minutes; Central Surveys, Inc. (questionnaire) and Charles Parker and staff (handbook); Dartnell Corporation. *
a) EMPLOYEE QUESTIONNAIRE. 1 form ('55, 4 pages); 1–99 copies, 15¢ each.
b) SUPERVISOR'S QUESTIONNAIRE. 1 form ('55, 5 pages, same as *a* above except for 11 additional items); 1–99 copies, 30¢ each.

RAYMOND A. KATZELL, *Professor of Psychology and Head of the Department, New York University, New York, New York.*

There are two separable features in this kit: a "do-it-yourself" handbook on the conduct of questionnaire surveys of employee attitudes, and a specific set of questionnaires for such purposes. The handbook or manual is devoted to the subjects of survey goals, planning, questionaires, procedures, tabulating and reporting, and follow-up implementation. It is the most detailed procedural guide on this subject that the reviewer has encountered, and should serve as a useful *vade mecum* even to the experienced professional. Its emphasis on the hows of its subject rather than the whys makes it essentially a cookbook, to be used only with great caution by the amateur unless bolstered with expert advice. As with all cookbooks, the greatest weakness lies in the domain of inference and interpretation.

The handbook contains specimens of the two Dartnell attitude questionnaires, one for supervisory and the other for nonsupervisory employees. The latter comprises 36 questions, most of which are multiple choice and several of which elicit opinions on more than one issue. The former has the same questions, plus 11 more which deal specifically with concerns of supervisors, particularly low level ones. Items may be scored by a key which allots points to each alternative on a scale of favorability from 0 to 4. By summing the results of a scant two to five items, a score may be obtained for each of 16 areas or categories of attitude; these categories are grouped under three main rubrics, Supervision, Company Policies and Practices, and Job Attitude (e.g., advancement, security, teamwork, etc.).

The handbook, so complete on survey procedures, is unfortunately quite devoid of psychometric data on the questionnaires. Among the missing are facts about the method of item construction and selection, the basis of the weights used for scoring each response as to favorability, the method of arriving at the 16 attitude categories and the allocation of items to them, reliability, and correlations with other variables. About the only data which the technically oriented reader can find in the manual are "national averages" of questionnaire responses, but even for these there are no indices of variability or information about the size and composition of the normative sample.

In the absence of technical data to the contrary, the questionnaires give the appearance of being rather superficial and amateurish instruments for assessing job attitudes. The procedures manual, on the other hand, is a useful distillation of practical experience in the conduct of employee attitude surveys. Fortunately, the latter can be purchased and used without the former, although its price may repel many individuals.

[1105]

★**Employee Opinion Survey.** Business and industry; 1956; opinions in 5 areas: management and the company, supervision, work conditions, pay and benefits, general; 1 form ['56, 6 pages]; no manual or other accessories; no data on reliability and validity; distribution restricted to clients; $7 per 25 surveys, postpaid; analysis and reporting fees vary and are additional; [20] minutes; R. W. Henderson; William, Lynde & Williams. *

[1106]

★**The Jenkins Job Attitudes Survey.** Industrial employees; 1959; derived from an unpublished form of *How Well Do You Know Yourself?*; identification of accident-prone individuals; Form AR-11 (6 pages); manual (6 pages); no data on reliability; $1 per test, postage extra; price includes scoring service; (25-40) minutes; Thomas N. Jenkins, Harold T. Fagin (manual), and John H. Coleman (manual); Executive Analysis Corporation. *

REFERENCES

1. JENKINS, THOMAS N. "The Accident-Prone Personality: A Preliminary Study." *Personnel* 33:29-32 Jl '56. * (*PA* 31:6752)

[1107]

★**The Organization Survey.** Employees in industry; 1958-61; formerly called *Organization Attitude Survey;* administered by the publisher's representatives; 11 scores: work organization, work efficiency, administrative effectiveness, leadership practices, communication effectiveness, personnel development, pay and benefits, immediate supervision, work associates, job satisfaction, organization identification, reactions to the survey; 1 form ('61, 4 pages, identical with form copyrighted in 1958 except for format); program description manual ('61, 25 pages); planning manual ('61, 37 pages); sample survey report ('61, 31 pages); survey analyzer ('61, 60 pages); manager's guide ('61, 23 pages); no data on reliability; distribution restricted to companies using the publisher's survey services; price information available from the publisher; specimen set not available; [30-40] minutes; [Richard Renck, Robert K. Burns, Melany E. Baehr, and Robert H. Waechter]; Industrial Relations Center. *

[1108]

*__The Tear Ballot for Industry.__ Employees in industry; 1944-62; job satisfaction questionnaire; 1 form ('44, 2 pages); revised manual ('62, 21 pages, hectographed); profile ('56, 1 page); $4 per 50 tests; $3 per 50 profiles; $5 per examiner's kit of 50 tests, profile, and manual; specimen set not available; cash orders postpaid; (3-5) minutes; Willard A. Kerr; Psychometric Affiliates. *

REFERENCES

1-4. See 4:783.
5. KERR, WILLARD A. "On the Validity and Reliability of the Job Satisfaction Tear Ballot." *J Appl Psychol* 32:275-81 Je '48. * (*PA* 23:1499)
6. TOPAL, J. R. *The Factorial Analysis of Job Satisfaction.* Master's thesis, Illinois Institute of Technology (Chicago, Ill.), 1950.
7. PRESSEL, G. L. *Pattern Analysis of Job Satisfaction Attitudes of Hospital Nurses.* Master's thesis, Illinois Institute of Technology (Chicago, Ill.), 1951.
8. KERR, WILLARD A. "Summary of Validity Studies of the Tear Ballot." *Personnel Psychol* 5:105-13 su '52. * (*PA* 27:4630)
9. SPEROFF, B. J. "Job Satisfaction Study of Two Small Unorganized Plants." *J Appl Psychol* 43:315 O '59. * (*PA* 34:6628)

RAYMOND A. KATZELL, *Professor of Psychology and Head of the Department, New York University, New York, New York.*

The core of this questionnaire consists of 10 five-alternative multiple choice items intended to elicit expressions of attitude toward major features of one's job, such as security, ability of supervisors, working conditions, and income. The item alternatives are arbitrarily scaled from 1 (least satisfied) to 5 (most satisfied). A total score may be obtained by adding the scores of the 10 items.

Split-half reliability coefficients have been calculated for the total score in a dozen small samples. The obtained coefficients range from .65 to .88, and average about .83. This is quite satisfactory for the determination of job satisfaction of groups, the use for which the questionnaire is intended.

The manual cites 10 sets of studies in support of the instrument's validity. These studies typically involved correlating the total score with some other variable. Without being labeled as such, the spirit in which these results are offered is in the nature of establishing the construct validity of the questionnaire. Some of these other variables (e.g., turnover or absenteeism) appear to be closer to the construct, "job satisfaction," than do others (e.g., empathic ability or hearing loss). Nevertheless, the general picture does suggest that the questionnaire reflects the construct of job satisfaction in most of the samples studied. This is hardly surprising since the questionnaire is essentially asking people 10 times how well they like their jobs. One important limitation should be noted: the samples all consisted of nonmanagerial, nonprofessional workers. It may be doubted that a questionnaire covering these particular topics would correlate as well with other indications of job satisfaction in a sample, say, of executives or of chemists.

In addition to summarizing the development of the instrument and available validity and reliability data, the manual furnishes several sets of percentile norms. The individual samples are too small and specialized to be of much use. However, the consolidated results, organized by sex and geographical region, may provide a helpful frame of reference. A table of item results is also provided, together with normative charts for profiling them; however, interpretation of the results of single items might be hazardous because of low reliability.

The author and publisher are to be commended for setting modest prices for the materials. However, the reviewer's copy of the hectographed manual was indistinct in places, and its stapled binding came apart promptly. It seems likely that most users of the manual would prefer to pay an extra 25 or 50 cents for higher quality production.

In summary, *The Tear Ballot for Industry* provides a quick and inexpensive way of obtaining a gross indication of general job satisfaction of workers in lower level occupations. The evidence is that the instrument possesses degrees of reliability and construct validity which are reasonably adequate for this purpose. Anyone interested in such an instrument may wish to compare this one with the Brayfield-Rothe Index of Job Satisfaction.[1]

For a review by Brent Baxter, see 4:783.

[1109]

★**[Tests A/9 and A/10.]** Applicants for technical and apprentice jobs; 1955–57; interest in scientific fields; 2 parts (English and Afrikaans editions in the same booklet); no manual; mimeographed norms ['57, 1 page]; separate answer sheets must be used; R40 per 100 sets of both parts; R5 per 100 answer sheets; 60c per specimen set; postpaid; National Institute for Personnel Research. *

a) TEST A/9: [TECHNICAL AND SCIENTIFIC KNOWLEDGE]. 1 form ['55, 7 pages]; 15(20) minutes.

b) TEST A/10: [TECHNICAL READING COMPREHENSION]. 1 form ['55, 7 pages]; 10(15) minutes.

1 BRAYFIELD, ARTHUR H., AND ROTHE, HAROLD F. "An Index of Job Satisfaction." *J Appl Psychol* 35:307–11 O '51. *

[1110]

★**Whisler Strategy Test.** Business and industry; 1959–61, c1955–61; "intelligent action"; 6 scores: 4 direct scores (number circled-boldness, number attempted-speed, number right-accuracy, net strategy) and 2 derived scores (caution, hypercaution); 1 form ('59, 8 pages); manual ('59, 4 pages); profile-supplementary norms ('61, 1 page); reliability data for net strategy score only; separate answer sheets must be used; $3 per 20 tests; $1 per 20 answer sheets; $1 per specimen set (must be purchased to obtain manual); cash orders postpaid; 25(30) minutes; Laurence D. Whisler; Psychometric Affiliates. *

REFERENCES

1. KERR, WILLARD A., AND ABRAMS, PETER. "Halstead Brain Impairment, Boldness, Creativity and Group Intelligence Measures." *J Clin Psychol* 18:115–8 Ap '62. * (*PA* 38:8458)

JEAN MAIER PALORMO, *Head, Industrial Test Research, Science Research Associates, Inc., Chicago, Illinois.*

To quote the test manual: "There is within the business community an explicit philosophy of intelligent action. There has been, however, no measurement technique directed to the measurement of intelligent action as so defined. The Strategy Test is presented as a venture in such measurement." The author distinguishes between the meaning of the term "intelligence" as used in the practical business setting, for example, and the meaning of the term when used by psychologists to describe mental capacity. The business man is judged as "intelligent" by his superiors and peers when "he makes wise use of the resources available to him at the moment."

This test contains 126 items of various types—vocabulary, general information, specific subject information, reasoning, checking, space, etc. Approximately 70 items are typical of those commonly found in traditional intelligence tests. The examinee's task is clearly stated in the instructions: he is to try for the highest possible score in the 25 minutes allotted by skipping about and answering the easiest blocks of questions first. If he is very certain of an answer, he should circle it; if it is right he receives a bonus point to reward him for his conviction, but if it is wrong he is heavily penalized.

The author reports a split-half reliability on college students and graduates of .56, which appears to be uncorrected. Two validity studies are cited. The first yielded a coefficient of .60 for 43 high school seniors, but the nature of the dependent variable is not given in the manual. The second study involved 63 university students who made self-ratings of their past success in 10 different decision or behavior areas. The summation of these ratings gave a "past strategy score," which when correlated with the Whisler test scores resulted in a Pearsonian coefficient of .29.

The norms published in the manual are based on 204 college students and graduates, most of whom "were in their twenties." This table presents percentile equivalents for four direct scores. A later supplement provides norms on 273 additional cases, described by the author as "key management and sales personnel." In addition to the four direct scores, percentile equivalents are given for the two derived scores, Caution and Hypercaution.

The information about the test presented in the manual is minimal at best, and the statistics that are given raise grave questions as to the adequacy of this "test" as a measurement device.

The reported reliability for *one score* only does not meet the accepted standard for an instrument to be used in individual classification. The method used in dividing the test is not given, but if alternate items were used to obtain the part scores, the coefficient is probably an overestimate because of the block arrangement of item types. The examinee does not have time (and perhaps knowledge) to answer all the items; his instructions are to *choose* those blocks of items which he thinks he can do best; and the items included represent only a small sampling of the universe of intelligent actions and knowledges. If an instrument is to yield a measure of an individual's strategy in utilizing his resources, the reliability of that measure should be based upon alternate test forms, each containing different samples of items from the universe. Such reliability studies should be extended to include *all* scores presented to the user in the norms tables.

The norms are not extensive, but manuals for new instruments frequently provide only minimum norms tables. The normative samples are not described as adequately as is desirable. A more serious problem, however, is the failure of the author to describe the rationale and the experimental operations which led to the presentation of a six-score profile. Without these, the user is at a loss to evaluate the scoring system or interpret test results.

Nor does the user receive help in his understanding of the test from the validity section of the manual. Again, few test manuals provide sufficient predictive validity information to meet the needs of all users. In the case of the Whisler test, the need for predictive validity data is perhaps secondary to the need for evidence of construct validity. The name of the test and the opening paragraphs of the manual in which the author describes "intelligent action" in the business situation are very appealing to the unsophisticated test user. Since every personnel man would welcome a measure of "practical judgment," it is imperative that the author who implies this measurement from his set of items provide evidence to substantiate his inferences.

Finally, it is necessary to question the appropriateness of the collection of items. About 40 per cent of the items are in the multiple choice format, calling for specific bits of information, and can be answered very quickly by the person who knows these facts. The remaining items, requiring reasoning and problem solving abilities, are much more time consuming. Thus, the examinee who happens to possess factual knowledge in the limited fields of specialization represented by items in the test has a tremendous advantage over the examinee whose factual knowledges are in other fields. The manual does not describe the research and results that led to the collection of this set of items to measure "strategy." The final paragraph of the manual recognizes that problems exist: "There are 'item-difficulty' problems. There are 'equivalent forms' problems. There are problems of factor analysis of kinds of items attempted. And there are problems of optimum composition."

It would seem to this reviewer that these are problems to be solved *prior* to the publication of a "test," and until they are solved no reliable and valid measurement of "intelligent action" can be achieved.

In summary, the *Whisler Strategy Test* cannot be recommended for operational use. It presents an interesting and unique measurement hypothesis which should be of interest to research people. However, the first research efforts might better be aimed at the investigation of test composition, rather than toward establishing validity of the collection of items presented in the current edition of the test.

PAUL F. ROSS, *Industrial Psychologist, Imperial Oil Limited, Toronto, Ontario, Canada.*

The *Whisler Strategy Test* is a 126-item, 25-

minute time limit test. Each item has two answers from which the respondent chooses the right one. The manual states that "three groups of vocabulary items and twenty-six other types of items are used in the Strategy Test." The reviewer finds vocabularly items, including a few in Spanish, French, and German; spatial relations items of puzzle parts, line length, map reading, and maze tracing types; general information items testing knowledge that does not go out of date; clerical skills items which seem related to checking and coding; and a few items which could be called number series and word series. There is little arithmetic and numerical content in the test. The respondent is instructed to "Try for the highest possible score; when you start the test, look it over. * See what kinds of questions seem easiest. * Start any place you wish, and skip around as much as you want to. Remember the time is only 25 minutes." The respondent marks his answers on an answer sheet, indicating his confidence in the correctness of his answer by circling the answers he is very sure are correct. Scores consist of (*a*) the number of items attempted, (*b*) the number of right answers, (*c*) the number of circled answers, and (*d*) a "net strategy" score which adds points for confidence in the correctness of right answers and subtracts points when the respondent is very sure a wrong answer is right. Two discrepancy scores—(*e*) items attempted minus circled answers, and (*f*) right answers minus circled answers—are computed and recorded on the answer sheet.

The manual does not say in a short, quotable statement what it is that the scores measure. The reader of one part of the manual understands that the test measures some aspect of intelligence. In another part, the discrepancy scores are referred to as a "plunger index," although "Experience will be needed to discover which discrepancy [score] will best serve as an index of style of performance." The manual reports reliability, validity, mean, and standard deviation *for only one of the six scores.* No information, other than norm tables, is reported for the other five scores. The net strategy score is reported to have a "split half reliability" of .56 when estimated from a sample of 204 college students. One of the two validity coefficients for the net strategy score is reported without any description whatsoever of the criterion. The other validity coefficient, based upon self-ratings of past success in a variety of activities, is reported as .29 when estimated from a sample of 63 university students. No intercorrelations of the six scores are reported. No mention of the use of item analysis techniques is made. No correlations of the scores from the test with scores from intelligence tests or personality tests are reported. In the reviewer's opinion, the net strategy score has a reliability adequate for only the crudest of test uses, and the evidence given as validity data amounts to *no* evidence for the valid use of this test for any purpose.

The manual is poorly organized and discouragingly incomplete. Instructions for administering the test are not adequate for accurate timing of the respondent's performance. The instructions are broken into two widely separated locations in the manual. No description is given of the qualifications of the test administrator or of the test interpreter. The manual cites no references to published research using the *Whisler Strategy Test.* Normative data for 204 people, "162 men and 42 women," are presented. By making an inference, the user of the manual can guess that these people were "college students or college graduates," but the guess may be wrong. Additional normative data published in 1961 are based on 273 "key management and sales personnel." The user does not know the ages, the educational level, or the occupation of the people in the norms groups. Test performance by men and by women is combined into one norm, in spite of the fact that the general information items in the test ask questions about metal working, plumbing, carpentry, mining, chemistry, and physics!

The reviewer wonders whether the publishers had an editorial review of this material before they undertook its publication. This test is an arresting example of poor practice in test design, test construction, and manual writing. Publication probably is not justified. The test should not be used, even for experimental purposes, until the instructions for administering it and perhaps the printed presentation of items and materials related to items are improved. The test is not ready for any practical use.

[1111]

★**Work Information Inventory.** Employee groups in industry; 1958; morale; 1 form (4 pages); manual (4 pages); mean score norms only; $3 per 50 tests; $1 per specimen set (must be purchased to obtain manual); cash orders postpaid; (15) minutes; Raymond E. Bernberg; Psychometric Affiliates. *

[**Other Tests**]

For tests not listed above, see the following entries in *Tests in Print:* 1952, 1960–1, 1963–4, 1966, and 1971; out of print: 1954, 1957, 1959, 1962, 1967–8; status unknown: 1969.

SELECTION & RATING FORMS

[1112]

★APT Controlled Interview. Applicants for employment; 1945–56; revision of *APT Quick-Screening Interview;* 19 ratings: job experience (2 ratings), work history, financial status (2 ratings), marital status, voice (3 ratings), appearance (4 ratings), health (2 ratings), family background, relations with the law, social history, total; 1 form ['56, 1 interview-rating card]; manual ['56, 24 pages]; no data on reliability; distribution restricted to clients; $2.50 per 50 interview-rating cards; $3 per manual; postage extra; [12–30] minutes; Associated Personnel Technicians, Inc. *

[1113]

★Career Counseling Personal Data Form. Vocational counselees; 1962; 1 form (11 pages); no manual or other accessories; no data on reliability and validity; $10 per 25 forms; $5.50 per specimen set of 10 forms; cash orders postpaid; [45–60] minutes; John B. Ahrens; Martin M. Bruce. *

[1114]

★[Cardall Interviewing Aids.] Adults; 1958–61; 3 record forms; no manual; no data on reliability and validity; specimen set free; postage extra; administration time not reported; Alfred J. Cardall; Cardall Associates. *
a) APPLICATION BLANK. 1958; 1 form (2 pages); $2.50 per 100 forms.
b) INTERVIEWING GUIDE. 1958; 1 form (2 pages); $2.50 per 100 forms.
c) CURRENT ACTIVITIES AND BACKGROUND INVENTORY. 1961; 1 form (2 pages); $3.50 per 100 forms.

[1115]

***Diagnostic Interviewer's Guide.** Applicants for employment; 1935–42; 1 form ('42, 4 pages, identical with form copyrighted in 1937); manual ('42, 4 pages); no data on reliability and validity; $8 per 100 forms; $1 per specimen set of 10 forms and manual; postage extra; E. F. Wonderlic; E. F. Wonderlic & Associates. *

REFERENCES

1. LAIRD, DONALD A. *The Psychology of Selecting Employees, Third Edition,* pp. 114–9. New York: McGraw-Hill Book Co., Inc., 1937. Pp. xiii, 316. * (*PA* 11:4726)
2. HOVLAND, CARL IVER, AND WONDERLIC, E. F. "Prediction of Industrial Success From a Standardized Interview." *J Appl Psychol* 23:537–46 O '39. * (*PA* 14:1039)

ALBERT K. KURTZ, *Fulbright Lecturer, Ein Shams University, Cairo, United Arab Republic.*

It is difficult to evaluate this interviewing guide in an objective manner. It shouldn't be. It came out in a revised edition in 1937 which was apparently copyrighted both in 1937 and in 1942. It provides for an objective score ranging between possible extremes of −34 and +34. A naïve reviewer might think that by now there would be many studies telling how well these scores correlate with some subsequently determined criterion of success. There is only one, published in 1939, which is somewhat out of date 25 years later. That report (*2*) gave reliability coefficients and validity information, but not a validity coefficient.

This lack of evidence does not mean that we should wait longer for it to appear. When 25 years have passed without any further data being made available, it is high time that potential users tried a competing device for which reliability and validity figures are available. Regrettably, this is sometimes easier said than done, but in the present case there are satisfactory alternatives. Perhaps the first choice, because validity figures are known and fairly high, is the set of patterned interview forms by Robert N. McMurry & Co. (see 1119).

Although validity is the most important single characteristic of a measuring device, let us consider some other aspects of this interviewer's guide, assuming that we may still wish to use it rather than its competitors.

This blank has four pages, each containing 6 to 14 questions for the interviewer to ask the job applicant about his work history, family history, social history, and personal history. At the bottom of each page, there are 5 to 12 yes-no questions (a total of 34) for the interviewer to answer about the applicant. These give the score.

Most of the questions seem relevant and well worded, although research on claims of various pseudo-sciences would not provide much justification for retaining the anachronistic "Can this applicant look you in the eye?"

The 4-page manual clarifies the use of the interviewer's guide and also gives a number of pertinent suggestions regarding the conduct of the interview, including references to some good, but now somewhat out-of-date, books and articles on the subject.

In conclusion, this is a form that was reasonably well constructed and well explained. It once had what was then a satisfactory reliability coefficient and a positive validity of unknown size in one company. If the author or anyone else had compiled more recent data on its validity, the form might have proved valid, thus justifying its continued use. Since this has not been done, but has been done for at least one competing device, there seems to be no reason for recommending the use of this somewhat aging form of unknown value.

For reviews by Clyde H. Coombs and Douglas H. Fryer, see 3:685.

[1116]

★**Employee Performance Appraisal.** Business and industry; 1962; 7 merit ratings by supervisors: quantity of work, quality of work, job knowledge, initiative, inter-personal relationships, dependability, potential; 1 form (4 pages); no manual or other accessories; no data on reliability and validity; $5 per 25 forms; $2.75 per specimen set of 10 forms; cash orders postpaid; [10-20] minutes; Martin M. Bruce; the Author. *

JEAN MAIER PALORMO, *Head, Industrial Test Research, Science Research Associates, Inc., Chicago, Illinois.*

This form is presented as an aid to "'force' the evaluator into being more critical, more analytical, more objective, and more of a thinker." While these are worthy aims, there is no evidence to show that the *Employee Performance Appraisal* achieves them. In view of the claims made by the author, one would expect that he would provide the user with at least a brief manual reporting intra- and inter-rater reliabilities and some evidence on scale intercorrelations. However, such is not the case.

Ratings are made on seven "factors" which have resulted from a "systematic outline of factors important in practically all jobs." What is meant by "systematic outline" is not known. These factors would certainly place high in a survey of popular use, for they are essentially those that have been used on hundreds of company-developed rating forms over the past 20 years. Some of these factors, or traits, have been shown to be highly susceptible to the constant errors of ratings. For example, Symonds demonstrated that the "halo effect" is most prevalent in rating traits of character and factors involving reactions with other people. Four of the seven factors on the form can be so classified.

The author has taken some steps to minimize rating errors. He has combined the numerical and graphic scales; the line is extended to include seven cue positions; most of the range is given to degrees of favorable report, which tends to counteract the leniency error. However, most investigators agree that the cues along the trait continuums contribute most to the control of rating errors, and the author appears to have neglected these in his developmental research.

The development of adequate rating forms involves a considerable amount of experimental work in the selection and placement of cues. There should be no doubt among raters as to the rank position of a cue among other cues. On the *Employee Performance Appraisal,* this reviewer finds many of these more confusing than helpful. For example, consider three adjacent cues on the factor "Quantity of Work":

Turns out a little more than most people in similar jobs.

Can be counted on to turn out more than most people. Does not need much supervision.

A superior employee. *Almost always can be counted on to do more than a full share.*

The italicized statements (italics the reviewer's) bear directly on the question of quantity. The other phrases in the second and third statements are not necessarily relevant, and certainly not unique, to the factor of "quantity," thus encouraging the rater to introduce errors of rating. If the rater ignores these phrases and considers only the statements relevant to the factor of quantity, he may be even more confused. There seems to be little difference between the first and second statements except in the words "more" and "little more"; both statements imply that this performance occurs 100 per cent of the time. Now, in the third statement the employee does "more," as he does in the first and second statements, but "almost always" instead of 100 per cent of the time. Yet, on the form these statements cover a numerical range of 19 through 35, with *the third statement being the highest!*

Similar confusions, at least for this reviewer, occur somewhere among the cues listed for every factor on the form. This leads one to wonder, particularly since no manual describing the form's development is available, about the method by which the scale positions for the cues were established.

In addition to careful experimental work in scale development, investigators have found the training of raters to be a very important factor in reducing errors of rating. The author of this form attempts to cover this in 10 points under "Directions." If, indeed, the raters follow the rules given in these brief statements, the author's claims for the form might be somewhat justified. However, it is doubtful whether a short direction telling the rater to "be fair, honest, impartial, and objective" will make him so.

The above paragraphs discuss technical inadequacies of the form. Perhaps the most important criticism, however, is the implication that the form can be used successfully for all employees in all jobs. In recent years many competent personnel research workers have reported studies pointing to the specificity of criterion factors. It is disturbing that this relatively new form, published in 1962, ignores so much of the research that has been done on performance evaluation and criterion development.

[1117]

*[**Employee Rating and Development Forms.**] Executive, industrial, office, and sales personnel; 1950–59; manual for *b* only; no data on reliability and validity in manual; postage extra; [5–30] minutes; Robert N. McMurry; Dartnell Corporation. *

a) [PATTERNED MERIT REVIEW FORMS.] 1950–59.

1) *Patterned Merit Review—Executive.* 1955–59; Form No. MR-407 ('59, 4 pages, identical with form copyrighted in 1955); 1–99 copies, 15¢ each.

2) *Patterned Merit Review Form—Plant and Office.* 1950–59; Form No. MR-405 ('59, 4 pages, identical with form copyrighted in 1950); 1–99 copies, 15¢ each.

3) *Patterned Merit Review—Sales.* 1955–59; Form No. MR-406R ('59, 2 pages, identical with form copyrighted in 1955); 1–99 copies, 10¢ each.

4) *Patterned Merit Review—Technical, Office, Special Skills.* 1956–57; Form No. MR-408 ('57, 2 pages, identical with form copyrighted in 1956); 1–99 copies, 10¢ each.

5) *Statement of Supervisory Expectancies.* 1958; Form No. ER-602 (2 pages); 1–99 copies, 10¢ each.

b) PATTERNED EXIT INTERVIEW. 1953–59; Form No. EX-501 ('59, 2 pages, identical with form copyrighted in 1953); manual ('53, 12 pages); 1–99 copies, 10¢ each; $2 per manual.

c) PERSONAL HISTORY REVIEW FORM. 1957; 1 form ['57, 4 pages]; 1–99 copies, 10¢ each.

RICHARD S. BARRETT, *Associate Professor of Management Engineering and Psychology, New York University, New York, New York.*

Since the forms and manuals discussed in this review represent about one fifth of the forms and manuals which are listed in the current catalogue of the Dartnell Corporation as having been prepared by Robert N. McMurry, they may be considered as a sample of his "Patterned" approach to personnel selection, appraisal, rating, and development.

Most of the forms are attractively printed in two colors. Black is used for the questions which are to be answered by an interviewer, a job incumbent, or an applicant. Colored ink is used to ask questions or to give instructions to the person who is interpreting the information to help him to get the most out of the material collected by the forms.

The Merit Review Forms, designed for use in the evaluation of employees on different types of positions, differ considerably from each other to reflect specific job duties and performance standards. They range in size from a single sheet used in sales and some office positions to a 4-page form for reviewing executive performance. The *Patterned Merit Review Form—Plant and Office* states, "A special manual on the 'Patterned Merit Review Plan' has been prepared"; yet the current (1961) order form lists no such manual, nor are manuals for the other Merit Review Forms listed.

In this reviewer's eyes, the questions on the most extensive form, *Patterned Merit Review —Executive,* start out in a sensible fashion but deteriorate toward the end of the form. In the beginning, the questions ask about functions of the executive's position, basic responsibilities, authority, and so forth. Specific questions are asked about his education, training, and experience, his demonstrated ability in such activities as analyzing work loads and market costs, holding meetings, speaking in public, and his attitudes toward the company and its supervisory and management policies. Then the questions become less specific, asking about leadership qualities, such as the ability to make decisions or to empathize. The last section asks questions which only the most sophisticated psychologist could be expected to answer adequately, and even he would be hard pressed to show how the answers would be related to a person's job performance. The rater is asked, for instance, to report on insecurity, defensiveness, impulsiveness, pleasure-mindedness, and other personality traits of dubious significance.

The *Patterned Exit Interview* is a single sheet which provides for identifying information, and for notes of an interview with the employee who is leaving, and of a related interview with his supervisor. A 16-page manual describes the benefits of the exit interview and provides suggestions for conducting the interview. There is illustrative material on how to chart an analysis of reasons for termination, but there is no explanation of how this material is prepared. There are no data from research studies which would support the claims in the manual that the use of the *Patterned Exit Interview* will help to salvage good employees, improve vertical communication, provide for catharsis on the part of the employee or his supervisor, or provide a continuing audit of personnel policies and practices.

The *Personal History Review Form* is a 4-page sheet which, in addition to identifying information, provides space for a report on the employee's performance with the company by which he is currently employed; previous employment, including part-time and school jobs; education; home and finances; domestic and social status; and health. There is no manual for the *Personal History Review Form* and no indication on the form itself of how the information is to be used. The reviewer assumes that the data are to be collected and up-dated periodically to help in planning each individual's career with the company. But just how the information is to be used is not clear.

These forms may provide a useful service to a personnel department by helping to record relevant information in a systematic way. Each follows a logical sequence, starting with adequate identifying information, followed with questions which the personnel specialist can ask directly or paraphrase. The additional questions and statements on interpretation give him some clues as to what can be gained from the answers to the questions and what areas should be probed if the original response is not completely informative. Some questions, as noted, require considerable psychological sophistication of the personnel specialist and may well provide information which is not relevant, even if it is correct.

An attempt to review forms which are designed to be placed in the hands of staff members in personnel departments or of supervisors who may not have any special personnel training highlights the inherent difficulty in evaluating personnel forms without knowing how they are used. These forms are well thought out and could provide a useful guide for systematic report by an astute observer. But, they could equally be used to report ill-considered prejudices of an inadequately trained observer who did not understand what he was looking for. Manuals are not available for several of the instruments being reviewed. Those which are available present instructions that could be useful if elaborated in an adequate training program but which may otherwise be no more useful than a collection of homilies.

The value of the forms is inherently researchable but there is no report in the manuals that any research has been performed on any of the forms since 1947. The lack of evidence makes it unfortunate that one manual so forthrightly states "actually the Patterned Exit Interview is a multi-purpose tool; it can make significant contributions in all of the following areas." The areas listed are important; it remains to be seen whether the form makes significant contributions toward them.

For reviews by Harry W. Karn and Floyd L. Ruch of a *(2 and 3), see 4:781.*

[1118]

★[Employee Rating Forms.] Employees; 1946–63; supervisors' ratings in 3 areas; human factor, work history, developmental factor; 3 rating forms; no manual; no data on reliability and validity; $8.75 per 25 forms, postage extra; specimen set not available; administration time not reported; Personnel Institute, Inc. *

a) EMPLOYEE RATING REPORT. 1950–62; 1 form ('62, 4 pages, identical with form copyrighted in 1950 except for format).

b) MANAGER RATING REPORT. 1946–63; 1 form ('63, 4 pages, identical with form copyrighted in 1946 except for format).

c) SALESMAN RATING REPORT. 1947–63; 1 form ('63, 4 pages, identical with form copyrighted in 1947 except for format).

[1119]

***[Executive, Industrial, and Sales Personnel Forms.]** Applicants for executive, office, industrial, or sales positions; 1949–62; most current forms are essentially the same as or identical with earlier forms; postage extra; Robert N. McMurry; Dartnell Corporation. *

a) [EXECUTIVE PERSONNEL FORMS.]

1) *Application for Executive Position.* 1949–59; Form No. EA-301 ('59, 4 pages); 1–99 copies, 10¢ each.

2) *Patterned Interview Form—Executive Position.* Applicants for management positions; 1949–62; Form No. EP-302 ('62, 6 pages); 1–99 copies, 30¢ each.

3) *Patterned Interview Form.* Applicants for positions of supervisor, foreman, engineer; 1955–59; Form No. EP-312 ('59, 4 pages); 1–99 copies, 15¢ each.

4) *Telephone Check on Executive Applicant.* 1950–59; Form No. ET-303 ('59, 1 page); 1–99 copies, 7¢ each.

5) *Selection and Evaluation Summary.* 1950–59; Form No. ES-404R ('59, 1 page, revision of form copyrighted 1955); 1–99 copies, 6¢ each.

6) *Position Analysis.* 1956–58; Form No. JA-601 ('58, 2 pages); 1–99 copies, 7¢ each.

7) *Physical Record.* 1958; Form No. PX-701 (4 pages); 1–99 copies, 15¢ each.

b) [INDUSTRIAL PERSONNEL FORMS.]

1) *Application for Position.* 1950–59; Form No. OA-201 ('59, 2 pages); 1–99 copies, 7¢ each.

2) *Application for Employment.* 1950–59; Form No. OC-200 ('59, 1 card); 1–99 copies, 6¢ each.
3) *Application for Office Position.* 1953–59; Form No. OA-205 ('59, 2 pages); 1–99 copies, 7¢ each.
4) *Patterned Interview (Short Form).* 1949–59; Form No. OP-202 ('59, 2 pages); 1–99 copies, 10¢ each.
5) *Patterned Interview Form.* Same as *a*(3) above.
6) *Telephone Check [With Previous Employers].* 1949–59; Form No. OT-203 ('59, 1 page); 1–99 copies, 6¢ each.
7) *Telephone Check With Schools.* 1949–57; Form No. OS-204 ('57, 1 page); 1–99 copies, 7¢ each.
8) *Selection and Evaluation Summary.* Same as *a*(5) above.
9) *Position Analysis.* Same as *a*(6) above.
10) *Physical Record.* Same as *a*(7) above.

c) [SALES PERSONNEL FORMS.]
1) *Application for Sales Position.* 1950–59; Form No. SA-101 ('59, 4 pages); 1–99 copies, 10¢ each.
2) *Patterned Interview Form—Sales Position.* 1950–58; Form No. SP-102 ('58, 4 pages); 1–99 copies, 15¢ each.
3) *Telephone Check on Sales Applicant.* 1949–59; Form No. ST-103 ('59, 1 page); 1–99 copies, 7¢ each.
4) *Sales Application Verification.* 1953–59; Form No. SV-104 ('59, 1 page); 1–99 copies, 6¢ each.
5) *Home Interview Report Form.* 1954–59; Form No. SH-114R ('59, 1 page); 1–99 copies, 7¢ each.
6) *Selection and Evaluation Summary.* Same as *a*(5) above.
7) *Sales Position Analysis.* 1962; 1 form (2 pages); 1–99 copies, 7¢ each.
8) *Physical Record.* Same as *a*(7) above.

REFERENCES

1. McMURRY, ROBERT N. *Tested Techniques of Personnel Selection.* Chicago, Ill.: Dartnell Corporation, 1961. Variously paged. *

JOHN P. FOLEY, JR., *President, J. P. Foley and Company, Inc., New York, New York.*

Prepared by the staff of the McMurry Company, the multilithed, looseleaf manual (*1*) covering this series of forms is divided into 12 sections, separated by appropriate index-tabbed dividers. Pages are numbered consecutively within each section. In addition to text material, the manual contains lists of tests, samples of charts, and other exhibits such as simple recruiting ads and diagrams of recommended space layouts for an efficient personnel department. The various selection forms—including position analysis, application, telephone and school check, physical record, patterned interview, as well as selection and evaluation summary forms—are classified into three types or groups for use with factory or office, sales, and executive personnel, respectively.

The purpose of the manual is to describe a comprehensive step-by-step selection program, to provide a practical reference source for personnel workers, and to furnish a text for the training of those engaged in the hiring process. Following a brief introduction highlighting the costly nature of selection errors, the manual presents a logical sequence of steps to be followed in the processing of job candidates. This sequence, as well as the essential content of the manual itself, can be best described by listing the consecutive sections: Why every business needs a planned selection program; Whom to hire, where to find them, how to screen them; What psychological tests contribute; Getting all the facts from and about the applicant; The patterned interview and how to use it; Interpreting the patterned interview; Motivation and emotional maturity in job placement; Matching the applicant and the job; Applying the step-by-step program to selecting plant and office employees; Applying the step-by-step program to selecting salesmen; Applying the step-by-step program to selecting executives and supervisors; and Using the step-by-step program effectively.

Three sections of the manual (9, 10, and 11) include a few briefly reported case histories of companies using the recommended program in the selection of different types of personnel. These are essentially *promotional testimonials,* however, and *cannot be accepted as validity data.* In fact, the reviewer finds in the manual no reported evidence of validity in the rigorous sense of the term.

Within the limitations necessarily imposed by a selection manual of this type, a number of *favorable features* deserve special notice. The need for extensive and effective recruiting is emphasized. Recognition is also given to the basic role of job specifications, the interviewer and others involved in the selection process being cautioned to think in terms of specific jobs and correlated requirements. Moreover, the tremendous diversity within the specifications for "selling" and other jobs bearing the same verbal tag is fully recognized.

Both the advantages and limitations of psychological tests are discussed. The reviewer was also impressed by the obvious, though all too frequently overlooked, distinction between the validities of personality tests applied in clinical or vocational counseling on the one hand, and personnel evaluation or selection situations on the other. Lip service is likewise given to the need for test validation.

In discussing the patterned interview, the authors commendably attempt to encourage the interviewer to dig beneath the surface facts, i.e., those reported by the applicant, in order to get at implications and other clues which are often the most significant findings of all. To this end, use is made of a "forcing technique" in which questions to be asked of the applicant are printed in black ink on the left hand side of the Interview Form, with space at the right of each question for the interviewer to record the applicant's answer—and with questions in red ink under each line which will force the interviewer to interpret (literally, to "question himself about") the applicant's answer. Use is also made of transparent overlays, each of which is geared to a key trait to which possible clues may be obtained from information supplied on different sections of the Interview Form. As indicated above, the purpose of such "forcing techniques" is commendable. And the techniques may—and undoubtedly do—work to a degree in some cases. But in the reviewer's opinion it is doubtful that such "canned procedures" represent the most effective approach to the depth interview.

Also commendable is the recognition of the fact that, irrespective of the accuracy and completeness of the applicant's rating on relevant job specifications, the final selection decision *cannot* be reached by summating or averaging the factor ratings. Thus, at the bottom of the Selection and Evaluation Summary the rater is cautioned: "Do not add or average these factors in making the over-all rating. Match the qualifications of the applicant against the requirements of the *particular position* for which he is being considered, and consider the importance of each mismatch." Although the manual omits much that could be said about compensating and other significant relationships within the makeup of an individual, there is at least some attempt to come to grips with the applicant's clinical makeup. The distinction between "can do" and "will do" factors represents an additional effort in the same desirable direction.

The techniques described in the manual are, of course, not limited to psychological tests. Rather, they encompass a variety of procedures to be followed in a comprehensive selection program. Most of these techniques have been utilized by companies for many years, although it is undoubtedly true that in many instances their application can be improved. It is precisely this role that the current selection manual is designed to serve. However, the purist might well question the use of the word "tested" in the manual's title.

One may also question the occasional loose or inconsistent use of terminology, as well as the confusion of degrees of abstraction. For example, the following are designated and discussed as "character traits": stability, industry, perseverance, ability to get along with others, loyalty, self-reliance, and leadership. With the possible exception of some aspects of "loyalty," one finds no reference to character as such. Rather, most of these traits fall within the motivational and personality spheres. Moreover, such a trait as "leadership" would seem to represent more of a composite trait than do others. One might likewise question why "manner" is listed under "can do" as opposed to "will do" factors. The reviewer would tend to feel that the latter distinction is essentially between "ability" and "motivational" considerations, in which case "manner" would fall within a very different category. Still another illustration of questionable terminology is found in the use of the term "empirical" in the following sentence: "Here the standards used are empirical —that is, by common sense analysis and judgment." As a matter of fact, psychologists use the term in exactly the opposite way, "empirical standards" being those established by experimentation rather than by a priori judgment and opinion.

"Diagnostic screening"—a technique employed in "go—no-go screening"—is described as being based upon careful scrutiny of the application form and any other written biographical material supplied by the candidate. With this in mind, it is difficult to see how "fine screens enable the rater to consider and weigh both favorable and unfavorable characteristics in the prospective employee." In the reviewer's opinion, such clinical-type judgments cannot—and should not—be made in the early screening stages of selection. Rather, they should be reserved for the final step of selection, viz., the intensive interview.

The "patterned interview" advocated by McMurry is little more than an orally administered questionnaire. True, certain "forcing techniques" are employed to encourage true evaluation, as noted above. However, the recommended technique is much too mechanical. Hence it loses many of the advantages of the true depth interview. Although one can certainly not criticize efforts to encourage the interviewer to penetrate beneath superficial information, one wonders if the procedures advocated provide the most effective answer to the problem. In the reviewer's opinion, the suggested technique is not sufficiently fluid or penetrating. Moreover, the impression is created that the "getting" and the "evaluating" of pertinent information are discrete temporal processes—an impression which is further accentuated by the use of the transparent overlays in interpreting information recorded in response to questions on the Interview Form.

When viewed overall, the selection program described in the present manual has much to commend it, providing the advocated procedures are utilized with both common sense and real skill. The manual fails to emphasize, however, that even careful study of such a printed program will not guarantee efficient selection. The real danger lies in blind application without understanding or skill. Certainly, no selection program will be any more effective than the way in which it is practiced.

For a review by Floyd L. Ruch, see 4:773.

[1120]

★Individual Background Survey. Business and industry; 1949–63; personal history and personality characteristics; 2 editions; no data on reliability; (25) minutes; Richardson, Bellows, Henry & Co., Inc. *

a) FORM S. 2 scores: part 1 (background), part 2 (self-description); 1 form ('49, 5 pages); manual ['63, 13 unnumbered pages]; $3.50 per 25 tests; 50¢ per key; $1 per manual; postage extra; $1 per specimen set, postpaid.

b) FORM T. 4 scoring scales: female clerical applicants and employees, male industrial applicants and employees, male clerical applicants and employees, male sales-supervisory-professional applicants and employees; 1 form ('52, 5 pages); manual ['63, 13 unnumbered pages]; $3.50 per 25 tests; 50¢ per set of keys; $1.25 per manual; postage extra; $1.50 per specimen set, postpaid.

[1121]

★Job Description Questionnaire. Employees; 1947–60; 1 form ('60, 8 pages, identical with form copyrighted in 1947 except for format); no manual; $8.75 per 25 forms, postage extra; specimen set not available; administration time not reported; Personnel Institute, Inc. *

[1122]

★The McQuaig Manpower Selection Series. Male applicants for office and sales positions; 1957; 4 parts in 2 booklets; no manual; 1–25 sets of *a* and *b*, 60¢ each; 1–25 copies of either *a* or *b*, 30¢ each; cash orders postpaid; Jack H. McQuaig; McQuaig Institute of Executive Training. *

a) [PARTS 1–3.] 1 form (6 pages).

1) *Part 1, The McQuaig Telephone Reference Check List.* [5–10] minutes.

2) *Part 2, The McQuaig Screening Interview Guide.* [30] minutes.

3) *Part 3, Personal History and Experience Record.* [20] minutes.

b) PART 4, THE MC QUAIG OCCUPATIONAL TEST. 1 form (6 pages); no data on reliability and validity; 15(20) minutes.

[1123]

***Merit Rating Series.** Industry; 1948–59; formerly called *Employee Evaluation Series;* 4–5 scores; 1 form (4 pages); 5 scales; manual ('53, 20 pages); mimeographed supplement ['59, 2 pages]; normal curve summary ('53, 4 pages); $5 per 20 forms; $5 per 20 normal curve summaries; postage extra; specimen set not available (forms and manual included in the complete set of the *Job-Tests Program*); (10–20) minutes; Joseph E. King; Industrial Psychology, Inc. *

a) PERFORMANCE: CLERICAL. 1956; 5 scores: quantity, accuracy, job knowledge, personal-work habits, overall; 1 form (some printings copyrighted in 1957).

b) PERFORMANCE: MECHANICAL. 1953–57; 5 scores: production, quality, job knowledge, personal-work habits, overall; 1 form ('57, identical with form copyrighted in 1953).

c) PERFORMANCE: SALES. 1953–57; 5 scores; volume, accuracy, job knowledge, personal-work habits, overall; 1 form ('57, identical with form copyrighted in 1953).

d) PERFORMANCE: TECHNICAL. 1953–57; 5 scores: same as for *b*; 1 form ('57, identical with form copyrighted in 1953).

e) PERFORMANCE: SUPERVISOR. 1953–57; 4 scores: department operation, employee relations, job knowledge, personal-work habits; 1 form ('57, identical with form copyrighted in 1953).

SEYMOUR LEVY, *Manager, Personnel Research and Manpower Development, The Pillsbury Company, Minneapolis, Minnesota.*

The *Merit Rating Series* is an elaborately designed and constructed set of instruments to measure job performance in five major job classifications. These measurement devices are part of an overall merit rating program that is described in a 20-page manual.

Materials fall into three categories: (*a*) a general description of a merit rating program as part of an overall personnel system, (*b*) the individual merit rating forms with scoring keys, and (*c*) a special form called the "Normal Curve Summary," to be used in providing some personnel controls on the evaluation process.

Rating forms have been developed for five major job families—clerical, mechanical, sales, technical, and supervisor. Each form is composed of 60 specific behavior statements to be answered either "yes" or "not true at present." The manual reports extensive data dealing with the item selection of each of these forms. For example, the frequency of endorsement of the item as listed for each of the five forms and phi coefficients are also presented for relating each item to the total score. The difficulty values have a mean of about .61 and the phi coefficients of .57. Items are given scoring weights based on the magnitude of the correlation with the total score. Each form consists of a number of specific statements that have been categorized into different performance areas. For example, the technical form includes items judged related to production, quality, job knowledge, personal work habits, and overall performance. Separate scores are provided for these subcategories.

Each merit rating scale contains three "bias" items that are comparable to the L scale items in the MMPI. In addition, there are several pairs of items of similar content with different phrasing designed to determine if the rater is consistent in his reporting on the subordinate. The bias items appear to be a very worthwhile contribution in the design of a measuring instrument. It is unfortunate that no specific data are reported relevant to their validity in screening out possible faking tendencies. Similarly, no data are reported with respect to the frequency of conflicting responses—the second control device.

There is considerable evidence with respect to the reliability of the different instruments and all the reliabilities appear to be quite satisfactory. Studies reporting satisfactory external validation are recorded for the clerical and for the mechanical scales. No validation data are made available for the other forms.

The Normal Curve Summary sheet is an elaborate control device to permit an overall evaluation of the ratings done by an individual supervisor and is a basis for a review of his personnel management practices. The scoring of the reports allows for a variety of different kinds of feedback to be made available to the rater, including such things as a tendency for his average rating to be too high or too low, insufficient variability, rating jobs rather than individuals, rating new employees too high or too low, salaries in relation to ratings, ratings out of line with aptitudes or with other personal records. This appears to be a possible and imaginative use of such kinds of data, but no information is provided to show what actually occurs when the material is used in this way.

The major value of these instruments is that they would appear to give some numerical estimate of the effectiveness of individuals. They represent, however, a point of view with respect to the merit rating process; namely, that it aims at defining individuals' behavior along specific kinds of traits or specific aspects of behavior. The difficulty with this concept is that it seems to be inconsistent with or in contradiction to the more recent thinking with respect to performance reviews, which emphasizes the goals for the future and the individual's development in his performance on the job, rather than measurement of his current performance level.

The test developer is to be congratulated on the intensiveness and care with which he has developed these instruments. From a technical design point of view, he has exhibited great care in developing this set of instruments; there has been care to insure that equal numbers of positive and negative statements appear in each of the performance reviews. It is unfortunate that he does not have more validation data. From his Normal Curve Summary sheet he should be able to develop, for example, some validation data with a salary criterion.

There is an increasing amount of research that raises some questions about this kind of instrument. In a series of recent studies conducted by the writer, as well as others, it has become clear that there are significant differences in the way that more and less effective managers describe the behavior of their subordinates on a series of specific behavior statements. It is evident that different kinds of behavior are valued and are elicited by different kinds of supervisors. These differences in supervisory style may limit the validity of specific statement rating forms and if these differences are ignored, they give greater weight and significance to these numerical scores than might be deserved.

For a review by Brent Baxter of the original series, see 4:770.

[1124]

★The Nagel Personnel Interviewing and Screening Forms. Job applicants; 1963; 4 forms; manual (12 pages plus sample copies of each form); no data on reliability and validity; $5 per 25 copies of *a* or *d*; $6.50 per 25 copies of *b* or *c*; $2.50 per manual; postpaid; Jerome H. Nagel Associates; Western Psychological Services. *

a) THE NAGEL INITIAL INTERVIEW FORM. 10 ratings: first impression, physical appearance, voice and speech, educational background, poise and self-confidence, ambition-motivation, intelligence, knowledge of

company, maturity, total impression; 1 form (2 pages); (15) minutes.
b) THE NAGEL PERSONAL HISTORY INVENTORY. 1 form (4 pages); [20–30] minutes.
c) THE NAGEL DEPTH INTERVIEW. Ratings in 8 areas: work factors, social and educational factors, economic factors and goals, personal factors, ability to do job, motivation to do job, likelihood to remain on job, suitability of personality; 1 form (4 pages); (30) minutes.
d) THE NAGEL EMPLOYMENT REFERENCE CHECK. 1 form (2 pages); [15–30] minutes.

[1125]

★[Performance Review Forms.] Employees, managers; 1960–61; 2 forms; no data on reliability or validity; cash orders postpaid; Seymour Levy; Martin M. Bruce. *
a) COUNSELING INTERVIEW SUMMARY. Employees, managers; 1960; for summarizing a performance review interview; 1 form (2 pages); 2 editions; counselor's manual (24 pages); preparatory manual for counselees (14 pages); form for employees: $2.50 per 25 forms, $1.50 per specimen set of 10 copies; form for managers: $3.00 per 25 forms, $1.75 per specimen set of 10 copies; $2.25 per counselee's manual; $2.50 per counselor's manual.
b) MANAGERIAL PERFORMANCE REVIEW. Managers; 1961; ratings by supervisors preparatory to performance review interview; 1 form (9 pages); $10 per 25 forms; $5.50 per specimen set of 10 forms.

[1126]

★Personal History Record. Applicants for executive and managerial positions; 1953; 1 form (9 pages); no manual; $5.50 per 25 copies, postage extra; 50¢ per specimen set, postpaid; Richardson, Bellows, Henry & Co., Inc. *

[1127]

★[Personnel Interviewing Forms.] Business and industry; 1956; no manual or other accessories; no data on reliability and validity; cash orders postpaid; Judd-Safian Associates; Martin M. Bruce. *
a) INITIAL INTERVIEW TABULATION. For recording ratings in 10 areas: appearance, voice and speech, poise, health, education, manner, responsiveness, experience, job stability, motivation; 1 form (1 page); $2.50 per 25 forms; $1.50 per specimen set.
b) PERSONAL HISTORY AUDIT. Job applicants; 1 form (4 pages); $5 per 25 forms; $2.75 per specimen set.
c) DEPTH INTERVIEW PATTERN. For interviewing in 5 areas: work evaluation, educational and social evaluation, economic evaluation, personality evaluation, ambitions evaluation; 1 form (4 pages); $6.25 per 25 forms; $3.50 per specimen set.
d) EMPLOYMENT REFERENCE INQUIRY. For securing employee evaluation from previous employers; 1 form (1 page); $2.50 per 25 forms; $1.50 per specimen set.

[1128]

★[Selection Interview Forms.] Business and industry; 1962; 2 parts; no data on reliability and validity; cash orders postpaid; Benjamin Balinsky; Martin M. Bruce. *
a) SELECTION INTERVIEW FORM. 1 form (6 pages); $6.25 per 25 forms; $3.50 per specimen set of 10 forms; [60–90] minutes.
b) INTERVIEW RATING FORM. 1 form (4 pages); $5 per 25 forms; $2.75 per specimen set of 10 forms; [15] minutes.

[1129]

★[Stevens-Thurow Personnel Forms.] Business and industry; 1951–64; 12 record and rating forms; postage extra; specimen sets not available; $7.50 per *Handbook on How to Hire* ('60, 121 pages) which contains copies of many of the forms and manuals listed below; Stevens, Thurow & Associates Inc. *
a) PERSONAL HISTORY RECORD. Applicants, employees; 1951–64; 2 forms: form for applicants ('64), form for employees ('62), (4 pages); manual ['51, 12 pages]; $3 per 25 forms; 50¢ per manual.
b) APPLICATION FOR POSITION. Applicants for clerical positions; 1951; 1 form ['51, 2 pages]; $1.50 per 25 forms.
c) APPLICATION FOR EMPLOYMENT. Applicants for shop or plant positions; 1951; 1 form (2 pages); $1.50 per 25 forms.
d) PRELIMINARY INTERVIEW. Prospective employees; 1954; 1 form (1 page); manual ['54, 3 pages]; $1.50 per 25 forms; (15) minutes.
e) INTERVIEWER'S GUIDE AND RATING FORM FOR PROSPECTIVE EMPLOYEES. Prospective employees; 1956–63; 1 form ('63, 4 pages, essentially the same as form published in 1956); manual ('62, 19 pages); $3 per 25 forms; $1 per manual.
f) EMPLOYMENT INTERVIEW SCHEDULE. Prospective employees; 1956; 1 form ('56, 2 pages); $1.50 per 25 forms.
g) WORK REFERENCE INVESTIGATION. 1951–63; 1 form ('63, 1 page); instructions ['63, 2 pages]; $1.50 per 25 forms.
h) JOB DESCRIPTION, [SHORT FORM]. 1956; 1 form (4 pages); $3 per 25 forms.
i) JOB DESCRIPTION QUESTIONNAIRE, [LONG FORM]. 1952; 1 form (8 pages); $6.25 per 25 forms.
j) APPRAISAL REPORT FOR MANAGEMENT PERSONNEL. Managers' rating of employees; 1959; 1 form ['59, 12 pages]; $6 per 25 forms.
k) APPRAISAL REPORT FOR MANAGEMENT PERSONNEL (SUPPLEMENTARY FORM FOR SALES MANAGERS). 1959; 1 form ['59, 4 pages]; $3 per 25 forms.
l) WORK BEHAVIOR INVENTORY. Supervisor's rating of employees; 1951–63; 2 forms ('63, 4 pages): *Employee Rating Report, Salesman Rating Report;* $3 per 25 forms.

[Other Tests]

For tests not listed above, see the following entries in *Tests in Print:* 1978, 1982, 1985, 1988–9, and 1991; out of print: 1979 and 1983.

SPECIFIC VOCATIONS

[Other Tests]

For tests not listed above, see the following entry in *Tests in Print:* 1993.

ACCOUNTING

[Other Tests]

For tests not listed above, see the following entries in *Tests in Print:* 1994–5.

DENTISTRY

[Other Tests]

For tests not listed above, see the following entries in *Tests in Print:* 1996–7.

ENGINEERING

[1130]

★AC Test of Creative Ability. Engineers and supervisors; 1953–60; 9 scores: quantity (parts 1, 2, 5), uniqueness (parts 1, 2, 3, 5), quality (part 4), total; parts 1, 2, and 5 may be administered alone for quantity scores only; Forms A ('53), B ('54), (12 pages); manual ('60, 25 pages); no data on reliability of subscores; norms for quantity scores only; scoring keys for uniqueness and quality scores must be developed locally; $6 per 20 tests; $1.25 per manual; postage extra; $1 per specimen set, postpaid; 80(90) minutes for full test, 45(50) minutes for parts 1, 2, and 5 alone; Richard H. Harris (test), A. L. Simberg (test), and Measurement Research Division, Industrial Relations Center, University of Chicago (manual); Education-Industry Service. *

REFERENCES

1. PARNES, SIDNEY J., AND MEADOW, ARNOLD. "Evaluation of Persistence of Effects Produced by a Creative Problem-Solving Course." *Psychol Rep* 7:357–61 O '60. * (*PA* 35:2700)

SAMUEL T. MAYO, *Associate Professor of Education, Loyola University, Chicago, Illinois.*

From an experimental sample of 14 short tests, the present test consists of 5 which held up under validation. Each of the original tests was based upon some facet of creativity as it was being discussed in 1953. Most of the hypotheses existing at that time had stemmed from Guilford's work, although the authors did not have access to his experimental tests. The above information was revealed in a private communication from one of the authors.

The scoring rationale was based upon the assumption that "more creative" persons would produce higher quantities of ideas, more unique ideas, and ideas of better quality. Unlike the *Owens' Creativity Test* and the *Purdue Creativity Test,* this test consists of verbal material rather than pictorial material. It is undoubtedly contaminated by a verbal fluency factor, judging from the correlations of .41 of the total score with the *Wonderlic Personnel Test* and .33 with the Kuder literary scale. Some of the specific content of Part 3 in both forms seems open to criticism as harboring potential biases associated with differing past experiences of individuals. For example, "Lawn Mower (Not motor driven)" is listed as one of several common machines or appliances. This device was much more common in 1953 than in 1963. Other devices which might be subject to bias would be "Gas Furnace" and "Electric Razor" (both in Form A), and "Table-model Radio" and "Gas Stove" (both in Form B).

The manual reports an unidentified Kuder-Richardson reliability coefficient of .92 for the total score without specifying the number of cases. An alternate form reliability coefficient of .75 is reported for 39 cases. The reliability estimates would seem to indicate that errors of measurement are larger than one would wish them to be for personnel selection or classification, especially on an individual basis.

Evidence of validity is presented in the manual in several sets of data, all of them based upon rather small samples which range in size from 35 to 56. It was disappointing to find that all the sets of data were in the form of tests of significance among means or medians or expectancy tables, to the exclusion of validity coefficients. Some of the mean or median scores on various subtests and total scores show significant differences between criterion groups judged as relatively high or low in creativity. In private communication with the author and some of his colleagues, it was reported that the test shows low to moderate correlations with two other tests associated with creative ability —*Word Fluency* and the *Cree Questionnaire.* It may also be revealing that the test correlates only .18 with Bennett's *Tests of Mechanical Comprehension* and shows predominantly nonsignificant correlations with a number of noncognitive measures. Taken as a whole, the statistical evidence in the manual is not very convincing.

In view of the disappointing statistical evidence for reliability and validity and also of the fact that the test has been administered to over 5,000 engineers and technical and supervisory personnel in industry, it seems unfortunate that correlational evidence of validity based upon much larger samples could not have been garnered.

When content validity is considered rationally, parts other than Part 3 seem satisfactory as stimuli to evoke divergent responses. The relevance of the item content to criteria seems intermediate between that of the *Owens' Creativity Test for Machine Design* and the *Purdue Creativity Test.*

This test cannot be recommended for application in predicting success in "tool design, gauge design, engineering, manufacturing, or process development," as the authors intended. The only kind of validity available in the manual is concurrent, while predictive validity studies are needed to support claims for generalizations from the test to the above work areas. Some doubt is also raised by unproved relevance of the highly semantic content of the test for the figural and symbolic content in the work areas. One hopes that the forthcoming revised manual promised by the publisher in a communication with the reviewer will report better norms and substantial statistical evidence on the adequacy of the test, as well as updated test content.

PHILIP R. MERRIFIELD, *Director, Bureau of Educational Research, Kent State University, Kent, Ohio.*

This test requires the examinee to write consequences of a described situation, explanations of statements assumed to be true, improvements of common appliances, solutions to situational problems, and uses of common objects. The similarity of these tasks to those used by other researchers in factor analytic studies is great; no reference to such research is made, nor is other factor analytic evidence adduced for the authors' interpretation of the results of their items and scoring procedures. The parts of this test do not appear to be measures of the same factor, although combining them into a composite called "creativity" is not illogical.

The procedures for scoring are, except for Part 4, quite mechanical. The quantity, or "Q," score is the total number of relevant responses, no guidelines being given in the manual as to relevance. The uniqueness, or "U," score is based on weights assigned inversely to frequency with which a response occurs. No guidelines are given to categorizing responses, so that a different verbalization of essentially the same idea would not necessarily count as a replication of that idea; further, the weighting procedure as described is quite sensitive both to size of sample used in establishing the weights and to the quantity of responses in that sample. This procedure induces experimental dependence of Q and U scores, and this accounts in part for the large correlation, .80 or greater, of the two scores from the same part. In the manual, this outcome is submitted as evidence for the "efficiency" of the Q scores at measuring U-performance, the latter apparently having some validity for the authors. Little information is lost using Q for U because so little was added in the measurement of U.

A reliability of .92 is claimed for the total test scores, based on Q and U scores from three of the five parts, U only from Part 3 and quality score from Part 4, all from a sample of size 36. Clearly this estimate is too high, due to the experimental dependence of Q and U scores from the same responses; it is unfortunate that the claim concludes a paragraph, apparently intended as tutorial, on the tendency of internal consistency estimates of reliability to be conservatively low. When the interpart correlations for Q are averaged and extended by Spearman-Brown procedures, the reliability estimate is .68; for the U scores, .74 seems a better estimate based on interpart correlations. As noted, the only reliabilities cited are based, apparently, on an early sample of AC Spark Plug Division engineers; other studies are cited, without additional reliability estimates reported. Perhaps the greatest question arises when one notes that the norms are based on 333 examinees; surely some estimate of reliability is available from so large a pool.

Validity is asserted on the basis of five studies, four from AC Spark Plug Division and one from Massachusetts Institute of Technology. Means of high and low criterion groups in two of the AC studies are, for every part, higher than the 99th percentile in the norms included in the manual. Unless the AC employees are indeed that much superior to the rest of the norms group, or the norms themselves are in error, the discrepancy requires explanation. In the MIT study, of 51 students with grades as a criterion, medians of the scores of A and B students are said to be significantly different, but no statistical test is named as being applied; the correlation between four grades—A, B, C, D—and rankings by quarters on the test is nearly zero; instructor's comments are referred to for 45 students in a table, but for 51 in a graph; quartiles for this graph differ from those used in the comparison of grades, although the examinees, and their scores, are presumably the same.

The only evidence of correlation between Form A and Form B, as published, is the report of a correlation of .75 between alternate forms before and after training.

In summary, the test items are ingenious and stimulating; they should educe interesting results in situations where semantic, not figural or symbolic, fluency is considered an appropriate measure. The uniqueness score adds little, partly because it is so mechanically derived; the user might consider developing a weighting scheme along more psychological lines, as in the recommended score for quality. However, he should not expect much help from the manual. Evidently the authors and publisher were aiming at an APA Level A test; with the present scoring procedures the test can be used as that, but with a sizable waste of potential information. Better tests for the factors implicit in these items are those by Guilford and his associates—*Consequences, Alternate Uses,* and *Christensen-Guilford Fluency Tests,* to name three. Norms for most of those tests are based on high school and college samples; the tests are factor analyzed; unfortunately, validation data are not extensive. The reviewer is involved as co-author of several of these tests, a fact the reader may wish to consider. Tests of other than semantic aspects of creativity, developed by Owens and by Lawshe and Harris, are reviewed elsewhere in this volume.

ALBERT S. THOMPSON, *Professor of Psychology and Education, Teachers College, Columbia University, New York, New York.*

This paper and pencil test of creative ability "is designed to give a measure of the quantity and the uniqueness of the ideas an individual can produce in a given situation." Each of the two parallel forms consists of five parts, requiring (*a*) listing possible consequences to problem situations as described, (*b*) giving reasons for a statement assumed to be true, (*c*) describing desirable improvements in common appliances, (*d*) giving solutions to specified problem situations, (*e*) listing possible uses of specified objects. Quantity scores are derived from Parts 1, 2, and 5, a "uniqueness" score from four of the parts, and a quality score from one.

The test materials are well printed and the instructions clear. Group administration is possible. Parts 1, 2, and 5 taken alone yield the quantity score based on 45 minutes of testing. The quantity score (Q) is standard and norms are provided based on 333 engineering and supervisory personnel. It is recommended in the manual that scoring keys and norms for the uniqueness and quality scores be developed for the specific situations and step-by-step procedures for developing such keys and norms are given.

This test was developed in the AC Spark Plug Division of General Motors Corporation for use in situations involving research, design, and development work. The data concerning the test are based on studies in this setting with various technical and engineering groups.

Although the test materials are oriented toward use in engineering-type situations, the items are sufficiently common in nature to be usable with a variety of groups. The procedures for developing scoring keys for the uniqueness and quality scores are designed to facilitate widespread use without danger of misinterpretation.

In summary, this test appears to be soundly constructed to yield a sample of the individual's productive behavior, for which quantity and quality scores can be derived. Except for the quantity score with engineering groups, norming and validation are required for other uses.

The reported research gives little insight into the nature of the characteristic being measured, except by a content analysis of the items and by noting the correlation with other tests and among the parts. No clear rationale as to the basic dimensions of creative behavior is presented or inferrable from the research data. In contrast to the Guilford and Purdue studies, the purpose is pragmatic prediction rather than analytic study. Further research and validation are necessary for the test to be useful in any ongoing employee appraisal program.

[1131]

***Engineering Aide Test.** Engineering aides; 1957–60; form 50-A ('57, 22 pages plus fold-out answer sheet); preliminary mimeographed manual ('57, 11 pages); general PPA mimeographed manual ['57, 7 pages]; norms ('60, 1 page); 10–49 tests, $1.20 each; $2 per specimen set; postpaid; 90(100) minutes; Public Personnel Association. *

[1132]

***The Graduate Record Examinations Advanced Tests: Engineering.** Grades 16–17; 1939–62; for more complete information, see 762; 180(200) minutes; Educational Testing Service. *

For a review of the testing program, see 5:601.

[1133]

***Minnesota Engineering Analogies Test.** Candidates for graduate school and industry; 1954–63; IBM; Forms E, F, ('54, 4 pages); preliminary manual ('55, 11 pages); bulletin of information ('63, 36 pages); revised procedures for testing center operation ('63, 8 pages); distribution restricted and test administered at specified licensed university centers; scoring and reporting handled by the local center; examination fee to centers: $1 per examinee; fees to examinees are determined locally and include reporting of scores to the examinee and to 3 institutions or companies designated at the time of testing; additional score reports may be secured from the publisher at a fee of $1 each; (45-60) minutes; Marvin D. Dunnette; Psychological Corporation. *

REFERENCES

1-6. See 5:933.
7. MacKinnon, Donald W. "Fostering Creativity in Students of Engineering." *J Eng Ed* 52:129-42 D '61. * (*PA* 36:4HD29M)
8. Spencer, George M., and Reynolds, Harlan J. "Validity Information Exchange, No. 14-04: D.O.T. Code 0-17, 0-19, Electrical and Mechanical Engineers." *Personnel Psychol* 14:456-8 w '61. *

For reviews by A. Pemberton Johnson and William B. Schrader, see 5:933.

[1134]

★National Engineering Aptitude Search Test: The Junior Engineering Technical Society. Grades 7-12; 1963, c1947-62; tests administered each spring at Junior Engineering Technical Society chapter centers; 5 scores: verbal reasoning, numerical ability, total, mechanical reasoning, space relations; IBM; 1 form ['63, c1947-62, 34 pages, special reprint of corresponding parts of *Differential Aptitude Tests,* Form M]; mimeographed directions for administering ['63, 2 pages]; information bulletin ['63, 5 pages]; score reports based on regular DAT norms; examination fee, $2 per student; postage extra; 115(130) minutes; Psychological Corporation. *

[1135]

★The Owens' Creativity Test for Machine Design. Engineers and engineering students; 1960; 4 scores: power source apparatus designs (workable solutions, total solutions), applications of mechanisms, weighted total; Form CT-1 (31 pages); manual (31 pages); no norms; publisher recommends use of local norms; $7.50 per 20 tests; 75¢ per manual; $1.25 per specimen set; cash orders postpaid; 160(170) minutes; William A. Owens; Iowa State University Press. *

REFERENCES

1. Owens, W. A.; Schumacher, C. F.; and Clark, J. B. "The Measurement of Creativity in Machine Design." *J Appl Psychol* 41:297-302 O '57. *

Samuel T. Mayo, *Associate Professor of Education, Loyola University, Chicago, Illinois.*

The present test consists of 15 problems of two kinds. Ten minutes are allowed for each problem. In Part 1 the task in each problem is to design as many mechanisms to connect two types of given motions as one can in the time allowed. In Part 2 the task in each problem is to list as many different devices in which each given connecting mechanism might function. Content of problems is specific to machine design and was chosen upon the advice of a panel of mechanical engineers at a university.

Actual construction of the test is not described either in the manual or in the one published article on the test (*1*). The article describes a study to determine the effectiveness of nine instruments in discriminating creative from noncreative design engineers. The present test, or "battery" as the author calls it, consists of two of the four instruments to survive item analysis and cross validation, and, it must be noted, the only cognitive instruments to survive. According to the article, the impetus behind the study, which culminated in the present test, was the critical shortage of creative machine designers during World War II and the fact that "an alarmingly small proportion of those present were either native born or the products of American Schools of Engineering."

Ease of scoring varies among the three component scores. Two of the scores—"total solutions" and "applications of mechanisms"—are arrived at quite easily and objectively by simple classification and counting processes guided by directions largely free of ambiguity. The "workable solutions" score of the Power Source Apparatus Test involves a considerable degree of subjectivity. The manual gives drawings for a number of more frequently occurring solutions. For drawings not shown, the examiner must use the instructions in the manual and his own best judgment. This would seem at first glance to be a decided disadvantage. However, the evidence on the reliability of the "workable solutions" score seems quite satisfactory. Furthermore, in spite of the high intercorrelation between the total and "workable" scores of the Power Source Apparatus Test for combined data for all companies (.89), the author seems justified in keeping both scores, in view of the evidence in the article from both simple and multiple biserial correlation coefficients and from discriminant analysis.

Only indices of equivalence are provided, and, according to the author, evidence as to the stability of test scores over time was not available at the time the manual was written.

Concurrent validity is reported but not predictive or construct validity. Content validity appears to be claimed on the basis of (*a*) the author's cautious statement that no validity for the battery is claimed outside the machine design field and (*b*) the fact that a panel of mechanical engineers screened the test content. In his article, however, the author did promise a predictive validity study with 1,500 students at 24 colleges and universities and in private communication with the reviewer he reported that the study was in progress at the time of the review. The author summarizes his quantitative evidence for validity in the following statement from the manual:

Let us assume two equal groups of engineers employed by a particular firm and matched for age, education, and relevant experience; let us further assume that one of the groups would be rated as "creative" by its immediate superiors and that the other would be rated as "non-creative." Based upon past experience, test scores obtained from the present battery would coincide with the posited ratings of creativity or non-creativity in about three-fourths of the cases.

No correlations with any outside tests are reported. However, some evidence is available, in the article and in personal correspondence with the author, against the hypothesis that relations between the scores and the criterion could be explained by common mental ability factors. In the study reported in the article, three aptitude tests—Space Relations, Figure Matrices, and Number Series—failed to discriminate the criterion groups. Furthermore, the author reported to the reviewer in private communication that engineers rated as creative were found to have had college averages typically of about C+.

The author is to be commended for his excellent reporting of evidence for concurrent validity, for his detailed and clear directions for scoring the more objective parts of the test, for his brave attempt at describing a scoring system for the more subjective parts, and for his clear operational definitions of the two criterion groups of creative and noncreative designers. Adversely, there seems to be much information which could well have been included in the manual, some of which is known by the reviewer to have been available at the time the manual was written. Examples of such information include a description of how the test problems themselves were constructed and tried out, more of the statistical results which are reported in the article, correlations with other tests, and evidence to discount the hypothesis that the test is heavily loaded with mental ability factors. The author also seems open to criticism in his use of the word "development" as indicating noncreative design work since the term is used to indicate creativity (the opposite) in two other tests, the *AC Test of Creative Ability* and the *Purdue Creativity Test*.

In summary, this appears to be a psychometrically good test. It has demonstrated its usefulness in differentiating creative from noncreative among experienced machine designers. When the results are available from the study of predictive validity, its usefulness as a predictor will be better known. Of the tests of creativity in engineering which are known to the reviewer, this would clearly be the best for use in machine design. It is not recommended for use outside machine design at the present time.

Philip R. Merrifield, *Director, Bureau of Educational Research, Kent State University, Kent, Ohio.*

The author states that his intention is to differentiate "creative designers in the machine design field from those better suited for development work." Within this specific area, his test should do a good job; however, it does require a certain amount of ability to sketch machine parts and to visualize spatial changes in the relations of objects. Presumably the level needed would have been attained by employed engineers in the course of their training, and thus differences in these abilities would not contribute much to the differences in scores on this test. Another source of unwanted differentiation, not emphasized by the author, is the tendency of scorers to reward neat, precise drawings which may be little better, in terms of creative solutions, than less skillful products. On the other hand, perhaps that difference is related to the value of the employee in terms of how well he can communicate his ideas in a hasty sketch.

The instructions for scoring the Power Source Apparatus Test (Part 1) items as "unworkable," "common and workable," or "unique and workable" are detailed and explicit, with sketches for each item. Nevertheless, as the author recommends, the scorer will need some knowledge of machine design terminology as a basis for judgment.

The item format for the Applications of Mechanisms Test (Part 2) could be improved by adding lines to guide the examinee's written responses. Perhaps more space would be enjoyed by the examinee and by the scorer, who must decide how many separate applications are suggested. The mechanisms might be more easily visualized were the sketches three-dimensional views instead of elevations.

Reliabilities were computed from odd-even scores, as the test appeared to be not speeded; the values given are .85 for PSA total, .83 for PSA workable, and .91 for the Applications of Mechanisms Test; AMT scores correlate about .40 with PSA workable and .50 with

PSA total; but there is a correlation of nearly .90 between the PSA total and PSA workable, induced at least in part by their mutual experimental dependence. Using both scores in a multiple regression problem, as the author did, may result in an inflated value for the multiple correlation, or, as in the present case, in a negative weight for one of the scores in the regression equation.

The validity studies are summarized by the author by combining the results from several (number not stated) companies for a total of 159 employed design engineers tested in 1953 and 1954. Validities are described in terms of per cent of correct predictions, assuming 50 per cent to be creative in computing the selection ratios. The validity for all examinees pooled was 66 per cent, compared to an average of 86 per cent for the within-company predictions. These data support the author's advice that each user should develop his own norms.

In summary, this is an interesting test, possessing both high face validity and some concurrent validity against supervisor's rating of creativity. The manual is excellent; the author categorizes the test as Level C in terms of APA standards, and the reviewer agrees.

[1136]

★**Purdue Creativity Test.** Applicants for engineering positions; 1960, c1957–60; test booklet title is *Creativity Test;* 3 scores: fluency, flexibility, total; Forms G, H, ('60, c1957, 21 pages); manual ('60, 10 pages); $7.50 per 25 tests, postage extra; 50¢ per specimen set, postpaid; 40(50) minutes; C. H. Lawshe and D. H. Harris; distributed by University Book Store. *

REFERENCES

1. Harris, Douglas Hershel, Jr. *The Development of a Test of Creativity in Engineering.* Doctor's thesis, Purdue University (Lafayette, Ind.), 1959. (*DA* 20:2374)
2. Harris, Douglas. "The Development and Validation of a Test of Creativity in Engineering." *J Appl Psychol* 44:254–7 Ag 60. * (*PA* 35:4032)

Samuel T. Mayo, *Associate Professor of Education, Loyola University, Chicago, Illinois.*

The stated purpose of this test is to find out how "fluent, flexible, and original" engineering personnel are in their thinking. According to the publisher's catalog, it is recommended for identifying design engineers who "have the capacity to be really creative in the designs they produce" and research and development engineers "whose success depends upon the production of new ideas." Furthermore, the catalog states, "This test measures creativity in engineering." The 20 items, each requiring two minutes, are of three kinds. In the first 8, one is asked to list as many possible uses as he can for each object alone as shown in a three-dimensional drawing; in the next 4 items one is asked to list as many uses as he can for two objects when used together as shown in a three-dimensional drawing; in the last 8 items one is asked to look at a line drawing and answer the question, "What is this?" and to "List as many possibilities as you can." Neither items nor pages are numbered. In administering the test the only oral instruction given when going on to the next item is the word, "Time," every two minutes. The flexibility score is obtained from the first 12 items by counting and summing the number of different categories of uses represented by responses, while the fluency score is obtained from the last 8 items by counting and summing the number of responses to each item. The total score is obtained by adding the flexibility subscore to one half of the fluency subscore. The manual does not explain the origin of the formula.

The authors recommend that each user accumulate his own applicant norms. The only norms reported in the manual are a set based upon 106 professional engineers. Norms are ostensibly given for fluency, flexibility, and total scores. Any test user would intuitively expect the total scores in the norms table to be based upon application of the formula for combining the two subscores. However, it is obvious that the norms for total score have not been derived from the formula. As an example, if we assume that a person places at the 95th percentile in both Fluency and Flexibility, he would place at only the 67th percentile on the published norms. Furthermore, a person at the median on both subtests would place at the 20th percentile on total score.

The reliability data reported are based upon a sample of only 64 professional engineers and leave much to be desired. The authors say that the two forms were "considered" to be comparable, although they do not report any empirical data on comparability. The split-half coefficients reported are .86 for Flexibility, .93 for Fluency, and .95 for total score. The two forms were used "interchangeably" in obtaining these coefficients, so that one does not know upon which form each coefficient was based. Separate coefficients should have been reported for the two forms. The second kind of reliability reported is that of interscorer agreement for two scorers; these coefficients are .87 for Flexibility and .97 for total score. Again, the authors' language is ambiguous. It is not clear whether the same form or alternate forms were used. The kind of coefficient which should have been reported is alternate form (once with same graders and again with different graders).

The only kind of validity reported for the published test is in the form of expectancy tables. From an earlier, experimental form of the test, cross validation on 29 machine design students, according to the manual, yielded validities of .16 for Fluency and .73 for Flexibility with a criterion of instructors' rating on the ability to produce original ideas for the development of machines to perform certain unusual functions. In view of the insignificant validity of the fluency score, the statement of the authors that "These correlations indicated....that the Creativity Scores showed considerable promise in the measurement of creativity" seems incredible. A series of expectancy tables in bar graph form is presented. Their effectiveness is weakened by the small samples involved. The samples range from 29 to 42 cases for three separate samples, with 104 cases for the samples combined. It would have been helpful if the manual had indicated that the intervals given under the column labeled "Test Scores" include equal numbers of persons. This information was reported in correspondence with one of the authors but does not appear in the manual. It is not at all clear how the two samples with odd numbers of cases (29 and 33) could have been split into two equal sized groups. Also, when percentages are computed from subgroups of around 15 cases each, a change of 1 case makes a change of nearly 7 per cent. Since the norms for total score were based upon scores which are not in accordance with the recommended scoring formula, one is led to suspect that the expectancy tables are also based upon such inappropriate scores.

Correlations with two other tests are reported, the *Wonderlic Personnel Test* and the *Tests of Mechanical Comprehension*. The coefficients for subtests and total score are all nonsignificant. Thus, this test appears to be measuring something different from general mental ability or mechanical aptitude. Correlations of creativity scores with age, education, and experience are not clearly demonstrated, but the wording of the manual suggests that these factors may not have been significantly related. One is left in the peculiar position of knowing some of the variables with which the test is not related but knowing little about what the test is actually measuring.

In summary, this test cannot be recommended for its intended purposes on the basis of the presently available data. It may very well be potentially an effective test for its stated purposes, but the manual does not adequately support these claims. It is to be hoped that the authors and publisher will see fit to gather some acceptable statistical evidence on the test's characteristics and will clarify the manual so that the user will know how and why he is using a particular score in a particular manner.

Philip R. Merrifield, *Director, Bureau of Educational Research, Kent State University, Kent, Ohio.*

The tasks in this test are three, all based on three-dimensional drawings of objects: list possible uses for a single object; list possible uses for two objects together; and list possible identifications for an object. There are 20 items in each form; each item is to be answered in two minutes. Close proctoring may be necessary to maintain time limits on items presented on facing pages.

Somewhat surprisingly, the authors obtain only two subscores from the three item types; perhaps a third score would add sensitivity to the test. More importantly, the fluency and flexibility scores are derived from disjoint sets of items, so there is no experimental dependence. Flexibility scores are based on items 1–12, eight of the first type noted above, and four of the second. The score for an item is the number of categories, specified in the manual, into which the examinee's responses fall; the flexibility score for the test is the sum of item scores; all items are scored using the same categories. This kind of scoring can verge on being a fluency score, if the examinee spreads his responses widely over the structure imposed by the scorer. In the reviewer's opinion, this procedure leads to a measure better called "sensitivity to dimensions of a problem" than the traditional "flexibility." However, it is a component of the composite behavior called "creative." The fluency score is the number of responses from items 13–20, all of the third type, after duplicate ideas have been eliminated. Examples of duplicates are given in the manual. Total score is defined as the score for flexibility plus one half the score for fluency; however, when used to combine the fluency and flexibility scores for given centiles in the "norms" in the manual, this formula gives results inconsistent with the given centiles for total score. It would appear that the score entry under Fluency is in fact the fluency component, i.e., one half the raw score for fluency. Under this assumption, the reviewer estimates the correlation between Fluency and Flexibility to be about .40; a value for this correlation is not reported in the manual. It is to be hoped that the authors will clarify this confusion in the next edition of the manual. In the meantime the user is well advised to follow their suggestion to develop his own norms.

Two kinds of reliability estimates are given for the flexibility score: an interscorer correlation of .87 and a split-half reliability coefficient of .86. Split-half reliabilities of .93 and .95 are reported for the fluency and total scores, respectively. The interscorer correlation for total score was .97. These values would be of greater use were the standard deviations of the scores presented; the standard error of estimate is more indicative of practical utility than is an average index of a relationship. No means or standard deviations are reported.

Concurrent validity is reported for total score only, using a group of 104 product, process, and project engineers rated by their supervisor on a criterion of creativity, defined as the ability to develop new solutions for problems. Better predictions were obtained in the product and process engineer groups than in the project engineer group; the criterion was applied in the first two by a paired-comparison technique, and in the third by a nomination technique, so there may be some confounding of procedure of criterion evaluation and the results. Users should, of course, investigate procedures for making criterion assessment both reliable and valid. The results are presented in bar graphs labeled "chances in a hundred of being superior." No statistical probabilities of the outcomes are given. In the composite graph for all three groups, five bars represent chances of groups which are separated approximately into fifths according to the norms in the manual; for the three kinds of engineers separately, the dichotomy point for scores varies. Perhaps it is the median for each group.

In summary, this test appears to have been soundly developed, with reliability adequate for use with group averages and perhaps with individuals, and with concurrent validity of some significance. Except for the matter of the norms discussed above, the manual appears to be carefully done, and contains references. One might wish for a more elaborate statistical treatment of the results of validation studies, and for some attempt by the authors to provide factorial validity for the constructs they claim to measure. However, in general, this test should be quite useful.

[Other Tests]

For tests not listed above, see the following entries in *Tests in Print:* 2001–2 and 2006–8.

LAW

[Other Tests]

For tests not listed above, see the following entries in *Tests in Print:* 2009–10.

MEDICINE

[1137]

***Medical College Admission Test.** Applicants for admission to member colleges of the Association of American Medical Colleges; 1946–64; 4 scores: verbal, quantitative, general information, science; administered 2 times annually (spring, fall) at centers established by the publisher; IBM; examiner's manual ('63, 11 pages); announcement ('64, 23 pages); examination fee, $15; fee includes reporting of scores to 1–6 schools designated at time of application; $1 per additional report; scores not reported to examinees; 210(255) minutes; Psychological Corporation. *

REFERENCES

1–11. See 4:817.
12–15. See 5:932.
16. SCOTT, J. ALLEN, AND BRENKUS, PEGGY M. "Medical College Admission Test Scores as an Aid in Teaching Medical Statistics." *J Med Ed* 29:39–43 Ap '54. * (*PA* 29:4644)
17. STALNAKER, JOHN M. "Report of the Director of Studies." *J Med Ed* 29:42–6 D '54. *
18. STALNAKER, JOHN M. "The Study of Applicants, 1954–1955." *J Med Ed* 30:625–36 N '55. * (*PA* 30:5243)
19. WATSON, ROBERT I. "Predicting Academic Success Through Achievement and Aptitude Tests." *J Med Ed* 30:383–90 Jl '55. * (*PA* 30:5248)
20. GEE, HELEN HOFER. "The Study of Applicants, 1955–56." *J Med Ed* 31:863–9 D '56. *
21. GLASER, ROBERT J. "Appraising Intellectual Characteristics." *J Med Ed* 32:31–43 O pt 2 '57. *
22. JACKSON, GEORGE GEE, AND KELLOW, WILLIAM F. "An Experiment With the Group Interview in the Selection of Medical Students." *J Med Ed* 33:491–500 Je '58. *
23. CROWDER, DOLORES GARCIA. "Prediction of First-Year Grades in a Medical College." *Ed & Psychol Meas* 19:637–9 w '59. * (*PA* 34:6563)
24. HILL, JOSEPH K. "Assessment of Intellectual Promise for Medical School." *J Med Ed* 34:959–64 O '59. *
25. KLINGER, ERIC, AND GEE, HELEN HOFER. "The Study of Applicants, 1957–58." *J Med Ed* 34:424–35 Ap '59. *
26. "Medical College Admission Test Data for 1959–60 Applicants." *J Med Ed* 35:1037–9 N '60. *
27. JOHNSON, DAVIS G. "An 'Actuarial' Approach to Medical Student Selection." *J Med Ed* 35:158–63 F '60. *
28. KLINGER, ERIC, AND GEE, HELEN HOFER. "The Study of Applicants, 1958–59." *J Med Ed* 35:120–33 F '60. *
29. LITTLE, J. MAXWELL; GEE, HELEN HOFER; AND NOVICK, MELVIN R. "A Study of the Medical College Admission Test in Relation to Academic Difficulties in Medical School." *J Med Ed* 35:264–72 Mr '60. *

30. "Application Activity and MCAT Data of Applicants to the Class of 1960–61." *J Med Ed* 36:1619–20 N '61. *
31. GARFIELD, SOL L., AND WOLPIN, MILTON. "MCAT Scores and Continuation in Medical School." *J Med Ed* 36:888–91 Ag '61. *
32. HUTCHINS, EDWIN B., AND GEE, HELEN HOFER. "The Study of Applicants, 1959–60." *J Med Ed* 36:289–304 Ap '61. *
33. RICHARDS, JAMES M., JR., AND TAYLOR, CALVIN W. "Predicting Academic Achievement in a College of Medicine From Grades, Test Scores, Interviews, and Ratings." *Ed & Psychol Meas* 21:987–94 w '61. *
34. SCHUMACHER, CHARLES F., AND GEE, HELEN HOFER. "The Relationship Between Initial and Retest Scores on the Medical College Admission Test." *J Med Ed* 36:129–33 F '61. *
35. SCHWARTZMAN, A. E.; HUNTER, R. C. A.; AND PRINCE, R. H. "Intellectual Factors and Academic Performance in Medical Undergraduates." *J Med Ed* 36:353–8 Ap '61. *
36. "MCAT Data of Applicants to the Class of 1961–62." *J Med Ed* 37:1130–1 O '62. *
37. BUEHLER, JOHN A., AND TRAINER, JOSEPH B. "Prediction of Medical School Performance and Its Relationship to Achievement." *J Med Ed* 37:10–8 Ja '62. *
38. CEITHAML, JOSEPH. "Student Selection in United States Medical Schools." *J Med Ed* 37:171–6 Mr '62. *
39. GEE, HELEN HOFER, AND SCHUMACHER, CHARLES F. "Reply to a Note on the Validity of the Medical College Admission Test." *J Med Ed* 37:787–9 Ag '62. *
40. GROFF, MORRIS, AND GRUBER, EDWARD C. *How to Score High on the Medical College Admission Test, Revised Edition.* New York: Arco Publishing Co., Inc., 1962. Pp. 278. *
41. HUTCHINS, EDWIN B. "The Student and His Environment." *J Med Ed* 37:67–82 D '62. *
42. HUTCHINS, EDWIN B., AND GEE, HELEN HOFER. "The Study of Applicants, 1960–61." *J Med Ed* 37:1203–12 N '62. *
43. JOHNSON, DAVIS G. "A Multifactor Method of Evaluating Medical School Applicants." *J Med Ed* 37:656–65 Jl '62. *
44. LEVITT, EUGENE E., AND TYLER, EDWARD A. "A Note on the Validity of the Medical College Admission Test." *J Med Ed* 37:395–6 Ap '62. *
45. MOORE, ROBERT A. "The Use of Objective Tests in the Selection of Medical Students." *J Med Ed* 37:455–62 My '62. *
46. RICHARDS, JAMES M., JR.; TAYLOR, CALVIN W.; AND PRICE, PHILIP B. "The Prediction of Medical Intern Performance." *J Appl Psychol* 46:142–6 Ap '62. *
47. SCHWARTZMAN, A. E.; HUNTER, R. C. A.; AND LOHRENZ, J. G. "Factors Related to Medical School Achievement." *J Med Ed* 37:749–59 Ag '62. *
48. SCHWARTZMAN, A. E.; HUNTER, R. C. A.; AND LOHRENZ, J. G. "Factors Related to Student Withdrawals From Medical Schools." *J Med Ed* 37:1114–20 O '62. *
49. WORK, HENRY H. "A Rationale for Grouping of Medical Students." *J Med Ed* 37:130–2 F '62. *
50. "Application Activity and MCAT Data of Applicants to the Class of 1962–63." *J Med Ed* 38:774–5 S '63. *
51. CONGER, JOHN J., AND FITZ, REGINALD H. "Prediction of Success in Medical School." *J Med Ed* 38:943–8 N '63. *
52. GOUGH, HARRISON G.; HALL, WALLACE B.; AND HARRIS, ROBERT E. "Admissions Procedures as Forecasters of Performance in Medical School." *J Med Ed* 38:983–98 D '63. *
53. HOFFMAN, E. LEE; WING, CLIFF W., JR.; AND LIEF, HAROLD I. "Short and Long-Term Predictions About Medical Students." *J Med Ed* 38:852–7 O '63. *
54. HUTCHINS, EDWIN B. "The Study of Applicants, 1961–62." *J Med Ed* 38:707–17 S '63. *
55. HUTCHINS, EDWIN B. "The Study of Applicants, 1962–63." *J Med Ed* 38:999–1003 D '63. *
56. HUTCHINS, EDWIN B., AND MORRIS, WOODROW W. "A Follow-Up Study of Non-Entrants and High Ability Rejected Applicants to the 1958–59 Entering Class of U.S. Medical Schools." *J Med Ed* 38:1023–8 D '63. *
57. RUDMAN, JACK. *How to Pass Medical College Admission Test: Questions and Answers, Second Edition.* Brooklyn, N.Y.: College Publishing Corporation, 1963. Pp. 298. *
58. SANAZARO, PAUL J., AND HUTCHINS, EDWIN B. "The Origin and Rationale of the Medical College Admission Test." *J Med Ed* 38:1044–50 D '63. *

ROBERT L. EBEL, *Professor of Education, Michigan State University, East Lansing, Michigan.* [Review of Forms Q and R.]

TEST CONTENT. The content of these forms is essentially the same as that of recent earlier forms. Items testing verbal and mathematical skills and knowledge in the areas of science and general culture are included. An outline of the current forms shows this composition: Part 1, Verbal (75 items, 20 minutes), Part 2, Science (86 items, 60 minutes), Part 3, Quantitative (50 items, 45 minutes), Part 4, General Information (75 items, 25 minutes), and Part 5, Experimental (86 items, 60 minutes). The fifth part does not contribute to the examinee's reported score.

For a test intended to assess aptitude for the study of medicine, this type of content seems quite appropriate. Verbal and mathematical skills are essential tools of learning, and items testing for these skills have established their value in tests of scholastic aptitude at all educational levels. A good foundation of knowledge of the sciences of biology, chemistry, and physics is clearly essential to the study of medicine. While a test of general culture, composed of items on history, literature, art, music, philosophy, economics, government, etc., may not have the highest relevance to success in the study of medicine, it can provide important information on the cultural backgrounds and prospects of future physicians. In the judgment of this reviewer, such a test is entirely appropriate in a battery intended to select medical students.

From time to time the *Medical College Admission Test* has been criticized for its emphasis on such conventional educational outcomes as knowledge and skills, presumably to the neglect of complex, higher mental abilities such as flexibility in thinking, balanced judgment, critical perception, and synthesizing ability. But these abilities are seldom defined in terms of operations that might be used to measure them. Further, the psychological soundness of speculations concerning their nature and functions often seems open to question. Until better evidence is available that such "higher" abilities do in fact exist as definite, significant, measurable factors of success in the study or practice of medicine, this test should not be criticized for seeming to neglect them.

ITEM STYLE. While the content of the current forms resembles that of earlier forms quite closely, there are perceptible differences in item style. The current items tend to be shorter, and perhaps simpler and more direct in statement. When an estimate of the total number of words in the test was divided by the number of items, a quotient of approximately 20 words per item was obtained for the current forms. The corresponding figure for earlier forms was 38 words per item. This verbal brevity is reflected in the size of the test booklet, currently 32 pages contrasted with 52 pages earlier. More of the shorter items (372) are included in the current 210-minute test than of the previous longer items (316) in a 215-minute test.

The increase in number of items obviously is not proportional to the reduction in number of words per item. Shortening the items probably reduces the time required for reading but may not reduce correspondingly the time required to choose a best answer. It is also possible that current forms have even more generous time limits than earlier forms. Limited data available to the reviewer tend to support this hypothesis. (Unfortunately, since there is little agreement among test specialists on a common, valid, easily interpretable measure of speededness, a common basis for comparing the speededness of two tests is not often available.)

Briefly stated items are likely to be regarded as more purely factual and, hence, less intellectually respectable than items based on more complex problems. But in spite of the current preference for test items which look nonfactual, there have been few cogent arguments, and there is surprisingly little experimental evidence, to support the view that such items measure something different from, or more useful than, that which factual items measure. The current forms of the test do require the examinee to use the factual knowledge he possesses to solve reasonably significant problems. This reviewer is not inclined to criticize the test on the ground that its items are excessively factual.

METRIC PROPERTIES. Analysis of the scores on Form R of the test, obtained from 2,960 applicants tested in May 1963 yielded these statistics.

Subtest	Items	Mean	SD	Reliability
Verbal	75	47 (47)	13 (9)	.91
Science	86	54 (54)	12 (11)	.89
Quantitative	50	32 (31)	8 (6)	.90
General Information	75	41 (47)	9 (9)	.79

The numbers in parentheses after the subtest means express hypothetical optimum values for the means, defined as scores midway between the maximum possible score and the expected chance score. It is apparent that, except for the general information test, the obtained means are very close to these hypothetical optima.

The numbers in parentheses after the subtest standard deviations express hypothetical minimum values for the standard deviations, defined as one sixth of the range between the maximum possible score and the expected chance score. Again, except for the general information test, the obtained standard deviations all exceed these minima.

Part of the reason for the somewhat high difficulty and the somewhat low reliability (K-R 20) of the general information subtest may be the heterogeneity and specificity of the item content. These characteristics are inherent in a test which asks for specific information over a broad area of knowledge. But it is also probable that more stringent selection of the best items from a larger pool of tryout items would result in a somewhat better test. In Form R of this test, 41 of the 75 items showed reasonably good item statistics (r of .20 or higher, and p between .35 and .80). But, 27 of the 75 items were below .20 in discrimination, and 8 more were either very easy (p above .80) or very difficult (p below .35). If these 34 weak items were replaced by items higher in discrimination and more appropriate in difficulty, this subtest would show somewhat better metric properties. Incidentally, the general information subtest of Form Q yielded a better spread of scores, and more reliable scores, than that of Form R.

Intercorrelations of the subtest scores, ranked from high to low, are as follows: .68, Verbal and General Information; .58, Science and Quantitative; .53, Verbal and Science; .48, Science and General Information; .34, Verbal and Quantitative; .31, Quantitative and General Information. In view of the content of the various subtests and their generally high reliabilities, these values are about what would be expected. None is high enough to cast serious doubt on the usefulness of separate subtest scores. There is no reason to believe that the intercorrelations have been inflated by test form factors or that any changes in the type of items used in the subtests would result in a useful reduction of the intercorrelations.

Since 1951, the reported scores on each subtest have been standard scores with a mean of 500 and a standard deviation of 100, with all standard scores for each new form presumably equivalent in meaning to those issued in 1951. Statistics of the distributions of standard scores actually issued since 1951 show a high degree of consistency. Scores from the May administrations tend to be higher than those from the October administrations, but the score levels from year to year show no appreciable change.

There are good reasons for equating scores on different forms of a test when students who have taken those different forms may be competing for admission to the same medical school class. If the job is done competently and carefully, as it has undoubtedly been done in the case of these tests, the equating is likely to be reasonably precise and dependable, in the short run. But it would be dangerous to claim, and there is really no need to claim, that the standard scores can retain identical meanings perpetually. Successive forms of the *Medical College Admission Test* change from year to year, as they must if they are to improve. The demands of medical schools on students also change, as they also must if they are to improve. So also must premedical education change. Many other changes may affect indirectly the kinds of students the medical schools need and are likely to get. In the face of all these complications, the question, "Did medical schools get better students in 1963 than they got in 1951?" becomes an essentially unanswerable question. About the only thing that can be said with reasonable certainty is that they probably did get, and probably should have gotten, a somewhat different kind of student.

VALIDITY. The tests comprising the *Medical College Admission Test* were selected and designed rationally and on the basis of considerable prior experience with similar tests intended to serve the same or closely related purposes. These tests thus possss the same kind of validity as do the curricula offered by medical schools in their efforts to develop the medical competence of their students. The best claim to validity that this or any similar test can have rests on the informed judgments of the experts selected to design and construct it. Their judgments, of course, are not infallible. If those who make higher scores on the test do not succeed in the study of medicine better than those of their classmates who made lower scores, the judgments may be called into serious question. But the essential validity of these tests is built into them. It is not something on which judgment must be completely suspended until after the test has been given, the students have earned some grades, and correlations between test scores and grades have been computed. Nor is it something simple enough to be adequately reported by a single coefficient of correlation between some composite of the test scores and some single set of imperfect criterion measures.

The content and form of this test battery seem well chosen in view of the purposes it is intended to serve. Various kinds of data from various sources confirm the expectation that students who receive high scores on the test succeed better in medical schools than those who receive lower scores. Some of these data are reported in a preliminary version of an MCAT handbook. Other data have been reported from time to time in various journals and newsletters. The medical school which cannot improve its selection of students by taking scores on these tests (or similar tests) into consideration will be a rare exception.

Some types of aptitude tests, particularly those composed of a few types of novel, unusual tasks, have proved to be subject to seriously invalidating influences of special coaching. But tests like the MCAT, which use more conventional types of test items and which sample more extensively in the fields of knowledge relevant to a broad area of professional study such as medicine, are less likely to be injured by special coaching. Students who repeat the test without special intervening study may expect to gain from 20 to 40 points on the standard score scale. Students who have not been studying science or mathematics just prior to taking the test will undoubtedly benefit from some careful reviewing in these areas. But the gain in score even on these tests is not likely to be spectacular. On the other tests, which measure verbal skills and general information, the amount of material to be reviewed is so large and diffuse that a very considerable effort in review would be likely to yield only a very small gain in score. On the whole, the test appears to be satisfactorily resistant to the invalidating effects of special coaching.

GENERAL EVALUATION. No doubt it is apparent that the reviewer looked for weaknesses in these tests where he thought they might be found, but that he found few of any degree and none that seemed serious. It should also be apparent that he was generously supplied by the publisher with descriptions and statistics on which to base his evaluations.

The *Medical College Admission Test* is a well

designed, expertly constructed test that serves its intended purposes admirably. Those who make the test and those who direct its use have recognized their responsibilities and discharged them competently. Better selections of students for admission to medical schools are being made with the help of this test than could possibly be made without it (or some test closely resembling it). All those who have been responsible for the development of these tests and of the supporting statistical data deserve high praise.

PHILIP H. DUBOIS, *Professsor of Psychology, Washington University, St. Louis, Missouri.*
[Review of Forms Q and R.]

The *Medical College Admission Test,* produced by the Psychological Corporation under contract with the Association of American Medical Colleges, is only for the eyes of bona fide applicants for admission to medical training, who, on an appointed day, are exposed to 286 functional items for exactly 2 hours, 30 minutes. For reasons of security, the test is not copyrighted, but rather controlled by an exact accounting for every copy. Two forms were seen; other forms exist or will be made.

In the present state of the art of psychometrics it is not difficult to produce a test of useful validity for any curriculum involving lectures and assigned readings. Reading comprehension will work; vocabulary (especially vocabulary close to the technical area) will work; a reasonably germane information test will work. Accordingly, it is not surprising that predictive validity against classroom success is considered to be satisfactory for a test having the following content: 75 verbal items (analogies, antonyms, synonyms), 86 science items (biology, chemistry, physics), 50 quantitative items (algebra, arithmetic, geometry), and 75 general information items (humanities, social science).

There is no doubt that the MCAT is competently prepared. The patina is right: precise instructions; carefully phrased item stems; four choices for each item; attractive decoys for the unknowing. The timing has been adjusted so that few candidates fail to finish, and the scoring formula is simply the number right. Such characteristics denote workmanship.

Statistical data rate the five stars awarded only to the best: a scaled score system (with expected mean of 500 and standard deviation of 100, which relate the present forms to their predecessors); norms in terms of percentages of applicants scoring below selected scaled scores by subtest, by sex, by college status, by undergraduate major, and by region; internal consistency reliabilities within subtests ranging from .79 to .93; consistent subtest intercorrelation patterns from administration to administration. (Correlations of the quantitative score with the verbal and general information scores are in the .30's; correlations of the science subtest are in the .50's; while the verbal and general information scores correlate in the .70's. The overall factor pattern is complex, just as the science subtest is reported to be internally.)

MCAT is the product of group planning and group evaluation. An impressive vector of talent—psychologists and medical educators from the Association of American Medical Colleges, and outside psychological and subject matter consultants—have advised the administrative and technical staff of the contractor in formal and informal conferences. Plans exist for the construction, refinement, and standardization of further alternate forms; for determining relationships with other high level tests; for finding predictive validities in medical education, school by school and course by course, and in the clinical years; and for modifications as premedical and medical curricula are changed and as new measurement approaches are conceived and perfected.

The MCAT handbook, seen by this reviewer in draft form, is intended for the use of members of admission committees of participating medical colleges. It discusses the use of selection devices currently available to medical schools, including the application form, letters of recommendation, interviews, interest and personality schedules, and college grades, all in relation to the MCAT, which is represented as the most objective, but not necessarily the most revealing, source of information about the applicant. The test is stated to be a uniform measure of aptitude and achievement, which makes possible direct comparisons of applicants with widely varying backgrounds. These claims are modest, and are well supported by validity data.

An important social problem is the recruitment and selection of doctors, just as it is of scientists, government administrators, military leaders, industrial executives, and hundreds of other varieties of top level personnel. Those who write selection tests and who sit on admission committees determine an appreciable portion of future variance within an occupation. Of course, with medicine we are dealing with an enlarging cluster of occupations—for which the common prerequisites have been judged by the MCAT makers to center around general intelligence and scientific knowledge.

Measurement techniques and the overall frame of reference being what they are, we can expect little better than the present MCAT. As criteria become better defined, and as selection materials are refined, validities may go up a bit, but no reviewer is likely to suggest changes that will radically improve the instrument.

He can, however, express surprise that the instrument has only three types of symbols: verbal, mathematical, and chemical-physical. In an instrument to select for occupations involving people and their health he had expected more pictorial content and graphical representation and more items reflecting knowledge of and interest in human beings. If doctors are to be physical scientists, the MCAT will pick them. On the other hand, if the bedside manner is worth conserving, the MCAT won't conserve it—that is left to the admission committees.

For a review by Alexander G. Wesman of forms previously published by Educational Testing Service, see 5:932; for a review by Morey J. Wantman, see 4:817.

[1138]

★Medical School Instructor Attitude Inventory. Medical school faculty members; 1961; 6 scores: democratic-autocratic attitude toward teaching, critical-complimentary attitude toward medical schools, liberal-traditional attitude toward medical education, appreciative-depreciative attitude toward medical students, favorable-unfavorable attitude toward full-time teachers, favorable-unfavorable attitude toward part-time teachers; 1 form (120 cards); manual (19 pages); 75¢ per set of cards; $2.50 per 100 sets of record sheets; manual free; $1 per specimen set; postpaid; (75) minutes; Edwin F. Rosinski; the Author. *

REFERENCES

1. Rosinski, Edwin F. "Changing the Attitudes of Medical School Instructors." *J Ed Res* 55:128–31 N '61. *

[1139]

***Veterinary Aptitude Test.** Veterinary school applicants; 1951–58; tests administered at centers established by the publisher; 4 scores: reading comprehension, science information, verbal memory, total; IBM; 1 form ('58); 4 parts in 3 booklets: Parts 1 (14 pages), 2 and 3 (11 pages, formerly called *Veterinary Achievement Test*), 4 (6 pages); directions for administering ['58, 8 pages, mimeographed]; examination fee, $10; fee includes reporting of scores to any 3 schools designated at time of application; $2 per additional report; postpaid; scores not reported to examinees; 135(165) minutes; Loyal C. Payne and William A. Owens; Psychological Corporation. *

REFERENCES

1–3. See 5:957.
4. Owens, William A. "An Aptitude Test for Veterinary Medicine." *J Appl Psychol* 34:295–9 O '50. * (*PA* 26:594)
5. Brown, Frederick G. "Predicting Success in the Clinical and Preclinical Years of Veterinary Medical School." *J Am Vet Med Assn* 137:428–9 O 1 '60. *
6. Ray, D. K. *A Validation Study of the Revised Veterinary Aptitude Test.* Master's thesis, Purdue University (Lafayette, Ind.), 1961.

[Other Tests]

For tests not listed above, see the following entry in *Tests in Print:* 2012.

MISCELLANEOUS

[1140]

★Card Punch Operator Aptitude Test. Prospective trainees on IBM card punch equipment; 1952–60; formerly called *Card Punch Aptitude Test;* 1 form ('52, 9 pages); revised manual ('60, 7 pages); no data on reliability; "reasonable quantities" and specimen sets free; 12(20) minutes; W. J. McNamara; distributed by International Business Machines Corporation. *

REFERENCES

1. McNamara, W. J., and Hughes, J. L. "The Selection of Card Punch Operators." *Personnel Psychol* 8:417–27 w '55. * (*PA* 31:1835)
2. Shott, Gerald L.; Albright, Lewis E.; and Glennon, J. R. "Predicting Turnover in an Automated Office Situation." *Personnel Psychol* 16:213–9 au '63. * (*PA* 38:6714)

[1141]

★Chemical Operators Selection Test, Revised Edition. Male high school students and applicants for positions of chemical operator; 1958–63; 6 scores: physical principles, tables, graphs, judgment, flow sheet, total; IBM; Forms [A] ('59, 21 pages, mimeographed), B ('63, 12 pages); no manual; no data on reliability; norms ['59, 9 pages] for total score only; separate answer sheets must be used; 30¢ per test; 50¢ per 25 answer sheets; 50¢ per scoring stencil; 25¢ per set of norms; postage extra; 60[70] minutes; M. A. Storr, J. H. McPherson, P. A. Maschino, and R. G. Garner (norms and Form B); Dow Chemical Co. *

REFERENCES

1. Coats, J. E.; with the assistance of R. G. Garner. *A Study of the Nature of the Chemical Operator's Occupation and the Personal Qualities That Contribute to Successful Operator Performance.* Midland, Mich.: Dow Chemical Co., March 1961. Pp. iv, 112. *

[1142]

★The Diebold Personnel Tests. Programmers and systems analysts for automatic data processing and computing installations; 1959; 5 tests; manual (19 pages); no data on reliability; no norms; scoring by the publisher only; $35 per set of tests (including scoring service), postpaid; John Diebold & Associates. *

a) SYMBOLS BLOCK DIAGRAM TEST. 1 form (16 pages); 60(85) minutes.

b) CODE INDEX TEST. 1 form (4 pages); 5(10) minutes.

c) RELATIONS IN NUMBERS TEST. 1 form (10 pages); 60(90) minutes.

d) CODE MATCHING TEST. 1 form (10 pages); 30(50) minutes.

e) WORD SEQUENCE TEST. 1 form (6 pages); 15(25) minutes.

[1143]

***Firefighter Test.** Prospective firemen; 1954–61; title on form 20-A is *Test for Firefighter;* forms 20-A ('54, 31 pages plus fold-out answer sheet), 20-B ('57, 26 pages plus fold-out answer sheet), 20-C ('61, 26 pages plus fold-out answer sheet); revised mimeographed manual ('61, 10 pages); general PPA mimeographed directions ['57, 7 pages]; no data on reliability of form 20-C; no data on validity; no norms for form 20-C; 10–49 tests, $1.60 each; $2 per specimen set; postpaid; 105(115) minutes; Public Personnel Association. *

[1144]

★[Firefighting Promotion Tests.] Prospective firemen promotees; 1960–63; IBM; 3 tests; manual ('63, 17 pages); no data on reliability; rental fee: 5 or fewer examinees, $25; specimen set of any one test loaned for fee of $5, which may be applied to rental fee; 210(225) minutes; McCann Associates. *

a) ASSISTANT FIRE CHIEF. 1961–63; 4 scores: firefighting knowledge, fire supervision, fire administration, total; 1 form ('61, 20 pages).

b) CAPTAIN. 1962–63; 5 scores: pre-fire practices, extinguishment practices, overhaul-salvage-rescue, fire supervision, total; 1 form ('62, 22 pages).

c) LIEUTENANT. 1962–63; 4 scores: pre-fire practices, extinguishment practices, fire supervision, total; 1 form ('62, 18 pages).

[1145]

★Fireman Examination. Prospective firemen; 1961–62; 8–9 scores: learning ability (verbal, quantitative, total), fireman aptitude (interest, common sense, mechanical, total), easy verbal learning (form 70 only), total; IBM; forms 62, 70; form 70, which is identical with form 62 except for easy verbal learning subtest, is recommended when a fixed passing score of 70 or 75 per cent is required; 2 parts: booklet 1 ('61, 7 pages, learning ability), booklet 2 ('61, 9–11 pages, fireman aptitude); separate manuals ('61, 17–19 mimeographed pages) for forms 62 and 70; candidate identification sheet ('62, 1 page); distribution restricted to civil service commissions and municipal officials; no data on reliability and validity; norms for subtotal and total scores only; separate IBM scoreable answer sheets must be used; 10–49 tests, $1.50 each; specimen set loaned free; postpaid; 50(60) minutes for booklet 1, 90(100) minutes for booklet 2 of form 62, 120(130) minutes for booklet 2 of form 70; McCann Associates. *

[1146]

★Memory and Observation Tests for Policeman. Prospective policemen; 1962; for use with *Police Examination;* IBM; 1 form; 2 tests; manual (8 pages); candidate identification sheet (1 page); no data on reliability; no description of normative population; distribution restricted to civil service commissions and municipal officials; separate IBM scorable answer sheets must be used; specimen set loaned free; postpaid; McCann Associates. *

a) MEMORY TEST FOR POLICEMAN. 1 form (5 pages); memory sheet (1 page); 1–49 tests, 25¢ each; 10(15) minutes for memory sheet, 10(15) minutes for test booklet.

b) OBSERVATION TEST FOR POLICEMAN. 1 form (6 pages); observation sheet (2 pages); 10–49 tests, 50¢ each; 10(15) minutes for observation sheet, 30(35) minutes for test booklet.

[1147]

★[NCR Test Battery for Prospective Check-Out Cashiers.] Prospective checkstand operators; 1961; 2 tests; battery manual (19 pages); $3 per set of 10 tests of *a* and 10 answer-scoring sheets for *b*; 30¢ per single copy of *a*; 75¢ per single copy of *b*; $1 per manual; postpaid; Ward J. Jenssen, Inc.; National Cash Register Co. *

a) PERSONNEL TEST FOR PROSPECTIVE CHECK-OUT CASHIERS. 3 scores: register tape checking, non-verbal reasoning, register key X-ing; 1 form (18 pages); 20(30) minutes.

b) PERSONAL OPINION BALLOT FOR PROSPECTIVE CHECK-OUT CASHIERS. Attitude and temperament survey; 1 form (9 pages); separate answer-scoring sheets must be used; (30) minutes.

DAVID O. HERMAN, *Staff Psychologist, The Psychological Corporation, New York, New York.*

This battery of four subtests has been designed for a specific employment situation, the selection of checkout cashiers. The first three tests measure perceptual and cognitive abilities in one booklet, called the Personnel Test. The fourth section is a single-purpose, single-score, personality device, entitled the Personal Opinion Ballot.

The manual and the reusable booklet of questions for the personality device are printed on durable stock. The manual is well written and organized, and the directions for administration and scoring are clear. On the other hand, the manual's omissions are unusual by current publishing standards, and make a full evaluation of the battery impossible.

Part 1, Register Tape Checking, of the Personnel Test reproduces pairs of cash register tapes which are to be compared, line by line. Part 2, Non-Verbal Reasoning, contains a variety of abstract and numerical problems of several types, such as series completion, analogy completion, and identifying which of several decimal numbers is the largest. Each item in Part 3, Register Key X-ing, consists of a printed representation of two columns of keys on a cash register, above which a price is written. The examinee marks the keys he would punch in ringing up the given price. These three tests are scored directly in the test booklet by means of strip keys.

The Personal Opinion Ballot consists of nine groups of 14 items each. For each block of items the examinee must check the seven which are more true of him and the seven which are less so. About two thirds of the items are keyed, each one adding from 1 to 5 points to an individual's score. The items' scoring weights were derived empirically by contrasting responses to individual items made by employed cashiers who were rated high in interpersonal relations, with the responses of those rated low in this area. Reading through the keyed items, one gathers that high scorers could be described as self-effacing, noncompetitive, uncomplaining, and inclined to mind their own business. To be sure, one is unlikely to locate managerial talent with this test, and the author's claim that it measures qualities shared by successful checkout cashiers has some face validity. Unfortunately, empirical evidence is not offered.

To score the Personal Opinion Ballot, the semitransparent answer sheet is laid over the key, which is essentially a replica of the working part of the answer sheet with scoring weights written into the answer spaces for the keyed responses. These weights are summed over all of the keyed responses which the examinee has checked to give the raw score. Instead of summing all item scores in one step, the raw score is obtained by summing nine subtotals (one for each item block) which are obtained and recorded separately, presumably to help minimize scoring errors. The scoring could be greatly simplified if item weights of only 0 or 1 were used instead of weights of 0 through 5. The manual mentions no study of the effect which unit weighting has on reliability and validity; since the effect has often been found negligible, the author should investigate this simplified procedure.

Percentile norms are presented for each of the three parts of the Personnel Test, and another table gives short verbal descriptions of people scoring at four levels on the Personal Opinion Ballot. In addition, the manual describes a single weighted composite of raw scores on all four parts, which was derived through multiple regression analysis. This combined score may be conveniently computed using a table printed on the cover of the Personnel Test booklet. The regression coefficients are not presented, nor can they be reconstructed, since the tests' standard deviations are also not given. Furthermore, the regression weights used for the total weighted composite appear not to have been cross validated, and "freezing" them at this point may be premature.

Since each test's influence on the battery composite is unknown, it may be that the three sections of the Personnel Test alone predict job performance nearly as well as they do in combination with the Personal Opinion Ballot. This issue is important because it appears that the item scoring weights for the Ballot were derived using one criterion—ratings of success in store-related interpersonal relations—while the Ballot's regression weight, which is used in computing the total weighted score for the entire battery, was derived using another criterion—a single score which may or may not have reflected interpersonal relations. Briefly, when a test is valid for one purpose, it may not be valid for another.

Although norms are not given for the composite predictor, the manual discusses the issues involved in setting a cutting score, such as personnel needs in relation to labor market conditions, the quality of current employees, and so on. An illustrative expectancy table is presented, which shows the chances of job success for those scoring in various ranges on the battery composite. The source of this table is not specified, however, and its entries, which are per cents, have apparently been rounded, for they are all multiples of 10 per cent.

Retest reliability coefficients for the four part scores of the battery, computed on a sample of 207 checkout cashiers, are said to range from .79 to .86. Surprisingly, the reliability of the recommended composite of these scores is not given.

The manual presents no evidence of the battery's validity, except for the questionable expectancy table mentioned above. One section of the manual does claim validity for each part of the battery; for instance it is said of Register Tape Checking that it "correlates extremely well with both accuracy of work and with speed of performance as a check-out cashier." Similar claims made for the other sections are at least consistent with what one would expect after examining the tests' content, but no supporting statistics whatever are offered to help the reader reach his own conclusions.

SUMMARY. This battery is an interesting example of a collection of tests constructed for a specific task. Its success in fulfilling its purpose cannot be evaluated, since not enough pertinent information is provided by the manual. Although the tests comprising the battery do have apparent face validity, until more detailed information, such as from a local validity study or an adequately revised manual, is available the battery must be considered experimental.

[1148]

★**Police Performance Rating System.** Policemen; 1964; ratings by immediate supervisors on 100 traits yielding 7 factor ratings (quality of work, interpersonal relationship traits, quantity of work, personality traits, character traits, quality of supervision given, quality of administrative work) and an overall rating; individual trait rating sheet (2 pages); summary form (1 page); manual (18 pages); no data on reliability and validity; $2 per 50 rating sheets; $2 per 100 summary forms; 50¢ per manual; specimen set loaned for rental fee of $2; postpaid; "more than an hour"; McCann Associates. *

[1149]

★**Police Promotion Examinations.** Prospective policemen promotees; 1960–63; IBM; 5 tests; manual ('63, 17 pages); no data on reliability; separate answer sheets must be used; rental fee: 5 or fewer examinees, $25; specimen set of any one test loaned for a fee of $5, which may be applied to rental fee; postpaid; 210(235) minutes; McCann Associates. *

a) CHIEF OF POLICE. 1960–63; 6 scores: police supervision, police administration, crime investigation, other police knowledges, law, total; 1 form ('60, 20 pages).

b) CAPTAIN. 1962–63; 6 scores: same as for *a*; 1 form ('62, 23 pages).

c) DETECTIVE. 1962–63; 4 scores: investigative judgment, crime investigation, law, total; 1 form ('62, 24 pages).

d) LIEUTENANT. 1962–63; 6 scores: patrol, other police knowledges, crime investigation, law, police supervision, total; 1 form ('62, 23 pages).

e) SERGEANT. 1962–63; 6 scores: same as for *d*; 1 form ('62, 23 pages).

[1150]

★**Policeman Examination.** Prospective policemen; 1960–62; IBM; 8–9 scores: learning ability (verbal, quantitative, total), police aptitude (interest, common sense, public relations, total), easy verbal learning (forms 70 only), total; forms 62A, 62B, 70A, 70B; forms 70A and 70B, which are identical with the corresponding forms 62A and 62B except for the easy verbal learning subtest, are recommended when a fixed passing score of 70 or 75 per cent is required; 2 parts: booklet 1 ('62, 7 pages, learning ability, common to forms 62 and 70), booklet 2 ('62, 11–14 pages, police aptitude); separate manuals ('60, 17–19 pages) for forms 62 and 70; candidate identification sheet ('62, 1 page); distribution restricted to civil service commissions and municipal officials; no data on reliability and validity; norms for subtotal and total scores only; separate IBM scorable answer sheets must be used; 10–49 tests, $1.50 each; specimen set loaned free; postpaid; 50(60) minutes for booklet 1, 90(100) minutes for booklet 2 of forms 62A and 62B, 120(130) minutes for booklet 2 of forms 70A and 70B; McCann Associates. *

[1151]

***Policeman Test.** Policemen and prospective policemen; 1953–60; forms 10-A ('53), 10-B, ('56), 10-C ('60), (30 pages plus fold-out answer sheet); mimeographed manual ['60, 12 pages]; general PPA mimeographed directions ['57, 7 pages]; no data on reliability and validity; 10–49 tests, $1.60 each; $2 per specimen set; postpaid; 95(105) minutes; Public Personnel Association. *

[1152]

★**The Potter-Nash Aptitude Test for Lumber Inspectors and Other General Personnel Who Handle Lumber.** Employees in woodworking industries; 1958; title on test is *The P-N Test;* arithmetic; 1 form ['58, 1 mimeographed page]; mimeographed description ('58, 2 pages); no data on reliability; no description of normative population; $2.50 per 4 tests, postpaid; specimen set not available; (30) minutes; F. T. Potter and N. Nash; N. Nash. *

[1153]

★**Revised Programmer Aptitude Test.** Applicants for programming training on IBM electronic computers; 1955–59; revision of *Programmers Aptitude Test;* IBM; 1 form ('59, 15 pages); manual ('59, 7 pages); "reasonable quantities" and specimen sets free; 60(75) minutes; J. L. Hughes and W. J. McNamara; distributed by International Business Machines Corporation. *

REFERENCES

1. McNamara, W. J., and Hughes, J. L. "A Review of Research on the Selection of Computer Programmers." *Personnel Psychol* 14:39–51 sp '61. * (*PA* 36: 4LD39M)

2. Oliver, Thomas C., and Willis, Warren K. "A Study of the Validity of the Programmer Aptitude Test." *Ed & Psychol Meas* 23:823–5 w '63. *

[1154]

★**Visual Comprehension Test for Detective.** Prospective police detectives; 1963; IBM; 1 form (7 pages); stimulus material presented by 16 mm. film; no manual; no data on reliability and validity; rental fee: 10 or fewer examinees, $50; specimen set (including film) loaned for fee of $35, which may be applied to rental fee; postpaid; (25) minutes for film, 45(50) minutes for test; McCann Associates. *

[Other Tests]

For tests not listed above, see the following entries in *Tests in Print:* 2014–5, 2017, 2019, 2021–2, and 2025–7.

NURSING

[1155]

***Achievement Tests in Nursing.** Nursing school students; 1952–63; tests administered at any time by individual schools; IBM; 12 tests; directions sheet ['57, 1 page]; technical data sheet ('63, 1 page); no charge to schools requiring *Entrance Examination for Schools of Nursing;* 35¢ per test per student for other schools; postpaid; fee includes scoring and reporting service; (40) minutes per test; Psychological Corporation. *

a) ANATOMY AND PHYSIOLOGY. 1953–63; 1 form ('60, 8 pages).

b) CHEMISTRY. 1954–63; 1 form ['54, 13 pages].

c) COMMUNICABLE DISEASES. 1953–63; 1 form ('61, 10 pages).

d) MEDICAL NURSING. 1952–63; 1 form ('61, 12 pages).

e) MICROBIOLOGY. 1952–63; 1 form ('61, 11 pages).

f) NUTRITION AND DIET THERAPY. 1952–63; 1 form ('57, 8 pages).

g) OBSTETRICAL NURSING. 1952–63; 1 form ('61, 12 pages).

h) PEDIATRIC NURSING. 1952–63; 1 form ('63, 11 pages).

i) PHARMACOLOGY. 1952–63; 1 form ('57, 10 pages).

j) PSYCHIATRIC NURSING. 1952–63; 1 form ('57, 11 pages).

k) PSYCHOLOGY AND SOCIOLOGY. 1957–63; 1 form ('57, 8 pages).
l) SURGICAL NURSING. 1952–63; 1 form ('57, 10 pages).

[1156]

★Entrance Examination for Schools of Nursing. Nursing school applicants; 1938–63; tests administered at centers established by the publisher; 13 scores: 7 ability scores (verbal, numerical, science, reading comprehension, arithmetic processes, general information, scholastic aptitude total) and 6 personality scores (achievement, orderliness, persistence, congeniality, altruism, respectfulness); IBM; Forms 1 ('62), 2 ('63), (30 pages); part 6, Personal Preference Schedule (formerly printed separately as *The Personal Preference Schedule for Student Nurses*) is an adaptation of *Edwards Personal Preference Schedule* and is common to both forms; manual ['62, 9 pages]; norms ['63, 1 page] for each form; interpretation leaflet ['62, 4 pages]; examination fee: $8 for initial testing, $10 for reexamination; fee includes reporting of scores to the school of nursing through which application for examination was made; $2 per additional report; postpaid; scores not reported to examinees; 155(210) minutes; Psychological Corporation. *

REFERENCES

1. CARRUTH, MARGARET SCRUGGS. *Predictive Value of Nursing School Tests.* Master's thesis, Southern Methodist University (Dallas, Tex.), 1944.
2. SARTAIN, A. Q. "Predicting Success in a School of Nursing." *J Appl Psychol* 30:234–40 Je '46. * (*PA* 20:4350)

[1157]

***NLN Achievement Tests for Basic Professional Nursing.** Students in state-approved schools of professional nursing; 1943–64; tests loaned to schools for their own use; IBM; 1 form; 2 levels; mimeographed manual ('63, 20 pages); directions for administering [no date, 4 pages]; interpretive manual for schools ('64, 45 pages, see *1* below); mimeographed norms ('61–63, 1–2 pages) for each test; examination fees: 75¢ per test where total score reported only, $1 where part scores reported; postpaid one way; [90–120] per test; National League for Nursing, Inc. *

a) [REGULAR ACHIEVEMENT TESTS.] Undergraduates completing courses in the subjects specified; 1943–63; 10 tests.
1) *Anatomy and Physiology.* 1943–55; Form 155 ('55, 19 pages).
2) *Chemistry.* 1943–63; Form 963 ('63, 24 pages).
3) *Microbiology.* 1943–61; Form 761 ('61, 21 pages).
4) *Normal Nutrition.* 1946–62; formerly called *Nutrition and Diet Therapy;* Form 662 ('62, 23 pages).
5) *Basic Pharmacology.* 1944–60; formerly called *Pharmacology and Therapeutics;* Form 960 ('60, 22 pages).
6) *Medical-Surgical Nursing.* 1956–62; 4 scores: medical nursing, surgical nursing, medical-surgical nursing, total; Form 862 ('62, 28 pages).
7) *Public Health Nursing.* 1956–61; for degree programs only; 4 scores: nursing practice and service, public health nursing, science and general information, total; Form 661 ('61, 36 pages).
8) *Obstetric Nursing.* 1945–61; 4 scores: antepartal care, partal and post-partal care of mothers, care of newborn, total; Form 361 ('61, 29 pages).
9) *Nursing of Children.* 1945–61; 4 scores: normal growth and development, pediatric nursing (psychosocial aspects, other aspects), total; Form 461 ('61, 29 pages).
10) *Psychiatric Nursing.* 1945–59; 3 scores: psychiatric nursing practices, facts and principles, total; Form 359 ('59, 34 pages).

b) [COMPREHENSIVE ACHIEVEMENT TESTS.] Seniors about to graduate; 1957–63; 8 tests.
1) *Diet Therapy and Applied Nutrition.* 1962; Form 762 ('62, 27 pages).
2) *Pharmacology in Clinical Nursing (Facts and Principles and Their Application).* 1960; Form 860 (29 pages).
3) *Natural Sciences in Nursing.* 1957; 3 scores: facts and principles (knowledge, application, total); Form 957 (28 pages).
4) *Maternal and Child Health Nursing.* 1958; 3 scores: psychological aspects, non-psychological aspects, total; Form 658 (34 pages).
5) *Disaster Nursing.* 1961; 3 scores: general nursing applied to disasters, facts and principles of disasters and disaster nursing, total; Form 261 (38 pages).
6) *Medical-Surgical Nursing, Part 1.* 1961; 4 scores: orthopedic nursing, neurological-neurosurgical nursing, eye-ear-nose-and-throat nursing, total; Form 262 (31 pages).
7) *Medical-Surgical Nursing, Part 2.* 1962; 3 scores: medical nursing, surgical nursing, total; Form 962 (35 pages).
8) *Communicable Disease Nursing.* 1946–63; 3 scores: prevention and transmission, disease manifestations and other aspects, total; Form 863 ('63, 31 pages).

REFERENCES

1. NATIONAL LEAGUE FOR NURSING. *The NLN Achievement Test, Third Edition.* The Use of Tests in Schools of Nursing Pamphlet No. 2. New York: National League for Nursing, Inc., 1964. Pp. iv, 41. *

[1158]

★NLN Achievement Tests for Psychiatric Aides. Hospital psychiatric aides and attendants; 1958–63; tests loaned to hospitals; either or both tests may be used; IBM; 1 form (22 pages); 2 tests; mimeographed manual ('63, 6 pages); guide for interpretation of score reports ('58, 2 pages); fee includes reporting results to hospitals; postpaid one way; (90) minutes per test; National League for Nursing, Inc. *

a) ELEMENTARY PSYCHIATRIC NURSING. Form 858; examination fee, 75¢.
b) BASIC NURSING PROCEDURES AND ELEMENTARY NUTRITION. 3 scores: basic nursing procedures, elementary nutrition, total; Form 958; examination fee, $1.

[1159]

***NLN Graduate Nurse Examination.** Registered professional nurses; 1945–62; formerly called *NLN Graduate Nurse Qualifying Examination;* tests administered throughout the year at centers established by the NLN; IBM; 1 form; 6 tests; manual ['60, 30 pages]; interpretive manual for schools ('62, 29 pages, see *4* below); mimeographed norms ('61, 11 pages); profile ['60, 1 page]; Plan A, all tests: examination fee, $10; Plan B, Nursing Tests and one other: examination fee, $9; Plan C, Nursing Tests only: examination fee, $8; Plan D, *NLN Test of Academic Aptitude* and *NLN Reading Comprehension Test:* examination fee, $4; fees include reporting results to 1 college; $2 per additional report; $1 per interpretive manual; postpaid; scores not reported to examinees; National League for Nursing, Inc. *

a) NLN TEST OF ACADEMIC APTITUDE. Special printing of level 1 (for grades 12–14) of *Cooperative School and College Ability Tests;* 3 scores: quantitative, verbal, total; Form B ('55, 12 pages): 70(85) minutes.

b) NLN READING COMPREHENSION TEST. Special printing of higher level (for grades 13–14) of *Reading Comprehension: Cooperative English Tests,* [*1960 Revision*]; 2 scores: speed, level; Form B ('60, 8 pages); 25(35) minutes.
c) [NURSING TESTS.] Earlier test called *Clinical Test;* 5 scores: total and 4 scores of tests listed below; 4 tests.
1) *Medical-Surgical Nursing Section.* Form 360 ('60, 31 pages); 105(115) minutes.
2) *Psychiatric Nursing Section.* Form 360 ('60, 21 pages); 60(70) minutes.
3) *Maternal and Child Nursing Section.* Form 360 ('60, 27 pages); 75(85) minutes.
4) *Science Section (Selected Areas of the Natural Sciences and Applications).* Form 360 ('60, 17 pages); 60(70) minutes.

REFERENCES

1. "The NLN Graduate Nurse Qualifying Examination." *Nursing Res* 3:21–5 Jl '54. *
2. NATIONAL LEAGUE FOR NURSING. *The NLN Graduate Nurse Qualifying Examination.* The Use of Tests in Schools of Nursing Pamphlet No. 3. New York: National League for Nursing, Inc., 1954. Pp. v, 39. *
3. CLELAND, VIRGINIA. "A Critical Inquiry Into the Use of the Graduate Nurse Qualifying Examination Clinical Test by One Institution." *Nursing Res* 8:202–6 f '59. *
4. NATIONAL LEAGUE FOR NURSING. *The NLN Graduate Nurse Examination, Second Edition.* The Use of Tests in Schools of Nursing Pamphlet No. 3. New York: the League Inc., 1962. Pp. iii, 27. *

[1160]

***NLN Practical Nurse Achievement Tests.** Students in approved schools of practical nursing; 1950–63; IBM; tests loaned to approved schools of practical nursing for their use; 1 form ('57); 2 tests; mimeographed manual ('63, 10 pages) for these tests and test 1161; directions for administering ['63, 4 pages]; examination fee, $1 for each test; postpaid one way; fees include reporting results to schools; National League for Nursing, Inc. *
a) PRACTICAL NURSE BASIC ACHIEVEMENT TEST. 1957–63; 4 scores: body structure and function, basic nursing procedures, nutrition and diet therapy, total; Form 857 (28 pages); mimeographed norms ('63, 2 pages); (90) minutes.
b) PRACTICAL NURSE ACHIEVEMENT TEST. 1950-63; 3 scores: medical-surgical, maternal-child, total; Form 856 (29 pages); mimeographed norms ('63, 1 page); (120) minutes.

[1161]

***NLN Pre-Admission and Classification Examination.** Practical nursing school entrants; 1950–63; tests administered throughout the year at centers established by the NLN; 8 scores: total and 7 scores listed below; IBM; 1 form ('58); 2 tests; mimeographed manual ('63, 10 pages) for this test and test 1160; norms ('63, 5 pages); profile ['58, 1 page]; examination fee, $6; fee includes reporting results to 1 school of nursing; $2 per additional report; postpaid; scores not reported to examinees; National League for Nursing, Inc. *
a) GENERAL INFORMATION AND JUDGMENT TEST. 4 scores: science and health, general information, arithmetic, total; Form 458 (24 pages); 90(95) minutes.
b) VOCABULARY AND READING TEST. 3 scores: vocabulary, reading, total; Form 458 (25 pages); 105(115) minutes.

REFERENCES

1. HESLIN, PHYLIS, AND KATZELL, MILDRED. "A Validation Study of the NLN Pre-Admission and Classification Examination." *Nursing Res* 11:26–9 w '62. *

[1162]

***NLN Pre-Nursing and Guidance Examination.** Applicants for admission to state-approved schools of professional nursing; 1941–63; tests administered throughout the year at centers established by the NLN; IBM; 1 form; 5 tests; manual ['61, 27 pages]; interpretive manual for schools ('61, see 7 below); report form ['63, 2 pages]; mimeographed norms ('63, 11 pages); examination fee, $10; fee includes reporting results to 1 school of nursing; $2 per additional report; $1.25 per interpretive manual; postpaid; scores not reported to examinees; 210(300) minutes in 2 sessions; National League for Nursing, Inc. *
a) NLN TEST OF ACADEMIC APTITUDE. Special printing of level 1 (for grades 12–14) of *Cooperative School and College Ability Tests;* 3 scores: quantitative, verbal, total; Form B ('55, 12 pages); 70(85) minutes.
b) NLN READING COMPREHENSION TEST. Special printing of higher level (for grades 13–14) of *Reading Comprehension: Cooperative English Test,* [*1960 Revision*]; 2 scores: speed, level; Form B ('60, 8 pages); 25(35) minutes.
c) NLN MATHEMATICS TEST. Abbreviated edition of an earlier form of *Cooperative Mathematics Test for Grades 7, 8, and 9;* Form B ('40, 7 pages); 35(40) minutes.
d) NLN NATURAL SCIENCE ACHIEVEMENT TEST. Special printing of *Cooperative General Achievement Tests: Test 2, Natural Science;* Form YZ ('51, 7 pages); 40(50) minutes.
e) NLN SOCIAL STUDIES ACHIEVEMENT TEST. Special printing of *Cooperative General Achievement Tests: Test 1, Social Studies;* Form YZ ('55, 8 pages); 40(50) minutes.

REFERENCES

1. SHAYCOFT, MARION F. "A Validation Study of the Pre-Nursing and Guidance Test Battery." *Am J Nursing* 51:201–5 Mr '51. *
2. BRUTON, FLORRIE ERB. "Some Implications of National Pre-Nursing Tests for the Selection of Students for Alabama Hospital Schools of Nursing." *Nursing Res* 3:60–73 O '54. *
3. NATIONAL LEAGUE FOR NURSING. *The NLN Pre-Nursing and Guidance Examination, Second Edition.* The Use of Tests in Schools of Nursing Pamphlet No. 1. New York: National League for Nursing, Inc., 1957. Pp. v, 42. *
4. MEYER, BURTON. "An Analysis of the Results of Pre-Nursing and Guidance, Achievement, and State Board Test Pool Examinations." *Nursing Outlook* 7:538–41 S '59. *
5. FERGUSON, RUTH H. *Predictive Study of Academic Success in the Freshman Term at a Selected Three-Year Hospital School of Nursing From Scores on the National Test for Nursing, Pre-Nursing and Guidance Test Battery.* Master's thesis, De Paul University (Chicago, Ill.), 1960.
6. HEYWARD, ROSALIND W. *Study of the Results of the National League for Nursing Pre-Nursing and Guidance Test in Relation to Performance in College and on the National State Board Test Pool Examination for a Selected Group of Students.* Master's thesis, Teachers College, Columbia University (New York, N.Y.), 1960.
7. NATIONAL LEAGUE FOR NURSING. *The NLN Pre-Nursing and Guidance Examination, Third Edition.* The Use of Tests in Schools of Nursing Pamphlet No. 1. New York: the League, Inc., 1961. Pp. v, 34. *
8. ROWE, HAROLD R. "Requirements for Admission to Basic Programs of Professional Nursing." *Personnel & Guid J* 42:155–9 O '63. *

[1163]

★PSB-Entrance Examination for Schools of Practical Nursing. Applicants for admission to practical nursing schools; 1961; test booklet title is *PSB-Aptitude for Practical Nursing Examination;* 5 scores: general mental ability, spelling, natural sciences, judgment in practical nursing situations, personal adjustment index; IBM; 1 form (22 pages); manual (29 pages); separate answer sheets must be used; $1 per test; $1 per manual (free with 25 tests); $1 per set of IBM answer sheets including scoring service; $1.50 per specimen set; postage extra;

180(190) minutes; Anna S. Evans, [George A. W. Stouffer, Jr.], and the Psychological Services Bureau of Indiana, Pa.; Educators'-Employers' Tests & Services Associates. *

[Other Tests]

For tests not listed above, see the following entries in *Tests in Print:* 2029 and 2031–2.

RESEARCH

[1164]

★Research Personnel Review Form. Research and engineering and scientific firms; 1959–60; for supervisor's evaluation of research personnel in preparation for a performance review interview; 1 form ('59, 6 pages); manual ('60, 13 pages); $4.95 per 20 forms; $1 per manual; $1.50 per specimen set; postage extra; tabulating service available; Morris I. Stein; [Morris I. Stein & Associates, Inc.]. *

[1165]

★Supervisor's Evaluation of Research Personnel. Research personnel; 1960; ratings by supervisors; 1 form (2 pages); manual (9 pages); $2.25 per 20 test-answer sheets; 25¢ per scoring stencil; 50¢ per manual; $1 per specimen set; postage extra; (15) minutes; William D. Buel; Science Research Associates, Inc. *

REFERENCES

1. Buel, W. D. "Stability of Preference Indices in Forced-Choice Rating Scale Items." *Eng & Ind Psychol* 1:134–7 w '59. * (*PA* 35:4046)
2. Buel, William D. "The Validity of Behavioral Rating Scale Items for the Assessment of Individual Creativity." *J Appl Psychol* 44:407–12 D '60. * (*PA* 35:3403)
3. Buel, William D., and Bachner, Virginia M. "The Assessment of Creativity in a Research Setting." *J Appl Psychol* 45:353–8 D '61. * (*PA* 37:1211)

John W. French, *Professor of Psychology, and College Examiner, New College, Sarasota, Florida.*

The *Supervisor's Evaluation of Research Personnel* (SERP) calls for the ranking of four statements in each of 13 tetrads of statements according to their descriptiveness of the ratee. These forced-choice items, according to the manual, were constructed by matching two statements "on high preference value and two [statements] on low preference value, one statement in each pair having significant discriminative ability and the other having little or none." This is the correct way to develop forced-choice items. The manual notes that the statements were also matched on standard deviation of preferences and on length. This is commendable. The idea behind the construction of SERP is good. However, this reviewer feels that more varied items would be desirable and some more convincing evidence of validity is required before the scale should be recommended for operational use. It seems desirable also that the manual not describe SERP as "a means of *objectively* comparing the research competence of staff members." This is a *subjective* instrument.

The 13-item scale requires about 15 minutes to complete. While this brevity has obvious administrative advantages, it is asking too much to expect 13 items to cover all important qualities in a research worker in any one field, much less the qualities that should be considered in evaluating research personnel in general, as this instrument claims to do. A few seemingly important characteristics of the researcher not covered by SERP are ability to write clearly, ability to make oral presentations of research results, and ingenuity in initiating ideas for research. This limitation in the scope of research activities covered by SERP occurs despite development activities which included the listing of 900 descriptive statements made by 20 research supervisors and the selection of statements from among these by means of cluster analysis including McQuitty's linkage analysis. Since the research supervisors were all on the staff of a single oil company, it seems likely that some kinds of research activities were insufficiently represented.

More data should be collected to establish validity, reliability, and norming statistics for the instrument. Until that is done, some of the statements made in the manual do not seem to be fully justified. Odd-even reliabilities, corrected by the Spearman-Brown formula, of .92 and .95 represent only that part of the measurement error resulting from item sampling. Even this source of error is not fully represented, because "halo" in the ratings made by a single rater tends to elevate reliability coefficients spuriously. A different and still greater source of error that should be considered when presenting evidence of reliability is the disagreement among raters. The manual quite rightly recommends that a research worker be rated by more than one rater whenever possible.

The validity data are limited to two rather small groups. Correlations between SERP and objective criteria concerned with patents are only in the low .20's. However, with some justification, the manual questions whether patents define a good criterion. Other validity coefficients given in the manual range from .61 to .72. These coefficients use other ratings as criteria. Unfortunately, the other ratings may not have any more "true" validity than the instrument itself. In addition, the manual does not make it clear whether the criterion ratings and SERP ratings were made by different people. Some further suspicion about what is actually being measured is aroused by the fact that the highest validity coefficient, .72, was found with the criterion "rating of mental qualifications," evidently a rating of general intelligence having no particular connection with research ability. Correlations between SERP and some personality and interest measures are presented in the manual and are found to be desirably low. It would be helpful, however, to see the correlation between SERP and scores on some general intelligence or aptitude tests.

J Counsel Psychol 10:100–1 sp '63. Laurence Siegel. This device was not really intended for counseling purposes. It was developed for those industrial applications wherein it is desirable to obtain objectively scored assessments of research competence. The *Supervisor's Evaluation of Research Personnel* (SERP) is briefly described here because of its possible implications for counseling graduate students and assessing their research competence. SERP is a forced-choice inventory completed by a supervisor (or faculty member) who is describing the ratee's research behavior. It contains thirteen tetrads and can be completed within 10 or 15 minutes. * Correlations between SERP and several personality, interest and values inventories tend not to be statistically significant. Also, SERP scores do not correlate either with age or length of service. SERP norms are exceedingly weak. Percentile conversions are presented for a total of only 149 cases. The failure to call attention to this deficiency in the Manual is extremely unfortunate. The inventory could use considerably more work before it can confidently be used in industry for the suggested applications of personnel evaluation and selection. However, the idea is an intriguing one. Without making a brief for its use as an operational tool, either in or out of industry, it should be interesting to use SERP on a *research* basis for attempting to improve our assessments of graduate students.

[1166]

★Surveys of Research Administration and Environment. Research and engineering and scientific firms; 1959–60; 2 forms for gathering information and opinions on the company and its research activities; manual ('60, 21 pages); no data on reliability and validity; no description of normative population; $1.50 per manual; $3 per specimen set; postage extra; tabulating service available; Morris I. Stein; [Morris I. Stein & Associates, Inc.].

a) STEIN SURVEY FOR ADMINISTRATORS. Supervisors and administrators; also part of *Technical Personnel Recruiting Inventory;* 1 form ('59, 12 pages); $9 per 20 forms; (30–40) minutes.

b) STEIN RESEARCH ENVIRONMENT SURVEY. Research and technical personnel; 1 form ('59, 12 pages); $9 per 20 forms; (90–120) minutes.

[1167]

★Technical Personnel Recruiting Inventory. Research and engineering and scientific firms; 1959–60; 3 parts; manual ('60, 20 pages); no data on reliability and validity; no norms; $1.50 per manual; $2.50 per specimen set; postage extra; (30–60) minutes per form; tabulating service available; Morris I. Stein; [Morris I. Stein & Associates, Inc.]. *

a) INDIVIDUAL QUALIFICATION FORM. Supervisors; description of an available research position; 1 form ('59, 4 pages); $2.75 per 20 forms.

b) PERSONAL DATA FORM FOR SCIENTIFIC, ENGINEERING, AND TECHNICAL PERSONNEL. Job applicants; 1 form ('59, 6 pages); $9 per 20 forms.

c) STEIN SURVEY FOR ADMINISTRATORS. Administrators; description of company's research environment; also part of *Surveys of Research Administration and Environment;* 1 form ('59, 12 pages); $9 per 20 forms.

SELLING

[1168]

***Aptitude Index Selection Procedure.** Prospective male ordinary life insurance agents; 1938–60; 2 tests; manual ['60, 4 pages]; recruiting diagnosis profile ['59, 2 pages] for maintaining records on candidates tested; separate scoring keys for United States and Canada; distribution restricted to home offices of member life insurance companies; details may be obtained from publisher; Life Insurance Agency Management Association. *

a) BIOGRAPHICAL PROFILE. 1960; preliminary screening test scored locally; 1 form ('60, 2 pages, also serves as mailing envelope for returning answer booklet for *b* for scoring); [5] minutes.

b) APTITUDE INDEX. 1938–60; 1 score combining an evaluation of life insurance information, personal background, interests, and attitudes; Form 7 ('60, 25 pages); scored by the publisher only; separate answer booklets ('60, 15 pages including information test, answer cards for remaining tests, and score report cards) must be used; French edition available; (60–90) minutes.

REFERENCES

1–5. See 40:1646.
6–19. See 4:825.
20. See 5:913.
21. FERGUSON, LEONARD W. "Ability, Interest, and Aptitude." *J Appl Psychol* 44:126–31 Ap '60. * (*PA* 35:4048)

For reviews by Donald G. Paterson and Albert S. Thompson of an earlier form of b, *see 4:825.*

[1169]

***Aptitudes Associates Test of Sales Aptitude: A Test for Measuring Knowledge of Basic Principles of Selling.** Applicants for sales positions; 1947–60; for a revision, see 1178; Form A ('47, 4 pages); revised manual ('60, 8 pages, identical with 1958 manual except for format, modification in some normative tables, and extension of bibliography); $5 per 25 tests; 25¢ per key; 75¢ per manual; $1 per specimen set; cash orders postpaid; (20-30) minutes; Martin M. Bruce; the Author. *

REFERENCES

1. BRUCE, MARTIN M. "Validity Information Exchange, No. 7-022: D.O.T. Code 1-86.11, Salesman, Commercial Equipment and Supplies." *Personnel Psychol* 7:157 sp '54. *
2. UNITED STATES EMPLOYMENT SERVICE. "Validity Information Exchange, No. 7-021: D.O.T. Code 1-57.30, Underwriter." *Personnel Psychol* 7:156 sp '54. *
3. GRAY, EDWARD J., AND ROSEN, JOHN C. "Validity Information Exchange, No. 9-7: D.O.T. Code 1-80.02, Salesman." *Personnel Psychol* 9:112 sp '56. *
4. HARLESS, BYRON B., AND BRUCE, MARTIN M. "Normative Data Information Exchange, No. 10-8." *Personnel Psychol* 10:104 sp '57. *
5. SPEER, GEORGE S. "Validity Information Exchange, No. 10-16: D.O.T. Code 1-86.01, Salesman, Wholesale (Steel Warehouse)." *Personnel Psychol* 10:206 su '57. *
6. *Normative Information: Manager and Executive Testing.* New York: Richardson, Bellows, Henry & Co., Inc., May 1963. Pp. 45. *

For reviews by Milton E. Hahn and Donald G. Paterson, see 4:824.

[1170]

★**Combination Inventory.** Prospective debit life insurance salesmen; 1954-59; 5 parts: arithmetic, mental alertness (items in parts 1 and 2 selected from tests developed by the Life Office Management Association), vocational interest (items selected from *Strong Vocational Interest Blank for Men, Revised*), personality (social desirability), personal history (economic maturity, same for both forms); Forms 1A, 1B, ('54, 14 pages); no manual; mimeographed scoring rules ['54, 5 pages] for each form; mimeographed scoring standards ('59, 7 pages) for personal history section; no data on reliability; separate answer booklets (which also contain personal history section) must be used; distribution restricted to home offices of member life insurance companies; details may be obtained from publisher; [90-120] minutes; Life Insurance Agency Management Association. *

REFERENCES

1. FERGUSON, LEONARD W. "Ability, Interest, and Aptitude." *J Appl Psychol* 44:126-31 Ap '60. * (*PA* 35:4048)

[1171]

★**The Dealer Inventory.** Manufacturers' distributors; 1956-58; attitudes and opinions about company represented; 11 scores: company relations, administrative services, company products, product services, sales promotion, distribution system, pricing policies, credit policies, administrative ability of company representative, technical competence of the company representative, reactions to survey; 1 form ('56, 8 pages); manual of general information ('56, 61 pages); program description manual ('56, 18 pages); survey analyzer ('56, 51 pages); profile ('58, 1 page); no data on reliability; distribution restricted to companies using the publisher's survey services; price information available from publisher; specimen set not available; [30-40] minutes; Richard Renck, George Y. Ogawa, David N. Larson, and Robert K. Burns; Industrial Relations Center. *

[1172]

★**The Evaluation Record.** Prospective life insurance agency managers; 1947-63; combination of evaluation procedures yielding a composite score; 3 parts; manual ('63, 4 pages); instructions-record folder ('55); revised scoring kit ('62, c1947); profile ('55, 1 page); rating form ('55, 1 page); no data on reliability; distribution restricted to home offices of member life insurance companies; details may be obtained from publisher; Life Insurance Agency Management Association. *

a) EXPERIENCE FORM. Completed by candidates; Form A ('58, 2 pages); [30] minutes.

b) STRONG VOCATIONAL INTEREST BLANK FOR MEN, REVISED. See 1070; scored for production manager only; special answer sheets must be used; (30) minutes.

c) HOME OFFICE RATING CHART. Ratings of personal qualities by 1-3 supervisors; Form B ('55, 2 pages); [10] minutes.

[1173]

Hanes Sales Selection Inventory, Revised Edition. Insurance and printing salesmen; 1954-55; 3 scores: verbal, personality, drive; 1 form ('55, 4 pages); manual ('55, 2 pages); no data on reliability and validity of drive score; $3 per 25 tests; $1 per specimen set (must be purchased to obtain manual); cash orders postpaid; (30-40) minutes; Bernard Hanes; Psychometric Affiliates. *

WILLIAM E. KENDALL, *Director, Personnel and Marketing Research Division, The Psychological Corporation, New York, New York.*

The *Hanes Sales Selection Inventory* is described as "designed to help select potentially successful insurance, printing and closely allied salesmen from the general run of applicants for such positions." Having made this statement, there is no further mention of printing and closely allied salesmen. The inventory is said to have been "constructed by an item analysis aimed at maximizing the differences between applicants and successful salesmen. The present edition is based upon a two-year follow up of successful salesmen." Since there is no indication of the criteria employed to measure success in sales positions, the reviewer has no basis for judging the degree to which the inventory does succeed in separating successful salesmen from among the applicants.

Part 1 of the inventory is a personal history form which resembles many application blanks commonly used in business. The responses to 10 of the items are scored as either favorable or unfavorable. The manual states, "In general, the author has found that three unfavorable responses indicate a poor risk regardless of other scores." In the light of the author's earlier statement about Part 1 that "what the man did in the past is one indication of his future performance," it is of interest to examine the seven responses which are rated as unfavorable. These are: age between 20 and 25; not now employed; employed on present job less than one year; started but did not finish college; single; no children; wife works. Of these responses only "started but did not finish college" appears to describe past behavior which may be an indication of future performance and even this response may require qualification. The remaining unfavorable responses are dependent to a significant degree on the age of the respondent, a fact which may account for their appearance in the course of doing an item analysis which failed to consider item interrelationships. Eight responses, e.g., married, member of two or more organizations, are considered favorable to the applicant, but there is no suggested use for this information.

Part 2 is described as "an excellent short yardstick of verbal knowledge." It consists of 18 items of which 3 are verbal analogies, 2 are simple verbal arithmetic items, and 13 require the respondent to pick a synonym for the stimulus word. Correct responses are given weights of 3, 2, or 1 so that a score of 33 is possible on this part of the inventory. Scores on Part 2 are converted into percentile ranks.

Norms are given for insurance salesmen ($n = 154$) and steel salesmen ($n = 30$). In a paragraph headed "Inventory Validity and Reliability" it is stated that Part 2 "was found to correlate .39 (Rho) with total PMA Intelligence on 30 college graduates applying for sales positions with a steel company." In the absence of evidence to the contrary, it seems reasonable to assume that the 30 college graduates referred to are the same 30 individuals whose scores appear in the Part 2 norm table.

The author states that "The best minimum qualifying score from the point of view of maximum selection of successful applicants and maximum rejection of poor bets" is the 55th percentile for Part 2. "Approximately 71 percent of the potentially successful salesmen will score 55 or better on Part 2." Split-half reliability for Part 2 is given as .84. No other data are presented.

Part 3, according to the manual, "provides some of the important personality variables. Successful salesmen are more similar in their personality than men in general and unsuccessful salesmen. The Drive Score (Items 25 through 30) of Part III is a good predictor of sales success—and its norms in Table 1 are based on 140 salesmen—seventy successful and seventy failures—within a year period."

Part 3 consists of 37 statements to which the respondent checks "yes" or "no" according to whether the statement is most often true or not. Only the "yes" answers are scored. Responses are differentially weighted; e.g., "Usually become a leader in social activities" is +3, "Most executives dodge the tough work" is +2, "Stop and think of consequences before acting" is −2, "Think out complicated problems" is −3, and "Depressed when criticized" is −4. The user is left to infer what the "important personality variables" are that are being measured in Part 3.

The weighting scheme produces negative scores in the normative groups for Part 3 (195 insurance and 31 steel salesmen) with a score of 0 being at the 95th percentile. A percentile rank of 65 is suggested as a minimum qualifying score. Approximately 65 per cent of the potentially successful salesmen will be at or above the 65th percentile on Part 3. The split-half reliability of Part 3 is reported to be .89.

The six items which constitute the Drive Score are so weighted that the range of possible scores is from −1 to +9. Norms based on 140 cases are given for this score. There is no comment on the Drive Score other than the statement that it "detects those few individuals in a hundred who receive a good score on Part 3 because they answer only a few questions in the affirmative."

In a personal communication the author reports that while he is using the inventory continuously, he has not had the occasion to compute other normative data.

Both the inventory and the manual are carelessly prepared. Copies of the forms appear to have been set in several type faces and printed, then after additional data had been gathered, to have been overprinted and rerun by offset. Thus, the appearance is not to the credit of either the author or the publisher.

In summary, whatever the basis on which one chooses tests, be it attractiveness of the layout, face validity of the items, or completeness of reporting of cross-validation studies, the prospective user will not find what he wants when he examines this product.

ALBERT K. KURTZ, *Fulbright Lecturer, Ein Shams University, Cairo, United Arab Republic.*

This sloppy test may have some validity and then again it may not. The entire validity information for Part 1 is presented in one sentence: "In general, the author has found that three unfavorable responses indicate a poor risk regardless of other scores." A 2 by 2 table gives the percentage of high and of low scores for "general applicants" and for "successful salesmen" on each of the other two parts. The sample sizes are given as 154 and 195, but on the other side of the single sheet manual, norms are given that may refer to 154 insurance salesmen for Part 2 and 195 such for Part 3. Where, or if, the "general applicants" come in is a minor puzzle that may not matter since the point that should be at issue is not the comparison referred to but rather whether the test will differentiate *at the time of hiring* between "successful salesmen" and *unsuccessful salesmen.* No information bearing in any way on either of these italicized requirements is supplied.

The two tables do show some differences which are not overly large (tetrachoric *r* cannot be computed because neither the cell frequencies nor the cell proportions are available), but it is neither surprising nor unusual that a test can differentiate between successful salesmen and general applicants. To be useful, the test must differentiate *in advance* between those who will later become successful and those who will later become *unsuccessful.* Such tests are not impossible to make; the reviewer was coauthor of one (4:825) for differentiating between potentially successful and unsuccessful life insurance salesmen as long ago as 1938.

In teaching testing courses, the reviewer has never placed much emphasis on face validity. Perhaps this was wrong. Maybe I should at least have mentioned that when changes are made, neither the test nor the manual should look so much like the patched up jobs they actually are. This test appears to have been set in type and used for some time, then a typist who didn't bother to clean the type (especially the letter a) added some material so that boxes (crudely drawn) could be inserted for answers to some of the items, and this altered test was reproduced by a photographic process.

The manual appears to have been patched up by the same typist, who included two uncorrected strikeovers. The directions for scoring are strewn around under "Administration and Scoring," "Scoring Interpretation," and "Mechanics of Scoring." One of these places rightly says to record the sectional scores, but it doesn't say where—possibly because there is no place on the test to record them. There is what appears to be a percentile grid on page 1 of the test, but it is not referred to anywhere.

The key for Part 1 counts age 20–25 as unfavorable, but the typed limits on the test are 18–25. This key also counts less than 1 year on the job as unfavorable, but the typed boxes correspond to 1, 2, 3, and 4 or more, with no way for the applicant to indicate anything less than 1 year.

In describing Part 2, the manual says, "Having a good vocabulary and being able to solve some simple problems is vital for success." If one believes this, will he be happy with only two mathematics problems? Some of the other items have dubious answers. How, for instance, would you answer item 5? It reads, "Sun is to Moon as Light bulb is to (a) lamp, (b) mirror, (c) light, (d) glass." The key gives (b), but the relation "is brighter than" seems fairly reasonable and yields a different answer.

Norms are given for "Insurance" and "Steel." Whether "Insurance" means successful insurance salesmen, applicants, or both is not clear. "Steel" probably means 30 college graduates applying for sales positions with a steel company.

In conclusion, this test has a poor appearance, appears to have been prepared carelessly, and has not yet been shown to be valid for picking successful rather than unsuccessful men in any selling field.

[1174]

***Information Index.** Life insurance agents; 1951–63; life insurance information; Forms A ('57), B ('61), (15 pages); revised manual ('63, 6 pages); directions sheet ['57, 2 pages]; separate answer sheets must be used; distribution restricted to home offices of member life insurance companies; details may be obtained from publisher; postage extra; Canadian edition available; 60(80) minutes; Life Insurance Agency Management Association. *

REFERENCES

1–3. See 5:927.
4. BAIER, DONALD E., AND DUGAN, ROBERT D. "Normative Data Information Exchange, Nos. 11-3." *Personnel Psychol* 9:277–82 su '56. *

[1175]

★Interviewer's Impressions—Sales Applicants. Adults; 1956; ratings following an interview; 6 scores: persuasiveness, industriousness, confidence, knowledge, social development, total; 1 form ['56, 1 page]; instructions-norms ['56, 2 pages]; no data on reliability; $4 per 10 forms, cash orders postpaid; specimen set not available; (5) minutes; [Eugene J. Benge]; [Management Service Co.]. *

[1176]

***Personnel Institute Hiring Kit.** Applicants for sales positions; 1954–62; manual ('57, 24 pages, same as manual copyrighted in 1956 except for one minor change); no data on reliability and validity; $15 per kit of manual and 10 copies each of *a–d*; postage extra; scoring service available: $15 per applicant when *e* is used, $45 per applicant when *f* is used; fee includes scoring, interpretation, and report of results; Personnel Institute, Inc. *

a) PRELIMINARY SCREENING INTERVIEW. 1 form ('57, 1 page); $1.50 per 10 copies; (10) minutes.

b) PERSONAL HISTORY INVENTORY. 1 form ('62, 6 pages, same forms also copyrighted in 1957); $2.50 per 10 copies; (30–45) minutes.

c) DIAGNOSTIC INTERVIEWER'S GUIDE. 1 form ('56, 4 pages); $3.50 per 10 copies; (30) minutes.

d) PERSONAL OR TELEPHONE WORK REFERENCE INVESTIGATION. Formerly called *Work Reference Investigation;* 1 form ('59, 1 page); $1.50 per 10 copies; (10) minutes.

e) SELECTOR TEST BATTERY. Applicants for routine selling jobs; 1955–57; directions sheet ('56, 2 pages); scoring by publisher only; (85–100) minutes.

1) *EM-AY Inventory.* Reprint of *Otis Employment Tests,* Test 2, Form A ('22), see 4:310; mental alertness; 1 form ('22, 4 pages); 30(35) minutes.

2) *ESS-AY Inventory.* Sales aptitude; 1 form ('57, 11 pages, same as test copyrighted in 1955); (40–45) minutes.

3) *The Personality Inventory.* See 157; 4 scores: extroversion, dominance, self-confidence, social dependence; 1 form ('35, 4 pages); (15–20) minutes.

f) COMPREHENSIVE TEST BATTERY. Applicants for complex selling jobs; 1955–62; directions sheet ('57, 2 pages); profile ('62, 2 pages); scoring by publisher only; (195–220) minutes.

1) Same as *e*(1) above.

2) Same as *e*(2) above.

3) Same as *e*(3) above.

4) *Vocabulary Inventory.* 1 form ('56, 4 pages, same as test copyrighted in 1954); (30) minutes.

5) *ESS-EYE Inventory.* Reprint of the SP (Special) Edition of the *Social Intelligence Test: George Washington University Series, Revised Form* ('47), see 176; 3 scores: social judgment, social observation, total; no norms for part scores; 1 form ('62, 8 pages); (40) minutes.

6) *B-B-ESS Inventory.* Business skills; 8 scores: comparing, computation, reading, spelling, vocabulary, arithmetical reasoning, English, total; no norms for part scores; 1 form ('56, 8 pages, same as test copyrighted in 1954); 40(50) minutes.

REFERENCES

1. BRUCE, MARTIN M. "The Prediction of Effectiveness as a Factory Foreman." *Psychol Monogr* 67(12):1–17 '53. * (*PA* 28:5019)

2. BRUCE, MARTIN M. "Validity Information Exchange, No. 7-004: D.O.T. Code 0-97.61, Manager, Sales." *Personnel Psychol* 7:128–9 sp '54. *

3. BRUCE, MARTIN M. "Validity Information Exchange, No. 7-076: D.O.T. Code 5-91.101, Foreman II." *Personnel Psychol* 7:418–9 au '54. *

[1177]

★**SRA Sales Attitudes Check List.** Applicants for sales positions; 1960; extension of *Sales Personnel Description Form;* 1 form (4 pages); preliminary manual (11 pages); no data on reliability; $4.95 per 20 tests; 25¢ per manual; 50¢ per specimen set; postage extra; (10–15) minutes; Erwin K. Taylor and the Personnel Research & Development Corporation; Science Research Associates, Inc. *

JOHN P. FOLEY, JR., *President, J. P. Foley and Company, Inc., New York, New York.*

A modification of the original *Sales Personnel Description Form,* which was designed to be used by sales supervisors or managers in rating their sales personnel, the present form is a self-description checklist intended to aid in salesman selection. The form consists of 31 forced-choice items, each comprising a tetrad of self-descriptive statements. From each set of four statements the examinee is to select the one statement he believes is most descriptive of his own behavior, as well as the one statement least descriptive. The test, given without time limit, is said to require from 5 to 15 minutes for completion. It can be administered individually or in groups. Utilizing a carbon insert sheet, the form is self-scoring.

Although it is recognized that sales positions vary widely in their requirements—and although emphasis is placed on the desirability of item analysis as a basis for maximizing validity within the local organization—it is maintained that the present instrument can contribute to the prediction of sales success when used as part of a sales selection test battery. In such a case, use is made of the established a priori key, which was developed on the basis of item analysis of the earlier form (*Sales Personnel Description Form*). However, users are encouraged to develop their own keys, reflecting the specifics of their sales situations, when justified by the size of their sales forces.

No evidence of reliability is provided in the manual, although it is claimed that "the repeated evidences of validity in various sales situations....indicate that the reliability is sufficiently high to make the *Check List* useful in predicting sales success."

Although it is recognized that the validity of the instrument has not been established for a wide variety of sales jobs, preliminary or suggestive indications of validity are reported in three instances, although the reader is cautioned against generalizing, even to seemingly similar situations. In one study, based on scores made by 197 new car automobile salesmen from four divergent geographical locations throughout the United States, checklist scores yielded a biserial correlation of .31 with average monthly earnings (corrected for locale) for a 12-month period, this correlation being significant at the .01 level of significance. In a second study, scores correlated .23 with average monthly sales for a group of 23 office equipment salesmen from widely different sales territories, but correlated only .04 with the average *number* of orders written monthly by the same group. In a third study based on the scores of several groups of railroad traffic salesmen, the criterion consisted of a rating of "over-all performance" by each man's superior. In the case of five separate subgroups, distinguished from each other on the basis of age and technical specialization, the correlation coefficients were .15, .44, .11, .37, and .02, respectively. It might be added that in all three of the studies cited the validities were concurrent, i.e., determined by testing current employees whose pretest performance was rated. Hence it is possible that "restriction of range" may have unduly lowered the validity coefficients obtained.

Based on the "a priori scoring" noted above, norms are presented in the manual on the following five groups: 197 automobile salesmen, 54 utility salesmen, 141 office equipment salesmen, 95 freight traffic salesmen, and 180 applicants for "sales and sales managerial positions." The variability among and within these groups illustrates the need for the empirical development of local norms as well as validation data.

Format of the test and manual is good. The self-scoring technique is very efficient. The reviewer is even more impressed by the emphasis on the a priori nature of the scoring key, the tentativeness of the reported norms, and the desirability of local validation whenever possible. Apart from the restrictions imposed by the relatively small number of groups on which normative data are currently available, the chief limitations of the present instrument are those inherent in any forced-choice test. Chief among these are the question of the degree to which distortion, faking, or falsification has actually been minimized or eliminated, the considerable cost and effort involved in local standardization or revalidation, and the lack of "face validity" evidenced by frustration and other negative reactions on the part of applicants tested. Moreover, in the present instrument, several of the items are awkwardly worded. A few involve the use of the "double negative." Lastly, one could question the appropriateness of the test's title. Although one might argue that the test is attitudinal in that each item necessarily involves a determination of salesman behavior as seen through the eyes of the salesman himself, it is nevertheless true that the test is not designed to measure salesman attitude, as the title implies, but rather, it attempts to measure different aspects of the salesman's on-the-job behavior.

[1178]

***Sales Comprehension Test.** Sales applicants; 1947–63; revision of the still-in-print *Aptitudes Associates Test of Sales Aptitude;* Form M ('53, 4 pages); revised manual ('63, 20 pages); profile ('62, 1 page); $5 per 25 tests; 25¢ per key; $2.75 per 25 profiles; $1.75 per manual; $2.50 per specimen set; cash orders postpaid; (15–20) minutes; Martin M. Bruce; the Author. *

REFERENCES

1–10. See 5:947.
11. Hecht, Robert, and Aron, Joel. "Normative Data Information Exchange, No. 12-16." *Personnel Psychol* 12:332 su '59. *
12. Murray, L. E., and Bruce, Martin M. "Normative Data Information Exchange, No. 12-17." *Personnel Psychol* 12:333 su '59. *
13. Murray, Lester E., and Bruce, Martin M. "A Study of the Validity of the Sales Comprehension Test and Sales Motivation Inventory in Differentiating High and Low Production in Life Insurance Selling." *J Appl Psychol* 43:246-8 Ag '59. * (*PA* 34:6609)
14. Ash, Philip. "Validity Information Exchange, No. 13-05: D.O.T. Code 1-86.12, Salesman, Typewriters." *Personnel Psychol* 13:454 w '60. *
15. Ash, Philip. "Validity Information Exchange, No. 13-06: D.O.T. Code 5-83.127, Typewriter Serviceman." *Personnel Psychol* 13:455 w '60. *
16. Dugan, Robert D. "Validity Information Exchange, No. 14-01: D.O.T. Code 0-98.07, Manager, Insurance Office." *Personnel Psychol* 14:213–6 su '61. *
17. Bass, Bernard M. "Further Evidence on the Dynamic Character of Criteria." *Personnel Psychol* 15:93–7 sp '62. * (*PA* 37:3906)

For a review by Raymond A. Katzell, see 5:947; for reviews by Milton E. Hahn and Donald G. Paterson of the original edition, see 4:824.

[1179]

★Sales Employee Inventory. Outside salesmen; 1958; attitudes and opinions about company represented; 14 scores: the company, management, supervisory administrative skills, supervisory communication skills, company products, pricing and credit, customer service, advertising, sales training, work goals, job satisfaction, pay, benefits, reactions to the survey; 1 form (8 pages); manual of general information (59 pages); program description manual (19 pages); survey analyzer (62 pages); supervisor's guide (20 pages); profile (1 page); no data on reliability; distribution restricted to companies using the publisher's survey services; price information available from publisher; specimen set not available; [30–40] minutes; Richard Renck, George Y. Ogawa, and David N. Larson; Industrial Relations Center. *

[1180]

***Sales Personnel Description Form.** Salesmen; 1953–60; forced-choice rating scale; 1 form ('53, 4 pages); manual ['60, 10 pages]; scoring by the publisher only; 50¢ per form including scoring service; 25¢ per specimen set; cash orders postpaid; [10] minutes; Personnel Research Institute. *

REFERENCES

1. Taylor, Erwin K.; Schneider, Dorothy E.; and Symons, Nancy A. "A Short Forced-Choice Evaluation Form for Salesmen." *Personnel Psychol* 6:393–401 w '53. * (*PA* 28:8152)
2. Taylor, Erwin K., and Hilton, Andrew C. "Sales Personnel Description Form: Summary of Validities." *Personnel Psychol* 13:173–9 su '60. * (*PA* 36:2LD73T)

Wayne K. Kirchner, *Manager, Personnel Research, Minnesota Mining and Manufacturing Company, St. Paul, Minnesota.*

This is not a test, but is a form for rating the performance of salesmen. It consists of three parts: one forced-choice rating of performance on 12 tetrads of sales behavior, and two graphic rating scales—one on present value to company and one on future potential as a salesman. It is not lengthy; even a slow reader would be hard pressed to spend more than 10 minutes on this form.

Operationally, the user must send the form to the publisher for scoring. This is supposed to be an advantage, according to the manual, but the reviewer suspects that it is more of a disadvantage. In any case, the graphic rating scales on the form do not seem particularly significant in value or different from any other graphic rating scale that might be made up. From the norms that were available to the reviewer (but not to the user of the form), it was evident that the two graphic rating scales produced two extremely skewed distributions. It appears that most salesmen are rated high on these two scales and that an average score is quite near the top end of the scale in both cases. The score obtained on the forced-choice section, however, is more normally distributed.

As far as reliability goes, the manual cites one test-retest study done on a group of 104 salesmen with an r of .71. This does not seem too bad for this kind of instrument. Validity, however, is another matter. Nine studies are cited in the manual with correlation coefficients listed which show the relationship between the scores on the SPDF and various other criteria of sales performance. Unfortunately, the reviewer is unable to tell from the table which of the three scores obtained on this form correlated with the particular criterion in question, so the table serves no particular useful purpose. Since correlations as high as .58 between this form and various criteria of sales performance are reported, however, it is reasonable to assume that the scores probably do correlate positively with most criteria of sales performance. From that standpoint, then, this would appear to be a valid instrument. The validity itself cannot be determined to any great extent by the information provided in the manual, however.

In summary, this is a sales performance rating form which cannot be scored by the user. It provides three separate scores: one from the forced-choice rating section, and two from graphic rating scales which produce extremely skewed distributions on the normative data that was provided. Whether or not this particular form is of any great value to any one in the sales field is markedly open to question. It is at best a substitute for any other measure of sales performance that might be available. It might be useful to check on present appraisal methods, for example, but this reviewer questions seriously whether or not this form actually produces much better information than might be obtained by a simple ranking of sales job performance.

[1181]

★**The Sales Sentence Completion Blank.** Applicants for sales positions; 1961; 1 form (3 pages); manual (25 pages); $5 per 25 tests; $1.75 per manual; $2.50 per specimen set; cash orders postpaid; (20–35) minutes; Norman Gekoski; Martin M. Bruce. *

William E. Kendall, *Director, Personnel and Marketing Research Division, The Psychological Corporation, New York, New York.*

The *Sales Sentence Completion Blank* consists of 40 sentence fragments constructed so as to elicit sales-oriented responses.

After a series of interviews with insurance salesmen and their supervisors, a preliminary form containing 54 sentence fragments was administered to 82 life insurance salesmen working in the Philadelphia area. The men were employees of three different insurance organizations. An unspecified number of the men were agency supervisors who, presumably, also sold insurance.

Of the 82 men, usable data were available on 60. These men were divided into high and low criterion groups. Average income of the 30 men in the high criterion group was $13,500 (sales experience averaged nine years, two months) while that of the 30 men in the low criterion group was $5,000 (average sales experience was two years, six months). In the manual, no mention is made of the relative proportion, in the two groups, of salesmen and supervisors. Supervisors, it must be assumed, have more service and higher incomes.

Responses to each sentence fragment were categorized and scoring values from 1 to 7 assigned, based upon the relative frequencies among high and low criterion cases. Scores of 7 are assigned to responses most typical of highly successful salesmen, while responses weighted 1 are typical of men found to be poorer salesmen. It should be noted that of the 40 items, 18 have a range of possible scores from 2 to 6. On only 4 items is it possible to obtain a score of 7. In order to score the blank, one must match completions against principles listed for each item. A total score is obtained by summing score values over all items.

Test-retest reliability (total score) based on administration to 30 college students is .84. The standard error of the total score based on the college student sample is 2.5 points.

The manual reports under the heading "Statistical Analysis" that the blank was validated against a group of 37 men for whom criterion data were obtained after the blanks had been scored. Product moment coefficients of .64 and .53 are reported between sales sentence blank total scores and actual earnings and sales index, respectively.

Percentiles are given for 37 life insurance salesmen, 64 auto insurance salesmen, 45 real estate salesmen, and 33 electrical parts salesmen, but there is no other mention in the manual of the source of these data or the use of the blank with these men.

The test catalog describes the blank as "valuable as an aid in evaluating applicants and employed sales personnel." There is no evidence of any kind presented in the manual to support the use of the blank in evaluating applicants. And, as is apparent from the preceding paragraphs, the fragments of data presented on the standardization group of employed sales personnel raise more questions than they answer.

The catalog also describes the *Sales Sentence Completion Blank* as a "projective form," "amenable to quantified, objective scoring as well as clinical interpretation," and says that it "combines the probing advantages of projective methods with scoring objectivity." If these claims are to be believed, it is clear, by APA standards, that the blank is a "Level C" instrument to be used only by qualified psychologists.

The reviewer tried, unsucccessfully, to obtain additional information from both author and publisher. Thus, based on the published data, this reviewer must conclude that in its present form, publication of the *Sales Sentence Completion Blank* is premature. It should be treated as an instrument suitable only for limited, experimental use by competent professionals.

J Counsel Psychol 8:374 w '61. John O. Crites. * The sentence stems....were developed primarily from interviews with a group of 82 life insurance salesmen from Philadelphia. There are 40 incomplete sentences in the Blank which were selected from 54 trial items because they seemed to elicit "sales-oriented responses." The Manual outlines fairly detailed scoring principles, with sample completions, for obtaining an over-all "sales achievement" score. Provision is also made for scoring omissions, simple responses of fact or opinion, stereotyped answers, ambiguous completions, multiple statements, and qualified responses. No data are reported, however, on inter-scorer agreement in using the scoring principles. The incomplete sentence stems which resulted from the initial standardization are generally adequate and provocative, although some of them are too long and introduce overly complex thought. The major question which the early work with the Blank raises concerns the validity of the scoring system. The scoring principles were developed from comparing the responses of the most and the least successful salesmen in the original sample, each group numbering 30 *S*s. The criteria of success were (1) income and (2) the ratio of the number of personal contacts made by the salesmen to the number of policies sold. The high criterion group had an average income of $13,500, with an average experience in selling life insurance of nine years and two months, whereas the low criterion group had a mean salary of $5,000, with an average of *only* two years and six months selling experience. Since income in life insurance sales is partly a function of the number of years in the occupation, due to the contribution of renewals, experience and ability were confounded in the success criteria. The high and low salesmen should have been matched on number of years in the field. Less serious, but still notable shortcomings of the Blank's development have to do with its reliability and norms. Although a test-retest reliability coefficient of .84 was obtained for a one-week period, the *S*s were a very small (and presumably statistically unstable) group of 30 college students of unknown characteristics (age, sex, college major, etc., were not specified). Norms are given for Auto Insurance Salesmen, Life Insurance Salesmen, Real Estate Salesmen, Electrical Parts Salesmen, and all groups combined, but the numbers in each are quite small, ranging from 33 to 64 for the occupational samples, with the general norms based upon 179 cases. The *Sales Sentence Completion Blank* represents a novel approach to the measurement of sales aptitude and has promise for further research, but at present it is not ready for practical use by counselors and personnel workers. Additional study of its validity is badly needed, with particular emphasis upon its correlation with criteria of sales success in a sample which is homogeneous in years of selling experience. Also, the objectivity of the scoring system has not been established, and the stability of scores in sales samples has not been determined. Finally, since one of the reasons for using incomplete sentences was to reduce the social (or "selection") response set, it seems important to gather some empirical evidence on how effectively this was done.

[1182]

***Steward Basic Factors Inventory (1960 Edition).** Applicants for sales and office positions; 1957–63; revision of *Steward Sales Aptitude Inventory;* originally called *Steward Vocational Fitness Inventory;* 14 scores: business knowledge (vocabulary, arithmetic, total), dominance, personal adjustment, occupational interests (clerical, artistic, supervisory, accounting, writing, selling, mechanical, total), total; 1 form ('60, 8 pages); manual, second edition ('60, 8 pages); technical report ['60, 8 pages, typewritten in part]; supplementary data ('63, 4 pages); no data on reliability; no norms for separate occupational interest scores; $4.35 per set of 5 tests and manual; $2.25 per manual; postage extra; (60–70) minutes; Verne Steward; Steward-Mortensen & Associates. *

LEONARD V. GORDON, *Chief, Behavioral Evaluation Research Laboratory, U.S. Army Personnel Research Office, Washington, D.C.*

The *Steward Basic Factors Inventory* is the latest in a series of instruments devised by the author for the selection of salesmen and office personnel. No particular background in personnel work or in the use of employment tests is specified as required of the user of the inventory. The author claims that the manual provides the necessary instructions for application of the inventory for selection purposes, and that skill in using the materials may be achieved by carefully reading the manual and by tryout appraisal of two or three persons well known to the user.

The Steward "system" involves, as a first step, the determination by the employer of the caliber of individual required for a given job (levels A through D). After the applicant has been administered the inventory, the vocabulary and arithmetic tests are used as a first test hurdle, cutoff scores being provided in the manual for each job level. Next, the employer checks, with the applicant's former employers, references, spouse, and with credit agencies, those personal data responses which he considers to be questionable. The remainder of the inventory is then scored, and raw scores on each test are converted into ratings of unqualified, borderline, acceptable, or superior, using tables provided in the manual. A final overall rating is then given the applicant. While standards are provided for giving "unqualified" final ratings, the employer is asked to use the "direct judgment method" in the assigning of acceptable, superior, or over-qualified ratings. The manual recommends that a standard personal data blank also be used in making the final employment decision, since applicants who are acceptable on the inventory may have other disqualifying weaknesses.

While the items in the tests appear to be relevant to their intended use, it is difficult to appraise the technical adequacy of the tests themselves because of the lack of statistical information in the manual. No reliability data are presented for tests in the present form. The standard errors of the means, which appear in the reliability section of the supplement, have no bearing on the stability of the tests for individual use.

The manual also is deficient in providing validity information. No validity data are presented for office jobs. Fragmentary concurrent validity data, obtained from 1934 through 1938 on the first form of the inventory, are reported for insurance salesmen, with tetrachoric coefficients ranging from .44 to .75. While group comparisons are presented for the 1960 form, these essentially show that insurance salesmen can be differentiated from college education majors on the basis of "dominance" and "selling interest." The authors estimate, on page 3 of the validity supplement, "that this Inventory with its Manual has 75 percent more value as a selection tool than their first 4-page Inventory." In the light of the validities reported for the first form, this is a most extravagant statement.

In view of the fact that the inventory is reported as having been administered in its present and earlier forms to more than a million persons for employment purposes, it would be expected that some longitudinal validity information, together with a range of descriptive statistics, would have been available for reporting in the manual. None is presented.

The manual as a whole is poorly written, and is deficient in a number of respects. For example, in the introduction, it states that "the materials have many features never before incorporated in sales personnel selection systems," citing as two of the six more important novel features, the use of objective scoring (scoring by keys), and the inclusion of instructions for administering, scoring, and interpreting the forms in one manual. Such a statement may have had some validity several decades ago.

The guidelines provided for deciding on the caliber of individual required for a given job are inadequate and, in places, appear not to have been carefully thought out. For example, the same level of arithmetic ability is prescribed for a typist and a bookkeeper; and the job of sales clerk is evaluated at one level in the text and at another level in the chart. Clear, objective guidelines for establishing job levels are important for the proper use of the system, since cutoff scores on which employment decisions are based differ for different levels of jobs.

No information is provided as to the basis on which the table for converting raw scores to categorical ratings was developed. It would be important to know, for example, the nature of the samples used in developing the tables, the number of cases, the nature of the jobs involved, the types of companies involved, whether the subjects were tested as applicants or as employees, and the criteria used in development of the table. The user of the inventory must accept, on blind faith, the universal applicability and universal validity of the conversion table.

In evaluating the interest test scores, the user is told that only the interest area relevant to the job under consideration need be scored. It would seem important to obtain scores on all interest areas, since the applicant may report a stronger interest in areas unrelated to the job under consideration, or even a strong interest in all areas.

A minor error in interpretation may be noted in the validity section. Business knowledge items were interpreted as being more valid than mental ability items, with respective coefficients of .59 and .44, where the lower quarter of the criterion group was not included in the latter analysis.

In the opinion of the reviewer, the *Steward Basic Factors Inventory* is inappropriate for industrial application in the manner outlined in the manual. It is entirely conceivable that the items comprising the inventory may be valid for certain selection purposes. However, it is incumbent on the author to prepare a manual which will provide the prospective user with sufficient statistical information to enable him to estimate the probable utility of the inventory for his employment purposes, and to restrict distribution of the materials to those individuals who have sufficient training to properly evaluate and apply them.

LYMAN W. PORTER, *Associate Professor of Psychology, University of California, Berkeley, California.*

This 8-page inventory contains three basic parts: Part 1, 55 "business knowledge" items, including 33 vocabulary and 22 business arithmetic computation items; Part 2, 70 "personality" items (answered "yes" or "no"); and Part 3, 98 "occupational interest" items (answered "like" or "dislike").

An 8-page manual is provided, which contains instructions on the administration and use of the test, scoring keys, and tables for converting scores on each part of the test into one of four possible ratings (unqualified, borderline, acceptable, superior). On the front page of the manual, the following statement is made: "These materials [the inventory plus the manual] have many features never before incorporated in sales personnel selection systems." Some of these features are, to quote the manual: (*a*) "This manual contains instructions for the objective scoring....[of] the tests." (*b*) "The Inventory contains one personality test which measures two factors, dominance and adjustment. The test is based upon personal data and cannot be 'fudged' by applicants without detection by alert employers." (*c*) "The Inventory's parts are published in one 8-page booklet; the instructions for administering, scoring and interpreting the form are included in one Manual." To say that these are features which have "never before been incorporated in sales personnel selection systems" is misleading at best and false at worst.

The manual turns out to be completely inadequate. Information is lacking on the following: the development of the test; how the items were obtained; how the tables for conversion of scores to ratings were developed; norms; reliability; and validity.

Two supplementary documents—one partly printed and partly typewritten—were made available to the reviewer. These documents supposedly supply information not contained in the manual itself concerning the "development and validation of the *Steward Basic Factors Inventory*." An opening statement on one of these documents makes the following claims:

The present *Inventory* and its predecessors has [*sic*] been the subject of research, revision and application for approximately forty years. * During these periods, the Steward tests have been the subject of continual experimental study and revision, offering present users objectively scored, concise, reliable and valid instruments for evaluating probable success in the insurance business.

Let us examine each of these claims in the light of the evidence presented:

a) Objective scoring: This is an accurate claim.

b) Conciseness: Since the authors state that the average time required to complete the inventory is about 60 minutes, the adjective "concise" is probably appropriate.

c) Reliability: The authors state, "The only meaningful estimate of reliability for a heterogeneous test such as the *Basic Factors Inventory* is a test-retest estimate." Ignored are the possibilities of obtaining reliability estimates for the supposedly homogeneous subparts of the test by either the comparable-half or Kuder-Richardson methods. At any rate, the authors imply that although test-retest reliability data would be most desirable, they were unable to obtain any sample which they could retest at a later date. Therefore, they make their reliability claims on the following basis:

To overcome this common problem in industrial test construction [the "problem" of not being able to retest particular samples], stability of sub-scores of the Inventory were [*sic*] examined with respect to their expected variability on retesting of the same or similar populations. Mean scores, standard deviations, and standard errors of the mean were computed on a sample of 100 successful life insurance salesmen. [The results, in terms of standard scores] show that mean scores obtained on the same or similar populations should vary very little. * This range of values [of standard errors of means for different subparts of the test for this sample of 100 life insurance salesmen] ....is well within acceptable limits of reliability and it can be assumed that on retesting, average scores of a similar sample population would vary very little from the obtained scores.

All of this ignores (*a*) the fact that the size of the standard error of a mean is partly a function of *n;* and (*b*) the fact that the size of a standard error of a mean says nothing at all directly about reliability. A test composed of items that produced completely random responses on the part of the individuals taking the test might produce consistent mean scores from sample to sample, and yet be a completely unreliable test instrument. It is obvious, therefore, that no acceptable data are provided concerning reliability.

d) Validity: The authors present mean scores for a sample of 63 life insurance salesmen and 26 college students on each of the various parts of the test. The college students scored significantly lower on all but one of the subparts of the test. From these results the authors conclude that there is "concurrent validity," even though there are no data presented on test scores in relation to differential sales performance on the job for any sample of life insurance salesmen or any other group of salesmen. Furthermore, even as "concurrent validity" data, a sample of 63 life insurance salesmen and 26 college students is not only small but hardly representative of either category of individuals (especially when no information is given as to where or how these two samples were obtained). The only conclusion possible is that adequate validity of the *Steward Basic Factors Inventory* has in no way been demonstrated.

In summary, this test is not recommended for use at the present time.

[1183]

***Steward Personal Background Inventory (1960 Revised Edition).** Applicants for sales positions; 1949–60; revision of *Personal Inventory of Background Factors;* ratings of 5 factors (caliber, aptitude, adjustment, survival, supplementary) in 7 areas (health, education, experience, financial status, activities, family status, miscellaneous); 1 form ('60, 8 pages); manual ('60, c1957, 11 pages, same as 1957 manual except for minor changes); no data on reliability and validity; $4.20 per 25 forms, postage extra; specimen set not available; [60–70] minutes; Verne Steward; [Steward-Mortensen & Associates]. *

LEONARD V. GORDON, *Chief, Behavioral Evaluation Research Laboratory, U.S. Army Personnel Research Office, Washington, D.C.*

The *Steward Personal Background Inven-*

tory is an information blank intended primarily for use, either by itself or as part of a battery, in the selection of salesmen. The inventory is reported to have been developed over a period of nearly 25 years. No particular level of training is specified for its use. According to the author, skill in using the materials is acquired by reading the inventory and manual, and by trying out the inventory on several persons well known to the prospective user.

The inventory elicits the type of information characteristically obtained on standard application forms and background data blanks. The 112 personal history items, which are of the completion type, are organized into seven content areas and are also examined by means of five "key to success" factors which cut across content areas. Fifty-four of the items, which are asterisked, reflect possible "danger signs."

Steps in evaluating the inventory include, in order: examining the completed form; going over questionable items with the applicant; checking the information with the applicant's former employer, references, wife (or parents); and finally, scoring the inventory itself. Scoring consists of marking favorable responses with a dash and unfavorable responses to each asterisked item with a double x (a danger sign). Responses that are neither favorable nor unfavorable are unmarked. The employer then is to "appraise the evidence" and assign a rating of unqualified, borderline, acceptable, superior, or over-qualified for each area and factor. No standards are provided for making the ratings.

The employer then evaluates each item marked with a danger sign "to determine whether a single weakness or handicap is sufficient for rejection." Applicants are rejected if they have six or more danger signs, if they have any rating of unqualified, or if certain combinations of borderline ratings are obtained. The employer is then to make hire or reject decisions for the survivors. "Here the decision will obviously be one in which the judgment of the employer plays the most important part." No guidelines for making the decision are provided.

The manual gives the impression of providing more guidance than it actually does. For example, objective scoring is claimed as a special feature of the system. Scoring of many of the items, however, is not objective, being based on the scorer's judgment. Furthermore, no scores are obtained for either the areas or the factors. The final ratings are for the most part arrived at judgmentally. The manual also purports to provide instructions for "appraising the evidence by section of the completed Inventory" and "rating the evidence for 'key to success' factors." However, these "instructions" are little more than statements that individuals differ in various respects.

An oddity appears in the ordering of the steps for using the inventory. The manual recommends that a personal investigation of the applicant be conducted *prior* to scoring his inventory. Since applicants are later eliminated on the basis of certain negative information obtained from the inventory, it would be preferable, as a first step, to "score" the inventory and eliminate those who are unqualified, with personal investigations being conducted for the survivors.

Information regarding the validity of the inventory is covered by the statement, "for our research groups [the system] has rejected more than half of unqualified and marginal persons without eliminating those of superior qualifications." No supporting data or references are provided. No information is given as to how the recommended standards for rating applicants as being "unqualified" were arrived at, and no statistical data are provided regarding their validity in application.

The *Steward Personal Background Inventory* is, in a sense, a hybrid of the keyed background information blank and the patterned interview form, but unfortunately lacks the primary advantage of each. It does not yield area or "factor" scores, nor does it provide the user with an indication of the significance of each response and guides for further probing. As an employment blank, the inventory does have the potential for providing the employer with useful information about the applicant. However, the utility of the inventory for selection purposes will depend entirely upon the skill of the user in developing techniques for assessing the significance of the applicant's responses for success or tenure in a particular type of job.

LYMAN W. PORTER, *Associate Professor of Psychology, University of California, Berkeley, California.*

This inventory, to quote from the manual, is "an 8-page form containing 112 personal history items which is to be completed by applicants for work and/or other persons whose qualifications are desired." Apparently, as one reads through the manual, the phrase "applicants for work" really means prospective salesmen, at least as far as the inventory authors are concerned.

The inventory attempts to gather data in seven areas of personal history (health, education, etc.) and five aspects of personal history (adjustment, aptitude for selling). In other words, each of the 112 items is cross-classified into one of the seven areas and one of the five factors.

Before discussing the data provided in the manual, it is necessary to say a few words concerning the nature of the 112 items. Some of them ask for objective and easily verifiable information (e.g., number of dependent children, number of college courses completed in economics, etc.) and others ask for semi-subjective responses which would be difficult to verify (e.g., "Have you ever spoken out in a group of adults on important business problems?"; "Are you enthusiastic with respect to the worth of the products or services to be sold?"). Although the applicant is supposed to be able to complete the form in 60 to 70 minutes, one wonders if this is realistic when one of the 112 questions asks the applicant to make out a budget allotment of monthly salary among 24 different items! It is clear, of course, that many of a respondent's answers are open to distortion on his part. This factor is recognized by the authors since they emphasize the importance of verifying the obtained data by use of interview, checking with former employers, checking with the applicant's wife, etc. However, since so many of the items are subject to easy falsification, it is doubtful that really adequate checking can be undertaken without a great deal of time and effort on the employer's part.

The manual provides scoring instructions for each item. The scorer is to give a "—" for a response indicating a "favorable clue," an "××" for a "danger sign," and no mark if the response is intermediate (neither a "favorable clue" nor a "danger sign").

Other than the instructions for scoring each item, the so-called manual was found by this reviewer to be highly inadequate. No information is given as to how the items were constructed. No information is given as to how the scoring procedures were developed (i.e., information as to why a particular response to a given item should be scored "××"). No method for calculating total scores on the inventory is provided other than the statement that if more than six items receive "××" scores the applicant is to be considered disqualified. (From looking back over the scored responses in a given section of the test, the administrator of the inventory is supposed to make a subjective rating from 1 to 4 as to the applicant's qualifications in that section of the test.) Since total scores are not possible to calculate, no norms are given in the manual. Finally, no reliability or validity data are supplied in the manual.

About all that can be said in a positive way about this inventory is that many of the items appear to tap useful areas of personal background information. But, until the authors can provide norms and adequate reliability and validity information, its use is not advocated by the reviewer.

[1184]

★**Word Check Forms.** Applicants for sales and managerial positions; 1952–62; series of sentence completion and checklist forms yielding a "motivational" profile of 49 scores in 5 categories: wants, working media, pattern of behavior, level of activity, occupational tie-in; author recommends use of *Cardall Test of Practical Judgment* as a check on wants score and for obtaining additional information on level of activity score; 12 parts: 4 occupational preference checklists (Forms 1, 4, 7, 10, '62, 1 page), 4 self-description checklists (Forms 2, 5, 8, 11, '58, 1 page), and 4 sentence completion forms (Forms 3, 6, 9, 12, '59, 1 hectographed page); Forms 13 ('58), 14 ('59), 15 ('62), (1 page) also available for checking purposes; hectographed directions for administering ('58, 6 pages); hectographed norms booklet ('58, 7 pages); profile explanation booklet ('59, 14 pages); hectographed scoring stencil booklet ('60, 23 pages); profile ('59, 1 page); no data on reliability and validity; no description of normative population; no norms for Forms 3, 6–9, and 12; distribution restricted to clients; $5 per set of all 12 parts (arrangements can be made with author for local reproduction), postpaid; [120–210] minutes; V. J. Swanson; the Author. *

[Other Tests]

For tests not listed above, see the following entries in *Tests in Print:* 2046, 2050, 2052, 2056–7, 2063–4, 2066, 2068–9, 2073, and 2075–6; out of print: 2053, 2059, 2072, and 2074.

SKILLED TRADES

[1185]

★**Automotive Mechanic Test.** Prospective automotive mechanics (especially master mechanics and journeymen); 1962–63; 9 scores: motor, transmission, rear end, brakes, front end, electrical system, tune-up, carburetor, total; IBM; 1 form ('62, 16 pages); manual ('63, 16 pages); no data on reliability and validity; separate IBM scorable answer sheets must be used; $25 per 10 tests; specimen set loaned for rental fee of $5; postpaid; 180(200) minutes; McCann Associates. *

[1186]

The Fiesenheiser Test of Ability to Read Drawings. Trade school and adults; 1955; 1 form (4 pages); hectographed manual (3 pages); $5 per 50 tests; $1 per specimen set (must be purchased to obtain manual); cash orders postpaid; 30(35) minutes; Elmer I. Fiesenheiser; Psychometric Affiliates. *

JOSEPH E. MOORE, *Regents Professor of Psychology, Georgia Institute of Technology, Atlanta, Georgia.*

The author states that this test was constructed "with the intent of sampling knowledge that might be obtained in both formal instruction and in shop experience." Four areas of information (information on the multiview projection method of drawing, reading of drawings, practice problems in drawing, and definitions) are sampled by 12 multiple choice questions, 3 drawings of different views of objects, 13 matching definitions for commonly used terms, and 22 written definitions of commonly used symbols.

The type and printing of the test material is clear; that is, it is bold and black and is easy to read. However, the section on definitions of commonly used terms appears to be unnecessarily crowded together. It would have helped the testee if one line had been skipped between the questions and the answers. The weakness here is in the arrangement of the material, rather than in the content. It might be better to say that this is a criticism more of the typist (the test is offset from typewritten copy) than of the author. The scoring key is certainly poorly prepared and in many places difficult to read. The drawings to be used as guides for scoring are very carelessly done and do not reflect credit on the author.

This is primarily a speed test with 50 items to be completed within 30 minutes. The statistical data on the test are rather skimpy. The split-half reliability of .88 for 139 cases is not very high but reasonably satisfactory. However, the basis for the validity data is not at all clear. The validity data were based on 32 mechanical engineers, 58 civil engineers, 9 individuals from other engineering disciplines, and 39 "liberal studies college students." The total is given as 136. This total is in error. It should read 138. The author also confuses the reader by stating that only "62 of these subjects had had no experience using prints and only 22 had never had a course in technical or engineering drawing in either high school or college," but he does not specify who these individuals are, whether the majority of them are students in the liberal studies college or whether they are engineers.

The normative group was composed of 32 mechanical engineers, 58 civil engineers, 39 nonengineers, and 136 who are called "total college." It would have been helpful to know whether the total college group included any engineering students or whether it is a composite group of individuals from many different college majors. The percentile table does not appear to warrant separating the two engineering groups. No data are presented to show the means and standard deviations of the two groups and the scores appear to be very similar.

In summary, one should not have much confidence in the value of this test to separate men with various degrees of experience in reading engineering drawings until its validity is established further. However, the test does appear to have sufficient value to be used as a rough screening device in selecting those who have as their task the reading of various kinds of architectural and engineering drawings.

[1187]

★Technical Tests. Standards 6–8 (ages 13–15); 1962; 5 scores: arithmetic, mechanical insight, spatial relations (2 scores), tool test; 1 form ['62, 36 pages, in Afrikaans and English]; mimeographed manual ['62, 22 pages, 11 pages each in Afrikaans and English]; separate answer sheets must be used; R7.66 per 100 tests; R0.50 per 100 answer sheets; R6.66 per 100 scoring keys; postpaid; manual free; specimen set not available; 72(92) minutes; National Bureau of Educational and Social Research. *

[1188]

★Written Trade Tests. Plumbers, electricians, carpenters, maintenance mechanics; 1962–63; IBM; tests designed primarily for master mechanics and journeymen; 4 scores: blueprint reading, identification of tools, trade practices and materials, total; 1 form ('62, 14 pages); 4 tests: Plumber, Electrician, Carpenter, Maintenance Mechanic; manual ('63, 18 pages); candidate identification sheet ('62, 1 page); no data on reliability; no description of normative population; separate IBM scorable answer sheets must be used; 10–49 tests, $2.50 each; $2 per 50 extra answer sheets; specimen set of any one test loaned for rental fee of $5, which may be applied to purchase price; postpaid; 150(165) minutes; McCann Associates. *

[Other Tests]

For tests not listed above, see the following entries in *Tests in Print:* 2080–8; out of print: 2079.

SUPERVISION

[1189]

How Supervise? Supervisors; 1943-48; Forms A ('43), B ('43), M ('48, consists of items from Forms A and B), (4 pages); revised manual ('48, 8 pages); $2.90 per 25 tests; 50¢ per specimen set; postpaid; administration time not reported; Quentin W. File and H. H. Remmers (manual); Psychological Corporation. * (Australian edition: Australian Council for Educational Research.)

REFERENCES

1-5. See 3:687.
6-13. See 4:774.
14-31. See 5:926.
32. Hilton, Andrew C.; Bolin, Stanley F.; Parker, James W., Jr.; Taylor, Erwin K.; and Walker, William B. "The Validity of Personnel Assessments by Professional Psychologists." *J Appl Psychol* 39:207-93 Ag '55. * (*PA* 30:5294)
33. Meyer, Herbert H. "An Evaluation of a Supervisory Selection Program." *Personnel Psychol* 9:499-513 w '56. * (*PA* 32:3394)
34. Albright, Lewis E.; Smith, Wallace J.; and Glennon, J. R. "A Follow-Up on Some 'Invalid' Tests for Selecting Salesmen." *Personnel Psychol* 12:105-12 sp '59. * (*PA* 34:3463)
35. Albright, Lewis E.; Smith, Wallace J.; and Glennon, J. R. "Normative Data Information Exchange, Nos. 12-11, 12-12." *Personnel Psychol* 12:154-5 sp '59. *
36. Decker, Robert L. "A Cross-Validation Study of a Test of Supervisory Ability." *Proc W Va Acad Sci* 29:105-9 My '59. * (*PA* 34:3496)
37. Neel, Robert G., and Dunn, Robert E. "Predicting Success in Supervisory Training Programs by the Use of Psychological Tests." *J Appl Psychol* 44:358-60 O '60. * (*PA* 35:4081)
38. Rosen, Ned Arnold. *The Revision and Validation of the How Supervise? Test—1960.* Doctor's thesis, Purdue University (Lafayette, Ind.), 1960. (*DA* 21:364)
39. Rosen, Ned A. "How Supervise?—1943-1960." *Personnel Psychol* 14:87-99 sp '61. * (*PA* 36:4LD87R)
40. Wiener, Daniel N. "Evaluation of Selection Procedures for a Management Development Program." *J Counsel Psychol* 8:121-8 su '61. * (*PA* 36:3LD21W)

Joel T. Campbell, *Research Psychologist, Educational Testing Service, Princeton, New Jersey.*

This test is designed to measure the supervisor's "knowledge and insight concerning human relations in industry." It is available in three forms, A, B, and M. Forms A and B each consist of 70 items, divided into the three areas of supervisory practices, company policies, and supervisor opinions. For supervisory practices and company policies, the person indicates whether he considers the item "desirable," "uncertain," or "undesirable." For supervisor opinions, the response is "agree," "uncertain," and "disagree." Form M, designed for higher levels of management, is composed of 100 items selected from the other two forms, and contains the same three sections.

Forms A and B were equated in construction. For Forms A and B, percentile and standard score equivalents of total raw scores on a single form and the two forms combined are reported. Comparison groups are (*a*) "higher level supervisors," defined as "top management, office supervisor, and producton supervisors above foreman level," and (*b*) "lower level supervisors," defined as "operating supervisors, foremen and below." For Form M, percentile and standard score equivalents are given for two comparison groups: "top management supervisors" and "office and middle management supervisors." The groups are large enough to provide stable comparisons. Since the manual was last revised in 1948, it is possible that there has been a change in "supervisory climate" since that time, with accompanying shift in percentile and standard scores. However, use of the norms table, even if it is outdated, probably does little damage in individual cases.

The single form reliability of Forms A and B is reported as .77, and the two forms combined have a reliability of .87. For Form M, the reported reliability is .87. These would appear to be adequate to warrant the use of the test.

Three different approaches were used to establish validity. First, mean scores on Forms A and B combined were compared for three different levels of supervisors. All critical ratios were significant at the 1 per cent level. Second, pre-training scores on one form were compared with post-training scores on the alternate form for the three management levels. These comparisons were uniformly significant. Third, for two small groups comparisons of test scores and executive ratings produced correlations between .50 and .60.

In addition to the material reported in the manual, a substantial body of research results has been reported in the psychological literature over the years. A number of aspects of the test have been controversial. One of these was the extent to which it was a disguised measure of verbal ability. Wickert (*20*) appears to have established fairly definitely that for those below high school level, the test measures largely verbal ability. For those above high school level, *How Supervise?* scores have little relationship with intelligence test scores.

A second aspect of controversy has been over whether the knowledge as measured by the test is reflected in supervisory behavior on the job. The published research on this point is contradictory. Rosen (*39*), who reviewed this literature, concludes: "On balance the literature contains more positive evidence supporting the proposition that *How Supervise?* scores are related to supervisory success than negative results."

A less controversial use has been to measure effectiveness of training programs. Here also a fairly large volume of research results is available in the literature, and, in general, results obtained are in the predicted direction. Scores after human relation or leadership training average higher than pre-training scores (*6, 12, 25*) while scores for control groups do not increase (*12*) or do not increase as much as the training group (*8*).

This reviewer was struck by the fact that he could not locate any study in the literature where the items were factor analyzed or the total score included in a factor analysis.

When this test was developed it was keyed by opinion of two groups of experts in the field of supervisory training and industrial relations or mental hygiene. Thus it was intended to measure knowledge of accepted supervisory practices as taught by supervisor training courses. It probably is not unfair to say that *How Supervise?* espouses the "democratic" leadership of the Lewin studies. Since that time the Ohio State leadership studies and others have emphasized a multifactor approach to supervision. This reviewer would hypothesize that *How Supervise?* measures the aspect of leadership Halpin and Winer [1] defined as "consideration" and fails to measure their "initiating structure" factor. At any rate, it would be interesting to see the items or scores from this test factor analyzed along with such measures as the social service score of the *Study of Values* and the nurturance score of the *Edwards Personal Preference Schedule,* as well as the consideration and initiating structure measures.

To summarize, the following points may be made: (*a*) The test probably should not be used for those with less than twelfth grade education. (*b*) The test probably measures knowledge of one aspect of supervisory behavior. (*c*) The test can be useful in evaluating results of a human relations type of supervisor training course.

1 HALPIN, ANDREW W., AND WINER, B. JAMES. Chap. 3, "A Factorial Study of the Leader Behavior Descriptions," pp. 39–51. In *Leader Behavior: Its Description and Measurement.* Edited by Ralph M. Stogdill and Alvin E. Coons. Ohio State University, Bureau of Business Research, Research Monograph No. 88. Columbus, Ohio: the Bureau, 1957. Pp. xv, 168. *

For a review by Milton M. Mandell, see 4:774; for reviews by D. Welty Lefever, Charles I. Mosier, and C. H. Ruedisili, see 3:687.

[1190]

★**Leadership Opinion Questionnaire.** Supervisors and prospective supervisors; 1960; 2 scores: structure, consideration; 1 form (4 pages); preliminary manual (12 pages); $4.95 per 20 tests; 35¢ per manual; 60¢ per specimen set; postage extra; (15–20) minutes; Edwin A. Fleishman; Science Research Associates, Inc. *

REFERENCES

1. FLEISHMAN, EDWIN A. "Leadership Climate, Human Relations Training, and Supervisory Behavior." *Personnel Psychol* 6:205–22 su '53. * (*PA* 27:3376)
2. FLEISHMAN, EDWIN A. "The Measurement of Leadership Attitudes in Industry." *J Appl Psychol* 37:153–8 Je '53. * (*PA* 28:3324)
3. FLEISHMAN, EDWIN A. Chap. 10, "The Leadership Opinion Questionnaire," pp. 120–33. In *Leader Behavior: Its Description and Measurement.* Edited by Ralph M. Stogdill and Alvin E. Coons. Ohio State University, Bureau of Business Research, Research Monograph No. 88. Columbus, Ohio: the Bureau, 1957. Pp. xv, 168. * (*PA* 32:1466)
4. BASS, BERNARD M. "Leadership Opinions as Forecasts of Supervisory Success: A Replication." *Personnel Psychol* 11:515–8 w '58. * (*PA* 34:2185)
5. STANTON, ERWIN S. "Company Policies and Supervisors' Attitudes Toward Supervision." *J Appl Psychol* 44:22–6 F 60. * (*PA* 34:8464)
6. FLEISHMAN, EDWIN A., AND PETERS, DAVID R. "Interpersonal Values, Leadership Attitudes, and Managerial 'Success.'" *Personnel Psychol* 15:127–43 su '62. * (*PA* 37:7321)

JEROME E. DOPPELT, *Assistant Director, Test Division, The Psychological Corporation, New York, New York.*

This questionnaire provides measures of two independent dimensions of supervisory leadership: structure and consideration. Structure (S) is defined as the extent to which an individual is likely to structure his own role and those of his subordinates toward goal attainment, and consideration (C) is the extent to which an individual is likely to have job relationships characterized by mutual trust, a certain warmth between supervisor and subordinates, and the like. The question booklet contains 40 short statements to which the examinee responds by expressing his opinion on how frequently he *should* do what is described, e.g., "Criticize poor work." For each item, scoring weights of 0 to 4 correspond to the five choices. Scores on the S and C scales, each based on 20 items, are readily obtained from an answer sheet cleverly embedded in the booklet.

The claim that the S and C scales are independent is based, in part, on the background of the questionnaire. Factor analysis studies revealed these two patterns as independent. Further evidence is offered in a table of correlations between S and C, reported in the manual. For 13 groups, the correlation coefficients varied between −.23 and .08. Low correlations are also reported between scores on the questionnaire and several measures of mental ability and of personality. It is unfortunate that the tables of correlation data suffer from poor description of the groups of subjects. The table relating questionnaire scores to personality measures does not identify the groups at all. Two tables include such incomplete descriptions as "22 Top Executives," "394 Industrial Employees," and "145 ROTC Cadets." None of the correlation tables shows means and standard deviations of questionnaire scores or of the other variables. The reader who is interested in determining the similarity between any of the reported groups and his own group, either in terms of description or of score distributions, will find it difficult to do so.

Reliability estimates, computed by the split-half method for four groups, vary between .79 and .88 for the S scale and between .62 and .89 for the C scale. Test-retest coefficients for two small groups (31 first-line employees who are not otherwise described and 24 Air Force noncommissioned officers) were .74 and .67 for S and .80 and .77 for C. The test-retest coefficients are low for the assessment of individuals although the odd-even coefficients are higher than would be expected of such short scales. It is possible the odd-even reliability estimates are increased by the inclusion of some items which are essentially alike. For example, "Be willing to make changes," and "Reject suggestions for changes," appear to be the same item with a change in polarity. (Again, the failure to show means and standard deviations for the reliability samples hinders generalization of the findings.)

Percentile norms for each scale are given for a group of 780 "General Supervisory Personnel" and for six "Special Manager Groups" which include foremen, college seniors majoring in engineering and industrial administration, executives, etc. Except for the college seniors, the sources of the norms groups are not made clear and it would be advisable to heed the manual's suggestion: "These may be used as guidelines for interpreting the LOQ scale scores until local normative and validity data are accumulated."

The author of the LOQ feels that the factor analysis and item selection procedures used to develop the consideration and structure measures support the construct validity of the instrument. Perhaps so, but even more important is this sentence in the same paragraph: "It is urged that validity studies, relating these dimensions to independent critera of effectiveness, be carried out in particular organizations." Two of the three studies reported in the manual are of interest: In one, 53 supervisors in a petrochemical plant were rated on performance two years after testing; in the second, 42 sales supervisors were rated three years after testing. The S scale showed no relationship to the criterion in either study. The C scale correlated .29 and .32 with the criteria of the two studies.

Supplementary unpublished materials sent to the reviewer summarized several additional studies of the questionnaire. One of these was a further follow-up of the second study noted above. Five years after the administraton of the questionnaire, ratings and C scores correlated .37 for the 26 people who remained in the group. The relationships between C and S scores and various types of ratings were studied in a pharmaceutical company, a shoe manufacturing company, and in three hospitals. Some of the findings were encouraging and some possible uses of the questionnaire were suggested.

In summary, the *Leadership Opinion Questionnaire* is a short, easily administered instrument which yields two scores. It is important to heed the author's caution, "If used for selection purposes, individual validity studies should be carried out first." The questionnaire may be useful as an aid in management training programs which want to concentrate on the encouragement or suppression of the attitudes exemplified by the items. The current manual is labeled "Preliminary Edition"; future editions would be improved by more generous description of the data.

WAYNE K. KIRCHNER, *Manager, Personnel Research, Minnesota Mining and Manufacturing Company, St. Paul, Minnesota.*

This questionnaire consists of 40 items related to supervisory or managerial behavior. It is scored on two dimensions or factors: structure and consideration. Essentially, structure characterizes the extent to which a person likes to direct group activities and, in a sense, is directed toward getting out the work. Consideration reflects the extent to which a supervisor is human relations oriented or how warm he is in dealings with subordinates. The basic use of the questionnaire is to determine an individual's leadership "style" in terms of the two dimensions. The two dimensions of supervisory behavior were identified in the well known Ohio State leadership studies of a few years ago and were derived through factor analytic techniques. Past research in this area is impressive.

Statistically, the instrument appears to be fairly reliable. Correlations are cited for a variety of groups for both the split-half and test-retest methods. Correlations range from .62 to .89 for the two scales. It seems likely, therefore, that this is a reasonably reliable instrument.

Several validity studies are cited. There is good evidence that consideration scores, for example, correlate with successful ratings of supervisory performance in a variety of different activities. It appears, therefore, that this questionnaire has some validity in determining leadership style or supervisory behavior.

Norms are available for several different groups. They encompass the range from the perennial college senior to such groups as educational supervisors. In addition, they contain norms for a sizable ($n = 780$) group of general supervisory personnel.

Does the questionnaire have defects? Certainly, one question that comes to mind is the degree of fakability of the questionnaire. Could a supervisor completing this questionnaire make himself appear much higher in consideration than he normally is? This is highly possible. In using the questionnaire with a group of people from his own company, the reviewer found some people, who by all external criteria were quite hard hearted and non-human relations minded, who scored high on consideration. Informal interviews with these people and a review of the items on the scoring key suggest that this might be a somewhat fakable instrument.

Its particular value ought to be in terms of use within the structure of a supervisory or managerial training program. Where persons fill out the questionnaire honestly, one can estimate how they stack up against other supervisors and managers. This should have some beneficial effect. Data relevant to this question are presented in the manual and in related material.

Overall, this is not a bad instrument. It has been developed through careful research and careful statistical techniques. It appears to be reliable, presents good evidence of validity, and presents reasonably good norms. It seems well suited for research activities and training activities, although it is probably not the best thing to use as an evaluative instrument of supervisory performance.

[1191]

★**Personal Development Record.** Supervisors; 1957–63; 5 parts: self-evaluation of abilities, self-evaluation of job performance, strengths and weaknesses, plans for improvement, summary; Form S ('57, 9 pages); manual ['63, 4 unnumbered pages]; no data on reliability; norms for males and for first three parts only; $6.75 per 25 records; 10¢ per key; postage extra; $1 per specimen set, postpaid; (30) minutes; Richardson, Bellows, Henry & Co., Inc. *

[1192]

★**Supervisory Index.** Supervisors; 1960; 5 attitude scores: management, supervision, employees, human relations practices, total; 1 form (4 pages); preliminary manual (11 pages); $4.95 per 20 tests; 25¢ per manual; 50¢ per specimen set; postage extra; (10–20) minutes; Norman Gekoski and S. L. Schwartz; Science Research Associates, Inc. *

REFERENCES

1. Schwartz, Solomon L., and Gekoski, Norman. "The Supervisory Inventory: A Forced-Choice Measure of Human Relations Attitude and Technique." *J Appl Psychol* 44:233–6 Ag '60. * (*PA* 35:4130)

Arthur H. Brayfield, *Executive Officer, American Psychological Association, Washington, D.C.*

The *Supervisory Index* poses a neglected ethical problem.

The instructions to the testee say: "Remember, this is NOT a test; there are no right or wrong answers. You should mark those statements which best describe how you feel about these things."

In the manual, there is a section on suggested uses of the index which includes selection, placement, and training. Thus: "The scores on the *Index* may be used, in conjunction with other appropriate instruments, for selecting from the pool of supervisory candidates those most likely to be 'successful.' In some companies the total score may be a significant predictor of success; in other company environments a composite score obtained by applying appropriate weights to the area scores may yield the best results." In short, personnel actions based on scores derived from the index are suggested.

In the light of the instructions on the front page of the index, these suggestions embrace a form of deception. I recommend that the index be withdrawn from the market pending clarification of this question.

ALBERT K. KURTZ, *Fulbright Lecturer, Ein Shams University, Cairo, United Arab Republic.*

This is a very carefully constructed test which has been shown to correlate with two somewhat different criteria of the success of 73 men already employed as supervisors. If it can show similar validity coefficients when given to new (and preferably larger) groups who are tested when appointed as supervisors and evaluated later, it will have shown itself to be a very worthwhile test.

Except for a few places where minor objections might be raised, the bulk of the manual is well written and sufficiently detailed to give the prospective test user an excellent description of the steps taken in constructing and validating the test. Further, the work appears to have been done well.

The *Supervisory Index* was cross validated against ratings made by plant psychologists on two criteria: (*a*) attitudinal characteristics and (*b*) administrative and production skills. The reviewer's work as an industrial psychologist may be responsible for his marked preference for the second criterion against which the total score gave a validity of .33 as opposed to .61 for the first criterion. Even though .33 does not appear to be very high, it is difficult to achieve high validities in industry, especially on supervisory jobs. (Besides, for people who prefer the other criterion, that validity of .61 is indeed high.) As hinted above, the crucial issue is whether or not these figures on concurrent validity are typical of the at present unknown predictive validity of the test.

The directions for giving the test are too casual. The test administrator is supposed to read the directions to "large groups," implying that this is not to be done for individuals tested singly or in small groups. He is to "emphasize" some points, "warn" the people taking the test, and check to see that each person "has filled in the information requested in the box on the cover of the booklet completely." The latter may be a bit difficult, both because the directions say nothing about filling in these blanks and because as soon as anyone starts answering the test, the box (completed or ignored) is no longer visible. In brief, the directions need to be clarified and standardized. This will necessitate changes both in the manual and on the test blank.

The difficulty which Science Research Associates had for years in getting the printer to so align his pages that the pinholes in the *Kuder Preference Record* would register properly for scoring is here again, even though no pinholes are used. This test is answered by blackening small circles. In 5 of the 24 forced-choice items, the answer circles for two of the alternatives are so close together (because some of the alternatives are only one instead of several lines long) that a tiny printer's error in alignment could (and on my copy of the test would) lead to errors in scoring. This is minor because it would be so easy to correct, but it is also a major criticism because it may lead to erroneous scores.

Another criticism, applying to this and several hundred other tests, is that the four part scores are not reliable enough to justify their use for differential diagnosis. The total score alone should be used.

The *Supervisory Index* is a well constructed and validated test. If it can be shown to have predictive validity as well as the concurrent validity it possesses, it will be a good test for selecting supervisors in industry. The test is badly in need of improved directions for administering it. Other aspects of the test could also be improved if the authors and publisher have the desire to do so.

[1193]

★Supervisory Inventory on Human Relations. Supervisors and prospective supervisors; 1960; 1 form (3 pages); revised manual (9 pages); $4.95 per 20 self-marking tests; 25¢ per manual; 50¢ per specimen set; postage extra; (15) minutes; Donald L. Kirkpatrick and Earl Planty; Science Research Associates, Inc. *

REFERENCES

1. KIRCHNER, WAYNE; HANSON, RICHARD; AND BENSON, DALE. "Selecting Foremen With Psychological Tests." *Personnel Adm* 23:27–30 N–D '60. *

SEYMOUR LEVY, *Manager, Personnel Research and Manpower Development, The Pillsbury Company, Minneapolis, Minnesota.*

This test asks the subject to indicate his agreement or disagreement with 80 items reflecting various principles and practices and attitudes related to supervisory behavior. Item content reflects concepts dealing with understanding and motivating employees, the supervisor's role in management, developing positive employee attitudes, some awareness of principles of learning and training, and, lastly, five items on problem solving techniques. The test is presented in an attractive format. It is easily readable and probably does not pose any technical difficulties in completion of the instrument. The language of the items is clear and the statements are short and should not pose undue difficulties in interpreting their meaning.

The inventory was originally developed as a measuring tool for evaluating institutes on human relations for foremen and supervisors at the Management Institute of the University of Wisconsin. The items thus reflect the course content of this program. Item scoring was developed by obtaining agreement of the instructors who presented the course.

The authors suggest this instrument may be used: (*a*) to determine needs for human relations training, (*b*) to provide information for on-the-job coaching, (*c*) as a device for conference discussions, (*d*) to determine the effectiveness of a human relations course, and (*e*) to assist in the selection of supervisors. Very few data are provided on the validity of the inventory in these different situations. The norms that are provided are clearly inadequate. While it is stated that the norm table includes scores of foremen, office supervisors, and middle and top management groups, no measures of standard deviation and no percentiles are provided. This leaves real ambiguity with respect to variability. The publisher reports that percentiles will be made available in a future manual.

A split-half reliability of .94 is reported. No data, however, are provided with respect to the number of persons involved in this sample and the nature of their backgrounds.

The validity and significance of this inventory is still to be determined. The instrument raises more questions than it answers. For example: Are there differences in scores at different job levels of supervisory responsibility? What is the correlation with intelligence and with experience? Are there differences among supervisors in different industries? Does change in score through teaching reflect itself in improved performance on the job?

[1194]

***Supervisory Practices Test.** Supervisors; 1957–64; 1 form ('57, 4 pages); revised manual ('64, 12 pages); $5 per 25 tests; 25¢ per key; $1.75 per manual; $2.50 per specimen set; cash orders postpaid; French, Portuguese, and Belgian editions available; (20–30) minutes; Martin M. Bruce; the Author. *

REFERENCES

1. BRUCE, MARTIN M. "Normative Data Information Exchange, No. 10-34." *Personnel Psychol* 10:369 au '57. * (*PA* 33:80)
2. BRUCE, MARTIN M., AND LEARNER, DAVID B. "A Supervisory Practices Test." *Personnel Psychol* 11:207–16 su '58. *
3. WATLEY, DONIVAN JASON. *Prediction of Academic Success in a College of Business Administration.* Doctor's thesis, University of Denver (Denver, Colo.), 1961. (*DA* 22:3527)
4. WATLEY, DONIVAN J., AND MARTIN, H. T. "Prediction of Academic Success in a College of Business Administration." *Personnel & Guid J* 41:147–54 O '62. * (*PA* 37:5656)

For reviews by Clifford E. Jurgensen and Mary Ellen Oliverio, see 5:955.

[1195]

★Test of Supervisory Judgment. Business and industry; 1949–63; Forms S ('49), T ('53), (9 pages); Form T is a revision of Form S (with 60 per cent of the items the same) rather than a parallel form; separate manuals for Forms S ['63, 13 unnumbered pages], T ['63, 6 unnumbered pages]; $5.50 per 25 tests; $1 per set of keys; $1.25 per manual for Form S; $1 per manual for Form T; postage extra; $2 per specimen set, postpaid; (30–35) minutes; Richardson, Bellows, Henry & Co., Inc. *

[1196]

★WLW Supervisor Survey. Supervisors; 1956–62; 2 scores: considerate attitudes, initiative; Form 3 ('62, 8 mimeographed pages); mimeographed manual ('62, 3 pages); mimeographed teaching manual ('57, 14 pages) for an earlier form; no data on reliability and validity; 15¢ per test, postpaid; teaching manual free; [35] minutes; R. W. Henderson; William, Lynde & Williams. *

[Other Tests]

For tests not listed above, see the following entries in *Tests in Print:* 2092 and 2098; out of print: 2093; status unknown: 2089.

TRANSPORTATION

[1197]

[Driver Selection Forms and Tests.] Truck drivers; 1943–55; part of White Motor Company's *Continuing Control System of Truck Management;* individual in part; no manual; postage extra; Dartnell Corporation. *

a) EMPLOYMENT APPLICATION. 1946; 3 editions: Form Nos. 111 (city delivery drivers), 211 (over-the-road drivers), 311 (long distance drivers), ['46, 2 pages]; 1–99 copies, 7¢ each.

b) TELEPHONE CHECK. 1946–53; Form No. OT-203 ('53, 1 page); 1–99 copies, 6¢ each; Robert N. McMurry.

c) DRIVER INTERVIEW. 1946; Form No. 13 ['46, 2 pages]; 1–99 copies, 10¢ each.

d) PHYSICAL EXAMINATION RECORD. 1946–54; Form No. 19 ('54, 1 page); 1–99 copies, 6¢ each.

e) SELECTION AND EVALUATION SUMMARY. 1950–55; Form No. ES-404R ('55, 1 page); 1–99 copies, 6¢ each; Robert N. McMurry.

f) STANDARDIZED TEST: TRAFFIC AND DRIVING KNOWLEDGE FOR DRIVERS OF MOTOR TRUCKS. 1946–54; Form No. 16 ['46, 4 pages]; directions sheet-scoring key ['46, 2 pages]; no data on reliability; 1–99 copies, 10¢ each; 7¢ per directions sheet-scoring key; administration time not reported; Amos E. Neyhart and

Helen L. Neyhart; also distributed by Institute of Public Safety, Pennsylvania State University.
g) ROAD TEST IN TRAFFIC FOR TESTING, SELECTING, RATING, AND TRAINING TRUCK DRIVERS. 1943–46; 3 scores: specific driving skills, general driving habits and attitudes, total; individual; 1 form ['45]; score sheet ['46, Form No. 18, 2 pages]; no manual; no data on reliability; no norms; 1–99 copies, 7¢ each; [30–60] minutes; Amos E. Neyhart.

JOSEPH E. MOORE, *Regents Professor of Psychology, Georgia Institute of Technology, Atlanta, Georgia.*

There are 10 forms in this series. The three employment application forms are identical except for the color of the paper. Form OT-203, Telephone Check, asks only one question concerning driving, "What accidents has he had?" Form 13, Driver Interview, is the typical patterned interview form with six specific questions concerning accidents. On the basis of replies to such questions as "What was the worst driving accident you ever had?" the interviewer is asked "Is he careless?" On the response to the question "How did it happen?" the interviewer is asked, "Does this indicate 'accident proneness'?" It is doubtful if many or perhaps any interviewer could ascertain significant behavior from such short questions. These forms are for interviewing and evaluating applicants but, as in using all such forms, the significant value comes from the skill, training, and clinical insight possessed by the interviewer. However, the patterned interview forms could very well suggest questions that the average interviewer is not competent to evaluate and thus do a disservice, if not a rank injustice, to the applicant.

Form 16 claims to be a standardized test of traffic and driver knowledge for drivers of motor trucks. This test is composed of 57 multiple choice questions, each containing four choices. Form 17 is the scoring key. There is no manual or other information pertaining to validity or reliability of the test. Form 18 is the road test. This is merely a checklist and score sheet for 16 areas of performance covering such things as starting the engine through signaling and positioning of the vehicle on the roadway.

Form 19 is a typical physical examination record for drivers.

Form ES-404R, the Selection and Evaluation Summary, contains certain items grouped under background, character traits, motivation, and emotional maturity. The rater assigns values from 1 through 4 and tries to match the applicant's qualities against the requirement for a particular position.

The forms are printed in clear legible type. The arrangement of items is, for the most part, logical and sequential. The users of these forms should be alerted to the fact that they will not, in and of themselves, improve selection procedures. The unsubstantiated claims set forth in the general booklet entitled *Developing a Better Personnel Selection Program* should be taken as just that. For example, the exaggerated statements "Even the addition of a telephone check plan may double the effectiveness of personnel selection in many organizations," and "the patterned interview has been designed to overcome the limitations and faults of ordinary interviewing" have no data whatsoever supporting them.

For a review by S. Rains Wallace, Jr., see 4:789.

[1198]

★[McGuire Safe Driver Scale and Interview Guide]. Prospective motor vehicle operators; 1961–62; 2 parts; driver selection guide ('62, 26 pages including copies of both parts and manual for *a*); $15 per set of 25 copies of *a*, manual for *a*, and 25 copies of *b*; $5 per driver selection guide; postpaid; Frederick L. McGuire; Western Psychological Services. *
a) THE MC GUIRE SAFE DRIVER SCALE. Title on test is *The McGuire S D Scale;* items selected in part from *Kuder Preference Record-Personal* and *Minnesota Multiphasic Personality Inventory;* 1 form ('61, 4 pages); manual ('62, 8 pages); reliability data for part 1 only; $6.50 per 25 tests; $3 per manual; (10–20) minutes.
b) THE MC GUIRE SAFE DRIVER INTERVIEW GUIDE. 1 form ('61, 4 pages); no specific manual; instructions contained in driver selection guide; no data on reliability and validity; $6.50 per 25 forms; [30–60] minutes.

REFERENCES

1. McGuire, Frederick L. "The Safe-Driver Inventory: A Test for Selecting the Safe Automobile Driver." *U S Armed Forces Med J* 7:1249–64 S '56. * (*PA* 31:3052)

WILLARD A. KERR, *Professor of Psychology, Illinois Institute of Technology, Chicago, Illinois.*

This well printed 4-page test of 78 temperament, value, and interest items is outwardly labeled simply *The McGuire S D Scale.* All items are objectively stated and scored, and the scoring process is simple.

The McGuire kit also contains a 4-page "Safe Driver Interview Guide," which is a conventional guide for making and recording one's impressions of the driver job applicant. The eight areas of guided discussion with an observation of the applicant are work history, school history, military record, health history, family history, marital history, social level, and aspiration level. The guide is concluded by a total summation rating of risk. The manual provides no supportive evidence of validity or even of specific research derivation.

The purpose of the test is to help detect the safe driver. Items employed have been found to discriminate between driver groups with good safety records and driver groups with weaker safety records. All items are of the voluntary commitment type, such as temperament test and interest test items. Content of the accompanying manual suggests a thoughtful and competent approach to the psychology of this difficult problem, including a provocative summary of characteristics of drivers with superior safety records. An odd-even reliability of .88 on 153 Navy personnel is reported.

The six validity studies which are briefly reported convince the reviewer that the test can discriminate between better and poorer drivers *when both are tested after already being hired*. Under this limited condition, using a raw cutting score of 46, the efficiency of prediction is reported to range between 61 and 88 per cent. Although some of these studies are referred to as cross validations and, in a sense, are, none of them seems to be based on pre-employment testing and later follow-up in service which is the crucial test of validity of all voluntary commitment devices.

The manual is weak specifically in that (*a*) no validity coefficients are given, and (*b*) although there is implication that the test is useful in selecting safe drivers, none of the validity evidence appears to be from pre-employment evaluation situations. Therefore, one can only speculate whether or not the test will predict driver safety when it is administered as part of the pre-employment evaluation. The motivation to "look good" to the prospective employer will probably reduce the test's usefulness substantially, as it does in current temperament and interest measures in pre-employment testing; nevertheless, the test shows ingenuity and deserves a fair trial in the pre-employment selection of taxi and truck drivers.

D. H. Schuster, *Staff Psychologist, Collins Radio Company, Cedar Rapids, Iowa.*

MC GUIRE SAFE DRIVER SCALE. According to the manual, the MSDS "is a paper-and-pencil test for use in selecting safe motor-vehicle drivers." In the test derivation, two assumptions were made about predicting motor vehicle accidents. The first was that "the largest and most important factor operating to produce motor-vehicle accidents is the attitude and personality pattern of the individual driver." The second was that "it is more productive and efficient to identify and select the safe driver than to identify the accident producer." The first assumption is subject to question, since the reviewer has found that motor vehicle accidents can be predicted at least as well on the basis of risks taken while driving (i.e., amount of night driving or annual mileage driven) as on the basis of the driver's attitude. The second assumption is justified in the context of the intended use of this test, that is, selection of the safe driver for commercial transportation organizations.

Many of the items in the MSDS were selected by item analysis from standard tests cited in the manual. Items retained were those which differentiated an accident group from an accident-free group at the 5 per cent level of significance. The accident group consisted of drivers (U.S. Marines) who reported that they had been involved within the previous two years in an accident and also had received a moving violation citation at the time of the accident. The tacit assumption is that the driver was, accordingly, responsible for the accident. The accident-free group consisted of drivers who claimed that they had never been involved in any accidents while driving, nor had they ever incurred any moving violation citations. Thus a considerable number of drivers with intermediate records were omitted from the item analysis; how many is not stated. This process conceivably could select just the more extreme problem drivers. It should be noted that the criterion for assigning drivers to the groups was a dual one, involving both accidents and moving violation citations. No information on the correlation between these two variables is reported in the manual, but, from unpublished studies made by this reviewer, the correlation would appear to be about .20 to .30. In the original sample used for item analysis, drivers reportedly could be assigned to the correct driver group with an accuracy of 88 per cent.

In one cross validation, the efficiency of correct assignment was 65 per cent versus a chance level of 50 per cent. In other cross validations with Marine Corps drivers, the accuracy varied from 61 to 70 per cent correct. These results are statistically significant at or beyond the 1 per cent level. Thus, in several cross validations, the MSDS appears to have some predictive validity for current accident records of drivers. It should be noted that the "prediction" was really postdiction, not prediction as would be obtained from a follow-up study after testing of the drivers.

The cutoff score is not reported in all cases for the cross validation studies. In a number of studies a raw cutoff score of 46 was used, corresponding to a centile score of 69 for "Private Operators," reasonably close to the percentage of accident-free drivers in a three-year period. A raw cutoff score of 54 should be used for professional drivers, as this corresponds to a centile score of 71. The cutoff score should be adjusted by the user, depending on the supply of applicants and on how confident he wishes to be about the future accident record of the applicants.

Norms for three groups are given in the manual, and these will be quite useful to the test user. The user is well advised to collect data and develop his own norms as soon as possible.

In two of the three studies in which accident and nonaccident groups were compared, there was an equal number of drivers in each of the groups; this is far from the accident distribution found in practice. Most drivers in a given one- or even three-year period have not had any accidents. Thus the prediction problem is particularly bad, since the aim of the MSDS is to weed out the rare driver with a poor record. The usefulness of the test can be judged by seeing how much improvement it produces above chance or existing selection procedures. In selecting civilian professional drivers in a transit company, the MSDS was able to produce an improvement of 16 percentage points (86 per cent correct selection compared to 70 per cent) over the established hiring procedure of the company. Thus the scale appears to have some merit for improving the chances of hiring a safe driver.

Reliability of Part 1 appears to be satisfactory (.88); no reliability data are given for Part 2. No figures are given for validity in terms of correlation coefficients.

MC GUIRE SAFE DRIVER INTERVIEW GUIDE. The manual for the interview guide (MSDIG) presents the background of the research in greater detail than the manual for the MSDS. The temperament and personality traits which have been found to be related to moving violation and accident-incurring drivers are reviewed. The MSDIG incorporates the MSDS as an important factor in the employment interview. In addition, an interview guide is provided to direct the questions asked of the applicant by the interviewer. The following areas are covered: work history, school history, military record, health, family history, marital history, social history, and aspiration level. In general, the interview guide is designed to elicit information of positive and negative factors with respect to hiring a good employee, as well as hiring a good and safe driver. The approach in using the MSDIG is clinical or global, and no validity data for the guide by itself are presented. Its use is justified by the important negative finding (such as a very poor attitude) it may uncover occasionally.

SUMMARY. The interview guide and MSDS appear to be worthwhile instruments in the selection of safe drivers. Actual data on predictive validity of the two instruments are not yet available. The test does offer some validity for locating accident-having drivers. The prospective user also should consider tests of driving performance, driving information, and driving aptitude in the selection of drivers. No data are given in the test manual, or are available anywhere—at least not to the reviewer's knowledge—that support this specific recommendation. The recommendation for using other tests is based on the general consideration that predictive validity is increased in general by sampling as many different relevant factors as possible.

[1199]

Truck Driver Test. Drivers of light and medium trucks; 1957–58; form 60-A ('57, 15 pages plus fold-out answer sheet); preliminary mimeographed manual ('58, 5 pages); general PPA mimeographed directions ['57, 7 pages]; no norms; 10–49 tests, $1 each; $2 per specimen set; postpaid; 90(100) minutes; Public Personnel Association. *

WILLARD A. KERR, *Professor of Psychology, Illinois Institute of Technology, Chicago, Illinois.*

A 14-page reusable test booklet with separable answer sheet is accompanied by a brief normless manual which states that the test is intended "to assist in the selection of light and medium truck drivers for the public service."

The test, which contains 75 multiple choice items arranged in ascending order of difficulty within each subject matter field, is primarily an information test. Most items have high face validity for light truck driving, but the manual is devoid of actual validity evidence. The items are relevant (safe driving practices, maintenance service and repairs, traffic regulations, mechanical aptitude and ability to understand written orders) and it is reasonable to believe that the test has validity for selecting individuals with appropriate knowledge for truck driving. It does not pretend to be a test of skill in actual driving.

D. H. SCHUSTER, *Staff Psychologist, Collins Radio Company, Cedar Rapids, Iowa.*

The items in the test were developed on the basis of task analysis of the typical duties and responsibilities for the job of truck driver. Many public personnel agencies were polled and only the items rated by two or more agencies as involved in the job of truck driver were retained. The trial form reflected the common core of subject matter included by most agencies in their own test for the truck driver class. The trial form of the test was administered to more than 800 applicants by eight public agencies throughout the United States and Canada. An item analysis was employed with the criterion apparently (not so stated) the total item score. Items retained were correlated at least .30 with the criterion. The validity of the test is essentially that of content validity plus face validity. The test, by agreement among the agencies originally polled, does measure the knowledge and abilities important in the selection of truck drivers. No predictive validity checks with an external criterion have been made. The reason given is that there is no global criterion or suitable yardstick to measure the success of truck drivers. Thus the validity of the test is qualitatively that agreed upon by personnel agencies and has no quantitative figure. In the opinion of the reviewer, a suitable external criterion might be merit ratings or driving record of violations and accidents.

The reliability, as estimated by the split-half technique, is "greater than 0.90." The development of the *Truck Driver Test* is yet to be completed. Although the manual is dated January 1958, no further validity or evaluation data have yet appeared.

In summary, the test appears to be valid for testing what a truck driver needs to know in terms of operating rules, procedures, and practices. It is not a driving performance test. The most notable lack is quantitative validity information. In addition, it seems the test could well be supplemented by tests involving personality variables or aptitudes pertinent to driver selection.

[1200 [1]]

★**Wilson Driver Selection Test.** Prospective motor vehicle operators; 1961; 6 scores (visual attention, depth visualization, recognition of simple detail, recognition of complex detail, eye-hand coordination, steadiness) and safety aptitude rating (based on number of subtests passed); 1 form (15 pages); manual (28 pages); $10 per 25 tests; 25¢ per key; $1.75 per manual; $2.50 per specimen set; cash orders postpaid; 26(50) minutes; Clark L. Wilson; Martin M. Bruce. *

WILLARD A. KERR, *Professor of Psychology, Illinois Institute of Technology, Chicago, Illinois.*

This test consists of a well printed 16-page booklet containing six chiefly nonverbal aptitude tests plus an unscored page of biographical information. It is intended to measure ability to operate vehicles with minimal risk. The six subtests are Visual Attention (5 minutes), Depth Visualization (5 minutes), Recognition of Simple Detail (4 minutes), Recognition of Complex Detail (5 minutes), Eye-Hand Coordination (2 minutes), and Steadiness (5 minutes). Reliabilities reported are, respectively, .59, .75, .79, .81, .84, and .93.

Perceptual speed and spatial relations form the central aptitude bases of this test, the rationale excluding personality variables. The specific measures have good face validity and seem well constructed.

The author notes consistent lack of predictive validity of paper and pencil tests for driver accident prevention published up to 1961. Why the present test content would perform better is not clear. Nevertheless, crude (null hypothesis rejection statistics) evidence is presented showing validity trends favoring the test for 71 bus drivers, 88 milk truck drivers in one group, 899 other milk truck drivers,

1 Because of the insertion of additional tests (8a, 74a, 74b, 84a, 146a, 230a, 307a, 313a, 342a, 716a, 844a, 867a, 872a, 887a, 909a, 931a, 951a, 1013a, and 1061a), the total number of test entries is 1219.

206 salesmen, and 85 police motorcycle officers. Without validity coefficients, however, the strength of these relations is unclear.

The manual makes deferential reference to the APA standards for test manuals and then proceeds to display seven pages of validity data without reporting a single validity coefficient. Nevertheless, this test apparently has *some* validity for screening low aptitude people away from driving jobs; a communicable validity study on it is needed.

D. H. SCHUSTER, *Staff Psychologist, Collins Radio Company, Cedar Rapids, Iowa.*

This is a battery of six short timed tests measuring four visual aptitudes listed above and two psychomotor tests. A cutoff score, established on the basis of a pass-fail dichotomy for the accident records of bus drivers, was established for each test. The battery score is simply the number of tests out of six that the driver passed (number of tests on which the driver's score was at or above the test cutoff score).

A number of validity studies were made with different types of drivers—bus drivers, milk delivery drivers, field salesmen, passenger car drivers, and motorcycle drivers. While most of the studies were concerned with postdiction, or the prediction of accident records of drivers in the immediate past, two of the validity studies were concerned with predicting the accident records of drivers subsequent to testing. Using at-fault accidents as the criterion, most of the studies showed that the final test battery score (0 to 6) does discriminate between drivers with and without accidents. The level of significance in these studies varied from close to the 5 per cent level to well beyond it. Even when the criterion was somewhat weaker, merely accident involvements, the test also provided significant discrimination. Since the battery score was not dichotomized, accuracy of prediction figures are not given. The reviewer took the liberty of establishing a cutoff score for one of the validity studies and determined that the battery score discriminated with an accuracy of 59 per cent between motorcylists with and without accident involvements, versus the 47 per cent discrimination expected by chance in this case.

The reliability for the battery as a whole is a satisfactory .84. The reliabilities for the six individual tests are lower but range from .59 to .93.

Missing from the manual are data that show the correlation between the battery score and number of accidents, or information about the factor structure of the six tests. Also missing is any information on the reliability of the accident criterion. In the experience of the reviewer, the reliability of accidents is fairly low, ranging from approximately .3 to .4, based upon communality estimates. While the prediction obtained with this test is thus likely close to the maximum attainable, the user ought to consider driver attitude, driving information, and performance tests in his selection battery.

In summary, the validity studies show that the *Wilson Driver Selection Test* does have a low but useful validity in discriminating between drivers with and those without accidents.

[Other Tests]

For tests not listed above, see the following entries in *Tests in Print:* 2100 and 2102–3.

Books and Reviews

* * * * *

The following roughly classified index has been prepared to assist readers to locate books on a particular subject. In addition to using this index, readers are urged to skim over titles and excerpts in search of works which otherwise may be overlooked.

[B1]

★Attitude Scaling. Publications of the Market Research Society, No. 4. London: Oakwood Press, 1960. Pp. vi, 76. 15*s*. * (*PA* 35:2090)

Brit J Ed Psychol 31:313 N '61. This is a symposium, three chapters of which—by Eysenck, Handyside and Trenaman—deal succinctly and usefully with scale construction. The other authors are concerned with attitude assessment in market research, and the two sections fail to integrate. Sofer and Menzies.... make a good case for so-called depth interviewing, projective techniques and group discussions, as being more sound, psychologically, than the formal questionnaire. But if this is so, why do not market researchers publish evidence of validity, for they have a much better criterion, namely rises in sales, than academic experimenters usually have? It would be useful, also, if they would define their terms. Eysenck considers attitudes as habits, not as drives, whereas R. P. Kelvin states that the object of attitude research is to discover the consumer's "needs" and how they can be met. D. Melvin is the most successful in bridging the gap, showing how qualitative procedures can be used to provide hypotheses which can then be tested by questionnaire surveys and statistical analyses.

[B2]

★The Canadian Tests, Grades 8, 9, and 10: Testing Instruments Used in the First Two Years of the Carnegie Study. Carnegie Study of Identification and Utilization of Talent in High School and College, Bulletin No. 5. Toronto, Canada: Department of Educational Research, Ontario College of Education, University of Toronto, 1964. Unnumbered pages. Paper, plastic binding. $5.00. *

[B3–4]

★Editors and Writers Conference on Testing, May 13 and 14, 1958, Princeton, New Jersey. Princeton, N.J.: Educational Testing Service, 1959. Pp. 78. Paper. Out of print. *

Personnel & Guid J 38:337–8 D '59. Thomas M. Magoon. This first conference of its kind brought specialists in tests and measurements together with a group of journalists interested in learning more about the development, use, and limitations of measurement and the means of communicating such information to the general public. The topics range from development and nature of modern tests, tests for identifying talent and for use in guidance, tests and organizations for testing services, to tests in teaching and in selection for scholarships. The papers are readable and quite general to the point of communicating little at times other than (hopefully) a favorable impression among the journalists that conscientious work is being done, that there are many problems involved, and that there are few pat answers. The paper by Traxler on tests and organizations for test services provides a useful, broad view of the nature and size of the testing movement, test publishers, and typical reference works regarding testing. * The discussion sessions following each address are printed in condensed form and make for some of the most interesting reading. All too infrequently do we have an opportunity to view and weigh the questions, observations, and inferences of interested nonspecialists.

[B5]

★Evaluation of Pupil Progress in Business Education. American Business Education Yearbook, Vol. 17, 1960. Estelle L. Popham, editor; Charles Hicks, associate editor. Published jointly by Eastern Business Teachers Association and National Business Teachers Association. New York: New York University Campus Stores, 1960. Pp. x, 399. Out of print. *

J Bus Ed 36:137 D '60. This volume....sets a new high standard for a series of publications of which business teachers can rightly be proud. * it is much more than a book on tests and measurements. It attempts with considerable success to develop a philosophy of evaluation. It asks why test? How evaluate the test itself? What is the relationship between formal and informal testing, and testing during the class presentation? * The final section on evaluation in job situations will be especially useful in giving teachers an insight into other uses for testing procedures. Such a good yearbook deserves an index.

[B6]

★Guidelines for Testing Minority Group Children. Prepared by a Work Group of the Society for the Psychological Study of Social Issues: Martin Deutsch, Joshua A. Fishman (Chairman), Leonard Kogan, Robert North, and Martin Whiteman. Supplement to the *Journal of Social Issues,* Vol. 20, April 1964. Ann Arbor, Mich.: the Society, April 1964. Pp. 127–45. Paper. $0.25. *

[B7]

★Hearing Testing of School Children and Guide for Hearing Conservation Programs: For Professional Use. Berkeley, Calif.: California State Department of Public Health, 1962. Pp. 54. Paper. Gratis. *

[B8]

★How to Pass Biology: Questions and Answers: Advanced Test No. 1, Graduate Record Examination. Brooklyn, N.Y.: College Publishing Corporation, 1964. Unnumbered pages. Paper, plastic binding, mimeographed. $3.00. *

[B9]

★How to Pass Chemistry: Questions and Answers: Advanced Test No. 2, Graduate Record Examination. Brooklyn, N.Y.: College Publishing Corporation, 1964. Unnumbered pages. Paper, plastic binding, mimeographed. $3.00. *

[B10]

★How to Pass Economics: Questions and Answers: Advanced Test No. 3, Graduate Record Examination. Brooklyn, N.Y.: College Publishing Corporation, 1964. Unnumbered pages. Paper, plastic binding, mimeographed. $3.00. *

[B11]

★How to Pass Government: Questions and Answers: Advanced Test No. 8, Graduate Record Examination. Brooklyn, N.Y.: College Publishing Corporation, 1964. Unnumbered pages. Paper, plastic binding, mimeographed. $3.00. *

[B12]

★How to Pass Guidance Counselor: Questions and Answers: Optional Examination No. 16, National Teacher Examination. Brooklyn, N.Y.: Technical Extension Service, Inc., 1964. Unnumbered pages. Paper, plastic binding, mimeographed. $3.95. *

[B13]

★How to Pass High on the American College Testing Program Exams. New York: Arco Publishing Co., Inc., 1960. Pp. iv, 128, plus supplements. Paper. $3.00. *

[B14]

★How to Pass History: Questions and Answers: Advanced Test No. 9, Graduate Record Examination. Brooklyn, N.Y.: College Publishing Corporation, 1964. Unnumbered pages. Paper, plastic binding, mimeographed. $3.00. *

[B15]

★How to Pass Literature: Questions and Answers: Advanced Test No. 10, Graduate Record Examination. Brooklyn, N.Y.: College Publishing Corporation, 1964. Unnumbered pages. Paper, plastic binding, mimeographed. $3.00. *

[B16]

★How to Pass Physics: Questions and Answers: Advanced Test No. 13, Graduate Record Examination. Brooklyn, N.Y.: College Publishing Corporation, 1964. Unnumbered pages. Paper, plastic binding, mimeographed. $3.00. *

[B17]

★Let's Look at Our Testing Program. Professional Series Bulletin No. 40. East Lansing, Mich.: Bureau of Educational Research Services, College of Education, Michigan State University, 1959. Pp. 11. Paper. $0.15. *

[B18]

★Mental Alertness Tests: Five Full Length Practice Tests for Civil Service Examinations Which Include Mental or General Tests, [New Edition]. Milwaukee, Wis.: Pergande Publishing Co., 1959. Pp. 139. Paper, $3.50; cloth, $4.50. *

[B19]

★Multiple-Choice Items for a Test of Teacher Competence in Educational Measurement. Collected and arranged by a committee of the National Council on Measurement in Education, Robert L. Ebel, Chairman. [East Lansing, Mich.: the Council, c/o Irvin J. Lehman, Secretary, Office of Evaluation Services, Michigan State University], May 1962. Pp. 35. Paper, lithotyped. $2.50. *

[B20]

★Multiple-Choice Questions: A Close Look. Princeton, N.J.: Educational Testing Service, 1963. Pp. 43. Gratis. *

[B21]

★Normative Information: Manager and Executive Testing. New York: Richardson, Bellows, Henry & Co., Inc., May 1963. Pp. 45. Paper, lithotyped. Gratis. *

[B22]

★Reviews of College Board Tests From The Fifth Mental Measurements Yearbook. Introduction by John A. Valentine. Comments on the reviews by William E. Coffman. New York: College Entrance Examination Board, 1959. Pp. 40. Paper. Gratis. *

[B23]

★A Scale for Evaluation of High School Student Essays. Prepared for the California State Articulation Conference under the direction of the Joint Subcommittee on Composition by Pat Nail, Rodney Fitch, John Halverson, Phil Grant, and N. Field Winn, Chairman. Sponsored by the California Association of Teachers of English. Champaign, Ill.: National Council of Teachers of English, 1960. Pp. 32. Paper. $0.50. *

[B24]

★**The Scottish Scholastic Survey, 1953.** Publications of the Scottish Council for Research in Education, [No.] 48. London: University of London Press Ltd., 1963. Pp. 218. 25*s.* *

Brit J Ed Psychol 34:99–100 F '64. R. R. Dale. This volume is worthy of the best traditions of the Scottish Council for Research in Education. It completes the Scottish Scholastic Survey which began in 1953, and provides national norms (1953) in Mechanical Arithmetic, Arithmetical Reasoning, English Usage and English Comprehension, for children aged 9 years 11 months to 10 years 10 months. The comparison between the sexes is of interest. * By no means the least valuable part of the survey is the item by item analysis of the test results and the consequent practical suggestions to the teaching profession about the specific topics or methods in Arithmetic and English which require more time and care or outright change of teaching method.

[B25]

★**Supplementary Test Suggestions.** Prepared by a Joint Subcommittee of the Tests and Measurements Committee and the Public Schools Advisory Committee with the assistance of the Educational Records Bureau Staff. Educational Records Bulletin, No. 81. New York: the Bureau, March 1962. Pp. iv, 36. Paper, lithotyped. $1.00. *

[B26]

★**Testing and the Freshman Year: A Handbook for Harvard Advisers.** Cambridge, Mass.: Office of Tests, Harvard College, September 1964. Pp. iv, 26. Paper, lithotyped. Gratis. * (A revision of *Interpretation of Placement Test Scores: A Handbook for Harvard Advisers* published in 1958.)

[B27]

★**Testing and the Schools.** *Theory Into Practice,* Vol. 2, No. 4. Columbus, Ohio: Bureau of Educational Research and Service, College of Education, Ohio State University, October 1963. Pp. 177–248. Paper. $1.00. *

[B28]

★**Testing Guide for Teachers.** Prepared by the Technical Subcommittee of the Independent Schools Advisory Committee, Raven O. Dodge, Chairman. New York: Educational Records Bureau, 1961. Pp. vii, 43. Paper. $1.00. *

[B29]

★**Testing, Testing, Testing.** Prepared by the Joint Committee on Testing established by the American Association of School Administrators, Council of Chief State School Officers, and National Association of Secondary-School Principals. Washington, D.C.: National Education Association, 1962. Pp. 32. Paper. $1.00. *

[B30]

★**The University of Kansas Conference on External Testing Programs.** University of Kansas Publications, School of Education, Kansas Studies in Education, Vol. 14, No. 2. Lawrence, Kan.: the School, January 1964. Pp. 24. Paper. $0.50. *

[B31]

★Adams, Georgia Sachs; in consultation with Theodore L. Torgerson. **Measurement and Evaluation in Education, Psychology, and Guidance.** New York: Holt, Rinehart & Winston, Inc., 1964. Pp. xiii, 654. $7.50. *

[B32]

★Ahmann, J. Stanley. **Testing Student Achievements and Aptitudes.** New York: Center for Applied Research in Education, Inc., 1962. Pp. viii, 118. $3.95. * (London: Prentice-Hall International, Inc., 1964. 32*s.*)

[B33]

Ahmann, J. Stanley, and Glock, Marvin D. **Evaluating Pupil Growth.** Boston, Mass.: Allyn & Bacon, Inc., 1958. Pp. xiii, 605. * For the second edition, see B34.

Ed & Psychol Meas 19:681–3 w '59. Sam Duker. * a valuable and worthwhile book * Part Two is particularly well-done and deals with the characteristics of a good evaluation instrument. The two chapters on validity and reliability are far superior to the treatment given these topics in similar books. * The fourth part....impresses the reviewer as lacking unity and being a catch-all for topics not previously considered. It deals only very peripherally with "improving learning." Each chapter is followed by an excellently-written summary * Appendices include....selected lists of various types of tests. The value of the latter lists seems doubtful. Such lists become dated almost immediately and it would seem to me that the frequent emphasis in the text on the importance of becoming acquainted with, and making use of the *Mental Measurement Yearbooks* would offer a much more desirable means of locating appropriate tests. * The authors state that, "This book was written for a one-term college course, whether at the undergraduate or graduate level...." * It is hard to see how the subject matter dealt with by Ahmann and Glock in this book can be considered as appropriate for the graduate level. * The second issue raised by this book is one that should also be faced frankly by educators and particularly by teachers of tests and measurements. Is a basic knowledge of elementary statistics and an understanding of the fundamental principles involved necessary to the study of evaluation procedures? The reviewer thinks so. The authors, apparently, do not. * To study evaluative procedures without a good working mastery of elementary statistics seems to be a futile expenditure of time which will not have any lasting beneficial results either for the student himself or for those who will be subjected by him to "evaluation" in the years to come. These two issues are not, of course, ones that it was the obligation of the authors of the book being reviewed, to solve. Their very excellent book which will, no doubt, win wide acceptance by teachers of courses in educational evaluation must, nevertheless in a larger sense, be judged on the basis that these major issues in teacher education are not faced up to by its authors.

Personnel & Guid J 38:158 O '59. John W. M. Rothney. * Two outstanding features....are the well-selected and well-annotated list of suggested readings at the end of each chapter and the excellent digesting of main ideas in the chapter summaries. * The authors tread a well-beaten path and they do it in very thorough fashion. If a student can master the usual discussions of validity, reliability, and norms he will be well prepared to examine test manuals. It is unfortunate, however, that the authors did not apply the standards they had set up in earlier chapters to their discussion of particular tests. They follow a common pattern of those who review and write about tests, inventories, and rating scales when they indicate limitations so serious that the instruments could not be used meaningfully but end up by endorsing them explicitly or by implication. The student is not made aware of the great gap that exists between theory and application in the testing movement. * students who are beginners in the field may find the going difficult. The thorough, scholarly, and lengthy treatment is not likely to be mastered by undergraduates in one semester. This book is a fine contribution to educational literature. If balanced with a heavy dose of the cynicism that critical examination of evaluation instruments should produce, the reader will be well prepared to approach the difficult processes of evaluating pupil growth.

[B34]

*Ahmann, J. Stanley, and Glock, Marvin D. **Evaluating Pupil Growth, Second Edition.** Boston, Mass.: Allyn & Bacon, Inc., 1963. Pp. xi, 640. Text price, $7.95; trade price, $10.60. * For reviews of the first edition, see B33.

[B35]

★Ahmann, J. Stanley; Glock, Marvin D.; and Wardeberg, Helen L. **Evaluating Elementary School Pupils.** Boston, Mass.: Allyn & Bacon, Inc., 1960. Pp. xviii, 435. Text price, $6.50; trade price, $8.65. * (*PA* 35:2688)

Personnel & Guid J 40:576–8 F '62. Blanche B. Paulson. * a thoughtful, carefully constructed book which, evaluated against its foreordained scope as set forth in the preface, deserves a high score * proceeds from a discussion of role and procedures of evaluation to a chapter on educational objectives and evaluation—one of the best chapters in the book. From there the outline turns to testing, *per se,* beginning with a chapter on validity and reliability and another, disappointing one, on scoring, disappointing because of its divorcement. Sections follow on evaluating knowledge and understanding, only to have interposed between them and a succession of chapters on content areas, chapters on achievement and aptitude testing. The logic of organization is not immediately apparent, but the coverage is complete. There are omissions and inclusions that are notable. The new Metropolitan Battery is listed in Appendix C, but stanines, offered by the Metropolitan and introduced some 15 to 20 years ago, are not included along with percentile ranks and grade equivalents in a chapter obviously designed as explanatory. One does not know how the authors decided upon the lists of tests given in the appendices. In the text considerable space is given to certain tests, apparently arbitrarily, since no superiority is accorded them. Readers, therefore, should not use this book to bolster choices among commercial tests but should regard the book as an attempt to provide a ground position on evaluation with specific tests as illustrative only and with much help to the classroom teacher faced with evaluation.

[B36]

Ahmavaara, Yrjö. **On the Unified Factor Theory of Mind.** Annals of the Academia Scientiarum Fennica, Series B, Vol. 106. Helsinki, Finland: Suomalainen Tiedeakatemia, Academia Scientiarum Fennica, 1957. Pp. 176. Paper. 7.50 mk. * (*PA* 33:1)

Cont Psychol 3:184–5 Jl '58. Charles Wrigley. The effort expended upon factor analysis will be worth while only if factors prove reasonably invariant, i.e., identifiable in other test batteries and other samples of persons; but as results have accumulated, factors have proliferated, so that it has now become hard to decide whether factors reported by different investigators are the same. This problem of the comparability of the different reported factors is the one to which Ahmavaara, a Finnish psychologist, has addressed himself. * Has factor analysis achieved unified results? The answer in terms of Ahmavaara's results is *No*. Indices of matching are reported for 26 pairs of factorial studies with sufficient tests in common to warrant applying his method. Many matchings are not at all good. * Most reported factors are obviously not easily replicated. * Ahmavaara has done a great service by publishing these results. They provide an urgent warning of the need to adopt methods which insure replicable factors. Perhaps the most valuable section....is the discussion of reasons for "noninvariance." Ahmavaara attributes it partly to factor fission (decomposition of factors into subfactors) and partly to indeterminancy of rotation. These pages should be required reading for every factorist. I do not think that Ahmavaara has taken sufficiently to heart the implication of his results. They demonstrate the instability of placement of reference axes, and yet he proceeds to use the indices to prepare a list of postulated invariant factors. One extreme example must suffice. Perceptual speed, included in his "first certainty class," has a mean index of .43 (derived from seven comparisons). How can any confidence be placed in a factor as variant as this? The search for invariant factors will be hazardous until factor analysis becomes a completely objective (i.e., nonjudgmental) technique. One would like to have seen Ahmavaara reanalyze the correlations in each case with uniform procedure for initial factoring, estimating communalities, and deciding upon the number of factors, and with use of an analytic rotational technique, before employing his transformation method. But reanalyses on this scale are probably more readily carried through in this country, at some center equipped with a high-speed computer, than in Helsinki. In some forty pages of Part I Ahmavaara reviews factorial logic and mathematics. This section is not easily appraised. On the one hand, the link with the topic of factor comparability to follow is tenuous, and the treatment is too brief and episodic to serve as a systematic introduction to the problems. On the other, the account is nevertheless a stimulating and provocative one, which by stressing the abstractive nature of factorial theories may persuade factorists to re-examine their logical presuppositions. To the ears of the American behaviorist, it may at first sound strange to hear the mind again assuming a central role, but factorists have always shown a particular partiality for mind; witness Thurstone's, Truman Kelley's, and Cyril Burt's use of the word in their titles. Let me summarize my impressions. The psychologist in search of a unified account of factorial results will be disturbed by Ahmavaara's results, but the trouble here is the fault of contemporary factor analysis, not of Ahmavarra himself, who is heroically trying to restore order in a jungle. Ahmavaara's analysis is one of several noteworthy factor-analytic contributions recently emanating from Scandinavia. One hopes there will be more.

Psychometrika 25:105–8 Mr '60. Rolf Bargmann. * the most careful and comprehensive accounts of the philosophical basis of factor analysis remain those contained in the books by L. L. Thurstone and Sir Godfrey Thomson. Ahmavaara, following the terminology of Cohen and Nagel, places factor analysis in the domain of abstractive theories which encompass, among others, the theories of relativity, evolution, and quantum theory, in contradistinction to mechanistic theories which include field theories, the theory of atomic structure of matter, and current theories of learning. * The first two pages....are directed strongly against statistics and statisticians. He claims on page 12 that "the validity of the whole factor theory has been questioned by statisticians"; the reviewer, who is a statistician, must take exception to that statement. * the statisticians have been rather cooperative and enthusiastic about factor analysis * The problem of comparing two factor studies by statistical techniques is essentially solved. * Testing equality of two factor matrices may be somewhat more difficult, but is still amenable to treatment by a minor extension of Lawley's approach. The maximum determinant solution which L. L. Thurstone suggested in 1953 on intuitive grounds....leads to results identical with the maximum likelihood solution, and is particularly easy to handle for the comparison of two factorial studies. Statisticians do have methods of solution, and also available is the computational equipment to find them in a relatively short time. Many statisticians appreciate the ideas of factor analysis and like to help. * This reviewer enjoyed reading the monograph, and while he is doubtful about the value of the author's transformation analysis, he is impressed by the clarity of the logical presentations of factor analysis as an abstractive theory. He preferred to view factor analysis as a method to identify principles of classification, and stands corrected by the author who would certainly regard even this unpretentious interpretation as mechanistic. While the reviewer would dissuade against use of the author's mathematical techniques, he would strongly recommend the monograph to philosophers, psychologists, and social scientists. He would also encourage the author to excerpt the monograph, leave out all mathematical formulation, and present such an article to a more general group of readers including, by all means, statisticians. [See original review for additional critical comments not excerpted.]

[B37]

AHMAVAARA, YRJÖ, AND MARKKANEN, TOUKO. **The Unified Factor Model: Its Position in Psychometric Theory and Application to Sociological Study.** Finnish Foundation for Alcohol Studies, Alcohol Research in the Northern Countries, Vol. 7. Stockholm, Sweden: Almqvist & Wiksell, 1958. Pp. 188. Paper. Sw. kr. 18. *

Cont Psychol 4:290–2 S '59. Jum C. Nunnally. * The best way to read the monograph is to start with Chapter 4 in Part I. The first three chapters, comprising nearly half of the entire monograph, are interestingly unrelated to the main issue presented in the succeeding pages. The first three chapters give a running description of a little bit of everything in psychometrics, including Guttman scaling, Rashevsky's mathematical models, Thurstone's "box problem," and so on. The account is sketchy, will provide little that is new to people in psychometrics, and will only confuse readers who are new to the problems. In addition, the first part of the monograph is written in a quaint English that is sometimes difficult to read. (In contrast, the second part of the monograph is written in crisp English.) The proposed method for studying the invariance of factors is spelled out in Chapter 4. The scene is set when the same battery of tests has been administered to two different samples of subjects and the results of each have been factor-analyzed separately. (The factors can be either rotated or unrotated, either oblique or orthogonal.) To study the invariance of factors in the two samples, a transformation matrix is sought such that the factor loadings (or "specification-equation" weights) from one study are made the same as those from the other study. The authors claim that if such a transformation matrix exists, it demonstrates the invariance of factors from one analysis to another. Further, they recommend that such transformation matrices be applied in practice to clarify factor rotations and interpretations. Because the whole monograph centers around the "transformation analysis," a number of points about the method should be considered. First, the method is not new: British and American psychologists have worked on similar methods for over ten years and have sought remedies for some loopholes not even mentioned in the monograph. * second ....even though one can write the equation to find a transformation, no exact transformation is likely to be found. Consequently, the factorist is thrown back on seeking an approximate transformation—a "least-squares" solution is the one most often recommended. Ahmavaara and Markkanen do not make the problem of statistical approximation explicit and leave unclear what they would do or recommend. Third, in order to use the method in practice, it would be necessary to find a *good* approximation by the transformation method. The results which the authors obtain are rather disappointing. (See the numerous large discrepancies in Table 6, p. 122.) A previous study by Ahmavaara of a broad range of factors of human ability produced equally disappointing results * Either the method is improper or the factors are less than invariant. Fourth, although the transformation method has some common-sense backing, it is not, as presently conceived, a complete solution to the matching of factors. It fails on a crucial counter example: there is nothing to prevent seeking a transformation of some of the factors in an analysis to other factors in the *same* analysis. It is not hard to compose examples of this kind in which the matching is, by current standard, reasonably good. This raises some serious questions about the method. In spite of the importance of what the authors are working so hard to accomplish and the notable contributions which they have made in previous publications, the present monograph does them little justice. Much of it is irrelevant to the main issue; the central problem of "transformation analysis" for the matching of factors is not presented adequately, and the empirical demonstration of the method is disappointing.

Psychometrika 25:109–13 Mr '60. Rolf Bargmann. This monograph consists of two parts. The first, by Ahmavaara, is entitled "A Treatise on Psychometric Models," and the second, authored by Markkanen, "On the Sociological Theory of Alcohol in Terms of the Unified Factor Analysis Model." The title of the first part is misleading. It is not at all a treatise of psychometric models * Instead, and much to the annoyance of the reader, it represents an exceedingly poor presentation of some selected techniques of scaling with severe criticisms attached, which verge on the polemic (pages 40 to 47 on Guttman's principal components), and a eulogy on the first author's own methods. The reviewer, who enjoyed the author's earlier *On the Unified Factor Theory of Mind* because of its interesting and compelling logical development, and in spite of its grotesque mathematics (transformation analysis), was not at all impressed by the present volume. * Ahmavaara's description of Guttman's principal components is no description at all. It is a highly loaded criticism, sometimes advanced with polemic technicalities. * It is indicative of the author's prejudice that he describes Thurstone's box problem without mentioning the fact that all measurements were normalized before correlations were computed. Failure to do so leads to serious distortions of the nonlinear combinations. The author's description of Guttman's simplex, radex, and circumplex is critical as indicated by the heading. Since Ahmavaara's treatise contains not a single constructive idea in this respect, his criticism lacks authority; however, the point which Ahmavaara raises regarding the indeterminancy of simplex or circumplex structures, when several of these are present, has received and may deserve further study. * The mathematics used by Ahmavaara in his transformation analysis is beyond the comprehension of this reviewer. How, from the fact implied by equation (43) (p. 82) that $A'_1A_1L = A'_1F_2$, he concludes any similarity between the matrices A_1L and F_2 (both are rectangular) is incomprehensible. * We read in the summary of Part I that this treatise has been a "systematic presentation of the theoretical thinking of the 'Finnish school.'" This reviewer suggests that the author gather some more experience with existing methods and literature before aspiring to the establishment of a new school. In Part II, T. Markkanen presents the results of a very extensive analysis of data....on alcohol sales experiments in rural Finland. * The first factor analysis was made for the general group which (see p. 108) represents all the interviewed persons ($N = 293$). The primary factor matrix after rotation is recorded and represents, according to the author, a satisfactory simple structure. The reviewer does not quite agree, with 25 variables and 9 factors, a total of 13 zero loadings ($\pm .10$) can be obtained in a hyperplane by a pure 50-50 chance, in the absence of any concentration. Only one of the factors (5) shows significant over-determination. This does not mean that the factors are spurious; as a matter of fact they show a fairly convincing high-low tendency. It only means that the authors may consider using some more effective rotation method to clean up and clearly define their structure. The method they used (Ahmavaara's cosine method) seems to be wanting in this respect. * There follows the transformation analysis of the two groups, and the agreement between the two patterns (graph on page 116) looks quite extraordinary. Equally extraordinary, however, is the agreement between the two correlation matrices (pp. 178 and 180). Most extraordinary, alas, is the composition of the two groups, for one of them ($N = 254$) represents the users of alcohol, whereas the other represents the general group ($N = 293$). Thus, the two groups which are compared in the "consistent and unique" transformation analysis, *have all 25 responses of 254 subjects in common* and differ only in that the general group has 39 subjects added to it. A beginning student in some scientific discipline may be forgiven for making this kind of error of comparison. It is less easy to be tolerant of the promoters of new, systematic, scientific theories. * In conclusion it must be said that this monograph places the users and defenders of factor analysis in an embarrassing position. Theirs is a mathematical model, well related to the real world, soundly formulated and, for the last 25 years, extensively studied. The results of many demonstration studies, starting with Thurstone's box problem, constitute strong evidence in favor of the method. * But how can anyone convince skeptics of the usefulness of factor analysis if authors, like the present ones, make a travesty of it? [See original review for additional critical comments not excerpted.]

[B38]

AINSWORTH, MARY D., AND AINSWORTH, LEONARD H. **Measuring Security in Personal Adjustment.** Toronto, Canada: University of Toronto Press, 1958. Pp. xiii, 98. $2.95. (London: Oxford University Press. 24*s*.) * (*PA* 32:5224)

Brit J Ed Psychol 29:176–7 Je '59. H. Phillipson. * describes....an attempt....to devise a series of tests that will measure the extent of a person's security or insecurity in five major areas of adjustment: intimate family relations, interpersonal relations outside the primary family, vocation and the preparation for it, leisure activities and philosophy of life. * This is a valuable piece of work, reported with considerable care and unusual clarity. It has particular value in that it presents, in a most difficult area of test construction, a model in which personality theory and statistical analysis have been brought into a working relationship. The result is a test that has a theoretical basis and a rationale which are widely acceptable, and which lend themselves to extension and refinement as the test is further developed.

Brit J Psychol 50:285 Ag '59. R. W. Pickford. * The book is a very interesting study in the steps, stages and processes of test construction and validation, and the tests themselves should be useful to practical psychologists.

[B39]

★ALBRIGHT, LEWIS E.; GLENNON, J. R.; AND SMITH, WALLACE J. **The Use of Psychological Tests in Industry.** Cleveland, Ohio: Howard Allen, Inc., Publishers, 1963. Pp. 196. $4.25. (Copenhagen, Denmark: Munksgaard Ltd. D.kr. 30; 31*s*. 6*d*.) * (*PA* 38:6700)

Cont Psychol 9:297–8 Jl '64. Wayne K. Kirchner. * Very little space is devoted (4 pages of 196, in fact) to the use of tests for such purposes as placement, promotion, upgrading, and vocational counseling. This is not a criticism, but rather an indication to the prospective buyer that this book will help him more if he is primarily concerned with selection problems. * The editors of this volume have "modestly" stated in the preface that the book should become the standard reference for personnel departments in industry and all employee institutions. To some degree they are correct. This book ought to be useful as a reference for people in personnel offices. The authors do a competent and professional job of covering the topics mentioned above. While it is difficult to empathize with this book's audience, the reviewer feels that people who know nothing of testing ought to be able to use this volume to their advantage. * some of the chapters and material covered are too difficult for the average personnel man. This may not necessarily be a particular criticism of the book as much as it is a criticism of the kind of person often found in personnel offices. In any case, although very compact, in many cases it also seems rather complex and overly academic in treatment. The statistical chapter, for example, should pose difficulties for a novice. Certainly, this book does provide a number of worthwhile tables, including one for prediction of the values of a multiple correlation coefficient from various pairs of predictor validities and from various inter-correlations among the two predictors. One suggestion to the authors, however, seems in order. In a book which is intended as a small handbook or reference source, it seems extremely desirable to have a glossary of terms. Over-all, the reviewer regards this book with much more pleasure than pain. The authors should be commended for cramming so much information into such a short volume. As indicated above, however, this cramming also creates its own problems. The reviewer does recommend this book to the literate and intelligent personnel man, however. It is not a book to be scanned, however; it has to be read.

[B40]

★ALCOCK, THEODORA. **The Rorschach in Practice.** London: Tavistock Publications, 1963. Pp. xii, 252. 63*s*. * (Philadelphia, Pa.: J. B. Lippincott Co., 1964. $12.50.)

Percept & Motor Skills 18:989 Je '64. C. H. Ammons. Alcock's is just another of those "how-to-do-it" books for the clinician. The method of scoring the Rorschach differs from those commonly used in the USA. Reliability and validity are not considered directly at all but illustrative examples are presented in considerable detail in the form of selected individual case studies and a comparison of Rorschachs obtained from 25 asthmatic and 25 normal children. The author provides some interesting reading but contributes little to scientific progress in understanding personality.

Rorsch Newsl 8:34–5 D 63. Jessie Francis-Williams. This is the first major publication on Rorschach practice in Britain and it is fitting that it should have been written by Miss

Alcock, the leading teacher of the use of Rorschach in this country. It is to her that we mainly owe the creation of a distinctively British tradition. * To the many who have benefited from her teaching, this book is especially welcome. * The author shows clearly how her work has led on from that of Bruno Klopfer and his associates and assimilated into the Rorschach tradition more recent findings from experimental psychological studies of perception as well as developments in psychoanalytic theory. * The final chapters of Part I discuss differential diagnosis of various pathological states. * Alcock has brought her own vast experience to bear on the use of Rorschach. Although in scoring she adheres fairly closely to Klopfer's method the few modifications or additions she herself has introduced are always shown to arise from her own experience and are thoughtfully and intelligently explained. Her own introduction of the Concept of "Sinister" responses brings a most useful addition to the Special Scoring categories. One of the most valuable and most brilliant chapters in the book is Miss Alcock's account of "Analysis and Assessment of Data." Here we see the rigorous discipline which she imposes on herself in analysing the data taken from a record. And it provides a solid base from which she moves to discussion of differential diagnosis in the later Chapters of Part I. It is unfortunate that in the reproduction of the blots in Chapter 2, there are such big discrepancies in colour and tone from the originals. * The author uses well-chosen cases to clarify her theoretical approach to the test. And it is through these that we can gain an illuminating insight into the principles governing her method. Her Chapter on "Conflict and Defence within the Healthy Personality" underlines Miss Alcock's basic teaching that an accurate assessment must match carefully control and conflict and that it is the *manner* of coping with inner stress that demonstrates personality health or sickness. After her presentation of a case study of a healthy personality, she presents further cases which demonstrate Rorschach indications of varying kinds and degrees of mental and emotional disturbance. In these presentations Miss Alcock's wisdom and insights are frequently demonstrated particularly in the adult cases where her touch is always sure. * This book represents a most important landmark for the British Rorschach Forum. For workers with the Rorschach it provides a handbook which gains in value the more it is studied and which they will wish to keep by them for constant reference.

[B41]

★ALLEN, CLIFFORD. **Passing Examinations: A Psychological Study of Learning, Remembering and Examination Techniques, and the Causes of Failure, for the Assistance of Students.** London: Macmillan & Co. Ltd., 1963. Pp. xiii, 146. 12*s.* 6*d.* (New York: St Martin's Press, Inc. $2.50.) *

[B42]

*ALLEN, ROBERT M. **Guide to Psychological Tests and Measurements, Third Edition.** Chapter on statistics by Raymond E. Hartley. Coral Gables, Fla.: University of Miami Bookstore, 1960. Pp. i, 68. Paper, plastic binding. $2.00. * For a review of the first edition, see 5:B33.

[B43]

ALLEN, ROBERT M. **Personality Assessment Procedures: Psychometric, Projective, and Other Approaches.** New York: Harper & Row, Publishers, Inc., 1958. Pp. xi, 541. Out of print. * (*PA* 32:4160)

Child Develop Abstracts 33:58 F–Ap '59. R. Wirt. * an excellent summary and critical review of all of the major methods and techniques for assessing personality. The author writes clearly and objectively at a level understandable and interesting to college undergraduates. It is a remarkable book in that the author has succeeded in fairly reviewing and evaluating scores of instruments and many of the studies undertaken to evaluate them in less than 500 pages. Furthermore, he includes short, well-written sections on the application of these testing procedures and the professional ethics governing their use. * The inclusion of life situation and group dynamics approaches as well as the polygraph and other physiological methods makes this work broader in scope than the usual survey of testing methods. The book contains a fine introduction to test theory and a valuable, exhaustive bibliography of over 600 titles, mostly recent. This carefully done volume should get wide acceptance as an undergraduate textbook.

Cont Psychol 4:148–9 My '59. Betty L. Kalis. * Included are tests to which, admittedly, no reference has appeared in the literature for at least twenty-five years. On the other hand, promising new methods such as Gough's California Psychological Inventory and Phillipson's Object Relations Technique—to name but two—are omitted entirely. The whole area of perceptual tasks in the assessment of personality is dismissed with a footnote, while space is given to graphology, the electroencephalogram, endocrinopathy, and other esoteric sidelines that are of limited interest to psychologists in general. * several chapters contain reports of tests listed in alphabetical order, with no transitional or organizing material and little reference to the relative usefulness of the various techniques. One feature of the organization that is certain to be confusing and frustrating to students is the fact that many of the chapter sections labeled "summary" contain not a resumé of the preceding material but new information. These comments, and some of the cogent footnotes, are frequently the most rewarding portions of the book, but the author is unduly reticent about his own contributions. * In the final chapters, Professor Allen belatedly discusses some of the uses of assessment procedures. Had the entire text been written from this standpoint, in answer to the question "Assessment for what?", then the organization could have been natural, rather than arbitrary, and the comments about test characteristics and validity would have fallen into a meaningful framework of personality theory and clinical applicability. * Allen's book, considered as a text and basis for lecture material, is not written in a fashion that will provoke interest and critical thinking in this important area.

[B44]

★Allen, Robert M., and Jefferson, Thomas W. **Psychological Evaluation of the Cerebral Palsied Person: Intellectual, Personality, and Vocational Applications.** Springfield, Ill.: Charles C Thomas, Publisher, 1962. Pp. xiii, 86. $5.00. * (*PA* 37:5391)

Am J Mental Def 68:291–2 S '63. L. Leon Reid. * This book is a significant compendium of significant facts important to the psychologist in the psychological assessment of the cerebral palsied individual. The most significant tests of importance with the cerebral palsied individual have been briefly outlined and discussed with suggestions concerning administration and scoring. The strong and weak factors relating to the various tests as used with the cerebral palsied are emphasized. The experiences of two able psychologists are briefly reviewed. A tremendous amount of invaluable information is immediately available to the professional concerned.

Brit J Psychol 54:98 F '63. J. A. L. Naughton. * The authors' personal experience of formal procedures with cerebral palsied appears to be chiefly in the use of the Rorschach. They deprecate the invention of cerebral palsy personality stereotypes, or their allocation to different types of neurological disability. The final chapter on Vocational Assessment Issues is excellent. It demonstrated the authors' firm comprehension and humane grasp of what is often the most difficult problem the "Spastic" has to face, and offers wise advice. * The book is well produced but seems rather dear for the 60 pages of letterpress which remain if the reproductions of forms, etc., are deducted.

Cont Psychol 8:397–8 O '63. Salvatore G. DiMichael. * There is much useful know-how brought together, heavy on the "how-to" and light on "what-it-means." The book will be most helpful to trained psychologists with little or no experience with....cerebral palsied persons. It assumes broad knowledge of psychological and vocational tests, and especially evaluation. Most of the manual is devoted to intelligence tests, 50 pages consecutively and 4 more under another chapter heading. This is the best part of the book. * The manual strives to be pithy and to the point. We can be sympathetic with the aim. It would have been more helpful, however, if the coverage on personality and vocational assessment, and especially the evaluation of test results had been substantially increased. The book makes it abundantly clear that skillful assessment of the cerebral palsied is difficult. *

[B45]

★American Academy of Pediatrics Committee on the Handicapped Child. **The Application of Psychological and Psychometric Testing Data to Pediatric Practice.** Evanston, Ill.: the Academy, 1962. Pp. 21. Paper. $0.25. * (*PA* 37:6670)

[B46]

★American Association for Health, Physical Education, and Recreation, Youth Fitness Project, Paul A. Hunsicker, Director. **AAHPER Youth Fitness Test Manual.** Washington, D.C.: the Association, 1958. Pp. v, 55. Paper. * For the latest edition, see B47; see also 715.

[B47]

★American Association for Health, Physical Education, and Recreation, Youth Fitness Project, Paul A. Hunsicker, Director. **AAHPER Youth Fitness Test Manual, Revised Edition.** Washington, D.C.: the Association, 1961. Pp. iv, 60. Paper. $0.75. * See also 715.

[B48]

★American Council on Education, Committee on Measurement and Evaluation, Paul R. Anderson, Chairman. **College Testing: A Guide to Practices and Programs.** Washington, D.C.: the Council, 1959. Pp. x, 190. $3.00. *

AAUP B 45:427–9 S '59. Joseph C. Heston. * Because of drastic contraction of significant materials, a major objective of the book has not been significantly achieved. Used by itself alone, the book will not serve as an adequate "how-to-do-it" manual for our colleagues who may feel themselves disconcertingly naive about testing practices. This first half performs an admirable service in enumerating the functions that tests can serve in educational institutions. Issues which demand consideration, knotty problems, and potential pitfalls are all carefully identified. The intelligent reader, inexperienced in testing procedures, will soon realize the volume raises a multitude of pertinent questions, for many of which he will recognize his lack of preparation. This is excellent —and for this reason alone the publication is completely justified. * in numerous instances it suggests many more questions than it answers. Study of the book will thus force one to seek more assistance, either through wider technical reading and/or consultation with testing specialists. * For the neophyte in measurement, Part II should prove a gold mine of ideas and suggestions. This second half offers well-written résumés of college testing programs at seven different institutions. * Interesting procedures, problems, and philosophies abound in all seven program summaries. No reader, sophisticate or novitiate, will study these sections without encountering at least something new, interesting, or challenging. Many testing program directors will seize upon these pages as a convenient device to help persuade higher-echelon administrators of the need for improvement or experimentation in their own school programs. In summary, *College Testing* is well written, full of useful suggestions. Because of space limitations, it does not answer all the questions it poses. Therefore, for its intended audience—the untrained among current college testers—it cannot serve as a full operations manual. Its prime contribution lies in the provocative way in which it will make them cognizant of more of the procedures and principles they *should* know.

J Higher Ed 31:293–4 My '60. Wilbur L. Layton. * The seven chapters of Part I are written with a simplicity which reflects the high level of sophistication of the authors. The chapter on "The Use of Tests in Instruction" is especially good. The section on growth is also very well done. In the discussion of the use of tests as growth measures, the treatment of the concept of regression toward the mean is an outstanding example of the ability of the authors to write about difficult statistical concepts in language which the layman can understand. The section on the use of tests to evaluate teaching materials and procedures would have benefited from some detailed examples illustrating how instructors were helped in evaluating their practices. The role of tests in stimulating and guiding learning is excellently handled. The sections on the development of local examinations and on the statistical analysis of student responses contain an informative discussion of the analysis of tests, including item analysis and the concepts of the difficulty and discriminating power of an item. Chapter V, "The Use of Tests in Educational Counseling," is also an excellent one. Particularly good is the use of the example of college X. The analysis of the causes of student difficulties there serves to make specific some of the ideas discussed in the chapter. * The interpretation of tests and other data in educational counseling is a little weak, too much space being devoted to the use of norms at the expense of a presentation of the integration of test data in the counseling process. * The discussion which deals with the reporting of test scores to students and faculty is inadequately handled. It underestimates the difficulty students, parents, and faculty encounter in trying to grasp the meaning of test scores as they are usually reported. * The seven chapters [in Part II]....are very well written and provide good descriptions of testing programs. It would have been helpful had the authors of Part I of this book chosen examples from the colleges written about in Part II. * This book deserves to be widely read. It is the best lay discussion the reviewer has seen of the use of tests in higher education. Professional testers will find it particularly useful on college campuses in their work with faculty members. It is excellent reading material for members of governing boards, as well as for high administrative officials in colleges and universities. Deans and department heads should have copies of this book to acquaint them with the way in which testing can help meet educational objectives.

[B49]

★American Educational Research Association, Committee on Educational and Psychological

Testing, Eric F. Gardner, Chairman. **Educational and Psychological Testing.** *Review of Educational Research,* Vol. 32, No. 1. Washington, D.C.: the Association, February 1962. Pp. 114. Paper. $2.00. *

[B50]

★American Educational Research Association, Committee on Educational and Psychological Testing, William B. Michael, Chairman. **Educational and Psychological Testing.** *Review of Educational Research,* Vol. 29, No. 1. Washington, D.C.: the Association, February 1959. Pp. 131. Paper. Out of print. *

[B51]

★Ames, Louise Bates, and Ilg, Frances L. **Mosaic Patterns of American Children.** New York: Hoeber Medical Division, Harper & Row, Publishers, Inc., 1962. Pp. xii, 297. $9.50. (London: Harper & Row Ltd. 72s.) *

Am J Psychother 17:142–3 Ja '63. Frederic Wertham. This is an excellent book that deserves careful attention. It is of importance not only for those interested in the Mosaic test itself, but also for psychologists and psychiatrists and all those concerned with the scientific study and treatment of children. This is the first book about the Mosaic test dealing exclusively with children. As Margaret Lowenfeld says in the introduction, it is a massive collection of information. The subjects were boys and girls from two to sixteen years of age. The tests were repeated so that responses were available for every year. The emphasis in the interpertation is on developmental changes and on the individuality of the child. * The book is illustrated with 32 plates, each containing six mosaic pictures. These designs are beautifully reproduced in color and are highly instructive. Quite apart from their value as productions of the Mosaic test, they are very interesting as children's art work. Some of these children can convey a theme remarkably well with the very restricted means of geometrical mosaic pieces * The book contains a good discussion of the literature and a full bibliography. * A minor correction to be made is that the term "slab" is not identical with the term "simple agglutination" used in my investigations. The Mosaic test has been very much neglected in clinical practice and in research. In cases of lobotomy, for example, I have found in every instance that there was—regardless of symptomatic outcome—definite evidence of organic cortical defect. In other tests this evidently does not show up so clearly, and therefore a severe consequence of lobotomy has not been sufficiently recognized. The Mosaic test has also been mostly overlooked in such important fields as the study of the brain-injured child and childhood schizophrenia. This book....can be most highly recommended as a signal contribution to the practice and theory of psychodiagnostic testing.

Brit J Med Psychol 36(1):95–6 '63. H. R. Schaffer. * It is good to see that some of the criticisms levied against the Rorschach work, such as small numbers and the neglect of longitudinal material, have been taken into account in the present volume. The old Gesellian language of the 1930's is, however, still retained: the almost magical power with which chronological age is endowed, the picture of development as progressing from one equilibrium to another, and the usage of such quaint phrases as "successive reorganization of energies." But a more serious charge that must be brought against the book concerns the limited applicability of its findings. No one will dispute the authors' point that the developmental component must be isolated from a child's test protocol before indicators of individual personality can be located, but the identification of this component involves the study of more than one highly specific sample. As Margaret Lowenfeld herself points out in the Foreword, the test is very susceptible to cultural factors, so that many of the features found by her in the Mosaic patterns produced by English children apparently do not occur in those reported on the present sample of American children. The latter, moreover, are of superior status both intellectually (mean I.Q. 118) and socially (mainly from professional parents) and come from what is surely the most intensively studied and hence most psychologically sophisticated child population in the world, New Haven in Connecticut. In reading this otherwise very careful and commendable study it is therefore important to bear in mind (as the authors themselves do not always appear to have done) that extrapolation to other groups is not justified without further investigation.

Cont Psychol 8:342–4 S '63. Austin E. Grigg. * So faithful are the authors to their examination of shifts in Mosaic patterns with age, that, as they admit, "the very thing which the Mosaic Test was set up to reveal—unique personality patterns in the individual subject—is scarcely mentioned in the present volume...." (p. 242). But the book provides complete summaries of the literature on the technique so that the readers can learn some of the kinds of things that the Mosaic is alleged to tell about personality. This is not fully satisfying, since the authors are quite frank about the generally negative results in the literature in regard to the validity of the test as an assessment of personality variables. Since the technique has not won an extensive bibliography as yet, there is some foundation for the optimistic stance that this is still a poorly researched gadget and that it is too early to have another test burning. As a matter of fact, Ames and Ilg have presented here impressive evidence that should gain a stay of execution. * A major portion of the book is devoted to detailed descriptions of the Mosaics at each age level from two through 16 years. Sometimes this format is frustrating to the general reader who would like to ask, "What does it all mean?" It must, of course, mean something more than simply that the child's age has changed. The authors are keenly aware of this, but they regard the study as a "beginning" and they are content to tabulate shifts in choice of color, in choice of shapes of pieces, in types of designs. * Unfortunately, the sample of children studied was above average in intelligence and from the top two socioeconomic levels, mostly from Level I. The major impression is that now we may really understand exactly how Mosaic patterns alter as age changes. It would have added to the book if the authors had drawn from their rich and penetrating insights into child development and had discussed what the Mosaic changes most likely reflect insofar as personality and cognitive functions are concerned. Perhaps this will make a future publication. It certainly should be communicated.

[B52]

★AMES, LOUISE BATES; MÉTRAUX, RUTH W.; AND WALKER, RICHARD N. **Adolescent Rorschach Responses: Developmental Trends From Ten to Sixteen Years.** New York: Hoeber Medical Division, Harper & Row, Publishers, Inc., 1959. Pp. xiii, 313. $8.50. (London: Harper & Row Ltd. 64*s*.) * (*PA* 34:1329)

Am J Orthopsychiatry 31:198–201 Ja '61. Samuel J. Beck and Anne G. Beck. * As a study of the adolescent years, this book contains many valuable observations about this important age phase; and concerning the changes of trends from each year to the next. The comments are illuminating rays about the states of mind of the children in coping with the problems that life presents to them * this investigation has the merits that its authors in the main orient themselves around normative concepts—all as is to be expected in a setting in which mental measurement has so consistently guided itself by empiric data * these authors do not consistently follow the behavioral method. They, too, commit the error of scoring movement—that important discovery of Rorschach's, the mirror of the unconscious—where the association involves using a verb, with the attendant interpretation of the response as indicating unconscious fantasy. It is the fallacy of begging the question. In this as in some other techniques, they, too, are phenomenological, whether they are aware of it or not, and again phenomenology and behavioral method just do not mix. This book, as does so much writing in the Rorschach test, points up the failure by investigators to formulate operational descriptions of the several test variables, descriptions that would define Rorschach test scorings so as to make of them operations that are public and repeatable. As one example, with reference to the whole response (W) the authors note (p. 9) that "Beck's students score W far more critically than we do (their mean W per cent for ages ten to thirteen is 15%, ours is 48%)." The question becomes: When is a whole is not a whole is a whole (with apologies to a certain Miss Stein)? Intelligent persons, meaning psychologists, ought to be able to get together on such simple operational definitions. But then, psychologists are human beings. The reviewers' point is: Rorschach investigators working in the behavioral-statistical orientation are really very little apart. They could iron out their small differences and advance the test as the empiric experiment which was its author's ambition. And talking about that author, Rorschach, he is being neglected in the present as in other American Rorschach test writings, to the detriment of the investigations which they report. His name appears really only once in this book (for pp. 84, 85) in the index, but he is referred to on other pages, not indexed. Oberholzer, the man most responsible for establishing the test on sound clinical foundations, does not appear in the index. The authors' citation of the literature is also remiss in ignoring some earlier Swiss or German study in the test in adolescence (Löpfe, Schneider). Löpfe's findings in adolescence are in disagreement with those of the present writers in relation to the introversion-extratension rhythm within both boys and girls. Other writings, not mentioned in the chapter reviewing the literature, are also germane. The importance of the book as these reviewers see it is principally in the light it throws on the personality course in adolescence. The writers make some stabs at suggesting clinical significance of findings but the sophisticated clinical psychologist will react to these as having an unripe ring. As a manual for using the test we must have the reservations incident to the differences, some noted above, and there are others, in technical processing of the associations. Correcting for such differences, its norms provide very useful compass points of reference whereby to evaluate test data. It is, in fact, one more tribute to the instrument which Rorschach has invented that one can so validly get the right answers with it even though in some respects not for the right reason. In providing points of departure for interpretation, the book is then a very useful one for any psychologist using the test in the adolescent age ranges, especially in the provocative thinking which it sets going with respect to personality development.

Cont Psychol 5:200–1 Je '60. Irwin J. Knopf. * In general the major contribution of this book lies in its practical value to clinicians as a source of reference on the normative and developmental aspects of children's Rorschach responses. The reader is given sufficient information about the procedural details and the outline of the study to permit replication, comparisons, and a more precise understanding of the interpretative limits of the results. Data on Rorschach variables are adequately presented in tabular form reflecting changes from age to age, as well as the over-all direction of change for the 7-year period. The developmental findings as evidenced in these over-all trends gives the reader a valuable perspective from which to view and interpret the Rorschach performance of children in the clinical situation. Such findings as the trend toward a slow increase in the number of responses with age, a decrease in $W\%$, an increase in $D\%$, no change in $Dd\%$, a slight decrease in $F\%$ with essentially no change in $F+\%$, a slight upward trend for M, and an increase in the use of controlled color responses as manifested in the increase of FC will be valuable guideposts for inexperienced and experienced Rorschachers alike. Sex differences in the years 10 to 16 in Rorschach responses are found to be relatively consistent and striking. Nevertheless, some limitations of the study tend to restrict its practical value and the extent to which its findings are generalizable. The work is based on 700 Rorschach records; those of 50 girls and 50 boys at each successive age. Many children, however, contributed records at more than one age, and only 271 children contributed single records. This distribution, in effect, resulted in 33 to 50 per cent overlap of subjects between adjacent ages and, consequently, confounded cross-sectional and longitudinal data in the statistical analysis of the results. Moreover the sample of subjects was not representative. The subjects were of predominantly above-average intelligence, and mostly (over 75%) from upper middle-class home backgrounds. It is likely that the reader will not be convinced by the authors' attempt at illustrating the similarity between the cross-sectional and longitudinal findings because these conclusions rest heavily on data from one pair of fraternal twins tested at yearly intervals for the 7-year period. Finally, readers who expect to see these latest findings discussed in light of the available data and integrated into the existing Rorschach literature will be greatly disappointed. The authors make some attempt to review the literature in the second chapter of their book, but this good start must be regarded merely as a token; from this point on reference to the relevant work of others is noticeably absent.

[B53]

*ANASTASI, ANNE. **Psychological Testing, Second Edition.** New York: Macmillan Co., 1961. Pp. xiii, 657. $7.95. * (London: Collier-Macmillan, Ltd. 60*s*.) (*PA* 36:1HA57A)

Cont Psychol 7:270–1 Jl '62. Andrew L. Comrey. * a scholarly guide * The chapters describing specific tests should be useful to graduate students and professional workers who wish to consult a less detailed source than the *Buros Mental Measurements Yearbooks.* The chapters containing general information should be helpful to the beginning student as an introduction to the field and to more advanced students for review and reference. Valuable discussions of current technical issues appear in the general chapters as well as in certain of the chapters devoted to specific tests. Throughout, the book gives extensive references to original and secondary sources. * The book reflects painstaking care in preparation and an extensive knowledge of the subject matter. The author has approached the evaluation of each test in terms of the extent to which it has demonstrated validity of one kind or another. She adopts a fair attitude, even leaning over backwards at times to give a test the benefit of the doubt. In the face of overwhelming negative evidence regarding a test's value, or exaggerated claims by a test author, however, she does not hesitate to call a spade a spade. Rationalizations and specious reasoning are not accepted as adequate substitutes for demonstrated validity. The reviewer's principal criticisms about the book have to do with its function as a text. * a textbook at the undergraduate level should give the big picture with extended discussion of major principles. Test materials should be introduced and discussed as illustrations of these principles. In many chapters of this book, one finds a step by step progression through specific test instruments, with a description of each, sometimes with critical comments, and sometimes not. Although this is valuable for the advanced student or professional worker who does not want to miss a specific test in use, it is less interesting and appropriate for the undergraduate student. From this standpoint, the first seven chapters of general background, the chapters on the Stanford-Binet, Wechsler tests, interest tests, projective tests, and the first chapter on achievement tests seem best suited for the college student. The others seem more appropriate for advanced students and professional workers. The reviewer was occasionally bothered by the appearance in the early chapters of phrases similar to "as we have already pointed out," and "this will be discussed more fully in a later chapter." The organization could be improved in some places by bringing together the material pertaining to a given topic. The section on elementary statistics should be eliminated, thereby making room for more advanced methodological topics. The student should have some knowledge of statistics before studying this book. If he has not, the material included is probably insufficient. On the other hand, the college student is not likely to have had a course in factor analysis, for example. Since important parts of the book deal with test materials developed through factor analysis, more than a cursory description of this technique should be given. In summary, the merits of this book far outweigh its flaws. Selected portions will serve adequately as a textbook for capable undergraduates majoring in psychology. As a whole, the book will be a valuable addition to the library of more advanced students.

Ed & Psychol Meas 21:1048–50 w '61. Richard E. Schutz. * extremely well written throughout. Anastasi is a master at condensing and summarizing complex topics. She makes every word count. However, this meaty style may appeal more to specialists than to students, particularly beginning students. The book is not easy reading. * The principal characteristic which distinguishes this book from other sound measurement texts is the greater attention given to discussions of specific tests. By rough index count, Thorndike and Hagen make reference to 110 test titles, Cronbach to 140, and Anastasi to 266. The "climate" of Anastasi's book is thus somewhat encyclopedic when compared with other texts. This is a strength if one is seeking a compendium. It is a weakness if one is looking for exhaustive coverage of topics.

Personnel Psychol 15:119–20 sp '62. Frederick G. Brown. * Part 1, Principles of Psychological Testing....is one of the best summaries of the basic principles of testing currently available. In short, this part of the book is excellent. The remaining two-thirds of the book (Parts 2–4) is primarily a survey of various types of tests. Tests of general intelligence, aptitudes, achievement, personality, and interests are all covered. Here Anastasi attempts to deal with an impossible task—to develop skill in evaluating and interpreting various types of tests through the use of examples within each area. What happens is that she succeeds neither in presenting major principles without becoming encyclopedic nor does she approach the degree of comprehensiveness needed to fully understand a test, i.e., that found in test manuals and technical publications. Thus the reader does not get enough information to evaluate particular tests, but he gets so many details about specific tests that he is liable to get bogged down. * What use would Anastasi's book be to personnel men and management? The only possible answer is very little. Industrial testing and selection get shortchanged in comparison to educational and clinical testing. Criterion problems are virtually ignored. The most common personnel tests are only briefly discussed. There is only incidental discussion of the problems and techniques of devising a selection battery. * To summarize, the book will be of little use to management and personnel men in business and industry. Because of its clear writing and technical competence it is a very good book for classroom use, particularly when supplemented by stimulating lectures and laboratory experiences. A book, as a person, cannot be all things to all people. In this case it will be business and industrial personnel who will be disappointed.

For reviews of the first edition, see 5:B42.

[B54]

★ANASTASI, ANNE; MEADE, MARTIN J.; AND SCHNEIDERS, ALEXANDER A. **The Validation of a Biographical Inventory as a Predictor of College Success: Development and Validation of the Scoring Key.** New York: College Entrance Examination Board, 1960. Pp. v, 81. Paper. $2.00. * (*PA* 35:5358)

[B55]

ANDERSON, CHARLES C. **Function Fluctuation.** British Journal of Psychology Monograph Supplements, No. 30. London and New York: Cambridge University Press, 1958. Pp. vii, 104. Paper. 21*s*.; $4.25. * (*PA* 33:9035)

Brit J Psychol 49:349 N '58. H. J. Eysenck. This monograph takes up an important problem in mental testing on which there is a surprising amount of speculation but relatively little evidence. As is well known, the fact that two tests of one and the same function fail to correlate perfectly is due partly to errors associated with the test, and partly to 'function fluctuation,' which is a term originally suggested by Thouless to denote a day-to-day quantitative variation in the function tested. The first half of this monograph reviews the literature on this and related concepts and tries to clarify the undoubted confusion of terms and concepts existing in this field. Also included in the first part is a chapter giving results of previous research. The review is clear and to the point, although at times it appears a little niggling and ungenerous to some of the earlier workers. There is also a superabundance of quotations more characteristic of a Ph.D. thesis than a monograph; these do not always contribute greatly to the argument. However, taken by and large, the reader of this section should have a fairly clear grasp of the problems and theories in this field. Not all relevant material is included; thus, no mention is made of the work of Fleischman, or of the Hartshorn and May studies. The second part of the monograph deals with the author's own experiments which appear to have been unusually extensive as far as the number of tests administered is concerned. Analysis, presentation and discussion are clearcut and incisive. The main results are that function fluctuation is active both in cognitive and in non-cognitive functions, but more extensively in the latter. Function fluctuation does not appear to be a characteristic feature of a given individual; correlations between function fluctuation on one test and function fluctuation on another appear to be nearly zero. From these results the author derives a number of conclusions which are sensible, and a theory of cognitive function fluctuation which does not seem a great advance to the reviewer and which, if true, would suggest that correlations of function fluctuation should be obtained between different tests. However that may be, we are in debt to the author for both his review and his experimental contribution to an important aspect of test psychology that has been somewhat neglected in the past.

Cont Psychol 4:183–4 Je '59. George A. Ferguson. * While many of the conclusions drawn are clearly substantiated by the data, some of the statistical procedures used are open to question. For example, the author, without explanation, applies a test of significance to Thouless's criterion. It is not clear to me what the appropriate test would be. Other points of statistical criticism may be made. Nevertheless the research itself was competently conducted, and many of the findings are of interest. About half of the monograph explores the concept of function fluctuation and reviews previous research. Here the author splits many a hair. He presents numerous quotations from the writings of other investigators, accompanied by his assorted commentary, evaluations, and argument. This dulls the reader when he attempts to follow the discourse in detail and exasperates him when he loses the thread. The author has even exhumed a number of dusty quotations from my own writing items that I hoped had been dead many a year. Surely the first half of the monograph could be substantially reduced without loss to the reader, and indeed with some gain. The discourse at times appears jumbled and unintelligible. Read this: "Function fluctuation, although a hypothetical construct, is not a fundamental psychological explanation, but a functional process, a kind of intervening hypothesis, which may be open to explanation by a resort to motivational terms." Do you understand? This monograph is an easy target for criticism, a circumstance which unfortunately makes difficult a fair evaluation of its research content. The fact is that Anderson has conducted a worthwhile piece of research, one which represents the most thorough investigation of the topic undertaken to date, but the account of which is poorly written and not clearly argued.

[B56]

*Anderson, Howard R., and Lindquist, E. F.; revised by David K. Heenan. **Selected Test Items in World History, Third Edition.** National Council for the Social Studies, Bulletin No. 9, Third Edition. Washington, D.C.: the Council, 1960. Pp. vi, 93. Paper. $1.50. *

[B57]

*Anderson, Howard R., and Lindquist, E. F.; revised by Harriet Stull. **Selected Test Items in American History, Fifth Edition.** National Council for the Social Studies, Bulletin No. 6, Fifth Edition. Washington, D.C.: the Council, 1964. Pp. ii, 126. Paper. $1.50. * For reviews of earlier editions, see 3:734-5 and 40:B827.

[B58]

★Anderson, Scarvia B.; Katz, Martin; and Shimberg, Benjamin. **Meeting the Test.** New York: Scholastic Book Services, 1963. Pp. vi, 185. Paper. $0.45. * (A reprint of a series of fifteen articles on standardized testing originally published in 1958-59 in *Senior Scholastic, World Week,* and *Practical English.*)

[B59]

★Arasarkadavil, Denis J. **The Secondary School Leaving Examination in India: A Case Study of the Validity of the Examination in Kerala State.** New York and London: Asia Publishing House, 1963. Pp. xx, 203. $8.50; 35*s.* *

[B60]

★Arnold, Magda B. **Story Sequence Analysis: A New Method of Measuring Motivation and Predicting Achievement.** New York and London: Columbia University Press, 1962. Pp. ix, 287. $7.50; 56*s.* *

Brit J Psychol 54:376 N '63. A. Kaldegg. * Arnold found empirically that the imports of "high achievers" were distinguishable from those of "low achievers" * To abstract the correct import may present difficulties even to the experienced psychologist. Provided the method can be mastered without tuition, it may well prove valuable for vocational selection and rehabilitation.

Lib J 88:110 Ja '63. George Adelman. * Arnold....has taken the Thematic Apperception Test....and has devised a method of scoring which shows great promise both as a measurement of motivation and predictor of achievement and as a diagnostic tool for psychiatry. * Arnold's method for scoring involves describing each story in terms of its outcome, moral, or "import" rather than in terms of detail or plot. Each "import" is taken by the reviewer and related to the import of the stories which precede it. The result is a sequence of imports which gives a picture of the subject's motivations, positive or negative, and usual outlook on life. The first part of the book is a theoretical rationale for this new method and is presented in the author's usual lucid and persuasive style. Highly recommended to all subject collections.

[B61]

★Arnold, Magda B.; Hispanicus, Petreolus; Weisgerber, Charles A.; and D'Arcy, Paul F. **Screening Candidates for the Priesthood and Religious Life.** Chicago, Ill.: Loyola University Press, 1962. Pp. x, 205. * For a 1964 edition with content apparently identical, see B248.

[B62]

★Austin, Mary C.; Bush, Clifford L.; and Huebner, Mildred H. **Reading Evaluation: Appraisal Techniques for School and Classroom.** New York: Ronald Press Co., 1961. Pp. v, 256. $4.50. *

Reading Teach 15:63 S '61. Harry T. Hahn. There has been an obvious need for a textbook which focused its attention on current procedures, materials, and practices for evaluating reading progress in the school and classroom. Austin, Bush, and Huebner offer this unique guide to satisfy this need. They have made a significant contribution. The first half of the text is devoted to specific practices for appraising group and individual reading skills. Informal tests receive considerable attention, and an informal reading inventory is included for the teacher's use. While standardized tests are not subjected to a critical evaluation, charts of selected tests are provided with a breakdown of the skills which they treat. School administrators will be particularly pleased with the final half of the text which gives detailed plans for conducting school-wide reading surveys. Information as to costs, preparation, interpretation, and follow-up is included, and examples are cited from school programs.

[B63]

★AUSTRALIAN COUNCIL FOR EDUCATIONAL RESEARCH. **Making the Classroom Test: A Guide for Teachers.** Hawthorn, Australia: the Council, 1962. Pp. 36. Paper. 3*s.* * (An Australian revision of *Making the Classroom Test: A Guide for Teachers* prepared by Quentin Stodola and published in 1959 by the Educational Testing Service.)

[B64]

★BALL, JOHN C. **Social Deviancy and Adolescent Personality: An Analytical Study With the MMPI.** Lexington, Ky.: University of Kentucky Press, 1962. Pp. xv, 119. $3.00. * (*PA* 37:8176)

Cont Psychol 9:263–4 Je '64. Louise J. Farnham. * an attempt to describe the relationship between various forms of deviation from middle class norms on one hand and adolescent personality on the other, as personality is measured by the MMPI. To test the hypothesis that social deviancy is linked with important personality differences, comparisons were made between delinquents and non-delinquents, school achievers and non-achievers, maladjusted and adjusted students, Negroes and whites, high and low socioeconomic status adolescents, and adolescents from stable and broken homes. * The author's aims are certainly important. Accurate personality descriptions of various subgroups of the adolescent population are necessary precursors to explaining behavioral concomitants of the various types of social deviation Professor Ball discusses. However....the author failed to achieve even the relatively limited goal of personality description. The basic design of the study was a simple one, involving the classification and reclassification of a sample of 262 Kentucky adolescents. Mean MMPI profiles and scale by scale comparisons were reported for each of the classifications by sex. Unfortunately, there is no way for the reader to be certain of the degree to which the reported differences were related to any of the particular classifications employed. For example, differences were reported between Negro and white girls on five MMPI scales, but these girls differed in social class membership and academic achievement as well. Can MMPI differences then be unambiguously related to the single independent variable, race membership? One would be hard-pressed to determine from the data presented which of the many independent variables are contributing to the variance for any reported difference. Some of the independent variables (academic achievement, family composition, socioeconomic status) are reported for each of the subgroups and the number of significant differences is distressingly high. From the data presented, it is virtually impossible to reconstruct the sample to check for differences on other independent variables. Multiple regression analysis would certainly have led to more definitive interpretations of the differences found between groups on each of the MMPI scales. The unambiguous findings that were reported were primarily replications of earlier findings. It will be no surprise to readers familiar with MMPI lore that 23 of the 30 mean profiles presented in the book have as their highest three scales 4 (psychopathic deviate), 8 (schizophrenia), and 9 (hypomania). It is also not surprising that "caught" delinquents score higher on scale 4 than other adolescents. There are few significant differences in the scale by scale comparisons, considering the number of comparisons made. This study would have been more enlightening had earlier findings been considered in its design and had the results of the study been discussed in relation to the earlier findings. Furthermore, the present results would have been easier to interpret had the author tempered his extreme empirical approach by making explicit what appears to be an implicit theoretical position. One wonders what function a construct such a social deviancy can serve when it subsumes both situational factors and behavioral responses to those situational factors. Certainly low socioeconomic status or being Negro cannot be considered "deviant behavior" on the part of an adolescent in the same way that delinquency or classroom maladjustment can be so considered. While the author makes much of his empirical approach, it would appear to have little value if it results in neither the clarification of existing problems nor the refinement of theories advanced by others.

[B65]

★BARNETTE, W. LESLIE, JR. **Readings in Psychological Tests and Measurements.** Homewood, Ill.: Dorsey Press, Inc., 1964. Pp. xi, 354. Paper, $3.00; cloth, $5.00. *

[B66]

★BARNHART, E. L., AND ANDERSON, KENNETH E. **A Study of the Relationships Between Grade-Point Averages, Placement-Test Scores, Semester Hours Earned, and Area of Major Interest for the Group Who Entered the University of Kansas in the Fall of 1954.** University of Kansas, School of Education, Kansas Studies in Education, Vol. 11, No. 1. Lawrence, Kan.: the School, January 1961. Pp. 36. Paper. Gratis. *

[B67]

★BARROW, HAROLD M., AND MCGEE, ROSEMARY. **A Practical Approach to Measurement in Physical Education.** Philadelphia, Pa.: Lea & Febiger, 1964. Pp. 560. $8.50. *

[B68]

★BASS, BERNARD M., AND BERG, IRWIN A., EDITORS. **Objective Approaches to Personality Assessment.** Princeton, N.J.: D. Van Nostrand Co., Inc., 1959. Pp. x, 233. $4.95. * (London: D. Van Nostrand Co., Ltd. *37s. 6d.*) (*PA* 33:9926)

Cont Psychol 5:68 Mr '60. W. Grant Dahlstrom. * It is possible for this book to serve as a text, but not in standard departmental offerings. It is not elementary. It is not just another "Introduction to" something. Some of the papers here are fine introductions to special areas of personological research. The papers are short, readable and discrete. The reader has available concise reviews of work on leadership (Bass), objective Rorschach methods (Holtzman), the deviation hypothesis (Berg), and social desirability (Edwards). Profile patterning (McQuitty), factor analytic methods (Cattell), and clinical judgment material (W. A. Hunt) get more parochial treatment. It must have been a difficult decision for the invited participants to allocate their brief time between definitions, resumés of the work of others, and their own work in progress. Since each participant arrived at a different resolution of this conflict, the book lacks the cohesiveness and balance necessary in a text. Pepinsky—perhaps carried away by the enthusiasm of this conclave of experts—describes the material here as "a new and abundant harvest of ideas and facts and methods of inquiry....for research workers and practitioners alike." The ideas are here in abundance. This is a series of methodological exercises and most of the current approaches are represented. Perhaps, of all the methods in vogue, only the Q-sorting, self-conceptualizing developments get scant treatment. The facts are, however, omitted, and the research worker is going to find this omission serious. Pepinsky also praises the "imaginativeness and productive originality" of these contributions. He may well be right, but the history of research reveals no dearth of ingenious approaches or techniques in any area of psychology. We scarcely need more variations; we need solid, substantiated findings. It was discouraging to find in the various projects reported here a lack of interest in incorporating some other men's procedures and data given in the interest of comparability. * Graduate students facing departmental examinations may seek this book out with profit for the recent developments it includes. Harassed teachers unable to keep up with the literature will find it a handy summary. The hard-pressed clinician looking for additional dependable means of assessing personality may well take the title of the work literally. The many good cooks are better than their broth.

Ed & Psychol Meas 20:409–11 su '60. S. B. Sells. * a volume of generally competent and interesting individual papers by a number of well-known and respected psychologists, each going his own way, preoccupied with his own idiosyncratic approach. The exceptions are two introductory presentations, one a historical review, the other a theoretical survey, and a concluding summary paper, intended to tie everything together. Since his critical remarks apply equally both to the symposium and to the field it discusses, Harold Pepinsky's brief but temperate, engagingly phrased, and wise summary is an excellent orientation to the problems of objective personality assessment. The historical review by Robert I. Watson is a valuable analysis of the growing concern in American psychology with problems of objectivity in measurement. * The reviewer is inclined to agree with Pepinsky on the following points: (1) There is much to read in this collection of papers that is rich and satisfying; (2) The unanimous conviction of the participants that "whatever assessment data are used must, in principle be capable of being defined empirically, measured in amount and recorded as scores in the public domain" was clearly a distinguishing characteristic of this symposium; and (3) Lack of concern with variations of interpretation on basic methodological issues defining objective measurement of behavior and with the problem of achieving some systematic closure on fundamental issues also characterized both the majority of the participants and the symposium as a whole. Perhaps such symposia serve a function toward breaking through the insulation and seeming indifference to other significant work manifested by representative participants, by obliging them to listen to each other. However, a much more interesting, novel, and long overdue symposium would be a follow-up session dealing with the unresolved issues after the already well-known positions have been expounded. * the entire spectrum of approaches to objective personality assessment is not represented. This volume may well be a useful reference for a graduate course in personality theory or assessment to provide students with a handy collection of readings, particularly where library journal collections are inadequate. Several such books are available, and this will be a worthy addition to their number.

Personnel Psychol 13:103–5 sp '60. Edwin C. Nevis. * the presentations of Raymond B. Cattell, Irwin A. Berg, Wayne H. Holtzman, William A. Hunt and James G. Miller are particularly stimulating. Cattell's long-term studies, his methods and results, are certainly impressive. His decisions to use at least three types of observation (behavior ratings, questionnaires, and performance in miniature situations), his use of variables found by others, his insistence upon replication and longitudinal studies, and his rigorous quantification together make an excellent model for others to follow. That his results tend to support many clinical findings and dynamic personality theory is also greatly encouraging. Berg's well documented argument questioning the importance of item content deserves wide circulation among those interested in developing new tests and research devices. His emphasis upon characteristic response patterns or "sets"—his deviation hypothesis—rather than clear content, opens up great possibilities for new types of items and tests. Following his conclusions would result in all kinds of stimulus conditions in tests, many or most of which would lack the face validity emphasized so much in currently popular tests. * The research psychologist....will find many stimulating techniques and suggestions in this collection of papers and the very relevant references appended to each paper. The clinical and industrial practitioner, however, will find little to comfort him immediately. Indeed, if the twelve experts whose papers are discussed are on the right track, many of the familiar tests and procedures are headed for the wastepaper basket. * this book gives us a glimpse into the future tools available to the practitioner. Exactly what kinds of techniques and measuring procedures we shall arrive at cannot be determined from these articles. Each of the twelve distinguished authors is going more or less his own way and seems to be too excited about what is emerging to stop and find agreement with the others. While this is unfortunate in some respects, the broad-gauge conception and dedication to programmatic work that is demonstrated should result in significant, integrated bodies of data. This reviewer has frequent fantasies about what would happen if we suddenly stopped using all currently available personality tests, perhaps even placed a moratorium on all such testing, and forced ourselves to be more creative and less rigid in our daily assessment practices. While the immediate result would be chaos, to say nothing of loss of income from our practice, ultimately we would be thinking more like these authors and using techniques like those they are developing. No open-minded psychologist who is engaged in the practice of personality assessment can afford not to study this book carefully and begin to better prepare himself for what lies around the corner, as well as to get some ideas on how to improve his current practices.

[B69]

★BAUERNFEIND, ROBERT H. **Building a School Testing Program.** Boston, Mass.: Houghton Mifflin Co., 1963. Pp. xvii, 343. $4.95. (*Instructor's Guide for Building a School Testing Program.* Pp. ii, 56. Paper.) *

J Counsel Psychol 10:410 w '63. Donald E. Super. * Despite the fact that the author espouses a position with which I cannot agree, he has written an excellent book. The position is stated on page 5 (and reiterated a few times later): "The typical school testing director is not a measurement specialist: the group testing program is usually decided by the school administrator, the school psychologist, the guidance director, or the curriculum coordinator." If this were stated as a lamentable but none-the-less true fact, we would have no quarrel, but it is also accepted as a principle, a *desideratum.* But as I see it, if the testing director doesn't know more about testing than three out of four of the people named, he and the school are in a bad way, and the good name of testing is likely to suffer! As it too often has. Having announced his intention to write for the uninitiated, Bauernfeind does a good job of it. If his test directors are stimulated to go and learn more about statistics and about psychometrics, as they may well be, his mistaken premise will do no harm. Basic concepts are well explained. Good questions, and answers in an instructor's guide, are supplied at frequent intervals. Current issues such as global intelligence versus multifactor tests, ipsative versus normative interest inventories, and the use of personality inventories in school testing programs, are discussed in detail, clearly, and with courage. * One important feature of the text is bothersome, but perhaps only because of one of my biases. A school testing program is discussed in Chapter 14, in a way which could make it seem to be a proposed model. Some of the tests chosen have been found lacking by quite a few critics, for reasons covered in Buros' and in other publications: for example, the SRA Primary Mental Abilities Tests are recommended for kindergarten use, as are the Davis-Eell Games in Grade 3; Cattell's Culture Fair Test appears in Grade 5, and the FACT Battery in Grade 10, with no mention of the GATB or the use of National Merit, College Board, or American College Testing Service tests at the higher levels. The wisdom of recommending, or even proposing, a master testing program when so many people deciding on the use of tests slavishly copy rather than finding out what they need in their schools, and how good the various possible tests actually are for their purposes, is questionable.

Personnel & Guid J 42:624–5 F '64. John R. Hills. * interesting little book * One of the high points of the book occurs in this chapter, between pages 212 and 224, where the author clearly displays some of the immense problems involved in accurately interpreting scores such as those from the Kuder Preference Record—Vocational. This is an exceedingly important discussion since counselors seem often to be indoctrinated to believe that the Kuder is especially useful because it is so *easy* to interpret. After reading these pages it can be anticipated that the Brainard Occupational Preference Inventory, which avoids ipsative scores, will see increased popularity. * Chapter 13 provides a good discussion of the role of subject-matter tests, especially those made by the teacher. * Two features of the organization of the book should be mentioned. First, throughout the book are inserted stimulating questions to the reader, questions which should provoke exciting class discussions if the students are at all eager. It seemed to the reviewer that some of the questions would be very difficult for people who needed the level of exposition of most of the book, but perhaps such questions will keep the reader from becoming overconfident. The second feature deserving mention is that in each chapter of the section on choosing tests there are short, detailed, evaluative descriptions of tests and test batteries which the author feels may be recommended. Frequent references are made to Buros' *Mental Measurements Yearbooks.* If the book has a weakness, it seems to the reviewer that it is in Section One on the statistics of tests and measurements. Bauernfeind states that he assumes that the reader has had or is taking a basic college course in educational measurements, but the level of discourse seems to vacillate between such levels as giving the reader credit for considerable sophistication about means and standard deviations in one passage and elsewhere assuming that he does not understand those tools sufficiently well to use them in developing local stanine scores. The author feels it necessary to tell what variance means in a footnote, but later talks about "standard deviation scores" with no discussion of what they are. While Section One is a noble effort to present an abbreviated beginning statistics course, it is the reviewer's impression that should he try to help an experienced teacher newly assigned to the status of testing director, he would need especially to help with this part of the book. Further, the reviewer predicts that the book is good enough to be revised, and that the revision will clear up much of the difficulty of Section One by picking one level of readership and writing entirely for that level. It was a pleasure to read a book which presented so clearly and unequivocally an informed, practical man's thoughtful opinions about tests and testing in schools.

[B70]

★BAUGHMAN, M. DALE, EDITOR. **Pupil Evaluation in the Junior High School: Review of Relevant Literature, Position Papers on Evaluation, Opinions on Aspects of Evaluation and Prevailing Practices in Representative Junior High Schools.** Sponsored by The Junior High School Association of Illinois. Danville, Ill.: Interstate Printers & Publishers, Inc., 1963. Pp. vii, 80. Paper. $1.50. *

Ed & Psychol Meas 24:736–7 f '64. Richard E. Schutz and James C. Moore. This publication is a....good example of what happens when a group of teachers and administrators discuss evaluation. The report is divided into eight chapters, individually authored, and one chapter in which many persons present brief pro and con positions on "unresolved issues." The chapters are overlapping, nonspecific, and superficial. They swing from overgeneralizations to overdiscriminations. * Unfortunately the authors present so little in the way of specific operational practices that the report is of little help to fellow school people. Test specialists may be interested in the contributions as a sample of the evaluation-related verbal behavior of what is likely a better than average group of professional educators.

[B71]

★Bayer, Leona M., and Bayley, Nancy. **Growth Diagnosis: Selected Methods for Interpreting and Predicting Physical Development From One Year to Maturity.** Chicago, Ill.: University of Chicago Press, 1959. Pp. xiv, 241. $10.00. *

Child Develop Abstracts 35:58 F–Ap '61. J. M. Tanner. * The authors evidently assume familiarity with the basic facts of growth and do not attempt to describe them here. * Some of the methods they advocate are not those thought best in more recent times; indeed, the book has a curiously old-fashioned air despite its excellent production. The standard tables date from 1931, and so, by the looks of things, does the instrument for measuring hip width. In charting weight deviation in terms of standard deviations rather than percentiles, the authors are clearly in error, though they break new and interesting ground in providing charts for height and weight against age which allow for advancement and retardation in maturity. The latter two-thirds of the book is occupied with descriptions of eight normal children and 22 children with growth disorders. These are of much interest; they are very well illustrated and followed over often prolonged periods of time with body measurements, photographs, and skeletal age determinations. Bayley's method of predicting adult height from age and skeletal maturity is fully tested and emerges very creditably indeed even from this trial by pathology. This is a book for pediatricians to ponder over, and for those—and not least those contemplating publishing, the layout is so excellent—to glance through. It invites criticism in detail but deserves nothing but praise in intention and general outline.

Cont Psychol 5:266–7 Ag '60. Edward E. Hunt, Jr. This handsome volume is the work of two justly respected authorities on the physical development of children. It defines a battery of somatic measurements and ratings which require some technical skill and equipment for radiography, anthropometry, and full-length photography in the nude. Norms for each variate are presented which apply best to American white children of North European ancestry who have been reared under conditions favoring early and rapid growth. In order to carry out the entire program on a child, an investigator would need both the present volume and the second edition of the *Radiographic Atlas of Skeletal Maturation (Hand)* by Greulich and Pyle. Anyone with a really broad interest in child development would do well to have both books within easy reach. From these volumes, an investigator can detect deviations of size and body breadth, unusual lengths of limbs, the appropriateness of a child's physique to his sex and age, and his progress in skeletal and genital maturation. He would not have a measure of maturity in terms of teeth present in the mouth or other features of the head, and could only indirectly observe caloric balance in terms of thickness of the subcutaneous adipose layer. It would have been well to have added a chapter on norms of caloric and protein intake for boys and girls of different ages, so that the investigator could transform the evidence of dietary questionnaires into evaluations of how efficiently a child transforms pabulum into protoplasm. * parts of the battery can act as a modest corrective against the excessive "mentalism" of a psychologist, but the entire procedure is too much to ask of him—at least, on his own. He may record stature and weight, and perhaps learn to count and classify teeth, but probably more important are the skill to evaluate outward facial maturity relative to age and being on the lookout for such things as excessive breast development in a pubescent boy. In other words, the relevance of somatic data to the psychologist might be to define a child's size, strength, and vitality alongside his peers, his "body image" and attitudes toward his developmental assets and liabilities, his adiposity and sexual maturation. Although the correction of physical deformities is not the psychologist's province, he should, nevertheless, be aware of such characteristics in his subjects and patients. In other words, somatic data often help the psychologist in encouraging his young clients to make successful transitions from one period of life to the next.

[B72]

★Beck, Samuel J. **The Rorschach Experiment: Ventures in Blind Diagnosis.** New York: Grune

& Stratton, Inc., 1960. Pp. viii, 256. $6.50. * (London: William Heinemann Medical Books Ltd. 46*s*.)

Am J Orthopsychiatry 31:433–5 Ap '61. Otfried Spreen. * introduces a new scoring of the Rorschach data, the Experience Actual (EA). The EA is an addition to Rorschach's *Erlebnistypus* (ratio of M:C) and consists simply of the sum of M plus C; this is interpreted as the subject's "total emotional reactivity." Although this reviewer agrees with Beck that careful and detailed blind analyses of Rorschach protocols are one valuable means of determining the diagnostic worth of the test, he feels that a new scoring like the EA should not be introduced without presentation of normative data and good evidence for, or at least sound reasoning about, its usefulness and validity. Normative data for the EA are not given and the few illustrations of low EA in depressives and mental defectives and high EA in manics seem to demonstrate no more than the well-known fact that depressives and mental defectives give few responses and manics give many. Statistical validation is not attempted and the reasoning in connection with *Erlebnistypus* and EA is hard to follow. * These early chapters seem to be the weaker parts of this book. However, two thirds of the book consists of eight case presentations and here Beck is at his best. The cases are well chosen and contain interesting comparisons of the Rorschachs of mother and son and of three records obtained during five years' development of a schizophrenic boy. * As many Rorschach workers do, Beck relies heavily on observational details such as sighs and body movements and on the analytic interpretation of content rather than on the numerical scoring. Surprisingly, he makes little use of his new EA scoring. The clinical notes given at the end of the case presentations, however, contain very few of the data the reader would hope for. They often consist of only a few lines or are altogether missing; data of other psychological tests are usually not given. It is hard to substantiate the Rorschach interpretations on the basis of so little data. * The value of this book would seem to lie in those parts which are written by the experienced clinician rather than by the theorist, i.e., the case presentations and the valuable survey of the evaluation of treatment and prognosis as reflected in the test.

Cont Psychol 6:438–40 D '61. Martin Mayman. * Beck is quick to warn the reader that the title of the book is something of a misnomer, for his "ventures in blind diagnosis" are not really "experiments." His effort here, he says, is not to prove the test's validity but to demonstrate its working processes. In accord with this intention, each test report is accompanied by a set of footnote explanations which trace the links between interpretive statements and the test data on which they were based. There are on the average 65 such explanatory annotations per report. It is regrettable that these annotated reports are no more a demonstration of the "clinician's working processes" than the blind diagnostic "experiment" is really an experiment. Beck takes only a first step toward explicating the intricacies of the inference process in clinical case studies. * for the clinician to be able to *demonstrate* the discipline and the science behind his clinical art, he must first develop a method for achieving what Beck set out to do. He must develop appropriate techniques for the study of his own "intuitive" working processes, techniques to pry into and make explicit the intricate network of inferences in order that he be able to establish convincingly the intrinsic reasonableness of some inferences (and the intrinsic arbitrariness of others). Surely, in time, clinical psychology will be able to demonstrate conclusively both the objective and the verifiable nature of its interpretive processes, but that day has not yet arrived. Beck's book provides some of the raw data for a study of the clinical art, but does not undertake the study itself. * In a comprehensive analysis of the process of clinical inference....other kinds of questions would be considered as well. What factors—what assumptions, thoughts, or impressions—influenced Beck to select this particular cluster of observations as the groundwork for his inference pyramid? Does his selection differ from that which would be made by other leading Rorschach workers? If so, why? Why do some observations become focal organizing points for the inference process and others not? Why does one put more reliance on some inferences than on others? To what extent does the report consist of only a few primary inferences and a large number of secondary inferences drawn not from one's test data but from the examiner's conceptual stereotypes and his personality theory? That is, to what extent does the report consist of deductive conclusions rather than inductive ones? These are only a few of the questions one could ask of the inference process if one were tracing the full development of Beck's thought from primary data to ultimate inferences, questions Beck does not attempt to consider in this book. * A word of warning concerning the use which may be made of the new score which Beck proposes in the introductory section of this book—*E-A* score (*Erlebnis-Actual*), which is computed by adding the sum *M* and sum *C* scores of a Rorschach protocol, that is to say, by adding the numerator and denominator of Rorschach's Experience Balance. There is no logical reason for objection when someone wants to add two oranges to one apple to make three pieces of fruit, or even two apples to one good idea, to make a total of three personal possessions. The only question is: How useful is the product of such summations? The seven case illustrations do not show convincingly the superiority of the *E-A* score over a more qualitative assessment of the dilation or constriction of a Rorschach protocol. There are, moreover, many conceptual objections which can be raised to the suggestion that the *E-A* score measures the "psychologic animation" or "reflects the inner state of total psychologic vitality" of the personality. There is much in the book, however, to balance its limitations. Sprinkled through all of the theoretical and case discussions are keenly expressive phrases which enrich the meaning of Rorschach variables for the experienced practitioner as well as the novice. If one wants to learn what observations Beck relies upon most heavily in his Rorschach work, and what kinds of inferences he is most inclined to draw, this is a valuable sourcebook and provides a useful supplement to his basic text. Beck's courage in exposing to public view the reasoning behind his blind diagnostic test statements would be sufficiently rewarded if it should indicate no more about the process of clinical inference than that clinicians have not yet found a way to make fully explicit all of the implicit "psycho-logic" of clinical inferences. With more publications by Beck and others directed to these engrossing and important problems, clinicians may finally succeed in developing an articulate science of clinical inference.

Psychoanalytic Q 31:411–3 Jl '62. Gertrud M. Kurth. Any major addition to the existing spate of Rorschach literature needs justification. The present volume has a double claim. First, it offers a novel contribution to the teaching of the Rorschach test. Each protocol and report is complemented by extensive and detailed notes on the author's "interpretive reasoning," exemplifying the path from administration to diagnosis. * The second new contribution is to Rorschach theory. It concerns Rorschach's concept of *Erlebnistypus,* which Dr. Beck himself originally translated as "experience balance." * Under the influence of Jungian type psychology, Rorschach supposed that this relation distinguishes between introvert and extrovert personalities, a terminology modified by Rorschach workers to introversive versus extratensive to indicate dominant dynamics rather than types. But although it has always seemed obvious that this relation is meaningful in practical work, it has remained ambiguous and undependable. Consequently, Dr. Beck suggests a new approach by making use not of the quantitative relations between the two types of responses but of their sum, which he calls the "experience actual" and compares to Freud's "psychologic economy." * This new approach to one of Rorschach's central but more elusive concepts appears as promising as Beck's contention that he based his test interpretations on "the major psychoanalytic hypothesis of personality as an accommodation of ego and id forces," or "as expressing results of an ego-affect give-and-take." It is somewhat disturbing that, in the same breath as it were, Beck calls on the Jacksonian concepts of brain and nervous system functioning as additional foundation for his own view of personality. It is to be expected that, in this context, Freud and Jackson may turn out to be not merely strange but even incompatible bedfellows. Upon getting immersed in the body of the book—the eight test records with interpretations and notes —one soon finds that a feeling of bewilderment is due not so much to the prolixity and heaviness of style of the text as to genuine obscurity of meaning. For instance, Beck speaks of a "neurosis marked by consciously held pathogenic defenses." He then elaborates on the patient's "ability to recover from shocks, reflecting reserves on which she can continue to call in spite of the ego's being constantly in action. This ego effort is likely to be the chief obstacle to early success in treatment." These are baffling statements and cannot possibly be understood on the basis of the freudian concept of ego. In fact, as one continues, Dr. Beck's ego emerges as a hybrid creature with strangely limited characteristics. For instance: "A first point of interest in appraising treatability is necessarily the state of the ego. How much wish does the patient show to hold on to established values? And to direct herself by them as a central, piloting set of dictates?" (Is this the superego?) Or: "The ego is strong but under pressure from defensive needs, and it limits its sights to those needs. The insecurity of the individual....urgently commands those defenses. Should they break, the anxiety and terror go out of bounds. Hence the sometimes desperate sticking to the defense pattern and the frightened resistance of any insight that disturbs or breaches them." Since this applies to emotional illness in general—though one might not want to express it in these anthropomorphic terms—one wonders what light such a statement can throw on an individual case. Furthermore: "Why had this patient not developed defenses? For ego resources were available to her....and defenses are an ego product." Here Dr. Beck seems to disregard the concept of deficiencies in separate ego functions as well as the concept of the unconscious ego. Actually, what he calls ego appears to be restricted to certain aspects of the conscious ego and of the conscious superego. Small wonder that, in spite of his courageous and honest revealing of his reasoning in the notes, both notes and reports make unrevealing reading for the psychoanalytically trained reader. Similarly, the concluding chapters which deal with the Rorschach aspects of prognosis reflect the confusion that results from the author's misunderstanding of freudian terminology as well as from his determination to force Freud and Jackson into a Procrustean bed. A liberal sprinkling, throughout the book, of references to writings of Anna Freud, Fenichel, and Federn, and to those of authors of other schools of thought tends to compound the confusion. The underlying assumption that entire theoretical frameworks, or even individual technical terms, are directly interchangeable proves a dangerous fallacy. * Finally, the author appears naïvely unaware of techniques of psychoanalytic treatment, and his personal attitude emerges as judicial rather than clinical * Summarizing, it may be stated with regret and disappointment that, with the exception of the concept of the "experience actual," this volume will not add to the knowledge or skill of the psychoanalytic psychologist.

Rorsch Newsl 6:34–5 Je '61. A. Kaldegg. * A blind analysis is given of....8 cases. In his "notes on interpretation" Dr. Beck thinks aloud. Blind analysis demands the greatest self-discipline and Dr. Beck with all his vast knowledge submits humbly to it. Nothing is left to hazard and hunches. Data are painstakingly checked against norms wherever available, viewed in perspective and in their inter-relationship. The basis of all reasoning is clearly and readably stated. It would be easy for Dr. Beck to speculate on the meaning of unusual responses but he carefully refers them to the psycho-therapist for exploration. All who put integrity above spectacular results are recommended to work through these notes. The method of references and cross-references used by Dr. Beck is somewhat cumbersome though it may have the advantage of avoiding repetitions. Strict scientists might object to Dr. Beck quoting almost exclusively norms derived from his own work. It is true that many of his norms are widely accepted but there are also norms put forward by other distinguished workers in the field and the book's teaching value might have been enhanced if he had taken cognizance of them. A drawback is the different scoring system which makes it necessary for younger Rorschach workers to familiarise themselves first with Dr. Beck's older books before they can enjoy the present one. A short recapitulation of the scoring system, of Dr. Levy's "movement scale" for which no reference could be detected (perhaps Zubin, Levy and Rust, 1947?) and the Lambda index frequently mentioned would have obviated these difficulties. But these criticisms are trifling. Dr. Beck sets out "not to test the test's validity but to demonstrate its working processes." He does it with the touch of the master. One is grateful to him for his book and its wisdom.

[B73]

*Beck, Samuel J.; Beck, Anne G.; Levitt, Eugene E.; and Molish, Herman B. **Rorschach's Test: I, Basic Processes, Third Edition.** New York: Grune & Stratton, Inc., 1961. Pp. x, 237. $6.00. (London: William Heinemann Medical Books Ltd. 42*s.*) * (*PA* 36:1HG37B)

Am J Orthopsychiatry 32:205–6 Ja '62. Adolf G. Woltmann. The first edition of Volume I of Beck's *Rorschach Test* appeared in 1944. At that time it was regarded as the most comprehensive treatise on the basic processes of the Rorschach test, and was treasured as a bible among Rorschach workers. Now, 17 years later, the third edition, fully revised, has appeared. It contains only 14 more pages than the first edition; but in terms of content, this book has grown, matured and benefited from the numerous continuing investigations, refinements and added applications. The most important revision is the determination of good and poor form, F+ and F− (Chap. 12). Since such discriminations are critically essential for the diagnostic value of the test, Beck absorbed into his already revised scoring the replies of 200 psychologists (Div. 12, A.P.A.) who responded to his request that doubtful F+ and F− responses be sent to him. This list, as Beck cautions, is only a tentative guide. It reflects "the fluidity of this instrument, as fluid as the variability of human mentalities which it probes." Another great improvement over the first edition lies in the fact that Beck uses the Small location charts, rather than his previous markings which delineated scoring areas out of context with the total inkblot. The scoring categories themselves are listed one underneath another. They can be located more easily than in the first edition, where they were grouped together in paragraphs. Although much of the original material has been retained, the third edition contains a number of timely and up-to-date revisions. Among these are the chapters on Approach, Sequence and Phantasy Association (M). Beck states in the Preface that this revision is intended for the initiate in the Rorschach test during his early years as a clinical psychologist. Yet the usefulness of this book should not stop there. The experienced Rorschach worker will also profit from the wealth of actual examples with which various aspects of this test are illustrated and clarified. The book accomplishes what the title promises. It introduces the reader to the necessary basic principles of this test in terms of test administration and scoring. How good he will be in terms of grasping the psychological significance of the test data depends on how accurately and impersonally he has observed and recorded; how soundly he knows the Rorschach test concepts; and how deeply, as well as broadly, he knows human nature. "The Rorschach test answers no questions. It is only 10 inkblots. It is never better than the brain of the psychologist using it."

Cont Psychol 7:252–4 Jl '62. Philip Roos. * Beck's third revision....introduces few modifications. Clinicians will welcome the revised and simplified F+ tables, which now include graphic outlines of the D and Dd locations, and which are based on a recent normative investigation. * Although the primary purpose of the book is to present Beck's scoring system, he skillfully relates scoring to empirical research, earlier writings, and the rationale of interpretation. It is regrettable that the principles of scoring are frequently not made explicit, so that the reader is forced to reach these principles through inductive reasoning from the many illustrative responses. The illustrative material would be of considerably more value if the inquiry were included. As it is, the reasons for scoring are frequently unclear and at times the scoring appears inconsistent. *

Mental Hyg 47:686–7 O '63. Zygmunt A. Piotrowski. * A new list of good form and poor form responses is the most significant change from the earlier editions. One-third of the book is devoted to a listing of good and poor form responses for each blot, preceded by a short explanation of the method used in compiling the long list. No doubt, the reliance on a list of this sort will standardize scoring and thus improve reliability. Whether it will also increase validity is debatable. For, not only does it matter what visual image the subject associates with a blot area and what proportion of the population samples also produce the same image; it is important how the subject relates the visual association to the blot area which elicited it. * This is an important introduction to the Rorschach test for beginners. It is a real contribution, especially in this period when so many psychologists avoid accurate scoring of the test responses and rely on their own free associations to interpret the test records in a rather unreliable and frequently haphazard manner. The formal, scorable aspects of the test responses as well as the anecdotal ("symbolic") verbal content are essentials. Beck rightly stresses this fundamental point.

For reviews of the first edition, see 3:75 and 3:77.

[B74]

★BENNETT, EDWARD. **Personality Assessment and Diagnosis: A Clinical and Experimental Technique.** New York: Ronald Press Co., 1961. Pp. xiv, 287. $8.00. * (*PA* 36:3HI87B)

Cont Psychol 7:133–4 Ap '62. John D. Black. Despite its imposing title, this book is essentially a manual for the use of a personality assessment technique called the "polydiagnostic method," in which subjects are forced to choose from sets of 15 adjectives the 3 most self-descriptive; then from the remaining 12, the next 3 most descriptive; from the remaining 9, the next 3, and so on. This process is repeated for 20 overlapping sets of 15 adjectives each with occasional changes in instructions; e.g., select the least descriptive adjectives, the ones you would most like to be, the ones which best describe other people. A slightly diabolical touch is added by providing only favorable adjectives for the "least descriptive" instructions, and unfavorable adjectives for all "most descriptive" choices. The lists are individually administered to one subject at a time. How adjectives were chosen for the sets is not explained. * the norms were meticulously corrected to reflect age and sex distributions of the urban white population. Unfortunately, nearly all subjects came from greater Boston and no information is given regarding their education or socio-economic status. * No attempt is made to show relationships between other tests and the "polydiagnostic." * There is no evidence that the "polydiagnostic method" can provide more useful information in assessment or diagnosis than, for example, the scoring of Gough's *Adjective Check List* for Heilbrun's need scales, which is far less time-consuming for both examiner and subject. As a test manual, Bennett's book is probably as good as many that are released these days; as a treatment of personality assessment and diagnosis, it misses the mark by being too technical for laymen, too superficial and naive for the professional.

Ed & Psychol Meas 22:249–50 sp '62. Harold Borko. * The polydiagnostic technique, as Bennett calls it, is based on the assumption that people can express their feelings and subjective experience in a fairly direct manner if they are given a minimum of structure and help. * what is being proposed is not a personality test but a method for obtaining quantifiable measures of subjective feelings. The question remains—what are the advantages of this technique? The author illustrates its value by means of case histories. These studies show that in the hands of a skilled technician the polydiagnostic technique provides a great deal of information on the subject's adjustment, conflicts, and anxieties. How valid are these interpretations? Well, no validity coefficients are presented, and possibly it is unfair to expect such data at this time. If the technique is used simply to gather data for later discussion in an interview situation, validity statistics may not be required. Bennett, in fact, suggests this use. * At the present time all that can be said is that....Bennett describes an original procedure for eliciting subjective feelings about the self and society and of scoring these feelings on a five-point scale by means of forced-choice judgments. The technique appears to have merit and should be examined by both experimental and clinical psychologists, for only through their use can its true value be determined.

J Proj Tech 26:371–2 S '62. Theodore H. Blau. * Data are handled in a variety of intensities, from means and variances for each item in the PM [Polydiagnostic Method] test to a perfunctory "As the pieces come together, some of these interpretations are in obvious disagreement; and they can be discarded." Hypotheses and conclusions are presented in an enthusiastic and decisive manner, while cautions are discernible, but soft-spoken. There are too many sweeping generalities, and unsupported enthusiasms to consider this a significant research contribution. It stands rather as an enthusiastic preliminary report. The word "enthusiastic," to the reviewer, seems appropriate in describing the author's style. Strikingly naïve and repetitious if intended for fully trained psychologists it would, on the other hand, seem hopelessly complex and unrelated as a graduate text. However, Doctor Bennett writes with clarity and energy. One would look forward to his report of cross-validation with the PM technique, or perhaps to the application of his pleasant style to some of the better-known but muddily communicated clinical techniques.

Psychoanalytic Q 32:124 Ja '63. Miriam G. Siegel. This book does not fulfil its intention. * The early chapters on mental health and maladjustment are shallow and superficial; they are followed by detailed descriptions of the technique, by which the subject is helped "to express his subjective feelings." The author claims that the only difference between traditional procedures of psychiatric and casework interviews and this device is that of quantification. In the discussion of the results, the reader is overwhelmed by a mass of data, much of it trivial and distorted. The application of this "polydiagnostic" method is described in several case histories and a research project. While the approach is vigorously objective, the findings are without psychological significance and the social and clinical implications are generalized and naïve. Current research emphasizes the need for translating clinical findings into quantitative data, subject to statistical analysis. However, experience has demonstrated that this can be accomplished within the framework of ego psychology, without overmathematical assessment and the destruction of basic principles.

[B75]

*Berdie, Ralph F.; Layton, Wilbur L.; Swanson, Edward O.; and Hagenah, Theda. **Counseling and the Use of Tests: A Manual for the State-Wide Testing Programs of Minnesota.** [Minneapolis, Minn.: University of Minnesota Press], 1959. Pp. xi, 178. Paper. * For the latest edition, see B77.

Personnel & Guid J 38:68 S '59. Thomas M. Magoon. This expanded and up-to-date edition of the Minnesota manual offers much to its readers, particularly those unfamiliar with earlier editions. Chapters include "Why Understand Pupils," "Learning about Pupils," "Tests," "The Uses of Tests," "State-Wide Testing Programs," "Administration of Tests," "Norms and the Use of Percentile Scores," and "Predictive Instruments." The Appendix includes a detailed section on procedures in choosing a college and the admission requirements of the colleges within the state. Also included are sections on guides to statistical computations useful to counselors and school administrators, and norms for both high school juniors and college freshmen for certain of the state-wide tests. The presentation is well illustrated and supported with tabled data on reliability and academic prediction studies. The total report very clearly illustrates the multiple advantage to the school systems in the state of a centralized state-wide testing, scoring, and reporting program. The occasionally voiced apprehensions about potential dangers ensuing from such a system find little support in this program. A greater value than centralization of testing and scoring is indicated by the many educational and psychometric research studies which have been made and reported in the manual. When there exists no centralized unit budgeted and staffed for such work, it is neither feasible nor economical to explore such data for its fullest implications and use by the cooperating school systems. The enactment of the National Defense Education Act, with its provisions for support of state-wide testing, makes the Minnesota program an even more vivid model of how cooperative relationships between colleges and school systems coupled with centralization of service functions can provide so much sound information for the educational systems in a state.

[B76]

★Berdie, Ralph F.; Layton, Wilbur L.; Swanson, Edward O.; and Hagenah, Theda. **Testing in Guidance and Counseling.** New York: McGraw-Hill Book Co., Inc., 1963. Pp. xiii, 288. $6.75. (London: McGraw-Hill Publishing Co. Ltd. 52*s.* 6*d.*) *

Cont Psychol 9:314–5 Ag '64. William C. Cottle. It is difficult to begin an appraisal of this material. It has taken such basic data as a beginning *high school counselor* needs to know about tests and presents these data in a simple and disarming fashion. At the same time there are places in the discussion that require considerable sophistication. * The Minnesota group under the leadership of Donald Paterson has been so immersed in the development and use of group psychological tests that they often overlook the more limited approaches and exposure of others in guidance and counseling who lack such an extensive and rich background. Thus it would be well for any college instructor planning to use this text to note carefully the spots where additional explanations are needed and to expand the material for beginning counselors. * Examples of this are included in the discussion of the "Nature of Counseling" on pages 9–13. Here the stress is on understanding the student as an individual in an educational setting but practically no mention is made of his having to function in groups. In developing knowledge about the individual the counselor needs as much ipsative or idiographic data as possible as well as competence in nonparametric statistics. Such competence is not discussed. In the context of a student's functioning in groups, there is no mention of the counselor's need for normative data and for the sociological background necessary to use such data effectively (although this is discussed in later chapters). In the same sense, if one were not personally acquainted with them, the authors might seem to be presenting an extremely authoritarian approach to counseling when they say (p. 12), "Seldom will we be able to form a picture that encompasses all of our information, *one that completely satisfies us* (italics mine) as adequately describing the pupil. At best, we can obtain a concept of each person that allows us to make some inferences regarding his goals and objectives and to help that person, his family, and his teachers explore means of reaching those goals or of finding new ones." At the same time the stress in succeeding chapters is on use of *all* data concerning the individual in helping him make effective life choices. * The body of the material is devoted to an excellent assessment of tests and test usage, with illustrative cases. * [The] last chapter contains a brief summary of selected tests judged useful to the high school counselor. The chapter is nowhere near as detailed as the discussion of these same tests in Buros, nor does it contain discussions of pertinent validating research such as those presented in Super and Crites. Perhaps it would have been wiser to omit this last chapter in favor of expanding earlier chapters dealing with the use of tests in guidance and counseling. * On the whole, the book presents basic information about the counselor's use of tests and it does so in a simple, readable fashion. One cannot help thinking that if the material had been broadened somewhat to emphasize use of tests in areas other than that of high school counseling, the text would be more usable in a general course on group tests.

J Counsel Psychol 10:409–10 w '63. Donald E. Super. * In one sense the title is descriptive: testing is dealt with in the context of guidance and counseling. In another sense the title might be misleading: this is not a book about tests. * In a book of 280 pages, of which only half is devoted to testing and tests, the treatment is of necessity brief. * The book is well written, and the ground covered is handled clearly and concisely. But it seems strange, in this year of grace, 1963, when many counselors are urging the extension and the intensification of counselor education, when other Minnesotans are providing leadership in raising standards, that this group should write a book on testing which assumes no background and which hardly deals with tests. Counselors taking a course on testing in counseling are generally, even in one-year programs, expected to have had a basic course in measurement, another in guidance, before they take this course. Berdie and his colleagues have written clearly and easily; it is regrettable that they have not written informatively on the central subject of their book. Not that the book is completely lacking in information on tests. The chapter on test administration is superior to most treatments of this subject, so often considered elementary and so generally dealt with too cavalierly. The inadequacy of the validity data on the Kuder is clearly pointed out, and the need for percentile tables for the Otis Quick-Scoring is noted—these critical notes are a pleasant departure from the blandness of the annotated test catalogues which too often appear in books on tests and which, in fact, constitute most of Chapter 15. For example, Otis' claim that his norms are nationally representative is cited, but the only criticism the authors make is that they are "not clearly defined," and the reliability of the Kuder is noted without indicating how the data were ascertained and with no mention of the very real problem of unreliability over the high school years. There are a number of unusual and good features, in addition to the chapter on test administration. Cases are worked into the text as illustrations. Expectancy tables are illustrated and explained. The role of parents is well handled. Follow-up studies are discussed (at proportionately too great length) and so is research by the counselor. There is a good treatment of the interview as an appraisal tool. This book will be welcomed by teachers who like to make testing courses painless for students by leaving out the scientific substance. It can hardly be welcomed, despite its many good features, by those who think that counselors should know something about tests as tests when using them with people.

Personnel & Guid J 42:716–7 Mr '64. Hugh M. Bell. * written primarily for counselors of secondary school pupils. The term "guidance" appears in the title, but is seldom referred to in the text. Evidently "counseling" is assumed to cover the same area as "guidance." This book has many excellent points to recommend it to the reader. The 15 chapters are logically arranged and the materials within each chapter well organized. A commendable feature is the integration of the materials on standardized testing with a discussion of personality dynamics and the counseling process. * An excellent discussion of the various national testing programs....is included. The book also contains a good chapter on counseling with parents and one on educational and occupational information. Another commendable feature is the inclusion of case studies of high school students in which test scores and other information on students' backgrounds and plans are interrelated. * A good discussion of the influence of physical and social factors on learning is included. A criticism of this book which should be directed toward secondary schools as well as the authors, grows out of the fact that high school counselors today are not doing, and probably won't be doing very soon, most of the things that are recommended in this text. The authors are familiar with this fact and cite studies which indicate that high school counselors today are basically clerks and administrative assistants. * Many would-be counselors who have received the kind of training recommended in this book suffer intense frustrations when they have to spend their time during the school year checking graduation requirements, recording pupil attendance, filing test information, and so forth. * A somewhat minor criticism has to do with the authors' use of the term "personality tests" so as to exclude measures of interest, aptitude, and achievement. Surely an individual's abilities and interest are as much a part of his total personality as are his feelings, attitudes, and values. * This is a scholarly book, attractive in format, and well written. It teaches something on every page. It gives dignity and stature to the field of counseling. One can only hope that soon practice in the schools will approximate the standards the authors have set for counselors.

[B77]

*Berdie, Ralph F.; Layton, Wilbur L.; Swanson, Edward O.; Hagenah, Theda; and Merwin, Jack C. **Counseling and the Use of Tests: A Manual for the State-Wide Testing Programs of Minnesota, Revised Edition.** Minneapolis, Minn.: University of Minnesota Press, 1962. Pp. xi, 192. Paper. $2.00. * For a review of an earlier edition, see B75.

[B78]

★Berger, Bernard; McCormack, James; Reiner, Harry; and Setzer, Charles J. **The Essay Test in Public Personnel Selection.** Personnel Brief No. 611. Chicago, Ill.: Public Personnel Association, 1961. Pp. iv, 21. Paper. $2.50. *

[B79]

★Bernard, William, and Leopold, Jules. **Test Yourself: A Handbook Based on Modern Psychological Methods, Fourth Edition.** Philadelphia, Pa.: Chilton Co., 1962. Pp. 99. $3.95. * (London: Souvenir Press Ltd. 16*s.*)

[B80]

★Bieliauskas, Vytautas J. **The House-Tree-Person (H-T-P) Research Review.** Beverly Hills, Calif.: Western Psychological Services, 1963. Pp. 50. Paper, spiral binding. $4.00. *

[B81]

★Birney, Robert C., and Teevan, Richard C., Editors. **Measuring Human Motivation: An Enduring Problem: Selected Readings.** Princeton, N.J.: D. Van Nostrand Co., Inc., 1962. Pp. ix, 181. Paper. $1.45. * (London: D. Van Nostrand Co., Ltd. 11*s.* 6*d.*)

Brit J Social & Clin Psychol 2:159 Je '63. W. R. Robinson. * the majority of....students should have access to most of the journals from which the nine articles in this volume are drawn. The articles are not supplemented by editorial comment and the unsupervised reader may well find it very difficult to integrate and evaluate the contents. Editorial reference to later theoretical and empirical work on the methods described would have been useful and brief passages to link the articles would have helped still further. As it is, this book can be really useful only to a limited section of the student body of this country. While the articles presented are all relevant to the measurement of human motivation, they do not constitute a representative sample of the field. As the title suggests the emphasis is upon methods of measurement rather than ways of thinking about motivation, while the projective methods command most attention. Further, the projective methods described are mainly of the intermediate type—imaginative stories told to fairly structured pictures. The four articles about this method are most useful: they show the manner in which the study of individual differences among the normal population has grown out of techniques originally designed to facilitate a clinical diagnosis, with a corresponding increase of concern about objectivity, reliability, and empirical validity in an experimental context. Psycho-analysis is directly represented by Freud, Jung and Ferenczi, whose article is devoted to Freud's theory of dreams. Freud's advice on the conduct of analytic interviews is a surprising selection, but not quite so surprising as the penultimate article by Taylor in which this author tests predictions from Hullian learning theory using a questionnaire for measuring motivation. The editors seem to have felt guilty suddenly about their limited frame of reference, but the isolated inclusion of an article using a more direct method of measurement is either inadequate or inappropriate. The final chapter mentions some of the limitations of projective techniques. The earlier chapters are well supported with sample protocols and their analysis. Thus no dominant theme is introduced, developed, and discussed. The editors set themselves an extraordinarily difficult task, and while their selections represent some excellent individual articles, the continuity can only be established by a reader already conversant with the problems of measuring human motivation.

Ed & Psychol Meas 24:165–6 sp '64. Edward Levonian. * This volume is intended to give the reader an overview of the origins of contemporary methods used in the measurement of human motivation. Yet this review has made no mention of the application of the psychometric method to this area, and this absence will be especially disturbing to the reader who does not find the term *measurement* entirely applicable to those chapters in this book which involved nothing more quantitative than content analysis. The editors explain this absence as reflecting the fact that the psychometric method of assessing human motivation deserves its own volume. Fine, but the remaining material presented in *Measuring Human Motivation* might then have been subsumed under a less inclusive title.

[B82]

★Bjerstedt, Åke. **Glimpses From the World of the School Child: Self and Other Explored in Dyadic Communication.** Sociometric Monograph No. 41. [Beacon, N.Y.: Beacon House, Inc., Publishers], 1960. Pp. 131. Paper. $3.50. * (*PA* 36: 1FC30B)

Am J Psychol 76:168–9 Mr '63. I. D. Steiner. What kinds of questions would you ask of a stranger if you wished to learn as many important facts as possible about him? What would you tell a stranger about yourself if you wished him to perceive you accurately? These two questions are the major tools with which Bjerstedt obtained data concerning children's self-perceptions and their perceptions of other people. * Although Bjerstedt acknowledges a debt to Murray for some of the concepts with which he approaches the task of analyzing his protocols, neither the content categories Bjerstedt employed nor the conclusions he reaches reflect great concern about elusive personality processes. This is primarily a book about a technique with which to investigate age and sex differences in the perceptions of children—or of adults. The author generally assumes that the manifest content of subjects' protocols reveals their tendencies to attach differential importance to various people, things, activities, and attributes; but no analysis of underlying personality mechanisms is undertaken. As might be expected, intercoder reliabilities tend to be high. But the validity of Bjerstedt's interpretations of his data remains in doubt, for he reports no systematic attempt to appraise the correctness of his conclusions. Probably this omission is not very serious because Bjerstedt tends to impute very little surplus meaning to his content categories, and he rarely editorializes about the possible implications of his data. Indeed, some readers will probably criticize him for failure to enumerate the theoretical questions for which his findings might be assumed to provide answers. This book does not attempt to rewrite anybody's theories or to prove that vast stores of new knowledge are soon to revolutionize our thinking. * The author has described a relatively simple but time-consuming technique by which it is possible to obtain and to categorize data about certain interesting and possibly critical behaviors of children. Presumably these data represent facets of interpersonal and intrapersonal perception. In view of the difficulties which have generally beset scholars in these areas of research, Bjerstedt's efforts should be regarded as a welcome contribution.

Cont Psychol 7:8–9 Ja '62. W. Cody Wilson. Contrary to the image that the title first aroused in the reviewer, *Glimpses from the World of the School Child* is directed to psychologists, not to teachers of school children. In it the author, a Swedish social psychologist who has visited and worked in the United States, presents a new data-gathering technique, a method for analyzing the data, and two empirical studies illustrating selected uses of the new technique. Bjerstedt is interested in both the individual with his phenomenological life space and the individual in interaction with others. He asks a subject first to tell what he would ask a stranger to find out quickly as many important things about him as possible, and secondly what he would tell another person about himself in order to give quickly as correct and complete a picture as possible; then two subjects, strangers, interview each other in turn to find out as much about each other as they can in a short specified time. The technique is simple enough to be used with children, yet interesting enough to be used with adults. * The technique shares in the advantages and disadvantages of many other relatively unstructured methods in current use; for example, it elicits a wealth of material that is self-selected by the respondent, but the material then has to be reduced to some more manageable form. The author provides a system for content analysis of the obtained protocols. The monograph has two weaknesses, both in the direction of incompleteness. First, the theoretical rationale provides neither sufficient context for the technique nor an adequate view of its relation to the variety of problems for which it might be useful. Secondly, the empirical examples, although they give a rich and interesting description of the kinds of data obtained by the technique, do not illustrate adequately its potential usefulness and breadth of application. The book will be of some interest to a wide variety of psychologists for it touches on a number of different areas: dyadic interaction, interpersonal perception, phenomenological life space, developmental changes, content analysis, communication across language barriers, and international attitudes. It would have been of greater interest had it been postponed until the technique had been explored more thoroughly, so that there could have been a more complete discussion of its relation to existing bodies of psychological knowledge and of its potential application in new investigations.

[B83]

★BLACK, HILLEL. **They Shall Not Pass.** New York: William Morrow & Co., Inc., 1963. Pp. ix, 342. $4.95. *

Personnel & Guid J 42:1037–8 Je '64. Charles A. Sukman. "Testing the Test Critics." Letter. * In a summing-up chapter, the author advocates the abolishment of all personality and career-choice questionnaires. He says this should be done, since, not only are the teachers and guidance counselors untrained in the use of such questionnaires, but these questionnaires can cause grievous harm to a child. Also, schools use these instruments simply because they have found a short cut method to handle large masses of students. He encourages parents to demand that these tests be abolished. What are we going to do about this anti-testing, anti-guidance counselor movement? Every effort must be made through in-service training, supervision, college courses, research, writings, public relations, and other means within our power to develop and maintain strong emphasis on accurate, logical, proper test interpretation and meaningful methods of imparting test results to teachers, students, parents, administrators, and others. We can't afford the risk of having *any* guidance counselor throw caution to the winds when interpreting test scores. Each and *every* counselor must be instilled with the realization that test results are influenced by many factors. Emotional disturbances, physical health deficiencies, home conditions, language barriers, are just a few of the many factors influencing test scores. The counselor must acknowledge and accept the philosophy that test scores are only partial indications of a student's behavior and such results must be used *only* in relation to *all* information about a student, not as ends in themselves. Only when we get this idea accepted and practiced by *all* counselors, can any fears and uncertainties we might have as to what effect we are having upon youngsters be allayed. Black's arguments are circumstantial and can be overcome, somewhat, by good, skillfully written publications describing the many accomplishments of guidance counselors in helping our youth. We need books of enough interest to get the kind of circulation and attention that books such as Black's and Gross's enjoy. Each of us objects strenuously, I am sure, to the innuendoes of this book, especially when we think of the lay person, who in reading such a book, gets only part of the *whole, real* story of testing and guidance counseling as practiced today. Of course, we are alarmed about what this book reveals. However, we are even more concerned about what this book hides. While Black warns parents they should be very disturbed by the fact that their child may be one of our victims, let us not allow these same parents to become victims of journalistic jargon, palpitating prose, glowing generalities, and sizzling semantics.

Personnel & Guid J 42:1044–5 Je '64. Joann Chenault. This is another bandwagon book, quasi anti-testing. A moderately well-read professional person is likely to find the issues and arguments old hat. But the author is writing to a lay public, not to APGA members. As might be expected, the implicit definitions of terms like intelligence, aptitude, and ability are not professional; there is a kind of naive TV-ad concept of what research data mean; and there are the usual anecdotes, generalizations, and unscientifically determined conclusions. * Even those who unequivocally abhor the use of tests may find this book unimpressive. Perhaps this is because the author's objections to testing are not primarily on philosophical grounds. It is easier to be indignant about something like deprivation of individuality than about the lack of face validity of "some" multiple-choice items. A sense of contradiction often overshadows the message. There is the inevitable, protective *however* following each argument (ACT may be unethical in hiring deans of admissions; *however,* a valid argument can be made for both ETS and SRA in that prominent educators can improve the quality of the product; mass testing is doing incalculable harm to thousands of students; *however,* tests can correct the fallibility of human judgment and may be truly beneficial; the admissions mania is deplorable; *however,* here are the ways you can get your child into college). Quotations from ETS and SRA staffs supporting each point somehow weaken the arguments. Parents, for whom the mystique of testing is supposedly exposed, may, happily, become more skeptical of the use of standardized tests; but many readers may be torn between contempt for testing and admiration for the well-informed remarks of the ETS staff. Certainly it is clear that the author's words are an intended attack against present practices in mass testing. Yet those same words leave little doubt that everything would be all right if only the testing Institution were in the capable hands of perceptive people like Mr. Black.

Sat R 46:56–7 D '63. Henry S. Dyer. * an interesting mixture of legitimate criticism, homely advice to parents, and propaganda. On the one hand, it gathers together some useful information about what tests can and cannot do and about the dangers of overinterpreting test results. On the other hand, its blurring of facts to make things look as bad as possible, its over-reliance on anecdotal evidence, its use of scare headlines for chapter titles (*e.g.,* "The Guillotine at the College Gate"), all add up to a performance more calculated to make the reader shudder than to help him get a balanced view of the field. This is unfortunate. The book says much to the general reader that has needed saying. But as an objective analysis of what is right and wrong with standardized testing, *They Shall Not Pass* flunks.

Sci 144:44 Ap 3 '64. M. H. Trytten. * a curious document, written by a layman in the testing world. At first blush (judging by the title and dust jacket), it would seem to promise to be a finger-pointing, "how terrible" exposé of the seamy side of testing. In actuality, one has the feeling that, although this may have been the author's original intent, he was more than a little persuaded that on the whole testing is necessary, inevitable, and only in certain respects occasionally vulnerable to attack. Much of Black's attack relates to undue rigidity in the use of test scores. Much of his comment, however, is aimed not at testing so much as at the unhappy psychological effects of the highly competitive situation with respect to admission to college. Most of his "viewing-with-alarm" is with respect to situations wherein testing is an element only. But, primarily, it seems to me that Black is speaking for common sense, and reasonably good judgment, in the selection and use of tests *

[B84]

★Black, John W., Editor. **Multiple-Choice Intelligibility Test.** Danville, Ill.: Interstate Printers & Publishers, Inc., 1963. Pp. 50. Paper. $1.50. *

[B85]

★Blau, Harold. **How to Write the College Entrance Examination "Writing Sample."** Philadelphia, Pa.: Chilton Co., 1961. Pp. xi, 100. Paper. $1.95. *

[B86]

★Bleifeld, Maurice. **How to Prepare for College Board Achievement Tests: Biology.** Great Neck, N.Y.: Barron's Educational Series, Inc., 1963. Pp. vi, 250. Paper, $2.25; cloth, $4.50. *

[B87]

★Block, Jack. **The Q-Sort Method in Personality Assessment and Psychiatric Research.** Springfield, Ill.: Charles C Thomas, Publisher, 1961. Pp. ix, 161. $6.75. * (*PA* 36:5HE61B) For reviews and excerpts from reviews, see 72.

[B88]

★Bloom, Benjamin S. **Stability and Change in Human Characteristics.** New York and London: John Wiley & Sons, Inc., 1964. Pp. xiv, 237. $7.00; 53*s*. *

[B89]

★Bloom, Benjamin S., and Peters, Frank R. **The Use of Academic Prediction Scales for Counseling and Selecting College Entrants.** New York: Free Press of Glencoe, 1961. Pp. xiii, 145. $5.95. *

Ed & Psychol Meas 24:428–30 su '64. Donivan J. Watley. The immediate attraction of this book is the statement...."With grade adjustments, the correlations (between high school and college grades) reach the level of +.70 to +.80 in contrast with the usual level of about +.50." * Three different methods for making adjustments are discussed—the Internal Method, the Aptitude Method, and the Achievement Method. Of the three, the first seems most interesting. This method involves finding the best fit between high school and college grades by first adjusting high school grades on the basis of college grades, and then in turn correcting college grades on the basis of high school grades. Bloom and Peters claim that by adjusting school and college grades for institutional variation they were able to increase the overall correlation between school and college grades from about .50 to .77. For a sample of 23 high schools they reported a median within-school correlation of .54 for unscaled school and college grades, and with scaled grades this was raised to .77. For 13 colleges they reported a median within-college correlation of .57 for unscaled school and college grades, and .68 for adjusted grades. Now, several factors must be considered in relation to grade adjustments. First, it must be remembered that the upper limit of predictive efficiency of internally scaled grades for any given college is determined by the average within-school-within-college correlation of school and college grades. Significant improvement from internal scaling cannot occur unless this average correlation is high, and unless large differences exist among schools in grading standards. It is important perhaps that Bloom and Peters obtained their data from the records of the National Registration Office for Secondary Schools, whose services are used primarily by private high schools. Since most students from these private schools then entered a relatively small number of rather selective colleges, the situation appears most conducive toward producing high within-school-within-college correlations. One wonders, however, how they were able to classify some of these secondary schools into a group on the basis of the students having earned "somewhat" higher average grades in college than they received in high school. These same remarks have been made elsewhere by Lindquist. Lindquist's research with the ACT Program is significant in relation to the question of Bloom and Peters' sampling. With 31 colleges and an average of over 300 students per college, Lindquist reported the median improvement after adjustments to be only .041. The improvement in medians for a sample of 608 high schools was only .008. Probably Lindquist's ACT sample was somewhat more representative of American high schools and colleges than was the sample used by Bloom and Peters, although the ACT sample is not free from bias either. The ACT research does, however, cast serious doubt upon any general and wholesale use of internal scaling methods. The individual college is interested primarily in increasing its own predictive efficiency. Bloom and Peters' data are extremely difficult to interpret in this connection. Of their sample of 13 colleges, 5 had less than 70 cases included. With *N*'s of this size the stability of the results is highly questionable. The inclusion of both more colleges and more students per college would have done much to ease the concern over sampling fluctuations. Another crucial point is that no attempt was made to crossvalidate their results within colleges. Also of much interest to the individual college is the value of adjusted school grades when they are used in a multiple correlation in conjunction with admission test scores. In other words, does an adjusted high school average contribute or add more to a multiple correlation than does an unadjusted high school average? Bloom and Peters did not deal with this question at all. Both Lindquist's research with the ACT Program and Willingham's results at Georgia Tech led to the conclusion that adjusting school grades increases multiple correlations such a small amount that the additional increase is impractical considering the amount of work required. Because of the criticisms mentioned above, and because of the results of other studies attempting to corroborate Bloom and Peters' findings, internal scaling methods do not seem to be so promising as Bloom and Peters would lead us to believe. One should think twice (and maybe more than that) before jumping on the Academic Prediction Scales bandwagon. Rather than setting up national or state programs for making school and college adjustments, as Bloom and Peters suggest, it appears much more reasonable for each college to continue to handle this problem individually.

[B90]

★BLUM, HENRIK L.; PETERS, HENRY B.; AND BETTMAN, JEROME W. **Vision Screening for Elementary Schools: The Orinda Study.** Berkeley, Calif.: University of California Press, 1959. Pp. xi, 146. Paper. $3.75. *

Am J Optom 36:449–50 Ag '59. Charles R. Stewart. * The results of the Orinda Study show how it is possible to overcome the serious deficiencies of several visual screening procedures currently used to identify children who need visual care. Included....is a realistic, practical, and efficient design for a vision program in elementary schools. Other valuable contents of this publication include an excellent review of the literature on school vision screening; a cost analysis of visual screening; an analysis of a questionnaire sent to optometrists and ophthalmologists concerning criteria for referral; and nearly 100 references. It is of interest to note that comparison of the results of ophthalmological and optometric examinations of the children used in this study revealed no significant differences. For several decades attempts have been made to devise tests which will rapidly and efficiently identify school children who need visual care. These tests have been administered by teachers, nurses, or mothers; sometimes by or with the help of optometrists and/or ophthalmologists. In reports of the results of such vision screening tests, none have a sufficiently high degree of efficiency: If a test picks out most of those who need visual care, it also fails many who do *not* need visual care; on the other hand, if the number of false failures is reduced, then many pupils who need visual care are missed. The procedures tested in the Orinda Study and reported in *Vision Screening for Elementary Schools* provide the basis for a vision testing program in which the efficiency of referral is exceptionally high. It is noteworthy that to attain a high degree of efficiency it is necessary to have a "qualified" professional examiner (optometrist or ophthalmologist) participate in the testing. None of several other procedures come close to producing the same high degree of efficiency. It appears also that accurate referral for refractive error requires retinoscopy as one of the screening tests. Because of the importance of school children and school screening programs to optometry, *Vision Screening for Elementary Schools* should be read and studied by every optometrist.

[B91]

★BOHM, EWALD. **A Textbook in Rorschach Test Diagnosis for Psychologists, Physicians, and Teachers.** Translated by Anne G. Beck and Samuel J. Beck. New York: Grune & Stratton, Inc., 1959. Pp. xiii, 322. $7.75. *

Am J Psychother 14:801–2 O '60. Daniel G. Brown. * Perhaps one of the main values of this book is that it provides American readers with a survey of the principles and clinical applications of the Rorschach in European psychologic and psychiatric practice and research. As such, it is an important supplement to such recognized references as Beck, Klopfer, Rapaport, Schafer, and others. Some idea of the relative proportion of European in contrast to American writers cited in this book, may be seen from an analysis of the references in three chapters ("Neuroses," "Psychoses," and "Depressions"). It shows approximately three-fourths of the references to be non-English publications, while about one-fourth are in English. * Bohm writes about the Rorschach with much enthusiasm and confidence, perhaps a little too much. * research findings, at least those reported by American workers, do not support such optimistic endorsements of the Rorschach or, for that matter, any other projective-type evaluative instrument * A particularly useful discussion is provided relative to the organization and presentation of a Rorschach summary. * Special mention should be made of the chapter entitled "Special Phenomena." This includes 67 different items, each briefly defined and interpreted, such as: Card Rejection; Various Kinds of Shock (Red, Dark, Blue, Brown, White, Kinesthetic); Symmetry; Confabulations; Contaminations; Perseveration; Infantile Responses; Self References; Disavowal; Fusion of Figure and Ground; Sexual Symbol Stupor; Mask Responses. Many interpretive insights are brought out in Bohm's analyses of these and other special phenomena. The book would have been justified on the basis of this chapter alone. This text may be highly recommended to all those who use or make use of the Rorschach in practice or research. It is relatively well documented, well organized, extremely well written and translated. It is a distinct contribution to projective psychology and should become a major companion volume to the standard Rorschach references.

Brit J Psychol 51:187 My '60. B. Semeonoff. * the most systematic and ambitious attempt yet published to produce a comprehensive guide to Rorschach diagnosis. It is systematic in that the author not only explicitly identifies himself with the psychoanalytic approach to personality study (as indeed most Rorschach practitioners do at least implicitly) but categorically states "we do not believe that a Rorschach test can be exhaustively interpreted without knowl- of psychoanalytic theory." * It is ambitious in so far as guidance—often avowedly "rule of thumb"—is given for much more refined diagnosis than Rorschach writers usually offer. * A further valuable and unusual feature....is its frequent reference to the work of European psychiatrists and Rorschach writers, notably Binder, Zulliger, Oberholzer and Loosli-Usterli, whose work is relatively unfamiliar, at any rate in detail, to British or American psychologists. Unfortunately the continental bias makes itself felt by the presence in the text of large numbers of pseudo-technical terms, some based on false etymology and nearly all open to condemnation by the authors of a recent psychological dictionary as examples of bogus erudition. Thus such words abound as amphithymia (and also *ambi*thymic), ixothymia (and ixophrenia), schizaffinic, pathotropic, encephalopathy, pfropfschizophrenia, sophropsychic (thus in the text; in the index—more correctly?—*sopro*psychic). One may perhaps be forgiven if one confesses that the vulgarism "baffling with science" comes to mind, and if one points out, by way of retaliation, that four mistakes appear in the printing of the six-letter Greek word from which "ixothymia" is derived. All this makes for heavy going, and—again regrettably—the translation itself has a marked continental flavour. Furthermore, although the book is intended for the beginner as well as for the specialist, some of the advice given to the learner seems to the reviewer to be positively harmful, e.g. the recommendation that locations should be noted in words rather than by the use of the location chart. The conclusion one seems to come to is that this is not a book for the beginner, nor for those only partially convinced of the value of the Rorschach method. For the advanced practitioner, on the other hand, it opens out new vistas.

J Proj Tech 22:462–3 D '58. Henry P. David. This is an important book * By incorporating most of the major European advances reported in the half-dozen years between the 1951 and 1957 editions, Bohm's volume has grown even more encyclopedic. It has been widely accepted as *the* standard text of classical Swiss Rorschach tradition * In these days of conflicting Rorschach systems, claims, and counterclaims, it is a richly rewarding experience to browse through Bohm's detail-laden but well organized and succinctly written text. Almost stubbornly, Bohm takes his stand with Rorschach, rejecting complex modifications or dilutions of basic premises, and warning students that productive research requires uniformity in administration and scoring as well as Rorschach's original inkblots. This seemingly conservative attitude is hedged by an acceptance of innovations which leave Rorschach's ideas intact and by a readiness to revise concepts unsupported by factual evidence. The second edition contains much additional information and fresh research suggestions, but follows the same excellent, systematic contents outline * There is an especially lucid subsection on the phychoanalytic theory of neuroses, noteworthy for its moderate views (in the Swiss and Rorschach's own tradition). * While his conclusions are frequently labelled "tentative" and are not guaranteed to survive the rigors of IBM type research, they are, at the very least, stimulating and provocative. For example, the material on constitutional factors, so representative of European interests, should open new vistas to Ph.D. candidates in search of thesis ideas. Regrettably, the same high caliber is not reflected in the survey of Rorschach work with children and the aged, or in the discussion of theoretical foundations, where recent American contributions are dismissed on the ground that the instrument used is no longer strictly comparable with that originated by Rorschach. The volume concludes with an extremely valuable cross-section of 31 illustrative Rorschach protocols, each complete with scoring and tabulation, diagnostic impression, brief personality analyses, and clinical summary. This important teaching aide is not in the American edition. Neither are the especially prepared, multicolored detail identification plates, nor the German-English-French-Latin glossary of Rorschach symbols, regrettable omissions. The translation, by Samuel and Anne Beck, was seen only in the galley proof stage. While we must be grateful to the Becks for introducing Bohm to the English language area, rejoicing is somewhat tempered by what seems to this reviewer an uncommonly stiff and pedantic version of Bohm's free-flowing style and by the publisher's unfortunate decision to cut corners and delete important material. * The loss of the historical introduction, the cautions on use and abuse, and the illustrative case protocols are unfortunate, but do not diminish the virtue of translating the work of a sensitive Rorschach teacher and his extensive review of European literature previously missed or dismissed in this country. The Becks have eminently succeeded in bringing to our attention Bohm's concepts of fundamental Rorschach principles, test procedures, and the clinical significance of materials obtained. All in all, what really matters is that Bohm is available in English and that another language barrier has been removed, facilitating international Rorschach communication. This translation of a Swiss Rorschach text, the first since the *Psychodiagnostik,* was well worth the long wait.

[B92]

★BORDUA, DAVID J. **Prediction and Selection of Delinquents.** Facts and Facets Series No. 17. Washington, D.C.: Children's Bureau, Welfare Administration, United States Department of Health, Education, and Welfare, 1961. Pp. ii, 29. Paper. Gratis. *

[B93]

★BOWER, ELI M. **Early Identification of Emotionally Handicapped Children in School.** Springfield, Ill.: Charles C Thomas, Publisher, 1960. Pp. xiii, 120. $5.50. * (*PA* 35:809) For related reviews, see 164.

Mental Hyg 46:141 Ja '62. Frederick H. Allen. This book on an important matter is pointed toward the opportunity of the schools to detect the early evidences in a child's behavior that he is emotionally disturbed or handicapped, the latter term preferred by the author. It outlines a way to utilize the extensive knowledge of the classroom teacher and of the children in the author's "class play" plan which includes a rather detailed form to be filled in. This sounds like a very useful approach and one that can be used in our schools. * The book should prove useful to schools making efforts not just at early detection but in modifying programs and services which are based on a deeper understanding of the child's special needs.

[B94]

★BOYDEN, BARTLETT W., AND HINDLE, PETER G. **How to Boost Your Marks in the S.A.T.** New York: Macfadden-Bartell Corporation, 1964. Pp. 143. Paper. $0.75. *

[B95]

★BRICKLIN, BARRY; PIOTROWSKI, ZYGMUNT A.; AND WAGNER, EDWIN E. **The Hand Test: A New Projective Test With Special Reference to the Prediction of Overt Aggressive Behavior.** Springfield, Ill.: Charles C Thomas, Publisher, 1962. Pp. x, 100. $5.00. * (*PA* 37:1191) For related reviews, see 216.

J Nerv & Mental Dis 137:405 O '63. Melvin Roman. In recent years we have seen a phenomenal growth in the creation of new "tailor-made" projective techniques. Some of these new techniques have been designed to test specific research hypotheses, while others have been developed to approach more directly a delimited diagnostic problem. The Hand Test is another of the "tailor-made" variety in that it has been designed with special reference to aggressive behavior. The technique is described by the authors as a quick (administration and scoring time: 15 minutes) and useful device for the detection of potentially aggressive behavior. The test consists of ten cards, nine of which depict the human hand in ambiguous poses, and a tenth which is blank. To the first nine cards the subject is asked to tell what each hand is doing. To the blank card the subject is asked first to imagine a hand and then to describe what the imagined hand might be doing. The scoring system yields an acting-out score which, according to the data presented, seems capable of differentiating overtly aggressive adult groups from non-aggressive groups. The data are inconclusive when it comes to differentiating groups of children. Since there is little evidence presented to indicate that *The Hand Test* does anything more efficiently or effectively than other techniques it is difficult to evaluate its specific clinical and/or research usefulness.

[B96]

★BROOKS, ROBERT J. **Andy and the IQ: A Guide to Intelligence for Correctional Workers.** Menard, Ill.: Illinois State Penitentiary, 1961. Pp. 47. Paper. Gratis. * (*PA* 36:1JO47B)

[B97]

★BROWNSTEIN, SAMUEL C., AND WEINER, MITCHELL. **Barron's How to Prepare for College Entrance Examinations, Third Edition.** Great Neck, N.Y.: Barron's Educational Series, Inc., 1962. Pp. 443. Paper, $2.50; cloth, $5.25. * (Earlier editions published in 1954, 1955, and 1958.)

[B98]

★BUCHORI, MOCHTAR. **Some Problems Pertaining to the Examination and the Selection of Prospective Students of the Teacher Training and Educational Sciences, Bandung (Academic Year 1958/1959).** Translated by Siti Aisah Adisapoetra. Bandung, Indonesia: Institute for Educational Research, Faculty of Teacher Training and Educational

Sciences, Padjadjaran State University, 1959. Pp. vi, 41. Paper. *

[B99]

★BUNGER, FRED ANTON. **Cultural Forces and Academic Success in College Freshmen.** Bulletin of the Bureau of School Service, College of Education, University of Kentucky, Vol. 33, No. 1. Lexington, Ky.: the Service, September 1960. Pp. 91. Paper. $1.00. *

[B100]

★BURGEMEISTER, BESSIE B. **Psychological Techniques in Neurological Diagnosis.** New York: Hoeber Medical Division, Harper & Row, Publishers, Inc., 1962. Pp. viii, 248. $7.50. (London: Harper & Row Ltd. 56*s*.) *

J Proj Tech 26:487–8 D '62. Walter G. Klopfer. * The general and most substantive part of the book is the first 60 pages. At the beginning there is a thorough and systematic review of current theory and knowledge concerning the psychological sequelae of neurological disorders. The difficulty in this area concerns the relatively picayune approach of neurophysiology with its concomitant difficulty in identifying large functional units as contrasted to the rather vague holistic approach of psychology with its reluctance to make specific predictions. The picture is confused by problems of definition and etiology. * The basic hypothesis in using intelligence tests is that organicity is measured by the estimated discrepancy between optimal and present functioning. * A review of the literature in this area is rather limited and disappointing, especially since little of the rather overwhelming negative evidence concerning the utility of Wechsler-type scales for the detection of organicity is mentioned. * Burgemeister's reaction to the failure of quantitative approaches, as illustrated by the Shipley-Hartford, Hunt, and Halstead, is to espouse qualitative approaches such as the Hanfman-Kasanin, Zaslow and Goldstein techniques. Her motto seems to be that a devil unknown is better than a devil known. Whether it is really true that qualitative observations which cannot be proved invalid are superior to quantitative approaches of doubtful validity is of course, a matter of taste. A discussion of projective methods is also a little disappointing. * In her discussion of the Rorschach she mentions the various lists of signs of which she seems quite enamoured. However, she does not mention some of the most frequent criticisms of the sign approach, such as the overlapping of groups, the lack of utility of signs based on extreme groups for borderline diagnoses, the frequent lack of behavioral referents, the unreliability of judgments, etc. * In a brief section on the neuropsychological examination, Burgemeister makes some suggestions for conducting the examination and integrating the findings. Her suggestions seem sound, but are rather sparse, and could well be elaborated. Little emphasis is given to the necessity of diagnosing not only the nature and degree of the organic disorder, but also the patient's particular emotional reactions to it. Emotions in this book are thought of more as signs of organicity rather than reactions to it. The discussion of various organic syndromes that follows is of a pattern. In each instance there is a sophisticated discussion of the syndrome, its neurophysiological characteristics, and its psychological sequelae. This is followed by brief remarks concerning expected behavior on psychological tests which are in turn illustrated by case histories. * In each one of these sections, the author does her best. The general description of these syndromes and the suggestions as to test indicators should certainly be useful to any clinical psychologist or clinical psychology trainee working for the first time in a setting where such pathology is apt to occur. * The book appears to be somewhat padded with the many case illustrations and test protocols, but these will undoubtedly be of value to students and instructors in illustrating the various points made. The over-all effect of the volume is that of modesty rather than grandiosity. The little knowledge that we possess concerning the utilization of psychological tests and observations for the diagnosis of organic brain damage is nicely brought together between two covers and the book will be of great value in both training students and reminding experienced clinicians of these areas when they run across them only infrequently. No one should be disappointed if Burgemeister can only review work that has been done. Her admonition to emphasize qualitative observations in the detection of neuropsychological disorders strikes a responsive chord, but begs the question as to the validity of diagnosis based on such unquantifiable criteria.

[B101]

★BUROS, OSCAR K. **Schematization of Old and New Concepts of Test Reliability Based Upon Parametric Models.** Highland Park, N.J.: Gryphon Press, 1963. Pp. 37. Paper, mimeographed. $1.00. *

[B102]

BUROS, OSCAR KRISEN, EDITOR. **The Third Mental Measurements Yearbook.** Highland Park, N.J.: Gryphon Press, 1949. Pp. xv, 1047. $18.00. * (*PA* 23:3523) For reviews, see 4:B71.

[B103]

BUROS, OSCAR KRISEN, EDITOR. **The Fourth Mental Measurements Yearbook.** Highland Park, N.J.: Gryphon Press, 1953. Pp. xxv, 1163. $20.00. * (*PA* 27:6280) For reviews, see 5:B84.

[B104]

★BUROS, OSCAR KRISEN, EDITOR. **The Fifth Mental Measurements Yearbook.** Highland Park, N.J.: Gryphon Press, 1959. Pp. xxix, 1292. $22.50. * (*PA* 34:78)

Am J Mental Def 64:928–9 Mr '60. James G. Foshee. This volume, like its predecessors, should continue to be the "Bible" for all test users. It is the eighth in Buros' well-known series of publications * another major contribution to all test users—whether one uses tests with mentally retarded individuals or with college students.

Austral J Psychol 12:138–9 Je '60. R. L. Want. * Reference to this book, if not undertaken lightly, is an intellectual and educational experience. When the reader closes it he cannot fail to be more critical of his own thinking, better informed about testing, and more sophisticated in the use of tests than he was before. The reader who hopes to find a test tailored for a particular purpose must, in the nature of things, very often be disappointed. Variations in educational methods, variations in occupational requirements, currency differences, and cultural differences of more subtle type limit the usefulness of tests for particular purposes. The book is therefore of less interest in telling us what tests are available for purchase than it is in keeping us informed about the broad field of testing and in giving us pointers as to where we may seek specific information about tests. From this point of view, its value would be increased if an index of tests in current use but not commercially available could be added. * However, the generous space allotted to Australian tests leads one to believe that the coverage is extremely broad. * One can think of no other single event that represents the mature status of psychology as a profession as effectively as does the publication of the volumes in this series. The *Yearbook* is more than a mere book of reference. It is a milestone in the history of psychology, and a bible for those who are interested in the theory of psychological testing.

Brit J Ed Studies 8:187–9 My '60. W. D. Wall. The successive *Mental Measurements Yearbooks* have proved themselves indispensable instruments for all who use tests. This and the preceding volumes are a testimony to Buros's remarkable and painstaking scholarship and devotion over nearly a quarter of a century. They are too a massive (quite literally) monument to the immense growth of the science of mental measurement, particularly in the inter- and post-war years. It is fitting that Buros should dedicate the present volume to Burt who, more than any other European except perhaps Binet, can be regarded as a founding father of psychometrics. The work behind this and preceding volumes is something more than that of a mere compiler. The editor's instructions to test reviewers have quite deliberately drawn attention to the various aspects of tests which should be evaluated. He has insisted that reviewers should be critical in the best sense, drawing attention in an impartial way to the good as well as to the bad points of the test in question and that full discussion should be given of the technical data supplied by the author. Because of this, the successive Yearbooks have played an important part, if not the principal part, in rescuing the mental measurements movement from the discredit into which it looked as if it might be led by over-enthusiasm (and sometimes lack of scientific scruple). The majority of tests are in English and of these the bulk are constructed in the United States. It is not surprising therefore to find that most of the entries and of the reviewers are American. Over the past years however, an increasing number of tests, books and reviewers have been drawn from all over the English speaking world. The present volume is now fully comprehensive so far as American, British and Commonwealth tests are concerned. In addition selected tests produced in non-English speaking countries likely to be of interest to English speaking psychologists are included. In a reference work which already lists over nine hundred tests and nearly five hundred books published since 1952, it is perhaps a mere cavil to regret that the coverage is not even more comprehensive and world-wide. However there is a small and steady production of tests and of books produced in Europe and elsewhere but not in English about which English-speaking psychologists should know. Moreover the science of psychometrics in Europe needs the normative influence which the successive Yearbooks have wielded. Thus this reviewer would plead for an extension in the scope of the work. Unhappily not merely is such an extension unlikely, but it seems that future volumes will not attempt to cover work appearing in Australia, Canada, New Zealand, South Africa and the U.K. The Sixth Yearbook (1962) will be a predominantly American one. The decision—in view of the growth of test production everywhere—is understandable; it is nonetheless to be regretted, unless it provokes the production of a companion volume. The present Yearbook supplements the Third and Fourth Yearbooks which remain indispensable. For the most part, the tests have been reviewed specially for this edition and the list of reviewers is impressive, including as it does, most of the leading English-speaking experts. For each test, full details are given including such necessary information as publisher, price, age levels for which it is intended, testing time, and an indication as to whether technical data on standardization are available. Each test reviewed is accompanied by a bibliography of published and unpublished research work concerned with it. Again, the present reviewer finds matter for regret in the editor's intention not to publish these bibliographies in the future. Annexed to the volume are lists of periodical publications, of test publishers, an alphabetic index of tests and books reviewed, an author index, and a list of tests carefully classified according to the field covered. The first two of these are in their own right valuable reference works. One hesitates to use superlatives but it is difficult to see how the present volume could be presented in a more useful way or how it could contain more practical information. In conception and execution, it ranks as a model for other fields of learning and shows what one scholarly mind can achieve in co-operation with colleagues in many different countries.

Brit J Med Psychol 32:303 pt 4 '59. Once again this monumental work presents an exhaustive review of the test literature in the seven-year period—1952 to 1958.

Brit J Psychol 51:186–7 My '60. B. Semeonoff. "Indispensable" is the word that comes most readily from one's pen in attempting to review a *Mental Measurements Yearbook.* The term Yearbook is of course strictly a misnomer, since this is, as the title tells us, only the fifth of the series * it seems inconceivable....that any psychologist concerned with mental measurement in its broadest sense (educational assessment, projective techniques and questionnaires are all included) should not know what can be found in the Yearbooks * Apart from the tenor of the reviews, no evaluation of the books or tests is offered. This may or may not be a good thing; the present reviewer is inclined to the former view. British psychometry is unusually adequately covered * It is pleasant, too, to note that the dedication of the book is "To Cyril Burt."

Brit J Stat Psychol 12:165–6 N '59. Charlotte Banks. * It is astonishing that these invaluable volumes are not better known. Almost every day the staff of psychological departments and the editors of psychological journals receive requests from many quarters inquiring about the existence or the merits of tests of various types; and the answer almost invariably is, "You will find all the information you want in the latest *Yearbook.*" * Psychologists on this side of the Atlantic will feel gratified to find that a yearbook coming from a country which has itself contributed so lavishly to test construction is dedicated to a British pioneer—Sir Cyril Burt. Since a vast amount of the labour, expense, and organization entailed by the selection and arrangement of the material for this volume has been borne personally by Professor and Mrs. Buros, test-users in every country are under an immense debt to them for their courageous and self-sacrificing enterprise. If only in his own interests, every psychologist and educationist should see to it that the series has his fullest support.

Child Develop Abstracts 34:214–5 O–D '60. R. E. Muuss. * The Fifth Yearbook again is monumental and its statistics surpass those of the previous isues. * contains an unusually well organized index and reference system * Test reviewers are asked to give "frankly critical" reviews that combine strength and weaknesses in a judicious manner. A few of the reviews are excessively critical and sometimes in real disagreement with other reviews of the same test. * Nevertheless, Buros has again produced another standard work on psychological testing, critical but comprehensive, well organized, interesting and informative. Since the yearbooks are not in competition with any other similar publication, they have become indispensable to many professional groups, especially psychologists, educators, counselling personnel, the student of tests and measurements, and are a "must" for the college library.

Cont Psychol 5:387–90 D '60. Charles R. Langmuir. [This review and the biographical note preceding it are being reprinted in full because they describe so well the historical development of *The Mental Measurements Yearbooks.*] *The editor and compiler of these test codices is well described by the reviewer. The volumes constitute the life-work of Professor Buros, who has worked at them compulsively for many years now, assisted by his wife, a loyal editorial associate, and a few others when the rush of a new volume is on, aided by the complacent support of Rutgers University, but with no other backing, for even the Gryphon Press is the Buroses'. Mr. Langmuir, the reviewer, is Director of Research and Special Projects in the Psychological Corporation of New York City. For a number of years he worked with the Carnegie Foundation for the Advancement of Teaching and was adjutant in the formation of the Graduate Record Examination.* Publication of *The Fifth Mental Measurements Yearbook* marks twenty-five years of remarkable editorial achievement. Actually, the *Fifth Yearbook* is the eighth item in a series of which the first three were bibliographies. Even though the early publications are not in any way comparable to the five yearbooks, they are part of the over-all development. The germ of Buros' unique creation in psychometric literature is found in the energizing ideas of his first bibliographical product. The 1935 and 1936 issues not only updated Gertrude Hildreth's *Bibliography of Mental Tests and Rating Scales* (1933), but also added practical aids to help the person searching for a test suitable for some purpose. Catalog information about the cost of the tests and the time required for administration was included and, most significantly, references to the literature reporting experimental studies about specific tests were cited. In these early publications the editor's extensive effort to make the information available in the practical, as well as the scholarly, sense can be seen in the elaborate care he gave to classification of entries, indices, and cross references. All of these germinal efforts have been brought to elaborate development in the five yearbooks. In the third bibliography (1937) the publication was expanded from the initial forty-four pages by an additional one hundred pages, most of which were given over to reprinting excerpts of reviews of books, monographs, and other publications related to educational and psychological measurement. In a prefatory paragraph, the editor turned on the lamp of missionary zeal that clearly motivated and energized the colossal development that followed. He stated that the book review section, among other values, was expected to aid readers to be more discriminating, to make available some of the provocative statements made by reviewers, and to raise the quality of reviewing. It was but a short step to the idea of disseminating in one publication descriptive and critical reviews of tests along with the bibliographical entries. In the following year, the first of the "frankly critical" yearbooks was born. In the mid-1930s, the state of psychometric publishing is indicated in the following comment included in a presentation to the annual conference of the Progressive Education Association. "Today, it is practically impossible....to make a thorough appraisal of the construction, validation, and use of most standard tests being published because of the limited amount of trustworthy information supplied by test publishers and authors....There is a greater immediate need for critical evaluations of existing tests and their uses than for the construction of new tests. If only 10% of the money which the foundations have granted to test makers in recent years could have been given to endow a test consumers' research organization, I am sure that the testing movement would be more advanced than it is today. Such an organization would have a tremendous effect on the quality of standard tests published." Sandiford offered a less grandiose proposal in his review of the third bibliography. He suggested, "Buros' annual publication would be made much more useful if he would mark with a prominent star those which were valid, reliable, and had satisfactory norms. Then busy workers could neglect the rest, or if they wasted their money on gold bricks, the fault would be their own." An attempt to start a test consumers' research organization was unsuccessful, but Buros was able to obtain financial support of the School of Education of Rutgers University to develop a cooperative test reviewing project and the contributing participation of more than one hundred professional workers who were willing to write "frankly critical reviews." At least half of the names on the original roster of cooperative reviewers would be widely recognized in educational circles today and most of them with recognition of some distinction. The idea of publishing evaluative commentary on the psychometric devices that were appearing by the hundreds leads to a result somewhere between the presumed objective standards of a consumers' research laboratory and an authoritative all-wise opinion. The onus of decision about the assignment of "prominent stars" could not be assigned to a single judge and it could not be tolerated by the editor. All the problems of critical reviewing are present—subjective judgment, personal bias, uncertainty about objectives, paucity of data, and many others. It should not be expected that these problems would vanish because the material under review happens to be named *objective tests.* Perhaps the most insidious difficulty is the semantic confusion that pervades psychology when applied to education, guidance, mental health, and adjustment. Buros was sensitive to the issues and he has lavished gargantuan effort on the problem of getting appropriate editorial decision not subject to valid charges of bias in a context that was dedicated to improving the state of affairs by frankly critical exposure. It is interesting to see how it worked out. If one is to engineer the publication of evaluative and hopefully definitive judgments without specific personal decisions, it is necessary to recruit a panel of qualified experts to do the job. Buros chose to select a "representative sampling of able test technicians, subject matter specialists, and psychologists." This editorial decision is a choice of policy. It escapes the need for the editor to assign or withhold prominent stars, but it does not settle the matter of qualifications since there is plenty of variation within and among the separate categories. It does, however, establish as a fact that Sandiford's hope for an authoritative judgment will not be satisfied. The end product will be instead a "representation of various viewpoints in American education." To assure the representative requirement, invitation to participate was sent to "conservatives and progressives, to users and non-users of the tests to be reviewed, and to friends and opponents of objective type tests." Having gone so far to avoid responsibility for absolute judgments, Buros introduced an important correction factor. He sought two or more reviews for each test. When he took this editorial posture, he found himself impaled on both horns of the democratic dilemma. Acceptance of the idea of broad representation of views on many discrete items like tests leads logically to the necessity for broad representation of opinion on each item. On the other hand, how can one know that a heterogeneous representation represents or even encompasses competence of evaluative judgment? The preface to the 1938 volume contained the conventional statement that "both favorable and unfavorable comments will be gratefully received." They were received and gratefully, too, as indicated by their inclusion to the extent of five full and delicious pages quoted in the 1940 *Yearbook,* the second of the series. It is hard to say whether an aggrieved author is more aggrieved than an aggrieved publisher, but the theme songs of both thrust the editor into an extension of his initial ideas and a more elaborate expression of them. The long and interesting introduction to the second *Yearbook* shows the results of tossing an editor from this horn to that, namely, the editor's problems of deciding who should review what and how to get broad representation of points of view while simultaneously supplying the unsophisticated test user with competent, well-qualified, fair, and unbiased judgments. Buros describes in full how he went about selecting reviewers for the second volume. The initial 133 contributors were solicited for suggestions of others and the others suggested others until a list of 600 potential reviewers was assembled. For each of these, objective information descriptive of education, professional position occupied, research interests, and bibliographies of recent writings was compiled in order to "increase the likelihood of securing reviewers who are especially competent to review a particular test." Invitations were finally sent to 400 prospective reviewers. Here the idea of competence was made explicit. On the other side, an effort was made to choose persons "representing a wide variety of positions and viewpoints....as a result, a very heterogeneous group of reviewers have cooperated—classroom teachers, city school research workers, clinical psychologists, curriculum specialists, guidance specialists, personnel workers, psychologists, subject-matter specialists and test technicians. Various groups and schools of thought within each of these classes of reviewers have cooperated. For example, the reviewers include Americans and Britishers, authors and non-authors of standard tests, conservatives and progressives, persons with and persons without experience in administering the tests reviewed, proponents and opponents of essay type tests, proponents and opponents of objective type tests, users and non-users of standard tests, and well-known and little-known persons." This is surely a classic example of a search for rampant representativeness. In the next paragraph Buros pointed out that all the qualifications required of the ideal reviewer rarely exist in any one person and consequently it is necessary to have each test reviewed by several persons who are considered especially competent in their fields and who have the courage to speak frankly and honestly. In the 1940 *Yearbook* this idea was fully extended; Buros wrote "this representation of various viewpoints can only be achieved by having each test reviewed three to six times and in the case of a few tests, even more." By 1940 the philosophical bases of the editorial policy with respect to selection of reviewers and choice of their assignments had fully matured. The publication in January 1941 of the second *Yearbook* included tests published up to September 1940. It represented an achievement of prodigious individual labor—scholarly and executive and clerical. Efforts to obtain financial support from the foundations most interested in the development of testing had been uniformly rejected. The WPA provided some clerical assistance, but the support of sponsorship was fundamentally lacking. The story of this interval is encapsulated in the little fact that the volume is not copyrighted and that the business address of the publisher happens to be the residence of the editor. The management of the project right down to and including the wrapping and mailing of packages to fill orders was the personal activity of the editor. The fact that the book achieved publication is startling. The publication of the 1940 *Yearbook* was startling, and the sequence of events in the next twenty years makes the whole development remarkable. The war interrupted the editor's projected plans. It is to the everlasting credit of Rutgers University that its School of Education and its University Research Council in the critical period after the war provided sponsorship, some financial assistance, and publication facilities to reactivate what had been proved to be an important and useful undertaking. The *Third Yearbook* covering the period 1940 to 1948 was published by the Rutgers University Press in 1949. The *Fourth Yearbook* published in 1953 and the current *Fifth Yearbook* which includes tests published through December 1958 were published without the benefits of official sponsorship, but with confidence that the reputation of the product would carry the project and with the cooperation and moral support of an ever-increasing group of professional friends. At the present time, the *Third, Fourth* and *Fifth Yearbooks* are in print and they are indispensable sources of factual information and professional opinion about educational and psychological tests. The information about the tests is more complete and more reliable than the information in most publishers' catalogs. It is the first and usually the final source of information short of examining a specimen set. It should now be clear that this reviewer has a high regard for the quality of the product under discussion and admiration for the persistent effort applied to its achievement. Next in order is a frankly critical comment about the future. The expansion in the size of the volumes together with the inflation in the costs of production may soon make these indispensable books available only in university reference libraries and in the personal libraries of a few hundred contributing reviewers who receive courtesy copies for their scholarly work. The 1940 volume of 700 pages sold for $7.00. The next volume was 1,062 pages and sold for $12.50. The *Fourth* and *Fifth Yearbooks* each increased in size by only 10%, but the most recent 1,322 page volume costs $22.50. Clearly, if the *Yearbooks* of the future are to be easily available to the choosers and users of tests, the price must come down. A first step could be a reduction in size of the volumes and correlated costs of editorial work as well as costs of manufacturing. This objective can be easily accomplished in substantial amount. Twenty percent of the printed pages can be eliminated by dropping the entire section devoted to reprinting book reviews that have appeared in sundry journals. The content that makes the *Yearbooks* indispensable, going all the way back to the volume published twenty years ago, is not the convenience of the encyclopedic packaging; the value resides in the fact that the factual information is not easily available anywhere else whereas the commentary of the test reviews is not available elsewhere at all. Reprinted reviews of books have no enduring value in this company of original contributions. Another 5% and possibly more could be saved by critical attention to the references to the professional literature that are appended to the bibliographical entries of the tests. The horrendous example is, of course, under the entry, *Rorschach.* Eighteen and one-half pages are occupied by 1,078 entries and these only supplement 1,219 entries which are listed in preceding *Yearbooks.* Buros suggests in the preface that the next *Yearbook* will eliminate all references. That decision is unfortunate. There is a better solution. Buros has erected a most substantial editorial pedestal on the theme of the frankly critical examination of the test products of authors and publishers. The treatment was, and remains, useful with respect to tests. A similar critical expression is sorely needed with respect to the literature reporting on tests. I do not mean to suggest the yearbook idea applied to reviews of the rehashes of theses in Education and Psychology that appear in the journals. I mean to suggest that Buros could properly, and profitably to all, exercise an editor's prerogative, indeed obligation, to delete. It would be constructively helpful if substantial references in the literature received the attention of a listing with the entry for the test. This reviewer would go even further. He wou'd suggest that Buros exercise his editorial stature to curtail the review space allowed to inconsequential products of test authors and publishers. The reader should not infer that the volume under review is burdened with inconsequential material. The significant contents of the *Fifth Yearbook* are the 698 original contributions prepared by 350 reviewers. Essentially every test published or revised in the period from 1952 to 1958 is included. These contents plus indices comprise more than one thousand pages. It is obviously impossible to document any generalizations about such a collection, but in a few minutes any reader can verify the following statements. The editing for factual accuracy and completeness reaches a high standard of merit. The organization of the contents, the classification of entries, the bibliographical conventions adopted, and the indexing are excellent. The book is well manufactured. It would take a great deal of time for a reader to comprehend the principal components of the human variability that endow the book with an interest quite independent of its utility as a reference. The clichés of the psychometric domain abound, especially "should be used with caution" and "more research is needed." The knowledgeable reader will enjoy the skilful grinding of axes. The student has much to gain from exposure to the differences of professional opinion and from the consistency with which his seniors apply fundamental ideas in their critique. Practically everyone will enjoy the frankly critical commentary which is liberally available, most frequently by implication, often direct but muted, and sometimes blunt and raucous. "Should not the do-it-yourself movement be stopped short of professional psychology," or "this test was published prematurely," or "it is recommended that the publisher remove the test from the market; users should encourage the publisher in this course of action by refusing to buy the inadequate product." The 350 contributors have done much more than polish such critical gems. They have done their work with devoted care—and they deserve a salute.

J Counsel Psychol 7:239–40 f '60. Irwin A. Berg. Another bone-and-muscle type volume ....edited by the felicitously initialed O. K. Buros. Every counselor has used the previous *Yearbooks* and the fifth edition is all that the others were and a lot more. There are more tests, more coverage, more everything of what the counselor wants to know in mental measurement, provided he can lift the book. * All counselors know the Buros *Yearbook,* so there is little point in dwelling upon the organization of the present edition. The comprehensiveness is there, the test reviews are as incisive as ever, the documentation is superb and, candidly, one wonders how Buros does it. It isn't often that an adequate commentary on a revised book may be expressed, "It is fully as good as the previous edition and even more extensive in coverage." But that's what the fifth *Yearbook* is, and somebody ought to give Buros a medal.

J Proj Tech 23:471–2 D '59. Bertram R. Forer. The latest achievement of Buros and his huge entourage of reviewers has given us another useful summary of tests and texts in the field of measurement. The eighth of an increasingly broad and intensive series * Generally, the reviews seem to be objective, insofar as this can be expected from persons who inevitably have their own convictions about what a test should be and do and requirements of validity, reliability and normative data. In some cases the background of one or more of the test reviewers may seem rather far afield from the kind of experience which would foster realistic and sophisticated appraisal of the test *in situ* rather than on sheer structural statistical grounds. Yet most such reviews are complemented by others written by appropriately specialized experts. All this is to the good. Out of the opposition of uncritical acceptance and overcritical insistence on formal structure can come only more ingenious tests and careful standardization. The coverage is restricted to the English language (though many reviewers are foreign), but broad in scope: achievement batteries, character and personality, non-projective tests (126 pp.), projective techniques (112 pp.), languages, arts, intelligence, sciences, skills, aptitudes, vocational tests. Previous editions have listed 1219 Rorschach references. The present volume adds another 918, presents original critical discussions of the Rorschach by Beck, Eysenck, McCall and Shaffer (certainly a healthily heterogeneous group) and describes variant forms and appurtenances that have been added to the Rorschach armamentarium. A similar kind of treatment is accorded the TAT. New and less popular tests are discussed with appropriate brevity. Here is a wonderful opportunity to obtain an overview of the field of projective techniques. * This reviewer is not in a position to evaluate either the coverage or treatment of the psychometric tests. If, however, the coverage of projective methods is an example, all is in fine order. We are impressed by Buros' heroic and successful efforts to present a picture of the entire field of English tests at both the descriptive and critically evaluative levels. Buros' goal of fostering the improvement of quality in the American testing movement can not fail to be achieved if those who build, validate, administer, interpret or perform research with tests will read this book and take it seriously. For those who wish to know where the testing movement is going, what has been done in the way of coping with recurrent problems, what new ideas and trends have sprung up, Buros' book is essential. Clinical psychologists would do well to refer to it frequently in order to achieve an informed perspective even on those tests which they feel they know well. There is simply no other source for such a rich smorgasbord of information in the field of measurement. The collaborative efforts of Buros' devoted staff have collected and organized information of such magnitude that they serve somewhat the same labor-saving role as purveyors of information that electronic computers have served in large-scale research. For his contribution as leader in this grand enterprise, Buros deserves our deepest appreciation.

J Speech & Hearing Disorders 25:213 My '60. Harold Seashore. Readers of this journal have an interest in this monumental addition to a distinguished series of volumes both because of their direct use of educational and psychological tests and because test scores crop up constantly in the records of students and clients with speech and/or hearing problems. * How....can professional workers in speech find Buros' MMYB useful? They will find it helpful to read the relevant reviews when they feel that they need a better understanding of the tests being used by fellow professionals—the administrators who typically give achievement and aptitude tests and the clinical psychologists who provide case work-ups for many of the persons with whom the speech clinician deals. Many speech clinicians will have occasion to sit in on conferences to plan for group testing and clinical testing programs in schools and in clinics. Although there are only two tests in this volume under the rubric of Speech, there are other tests concerned with Hearing, Listening Comprehension, and Oral Reading, which are clearly in the domain of the speech specialists. With the Fourth MMYB and the Fifth MMYB at hand in his personal or institutional library, the speech and hearing specialist will have ready access to critical evaluations of nearly all currently available tests. Buros himself would agree that this competently prepared and comprehensive volume provides only supplementary help to those who wish to learn more about the complex field of educational and psychological measurement. We need to study the original sources, the tests and their manuals; even before that, we need to have sound training in psychometrics or have access to advisers who are so trained.

Psychiatric Q 34:584 Jl '60. Once again Buros has prepared a monumental volume that will be of immense value to psychologists, educators and other test-users. * No educational institution can afford to be without this reference book; and as a guide it is, of course, a must for all users of tests.

Psychol Rep 5:797 D '59. To review and document the tests developed for use in research and in the practice of psychology is a monumental task, but one which....Buros has courageously undertaken repeatedly. The results of his latest effort are certainly impressive. The value of the volume far exceeds the price; indeed, one wonders at finding such a bargain.

Reading Teach 14:197–9 Ja '61. Agatha Townsend. * The best known reference on the selection of reading tests will undoubtedly prove to be the current edition of Buros. This series—which has achieved the distinction of being known by its producer's name, like Dun and Bradstreet or Webster's—is represented in the bibliography by *The Fifth Mental Measurements Yearbook.* It is, in essence, a comprehensive listing of current tests with reviews written by specialists in the subject field covered by the test, or by measurement experts, or both. The reading teacher should be cautioned that the fact that the Fifth Yearbook is the most recent does not mean that it supersedes earlier volumes. Certain tests which are in wide use, but which have been in print for a number of years, may not be reviewed in the 1959 edition, and should be sought in the Fourth Yearbook. Useful as it is, Buros should be approached with some caution. Remember that a test reviewer may be applying criteria to the test which reflect *his* needs, not *yours.* Every effort is made to include reviews representing different points of view, but use of the Yearbook should not preclude careful judgment in interpretation. Sheer accessibility of test listing is extremely important, however. Nowhere else can one locate in a single reference as complete information on the sixty or more tests reviewed under the main heading of reading. *

[B105]

★Buros, Oscar Krisen, Editor. **Tests in Print: A Comprehensive Bibliography of Tests for Use in Education, Psychology, and Industry.** Highland Park, N.J.: Gryphon Press, 1961. Pp. xxix, 479. $7.00. * (*PA* 36:5HB79B)

Am J Psychol 76:714–5 D '63. Jum C. Nunnally. * essentially a list of every test published in English which the author could find in an exhaustive search of the *Mental Measurement Yearbooks,* test catalogues, professional journals, and other sources * An introduction provides (a) an overview of the purpose and scope of the book, (b) statistical breakdowns of the types of tests included, and (c) some sardonic, bittersweet comments about the dogmatically superstitious behavior of the average test user. * How will the book be useful? It will be useful for locating critical reviews for particular tests. The book would be valuable if for no other reason than serving as a master index to reviews in the five *Mental Measurement Yearbooks.* It will be useful for the person who, with no particular test in mind, is searching for those available in a particular area, e.g. measures of socioeconomic status. Finally, the book will be valued by those omnivorous fact-gatherers who would, for example, enjoy remembering that a Hebrew Aptitude Test is available. Who will want the book? It will be a valuable reference book for university libraries. In addition, the book inevitably will rest on the bookshelves of all those who deal extensively with tests: measurements specialists in research centers, school programs, clinics, industry, and the armed forces. Now that the book is available it is hard to see how we ever did without it.

Brit J Ed Studies 10:193 My '62. C. M. Fleming. This is a fitting supplement to the work undertaken by Professor Buros many years ago when he set himself the task of improving the quality of tests through the publication of authoritative reviews of material already on the market as well as of each new test as it appeared. The series....has done much to direct attention to the desirability of discrimination in selection and use; and this new volume facilitates reference to information on the quality and contents of more than two thousand tests. * skilfully printed, pleasantly presented and easy to handle. This is a book to buy and to treasure.

Cath Ed R 60:277–8 Ap '62. Raymond J. Steimel. Buros has long been known in the field of psychological testing for the practicality and the thoroughness of his work. For the last twenty years, the *Mental Measurement Yearbooks,* which contain critical evaluations of current tests, have served as the bible to busy test users. *Tests in Print* reflects this same thoroughness. It is a comprehensive bibliography of psychological tests both in and out of print. In this regard it is a godsend to test specialists. Anyone who has spent hours searching for the source of some test will be deeply appreciative of the information contained in this volume. The author has taken great pains to include a complete listing of all tests which are or have been used in English-speaking countries. * The book fills a real need in the field of testing; it is a basic source-book of all in print and out of print tests. It will most logically have a place on the shelf of the university professor and the test specialist, and in the library of the central guidance offices. What *Webster's Unabridged Dictionary* is to the writer, *Tests in Print* is to the test user. It would be of only occasional use to the average school counselor or personnel director since seldom is he concerned with tests not readily available. The technical recommendations are probably somewhat too complicated for the ordinary test user. The purpose of the book is simple and straightforward, to serve as a comprehensive bibliography and companion to the *Yearbooks*. In this it is an excellent book. It, however, will be of only limited use to most school personnel.

Cont Psychol 7:397–8 N '62. Harold Seashore. How can one do a regular review of Oscar K. Buros' *Tests in Print?* The distinguished author of the series of *Mental Measurements Yearbooks* has put together an almost complete annotated listing of tests which, as of 1961, were available for operational use. There is more to the book, but this is the gist of it. I like to think that Buros would have preferred to do a volume called *Tests Fit to Print*. On reading the preface and introduction to this volume (and the earlier Yearbooks) one will see that the editor's professional goal is clearly to drive, cajole, lure, and shame test makers to greater excellence. In the process, he informs. I commend the Preface and Introduction to all psychologists—for history, facts, and hair-shirting sermonettes from a man whose role it is to be the esteemed conscience of all testers. Buros briefly describes 2126 different tests which are verified as being available in 1961. He names the authors and publishers, gives dates and ages or grade levels, and tells where to find reviews of those which have been evaluated in the MMY series. As a publisher, I know how he prodded for facts about dead, dying, living, and aborning tests. He tells us that 23 per cent of these titles have not appeared in the MMY series—because they are new or failed to show up in his earlier screenings of the universe of measurement. Another 20 per cent of the entries show revisions of test content, manual, or supplementary material since they were last described in a MMY. Eighty per cent are published in the USA. The list, however, is a worldwide coverage of tests usable by English-speaking people. Buros' compulsive search for completeness is an historical *tour de force*. Then we are taken into the psychometric graveyard to ponder a list of 841 tests in a section called *Out of Print Tests*. These are tests which were once generally available and now either are really dead or at least in such a comatose condition that they have been withdrawn from distribution. Who publishes tests? The Publishers Directory and Index lists companies and individuals whose products are in the book in either the live or dead section. Many of these publishers are individual authors who act as their own publishers. Some are dead commercial publishers of dead tests. Forty companies or agencies issue catalogs, eight of these being foreign. Deeply involved as I am in the test business, I found that on checking the fifth and tenth entries in each of the 26 columns of listings, only 22 companies, agencies, or author-publishers were known to me as publishers of one or more tests; there were 30 entries which I in no way have associated with test publishing. Imagine checking about three thousand test titles with over four hundred sources of publication, living and dead! All this for seven dollars from Gryphon Press, Highland Park, New Jersey. Frankly, I think Buros should have added about two dollars to the sales price, the extra dollars to be set aside to render more likely the publication of the *Sixth MMY*. An incidental contribution of some merit is a six-page listing of foreign agencies with the names of American test companies and agencies or individuals they represent as distributors. This list will guide psychologists in advising their colleagues and others in foreign countries who ask about American tests available in those countries. Many of these firms also are publishers of both indigenous tests and adaptations of American tests. Reproduced also are the Technical Recommendations of the American Psychological Association and the American Educational Research Association on matters of test construction. So, Buros begins the book with his tenacious prodding towards quality and ends by making easily available the concrete recommendations and standards which aim to push psychometricians and consumers forward on the road toward better performance. Division 5 has cited Buros for his role as a keeper of the psychometric conscience. Let us add an oak leaf to the medal. Standing on a hard statistical rock and surveying much of the incompetence in the fields about him, Buros steadily preaches that in psychometrics as in other endeavors, excellence is a reasonable goal.

Ed & Psychol Meas 24:155–6 sp '64. William B. Michael. Again Oscar Buros has prepared a volume that will be of immense value and service not only to research workers in education and psychology, but also to counselors, school administrators, teachers, personnel directors, editors, and graduate students who wish information about tests. * The reviewer was greatly impressed with the extreme care that was taken to assure accuracy of each entry and to "track down" every possible test that could be included in terms of the criteria set forth. The tests in print represented those which could be "....bought, borrowed, rented, or obtained upon request." Many are labeled as experimental and/or research tests—a fact which Buros warns should be kept in mind for other tests listed but not so identified by their publishers. Thus he stated that the discriminating user of his volume will employ it as "....a source of 'leads' to tests." Incidentally, the introductory pages should be studied with care before one makes extensive use of the volume. The four indexes are most helpful. In addition to a directory for publishers combined with an index, which enumerates the entries for their tests, there is a directory for distributors arranged by country, a separate index for titles of tests, and a separate index for names. Frequent reference to the material cited in these indexes will contribute to the effective use of the volume. One can find little to criticize in this most helpful book which indeed has represented a "labor of love," if not a "love of labor." To the dedicated scholar and his editorial staff who painstakingly compiled a storehouse of information both publishers and consumers of tests should express their appreciation at every opportunity. It may be expected that the readers and subscribers of *Educational and Psychological Measurement* will make a place on their shelves for this new volume next to their copy of the latest edition of *The Mental Measurements Yearbook.*

J Proj Tech 26:488 D '62. Bertram R. Forer. Buros' most recent volume is a handy index and supplement to his Mental Measurements Yearbooks. * Buros has devoted his professional life to the development, implementation and communication of psychological testing, information and methodology, and his volumes have added tremendously to the organization and structuring of our knowledge. Most importantly, he consistently reminds us of the limitations of tests and refuses to indulge our needs to select and use tests mechanically in order to avoid the time and effort of critical thinking and evaluation. An added bonus is his inclusion of the Technical Recommendations for Psychological Tests and Diagnostic Techniques prepared originally by the APA Committee on Test Standards plus Technical Recommendations for Achievement Tests developed by the American Educational Research Association and the National Council on Measurements. Newcomers to clinical psychology are likely to be less familiar with these reports than they ought to be. Their republication gives this book a greater degree of integration and autonomy than it would have had without them. The book has several unique features that make it virtually indispensible to persons in counseling and educational measurements as well as to the clinician who performs research or who wishes to increase his diagnostic armamentarium with both projective and nonprojective techniques, in order to deal with special issues not adequately assessable with global psychodiagnostic techniques. It lists all known available tests, experimental as well as standardized. It provides references to reviews and bibliographies. It indicates existing variants of well-known tests. Hence it is essentially the only source to which one can go in search of specialized techniques. It includes an exhaustive directory of test publishers and distributors, foreign as well as domestic, a title index of the tests and an index of test authors. What more could one wish for in a catalog of tests? And why in the world would anyone who uses tests not want a copy?

J Teach Ed 13:365–6 S '62. James Lumsden. Professor Buros has for almost thirty years made a monumental contribution to psychology and education by providing extensive, accurate, and critical information about tests. This is a further example of his careful, scholarly, and helpful work. * An indication of the care with which this book was prepared is the statement that the entries for all the tests (except six apparatus tests) were based on a firsthand examination of at least part of the test materials. Extremely valuable additions to the main test sections are reprints of the *Technical Recommendations* for both psychological and achievement tests, publishers' directory and index, distributors' directory and index, title index, and name index. An introduction describes the purpose of the book and the manner in which the test information is recorded. This is well enough done but *Tests in Print,* like the MMY, will prove a little inconvenient for users because the section describing the meaning of the stars, asterisks, etc., has to be searched for each time the book is used. A cross reference at the beginning of each test section and, perhaps, a solid bookmark with a brief key would be useful. Buros expresses some disappointment that his work and that of the American Psychological Association committees who prepared the *Technical Recommendations* have not proved more fruitful in producing the withdrawal or amendment of bad or inadequately prepared tests and manuals. In my opinion, he correctly ascribes this to the ignorance of test users, but there probably has been much more progress than he thinks. It is true that bad tests are still published and sold, but the average, thanks to Buros, has improved greatly. *Tests in Print* is essential for all those who evaluate or advise on the use of tests for psychology, education, or industry. It should form part of every test collection and it should be purchased by every general library that has any pretensions to being more than a heap of books.

Personnel & Guid J 41:72–3 S '62. Frank B. Womer. Tests in Print is, primarily, a bibliography of standardized tests. As such it fills a definite need for a basic concise reference list of both available and out-of-print tests. Of course, it has been possible previously to use the various *Mental Measurements Yearbooks* (same editor) for reference purposes, but using from three to five dictionary-sized books when searching for some test information is much less convenient than having it readily available in a single book. To the reviewer, this book's primary usefulness is as a bibliography. However, the editor had additional purposes in mind. He feels that *Tests in Print* can serve as an index and supplement to the *Mental Measurements Yearbooks* (MMY) and can help to upgrade test use. It certainly can serve as an index, but the fact that 23 per cent of the entries are not listed in any of the MMY makes it much more than an index. It is a supplement to the extent that it provides information about the existence of those 23 per cent, but it does not provide reviews of them. The book can help to upgrade test use as it provides bibliographic information; it is not, in the reviewer's opinion, going to be as valuable for that purpose as the MMY. The APA and AERA-NCME (not NCMUE any more) technical recommendations for test production and evaluation have been reprinted in the book, and this may contribute to their general dissemination. They are included, no doubt, to help upgrade test use. The reviewer feels that anyone working regularly with standardized tests will find this book indispensable. Certain characteristics are worthy of special note: (1) Out-of-print tests are included, but in a separate listing. There probably is no other such source in print. (2) The criterion for inclusion or exclusion of an entry was commercial availability. (3) In addition to the 23 per cent of entries not previously included in any MMY, 20 per cent represent tests that have been revised since the fifth MMY. Thus, 43 per cent of the entries represent some new information about tests that is not available in the MMY. (4) Although *Tests in Print* can serve as an index to the MMY, test numbering is different. A test is not identified by a common number in this book and the MMY. (5) The extreme detail and care in producing the book is indicated by the use of an asterisk after an entry to indicate that a complete set of the materials are in the physical possession of the editor. Catalogue listings were not considered sufficient evidence of a test's existence. If one considers how this book might have been or might be made even more useful, the most obvious suggestion would be the inclusion of a detailed subject index. There are detailed indexes for publishers, distributors, test titles, and test authors and reviewers. The only subject index is the table of contents. The editor mentions this omission and explains that the effort to produce such an index could have held up publication significantly. The reviewer would hope that the necessary effort could be made before the next edition is published. The rapid growth in test publication indicates the potential usefulness of some plan to keep *Tests in Print* up to date. Perhaps a yearly supplement, even in mimeographed form, could be produced for those who find it imperative to keep abreast of available test materials. There are a number of specific points that a potential user of this book might find helpful: (1) It is most important that a user read the introduction very carefully. Familiarity with the MMY does not provide all the information gleaned from the introduction. (2) Perhaps the best way to use *Tests in Print* is as a supplement to the MMY, not as a replacement. *Tests in Print* is not a short-form, less-expensive edition of the MMY. It should be purchased after or with the MMY, not in place of. (3) *Tests in Print* is particularly useful for a quick scanning of available tests in order to discover those that may, not necessarily will, fit one's own needs. (4) *Tests in Print* is indispensable for anyone attempting to maintain a test file of his own. Buros and his staff are to be commended for producing a much needed bibliography of standardized tests.

[B106]

*Burt, Cyril. **Mental and Scholastic Tests, Fourth Edition.** London: Staples Press Ltd., 1962. Pp. xxxi, 549. 65*s*. * (Toronto, Canada: Ambassador Books, Ltd. $13.00.) ["A few minor emendations have been made in the text either to remove slips and ambiguities or to incorporate references to recent work. In the arithmetic tests the wording has been occasionally modified in order to bring the setting of the problems more nearly into line with the prices or practices of the present day. The most important change has been the substitution of fresh specimens of children's drawings on pages 489–500, where the persons represented and their style of dress were plainly out of date."—Preface to the Fourth Edition.]

Brit J Stat Psychol 15:102–3 My '62. E. R. Jennings. There can be few books on psychological topics, published over forty years ago, which, after six or seven reprintings, are still sufficiently in demand to warrant being set up afresh and re-issued. The studies which form the basis of this volume were undertaken when mental and scholastic testing was still in its infancy. The author was the first psychologist to be appointed to an official position as consultant to an education authority; and the educational area covered by that authority was the largest in the world. Many of the new and ingenious devices introduced in the course of these researches have since given rise to a long series of developments in statistical psychology. Here we encounter the first survey of an entire school population, the first attempts at absolute scaling, the first assessments by item analysis, the first demonstration that the distribution of intelligence is approximately normal and yet significantly non-normal, and some of the first applications of factor analysis using what has since become known as the "centroid" method. But the book is much more than a historical landmark. For teachers, educationists, educational psychologists, and psychological students generally, it provides an admirable introduction to the techniques of which it treats, and a model for further researches. Where the content of the test problems has become somewhat antiquated, new problems have now been substituted. Fresh specimens for the norms for children's drawings at various ages have been obtained by a new investigation. A good deal of material that would today seem irrelevant owing to altered conditions in the schools has been omitted. And the whole volume has been revised and brought up to date. In resetting the pages a new and more attractive type-face has been adopted; and the production of the whole book greatly improved. One or two criticisms are perhaps called for. The printer has apparently changed the method used in reproducing the children's drawings. In the original edition the appearance of actual pencil work was skilfully preserved; in the new this effect has unfortunately been lost. It seems a pity too that Professor Burt did not include the age-assignments for the London Revisions of the Stanford-Binet and Terman-Merrill scales. May we hope that when another reprinting is called for, these minor shortcomings will be removed? In all other respects both publishers and authors deserve the warmest congratulations from teachers and psychologists alike.

For reviews of the second edition, see 4:B74.

[B107]

*Byrne, John, and Byrne, Katharine. **You and Your Abilities.** Chicago, Ill.: Science Research Associates, Inc., 1959. Pp. 64. Paper. $0.50. * (Revision of *You and Your Mental Abilities* by Lorraine Bouthilet and Katharine Mann Byrne. See 4:B54.)

[B108]

★Cabat, Louis, and Godin, Jacob D. **How to Prepare for College Board Achievement Tests: French.** Great Neck, N.Y.: Barron's Educational

Series, Inc., 1960. Pp. vi, 110. Paper, $1.50; cloth, $3.95. *

[B109]

★CABAT, LOUIS, AND GODIN, JACOB D. **How to Prepare for College Board Achievement Tests: Spanish.** Great Neck, N.Y.: Barron's Educational Series, Inc., 1960. Pp. vi, 107. Paper, $1.75; cloth, $3.95. *

[B110]

★CALDWELL, EDSON. **Creating Better Social Climate in the Classroom Through Sociometric Techniques.** San Francisco, Calif.: Fearon Publishers, Inc., 1959. Pp. iv, 76. Paper. Out of print. *

[B111]

CALIGOR, LEOPOLD. **A New Approach to Figure Drawing: Based Upon an Interrelated Series of Drawings.** Springfield, Ill.: Charles C Thomas, Publisher, 1957. Pp. xii, 149. $4.50. * (*PA* 31:7902) For reviews, see 211 and 5:131.

[B112]

★CALLIS, ROBERT; WEST, DORAL N.; AND RICKSECKER, E. L. **The Counselor's Handbook: Profile Interpretation of the Strong Vocational Interest Blanks.** Urbana, Ill.: R. W. Parkinson & Associates, 1964. Pp. 100. Paper. $3.00. *

[B113]

★CARKHUFF, ROBERT R. **The MMPI: An Outline for General Clinical and Counseling Use.** Lexington, Ky.: the Author, University of Kentucky, 1961. Pp. vi, 60. Paper, mimeographed. $2.00. * (*PA* 37:6811)

Personnel & Guid J 40:836 My '62. Thomas M. Magoon. * This handbook is called on "outline," probably because its format is in outline form and its entries are terse and to the point. What the author has done is to compile and classify findings in the literature regarding the Minnesota Multiphasic Personality Inventory. The findings are presented separately for each of the three validity scales and the 10 clinical scales. The materials are further organized under the following headings: item content; general scale meaning; clinical interpretation of high and low scores; and educational and vocational meanings of high and low scores. The appendices include three coding systems (Hathaway, Welsh and Drake and Oetting's), a page of interrelationships among the scales and an 87-item bibliography. The interrelation section is quite weak and would have profited from a reproduction of the scale intercorrelations. Also included are graphic presentations of different response set patterns, neurotic patterns, conduct disorder profiles, and psychotic patterns. This kind of organization of evidence should serve as a valuable teaching aid to students and as a resource guide to practitioners, particularly in that its format is such that the user can subsequently add future data as he encounters them.

[B114]

★CARLSON, ROBERT E.; DAWIS, RENE V.; ENGLAND, GEORGE W.; AND LOFQUIST, LLOYD H.; WITH THE ASSISTANCE OF LOIS L. ANDERSON AND DAVID J. WEISS. **The Measurement of Employment Satisfaction.** University of Minnesota, Industrial Relations Center Bulletin 35; Minnesota Studies in Vocational Rehabilitation 13. Minneapolis, Minn.: the Center, May 1962. Pp. v, 189. Paper. Gratis. * (*PA* 38:6328)

[B115]

★CARLSON, ROBERT E.; DAWIS, RENE V.; ENGLAND, GEORGE W.; AND LOFQUIST, LLOYD H.; WITH THE ASSISTANCE OF LOIS L. ANDERSON AND DAVID J. WEISS. **The Measurement of Employment Satisfactoriness.** University of Minnesota, Industrial Relations Center Bulletin 37; Minnesota Studies in Vocational Rehabilitation 14. Minneapolis, Minn.: the Center, December 1963. Pp. vi, 74. Paper. Gratis. *

[B116]

★CARR, ARTHUR C.; FORER, BERTRAM R.; HENRY, WILLIAM E.; HOOKER, EVELYN; HUTT, MAX L.; AND PIOTROWSKI, ZYGMUNT A. **The Prediction of Overt Behavior Through the Use of Projective Techniques.** Springfield, Ill.: Charles C Thomas, Publisher, 1960. Pp. xii, 177. $6.75. * (*PA* 36:2HG77C)

Brit J Psychol 52:410 N '61. B. Semeonoff. * The result is on the whole disappointing. Theoretical and other systematic points are developed very briefly and almost exclusively as an introduction to the consideration of the case material, and interpretation is in terms of personality dynamics in general, rather than of actual prediction of behaviour. Evaluation is also hampered by what Dr Hooker describes as "lack of a common framework of predictive language." That being so, it is not surprising that in respect of different "behavioural dimensions" three of the techniques (Bender-Gestalt was discounted here because of incomplete data) line themselves up, two against one, in all three possible combinations. There is, nevertheless, substantial agreement, particularly on the main point that emerged, namely that the homosexual twin appeared, both clinically and in terms of test results, to be better adjusted than the heterosexual twin. This is in itself an interesting finding which might perhaps have been discussed more fully. Whether this could have been done satisfactorily within the framework of a report of a symposium is another matter, and one which casts doubt on the wisdom of this sort of publication. This particular instance represents poor value for money—less than 90 pages of actual text, the remainder being an Appendix of Test Protocols. One must also register a mild protest against the misleadingly general title of the book, and the exaggerated nature of some of the claims set out on the dust-jacket.

Cont Psychol 7:32 Ja '62. Thomas W. Richards. * The title of this small book would suggest that something might be concluded about the predictive efficiency of some projective techniques. Unfortunately this is not the case. Four excellent clinicians give here an extremely interesting demonstration of their thinking and methods of operation in developing guesses about two persons whose test protocols had been submitted to them. * This book is an interesting picture of how clinicians work and verbalize their operations. Test protocols are given verbatim and the reader may work over them as he will. The book is in no sense a demonstration of the validity or invalidity of projective techniques. It shows that Forer and Henry and Hutt and Piotrowski—individuals all—have a high degree of communality and for this we are grateful if not surprised. The nomothetic psychologist will feel that this study proves nothing about the validity of projective techniques, while the idiographic psychologist will find some reassurance that these techniques are valuable resources in clinical study.

J Proj Tech 25:481–3 D '61. Stephanie Z. Dudek. * The material consists of Sentence Completion, Thematic Apperception test stories, Rorschach, Figure Drawings and Bender Gestalt patterns of two male identical twins, one of whom is heterosexual and the other an overt homosexual. The protocols of the twins were identified for the authors as to type of sexual adjustment (which is perhaps regrettable). The original test-retest data is presented at the back of the book. The case history includes also a brief and inadequate summary of the free associational material of approximately 300 hrs. of psychoanalysis of the heterosexual twin. The compilation of this material provides an exceptional and valuable opportunity for the clinician to study many factors beyond those covered by the authors, who have restricted themselves to the problems of predicting overt behavior from projective test material. We have the records of identical male twins with divergent patterns of overt sexual behavior but essentially the same development histories. One of the twins went into therapy while the other did not, and we have test-retest data allowing for a comparison of the effects of psychoanalysis versus time on the psychodynamics of these young men. Finally, we have the demonstration of the idiosyncratic and brilliant methods of analysing the test data by four outstanding clinicians using four different techniques. This is indeed a unique publication. However, as a book, the "Prediction of Overt Behavior" demonstrates only too clearly the weaknesses of much of clinical writing today. The case history material is so loosely documented that it fails to either corroborate or deny many of the statements made about the twins by the clinicians. It therefore again demonstrates the extent to which the clinicians operate within a tautological system. If the case history does not agree with the clinician's opinion, so much the worse for the case history. In practice we end up by dispensing with the case history entirely. If the findings of one test agree with those of another about some vaguely described and loosely defined characteristic such as the patient is "labile," or "outgoing" we assume that our inferences are valid and the test "works." If, on the other hand, the findings of, for example, the TAT disagree with those of the Rorschach for some personality dynamic, we say that the Rorschach measures a deeper level of the personality. This may be the correct explanation. However, such an attitude does not achieve for us a greater degree of confidence in our techniques for describing, to say nothing of predicting, behavior. Nor does it help us to identify the cues we use in making inferences, which may in fact be different from the ones we assume we are using. In effect, this attitude encourages loose and circular reasoning, and discourages experimental validation. * in allowing this book to appear, so strikingly lacking in relevant validating material as it is, they end up in the position of paying only lip service to the urgent methodological and validational needs they have outlined. It would seem that the demands of a symposium with its rigid time limits are inappropriate when extended to published material which we are told the authors had ample opportunity to evaluate and amplify. The problems inherent in the prediction of overt behavior by psychological tests are most cogently stated by Dr. B. R. Forer. * The most concrete definition of rules for inferring overt behavior is presented by Zygmunt Piotrowski. * He demonstrates his rules brilliantly in an analysis of the test-retest Rorschach protocols of both twins. * Between the four projective analysts and the discussant the problem of predicting overt behavior receives a thorough analysis. However, for this reviewer, one difficulty remains. It resides in the fact that prediction as it relates to routine psychological reporting in daily clinical practice is never defined. Prediction of overt behavior is dealt with as something we do not normally do, and for which a methodology must be worked out. That is, how relevant is the question raised by W. Henry as to whether we should concern ourselves with prediction of overt behavior at all (which he answers affirmatively) and does it perhaps apply differently to different projective techniques? What is it we do when we write a psychological report and make inferences about a patient's behavior? How much of the psychological report consists of a description (prediction?) of overt behavior and how much refers to unconscious or overt processes (facets of the personality organized or functioning and recognizable on different levels)? What are we diagnosing when we call a patient a latent homosexual or a borderline schizophrenic? Do these terms infer something (or can they) about the overt behavior in the same way that a statement such as the following made by Dr. Piotrowski about one of the twins: "Tom is competitive, plainly sadomasochistic, argumentive and assertive and more frankly exhibitionistic," (p. 58). Is Dr. Piotrowski here describing potentialities or actualities? In other words, when a descriptive statement applied to a patient's behavior is not readily recognized in overt behavior, is the fault due to inaccurate and unsophisticated observations and/or faulty interpretation, or are we dealing with something that is truly covert, or possibly only a behavioral potentiality? Is the main problem one of improving our observational and interviewing techniques or our diagnostic tools? It would seem that we cannot improve the latter without refining the former. In short, this is a unique book and well worth careful analysis. It offers a positive contribution, whether it is considered as an approach to the study of overt behavior, as was its intention; or as a guide to projective test interpretation; or as an elucidation of the possible etiology and psychodynamics of overt sexual psychopathology.

[B117]

★CARRUTHERS, ROBERT B. **Building Better English Tests: A Guide for Teachers of English in the Secondary Schools.** Champaign, Ill.: National Council of Teachers of English, 1963. Pp. 32. Paper. $1.00. *

Engl J 53:381–2 My '64. Oscar M. Haugh. * For many teachers of English this leaflet will provide a liberal education in test construction. To the inexperienced teacher it will reveal new types of questions as well as more effective ways to construct the most common types. The more experienced teacher will find new understandings emerging as the limitations of certain familiar types of questions are examined. Even the sophisticated will find value in learning a simplified type of item analysis which will determine the discriminating power of test questions. Too, a valuable bibliography has been added for those who would like to venture into deeper and swifter waters. The many examples of test questions are unquestionably the strongest feature of the leaflet. First, since examples are chosen from the content of secondary school English, teachers will find the principles especially meaningful and easy to apply. Second, both "poor" and "improved" sample questions are given with accompanying explanations so that the teacher can understand what to do as well as what to avoid. Finally, the explanations are relatively nontechnical. Brevity is both a strength and a weakness. The overworked or faint of heart who have been discouraged in their previous efforts to understand involved and voluminous discussions about test-making will find a measure of hope in a leaflet of this size. But brevity does not permit the author to discuss fully all important phases of test-making, or to give much attention to the problem of scoring tests. What has been included about the grading of essay test questions is good, but more explanation would be helpful, as would an example of the grading of an essay question or two. Nevertheless, this reviewer knows no pamphlet that will be as helpful to high school English teachers interested in preparing tests which will more effectively measure classroom achievement. It should not be overlooked.

[B118]

*CATTELL, PSYCHE. **The Measurement of Intelligence of Infants and Young Children, Revised Edition.** New York: Psychological Corporation, 1960. Pp. 274. $6.00. * (Although "Revised 1960" appears on the title page, the author has added little new material; it is essentially a reprinting with "changes in language here and there.") For reviews of the first edition, see 3:282.

[B119]

CATTELL, RAYMOND B. **Personality and Motivation Structure and Measurement.** New York: Harcourt, Brace & World, Inc., 1957. Pp. xxv, 948. $11.50. * (London: George G. Harrap & Co. Ltd. 85*s*.) (*PA* 32:3918)

Am J Psychol 71:620–8 S '58. S. B. Sells. This book has been difficult to review, partly because of the sheer length of its detailed presentation, but also because it invites both admiration and criticism. It is unquestionably a major contribution to the theory, taxonomy and quantitative study of human personality and motivation. Since it is presented as a progress report and the author carefully points out what still needs to be done, he cannot be taken to task for the fact that the work ahead is extensive. Actually he has been a leading contributor to knowledge and capability in these areas. One may, however, note a tendency to overstate the case that is perhaps most apparent in the final chapters, which outline applications to clinical and industrial psychology. The tolerance of his readers with this exuberance of an innovator and pioneer in the development of new concepts and methods will vary. Unfortunately, the author's familiar polished and lucid exposition is as aggressively and even contentiously outspoken in disparagement of divergent viewpoints as it is in support of his own. * Several aspects of this book stand out even on casual reading. First, both in conception and execution it represents one of the most prodigious efforts undertaken in psychology. The tremendous amount of data gathering reflects generous financial support and the analyses could probably not have been accomplished without extensive exploitation of modern electronic computing facilities. Second, the systematic classification of masses of data and the Universal Index, providing symbols for identification of data media, population sample, factor analytic design and factor order, reflect Cattell's genius for organization and structure. Third, his careful scholarship, combined with generous amounts of clinical and theoretical insight, have produced a text abounding in elegant detail illustrating, interpreting and integrating the research results presented. Finally, his invention of large numbers of objective tests to measure personality and motivation traits is a creative contribution of importance. * Chapter 9 is an excellent summary of a number of important psychometric concepts. It includes the variations of reliability and validity formulations; the relations among factor-pure, homogeneous and difficulty-vectored scales; the varieties of type definitions; and current approaches to pattern and profile analysis. The survey is extended in Chapter 10 which deals with measures of pattern similarity and related issues involving group functions and culture effects. These discussions will be found useful by investigators and graduate students and can be read profitably without reference to the remainder of the book. The last section of Chapter 10, entitled "The Taxonomy of Situations and Criteria in Relation to Psychophysics" is a highly important commentary on most current practice in psychology, including the present book. * In many respects Part IV, "The Measurement of Attitudes, Motivation, and Conflict Adjustment," is the most exciting part of this book. It reports a truly original approach, using techniques derived from earlier work in objective personality measurement, that has been brought to bear on the measurement of motivation. * The five Parts are a monumental summary of the major portion of Cattell's life work to date. He appears throughout in the scientific roles of theorist, innovator, test creator and systematist, and as an important contributor to the fields of personality and motivation-structure and measurement. It is only when he adopts a fifth role, namely that of protagonist, that his star fails to shine. As a scientist he has reported and interpreted his data accurately and objectively, although this may be better appreciated if the reader understands some of the idiosyncrasies of the author's writing style, as when he uses phrases such as "not yet clearly established" to describe inconclusive results. As a protagonist, however, he has indulged his own (previously expressed) faith and enthusiasm with the result that many of his introductory and summary statements tend to create impressions which reach beyond the limitations of his data. A tendency has also been noted to expand at subsequent points conclusions which were carefully qualified where they first appeared. These embellishments are all the more to be regretted because the work reported is impressive enough to stand on its own merits. Unfortunately, Part IV, in which the tests and concepts developed are "made available" to the applied fields of clinical, educational and industrial psychology, appears to have been written principally by the protagonist. The critique of current practices with regard to psychological measurement in these fields gives an exaggerated picture of prevailing levels of sophistication such as are reflected, for instance, in the chapters of the Annual Reviews. Doubtless, many of the abuses and inadequacies pointed out abound among unsophisticated practitioners, but that will not be changed by this or any other book. The principal point of criticism, however, is that the sweeping reforms advocated by Cattell are inadequately supported by present evidence, including that reported in the earlier parts of this book. His critical analyses of non-structured tests and particularly of projective (or "mis-perceptive") tests are trenchant, but, rationale apart, the tests he proposes for use are subject—in their present form and stage of development—to the same objections. As implied earlier, in review of the research, there is a great need for further research and development with these approaches. There is a specific need for applied psychologists to work with these materials on a research basis, principally to develop needed criterion relations. But neither the uncritical adoption of the various tests described nor the uncritical acceptance of the numerous application procedures advocated, particularly in personnel selection, is indicated on the basis of present knowledge. In brief, the reviewer is impressed with the potentialities of Cattell's tests and plans for using them and would encourage research to try them out and to contribute to their further development. On the other hand, he feels that a case for their immediate general adoption for operational use has not yet been made. * Cattell's methodological position, often reiterated, is that predictions should be based on well established factors, covering the entire range of ability, personality and dynamic trait modalities, and that *ad hoc,* non-factored, special purpose tests are inferior. For example, he estimates that employee profiles, to be complete, need about 50 factor measures: 14 abilities, 16 personality factors and 20 interest-motivation factors. To the extent that such profiles sample a wider range of functions relevant to the criterion than special purposes batteries ordinarily cover, his position may be found empirically to carry weight. However, at the present time, professionally developed, tailored selection batteries based on discerning job analysis have the advantage of demonstrated superiority (as in the case of the USAF aircrew selection batteries), whereas factor-based prediction is still an unproven alternative. Theoretically, a factor can never be measured directly (it is a concept) and must be estimated from tests which measure a) factors, b) specific (often unidentified) variance and c) error, in varying proportions. Until defining variables, having factor loadings in excess of .9, can be developed for at least a substantial portion of the factor spectrum, factor estimates by different combinations of salient variables, having non-common-factor (specific) variances with varying correlations with criteria, may show variations in validity which favor certain estimates significantly over others. This state of affairs actually reduces to an argument in favor of special purpose tests. In summary, this book is a contribution of major importance of psychology. In addition to the progress reported on the specific topics of personality and motivation-measurement and structure, it contains original methodological, theoretical and factual information of significance to every branch of theoretical and applied psychology. It will be found a rich source of research problems and is overall a challenge to research volunteers for a project with excellent prospect of eventual payoff. The criticism presented in this review has been directed principally toward the expository aspects of the author's generalization of his results and suggestions for their use by applied psychologists. The research report, presented in Parts I and through V and 12 appendices, is a magnificent achievement which need not be devalued by the criticism of the applied section. However, critical reading is required to avoid being swept along by the author's eloquence in generalizing his position. [See original review for critical comments not excerpted.]

Austral J Psychol 12:241–9 D '60. A. G. Hammer. Cattell writes faster than I am able to read. This is a discouraging thought, for (i) Cattell seems to be writing most of the time, (ii) what he writes is, though uneven in quality, very well worth consideration, and (iii) one still needs to read others since, despite Cattell's over-enthusiastic leaning to a contrary view, what he writes about is not a system of psychology but only a particular approach to a limited area of psychological study

—i.e. the factorial analysis of individual differences in personality. However that may be, any serious student of personality theory and indeed any student interested in fitting personality theory into the framework of general psychology should certainly be informed of Cattell's contributions; and if he is willing to do some real work, he might well be advised to acquire this information by concentrated study of this impressive volume. The book gives a coherent and systematic survey of personality dimensions, although for the most part the quite extraordinary amount of empirical work reported comes from Cattell's own laboratory. Cattell has made use of findings he has previously published and makes constant reference to them, but it is my impression that this book can stand alone. References are also made to articles still in press at the time of publication. Inspection of current journals will show that the issues raised in the book are still being actively worked on. We can say, therefore, that the book serves to summarize and coordinate previous material, to present a great deal of new material, and to provide a jumping off platform for further advance. * The English style is evidence of the author's high score on the fluency factor, but I think many students would find the book easier to read, and just as precise, if rather more use had been made of short, simple, Anglo-Saxon words. Cattell has expressed his fear that the book will not be used in undergraduate courses because it is too mathematical. It is not in fact particularly mathematical, but I doubt its suitability for undergraduate courses. It is too difficult, too specialized, too long, and too demanding of unremitting, critical scrutiny. On the other hand, I deem it an excellent basis for post-graduate study. For 15 months now I have used it in a seminar group consisting of Ph.D. students. So far, meeting once weekly, we have reached page 330! Members of the group will no doubt forgive me if I say that they are probabaly no better and no worse than other post-graduate groups I have known; but the seminar is the best I have participated in. It is my conviction that this happy state of affairs springs from the suitability of the book—from the importance of the questions considered, the excellent blend of methodology and content, the provocativeness and the strong arguments for certain positions which to some members of the group are bound to seem in error. * I want now to turn from these trifles to much larger issues, not in a spirit of carping criticism but rather to show that this is a book which merits serious criticism. Actually to do the book justice one would have to write a review almost as long as the book. Consequently I shall be able to do little more than mention the issues in cursory fashion and take up only one in some detail. Although Cattell is genuinely erudite, the picture he sketches is overmuch determined by his own results. He is not unaware of the findings of others, but as it were fits them to his findings rather than arriving at a compromise. There are one or two contributions to which surprisingly he does not refer; for example, the work of Witkin. Although this is in a way a charge of inbreeding, it has to be conceded that there has not resulted any sterility. It is possible that the somewhat circumscribed character of the Illinois findings arises out of the basic conviction that the initial dictionary study of personality traits adequately sampled the personality sphere (i.e. all conceivable non-trivial ways in which persons may differ from others). This assumption is one with which many people might well disagree. Cattell is confident that oblique simple structure is the solution to the problem of the indeterminacy of factorial solutions. I am not. It seems to me far more probable that phenomena as they occur in nature will be maximally rather than minimally complex. The replication of factors arrived at by way of oblique simple structure provides necessary but not sufficient evidence of their validity. Cattell often hovers on, and in my opinion sometimes slips over, the brink of reification. In particular, he writes as if factors must correspond to something having a real and independent existence in nature, instead of being merely any set of circumstances giving rise to a pattern of correlations. Factor C is defined as "the *capacity* (my italics) to express available emotional energy along integrated as opposed to impulsive channels." What is the value of inventing a capacity here? What factor C shows is that there is a pattern of stimulus generalizations and response generalizations such that people who respond complainingly in some situations and ways tend to do likewise in others. Nothing is gained by the invention of a capacity as an explanation. The factor is what has to be explained. This criticism of course does not in any way detract from the merits of having demonstrated the pattern. Cattell overdoes the importance of measuring, and of measuring personality. Attempts to quantify psychology deserve support, but they are not a necessary condition for progress. Cattell argues that psychiatric advance is hampered by the absence of measures of neuroticism taken before and after treatment. I think to the contrary that it is fairly easy to detect changes in patients and that our real problem is still to discover how to bring them about and to understand them. Further, it is not always traits—i.e. properties of the organism—that the psychologist has to deal with, but properties of the response. For example, it would be good to measure experiences along the dimensions of, say, colour or of emotion. Psychiatrists may need to measure not a patient's neuroticism, but how much the patient is *"obsessing"* at the moment. * [See original review for critical comments not excerpted.]

Cont Psychol 3:323–5 N '58. Charles Hanley. * an omnibus of ideas regarding traits, attitudes, drives, conflict, fatigue, anxiety, typology, personality structure, test theory, plus applications in clinical and industrial psychology. The author approaches his topics with a firm belief in factor analysis as the preferred method of organizing data, and an unswerving allegiance to the principle that oblique simple structure is the essential characteristic of dimensions worthy of scientific attention. His innovations almost always concern testing and are designed to obtain precise evidence on theories derived from Freud, Jung, McDougall, Kretschmer and lesser figures, from general psychology, and from his own insights. His position on personality theory is thus both eclectic and conservative. * The book summarizes a host of technical and theoretical publications * It has as well the character of an advanced text and a proselyting tract. The energy, audacity, and enthusiasm displayed cannot fail of admiration, yet it is an unfortunate fact that Cattell, the writer, is hardly the equal of Cattell, the psychologist. The simplest material is made extraordinarily difficult while, paradoxically, some of the mathematically demanding sections are clear and neat. The chief difficulty in the writing lies not in the neologisms, the technical jargon, and the Graduate-School English, but rather in details that careful revision could have eliminated. * Cut and dried tasks, such as the description of each factor, are confounded by the intrusion of hypotheses, observations, anticipations, and postponements. At its worse, the narrative becomes an alphabet soup so thick a parenthesis drowns * [The] writing cannot be praised; the content is another matter. Cattell's modern conservatism will be admired in proportion to a reader's pleasure in finding giants and dwarfs living together under one roof. Psychologists who like heterogeneous results painted on a broad canvas will be delighted with Cattell's achievement; those who wonder how the brushwork was managed will find little to go on. * (Narrow-gauge psychologists may balk at the manner in which self-ratings on Physical Energy are translated as Surgency, Voice Quality as Cyclothymia, Breadth of Interest as Comention. The fact that graphs illustrating changes in test-retest correlations over time are scaled to *square roots* of coefficients, instead of *squares,* as the text asserts, does not help.) The Objective Tests should arouse great interest, but their description is sketchy. The chapters on clinical and industrial psychology are full of ideas, but evidence of their utility is presented in findings of "statistical significance" rather than "amount of criterion variance accounted for." A general problem arises from Cattell's investment in the linear "specification equation" * Readers who dimly remember the curved and wiggly lines in natural science textbooks may wonder why human behavior is so simple. Cattell ignores this question for nearly 400 pages, then admits that more complex relationships are possible. After a short section describing a few such equations, he pulls the rug from under himself: "The shrewd reader may interject at this point: 'If the simple specification equation is abandoned, so also is the factor method of *finding* functional unities, for they are mutually interdependent, factors being consistent with linear relationships.' This is logically correct; but...." Then follows a chain of lawyer's arguments: new methods might be discovered (but nothing much is to be expected from them), the linear model always approximates complex functions, skillful manipulation will uncover such cases, and there are no S-shaped relationships anyway. Strict adherence to Cattell's position would seem to guarantee overlooking nonlinear relations, whereas any stable equation involving test and nontest behavior is welcome in science, regardless of one's preference for straight lines. *Personality* *and Motivation Structure and Measurement* is aimed at informing and converting psychologists, and its author hopes it will be used as a text for graduate students and undergraduate majors. (For this reason, a list of bloodcurdling problems follows each chapter.) Readers are bound to be simultaneously stimulated and irritated by this book.

J Counsel Psychol 7:312–3 w '60. Irwin A. Berg. * every counselor should know....what Cattell is striving to achieve; for a steadily growing number of psychologists believe that his work will revolutionize the study of personality. The curious thing is that relatively few persons seem to recognize the galactic scope of his notions. The reason for this is probably Cattell himself. * Cattell is a dedicated empiricist. He wants to measure and classify behavior carefully and establish appropriate laws of relationship. Then, and only then, he is convinced, will psychology be ready for a genuine theoretical structure to replace the pasteboard edifices which currently masquerade as modern psychological theory. In Cattell's view, the most important approach to the measurement problem is multivariate statistical analysis, particularly factor analysis. His current book is a critical statement and application of his convictions of how one goes about measuring personality and motivation and what has been done thus far in this research area by himself and others. * It is....Cattell at his urbane best, complete with facile writing and bespangled with colorful phraseology. The aims of the book, the scope and handling of its subject matter should cause it to be hailed as truly *monumental.* But if the past reception of Cattell's work is a guide, no such accolade will be bestowed at the present time. This is curious; for in many ways I think an excellent case could be presented as to why Cattell should be recognized as one of the half-dozen who have contributed most to modern psychology. He may win such full recognition eventually but not in the foreseeable future. * Of course this is not to say that Cattell is unknown. No man who has written 15 books, 200 articles, etc. can ever be completely ignored. He has received a fair amount of recognition but not the lavish praise which, in my judgment, he merits. The bibliographic lists of many books and articles record his name; however, such references to his work are often to some trifling point which he makes incidentally, not to his main concept which is of far greater significance. Cattell is often cosmic in his grasp; and with a chirpy insouciance, he will sail into a research problem of tremendous magnitude with a "damn the torpedoes" swagger. Thus he usually leaves people behind and intellectually awash. * Cattell has "new eras in his brains," as the poet said; and I believe he is ahead of his time in psychological research. The man is brilliant; however, many cannot wield concepts of the magnitude he often deals with, and in consequence, seize upon trivia as a rebuttal to his efforts. * Cattell flabbergasts his colleagues in other ways as well as by the breadth of some of his ideas. He makes up words and gives a new twist to old ones. * one must be competent in mathematics to understand just what he is up to; for Cattell, quite appropriately, sometimes uses a mathematical statement with little or no verbal commentary. This fondness for neologisms and quantitative expression is beyond the ken of most clinical and counseling psychologists, particularly the older and influential ones. Yet these are the very persons who could help in hoisting his ensign to the top of the mast. Furthermore, Cattell is not one to spend much time with those who cannot follow him. Indeed, he is likely to give them the back of his hand. * because of his neologisms, mathematics, and an occasional snarl, a number of psychologists recoil from putting forth the considerable and necessary effort to understand Cattell's work * There is a paradoxical quality in Cattell's attitude toward details which puzzles persons who know him. At times, he can airily dismiss what most people would regard as an important item and, at other times, hang on like a bulldog to an insignificant detail in an unimportant context. * In summary, I would say that Cattell is truly *avant garde* in his research program. He has won a measure of recognition for his work; however, in my judgment he deserves resounding acclaim, not merely scattered applause. There are undoubtedly many factors which account for the lack of appropriate response to his efforts. Those mentioned here are some of them which, to me, seem to have served as barriers to an understanding of what he is doing. In the future, I would assert that he will be recognized for superb contributions to psychology.

For additional reviews, see 5:B91.

[B120]

★CATTELL, RAYMOND B., AND SCHEIER, IVAN H. **The Meaning and Measurement of Neuroticism and Anxiety.** New York: Ronald Press Co., 1961. Pp. ix, 535. $12.00. * (*PA* 36:1HK27C)

Brit J Social & Clin Psychol 2:73–5 F '63. H. R. Beech. We are told that this book is directed toward two kinds of people, the clinician and the researcher. The authors say that their work will assist the former group by increasing the reliability of diagnosis and treatment by using and understanding precise scientific instruments to measure levels of anxiety and severity of neurosis, while those interested in research will be given a "firmer basis of enquirical findings about personality structure." In their preface....the authors also hold out the hope to the reader that he will find in it "....conceptually clear and precise instruments of measurement for use in research and routine practice." However, we are warned that the proper import of the techniques and procedures referred to can only be grasped by the reader who is prepared to accept radically new ideas. * the book falls far short of the achievements confidently referred to in the preface. In fact the "new ideas" we are asked to grasp turn out to be time-worn, and the new techniques and procedures amount to nothing more than the multivariate analysis of old and new data gathered by Cattell and other workers—the principle of selection employed in the case of the latter being undisclosed. As for the "precise scientific instruments," these are, it seems, questionnaires and objective tests apparently characterized by poor reliability and doubtful validity, and of virtually unknown clinical value. One is also left with the impression that an adequate presentation, or even in some cases the bare mention of a particular piece of information would have greatly contributed to the meaningfulnes of this book. Sometimes the compression of material has resulted in near incomprehensibility, a feature which is not lessened by Cattell's predilection for neologisms in labelling his factors. However, the evaluation of this work really hinges upon two main points; the procedures used and other technical matters related to the statistical analysis, and the contribution made by this book to clinical understanding and know-how. So far as the first of these points is concerned Cattell is open to criticism for precisely those reasons given in papers by Sir Godfrey Thomson and Dr Charlotte Banks. Indeed, the discussion of Cattell's earlier contributions by these two authors seems to be as apt today as they were fifteen years ago, and suggests that his work has a less secure statistical foundation than one is asked to believe. It is, however, the second main point, concerning the clinical value of the book, which most readers will be anxious to appreciate. Certainly Cattell will carry all clinicians with him in stating that there is a "....need for more effective treatment and more adequate theories, a genuine dissatisfaction and search for new possibilities....," but it is unlikely that many readers will endorse the solution offered. For example, it seems reasonable to ask questions concerning the way in which an individual's factor profile is obtained. Basically this depends upon the satisfactory nature of the 16 PF questionnaire, although the authors refer to the Objective-Analytic battery of tests which is apparently being revised to improve its validity. In general the position respecting personality questionnaires of a conventional character seems not to have changed much in recent years. Kronhauser (1945) sounded the opinions of psychologists on questionnaires and discovered, not surprisingly, that 85 per cent of the sample considered such procedures doubtfully satisfactory or worse. Cattell's data does little or nothing by way of converting this large majority. The reliability coefficients are not at all comparable with those obtained from cognitive tests, and indeed in the 1957 IPAT manual no information is given concerning test-retest reliabilities because certain traits "fluctuated in level a good deal." This may be the case but such a conclusion must necessarily limit the clinical usefulness of the knowledge derived from the test. Further difficulties might be envisaged by the more cautious clinician in adopting the procedure of correlating an individual's profile with the "standard profile" obtained by various diagnostic groupings. In effect this would mean offering the statement that patient *x* is obsessive-compulsive to the extent of *r* 0.78, fits the depressive reaction category to the extent of *r* 0.58, etc. This technique could not only be faulted on the grounds that the unreliability is being multiplied, but that the end result is tied up with what are commonly regarded as unsatisfactory diagnostic categories and that the profile itself has no obvious implications for treatment and disposal. Perhaps just as important an issue is the degree of differentiation between groups on the various factors. Here the criticisms of the interested reader of this book might range from doubting the logic of some of the arguments advanced to astonishment at the conclusions drawn from the data provided. But in justice to Cattell and Scheier it must be said that a note of caution enters the discussion from time to time, indeed, in treating of diagnosis and therapy it is admitted that half of what is being said is only a statement of things to come. It must also be said that bringing together the mass of data presented represents an enormous task, and clearly a great deal of work has gone into the preparation of the book. However, clinicians and researchers alike are likely to be somewhat sceptical about the procedures employed, the conclusions drawn, and the rather extravagant claims made for the contents of the book. It is probable that the volume could be re-written and carefully edited to eliminate obscurities and present a more balanced evaluation of the contribution made by this material; it is more difficult to see how the techniques and procedures used in obtaining the material could be improved by such a revision.

Brit J Social & Clin Psychol 2:224–6 O '63. Raymond B. Cattell. [A reply to the above review by H. R. Beech.] A good review commonly brings out clearly what new experimental or theoretical contributions the author has to make and then critically evaluates them. Unfortunately, Beech's recent and apparently maiden review effort on the above book dispenses with the first. Somewhere in his peer group he has heard a voice cry "Havoc," and has so eagerly let loose the hounds of destruction that he has forgotten to describe the victim. On behalf of my fellow author, Dr Ivan Scheier, and myself, I should like to state soberly, and in the brief space allotted, the theoretical points and factual findings at issue. * When one of the greatest needs of our time is to transcend those differences in professional education which block the integration of clinical psychology, on the one hand, with the resources of psychometric personality structure analysis, on the other; when one or two books, at most, appear in this area in a year (as contrasted with two or three hundred of the Freud-to-Fromm variety) one might hope that a thorough airing would be given, in knowledgeable circles, to the strange ideas and methods involved. Instead, this book seems merely to have been exposed to a piece of juvenile vandalism. [See original reply for critical comments not excerpted.]

Cont Psychol 8:467–8 D '63. Sanford J. Dean. * This volume, taken together with previous work by the authors, is the most sophisticated and far reaching attempt yet reported to apply the factor analytic method to the study of human behavior. It is a contribution deserving the serious attention of all psychologists. The case for factor analysis is forcefully and convincingly presented and the results it has yielded are presented in detail. This reviewer's main criticism is that the authors are carried away by their own enthusiasm for and commitment to their method. Perhaps this is as it should be and authors should leave to others the adding of the grain of salt. The fact that factors only reflect relationships among responses causes little concern. For these enthusiasts, factors exist, they are real, and they operate as determinants of personality and of behavior pathology. Some factors are inherited, others are acquired; some are conscious, others are unconscious. It is not always clear which of two related factors causes the other, but further factor analysis will tell. While the desirability of employing factorially defined variables in experiments is recognized, few if any, of the interpretations are based on experimental results. Some idea of the authors' unbounded faith in their measures may be conveyed by the following example. In discussing the factor profiles that differentiate neurotics from normals, the authors conclude that neuroticism is distinct from psychoticism because the same profile also differentiates neurotics from psychotics. However, psychotics do not differ from normals. "Practically every questionnaire and objective test dimension measured thus far shows psychotics at about the same level as normals. This suggests, for further study, the hypothesis that psychoticism is in many respects functionally closer to normalcy than neuroticism is" * Researchers have been finding no differences between psychotics and normals on many measures for many years. The usual interpretation, however, is that the measures are not adequate or appropriate, not that no differences exist. The authors recognize that certain factors may have operated with the psychotics which would result in random responding an artifactual flattening of the profile, but this is not seen as bearing on the validity of the first conclusion. However, if the measures on the psychotics are not valid, the comparisons with the neurotics are as questionable as the comparisons with the normals and neuroticism and psychoticism may not be separate and distinct processes. Considering the authors' critical treatment of single tests developed as operational definitions of concepts without benefit of factor analysis, the correlation between the anxiety factor and the Taylor Manifest Anxiety Scale is of some interest. The correlations of .82 and .85 are the highest reported for the anxiety factor—much higher than the correlations, ranging from .20 to .42, with clinically judged anxiety. Researchers who have been using the Taylor scale now can feel either less guilty because it is factorially respectable, or more guilty because it has little to do with clinically judged anxiety. This is not an easy book to read. Not only is a large array of data presented in a very compact style, but the uninitiated will find that a whole new vocabulary is required. At times the reader will be slowed to a crawl while he backtracks to identify and reidentify variables. While the authors advance a defensible rationale—that a science of behavior cannot be expected to be simple—it is equally true that complexity and validity are not synonymous and it is unfortunate that many potential readers may be lost when a more fluent style would have served equally well. In summary, this report of a systematic, continuing attempt to explore personality through factor analysis is highly recommended for all those involved in personality theory and research. It is hoped that some of the variables defined factorially by the authors will be taken up and investigated experimentally. The authors' suggestion that their measures be adopted by practitioners in the clinical setting is likely to go unheeded, at least for some time. The approach is an alien one to most clinicians, many of whom have heavy investments in other methods offering greater intuitive freedom, if not so much objectivity and validity.

Occup Psychol 35:253–6 O '61. H. J. Eysenck. * The book is difficult to review * The contents cover such a wide variety of subjects, and are strung together so loosely in conformity with an over-all plan which is not always apparent to the reader, that any attempt to discover precisely what the evidence is for a given statement, or how it fits in with the general scheme, becomes extremely difficult. The task is not made easier by Cattell's dualistic habit of referring to factors sometimes in terms of a numerical system, sometimes in terms of a verbal system which requires almost as much acquaintance with his previous writings to understand. Indeed, it would probably be true to say that this book would be almost unintelligible on its own and without extensive familiarity with Cattell's previous writings. This is not to say that it would not be extremely rewarding for the expert reader, but for the average student, attracted by the title and imagining that he will find some general discussion and consideration of its facts and viewpoints, the impact is liable to be traumatic. * it is very encouraging for the reviewer to note that the two quite separate streams of research represented by the work of Cattell's unit and that at the Maudsley Hospital have now agreed in their main conclusions. Through the further analysis of second-order factors Cattell has finally come to the conclusion that the two main and most easily reproducible factors in the personality field are extraversion-introversion and neuroticism (which he prefers to call "anxiety"). * This agreement, as will be seen from the top diagram on page 132, also extends to the position of psychiatric nosological groups in the framework provided. * Results from the Maudsley have always shown that psychotic reactions are entirely dissimilar to neurotic ones, and it has been proposed that psychoticism as a personality dimension is orthogonal to neuroticism. Cattell confirms this view * What is normally called "neuroticism," Cattell calls "anxiety"; he finds that what amounts to random sample of neurotics cannot be characterized by a single primary or second-order factor. This, however, is hardly surprising. * It is unfortunate that Cattell has chosen to use the terms ("neuroticism" and "anxiety") which play such a large part in the work of other investigators, but has changed their meaning around in such a way that what they call neuroticism, he calls anxiety, and what they would call anxiety he calls neuroticism. The innocent reader might be sorely perplexed to understand Cattell's work and that of others if he failed to pay attention to this important point. * Cattell relies very much on factor analysis, occasionally attempting to integrate it with psychoanalytic concepts. This integration, being almost purely semantic, does not strike one as very convincing, and psychoanalysts have been rather chary of accepting the olive branch held out by this otherwise resolute empiricist. To the reviewer the lack of any theoretical concepts and development is the weakest point in Cattell's work and probably marks the strongest contrast between it and the kind of research carried out at the Maudsley. "A correlation coefficient is a confession of ignorance," Thurstone once said, meaning that the knowledge that a relationship exists between two variables tells us nothing about the all-important causal relations between them. Much the same comment may be made about a factor loading, and the failure of Cattell's work to be more widely accepted by personality theorists and others is possibly due, in part at least, to his failure to link up his descriptive factors with causal theories culled from learning theory. * Cattell uses many physiological, autonomic, biochemical and other measures in his work, but he never publishes sufficient detail to make it possible to duplicate the work or to judge it properly. Physiological measures in particular are so dependent on the precise conditions of measurement (temperature, electrode paste, wiring diagram, *et cetera*) that failure to specify these in the greatest possible detail presents the reader with considerable difficulties of interpretation. It is difficult to find an answer to this problem; giving all the required detail would make the book at least twice as long, and would probably make it impossible to publish at all. Possibly the next book will give details of the kind required. Even then, however, there are many questions and doubts that remain in one's mind. The precise details of many of Cattell's objective tests (length of practice, length of rest pause, *et cetera*) seem to have been arrived at on an almost arbitrary basis; yet they may profoundly determine the actual results obtained. One would often like to have a detailed discussion of the reasons for choosing one set of values for the experiment rather than another, and indeed one often feels that a test should not be made part of a large battery before it has been investigated for its own sake in very considerable detail. The slightly critical tone of this review should not mislead the reader into thinking that Cattell's new book is anything but a truly important and exciting contribution to the literature on the objective measurement of personality. * Cattell is in the very forefront of all those attempting to make the study of personality into a scientific branch of psychology * this new volume represents an important step in this endeavour.

[B121]

★Chase, Clinton I.; Ludlow, H. Glenn; and Pugh, Richard C. **Predicting Success for Master's Degree Students in Education.** Indiana Studies in Prediction No. 5. Bloomington, Ind.: Bureau of Educational Studies and Testing, Indiana University, 1964. Pp. v, 25. Paper. $0.50. *

[B122]

★Chase, Clinton I.; Ludlow, H. Glenn; Pomeroy, Martha C.; and Barritt, L. Spencer. **Predicting Individual Course Success for Entering Freshmen.** Indiana Studies in Prediction No. 2. Bloomington, Ind.: Bureau of Educational Studies and Testing, Indiana University, 1963. Pp. v, 41. Paper, lithoprinted. $0.50. *

[B123]

★Chase, Clinton I.; Ludlow, H. Glenn; Pomeroy, Martha C.; and Barritt, L. Spencer. **Predicting Success for University Freshmen.** Indiana Studies in Prediction No. 1. Bloomington, Ind.: Bureau of Educational Studies and Testing, Indiana University, 1963. Pp. vi, 47. Paper, lithotyped. $0.50. *

[B124]

★Chase, Clinton I.; Ludlow, H. Glenn; Pugh, Richard C.; and Pomeroy, Martha C. **Predicting Success for Advanced Graduate Students in Education.** Indiana Studies in Prediction No. 4. Bloomington, Ind.: Bureau of Educational Studies and Testing, Indiana University, January 1964. Pp. v, 36. Paper, lithotyped. $0.50. *

[B125]

★Chauncey, Henry, and Dobbin, John E. **Testing: Its Place in Education Today.** New York: Harper & Row, Publishers, Inc., 1963. Pp. xiii, 225. $4.00. (London: Harper & Row Ltd. 30*s*.) * (*PA* 38:9257)

Sat R 47:73 Ja 18 '64. Paul Woodring. * Most of the scholarly books on testing are too technical for the lay reader. For parents and school board members, as well as for the many teachers who lack a sophisticated knowledge of statistics, the most readable and authoritative discussion of testing to have appeared in many years is *Testing: Its Place in Education Today* * By analyzing examples of questions from standardized tests, the authors effectively refute the charge that multiple choice questions measure only factual knowledge. They cite many examples of items that require logical thinking and could not possibly be answered from memory alone. They also offer convincing evidence that many of the other criticisms directed against standardized tests are without foundation. But the authors are alert to the danger that test scores will be misused. * This book is a useful antidote to the many recent volumes critical of testing. Although much of the criticism has some basis in fact, the vast and complex educational enterprise of 1964 could not operate effectively without standardized testing of some kind. Since tests must be used, the task facing educators is to learn to use them more wisely. To this task, Chauncey and Dobbin have made a significant contribution.

Sci 144:44 Ap 3 '64. M. H. Trytten. * a very timely book * there is a philosophy of criticism and dissent, and at times of revolt, against the whole testing movement, as well as criticism of specific tests and test procedures. Thus, an authoritative book on testing is needed. Chauncey and Dobbin have been admirably restrained, factual, and objective in their book. A brief history of testing constitutes the first chapter. The second chapter deals with tests of learning ability. These chapters form an indispensable background for anyone seeking orientation with respect to the understanding and use of tests. They should be required reading in many contexts. * *Testing* should be of great value to the manifold users of tests, and it should become a landmark as well as a point of departure for future literature on testing. *

[B126]

★CLARK, KENNETH E. **The Vocational Interests of Nonprofessional Men.** Minneapolis, Minn.: University of Minnesota Press, 1961. Pp. xi, 129. $3.75. (London: Oxford University Press. 30s.) *

Cont Psychol 7:398–9 N '62. Robert Callis. Some psychologists have suggested that the vocational interest of non-professional men is essentially undifferentiated, and, therefore, cannot be adequately measured for purposes of classification and occupational choice. Clark challenged this notion and proceeded to investigate the nature of vocational interest of skilled tradesmen both civilian and military. * One of the most interesting sections of the book has to do with the length of a scale in relation to validity. * His data suggest (to the reviewer) four major clusters of occupational groups. * The author has not done justice to his 16 years of intensive research. He was liberal with numbers and stingy with words (56 tables in 129 pages). A fuller interpretation of his findings would have markedly improved the book. However, Clark has made a major contribution to professional literature on vocational interest. It is a fascinating landmark, but a difficult book.

J Counsel Psychol 9:401 w '62. Donald E. Super. * In this slim monograph Clark reports more than ten years of painstaking work in the measurement of the vocational interests of men in occupations hitherto slighted, together with the development of the Minnesota Vocational Interest Inventory and its scales. He provides better answers than any hitherto available on the questions of homogeneous versus empirical or occupational keys, and throws light on the structure of interests at the skilled occupational levels. He still does not deal with the problem of the interests of unskilled workers, nor even those of the semiskilled, but we may rejoice in being able to move one step further down the scale. There is not much here for the practitioner, until the MVII is published as such, but this is a must for those who would understand better the structure of interests and the nature of interest inventories.

[B127]

*CLARKE, H. HARRISON. **Application of Measurement to Health and Physical Education, Third Edition.** Englewood Cliffs, N.J.: Prentice-Hall, Inc., 1959. Pp. xv, 528. $7.95. * (London: Prentice-Hall International, Inc. 64s.) For reviews of the earlier editions, see 4:B92 and 3:805–6.

[B128]

★CLAWSON, AILEEN. **The Bender Visual Motor Gestalt Test for Children: A Manual.** Beverly Hills, Calif.: Western Psychological Services, 1962. Pp. ii, 29, 43. Paper, spiral binding. $6.50. *

[B129]

★CLIFTON, JAMES A., AND LEVINE, DAVID. **Klamath Personalities: Ten Rorschach Case Studies.** [Lawrence, Kan.: James A. Clifton, University of Kansas], 1961. Pp. iv, 80. Paper, lithotyped. Gratis to libraries and specialists. *

Am Anthrop 64:1342–3 D '62. Roy G. D'Andrade. * The Rorschach analyses by David Levine were made "initially without information concerning the subject's life history." The subjects were selected to represent the most varied types of cultural and psychological adjustment. Use of group averages, either by mean, median, or mode, is completely rejected as sterile and mechanical. (In the reviewer's opinion, while statistics *can* be used in "sterile" and "mechanical" fashion, they can also be used in a constructive and creative fashion. Certainly some use of averages would have been helpful in this study to allow comparisons with other cultural groups.) Levine has relied extensively on Piotrowski's method of percept analysis and has focused primarily on the way in which both impulses and the external world are managed by the individual, rather than "probing unconscious depths." In a sense, this brief monograph serves as an example of the present and past dilemmas of culture and personality research. The strong reliance on Rorschach rather than observational data to establish personality characteristics; the formation of generalizations based on subjective impressions which have at most the status of a hypothesis; the attempt to formulate "typical" personality types in the face of a wide range of personality characteristics; the failure to find a general model which can be used to predict relevant personality characteristics; all these seem to leave culture and personality studies marking time. Clifton deserves some commendation for attacking these problems in his thesis. The outcome of his work, however, seems valuable mainly as additional documentation concerning the plight of reservation life.

J Proj Tech 26:251–3 Je '62. Sohan Lal Sharma. * The aim of this study is to record variant attributes of personality, understanding of the psychological, especially the interpersonal aspects of Klamath personality, and the synthesis of the psychological and cultural data which may throw additional light on psychological consequences of acculturation. * had the psychologist used more of an eclectic approach to the interpretation of the Rorschach records, rather than sticking so closely to Piotrowski's method, he might have been able to pick up many other facets of the Klamath personality structure and their interpersonal relationships, e.g., the role of aggression and passivity. The present study, contrary to certain prevailing beliefs, shows that the more the Rorschach interpreter is familiar with the culture that is being studied, the better the chances of his arriving at meaningful interpretations of the records. It is, therefore, unfortunate that the interpreter, although extremely familiar with Klamath culture, did not make much use of the content of the records. To this reviewer, it appears that the use and the interpretation of the test contents provides one of the more reliable guides to the subjects' acculturation level. Although no comparison within the same culture is made, the records of these ten Klamath cases are compared with the other Red Indian tribes of the United States who are going through a similar process of acculturation. Thus, the study shows clearly the strains and effect of acculturation. *

[B130]

★College Entrance Examination Board. **College Board Score Reports: A Guide for Admission Officers.** New York: the Board, 1962. Pp. 20. Paper. Out of print. * For the lastest edition, see B132.

[B131]

★College Entrance Examination Board. **College Board Score Reports: A Guide for Counselors: Preliminary Scholastic Aptitude Tests, Scholastic Aptitude Test, and Achievement Tests.** New York: the Board, 1963. Pp. 44. Paper. Out of print. * For the latest edition, see B132.

[B132]

★College Entrance Examination Board. **College Board Score Reports: A Guide for Counselors and Admissions Officers: Preliminary Scholastic Aptitude Test, Scholastic Aptitude Test, Achievement Tests.** New York: the Board, 1964. Pp. 58. Paper. $0.25. *

[B133]

*College Entrance Examination Board. **A Description of the College Board Achievement Tests.** New York: the Board, 1964. Pp. 119. Paper. Gratis. * (Earlier editions published in 1956, 1958, 1959, 1960, 1962, and 1963.)

[B134]

*College Entrance Examination Board. **A Description of the College Board Scholastic Aptitude Test.** New York: the Board, 1964. Pp. 55. Paper. Gratis. * (Earlier editions published in 1956, 1960, 1962, and 1963.)

[B135]

★College Entrance Examination Board. **A Description of the College Board Supplementary Achievement Tests.** New York: the Board, 1963. Pp. 62. Paper. Gratis. *

[B136]

★College Entrance Examination Board. **Manual of Freshman Class Profiles, 1964 Edition.** New York: the Board, 1964. Pp. xiv, 584. Paper. $7.00. * (Earlier editions published in 1961, 1962, and 1963.)

Col & Univ 37:302–4 sp '62. Jean Reiss. [Review of the 1961 edition.] * This *Manual* is an excellent type of basic textbook and should be on every college counselor's bookshelf, readily available as a reference. Probably the two most important benefits to be derived are (1) that it gives counselors increased knowledge which should enable them to do a better job of counseling with all students, and (2) that it serves as an aid in cutting down multiple applications, especially the applications from those clearly unqualified candidates who are certain to be rejected at the colleges they and their parents are considering. *

[B137]

★COLLEGE ENTRANCE EXAMINATION BOARD. **Review of College Board Research, 1952–60.** New York: the Board, 1961. Pp. iv, 67. Paper. Gratis. * (A revision of *Review of the Research Activities of the College Entrance Examination Board, 1952–57* by Joshua A. Fishman.)

[B138]

★COLLEGE ENTRANCE EXAMINATION BOARD, COMMISSION ON ENGLISH, HAROLD C. MARTIN, CHAIRMAN. **End-of-Year Examinations in English for College-Bound Students Grades 9–12: Sample Questions in Language, Literature, and Composition; Sample Responses by Students; Evaluations of the Responses.** New York: the Board, 1963. Pp. viii, 193. Paper, spiral binding. $2.00. *

Col Engl 25:231 D '63. Charles D. O'Connell. The project of which this volume is the report began in 1960 when the Commission on English of the College Entrance Examination Board prepared and pre-tested on about 1,200 college freshmen an experimental year-end examination for the twelfth grade. Similar materials were then developed and tested for grades 9, 10, and 11. The result is a significant contribution to the field of college preparatory English * Each examination consists of three questions. The first tests the ability to read and analyze an unfamiliar literary passage (admirably chosen, by the way). The second requires the writing of a well-organized essay based upon literary works already known. The third measures achievement in some aspect of language study. All the questions test competence in writing clear, correct English. But this book is much more than a set of "model examinations." More helpful than the questions to the new or even the veteran teacher of high school English are the sample student answers that are presented, followed by the genuinely illuminating critical comments of experienced teachers. Answers, for the most part, are graded on a five-point scale, with generous examples of the sublime and the ridiculous; careful, evaluative comments follow, written not as if for students, but by English teachers for other English teachers. It is here that the report may well provide the "precise and practical" help for which it is intended, for most teachers will surely profit (I know I did) from the kind of insights not only into effective teaching that the comments provide but into the kind of literary analysis that is possible at even the secondary school level. All in all, the book is graced by an orderly, beautifully simple, and eminently helpful organization. It manages with some success to walk the very narrow line between the real and the ideal, to show us what students are like and at the same time to hint what they are capable of becoming. The effect, the Commission rightly hopes, will be stimulating to teachers rather than disheartening. The Commission and the College Board emphasize that the examinations in the report *"have absolutely no bearing on college admissions. The College Board has no intention of using them for that purpose"* (italics in original). Their concern is misplaced, I think. It would be most comforting, at least to this admissions officer, if schools were to begin teaching with such goals in mind as these examinations test rather than the Scholastic Aptitude Test or English Composition Achievement Test. Most models that are provided for teaching English effectively are good enough in themselves but by their nature sterile; the virtue of this report is that it has obvious powers of reproduction that may stimulate not only teachers of college-bound students but even the secondary school curriculum. It is enough to make us look forward with enthusiasm and confidence to further help from the Commission on English.

Engl J 52:717–8 D '63. Edmund J. Farrell. * One might question the suitability of at least two questions, Question 1, Grade 9, and Question 2, Grade 12. The first requires the student to analyze a paragraph about a father's perceptions of his son's typical days while attending a private school in New York. In ghetto schools, in metropolitan areas, and in rural secondary schools, the content and concerns of the paragraph would seem beyond the ken of many intelligent ninth graders. The second question solicits sweeping generalizations from the students * But one shouldn't cavil. Certainly the questions are superior to those composed by most harassed teachers at the end of a school year. The poems to be analyzed are twentieth-century poems and not from those usually anthologized; the literary works to be discussed are those of the student's choosing. If there is an Achilles' heel, it is to be found in the examinations on language, from which one cannot infer a sequential program of instruction for students. If the heel is exposed, it is exposed throughout the profession, however; the Commission may be forgiven for failing to create examinations which would simultaneously please the traditional, descriptive, and generative grammarians, as well as the philologists and semanticists among us. Certainly this report should be read by every teacher and discussed in every department of secondary English in the country. With rare exceptions the questions are judiciously composed; the student answers are revealing, sometimes profound, occasionally delightful; the readers' analyses and commentaries are insightful and, thankfully, unsplenetic. Teachers who initially feared that the Commission, working under the aegis of the powerful College Entrance Examination Board, would impose a curriculum in secondary English should be reassured, not only by Mr. Rinker's introduction to the examinations but by the examinations themselves. Those seeking prescription and proscription must continue to seek elsewhere.

[B139]

★College Entrance Examination Board, Committee on Advanced Placement, 1962, Thomas C. Mendenhall, Chairman. **Advanced Placement Program: Course Descriptions.** New York: the Board, 1963. Pp. 152. Paper. $1.50. *

[B140]

★Committee on Measurement in Physical Education, Anna Espenschade, Chairman. **California Physical Performance Tests.** Sacramento, Calif.: California State Department of Education, 1962. Pp. vii, 109. Paper. $0.35. *

[B141]

★Coombs, Clyde H. **A Theory of Data.** New York and London: John Wiley & Sons, Inc., 1964. Pp. xix, 585. $14.95; 113s. * (*PA* 39:53)

[B142]

Coombs, Clyde H., and Kao, R. C. **Nonmetric Factor Analysis.** University of Michigan, Engineering Research Institute, Bulletin No. 38. Ann Arbor, Mich.: University of Michigan Press, 1955. Pp. vii, 63. Paper, lithotyped. Out of print. * (*PA* 32:2288)

Psychometrika 24:93–4 Mr '59. Samuel Messick. Following a brief description of Coombs' theory of data, this slender technical monograph treats two classes of models for the resolution of behavior into components. These models, conjunctive-disjunctive and compensatory, are intended for scaling dichotomous monotone items collected by the method of single stimuli. The models are not competitive with Guttman scalogram analysis but are offered as multidimensional formulations which might be appropriate when unidimensional solutions are not obtained. A general axiomatic basis for the approach is presented, and theorems specific to each model are derived separately. Some very helpful interpretive material is interspersed throughout the mathematical development. * Several advantages may accrue from a mathematically precise formulation of a measurement model, not the least of which is the clarity gained from an explicit statement of assumptions and inferences. For example, the precise formalization of a model might stimulate theory construction in measurement by providing the foundation for further generalizations and by making it possible to compare the exact properties of different methods. A more important contribution is sometimes made, however, in that the models underlying various measurement methods frequently have implications for theorizing in psychology. Some such implications, a few of which are briefly illustrated in the Introduction, are attendant upon the distinctions made by Coombs and Kao in formulating the models of *Nonmetric Factor Analysis.* These implications may be derived in spite of the fact that statistical machinery has not yet been developed for practical applications of the models. The elegance and precision gained through the axiomatic presentation has an accompanying difficulty of reading, so that the audience for this technical monograph seems limited to measurement specialists interested in the theory of models.

[B143]

*Cornell University, University Testing and Service Bureau. **Cornell University Test List, 1960 Revision.** Ithaca, N.Y.: the Bureau, 1960. Pp. v, 98. Paper, mimeographed. Out of print. *

[B144]

★Craven, Ethel Case. **The Use of Interest Inventories in Counseling.** Chicago, Ill.: Science Research Associates, Inc., 1961. Pp. iv, 44. Paper. $1.50. *

[B145]

*Cronbach, Lee J. **Essentials of Psychological Testing, Second Edition.** New York: Harper & Row, Publishers, Inc., 1960. Pp. xxi, 650. $7.50. * (London: Harper & Row Ltd., 1961. 56s.) (*Test Items to Accompany Essentials of Psychological Testing, Second Edition.* By Douglas McKie and Lee J. Cronbach. 1964. Pp. i, 75. Paper. Gratis to instructors using the book as a text. *) (*PA* 36:1HA50C)

Am J Psychol 73:323–4 Je '60. Benjamin Rosner. * among the most teachable introductions to psychometric theory and practice currently available to students of testing * Several comments may be made regarding....Part I * First, while much space is devoted to specific delineation of the APA code for test distribution, reference to the APA *Technical Recommendations* is rather casual. Secondly, considering Cronbach's statement that "A decision about the merit of a test must come after study of the test manual and accompanying information, the Buros yearbook reviews, and other sources," the treatment of sources of test information seems rather cursory. Lastly, and perhaps out of concern for elementary and secondary school teachers who are likely to study the text, there is a lack of treatment of the mechanics of item-writing and too little on the general test construction process. * Although parts I and II are clearly written and highly stimulating, part III generates and sustains an even higher level of interest. This is due, no doubt, to the intrinsic character of the material, but still more to the excellent quality of the analytic and evaluative commentary. Particularly appealing is the discussion of the bandwidth-fidelity dilemma in the summary chapter appraising clinical and actuarial approaches to the assessment of personality. In brief, here is an outstanding introduction to current psychological testing. There is no question that the present edition adds to the quality of its almost classic predecessor.

Austral J Psychol 13:125–7 Je '61. J. A. Radcliffe. Following substantial changes in organization and content and the inclusion of much new material this book more effectively realizes its aim to show the student how "to choose tests wisely" than did the earlier edition. * It is a pity that he repeats the popular view that K-R 21 is "less accurate" than K-R 20, whereas in fact it involves a different concept of "error," treating variance of item difficulties as a component of "error" variance. * Choice among personality trait measures "can be made only on aesthetic grounds" and the Guilford-Zimmerman and Cattell questionnaires are relegated to inclusion in the list of other tests available. In fact, the 16 PF test is "not recommended for assessment of individuals"! Cronbach seems to be able to make "decisions" independently of institutional affiliations! * the most interesting chapter is that on "Performance Tests of Personality." Here is an excellent review of "structured" tests (especially of perceptual and cognitive styles), tasks involving "complex performance" (problem solving, perception, and group behaviour), and "thematic projection" techniques. The Rorschach receives much less space than formerly and it is noticeable that with all its empirical emphasis the chapter contains no reference to Cattell's "objective" tests of personality. The layout is more attractive than before, tables and illustrations are clearer, and better discussion exercises are included. In all, it is a good *textbook* on how to choose, how to give, and how to interpret tests, especially for "decision making." There is a healthy empirical emphasis, tempered by the recognition that the psychometric approach must be supplemented by "judgment." It is not a book on assessment techniques generally but could well serve as a foundation for such a course. On selected topics it could also be a useful reference book.

Can J Psychol 14:287–8 D '60. R. W. Payne. * a good text for an introductory undergraduate course in psychological testing, although even for this purpose some teachers might find it unnecessarily simplified. It is far too elementary for a postgraduate course. As a textbook on psychological testing, it has two very considerable advantages. First of all, no statistical or mathematical demands are made on the reader at all. However this advantage has not been obtained at the expense of the discussion of the fundamental psychometric problems of reliability, validity, and standardization. Also, each statistical procedure is explained to the reader very competently indeed with the aid of easily understandable diagrams, and the implications of these statistics are made quite clear. If this book errs at all, it is in underestimating the capacity of the under-graduate student approaching psychological tests for the first time, even without prior statistical knowledge. The 1937 revision of the Stanford-Binet test was in many ways a landmark in the history of psychometrics * none of the technical difficulties involved in this Binet revision are discussed by Cronbach, and age scales in general are made to sound deceptively simple to construct and standardize. Occasionally, in an attempt to simplify, the author is guilty of misleading the reader seriously. For example, on page 223, when discussing speeded *versus* unspeeded tests of intelligence he writes: "The trend in recent American tests is to provide ample time for nearly everyone to finish. This point of view is not universally accepted. Eysenck (1953) and Furneaux in England argue that the speed with which the mind produces hypotheses is the essence of good problem solving, and that a speeded test is therefore the best measure of mental ability."

This is to misrepresent Furneaux's position completely, since Furneaux has argued strongly that measuring any single intellectual characteristic (speed, error, or persistence) gives a completely inadequate description of intellectual capacity, and that what is needed are various tests, each producing relatively pure measures of each of these aspects of cognitive function. Indeed what Furneaux means by a test of intellectual speed is not simply a speeded test, since this is an impure measure. In spite of these minor defects, this text is one of the best introductory books on this subject which I have so far read.

For reviews of the first edition, see 4:B101.

[B146]

★Dahlstrom, W. Grant, and Welsh, George Schlager. **An MMPI Handbook: A Guide to Use in Clinical Practice and Research.** Minneapolis, Minn.: University of Minnesota Press, 1960. Pp. xx, 559. $8.75. * (*PA* 35:2217) (London: Oxford University Press, 1961. 70*s*.)

Cont Psychol 6:167–8 My '61. E. R. Oetting. * The *Handbook* is obviously destined to be the basic text on what has proved to be the most adequate and most widely used instrument for personality assessment today. The authors' opinions and ideas not only have the weight of their considerable authority in this field but also are thoroughly documented and based on experimental evidence and sound theoretical concepts. The work is encyclopedic, particularly in the area of clinical applications, where the mass of reported studies and references becomes almost overwhelming. * The brief section on administration will be of some value to the initiate and the psychometrist. The discourse on the basic scales is clear and concise, providing a foundation for the student and a refreshing review for the experienced. The true core of this book, which begins with Chapter 4, is the precise, rational introduction to the use of patterns and configural analysis in the interpretation of the MMPI. The authors not only describe and illustrate the common types of psychograph but succeed in providing a clear and logical approach to interpretation of profile characteristics beyond the individual scales. We might hope that the text would serve to suppress the prolification of further scales. The richness and depth of the configural approach is strongly emphasized and should yield some repugnance toward the abstraction of a 214th MMPI scale to add to Appendix I. * Starke Hathaway, in the *Foreword,* comments succinctly on item validity and the value of identifying, rather than of eliminating, the "K" attitudes, the motivated distortion of response. The base-rate problem, relating particularly to the difficulty of predicting any rare event, is also placed in its proper perspective, not as a destroyer of validity, but as a limitation on utility. The "Barnum" and "Aunt Fanny" effects on test interpretation are lucidly presented and should arouse some guilt-produced anxiety in a few complacent clinicians. Included as well are the previously unpublished Meehl-Dahlstrom rules, a "multi-stage, sequential system to typify profiles as neurotic, psychotic or indeterminate." Despite the caution that the "rules" themselves are still in the research stage, this publication is likely to lead to their widespread clinical use. Any risk due to premature application should be more than offset by increased circulation of a new methodology for classifying and using pattern relationships in an actuarial device. The only disappointed reader will be the one who is seeking "the way" of interpreting the MMPI. At times the authors extend an hypothesis with some confidence. Most often, the reader is left to build his own ideas from the evidence and to test them through experiment or experience. In short, we find that, as expected, Dahlstrom and Welsh have given us a *Handbook,* not of constants, but of constructs, earnestly soliciting additions and modifications of the nomological nets they represent.

[B147]

★Dailey, John T., and Shaycoft, Marion F. **Types of Tests in Project Talent: Standardized Aptitude and Achievement Tests.** United States Office of Education, Cooperative Research Monograph No. 9. Washington, D.C.: United States Government Printing Office, 1961. Pp. v, 62. Paper. $0.25. * (*PA* 36:4KK62D)

[B148]

★Darley, Frederic L., Editor. **Identification Audiometry.** A Report Prepared With Support of the Children's Bureau, United States Department of Health, Education, and Welfare by the Committee on Identification Audiometry, American Speech and Hearing Association, William G. Hardy, Chairman. The Journal of Speech and Hearing Disorders Monograph Supplement Number 9. Washington, D.C.: American Speech and Hearing Association, September 1961. Pp. iv, 68. Paper. $1.90. *

[B149]

★Darley, John G. **Promise and Performance: A Study of Ability and Achievement in Higher**

Education. Berkeley, Calif.: Center for Study of Higher Education, University of California, 1962. Pp. vii, 191. Paper. $2.00. *

Cont Psychol 9:51–3 F '64. Paul S. Burnham. * a masterful handling of a tremendous amount of statistical information * The data were drawn from 200 institutions enrolling some 60,000 students entering in 1952 and are presented in 89 different tables, not including those in the Appendix. * In order to make comparisons between and within groups of institutions, Darley had not only to establish transmutation scales between the various editions of certain aptitude tests but also across the board, so to speak, among the following eight measures: ACE, SAT, SCAT, CQT, AGCT, OTIS, OSUPE, and NSF. His Appendix C gives the basic assumptions involved in these various conversions and follows it up with presentation of conversion tables so developed. In summary, all available Aptitude Test Scores were converted to the 1952 ACE basis. The 1952 edition of the American Council on Education Psychological Examination had been chosen as the bench mark since it was the measure most generally available in statewide surveys. Other workers who encounter the same problem will welcome the conversion tables that Darley provides. Any user of them, however, will be well advised to heed William Angoff's admonitions (ETS Invitational Conference, 1962) on the difficulties involved in establishing statistically adequate transmutation scales. * The major research reported is based on longitudinal studies of large samples of students in four states. Measures of academic ability were related to socio-economic factors, types of institutions, survival and withdrawal rates and to occupational choices. * one of the most provocative findings was that in none of the four states studied intensively did as many as 50% of the students graduate within the time limits of the follow-up studies; and in each state the percentages withdrawing before graduation closely paralleled the percentages graduating. * *Promise and Performance* is a major contribution to the literature on higher education. It raises questions that should leave many people disturbed by the status quo.

[B150]

★Davis, Frederick B. **Educational Measurements and Their Interpretation.** Belmont, Calif.: Wadsworth Publishing Co., 1964. Pp. ix, 422. Text price, $7.50; trade price, $10.00. *

[B151]

*Dearborn, Walter F., and Rothney, John W. M.; with the cooperation of Howard H. Long, John M. Ratcliff, William J. Crissy, Helen E. Donnelly, and Grace McGlinchey. **Predicting the Child's Development, Second Revised Edition.** Cambridge, Mass.: Sci-Art Publishers, [1963]. Pp. 368. Paper, $3.95; cloth, $9.50. * (A reprinting of the original 1941 edition with the addition of a preface and a 7-page supplement, "Twenty-Two Years Later," by John W. M. Rothney.) (*PA* 38:636)

Child Develop Abstracts 38:57–8 F–Ap '64. G. T. Kowitz. * a paperback edition of the classic report on the monumental Harvard Growth Study. Very little has been added to this standard work on child development. * The final section, entitled "Twenty-Two Years Later," restates the position of the original study: the behavior of individuals is not the same as the behavior of groups. However, no hint is given on why most of the data is presented on groups or how the results can be interpreted for individuals. The only general conclusion is that the growth process is far more complex than the pioneers of child study had suspected. The Harvard Growth Study, which was started in 1922, involved over 3500 children. Hundreds of them were retested throughout their school life. Measures of physical growth, intelligence, and scholastic achievement were obtained. The data are explored in every conceivable way—in terms of actual magnitude, in ratios to other dimensions and in ratios of the same dimensions at different times in the child's life. Perhaps the most interesting thing about the book is that it was reprinted at a time when there is little respect for broad, empirical research. In an era when research must be theoretically based with complex and even exotic statistical tests of specific hypotheses, it is strange to find a volume of a posteriori explorations of a massive collection of data. The conclusion posts a challenge to more recent and sophisticated efforts: Very few generalizations of the original analyses of the Harvard Growth Study have been discarded and even fewer ones have emerged. It is suggested "there has been little coordination of the efforts of investigators, and the research reports too frequently contain too little data about too few persons over too short a period to permit generalizations." On the other hand, this classic report has not been the foundation of a theory of knowledge about human development. It has been, and probably will continue to be, an important historical benchmark for the study of child development.

For reviews of the first edition, see 3:837.

[B152]

DELAY, J.; PICHOT, P.; LEMPÉRIÈRE, J.; AND PERSE, J. **The Rorschach and the Epileptic Personality.** New York: Hoeber Medical Division, Harper & Row, Publishers, Inc., 1958. Pp. xx, 265. $6.00. * (*PA* 33:8866)

Brit J Med Psychol 32:298 pt 4 '59. Theodora Alcock. This book, first published in the original French in 1955, has already proved its value, and this admirable translation is greatly to be welcomed by those interested in either aspect of its subject. The methodology of the research project which the authors describe appears quite admirable, precisely planned and most faithfully carried out. They survey the literature of not less than eight countries on the epileptic personality, and discuss the published findings critically from various standpoints. * To quote Piotrowski's foreword, "this volume presents a model of what the Rorschach approach to a diagnostic problem should be." The results are both impressive and useful. The authors make a highly significant contribution to the vexed question of the epileptic personality by demonstrating this as bi-polar, on the basis of systematic study of the inter-relationship of variables. They distinguish two different types, subjects with a coartative personality being at the first pole, those with an extratensive personality at the second. * a study carried out at the highest level of professional integrity.

J Nerv & Mental Dis 131:172-4 Jl '60. Benjamin Pope. * Although this is a dedicated work, it embodies a realistic awareness of the tentativeness and instability of our knowledge of this subject. * This reviewer cannot refrain from expressing some disappointemnt in the overall findings of this elaborate and carefully conducted investigation. The results do no more than iterate—perhaps in somewhat more specific terms than is usually the case—what has been generally known about various trends in the personalities of people who have epilepsy. The proof in this study regarding the relationship of specific personality deviation to etiology and localization is not very convincing, especially in view of the small number of subjects in the subgroups. The conclusion that the epileptic personality is in many respects similar to the organic non-epileptic personality is, of course, also consistent with previous knowledge. In view of this similarity between epileptic and non-epileptic organic patients it is difficult to understand the rather exuberant claim of the authors regarding the usefulness of the Rorschach in the differential diagnosis of epilepsy. It need hardly be added that this study adds nothing to the settlement of such controversial questions as the hereditary or acquired nature of the epileptic personality and its reactive or primary role in relation to the disease. Nevertheless, if one is interested in a description of the kinds of personality trends that are likely to be encountered in epileptic patients, this book adds considerable descriptive detail, rather more carefully classified and organized than is found elsewhere. Moreover, it is a meticulously organized abstracted report of the current state of knowledge regarding the epileptic personality, both in terms of general theory, and more specifically in terms of Rorschach findings. No one working in this area can afford to overlook this volume.

[B153]

★DE RIDDER, J. C. **The Personality of the Urban African in South Africa: A Thematic Apperception Test Study.** London: Routledge & Kegan Paul Ltd., 1961. Pp. xvi, 180. 25*s*. * (New York: Humanities Press, Inc. $5.00.) (*PA* 37:4811)

Am Anthrop 64:865-6 Ag '62. Leonard W. Doob. The title of this book raises keen expectations because psychological information concerning urban Africans is scarce; but, alas, its content is methodologically disappointing with respect to the very instrument indicated in its subtitle. * The main body of the book consists of results inspired by an analysis of the T.A.T.'s of 2,500 males living for the most part in Johannesburg. The word "inspired" in the last sentence has been chosen deliberately: the author makes no attempt to show how the generalizations have been derived from the data, and no statistical analysis is offered; instead, copious, fascinating illustrations from the protocols are cited. "The urban Africans are an extraordinarily imaginative people," it is stated, but neither the mode of scoring nor the distribution of the attribute is revealed: does every African possess the gift? Even a comparison between Africans from two cities, which suggests that those in Durban are less "sophisticated," less "unrestrained in the expression of their emotions," and less anxious and insecure than those in Johannesburg, contains not a shred of quantitative evidence. Unquestionably the investigator is able to employ his T.A.T. most skillfully. In the introduction he has provided data indicating that he himself achieved remarkable success in identifying, by means of a "blind analysis" of the protocols, which of 163 bus drivers had objectively satisfactory accident and disciplinary records. His categories of analysis are sophisticated and ingenious. The ensuing generalizations are provocative and often original. The failure to show how that skill and those methods have achieved such results is thus particularly regrettable: at the present stage of methodological development it is no longer useful merely to demonstrate an artistic or clinical aptitude in the use of a technique, rather an explicit, objective procedure should be faithfully described. Although the informants composing the sample come from five major societies, no breakdowns even of a qualitative sort are offered. Instead, reference is always made to a statistically defined entity called "the urban African." *

Brit J Social & Clin Psychol 1:156–7 Je '62. S. G. Lee. In the blurb we are told, with unexpected and accidental candour that: "This is a study of these people—their make-up personality...." I find myself in full agreement with this statement, but with little else in this appallingly bad book. Dr de Ridder gave his own version of a T.A.T. to "some 2,500" urban African subjects, to most of whom, apparently, the test was part of a commercial selection procedure. The effect of this "set" is nowhere taken into account, and the crude assumption is made that the subjects' protocols represent, without distortion, "the personality of the Urban African." * The book is truly autistic psychology, the reality check, throughout, being held strictly in abeyance. No attempt is made to produce independent criteria for the individual interpretations made. Any validity rests on stereotyped ideas of the social background derived, sketchily, and at second or third hand, from ethnography based on nineteenth-century reality or, for present day urban conditions, from accounts supplied by literate African informants. These latter have the great advantage, which they share with the T.A.T. protocols quoted, of being written in vivid and readily understandable prose—unlike most of the rest of the book which is filled with wordy and pretentious jargon. The picture stimuli were apparently arbitrarily chosen and no reference is made to previous work in this specific field—e.g. the research by E. T. Sherwood, in Johannesburg, using an African T.A.T. Again, no reference is made to the work of McCrone whose investigations of race attitudes in the area are highly pertinent. The "selected bibliography" is most inadequate. Usually, in the text, one reads that "X says....," followed by some more or less apposite quotation. Nowhere is there further reference to where or when X said it, and the imagination of this reviewer has been enriched by several hitherto unknown, but unfortunately rather vague, declamatory figures. But the chief disservice of the book to psychology and to African studies lies in the pseudo-scientific reinforcement of commonly held lay stereotypes. Most South African whites think that "town kaffirs" show off too much in public and the author of this book is no exception. Again and again the "exhibitionism" of his subjects is claimed: "His fantasy reproductions are remarkably blatant, and his exhibitionism naive and unsophisticated. This aspect of personality immaturity, this outspoken personal selling, this blatant exhibitionism, is typical of the urban African personality. If he decides that the best way to obtain work is to curry favour, he will proceed to 'butter-up' his potential employer in his T.A.T. stories, without any semblance of tact, delicacy or finesse." Indeed, later in the text, this "exhibitionistic trend" is apparently shown in the tendency for African nationalists to "apperceive well-meaning European motives in a totally wrong light." Throughout the penultimate chapter the headings in italics—strangely reminiscent of a mediaeval bestiary—bear little relation to the statements in the text around them. For example: *Male-Female Relations amongst the Younger People of the Urban Areas are an Aggressive, Morally Lax Association, Characterized by Uninhibited Primitivism and Sexual Licentiousness'* (sic) is followed by a general statement that the urban African is not completely emancipated from tribal influence—but sex is not mentioned therein. One gathers that, "The problem which the Europeans in South Africa must face, is what to do with those Africans whose learning has given them ambitions beyond the industrial colour bar." This is true, and the problem is a difficult one, but any reader may or may not be cheered by the assurance that, "The urban African tends towards immature attitudes and an exhibitionistic approach, but such functions in no way imply that he will not respond to understanding and tactful handling." One may even hope that the emergent African may avoid "tribal sectionarism" (sic). In the text we are told that, "When an individual is exposed to a particular culture, a process occurs which can be defined as socialization." A process from which the author of this book, obviously, has not been exempt.

Cont Psychol 8:147–8 Ap '63. Robert A. LeVine. * This study by de Ridder, however, is below the usual standard of South African psychology, lacking the methodological rigor of Biesheuvel's group and the theoretical insight and sophistication of a personologist like Lee. Mr. de Ridder designed a T.A.T. of nine cards to help a Johannesburg bus company select drivers; it was administered to 163 drivers and the results were analyzed blind to predict which men were good accident and disciplinary risks. Against objective criteria of accident liability and disciplinary record, the T.A.T. predictions were (we are told) successful. No details of this study are given in the book. Subsequently, the T.A.T. was administered to 2500 African job applicants. In this book Mr. de Ridder purports to summarize the common personality characteristics of these 2500 male subjects in relation to their cultural environment and social system. This could have been a most interesting and significant study. However, it is so unsystematic—with an alternation of anecdotal material and obscurely founded global generalizations—that it could not be judged successful in the most modest definition of its purpose. Among the more serious flaws of the volume are: the complete absence of quantitative evidence, the journalistic quality of the account of urban African life, the failure to relate ethnographic background meaningfully to test results, the lack of any mention of previously published T.A.T.'s designed for use with Africans in South Africa, viz., those of Lee (1953) and Sherwood (1957). Eighty pages are devoted to illustrative excerpts from the T.A.T. protocols, with comments which point out gross behavioral themes in the social life of Johannesburg Africans: gang violence, racial discrimination, striving for money, the use of American slang, sexual promiscuity. Rarely does the author attempt to analyze in any depth the personalities of the individuals in this social setting, and when he does he produces a spate of ethnocentric clichés: the urban African is "immature," "exhibitionistic," "easily led" (p. 111), and "retains within himself a great deal of the uninhibited, uncontrolled primitive" (p. 158). Although he does not cite any previous psychological studies of Africans, there is evidence that Mr. de Ridder has been influenced by one of them. In the 1959 Hoernle Memorial Lecture in Johannesburg, Biesheuvel applied Riesman's typology of character structure to urban Africa and coined the term "id-directed self" to characterize the transitional state of township dwellers. Mr. de Ridder concludes a year later: "In this cultural reformation, the tradition-directed society of the rural areas....is being supplanted by what may be called an individually-directed society with a predominating id-complex" (p. 154). How unfortunate that his analysis of 2500 T.A.T.'s did not enable the author to go beyond the sweeping, surface formulation of Biesheuvel!

[B154]

★DIEDERICH, PAUL B. **Short-Cut Statistics for Teacher-Made Tests, Second Edition.** Evaluation and Advisory Service Series, No. 5. Princeton, N.J.: Educational Testing Service, 1964. Pp. 33. Paper. Gratis. * (A first edition of 44 pages was published in 1960.)

[B155]

★DODSON, C. J. **Oral Examinations.** Pamphlet No. 12. Aberystwyth, Wales: Faculty of Education, University College of Wales, 1963. Pp. 19. Paper. 2*s.* 6*d.* *

[B156]

DOWNIE, N. M. **Fundamentals of Measurement: Techniques and Practices.** New York and London: Oxford University Press, 1958. Pp. xi, 413. $6.00; 48*s.* * (*PA* 33:9038)

Brit J Ed Psychol 29:271 N '59. P. E. Vernon. Downie's book is misnamed: it has little to do with fundamentals. Rather, it is a sound and useful textbook for an elementary course on intelligence, attainment and personality testing. It is particularly directed to teachers and school or college counsellors, and is extremely practical in its advice throughout. * For British readers perhaps the most useful portion is the summary descriptions of some of the better-known American tests.

Ed & Psychol Meas 19:119–20 sp '59. M. Jacinta Mann. This reviewer, a teacher of a first course in educational measurement, has been searching for an up-to-date text which would provide the happy combination of terseness in theory and practicality in pedagogy. She has found it. Mr. Downie has written it. *

[B157]

★D'OYLEY, VINCENT R. **Technical Manual for the Canadian Tests: Statistical Data on the Carnegie Study Tests of Academic Aptitude and Achievement in Grades 8, 9, and 10 in Ontario Schools and Grades 7 and 8 in Toronto Schools.** Carnegie Study of Identification and Utilization of Talent in High School and College, Bulletin No. 4. Toronto, Canada: Department of Educational Research, Ontario College of Education, University of Toronto, 1964. Pp. viii, 50. $1.00. *

[B158]

★D'OYLEY, VINCENT R. **Testing: The First Two Years of the Carnegie Study 1959 to 1961: Analysis of Scores by Course, Sex, and Size of Municipality.** Carnegie Study of Identification and Utilization of Talent in High School and College, Bulletin No. 6. Toronto, Canada: Department of Educational Research, Ontario College of Education, University of Toronto, 1964. Pp. ix, 53. $1.00. *

[B159]

★DRAKE, L. E., AND OETTING, E. R. **An MMPI Codebook for Counselors.** Minneapolis, Minn.: University of Minnesota Press, 1959. Pp. vii, 140. $3.75. * (London: Oxford University Press. 30*s*.) (*PA* 34:6013)

Brit J Psychol 51:178 My '60. B. Semeonoff. * Standardization of the Codebook was based on work with more than 4000 counselling cases at the University of Wisconsin, which on *prima facie* grounds suggests high probability of validity for a student population. Lacking experience, one cannot form an opinion of the actual validity of the hypotheses, but it may be worth recording that in an informal try-out with about a dozen psychology students two apparently contrasted female profiles each evoked the single hypothesis "mother conflict." By contrast, certain other profiles seem to be associated with such a wide variety of hypotheses that one feels one has arrived nowhere. One is left with the impression that this is not yet the handbook of MMPI diagnosis one had been hoping for. A need for something more universally applicable than this book and less cumbersome than the *Atlas* seems to be indicated.

J Counsel Psychol 7:239 f '60. Irwin A. Berg. * To utilize the codebook, it is essential that the counselor know the MMPI thoroughly and have at least several years of counseling experience behind him. The inexperienced counselor simply cannot use the codebook effectively, because, until additional validity is established, it is essential that the counselor utilize his knowledge of past clients as a kind of "horseback validity" checkout. Those who can do this will benefit considerably from the codebook while those who cannot are likely to be led astray. The inexperienced counselor, however, will benefit from the neatest, most succinct description of the MMPI scales and the rationale for them which has ever been presented. *

Personnel & Guid J 38:510-1 F '60. Florian J. Hering. * In this codebook the three highest and the two lowest scales were placed in the *numerical* order of the coding system irrespective of the deviation magnitude. * The method....does not permit one to speak of a particular profile configuration. The authors, therefore, had to proceed with limited profile data. Hathaway made the same error, but pointed out that the instrument necessitates a compromise in order to convey most of the useful meaning. This compromise is repeatedly questioned in the scientific literature. * The authors' major contribution in this manual is that they describe in positive terms what the college population is in terms of the MMPI profile. They give some more normative data on a normal population. The major criticism of this codebook is that the results of the study need to be cross-validated. In fact, this should have been done before the decision was made to present the manual for use by counselors and as a basic text. Until validity is definitely established, its use by counselors certainly should be limited to the college population and with extreme limitations and caution, and as another hypothesis succinctly emphasized by the authors. It should be used basically as a research tool until there is more empirical validity built into it, and it should be cross-validated on other normal populations before using it as a "cookbook." Until this is accomplished it is wrought with danger because the code section will sometimes be used routinely for positive interpretation of the profile and thus giving it the "P. T. Barnum" effect. This study should have been published as a psychological monograph in order that researchers might bat it around for awhile before presenting it for use in counseling. Contaminations are clearly admitted in this study (pp. 12, 13). The authors stated that "most of the deficiencies in the data do not detract from the positive findings but may have prevented identification of other categories for which the data were too few for statistical analysis" (p. 13). This is pure rationalization. Hathaway made the same error in the early days. Psychiatrists started using the MMPI, having it in front of them while making the diagnosis, and so it made it impossible to use the MMPI as a validity criterion. In the Code Sections the phrase "was infrequently associated with" appears 214 times in the Male Code Section and 336 times in the Female Code Section. It would not be a semantic problem if the repetition contributed to the scientific approach, but it is highly problematical when the code pattern can at times be based upon even a minimum of one interview. There is danger in emphasizing the positive and eliminating the negative which happened in this study. The authors report only the statistically significant code patterns in the tables used in this study. The code sections appear to take into consideration the complete data of the study. There was ample room to show this complete data in the two frequency tables. What are the means and the standard deviations for this study? Are they the same as for the original study which was based upon a clinical population? There are studies showing that the college population achieves considerably higher mean scores. Is the Drake-Oetting opus a product of *"parturient monte, nascetur ridiculus mus,"* or could it be that the manual with its cookbook is what Meehl has in mind when he makes the plea: "Wanted—A Good Cookbook"? Despite its limitation it may serve as part of the link towards an improvement in construct validation. The codebook sections may be the beginning of the end for what Meehl suggests "that for a rather wide range of clinical problems involving personality description from tests, the clinical interpreter is a costly middleman who might better be eliminated." Personality assessment would then be in the field of physics. And until this physical conception of psychology is a fact, "counselors can continue" what Williamson labels "the 'hand-holding' function and thereby temporarily postpone their unemployment." I cannot believe that the human cortex is so simple a structure that it can be reduced completely to the profile language by our present knowledge of measurement.

[B160]

DRESSEL, PAUL, EDITOR. **Evaluation in the Basic College at Michigan State University.** New York: Harper & Row, Publishers., Inc., 1958. Pp. viii, 248. $4.00. *

J Higher Ed 29:407–8 O '58. H. Taylor Morse. This volume assuredly has considerably broader significance for other colleges and other faculties than the title would suggest. While it is, in fact, an account of numerous deep-probing evaluation studies conducted at a single institution, the implications are clear indeed for any college desiring to conduct its own evaluative studies. It would be an invaluable reference for any faculty committee wishing to consider various ways in which it might go about the job for itself. The style is clear, concise, and nontechnical, and the presentation is readily comprehensible. Even a lay reader would find much of interest in the book. The titles of parts and chapters, phrased in sprightly terms, provide initial evidence that this is by no means an ordinary textbook on measurement. * This volume is unquestionably one of the most comprehensive, incisive, and thoughtfully integrated accounts of evaluation of numerous and often complicated aspects and elements of the college learning situation to be found in the literature in the field. Mr. Dressel and his colleagues are refreshingly modest in their discussion of the rôle of evaluation. They freely admit the limitations faced in the course of their investigations, yet they give a clear and decisive account of the crucial part good evaluation studies can play in helping to keep a college program well geared to its objectives and operating within the realities of day-to-day classroom activities. The volume as a whole is well structured to meet the broad purpose stated by its editor: "An evaluation and interpretation of the significance of our accumulated efforts." The task involved is a difficult one, but it is performed at a high level of sincerity, integrity, and effectiveness. * *Evaluation in the Basic College* sets a high standard, indeed, in terms of its comprehensiveness, its sensitiveness to the limitations of evaluative studies and techniques, together with a recognition of their positive contributions, its openmindedness on issues concerning which no clear-cut conclusions have been reached, and its continuous forward movement with further investigations, to keep the data constantly fresh and relevant to the major problems facing an instructional program in higher education. The competence with which these studies were made and the spirit of honest inquiry in which they were undertaken make this volume serviceable to higher education in general. More studies of this kind would be increasingly useful to us in providing new insights into the total function and impact of higher education in our society.

[B161]

★Dressel, Paul L., and Associates. **Evaluation in Higher Education.** Boston, Mass.: Houghton Mifflin Co., 1961. Pp. xvi, 480. $6.50. * (*PA* 36: 4KA80D)

J Higher Ed 33:404–5 O '62. C. E. Ayres. * I find discussions such as this one vaguely alarming * I find my temperamental demurrer taking fairly definite form under three distinct but related issues. First, with regard to educational evaluation generally, it seems to me that there is no getting away from the exercise of judgment. Doubtless a hundred passages could be culled from this book to prove that its authors are well aware of this. That, perhaps, is the study's saving grace. Nevertheless, the several authors seem to agree in favoring so-called objective tests, the sole advantage of which has always seemed to me that they obviate the necessity of passing judgment. Times without number I have heard colleagues say that although the time and effort required to design a satisfactory objective test are at least as great as are involved in giving and grading an essay-type test, they prefer to invest their energy in designing the test rather than in grading papers; and most especially they prefer the precision of the scores. It is most satisfactory to be able to tell a student "You made so-and-so," rather than "I judge your paper thus-and-so." Dressel and his associates are well aware of this foible, and in discussing particular questions they show great acumen. But the precision of objective-test grading still attracts them, and the imprecision of teachers' judgments of essay-type answers still repels them; and this seems to me to mean that their objective is to detach "evaluation" from judgment. Another equally well-known and obvious issue is that of method and content. Is it possible even to discuss evaluation meaningfully in isolation from the nature of what is being evaluated? I am sure that Dressel and all his associates would give a resounding negative answer to such a question. At almost every particular point in the book they do so. But the net effect of the whole is that of a divorce of teaching methods and processes from the widely varying content of the different fields of learning and enquiry. I can think of no better way to designate my third issue than as that of intellectual, and educational, pluralism. Scholars and teachers are not all alike. What one approves, another disapproves—and this is probably a good thing. I have long regarded grade-giving as a voting procedure, and a very good one. Each of us votes whether to encourage a student to go on, or to advise him to leave and get into another occupation (or at least another subject), or whether to give him a *C* and thereby abstain from voting. This means that although each of us must make responsible judgments, no one of us has the power to decide any student's fate. That decision is a collective one. * The implication of this whole evaluational rationale seems to be contradictory of the pluralism which in fact exists. The implication of all these evaluational procedures, including most particularly evaluation of faculty members and institutions, seems to be that there is only one scale on which each of us is either high or low. This is a proposition with which I would readily agree on condition that I stipulate the scale. Like my colleagues, I know a number of people who ought not to be on a university faculty at all. The trouble is, they have lists too, and I am quite likely to be on some of them. Such being the case, we, like the Great Society of which we are a part, have to struggle along on the basis of mutual tolerance and let the future determine which of us is right. At all events, I prefer the future to any evaluation scale I have yet seen.

Teach Col Rec 64:517–8 Mr '63. Richard H. Lindeman. * unique and important contribution to the literature dealing with higher education. While many of the topics included have appeared elsewhere, the sources are either too diffuse to afford reasonable availability, or they are generally inaccessible except to specialists in the areas concerned. * a well organized, highly readable volume * It is decidedly nontechnical, but is necessarily so because of the heterogeneous group at which it is directed. * Perhaps the most important of this book's assets is its broad coverage of diverse but related topics and its synthesis of them in the context of evaluation in higher education. * the book....suffers to some extent from a lack of balance in the topics considered. The case for separate discussions of evaluation in the four content areas mentioned is not convincing. This material comes close to the how-to-do-it type of presentation which is meticulously avoided in the remainder of the volume. It is doubtful whether differences in the principles involved are great enough to warrant separate treatments in this type of volume. These four chapters might well have been reduced to one, with less emphasis on cognitive and more on affective objectives. Such a reduction would have permitted greater attention to the overall evaluation methods considered too briefly in the last two chapters. In spite of this criticism, this is a book which helps significantly in meeting a manifest need. It should be extremely useful to all who are concerned either directly or indirectly with higher education.

[B162]

★DUGGAN, JOHN M., AND HAZLETT, PAUL H., JR. **Predicting College Grades: A Computation Workbook for Estimating Freshman Grade Averages From High School Records and College Board Scores.** New York: College Entrance Examination Board, 1963. Pp. vi, 70, plus inserts. Paper, loose leaves. $2.00. *

[B163]

★DUNN, S. S. **Testing in the Primary School.** Melbourne, Australia: Australian Council for Educational Research, 1962. Pp. v, 30. Paper. 3*s*. *

[B164]

★DUROST, WALTER N., AND PRESCOTT, GEORGE A. **Essentials of Measurement for Teachers.** New York: Harcourt, Brace & World, Inc., 1962. Pp. vii, 167. $3.95. *

Ed & Psychol Meas 22:625–6 au '62. Gilbert Sax. * a concise and readable text * any text which covers the content that the present authors have attempted....can but briefly cover many important topics in educational measurement. Thus, the authors can afford to spend but one paragraph on personality and interest inventories, less than one page on essay examinations, and nothing at all on item analysis. On the other hand, perhaps the authors spent an inordinate amount of time on such concepts as modal-age equivalents (3 pages), techniques for grouping students (11 pages), and the meaning, computation, and uses of stanines (13 pages). The reviewer also believes that some of the tables in the appendices could be eliminated. For example, reciprocals and reciprocals of square roots, products of deviations from 1 to 35 and their square times numbers from 1 to 15, and reciprocals and *f* times the reciprocals (*f* from 1 to 10) for numbers 25 to 120 could easily have been eliminated. The relatively long discussion of how to extract fourth roots from one table could also have been eliminated to make room for more useful material. Considering the size of the text, the authors have done a commendable job in maintaining accuracy without being overly complex. However, a few inaccuracies and overly complicated material are likely to creep into even the very best manuscripts. For example, teachers may experience some difficulty understanding what reliability means when it is first defined as the obtaining of "an identical score on repeated measurements" and later as the "degree of rank-order agreement between two sets of scores." More advanced readers may be concerned about such statements as "split-half and Kuder-Richardson coefficients are....measures of the stability of the test...." or that intelligence tests may be used "to identify individuals who have latent mental capacity," or that Thorndike's three aspects of intelligence are "level, extent, and spread." It seems to the reviewer that the use of the term capacity and the subsequent discussion in the text of under-achievement and over-achievement tends to perpetuate anachronisms in measurement. Indeed the authors state that "an overachiever....is achieving at a level beyond his measured capacity." In general, the text might have been greatly improved by covering fewer topics but in more detail. However, if the text is used by teachers who already have some background in measurement, it may well prove to be of value as a general review.

Personnel & Guid J 41:556–8 F '63. Dugald S. Arbuckle. * The minute size of the book is probably the reason for the major criticism that this reviewer would offer: it is too small really to get at some of the difficulties that it raises, and yet, as a book, one might expect more from it than one would from a chapter on measurement in a book on pupil personnel services. * Another deficiency in the book is its astonishing lack of references and documentation. * This makes the book read, sometimes, like a collection of authors' instructional notes, and the lack of documentation does tend to make for a rather parochial work. * Nevertheless, this is a worthwhile book, and about half of the chapters can be read with profit by the average teacher who has little or no background in measurement or statistics. The authors' ideas are pertinent, functional, and to the point. On the other hand, the authors join a large company of others who have yet to produce a book on the "simple" statistical treatment of tests that can be read and understood, without the aid of an instructor, by one who knows next to nothing about measurement and statistics.

Teach Col Rec 65:463–5 F '64. Frederick B. Davis. * The authors are very familiar with practical problems in measurement and have drawn on their experience to provide useful solutions. Their descriptions and explanations of various types of norms (ch. 5), of methods for grouping pupils (ch. 7), of interpreting test scores to parents (ch. 9), and of simple statistical techniques (ch. 11) should prove helpful to teachers. The materials on tests of intelligence and aptitude (ch. 3) and on the construction and use of tests by the teacher in her own classroom (ch. 4) may also provide needed aid. Because teachers need to judge the accuracy of test scores, the authors have provided (ch. 2) a discussion of the reliability coefficient and of the standard error of measurement. The latter is defined on p. 19 as "an estimate of the amount of variation (change) that would be expected in a test score if another form of the test were administered to the same pupil under comparable conditions...." This sounds like the conventional definition of the standard error of estimate * A good approach to interpreting obtained scores in the discussion on pp. 20–21 might have been to illustrate the use of the standard error of measurement for establishing a range of obtained scores that has a defined probability of including the pupil's true score. *

[B165]

★Dutton, Wilbur H. **Evaluating Pupils' Understanding of Arithmetic.** Englewood Cliffs, N.J.: Prentice-Hall, Inc., 1964. Pp. iv, 153. Paper. $2.95. * (London: Prentice-Hall International, Inc. 20s.)

[B166]

★Educational Testing Service. **ETS Builds a Test.** Princeton, N.J.: the Service, 1959. Pp. 24. Paper. Gratis. *

[B167]

Edwards, Allen L. **The Social Desirability Variable in Personality Assessment and Research.** New York: Holt, Rinehart & Winston, Inc., 1957. Pp. xv, 108. $3.25. * (*PA* 32:464)

Cont Psychol 3:326–8 N '58. Jerry S. Wiggins. * When judges are instructed to rate the desirability or undesirability of traits implied by personality statements, they do so in terms of a continuum that Edwards feels is "the most important single dimension on which to locate personality statements." A social-desirability value may be obtained for any such item by application of one of the conventional psychological scaling methods. People tend to evaluate these items consistently, whether they be college students, Japanese-Americans, high or low status adolescents, Norwegians, psychiatric patients, or "Skid-Row" alcoholic TB patients. More striking than cross-cultural psychophysics, however, is the use to which the scale values themselves can be put. Armed with the values on a social-desirability scale for a group of personality statements, one can account for about 76% of the variance involved when the same items are administered to subjects or patients in inventory, Q-sort or adjective check-list format. This is a dramatic way of saying that the correlation coefficient between the number of people who answer "true" to an item in a personality inventory and the independently judged social-desirability scale value of that item is about .87. This finding has been replicated with such regularity that one has no alternative to accepting it as a fact. It is the implications of this fact for personality assessment and research that constitute the main body of this monograph. Edwards makes a pallid correlational result come to life and subsume such unquestionable techniques as the Q-sort and the mighty MMPI. One is tempted, at points, to view all self-report devices as simply crude measures of social desirability "set" and even to view psychological illness as a kind of pathology of this set. Nor would this kind of expansive extrapolation be discouraged by the tone of the monograph. The weighty evidence, moreover, produces such a sense of urgency that one almost becomes receptive to any proposed solution of this dilemma. Yet there are many points in the fast moving argument at which some will drag their feet. To what extent do these group correlations reflect individual tendencies to answer items in terms of their perceived social desirability? A study by Rosen, which is discussed in the present monograph, may provide insight into this problem, but some would say that the amount of space devoted in the monograph to arguing away Rosen's findings might have been better employed in presenting a more complete picture of what he did. What are the psychological components of the social desirability set? Distinctions between conscious and unconscious distortion, subtle and obvious items, faking "good" and "bad" are soft-pedaled here. We are told only that this set is all that is "purely" measured by the K-scale of the MMPI as well as other unspecified things. At times, the trait becomes so pervasive that one wonders if he might anticipate individual differences in it. Certainly the concept would benefit from a sharper delineation of the defensive tendencies involved, and certainly the specific clinical and personality scales that are correlated with this tendency suggest something about it as well as revealing their own susceptibility to it. On the other hand, one wonders why an author who is so favorably disposed to "operationism" chooses to ignore the metaphysically pure "deviant response-set" interpretations of personality inventories that have been offered by Berg (1955) and Barnes (1956). Does the forced-choice item format suggested by the author really control for this tendency? The evidence presented clearly supports the contention that this format (as exemplified in the *Personal Preference Schedule*) does much to control this insidious test-taking attitude. Evidence from other quarters is just beginning to appear in the psychological journals, however, and the final judgment may be close to a draw. Much of the burden of proof for the assertions made appears to rest on studies that have employed a "social desirability scale" (SD) which purports to measure the test-taking attitude under discussion. This scale, which appears to be essentially an anxiety scale with reverse keying, fails to satisfy the three criteria that the author emphasizes throughout the monograph: (1) the judges' ratings were not obtained under the standard instructions; (2) no attempt was made to scale the items in the suggested manner; (3) the items do not appear to be heterogeneous or independent of the trait of "anxiety." This is the scale that led Edwards to the questionable position that subjects who obtain low scores on the Taylor Anxiety Scale are more "anxious" than subjects who score high. Despite the fact that many of the author's assertions are of relatively low "social desirability value" in the present psychological scene, this little monograph seems likely to have an impact on current conceptions of the devices that depend on self-report. It is a *must* for all who are directly or peripherally concerned with such tests. Some knowledge of MMPI and other scales is required to thread one's way meaningfully through the maze of intercorrelations present. Some empathy with the problems of the constructor of paper-and-pencil tests is also required to appreciate a theoretical argument that "predicts" *signs* of correlation coefficients. Nevertheless those whose research makes them vulnerable to the currently fashionable bit of seminarmanship: "But couldn't you account for your findings equally well in terms of social desirability?" should familiarize themselves with the full implications of the charge.

Ed & Psychol Meas 19:451–4 au '59. Samuel Messick. This slender monograph reviews most of the recent research and thinking about the social desirability variable and its pervasive effects upon personality assessment. Edwards builds his case rapidly, marshalling evidence with cumulative effectiveness, until he leads the reader to an inexorable conclusion that social desirability is an important component, if not a major determinant, of responses to structured personality items. The book reports a program of research directed toward the measurement and control in personality inventories of the tendency to respond in a socially desirable way, which Edwards calls the *SD set.* With the benefit of hindsight and the extensive groundwork laid by Edwards, certain aspects of this research program may be criticized and some of the interpretations questioned, as will be mentioned briefly in the body of this review, but the scope and importance of the implications stemming from Edwards' work should not be minimized. Edwards begins by distinguishing between the *judged* desirability of a personality item and the tendency to *respond* in a socially desirable manner. By means of the psychological scaling method of successive intervals, the judgments of desirability provide a scale, "the most important single dimension on which to locate personality statements," in terms of which items may be equated in desirability. To assess the stability of this scale across several different samples of judges, desirability values were compared for....diverse groups....and generally high correlations were obtained among the various scales. In evaluating this striking similarity in group opinion....it must be remembered that successive intervals scale values represent a kind of average rating for the group involved. * Differences in judging desirability might be studied better at the individual level, for there may exist, within a single judging group, consistent individual differences with sufficient structure to warrant their consideration as different "points of view" with respect to desirability. When social desirability scale values of personality items were correlated with the proportion of individuals endorsing each statement in an independent sample, the coefficients ranged in the high eighties and low nineties for such materials as inventory items, check lists, and Q-sorts. As Edwards points out, this high correlation suggests the possibility that traits judged to be desirable are prevalent or dominant in the group under study, or it might also reflect a tendency to create a good impression or to respond, either deliberately or unintentionally, in a socially desirable manner. * Edwards felt that the tendency to respond in a socially desirable way was, on one hand, a fairly stable personality characteristic, and, on the other, a source of "error" in responding to items dealing with other personality traits. He attempted to measure this response tendency by selecting 79 MMPI items, called the SD Scale, which had been unanimously judged to be desirable or undesirable by 10 judges. This scale, and a shorter form composed of 39 discriminating items, was found to have significant correlations with a variety of MMPI, Guilford-Martin, and other inventory scales. The interpretation of results with this scale, however, should be tempered by the following considerations: (a) The SD scale is not independent of MMPI correction scales (48 of the 79 items are from the F scale with reversed keying); (b) it is not independent of MMPI content scales (22 out of 39 items on the shorter version are from the Manifest Anxiety scale with reversed keying); (c) only 9 out of 39 items are keyed "true," permitting the possible influence of acquiescent response set. Edwards, being cognizant of these difficulties, spent several pages, for example, arguing away the possible contribution of acquiescence in his findings. His arguments are impressive: When the action of social desirability would lead to a negative correlation between two scales and the pure action of acquiescence would lead to a positive correlation, the actual finding of a negative correlation, even a smaller one than might be expected, indicates that acquiescence cannot completely account for the results. However, the possibilities of supporting and interactive effects between acquiescence and SD set should also be considered. * Edwards....selected pairs of items with approximately equal social desirability scale values and arranged them in a forced-choice paired-comparison format. In this manner a personality inventory was constructed to measure 15 of Murray's "needs," each need being compared with every other need twice. Much research is needed to evaluate the effectiveness of this control procedure and to investigate the possibly peculiar properties of forced-choice ipsative scales. There is some evidence that social desirability still effects choices in this paired-comparison situation (cf. J. Consult. Psychol., 1958, *22*, 70–72), so that at least some tightening of control seems likely, but Edwards' initial attempts seem to have decreased the SD variance significantly. This forced-choice format has other restrictions, however, which should be evaluated in using Edwards' inventory. For example, 28 item-pairs are used to measure each need, and scale reliability is computed in terms of 28 items. Yet only nine personality statements are involved as need referents; eight statements appear three times each and one appears four times in constructing the 28 item-pairs. The effect of this replication on scale reliability and, indeed, the precise interpretation of scale reliability under these circumstances needs clarification. Also, under the forced-choice arrangement, the attainment of a high score on one scale somewhat restricts performance on other scales. However, with only two items overlapping for any two scales, the attendant forced negative correlation seems negligible for practical purposes. The psychometric properties of such forced-choice scales need elucidation, and unfortunately the chapter on The Forced-Choice Inventory is rather short and sketchy. Since most of the material discussed has already appeared in psychological journals, the separate publication of this small monograph will probably serve a limited audience. However, the appearance of a bound volume devoted entirely to social desirability tends to emphasize the importance of the variable, although this emphasis might have been achieved almost as well and more economically by a chapter in a text on personality assessment. It is interesting to note that the book attempted a broad survey and integration of research findings on social desirability, but at the same time it seems to be based primarily upon original work by Edwards and his students. This apparently paradoxical coverage is actually a fairly honest reflection of Edwards' considerable contribution to research and thinking on this topic.

[B168]

★Elmgren, John. **Some Fundamental Problems in Psychological Factor Analysis.** Acta Universitatis Gothoburgensis, Göteborgs Universitets Årsskrift, Vol. 64, No. 3. Stockholm, Sweden: Almqvist & Wiksell, 1958. Pp. 44. Paper. Sw. kr. 5. *

[B169]

★Endler, Norman S.; Hunt, J. McV.; and Rosenstein, Alvin J. **An S-R Inventory of Anxiousness.** American Psychological Association, Psychological Monographs: General and Applied, Vol. 76, No. 17, Whole No. 536. Washington, D.C.: the Association, Inc., 1962. Pp. 33. Paper. $2.00. * (*PA* 38:2711)

[B170]

★England, George W. **Development and Use of Weighted Application Blanks.** Dubuque, Iowa: Wm. C. Brown Co., 1961. Pp. xi, 55. $2.50. * (Revision of *How to Develop a Weighted Application Blank* by Josephine Welch, C. Harold Stone, and Donald G. Paterson. See 5:B466.)

[B171]

★Engler, David. **How to Raise Your Child's IQ.** New York: Ballantine Books, Inc., 1961. Pp. 153. Paper. $0.50. * (Reprint of 1958 edition published by Criterion Books, Inc.)

Cont Psychol 7:263 Jl '62. Edward J. Murray. A school teacher attacks educators who use group tests in rigid and ignorant ways. The book is technically poor and sensationalistic, but it does raise important issues. However, his solution (practice exercises) left me feeling a little disturbed. The real solution is to train more and better school psychologists. No index.

[B172]

★Evans, K. M. **Sociometry and Education.** London: Routledge & Kegan Paul Ltd., 1962. Pp. vii, 149. 18*s*. (New York: Humanities Press, Inc. $3.75.) *

Brit J Ed Psychol 32:311–2 N '62. P. K. Poppleton. * teachers will find a great deal to interest them in the results of sociometric studies which have investigated aspects of popularity and leadership in a school setting * the teacher who wishes to use a sociometric test would have been helped by the inclusion of an actual example * whilst teachers will be quick to recognise the value of applying the information revealed about interpersonal relationships, they may find their suspicions confirmed that the social sciences tell us little that we do not already know. To overcome this, long-term studies would be required which would demonstrate that the manipulations made as a result of applying sociometric techniques have some lasting effect in terms of learning and adjustment. Dr. Evans cannot be blamed for the absence of such studies but more might have been said about the failure of many investigators to relate sociometric measures to fundamental variables in a systematic way. The later chapters of the book are occupied with a more general discussion of problems of communication and social perception which have been investigated by means of rating scales, personality inventories and questionnaires. * Here again, studies reveal some interesting information about the way in which teachers regard pupils and *vice versa,* yet we know comparatively little about the variables which determine these impressions and whether social perception follows the same laws as the perception of non-social objects. It is the absence of central hypotheses of the kind mentioned that makes a record of the empirical findings in this field somewhat tedious reading. There is no doubt, however, that teachers and students will find much in this book which will enlarge their understanding of classroom relationships.

Brit J Ed Studies 11:83 N '62. W. A. L. Blyth. It is appropriate that this timely book, the first of its kind in Britain, should be written by Dr. Kathleen Evans, who has herself played a distinguished part in the work which she describes. * she writes succinctly enough for the beginner but comprehensively enough to satisfy the more advanced scholar too * a serviceable compendium of sociometric techniques, supplemented by a fairly exhaustive survey of the British and much of the relevant American research * It might....have been worth while to include some reference to European sociometric studies, notably the work of Bjerstedt in Sweden, for sociometry is not an Anglo-American monopoly. * the cohesion of the work is somewhat impaired....as there is no definite concluding chapter * it is surprising that a chapter on "Judging Ourselves and Others" includes no reference to Tagiuri's methods of relational analysis which are derived directly from sociometry. The actual writing preserves an admirable balance between the results of scientific investigation and the needs of classroom practice. * deserves wide recognition *

[B173]

★Eyde, Lorraine Dittrich. **Work Values and Background Factors as Predictors of Women's Desire to Work.** Ohio State University, College of Commerce and Administration, Ohio Studies in Personnel, Bureau of Business Research Monograph No. 108. Columbus, Ohio: the Bureau, 1962. Pp. xi, 88. Paper. $2.00. *

Personnel Psychol 16:406–8 w '63. Edwin C. Lewis. * Not only does her study provide some valuable data concerning working women; she has also succeeded in presenting her material so that it can be read and understood by non-specialists. The major purpose was to locate attitudinal and biographical variables which would predict work motivation among college women. Two instruments were designed for use in this study. The first was a Work Value Scale, based on six factors: a general factor, dominance-recognition, economic, mastery-achievement, independence, interesting activity-variety, and social value. The criterion was a Desire to Work scale, on which the women rated their attitude toward working under 17 different conditions, involving variables such as marital status, number and age of children, and husband's income. * One of the major benefits of this study is the carefully constructed Work Value Scale, which should be a useful contribution to further research in this area. Apparently such values change within several years after college, so that alumnae value work for different reasons than do college seniors. This has long been suspected, but up until now with little confirmation. Dr. Eyde provides a clear description of the Wherry-Winer technique of factor analysis, by which the scale was constructed. It would make instructive reading for anyone who wants to become more familiar with this technique. The data are presented in easy-to-read tables, and the author's conclusions seem for the most part to be reasonable and warranted. She has a tendency to rely perhaps too much on the ten per cent level of significance: many variables in her study "approach significance" on this basis. She is also too quick to conclude that the nonrespondents in her population did not differ in any important way from the respondents. In most respects this seems to be true, but a reanalysis of Table 4 (p. 29) shows that, if the Social Studies majors are compared with a single combined group of non-Social Studies majors (Sciences plus Humanities), the respondents contain a significantly greater proportion of Social Studies majors (chi-square = 4.72, significant at the .05 level with one degree of freedom). The major difficulty with this study, as with all studies of work motivation among women, lies in the criterion. Dr. Eyde's criterion is better designed than most, but its interpretation is still subject to question. For example, "work" is apparently considered to be a unitary concept; no provision is made for full-time vs. part-time, or other such distinctions which are quite important to many women. The idea that work motivation is a unidimensional concept may be fallacious. It is likely that "desire to work" is only one determiner of whether a woman will actually work or not, and how important a determiner is hard to say. * Employers need to know not only why women *want* to work but also why they actually *do*. For research purposes we need to know more about the actual relationship between women's attitudes and behavior concerning work, in order that a motivation criterion can be meaningful. Nevertheless, it's a good study and we need more like it. *

[B174]

★EYSENCK, H. J. **Know Your Own I.Q.** London: Penguin Books, Ltd., 1962. Pp. 192. Paper. *3s. 6d.* (Baltimore, Md.: Penguin Books, Inc. $0.85.) *

Brit J Psychiatry 109:835 N '63. Max Hamilton. * As far as it goes, the account of intelligence testing is reasonably good, though it is a great pity that the author did not take the opportunity to explain why the I.Q. is a very unsatisfactory way of measuring intelligence and to point out that the use of standard units would solve many difficulties. * He discusses the arguments for and against intelligence testing and, as is his custom, gives the arguments defending his views in great detail and those opposing them at minimal length. He has no hesitation at times in bolstering his opinions with speculation, e.g. page 29 and page 34, which contrasts with what he has written on pages 17 and 18. The second part of the book consists of a series of tests designed to enable the reader to assess his own intelligence. The best that can be said for these tests is that they are a bad joke. Anybody with a little sophistication in the design of tests can discover any number of items to which perfectly legitimate alternative answers can be found. It may well be that these tests will survive in the literature chiefly as "awful examples" of how not to devise intelligence tests.

Brit J Stat Psychol 15:221–3 N '62. G. R. Roberts. This book has already evoked considerable criticism both from educationists and from psychologists. The educationists deplore the encouragement which they suppose it offers to parents and others who are only too eager to coach their children in devices of intelligence-testing in the hope of squeezing them into schools or occupations for which they may scarcely be fitted. The psychologists protest against the idea that an untrained reader can determine his own I.Q. by answering questions like those contained in this and similar publications. Both criticisms can perhaps be pressed too far; and both have been to some extent met by Professor Eysenck himself. He warns his readers, with all the emphasis that italics can bestow, that they "should not base any decisions on the results." * The bulk of the book consists of eight half-hour tests, each containing forty questions. These are undoubtedly highly entertaining in themselves. To the psychologist their chief interest lies in the fact that to a large extent they succeed in breaking away from the stock types of problem—syllogisms, reasoning tests, completion tests, and such hardy annuals as opposites, synonyms, analogies, etc.—or at any rate in presenting them in an entirely novel guise. The attempt, however, has at times been made at the cost of genuine efficiency. A few trials will quickly show that in certain cases the most intelligent persons do not give the somewhat far-fetched answers that the key rather surprisingly enjoins. * Most of these objections could easily be dispelled by a few slight changes when revising the book for a future edition. They are objections too that are likely to weigh more with the lay reader than with the psychological specialist. The psychologist realizes that the proper way to judge a test is by the statistical data obtained to demonstrate its efficiency, not by mere armchair introspection. But here again the book is disappointing. What the psychologist would like to know is the actual evidence showing that these novel types of test are at least as effective as the older types. How many people have been tested with them in the preliminary studies of reliability, validity, and item-analysis, and what precisely were the results? How were the marks standardized in terms of an I.Q.? A very rough trial suggests that many of the items are exceptionally difficult. Indeed, we actually learn that, in general, to score half the total marks you must have an I.Q. of 135 or thereabouts, which means you must be among the top 1 per cent of the population. I wonder how many readers will score, shall we say, three-quarters of the total number. It is therefore not surprising to find that a good many psychologists have been inclined to criticize the project as a whole. They not unnaturally fear that, in spite of the incidental warnings, a large number of uninstructed readers will suppose from the title and the author's name that here they have a scientific method of assessing their own intelligence, and, when they fail, will either conclude that they are hopelessly incompetent or alternatively that the whole technique of mental testing is devoid of any sound basis.

[B175]

★Eysenck, H. J. **The Structure of Human Personality, Second Edition.** London: Methuen & Co. Ltd., 1960. Pp. xix, 448. 55*s*. (New York: John Wiley & Sons, Inc. Out of print.) *

Brit J Ed Psychol 31:217 Je '61. P. E. Vernon. The factorial approach to personality is not the only, nor, probably, the most fruitful one. But it is a necessary adjunct as may be seen from the sorry history of perseveration, rigidity and other popular constructs which have failed to show any useful functional unity, by the lack of precision of "authoritarianism" and "anxiety," and many other examples. Thus, few psychologists who are interested in human beings (and there are many who aren't) can afford to neglect factorial work in the personality field; and Eysenck's book provides an invaluable, even if perhaps sometimes a too optimistic, compendium. In this second edition a large amount of work published between 1953 and 1960 has been incorporated, including a useful survey of Cattell's numerous contributions. There are two new chapters—one on methods of analysis, which is perhaps rather too advanced for non-specialists and deals more with the logical basis of factorization than with techniques; the other is on projective techniques, mostly Rorschach. Eysenck still maintains the general position that most of the primary factors claimed by other workers represent "traits" that are subsidiary to the major "types" of neuroticism, extraversion-introversion and psychoticism. He brings out clearly the great variability in different investigations resulting from slight changes in the settings of the tests, or changes in the populations tested. But he does not appear to admit that the same kind of variability occurs in studies by himself or his students, whereby the loadings of tests hypothesized to measure neuroticism, etc., are highly unstable. Another weakness seems to be his acceptance of factors extracted from ratings or from questionnaire responses, although he draws attention to recent work on "response bias" which would suggest that such factors represent conceptual stereotypes in the raters rather than fundamental unities in personality. However, he agrees that a good deal of factorial work is open to criticism for its blind empiricism, and insists that fruitful advances are made only by designing factorial studies to test definite hypotheses, i.e., by linking this approach with the approach of the experimental and the developmental psychologist. Considering the complexities of the topic, the descriptions of the tests studied by factorists and their results are remarkably clear, and the book is well-organised and eminently readable. It is a pity it is so expensive.

For reviews of the first edition, see 5:B144.

[B176]

★FEIN, LEAH GOLD. **The Three-Dimensional Personality Test: Reliability, Validity and Clinical Implications.** New York: International Universities Press, Inc., 1960. Pp. xii, 324. $6.75. * (London: Bailey Bros. & Swinfen, Ltd., 1961. 58s.) (*PA* 35:3393)

Brit J Psychol 52:307–8 Ag '61. B. Semeonoff. * Readers who have been privileged to be present at one of Dr Gold Fein's engaging demonstrations of the "3-DPT" are likely to have formed a clearer and more favourable impression of the technique than the book affords. To find out what it is all about one has to read the last chapter first, and even so one can obtain only a poor idea of the material, since the only illustration is a crudely executed line drawing which does scant justice to the rather attractive "forms." These are small plastic objects, some of which are vaguely reminiscent of Henry Moore sculptures, some have geometric properties, while others suggest nothing more than blobs of clay or plasticine. The subject is invited to choose some of the pieces, to arrange them on a table, and to tell a story around them. To attempt to follow the author's exposition without the material at hand is a frustrating experience, with the result that while the author succeeds to some extent in communicating her enthusiasm, one finds it difficult to project oneself into the test situation or to find the interpretative material wholly convincing. The statistical data are not very impressive: "reliability coefficients" of 0.4 or less are quoted as "significantly consistent." Nevertheless, one feels that the method has possibilities, particularly if treated as an exploratory tool rather than as a "test" in the psychometric sense. *

Cont Psychol 7:46 F '62. Austin Grigg. This is a mixture of statistical analysis of research data, clinical impressions not submitted to impartial test, extensions of interpretations from one test (Rorschach) to another (3-DPT), and occasional lapses into superficiality even while insisting that the material under consideration "derives from a deep layer" of personality. Not deep, for example, is this judgment: "The 3-DPT is designed to measure personality functions. Rate of production and language variables are functions of personality. Therefore, if the 3-DPT measures these variables consistently it is a valid instrument for measuring personality functions" (p. 124). * Reliabilities, usually reported here as *r*-squared, are unimpressive: the highest is .55 for normals for one scoring category and .90 for 6 catatonics (*r*). There is confusion for the reader about the tables: beginning with Table 22, all N's for various normal and clinical samples have been doubled, but with Table 26, earlier N's are again reported. Rich clinical examples and the author's interpretations of what various responses may reflect allow the book to be used as a manual for the test. Despite numerous statistical tables, and even a multiple regression, the reviewer judges that the book is intended for the clinician's clinician.

J Proj Tech 25:484–5 D '61. Theodore H. Blau. * a significant contribution to the field of projective techniques * A number of projective techniques have achieved wide usage and popularity long before publication of substantial research or clinical data (MAPS, Blackie, etc.). The 3-DPT has won no popularity contest, perhaps because it is not "cute" or simple. The 3-DPT materials and procedures are complex and, interestingly enough, threatening to some psychologists. Among the relatively few psychologists who have examined this technique one should not be surprised to hear rather heated or defensive comments. These comments seem to be directed toward the absence of face validity in the 3-DPT. One wonders why such a reaction is not readily identified as a tribute to the stimulus value of the instrument. Dr. Fein presents data to demonstrate both reliability and validity in the use of the 3-DPT with normal and clinical populations. Chapters II through VII present data derived from a population of 108 normals, including 53 children and 81 clinical patients. It is questionable whether the size of the sample and its heterogeneous content justifies the intensive statistical treatment reported, but the effort to treat the data objectively is certainly commendable. * Students will find the book as a whole wearisome and involved. It is likely that clinical psychologists with a deep interest in diagnostic procedures will enjoy sharing Dr. Fein's experience of trying to apply parametric statistics in research with projective techniques. Some who read this book will be curious enough to learn the 3-DPT technique and thus broaden their diagnostic armamentarium with a culture-free, subtle technique that is quite promising. Hopefully, this book will stimulate the interest, familiarity and critique that is necessary to bring forth extensive cross-validation of new techniques. Should this occur, I hope that Dr. Fein will produce a companion volume, extending and enriching Chapters VIII, IX, and X which present a clear description of administration procedures and interpretation. The richest and most dynamic elements of this work are to be found in those chapters reflecting Dr. Fein's broad and insightful experience with the clinical application of the 3-DPT.

[B177]

★FERRIS, BRIAN. **Mark Scaling Tables.** London: Sir Isaac Pitman & Sons, Ltd., 1961. Pp. 48. Paper. 5*s*. *

[B178]

★FLANAGAN, JOHN C.; DAILEY, JOHN T.; SHAYCOFT, MARION F.; GORHAM, WILLIAM A.; ORR, DAVID B.; AND GOLDBERG, ISADORE. **Design for a Study of American Youth: 1, The Talents of American Youth.** Boston, Mass.: Houghton Mifflin Co., 1962. Pp. 240. Paper, $1.95; cloth, $4.00. * (*PA* 37:2001)

Cont Psychol 9:312–3 Ag '64. David V. Tiedeman. * Project Talent....is neither census nor convincing research, because it attempts both tasks simultaneously with scant demarcation and therefore carries off neither clearly and resolutely * The manuscript is a loosely linked set of nine studies of the American high school. The set: 1) portrays the nature of the variation in organization, support, expectation, and location of secondary education in this country; 2) indicates the existence, program, and expected growth of services in guidance; and 3) relates community characteristics, services, and organization to aptitude and achievement in high school. The information offered in each of these sets is: 1) novel; 2) important; 3) extensive yet concisely and ingeniously represented; and 4) undoubtedly extremely accurate. And yet, the report is not now a complete census. The values of all the statistics are not always reported for all of the 17 groups of schools in the adopted taxonomy. Not all variables are interrelated. The test scores for each of the grades tested are not included in each of the analyses. * the authors address themselves to two more general issues. The first general issue is the adoption of a taxonomy of a few classes which effectively carries the evident heterogeneity among the statistical series under study. The credibility generated for the proferred taxonomy suffers, however, because little effort is made, in any of the numerous and often disparate references to the taxonomy, to consolidate the conclusion that the solution adopted indeed achieves, for many variables, a uniquely valuable homogeneity within subsequent classes. The second general issue is the effect of community and school organization upon the achievement of pupils. Despite the evident importance of this issue for the authors, the observations from such relationships are not: 1) complete for all of the data collected at a school; 2) closely intertwined from chapter to chapter or within a specific section; 3) placed into a context in which the findings are made to bear directly upon important and well developed issues which have remained unresolved for a number of years; 4) based upon demonstration that the tasks tested are in direct relation to the intentions of the schools whose organizations are being assessed; and 5) always made with direct allowance for differences in aptitude among the pupils. * I believe that the authors can make more lasting contributions in future reports of Project Talent by publishing a census before they engage alone in research on census-like data which are of such import both to the public and to those who make their livelihood in education. * despite difficulty, the present report provides aspects of a benchmark deserving of wide reference. I sincerely hope that interested parties can use the report as a partial census without violent reaction to the proferred observations on the efficiency of instruction, vocational education, and guidance services. Many of those interpretations are not offered for, nor yet worthy of, other than speculative consideration.

Teach Col Rec 64:433–4 F '63. Julian C. Stanley. * semi-popular, semi-technical report of the design of a huge nation-wide testing project conducted in the spring of 1960 * measurement specialists and educational researchers do not yet have a technical enough presentation of PROJECT TALENT to evaluate its promise fully * One may call this project a mixture of splendid psychometrics and ambitious correlational analysis. To test almost half a million students in Grades 9 through 12 in 1,353 schools in 49 states with nearly 2,000 questions for two days is no small achievement. PROJECT TALENT required and got the most careful planning and development probably ever given a measurement undertaking. * I admire the testing operation itself. The American Institute for Research and the University of Pittsburgh have good cause to be proud of it, despite a few inevitable flaws in design and execution. It is the promised attempt to tease out "causation" from essentially correlational data that gives me pause. * Because of the semi-popular level of this volume, we are not told just how causation is to be inferred from associational data. It is implied that much statistical partialing out of confounded variables will be attempted, but how will the analyzers stop short of throwing away the baby with the dirty bath water? The partialed-out variables are not antecedent to the independent variable (class size), as they typically are in the analysis of covariance as applied to the results of controlled experiments, but instead they are concurrent with it or even subsequent to it. How much should one partial out in order to remove confounding influences of per-pupil expenditures, educational level of parents, verbal ability of students, and the like, without partialing out the independent variable itself? We shall look to the PROJECT TALENT staff for penetrating insight into these perplexing issues. It is well known that correlation is not necessarily indicative of causation. This is the dilemma which all analyzers of concomitant variation face. They must decide whether a causative relationship exists and, *if so,* in which direction it goes. A brief review is not the right place, however, to examine complex aspects of correlational analysis, except to state that they will be highly relevant to attempts at answering the ten questions on pages 40–41. Partial correlation is not, in general, logically equivalent to the analysis of covariance of results from a controlled experiment, but by conducting their analyses within the four sampling strata used (type of school, geographical unit, school size, and school holding power) and by considering other factors judiciously, the PROJECT TALENT staff may be able to rule out plausible alternative hypotheses sufficiently to make their findings—*e.g.,* about the effect of class size on achievement—supplement previous studies helpfully. Already we are indebted to PROJECT TALENT for beautiful psychometrics. I look forward hopefully to ingenious analyses of the data. At least, they should generate hypotheses for controlled experimentation.

[B179]

★FLANAGAN, JOHN C.; DAILEY, JOHN T.; SHAYCOFT, MARION F.; ORR, DAVID B.; AND GOLDBERG, ISADORE. **Studies of the American High School.** Cooperative Research Project No. 226. Pittsburgh, Pa.: University of Pittsburgh Project Talent Office, 1964. Pp. [375]. Paper. $5.00. *

[B180]

★FLANAGAN, JOHN C.; DAVIS, FREDERICK B.; DAILEY, JOHN T.; SHAYCOFT, MARION F.; ORR, DAVID B.; GOLDBERG, ISADORE; AND NEYMAN, CLINTON A., JR. **The American High School Student.** Technical Report to the United States Office of Education, Cooperative Research Project No. 635, Project Talent: The Identification, Development, and Utilization of Human Talents. Pittsburgh, Pa.: University of Pittsburgh Project Talent Office, 1964. Pp. xxiii, [700]. Paper. $8.50. *

[B181]

★FLEISHMAN, EDWIN A. **The Structure and Measurement of Physical Fitness.** Englewood Cliffs, N.J.: Prentice-Hall, Inc., 1964. Pp. xv, 207. $6.95. * (London: Prentice-Hall International, Inc. 56*s*.)

[B182]

★FLEMING, W. G. **The Kuder Preference Record —Vocational as a Predictor of Post-High School Educational and Occupational Choices.** Atkinson Study of Utilization of Student Resources, Supplementary Report No. 2. Toronto, Canada: Department of Educational Research, Ontario College of Education, University of Toronto, 1959. Pp. vii, 49. Paper. $1.00. *

[B183]

★FLEMING, W. G. **Personal and Academic Factors as Predictors of First Year Success in Ontario Universities.** Atkinson Study of Utilization of Student Resources, Report No. 5. Toronto, Canada: Department of Educational Research, Ontario College of Education, University of Toronto, 1959. Pp. xi, 137. Paper, lithotyped. $2.50. *

[B184]

★FLEMING, W. G. **The Use of Predictive Factors for the Improvement of University Admission Requirements.** Atkinson Study of Utilization of Student Resources, Report No. 9. Toronto, Canada: Department of Educational Research, Ontario College of Education, University of Toronto, 1962. Pp. xi, 76. Paper, lithotyped. $2.50. *

[B185]

★FLOWERS, JOHN F. **An Evaluation of the Kuder Preference Record—Personal for Use in Ontario.** Atkinson Study of Utilization of Student Resources, Supplementary Report No. 4. Toronto, Canada: Department of Educational Research, Ontario College of Education, University of Toronto, 1961. Pp. viii, 31. Paper. $1.00. *

[B186]

★FRANKE, WOLFGANG. **The Reform and Abolition of the Traditional Chinese Examination System.** Distributed for the East Asian Research Center, Harvard University. Cambridge, Mass.: Harvard University Press, 1960. Pp. viii, 100. Paper, lithotyped. $2.50. (London: Oxford University Press. 20*s*.) *

[B187]

★FREDERIKSEN, NORMAN. **Factors in In-Basket Performance.** American Psychological Association, Psychological Monographs: General and Applied, Vol. 76, No. 22, Whole No. 541. Washington, D.C.: the Association, Inc., 1962. Pp. 25. Paper. $1.50. * (*PA* 38:6692)

[B188]

★FREDERIKSEN, NORMAN, AND GULLIKSEN, HAROLD, EDITORS. **Contributions to Mathematical Psychology.** Chapters by Robert P. Abelson, Clyde H. Coombs, J. P. Guilford, Harold Gulliksen, Paul Horst, Ledyard R Tucker, and Dorothy C. Adkins. New York and London: Holt, Rinehart & Winston, Inc., 1964. Pp. x, 189. $6.50; 52*s*. *

[B189]

*FREEMAN, FRANK S. **Theory and Practice of Psychological Testing, Third Edition.** New York and London: Holt, Rinehart & Winston, Inc., 1962. Pp. xix, 697. $7.95; 64*s*. *

Ed & Psychol Meas 23:607–8 au '63. Richard E. Schutz. This text is short on theory and long on clinical practice. The imbalance is more obvious now than when the first edition appeared in 1950—not because the contents have changed markedly but because the psychometric theory developed since this date has not been incorporated into the revised editions. The present revision is not a radical one. The text has been expanded in terms of both the number of pages and the page size. Two new chapters have been added at the beginning of the book, the first titled "Historical Background" and the second "Elementary Statistical Concepts." The contribution of these additions to the effectiveness of the book as a text is not great. Although the historical review is competent, it is not an effective "grabber" for students beginning a course in measurement. The statistics chapter, which was deleted from the second edition of the book, is back in the third. However, the chapter is so condensed that its chief value is as a review reference for students who sold their statistics text after completing the descriptive course. The discussion of validity and reliability has been expanded. The *Technical Recommendations* validity categories are treated briefly. The discussion of construct validity, which is extremely weak, will mislead the student. Freeman implies that construct validity can be established simply by rational analysis of "the degree to which the test items individually and collectively sample the range or class of activities or traits, as defined by the mental process or the personality trait being tested." Since Freeman does not make consistent application of the validity terminology in his discussion of specific instruments in later chapters, much of the impact of the expanded validity treatments is lost. More than three-fourths of the book is devoted to a discussion of various testing instruments in terms of their content and clinical usage. The analysis of each test is descriptive rather than critical. Although evaluations are included, these apply to all of the tests in a given category such as "Group Scales" or "Aptitude Tests." This commits the discussion to a general level in which the sting that might be imposed by the criticism of any single test is lost completely. Although a large number of tests are discussed, many of the more recently constructed instruments are not included. * Moreover, the failure to cite the publishers of each test is a limitation to students desiring to use the book as a reference in later years. The book is well edited and better produced than were earlier editions. * As far as text usage is concerned, the book should appeal more to instructors looking for an overview of available psychological tests than to those seeking a rigorous undergirding in psychometric principles.

For reviews of the earlier editions, see 5:B158 and 4:B155.

[B190]

★FRIEDENHAIN, PAULA. **Write and Reveal: Interpretation of Handwriting.** London: Peter Owen Ltd., 1959. Pp. 184. 30*s*. * (Hollywood-by-the-Sea, Fla.: Transatlantic Arts, Inc., 1960. $8.25.)

Brit J Ed Psychol 30:192 Je '60. P. E. V[ernon]. Like many recent books on graphology, this one protests that specific features of the script are no longer supposed to have fixed significance for personality, and that modern graphology—based on Saudek's principles—is an exact and reliable method; and then proceeds to draw large numbers of conclusions from signs, or from intuitive guesses, and to validate these merely by presenting specimen analyses which somebody certifies to be a faithful picture of the writer. This example is well written and attractively put together, with numerous illustrations. It includes a number of interesting pathological cases, and of instances where the graphological diagnosis is said to have helped in vocational guidance. One's doubts are, if anything, enhanced by the claim that the scripts of children as young as 9 years provide valuable material for educational guidance. Fortunately, the author does not encourage amateurs to undertake graphological analyses on their own, and she stresses the need for further research.

[B191]

★FRISBY, C. B.; VINCENT, D. F.; AND LANCASHIRE, RUTH. **Tests for Engineering Apprentices: A Validation Study.** National Institute of Industrial Psychology Report 14. London: the Institute, 1959. Pp. iii, 24. Paper. 5s. 4d. *

[B192]

*FROEHLICH, CLIFFORD P., AND HOYT, KENNETH B. **Guidance Testing and Other Student Appraisal Procedures for Teachers and Counselors, Third Edition.** Chicago, Ill.: Science Research Associates, Inc., 1959. Pp. xviii, 438. $5.25. * For reviews of the earlier editions, *Studying Students* by Clifford P. Froehlich and John G. Darley and *Testing and Counseling in the High School Program* by John G. Darley, see 5:B162 and 3:828.

[B193]

FURST, EDWARD J. **Constructing Evaluation Instruments.** New York: David McKay Co., Inc., 1958. Pp. xv, 334. $5.50. * (*PA* 32:3343)

Cont Psychol 4:57 F '59. Elizabeth Hagen. * the problem of interpreting the results of evaluation is not given any consideration. Validity and reliability are discussed but not in any really logical fashion. The discussion of validity is confusing and would tend to mislead a beginner in the field. The other so-called problems that are discussed are really superficial aspects of validity and reliability. The tendency of the author to use terminology that is somewhat different from that commonly used and to try to make distinctions without any existing true differences troubles this reader. In general, Part I would have very little value for the classroom teacher. The good points that are made are so deeply imbedded in irrelevant and marginal material that they are difficult for even an experienced person to pick out. Many of the suggested procedures for teachers to follow are unrealistic from the standpoints of the time, training, and facilities available to the classroom teacher. Although the author makes passing mention of evaluating devices other than paper-and-pencil tests, the classroom teacher is likely to come away with the idea that the only dependable and true evaluation device is the essay or short-answer test. Since many teachers already hold this misconception, this reviewer is sorry to see it reinforced. Part II of the book appears to be either an afterthought or an attempt to add to a manuscript that was originally too short. The inexperienced person will find it difficult to relate the material on test construction to the principles set forth in Part I. The suggestions for constructing different kinds of test items are too brief to be helpful to the neophyte and the examples used are generally not too good. Too much of the material in Part II is directed toward large-scale testing programs and not to the person who must make up his own tests for classroom use. There are other annoying things in this volume. One is the poor proofreading that resulted in whole sentences being omitted in the text as on page 121 and in the inaccurate citing of bibliographical references. Another is the tendency of the author to make somewhat vague and unjustified generalizations without adequate explanation. A third is the repetitiousness of many of the chapters and the lack of organization in the book as a whole. It is this reviewer's opinion that *Constructing Evaluation Instruments* does not achieve its purpose. It is not a book that one would want to put in the hands of a classroom teacher since there is too great a danger that the teacher will be misled or will pick up some erroneous ideas about evaluation.

Ed & Psychol Meas 19:450–1 au '59. Wimburn L. Wallace. Tucked away in a late chapter of this book is a list of relatively clear, useful, conventional suggestions for writing multiple-choice type test items. Deliberate rereading of earlier chapters reveals a few other kernels of worthwhile material, but they are so lost in extraneous, meandering verbiage that the winnowing process is a difficult one even for a person well acquainted with the topics considered. * Part I is intended to deal with "the really fundamental problems," and it is postulated that "these problems are to: (1) determine what to evaluate . . . , (2) define the *what* in terms of behavior, (3) select appropriate situations for calling forth this behavior, (4) devise some method for getting a record of this behavior, (5) devise some method for summarizing or evaluating the behavior so recorded." * The thesis that most processes in education should be integrated and are inevitably interdependent should not lead to a confusion or conglomeration of an array of topics loosely strung together on strands of philosophical discussion. It is almost inconceivable how Part I could contribute to the aim of rendering existing evaluation techniques readily useful to the classroom teacher. The chapter entitled "Getting a Record" should be the heart of this exposition intended to describe the construction of evaluation instruments, since it is in this section that the author discusses the instruments themselves. However, the types of records described are anecdotes, check lists, photography, sound recording, other mechanical recording devices, self reports, and questionnaires. Although tests surprisingly are not mentioned among the methods of getting a record of what is to be evaluated, the last part of the chapter dealing with the validity and practicability of the record uses standardized tests as the illustration of good technique. Part II of the book, called "Constructing Achievement Tests," bears little if any apparent relation to the "basic problems" in Part I. The suggested requirements or features of a good achievement test are better suited to the construction of instruments to be standardized, published, and widely used than they are to the practical problems the teacher must face in making class tests. Most of the refinements recommended are beyond feasible application in the single-course situation. At the same time it is implied that the essay or short-answer type of test is superior to other types in most instances. It is unfortunate that such a bias is communicated by the text. Some other features of the book which merit criticism are errors in bibliographical references, omitted lines of type, study questions which interrupt the flow of the text instead of contributing to understanding, an index which is incomplete, inconsistent, and inaccurate, and the lack of reference to several of the best recent books in the immediate area such as those by Travers, Anastasi, and Thorndike and Hagen.

[B194]

★Gannon, F. B., and Telschow, Earl. **Tests and Interpretations: A Teacher's Handbook.** Rochester, N.Y.: City School District, June 1960. Pp. iii, 31. Paper, lithotyped. $0.35. *

[B195]

★Garrett, Henry E. **Testing for Teachers.** New York: American Book Co., 1959. Pp. x, 262. $3.75. *

Ed & Psychol Meas 19:683–6 w '59. Samuel T. Mayo. * It might be that the appeal of the book will be related inversely to the sophistication of the reader; that is, the naive student or instructor of a measurement course may feel more secure because the book does appear to simplify the field of educational measurement, while the sophisticate will find much that conflicts with his previous background. The disadvantages of the book seem to far outweigh the advantages. Something seems to have been lost with brevity. * The present volume could be used effectively as a text, it would seem, only under certain limiting conditions. As a text for the introductory course, it could be used only when supplemented by clarification and elaboration by the instructor of certain doubtful points or in conjunction with outside reading in more comprehensive texts. It might, however, be used for a second course in which standardized tests were emphasized a great deal. Such criticisms as the foregoing do not serve to instill confidence in this as a promising text for measurement courses or for the in-service teacher.

[B196]

★Gayen, A. K.; Nanda, P. B.; Duari, P.; Bhattacharyya, N.; Mukherjee, H. N.; and Mathur R. K. **Measurement of Achievement in English: A Statistical Study on Effectiveness of Board or University Examinations.** Report No. 2 of the Research Project on Examinations sponsored by the National Council of Educational Research and Training, New Delhi. (New Delhi, India: National Council of Educational Research and Training, 1962.) Pp. xix, 208, xxviii. Rs. 12.50; $3.50; 25*s.* * (Separately published "Appendix Tables," 164 pages.)

[B197]

★Gayen, A. K.; Nanda, P. B.; Mathur, R. K. Duari, P.; Dubey, S. D.; and Bhattacharyya, N. **Measurement of Achievement in Mathematics: A Statistical Study on Effectiveness of Board and University Examinations in India.** Report No. 1 of the Research Project on Examinations Sponsored by the Ministry of Education, Government of India, New Delhi. [New Delhi, India: National Council of Educational Research and Training, 1961. Pp. 246. Rs. 12.50; $3.00; 20*s.* * (*PA* 37:7187)

Ed R 16:77–8 N '63. R. Beard. This report is the first of a series on student achievements in the major subjects of Board and University examinations in India. * The writers find that in the compulsory paper for the School Final Examination the syllabus is unequally represented, many alternative questions cause confusion to both candidates and examiners; alternatives differ in subject matter and difficulty, and the variety of choices combined with a low pass mark enable a student ignorant of two thirds of the syllabus to scrape a pass. * If the recommendations of this careful inquiry are followed many of the causes of present dissatisfaction will disappear; and, since teaching is influenced considerably by public examinations, review of future results on similar lines should ensure a steadily rising standard of achievement.

J Royal Stat Soc 125:658–9 pt 4 '62. D. J. Finney. This report....relates primarily to a detailed analysis of a 10 per cent. sample (3,700 candidates) of results from the compulsory mathematics paper in a School Final Examination. The question paper is deplorably old fashioned, and demanded of the candidate very careful reading in order to understand the system of options and the marking scheme; it appears in need of so much improvement of an elementary kind as to make the authors' efforts to study relative difficulties and discriminatory powers of individual questions scarcely worth while. There is little to interest the statistician here, either in methods or in conclusions. The extensive discussions of discriminating power contain nothing of importance that is new, but perhaps the suggestion that maximum marks ought to be in proportion to the difficulty of a question deserves further attention. One may agree strongly with the authors' views that more research into the setting and marking of examinations is needed, without feeling that this quite excessively long report has any importance outside India.

[B198]

★Gekoski, Norman. **Psychological Testing: Theory, Interpretation, and Practices.** Springfield, Ill.: Charles C Thomas, Publisher, 1964. Pp. xiii, 300. $8.50. * (*PA* 39:1662)

[B199]

★Genua, Albert J. **How to Score High on the Scholastic Aptitude Test and Other College Entrance Tests.** New York: John F. Rider, Publisher, Inc., 1962. Pp. vi, 218. Paper. $2.10. *

[B200]

*Gerberich, J. Raymond; Greene, Harry A.; and Jorgensen, Albert N. **Measurement and Evaluation in the Modern School.** New York: David McKay Co., Inc., 1962. Pp. xviii, 622. $6.95. *

Cont Psychol 8:355–60 S '63. Theodore R. Husek. This volume was prepared as a comprehensive first text in measurement and evaluation for the prospective teacher who knows little about measurement and less about statistics. It is not a success. The book has some important virtues. There is an extensive and useful section on the construction of classroom tests. The last section of the book, "designed to deal briefly with the appraisal of pupil learning in ten broad instructional areas and in general education," contains much valuable material. There is a simple outline of each chapter at its beginning, and there is a wealth of useful illustrative test material. But the faults of the book are also important. Considering that the word "evaluation" is used in the title, the treatment of evaluation in the text is woefully inadequate. Too much of the terminology is not consistent with that of other comparable texts and, furthermore, it is confusing. * The writing is almost always dull, and it is often unclear. * Outlining and the use of italics to separate topics are carried to the point where they sometimes distract rather than assist. * The number of tests treated makes the absence of some common and important tests stand out. * This last fault is particularly important, since the reasons for the choices of tests to be included are not given. As a final criticism, some drawbacks of the generally excellent last section on measurement and evaluation in specific school subjects should be mentioned. The sections on mathematics and science suffer by taking inadequate account of the impressive changes presently occurring in these areas. As an extreme example, (most of the material is quite good) the list of principles and generalizations of science at the beginning of that chapter are taken from a 1932 publication. In general, this book possesses many of the virtues and faults of its parent volumes, by the same authors, on measurement and evaluation in the secondary school and in the elementary school. The authors indicate that it is not a revision of the two previous books, and much of the material in the present volume is identical to that of the previous volumes. Instructors who liked the previous volumes will probably like this one.

However the reviewer feels that a one-volume revision of the parent books would have been much more valuable than the present offspring.

Ed & Psychol Meas 23:393–4 su '63. David A. Payne. * Although the text is brief, one wonders what functions are served by the inclusion of chapters on the measurement of (a) socioeconomic status and (b) health and physical fitness. Space might better have been devoted to an extended discussion of possible interaction effects of the socioeconomic variable with the measurement process. * Chapters 9 and 10 provide a lucid presentation of basic test and item types with numerous examples and helpful suggestions for test construction. This material finds excellent expression and application in ten chapters devoted to measurement and evaluation in specific subject-matter areas. In summary, this excellent text, which obviously synthesizes the considerable experience and knowledge of its authors, should find a wide audience in introductory measurement and evaluation courses.

Psychol Rep 12:619 Ap '63. The authors have described quite a few tests available for measuring various skills, aptitudes, personality, etc., but they fail to discuss the process of standardization so as to develop a basis for the prospective teacher's evaluating the adequacy of a test. Teachers are told that IQ tests are probably unreliable for the retarded and very bright, so such children (note that the teacher has already discriminated these) should be examined by the school psychologist. Many pages are spent explaining how to calculate the MA, percentile, etc., and very few on cautions concerning interpretation by whom, to whom and for what purpose. It is no wonder teachers may often find themselves in hot water!

For reviews of earlier editions, see 5:B181–2 and 3:914–5.

[B201]

★GETZELS, JACOB W., AND JACKSON, PHILIP W. **Creativity and Intelligence: Explorations With Gifted Students.** New York and London: John Wiley & Sons, Inc., 1962. Pp. xvii, 293. $5.95; 45*s*. *

Am J Psychol 77:153–4 Mr '64. E. Paul Torrance. * this book will probably go down in the history of psychology and of education as an important link in our expanding concept of giftedness * The authors do not take a position emphasizing creativity over intelligence (IQ), as some critics have interpreted. Neither do they emphasize the importance of morality over adjustment. They simply show that intellectual giftedness may be viewed in *at least* two ways, in terms of creativity and in terms of intelligence and that psychosocial excellence may be viewed in *at least* two different ways, in terms of adjustment and in terms of moral standards. Furthermore, they show that "creativity" and "intelligence" actually are two ways of viewing intellectual giftedness and that "adjustment" and "moral standards" provide two different ways of regarding psychosocial excellence. In doing this, we cannot conclude that creativity and intelligence are antithetical nor that adjustment and morality are antithetical. Perhaps it is in this respect that the presentations of the authors have misled some students of their work. They have said little about those who rank high *both* in creativity and in intelligence, *both* in adjustment and moral standards. While they call for increased emphasis on creativity and moral standards, they do not call for a de-emphasis on intelligence and adjustment. Although this reviewer has found through numerous partial replications of the study of creativity and intelligence that the results reported by Getzels and Jackson do not hold in all schools, he knows of no data which are in conflict with the fundamental concepts developed. The Getzels and Jackson study simply does not tell the entire story. No single study can answer all of the important questions about such a complex problem as "giftedness." The phenomena do occur in most schools and other learning situations thus far studied. *

Am J Psychother 16:714–6 O '62. Ariel Mengarini. * The authors are to be commended for an inspiring start * One can only applaud the demonstration that the traditional IQ is but a scanty sampling of the abilities that make for achievement. However, in delimiting their groups the authors had to select *negatively* for creativity in the one and for intelligence in the other, so that the composite personality profiles which emerge are at best tainted pictures: this is what an intelligent person *who is not* similarly creative looks like, and vice versa. Nor do the authors favor us with figures to show how many students they had to exclude to obtain their mutually independent groups, nor with personality sketches of those students who happened to combine the traits. *

Perhaps a clue to the underlying fault appears in the authors' use of the phrase "to educate for creativity" (p. 130). Though used but once and incidentally, the impression persists that this is what the authors may have had in mind all along, and that the desire to suggest developments along this line introduced an unconscious bias. I would venture to suggest a contradiction inherent in this seemingly innocuous phrase. The creative person has a need to take the extant pattern apart and rearrange it in individual fashion. Make it an aim of education, and you tend to smother originality in the horrible conformity of pseudononconformism. We already have too much phony self-expression and forced "creativity" in television, advertising, and the like. Creativity is the leaven in the loaf of culture. Considering that the need to live a preeminently creative existence is most often a sublimated neurotic drive, one suspects that pushing "education for creativity" would result in a precisely opposite effect, or at best would prove to be quite irrelevant to eventual achievement. * This is a book which needed to be written, and it is a success from the standpoint of readability and stimulation. While greater breadth of observation in both space and time is indicated to carry conviction, the authors have opened up magnificent vistas for exploration.

Am J Sociol 68:278–9 S '62. Lee J. Cronbach. * The report is fascinating and deplorable; fascinating because it contains provocative results, deplorable because faulty design and inadequate reporting convey false impressions and leave one uncertain of which findings to trust. * The authors have been admirably ingenious in their selection and handling of dependent variables. But almost everything is wrong with the selection and description of the groups. The A's are selected as high in IQ and low on creativity measures; B's have the reverse pattern. Intelligence is appraised by a not necessarily recent Binet test. Where this was not available, a regressed Henmon-Nelson score is substituted, which introduces a systematic distortion (an equipercentile conversion is required). The five "creativity" measures include unusual uses, hidden figures, and a test in which pupils invent arithmetic problems using given data. These tests do not cohere and cannot all be measures of the same thing. It is regrettable that the authors did not investigate which of the tests is associated with the main group differences. These tests have much in common with mental ability: The authors obtain unduly low correlations by correlating the separate tests with IQ, thus partialing age out of one variable and not the other. Groups A and B are more similar in *true* IQ than the authors recognize. The characteristics of the A and B groups are inadequately reported; we know nothing, for example, about their age distributions, which perhaps differ. For no good reason, all high-morality and high-adjustment cases were culled from the groups before proceeding. Finally, the decision not to investigate the sixty children high on *both* tests impoverishes the study: It is this group, if any, that promises genuine creativity. The authors continually speak of differences between "highly creative" and "highly intelligent" adolescents, in a manner certain to mislead a large part of their audience. There is no population to which their design permits them to generalize, and they have left out of consideration the more typical gifted cases in the high-high cell. They give quite inadequate attention to the fact that validity for the creativity tests is purely an assumption. One contribution is their exploration of two syndromes, but their presentation is marred by the undefended implicit judgment that the B's are highly commendable. The *Mad Magazine* mentality of the B's could easily be called childish and irresponsible; they are strongly reminiscent of the ill-adjusted late maturers of Jones and Bayley. If the study had included pupils high on both tests, the reader might be left wondering how the syndrome of the B's could be cured rather than how it could be "fostered." By the same token, the authors' A syndrome is atypical of high intelligence; they have studied force-fed and sterile conformers who would surely suffer by comparison to the high-high group. Subsequent investigators can be counted upon to determine what ideational fluency tests measure and what social value if any this talent has. They will be helped by the techniques Getzels and Jackson have invented and by the truly striking hypotheses offered by their work. But there is a larger issue to consider. We see with increasing frequency books which serve as primary outlets for research studies and at the same time try to reach a non-scholarly public. This book is not atypical, with its catchy title, its failure to dispel the connotations that arise in the lay mind when Group B is labeled "highly creative," and its failure to present sufficient data to permit another scholar to evaluate the conclusions. Is it too much to ask that publishers who publish primary reports of research impose editorial standards equal to those of a scholarly journal?

Ed & Psychol Meas 22:803–8 w '62. Richard de Mille and Philip R. Merrifield. Despite the enthusiasm of the publisher and the quick public acceptance of this book, a rather discouraging evaluation of it must be made in a journal devoted to measurement problems. Its success is quite understandable as a consequence of the readable style and wealth of anecdotal material. * Naïve readers, of whom there will be many, will take pleasure....in the measurement portions of the book. Informed readers are in for a disappointment. Of the various possible approaches to research problems, some are incompatible with others. Attempts to combine the incompatibles run the risk of disaster. Two such dichotomies are: trait versus type psychology, and exploration versus hypothesis testing. In trait psychology, of which factor-analytic studies offer familiar examples, attention is focused on traits that are assumed to be common to all members of a given population, in greater or lesser degree. A goal of research is to differentiate the traits, providing operational definitions for them that are distinct or mutually exclusive. In type psychology attention is focused on categories of people. It is assumed that persons in general fall naturally into classes distinguished by unique combinations of attributes. The purpose of classification is to reflect the natural attribute clusters, which may then be studied as unitary entities, or types. Type psychology has been found less fruitful than trait psychology in the study of personality. * Instead of pursuing the relationships between traits of creativity and other intellectual and personality traits—knowledge about which would be valuable indeed—they attempted to distinguish between creative and intelligent types of students and to discover clusters of attributes proper to each type. The tools they used to effect this classification were those very tests that had been developed as measures of traits common to all, and the classification was achieved by discarding a sizable group of students who were high scorers on both measures. Such a procedure is not comparable to taking groups of extreme scorers, high and low, on the same measure, which is a conventional research procedure. It is rather more like studying two types of people, parents and married people, while leaving out the group composed of married parents. * The creativity measure was a summated score from a somewhat redundant and not entirely appropriate collection of five tests representing a very limited array of factors of creative thinking. The descriptions of the test items as well as the test intercorrelations indicate that verbal meaning, the chief component of most IQ measures, was an important factor in every test. Recent observations reported by Guilford suggest that, at these high levels of ability, IQ is hardly correlated with creativity measures. Three of Getzels and Jackson's creativity tests were substantially correlated with their IQ measure, suggesting that the selection of creativity tests was not a very good one, especially for their purposes. By dichotomizing both the IQ and the composite creativity measure at the 80th centile the investigators made a two-way classification of the 449 students. This resulted in the creation of four groups: a high-high group who were in the upper 20% on both measures; a low-low group who were in the lower 80% on both measures; a high-low group who were in the upper 20% on the IQ measure and the lower 80% on the creativity measure; and a low-high group who were in the lower 80% on the IQ measure and the upper 20% on the creativity measure. In such studies, as Torrance has reported, the high-highs may be as numerous as the high-lows or the low-highs. Analysis of the incomplete figures presented by Getzels and Jackson indicates that their high-high group could have been as numerous as the high-low and the low-high groups combined. Nevertheless, no report of the number of students in either the high-high group or the low-low group is given. This strange omission becomes even stranger when it is realized that if the high-highs were numerous, as they were reported to be in an earlier paper, then the creation of two types of students by the selection of small groups that did not overlap was arbitrary and essentially meaningless. It is not type psychology at all, in the best sense, and it entails a serious loss of information besides. By confining their attention to the "highs," the investigators denied themselves the use of about three-quarters of their subjects. The exclusion of the high-high group further restricted the study, so that ultimately only one-ninth of the subjects were used. The stated purpose of this drastic reduction was to isolate two types of cognitive excellence, but its effect was to manufacture two fictitious types of people. Both the loss of information and the unnatural classification could have been avoided by a trait psychology approach using a correlational analysis. This would have necessitated gathering non-aptitude data for more than the 52 students studied, but the results might have been well worth the labor. Getzels and Jackson dealt with some very interesting non-aptitude variables, both psychological and sociological, and a successful analysis of all the interrelationships might have made a valuable contribution to psychology, sociology, and education. The high-low group was inappropriately labeled the "high intelligence group," giving the impression that all those at the highest IQ levels were included. Likewise, the low-high group was misnamed the "high creativity group," giving the impresion that all those at the highest creativity levels were included. A scant footnote (p. 21) to the effect that the high-highs were "of course" excluded does not prevent the reader from losing track of the high-high group entirely (if indeed he ever realized their existence) as the labels "high IQ" and "high creative" are repeated on page after page. An additional source of confusion against which the reader is not adequately protected is the fact that in comparison with ordinary school populations almost all of these students were "highs." The reader is forced to keep reminding himself that about half of what are implied to be low-IQ subjects actually had IQ scores above 130. In spite of a warning—possibly an afterthought—that the results may not be representative or repeatable, a misleading impression of generalizability is created throughout the book. The informed reader will find it difficult to resist. The naïve reader is sure to find it overwhelming. A second general criticism involves the confounding of descriptive and predictive methodology. As the title reveals, the study was exploratory. The authors speak of being "lost in phenomena without relevant explicit concepts to guide [their] needs" (p. ix). Assuredly there is nothing wrong with doing a purely descriptive study. Getzels and Jackson, however, attempted to improve on exploration by bringing in statistical tests at every opportunity, as though to test hypotheses, when no hypotheses had been stated. In many instances a significant finding could be reported only by dropping the acceptable level of significance to the 10 per cent or even the 20 per cent level. In the absence of previous predictions, such "significance" has no meaning. The procedure improperly imparts an appearance of generality to observations that may be largely or entirely unrepeatable. The fact that this problem is acknowledged in a tardy footnote (p. 62) does not help matters. If the investigators knew the procedure was inappropriate, they should have been even less ready to make use of it. The same results could have been presented with complete propriety and clarity using confidence intervals, as is commonly done in descriptive studies where parameters are to be estimated. Thus far criticism has been aimed at the general design of the study. Even within the investigators' frame of reference, however, unjustified procedures were used and consequent erroneous findings were made. A discovery widely attributed to Getzels and Jackson is that teachers prefer "high IQ's" to "high creatives." This may be true, but it was not indicated by Getzels and Jackson's observations, even though they do report something that sounds very much like it. Their exact wording is: "the high IQ students are preferred over the average students by their teachers, the creativity students are not" (p. 30). This statement, the import of which is not immediately clear, arises from a comparison of each of the subgroups in turn with a larger group of 449 (or 395—the table is ambiguous) "average students." It is reported that the teachers took a significantly greater degree of pleasure in teaching the "high IQ's" than in teaching the "average students." There is nothing surprising in that. They also took a greater degree of pleasure in teaching the "high creatives" than in teaching the "average students," but the result was not statistically significant. The fact that both of these preferences were in the same direction and of nearly the same magnitude is ignored. The reader is left with the unjustified impression that the teachers prefered the "high IQ's" to the "high creatives." If this questionable logic is not enough, a closer inspection reveals that the reported significant difference in teacher reaction to "high IQ's" and "average students" was itself illusory. This "significant" finding was based on a *t* test requiring homogeneity of variance, while the table reveals that the variances were not homogeneous at all. The *F* ratio exceeds five-to-one. When the *t* test is appropriately made with an estimate of population variance, the significance vanishes. Analysis indicates, moreover, that a difference between the "high IQ's" and the "high creatives" as great as the one reported would occur through chance sampling at least one time in four. Contrary to their report, Getzels and Jackson's results suggest that teachers do not prefer any group of students to any other group. If there were actual differences in the teachers' preferences, they were overlooked by this method of analysis. A more sober and thorough appraisal would have resulted from using median dichotomies, establishing four groups of students, and performing an analysis of variance of the teachers' ratings. The matter would seem to end there, but one point remains. The group of "average students" included an unspecified but certainly substantial number of students who were in the upper 20 per cent on both measures. They were outstanding in both creativity and intelligence. The group included also a large number of students who were in the lower 80 per cent on both measures. This lumping together of high-highs and low-lows entirely obscured the feelings of the teachers toward the high-highs. It is just possible that, given the chance, the teachers might have said their greatest pleasure was in teaching students who were excellent in every way. In their long promised study of the high-high group, Getzels and Jackson have an opportunity to test this hypothesis. Limitations of space forestall an exposition of every misstep, but one additional kind of error is worth noting. In a table (p. 39) presenting supposed differences in fantasy production between "high IQ's" and "high creatives," six successive chi-square tests are shown on different scorings of the same fantasy responses. The usual probability tables for chi square assume that the test will not be repeated on correlated aspects of the same observations. Were hypothesis-testing techniques justified at all here, almost any multivariate analytic technique would have yielded more interpretable results than this insupportable repetition of a univariate model. In the absence of hypotheses, perhaps the best presentation would have employed confidence intervals for proportions or for differences between proportions. Throughout the book the reader encounters questionable clinical interpretations, incongruous theoretical statements, and gratuitous research conclusions. An example of the last is a description of the attributes supposedly held in common by the "high creatives" and a so-called highly moral group. The commonality of some of these attributes could have been tested by an analysis of data available in the study, but the analysis is not presented. Minor errors, ambiguities, and inconsistencies in text and tables are frequent enough to cause the reader to question the care with which the study was done. The groups of subjects fluctuate in size from comparison to comparison, and the reasons given do not always seem entirely appropriate. However, it is not the little inconsistencies that make this a remarkable piece of research. It is the bald manner in which incompatible and inappropriate procedures have been mixed into a muddle whose meaning is largely incomprehensible, whose relevance is frequently doubtful, and whose effect more often than not is to exasperate the expert and lead the layman astray.

Psychoanalytic Q 32:423–5 Jl '63. Victor H. Rosen. * The study seems to have been well conceived and carefully executed. It should be of considerable interest especially to educators and social psychologists. The occasional polemical undercurrent which makes a special plea for the understanding and educational assimilation of the nonconforming "creative" child can easily be forgiven. Where a stand is taken on theoretical issues the authors reveal a firm grasp of general formulations and of the conflicting approaches to the subject including the psychoanalytic one. They are impressed with Kris's concept of "controlled regression" and the role of preconscious processes in the creative process and suggest a supplementary alternative in Schachtel's theory of "perceptual modes." The discussion of these viewpoints as if they were antithetical overlooks Greenacre's emphasis on "collective alternatives" and the unusual receptivity to external stimuli on the part of creatively gifted individuals. * Of special interest to the whole problem of the psychology of creativity is the study's implicit and inevitable involvement in the ambiguities of circular reasoning. In his Psychoanalytic Explorations in Art, Kris in particular has emphasized the insidious interpolation of the circular fallacy wherever the psychologist has attempted to study the creative process. By their own admission and in felicitous terms the authors note that they are comparing groups of adolescents with different "cognitive styles." These "cognitive styles," although similar, may bring together individuals with diverse characteristics in other respects when they are used as a basis for classification. The group that is described as "creative" shows an unusual capacity for imagination, humor, and originality in the handling of test material. Since we have not yet agreed upon a precise definition of the meaning of the term "creative" it may be plausible for the authors to define this characteristic as a synonym for a "cognitive style" which combines the aforementioned elements. They admit, however, that these are the apparent prerequisites for creative activities and do not in themselves insure creative achievement. Thus in reality the so-called "creative" group is one with a presumed potential for creativity which may or may not become fulfilled. No matter how plausibly presented, there is a *petitio principii* in treating originality, for example, as both an evidence of creativity and a prerequisite for its emergence. Only careful follow-up studies of both the "high IQ group" and the "creative group" can further elucidate the data. There may be surprises. One might find in later life, for example, that some adolescents without the favorable "cognitive style" of what I would prefer to call the "imaginative" rather than "creative" group will still achieve significant artistic or scientifically creative goals. In fact, utilizing their own original approach to the problem, could the authors now begin to examine other groups of subjects to determine whether some may achieve high test scores for imagination and originality yet show very little creative achievement and vice versa? These critical comments are not meant to detract from the value of the study as it now stands, nor from the care and industry which it reveals. *

Sci 138:673 N 9 '62. Frank Barron. * an important piece of psychological research * The Getzels and Jackson study is also, and perhaps this is its greatest significance, an astringent corrective to the oversold concept of the I.Q. and its accompanying test paraphernalia. * Getzels and Jackson were by no means the first psychologists to recognize the folly of this system, nor for that matter were they first to carry out investigations establishing the relationship of measures of general intelligence to measures of creativity. Their contribution lies rather in their dramatic use of the test results, especially in the telling individual cases they report, and in their informed and penetrating discussion of the issues upon which their data shed some light. * The data are slight in themselves and would not warrant the far-reaching interpretations the authors have placed upon them were it not for their internal consistency and sensibleness as well as their neat dovetailing with a host of other findings that are emerging from an impressive volume of recent research on creativity in a wide variety of settings. Getzels and Jackson seem to have summed up the tenor of much of this recent work in their own study.

[B202]

★GEWIRTZ, HERMAN. **How to Prepare for College Board Achievement Tests: Physics.** Great Neck, N.Y.: Barron's Educational Series, Inc., 1963. Pp. iv, 147. Paper, $2.25; cloth, $4.50. *

[B203]

★GHISELLI, EDWIN E. **Theory of Psychological Measurement.** New York: McGraw-Hill Book Co., Inc., 1964. Pp. xi, 408. $8.95. * (London: McGraw-Hill Publishing Co. Ltd. 69*s.* 6*d.*)

[B204]

★GILBAUGH, JOHN W. **A Teacher's Guide for Test Construction With Percentage Tables for Computing Test Scores.** San Jose, Calif.: Modern Education Publishers, 1960. Pp. 28. Paper. $1.00. *

[B205]

★GOLDMAN, LEO. **Using Tests in Counseling.** New York: Appleton-Century-Crofts, 1961. Pp. xix, 434. $7.00. * (*PA* 36:4KI34G)

Cont Psychol 7:158–9 Ap '62. John O. Crites. * the coverage and organization of the book is comprehensive and logical, the only possible omission being a treatment of how to write test reports for case summaries, clients, and referrals * the bulk of the book is devoted to test interpretation and communication * the author....sees counseling as primarily concerned with the client's difficulties in occupational selection and educational achievement. The role of the counselor is to use tests to facilitate the client's problem-solving and decision-making processes as they relate to future goals and objectives. Although reasonable in its intent and purpose, this formulation suffers from two conceptual difficulties which limit its usefulness and applicability. First, despite the cogency of the decision model for certain components of vocational-educational counseling, the discussion of the relationship between theory and practice is too general and superficial: the connections are implied and vague rather than explicit and specific. As a result, the analogue has less meaning and significance than its initial presentation promises. Second, the decision model, although appropriate for counseling conceived largely as problem-solving, is too restrictive in scope for counseling designed to further personal development as well. Consequently, acceptance of the author's conceptualization of counseling leaves the counselor with both an inexact and an incomplete theoretical foundation for the various uses and interpretations of tests. Another formulation, also having shortcomings, pertains to the inductive-deductive process of reasoning pursued by the counselor in drawing conclusions from test data and stating them as predictions of future choice and performance. Dr. Goldman points out that there are two "bridges," the statistical and the clinical, by which the counselor moves from test results to their interpretation. His explanations of these methods, however, lead to two ambiguities which require clarification. First, he classifies normative data on unselected samples as a statistical bridge, along with regression equations and expectancy tables. Norms derived from samples which are unselected with respect to occupation or college major involve only *one* variable, the test scores, and offer no basis for the prediction of other behaviors. As Dr. Goldman points out, test validity rests upon the demonstration of relationships between predictor *and* criterion variables. Second, and more important, in the exposition on clinical bridges, the author outlines the steps in the process of "nonmechanical" test interpretation but not how to make them. There is no discussion of the rules of logic, particularly as they apply to the formation of hypotheses and the verification of syllogisms, as aids to the counselor in making inferences and predictions from the test data. These comments highlight the weaknesses of *Using Tests in Counseling* rather than its strengths, which are equally notable but far more numerous. Well-organized, interestingly written, and sound in precept, if not especially in concept, Dr. Goldman's book deserves the counselor's attention and acceptance as an authoritative guide to the appraisal of clients and as a contribution to the distinctive subject-matter of counseling psychology.

J Counsel Psychol 8:287 f '61. Irwin A. Berg. * something of a model for books of its kind * like Super, Goldman has organized in scholarly fashion an astonishing mass of research data which bears on the use of tests. The end result is a clear distillate of testing in relation to counseling. It's all there, from the purpose of testing to reporting the tests with test selection, scoring, interpreting, and so on placed in between and in logical sequence. All counselors understand tests and their use, of course; hence a detailed statement of what Goldman covers would not be new to them. But your column editor will wager that the research evidence which supports the *tests-and-counseling* practices presented by Goldman will have much that is new for any counselor. Equally educative is the author's habit of pointing out areas where little or no research evidence is available.

Personnel & Guid J 40:738–9 Ap '62. Barbara Kirk. * a volume which makes a major contribution to its field. This book is a much needed one. It fills a sizable gap in counseling literature. * Goldman has succeeded admirably in his comprehensive approach to his subject. He has evolved a scholarly scientific work which also offers a wealth of practical ideas. It brings research and measurement findings to bear upon each topic or problem, combined with the author's knowledge and experience of clinical practice. Especially is this important in the very difficult area of diagnosis or formulation where his approach is to lay "statistical bridges" and "clinical bridges," subsequently evaluating both, providing illustrative cases, and devoting considerable attention to the special problem of contradictory or inconsistent test results. Further, detailed treatment is given such common problems as overachievement and underachievement, quantitative versus linguistic abilities, and differential prediction of school grades. Especially excellent is the section on improving clinical prediction. The author's choice of terminology may well become standard language for these processes: He uses "test interpretation" to signify the counselor's synthesis of test results into his diagnosis or formulation of the case, and "test reporting" for the counselor's communication of test results to the counselee. An important value of this book, also, is the standard implied throughout. The author expects high professional performance of both the counselor and psychometrist—and provides in most instances full specifications for implementation. There are a few matters which can be pointed to as limitations and which may be hoped can be improved in future revisions. The emphasis throughout is upon the counselor's role as answering a specific question rather than upon helping to develop the best or optimum plan with the counselee. There is some tendency to regard techniques as dichotomized rather than interactive, as, for example, in test reporting "the counselor (must be) flexible enough to shift from reporting scores to helping his client to talk," and when directive-nondirective methods are regarded as alternative rather than variably interactive depending upon counselee. One would hope for more illustration in "how to" select tests, intensification in interpretation of interest tests, but this is veritably quibbling in view of the advancement to the field of counseling provided by this book. It belongs indispensably on the desk or shelf of each and every worker and student in the field, be he counselor, psychometrist, counseling psychologist, counselor trainer, in all schools, colleges, agencies, hospitals, etc., to be read and re-read, and referred to innumerable times in his professional life.

[B206]

★Good, Patricia King-Ellison, and Brantner, John P. **The Physician's Guide to the MMPI.** Minneapolis, Minn.: University of Minnesota Press, 1961. Pp. 69. Paper. $1.85. (London: Oxford University Press. 15*s.*) *

Psychiatric Q Sup 35:361 pt 2 '61. * As a short discussion for somebody who knows something about the MMPI, it is excellent. For one who knows nothing about the test, it would be completely baffling.

[B207]

★Goslin, David A. **The Search for Ability: Standardized Testing in Social Perspective.** Volume 1 of a Series on the Social Consequences of Ability Testing. New York: Russell Sage Foundation, 1963. Pp. 204. $4.00. *

Am J Sociol 70:125–6 Jl '64. Alexander W. Astin. * At a time when testing practices are being subjected to a series of sensationalistic and poorly considered attacks, Goslin's scholarly and dispassionate view of the problems concerned with standardized ability-testing comes as a welcome change. * presents a lucid and comprehensive analysis of the nature, extent, and possible effects of ability testing as it is currently practiced. It is recommended reading for all.

Child Develop Abstracts 38:60–1 F–Ap '64. J. Beker. * Particularly useful paradigms for the analysis of variables influencing test performances and for the analysis of the social and individual impact of testing are provided. Also included is an interesting and provocative comparison of the development and antecedents of the standardized aptitude and ability testing movement in the United States with the development and antecedents of its counterparts in Great Britain and Russia. Probably the greatest value of the book to behavioral scientists lies in its explicitness in formulating and stating many of the significant social questions relating to the testing movement that are currently in need of objective study through research. * Many new and critical questions are raised and implied, and old questions restated in a sociological context, almost always in researchable terms. * Perhaps the most important contribution....lies....in its recurrent, expressed and implied, demand for sober, objective, unemotional analysis of the testing movement to replace the veritable flood of largely "popular" attacks on testing with which professionals in the field have been inundated in the last few years. It would seem to behoove both the pro-testers and the protesters to study responsibly and critically the issues posed by Goslin before adapting dogmatic and absolute positions on the standardized aptitude and achievement testing issue.

J Counsel Psychol 10:410–1 w '63. Donald E. Super. * a refreshing change among books about testing by nonspecialists—even though I did have to buy a copy! The author is a Ph.D. in sociology, and his project is part of a serious Foundation attempt to examine testing programs in perspective. The objective is to clear up some of the confusion about standardized tests and to raise questions concerning their impact on society in ways which will lead to research on the important issues. Most of the material in the book, the first in a proposed series on this subject, will be familiar to psychologists who keep up with testing. But the perspective in which Goslin puts testing for guidance and for selection is somewhat new, and will prove helpful to test users. By raising most questions as questions, and seeking answers, he does the field a real favor; the answers, when provided, tend to be the result of balanced judgment. Only occasionally does a negative set show: for example, on page 55 and

56, and again in Chapters VII and VIII, the "self-fulfilling prophecy characteristics of ability tests" are discussed as though their purpose were self-fulfillment, with no recognition of what psychologists have so long pointed out, that prophecy is often designed to avert rather than to bring about failure! The placement of a low-ability child in a slow-moving group is designed to enable a teacher to give him the kind of instruction he needs in order to progress, not to condemn him to slow movement. Ability to look at all aspects of a question is shown in connection with duplication in testing programs. In addition to the practice and second-chance arguments in favor of some duplication, Goslin reminds the reader that two or three days of testing to evaluate learning during the course of a year involves less in the way of interference with learning than do athletics, senior plays, yearbooks, and many other school activities. At the same time, limits to the extent of duplication are considered desirable. One of the strong features of the book is the tendency to identify researchable problems in the social consequences of mass testing. We should see important work in this area in the future, and Goslin notes the openness of test specialists to answering questions by looking for relevant facts. A few errors, most of no consequence, have crept into this book, as they tend to do when a specialist in one field writes about another specialty. One we are too often guilty of ourselves is a reference to the "Wechsler-Bellevue IQ Test"; more serious is the statement that the Psychological Corporation has specialized in non-academic testing (despite the DAT); there is no mention of the APA *Ethics Code* and of its role in testing, nor of the effect of APA's *Technical Recommendations* on test publication and distribution (p. 33). Goslin is apparently unaware of the studies of the effects of test interpretation on self-knowledge (p. 179), and Lee Cronbach, who is certainly many things in psychometrics, is hardly a "pioneer" (p. 183) in the sense of an early explorer—but perhaps Goslin meant to characterize him as a current explorer, and I got the wrong connotation. Finally, some sources which I would have expected to find in the references are not there; they are mostly the student and pupil personnel specialists such as Williamson, Darley, and Froelich, but include also the NIIP studies, highly relevant to such an enterprise as this. Counseling psychologists will await the other Russell Sage books in this series with great interest. In the meantime, we can be pleased that such a careful, thoughtful, and unbiased approach is being taken to a vital subject.

[B208]

★GOUDE, GUNNAR. **On Fundamental Measurement in Psychology.** Stockholm Studies in Psychology 2. Stockholm, Sweden: Almqvist & Wiksell, 1962. Pp. 176. Paper. Sw. kr. 18; 24*s*. 9*d*. * (*PA* 38:43)

Cont Psychol 8:442+ N '63. Andrew Comrey. * The book is a small volume translated from Swedish. The treatment of the theory of measurement is brief, based primarily, according to the author, on four works by Campbell, Hempel, Stevens, and Torgerson. It is not suitable as a text book. The book's greatest value would seem to be in the many experiments reported to illustrate the possibilities of different methods of psychological measurement. Particularly novel are the author's attempts to provide a physical interpretation of addition. * Still another series of experiments determines estimates of the ratios among five weight stimuli by means of the ratio-estimation, addition, and part-sum methods. * Whether the author's line of evidence is adequate to demonstrate that fundamental measurement has taken place in his various examples is open to question. Regardless of the conclusion on this issue, however, it must be pointed out that a method of measurement cannot be validated as such. Each psychological property in which we are interested must be shown individually to be measurable. Whether the techniques used by Goude will be helpful in improving psychological measurement remains to be seen. At any rate, his book should be read by the measurement specialist.

[B209]

★GRAHAM, GRACE. **Teachers Can Construct Better Tests.** University of Oregon, School of Education, Curriculum Bulletin, Vol. 12, No. 170. Eugene, Ore.: Curriculum Bulletin, the University, December 10, 1956. Pp. 11. Paper, mimeographed. $0.50. *

[B210]

★GREEN, DONALD A. **Cumulative Records in Ohio High Schools.** Ohio University, College of Education, Center for Educational Service, Pupil Services Series, No. 3. Athens, Ohio: the Center, 1960. Pp. 28. Paper. $1.00. * (*PA* 36:1KJ28G)

[B211]

★GREEN, JOHN A. **Teacher-Made Tests.** New York: Harper & Row, Publishers, Inc., 1963. Pp. ix, 141. Paper. $1.95. (London: Harper & Row Ltd. 15*s*.) *

Peabody J Ed 41:126–7 S '63. William S. Graybeal. * A major strength of this book is its emphasis upon measuring the accomplishment of all instructional objectives. * The author....has realistic suggestions for assessing pupil accomplishment in such areas as critical thinking, social adjustment, acquirement of interests, attitudes, and appreciations, in addition to the more commonly measured skills and facts. Following the discussion of each type of tests, the author evaluates the type being discussed and identifies purposes for which it may be used effectively. Review of these sections should broaden the scope of testing instruments available to any teacher. * Many helpful suggestions are given regarding bases for assigning course marks. * The final chapter discusses statistical treatment of test score data. This is the weakest part of the book. * The book is a valuable document which should be placed in the professional library of every school. In addition to use as a resource for planning coordinated grading procedures, the book may be used to assist a "factual achievement" centered teacher to broaden the base of her teaching and evaluation.

[B212]

★GREER, EDITH S. **Pupil Marks and School Marking Systems.** Washington, D.C.: United States Government Printing Office, 1963. Pp. 22. Paper. $0.20. *

[B213]

★GROFF, MORRIS, AND GRUBER, EDWARD C. **How to Score High on the Medical College Admission Test, Revised Edition.** New York: Arco Publishing Co., Inc., 1962. Pp. 278. Paper, $4.00; cloth, $6.00. *

[B214]

★GRONLUND, NORMAN E. **Sociometry in the Classroom.** New York: Harper & Row, Publishers, Inc., 1959. Pp. xix, 340. Out of print. *

Brit J Ed Psychol 30:193 Je '60. K. M. Evans. * Too often sociometric writers have been more noted for their enthusiasm than for their powers of criticism. The present author is to be commended for showing both the importance of the technique and its limitations; for it must be admitted that the very ease with which a sociometric test can be applied has induced what can only be described as "test happiness" in many devotees. The sane and judicious account of the ways in which the results of a sociometric test can add to our knowledge of a group of children and give guidance for their future treatment should do much to ensure that those who adopt the methods described do so with a full appreciation of what the test does and does not tell us. If the book has a weakness, it is the fewness of the sociometric diagrams shown. A large part of the appeal of sociometry has always been the clarity with which a sociogram portrays the relationships within a group of people. A book which sets out to describe the basic techniques of sociometry should surely base more of its exposition on a study of sociograms than is done here. This, however, is a minor point, and the book can be strongly recommended as satisfying a real need. It should find a place in all training college libraries.

El Sch J 60:47–8 O '59. Britomar J. Handlon. * the author provides a guide for the construction, administration, and analysis of sociometric tests; he offers a critical interpretation of the use of these tests in the classroom; and for good measure, he throws in a comprehensive review of the literature. So far as this reviewer knows, not one of these tasks has been seriously attempted before. * Part I is essentially a manual, and an excellent one. The chapter on construction and administration of sociometric tests deals with "strong" and "weak" criteria, specific and general criteria, number of choices, and negative choices. The advice is sound and sensible at every point. The chapter on analysis and presentation of results is based primarily on a combination of Northway and Bronfenbrenner's methods, though other methods are also referred to. The researcher might prefer more sophisticated methods, but the combination of methods chosen by Gronlund is undoubtedly the wisest for the teacher. It is relatively simple and yet comparatively free from coding or interpretive unreliability, a criticism to which Moreno's original sociograms are highly susceptible. The chapter on typical results is just that. One wishes that Gronlund had said something about the cultural significance of these results. If he had no data for drawing conclusions, one wishes that he had at least speculated. Part II is primarily a review of sociometric studies. The author seems to think that the problems of reliability and validity are more difficult to solve for the sociometric test than for any other psychological test, an opinion not shared by this reviewer. * The real contribution of this excellent book lies in Part III, which is a discussion of the applications of the sociometric test in the school. Gronlund never makes the mistake of assuming that the sociometric test is a test of personal adjustment. He nowhere declares that being an "isolate" is necessarily bad or being a "star" necessarily good. At every point, he shows the test as part of a battery of tools for understanding a classroom, a school, or a child. Sociometric responses are never to be interpreted in isolation from other data about a classroom, a school, or a child, any more than any other psychological test should be interpreted in isolation from other relevant data. I wondered about Gronlund's suggestion that a pupil's sociometric scores should be made as much a part of the pupil's permanent record as his achievement scores. If Gronlund were administering the procedure, I shouldn't worry. But how would it work out in the field? I can see college-admissions boards and prospective employers weighting peer-status scores in their formulas, and the prospect gives me 1984 shudders. This is an unusual book. One wonders why someone didn't write it a long time ago. It certainly needed to be written, and this reviewer is glad that the author who took the assignment is someone with a style as clear and lucid as Gronlund's.

Harvard Ed R 31:115–6 w '61. Renato Tagiuri. * The contents of the book are well balanced. * The author does not spare any effort in forwarding the idea that sociometric data are susceptible to a great many factors. * Not given the attention it deserves is the relationship the teacher has with the pupils and its effect upon sociometric results. This issue merits some discussion, even if (as is the case with other topics discussed in the book) little empirical documentation exists on it. There are some other places where the reviewer felt more should have been said. Neglected, for example, is the possibility of using a combination of free and fixed choices, so useful in keeping the door open to statistical analyses, yet generating information on such variables as social expansiveness. Probably because of the reviewer's own interest and work in dyadic analysis of sociometric data, it was felt that more should have been said about this, too. * All along, care is taken to distinguish the sociometric data from the "actual" relationships among pupils. This distinction is, of course, crucial for a sophisticated approach to any form of measurement. * Glossing over the questionable reference to "actual" relations (whatever these might be), the author himself, however, slips occasionally. * One of the most undesirable consequences of a good exposition of a methodology and the action implications of its results is that it tends to produce pseudo-experts. In social and personality psychology this is definitely to be discouraged. Yet, without some selection and interpretation by the experts it is very difficult for others to benefit from available technical resources. Gronlund's book will, inevitably, produce the less desirable result in some cases. But for those more interested in understanding the child than in playing the expert, for those, that is, who will read carefully what is in the book, Gronlund has exposed a good many of the complexities and uncertainties of the use and interpretation of sociometric methodology. A balanced interpretation of method, analysis and results, though placed in the school setting, this book is not only for teachers, but for anyone who wishes a good overview of sociometry and its applications to children.

[B215]

★Gross, Martin L. **The Brain Watchers.** New York: Random House, Inc., 1962. Pp. x, 305. $4.95. * (New York: New American Library of World Literature, Inc., 1963. Pp. 256. Paper. $0.75.) (*PA* 38:4809)

Cont Psychol 8:228–9 Je '63. W. J. E. Crissy. This is a book about tests, testing and testers. In content and organization it is more of a mishmash than a potpourri. It certainly is neither a systematic treatise, text book, nor research work on the subject. The viewpoint can be inferred from the very first sentence, "This book is about brain watching, the art, its practitioners, and its subjects, some 50,000,000 hapless Americans." The professional practitioner engaged in personal evaluation is going to be irritated to find himself indiscriminately grouped with proprietary firms doing testing by mail. He is likely to be confused when he finds his own metalanguage invaded and many of his carefully qualified terms bandied by the author in cavalier and dogmatic fashion. What is the mission of the book? It seems to be to set the American public straight on that dreadful evil, testing. The indictments are many. First, with regard to the tests themselves, it is alleged that few are reliable and none valid. Second, the testers have become all-powerful Machiavellian wielders of influence, changing men's lives and firms' destinies. Third, the influence of the testers is all-pervasive. Their machinations are taking the creativity out of Madison Avenue, the ingenuity out of our schools, and entrepreneurial aspirations out of our salesmen. Fourth, as a culminating indictment, tests are seen as an invasion of privacy. The book places in public purview some truly serious issues with regard to tests, ones which psychologists have been grappling with for a long time. Certainly the empirical evidence on validity of inventory-type personality and motivational measures is controversial at best. Few if any of them have a predictive preciseness that warrants their use in definitive selection decisions. Another unresolved problem is that of keeping tests out of the public domain. Many widely-used measures are readily available to the layman. Indeed paperbacks containing scoring keys of some tests are available at newsstands. Still another issue stems from man's unending quest for a simple way of understanding himself better. This has provided an almost limitless market for the test charlatan. Another problem, only too well known to psychologists, is that test results are certainly vulnerable to misinterpretation. The Gross book contains some horrible examples of this. Yet another problem, related more to testers than to tests, is that of dual allegiance. For example, if the psychologist is retained to screen candidates for a prospective employer or to assist a corporate client in upgrading employees, he must uphold the best interests of the business which he serves. On the other hand, he has an ethical as well as a professional obligation to try to help the applicant or the employee involved. Should he become privy to personal information that might from a managerial viewpoint eliminate considering an applicant further or cause serious doubts about an employee's promotability, he must determine whether or not it was provided on a confidential basis by the person involved. The stickiness of this issue is reflected in part by the treatment of it in the A.P.A. *Code of Ethics* which, incidentally, is not referred to in the book. * What will be the impact of the book on the general public? It is certainly likely to raise questions about the utility and value of tests. Some people may without further evidence discontinue testing. More sophisticated readers are likely to discern an axe-grinding in the diatribe. Perhaps in the long run the very attention focused on testing may be beneficial.

Cont Psychol 9:190–1 Ap '64. John Nickols and Marcia Nickols. [Criticism of above review by W. J. E. Crissy.] * Crissy's review of....*The Brain Watchers*....represents an unfortunate position for *CP* to have taken. First, *CP* gives recognition to Gross as a feature writer and commentator, one whose function includes questioning current issues for the lay public. *CP* then proceeded to present a review which designated the author's book as "neither a systematic treatise, text book, nor research work," as if such achievements were expected of a commentator, while referring to the "professional practitioner" having his "metalanguage invaded" and many terms "bandied....in cavalier and dogmatic fashion." The question emerges whether psychology can expect to remain unchallenged by the very public it presumes to assess. Perhaps even more basic, can *CP,* as the designated journal for review and evaluation, limit articles to the role of protecting the scientific status of psychology in such a pontifical manner? Secondly, it would appear ill-advised to base the rebuttal of a book capitalizing upon emotional appeals by falling prey to the same error. We refer to the use of such loaded phrases as "mishmash," "that dreadful evil," "hapless Americans," "all-powerful Machiavellian wielders of influence." Perhaps Gross reflected some opinions gaining root in society, but we do not become exonerated through possessing equal facility in an exhibition of incendiary vocabulary. Such tactics, and the mere statement that we are already "grappling" with the "serious issues" without concrete evidence of doing so, make psychologists look like pompous book-readers, long on shallow comments and short on scientific attitude. Contradictions, within the review, itself, are apparent. In one paragraph, Crissy mentioned the strictness of the APA Code of Ethics as a safeguard against invasion of privacy; whereas in the next paragraph, the review went beyond the content of the book to refer to the "adjustment mechanisms of the author," and to inquire whether he had had "a traumatic experience with tests." The term "dreadful evil" would not seem appropriate in a scientific review, since it might appear to exaggerate the nature of testing to an absurd degree. Applying the terms "irritated" and "confused," along with the phrase, "stronger drive to counteractions," to the anticipated reactions of psychologists could foreclose hope that psychologists would approach subject matter (or a book) with an open mind. Has anyone attempted truly impartial investigations into the specters Gross might have raised? Can we ignore the possibility of truth underlying his axe-grinding bent? If the professional practitioner should be indiscriminately grouped with the mail-order level of testing in the mind of the lay public, can it be that psychologists have not engaged in sufficient endeavors to inform the public about qualified services? How much actual danger to individual rights and potential development occurs through testing and, more pointedly, how many parents and children would wish to burn the test papers, given access to them? Testers might not be "all powerful," but how many merely misuse tests? How much potential individuality is hampered directly or indirectly by the mental test movement? How much invasion of privacy actually occurs? We cannot answer such questions; thus we cannot justifiably negate the source. Rather than negating the voices of discontent, why can't *CP* encourage greater perspective in handling reviews? In the case of *The Brain Watchers,* the author might be extending a challenge for better safeguards to the welfare and privacy of the subject; he might legitimately demand more effective validation of tests in relation to specific purpose and subject population. Perhaps the book, itself, can serve as a test of whether psychology has progressed sufficiently on scientific merit for psychologists to be confident that their instruments can withstand potently expressed challenges. If psychologists really require defending, *CP* might provide the opportunity for the presentation of pro-and-con data. Or at least provide the author with an appropriate expert to serve as his defense attorney. This seems to be in line with Eysenck's position in relation to another matter (*CP,* Oct. 1963, 8, 414). Is it necessarily an unacceptable position? Personally, we appreciated reading *The Brain Watchers.*

Cont Psychol 9:238 My '64. W. J. E. Crissy. [Reply to above criticism by John Nickols and Marcia Nickols.] * I have reread my review and think that it reflects my perception of the book. *

N Y Times Book R 6 O 21 '62. John Dollard. The American public has been in need of a blast against the use of invalid personality tests, and this is provided, in fact with a vengeance, by this angry journalist. The hard-nosed among academic psychologists have deplored the mushrooming use of unproved personality tests, but their disapproval has not restrained the promoters among psychologists from making a considerable business out of selling such tests. There may be exceptions unknown to me, but generally speaking projective tests, trait scales, interest inventories or depth interviews are not *proved* to be useful in selecting executives, or salesmen, or potential delinquents, or superior college students. If not *known* to be reliable and valid, personality tests should be resolutely avoided because they can do much harm. Since we are all a little soft toward our own professions, I doubt that any psychologist could have made as telling a case against test abuses as Martin L. Gross has done. He reminds us of the over-selling done by some commercial test organizations. He points out that unreliable tests are a grave danger to those whom they exclude from employment or promotion. The judgment of business users that "the tests work" may be, he says, only an emotional evaluation and not a matter of proved fact. He declares that the taking of tests in the business setting is generally not a voluntary act and is thus an infringement on privacy. Mr. Gross questions whether a depth interviewer can with good conscience work for management since he must of necessity betray his subject in making his report. Mr. Gross fears that the tests tend to weed out the cultured, liberal or artistic people and hand over to the corporations using the tests only the sodden conformists. He repeats the excellent sentence pronounced by Prof. Lee Cronbach of the University of Illinois, "The names given to traits by test authors cannot be trusted"; in plain English, the test called "Honesty Test," if there is one, doesn't necessarily test honesty. Mr. Gross notes, truly, that there is no general theory of personality agreed on by psychologists which could provide the theoretical basis for personality tests. What Mr. Gross brings to his task is righteous indignation at puffery and error. However, he overdoes it. His attitude seems to be one of hatred of tests and testing. One feels that he would, if he could, abolish all kinds of testing and even perhaps research toward finding better tests. His book abounds in invective and slanted judgments. Such a one-sided speaker makes even the truth seem odious. A good example of the hating is the name he gives to personality testers, i.e., "brain watchers." It suggests "bird watchers," something trivial if you are not a bird-watcher, and "brain washers," something very menacing whatever you are. In other words, he uses a trick, that is a biased name, to get his opinion across. The same trick is used by right-wing groups who call every liberal man who disagrees with them a "commie" or a "pinko." It is a sorry trick wherever used. The appearance of this one-sided but useful book should cause psychologists to pause. Our profession has a code of ethics forbidding "excessive claims" which might be expected to prevent anyone from selling an invalid test. But we have no policing organization for this code. Should psychologists be more active in protecting the public? Should tests not known to be valid be prohibited as rigorously as drugs not known to be useful and harmless?

Personnel & Guid J 41:824–5 My '63. Leo Goldman. This book....is a full-length treatment of the....abuses and dangers in the use of personality tests for selection in business and education. Many psychologists have felt for some time that there are such abuses and dangers and that the topic warrants a thorough and critical assessment. The pity is that Mr. Gross's book is so bad that the good ideas it does contain may be rejected by those in the field who should take them seriously. And it is just possible that the layman will be unable to distinguish the good ideas from the others and will end by believing even more incorrectly than he does now. Essentially Gross is saying that personality tests, both the multiple-choice inventories and the projective devices, are extremely low in reliability and unproved in validity. Furthermore, their users, whether management consultants or the employers themselves, rarely do the local research needed to establish validity for the jobs in question. Even when they do the research and work from an empirical image of the successful worker, they are guilty of perpetuating this image and blocking healthy change. So you can't win: If your test is invalid, you are a charlatan; if it is valid, you are a conspirator against Gross's good guys, the introspective and nonconforming people of the world. Gross has put his finger on a number of really serious problems which we in the field have either failed to recognize or have chosen to ignore: Often personality (and interest) tests are used for selection which were intended only for counseling use. Certainly he is correct in saying that test users rarely do local validation studies. It is also well known that several major consulting organizations do a land-office business in blind interpretations of tests, without much information about the subject and without ever seeing him. Most troubling of all is the question as to whether it is ethical for psychologists to consider the employer (or school) their client, and the individual applicant or employee or student as merely a subject, from whom they pump as much as possible of what the employer wants to know and in whom they seek whatever qualities the employer deems desirable. Lest counselors in schools feel untouched, Gross focuses his bright lights on some of their ethical and moral flaws also. Inadequate training to interpret personality tests is certainly the rule rather than the exception. But even the well-trained ones have very questionable legal and moral justification for their probes into children's deep feelings and attitudes, and their family relationships, sex behavior, and other facets of their lives which personality measures get at, directly or indirectly. These are legitimate criticisms. They compel us to ask whether some current practices are indeed an unconscionable invasion of personal privacy and a curtailment of the right to a job without regard to one's political or religious beliefs or his family squabbles. Perhaps in our role as testers we don't see things quite the way we would if these were our own children or friends being tested by people who were strangers to us, and about whose qualifications we had some reasonable doubt. Unfortunately, the criticisms in this book are presented so unfairly as to represent poor scholarship and poor journalism. Not that Gross hasn't read; he cites many studies, and he also reports many interviews with people in the field. But the studies and the opinions which support his position are presented straightforwardly; the others are ridiculed. If the results of a study are not to his liking, he highlights the flaws in the research methods (in the studies which support his conclusions, he ignores the very same flaws) and attributes either stupidity or maliciousness to the researcher. For example, the people for whom the predictions from a test turn out to be in error (as if there has ever been a prediction study without errors) are "victims of an unholy conspiracy." Gross reports with delighted dismay the percentages of false positive and false negative test predictions, but he doesn't mention what these rates would have been without the test. There are many, many errors of fact and of interpretation, but even a certain number of these can be excused if an author gives a balanced and fair analysis of the situation. Gross uses the weapons of the propagandist more often than the tools of the responsible journalist. For example, the treatment he gives the Strong Vocational Interest Blank is typical. He characterizes it as a way of getting at prejudices and proves his point by selecting for illustration those few items which look like prejudice items (liking foreigners and people with hooked noses). He also selects for illustrations those few items which have political relevance, again implying that these are typical. And so he flails away, chapter after chapter, disregarding contradictions in his own arguments. He is convinced that most people lie on their tests and in their interviews and thereby outwit the brain watchers. Yet he reaches the conclusion, with practically no evidence, that testing "has personally injured and threatened untold numbers of individual lives." (Whenever you don't know how many of anything, "untold" is pretty safe.) He alternates between scoring the futility of obtaining valid information through testing, and warning that testers will learn your innermost secrets if you don't watch out. It may be that Martin Gross felt that this kind of approach is necessary to get public attention. He has certainly achieved that goal, probably more so than if he had given a properly balanced treatment in the best traditions of journalism. One wonders what effects this book will have. Counselors and psychologists had better be ready to deal with some badly misinformed and angry readers of the book. They should also get to work and clean house.

Psychol Rep 12:295 F '63. C. H. Ammons and R. B. Ammons. This is a naive treatment of psychological testing such as one might well expect from a person without technical training in the standardization and clinical use of psychological tests. As yet, it is not possible to assess what damage the author's "crusade" may do to individuals in need of the best in testing. For those who understand problems in the use of psychological tests, it calls attention again to the need for continual effort toward establishment of intelligent and practical standards for tests and testers. The writing has the sound and taste of a rigged authoritarian political rally, which may help the sale of the book, but clearly shows that the author's "more than three years of extensive study and original research" reflect limited reading (which is difficult to check because references are little more than appeals to authority, i.e., journal names) and little or no scientific research such as the psychologist traditionally would perform. One is reminded unpleasantly of the confused and distorted logic evident in the legal conduct of the Nuremberg trials. One might conclude that this book represents a perversion of intellectual processes in the services of a most violent and destructive anti-intellectualism.

[B216]

★GRUBER, EDWARD C. **Graduate Business Admission Test.** New York: Arco Publishing Co., Inc., 1963. Pp. 262. Paper, $4.00; cloth, $6.00. *

[B217]

★GRUBER, EDWARD C. **High School Entrance Examinations: For Private High Schools and Special High Schools.** New York: Arco Publishing Co., Inc., 1963. Pp. vii, 236. Paper, $3.00; cloth, $5.00. *

[B218]

★GRUBER, EDWARD C. **How to Score High on the Catholic High School Entrance Examination.** New York: Arco Publishing Co., Inc., 1962. Pp. 117, plus supplements. Paper, $2.50; cloth, $4.00. *

[B219]

★GRUBER, EDWARD C. **How to Pass High on the Graduate Record Examination.** New York: Arco Publishing Co., Inc., 1962. Pp. iv, 164, plus supplements. Paper. $4.00. *

[B220]

★GRUBER, EDWARD C. **How to Score High on the Law School Admission Test.** New York: Arco Publishing Co., Inc., 1962. Pp. viii, 117, plus supplements. Paper. $4.00. *

[B221]

★GRUBER, EDWARD C. **How to Score High on the National Teacher Examination.** New York: Arco Publishing Co., Inc., 1962. Pp. vi, 167, plus supplements. Paper. $4.00. *

[B222]

★GRUBER, EDWARD C. **Practice for Scholastic Aptitude Tests: Complete Preparation.** New York: ARC Books, Inc., 1963. Pp. vi, 277. Paper, $0.95; cloth, $2.50. *

[B223]

★GRUBER, EDWARD C. **Science Scholarship Exams.** New York: Arco Publishing Co., Inc., 1963. Pp. 266. Paper, $3.00; cloth, $5.00. *

[B224]

★GRUBER, EDWARD C., EDITOR. **Biology: Advanced Tests for the Graduate Record Examination.** New York: Arco Publishing Co., Inc., 1963. Pp. 46, 16. Paper. $1.95. *

[B225]

★GRUBER, EDWARD C., EDITOR. **Geology: Advanced Tests for the Graduate Record Examination.** New York: Arco Publishing Co., Inc., 1963. Pp. 49, 16. Paper. $1.95. *

[B226]

★GRUBER, EDWARD C., EDITOR. **Psychology: Advanced Tests for the Graduate Record Examination.** New York: Arco Publishing Co., Inc., 1964. Pp. iii, 63, 8. Paper. $1.95. *

[B227]

★GRUBER, EMANUEL C., AND GRUBER, EDWARD C. **Dental Aptitude Tests.** New York: Arco Publishing Co., Inc., 1963. Pp. vii, 184, 96. Paper, $4.00; cloth, $6.00. * (Earlier editions published in each of the years 1958–62.)

[B228]

★GUILFORD, J. P. **Personality.** New York: McGraw-Hill Book Co., Inc., 1959. Pp. xiii, 562. $7.95. (London: McGraw-Hill Publishing Co. Ltd. 62s.) *

Am J Psychol 73:650–1 D '60. Julius Wishner. * Guilford grapples courageously and in deceptively simple language with the basic problems of definition and approach in the first five chapters. The discussion is always straightforward. Many teachers will want to refer their students to these chapters even if they prefer a different organization of the area and an emphasis on other variables. Particularly helpful for the professionally naïve student will be the sections dealing with the varying goals of divers professional groups in their respective studies of personality, and the clarification of the aims of the scientist. Nevertheless, the current state of the field is reflected in that definitions continue to be imprecise and aims not always clear. * in the last thirteen chapters....Guilford's biases have a decidedly narrowing effect on the kinds of data he considers, and result in a peculiarly static, descriptive organization of research finding—taxonomy carried to an extreme, without the redeeming feature of the kind of hierarchical structure that could lead to the hypothetical formulation of functional relations for research purposes. All that seems to be left is to seek endless new dimensions through factor analysis. Presumably, more and more detailed compendia of the results of such analysis will appear in the future. It is certainly true that this book contains the most thorough summary available to this point of the important research which uses the correlation coefficient as the basic statistic. One searches in vain, however, for a statement concerning a *chain* of behavior, and the necessary and sufficient conditions for its occurrence. * Generally, there seems to be reluctance to refer to overt behavior as the final testing ground for the validity of proposed dimensions. In this respect, we see revealed the ultimate weakness of the basic data on which many factor analyses are based. As has been pointed out so often before, no amount of statistical manipulation can convert a response (*e.g.* to a questionary), the determinants of which are unknown, into part of a meaningful factor. There is reliance on factor analysis as the sole method of organizing and interpreting research data in this book. There is insufficient evaluation of the worth of the raw data and of the relevance of the final factor matrix to behavior. Instead, Guilford has frequent recourse to the notion of "factorial validity," defined as the validity of a trait found by factor analysis. "The degree of factorial validity of a test is indicated by its factor loading" (p. 112). One wonders if the circle described by this perpetual circularity of the factor analytic methods is large enough to be useful for very much longer. To sum up, this is among the very best textbooks based on factor analytic studies of personality yet produced. The overall orientation is probably too narrow for most introductory courses in personality. The book should prove very useful, however, as auxiliary to a more broadly-gauged text, particularly the first five chapters, but also, for discussion of selected samples of the factor analytic literature. Every psychologist can learn something from this book, and those in the area of personality will certainly want to be familiar with it. The final picture of personality offered seems thin and static, but reflects more rigorous thinking than is usually found in books on personality. There is little discussion of serial behavior linked by functional relations.

Cont Psychol 5:126–8 Ap '60. Ronald Taft. * Many teachers will adopt this new book for their course on personality, sight unseen on the author's reputation alone, but quite a few of them will be disappointed with it, for it lacks the balanced and comprehensive coverage required. It seems likely that Guilford's involvement with his own important contributions to the study of personality have contributed to this defect. He claims that he has attempted to present the picture of personality from the one point of view of the statistical and experimental, and much of the subject matter that is conventionally included under the rubric

Personality he has deliberately excluded or dealt with only summarily. Some of his notable omissions are: the development of personality, hereditary factors in personality, personality in relation to culture and social structure, the dynamics of abnormal behavior, the interplay and integration of dynamic aspects (Guilford calls them *hormetic traits*), and the self. What does this book called *Personality* contain, then? It includes a general introduction on the nature of the concepts of personality and the meaning of traits, a discussion of various methods of assessment and their validity, and an integration of the literature on the dimensions of personality. This treatment clearly brings Guilford's work into the group of personality theories described by Hall and Lindzey as *Factor Theories* and its scope resembles most that of Eysenck's * It differs, however, from Eysenck's contributions in two important ways: in its preference for many specific rather than a few broad, independent traits and in its avoidance of an attempt to explain traits in terms of some other constructs. Guilford specifically withholds his apologies for giving his book such a comprehensive title. To him the scope of the book correctly represents *personality* which he defines as an individual's unique pattern of traits. * Guilford objects to the very appropriate title *Description and Measurement of Personality* on the grounds that this title has been pre-empted, but other apt ones are available—for example, *Personality, its Structure and Measurement*. In any case the title *Personality* has also been used before. As a text, the book is not coordinate with the typical upper-division course in personality, but it will fit adequately the minority of such courses as are oriented towards the phenotypical structure of personality, and especially those personality courses that are related to problems of assessment and vocational selection. It will also serve as a useful supplementary text for more orthodox courses. * The section on various methods of assessing personality is a valuable critical review which varies in quality from a rather weak treatment of attitude measurement to excellently balanced chapters on somatic measurements (morphological and physiological), inventory tests and general clinical methods. In these sections Guilford's long experience as a constructor of factor-based tests, and as an aviation psychologist working on problems of selection, lend a refreshing sense of reality to the discussions. The book concludes with an extremely useful pulling together of the various superficial personality dimensions that have been identified in the experimental literature. The writing is at a level of psychological and statistical sophistication that is appropriate for the average upper-division student. The introduction of necessary statistical concepts, like analysis of variance, is handled with a delicacy that is most unusual in a writer who is a heavyweight in this field, and there is an eight-page appendix that appears adequately to serve the purpose of reminding the student of what he learnt in his introductory course in statistics and of introducing him to factor theory. The student who uses the book will emerge from his course with a healthy respect for rigor in the study of personality, but a somewhat biased perspective on the position enjoyed by multiple factor techniques in the scientific study of personality. In this connection the tyro may well be misled by the hoary semantic fallacy "that many obtained factors should be taken seriously as representing psychological reality." Guilford confesses that factor analysis has its deficiencies for providing "a general, rational basis for the description of personality," but he does not discuss these limitations with the reader in any detail. There are several unexpectedly imprecise expressions and arguments in the book that may leave a thoughtful reader saying to himself, "Just what does he mean by that?" * One confusion in definition is worth mentioning. In defining *scalability* he mixes the usually accepted meaning of unidimensionality with that of continuity. A trait is described as scalable when "different individuals have different degrees of it," and unscalable when it is either present or absent as, for example, having a phobia or a tic. In practice it is possible to describe the presence or absence of any trait in the process of measurement, for example, extraverted or not extraverted, and it is also possible to describe degrees of having a phobia or a tic. The scalability of a trait surely could not rest on this measurement fiat. * So much for this book as a text. The reviewer considers that it will also find extensive use as a handbook for psychologists who are working with personality concepts in research or assessment. It offers the assessor a vast catalogue of empirically established dimensions—physical, intellectual, temperamental, motivational and pathological—from which to choose in order to describe personality in a coherent fashion, and it thus provides an alternative to the work of Eysenck and Cattell. Eysenck's factors are, as Guilford points out, too broad for practical value in assessment, although breadth has its virtues for explanation in personality theory. Cattell's factors can less easily be dismissed on these grounds and Guilford's objections to them is that confusion can arise from his "use of experimental variables from different levels in the hierarchy," most of them at a higher level of generality than Guilford's preferred level. Nevertheless Guilford makes use of Cattell's findings where he considers them to be applicable. This extremely atomistic approach to personality has further advantages. It avoids such irksome issues as the correlation between the factors and the question of surface versus source traits. The approach serves as a launching pad for systematic probes into personality, but in the endeavor to use empirical methods to understand personality—Guilford has left off very close to the point where Cattell started, that is to say, at the definition of surface traits. Perhaps he has done so advisedly, but, if so, he seems to have had mixed feelings about it. Guilford pays tribute to the "great advantages to finding dimensions located in the personality sphere that are independent or nearly independent." To apply this principle would lead him to a few high-level traits rather than many low-level ones. He also argues that in the trait hierarchy "determination is downward" and one might therefore expect him to pay more respect to the study of higher-level traits (or "types"). He seems finally to rest his case on the fact that lower-level traits are more valuable to the vocational psychologist. In taking this point of view he has produced a valuable introduction to the study of the structure and measurement of personality, but his contribution to the understanding of personality is necessarily limited thereby.

[B229]

★GULLIKSEN, HAROLD, AND MESSICK, SAMUEL, EDITORS. **Psychological Scaling: Theory and Applications.** New York and London: John Wiley & Sons, Inc., 1960. Pp. xvi, 211. Lithotyped. $5.00; 38s. * (*PA* 35:1470)

Am J Psychol 74:655–6 D '61. William B. Michael. * Throughout this broad survey of recent thinking in scaling theory numerous applications are cited with respect to measurement of sensory magnitudes, cognitive abilities, utility, and attitudes. Several of the examples, however, constitute rather specialized illustrations, the immediate utility of which many an applied psychologist and even research worker in industrial and educational psychology would find difficult to see. All in all, the volume affords both a broad perspective of recent developments in scaling theory and an appropriate balance in the types of models and sorts of applications being made. * Despite the diversification of interests and emphases of the writers the volume is well organized and well written. Particularly helpful and pleasing are the numerous captions that serve to guide the reader in his grasp of countless concepts that could readily be lost in a less suitable format. Although by no means exhaustive, the bibliography of more than 150 references does include references covering much if not most of the significant work done during the past fifteen years in scaling and in theory of measurement. In short, the reviewer found the volume to be informative, well organized and clearly written, representative of current research thinking in psychological scaling, and useful as a reference source. Although highly specialized in coverage, it should find its way to the shelves of most students and research psychologists who are concerned with scaling theory, sensory psychology, decision making and choice behavior, and factor analysis. Its excellence should stimulate many to think about several of the problems posed, to formulate additional problems, and to make important original contributions to their solution.

Austral J Psychol 13:131–2 Je '61. J. A. Keats. * A serious examination of the extent to which present scaling methods provide adequate, practical, quantitative methods for workers in other areas of psychology might well indicate that the obvious lack of application is due mainly to the fact that research workers in general do not appreciate the relevance of these methods. The present publication has done little for such psychologists. Unfortunately this conference also does little to clarify the terminology of scaling. The fact that there is a problem is demonstrated by Lazarsfeld's difficulties when discussing test theory. Stevens who uses terms like metathetic and prothetic refers to "Thurstone's penchant for novel but misleading terminology" and gives examples such as "discriminal dispersion." A suggestion that a working group be established to standardize terminology with a view to both consistency and simplicity seems pertinent. For most psychologists the subject of scaling is difficult enough without having to remember two or more polysyllabic names for the same operation. Gulliksen and Messick have, however, provided a very useful book for honours and graduate students as well as specialists in this field. In less than two hundred pages examples of the recent work of most of the major contributors to scaling theory are presented. The extension of these examples to provide a worthwhile course in scaling should not be difficult.

[B230]

★HAEUSSERMANN, ELSE. **Development Potential of Preschool Children: An Evaluation of Intellectual, Sensory, and Emotional Functioning.** New York: Grune & Stratton, Inc., 1958. Pp. xvii, 285. $8.75. *

Cont Psychol 4:232–3 Ag '59. Charles D. Smock. * Brief introductory chapters contain discussions of the purpose of an educational evaluation, special problems in testing handicapped children, limitations of standardized psychological tests, and a general description of a new structured interview procedure designed to evaluate the intellectual functioning of handicapped children. The remainder of the book (200 pages) contains directions for administering the *Educational Evaluation,* the test items utilized in the evaluation, and interpretation of the obtained data. The beginning chapters are "deliberately designed as a training opportunity which will serve to prepare the serious reader to apply the directions given in the latter" section of the book. The discussion of the concepts and principles of testing and of clinical predictions are, however, brief and superficial. In addition, the flexibility of the interview is such as to demand much more "judgment, sensitivity, ingenuity and experience of the examiner" than is true of the usual standard test. Therefore, the book is likely to have limited value as a training manual per se. Nevertheless advanced students and experienced clinicians will find some valuable suggestions in both the structure and content of the new procedure. The *Educational Evaluation* consists of a standard set of materials designed to tap sensory, perceptual, conceptual and motor abilities. An estimate of the level of functioning is obtained from the items of varying difficulty within each area. Items are presented in increasing chronological order (2 to 6 years). The testing materials are, for the most part, familiar to clinical psychologists. Selection of items was based on clinical "trial and error" procedures. Reliability and validity are not discussed. No normative data are provided. The evaluation procedure departs from the usual standardized methods of intellectual evaluation ways in two important ways. First, the author has modified the test materials and the responses demanded so that motor manipulation and verbal response are not necessary to "pass" many of the items. Secondly, failure on a standard test item is followed by the introduction of a series of modifications of that item (as discussed in a separate chapter). The purpose of the latter procedure is to provide further information regarding the maximum level of functioning in the area of impairment. This procedural flexibility—"experimental exploration," the author terms it—is justified on the basis of the kinds of predictions that are required. That is to say, in order to predict the educational potential of a handicapped child, it is necessary to have an estimate of the kinds of training and experience that will best promote the child's adaptive functioning. Available standardized test procedures, if followed precisely, yield limited information on which to base such predictions. The implication that standardized tests preclude "experimental exploration" will, however, surprise many practicing clinicians. Even celebrated cookbook clinicians would admit that useful clinical predictions sometimes are those which go beyond a statement of a quantitative score. The standardization of a "systematic experimental exploration" merely displaces the problem of validity to a different level; it does not remove the problem. The question of the validity of the clinician's predictions is, in fact, most pertinent and is neglected in this text. The failure to discuss these issues, which are central to the problems of clinical prediction, seriously limits the usefulness of this book as a general training manual. Nevertheless, students in clinical psychology will benefit from reading the chapters on problems of testing physically handicapped children and the excellent discussion of procedures for conducting the testing interview.

[B231]

★HALLER, ARCHIBALD O., AND MILLER, IRWIN W. **The Occupational Aspiration Scale: Theory, Structure and Correlates.** Michigan State University, Agricultural Experiment Station, Department of Sociology and Anthropology, Technical Bulletin 288. East Lansing, Mich.: the Station, 1963. Pp. 132. Paper. Gratis. *

J Counsel Psychol 11:204–5 su '64. C. Gilbert Wrenn. * includes a review of the literature and previous research on Level of Occupational Aspiration * the study....has marked originality including a theoretical model of LOA (Level of Occupational Aspiration) and eight hypotheses which are to be tested in the determination of any instrument's ability to measure LOA. The bulk of the bulletin is devoted to the development and standardization of the Occupational Aspiration Scale (first presented by Haller in 1957). The standardization job is thorough and workmanlike but most appealing is their blending of theoretical, statistical, and practical dimensions of the project. Much remains to be done on the scale the authors say—its predictive validity is unknown although its relation to many personal variables, including 16 P-F scores, is shown; its fakeability is untested, etc. The OAS is not yet a counseling instrument. As a research tool it has real promise. Counseling could learn much about the *structure* of LOA and its correlates by browsing this short study. The important North-Hatt occupational prestige tables are also given a good bit of additional meaning.

[B232]

HAMMER, EMANUEL F., EDITOR. **The Clinical Application of Projective Drawings.** Springfield, Ill.: Charles C Thomas, Publisher, 1958. Pp. xxii, 663. $13.50. * (*PA* 33:1177)

A.M.A. Arch Neurol & Psychiatry 80:401–2 S '58. Robert I. Yufit. This 688 page book fills a much-needed gap in presenting a comprehensive survey of drawing techniques used to study personality. * the shortcomings of this youthful (20-year-old) technique are reflected by the frequently unverified interpretations made by some of the contributors, especially Hammer. To this reviewer it seems that too many of the drawing analyses represent only so faithfully the astute observation made by Gordon Allport and cited by Hammer: "The greatest failing of the psychologist at the present time is his inability to prove what he knows to be true." Many correlative statements of something-standing-for-something-else were noted, and the sophisticated reader should evaluate their validity with more caution than is adequately exercised by the writers who made such statements. It seemed that sheer quantity ("....in 5500 drawings....") and personal experience too often were substituted uncritically for reasoned interpretations based on existing research or theory. In spite of this rather serious flaw (which several of the contributors did not commit), the book is otherwise well written, at times with flowery phraseology, and excellently documented as to original studies. As a reference source it brings up-to-date much of the relevant literature and will be of use to those contemplating research in this area. The material is well organized; the index is good. There are numerous drawings illustrating the raw data. Many of the drawings are quite dramatic. It is too bad that the editor did not see fit to sacrifice the expensive glossy pages in order to publish the chromatic drawings in color. The case studies are comprehensive in scope and illustrate well the usefulness of the drawing technique as a diagnostic tool. Also, its value as an index of psychotherapeutic progress is demonstrated. It is interesting to compare the various approaches used by the contributors of case material. This reviewer was rather concerned at the analyses forwarded by Buck. His interpretations seemed highly idiosyncratic and lacking in empirical verification, or even theoretical relevance. Hammer leans heavily to Buck's work and commits similar errors in interpretive thinking. Lack of theory is another shortcoming of the book. In spite of the clinical orientation of the book, a technique which has barely passed the infant stage of development needs the structure of theoretical formulations. The theoretical offerings of the book are considered meager. For example, there is proportionately little discussion given to the mechanisms of defense in relation to drawings. Another limitation is that there are too few data cited for nonclinical groups. The section on formal scoring and interpretation is comprehensive in scope but will not be very helpful to the novice. Although qualitatively rich in presenting an array of signs and symbols, it does not provide a quantified schema by which to assess the multidimensionality of personality as captured on paper by drawings. Admittedly, few techniques accomplish this important but complex task. Perhaps a book like this must have such shortcomings, and, hopefully, further research will be thereby stimulated to put the Draw-A-Person Test more firmly on its feet as a diagnostic instrument. Hammer admits that this book is "not yet the full-dress debut of a wholly mature scientific instrument." Over-all, the book can be recommended to students and practitioners in psychiatry and psychology as a useful reference source about projective drawings, and successive revisions will perhaps reveal the further growth of this unique clinical technique.

Can J Psychol 15:119–20 Je '61. R. W. Payne. * By and large, the contributions appear to have been carefully co-ordinated, and the repetitions which commonly occur in books of this sort are minimized. Nevertheless, as a drawing test manual, it is unbalanced. Too little space is taken up with the practical problems of the method of administering the tests discussed, and the details of their interpretation. The beginner would need to do considerable supplementary reading were he desirous of acquiring these techniques. * Generally speaking, no objective validation data are offered in support of their beliefs. There is, however, one section by Everett Heidgerd devoted to a general discussion of the validity of drawing tests, with a short review of the literature. Heidgerd, like the other contributors, regards these techniques as "personality" tests. He does not discuss what he means by the term "personality." It is usually taken to mean the sum of individual differences, so that the term "psychological tests" would be equally appropriate. It is clear that the tests are conceived of as being somehow relevant to a wide range of behaviour, as the "validation" studies quoted are heterogeneous in the extreme. For example, studies which demonstrate that the age and sex of the subjects significantly influence the drawings made, and studies which show that fat people draw fatter people than thin people are all held to be relevant to the "validity" of the tests. In fairness to Heidgerd, he concludes that these tests have not yet been shown to be valid. Nevertheless, he completely begs the question of what the tests are supposed to be valid *for*. If their purpose is left so vague, validation becomes impossible to discuss. Most of the contributors emphasize the practical value of these procedures. Many are willing to accept that they have not been validated in any scientific sense. However, they feel this does not detract from their usefulness. Yet many readers will ask, "useful for what?" Are these tests intended to be used to predict how a specific psychiatrist might diagnose a patient (thus predicting the behaviour of the psychiatrist rather than the patient)? Are they to tell us what unconscious conflicts motivate patients? Are they to be used prognostically? Can they be used to determine what type of treatment will cure certain mental disorders in certain patients? Most of the contributors remain vague on these more practical issues, and when they are discussed, no evidence is presented which supports the claims made.

J Proj Tech 23:93–5 Mr '59. Walter G. Klopfer. * This book should find a place in the library of every clinical psychologist. As a casebook governing the clinical use of projective drawings it has no equal. From a scientific view it seems rather unnecessarily defensive and pretentious. Presentation of the many excellent cases here would seem to be sufficient *raison d'etre,* without the quasi-scientific sections interlarded throughout. There is no question that expressive techniques are an important adjunct of clinical assessment and that drawings are useful in this regard. Whether the clinical utility of this approach will stand the test of time is difficult to tell before reading this book, and it is just as difficult afterwards. [See original review for additional critical comments not excerpted.]

[B233]

★HARMAN, HARRY H. **Modern Factor Analysis.** Chicago and London: University of Chicago Press, 1960. Pp. xvi, 469. $10.00; *72s.* * (*PA* 35:2904)

Austral J Psychol 14:72–3 Ap '62. J. A. Keats. The title Modern Factor Analysis is a little misleading as Harman's book deals at great length with most factor analytic methods since the invention and application of the method. Indeed each method is treated both theoretically and with excellent tabulations of computational steps for students to follow. The book is very well planned for the introduction of matrix algebra in that the simpler methods, which are presented first, are left in ordinary algebra as much as possible, but more complex methods rely more and more on the matrix form. * The reviewer's chief criticism refers to Harman's attitude to Lawley's methods. Reference to these methods in early chapters suggests that they are too lengthy even for electronic computers. This seems to be an exaggeration of the position. The collection of data involves costs of planning, testing, marking and initial tabulation which far exceed any likely cost of computer time. Furthermore, the more often this method is used the more attention will be given to the problem of reducing computer time by applying more efficient iterative procedures than those used at present. A method which solves the problems of when to stop factoring and how to estimate communalities, as well as providing the most efficient estimates of factor loadings, cannot be discarded simply because insufficient attention has been given to a mathematical problem of increasing the rate of convergence. Problems of rotation of factors should be carefully separated from those of extracting factors. Harman concedes this but does not give it sufficient emphasis. * In his illustrative examples he rotates from centroid and averoid solutions but not from the principal component solution which was available. However, in discussing rotation methods the objective solutions are brought together in the one volume for the first time and the synthesis and evaluation of these methods is a very valuable contribution. * Harman's positive contribution lies in presenting some of the modern approaches to this subject in one volume. His computational routines for almost all of the methods he discusses should be very valuable to students and research workers. The orderly presentation of ideas leads the student on to the more subtle problems of the subject and so makes this a valuable text for students who wish to specialize in this work. The work suffers from an over-emphasis on American contributions; the simple structure notion and variations on this theme receive considerable attention, but overlapping group factors are not mentioned, nor is the reappearance of the general factor through factoring of oblique simple structure solutions. In the reviewer's opinion far too much space is devoted to methods of extracting factors which should never be used now that "modern" facilities are available.

Cont Psychol 6:374–6 O '61. Henry F. Kaiser. * this penetrating and up-to-date treatise of factor analysis will undoubtedly provide thoroughgoing insight into the fundamentals of factor analysis for the rising generation of mathematically sophisticated psychologists, for not only is Harman's book a modern treatise on factor analysis, it is also an excellent textbook for serious students of the subject * The first part....develops the entire mathematical model with unusual clarity and perception. * this first part is....likely to make mathematically timid souls shudder. Even old pros will study hard. Nevertheless the reward is well worth the effort: a mastery of these first 116 pages yields the dividend of as penetrating an outline of the fundamentals of factor analysis as is obtainable. Subsequent parts of the volume deal with more specialized aspects, how and *why* to do what you do to obtain particular solutions. * As one of the leaders in the application of electronic computers to psychological problems, Harman has throughout interspersed his text with detailed outlines of potential computer programs. His choice of computer applications is excellent * Harman's consideration of the traditional rotation problem is extensive, but perhaps a little overpartial to the newer, scientifically more desirable, analytic methods. The conventional subjective procedures—particularly Thurstone's—are given a limited treatment, while those analytic methods with the pharmaceutical names—*quartimax, varimax, oblimax, quartimin, biquartimin, binormamin*—are treated in minute detail. Unfortunately, it would seem that in the oblique case these desirable new methods are not always completely satisfactory—if we are to accept the wisdom of senior factor analytic citizens like Cattell, Guilford, and Tucker. * He presents much of his material dispassionately, sometimes presenting contradictory points of view without making a case for the "better." An example is his consideration of the classic, knotty, and profoundly difficult problem of the "number of factors." Sometimes he gives mutually contradictory algebraic, psychometric, psychological, and statistical considerations of this traditional question with tactical excellence, yet possibly with strategic inadequacy. A feature which makes this book an excellent text is the large number of problems (with answers). Because of this and the general excellence of the text, it will be useful to a large number of senior people and to first-rate graduate students. * I might compare Harman's text with the two previous masterpieces in factor analysis—Thurstone's and Thomson's. Although the book under review does not show Thurstone's flashes of genius (*Multiple-Factor Analysis,* Univ. Chicago

Press, 1947) it is much more even, accurate, and desirable as a textbook. Thurstone, of course, is perhaps the primary contributor to the theory of factor analysis, but his book is never quite to be trusted, for we never know whether we are reading Thurstone the genius or Thurstone the zealot. Thomson's text (*Factorial Analysis of Human Ability,* Houghton Mifflin, 1939) is now somewhat out of date. Thomson wrote with rare beauty on a difficult subject and with much less mathematics than Harman; thus, I would suggest that Harman's text for modern mathematical sophistication, and Thomson's for a psychologically insightful presentation and a mathematically gentler introduction....would provide an ideal pair for graduate courses. What, in general, has Harman accomplished? He has written the most modern and mathematically sophisticated textbook available on the subject of factor analysis. With admirable clarity and almost uncanny accuracy, his book outlines in an unbiased fashion this mathematical model—peculiarly developed by psychologists—for an audience of mathematically well-trained psychologists, statisticians, and mathematicians.

[B234]

★HARPER, A. EDWIN, JR. **Interpreting Test Profiles: A Programmed Text Book for Teachers, School Counsellors and Students.** Allahabad, India: [Delhi, India: Manasayan], 1963. Pp. ii, 78, plus 14 response sheets. Rs. 5.95; $1.50. *

[B235]

★HARRIS, CHESTER W., EDITOR. **Problems in Measuring Change.** Proceedings of a Conference Sponsored by the Committee on Personality Development in Youth of the Social Science Research Council, 1962. Madison, Wis.: University of Wisconsin Press, 1963. Pp. x, 259. $7.50. *

Harvard Ed R 34:477–9 su '64. William W. Cooley. * this very valuable collection of papers will have much impact upon psychological and educational research. This is the first significant book of its kind, and it is encouraging to find this kind of talent concerned with the important problem of studying behavioral change over time. * Although Professor Harris is listed as editor of this volume, his main contribution seems to have been selecting the conference participants and securing a publisher, for there is no attempt to link together the several papers. Even the notation varies greatly from chapter to chapter. * Harris claims that "these authors can speak for themselves," so he makes no effort to discuss the papers, their relationships, or research implications. However, these authors speak only to those who have mastered measurement theory, matrix algebra, and multivariate statistical theory. * In spite of this progress in recent years, two major research principles still seem valid today. One is that regardless of this book's title, one does not measure change; change must be computed from multiple measurements over time. The other is that the types of behavioral measurements which we are able to make require us to focus on relative change, on making contrasts among groups or individuals. Absolute estimates of change for a single group or individual are still apparently impossible or unrewarding. What research workers need today is a book which spells out the *new* ways in which these two basic principles can now be implemented. This will be a very difficult undertaking, but a necessary one if actual research on change is to be improved. The first large task of that author will be to master the contents of the book reviewed here. [See original review for critical comments not excerpted.]

[B236]

★HARRIS, DALE B. **Children's Drawing as Measures of Intellectual Maturity: A Revision and Extension of the Goodenough Draw-a-Man Test.** New York: Harcourt, Brace & World, Inc., 1963. Pp. xv, 367. $8.95. * (London: George G. Harrap & Co. Ltd. 70s.)

[B237]

*HARROWER, MOLLY. **Appraising Personality: An Introduction to Projective Techniques, Revised Edition.** New York: Franklin Watts, Inc., 1964. Pp. xix, 302. $7.95. * For reviews of the first edition, see 5:B197.

[B238]

★HARROWER, MOLLY. **Personality Change and Development as Measured by the Projective Techniques.** New York: Grune & Stratton, Inc., 1959. Pp. vii, 383. $10.50. *

A.M.A. Arch Gen Psychiatry 2:122–4 Ja '60. Sheldon J. Korchin. * Harrower has struck a happy balance between the excessively detailed and quantitative approach, so common in test "validational" research, and the overly global and clinical approach, so common in psychiatric research * Whatever its limitations —redundance and excessive length, on the stylistic side, and a complete avoidance of even minimal statistical tests of reliability, on the methodological—this book is a distinct contribution to the test validational literature and should increase confidence in the clinical value of projective testing. At the same time, Harrower may inspire some of the rest of us to dig into the wealth of material, old test protocols and therapy notes, moldering in bottom desk drawers in order to test in retrospect the predictions made initially, to evaluate the effect of one or another action in therapy, and to answer the many other questions in this field. Quite aside from all else, Harrower illustrates a kind of research which can only—and must—be done by working clinicians.

J Proj Tech 23:473–4 D '59. Theodore H. Blau. * Described as a study, the book proposes a number of extremely general hypotheses such as the existence of a "core personality" and the consistency of test-re-test changes with life situation changes. These hypotheses were tested by rating projective techniques and therapists' opinions on 50 or 60 individuals referred to the author by physicians, therapists, school authorities, and parents. The method of study is substantiated by reference to a few, rather doubtful authorities. In a very limited review of the literature, the author deals with contrary opinions like Alice's Queen of Hearts. In discussion of procedure, it is noted that the projective data are validated in light of therapists' opinions. It is further suggested that in the next volume, the therapeutic process will be validated by projective data. This predictor-validator ping-pong is characteristic of the uncritical, diffuse nature of the book, which is unimpressive even as a collection of interesting projective protocols. Occasional examples of Dr. Harrower's excellent descriptive analysis of test material are refreshing but infrequent. As a descriptive study, the book is inadequate, even confusing. The author emphasizes the preliminary nature of this work in the Introduction. The book as a whole certainly reflects this.

[B239]

★Harrower, Molly; Vorhaus, Pauline; Roman, Melvin; and Bauman, Gerald. **Creative Variations in Projective Techniques.** Springfield, Ill.: Charles C Thomas, Publisher, 1960. Pp. viii, 138. $8.50. * (*PA* 35:963)

J Proj Tech & Pers Assess 27:481–2 D '63. Albert I. Rabin. * Workaday-world clinicians will find many of the ideas suggested in this volume fruitful and practical. The techniques or modifications of existing methods are primarily empirical; theory is, at best, implicit. However, the researcher, as often is the case, may find useful suggestions and ideas in this "raw" material, based on the experience, and emanating from the minds, of imaginative clinicians.

[B240]

★Hathaway, Starke R., and Monachesi, Elio D. **Adolescent Personality and Behavior: MMPI Patterns of Normal, Delinquent, Dropout, and Other Outcomes.** Minneapolis, Minn.: University of Minnesota Press, 1963. Pp. xiii, 193. $5.75. * (*PA* 38:8110) (London: Oxford University Press. 46*s*.)

[B241]

★Hathaway, Starke R., and Monachesi, Elio D. **An Atlas of Juvenile MMPI Profiles.** Minneapolis, Minn.: University of Minnesota Press, 1961. Pp. xviii, 402. $8.50. * (London: Oxford University Press. 64*s*.) (*PA* 36:2HF02H)

Am J Orthopsychiatry 31:846–8 O '61. Richard L. Jenkins. * To this reviewer the distressing thing is how little he is able to find in common in the narrative descriptions of cases with the same MMPI code. Whenever a useful approximation is found in an important but "fuzzy" area of work, there develops a tendency dogmatically to accept it as an ultimate reality and to find special reasons to account for all instances in which experience does not support its predictions. These scale scores are, of course, no exception to this rule. We are seeing minor refinements of what is necessarily a rather crude clinical instrument. Everyone would be happier to see a more accurate instrument developed. In the meantime it seems virtuous to do our best with what we have but to keep a salt shaker within easy reach. It is of great interest that the adolescent population shows, compared with the standardizing population, conspicuously high average scores on scale 8 (Sc), scale 4 (Pd), and scale 9 (Ma), and on scale 7 (Pt). This apparently is the picture of adolescence and should be considered clinically in evaluating the profiles of this age group. As might be expected, the code stability leaves something to be desired. Of the 18 per cent of the boys who had their highest score on scale 4 on this first test, 60 per cent scored either their highest or second highest score on this scale at retest, which was usually in the twelfth grade. No other group maintained this high a percentage, and the degree of correspondence which would be accounted for by chance expectancy would be not 60 per cent, but only 36 per cent. There is clearly a significant correspondence but one which is far from satisfying for predictive purposes.

Cont Psychol 7:93 Mr '62. Alfred B. Heilbrun, Jr. * The usefulness of the system is plainly dependent upon whether the user of the *Juvenile Atlas,* once having found the case history descriptions appropriate to the high-point class in which he is interested, can generate valid statements about the case in question. In this regard, two serious issues merit comment. For one, Hathaway and Monachesi deliberately avoided culling out common features associated with membership in the various adolescent classes, leaving the user the task of scanning multiple case histories in search of some common interpretable feature of the code-type in question. Since the case histories for the same code-type class are often quite variable, this provides a temptation for certain users to "shop around" until a case history is found which fits his *a priori* convictions. This reviewer would have preferred the safer guidelines of having Hathaway and Monachesi, as experts, assume the responsibility for deducing lawful relationships between class membership and other variables using their basic pool of 11,000 cases. The second issue has to do with the reliability of the MMPI high-point codes for adolescents. Hathaway and Monachesi acknowledged the "rapid shifts in personality" which occur in adolescence and the resultant limitation of validity. However, one finds that in only about five per cent of the over 600 reported cases who were retested three years later was the adolescent a member of the same two-point code class. Elusive class membership remains an interpretive headache for the *Juvenile Atlas* user. Criticism is easy, accomplishment difficult; this brief review has given short shrift to the conscientious work that has gone into this book. I have no doubt that, used cautiously as Hathaway and Monachesi advise, the *Juvenile Atlas* will be of considerable assistance to those interested in the behavior of adolescents. Someday a better adolescent cookbook may appear but, if so, it will probably have its inception in Minneapolis.

[B241a]

★Hawes, Gene R. **Educational Testing for the Millions: What Tests Really Mean for Your Child.** New York: McGraw-Hill Book Co., Inc., 1964. Pp. xii, 291. $6.50. *

[B242]

★Heath, Robert W. **The Development of a Measure of Social Class Identification.** Purdue University, Division of Educational Reference, Studies in Higher Education 87; Further Studies in Attitudes Series 25. Lafayette, Ind.: the Division, January 1958. Pp. 41. Paper. $1.00. *

[B243]

★Helmstadter, G. C. **Principles of Psychological Measurement.** New York: Appleton-Century-Crofts, 1964. Pp. xxi, 248. $5.00. *

[B244]

★Hemphill, John K. **Dimensions of Executive Positions: A Study of the Basic Characteristics of the Positions of Ninety-Three Business Executives.** Ohio State University, College of Commerce and Administration, Ohio Studies in Personnel, Bureau of Business Research Monograph No. 98. Columbus, Ohio: the Bureau, 1960. Pp. xiv, 103. Paper. $2.00. * (*PA* 36:1LI03H)

Ed & Psychol Meas 22:413-4 su '62. Harold Borko. * Ninety-three executives were selected as representative of different managerial positions. They were given a questionnaire of 575 items, each of which is scored as an 8-category scale—0 if the item is definitely not part of the position, and 7 if it is a most significant part of the position. Product moment correlation coefficients were computed for each pair of the 93 positions. The matrix was divided and factor analyzed, using a procedure described by Tucker for the determination of inter-battery factors. Ten factors were extracted and rotated orthogonally for simple structure. These factors were interpreted as dimensions characterizing executive performance and labeled as staff service, supervision of work, business control, and the like. The study continues beyond the routine factor analysis through the construction of a new questionnaire consisting of 191 of the 575 items. The choice of items was determined by the factor weights of these items on the two batteries. This new shortened scale is available for use, together with a profile for plotting the executive position. * A few technical details in the study are not reported with sufficient clarity to facilitate replication. For example, it is stated that the computations were "carried out with the aid of electronic data processing machines," but the type of computer and programs are not mentioned. In the factor analysis program, the value substituted into the diagonals is left in doubt. We are told that the ten factors were rotated orthogonally, but it is not clear as to whether an analytic or graphic method of rotation was used. Of somewhat more importance is the unresolved question as to whether the 8-point scale responses to the 575 items were normalized prior to the computation of the correlation coefficient. Finally, the factor scoring procedures for developing the revised questionnaire are quite vague. These, however, are mild criticisms, for it is recognized that the author is writing a monograph and that information of a highly detailed and specific nature would be available, if requested. The research is a good solid piece of work and a significant addition to the literature. It contributes to the understanding of the dimensions of executive performance and outlines a methodology which will be useful for further studies in this and related areas.

[B245]

★HEMPHILL, JOHN K.; GRIFFITHS, DANIEL E.; AND FREDERIKSEN, NORMAN; WITH THE ASSISTANCE OF GLEN STICE, LAURENCE IANNACCONE, WILLIAM COFFIELD, AND SYDELL CARLTON. **Administrative Performance and Personality: A Study of the Principal in a Simulated Elementary School.** New York: Bureau of Publications, Teachers College, Columbia University, 1962. Pp. xix, 432. $8.00. *

Cont Psychol 8:454–5 N '63. William E. Kendall. * an in-basket test is a situational test which seeks to simulate aspects of the task of the administrator. The examinee is presented with a collection of items which have presumably accumulated in the administrator's in-basket and are awaiting his attention. The examinee is given necessary background information and is told that he is the new incumbent of the administrative position and is to deal with the material in the in-basket. The items in the basket are the test items and the actions taken by the examinee with respect to the items in the basket are his responses to the test. * The research reported....represents an attempt to utilize the in-basket test as a device for making observations of administrative behavior, specifically, the administrative performance of the elementary school principal. * the title chosen by the authors, namely, *Administrative Performance and Personality* is....inappropriate. The data reported were collected in 1958–59 on 232 elementary school principals (137 men and 95 women) brought together in small groups for a one week testing session. * each participant completed the Strong Vocational Interest Blank for Men, the Symonds Educational Interest Inventory, the Sixteen Personality Factor Questionnaire, four measures of professional and general knowledge, and tests purporting to measure thirteen "basic mental ability" factors, *e.g.,* deduction, flexibility of closure, ideational fluency, associative memory * It would have been of interest....if the authors had explained why, other than for reasons of "factorial purity," they had chosen the particular tests and questionnaires employed. The authors (p. 80) concede, insofar as the basic mental ability battery is concerned, that meaningful normative data obtained from comparable groups under similar conditions are not available. The descriptions given by Cattell for factor scores of the 16 PF Questionnaire were adopted without qualification. It is relevant here to note that the "appearance of many orderly relationships between personality factors and performance of the principals" on the in-basket test was, in the words of the authors, "somewhat unexpected." There is no mention of treatment of the Symonds Interest Inventory data. The Strong VIB Scores were handled in the same manner as those of the 16 PF Questionnaire, that is, scores of men and of women are not separated in the analysis. This leads to some dubious interpretations of relationships of SVIB Scales, *e.g.,* (p. 271) with respect to in-basket composite Score A: Exchanging Information; high communication principals are said to "tend toward the feminine side of the masculinity-femininity continuum" (r with M-F Scale = −.20). After scoring the in-baskets using 68 scoring categories developed for the purpose, intercorrelations were computed among the 40 highest frequency in-basket scoring categories and used for purposes of factor analysis. Eight first-order factors and two second-order factors were identified and "interpreted as basic concepts of administrative performance in the in-basket test situation" (p. 147). The first-order factors were labeled: A. Exchanging Information; B. Discussing With Others Before Acting; C. Complying With Suggestions Made by Others; D. Analyzing the Situation; E. Maintaining Organizational Relationships; F. Organizing Work; G. Responding to Outsiders; H. Directing the Work of Others. The second-order factors were called: X. Preparation for Decision *vs* Taking Final Action and Y: Amount of Work Expended in Handling the Item. Having identified and labeled these factors the authors treat them throughout the balance of the report as though they were criterion measures, that is, correlations with test scores and personal and demographic data were computed, analyzed and interpreted. In the final chapter the authors discuss the implications of their research for selection of administrators. They observe, for example, (p. 337) that correlations between ratings of principals and personality questionnaire scores were "too low to be of much value in selection." However, when the "unique components of the eight factors were used as criterion measures....very interesting patterns of relationships with personality test scores were obtained for each of the eight factors." The authors illustrate how these interesting patterns of relationships might be utilized by a school board in selecting principals. Thus, if it were desirable to employ principals who "are proficient at maintaining organizational relationships" 16 PF Scores should be such that the principals are: "1. Friendly, socially responsive; 2. Lively and enthusiastic; 3. Bold, warm-hearted, and spontaneous; 4. Self-confident and accepting; 5. Free from worry and anxiety." If on the other hand, the school board desired principals "whose forte was responding to outsiders" the 16 PF attributes should include "1. submissiveness, modesty, and obedience; 2. simple sentimental naivete; 3. lack of enthusiasm; 4. shyness and timidity; 5. persistence and stability; 6. lack of anxiety." Similar suggestions are made for the use of the mental ability tests and for the SVIB. The authors tell us, for example, "Principals of high general mental ability are characterized more by preparation for decision than by taking terminal action" and that high work output is "typical of high mental ability principals." They suggest, "If a district determines the factors it wants in a principal," SVIB "scores might be of some help in making a choice." Thus, interest scores could help to pick a principal high on Factor A; Exchanging Information, since persons high on Factor A "have interests unlike those keyed for policemen, but positively related to the interests of city school superintendent, lawyer, and psychologist." In the opinion of this reviewer, while the in-basket test may have a place as a research device, e.g., in training and training evaluation, the case for the use of in-basket test scores as criterion measures of on-the-job performance is not convincing. This opinion plus a negative reaction to the proposed use of mental ability, personality, and interest scores, leads this reviewer to the conclusion that this volume should never be allowed to fall into the hands of a school board. For the psychologist who is involved in the selection of administrators, this volume, despite its title, will be disappointing.

[B246]

★Henry, William E., and Farley, Jane. **The Validity of the Thematic Apperception Test in the Study of Adolescent Personality.** American Psychological Association, Psychological Monographs: General and Applied, Vol. 73, No. 17, Whole No. 487. Washington, D.C.: the Association, Inc., 1959. Pp. 40. Paper. * (*PA* 35:694)

[B247]

Henrysson, Sten. **Applicability of Factor Analysis in the Behavioral Sciences: A Methodological Study.** Stockholm Studies in Educational Psychology 1. Stockholm, Sweden: Almqvist & Wiksell, 1957. Pp. 156. Paper. Sw. kr. 15. * (*PA* 31:6916)

Am J Psychol 71:476–8 Je '58. Raymond B. Cattell. * substantial scholarly contribution * Henrysson....has set out to sum up the present situation in factor analysis, to indicate the more promising solutions at points where technical progress has met difficulties, and to help investigators in various psychological fields to take advantage of the method, appropriately to their needs. He begins with a chapter on "The Basic Theory of Factor Analysis" which is excellent in its balance, and elegant in its condensation. The ensuing chapter on "The Most Important Factor Models" gives a similarly well-condensed view of historical developments according to the particular emphases of Spearman, Burt, Thomson, Thurstone and others. It is in the next chapter—"The Different Applications of Factor Analysis"—that one encounters evidence not only of the writer's scholarly competence and gift for getting to essentials—already shown in the first chapters—but of an intellectual enterprise and alertness to new possibilities which comparatively few of the British and American writings on this topic in the last few years have shown. For example, he at once explodes the tiresomely repeated error that factor analysis is restricted to descriptive statistics and shows its potentially very great rôle in the hypotheticodeductive method. This involves stating hypotheses in the form of an expectation that a particular factor pattern will emerge, and checking on its appearance. Similarly he perceives the virtue of starting, from the very beginning, with the oblique factor model, which readily admits orthogonal factors as a special case. This is preferable to arresting psychological thought with a pointless antithesis of oblique and orthogonal factor systems. Again, in view of the fact that so many psychometrists have thought of factor analysis only as an actuarially-convenient condensation device, permitting prediction from a single estimated factor instead of a host of tests, it is refreshing to find the clearly stated perspective that the primary function of factor analysis is as a research instrument for determining relatively permanent psychological structural concepts. * The section on applications of factor analysis in psychometric prediction, job classification and analysis, differential prediction, etc., seems to the present reviewer somewhat less satisfactory than the chapters concerned with basic research, largely because of its acceptance, with relatively little criticism, of all the expediencies, short cuts and short sighted practices so prevalent in writers on applied psychometry. To give the author his due, this is partly the result of his very catholicity, and the thoroughness with which he culls every novel idea in the field. However, the cleverness of these ideas inclines to the bizarre. Their originators blithely sacrifice the organic connection and meaning of factors, in the general matrix of scientific psychology, for, perhaps, a 3% gain in multiple correlation with the criterion, on the particular sample at the particular moment. More valuable is the writer's discussion of the rationale for changing factor weights for prediction at different stages of a learning process, adequately worked out, so far, only in the important study of Fleishman and Hempel. The book concludes with four more theoretical chapters, which are again quite outstanding in their success in doing justice in a comparatively small space to most of the important contributions. The treatment of factors as intervening variables and hypothetical constructs, and particularly as generators of hypotheses, is especially clear and constructive, and could be read with advantage by a substantial number of psychometrists now using factor analysis without utilizing its full repertoire. Toward the end of this examination of the scientific, explanatory functions of factor analysis Dr. Henrysson gets his teeth into the vexed question of "invariance" of factor solution, on which so much hinges. His treatment is again broad but incisive, dealing with simple structure, proportional profiles, effects of selection, communality estimation, and non-factorial guides to uniqueness of solution. Although his handling of the present reviewer's "proportional profiles" method of determining a unique resolution is very fair and adequate, he leaves the reader liable to two misconstructions which, because they are very common, need to be pointed out. First, it is not strictly "an analytical method for simultaneous rotation (of two studies) to simple structure" (p. 119). The simple structure is a common but incidental consequence of the principle, which primarily rests on a test of "factor reality" totally independent of simple structure. Secondly, though it uses matrix operations rather closely parallel to those in Tucker's device for simultaneous rotation (of two studies) to congruent results, it is radically different in assumptions and aims. Tucker aims to get the two matrices as congruent as possible and to move them together to a position which must finally be decided by simple structure, whereas proportional profiles aims to find the unique position, in which a relation, not of congruence but of complex proportionality, arises between the two studies. The final chapter deals with the furnishing of factor analysis with the necessary distribution formulas for its proper use as a tool of statistical inference. Inevitably it comes to the unhappy conclusion that we do not yet possess expressions for the significance of factor loadings, and factors, that are as free of undesirable assumptions as we should like. * Although it would be ideal to have every graduate student possessed of the clear perspective and up-to-date statistical information which this little book supplies, it is unfortunately true that he would not understand it until he has read one of the larger standard textbooks on multivariate methods. Thus, while this elegant, condensed treatment cannot be offered as a "brief introduction," it is to be hoped that it will have a wide circulation as a supplement or "finishing off" course for those already basically trained in the subject.

Cont Psychol 3:129–30 My '58. Edwin A. Fleishman. * The reader who thinks the word *applicability* in the title means *applications* is going to be disappointed. Henrysson wants to know, mainly, where factor analysis fits into general scientific method and theory, what is the status of the mathematical assumptions underlying the technique, on what basis we choose this factorial model or that one, how we may consider factor analysis as a method of statistical inference. He does not ignore specific applications but summarizes them in terms of general classes of problems in the behavioral sciences within which, in his view, factor analysis has or has not made a contribution. To this reviewer, the product represents one of the most thoughtful recent efforts to bring into focus in a single publication the variety of conceptual, practical, and mathematical issues involved. There is little doubt that factor analysis has a controversial place in the scheme of psychological science, and this book does much to sharpen, clarify, and sometimes even resolve some of the issues involved. The volume is ideal, for example, for the experimental psychologist whose contact with factor analysis has been limited to the many poorly conceived "shotgun" studies in the journals. It will not necessarily convince him that factor analysis has a place in the scientific study of behavior (nor does it try to) but it will present him with some serious thinking by a competent person who concludes that it has. The crux of the book appears to lie in Henrysson's discussion of "explanatory factor analysis." Descriptive factor analysis is, in principle, only a deductive procedure which gives operationally defined factors related to a given set of data. Explanatory factor analysis is more an inferential procedure, whose object is to find factors that "explain" as many regularities as possible, even outside an actual factorial study. The distinction between descriptive and explanatory factor analysis is seen as a facet of the lively discussion of intervening variable and hypothetical construct a few years ago. * Explanatory analysis *is* possible and is simply a link in an inferential procedure which includes data from other sources. Under certain conditions, factor analysis can be used for testing hypotheses formulated on the basis of other methods as well as for generating hypotheses that are verified by other methods. The reader who thinks he has this distinction firmly in mind will do well to read this treatment of the topic. The key concepts in this discussion are those of simple structure and factorial invariance. Perhaps Henrysson does not go far enough in stressing the need for programmatic factor analysis research in other areas and the interdependence of the formulation of hypotheses, the development of measures of behavior, and the method of analysis. Especially in view of the unresolved statistical problems, the problem of replication under certain prescribed conditions needs to be stressed. More attention could have been given to specific approaches to nonfactorial validation of factors. It is the reviewer's opinion that the contribution of factor analysis really cannot be adequately assessed until more psychologists conduct studies which combine experimental laboratory methods with designs that use factor analysis. There have been some attempts at this union, but rarely has the undertaking been of a programmatic nature. There are, moreover, vast barriers between investigators' using correlational approaches and others' using experimental techniques, even in the same general areas. For example, Guilford's factor analysis studies have made notable contribution in describing the dimensions of intellectual functioning. Yet how many psychologists, conducting experiments on problem-solving, have used Guilford's factors to describe their task variables? How many have tried to see if Guilford's factors are useful or not useful in "accounting for" certain of their own results? We do not even know if measures of these problem-solving factors predict performances in the kinds of laboratory tasks used to study problem-solving. We certainly need to know this in order to assess the power and generality of the concepts provided by the factor analysis research. Thus the psychologist who is interested in factor theory will find this monograph a valuable addition to his library. It is appropriate for supplementary reading in advanced courses in statistics and in courses in factor analysis, research methodology, and psychological measurement. Henrysson has restricted his audience by placing his heavy load of mathematics in the first chapter; yet the reader who prefers his factor analysis without mathematics can skip this chapter and find much left to stimulate him.

[B248]

★Herr, Vincent V.; Arnold, Magda B.; Weisgerber, Charles A.; and D'Arcy, Paul F. **Screening Candidates for the Priesthood and Religious Life, [1964 Edition].** Chicago, Ill.: Loyola University Press, 1964. Pp. x, 205. $2.80. * (The original edition, see B61, was published in 1962 with apparently identical content but with a different authorship listing.)

[B249]

*Hertz, Marguerite R. **Frequency Tables for Scoring Rorschach Responses, Fourth Edition.** Cleveland, Ohio: Press of Western Reserve University, 1961. Pp. ii, 253. Paper, lithotyped. $4.50. *

[B250]

★Heyel, Carl. **Appraising Executive Performance.** New York: American Management Association, Inc., 1958. Pp. 189. $4.50. *

[B251]

★Hill, George E. **Evaluating the School's Testing Program.** Ohio University, College of Education, Center for Educational Service, Pupil Services Series, No. 2. Athens, Ohio: the Center, 1959. Pp. 28. Paper. $1.00. *

[B252]

★Hill, George E. **The Staff Evaluate the School's Testing Program.** Ohio University, College of Education, Center for Educational Service, Pupil Services Series, No. 1. Athens, Ohio: the Center, 1960. Pp. 30. Paper. $1.00. *

[B253]

★Hills, John R.; Emory, Linda B.; and Franz, Gretchen. **Freshman Norms for the University System of Georgia, 1958–59.** Atlanta, Ga.: Office of Testing and Guidance, Regents of the University System of Georgia, March 1960. Pp. ix, 91. Paper, lithotyped. Gratis. *

[B254]

★Hills, John R.; Emory, Linda B.; and Masters, Pauline B. **Freshman Norms for University System of Georgia, 1959–60.** Atlanta, Ga.: Office of Testing and Guidance, Regents of the University System of Georgia, September 1961. Pp. vii, 65. Paper, lithotyped. Gratis. *

[B255]

★Hills, John R.; Emory, Linda B.; and Masters, Pauline B. **Freshman Norms for the University System of Georgia, 1960–61.** Atlanta, Ga.: Office of Testing and Guidance, Regents of the University System of Georgia, January 1962. Pp. xi, 65. Paper, lithotyped. Gratis. *

[B256]

★Hills, John R.; Franz, Gretchen; and Emory, Linda B. **Counselor's Guide to Georgia Colleges.** Atlanta, Ga.: Office of Testing and Guidance, Regents of the University System of Georgia, December 1959. Pp. 32. Paper, lithotyped. Gratis. *

[B257]

★Hills, John R.; Klock, Joseph A.; and Bush, Marilyn L. **Freshman Norms for the University System of Georgia, 1962–63.** Atlanta, Ga.: Office of Testing and Guidance, Regents of the University System of Georgia, March 1964. Pp. xi, 65. Paper. Gratis. *

[B258]

★Hills, John R.; Klock, Joseph A.; and Lewis, Sandra C. **Freshman Norms for the University System of Georgia, 1961–62.** Atlanta, Ga.: Office of Testing and Guidance, Regents of the University System of Georgia, June 1963. Pp. xi, 65. Paper, lithotyped. Gratis. *

[B259]

★Hills, John R.; Masters, Pauline B.; and Emory, Linda B. **Supplement: Counselor's Guide to Georgia Colleges.** Atlanta, Ga.: Office of Testing and Guidance, Regents of the University System of Georgia, 1961. Pp. ix, 35. Paper, lithotyped. Gratis. *

[B260]

★Hirt, Michael, Editor. **Rorschach Science: Readings in Theory and Method.** New York: Free Press of Glencoe, 1962. Pp. ix, 438. $8.50. * (*PA* 37:6737)

Cont Psychol 9:31–2 Ja '64. Bernice T. Eiduson. * In an introduction and a second chapter written especially for the volume—the only two contributions hitherto unpublished—Hirt and Mooney respectively point to the need to study and clarify the role of the Rorschach test as a perceptual device that reveals personality processes. * The selection of articles for this volume is unfortunately dated, with the references cited at the end of each article as it originally appeared in publication limiting the bibliography on Rorschach almost exclusively to material published before 1956. All recent studies of the Rorschach—and especially many which have been influenced by recent work in the field of perception—have been excluded. No mention is made, for example, of studies on the change in stimulus properties of the cards, as with elimination of color; nor of studies on verbal reinforcement of responses, and the effects of such reinforcement on such specific categories as M. Such omissions loom as particularly significant, since the editor has directed attention to the Rorschach as a perceptual tool, and since Mooney elaborates very interestingly the need for clarification of the Rorschach as a perceptual instrument. * One would have hoped that through editorial integration Hirt might have brought the intended perceptual focus of the volume more directly into relationship with the articles included. It seems quite feasible that these evaluative and experimental articles could be freshly reviewed with benefit, as the projectives are being viewed as perceptual devices whose very complexity and ambiguity give them some of the same properties that are now being systematically investigated in experimental studies of other perceptual stimuli under conditions of partial sensory deprivation or under subliminal thresholds, or under unusual pathological states, as created by drugs. However, Hirt did not take this opportunity, and one is left, therefore, with the feeling that the volume will serve mainly to permit students easy access to this group of now classic studies whose significance rests in the work that they subsequently influenced and in their historical importance. * the title of the book seems out of context with the experimental emphasis within. To use the word "science" with Rorschach data at this time is so inappropriate that one can only wonder if the editor was being satirical.

Psychosom Med 26:91 Ja–F '64. James J. Muller. * In view of the publisher's claim that this is "a milestone in the development of scientific personality assessment," readers should note that most of the articles, including that on the "current" status of the Rorschach, have been in print for more than a decade. Introductory statements....propose that the Rorschach is not an adequately objective measuring device, but may be improved in this regard by greater research efforts. The narrow emphasis, in selecting studies for inclusion in this collection, on statistical demonstrations of reliability and validity of the existing test, reflects the view that these particular 10 inkblots provide necessary and sufficient conditions for personality appraisal. Readers who are seriously concerned with research in perception and cognition will recognize the anachronistic plea for a "Rorschach Science," or a "psychology" based on the Rorschach, as an embarrassing reminder of past enthusiasms. For experienced clinicians, the immediate, practical value of the "test," as a peculiarly flexible and productive medium for eliciting behavior in a form hospitable to metapsychological interpretations, is sufficient justification for its use. Further, it provides many provocative ideas about relationships between phenomenal experience and personal development. But the research task which most clinical psychologists currently address themselves to is that of independent, experimental explorations of parameters of behavior only narrowly and unsystematically sampled by the Rorschach itself. For this reason, the omission of even such work as Holtzman's systematic variations of Rorschach determinants restricts the usefulness of the book to those interested in a basic, historical introduction to Rorschach criticism.

[B261]

★Hitchcock, William L.; Christensen, O. C., Jr.; Weaver, Glen L.; Thomas, Robert L.; and Hall, Joseph I. **Selection and Use of Standardized Tests.** Salem, Ore.: Guidance Service, State Department of Education, 1961. Pp. 59. Paper. $0.75. *

[B262]

★Hoeflin, Ruth, and Kell, Leone. **The Kell-Hoeflin Incomplete Sentence Blank: Youth-Parent Relations.** Monographs of the Society for Research in Child Development, Vol. 24, No. 3, Serial No. 72. Lafayette, Ind.: Child Development Publica tions, 1959. Pp. 64. Paper. $2.25. * (*PA* 35:767)

[B263]

★Hoffmann, Banesh. **The Tyranny of Testing** New York: Crowell-Collier Press, 1962. Pp. 22 Paper, $0.95; cloth, $3.95. * (London: Collier-Mac millan, Ltd., 1963. Paper, 7*s.* 6*d*; cloth, 30*s.*)

Personnel & Guid J 42:76–8 S '63. Lawrenc Beymer. * it is refreshing to discover on who can state his case within a framework o reasonableness and responsibility. This boo can be set apart from the typical tirades a several points. First of all, the author resist the temptation to write on an emotional leve preferring a more intellectual battlefield. H refrains from the name-calling that so ofte characterizes this type of book. Second, h bends over backward to present the other sid of the controversy in the words of the oppo sition, avoiding the frequent pattern of argu mentative deck-stacking. Third, he directs hi fire at the strong points, not the weak ones, o his opposition. Instead of flailing away at som vague personality inventory published by som obscure firm, he directs his criticism towar objective tests of aptitude and achievemen developed by one of the best test-constructin organizations. Hoffmann concentrates upo multiple-choice questions, dismissing true-fals items with the comment that their range o legitimate use is so narrow that almost ever time they are used they are misused. He charge that multiple-choice questions are concerne with the choice of answer only and not the qual ity of reasoning that led to it: that they do no measure either creativity or motivation; an that because of the "virtual inevitability o ambiguity" the so-called "deep" student see more in a question than his more superficia competitors and is thusly penalized unjustly. One can imagine some potential Einstein be ing overlooked and forever remaining an undis covered diamond-in-the-rough, but this hardl seems likely. Perhaps the seeds of rebuttal ca be found in Hoffmann's own text. On pages 2 and 30 he says, "Two facts dominate the prob lem. One is that testing must take place. An the other is that, except in the simplest situa tions, there is no satisfactory method of testin —nor is there likely to be." And on page 21 he admits that "All methods of evaluating peo ple have their defects—and grave defects the are." * Hoffmann proposes no solution to th problem. * One wonders if he is serious abou the establishment of a national committee of inquiry to serve as a sort of psychological test "pure food and drug administration." He would have only a minority of this group drawn from experts in measurement, and it is at this point that the reviewer feels the author is more than a little inconsistent. * The reader will not always agree with the author of this book, but he deserves to be heard. We may find it easier to stay in the middle of the road if we allow ourselves to see both sides.

Teach Col Rec 64:510–4 Mr '63. John L. Holland. * [This and Gross's book (see B215)] have much in common. Both were written by men who lack the training and perspective for the tasks they attempted. Both wear the trappings of scholarship, but frequently violate its ideals by distortion and by biased selection of evidence. Gross's shortcomings in this respect may be forgivable, since he is a magazine writer and not a trained scholar. Hoffmann's are not. Although Hoffmann is a physicist and mathematician, his methods reflect some of the anti-intellectual attitudes that we would expect from an uneducated person—reliance on anecdotal evidence, the substitution of invective and insinuation for information, misinterpretation of the role of statistical procedures in test construction, and even at times an apparent disregard for scientific method itself. Both books are more concerned with inciting rather than informing the reader. Except for some new anecdotes, neither adds anything to our present knowledge about tests. If they had been scholarly, they might have helped to clarify some of the real issues connected with the use of tests, and perhaps they could have outlined some constructive action. Too often, both authors display a predilection for the sheerly peripheral. * Twenty-seven of the 31 items which Hoffmann takes us through in his review were never used in any published test. And of these twenty-seven, 16 were written by Hoffmann himself. Hoffmann then suggests, by loaded diction and by an odd statistical and sampling procedure, that "defective" questions ("defective" in that they fail to meet his rational analysis) exist in large quantities * Hoffmann makes two fundamental errors. First, he assumes that his little sample of test items is representative of all published objective test items. This inference cannot be made, since only four of 31 items were taken from published tests. Second, Hoffmann fails to realize that even if he could prove his first assumption that the test items are ambiguous, he would still not have disproved their empirical validity. In short, a test question may work empirically even though we lack approving agreement on its wording or an understanding of the reasons for its working. Hoffmann's extended harangue about "defective" items—indeed, most of his book—seems inconsistent with his earlier statement that "The majority of the questions that testers ask are clear-cut and straightforward" (p. 21). Some of Hoffmann's attempts to document his charges display an amateurish handling of a few selected studies. Like Gross, when he cannot find evidence, he cites anecdotes or misinterprets the available evidence. His belief that testers and testing agencies "are already too powerful," and therefore evil, receives only anecdotal illustration. Most readers will be bored by his lengthy account of correspondence between himself, testing agencies, and two students who didn't like certain test items. *

[B264]

★HOLTZMAN, WAYNE H.; THORPE, JOSEPH S.; SWARTZ, JON D.; AND HERRON, E. WAYNE. **Inkblot Perception and Personality: Holtzman Inkblot Technique.** Published for the Hogg Foundation for Mental Health. Austin, Tex.: University of Texas Press, 1961. Pp. xi, 417. $8.00. * (*PA* 36:5HB17H)

Cont Psychol 7:250–2 Jl '62. Norman D. Sundberg. At long last, someone has set out to produce an assessment device possessing both the rich complexity of the Rorschach and the statistical precision of psychometric tests. Holtzman....after a number of earlier studies with the old Rorschach, started around 1955 to develop a new technique. * The technique, despite some drawbacks, possesses great attractiveness for both clinical and psychometric camps, and I should not be surprised if in ten years it would rival the formidable Rorschach itself in annual number of publications. * Why develop a new technique? Very simply, because the Rorschach method, basically unchanged since its inception in 1921, is lacking in many of the characteristics that make a test reliable and objective. It is too short (10 stimulus blots) and too permissive and variable in administration and scoring, and it does not have an equivalent form for retesting. Earlier and little used facsimiles, such as the Behn and Howard Inkblots, have not provided adequate psychometric correctives. Holtzman has developed two parallel forms of 45 inkblots each. The subject must report only one percept for each card, after which there is a rather specific inquiry. Through painstaking efforts, Holtzman and his colleagues have produced fair to excellent reliability on 22 scores, all of which can be punched into IBM cards for analysis by computers. Norms for children, normal adults and some hospitalized patient groups are presented, as are correlations with other tests and one illustrative case. The book would be a necessary reference for those interested in working with this new technique. The numerous tables and the wealth of detail on scoring and preparation of results for analysis would speed the work of the person wishing to do research. Administration of the test is not difficult to learn. Disappointingly, the Holtzman test has not removed much of the looseness of the Rorschach inquiry nor the susceptibility to examiner influence. Although the book reports only on research with individual administration, group administration is possible with some modifications, and early results suggest close similarities with the individual form. * Scoring still requires quite a bit of judgment, although the book indicates that clerks can be satisfactorily trained to administer and score the test with only a few weeks of training. * Research on validity has been mainly confined to correlations with concurrent variables and to group differences. Similar Rorschach and Holtzman scores correlate moderately (ranging from .30 to .79). * Very few significant correlations were found with personality inventories. Holtzman anxiety and hostility are unrelated to Taylor, Sarason, and Siegel paper-and-pencil anxiety. (When will we get an adequate theory for clearing up this confusion of measures bearing the same label but sampling different kinds of behavior at different levels of communication?) * There seems to be little doubt about the strength of the psychometric underpinnings of the Holtzman Inkblot Technique developed so far. The Rorschach-type protocol is still there to delight the clinician and stimulate his dynamic hypothesizing. The greatest limitations, on which future work might well concentrate, lie in two areas—the theoretical and the practical. In reading the book I was torn between admiration for its psychometric care and constraint and a wish for some of the European conviction and clinical speculation that has characterized the Rorschach of the past. This conflict can be resolved if it is possible to relate Holtzman variables and configurations to testable theory. At the present time, one searches in vain for an integrated rationale for the choices the test developers have made along the way and for a guide to interpretation. The work has concentrated on developing a good technical instrument simply appropriating the theoretical concepts from the hodgepodge of ideas that have grown up around the Rorschach. It is hard to imagine that the Rorschach, which has generated thousands of publications and unrestrained clinical enthusiasm, does not relate to some important underlying constructs. This new version may provide just the right assistance to prove (or disprove) these ideas. The practical side of the Holtzman needs much development. The paucity of conceptual framework is reflected in the interpretation of the test. A great deal of attention needs to be devoted to the manner in which the test is to be interpreted clinically as well as statistically. What sort of adjectival and Q-sort descriptions are related to its patterns? How consistent are they? The interpretations in the one illustration in the book strike one as weak and unconvincing, especially if they are separated from the case history. Perhaps the authors are just being properly cautious at this stage. Many studies of predictive validity (not concurrent validity) are needed. It remains to be demonstrated how much "incremental validity" the test possesses—does it add anything above and beyond the clinical base rates, the case history, the MMPI? Is the increase worth the time to administer and score and interpret the test (probably at least the Rorschach's estimated four hours) as compared with other assessment techniques? No technique can be expected to be useful in measuring all aspects of personality. The Holtzman, on the basis of very limited research so far, seems to be related to perceptual, cognitive and conceptual aspects of a person, but possibly not to social interaction nor to some levels of self-description. Where in the realm of personality will it fit most efficiently? The history of initial enthusiasm and later disillusionment with projective techniques tells us that the answers to these questions will require many years of well-coordinated research. But if ever the line of inquiry started by Rorschach is to be put on a sound scientific basis, it will be in the direction taken by the Holtzman Inkblot Technique.

J Proj Tech 26:248–9 Je '62. A. Barclay. * a scholarly treatise, providing a cogent analysis of psychometric weaknesses of the Rorschach Method and offering an alternative approach to inkblot perception that circumvents these psychometric inadequacies while retaining the unique projective approach to personality assessment that the Rorschach Method offers. Those who are aware of the often caustic criticisms that have been leveled at inkblot techniques from the standpoint of their psychometric imperfections will welcome the advent of an approach to inkblot techniques that promises to obviate the greater majority of these difficulties. * the psychometric soundness of the technique will encourage clinicians to explore its research possibilities and the provision for translating from Holtzman variables to Rorschach variables ought to encourage comparisons of the clinical utility of both instruments. The limited comparative research already accomplished suggests that there is a relatively high degree of commonality for both techniques and it is probable that the usefulness of each technique can be enhanced by further research into their mutual contributions one to another. With respect to other considerations generated by a review of the present work it should perhaps be noted that many clinicians have considered that the Rorschach is in reality two separate techniques; first, the truly projective aspects of an individual's spontaneous associations to such inkblot materials; and, second, the more formalized interrogative aspects of the inquiry for the determination of scoring categories. Thus, the Rorschach has had both projective as well as psychometric aspects and it has been in the latter area that the majority of criticisms have arisen. The Holtzman Technique by virtue of its basic psychometric soundness should offer the possibility of validating, on an experimentally demonstrable basis, certain Rorschach findings that have heretofore been equivocal because of the statistical inadequacies of the Rorschach Method. Similarly, as a body of knowledge accrues around the Holtzman Technique, it should become apparent from what areas the Holtzman Technique can be implemented by drawing upon the Rorschach literature. Such mutual enrichment will represent a distinct advance in the establishment of sound foundations for the assessment of personality through projective methods.

For additional reviews, see 217.

[B264a]

★Horrocks, John E. **Assessment of Behavior: The Methodology and Content of Psychological Measurement.** Columbus, Ohio: Charles E. Merrill Books, Inc., 1964. Pp. xv, 736. Text edition, $8.50; trade edition, $11.35. *

[B265]

★Howitt, Lillian C. **Practical Classroom Testing.** Englewood Cliffs, N.J.: Prentice-Hall, Inc., 1961. Pp. 64. Paper. $2.00. *

[B266]

★Hubbard, John P., and Clemans, William V. **Multiple-Choice Examinations in Medicine: A Guide for Examiner and Examinee.** Philadelphia, Pa.: Lea & Febiger, 1961. Pp. 186. $3.75. * (London: Henry Kimpton, Medical Publisher and Bookseller. 28*s.*)

Ed & Psychol Meas 22:408–9 su '62. Peter G. Loret. * Hubbard and Clemans are to be congratulated on their success in achieving a comprehensive and informative presentation of an aspect of evaluation which has come to play an increasingly important part in the medical schools of the United States in the past two decades. There has long been a need for such a systematic guide, particularly one which is directed primarily to a medical audience. * The illustrative items presented should prove particularly helpful to the reader, as should the discussion dealing with the rewriting of items. This section concludes with a list of standards which each test item should satisfy; however, this reviewer wishes that some specific comment might have been made about the use and abuse of "None of the above" as an option, since the novice item-writer frequently falls into the trap of using this option much too frequently. It would also seem desirable to have included in this section some discussion of the need for including as much information as possible in the stem (leading clause) of an item. Unfortunately, several of the examples in the appendix are characterized by the use of a stem which requires that the examinee read each and every option in order to determine what is really being asked; for example, "The etiologic agent of infectious hepatitis" or "As a result of cutting one hypoglossal nerve." It might have been valuable to point out this pitfall to the reader and to stress the "rule" that the stem of an item ought to present either a complete question or as much of the problem as is possible. A brief but excellent discussion relative to the scoring and analysis of multiple-choice tests is presented in Chapters 4 and 5. Chapter 6, which is devoted to a discussion of multiple-choice and essay tests is, with its annotated bibliography, an excellent résumé of the pros and cons of the two types of tests; the presentation of an essay question in pathology with the criteria used for grading, followed by a series of multiple-choice questions covering the same material, is particularly illuminating. * This book will undoubtedly prove to be extremely valuable to the examiner who seeks to construct and administer multiple-choice examinations in medicine and related fields. Its value as a guide to the examinee, however, may be somewhat overemphasized; this latter function might perhaps be more appropriately fulfilled by a brief but comprehensive bulletin of information for the candidate.

[B267]

★ HUFF, DARRELL. **Score: The Strategy of Taking Tests.** New York: Appleton-Century, 1961. Pp. ix, 148. $3.75. * (London: Victor Gollancz, Ltd., 1962. 15*s*.) (Harmondsworth, Middlesex, England: Penguin Books, Ltd., 1964. Paper. 3*s*. 6*d*.)

Personnel J 41:33 Ja '62. W. Porter Swift. * Although written in a light vein and humorous in part, his essay yields practical advice which, if wisely followed, would not only serve to equalize the opportunity of testees but would also tend to increase the validity of test results. * The total content of the book is helpful and has its amusing highlights; it is sometimes derisive of the test-makers and at other times appreciative and explanatory. Its chief limitation is in what it leaves unsaid and the half-truths which remain with the reader as the last page is turned. The efficient construction, administration, interpretation, and use of results is minimized in displaying some faulty procedures. *

[B268]

★HUTT, MAX L., AND BRISKIN, GERALD J. **The Clinical Use of the Revised Bender-Gestalt Test.** New York: Grune & Stratton, Inc., 1960. Pp. viii, 168. $5.00. * (London: William Heinemann Medical Books Ltd. 35*s*.) (*PA* 35:3384) (An erratum slip is currently being included with all volumes distributed stating that, in accordance with an agreement with the American Orthopsychiatric Association and Lauretta Bender, to avoid confusion with the latter's *A Visual Motor Gestalt Test and Its Clinical Use,* the title has been changed to *The Hutt Adaptation of the Bender-Gestalt Test.* Future reprintings will bear the new title.)

Am J Mental Def 66:591–2 Ja '62. Clifford H. Swensen, Jr. * There are some characteristics of the book that will bother some people. First, the authors interpret consistently in terms of Freudian theory. Psychologists of a different theoretical persuasion may find this bias a little distasteful. Second, the authors habitually present interpretations without any factual evidence to support the interpretation. For example, in discussing the meaning of the placement of the first figure (Figure A) on the Test, they state: "Placement of figure A in the lower right-hand corner of the page, for example, almost invariably is indicative of eccentricity, anxiety, and ego disturbance of psychotic proportions." There is no elaboration of what is meant by "almost invariably" nor is there any clearer definition of what is meant by "eccentricity," "anxiety," or "ego disturbance." One of the biggest problems in psychological theory and diagnosis is the problem of clear definition of terms. This kind of statement is fairly characteristic of the kinds of assertions made throughout the book, and I think, is the kind of statement that is most apt to arouse the criticism of the empirically-minded. But these criticisms should not detract from the basic value of this book. Wherever pertinent research evidence was available, the authors cited it. Where research evidence was not available the authors present their best judgment without apology. Their judgment is not infallible, but it has produced what, in the opinion of this reviewer, is the best available manual on the Bender-Gestalt Test.

J Proj Tech 25:239–41 Je '61. S. Z. Dudek. * a commendable though not complete job * The authors present a system of interpretation based on projective principles which makes it possible for the psychologist to arrive at a full personality description and an evaluation of the underlying process phenomena and they do this in an orderly methodical sequence. In addition to this they contribute a valuable extension to the test in adding the elaboration and association phases. These help to ease the interpretative problems by often revealing the personal or symbolic meaning of the design to the subject. There is an excellent chapter on general problems of diagnosis stressing the dynamic as opposed to the structural (Kraepelinian) approach. * one gets the impression that the authors have been so carried away by their conviction of the existence of this nebulous substantial body of already validated data that the question of validation has gone by relatively unnoticed. There are references throughout the book to a few validational studies but far too many interpretative statements are made without either an explanation of why or how the principle "works"; or of statistics on how the confidence in any particular interpretative principle became established. There are also frequent references to normative studies but no norms are presented. There is no doubt that the authors feel very sure of their ground, so their confidence must be built on considerable clinical validation. If this is so, surely it would have been worth the effort to go through the files to compile the pertinent statistical data. * there are too many inferences drawn without reference to empirical finding. Since this is presumably intended as a textbook, something more is needed. * In every projective technique each sign or determinant has a fixed and fundamental meaning, and a provisional one, in which case the meaning is modified by the rest of the configuration. This is precisely what makes validation such a difficult problem. However, to the extent that each sign has a fundamental meaning, it is possible to validate it, whether singly or within its configuration. The authors have not felt it necessary to bother with this or, if they have, they have not given us the data. They have used experimental evidence where this existed and have allowed the remainder to rest on their clinical experience and knowledge. Since the book is intended to give the rationale and principles of interpretation, and is therefore to be used as a textbook, much more than this is necessary to give the beginning student, and even the experienced clinician, a confidence in the universal validity of the authors' statements. Considering the vagueness of many concepts in clinical psychology and the idiosyncratic quality of many of the interpretative signs, it is time clinicians made some serious attempts at validation instead of referring to the substantial body of evidence which becomes more nebulous and tautological with the addition of each new projective technique and each new interpretative sign. The feeling of scepticism is reinforced in the second part of the book which deals with case presentation. While the interpretations are brilliant and reportedly correct they fail to exemplify the methods and problems of interpretation. At times, as in case 1, the inferences come too quickly and perhaps too brilliantly so that the connections between inference and evidence is either lacking or too difficult to follow, and it is difficult to combat scepticism and annoyance. At times the case analysis consists of no more than an enumeration of the perceptual distortions ending up in a diagnostic statement. Although this technique is apparently deliberate, it is not satisfactory. The impression one gets is that the book was written in great haste and the authors were too pressed for time to look into the background material or to compile the necessary statistics. The case histories are generally frustratingly inadequate—a tendency only too common among clinical writers. However, in spite of all the shortcomings, this is a valuable book. It deepens and broadens our understanding of the Bender Gestalt and of the inferential and configurational approach. It raises many interesting problems for research, and on the whole it does a service to the practising clinician who uses the Bender Gestalt. It is a book worth careful study.

[B269]

★INVITATIONAL CONFERENCE ON TESTING PROBLEMS. **Proceedings of the 1958 Invitational Conference on Testing Problems, November 1, 1958.** Roger T. Lennon, Chairman. Princeton, N.J.: Educational Testing Service, 1959. Pp. 130. Paper. $1.00. *

[B270]

★INVITATIONAL CONFERENCE ON TESTING PROBLEMS. **Proceedings of the 1959 Invitational Conference on Testing Problems, October 31, 1959.** Dorothy Adkins Wood, Chairman. Princeton, N.J.: Educational Testing Service, 1960. Pp. 99. Paper. $1.00. *

Personnel & Guid J 39:423 Ja '61. Thomas M. Magoon. This report....is wide in its coverage and perhaps more stimulating than many of its predecessors. * The Conference report is indeed a stimulating one. The reader should find much food for thought and those *Journal* readers affiliated with educational institutions will find much to consider in terms of application to their local problems and procedures.

[B271]

★INVITATIONAL CONFERENCE ON TESTING PROBLEMS. **Proceedings of the 1960 Invitational Conference on Testing Problems, October 29, 1960.** John B. Carroll, Chairman. Princeton, N.J.: Educational Testing Service, 1961. Pp. 136. Paper. $1.00. * (*PA* 36: 4KJ36C)

[B272]

★INVITATIONAL CONFERENCE ON TESTING PROBLEMS. **Proceedings of the 1961 Invitational Conference on Testing Problems, October 28, 1961.** Paul L. Dressel, Chairman. Princeton, N.J.: Educational Testing Service, 1962. Pp. 108. Paper. $1.00. * (*PA* 37:3866)

[B273]

★INVITATIONAL CONFERENCE ON TESTING PROBLEMS. **Proceedings of the 1962 Invitational Conference on Testing Problems, November 3, 1962.** Eric F. Gardner, Chairman. Princeton, N.J.: Educational Testing Service, 1963. Pp. 131. Paper. $1.50. * (*PA* 38:2622)

[B274]

★INVITATIONAL CONFERENCE ON TESTING PROBLEMS. **Proceedings of the 1963 Invitational Conference on Testing Problems, November 2, 1963.** Alexander G. Wesman, Chairman. Princeton, N.J.: Educational Testing Service, 1964. Pp. 164. Paper. $1.50. *

[B275]

★IRWIN, ORVIS C. **A Manual for Testing the Articulation of Children With Cerebral Palsy.** Wichita, Kan.: Institute of Logopedics, Inc., 1961. Pp. 24. Paper. $1.50. (Reprinted from *Cerebral Palsy R* 22:1–24 My–Je '61.) *

[B276]

★JACKSON, DENNIS B. **The Exam Secret: How to Shine in Examinations and Life! Second Edition.** Kingswood, Surrey, England: Elliot Right Way Books, 1960. Pp. 127. Paper. 3*s.* 6*d.* (Hollywood, Calif.: Wilshire Book Co. $1.00.) *

[B277]

★JANSEN, UDO H. **Marking and Reporting Procedures in the Secondary Schools of Texas.** Texas Study of Secondary Education, Research Bulletin No. 32. Austin, Tex.: the Study, University of Texas, 1960. Pp. 30. Paper. $1.00. *

[B278]

*JENNINGS, HELEN HALL. **Sociometry in Group Relations: A Manual for Teachers, Second Edition.** Washington, D.C.: American Council on Education, 1959. Pp. xi, 105. $1.50. * (*PA* 33:10963)

Cath Ed R 57:356–7 My '59. Robert B. Nordberg. * The book begins with a good theoretical discussion of group relations and of sociometry as a technique for studying same. Then it gets down to specific ways of making sociometric tests, administering them, following them up, and so forth. In the last chapter, a provocative theory of sociometric choices is offered. There are abundant illustrations of sociograms. * The last chapter went beyond the usual, rather superficial level of theorizing about group phenomena. The only weakness noted was this: while the operational character of sociometry was noted in the abstract, this tended to be forgotten when the author was drawing certain conclusions. For instance, she is apparently against academic "segregation," and says: "Separation in seating, such as placing the best students near the teacher....sets up choice patterns in which both the good and the bad students tend to reject those with whom they are grouped...." This, surely, is not a *total* rejection. Let us say, they reject them at certain times, for certain purposes, under certain circumstances. * Nowhere is the need for operational definitions more acute than in sociometry. Responses are made to a specific question. A slight variation in the wording of the question, or even the tone of voice in which it is asked, often produces strikingly different results. It seems very questionable to condemn major policies, such as ability-grouping, on such tenuous evidence. Aside from this one weakness, the reviewer felt this was a very good and practical manual on an important educational technique.

For reviews of the first edition, see 4:B217.

[B279]

★JENSEN, OLLIE A. **Improving Multiple-Choice Test Items: A Manual for Examiners.** Personnel Brief No. 603. Chicago, Ill.: Public Personnel Association, 1960. Pp. 53. Paper. $3.00. *

[B280]

★JEX, FRANK B. **University of Utah Studies in the Prediction of Academic Success.** University of Utah Research Monographs in Education, Vol. 1, No. 1. Salt Lake City, Utah: the University, July 1957. Pp. ix, 51. Paper. $1.00. *

[B281]

★JOHNSON, WENDELL; DARLEY, FREDERIC L.; AND SPRIESTERSBACH, D. C. **Diagnostic Methods in Speech Pathology.** New York: Harper & Row, Publishers, Inc., 1963. Pp. xvii, 347. $7.50. (London: Harper & Row Ltd. 56*s.*) * (*PA* 38:2967) For a listing of forms, see 308.

Cont Psychol 9:201–2 My '64. Harry Hollien. Although this book was written primarily for students of speech pathology, it is of interest and value to workers in other clinical specialties. In fact, clinical psychologists, audiologists, physicians, nurses, and both physical and occupational therapists should find the work an excellent reference. * the authors.... provide a wealth of tables that contain information on birth, physical size, motor development, and disfluencies of speech; on vocabulary, sleeping time, bowel and bladder control, nail biting, language development, and so on. While all these tables have some pertinency to the diagnostic task in speech pathology, the simple compilation of such extensive reference materials would alone seem to justify the price of the book. Moreover, the normative data provided allows the clinician to assess and evaluate the client's performance and status at the time of diagnosis. This, in turn, permits a more sophisticated diagnosis and enhances the effectiveness of the therapeutic program. * The bulk of the text is devoted to the problems encountered in testing and assessing articulation, voice, language and stuttering. Consideration is also given to evaluating general speech behavior, assessing the speech mechanism and carrying out supplementary diagnostic procedures. Although step-by-step procedures are provided, this is not a "cookbook." The authors attempt to assist the clinician in acquiring the skills necessary for intelligent and competent diagnostic work. For example, they point out that not only should the clinician be able to assess the kind and severity of stuttering but also he should understand such matters as normal disfluencies, the many ways stuttering is measured, the attitudes of the stutterer toward his speech and so on. The reviewer's over-all reaction to the book is quite positive. In general only minor criticism can be made. First, in several instances the results of a number of investigations have been combined into a single table which then contains almost too much information for easy use. In other tables, the use of different scaling systems could create some confusion unless the reader takes the time to convert values. Another criticism is that some of the diagnostic materials and techniques seem to be almost too detailed; some of the tests obviously are very time-consuming. Quite naturally certain workers will feel that such time could be more profitably expended on therapy. On the other hand, the reviewer agrees with the authors' philosophy that effective therapy results from systematic and competent evaluation of the client and his problems. Moreover, it is obvious that detailed evaluation is recommended only when *appropriate* to the nature of the disorder. In summary, this text is clearly the best of its kind and of unquestioned value to the speech pathologist. The materials and procedures provided are presented systematically and thoroughly, and are based on both clinical experience and research. Moreover, in developing their own specialties, the authors have learned from other disciplines and are not afraid to utilize the resulting skills and concepts appropriately.

[B282]

★JONES, MARSHALL B. **Simplex Theory.** U.S. Naval School of Aviation Medicine Monograph Series, No. 3. Pensacola, Fla.: the School, U.S. Naval Aviation Medical Center, June 1959. Pp. v, 196. Paper. Gratis. *

[B283]

★JÖRESKOG, K. G. **Statistical Estimation in Factor Analysis: A New Technique and Its Foundation.** Stockholm, Sweden: Almqvist & Wiksell, 1963. Pp. 145. Paper. Sw. kr. 24. *

Brit J Stat Psychol 17:95–6 My '64. M. S. Bartlett. * essentially a research monograph, and requires careful consideration before it could be recommended to a wider audience than statisticians and psychologists actively concerned with the methodology of factor analysis. Broadly speaking, the model assumed is still the orthodox linear multiple factor model, but a new restrictive assumption is introduced, *viz.* that the residual variances, after removing the effects of the group factors, are proportional to the reciprocal values of the diagonal elements of the inverted population dispersion matrix. This assumption, while it is claimed to lead to simplification in the inference problem (such as the avoidance of iterative techniques of the kind necessary in Lawley's maximum likelihood method), appears to be quite arbitrary, and to be advocated not so much for any intrinsic plausibility as for technical convenience. * However, the technique appears to give a very good account of itself when tried on actual data, so that it can hardly be dismissed offhand. The data tested out are of two kinds, artificial and empirical. The use of artificial data is not of course to be deprecated, as it enables the analysis to be tried out under conditions which are precisely known. An extensive series of experiments was made, ranging from 10 to 30 tests and 2 to 6 group factors. It is important to notice that these artificial series were not necessarily restricted to satisfy the extra assumption, a restriction which would have been open to criticism. * What seems less conclusive is the effect of the specification error on the testing procedure discussed in Chapter IV. One would expect the goodness of fit test for the number of factors required to break down for *large* samples, but if this point was discussed the reviewer did not notice it. In the final comparisons on empirical data, the most interesting comparison is with Lawley's maximum likelihood method, using two sets of data: (i) the data used by Emmett with 9 tests and three apparent factors (sample of 211 children); (ii) a battery of 33 tests used by Lord with at least ten apparent factors (sample of 649 students). There is no doubt that the new method does extremely well on these two examples, so that as a "working method" the value of the new technique seems established. How will it compare ultimately with Lawley's maximum likelihood method? The author himself says of this latter method (p. 129): "This method is definitely the best available method for anyone who could afford to carry it through." Thus the value of the new technique would seem at present to lie either as a useful self-contained procedure for those unable to embark on the full maximum-likelihood method, or perhaps as an initial computation that could be used as a convenient starting point for the more laborious method. Before it can be assessed as a foolproof final procedure in its own right, some further elucidation and discussion of the effects of the specification error resulting from the extra assumption would still appear to be needed.

[B284]

★JURGENSEN, CLIFFORD E.; LOPEZ, FELIX M., JR.; AND RICHARDS, KENNETH E. **Employee Performance Appraisal Re-examined.** Personnel Brief No. 613. Chicago, Ill.: Public Personnel Association, 1961. Pp. 29. Paper. $2.50. *

Personnel Prac B 18:58–9 S '62. P. L. Mason. * interest in how to develop better ways of appraising workers continues to run high. However, the subject remains complex, difficult to fathom, and full of contention. This report provides a three-pronged approach to a re-examination of the problem. Part I describes some of the discernible recent trends in the field, and incorporates a useful reference list; Part II contains a case study of the experience of a public agency; and Part III deals with facts, fears and fallacies about performance appraisal. The report ends with a comprehensive bibliography with respect to evaluation of employee work performance. Although the three articles are very clearly written, their usefulness for the practitioner decreases in order of their appearance in the report. Collectively, however, they provide a deeper understanding of this important facet of personnel management—no mean achievement in a work of only 29 pages.

[B285]

★KAGAN, JEROME, AND LESSER, GERALD S., EDITORS. **Contemporary Issues in Thematic Apperceptive Methods.** Springfield, Ill.: Charles C Thomas, Publisher, 1961. Pp. xiv, 328. $12.00. * (*PA* 36:1HG28K)

Am J Psychother 16:327–8 Ap '62. Bernard Landis. * little information is provided that is not available elsewhere. Were this material better integrated, its compilation between one set of covers might be quite useful. As it is, the book does not hold together well; it is a collection of different papers not clearly related to each other. Nor is there as much clarification of key issues as one might expect from this volume, with a few noteworthy exceptions. For example, Bernard Murstein discusses the important, and often overlooked, distinction between *structure* and *ambiguity* of the stimulus. Robert R. Holt presents a valuable, detailed analysis of the differences and similarities between fantasy and stories to pictures. * the editors clarify neither term when they distinguish between "apperception" and "projection" * While there are a number of interesting presentations in this book, these are not brought together, and one has to do a good deal of sifting and sorting to benefit from the collection, as a whole. The publisher must take some of the responsibility, especially when he states that "careful attention is given to all details of manufacturing and design." For this book, in spite of its high price, is technically unsatisfactory. The relationship of type faces is poor; the copy is crowded together with headings hard to distinguish from the body type; and the layout is haphazard—making the book difficult to read.

Brit J Psychol 53:218 My '62. A. Kaldegg. * Each lecture taken in isolation has something to offer. The cumulative result is, however, intellectual indigestion. For research and references the compilation has its uses but, had they been rigorously edited and judiciously distributed over the technical journals, the papers might have been more effective.

Cont Psychol 7:28–30 Ja '62. Edith Weisskopf-Joelson. * Somewhere among the multitude of quantitative variables in the book the individual has been lost. The clinician who expects immediate gains regarding his interpretative sensitivity will profit little from this volume. Perhaps the greatest value of the book lies in its potential power of stimulating research. This is especially true for Lazarus' interesting chapter "A Substitutive-Defensive Conception of Apperceptive Fantasy." The book should be a gold mine for topic-hungry thesis writers. The most striking shortcoming of the book is its....lack of integration of the chapters with each other and lack of integration of the material of the book with the body of knowledge in the field of psychology. * the volume could use some more editing. It is a potpourri of some very relevant issues and some personal preoccupations of eight authors and a number of discussants. But it is, at least, a stimulating potpourri.

[B286]

★KAHN, THEODORE C., AND GIFFEN, MARTIN B. **Psychological Techniques in Diagnosis and Evaluation.** Oxford, England: Pergamon Press Ltd., 1960. Pp. xi, 164. 40*s*. * (New York: Macmillan Co. $6.50.)

Am J Orthopsychiatry 32:207–9 Ja '62. Max L. Fogel. * The book is clearly written and most of the psychological terms used are satisfactorily explained for the intended level of readership. However, the aim of providing a review of psychological method for those without formal training in psychology has been achieved with only partial success. The contents include a mixture of valuable information for the nonpsychologist along with material either too sophisticated or irrelevant for this type of reader. The result is a book which seems somewhat lacking in focus. The section on general test concepts (validity, reliability, etc.) is well written. The treatment of specific tests, however, exemplifies the inconsistencies present in the volume. The authors plunge into verbal descriptions of Rorschach determinants (e.g., C = impulsive and explosive) with no explanation given of what the symbols refer to in a stricted sense (i.e., C = color). Nor is there any exposition of the fundamental nature and purpose of the Rorschach method. The Kahn Test of Symbol Arrangement is also presented, without adequate description of instructions and scoring, or explanation of the interpretative symbols employed. * The authors might have been more emphatic in stressing that many of the generalizations advanced lack strong empirical support and should be considered as tentative. * more careful editing would have benefited the book and corrected questionable statements (e.g., that a nonelevated psychopathic deviate scale score on the MMPI is consistent with the absence of signs of character and behavior disorder) as well as factual errors (e.g., the WAIS appeared in 1955, not 1958 as is stated). It is unfortunate that a more favorable assessment cannot be made of a book which is designed to close an obviously large gap in psychological writing, that between psychology and bordering disciplines. In its favor, it can be stated that the book is certainly easy to read and that much of it will be useful to the readers for whom it is intended.

Brit J Psychol 52:307–8 Ag '61. B. Semeonoff. * one must admit....serious disappointment in the Kahn and Giffen book. Reference to the preliminary material reveals that it is intended not for the psychologist, but for people "who on account of their work, come into contact with psychological evaluations." Since the first-named author is himself a psychologist, the curious mixture of awe and condescension with which the work of the clinical psychologist is introduced strikes a disconcertingly false note. The plan of the book is interesting: following some general chapters on tests, the concept of "normalcy," intelligence etc., separate chapters are devoted to the identification and assessment of psychiatric disorders and to the application of psychological techniques to child study and in occupational guidance. The specific contribution in each context of the various projective and other techniques covered is described, but unfortunately in such a way as to presuppose a degree of familiarity with these totally at variance with the elementary level of other parts of the book. This is particularly the case in relation to Dr Kahn's little-known "Test of Symbol Arrangement" (KTSA) detailed findings from which are discussed without any indication of what the subject is required to do. One is left with the impression that the authors, both of whom are attached to the U.S. forces in Germany, have been working in isolation, and that a potentially valuable work has been spoiled by lack of facilities. The book is attractively produced, but seems unnecessarily expensive.

J Nerv & Mental Dis 136:91 Ja '63. Herbert J. Schlesinger. Psychologists who have wished for a well written, non-technical book to inform colleagues about how the clinical psychologist contributes to psychiatric diagnosis will have to go on wishing. The present book, which is offered to fill that need, is not the answer. The major part of the book is arranged under such chapter headings as "Normals, Character Disorders, and Differential Diagnosis," "Identification of Schizophrenia," "Assessment of Neurosis" and "Methods for Testing and Evaluating Organic Brain Impairment." In each of these chapters a number of tests, mostly popular, are briefly described together with a list of "signs" to lead the psychologist to suspect the presence of the rubric condition. Thus the same tests (with somewhat different lists of signs) appear in several chapters. The lists of signs, larded with cautions, are of highly dubious validity and in any case are out of place in a book intended for nonpsychologists. The picture the reader might infer is that the psychologist picks over his tests one by one looking for "signs" of one or another static pathological condition and then balances his lists to discover the name of the patient's disease. In regard to labeling, the authors urge the psychologist who might prefer to present his test findings without jargon to use psychiatric labels freely, not to be "too fearful or too proud to speak the language of the people with whom he deals....Naturally, when he reports to persons who are not psychiatrically oriented he must use terms and descriptions *which can be understood*" (italics added). The authors say nothing about the importance of understanding thought processes, affective processes and interpersonal processes, for instance, in drawing diagnostic inferences. An even more elementary failing is a lack of any simple and straightforward description of such important tests as the Rorschach, TAT and Lowenfeld Mosaic, even though there are many scattered, often technical references to the significance of findings obtained with them. On the other hand, quite meticulous descriptions are offered of several tests devised by one of the authors, even though in several instances the test itself or the application to which it is put is in an experimental stage. In addition, claims are made for the author's tests which could hardly be justified if the tests are indeed still experimental. One can question as well the propriety of giving a far more detailed presentation of a test which is still under development, let alone one by the author, than to tests which are well established and widely used and which a reader might have more reason to want to know about. Among the book's redeeming features are a discussion of intelligence which would be suitable for one not professionally concerned with this area and a superficial, but in this context adequate, discussion of psychological tests in vocational and educational guidance. Quality aside, at $6.50 this 164-page book is much overpriced.

[B287]

★Karp, Stephen A. **Kit of Selected Distraction Tests.** Brooklyn, N.Y.: Cognitive Tests, 1962. Pp. i, 18. Paper, mimeographed. Gratis. * (*PA* 37:7983)

[B288]

★Kasper, Sidney. **Measurement of Adjustment in Adolescents: An Extension of Personal Construct Theory and Methodology.** American Psychological Association, Psychological Monographs: General and Applied, Vol. 76, No. 6, Whole No. 525. Washington, D.C.: the Association, Inc., 1962. Pp. 32. Paper. $1.50. * (*PA* 37:6506)

[B289]

*Katz, Martin. **Selecting an Achievement Test, Second Edition.** Evaluation and Advisory Service Series, No. 3. Princeton, N.J.: Educational Testing Service, 1961. Pp. 32. Paper. Gratis. * (The second edition is very nearly identical to the first edition published in 1959.)

Personnel & Guid J 37:608 Ap '59. Thomas M. Magoon. [Review of the first edition.] * The content goes beyond the do and don't generalizations that are common in the measurement field. Rather, the authors have liberally spiced the guide with illustrative material as to the reasons for and implications of each topic considered. The topics include definitions and properties of achievement tests (validity, reliability, and norms), characteristics of the school population, curriculum content and objectives, related purposes of testing (diagnosis, assessment of change, prediction, and evaluation), and the use of test scores in terms of the purposes of testing. * The author's....guidance is concrete and sound. * a very valuable reference for those personnel workers concerned with test construction, selection, and usage.

[B290]

★Kelly, E. Lowell, and Goldberg, Lewis R. **Correlates of Later Performance and Specialization in Psychology: A Follow-Up Study of the Trainees Assessed in the VA Selection Project.** American Psychological Association, Psychological Monographs: General and Applied, Vol. 73, No. 12, Whole No. 482. Washington, D.C.: the Association, Inc., 1959. Pp. 32. Paper. $1.00. * (*PA* 34:7952)

[B291]

★Kennedy, Wallace A.; Van de Riet, Vernon; and White, James C., Jr. **A Normative Sample of Intelligence and Achievement of Negro Ele-**

mentary School Children in Southeastern United States. Monographs of the Society for Research in Child Development, Vol. 28, No. 6. Lafayette, Ind.: Child Development Publications, 1963. Pp. 112. Paper. $3.00. *

[B292]

★KENT AREA GUIDANCE COUNCIL. **A Proposed 12 Year Testing Program.** Columbus, Ohio: Ohio Scholarship Tests, State Department of Education, 1959. Pp. vi, 57. Paper, lithotyped. $1.00. *

[B293]

★KETTNER, NORMAN W.; GUILFORD, J. P.; AND CHRISTENSEN, PAUL R. **A Factor-Analytic Study Across the Domains of Reasoning, Creativity, and Evaluation.** American Psychological Association, Psychological Monographs: General and Applied, Vol. 73, No. 9, Whole No. 479. Washington, D.C.: the Association, Inc., 1959. Pp. 31. Paper. $1.00. * (*PA* 34:7333)

[B294]

★KIMBALL, REGINALD, AND VAN DE WATER, HOPE S. **How to Prepare for High School Entrance and Scholarship Examinations, Revised Edition.** Stamford, Conn.: Youth Education Systems, Inc., 1960. Pp. 293, 25. Paper. $2.50. *

[B295]

★KLOPFER, BRUNO, AND DAVIDSON, HELEN H. **The Rorschach Technique: An Introductory Manual.** New York: Harcourt, Brace & World, Inc., 1962. Pp. viii, 245. $8.50. (London: George G. Harrap & Co. Ltd. 60*s.*) *

Brit J Psychol 54:376–7 N '63. Theodora Alcock. * This up-to-date introductory manual provides a pleasant contrast to that of 1942 in its greatly increased clarity and precision of phrase, which make for easy reading and assimilation. * The clinical sensitivity of Klopfer, and perhaps the skill which he has acquired as a Jungian analyst, seem reflected better than in any of his previous text-books when he discusses interpersonal relationships briefly under the heading "The Examination Atmosphere." Indeed, many of his admirers, including the present writer, could wish that he had allowed himself more space to expand upon this subject. Many examples of scoring are given, and will be useful to students. * In the section on scoring, the advice to give all additional determinants a common rating of 0.5 may not be universally acceptable, since these additionals vary so greatly in their perceptual significance. In a response such as leaping flames, directed to a red area, the determining factors of movement and colour are usually inseparable and apparently of equal importance to the perceiver, in contrast to other percepts which are scored as additions either because they refer only to a small part of the area used, or because they are not seen until the second showing. However, the question as to whether additionals should be weighted is another story. Disagreement on this small point should in no way detract from appreciation of a contribution to Rorschach literature upon which its authors are indeed to be warmly congratulated.

J Proj Tech & Pers Assess 27:369 S '63. Mortimer M. Meyer. * The content covers a brief introduction followed by Administration, Scoring, Interpretation, and two case studies. * The discussion of scoring is presented clearly and with many helpful illustrations which are annotated. The interpretation is also presented with a simple clarity and in a format that makes for ready access to the material. The two case studies included are an excellent aid to the student and intriguing because they represent average people and not psychiatric patients. * The presentation of the material is most carefully organized so that a beginner can follow the substance easily and also find it most useful for ready reference about specific aspects of the scoring and interpretation. It will serve well as a text where, as suggested in the preface, elementary knowledge and general acquaintance is the goal.

[B296]

★KOLTUV, BARBARA BLACK. **Some Characteristics of Intrajudge Trait Intercorrelations.** American Psychological Association, Psychological Monographs: General and Applied, Vol. 76, No. 33, Whole No. 552. Washington, D.C.: the Association, Inc., 1962. Pp. 33. Paper. $2.00. *

[B297]

★KOPPITZ, ELIZABETH MUNSTERBERG. **The Bender Gestalt Test for Young Children.** New York and London: Grune & Stratton, Inc., 1964. Pp. xi, 195. $6.75; 48*s.* * (*PA* 39:1740)

Percept & Motor Skills 18:325 F '64. C. H. Ammons. * As a test for screening first graders, children with organic damage, etc., is needed (especially for the age range of 5 to 10 years), this work merits careful evaluation. All one may say, however, is that the present development is promising. This reader was disturbed by such items as: failure to report separately scores for boys and girls; lack of control for socio-economic level; use of teacher ratings of adjustment and achievement without indicating reliabilities; grossly uneven *N*s over age levels (norms for children in first two grades are based on more than 150 cases each but for levels 10 years, 0 months to 10 years, 11 months *N*s range from 27 to 30).

When reliabilities *are* reported, these tend to be fairly high; *r*s for scorers of .88 to .96; *taus* (test-retest over 4 mo.) of .54 to .66 (for an unknown number of children). The study is better than many, but in several ways below standards set up by the APA committee on test standardization. Further research *is* needed, as the author suggests.

[B298]

★KRAMER, HARVEY J. **Stimulus Variables in Auditory Projective Testing: 1, An Information Theory Method for Measuring Psychological Ambiguity; 2, Effects of Varying Ambiguity and Type of Content Upon Projection With Blind and Sighted.** AFB Publications, Research Series No. 9. New York: American Foundation for the Blind, Inc., 1962. Pp. 81. Paper. $1.00. * (*PA* 37:5028)

[B299]

★KRATHWOHL, DAVID R.; BLOOM, BENJAMIN S.; AND MASIA, BERTRAM B. **Taxonomy of Educational Objectives: The Classification of Educational Goals: Handbook 2, The Affective Domain.** New York: David McKay Co., Inc., 1964. Pp. xiv, 196. Paper. $2.50. *

[B300]

★LADO, ROBERT. **Language Testing: The Construction and Use of Foreign Language Tests: A Teacher's Book.** London: Longmans, Green & Co. Ltd., 1961. Pp. xxiii, 389. 35*s*. (New York: McGraw-Hill Book Co., Inc., 1964. $6.00.) *

Engl Lang Teach 17:97–9 Ja '63. This is an important and welcome book for the language-teaching profession as a whole, including the individual teacher of English as a foreign language. The reader should be aware in advance that it is written in the recent traditions of American language teaching as practised at Michigan, yet although these are different in some ways from British practice it is important that the extraordinary value of that which is universal and relevant to Britain and the United States alike should not be overshadowed by what is more controversial. * Part I, of 37 pages, is entitled "General Introduction and Theory of Foreign Language Learning," and provides a groundwork of views on language, language learning, language testing and the variables that are encountered, and a guide to the critical evaluation of tests. Part II, "Testing the Elements of the Language," covers 166 pages and is the central section of the book, covering these subjects: pronunciation; testing recognition of the sound segments; testing production of the sound segments; the testing of "stress"; the testing of intonation; testing control of the grammatical structure of a foreign language; testing vocabulary. Part III is entitled "Testing the Integrated Skills." It covers 70 pages and deals with comprehension (both auditory and through reading), speaking, writing, translation, and "over-all control" of the language. In Part IV (23 pages) the author goes "Beyond Language" and considers the relation of language to culture and "the higher values." Finally, Part V, "Refining and Using Foreign Language Tests," provides 90 pages of essential description of the technical aspects of test construction: norms, validity, reliability, item analysis and scoring, different kinds of test, and the design of experiments in foreign-language learning. All this amounts to a treatment of the subject which is by far the most comprehensive of those available to language teachers at the present time. * Lado's allegiance is to a kind of linguistics which has never been accepted by British linguists or language teachers and this means that British readers of his book must expect to find and to make allowances for a degree of "phoneme-worship" that they do not share. Similarly, most of the examples are from American varieties of English, even though the text contains some additions which have the aim of meeting the British reader. Many important references are given to works on test construction, statistics, and linguistics, but there is little mention anywhere in the book of British contributions. It is true that America has been ahead of Britain in this field, but one would have expected a reference to Catherine McCallien's *Oral English Test for West Africa,* for example, which has made a great contribution towards "objectivizing" the difficult task of conducting an oral examination over a vast area with inadequate numbers of examiners. The references to linguistics, similarly, almost ignore work outside America, except for a passing mention of Jespersen. A British author writing in this field for an American readership might perhaps *criticize* recent American work, but one hopes that he would not *ignore* it. The area where possibly the least overlap occurs between the British reader's experience and the author's illustrations is in the chapters on stress and intonation. But this is not their main point: these pages embody the vital argument justifying the use of paper-and-pencil tests for testing some parts even of speech production. If this book can help more teachers to accept the validity of this kind of testing, it will have contributed a great deal to the profession. * Lado's book, then, has some drawbacks and limitations for the British reader, but these are far outweighed by the value and importance of the book as a whole. In particular, it takes too little account of British progress in the field of applied linguistics. But against this it is an extremely valuable explanation of important new methods and techniques; it gives an excellent introduction to the special problems of constructing, administering, and developing language tests; and it provides good references to American work in this field. Above all, it illustrates two of the crucial notions in modern language-teaching theory: first, that the teaching of English as a foreign language is a single case of the general category of teaching foreign languages, and that therefore the various branches of the profession may be able to learn from each other; and second, that among the many areas where linguistics may be applied to help the language teacher, testing is one of the most fruitful.

Int R Ed 10(1):116 '64. H. H. Stern. * an excellent American book on language testing which has already become a landmark in the international literature on foreign language teaching * This book is....more than a manual on testing; it relates, at all stages, language testing to the theory of language teaching. It clarifies issues which in the past have been rather muddled. Lado regards the task of language testing as threefold: (1) testing the elements of a language (sounds, intonation, stress, grammar, etc.), (2) testing the integrated skills, and (3) testing cultural understanding and educational values. The book is at its best on the first two. It shows how tests should be designed so as to make the assessment of proficiency in a language more diagnostic and more objective than conventional language examinations can be. The final part deals in a more general way with test construction and experimental design. While this is not new to those familiar with works on mental testing, linguists may welcome this helpful introduction to procedures on which they are not usually as well informed as they might like to be. The book is, of course, based on American experience and therefore does not provide ready-made solutions for language testing elsewhere. But readers in any country will find that it stimulates productive thinking on language teaching and that it clarifies the problems of testing. It may save weeks and months of futile groping and searching wherever language teaching is under review.

[B301]

★LANDMARK, MARGRETE, AND GRINDE, TURID. **Children's Bender Drawings From 1938 to 1962: A Study of the Literature.** Nordisk Psykologi's Monografiserie No. 16. Copenhagen, Denmark: Munksgaard Ltd., 1964. Pp. iv, 69–104. 8 kr. * (Reprinted from *Nordisk Psykologi* 16:69–104 Jl '64.)

[B302]

★LATCHAW, MARJORIE, AND BROWN, CAMILLE. **The Evaluation Process in Health Education, Physical Education, and Recreation.** Englewood Cliffs, N.J.: Prentice-Hall, Inc., 1962. Pp. xiv, 267. Text price, $6.95; trade price, $9.25. * (London: Prentice-Hall International, Inc. 46s.)

[B303]

★LAWLEY, D. N., AND MAXWELL, A. E. **Factor Analysis as a Statistical Method.** London: Butterworth & Co. (Publishers) Ltd., 1963. Pp. viii, 117. 21s. (Washington, D.C.: Butterworth Inc. $4.25.) *

Brit J Stat Psychol 16:219–21 N '63. M. G. Kendall. For twenty years Dr. Lawley has been wrestling with the problems of statistical estimation and significance which arise in factor analysis; and with a considerable measure of success. This brochure, written in conjunction with Dr. Maxwell, summarizes the position as it now stands. Since much of the work which has been done to bridge the gap between the statistician and the psychologist lies in learned journals it is very useful to have a unified presentation of such authority. * The treatment, by design, has to be condensed and assumes that the reader already has a fair knowledge of theoretical statistics; for instance, that he knows the method of maximum likelihood and recognizes the Wishart distribution of variances and covariances in a multivariate normal system. Nevertheless room has been found for illustrative arithmetical examples and a few exercises. The reader will probably need to follow some of the mathematics with pencil and paper but should not encounter any real obscurities. On the whole, I think this is a very useful book, and most of the suggestions I would have to make could only be satisfactorily covered by doubling its size. However, here they are: (1) At various points the authors contrast the method of factor analysis unfavourably with the method of principal components on the grounds that, in the former, factor loadings are invariant under changes of scale, whereas in the latter they are not. This distinction, in my opinion, is largely illusory, and in practice is not a consideration which should influence the preference of a research worker for one method against the other. In factor analysis we are, in effect, seeking for a subspace and can only select factors with precision by using a supplementary convention or rotation techniques based on extraneous knowledge. In component analysis we do not need these extra assumptions, but seek for those components which explain most of the variation. The price we pay for this is that component weightings are not invariant. It is not a question of methodological superiority but of choice in assumptions. (2) The chapter on the estimation of factor loadings refers to the fact that, with the advent of the electronic computer, the solution of the maximum likelihood equations has lost much of its terror. But not all of it. There seems to be some curious properties in the convergence of iterative solutions to the likelihood equations which have not yet been elucidated. There is also an important gap in that the book does not touch on the difficult problem of determining standard errors in factor loadings or estimates of residual variance. An example from the book itself may make clear the kind of difficulty involved. A numerical example on p. 16 analyzes observations of nine variates (which, incidentally, are not specified). A test indicates that no more than three factors are required. They contribute to the total variation 47.3 per cent, 10.7 per cent, and 4.1 per cent respectively. The residual variance is 37.9 per cent. Without any sophisticated tests, would anyone place any confidence at all in a factor contributing 4.1 per cent where the residual is nine times as large? For that matter, the second factor is not particularly strongly indicated. (3) The chapter on the estimation of factor *scores* appears to me to evade a fundamental difficulty. The problem is that, if we wish to estimate factor loadings and factor scores, we are setting ourselves an impossible task, however large the sample, because there are more parameters under estimate than observations. The situation is essentially underdetermined. The authors (p. 88) recognize this but proceed: "We can, however, find linear functions of the x_i (the variates) which in some sense provide reasonable estimates of the f_r (the factor scores)." They do not say in what sense, but proceed to give the Thomson-Bartlett methods, which lead to the regression of the f's on the x's. Personally I am convinced that this is not a solution of the problem. Regression equations, used as estimators or predictors, will only give average results, not individual factor scores. (4) The examples presented in the book are, naturally enough, based on psychological tests. It would have been instructive to see an example or two from nonpsychological fields, for a reason which is not generally appreciated. It is customary to assume multivariate normality in test scores, at least until somebody can bring forward contrary evidence. The whole of the system of estimation developed by maximum likelihood methods depends on normality, and seeks for estimates of the parameters of underlying variables, not the observed variables themselves. It appears to be required that the selection of the sample is carried out with reference to these underlying variables, not the linear transforms of them which are actually observed, and this raises some curious problems of interpretation which may require a good deal of explanation in non-psychological applications. Some of these topics, however, are for the future. The present book provides an admirable summary of what is known and will be an indispensable starting point for further study.

[B304]

LAYTON, WILBUR L. **Counseling Use of the Strong Vocational Interest Blank.** Minnesota Studies in Student Personnel Work, No. 8. Minneapolis, Minn.: University of Minnesota Press, 1958. Pp. 40. Paper. $1.25. * (*PA* 33:4702)

J Counsel Psychol 6:169 su '59. Robert Callis. * It was a disappointment not to find a more scholarly discussion of the stability of interest. Practical experience suggests that Strong's findings concerning the stability of interest may hold true for students coming from middle to high socio-economic backgrounds, but that these findings may not hold true for students who come from lower economic backgrounds and achieve professional occupational status. Perhaps research is not yet available to attack this problem with more precision. However, this is a problem that should not be ignored any longer and any new treatise on the measurement of vocational interest certainly should deal with this problem head on. The meat of this treatise in terms of new data is included in Chapter 4. Layton presents six information-loaded tables of distribution of scores on the various scales of the Blank for male and female high school seniors and college freshmen. These tables deserve careful and intensive study by any user of the Strong Vocational Interest Blank. Differences in interest pattern between a general high school group and a college group are observed in these tables. The section on concurrent and predictive validity of the Blank is much too short. It was a disappointment not to find more of Strong's monumental 18-year follow-up study abstracted here for the benefit of the school counselor. In summary evaluation of this booklet it must be recognized that it cannot stand alone as a single reference for the school counselor. The manual for the Blank must be referred to for accurate descriptions of the criterion occupational groups. Strong's *Vocational Interests of Men and Women* must be used to understand the intricacies of construction of the Blank. Strong's *Vocational Interests 18 Years After College* must be consulted for the best validity data and Darley and Hagenah's *Measurement of Vocational Interests* must be consulted for a more theoretical orientation to the nature of vocational interest. However, all of this does not detract from the utility of Layton's booklet. It provides a short, easy stepping stone between the manual and more intensive studies of the Blank for the beginning counselor. This, of course, was his purpose in writing this booklet. The purpose has been achieved.

Personnel & Guid J 37:396–7 Ja '59. Thomas M. Magoon. * The material on differential "popularity" of interest profiles for high school males and females, as well as for males and females in different colleges of the University of Minnesota, is particularly revealing. High school-college differences are noteworthy as are the intercollege differences, many of which present empirical evidence that would jibe with the reader's expectations. A relatively short (27 items) bibliography will lead the counselor into considerable elaborations of the topics so readably presented here. It is unfortunate that, with the focus on high school counseling use of this instrument, more attention is not paid in the next to last chapter to age correlates of inventoried interests. Such information as test-retest changes from high school to college years would encourage a more understanding use of the Blank than warnings to use the Blank with caution with individuals below the age of 20. In sum, an essential publication for any high school counselors making use of the SVIB.

[B305]

★LAYTON, WILBUR L., EDITOR. **The Strong Vocational Interest Blank: Research and Uses: Papers From the Institute on the Strong Vocational Interest Blank Held at the University of Minnesota in February 1955.** Minnesota Studies in Student Personnel Work, No. 10. Minneapolis, Minn.: University of Minnesota Press, 1960. Pp. viii, 191. Paper. $3.50. * (*PA* 36:1LC91L)

Am J Psychol 75:350 Je '62. Lawrence H. Stewart. * The psychologist who has kept up with the literature on interest measurement will find very little new information in this book. Many of the findings on which these papers were based have been published in other sources. The reader will, nevertheless, probably be interested in the somewhat informal observations and comments by these "pros" which are not usually included in published technical reports. Strong's reflections on the use of the Strong Blank will be of particular interest.

Ed & Psychol Meas 21:1075–6 w '61. Peter F. Merenda. * This excellent report....is perhaps as complete an account of the historical and operational use of the instrument and research studies conducted with it as one can imagine for a volume of its size. The report is the last of the Minnesota Studies in Student Personnel Work and, perhaps, the best of the series. * Professors as well as students of measurement, school counselors, personnel workers in business and industry, and all who are concerned with the assessment of vocational interests will find this volume both informative and instructional, and this reviewer feels that none should be without this ready reference both in his professional and personal libraries. The volume is extremely well documented. * A particularly valuable paper is that by Ralph Berdie, who....reports on the validities of the SVIB, or as he poetically states, "the verities and varieties of validities" of the SVIB. * Another especially important paper is that by John Darley, who discusses the theoretical basis of interests. This reviewer recommends this provocative paper as required reading for all users of the SVIB. * The remaining papers in this volume are of equally high caliber and serve to round out rather well what has been undoubtedly the most complete and comprehensive symposium on the research and uses of the Strong Vocational Interest Blank.

[B306]

★LEDWITH, NETTIE H. **Rorschach Responses of Elementary School Children: A Normative Study.** Pittsburgh, Pa.: University of Pittsburgh Press, 1959. Pp. xi, 185. Out of print. * (*PA* 34:1385)

Am J Orthopsychiatry 31:198–9 Ja '61. Samuel J. Beck and Anne G. Beck. * The question in judging this book, or any book that statisticizes Klopfer technique data is: What do these statistics mean for purposes of establishing spheres of reference? Klopfer and his colleagues have made it clear that their orientation is phenomenologist. Consistent with this position they reject statistics in evaluating their Rorschach test data. They are, of course, logical in so doing since statistics derived for behavioral data do not apply to phenomenological observations. Dr. Ledwith commits then the logical fallacy of using behavioral statistics for her phenomenological data. It is an error which has bedeviled the test since its use began to spread in America. Trained as our psychologists are in behavioral method, they follow the statistical scents even when they are pursuing phenomenological game. It is as though they are trying to travel at the same time in two universes that do not intersect. Actually, Dr. Ledwith's figures are results of processing, in statistical language, the phenomena in her children's minds as she judged these to be from their Rorschach test associations. Such figures are a tabular compendium of one person's judgments. Norms they are not. The present reviewers, rooted as their own habits are in the Rorschach-Oberholzer empiric-statistical approach, are aware of the valid personality descriptions which the phenomenologist technique achieves. There are more ways than one of applying Rorschach's ink-blot figures in the field of personality. But phenomenologists cannot throw out their statistical apples and have them too. * the most valuable part of the book is the sixth chapter with the full test protocols. Dr. Ledwith has justly allotted to it as much space as to the first five chapters put together. These, together with the chapter of the most frequent responses, will serve other students of the test as the raw ore out of which to help canalize the certainly all too fluid standards now at hand. All this is material out of which to construct norms. But the investigator who uses the book as it is must first decide that the quality of children's "norms" here published is such as he is willing to use.

Am J Psychol 72:653 D '59. Wayne H. Holtzman. * A somewhat cursory comparison is made between the children's norms and the rough adult "norms" suggested by Klopfer, revealing a general tendency for the later age-levels to approach the adult figures. Most Rorschach workers will find the tables and sample case presentations simple and straightforward to apply. In view of the care that went into the sampling and testing of children, it is disappointing to find no statistical analysis beyond some group comparisons and simple normative tables. No attempt is made to investigate the nature of intra-individual variability through time, a crucial question for which Ledwith's data could provide an answer. Nor has the author presented any findings of relationships between the Rorschach scores and any other test data or personality assessments. *

J Proj Tech 23:474 D '59. Mortimer M. Meyer. * The presentation is of little value to those who are seeking "ways of interpreting" records. However, there is a great deal of usefulness in terms of the opportunity to become familiar with the records of normally functioning children, especially in terms of the developmental process. This is, of course, not unique to this book. The limitation is, obviously, that the norms are based on a relatively small and homogeneous population. Nevertheless it has value in that enough of such studies will make it possible for the users of the Rorschach to get objective data to compare subjective impressions. *

[B307]

★LEDWITH, NETTIE H. **A Rorschach Study of Child Development.** Pittsburgh, Pa.: University of Pittsburgh Press, 1960. Pp. ix, 336. $6.50. * (*PA* 35:1998)

Am J Orthopsychiatry 32:564 Ap '62. Erika Fromm. * The blind interpretations included an amazing number of correct statements about the dynamics of these children and their life situations at the times when the Rorschachs were administered to them. Most of the interpreters, however, do not state *what,* specifically, in these particular Rorschach protocols provided the clues for their hypotheses nor how they critically evaluated the evidence. Therefore the cases—which form the bulk of the book—are of little value to those who want to learn to understand children's Rorschachs. Notable exceptions are the cases of Eileen (Chap. XI), Anna (Chap. XII), and Amy (Chap. XIV). The author indicates that there were no publications dealing with normal children's Rorschach responses at different age levels prior to her 1959 book, and that her present book is the first longitudinal Rorschach study published. One is puzzled by her failure to mention the normative standard work by Ames, Learned, Métraux and Walker published in 1952, and by her disregarding Halpern's publications. And one wonders why she overlooks Paulsen's "Personality Development in the Middle Years of Childhood: A Ten-Year Longitudinal Study of Thirty Public School Children by Means of Rorschach Tests and Social Histories" published in this Journal in 1954. This book contains but one reference in the text to work other than the author's own previous publication, and no bibliography.

Cont Psychol 6:298–9 S '61. Bruno Klopfer. * Any associations of the word "study" with efforts of validation or other nomothetic approaches would here be entirely misleading. In fact, one of the main values of Ledwith's book is the frankly idiographic approach to her subjects, tinged, as it is, with a warm humanitarian feeling. * The quantitative and qualitative observations contained in Chapter 17, *Some Significant Aspects of Children's Rorschachs,* will certainly be very helpful to the Rorschach worker. They are most carefully chosen. Their "phenomenological" character should have been more consciously stressed so as to emphasize the fact that they are not meant to be a substitute for validation research. Normative data, as one of the reviewers has pointed out, are not the same as validating data. Ledwith's book keeps to a careful middle ground between the frankly clinical approach of Florence Halpern's, which dispenses with normative data, and the unfortunate attempt of Ames and her group to put data into a schematic validation procedure, which actually often thwarts the interpretative meaning of the record * The eleven case studies will be of invaluable help to any school psychologist or to other workers trying to master the intricacies of the Rorschach technique with children.

J Proj Tech 24:445–6 D '60. Mortimer M. Meyer. * The title of the book is a promising one. Unfortunately the contents, although valuable, are disappointing because they do not really fulfill the promise: the "Study" promised in the title is missing. What is presented is a reporting of a series of Rorschachs with their interpretations and brief case history. The author writes as if the presentation of the series of Rorschachs with their interpretations and the associated life information is a study of child development whereas at best it is a picture of it. * It is interesting to read the series of interpretations made but no evidence is offered to verify many of the interpretations and nowhere in the book is there any reference to research or to the fact that there may be some questions as to the validity of some of the current ways of using the Rorschach. At times it seemed....as though the author were confusing raw data with validity and assumed that presentation of such data is the same as the development of theoretical concepts from data. There are some statements that appear to suggest that having Rorschach normative data is the same as validating data. On the whole, this book....has a dilettante flavor in that it contains a little bit about the children, a little bit about the way some skilled people interpret children's Rorschachs, and a little bit about the author's findings about children's Rorschachs. Any of these areas, if explored in detail would be a contribution, but the small and unexplored sampling of them, robs the book of its real potential.

[B308]

★LEFTWICH, WILLIAM H., AND REMMERS, HERMANN H. **A Comparison of Graphic and Forced-Choice Ratings of Teaching Performance at the College and University Level.** Purdue University, Division of Educational Reference, Studies in Higher Education 92. Lafayette, Ind.: the Division, June 1962. Pp. 35. Paper. $1.00. *

[B309]

★LEVINE, EDNA SIMON. **The Psychology of Deafness: Techniques of Appraisal for Rehabilitation.** New York and London: Columbia University Press, 1960. Pp. xii, 383. $7.50; 56*s*. * (*PA* 35:1003)

Am J Psychol 76:521–4 S '63. Carl W. Fuller. * The principal emphasis of the book is consistent with the author's stated purpose, namely, "to provide guides for the psychological appraisal of adults and children with impaired hearing" * The psychological examiner inexperienced in testing the deaf often finds it difficult to appreciate the stultifying influence of severe hearing loss upon language development and usage. The pervasive effects of language deprivation on examination procedures and test interpretation are carefully detailed by Levine. * Despite these difficulties Dr. Levine makes it clear that with the observance of appropriate precautions clinicians can usually enjoy the comfort of verbal communication with deaf subjects and utilize tests and test procedures with which they are already familiar. The lists of tests in Chapters 8 (adults) and 9 (children) and in Appendix H comprise a library which ought to satisfy any of the routine needs of "appraisal for rehabilitation." Part Three, which represents the book's sub-title, includes 167 of the 308 pages of main text; the subject-matter of the main title is presented in the 61 pages of Part One: "The Implications of Hearing and Impaired Hearing." The disparity in the quantity of discussion devoted to the latter topic unfortunately entails a comparable disparity in quality. A major deficiency of this section is its lack of a clear-cut definition of what "deafness" is. * To sum up, the book's discussion of the psychology of deafness is essentially a generalized introduction to an incomplete bibliography. As a "short course" in the psychometry of deaf persons, particularly adults, Dr. Levine has written one of the most helpful guides in print.

Psychiatric Q 35:197 Ja '61. * The book tends to be very repetitious; and, although the author mentions the organic nature of deafness, nowhere does she express the need for medical and psychiatric evaluation of the patient or for the medical answer to such questions as the possibility of arrest or improvement of the deafness, the effect of tinnitus, vertigo and otorrhea, the presence of psychogenic as well as central nervous system factors, and the effect of the physical environment. A useful part of the book deals with various tests which can be used at different ages and in different forms of deafness. The reviewer feels that the author's assigning of the psychologist to the center of the rehabilitation team is misplaced. For adequate treatment, vocational worker, psychologist, speech therapist, and others must remain secondary to proper medical diagnosis and therapy. For a purely psychological interpretation, however, the book is adequate and expresses the need for continued study of an important segment of the handicapped population.

[B310]

★Levine, Murray, and Spivack, George. **The Rorschach Index of Repressive Style.** Springfield, Ill.: Charles C Thomas, Publisher, 1964. Pp. xvi, 164. $7.50. * (*PA* 39:1747)

[B311]

★Liebers, Arthur. **How to Pass Employment Tests.** New York: Arco Publishing Co., Inc., 1959. Pp. ii, 99, 222, plus supplements. Paper. $3.50. *

Personnel & Guid J 39:240–1 N '60. Lyle D. Schmidt. The purpose....seems to be to acquaint readers with various types of tests used in employing or promoting people in industry, and the qualities or characteristics these tests are intended to measure so that they might have an advantage when their time comes to be tested. * In examining material of this type, one may view it from different perspectives: on the one hand, it may well give an individual an advantage on certain tests but if the tests are valid and employed properly, the persons selected will be expected to fulfill certain expectancies which no test-taking knowledge will develop. Also, everyone should have equal opportunity for knowing what to expect on tests as well as understanding test marking procedures, but how far should one go in indicating attitudes to try to convey and personality types to assume in answering tests. In general, many *Journal* readers may find themselves with some feelings of skepticism and reservation as to the actual contribution of various "How to...." publications. In any case, one might ponder the effects such publications may work on present validities, reliabilities, and predictabilities.

[B312]

★Lindvall, C. M. **Testing and Evaluation: An Introduction.** New York: Harcourt, Brace & World, Inc., 1961. Pp. viii, 264. $4.50. *

Personnel & Guid J 42:305–7 N '63. Robert H. Bauernfeind. * in Chapters 1–8 the author provides a series of excellent guidelines for teachers in preparing classroom tests. He stresses the need for using *action verbs* in setting instructional objectives; he stresses the desirability of instructional objectives stated (a) in terms of the pupil, (b) in terms of observable behaviors, and (c) in terms of the behavioral process and the specific content to which the process is to be applied (pp. 23–25). He provides an excellent discussion of content validity (pp. 39–41), and in Chapters 4–6 the author develops a highly useful discussion of the uses, advantages, and limitations of various types of teacher-made tests—essay, fill-in, true-false, multiple-choice, and matching. These are fairly short chapters, but they are highly provocative, and an instructor should be able to use them effectively as starting points for class discussions and for student projects in test-item writing. Later in the book, on pages 200–201, the author briefly introduces the idea of the behavior check list (or goal card), but he leaves this idea too quickly. Goal cards show great promise for leading teachers out of the jungle of ambiguities in the measurement field —notably problems of interpreting raw scores, norms scores, and teacher grades. The goal card shows us precisely what the pupil can and cannot do in a given field at a given time. One wishes that the author had elected to develop these two pages into a much more extensive exposition. In general this reviewer approves highly of the author's work in Chapters 1–8, as indicated above. But Chapters 9, 10, and 12 come as a series of disappointing anticlimaxes to the first eight chapters. In Chapter 9 the author presents the seemingly inevitable chapter on statistics for teachers, which almost invariably chills the teacher's enthusiasm for becoming deeply involved in better testing efforts. The reader is shown the functional notions of mean, median, and percentile rank, but he is then subjected to ways and means of computing standard deviations and T-scores—as if any sensible teacher would compute either in his day-by-day classroom work. Similarly, the notion of stanines is not introduced in Chapter 9, although many teachers do keep pupil records in terms of classroom stanines and many schools, especially in Western states, keep total school test records in terms of schoolwide stanine norms. Chapter 10, "Standardized Achievement Tests," leaves the reader with a false sense of security in several respects. He is told that the published norms for achievement tests should be "adequate," and that the claimed reliability of the scores should be "0.85 or higher." But there is no mention of schoolwide norms (which are probably most "adequate") nor of the desirability of conducting schoolwide spread-of-raw-score studies as a check on the local reliability of test scores. In short, the beginning teacher is encouraged to judge these technical qualities of published tests solely in terms of the non-comparable studies reported in test manuals. Chapter 12 presents an anemic rationale for intelligence testing in schools. The author ignores the troublesome problems of the *jangle fallacy* as, for example, in encouraging the beginning teacher to consider the Otis Beta as somehow being different from the Stanford Achievement Tests. Pages 223–226 suggest that so-called "intelligence tests" are highly useful tools for placement and programming and for individual diagnosis and guidance. Readers who accept these contentions will probably join the teacher cult of IQ devotees. Those who recognize that carefully selected achievement tests can serve each of these purposes much more effectively will probably end up wondering what Chapter 12 was all about. The Appendix, "Assigning Marks or Grades," is also weak. This chapter concentrates on techniques for "grading on the curve" while largely ignoring the alternate possibilities of assigning grades in terms of pupil growth or in terms of teachers' standards. The materials presented in Chapters 13 and 14 of Thomas' 1960 textbook *Judging Student Progress* (to cite just one example) are much more challenging than those presented in the appendix to Lindvall's book. Two further criticisms of this book should be noted. First, while the book was copyrighted in 1961, most of the writing seems to have been accomplished prior to 1959. Buros' *Fourth Mental Measurements Yearbook* (1953) is cited as the current yearbook; Cronbach's first edition (1949) is cited as current; and Thomas' first edition (1954) is cited as current. Second, there is an inordinate stress on Harcourt, Brace and World test publications in this text. Of some 61 exhibits, 57 show test materials or test data pertaining directly to this one publisher's test offerings. The reader will find *no materials* illustrating test publications of Science Research Associates, California Test Bureau, Educational Testing Service, or other prominent and ethical test publishers. The implication for the beginning teacher would seem to be that Harcourt, Brace and World has both the best and the best-known test offerings, and one wonders if the author would want to support this implication from a professional point of view. A revision of this book—improving its latter sections, correcting its present test-publisher bias, and updating its references—could well prove to be one of the best books available in the field of testing for teachers. As for the present edition, this reviewer would be glad to assign students to readings in the first eight chapters, but he would not want them to purchase it as a professional reference book for the reasons cited above.

[B313]

★LINDZEY, GARDNER. **Projective Techniques and Cross-Cultural Research.** New York: Appleton-Century-Crofts, 1961. Pp. xi, 339. $6.00. * (*PA* 37:3199)

Am Anthrop 64:1326–8 D '62. George D. Spindler. This....summary and critique of the projective techniques in their cross-cultural applications....is unparalleled in its thoroughness and in its thoughtfulness and objectivity of criticism. The result is certainly not an optimistic evaluation of the projective techniques and their cross-cultural utilization, but it leaves room for optimism. Reading it will be an absolute requirement for anyone who has any aspirations towards using projective techniques in cross-cultural research, or for that matter, in any research that uses the techniques. Lindzey begins with a concise and thoughtful overview of the reasons why anthropologists have been interested in projective techniques, some of the early studies that are particularly diagnostic of the difficulties that have been encountered, and some of the particularly important reasons for unrest about these usages among anthropologists and psychologists. * Lindzey is consistently fair and objective. He presents the pros and cons on every issue and provides a broad summary statement for each discussion. One conclusion that emerges very clearly is that anthropologists using the techniques, particularly the Rorschach, have made less progress than they should because these techniques have little systematic, accepted psychological theory to back them, and because they originated with a highly specialized and somewhat esoteric group in psychology and psychiatry who were quite removed from the domain of "respectable" academic psychology. * The needs of anthropologists are different than those of psychologists. For example, the fact that culture is revealed in the response to the Rorschach and in the way the response is made, and not always "personality structure," is not a handicap for the anthropologist as it might be for the psychologist. In many cases of cross-cultural usage the "impact of the culture" (Lindzey's term), mediated through individual responses to ambiguous but standardized stimuli under semi-controlled conditions, is precisely what we are after. In an acculturation study, for instance, the covert, less manifest level of culture than that revealed directly in house type, clothing, subsistence patterns, or ceremonial, is "projected" in Rorschach responses, and such projections are crucial if one is interested in cultural persistence exhibited in groups representing different degrees of overt acculturation. It should also be remembered that much anthropological usage of projective techniques was motivated by a search for behavioral indices that would be operationally and conceptually equivalent cross-culturally. * Much of what Lindzey has written, and that which is said in this review, points to the failure of anthropologists to develop theories and methodologies of their own relevant to the use of projective techniques in cross-cultural research. Perhaps they have been too awed by the obstructions they see in psychological theory. Or perhaps they have been confused by the confusion in personality and culture theory. In either case, it is time for another round of rigorous work on cross-cultural applications of projective techniques, for as Lindzey points out, the alternatives to the use of such techniques are no more reliable or valid and, in many cases, not as promising for the eliciting of rich, pertinent data.

Am J Sociol 68:386–8 N '62. William E. Henry. * As Lindzey comments, the book is somewhat of a survey, in that it summarizes a great deal of research in this area; it is in part a critique, in that it identifies misuses and special problems of the techniques; and it is also a cookbook, in that it provides the research person with information about the advantages and the hazards of undertaking cross-cultural research with these methods. * The treatment of review, criticism, and advice has been excellently integrated around a well-developed, and interestingly written, plot line which leads the specialist, as well as the non-specialist, through this complex field with surety. * Lindzey presents a fully developed discussion of the characteristics of the projective techniques as stimulus situations and a categorization and description of various available instruments. These two sections will be of importance for the specialist as well as the novice. * In his longest and most detailed chapter on the actual applications in cross-cultural work, the author reviews a large body of published studies. His list is extensive but is limited to studies using projective techniques in a non-literate or cross-cultural setting, excepting those studies which deal exclusively with European or modern American Societies. In this analysis he uses the issues which developed from his previous commentaries on the nature of projective techniques and of the various factors possibly determinant of response. * This chapter gives the fullest and most explicit summary of such work available in the literature * In a volume so exhaustive in its inclusions and in its analysis of the pros and cons, criticism seems almost pointless, as well [as] redundant. The reviewer would, however, call attention to three points which seem to him undertreated by Lindzey. The first is that the analysis of the situational and other non-personality contributions to response deals primarily with studies in which the variations noted stem from counts of specific content variables and not from studies in which situational variations produce inconsistent *interpretation* differences. While the evidence for it is lacking, it seems possible to wonder to what degree some, but only some, of the variations would disappear where the criterion for sameness or difference resided in personality interpretations as opposed to response content. Related to this is a second broader issue of the contribution to validity (or its absence) made by the conceptual framework of personality or social variables in terms of which the projective technique is analyzed. This framework, intervening between response and finding, becomes particularly crucial when data from another source are to be compared for purposes of determining the interrelations of instruments or the soundness of findings. Third, and perhaps ungraciously considering the tremendous task actually so successfully done, the volume is essentially psychological in nature rather than anthropological. This is entirely reasonable in the light of the discipline base in psychology of the projective techniques and of many of the investigators whose work is reviewed. However, ethnographic data have most frequently been used as criteria for validity, and Lindzey points specifically to the desirability of the tie-in to ethnographic data. In fact, prominent among the studies which he views as most successful are those characterized by a systematic relating of personality and ethnographic information. The nature and problems inherent in these criterion data and in the fieldwork setting in which they are collected, however, seem somewhat lightly treated. This book is an important one for the cross-cultural research field and for projective techniques, both in their cross-cultural and domestic use. It points up, mercilessly but without malice, the past faults and inadequacies. At the same time it describes precisely the desiderata for future work. These faults and desiderata reside within both the projective and the anthropological fields. Their presentation in this pointed and lucid form should result in future collaborative work more specific and purposeful with regard to the scientific issues in the area of culture and personality.

Cont Psychol 8:102–4 Mr '63. Bert Kaplan. * Lindzey has provided what in many respects is a classical stocktaking; the only limitation to my enthusiasm is that his critical comments have been confined mostly to methodological issues. With wisdom, thoroughness and exemplary fairness he has reviewed the bulk of the significant work in the field, given an account of methods and findings and weighed values and faults. This is undoubtedly the best methodological review that these studies have received, and it is an invaluable resource for anyone planning cross-cultural research of any kind. In preparing the groundwork for his critique, Dr. Lindzey has, incidentally, produced one of our most valuable introductions to the projective techniques themselves. Covering a span of 150 pages, his four preliminary chapters constitute both an excellent introduction to the study of projective techniques and a very sophisticated treatment of projective technique theory for advanced workers. This book then is destined to join the small handful of works that contribute significantly to the clarification of projective theory and practice. The main focus of the book, however, is the critique of the cross-cultural use of projective techniques. In summarizing what he finds wrong with this body of research, Dr. Lindzey describes the following "modal flaws": 1) the doubtful independence of many of the personality inferences; 2) the lack of objectivity in relating projective technique to ethnological sources; 3) a peculiar failure of anthropologists to provide a full description of the circumstances under which the tests were administered; 4) a failure to explore the possible contribution of nonpersonality factors; 5) an apparent unawareness of the examiner's influence on the test performance; 6) a failure to select well-matched samples where cultural groups are being compared; 7) the tendency to take group averages and treat them as descriptive of the group as a whole; and perhaps most damaging of all....the fact that there has apparently been little accumulation of sophistication and wisdom in carrying out such studies. Taken together these findings constitute a damaging criticism of the whole body of research, a damage which is not mitigated by Lindzey's corresponding list of contributions. As someone identified with cross-cultural personality research I would like to be able to controvert Dr. Lindzey's critique and defend the legitimacy of what has been done. In all honesty, however, I must say that his points seem to me to be essentially just and correct. If his demands are occasionally contradictory, as when he seems to ask for both independence from contamination by *and* full consideration of relevant ethnographic materials, or occasionally somewhat rigid as when he asks people to produce materials or analyses that are irrelevant to their particular problems, there can be little doubt that his charges are substantially correct. In mitigation it can be claimed that some of these problems are inherent in the use of projective techniques anywhere, something Dr. Lindzey acknowledges, and that other problems have to do with the fact that cross-cultural personality research has been done largely by anthropologists who are relatively untrained in the more rigorous criteria of psychological research and, more significantly, are professionally unequipped to deal with the extremely difficult problems encountered in this kind of research. We are still awaiting the serious entry of the psychologist into this field and while Dr. Lindzey's critique correctly represents the psychologist's understanding of all that is wrong with what has been going on, it also represents our failure thus far to make any significant positive contribution to the solution of problems. We can expect the anthropologist to do more careful research work, but it is not reasonable that we expect him to solve our basic problems for us.

[B314]

★Lindzey, Gardner; Bradford, Jean; Tejessy, Charlotte; and Davids, Anthony. **Thematic Apperception Test: An Interpretative Lexicon for Clinician and Investigator.** Journal of Clinical Psychology Monograph Supplement No. 12. Brandon, Vt.: Journal of Clinical Psychology, April 1959. Pp. iv, 98. Paper. $2.50. *

[B315]

★Little, Kenneth B., and Shneidman, Edwin S. **Congruencies Among Interpretations of Psychological Test and Anamnestic Data.** American Psychological Association, Psychological Monographs: General and Applied, Vol. 73, No. 6, Whole No. 476. Washington, D.C.: the Association, Inc., 1959. Pp. 42. Paper. $1.50. * (*PA* 34:3010)

[B316]

★Loevinger, Jane. **Objective Tests as Instruments of Psychological Theory.** Psychological Reports Monograph Supplement 9. Missoula, Mont.: Psychological Reports, 1957. Pp. 635–94. Paper. $2.50. (Reprinted from *Psychol Rep* 4:635–94 D '57.) *

Psychometrika 24:375–6 D '59. Robert M. W. Travers. * The mission of the monograph is to present the point of view that....such concepts as predictive, concurrent, and content validities be swept aside as mere handmaidens of a psychotechnology of dubious scientific status. The clean sweep would also include such off-brand varieties of validity as factorial validity. In their place, it is proposed, the only concept of validity which be retained is that of construct validity, a concept which is developed more fully in this monograph than it has been developed elsewhere. It is argued that predictive, concurrent, and content validity are ad hoc concepts which have little to do with what the scientist does or what he needs to know. * The central purpose of the monograph is to clarify the concept of construct validity and to begin to establish it as an idea of central importance in the development of a science of behavior. Jane Loevinger is attempting to initiate a revolution in thinking in the area of psychometrics so that the instruments that evolve will be instruments for scientific advance rather than gadgets in a technology. Objective tests, she believes, are to play a central role in the development of psychological theory. Tests must be based on a theory of test behavior which is to be related to a theory of behavior in nontest situations. The elements in a psychological theory, it appears, are variables, but it is not clear whether these are or are not to be defined by objective tests. The monograph proposes that the concept of validity be considered to include two components. One of these is the substantive component which is "the extent to which the content of the items included in (and excluded from?) the test can be accounted for in terms of the trait believed to be measured and the context of measurement." * the reviewer is left with the uneasy feeling that Loevinger is concerned with intuitively derived psychological theory rather than that in which the constructs are hypothetical and include unobservables * The second major component of validity proposed in the monograph is the structural component, which is a much better defined concept than is the substantive component. The structural component refers to "the extent to which structural relations between test items parallel the structural relations of other manifestations of the trait being measured." Interpreted in terms of the language of systematic psychology, one might say that structural validity implies that relations between responses within test situations should parallel in some way the relations discovered between responses in nontest situations. * The monograph provides an overview of various structural models that have been used and the problems which they involve. Under this heading the author has included quantitative models, class models, and dynamic models. The material could be dry to read, but it is not. Novel ways of looking at the problems involved add a continuous source of freshness to the discussion. Indeed, the incidental comments alone make this monograph worth reading, but it contains much more than incidental material. Loevinger writes with a contagious enthusiasm for her subject. Whether the reader agrees or disagrees with the arguments presented, he will come away from the monograph with the feeling that he has lived through a refreshing and worthwhile experience.

[B317]

★Long, Nicholas J.; Cook, Anne R.; Evans, Ellis D.; Kerr, Joan; Linke, Linda A.; Neubauer, Barbara; and Payne, David C. **Groups in Perspective: A New Sociometric Technique for Classroom Teachers.** Bulletin of the School of Education, Indiana University, Vol. 38, No. 6. Bloomington, Ind.: Indiana University Bookstore, 1962. Pp. xi, 112. Paper. $1.25. * (*PA* 37:7212)

[B318]

★Lyman, Howard B. **Test Scores and What They Mean.** Englewood Cliffs, N.J.: Prentice-Hall, Inc., 1963. Pp. xv, 223. Text price, $3.75; trade price, $5.00. (London: Prentice-Hall International, Inc. 32s.) * (*PA* 37:7973)

Cont Psychol 9:64+ F '64. Arthur P. Coladarci. * It is understandably disturbing, particularly to a psychometrician like Lyman, to observe that approximately one million tests per school day are used in American schools and....to realize that the personnel of that institution modally have very little preparation for the task of selecting, constructing, administering, and interpreting the measures they employ. * Nor is the picture any more reassuring if one looks at other groups that have significant recourse to tests: social workers, admissions officers, personnel specialists, etc. * The author has a long line of predecessors who have tried to raise the level of psychometric sophistication among experienced professional workers by providing them a brief, simplified, and "practical" guide to the use and interpretation of tests. My impression is that such ventures have produced very little effect (as distinguished from sales volume). If the impression is correct, it is not surprisingly so since "the complete tester" approach appears to involve two fallacies: (1) assuming that the in-service person feels the need for the understanding promised by the little book, and (2) the assumption that any intelligently usable and critical understanding of tests and their interpretation can be provided *briefly* and *simply.* Although Lyman has provided a book which is a notable and rewarding exception among those with similar general intent, a considerable portion of its content seems to commit both fallacies—and almost certainly the second. What, for example, can be communicated effectively about "content validity" in a half-page? Or, again, what consequents can be expected to follow from a presentation of the total gamut of reliability-determination, when that presentation must be limited to a little more than five pages of text? In short, brevity and simplification have been accomplished at the expense of understanding and applicability. The second half of this book, however, fully justifies its publication and comprises a genuine contribution to the literature of educational measurement. Lyman offers classification systems for norms and for derived scores—the latter so systematic and suggestive as to approach a taxonomy. It is likely that anyone who has dealt with norms tables will profit from distinctions offered by Lyman, which make it possible quickly to distinguish the conceptual and technical differences among various norming approaches and formats. The classification scheme for derived scores which, like the classification for norms, is apparently original with the author, goes far beyond the usual and rather coarse distinction between (1) comparison with an absolute standard, (2) inter-individual comparisons, and (3) intra-individual comparisons. The author has ordered inter-individual comparisons, in terms or derived scores utilizing primarily mean and standard deviation, rank, range and same-score-status schemes (e.g., age scores). Indeed, so heuristic is Lyman's original classification system that one wishes that it had been (and will be) included in the standard textbooks in educational measurement and, thereby more likely....get the attention of the masses of potential professional people in conventional training programs. * That is, the student in a usual course may need a frame of reference for thinking about scores (and for implying the technical procedures that produce scores); a frame of reference that permits him to identify or innovate a scoring system and interpretation *relevant to a given purpose* and, conversely, interpret meaningfully any given score or set of scores in terms of the score-producing operations. Lyman's schemata seem worthy of consideration as tools to this end.

Ed & Psychol Meas 24:153–4 sp '64. Richard E. Schutz and James C. Moore. * Lyman ....follows the lead of previous authors of "simplified" measurement and statistics books in equating a condensed treatment with an easily-learned treatment. Unfortunately, an incomplete presentation is as unsuitable for the novice as an exhaustive one. The beginning student whose limited objective is to increase the accuracy of his classroom decisions is left stranded and confused by either approach. Although well-intentioned, there is some danger that the book will foster a negative attitude toward testing in general. In keeping with the informal style in which the book is written, Lyman sprinkles in numerous short illustrative examples, set off from the context in smaller type. Almost without exception these illustrations describe faulty test practices. While the text clearly emphasizes that this is "what not to do," the novice may well conclude that testing is so complicated and risky that he had best avoid it altogether. In using the book instructionally, we would suggest "starting at the back." The appendix contains a well-designed table for converting derived acores from one mode to another. Comparable scores for z, T, AGCT, CEEB, Wechsler, Stanford Binet, stanine, C, sten, and percentile ranks are given. Following the table is a chart summarizing the rationale, advantages, and limitations of each score. A carefully guided inspection of the relationships among these score systems would provide a basis for considering the chapter on profiles and the final three chapters dealing with rule-of-thumb aspects of reporting test results. This material will at least be intelligible to the intelligent but uninformed adult to whom the entire book is directed. Such a person should profit from this semi-technical material and should be a better test-user because of it. This is likely a more limited objective than Lyman hoped to attain, but one for which the reviewers would happily settle.

Personnel & Guid J 42:524–5 Ja '64. J. O. Crites. There has been a need for a book like this one for some time and now the need has been largely filled. Lyman set himself the task of analyzing, classifying, and explaining the meaning of the various kinds of scores which are used in psychological testing. * The chapter on types of scores is the major contribution of the book, and one which should be read and re-read by counselors and others who interpret tests, but there are other chapters which deal with related subjects. Some of these are excellent, whereas others are only mediocre. The chapter entitled "A Few Statistics" is one of the best which has been written as a background for a discussion of test scores. * Particularly noteworthy in this chapter is the clarity of the examples which are used to illustrate statistical concepts. Also valuable is the inclusion of the discussion of expectancy tables in this chapter, which follows naturally from the preceding section on the standard error of estimate. It is unfortunate, however, that a fuller, more detailed comparison of expectancy tables with norms was not made in the chapter on the latter topic. Lyman briefly mentions their similarities and differences but does not emphasize strongly enough the basic difference between them. Expectancy tables are derived from the relationship between *two* variables, whereas norms are based upon only *one* variable. * Certain cautions in the use of norms are made, such as not comparing percentile ranks for tests with different norm groups, but more could have been said about the selection of the appropriate norm group to use for particular counseling or selection problems. * The other major chapter of the book is on "Basic Attributes of the Test," in which Lyman discusses the validity, reliability, and usability of tests. Perhaps it is because of the present lack of agreement and clarity in conceptualizing the validity and reliability of tests, but whatever the reason, this chapter is more confusing than it is informative. Lyman differentiates between "face" and "content" validity by the unconvincing criterion that the latter is more sophisticated, in the sense that "the test content is examined in detail." Concurrent and predictive validity are lumped together under the rubric "empirical validity," but with no explanation of why factorial and construct validity are not also "empirical." Construct validity is simply described as being like empirical validity, because "it typically involves a correlation between test scores and values of another variable," but it is distinguishable because "the outside variable is not really a criterion, even though it is a variable which should relate logically to the test" (p. 30). From these comments, it is difficult to know exactly what construct validity is, which is disturbing because Lyman considers it "the most important type in psychological theory" (p. 30). In short, a chapter such as this one on the basic concepts in test construction, which is only 12 pages in length, might have profitably been expanded and other chapters shortened or omitted. In particular, the chapters "Common Sense," "What Can We Say," and "Experts Still Needed" are largely superficial and superfluous. * The implication is that the book is probably better designed for additional readings in course assignments or selective reading in in-service training rather than as a primary text in a course on test scores and their meaning. As such, it is excellent and should find widespread acceptance among test users.

[B319]

★MacArthur, R. S., and Hunka, S. **School Examination Practices and Standards in Alberta: Condensed From a Report Submitted to the Royal Commission on Education in Alberta in February, 1959.** University of Alberta Monographs on Education, Monograph No. 2. Edmonton, Alta., Canada: Alberta Advisory Committee on Educational Research, Faculty of Education, the University, 1958. Pp. v, 66. Paper. $2.00. *

[B320]

★MacArthur, R. S.; Irvine, S. H.; and Brimble, A. R. **The Northern Rhodesia Mental Ability Survey 1963.** Rhodes-Livingstone Communication No. 27. Lusaka, Zambia: Rhodes-Livingstone Institute, 1964. Pp. ix, 100. Paper. 21*s.* *

[B321]

★McCann, Forbes E. **The Flexible Passing Point.** Personnel Brief No. 10. Chicago, Ill.: Public Personnel Association, 1959. Pp. 15. Paper, lithotyped. $2.00. *

[B322]

*McIntosh, Douglas M.; Walker, David A.; and Mackay, Donald. **The Scaling of Teachers' Marks and Estimates, Revised Edition.** Edinburgh, Scotland: Oliver & Boyd Ltd., 1962. Pp. xii, 182. 18*s.* 6*d.* *

Ont J Ed Res 5:188–9 sp '63. Dormer Ellis. * Outside of research, scaling of marks is rarely undertaken. The authors....reiterate the plea for between-subject and between-school comparability of marks and advocate certain procedures by which this could be accomplished. They hold that the neglect of scaling is largely due to the widespread belief among classroom teachers, principals, and supervisors that it demands a level of mathematical sophistication and perhaps also an amount of computational drudgery that it is unreasonable to expect of the practical worker in education. The book under review is an attempt to dispel this belief. * a useful contribution to the literature on scaling in that it includes applications of the theory to actual sets of teachers' marks. The calculations are shown in detail. Numerous exercises are provided, the answers to which are given at the back of the book. The reader needs no knowledge of mathematics beyond the elementary operations of arithmetic. Rigorous proofs are avoided but some attempt has been made to make the formulae and procedures appear reasonable. * As the book is intended primarily for use in the United Kingdom, the scaling methods recommended by the authors are applied to the "Primary to Secondary Transfer Stage" and to the "Leaving Certificate" level. However, the statistical procedures that are advocated are not inherently limited to these applications but could be generalized to include many other situations. * a suitable text for an in-service course in educational measurement for practising teachers.

For reviews of the first edition, see 4:B255.

[B323]

★McLaughlin, Kenneth F., Editor. **Understanding Testing: Purposes and Interpretations for Pupil Development.** Prepared by the Guidance, Counseling, and Testing Section, Division of State and Local School Systems, United States Department of Health, Education, and Welfare. Washington, D.C.: United States Government Printing Office, 1960. Pp. v, 24. Paper. $0.25. * [A reprinting of articles from the September 1959 issue of *School Life.*]

[B324]

★McMurry, Robert N. **Tested Techniques of Personnel Selection.** Chicago, Ill.: Dartnell Corporation, 1961. Variously paged. Loose leaf binding.

$24.00. * For a listing and review of the rating forms, see 1119.

[B325]

*MAGNUSON, HENRY W.; GIPE, MELVIN W.; AND SHELLHAMMER, THOMAS A. **Evaluating Pupil Progress, 1960 Edition.** California State Department of Education Bulletin, Vol. 29, No. 14. Sacramento, Calif.: the Department, 1960. Pp. vii, 229. Paper. $1.00. * For reviews of the first edition, see 5:B283.

[B326]

★MAGNUSSON, DAVID. **A Study of Ratings Based on TAT.** Swedish Council for Personnel Administration, Report No. 22. Stockholm, Sweden: Almqvist & Wiksell, 1959. Pp. 176. Paper. Sw. kr. 26. * (*PA* 34:1394)

Percept & Motor Skills 9:336 S '59. C. H. Ammons. A most stimulating and valuable study of inter-rater reliability and concurrent validity of the TAT responses of 65 21-yr.-old male students. Two measures of intelligence (F-test by Haernquist and the Cornell Index), a sentence completion test, Rorschach, a color test, a questionnaire, and the TAT were administered. Students also rated each other. A factor analysis and a cluster analysis of student ratings were made. Comparison of scoring by four examiners was made for a number of variables. Despite less than desirable English, psychologists will find the data presented useful and well organized.

[B327]

★MAHER, T. F. **Ability Tests for Transition Classes.** Leeds, England: E. J. Arnold & Son Ltd., 1960. Pp. 62. Paper. 3*s.* 6*d.* (*Answer Book.* Pp. 12. Paper. 1*s.*) *

[B328]

★MALTZMAN, IRVING; SIMON, SEYMORE; RASKIN, DAVID; AND LICHT, LEONARD. **Experimental Studies in the Training of Originality.** American Psychological Association, Psychological Monographs: General and Applied, Vol. 74, No. 6, Whole No. 493. Washington, D.C.: the Association, Inc., 1960. Pp. 23. Paper. $1.00. *

[B329]

★MANDELL, MILTON MICHAEL. **The Employment Interview.** AMA Research Study 47. New York: American Management Association, Inc., 1961. Pp. 110. Paper. $4.50. *

[B330]

★MARKKANEN, TOUKO. **An Exact Factor Analytical Approach to Differences in Personality Structure Between Alcoholics and the Normal Group.** Reprint from *Drinking and Drinkers,* Publication No. 6 of the Finnish Foundation for Alcohol Studies. Helsinki, Finland: the Foundation, 1957. Pp. 37. Paper. $1.50. *

[B331]

★MARKS, PHILIP A., AND SEEMAN, WILLIAM. **The Actuarial Description of Personality: An Atlas for Use With the MMPI.** Baltimore, Md.: Williams & Wilkins Co., 1963. Pp. xxv, 331. $7.50. * (London: Baillière, Tindall & Cox, Ltd. 60*s.*)

[B332]

*MATHEWS, DONALD K. **Measurement in Physical Education, Second Edition.** Philadelphia, Pa. and London: W. B. Saunders Co., 1963. Pp. xi, 373. $6.75; 47*s.* *

[B333]

★MAXWELL, JAMES. **The Level and Trend of National Intelligence: The Contribution of the Scottish Mental Surveys.** Publications of the Scottish Council for Research in Education 46. London: University of London Press Ltd., 1961. Pp. 77. Paper, 5*s.*; cloth, 7*s.* 6*d.* *

[B334]

★MEHDI, BAQER. **Guide to Reference Materials in Educational Measurement and Evaluation.** Delhi, India: Central Institute of Education, National Council of Educational Research and Training, 1962. Pp. viii, 27. Paper. Gratis. *

[B335]

★MEHDI, BAQER. **Guide to Reference Materials in Tests and Measurements.** Delhi, India: Central Institute of Education, National Council of Educational Research and Training, 1962. Pp. vii, 51. Paper. Gratis. *

[B336]

*MENDEL, A. O. **Personality in Handwriting: A Handbook of American Graphology, Second Edition.** New York: Stephen Daye Press, 1958. Pp. 376. $5.00. (London: Peter Owen Ltd. 35*s.*)

Occup Psychol 33:64–5 Ja '59. P. E. Vernon. In a promising introductory chapter, Mr Mendel points out that the deviations in a person's handwriting from the pattern he was originally taught represent a type of expressive movement which, like his gestures, depend on central nervous organization, not merely on peripheral musculature. In theory, then, handwriting should reflect personality trends in much the same way as do responses to Rorschach, or drawings. Though their interpretation, like that of most projective devices, is likely to remain largely an artistic, intuitive process, the author sets out to provide a logical and complete system of analysis, based on the principles established by the great European graphologists, such as Klages, Saudek and Pulver. However, as soon as the exposition begins, we find that many of the qualities of handwriting on which interpretation is based are highly subjective and insusceptible of exact definition—for example "rhythm" and "symmetry." And it is not long before we meet such obviously questionable claims as: "A wide lower margin may be interpreted as superficiality (of character) as well as fear of a sexual or emotional trauma." At no point is any scientifically acceptable evidence offered for any of these hunches, nor any proof that graphology can provide valid diagnoses for vocational, psychiatric or other purposes. The book is well-written and illustrated, and it does bring out that the graphologist takes his job seriously; he conducts an extraordinarily detailed analysis of innumerable features of a script, and weighs up the inferences he draws from these against one another in somewhat the same way as does the clinical psychologist or psychiatrist. But it is clear that no progress whatever has been made towards putting graphology on a scientific footing. Despite the good work of Saudek, and the sympathetic attitude of such psychologists as Gordon Allport, Gardner Murphy, and Wolff, we are forced to treat graphological claims with even greater caution than we do those of devotees of Rorschach and T.A.T.

For reviews of the first edition, see 4:B268.

[B337]

★MESSICK, SAMUEL, AND ROSS, JOHN, EDITORS. **Measurement in Personality and Cognition.** New York and London: John Wiley & Sons, Inc., 1962. Pp. xi, 334. $5.75; 45s. * (*PA* 38:2638)

Cont Psychol 9:88–9 F '64. Walter Mischel. * many of the viewpoints and research reports are already well-known and a number have been seen published in other sources. There is no single focus to the conference: rather, a sampling of views and research efforts is presented. The main topics that emerge include psychometric paper and pencil tests, response sets, and individual differences in "cognitive styles." * Perhaps most interesting are the commentary chapters by authors who do not concentrate on presentations of their own research findings. These chapters point out fundamental methodological problems which bedevil much of the reported research. Although the points frequently seem fairly obvious, they clearly need to be remembered and incorporated into new research designs. *

[B338]

★MEYERS, C. E.; ORPET, R. E.; ATTWELL, A. A.; AND DINGMAN, H. F. **Primary Abilities at Mental Age Six.** Monographs of the Society for Research in Child Development, Vol. 27, No. 1, Serial No. 82. Lafayette, Ind.: Child Development Publications, 1962. Pp. 40. Paper. $1.50. * (*PA* 38:8462)

[B339]

★MEYERS, CARLTON R., AND BLESH, T. ERWIN. **Measurement in Physical Education.** New York: Ronald Press Co., 1962. Pp. vii, 473. $6.50. *

[B340]

★MEYERSON, LEE. **Hearing for Speech in Children: A Verbal Audiometric Test.** Acta Oto-Laryngologica Supplementum 128. Stockholm, Sweden: Almqvist & Wiksell, 1956. Pp. xv, 165. Paper. Out of print. *

[B341]

★MILLER, ARTHUR L., EDITOR. **Tests and Measurements in Lutheran Education.** Lutheran Education Association, Fourteenth Yearbook, 1957. River Forest, Ill.: the Association, 1959. Pp. xi, 115. Paper. $2.00. *

[B342]

MINER, JOHN B. **Intelligence in the United States: A Survey—With Conclusions for Manpower Utilization in Education and Employment.** New York: Springer Publishing Co., Inc., 1957. Pp. xii, 180. $4.75. * (*PA* 32:1344)

Cont Psychol 3:69–70 Mr '58. Dorothy Ransom. * Introductory chapters on the nature and measurement of intelligence, and concluding chapters on implications for manpower utilization * they reflect more the ideologies of military and industrial management (with overtones of racialism) than of the conservation of human resources. Advertisements inform us that "this study of intelligence testing and the concept of intelligence gives substance to the growing debate on the validity of existing standards." The standards in question are those that include the developmental and evolutional aspects of psychological concepts of intelligence. Here Miner follows and goes beyond Wechsler in dispensing with measurements of rate of learning. For him the standard deviation goes the way of the mental age and the intelligence quotient. The accumulated scientific knowledge of how the individual and the species progress slowly toward fuller degrees of consciousness is separated off from the scientific psychology by the psychometric device of measuring intelligence in terms of a single score on an abbreviated form of the Thorndike Vocabulary Test. In this choice Miner follows, and again goes beyond, R. L. Thorndike in the scope of application of one part of the research methodology Thorndike has been developing over the years. Miner demonstrates that the scope of predictions for purposes of control is not confinable to the limits of available knowledge. To predict that it is "less probable that any given Negro student (than any white student) will score above the 10th percentile," only 25 Negro students' scores on the vocabulary test, administered by public-opinion-poll interviewers, were required. If enough people read and believe the prediction, educational opportunities for Negroes could eventually become limited enough to make the prediction come true. Only a slightly larger number of such test scores for employed adult Negroes were required for the prediction that "there are apparently very few Negroes who left school at an educational level markedly below that which they might have attained." The becoming true of this prediction might be slower, since it would involve some suppression of the biological inheritance of intelligence in Negroes. Miner presents the scientist whose "ultimate aim [in George A. Kelly's words] is to predict and control." By substituting group constructs for "personal constructs," and the management of the psychological factors that determine the governmental processes of a nation for "client management," this vigorous and purposeful younger member of the profession has condensed Kelly's 1218 pages into a slender 180 pages. It might be possible to shrug off the book as not very important, as perhaps an ill-timed and not scientifically accurate work, did it not so clearly reflect, and so greatly magnify, the flaws inherent in that philosophy of science which serves as the frame of reference for an increasing number of present-day American psychologists. With the cutting off of the biological concepts of slow maturation and evolution of human mental processes, something goes wrong with the time element in human planning. Processes of maturation and evolution give way to planned processes of a revolutionary nature, both in the planning of controls over the minds of individuals (as in "client management") and in the planning of controls over the distribution of the population, a process upon which the democratic governmental process is dependent. (Miner recommends a psychometric model of manpower management, one which by his definition of the conditions under which it could be carried out would of necessity change a democratic into a totalitarian regime.) Within the frame of reference of a philosophy of science that denies the value of knowing for the sake of knowing, and of communicating knowledge for the sake of increasing the sum of human consciousness, "scientific" predictions of a propagandistic nature are just as scientific as those that give knowledge of natural laws, for each can equally well be proved to have come true at some later date. Because of that philosophy of science, it is not inconsistent for the volume to give liberal space in its bibliographical references to the notoriously racially prejudiced writers, J. C. F. McGurk and Henry E. Garrett, while omitting mention of other workers—Gilliland, Benedict, Weltfish, Marcus, Bitterman—who have cast doubt on differences between Negro and white intellectual capacities. Nor was it a non sequitur for it to use, for analysis of the data, statistical procedures that have no logical explanation for their choice other than that they give the impression of a greater than real difference between Negro and white intellectual capacities.

Cont Psychol 3:207 Jl '58. Henry E. Garrett. [A reply to the above review by Dorothy Ransom.] The review....violates the letter as well as the spirit of good reviewing in the field of science. Miner's study is concerned with factors related to adult intelligence in the U.S. with a view toward a better utilization of American manpower. From this review, *CP*'s readers would never discover what the author set out to do and how well he did it. But they would be able to make several inferences with regard to the temper and good judgment of the reviewer. The Editor says in his blurb describing Miss Ransom that "she is a strong believer in scientific measurement and in political democracy and she sees no reason why one cannot support the other." This is all very fine, but it hardly justifies her using Miner as a soapbox. Miss Ransom writes that "Miner recommends a psychometric model of manpower management, one which by his definition of the conditions under which it could be carried would of necessity change a democratic into a totalitarian regime." This is as unequivocably false as it is badly written. I am, of course, interested in the gratuitous insult which Miss Ransom tenders to Dr. F. C. McGurk and me. The issue here is quite simple. McGurk and I believe that the mental-test data indicate the existence of racial differences which are probably genetic. Others, whom Miss Ransom evidently favors, hold the opposite view. Heretofore, clashes of opinion in science have been resolved by appeals to the evidence, re-analysis of the existing data, and the suggestion of new experiments. To settle a controversy by invective and name-calling is a new approach. For *CP*'s reviewer to refer to Dr. McGurk and to me as "notoriously racially prejudiced writers" is uncalled for, untrue, and, I suspect, malicious. The Editor of *CP* is just as culpable as his reviewer.

Cont Psychol 3:207 Jl '58. John B. Miner. [A reply to the above review by Dorothy Ransom.] * Dorothy Ransom has made certain statements about my intent in writing the book and my attitudes toward Negroes, democratic government, science, etc., which I cannot permit to go unchallenged. It is frankly almost unbelievable to me that any reviewer, after reading the book, could come to the conclusions that Miss Ransom has reached. * I....hope that the following statements will serve to eradicate from the minds of *CP*'s readers any notion that *Intelligence in the United States* was a deliberate attempt to clothe anti-Negro and totalitarian motives in scientific garb. 1. Far from being anti-Negro in orientation, I am, if anything, biased in the opposite direction. In fact, it was my private wish during the initial stages of the data analysis that the Negro group would turn out to be as intelligent as the whites. When this proved not to be the case and it became obvious that I must report results similar to those obtained by so many other psychologists, I decided to devote a small section of the book to a discussion of the factors that might account for my findings. In thus briefly outlining the nature of the problem as I saw it, I hoped to contribute in some small way to increased understanding and perhaps an ultimate solution. Certainly any idea of making the lot of American Negroes any more difficult than it already is, was furthest from my mind. 2. With regard to Miss Ransom's assumption that I favor totalitarian methods of manpower control, I can only once again state that she could not be more wrong. It is my belief that effective manpower utilization can be and should be achieved within a democratic framework and I have so stated throughout the book. Nor can I accept the view that research of this type necessarily fosters a totalitarian system. The democratic process cannot operate to produce change unless the society has an opportunity to become aware of any deficiencies that may exist as a result of present policies. For this reason I believe that continued study in the area of manpower utilization is essential to the survival of our democracy in a changing world. We do not solve manpower problems by refusing to study them any more than we eliminate the threat of Russian communism by closing our eyes to the factors which perpetuate it. In writing a book about manpower utilization, I have no doubt exposed myself to the risk of being called undemocratic, just as students of Russian history and thought have faced the danger of being termed pro-communist. Contrary to Miss Ransom's assumptions, however, the conduct of research in the manpower field is not sufficient grounds for labeling a man as a proponent of totalitarian government. In fact quite the contrary may well be the case. 3. Perhaps most disturbing of all is my reviewer's accusation that I have perverted the scientific process to achieve preconceived objectives. I feel strongly that any scientist must strive to design his research and analyze his data in the manner which he believes is most likely to produce valid results. This should be the sole criterion. Whatever the shortcomings of my research procedures, I can assure *CP*'s readers that their choice was not motivated by a desire to foster racialism and a totalitarian system of government in this country. The study was conducted and the findings were interpreted with every effort to achieve as objective a research product as possible. Finally, may I suggest that those of *CP*'s readers, who read Miss Ransom's review and believed what they found there, glance through the book itself, especially the 7 or 8 pages on the Negro, and see for themselves whether there is any truth in her accusations. I believe they will find that there is not.

Cont Psychol 3:280 S '58. Frank C. J. McGurk. [A reply to the above review by Dorothy Ransom.] * Miss Dorothy Ransom refers to me as one of two "notoriously racially prejudiced writers." Miss Ransom does not say why she so regards me, but by her suggestion to Dr. Miner that he could have done better by referring to the publications of Gilliland, Benedict, Weltfish, Marcus, and Bitterman, Miss Ransom seems to imply that their work on the problems of the Negro-white difference was more preferable to her than was mine. To me there is only one reason why a critic indulges in name-calling, and that is because the critic dislikes something, but has no other basis for criticizing it. If there is factual objection to a published point of view, the critic need not call names, but needs only to state the factual objection. In this way, students of the problem may check the factual objection for its accuracy. But by name-calling, the critic masks the objection, and neither the impugned writer nor students of the problem know where to begin to correct the implied error. The problem of the Negro-white test-score difference needs a factual solution. It cannot be solved merely by saying that it does not exist, nor by the opinions of distinguished social scientists who do not wish to have it exist. The shape and size of the earth would never have been known had the opinions of the distinguished geographers and astronomers of the time been heeded; the sun would have continued to revolve around a flat disc supported by four gigantic elephants standing firmly in the heavens. If we continue to invest the race difference problem with moral considerations, we shall continue to live on a flat disc. I should appreciate it if Miss Ransom would do what scientists are expected to do with each other's works. I should like to have her point out the factual errors in my studies. Students of the problem would consider that a very constructive deed.

For additional reviews, see 5:B293.

[B343]

★Mira y Lopez, Emilio. **M.K.P.: Myokinetic Psychodiagnosis.** Translated by Mrs. Jacques Dubois from the 1951 French Edition. New York: [Hoeber Medical Division, Harper & Row, Publishers, Inc.], 1958. Pp. xx, 186. $6.75. (London: Harper & Row Ltd. 51*s.*) * (*PA* 33:7261)

A.M.A. Arch Gen Psychiatry 1:558–9 N '59. Sidney J. Blatt. * This is an all-too-short introduction to an ingenious and fascinating technique. Although in large measure the book is devoted to details of administration, scoring, and normative data, the few pages that deal with theoretical rationale and the presentation of clinical findings suggest that this procedure has great promise. Many questions can be raised about the lack of theoretical rationale, the questionable and sometimes esoteric interpretative assumptions, the brevity of the clinical summaries, and the limited and inadequate data on reliability and validity. These shortcomings, however, do not detract from the intrinsic value of the procedure or from the significance of the findings that are presented. * Though it would have been helpful to have seen empirical data on these findings, and to know more about the criteria used in differentiating the types of schizophrenias and depressions, it is apparent that Professor Mira y Lopez has developed a valuable diagnostic technique. The procedure takes on even greater significance, since it fills a gap in the types of psychodiagnostic procedures that are available. * The M.K.P. may not assume a predominant role in the usual clinical battery, for it gives little insight into the dynamic and structural aspects of personality. However, it should prove to be invaluable in situations where nonverbal diagnostic procedures are required. More important, however, is the fact that now motor correlates of nonverbal, and hopefully preverbal, experiences can be systematically studied by this technique and integrated with observations made on higher levels of psychological development. The integration of these various levels of psychological functioning should aid in refining diagnostic procedures, as well as in making significant contributions to psychological theory. The introduction of the M.K.P. in its present form should stimulate necessary research to examine the theoretical assumptions and clinical utility of the test.

Cont Psychol 5:362–4 N '60. David Wechsler. * Professor Mira, once Spain's distinguished psychologist at Barcelona and now Director of the Institute for Professional Selection and Guidance at Rio de Janeiro, has long been interested in the development of expressive techniques for the study of the personality. His Myokinetic test (M.K.P.) is a new effort in this direction, and one of the most promising. Like other quantitative measures of expressive movement, the M.K.P. has an initial appeal of being "objective," that is to say, of requiring minimal interaction between investigator and subject. It furnishes a motor approach to the appraisal of personality and, because of its simplicity, offers the beleaguered clinician a less tortuous road to psychodiagnosis. For any or all of these reasons, one would have expected Professor Mira's ingenious test to have attracted American psychologists. Actually it has not. Professor Gordon Allport, in his foreword to the present volume, expresses the view that the lack of American interest in the M.K.P. may be due in part "to the aura of charlatanry" with which graphological methods have been viewed in this country and, in part, "because studies in this area are difficult to execute." These factors, however, are at most but a small part of the story.

A more immediate reason for the scant attention which the M.K.P. has received in America arises from the competition it has had to meet from already espoused projective techniques, particularly the TAT and the Rorschach. American clinicians have not only been thoroughly "sold" on the latter, but, in this reviewer's opinion, have been unduly impressed by the role which perception plays in the structuring of personality. They have seemingly lost sight of the fact that the *persona* is determined not only by how one takes in the world but also by what one does to it. Professor Mira's researches do a great deal to reinstate the motor components of behavior as correlates of human personality. * The current volume is a definitive exposition of the present status of the M.K.P. as a systematic technique for appraising various aspects of personality. It is also organized to serve as a manual for the administration and interpretation of the test. * the M.K.P. consists essentially of a number of simple motor tasks in which the subject is required to make a series of movements "in the fundamental directions of space." This requirement is met by having the subject first trace lines of set length in different spatial planes (later, also some supplementary figures) and then requiring him to continue drawing the same lines with his vision occluded. He does this alternately with the right and the left hand, and in the case of several of the figures, with both hands simultaneously. The general assumption of the test procedure is that the movement of each hand "has a particular significance according to the way it is executed" and that "disturbances of psychic tension should be transferred into the domain of muscular tension provided we can eliminate the voluntary correction of the subject." Evaluation of the subject's productions is made in terms of the differences in the length of his drawn lines in comparison with the standard. * According to Mira, movements of the dominant and nondominant hands are related to the different levels of conscious and unconscious control respectively. The right is the educated, the left the uneducated hand. The former represents the acquired, the controlled; the latter, the primitive and instinctive trends. Concomitantly, deviations in the different planes (vertical, horizontal, sagittal) are associated with temperament and characterological traits. Thus, positive primary deviations in the vertical plane signify elation, negative deviation signifies depression. A positive deviation in the horizontal plane shows extratension, a negative deviation reveals intratension. Positive deviation in the sagittal plane is indicative of heteroaggression, negative deviation of autoaggression. Interpretation of these indicated traits depends, in addition, upon whether the deviations are manifested more intensively by the left or right hand. In general, traits inferred from the movements of the left hand are interpreted as constitutional and deep-rooted; those of the right hand as temporary and culturally determined. The foregoing trait assessments are derived primarily from the execution of the initial portion of the test, namely, from the drawings of the lines in the different planes, and are referred to as the *lineograms.* The other parts of the test involving reproduction of various figures such as the *zigzag, chains, staircase,* etc., are used primarily to confirm the information already obtained from the lineograms, although in some instances they also furnish additional diagnostic material. In the reviewer's experience, execution of the added figures consumes much more time than the basic lineograms, and his feeling is that most of the supplementary figures could be omitted without seriously impairing the value of the test. The time factor is of moment not only in the matter of administration but also in the scoring of the test. Mira mentions some 79 recommended measurements, many of which are difficult to make and for the most part are unsupported by available norms. Some of the recommended measures may be of value for research purposes, but in the practical application of the test the reviewer has not found most of them utilizable. The test would gain much as a clinical instrument if substantially shortened. One regrettable weakness of the book is the author's somewhat cavalier presentation of his theoretical formulations, which are often cryptic and not infrequently hard to follow. Some of the difficulty in comprehending parts of the text may be due to strict linguistic fidelity to which the editors seemingly committed themselves in translating from the original Spanish or French versions. * the author and the editors could have made out a better case for the predictive potential of the test by presenting in some detail the findings of other investigators. The book has a bibliography of some 127 titles, but very few of them are effectively utilized or referred to in the text. * Altogether, the M.K.P. constitutes a basic contribution to the evergrowing field of projective tests. It is rooted more firmly on the objective performance of the examinee and less subject to arbitrary interpretations by the examiner than are most other projective techniques. Moreover it deals with and brings to light aspects of the personality which sensory-perceptual approaches often fail to reveal. M.K.P. has the important virtue of being independent of content and relatively unfettered by interjacent symbolism. While Mira states that the test is influenced by cultural factors, that can be true only in a small degree. Many of his claims for M.K.P. need to be confirmed and, while some of the findings reported, like the high correlations (.75) of the M.K.P. and intelligence, seem spurious, the over-all validity of the test as a clinical tool is amply supported.

For additional reviews, see 232.

[B344]

★MOGENSEN, ALAN; FENGER, GJERTRUD; AND LANGE, BENT. **Rorschach on 122 Ten-Year Old Danish Children: A Standardizational and Structural Study: A, The Normative Results.** Psychological Research Report 2A. Risskov, Denmark: Institute of Psychiatry, State Mental Hospital, [1960]. Pp. 54. Paper, mimeographed. Gratis. * (*PA* 36:4HG49M)

Am J Orthopsychiatry 32:565 Ap '62. Max L. Fogel. This short but concise, carefully reasoned and carefully prepared monograph reports the results of one aspect of a group of Danish psychiatric, psychological and demographic studies carried out by a staff attached to the Institute of Psychiatry, University of Aarhus, and the State Mental Hospital, Risskov, Denmark. The particular findings herein reported are from a cross-sectional investigation of a complete sample of the ten-year-old children from the island of Samsoe, which has a population of about 6600 and lies in the middle of the Danish inland sea, Kattegat. * The monograph has been very carefully written and the material is well analyzed and interestingly presented. Such a comprehensive investigation of an entire homogeneous cultural subgroup has rarely been achieved and certainly merits attention, despite the restricted size of the sample. American workers will want to compare these results with those obtained in the Yale studies (Gesell Institute), reported in *Child Rorschach Responses* and *Adolescent Rorschach Responses* by Ames et al.

[B345]

★MORENO, J. L., EDITOR. **The Sociometry Reader.** New York: Free Press of Glencoe, 1960. Pp. xxiv, 773. $10.00. * (*PA* 36:1GE73M)

Am J Psychiatry 119:189 Ag '62. Henry A. Davidson. * To the clinician, many of the articles will seem turgid with abstract concepts, hard-to-follow sociograms, and a rather esoteric jargon. (Example: "Cultural conserves are products of creativity, antipodal to spontaneous matrices which emerge in the intensive heat of status nascendi.") * Some of the chapters are written with transparent clarity; others are utterly obscure. Little of the material is of everyday clinical value, but a mastery of the sociometric concepts will give any psychiatrist a better philosophic foundation. On the whole, this book makes hard reading. To grasp it, you have to sweat over some of the pages. But it is loaded with ideas. It is a volume to be tasted. It certainly cannot be gulped.

Am J Psychother 16:337–8 Ap '62. Nathaniel H. Siegel. * a useful book for what it is, namely, reflections on Moreno's approach to some areas of sociometry * The reader, however, who identifies the term *sociometry* with the more generic application of quantitative study techniques to interpersonal behavior may be disappointed with this volume. The contributions of Asch, Bales, Cartwright, Lippitt, and Strodtbeck, to name but a few, are not represented. What is represented, for the most part, is material from *Sociometry* before the Journal passed from Moreno's hands to those of the American Sociological Association. The *Reader* is a collection of papers to which Moreno has written the preface and appendix (the first and last words); he has also authored 13 of the 14 papers on sociometric foundations which open the text paper. * the reader may wonder why a book published in 1960 contains reprints of only three 1956–1957 papers with all other reprints being of an earlier vintage. Certainly, meaningful contributions have been made in more recent years. The book is recommended to those who wish to know more about an important area of sociometric study. Its contribution, however, is a limited one and certainly this reader would not agree with the publisher's blurb which calls the book "....a collection of the most important articles in the field of sociometry," unless one wishes to equate sociometry with Morenometry.

[B346]

★MORRISON, WILMA. **The School Record: Its Use and Abuse in College Admissions.** New York: College Entrance Examination Board, 1961. Pp. 15. Paper. $1.00. *

[B347]

*MORSE, HORACE T., AND MCCUNE, GEORGE H. **Selected Items for the Testing of Study Skills and Critical Thinking, Fourth Edition.** National Council for the Social Studies, Bulletin No. 15, Fourth Edition. Washington, D.C.: the Council, 1964. Pp. vii, 91. Paper. $1.50. * For reviews of earlier editions, see 4:B280 and 3:1039.

[B348]

★MOULY, GEORGE J., AND WALTON, LEWIS E. **Test Items in Education.** New York: Schaum Publishing Co., 1962. Pp. xi, 290. Paper. $2.50. *

[B349]

★MURSTEIN, BERNARD I. **Theory and Research in Projective Techniques (Emphasizing the TAT).** New York and London: John Wiley & Sons, Inc., 1963. Pp. xiii, 385. $8.50; 64s. * (*PA* 38:6098)

[B350]

★MYERS, SHELDON S. **Mathematics Tests Available in the United States.** Washington, D.C.: National Council of Teachers of Mathematics, 1959. Pp. ii, 12. Paper. $0.50. *

[B351]

★NATIONAL COUNCIL OF TEACHERS OF MATHEMATICS. **Evaluation in Mathematics: Twenty-Sixth Yearbook.** Washington, D.C.: the Council, Inc., 1961. Pp. iv, 216. $3.00. *

Arith Teach 9:344–5 O '62. Jens L. Lund. * Some unnecessary duplication of material can be observed, as, for example, the repetitious concern for such concepts as validity, reliability, and objectivity. The importance of objectives and the need for treating evaluation in terms of established objectives is discussed in several places. * Most of the aspects of evaluation treated in this book have been discussed in other educational references. In this sense the material is basically not new. * Of real and significant value, though, is the directing of these ideas to mathematics education and the bringing together into one volume that material which should prove of real help to the classroom teacher. Fresh viewpoints taken by the several authors add interest and stimulation to the subject of evaluation. * The Committee recognized the need for the development of appropriate evaluation instruments for new curricula, but, outside of general evaluation principles and a good discussion of evaluation of attitudes and appreciations, few suggestions were offered in this regard. This book should prove to be a helpful reference for teachers. A study of parts or all of the book by a mathematics teacher could only serve to enhance the classroom teaching and learning situation. Of particular value to administrators, as well as teachers, is Chapter 8 describing the evaluation practices carried out in eighteen selected schools. *

[B352]

★NATIONAL COUNCIL ON MEASUREMENTS USED IN EDUCATION. **The Sixteenth Yearbook of the National Council on Measurements Used in Education, 1959.** Edited by Edith M. Huddleston. [East Lansing, Mich.: the Council, c/o Irvin J. Lehmann, Secretary, Office of Evaluation Services, Michigan State University], 1959. Pp. vi, 204. Paper, lithotyped. $3.00. * (*PA* 34:8402)

[B353]

★NATIONAL COUNCIL ON MEASUREMENTS USED IN EDUCATION. **The Seventeenth Yearbook of the National Council on Measurements Used in Education, 1960.** Edited by Edith M. Huddleston. [East Lansing, Mich.: the Council, c/o Irvin J. Lehmann, Secretary, Office of Evaluation Services, Michigan State University], 1960. Pp. vi, 180. Paper, lithotyped. $3.00. *

[B354]

★NATIONAL COUNCIL ON MEASUREMENT IN EDUCATION. **The Eighteenth Yearbook of the National Council on Measurement in Education, 1961.** Edited by Edith M. Huddleston. [East Lansing, Mich.: the Council, c/o Irvin J. Lehmann, Secretary, Office of Evaluation Services, Michigan State University], 1961. Pp. vi, 176. Paper, lithotyped. $3.00. * (*PA* 36:5KJ76H)

[B355]

★NATIONAL COUNCIL ON MEASUREMENT IN EDUCATION. **The Nineteenth Yearbook of the National Council on Measurement in Education, 1962.** Edited by Martin Katz. [East Lansing, Mich.: the Council, c/o Irvin J. Lehmann, Secretary, Office of Evaluation Services, Michigan State University], 1962. Pp. vi, 178. $3.00. *

[B356]

★NATIONAL COUNCIL ON MEASUREMENT IN EDUCATION. **The Twentieth Yearbook of the National Council on Measurement in Education, 1963.** Edited by Martin Katz. [East Lansing, Mich.: the Council, c/o Irvin J. Lehmann, Secretary, Office of Evaluation Services, Michigan State University], 1963. Pp. v, 198. Paper. $3.00. * [This is the last volume in the NCME yearbook series. The yearbook series has been replaced by the *Journal of Educational Measurement,* which started publication with Vol. 1, No. 1, June 1964.]

[B357]

★NATIONAL EDUCATION ASSOCIATION, COUNCIL ON INSTRUCTION. **Toward Better Evaluation of Learning: A Brief Guide for Teachers and Administrators and Others Concerned With Testing and Evaluation in Our Schools.** Washington, D.C.: the Association, 1962. Pp. vii, 36. Paper. $0.50. *

[B358]

*NATIONAL LEAGUE FOR NURSING. **The NLN Achievement Tests, Third Edition.** The Use of Tests in Schools of Nursing Pamphlet No. 2. New

York: the League, Inc., 1964. Pp. iv, 41. Paper. $1.25. *

[B359]

*NATIONAL LEAGUE FOR NURSING. **The NLN Graduate Nurse Examination, Second Edition.** The Use of Tests in Schools of Nursing Pamphlet No. 3. New York: the League, Inc., 1962. Pp. iii, 27. Paper. $1.00. *

[B360]

*NATIONAL LEAGUE FOR NURSING. **The NLN Pre-Nursing and Guidance Examination, Third Edition.** The Use of Tests in Schools of Nursing Pamphlet No. 1. New York: the League, Inc., 1961. Pp. v, 34. Paper. $1.25. *

[B361]

★NATIONAL SCIENCE TEACHERS ASSOCIATION, COMMITTEE ON EVALUATION, PAUL L. DRESSEL, CHAIRMAN. **Analyses of Science Tests.** Washington, D.C.: the Association, 1959. Pp. iv, 57. Paper. $0.50. *

[B362]

★NATIONAL SOCIETY FOR THE STUDY OF EDUCATION. **The Impact and Improvement of School Testing Programs.** The Sixty-Second Yearbook of the National Society for the Study of Education, Part II. Edited by Warren G. Findley. Chicago and London: University of Chicago Press, 1963. Pp. xii, 304, ciii. $4.50; 33*s.* 6*d.* *

Am Ed Res J 1:137–8 Mr '64. John C. Gowan. * a capable and authoritative treatise on the subject. Contributors include a dozen of the most knowledgeable specialists in the field. * The editor has set the tone for the book in the first chapter and has evidently been able to guide the contributors to the extent that little unevenness is apparent. Most of the chapters are organized in terms of recommendations or generalizations. As a result, the book contains specific prescriptions, which, if followed by school districts, will do much to solve problems related to testing and lead to advances in the field. The chapter by Ohlsen on the interpretation of test scores is probably the most scholarly and well researched, but it is closely followed in this respect by the penetrating report by Traxler and North on the selection and use of tests. In the reviewer's opinion, the weakest contribution is perhaps that of Wrightstone, which includes few up-to-date bibliographical references and discusses the contributions of Guilford and Torrance in a single final paragraph without any references at all. This chapter illustrates a general shortcoming of the book; namely, that in a decade when a great deal of new information about human intellectual abilities has become available and when marked changes in methods and curricula have followed the researches of Skinner, Bruner, Piaget, Hebb, Bloom, and others, ideas in the field of testing seem to have changed very little. Yet they will have to if adequate appraisals are to be made of new procedures in education. If education is the stimulation of man's abilities and if new abilities and new methods of stimulating them are found, new methods of assessment need to be devised. It is a pity that some of the suggestions in Bloom's *Taxonomy of Educational Objectives* have not been taken more to heart. Despite a tendency to rehearse the old and the obvious, the book has considerable merit and will be useful in every school-district office and, indeed, in many courses in educational measurement. The book contains an abundance of practical material and makes many sensible recommendations on what testing programs can and cannot be expected to do. The Society for the Study of Education deserves thanks for sponsoring this yearbook. To Dr. Findley should go special praise for the clear organization and skillful direction that the book displays. The fact that he was for many years involved in the testing program of a large school district is no doubt at least partly responsible for the practical tone of the book. It is, in short, a serviceable and useful addition to the literature of measurement.

Cont Psychol 9:329 Ag '64. Carmen J. Finley. * Particularly well done....was the chapter by Mahlev and Smallenberg on "Effects of Testing Programs on the Attitudes of Students, Teachers, Parents, and the Community." * Ebel also presents an interesting argument that is contrary to the much quoted contention that "intangible outcomes of education are difficult to measure and may be entirely unmeasurable" * This reviewer's main criticism concerns an omission. In the last five years there has been a great deal of activity in the application of electronic data processing procedures to pupil personnel areas. A good segment of this general interest applies to test scoring, recording of pupil information and analysis of pupil data. While brief mention of improved processing methods was made by several contributors to this volume, it now seems entirely in order that an expanded treatment of this rapidly developing field enter current texts on measurement and evaluation.

[B363]

★NELSON, CLARENCE H. **Let's Build Quality Into Our Science Tests.** Washington, D.C.: National Education Association, 1958. Pp. 25. Paper. $1.00. *

[B364]

★NEVIS, EDWIN C.; WALLEN, RICHARD W.; AND STICKEL, ERNEST G. **The Thematic Evaluation of Managerial Potential: An Experimental Manual for the Use of the Thematic Apperception Test in Assessment of Vocational Adjustment.** Cleveland, Ohio: Personnel Research & Development Corporation, 1959. Pp. iii, 283, xx. Paper, spiral binding. Out of print. *

[B365]

★NEWMARK, MAXIM, AND SCHERER, PHILIP. **How to Prepare for College Board Achievement Tests: German.** Great Neck, N.Y.: Barron's Educational Series, Inc., 1962. Pp. viii, 134. Paper, $2.25; cloth, $4.50. *

[B366]

★NICHOLS, ROBERT C., AND HOLLAND, JOHN L. **Prediction of the First Year College Performance of High Aptitude Students.** American Psychological Association, Psychological Monographs: General and Applied, Vol. 77, No. 7, Whole No. 570. Washington, D.C.: the Association, Inc., 1963. Pp. 29. Paper. $1.50. *

[B367]

★NICHOLSON, R. J., AND GALAMBOS, P. **Performance in G.C.E. (Advanced Level) Examinations and University Examinations.** Hull, England: University of Hull, February 1960. Pp. 22. Paper. 2*s*. *

Brit J Ed Psychol 30:290 N '60. This investigation is similar to several other follow-up studies of the predictive value of secondary school examinations for university courses, and yields the same depressing results. Among groups of around a hundred students in the University of Hull, the correlation between A-level and first-year results in English was .16; Economics .22; and with Finals the figures were even lower. However, in French and Chemistry the coefficients reached .33 and .41. But these, as the authors point out, hardly justify the use of A-level passes as the main basis for admission. There are several other points of interest to those concerned with university selection. The reviewer would disagree with the author's rejection of corrections for homogeneity; for surely what one wants to know is the success of A-level in differentiating *candidates* who will perform reasonably at university from those who are rejected because they are likely to get very low marks, rather than in differentiating the better from the poorer *acceptances.*

[B368]

★NIELSEN, HELLE H. **Visual-Motor Functioning of Cerebral Palsied and Normal Children.** Nordisk Psykologis Monongrafiserie, Nr. 14. Copenhagen, Denmark: Munksgaard Ltd., 1962. Pp. 41–103. Paper. D.kr. 10. (Reprinted from *Nordisk Psykologi* 14(2):41–103 '62.) *

[B369]

NOLL, VICTOR H. **Introduction to Educational Measurement.** Boston, Mass.: Houghton Mifflin Co., 1957. Pp. xxi, 437. $6.95. (*PA* 32:5975) (*Instructor's Manual to Accompany Introduction to Educational Measurement.* By Victor H. Noll and Joe L. Saupe. Pp. vi, 84. 1959. Paper.) *

Austral J Ed 6:71 Mr '62. S. S. Dunn. * This is a disappointing and superficial book. It attempts too much. It scatters the names of tests around with gay abandon over the whole field of achievement, intelligence, aptitude and personality testing but fails to come to grips with the fundamental problems of measurement as they affect the classroom teacher. It would serve little purpose in this review to write paragraph after paragraph of detailed criticism. A few major criticisms will be made and the remainder, many of which are still important, will be left unstated. We find a chapter headed "Objectives as the Basis of All Good Measurement," but this is Chapter 5. Surely a chapter on the basis of all good measurement should come before ones on "A Little Statistics" and "Finding and Selecting Good Measuring Instruments." In the section dealing with "Characteristics of a Good Measuring Instrument" it is unfortunate that reliability is discussed before validity, which is the more important basic concept. When dealing with evaluation, Noll completely misses the essential difference between *measurement* and *evaluation* although this is made clear in some of the books he quotes in his bibliography. Evaluation asks "what value?" as well as "how much?" A topic as fundamental to the classroom teacher as diagnostic testing (including remedial work) receives a mere three and a half pages. Since most intelligence tests are based on the use of deviation I.Q.'s, the constant use in this book of ratio I.Q.'s without critical comment on the difficulties involved is misleading to students. The discussion of educational and achievement quotients is also uncritical. In fact, the approach of the book throughout is naive and uncritical, and it is no defence to say that this is an Introduction. It is misleading and dangerous to introduce concepts which have serious limitations without giving some hint, at least, of these limitations.

Cont Psychol 3:169 Je '58. John B. Morris. * a textbook for the undergraduate student in education. The ease with which the proposed audience is recognized represents a refreshing departure in a field in which most authors try to write to teachers, psychologists, and guidance workers as though they were a homogeneous group. The author, moreover, seems well aware of the intellectual level of those likely to be exposed to his book and has written in an easily read style. He makes a worthy attempt to allay the fear with which many students of education approach courses in measurement and to stimulate interest in the field. In fact, the goal of writing specifically for the prospective elementary and secondary school teacher is so well achieved that psychology students and psychologists will find little of interest to them in this volume. The book is oriented frankly and consistently for teachers and should be well received in teachers' colleges. * Noll has chosen well and restricts himself in admirable fashion. The first seven chapters represent a particularly good selection of the fundamentals of test construction. * The weakest chapter in this group is that entitled *A Little Statistics,* an attempt to introduce the student to statistics painlessly. * One of the goals of this book is to make the introductory measurement course functional, to prepare teachers to use measurement. If this book has a unique contribution, it is the thoroughness with which the effort is maintained to achieve this objective. The last two chapters, *The Measurement Program* and *Using the Results of Measurement,* are virtually a manual for instituting a testing program and cover many of the minute aspects of such a program, including many things that most authors assume the student should know. *

For an additional review, see 5:B321.

[B370]

★NUALLÁIN, C. Ó. **Personnel Assessment and Selection.** Administrative Procedures: 2. Dublin, Ireland: Institute of Public Administration, 1961. Pp. 32. Paper. 7*s.* *

Pub Adm 40:239 su '62. This little pamphlet reflects the wisdom of the "seven point plan" for staff selection pioneered and published by the National Institute of Industrial Psychology in Britain. It devotes a rather sketchy chapter to intelligence and personality and finally recommends the setting up of a central testing and selection Commission to serve all public authorities in Ireland. This suggestion seems logical if modern selection techniques are to be developed in that country, but the pamphlet itself adds little if anything to the existing published material on this important subject. In fairness, the publication started as a lecture and the author pays proper tribute to the work of the N.I.I.P.—but like so many short publications it can only scratch the surface of the subject.

[B371]

★NUNNALLY, JUM C. **Educational Measurement and Evaluation.** New York: McGraw-Hill Book Co., Inc., 1964. Pp. xv, 440. $7.50. * (London: McGraw-Hill Publishing Co. Ltd. 58*s.*) (*Teacher's Manual to Accompany Educational Measurement and Evaluation.* Pp. 51. Paper. $1.50; 12*s.* *)

[B372]

★NUNNALLY, JUM C., JR. **Tests and Measurements: Assessment and Prediction.** New York: McGraw-Hill Book Co., Inc., 1959. Pp. x, 446. $7.50. * (London: McGraw-Hill Publishing Co. Ltd. 58*s.*)

Ed & Psychol Meas 21:506–10 su '61. William E. Coffman. The author....has undertaken a monumental task—to write a single volume which can at the same time "serve as a comprehensive text for use of students in tests and measurements courses, whether in the field of psychology or education" and "also serve as a helpful adjunct to graduate courses in measurement, and as a practical guide to psychological testing for teachers and administrators." By trying to serve such a heterogeneous audience, he actually serves none of them well; however, certain aspects of his presentation will prove worthy of attention by each class of consumer he mentions. Furthermore, he has provided a stimulating document for a class of consumer he fails to mention in the preface—the specialist in measurement who wishes to take a fresh look at the ever expanding field in which he works. The specialist has enough sophistication to avoid the traps implicit in the oversimplifications which are the inevitable results of attempting to make the text comprehensive and elementary at the same time. He will find Nunnally's treatment of the statistical aspects of testing fresh and illuminating. * Where he is writing out of a deep well of experience, as in the statistical sections and in the sections dealing with applications within the general field of psychology, the result is enlightening even to the sophisticated reader. Where he is apparently relying on less formidable background, as in the sections devoted to assessment and to the details of test construction—particularly the construction of educational achievement tests—his treatment may prove something less than a "helpful guide." Nunnally repeats a number of cliches regarding the construction of achievement tests which have served as rules of thumb in the absence of adequate theory but which are of doubtful validity. * As a survey of the field of tests and measurements the text will be useful to "teachers and administrators"; however, they should be cautioned to look elsewhere for advice on the details of test construction. As an introduction to the field for "students....of psychology or education," it provides an excellent framework on which to hang increasing insights; however, they should be informed that the sharp distinction drawn between assessment and prediction is seldom encountered in the field of education. As "a helpful adjunct to graduate courses in measurement" it offers the same fresh view as that experienced by the reviewer; however, the field is moving rapidly, and such new developments as multi-dimensional scaling and recent refinements in factor analysis will have to be traced from sources other than this.

Personnel Psychol 13:366–7 au '60. Marvin D. Dunnette. Here is a book that is bound to be useful to persons in industry or in education who wish to gain an accurate and fairly rapid overview of psychological testing and measurement methods and practices. It is a well written book—nicely suited to self study by the busy businessman or school administrator. It is a practical book—Dr. Nunnally obviously has had broad experience in using tests and measurements, and he manages reliably to convey these experiences and practical hints to the reader. In addition to practicality, Nunnally has provided scholarship; certainly the book merits consideration as a text for beginning courses in testing. The subject matter is not treated in depth, however, and anyone seeking more than an overview of the field would be better advised to turn to Cronbach's latest edition of *Essentials of Psychological Testing.* * The chapters on test construction and on multivariate prediction are particularly good. * An excellent chapter....gives a fine overview of some of the "newer" measurement techniques such as Q-sort, Semantic Differential, Communications analyses, etc. * Nunnally has provided the beginning student with a well-written, fairly comprehensive overview of psychological testing and its uses. *

[B373]

★OJEMANN, RALPH H.; ASSISTED BY SHELDON C. FRIEDMAN AND ESTHER B. TUTTLE. **Tests and Evaluation Methods Used in Driver and Safety Education: An Analysis to Help Teachers Measure Instructional Outcomes.** Washington, D.C.: National Commission on Safety Education, National Education Association, 1959. Pp. 48. Paper. Out of print. *

[B374]

★OLIVER, R. A. C. **An Experimental Test in English.** Joint Matriculation Board, Universities of Manchester, Liverpool, Leeds, Sheffield, and Birmingham, Occasional Publication 13. [Manchester, England: Joint Matriculation Board], 1963. Pp. 56. Paper. Gratis. *

Brit J Ed Psychol 34:97 F '64. James Britton. * a valuable report * The test represents an interesting compromise. In the year when the American College Entrance Board took one step in our direction by replacing one-third of their objective tests by essay questions.... Oliver has taken two steps in the opposite direction by including two hours of objective questions in this three-hour Use of English paper. The remaining hour is given to two samples of the candidates' continuous writing, and an attempt is made to differentiate between them by providing in the question paper material for the first piece of writing and inviting personal views in the second. Each of a candidate's two compositions was marked by a different team of two markers. * It would have been valuable to know how much would have been gained by having a third or fourth marker for each composition. The differentiated double sample of a candidate's writing is an interesting feature of the experiment and might have been more fully reported on. Correlation between the two sets of marks was no higher than .319 and yet no reference is made to this as an aspect of reliability. Reliability of the test as a whole is, in fact, considered only in the form of mark/re-mark coefficients for a sample of 148 scripts. * some form of test/re-test coefficient would surely be a more realistic indication of reliability * We are not told whether the inclusion of the compositions raised or lowered the validity of the test as a whole, and this omission may perhaps hint at the uneasy basis of the whole compromise. The objective questions are more reliable and more valid and are clearly included for that reason: the compositions seem to be included on quite different grounds: "It is universally agreed that the writing of continuous prose is an essential element in the use of English" (p. 40). * Today, for the first time, it is being recognised that examining boards must accept responsibility for the "backwash effect"—the effect of examination upon teaching. The pattern of this experimental test, and the explicit terms of its justification (p. 38), represent a setback at a particularly dangerous point. Few can suppose (and they do not appear to include Professor Oliver) that this examination has been introduced simply as an additional selection device: in which case it represents, in fact, a deliberate attempt to *have an effect* upon the teaching in schools. The effect of the test in the form used here will inevitably be the publication and the use in many sixth forms of collections of interlinear tests and multiple-choice vocabulary and comprehension tests. This is not America—ours is, in fact, a unique situation, with its free choice of syllabus for teachers and free enterprise in textbook publishing, and we must face the consequence that wherever there are external examinations they will inevitably call the tune—not in all schools but in the majority.

[B375]

★OLIVER, R. A. C. **General Studies (Advanced) in the G.C.E.** Joint Matriculation Board, Universities of Manchester, Liverpool, Leeds, Sheffield, and Birmingham, Occasional Publication 9. [Manchester, England: Joint Matriculation Board], November 1960. Pp. iv, 48. Paper. Gratis. *

[B376]

★OLIVER, R. A. C. **General Studies (Advanced) 1960.** Joint Matriculation Board, Universities of Manchester, Liverpool, Leeds, Sheffield, and Birmingham, Occasional Publication 11. [Manchester, England: Joint Matriculation Board], June 1961. Pp. ii, 34. Paper. Gratis. *

[B377]

★OLYANOVA, NAYDA. **The Psychology of Handwriting.** New York: Sterling Publishing Co., Inc., 1960. Pp. 224. Paper. $1.35. *

[B378]

★ORGEL, JOSEPH R. **Reading Comprehension: A Testing Program for College Entrance Scholastic Aptitude Tests, New York State Regents Examinations, Westinghouse Science Aptitude Examinations, Other Terminal and Scholarship Examinations.** New York: Oxford Book Co., Inc., 1960. Pp. x, 269. Paper, $1.35; cloth, $2.15. *

[B379]

★ORGEL, JOSEPH RANDOLPH. **Preparing for American College Test Program Examinations.** Cambridge, Mass.: Educators Publishing Service, Inc., 1963. Pp. vi, 314. Paper. $3.00. *

[B380]

★OSGOOD, CHARLES E.; SUCI, GEORGE J.; AND TANNENBAUM, PERCY H. **The Measurement of Meaning.** Urbana, Ill.: University of Illinois Press, 1957. Pp. vii, 342. $7.50. *

Cont Psychol 3:113–5 My '58. Roger W. Brown. * a distinguished contribution to psychology. There are two kinds of research described in this book; the first uses factor analysis to discover the dimensions of meaning. An original group of 100 subjects was given a list of concepts, an odd lot including *lady, boulder, sin* and 17 others, and also a list of 50 bipolar, 7-point scales whose extremes were labeled with such familiar adjective antonyms as *good-bad, sweet-sour,* and *active-passive.* The job was to place each concept on each scale. A few of these 1,000 judgments (50 scales x 20 concepts) were quite prosaic; e.g., deciding whether *boulder* is *light* or *heavy.* In the majority of cases, however, the scales could not be said to have any "literal" application to the concepts and subjects had to extend themselves to think in metaphors and difficult-to-explain associations. Does *sin* seem to be *red* or *green?* Is a *boulder sweet* or *sour?* When the data were examined, it could be seen that some scales functioned as near synonyms, with judgments on one scale being highly predictable from judgments on another. Using Thurstone's Centroid Method, the authors analyzed the matrix of intercorrelations and extracted three identifiable factors. Such scales as *good-bad* and *beautiful-ugly* were heavily loaded with the first factor and so it was called *evaluation.* The second factor was named *potency,* since it was identified with such scales as *strong-weak* and *large-small.* The third factor was called *activity;* for it the most distinctively loaded scales included *fast-slow* and *active-passive.* There are many similar factor analyses described in this book. The most elaborate of these made use of 76 scales selected to represent the dimensions of meaning utilized in Roget's *Thesaurus.* In this case there were eight identifiable factors but the first three were the reliable trio—*evaluation, potency,* and *activity.* The second kind of research described in this book builds on the factor analytic studies. Since the meanings of concepts appear usually to have three major dimensions, it should be possible to devise an instrument for the economical measurement of meaning by selecting a small number of scales to represent each factor. Such an instrument is called a *Semantic Differential.* Researchers have most commonly used four scales to represent evaluation, three for potency, and three for activity. Subjects have been asked to place concepts (or pictures from the Thematic Apperception Test, the names of political candidates, representational paintings, even sonar signals) on each of these ten scales. The data are usually summarized as a score for each scaled item on each of the three factors, a three-dimensional meaning score. The investigator is sometimes interested in differences of meaning from one concept to another, sometimes in differences between groups or persons and sometimes in differences over time. * While the 10-scale form of the differential has been used more than any other, it is important to understand that there is no one differential which can be considered a standard test to be used whenever meaning is to be measured. There are many reasons why this is so. The most important of these is the fact that the factor loadings of particular scales can change with a change in the items scaled; e.g., whereas *deep-shallow* is not heavily loaded with evaluation for a miscellany of concepts, it is so loaded when sonar signals are scaled. The authors give the potential researcher all possible guidance on the problem of selecting *a* Semantic Differential for his particular purpose. For all their vital empiricism the authors have not neglected theory construction. Osgood's original article on the logic of the measure was accompanied by a paper setting forth a behavioral interpretation of meaning as a mediating reaction (a near relative of Hull's pure-stimulus act). In the present book the authors elaborate their theoretical construct so as to improve its coordination with meaning as it is now measured. They suggest that the mediating process has bipolar components corresponding to the dimensions of semantic space. Mediating processes are conceived to vary, therefore, in the components activated and in the intensities of activation. Several experimental results are said to "validate" this coordination; e.g., extremity of placement of a concept on a scale is inversely related to the latency of the scaling response. While I find these results and all the others in the book *consistent* with the amended theory, I cannot see that they have been predicted by it. This conclusion does not, of course, exclude the possibility that the researches have been *inspired* by the theory for reasons that have to do with the personal psychology of the researchers. Differential research is much closer to the literature on synesthesia and metaphor than it is to the semantic analyses of logicians. The authors say that the meaning measured by the differential is "connotative," but, in terms of any standard semantic analysis, the differential must be considered a mixture and a mixture that changes with the problem at hand. * The differential solves none of the problems of meaning posed by philosophers and does not even observe the distinctions of which they feel most confident. This may be just the bold step needed to advance the empirical study of meaning whose movement until now has been glacier-like in its imperceptibility. However, the uncertainty about the sort of meaning measured by a differential sometimes causes uncertainty about the precise interpretation of a research result. *

Cont Psychol 3:115–9 My '58. Harold Gulliksen. * Each semantic scale is defined by a pair of antonyms with seven possible locations between them. Each concept in the set to be scaled is assigned a location (1 to 7) on each of the scales utilized for differentiating that set of concepts. * The book presents an impressive series of studies showing both originality in developing the semantic differential as a measuring device, and ingenuity in applying this device to various problems in a broad range of psychological fields. These studies make a definite contribution in showing that one can obtain consistent and stable results when investigating meaning by scaling methods. I have been asked to review the methods used in this work with particular reference to desirable lines of further experimentation. It seems to me that the results so far reported indicate certain critical points that should be carefully explored in subsequent studies. * [In my review,] five major points have been stressed. 1. It is desirable to use scaling methods that will give better discrimination, particularly for the more homogeneous concepts, than is furnished by the present 7-category scales. Repeat measures should give, let us say, not more than 20% identical results. It might be possible to achieve such a goal by using a 15-point or 25-point scale. Or it might prove necessary to use other scaling methods. 2. In view of the significant concept-scale interaction, the methods of factor analysis may give misleading conclusions regarding dimensionality of the semantic space. Other methods should be tried out, such as covariance analyses or a multidimensional scaling of concepts that show low intersubject variance. 3. The development of parallel sets of scales would help to solve the problem of differentiating between low reliability and a change in attitude. 4. Nonsignificant differences found with small numbers of cases should not be interpreted as a reliable indication of similarity of the groups or variables tested until the results have been duplicated with a reasonably large number of cases. 5. Scales which are significantly curvilinearly related to each other cannot be regarded as interchangeable for all purposes, even though there is a high correlation between them. The studies reported in the book under review form an impressive demonstration of the potential value of the measurement of meaning from the point of view of both basic research and practical applications. [See original review for additional critical comments not excerpted.]

[B381]

★O'SHAUGHNESSY, MARY MICHAEL. **Some Effects of Praise and Reproof on Test Performances on School Ability and Reading Achievement Tests.** Catholic University of America, Educational Research Monograph, Vol. 24, No. 2. Washington, D.C.: Catholic University of America Press, December 2, 1960. Pp. x, 114. Paper. $2.00. *

[B382]

★PALERMO, DAVID S., AND JENKINS, JAMES J. **Word Association Norms: Grade School Through College.** Minneapolis, Minn.: University of Minnesota Press, 1964. Pp. xviii, 469. $7.50. *

[B383]

★PARKER, JAMES F., JR., AND FLEISHMAN, EDWIN A. **Ability Factors and Component Performance Measures as Predictors of Complex Tracking Behavior.** American Psychological Association, Psychological Monographs: General and Applied, Vol. 74, No. 16, Whole No. 503. Washington, D.C.: the Association, Inc., 1961. Pp. 36. Paper. $1.50. * (*PA* 36:2CD36P)

[B384]

★PASCAL, G. R., AND JENKINS, W. O. **Systematic Observation of Gross Human Behavior.** New York: Grune & Stratton, Inc., 1961. Pp. ix, 126. $4.75. * (London: William Heinemann Medical Books Ltd. 34*s*.) (*PA* 36:1HE26P)

Cont Psychol 7:192–3 My '62. John A. Stern. This book....attempts to give the student a theoretical position and methodology for exploring human behavior. Its strength, the presentation of one and only one position, is at the same time its principal weakness. * One of the major assets of this book lies in the detailed exposition of the classes of behavior to be observed, the stimulus categories and the responses to be recorded. The development of the observational scales is systematic and logical in approach and has generated some interesting findings as described in a later section of the book. Though the book is entitled *Systematic Observation of Gross Human Behavior,* only some 30 or so pages are devoted to the exposition of this approach. Had the title been based on the remainder of the book it might better have been entitled *Systematic Recording of Self-Observations of Gross Human Behavior.* * According to the authors the chief instrument to be used in this investigation is the "fallible observer." After reading the book it appears to this reviewer that there is more fallibility in the recommended procedures than the authors are willing to state. * The book's approach to the study of behavior is avowedly behavioristic. The major concern expressed is for a study of man as he responds to "stimuli in his natural environment," the most important of which is considered to be other people. Some restrictions are made as to what may be a stimulus. Early in the book the content of the subject's verbalizations are not considered legitimate stimuli while the non-content or nonverbal aspects of his verbal behavior such as rate and intensity of speech are acceptable data. In the final analysis we unfortunately find that the elicitation of reports about the behavior of the subject by the subject rather than the direct observation of the subject constitutes the data on which a science of human behavior is to be based. Thus content, as long as it does not concern itself with unobservable behavior such as feelings, hopes, and attitudes is the data we end up with. Why reports of feelings, etc., are attributed to the organism and thus excluded while other experiences are freely attributed to the stimulus is not explained although one is left with the feeling that feelings, hopes, attitudes, and pain associated with ingrown toenails are not fit subjects for a science of human behavior. Though they state that paper and pencil tests and "responses to questionnaires become for us merely paper marking responses to a stimulus situation which consists of paper, pencil, examiner, etc." (p. 23), it seems that the data obtained by their approach is but one step removed from questionnaires and paper and pencil tests. Instead of feeding the subject questions through visual means and obtaining a response mediated through the use of a pencil by the respondent these authors substitute an oral presentation, an oral report, and the pencil is wielded by the questioner. Admittedly, this may lead to somewhat greater flexibility in the investigative procedure but there is little evidence that it leads to more valid, or even more reliable information. In the final analysis one must decide whether a science of human behavior can be based on observations as limited as those described in this book. These authors are willing to make a case for this approach. Their procedure for obtaining their data are well described and the approach deserves a full trial. This reviewer has some qualms about developing a science of human behavior utilizing only one technique. It is our pessimistic conviction that what a person says and what he does are far from perfectly correlated, and that what he says he did is even more poorly correlated with what in fact he did in the past. It would seem to us that a science of human behavior, however gross, must have a broader base of observation than suggested by this book. I would recommend this book for use in a course devoted to the development of techniques for assessing human behavior. It should, however, be placed amongst a series of books or articles describing different approaches to this admittedly complex problem. By itself, it is rather meager fare.

[B385]

★Pedley, F. H. **A Parent's Guide to Examinations: From Primary School to University.** Oxford, England: Pergamon Press Ltd., 1964. Pp. xiii, 224. 15*s*. (New York: Macmillan Co. $2.45.) *

[B386]

★Peek, Roland M., and Olson, Gordon W. **Organization and Internal Structure of the MMPI, Second Edition.** St. Paul, Minn.: Department of Public Welfare, State of Minnesota, 1959. Pp. vi, 66. Paper. Gratis. * (*PA* 35:793)

[B387]

★Pemberton, W. A. **Ability, Values, and College Achievement.** University of Delaware Studies in Higher Education, No. 1. Newark, Del.: University of Delaware Bookstore, 1963. Pp. xii, 77. Paper. $2.00. * (*PA* 38:6573)

Personnel & Guid J 42:932–4 My '64. Irvin J. Lehmann. * This....monograph "is an attempt....to describe the relationship of ability and values to college achievement for one senior class." * reference to college achievement is made in terms of four dimensions or facets of personality: (a) intellect, (b) motivation, (c) temperament, and (d) environment. * Viewed as a research project, this is an important work which is characterized by careful, thoughtful analysis and interpretation. The author is constantly aware of the possibility of misinterpretation of the data. He goes on to mention that although the factors extracted are uncorrelated, the personality dimensions discussed in this and other studies "function in interaction." Despite this caution....some of the interpretations made are done in the light of isolation rather than interaction. * does not completely satisfy the criterion of careful design. This reviewer feels that the study's greatest potential value has not been realized because only graduating seniors were used. * The college graduate is rather atypical not only in terms of cognitive skills but in affective variables. * it would have been desirable and the study's over-all value would have been enhanced if these seniors had been studied in a longitudinal fashion from their freshman to senior year. In this way, the predictive power of certain variables could have been studied in an attempt to ascertain whether or not they are more powerful at one stage than another. Because seniors were used for the major analyses (although reference is made to freshmen, sophomores, and juniors, at various stages), it is also conceivable that some of the interpretations made reflect an inherent bias. For example, "differences in general intelligence and in cultural background seem to become less important, and motivation seems to assume a more important role at each higher educational level" is not something unexpected. In fact, we would be at a loss to explain contradictory results. * Another methodological defect....is the failure of the researcher to analyze the data separately for males and females. It is universally agreed that there are marked sex differences not only in certain selected cognitive areas but in some of the affected areas as well. Despite this, this study as well as many others in this area have tended to treat the data in terms of total responses. * Finally, the nature or composition of the sample of seniors may have been such that the obtained results were biased. Although two-thirds of this group of seniors "....completed their degrees in four years....the remaining one-third entered from five to twenty years before graduation." It is quite conceivable that this latter group differed significantly from the other on the very variables that were being investigated. This being the case, prior tests should have been made to ascertain this, and, if the two groups differed markedly, should have been considered separately in the data analysis. As it stands now, it is difficult to know whether the observed differences are real differences or are only a reflection of this "atypical" group of seniors. * In summary, it can be reiterated that a more parsimonious design, *viz.,* multiple discriminant function analysis, would have resulted in more meaningful data being obtained. This is especially true in those sections where rank-order correlations were employed to conclude that two or more groups could be distinguished on the basis of certain characteristics. In addition, the nature of the sample and the failure to analyze the data separately for males and females might have clouded the findings. Despite these technical flaws....the data *do* contribute something to the gradually accumulating body of knowledge with respect to the prediction of college success. This monograph dramatically emphasizes the role of non-cognitive characteristics in the learning process and the continual interaction of a variety of factors. *

[B388]

★Perlman, Leonard A. **Preparing for High School Entrance and Scholarship Examinations: With Separate Answer Key, Revised Edition.** Stamford, Conn.: Youth Education Systems, Inc., 1959. Pp. vi, 178. Paper. $2.50. *

[B389]

★Petch, J. A. **G.C.E. and Degree, Part 1.** Appendix by T. Lewis. Joint Matriculation Board, Universities of Manchester, Liverpool, Leeds, Sheffield, and Birmingham, Occasional Publication 10. [Manchester, England: Joint Matriculation Board], April 1961. Pp. ii, 85. Paper. 5*s.* *

[B390]

★Petch, J. A. **G.C.E. and Degree, Part 2.** Joint Matriculation Board, Universities of Manchester, Liverpool, Leeds, Sheffield, and Birmingham, Occasional Publication 14. [Manchester, England: Joint Matriculation Board], September 1963. Pp. iii–iv, 87–138. Paper. 5*s.* *

[B391]

★Petch, J. A. **Marks and Marking.** Joint Matriculation Board, Universities of Manchester, Liverpool, Leeds, Sheffield, and Birmingham, Occasional Publication 8. [Manchester, England: Joint Matriculation Board], October 1960. Pp. ii, 32. Paper. Gratis. *

[B392]

★Petch, J. A. **State Scholars 1962 and General Studies (Advanced).** Joint Matriculation Board, Universities of Manchester, Liverpool, Leeds, Sheffield, and Birmingham, Occasional Publication 12. [Manchester, England: Joint Matriculation Board], February 1963. Pp. ii, 17. Paper. Gratis. *

[B393]

★Peters, Max; Coleman, Jerome; Shostak, Jerome; and Gunsher, Daniel. **Barron's How to Prepare for High School Entrance Examinations.** Great Neck, N.Y.: Barron's Educational Series, Inc., 1961. Pp. x, 502. Paper, $2.98; cloth, $4.95. *

[B394]

★Pettit, Lincoln. **How to Study and Take Exams.** New York: John F. Rider, Publisher, Inc., 1960. Pp. vii, 87. Paper. $1.00. *

[B395]

★Pickford, R. W.; with the assistance of Ruth Bowyer and John Struthers. **Pickford Projective Pictures.** London: Tavistock Publications, 1963. Pp. xi, 122. 30*s.*; accompanying pictures, 25*s.*; the set, 50*s.* (New York: Springer Publishing Co., Inc., $4.00; accompanying pictures, $5.00.) * For reviews, see 234.

[B396]

★Pinneau, Samuel R. **Changes in Intelligence Quotient: Infancy to Maturity: New Insights From the Berkeley Growth Study With Implications for the Stanford-Binet Scales and Applications to Professional Practice.** Boston, Mass.: Houghton Mifflin Co., 1961. Pp. xi, 233. $4.60. * (*PA* 37:6706)

Cont Psychol 7:285–6 Ag '62. Dale B. Harris. Pinneau's volume is a useful addition to the literature on psychology's most widely known concept and tool. It admits and documents the mutability of intelligence as measured by a single index—IQ. It goes some small way behind the index to examine the composition of intelligence, developmentally considered. It offers the working psychologist new tables for his armamentarium of manuals and norms. Because the monograph treats intelligence as a built-in aspect of the organism, it belongs in the older tradition (and an honorable one it is) of the intelligence concept. It discusses the "prediction" of intellectual growth from earlier status and charts the course of such growth, regardless of schedules of reinforcement, programs of learning, or patterns of experience. The research reported here shows how even the most extensively developed concepts and instruments can be tightened by painstaking conceptual and statistical treatment. The major part of this report is based on data from Nancy Bayley's Growth Study at the University of California's Institute of Child Welfare, now the Institute of Human Development. Only a small number of cases were involved (36 to 61) depending on the test comparisons made, but they were the same individuals retested periodically from infancy to maturity. While the N was small, the fact that the study was truly longitudinal enhances its value for the study of the consistency of the IQ over time. * Pinneau concluded that values tabled from the Berkeley Growth Study can be used, with caution, to estimate the amount of change one may generally expect in IQ from any age to any other age. * The usefulness of the prediction tables depends on one's framework of thinking concerning the measurement of intelligence and his understanding of the logic of probability. These tables essentially assume a conventional definition of intelligence and its measurement and will appear most useful to those who define intelligence as a relatively fixed entity or stable quality of behavior. If we believe intelligence tests are achievement tests rather than estimates of aptitude, and if we believe the course of intellectual development can be closely regulated by controlling experience input, such tables have little value. Since the definition of intellectual development just implied is still undemonstrated empirically, the means of manipulating mental growth still largely undescribed, and the parameters of such induced change quite unknown, this reviewer believes Pinneau's tables may be used for some years at least! The second major contribution is a set of tables for Deviation IQ's for the 1960 revision of the Stanford-Binet tests, based on data provided by that revision. Pinneau has shown that McNemar's corrections in the 1937 revision for irregular variability from age to age were justified but did not go far enough. * While Pinneau has in effect conceded Wechsler's point on the usefulness of a relative measure of brightness, he seeks to preserve the mental age concept as a measure of mental *level*. * The third significant contribution of this monograph is theoretical, bearing on the nature of mental growth. John E. Anderson pointed out years ago that children may show a relatively stable IQ, even though increments in their mental growth are random in character from year to year. That is, the constancy of the intelligence quotient is in large measure a matter of the part-whole or overlap relation, because the individual never loses what he has already gained, but adds to it. Pinneau considers, however, that the present study does not support a theory of random increments. Bright children consistently make larger gains than do average children from year to year. Moreover, as they grow older their conventional IQ scores become less stable than are those of children with lesser ability in the same age groups. By a careful analysis of standardization data Pinneau shows that this instability results from increased weighting given items at later ages as compared with earlier mental ages (on which brighter children achieve their higher scores), as well as from age changes in the means and standard deviations of the conventional IQ. The latter part of the book contains a number of useful suggestions for practical interpretations of intelligence test scores, as well as guides for interpreting the tables Pinneau has provided for the new Stanford-Binet. The practitioner should keep these tables with his test manual and will find Pinneau's suggestions helpful. However, these materials cannot possibly substitute for a fundamental understanding of the statistical thinking involved in averages and standard deviations. Until we have more adequate and well-standardized differential tests that are suitable for children, and until professionals who use test results are considerably more knowledgable about statistics, the Binet will continue to be used as a general measure. It remains one of psychology's great achievements and promises to bear up under another generation of criticism.

J Nerv & Mental Dis 135:270–1 S '62. A. B. Silverstein. * [the author] appears to have become so involved in the methodological aspects of his research that in one sense, he has failed to do justice to the substantive findings of the study. In another sense, however, Pinneau has made altogether too much of his results. The size of the BGS sample (over a period of 18 years, the original 61 cases dwindled to 40), and particularly its unrepresentativeness (geographically and in terms of socio-economic status), place rather severe limitations on the generalizability of the findings. Yet on the basis of these findings, Pinneau presents tables for predicting IQ changes not only on the Stanford-Binet, but also on the Wechsler Intelligence Scale for Children, which was not even used in the BGS. Pinneau's statistical handling of the BGS data was a very workmanlike job. His development of revised IQ tables for the Stanford-Binet is a boon to thousands of psychologists and members of other professional groups who use this test.

Unfortunately, the reviewer cannot agree with the author's introductory remarks to his book, that (italics added) "the study reported here reveals *new* information which is critical in reading and using this number, *the IQ*...."

[B397]

★PINSENT, A. **The Construction and Use of Standardised Tests of Intelligence and Attainment: With Special Reference to the Problems of a Mixed Language Area.** University College of Wales, Faculty of Education, Pamphlet No. 3. Aberystwyth, Wales: the Faculty, 1963. Pp. 51. Paper. 3*s*. *

[B398]

PIOTROWSKI, ZYGMUNT A. **Perceptanalysis: A Fundamentally Reworked, Expanded, and Systematized Rorschach Method.** New York: Macmillan Co., 1957. Pp. xix, 505. $7.95. (London: Collier-Macmillan, Ltd. 60*s*.) * (*PA* 32:501)

Am J Psychol 71:628–30 S '58. Bruno Klopfer. * Piotrowski has used the Rorschach technique as a clinical and as a research tool as skillfully and as devotedly as anybody in this country. This concentrated effort has created in his fertile and facile mind a flood of observations, hypothetical ideas and literary analogies, which fill the 490 pages of text in this book to the brim. In fact, at times they brim over to such an extent that some of his chapters read more like stream-of-consciousness writing than like a cut and dried textbook. * The major methodological weakness of Piotrowski's book is his tendency to consider only his own ideas as objective and scientific: he speaks, for example, about the "impersonal banner of perceptanalysis" (p. 3). Conversely, he is too easily inclined to consider divergent opinions as specious. The most unfortunate such instance is his attitude toward Roy Shafer's attempt at a "psychoanalytic interpretation of the Rorschach method." * it seems to me that Shafer's contribution is as constructive as it is because it fulfills Piotrowski's postulate particularly well. Chapters 3 to 11 contain Piotrowski's description of the administration, scoring and interpretation of Rorschach records. In line with his phenomenological orientation, he makes an intriguing attempt to combine the description of scoring categories with their interpretative meaning. The many hypothetical ideas emerging from his phenomenological fusion are undoubtedly the most valuable contributions of his book. The price Piotrowski has to pay for this achievement, in order to contain his material within the covers of one book, is an almost complete disregard of the technical explanations and administrative preparations for the beginning Rorschach student and of all the published research efforts to clarify to some extent the interpretative meanings claimed. Fortunately, the previously mentioned combination of nonconformist and traditionalistic tendencies limits Piotrowski to the introduction of relatively few new scoring categories: they are to be found mostly in the area of shading responses. The many new interpretative ideas connected with practically every one of the scoring categories will remain a challenge to Rorschach workers for some time to come. Piotrowski's most original contribution is contained in the last two chapters, "Principle of Interdependence of Components" and "Individual Case Studies." In the latter chapter, Piotrowski brings first a most detailed interpretation of one of his own cases, and follows this with a re-interpretation of one of the two detailed case studies published so far from Rorschach's own material. The careful 18-page index is also worth mentioning. Although this book is....probably not the easiest way to establish a first familiarity with the Rorschach technique, certainly any clinical psychologist interested in diagnostic and prognostic testing will do well to expose himself at some time during his pre- or post-doctoral training to the provocative charm of this book.

Cont Psychol 3:189–92 Jl '58. Herman B. Molish. This volume is one of the most provocative revisions and expansions of Rorschach's *Psychodiagnostics,* originally published in 1921. * It is evident from the early pages of this volume that Piotrowski does not feel bound to the traditional thinking of the master, Rorschach. * This volume is....one of the few contemporary texts on the Rorschach Test in which the reader will have no doubt that the author has read and re-read Rorschach's original text from cover to cover. Piotrowski develops each of his own concepts within the framework of Rorschach's thinking, demonstrating the manner in which his thinking differs from the master's and the logical reasoning behind the divergence. The care with which these points are made reflects the thoroughness of a scholar and expert. The term *perceptanalysis* extends Rorschach's original thinking of the procedure as a "diagnostic test based on perception." The author justifiably notes an ever-increasing trend, among those using the test today, to neglect the formal and structural aspects of the Test Figures, and to rely too much upon interest content. He hopes that through the science of perceptanalysis, he may "return to the fold" those who are tempted to study personality in the erring ways of the pre-Rorschach period. The title of this volume is unique insofar as it does not even include the term *Rorschach* in its main heading. Indeed this book *is* more than just a volume on the Rorschach Test. Packed into its 474 pages are philosophy, methods of science, personality theory, logic, physics, geometry, and many historical references pertinent to the development of the test. Some readers may feel, at times, burdened by this elaboration of concepts, carried to a degree approaching pedantry and tautology. * It is....disturbing to find the author so greatly preoccupied with the goal of developing the Rorschach Test as a science in itself, and further developing "the new science Rorschach created." Rorschach did not in essence create a "new science." What he devised was an experimental procedure that can be applied within the framework of a science of personality. * Although Piotrowski is fully cognizant of the importance of the interdependence of Rorschach components, some of his generalizations concerning the "prototypal role" of the *M* response appear to deny this concept. There is much in this approach that resembles the confusion that results when phenomenological data are treated as behavioral. Indeed the author may be aware of this difficulty; yet some of the generalizations that he makes with reference to the "prototypal roles" of *M* responses seem to reflect a painful attempt to bridge the gap between psychological and social data. * The diversity of opinion among Rorschach workers in the use of shading responses has always been acute. The chapter dealing with this issue presents the most replete modification and application of the shading responses ever published in recent literature. Its didactic value alone is of value, since it gives a thorough historical account of the use of this Rorschach component. For the shading responses, Piotrowski refers to his "simplified scoring system"; nevertheless the reader may here find himself lost in a series of symbols which are explained in almost axiomatic-like language of geometry. The issues presented in relating shading responses to anxiety are many. Often these issues become confused with the author's own concept of anxiety. Little or no reference is made to the classical literature on this topic. It is difficult to determine the exact nature of Piotrowski's own theoretical aspect of anxiety. It is equally difficult to see how he relates the interpretation of the shading responses to other formal aspects of the Rorschach Test. * some of the thinking in regard to *Sex Shock* (Plates VI, VII, IX) is somewhat "free-wheeling." The author should have addressed himself to his own expressed cautious attitude in the use of "Universal Symbols" and the overinterpretation of "psychosexual inadequacies." The same criticism applies to his comment: "*M* shock points to a conflict over the subjects' homosexual tendencies, or, to be exact, over his or her insufficiently strong heterosexual tendencies." Likewise his thinking, in relation to Plate IX ("Shock") as "an indicator of a very acute ambivalence regarding sexual intercourse," appears overextended in its generalization. It is disappointing to find the chapter on *Principles of Interdependence of Components* left until the end of the book. It is upon this chapter that the scientific status of perceptanalysis must be based. Yet only 23 pages are devoted to this topic. One fact, however, is evident early in this chapter. There is recognition of the limitations of the author's painful attempts to bridge the gap between psychological and social aspects of behavior * The last chapter on *Individual Case Studies* is too limited in scope. Examples of several cases from a variety of nosological groupings to which the principles of *perceptanalysis* were applied would have been of great value to those interested in differential diagnosis. What is the status of this volume in contemporary Rorschach literature? Any volume which stimulates new ideas based on independent thinking and investigation in any branch of science is of value. In this sense, Piotrowski has beyond doubt achieved a success. His experience as a clinician, his obvious knowledge of traditional Rorschach method, and his research pursuits, qualify him to make these bold departures from "the footsteps of the master." Yet one may ask: Has he achieved one of his main goals of "tidying up and tightening perceptanalysis as a scientific procedure"? In what way has he improved upon the Rorschach Test as a scientific method? In spite of his courageous efforts, only further exploration of the concepts he proposes will answer these questions. He himself recognizes that validation on many of these issues is needed. His tendency to attempt the cross-over from psychological to social data will make this task even more difficult. His goal is expressed more conservatively in the closing pages of the book: "The purpose of this book is primarily to contribute to a more productive and more systematized interpretation of perceptanalytic data. Any validation of the rules of interpretation is beyond the scope of this enterprise." But "rules" alone do not make science, no more than mere ritual implies scientific method. Nor does the description of such "rules" in axiomatic language of logic and of the physical sciences necessarily enhance their scientific value. *

For additional reviews, see 5:B340.

[B399]

★PIOTROWSKI, ZYGMUNT A., AND ROCK, MILTON R.; WITH THE ASSISTANCE OF JOHN J. GRELA. **The Perceptanalytic Executive Scale: A Tool for the Selection of Top Managers.** New York and London: Grune & Stratton, Inc., 1963. Pp. iv, 220. $6.00; 42*s*. * (*PA* 38:9357)

Personnel 41:74–5 Jl–Ag '64. John A. Bromer. * a provocative book, but it's not for the personnel manager who lacks considerable training and experience in the uses of projective tests. Two chapters, however, will be of interest to the general business reader, whether or not he is trained in psychology. In Chapter 2, the authors provide a useful (though uncritical and incomplete) survey of the literature on identification of the characteristics of successful business executives; and in Chapter 7 they summarize the personality differences between successful and unsuccessful executives as seen by the clinician. Another chapter apparently aimed at the broad business audience fails in its purpose. This is Chapter 8, a how-to discussion of executive selection; very sketchy, it suggests some hypotheses for future research but is much too incomplete to be of practical value. * I cite two examples of a laxity in developing hypotheses and reporting research results: On page 16 the authors report a finding from their research before they have begun to describe their research hypotheses and procedure. On pages 27–28 they say, "He who seeks more goals and pursues them more intensely, perceives and imagines more than he who seeks little and is less active." This dubious assumption is supported by no data whatsoever. Further, there is reason to believe that many of the subjects had already been identified as "successes" or "failures" before the Perceptanalytic scale was applied and/or interpreted. Consequently, it seems to me that the impact of their experience in top management colored their emotional lives and their reactions to the inkblots, and the clinician's interpretations might have been influenced by his previous knowledge of the "success" or "failure" status. In describing the effect of training of "raters" on reliability of test observations, on pages 90 and 91 the authors are guilty of several imprecise statements and what seems to me to be a questionable statistical procedure. At the beginning of Chapter 7 they recognize the need for cross-validation of their findings, but elsewhere in their text they are much less critical in the way they generalize from the findings of their research. One of the interesting questions this research raises is that of cause and effect. Did the personality characteristics revealed by the Perceptanalytic scale contribute to the executives' downfall—or success—or are some of them affected or reinforced by recent experience? The authors suggest that the characteristic is there *before* success or failure, since "none of the psychological traits measured by the scale signs can be readily acquired, assumed by an act of will, or erased in a deliberate manner. The personality weaknesses precede the downfall and are not caused by the failure, although they may be reinforced by it." (Pages 199–200.) Perhaps, even probably, this assumption is true, but no data are presented that clearly support it. In summary, this is a stimulating book; much of it will not be readily understood by nonpsychologists, but for the personnel research man, it can be a useful source of hypotheses for future testing.

[B400]

★PORTEUS, STANLEY D. **The Maze Test and Clinical Psychology.** Palo Alto, Calif.: Pacific Books, 1959. Pp. vii, 203. Out of print. *

Am J Psychiatry 118:572–3 D '61. A. James Gregor. * one of the most sensitive measures of brain damage available. In use since 1915, the Maze Test has been variously conceived and employed as a test of generalized planning capacity (prehearsal and prevision), testing a segment of general intelligence neglected or inadequately assessed by any other series of tests (*cf.* p. 42)—a performance test of considerable diagnostic significance in the classification of psychoneurotics as dysthymics on the one hand, and hysterics and psychopaths on the other (*cf.* pp. 95 ff.)—a prognostic test which serves at least as a partial index of social adaptation (p. 84) having considerable predictive value in the identification of delinquent and protodelinquent disposition (*cf.* particularly pp. 90, 94) as well as potential industrial efficiency (p. 91). * To the clinician and the psychiatrist the effectiveness of the Maze as a sensitive indicator of brain damage is perhaps its prime importance. Postoperative examination, employing such standard testing devices as the Kohs Block Design Test, the Rorschach Test and the Wechsler-Bellevue afforded only negative or indifferent results (*cf.* pp. 53, 62 f.) while the Maze revealed extensive and apparently lasting impairment of the critical functions of initiative and response (pp. 54, 62), results which accorded themselves well with the intuitive estimate of the results of lobotomy tendered by qualified observers. * The continued and increased usefulness of the Porteus Maze as a testing device mark it a hardy growth in the hothouse of psychometric techniques. * Interestingly enough, while Professor Porteus alludes, several times throughout the text, to the usefulness of the Maze in the study of primitive mentality.... as well as racial temperament....there is no systematic exposition of the findings in the present volume similar to that which appeared in his earlier work, *The Porteus Maze Test and Intelligence* * The omission of these findings is to be lamented. So little has been forthcoming in these areas that each failure to at least review the established findings is a serious loss. It is to be hoped however, particularly with respect to available primitive subjects, that maze testing be, in the future, conducted with the more expanded series of tests (*cf.* Chapter VIII, Extension Maze Series), in order to mitigate one of the cardinal objections raised against the testing of primitives. The employment of a single test series, particularly where there is a paucity of available subjects (as is often the case in primitive populations) make chance deviations disproportionately significant. * Lucidity of presentation, a ready command of language, and a well-turned metaphor make the volume a model piece of professional literature. Unfortunately there is no index.

Brit J Psychol 52:202 My '61. J. Drewery. It is 45 years since Dr Porteus introduced his Maze test, and these years have seen the slow but progressive development of the test as a diagnostic instrument. His loyalty to the Maze test is a unique example of how rich the rewards can be when a basically simple procedure is fully exploited. In....the present volume the author introduces us to the possibilities of his test as a vehicle for the study of expressive behaviour. * Of particular interest is the chapter describing the performance decrement which follows the therapeutic administration of chlorpromazine. * The present volume supersedes all earlier handbooks for the administration and interpretation of the test. For those working in the clinical field, this is a necessary and very welcome standard text.

Cont Psychol 5:308–9 S '60. Henry N. Peters. * This test is certainly among the top ten in terms of quantity of articles about it. Among tests which psychologists use to assess maladjustment, Porteus' has been in active use longer than any other. * the tenacity of the maze test has not been a result only of Porteus' persistent expressions of interest in it for over 40 years. It is a good test. The research material summarized in this volume is convincing support for this opinion. * Porteus is....primarily concerned with practical conclusions and is impatient with a cautious assessment of data. The remarkable thing is how consistently his conclusions have withstood the test of time. Thus many cautious psychologists, although questioning Porteus' treatment of data and interpretation of evidence, still find themselves in agreement with his conclusions.

[B401]

★PRELINGER, ERNST, AND ZIMET, CARL N.; WITH THE COLLABORATION OF ROY SCHAFER AND MAX LEVIN. **An Ego-Psychological Approach to Character Assessment.** New York: Free Press of Glencoe, 1964. Pp. ix, 211. $4.95. * (London: Collier-Macmillan, Ltd. 38*s.*)

[B402]

★RABIN, ALBERT I., AND HAWORTH, MARY R., EDITORS. **Projective Techniques With Children.** New York: Grune & Stratton, Inc., 1960. Pp. xiii, 392. $11.75. * (London: William Heinemann Medical Books Ltd. 83*s.*) (*PA* 35:2229)

Cont Psychol 6:364–6 O '61. Robert D. Wirt. * Rabin and Haworth....and their authors have accomplished a remarkable feat. While there is an extensive literature, and there are many psychologists familiar with projective techniques, no single person could hope to become competent to write such a book. Even two such highly qualified persons as these editors are could not have done the job alone. It required expert contributors and expert editors. * Good editors choose contributors wisely and then work carefully to provide a well-integrated volume. Rabin and Haworth are good editors. * The book has a unity rarely found in edited volumes. Most of these chapters begin with a discussion of the theoretical rationale for a given technique, which is followed by systematic coverage of methods for administration, scoring, and interpretation, and then by selected case examples, a survey of research findings, and a summary. Every chapter includes an excellent list of references. * The editors and their contributors steer a sensible course between factual reporting of research findings and honest assertion of clinical interpretation. * The book is intended for the clinical student, the practicing clinician, and the research worker. It will be useful to all of these persons, but of most use to the clinical student who has already had some course work in projective techniques and some clinical experience.

J Proj Tech 25:241–4 Je '61. Walter G. Klopfer. * The book is certainly representative in that all sorts of views are presented between its covers. * the quality of the material is exceedingly uneven * Siegel presents some excellent criteria for determining whether a projective technique can be used as a research tool. It would have been interesting to instruct the authors dealing with the specific technique to evaluate their tools according to this sort of framework. However, since the authors were apparently given no structure but allowed to proceed entirely on their own, the question of operational statements, reliability, validity, and predictive efficiency are taken up only when the author is so inclined. In general, the book makes very interesting and stimulating reading, the bulk of existing knowledge concerning the application of projective techniques to children is probably contained or referred to in the chapters, and the many interesting case illustrations are always helpful to the practicing clinician as well as the novice. * There is a useful chapter by Fromm....on the projective elements of intelligence testing. * Fromm supplies a list of personological categories and variables with hints as to how they can be applied to standard intelligence tests. Regrettably these are exclusively psychoanalytic in nature, and are therefore limited to settings in which this is the sole frame of reference. * In general....the book is a very worth while one and quite representative of the present status of the field it purports to cover. The clinical and theoretical approaches covered are representative of people working in the area of child clinical psychology. * The editors.... are to be commended for their bringing together....so much useful information from so many divergent points of view. * [See review for additional critical comments not excerpted.]

Psychiatric Q Sup 35:366–7 pt 2 '61. * The editors and most contributors to this volume try hard to provide a psychoanalytic theory for their procedures, but it is a very highly edited form of psychoanalysis which might be acceptable even to Queen Victoria. Projection is defined simply as "externalization." Moreover, the link between the theory and the results of the tests presented in this book is so weak that one does not miss anything by skipping the theory. The reason is emphasis on ego-psychology with no meaningful reference to the unconscious. Freudian ego-psychology does not differ from the pre-Freudian psychology of conscious personality except that in it, the ego has to get along with the id and the super-ego. The complex interrelationship among these three Freudian "institutions" of personality cannot be reliably inferred from projective test data, and this difficult problem is not discussed, let alone solved, in this series of presentations. The historically first projective technique, the word association test, is included, but its author's name, C. G. Jung, is absent from this book, which aims at completeness and is replete with names. The volume contains some misinformation. For example, it is not true that the Rorschach test requires the subject to respond with the first image or idea and to do so as soon as possible. It is not true that Rorschach used "a vague psychoanalytic background" for his test. Not only is there no trace of psychoanalysis in the *Psychodiagnostics,* but Rorschach plainly stated that "the test cannot be used to probe into the content of the subconscious." He added that the test "can be of some service to the psychoanalyst" as a diagnostic aid and thus "can clear up those unpleasant situations arising when one has an analytic patient in whom there is a suspicion of schizophrenia." The theory offered in the present book is vague, sketchy and confusing rather than helpful. The best aspects of this volume are in its factual review of projective personality tests and its illustration of some of the applications of these tests to the understanding of children's personalities.

[B403]

*RAND, HENRY A. **Graphology: A Handbook, Second Edition.** Cambridge, Mass.: Sci-Art Publishers, 1961. Pp. 208. Paper. $1.90. * (London: Peter Owen Ltd., 1962. 25*s.*)

Brit J Psychol 53:105–6 F '62. H. Wallerstein. * A well-organized system for relating graphic signs to personality traits is presented but the system's validity appears dubious. Demonstration of trait deviations in terms of handwriting deviations from "....the copybook model letters...." (p. 36) probably must await more adequate understanding of personality dynamics.

Occup Psychol 37:162 Ap '63. H. J. Eysenck. Many psychologists are opposed to graphology almost on principle; this attitude seems to be mistaken, because there is much evidence to show that expressive movements are related to personality traits, and what is writing but a kind of expressive movement? However, the experimental evidence to date certainly does not encourage optimism; well controlled trials have almost always given negative results. This fact tends to be disregarded by writers on graphology; thus Mr Rand says that "only one experiment has shown negative results.... all the other experiments have yielded positive results." This is simply untrue, and reflects the obvious naivety of the writer as far as the experimental literature and procedures are concerned. This is also shown in a list of 129 traits he gives, together with their "graphological signs." This list goes from acquisitiveness through beneficence, ceremoniousness, diplomacy, *ennui,* fickleness, instability, love of luxury, procrastination, sensuousness and vulgarity to zealousness! According to this list, if you possess a trait called "humour" then your writing will show "i" dots and wavy "t" bars! As a serious contribution to the subject this book is valueless; its only function will be to indicate to Ph.D. students in search of a topic that perhaps some interesting and promising leads for research might be found in this field.

For reviews of the first edition, see 4:B315.

[B404]

★RASCH, G. **Probabilistic Models for Some Intelligence and Attainment Tests.** Danish Institute for Educational Research, Studies in Mathematical Psychology 1. Copenhagen, Denmark: Danish Science Press, Ltd., 1960. Pp. xiii, 184. Kr. 48. * (*PA* 36:5HB84R)

Cont Psychol 8:7–8 Ja '63. Eric F. Gardner. * Rasch attempts to set up and illustrate the use of models which take into account two very old issues associated with the role of the examinee population. They are 1) the extent to which most statistics, being group-centered, are appropriate or adequate for answering questions about individuals and 2) the desirability of being able to make comparisons between individuals independent of the particular instruments used and, symmetrically, the desirability of being able to compare stimuli measuring the same thing independent of which particular individuals were used in the comparison. Stochastic models based upon the probability that a subject responds incorrectly are developed for several types of tests in the application of which the role of the populations are eliminated. Each model implies two types of parameters, a "difficulty" for each test (or item) and an "ability" for each person. * A third major topic is the presentation of a structural model for scaling items of a test. The approach is somewhat similar to Guttman's work on scaling (1941) and to Ebel's "test scores having content-meaning" (1962). Although there are a number of shortcomings of these models, including the extent to which data in most practical situations would meet the necessary assumptions, the approach is very interesting and provocative. However in defense of Dr. Rasch some of the assumptions appear to be no more violent than some currently used by psychometricians, e.g. the assumption that the distribution of errors of measurement of a number of individuals estimated from scores based on odd-even responses can be used as an approximation for the distribution of errors of measurement of a particular individual on an infinite number of comparable forms of a test. Although the empirical data presented conform well to the models, it would be premature to assume that we now have available new techniques to replace the currently used procedures. The success of the model even in the special cases cited seems to me to be due in no small measure to the apparently extremely careful work which must have been done to obtain the comparable forms of the instruments used. As Dr. Rasch says, "Psychologists wishing to use the methods in practice will miss a careful discussion of how to do so. I consider, however, that it is as yet a little early to go right ahead to practice." This volume, presenting an interesting and somewhat different approach, deserves careful study by theoretical psychometricians.

Psychometrika 28:219–20 Je '63. Rosedith Sitgreaves. This is an extremely interesting and well-written book in which three mathematical models are developed and discussed, two for oral reading tests and one for the structure of items of a test of ability. * The two models for oral reading are beautifully presented, the development progressing logically from the probability assumptions to the testing of the models against reality. The presentation of the third model is somewhat less satisfying since it is more discursive and heuristic, but the model proposed and the questions that it raises are extremely interesting. Over-all, the author has made a substantial contribution to model building in tests of ability.

[B405]

★REDFERN, GEORGE B. **How to Appraise Teaching Performance.** Columbus, Ohio: School Management Institute, Inc., 1963. Pp. 100. Paper. $2.50. *

[B406]

*REMMERS, H. H.; GAGE, N. L.; AND RUMMEL, J. FRANCIS. **A Practical Introduction to Measurement and Evaluation.** New York: Harper & Row, Publishers, Inc., 1960. Pp. xiii, 370. $4.75. * (London: Harper & Row Ltd. 36s.)

Personnel & Guid J 39:417–8 Ja '61. John W. M. Rothney. * The authors have attempted to be both practical and theoretical in a book that is much shorter than others with similar titles. How well have they succeeded? Generally very well is the judgment of this reviewer. But the authors have warned the readers that something must be lost when maximum brevity is sought. The loss in this book is in the latter chapters where discussions of sociometry, rating scales, anecdotal records, inventories and projective techniques are presented. It is clear that the authors are much more concerned with statistics and methods of handling objectively-scored tests than with materials that cannot be scored with a key. The authors' enthusiasm for tests has not apparently led them to detailed reading of test manuals. They recommend and use for illustration tests which violate the very principles presented throughout the book. The practical teacher is going to be in a dilemma when she, having learned what is desirable from this textbook, sets out to select a test and finds in the manuals that test authors and publishers seem not to have read the same book. The authors have not done the critical job that seems essential if the readers are to become intelligent consumers of tests. Is it really true that the best tests are developed commercially and that, other things being equal, the best tests are the cheapest tests? The authors suggest that the book might be "focally relevant to the professional role of the counselor" but the term predictive validity appears only once in a short paragraph. Attempts are made to suggest implications for professional counselors but it seemed clear to this reviewer that the book was written for use in the pre-service and in-service education of classroom teachers. If one has to give or take short courses on measurement and evaluation and one is willing to sacrifice thorough and critical discussions for a concise rather traditional treatment of the field, this is as good a book as one can find. The counselor may wish, however, that his colleagues had read more deeply and critically in this important area.

Teach Col Rec 62:258–9 D '60. Robert L. Thorndike. * devoting eight pages to computation procedures for the correlation coefficient while making no mention of informal techniques of item analysis by which a teacher can improve his own tests seems a serious imbalance. Furthermore, in order to save space there is pressure to present general principles in broad outline, while cutting down on the illustrations and explanations that give them substance and meaning. Some of this appears to have occurred in the present volume. The book is a sound one, none the less, but this reviewer prefers the fuller *Educational Measurement and Evaluation* from which it has been abridged.

For reviews of the earlier editions, see 5:B350 and 3:1112.

[B407]

★RICHMAN, ELI. **College Admissions Based on S.A.T. Scores, 1960–1961.** [Chelsea, Mass.: the Author, School Department, 1961.] Pp. v, 43. Paper, mimeographed. * For the latest edition, see B408.

Personnel & Guid J 40:201–2 O '61. Thomas M. Magoon. * The author....has sought such information from more than 300 higher educational institutions throughout the United States which employ the S.A.T. For 259 of these distribution data were received. The....content is quite detailed in some instances, such as the number of places to which decimals are carried, so detailed as to delay grasp of the data and imply a degree of accuracy which is more apparent than real. To what use can such material be put? The author hopes that the degree of reality in educational planning will be increased and that one consequence might be the reduction of number of applications made to different institutions. A companion publication which would be of considerable value to personnel workers would be one directed at the differential weight (albeit perhaps more subjective than statistical) which institutions give to both psychometric and other application data. Review of the tables in this report indicates a considerable range of accepted students' scores within institutions. The percentage of accepted students in each score range provides a gross index of the degree of weight accorded the test data.

[B408]

★RICHMAN, ELI. **College Admissions Based on S.A.T. Scores, 1962–1963.** [Chelsea, Mass.: the Author, School Department, 1963.] Pp. i, 63. Paper, mimeographed. $1.50. * For a review of the first edition, see B407.

[B409]

★RICKERS-OVSIANKINA, MARIA A., EDITOR. **Rorschach Psychology.** New York and London: John Wiley & Sons, Inc., 1960. Pp. xvi, 483. $8.95; 68*s*. * (*PA* 35:2231)

Am J Orthopsychiatry 32:206–7 Ja '62. Erika Fromm. This is one of the most important and scientifically most stimulating books ever published on the Rorschach method. Immersing oneself in it is an exciting experience—and a must—for theory-minded readers in the clinical field and in experimental psychology. The authors probe, and hypothesize, and evaluate. They draw on hunches and on their great store of knowledge. They are eagerly pushing ahead at the frontier of the theoretical and the research potential of the Rorschach technique. * Rickers-Ovsiankina....wrote the excellent introductory chapter "Synopsis of Psychological Premises Underlying the Rorschach." * In a fascinating chapter on the "White-Space Response," Fonda gives new meaning to the S response. For too long a predominantly negative connotation ("oppositional trends") has been attributed to it. Similarly, the concept of aggression had only a negative, destructive meaning in psychoanalytic theory until recently. We now know that not all aggression is destructive. * A well-organized chapter by Korchin on "Form Perception and Ego Function" * David Shapiro in his highly stimulating chapter "A Perceptual Understanding of Color Response" examines the puzzling question of the linkage between color perception and affect with which experimental psychologists and Rorschach theoreticians alike have struggled. * Holt and Havel present a supplementary method for scoring content which Holt has recently developed. * Holt's scoring system is elaborate and well thought out. It will meet with resistance from those of our confreres who like to do their Rorschach interpretations on an impressionistic "quickie" basis and fail to subject their intuitive hypotheses to a careful deliberative critical scientific evaluation. This reviewer feels that Holt's system represents a major break-through in Rorschach theory and practice. * The editor invited the Swiss psychiatrist Roland Kuhn to contribute a chapter on Rorschach and existentialism. Unfortunately this paper was put together haphazardly, and thus lends stature neither to modern Rorschach psychology nor to existentialism. * This book abounds in new ideas related to personality research, to perception, and to cognition. It shows how the Rorschach method can be understood from the viewpoint of psychoanalytic psychology, of Gestalt theory, of contemporary developmental psychology, and of phenomenology and existentialism. It is a creative book and opens up many new vistas for future research.

Am J Psychiatry 118:859–60 Mr '62. Stephanie Z. Dudek. This is a well-written, thought-provoking book which assumes a sophisticated knowledge of the Rorschach technique of personality analysis. It is mainly intended for the experienced clinician who wants to go beyond the use of the Rorschach as a purely diagnostic and personality descriptive tool. In this respect it is a valuable contribution to his thinking and theorizing. Sixteen contributors, all experts in the areas they explore, have done an excellent job of meeting the challenge set for them. What emerges is a book with exciting theories about feeling, about cognition, about relationships—in short a book with exciting theories about personality, theory, research, and clinical practice. There is an excellent chapter by Piotrowski on the human movement response, an area which has been enriched by his original thinking and research over many years. Shapiro provides a fascinating interpretation of colour from the point of view of perception, which will undoubtedly stimulate important experimental work. The research and theorizing about the experience balance is very well summarized by Singer, including his own practical research oriented reformulation of it. Bohm does a service to the clinician who is unable to read German in presenting Binder's theories about the shading determinant. Havel and Holt contribute an interesting, if highly complicated, research tool for gauging primary and secondary processes in the Rorschach from the point of view of adaptive and maladaptive regression (regression in the service of the ego). All the contributions are useful and tie together many cross segments of research and information which otherwise would not be so readily available. In the last chapter Harris succeeds in casting the depressive light of a grey day on the provocative theorizing with a summary of the status of research on validity in which he attempts to examine the inconsistencies in the Rorschach literature. For all his pessimism he is able to end with the firm conviction that "the inkblots do have something meaningful to say about personality which no other method of depth analysis quite succeeds in tapping." * highly recommended for the experienced Rorschach clinician and for the personality theorist who may be interested in using the Rorschach as a method of personality investigation. It brings together the most relevant research on the many Rorschach hypotheses that are used in clinical interpretation and for this alone the editor....is to be highly commended.

Cont Psychol 6:420–2 D '61. Laurance F. Shaffer. * The good chapter on developmental theory (Laurence Hemmendinger) draws extensively from Werner. * Another theory of great generality, psychoanalysis, is not so well represented. It appears, meagerly and not too successfully, only in a chapter on assessing primary and secondary process through the Rorschach content (R. R. Holt and Joan Havel). * The other "theories" are more Rorschach-bound. The chapter on organizational activity (Marguerite R. Hertz) is a scholarly and useful summary of Rorschach methods but does not draw on other approaches to cognitive functions. * Every theory that deserves the designation should produce a series of testable hypotheses which generate empirical research. All contributors (except the two European ones) accept the intimate relationship between theory and evidence and cite from 19 to 118 references, mainly to research studies. The amount of empirical research is impressive, but its quality often is not. A reviewer should treat a slip or two with charitable silence, but the shortcomings are numerous enough to require a warning that the reader should examine with a critical eye the original articles cited. The chapter on the white-space response says, "The most clear-cut findings show that the higher a person's rate of *S* emission, the more likely he is to be bright (21....)....ingenious (21....), and self-sufficient (21)" (p. 93). The thrice cited article designated by "(21)" reported, among other data, the correlations of 37 non-Rorschach variables with *S*. Two of these 37 correlations were significant, about what one would expect by chance. The original authors wisely drew no positive conclusion. The present chapter extracts two conclusions, "bright" and "ingenious" from an r of .197 with PMA reasoning when five other PMA scores are not significantly related, and a conclusion of "self-sufficient" from an r of $-.251$ with the number of sociometric choices made. The chapter on form perception, in support of the proposition that good form is a measure of ego strength, cites a nonsignificant r as positive evidence, and gives in some detail the findings of an apparently positive study not confirmed by two replications (p. 118). An article cited as evidence for the meaning of flexor and extensor *M* suffers from such severe inconsistencies in its tables as to raise grave doubts about its competency (p. 137). In another instance, a finding on the internal-consistency reliability of the Rorschach is reported without qualification as "an average correlation of .85 for three groups" (p. 371) when the original research was concerned only with the reliability of *R*, the number of responses. Two chapters give results of their authors' original studies not reported fully elsewhere. Neither presentation would have passed an editorial screen. Two reported studies of the movement response are *post hoc* analyses lacking cross-validation (pp. 139–141). An elaborate study of the scoring of content for primary and secondary processes seemed strikingly confirmed for a group of 15 men and not confirmed at all for a group of women (pp. 311–314). Do the results show a sex difference, or a failure of cross-validation that negates the method? Only further research can answer that question, and, pending the emergence of such evidence, the publication of 40 pages of detailed scoring instructions has perhaps been premature. Another striking characteristic of the book is the scarcity of negative evidence until the final chapter. A reader not already well informed might receive the impression that almost all research confirms the positions presented by the authors. Rorschach research is complex and much of it is conflicting. Many of the generalizations would be challenged by worthy studies that are not even listed in the bibliographies or the name index. Two chapters near the end of the volume supply the book's most substantial contributions. The reviewer engaged in a fantasy of what might have happened if these chapters had been written first and made required reading for the other contributors. Lois and Gardner Murphy, after a sensitive appraisal of Hermann Rorschach's place in the development of psychological thought, develop a theory of considerable generality in terms of levels and functions, and the interdependence of functions. To sample all these might require a formidable instrument capable of evoking hundreds of responses. Rorschach's unique insight was that a single response might give multiple information about several levels and functions; but this attractive economy, basic to the widespread clinical use of the instrument, has its hazards for a genuine understanding of personality through research: "....sampling so much with so little gets one involved in contamination, in problems of low reliabilities which cannot be explained away...." (p. 353). Rorschach's pioneering work might evoke three attitudes, write the Murphys, to revere him, to standardize and codify him, or to push on to new accomplishments which require a blending of earlier and contemporary methods. The authors favor the third course, which demands the development of new techniques that retain the merits and correct the faults of *the* Rorschach. A similar conclusion is reached in the long and useful final chapter on validity, by Jesse G. Harris, Jr. Here at last, many technical problems of the Rorschach receive the frank recognition they demand—the language of the examinee and examiner, the sufficiency of sampling, the nature of criteria, and the effects of variations in conditions, materials, and examiners. The chapter looks to the future. The Rorschach is neither as dead as its opponents aver, nor as eternal as its faithful adherents believe. It is a prelude to research on personality that has hardly begun. *Rorschach Psychology* is an honest representation of the contemporary state of its field, with all of its inspirations and confusions, all of its good and bad theory and research. As such it is a successful book that will stimulate both thoughts and feelings in the informed and critical reader and in the graduate student under appropriate guidance. It deserves to be read.

[B410]

★Rines, Alice R. **Evaluating Student Progress in Learning the Practice of Nursing.** Nursing Education Monographs, No. 5. New York: Bureau of Publications, Teachers College, Columbia University, 1963. Pp. xi, 76. Paper. $2.50. *

[B411]

Robinson, Helen M., Editor. **Evaluation of Reading: Proceedings of the Annual Conference on Reading Held at the University of Chicago, 1958.** Supplementary Educational Monographs, Vol. 20, No. 88. Chicago, Ill.: University of Chicago Press, 1958. Pp. vii, 208. $3.50. *

J Develop Read 2:49–51 su '59. Gladys L. Persons. * A noteworthy contribution is the frank and illuminating discussions of the values and limitations of standardized reading tests. Dr. Arthur E. Traxler's discussion of this topic is especially provocative and helpful. With all their weaknesses, standardized tests are better for determining points of approach to instruction than any other single measure. The conference tried to include discussion of the part the entire school should play in its reading program. Teachers, principal, administrator, reading consultant—the duties of each are suggested and discussed. Of course, the teachers are the ones on whom the burden is heaviest. If a teacher were to read the monograph through from cover to cover and list all the suggestions made for teachers, he would feel that no day is long enough nor any teacher energetic enough to do all that is suggested for each one of his pupils. The speeches.... which are most helpful are those which propose concrete suggestions. June Oppenheim's contribution on Appraising Interests and Attitudes is excellent for its specific help. Gertrude Whipple is good on Identifying Needs and Providing Guidance in Appraisal of Reading in Content Areas. *

[B412]

★Rogers, L. Edna. **Measurement of Status Relations in a Hospital.** Ohio State University, College of Engineering, Engineering Experiment Station, Vol. 28, No. 3. Columbus, Ohio: the Station, May 1959. Pp. vii, 55. Paper. $2.00. *

[B413]

Roman, Klara G. **Handwriting: A Key to Personality.** New York: Pantheon Books, Inc., 1952. Pp. xi, 382. $6.50. * (London: Routledge & Kegan Paul Ltd., 1961. Paper. 11*s.* 6*d.*) For reviews, see 5:B360.

[B414]

★Rosen, Albert. **Development of MMPI Scales Based on a Reference Group of Psychiatric Patients.** American Psychological Association, Psychological Monographs: General and Applied, Vol. 76, No. 8, Whole No. 527. Washington, D.C.: the Association, Inc., 1962. Pp. 25. Paper. $1.50. * (*PA* 37:3098)

Personnel & Guid J 41:828–30 My '63. L. E. Drake. * this monograph....should be a contribution to the literature on structured personality inventories. Rosen hypothesizes that many of the items on the original scales were differentiating normals from abnormals rather than contributing to diagnostic categories as such. This hypothesis was derived from the fact that the original clinical scales were obtained by the comparison of item responses of normals with item responses of individuals who were considered abnormal and assigned to various diagnostic categories. * The author used as a basic reference group psychiatric patients in general rather than normals in general. Then he drew cases from the files that were classified into five different categories. These were male patients and were categorized according to the VA psychiatric nomenclature as follows: (1) anxiety reaction, (2) conversion reaction (hysteria), (3) depressive reaction (neurotic depression), (4) somatization reaction (psychophysiological reaction), and (5) schizophrenic reaction, paranoid type. The conversion reaction (Cr) scale will serve to illustrate his procedures with all the scales, and is especially pertinent since the original Hy scale was derived from a clinical group diagnosed as conversion hysterics. Seventy-seven items were found to differentiate between patients in general and the group showing conversion reactions at the 0.05 confidence level. These items constituted the scale. * The items on the scale were subjectively classified by Rosen. The major classifications were: (1) denial of emotional disturbance, (2) gregariousness, and (3) religiosity. There was only one somatic item on the scale and practically no items in common with the Hy scale. It was noted that there is a considerable overlap in a positive direction of Hy items with original scales. There was a slight overlap of items on the new Cr scale with the original scales but they were usually scored in the opposite direction. It appears that Cr and Hy are markedly different in content and that Cr differs more from the other original scales than does the Hy scale. This is further born out by correlations of the Cr and Hy scales with the other scales. Whereas the Hy scale correlates positively with the original scales, the Cr scale correlates negatively with all the original scales except for L and K which are positive. Of special significance is the coefficient of −0.24 between Cr and Hy. Rosen explains this negative relationship as follows: "Since somatic complaints, anxiety, tension, depression, and similar symptoms are common among all groups of psychiatric patients, conversion cases as well as a general sample of psychiatric patients will respond to 'somatic' and 'anxiety' items in a similar manner. In an item analysis within a psychiatric population, therefore, these items will not be differentiating. When the comparison is made between conversion cases and *normals,* however, these items will emerge as discriminating ones, as in the Hy scale. Within a psychiatric population, on the other hand, the great majority of items differentiating conversion cases from other patients are those answered in the 'normal' direction." This reviewer agrees in general with Rosen's explanation of the negative relationship, however; Hy does measure something other than merely the differentiation of abnormal and normal. Rosen reports correlation coefficients for Hy with Pr, Pa, Pt, Sc, and Ma of +0.30, +0.30, +0.34, +0.22, and +0.08. These coefficients should be higher if the differentiating factor is merely abnormality. Furthermore, studies using adjective check lists to describe people with elevated Hy scores frequently report descriptions which would indicate favorable characteristics for such persons. * Rosen has made his point well. If the clinician dealing with abnormals desires to diagnose cases by means of a structured personality instrument, he can differentiate better by using scales derived from an abnormal population. However, this may not be the only way of improving the diagnosis. A pattern analysis might do as good a job and be simpler. Nevertheless, Rosen has made a contribution that goes beyond the derivation of scales and the methodology used. The added insight into the reactions of abnormals to the items is not only interesting but should also stimulate further research. Finally, it will be interesting to determine what these scales will do with a normal population.

[B415]

★Rosen, Ned A. **A Validation Study of the College Entrance Examination Board Examinations and Other Predictors at Purdue University.** Purdue University, Division of Educational Reference, Studies in Higher Education, No. 90. Lafayette, Ind.: the Division, August 1960. Pp. 26. Paper. $1.00. * (*PA* 35:2788)

[B416]

★Rosenfeld, Sam. **30 Days to a Higher I.Q. for Your Child.** New York: Crown Publishers, Inc., 1961. Pp. iv, 188. Paper. $2.95. *

[B417]

★Rothney, John W. M.; Danielson, Paul J.; and Heimann, Robert A. **Measurement for Guidance.** New York: Harper & Row, Publishers, Inc., 1959. Pp. xiii, 378. $5.50. * (London: Harper & Row Ltd. 37*s.* 6*d.*)

Ed & Psychol Meas 19:454–7 au '59 J. C. Gowan. This book is perhaps mistitled; a better name might be: "No Measurement for Guidance." The introduction states that: "This refreshing and stimulating book deals with the appropriateness, selection, use, recording and interpretation of tests with respect to their value in the counseling process. Weaknesses as well as strengths of tests are treated with the delicate discrimination and judgment which comes from years of work with tests in relation to individual counseling * All those who work with tests will experience pleasure as well as professional improvement from using and pondering this work." A more accurate introduction might have read: This stimulating book deals with the inappropriateness of tests and their lack of value in the counseling of individuals. Strengths of tests are treated with delicate discrimination and faint praise, while weaknesses are clobbered with a heavy hand. All those who work with tests will experience pain, but most will derive professional improvement from using and pondering this work. * It may be permissible to wonder whether the over-all lambasting which testing takes in the volume may not have the general effect of prejudicing teachers and counselors against all tests instead of just the poor ones. While it is obvious that we work with imperfect tools, they are perhaps better than none at all. The book constitutes a scathing and well written polemic against abuses in mental testing. That the indictment is deserved is incontestable; that the prosecution is relentless is obvious; that the result is overstatement is inevitable. Despite the soundness of their position, the tone of the authors is often unnecessarily angry * The book is certainly a salty antidote for the excesses of testing as exploited by some commercial houses. It comes down hard on some of the more vulnerable spots, and in this respect offers a much needed commentary to counterbalance the blurbs of the manuals. While criticism, much of it highly justified, is scattered abroad with little regard as to where it falls, one may note that it is more tempered with regard to SCAT and other offerings of ETS than with regard to the CTMM and other offerings of the California Test Bureau. The Psychological Corporation comes out better than Science Research Associates. * The first several chapters on sources, kinds, criteria of selection, and meaning of test scores have some very sound things to say about reliability, norms, and validity. The IQ is damned and buried at the crossroads with a lance through its standard deviation, which is probably as it should be, but perhaps too little is said about the possibilities of band scoring, or the use of stanines or deciles or of other units of such a size that the standard error of measurement for an individual will be less than half such a unit interval. The authors really "tee off" on personality questionnaires and interest inventories, which they do not even dignify by the name of "test." Admitting that there is much to blame and little to praise in this newest and most difficult area, it may fairly be asked whether the authors have not tarried too long in beating a dead horse to have noticed some of the newer vehicles. * Some other odds and ends which this reviewer missed were any detailed discussions or other assessment methods, especially the sociometric ones. The relationship between the way a person is seen by himself (in the self report of tests) and the way he is seen by others (in his behavior) is an important validation area which might have received more emphasis. The authors come down rather hard on the forced choice approach—an attack which is perhaps to the good. Yet there is little said on the Q-technique which, as a related method, may perhaps have certain advantages without the same flaws. Another area of validation of testing concerns replications of tests with growth study subjects. Again this engaging line of research is not adequately discussed. * The authors in their frequent appeals to authority find it often necessary to quote themselves. While their eminence well qualifies them for this useful privilege, the result is often the opposite of what they wish to produce. For by wearing both the hats of the prosecutor and jurist, they induce in us the jury an underdog sympathy for the defendant testmaker which he probably does not always deserve. * To the large extent that this book will make such workers more sophisticated and discriminating, it will serve this function. To the small extent that it may tend to produce in them disdain and apathy for testing as a method of helping to understand individual differences, it may do a disservice.

J Counsel Psychol 6:325–6 w '59. Donald E. Super. * might well have been subtitled "An Idiosyncratic Approach" * This book *is* different. But, come to think of it, what book on measurement in guidance is not unique, if it departs from the sad pattern of an annotated catalogue of published tests? * a text for an *advanced introductory* course * Test administration, slighted elsewhere, is well treated here. This material is good but it does not familiarize the counselor with the specific tools which he may use. * They characterize a predictive validity of .60 to .65 as "low" in condemning the Aviation Cadet Classification Tests of World War II, although most psychologists consider such predictive validities rather high * Interests and personality inventories are viewed with a skepticism which Rothney and his colleagues consider "healthy," but which, since it rejects Strong's 18-year follow-up in a cavalier manner and states categorically that no other validity studies have been made with interest inventories, must at least be characterized as deviant and may therefore be suspected of being *un*healthy. * great stress is put on the need to make clinical interpretations of tests rather than using them mechanically, but virtually no attention is paid to the massive evidence accumulated in Meehl's book on *Clinical vs. Statistical Prediction* and in subsequent studies to the effect that clinical interpretation spoils valid tests. If much use were made of the Koester-Meehl-McArthur research and discussions of how to improve clinical procedures when actuarial data are lacking one would not be disturbed by this approach, but when important evidence and discussions are neglected one cannot but suspect that the omissions result from failure of the data to fit the authors' biases. These evidences of bias are, in my judgment, serious defects, and combined with the lack of attention to specific tests make the book unsuitable for use as a text in most courses. As a source of supplementary reading, with suitable discussion in class, it could prove very valuable.

[B418]

★Rudman, Jack. **Graduate Record Examination: How to Pass Aptitude Test: Questions and Answers.** Brooklyn, N.Y.: College Publishing Corporation, 1963. Pp. v, 294. Paper. $3.50. *

[B419]

★Rudman, Jack. **How to Pass Common Examinations: 1, Professional Information; 2, English Expression; 3, Social Studies, Literature, and Fine Arts; 4, Science and Mathematics; 5, Nonverbal Reasoning: Questions and Answers: National Teacher Examinations.** Brooklyn, N.Y.: College Publishing Corporation, 1964. Pp. 304. Paper. $3.95. *

[B420]

★Rudman, Jack. **How to Pass Dental Aptitude Test: Questions and Answers.** Brooklyn, N.Y.: College Publishing Corporation, 1962. Pp. 301. Paper. $3.95. *

[B421]

★Rudman, Jack. **How to Pass Law School Admission Test: Questions and Answers.** Brooklyn, N.Y.: College Publishing Corporation, 1963. Pp. v, 295. Paper. $3.95. *

[B422]

★Rudman, Jack. **How to Pass Medical College Admission Test: Questions and Answers, Second Edition.** Brooklyn, N.Y.: College Publishing Corporation, 1963. Pp. 298. Paper. $3.95. *

[B423]

★Rudman, Jack. **How to Pass Nonverbal Reasoning: Questions and Answers: Common Examinations No. 5, National Teacher Examinations.**

Brooklyn, N.Y.: Technical Extension Service, Inc., 1962. Unnumbered pages. Paper, mimeographed, plastic binding. $3.50. *

[B424]

★RUDMAN, JACK. **How to Pass the Admission Test for Graduate Study in Business.** Brooklyn, N.Y.: College Publishing Corporation, 1963. Pp. 308. Paper. $3.95. *

[B425]

★RUPIPER, OMER JOHN. **Item Writing: A Programed Text of Rules for Writing Objective-Type Test Items.** Norman, Okla.: Harlow Publishing Corporation, 1964. Pp. vii, 352. Paper. $2.50. *

[B426]

★SARA, DOROTHY. **Handwriting Analysis.** New York: Pyramid Books, 1956. Pp. 160. Paper. $0.35. *

[B427]

★SAVAGE, H. W. **An Evaluation of the Brown-Holtzman Survey of Study Habits and Attitudes for Use in Ontario.** Atkinson Study of Utilization of Student Resources, Supplementary Report No. 3. Toronto, Canada: Department of Educational Research, Ontario College of Education, University of Toronto, 1961. Pp. viii, 34. Paper. $1.00. *

[B428]

★SCHIAVONE, JAMES. **How to Pass Exams.** New York: Grosset & Dunlap, Inc., 1964. Pp. 96. Paper. $1.00. *

[B429]

★SCHMEIDLER, GERTRUDE RAFFEL. **ESP in Relation to Rorschach Test Evaluation.** Parapsychology Monographs, No. 2. New York: Parapsychology Foundation, Inc., 1960. Pp. iii, 89. Paper. $1.75. *

[B430]

★SCHNEIDERS, ALEXANDER A.; ANASTASI, ANNE; AND MEADE, MARTIN J. **The Validation of a Biographical Inventory as a Predictor of College Success: Part 2, The Role of Contingency Factors in College Success; Part 3, Description and Analysis of Discordant Cases.** New York: College Entrance Examination Board, 1960. Pp. iii, 56, iii, 22. Paper, plastic binding, mimeographed. $2.00. *

[B431]

★SCHUCMAN, HELEN. **Evaluating the Educability of the Severely Mentally Retarded Child.** American Psychological Association, Psychological Monographs: General and Applied, Vol. 74, No. 14, Whole No. 501. Washington, D.C.: the Association, Inc., 1960. Pp. 32. Paper. $1.00. * (*PA* 36:1KG32S)

[B432]

SCHUTZ, WILLIAM C. **FIRO: A Three-Dimensional Theory of Interpersonal Behavior.** New York: Holt, Rinehart & Winston, Inc., 1958. Pp. xiii, 267. $6.50. * (*PA* 33:2479) For test materials, see 94.

Am J Sociol 66:543–4 Mr '61. Jack D. Douglas. * *FIRO* (meaning "Fundamental Interpersonal Relations Orientation") is one of the recent theoretical works to come out of small-group work (and as such can be very fruitfully compared with other theoretical works depending primarily on small-group data for inspiration and support, such as Thibaut and Kelley's *The Social Psychology of Groups*). It differs from most of the other theories in that it makes an attempt at "coming-out." Its paucity of references to other data might be laid to a certain shyness inevitable in any theoretical coming-out, but it is nonetheless striking. Schutz has tried to show that the three primates—inclusion, control, and affection—which are measured by the FIRO questionnaire, assume dominance in a sequential phase-shift of group, as well as individual and cultural, development and dissolution. First the problem of inclusion dominates interpersonal behavior; then control dominates; then affection. The similarity of this phase-shift model to Parsons and Bales's phase-shift model in the *Working Papers* is striking, but somehow the *Working Papers* escape reference. During the dissolution of a group the order of dominance (of ultimate concern) is reversed: from affection to control to inclusion —which is something-more-than-Parsons-and-Bales. Group compatibility, treated largely as a function of complementarity of desired and expressed role behavior, is considered at length, but primarily relative to group productivity. Finally, the subtheories are collected into a proposed formal general theory, which is not totally synthesized into a *system* of equations. *FIRO* seems to be a theory built around and for instrumental task groups; its relevance for the entire range of interpersonal behavior is more an assertion than a description of what the work attempts. Quite possibly this chasm between aspiration and serious attempt is due primarily to a failure to grasp fully the fundamental question underlying every theory in process of being constructed: precisely what are the important questions to ask nature about this universe of phenomena? One of the consequences of the failure adequately to face this question is the lack of any variable representing communication (how are inclusion, control, and affection to get around without communication?) or learning (and thus no "values") unless in some way one can get "learning" out of "control." The major potential contribution of *FIRO* to sociology is its consideration of affection as a basic variable of interaction—a variable generally completely left out of sociology, though Homans gave it far more adequate treatment—and its development of a formal theory of interaction that demonstrably generates specific, quantitative hypotheses to be tested by measuring devices developed as an integral part of the theory. The formal theory of *FIRO* seems largely an attempted synthesis of interpersonal behavior under a basic theory of three interrelated quantitative variables—an undertaking strikingly Newtonian in its grandiose aspirations, if not in its achievements. Schutz's failure to consider such closely related and frequently competing theories as Homans' interaction-friendliness theory, Heider's structural-balance theory, Newcomb's A-B-X model, etc., is disturbing. But the terrible audacity of the work is captivating and its empirical theorizing most exemplary for sociology.

Ed & Psychol Meas 20:210–1 sp '60. Harold Borko. * one major criticism....is that the author lays the entire field of psychology on the Procrustean bed of his theory and forces it to fit. He reviews approximately 16 studies and all can be made to fit the ICA framework. No reported study fails to fit! Freud, Fromm, and Horney became Procrustean bedfellows among themselves and with the factor analysts! * FIRO-B....is the key measuring instrument for this theory of interpersonal behavior. The test attempts to measure how an individual characteristically behaves as he relates to other people. In describing this instrument, Schutz states: "The primary purposes for developing FIRO-B are (1) to construct a measure of how an individual acts in interpersonal situations, and (2) to construct a measure that will lead to the prediction of interaction between people, based upon data from the measuring instrument alone. In this second regard FIRO-B is somewhat unique among personality tests (p. 58)." This claim of uniqueness is an understatement. Few psychologists expect to predict overt behavior solely on the basis of test scores. On the other hand, the validation data look promising, and the test is interesting. It deserves to be used and evaluated by other researchers in this area. A decision as to whether the text is a valuable and meritorious attempt at system building, or simply a premature and pretentious effort will, in part, be determined by the quality and quantity of the research it stimulates. In any case, the author deserves credit for trying to derive a theory of interpersonal behavior that is based upon the hypothetical-deductive philosophy. In summary, FIRO is an unusual book, quite different from other texts on personality theory, and one which experimentally-oriented psychologists interested in interpersonal relationships may find especially challenging. It is hoped that this work will be only the first of a series of publications by William C. Schutz.

[B433]

SCHWARTZ, ALFRED, AND TIEDEMAN, STUART C.; WITH THE ASSISTANCE OF DONALD G. WALLACE. **Evaluating Student Progress in the Secondary School.** New York: David McKay Co., Inc., 1957. Pp. xiii, 434. $5.25. * (*PA* 31:6683)

Cont Psychol 3:90–1 Ap '58. Roger T. Lennon. * Chapter 5 offers a systematic treatment of the concepts of *validity, reliability, objectivity, efficiency,* and *usefulness* as applied to evaluative techniques. The discussion of these concepts is, on the whole, undistinguished and marked at times by a looseness that is not to be excused on grounds of simplicity or readability. * The discussion of topics....essential to proper understanding and conduct of evaluation activities is sketchy. For example, scarcely a page of text is devoted to the matter of norms. The central role of teacher-made tests as sources of evaluative data is reflected in a three-chapter treatment of the construction of such tests. * This section should prove one of the most useful in the book. * the facts of current school practice would have suggested a somewhat different apportionment of the space allotted to standardized tests and to other evaluative devices such as sociograms, check lists, questionnaires, observation, and anecdotal records. For good or ill, these latter devices are used with far less frequency by the secondary school teacher than are standardized tests. Surely it would be advantageous in a book on evaluation to describe in some detail at least a few of the more widely used achievement batteries and subject tests. Lists of some such tests are given, but there is little discussion or critical analysis of them. By contrast, the treatment of sociometry, the case study, and the interview is extensive beyond the needs—and probably beyond the interest—of most teachers. * There is little in the book that makes it uniquely appropriate for the *secondary* school teacher. * For a book which makes special claim to "readability" and clarity, *Evaluating Student Progress* seemed to this reviewer to fall short of excellence. Needless repetition and duplication is to be found. The book teems with lists of advantages, disadvantages, observations, rules, and dangers. * Not only does such cataloging make for dull reading; it is also symptomatic of a general weakness of the book—a tendency to "tell," to seek to convey information rather than to develop understanding or skills. There is no provision for student involvement or activity—no exercises, no problems, no questions, only the briefest of bibliographies. Greatly will this book need an instructor to supplement it.

For additional reviews, see 5:B376.

[B434]

★SCHWARTZ, PAUL A. **Aptitude Tests for Use in the Developing Nations.** A research report submitted to the International Cooperation Administration. Pittsburgh, Pa.: American Institute for Research, 1961. Pp. v, 101. Paper. $2.00. *

[B435]

★SCHWIER, MILDRED E., AND DAVIDSON, E. RITA. **Improving Test Construction: Report of a Workshop Conducted by and for the Faculties of the Hospital Schools of Nursing and Cooperating Agencies in Rhode Island, January 4–5, 1961.** New York: National League for Nursing, Inc., 1962. Pp. vii, 56. Paper, mimeographed. $1.25. *

[B436]

★SCOTT, M. GLADYS, AND FRENCH, ESTHER. **Measurement and Evaluation in Physical Education.** Dubuque, Iowa: Wm. C. Brown Co., 1959. Pp. xvi, 493. $6.25. *

[B437]

★SEASHORE, STANLEY E. **Assessing Organization Performance With Behavioral Measurements.** Ann Arbor, Mich.: Foundation for Research on Human Behavior, 1964. Pp. vi, 92. Paper. $3.00. *

[B438]

★SECONDARY SCHOOL EXAMINATIONS COUNCIL. **The Certificate of Secondary Education: Notes for the Guidance of Regional Examining Bodies.** Fifth Report of the Secondary School Examinations Council, 1962. John Lockwood, Chairman. Prepared for the Minister of Education. London: Her Majesty's Stationery Office, 1962. Pp. x, 17. Paper. 1*s.* 9*d.* *

[B439]

★SECONDARY SCHOOL EXAMINATIONS COUNCIL. **The Certificate of Secondary Education: A Proposal for a New School Leaving Certificate Other Than the G.C.E.** Fourth Report of the Secondary School Examinations Council, 1961. John Lockwood, Chairman. Prepared for the Minister of Education. London: Her Majesty's Stationery Office, 1961. Pp. iv, 20. Paper. 1*s.* 6*d.* *

[B440]

★SECONDARY SCHOOL EXAMINATIONS COUNCIL. **The Certificate of Secondary Education: Some Suggestions for Teachers and Examiners.** Examinations Bulletin No. 1. London: Her Majesty's Stationery Office, 1963. Pp. xi, 139. Paper. 10*s.* *

[B441]

★SECONDARY SCHOOL EXAMINATIONS COUNCIL. **Examinations in Secondary Schools.** Report of the Secondary School Examinations Council, 1947. Philip Morris, Acting Chairman. Prepared for the Minister of Education. London: Her Majesty's Stationery Office, 1947. Pp. 8. Paper. 6*d.* *

[B442]

★SECONDARY SCHOOL EXAMINATIONS COUNCIL. **Examinations in Secondary Schools.** Second Report of the Secondary School Examinations Council, 1952. J. F. Wolfenden, Chairman. Prepared for the Minister of Education. London: Her Majesty's Stationery Office, 1952. Pp. 4. Paper. Out of print. *

[B443]

★SECONDARY SCHOOL EXAMINATIONS COUNCIL. **The Examining of English Language.** Eighth Report of the Secondary School Examinations Council, 1964. John Lockwood, Chairman. Prepared for the Minister of Education. London: Her Majesty's Stationery Office, 1964. Pp. ix, 69. Paper. 5*s.* *

[B444]

★SECONDARY SCHOOL EXAMINATIONS COUNCIL. **The General Certificate Education and Sixth Form Studies.** Third Report of the Secondary School Examinations Council, 1960. John Lockwood, Chairman. Prepared for the Minister of Education. London: Her Majesty's Stationery Office, 1960. Pp. v, 29. Paper. 2*s.* 6*d.* *

[B445]

★SECONDARY SCHOOL EXAMINATIONS COUNCIL. **Scope and Standards of the Certificate of Secondary Education.** Seventh Report of the Secondary School Examinations Council, 1963. John Lockwood, Chairman. Prepared for the Minister of Education. London: Her Majesty's Stationery Office, 1963. Pp. ix, 18. Paper. 2*s.* *

[B446]

★SECONDARY SCHOOL EXAMINATIONS COUNCIL. **Secondary School Examinations Other Than the G.C.E.** Report of a Committee Appointed by the Secondary School Examinations Council in July 1958. John Lockwood, Chairman. Prepared for the Minister of Education. London: Her Majesty's Stationery Office, 1960. Pp. vi, 73. Paper. 4*s.* 6*d.* *

[B447]

★SECONDARY SCHOOL EXAMINATIONS COUNCIL. **Sixth Form Studies and University Entrance Requirements.** Sixth Report of the Secondary School Examinations Council, 1962. John Lockwood, Chairman. Prepared for the Minister of Education. London: Her Majesty's Stationery Office, 1962. Pp. viii, 36. Paper. 3*s.* *

[B448]

★SELIGSON, HENRY, AND SIMON, LEONARD. **Evaluation: A Memorandum for Curriculum Workers.** Board of Education of the City of New York, Bureau of Curriculum Research, Curriculum Research Report. New York: Curriculum Center, the Bureau, [1959]. Pp. iii, 61. Paper. $0.25. *

Reading Teach 13:814 Ap '60. Berj Harootunian. This pamphlet is concerned with the nature and function of evaluation and with specific evaluation techniques. In addition, it attempts in twenty-seven pages to explain the complexities of the analysis of data, sampling, and other topics in statistics. It is questionable whether this booklet will be much help to the curriculum worker who is unfamiliar with evaluation or statistics. Perhaps by reading it one will be encouraged to consult some of the excellent references listed in the bibliography. For the person with some sophistication in evaluation and measurement, *Evaluation: A Memorandum for Curriculum Workers* is overly simple, overly general, sometimes incorrect, and often inappropriate for students of educational problems. Here is an excellent example of how short-cuts to an understanding of evaluation can confuse rather than clarify.

[B449]

SEMEONOFF, BORIS, AND TRIST, ERIC. **Diagnostic Performance Tests: A Manual for Use With Adults.** London: Tavistock Publications, 1958. Pp. xvi, 176. 32*s*. *

Brit J Ed Psychol 29:183–4 Je '59. B. Clarke. This manual describes adaptations of some individual exploratory procedures: the originals were the Vigotsky, Weigl, Kohs, Carl Hollow Square, and Passalong tests. Half the book is devoted to norms, statistical analyses, and appendices. Most of the work was done about twelve years ago. These procedures study the detailed cerebration of the individual, how he perceives, categorises, surmounts difficulties, perseveres, perseverates, or peters out: all as practically important as any global intelligence index. This volume is recommended to those who wish to extend their testing skills in this direction; these adaptations are sensible, and the materials can be bought easily. Some parts could, with discrimination, be used with children: there is a plain opportunity to devise an analogous series, particularly for handicapped children. The dilemma with this type of test is whether one gets more by observational recording or by the more cramping conditions necessary if standard norms are used. The authors' own approach is not rigid, but the elaborate marking systems may tempt some to concentrate on summed scores rather than study individual problem-solving patterns, wherein the value of these methods lies. (Ultimately, perhaps, test-norms will be used as an incidental sighting-point, not to give a final "social placing" (like an I.Q.); as in physical medicine tables of normal heights and weights are for initial orientation, not for diagnosis). More of the book (overloaded with minutiae) might have been given to discussion of the psychological concepts involved. * the book is excellently produced * It will be a standard British reference manual for such tests for some time to come.

Brit J Psychol 50:80–1 F '59. Cyril Burt. * intended to serve as a practical manual * Its primary purpose is to furnish instructions for the use of a set of five performance tests, some entirely new, others based on well-established procedures, all carefully standardized and combined in a battery for assessing the psychological efficiency of adults. * The whole book is based on a vast amount of accumulated experience and represents an important advance in the technique of psychological assessment. It forms a most valuable addition to the psychologist's equipment for exploring adult personality and assessing adult intelligence; and can be warmly recommended to psychologists, psychiatrists, and all who are interested in the problems of individual diagnosis.

Q J Exp Psychol 11:128 My '59. Florence E. MacNeill. * Because of the fullness of the material, one very valuable aspect of the book is that the reader can see what amounts to research as it is taking place. The suggested interpretations are not dogmatic, and at several points opportunities arise for the reader to develop his own ideas. One might call it a refreshingly open-ended book, having something of the quality associated with the testing standpoint of the authors. It is not a book for beginners, but it could be a very important undergraduate and postgraduate text, and an absolute "must" for anybody contemplating research in this field.

For an additional review, see 519.

[B450]

★SHAW, JACK, AND ANFINSON, OLAF P. **Using Measurement in Education.** Greeley, Colo.: Educational Projects, 1961. Pp. iv, 155. Paper, looseleaf. $4.00. *

[B451]

★SHAYCOFT, MARION F.; DAILEY, JOHN T.; ORR, DAVID B.; NEYMAN, CLINTON A., JR.; AND SHERMAN, STUART E. **Studies of a Complete Age Group, Age 15.** Cooperative Research Project No. 566, The Identification, Development, and Utilization of Human Talents. Pittsburgh, Pa.: University of Pittsburgh Project Talent Office, 1964. Pp. [270]. Paper. Out of print. *

[B452]

★SHERMAN, MURRAY H., EDITOR. **A Rorschach Reader.** New York: International Universities Press,

Inc., 1961. Pp. xvi, 440. $7.50. * (London: Bailey Bros. & Swinfen, Ltd. 64s.) (*PA* 36:4HG40S)

Am J Orthopsychiatry 32:563–4 Ap '62. Max L. Fogel. * A number of the papers are provocative in concept, provide sound experimental technique, and are well documented by statistically reliable findings. A few may be considered as minor classics in this area, e.g., Furrer's "The Meaning of M in the Rorschach Test" and Schachtel's "On Color and Affect," and easily warrant inclusion in any collection of distinctive Rorschach contributions. Papers on content analysis such as F. Brown's "An Exploratory Study of Dynamic Factors in the Content of the Rorschach Protocol" are also valuable because of their scarcity. However, just as many seem to be unworthy of republication in book form, because of triviality of content or inadequacy of research methodology. Moreover, one might suspect that the book will appeal primarily to beginning Rorschachers, or to those who have at least become familiar with basic scoring techniques. Older or more experienced workers will already be familiar with many of the articles, or with a comparable selection of articles which may be equally as representative of the various fields of Rorschach usage as are those in the current volume. Some coverage of the fields is indeed offered, but owing to necessary limitations of space each is treated rapidly and often superficially. The shortcoming of this collection may be that it is too variegated; better would have been a more limited range of topics with each thereby more adequately canvassed. However, for the beginning Rorschach worker who may desire a handy source book of representative references, there is much in this collection which will be stimulating and instructive.

Cont Psychol 7:252–4 Jl '62. Philip Roos. * The book is divided into five main parts. The first part includes 8 papers dealing with psychopathology. * The second section....consists of 5 articles focussing on the implications of Rorschach findings for vocational choice. The articles selected are generally sound and appropriate, but might lead to a spuriously optimistic evaluation of the Rorschach as a predictor of vocational success. Of particular interest are the somewhat conflicting studies of creativity by Anne Roe and Walter Myden. * In the fourth section....Sherman has included five experimental investigations of the Rorschach, including Anne Munroe's study of the relationship between Rorschach findings and A. C. E. constellations and the excellent paper by Julian Meltzoff *et al* on motor inhibition and the M response. The papers are of uniformly high quality, but it is somewhat surprising to note the absence of any of the many studies reporting clearly damaging results to the Rorschach, such as the work on "color shock" by Lazarus, Siipola, etc. The final section of the volume is devoted to seven papers on Rorschach interpretation. A. Furrer's paper on the meaning of M and Ernest Schachtel's discussion of color responses are classics in expounding the rationale behind formal Rorschach interpretation. Fred Brown's study of dynamic factors in content is representative of the "clinical-qualitative" approach to interpretation. Perhaps the most sobering paper in the entire book is Richard Wittenborn and Seymour Sarason's telling presentation of exceptions to Rorschach indications of pathology. Because of the very broad area covered by this anthology and the relative lack of clinically applicable material, it will probably prove to be of limited use to the practicing clinician. On the other hand, these very factors suggest that the book should be of value to students as an introduction to the unwieldy literature on the Rorschach. It might be a valuable supplemental text in introductory Rorschach courses.

[B453]

★Shneidman, Edwin S.; Hooker, Evelyn; Forer, Bertram R.; Meyer, Mortimer; Fine, Reuben; and Murray, Henry A. **The Case of El: A Demonstration of Diagnostic Methods in Clinical Psychology.** Glendale, Calif.: Society for Projective Techniques, Inc., 1961. Pp. ii, 81. Paper. $2.50. * [Reprinted from *J Proj Tech* 25:131–54, 252–67, 371–411 Je, S, D '61.] (*PA* 36:2IK31S)

[B454]

★Shostak, Jerome. **How to Prepare for College Board Achievement Tests: English, English Composition, The Writing Sample.** Great Neck, N.Y.: Barron's Educational Series, Inc., 1964. Pp. vi, 116. Paper, $1.75; cloth, $4.50. *

[B455]

Shuey, Audrey M. **The Testing of Negro Intelligence.** Lynchburg, Va.: J. P. Bell Co., Inc., 1958. Pp. xv, 351. $4.00. * (*PA* 32:3907)

Am Anthrop 62:544 Je '60. Ina C. Brown. This volume is a review and interpretation of approximately 288 publications having to do with the intelligence of Negroes. * In her Introduction Dr. Shuey says of the studies, "The results are objective, verifiable, and presumably accurate within the limits of each experiment; the interpretations or comments are relatively subjective and may not necessarily be accurate." She then proceeds to ignore the interpretations and comments of the testers while using their "results" as the basis of her own interpretations with which many of the testers would most certainly disagree. In a concluding statement the author lists a number of "facts" which she says "all point to the presence of some native differences between Negroes and whites as determined by intelligence tests." With one or two exceptions her "facts" are not only verifiable but are common knowledge to persons working in the field. These facts, however, together with some other facts which Dr. Shuey ignores, point much more clearly to something other than differences in native intelligence and that is to the very great differences between Negroes and Whites in economic and educational opportunities, home backgrounds, civic and community participation, motivation, cultural expectation and self image. There may, of course, be some native differences between Negroes and Whites but as of now we have no way of proving that such differences do exist while the evidence of socio-cultural differences is overwhelming. The book really adds up to much ado about nothing. No informed person questions the fact that on the average Whites perform better than Negroes on the tests or that northerners perform better than southerners or urban subjects better than rural subjects. It is the why that is important and Dr. Shuey's brushing aside the interpretations of most of the recent testers in favor of her own conclusions adds nothing to our knowledge. One can, however, predict wide use of the book by White Citizens' Councils and others who are in search of material which they can interpret as "scientific" support for their point of view.

Brit J Psychol 49:347–9 N '58. A. E. Maxwell. As the author herself says, this book might properly be called *A Comparative Study of the Intelligence of American Negroes and Whites.* Her address, *Lynch*burg, Virginia, and her acknowledged indebtedness to her students in the *"Racial* Psychology Classes" (at Randolph-Macon College) are sufficient indicators of her motivation and purpose in writing a book on this subject of lively debate in the United States. The book is a painstaking and careful review of approximately 240 experimental studies, over 44 years, of negro intelligence, of which all but two were carried out in the States. * Having assembled the data, Dr Shuey attempts an evaluation of them. The conclusions to be reached from this evaluation are inescapable. Everywhere, and with remarkable consistency, the results indicate a discrepancy between the average intelligence of negroes and of whites in favour of the latter, irrespective of whether the comparison is between actual groups of negroes and whites tested, or between negroes and general population norms. * Now there is no reason why negroes should not differ from whites in intelligence. They differ from whites in pigmentation, in bone structure, in distribution of blood groups, and no doubt in other ways. But where intelligence is concerned we must be careful, not only because of the slur likely to be cast since high intellectual potential is at a premium in the world today, but also because intelligence, since it can only be measured indirectly, is difficult to measure accurately. To compare negroes and whites impartially where intellectual ability is concerned would require the construction of special batteries of tests for which an item analysis would require to be carried out separately on equal stratified samples of negroes and whites and the items subsequently chosen so as to give both races an equal chance of success. Some of the investigators whose work is reported were aware of this; Young and Bright, for example, in their 1954 study, question the suitability of the W.I.S.C. for southern rural negro children. Although Dr Shuey reports this and draws attention to a few investigators who noted some test-item differences between the racial groups, she does not lay sufficient emphasis anywhere on the possible limitations of the tests employed. Possible bias on the part of testers is another factor which, in a well-planned investigation, would require to be taken into account: a careful examination of the data which Dr Shuey presents suggests that bias may well exist. However, these are points to be kept in mind when evaluating future studies: for the present, we must congratulate Dr Shuey on the interesting review she has given us of the literature to date.

Cont Psychol 5:196–7 Je '60. Roger K. Williams. This is a timely book. It will interest some psychologists, social workers, and school officials because it cumulates statistics on the topic. It is primarily a summary of "the results" of some 240 separate investigations, not of "the comments and conclusions" of the original investigators, and it ends up with what the author regards as an inescapable conclusion: that all Negro-white differences in psychometric test performance "point to the presence of some native differences." * Summarizing all the published research in racial differences should entail the evaluation of the problems that the original investigators faced. In this volume presentation of the results of the experiments—to the exclusion of the original experimenters' comments and conclusions—seems to have led to an avoiding of the scientist's responsibility. If there be generally recognized limitations to straightforward conclusions, then the summarizer-evaluator should counsel scientific caution. Results should be distinguished from their meanings. The latter, in turn, demand that there should have been suitable selective criteria for the experimental comparisons, relentless care, and defensible value-judgments. In this area of research, there are many gaps which force the psychological researcher to question the legitimacy of his initial hypotheses. There can be seen a kind of bimodality of "conclusions" among the investigators who have sought to explain, and not simply to describe, certain types of results. Whether the researcher emerges an environmentalist or a hereditarian depends in large part upon how thoroughly he is aware of the probable gaps in his hypothetical structure and subsequent methods. * If racially mixed ancestry precludes determining how "Negro" a Negro is, or how "white" a white, of what scientific value is it to assume that "the American Negro constitutes a recognizable and clearly defined group, the criterion of membership in which group being that of more-or-less African ancestry"? If the environments of the groups referred to in the various studies were improperly or unsatisfactorily equated, of what scientific value was it to speak as if they were? The volume may, therefore, be described as a study of testing and intelligence. It may not be considered as a study of race. Its treatment of the effect on prediction of considerable and varying degrees of overlapping seems to have resulted from too heavy a dependence upon the significance of mean differences. Assuming all other elements in the compositions of the various experiments originally reported to have been controlled satisfactorily, this oversight would, singly, vitiate any broad generalization of a difference between the two groups. In a sense, nevertheless, *The Testing of Negro Intelligence* is timely. It is timely because it is a study in the areas of untested assumptions, a demonstration of the need for interdisciplinary insights in research design, and an exhibit of the futility of confusing summaries of data with the critical evaluation of what the data are supposed to represent.

Eug R 52:174 O '60. P. E. Vernon. * a valuable and scholarly survey * The essential data of some 170 studies are given in convenient tabular form, and the text provides a balanced critique and interpretation of the evidence. As Professor H. E. Garrett points out in his introduction, American negroes and whites constitute particularly fruitful groups for the study of racial differences. For even if the former can hardly be called a pure "race," they are a largely distinctive minority, who speak the same language, and are brought up in much the same cultural environment, as the majority. Nevertheless their living conditions, jobs and schooling, especially in the Southern States, are so often inferior that psychologists and anthropologists have tended to explain away the marked differences which are practically always found in terms of environment alone. Far too many writers, for example, quote Klineberg's study of the effects of length of residence in New York on the I.Q. as if this disproved the existence of any genetic differences. Shuey's survey indicates that at least one-third, possibly half, of the difference between Northern and Southern negroes is attributable to selective migration of the brighter stocks. Averaging a large number of researches she concludes that the mean I.Q.s of these groups are 87 and 78, in contrast to the white 100. However good the environment, the Northern figure is seldom much exceeded. Perhaps the most striking evidence of genetic differences is provided by the inferiority of negro to white college students, despite the considerably greater selectivity of the former. In general the differences seem to increase with age, though the researches on pre-school children are particularly unreliable, and this phenomenon might well be held to reflect the progressive effects of poor environment. Most interesting, again, are the differences on different kinds of tests. Negroes do not necessarily do better on non-verbal or performance than on verbal tests. They seem to be strongest in rote memory and in commonsense concrete tasks, least good in abstract reasoning. Probably further research along these lines will be more fruitful than more studies of the genetics of a poorly defined general intelligence. Some readers may judge Shuey, and her sponsor, Professor Garrett, to be somewhat biased, though they do not in fact deny that much of the observed difference arises from poor upbringing. To the present writer this seems as impartial a study as any that have been made in the racial field, and an important corrective to extremist views on both sides.

Personnel & Guid J 38:333–4 D '59. W. L. Cash, Jr. * The author must be commended for bringing together such a wealth of material, and the average reader would be amazed to learn that so much has been done in this area. The evidence presented by the studies Shuey has assembled substantiates without a doubt her concluding phrase that the remarkable consistency in test results, regardless of location, age status, environment, or the kind of tests, verbal and non-verbal, *et al,* "all point to the presence of some native difference between Negroes and whites as determined by intelligence tests." This is the point the book set out to present, but the more critical reader may raise some questions regarding the sampling procedures employed by those who did the studies and why the differences in size of the S.D.'s between the two racial groups "were typically small and the significance of the differences rarely determined." This also applies to the mean differences.

For an additional review, see 5:B396.

[B456]

★SILVERMAN, LLOYD H. **A Q-Sort Study of the Validity of Evaluations Made From Projective Techniques.** American Psychological Association, Psychological Monographs: General and Applied, Vol. 73, No. 7, Whole No. 477. Washington, D.C.: the Association, Inc., 1959. Pp. 28. Paper. $1.00. * (*PA* 34:3030)

[B457]

★SMILANSKY, M., AND ADAR, L., EDITORS. **Evaluating Educational Achievements: Summaries of Some Studies Carried Out by the Henrietta Szold Institute on Schooling in Israel.** Unesco Educational Studies and Documents, No. 42. New York: UNESCO Publications Center, 1961. Pp. 46. Paper, lithotyped. Out of print. (London: Her Majesty's Stationery Office. 2*s.* 6*d.*) *

[B458]

★SMITH, ARTHUR E. **What Tests Can Tell You About You.** Guidance Series Booklets 103. Chicago, Ill.: Science Research Associates, Inc., 1961. Pp. 49. Paper. $0.50. *

[B459]

★SMITH, DONALD C., EDITOR. **The Use of Projective Techniques With the School-Aged Child.** Columbus, Ohio: Child Study Center, Department of Psychology, Ohio State University, December 1962. Pp. 96, unnumbered. Paper, mimeographed. $1.00. *

[B460]

★SMITHELLS, PHILIP A., AND CAMERON, PETER E. **Principles of Evaluation in Physical Education.** New York: Harper & Row, Publishers, Inc., 1962. Pp. x, 478. $6.75. * (London: Harper & Row Ltd. 51*s.*)

[B461]

★SOLOMON, HERBERT, EDITOR. **Studies in Item Analysis and Prediction.** Stanford Mathematical Studies in the Social Sciences, No. 6. Stanford, Calif.: Stanford University Press, 1961. Pp. ix, 310. $8.75. * (London: Oxford University Press. 70*s.*) (*PA* 36: 3AE10S)

Brit J Ed Psychol 33:336 N '63. D. M. Lee. This is definitely a book for those interested in mathematical theory. It brings together a number of recent contributions to the fields of Item Analysis and Prediction, and develops a coherent picture of the statistical background involved. But the reader must, in general, apply the theory for himself. Apart from a rather brief Editor's introduction, there is little practical help or guidance as to the types of problems which might be solved by the use of the various theoretical aspects discussed. Whilst such volumes as this could play a considerable role in improving and developing techniques for educational research, they will not achieve their goal until the writers generate a better synthesis of theory and practice. Most practising research workers have neither the background knowledge nor the time to unravel the complexities of advanced statistics before applying it to the problem in hand. Theories of as complex a nature as those propounded in this book need to be illustrated by a variety of very suitable and careful applications.

Occup Psychol 37:86–7 Ja '63. A. E. Maxwell. * This is a book for the mathematically minded reader, but even he is likely to sample it in small doses. The editor has done a good job in the arrangement of the material at his disposal but he has been altogether too lax in editing it. Some chapters contain page after page of dreary algebraic derivations and formulae (Sitgreaves is the principal offender in this respect) which could have been presented more succinctly, or briefly summarized, or even omitted—for example, in chapter three after numerous pages of algebraic manipulation we are told that "these results are not very useful." Other chapters, however, are written with an economy of expression reminiscent of the best traditions of statistical essays. This is true especially of Elfving's contributions and of a chapter by M. V. Johns entitled "An empirical Bayes approach to non-parametric two-way classifications," though the content of the latter chapter has already been superseded by other published work. There is a lucid chapter too by H. Raiffa introducing the reader to concepts from statistical decision theory. But the overall impression which the present reviewer got from reading the book was one of unreality. It is relatively easy for a mathematician to construct mathematical models for one purpose or another, but such exercises are not very useful unless he has a clear-cut practical application in mind and, if possible, supplies a practical example. I was not convinced that the contributors to this book, with the exception of Solomon himself, had any very extensive first-hand knowledge of the practical problems involved in the construction of tests and inventories. Primarily for this reason it is unlikely that this book will have much influence on the development of psychometrics.

Psychometrika 27:207–13 Je '62. Frederic M. Lord. * The term "item analysis" in the title carries connotations that may mislead many testers. Most of the first twelve chapters are concerned with the basic problems that arise when we want to select items so as to produce a test with optimum properties. The last five chapters are concerned with a particular classification problem that transcends the field of mental testing. The reader will find some knowledge of decision theory helpful in reading most of the chapters. Herbert Solomon's *Introduction* provides an indispensable perspective, sometimes explaining the motivation, the interrelations, and the significance of the individual papers much more clearly than do the papers themselves. It also provides a partial history and perspective view of mental test theory. Although it is easy to see how someone reading certain parts of the literature could arrive at Solomon's conclusions about mental test theory, these conclusions require some correction, as follows: (*a*) Most mental test theorists do *not* assume that "the human trait of mental ability is a unidimensional trait." (*b*) Nor, in general, that this trait is normally distributed. (*c*) Birnbaum does not use the assumption of a "logistic distribution" of ability except in the most ancillary fashion. (*d*) The "classical mental-test theorist" relies on the "local independence" assumption; he does *not* rest his theory on the less general single-factor assumption, although he may sometimes use this assumption or the normality assumption, as is also done throughout the first three chapters of the present book. * Considered as a whole, the book is mainly concerned with finding optimum test designs and optimum ways of prediction from the test responses. These are the most basic and important problems both in practical testing and in test theory. At least two very different mathematical models for the test responses are described and used for finding and evaluating optimum test designs. It has frequently been pointed out that the design of a strictly optimum test becomes computationally too burdensome when there are more than a very few items. This fact will discourage many readers who are interested only in simple, immediate applications for 25-item and longer tests. Other readers will find the book very valuable. The reviewer expects that the difficulties encountered in designing longer tests will be overcome. One possible solution has already been mentioned here. Any appreciable progress in test design in the future must surely be based on the application of decision theory and related techniques to appropriate mathematical models for the test responses. The present book shows clearly how this is done. Solomon and all the other authors have performed a valuable service in writing this book and in the several years of work and planning that preceded the final writing. The serious student who is interested in the content of the book but finds himself unable to follow the mathematics will have to consider whether he is receiving the mathematical training necessary for creative professional work in the field of his interests. [See original review for additional critical comments not excerpted.]

[B462]

★SPEARRITT, DONALD. **Listening Comprehension—A Factorial Analysis.** A.C.E.R. Research Series No.

76. Hawthorn, Australia: Australian Council for Educational Research, 1962. Pp. x, 149. 42s. Austl. *

Brit J Ed Psychol 33:209 Je '63. F. W. Warburton. * This book....not only makes an original contribution to our knowledge, about listening comprehension, but also serves as a model to research students, particularly in the factorial field, preparing to write an account of their own investigation. * It is interesting to find that the human rotations give a poorer simple structure than the Biquartimin rotation, yielding hyperplanes of something like 10 per cent. less density, with very little compensating advantage in the number of relatively high loadings. The results, based on thirty-four tests, are most informative, as few of the hypotheses put forward by the author were fully verified. For example, the suggestion that there is no factor of listening comprehension separate from reasoning, verbal comprehension, attention and memory was rejected. * There is little to fault in this book except perhaps the statistical appendix, which will surely be too elementary for the cognoscenti and too difficult for everyone else. In summary, this book is recommended, not only for readers interested in listening comprehension, but also for those concerned with the design of theses on experimental topics, particularly in the area of factor analysis.

[B463]

★STAFFORD, MURIEL. **You and Your Handwriting.** New York: Dell Publishing Co., Inc., 1963. Pp. 158. Paper. $0.50. *

[B464]

*STANLEY, JULIAN C. **Measurement in Today's Schools, Fourth Revision.** Englewood Cliffs, N.J.: Prentice-Hall, Inc., 1964. Pp. xviii, 414. $7.50. (London: Prentice-Hall International, Inc. 56s.) * [First edition and second revision by C. C. Ross; third revision by Julian C. Stanley with C. C. Ross's name on the title page.] For reviews of previous editions, see 5:B361, 4:B325, and 3:1131.

[B465]

★STEIN, MORRIS I. **Personality Measures in Admissions: Antecedent and Personality Factors as Predictors of College Success.** New York: College Entrance Examination Board, 1963. Pp. vii, 69. Paper. $2.50. *

[B466]

★STODOLA, QUENTIN. **Making the Classroom Test: A Guide for Teachers, Second Edition.** Evaluation and Advisory Service Series, No. 4. Princeton, N.J.: Educational Testing Service, 1961. Pp. 27. Paper. Gratis. * (First edition published in 1959.)

Personnel & Guid J 38:69 S '59. Thomas M. Magoon. * a very readable and clearly illustrated pamphlet on achievement test development, scoring, and interpretation. The material is focused on and illustrated with 5th, 8th, 10th, and 12th grade teaching situations and covers a wide range of coursework content. The practical suggestions and underlying principles are not limited to any grade level or subject matter area, however. For this reason the pamphlet should be of considerable use for both self-study and for consultative relationships with any interested faculty members, for workshops, and as supplementary material in tests and measurements coursework. *

[B467]

★STOUGHTON, ROBERT W. **The Testing Service: A Design for Program Development.** Hartford, Conn.: Bureau of Pupil Personnel and Special Educational Services, State Department of Education, June 1959. Pp. 160. Paper. $1.00. *

[B468]

★STRAUS, MURRAY A. **Direct, Indirect, and Disguised Measurement in Rural Sociology.** State College of Washington, Washington Agricultural Experiment Stations, Institute of Agricultural Sciences, Technical Bulletin 26. Pullman, Wash.: the Institute, August 1957. Pp. ii, 29. Paper. $0.20. *

[B469]

★STRAUS, MURRAY A. **A Technique for Measuring Values in Rural Life.** State College of Washington, Washington Agricultural Experiment Stations, Institute of Agricultural Sciences, Technical Bulletin 29. Pullman, Wash.: the Institute, August 1959. Pp. ii, 34. Paper. Out of print. * For an excerpt of a review of the manual, see 181.

[B470]

★STRONG, ALAN. **Pass That Exam!** Preston, Lancs., England: A. Thomas & Co., 1963. Pp. 206. 20s. *

[B471]

★STUCKY, MILO O., AND ANDERSON, KENNETH E. **A Study of Persistence in College Attendance in Relation to Placement-Test Scores and Grade-Point Averages.** University of Kansas, School of Education, Kansas Studies in Education, Vol. 9, No. 2. Lawrence, Kan.: the School, April 1959. Pp. 58. Paper. Gratis. *

[B472]

*SUPER, DONALD E., AND CRITES, JOHN O. **Appraising Vocational Fitness by Means of Psychological Tests, Revised Edition.** New York: Harper & Row, Publishers, Inc., 1962. Pp. xv, 688. Text price, $8.75; trade price, $12.00. * (London: Harper & Row Ltd. 66s.) (*PA* 37:2038)

Austral J Psychol 15:75 Ap '63. J. F. Clark. * an authoritative, comprehensive, and thorough treatment of the subject, and discusses critically the issues with which a tester must be familiar if he is to make the most effective use of his tools. Super, one of the most experienced workers in the guidance field, is well qualified to advise on these matters. * Little attention is given to promising new types of tests which might be of interest to the test experimenter rather than the practitioner. * From his more recent work on career patterns and the importance of situational factors at work one might have expected a change in emphasis and a departure from interpretations based on the direct relationship between test results and occupational success. This book is sound, thorough, and traditional. It is written in as lively a way as this kind of material will allow but is still dull. One wonders if this is the best way to teach the use of psychological tests in vocational counselling or if this material should be separated out to be taught as a special subject. It is hard to prevent it from becoming a mere catalogue of information.

Cont Psychol 8:240–1 Je '63. William C. Cottle. This book, like the earlier edition, is essential for the library of the counseling psychologist. It would make a useful companion text for a book like that of Cronbach or Anastasi in a course dealing with understanding and using group psychological tests in vocational appraisal and counseling. It can also serve as a review for psychologists working in other specialties of major developments in the area of vocational testing. The authors of the revised edition have wisely elected to change as little as possible of the excellent material in the 1949 edition. Only those changes required to make the text current have been introduced. Many changes have been made in the chapter dealing with multifactor batteries, in the one on measurement of interests, and in the treatment of measurement of personality, attitudes and temperament; the revisions reflect the changes in vocational testing over the last twelve years. * Most of the material in Chapters 1 to 13, and in Chapter 15, is the same as that of the earlier edition with the change of a sentence here or there. The same is true for Chapters 20–22, although four new pages are added at the end of Chapter 20 to bring the discussion of "appraising individual vocational promise" up to date. * Appendix B is old Chapter 24 with minor changes. * Chapter 14, dealing with multifactor test batteries, still discusses only the General Aptitude Test Battery and the Differential Aptitude Tests as the two batteries in general use * What amounts to a major rewriting has been done on the chapters on vocational interests in order to include the extensive research that has been published since 1949. The discussion and conclusions are generally appropriate for these data with perhaps a little too much emphasis on the relation of interests and endocrine factors in light of the limited data available. The authors do a professional job of reviewing the research they have chosen to include in these chapters. They include a synthesis of "inherited neural and endocrine factors, on the one hand, and opportunity and societal evaluation of the other" (p. 410) as the multiple elements interacting in the development of vocational interests. This synthesis could well have had more space than one page devoted to it. The effect of response set on inventoried interests could have been indicated. * The major research on measurement of vocational interests has been covered adequately. The treatment of personality, attitudes and temperament in Chapter 19 is based on the statement (p. 517) that, "personality as defined in this discussion determines the kinds of adjustment problems which the worker will encounter and the role he will play in any occupation he enters." * The synthesis of research on the MMPI and the EPPS contains the major points the counselor needs to consider. The content of the chapter highlights the current trend toward more sophisticated self-report instruments while it attempts to forecast increasing use of projective devices in vocational counseling. However, after devoting fifteen pages to a discussion of the Rorschach, the authors conclude (p. 575), "the technique can be considered only an instrument which may be worth using in validation studies, as one which research may yet prove valuable in vocational counseling and selection, but about which too little is now known to justify its use in practical counseling or personnel work." One could not help wishing that the Rorschach had been given the minor treatment of the other projective devices which would have left space for a discussion of the California Psychological Inventory and the Guilford Zimmerman Temperament Scale which Super and Crites say they wished they could have included.

For reviews of the first edition, see 4:B368.

[B473]

★Symonds, Percival M.; with Arthur R. Jensen. **From Adolescent to Adult.** New York and London: Columbia University Press, 1961. Pp. x, 413. $8.75; 65*s*. * (*PA* 35:2021)

Am J Psychol 76:166–8 Mr '63. Dale B. Harris. * As a scientific investigation of the fantasy life of young adults, or as a study of the predictive power of adolescent adjustment for adult status, this study is unconvincing. As a collection of detailed data on the fantasies and experiences of clinically unselected young people, the book is highly interesting. The authors are imaginative but plausible in their essentially subjective interpretations. * the most valuable contribution of the present volume is the survey of fantasy themes in young adults' responses to thematic pictures. This survey suggests that young adults do not differ greatly from adolescents. * By a selective review of individual cases the authors satisfy themselves that in many instances the themes of adolescent fantasy work themselves out in adult behavior and adjustment. The present volume attempts to study the transition from adolescence to adulthood. No new insights into this process appear, however. * From the standpoint of nomothetic science, the study leaves much to be desired methodologically. Although the authors make appropriate cautionary statements at many points, they cheerfully go on to assertions and conclusions of which they seem quite convinced. For instance, they point out that it is very difficult to distinguish between a coincidence and a correspondence in selected anecdotal materials, yet they find many correspondences and recognize no coincidences. They say, conservatively, their method cannot truly *predict,* yet they conclude that adult adjustment was quite well predicted by the adolescent data. * The danger in treating such material as scientific data is well illustrated by the following: The authors successfully match thematic protocols taken in adolescence with protocols taken from the same persons 13 yr. later. Early in the volume they note (p. 45) that "actually the formal factors (of expression) were more reliable indicators on which to base matching. Apparently manners of style, language, special comments, fidelity to the picture, emotional tone, and the like are somewhat more prominent characteristics of an individual than are his fantasy themes." Later, this fact—that formal characteristics of language and expression are the principal cues in matching protocols—is forgotten: "There is a marked persistence of themes and fantasy over the 13-yr. interval between this study and its predecessor, enough to make it possible to identify the narrator and match stories told 13 yr. apart when they have been mingled indiscriminately with the stories of other narrators" (p. 209). The wish is father to the thought.

Brit J Psychol 53:348–9 Ag '62. H. H. Stern. * an intelligent and civilized book which will be read with interest by many psychologists and students. Its merits are several. Above all it contributes to an understanding of the growth from adolescence to adulthood. Here the concept of adolescence as a distinct period, completely different from other stages of life, recedes. The persistence of individual characteristics, the stability of fantasy, the living-out of fantasy in life experience are strikingly observed. * The absence—even in outline or reduced form—of the pictures which play such an important part in the study is a disadvantage. Apart from that the work can be entirely recommended as a sensitive, searching and balanced contribution to the psychology of development and personality.

Personnel & Guid J 41:73–4 S '62. Merle Ohlsen and Ray Thompson. This book fills a gap in the literature. Much has been written about adolescence, but too little is known about the transition from adolescence to adulthood. However, the prospective reader must not be mislead by the title and assume that the volume provides a comprehensive treatise on all facets of development from adolescence to adulthood. This book is limited to the treatment of fantasy and its importance in appraising personality development. * One of the obvious weaknesses of this study is the fact that it included only 28 subjects. Though the authors recognize the weakness of a small sample, they assumed that their population was a fair sample of an urban population; this is a questionable assumption. Nevertheless, they did point out that their results must be looked upon as only tentative and perhaps most fruitful in hypothesis building for future studies. Had the book been limited strictly to the author's major findings, it could have been condensed into a professional paper. Throughout their 12 chapters (212 pages), they presented an excellent discussion of their results, including significant and interesting case material. * Throughout the volume the authors were careful and honest in reporting their findings. * Other strengths of the book were detailed descriptions of methodology and careful documentation with reference to other relevant studies. *

[B474]

★SZONDI, LIPOT; MOSER, ULRICH; AND WEBB, MARVIN W. **The Szondi Test: In Diagnosis, Prognosis and Treatment.** Philadelphia, Pa.: J. B. Lippincott Co., 1959. Pp. xv, 309. $12.00. * (London: Pitman Medical Publishing Co., Ltd. 96s.) (*PA* 33:10370)

A.M.A. Arch Gen Psychiatry 1:450 O '59. Robert I. Yufit. This book, while filling a gap in American literature on this infrequently used technique, is difficult to assess. The authors seem to believe what they are saying, yet offer little evidence, empirical or otherwise, to support their claims. Some of their statements seem to evolve from the mystics of occult more than from sound scientific inferences. * The Szondi Test is a projective technique based on a person's reaction to a series of 48 photographs of psychotic patients. The photographs were chosen in accordance with the principle of genic relationship; that is, the person assumedly selects a photograph which portrays a psychiatric disorder also inherent in the subject's own familial genealogy. * While trying to be open-minded in seriously considering this rationale, this reviewer found little evidence to substantiate its validity. The authors work hard in attempting to quantify their diagnostic device, but are oftener than not carried away by their intensely positive identification with the Szondi Test, and objective conclusions are lacking, in spite of the authors' claims. * The book answers most questions for anyone wanting to know something about the test, but this reviewer questions how much of this material is logical, in terms of current research in the behavioral sciences. In fact, there are several psychological studies in the ten years since the test was introduced in America which discount the assumed relationship between the subject's response and the diagnostic classification of the persons pictured in the photographs. None of these studies is mentioned. Another major disappointment is that the book's senior author, Lipot Szondi, contributed only 51 pages of the 309 comprising the book. Although comprehensive in presenting the structure and content of the Szondi Test, the book is difficult to read, mainly because of its unique terminology, which demands careful study, and also because of its numerous charts and graphs, which this reviewer found to be tedious reading. The book has many interesting statements which must be tested more rigorously, but the high price of the book will likely discourage wide readership. If the authors' hope was to place their technique higher on the frequency scale of use among American diagnosticians, their mission is not considered successful. Possibly there is a cultural factor in the nature of the photographs which Americans do not identify with; but, whatever the case, research, oriented to testing concurrent validity, construct validity, and content validity, is much needed.

Brit J Psychol 51:187–8 My '60. Mary Williams. * The authors have made their task more difficult, and the book less readable, by their anxiety to prove the superiority of their theory and method to others, and by trying to confound those psychologists who rejoice in making nonsense of tests and theories which rely on the concept of a dynamic unconscious. The somewhat messianic attitude goes with the scolding meted out to the unconverted and seems more likely to put people's backs up than to induce them to take an interest in the material presented. Unfortunately, clarity is further impeded by the language used, which is mainly in the Teutonic style, heavy, often florid and sometimes obscure. Reading is made difficult by the Szondian terminology which, in his own works, is explained at length as he builds up his concepts, but in this book is piled upon the reader in a more or less arbitrary manner. *

Cont Psychol 5:160–1 My '60. Walter G. Klopfer. * It is evident from the beginning that in the world of Szondi there are but two kinds of psychologists. First, there is the "materialist" who is interested in somatic therapy, statistical methods of research, and the discovery of organic etiology for personality disorders. This psychologist is the villain of the piece. The hero is the "clinician" who is interested in psychotherapy, prefers depth analysis as a research method, and feels that personality disorders are mainly the result of unconscious factors. It may be difficult for the American psychologist to accept these as two syndromes. In the part of the book dealing with history, rationale, and therapy, American studies are referred to obliquely, but never cited. Henry David in his 1954 Szondi bibliography cited 332 studies. Only two of these are mentioned in this book. The selection of the pictures is described without reference to pertinent research which has challenged the validity of such procedures, but the chapter is accompanied by the statement, "The language of choice has stood the test of clinical validity." Much case material is presented with the explicit implication that this constitutes irrefutable evidence. * Validity is given short shrift in two pages. Studies contemptuously referred to as "statistical" are not presented since the authors assume that they are based either on false premises or inadequate methodological assumptions. An adequate study of the Szondi Test could be operationally defined as one which tends to support the assertions made by the authors. * This volume is aimed directly at the American reader with a "chip-on-the-shoulder" attitude being evident throughout. The authors realize the potential unpalatability of their approach to someone whose training has emphasized the scientific method. It was disappointing to find that Szondi and his disciples in 1959 could continue to ignore all of the pertinent questions raised by American investigators and summarized by Borstelmann and this reviewer in 1953, and to find the empirical method still so distasteful. Nevertheless, in spite of this bias, the theory and the therapeutic methods appear to be unique and ingenious, and as such worthy of greater familiarity on the part of the reader. Careful case illustrations are always instructive to the clinician. However, the gap between European armchair psychology and American empirical psychology seems just as wide in 1959 as it was in 1947.

[B475]

★TAKALA, MARTTI; ASSISTED BY MATTI KAASINEN, ERKKI JANHUNEN, VOITTO VUORINEN, AND SINIKKA OJANEN. **Studies of the Wartegg Drawing Completion Test: Studies of Psychomotor, Personality Tests II.** Annals of the Academia Scientiarum Fennica, Series B, Vol. 131, No. 1. Helsinki, Finland: Suomalainen Tiedeakatemia, Academia Scientiarum Fennica, 1964. Pp. 112. Paper. 5.60 mk. *

[B476]

★TARR, HARRY A. **How to Pass National Merit Scholarship Tests.** New York: Arco Publishing Co., Inc., 1960. Variously paged. Paper. $3.00. *

[B477]

★TAYLOR, EDITH MEYER. **Psychological Appraisal of Children With Cerebral Defects.** Cambridge, Mass.: Harvard University Press, 1959. Pp. xvii, 499. $8.50. (London: Oxford University Press. 68*s.*) * (*PA* 34:4756)

Cont Psychol 6:13–4 Ja '61. Alan O. Ross. * Taylor's description of her work gives the reader the sense of being in the presence of a master craftsman. She commands more than one hundred different techniques, each with a number of variations and modifications, and uses these tools with the flexibility and resourcefulness which alone make it possible to test the "untestable." Critical of the emphasis on "rigid statistical measurements," she is more interested in the process the child uses in approaching a task than in the score he achieves. She holds that qualitative aspects of the performance are often the sole indicators of cerebral pathology and repeatedly points out that numerical results obscure the essence of a child's test behavior. This book is a valuable vade mecum for the psychologist who encounters brain-injured children in his clinical work. It derives its strength from the fact that the author has had personal clinical experience with every test she discusses. Yet this fact is also the source of one of the book's weaknesses for it leads to the omission of some of the more recently introduced techniques * The field of testing children suspected of having a cerebral defect is beset by three difficulties: The lack of well-standardized developmental norms; the absence of a valid, independent criterion (short of a post mortem); and the want of a workable theoretical framework. * Many of the techniques she finds most useful have had little or no standardization, despite their long life. * Occasionally the author draws on her extensive experience to tell us that, on a specific test, "eight-year-old handicapped children may do at least as well as normal six-year-olds." The practicing clinician would gladly accept more statements beginning with "experience shows," were they to introduce such valuable, though informal and undocumented, norms. * Taylor is of little help in the borderline case where the question is not one of extent of damage but of the presence or absence of injury. Our author admits that this differentiation is "sometimes impossible" * one cannot help wondering whether there might not be some central themes which could help to unify the diverse findings. There are a few points where the author attempts to explain why certain defects are repeatedly found in brain-injured children, and the reader who likes a theory on which to hang his facts will welcome these passages and wish there were more. *

[B478]

★TAYLOR, STANFORD E. **Eye-Movement Photography With the Reading Eye, Second Edition.** Appendices (EDL Research and Information Bulletins Nos. 2 and 3) by Stanford E. Taylor, Helen Frackenpohl, and James L. Pettee. Huntington, N.Y.: Educational Developmental Laboratories, Inc., 1960. Pp. 69, 12, iv, 22. Paper, spiral binding. $3.75. * For reviews of the *Reading Eye,* see 838.

J Develop Read 5:120–3 w '62. N. Dale Bryant. This detailed and well written book, in a brief one hundred pages, provides (1) a review of previous work with eye movement photography, (2) a theoretical framework for understanding measurements obtained from eye records, (3) a detailed manual for using the reading eye camera, (4) a guide to scoring and interpreting eye movement records, and (5) the normative and research results which provide the basis of the entire field of eye movement photography. Some parts of the book, particularly an appendix (which is available independently as EDL Research and Information Bulletin No. 2 and No. 3), contain major research contributions of value to every serious worker in the field of reading. To anyone beginning to use the tremendous potentialities of eye movement photography for research or diagnosis, this detailed manual is essential. However, this volume clearly shows that the values of eye movement photography are not achieved easily. * The standardized materials, substantial norms, and clearly defined indices of fundamental reading skills that are the bases of this system of eye movement photography are supported by impressive data and competent research. While the norms are not based upon a carefully stratified sample, they are adequate both in number and representativeness of cases. * Eye movements are not presented as the major controlling factor and most valid measure of good reading, a position at one time vigorously expressed by the author's father, Earl A. Taylor. * Eye movement analyses are considered a supplementary, but powerful, tool to provide a clear picture of a reader's performance, capabilities, and limitations rather than a substitute for other standardized tests. It is refreshing to find the president of a company....which manufactures equipment for control reading, producing a book which contradicts claims often made by equipment salesmen and users: that good readers cover four to five words per fixation. Taylor reports that the average span of recognition (in reading, not in flash exposure) for college students is about one word per fixation and has been so since high school. * In summary, this book and the system of eye movement recording and analysis it presents is a major contribution that deserves study by anyone doing diagnostic or research work in the field of reading.

[B479]

★Taylor, Vernon R. **Guide for Setting Passing Points.** Personnel Brief No. 20. Chicago, Ill.: Public Personnel Association, 1959. Pp. 15. Paper, lithotyped. $2.00. *

[B480]

★Thomas, Caroline Bedell; Ross, Donald C.; and Freed, Ellen S. **An Index of Rorschach Responses: Studies on the Psychological Characteristics of Medical Students—I.** Baltimore, Md.: Johns Hopkins Press, 1964. Pp. xlv, 741. $15.00. * (London: Oxford University Press. 120*s*.)

[B481]

*Thomas, R. Murray. **Judging Student Progress, Second Edition.** New York: David McKay Co., Inc., 1960. Pp. x, 518. $5.50. *

Cont Psychol 6:367–8 O '61. Harold F. Bligh. * Thomas' approach is interesting and quite effective. He sees his text as having the same general functions as a class in school, the book is the teacher, the reader is the learner. * Regularly he utilizes for illustration actual classroom or school incidents which might occur in any American school. * The incidents are carefully chosen and relate directly to realistic problems which must be faced by teachers as they assume more active roles in appraising the progress of their students. * In his discussion of some of the more technical aspects of measurement and statistics, the author may be challenged for looseness of terminology and for statements which, though not entirely inaccurate, may nevertheless lead to misinterpretation and faulty generalization. * the discussion of norms (p. 107–109) [is] very sketchy. The author makes no attempt....to define and give illustrative examples of the conventional ways of reporting scores. * Nor is definition of basic statistical terms as precise as this reviewer would like. * Despite shortcomings resulting from the presentation of complex concepts in simple, nontechnical language, this well organized text meets a definite need. Anyone seeking a clear, simple presentation of basic concepts would profit from reading it. It should prove increasingly popular with teachers and other school personnel who are facing the challenge of the *movement for testing for guidance* which has been given impetus by national concern over the effectiveness of our schools.

For a review of the first edition, see 5:B422.

[B482]

★THORNDIKE, ROBERT L. **The Concepts of Over- and Under-Achievement.** New York: Bureau of Publications, Teachers College, Columbia University, 1963. Pp. ix, 79. $3.25. *

Personnel & Guid J 42:828–9 Ap '64. William W. Farquhar. * a welcome clarification of the ever-expanding study of discrepant achievement. It is an excellent source of ideas for those who plan to research the over- and underachiever, or for those who want a review of elementary measurement principles. * Thorndike has an unusual ability to hold the interest of his reader. His style is clear and his abstractions are undergirded with pertinent examples. * The emphasis....is not what the title promises. True, most of the basic "concepts of over- and underachievement" are touched upon at one point or another, but the organizational theme is research *design.* * I felt disappointed because Thorndike did not dig into some of the unique methodological problems that harass the researcher of over- and underachievement. * My disappointment was further heightened because Thorndike did not take a stand on which of the variety of techniques available for identifying over- and underachievers he would actually advocate. * I would hope that his advocating a matched-pair design (see page 28) does not imply discarding members of the sample. * The testing of beta's ....to determine if a particular variable adds anything to the prediction of final achievement is questionable * Beta's found to be significantly different from zero may be adding nothing new because the magnitude of a beta depends on the intercorrelation of the predictor variables. Testing the increase of the multiple over the zero order coefficient seems more appropriate in answering this question. * This is an excellent book and, if read carefully, will do for the area what Thorndike hopes it will do—"lead to fewer and better publications in the future." However, my over-all reactions were a mixture of admiration and disappointment—admiration for the precision and clarity of logic of what was presented, disappointment with the lack of new solutions to some persistent problems.

[B483]

*THORNDIKE, ROBERT L., AND HAGEN, ELIZABETH. **Measurement and Evaluation in Psychology and Education, Second Edition.** New York and London: John Wiley & Sons, Inc., 1961. Pp. viii, 602. $7.75; 59*s*. * (*PA* 36:2KJ02T) (*Teacher's Manual for Measurement and Evaluation in Psychology and Education, Second Edition.* 1962. Pp. iii, 73. Paper. $1.75; 14*s*.) *

Cath Ed R 59:565–6 N '61. Robert B. Nordberg. * Their stated purpose....is "the hope of developing more restrained, discriminating, and insightful testers...." If the purpose had been to present an effective case for objective tests of all kinds, one could say they had succeeded. As it is, reservations must be expressed. * The most noteworthy change is the section on validity, which now includes a greater variety of modes of same, but still stops short of the emerging notion of relevance. * The authors seemingly have not probed the fundamental principles of what they are doing. One senses this, for instance, in a certain unspoken horror of anything "subjective." The authors admit that those who teach for important ideas will have difficulty in using the kinds of tests they advocate; but they seem to feel that this kind of teaching is something invented to make trouble for would-be objective testers. The section on essay tests complains that "The student who is able to write effectively will often get a higher grade...." with no suggestion that perhaps he writes better because he thinks better. A check-list on the comparative merits of objective and essay tests (which, of course, already begs the question) lists as an advantage of the objective test that it "Is free from factors of skill in expression...." Distaste is expressed for "the laborious and subjective operation of evaluating the answers" on essays. The book, in short, seemingly is opposed to thought and the expression of thought. If one can overlook that tiny bias, it should be a helpful volume.

Cont Psychol 7:270–1 Jl '62. Andrew L. Comrey. * The authors have a direct, readable style. The book is well organized. In treating a topic, the authors blend the material from their various sources of information and present a coherent, unified statement. They seldom resort to leapfrogging from the findings of one investigator to another through the medium of brief, self-contained summaries of research studies. Questions for discussion are given at the end of each chapter. A useful, but selective (mention of R. B. Cattell's tests, for example, is lacking) annotated bibliography of current tests is given in an appendix. A novel and practical appendix item is the method of extracting a square root. Several parts of the book are particularly well done: analysis of testing from the standpoint of what kinds of products are called for, how to prepare classroom examinations, where to find information about specific tests, interpreting intelligence test scores, philosophy of test use in school programs, ratings, the school testing program, and what can be done with scores in the counseling situation. On the negative side, discussion of technical issues is either superficial or avoided entirely. Although the concept of correlation, for example, is discussed, calculation of the coefficient itself is considered to be so technical that it is put in an appendix. Even though it underlies much of the test development for instruments discussed, factor analysis is just one of those advanced topics too complicated to be considered. One wonders how long those who aspire to be competent in the use of tests can be sheltered from technical essentials. Discussion of the Wechsler, Stanford-Binet, and other tests is superficial for the most part. References to primary sources are scanty. Although technically accurate as a rule, the authors convey the mistaken impression that an equal-unit scale is obtained by using normalized standard scores. Although they may not wish to go into such a technical matter, the text material should be consistent with more profound sources. From the discussion of multifactor batteries, the mistaken impression could be obtained that one can assess the value of a battery, in comparison with that of a single complex test, by inspecting the magnitude of individual validity coefficients of the component tests in the battery. It should be heavily emphasized beyond possible misinterpretation that it is the multiple R of the battery which must be compared with the validity coefficient of the complex test. * In the discussion of school marks, the authors vacillate. At times they seem to side in with those educationists who would do away with school marks (because failure is distressing to poor students) while at other times they seem to be in favor of curbing professors who give too many A's. The final chapter on tests in the selection of personnel attempts to reduce a good technical book to a non-technical treatment in a brief space. The result fails to match the style and level of the other chapters. In summary, the book appears insufficiently exhaustive in technical matters and detail to serve as a suitable text for psychology majors in first rate colleges or universities. Nor is the choice of topics particularly appropriate for this group. The word "psychology" should be dropped from the title. On the other hand, judging from the book content alone, it appears to have been written primarily for prospective school teachers with no previous background in statistics. For this audience, the book is particularly well suited since the non-technical discussions, designed to guide the lay person in the use of tests, are excellent.

Personnel & Guid J 40:486–8 Ja '62. Ralph F. Berdie. * an excellent teaching text * The revised edition of the text is equally as good as the original and in some ways has been improved. The book maintains its position as one of the best testing texts and the reviewer knows of none that can be better used for beginning undergraduate and graduate courses in measurement. * A major change has been made in the discussion of validity and where the first edition discussed content validity, the second edition discussed rational or representing validity. Predictive validity has been renamed statistical or empirical validity and although the discussion of this validity may have become more meaningful to students, it is not as precise as the corresponding discussion in the original text. The concept of congruent validity has been renamed describing or signifying validity. * The only thing in this text to which the reviewer had a definitely negative reaction was the discussion of personality and interest inventories and here the reviewer's and the authors' biases are quite different. The authors assume that personality and interest inventories can be misused and perhaps will be misused more easily than will achievement or aptitude tests. They assume that high intercorrelations between scales on personality and interest inventories limit their usefulness, but emphasize no such assumption regarding high intercorrelation of scores on achievement or aptitude test batteries. They apparently assume that aptitude and achievement tests can be used by relatively untrained teachers but feel that interest and personality inventories must be used by highly skilled clinical counselors. Partly the authors' biases reflect the classroom teaching orientation apparent throughout the text. The authors know much more about teaching and curricula than they know about counseling, and, consequently, they write more skillfully about aptitude and achievement tests as related to teaching than they do about tests which are more relevant for counseling. The authors reveal another bias, this time one with which the reviewer agrees, when they discuss projective tests. The discussion in this text of the Rorschach and other projective techniques will serve to make the beginning student properly skeptical and cautious when it comes to using these tests. The authors' style is readable and literate. The examples are well chosen; the book is well manufactured; and the entire work shows careful attention and devotion. Instructors in courses of measurement in psychology and education must give careful consideration to this text when they are considering the many well-written texts that are available.

For reviews of the first edition, see 5:B424.

[B484]

★THORPE, LOUIS P.; WHITSON, MILO E.; BARON, DENIS; AND ADAMS, GEORGIA SACHS. **Studying Social Relationships in the Classroom: Sociometric Methods for the Teacher.** Chicago, Ill.: Science Research Associates, Inc., 1959. Pp. 49. Paper. $1.00. *

[B485]

★THROWER, ARTHUR H. **The New Guide to I.Q. Tests.** Preston, Lancs., England: A. Thomas & Co., 1963. Pp. 191. 20*s*. *

[B486]

★THURSTONE, L. L. **The Measurement of Values.** Chicago, Ill.: University of Chicago Press, 1959. Pp. vii, 322. $7.50. (London: University of Chicago Press, Ltd. 56*s*.) * (*PA* 33:9357)

Brit J Psychol 50:377–8 N '59. H. J. Eysenck. This book contains twenty-seven of Professor Thurstone's papers on psychological measurement and its application in the behavioural sciences. * Thurstone did not write much but every one of the papers included here reaches a very high standard indeed; there is no dead wood at all. He also preserved throughout his life an abiding interest in the topic which is reflected in this series of papers, the measurement of subjective qualities by rational methods. Quite apart from his later monumental work on factor analysis, his fame rests securely on such contributions as his Law of Comparative Judgement, his Phi-Gamma Hypothesis, his Measurement of Value and his Theory of Attitude Measurement. These, as well as other contributions contained in this book, are absolutely basic and should be familiar to all students of psychology; the publication of this book will make them more easily available to students in small departments without the necessary library facilities. But quite apart from any utilitarian function, the book affords a welcome opportunity of reviewing between two covers the work and contributions of one of the leading psychologists of our time who has left an indelible imprint on our ways of looking at the problems of measurement and our methods of dealing with them in our research. *Si vis monumentum, circumspice.*

[B487]

★TOLOR, ALEXANDER, AND SCHULBERG, HERBERT C. **An Evaluation of the Bender-Gestalt Test.** Foreword by Lauretta Bender. Springfield, Ill.: Charles C Thomas, Publisher, 1963. Pp. xxiii, 229. $9.50. * (*PA* 38:967)

Am J Orthopsychiatry 34:170–1 Ja '64. Adolf G. Woltmann. * [this book] is truly outstanding * Tolor and Schulberg speculate whether "the simplicity of the technique has not prompted a deluge of ill-conceived research with relatively little concern for theoretical and methodological considerations." Dr. Bender regards her work on the Gestalt Test as a result of neuropsychiatric clinical observations, not psychological research. She also feels that many of the disappointing results are due to the fact that "the original meaning and value of the Gestalt Test have been lost sight of by many of these investigators and their followers." Tolor and Schulberg's book is more than a summation of research * they systematically examine the validity or reliability of the research design of each study. They scrutinize methodology and sampling. They indicate where lack of proper research design, poor diagnostic criteria, inadequate or inconsistent use of data or scoring methods fail to produce meaningful results. At the end of each chapter they clearly indicate where more clarifying research is needed. In other words, they painstakingly separate the wheat from the chaff. For this monumental work they deserve the thanks and gratitude of all workers and students in the field. * The book is well put together. The type is clear and the style easily readable. Subject and author indexes greatly facilitate the reading. The importance of this book cannot be stressed too highly. I wholeheartedly agree with the authors' conclusions: "The results of some of the more sophisticated studies offer considerable promise that this method may yet find its rightful place when used selectively for specific problems for which it has demonstrated utility."

Cont Psychol 9:85–6 F '64. Read D. Tuddenham. * the authors undertake a conscientious evaluation of both intuitive and objective approaches. If not quite as "brilliantly evaluated" and "monumental" as Bender judges their review to be, it is nevertheless a substantial contribution. It is clearly written, and the frequent summaries help keep the reader afloat in a sea of detail. While the recurrent discussion of the same studies in different connections make the book repetitious the comprehensive coverage in each chapter adds to the book's reference value. Throughout the volume, Tolor and Schulberg, incorruptible as restaurant investigators for the Guide Michelin, parcel out conscientious and usually justified criticism to nearly everyone. Even Dr. Bender, who heaps encomiums on them in her foreword, is not immune. Yet the book is not wholly satisfying. Too long for a journal article, it is not long enough to provide a really exhaustive treatment. The reader will find here an excellent summary and bibliography; but if he is unfamiliar with the commoner administrative and scoring procedures, or even with the appearance of the designs, he will have to turn to original sources. Comparison with Billingslea's parallel review which appeared almost at the same time is inevitable. (Billingslea, F. Y., The Bender-Gestalt: a review and perspective. Psychol. Bull., 1963, 60, 233–251). The Tolor and Schulberg reference list is about twice as long, and covers publications both earlier and later than the span 1950–1960 incl., which Billingslea sets for himself, but excludes a few non-English studies which Billingslea lists. The Tolor and Schulberg book is the more comprehensive, more repetitious, and much more frankly evaluative. Yet the scope, level of discussion and conclusions of the two treatments are very similar despite a disparity in length of text of about seven to one. The only sharp difference in interpretation concerns the validity of the Bender-Gestalt as a measure of intelligence for children aged four to twelve. Billingslea takes the affirmative, while Tolor and Schulberg, who apparently had access to a prepublication copy of his paper, argue that the test is valid "only when there is at least moderate ego impairment." * The non-clinician who encounters the Tolor and Schulberg volume may find in it a representative sample of the present state of the diagnostic art. He is likely to be equally astonished at the range of Bender-Gestalt research,—from psychoanalysis to factor analysis, from LSD to reading-readiness,—and at the perennial optimism of Bender-Gestalt researchers in the face of persistently meager and contradictory findings. If he invokes the theory of partial reinforcement to account for the resistance to extinction of the Bender user's enthusiasm, he may find a corrective for scientific smugness in the evidence that at least in some circumstances, the objective, quantitative approach does not improve upon the accuracy of the clinician's subjective impressions! As usual, more research is needed to establish the rightful place of this tool,—but of what kind? In 1951, the reviewer recommended for tests like the Bender "smaller, more precisely formulated investigations" and validation goals phrased as testable hypotheses. The advice is still good as far as it goes, but is not enough. Bender research has not lacked for well-planned studies along with many poor ones. Yet with curious rigidity, investigators have taken the nine designs as given and made no attempt to broaden the sampling basis for measuring variables hopefully so fraught with significance. We need more studies of the *processes* involved in such tests. Above all, we need a sound theoretical rationale to integrate what has been established and to give direction to future work. Tolor and Schulberg are quite right. Empiricism is not enough!

[B488]

★Tomkins, Silvan S., and Miner, John B. **PAT Interpretation: Scope and Technique.** New York: Springer Publishing Co., Inc., 1959. Pp. vii, 184. $5.50. * (*PA* 34:1430) For reviews, see 246.

[B489]

Torgerson, Warren S. **Theory and Methods of Scaling.** New York and London: John Wiley & Sons, Inc., 1958. Pp. xiii, 460. $9.50; *72s.* * (*PA* 33:7320)

Austral J Psychol 13:123–5 Je '61. S. B. Hammond. * Torgerson does more than provide a review of the field. He makes three contributions that help to bring order to what has been an extremely diversified field of study. First, he provides an acceptable general classification of scaling methods. In the past we have tended to identify methods by their authors or by their purposes or by their special features; but Torgerson sets out a general classification * The author's second contribution lies in a number of methodological inventions. These help to provide a compact and impressive presentation of Thurstone's judgment methods, and an illuminating but difficult treatment of methods of inferring more than one dimension at a time. A third and most important contribution by the author is his consistent attempt to evaluate scaling methods in terms of how far they allow us to test the assumptions on which they are based. He has no time for scales which are such only by definition, nor for easy solutions such as those which make assumptions about the overall score distributions. He goes to considerable trouble to examine whether a method provides some check upon its underlying assumptions. It is because of this that Torgerson has been able to go beyond making a review of methods and to give us a unitary enquiry into the premises of psychological scaling. It would be too much to expect that a first attempt of this kind would meet all our needs equally well. It seems likely that this book will be used as a text for teaching graduate groups, and from this point of view it has a number of faults. The book is difficult not simply because it uses mathematics, but because it assumes a fairly high level of psychometric sophistication from the reader and because of the lack of any but the most abstract examples. This is a text that will only repay close study. Some of the difficulty with the book arises from the fact that it is simply not possible to deal adequately with all the scaling techniques available in Psychology. For one reason or another, Torgerson has little to say about classical psychophysical scaling, about test construction, or about factor analysis; but he assumes the knowledge of them on the part of the reader. The omission of these topics may be excused when we remember that there are many other texts dealing adequately with them; but their omission leaves us with a set of methods which appear powerful and sophisticated but which are as yet rather remote from the everyday problems of Psychology.

J Am Stat Assn 56:430–3 Je '61. Joseph L. Zinnes. * The scaling methods covered are restricted to those which are "fundamental." These are methods "whose general rationale involve the construction and application of a self-contained testable theory" (p. 418). Measurement by definition or by a derived process is specifically excluded. Excluded, therefore, is the problem of selecting and weighting indicants and the mental testing or individual-difference methods. The latter are excluded because they involve at the most a weighted sum of items answered correctly and this, it is argued, is essentially measurement by definition. * In addition to the "fundamental" criterion two other explicit criteria govern the author's selection of scaling methods. Firstly, the methods must be general, not solely applicable to a single attribute or context. The problem of estimating parameters within a given theory is therefore excluded. And secondly, the methods must yield at least an ordering of the objects (i.e., an ordinal scale) so that classification procedures or measurement procedures leading to a nominal scale are also excluded. Within the area mapped out by these self imposed restrictions there appear to be further omissions. The huge literature on scaling utility, for example, is completely ignored although much of this literature has both direct and broad implications for scaling theory. * The author has....at least two basic aims in this book: to provide a clear presentation of each method, making the assumptions and character of the method evident, and to provide a theoretical framework or basis for comparing and integrating the methods. * Torgerson's main contribution....lies in his handling of the first problem. His writing is thoroughly and amazingly lucid without any sacrifice in detail and completeness. At the same time the text does not have a cookbook quality about it. No magic formulas or prescriptions are offered. The writing is serious and where necessary, which is often, conclusions are reached tentatively. The author has for the most part even refrained from reporting many of the standard practices of scaling theories without first subjecting them to some critical analysis. In short, the tone of the book is altogether consistent and fitting with the present tentative state of the field. Of course, occasional slip-ups do occur over which one could quibble. There are some errors of reporting (e.g., Coombs' Task A and Task B are incorrectly identified as the author's judgment and response methods, respectively, rather than vice versa); some inconsistencies in notation (e.g., population and sample values are indicated in at least three distinctly different ways at various points of the book); and some uncritical descriptions of dubious conventions (e.g., the least squares fitting procedure and the goodness of fit test for the Thurstone methods are related without discussing the nature of the approximations involved). Despite the fact that this book is not wholly free from defects, it is, and probably will remain for some time, the best single reference book of scaling methods. Its only major deficiency as a reference book is its minor treatment of the Bradley-Terry methods which have recently come into much prominence among psychologists, primarily as a result of the work of R. D. Luce. The author fares less well with the more difficult problem of providing a theoretical basis or organization. Although there is a clear attempt to provide a unified or abstract treatment of scaling methods, for example, by grouping together different experimental procedures which employ the same scaling model, the level of unity which is achieved is still fairly minimal. All too often the distinctions which are made appear arbitrary and tend to emphasize what is conventional rather than what is basic. The Thurstone theory is described as a judgment method although it could equally well be employed as a response or subject centered method. In fact much the same could be said for most of the scaling models which are classified in one way rather than another. Furthermore the properties which are attributed to these various classes of scaling methods do not appear to be intrinsic to them. The judgment method is characterized as a method in which the attribute is clearly specified a priori, although in the case of the multidimensional methods this is certainly not the case. Also the fact that two long chapters (Chapters 9 and 10) are devoted to methods which employ the same scaling model does not help to increase the general level of abstraction. More serious than the lack of unity is the absence of an adequate scaling model in many cases. This is particularly true of the three chapters on quantitative judgment methods. No theory is developed which rigorously justifies the numerical assignments obtained by these methods. It is for this reason that the goodness of fit tests are so difficult to formulate. It is not obvious what properties these numerical assignments must satisfy to constitute a scale and hence what properties can form the basis of a goodness of fit test. The list of properties which the author gives for each scaling method does not distinguish between those properties which make the scale stable (and hence desirable) and those which are in fact necessary for the existence of the scale. (In one instance a scale is ruled out because no properties could be found which could form the basis of a goodness of fit test although this scale of interpoint distances would nevertheless prove useful if, in a particular context, it led to an Euclidean space of few dimensions.) Apart from the lack of adequate scaling models underlying the quantitative judgment methods, what is needed is a general discussion of the nature of scales, a discussion that highlights the essential elements involved in the construction of a scale or in determining the existence of a scale. The general discussion of science and measurement in the first three chapters do not, as one would hope, perform this function. There is little connection between the general considerations in these early chapters and the scaling methods described in the later chapters. By and large the deficiencies of this book are those which are characteristic of the scaling field. One cannot refrain from hoping that the major impetus of this book will be in directing scaling researchers to these gaps of knowledge and in goading the researcher into the job of filling them in, both at the top and at the bottom, rather than in providing a handy file for the practitioner.

[B490]

★TURNER, DAVID. **How to Pass High on High School Entrance and Scholarship Tests, 1959 Edition.** New York: Arco Publishing Co., Inc., 1959. Pp. 256. Paper. $2.50. *

[B491]

★TYLER, LEONA E. **Tests and Measurements.** Englewood Cliffs, N.J.: Prentice-Hall, Inc., 1963. Pp. xi, 116. Paper. Text edition, $1.50; trade edition, $3.95. * (London: Prentice-Hall International, Inc. *12s. 6d.*) (*PA* 38:937)

Austral J Psychol 15:133–4 Ag '63. C. A. Gibb. * Tyler begins with a clear and concise discussion of the nature and function of measurement in psychology. She passes then to a short chapter on Basic Statistics which, while it is well done, would not meet the text needs in this area for any introductory course in Australia. Subsequent chapters deal with principles of testing, Intelligence Tests, tests of

Special Ability, Personality Tests and the applications of tests to the making of decisions about people and by people, and to research. * There are few introductory texts to which it would be a useful supplement and there is very little likelihood indeed that it would serve any course other than the introductory. *

Brit J Ed Psychol 34:102–3 F '64. E. Fisk. * attempts to convey no more information than do the relevant sections of some general texts of educational psychology * the essential principles underlying psychological measurement are clearly explained, the treatment of the concepts of validity and reliability being particularly well developed. The section on factor analysis omits any reference to British work, apart from the pioneer contributions of Spearman. * The classification of different types of tests with a consideration of the purposes and limitations of each is straight-forward and acceptable, whilst the detailed description of one or two major tests of each type will doubtless be helpful. The omission of any reference to tests constructed in Britain is one obvious disadvantage for students in this country. The omissions referred to make it unlikely that this book will be widely used in this country but it is worth consideration because it does appear to be a book that virtually all students could read and understand without tutorial assistance and one which makes a valiant effort to stress the need for "clear thinking and a dash of cautious scepticism" on the part of all who make use of tests and measurements.

Ed & Psychol Meas 23:848–9 w '63. Herbert Zimiles. * Written in a clear, interesting style, the book offers more content and better perspective than that provided by the omnibus introductory text. In fact the presentation of some topics is superior to that encountered in many larger texts written for a whole course in testing. * Following an elementary introduction which is almost too simple, the remainder of the first and the second chapters is given over to concepts of measurement and statistics which are beyond the scope of the beginning student. The section which distinguishes among nominal, ordinal, interval, and ratio scales of measurement establishes a distinction which bears little relation to the pages that follow; it is more likely to distract and to confuse than to edify. Basic statistics are presented in the best tradition of such one-chapter presentations; this section is much too concentrated for all but the most gifted students. Important statistical concepts are frequently presented almost casually, with off-hand computational illustrations which are not sufficiently explained. An excellent but remarkably concise discussion of statistical inference is included. In fact almost an entire semester of work is summarized in thirteen pages! The elements of psychometric theory are presented lucidly, and in terms of the most current thinking. * The treatment of intelligence and aptitude testing is good, that of personality testing superior, in some respects, to what is usually found in more advanced textbooks. * None of the serious problems which beset psychological testing is overlooked; yet the overall effect is constructive. For a brief presentation of psychological testing, the book affords an unusually complete and intelligent statement.

[B492]

*United States Army Personnel Research Office. **Army Personnel Tests and Measurement.** Department of the Army Pamphlet No. 611–2. Washington, D.C.: Publications Branch, The Adjutant General's Office, Department of the Army, June 22, 1962. Pp. iv, 114. Paper. Restricted distribution. * [Revision of Pamphlet No. TM 12-260, April 9, 1953.] For reviews of the first edition, see 5:B1.

[B493]

★Valin, E. **The Value of Examinations: A Technical Study Carried Out in the Lebanon.** Unesco Educational Studies and Documents, No. 40. New York: UNESCO Publications Center, 1961. Pp. 38. Paper, lithotyped. $0.50. (London: Her Majesty's Stationery Office. *2s. 6d.*) *

[B494]

★Vandenberg, Steven G. **The Primary Mental Abilities of Chinese Students: A Comparative Study of the Stability of a Factor Structure.** Annals of the New York Academy of Sciences, Vol. 79, Art. 9. New York: the Academy, 1959. Pp. 257–304. Paper. $2.50. * (*PA* 35:3420; 36:3HD57V)

[B495]

★Vernon, P. E. **Intelligence and Attainment Tests.** London: University of London Press Ltd., 1960. Pp. 207. *20s.* * (New York: Philosophical Library, Inc., 1961. $7.50.) (*PA* 35:3421)

Am J Psychol 75:343–4 Je '62. J. Stanley Ahmann. * The outstanding feature....is the heavy emphasis on intelligence tests and the very light emphasis on attainment tests. * In addition to the lack of emphasis on attainment tests, the reader will quickly notice the failure of Professor Vernon to devote sufficient space to validity, reliability, and norm considerations. The weakness of the treatment in these three areas probably stems in part from the fact that Professor Vernon attempted to restrict his consideration of statistical aspects of testing to a minimum. On the other hand, it is disappointing to note that Professor Vernon devoted considerably more pages to the question of the effects of coaching and practice on intelligence test results than he did to the determination and evaluation of the validity and reliability of those tests. A relatively large part of the volume is devoted to descriptions of individual and group intelligence tests used in Great Britain. Little is provided here which cannot be found in test manuals or in standard references concerning commercially available tests. On the other hand, his treatment is concise and provides a convenient first step for a person interested in enlarging his knowledge of popular intelligence tests. In summary, it is clear that the material prepared by Professor Vernon will, in general, be quite useful to the unsophisticated student of psychological testing. The more sophisticated reader will not, however, find this volume helpful in his efforts to enlarge his grasp of the present status of psychological testing, except in so far as it is applied in Great Britain.

Cont Psychol 7:378–9 O '62. Julian C. Stanley. In just 185 small pages of text this British educational psychologist....discusses mental ability so lucidly and insightfully that intelligent laymen, students, and specialists will all find much of interest. Vernon communicates well without oversimplification. His style is straightforward and declarative, but typically he tries to include several points of view. * He stresses "intelligence" testing throughout, despite the title, except for the lonesome ten pages that constitute Chapter 6, "Educational Attainment Tests," in which some popular topics, largely irrelevant to his main theme, are dispensed with quickly. * In the excellent chapter on heredity and environment, he judiciously explores the nature-nurture balance hinted at above, emphasizing "the importance of upbringing, social differences and education." Vernon is by no means an extreme environmentalist, however. His statement on pages 175–176, citing Shuey's 1958 book favorably, may discomfit some SPSSIites: "From such results, it seems quite probable that genetic differences between racial and ethnic groups do exist—at least in some aspects of intellectual ability—though we have no satisfactory way of proving it." All in all, nearly every thoughtful adult would find something worth-while in this little volume. It could do much to counteract the superficial, stereotyped criticisms of "IQ tests" rampant in the popular press of his country and ours. Present and prospective teachers particularly need Vernon's balanced evaluations.

Personnel & Guid J 41:278–80 N '62. Carl Bereiter. * The book is pretty much eliminated from consideration as a regular measurement text by the fact that large portions of it are devoted to British tests which the American user probably will never see. However, the chapters on the history of intelligence testing, heredity and environment, and the educational and vocational implications of intelligence tests can be recommended as supplementary reading, either for measurement courses or for introductory education or guidance courses. They are brief and unusually lucid. The heredity-environment chapter will make good reading also for professionals whose taste for the subject may have been jaded by the pretentious manner in which it has been treated by devotees of this paradox. A chapter on the effects of coaching and practice on intelligence tests may be highly recommended to all people who work with intelligence tests. *

[B496]

VERNON, PHILIP E. **The Measurement of Abilities, Second Edition.** London: University of London Press Ltd., 1956. Pp. xii, 276. 21*s*. * (New York: Philosophical Library, Inc., 1961. $7.50.) (*PA* 37:1189)

Personnel & Guid J 41:75–6 S '62. S. B. Sells. * well written * The first seven chapters explain the statistics necessary to deal with mental measurement and marking. These contain practical and extremely valuable discussions of problems that are often overlooked in statistics texts and that reflect both the extensive experience and wisdom of the author. While matters of handling frequency distributions, interpretation of school marks and tests scores, reliability, and correlation are often regarded as "elementary," the treatment of these topics by Vernon contains much that the professional psychometrician will find of value in dealing with practical situations. The second half of the book is an equally valuable, practical-oriented survey of mental tests, primarily for ability measurement. Vernon's devotion to Spearman's viewpoint in the discussion of mental organization may appear strange to present-day American factor analysts. Nevertheless his discussion is worth reading. Even as advanced a field as this is far from settled, and many of the contemporary problems are fairly discussed at the level of the lay reader to whom the book is addressed. The inclusion of much material which is culturally oriented to British schools and British publications is both an advantage and a handicap vis-a-vis the American reader. To many it should serve as a valuable reference to the contemporary practices of our British colleagues, prepared by an outstanding British spokesman. Unfortunately, however, the same emphasis may restrict its use as a text in American schools.

For additional reviews, see 5:B445; for reviews of the first edition, see 3:1219 and 40:B1115.

[B497]

★VERNON, PHILIP E. **Personality Assessment: A Critical Survey.** London: Methuen & Co. Ltd., 1964. Pp. ix, 333. 42s. (New York: John Wiley & Sons, Inc. $7.50.) *

[B498]

*VERNON, PHILIP E. **The Structure of Human Abilities, Second Edition.** London: Methuen & Co. Ltd., 1961. Pp. x, 208. Out of print. * (John Wiley & Sons, Inc. published only the original 1950 edition which is still in print.) For reviews of the first edition, see 4:B406.

[B499]

VIITAMÄKI, R. OLAVI. **Personality Traits Between Puberty and Adolescence: Their Relationships, Development and Constancy With Reference to Their Relation to School Achievement.** Annals of the Academia Scientiarum Fennica, Series B, Vol. 104. Helsinki, Finland: Suomalainen Tiedeakatemia, Academia Scientiarum Fennica, 1956. Pp. 183. Paper. 7 mk. * (*PA* 32:3300)

Psychometrika 25:120–1 Mr '60. J. A. Radcliffe. This is a report on the relationships betweeen scholastic achievement and "certain ability, temperament and dynamical traits." A battery of ability tests, the Wartegg drawing completion test, and the Zulliger shortened variation of the Rorschach test were given to a sample of high school boys and girls, some of whom took the projective tests again at college three years later. Almost everything that could have been done with the data has been done. Reported for the sexes separately are multiple correlations with high school and college achievement, combined and separate factor analyses, and differences between the means and correlations between the two testings with the projective devices. There is also a Q-technique analysis for those with the best matriculation results. The ability tests are too restricted in content and too inadequately described for the factorial results to be of any interest outside Finland. * To those who don't speak the projective language or who lack the necessary intuition, the results will have little appeal. Some developmental psychologists may find merit in the evidence concerning personality changes between ages 15 and 18, provided they can interpret and justify the changes and disregard that out of enough differences considered some must turn out to be statistically significant. Consistently overlooked are the need for cross validation in such a fact-finding study, and the role of experimental dependence between variables in the use of factor analysis. Interpretation of factorial differences between boys and girls and between ages 15 and 18 in terms of *differentiation* is questionable, especially considering that methods of communality estimation and of deciding the number of factors are not given. Too much of the report consists of mention of material for its own sake rather than for its relevance. * Viitamäki insists that factor analysis is a hypothesis-testing technique, yet uses it in a fact-finding way. Perhaps of most interest is the application of a method of rotation suggested by Ahmavaara, but not elsewhere reported, though it is implied in Ahmavaara's writings. The primary factor axes are located through those tests which have the lowest ratios of their first centroid loadings to the lengths of their vectors, that is, along those vectors furthest from the first centroid. Rotation is made directly to oblique primary factor pattern. In the analysis reported, this method of rotation yields a fair simple structure. But it may overemphasize single variables in the location of hyperplanes and might better be used for selection of the first trial vectors in the single plane method of rotation. * All in all, there has been a lot of busy-work and much being wise after the event. One gets lost in the wealth of data, and this is aggravated by the highly intuitive interpretations. The report is below the standard of others in the *Series* and will interest a limited audience only.

[B500]

★VIITAMÄKI, R. OLAVI. **Psychometric Analysis of the Thematic Apperception Test: With Reference to Personality Structure and School Success in Adolescence.** Annals of the Academia

Scientiarum Fennica, Series B, Vol. 115, Part 2. Helsinki, Finland: Suomalainen Tiedeakatemia, Academia Scientiarum Fennica, 1959. Pp. 61. Paper. 3 mk. *

[B501]

★WALDER, HANS. **Drive Structure and Criminality: Criminobiologic Investigations, Revised Edition.** Translated by Marvin W. Webb. Springfield, Ill.: Charles C Thomas, Publisher, 1959. Pp. xvii, 174. $7.50. *

Am J Psychother 14:611–3 Jl '60. Frederic Wertham. * a treatise on the application of the Szondi test to practical and theoretical problems of criminology. The original German edition was published in 1952. The author is attorney-general of the Canton of Zurich in Switzerland. He feels that the Szondi method is of great value not only in crime detection and penology but also as the foundation for a theory of crime causation. * It would seem that much more work is necessary on the application of the Szondi test to individuals who have not committed any crimes or delinquencies before it can be used safely in the criminological field. The author feels it can be of great help, as part of the "evidence," to help evaluate suspects, to determine what the sentence should be, or who should be put on parole or probation. As applied by the author however, the test seems to constitute a considerable danger to anybody who is accused and has to submit to the test. In fact, there is a Kafka-like atmosphere in some of the case discussions. To be called a "latent exhibitionist" or a "repressor of a latent Cain nature," or a "killer" would seem to me to be prejudicial for any accused. The author claims that with the Szondi test one can "experimentally determine those individuals who are potential arsonists or perpetrators of homicide, robbers, homosexuals or pedophiliacs, exhibitionists, thieves, etc." And all this without "any information relating to the previous life of the accused or knowledge concerning the nature of the deed."

J Proj Tech 25:245 Je '61. F. Ferracuti. * The chapters reflect classical German thought, taken from Exner and Mezger, and appear incomplete and naive to any reader familiar with the complex contemporary discussions on the subject matter, the methodology and the aims of modern criminology. * The author has constructed a criminobiologic typology upon the basis of the Szondian theory of drives and, in pursuing this outmoded aim, has assumed a close correspondence between character traits, or drives, and type of offence. This is in contrast with modern approaches of clinical criminology, which try to underline the need for individual examination and state the possibility that, in given circumstances, the same drive constellation can motivate quite different external criminal (as well as non-criminal) behaviors. Some of the types presented by the author are described in an unusual terminology (e.g.: the "Misunderstood Genius" and the "latent acquirer of valuable objects") which does not help to clarify his concepts. Also, his "significant criminobiologic types" are not in any sense, demonstrated. The book has a tautologic approach and makes no use of statistical analysis. The author goes as far as to state (p. 128) that the Szondi test can be used as a method of *criminal inquiry,* to rule out those suspects whose drive structure does not conform to the criminal behavior under investigation. The large literature, other than Swiss or German, discussing the Szondi test and challenging its validity is completely ignored. * More recent investigations (W. M. Coulter: The Szondi test and the prediction of antisocial behavior, *J. proj. Tech.,* 1959, *23,* 24–29) disprove the validity of the Szondi procedure in criminology and makes it very difficult to accept the overenthusiastic conclusions of Dr. Walder. The book, however, presents a number of criminal cases studied with the Szondi test and can be used as an anthology of clinical criminal cases. The use of the Szondi test in criminological examinations, together with other tests, is certainly justified, but unwarranted generalizations and statements, such as those presented in this book, are contrary to a scientific approach to and a valuable understanding of the field of criminal psychology.

[B502]

*WARNER, W. LLOYD; WITH MARCHIA MEEKER AND KENNETH EELLS. **Social Class in America: A Manual of Procedures for the Measurement of Social Status, [1960 Edition].** New York: Harper & Row, Publishers, Inc., 1960. Pp. xiii, 298. Paper. $1.60. * (Identical to the original 1949 edition except for the replacement of the appendix with two chapters and a bibliography previously published in *Review of Sociology* edited by Joseph Gittler.) For reviews, see 4:B409.

[B503]

WECHSLER, DAVID. **The Measurement and Appraisal of Adult Intelligence, Fourth Edition.** Baltimore, Md.: Williams & Wilkins Co., 1958. Pp. ix, 300. Cloth. $5.00. * (London: Baillière, Tindall & Cox, Ltd. 40*s.*) (*PA* 33:796)

Cont Psychol 4:210+ Jl '59. Read D. Tuddenham. * a far more thorough revision than those that preceded it * New are chapters on the factorial composition of W-B I and WAIS, on age-changes in intelligence, and on sex differences. In addition, there are special chapters on the clinical evaluation of brain damage and on the use of the tests in counseling and guidance. Throughout the volume there is considerable rewriting and expansion of particular sections, and a consistent integration of findings on WAIS with the older material on W-B I. No mention is made of W-B II, nor of WISC. * after fifty years of "clarification," intelligence as a concept remains muddled, in spite of the enormous popular success of tests purporting to measure it. Wechsler has not changed his position on the fundamental issue. For example, he has modernized his definition of intelligence as an aggregate or global capacity to act purposefully, etc., only by adding the phrase "operationally defined." Operational or not, this formulation, like most such, is too all-embracing to help much in evaluating specific test content. In another place, he describes intelligence "as an effect rather than a cause, a resultant of interacting abilities—non-intellective included," and distinguishes between intelligence (adequacy of functioning) and intellectual ability (capacity to function). The specification of intellectual abilities, he thinks, is the task of factor analysis. Intelligence cannot, however, be inferred directly from summations of factor scores, both because it involves complex interactions among abilities and because it comprises such non-intellective components as drive and experience. Although Wechsler regards factors as real—"factors are facts, not just theoretical categories"—there are too many of them (and too many ways of calculating them) for factor analysis to constitute an ultimate answer to the resolution of intelligence into its components. Where does this leave us with respect to the construction of intelligence tests? Our choices of content must be founded on judgment and experience. Wechsler thinks his scales measure general intelligence, and most clinicians would agree. He concedes they do not measure all that goes to make it up. "The only thing we can ask of an intelligence scale is that it measure sufficient portions of intelligence to enable us to use it as a fairly reliable index of the individual's global capacity." But what is sufficient? How may we determine whether the test is not only a long enough but also an ecologically representative enough sampling of the demands for intelligence imposed by our physical and cultural milieu? There is no real criterion, but only Spearmanites would expect so much from ten or eleven item-types selected on other grounds. Absence from the factorial data of several commonly identified factors suggests that the Wechsler scales cover none too thoroughly even the more limited domain of general intelligence tests. Perhaps the most interesting chapter for the general reader concerns changes in intelligence with age. Wechsler's report in his first edition of a systematic decline in tested adult intelligence, following a maximum between 20 and 25 years, was at once a *raison d'être* for the Wechsler-Bellevue scale and a research finding of the greatest significance for gerontology and for society generally. Wechsler's data confirmed earlier cross-sectional studies on aging (e.g., Jones and Conrad, 1933), and his conclusion was generally accepted that detectable mental deterioration in human beings begins in early adulthood and parallels decline in such anatomical and physiological characteristics as brain weight and vital capacity. This view has recently been challenged by Bayley (1955) and Owens (1953). These workers found clear evidence that abstract and verbal skills, at least among the intellectually superior, continued to *increase* up to age 50, and perhaps longer. Equally serious for Wechsler's contention are his own findings, reported in the present edition, that on WAIS the maximum is not reached until 25–29, and that the decline is appreciably less marked up to age fifty than he previously believed. Wechsler attempts a conscientious reconsideration of the problem, but in this reviewer's opinion dismisses much too summarily the argument that cross-sectional data provide an insecure basis for longitudinal inferences. For example, the difference between the older and younger generations, which Wechsler attributed to biological decline, was observed in the comparison of World War I and World War II soldiers tested at the same age (Tuddenham 1948). There can be little doubt that Wechsler's age curves are correct as descriptions of the mean level of test performance in different age brackets of today's population. The observed phenomenon can, however, be as readily explained by secular changes in the education, the test sophistication, and the health of the samples compared, as by the decline in some biological substrate of the test score. Wechsler is reluctant to abandon his earlier position. He states flatly that most intellectual abilities decline with age and at a systematic and linear rate. General intelligence, however, "as evaluated by pragmatic criteria," appears to maintain itself unimpaired over a much greater portion of adult life and to decline at a much slower rate than do the mental abilities by which it is measured. In this context, Wechsler seems to imply that his test measures intellectual abilities which decline, not intelligence, some of whose aspects (e.g., sagacity) may actually increase. A vagrant question arises whether tests which show increases are thereby better measures than Wechsler's of intelligence in older people. In any case, those now entering the middle years seem entitled to face their futures with considerably more equanimity than could the corresponding age group in 1939. There are many novel features in this edition. Noteworthy among them is a stimulating discussion of sex differences in intelligence, and a method for scoring psychological masculinity and femininity based on differences between subtest scores. The value of such scores is not established. The writing of the clinical chapters is somewhat more cautious than heretofore but not fundamentally different. Minor changes have been introduced in the calculation of deterioration ratios. The controversial "sign" lists for psychiatric syndromes are carried over almost without alteration, despite a vehement disclaimer of them as patterns. The volume concludes with an excellent chapter on changes in intelligence consequent to brain damage, and a somewhat thinner discussion of the applications of the tests in counseling. In reading the last section of the book, the reviewer's reservations about ratios, "signs," and the like did not diminish his admiration for the clinical wisdom and rich experience which illuminate Wechsler's discussion of specific cases and responses. Wechsler describes himself as "a reformed but unchastened Spearmanite." On the evidence of this volume he might also have described himself as a reformed but unchastened clinician—and for this, several thousand clinical psychologists deeply in his debt should be profoundly grateful.

Ed & Psychol Meas 19:120–2 sp '59. William D. Altus. * Wechsler has been put somewhat on the defensive by the multitude of studies concerning his clinical "signs" and various nosological categories. Wechsler characteristics of the various nosologies remain about the same, but now Wechsler says, and says again, "....these lists *are not patterns*." These lists are merely bases from which patterns may be evolved. Despite these *caveats*, one fears that the psychometrician who is poorly trained or naive will continue to regard the newly-named "characteristics" as invariant patterns. The problem of urban-rural differences in intelligence test performance is quite frankly faced: The mean full-scale IQ is about one-half sigma higher for the city dweller. Wechsler does not try to offer any new explanation for this differential which has been known for so long. Nor does he offer any empirical evidence from the WAIS standardization for the racial and group differences which were undoubtedly found. It is too bad that the latter were not offered. Let us hypothesize a group we shall call X, which has an IQ about one-half sigma below the full-scale WAIS IQ norms. Let us further assume that the urban-rural differential, blazoned forth in the book under consideration, also holds for hypothesized group X. In this event the rural X's are one full sigma below the national norms. To the unwary, naive, urban-reared psychologist, differential norms would probably be of considerable aid—in military installations, in educational work, in mental hospitals. For example, the reviewer found that a certain cutting score for the Wechsler Mental Ability Scale, Form B, IQ's would give these anomalous effects in a military school for illiterate soldiers in World War II: Four out of five American Indians with IQ's below this point would succeed in the school, pass the final tests and graduate; conversely, four out of five old-line Whites with similar IQ's on the same scale would fail. The reviewer developed differential norms and markedly sharpened his predictive efficiency thereby. Perhaps Wechsler's overall IQ's should be retained but with differing interpretations and expectancies for certain social groups. One could well conclude by strongly recommending the Fourth Edition to all who have more than a cursory interest in the testing of intelligence and in some very stimulating speculation about that which is being tested, even though the latter is still seen as through a glass darkly. The author is to be commended for his thought-provoking summation of data relevant to intelligence testing and for his own unique contributions to theory and practice in that incompletely-explored province.

Psychoanalytic Q 27:592–4 O '58. Philip S. Holzman. * In a major revision of a book, the reader expects the author to take notice of new relevant data and novel views of his topic even if they tend to contradict the author's own interpretations. Here lies the glaring omission in Wechsler's current text. His ideas about intelligence, tightly tied to Spearman's, remain essentially unrevised. The author is certainly entitled to his commitment. His steadfastness, however, becomes parochial when he ignores completely the recent theoretical contributions to the problem of intellectual functioning and development from sources other than studies utilizing traditional intelligence tests. Psychoanalytic ego psychology, as represented by the contributions of Hartmann and Rapaport (including studies of conflict-free structures, processes of automatization, and the delaying function of thought), and Piaget's investigations of the development of intelligence are unmentioned. It is particularly unfortunate that the author of a test which is so useful in appraising the uniqueness of a person's intellectual functioning should shun the efforts to understand intellectual functioning within the context of a general theory of personality. Wechsler's efforts to maintain the insularity of intelligence force him to ignore the implications of many of his own statements. When he defines intelligence as "the aggregate or global capacity of the individual to act purposefully, to think rationally, and to deal effectively with his environment," he implicates the processes of adaptation and the defensive delaying of impulse discharge. Yet he nowhere follows his definition to its significance for reality testing, control over affects, and detours for impulse discharge. Although Wechsler defines intelligence as a "global capacity," intelligent behavior is discussed by him as if it were empirically separable from nonintellective behavior. Thus, he writes, "more challenging, at least for diagnostic purposes, are the failures and successes....usually on individual test items which are seemingly due to the individual's personality and emotional conditioning." The author implies that personality enters into intelligent behavior only in so far as the *content* of a person's response is concerned. The formal organization of thought and the patterning of abilities are treated as if they did not reflect the personality organization of the person. It becomes clear that to the author, personality organization consists of drives, motives, and affects that *disrupt* test performance. "In the writer's opinion," Wechsler writes (p. 179), "both the oversensitized clinician and the matter-of-fact statistician are likely to overestimate impact of personality variables on test performance. This does not mean that these variables are of no importance....emotionality, anxiety, motivation, etc. can influence test scores, but only seldom do they influence performance to such a degree as to invalidate the test findings as a whole." The author has expanded the chapter on Diagnostic and Clinical Features from twenty-two pages in the third edition to forty-four pages in the fourth edition, indicating his increased appreciation for the diagnostic yield of his test. Yet his view of diagnosis is unfortunately primitive, borrowing from the worst features of psychiatric nosology. Wechsler presents "typical" test score patterns of such mythical groups of people as "the schizophrenic," "the anxiety reaction type," "the sociopath." It is a pity that Wechsler's skill as a test constructor is not matched by his sophistication as clinician. He gives scant consideration to the psychological problems a person must confront when solving the test items, to the cognitive functions tapped by the tests. The W-B I and the WAIS are excellent instruments for gathering information about the cognitive organization of the person tested; but one can make optimal diagnostic use of the tests by reasoning from the psychological functions tapped by the test rather than from a blind application of signs such as, "a very high Similarities along with a very low Picture Completion is definitely indicative of schizophrenia, *because* [italics added] no other type of patient, so far as we have been able to determine, shows this combination." A similar kind of reasoning from signs and classes rather than from psychological processes pervades the discussion of brain damage and the potentially useful chapter on Sex Differences. By confining his discussion to the statistical evidence for a decline in "mental ability" in the chapter on Mental Deterioration, Wechsler misses a fine opportunity to discuss the possible effects of such a decline on well-established control processes, on affect expression, and on adaptive efforts. The publishers have done a slipshod job of typesetting. Margins in the bibliography are violated and there are numerous typographical errors. The test, not the text's the thing.

For reviews of earlier editions, see 3:299–301 and 40:B1121; for related reviews, see 5:414–5, 4:361, 3:298, and 40:1429.

[B504]

★Wechsler, Louis K.; Blum, Martin; and Friedman, Sidney. **College Entrance Examinations, Revised Edition.** New York: Barnes & Noble, Inc., 1964. Pp. x, 310. Paper. $2.25. * (First edition published in 1960.)

[B505]

★Weiss, David J.; Dawis, Rene V.; England, George W.; and Lofquist, Lloyd H. **Validity of Work Histories Obtained by Interview.** University of Minnesota, Industrial Relations Center 34; Minnesota Studies in Vocational Rehabilitation, 12. Minneapolis, Minn.: the Center, September 1961. Pp. ii, 47. Paper. Gratis. * (*PA* 36:5LD47W)

[B506]

★Weiss, David J.; Dawis, Rene V.; England, George W.; and Lofquist, Lloyd H.; with the assistance of Lois L. Anderson, Robert E. Carlson, and Richard S. Elster. **The Measurement of Vocational Needs.** University of Minnesota, Industrial Relations Center Bulletin 39; Minnesota Studies in Vocational Rehabilitation 16. Minneapolis, Minn.: the Center, April 1964. Pp. vi, 101. Paper. Gratis. *

[B507]

★Wellman, Frank E., and Twiford, Don D. **Guidance Counseling and Testing Program Evaluation: Suggestions for Secondary Schools: Title V-A, National Defense Education Act of 1958.** Sponsored by the United States Office of Education. Washington, D.C.: United States Government Printing Office, 1961. Pp. v, 37. Paper. $0.30. *

[B508]

★Western Regional Conference on Testing Problems. **The Eighth Annual Western Regional Conference on Testing Problems, May 1, 1959: Measurement Implications of Recent Curriculum Developments.** Arthur P. Coladarci, Chairman. Berkeley, Calif.: Educational Testing Service, [1959]. Pp. ii, 78. Paper, plastic binding, lithotyped. $1.00. *

[B509]

★Western Regional Conference on Testing Problems. **The Ninth Annual Western Regional Conference on Testing Problems, May 6, 1960: Convergence of Measurement and Instruction.** Henry W. Magnuson, Chairman. Berkeley, Calif.: Educational Testing Service, [1960]. Pp. ii, 71. Paper, plastic binding, lithotyped. $1.00. *

[B510]

★Western Regional Conference on Testing Problems. **The Tenth Annual Western Regional Conference on Testing Problems, May 5, 1961: Changes in Education and Measurement Since Sputnik.** Virgil J. O'Connor, Chairman. Berkeley, Calif.: Educational Testing Service, [1961]. Pp. ii, 87. Paper, plastic binding, lithotyped. $1.00. *

[B511]

★Western Regional Conference on Testing Problems. **The Eleventh Annual Western Regional Conference on Testing Problems, May 4, 1962: Creativity, Its Assessment and Measurement.** Merle H. Elliott, Chairman. Berkeley, Calif.: Educational Testing Service, [1962]. Pp. ii, 59. Paper, plastic binding, lithotyped. $1.00. *

[B512]

★Western Regional Conference on Testing Problems. **The Twelfth Annual Western Regional Conference on Testing Problems, May 3, 1963: The Evaluation of Education Today: Measurement's Contribution.** T. Leslie MacMitchell, Chairman. Berkeley, Calif.: Educational Testing Service, [1963]. Pp. ii, 42, 16. Paper, plastic binding, lithotyped. $1.00. *

[B513]

★Western Regional Conference on Testing Problems. **The Thirteenth Annual Western Regional Conference on Testing Problems: Testing in Learning and Teaching.** Carl A. Larson, Chairman. Berkeley, Calif.: Educational Testing Service, 1964. Pp. iii, 60. Paper. $1.50. *

[B514]

★Whisler, Thomas L., and Harper, Shirley F., Editors. **Performance Appraisal: Research and Practice.** New York: Holt, Rinehart & Winston, Inc., 1962. Pp. xiii, 593. $9.75. *

Cont Psychol 8:114 Mr '63. Wayne K. Kirchner. This is an excellent book, not only for people who know nothing about performance appraisals and ratings, but also for people who do. At first glance, the book appears to be another collection of readings, but in addition to the readings that have been collected, the authors also spend some time putting across their own viewpoint on performance appraisals and also present case history information about actual company experience with performance appraisals. It is a handy reference source, yet it is also a book that presents some interesting thoughts on the future of performance appraisals in industry. The readings range from articles written by such stalwarts as Donald G. Paterson and Arthur Kornhauser back in the early 20's to modern critiques of performance appraisals such as Doug McGregor's. There is no particular quarrel on the part of the reviewer with the readings that were selected. It is interesting, however, while browsing through these readings to discover that many of the things that we talk about today in the rating and appraisal area were talked about forty years, and in some cases considerably longer, ago. * the authors....make some suggestions as to how performance appraisals might be used more effectively and it is here that the serious psychologist is probably going to find his most enjoyment * Again, then, this book is a well collected set of readings, with fairly well done case history materials, plus a thoughtful summary statement of the authors' thoughts and predictions concerning the general field of performance appraisal. This reviewer liked it; he thinks most industrial psychologists and most personnel people, in fact, will too.

[B515]

★Whybrew, William E. **Measurement and Evaluation in Music.** Dubuque, Iowa: Wm. C. Brown Co., 1962. Pp. ix, 184. Paper. $3.50. *

[B516]

★Willgoose, Carl E. **Evaluation in Health Education and Physical Education.** New York: McGraw-Hill Book Co., Inc., 1961. Pp. x, 478. $7.50. (London: McGraw-Hill Publishing Co. Ltd. 58*s.*) *

[B517]

★Wiseman, Stephen, Editor. **Examinations and English Education.** Manchester, England: Manchester University Press, 1961. Pp. xx, 188. 21*s.* *

Brit J Psychol 53:104 F '62. James Maxwell. It is an excellent custom of Manchester University School of Education to hold annually a series of lectures on educational topics. This volume is based on a series about examinations. The seven chapters cover the historical developments of English school examinations, their relation to Grammar, Secondary Modern and Primary Schools, their efficiency, with particular attention to selection, and the questions arising out of attempts to examine "general education." The interests of the writers vary, the administrative, the educational and the psychological all being represented. In each a workman-like presentation has been achieved. The "11-plus" is discussed, in a commendable objective way, but is not allowed to dominate. The main centre of interest is rather in examinations at school leaving and University entrance level. In such a wide survey, certain shortcomings are unavoidable. Some of the writers seem to find themselves cramped for space in dealing with the ramifications of the English examination system; the uninitiated may occasionally be confused among the G.C.E.s, the J.M.B.s, the S.S.E.C.s, etc.; and the major question, the effects of examinations on the manner and content of school education, is discussed in terms of hopes and opinions—in any case, solid information is just not available. Nevertheless, these lectures contain much of value and interest, and fully justify their publication for a wider audience.

[B518]

Wolf, William B. **Merit Rating as a Managerial Tool: A Simplified Approach to Merit Rating.** Seattle, Wash.: Bureau of Business Research, College of Business Administration, University of Washington, 1958. Pp. ix, 91. Paper, lithotyped. $1.75. *

Personnel Prac B 15:61-2 S '59. B. L. White. * Wolf....developed the "Performance Sample System" (P.S.S.), a simplification of Flanagan's Critical Incident method. The author criticizes currently used formalized rating systems, and emphasizes their intrinsically subjective nature by noting that reliability coefficients seldom exceed +0.50. He concludes that at the best merit rating can be no more than a "useful guide" in determining workforce adjustments. Wolf then describes in detail the P.S.S. Each supervisor is required to make daily entries on a form, briefly describing under a number of headings any incidents of either exceptionally good, or very poor behaviour on the part of an employee. These entries are to serve as "memory joggers" at a subsequent evaluation interview; no attempt is made to assign point scores on their basis. The author suggests that this method of rating increases the supervisor's powers of observation, and that it is objective because actual happenings are recorded, rather than vague, subjective judgments. Some pitfalls and possible abuses are discussed. Wolf concludes with a brief outline of personality theory, and indicates how this knowledge can be of value to the supervisor. The latter part of the book is devoted to a discussion of interviewing techniques, and the use of the manual in a training programme. The text is well documented and very clearly set out, with numerous sub-headings and summaries at the conclusion of each chapter. A criticism may be levelled at the lack of sufficient elaboration of details of the system; a consequence of this could be that the reader would have inadequate information on which to base use of the system. However, no pretence is made that the book should be regarded as anything other than a training guide.

[B519]

★Womer, Frank B. **Testing Programs in Michigan Schools.** A study conducted by the Michigan

School Testing Service, Bureau of School Services, The University of Michigan. The University of Michigan Official Publication, Vol. 65, No. 31. Ann Arbor, Mich.: the Bureau, September 1963. Pp. iv, 64. Paper. Gratis. *

[B520]

★WOMER, FRANK B. **Testing Programs in Michigan Schools.** A study conducted by the Testing and Guidance Committee, Michigan Association of Secondary School Principals. The University of Michigan Official Publication, Vol. 60, No. 137. Ann Arbor, Mich.: Bureau of School Services, the University, June 1959. Pp. vii, 62. Gratis. * For a sequel to this report, see B519.

Personnel & Guid J 39:524 F '61. Thomas M. Magoon. * The purpose of the study was to depict the current testing and guidance practices in the state's school systems. The contents include: incidence of testing programs; personnel involved in development of testing programs; tests used; personnel who administer, score and record tests; personnel who interpret test results and the methods employed; use of test results; financing of testing programs; scholarship testing; and the use of GED diplomas. Three impressions this reviewer gained from this report were: (a) these types of inquiries are essential, particularly the more diversity there is in the state system; (b) there is clear evidence of continued use of personnel trained for such highly demanded services as teaching and counseling for test scoring and recording (the teacher aid plan should have much to offer in this regard); and (c) the need for a companion piece on guidance and counseling programs in the state's school systems.

[B521]

★WOOD, DOROTHY ADKINS. **Test Construction: Development and Interpretation of Achievement Tests.** Columbus, Ohio: Charles E. Merrill Books, Inc., 1960. Pp. ix, 134. Paper, $1.95; cloth, $3.95. * (London: Prentice-Hall International, Inc. 16s.) (*PA* 35:2801)

Brit J Ed Psychol 31:306 N '61. * a very practical, though rather conventional, survey which will be useful to teachers who try to construct their own new-type attainment tests, or to students on a Diploma or M.A. course. It covers very clearly the essentials of psychological measurement, reliability and validity, test planning, item writing, and item analysis, and contains very little statistical matter. The hints on unintentional clues in test items are particularly useful. A final chapter discusses the essay examination, and strongly criticises the common practice of providing optional questions. Probably this arises because the examiner realises the inadequacy of his sampling of the field by a few long questions; and she suggests that he would do better to set a lot of shorter questions. Though emphasizing the scorer-unreliability of the essay exam., she fails to mention the correspondingly high author-unreliability of the new-type test. One other minor criticism is that she does not sufficiently warn testers of the variability of item-statistics based on small numbers of testees.

Cont Psychol 6:227–8 Jl '61. Jerome E. Doppelt. * When the purpose of a book is to make technical knowledge available to nonspecialists, two dimensions of criticism are possible: the acceptability of the information imparted, and the effectiveness of communication with the reader. On both of these dimensions the book deserves considerable praise. Dr. Wood's knowledge of the field and her experience in test construction are reflected in her selection of topics and the clear manner in which they are treated. * two topics might have been further elaborated * more examples of different types of poorly written items and how such items could be improved would have been helpful * Since a simple but useful procedure for obtaining indices of item discrimination is presented, it would have been helpful if the author had discussed the question of how high discrimination indices should be. Although a simple answer cannot be given, that question is often asked by initiates in the procedures of item analysis. Some discussion of this specific point would have been desirable, if only to indicate the problems. It is to the author's credit that she has kept to her avowed purpose of presenting a brief, useful treatment of the techniques of measurement. Most teachers, including those with some training in measurement, will find it profitable to take time to study this book.

Psychometrika 27:215–6 Je '62. Elizabeth Hagen. * The first five chapters could have been more effectively organized into one or two chapters which would more clearly have shown the relationship among the topics being discussed. Chapter 6....contains a good discussion of why a test plan should be made but gives the reader very little help in how to make a blueprint. Since this step in test construction is one most frequently omitted by classroom teachers, it could have been given greater emphasis. Chapter 7....gives general principles for writing any kind of objective items but does not give specific instructions for writing each kind of item. Although the principles given are sound ones, some of the most common faults found in items constructed by classroom teachers are not included. The unsophisticated reader....may have difficulty in applying the abstract principles to the actual writing of items because of the scarcity of illustrative examples. Two appendices....are devoted to sample items, but these are not related to the principles of item writing in Chapter 7. Chapter 8....has one of the best discussions of the translation of raw scores on a test to letter grades and of the method of combining several grades into an over-all average score that this reviewer has seen. This is an excellent presentation and is written with such clarity that anyone could understand it. * Chapter 10....has a good discussion on the presumed advantages of the essay test and the usual material on the writing and scoring of essay type items. This is a good little book, but a person inexperienced in testing might have difficulty understanding many of the concepts presented if he did not have an instructor to help him interpret the material. In part this is due to the brevity of the book and in part it is due to the author's use of some rather difficult measurement concepts before they are explained.

[B522]

★Woodley, Colin E. **How to Study and Prepare for Exams.** New York: New American Library of World Literature, Inc., 1961. Pp. 127. Paper. $0.50. *

[B523]

★Young, Michael. **The Rise of the Meritocracy 1870–2033: An Essay on Education and Equality.** London: Thames & Hudson, Ltd., 1958. Pp. 160. 15*s*. (Baltimore, Md.: Penguin Books, Inc., 1961. Pp. 190. Paper. $0.95.) *

Cont Psychol 7:205–6 Je '62. Harry Laurent. This essay is a satirical social history of England from 1870 through 2033 with particular emphasis on changes in the educational system and their effects. The stated purpose is to present the historical causes of workers' grievances in the early part of the twenty-first century; however, the underlying purpose is quite clear. The author cleverly projects current trends in order to argue against a) testing as a means of predicting and controlling behavior and b) to the segregation of students on the basis of ability. He also argues for a classless society. * Today (2033, that is) every member of the meritocracy has a minimum IQ of 125, the 5% of the nation who know what 5% means. Intelligence is defined operationally: the ability to raise production, directly or indirectly. Effort is measured as precisely as intelligence, and intelligence plus effort equal merit (I + E = M). The aristocracy has been replaced gradually by the meritocracy. * The essay's thesis is summarized in a manifesto issued by the Technicians' Party in 2009. The Technicians' goal is a classless society. They seek equality in the sense that they want every man to be respected for the good that is in him. They would consider not only one's intelligence, education, and power but also his kindness, courage, sensitivity, and as many other qualities as necessary. Everyone, then, would have equal opportunity, not to rise up in the world in the light of any mathematical measure, but to develop his own special capacities for leading a rich life. This is a persuasive book. Most readers will probably agree with many points ably made. However, the major thesis is difficult to accept. Consideration of qualities other than intelligence, education, and power is no guarantee of a classless society, an observation illustrated by various cultures throughout the world. It is also unlikely that such sharp class distinctions would exist unless one were willing to draw fine lines through the merit continuum. Then, too, industry has not been, nor is it likely to become, the sole determiner of class status. Other organizations—church, family, community—do, and will continue to, reward other qualities. Another questionable feature lies in the projections. Trends in measurement and education seem to be projected on a straight line; educational and industrial psychologists have attained outstanding success in the measurement of intelligence and effort. If this is so, it would seem reasonable that social psychologists and sociologists should be equally successful in solving the resulting social problems. Perhaps during the next 70 years the described accuracy of intelligence measurement will be reached, but this is questionable. Even so, it is doubtful whether intelligence test scores alone will predict perfectly a realistic criterion of success unless considerable self-validation of the results is built into the situation. There is no evidence so far that managers will allow this to happen. They will probably insist on comparable efficiency in the measurement of additional variables which they consider important. It is unfortunate that the author of this essay was killed in the Peterloo uprising in 2033. Fortunately, however, no one took the liberty of revising his manuscript. The book is excellently written and makes delightful and provocative reading. It is recommended for anyone with an interest in trends in education or in the reward systems of business and industry.

[B524]

★YUZUK, RONALD PAUL. **The Assessment of Employee Morale: A Comparison of Two Measures.** Ohio State University, College of Commerce and Administration, Ohio Studies in Personnel, Bureau of Business Research Monograph No. 99. Columbus, Ohio: the Bureau, 1961. Pp. ix, 67. Paper. $2.00. * (*PA* 36:1LH67Y)

Personnel Psychol 14:473–5 w '61. V. J. Bentz. * a contribution that will be of interest to measurement-oriented psychologists. It is a carefully produced, well turned out piece of work, representing sound design and sophisticated use of factor analytic techniques. The work is technical in nature; the personnel administrator will not find this rewarding reading. One might be stuffy and object to the title. When a book represents itself as THE ASSESSMENT of anything, the reader expects extensive, generalized treatment. The current monograph is no such grand-scale project. Instead, it reports an intensive investigation in which two paper-and-pencil devices for the measurement of employee reactions are contrasted. Though this reviewer expresses admiration for the professional craft represented, it is disturbing that the instruments were constructed on information gained from nonstructured interviews with 15 employees and that all this effort was expended upon data from only 130 subjects (65 being represented in each group). Thus, one does not view this as the definitive work in the assessment of employee morale, but rather as highly stimulating pilot study in this elusive area of measurement. The two paper-and-pencil instruments differ in format. One is called Evaluative, the other Descriptive. In the Evaluative questionnaire subjects make agree-disagree responses to such items as: "It takes a long time to get a raise around here." The Descriptive device asks subjects to respond by giving an objective count of experiences, such as "I received (0, 1, 2 or more) pay raises in the past six months." Yuzuk apparently assumes that each instrument is a variant approach to a single phenomenon: morale. Though this premise is open to the serious questions that arise whenever a strict tabulative technique (the criticisms of Kinsey's counting come to mind) is utilized for measuring emotionally or attitudinally toned responses, the results that emanate from these contrasting instruments are interesting. * When the factorial structures for the two inventories are compared, the structure resulting from the Descriptive, or tabular, approach is cleaner and freer from the influence of a general (bias) factor than is the structure of the Evaluative inventory. Yuzuk states that this "vast difference in biasability is largely a function of the basic difference between inventories." One wonders if this is the case, or if he is measuring two classes of phenomena with essentially different instruments rather than a single class with contrasting measurement methods. Yuzuk ascribes to the latter view and offers the opinion that "the relatively general and ambiguous nature of the Evaluative items accounts for the bias factor....the more objective and specific the approach, the more pinpointed and meaningful the item, the less the bias." There can be little argument over this point, except that the more ambiguous items may come closer to measuring morale while the specific items may be measuring organizational behavior. This leads to a consideration of validity. Yuzuk developed eight criteria taken from employee records, representing organizational values (other than morale). These were worked into single indices for such things as supervisory ratings, labor grades, absenteeism, production, etc. Criteria factor scores were obtained and criterion factors were correlated with morale factor scores for both Evaluative and Descriptive inventories. *Both inventories yielded 17 significant correlations with the criteria.* The nature of these correlational patterns do not yield new insights, though it does indicate that *both* kinds of instruments "relate to selected facets of employee performance." However, in this reader's opinion these relationships do not make a good case for the validity or non-validity of either type of inventory as a valid assessment of morale. One wishes that a more direct morale-type criteria had been employed to this end. Despite its obvious shortcomings, Yuzuk's monograph cannot be read without generating a series of highly pertinent questions; it might also serve as model of elegant design in a field so often visited by work of considerably less rigor.

[B525]

★ZANDER, ALVIN F., EDITOR. **Performance Appraisals: Effects on Employees and Their Performance.** Ann Arbor, Mich.: Foundation for Research on Human Behavior, 1963. Pp. ii, 64. Paper. $3.00. * (*PA* 38:6718)

Personnel Psychol 17:226–8 su '64. Carl J. Kujawski. * In spite of its title, this is a treatise against employee performance appraisal—not about it. The papers cast some reflections which will probably provoke the high priests, practitioners, and believers in the rituals and sacred theology of performance appraisals as they are generally known. The contributors, in concert, add to the increasing body of evidence that trait-oriented, merit-rating type employee performance appraisal plans are ineffective and tend to produce some unfortunate human and organizational consequences. Further, they seem to indicate that there are more effective ways of planning, reviewing, and improving performance. This is a message that could be profitably read by business managers whose relations with and decisions about people now depend upon these "greasy kid stuff" merit ratings and appraisals. Unfortunately, this booklet seems to be designed more as a souvenir for the participants than it is for educating and informing the business public. Much of the savor of the spoken give-and-take of the seminar setting appears to have been lost in its abbreviation to paper. The average layman, unfamiliar with psychological jargon, may easily get lost in the welter of symbols such as *O* and *P* which really have meanings like rater and ratee or supervisor and subordinate. The thoughtful business man may wonder about the appropriateness of applying the findings of research done in nonbusiness surroundings and involving students, teachers, volunteers, and the like directly to the business scene. On the other hand, psychologists in industry are likely to find much of this material old hat. It is a rehash of research findings and other information already reported in greater detail in professional and business journals, books, and meetings. After castigating traditional rating and appraisal activities in the early chapters, the later chapters report the research background and format of a modified system of work planning and performance review within a General Electric plant. * the General Electric work planning and performance review system represents a promising marriage of behavioral science research findings and practical business objectives. * The General Electric system may require excessive commitments of productive time and manpower in some businesses. There is also a question of whether or not the General Electric system....would be as effective in other companies with different processes and operations and with employees in such functions as marketing, finance, and industrial relations. * Work planning and performance review programs may not always result in favorable changes in employee attitudes and performance. * This is sort of an everybody pamphlet. It has something old, something borrowed, and something blue. It doesn't seem to have very much that's new.

[B526]

ZULLIGER, HANS. **Behn-Rorschach Test: Text.** Bern, Switzerland: Hans Huber, 1956. Pp. 200. Fr. 25. (New York: Grune & Stratton, Inc., 1956. $8.00.) * (*PA* 35:773)

Am J Psychother 15:178–9 Ja '61. Horst Rodies. * the manual for the administration, scoring, and interpretation of the parallel series of inkblots chosen by Hermann Rorschach and Hans Behn-Eschenburg in 1920. Zulliger states, "These ten plates were standardized against the plates of the Rorschach series." The first publication of the "Behn" plates and manual appeared in 1941. Whether this present English edition is a translation of the original manual or whether the material has since been re-worked, is not explicitly stated. Half of this 200-page manual is allotted to the technique of the "Form Interpretation Test," as Zulliger calls it. The second half is given over to a presentation of actual psychologic evaluations, many of them cases of adolescents who were tested for educational counseling or who had been referred by the courts. Of particular interest is the problem of "thieving or thievish impulses" which is mentioned frequently. * While there are many similarities in techniques of administering, scoring and interpretation, the experienced clinician in this country will find significant variations. Decades of Rorschach research and scoring seminars here seem to have caused little feedback within the Behn-Rorschach system. Zulliger feels that the Behn and the Rorschach plate series are equal alternates. He uses extensive comparisons of both psychograms to prove his case. He emphasizes the usefulness of his test both as a control and as a complement to the Rorschach. Published attempts in this country, using the Behn plates on an alternate basis, indicate many similarities, but stress unanimously statistically significant differences with the Rorschach plates, concluding that the Behn plates cannot be considered an equivalent form of the Rorschach. Perhaps of greatest interest to the active clinician is the section on psychologic and characterologic symptomatology, in which overall interpretive conclusions and some unique generalizations are made. Also, the supplement on "Intelligence, Fantasy, and Originality," in which Zulliger discriminates different types within each category, is of special interest. Summary: Zulliger's brand of Rorschach with a different set of plates.

J Proj Tech 24:447–8 D '60. Murray Levine. * Ostensibly a manual to accompany the Behn blots, the book has very little to do with the "Bero" inkblots as such, but it is more like a combination casebook and notebook on "form interpretation tests," with the focus happening to be upon the "Bero" blots. The book might better have been titled "Zulliger at Work." The Bero inkblot series "....were standardized against the plates of the Rorschach series." The blots were apparently never printed until the original publication date of this volume, 20 years after they were developed. The reader who approaches this volume looking for standardization data, normative tables, reliability coefficients, or validation studies, or for any of the usual statistical paraphernalia we expect in a test manual will be severely disappointed. There is none. There is a listing of about 500 responses, broken down by Bero card location, and scored by Zulliger. These are frequently appearing responses, but Zulliger cautions against using these as a "pure answer table." Also the reader who approaches the volume looking for detailed comparisons between the Bero and Rorschach blots will be disappointed. About two pages are devoted to indicating certain differences which he finds in the two series, but the differences are minor in nature. Zulliger's clinical experience indicated that the blots constituted a parallel series, and for him (in 1941) this was sufficient. When the results were not parallel, it meant the subject was a labile individual, and the differences in response to the two inkblot series suggested something of the changeable nature of his personality. In fact Zulliger recommends using both series just for the added depth of analysis the comparison sometimes provides. The bulk of the book is devoted to his scoring system (little advanced from Rorschach's), to interpretations for the various scoring features, and for combination of these features, and to case studies which demonstrate Zullig r's virtuosity as a clinician. Many of the interpretations, referring to both Bero and Rorschach blots, will be familiar to an older breed of psychologist who still scores the Rorschach test, but they will appear quite novel to moderns who interpret test content only. The manner in which Zulliger develops interpretations based on combinations of features, or modifies the significance of test features in different contexts, should give pause to, and intrigue those researchers who still tabulate Ws, Fc's, A % etc., run simple statistical tests, and thus arrive at conclusions. While more in the nature of notes than exhaustive system. Zulliger's version of "holistic interpretation of the formal scoring" seems to me to be among the most articulate to be found. If one were interested in deriving a "cookbook" for ink blot tests, Zulliger's manual would be an excellent place to start. * Zulliger's interpretations and comments are neat, sensitive, and often stated in highly picturesque terms. He is obviously a keen observer, and his all too brief comments on intellectual types in particular are quite worthwhile, especially if read in light of current interest in "styles" of thought. While the material is incomplete, and scattered, there is stuff of interest here, even though the volume is some 20 years old. Zulliger, one of Europe's foremost clinicians, and author of a three card ink blot test (compare with Holtzman's 40 card test!), is worth "watching at work."

Periodical Directory and Index

* * * * *

References are to test and book entry numbers under which review excerpts from the given journal will be found, not to page numbers. Book entry numbers begin with the letter B. *The name and address of the editor and the review editor are given for each journal. Test references are not indexed.*

ED & PSYCHOL MEAS—Educational and Psychological Measurement: A Quarterly Journal Devoted to the Development and Application of Measures of Individual Differences. 4 issues; vol. 24 started spring '64; $10 per year; $2.50 per issue; G. Frederic Kuder, editor, Box 6907, College Station, Durham, N.C. 27708; William B. Michael, review editor, University of California, Santa Barbara, Calif. 93101: 72, B33, B53, B68, B70, B74, B81, B89, B105, B156, B164, B167, B189, B193, B195, B200–1, B244, B266, B305, B318, B372, B417, B432, B491, B503

Ed R—Educational Review. Journal of the Institute of Education, University of Birmingham. 3 issues; vol. 16 started N '63; 20*s.* per year; 6*s.* 8*d.* per issue; E. A. Peel, H. J. Hallworth, and A. M. Wilkinson, editors; The University, Edgbaston, Birmingham 15, England: B197

El Sch J—The Elementary School Journal. A publication of the Department of Education, University of Chicago. 8 issues (omitting Je, Jl, Ag, S); vol. 65 started O '64; $4.50 per year; $1 per issue; Kenneth J. Rehage, editor, University of Chicago, 5835 Kimbark Ave., Chicago, Ill. 60637: B214

Engl J—English Journal. The high school organ of the National Council of Teachers of English. 9 issues (omitting Je, Jl, Ag); vol. 53 started Ja '64; Richard S. Alm, editor, University of Hawaii, Honolulu, Hawaii 96822: B117, B138

Engl Lang Teach—English Language Teaching. 4 issues; vol. 18 started O '63; 8*s.* per year; 2*s.* 6*d.* per issue; W. R. Lee, editor, 16 Alexandra Gardens, Hounslow, Middlesex, England: B300

Eug R—The Eugenics Review. A publication of The Eugenics Society. 4 issues; vol. 56 started Ap '64; 40*s.* per year; 10*s.* per issue; K. Hodson, editor, 69 Eccleston Square, London S.W. 1, England: B455

FRENCH R—French Review. A publication of the American Association of Teachers of French. 6 issues (O, D, F, Mr, Ap, My); vol. 38 started O '64; $5 per year; Leon S. Roudiez, editor, 517 Philosophy Hall, Columbia University, New York, N.Y. 10027: 357

HARVARD ED R—Harvard Educational Review. 4 issues (w, sp, su, f); vol. 34 started winter '63; $5 per year; $1.75 per issue; Stanley Goldberg, chairman, editorial board; K. Gerald Marsden and Peter S. Rosenbaum, review editors; Longfellow Hall, 13 Appian Way, Cambridge, Mass. 02138: B214, B235

INT J GROUP PSYCHOTHER—International Journal of Group Psychotherapy. Official publication of The American Group Psychotherapy Association, Inc. 4 issues; vol. 14 started Ja '64; $8 per year; $2 per issue; Harris B. Peck, editor, 11 East 68th St., New York, N.Y. 10021; Irving A. Goldberg, book review editor, 755 Medical and Dental Bldg., Seattle, Wash. 98111: 233

Int J Social Psychiatry—The International Journal of Social Psychiatry. A publication of The International Association of Social Psychiatry. 4 issues (w, sp, su, au); vol. 10 started winter '64; 42*s.* per year; Joshua Bierer, editor, 7 Hollycroft Ave., London N.W.3, England: 211

Int R Ed—International Review of Education. Publication of the Unesco Institute for Education. 4 issues; vol. 10 started no. 1 '64; 21 guilders ($5.85) per year; 6 guilders ($1.68) per issue; G. Hausmann, managing editor, Unesco Institute for Education, Feldbrunnenstrasse 70, Hamburg 13, Germany: B300

J AM STAT ASSN—Journal of the American Statistical Association. 4 issues; vol. 59 started Mr '64 (No. 305); $10.50 per year; $3 per issue; John W. Pratt, editor, Harvard Business School, Boston, Mass. 02163: B489

J Bus Ed—Journal of Business Education. 8 issues (omitting Je, Jl, Ag, S); vol. 40 started O '64; $4 per year; 60¢ per issue; Elizabeth T. Van Derveer, editor, 15 South Franklin St., Wilkes-Barre, Pa. 18701: B5

J Chem Ed—Journal of Chemical Education. Published by the Division of Chemical Education, American Chemical Society. 12 issues; vol. 41 started Ja '64; $4 per year; 60¢ per issue; William F. Kieffer, editor, College of Wooster, Wooster, Ohio 44691: 898, 900, 903, 905–6, 908

J Child Psychol & Psychiatry—Journal of Child Psychology and Psychiatry and Allied Disciplines. Official organ of the Association of Child Psychology and Psychiatry. 4 issues; vol. 5 started Je '64; 105*s.* ($15) per year to individuals; 200*s.* ($30) per year to libraries and institutions; 50*s.* per issue; joint editors: C. B. Hindley, 41 Brunswick Square, London W.C.1, England; L. A. Hersov, 33 Daleham Gardens, London N.W.3, England: 68

J Consult Psychol—Journal of Consulting Psychology. Published by the American Psychological Association, Inc. 6 issues; vol. 28 started F '64; $10 per year; $2 per issue; Jules D. Holzberg, editor, Wesleyan University, Middletown, Conn. 06458: 68, 87, 118, 138, 160, 186, 190, 201, 211, 242, 357, 442, 525, 773, 857

J Counsel Psychol—Journal of Counseling Psychology: A Quarterly Journal for Psychologists and Personnel Workers Concerned With the Counseling of Clients, Students, and Employees. 4 issues; vol. 11 started spring '64; $8 per year; $2.25 per issue; Francis P. Robinson, editor, The Ohio State University, 1945 North High St., Columbus, Ohio 43210; C. Gilbert Wrenn, review editor, College of Education, Arizona State University, Tempe, Ariz. 85281: 59, 118, 147–50, 170, 184, 197, 220, 242, 256, 357, 442, 462, 495–6, 769, 776, 800, 857, 980, 1024, 1059, 1066, 1165, 1181, B69, B76, B104, B119, B126, B159, B205, B207, B231, B304, B417

J Develop Read—Journal of Developmental Reading: A Quarterly for the Improvement of Reading in High School, College, and Adult Programs. Title changed to *Journal of Reading* and publication taken over by the International Reading Association, Inc. beginning with vol. 8, O '64; 6 issues (O, N, Ja, Mr, Ap, My); $4.50 per year; $1 per issue; George B. Schick, editor, 314 Heavilon Hall, Purdue University, Lafayette, Ind. 47907: B411, B478

J Higher Ed—The Journal of Higher Education. 9 issues (omitting Jl, Ag, S); vol. 35 started Ja '64; $6 per year; 75¢ per issue; Franklin J. Pegues, editor, Ohio State University Press, 164 West 19th Ave., Columbus, Ohio 43210: B48, B160–1

J Mental Sci—Journal of Mental Science. Title changed to *British Journal of Psychiatry* (*q.v.*) beginning with vol. 109, no. 458, Ja '63.

J Nerv & Mental Dis—Journal of Nervous and Mental Disease. 12 issues in 2 volumes; vol. 138 started Ja '64; vol. 139 started Jl '64; $15 per year; $2 per issue; Lawrence S. Kubie, editor-in-chief; H. A. Robinson, managing editor; The Psychiatric Institute, University of Maryland, Baltimore, Md. 21201: B95, B152, B286, B396

J Proj Tech—Journal of Projective Techniques. Title changed to *Journal of Projective Techniques and Personality Assessment* (*q.v.*) beginning with vol. 27, no. 2, Je '63.

J Proj Tech & Pers Assess—Journal of Projective Techniques and Personality Assessment. Published by the Society for Projective Techniques, Inc. Title was *Journal of Projective Techniques* through vol. 27, no. 1, Mr '63. 4 issues; vol. 28 started Mr '64; $8 per year; $2 per issue; Bruno Klopfer, editor, Bertram R. Forer, executive editor, 2170 East Live Oak Drive, Los Angeles, Calif. 90028: 211, 216, 240, 246, B74, B91, B100, B104–5, B116, B129, B176, B232, B238–9, B264, B268, B295, B306–7, B402, B501, B526

J Psychosom Res—Journal of Psychosomatic Research. 4 issues; vol. 8 started Jl '64; 105*s.* ($15) per year to individuals; 200*s.* ($30) per year to libraries; Denis Leigh, editor-in-chief, The Maudsley Hospital, Denmark Hill, London S.E.5, England:138

J Royal Stat Soc—Journal of the Royal Statistical Society, Series A (General). 4 issues; vol. 127 started part 1 '64; 104*s.* per year; 31*s.* per issue; Royal Statistical Society, 21 Bentinck St., London W.1, England: B197

J Speech & Hearing Disorders—Journal of Speech and Hearing Disorders. 4 issues; vol. 29 started F '64; $7 per year; $1.90 per issue; William R. Tiffany, editor, Parrington Hall, University of Washington, Seattle, Wash. 98105: 315, B104

J Teach Ed—The Journal of Teacher Education. Published by the National Commission on Teacher Education and Professional Standards, National Education Association. 4 issues; vol. 15 started Mr '64; $3 per year; $1 per issue; D. D. Darland, editor, 1201 Sixteenth St., N.W., Washington, D.C. 20036; Willard B. Spalding, book review editor, Room 4184, 455 Golden Gate Ave., San Francisco, Calif. 94102: B105

LIB J—Library Journal. 22 issues (1st and 15th from S to Je, monthly Jl and Ag); vol. 90 started Ja 1 '65; $10 per year; 55 ¢ per issue; Eric Moon, editor; Margaret E. Cooley, book editor; 1180 Avenue of the Americas, New York, N.Y. 10036: B60

MANAS—Manas: A Journal of Scientific Psychology. 2 issues (1 issue in '61, and 1 issue in '62); vol. 11 started '64; Rs. 15 ($5.00) per year; Rs. 7.50 ($2.50) per issue; J. M. Ojha, Udai Pareek, and Prayag Mehta, editors, 32 Netaji Subhash Marg, Delhi 6, India: 672, 757

Mental Hyg—Mental Hygiene. Quarterly journal of the National Association for Mental Health, Inc. 4 issues; vol. 48 started Ja '64; $6 per year; $1.50 per issue; George S. Stevenson, editor, 10 Columbus Circle, New York, N.Y. 10019: B73, B93

N Y TIMES BOOK R—The New York Times Book Review. 52 issues; vol. 69 started Ja 5 '64; Sunday issues of *The New York Times* must be purchased to obtain the book review section; the Editor, Times Square, New York, N.Y. 10036: B215

OCCUP PSYCHOL—Occupational Psychology. Published by the National Institute of Industrial Psychology. 4 issues; vol. 38 started Ja '64; 50*s.* per year; 12*s.* 6*d.* per issue; Alec Rodger, editor, 14 Welbeck St., London W.1, England: 246, B120, B336, B403, B461

Ont J Ed Res—Ontario Journal of Educational Research. Published by the Department of Educational Research, Ontario College of Education, University of Toronto. 2 issues (au, sp); vol. 7 started autumn '64; $2 per year; $1 per issue; Kathleen M. Hobday and E. Brock Rideout, editors, Suite 500, 344 Bloor St., West, Toronto 5, Ont., Canada: B322

PEABODY J ED—Peabody Journal of Education. A publication of the George Peabody College for Teachers. 6 issues; vol. 42 started Jl '64; $3.50 per year; 60¢ per issue; A. L. Crabb, editor, the College, Nashville, Tenn. 37203: B211

Percept & Motor Skills—Perceptual and Motor Skills. 6 issues in 2 volumes; vol. 18 started F '64; vol. 19 started Ag '64; $20 per year; $5 per issue; R. B. Ammons and C. H. Ammons, editors, Box 1441, Missoula, Mont. 59801: 234, B40, B297, B326

Personnel—Personnel. A publication of The American Management Association, Inc. 6 issues; vol. 41 started Jl–Ag '64; $10 per year; $1.75 per issue; Juliet M. Halford, editor, 135 West 50th St., New York, N.Y. 10020: B399

Personnel & Guid J—Personnel and Guidance Journal. 10 issues (omitting Jl, Ag); vol. 43 started S '64; $10 per year; $1 per issue; Roger C. Bowman, managing editor, 1605 New Hampshire Ave., N.W., Washington, D.C. 20009: 1, 26, 246, 292, 357, 466, 536, 1054, 1075, B3, B33, B35, B69, B75–6, B83, B105, B113, B159, B164, B205, B215, B263, B278, B289, B304, B311–2, B318, B387, B406–7, B414, B455, B466, B473, B482–3, B495–6, B520

Personnel J—Personnel Journal: The Magazine of Labor Relations and Personnel Practices. 11 issues (combining Jl–Ag); vol. 43 started Ja '64; $7 per year; 75¢ per issue; Arthur C. Croft, editor, 100 Park Ave., Swarthmore, Pa. 19081: 246, B267

Personnel Prac B—Personnel Practice Bulletin. Prepared by the Personnel Practice Section, Department of Labour and National Service, Commonwealth of Australia. 4 issues; vol. 20 started Mr '64; 20*s.* per year; 5*s.* per issue; Commonwealth Department of Labour and National Service, 125 Swanston St., Melbourne C.1, Vic., Australia: B284, B518

Personnel Psychol—Personnel Psychology: A Journal of Applied Research. 4 issues; vol. 17 started spring '64; $8 per year; $2.50 per issue; John A. Hornaday, editor, P.O. Box 1633, Boston, Mass. 02105; Theodore Kunin, review editor, Psychological Consultants to Industry, 210 Grant St., Pittsburgh, Pa. 15219: B53, B68, B173, B372, B524–5

Psychiatric Q—The Psychiatric Quarterly. A publication of the New York State Department of Mental Hygiene. 4 issues; vol. 38 started '64; $8 per year; $2.25 per issue; Newton Bigelow, editor, Utica State Hospital, Utica, N.Y. 13502: B104, B309

Psychiatric Q Sup—The Psychiatric Quarterly Supplement. A publication of the New York State Department of Mental Hygiene. 2 issues; vol. 38 started part 1 '64; $4 per year; $2.25 per issue; Newton Bigelow, editor, Utica State Hospital, Utica, N.Y. 13502: B206, B402

Psychoanalytic Q—Psychoanalytic Quarterly. 4 issues; vol. 33 started Ja '64; $10 per year; $3 per issue; Bertram D. Lewin, editor, 57 West 57th St., New York, N.Y. 10019: B72, B74, B201, B503

Psychol B—Psychological Bulletin. Published by the American Psychological Association, Inc. 12 issues; vol. 62 started Jl '64; $20 per year; $2 per issue; Lloyd Humphreys, editor, Department of Psychology, University of Illinois, Urbana, Ill. 61803: 203

Psychol Rep—Psychological Reports. 6 issues in 2 volumes; vol. 14 started F '64; vol. 15 started Ag '64; $20 per year; $5 per issue; R. B. Ammons and C. H. Ammons, editors, Box 1441, Missoula, Mont. 59801: B104, B200, B215

Psychometrika—Psychometrika: A Journal Devoted to the Development of Psychology as a Quantitative Rational Science. Official journal of the Psychometric Society. 4 issues; vol. 29 started Mr '64; $14 per year; $3.50 per issue; B. J. Winer, managing editor, Department of Psychology, Purdue University, Lafayette, Ind. 47907; John E. Milholland, review editor, 122 Rackham Bldg., University of Michigan, Ann Arbor, Mich. 48104: B36–7, B142, B316, B404, B461, B499, B521

Psychosom Med—Psychosomatic Medicine: Journal of the American Psychosomatic Society. 6 issues; vol. 26 started Ja–F '64; $10 per year; $2 per issue; Morton F. Reiser, editor-in-chief; John C. Nemiah, book review editor; 265 Nassau Road, Roosevelt, N.Y. 11575: B260

Pub Adm—Public Administration: Journal of the Royal Institute of Public Administration. 4 issues (sp, su, au, w); vol. 42 started spring '64; 35*s.* per year; 10*s.* per issue; D. N. Chester, editor, 24 Park Crescent, London W.1, England: B370

Q J EXP PSYCHOL—The Quarterly Journal of Experimental Psychology. A publication of The Experimental Psychology Society. 4 issues; vol. 16 started F '64; 60*s.* per year; 20*s.* per issue; O. L. Zangwill, editor, Psychological Laboratory, Downing St., Cambridge, England: 68, B449

READING TEACH—Reading Teacher. A publication of the International Reading Association, Inc. 8 issues (omitting Je, Jl, Ag, S); vol. 18 started O '64; $4.50 per year; $1 per issue; Russell G. Stauffer, editor, University of Delaware, Newark, Del. 19711; George Spache, review editor, University of Florida, Gainesville, Fla. 32603: B62, B104, B448

Rorsch Newsl—The Rorschach Newsletter. Journal of The British Rorschach Forum and Society for Projective Techniques. 2 issues; vol. 9 started Je '64; 10*s.* per year; 6*s.* per issue; Celia Williams, editor, 2 Beaumont St., London W.1, England: B40, B72

SAT R—Saturday Review. 52 issues; vol. 47 started Ja 4 '64; $8 per year; 25¢ per issue; Norman Cousins, editor; Rochelle Girson, review editor; Paul Woodring, education editor; 380 Madison Ave., New York, N.Y. 10017: B83, B125

Sci—Science. A publication of the American Association for the Advancement of Science. 52 issues in 4 volumes; vol. 142 started O 4 '63 (3588); vol. 143 started Ja 3 '64 (3601); vol. 144 started Ap 3 '64 (3614); vol. 145 started Jl 3 '64 (3627); $8.50 per year; 35¢ per issue; Philip H. Abelson, editor; Sarah S. Dees, book review editor; 1515 Massachusetts Ave., N.W., Washington, D.C. 20005: B83, B125, B201

Scottish Ed J—The Scottish Educational Journal: The Official Organ of the Educational Institute of Scotland. 52 issues; vol. 47 started Ja 3 '64; 26*s.* per year; 6*d.* per issue; Raymond H. K. Thomasson, editor, 46 Moray Place, Edinburgh 3, Scotland: 234

Sociol & Social Res—Sociology and Social Research: An International Journal. A publication of the University of Southern California. 4 issues; vol. 49 started O '64; $5 per year; $1.50 per issue; Martin H. Neumeyer, editor; Milton Bloombaum, book review editor; the University, Los Angeles, Calif. 90007: 181

Speech Teach—Speech Teacher. A publication of the Speech Association of America. 4 issues (Ja, Mr, O, D); vol. 14 started Ja '65; $10 per year; $2.50 per issue; Hugh F. Seabury, editor, 8 Shaeffer Hall, State University of Iowa, Iowa City, Iowa 52240: 315

TEACH COL REC—Teachers College Record. A publication of Teachers College, Columbia University. 8 issues (omitting Je, Jl, Ag, S); vol. 66 started O '64; $7.50 per year; $1.50 per issue; Edward Joseph Shoben, editor, 525 West 120th St., New York, N.Y. 10027: B161, B164, B178, B263, B406

Publishers Directory and Index

* * * * *

References are to test and book entry numbers, not to page numbers. Stars indicate test publishers which issue catalogs devoted entirely or in large part to tests; asterisks indicate other publishers of one or more tests listed in this volume. Book entry numbers begin with the letter B.

ARC Books, Inc., Subsidiary of Arco Publishing Co., Inc., 219 Park Ave., South, New York, N.Y. 10003: B222

Arco Publishing Co., Inc., 219 Park Ave., South, New York, N.Y. 10003: B13, B213, B216–21, B223–7, B311, B476, B490. See also ARC Books, Inc.

Arnold (E. J.) & Son Ltd., Butterley St., Leeds 10, England: B327

Asia Publishing House, 119 West 57th St., New York, N.Y. 10019: B59; 447 Strand, London W.C.2, England: B59

*Associated Personnel Technicians, Inc., 815 Beacon Bldg., Wichita, Kan. 67202: 40, 1076, 1112

*Associated Publishers, 355 State St., Los Altos, Calif. 94022: 76

*Association Press, 291 Broadway, New York, N.Y. 10007: 154

*Audivox, Inc., 123 Worcester St., Boston, Mass. 02118: 942

★Australian Council for Educational Research, Frederick St., Hawthorn E.2, Vic., Australia: 194, 282, 327, 432–6, 471, 490, 538–40, 592, 644, 782, 806, 819, 845, 886, 978, 1030–1, 1082, 1092, 1189, B63, B163, B462

*BADGER Tests Co., Ltd., 17–18 St. Dunstan's Hill, London E.C.2, England: 227–8

Bailey Bros. & Swinfen, Ltd., Warner House, 48 Upper Thames St., London E.C.4, England: B176, B452

Baillière, Tindall & Cox, Ltd., 7 & 8 Henrietta St., Covent Garden, London W.C.2, England: B331, B503

Ballantine Books, Inc., 101 Fifth Ave., New York, N.Y. 10003: B171

Barnes & Noble, Inc., 105 Fifth Ave., New York, N.Y. 10003: B504

Barron's Educational Series, Inc., 343 Great Neck Road, Great Neck, N.Y. 11021: B86, B97, B108–9, B202, B365, B393, B454

*Bausch & Lomb Inc., Rochester, N.Y. 14602: 958

Beacon House, Inc., Publishers, P.O. Box 311, Beacon, N.Y. 12508: B82

Bell (J. P.) Co., Inc., 816 Main St., Lynchburg, Va. 24505: B455

*Beltone Electronics Corporation, Special Instruments Division, Beltone Bldg., 4201 West Victoria St., Chicago, Ill. 60646: 943

*Better Reading Program, Inc., 230 East Ohio St., Chicago, Ill. 60611: 837

★Bobbs-Merrill Co., Inc. (The), 4300 East 62nd St., Indianapolis, Ind. 46206: 2, 19, 131, 248–9, 286, 320, 326, 342a, 364, 418, 439, 453, 488, 605–6, 612, 615, 783, 798, 807, 842, 963, 1013a

*Book Society of Canada Ltd., 4386 Sheppard Ave., Agincourt, Ont., Canada: 851

*Brandywine Achievement Test, Box 526, Coatesville, Pa. 19320: 990

*Briggs (Peter F.), University of Minnesota, Minneapolis, Minn. 55414: 136

Brigham Young University. See University Press.

Brown (Wm. C.) Co., 135 South Locust St., Dubuque, Iowa 52003: B170, B436, B515

★Bruce (Martin M.), 340 Oxford Road, New Rochelle, N.Y. 10804: 160, 190, 201, 222, 329, 560, 1101, 1113, 1116, 1125, 1127–8, 1169, 1178, 1181, 1194, 1200

*Bruce Publishing Co. (The), 400 North Broadway, Milwaukee, Wis. 53202: 296

*Brye (Edvin), 7914 South Oglesby Ave., Chicago, Ill. 60617: 663

Bureau of Business Research, College of Business Administration, University of Washington, Seattle, Wash. 98105: B518

Bureau of Business Research, College of Commerce and Administration, Ohio State University, 1775 South College Road, Columbus, Ohio 43210: B173, B244, B524

★Bureau of Educational Measurements, Kansas State Teachers College, Emporia, Kan. 66801: 31, 34, 38, 54, 250, 257, 297, 301, 325, 339, 408, 411, 498, 563, 575, 599, 608, 630, 634, 648, 659, 721, 726, 732–3, 735, 737, 744, 788, 803, 871, 873, 888, 910, 932, 965, 972, 981, 991, 993, 995–6, 999, 1004–5, 1011, 1015–6, 1022

Bureau of Educational Research and Service, College of Education, Ohio State University, 191 Arps Hall, Columbus, Ohio 43210: B27

★Bureau of Educational Research and Service, University of Iowa, Iowa City, Iowa 52240: 315, 322, 346

Bureau of Educational Research Services, College of Education, Michigan State University, East Lansing, Mich. 48823: B17

Bureau of Educational Studies and Testing, Indiana University, Bloomington, Ind. 47405: B121–4

★Bureau of Publications, Teachers College, Columbia University, New York, N.Y. 10027: 156, 318, 355, 790–3, 824, 828, 845, 859, B245, B410, B482

Bureau of Pupil Personnel and Special Educational Services, State Department of Education, Hartford, Conn. 06115: B467

Bureau of School Service, College of Education, University of Kentucky, Lexington, Ky. 40506: B99

Bureau of School Services, The University of Michigan, Ann Arbor, Mich. 48104: B519–20

*Bureau of Special Education, State Department of Education, 721 Capitol Mall, Sacramento, Calif. 95814: 164

Burgess Cellulose Co. See Grade-O-Mat Division.

*Burke (Charles), Box 494, Westport, Conn. 06881: 1048, 1051

Butterworth Inc., 7235 Wisconsin Ave., Washington, D.C. 20014: B303; Butterworth & Co. (Publishers) Ltd., 88 Kingsway, London W.C.2, England: B303

*C.P.S. Inc., P.O. Box 83, Larchmont, N.Y. 10538: 206

California State Department of Education, Sacramento, Calif. 95814: B140, B325. See also Bureau of Special Education.

California State Department of Public Health, 2151 Berkeley Way, Berkeley, Calif. 94704: B7

★California Test Bureau, Del Monte Research Park, Monterey, Calif. 93940: 3–4, 73, 130, 141, 242, 251, 280, 283, 352, 371, 388, 424, 442–4, 503, 564, 591, 602, 616, 622–3, 638, 647, 723, 776, 784, 795, 815, 820–1, 846, 857, 884–5, 897, 994, 1010, 1064, 1066

Cambridge University Press, Bentley House, 20[illegible] Euston Road, London N.W.1, England: B55; 3[illegible] East 57th St., New York, N.Y. 10022: B55

*Campus Stores, University of Iowa, Iowa City, Iowa 52240: 202

*Cardall Associates, Yardley, Pa. 19068: 446, 580, 617, 1033, 1067, 1102, 1114

Carkhuff (Robert R.), University of Kentucky, Lexington, Ky. 40506: B113

Catholic University of America. See Program of Affiliation.

Catholic University of America Press (The), 62[illegible] Michigan Ave., N.E., Washington, D.C. 20017: B381

Center for Applied Research in Education, Inc., 7[illegible] Fifth Ave., New York, N.Y. 10011: B32

Center for Educational Research and Service, Ohio University. See Center for Educational Service.

Center for Educational Service, College of Education, Ohio University, Athens, Ohio 45701 (name of Cen

★Educational Testing Service, Princeton, N.J. 08540: 9, 24, 28–9, 67, 105, 144, 147, 164, 254, 259–60, 287–9, 299, 309, 344–5, 348, 350–1, 356, 366–70, 374, 376–7, 379, 383–7, 391, 393–6, 398–401, 403–6, 412–5, 417, 419–23, 425, 427, 430, 449, 461, 487, 551, 568–72, 578, 583–4, 695, 698, 700, 708–9, 722, 727–8, 734, 736, 738, 741–3, 759–62, 868–9, 878, 887, 892–4, 896, 914–6, 919, 921–2, 924–8, 931, 966–7, 974–5, 987, 1000–1, 1003, 1018, 1021, 1084, 1132, B3, B20, B63, B154, B166, B269–74, B289, B466; 1947 Center St., Berkeley, Calif. 94704: 814, B508–13. See also Cooperative Test Division.

★Educators'-Employers' Tests & Services Associates, 120 Detzel Place, Cincinnati, Ohio 45219: 158, 696, 1025, 1163

Educators Publishing Service, Inc., 301 Vassar St., Cambridge, Mass. 02139: B379

*Eidsmoe (Russell M.), Morningside College, Sioux City, Iowa 51106: 702

*8CRT, Box 31, Gracie Station, New York, N.Y. 10028: 211

*Electronics for Education, Inc., 10582 Metropolitan Ave., Kensington, Md. 20795: 665

Elliot Right Way Books, Kingswood Bldg., Kingswood, Surrey, England: B276

Engineering Experiment Station, College of Engineering, Ohio State University, 156 West 19th Ave., Columbus, Ohio 43210: B412

*English Language Institute, The University of Michigan, Ann Arbor, Mich. 48104: 360, 362

*Essay Press, P.O. Box 5, Planetarium Station, New York, N.Y. 10012: 830–1

*Evaluation Institute of Canada (VALCAN) (The), 2733 West Broadway, Vancouver 8, B.C., Canada: 1072

★Examinations Committee, Division of Chemical Education, American Chemical Society, University of South Florida, Tampa, Fla. 33620: 898–909

*Executive Analysis Corporation, 76 Beaver St., New York, N.Y. 10005: 118, 1059, 1106

*Expression Co., Magnolia, Mass. 01931: 938

FACULTY of Education, University College of Wales, Aberystwyth, Wales: B155, B397

*Family Life Publications, Inc., P.O. Box 6725, College Station, Durham, N.C. 27706: 175, 675–6, 681, 684–5, 687

Fearon Publishers, Inc., 828 Valencia St., San Francisco, Calif. 94110: B110

*Fetler (Daniel), Department of Government and International Relations, New York University, New York, N.Y. 10003: 183

Finnish Foundation for Alcohol Studies, Pitkänsillanranta 3B, Helsinki, Finland: B330

*Fischer (Carl), Inc., 56–62 Cooper Square, New York, N.Y. 10003: 349

*Follett Publishing Co., 1010 West Washington Blvd., Chicago, Ill. 60607: 834

*Follett's Michigan Book Store, Inc., 322 South State St., Ann Arbor, Mich. 48104: 360, 362

Foundation for Research on Human Behavior, 1141 East Catherine St., Ann Arbor, Mich. 48106: B437, B525

Free Press of Glencoe (The), 60 Fifth Ave., New York, N.Y. 10011: B89, B260, B345, B401

*Freund Brothers, 1514 Pacific Ave., Atlantic City, N.J. 08401: 954

*Frostig (Marianne) School of Educational Therapy, 7257 Melrose Ave., Los Angeles, Calif. 90046: 553

*GALLAGHER (Ralph), 613 North Mountain Ave., Bound Brook, N.J. 08805: 106

*Gibson (Robert) & Sons (Glasgow), Ltd., 2 West Regent St., Glasgow C.2, Scotland: 81

*Gilbert & Co., 3701 Dundas St., West, Toronto 9, Ont., Canada: 114

*Ginn & Co., Statler Bldg., Park Square, Boston, Mass. 02117: 826

Gollancz (Victor), Ltd., 14 Henrietta St., Covent Garden, London W.C.2, England: B267

*Grade-O-Mat Division, Burgess Cellulose Co., P.O. Box 560, Freeport, Ill. 61033: 666

*Graham-Field Surgical Co., Inc., 32–56 Sixty-Second St., Woodside, N.Y. 10077: 962

*Grason-Stadler Co., Inc., West Concord, Mass. 01781: 946

Gregory (C. A.) Co. See Bobbs-Merrill Co., Inc.

*Griffiths (Ruth), Child Development Research Centre, 47 Hollycroft Ave., London N.W.3, England: 523

Grosset & Dunlap, Inc., 1107 Broadway, New York, N.Y. 10010: B428

*Grune & Stratton, Inc., 381 Park Ave., South, New York, N.Y. 10016: 84a, 99, 203, 237, 243, B72–3, B91, B230, B238, B268, B297, B384, B399, B402, B526; 23 Bedford Square, London W.C.1, England: B297, B399

Gryphon Press (The), 220 Montgomery St., Highland Park, N.J. 08904: B101–5

★Guidance Centre, Ontario College of Education, University of Toronto, 371 Bloor St., West, Toronto 5, Ont., Canada: 5, 100, 252–3, 337, 365, 445, 493, 565–7, 662, 747, 1032, 1041, 1053

Guidance Service, State Department of Education, Salem, Ore. 97310: B261

*Guidance Testing Associates, 6516 Shirley Ave., Austin, Tex. 78752: 507, 818

*HRB-SINGER, Inc., Science Park, P.O. Box 60, State College, Pa. 16801: 674

*Hammond (C. S.) & Co., Maplewood, N.J. 07040: 851

★Harcourt, Brace & World, Inc., 757 Third Ave., New York, N.Y. 10017: 11, 15, 26, 66, 102–3, 113, 186, 237, 270, 279, 330, 460, 480–1, 517, 527, 537, 586, 601, 624, 627, 637, 739, 794, 797, 813, 864, 867, 877, 883, 955–6, 970, 977, 1019, 1056, B119, B164, B236, B295, B312

Harlow Publishing Corporation, 212 East Gray St., Norman, Okla. 73069: B425

*Harper & Row, Publishers, Inc., 49 East 33rd St., New York, N.Y. 10016: 308, B43, B125, B145, B160, B211, B214, B281, B406, B417, B460, B472, B502; Harper & Row Ltd., 35, Great Russell St., London W.C.1, England: B51–2, B100, B125, B145, B211, B281, B343, B406, B417, B460, B472. See also Hoeber Medical Division.

★Harrap (George G.) & Co. Ltd., 182 High Holborn, London W.C.1, England: 455, 465, 480, 501–2, 532, 536, 631, B119, B236, B295

*Harrower (Molly R.), 1040 Park Ave., New York, N.Y. 10028: 237e

Harvard College. See Office of Tests.

*Harvard University Press, 79 Garden St., Cambridge, Mass. 02138: 245, B186, B477

*Haskins (Mary Jane), Department of Physical Education for Women, Ohio State University, Columbus, Ohio 43210: 716

★Hayes Educational Test Laboratory, 7040 North Portsmouth Ave., Portland, Ore. 97203: 587–8

Headquarters, United States Air Force Recruiting Service (ATC). See United States Air Force Recruiting Service (ATC).

Heinemann (William) Medical Books Ltd., 15–16 Queen St., Mayfair, London W.1, England: B72–3, B268, B384, B402

*Hellersberg (Elizabeth F.), P.O. Box 104, Harvard, Mass. 01451: 218

McKay (David) Co., Inc., 750 Third Ave., New York, N.Y. 10017: B193, B200, B299, B433, B481
*Macmillan Co., 60 Fifth Ave., New York, N.Y. 10011: B53, B286, B385, B398; Macmillan & Co. Ltd., 10 St. Martin's St., London W.C.2, England: 843, B41. See also Collier-Macmillan, Ltd.
*McQuaig Institute of Executive Training, 541 Lexington Ave., Suite 350, New York, N.Y. 10022: 1122
*Maico Electronics, Inc., 21 North Third St., Minneapolis, Minn. 55401: 947–8
★Management Service Co., 354 Lancaster Ave., Haverford, Pa. 19041: 340, 1088, 1175
*Manasayan, 32 Netaji Subhash Marg, Delhi 6, India: 284, 672, 757, 1050, B234
Manchester University Press, Manchester 13, England: B517
*Mark James Co., Publishers, P.O. Box 5128, Akron, Ohio 44313: 216
*Mason (Clarence E.), Jr., Philadelphia College of Bible, 1800 Arch St., Philadelphia, Pa. 19103: 753
*Massachusetts Department of Public Health, Division of Maternal and Child Health Services, 88 Broad St., Boston, Mass. 02110: 949–50
Measurement and Research Center, Purdue University. See Division of Educational Reference.
*Measurement Research Center, Inc., P.O. Box 30, Iowa City, Iowa 52242: 670
Meredith Publishing Co. See Appleton-Century; and Appleton-Century-Crofts.
Merrill (Charles E.) Books, Inc., 1300 Alum Creek Drive, Columbus, Ohio 43216: B264a, B521
*Merrill-Palmer Institute, 71 East Ferry Ave., Detroit, Mich. 48202: 678
Methuen & Co. Ltd., 36 Essex St., Strand, London W.C.2, England: B175, B497–8
Michigan State University. See Agricultural Experiment Station; and Bureau of Educational Research Services.
*Midwest Psychological Services, 1195 Commerce Blvd., N.W., Mound, Minn. 55364: 247
*Mills Center, Inc., 1512 East Broward Blvd., Ft. Lauderdale, Fla. 33301: 836
*Ministry Studies Board, 1810 Harvard Blvd., Dayton, Ohio 45406: 755
Modern Education Publishers, P.O. Box 651, San Jose, Calif. 95106: B204
*Morrison (James H.), 6415 West 83rd St., Overland Park, Kan. 66212: 188
Morrow (William) & Co., Inc., 425 Park Ave., South, New York, N.Y. 10016: B83
Munksgaard Ltd., Prags Blvd. 47, Copenhagen S, Denmark: B39, B301, B368

*NEA SERVICE, Inc., 1200 West Third St., Cleveland, Ohio 44113: 731
*Nash (N.), Great Eastern Lumber Co., Inc., 2315 Broadway, New York, N.Y. 10024: 1152
*National Association for Mental Health, 39 Queen Anne St., London W.1, England: 165
*National Association of Independent Schools, 4 Liberty Square, Boston, Mass. 02109: 464
*National Bureau of Educational and Social Research, Department of Education, Arts and Science, Private Bag 122, Pretoria, Republic of South Africa: 477, 619, 629, 777, 799, 811, 1028, 1187
*National Business Education Association, 1201 Sixteenth St., N.W., Washington, D.C. 20036: 30, 32–3, 36, 39, 47, 55
National Cash Register Co. See Data Processing Systems and Sales Department.
National Commission on Safety Education, 1201 Sixteenth St., N.W., Washington, D.C. 20036: B373
*National Computer Systems, 1015 South Sixth St., Minneapolis, Minn. 55415: 92, 180, 671
National Council for the Social Studies, 1201 Sixteenth St., N.W., Washington, D.C. 20036: B56–7, B347
National Council of Educational Research and Training, 16 Ring Road, New Delhi, India: B196–7. See also Central Institute of Education.
National Council of Teachers of English (The), 508 South Sixth St., Champaign, Ill. 61822: B23, B117
National Council of Teachers of Mathematics, 1201 Sixteenth St., N.W., Washington, D.C. 20036: B350–1
National Council on Measurement in Education, Irvin J. Lehmann, Secretary, Office of Evaluation Services, Michigan State University, East Lansing, Mich. 48832: B19, B352–6
National Curriculum Research Institute. See American Association for Jewish Education.
*National Education Association, 1201 Sixteenth St., N.W., Washington, D.C. 20036: 748, B29, B357, B363. See also American Association for Health, Physical Education, and Recreation; American Educational Research Association; National Commission on Safety Education; National Council for the Social Studies; National Council of Teachers of Mathematics; National Business Education Association; and National Science Teachers Association.
★National Foundation for Educational Research in England and Wales, the Mere, Upton Park, Slough, Bucks, England: 86, 212, 261–2, 264, 354, 458, 473, 479, 486, 489, 499, 506, 510–1, 514, 519–20, 538, 585, 610, 614, 621, 626, 768, 785, 809, 952, 960, 1093
*National Institute for Personnel Research, South African Council for Scientific and Industrial Research, P.O. Box 10319, Johannesburg, Republic of South Africa: 459, 539, 618, 639, 778–9, 1026, 1109
National Institute of Industrial Psychology, 14 Welbeck St., London W.1, England: B191
*National League for Nursing, Inc., 10 Columbus Circle, New York, N.Y. 10019: 1157–62, B358–60, B435
National Science Teachers Association, 1201 Sixteenth St., N.W., Washington, D.C. 20036: B361
*Netherlands Institute of Industrial Psychology, Utrecht, Holland: 213
*Nevins (C. H.) Printing Co., 311 Bryn Mawr Island, Bayshore Gardens, Bradenton, Fla. 33505: 825
New American Library of World Literature, Inc., 501 Madison Ave., New York, N.Y. 10022: B215, B522
New York Academy of Sciences, 2 East 63rd St., New York, N.Y. 10021: B494
*New York Times, School and College Service, Times Square, New York, N.Y. 10036: 983–4
New York University. See Center for Safety Education.
New York University Campus Stores, 18 Washington Place, New York, N.Y. 10003: B5
★Newnes Educational Publishing Co. Ltd., Tower House, 8–11 Southampton St., Strand, London W.C.2, England: 261–2, 264, 458, 479, 486, 489, 499, 510–1, 585, 610, 614, 621, 626, 809, 1093
*Newsweek Educational Division, 444 Madison Ave., New York, N.Y. 10022: 985–6
*Nijhoff (Martinus), P.O. Box 269, The Hague, Holland: 213
*Norman (J. H.), 726 Austrian Way, Grand Prairie, Tex. 75050: 45, 56, 185, 437, 482, 805, 1027, 1047, 1065

*OAIS Testing Program, Box 388, Ann Arbor, Mich. 48107: 151
*OPI Research Program, Center for the Study of Higher Education, 4606 Tolman Hall, University of California, Berkeley, Calif. 94720: 150

Index of Titles

* * * * *

In addition to listing all tests and books in this volume, this index lists all other tests known to be in print as of late 1964. References are to entry numbers, not to page numbers. Entry numbers for books begin with the letter B; *entry numbers for tests listed in* Tests in Print *but not in this volume begin with the acronym* TIP; *all other references are to tests in this volume. Test references are not indexed; neither are tests which were listed as out of print in* TIP *or which have gone out of print since they appeared in* TIP. *Also excluded are a few tests whose status is unknown. For tests not listed in this volume,* Tests in Print *must be consulted for further information and for references to entries, reviews, and bibliographies in earlier* MMY's.

Index of Names

* * * * *

References are to test and book entry numbers, not to page numbers. The abbreviations and numbers following the names may be interpreted thus: "rev, *68*" *indicates authorship of an original review of test 68;* "test, *73*" *indicates authorship of test 73 or of some accessory mentioned within the entry for test 73;* "bk, *B16*" *indicates authorship of book 16;* "exc, *112*" (*or* "exc, *B213*") *indicates authorship of an excerpted review of test 112 (or book 213);* "ref, *126(34)*" *indicates authorship of reference 34 for test 126;* "cross ref, *347*" *indicates authorship of an earlier review of test 347, to which a cross reference appears under test 347;* "f, *164*" *indicates that the person is mentioned in a footnote to a review of test 164;* "other, *466*" (*or* "other, *B510*") *indicates that the person is mentioned under test 466 (or in the entry for book 510) in a manner not classifiable under any of the above categories.*

Classified Index of Tests

* * * * *

In addition to presenting a classified listing of all tests in this volume, this index lists all other tests known to be in print as of late 1964. References are to entry numbers, not to page numbers. Under each category the tests which appear in this volume are listed first along with the names of the test reviewers and the number of review excerpts. Stars indicate tests not previously listed in an MMY; *asterisks indicate tests revised or supplemented since last listed in an* MMY. *In each category a smaller type size is used to list all other tests known to be in print as of late 1964. Numbers preceding these titles indicate* Tests in Print *entry numbers to be consulted for further information and for references to entries, reviews, and bibliographies in earlier* MMY's.

ACHIEVEMENT BATTERIES

1. ★The American College Testing Program Examination. Reviews by Max D. Engelhart and Warren G. Findley; and an excerpt from a review.
2. *American School Achievement Tests. Reviews by Robert H. Bauernfeind and Frank B. Womer.
3. *California Achievement Tests, 1957 Edition With 1963 Norms. Reviews by Jack C. Merwin and Robert D. North.
4. California Basic Skills Tests. Review by Robert D. North.
5. ★Canadian Test of General Information (CTGI). Reviews by J. Douglas Ayers and Robert J. Solomon.
6. *Closed High School Placement Test. Reviews by Marion F. Shaycoft and James R. Hayden.
7. Cooperative General Achievement Tests. Review by Willard G. Warrington.
8. *Eighth Grade Test.

8a. *General Scholarship Test for High School Seniors.

9. *The Graduate Record Examinations: The Area Tests. Reviews by Paul L. Dressel and Everett B Sackett.
10. *The Gray-Votaw-Rogers General Achievement Tests. Reviews by Kenneth D. Hopkins, Victor H. Noll, and Ellis Batten Page.
11. ★High School Classification Examination. Reviews by Thomas W. Mahan, Jr. and David V. Tiedeman.
12. *High School Fundamentals Evaluation Test. Reviews by George D. Demos and Jason Millman.
13. Iowa Tests of Basic Skills.
14. *The Iowa Tests of Educational Development. Reviews by Ellis Batten Page and Alexander G. Wesman.
15. *Metropolitan Achievement Tests. Reviews by Paul L. Dressel, Henry S. Dyer, and Warren G. Findley.
16. *National Achievement Tests.
17. ★National Educational Development Tests. Reviews by Willis W. Clark, Arthur E. Traxler, and Alexander G. Wesman.
18. *National Merit Scholarship Qualifying Test. Reviews by Dorothy C. Adkins, George K. Bennett, and J. Thomas Hastings.
19. *Public School Achievement Tests.
20. ★Pupil Record of Educational Progress. Reviews by George D. Demos and Jack C. Merwin.
21. *SRA Achievement Series. Review by Jacob S. Orleans.
22. *SRA High School Placement Test. Reviews by Walter N. Durost and Charles O. Neidt.
23. *Scholastic Achievement Series. Reviews by J. Stanley Ahmann and Thomas W. Mahan, Jr.
24. ★Secondary School Admission Tests: General School Ability and Reading Test. Reviews by Charles O. Neidt and David V. Tiedeman.
25. *Sequential Tests of Educational Progress. Reviews by Harold Seashore and John E. Stecklein.
26. *Stanford Achievement Test, [1964 Revision]. Review by Miriam M. Bryan; and an excerpt from a review.
27. Wide Range Achievement Test: Reading, Spelling, Arithmetic From Kindergarten to College, 1946 Edition.

BUSINESS EDUCATION

BOOKKEEPING

MISCELLANEOUS

SHORTHAND

TYPEWRITING

CHARACTER & PERSONALITY

NONPROJECTIVE

73. California Test of Personality, 1953 Revision.
74. The Cassel Psychotherapy Progress Record. Review by William Schofield.
74a. ★The Child Behavior Rating Scale.
74b. ★Children's Embedded Figures Test.
75. ★The Children's Hypnotic Susceptibility Scale. Reviews by C. Scott Moss and John G. Watkins; and an excerpt from a review.
76. *Client-Centered Counseling Progress Record. Review by William Schofield.
77. The College Inventory of Academic Adjustment. Review by Leonard D. Goodstein.
78. Concept Formation Test.
79. ★Constant-Choice Perceptual Maze Attitude of Responsibility Test.
80. Cornell Word Form 2. Review by S. B. Sells.
81. ★Cotswold Personality Assessment P.A. 1. Reviews by Ralph D. Dutch and G. A. V. Morgan.
82. ★Cowell Personal Distance Scale.
83. ★Cowell Social Behavior Trend Index.
84. ★Cree Questionnaire. Reviews by Allyn Miles Munger and Theodor F. Naumann.
84a. ★Developmental Potential of Preschool Children.
85. *Diplomacy Test of Empathy. Reviews by Arthur H. Brayfield and Richard S. Hatch.
86. ★Dynamic Personality Inventory. Review by S. B. Sells.
87. *Edwards Personal Preference Schedule. Reviews by John A. Radcliffe and Lawrence J. Stricker; and an excerpt from a review.
88. The Ego Strength Q-Sort Test. Reviews by Allen L. Edwards and Harrison G. Gough.
89. *Embedded Figures Test. Reviews by Harrison G. Gough and Leona E. Tyler.
90. ★Emo Questionnaire. Reviews by Bertram D. Cohen and W. Grant Dahlstrom.
91. *The Empathy Test. Review by Wallace B. Hall.
92. ★[Environment Indexes.]
93. ★Eysenck Personality Inventory. Review by James C. Lingoes.
94. ★FIRO-B: [Fundamental Interpersonal Relations Orientation—Behavior].
95. Family Adjustment Test. Review by John Elderkin Bell.
96. ★Famous Sayings. Reviews by Wesley C. Becker and Robert L. Thorndike.
97. Fatigue Scales Kit. Review by Richard S. Barrett.
98. ★The Forty-Eight Item Counseling Evaluation Test.
99. The Freeman Anixety Neurosis and Psychosomatic Test. Reviews by Gerald A. Mendelsohn and Robert C. Nichols.
100. ★G. C. Personality Development Record.
101. Goldstein-Scheerer Tests of Abstract and Concrete Thinking. Review by R. W. Payne.
102. *Gordon Personal Inventory. Reviews by Charles F. Dicken and Alfred B. Heilbrun, Jr.
103. *Gordon Personal Profile. Reviews by Charles F. Dicken and Alfred B. Heilbrun, Jr.
104. Group Cohesiveness: A Study of Group Morale. Reviews by Eric F. Gardner and Cecil A. Gibb.
105. ★Group Dimensions Descriptions Questionnaire.
106. ★Guidance Inventory. Review by John W. M. Rothney.
107. ★Guilford-Holley L Inventory.
108. The Guilford-Martin Inventory of Factors GAMIN, Abridged Edition.
109. The Guilford-Martin Personnel Inventory.
110. The Guilford-Zimmerman Temperament Survey.
111. ★The Handicap Problems Inventory. Revie by Dorothy M. Clendenen.
112. ★Harvard Group Scale of Hypnotic Suscept bility. Review by Seymour Fisher.
113. Heston Personal Adjustment Inventory.
114. ★The Hoffer-Osmond Diagnostic Test (HOD Reviews by Maurice Lorr and William Schofield.
115. ★Holland Vocational Preference Inventory, Re search Edition, Third Revision. Reviews by Robert I French and H. Bradley Sagen.
116. ★The Hooper Visual Organization Test. Re views by Ralph M. Reitan and Otfried Spreen.
117. Hospital Adjustment Scale. Review by Wilso H. Guertin.
118. ★How Well Do You Know Yourself? Review by Lee J. Cronbach and Harrison G. Gough; and ex cerpts from two reviews.
119. *Human Relations Inventory.
120. *The Humm-Wadsworth Temperament Scale Reviews by James R. Glennon and Floyd L. Ruch.
121. *The IPAT Anxiety Scale Questionnaire. Review by Jacob Cohen.
122. ★IPAT Children's Personality Questionnaire Reviews by Anne Anastasi, Wilbur L. Layton, anc Robert D. Wirt.
123. IPAT Contact Personality Factor Test.
124. ★IPAT 8-Parallel-Form Anxiety Battery. Reviews by Jacob Cohen and Paul M. Kjeldergaard.
125. *IPAT Music Preference Test of Personality. Reviews by Kenneth L. Bean and Paul R. Farnsworth.
126. ★Inpatient Multidimensional Psychiatric Scale (IMPS).
127. Interpersonal Check List. Review by P. M. Bentler.
128. An Inventory of Factors STDCR.
129. ★It Scale for Children. Reviews by Philip L. Harriman and Boyd R. McCandless.
130. Johnson Temperament Analysis.
131. *Jr.-Sr. High School Personality Questionnaire. Reviews by C. J. Adcock and Philip E. Vernon.
132. *Kuder Preference Record—Personal. Reviews by Dorothy M. Clendenen and Wilbur L. Layton.
133. ★The Leadership Ability Evaluation. Reviews by John D. Black and Cecil A. Gibb.
134. ★The Leadership Q-Sort Test (A Test of Leadership Values). Reviews by Joel T. Campbell, Cecil A. Gibb, and William Stephenson.
135. *The MACC Behavioral Adjustment Scale: An Objective Approach to the Evaluation of Behavioral Adjustments of Psychiatric Patients. Review by Wilson H. Guertin.
136. ★M-B History Record.
137. The Manson Evaluation. Review by Dugal Campbell.
138. ★Maudsley Personality Inventory. Reviews by Arthur R. Jensen, James C. Lingoes, William Stephenson, and Philip E. Vernon; and excerpts from three reviews.
139. ★Maxfield-Buchholz Scale of Social Maturity for Use With Preschool Blind Children.
140. *Memory-For-Designs Test. Review by Otfried Spreen.
141. *Mental Health Analysis, 1959 Revision. Review by J. Robert Williams.
142. Minnesota Counseling Inventory. Reviews by Norman Frederiksen and John W. M. Rothney.
143. Minnesota Multiphasic Personality Inventory, Revised Edition. Reviews by C. J. Adcock and James C. Lingoes.
144. *Minnesota T-S-E Inventory.
145. Mooney Problem Check List, 1950 Revision. Review by Thomas C. Burgess.
146. ★The Mother-Child Relationship Evaluation. Reviews by John Elderkin Bell and Dale B. Harris.

146a. ★Motivation Analysis Test.
147. ★Myers-Briggs Type Indicator. Reviews by Gerald A. Mendelsohn and Norman D. Sundberg; and an excerpt from a review.
148. ★The Neuroticism Scale Questionnaire. Reviews by E. Lowell Kelly and Jerome D. Pauker; and excerpts from two reviews.
149. ★Objective-Analytic (O-A) Anxiety Battery. Review by Harold Borko; and an excerpt from a review.
150. ★Omnibus Personality Inventory. Reviews by Paul M. Kjeldergaard and Norman E. Wallen; and an excerpt from a review.
151. ★Opinion, Attitude and Interest Survey. Reviews by John O. Crites and Harold Webster.
152. ★Organic Integrity Test.
153. ★The Orientation Inventory. Reviews by Richard S. Barrett and H. Bradley Sagen.
154. *Personal Adjustment Inventory. Reviews by Norman D. Sundberg and Robert D. Wirt.
155. ★Personal Qualities Inventory.
156. *Personality and Interest Inventory: Elementary Form, Revised.
157. The Personality Inventory. Reviews by Wesley C. Becker and Donald J. Veldman.
158. *Personality Rating Scale. Review by Laurance F. Shaffer.
159. Personality Schedule, 1929 Edition.
160. ★Polyfactorial Study of Personality. Reviews by Bertram D. Cohen and Donald R. Peterson; and an excerpt from a review.
161. ★Position Response Form and Response Form.
162. The Power of Influence Test. Reviews by Åke Bjerstedt and Eric F. Gardner.
163. ★The Press Test. Reviews by William H. Helme and Allyn Miles Munger.
164. ★A Process for In-School Screening of Children With Emotional Handicaps. Reviews by Alan O. Ross and J. Robert Williams.
165. ★Progress Assessment Chart (P-A-C).
166. ★Psychometric Behavior Checklist.
167. ★The Psychotic Reaction Profile (PRP): An Inventory of Patient Behavior for Use by Hospital Personnel. Review by Wilson H. Guertin.
168. *The Purdue Master Attitude Scales. Review by Donald T. Campbell.
169. ★Rutgers Social Attribute Inventory. Reviews by David B. Orr and John Pierce-Jones.
170. *SRA Youth Inventory. Review by Forrest L. Vance; and an excerpt from a review.
171. ★A Scale to Measure Attitudes Toward Disabled Persons.
172. ★Self-Interview Inventory. Reviews by Andrew R. Baggaley and David T. Lykken.
173. Shipley-Institute of Living Scale for Measuring Intellectual Impairment.
174. *Sixteen Personality Factor Questionnaire. Review by Maurice Lorr.
175. ★A Social Competence Inventory for Adults. Reviews by William J. Eichman and Jerome D. Pauker.
176. *Social Intelligence Test: George Washington University Series, Revised Form.
177. ★Spiral Aftereffect Test. Reviews by William J. Eichman and Ralph M. Reitan.
178. ★Stanford Hypnotic Susceptibility Scale. Reviews by Milton V. Kline and C. Scott Moss.
179. ★Stanford Profile Scales of Hypnotic Susceptibility. Reviews by Seymour Fisher and Eugene E. Levitt.
180. ★Stern Activities Index.
181. ★Straus Rural Attitudes Profile. Excerpt from a review.
182. *Study of Values: A Scale for Measuring the Dominant Interests in Personality, Third Edition. Reviews by John D. Hundleby and John A. Radcliffe.
183. ★Style of Mind Inventory: Trait, Value and Belief Patterns in Greek, Roman and Judeo-Christian Perspectives.
184. ★Survey of Interpersonal Values. Reviews by Lee J. Cronbach, Leonard D. Goodstein, and John K. Hemphill; and an excerpt from a review.
185. ★Survey of Personal Attitude "SPA" (With Pictures): Individual Placement Series (Area III).
186. ★Syracuse Scales of Social Relations. Review by Åke Bjerstedt; and an excerpt from a review.
187. ★Temperament Comparator. Reviews by Lawrence J. Stricker and Robert L. Thorndike.
188. ★Test of Basic Assumptions.
189. ★Test of Behavioral Rigidity, Research Edition. Reviews by Douglas P. Crowne and Benjamin Kleinmuntz.
190. ★Test of Social Insight. Reviews by John D. Black and John Pierce-Jones; and an excerpt from a review.
191. ★Test of Work Competency and Stability.
192. Thurstone Temperament Schedule.
193. ★Triadal Equated Personality Inventory.
194. Vineland Social Maturity Scale.
195. ★The Visual-Verbal Test: A Measure of Conceptual Thinking. Reviews by R. W. Payne and Donald R. Peterson.
196. ★WLW Personal Attitude Inventory.
197. ★Welsh Figure Preference Test, Research Edition. Review by Harold Borko; and an excerpt from a review.
198. *The Western Personality Inventory.
199. ★William, Lynde & Williams Analysis of Personal Values, Second Edition.

FOR OTHER TESTS, see in *Tests in Print*:

235. Objective-Analytic Personality Test Batteries.
235a. Ohio College Association Rating Scale.
235b. P-S Experience Blank: Psycho-Somatic Inventory.
236. The Pauli Test, [N.I.P.R. Edition, Experimental Form].
238. Personal Audit.
239. Personal Experience and Attitude Questionnaire.
241. The Personal Preference Scale.
242. Personal Relations Inventory.
244. The Personality Evaluation Form: A Technique for the Organization and Interpretation of Personality Data.
247. Carlile's Scoring Bars.
248. Personality Record (Revised).
249. Personality Report.
251. The Personnel Reaction Blank.
252. The Philo-Phobe.
253. Pictorial Study of Values: Pictorial Allport-Vernon.
257. Practical Policy Test.
258. Pre-Counseling Inventory.
260. Problem Check List: Form for Rural Young People.
261. Problem Check List: Form for Schools of Nursing.
262. Problems Inventory (For Guidance Purposes Only).
266. Pupil Adjustment Inventory.
268. The Purdue Rating Scale for Administrators and Executives.
271. Russell Sage Social Relations Test.
273. SAQS Chicago Q Sort.
278. The School Inventory.
279. School Motivation Analysis Test, Research Edition.
280. Schrammel-Gorbutt Personality Adjustment Scale.
281. The Science Research Temperament Scale.
282. Security-Insecurity Inventory.
283. Self-Analysis Inventory.
286. Sense of Humor Test, Second Edition.
287. The Sherman Mental Impairment Test.
292. Social Personality Inventory for College Women.
295. [Stereopathy-Acquiescence Schedule.]
298. A Study of Choices.
303. Temperament and Character Test.
310. Tucson YMCA Character Rating Scale.
311. Tulane Factors of Liberalism-Conservatism.
312. [VC Personality Test Battery.]
317. Washburne Social-Adjustment Inventory.
318. A Weighted-Score Likability Rating Scale.
320. What I Like to Do: An Inventory of Children's Interests.
323. The Wishes and Fears Inventory.
324. Wittenborn Psychiatric Rating Scales.

PROJECTIVE

200. ★The African T.A.T.

201. ★Association Adjustment Inventory. Reviews by W. Grant Dahlstrom and Bertram R. Forer; and an excerpt from a review.

202. *The Behavioral Complexity Test: A Test for Use in Research. Review by John Elderkin Bell.

203. *[Bender-Gestalt Test.] Review by C. B. Blakemore; and an excerpt from a review.

204. *The Blacky Pictures: A Technique for the Exploration of Personality Dynamics. Review by Bert R. Sappenfield.

205. ★Buttons: A Projective Test for Pre-Adolescent and Adolescent Boys and Girls.

206. *Children's Apperception Test. Reviews by Bernard I. Murstein and Robert D. Wirt.

207. Controlled Projection for Children, Second Edition. Review by John Liggett.

208. Curtis Completion Form. Reviews by Irwin G. Sarason and Laurance F. Shaffer.

209. ★The Draw-A-Person.

210. ★The Driscoll Play Kit.

211. The Eight Card Redrawing Test (8CRT). Excerpts from four reviews.

212. ★The Family Relations Indicator: A Projective Technique for Investigating Intra-Family Relationships. Reviews by C. B. Blakemore and Walter Katkovsky.

213. *Four Picture Test (1930), Second Edition. Reviews by S. G. Lee and Johann M. Schepers.

214. ★The Group Personality Projective Test.

215. *H-T-P: House-Tree-Person Projective Technique. Review by Mary R. Haworth.

216. ★The Hand Test. Review by Goldine C. Gleser; and an excerpt from a review.

217. *The Holtzman Inkblot Technique. Reviews by Richard W. Coan, H. J. Eysenck, Bertram R. Forer, and William N. Thetford.

218. *Horn-Hellersberg Test.

219. *The Howard Ink Blot Test. Reviews by Jesse G. Harris, Jr. and Bernard I. Murstein; and an excerpt from a review.

220. ★The IES Test. Reviews by Douglas P. Crowne and Walter Katkovsky; and an excerpt from a review.

221. *An Incomplete Sentence Test.

222. ★The Industrial Sentence Completion Form.

223. Interpersonal Diagnosis of Personality. Review by Jerry S. Wiggins.

224. *Kahn Test of Symbol Arrangement.

225. ★The Kell-Hoeflin Incomplete Sentence Blank: Youth-Parent Relations.

226. Kent-Rosanoff Free Association Test. Review by Jerry S. Wiggins.

227. The Lowenfeld Kaleidoblocs. Reviews by T. R. Miles and George Westby.

228. Lowenfeld Mosaic Test. Reviews by T. R. Miles and George Westby.

229. Machover Draw-A-Person Test. Review by Philip M. Kitay.

230. Make A Picture Story. Review by Arthur R. Jensen.

230a. ★Miner Sentence Completion Scale.

231. ★Minnesota Percepto-Diagnostic Test. Reviews by Richard W. Coan and Eugene E. Levitt.

232. ★Myokinetic Psychodiagnosis (MKP). Reviews by Philip L. Harriman and Irwin G. Sarason.

233. The Object Relations Technique. Review by H. R. Beech; and an excerpt from a review.

234. ★Pickford Projective Pictures. Review by Stanley J. Segal; and excerpts from three reviews.

235. ★Psychiatric Attitudes Battery.

236. ★Rock-A-Bye, Baby: A Group Projective Test for Children.

237. *Rorschach. Reviews by Richard H. Dana, Leonard D. Eron, and Arthur R. Jensen.

238. *Rosenzweig Picture-Frustration Study. Review by Åke Bjerstedt.

239. The Rotter Incomplete Sentences Blank.

240. ★The South African Picture Analysis Test. Reviews by S. G. Lee and Johann M. Schepers; and an excerpt from a review.

241. ★Structured Doll Play Test. Reviews by Terence Moore and Alan O. Ross.

242. Structured-Objective Rorschach Test: Preliminary Edition. Reviews by Jesse G. Harris, Jr. and Boris Semeonoff; and excerpts from two reviews.

243. *Szondi Test.

244. ★Ten Silhouettes.

245. Thematic Apperception Test. Review by C. J. Adcock.

246. *The Tomkins-Horn Picture Arrangement Test. Review by Robert C. Nichols; and excerpts from three reviews.

247. ★Visual Apperception Test '60. Reviews by Bert R. Sappenfield and Stanley J. Segal.

For other tests, see in *Tests in Print:*

325. The Auditory Apperception Test.
333. Draw-A-Person Quality Scale.
334. The Drawing-Completion Test: A Projective Technique for the Investigation of Personality.
337. Family Relations Test: An Objective Technique for Exploring Emotional Attitudes in Children.
338. The Five Task Test: A Performance and Projective Test of Emotionality, Motor Skill and Organic Brain Damage.
339. The Forer Structured Sentence Completion Test.
340. The Forer Vocational Survey.
342. Franck Drawing Completion Test.
344. The Graphoscopic Scale: A Multi-Dimensional Projective Test of Personality.
346. [Group] Picture Impressions.
347. Group Projection Sketches for the Study of Small Groups.

359. The Kessler Structured Sentence Completion Test.
364. Make A Sentence Test.
365. The Michigan Picture Test.
368. Pain Apperception Test.
369. The Picture Impressions: A Projective Technique for Investigating the Patient-Therapist Relationship.
370. The Picture World Test.
376. The Ruth Fry Symbolic Test.
378. Sentence Completions Test.
380. Spatial Comprehension Schedule.
383. Symbol Elaboration Test.
384. Symonds Picture-Story Test.
391. Thematic Apperception Test for African Subjects.
392. Thematic Apperception Test: Thompson Modification.
394. The Toy World Test.
395. The Travis Projective Pictures.
396. The Tree Test.
397. Twitchell-Allen Three-Dimensional Personality Test.

ENGLISH

248. *American School Achievement Tests: Part 3, Language and Spelling.
249. *Analytical Survey Test in English Fundamentals. Reviews by Leonard S. Feldt and Roger A. Richards.
250. *Barrett-Ryan English Test. Review by Clarence Derrick.
251. *California Language Test, 1957 Edition With 1963 Norms. Review by Richard E. Schutz.
252. ★Canadian Achievement Test in English (CATE). Review by Bernard Spolsky.
253. ★Canadian English Achievement Test (CEAT). Reviews by J. Douglas Ayers and Bernard Spolsky.
254. *College Entrance Examination Board Advanced Placement Examination: English.
255. *Cooperative English Test: Usage, Spelling, and Vocabulary. Reviews by Margaret F. Lorimer and John M. Stalnaker.
256. *Cooperative English Tests, [1960 Revision]. Reviews by Leonard S. Feldt and Margaret F. Lorimer; and an excerpt from a review.
257. *English: Every Pupil Scholarship Test.
258. *English Expression: Cooperative English Tests [1960 Revision]. Reviews by John C. Sherwood and John M. Stalnaker.
259. *English Language and Literature: National Teacher Examinations. Review by Holland Roberts.
260. English Language and Literature: Teacher Education Examination Program.
261. *English Progress Tests.
262. *English Test (Adv.). Review by A. E. G. Pilliner.
263. ★English Test (Four-Year Course): Affiliation Testing Program for Catholic Secondary Schools. Review by Henry Chauncey.
264. *English Tests 1, 3–13. Reviews by Stanley Nisbet and H. J. Sants.
265. *English Usage: Every Pupil Test.
266. *Essentials of English Tests, Revised Edition. Review by J. Raymond Gerberich.
267. *The Iowa Tests of Educational Development: Test 3, Correctness and Appropriateness of Expression.
268. *Language Arts: Minnesota High School Achievement Examinations. Review by Marvin D. Glock.
269. ★Language Perception Test.
270. ★Metropolitan Achievement Tests: High School Language Tests.
271. ★[Moray House English Tests.] Review by M. Alan Brimer.
272. ★Nationwide English Grammar Examination.
273. *Novelty Grammar Tests, Second Revision.
274. ★The Pribble-Dallmann Diagnostic Tests in Elementary Language Skills. Reviews by William H. Lucio and George D. Spache.
275. ★The Pribble-McCrory Diagnostic Tests in Practical English Grammar. Review by Clarence Derrick.
276. *The Purdue High School English Test. Reviews by Charlotte Croon Davis and Benjamin Rosner.
277. *SRA Achievement Series: Language Arts. Review by Miriam M. Bryan.
278. *Scholastic Achievement Series: English-Spelling.
279. *Stanford Achievement Test: Spelling and Language Tests.
280. ★Survey of Language Achievement: California Survey Series. Review by Miriam M. Bryan.
281. *Survey Tests of English Usage. Review by Holland Roberts.
282. ★T.C. English Test.
283. Test of English Usage. Review by John C. Sherwood.
284. ★A Test of English Usage [Manasayan].
285. ★Test of Language Skill.
286. Tressler English Minimum Essentials Tests, Revised Edition. Reviews by Osmond E. Palmer and Roger A. Richards.

FOR OTHER TESTS, see in *Tests in Print:*

398. A.C.E.R. English Usage Tests.
403. Barrett-Ryan-Schrammel English Test, New Edition.
404. Basic Language Skills: Iowa Every-Pupil Tests of Basic Skills, Test C.
407. The Clapp-Young English Test: The Clapp-Young Self-Marking Tests.
408. College English Test: National Achievement Tests.
410. College Placement Test in English.
411. College Preparatory Test in English.
417. Correctness and Effectiveness of Expression.
418. Cotswold Junior English Ability Test.
419. Cotswold Measurement of Ability: English.
420a. Diagnostic Tests in English Composition.
421. The Eaton Diagnostic-Accomplishment Tests in English.
422. Eleventh Year English Fundamentals: Manchester Semester-End Achievement Tests.
425. English IX–XII: Final District-State Scholarship Test.
426. English IX–XII, Form 4: Achievement Examinations for Secondary Schools.
427. English IX–XII: Preliminary District-State Scholarship Test.
428. English: Northumberland Standardised Tests (1925 Series).
432. English Test: Municipal Tests: National Achievement Tests.
433. English Test: National Achievement Tests.
435. English Test 2.
436. English: Thanet Mental Tests.
440. Greene-Stapp Language Abilities Test.
442. Iowa Grammar Information Test.
444. Iowa Placement Examinations: English Aptitude: Series EA1, Revised.
445. Iowa Placement Examinations: English Training.
446. Iowa Primary Language Test.
448. Kirby Grammar Test: University of Iowa Standard Tests and Scales.
455. Mechanics of Written English: State High School Tests for Indiana.
457. Nelson's High School English Test: The Clapp-Young Self-Marking Tests.
459. Ninth Year English Fundamentals: Manchester Semester-End Achievement Tests.
461. Objective Test in Constructive English.
462. Objective Test in Grammar.
463. Objective Tests in English [Grammar].
464. Objective Tests in Punctuation.
467. The Purdue Placement Test in English: The Clapp-Young Self-Marking Tests.
468. Rinsland-Beck Natural Test of English Usage.
471. The Schonell Diagnostic English Tests.
472. Senior English Fundamentals: Manchester Semester-End Achievement Tests.
475. Tenth Year English Fundamentals: Manchester Semester-End Achievement Tests.
477. Tests of Language Usage: Active Vocabulary and Expression: Cooperative Inter-American Tests.
479. 20th Century Test for English—9th Grade.
480. 20th Century Test for English—10th Grade.

COMPOSITION

287. *College Entrance Examination Board Achievement Test: English Composition. Reviews by Charlotte Croon Davis, Robert C. Pooley, and Holland Roberts.

288. ★College Entrance Examination Board Placement Tests: English Composition Test.
289. ★College Entrance Examination Board Writing Sample. Review by Robert C. Pooley.
290. ★Nationwide English Composition Examination.
291. *Sequential Tests of Educational Progress: Essay Test.
292. *Sequential Tests of Educational Progress: Writing. Reviews by Hillel Black and Albert N. Hieronymus; and an excerpt from a review.
293. ★Writing Skills Test. Reviews by William E. Coffman and Osmond E. Palmer.

LITERATURE

294. *American Literature: Every Pupil Test.
295. ★Book Review Tests.
296. ★Catholic Book Tests.
297. *Davis-Roahen-Schrammel American Literature Test.
298. *English Literature: Every Pupil Test.
299. *The Graduate Record Examinations Advanced Tests: Literature.
300. *The Iowa Tests of Educational Development: Test 7, Ability to Interpret Literary Materials.
301. *Literature: Every Pupil Scholarship Test.
302. ★Objective Tests in American Anthology.
303. ★Objective Tests in English Anthology.
304. *Objective Tests in English.
305. ★Outside Reading Tests for Freshmen and Sophomores.
306. ★Outside Reading Tests for Juniors and Seniors, Third Edition.
307. ★Outside Reading Tests for Junior High Schools.

For other tests, see in *Tests in Print:*

487. An Awareness Test in 20th Century Literature.
495. The Eaton Book-Report System.
496. The Eaton Literature Tests and The New Eaton Literature Tests.
501. English Tests for Outside Reading.
505. Interpretation of Literary Materials.
507. Literature Appreciation Tests.
509. Literature Test: National Achievement Tests.
512. Objective Tests in American Literature.
513. Objective Tests in English Literature.
515. Objective Tests in English [Turner E. Smith & Co.].
517. Rigg Poetry Judgment Test.
518. Survey Test in American Literature.
519. Survey Test in English Literature.
521. Ullman-Clark Test on Classical References and Allusions.

SPEECH

307a. ★The Arizona Articulation Proficiency Scale.
308. ★Forms From Diagnostic Methods in Speech Pathology.
309. The Graduate Record Examinations Advanced Tests: Speech.
310. ★The Houston Test for Language Development.
311. ★An Integrated Articulation Test for Use With Children With Cerebral Palsy.
312. ★Language Modalities Test for Aphasia. Review by T. R. Miles.
313. ★Nationwide Speech Examination.
313a. ★The Orzeck Aphasia Evaluation.
314. ★Speech Articulation Test for Young Children (Revised Edition).
315. ★Templin-Darley Screening and Diagnostic Tests of Articulation. Excerpts from two reviews.
316. ★Verbal Language Development Scale.

For other tests, see in *Tests in Print:*

526. [Speech Correction Records.]
527. Speech Defect Questionnaire.
528. Speech Diagnostic Chart.
530. Weidner-Fensch Speech Screening Test.

SPELLING

317. Ayer Standardized Spelling Test. Review by Gus P. Plessas.
318. *Gates-Russell Spelling Diagnostic Tests.
319. ★Group Diagnostic Spelling Test.
320. *Lincoln Diagnostic Spelling Tests. Review by Gus P. Plessas.
321. ★Nationwide Spelling Examination.
322. ★The New Iowa Spelling Scale.
323. *Spelling and Vocabulary: Every Pupil Test.
324. ★[Spelling and Word Meaning Tests.]
325. *Spelling: Every Pupil Scholarship Test.
326. Traxler High School Spelling Test. Review by Gus P. Plessas.

For other tests, see in *Tests in Print:*

531. A.C.E.R. Spelling Test (Form C).
532. A.C.E.R. Spelling Tests.
534. Buckingham Extension of the Ayers Spelling Scale.
538. Graded Word Spelling Test.
539. [Iowa Dictation Exercise and Spelling Test.]
540. The Iowa Spelling Scales.
542. Kelvin Measurement of Spelling Ability.
545. Morrison-McCall Spelling Scale.
547. The New Standard High School Spelling Scale.
552. Spelling Errors Test.
555. Spelling: Seven Plus Assessment: Northumberland Series.
556. Spelling Test for Clerical Workers: [Personnel Research Institute Clerical Battery].
557. Spelling Test: National Achievement Tests.
559. Wellesley Spelling Scale.

VOCABULARY

327. *A.C.E.R. Word Knowledge Test—Adult Form B.
328. ★American Literacy Test. Review by Victor H. Noll.
329. ★Bruce Vocabulary Inventory.
330. Durost-Center Word Mastery Test: Evaluation and Adjustment Series. Review by George P. Winship, Jr.
331. ★Gulick Vocabulary Survey. Review by George P. Winship, Jr.
332. *The Iowa Tests of Educational Development: Test 8, General Vocabulary.
333. *Johnson O'Connor English Vocabulary Worksamples.
334. ★Johnson O'Connor Vocabulary Tests.
335. ★Nationwide English Vocabulary Examination.
336. *New Standard Vocabulary Test.
337. Quick-Scoring Vocabulary Test: Dominion Tests. Review by Stephen Hunka.
338. ★A Test of Active Vocabulary.
339. *Vocabulary: Every Pupil Scholarship Test.
340. ★Vocabulary Test [Management Service Co.].
341. ★Vocabulary Test [Richardson, Bellows, Henry & Co.].
342. ★Vocabulary Test—GT. Review by Robert E. Stake.
342a. ★Vocabulary Test for High School Students and College Freshmen.
343. ★Word Clue Test.

For other tests, see in *Tests in Print:*

562. The College Vocabulary Test.
563. Cooperative Vocabulary Test.
566. Holborn Vocabulary Test for Young Children.
567. The Inglis Tests of English Vocabulary.
570. Kansas Vocabulary Test.
571. A Lower Extension of the Inglis Tests of English Vocabulary.
572. Michigan Vocabulary Profile Test.
574. Purdue Industrial Supervisors Word-Meaning Test.
578. Survey Test of Vocabulary.
582. Vocabulary Test: National Achievement Tests.
583. Wide Range Vocabulary Test.

ment Test: German Listening Comprehension. Reviews by Harold B. Dunkel and Herbert Schueler.

385. *College Entrance Examination Board Advanced Placement Examination: German.

386. ★College Entrance Examination Board Placement Tests: German Listening Comprehension Test.

387. ★College Entrance Examination Board Placement Tests: German Reading Test.

388. ★Common Concepts Foreign Language Test: German, [Research Edition].

389. ★German: Every Pupil Test.

390. *German I and II: Minnesota High School Achievement Examinations.

391. ★Graduate School Foreign Language Test: German. Review by Jack M. Stein.

392. ★MLA-Cooperative Foreign Language Tests: German.

393. ★MLA Foreign Language Proficiency Tests for Teachers and Advanced Students: German. Reviews by Harold B. Dunkel and Herbert Schueler.

FOR OTHER TESTS, see in *Tests in Print:*

654. First Year German Test.

655. German I and II, Form 4: Achievement Examinations for Secondary Schools.

GREEK

394. *College Entrance Examination Board Achievement Test: Greek.

395. ★College Entrance Examination Board Placement Tests: Greek Test.

HEBREW

396. ★College Entrance Examination Board Achievement Test: Hebrew.

397. ★Test on the Fundamentals of Hebrew.

ITALIAN

398. ★College Entrance Examination Board Achievement Test: Italian Listening Comprehension.

399. *College Entrance Examination Board Achievement Test: Italian Reading and Essay.

400. ★College Entrance Examination Board Placement Tests: Italian Listening Comprehension.

401. ★College Entrance Examination Board Placement Tests: Italian Test.

402. ★MLA-Cooperative Foreign Language Tests: Italian.

403. ★MLA Foreign Language Proficiency Tests for Teachers and Advanced Students: Italian.

LATIN

404. *College Entrance Examination Board Achievement Test: Latin.

405. *College Entrance Examination Board Advanced Placement Examination: Latin.

406. ★College Entrance Examination Board Placement Tests: Latin Reading Test.

407. *First- and Second-Year Latin: Every Pupil Test.

408. *First Year Latin: Every Pupil Scholarship Test.

409. *Latin I and II: Minnesota High School Achievement Examinations.

410. ★Latin Test (Two-Year Course): Affiliation Testing Program for Catholic Secondary Schools. Review by Henry Chauncey.

411. *Second Year Latin: Every Pupil Scholarship Test.

FOR OTHER TESTS, see in *Tests in Print:*

665. Cicero Test.

668. Cooperative Latin Test.

670. First Year Latin: Manchester Semester-End Achievement Tests.

671. Holtz Vergil Test.

672. Kansas First Year Latin Test.

673. Kansas Second Year Latin Test.

675. Latin I and II: Final District-State Scholarship Test.

676. Latin I and II, Form 4: Achievement Examinations for Secondary Schools.

678. Latin I and II: Preliminary District-State Scholarship Test.

679. Latin Test: State High School Tests for Indiana.

680. Orleans-Solomon Latin Prognosis Test.

683. Second Year Latin: Manchester Semester-End Achievement Tests.

684. Ullman-Kirby Latin Comprehension Test.

RUSSIAN

412. ★College Entrance Examination Board Achievement Test: Russian.

413. ★College Entrance Examination Board Achievement Test: Russian Listening Comprehension.

414. ★College Entrance Examination Board Placement Tests: Russian Listening Comprehension Test.

415. ★Graduate School Foreign Language Test: Russian.

416. ★MLA-Cooperative Foreign Language Tests: Russian.

417. ★MLA Foreign Language Proficiency Tests for Teachers and Advanced Students: Russian. Review by Wayne D. Fisher.

SPANISH

418. ★Baltimore County Spanish Test. Review by Mariette Schwarz.

419. *College Entrance Examination Board Achievement Test: Spanish.

420. ★College Entrance Examination Board Achievement Test: Spanish Listening Comprehension.

421. *College Entrance Examination Board Advanced Placement Examination: Spanish.

422. ★College Entrance Examination Board Placement Tests: Spanish Listening Comprehension Test.

423. ★College Entrance Examination Board Placement Tests: Spanish Reading Test.

424. ★Common Concepts Foreign Language Test: Spanish, [Research Edition].

425. The Graduate Record Examinations Advanced Tests: Spanish.

426. ★MLA-Cooperative Foreign Language Tests: Spanish.

427. ★MLA Foreign Language Proficiency Tests for Teachers and Advanced Students: Spanish. Review by Walter V. Kaulfers.

428. ★National Spanish Examination.

429. *Spanish I and II: Minnesota High School Achievement Examinations.

430. Spanish: Teacher Education Examination Program.

431. ★Spanish Test (Two-Year Course): Affiliation Testing Program for Catholic Secondary Schools. Review by Henry Chauncey.

FOR OTHER TESTS, see in *Tests in Print:*

691. First Year Spanish Test: State High School Tests for Indiana.

692. Furness Test of Aural Comprehension in Spanish.

694. Iowa Placement Examinations: Spanish Training: Series ST1, Revised.

695. Kansas First Year Spanish Test.

696. Kansas Second Year Spanish Test.

699. Spanish and Latin American Life and Culture.

700. Spanish I and II: Final District-State Scholarship Test.

701. Spanish I and II, Form 4: Achievement Examinations for Secondary Schools.

703. Spanish I and II: Preliminary District-State Scholarship Test.

INTELLIGENCE

GROUP

432. *A.C.E.R. Higher Tests.
433. *A.C.E.R. Intermediate Test A.
434. *A.C.E.R. Junior A Test.
435. *A.C.E.R. Junior B Test.
436. ★A.C.E.R. Test W.N.V.
437. ★Academic Alertness "AA": Individual Placement Series (Area I).
438. American Council on Education Psychological Examination for College Freshmen.
439. ★American School Intelligence Test. Reviews by David A. Payne and Frank B. Womer.
440. ★Analysis of Relationships. Reviews by Gustav J. Froehlich and Wimburn L. Wallace.
441. *Army General Classification Test, First Civilian Edition. Reviews by Bert A. Goldman and Howard B. Lyman.
442. California Analogies and Reasoning Test. Reviews by John R. Hills and Wimburn L. Wallace; and excerpts from two reviews.
443. *California Short-Form Test of Mental Maturity, 1963 Revision. Review by Julian C. Stanley.
444. *California Test of Mental Maturity, 1963 Revision.
445. ★Canadian Academic Aptitude Test (CAAT). Reviews by Donald B. Black and George A. Ferguson.
446. ★Cardall-Miles Test of Mental Alertness.
447. ★The Carlton Picture Intelligence Test. Reviews by Elizabeth D. Fraser and S. Rachman.
448. *Classification Test 40-A. Reviews by N. M. Downie and David G. Ryans.
449. *College Entrance Examination Board Scholastic Aptitude Test. Reviews by John E. Bowers and Wayne S. Zimmerman.
450. *College Qualification Tests. Reviews by Ralph F. Berdie and Warren G. Findley.
451. Concept Mastery Test.
452. *Cooperative School and College Ability Tests. Review by Russel F. Green.
453. *Culture Fair Intelligence Test. Reviews by John E. Milholland and Abraham J. Tannenbaum.
454. ★The D48 Test. Reviews by Paul C. Davis and S. S. Dunn.
455. ★Deeside Non-Verbal Reasoning Test: English-Welsh Bilingual Version.
456. *Doppelt Mathematical Reasoning Test. Review by W. V. Clemans.
457. *Figure Reasoning Test: A Non-Verbal Intelligence Test, Second Edition. Review by A. W. Heim.
458. *General Verbal Practice Tests.
459. ★Gestalt Continuation Test.
460. *Goodenough-Harris Drawing Test.
461. *The Graduate Record Examinations Aptitude Test. Reviews by Robert L. French and Warren W. Willingham.
462. *The Henmon-Nelson Tests of Mental Ability, Revised Edition. Review by Norman E. Wallen; and an excerpt from a review.
463. ★Inventory No. 2.
464. *Junior Scholastic Aptitude Test, Revised Edition. Review by Jerome E. Doppelt.
465. *The Kingston Test of Intelligence. Review by H. J. Sants.
466. *Kuhlmann-Anderson Intelligence Tests, Seventh Edition. Reviews by William B. Michael and Douglas A. Pidgeon; and an excerpt from a review.
467. *The Lorge-Thorndike Intelligence Tests.
468. ★Lowry-Lucier Reasoning Test Combination. Reviews by Andrew R. Baggaley and Russel F. Green.
469. ★Maddox Verbal Reasoning Test. Reviews by T. R. Miles and A. E. G. Pilliner; and an excerpt from a review.
470. *Manchester General Ability Test (Senior). Reviews by A. W. Heim and Arthur B. Royse.
471. *Mill Hill Vocabulary Scale. Review by Morton Bortner.
472. *Miller Analogies Test. Reviews by Lloyd G. Humphreys, William B. Schrader, and Warren W. Willingham.
473. ★Mitchell Vocabulary Test.
474. *[Moray House Intelligence Tests.]
475. *Moray House Picture Test 2.
476. ★Multi-Racial Picture Intelligence Tests Suitable for Use in African and Asian Schools.
477. ★[N.B. Group Tests.]
478. ★Non-Verbal Reasoning Test. Reviews by James E. Kennedy and David G. Ryans.
479. *Non-Verbal Tests. Reviews by T. R. Miles and John Nisbet.
480. Otis Group Intelligence Scale. Review by D. Welty Lefever.
481. *Otis Quick-Scoring Mental Ability Tests.
482. ★Performance Alertness "PA" (With Pictures): Individual Placement Series (Area I).
483. ★Personal Classification Test.
484. Personnel Research Institute Classification Test. Reviews by James R. Glennon and Melvin R. Marks.
485. Personnel Research Institute Factory Series Test. Review by N. M. Downie.
486. *Picture Test 1.
487. ★The Preliminary Scholastic Aptitude Test. Review by Wayne S. Zimmerman.
488. ★[Pressey Classification and Verifying Tests.] Review by Walter N. Durost.
489. *Primary Verbal Tests.
490. *Progressive Matrices. Review by Morton Bortner.
491. Purdue Non-Language Test. Reviews by John D. Hundleby and Benjamin Rosner.
492. ★Quantitative Evaluative Device.
493. *Quick-Scoring Group Test of Learning Capacity: Dominion Tests. Reviews by Donald B. Black and George A. Ferguson.
494. Revised Beta Examination. Review by Bert A. Goldman.
495. *SRA Tests of Educational Ability, 1962 Edition. Reviews by J. Stanley Ahmann and John E. Horrocks; and an excerpt from a review.
496. ★[SRA] Tests of General Ability. Reviews by John E. Horrocks and Richard E. Schutz; and an excerpt from a review.
497. ★Safran Culture Reduced Intelligence Test.
498. *Schrammel General Ability Test.
499. ★Secondary Verbal Tests. Review by Stanley Nisbet.
500. Ship Destination Test. Review by William B. Schrader.
501. The Simplex GNV Intelligence Tests. Review by Philip M. Levy.
502. *Sleight Non-Verbal Intelligence Test.
503. ★Survey of Mental Maturity: California Survey Series. Review by Naomi Stewart.
504. ★Test of Learning Ability.
505. ★Test of Non-Verbal Reasoning.
506. Tests AH4 and AH5. Review by John Liggett.
507. *Tests of General Ability: Cooperative Inter-American Tests.
508. ★The Verbal Power Test of Concept Equivalence.
509. ★Verbal Reasoning. Reviews by James E. Kennedy and David G. Ryans.
510. *Verbal Test (Adv.). Reviews by J. S. Lawes and John Nisbet.

511. *Verbal Tests 1–2, 4–13. Review by Arthur B. Royse.
512. ★The Western Personnel Tests. Reviews by Lewis E. Albright and Erwin K. Taylor.
513. *Wonderlic Personnel Test. Reviews by N. M. Downie and Marvin D. Dunnette.

FOR OTHER TESTS, see in *Tests in Print:*

706. A.C.E.R. Advanced Test B40.
707. A.C.E.R. Advanced Tests AL and AQ.
710. A.C.E.R. Intermediate Test D.
713. A.C.E.R. Junior Non-Verbal Test.
715. APT Performance Test.
717. Academic Aptitude Test: Non-Verbal Intelligence: Acorn National Aptitude Tests.
718. Academic Aptitude Test: Verbal Intelligence: Acorn National Aptitude Tests.
719. Adaptability Test.
721. Advanced Test N.
726. Army Group Examination Alpha.
727. Army Group Examination Alpha: Schrammel-Brannan Revision.
730. California Capacity Questionnaire.
734. Cattell Intelligence Tests.
735. Chicago Non-Verbal Examination.
737. Cole-Vincent Group Intelligence Test for School Entrants.
741. Comprehension Tests: Supplementary Mentality Tests for Superior Adults.
744. Cotswold Junior Ability Tests.
745. Cotswold Measurement of Mental Ability.
746. Daneshill Intelligence Test.
748. Dawson Mental Test.
749. Deeside Picture Puzzles.
750. Detroit Advanced First-Grade Intelligence Test.
751. Detroit Beginning First-Grade Intelligence Test (Revised).
752. Detroit General Intelligence Examination.
753. [Detroit Intelligence Tests.]
754. The Dominion Group Test of Intelligence.
757. Easel Age Scale.
758. The Essential Intelligence Test.
760. General Intelligence: Northumberland Standardised Tests (1925 Series).
765. Group Tests 33 and 33B.
766. Group Test 36.
767. Group Test 70.
768. Group Test 75.
770. Group Test of Learning Capacity: Dominion Tests.
771. Henmon-Nelson Tests of Mental Ability: The Clapp-Young Self-Marking Tests.
774. Inductive Reasoning Test.
775. Jenkins Non-Verbal Test.
776. Job Alertness Tests.
778. Junior School Grading Test.
779. Kelvin Measurement of Ability in Infant Classes.
780. Kelvin Measurement of Mental Ability.
781. Kentucky Classification Battery.
783. Kuhlmann-Anderson Intelligence Tests, Sixth Edition.
785. Kuhlmann-Finch Tests.
796. Modified Alpha Examination Form 9.
801. New Rhode Island Intelligence Test.
802. New South African Group Test.
803. Non-Language Multi-Mental Test.
805. The "Northern" Test of Educability.
806. The Northumberland Mental Tests.
807. The Ohio Penal Classification Test.
808. Ohio State University Psychological Test.
809. An Orally Presented Group Test of Intelligence for Juniors.
810. O'Rourke General Classification Test, Senior Grade.
811. The "Orton" Intelligence Test, No. 4.
812. Otis Classification Test, Revised.
813. Otis Employment Tests.
818. Otis Self-Administering Tests of Mental Ability.
819. Pattern Perception Test.
824. Personnel Tests for Industry.
826. Pintner General Ability Tests: Non-Language Series.
827. Pintner General Ability Tests: Verbal Series.
832. Proverbs Test.
835. Reasoning Tests for Higher Levels of Intelligence.
837. Roback Mentality Tests for Superior Adults, Eighth Edition.
838. The Ryburn Group Intelligence Tests.
840. SRA Non-Verbal Form.
843. SRA Verbal Form.
845. School Aptitude Test: Thanet Mental Tests.
847. Schubert General Ability Battery.
848. Scientific Ingenuity and Juristic Aptitude Test.
849. Scott Company Mental Alertness Test.
854. The Simplex Group Intelligence Scale.
855. [The Simplex Junior Intelligence Tests.]
857. The Southend Test of Intelligence.
860. Terman-McNemar Test of Mental Ability.
862. Test of Word-Number Ability.
865. Thurstone Test of Mental Alertness, Revised Edition.
866. The Tomlinson Junior School Test.
867. Verbal and Non-Verbal Test 1.
868. Verbal Capacity Sampler.
871. Vocabulary Tests.
872. Wesman Personnel Classification Test.
873. The "West Riding" Tests of Mental Ability.
874. "West Yorkshire" Group Test of Intelligence.

INDIVIDUAL

514. *Alexander Performance Scale: A Performance Scale for the Measurement of Practical Ability. Review by H. Gwynne Jones.
515. *Cattell Infant Intelligence Scale.
516. ★Children's Picture Information Test. Reviews by Dorothy Eichorn and T. Ernest Newland.
517. *Columbia Mental Maturity Scale, Revised Edition. Reviews by Marshall S. Hiskey and T. Ernest Newland.
518. Crichton Vocabulary Scale. Review by Morton Bortner.
519. ★Diagnostic Performance Tests. Review by H. Gwynne Jones.
520. ★English Picture Vocabulary Test. Reviews by L. B. Birch and Philip M. Levy.
521. Full-Range Picture Vocabulary Test.
522. Gesell Developmental Schedules, 1940 Series. Review by Emmy E. Werner.
523. The Griffiths Mental Development Scale for Testing Babies From Birth to Two Years. Review by C. B. Hindley.
524. ★Kahn Intelligence Test: Experimental Form.
525. *The Leiter Adult Intelligence Scale. Reviews by Paul C. Davis and Frank B. Jex; and an excerpt from a review.
526. Leiter International Performance Scale. Review by Emmy E. Werner.
527. Merrill-Palmer Scale of Mental Tests. Review by Marjorie P. Honzik.
528. Minnesota Preschool Scale. Review by Marjorie P. Honzik.
529. *Non-Verbal Intelligence Test for Deaf and Hearing Subjects. Review by J. S. Lawes.
530. ★Peabody Picture Vocabulary Test. Reviews by Howard B. Lyman and Ellen V. Piers.
531. ★Pictorial Test of Intelligence.
532. *The Porteus Maze Test.
533. ★Quick Screening Scale of Mental Development. Review by Boyd R. McCandless.
534. ★The Quick Test. Reviews by Boyd R. McCandless and Ellen V. Piers.
535. ★Slosson Intelligence Test (SIT).
536. *Stanford-Binet Intelligence Scale, Third Revision. Review by Elizabeth D. Fraser; and excerpts from five reviews.
537. *Van Alstyne Picture Vocabulary Test. Reviews by Mary R. Haworth and Ellen V. Piers.
538. Wechsler Adult Intelligence Scale.
539. Wechsler-Bellevue Intelligence Scale.
540. Wechsler Intelligence Scale for Children. Review by Alvin G. Burstein.
541. ★Williams Intelligence Test for Children With Defective Vision. Review by T. Ernest Newland.

FOR OTHER TESTS, see in *Tests in Print:*

877. Arthur Point Scale of Performance Tests.
878. Canadian Intelligence Examination, 1947 Revision.
879. Carl Hollow Square Scale.
884. Detroit Kindergarten Test.
885. Detroit Tests of Learning Aptitude.
891. The Immediate Test: A Quick Verbal Intelligence Test.
892. Intelligence Tests for Children.
894. Kent Series of Emergency Scales.
900. Nebraska Test of Learning Aptitude.
903. Ontario School Ability Examination.
904. The Passalong Test: A Performance Test of Intelligence.
906. Performance Tests of Intelligence: A Series of Non-Linguistic Tests for Deaf and Normal Children, Third Edition.

SPECIFIC

MATHEMATICS

ALGEBRA

601. Seattle Algebra Test: Evaluation and Adjustment Series. Reviews by Sheldon S. Myers and Willard G. Warrington.
602. ★Survey Test of Algebraic Aptitude: California Survey Series. Reviews by Cyril J. Hoyt and Donald L. Meyer.
603. *The Votaw Algebra Test: Elementary Algebra. Review by Kenneth F. McLaughlin.

FOR OTHER TESTS, see in *Tests in Print:*
979. Advanced Algebra, Form 4: Achievement Examinations for Secondary Schools.
981. Advanced Algebra (II): Final District-State Scholarship Test.
982. Advanced Algebra (II): Preliminary District-State Scholarship Test.
983. Advanced Algebra Test: State High School Tests for Indiana.
984. Algebra Readiness Test.
986. Blyth Second-Year Algebra Test.
987. Breslich Algebra Survey Test.
988. California Algebra Aptitude Test.
992. Diagnostic Test in Basic Algebra.
994. Elementary Algebra, Form 4: Achievement Examinations for Secondary Schools.
997. First Year Algebra: Manchester Semester-End Achievement Tests.
998. First-Year Algebra (I): Final District-State Scholarship Test.
999. First-Year Algebra (I): Preliminary District-State Scholarship Test.
1001. First Year Algebra Test: State High School Tests for Indiana.
1002. Garman-Schrammel Algebra Test.
1003. Illinois Algebra Test.
1004. Iowa Algebra Aptitude Test, Revised Edition.
1005. Lankton First-Year Algebra Test.
1006. Larson-Greene Unit Tests in First-Year Algebra.
1007. Lee Test of Algebraic Ability.
1008. Orleans Algebra Prognosis Test, Revised Edition.
1010. Second Year Algebra: Manchester Semester-End Achievement Tests.
1012. 20th Century Test for First Year Algebra.

ARITHMETIC

604. ★American Numerical Test. Reviews by Marvin D. Glock and Richard T. Johnson.
605. *American School Achievement Tests: Part 2, Arithmetic.
606. *Arithmetic Computation: Public School Achievement Tests.
607. ★Arithmetic: Cooperative Mathematics Tests. Review by O. F. Anderhalter.
608. *Arithmetic: Every Pupil Scholarship Test.
609. *Arithmetic: Every Pupil Test.
610. *Arithmetic Progress Test.
611. ★Arithmetic Reasoning.
612. *Arithmetic Reasoning: Public School Achievement Tests.
613. *Arithmetic Test: National Achievement Tests.
614. *Arithmetic Tests 1–2, 4–13.
615. ★Bobbs-Merrill Arithmetic Achievement Tests.
616. *California Arithmetic Test: 1957 Edition With 1963 Norms.
617. *Cardall Arithmetic Reasoning Test.
618. ★Computation Test A/67.
619. ★Diagnostic Arithmetic Tests.
620. ★Diagnostic Tests in Money. Reviews by Kenneth Lovell and G. A. V. Morgan.
621. ★Intermediate Diagnostic Arithmetic Test. Review by Stanley Nisbet.
622. Los Angeles Diagnostic Tests: Fundamentals of Arithmetic.
623. Los Angeles Diagnostic Tests: Reasoning in Arithmetic.
624. Madden-Peak Arithmetic Computation Test: Evaluation and Adjustment Series.
625. ★Manchester Mechanical Arithmetic Test (Sen.).
626. *[Mechanical Arithmetic Tests.]
627. *Metropolitan Achievement Tests: [Arithmetic]. Reviews by O. F. Anderhalter and E. W. Hamilton.
628. *[Moray House Arithmetic Tests.]
629. ★N.B. Arithmetic Tests.
630. *Primary Arithmetic: Every Pupil Scholarship Test.
631. *Revised Southend Attainment Test in Mechanical Arithmetic.
632. *SRA Achievement Series: Arithmetic. Review by E. W. Hamilton.
633. *Scholastic Achievement Series: Arithmetic.
634. *Schrammel-Otterstrom Arithmetic Test.
635. ★Seeing Through Arithmetic Tests. Review by William H. Lucio.
636. ★Shop Arithmetic Test.
637. *Stanford Achievement Test: Arithmetic Tests. Review by C. Alan Riedesel.
638. ★Survey of Arithmetic Achievement: California Survey Series. Reviews by C. Alan Riedesel and Harold C. Trimble.
639. ★Test A/8: Arithmetic.
640. ★Test of Arithmetic Fundamentals.
641. ★Understanding the Meanings in Arithmetic: A Diagnostic Test. Reviews by Richard T. Johnson and Harold C. Trimble.
642. ★The Wirral Mechanical Arithmetic Tests. Review by John Sutherland.

FOR OTHER TESTS, see in *Tests in Print:*
1014. A.C.E.R. Arithmetic Tests.
1015. A.C.E.R. Arithmetic Tests: Standardized for Use in New Zealand.
1016. A.C.E.R. Number Test.
1017. American School Achievement Tests: Arithmetic Readiness.
1020. Analytical Survey Test in Computational Arithmetic.
1022. Arithmetic Essentials Test.
1025. Arithmetic Fundamentals Test: State High School Tests for Indiana.
1026. Arithmetic: Northumberland Standardised Tests (1925 Series).
1028. Arithmetic Reasoning.
1030. Arithmetic Reasoning Test: [Personnel Research Institute Clerical Battery].
1031. Arithmetic: Seven Plus Assessment: Northumberland Series.
1032. Arithmetic Test: Fundamental Operations: Dominion Tests.
1033. Arithmetic Test (Fundamentals and Reasoning): Municipal Tests: National Achievement Tests.
1036. Arithmetic: Thanet Mental Tests.
1038. Basic Arithmetic Skills: Iowa Every-Pupil Tests of Basic Skills, Test D.
1040. Basic Skills in Arithmetic Test.
1041. A Brief Survey of Arithmetic Skills, Revised Edition.
1042. [Brueckner Diagnostic Arithmetic Tests.]
1045. The Clapp-Young Arithmetic Test: The Clapp-Young Self-Marking Tests.
1046. Commercial Arithmetic: Manchester Semester-End Achievement Tests.
1047. Commercial Arithmetic Test: State High School Tests for Indiana.
1050. Cotswold Junior Arithmetic Ability Test.
1051. Cotswold Measurement of Ability: Arithmetic.
1053. Diagnostic Chart for Fundamental Processes in Arithmetic.
1054. Diagnostic Tests and Self-Helps in Arithmetic.
1055. Diagnostic Tests in Arithmetic Fundamentals, Revised Edition: Dominion Tests.
1057. Diagnostic Tests in Vulgar Fractions, Decimal Fractions and Percentages.
1058. Easy Steps in Arithmetic.
1059. [Essential Arithmetic Tests.]
1060. Gilbert Business Arithmetic.
1061. Group Test of Speed and Accuracy in Arithmetic Computation: Dominion Tests.
1062. Hundred Problem Arithmetic Test.
1066. Kelvin Measurement of Ability in Arithmetic.
1067. Lee-Clark Arithmetic Fundamentals Survey Test: High School Edition.
1075. New York Test of Arithmetical Meanings.
1077. Oral Diagnostic Test in Addition: Analysis of Errors in Addition: Dominion Tests.
1078. Otis Arithmetic Reasoning Test.
1084. Schonell Diagnostic Arithmetic Tests.
1087. Southend Attainment Test in Mechanical Arithmetic.

1088. Speed and Diagnostic Tests of Arithmetic.
1089. The Staffordshire Arithmetic Test.
1092. Survey Test of Arithmetic Fundamentals: Dominion Tests.
1094. Test A/68: Arithmetical Problems.
1096. The Tiedeman Arithmetical Knowledge and Information Test.
1098. The Wilson General Survey Tests in Arithmetic.
1099. The Wilson Inventory and Diagnostic Tests in Arithmetic.

GEOMETRY

643. ★Analytic Geometry: Cooperative Mathematics Tests.
644. ★Diagnostic Test in Basic Geometry.
645. ★Geometry: Cooperative Mathematics Tests.
646. *Geometry: Every Pupil Test.
647. *Lee Test of Geometric Aptitude, 1963 Revision. Reviews by Kenneth F. McLaughlin and Lynnette B. Plumlee.
648. *Plane Geometry: Every Pupil Scholarship Test.
649. *Plane Geometry: Minnesota High School Achievement Examinations.
650. ★Plane Geometry: National Achievement Tests.
651. ★Plane Geometry Test: Affiliation Testing Program for Catholic Secondary Schools. Review by Henry Chauncey.
652. *Solid Geometry: Minnesota High School Achievement Examinations.
653. ★Solid Geometry: National Achievement Tests. Review by Sheldon S. Myers.

For other tests, see in *Tests in Print:*

1105. Geometry Attainment Test.
1107. Geometry Survey Test.
1108. Illinois Plane Geometry Test.
1109. Iowa Plane Geometry Aptitude Test, Revised Edition.
1110. Lane-Greene Unit Tests in Plane Geometry, 1944 Edition.
1112. Orleans Geometry Prognosis Test, Revised Edition.
1114. Plane Geometry: Final District-State Scholarship Test.
1115. Plane Geometry, Form 4: Achievement Examinations for Secondary Schools.
1116. Plane Geometry: Manchester Semester-End Achievement Tests.
1119. Plane Geometry: Preliminary District-State Scholarship Test.
1120. Plane Geometry Test: State High School Tests for Indiana.
1121. Schrammel-Reed Solid Geometry Test.
1122. Seattle Plane Geometry Test.
1123. Seattle Solid Geometry Test Series.
1124. Shaycoft Plane Geometry Test.
1125. Solid Geometry, Form 4: Achievement Examinations for Secondary Schools.
1126. Solid Geometry: Manchester Semester-End Achievement Tests.
1129. Solid Geometry Test: State High School Tests for Indiana.
1130. 20th Century Test for Plane Geometry.

MISCELLANEOUS

654. ★Calculus: Cooperative Mathematics Tests.
655. ★Structure of the Number System: Cooperative Mathematics Tests.

TRIGONOMETRY

656. ★Plane Trigonometry: National Achievement Tests.
657. ★Trigonometry: Cooperative Mathematics Tests.
658. ★Trigonometry: Minnesota High School Achievement Examinations.

For other tests, see in *Tests in Print:*

1134. Rasmussen Trigonometry Test.
1135. Trigonometry: Manchester Semester-End Achievement Tests.
1137. Trigonometry Test: State High School Tests for Indiana.

MISCELLANEOUS

For tests, see in *Tests in Print:*

1138. Creative Ability Inventory (Preventive-Imagination and Constructive-Imagination).
1139. How Well Can You Read Lips?
1140. Inventory of Satisfactions in Home Life.
1141. What Do You Know About Photography?
1142. Worth of People to Each Other Inventory.

AGRICULTURE

659. *Agriculture: Every Pupil Scholarship Test.

COMPUTATIONAL AND SCORING DEVICES

660. ★Chronological Age Computer.
661. ★Digitek Optical Test Scoring and Document Scanning System.
662. ★Dominion Table for Converting Mental Age to I.Q.
663. ★The EB Punch-Key Scoring and Answer Sheet System.
664. ★[Grade Averaging Charts.]
665. ★Grade Master.
666. ★Grade-O-Mat.
667. *Hankes Answer Sheets.
668. ★IBM Optical Mark Scoring Reader.
669. *IBM Test Scoring Machine.
670. ★[MRC Test Processing Service.]
671. ★NCS Digital Test Scoring and Data Processing.
672. ★Psychometric Research and Service Chart Showing the Davis Difficulty and Discrimination Indices for Item Analysis. Excerpt from a review.
673. ★The Rapid-Rater.
674. ★STAR Score Teach Answer Record.

For other tests, see in *Tests in Print:*

1148. The Bowman I.Q. Kalculator.
1151. Hammond Matrix Sorter.
1154. I.Q. Calculator.
1158. The Multiple Purpose Self Trainer.
1159. Normal Percentile Chart.
1160. The Tweeddale I.Q. Conversion Tables.

COURTSHIP AND MARRIAGE

675. ★A Courtship Analysis. Review by William R. Reevy.
676. ★A Dating Problems Checklist. Reviews by Clifford R. Adams and Robert A. Harper.
677. ★The El Senoussi Multiphasic Marital Inventory.
678. ★Individual and Marriage Counseling Inventory.
679. ★The Male Impotence Test.
680. ★Marital Roles Inventory. Review by Robert A. Harper.
681. ★A Marriage Adjustment Form. Review by Lester W. Dearborn.
682. ★The Marriage Adjustment Inventory. Reviews by Clifford R. Adams and Albert Ellis.
683. ★The Marriage Adjustment Sentence Completion Survey. Review by Albert Ellis.
684. *A Marriage Prediction Schedule. Review by Lester W. Dearborn.
685. ★Marriage Role Expectation Inventory. Review by Robert C. Challman.
686. ★Otto Pre-Marital Counseling Schedules. Reviews by Robert C. Challman and William R. Reevy.
687. *Sex Knowledge Inventory, Experimental Edition. Review by Clifford R. Adams.
688. ★Sex Knowledge Test.

For other tests, see in *Tests in Print:*

1288. Information Test on Human Reproduction.

DRIVING AND SAFETY EDUCATION

689. ★Driver Attitude Survey.
690. ★Hannaford Industrial Safety Attitude Scales. Review by David O. Herman.
691. ★The McGlade Road Test for Use in Driver Licensing, Education and Employment.
692. ★National Test in Driver Education (Preliminary Form).
693. *Siebrecht Attitude Scale.
694. ★Student Record in Driver Education.

For other tests, see in *Tests in Print:*

1162. [American Automobile Association Driver Testing Apparatus.]
1162a. Bicycle Safety Performance and Skill Tests, [1958 Revision].
1164. Examination for Driving Instructors.
1165. General Test on Traffic and Driving Knowledge.
1169. Rating Scale for Automobile-Driver Skills: The Abercrombie Driver Test.
1171. Road Test Check List for Passenger Car Drivers.
1173. Safety Education: Manchester Semester-End Achievement Tests.
1176. Test of Safety Mindedness.

EDUCATION

695. ★College and University Environment Scales (CUES).
696. Diagnostic Teacher-Rating Scale.
697. *Faculty Morale Scale for Institutional Improvement.
698. *The Graduate Record Examinations Advanced Tests: Education. Review by D. Welty Lefever.
699. Minnesota Teacher Attitude Inventory.
700. *National Teacher Examinations. Review by Harold Seashore.
701. Pictographic Self Rating Scale. Reviews by Stanley E. Davis and John D. Krumboltz.
702. *A Pupil's Rating Scale of an Instructor. Review by James R. Hayden.
703. ★Purdue Instructional Television Attitude Scale.
704. ★The Purdue Instructor Performance Indicator. Review by C. Robert Pace.
705. *The Purdue Rating Scale for Instruction. Review by C. Robert Pace.
706. ★The Purdue Teacher Morale Inventory.
707. ★Remmlein's School Law Test.
708. ★Sizing Up Your School Subjects.
709. *Teacher Education Examination Program.
710. A Test on Adult Attitudes Toward Children. Review by Elizabeth Hagen.
711. *The Wilson Teacher-Appraisal Scale. Review by James R. Hayden.

For other tests, see in *Tests in Print:*

1177. Academic Freedom Survey.
1180. Case Study Tests in Human Growth and Development, Revised Edition.
1181. Class Activity-Analysis Chart.
1183. Educational Aptitude Test: George Washington University Series.
1187. How I Counsel.
1188. How I Teach: Analysis of Teaching Practices.
1193. Ohio Teaching Record: Anecdotal Observation Form, Second Revised Edition.
1194. Problem Check List for Student Teachers and Intern Teachers, [Experimental Edition].
1201. A Self Appraisal Scale for Teachers.
1203. Survey of Educational Leadership Practices.
1204. Syracuse Test Series in Human Growth and Development.
1206. Teacher Opinionaire on Democracy.
1207. Teacher Preference Schedule.
1208. Teaching Aptitude Test: George Washington University Series.
1209. The Teaching Evaluation Record.
1211. What Would *You* Do? Perplexing Incidents in Human Relations.

ETIQUETTE

For tests, see in *Tests in Print:*

1213. Furbay-Schrammel Social Comprehension Test.
1214. The New Century Social Conduct Test.
1215. Parsons Social Comprehension Test.
1216. Test on Social Usage.

HANDWRITING

712. ★The American Handwriting Scale. Review by Theodore L. Harris.
713. Evaluation Scales for Guiding Growth in Handwriting. Review by Theodore L. Harris.
714. Normal Handwriting Scale. Review by Theodore L. Harris.

For other tests, see in *Tests in Print:*

1218. Ayres Measuring Scale for Handwriting.
1220. Metropolitan Primary Cursive Handwriting Scale and Metropolitan Primary Manuscript Handwriting Scale.

HEALTH AND PHYSICAL EDUCATION

715. ★AAHPER Youth Fitness Test.
716. ★Action-Choice Tests for Competitive Sports Situations.
716a. ★Basic Fitness Tests.
717. ★Belmont Measures of Athletic Performance: Field Hockey Scale.
718. *College Health Knowledge Test, Personal Health. Reviews by James E. Bryan and Peter G. Loret.
719. Cornell Medical Index—Health Questionnaire.
720. ★Cowell Test of Ability to Recognize the Operation of Certain Principles Important to Physical Education.
721. *Elementary Health: Every Pupil Scholarship Test.
722. ★The Graduate Record Examinations Advanced Tests: Physical Education.
723. ★Health Behavior Inventory. Reviews by James E. Bryan and Peter G. Loret.
724. *Health and Safety Education Test: National Achievement Tests.
725. *Health Education and Hygiene: Every Pupil Test.
726. *High School Health: Every Pupil Scholarship Test.
727. *Physical Education: National Teacher Examinations.
728. Physical Education: Teacher Education Examination Program.
729. ★Smoking Habits Questionnaire.
730. ★Veenker Health Knowledge Test for the Seventh Grade.
731. [Wetzel Grid Charts.] Review by Dorothy Eichorn.

For other tests, see in *Tests in Print:*

1223. Attitude Inventory.
1225. Byrd Health Attitude Scale.
1229. Gill-Schrammel Physiology Test.
1231. Health and Safety Education Test: State High School Tests for Indiana.
1233. Health Education Test: Knowledge and Application: Acorn National Achievement Tests, Revised Edition.
1235. Health Knowledge Test for College Freshmen: National Achievement Tests.
1236. Health: Manchester Semester-End Achievement Tests.
1237. Health Practice Inventory.
1238. Health Test: National Achievement Tests.
1241. Kilander Health Knowledge Test.
1242. Kilander Health Knowledge Test [for College Students].
1243. Patient's Self-History Form, Second Edition.
1248. Stimulants and Depressants.
1252. Width-Weight Tables, Second Revised Edition.

HOME ECONOMICS

732. *Clothing: Every Pupil Scholarship Test.
733. *Foods: Every Pupil Scholarship Test.

INDUSTRIAL ARTS

LISTENING COMPREHENSION

PHILOSOPHY

PSYCHOLOGY

RECORD AND REPORT FORMS

RELIGIOUS EDUCATION

SOCIOECONOMIC STATUS

TEST PROGRAMS

1362. Ohio District-State Scholarship Tests.
1365. Purdue Personnel Tests.
1366. State High School Tests for Indiana.

MULTI-APTITUDE BATTERIES

766. ★Academic Promise Tests. Reviews by Julian C. Stanley and William W. Turnbull.
767. *Differential Aptitude Tests. Reviews by J. A. Keats and Richard E. Schutz.
768. *Differential Test Battery.
769. *Employee Aptitude Survey. Reviews by Paul F. Ross and Erwin K. Taylor; and an excerpt from a review.
770. *Flanagan Aptitude Classification Tests. Reviews by Norman Frederiksen and William B. Michael.
771. *General Aptitude Test Battery. Reviews by Harold P. Bechtoldt and John B. Carroll.
772. *The Guilford-Zimmerman Aptitude Survey.
773. *The Jastak Test of Potential Ability and Behavior Stability. Reviews by Anne Anastasi and Benjamin Kleinmuntz; and excerpts from two reviews.
774. *Job-Tests Program. Reviews by William H. Helme and Stanley I. Rubin.
775. ★Measurement of Skill: A Battery of Placement Tests for Business, Industrial and Educational Use. Reviews by Dorothy C. Adkins, Lloyd G. Humphreys, and Joseph E. Moore.
776. *Multiple Aptitude Tests, 1959 Edition. Reviews by S. S. Dunn and Leroy Wolins; and an excerpt from a review.
777. ★N.B. Aptitude Tests (Junior).
778. ★National Institute for Personnel Research High Level Battery.
779. ★National Institute for Personnel Research Normal Battery.
780. *SRA Primary Mental Abilities, Revised. Review by John E. Milholland.
781. ★Vocational Guidance Program. Review by Leo Goldman.

FOR OTHER TESTS, see in *Tests in Print:*

1368. Aptitude Tests for Occupations.
1369. Detroit General Aptitudes Examination.
1378. Holzinger-Crowder Uni-Factor Tests.
1380. The Multi-Aptitude Test.

READING

782. *A.C.E.R. Silent Reading Tests, Forms C and D.
783. *American School Achievement Tests: Part 1, Reading.
784. *California Reading Test, 1957 Edition With 1963 Norms.
785. ★Comprehension Test for Training College Students.
786. *Davis Reading Test. Reviews by William E. Coffman and Alton L. Raygor.
787. *Developmental Reading Tests. Reviews by Edward Fry and Agatha Townsend.
788. *Elementary Reading: Every Pupil Scholarship Test.
789. *Elementary Reading: Every Pupil Test.
790. Gates Advanced Primary Reading Tests. Review by Kenneth D. Hopkins.
791. Gates Basic Reading Tests. Reviews by Albert N. Hieronymus and Arthur E. Traxler.
792. Gates Primary Reading Tests. Reviews by William Eller and Coleman Morrison.
793. *Gates Reading Survey. Reviews by George D. Spache and Morey J. Wantman.
794. *Iowa Silent Reading Tests: New Edition. Review by Worth R. Jones.
795. Lee-Clark Reading Test, 1958 Revision. Reviews by Thomas C. Barrett and Coleman Morrison.
796. ★Manchester Reading Comprehension Test (Sen.) 1.
797. *Metropolitan Achievement Tests: [Reading]. Review by H. Alan Robinson.
798. *Monroe's Standardized Silent Reading Test. Reviews by Charles R. Langmuir and Agatha Townsend.
799. ★N.B. Silent Reading Tests (Beginners): Reading Comprehension Test.
800. *The Nelson-Denny Reading Test: Vocabulary-Comprehension-Rate. Reviews by David B. Orr and Agatha Townsend; and an excerpt from a review.
801. Nelson-Lohmann Reading Test: Coordinated Scales of Attainment. Review by Jason Millman.
802. *The Nelson Reading Test, Revised Edition: Vocabulary-Paragraph Comprehension. Review by H. Alan Robinson.
803. *Primary Reading: Every Pupil Scholarship Test.
804. *Primary Reading: Every Pupil Test.
805. ★Reading Adequacy "READ" Test: Individual Placement Series.
806. *Reading Comprehension: Cooperative English Tests, [1960 Revision]. Reviews by W. V. Clemans and W. G. Fleming.
807. *Reading: Public School Achievement Tests.
808. *SRA Achievement Series: Reading. Review by Edward B. Fry.
809. *Sentence Reading Test 1.
810. *Sequential Tests of Educational Progress: Reading. Reviews by Emmett Albert Betts and Paul R. Lohnes.
811. *Silent Reading Tests.
812. ★Southgate Group Reading Tests. Reviews by M. L. Kellmer Pringle and Magdalen D. Vernon; and an excerpt from a review.
813. *Stanford Achievement Test: [Reading Tests].
814. ★Survey of Primary Reading Development. Reviews by Thomas C. Barrett and Russell G. Stauffer.
815. ★Survey of Reading Achievement: California Survey Series. Reviews by Clarence Derrick and J. Raymond Gerberich.
816. *Techniques in Reading Comprehension: Every Pupil Test.
817. ★Test of Reading Comprehension.
818. *Tests of Reading: Cooperative Inter-American Tests.
819. ★W.A.L. English Comprehension Test.

FOR OTHER TESTS, see in *Tests in Print:*

1387. A.C.E.R. Silent Reading Tests, Forms A and B.
1389. A.C.E.R. Silent Reading Tests: Standardized for Use in New Zealand.
1390. Achievement Test in Silent Reading: Dominion Tests.
1392. American School Reading Tests.
1393. Buffalo Reading Test for Speed and Comprehension.
1397. Commerce Reading Comprehension Test.
1399. Detroit Reading Test.
1400. Detroit Word Recognition Test.
1406. Emporia Silent Reading Test.
1412. High School Reading Test: National Achievement Tests.
1415. Kelley-Greene Reading Comprehension Test.
1416. Kelvin Measurement of Reading Ability.
1417. The Kingston Test of Silent Reading.
1419. Los Angeles Elementary Reading Test.
1422. Minnesota Reading Examination for College Students.
1424. The Nelson-Denny Reading Test: Vocabulary and Paragraph: The Clapp-Young Self-Marking Tests.
1428. Pressey Diagnostic Reading Tests.
1431. Primary Reading Test.
1432. Primary Reading Test: Acorn Achievement Tests.
1433. The Purdue Reading Test.
1434. Purdue Reading Test for Industrial Supervisors.
1437. Reading Comprehension Test: National Achievement Tests [Crow, Kuhlmann, and Crow].
1438. Reading Comprehension Test: National Achievement Tests.

1440. Reading: Seven Plus Assessment: Northumberland Series.
1441. Reading Test (Comprehension and Speed): Municipal Tests: National Achievement Tests.
1443. SRA Reading Record.
1446. The Schonell Reading Tests.
1447. Schrammel-Gray High School and College Reading Test.
1450. Silent Reading Comprehension: Iowa Every-Pupil Tests of Basic Skills, Test A.
1456. Survey Tests of Reading.
1459. Traxler High School Reading Test.
1460. Traxler Silent Reading Test.
1461. Williams Primary Reading Test.
1462. Williams Reading Test for Grades 4–9.

DIAGNOSTIC

820. ★California Phonics Survey. Review by Thomas E. Culliton, Jr.
821. ★Diagnostic Reading Scales. Review by N. Dale Bryant.
822. *Diagnostic Reading Test: Pupil Progress Series. Review by Agatha Townsend.
823. *Diagnostic Reading Tests. Reviews by Albert J. Kingston and B. H. Van Roekel.
824. *Gates-McKillop Reading Diagnostic Tests. Reviews by N. Dale Bryant and Gabriel M. Della-Piana.
825. Group Diagnostic Reading Aptitude and Achievement Tests.
826. ★McCullough Word-Analysis Tests, Experimental Edition. Reviews by Emery P. Bliesmer and Albert J. Harris.
827. ★OC Diagnostic Syllable Test.
828. ★Phonics Knowledge Survey.
829. *Phonovisual Diagnostic Test. Reviews by Charles M. Brown and George D. Spache.
830. ★Roswell-Chall Auditory Blending Test. Reviews by Ira E. Aaron and B. H. Van Roekel.
831. *Roswell-Chall Diagnostic Reading Test of Word Analysis Skills. Reviews by Ira E. Aaron and Emmett Albert Betts.
832. Silent Reading Diagnostic Tests: The Developmental Reading Tests. Reviews by Emery P. Bliesmer and Albert J. Kingston.
833. The Standard Reading Tests. Review by L. B. Birch.

For other tests, see in *Tests in Print:*

1445. Scholastic Diagnostic Reading Test.
1465. Diagnostic Reading Examination for Diagnosis of Special Difficulty in Reading.
1466. Doren Diagnostic Reading Test of Word Recognition Skills.
1467. Durrell Analysis of Reading Difficulty, New Edition.
1474. Primary Reading Profiles, [Revised Edition].
1476. Reading Diagnostic Record for High School and College Students.

MISCELLANEOUS

834. ★Botel Reading Inventory. Reviews by Ira E. Aaron and Charles M. Brown.
835. ★Functional Readiness Questionnaire for School and College Students.
836. ★Learning Methods Test. Reviews by Thomas E. Culliton, Jr. and William Eller.
837. ★The Reader Rater.
838. ★The Reading Eye. Reviews by Arthur S. McDonald and George D. Spache.
839. ★Reading Versatility Test.
840. ★Understanding Communication (Verbal Comprehension). Reviews by C. E. Jurgensen and Donald E. P. Smith.

For other tests, see in *Tests in Print:*

1463. Basic Sight Word Test.
1464. Cumulative Reading Record, 1956 Revision.
1468. Durrell-Sullivan Reading Capacity and Achievement Tests.
1471. Individual Reading Test.

ORAL

841. ★Flash-X Sight Vocabulary Test.
842. ★Gray Oral Reading Test. Reviews by Emery P. Bliesmer, Albert J. Harris, and Paul R. Lohnes.
843. ★Neale Analysis of Reading Ability. Reviews by M. Alan Brimer and Magdalen D. Vernon; and an excerpt from a review.
844. ★Slosson Oral Reading Test (SORT).

For other tests, see in *Tests in Print:*

1483. Gilmore Oral Reading Test.
1484. Graded Word Reading Test.
1485. Holborn Reading Scale.
1488. Oral Diagnostic Test of Word-Analysis Skills, Primary: Dominion Tests.
1489. Oral Word Reading Test.
1490. Standardized Oral Reading Check Tests.
1491. Standardized Oral Reading Paragraphs.

READINESS

844a. ★The Anton Brenner Developmental Gestalt Test of School Readiness.
845. *Gates Reading Readiness Tests.
846. *Lee-Clark Reading Readiness Test, 1962 Revision.
847. *Maturity Level for School Entrance and Reading Readiness.
848. *Perceptual Forms Test. Review by Mary C. Austin.
849. Reading Readiness Test. Review by David A. Payne.
850. *Scholastic Reading Readiness Test. Review by David A. Payne.
851. ★Watson Reading-Readiness Test.

For other tests, see in *Tests in Print:*

1492. American School Reading Readiness Test.
1493. Binion-Beck Reading Readiness Test for Kindergarten and First Grade.
1496. Group Test of Reading Readiness: Dominion Tests.
1497. The Harrison-Stroud Reading Readiness Profiles.
1500. Metropolitan Readiness Tests.
1502. Reading Aptitude Tests.
1504. Reversal Test.

SPECIAL FIELDS

852. *The Iowa Tests of Educational Development: Test 5, Ability to Interpret Reading Materials in the Social Studies.
853. *The Iowa Tests of Educational Development: Test 6, Ability to Interpret Reading Materials in the Natural Sciences.
854. ★Lorimer Braille Recognition Test: A Test of Ability in Reading Braille Contractions.
855. ★Tooze Braille Speed Test: A Test of Basic Ability in Reading Braille.

For other tests, see in *Tests in Print:*

1508. Interpretation of Reading Materials in the Natural Sciences.
1509. Interpretation of Reading Materials in the Social Studies.
1512. [Robinson-Hall Reading Tests.]
1513. Tests of Natural Sciences: Vocabulary and Interpretation of Reading Materials: Cooperative Inter-American Tests.
1514. Tests of Social Studies: Vocabulary and Interpretation of Reading Materials: Cooperative Inter-American Tests.

SPEED

For tests, see in *Tests in Print:*

1516. Minnesota Speed of Reading Test for College Students.
1518. Tinker Speed of Reading Test.

STUDY SKILLS

856. Brown-Holtzman Survey of Study Habits and Attitudes.
857. California Study Methods Survey. Reviews by

John D. Krumboltz and Donald E. P. Smith; and excerpts from two reviews.

858. *The Iowa Tests of Educational Development: Test 9, Use of Sources of Information.

859. *A Library Orientation Test for College Freshmen, 1955 Edition. Review by Morey J. Wantman.

860. ★Nationwide Library Skills Examination.

861. ★OC Diagnostic Dictionary Test.

862. *SRA Achievement Series: Work-Study Skills.

863. ★Senior High School Library and Reference Skills Test.

864. Spitzer Study Skills Test: Evaluation and Adjustment Series. Review by Alton L. Raygor.

865. ★The Study Skills Counseling Evaluation. Reviews by Stanley E. Davis and W. G. Fleming.

866. ★A Test on Use of the Dictionary.

867. *Watson-Glaser Critical Thinking Appraisal.

For other tests, see in *Tests in Print:*

1519. Ability to Learn (Exploratory and Corrective Inventory).
1520. Bennett Use of Library Test.
1525. Evaluation Aptitude Test.
1529. Logical Reasoning.
1530. Peabody Library Information Test.
1536. Stanford Achievement Test: Study Skills.
1537. Study Habits Inventory, Revised Edition.
1538. Study Performance Test.
1539. Survey of Study Habits, Experimental Edition.
1541. A Test of Study Skills.
1542. Tyler-Kimber Study Skills Test.
1544. Work-Study Skills: Iowa Every-Pupil Tests of Basic Skills, Test B.

SCIENCE

867a. ★Advanced General Science: Cooperative Science Tests.

868. *Biology and General Science: National Teacher Examinations.

869. *Chemistry, Physics and General Science: National Teacher Examinations.

870. Cooperative General Achievement Tests: Test 2, Natural Science.

871. *Elementary Science: Every Pupil Scholarship Test.

872. *Elementary Science and Health: Every Pupil Test.

872a. ★General Science: Cooperative Science Tests.

873. *General Science: Every Pupil Scholarship Test.

874. *General Science: Every Pupil Test.

875. *General Science: Minnesota High School Achievement Examinations.

876. *The Iowa Tests of Educational Development: Test 2, General Background in the Natural Sciences. Reviews by Lloyd H. Heidgerd and Jacqueline V. Mallinson.

877. *Metropolitan Achievement Tests: [Science]. Reviews by William W. Cooley and George G. Mallinson.

878. Physical Science: Teacher Education Examination Program.

879. ★Purdue Physical Science Aptitude Test. Review by William W. Cooley.

880. ★Science Background: A Science Service Test to Identify Potential Scientific and Technical Talent.

881. ★Science: Minnesota High School Achievement Examinations. Reviews by Elizabeth Hagen and Jacqueline V. Mallinson.

882. *Sequential Tests of Educational Progress: Science. Reviews by John C. Flanagan and George G. Mallinson.

883. *Stanford Achievement Test: Science.

884. *Survey Test in Introductory Science: California Survey Series. Reviews by Kenneth E. Anderson and Lloyd H. Heidgerd.

885. *Survey Test in Physical Science: California Survey Series. Review by Irvin J. Lehmann.

886. ★T.C. General Science Test.

For other tests, see in *Tests in Print:*

1554. Elementary Science Test: National Achievement Tests.
1557. General Science: Final District-State Scholarship Test.
1558. General Science: Preliminary District-State Scholarship Test.
1560. General Science Test: National Achievement Tests.
1561. General Science Test: State High School Tests for Indiana.
1562. General Science III, Form 4: Achievement Examinations for Secondary Schools.
1567. Physical Science Aptitude Examination, Special Edition.
1570. Read General Science Test.

BIOLOGY

887. Biological Science: Teacher Education Examination Program.

887a. ★Biology: Cooperative Science Tests.

888. *Biology: Every Pupil Scholarship Test.

889. *Biology: Every Pupil Test.

890. *Biology: Minnesota High School Achievement Examinations. Review by Barbara F. Esser.

891. ★Biology Test: Affiliation Testing Program for Catholic Secondary Schools. Review by Henry Chauncey.

892. *College Entrance Examination Board Achievement Test: Biology.

893. *College Entrance Examination Board Advanced Placement Examination: Biology. Review by Clarence H. Nelson.

894. ★College Entrance Examination Board Placement Tests: Biology.

895. *Cooperative Biology Test: Educational Records Bureau Edition.

896. *The Graduate Record Examinations Advanced Tests: Biology.

897. *Survey Test in Biological Science: California Survey Series. Reviews by Barbara F. Esser and Clarence H. Nelson.

For other tests, see in *Tests in Print:*

1580. Biology: Final District-State Scholarship Test.
1581. Biology, Form 4: Achievement Examinations for Secondary Schools.
1582. Biology: Manchester Semester-End Achievement Tests.
1584. Biology: Preliminary District-State Scholarship Test.
1585. Biology Test: State High School Tests for Indiana.
1590. General Biology Test: National Achievement Tests.
1592. Nelson Biology Test.
1593. Semester Test for Biology.

CHEMISTRY

898. *A.C.S. Cooperative Examination: Biochemistry. Excerpt from a review.

899. ★A.C.S. Cooperative Examination for Graduate Placement in Analytical Chemistry.

900. ★A.C.S. Cooperative Examination for Graduate Placement in Organic Chemistry.

901. ★A.C.S. Cooperative Examination for Graduate Placement in Physical Chemistry.

902. *A.C.S. Cooperative Examination in General Chemistry. Reviews by J. A. Campbell and William Hered; and an excerpt from a review.

903. ★A.C.S. Cooperative Examination: Inorganic Chemistry. Review by Frank J. Fornoff; and an excerpt from a review.

904. *A.C.S. Cooperative Examination in Physical Chemistry.

905. *[A.C.S. Cooperative Examinations in Organic Chemistry.] Excerpt from a review.

906. *[A.C.S. Cooperative Examinations in Qualitative Analysis.] Excerpts from two reviews.

907. *A.C.S. Cooperative Examination in Quantitative Analysis.

MISCELLANEOUS

PHYSICS

SENSORY-MOTOR

HEARING

MOTOR

VISION

959. Spache Binocular Reading Test. Review by Helen M. Robinson.
960. ★Stycar Vision Test.
961. ★T/O Vision Testers.
962. ★Test for Colour-Blindness.

FOR OTHER TESTS, see in *Tests in Print:*

1677. A-B-C Vision Test for Ocular Dominance.
1678. AO H-R-R Pseudoisochromatic Plates, Second Edition.
1680. AO Sight Screener.
1681. Burnham-Clark-Munsell Color Memory Test.
1683. Dvorine Animated Fusion Training Charts.
1686. Eye Movement Camera.
1687. Farnsworth Dichotomous Test for Color Blindness: Panel D-15.
1688. The Farnsworth-Munsell 100-Hue Test for the Examination of Color Discrimination.
1689. Freeman Acuity-Tester.
1690. Freeman Protometer.
1691. The Illuminant-Stable Color Vision Test, Second Edition.
1692. Inter-Society Color Council Color Aptitude Test, 1953 Edition.
1694. [Keystone Visual Tests.]
1695. Massachusetts Vision Test.
1698. Ortho-Rater.
1705. Visual Reaction Timer.

SOCIAL STUDIES

963. *American School Achievement Tests: Part 4, Social Studies and Science.
964. ★Christian Democracy Test (Civics, Sociology, Economics): Affiliation Testing Program for Catholic Secondary Schools. Review by Henry Chauncey.
965. ★Citizenship: Every Pupil Scholarship Test.
966. *College Entrance Examination Board Achievement Test: American History and Social Studies. Review by Howard R. Anderson.
967. *College Entrance Examination Board Achievement Test: European History and World Cultures. Review by David K. Heenan.
968. Cooperative General Achievement Tests: Test 1, Social Studies.
969. *The Iowa Tests of Educational Development: Test 1, Understanding of Basic Social Concepts. Review by Morey J. Wantman.
970. *Metropolitan Achievement Tests: [Social Studies]. Reviews by Richard E. Gross and Robert J. Solomon.
971. *Sequential Tests of Educational Progress: Social Studies. Reviews by Jonathon C. McLendon and Donald W. Oliver.
972. *Social Studies: Every Pupil Scholarship Test.
973. ★Social Studies: Minnesota High School Achievement Examinations.
974. *Social Studies: National Teacher Examinations. Review by Harry D. Berg.
975. Social Studies: Teacher Education Examination Program.
976. *Social Studies 12 (American Problems): Minnesota High School Achievement Examinations.
977. *Stanford Achievement Test: Social Studies Test.
978. ★T.C. Social Studies Test.

FOR OTHER TESTS, see in *Tests in Print:*

1706. American History—Government—Problems of Democracy: Acorn Achievement Tests.
1711. Cooperative Social Studies Test for Grades 7, 8, and 9.
1712. The Greig Social Studies Test.
1713. History and Civics Test: Municipal Tests: National Achievement Tests.
1717. Senior Social Studies: Final District-State Scholarship Test.
1718. Senior Social Studies: Preliminary District-State Scholarship Test.
1724. Social Studies Test: Acorn National Achievement Tests.
1725. Social Studies Test: National Achievement Tests.

CONTEMPORARY AFFAIRS

979. *Contemporary Affairs: Every Pupil Test.
980. ★Cooperative Test on Foreign Affairs. Review by Christine McGuire; and an excerpt from a review.
981. *Current Affairs: Every Pupil Scholarship Test.
982. ★Nationwide Current Events Examination.
983. ★New York Times Current Affairs Test.
984. ★New York Times Current Affairs Test for Colleges.
985. ★Newsweek Current News Test.
986. ★Newsweek NewsQuiz.

FOR OTHER TESTS, see in *Tests in Print:*

1731. Current Affairs Test.

ECONOMICS

987. *The Graduate Record Examinations Advanced Tests: Economics.
988. ★A Standard Achievement Test in Economic Understanding for Secondary Schools, Sixth Revision.
989. ★Test of Economic Understanding, Preliminary Edition No. 2.

FOR OTHER TESTS, see in *Tests in Print:*

1736. Economics Test: State High School Tests for Indiana.
1738. High School Economics: Manchester Semester-End Achievement Tests.
1739. Hills Economics Test.

GEOGRAPHY

990. ★Brandywine Achievement Test in Geography for Secondary Schools.
991. *Geography: Every Pupil Scholarship Test.
992. *[Geography]: Every Pupil Test.
993. ★Physical Geography: Every Pupil Scholarship Test.
994. *Survey Test in Geography: California Survey Series. Review by Jonathon C. McLendon.
995. ★World Geography: Every Pupil Scholarship Test.

FOR OTHER TESTS, see in *Tests in Print:*

1742. Economic Geography, Form 4: Achievement Examinations for Secondary Schools.
1747. Geography Test: Municipal Tests: National Achievement Tests.
1748. Geography Test: National Achievement Tests.
1751. Tate Economic Geography Test.

HISTORY

996. *American History: Every Pupil Scholarship Test.
997. *American History: Every Pupil Test.
998. ★American History Test: Affiliation Testing Program for Catholic Secondary Schools. Review by Henry Chauncey.
999. ★Ancient History: Every Pupil Scholarship Test.
1000. *College Entrance Examination Board Advanced Placement Examination: American History. Review by Harry D. Berg.
1001. *College Entrance Examination Board Advanced Placement Examination: European History.
1002. ★Cooperative Topical Tests in American History.
1003. *The Graduate Record Examinations Advanced Tests: History.
1004. *History: Every Pupil Scholarship Test.
1005. *Kansas United States History Test.
1006. ★Objective Tests in American History.
1007. ★Objective Tests in World History.
1008. *Social Studies 10 (American History): Minnesota High School Achievement Examinations.

1009. *Social Studies II (World History): Minnesota High School Achievement Examinations.
1010. *Survey Test in Introductory American History: California Survey Series. Review by Richard E. Gross.
1011. *World History: Every Pupil Scholarship Test.
1012. *World History: Every Pupil Test.
1013. ★World History Test: Affiliation Testing Program for Catholic Secondary Schools. Review by Henry Chauncey.

For other tests, see in *Tests in Print:*

1755. American History: Final District-State Scholarship Test.
1757. American History: Preliminary District-State Scholarship Test.
1758. American History Test: National Achievement Tests.
1759. American History Test: State High School Tests for Indiana.
1763. Cooperative American History Test.
1764. Cooperative Ancient History Test.
1765. Cooperative Modern European History Test.
1766. Cooperative World History Test.
1768. Crary American History Test.
1769. Cummings World History Test.
1775. Kansas Modern European History Test.
1777. Modern World History, Form 4: Achievement Examinations for Secondary Schools.
1779. Ohio History: Every Pupil Test.
1780. Semester Test for American History.
1781. Semester Test for High School World History.
1787. United States History: Manchester Semester-End Achievement Tests.
1790. World History: Final District-State Scholarship Test.
1791. World History: Manchester Semester-End Achievement Tests.
1792. World History: Preliminary District-State Scholarship Test.
1793. World History Test: Acorn National Achievement Tests.
1794. World History Test: State High School Tests for Indiana.

POLITICAL SCIENCE

1013a. American Civics and Government Tests for High Schools and Colleges, Revised Edition. Review by John H. Haefner.
1014. *American Government and Citizenship: Every Pupil Test.
1015. *American Government: Every Pupil Scholarship Test.
1016. *Constitution: Every Pupil Scholarship Test.
1017. ★Duke University Political Science Information Test (American Government).
1018. *The Graduate Record Examinations Advanced Tests: Government.
1019. Peltier-Durost Civics and Citizenship Test: Evaluation and Adjustment Series. Reviews by Howard R. Anderson and Christine McGuire.
1020. ★Principles of Democracy Test. Reviews by William C. Bingham and John H. Haefner.

For other tests, see in *Tests in Print:*

1801. Cooperative American Government Test.
1805. Junior High School Civics Test: State High School Tests for Indiana.
1808. Patterson Test or Study Exercises on the Constitution of the United States.
1810. Patterson's Tests on the Federal Constitution.
1812. Senior High School Civics Test: For a One-Semester Course: State High School Tests for Indiana.
1813. Senior High School Civics Test: State High School Tests for Indiana.
1814. 20th Century Test for Civics.
1815. United States Government: Manchester Semester-End Achievement Tests.

SOCIOLOGY

1021. *The Graduate Record Examinations Advanced Tests: Sociology. Review by J. Richard Wilmeth.
1022. Sare-Sanders Sociology Test. Review by J. Richard Wilmeth.

VOCATIONS

1023. ★Airman Qualifying Examination.
1024. ★[Aptitude Inventory.] Reviews by Leonard W. Ferguson and C. E. Jurgensen; and an excerpt from a review.
1025. ★ETSA Tests. Reviews by Marvin D. Dunnette and Raymond A. Katzell.
1026. ★General Adaptability Battery.
1027. ★Individual Placement Series.
1028. ★Screening Tests for Apprentices.
1029. ★Steward Personnel Tests (Short Form), 1958 Edition. Reviews by Leonard V. Gordon and Lyman W. Porter.

For other tests, see in *Tests in Print:*

1819. [APT Test Batteries.]
1824. Personnel Selection and Classification Test.
1826. Thurstone Employment Tests.
1827. Vocational Aptitude Examination, Type E-A, Revised 1946.

CLERICAL

1030. *A.C.E.R. Short Clerical Test.
1031. *A.C.E.R. Speed and Accuracy Tests.
1032. ★Beginner's Clerical Test. Reviews by Stephen Hunka and Harry L. Stein.
1033. ★Cardall Test of Clerical Perception.
1034. ★Checking Test.
1035. ★Classifying Test.
1036. ★Clerical Tests, Series N.
1037. ★Clerical Tests, Series V.
1038. ★Clerical Worker Examination.
1039. ★Cross Reference Test. Review by Philip H. Kriedt.
1040. *Minnesota Clerical Test.
1041. *National Institute of Industrial Psychology Clerical Test (North American Revision). Review by Harry L. Stein.
1042. ★Number Checking Test.
1043. ★Office Skills Achievement Test. Reviews by Douglas G. Schultz and Paul W. Thayer.
1044. *Office Worker Test. Reviews by Ray G. Price and Douglas G. Schultz.
1045. The Short Employment Tests. Review by Leonard W. Ferguson.
1046. ★Short Tests of Clerical Ability. Reviews by Philip H. Kriedt and Paul W. Thayer.
1047. ★Survey of Clerical Skills (SOCS): Individual Placement Series (Area IV).

For other tests, see in *Tests in Print:*

1831. Clerical Aptitude Test: Acorn National Aptitude Tests.
1834. Clerical Tests 1 and 2.
1836. Detroit Clerical Aptitudes Examination.
1837. Group Test 20.
1838. Group Test 25 (Clerical).
1839. [Hay Tests for Clerical Aptitude.]
1844. O'Rourke Clerical Aptitude Test, Junior Grade.
1845. Personnel Institute Clerical Tests.
1846. [Personnel Research Institute Clerical Battery.]
1847. Psychological Corporation General Clerical Test.
1848. Purdue Clerical Adaptability Test, Revised Edition.
1849. SRA Clerical Aptitudes.
1853. Survey of Working Speed and Accuracy.
1854. Turse Clerical Aptitudes Test.

INTERESTS

1048. ★Burke Inventory of Vocational Development.
1049. ★Career Finder. Reviews by Arthur C. MacKinney and Charles F. Warnath.
1050. ★Chatterji's Non-Language Preference Record.
1051. ★College Planning Inventory, Senior College Edition.
1052. ★Curtis Interest Scale. Reviews by Warren T. Norman and Leona E. Tyler.
1053. ★Fowler-Parmenter Self-Scoring Interest Rec-

ord. Reviews by David P. Campbell and John W. French.

1054. ★The Geist Picture Interest Inventory. Reviews by Milton E. Hahn and Benjamin Shimberg; and an excerpt from a review.

1055. ★Geist Picture Interest Inventory: Deaf Form: Male.

1056. ★Gordon Occupational Check List. Reviews by John O. Crites and Kenneth B. Hoyt.

1057. ★The Guilford-Zimmerman Interest Inventory. Review by Kenneth B. Hoyt.

1058. ★Hackman-Gaither Vocational Interest Inventory.

1059. *How Well Do You Know Your Interests. Review by John R. Hills; and an excerpt from a review.

1060. *Inventory of Vocational Interests: Acorn National Aptitude Tests. Review by John W. French.

1061. ★Job Choice Inventory.

1061a. *Kuder General Interest Survey.

1062. *Kuder Preference Record—Occupational. Review by David P. Campbell.

1063. *Kuder Preference Record—Vocational. Review by Martin Katz.

1064. *Occupational Interest Inventory, 1956 Revision.

1065. ★Occupational Interest Survey (With Pictures): Individual Placement Series (Area II).

1066. Picture Interest Inventory. Reviews by Ralph F. Berdie and Donald E. Super; and an excerpt from a review.

1067. Primary Business Interests Test.

1068. *Qualifications Record, 1961 Revision. Reviews by Arthur C. MacKinney and Charles F. Warnath.

1069. ★Safran Vocational Interest Test.

1070. *Strong Vocational Interest Blank for Men, Revised. Reviews by Alexander W. Astin and Edward J. Furst.

1071. *Strong Vocational Interest Blank for Women, Revised.

1072. ★VALCAN Vocational Interest Profile (VIP).

1073. ★Vocational Sentence Completion Blank, Experimental Edition.

1074. ★William, Lynde & Williams Analysis of Interest.

1075. ★Your Educational Plans. Review by Leo Goldman; and an excerpt from a review.

FOR OTHER TESTS, see in *Tests in Print:*

1856. Brainard Occupational Preference Inventory.
1859. Cleeton Vocational Interest Inventory, Revised Edition.
1862. Devon Interest Test.
1864. Fields of Occupational Interest.
1867. Gregory Academic Interest Inventory.
1868. The Guilford-Schneidman-Zimmerman Interest Survey.
1869. Henderson Analysis of Interest, [Second Edition].
1871. Interest Check List.
1877. Occupational Interest Comparisons.
1881. Occupational Satisfactions Inventory.
1882. Office Occupational Interests of Women.
1883. Pictorial Interest Inventory.
1886. Rothwell-Miller Interest Blank.
1889. Thurstone Interest Schedule.
1890. The Vocational Apperception Test.
1891. Vocational Interest Analyses: A Six-Fold Analytical Extension of the Occupational Interest Inventory.

MANUAL DEXTERITY

1076. ★APT Manual Dexterity Test.

1077. *Minnesota Rate of Manipulation Test, [1946 Edition].

1078. O'Connor Finger Dexterity Test.

1079. O'Connor Tweezer Dexterity Test.

1080. ★Purdue Hand Precision Test.

1081. Purdue Pegboard.

FOR OTHER TESTS, see in *Tests in Print:*

1898. Crawford Small Parts Dexterity Test.
1899. Hand-Tool Dexterity Test.
1902. Minnesota Manual Dexterity Test.
1903. Minnesota Rate of Manipulation Test, [1933 Edition].
1905. Motor Skills Tests Adapted to the Blind.
1908. Pennsylvania Bi-Manual Worksample.
1911. Stromberg Dexterity Test.

MECHANICAL ABILITY

1082. *A.C.E.R. Mechanical Reasoning Test.

1083. *Chriswell Structural Dexterity Test, 1963 Revision.

1084. ★College Entrance Examination Board Placement Tests: Spatial Relations Test.

1085. ★[Curtis Object Completion and Space Form Tests.] Reviews by Richard S. Melton and I. Macfarlane Smith.

1086. ★Flags: A Test of Space Thinking. Review by I. Macfarlane Smith.

1087. ★Hazlehurst Primary Mechanical Ability Tests.

1088. ★Mechanical Information Questionnaire.

1089. ★Mechanical Movements: A Test of Mechanical Comprehension. Review by William A. Owens.

1090. ★Moray House Space Test 2. Review by E. Anstey.

1091. O'Connor Wiggly Block.

1092. Revised Minnesota Paper Form Board Test.

1093. *Spatial Tests 1, 2, and 3.

1094. Tests of Mechanical Comprehension.

1095. ★Three-Dimensional Space Test.

1096. ★Tool Knowledge Test.

1097. ★Two-Dimensional Space Test.

1098. ★Weights and Pulleys: A Test of Intuitive Mechanics. Review by William A. Owens.

FOR OTHER TESTS, see in *Tests in Print:*

1912. A.C.E.R. Mechanical Comprehension Test.
1915. [Cox Mechanical and Manual Tests.]
1917. Detroit Mechanical Aptitudes Examination, Revised.
1919. Form Relations Group Test.
1920. Group Test 80A.
1921. Group Test 81.
1922. MacQuarrie Test for Mechanical Ability.
1923. Mechanical Aptitude Test: Acorn National Aptitude Tests.
1925. Mechanical Knowledge Test.
1927. Mellenbruch Mechanical Motivation Test.
1929. Minnesota Paper Form Board Test.
1930. Minnesota Spatial Relations Test.
1932. N.I.I.P. Squares Test.
1934. O'Rourke Mechanical Aptitude Test.
1936. Prognostic Test of Mechanical Abilities.
1937. Purdue Mechanical Adaptability Test.
1940. SRA Mechanical Aptitudes.
1943. Survey of Mechanical Insight.
1944. Survey of Object Visualization.
1945. Survey of Space Relations Ability.
1947. Tool Knowledge Test [A.C.E.R.].
1950. The Vincent Mechanical Models Test A (Industrial).

MISCELLANEOUS

1099. ★The Biographical Index. Reviews by John K. Hemphill and Richard S. Melton.

1100. ★Breadth of Information.

1101. *Business Judgment Test.

1102. *Cardall Test of Practical Judgment.

1103. ★Conference Meeting Rating Scale.

1104. ★Dartnell Self-Administered Employee Opinion Unit. Review by Raymond A. Katzell.

1105. ★Employee Opinion Survey.

1106. ★The Jenkins Job Attitudes Survey.

1107. ★The Organization Survey.

1108. *The Tear Ballot for Industry. Review by Raymond A. Katzell.

1109. ★[Tests A/9 and A/10.]

1110. ★Whisler Strategy Test. Reviews by Jean Maier Palormo and Paul F. Ross.

1111. ★Work Information Inventory.

SELECTION AND RATING FORMS

SPECIFIC VOCATIONS

ACCOUNTING

DENTISTRY

ENGINEERING

LAW

MEDICINE

MISCELLANEOUS

NURSING

FOR OTHER TESTS, see in *Tests in Print:*

2029. Achievement Tests in Practical Nursing.
2031. Entrance Examinations for Schools of Practical Nursing.
2032. George Washington University Series Nursing Tests.

RESEARCH

1164. ★Research Personnel Review Form.
1165. ★Supervisor's Evaluation of Research Personnel. Review by John W. French; and an excerpt from a review.
1166. ★Surveys of Research Administration and Environment.
1167. ★Technical Personnel Recruiting Inventory.

SELLING

1168. *Aptitude Index Selection Procedure.
1169. *Aptitudes Associates Test of Sales Aptitude: A Test for Measuring Knowledge of Basic Principles of Selling.
1170. ★Combination Inventory.
1171. ★The Dealer Inventory.
1172. ★The Evaluation Record.
1173. Hanes Sales Selection Inventory, Revised Edition. Reviews by William E. Kendall and Albert K. Kurtz.
1174. *Information Index.
1175. ★Interviewer's Impressions—Sales Applicants.
1176. *Personnel Institute Hiring Kit.
1177. ★SRA Sales Attitudes Check List. Review by John P. Foley, Jr.
1178. *Sales Comprehension Test.
1179. ★Sales Employee Inventory.
1180. *Sales Personnel Description Form. Review by Wayne K. Kirchner.
1181. ★The Sales Sentence Completion Blank. Review by William E. Kendall; and an excerpt from a review.
1182. *Steward Basic Factors Inventory (1960 Edition). Reviews by Leonard V. Gordon and Lyman W. Porter.
1183. *Steward Personal Background Inventory (1960 Revised Edition). Reviews by Leonard V. Gordon and Lyman W. Porter.
1184. ★Word Check Forms.

FOR OTHER TESTS, see in *Tests in Print:*

2046. Detroit Retail Selling Inventory.
2050. Hall Salespower Inventory.
2052. Hiring Kit.
2056. LIAMA Inventory of Job Attitudes.
2057. Measure of Consociative Tendency.
2063. Sales Method Index.
2064. Sales Motivation Inventory.
2066. Sales Situation Test.
2068. Steward Life Insurance Knowledge Test.
2069. Steward Occupational Objectives Inventory, 1957 Edition.
2073. Test for Ability to Sell: George Washington University Series.
2075. The Test of Sales Insight.
2076. Test of Sales Judgment.

SKILLED TRADES

1185. ★Automotive Mechanic Test.
1186. The Fiesenheiser Test of Ability to Read Drawings. Review by Joseph E. Moore.
1187. ★Technical Tests.
1188. ★Written Trade Tests.

FOR OTHER TESTS, see in *Tests in Print:*

2080. Purdue Blueprint Reading Test.
2081. Purdue Industrial Training Classification Test.
2082. Purdue Interview Aids.
2083. Purdue Test for Electricians.
2084. Purdue Test for Machinists and Machine Operators.
2085. Purdue Trade Information Test for Sheetmetal Workers.
2086. Purdue Trade Information Test in Carpentry.
2087. Purdue Trade Information Test in Engine Lathe Operation.
2088. Purdue Trade Information Test in Welding, Revised Edition.

SUPERVISION

1189. How Supervise? Review by Joel T. Campbell.
1190. ★Leadership Opinion Questionnaire. Reviews by Jerome E. Doppelt and Wayne K. Kirchner.
1191. ★Personal Development Record.
1192. ★Supervisory Index. Reviews by Arthur H. Brayfield and Albert K. Kurtz.
1193. ★Supervisory Inventory on Human Relations. Review by Seymour Levy.
1194. *Supervisory Practices Test.
1195. ★Test of Supervisory Judgment.
1196. ★WLW Supervisor Survey.

FOR OTHER TESTS, see in *Tests in Print:*

2092. Managerial Scale for Enterprise Improvement.
2098. Test of Supervisory Ability.

TRANSPORTATION

1197. [Driver Selection Forms and Tests.] Review by Joseph E. Moore.
1198. ★[McGuire Safe Driver Scale and Interview Guide.] Reviews by Willard A. Kerr and D. H. Schuster.
1199. Truck Driver Test. Reviews by Willard A. Kerr and D. H. Schuster.
1200. ★Wilson Driver Selection Test. Reviews by Willard A. Kerr and D. H. Schuster.

FOR OTHER TESTS, see in *Tests in Print:*

2100. [American Transit Association Tests.]
2102. Road Test Check List for Testing, Selecting, Rating, and Training Coach Operators.
2103. Road Test in Traffic for Testing, Selecting, Rating and Training Truck Drivers, [1955 Revision].